ENCYCLOPEDIA OF WORLD CRIME

ENCYCLOPEDIA OF WORLD CRIME

Criminal Justice, Criminology, and Law Enforcement

Volume IV
S-Z
Supplements

Jay Robert Nash

CrimeBooks, Inc.
Wilmette, IL 1990

Publisher and **Editor-in-Chief**: Jay Robert Nash; **Associate Publisher** and **Executive Editor**: Oksana L. Creighton; **Managing Editor:** Joseph Anthony Reich (Production/Database/CD-ROM Services); **Senior Editors:** Jim McCormick, Richard C. Lindberg, Jennifer S. Harris, Richard E. Stark, Jean Blashfield Black; **Associate Editors**: Cordelia Maloney, Marck L. Bailey, Kristina Lawson, C.R. Green, Laura A. McKee, Bill Young, Eric Murphy; Jeff Carlson, Mary Anne Maloney; **Art Director:** Curtis W. Randell; **Art Consultants:** Cathy Anetsberger-Edens, Wm. O. Boze Harz; **Art Production Assistant**: Doreen J. Kozak; **Assistant Editors:** Marydeanne Wildman, John Leacock, Lawrence Eric Buhl, Marcy Firmiss, Constance Kuehn, David Foe, Amy Schroeder, Vincent M. Tornatore, John A. Koehlinger, Andrew D. Schmit, Leslie A. Krampf, Bennett H. Merens, Carol Hanson, Annie C. Higgins, Joni Overton, Clifford Tarrance, Mary Keegan Mathie, Joe Scheringer, Elizabeth Hansen, Katie Maloney, Jodi L. Schenck; **Research** and **Editorial Assistants**: Paul Adee, Martha Keefe, Kevin P. Pierce, Chad R. Well, Timothy A. Walsh, Angela L. Johnson, Andrea Nash, Carmel Carroll, Celia Carroll, Kymber Whitney, Inga Johnson, Leslie Haines, Daniel P. Bakula, Darryl Fox, Aaron Epstein, Christopher B. DeZutter, Michael Doorley, M. Andrew Conaway; **Bureau Chief** (Washington, D.C.): John E. Vetter; **Foreign Correspondents:** Paul Allen (Paris), Roger Madden (London), David Halliday (Berlin), G. Caetani (Rome); **Editorial Consultants:** Mitchel H. Tobin (Legal Editorial), Robert A. Janet (Law Enforcement).

Business Group: Judith A. Nash, Business Director and Associate Publisher; Patrice Tracy, Business and Sales Manager; Cordelia Maloney, Publicity and Promotion; **Consultants**: Robert Lee Ganchiff, Associate Publisher/Finance; Marc Davis, Advertising and Marketing; George C. de Kay, Publishing and Distribution; E. Leonard Rubin, David Canmann, Legal; **Associate Publishers**: Stanley Ralph Ross, Lawrence Ferguson, Barbara Browne Cramer, Marc B. Benson, Robert D. and Claudette Endacott, Peter Barrett, Lynn C. Maddox, James Baxter, Robert Champion, Ralph E. Dieckmann, James L. Anderson, Marsh Blackburn, Jeanne Nathan, Ira N. Kudish, Helen C. Creighton, James and Carole Creighton, Michael and Susan Creighton, David and Marilyn Wallace, Jeffery A. Harris, Stephanie Bemler, Jean E. Oyen, George Manny.

Editorial and **Sales Offices**: CrimeBooks, Inc., 1213 Wilmette Avenue, Wilmette, IL 60091-2557. Telephone: 1-708-251-8350. FAX: 1-708-251-5289.

Library of Congress Catalog Card Number: 88-92729
ISBN:0-923582-00-2 ENCYCLOPEDIA OF WORLD CRIME (6 Vols.)
0-923582-04-5 ENCYCLOPEDIA OF WORLD CRIME, Vol. IV (S-Z, Supplements)

Printed in the United States
First Edition

1 2 3 4 5 6 7 8 9 10

HOW TO USE THIS ENCYCLOPEDIA

ALPHABETICAL ORDER

Each entry name in the ***Encyclopedia of World Crime*** is boldfaced and listed alphabetically. Biographical entries are alphabetized by the subject's last name. Everything preceding the comma is treated as a unit when alphabetizing. Hyphens, diacritical marks, periods following initials, and spaces do not influence its alphabetization. For example, **La Pietra** follows **Lang**, and **Black Bart** follows **Black, Robert**. Names with prefixes such as **de**, **von**, or **le** are listed under the most common form of the name, such as **de Gaulle, Charles** and **Ribbentrop, Joachim von**. Names beginning in **Mc** or **M'** are treated as if spelled **Mac**; thus **McManus, Fred** appears before **MacMichael,** Sir **Harold**. Asian names, in which the family name comes first, are alphabetized by the family name, omitting the comma. Identical names are alphabetized chronologically. Monarchs commonly known by one name, such as **Elizabeth I** or **Louis XIV**, are usually listed under that name only and would precede an identically spelled surname in entry order. Entries with numbers or abbreviations in them are alphabetized as though spelled out. When an entry heading refers to an event rather than to a person, it is alphabetized according to the first key word in the commonly used title, as in **Popish Plot** or **King Ranch Murders**. When the names of two or more people head an entry, it is usually alphabetized according to the most prominent person's last name.

ENTRY HEADINGS

Appearing in boldface type at the beginning of each ***Encyclopedia of World Crime*** entry is the name by which that entry is most commonly known. Entries are categorized alphabetically under the name of the offender, criminal event, or the professional in the field of crime. If a crime remains unsolved, the entry is found under the victim's name, and is denoted by the abbreviation **unsolv.** in parentheses immediately preceding the crime category. Other entries appearing under the victim's name include **assassinations**; thus, information concerning the assassination of President Abraham Lincoln would be found under Lincoln and not John Wilkes Booth. The royal or political title or military rank held by the assassination victim precedes the category abbreviation. Parenthetical remarks immediately following an entry name indicate an alternate spelling, that person's original or maiden name, or the entry's alias if preceded by **AKA:**. These names also appear in boldface.

Following the name are **date**(s) relevant to that entry. The letter **b.** preceding the date signifies that only the person's date of birth is known, while the letter **d.** signifies that only the person's date of death is known. The letter **c.** (circa) signifies that the date which immediately follows is approximate. In some cases **prom.** (prominent) is used to denote the year(s) in which that entry was noteworthy. All years B.C. are designated as such.

In a number of entries the phrase **Case of** follows the date, designating that the person named was tried for the crime which follows but found Not Guilty.

The **country** designation in each entry heading refers to the country in which the crime was committed or the country in which persons in the field of crime are known professionally. The country is named as it was known at the time the crime was committed; thus, Russia is referenced prior to the Russian Revolution, while U.S.S.R. is used for crimes committed since that time. Entries where crimes are committed in more than three countries or committed on the high seas are designated as Int'l (International).

The last piece of information contained in the Entry Heading is the **crime category**, designating the crime(s) the subject was convicted of, or the professional field of crime with which the subject is associated. For persons wrongly convicted of a crime, prior to the crime category is the designation **(wrong. convict.)**. If however, the subject's conviction was overturned on a legal technicality or there is some doubt as to his actual innocence, then the designation **(wrong. convict.?)** is used. In some cases a question mark may follow the crime category. This denotes that there is uncertainty as to whether the crime in question actually occurred; e.g., **mur.?**, might denote that there is some doubt as to whether a person was killed, committed suicide, or died from other causes.

A number of entries may include more than one person if the criminals or professionals worked together. When the relevant dates of a **multiple name entry** coincide, one date will follow the last person named in the entry heading.

REFERENCES

After each **Encyclopedia of World Crime** entry, the references used in compiling it are cited. The abbreviation **CBA** denotes **CrimeBooks Archives**. Other sources are cited in four categories: nonfiction, fiction, drama, and film. Nonfiction works are listed first, alphabetically by the author's last name. If two or more works by the same author are used, the second and all following citations are indicated by a blank line and are alphabetized by the first word (ignoring articles A, An, The). If a source is anonymous, this is indicated in parentheses after the title. Sources without a specific author (pamphlets, reports, tracts, trial transcripts, compilations, etc.) are listed alphabetically by the title. Plays based on a case appear after **(DRAMA)** and are listed alphabetically by author. Fictional accounts of a case appear alphabetically by author after **(FICTION)**. Films based on the case appear after **(FILM)**, and are listed chronologically, each title followed by the year of its U.S. release. Silent films are denoted by the letters preceding the year of release. Often alternate titles **(alt. title)** of films follow U.S. titles in parentheses.

Cross references immediately following an entry refer the reader to entries containing additional information relevant to the case, person, place, or event being consulted. Direct references are also used frequently throughout the volumes to lead the readers from a well known name (alias, victim, event) to the name under which that entry appears (**Bonney, William H.**, See: **Billy the Kid**).

KEY TO ABBREVIATIONS USED IN THE *ENCYCLOPEDIA OF WORLD CRIME*

2d lt.	= second lieutenant
abduc.	= abduction
abor.	= abortion
accom.	= accomplices
adm.	= admiral
adult.	= adultery
Afg.	= Afghanistan
Ala.	= Alabama
Alb.	= Albania
Alg.	= Algeria
Arg.	= Argentina

Ariz. = Arizona
Ark. = Arkansas
assass. = assassination
asslt. = assault
asslt.&bat. = assault and battery
attempt. = attempted
atty. gen. = attorney general
Aus. = Australia
Aust. = Austria
banish. = banishment
Bav. = Bavaria
Belg. = Belgium
Ber. = Bermuda
big. = bigamy
blk. = blackmail
Bol. = Bolivia
bomb. = bombing
boot. = bootlegging
Braz. = Brazil
brib. = bribery
Brit. = Britain/England including Wales
Bul. = Bulgaria
burg. = burglary
Calif. = California
can. = cannibalism
Can. = Canada
cap. pun. = capital punishment
capt. = captain
coin. = coining
col. = colonel
Col. = Columbia
Colo. = Colorado
comdr. = commander
Conn. = Connecticut
consp. = conspiracy
cont./ct. = contempt of court
corr. = corruption
Cos. = Costa Rica
count. = counterfeiting
cpl. = corporal
crim. insan. = criminal insanity
crim. just. = criminal justice
crim. law. = criminal lawyer
crim. neg. = criminal negligence
crime preven. = crime prevention
crime&punish. = crime and punishment
criminol. = criminologist or criminology
ct. mar. = court-martial
Czech. = Czechoslovakia
Del. = Delaware
del. = delinquency
Den. = Denmark
det. = detective
Dom. = Dominican Republic
Dr. = doctor
duel. = dueling
Ecu. = Ecuador
El Sal. = El Salvador
embez. = embezzlement
emp. = emperor or empress
esc. = escape
esp. = espionage
Eth. = Ethiopia
euth. = euthanasia
execut. = executioner
extor. = extortion, extortionist
fenc. = fencing
Fin. = Finland
fing. ident. = fingerprint identification
Fla. = Florida
forg. = forgery
Fr. = France
Ga. = Georgia
gamb. = gambling, gambler
gen. = general
geno. = genocide
Ger. = Germany
Gr. = Greece
Guat. = Guatemala
harass. = harassment
her. = heresy
hijack. = hijacking
Hond. = Honduras
host. = hostage
Hung. = Hungary
Ice. = Iceland
Ill. = Illinois
impris. = imprisoned
Ind. = Indiana
Indo. = Indonesia
Int'l. = International
Ire. = Ireland
Isr. = Israel
Jam. = Jamaica
Jor. = Jordan
jur. = jurist
Kan. = Kansas
kid. = kidnapper, kidnapping
Kor. = Korea
Ky. = Kentucky
La. = Louisiana
law enfor. off. = law enforcement officer or official
Leb. = Lebanon
loot. = looting
lt. = lieutenant
lt. col. = lieutenant colonel
lt. comdr. = lieutenant commander
lt. gen. = lieutenant general
lt. gov. = lieutenant governor
Lux. = Luxemburg
lynch. = lynching
Mac. = Macedonia
maj. = major
mansl. = manslaughter
Mass. = Massachusetts
Md. = Maryland
med. mal. = medical malpractice
Mex. = Mexico
Mich. = Michigan
Mid. East = Middle East
milit. = military
milit. des. = military desertion
Minn. = Minnesota
Miss. = Mississippi
miss. per. = missing persons
Mo. = Missouri
mob vio. = mob violence
Mont. = Montana
Mor. = Morocco
mur. = murder, murderer
mut. = mutiny
mutil. = mutilation
N. Zea. = New Zealand
N.C. = North Carolina
N.D. = North Dakota
N.H. = New Hampshire
N.J. = New Jersey
N.M. = New Mexico
N.Y. = New York
Neb. = Nebraska

necro.	= necrophilia
Neth.	= Netherlands
Nev.	= Nevada
Nic.	= Nicaragua
Nig.	= Nigeria
Nor.	= Norway
obsc.	= obscenity
Okla.	= Oklahoma
Ore.	= Oregon
org. crime	= organized crime
P.R.	= Puerto Rico
Pa.	= Pennsylvania
Pak.	= Pakistan
Pan.	= Panama
Para.	= Paraguay
path.	= pathologist
penal col.	= penal colonies
penol.	= penology, penologist
Per.	= Persia
perj.	= perjury
Phil.	= Philippines
pick.	= pickpocket
pir.	= piracy
Pol.	= Poland
pol.	= police
pol. mal.	= police malpractice
polit.	= politician
polit. corr.	= political corruption
poly.	= polygamy
porn.	= pornography
Port.	= Portugal
pres.	= president
pris.	= prison
prof.	= professor
prohib.	= prohibition
pros.	= prostitution
R.I.	= Rhode Island
rack.	= racketeering
rebel.	= rebellion
rev.	= reverend
rob.	= robbery
Rom.	= Romania
Roman.	= Roman Empire
Rus.	= Russia (prior to 1918)
S. Afri.	= South Africa
S.C.	= South Carolina
S.D.	= South Dakota
sab.	= sabotage
Saud.	= Saudi Arabia
Scot.	= Scotland
sec. firm	= security firm
secret crim. soc.	= secret criminal societies
secret soc.	= secret society
Sen.	= Senegal
sgt.	= sergeant
Si.	= Sicily
Sing.	= Singapore
skyjack.	= skyjacking
sland.	= slander
smug.	= smuggling
sod.	= sodomy
Sri.	= Sri Lanka
Sudan	= Sudan
suic.	= suicide
supt.	= superintendent
Swed.	= Sweden
Switz.	= Switzerland
Tai.	= Taiwan
Tan.	= Tanzania
tax evas.	= tax evasion
Tenn.	= Tennessee
terr.	= terrorism, terrorist
Thai.	= Thailand
tort.	= torture
toxicol.	= toxicologist
treas.	= treason
Tun.	= Tunisia
Turk.	= Turkey
U.A.E.	= United Arab Emirates
U.K.	= United Kingdom
U.S.	= United States of America
U.S.S.R.	= Union of Soviet Socialist Republics (after 1918)
unsolv.	= unsolved
Urug.	= Uruguay
Va.	= Virginia
vandal.	= vandalism
Venez.	= Venezuela
vice dist.	= vice district
vict.	= victim
Viet.	= Vietnam
vigil.	= vigilantism
Vt.	= Vermont
W.Va.	= West Virginia
Wash.	= Washington
west. gunman	= western gunman
west. lawman	= western lawman
west. outl.	= western outlaw
wh. slav.	= white slavery
Wis.	= Wisconsin
Wyo.	= Wyoming
Yug.	= Yugoslavia

TYPES OF ENTRIES

Biographical; case studies; celebrated trials; criminal secret organizations; direct references; historic and current techniques in police science; historical events and places; literary fiction based on criminals or crime events; unsolved crimes.

DICTIONARY

More than 20,000 terms used in America, U.K., and elsewhere by the underworld and law enforcement, from ancient times to the present, are listed in a dictionary (Vol. V).

TYPES OF SUPPLEMENTS

VOL. IV: Arson; Assassination; Bombing; Burglary; Capital Punishment; Computer Crime; Detectives, Notable; Drugs; Dueling; Firearms and Ballistics; Forensic Sciences, Notable Experts; Fraud; Hijacking; Identification Systems; Kidnapping; Looting; Lynching and Vigilantism; Mob Violence (Riots); Organized Crime; Police; Prisons; Robbery; Skyjacking; Terrorism; Toxicology; War Crimes and Criminals; Western Lawmen; Western Outlaws and Gunmen.

DICTIONARY (VOL. V): International Acronyms for Prominent Organizations and Operations; U.S. Correctional Systems; Landmark U.S. Crime Legislation; Landmark U.S. Federal and State Court Decisions; U.S. Correctional Systems; U.S. Crime Commissions; U.S. Federal Bureau of Investigation Offices by City.

INDEX

The index contains the following: Bibliography; Subject Index; Proper Name Index.

SUPPLEMENTS
TABLE OF CONTENTS

Saada, Antun, 1904-49, Syria, treas. Originated secret association later known as Syrian National Party in 1932, with goal of consolidating Syria with adjacent geographical areas. He was arrested, convicted, and executed for treason following a conflict in Beirut with a rival faction.

REF.: *CBA;* Paine, *The Assassins' World.*

Saavedra Ramirez de Baquendano, Angel de (Duque de Rivas), 1791-1865, Spain, treas. Sentenced to death in 1823 for espousing radical leftist beliefs. He fled custody and lived in exile until receiving amnesty in 1834. He served as minister of interior two years later, but was exiled for supporting conservative views from 1837-38. He joined the senate in 1838, and served as president of the government in 1854. REF.: *CBA.*

Sacco, Nicola, 1891-1927, and **Vanzetti, Bartolomeo,** 1888-1927, U.S., rob.-mur. The Sacco-Vanzetti case in the U.S. rivaled the sensational French *cause célèbre,* Alfred Dreyfus. The case became a state of mind and an intellectual point of view that captivated the U.S. for six years, following a blatantly biased trial and conviction of two illiterate Italian immigrants, Nicola Sacco and Bartolomeo Vanzetti. Sacco worked in a factory making shoes, Vanzetti was a self-employed fishmonger. Both men were ardent radicals and devout anarchists, who went armed on the streets and gave rabble-rousing speeches in which they urged the violent overthrow of the U.S. government. To the police in Massachusetts, along with leading members of the judiciary, these men were dangerous, capable of any crime. When the pair stood accused of a brutal robbery involving the murders of two innocent men, establishment forces in the state at the time had no qualms in judging Sacco and Vanzetti out of hand.

At the time, the nation was undergoing emotional trauma created by radicals who, in 1919, had tried to blow up dozens of U.S. political leaders. In response to these anarchist attacks, U.S. Attorney A. Mitchell Palmer had ordered federal agents to arrest every radical in the country. The agents ran amuck, illegally breaking into homes and offices, beating up suspects, and arresting thousands of persons, many of whom were innocent. These wholesale arrests were known as the infamous Red Raids, and the publicity attending them frightened the U.S., which saw through the eyes of the press all radicals as dark-complexioned immigrants bent on mass destruction and death, the—very image of Sacco and Vanzetti.

Two crimes, each occurring four months apart, sealed the fate of Sacco and Vanzetti. The first of these happened on the morning of Dec. 24, 1919, in Bridgewater, Mass., a manufacturing center about thirty miles south of Boston. On that day a party of men, all "foreign-looking" to witnesses testifying later, stopped a truck carrying the payroll of the White Shoe Company. Two men got out of a car and fired at the truck, one blasting it with a shotgun, when the driver refused to turn over the payroll. The driver, however, was armed and fired back. With that, the two men leaped back into the car with the other robbers and the auto sped off. An Overland car, which was thought to be the auto in which the robbers escaped, was later found in a Bridgewater garage. Attendants stated that it was owned by a man named Boda. Police ordered the garage owner to contact them when Boda came to pick up his car.

On Apr. 15, 1920, Frederick A. Parmenter, cashier for the Slater and Morrill Shoe Company, and a guard, Alexander Berardelli, were transferring almost $16,000 in cash from one company building to another along the main street of South Braintree, Mass. It was 3 p.m. on a sunny afternoon and few people were around. Some workers moved along the street conducting business, and two men idled next to a fence separating the two shoe company buildings. They stood in the path of Parmenter and Berardelli, and as the cashier and guard came abreast of them carrying the payroll, the two men blocked the sidewalk. Berardelli, carrying a bag with payroll money inside, stepped into the gutter to avoid them, but one of the men suddenly jammed a gun into his ribs and fired several times, killing him. The gunman picked up the money bag.

Parmenter, who had been walking behind the guard by some ten feet, saw the cold-blooded murder and dropped his money bag. He immediately ran across the street, the other gunman running after him, firing two bullets which struck the cashier in the back and killed him on the spot. The second murder was probably committed to prevent Parmenter from later identifying the robbers. The killers then picked up the second bag of money, and both men ran to the street. At that moment a car, later identified as a Buick, roared around a corner, raced up to the two waiting men, and stopped for a few seconds as the robbers tossed the money bags inside and dove into the back seat. The Buick roared down the street and out of sight. The robbery and murders took place in less than four minutes, but it proved to be one of the most shocking crimes in Massachusetts history to that date. Like the abortive Bridgewater robbery months earlier, the robbers and thieves were described as a group of "foreign-looking" men.

The Buick used in the South Braintree robbery had been stolen and was found two days later in a rural area. Tracks from another car led away from the area where the Buick was found and detectives concluded that these tire tracks belonged to the Overland parked in the Bridgewater garage. On May 5, 1921, Boda and three other men later identified as Sacco and Vanzetti and a man named Orciani, appeared at the garage, asking for the Overland. The owner, Johnson, told the men that his wife had to perform an errand before he could release the car to them. Mrs. Johnson ran next door to a neighbor's house to call police, as detectives had earlier instructed the owner to do when Boda called for his car (this had been done on previous occasions because the Bridgewater raid without police response). Meanwhile, Johnson chatted with the Italians who seemed to grow increasingly nervous. The garage owner pointed out to Boda that the Overland had improper plates. The men began to talk quietly in Italian and then abruptly left the garage, Boda and Orciani riding away on a motorcycle, the other two men, reportedly Sacco and Vanzetti, on foot.

Several cars full of armed police officers arrived a few minutes later. Learning that the suspects had left, the police fanned out in all directions, searching for them. More police were called into the dragnet, and that evening an officer got aboard a streetcar and noticed two swarthy-looking men sitting together. He took no chances, drawing his gun and ordering the two men off the streetcar. Both men were armed with guns, and these weapons were pocketed by the arresting officer. They gave no resistance and identified themselves as Nicola Sacco and Bartolomeo Vanzetti.

Inside one of Sacco's pockets, police found some radical literature, including a leaflet written by Sacco which was later used against him at his trial. The compromising document read: "Fellow workers, you have fought all the wars. You have worked for all the capitalists. You have wandered over the countries. Have you harvested the fruits of your labors, the price of your victories? Does the present smile on you? Does the future promise you anything? Have you found a piece of land where you can live like a human being?

"On these questions, on this argument, and on this theme the struggle for existence Bartolomeo Vanzetti will speak. Admission free. Freedom of discussion to all. Take the ladies with you." Charged with carrying concealed weapons, both men pleaded guilty. They were then asked what they were doing in Bridgewater, and they said they were going to see a friend. They were held on suspicion of committing the Bridgewater and South Braintree robberies. Sacco was able to prove that on the day of the Bridgewater robbery he was at work but unfortunately had no alibi for Apr. 15, 1920, the day of the South Braintree robbery, which was his day off work. Sacco was charged with the South Braintree robbery. Vanzetti could provide no alibi for the dates of either robbery and he was charged with both crimes.

Vanzetti was tried first, for the Bridgewater robbery, appearing before Judge Webster Thayer at Plymouth, Mass., on June 22, 1920. He was convicted on questionable evidence, and Judge Thayer, an avowed foe of radicals, gave Vanzetti the maximum sentence of between ten and fifteen years in prison. Then both Sacco and Vanzetti were tried together in Dedham, Mass., in June 1921. Their conviction was almost a certainty from the outset. The same judge who had presided over Vanzetti's trial in Plymouth and had sentenced him to prison was the presiding judge in the Dedham trial. He was one of the most conservative jurists on the Massachusetts bench, an outspoken foe of liberals, and he saw the radical movement in the U.S. as a dangerous threat to democracy. He was openly prejudiced in the case but he refused to remove himself from the bench. It was later stated that, either during or following the Dedham trial, Judge Thayer boasted: "Did you see what I did with those anarchist bastards?"

The prosecutor, Frederick Katzmann, hated anarchists as much as the Back Bay Webster Thayer. Said Katzmann: "I will crucify those damned God-hating radicals!" Twelve arch conservative jurors helped Katzmann drive the nails into Sacco and Vanzetti. Facing a hostile judge and jury, Sacco and Vanzetti made a crucial error in the selection of their defense attorney. On advice from friends, the two anarchists chose Fred Moore to defend them. Moore was a wild Bohemian from California and supporter of leftist causes. He wore long hair, rumpled clothes, and arrogantly flaunted his radical views in front of Thayer and the jury, whose members later stated they found the defense attorney "repulsive." Moore challenged the court at every opportunity and used Sacco and Vanzetti for his own political cause and ends. He wore garish ties and outlandish clothes that seemed as if he had rented them in a costume shop. On more than one occasion, Moore relaxed outside the courtroom, standing in his dirty, bare feet.

Moore set a pattern of open confrontation with the court that immediately put his clients into jeopardy. He fought every minor rule and regulation, and his remarks to the bench were provocative and insulting, quickly arousing Judge Thayer's considerable ire. Before the trial commenced, Moore retained additional counsel in the form of John and Thomas McAnarney, but even these respectable and able lawyers could do little to help Sacco and Vanzetti since Moore continued to be the lawyer of record and controlled the defense.

Every move Moore made was political and he disregarded the advice of his fellow attorneys. Moore exhausted the jury system in Dedham for weeks as he dismissed more than 700 prospective jurors. If a prospective juror wore a conservative suit, he was dismissed. Anyone who worked in a bank or a brokerage house was dismissed. Said a disgusted Thomas McAnarney after the trial: "Every time I wanted a man on the jury whom I felt to be honest, he (Moore) would make an exception to it. Whenever he was addressing the court, it was quite similar to waving a red flag in the face of a bull!"

John McAnarney realized after the first disastrous day that Moore's unpredictable and flamboyant actions would certainly send his clients to the death chamber. McAnarney went to the noted trial lawyer William G. Thompson and pleaded with him to take over the defense. "I told him that the lives of two innocent men were at stake," McAnarney later said. Thompson agreed to take on the case. When Thompson appeared the next morning, Moore adamantly refused to withdraw from the case and became hysterical, screaming: "You will not deny me my shining hour!"

Moore stayed on, taking a week to impanel the jury. The trial finally opened with Katzmann relating in detail the robbery and murders that occurred in South Braintree. Meanwhile, the defendants fidgeted and whispered to each other, glancing furtively at the judge and jury. They spoke broken English and communicated poorly with their attorneys. Sacco, the shoemaker, was thought to be the more suspicious of the pair. Even the fact that he made shoes and that both the South Braintree and Bridgewater robberies were of shoe firm payrolls seemed to implicate him.

Born on Apr. 22, 1891, Sacco was married and had one child. Vanzetti, a fishmonger, was a confirmed bachelor, born on June 11, 1888. They had been lifelong friends, had emigrated from Italy to the U.S. in 1908, and were bonded by their common zeal for anarchy. The prosecution pointed out that in 1917 and 1918 both men shirked their duty by evading the draft in WWI, fleeing to Mexico and remaining there until the war was over. Even their own defense attorneys admitted that their clients acted suspiciously; this was no doubt due to their precarious political posture. The attitude of the accused was later described as "the consciousness of guilt." In other words, the defendants looked and acted guilty. Therefore, the illogical conclusion was that they *were* guilty. The prosecution then brought forth a small army of witnesses who positively identified both Sacco and Vanzetti as being members of the South Braintree robbery gang. Immediately after the robbery these same witnesses could not give a clear description of the killers. But, after careful coaching and prodding on the part of Katzmann and his aides, these very witnesses suddenly recalled, thirteen months after the crime, the exact identities of Sacco and Vanzetti.

Michael Levangie, a gate keeper at a South Braintree railroad crossing, was typical of those who bore witness against the defendants. Following the robbery he stated: "I saw nobody. I was too damned scared to see anyone. All I saw was the muzzle of that damned gun and I turned and ran for the shanty and they put a bullet through the shanty." In court, however, it was a different matter. Levangie described one of the killers in precise detail, saying that the driver of the getaway car was "dark complected, with cheekbones sticking out, black hair, heavy brown mustache, slouch hat and an army coat." Assistant Prosecuting Attorney Harold P. Williams asked Levangie if he had seen that man since, and the witness, without hesitation, pointed at the defense table and replied: "Yes, sir. Right there!" Levangie's testimony was attacked vigorously by the defense who pointed out that other witnesses had described the driver as blond and sallow-complected. This meant very little to a judge and jury who had already come to a decision.

Dozens of witnesses were company employees who swore that Sacco and Vanzetti were the culprits. Lewis L. Wade was the exception. He testified for the prosecution, but when he was asked to identify Sacco as one of the bandits, Wade said: "Well, I ain't so sure now. I have a little doubt." Two weeks later, after having worked for Slater and Morrill for sixteen years, Wade was fired.

Fifty-nine witnesses testified for the prosecution. Many of these were ballistic experts. One firearms expert positively identified the bullets that killed Parmenter and Berardelli as having come from the gun taken from Sacco when he was arrested in Bridgewater. Another ballistics expert testified that the bullets were "consistent," therefore having been fired by the same weapon.

The defense called ninety-nine witnesses to the stand, many stating that they had seen Sacco and Vanzetti on the day of the murder. A clerk in the Italian consulate in Boston swore in a deposition that Sacco had been there on the day of the robbery, filling out a form to obtain a passport for a return trip to Italy. Others came forth to say that at the time of the robbery they were buying fish from Vanzetti in Boston. After thirty-seven grueling days, the trial came to an end. Judge Thayer, for all of the bad press he had received, summed up the trial fairly and impartially for the jury. The jury returned a verdict of Guilty on July 14, 1921, convicting both men of first degree murder. When hearing the verdict Sacco leapt to his feet shouting: "*Siamo innocenti!* They kill an innocent man! They kill two innocent men!" On Nov. 1, 1921, Judge Thayer sentenced both men to death.

Thus began a seven-year ordeal for the condemned men as their attorneys, friends, relatives, and the legions of supporters they had collected fought battle after battle to save their lives. Continual appeals were filed, and stays of executions were granted. Thousands picketed the Massachusetts state house and government buildings, demanding a pardon for Sacco and Vanzetti. On

Bartolomeo Vanzetti and Nicola Sacco, accused murderers.

Judge Webster B. Thayer.

Robert Benchley

Edna St. Vincent Millay

Dorothy Parker

Columnist Heywood Broun arguing for the lives of the accused.

Vanzetti and Sacco following their conviction for murder.

The funeral cortege in Boston for the executed Sacco and Vanzetti.

the literary front, the fires blazed for the pair. Heywood Broun, the giant columnist for the New York *World,* wrote so many columns defending the pair that his boss, Herbert Bayard Swope, fired him for a brief period. Joining the cause were such distinguished literary lights as poet Edna St. Vincent Millay and writer Dorothy Parker. Robert Benchley, the humorist, also mounted podiums in defense of the convicted anarchists. Many, like Katherine Ann Porter, were arrested and jailed for their picketing and protests. Porter later related how many of the political groups supporting Sacco and Vanzetti used the pair for their own ends, calling to mind leftist Rosa Baron. Porter had stated to Baron in Boston, before joining a picket line, that she hoped they could save the lives of the shoemaker and the fishmonger. Snapped Baron: "Alive—what for? They are no earthly good to us alive!"

Year after year, petitions and letters from famous persons around the world flooded the offices of Governor Fuller of Massachusetts, all asking for a new trial, for clemency, for parole, or for pardon. The letter writers included George Bernard Shaw, John Galsworthy, John Dos Passos, H.G. Wells, President Tomás Garrigue Masaryk of Czechoslovakia, Captain Alfred Dreyfus, and even Italian dictator Benito Mussolini. Governor Fuller, in turn, appointed a special independent committee to reinvestigate the case, a committee headed by President Lowell of Harvard University and Judge Robert Grant. The Lowell Committee's task was to review the entire case and report to Fuller, to help guide him in his decision regarding clemency. The Lowell Committee found that there was substantial bias on the part of trial judge Thayer but that the jury's verdict could not be challenged, and that the condemned men were guilty "beyond all reasonable doubt."

At the same time the Lowell Committee was sifting through already yellowing archives and affidavits, Celestino Madeiros, a youthful Portuguese gunman, confessed to having taken part in the South Braintree robbery and told police that Sacco and Vanzetti had nothing to do with it. Examining this confession was Judge Thayer. He concluded that Madeiros' confession had not established a "reasonable doubt" as to the guilt of either Sacco or Vanzetti. The Massachusetts State Supreme Court upheld Thayer's decision. Judge Thayer brought them before his bench on April 5, 1927, and confirmed the death sentence.

"You know I am innocent," Sacco shouted from the dock. "That is the same words I pronounced seven years ago. You condemn two innocent men!"

Said Vanzetti: "Never in our full life could we hope to do such work for tolerance, for justice, for man's understanding of man as we do now by accident. Our words—our lives—our pains... nothing! The taking of our lives—lives of a good shoemaker and a poor fish-peddler—all! That last moment belongs to us—that agony is our triumph!"

The two men returned to the Charlestown Prison, once more to await the end in the same death house cells they had occupied for seven years. At midnight on Aug. 22-23, 1927, Madeiros, who had been condemned for another murder, then Sacco, then Vanzetti, were electrocuted. After being strapped into the electric chair, Nicola Sacco cried out in Italian: "Long live anarchy!" In English, he added: "Farewell my wife and child and all my friends. Farewell, Mother." Vanzetti claimed innocence to the last, saying calmly: "I have never committed a crime but sometimes sin. I am innocent of all crime, not only of this, but all."

The deaths of these two men resulted in nationwide mourning among the liberal-leftist camp because it had lost a great cause, and the public in general was sickened by the executions because the condemned men had been put through an agonizing and interminable process before meeting a fate that had been judicially decreed years earlier. The waiting for death was, indeed, cruel and unusual punishment, let alone the execution itself. The funeral procession in Boston for the pair was attended by tens of thousands.

The Sacco and Vanzetti case remains today almost as hotly debated as it was in its long-ago era. Were the two men guilty? After thorough examination of all the evidence, the author believes Vanzetti was innocent but that Nicola Sacco was most probably guilty, that he had been in South Braintree on the day of the robbery and murders and was part of the gang that slew the cashier and guard. The testimony of ballistics experts is the strongest evidence to support this conclusion, along with Sacco's own peculiar statements, crying out to the court when first convicted: "They kill an innocent man," then amending that blurted thought with "they kill *two* innocent men." No one could read Sacco's mind at the time, of course, but the inference that can be drawn was that his first statement was a plea for Vanzetti, and then, to maintain their umbilical defense, he added himself, a telling slip of the tongue. The entire case, irrespective of guilt or innocence, was a miserable shambles, leaving an ugly stain on U.S. jurisprudence. See: **Berkman, Alexander**; **Goldman, Emma**; **Palmer, A. Mitchell**; **Red Raids**.

REF.: Adams, *Incredible Era;* Admic, *Dynamite;* Allen, *Only Yesterday;* Amory, *The Proper Bostonians;* Baldwin, *We Saw It Happen;* Bechhofer-Roberts, *Famous American Trials;* Block, *Science vs. Crime;* Borchard, *Convicting the Innocent;* Brooks, *The Flowering of New England;* Broun, *Collected Edition;* Busch, *Prisoners at the Bar; CBA;* Commanger, *The American Mind;* Cooke, *A Generation on Trial;* Ehrmann, *The Case That Will Not Die;* ____, *The Untried Case: The Sacco and Vanzetti Case and the Morelli Gang;* Elliott, *Agent of Death;* Fast, *The Passion of Sacco and Vanzetti;* Felix, *Protest: Sacco-Vanzetti and the Intellectuals;* Fraenkel, *The Sacco and Vanzetti Case;* Frankfurter, *The Case of Sacco and Vanzetti;* ____ and Gardner, *The Letters of Sacco and Vanzetti;* Furneaux, *Courtroom USA;* Goodman, *The Correspondence of Murder;* Hastings, *The Other Mr. Churchill;* Heppenstall, *Bluebeard and After;* Hibbert, *The Roots of Evil;* Hoffman, *The Twenties;* Joughin and Morgan, *The Legacy of Sacco and Vanzetti;* Leighton, *The Aspirin Age, 1919-1941;* Lowenthal, *The Federal Bureau of Investigation;* Luhan, *Intimate Memories;* Lyons, *Assignment in Utopia;* ____, *The Life and Death of Sacco and Vanzetti;* Marks, *Thirteen Days;* Massachusetts General Court, *Record of Public Hearing Before Joint Committee on the Judiciary of Massachusetts Lesislature on the Resolution...Recommending a Posthumous Pardon for Nicola Sacco and Bartolomeo Vanzetti;* Mencken, *The Days of H.L. Mencken;* Montgomery, *The Twenties;* Montgomery, *Sacco-Vanzetti: The Murder and the Myth;* Musmanno, *After Twelve Years;* ____, *Verdict;* Nash, *Crime Chronology;* Playfair, *Crime in Our Century;* Powers, *Secrecy and Power;* Raby, *Fifty Famous Trials;* Reynolds, *Courtroom;* Roberts, *Famous American Trials;* Robinson, *Science Catches the Criminal;* Runyun, *Trials and Other Tribulations;* Russell, *Tragedy in Dedham;* Sann, *The Lawless Decade;* Scott, *The Concise Encyclopedia of Crime and Criminals;* Sheridan, *I Killed for the Law;* Shore, *Crime and Its Detection;* Snyder and Morris, *A Treasury of Great Reporting;* Thorwald, *The Century of the Detective;* ____, *Marks of Cain; Transcript of the Record of the Trial of Nicolo Sacco and Bartolomeo Vanzetti in the Courts of Massachusetts and Subsequent Proceedings, 1920-27;* Watters and Gillers, *Investigating the FBI;* Weeks, *Commonwealth vs. Sacco and Vanzetti;* Whitehead, *The FBI Story;* Wilson, *Encyclopedia of Murder;* (DRAMA), Anderson, *Gods of the Lightning;* ____, *Winterset;* Rice, *We the People;* (FICTION), Sinclair, *Boston.*

Sach, Amelia, 1873-1903, and **Walters, Annie**, d.1903, Brit., mur. Along with an accomplice, Annie Walters, Amelia Sach operated a home in London for unwed mothers. Sach ran advertisements offering their services before and during the birth stating the "baby can remain", leading the mothers to believe Sach and Walters would arrange for adoption.

In addition to paying the basic fees, unwary mothers who did not wish to keep their children were usually charged from £25 to £30 to arrange for adoption. The sad reality was that once the child was born and an "arrangement" agreed upon, Sach turned the baby over to Walters who would poison the infant and then dispose of the body. They would then split the fees.

For an unknown reason, in 1902 Walters took two of the children home with her where each of them unfortunately "died." Her landlord happened to be a policeman whose wife became suspicious when still a third child Walters brought home disappeared. Annie Walters told authorities a "boutful" woman in a coach took the children. Sach's role as "baby farmer" was revealed, and both women were tried and found Guilty of murder.

They were hanged in January 1903 in Holloway Prison.

REF.: *CBA; Jesse, Murder and its Motives;* Laurence, *A History of Capital Punishment;* Nash, *Look For the Woman;* O'Donnell, *Should Women Hang?;* Shew, *A Companion to Murder; Taylor's Principles and Practice of Medical Jurisprudence.*

Sacheverell, William, 1638-91, Brit., jur. Helped lead investigation of Titus Oates' Popish Plot. He joined Parliament in 1670. He also helped create the British Bill of Rights. REF.: *CBA.*

Assassins firing into President Sadat's party as he reviews the military parade.

Sadat, Anwar, 1918-81, Egypt, pres., assass. The murder of Egypt's president Anwar Sadat on Oct. 6, 1981, was almost as spectacular as the massive military parade Sadat was reviewing at that moment. In fact, many of those in the reviewing stand, Sadat included, thought that the soldiers rushing toward them with automatic weapons raised in their direction were actually part of the celebration. Moments before he was fatally shot, President Sadat, one of the most enlightened leaders in Egypt's history, raised his arm and snapped a salute at the man about to send four bullets into his body.

The assassination of Sadat was not an impulsive act, but one that had been some time in the making. Many plots had been fermenting for several years, with some nearing completion almost two years earlier. Sadat knew that he had been marked for death by Islamic extremists and other radical groups infesting a Middle East in almost constant revolution for a decade. But this was an accepted way of life for Arab leaders throughout the century. In Egypt, one coup followed another, as one might expect regular elections in Western countries. But in Egypt, the coups were invariably at gunpoint while in neighboring states blood flowed as one despotic rule replaced another in a weary system that saw the names of tyrants change but oppressive tyranny remain. Anwar Sadat was one of the few Arab leaders to alter that system, to break the political shackles worn for generations in his impoverished country.

Sadat came from a middle-class background and early on entered the military, becoming a cadet in the Egyptian Army in 1937. While still in his late teens he befriended another cadet, Gamal Abdel Nasser. Both youths believed that Egypt suffered under two corruptive influences, that of their own rulers and those their rulers took orders from—the British. Upon entering the Egyptian Officer Corps, Sadat organized a group he called the Free Officers corps, an organization bent on establishing an Egypt free of foreign colonialism. In 1942, Sadat was arrested for seditious activities, although he had never planned a violent overthrow of the government. Released in 1948, Sadat emerged to find that his Free Officer Corps was still intact and had been nurtured to a potent force by his close friend Nasser.

Reinstated in the army, Sadat worked as Nasser's top aide. Both men planned a bloodless coup in Egypt, one which would finally overthrow the venal King Farouk and cause the overpowering influence of the British to cease. As Sadat would later point out, the British secretary for oriental affairs situated in the British Embassy in Cairo was the real ruler of Egypt, dictating policy and procedure at the country's highest level. At Nasser's right hand during the July 23, 1952, revolution was Anwar Sadat. Nasser sent Sadat, then a full colonel in the army, to Alexandria to confront King Farouk and order the bloated, utterly corrupt sovereign to abdicate and leave the country. With the army and Nasser in complete control of Egypt at the time, Farouk had no choice but to go into lavish exile. The departure of Farouk, according to Sadat, was his boyhood dream of Egyptian freedom come true. Yet it would be four more years before the British evacuated the country, and still independence did not bring about democracy.

Sadat soon learned that Nasser, despite all his well-intentioned plans and promises, never had any intention of setting up a free electorate. He presided over a one-party system—a form of socialism that disguised a regime as totalitarian as that of the deposed Farouk. Nasser kept Sadat as his top aide, confiding to him his worst fears, for he was a man plagued by nightmares and ghosts of assassins. He saw plotters and conspirators everywhere and distrusted all but Sadat who served him loyally, if too silently. Sadat, by his own later admissions, never argued with his boyhood friend but carried out his policies without voicing opposition or criticism. For eighteen years, Sadat dutifully acted as Nasser's liege man but only toward the end of Nasser's life did Sadat realize that he was expected to replace Nasser. This Nasser told him only a few months before he died of a heart attack in September 1970.

When Anwar Sadat was sworn in as president of Egypt, he inherited a nation in economic ruin. Worse, Nasser had indentured Egypt to the U.S.S.R., and the Soviets dictated policies and procedures that went far beyond what the British had practiced for dozens of years. The Soviets made daily demands on Sadat without ever fulfilling their promises of economic support. Sadat could turn to no other major country for support as Nasser had all but severed relations with most of the Western powers—especially alienating the U.S. by his pro-Soviet policies. This stance had left Egypt on the verge of perpetual bankruptcy and Sadat desperately tried to extricate himself from Soviet domination. Further, the 1967 defeat of Egypt by Israel had brought the country's image to an all-time low. Internally, thanks to Nasser's half-baked socialistic movement, the country was overrun with scores of Marxist groups planning their own coups. In July 1972, Sadat broke with the U.S.S.R., expelling more than 15,000 Soviet engineers and workers. He immediately opened friendly talks with the U.S. in an effort to strengthen Egypt's economic position.

In October 1973, Sadat sent Egyptian forces in a swift tank attack which captured the Suez Canal and tore through the Israeli-occupied Sinai. This later became known as the Yom Kippur War, one which ended with Egypt at a slight military disadvantage but one which considerably boosted the image of Egypt and Sadat as a decisive leader. At home Sadat had instituted many reforms, closing detention centers and prohibiting arbitrary arrests. He became as popular a leader as Nasser, and the Egyptian parliament universally re-elected him to his post as president for another six years in 1976. Though Sadat had paid lip service to Arab nationalists and Islamic radicals such as PLO (Palestine Liberation Organization) leader Yassar Arafat, he sought the friendship of Western countries, particularly the U.S., and in November 1977, made the surprising step of approaching Israel with offers of a long-lasting peace between the two continually-warring countries. This move shocked and angered the radical Arab countries and incensed the Islamic fundamentalists, but Sadat proceeded to cement relationships with Israel, going to that country to publicly embrace Prime Minister Menachem Begin.

Meeting with Begin and U.S. president Jimmy Carter at Camp David, Md., in September 1978, Sadat signed the peace accords that finally brought peace between Egypt and Israel, a truly historic agreement. For this heroic and far-sighted act, Sadat and Begin were awarded the Nobel Peace Prize. This act, more than any other by the liberal Sadat, so angered Islamic radicals and terrorists that many underground groups vowed to kill him. When the ousted shah of Iran sought refuge in Egypt in June 1979, Sadat offered him sanctuary. The shah, despite the demands of radicals in Teheran for his return for trial, remained in Egypt where he died. This act of kindness on Sadat's part further infuriated his growing number of enemies, not the least of whom was Colonel Muammar Qaddafi, the leader of Libya and financier of world terrorists who had long lobbied for Sadat's assassination, calling him "a traitor to Islam." In Spring 1980, Sadat flew to Washington, D.C., to confer with President Carter. His plane was to stop over in the Azores for refueling but intelligence agents spotted some of Qaddafi's known assassins arriving in the Azores some days before Sadat's plane was to land. The U.S. agents notified Washington and Sadat's plane was rerouted, the would-be assassins left with no one to shoot.

Though Sadat appeared to many Arabs as a compromiser, he nevertheless attempted to advance the Palestinian cause by meeting with President Ronald Reagan in August 1981, urging the U.S. to enter negotiations with the PLO. Upon his return to Egypt, Sadat was confronted with a mounting resistance to his regime, causing him to imprison more than 1500 political dissidents. Among these was the brother of an Islamic fanatic, Khaled Ahmed Shawki el Islambouli, a lieutenant in the Egyptian Army and leader of an extremist sect called Takfir Wal-Hajira ("Repentance of the Holy Flight"). Oddly enough, the founder of this sect, Sayyed Kotob, had plotted the assassination of Nasser in 1966 and had been caught and hanged before putting his plan into action. The 30-year-old terrorist organization, nurtured by a few members up to the time of Sadat's death, was an offshoot of the outlawed Muslim Brotherhood dedicated to the killing of any Muslim leader branded as a heretic and traitor to Islamic fundamentalism. The Brotherhood proudly traced its own origins back to the eleventh century, claiming to have historic links with the dreaded Order of the Assassins. Stranger still is the fact that upon assuming power, Sadat pardoned several members of Takfir Wal-Hajira and released them from prison. Islambouli vowed revenge against Sadat for the 1981 imprisonment of his brother and began planning his assassination of the president. He selected Oct. 6, 1981, as his target date, pinpointing an event upon which all Egypt would be focused. Islambouli chose Oct. 6 as the attack day, when Sadat would be reviewing troops in Cairo in celebration of the anniversary of the Yom Kippur War.

It was a bold plan in that Sadat would be exposed to public view, and the conspirators would have instant access to him. But Sadat would also be extremely well guarded as he stood in the reviewing stand to take the salutes from his passing legions. In front of the stand and flanking it would be his special palace guard, commanded by General Mohammed Abdel-Halim Abu Ghazala, defense minister and the man who had planned the sneak attack in 1973 when Egyptian troops attacked and overran Israeli positions in the Suez. Plainclothes detectives would be planted throughout the crowd in the reviewing stand. Sadat himself was aware that there was an assassination plot afoot in recent weeks, one that he considered serious, but he was a charismatic, open man who refused to shelter himself behind phalanxes of guards and barred palace doors. That had been Nasser's way, Farouk's way, and the way of dozens more of Egypt's despotic rulers. He felt he had brought a new open society to his country and that the more visible he was the more confidence his people would have in his administration.

Islambouli knew and planned to take advantage of Sadat's willingness to expose himself; he had studied the man, he later admitted, and realized that he could almost strike at will against a man he considered to be a traitor to the fundamentals of Islam. Moreover, Islambouli chose the day of the big military parade to make sure that the assassination would be well covered by the nation's press, and the impact of the killing would, he assumed, bring about sympathy for the murderers and help to more quickly establish the kind of religious government Ayatollah Ruhollah Khomeini had created in Iran. The young lieutenant, who was, ironically, about the same age as Sadat when Sadat created *his* revolutionary cadre, estimated that he would need four others to complete the job of killing the president. His right hand man, Hussein Abbas Muhammad, was already in the army, a reservist who would have the right to appear in the parade. Three others, however, were civilians, and it would be difficult for Islambouli to smuggle these men onto the Cairo parade grounds. The master assassin solved the problem a few days before the parade by sending three of his regular soldiers on sick leave and, at the last minute, substituting his own civilian killers whom he dressed in army fatigues like himself and Muhammad. These five men were to perform the actual murder, but at least seventeen others were involved in the plot one way or another. All of these extremists belonged to the terrorist group Takfir Wal-Hajira. Though small, Islambouli's group had the endorsement of powerful Islamic fundamentalist terrorist groups throughout the Middle East—spiritual if not financial.

Normally no ammunition was ever issued at any military parade (in Egypt as well as anywhere else), but somehow Islambouli obtained ammunition for his Kalashnikov submachine gun and the three AK47 assault rifles his men were to use. He also obtained two grenades and some stun bombs and then loaded his men into the back of a Russian-built army truck which was to appear in that section of the parade displaying heavy artillery, scheduled for the end of the parade. As had been the custom with the Order of Assassins nine centuries earlier when preparing to commit a political assassination, Islambouli passed small doses of hashish to his men, ordering them to inhale and chew the drug to prepare their minds for what they were about to do. The parade began before noon and Islambouli sat sweating in the rear of the truck for ninety minutes as the massive parade, with bugles blaring and drums beating, filed past the large reviewing stand where Sadat and other dignitaries sat casually chatting. The president was in the front row of the reviewing stand, flanked by his 52-year-old vice president, Hosni Mubarak, and General Ghazala. The 62-year-old Sadat was unmistakable in the crowd. He wore a distinctive black army uniform and black boots and spurs. Around his neck shone his Star of Sinai medal. He appeared calm and happy in taking the salutes from his soldiers as they swung past in strict military order. This was the kind of event Sadat relished. He enjoyed showing himself to his people, especially his troops, believing, and rightly so, that he had restored Egypt's self-pride and increased its status as a Middle East power.

At a little after 1 p.m., a roaring flight of F-4 Phantom jets, followed by Mirage trainer planes, began passing over the reviewing stand. Sadat and his retinue stood up, looked skyward, pointing at the air show. At that precise moment, the truck carrying Islambouli and his men stopped right before the reviewing stand. Inside the truck Islambouli suddenly turned to the driver and ordered him to halt. The lieutenant and his men then jumped from the rear of the vehicle. Those in the stands who bothered to take their eyes from the skies thought the truck had broken down and that the men were preparing to push it. They turned, however, away from the truck, slung down their weapons and began to move toward the reviewing stand which was only twenty yards away. Islambouli shouted at his men: "Kill the traitor! Kill the traitor! Attack!"

He threw a grenade that landed far short of the stand and exploded without causing any injuries. Another assassin tossed the second grenade but this failed to go off. Islambouli and the others than charged the reviewing stand. In a split second Sadat took his eyes from the passing jets and glanced at his attackers, confused by their actions. Whatever he was thinking at that deadly moment somehow fused the thought into a final military gesture. He brought his hand to the bill of his cap and saluted Islambouli and his men. Perhaps he thought this might cause the attackers to pause and instinctively revert to military protocol, ceasing their attack. If so, Sadat did not reckon that three of his attackers were not soldiers but dedicated assassins bent on his death. Their gunfire riddled the crowd which was now in pandemonium, those in the stands throwing themselves to the ground. Sadat remained standing, a stoic figure, as his killers ran forward. His personal secretary, Fawzi Abdul Hefez, leaped forward holding a chair, attempting to place this in front of Sadat and the hail of bullets now striking the reviewing stand. Hefez was sent crashing to the floor of the reviewing stand with a bullet in his leg.

Sadat was then struck by four bullets, two entering the left side of his chest, one striking near the collarbone that lodged in his neck, and one that smashed into his right leg above the knee. (Doctors later discovered a huge gash in the right leg that they could not explain.) For a second or two the president swayed glassy-eyed and then collapsed into his chair. At that moment General Ghazala, receiving a slight head wound which caused his entire face to run blood, jumped for the microphone and began barking orders to his troopers to shoot down the assassins. But the palace guard had already been shot to pieces, several of these troopers lying dead in front and around the reviewing stand. Ghazala kept shouting at his men to strike down the killers and, at one point, Islambouli faced him squarely but did not fire his weapon; either it was jammed or he had hesitated for arcane reasons. In the confusion guards and assassins mixed in front of the stand, the loyal troopers unable to make out the assassins from their own men because of the khaki uniforms they wore. One guard reportedly picked up a pike and raced toward a man he thought was one of the assassins, skewering the man on the spot. Within minutes of General Ghazala's microphone orders to his troops, waves of soldiers washed over the frantic gunmen, disarming them and beating them to the ground. In the stands all was havoc and death. Eleven in the reviewing stands were dead, including Omani prince Shabeb bin Teymour, Bishop Samuel of the Coptic church, Major-General Hassan Allam, and Mohammed Rashwan, Sadat's personal photographer who had just finished snapping a photo of a skyward-looking and smiling President Sadat before the fusillade killed him. Four Egyptian soldiers who had put their bodies in front of Sadat and faced the charging killers were also dead. Thirty people were wounded and these included Said Marei, presidential adviser; Belgium ambassador Claude Ruelle; Australian first secretary John Woods; Irish defense minister Jim Tully; Abd Rabb Enabi Hafex, Sadat's military chief-of-staff, and Vice President Mubarak who immediately went to the fallen Sadat and discovered that he was still alive.

As Islambouli and the other assassins were led away, a helicopter quickly landed at the parade grounds, and Sadat was removed to Maadi Hospital where Egypt's chief surgeon, Major-General Karim, along with a dozen other top medical specialists, began a two-hour battle to save the president's life. Sadat, with blood gushing from his mouth, arrived at the hospital twenty minutes after he had been shot. Physicians began giving Sadat blood transfusions and later performed heart massages, but the president grew steadily weaker and died two hours later. Cause of death was listed as "violent nervous shock, internal bleeding in the chest cavity, with the left lung and major blood vessels at the bottom of the left lung torn."

Egypt had lost its most significant leader of the century. Mubarak, a competent and loyal Sadat stalwart, took over the reigns of government while more than 800 dissidents were arrested on suspicion of having been involved in the assassination. This number soon dwindled to twenty-four who were indicted on premeditated murder and conspiracy. This group was tried en masse on Nov. 21, 1981, in Cairo in an open court where the prisoners were held in a large cage. They clung to the wires and shouted slogans, obscenities, and threats at their accusers and prosecutors. The five assassins were identified as Muslim fundamentalist fanatics who had sought to overthrow the civilian government, replacing it with a Khomeini-style religious regime. They each loudly proclaimed that it had been their ambition to end "permissive Western influence" in Egypt by killing Sadat. The arrogant Islambouli freely admitted to plotting the assassination and carrying it out with Muhammad and the others but he emphatically denied that his acts had anything to do with eliminating the entire Egyptian administration. He demanded that Egypt's defense minister testify so that he could report Islambouli's conduct during the assassination. "Get Abu Ghazala here to testify," Islambouli shouted. "Ask him. During the shooting I looked him in the eyes and said, 'I don't want you, I want your dog (Sadat)!'"

Five of the defendants, including Islambouli and Muhammad, were condemned to death, while seventeen others were given sentences ranging from life at hard labor in prison to smaller sentences. Two of the defendants were acquitted. Islambouli and Muhammad, having been Egyptian soldiers, were afforded the military style of execution by firing squad while the other three civilian assassins were ignominiously hanged, all of them dying on Apr. 15, 1982. Islambouli, according to witnesses at his execution, went to his death calmly, stoically proclaiming the righteousness of his cause. Many curious and unexplained facts about the assassination were lightly touched upon at the mass trial of the assassins or not at all. It was never explained how Islambouli knew exactly when Sadat's attention and that of most others in the reviewing stand would be riveted upon the skies to watch the air show. Even more puzzling was the fact that the bodies of two plainclothes detectives, part of a contingent of private guards who protected Sadat, had been found shot to death in the rear of the reviewing stand a few minutes *before* Islambouli and his men alighted from the truck to open fire on their prey. This, coupled to some of Sadat's strange wounds, tended to support the theory that there had been others in the reviewing stand who were part of the plot and had opened fire from behind the dignitaries to coordinate the attack being made from the front by Islambouli and others. President Mubarak later confirmed that the Sadat assassination had, indeed, been a concerted attack aimed at eradicating the entire administration. The question was also raised repeatedly by Western journalists how Qaddafi's government-controlled radio station in Libya had announced Sadat's assassination with exact details long before the Egyptian authorities had even put those details together.

The triumphant Islambouli behind bars during his trial.

In the heart of Islam, for days following Sadat's murder, there was jubilation in Beirut, Teheran, and other Middle Eastern cities, with Islamic fanatics firing automatic weapons in the air, performing bizarre dances, and giving street fetes. Sadat was considered by these violent terrorists to be an arch foe of anachronistic fundamentalism, the very reason why Sadat was heralded in the West as one of the most enlightened leaders of the Arab world. Sadat was, in the world view, a paradoxical and unpredictable man who led not only his own people with resolution and firmness but one who could put aside his own vanity and national pride for a greater good. To the fundamentalist Arab, Sadat's embrace of Israel was a sign of degenerate weakness, but to the rest of the world it was a sign of towering, inner strength. Sadat had made the first move toward peace in a region of the earth where peace had not been known in decades. Sadat pushed for peace and obtained it, though it cost him his life. See: **Order of the Assassins, The; Qaddafi, Muammar al.**

REF.: *CBA;* Cremeans, *The Arabs and the World: Nasser's Arab Nationalist Policy;* Demaris, *Brothers in Blood: The International Terrorist Network;* Dobson and Payne, *Counterattack—The West's Battle Against the Terrorists;* ____, *The Terrorists—Their Weapons, Leaders and Tactics;*

Franzius, *History of the Order of Assassins;* Lewis, *The Assassins, A Radical Sect in Islam;* O'Ballance, *Language of Violence—The Blood Politics of Terrorism;* Sadat, *Revolt on the Nile;* St. John, *The Boss: The Story of Gamal Abdel Nasser;* Wheelock, *Nasser's New Egypt;* Wilson, *Encyclopedia of Modern Murder;* Wynn, *Nasser of Egypt.*

Sade, Donatien Alphonse François Comte **de** (Marquis **de Sade**), 1740-1814, Fr., asslt.-kid.-rape. The old and respected name of de Sade was given new meaning in France following the death of the marquis in 1814. Sadism, meaning the sexual pleasure derived from inflicting pain, entered the language due to the libertine habits of the marquis, who was born into the family of Louis Joseph de Bourbon, the Prince of Condé.

At the age of fourteen, de Sade went off to fight in the Seven Years' War against Germany. He served in the military for nine years, rising to the rank of captain of the Burgundy Horse, but the life of a soldier was not to his liking. De Sade resigned his commission in 1763 and spent much of his time in Paris brothels, where he encouraged his young charges to flog him as a means of sexual gratification. His conduct piqued the sensibilities of King Louis XV, who had him jailed for his debaucheries, but following his release, de Sade began a career of unbridled orgy that did not let up until he died at the Charenton Lunatic Asylum in December 1814.

De Sade hired a baker's widow, Rose Keller, to work as his housekeeper at the Arcueil estate on Easter 1768. He bound, gagged, and flogged the woman until she was nearly dead. He locked her up and promised to kill her the next day, but Keller escaped by lowering herself from a window by a bed sheet. She reported the attack to the gendarmes, who arrested de Sade for kidnapping and assault. He was sentenced to six months in the prison at Lyons. When he was released, de Sade faced an even unkinder fate: the relentless pursuit of his mother-in-law, Madame de Montreuil who vowed to avenge her family name at all costs. She would not be happy, she said, until "I have had the beast cast away in prison—or in a madhouse—for the rest of his evil life."

In June 1772, the "affair of the poisoned sweetmeats" commenced when de Sade and his hulking servant Latour engaged four Marseilles prostitutes. To encourage the women to beat him with a grotesque, nail-studded whip, de Sade offered them a sampling of sweets from a metal tin. The bonbons contained a mixture of aniseed and cantharides, believed by de Sade to be a powerful sexual stimulant known as "Spanish Fly." Two of the women, including the city's most famous prostitute Marguerite Coste, suffered stomach cramps. When she recovered sufficiently, she swore out a warrant for de Sade's arrest. He fled the province with his sister-in-law, Mademoiselle de Launay, and his faithful servant. De Sade's property was confiscated and his wife was made the guardian of his children.

For the rest of his life, the marquis was forced to run from his vengeful mother-in-law and the authorities. He spent many years in and out of the Bastille and the fortress of Vincennes. In his gloomy cell in the Bastille, de Sade wrote *Les 120 Journées de Sodome* (1784) on a single role of paper thirty-nine feet long, and *Les Crimes de l'amour* (1788). During the French Revolution, de Sade was revered as a hero of the Republic for the many indignities he suffered at the hands of the ancien-regime. He was appointed the head of one of Paris's ruling revolutionary committees, but he was adjudged to be "too lenient" by the Jacobins. His many profligacies proved too much for Robespierre, who had him thrown in prison and sentenced to death, but when the radical leader of the Convention was himself guillotined, de Sade's life was once again spared. For thirteen years beginning in 1801, de Sade languished in the lunatic asylum at Charenton. Emperor Napoléon Bonaparte ordered that he never see the light of day again, but this experience provided de Sade with ample opportunity to reflect on his misspent life and sexual adventures. What emerged from those long periods of incarceration were such classics of erotic literature as *Justine,* or *Virtue Unpunished* (1791), and *Juliette,* or *Vice Rewarded* (1798). He died on Dec. 2, 1814, leaving behind thirteen years of writings which were burned by his embarrassed offspring.

REF.: Blanchet, *Lautrémont et Sade; CBA;* Scott, *The Concise Encyclopedia of Crime and Criminals;* (FICTION), Endore, *Satan's Saint: A Novel About the Marquis de Sade;* Lely, *The Marquis de Sade;* Summers, *The Geography of Witchcraft;* Wilson, *Witches;* (FILM), *The Persecution and Assassination of Jean-Paul Marat as Performed By, 1967, the Inmates of the Asylum of Charenton under the Direction of the Marquis de Sade,* 1967; *De Sade,* 1969; *Justine,* 1969.

Sadler, Dora Martha Spalding, b.1886, Brit., mur. Dora Sadler was a nanny for two children in a family in West Kensington. She became so possessive of the children that she developed an insane jealousy of the children's mother. The mother, upset by the developing situation, gave Sadler a notice.

Later that night of Nov. 11, 1923, Sadler, distraught over losing her beloved charges, put them to bed, turned the heater on, and laid down beside them to die. The children died but Sadler lived.

Charged with murder, Sadler was found Guilty and sentenced to death. She later was given a reprieve because her sanity at the time of the murders was questioned.

REF.: *CBA;* Nash, *Look For the Woman;* Shew, *A Second Companion to Murder.*

Sadler, Fern L. (AKA: **Frank Craig**), b.c.1899, and **Rankin, Gilman D.**, and **Wagoner, Frank**, and **Schlagle, Harvey**, prom. 1927-28, U.S., rob. In July 1927, Fern L. Sadler, an employee of the Bureau of Power and Light in Los Angeles, placed a want-ad in a local newspaper.

BIG MONEY FOR MAN WITH PLENTY OF NERVE AND GOOD HEAD. BOX NUMBER 6666

Many people responded to the ad. Sadler decided on Gilman Rankin as the man who should help him carry out a daring daylight robbery of his employers. A friend of Sadler's, Frank Wagoner, was hired to kidnap the watchman the morning of the robbery, for two hours. After considerable preparation, Sadler, Wagoner, Gilman, and a fourth accomplice, Harvey Schlagle, carried out the plan on Sept. 26, 1927.

Using a pair of borrowed and unloaded handguns, Sadler burst in on his own office heavily disguised. It was payday for his coworkers in the Distribution Department. The robbers casually strode into the teller's cage and ordered the contents of the safe removed. Within ten minutes, the frightened cashiers loaded $73,600 in cash into two white canvas bags. The crime was carried off flawlessly while outside, dozens of Los Angeles pedestrians walked by oblivious to what was happening inside.

For the next four months detectives were baffled. Finally, on Jan. 20, 1928, acting Captain Jack Trainor of the Georgia Street station reported the arrest of a suspect: 29-year-old Fern Sadler who had masterminded the robbery while on his company-paid vacation. The facts of the case came to light when Captain William Cahill interrogated the suspect at length, finagling a confession out of him that implicated the other accomplices. The $73,600 had been split four ways he explained. But the chief beneficiary was Sadler who had pocketed $58,600. All but Rankin were convicted of second-degree robbery. They were sentenced to one year to life imprisonment at San Quentin Penitentiary. Rankin, who had steadfastly refused to cooperate with prosecutors, was tried for first-degree robbery, found Guilty, and sentenced to seven years to life in prison. REF.: *CBA.*

Sáenz, Manuela (AKA: **La Sáenz**), 1797-1856, Col., rebel. Entered romantic relationship with South American revolutionary leader Simon Bolivar in 1822, and backed his efforts throughout remaining eight years of his life. She worked as a candy vendor in Paita, Peru, following her exile from Bogotá in 1834. REF.: *CBA.*

Saffran, Fritz, b.c.1899, and **Kipnik, Erich**, and **Augustin, Ella**, prom. 1930, Ger., arson-mur. Fritz Saffran was well-liked by his employees at the Platz Furniture Store in Rastenburg, Prussia. By all appearances, Saffran was a successful young businessman. But actually the reverse was true. The Platz Company teetered on the verge of bankruptcy. Attempts to stave off creditors included falsification of the ledgers, but Saffran finally decided on more drastic measures after hearing about a burning car murder.

Saffran decided that he should fake his own death and then collect on an insurance policy valued at £7,000 British currency. First he needed to find a body, so he enlisted the help of his clerk Erich Kipnik, and a young woman with whom he having an affair, Ella Augustin. They organized a "murder camp" in the Nikolai Forest, where they planned to waylay the intended victim. On Sept. 12, 1930, they met unemployed dairyman Friedrich Dahl, twenty-five, outside Luisenhof. Either Saffran or Kipnik killed Dahl. It was never clearly established who the culprit actually was. Three days later the body was placed inside the furniture store which was doused in gasoline and set on fire. Thirty employees dashed out the door to safety. Kipnik escaped through the flames and notified the fire department that his boss, Saffran, had perished.

The insurance company and the fire department sifted through the remains and found the body, and a watch which belonged to Saffran. The insurance company seemed reasonably satisfied. However, two days later Augustin hired a chauffeur to take her sick mother to Konigsberg. The ailing woman turned out to be Saffran, who was well known to the driver, a former furniture store employee. A friend of the driver reported the tale to the police, and Saffran and his conspirators were soon arrested. Through dental charts, Dahl was identified as the victim. The three were put on trial in Bartenstein on Mar. 23, 1931. Saffran and Kipnik accused one another of firing three bullets into Dahl's head. The jury sentenced both men to death, and Augustin to five years in prison for her part in the crime. The death sentences were commuted to life imprisonment.

REF.: Boar, *The World's Most Infamous Murders; CBA;* Wilson, *Encyclopedia of Murder.*

Saft, Howard E., and **Fialkow, Norman**, prom. 1977, U.S., fraud. In a twenty-three count indictment handed down in April 1976, Howard E. Saft, president of Adlay Jewelry Inc., was charged with misrepresenting his firm's financial status to secure a $5 million loan to stave off bankruptcy. Norman Fialkow, an accountant, was indicted for falsifying bank statements on Saft's behalf.

The business eventually was declared bankrupt in 1974. A portion of the $2 million that Saft received in 1973 had been diverted to his own private use, in order to refurbish his East Hampton home on Long Island, N.Y.

Saft, who pleaded guilty to tax evasion and two counts of fraud, was sentenced to three years in prison by Judge Lawrence Pierce in the Manhattan Federal District Court in March 1977. Norman Fialkow pleaded guilty to falsifying bank loan statements and received a year and a day in prison and was forced to relinquish his license as a public accountant. REF.: *CBA.*

Sager, Harold G. (AKA: **Colonel Harold S. McClintock**), prom. 1967, U.S., fraud. In 1967, a charitable organization known as the Disabled American Veterans (DAV) hired a Chicago businessman, Harold G. Sager, to solicit leading corporations for merchandise contributions with the understanding that the DAV would get 51 percent of the sale of these proceeds. In return for doing business with Sager and the DAV, donors could write off the contribution as a tax deduction.

Sager sold the items to an accomplice at low prices. Then, he turned over the 51 percent to the veterans organization, and then secretly resold the goods at inflated prices. Sager realized a handsome profit on the merchandise, originally valued at $2 million. The self-described "colonel" was convicted of mail fraud and given a five-year probationary sentence.

REF.: *CBA;* Kahn, *Fraud.*

Said Halim Pasha, Mehmet, 1863-1921, Turk., pres., assass. Senator and president of Council of State following Turkish Revolution. He served as grand vizier of the Ottoman Empire from 1913-16, and signed a covert treaty allying Turkey and Germany, despite personal opposition to having the empire enter WWI. He was jailed in Malta by the British from 1918-21, and assassinated in Rome shortly after his release. REF.: *CBA.*

Said Mohammed Pasha, d.1928, Egypt, prime minister, attempt. assass. Succeeded Boutros Pasha as prime minister in 1910 and worked with British for reforms. While prime minister he narrowly escaped an assassination attempt. REF.: *CBA.*

Saietta, Ignazio (AKA: **Lupo the Wolf**), 1877-1944, U.S., org. crime. Most of the many Black Hand gangsters in New York and other large U.S. cities at the turn of the century operated independently, shaking down local businessmen and upscale residents of the ghetto for a few dollars, but Ignazio Saietta, better known as Lupo the Wolf, was ten times deadlier. The mere mention of Lupo the Wolf in the crowded tenement district of Italian Harlem would strike terror into the hearts of the fearful peasants, who dreaded the day when they might become victims. This cold-blooded Black Hander never hesitated to assassinate an enemy, real or imagined.

Black Hander Ignazio Saietta.

Saietta arrived in New York from his native Sicily in 1899. Over the next two years he acquired a reputation as the murderous leader of the Morellos, then the foremost Mafia power in "Little Italy." His "soldiers" were made to understand that anything less than unswerving loyalty to him was punishable by death. It was long rumored that Saietta had personally done away with a family member on the mere suspicion that he was going to betray him.

The killings were done at the Murder Stable, located on East 107th Street in Italian Harlem. Neighborhood residents soon became accustomed to the anguished screams of the victims, who often underwent ghastly tortures before being put to death. The police seldom ventured into this area. There were few Italians courageous enough to report the goings-on here, lest they become a victim themselves. After years of operating above the law Saietta was at last arrested for a counterfeiting ring he ran in the Catskill Mountains. Sent to prison for thirty years in 1910, Saietta was paroled in June 1920. A year later, Attorney General Harry M. Daugherty granted him permission to travel to Italy in hopes that he would find the surroundings so pleasant that he wouldn't come back. To the dismay of the federal authorities, however, he returned to New York in 1922 to enter into the wholesale fruit and bakery business with his son. As the Prohibition gang wars heated up in the 1920s, Saietta became less and less of a factor in New York organized crime. His methods were deemed obsolete by younger Mafia leaders, who preferred to bribe their adversaries rather than face reprisals from the police and district attorney. Squeezed out of the picture by the crooks in the silk suits, Saietta retired to Brooklyn where he ran a lottery that Charles "Lucky" Luciano and the other overlords of the national crime syndicate regarded as strictly penny-ante. Later, he organized a "protection" racket that extorted sums of money from the Brooklyn bakers.

In 1936, New York governor Herbert Lehman sought the assistance of President Franklin D. Roosevelt to have Saietta sent back to prison on federal racketeering charges. Saietta was returned to prison in Atlanta, where he served a few more years before being granted his freedom. He retired to Brooklyn, where he lived out his last years quietly, no longer a force in the underworld. See: **Black Hand; Petrosino, Joseph.**

REF.: Asbury, *The Gangs of New York; CBA;* Eisenberg and Landau, *Meyer Lansky;* Kobler, *Al Capone;* Lait and Mortimer, *Chicago: Confidential;* McPhaul, *Johnny Torrio;* Nash, *Bloodletters and Badmen;* Peterson,

The Mob; Reid, *The Grim Reapers;* Thompson and Raymond, *Gang Rule in New York.*

St. Albans (Vt.) Robbery, 1864, U.S., rob. In a desperate attempt to bolster the fading hopes of the South during the waning days of the Civil War, twenty-two Confederate soldiers galloped into the town of St. Albans, Vt., on Oct. 18, 1864, to rob the local banks. They succeeded in looting the vaults of three banks of $114,522 in gold and currency. The soldiers fled the town and crossed over into Canada where the loot was presumably buried. Fourteen of the men were eventually hunted down and arrested, but the money, earmarked for the Confederate war effort, was never recovered—the robbers could not remember where they had buried their treasure.

REF.: *CBA;* Nash, *Open Files.*

St. Bartholomew's Day Massacre, See: **Charles IX**.

St. Bude, David, prom. 1929-30, Brit., burg. Like the famous American actor Lon Chaney, David St. Bude was a man of a thousand disguises. Beginning in 1929, St. Bude, a thespian of modest talents, committed a string of hotel burglaries in London. Each time the proprietor of the establishment described a different sort of individual. There were no fingerprints that could suggest to police who the culprit might be, just a collection of full beer bottles which the thief had used to weigh down his suitcases.

The robberies of the posh hotels continued for nearly a year, until Spring 1930 when the owner of a boarding house near Madame Tussaud's Waxworks reported to the Marylebone Police that her lodgers had been burgled. Detectives from the CID discovered a beer bottle, but this time there was a small identifying stamp mark on the glass, which had been put there by the Queen's Head and Artichoke pub on Albany Street.

The proprietor of the pub identified St. Bude, a repertory actor, as the man who routinely purchased three quart bottles of beer each night. The detective-sergeant investigating the case, Robert Fabian, captured St. Bude at an actor's party held in the upstairs flat of the Albany Street pub. St. Bude was convicted and sentenced to five years of penal servitude at Wandsworth Prison where he joined the amateur theatrical society.

REF.: *CBA;* Fabian, *Fabian of the Yard.*

St. Claire, Ruth (AKA: **Ruth Laeger**), 1900- , U.S., theft. When the Baumes Law was passed in New York State, the intention was to put away habitual offenders convicted of at least four felonies. When Ruth St. Clair, thirty, was sentenced to life imprisonment in March 1930, after pilfering small items valued at $121 from Manhattan's John Wanamaker department store, there was a public outcry against the injustice of the court system. The attractive ex-chorus girl said she did not need the shoplifted items, but that she was a kleptomaniac.

A blistering 500-page report submitted to Governor Franklin D. Roosevelt by John C. Maher of the New York Parole Commission, detailed St. Claire's unfortunate, if not sordid past. Ruth St. Claire was the daughter of a poor Russian Jew who settled in the squalid slums of Manhattan's lower East Side. She had been raped at age eleven by a 55-year-old grocer—an experience that put her firmly on the road to juvenile delinquency. Between 1914-30, Ruth had been arrested numerous times on shoplifting charges. Then, while serving an eight-year sentence, she developed a drug habit. Prison officials dismissed her as a "moral imbecile" who had demonstrated "anti-social" behavior. REF.: *CBA.*

St. Clair, Stephanie (AKA: **Madam Queen, Tiger from Marseilles**), prom. 1920s-30s, U.S., gamb.-org. crime. When organized crime figure Dutch Schultz lay dying in Newark City Hospital, a telegram arrived for him. It read, "As ye sow, so shall ye reap," and was signed "Madam Queen of Policy." Madam Queen, as Stephanie St. Clair like being called, was the tenacious black woman who became the numbers racket boss in Harlem in 1923. Schultz continually tried to wrest St. Clair's territory. St. Clair went to city hall. As a result of her complaints, she received special police protection from attacks by Schultz's men. When Schultz finally died, Madam Queen had secured her throne. See: **Schultz, Dutch.** REF.: *CBA.*

St. Clair, Thomas, and **Hansen, Hans**, d.1895, U.S., mur. A mutiny was scheduled aboard the Australian bark *Hesper* for the night of Dec. 22, 1892. It was to begin at midnight, when the second mate Maurice Fitzgerald took over the watch. The *Hesper* bobbed wildly on the choppy ocean waves. The wind whistled through the sails, drowning out all sounds except one—the sudden shriek of a man. The ship's officers searched the deck for a sign of the first mate, but he had vanished. Afterward, they found blood stains on the deck. A hatchet found nearby attested to the fact that Fitzgerald had been murdered and then thrown overboard.

Seamen Thomas St. Clair, Herman Sparf, and Hans Hansen were arrested and charged with murder. Under questioning they revealed their mutinous plan to seize control of the ship, kill all the officers, and sell the ship's cargo in Chile. St. Clair and Hansen were placed under ship's arrest until the vessel steamed into the port of San Francisco. The pair were convicted in the federal courts, and hanged in San Quentin yard on Oct. 18, 1895.

REF.: *CBA;* Duke, *Celebrated Criminals Cases of America.*

St. George, Anthony (Arthur Hazel, AKA: Raffles of the River), 1894-1945, Brit., fraud. Born in Liverpool in 1894, Arthur Hazel was poor and uneducated with big ambitions. When war broke out in Europe in 1914, he joined the Coldstream Guards, and changed his name to Anthony St. George.

Until 1923, St. George had tried to carve out an honest living for himself, but failed both as a teacher and as an insurance agent. In 1923, he was sent to prison for six months for stealing his employer's money. Thereafter, the lure of easy money proved to be too great a temptation. St. George singled out England's upper classes for burglary. He fancied himself an officer and a gentleman, and therefore concentrated only on the "big score." In Summer 1924, a spate of country-house burglaries in Surrey had the police up in arms. Each day there were new reports of someone breaking and entering the elegant homes of the local gentry. St. George was caught on Aug. 14 by Constable P.C. Elkins who found a torn piece of a matchbook at the home of Mr. T.G. Lucas. "Got a light?" Elkins asked the wily St. George who happened to be passing on the road. The other half of the yellow matchbook was produced and it was a perfect fit. "That's not very sporting," St. George said. He was sentenced to five years of penal servitude, just one of many prison sentences St. George would serve in his forty-six years of burglaries.

REF.: *CBA;* Cherrill, *Cherrill of the Yard.*

St. George's In the East Rituals Disturbance, 1859-60, Brit., riot. In August 1859, and again in July 1860, Scotland Yard was called on to help quell a disturbance at St. George's Church, a Protestant church in London that had been the scene of riotous behavior after the rector introduced incense, unusual images, and ceremonial robes to his service. A clergyman eventually convinced the controversial reverend to take a year's leave. A new reverend with more moderate beliefs, and one not inclined toward "ritualism," was installed as rector. His first sermon was attended by 300 on-duty policemen in case of another outbreak. REF.: *CBA.*

Saint-Germain, Comte de, c.1707-84, Fr., consp. Assigned to secret missions as diplomat under Louis XV and involved in numerous political conspiracies. He joined Landgrave Charles of Hesse in probing the occult after retiring in c.1775. REF.: *CBA.*

St. Germain, M. and **Boudin, M.**, prom. 1800s, Fr., rob.-mur. Vidocq, the criminal turned government spy who founded the French Sûrete, met two thieves named St. Germain and Boudin, who suggested that he join them in robbing the house of two old men. As St. Germain and Boudin discussed their plans over several days, they heard a rumor that Vidocq worked for the police. They changed their plan and insisted that Vidocq spend the entire day with them before they carried out the new plan of robbing a banker. Vidocq had his mistress follow them wherever they went, and once he learned the details of the plan, he dropped a note on the pavement which she picked up and took to the police. The thieves found themselves ambushed at the banker's house. Vidocq pretended to have been killed by a bullet and when St. Germain and Boudin were tried and sent to prison, they still did not know they had been expertly trapped. See: **Vidocq, Francois Victor.**

REF.: *CBA;* Dilnot, *Great Detectives and Their Methods.*

St. James, George L., See: **Therrien, Joseph W.**

St. Jean, Harvey, d.1975, U.S., (unsolv.) mur. Who wanted to kill Harvey St. Jean? The Miami Police struggled wtih this question for many days after finding his bullet-riddled body in a parking lot near the convention center on Dec. 17, 1975. Everyone in town knew St. Jean. As one of Miami's most famous criminal lawyers, he belonged to some of the most exclusive private clubs in the city, and associated with the movers and shakers of politics, entertainment, and the underworld.

St. Jean arrived penniless in Miami Beach from Holyoke, Mass., in 1939. He took a test for the police department, and secured a job as a part-time patrolman. He spent the rest of his waking hours digging ditches for the city. He later studied law and still later, in 1951, was admitted to the Florida bar. Over the next few years he built up his practice, which mostly catered to the gliterati: Harvey St. Jean enjoyed the company of celebrities. One of his clients was Jack Murphy, who pilfered the Star of India sapphire in one of the most celebrated jewel heists of the 1960s.

St. Jean was well-liked by judges and politicians, and few people had anything bad to say about this self-made man from Holyoke. It has been suggested that his assassination was ordered by Cuban drug traffickers who had retained him as legal counsel. Unhappy with certain financial arrangements, the drug kingpins may have ordered St. Jean killed. At least this is the theory Miami Police have advanced for this still-unsolved gangland killing. See: **Murphy, Jack.**

REF.: *CBA;* Trillin, *Killings.*

St. John, Oliver, c. 1598-1673, Brit., jur. Served as solicitor general from 1641-43, and acted as attorney general in 1644. He served on the Uxbridge peace commission in 1645, and as chief justice of the court of common pleas in 1648. He wrote *Case of Oliver St. John* in 1660 to protect himself from being implicated in the beheading of Charles I. REF.: *CBA.*

Saint-Just, Louis Antoine Léon de, 1767-94, Fr., consp. Joined National Convention in 1792 and Committee of Public Safety in 1793. He was a top associate of Maximilien Robespierre, with whom he was jailed and guillotined. REF.: *CBA.*

St. Laurent, Louis Stephen, 1882-1973, Can., atty. gen. Held office in House of Commons from 1942-58, and served as minister of justice and as attorney general from 1941-46 and 1948. He also served as Liberal prime minister of Canada from 1948-57. REF.: *CBA.*

St. Lawrence, Napoleon, prom. 1910, U.S., wh. slav. The glib and persuasive Napoleon St. Lawrence was a 24-year-old white slave trafficker who induced a young woman from Providence R.I., to leave the Lancaster School, in Lancaster, Mass., to become a prostitute. From April until July of 1910, St. Lawrence lived off of her earnings until the authorities caught up with him. He was sentenced on July 28, 1910, by the judge of the Sixth District Court of Rhode Island, to serve one year in the state work house. The girl was sent back to school.

REF.: *CBA;* Roe, *The Great War on White Slavery.*

St. Leger, Sir **Anthony (Sentleger)**, c.1496-1559, Brit., polit. corr. Lord deputy of Ireland from 1540-46, 1550-51, and from 1553-56. He avoided religious disputes by promising titles of nobility to leaders willing to answer to Henry VIII and reject the pope. REF.: *CBA.*

St. Leon, Ernest (AKA: **Diamond Dick**), d.1891, U.S., west. lawman. The son of a refugee from France, Ernest St. Leon was raised in San Antonio, Texas. He studied law but later joined the U.S. Cavalry, participated in a number of Indian campaigns, and eventually was promoted to sergeant. He was alleged to have shot and killed three Indians who had slain one of his men. St. Leon left the army in the 1880s and joined the Texas Rangers' Company D, where he gained the nickname "Diamond Dick" because he enjoyed decorating himself with large diamonds.

A drinking problem got St. Leon kicked out of the Rangers, but Corporal John Hughes sent him on an undercover mission which he managed so well that he was soon reinstated and given other clandestine assignments. In 1889, in Shafter, Texas, St. Leon, pretending to be an ore thief, went with three criminals and a mule train to an abandoned mine shaft. Rangers Lon Oden and John Hughes were waiting in the darkness and called to the criminals to surrender. A fight erupted, with St. Leon opening up on the thieves at close range. All three criminals were slain and buried on the mountainside. In 1891, St. Leon and a deputized citizen arrested three cowboys, but St. Leon decided to release them. All five man went to a bar to drink together. There a fight erupted and St. Leon and the deputy were shot. The deputy died immediately, St. Leon the next day.

REF.: *CBA;* Martin, *Border Boss.*

St. Osyth Witches, 1582, Brit., witchcraft. Fourteen women living in St. Osyth, England, were brought before the county session at Chelmsford in 1582 accused of witchcraft. The trial was a notable one, given the fact it was a marked departure from the customary practice of indicting women on witchcraft charges based on a single offense, or the hearsay of a neighbor. In the case of the fourteen women of St. Osyth, the crimes had more to do with a village vendetta stemming from personal jealousies, and ancient feuds that had existed among the townspeople.

The charges of witchcraft were eagerly received by Judge Bryan Darcy, who stated in his pamphlet published after the trial that he had uncovered a "nest of witches." The testimony of children ranging in age from six to nine was accepted as reliable evidence. Given the zealous attitude of the prosecutors and their willingness to accept as fact the imaginative tale spun by 9-year-old Henry Celles, it was remarkable that only two of the fourteen accused witches suffered the prescribed penalty of the law. Elizabeth Bennet, who had been indicted for murdering a married couple, and Ursula Kempe who had confessed to killing three people between October 1580 and February 1582 were found Guilty and hanged. The rest were either reprieved, acquitted, or discharged.

REF.: *CBA;* Ewen, *Witchcraft and Demonianism;* ____, *Witch Hunting and Witch Trials;* Kittredge, *Witchcraft in Old and New England;* Linton, *Witch Stories;* Notestein, *History of Witchcraft in England from 1558 to 1718;* Robbins, *The Encyclopedia of Witchcraft and Demonology;* Seth, *Witches and Their Craft; A True and Just Record of the Information, Examination and Confession of All the Witches Taken at St. Oses.*

St. Valentine's Day Massacre, 1929, U.S., org. crime. The gang wars of Chicago had taken their massive toll by the beginning of 1929. Al Capone had managed to dominate or crush all rival gangs in the city by that time, becoming the supreme overlord of crime and the king of the bootleggers, his underworld empire producing by then more than $50 million in illegal revenues. The only thorn in his side was the stubborn North Side gang that he had been battling for almost a decade. This gang, which controlled the lucrative 42nd and 43rd wards of the city, had been headed by Charles Dion O'Bannion, whom Capone had murdered in 1924, then Earl "Hymie" Weiss, whom Capone had killed in 1926. In early 1929, the North Siders were under the command of George "Bugs" Moran, last of the old North Side gang leaders.

Moran was Capone's sworn enemy and though his gang members were greatly outnumbered by Capone's legions, the feisty North Side boss refused to yield to the "beast," as he called Capone. Moran gunmen raided Capone's warehouses, hijacked his trucks, and regularly killed his best strong-arm men. Moran had tried to have Capone murdered on many occasions, by having prussic acid dropped in his soup, by ambushing his chauffeur-driven, bullet-proof car, and by bribing his own bodyguards to slay Scarface. Capone, nervous, finally moved to his Palm Island, Fla., estate to direct his Chicago operations long-distance and plan the extermination of his last gangster rival, Bugs Moran.

The North Side gang chief had his headquarters in a garage with a truck entrance at the rear, located at 2122 N. Clark Street.

The front entrance consisted of a single door and an opaque front window bearing the title S-M-C Cartage Co. Moran's men met here every day to receive their assignments—shipments of illegal liquor and beer which, in turn, were distributed to saloons and clubs throughout the North Side. The area dominated by Moran was extremely lucrative, and Capone had for many years eyed the area covetously. He not only wanted to take over the bootlegging operations there but planned to install widespread gambling dens and especially brothels. Moran, like O'Bannion and Weiss before him, refused to allow whorehouses to operate in the area, believing that such vice operations would bring on the wrath of civic leaders and religious reformers. Moreover, Moran thought such operations beneath him, such criminal pursuits being the province of "Dago pimps like Capone."

Capone took weeks developing a plan with his top aides, one that would forever end the problem of George "Bugs" Moran. Frank Nitti and "Machine Gun" Jack McGurn finally developed a plan that was devilishly simple. They knew, of course, that Chicago police routinely raided Moran's headquarters, as they did many of Capone's operations. Because most of the police force was then on mob payrolls, such raids were merely face-saving measures. Invariably, the raiding officers would arrest a few minor gang members, receive their payoff, and the gang members would later be released.

There would be another such raid targeted for Moran's North Side garage, but this time the police officers would be Capone's killers. Their uniforms would allow them uncontested entrance to the garage, McGurn told Capone, but they must be out-of-town killers because Capone's own thugs would be easily identified by Moran's men. To that end, Fred R. "Killer" Burke, an independent gunman who operated mostly in Missouri, Indiana, and Michigan, was enlisted, as was one other man whose identity has never been fully determined. He may have been Fred Goetz, also known as Shotgun Ziegler, or Vincent Leo Brothers, a St. Louis gunman Capone later used to murder Chicago *Tribune* editor Jake Lingle. Three other men were involved, a uniformed cop at the wheel of the police car—a detective's car—with a special insignia to identify it as such. The driver would be McGurn. Two other men, dressed in civilian clothes, would pretend to be plainclothes detectives. They would remain in the car until the fake uniformed officers lined up Moran and his men in the back of the garage and would then enter with submachine guns beneath their long coats. They would then shoot down the unsuspecting Moran men, and the North Side gang would no longer trouble Al Capone. The two phony detectives would be Scarface's top murder men, Albert Anselmi and John Scalise. Because both were known to Moran and his men, they would enter the garage last.

Nitti and McGurn planned the crime weeks in advance. One of their men, Sam "Golf Bag" Hunt, using an alias, rented the type of car used by Chicao Police Department detectives and took it to a rented garage on the North Side where police insignias were painted on its doors. Next, another plan was put into effect, one which would assure Moran's presence on the day of the intended massacre, Feb. 14, 1929—St. Valentine's Day—a day personally picked by Capone for the killings ("I'm gonna send Moran a Valentine he will never forget," Capone reportedly told McGurn, Nitti, and others at Palm Island during the planning stage).

Nitti contacted Abe Bernstein, head of Detroit's Purple Gang and a Capone ally, asking him to select someone in the area that Moran would trust. That person would then contact Moran and tell him he had a special shipment of bonded whiskey from Canada that he would deliver to Moran's North Side garage late in the morning of Feb. 14, 1929. The contact person in Detroit called Moran on Feb. 13, 1929, telling him he had a "load of booze, the best there is, right off the river."

"How much?" asked Moran.

"Fifty-seven dollars a case," the caller told him.

"Okay," snapped Moran. "Deliver it to the garage." He told the caller to have his truck there by 10:30 the next morning. He added that he would be present to pay the delivery man, this in response to the caller's request. Moran told the caller that all his men would be present. "We're short, and they'll want a cut."

The next morning the Moran gang assembled in the garage, or most of what was left of the gang after years of gang wars. Adam Heyer, who owned the garage and was a Moran front-man, was present. So, too, were John May, truck repairman, safecracker, and thief; speakeasy owner and Moran's bookkeeper Albert Weinshank; bootlegger, bankrobber, and Moran strong-arm man James Clark; Peter and Frank Gusenberg, Moran's top gunmen; and an odd little man, Dr. Reinhardt H. Schwimmer, an optometrist who lived in the area and was, like many in that machine-gun era, obsessed with gangsters. Schwimmer liked to drop by the garage, sip coffee, and gossip with the gangsters, thrilling to their presence. The gang tolerated him, almost as a mascot. But the gang also had a real mascot, a German shepherd named Highball, which belonged to May.

At 10:30 a.m. all these men were present in the rear of the building, waiting for Moran to appear with his two ever-present bodyguards, Willie Marks and Ted Newberry. At that moment, the phony detective car pulled up to the garage and parked at the curb. The two uniformed police men got out and walked into the building. Just then, Moran and his two bodyguards were approaching the garage. "Cops," Moran whispered to his men, "a raid. Let's go into the coffee shop on the corner. You can bail the boys out later."

As Moran, Marks, and Newberry sipped coffee in the nearby shop, the two plainclothes detectives—Anselmi and Scalise—entered the garage. What happened next can only be imagined, for no eyewitnesses to the terrible slaughter ever came forward. From what was found inside the garage a short time later, the seven men apparently had been lined up against a brick wall of the garage and were told to face the wall. The Moran gangsters believed, apparently, that they were about to be searched in a routine arrest, and they submitted freely to the orders of the fake cops, their hands stretched above their heads on the wall.

Unseen by them were the two machine gunners, Anselmi and Scalise, who then entered the garage and opened up a terrible fusillade, peppering the backs of the Moran men, spraying their deadly barrage back and forth at head, waist, and knee level, firing hundreds of bullets that smashed the North Side men to pieces. The victims fell from the wall like rag dolls, crushed and bleeding, streams of blood from each body joining to form a dark pool of blood.

The two uniformed killers then produced sawed off shotguns and went to those fallen gangsters who still showed twitching signs of life. They fired shotgun blasts into the heads of these men, tearing away the tops of their skulls so that their brains spilled onto the cement floor of the garage. With that, the four killers left, the uniformed policemen marching the plainclothes men in front of them at gunpoint, pretending that those in civilian dress were members of the Moran gang and under arrest. The four went to the street and got into the detective car, which slowly pulled into traffic and went southward on Clark Street. The racket created by the submachine guns had been heard by neighbors, who thought the sound was caused by pneumatic drills, the result of construction work inside the garage.

Inside the garage, the only living creature was Highball, the German shepherd. The dog began to howl. Mrs. Jeanette Landesman, the landlady in the building just north of the garage, heard the dog howling, and asked one of her tenants, C.L. McAllister, to go into the garage and see what was wrong. Within two minutes McAllister appeared, his face ashen, his mouth gaping. He gasped: "The place is full of dead men!"

Mrs. Landesman called the police, who arrived minutes later with a few news photographers in tow; they stepped into the garage and then shrank back in horror at the sight of the human gore littering the garage floor. The photographers, grimacing, began taking photos of the seven men heaped on the floor. While police called for the morgue wagon, a reporter appeared and re-

Left to right, George "Bugs" Moran, who missed death by minutes, and Peter and Frank Gusenberg, James Clark, who were killed.

Left to right, more massacre victims: Al Weinshank, Adam Heyer, John May, and Dr. Reinhardt Schwimmer, all machine-gunned to death.

"Machine Gun" Jack McGurn, one of the killers in the garage.

The front of Moran's headquarters, the S-M-C Cartage Company.

The carnage: seven men shot to pieces by Al Capone's killers, 1929.

corded how the police took inventory of the dead. He described the gangsters as models of "upkeep and dress—shave, hair trim, manicure; the silk shirt, the flashy tie; here and there a diamond stickpin and ring; in Dr. Schwimmer's case a carnation boutonniere; fedoras with brims slanted down over the right eyes; spats; tailored suits and overcoats; each with the customary bank roll—Heyer, $1,135; Weinshank, $1,250; May, $1,200..."

The motive for the mass killing was not money, since the killers never bothered to rummage the pockets of their affluent victims. The object was mass murder, and the assignment was completed with professionalism the police immediately identified as a gangster slaying. Yet the killers had not been as thorough as Capone would have expected. While coroner's assistants and detectives examined the corpses, one of the victims stirred, and a low moan came from him. Startled officials soon realized that Frank Gusenberg, who was found some distance from the other six men, was still alive. With a half dozen bullets in him, the tough gangster was rushed to Alexian Brothers Hospital. A short time later, CPD Sergeant Frank Sweeney, a boyhood pal of Gusenberg's sat at the bedside of the dying gangster, questioning him.

"Who shot you, Frank?" asked Sweeney.

"No one," whispered Gusenberg, "nobody shot me."

"Your brother Pete is dead, Frank. Everybody in that place is dead," Sweeney told Gusenberg. "Who did this thing? Tell us, we'll get them for you."

Half-conscious, the fading gangster who had been involved in the gang for more than a decade, who had started as a hijacker for O'Bannion, who had worked as a gunman for Weiss and Moran, who had himself shot and killed an estimated twenty men, was determined to keep the code of the underworld. He would inform on no one, not even his own killers. He opened his eyes for a moment and stared at the policeman, saying in a low voice: "Nobody shot me."

"Do you want a preacher, Frank?"

Frank Gusenberg's lips moved slightly as his last breath and a single word left his body: "No."

With Gusenberg's death the toll rose to seven, the worst single gangland slaughter in the history of the U.S. underworld. The city of Chicago, which was used to killings, bombings, and gun battles, was shaken at its roots by the terrible carnage. Capone badly underestimated civil reaction to his mass murder of the North Side gang. This crime proved to be his undoing. Its infamy spread across the pages of the nation's newspapers, and in Washington, D.C., President Herbert Hoover gave orders to have Capone arrested and jailed, no matter what the cost, no matter how long it took. Several years passed before IRS agents led by Elmer Irey prepared enough evidence to convict Capone of tax evasion and send him to a federal penitentiary, but the slow process really began with the slaughter of the Moran gang in 1929.

Moran had been spared by accident, merely because he was late for an appointment. He checked himself into a hospital, and newsmen finally tracked him there. Moran lay in a bed with his bodyguards, Marks and Newberry flanking him, guns tucked beneath their coats.

"What about your boys getting knocked off like that, Moran?" one of the newsmen asked the gang leader.

"Yeah," Moran answered slowly, "I knew them, friends of mine."

"Who did it, Moran?" another asked.

"I dunno," mumbled the gang leader.

"C'mon, George, who bumped your boys?"

Suddenly George "Bugs" Moran exploded, forsaking the code of the underworld, and shouted: "Only Capone kills like that!"

Moran's power on the north side was broken. He and the remnants of his gang clung to power for a few more years, but by the 1930s Moran had quit the rackets, or so it was thought. Yet the very mastermind of the St. Valentine's Day Massacre, Machine Gun Jack McGurn, was killed seven years later on the anniversary of the 1929 slaughter, shot to death in a Chicago bowling alley. His killers were reported to have been George "Bugs" Moran and two other men. See: **Brothers, Leo Vincent**; **Burke, Fred**; **Capone, Alphonse**; **Goetz, Fred**; **McGurn, Jack**; **Moran, George**; **Nitti, Frank**; **O'Bannion, Charles Dion**; **Purple Gang**; **Weiss, Earl**.

REF.: Asbury, *Gem of the Prairie;* Asbury, *The Great Illusion;* Bennett, *Murder Is My Business; CBA;* Demaris, *Captive City;* Fox, *Mass Murder;* Gage, *The Mafia is not an Equal Opportunity Employer;* Gribble, *Murders Most Strange;* Haskins, *Street Gangs;* Hynd, *We are the Public Enemies;* Kobler, *Al Capone;* Lustgarten, *Story of Crime;* Lynch, *Criminals and Politicians;* McPhaul, *Johnny Torrio;* Messick and Goldblatt, *The Mobs and the Mafia;* Moorehead, *Hostages to Fortune;* Morgan, *Prince of Crime;* Nash, *Bloodletters and Badmen;* ____, *People to See;* Ness, *The Untouchables;* Peterson, *The Mob;* Robinson, *Science Catches the Criminal;* Reppetto, *The Blue Parade;* Sann, *The Lawless Decade;* ____, *Kill the Dutchman;* Scott, *The Concise Encyclopedia of Crime and Criminals;* Smith, *Syndicate City;* Spiering, *The Man Who Got Capone;* Thorwald, *The Century of the Detective;* Whitehead, *The FBI Story;* (FILM), *Dance, Fools,* 1931; *Some Like It Hot,* 1959; *Saint Valentine's Day Massacre,* 1967.

Saisset, Bernard, c.1232-c.1311, Fr., her.-treas. Served as first bishop of Pamiers in 1295. He was condemned for blasphemy and treason and his personal property was seized by King Philip IV in 1301. He was exiled to Rome in 1302, following orders for his release by his mentor, Pope Boniface VIII. He reportedly returned to France three years later. REF.: *CBA.*

Sakai Toshihiko (AKA: **Shiburoku Kaizuka, Kosen**), 1870-1933, Japan, impris. Jailed in 1923 for role in founding of Japanese Communist Party in 1922. A former teacher, he later returned to education and started a school of agriculture. REF.: *CBA.*

Sakamoto Ryoma, 1835-67, Japan, rebel.-assass. Instrumental in reinstating powers of emperor in 1668 by forming union between fiefs owned by Choshu and Satsuma. His plans to set up a conspiracy to remove the shogun were halted by his assassination. REF.: *CBA.*

Sakuma Shozan (Sakuma Zozen), 1811-64, Japan, jur., assass. Author of phrase "Eastern ethics and Western science" encouraging nineteenth century efforts to modernize Japan, including changes brought on by ascension of Mutsuhito in 1868. He was killed by samurais seeking to halt the changes. REF.: *CBA.*

Sala, Peter, and **Ouyerack, Charlie**, prom. 1941, Can., mansl. On the craggy, windswept Belcher Islands in the Hudson Bay, two native Eskimos went on trial for murder in August 1941. The two defendants, Peter Sala and Charlie Ouyerack, were accused of killing three other Eskimos who ridiculed their contentions that they were both Christ returned to Earth. Sala and Ouyerack became convinced they were both messiahs during Winter 1940. During a fierce snowstorm, a female accomplice—or disciple—named Mina led a weary band of Eskimos out onto the Bay to await the coming of their "Jesus." Two women and four children later died from exposure.

Sala and Ouyerack were convicted of manslaughter before Justice C.P. Plaxton. Each received two years in prison, and Mina was declared insane. REF.: *CBA.*

Salabarria, Mario, 1914- , Cuba, mur. As the head of Havana's Police Investigation Bureau, Major Mario Salabarria, thirty-four, was a vain and jealous leader who felt threatened by the presence of the popular young war hero, 29-year-old Emilio Tro, who had fought with distinction on the side of the Loyalists during the Spanish Civil War. In 1947, Tro accused Salabarria's office of malfeasance and running a black market operation, a serious charge that compelled the major to seek an arrest warrant for Tro and his supporters.

With two carloads of armed men, Salabarria descended on Tro's residence in suburban Marianao in late September 1947. Without warning, the uniformed men strafed the house with nonstop machine gunfire, killing Tro, four of his supporters, and a pregnant woman. The killing was stopped by a tank crew and an armored personnel carrier. The atrocity had been filmed by Army Chief Genovevo Pérez Dámera who submitted it in court as evidence. A roundup of Salabarria partisans was ordered by President Ramón Grau San Martin, who attempted to placate the grieving Tro supporters.

On Mar. 8, 1948, a military court martial sentenced Salabarria to thirty years' imprisonment for murder, and a year for creating a public disorder. Ten other men who participated in the attack received varying terms of six months to twenty-five years. REF.: *CBA.*

Salamanca Place Mystery, 1902, Brit., (unsolv.) mur. Thirteen years after Jack the Ripper terrorized London, Scotland Yard thought for a moment the madman had returned. In that year, two laborers returning home from work at the Doulton's Works made a gruesome discovery. They found on the pavement some scattered human remains and a severed head. It was a woman, and the body parts had apparently been cooked. The identity of the woman remained a mystery, as well as that of her killer.

REF.: Brock, *A Casebook of Crime; CBA.*

Salameh, Ali Hassan (AKA: **Abu Hassan, Red Prince**), 1943-79, Leb., terr.-assass. To Western observers who knew him, Ali Salameh was a man of considerable breeding and refinement. The Israeli Mossad considered Salameh in different terms. For nearly two decades he was one of the most feared Palestinian Liberation Organization (PLO) terrorists, who was believed to have been the principle architect of the 1972 raid on the Olympic Village in Munich which claimed the lives of eleven Israeli athletes,

The son of a Palestinian who was killed by Haganah terrorists in 1948, Salameh extracted revenge on his father's killers twenty years later when he drove a beer truck laden with dynamite into a crowded street in the Jerusalem marketplace. The explosion killed twelve people. After the Jordanians drove the PLO out of their country in 1970, the Black September movement was organized by Yasir Arafat as an instrument of retaliation against the enemies of the displaced Palestinian people. Salameh became its director of intelligence and third in command. He proved to be an expert organizer, and especially skilled at dodging the agents of Mossad sent out to kill him. The Israelis labeled him the "Red Prince" for his jet-setting lifestyle.

The end came on Jan. 21, 1979, when a car bomb planted inside a Volkswagen deep inside war-torn Beirut was detonated by a radio signal at the moment Salameh and four bodyguards were driving by in their Simca sedan. The assassins were believed to be Peter Scriver and Roland Kolberg, Israeli agents who posed as British businessmen. They had carefully planned the operation for months. See: **Black September Organization; Arafat, Yasir**. REF.: *CBA.*

Salan, Raoul Albin Louis, 1899-1984, Fr., consp.-terr. Born in a small town outside Toulouse, Fr., Raoul Salan became one of France's most decorated war heroes. He won the prestigious Croix de Guerre in 1917, one of thirty-five military decorations he would eventually receive. After France fell to the Germans in 1940, Salan sided with the Vichy government but later changed sides when the tide of victory appeared to be in the Allies' favor.

From 1945 until 1950, Salan was the supreme commander of the French colonial troops. In 1950, he accepted an appointment to serve as commander-in-chief of the French forces headquartered in Indo-China (Vietnam). He remained in command until the French were driven out in 1954, at which time Salan was assigned to Algeria. Two years later General Salan assumed command of forces in Algeria who were fighting against rebel forces seeking to evict the French colonial settlers from their land.

Salan headed the Committee of Public Safety established to preserve French colonial rule in the region. The new prime minister, Pierre Pflimin, indicated in 1958 that he favored a negotiated settlement. After Charles de Gaulle acceded to the presidency, Salan plotted with three other generals to keep Algeria in French hands.

Exiled to Spain for his part in the famous "revolt of the generals," Salan formed the Secret Army Organization. In May 1961, the underground movement instigated a coup in which they held Algiers for four days. Their actions followed continued acts of bombing and terrorism in the Algerian city. President de Gaulle appealed to the patriotism of the military and within days the coup collapsed. General Salan was forced into hiding and was sentenced to death in absentia. He was arrested in 1962 and was imprisoned for life after an assassination plot against de Gaulle was foiled by the French security. In 1968, Salan was pardoned by de Gaulle, and two years before his death, President François Mitterrand restored him to the rank of general with full military honors. See: **de Gaulle, Charles**. REF.: *CBA.*

Salaverry, Felipe Santiago, 1806-36, Peru, gen., assass. Headed military drive against General Agustin Gamarra in 1834, and gave himself title of chief of Peru from 1835-36. He was shot and killed by Bolivian president Santa Clara in 1836 after he lost a battle and was seized. REF.: *CBA.*

Salazar, Enrique Camarena, See: **Camarena, Enrique.**

Salazar de Frias, Alonzo, prom. 1611, Spain, witchcraft. Alonzo Salazar effectively refuted the findings of the Spanish Inquisitors who executed six suspected witches near Cigarramundi on Nov. 7, 1610. The judges in these cases accused 280 adults and children of worshipping the devil. The evidence of sorcery was accumulated mostly from children between twelve and fourteen. When Salazar arrived on May 22 to administer an edict which permitted the accused to confess their crimes without penalties, he found that 1,384 supposed witches were adolescents.

Salazar concluded in his report that the hysteria had been provoked by the presence of the eager inquisitors. His list of recommendations included instructions to inquisitors that in the future they should only seek external evidence to confirm accusations of witchcraft. As a result, witchcraft hysteria was virtually ground to a halt in Spain. The more relaxed views of Salazar, himself an inquisitor, helped usher in a period of enlightened tolerance in Spain.

REF.: *CBA;* Lea, *History of the Inquisition of the Middle Ages;* Robbins, *The Encyclopedia of Witchcraft and Demonology;* Williams, *Witchcraft.*

Salcido Uzeta, Manuel (AKA: **Cochi Loco**), 1947- , Mex., drugs-org. crime. Manuel Salcido Uzeta began his underworld career as an enforcer for Alberto Sicilia Falcón and quickly rose through the ranks to become one of the leaders of the Guadalajara drug cartel. Based in Mazatlán, Mex., Salcido Uzeta is regarded as one of the most cold-blooded members of the drug ring. His personal holdings in Mazatlán are estimated at $35 million. Salcido Uzeta owns several tourist hotels and restaurants, movie houses, an office building, and a disco. While his contemporaries in the Mexican drug trade expanded into South America, Salcido Uzeta had amassed a fortune based on marijuana and cocaine distribution in southern Sinaloa.

Salcido Uzeta did not come by his nickname "Cochi Loco" or Crazy Pig by chance. Between 1985 and 1986, three men were murdered—two U.S. tourists suspected of being DEA informants on Jan. 30, 1985, and a DEA informant on June 22, 1986—in Guadalajara, Salcido Uzeta's territory. There was strong evidence that DEA informant Martin Aguirre Orzoco, and tourists John Walker, and Alberto Radelat, had been tortured by their captors. Salcido Uzeta retreated to Mazatlán where he continued to run his marijuana wholesale operation, and was seen driving around the city guarded by two dozen Sinaloa state judicial police. Following the imprisonment of Rafael Cáro Quintero and Ernesto Fonseca Carrillo, Salcido Uzeta took on an even greater role in the Guadalajara cartel, of which he and Miguel Angel Félix Gallardo were the most eminent—and most wanted. Salcido Uzeta is believed to be responsible for the Feb. 22, 1988, murder of journalist Manuel Burgueno Orduno, who had criticized lawlessness in the region; and the wounding of Mazatlán police chief Lorenzo Groztiza Castro on Mar. 16, 1988.

REF.: *CBA;* Shannon, *Desperados.*

Saldanha Oliveira e Daun, Joao Carlos de (Duque de Saldanha), 1790-1876, Port., rebel. Minister of war and president of the council in 1835. He helped spark a counterrevolution against the Septembrists, for which he was exiled from 1836-46. REF.: *CBA.*

Salem (Ind.) Bomb Scare, 1988, U.S., (unsolv.) attempt. bomb. The quiet little hamlet of Salem, Ind., was known only for its small cabinet making factory and automobile parts company that provided jobs for many of the town's 6,000 residents.

But the town was stunned on July 5, 1988, when thirteen homemade bombs wrapped in paper bags were found near bridges and arterial gas lines. In all, 400 pounds of dynamite had been placed there. If the bomb maker had not erred in constructing the blasting caps, it is likely that the town would have been destroyed, or at least cut off from the outside world. "You can talk about anarchists, terrorists, but in Salem?" said Mayor Frank Newkirk, Sr. "The only thing we can think of is it's some kook."

The explosives were traced to the theft of dynamite from the Mulzer Crushed Stone Company in English, Ind., between June 6-13, 1988. The identity of the suspects, and the motive for the attempted bombings have not been established. REF.: *CBA*.

Salem Murder Case, See: **Crowninshield, Richard**.

Cotton Mather praying for the Salem "witches."

Salem Witchcraft Trials, 1692, U.S., witchcraft-her. Feeding upon the superstitious, the elders of Salem, Mass., were overwhelmed with a witchcraft craze that swept their little community into the very real horrors of heresy and wholesale executions. Salem was to become forever linked with supernatural evils and importing the brutal customs of the Inquisition to the New Land to exterminate the sinister spirits in its midst. The colony of Salem and surrounding communities operated as a theocracy, governed after 1690 by Mosaic laws applied to the temporal and the spiritual alike.

Inhabitants lived by a rigid code of laws that not only regulated their every physical move but attempted to govern their very thoughts. Though the pursuit of the witches in Europe was all but non-existent by the time of the New England mania (the last witch in England was burned in 1685), the Puritans were suddenly awash with witches and witch-hunts that would see the imprisonment of close to 200 suspected witches and the executions of nineteen alleged witches and one lone wizard before the madness waned.

It began in Salem in February 1692 in the home of the Reverend Samuel Parris, who, since 1689, was the pastor of the First Church at Salem. Parris had been a merchant in the West Indies (some later rumored that he had trafficked in slaves along the Spanish Main) and financial reverses brought him to the ministry. Coming from Boston to Salem, which then boasted a population of 1,700, Parris brought along two slaves he had acquired in the West Indies, a man called John Indian and his wife, Tituba.

When not performing her more arduous chores of scrubbing floors, washing, slaughtering farm animals for meals, and emptying the slops, Tituba whiled away the tedious hours by telling ghost stories to Parris' 9-year-old daughter, Elizabeth, and her cousin Abigail Williams, eleven. So provocative were Tituba's tales that the girls invited their friends to gather each evening at the parsonage to hear the slave's twaddle. These included Ann Putnam, twelve, Mercy Lewis, seventeen, Mary Walcott, seventeen, Elizabeth Hubbard, seventeen, Elizabeth Booth, eighteen, Susan Sheldon, eighteen, Mary Warren, twenty, and Sarah Churchill, twenty. The group, later known as the "Circle Girls," were entranced and terrified by Tituba's antics.

The slave told their fortunes in ominous tones, working her voice into strange pitches. She seemed to induce tables to tip crazily and bring about strange rappings and other noises the girls unhesitatingly ascribed to spirits and the Devil, many of the younger girls falling into hypnotic trances. As the meeting went on, the conduct of the girls became unpredictable and wild. (Most of these girls were lonely sorts, unattended by young men, embittered by their lots in life. They were unschooled and only two of them could write their names. Ann Putnam, who would wreak the most havoc, was epileptic. Three of the girls were domestic workers who later willingly testified against their employers, bringing about their gruesome deaths.)

Pastor Parris, who was later described as a man "narrow and bigoted," became alarmed at his daughter's odd behavior. Elizabeth Parris and Abigail Williams appeared to throw fits at all hours of the day. They became hysterical and pulled at their hair. They went into uncontrollable convulsions. The Reverend called in a friend, Pastor Deodat Lawson, who sat in the Parris home one night and watched horrified as Abigail Williams became nearly insane. In his account of the Salem Witch trials, *A Brief and True Narrative,* Lawson recalled how he watched the Williams child "run to the fire, and begin to throw fire brands about the house and run against the back as if she would run up the chimney."

Lawson was also present on Mar. 20 when Abigail Williams went berserk during a prayer meeting at the parsonage. She interrupted the meeting many times by shrieking and stamping the floor. In tandem, little Elizabeth Parris shouted incoherent phrases interpreted as obscenities. Elizabeth hurled a Bible across the room, striking her strict and startled father.

Much disturbed, Lawson later wrote that: "After psalm was sung, Abigail Williams said to me, 'Now stand up and name your text.' And after it was read, she said, 'It is a long text.'" In the afternoon, Lawson remembered that Abigail, "upon my referring to my doctrines, said to me, 'I know of no doctrine you had. If you did name one, I have forgot it.'"

This was, of course, heresy and, the baffled adults concluded, the certain workings of the Devil. A local doctor named Gregg was summoned and he observed the girls go through their tantrums. "I know of nothing else to say save to declare them both bewitched," pronounced the good doctor.

"Who bewitched you?" demanded Parris of his daughter and niece. They stood mute before him with staring eyes and tightly closed lips. The slave Tituba stepped forward, the sinister catalyst of the horrors to come, and offered a remedy, saying: "Take four ounces of rye meal, mix it with children's water (urine), roll it in a biscuit, bake it in ashes, and feed it to the dog. If the dog gets sick, the girls will tell who bewitched them."

Parris ordered this repugnant concoction fed to the family dog, and the animal vomited. Then, with Tituba coaching the two girls, a plethora of names spilled forth from their mouths. The first person named in their chatter as a witch was, quite naturally, Tituba, who made no denial and added that Satan compelled her to sign her name in his book and vow to work mischief upon all children. The demented slave was thrown into jail where she remained throughout the fear-clutching witchcraft trials. (How Tituba, an illiterate who could not write, managed to sign her name in the Devil's book was never revealed; the fact that she enjoyed her stay in jail with no labors to perform was well recorded.)

The cane-wielding demagogue, Sir William Phips, the first governor appointed to rule the newly reorganized Massachusetts Colony, took a coat-flying tour of the jails in Boston, Ipswich, Cambridge, Andover, and Salem and found them brimming with accused felons and witches. He wasted no time in establishing a witchcraft court, appointing four Boston and two Salem men to preside over this court as judges. The court's only reason for existing was to rid the colony of witches. That the governor had no power to create courts and that this court was illegal was ignored. Deputy Governor William Stoughton was made chief justice. The other judges were John Hathorne, Jonathan Corwin, Major Bartholomew Gedney, Wait Winthrop, Peter Sargent, Major John Richards, and Captain Samuel Sewall. The trials ensued in late February 1692, and those brought before the judges stood accused by girls whose parents and relatives had old scores to settle. Most of those tried and convicted of witchcraft were avowed enemies of Ann Putnam, mother of the 12-year-old who testified in all but one of the cases, which resulted in the death penalty. The mother coaxed and counseled her daughter in every instance.

The first "witch" tried in Salem (those accused in Boston and other communities were sent to Salem to stand trial) was a 60-year-old woman, three times married, Bridget Bishop. As the keeper of a rowdy inn between Salem and Beverly, Bishop's reputation was somewhat soiled, and she had been tried as a witch but freed for lack of evidence twelve years earlier. Bishop was brought into court on June 2, 1692, following an examination in which nine Puritan women stripped her in her jail cell in a fruitless search for "witchmarks" (marks on the flesh such as birthmarks that could be interpreted as brandings by the Devil).

The moment this hapless woman appeared, those who accused her of being a witch—Ann Putnam, Abigail Williams, Mercy Lewis, Elizabeth Hubbard, and Mary Walcott—fell from their benches and rolled in paroxysms of pain, screaming and ranting that Bridget Bishop was pinching them and thrusting long needles into their flesh. Such a hysterical display greatly moved the Puritan throng and visibly upset the dour-faced judges.

Judge Hathorne began the inquisition with: "Bridget Bishop, what do you say? You here stand charged with sundry acts of witchcraft made upon the bodies of Mercy Lewis and Ann Putnam and others."

"I am innocent," Bishop replied. "I know nothing of it. I have done no witchcraft."

Hathorne addressed the girls, many of whom were still in spasms, rolling their eyes and wincing in what appeared to be intense pain. "Look upon this woman and see if this be the woman that you have seen hurting you." The judge turned to Bishop: "What do you say now that you see they charge you? Do you confess?"

"I never hurt them in my life. I never saw these persons before. I am innocent as the child unborn."

"What contract have you made with the Devil?"

"I have made no contract with the Devil. I never saw him in my life."

One of the bewitched accusers, Mercy Lewis, jumped to her feet and shouted: "Oh Goody Bishop (most women in this formal era were referred to as goodwife, "goody" for short, and men goodman), did not you come to my house the last night and did you not tell me that you would torment me?"

Hathorne let the interruption stand without rebuke, a technique of the cabalistic girls that was consistently tolerated during all the trials. The judge then turned back to the accused: "Tell the truth in this matter. How come this person to be tormented and to charge you with doing it?"

"I am not come here to say I am a witch and to take away my life."

As the mania spread throughout the courtroom, spectators succumbed to the swelling fever. Marshall Herrick claimed that Bridget Bishop had once entered his bed chamber as a ghost and added: "She is by some of the afflicted persons charged with murder."

To this hearsay, Hathorne persisted: "What do you say to these murders you are charged with?"

"I am innocent," cried the exasperated woman. "I know nothing of it."

Witnesses full of suspicion, fear, and overcome by their own nightmares came forward to testify against Bridget Bishop. William Stacey claimed that "about fourteen years gone I had the small pox and Bridget Bishop did visit me and profess a great love for me in my affliction. After I got well, Bridget Bishop got me to do some work for her for which she gave me three pence which seemed to me as if it had been good money, but I had not gone over three or four rods before I looked into my pocket where I put the money but could not find it.

"Sometime afterwards I met the said Bishop in the street going to the mill. She asked me whether my father would grind her grist. I asked her why she asked me that and she answered: 'Because folks count me a witch.' Then I told her I knew my father would grind it. But being gone about six rods from the said Bishop suddenly my off wheel here sunk down into a hole upon plain ground and I was forced to get one to help me get out. Afterwards I went back to look for the hole where the wheel sunk in but could not fine any hole.

"After that in the winter about midnight I felt something between my lips pressing hard against my teeth and it was very cold insomuch that it did wake me, and I got up and set upon my bed and at the same time I did see the said Bridget Bishop at the foot of the bed and it was as light as if it had been day. It was either the said Bishop or her shape she having then a black cat and a black hat and a red coat. And the said Bishop or her shape clapped her coat close to the legs and hopped upon the bed and about the room and then went out.

"Sometimes afterwards I met the said Bishop by Isaac Stone's hill and after I had passed by her my horse stood still with a small load going up the hill, and the cart fell down. Then I went to lift a bag of grain of about two bushels but could not budge it with all my might.

"I fully believe that the said Bishop was instrumental in the death of my daughter Pricilla about two years ago. The child was a likely, thriving child and suddenly screached out and so continued in this unusual manner for about a fortnight and so died in a lamentable manner."

A Salem man, Samuel Gray, then testified that Bridget Bishop had entered his bedroom as a specter in 1678. The ghostly apparition, Gray stated, stood between his bed and the cradle of his child. He called out to her: "In the name of God what do you come for?" The phantom departed, he said, and, thinking it all a dream, Gray went back to sleep. "Then I felt something come to my lips cold and thereupon I started and looked up and again I did see the same woman with something between her hands holding it before my mouth and the child in the cradle gave a great screach as if it were greatly hurt and she disappeared, and when I took the child I could not quiet it in some hours." Gray added, almost in tears, that his once healthy child "pined away and was never well although it lived some months in a sad condition and so died." And Gray raised an arm and pointed a finger. He identified that ghost of fourteen years earlier as one and the same Bridget Bishop.

John Hale testified that Bishop kept her inn open at all hours of the night to those "who were drunk and played at shovel board," and when a neighbor, John Trask, at the request of his wife, entered the inn to complain of the noise, he was insulted. After Trask threw the pieces of the game into the fire, his wife

Christiane, became bewitched, a spell that was broken only after many months of intense prayer and church communion.

Trask's wife then suddenly died. Of this, Hale stated: "As to the wounds which Christiane Trask died of I observed three deadly ones. A piece of her windpipe was cut out and other one about through the windpipe and gulle to the veins they call jugular so that I then judged and still do believe it impossible for her to do so without some extraordinary work of the Devil or witchcraft."

Sam Shaltoch insisted that his fitful, sick child had been made ill by Bridget Bishop who cast a spell over him. An argument with the accused, stated John Lauder, caused Bishop to enter his bedroom late at night in 1684 and sit upon his stomach. "She presently laid hold of my throat and almost choked me and I had no strength or power in my hands to rise or help myself and in this condition she held me." One of the innkeeper's employees, John Blye, testified that she kept "poppets (puppets) made up of rags and hoggs brussels with headless pins in them" in holes in the basement walls of the inn's cellar. A half dozen more, including Bishop's husband, Edward, damned her as a witch.

Susan Sheldon was one of the "witch bitches," as the original accusing coterie of girls was labeled by old George Jacobs, whom they accused of being a witch. Susan Sheldon claimed that "on the second day of June 1692, I saw the apparition of Bridget Bishop and immediately appeared two little children and said they were twins and told Bridget Bishop to her face that she had murdered them by setting them into fits whereupon they died."

A solemnly convinced jury found Bridget Bishop Guilty. Chief Justice Stoughton did not pause in signing her death warrant, which read: "Whereupon Bridget Bishop, alias Oliver, at a special court held at Salem the second day of this month of June before William Stoughton, Esquire and his Associate Justices of the said court, was indicted for practicing and exercising on the nineteenth day of April last past and diverse other days and times certain acts of witchcraft in and upon the bodies of Abigail Williams, Ann Putnam, Mercy Lewis, Mary Walcott, and Elizabeth Hubbard of Salem whereby their bodies were greatly afflicted, pined, consumed, wasted, and tormented. To which indictment Bridget Bishop pleaded not guilty and put herself upon God.

"Whereupon she was found guilty of the offense and witchcrafts and sentenced to death. Therefore, in the name of their majesties William and Mary, now king and queen of England, we command you Sheriff George Corwin that on Friday next, being the tenth day of June to conduct the said Bridget Bishop from their majesties' jail in Salem to the place of execution and there cause her to be hanged until she be dead."

Corwin carried out the order on June 10, 1692, and, confirming the convicted witch as being dead, cut down her body and buried her next to the scaffold. On hand for the execution was the witch-hunter, Cotton Mather. He claimed that a moment before Bridget Bishop hanged, she looked toward the church and her withering, evil glance caused a giant timber to be torn loose from the building and slam through a distant wall. Mather failed to record how the pathetic woman turned into a raving lunatic on the gallows. Soon after the first Salem witch was executed, her husband, Edward, who "gladly followed her to the gallows," took his third wife. The trials ground on all summer. On July 19, five more convicted witches—Sarah Good, Elizabeth How, Susanna Martin, Rebecca Nurse, and Sarah Wilds—were taken to the Salem scaffold and hanged on July 19, 1692. Sarah Good was a 70-year-old beggar woman no one liked. When she was refused alms, she would curse the niggardly passerby. She was the first person arrested for witchcraft in Salem. Her husband, John Good, a known drunk, testified that "my wife often appears to be possessed of the Devil." Elizabeth How of Topsfield was also seventy and she escaped from the Salem jail, later to be found walking in a daze through the forests around Boston. Susanna Martin came from Amesbury and she was seventy-two years old. Rebecca Nurse, seventy-one, had been involved in many lawsuits with the Putnam family. All of these people were accused of "tormenting" the "witch bitches" and were hanged for it.

Seventy-five-year-old George Jacobs was the first male witch to be convicted. Jacobs had to struggle against his own senility while combating the dozens of "bewitched" girls and men accusing him. In the preliminary hearing of Jacobs, the judge pointed to several of the Circle Girls and stated: "Here are them that accuse you of witchcraft."

"Well," Jacobs replied quietly, "let us hear who they are and what they are."

"Abigail Williams," announced the judge.

Jacobs looked at the wide-eyed 11-year-old and laughed.

"Why do you laugh?" the judge asked,

"Because I am falsely accused. Do you think this is true?"

"What do you think?" the judge queried.

"I never did it."

"Who did it?"

"Don't ask me."

The judge pointed to one witness. "Sarah Churchill accuses you. There she is."

"I am as innocent as a child born tonight. I have lived in Salem thirty-three years. If you can prove that I am guilty, I will lie under it."

Sarah Churchill then spoke in a monotone as one would in a trance: "Last night I was afflicted at Deacon Ingersoll's and Mary Walcott said it was a man with two staves, it was my master." (Jacobs walked on two canes and he was Sarah Churchill's employer.)

Jacobs would not look at the lonely girl who worked for him on his ten-acre farm but turned to the judge, pleading: "Pray do not accuse me, your worship. You must judge rightly."

The trial of George Jacobs.

He was ignored, the judge concentrating on the witness. "What book did he bring to you, Sarah?"

"The same the other women brought."

"The Devil can go in any shape," the judge prompted.

"He appeared to me on the other side of the river and hurt me."

"Look here," the judge pointed out, "she accuses you to your face. It is not true?"

"I never wronged no man in word or deed."

"Here are three evidences."

Jacobs grew disgusted with the farce. "You tax me for a wizard, you may as well tax me for a buzzard!"

"Is it no harm to afflict these?"

"I never did it."

"But how comes it to be in your appearance?"

"The Devil can take any likeness."

"Not without their consent."

"Please, your worship. I am silly about these things as the child born last night."

"You argue you have lived so long, but Cain might have lived long before he killed Abel and you might have lived long before the Devil got you."

"Christ hath suffered three times for me."

"What three times?"

"He suffered the cross and the gale."

Sarah Churchill, in keeping with the brazen conduct of all the allegedly bewitched girls, stepped closer to the accused and shouted: "You might as well confess if you are guilty."

"Have your heard that I have any witchcraft?"

"I know that you live a wicked life," Sarah offered.

"Let her make it out."

"Does he ever pray in his family?" the judge asked Sarah Churchill.

"Not unless by himself."

"Why do you not pray in your family?" the judge admonished Jacobs.

"I cannot read."

"Well," harrumphed the judge, "but you may pray for all that. Can you say the Lord's Prayer? Let us hear you!"

Old George Jacobs glared at the judge, and following more statements by Sarah Churchill that he compelled her to write her name in the Devil's book, Jacobs turned angrily toward the judge and said: "Well, burn me or hang me, I will stand in the truth of Christ."

When Jacobs was examined in court for a second time, Ann Putnam, Abigail Williams, and Mercy Lewis, who were all to testify that he was a witch, fell upon the floor when he appeared, going into frothy fits.

The judge wasted no time in asking the girls: "Is this the man who hurts you?"

"This is the man!" Abigail Williams screeched and sank back into her fit.

Ann Putnam shouted: "This is the man that hurts her and brings her the book, and she should be as well as his granddaughter!" (It is important to note that one of Ann's relatives was involved in a suit with Jacobs some time before, and it was her father, Thomas Putnam, who accused Jacobs of bewitching his daughter.)

The judge pointed his finger at the accused. "Mercy Lewis! Is this the man?"

Mercy Lewis could barely manage to interrupt her fit to bubble: "This is the man...He almost kills me." She then resumed her eye-rolling and body twisting on the floor.

Mary Walcott, too, had to struggle against the fit she claimed Jacobs was then imposing upon her to burst forth with: "This is the man! He used to come with two staves and beat me with one of them!"

The judge spun around to Jacobs. "What do you say? Are you not a witch?"

"No," the old man mumbled, tired, "if I were to die presently." Asked by the court if Mercy Lewis' statement was correct, Jacobs responded, "Why, it is false."

Vicious little Ann Putnam shouted: "Yes, you told me you had been so (a witch) for forty years." Then she and Abigail Williams held out their hands, palms upward. There were pins sticking in their palms, and they cried out that Jacobs had caused this to happen during the testimony.

The judge took the pins as conclusive evidence. "Are you not the man that made a disturbance at a lecture in Salem?" he asked Jacobs.

"No great disturbance. Do you think I use witchcraft?"

"Yes, indeed," the judge snapped.

"No, I use none of it!"

The remainder of the testimony in the trial of George Jacobs no longer exists. It is known that his granddaughter Margaret was badgered into confessing that she was bewitched by her grandfather. A day before Jacobs was executed, the child became violently insane. Only hours after Jacobs and four other convicted witches were hanged, the ten-acre Jacobs farm was seized by Sheriff Corwin. Sarah Jacobs, George's ailing wife, had her wedding ring torn from her finger. She, too, was convicted of being a witch, but her execution was delayed until the witchcraft delusion was over. When released, Sarah Jacobs married John Wilds, whose own wife had been hanged.

It soon became apparent that the authorities were more lenient with those who confessed to being a witch than those who denied it. In fact, the twenty victims of the Salem madness were executed because they refused to admit they were witches. Dozens, and then hundreds from the area around Boston were rounded up and imprisoned for suspicion of practicing witchcraft, which was also treason against the theocratic government. Cotton Mather clearly defined witchcraft and treason as one and the same offense, writing that such acts meant "a renouncing of God and advancing a filthy Devil into the throne of the Most High; 'tis the most nefandous high treason against the majesty on high."

Rather than suffer execution, those Puritans who stood accused confessed to anything demanded of them. Their admissions were, they knew, along with the judges and juries who heard them, quite ridiculous, but such confessions functioned to cleanse the spirit and thereby exonerate the living flesh. And to confess was to live. Deliverance Hobbs and her daughter, Abigail, were both accused, and they both readily confessed and were spared the hangman's rope.

Deliverance Hobbs taxed her imagination to the utmost with: "I was at a meeting of witches yesterday morning and there were present Proctor and his wife, Goody Nurse, Giles Corey and his wife, Goody Bishop, and Burroughs, the preacher. He (Burroughs, who was hanged later as a conjurer, a wizard) told us to bewitch all the village, but to do it gradually, assuring us we would prevail. He administered the sacraments with red bread, and red wine like blood. I saw Osborne (Sarah Osborne, convicted witch who died in jail), Sarah Good, Goody Wilds, and Goody Nurse distribute the bread and wine, and a man in a long crowned hat (the Devil) sat next to the minister (Burroughs), and they sat at a table and filled out the wine in tankards.

"I did not eat or drink but all the rest did, therefore they threatened to torment me. The meeting was in the pasture by Mr. Parris' house. I saw Abigail Williams run out to speak to the others, then I was struck blind and could see no more. Goody Wilds told me if I would sign the book she would give me some clothes and would not afflict me any more. I saw Goodman Corey and a woman from Boston trying to break my daughter's neck."

The case against the Reverend George Burroughs, a graduate of Harvard in the class of 1670 and one-time pastor of the First Church in Salem (in 1680), was wholly trumped up by the scheming Putnam family. He was made the chief wizard in the witch trials, the man who conducted black witch masses and administered the witch's sacrament in the dark of night in the Reverend Parris' pasture. When Burroughs' first wife died in 1681, he ordered some rum from John Putnam to be used at her funeral. Burroughs never paid for the rum, moving to Maine some years later. Thomas Putnam, John's brother, was the constable who traveled to Maine and arrested Burroughs for witchcraft and brought him back to Salem to stand trial.

The one-time Salem minister had been married three times and his first two wives had died mysteriously; it was the belief of the Circle Girls, or so they told the court, that the Reverend Burroughs had murdered them, as well as organized the great witch coven of Massachusetts. It was to the sinister pasture meeting that Burroughs summoned Ann Foster and a host of others. Foster was a widow from Andover who herself was a confessed witch.

To save herself from the gallows, Foster created the impossible broomstick legend. Her testimony and that of many others, all intimidated, some tortured by being tied hand and foot and hung upside-down until blood ran from their noses, sealed the fate of George Burroughs, wizard.

Ranted Foster: "The Devil appeared to me several times in the shape of a bird as I never saw the like before, and I have had the gift of striking the afflicted down with my eye ever since. I know the bird was the Devil, because he came white and vanished away black. The Devil told me I should have this gift if I would believe him, and he told me I should have prosperity. He came to me three times, always as a bird, and the last time was about a half a year since and sat upon a table. He had two legs and great eyes, and Carrier's wife (Martha Carrier, another accused witch) came to me about three weeks ago and persuaded me to hurt these people. One time I bewitched a hog of John Lovejoys to death, and I hurt some persons in Salem. Goody Carrier wanted me to bewitch two children of Andrew Allins, and she had two poppets made and stuck pins in them to bewitch the said children by which one of them died and the other was very sick.

"Carrier came to me and wanted me to go to the meeting of witches. So we got upon sticks and went said journey; and I saw Burroughs, the minister, there, and he spake to all of us. There was about twenty-five persons there met together and I tied a knot in a rag and threw it into the fire to hurt Timothy Swan, and I hurt the rest by squeezing poppets and almost choked them. When we rode on a stick to the meeting the stick broke as we were carried in the air above the tops of the trees and we fell, and I hung fast about the neck of Goody Carrier and we were presently in the village and my leg was much hurt. I heard some of the witches say there was 305 in the whole country, and that they would ruin this village.

"There was present at the meeting two men besides Burroughs. One of them had gray hair and used to attend public meetings (Jacobs) to worship God. About three or four years ago, Martha Carrier told me she would bewitch James Hobbs' child to death, and the child died in twenty-four hours."

For these absurd tales, couched against Burroughs and Martha Carrier, who were both hanged and for whom the Salem witch-hunters harbored special animosities (those who confessed were well aware of such animosities and thoroughly briefed by the accusers as to events, people, and places), Foster was reprieved from the gallows only to die in jail.

The confession of the hysterical Abigail Hobbs, daughter of Deliverance, was also used against Burroughs to convict him. A judge leaned over the frightened girl and asked her: "Did Burroughs bring you any of the poppets of his wives to stick pins into?"

"I don't remember."

It was them established that Burroughs provided poppets of his wives for Abigail Hobbs to stick pins into and when the judge inquired "Did you know of any poppets pricked to kill her (one of Burroughs' deceased wives)?" the girl provided the rationale for all of those who stood accused and saved their lives through lies.

"No, John Proctor told me better to afflict than be afflicted, and then I should not be hanged. He brought me a poppet and a thorn to afflict Ann Putnam last Friday." This pathetic girl later committed suicide.

In jail, the heavyset Burroughs was thoroughly examined for witch marks but none were found. When entering the court he became so angry that he jumped backward and knocked down many of those who were prepared to bear witness against him. The testimony of Ann Putnam damned him completely.

The 12-year-old stated: "On Apr. 20, 1692, at evening I saw the apparition of a minister at which I was grievously affrightened and cried out, 'O, dreadful, dreadful, here is a minister come! What are ministers converts to? Whence come you and what is your name for I will complain of you, though you be a minister, if you be a wizard?' Immediately I was tortured by him, being racked and almost choked by him and he tempted me to write in his book which I refused with many outcries. And I told him I would not write in his book though he tear me all to pieces, but told him that it was a dreadful thing for him which was a minister that should teach little children to fear God should come persuading poor creatures to give their souls to the Devil.

"'Tell me your name that I may know who you are?' Then he told me his name was George Burroughs, and that he had three wives and that he had bewitched the first two of them to death, and that he killed Mrs. Lawson, and also killed Mr. Lawson's children because he went to the Eastward with Sir Edmon and preached to the soldiers and that he had bewitched a great many soldiers to death at the Eastward, and that he had made Abigail Hobbs a witch and several more, and he also told me that he was above a witch; that he was a conjurer."

Five more terrible examples of witchcraft—Martha Carrier, George Jacobs, John Proctor, John Willard, and the "wizard" George Burroughs—were solemnly escorted to the gallows on Aug. 19, 1692, and hanged until dead. Burroughs made a very moving speech, claiming his innocence. He denounced the witch-hunting in such a convincing manner that many in the crowd had second thoughts. According to one story, his avowed foe, Cotton Mather, saw a threat to his master scheme of purging the land of evil, and, riding wildly through the dense gathering on horseback, he shouted down the minister and ordered the hangman to perform his duty, which he did.

Families and relatives of those condemned were compelled to pay the hangman's fee, as well as fees for maintaining the accused in jail. Fees for discharges and reprieves were also charges, meaning that many of the less notorious who were suspected of witchcraft could buy their way to freedom from the money-loving Puritans.

Following the execution of George Burroughs, the witch trials became more bizarre. Giles Corey and his wife Martha were accused of being witches, some said so that the Putnams and others could seize their sizeable property. The general rule of thumb in Massachusetts at that time seemed to be that if one admitted one was a witch, death was not the penalty, but the loss to the state of any personal possessions was assured. Corey owned a considerable tract of land and when he was tried for witchcraft, rather than admit or deny anything, he stood mute.

Corey, an enfeebled 81-year-old, angered the entire court by constantly protesting Judge Hathorne's treatment of his wife Martha. In jail he was tortured until he agreed to testify against her. She was sentenced to death. At his own trial, Corey shrewdly refused to utter a word. He repeatedly resisted either admitting or denying he was a witch. He intended to preserve his land for his sons and daughters.

The old man bravely stood up to Judge Hathorne, making only this statement before the farce of a trial ensued: "I will not plead. If I deny, I am condemned already in courts where ghosts appear as witnesses and swear men's lives away. If I confess then I confess to a lie, to buy a life which is not life, but only death in life. I will not bear false witness against any, not even against myself, whom I count least."

Corey was promptly convicted of witchcraft and treason. As if to place emphasis on the entire exaggerated sequence of nightmare events in Salem, a death penalty of the Dark Ages was resurrected, that of *peine forte et dure*. This was the only execution of that medieval custom ever carried out in America. Giles Corey was pressed to death.

Although no complete description of Corey's execution has survived, this traditional torture death is thus described in John Swain's *History of Torture*: "The victim was stripped and tied to the ground with his arms and legs extended; a square board was then placed on his chest, upon which weights were laid until he pleaded or life became extinct. The torture occasionally lasted three days. A triangular board was sometimes placed under the victim's back which had the effect of breaking his spine, thus bringing the torture to a more rapid termination." In Corey's case, the board was dispensed with and rocks were piled directly on top of his chest, his hands and feet stretched and staked down. He died silently and in much pain. According to later apocryphal reports, every now and then through the long hours of his dying, Corey cried out in irony: "More weight!"

The hatred and vengeance in Cotton Mather waned considerably when he viewed the old man's body, which had been placed in Potters' Field in Salem, a huge boulder still atop his crushed chest. He realized for once the inhumanity of the trials and executions and was quoted as saying over Corey's body: "O sight most horrible! In a land like this spangled with churches Evangelical inwrapped in our salvations, must we seek in mouldering statute books of English court some old forgotten law, to do such deed?...This poor man, whom we have made a victim hereafter will be counted as a martyr!"

Yet the last insane acts of the Puritans in their spectacular witchcraft trials, not unlike the McCarthy era some 250 years later, were grotesque and unconscionable. Robert Calef, in his *More Wonders of the Invisible World Discovered,* states that two dogs were tried at Salem for witchcraft, one being the familiar of John Bradstreet, who rode on the dog's back as would a witch upon a broomstick. The dog was convicted for "afflicting them and they all would fall into fits at the dog looking upon them. Whereupon the said dog was tried and hung for a witch."

No records of these dog trials now exist (the Puritans no doubt found them then as inhuman as we do today); the ledgers of record were destroyed. It is known that the animals were held in halters by bailiffs before the judge and made to answer charges by barking, which was produced by goads and prongs rammed by the bailiff up the animal's anus. The dogs were always hanged head downward.

The last of the executions occurred on Sept. 22, 1692, when Martha Corey, Mary Esty, Alice Parker, Mary Parker, Ann Pudeator, Wilmot Reed, Margaret Scott, and Samuel Wardwell were hanged as witches. There remained almost 200 people in various jails, many of whom, like the Coreys, had been constantly moved from Andover to Boston to Salem in an "around the horn" technique later popular with certain police departments to prevent relatives and friends from contacting the accused, another Puritan "first."

Before most of the accused were permanently freed in early 1693, several notable prisoners escaped, one of them John Alden of Boston, whose father would be immortalized by Henry Wadsworth Longfellow. The Circle Girls were brought to Alden's Boston trial and committed all sorts of slanders against this esteemed hero of the Indian wars. One of his accusers screamed in court: "There stands Alden! A bold fellow with his hat on before the judges. He sells powder and shot to the Indians and French, and lies with Indian squaws and has Indian papooses!"

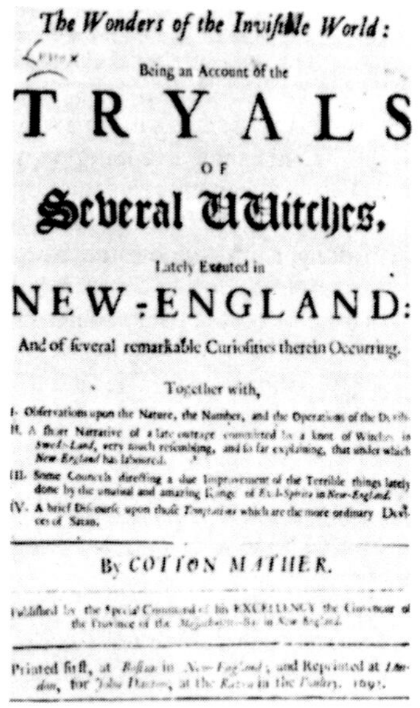
The Wonders of the Invisible World:
Being an Account of the
TRYALS
OF
Several Witches,
Lately Executed in
NEW-ENGLAND:
And of several remarkable Curiosities therein Occurring.
Together with,
I. Observations upon the Nature, the Number, and the Operations of the Devils.
II. A short Narrative of a late outrage committed by a knot of Witches in *Swede-Land*, very much resembling, and so far explaining, that under which *New England* has laboured.
III. Some Councils directing a due Improvement of the Terrible things lately done by the unusual and amazing Range of *Evil-Spirits* in *New-England.*
IV. A brief Discourse upon those *Temptations* which are the more ordinary Devices of Satan.

By COTTON MATHER.

Published by the Special Command of his EXCELLENCY the Governour of the Province of the [illegible] in New England.

Printed first, at *Boston* in *New-England*; and Reprinted at *London*, for *John Dunton*, at the *Raven* in the *Poultry*. 1693.

Mather's own account of the events that occurred in Salem in 1692.

Alden was forced to stand on a chair and face the girls; the accusers went into their tired act, falling into faints. Alden's hand was placed upon each apparently unconscious girl and they revived immediately. Revolted by such shamming, the logical Alden turned to the judge and said: "What's the reason *you* don't fall when I look at you? Can you give me one?" The judge grew red-faced and nonplussed. Alden was sent to Boston prison where he remained for fifteen weeks until he escaped. He was later recaptured in New York but released.

Though many sued the government for private lands and possessions seized during the hysteria, petitioners had to wait until 1711 before damages were awarded. The State of Massachusetts, however, has never reversed the witchcraft convictions.

The relatives of Giles and Martha Corey were eventually given £79 for their property loss. The Burroughs family received £50. These payments were forthcoming almost twenty years after the trials had become an ugly, unwanted memory. Abigail Faulkner and Elizabeth Proctor, who were both sentenced to death and reprieved because of pregnancy, were released to find that they had been legally declared dead and therefore cut off from their property and inheritances.

The Salem jury repented its convictions in 1696, four years after it had found twenty persons guilty of witchcraft. In a petition signed by all twelve members, the jury stated that they "were not capable to understand, nor able to withstand (thus stating that the Devil brought about the trials), the mysterious delusions of the Powers of Darkness and Prince of the Air, but were, for want of knowledge in ourselves and better information from others, prevailed with to take up such evidence against the accused, as on further consideration and better information we justly fear was insufficient...We fear we have been instrumental with others, though ignorantly and unwittingly, to bring upon ourselves and this people of the Lord the guilt of innocent blood...

"We do therefore hereby signify to all in general, and to the surviving sufferers in especial, our deep sense of, and sorrow for our errors, in acting on such evidence to the condemnation of any person. And we do hereby declare that we justly fear that we were sadly deluded and mistaken, for which we are much disquieted and distressed in our minds...

"We do heartily ask forgiveness of you all whom we have justly offended, and do declare according to our present minds we would none of us do such things again on such grounds for the whole world..."

Only one of the judges, Samuel Sewall, who later helped to disperse damage funds to the families of the trial victims, admitted his error. He confessed the total guilt of the court and took "the blame and shame of it, asking pardon of all men" in 1702. The despicable Judge Hathorne held fast unto death his belief in the witchcraft convictions and executions as did Stoughton and others. Hathorne's great-great grandson, author Nathaniel Hawthorne (who added a "w" to his name to avoid the stigma of his murderous ancestor) branded his Puritan forefathers for the superstitious bigots they were in *The Scarlet Letter.*

The Reverend Samuel Parris in whose home the great religious pogrom of Salem began was eventually driven from the town's precincts by enraged citizens. The ten girls who first pointed their accusatory fingers at the old, the feeble-minded, and, in particular, those whom their parents and adult counselors wanted to get rid of, were separated in late 1692 and with the separations came silence. Most of these girls married and settled into obscure lives. Ann Putnam was reinstated into her church in 1697.

In 1706, Putnam confessed to the gigantic fraud and deception she and her friends practiced during the witch trials. This confession was read in the First Church of Salem by the new pastor, Joseph Green. It read: "I desire to be humbled before God for that sad and humbling providence that befell my father's family in the year about 1692; that I, then being in my childhood, should by such a providence of God be made an instrument for the accusing of several persons of a grievous crime, whereby their lives were taken away from them, whom now I have just ground and good reason to believe they were innocent persons. And that it was a great delusion of Satan that deceived me in that sad time, whereby I justly fear I have been instrumental, with others, though ignorantly and unwittingly, to bring upon myself and this land the guilt of innocent blood...I desire to lie in the dust, and to be humbled for it, in that I was a cause, with others, of so sad a calamity to them and their families, for which cause I desire to lie in the dust and earnestly beg forgiveness of God, and from all those unto whom I have given just cause of sorrow and offense whose relations were taken away or accused."

The following wrongly convicted persons were tried and condemned at the Salem Witch Trials in 1692 (twenty being executed): Bishop, Bridget, hanged, June 10; Bradbury, Mary, convicted, Sept. 6, escaped; Burroughs, Reverend George, hanged, Aug. 19; Carrier, Martha, hanged, Aug. 19; Cloyce, Sarah, convicted, Sept. 6, reprieved; Corey, Giles, pressed to death, Sept. 19; Corey, Martha, hanged, Sept. 22; Eames, Rebecca, convicted, Sept. 17, reprieved; Esty, Mary, hanged, Sept. 22; Faulkner,

Abigail, convicted, pleaded pregnancy; Foster, Ann, died in jail; Good, Sarah, hanged, July 19; Hoar, Dorcas, convicted, Sept. 6, reprieved; Hobbs, Abigail, convicted, Sept. 6, reprieved, later committed suicide; Howe, Elizabeth, hanged, July 19; Jacobs, George, hanged, Aug. 19; Lacy, Mary, convicted, Sept. 6, reprieved; Martin, Susanna, hanged, July 19; Nurse, Rebecca, hanged, July 19; Osborne, Sarah, died in jail; Parker, Alice, hanged, Sept. 22, Parker, Mary, hanged, Sept. 22; Proctor, Elizabeth, convicted, pleaded pregnancy; Proctor, John, hanged, Aug. 19; Pudeator, Ann, hanged, Sept. 22; Reed, Wilmot, hanged, Sept. 22; Scott, Margaret, hanged, Sept. 22; Tituba, held in jail; Wardwell, Samuel, hanged, Sept. 22; Wilds, Sarah, hanged, July 19; Willard, John, hanged, Aug. 19.

REF.: Adams, *Emancipation of Massachusetts: The Dream and the Reality;* Akagi, *The Town Proprietors of the New England Colonies: A Study of Their Development, Organization, Activities, and Controversies, 1620-1770;* Andrews, *The Colonial Period of American History;* Bailey, *Historical Sketches of Andover;* Beard, *Psychology of the Salem Witchcraft Excitement of 1692;* Boas, *Cotton Mather, Keeper of the Puritan Conscience;* Bradford, *Of Plymouth Plantation;* Bridenbaugh, *Cities in the Wilderness;* Burr, *Narratives of the Witchcraft Cases, 1648-1706;* ____, *Papers of the American Historical Association;* Calef, *More Wonders of the Invisible World;* Canning, *Fifty True Tales of Terror;* Carroll, *Puritanism and the Wilderness: The Intellectual Significance of the New England Frontier; CBA;* Chandler, *American Criminal Trials;* Demos, *Entertaining Satan, Witchcraft and the Culture of Early New England;* Drake, *Annals of Witchcraft in New England;* ____, *The Witchcraft Delusion in New England;* Felt, *The Annals of Salem from Its First Settlement;* Garcon and Vinchon, *The Devil, An Historical, Critical and Medical Study;* Gemmill, *The Salem Witch Trials;* Hall, *The Faithful Shepherd: A History of the Puritan Ministry in the Seventeenth Century;* Hanson, *Witchcraft at Salem;* Haskins, *Law and Authority in Early Massachusetts: A Study in Tradition and Design;* Hibbert, *The Roots of Evil;* Jackson, *The Witchcraft of Salem Village;* Kittredge, *Witchcraft in Old and New England;* Konig, *Law and Society in Puritan Massachusetts, Essex County, 1629-1692;* Lawson, *A Brief and True Narrative;* Levin, *What Happened in Salem?;* Lewis, *Witchcraft Confessions and Accusations;* Love, *The Fast and Thanksgiving Days of New England;* Macfarlane, *Witchcraft in Tudor and Stuart England;* Marsden, *History of the Early Puritans;* Mather, *Diary;* ____, *Magnalia Christi Americana;* ____, *Memorable Providences Relating to Witchcrafts and Possessions;* ____, *Wonders of the Invisible World;* Maule, *The Truth Held Forth and Maintained;* Middlekauff, *The Mathers: Three Generations of Puritan Intellectuals, 1596-1728;* Moore, *Final Notes on Witchcraft in Massachusetts;* Neal, *History of the Puritans;* Nevins, *Witchcraft in Salem Village in 1692;* Orians, "New England Witchcraft in Fiction"; Palfrey, *History of New England;* Perley, *The History of Salem, Massachusetts;* ____, *Salem Witchcraft Trials;* Phillips, *Salem in the Seventeenth Century; Plymouth Church Record, 1620-1859;* Powers, *Crime and Punishment in Early Massachusetts, 1620-1692;* Powers, *Secrecy and Power;* Prince, *A Chronological History of New England in the Form of Annals;* Putnam, *Witchcraft of New England Explained by Modern Spiritualism;* Robbins, *The Encyclopedia of Witchcraft and Demonology;* Roberts, *Famous American Trials;* Sawyer, *History of the Pilgrims and the Puritans;* Schneider, *The Puritan Mind;* Seth, *Witches and Their Craft;* Silverman, *The Life and Times of Cotton Mather;* Smith, *Man and His Gods; Some Miscellany Observations on Our Present Debates Respecting Witchcraft;* Starkey, *The Devil in Massachusetts;* Summers, *Discovery of Witches;* ____, *The Geography of Witchcraft;* ____, *The History of Witchcraft;* ____, *Popular History of Witchcraft;* ____, *Witchcraft and Black Magic;* Swain, *History of Torture;* Tapley, *Rebecca Nurse;* Upham, *Lectures on Witchcraft;* ____, *Salem Witchcraft;* Wagenknecht, *The Supernatural of New England;* Washburn, *Sketches in the Judicial History of Massachusetts;* Waters, *Ipswich in the Massachusetts Bay Colony;* Weeden, *Economic and Social History of New England;* Wendell, *Cotton Mather, The Puritan Priest;* Willard, *Some Miscellany Observations on Our Present Debates Respecting Witchcraft;* Willison, *Saints and Sinners, Being the Lives of the Pilgrim Fathers & Their Families & Their Friends and Foes;* Wilson, *Witches;* Woodward, *Records of the Salem Witchcraft;* (FICTION), Baker, *Peace, My Daughter;* Castleton, *Salem;* Forbes, *A Mirror for Witches;* Garis, *With Force in Arms;* Hammond, *Road to Endor;* Hawthorne, *The House of Seven Gables;* Reid, *The Devil's Hand Maidens;* (FILM), *Witchcraft Through the Ages,* 1921, silent; *Maid of Salem,* 1937; *Witches of Salem* (Fr., *Les Sorcieres de Salem*), 1957; *Witchcraft,* 1964.

Salerno, Anthony (**AKA: Fat Tony Salerno**), 1911-   , U.S., org. crime. On May 3, 1977, Mafia figure Anthony "Fat Tony" Salerno was indicted with his brother and five others on federal charges of running a New York City gambling ring that allegedly took in $10 million a year. As principal defendant, Salerno was charged with controlling and managing the operation which employed 200 people. Salerno, sixty-five at the time, was a key figure in the gambling business of the late Vito Genovese's crime family then under the leadership of Frank "Funzi" Tieri. Though Salerno had a long record of arrests he had suffered no major convictions and so in 1978 was convicted and sentenced to a six-month jail term on first-time charges of gambling and tax evasion. U.S. Attorney Robert B. Fiske, Jr. said the tax evasion charge accompanying the indictment accused Salerno of failing to report over $130,000 in income from 1971 to 1974, and credited the FBI, the IRS, and the New York City Police Department for gaining the indictment. Also charged were Salerno's brother, Cirino Salerno, and Vincent Cafaro, Gaetano Cirillo, Nicholas Cirillo, Anthony Napoli, and Michael DeSalvo.

In October 1986, *Fortune* magazine rated 75-year-old Salerno as America's top gangster in terms of power, wealth, and influence. In a kind of hit parade of mob bosses, *Fortune* classified a number of Mafia and other criminal figures in the $50-billion-a-year organized crime industry. Under Genovese family boss Tieri, Salerno functioned as consigliere while leading the Harlem number rackets, which earned $50 million annually. When Tieri died in 1981 Salerno came into full power. Under his leadership the Genovese family expanded its involvement in narcotics, loan sharking, extortion, pornography, gambling, waterfront activities, union racketeering, and vending machines.

On Nov. 19, 1986, in a Manhattan Federal District Court, Salerno and several other defendants were convicted of conducting the affairs of "the commission of La Cosa Nostra." At the sentencing on Jan. 13, 1987, Judge Richard Owen called the defendants vicious racketeers who operated the Mafia's board of directors. Owen gave 100-year sentences to seven of the convicted crime leaders, including Salerno, Anthony "Ducks" Corallo, seventy-three, of the Lucchese family, Carmine "Junior" Persico, fifty-three, of the Columbo group, Ralph Scopo, fifty-eight, a Colombo family member, Salvatore "Tom Mix" Santoro, seventy two, and Christopher "Christie Tick" Furnari, sixty-two. The last two were sentenced as the underboss and counselor of the Lucchese family. Defendant Anthony "Bruno" Indelicato, who had been convicted of participating in the 1979 slaying of crime boss Carmine Gallante, received a forty-year sentence. Gennaro "Gerry Lang" Langella, forty-eight, convicted in a separate racketeering case along with Persico, had already been given a sixty-five-year jail term. In sentencing Salerno, Judge Owen said, "You have essentially spent a lifetime terrorizing this community to your financial advantage."

Except for Indelicato, all of the defendants were convicted of operating a ring that extorted payoffs from contractors in the process of allocating concrete contracts. Two other crime bosses were also charged in the case, Paul Castellano of the Gambino group, who was killed in 1985, and Bonanno family member Philip Rastelli who was convicted in a separate 1986 trial.

REF.: Alexander, *The Pizza Connection; CBA;* Demaris, *The Last Mafioso;* Gage, *The Mafia is not an Equal Opportunity Employer;* Reid, *The Grim Reapers;* Velie, *Desperate Bargain: Why Jimmy Hoffa Had to Die;* Zuckerman, *Vengeance Is Mine.*

Salii, Lazarus, 1936-88, Palau, polit. corr.-suic. Since the end of WWII, the island of Palau in the western Pacific Ocean has been a U.S. protectorate. Succeeding Palau governments had committed to a policy of "free association" in which the U.S. was permitted to maintain military bases while Palau obtained self-rule and the right to chart its own political destiny.

This was the policy followed by President Lazarus Salii, who was elected to office in August 1985 following the June 30 assassination of Haruo Remeliik. Salii was popular with U.S. diplomats, despite growing allegations of official corruption within his administration and an increased reliance on marijuana as the chief agricultural export in the region. In 1987, President Salii was accused of receiving $200,000 in kickbacks for the costly construction of a powerplant that proved to be ineffective. In August 1988, Salii was notified that the General Accounting Office was sending in officials from Washington to investigate these charges. At the same time, the president had outlined plans to announce his plans for re-election.

But on Aug. 20 Salii was shot and killed, apparently by his own hand. According to U.S. government officials, Salii shot himself in the head, although earlier unconfirmed reports listed the cause of death as political assassination. Vice-President Thomas Remengesau assumed control of the island nation, which has a population of 15,000. REF.: *CBA.*

Salinas, F.A., prom. 1922, U.S., consp.-smug. In March 1922, the U.S. Customs Service sent one of their top agents, Al Scharff, into Yuma, Ariz., to investigate a liquor smuggling operation run by the proprietor of a large general store, F.A. Salinas. Scharff and his men discovered that the store was the drop-off point for illegal liquor smuggled in from Algodones, Mex., by the Torres brothers. Each night the Mexicans dropped off sacks of liquor on the California border, which were retrieved by Salinas' agents. The booze would then find its way into the saloon operated by Salinas.

In May, after weeks of extensive surveillance of the adjoining areas, Scharff and his men intercepted a load of the contraband liquor that had been placed on a wooden raft and sent up the Colorado River. They arrested the three smugglers who manned the raft and took them to Yuma where they swore that it was Ernesto Torres who had loaded the liquor on the raft. The license plates of the cars that were used to run the liquor were listed under the name of F.A. Salinas, who was charged with conspiracy. The Torres brothers and Salinas appeared before a grand jury in Phoenix, where they heard the arrested rum-runners give testimony against them. The case was eventually brought to trial several times, but in each instance Salinas failed to appear. He became a fugitive from justice by forfeiting his bond.

REF.: *CBA;* Roark, *The Coin of Contraband.*

Salisbury, Francis, d.1697, Brit., count.-forg. Francis Salisbury was about to embark on a career in the clergy when he met counterfeiter Thomas Houghton, who worked as a candle lighter at St. Margaret's, Westminster.

Salisbury and Houghton decided to go into business forging the sixpenny stamps used on legal documents. On Sept. 12, 1697 they ran off 500 sheets of stamped paper expert enough to fool the chief engraver of the mint, Henry Harris.

Salisbury and Houghton then sold the paper at the Fountain Tavern in High Holborn, London, and at the Thatched House Tavern in Charing Cross for £5 to £6 a ream. Eventually the two were caught and on Oct. 15, 1697, they were indicted at the Old Bailey for forgery. They were convicted and sentenced to die at Tyburn on Nov. 3. See: **Houghton, Thomas**.

REF.: *CBA;* Smith, *Highwaymen.*

Salisbury, Steven A., 1953- , U.S., kid. In debt and rejected by his girlfriend, Steven A. Salisbury, twenty-four, took six persons hostage at an Aurora, Ill., bar on June 7, 1977, and held them in a five-hour siege. Salisbury's former girlfriend, Mary Hamm, twenty-eight, said, "I know he did it because of me." Aurora Police Chief Victor Puscas explained that Hamm had made admiring remarks to Salisbury about a similar siege that took place in Aurora on May 26, when 27-year-old David Kimes, a Kane County Jail prisoner, escaped and took two persons hostage. He released both eleven hours later.

Salisbury, a machinist at a Montgomery, Ill., metal products company, entered Bernie's Cheerio Inn, a tavern on New York Street in Aurora, just after 10 a.m., leaving an hour later only to return with a shotgun. After trying to sell his pickup truck, on which he owed $4,000, his motorcycle, and his gun to bar customers, he pointed the shotgun at them saying, "If nobody wants to buy my stuff, I'll just turn this into a holdup." The six hostages, all from Aurora, included Don M. Davis, sixty-four, Vernon Vawter, fifty-nine, Shirley M. Coffey, forty-one, Robert G. Sartan, forty-three, Eldon Lee Minor, thirty-five, and Ralph Bahe, fifty. Two were bar employees and the others patrons. A seventh hostage, flower shop owner Phil Reuland, was freed when he told Salisbury he had heart trouble. Reuland then told police of the incident at approximately 11 a.m. The area was blocked off by police and a large crowd gathered to watch.

The hostages were allowed to continue drinking, listening to the jukebox, playing shuffleboard, and ordering out for pizza during the five hour siege. Salisbury took twenty-five phone calls from police and reporters but made no demands. According to Bahe the kidnapper "threatened to blow all our brains out—he threatened to kill everyone constantly. He pointed the shotgun up against my head." When asked by a reporter what he was trying to accomplish Salisbury replied, "Oh, nothing." He held off police, FBI agents, chaplains, and relatives until he was overpowered by hostages Minor and Davis. According to one hostage, the two men tackled Salisbury not long after he warned them, "If you keep fooling around, you're going to get it." The two men tackled Salisbury as he talked to his brother Kevin through a rear door of the tavern. FBI agents and police then burst into the tavern, discovering that Salisbury's 12-gauge shotgun was not loaded.

Salisbury pleaded guilty on Dec. 5, 1977, to armed violence and was given a one-to-three year prison sentence the same day. REF.: *CBA.*

Salmon, Sheldon J., 1942- , and **Helman, William**, 1947- , and **Truen, Jerome**, 1946- , U.S., consp.-fraud. Sheldon Salmon and two business associates, William Helman and Jerome Truen were among nine executives of the defunct S.J. Salmon brokerage firm accused of manipulating over-the-counter stock sales that bilked investors out of millions of dollars.

The one-count federal indictment, handed down on Jan. 27, 1977, charged the investors with artificially raising the price and controlling the market for nine over-the-counter stocks that were underwritten by the firm. The scheme was carried out over a three year period, from 1969 until 1972, until Salmon & Company was forced to liquidate because of repeated security violations. On May 5, 1988, Sheldon Salmon and William Holman were sentenced to eighteen months in prison. Truen, who had served as the company's principle officer, was sentenced to two years. The three had pleaded guilty before judges Charles E. Stewart and John Cannella on separate charges involving securities law violations. REF.: *CBA.*

Salmon, Thomas, 1833-85, U.S., arson-mur. Thomas Salmon committed the first triple murder in New Hampshire on Nov. 24-25, 1883, and then tried to hide the crime by setting fire to the victim's residence. Salmon, an unbalanced man and nervous by nature, was arrested and almost lynched by the townspeople of Laconia.

Salmon was born in Dublin, Ire. He sailed to Boston with his brother John during the first great wave of Irish immigration to the U.S. in the 1840s, a time when thousands of young Irishmen, impoverished by the potato famine crossed over to seek their fortune. The Salmon brothers opened a wholesale liquor dealership in the city and did well. Later, Thomas moved to New Hampshire where he worked as a cook in some of the state's finest hostelries. He married Johanna Welch, a widow, on July 27, 1882. The couple set up housekeeping in a crowded tenement building in Laconia, upstairs from Mrs. Jane Ford.

On the morning of Nov. 24, 1883, Jane Ford entered Salmon's apartment. Both had been drinking the night before and still were at it. Ford demanded more beer from Salmon, but he had exhausted his supply. Angry words passed and in a moment of unbridled anger Salmon flung the woman to the floor and crushed her chest with the soles of his feet. "When I flung her to the floor

I felt mad and discouraged, but I had no thought of killing her," Salmon said in his confession to police. "I don't know what I did. I went round the house completely bewildered, leaving her on the floor." His mind racing, Salmon pulled out a large trunk, but the woman's body barely fit inside. Taking his ax, he tried to sever the corpse at the knees. After an hour Salmon succeeded in cramming the remains into the trunk. He pulled the cumbersome parcel down the stairs and transported it by wheelbarrow to the home of James Reddy.

Salmon explained to Rosa Reddy that he had been directed to deliver the trunk to the front yard. Since her husband was not home at the time Rosa suggested that Salmon leave the trunk by the side of the house until he arrived. Thomas Salmon obliged and went on his way. Later that afternoon he returned with James Reddy. Since Salmon's wife was visiting friends in Plymouth, the Reddys suggested that Salmon and spend the night with them. The evening passed quietly, nothing was said about the trunk sitting in the yard. Salmon retired to his bedroom and the house remained quiet until midnight.

Late that night Reddy was awakened by the sound of Salmon's footsteps. He entered his guest's room and asked him what troubled him. Salmon and Reddy spoke in low tones for several minutes, Salmon explaining that he thought he heard the sounds of a prowler and was nervous. At one point Mrs. Reddy peered in. Assured the matter was under control, Rosa returned to her room. A short time later she was awakened by a loud crash in the kitchen. "I sprang from my bed," she recalled, "went into the kitchen, and saw my husband in a chair with his head hanging over the back and apparently dead. Before I could touch him, Salmon rushed upon me and struck me with an ax, cutting my left hand nearly off." Rosa attempted to run away, but Salmon brought the hatchet down on her head and on that of her son Frank. The woman fell to the floor but did not lose consciousness. She feigned death while the madman covered the bodies of her son and husband with feather pillows. Salmon went into the other room and doused the straw bed with kerosene. What was left was poured over the three Reddys. "I could feel the oil as it struck my face and ran down my neck," she said. "Salmon then set the feather bed on fire and ran out of the house." Mrs. Reddy struggled to her feet and made it to the front yard where she collapsed. A neighbor, Stephen Andrews, heard the screams and summoned the police. Rosa, who survived, provided an accurate narrative of what had happened. The town's selectmen posted a $300 reward for the capture of Salmon, which was easily accomplished later that same day. Under questioning the murderer confessed to his crime and was arraigned at the county jail on Dec. 6 before Judge John G. Jewett. When asked of his guilt or innocence, Salmon stared straight ahead and without the slightest hesitation answered "Guilty."

Salmon was found Guilty of first-degree murder and given the death sentence on Apr. 11, 1884. He was hanged on Apr. 17, 1885, at the state prison in Concord, N.H.

REF.: *CBA; Particulars of the New Hampshire Horror, with Sketches of the Murderer and His Victims.*

Salmon Falls (Maine) Assaults, 1683, U.S., witchcraft. The account of a demonic poltergeist that plagued Mary Hortado in Salmon Falls, Maine, was described by Increase Mather in his *Illustrious Providences,* published in 1684. In June 1682, Hortado claimed that she heard voices outside her dwelling, and that a mysterious object struck her in the temple as she stood outside her door, and a large stone had mysteriously appeared, and then vanished into the chimney.

Hortado later claimed that she and her husband saw a floating head and a cat's tail while sailing in their canoe. These and other unearthly apparitions were assiduously recorded by Mather as proof of the existence of witchcraft in New England. See: **Mather, Increase**.

REF.: *CBA;* Mather, *An Essay for the Recording of Illustrious Providences;* Robbins, *The Encyclopedia of Witchcraft and Demonology;* Summers, *The Geography of Witchcraft.*

Salomen, Edith (AKA: **Ann O'Delia Diss Debar, Vera P. Ava, Countess Landsfeldt, Sister Mary, Theo the Swami**), b.1849, U.S.-Brit., fraud. For a stiff price Edith Salomen promised to conjure up the long departed spirits of Shakespeare, Cicero, Frederick the Great, or anyone with whom people, with the ability to pay, cared to speak. Salomen was one of the nineteenth century's most famous con artists, having learned the technique at an early age from her father, who passed himself off as a learned professor.

Born in Kentucky, Salomen left home when she was twenty. She caused an immediate stir in Baltimore by claiming to be the illegitimate daughter of the famous dancer Lola Montez and her lover, Ludwig I of Bavaria. The local newspapers were filled with stories about the long-lost heiress and scion. Eager to make her acquaintance, many of the city's most eligible young bachelors asked for her hand in marriage. One man in particular, whose family was a pillar in local society, turned over nearly $200,000 to the swindler, and then Salomen was exposed as a fraud by his parents. While awaiting her fate, Salomen began smoking opium in such large amounts that she had to be hospitalized. One morning she arose from her bed, seized a knife, and stabbed an orderly. Salomen ran screaming through the corridors trying to convince the doctors that she was indeed insane. They were easily fooled.

Committed to an asylum, Salomen enticed a physician named Mesant into marriage. The doctor agreed to sign her release papers and in the following year Salomen was back on the streets. Mesant conveniently passed away which afforded the widow a chance to branch out to a more lucrative field, hypnotic mysticism. In New York she married General Diss Debar, taking the name "Ann O'Delia Diss Debar" for her alias. She set up shop on Madison Avenue, advertising séances on demand. Salomen would lapse into a semi-hypnotic trance, bringing back the souls of the dearly departed. Her most famous victim was Luther R. Marsh, an aging lawyer whose lifelong dream was to become a famous painter. Salomen put him in touch with the sixteenth century master Raphael after Marsh had given her a sizable amount of cash. In ten days, she promised, Raphael would produce an original oil on canvas. The famous Italian artist was a man of his word. Marsh viewed the original work in a locked cabinet ten days later. As an added touch, the paint was still wet.

The astonished lawyer became a true believer. Next he wanted to commune with Shakespeare, Charlemagne, and Cicero. Once his money was gone Marsh signed over the deed to his house on Madison Avenue. Finally, relatives came to his rescue and had Salomen and her confederates arrested. She served six months in jail and was released. At this point the seer had no further need of a husband. She divorced the general and with a new identity as Madame Vera P. Ava took to the lecture circuit, combining her talks on the spiritual world with a crude vaudeville routine. She was hooted off the stage. A series of bigamous marriages followed. In Kansas City she married a man named Smith, but abandoned him after picking his bank accounts clean. Salomen moved on New Orleans, taking for her husband a man named Mr. Jackson. He became her trusted assistant, helping her set up a series of "psychic lectures" in which she again brought forward the famous and the obscure from the spirit world. The Countess Landsfeldt, as she now called herself, was soon exposed. "The most popular ghost was that of Frederick the Great," commented one journalist, "and for an extra charge of two dollars per head he appeared wearing the Imperial Crown of Germany, oblivious to the fact that that particular crown was in the possession of the Austrians."

Forced to flee New Orleans, she continued to Chicago, where she was dubbed Sister Mary. This time the scam involved raising money for a fictitious orphanage. From there, Salomen and her husband traveled to Capetown, S. Afri. She opened up a "Theosophical University," which handed out degrees in the field of "higher mysticism." When the university was forced to close down, Salomen took her show to England where she was known as "Theo the Swami," a new variation on the Theosophical University swindle. Jackson and Salomen were exposed as frauds by Chief Detective Inspector Kane of Scotland Yard. The self-styled Swami was placed on trial in 1901, found Guilty, and sentenced to seven years in prison. After completing her sentence, Salomen left England for the U.S. where she faded into obscurity.

REF.: *CBA;* Nash, *Look for the Woman.*

Salter, Sir **Arthur Clavell,** 1859-1928, Brit., jur. Successfully prosecuted Leo George O'Donnell for murder, and prosecuted Georges Codère. He served on the High Court, King's Bench, from 1917-28, presiding over the murder trials of Lieutenant-Colonel Norman Cecil Rutherford, Henry Griffin (second trial), and Alfred Solomon. REF.: *CBA.*

Saltis, Joseph (AKA: **Polack Joe**), prom. 1920s, U.S., org. crime. In the years before Al Capone consolidated his holdings at the expense of his hoodlum rivals, Chicago was partitioned into "spheres of influence," where territorial rights were strictly observed. The Southwest Side for example, was the domain of "Polack" Joe Saltis, a beefy gangster and bootlegger who owned a saloon in Joliet, Ill., before WWI. With the advent of Prohibition in 1920, Saltis teamed up with John "Dingbat" O'Berta, a state senatorial candidate with political ambitions, to supply bootleg liquor to some of the 200,000 residents of the Southwest Side.

Saltis and O'Berta made a fortune in a few short years. By 1925, the Polish bootlegger was a wealthy, self-made man who celebrated his notoriety by purchasing an estate near Eagle River, Wis. (Saltis' ego knew no bounds. He employed thirty-one of the sixty residents of a nearby community, thus ensuring their loyalty on election day when a referendum came asking the voters whether the town shall be renamed Saltisville.) Back in Chicago Joe Saltis paid lip service to Al Capone, his powerful neighbor on the South Side. At the same time he concluded a secret "treaty" with North Side mobster Earl "Hymie" Weiss to drive Capone out of Chicago.

Chicago bootlegger Joe Saltis.

Saltis fortified his empire by recruiting such gunmen as Frank "Lefty" Koncil, Charlie "Big Hayes" Hubacek, and Frankie McErlane, who would become a full partner in the operation shortly. In 1925, John "Mitters" Foley was silenced by O'Berta, Koncil, and Saltis, after he meddled in the Southwest Side. O'Berta and his associates were indicted for murder, but the case was dropped, in part due to the Dingbat's considerable political clout. The next year, O'Berta arranged a conference of all of Chicago's powerful gangsters at the Hotel Sherman. Present at the Oct. 20, 1926, meeting were Capone, George "Bugs" Moran, Vincent "Schemer" Drucci, Jake "Greasy Thumb" Guzik, Ralph Sheldon, William Skidmore, Maxie Eisen, Jack Zuta, and Christian P. "Barney" Bertsche. Pledging to respect each other's turf, a cease fire was declared with Madison Avenue established as the boundary line between the Capone interests and the North Side Moran gang. The fragile peace barely lasted two months. It was shattered on Dec. 30, 1926, when Saltis bullets tore apart Hillary Clements, a member of the Ralph Sheldon gang. Saltis and Sheldon had wrangled over the Southwest Side territory for over a year. Capone had been using Sheldon to gain a foothold in Saltis' neighborhoods. Eight months earlier, in April 1926, two of Sheldon's beer runners, John Tucillo and Frank DeLaurentis were stopped by Saltis gunmen. The murder of Clements contributed to an already tense and difficult situation. On Mar. 11, 1927, Frank "Lefty" Koncil, and Charlie Hubacek were lured into a trap and machine gunned to death. Saltis deemed it prudent to make his peace with Capone.

Frankie McErlane, who pioneered the use of the Thompson sub-machine gun in Chicago, quit Saltis in late 1929. He was disgruntled by his share of the bootleg profits after being denied a bigger cut. Then on Jan. 28, 1930, McErlane was shot at, presumably by Saltis' men. The police questioned him from his hospital bed. But all they could get out of him was characteristic indifference. "Shoo, shoo!" he laughed. "Just say the war's on again. It's been brewing since last November. You'll all know about it in two weeks." The police were not disappointed. On Mar. 25, 1930, O'Berta and his chauffeur Sam Malaga were taken for a "one way ride." They found O'Berta with his head blown off.

All this was too much for Joe Saltis, who retired to his lavish Wisconsin estate a year later. "I'm out of the racket," he told Chief of Detectives John Stege. "I got a fine country home and farm at Saltisville on Barker Lake, Wisconsin." Saltis' Southwest Side territory was swallowed by Capone, and the remnants of his old mob dispersed. See: **Capone, Alphonse; Sheldon Gang; Eisen, Maxie; Moran, George; Drucci, Vincent.**

REF.: Asbury, *Gem of the Prairie; CBA;* Kobler, *Al Capone;* Landesco, *Organized Crime in Chicago;* McPhaul, *Johnny Torrio;* Morgan, *Prince of Crime;* Nash, *Bloodletters and Badmen;* Smith, *Syndicate City*

Salute to a Hero, 1942, a novel by Constance Robertson. Daniel Sickles' fatal shooting of Philip Barton Key (U.S., 1859), Sickles' wife's secret lover, is the basis of this work of fiction. See: **Sickles, Daniel.** REF.: *CBA.*

Salvage, Arthur James Farraday, 1908- , Brit., mur. On July 5, 1931, Arthur Salvage, a poultry farmer from Ruckinge, Kent, murdered an 11-year-old neighbor girl, Ivy Mary Godden, and then buried her in the woods. Salvage joined the search party which was unable to locate the remains of the child for two full days. On the third day Ivy's body was found in a shallow grave. A bloodhound was brought to the scene of the crime, and while Salvage amused himself in a game of cricket, the dog traced a path back to his residence in Sunningdale.

Salvage offered a hasty confession, and was brought before Justice MacNaghten at the Old Bailey the following September. A Guilty verdict was returned after Salvage had recanted his earlier confession on the grounds that the constables had made him certain guarantees. He was given the death sentence, but upon further examination by psychiatrists Salvage was declared insane. Under the terms of the Criminal Lunatics Act of 1884, he was committed to the Broadmoor Asylum for life. The murder might have been avoided if authorities had listened to earlier recommendations by doctors. Prison doctors recommended his committal after Salvage served time in prison for theft in 1927, but authorities released Salvage.

REF.: Adam, *Murder Most Mysterious; CBA;* Neil, *Manhunters of Scotland Yard;* Shew, *A Second Companion to Murder;* Woodhall, *Secrets of Scotland Yard.*

Salvator, Johann (AKA: **John Orth**), 1852-90, Aust., miss. per. Archduke Johann Salvador of Austria, the youngest son of Leopold II of Tuscany and a second cousin of Emperor Franz Josef of Austria-Hungary, set sail from Ensenada on the southern shore of Argentina on July 14, 1890. The day before, the archduke dispatched a message to his attorney in Vienna that he was leaving for Valparaiso on board his vessel the *Santa Margarita.* He said that he expected to reach port in about sixty days, and had taken personal command of the ship.

With a crew of twenty-six, Salvator and his wife Ludmilla Stübel, a former star of the Viennese stage, embarked on the fatal voyage. Two months passed, without a word from the vessel which should have passed through the treacherous Straits of Magellan. Through diplomatic channels, the Argentine government sent out a fleet of forty vessels at the behest of Austria to search for the doomed ship. A Chilean steamer named the *Toro* assisted in the futile hunt, but there was no trace of the *Santa Margarita,* which by all accounts simply vanished.

The disappearance of the Archduke created a sensation. The 38-year-old monarch had been cashiered out of the Austrian Army just three years earlier, after publishing a pamphlet that was critical of training methods employed by the high command. In 1889 he petitioned the emperor for permission to relinquish all titles and formal connections to the royal house. Accordingly, Salvator assumed the name of John Orth, after the family estate on the Gmüdensee. His marriage to an actress further scandalized the Hapsburg empire and led to speculation that the couple had met with foul play.

By 1912, it was rumored that he had not dissappeared, but in fact had gone into hiding in South America with his wife. As the years passed there were dozens of unsubstantiated reports that Orth was alive in Canada, South Africa, and the U.S. On Mar. 31, 1924, a death report was filed by the Department of Health in New York City, attesting that a man who identified himself as the missing archduke had died at Columbus Hospital. The story was confirmed by eyewitnesses, and it was given credence by the sensational suicide of Grace Wakefield in her Fifty-ninth Street apartment that afternoon. The woman's claim to be the ward of the archduke, could be neither proven nor completely discounted.

REF.: *CBA;* Smith, *Mysteries of the Missing.*

Sam, Vilbrun Guillaume, d.1915, Haiti, pres., assass. Assumed short-lived presidency after leading revolution in 1915. After several months, he was ousted and killed by a throng of attackers, opening the way for intervention by the U.S. REF.: *CBA.*

Sambhaji, Raja, d.1689, India, raja, assass. Second ruler of India's Maratha kingdom. He was seized and put to death by Aurangzeb. REF.: *CBA.*

Samory (Samory Toure), c.1830-1900, Guinea, exile. Formed Mandingo kingdom located in the Kankan region of Guinea in 1868, and expanded realm to Fouta Djallon from Upper Volta region. He frustrated attempts by the French to colonize West Africa, but was seized and exiled by the French in 1898. REF.: *CBA.*

Samples, Duane, 1942- , U.S., mur. Duane Samples was a seemingly normal college student in Salem, Ore., until he left school to serve in Vietnam. In 1975 he viciously attacked two women with a ten-inch knife. One of them died; the other, Diane Ross, narrowly escaped death.

Samples was convicted of murder and sentenced to life imprisonment at the Oregon State Penitentiary. In 1980, Governor Vic Atiyeh commuted the sentence to twenty years in prison after reviewing psychiatric reports that described Samples as suffering from a delayed-stress syndrome caused by his experiences in Vietnam, which compelled him to act out a lurid sexual fantasy involving violence and murder.

A year later, on Sept. 3, 1981, Governor Atiyeh rescinded his commutation order after hearing conflicting opinions about the original prognosis. A previously unpublished 1971 report alleged that Samples had beaten up a woman, which cast some doubts on his "delayed" stress syndrome. In May 1970, Samples had written a letter to his girlfriend, in which he discussed the ways and means of disemboweling women. Marion County district attorney Chris Van Dyke described Samples as a sexual sadist, and a danger to the community. In his own defense, Samples pointed out that after he returned from Vietnam he had opened a clinic in Salem to help troubled youths. "No one can claim Vietnam takes away their responsibility for what they did, but there were some things in me not strong enough. I reacted poorly to that experience," he said. REF.: *CBA.*

Sampson, Nicos, 1934- , Cyprus, terr.-treas. After a brief but bloody military coup, Nicos Sampson was proclaimed President of Cyprus in 1974. It was the culmination of a political struggle that began years earlier when he joined the radical EOKA nationalist movement, which sought unification of Cyprus with the Greek mainland. Sampson is alleged to have commanded an elite group of assassins who carried out the systematic murder-executions of twenty people in Nicosia between August 1956 and January 1957 on Ledra Street—known as the "murder mile."

In 1963 he carried out additional attacks against various Turkish villages. By 1974 Sampson was a part of the Cypriot mainstream, having been elected to the House of Representatives as the principle spokesman for Greek nationalism. After his government was toppled, the ex-president was imprisoned in Nicosia on a charge of treason.

REF.: Bell, *Assassin; CBA.*

Samuels, Joseph, prom. 1803, Aus., (wrong. convict.) mur. Joseph Samuels was transported to New South Wales for the murder of a police constable. He steadfastly maintained his innocence until the moment he faced the hangman on the gallows in Sydney. The assembled crowd took pity on Samuels, who said the actual murderer, a man named Simmonds, stood among them. The noisy mob demanded that Samuels be set free. The provost marshal however, ordered the "drop." The rope broke and Samuels fell to the ground unconscious.

After two more exeuction attempts failed, the marshal petitioned the governor for a reprieve. Simmonds was arrested and convicted of murder, and hanged with a rope that was tested before the execution.

REF.: Atholl, *Shadow of the Gallows; CBA.*

Samuelson, Victor, prom. 1974, Arg., kid. (vict.). In the mid-1970s, Argentina was a dangerous country for international business executives. The *Ejercito Revolucionario del Pueblo* (People's Revolutionary Army, or ERP) was at constant war with the government headed by President Juan Peron. On Dec. 6, 1973, the ERP abducted Victor Samuelson, director of Esso-Argentina Inc., a subsidiary of Exxon. The company paid a record sum of $14.2 million to secure the release of Samuelson from the hands of the Argentine guerrillas after five months of negotiation. He was freed unharmed on Apr. 30, 1974. Two Exxon shareholders later brought a suit against the company by charging that it had breached its fiduciary obligations, but the case was dismissed by the Manhattan Supreme Court on July 27, 1988. REF.: *CBA.*

Sanchez, Hector Reuben, 1946- , and **Peters, Warren, Jr.,** 1955- , U.S., kid.-mur. On Feb. 4, 1984, Michelle Thompson was sitting with a male companion named Rene Valentine in a parked car outside a popular nightspot in Gurnee, Ill., north of Chicago, when Hector Sanchez, thirty-eight, and Warren Peters, twenty-nine, accosted them. Sanchez shot and wounded Valentine, who was believed to have been involved in a drug deal, then he and Peters dragged Thompson back to Sanchez's deluxe $200,000 home in nearby Zion where thet raped and killed her. The body was found in a ditch near Milwaukee, Wis.

The 21-year-old victim was a former cheerleader, aspiring model, and the daughter of a prominent Zion family. Her companion was a cousin of her boyfriend's. Two days after the murder, Sanchez visited the Kenosha, Wis., home of Daniel Mika, seeking an alibi. According to Mika's statements to the FBI, Sanchez said that Valentine had held an ice pick to the back of his neck and that Peters had shot him. Mika felt uneasy about the whole matter and approached the FBI with the story.

Sanchez was arrested and charged with kidnapping, deviant sexual assault, attempted murder, and murder, and Peters was charged with kidnapping and attempted murder. Peters was convicted on Feb. 17, 1984, and sentenced to a total of 140 years in prison. On Aug. 30, 1984, a Lake County Jury returned a verdict of Guilty against Sanchez, amidst tearful pleas from the defendant that he had been mistreated as a child by his father. Two days later, the court passed a death sentence for what Assistant State's Attorney Raymond McKoski called a "brutal, heinous, and vicious" crime. REF.: *CBA.*

Sanchez, Ilyich Ramirez (AKA: **Carlos, The Jackal**), 1949- , Aust.-Libya, terr. The character of Carlos in Frederick Forsyth's novel the *Day of the Jackal* was loosely based on Ilyich Sanchez, a multinational terrorist leader.

Sanchez allied himself with the PFLP (Popular Front for the Liberation of Palestine) factions in Lebanon where he personally directed a number of terrorist campaigns against the West and its allies in the oil-producing regions of the Middle East. The most sensational attack carried out by Carlos and his pro-Palestinian guerrillas involved eighty-one OPEC (Organization of Petroleum Exporting Communities) delegates who gathered in Vienna on Dec. 21, 1975. The conference was in its second day when six terrorists, led by Carlos, seized the OPEC ministers and demanded safe passage out of the country in the name of the "Arm of the Arab Revolution."

Austrian Chancellor Bruno Kreisky and Algerian Foreign Minister Abdul Aziz Bouteflika negotiated the safe release of the forty-one Austrians taken during the raid, permitting Sanchez to fly to Algiers with the remaining contingency of African, South American, and Arab delegates. On Dec. 22, a number of neutral hostages were released, before the plane was forced to fly on to Tripoli. There, King Khaled of Saudi Arabia and the Shah of Iran paid a ransom estimated to be as high as $50 million to secure their release. Carlos freed the remaining hostages and disappeared into Libya, via Algiers, on Dec. 30. Carlos is still at large.

Terrorist Ilyich Ramirez Sanchez.

REF.: Bell, *Assassin; CBA;* Dobson and Payne, *The Carlos Complex;* ____, *The Terrorists—Their Weapons, Leaders and Tactics;* Hacker, *Crusaders, Criminals, Crazies: Terror and Terrorism in Our Time;* Schreiber, *The Ultimate Weapon—Terrorists and World Order;* Smith, *Carlos, Portrait of a Terrorist;* Wilson, *The Encyclopedia of Modern Murder.*

Sanchez Cerro, Luis M., 1889-1933, Peru, pres., assass. Coerced resignation of dictatorial Peruvian President Augusto Bernardino Leguia y Salcedo by heading successful revolution in 1930. He served as provincial president from 1930-31. He was temporarily ousted by a coup in 1931, but was elected to the presidency several months later. He held the office until his assassination. REF.: *CBA.*

Sanchez de Bustamante y Sirven, Antonio, 1865-1951, Cuba, jur. Served as delegate to second Hague International Conference in 1907, and to Paris Peace Conference ending WWI in 1919. He served as a judge on the Permanent Court of International Justice from 1921-39. He authored the Bustamante Code concerning international private law, approved in 1928. REF.: *CBA.*

Sancho II (AKA: The Strong), d.1072, king, assass. Son of Ferdinand I. He was defeated by Sancho IV of Navarre in 1071, and assassinated during a storming of Zamora. REF.: *CBA.*

Sancho IV (AKA: El Noble), c.1039-1076, king, assass. Battled Moors and the king of Castile. He used his great intellect to coax the King of Saragossa, who supported the Moors, to be his puppet. He was probably killed by his brothers. REF.: *CBA.*

Sancroft, William, 1617-93, Case of, Brit., libel. Named archbishop of Canterbury in 1678. He and six bishops were acquitted of seditious libel charges in 1688. He was stripped of his authority after refusing to accept the sovereignty of William III in 1690. REF.: *CBA.*

Sand Bar Gun Battle, 1827, U.S., duel.-mob vio. Following a duel between Dr. Thomas H. Maddox and Samuel L. Wells on Sept. 18, 1827, near Concordia Parish, La., the seconds and friends of each, all "gentlemen" of good social standing, became involved in a brawl in which two men were killed and two wounded. Wells, the brother of the Governor of Louisiana, was seconded by Robert A. Crain, who wrote a detailed report of the fray to his friend, General Joseph Walker.

In the letter written on Oct. 3, 1827, Crain explained how Wells and Maddox had fired two shots each, neither being wounded, and had then agreed that the matter was honorably settled, with Wells withdrawing earlier negative remarks he had made to Maddox. Included among the twelve men present besides Crain, Wells and Maddox, were Jim Bowie, Sam Cuney, Jeff Wells, a Dr. Denny, a man named McWhorter, a man named Wright, and two men named Blanchard. After the duel Wells suggested to Crain that they go for a glass of wine, and Crain said they would be better off going downriver to a friend's house to drink and "bury the hatchet." Wells agreed, collected the pistols, and they hiked down to the Sand Bar, with Bowie, Cuney, and Jeff Wells running after them. They intercepted Crain and Cuney pulled a gun on him saying, "Now is the time to settle our affair." Bowie and Crain both drew guns, after which Crain and Cuney fired simultaneously. Cuney was wounded. Bowie raised his knife—later known as a "Bowie knife" when he became a colonel and gained fame for his fighting exploits—but was hit in the head with the butt of Crain's pistol before he could use it. Wright and Bowie exchanged shots and Wright was mortally wounded, hit by a bullet and then by the hunting knife. Bowie was wounded by Wright's bullet. When Wright fell dead the fighting stopped. The action had taken place in a space less than thirty yards square, according to Crain. REF.: *CBA.*

Sand Creek Massacre, 1864, U.S., mur. John Chivington was the minister and soldier who commanded the slaughter of 450 Indian men, women, and children in the Sand Creek Massacre of Nov. 29, 1864, in the Cheyenne Territory in Colorado. Following the mass murder he was court-martialed but won acquittal. According to most authorities Chivington allegedly was never able to work again, tainted by the stigma of the massacre. In reality he moved to Denver, Colo., and got a job as an under-sheriff, a post he held for several years until his death in 1894. Chivington was said to have performed honorably and won the respect of those who worked with him, despite his notorious past. See: **Reynolds Gang**. REF.: *CBA.*

Sander, Hermann N., 1908- , Case of, U.S., mur. In 1941, Dr. Hermann Sander and his wife settled in Manchester, N.H., and he established a private practice. Regarded as a kind and compassionate physician, Sander provided free care to his poorest patients. In 1950, however, he became the center of an ethical controversy.

Mrs. Abbie C. Borroto, fifty-nine, was in the final stages of cancer. As she lay dying at Hillsborough County General Hospital in Goffstown, N.H., Dr. Sander was deeply moved by her plight. Mrs. Borroto's husband, Reginald Borroto, begged the doctor to ease her pain and, if necessary, "eliminate her life."

Sander wrestled with his conscience and remembered the vows he had taken. But the anguish of his patient drove him to commit euthanasia on Dec. 4, 1949. "Something snapped," he said. "Why I did it, I can't tell. It was just the appearance of her face and the remembrance of her long suffering that might have touched me off."

Dr. Sander ended Mrs. Borroto's life by administering four ten-cc injections of air into her veins, which brought on embolism within minutes. Nurse Elizabeth Rose later testified that she was certain Mrs. Borroto was already dead before Sander entered the room. "She had death pallor," Rose explained. "She was not breathing." The following week Dr. Sander had the records librarian, Josephine Connor, enter the notation describing his action and the resulting death into the ledger.

Two more weeks passed before the medical librarian reported the entry to her superiors. "It kind of slipped my mind," she explained. Dr. Sander was arrested on Dec. 29 and indicted on a charge of first-degree murder. He was tried at the Hillsborough County Courthouse in March 1950. The people of Manchester were divided in their opinions. A brother of the victim said her suffering "should have been left to the will of God." County Solicitor William Craig expressed the belief that "mercy killing is an act similar to murder." This view was also held by State's Attorney General William Phinney, who added, "simply because the adjective 'mercy' is inserted before 'killing' does not alter the situation."

Attorneys interviewed over seventy potential jurors and finally impaneled a jury including nine Roman Catholics. The prosecution tried to portray Dr. Sander as a killer who not only violated medical ethics, but flagrantly disregarded the law. Defense attorney Louis Wyman said there had been no murder, since Mrs. Borroto was probably dead at the time of the injection.

The jury agreed with the defense. After deliberating just seventy minutes, they returned a Not Guilty verdict. The State Board of Registration in Medicine considered the case in broader ethical terms and revoked Sander's license to practice medicine in the state of New Hampshire. On June 28, 1950, the board restored his license.

REF.: *CBA;* Harrison, *Criminal Calendar;* Rowan, *Famous American Crimes.*

Sanders, Albert, d.1918, and **Brooks, Fisher**, d.1917, U.S., (wrong. convict.?) mur. In May 1917 Mrs. Julia May Hess, a visitor to the city of Mobile, Ala., was robbed and murdered by strangulation and/or drowning. The cause of death was never completely ascertained, and there is still doubt about who committed the crime. Two men died for it, but only one claimed he killed her.

Fisher Brooks and Albert Sanders, two black men, matched a description of the cab drivers who picked up Mrs. Hess, and were indicted for murder. Both men were sentenced to death, despite Sanders' protestations that he was innocent. Brooks confessed, and told the court that his friend had nothing to do with the crime. Fisher Brooks was hanged in August 1917. Sanders followed nearly a year later on July 19, 1918. Up to the last minute Sanders maintained his innocence, giving an hour by hour description of his movements the night of the murder. But the court did not budge. Commenting on the affair, the Mobile *Register* said that the city "is to be praised and congratulated that it passed through the long and trying ordeal with self-control, satisfied that the law would serve and that the guilty would be punished." REF.: *CBA.*

Sanders, Howard L., b.1896, U.S., law enfor. off. Howard Sanders joined the Indianapolis Police Department on May 10, 1921. During his thirty-two year career on the force, he held a number of positions in the uniform patrol and as courthouse bailiff. On Jan. 22, 1947, he was promoted to chief of police and served in this position until he resigned on Dec. 31 of that year. Sanders was demoted to captain the next day of business. He permanently resigned from the department on Feb. 13, 1953. He was cited for neglect of duty only once during his lengthy career, and at a formal hearing six days later the trial board exonerated him of all charges. REF.: *CBA.*

Sanders, Lindberg, d.1983, U.S., mur.-suic. Lindberg Sanders called himself the "black Jesus." He convinced nine people in the Hollywood section of Memphis, Tenn., that the end of the world was at hand. Sanders and his fellow cult members holed up in a house to await Armageddon. When it did not come, Sanders declared the Antichrist had arrived in its place.

The devil had manifested himself in the form of white policemen, he told his followers. On Jan. 7, 1983, the group placed a call to the police to complain about a purse snatcher. When patrolmen came to their house, the cultists opened fire, severely wounding another officer and Robert Hester, who was dragged into the house and tortured.

After a period of useless negotiations, police stormed the house on Jan. 12 when eavesdropping devices tipped them that Hester had been killed. Inside, they found the bodies of Sanders and his six remaining followers, some of them dead from apparent suicide.

REF.: *CBA;* Wilson, *Encyclopedia of Modern Murder.*

Sanders, Nicholas (Sander), c.1530-81, Ire., consp. Assigned to help Cardinal Hossius to prevent expansion of heretic acts. From 1573 he lived in Madrid, participating in the effort to make England a Roman Catholic country. Six years later, he was sent by the pope to Ireland to incite insurgency. He was found dead in the wild within two years after his Italian and Spanish benefactors were ruined by Lord Grey. REF.: *CBA.*

Sanders, Robert, and **Jenkins, Thomas**, and **Cracknell, John**, prom. 1953, Brit., attempt. rob. Two weeks after Robert Sanders escaped Wakefield prison, he planned his next crime—the robbery of a wage clerk of a large industrial factory in Chatham Place, Hackney. The manager of the factory noticed Sanders, Thomas Jenkins, and John Cracknell loitering about the factory the afternoon of Feb. 6, 1953. Becoming suspicious, he called the police.

The manager lunged at them with an iron crowbar just as the hold-up gang made their move. Sanders escaped, speeding away in his car, but the police constables were in hot pursuit. After an exchange of gunshots, Sanders was forced to surrender. The three men were taken before the Central Criminal Court on Mar. 30, 1953, and charged with attempted robbery. Sanders received a life sentence. Jenkins was sent to prison for five years, and Cracknell for three.

REF.: *CBA;* Scott, *Scotland Yard.*

Sandino, Augusto César, 1893-1934, Nic., (unsolv.?) assass. Augusto Sandino was the son of a Nicaraguan landowner and an Indian peasant woman. His father instilled strong liberal convictions in him, which translated into a lifelong committment to securing political autonomy from the U.S. government, which occupied Nicaragua for most of the first third of the twentieth century.

Returning from the oil fields of Tampico, Mex., in 1926, Sandino joined the liberal revolt led by Dr. Juan Bautista Sacasa, which waged a continuous guerilla war against U.S. troops. On May 5, 1927, Sacasa negotiated a peace with envoy Henry L. Stimson, which Sandino and his rebel band found unsatisfactory. They continued to defy the Marine garrisons stationed at Ocotal. When asked to surrender his forces on July 15, 1927, Sandino replied: "I want a free country or death." The U.S. government proclaimed him an outlaw.

In 1932, Sacasa was elected president of Nicaragua, and the marines withdrew a short time later. Sandino proclaimed his intention to forge a lasting peace with the newly installed leader. To meet this objective, he traveled to Managua and met with President Sacasa several times in February 1934. On the night of Feb. 21, Sandino, his brother Socrates, his father, and two military generals left the presidential palace. Without warning, members of the Guardia Nacional pulled up to the gates, and forced Sandino, his brother, and the two generals into a truck. The Guardia, a force of about 2,500, was commanded by General Anastasio Somoza, who later became dictator. The vehicle drove through the streets of Managua, past the airport, to the crossroads of La Reynaga.

There, the guardsmen killed Sandino and his party with machine guns and left them on the side of the road. They buried the bodies secretly later that night, afraid of a public funeral. Sandino's assassination and his unwavering opposition to U.S. colonialism made Sandino a martyr to the insurgents who toppled the regime of the U.S.-backed military dictator Anastasio Somoza in 1979. The leaders of the revolutionary movement called themselves "Sandinistas" in his honor.

REF.: *CBA;* Hacker, *Crusaders, Criminals, Crazies: Terror and Terrorism in Our Time.*

Sands, Gulielma, See: **Weeks, Levi.**

Sands, The, prom. 1850s, U.S., vice district. The hottest crime district in Chicago in the 1850s was the Sands, a sin belt located where the Chicago Tribune and Wrigley buildings now stand on North Michigan Avenue. Composed of about forty buildings, the Sands housed gambling parlors, brothels, and combination saloon-whorehouses. The Chicago *Tribune* reported that "a large number of persons, mostly strangers in the city, have been enticed into the dens there and robbed, and there is but little doubt that a number of murders have been committed by the desperate characters who have made these dens their homes. The most beastly sexuality and darkest crimes had their homes in the Sands."

One Sands establishment, a saloon-bagnio run by Freddy Webster, housed a prostitute named Margaret McGuinness, who was said not to have been sober or outside of Webster's establishment for five years, and to have been altogether naked for three years. McGuinness, who serviced between fifteen and forty men nightly, died on Mar. 8, 1857, of "intemperance." Her death was the seventh in one week at the Sands. A "Whore War" in 1857 was provoked when a group of State Street madams tried to lure some of the most popular Sands prostitutes away from Michigan Avenue. A battle against the State Streeters, led by a vicious young hooker ironically known as "Gentle" Annie Stafford, kept the State Street faction away. Though several political and moral factions attempted for years to destroy the Sands it was not until 1857 that the district was demolished. Mayor John Wentworth waited until a day when all of the inhabitants of the crime dens had gone to attend a highly publicized dog fight at a nearby racetrack. With thirty policemen and two horse-drawn wagons, Wentworth ordered the dilapidated buildings pulled down. A fire company destroyed several more shacks with hoses, and others were set on fire. The hundreds of homeless criminals then relocated throughout the city and the one-time sin strip evolved into a prime business district. See: **Stafford, Annie.**

REF.: Asbury, *Gem of the Prairie; CBA.*

Sandys, Sir **Edwin**, c.1561-1629, Brit., impris. Member of Parliament from 1586-93 and from 1604-26. He served on the Virginia council in 1607. He improved the organization of the new colonial government, and helped secure the charter for the *Mayflower.* He was jailed in 1621 for seeking to establish a republican, puritan state in the new land. REF.: *CBA.*

Sanford, Edward Terry, 1865-1930, U.S., jur. Ended seventeen-year law practice in Knoxville, Tenn., after being appointed assistant attorney general by President Theodore Roosevelt in 1907. He left that post for a judgeship on the U.S. district court in Tennessee, serving from 1908-23. He was nominated associate justice of the U.S. Supreme Court by President Warren G. Harding in 1923. The majority of cases he reviewed in his seven-year tenure regarded civil rights. In *Gitlow v. New York* in 1925 he wrote the court decision supporting a New York law forbidding speech or publication of materials promoting an illegal overthrow of the government. He served on the court until his death. REF.: *CBA.*

San Francisco Anti-Squatter's League, prom. 1854, U.S., law enfor. agency. To combat the lawless forces who believed "possession was nine-tenths of the law," a group of prominent San Francisco citizens organized the Anti Squatter's League, a vigilante organization, on June 6, 1854.

They took action in response to violence caused by the vague and contradictory U.S. property laws passed between 1849 and 1864 that permitted anyone to lay claim to a piece of property provided he could hold on to it. The situation became acute following the fire of 1851, in which legitimate claimants defended their land with guns and many people died. See: **San Francisco Vigilance Committee**. REF.: *CBA.*

San Francisco Vigilance Committee, prom. 1851-56, U.S., law enfor. agency. The state of lawlessness brought on by the discovery of gold in California became a growing concern among the peaceful citizens of San Francisco. In 1851 the population of the city was estimated to be 30,000, with a relative amount of saloons and gambling halls. Yet only twelve policemen were assigned to safeguard the lives and property of the San Francisco citizens. Alarmed that the criminal element was poised to take over the city, William T. Coleman and eleven other civic leaders organized the Vigilance Committee in June 1851. They wrote a controversial five-point constitution that essentially allowed members to take the law into their own hands when the situation demanded.

The committee took its first ation June 10, 1851, when burglar John Jenkins attempted to cross the Bay towing a stolen safe. Jenkins was arrested and housed in the headquarters of the Vigilance Committee on Battery Street. The committee passed the death sentence and gave warning to all by ringing the bell on the Monumental Engine Company firehouse. The execution of Jenkins had an immediate effect. The criminal classes paused, and for a short time the city was quiet.

California Governor John McDougall issued a written protest, but privately, he applauded their efforts. Nevertheless, the committee temporarily disbanded operations on Sept. 16, only to quietly reorganize some months later. The shooting of newspaper publisher James King on May 14, 1856, instigated a renewal of vigilantism in the city. Armed with artillery pieces, the vigilantes forced the sheriff to hand over the two murderers, Charles Cora and James Casey, who were promptly taken to the scaffold and hanged. By August, support for the Vigilance Committee waned. Gradually the movement evolved to one of political activism through more legitimate channels. They renamed the committee the People's Party, and remained a force in local politics for many years. See: **Cora, Charles; San Francisco Anti-Squatter's League**. REF.: *CBA.*

Sanger, Lord **George**, See: **Cooper, Herbert**.

Sanger, Margaret, prom. 1883-1966, and **Byrne, Ethel**, prom. 1916, and **Mindall, Fania**, prom. 1916, and **Stuyvesant, Elizabeth**, prom. 1916, U.S., cont./ct. In 1914, an American feminist named Margaret Sanger published a magazine called *The Woman Rebel,* which espoused universal suffrage and advocated contraception. Censorship crusader Anthony Comstock and other moralists of the day had her husband, William Sanger, arrested and convicted for disseminating information that was in violation of civil and moral laws. The case attracted much attention and stirred public opinion on both sides. In defiance of Comstock and his people, Sanger, Ethel Byrne, Fania Mindell, and Elizabeth Stuyvesant opened a birth control clinic in the Brownsville neighborhood of Brooklyn, N.Y., in October 1916.

The clinic stayed open for ten days before it was closed by court order. Byrne was sentenced to thirty days in jail, but she went on a hunger strike that rallied public opinion to her cause. After spending eleven days in jail, she was pardoned by the governor of New York. Fania Mindell was fined $50, and Margaret Sanger was told that the charges against her would be dropped if she agreed not to re-open the clinic. She refused, and the court sentenced her to thirty days in jail. An appeals court ruled that contraceptive information could be distributed for the "cure and prevention of disease." However, it wasn't until the U.S. Supreme Court handed down a favorable decision in *Griswold vs. Conn.* in 1965, that birth control information could be printed and distributed in all fifty states free of censorship.

REF.: Bullough, *An Illustrated History of Prostitution; CBA.*

Sanger, Dr. **William W.**, prom. 1855-57, U.S., criminol. The first through study on American prostitution was made by Dr. William W. Sanger who interviewed about 2,000 prostitutes in New York City between 1855-57. Sanger found that half were between twenty and thirty years old, with another 750 under twenty. About five-eighths of the prostitutes were foreign born, and three-eighths were American. Nearly two thirds were illiterate or semi-illiterate. About a quarter of those interviewed gave inclination as the reason they chose that line of work, another quarter said destitution had motivated them, and the rest attributed their professional status to seduction, abandonment, drinking, or abuse by near relatives. One hundred twenty-four said they chose prostitution because it was "an easy life." Nearly half said they had been formerly employed as servants; the others had worked as seamstresses or in other occupations, and twenty-five percent had lived with their families. Earnings ranged from $1 to $7 weekly. Half admitted to drinking excessively.

The 2,000 prostitutes interviewed were thought to represent about one third of the number in New York City at that time. Dr. Sanger estimated that almost $4,000,000 was invested in prostitution and that the annual expenditure was more than $7,000,000. REF.: *CBA.*

Sangret, August, c.1913-43, Brit., mur. A young woman, Joan Pearl Wolfe, who was living a gypsy-style existence near an army camp in Surrey, England, met and fell in love with August Sangret, a French-Canadian soldier stationed at the nearby camp at Godalming. Sangret helped Wolfe build shelters in the woods near his military post, where she lived and they met frequently as lovers. The wigwam-style huts and Sangret's American Indian heritage caused this case to be known as the "Wigwam Murder."

Wolfe became pregnant, and in September 1942, she insisted that Sangret marry her. He attacked and killed her and buried her body on a ridge in Hankley Common. Two soldiers walking in the vicinity several weeks later discovered the body. She had been stabbed repeatedly with a knife with a peculiar shaped blade and bludgeoned over the head. A log found nearby was determined to be one of the weapons, and a knife, eventually found in the drain of a washroom on the army base because the drain was not working properly, was identified as the other weapon. Sangret, waiting to be interviewed early on in the investigation, had asked permission to go to the washroom and had probably hidden the knife then.

August Sangret and his American Indian lover Joan Wolfe, killed by Sangret in 1942.

Sangret's clasp knife was missing and blood stains were found on his clothing. He was found Guilty and was hanged at Wandsworth Prison on Apr. 2, 1943.

REF.: Bailey, *The Fatal Chance;* Butler, *Murderers' England; CBA;* Greeno, *War on the Underworld;* Gribble, *Great Manhunters of the World;* Jacobs, *Cavalcade of Murder;* Lefebure, *Evidence for the Crown; Notable British Trials;* Sanders, *Murder in Lonely Places;* Shew, *A Second Companion to Murder;* Simpson, *Forty Years of Murder;* Tullett, *Strictly Murder;* Wilson, *Encyclopedia of Murder.*

Sanhuber, Otto, See: **Oesterreich, Walburga**.

Sanjar (Mu'izz ad-Din Sanjar), c.1084-1157, Khorasan, kid. (vict.) Headed Seljuq dynasty from 1118. During the successful first half of his reign he established suzerain authority over the Transocanian princes and India's Ghaznavids. But later he lost Transoxania to the Turkish Qarlugs and the Karakitai, and narrowly escaped a rebellion headed by Atsiz. He was seized and jailed by Oguz tribes who lived in his domain. REF.: *CBA.*

Sankey, John, 1866-1948, Brit., jur. Served as king's counsel in 1909 and as judge on High Court, King's Bench, from 1914-28. He held office as lord chancellor of England from 1929-35, and represented Britain at the Tribunal in Hague from 1930. REF.: *CBA.*

Sankey, Verne d.1934, and **Alcorn, Gordon,** prom. 1933, U.S., kid. A rash of kidnappings in 1933 severely tested the resources of the U.S. Department of Justice which proved ill-equipped to meet the crisis head on. No fewer than twenty-seven major cases were investigated in the wake of the Lindbergh kidnapping. The "snatch racket," as kidnapping came to be called, became a new source of revenue for the Midwest gangs. In 1932, the Gordon Alcorn-Verne Sankey bank robbery gang got into the act when they abducted millionaire financier Charles Boettcher III outside his Denver, Colo., home on Feb. 12.

In the presence of his wife, Boettcher was carried away by the gang of six. A ransom note was left behind threatening the life of Boettcher unless $60,000 was paid. By the terms of the 1932 federal legislation, the Justice Department could not intervene in a case until a seven-day waiting period had elapsed. J. Edgar Hoover, however, ordered his men into the case after only three days. Meanwhile, Denver legislators began drafting a bill that would make kidnapping a capital offense.

On Feb. 20, the Boettcher family paid the $60,000 ransom, and the victim was released unharmed. On Mar. 6, informants led the authorities to the location of the gang in Denver and South Dakota. Four persons were taken into custody but Sankey and Alcorn remained at large. In May, two of the gang members pleaded guilty. One was given a twenty-six year sentence for conspiracy, while the other received two terms of sixteen years for conspiracy and kidnapping, and was fined $1,000 for extortion. No action was taken against one of two female defendants, while Sankey's wife was tried only for using the mail for extortion. Meanwhile, Sankey earned the dubious distinction of becoming "America's public enemy No. 1." Sankey was picked up by federal agents on Jan. 31, 1934, but hanged himself in his jail cell before he could go to trial. Alcorn, who was also arrested in Chicago, was sentenced to life in prison on Feb. 9 after pleading guilty to kidnapping charges.

REF.: Alix, *Ransom Kidnapping in America; CBA;* Cooper, *Ten Thousand Public Enemies.*

Sanson Family, prom. 1688-1847, Fr., execut. For more than 150 years, the Sanson family of executioners operated the French guillotine. The trade was handed down through seven generations; from father to son to grandson. In 1688, Charles Sanson, also known as Longval, was appointed by the Court of the Parlement of Paris to succeed Nicolas Lavasseur as executioner. Charles Sanson was succeeded by his namesake in 1707. The second Charles had two sons. The youngest, Charles Jean Baptiste, was appointed executioner in 1726 when he was only seven years old.

During his childhood, François Prudhomme assumed the duties of executioner until Charles Jean was ready to take over his duties in 1740. He in turn, had seven sons and three daughters. The most famous Sanson was the eldest son, born Charles-Henri. He succeeded his father on Feb. 1, 1778, and became known as "Monsieur de Paris," a macabre French custom whereby the executioner often took the name of the city to which he was assigned. Charles-Henri was present for the execution of King Louis XVI on Jan. 21, 1793. It was reported that the guillotining of the French monarch greatly affected Charles-Henri Sanson, who became afflicted with an illness shortly afterward and died six months later. This was not the case. Nor did Charles-Henri die during a fall from the scaffold while picking up a decapitated head. This accident befell a younger son who assisted the executioner. He did, therefore, carry out the executions of Marie-Antoinetten her sister-in-law Elizabeth, Malesherbes, and the Duc d'Orléans, among others.

Charles-Henri was succeeded in 1795 by his son Henri Sanson, who had assisted with many executions during the Reign of Terror.

Henri continued in his post until 1840 when, upon his death, he was succeeded by his son, Clement-Henri Sanson. The family dynasty ended ignobly in 1847 when Clement-Henri was dismissed for pawning the guillotine. The story of this remarkable family of executioners is well told in a six volume work published in 1863, titled *Seven Generations of Executioners, 1688-1847.*

REF.: *CBA;* Laurence, *A History of Capital Punishment;* Lenotre, *The Guillotine and Its Servants.*

Santa Anna (Antonio Lopez de Santa Ana), c.1795-1876, Mex., consp.-rebel. Headed revolts against Emperor Agustin I in 1822 and against Vicente Guerrero in 1828. He ousted Mexican President Anastasio Bustamante, with whom he defeated Guerrero, in 1832. He held office as president of Mexico from 1833-35, and led troops in the capture of the Alamo in 1836, although he later was captured by Texan leader Sam Houston. He ruled Mexico without official title from 1839-42, and was named dictator in accordance with the constitution in 1844. He was stripped of authority and exiled in 1845, but was brought back and named provisional president in 1847. During the U.S.-Mexican War he suffered great losses leading his forces, and was badly defeated by U.S. General Winfield Scott in 1847, and was exiled in 1848. He was reinstated as president from 1853-55, but was once again exiled during the revolution of Ayutla in 1855. From then on he lived variously in Cuba, Venezuela, St. Thomas, and the U.S., finally returning to Mexico City where he died in poverty. REF.: *CBA.*

Santa Claus Bank Robbery, See: **Ratliff, Marshall.**

Santa Cruz, Marta, 1938-61, U.S., (unsolv.) rape-mur. The nude body of 22-year-old Marta Santa Cruz was found floating in a stream the first week of July 1961, in Fairfax County, Va. The former clerk-typist at the Washington, D.C., Hospital Center had been raped and then strangled. She was the daughter of a former Bolivian army colonel, and a frequent guest at embassy parties. Her murder remains unsolved. REF.: *CBA.*

Santana, Frank, c.1937- , U.S., mur. Frank Santana was born in Puerto Rico, but had moved with his widowed mother and two younger brothers to the Bronx, N.Y. Frequently truant from school, young Santana fell in with a tough street gang known as the Navajos that was almost always warring with another group of undisciplined teenagers who called themselves the Golden Guineas. Outside a Bronx movie house on Apr. 30, 1955, Santana shot and killed Willaim Blankenship Jr.. Blankenship, who did not belong to any gang was accosted by Santana and his friends who demanded to know what he was doing on their turf. The Navajos believed that the 15-year-old white boy was a member of the Guineas. "Don't you point that thing at me!" Blankenship said, when one of the gang members brandished a pistol. Santana seized the gun and fired one shot and killed the boy.

Santana was indicted on a first-degree murder charge, but was allowed to plead guilty to second degree murder at the behest of the victim's father, who was a member of the Bronxwood Community Council, which was determined fight crime in the neighborhood. Santana was sentenced to twenty-five years to life by Judge William Lyman who characterized the youth as a "wanton murderer." This description was challenged by Assistant District Attorney Andrew McCarthy who did not readily accept the notion that Blankenship was entirely blameless.

REF.: *CBA;* Wertham, *The Circle of Guilt.*

Santarosa, Santorre di, 1783-1825, Italy, consp. Served Napoleon as subprefect of La Spezia from 1812-14. Later he formed a conspiracy plot against the Austrians in 1821. He went into exile to escape a death sentence, and was killed in action fighting for Greek independence in Sphakteria. REF.: *CBA.*

Santerre, Antoine-Joseph, 1752-1809, Fr., law enfor. off. Participated in attack on Bastille in 1789. He protected the royal family from possible mob attack as commander-in-chief of the Parisian Garde Nationale in 1792, and guarded them in jail prior to their executions. He led a failed army of volunteers in a doomed effort against the Vendeans in 1793, and was jailed from 1793-94. He regained his liberty upon the defeat of Maximilien Robespierre. REF.: *CBA.*

Santini, Donald Michael (AKA: **Joseph Brewster, Steve Buice, Donald Chapman, Brian Lewis, Charles Michael Stevens, Chuck Trimble, John Trimble, Michael Triple**), 1958- , Case of, U.S., rob.-mur. Donald Santini, born in Springfield, Mass., in 1958, is currently wanted for the murder of a Riverview, Fla., woman. With a record of aggravated robbery, Santini is considered to be an armed and dangerous felon. At this writing Santini is still at large. REF.: *CBA.*

Sapieha, Leon, 1803-78, Rus., rebel. Took part in November Insurrection against Russia in 1830. He served as chairman of the Austrian Galician Sejm from 1861-75. REF.: *CBA.*

Sapronov, Timofey Vladimirovich, 1887-c.1939, U.S.S.R., rebel. Took part in Bolshevik Revolution and served as official for Soviet government and Communist party. He headed the Democratic Centralist movement supporting more democracy and opposing growing centralization in the party. He was arrested during Joseph Stalin's purge of Old Guard Bolsheviks, and disappeared in the 1930s. REF.: *CBA.*

Sapru, Sir Tej Bahadur, 1875-1949, India, jur. Served on Imperial Legislative Council from 1916-20, and as law member on viceroy's council from 1920-23. REF.: *CBA.*

Sapwell, William (AKA: **John Smith**), d.1830, Brit., mur. The London Metropolitan Force was barely a year old when one of its members died in the line of duty. The murder of John Long of the Finsbury Division occurred on Aug. 18, 1830, while he was making his rounds at Gray's Inn Lane, a darkened street known to be a favored haunt for the criminal classes. On this night, Long and his partner, John Newton, noticed several suspicious men loitering near the Mecklenburg Square. When Long asked what the men were doing, one pulled out a shoemaker's knife and plunged it into the constable's chest. He died instantly. A man running from the direction of the scene was arrested. He said his name was John Smith, and claimed he was innocent. Several days later, Charles Baldwin gave himself up to police. He was arraigned on a murder charge with Smith, and a third suspect named Lawrence Summers.

Summers and Baldwin were discharged but Smith was bound over for trial. In court he was recognized as William Sapwell, who had been charged with burglary ten years earlier. He had escaped a prison sentence then by turning King's evidence. This time he was not so fortunate. He was found Guilty on Sept. 20 and hanged before a large assembly three days later. Afterward a public subscription was taken for the family of the slain officer.

REF.: Browne, *The Rise of Scotland Yard; CBA;* Cobb, *The First Detectives;* Thomson, *The Story of Scotland Yard.*

Sardinian Shepherds, prom. 1720-1970, Sardinia, kid.-mur. For 2,000 years the island of Sardinia in the Mediterranean Sea has been governed by succeeding generations of military conquerors who have imposed their own customs and laws upon the hapless shepherds who have tried to subsist on the harsh, uncompromising land. To fend off starvation, the shepherds of Sardinia turned to banditry, kidnapping, and violence. With each new crime wave, the government in power at the time—whether it was the Greeks, Carthaginians, Romans, Byzantines, Spanish, or Italians—have imposed harsh measures to attempt to control the peasants. Taken as a whole, the government mandates have not been successful.

In 1820, the Law of Enclosures cut off the grazing lands of the sheep herders by allowing the peasants in the foothills to construct large stone fences around their property. After this measure was passed, there were, on the average, a thousand murders a year on an island whose population was less than a half-million. In addition, a unique Sardinian crime called the "bardane," in which armed men on horseback would ride into villages to murder and pillage everyone in sight, was first practiced.

Since the 1880s, kidnapping has become quite popular on Sardinia especially in the regions surrounding the city of Nuoro. Between 1880 and 1889, 873 people were abducted and held for ransom. This sparked an official government inquiry launched by

Italian Prime Minister Francesco Crispi. The recommendations for improving relations between the nomadic shepherds and the peasant population were largely ignored. In 1962, Italy pledged 400 billion lire to stimulate economic development on the island, but the money was diverted to tourism and the petro-chemical industries instead. As a result, there was a fresh outbreak of kidnappings between 1966 and 1969, again primarily concentrated in the central mountains of Barbagia in Nuoro.

In 1967, a second Commission of Inquiry was launched by President Saragat of Italy, after the government had pumped one billion lire into the fight against the kidnappers. The Commission concluded that: "banditry in Sardinia is a problem not for the police but for society itself; until the economic and social gaps that divide shepherds and their traditions from modern industrial society are bridged, it is more than likely that the shepherd and the fugitive will continue to be one and the same." See: **Mesina, Graziano.**

REF.: *CBA;* Moorehead, *Hostages to Fortune.*

Sargent, John Garibaldi, 1860-1939, U.S., atty. gen. Served as state's attorney, Windsor Co., Vt., from 1898-1900, and as Vermont attorney general from 1908-12. He was appointed U.S. attorney general by President Calvin Coolidge in 1925 and avidly enforced Prohibition throughout his four-year tenure. He also supported wiretapping as a means to obtain evidence. REF.: *CBA.*

Sarit Thanarat, 1908-63, Thai., law enfor. Ousted Pibul Songgram in 1957 and unseated full government in 1958. He made himself prime minister in 1959, and focused his dictatorial reign on drives against organized crime, corruption, and on quelling Chinese control over the Thai economy. REF.: *CBA.*

Sarkiyev, Ilyas (AKA: **Vovchik-Syra**), prom. 1980s, USSR, org. crime. The menace of organized crime is not unique to Western nations or the southern tip of Italy. In Russia the existence of an extensive criminal network not unlike the Sicilian Mafia has come to light in the wake of *glasnost* (the new openness.) In the Republic of Turkmenia the Russian "Mafia" boss, Ilyas Sarkiyev, oversaw a powerful extortion racket that shook down the local construction trades. According to published reports in *Pravda,* Sarkiyev and his henchmen enjoyed the protection of the local police force and corrupt bureaucrats who were easily paid off.

In one instance the gang demanded an extortion payment of 100,000 rubles from a construction foreman named Gavrush Sarkisya under threat of death. When he could not meet this unreasonable demand, Sarkisya fled to the city of Krasnodar. The gangsters tracked him down and demanded immediate payment or else a brother—Genrikh Sarkisya—would also be killed. Hearing of this, an incorruptible police official, Alexander Udalov, organized a special "rackets squad" to break the power of the mob. Using techniques much like those of the FBI, the team of investigators attended the funeral of one of Sarkiyev's lieutenants. Disguised in native folk dress, they rounded up twenty gang members. Sarkiyev attempted to bribe Udalov, who had been purged from the Communist party several years earlier after failing to eradicate official corruption in the town of Sochi along the Black Sea. This time, however, Inspector Udalov was more successful. Three days after receiving the bribe offer, Udalov arrested Sarkiyev, thus breaking the power of the mob.

The loosening of Soviet society has afforded honest party officials and the Russian citizenry an opportunity to openly discuss these matters. It is now known that smaller, but no less deadly "Mafia" gangs flourish in Moscow, Leningrad, and other cities. They exert control over the cemetery business, taxi companies, and other related ventures, often through the connivance of corrupt party chieftains. REF.: *CBA.*

Sarrejani, Georges Alexander, See: **Sarret, Georges.**

Sarret, Georges (Georges Alexander Sarrejani), d.1934, and **Schmidt, Catherine** (AKA: **Mageli Herbin**), and **Schmidt, Philomena**, prom. 1934, Fr., mur. Georges Sarret was a Greek born in Trieste, Italy, who emerged as Frances' most notorious criminal in the early 1930s. Answering to the name of "Sarret," he prepared for his murderous profession by studying chemistry, medicine and law at the university in Marseilles. Afterward, he selected two vulnerable women to act as confederates in his murder schemes.

Sisters Catherine Schmidt and Philomena Schmidt were suspected of carrying out acts of espionage on behalf of the German government during WWI. They had moved to France from their native Bavaria before the war, and had worked for a time as governesses for a prominent family. While in domestic service, they met the young lawyer Sarret. After the war, the sisters remained in France, which proved to be a tragic mistake.

Threatened with exposure and arrest, the wily Sarret blackmailed them into marrying a succession of feeble, but wealthy old men. After the ceremonies had been duly performed, Sarrejani saw to it that the men died premature deaths and that the insurance money wound up in his pocket. The killings continued for some time, and nobody was the wiser. Then Catherine insured herself for the sum of a million francs, taking on the identity of Mageli Herbin who soon died of pneumonia. The insurance companies became very suspicious and began nosing around Sarret's property.

A pit of decomposed animal remains that had been saturated with acid was found in the garden of a home that Sarret had rented in Marseilles. Then Sarret made the mistake of doing away with Louis Chambon, a defrocked priest who had acted as a third accomplice to Sarret's many crimes. Chambon and his mistress, Noemie Ballandraux, were shot and the bodies disposed of in a vat of sulfuric acid. Catherine finally confessed to police her knowledge of Sarret's gruesome deed. He was arrested and condemned to die on the guillotine following a lengthy trial in October 1933. The Schmidt sisters each received ten years' hard labor.

The execution was carried out at Aix-en-Provence in April 1934 after some trepidation on the part of Anatole Joseph Deibler, France's notorious master of the guillotine who presided over 300 beheadings. This time, the blade was slow to fall. "Imbeciles!" yelled Sarret, "Be quick can't you!" For ten minutes the condemned man's head rested on the block while Deibler tried to correct the problem. Finally it was done, and the village square was hosed down so the blood would not offend the breakfasters. REF.: *CBA.*

Sartain, Albert E., prom. 1924-28, U.S., brib. When it was discovered that a prisoner named Remus, convicted of graft, received special privileges in the Atlanta Federal Penitentiary, the prison warden, Albert E. Sartain, was investigated. Remus' cell was supplied with fresh flowers and cleaned daily by a maid, and he ate all of his meals in the chaplain's home. He performed light work in the prison library and then only when he felt like it. Yet during a grand jury hearing Remus said he had never bribed Sartain, and then added cavalierly, "What did it matter if I did give Sartain a little money for the few comforts I was allowed? Anything that makes the awful grind of the penitentiary a little easier is all right, it seems to me. You know the government doesn't lash your back with rawhide—it breaks you mentally...If I'm allowed a handful of comfort, the other prisoners get a finger. It lets down the bars at least a little bit for all."

Sartain was convicted of accepting bribes and became an inmate in his own jail. On July 25, 1925, federal judge Robert T. Ervin decreed that a new trial would not be granted to Sartain and his sentence was upheld. He was granted a parole for good conduct on Feb. 2, 1928, three months before his sentence expired.

REF.: *CBA;* Kobler, *Ardent Spirits.*

Saruco, Charles, and **Slatter, Herbert Shorland**, prom. 1899, Brit., fraud. Charles Saruco and Herbert Shorland Slatter were the two principal partners in the Duncan Forbes Company which was put out of business in 1911 for engaging in investment swindles that netted the firm £80,000. Long before this time, Saruco and Slatter had concerned themselves with a "Grocer & Provision Shops Association" which acquired various small stores in the heart of London. Investors supplied the necessary cash on the promise of a 26 percent interest return.

The partners acquired eight stores, but because no rent was paid on these establishments, they were quickly repossessed. Saruco was sentenced to four years' penal servitude and Slatter to a term of hard labor. The ultimate losers in this venture were the women from the organized charities who had been induced to sink their meager incomes on the vague promise of a lucrative return. It was later revealed that Saruco had a long history of criminal fraud behind him. He was a racketeer and con man, pushing worthless shares for several bogus companies. See: **Forbes, Robert Duncan.**

REF.: *CBA;* Nicholls, *Crime Within the Square Mile.*

Sasakawa Ryoichi, prom. 1940s-80s, Japan, gamb.-org. crime. In a classified report by U.S. occupation forces in Japan after WWII, military officials described Sasakawa Ryoichi as someone who should be kept under close scrutiny. "Sasakawa appears to be a man potentially dangerous to Japan's political future," the report said. "He has been squarely behind Japanese military policies of aggression and anti-foreignism for more than twenty years. He is a man of wealth and not too scrupulous about its use. He chafes for continued power."

In the 1930s, Sasakawa openly supported the policies of Italian Fascist dictator Benito Mussolini and ordered his thugs to wear the traditional black shirts favored by the Italians. One of the young rightists under Sasakawa, Kodama Yoshio, became Japan's most famous "kuromaku" (or power broker) in the 1950s and 1960s. Sasakawa was imprisoned by the Americans in 1945. When he was freed in December 1948, Sasakawa approached several government officials in Japan, offering to give them a share of the proceeds from motorboat races he planned to sponsor. The cash-poor government ministers accepted and in the next few years the Japan Motorboat Racing Association grew into a lucrative sports-gambling empire with Sasakawa serving as its titular head. By 1980, his company's gross revenues were estimated at $7.4 billion.

Sasakawa bragged about his friendship with Taoka Kazuo, ruler of the *Yamaguchi-gumi* gang. When warfare between the yakuza gangs threatened the stability of the regime, Sasakawa was frequently called on to arbitrate disputes. Like other prominent businessmen caught up in the post-war nationalist fervor, Sasakawa supported right-wing causes. The *Zenkoku Kinrosha Domei,* or All-Japan White Collar Workers' League, was founded by Sasakawa to countermand the threat from the left. In 1963, he became a personal advisor and confidant of the Reverend Sun Myung Moon and his Unification Church. Together, Moon and Sasakawa allied the various right-wing groups into the *Kokusai Shokyo Rengo* (The International Federation for Victory Over Communism). By the end of the 1970s, Sasakawa claimed to have eight million followers and his face was familiar to television viewers. Regarding his past association with gangsters, Sasakawa said, "Formerly I had Kodama Yoshio and many other roughnecks around me. I was their leader. So, some may call me a rightist. But I am not a rightist. I am a humanitarian." However, in 1974, he bragged to *Time* Magazine of being the "world's richest Fascist." See: **Inagawa Kakuji; Kimura Tokutaro; Kishi Nobusuke; Kodama Yoshio; Machii Hisayuki; Nakasone Yasuhiro; Ogawa Kaoru; Osano Kenji; Taoka Kazuo; Toyama Mitsuru; Yakuza.**

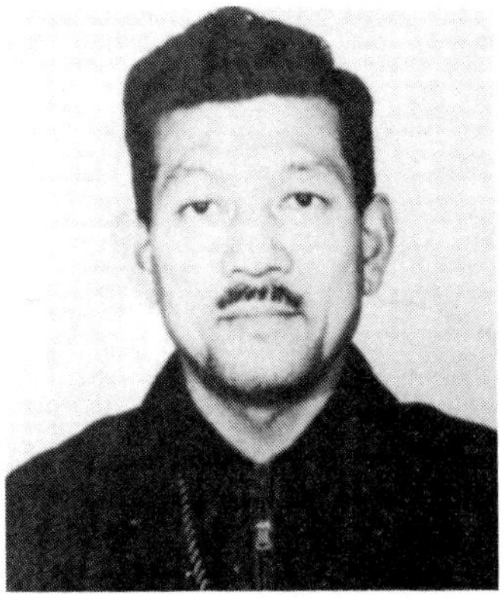

Japanese gangster Sasakawa Ryoichi.

REF.: *CBA;* Kaplan and Dubro, *Yakuza.*

Satan Was a Man, 1935, a novel by Edward Hale Bierstadt. This work is based upon the notorious Lizzie Borden case (U.S., 1892). See: **Borden, Lizzie.** REF.: *CBA.*

Satyricon Hoax, prom. 1668-1808, Italy, hoax. Titus Petronius Niger has been widely regarded as the author of *Satyricon,* a first century tract published in Rome during the reign of Emperor Nero. The wistful romantic prose survives only in fragments, but from time to time, individuals have come forward claiming to have "discovered" the missing pieces.

In 1668, Roman experts attested to the authenticity of thirty new pages, allegedly uncovered in a library at Trau, Dalmatia, by Martinus Statilius. These experts did not account for the textual and grammatical errors however, which shed grave doubt on the validity of Statilius' claim. The issue still remains in doubt. In 1693, a French soldier named François Nodot announced that he had found additional missing text in Belgrade while on military maneuvers. His claim was dismissed as a hoax when he failed to produce more than a facsimile of the original.

A century later, Spanish writer Joseph Marchena passed off a bogus Petronius text which he claimed to have located in a Swiss monastery. In 1808 Professor Heinrich Eichstädt of Jena demonstrated that Marchena's research was fraudulent. He had borrowed the text from an ancient manuscript at the university library. REF.: *CBA.*

Sauckel, Fritz, 1894-1946, Ger., war crimes. On Oct. 1, 1946, nineteen high-ranking Nazis were found Guilty of war crimes by the International Military Tribunal at Nuremberg. Found Guilty of crimes violating the laws of war and crimes against humanity was Fritz Sauckel, one-time Nazi labor boss. During his three days on the witness stand, prosecutors questioned Sauckel about his various efforts as Chief Commissioner for the Utilization of Manpower.

Testimony indicated that Sauckel had deported hundreds of thousands of young Russian girls into Germany on Hitler's orders. Other evidence showed that Sauckel had once urged that 1,000,000 Russian slave workers be handled "so roughly in the East they will feel they would rather come to Germany to work." Sauckel, along with ten other Nazis, was hanged at the Nuremberg prison on Oct. 16, 1946. According to witnesses at the execution, Sauckel said just before he was hanged, "I am dying innocent...I pay my respects to U.S. officers and soldiers, but not to U.S. justice." REF.: *CBA.*

Nazi war criminal Fritz Sauckel.

Saul, Nicholas, 1833-53, U.S., org. crime-rob. As leader of the Daybreak Boys, Nicholas Saul led the group of gangsters in their frequent raids on the docks of New York City's Hudson and East rivers in the 1850s. The gang included some of New York's most hardened criminals such as Saul's partner William Howlett, Bill Johnson, "Slobbery Jim," Cowlegged Sam McCarthy, Sow Madden, and Patsy the Barber. The Daybreak Boys got their name from their forays, made in the hours just before dawn. Membership in the gang was gained by committing at least one murder, a qualification most initiates met with ease.

During the two years that Saul served as their leader, the Daybreak Boys did well—stealing approximately $200,000. After stealing a ship's cargo and the captain's chest, Saul's crew generally killed the crew and sank the ship. But on Aug. 25, 1852, when Saul, Johnson, and Howlett set out to rob the *William Watson,* anchored in the East River, gunfire between the robbers and a watchman attracted the attention of a detective. A team of twenty heavily-armed policemen followed the three criminals to Pete William's Slaughter House Inn. After a three-hour siege, Saul, Johnson, and Howlett were arrested. Saul and Howlett were convicted of the murder of the ship's watchman, Charles Baxter, and sentenced to be hanged. On Jan. 28, 1853, as the men were brought out for execution, 200 fellow gangsters and politician friends, including Butcher Bill Poole and Tom Hyer, filed past them shaking hands and paying their respects. Saul and Howlett were then hanged in the Tombs Courtyard.

REF.: *CBA;* Haskins, *Street Gangs;* Nash, *Bloodletters and Badmen.*

Saunders, Howard Donald, 1952- , U.S., rob.-mur. Fluent in German, French, and several Asian languages, Howard Saunders is not a run-of-the mill killer. A former U.S. Army sergeant, he is wanted for robbery and murder. His extensive knowledge of firearms and explosives would make him a likely candidate for security jobs and paramilitary types of work. At this writing, Howard Donald Saunders is still at large. REF.: *CBA.*

Saunders, Raymond, prom. 1929, U.S., mur. Elliott Howe of the Virginia State Police was faced with a 16-year-old murder in July 1945 when he was called to investigate the discovery of a skeleton found in an abandoned well near Alexandria, Va. Scattered around the bones were bits of clothing and jewelry. The body was turned over to the coroner who, after calling upon several experts, was able to determine the sex, height, shoe size, and even hat size of the victim. Surmising that a piece of khaki cloth and a button found with the body were military in origin, he checked with the Marine base at Quantico. Their records, along with a dental chart of the skull, identified the remains as those of a missing ex-marine, Brad J. Ellison, who had disappeared sixteen years earlier.

Howe then checked local Quantico police records and found that the police officer, Sergeant Richard Duvall, since deceased, had investigated Ellison's disappearance and suspected two local men of killing Ellison but had lacked the evidence to act. Interviewing neighbors in the area, Howe learned that Ellison had moved in with Frenchy Carney, a local bootlegger, and soon started an affair with Carney's wife, Effie.

Frenchy had later been murdered, but Howe was able to locate Effie Carney. She admitted the relationship with Ellison and that Frenchy had become enraged when she informed him that she was planning to leave him for Ellison and he had offered $500 to anyone who would kill Ellison. Ellison had moved in with two local fellows named Dooley Dent and Raymond "Scissors" Saunders.

Howe located a man named Robert B. Leitch, a local tramp, who had lived in the area in 1929 and knew all about Ellison's disappearance. He said that he had seen Saunders the day after with a cut on his head. Saunders had said that "he had knocked hell out of Ellison and put him where he wouldn't bother anybody else."

Working on these leads, Howe finally located Scissors Saunders, by then an alcoholic, and arrested him. Saunders was tried for murder on Nov. 25, 1945, and found Guilty. He was sent to prison.

REF.: *CBA;* Nash, *Murder, America;* Reynolds, *Murder 'Round the World.*

Savage, Arthur William, 1857-1938, U.S., firearms and ballistics. Born in Kingston, Jam.; became naturalized U.S. citizen in 1895. He founded the Savage Arms Company in Utica, N.Y., in 1893. He is credited with improving magazine rifles and inventing a dirigible torpedo. REF.: *CBA.*

Savage, Richard, 1698-1743, and **Gregory, James**, and **Merchant, William**, prom. 1727, Brit., mur. Richard Savage was the son of Anne, Countess of Macclesfield, and Captain Savage, the Earl of Rivers. The countess had little use for either son or husband, and claimed that Richard, born in 1698 in England, was the result of an adulterous relationship.

After the Countess failed in her attempt to have him sent to the American colonies to work on a plantation, Savage was apprenticed to a shoemaker in Holborn, outside London. Deprived of his inheritance and declared legally dead by his mother, Savage became a playwright. In 1723, his first success, a tragedy, won him recognition and a royalty of £200. He appeared to be well on his way to literary fame.

Savage's career was cut short in December 1727 when he was implicated in a murder at Robinson's coffeehouse in Charing Cross. With his friends James Gregory and William Merchant, Savage stumbled drunk into the restaurant late one night. Merchant began harassing a patron named James Sinclair. In the scuffle that followed, Gregory demanded that the man draw his sword. Richard Savage inflicted the wound that claimed Sinclair's life the next day. The three assailants were brought before the magistrate and indicted for murder.

At the trial, it was proved that the defendants had acted in a capricious, aggressive manner. Sinclair had done nothing to provoke the attack. After eight hours of deliberation, on Dec. 11, 1727, a Guilty verdict was returned. Savage and Gregory were sentenced to die, but Merchant, who started the ruckus, was discharged.

The Countess heard of her son's troubles and used her position to thwart the appeal process. The queen learned of Richard Savage's plight from the Countess of Hertford, and granted him a royal reprieve. He and Gregory were freed on Mar. 5, 1728. But Savage's freedom carried with it new hardships. He was ruined as an author, and quickly fell into debt. He died in debtor's prison in August 1743.

REF.: *CBA;* Hibbert, *The Roots of Evil;* Mitchell, *The Newgate Calendar.*

Savage, Thomas, 1651-68, Brit., rob.-mur. At the age of fifteen, Thomas Savage was apprenticed to a wine merchant at the Ship Tavern in Ratcliff Cross. He disappointed his parents and his master by consorting with a local prostitute named Hannah Blay, whom he supplied with some of the merchant's best wines.

Savage fell in love with Blay, who threatened not to see him unless he provided well for her. She encouraged him to steal his master's money, but Savage protested, saying the house maid was always in the way. "Knock her brains out and I'll receive the money and go anywhere with you beyond the sea to avoid the stroke of justice," Blay promised.

The next day Savage carried out her plan. He entered through the kitchen window and bludgeoned the unsuspecting maid with a hammer. He then made off with £60 hidden in a cabinet. Savage fled to Greenwich, where he spent the night at an inn. Noticing the sack of money, the proprietor asked Savage where he planned to take it. Savage said he was going to Gravesend to deliver the bundle to his master. To allay the innkeeper's suspicions, Savage volunteered to leave the money with her until he returned from an errand in Woolwich.

Soon, news of the robbery and murder of the Ratcliff servant girl reached the inn. The innkeeper told the watchmen about Savage's mysterious money pouch. They found the apprentice sleeping off a drunken stupor under a table in an alehouse. He was brought back to Ratcliff, presented to the justice of the peace, and committed to Newgate.

Thomas Savage was found Guilty of murdering his master's kitchen maid and was sentenced to hang at Ratcliff Cross. Hannah Blay visited him each day and brought him alcohol and spiritual comfort, but was never charged with being an accomplice to the murder. On the execution day, Savage murmured a prayer before he was hanged. A few moments after he was cut down, the body suddenly began to show signs of life. His friends carried him to a soft bed and watched in amazement as Savage tried to form words. However, he was not able to regain his voice or the use of his tongue.

Within an hour, the sheriff arrived to take him back to the noose. This time it was fitted properly. Thomas Savage died on Oct. 28, 1668. His body was buried at Islington.

REF.: *CBA;* Smith, *Highwaymen.*

Savarkar, Vir Vinayak Damodar, 1883-1966, India, consp.-assass. Jailed from 1911-37 for supposed involvement in London assassination of Indian official. He presided over the Hindu Mahasabha group from 1937-43. He and seven other conspirators were charged with assassinating Mohandas Gandhi, but he was acquitted. REF.: *CBA.*

Savary, Henry, prom. 1825, Brit., forg. Henry Savary, a young London businessman, was brought before Lord Gifford on Apr. 4, 1825, charged with forging a £500 note. His plea of guilty caught the judge and the court by surprise because the crime carried with it an automatic death penalty. With no other choice, Lord Gifford donned the black hat and passed the death sentence. Savary's honesty in the matter impressed the prosecutor who implored the judge to exercise mercy in this case.

Lord Gifford said nothing, and the prisoner was led from the docket amidst profound silence. Savary's sentence was eventually commuted to one of transportation to the British penal colony in New South Wales, according to reports published in *The Times* on June 24, 1825.

REF.: *CBA;* Poynter, *Forgotten Crimes.*

Savasta, Antonio, 1955- , Italy, terr.-kid. The son of a Rome policeman, Antonio Savasta abandoned his law studies to join the infamous radical Red Brigades, an Italian terrorist group responsible for the 1978 kidnap-murder of Italian Prime Minister Aldo Moro. As leader of the Rome faction, Savasta masterminded the Moro abduction, and those of chemical company executive Giuseppe Taliercio and Ciro Cirillo, a political leader of the ruling Christian Democratic Party. In 1980, Savasta shot his way out of a police trap in the Sardinian City of Cagliari—a long-time stronghold of kidnap operations.

Savasta was an unrepentant revolutionary until he was captured in Padua on Jan. 28, 1982, by Italy's crack anti-terrorist squad, the Nucleo Operativo Centrale di Sicurezza (NOCS), more commonly known as the "Leatherheads." Arrested along with six other Brigadists for the Dec. 17, 1981, abduction of Brigadier General James L. Dozier, Savasta readily agreed to cooperate with the Italian police. He supplied the names of dozens of Red Brigades members, and signed an open letter which implored them to come out of hiding and surrender to the police. He revealed new information about long-suspected ties to the Palestine Liberation Organization (PLO), and various emissaries from Soviet block countries.

The daring rescue operation of Dozier from the Padua apartment building where he had been held captive for forty-two days underscored the determination on the part of the Italian government to break the stranglehold of Red Brigade terror. It was the first time since 1975 that a Red Brigades kidnap victim had been successfully rescued. Seconds before Dozier was released from his bindings, Savasta was poised to shoot him through the head. An armed commando burst into the apartment and bludgeoned the terrorist with a rifle butt before he could so much as get a shot off. In the general roundup that followed, 400 Red Brigades suspects were taken into custody and interrogated. The forty-two-day police operation was thought to have broken the back of the organization.

Savasta and sixteen other persons were charged with kidnapping and placed on trial in Rome, on Mar. 14, 1982. After eleven days of testimony, a Guilty verdict was returned against all seventeen. Savasta's co-defendants received varying terms of two to twenty-seven years; Antonio Savasta was sentenced to sixteen years and six months. See: **Red Brigades; Moro, Aldo; Dozier, James L.** REF.: *CBA.*

Savides, Christ, 1933- , U.S., org. crime.-gamb.-drugs. Christ Savides violated a basic tenet of the Chicago crime family: "Never get mixed up in the drug rackets, because you are sure to bring the heat down." The 54-year-old Savides operated several sports betting wire rooms out of his suburban Park Ridge apartment before attempting to cash in on the Columbian drug trade. During a routine raid on Mar. 8, 1986, that netted police $63,000 in cash and illegal gambling devices, the raiders uncovered ten kilos of uncut cocaine.

A month later, officers from the Chicago Police Department Organized Crime Unit discovered another ten kilos of Columbian cocaine in the trunk of a Mercedes belonging to a pair of suspected hitmen in Savides' employ, Robert Wilson and Donald Smith, both fifty-six.

In September 1987, U.S. District Judge Nicholas Bua sentenced Savides to twenty years in prison, coupled with a $500,000 fine. Government attorneys charged the Chicago racketeer with running a multi-million dollar drug ring. Added precautions were taken to ensure his safety from vengeful mobsters who would seek retribution for carrying on an independent operation in defiance of the local "rules." Unlike their counterparts on the East Coast, the Chicago contingency of the Mafia has frowned on drug trafficking because of the undue police attention it invariably causes. REF.: *CBA.*

Savidge Affair, prom. 1928, Brit., morals. The issue of a woman's chastity was at the forefront of a British sex scandal that rocked Scotland Yard in 1928 and led to the ouster of its commissioner, Sir William Thomas Francis Horwood, accused of sanctioning a third-degree interrogation against schoolgirl Irene Marjory Savidge.

Savidge was arrested on a morals charge by two Scotland Yard detectives after her alleged affair with Sir Leo Chiozza Money, parliamentary secretary to David Lloyd George was made public. At the forefront of the issue was the rightful age of Savidge, who was actually twenty-two at the time of her dalliance with Sir Leo, a married man. The police thought she was only sixteen. Savidge was examined by the medical examiner who certified that she was still a virgin. Placed on trial for improper conduct in Hyde Park, the young woman was acquitted of any moral wrongdoing. This did not placate the police however.

Determined to find the "truth," Inspector Collins, a thirty-two-year veteran of Scotland Yard subjected Savidge to an interrogation about her moral habits and past affairs with men. The police were censured for their conduct by an "Extraordinary Tribunal" appointed to investigate the matter. The two arresting constables were fined £10 each for making a false arrest and Commissioner Horwood was forced to step down in the ensuing scandal that occupied the front page of the British tabloid press for weeks. The official inquiry consumed some 2,000 pages of testimony.

With public opinion decidedly against Scotland Yard, the government took steps to restore a measure of confidence in the agency. Julian Hedworth George Byng, a military hero and grandson of Field Marshal John Byng, who fought along side of the Duke of Wellington at Waterloo, was appointed head of Scotland Yard. Meanwhile, Irene Savidge's father seemed pleased with the press attention his daughter had received. "I was vain enough to be pleased that I had a daughter who could be sufficiently interesting to attract a gentleman like Sir Leo. I have a jolly good girl for a daughter." See: **Byng, Julian Hedworth.** REF.: *CBA.*

Savigny, Friedrich Karl von, 1779-1861, Ger., jur. Served on Prussian Privy Council in 1817. He supervised the revision of Prussian statutes from 1842-48. He is credited with taking a major role in forming the historical school of jurisprudence. Also authored legal works. REF.: *CBA.*

Saville, William, 1815-44, Brit., mur. William Saville attempted to deceive his wife and mistress, and in the end, paid for it with his life. Saville was a 29-year-old framework knitter who lived in the town of Radford, east of Nottingham, England. His wife, Ann Saville, cared for their three children in a workhouse he had placed them in. Saville was ashamed of his marital status, and desired to hide it from his mistress, Miss Tait. When the facts came to light, he offered a feeble explanation. "She's not my wife. She has never troubled you and never will. She is safe and the children are provided for."

Seeking an explanation from her husband, Mrs. Saville went with him to the country where she was knifed to death with a razor. Saville was quickly arrested and convicted of murder. He was hanged in front of the Nottingham County Jail on Aug. 7, 1844, before a large unruly mob that pushed and shoved to get a better view of the proceedings. Twelve people were actually killed in the melee, and another sixteen were hospitalized. The mayor of Nottingham wrote a letter to Sir James Graham in Sir Robert Peel's cabinet saying he believed the area in front of the jail was unsuitable for public hangings.

REF.: Butler, *Murderers' England; CBA.*

Savina, Richard, 1952- , U.S., attempt. bomb. Richard Savina was an unemployed truck driver from Catonsville, Md., who belonged to the local chapter of the Ku Klux Klan. In May 1981, he attempted to firebomb the Baltimore County headquarters of the National Association For the Advancement of Colored People (NAACP). He was arrested and convicted on Aug. 28 by an all-white jury of manufacturing and possessing a bomb, a crime that carried with it a possible twenty-year prison sentence and $20,000 fine.

On Sept. 26, Federal District Judge Frank Kaufman sentenced the 29-year-old defendant to fifteen years in prison. See: **Ku Klux Klan**. REF.: *CBA.*

Savinkov, Boris Viktorovich (AKA: **Ropshin**), 1879-1925, Rus., consp.-suic.-mur. Led terrorist activities perpetrated by Social Democratic party. He was the ringleader of successful plots to kill V.K. Plehve in 1904, and Grand Duke Sergey Aleksandrovich in 1905, for which he was arrested and sentenced to death. He escaped the sentence and fled to Switzerland in 1906. Upon his return to Russia in 1917, he served under Alexander Kerenski as vice-minister of war. He fought the Bolsheviks in Russia, Poland, and Paris, and was arrested in Russia in 1924 and again sentenced to death. He killed himself in prison after his sentence was commuted to life.

REF.: *CBA;* Laquer, *Terrorism.*

Savino, James, 1955- , Case of, U.S., mur. While on an Army R.O.T.C. training exercise at a secluded nature sanctuary on Indian Island, located off of Long Island, N.Y., a 20-year-old cadet named Thomas Fitzgerald was killed in what was described as a "hazing ritual." The incident occurred around midnight on Nov. 5, 1976, near the R.O.T.C. campsite. Fitzgerald was playing the part of the "prisoner" during a war game exercise and was allegedly learning how to react when confronted by intimidation techniques, according to the story told to the Suffolk County district attorney's office. James Savino, a second lieutenant in the elite Pershing Rifles, a military fraternity, was accused of stabbing Fitzgerald to death in a case that raised serious questions concerning the need for validity of such R.O.T.C. programs during peacetime.

Savino was arraigned on a charge of second-degree murder. He was acquitted on June 23, 1978, following a four-week trial in which the judge had instructed jurors to disregard the prosecution's charge that Fitzgerald's death had resulted from an illegal hazing. REF.: *CBA.*

Savitt, Samuel Norman (AKA: **Samuel Savatsky**), 1919- , U.S., forg.-fraud-tax evas. Despite early success and a relatively high income, Sammy Savitt (legally changed from Samuel Savatsky) of Rochester, N.Y., lived beyond his means. That trait ultimately forced him into the French Foreign Legion. A big spender, gambler, and womanizer, he financed his high living through fraud and forgery in his dealings with his clients.

After successfully fleecing his gullible clients and avoiding prosecution for a number of years, Savitt was wanted in 1949 by the Securities and Exchange Commission, the Internal Revenue Service, and the U.S. Postal Service on a variety of charges including fraud, forgery, use of the mails to defraud, and tax evasion. In addition, he was arrested for refusing to make restitution on three bad checks.

Deciding that he could no longer evade the law, Savitt took what cash he could lay his hands on, passed a few more bad checks, obtained a passport under the name of Savatsky, and fled the country. Eventually, seeking what he thought was complete anonymity, he joined the French Foreign Legion, trained in North Africa, and then was sent to Vietnam, where he tramped through swamps for many months. In 1951, apparently in ill health, he left the legion.

After several years of diligently searching for Savitt throughout United States and Canada, the U.S. Postal Service was finally able to trace him down in Paris where he had made the mistake of applying for a job at an American company, giving a Rochester firm as a reference. After spending six months in a French jail while extradition proceedings went on, he was returned to the U.S. in March 1953. Savitt was tried on several of the outstanding charges, found Guilty, and sent to prison. REF.: *CBA.*

Savoy Hotel Murder, 1980, Brit., (unsolv.) mur. On Oct. 1, 1980, a woman was heard screaming in room 853 of the Savoy Hotel in London. Hotel employees found a woman bleeding to death from ten stab wounds. The woman, who was never identified, was thought to be a prostitute taken to the room by a man. A man who had checked into that room at the Savoy earlier that day was never located. Another man dressed in black was seen running from the hotel at the time of the incident. But those leads came to nothing and the murder was never solved.

REF.: *CBA;* Nash, *Open Files.*

Saw, U. (Galon U Saw), 1900-48, Burma, consp.-mur.-assass. Owned and edited nationalist newspaper *Thuriya,* and originated Myochit party. He employed his own private army to depose prime minister Ba Maw in 1939. He was prime minister from 1940-42, but was jailed from 1942-45 by the British on charges of negotiating with the Japanese. He traveled to London with competitor Aung San to negotiate Burmese independence, but balked at the treaty eventually signed by others in 1947. He ordered the political killing of Aung Sang shortly after the treaty was approved, for which he was convicted of conspiracy to murder and put to death. REF.: *CBA.*

Saward, James Townsend, See: **Jim the Penman**. REF.: *CBA.*

Sawtell, Isaac, d.1891, U.S., mur. On Feb. 5, 1890, Hiram F. Sawtell alighted from a passenger train in Rochester, N.H., where he was greeted by his brother Isaac. A few days prior Hiram had received a letter saying that his daughter Marion, who had been staying with Isaac, was sick and asking him to come immediately. The two brothers climbed into a buggy for what was ostensibly a short ride to the house.

Isaac Sawtell drove to a general store where he went in to pick up a few items, and reappeared a few minutes later carrying some packages. He continued to drive along the road away from town and finally pulled off heading toward an abandoned shack. There Isaac confronted his brother about two parcels of land in Boston, valued at $14,000, that had belonged to their mother. When Isaac was sent to prison, Hiram had taken control of the property. Upon his release, Isaac persuaded his mother to renege on the earlier agreement and deed the property to him. Hiram, in turn, had started legal proceedings to regain control.

Isaac pulled a gun on Hiram and demanded that he sign a document forfeiting all claims to the property. Hiram jumped from the wagon and ran toward a wooden shanty off the side of the road. As Hiram ran away Isaac shot him in the back. Isaac severed his brother's head and hands with an ax and buried all of the remains except the head in a shallow grave. After disposing of Hiram's clothing, Isaac proceeded to Boston and then to Maine, where he buried the head. On Dec. 5, a team of police and volunteers uncovered the body parts in the East Lebanon Woods near Berwick. Isaac Sawtell was indicted for murder in the first degree, accessory to murder in New Hampshire, accessory to a murder in Maine. The question then became where had the murder actually been committed? When the trial opened in Dover on Dec. 16, 1890, defense counsel James A Edgerly first tried to show that the body was not that of Hiram Sawtell. Failing in this, Edgerly argued that the murder was not committed in New Hampshire but in Maine. Sawtell refused to testify on his own behalf.

The prosecution, headed by Attorney John Kivel, produced items of clothing worn by the deceased on the day of his murder. Mrs. Janet Sawtell identified a pair of shoes as her husband's. The state rested its case on Dec. 23 after Marion Sawtell testified that her uncle had given her some medicine which made her ill. On Dec. 25 after two hours of deliberation, the jury found Isaac Sawtell Guilty of murder in the first degree and sentenced him to be hanged at the Concord Prison in January 1892. On Dec. 24, 1891, Sawtell was found unconscious in his cell. He was diagnosed as suffering from apoplectic shock and died on Dec. 26.

REF.: *CBA; The History of the Murder of Hiram Sawtell by his Brother, Isaac Sawtell.*

Saxbe, William, 1916- , U.S., atty. gen. Served as Ohio attorney general from 1957-58 and from 1963-68. He was appointed U.S. attorney general by President Richard Nixon in 1974. As attorney general, he backed capital punishment, heavier sentences for crimes involving guns, and legislation that would limit access to arrest and conviction records. He resigned in December 1974 after being appointed ambassador to India. REF.: *CBA.*

Saxe, Susan Edith, 1949- , U.S., rob.-mur. Susan Saxe was placed on the FBI's Ten Most Wanted List on Oct. 17, 1970, twenty-four days after she participated in an armed robbery of the State Street Bank and Trust Company in Boston, that left one policeman dead. The 21-year-old honor student from Brandeis University, Waltham, Mass., was a campus activist who had coordinated the National Strike Center in the wake of the Kent State shootings when four university students were slain by National Guardsmen in May 1970.

Armed bank robber and Brandeis University student Susan Saxe.

To fund radical activity, Saxe and four other Brandeis students masterminded the daylight robbery of the Boston bank which netted the gang $26,000. The shot that killed Officer Walter Schroeder was allegedly fired by William Gilday, forty-one. A communique issued by "Commander-in-Chief" Stanley Bond, of the "Revolutionary Action Force East," claimed responsibility for the hold-up. Bond, Gilday, and Robert Valeri of Sommerville, Mass., were arrested within a week of the shooting, but Saxe and a second woman, Katherine Power, eluded capture and were added to the FBI list of fugitives.

On Mar. 27, 1975, Saxe was arrested in downtown Philadelphia after being recognized by a policeman. She had eluded the authorities through her extensive contacts in the radical feminist movement. Saxe criss-crossed the country earning her living from various menial jobs. She was arraigned on separate charges of armed robbery and manslaughter, stemming from the Boston bank robbery and an earlier attack on the Bell Federal Savings and Loan in Philadelphia. According to the FBI, Saxe and Power also had participated in the theft of government property at the National Guard Armory in Newburyport, Mass., on Sept. 1, 1970.

Susan Saxe pleaded guilty in Suffolk Superior Court to manslaughter and two counts of armed robbery. She was sentenced to twelve years in prison by Judge Walter McLaughlin on Jan. 17, 1977. On Feb. 11, Federal District Judge Alfed Luongo in Philadelphia sentenced her to an additional ten years for the savings and loan robbery and the National Guard armory break in. The sentences were to be served concurrently.

REF.: *CBA;* Nash, *Bloodletters and Badmen;* ____, *Look for the Woman.*

Saya San, d.1931, Burma, treas. Buddhist monk who formed army of peasants, named himself king, and organized uprising against British in Lower Burma from 1930-31. The revolt was a failure and he was hanged. REF.: *CBA.*

Sayadian, Aruthin (AKA: **Sayat Nova**), 1712-95, Armenia, minister, assass. Served as court minister under Irakli II. He became a monk in 1770. He was killed by invaders from Persia. REF.: *CBA.*

Sayers, Dorothy Leigh, 1893-1957, Brit., writer. Created fictional detectives Lord Peter Wimsey and Montague Egg. Books authored: *Whose Body?, Strong Poison, Murder Must Advertise, Gaudy Night, Busman's Honeymoon, In the Teeth of the Evidence,* among other works. REF.: *CBA.*

Scaevola, Gaius Mucius, prom. 509-10 B.C., Roman., mansl.-attempt. assass. Accidentally killed bystander in attempt to assassinate Lars Porsena, the king of Clusium, in 509 B.C., according to legend. When threatened with execution by burning during an interrogation, he allegedly placed his right hand into the flames until it was burned off. This bravery persuaded Porsena to release his prisoner and negotiate a peace pact with Rome. REF.: *CBA.*

Scaevola, Quintus Mucius, prom. 95-82 B.C., Roman., consul, assass. Served as consul in 95 B.C. and later as governor of Asia and as pontifex maximus. He co-sponsored troublesome legislation refusing Roman citizenship to future allies, precipitating the Social War. He was censured by the Marian party in 82 B.C., and assassinated. REF.: *CBA.*

Scaffa, Noel Charles, prom. 1935, U.S., rob. Private detective Noel Scaffa might have served as an inspiration for one of Dashiell Hammett's brooding gumshoes—aloof, cynical, and calculating. Scaffa, however, proved in 1935 that he was hardly the incarnation of the noble Sam Spade. The swarthy, dark complected Scaffa was the son of a Sicilian contractor. He launched his career in private investigation in 1914, when he went to work for the Pinkerton agency as an office boy. After a few years had passed, he earned the right to become an investigator and then with six years of experience under his belt, he opened a Manhattan agency in 1920. In time Scaffa earned a reputation as a brilliant investigator who left the gun play for others. But he always managed to come up with the stolen merchandise, especially if the goods happened to be priceless jewelry.

On Sept. 30, 1925, dime-store heiress Jessie Woolworth was robbed of $683,000 in jewelry while she lounged in a bathtub at her fancy Manhattan apartment. Scaffa, hearing about the woman's misfortune, promised to locate the jewels for $65,000—a sum eagerly put forward by Woolworth's insurance company. On Oct. 13, Scaffa calmly strode into police headquarters and dropped a plain brown parcel on the desk. Inside were the stolen Woolworth jewels. Scaffa told the police he received them from a Broadway character named "Sam Layton," who he had met at the Prince George Hotel. Ten days later Chief Assistant District Attorney Ferdinand Pecora secured an indictment against Scaffa for allowing the mysterious Mr. Layton to escape. Scaffa's first trial ended in a hung jury, the second in acquittal. The sobering experience taught the private eye a valuable lesson: cooperation with the police in future matters was desirable.

In the next few years Scaffa took on a number of important clients including Wanamaker's Department Store, for which he recovered $200,000 in stolen merchandise, and a socialite Mrs. Joshua Cosden, whose missing jewels were valued at $81,000. By 1935, Scaffa was raking in $25,000 a year. His staff of twenty operatives lent valuable assistance to the local police, and the mild-mannered Scaffa, who lived a quiet life with his mother in the Bronx, was recognized as one of Manhattan's most influential private detectives. By his own account he had personally recovered $149 million in stolen property, all returned to the rightful owners.

Scaffa and other private detectives like him relied on their close contacts with the underworld and the insurance claims investigators in order to arrive at a mutually agreeable solution. For a large insurance company it was more economical to pay a reward, typically ten percent of the value of the item, than to reimburse the policyholder for the entire amount of the loss. For their part, skilled jewel thieves preferred to deal with someone like Scaffa than to have to go through a criminal fence, where the likelihood of police detection was greater. It was a shady arrangement but in the long run the victim, the burglar, the detective, and even the insurance company came out ahead.

Such was the case when two masked men robbed Mrs. Margaret Hawkesworth Bell, former Ziegfeld dancer, of jewels valued at $185,000. Bell and her companion, Harry Content, a Wall Street banker, were robbed of her necklaces and a thirty-two carat diamond ring at the Biltmore Hotel in Miami, Fla., on Jan. 26, 1935. Nicholas Montone and Charles Call were identified and arrested by Miami police. They were subsequently convicted and sentenced to twenty-five years in prison. A portion of the stolen loot was recovered on Mar. 18, 1935. Chief of detectives Eugene F. Bryant sheepishly explained that the thieves had left them in his car, which later proved to be a concocted story. The loot was actually removed from a numbered locker at the Union Bus Depot in Miami by Scaffa. The affair might have ended quietly if not for the assistance provided by Henry Latham Doherty, owner of the Biltmore Hotel, who recalled the National Stolen Property Act passed into law in 1934 which made the transportation of stolen merchandise across state lines a federal offense. The case was re-opened and Detective Bryant was summoned before a federal grand jury in April 1935. He testified that it was Scaffa who delivered the jewels, promising to split the insurance reward posted by Lloyd's of London for the safe return of the stolen property.

Scaffa was subpoenaed to appear before the grand jury, but he denied having seen the jewelry before it turned up on Mar. 18. The detective went on to say that he had no recollection of how the jewels had turned up at the bus depot, nor did he recognize the person who had given him the key to the locker. Scaffa was arrested on May 29 by Department of Justice agents and taken to the Federal House of Detention in New York where he was questioned at length. The next day he was formally charged with violation of the Federal Stolen Properties Act and four counts of perjury. The government accused him of entering into a conspiracy with five other men, including Benjamin Cohen, legal counsel for the convicted burglars, Chief Bryant, Fred Pine, former prosecutor in Dade County, his assistant Jack Kehoe, and C. Harrington, an associate of Scaffa's. The $15,000 reward money was to be divided among these men, with $7,000 split evenly between various other law enforcement officers in Miami who worked the case. Scaffa, the FBI charged, received $2,500 from the insurance company after a confederate returned the jewels to Miami on Mar. 8.

Caught in a web of lies, Scaffa was convicted on three counts of perjury on July 26, 1935. He was sentenced to six months in prison by Judge Carroll C. Hincks, following a plea for leniency from Defense Attorney George Z. Medalie, who presented letters and testimonials on Scaffa's behalf. In passing sentence, Judge Hincks observed: "It does appear, however, from the verdict of the jury confirmed by the defendant himself, that in the proceedings before the grand jury the defendant failed to recognize his paramount duty to tell the truth, but instead held another duty, to other individuals, to be higher than his duty as a witness." On Oct. 1, the state revoked Scaffa's private detective license. REF.: *CBA.*

Scalera, Ralph Francis, 1930- , U.S., jur. Served on Pennsylvania Crime Commission from 1969-70. He was appointed to the western district court of Pennsylvania by President Richard Nixon in 1971. REF.: *CBA.*

Scales, James I., c.1924-44, U.S., lynch.-mur. James Scales was an inmate at a correctional facility for black convicts sixty-nine miles northeast of Chattanooga, Tenn. One morning in late November 1944, Scales crossed the prison yard and knocked on the door of the residence belonging to Superintendent H.E. Scott. He was admitted to the bungalow, as was the usual custom. As a trusted prisoner, Scales assisted the women with the early morning chores. On this particular morning, the inmate had different ideas. With Warden Scott in Nashville on business, Scales decided the time was right to attempt a prison break. Four hours later, a bloody hammer, two butcher knives, and an ax were found adjacent to the battered corpse of Scott's 19-year-old daughter. Mrs. Scott was found nearby, also mortally wounded. Scales was apprehended ten miles away and was transported to the Bledsoe County Jail. The sheriff was away, so the prisoner was received by a young female cook. About an hour later three men appeared at the jail asking for the prisoner.

Scales was taken back to the reformatory where he was placed on an upright oil drum. A thirty-man firing squad appeared in the courtyard to exact "southern justice." Tennessee governor Prentice Cooper offered a $500 reward for the perpetrators of the lynching, but no one claimed the money. Scales became the second man in the U.S. to be lynched in 1944. Between 1900 and 1941, there were 4,699 lynchings in the country: 1,291 whites, and 3,408 blacks. REF.: *CBA.*

Scalia, Antonin, 1936- , U.S., jur. Antonin Scalia, was appointed to the Supreme Court by President Ronald Reagan in September 1986. Scalia, who was graduated from Georgetown University in 1957 and from Harvard Law School in 1960, entered a private law practice in Cleveland before leaving for a teaching post at the University of Virginia Law School. In the 1970s, Scalia served as general counsel of the White House Office of Telecommunications Policy and as head of the Administrative Conference of the U.S., a group that advises the government on questions of administrative law and procedure.

In 1974, Scalia became head of the Office of Legal Counsel in the Justice Department. Although he returned to academic life at the University of Chicago, he remained a presence in Washington through his active criticism of the legislative veto and as editor of *Regulation,* a magazine published by a Washington-based think tank. In 1982, Reagan named Scalia to the U.S. Court of Appeals. Before his appointment to the Supreme Court, Scalia already had demonstrated a restrictive view of the role of the courts, a clear opposition to "affirmative action" preferences for minorities, and impatience with judicial over-reaching—all positions likely to make him a favorite of, and comfortable choice for, conservative lawyers and activists. REF.: *CBA.*

Scalise, Frank (Frank Scalice, AKA: Don Cheech, Sceech), d.1957, U.S., org. crime-drugs. Frank Scalise was a made member of a Bronx organized crime family. He ran a large percentage of the mob-controlled construction firms in the Bronx and was a well known international drug trafficker. For years he was closely identified with Frank Costello and the exiled rackets boss Charles "Lucky" Luciano. During his many trips to Italy to procure heroin for his drug-running operation, Scalise was often a guest of Luciano. It was apparent, though never proven by government agents watching Luciano, that Scalise would deliver mob money to Luciano, who arranged drug shipments to the U.S.

Crime boss Frank Scalise.

Sacalise was a top lieutenant of Albert Anastasia, whom he joined in shooting to death Pete Morello on Aug. 15, 1930, outside Morello's loansharking office in East Harlem, N.Y. In 1957, a twenty-kilo shipment of heroin was seized. When Scalise refused to reimburse his partners for the financial loss they incurred, he was gunned down outside his favorite Bronx fruit and vegetable stand on June 17, 1957 (Scalise's death was also ordered for his selling of Mafia membersips at $50,000 a piece). The killer was reported to be Jimmy Jerome Squillante, an associate of Anastasia. The dead gangster's brother, Joseph Scalise, sought to avenge the murder but realized the mistake in his boasting and went into hiding. Squillante, however, convinced Joseph Scalise to return. On Sept. 19, 1957, a welcome home party was given for Scalise.

Afterward, he was allegedly murdered and his body dismembered into small, untraceable pieces. See: **Costello, Frank; Luciano, Charles.**

REF.: *CBA;* Gage, *Mafia, U.S.A.;* Gosh and Hammer, *The Last Testament of Lucky Luciano*; Maas, *The Valachi Papers*; Peterson, *The Mob*; Sodern, *Brotherhood of Evil*; Servadio, *Mafioso*, Velie, *Desperate Bargain*; *Why Jimmy Had to Die*; Zuckerman, *Vengeance Is Mine*

Scalise, George, prom. 1940, U.S., wh. slav.-rack. When labor racketeer Willie Bioff was sent to prison for extorting millions of dollars from leading Hollywood studios, much of the credit went to Westbrook Pegler, crusading columnist for the Scripps-Howard Newspaper chain. Pegler went after many a big fish in his day, including Governor Huey Long of Louisiana, Postmaster James Farley, and George Scalise, the truculent head of the AFL's Building Service Employee's International Union.

In January 1940 Pegler wrote a letter to President William Green of the AFL revealing for the first time Scalise's shady past. "I am going to tell you today that the head of one of your big international unions was sentenced to Atlanta Penitentiary for four years and six months for white slavery. The man I mean is George Scalise...a criminal of the vilest type." Pegler went on to say that Scalise had acquired a lavish twenty-seven room mansion from monies received through various crooked enterprises. Scalise defended himself against the attack by approaching Green with the names of officials within his own union whom he had accused of misappropriation of funds. These individuals, Scalise charged, were responsible for the smear campaign initiated by Pegler.

In April, Manhattan district attorney Thomas Dewey ordered the arrest of Scalise on extortion and conspiracy charges. Dewey accused Scalise and his henchmen of shaking down various local businesses in New York, including hotels, exterminators, and cleaning companies. "The union is to Scalise what a jimmy is to a burglar," said Assistant District Attorney Murray Grufein. The allegations of wrongdoing led to Scalise's resignation. "I've been Peglerized," he sighed. REF.: *CBA.*

Scalise, John, See: **Anselmi, Albert.**

Scalise, Joseph Jerome, 1938- , and **Rachel, Arthur** (AKA: **The Genius**), 1938- , Brit., theft.-org. crime. After a stint in the automobile "chop-shop" racket, a pair of syndicate gunmen from Chicago named Joseph Scalise and Arthur Rachel, became international jewel thieves. Scalise was particularly well-versed in this field. As a top triggerman for Albert "Caesar" Tocco, boss of the south suburban crime rackets, his criminal record included a number of jewel thefts. Scalise was believed to have been the triggerman who killed William Dauber as he drove away from the Will County courthouse on July 2, 1980.

The murder of Dauber, who was also a player in the lucrative "chop-shop racket," caused federal scrutiny of the operations of the Chicago mob. Knowing this, Scalise and Rachel traveled to London where they burst into the Graff Jewelry store in the fashionable Knightsbridge section of the city, armed with a revolver and a hand grenade. The Sept. 11 robbery was run with skill and precision. While five employees and two customers were forced to lie still on the floor, the gunmen removed twenty precious jewels from the display cases, including the famous Marlborough diamond valued at $960,000. The total value of the stolen jewelry exceeded $3.6 million.

Store employees attempted to follow the pair but quickly lost them in the traffic. Detectives from Scotland Yard traced their movements to Heathrow Airport where Scalise and Rachel had booked a flight to Chicago. FBI agents were there to greet them upon arrival at Chicago's O'Hare Field the next day. The Marlborough diamond, and the rest of the loot was not recovered however. FBI and mob efforts to locate the Marlborough diamond proved fruitless. According to statements given by Gerald Scarpelli, a top mob chieftain turned informant, Scalise had mailed the diamond to his sister in New York. It was later established that a London cabdriver had mailed a small package at the behest of the two thieves.

Rachel and Scalise were extradited to London to stand trial in July 1983. On Aug. 6, 1984, the two Chicagoans were sentenced to fifteen years a piece for the Graff's robbery. The stolen goods were never recovered. See: **Dauber, William E.; Scarpelli, Gerald Hector; Tocco, Albert Caesar**.

REF.: *CBA;* Servadio, *Mafioso.*

Scalish, John, b.1912, U.S., org. crime. Now deceased, labor racketeer John Scalish served as the nominal head of the Cleveland Mafia family from 1953 until 1975. He was one of sixty-seven mobsters present at the November 1957 "sit down" meeting at the estate of Joseph Barbara in Apalachin, N.Y. See: **Apalachin Conference**.

REF.: *CBA;* Demaris, *The Last Mafioso;* Gosch and Hammer, *The Last Testament of Lucky Luciano;* Sodern, *Brotherhood of Evil;* Servadio, *Mafioso;* Velie, *Desperate Bargain: Why Jimmy Hoffa Had to Die;* Zuckerman, *Vengeance Is Mine.*

Scampton, Thomas, prom. 1879, Brit., (wrong. convict.) arson. In 1866, Daniel Hands opened a hosiery factory in the city of Leicester, England. The business was not very profitable and Hands frequently found himself in financial trouble. To meet the daily expenses, he convinced one of his employees, Thomas Scampton, to invest £500 in the business and thus become a senior partner. Even with new capital, however, the business continued to suffer financial reversals. Still, Hands was always careful to pay his insurance premiums on the factory and machinery.

On the night of Feb. 17, 1875, a fire gutted the entire building and ruined the bulk of the equipment. Since this was the second fire at the factory, the insurance company refused to honor the claim. Shortly afterward, Hands charged Scampton with willful arson. Scampton was not permitted to testify in his own defense. Based on the fact that he had been quoted as saying that a fire would "do some good," he was convicted of arson and sentenced to twelve years' hard labor.

Scampton served four years at Brixton and Portland prisons before his family could secure a new trial for him. Finally, with the help of sympathetic attorneys, a move was made to have Hands indicted on a charge of perjury and Scampton released. The case went before the courts in 1879, and it was demonstrated that when Scampton refused to be a part of any scheme to defraud the company's creditors, Hands maliciously turned on his partner. At the suggestion of the police that someone had set fire to the factory, Daniel Hands had gone to the police with the story that his partner was responsible. When a new trial convened, Scampton was granted an unconditional pardon.

REF.: *CBA;* Cobb, *Trials and Errors.*

Scanlan, John, 1793-1819, and **Sullivan, Stephen**, c.1787-1820, Ire., mur. The murder of the young Irish bride Ellie Hanley in July 1819, became the inspiration for several notable works of literature, including Gerald Griffin's best selling novel *The Collegians.* Hanley was later immortalized in the *Lily of Killarney,* a light opera written by Sir Julius Benedict who was captivated by the innocence and beauty of the girl, who was killed by her bored husband and his man servant.

From the very first moment that 26-year-old John Scanlan laid eyes on her, he was captivated. After finally inducing the girl to steal her uncle's life savings and run off with him to be married, Scanlan became bored. He was accustomed to a bachelor's life and his servant Stephen Sullivan preferred to keep it that way. In the village of Glin on the Shannon River, the pair formulated a plan to murder Ellie and return to Castle Ballycahane with what was left of her small fortune.

Sullivan agreed to carry out the murder in his master's presence. On a moonlit night they sailed out on to the river, but Sullivan lost his nerve when Ellie suddenly broke out into uncontrollable laughter at the sight of him brandishing a club. The next attempt was successful. The servant asked her to accompany him on a second boat ride, without Scanlan. When she fell asleep, Sullivan struck her over the head with the butt of his pistol. Her body was dumped overboard, but washed ashore eight weeks later, on Sept. 6, 1819. A coroner's jury returned a verdict of willful murder against the pair, who by this time had disappeared.

Scanlan was found hiding in Ballycahane Castle, but Sullivan remained a fugitive until the following March. Though he was not present for the murder, Scanlan was found Guilty and hanged at the Gallows Green in Limerick. Sullivan was arrested on a charge of passing forged money, but was hanged for murder on the same gallows that his master had suffered, on July 27, 1820. REF.: *CBA.*

Scannell, John, prom. 1869, Case of, U.S., mur. In the 1860s, New York City was paralyzed by the corrupt political administration of Mayor William Marcy Tweed that comprised the powerful Tammany Hall organization. Political opponents were few in number and virtually powerless at election time. Alderman Florence Scannell and his older brother John fought the ring head on, and despite offers of bribes, the Scannells could not be corrupted.

The word on the streets in 1869 was that the Scannells must die. The ring met at Donahue's saloon on Second Avenue and Twenty-Second Streets. It was here that Florence Scannell imprudently ventured one afternoon in December 1869. There was a near riot, and pistol shots were heard on the streets. Florence Scannell was shot by barkeep Donahue, who then fled down the street. Scannell lingered eight months in the hospital and then died.

The Tweed-run newspapers attributed the blame for the shooting on John Scannell, who, they alleged, shot his own brother by accident. The older Scannell claimed innocence and swore revenge against the real murdererer. First, he took steps to insure his brother's election would not be invalidated by the Tammany Hall bosses. At gunpoint Scannell ordered the city chamberlain, Peter Barr Sweeney, to validate his brother's rightful election. The scheming political boss saw to it.

Three years after his brother's murder, Scannell tracked Donahue down and shot him to death. In the presence of 200 onlookers in a New York poolroom, the saloon keeper was cut down in his tracks. Scannell stood on trial for murder twice. The first jury could not agree on a verdict. They were split down ethnic lines. The second jury, composed of twelve native-born Americans, acquitted Scannell. See: **Tweed, William Marcy**.

REF.: *CBA;* Lewis, *Nation-Famous New York Murders.*

Scarborough, George W., d.1900, U.S., west. lawman. The son of a Baptist preacher, George W. Scarborough became a Texas cowboy, a lawman, and a range detective. He served as Jones County sheriff and as a U.S. deputy marshall in the El Paso area in the 1890s, dealing with gunmen John Selman, Wes Hardin, and Jeff Milton. Scarborough played his part in a plan to lure fugitive cattle rustler Martin Morose back across the Texas-Mexico border, when he met Morose on a bridge over the Rio Grande late on the night of June 21, 1895. As Scarborough and Morose crossed over the bridge into Texas, Deputy Marshall Jeff Milton and Texas Ranger Frank McMahon opened fire and killed Morose.

Western lawman George Scarborough.

John Selman, Scarborough's fellow lawmen and also his friend, accused Scarborough of stealing money from Morose's corpse. At 4 a.m. on Easter Sunday, Apr. 2, 1896, Scarborough came into El Paso's Wigwam Saloon where Selman sat drinking himself into a stupor. They went into the alley to quarrel and Scarborough drew his gun and fired, hitting Selman and then shooting into the prostrate form of the old gunman three more times. As he lay dying, Selman gasped out to a gathering crowd, "you know I am not afraid of any man; but I never drew my gun." Scarborough was found Not Guilty of murdering his one-time friend.

In July 1898 he assisted Jeff Milton in a search of eastern Arizona for outlaw Bronco Bill Walters. Finding him near Solomonville the officers shot it out with Walters and his companions Red Pipkin and Bill Johnson. Walters, who lived only to be sent to jail, was shot out of his saddle, Pipkin fled to safety on foot after his horse was killed, and Johnson was mortally wounded.

Scarborough later resigned from his post as deputy and became a detective for the Grant County Cattleman's Association. On Apr. 5, 1900, he was working near San Simon, Ariz., assisted by rancher Walter Birchfield as they traced some rustlers associated with Butch Cassidy's notorious Wild Bunch. The two detectives chased the outlaws into a canyon where a bullet from bandit Harvey Logan's gun tore through Scarborough's leg and killed his mount. Abandoning the hunt, Birchfield rode to San Simon to get a wagon. That night he transported Scarborough to the railroad and sent him to Deming, N.M., where his leg was amputated. Scarborough died the next day. See: **Selman, John.**

REF.: Bartholomew, *The Biographical Album of Western Gunfighters;* ____, *Black Jack Ketchum;* ____, *Kill or Be Killed;* Black, *The End of the Long Horn Trail;* Breakenridge, *Helldorado;* Casey, *The Texas Border; CBA;* Collison, *Life in the Saddle;* Dils, *Horny Toad Man;* Haley, *Jeff Milton;* Hardin, *The Life of John Wesley Hardin;* Harkey, *Mean as Hell;* Holloway, *Texas Gun Lore;* Horan and Sann, *Pictorial History of the Wild West;* House, *Cowtown Columnist;* ____, *Oil Field Fury;* Hunter, *Peregrinations of a Pioneer Printer;* ____, *The Story of Lottie Deno;* ____ and Rose, *The Album of Gun-Fighters;* Kemp, *Cow Dust and Saddle Leather;* King, *Mavericks;* Mangan, *Bordertown;* Metz, *John Selman;* Middagh, *Frontier Newspaper;* Parrish, *Coffins, Cactus and Cowboys;* Raine, *Famous Sheriffs & Western Outlaws;* ____, *Guns of the Frontier;* Scobee, *The Steer Branded Murder;* Sonnichsen, *Pass of the North;* Waller, *Last of the Great Western Train Robbers;* White, *The Autobiography of a Durable Sinner;* ____, *Lead and Likker;* ____, *Out of the Desert;* ____, *Them Was the Days;* ____, *Trigger Fingers.*

Scarfo, Nicodemo (AKA: **Little Nicky**), c.1929- , U.S., org. crime-drugs. On Dec. 12, 1987, Nicodemo Scarfo was acquitted of federal drug conspiracy charges. But, the reputed boss of the Philadelphia-southern New Jersey crime family faced a much stiffer charge; one of first-degree murder in the shooting death of rival mobster Frank D'Alfonso on a Philadelphia street, July 23, 1985.

Scarfo and six of his lieutenants were convicted of murder in Common Pleas Court on Apr. 5, 1989. He was already serving a fourteen-year sentence for extorting a "street tax" from wholesale drug dealers. Scarfo was accused of running three large drug operations that distributed phenyl-2-propanone, the key element of methamphetamine or speed.

On Apr. 6, 1989, Scarfo recieved a life sentence from Judge Eugene Clarke. Scarfo was fortunate to escape the death penalty. Had the death penalty been allowed to go through, it would have marked the first time since the execution of Louis Buchalter that a high-ranking member of organized crime went to the electric chair. See: **Murder, Inc**. REF.: *CBA.*

Scarlett, James (Baron Abinger), 1769-1844, Brit., atty. gen.-jur. Served as attorney general under George Canning and Wellington. He also played an essential role in reforming judicial processes. REF.: *CBA.*

Scarlisi, Sam Anthony, prom. 1970s-80s, U.S., org. crime. With Joseph "Doves" Aiuppa currently in prison, and Anthony "Big Tuna" Accardo in semi-retirement at his estate in Palm Springs, Calif., control of the Chicago "outfit" reverted to Sam Anthony Scarlisi, a low-profile mobster who receives guidance from North Side boss and Mafia elder statesman Gus Alex. See: **Accardo, Anthony Joseph; Aiuppa, Joseph; Alex, Gus.** REF.: *CBA.*

Scarlow, Sam (AKA: **Sam the Torch**), b.c.1888, U.S., arson. The Stock Market Crash of 1929 took its toll on Sam Scarlow, a Russian Jew who had opened up a fur business on the Lower East Side of New York in the 1920s. With no money to spare, people were unable to buy his dyed-squirrel-for-mink coats. Scarlow had a large inventory and no customers, which prompted a friend to suggest that what Scarlow really needed was a fire. A professional arsonist was hired.

It was a smooth, faultless operation. Scarlow became convinced that there was money to be made in this racket. Accordingly, he went to the New York Public Library and read up on arson, learning what pitfalls should be avoided. He realized that the only foolproof way of torching a building without being detected was to use a candle and some celluloid. When the candle burned down it left barely a trace. He also realized that timing was everything; never set fire to a warehouse during seasonal business slumps.

Armed with this information, Scarlow went into the arson-for-profit racket with Samuel J. Wurzberg, a free-lance insurance investigator, and Abe Goldner, a salesman who specialized in locating likely customers on the verge of bankruptcy. Goldner would insure the business for upwards of $30,000, ten percent of which went to Scarlow. Within a year, the arson gang was responsible for aggregate losses of $1,000,000 of commercial property in Brooklyn. Statistics showed a twenty percent increase in the number of fires in 1932 alone. The National Board of Fire Underwriters, working in conjunction with the fire marshal of Greater New York, initiated an investigation.

After 150 fires and $2,000,000 in lost property, Scarlow was nabbed by A. Bruce Bielaski, the chief of the Underwriter's Arson Unit and several police officers. "Sam the Torch" was induced to give evidence against his two confederates after learning that they had been holding out on him. However, the judge was not lenient. Scarlow served twelve years in prison before Governor Thomas Dewey recommended clemency in 1946. When Scarlow, fifty-eight, was released, he opened a laundromat.

REF.: *CBA;* Hynd, *Murder, Mayhem and Mystery.*

Scarne, John, 1930-85, U.S., org. crime. An internationally renowned expert on gambling, John Scarne's consulting brought him into intimate contact with leading figures in organized crime, whom he helped set up cheat-proof casinos. He repeatedly claimed that his skills barred him from gambling in Las Vegas, a testimonial that brought business to the mob by convincing the public that the casinos were beatable.

Scarne's list of mob acquaintances read like a "who's who" of crime and included Bugsy Siegel, Frank Costello, Arnold Rothstein, Meyer Lansky, Joe Adonis, Albert Anastasia, Jake Lansky, Willie Moretti, Frank Erickson, Santo Trafficante, and Abe Reles, but he repeatedly denied that the Mafia or a national crime syndicate existed. His 1976 book, *The Mafia Conspiracy,* theorized that all attacks on Italian organized crime figures were a conspiracy of the federal government to deprive Italian-Americans of their civil rights. Though Scarne was a best-selling author with eighteen previously published books, he could not find a publisher for his conspiracy book, which presented crime family mogul Joseph Colombo as "the great Italian-American civil rights leader." The author said he had even paid $50,000 of his own funds to have the book published, but some people saw it as a mob apology which the mob had probably financed.

The Mafia Conspiracy detailed Scarne's fascination with crime boss Meyer Lansky, and also revealed his frustration with the Jewish faction of organized crime which for some time had dominated big-time gambling through casinos in Florida, New York, Las Vegas, and Cuba. Scarne said that crime boss Santo Trafficante was only a part owner of several gambling establishments in Cuba, and that Havana's casino Hotel Capri was "the only one of the nineteen Havana casinos operated by an Italian-American group." To minimize the Mafia's importance in Cuba, Scarne conveniently overlooked the reality that many Italian-American "civil rights leaders" were given cuts of Lansky's many enterprises. He also defended Lansky from charges by informer Vinnie Teresa that Lansky bankrolled a number of lucrative gambling junkets and was involved in English casinos. Lansky himself may have condoned or even aided in the publication of *The Mafia Conspiracy,* realizing that a denouncement of harassment of the mob as bigotry might not be bad for business.

Scarne identified the Ohio gambling syndicate as the "Jewish Mob," pointing the finger at leaders Moe Dalitz, Morris Kleinman, Louis Rothkopf, Thomas J. McGinty, and Samuel Tucker, reasonably referring to the latter two as "non-Italians." According to Scarne, the conspiracy of Italian-American harassment was underscored when "Senator McClellan and Senator Lausche introduced the Senate bill to outlaw the mythical Mafia simply as a diversionary tactic to protect the non-Italian mobsters operating in their home states of Arkansas and Ohio." Scarne's claim of Jewish control of gambling may have been marginally accurate in the sense that the national crime syndicate, in its early 1930s beginnings, was chiefly a mixture of the two ethnic groups, and the Jewish faction may have been dominant. But as Jewish gangsters died out they did not establish a succession for their empires. And as their ranks grew thinner, the highly structured Italian Mafia moved in and expanded its influence. REF.: *CBA.*

Scarpelli, Gerald Hector, 1938-89, U.S., org. crime-suic. Fearing retribution at the hands of his former mob associates, Gerald Scarpelli, fifty-one, asphyxiated himself on May 2, 1989, at the Chicago Metropolitan Correctional Center where he was being held on interstate robbery charges. Before he ended his life, the one-time hitman for Joseph Ferriola provided a fascinating inside account of mob operations in the Chicago area to FBI agents. The sixty-two page transcript detailed how mob collection agents receive "street taxes" from bookmakers and owners of suburban houses of prostitution.

Scarpelli rose to prominence during the brief reign of Joseph Ferriola (1985-88) as a "juice" collector and gambling boss of the Southwest Chicago suburbs. He decided to turn informant after being arrested by FBI agents on July 16, 1988, just as he was leaving his home to rob a jewelry store in Kankakee County. Wire-tapped conversations between informant James "the Duke" Basile and Scarpelli in which the ways and means of syndicate assassination were discussed led to his arrest.

In his statements to federal authorities, Scarpelli admitted that he was one of five men who carried out the July 1980 murders of William and Charlotte Dauber, who were associated with south suburban crime boss Albert Caesar Tocco in the automobile "chop-shop" rackets. With a record of eighteen arrests and three prison terms behind him, Scarpelli had hoped to cut a deal with Judge Milton Shadur whereby he would be released from custody in return for his cooperation with the FBI. Two days before Judge Shadur was to rule on a defense motion to suppress all evidence relating to the robbery indictments, including videotaped statements to federal agents, Scarpelli committed suicide. See: **Dauber, William E.; Ferriola, Joseph; Tocco, Albert Caesar**. REF.: *CBA.*

Schacht, Hjalmar (Horace Greely Hjalmar Schacht), 1877-1970, Case of, Ger., war crimes. Before WWII, Schacht was a respected German financier who served as the director of the Nationalbank für Deutschland. A year after Adolph Hitler came to power in 1933, Schacht was appointed the Reich's minister of economics, a position he held until 1937. In 1945, he was arrested as a war criminal and placed on trial at Nüremberg. Given the precarious state of his health, he was acquitted by the War Crimes Tribunal in February 1947. REF.: *CBA.*

Schaefer, Gerard, prom. 1968-72, U.S., mur. Gerard Schaefer was a serial killer who deceived a number of young Florida girls to accept rides in his car. Then, he would take them to a secluded spot, usually on Hutchinson's Island near Fort Lauderdale, where he would fashion a noose and tie it to the limb of a tree. Schaefer enjoyed watching his victims expire by the rope. Afterward, he would collect personal artifacts of clothing or jewelry and store them in a trunk at his mother's home. After each murder, Schaefer chronicled his exploits in a diary.

Schaefer began his killing spree a year after his graduation from Florida Atlantic University. His real ambition was to become a police officer, a goal he realized by becoming deputy sheriff of Martin County. Because there were so many teen-age runaways, the local police did not bother following up every missing person's report. Schaefer covered his tracks well, and had diverted suspicion from himself by virtue of his position in the police department. In September 1973, however, he made his first mistake. He picked up a girl named Susan Place at her home and then drove off. Worried about her daughter's dating a man at least ten years her senior, Mrs. Place carefully noted the man's appearance and license plate number.

A month passed, and by this time Schaefer had gotten himself arrested on a charge of abduction. Mrs. Place came forward to identify not only Gerard Schaefer, but the Datsun automobile she had watched her daughter drive off in. The remains of Susan Place and her friend Georgia Jessup were found in a desolate location on Hutchinson's Island. Doctors determined that Schaefer was sane to stand trial. Gregarious and outgoing with the press, he became a media darling at his 1972 trial, which masked the darker crimes he was suspected of committing. Police theorized that he was responsible for close to twenty murders in south central Florida. Schaefer was found Guilty of the Place-Jessup murders and was sentenced to two life sentences, to be served concurrently at the Avon Park Correctional Institute in St. Lucie County.

Police photo of deputy sheriff and serial murderer Gerard Schaefer.

REF.: Cartel, *Serial Mass Murder; CBA.*

Schaeffer, Walter, prom. 1935, Case of, U.S. mur. On an evening in October 1935, Willie "Smokey" Saunders, the jockey who won the Kentucky Derby in May of the previous year, visited several bars with Walter Schaeffer, a horse track exercise boy, and two women, Agatha Mackison and Evelyn Sliwinski. At some point during the evening, Sliwinski was run over by Saunders' car. Murder charges were brought against Schaeffer, who was driving, and against Saunders as accessory to murder. The state's chief witness was Mackison, who testified that Sliwinski had been ordered out of the car, knocked down, and deliberately run over twice. Saunders testified that Sliwinski had too much to drink and had voluntarily gotten out of the car. He said that if they had run her over, it was without his knowledge. On Jan. 8, 1936, Schaeffer was acquitted of the murder charges. Subsequently the accessory to murder charge against Saunders was dismissed. REF.: *CBA.*

Schafer, James B. (AKA: **The Messenger**), c.1901- , U.S., fraud. Not even the Michigan chapter of the Ku Klux Klan was immune to James Schafer's many swindles. At his fraud trial in 1942, it was alleged that Schafer had "stole their money and sold them out," a charge hotly denied by the defendant.

Schafer, sometimes called the "Messenger," was a self-made man who decided the quickest way to a pot of gold was through religion. In 1935, the former advertising salesman founded the "Royal Fraternity of Master Metaphysicians," which attracted people who were willing to pump enough money into the racket so that Schafer could purchase the one-time Vanderbilt mansion on Oakdale, L.I., for $2,500,000.

Many of Schafer's followers went to live with him at the mansion which he had renamed "Peace Haven." For two years, he fed them a vegetable diet and a steady stream of "prophecy." The press picked up on the story, and publicized his efforts to raise Baby Jean Gauntt in this "pure" environment. However, Baby Jean was returned to her mother in Manhattan soon afterwards. The inhabitants of Peace Haven were evicted when Schafer was not able make the payments on the 110-room mansion.

Suspicious that the "Messenger" was not everything he said he was, several followers filed suit. Schafer was indicted for fraud and brought to trial. Among other things, it was alleged that he had swindled the Ku Klux Klan while he was a member of the Michigan contingent. Defense attorney Raymond Wise denied the charge. Nevertheless, Schafer was sentenced to a prison term of two-and-one-half to five years in Sing Sing for the theft of $9,000 from one of his parishioners. The sentence was imposed by Judge Owen Bohan of the General Sessions Court of Manhattan on May 5, 1942. REF.: *CBA.*

Schaft, Hannie, c.1921-45, Neth., mur. In 1945, Hannie Schaft became a martyr of the Dutch resistance movement. After her boyfriend's death, and the imprisonment of her parents at the hands of the Nazis, Schaft engaged in guerrilla tactics against the German occupiers of Holland. She was arrested for murder after pushing a German officer in an Amsterdam canal. She was taken prisoner and locked in a cell with the sign "murderess" tacked on the door. Following a relentless interrogation, Schaft, twenty-four, was taken to the dunes near Haarlem and shot. REF.: *CBA.*

Schall von Bell, Johann Adam (AKA: **T'ang Jo-wang**), 1591-1666, Ger., consp. Born in Germany but moved to China in 1619, concentrating on revising calendar in China and translating astronomy books to Chinese. From 1644-61 he served as an adviser under Emperor Shun-chih, and was promoted to mandarin. He was stripped of his command after the emperor died in 1661. Three years later he was convicted of scheming against the government and emperor. REF.: *CBA.*

Scharn, Kathryn, 1877-1900, U.S., (unsolv.) mur. Factory worker Kathryn Scharn was murdered in her boarding house room in August 1900. Police found the body of the 23-year-old fully dressed and draped across her bed. Her eyes had been blackened and there were ugly wounds at the back of her head, her temples, and jaw. These had been made by a carpenter's hammer, which was found on a nearby bureau. The drawers of the bureau had been rifled. On the floor was an empty purse and a torn mask. A little money had been stolen and four rings the girl had been known to wear had been wrenched from her fingers. The murder weapon belonged to Kathryn's brother Fred, who found her body and was first suspected of the crime and then exonerated. Several of Kathryn's beaus were questioned, but the police investigation petered out along dead trails. The Scharn case had its share of the fantastic.

In September, a wild-eyed man scurried into the Coney Island Police station, shouting: "Help, quick! I've located the murderer of Kate Scharn!" Captain Driscoll heard the yelling and stepped from his office to view a shabbily dressed man whose shoulder-length hair swept past a high forehead. The stranger identified himself as Professor Ernest Twigler, a 44-year-old native of Brooklyn. Puncturing this blurted explanation, Twigler frantically urged Driscoll to send a detective with him to apprehend the factory girl's killer.

Driscoll looked about the station and, seeing no detectives present, offered Officer James Tisdale, who was sweeping the floor, to "get a revolver and nightstick. Go with this man and bring in the murderer." Tisdale quickly shed the overalls covering his uniform, scooped up his weapons, and dashed off with the professor. Policeman and teacher soon reached the waterfront and, as the two crouched in the shadow of a frankfurter stand, Twigler pointed at a young man calmly smoking a pipe and sitting on one of the clam boats tied to a pier.

Officer Tisdale, gripping his revolver, rushed onto the boat, grabbed the young man by the collar, jerked him up and slammed him against a coal box at the stern of the boat. Perplexed, the young man gaped down at the revolver jammed into his stomach and made no movement to resist. Tisdale led him back to the station with Professor Twigler following at a discreet distance.

Captain Driscoll learned that the young man was a foreigner, hardly able to speak English. He did manage to find out that the man under arrest was 33-year-old Robert Holmes, newly arrived from Sweden. He was a fisherman who lived at 85 Wyckoff Street in Brooklyn. When Driscoll attempted to grill the prisoner, Holmes remained mute, a sign, the captain thought, indicating his guilt. "Take this man to Magistrate Voorhees in the police court," Driscoll ordered Tisdale. The prisoner was removed to the court.

Standing before Major Cooney, clerk of the court, Tisdale said: "I want this man held on a drunk charge."

Cooney looked Holmes over. "This guy is sober," he told Tisdale.

"He's drunk."

"No. He's sober. I won't charge him."

Professor Twigler, who had accompanied the prisoner and Tisdale to court, stood close by, obviously appreciating the scene.

Tisdale next took the Swede before Judge Voorhees. The patrolman asked that Holmes be held on a technical charge before he was officially charged with murder.

"What's your evidence?" Voorhees inquired.

Tisdale turned expectantly to the professor.

"Oh, I have it all," Twigler announced dramatically. A crowd in the courtroom pressed close to the bench as the professor began to speak in a stentorian tones, solemnly staring at the magistrate. "I am a hypnotist and I have been working on the Scharn case to get the thousand-dollar reward. I dreamed of the murderer and when I saw this man walk past me this morning, I knew him for the murderer of Katie Scharn, by the clothes he wore and by the pipe he was smoking. As he walked away from me I shut my eyes. So." Twigler pressed his eyes shut. "I held my hands over them. So." Twigler held his hands over his eyes. "And then I saw that he was really the man. I turned around and followed him until I saw him sit down, and then I went to the police station.

Judge Voorhees leaned as far forward as he could on the bench, his eyes almost popping from his skull. "I think you're insane," he said.

Professor Twigler looked as if he had been slapped in the face with a dead fish. "What! Insane! How dare you! I risked my life to bring in this slaughterer of women and that's the thanks I get for it! Why, I'll have you and all the clerks removed!"

"Get this lunatic out of here," Voorhees commanded. Twigler almost threw a fit and had to be restrained by court officers who seized him and hustled him aside. The magistrate told suspect Holmes that he was free to go. The fisherman blinked. He did not understand. The situation was patiently explained to Holmes and when he finally did realize what had happened, he became enraged, lunging for Twigler. Both men were ordered removed from the courtroom and escorted a block in opposite directions before being turned loose. Tisdale walked Professor Twigler to the end of a block and disgustedly said, "Thanks." Twigler gave a furtive glance over his shoulder, obviously looking for the offended Swede and then, according to Tisdale, "ran like hell." The murderer of Kathryn Scharn was never found. REF.: *CBA.*

Scheetz, Robert E., 1927- , U.S., law enfor. off. Robert Scheetz was appointed chief of the St. Louis Police Department on Sept. 28, 1985. Since taking over the city's principle law enforcement agency, Scheetz has implemented a number of noteworthy reforms, including an ambitious anti-drug campaign on the elementary school level known as WAR (We Are Responsible).

Through his efforts, the city purchased a BATmobile, the first of its kind in Missouri, in which police officers are able to screen intoxicated drivers at the time of arrest. Chief Scheetz has attempted to deal with escalating crime rates by re-instituting the Mobile Reserve and foot patrols in key city neighborhoods. A "Most Wanted Fugitive List" has also been introduced during his tenure of office. REF.: *CBA.*

Scheible, Mae (AKA: **Billie**), prom. 1925-34, U.S., tax evas.-wh. slav. Mae Scheible, a woman plagued with tuberculosis during much of her early years, moved to Pittsburgh, Pa. from her native Ohio in 1916. Within a few years, she opened a luxurious brothel on Fifth Avenue in the fashionable Oakland neighborhood. Her clientele included Pittsburgh's elite: judges, politicians, and show people.

During the first two years of business Scheible earned $100,000. She allegedly paid the Pittsburgh Police Department $900 a month to ensure their cooperation. Her clients were kept in line with the threat of exposure to their wives. The sexual preferences of her customers, and the number of times they called on her establishment were assiduously documented in a ledger. During her 1938 trial for income tax evasion, Assistant District Attorney John D. Ray threatened to publicize the names of the men who had frequented the resort unless Scheible plead guilty to the tax evasion charge.

Scheible's tax problems were only one of many legal entanglements she encountered over the years. In 1936, two years after she had left Pittsburgh, federal agents arrested her in Manhattan on a charge of white slavery. She had made the mistake of taking several of her girls with her—across state lines, a violation of the Mann Act. Scheible served only two years of a four year sentence when she was removed to Pittsburgh to stand trial for tax evasion. She received another two year sentence after gallantly agreeing to plead guilty. "I am doing this," she said, "in order to protect some very fine gentlemen who were very good friends of mine in days gone by."

REF.: *CBA;* Hynd, *The Giant Killers.*

Scheidemann, Philipp, 1865-1939, Ger., rebel. Served in Reichstag from 1898. Throughout WWI he fruitlessly recomended a compromise between forces. He served in the national cabinet under Prince Max. After the kaiser escaped to the Netherlands, he decreed without authority or party the formation of the Weimar Republic, in 1918. He served as the republic's first chancellor for five months before resigning in 1919 after the Treaty of Versailles was approved by the National Assembly. He escaped into exile after the Nazis assumed authority, and died in Copenhagen. REF.: *CBA.*

Scheveningen Prison Siege, 1974, Neth., host. Four convicts from the Scheveningen Prison in Holland seized fifteen hostages in the prison chapel on Oct. 26, 1974, and demanded safe passage out of the country in return for the lives of their captives. Two of the gunmen were Arab, and they requested a plane to take them back to the Middle East. The hostage ordeal lasted five days. Relying on the advice of an expert psychiatrist, the Dutch government wore down the convicts with constant dialogue. By the fifth day, the kidnappers had had enough. They offered only token resistance when the Dutch marines broke through the chapel's locked doors to free the captives. No one was hurt.

REF.: *CBA;* Clutterbuck, *Kidnap and Ransom.*

Schiff, Jack, and **Bertolotti, Freddy**, and **Borstein, Sydney**, prom. 1950, U.S., extor.-rack. A lucrative loan-sharking racket, operated out of the Abrams Delivery Company in New York City, was broken up by special agents of the district attorney's office in September 1950. By searching through a directory of unpublished phone numbers, the identity of Jack Schiff was established. It was learned that Schiff owned a garage. Employees and associates provided the name of an accomplice, Freddy Bertolotti, who was known around town as a notorious "juice" man and racketeer.

Schiff and Bertolotti were trailed to their usual haunts which soon led to the doorstep of the Abrams Company, where the confidential records of the loan sharking business were stored. The building was raided, and the documents seized. All that was left to do was extract a confession from the suspects. It took almost thirty-two hours of non-stop interrogation to get one of them to come clean, but it was at last accomplished. The three suspects pleaded guilty. Bertolotti drew a two-year prison sentence and $2,000 fine. Schiff was sentenced to eighteen months and assessed $2,500 in fines. Sydney Borstein, another accomplice, was given six months, and a $1,500 fine; and Abrams, the expressman, received a $1,000 fine.

REF.: *CBA;* Danforth, *The D.A.'s Man.*

Schild, Anabella, 1965- , Italy, (unsolv.) kid. A gang of Sardinian kidnappers seized a British electronics engineer named Rolf Schild, his wife Marta, and their 14-year-old daughter on Aug. 21, 1979, from their Porto Rafael, Sardinia, home. It was another in a long series of kidnap-for-ransom crimes allegedly carried out by Sardinian shepherds.

Rolf Schild was released on Sept. 5 and ordered to secure $600,000 ransom money to ensure the release of his wife and daughter. He paid the ransom and his wife Marta was freed on Jan. 15, 1980, but the shepherds held on to the girl Anabelle, demanding an additional $250,000 for her safe return. This latest demand followed the arrest of eight Sardinian farmers and shepherds on Dec. 17 in the countryside of Orune. Two men were killed in a gun battle between the kidnappers and carbinieri.

Following an appeal from Pope John Paul II for the safe return of Anabelle, the kidnappers, who were still at large, freed the girl on Mar. 22 without receiving any additional ransom money. By this time, six Sardinian shepherds were serving jail sentences of up to fifteen years for attempted murder. They all denied any connection with the Schild abductions. See: **Sardinian Shepherds**. REF.: *CBA*.

Schild, John, d.1813, U.S., mur. A farmer in Reading, Pa., went berserk on Aug. 12, 1812. First he accused his wife of putting poison in his tea. Then he grabbed an ax, rushed outside, and started chasing chickens with blade ready to chop at any available neck. He returned to the house where he killed both his father and mother. Smashing the furniture, he finished his insane display by setting the house on fire. Although he pleaded insanity at his trial, he was found Guilty of murder and was hanged on Jan. 20, 1813.

REF.: *CBA;* Nash, *Bloodletters and Badmen.*

Schildbach, Gertrude, See: **Reiss, Ignace.**

Schiller, Johann Christoph Friedrich von, 1759-1805, Ger., milit. des. Noted playwright and poet, taken into custody by Duke of Württemberg for fleeing military unit in which he served as surgeon. As punishment, he was prohibited from publishing any works but studies on the field of medicine. He escaped Württemberg, however, and was able to utilize his creative talents while living in Mannheim and Weimar. REF.: *CBA*.

Schindler, Michael, 1962- , and **Thompson, Anthony**, 1952- , and **Robertson, David**, 1961- , U.S., consp.-mur. With an eye on inheriting an estate valued at $40,000, Anthony Thompson of Baltimore, asked two of his classmates in a karate school he was attending, if they might be interested in a murder-for-hire scheme. Michael Schindler, a former class president of Patapsco High School and David Robertson, a varsity football star, replied in the affirmative.

The murder of Thompson's wife Mary, 23, and her grandmother Maria Zisser, eighty-three, was carried out on Nov. 24, 1979 while Anthony was away on a hunting trip to the Eastern Shore with his father-in-law. Police discovered that the two women were bludgeoned and stabbed repeatedly. Robertson, a deeply religious youth who belonged to a church choir was found Guilty of murder on Nov. 14, 1980. A year later he filed a writ of certiorari and was granted a new trial. He was subsequently judged Not Guilty on Apr. 26, 1984.

Michael Schindler of Dundalk, Md., was convicted of first-degree murder and sentenced to life imprisonment by Judge Joseph Pines on Sept. 8, 1980. Thompson, who pleaded guilty on two counts of conspiracy to commit murder also received a life sentence. REF.: *CBA*.

Schivarelli, Peter, c.1946- , U.S., asslt.-org. crime. An article in the *Wall Street Journal* during the week of Jan. 29, 1979, described mob efforts to influence the popular rock group *Chicago* to agree to an exclusive contract for concert bookings. The story went on to say that two Chicago mob figures, Anthony Spilotro and Peter Schivarelli, had discussed a possible deal with the group's manager. A small blurb on one of the group's albums expressed thanks to Schivarelli, who, in addition to this and other business interests, was serving as the $39,700-a-year deputy commissioner for the department of streets and sanitation in Chicago.

Schivarelli's ties to organized crime figures brought him under intense scrutiny by the press. Among other things, it was revealed that his uncle was John "the Bug" Varelli, identified by the Senate Rackets Committee in 1963 as a prominent member of the ruling "inner circle" that controlled gambling and loan sharking operations on the city's West Side. Schivarelli reportedly doubled as manager of a popular syndicate hangout called B. Ginnings in the Northwest suburb of Schaumburg. Danny Seraphine, the drummer for the band Chicago, and a close friend of Schivarelli, was the major owner of the club.

On Nov. 23, 1974, Schivarelli was with Michael Spilotro and Rocco Lombardo, brother of syndicate hitman Joseph "the Clown" Lombardo, at a Chicago cocktail lounge when a fight erupted with a patron, James V. Gandolfo. Gandolfo's only crime was that he accidentally knocked over Spilotro's drink, an offense that landed him in the hospital with broken bones. Indicted on an assault and battery charge, Schivarelli and his friends were eventually acquitted in April 1975, after extensive legal maneuvering by attorney Frank Whalen. Schivarelli's arrest record was later expunged.

Commenting on the political fortunes of the commissioner, columnist Mike Royko sarcastically noted: "Considering that he isn't even an alderman he lives remarkably well. His home is a twenty-two room mansion on the North Side and he regularly parks his $20,000 Mercedes Benz in a no-parking zone outside City Hall. In fact, Schivarelli himself is a prime example of the benefits to be gained by giving fine opportunities to a local boy." REF.: *CBA*.

Schlekat, Ludwig R., prom. 1951, U.S., embez. The president of the Parnassus National Bank in New Kensington, Pa., Ludwig R. Schlekat was a self-made man who rose from clerk to president by embezzling $600,000 to buy control of the bank. An investigation began in early August 1951, when a bank examiner discovered that the bank's "cash on hand" was listed as $719,651.95. The actual sum in the vault was $119,651.59. On Aug. 17, Schlekat was charged with misapplication of funds and making false entries. By 1947, Schlekat had risen to assistant cashier, and when former bank president Charles C. Alter retired, a local real estate man approached Schlekat on behalf of H.A. McDevitt and J.H. McKeown, two Ohio businessmen who offered $254,000 for 540 of the bank's 750 stock shares. Alter accepted, and the new stockholders soon elected Schlekat president. Investigation revealed that "McKeown" and "McDevitt" were fictional, and that the assistant cashier had stolen the bank's money to buy the bank. Schlekat pleaded guilty on Jan. 26, 1953. On Jan. 30, Judge Wallace S. Gourley sentenced Schlekat to twenty years in prison, telling him that he would only have to serve ten years if he paid a $35,000 fine. REF.: *CBA*.

Schlichler, Andreas, prom. 1908, Ger., mur. The body of Margarethe Filbert was found in the Schelmenkopf state forest near Rochenhausen, Ger. Dr. Zahn performed an autopsy assisted by a barber-surgeon, Herr Müller, and concluded that Filbert had been strangled before her head was severed. Corporal Schmidt, of Winnweiler, was directed to Andreas Schlichler, who was once charged with poaching. The 40-year-old father of five sullenly denied any involvement. A neighbor, Philipine Fluhr, anxiously confirmed Schlichler's alibi. All villagers who were interviewed seemed suspicious and fearful of the probable poacher; only one, Frau Zabaroff, would talk. She admitted to hearing cries for help from the direction of Schlichler's fields the day of the killing.

A Frankfurt commercial chemist, Dr. Georg Popp, was called in by District Attorney Sohn. Sohn had received an anonymous, semi-literate letter telling him that the entire village believed Schlichler guilty. Popp identified human blood under Schlichler's fingernails, and later found traces of blood on his trousers. In addition, minute hairs from the deceased's petticoat, which were found on Schlichler's shoes. On Dec. 1, 1908, Popp's final report was given to Sohn and Counselor Seeberger. Schlichler was tried in the Kaiserlautern district court, and was convicted and sentenced to death. After his sentence was commuted to life imprisonment, he admitted that he had accidentally encountered the well-dressed Filbert, presumed she had money, and strangled her. Finding no cash or valuables, he took revenge on the corpse by beheading it.

REF.: *CBA* Thorwald, *Crime and Science.*

Schlüter, Otto, d.1957, Ger., attempt. mur. In June 1957, a car bomb claimed the life of Otto Schlüter's 62-year-old mother, moments after he stepped out to buy a package of cigarettes. Schlüter, a West German arms dealer, had been targeted for assassination before, and had also survived an earlier bombing attempt. Schlüter's firm was a regular supplier of arms to the radical FLN (French National Liberation Front). REF.: *CBA.*

Schmerling, Anton von, 1805-93, Aust., jur. Held office as imperial minister of justice from 1849-51, and as premier of Austria from 1860-65. He was also the first to preside over the supreme court of Austria, from 1865-91. REF.: *CBA.*

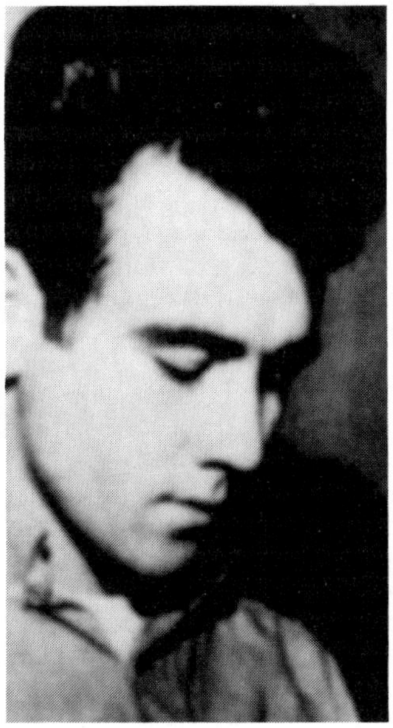

Convicted murderers John Saunders and Charles Schmid.

Schmid, Charles Howard, Jr. (AKA: **Smitty**), 1942- , and **Saunders, John**, prom. 1964, U.S., mur. Charles Schmid, five feet, three inches tall, was bothered by his short stature. To improve his image, he became a devoted gymnast, winning a state championship in high school. Uncomfortable with his peers in his twenties, he enchanted teenagers in Tucson, Ariz., with fantastic tales. "Smitty" Schmid's fantasies turned to terrible reality in Spring 1964. His teenage friends apparently knew when their hero turned to murder, but they told no one.

Smitty's main female devotee was Mary Rae French, an 18-year-old who worked at his mother's nursing home and turned most of her pay over to him. She never minded when he used his small cottage for orgies, and she often joined in. On the evening of May 31, French, Smitty, and a friend, John Saunders, were talking about Smitty's exploits with girls, when he suddenly got a different look on his face and announced, "I want to kill a girl...I think I can get away with it." French suggested that as their victim 15-year-old Alleen Rowe, whom she knew would be alone because her mother worked late in the evening. French called the girl and got her to agree to sneak out of her house and meet the threesome.

They drove into the desert where French stayed in the car while the men took Alleen off into the shadows and raped her. Then they killed the terrified, struggling girl by bashing in her head with rocks. French and the men dug a shallow grave and buried her. Everyone who knew Alleen Rowe was soon questioned about her disappearance, but Schmid just said in puzzled tones that he was supposed to have met her that night but that she was not home when he arrived.

Schmid soon started dating 17-year-old Gretchen Fritz, whose wildness seemed to match his own. Schmid was furious, though, when the doctor's daughter let him know that she had "gone all the way" with a boy in California. "I really loved that girl! I'll kill her!" he told a friend. On Aug. 16, 1965, Gretchen and her 13-year-old sister, Wendy Fritz, went to a drive-in movie. Schmid met them, enticed them out to the desert, and killed both girls, leaving their bodies out in the open along an unfrequented road. After he bragged to his friend Richard Bruns that he had killed them, the two returned to the desert and buried the already-decomposing bodies.

Friends of the Fritzes hired some "Mafia types" to investigate their daughters' disappearances. The men, hearing Schmid's story that the girls had run away to San Diego, insisted that he go with them to hunt for the girls. Schmid stayed there several months, until he was arrested for impersonating an FBI agent questioning girls on the beach.

Although the police suspected Schmid, they had no direct evidence, and the teenagers who had heard Schmid bragging delighted in protecting their hero. However, Schmid began to crack under the pressure of his murders. He once drove his fist through the wall of his small cottage, then ran outside shouting, "God is going to punish me!" Bruns, too, was feeling it—he was beginning to get terrified that his so-called friend would go after Bruns' girlfriend, Kathy Morath, who had previously been enamored of Schmid, though not as uncritically adoring as Schmid liked his girls. With that possibility preying on his mind, Bruns went to visit his grandmother in Ohio, and from there called the Tucson police and told them everything he knew.

On Nov. 11, 1965, Schmid was arrested for the murders of the Fritz sisters. Mary Rae French and John Saunders, under arrest for abetting the murder of Alleen Rowe, turned state's evidence against him. Schmid was found Guilty and sentenced to death, though the punishment was never carried out because of the U.S. Supreme Court decision against capital punishment in 1971. Saunders received a sentence of life in prison, and French was sent up for four to five years. Schmid was later tried for the murder of Alleen Rowe. He was convicted and received an additional fifty-five-year sentence on top of his life sentence.

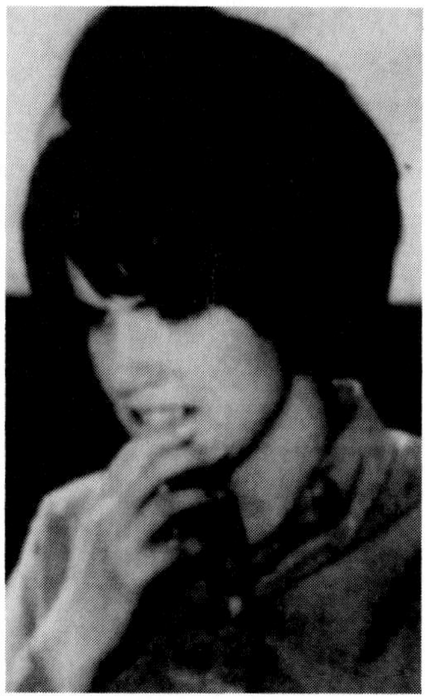

Mary French, who, with Saunders and Schmid, killed three teenagers.

Held in the Arizona State Prison, Schmid escaped on Nov. 11, 1972, along with Raymond Hudgens, a convicted three-time killer. Schmid and Hudgens held four people hostage on a ranch near Tempe, Ariz., before deciding to separate. Both were caught again within days and returned to prison.

REF.: *CBA;* Gilmore, *The Tucson Murders;* Nash, *Bloodletters and Badmen;* Wilson, *Encyclopedia of Modern Murder.*

Schmidbauer, Elizabeth, prom. 1954, Ger., smug. Elizabeth Schmidbauer became the unwitting dupe of a gang of West German watch smugglers during a vacation to the U.S. in 1954. She was promised free passage on the British cruise ship *Queen Elizabeth* in return for transporting a parcel of watch movements through U.S. Customs.

The ocean liner docked in New York Harbor on Dec. 14, 1954. Customs inspectors searched her luggage, but did not notice anything unusual. When the bags passed through electronic detection an alarm sounded. Agents discovered a false bottom suitcase containing 759 watch movements with an estimated value of $10,000. Schmidbauer explained through her tears that a man named Moritz, living in Munich, had approached her with an offer of free fare. She claimed she did not know what she was doing was illegal.

The agents laid a trap for the smugglers at Schmidbauer's aunt's residence in New York. Upon hearing that Schmidbauer had "cleared" customs, a man identified as Hans Berger arrived at the home. The customs agents emerged from hiding to take the man into custody. They learned that Berger also was only doing a "favor" for the elusive Mr. Moritz. Berger was released, and Schmidbauer received a six-month suspended sentence. REF.: *CBA.*

Schmidt, Franz, prom. 1580, Ger., execut. It was customary in Germany during the Middle Ages to execute female offenders by drowning them. This struck hangman Franz Schmidt as rather barbaric. He believed that a more compassionate way to end the life of the female criminal was beheading. In his journal, he recorded dozens of instances where he had chopped the heads off of the women "as a favour." Schmidt also considered hanging an unsuitable punishment for women.

REF.: Atholl, *Shadow of the Gallows; CBA.*

Schmidt, Hans (AKA: **Dr. Emil Moliere, George Miller, A. Van Dyke**), 1881-1916, U.S., count.-mur. On the morning of Sept. 5, 1913, a woman spotted a parcel floating in the Hudson River near an abandoned dock on the New Jersey side. The parcel was fished out and unwrapped, revealing the upper torso of a woman's body. The police investigated and discounted several false identifications of the corpse. Then, on Sept. 7, the lower part of the torso washed ashore near Weehawken. Still coming up empty-handed after exhausting their other leads, the police pursued a long shot. The distinctive, hand-crafted pillowcase in which the upper torso had been wrapped bore the name of its manufacturer, the Robinson-Rodgers Company of Newark, N.J. When police inquired at the firm, they found that only a small quantity of the cases had been produced, and the manufacturer therefore, was able to send them to the sole distributor. The distributor, located in New York City, had sold only two pillowcases and still had the receipt for the sale.

Along with several other household items, the pillowcases had been delivered to an apartment at 68 Bradhurst Avenue rented by a Hans Schmidt. Schmidt, who turned out to be the assistant pastor of St. Joseph's Church on West 125th Street, claimed that he had rented and furnished the apartment for a relative, a young woman soon to be married. After watching the apartment for several days and growing suspicious when no one came or went, the police broke in and found considerable evidence that a murder had been committed on the premises. In addition to bloodstains on the bedroom wall and on the floor, police found a newly sharpened butcher knife and saw. Except for a man's coat marked with the name A. Van Dyke, the only clothes in the apartment belonged to a woman. A stack of letters addressed to Anna Aumüller led police to the rectory of St. Boniface Church on 47th Street and Second Avenue where the woman had apparently worked as a housekeeper. There, police gathered information which began to tie the case together. The pastor of St. Boniface said that Aumüller had worked for him for a brief period in 1912. During that time, the pastor informed police, he became suspicious that Aumüller was becoming romantically involved with one of his parish priests, Father Hans Schmidt.

Anna Hirt, a woman who had worked at the St. Boniface rectory with Aumüller, told police she remembered a distinctive birthmark on Aumüller's chest. Police had Hirt view the body, which in fact bore a mark similar to the one she had described. Although unorthodox, the identification was accepted by police. Now armed with a positive identification, the police approached Schmidt at St. Joseph's and questioned him about the crime. Schmidt did not confess immediately although he did display great anxiety. However, when police began to press him with specific details of the murder, Schmidt broke down and admitted killing Aumüller, claiming he had done so "because he loved her." Police thwarted an attempt by Schmidt to kill himself with a razor he had concealed on his person and took him into custody. After his initial confession, Schmidt freely discussed the murder with police. He and Aumüller had obtained a marriage license, and he had performed a ceremony that they both apparently considered a valid marriage. Schmidt said he decided to kill Aumüller on Aug. 31. The only reason he gave for the decision was his love for her, saying that "sacrifices should be consummated in blood." Although it was never proved, evidence uncovered later caused police to suspect that Schmidt's decision to murder his "wife" came when he learned she was pregnant.

Schmidt told police in detail how he had gone to the apartment at night and entered quietly. He turned on only the bathroom light so as not to awaken the sleeping woman. With a butcher knife he had purchased several days earlier, cut her throat as she slept. In a detailed confession Schmidt gave to police inspector Faurot, he said he then put Aumüller's body in the bathtub and began dismembering it. When questioned about the precision with which the body had been mutilated, Schmidt told Faurot that he had once studied surgery in his native Germany. After dismembering and decapitating the body and cutting the torso in two, Schmidt wrapped the body parts in linens from the apartment, weighted them with rocks, and, in what he recalled to be four or five trips, took them across town to the Fort Lee ferry and dropped them into the river. Schmidt also attempted to destroy other evidence of the murder by scrubbing the bloodstained carpet and wall and burning the bloody mattress in a nearby vacant lot.

As word of Schmidt's confession spread, his superiors in the church hinted that Schmidt was an impostor and perhaps had never been ordained. Responses to police inquiries from officials in Schmidt's hometown of Aschaffenburg, Ger., and from church officials in Mainz where Schmidt claimed he was ordained in 1904, confirmed much of what Schmidt had told police. He was born in Aschaffenburg in 1881 and was educated there and in Mayence. He entered the seminary at Mayence on the wishes of his extremely religious mother. Schmidt's own preference for a more secular life was borne out by his fellow seminarians' reports that he led a "notoriously dissolute" life while at the seminary. Shortly before Schmidt was ordained at the age of twenty-four, he forged the documents required for a doctorate and received that title following his ordination. Schmidt used his skills as a forger to produce similar documents for other young priests who wanted titles they had not legitimately earned. In 1907, Catholic authorities who had learned of his "moonlighting" as a forger, deprived Schmidt of his rights as a priest.

In 1909, Schmidt had been arrested for fraud but he had escaped imprisonment on the grounds of insanity. (Further investigation revealed that numerous cases of insanity appeared in Schmidt's ancestry.) As soon as he was able to obtain his release, Schmidt emigrated to the U.S., where he used his prowess as a forger to obtain an assignment as the temporary pastor of St. Francis Church in Trenton, N.J. From the Trenton parish, Schmidt moved to St. Boniface where he met Aumüller.

During his confession, Schmidt told police that he had frequently posed as a physician under various names, and a search of his room uncovered evidence indicating that he was interested in the sale of substances particular to criminal medical practice. Police also found 500 business cards bearing the inscription: "Dr. Emil Moliere, formerly Assistant Surgeon of the Municipal Women's Hospital, Paris, France. Representative of the Chemical Hygiene Manufacturing Company." Schmidt told Faurot that he had used the name of Dr. Emil Moliere (Moliere being Schmidt's mother's maiden name) frequently when masquerading as a physician. Also found in Schmidt's room were certificates of stock in companies that manufactured patent medicines. The already amazing breadth of Schmidt's criminal activity took another leap when receipts police found in his apartment led them to a counterfeiting plant in an apartment on West 134th Street in New

York City. In the apartment, rented by Schmidt under the alias of George Miller, police found color printing presses, engraving plates, and cameras. They also found a stack of partially printed ten dollar bills and an unused set of twenty dollar plates. The building superintendent gave police a description of Schmidt's accomplice in the counterfeiting operation that led them to Dr. Ernest Arthur Muret. Muret, who police discovered had been practicing dentistry without a license, denied any complicity in the counterfeiting operation. Police learned that Muret had fled England in April 1911 rather that face charges of falsely representing himself as a medical man under the name of Dr. Ernest Stein. Inspector Faurot noted a strong physical resemblance between the two men and began to suspect that they were brothers, a fact which both vehemently denied. However, investigation into the matter revealed that Muret was most likely Adolph Mueller, Schmidt's cousin. Muret was arrested and, along with Schmidt, was charged with counterfeiting.

A continuing police investigation uncovered other evidence suggesting the two men had been jointly engaged in criminal activities. Muret also had apparently used the aliases of Emil Moliere and George Miller, as indicated by business cards and receipts found in his apartment. Schmidt accepted sole responsibility for both the murder and the counterfeiting operation. He told police that he intended to use the counterfeited money to help the poor and unfortunate. When police found forged blank death certificates among his belongings, Schmidt admitted that he had intended to continue murdering people and would have used the certificates to more easily dispose of the bodies. He claimed to believe in euthanasia and intended to put suffering people out of their misery.

Because Schmidt refused to implicate Muret, police were only able to charge him with illegal possession of a firearm. On Sept. 19, a coroner's jury found Hans Schmidt Guilty of the murder of Anna Aumüller. Schmidt was sentenced to die in the electric chair, a fate he said he welcomed. He was electrocuted in the prison at Ossining, N.Y., on Feb. 18, 1916.

REF.: *CBA;* Rodell, *New York Murders.*

Schmidt, Helmuth (AKA: **American Bluebeard, Herman Neugebauer, Carl Ulrich, F. Helmuth, C. Hamann**), d.1918, U.S., suic.-mur. Known in the press as the "American Bluebeard," Helmuth Schmidt preyed upon poor immigrant German girls employed as domestic servants. In the years before WWI, Schmidt took out newspaper ads in Missouri, New York, Lakewood, N.J., and Royal Oak, Mich., looking for a "suitable lady to marry soon." The lonely hearts lure attracted several young women seeking to better themselves with the presumably wealthy man. Using various aliases, Schmidt would invite the women to his residence, murder them for what little money they had, and bury the remains under cement.

Schmidt carried out these grisly crimes in New York and Michigan. After moving to Royal Oak, he went to work in a Ford plant outside Detroit. While in Ford's employ, he was arrested for the murder of 38-year-old Augusta Steinbach, who had answered his ad in the New York *Herald.* The police were tipped off by her companion Agnes Dominicki who had immigrated with Steinbach from Europe eleven years earlier.

Schmidt was taken into custody on Apr. 23, 1918, after blood-soaked clothing was found under his porch. Before Schmidt could provide an estimate of just how many women he had lured to their deaths, he killed himself in his prison cell by pulling a heavy iron bed railing down on himself, crushing his skull.

REF.: *CBA;* Willemse, *Behind the Green Lights.*

Schmidt, Johann, prom. 1897, Ger., fraud. For Maria Hussmann, a simple housekeeper from Essen, Germany, her whirlwind courtship in August 1897 was a storybook romance. Hussmann thought that the gallant young man she met while on holiday in Aix-en-Chapelle was Archduke Francis Ferdinand. But her fiancé was not the Archduke, he was not the nephew of Emperor Franz Joseph and the crown prince of the Austro-Hungarian Empire. Hussmann's gallant was Johann Schmidt. Schmidt flattered Hussmann's vanity and told exciting stories about royal life. His interest in Maria seemed genuine, and within a fortnight he had asked her to accompany him to London where they would be married. He only asked that she keep their marriage a secret until accounts with other members of the royal family could be squared. A reporter leaked the story to the press that a commoner had married the Archduke. At the palace in Hungary the real Francis Ferdinand was amused when he read the published accounts of his non-existent affair.

Detectives from Scotland Yard were sent to call on Maria at her honeymoon hotel, but she tearfully told them that her husband had disappeared. It was no wonder, because Johann Schmidt was an escaped inmate from a mental institution. He had fled from the hospital by posing as one of the staff doctors. Maria was returned to Essen through the kindness of a London woman who took pity on her. Schmidt was never brought to trial as Maria refused to press charges against him.

REF.: *CBA;* Kingston, *A Dictionary of Remarkable Rogues.*

Schmidt, John, See: **Hoch, Johann Otto.**

Schmidt, Kitty, c.1883-1954, Ger., pros. "Operation Salon Kitty" commenced on Apr. 8, 1940. The story began in the 1930s, when Madame Kitty Schmidt ran one of the most opulent brothels in Berlin. Her clientele included financiers, diplomats, and government officials. The watchword of the day was discretion, and the modest looking house on the Giesebrechtstrasse provided just that for Kitty's customers.

After the Nazis rose to power in 1933, the situation changed. The Berlin Police were no longer satisfied with the usual payoffs. Suspicious that Kitty was helping Jews escape from Germany, the SS selectively harassed her with raids. Sensing that the climate was no longer conducive to her type of business, she began transferring funds to a London bank account and formulating plans to flee the country. But SS-Obersturmfuhrer Walter Schellenberg had her arrested for treason.

She was given two choices: death, or cooperation with the Nazi SD, the central security organization. Schellenberg and his superior, Reinhard Heydrich, conceived the idea of converting the brothel into a secret intelligence compound with listening devices implanted in the walls. A team of specially-trained agent-prostitutes would be assigned to elicit information from suspected traitors and political leaders who frequented the resort. Kitty was permitted to run the brothel, and receive the "guests" who had been sent to her door by the Nazis. "I come from Rothenburg," they would say. The pre-determined code meant that Kitty had to show them the photographs of the twenty women assigned by the SD to work as prostitutes. Then, while the man was closeted with his choice, his every word would be recorded and stored by the Gestapo. Between 1940 and 1943, before the Nazis lost interest in the project, some 25,000 records were made, and countless German officers were brought before trial boards and court-martialed or shot. Foreign Minister Joachim von Ribbentrop, who had negotiated the peace treaty with Russia, was "bugged" while having sex with one of the women.

In 1943 the salon was returned to Kitty, just as the tide of Germany's war losses began to mount. Kitty Schmidt, who remained silent about the nature of the operation, died in 1954. The true circumstances of "Operation Salon Kitty" were finally revealed in Peter Norden's book, *Madam Kitty.* REF.: *CBA.*

Schmidt, Patricia (AKA: **La Satira**), 1926- , U.S., mur. Patricia Schmidt, an exotic dancer from Toledo, Ohio, used the stage name La Satira. She was touring the Caribbean with five other strippers in 1947 when she abruptly cut short her engagements to rendezvous with John Lester Mee, a philandering former PT boat commander whose long-suffering wife kept house in the posh lakefront suburb of Wilmette, Ill.

Mee had been expelled from Northwestern University in 1933, and then practiced law and learned Spanish, French, and Italian. After their discharge from active combat duty in WWII, Mee and his friend Charles Jackson bought a 75-foot yacht for $750 at a war assets sale. They outfitted the craft for a winter cruise and christened it *La Tirana,* the stage name of one of Mee's numerous girlfriends.

In Panama, Mee and Jackson met Patricia Schmidt during one of her performances. Mee's romance with her began in Chicago nearly a year earlier. The men invited Schmidt to join them aboard the yacht, and anchored in Havana harbor.

In honor of Patricia Schmidt, the *La Tirana* was re-christened *La Satira.* Jackson moved out of the cabin and Schmidt settled in. It was not until then that Schmidt discovered that Mee was married. During an early morning quarrel on Apr. 8, 1947, Mee ordered Schmidt off the yacht in a threatening manner. Fearing the worst, Schmidt pulled a .22-caliber handgun from the cabin drawer and fired it wildly, shooting Mee in the head. "Then I rushed to Jack's side," she later recalled. Moaning in pain, Mee said to her, "Kill yourself. I'm going to die and I want you to die in my arms."

Jackson then burst into the cabin and seized the gun from Schmidt's hand just as she was about to carry out Mee's request. Jack Mee was taken to the hospital where he hovered near death for the next five days. When his father arrived from Chicago, Patricia Schmidt was identified as the assailant and Cuban police arrested her. Until then time she had posed as Mee's wife so she could stay at his bedside. With Dr. Mee present, Jack finally named Satira as the one who pulled the trigger.

On Apr. 13, two weeks before he was scheduled to meet his wife in Florida, John Mee died. Patricia Schmidt was charged with homicide on Apr. 15, 1947, and held without bond by order of Judge Santiago Mencia. Her story touched Cuban hotel magnate Amleto Battisti, who paid her legal expenses. Schmidt maintained throughout her long ordeal that the shooting was accidental.

The trial dragged on for nearly eight months. On Dec. 16, 1947, Jackson was acquitted of being an accessory to murder. A week later, on Dec. 22, 1947, Schmidt received fifteen years imprisonment and was assessed a $5,000 fine to be paid to the family of John Mee. Patricia Schmidt remained in the Guanabacoa Woman's Prison until Oct. 7, 1948, when President Ramon Grau San Martin issued a formal pardon. REF.: *CBA.*

Schmidt, Siegfried, 1944- , Ger., embez. For nine years, German Air Force sergeant Siegfried Schmidt served as the paymaster for a Luftwaffe supply battalion, at the Mechernich Air Base in Bonn. He performed his duties with alacrity, dispatching the pay to 125 Air Force personnel, and cashing their checks for them at the nearby bank. His superiors found little fault with the quality of his work, and frequently praised his efforts.

In his private life Schmidt was a free-spending playboy who enjoyed the company of many beautiful women. He indulged them with gifts of fine clothing and jewelry. How he did it on a sergeant's pay came into question and the truth was uncovered in 1977 when Schmidt confessed to having "invented" 5,000 imaginary soldiers which he had "stationed" throughout the country. Their names were randomly selected from telephone books, and Schmidt collected their pay each week. By the time the fraud was detected, the sergeant had grossed over $500,000. The German military sentenced the high living playboy to a three-and-a-half-year prison term in April 1977. REF.: *CBA.*

Schneider, Anna, prom. 1910, Ger., big.-fraud. Anna Schneider had convinced the dashing young nobleman Count Renenski that she was the long lost daughter of William II, emperor of Germany and king of Prussia from 1888-1918. She presented her credentials to the count, and to him, the claim seemed to be legitimate. She said that the kaiser had secretly married her mother, Vera Savanoff in 1880, and had given her a daughter, Anna. The next year he married Princess Augusta Victoria, a member of the Royal House.

Count Renenski was deeply moved by the story and agreed to help her establish her claim. In the process, he fell deeply in love with the young woman and proposed marriage. She accepted, and the ceremony was scheduled for July 10, 1910. But the count had been swindled. Anna Schneider quietly fled with £3,000 and a large quantity of the family jewels.

Schneider was a Bonn beer-hall waitress who had researched her victim thoroughly before taking action. By the time her crime was detected she had moved to Hamburg, where she took on a new identity as a well-heeled society woman. Here she deceived Colonel Bernstorff, a cousin of Johann Heinrich Bernstorff, the famed German diplomat to the U.S. They became lovers, but the colonel was saved further embarrassment when the Berlin police arrested Schneider after she tried to get 100,000 francs for a check written for 1,000. Sent to a bleak prison in West Gradenz, Schneider discovered to her surprise that the governor was none other than Colonel Bernstorff. A few days after her arrival, Bernstorff forgave her for her past transgressions and they were married. The honeymoon lasted only three weeks, long enough for him to establish that Anna Schneider was already married. She was returned to prison, and ordered to finish out her original sentence, plus five years for bigamy.

REF.: *CBA;* Kingston, *A Dictionary of Remarkable Rogues.*

Schneider, E.L., d.1939, U.S., (unsolv.) mur. E.L. Schneider came to the attention of federal authorities in 1939, while they were investigating the tax records of corrupt Kansas City political boss Thomas Joseph Pendergast. Schneider was listed on various ledgers as the principal stockholder, secretary and treasurer for various construction firms that Pendergast controlled.

Schneider was hired by Pendergast in 1929 to manage his financial affairs. Schneider lived modestly and did not appear to have the money befitting the status of a wealthy magnate. Further investigation showed that Schneider did not own any stock, but only controlled it on behalf of Pendergast. Authorities learned that more than $1 million in assets had been artfully concealed through Schneider's financial manipulations.

On May 1, 1939, one of Pendergast's operatives, Higgins, paid a visit to Schneider. With the boss under federal indictment, the nature of the visit, and the discussion between the men can only be surmised. Four days later, Schneider's body was found floating in the Missouri River, two miles from the Fairfax Bridge. In view of the avaricious, corrupt nature of the political regime, public opinion accepted the notion that the bookkeeper had been murdered. Pendergast meanwhile, was sentenced to fifteen years in Leavenworth Penitentiary for tax evasion. See: **Pendergast, Thomas Joseph**.

REF.: *CBA;* Hynd, *The Giant Killers.*

Schneider, Jerry Neal, prom. 1971-72, U.S., fraud. On his way home from his Los Angeles high school, Jerry Neal Schneider frequently passed by the warehouse of Pacific Telephone & Telegraph (PT&T). Sifting through the trash bins one day, he came across operating manuals and detailed instruction guidebooks on how to order computer equipment by phone. After graduation, Schneider studied engineering at UCLA, and using the instruction books picked out of the garbage, he began a small business. He posed as a company supplier, ordered sophisticated computer equipment by phone, and delivery men brought the consignment merchandise to a specified drop-off point.

By 1972, Schneider was operating a 6,000 square-foot warehouse staffed by ten people. He was processing so much computer hardware that the company, at least on the surface, appeared to be a highly respectable venture. But the young entrepreneur was tripped up by a disgruntled employee who was refused a raise. The employee reported the operation to PT&T officials who filed a lawsuit against Schneider's operation. Schneider was sentenced to a prison farm for sixty days. Meanwhile, PT&T agreed to settle out of court for $8,500, a small sum for Schneider, who recently sold the rights to his story to a Hollywood studio. REF.: *CBA.*

Schneider, Marie, b.1874, Ger., mur. Marie Schneider, twelve, lived with her widowed mother in Berlin. She was a rebellious child with a decidedly mean streak. In later statements to the court, Marie described the tortures she inflicted upon younger school children and delighted in the cruelty she administered.

On July 7, 1886, while on an errand for her mother, she met 3-year-old Margarete Deitrich, who was wearing a pair of fancy earrings that Marie believed she could sell. Marie took the little girl back to her home and led her up a flight of stairs. After taking the earrings, Marie opened the window and forced the girl onto the ledge. She then pushed her off and went on her way to complete her mother's errand. She planned to use the money she received from the sale of the jewelry to buy some sweet cakes.

Examining doctors determined that Marie Schneider was intelligent beyond her years, but was a moral imbecile. She was sentenced to eight years in prison.

REF.: Brooke, *Murder in Fact and Fiction; CBA;* Hibbert, *The Roots of Evil;* Wilson, *Children Who Kill.*

Schnick, James Eugene, 1951- , U.S., mur. At first, police investigators believed that 14-year-old Kirk Buckner killed seven members of his family and himself in Elkland, Mo., on Sept. 25, 1987. The family's financial hardships troubled Kirk, a sophomore at Marshfield Junior High School.

Shortly before dawn on Sept. 25, a man armed with a .22-caliber pistol shot and killed 8-year-old Dennis Buckner, and his brothers Timothy and Michael, ages seven and two, as they slept in their bedroom. Outside the farmhouse, the gunman killed the parents, Steven Buckner, thirty-five, and his wife Jan, thirty-six. Then he drove to a dairy farm owned by Kirk's aunt Julie Schnick and her husband James Schnick. According to James, Kirk shot and killed Julie, and before Kirk was able to murder James, he was hit by an errant bullet during the struggle.

At first police had no reason to doubt Schnick's story. He had suffered severe abdominal wounds during the struggle, and his wife was dead. It seemed like an open and shut case of a troubled teenager on a rampage, until the facts came to light. "Some other evidence surfaced after investigators for the Missouri Highway Patrol were called in, and one lead led to another, and they all had to be followed up," explained Bill Bowers, an officer for the sheriff's department. The murder weapon was found in the dead boy's right hand. Kirk Buckner was left-handed.

On Oct. 5, 1987, James Schnick, a man with no prior criminal record, was arrested by local police and charged with seven counts of first-degree murder. His confession was videotaped at Missouri State Highway Patrol headquarters.

Six months later, on Apr. 14, 1988, Schnick was convicted. Judge John Parrish imposed the death sentence. Schnick joined fifty-nine other inmates awaiting execution in Missouri. Pending compulsory Supreme Court review, he remains on Death Row. REF.: *CBA.*

Schober, Johann, 1874-1932, Aust., law enfor. off. Joined imperial police service of Austria in 1898, and eventually served as service president from 1918-29. As chancellor of Austria from 1921-22 he signed the Treaty of Lány with Czechoslovakia in 1921. He also held office as vice chancellor and minister of foreign affairs from 1930-32. REF.: *CBA.*

Schoenfeld, James and Richard, See: **Woods, Frederick N.**

Schoeppe, Paul, prom. 1869, Case of, U.S., mur. In the late 1860s, a young German-born physician, Dr. Paul Schoeppe, was practicing general medicine in Carlisle, Pa. One of his patients was a wealthy woman named Maria Stennecke, who had a romantic interest in the doctor and offered him a great deal of money to marry her. On the evening of Jan. 27, 1869, Stennecke died shortly after taking medicine prescribed by Dr. Schoeppe. The doctor then produced a will, which bequeathed Stennecke's entire fortune to him, but her relatives balked, and the document was discovered to be a forgery, written in the doctor's hand. Stennecke's body was exhumed, prussic acid was found in the corpse, and Schoeppe was brought to trial for murder. When found guilty, he was sentenced to death. However, medical experts stated that their colleague had been convicted by faulty test results, that any evidence of acid was due to a reaction with the atmosphere, not to internal consumption. There was still the question of the forged document, but Schoeppe appeared to be an opportunist rather than a murderer. The court ordered a retrial, and on Sept. 8, 1872, in the courtroom of Judge Junkin, Dr. Paul Schoeppe was acquitted of all charges surrounding the death of Maria Stennecke. REF.: *CBA.*

Schonleben, Anna Maria (AKA: Anna Maria Zwanizer), d.1811, Ger., mur. Married at twenty, and widowed a short time later, Anna Schonleben of Nüremberg drifted through Bavaria working as a dollmaker, a confectioner, and a cook in a traveling circus. In Rosendorf, she went to work as a housekeeper for Judge Glaser, a well-respected man who was separated from his wife. Schonleben effected a reconciliation between Glaser and his wife, and then poisoned the woman with arsenic when she returned home.

Failing in her attempt to land Glaser, Anna moved on to Sanspareil where she found a similar job in the home of Judge Grohmann. The judge was engaged to be married, which greatly distressed Schonleben, so she slowly poisoned him. His death did not seem to cause great alarm in the community, so Schonleben moved in with an invalid, Frau Gebhardt. Without apparent motive, Schonleben poisoned her the same way, still not arousing any suspicions.

She remained in the Gebhardt household, serving the husband for a time, but the other servants became convinced that Schonleben had killed her mistress. Furious that they were casting aspersions on her, Schonleben mixed a quantity of arsenic in their coffee, and then took particular delight in watching them suffer. At this point, the magistrate ordered an investigation. Judge Grohmann's remains were exhumed, and traces of arsenic found in his digestive tract. Schonleben was arrested on Oct. 18, 1809, and charged with murder. At her trial, jurors learned that the mixing of the deadly powder and the anticipation of the crime gave Schonleben a type of sexual gratification. In July 1811, she was found Guilty and sentenced to die by decapitation. She later told the judge that it would have been impossible for her to give up poisoning, had she been reprieved.

REF.: *CBA;* Hibbert, *The Roots of Evil;* Thompson, *Poison and Poisoners.*

Schorpf, Georg, prom. 1581, Ger., sod. Georg Schorpf of Ermb, Ger., was found Guilty of engaging in unnatural sexual acts with four cows, two calves, and a sheep. He was beheaded at Vellin, and his remains were burned with those of a cow. REF.: *CBA.*

Schrank, John N., See: **Roosevelt, Theodore.**

Schreuder, Frances Bernice, 1939- , and **Schreuder, Marc Francis**, 1961- , U.S., mur. On July 13, 1978, millionaire Franklin Bradshaw, seventy-six, was shot to death in his Salt Lake City, Utah, car parts warehouse. Four years later, his daughter, Frances Bernice Schreuder, was arrested and charged with persuading her then 17-year-old son, Marc Francis Schreuder, to murder his grandfather before the man could cut them out of his will and his estate, estimated at $10.4 million. Marc Schreuder was arrested on Oct. 26, 1981, in Manhattan. His grandmother posted $100,000 bail which he forfeited in early March 1981, when the young man failed to show up for a lineup scheduled by his attorneys. He was arrested again two weeks later. By the end of April 1982, Frances Schreuder was released on a $500,000 bail.

During a two week non-jury trial, heard by Third Judicial District Court Judge James S. Sawaya, psychiatrists gave conflicting testimony. Dr. Louis G. Moench, University of Utah psychiatrist, painted Marc Schreuder as having an "extremely pathological" relationship with his mother, but Dr. Lee Stewart Coleman contended that psychiatrists had no better tools for assessing a criminal's state of mind than did laymen. On July 7, Marc Schreuder was found Guilty of second-degree murder and was given the maximum sentence of five years to life at the Utah State Prison and was fined $10,000.

Frances Schreuder's trial began in Salt Lake City on Sept. 20, 1983, before Judge James F. Baldwin. Her son testified that he had shot his grandfather because "my mother asked me to" so that she could inherit a great deal of money very quickly. A week later, on Sept. 27, the jury found Frances Schreuder Guilty of first-degree murder. Prosecutor Ernie Jones sought the death penalty, but Judge Baldwin decided that Schreuder would not be sentenced to death. On Nov. 18, 1984, the New York *Times* reported that Schreuder had been moved from Utah State Prison because she was suffering from "culture shock."

In December 1988, a New York State Supreme Court reversed a libel ruling against author Shana Alexander, who had written *Nutcracker: Money, Madness, Murder—A Family Album,* about the Schreuder case. New York psychologist Dr. Herman Weiner had sued because Alexander claimed that Weiner had an intimate affair with Frances Schreuder. Alexander's disclaimer at the beginning of her book said that many of her accounts were from family members who should not be considered "the best sources in any circumstances." The court ruled that this statement gave the author additional leeway that discounted Weiner's defamation claim. REF.: *CBA.*

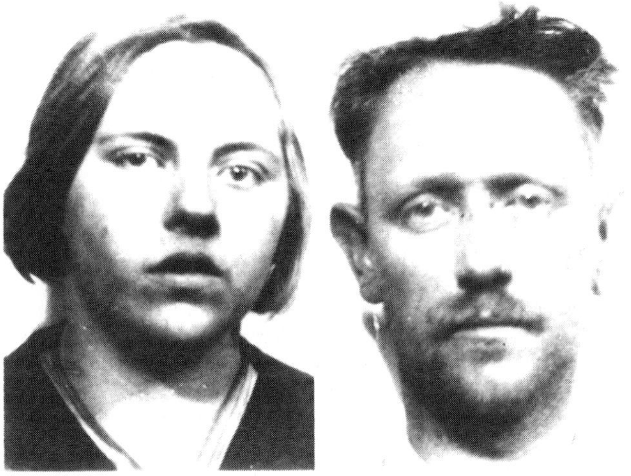

Husband and wife murderers Irene Schroeder and Walter Dague.

Schroeder, Irene, 1909-31, and **Dague, Walter Glenn**, 1894-1931, U.S., theft-mur. Irene Schroeder's life was drab until she met Sunday school teacher Walter Glenn Dague in 1929. Until the unassuming housewife fell in love with Dague she lived modestly in a small West Virginia town with her husband and 4-year-old son Donnie. At Dague's encouragement Schroeder took her son and left West Virginia with him to begin what she hoped would be an exciting new life. The couple held up a number of small stores and several banks in Pennsylvania for money to feed themselves and the boy. Most of the time they slept in a stolen roadster on the side of the highway. Dague and Schroeder ran into trouble in Butler, Pa. when they robbed a grocer. As two highway patrolmen Ernest Moore and Corporal W. Brady Paul chased their car Irene began shooting. One of her bullets struck Corporal Paul who was killed instantly. Dague shot at and injured Moore and the squad car veered into a ditch.

Schroeder and Dague set out for Arizona and succeeded in evading a number of road blocks before they eventually were cornered by a large posse. They surrendered after using up all their ammunition. Little Donnie, who viewed the high-speed chase as a game, testified against his mother in court. Pointing to a policeman he said, "My mother killed a cop like you!" Dague and Schroeder were convicted of murder and sentenced to die at the Rockview Penitentiary in Pennsylvania.

Irene accepted the court's judgment with such stoicism, that the press began calling her "Iron Irene." On the day of her execution—Feb. 23, 1931—she advised the prison chaplain to attend to her lover. "Don't worry about me," she said. "I'll be all right. You'd better go back to Glenn. I think he needs you more than I do." Concerned only with her lover's welfare, her last request was that the prison cook fry Dague's eggs on both sides. "He likes them that way," she said. A few minutes later Irene Schroeder became the first woman to be electrocuted in Pennsylvania as well as the first woman executed in that state since 1890.

REF.: *CBA;* Nash, *Look For the Woman.*

Schrotel, Stanley Russell, 1914- , U.S.. law enfor. off. Known as a reformer who ran a polished, professional force, Stanley Russell Schrotel began his law enforcement career when he became a police officer in 1934, and rose from night patrol duty to chief of the Cincinnati, Ohio, police department. Earning a law degree taking night classes at the local YMCA college, Schrotel became a captain. Posting the highest score on a competitive exam, he succeeded retiring Chief Eugene T. Weatherly in 1948.

Detailed and demanding about all aspects of police behavior, from uniforms and fitness to strict rules for outside jobs, Schrotel initiated a public relations campaign, forbade officers to argue with citizens, and sent a cop to visit anyone who made a complaint. During his sixteen-year term, from 1951 to 1967, Schrotel promoted extensive reforms, eliminating precincts and encouraging officers to gain public confidence and support. Like many other reformers at that time, Schrotel was against unionization of the police force, believing it undermined professional status, infringed on managerial perogatives, and introduced partisan politics into departmental affairs.

In a 1963 television interview on *Meet The Press,* Schrotel criticized officers for not working harder to stimulate public interest in crime prevention and to win public support. In 1966, he spoke at a civil rights and law enforcement seminar and called for more conferences with civil rights groups. After his retirement in 1967, Schrotel worked as an advisor and consultant for several law enforcement groups. REF.: *CBA.*

Schuessler, John, 1942-55, and **Schuessler, Anton,** 1944-55, and **Peterson , Robert**, 1941-55, U.S., (unsolv.) mur. On the evening of Oct. 16, 1955, 13-year-old John Schuessler, his 11-year-old brother Anton, and their friend, 14-year-old Robert Peterson, went bowling together. They were still together when their bodies were found two days later in a ditch in a nearby forest preserve.

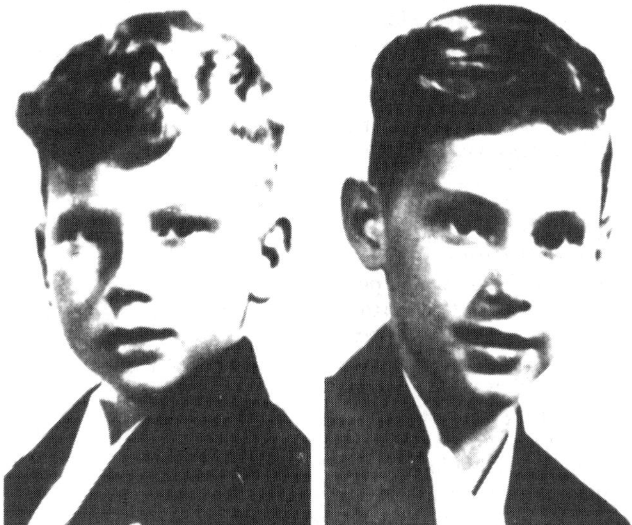

Anton and John Schuessler, found dead in 1955.

In spite of a months-long investigation and a nationwide search, and the fact that over forty persons confessed to the crimes, no valid suspects or clues were found in what came to be called "The Chicago Child Murders." Shortly thereafter, several other sensational slayings of young girls occurred. It was suggested that the same person committed all of them, but the killer has never been found.

REF.: *CBA;* Nash, *Open Files.*

Schuetz, Hans, 1933- , Ger., mur. An unemployed house painter on his way to France to look for work murdered 48-year-old Erna Riedel and her 20-year-old daughter Heidrun inside their home in Darmstsdt, W. Ger., on Apr. 19, 1967. Hans Schuetz later told police that he was desperate for sex, and he could not afford to pay a prostitute.

Schuetz had been hired to do some work in the house. Believing that there was sufficient interest on Mrs. Riedel's part, he propositioned her. When she resisted, he bludgeoned her to death, and then attacked her daughter upstairs. Arriving on the scene, the police concluded that the motive was sex. The killer had undressed the women after slaying them. Several suspects were arrested, but the trail led back to Schuetz, who had withdrawn fifty marks from the Riedel savings account the day of the murder. Interpol agents located the suspect in Paris where he was working as a laborer. Schuetz was arrested and brought back to Germany where he issued a guarded confession, saying only that "he lost his head" when Mrs. Riedel brushed against him in the cellar.

On the strength of this statement, coupled with the discovery of blood-stained clothing at his home, Hans Schuetz was convicted of murder and sentenced to life imprisonment on Oct. 13, 1968.

REF.: *CBA;* Dunning, *The Arbor House Treasury of True Crime.*

Schuldig, Winfried, prom. 1970, Case of, Ger., mur. Towards the end of 1969, Gertraude "Sisi" Braeuer moved in with her boyfriend Burkhard Stern in his father's home in Groot Osterfeld, outside Hamburg. She was a former prostitute who had defected from East Germany in 1956. On Jan. 20, 1970, the Sterns' next-door neighbor Winfried Schuldig (whose name means "guilty" in German), invited his neighbors over for a drink. Though Sisi Braeuer had renounced her former life as a prostitute, and was engaged to be married to Stern, she engaged in sex with Schuldig in full view of her astonished fiancé. The drunken orgy ended in violence. Stern tried to defend his honor against his brutish host, but Schuldig beat Stern to death with a wooden leg torn from a sofa. Schuldig claimed he was only acting in self-defense.

By this time, Sisi Braeuer had absconded with a large amount of her dead fiancé's cash. Without a reliable witness to refute Schuldig's story, the defendant was found Not Guilty of murder on Sept. 7, 1970. The following year, Gertrude Braeuer was found dead, her limbs severed and cut into small pieces. The case was filed under "unsolved." The police surmised that she was a victim of one of her sadistic clients.

REF.: *CBA;* Dunning, *The Arbor House Treasury of True Crime.*

Schüler, Johann, prom. 1663-64, Ger., witchcraft. The most brutal witch persecution in Germany during the latter half of the seventeenth century involved a prosperous miller in the town of Lindheim, in the district of Hesse-Darmstadt. The motive of Chief Magistrate Geiss was tied purely to profit. In 1661, he convinced Baron Oynhausen that the town of Lindheim was a witches' coven, and that a vigorous prosecution of the "guilty" parties would return a great deal of money to the village coffers and to the private account of the Baron.

The first witch trials to be held in this region in nearly eight years began in July 1661, with Geiss serving as the presiding magistrate and four local criminals as his duly appointed assistants. In 1663, Johann Schüler was singled out for harassment by Geiss, who wanted to confiscate his property. The midwife who had attended Frau Schüler said that she had used witchcraft to kill her own infant child. The remains of the infant were exhumed and found to be unviolated, but this did not placate Geiss.

Schüler was tortured on the rack for five days. When the townspeople revolted against the heavy-handed methods of Geiss, the miller fled the village for the safety of Speyer where he sought relief from the Supreme Court. Back in Lindheim, Frau Schüler was burned at the stake on Feb. 23, 1664. The Supreme Court ordered that the persecutions cease, and Oynhausen removed Geiss from power. Geiss was not held accountable for the deaths of thirty innocent people. Official records show that Geiss had received 188 thalers, eighteen albus, and some livestock from the confiscated estates of the victims.

REF.: *CBA;* Horst, *Daemonomagie, oder Geschichte des Glaubens an Zauberei und Daemonische Wunder;* Köppen, *Hexen und Hexenprozesse;* Lea, *Materials Toward a History of the Inquisistion in Spain;* Robbins, *The Encyclopedia of Witchcraft and Demonology;* Soldan, *Geschichte der Hexenprozesse aus der Quellen dargestellt;* Summers, *The Geography of Witchcraft.*

Schultheis, Heinrich von, prom. 1634, Ger., witchcraft-jur. In 1634, Heinrich von Schultheis published his *Detailed Instructions (on) how to proceed in the inquisition against the horrible vice of witchcraft,* of which only one copy is known to have survived, which is currently housed at Cornell University Library. Von Schultheis was a doctor of civil and ecclesiastical law, and his epic tome established new standards of harshness and severity against suspected witches.

The book sanctions the use of torture to extract confessions, and permits evidence that in any other civil or criminal trial would be dismissed outright. A bitter opponent of the Jesuits, von Schultheis was assailed as a "false witch judge" by Löher, and was bitterly criticized by Adam Tanner in his *Theologia Scholastica,* published in 1617.

REF.: *CBA;* Lea, *Materials Toward a History of Witchcraft;* Robbins, *The Encyclopedia of Witchcraft and Demonology;* Schultheis, *Eine ausführliche Instruction wie in Inquisitions-Sachen des grewlichen Lästers der Zauberei...zu procediren.*

Schultz, Arden (AKA: **Butch Schultz**), 1950- , drugs-mur. On Feb. 1, 1982, a Lake County, Ind., jury found Arden Schultz, thirty-two, Guilty of murdering an associate after a drug deal went awry. The key witness for the prosecution, headed by Jack Crawford, was Stanley McKnight, twenty-seven, the defendant's alleged partner in the murder. McKnight, who was sentenced to twelve years in jail for his part in the murder, testified against Schultz. He said that the victim, Tommy R. Melcher, thirty-two, acted as a go-between in several 1980 heroin deals. Schultz and McKnight suspected that Melcher had kept $900 from a drug sale. Melcher said he had thrown away the heroin when he was arrested for a traffic violation. Schultz and McKnight took him for a ride on Nov. 5, 1980, robbed him of $110, and stopped on a dirt road where Schultz shot and killed him. Schultz later dismembered the body with a hacksaw and a knife, cutting off the hands and head, which were never found. Schultz, denied killing Melcher, but was sentenced to fifty-five out of a possible maximum sixty years for the murder. REF.: *CBA.*

Schultz, Dutch (Arthur Flegenheimer, Fleggenheimer), 1902-35, U.S., org. crime. Born on Aug. 6, 1902, to Emma and Herman Flegenheimer, Dutch Schultz grew up in the Bronx and attended public school through the fourth grade and then dropped out. Arthur Fleggenheimer joined the Bergen Gang of pickpockets and store thieves and was soon looting the pockets of the unsuspecting and the counters of small shops. Schultz's father deserted the family when Schultz was fourteen. His mother, doting and kindly, took in washing to keep her son in good clothes and pocket money. She lectured him about returning to school, and even had the local principal visit him. The principal, Dr. J.F. Condon, could not persuade him to leave the streets. Condon, ironically, became a player in one of the greatest crimes of the century, serving as a go-between in the sensational Lindbergh kidnapping of 1932.

Schultz was a hopeless case. Instead of picking up his school books, he began carrying a set of burglar's tools, and he briefly worked as a printer to establish a cover for his illegal activities. For three years, Schultz committed many holdups and burglaries. The blue-eyed, five-foot-nine-inch Schultz, at age seventeen, was arrested for burglary in 1919. Convicted, he was sent to prison for fifteen months. He served the full time and emerged an even tougher hoodlum, one who had acquired a bloodlust and an ambition that would lead him into many gang wars, a personal fortune of millions of dollars, and a premature, bullet-ridden death.

A few months after his release from prison, Schultz purchased a sprawling Bronx saloon with the loot of several recent robberies. He announced that he was to be called Dutch Schultz, the name of a once-feared gangster who had led the Frog Hollow Gang in the Bronx before the turn of the century. Schultz began to put together a gang of some of the toughest criminals in the Bronx, including Joey Rao, George and Abe "Bo" Weinberg, Julie Martin, Abe Landau, and Lulu Rosencranz. At the beginning of Prohibition, Schultz quickly realized that a fortune awaited those who peddled beer and liquor. He opened several more saloons and supplied them with hijacked whiskey, smuggled liquor from Canada and Europe, and his homemade brew, considered the worst needle beer in the Bronx.

A homebody, Schultz married a quiet, unassuming woman. Frances Flegenheimer proved to be a tolerant wife who never interfered with her husband's illegal and lethal business. As Schultz's bootleg empire spread throughout the Bronx and into Manhattan, many rival gang members were eliminated by Schultz gunmen, including the Shapiro Brothers and the Amberg Brothers. During the late 1920s, Schultz branched out into other rackets, especially after he discovered that the numbers racket, also called policy, was reaping millions in Harlem and elsewhere. Schultz and his men approached Stephanie St. Clair, the queen of numbers in Harlem, and told her that she either turn over her operations to them, or be killed. St. Clair capitulated, causing all the other Harlem policy kings to fall into the Schultz camp.

By 1930, Schultz was reaping millions from his vast bootlegging activities and the Harlem numbers game. Everyone played every day, spending nickels and dimes on the chance that their number might come up. Next Schultz went into the slot machine business with Frank Costello and Joey Rao. The Schultz gang, by then numbering in the hundreds, distributed slot machines throughout New York City, and more millions poured into the Schultz coffers. To protect his sprawling underworld kingdom, Schultz hired top gunmen like Jack "Legs" Diamond and Vincent Coll. Diamond had a gang of his own and a large slice of the best Manhattan territory for his bootlegging operations, but he and his men worked in liaison with Schultz. Coll and a group of younger hoodlums began as errand boys and soon were delivering Schultz beer and liquor to hundreds of speakeasies.

By 1930, Schultz began to have serious trouble with Diamond. Schultz's beer trucks began to disappear with alarming regularity, and Schultz learned that Diamond, who had quit some time earlier, was behind the hijackings. A gang war erupted, and several members of the Schultz and Diamond gangs were taken for the traditional one-way rides, their bodies dumped throughout Manhattan and the Bronx. The war finally ended with Diamond's demise.

Diamond, the wiry gang leader, had been shot so many times that the press had dubbed him "the Clay Pigeon of the Underworld." After surviving many attempts on his life, Diamond's luck ran out on Dec. 19, 1931. Diamond had recently been acquitted of a kidnapping charge and had celebrated most of the evening with his wife and relatives, and later, his showgirl mistress, Marion "Kiki" Roberts. He arrived drunk at his Albany, N.Y., rooming house and collapsed into bed. Bo Weinberg and Julie Martin reportedly trailed Diamond that night and followed him to his room. The two Schultz gunmen kicked open the door to Diamond's bedroom and fired fourteen shots, killing him. When the press caught up with Schultz to ask him about the demise of his long-standing enemy, the gang lord barked: "Diamond was just another punk with his hands in my pockets."

Schultz boasted over the years that he paid his men well and cut them in on many of his rackets. He could therefore not abide any of their stealing from him. His position was emphasized by his lickspittle lawyer, Dixie Davis, who once stated: "You can insult Arthur's girl, spit in his face, push him around—and he'll laugh. But don't steal a dollar from his accounts.. If you do, you're dead."

In 1931, Vincent Coll, his brother, Peter Coll, and others, attempted to do just that. They began beating up speakeasy owners who bought Schultz beer and liquor, and Coll ordered them to take his own booze and beer. Coll invaded Schultz's numbers rackets and then boasted that he intended to take over Schultz's entire $20 million-a-year empire. Though hopelessly outnumbered, Coll and his gang of about ten men began killing Schultz's top lieutenants. While trying to machine-gun Joey Rao to death on a crowded Manhattan street in 1931, Coll and others fired hundreds of rounds at the fleeing Schultz gunman. They wounded several passersby and killed a child, a senseless slaying that earned Coll the sobriquet "Mad Dog."

In June 1931, Schultz, accompanied by his bodyguard, Danny Iamascia, spotted two figures lurking in the shadows of an alley as he walked along a Manhattan street. Schultz thought the men were the Coll Brothers, and he and Iamascia drew their guns and began firing at the two men, who also drew guns and returned the fire. The men in the alley proved to be two NYPD detectives, Steve DiRosa and Julius Salke, who had been tailing the booze baron. Iamascia fell mortally wounded. Schultz, realizing that he was alone and that his adversaries were advancing upon him, threw away his gun and raced down the street. DiRosa ran after him, tackling him in an alley.

When DiRosa identified himself to Schultz as a police detective, the gang leader yanked $18,600 from his pocket and offered it to DiRosa to let him go free. "Here, take it all!" Schultz told him.

DiRosa exploded: "You miserable bum! I'll shove that dough down your throat!" He knocked Schultz to the pavement and leaped on him. When Detective Sergeant Salke rushed up, he found DiRosa attempting to jam the wad of money into Schultz's mouth. Schultz was later booked for attempted murder, resisting arrest, and carrying a concealed weapon, but the reliable Dixie Davis soon had him released on bail and through one of the dozens of judges on Schultz's payroll, he was later released.

The cause of Schultz's apprehensions, Vincent "Mad Dog" Coll, for whom he mistook Detective DiRosa, continued to plague Schultz. So Schultz devised a clever murder plan to rid himself of "the Mick," as Schultz often called Coll. In 1932, one of Schultz's men trailed Coll for weeks and discovered that Coll made most of his business calls from a phone booth inside a drugstore on West Twenty-Third Street. Coll was busy blackmailing and extorting Owney "The Killer" Madden, kidnapping Big Frenchy DeMange, Madden's partner, and dealing on the drugstore phone for the ransom money.

During one of these kidnapping calls, Schultz's man spotted Coll in the phone booth and immediately called Abe and George Weinberg. The two gunmen brothers, accompanied by two other men, drove up to the drugstore and parked at the curb. The Weinberg brothers entered the drugstore. As George herded the clerk behind the counter and two patrons into a back room, Abe pulled a submachine gun from beneath his long coat and opened up on the phone booth, sending ribbons of fire through it. Dozens of steel-jacketed .45-caliber bullets smashed the glass door and riddled Coll, who crumpled dead inside the booth.

No sooner had Schultz eliminated this last rival than he was faced with income tax evasion. The state of New York claimed he owed millions in back taxes. Dixie Davis, Schultz's lawyer, managed to get a change of venue to a small town in upstate New York. Next, Schultz hired a public relations firm that made a great show of giving large donations from Schultz to local charities. Frances joined her husband, and the two played the part of the happily married couple, attending small town dances, bingo parties, and carrying the favor of local authorities. Within a week, Schultz was known in town as a "nice guy."

One admirer asked Schultz why he was wearing such cheap suits, a man of his wealth. Why did he not wear tailor-made pinstripe suits and silk shirts. "Such displays are vulgar," Schultz said, pretending to be the down-home type. "Personally I think only queers wear silk shirts....I never bought one in my life. A guy's a sucker to spend $15 or $20 on a shirt. Hell, a guy can get a good one for two bucks." The gullible rural jury that sat in judgment of Schultz pronounced him Not Guilty of tax evasion, and he quickly returned to his rackets.

By then there were fewer rackets left in his control. Charles "Lucky" Luciano and Vito Genovese, who had long coveted Schultz's numbers rackets among other enterprises, had moved

Dutch Schultz, 1935.

Thomas E. Dewey, 1935.

Dutch Schultz and his slavish lawyer, Richard "Dixie" Davis.

Stephanie St. Clair, the Numbers Queen of Harlem.

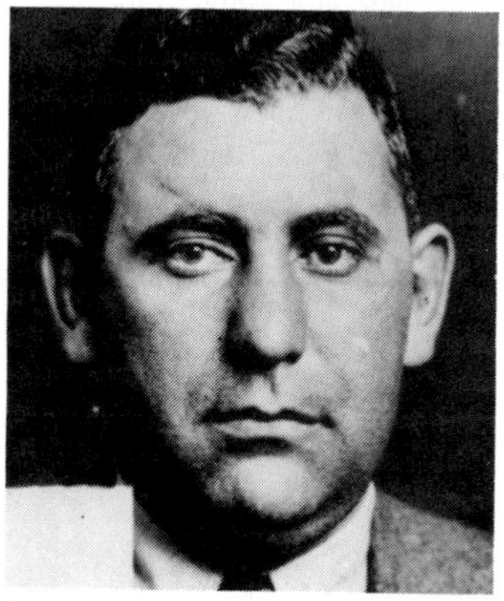

Schultz gunman Abe Bo Weinberg.

Schultz gunman Jules Martin.

Schultz awaiting tax trial.

Schultz gunman Abe Landau.

Schultz gunman George Weinberg.

Schultz gunman Lulu Rosenkrantz.

in while he was battling against a conviction in upstate New York, and seized many of his operations. Schultz Lieutenant Bo Weinberg had been a willing pawn in the hands of Luciano, helping the Italians to take over a good portion of the Schultz empire. Weinberg had been apprehensive over this takeover. "What if Schultz comes back?" he had reportedly asked Luciano.

"The loudmouth is never coming back," Luciano told Weinberg, but Schultz, to everyone's surprise, was soon back in Manhattan bragging about his acquittal and how he had hoodwinked a smalltown jury. When he discovered that Luciano and Genovese had siphoned off a large section of his numbers racket, he ordered his most trusted aide exterminated. Bo Weinberg was stabbed to death, his body thrown in a river.

Rather than go to war with the powerful forces of Luciano and Genovese, Schultz relocated his headquarters from the Bronx to Newark, N.J. He began to rebuild his rackets and beef up his underworld legions. By this time, the national crime syndicate had been born, with Luciano, Genovese, Costello, Meyer Lansky, Albert Anastasia, Louis "Lepke" Buchalter, and others controlling nationwide rackets. Schultz was too powerful a figure to ignore, even in decline, so he was made a member of the board of directors. He was argumentative and truculent, ignoring the common good of the syndicate in favor of his own rackets' well-being.

By 1935, Schultz's underworld operations were being scrutinized by New York district attorney Thomas E. Dewey who, with the backing of New York's colorful mayor, Fiorello LaGuardia, systematically destroyed Schultz's slot machine empire. These machines were gathered up by the hundreds in raids, dumped on barges in the East River, and smashed with sledgehammers. Mayor LaGuardia himself took great pleasure in being photographed while swinging a sledgehammer at these machines. So devastating was Dewey's attack on Schultz's slot machine operations that Schultz's partners, Frank Costello and Phillip "Dandy Phil" Kastel, moved their entire organization to Louisiana, shipping thousands of slot machines from New York to New Orleans, where the corrupt dictator of the state, Huey Long, shared the enormous spoils from the "one-armed bandits."

The destruction of his slot-machine empire enraged Schultz, who began making plans to murder Dewey. He brought the matter before the crime syndicate board. Elder statesman Johnny Torrio told Schultz that the plan was lunatic. "You can't go around bumping off big shots like him, Schultz," Torrio told Schultz.

"It will bring down the heat on all of us," Luciano added. Luciano, however, had thought seriously about doing the same thing. Dewey had been probing Luciano's far flung prostitution operations and was building a case against him that would later result in a conviction and a long prison term. But at the time, Luciano preferred a subtler approach. Joe Adonis, who had taken over many of Schultz's rackets in the Bronx, told Schultz the syndicate would not approve of his killing Dewey. One by one the board members lined up with Torrio, Luciano, and Adonis.

Schultz exploded, reportedly shouting at these powerful underworld bosses: "You guys stole my rackets and now you're feeding me to the law! Dewey's gotta go! He's my nemesis! He's gotta go! I'm hitting him myself and in forty-eight hours!" With that Dutch Schultz stormed out of the meeting.

The syndicate board was stunned. Their edict had been ignored, and their authority had been challenged by the maverick Schultz. Albert Anastasia, the newly appointed head of Murder, Inc., was quickly consulted. Murder, Inc., was the enforcement arm of the syndicate, its job being to liquidate any unruly member who went against syndicate decisions. The board voted to kill Schultz, to preserve its rackets and avoid a law-and-order crusade that would see the infant syndicate's destruction, which would undoubtedly occur if Dewey were killed. Here was one of the great ironies in the history of American organized crime, that its leaders voted to save the life of one of its sworn enemies and take the life of one of its own crime czars. Anastasia promised the board Schultz would be dead that night, Oct. 23, 1935.

That evening Dutch Schultz and three of his minions gathered in the back room of the Palace Chophouse in Newark, N.J. Schultz outlined his plans for killing Dewey to Otto "Abbadabba" Berman, his accountant, a wizard with figures, which explained his unusual sobriquet. Berman was opposed to the murder of Dewey, but Schultz brushed aside his objections. His two top gunmen, Abe Landau and Lulu Rosecranz, listened avidly to their boss' plan to ambush Dewey outside his home. While Schultz was going over the murder plans, a car drove up to the curb outside the chophouse. Inside sat Emmanuel "Mendy" Weiss, Charles "The Bug" Workman, and a man later identified only as Piggy. Because Piggy was not known, Weiss and Workman sent him into the restaurant-saloon to see if Schultz was present. He returned to the street within a few minutes, saying: "He's in there and he's got some men with him."

Workman, a cold-blooded member of the New Jersey branch of Murder, Inc., turned to Weiss and Piggy and said: "You guys wait here. I'll hit those guys alone." He sauntered into the Chophouse. The bar was deserted, and Workman pulled out two .38-caliber revolvers. He waved the terrified bartender into a side room, then stopped before the men's room. Workman pushed open the door and saw a heavyset man he did not recognize washing his hands, but he took no chances. Workman shot the startled man twice, then wheeled around and raced into the rear of the saloon, firing both revolvers, hitting Landau, Berman, and Rosencranz several times.

Workman, looking over the fallen gangsters, realized that Schultz was not among them. He returned to the washroom to see the man inside slumped to the floor, apparently dead. The Bug rifled his pockets, taking thousands of dollars in cash, and fled the restaurant. Once on the street, Workman saw that both Piggy and Weiss had fled. He began running and did not arrive at his New York hideout until hours later. Weiss later claimed that Piggy had panicked as he sat behind the wheel of the getaway car and had simply driven off. He then went inside and saw the three dying men in the rear of the restaurant and left, not knowing that Workman was inside the washroom, stealing Schultz's bankroll.

Workman later complained to syndicate board members that his fellow killers had deserted him, and he demanded that they be punished. Weiss was exonerated in that he had checked on Workman and then left and, had Workman not stopped to take Schultz's money, he could have left with Weiss. Piggy was another matter. The minor hoodlum was found a week later and taken to a remote spot in Brownsville where he was tortured, shot, and his body set afire for betraying the mob. His killers were Murder, Inc., slayers Abe "Kid Twist" Reles, Harry "Pittsburgh Phil" Strauss, and Harry "Happy" Maione.

But thorough as Workman was purported to be, he had slain none of his victims. The mortally wounded Rosencranz, Landau, and Berman, along with Schultz, were rushed to the Newark City Hospital, where they died within hours, one after another. Schultz lingered the longest, raving incoherently with bullets in his back and side. More than 500 cubic centimeters of blood were given to him in massive, useless transfusions. Police officers kept a vigil at his bedside, trying to learn the name of the killer who had so boldly invaded the Palace Chophouse. Police stenographer F.J. Long wrote down every senseless word Schultz uttered, a fascinating litany of paranoia, power, and fear.

"George, don't make no full moves," raved Schultz. "What have you done with him? Oh mama, mama, mama. Oh, stop it, stop it; oh, oh, oh. Sure, sure mama. Now listen, Phil" (perhaps referring to Dandy Phil Kastel, Schultz's slot machine partner), "fun is fun. Ah, please, papa. What happened to the sixteen? Oh, oh, he done it, please. John, please, oh, did you buy the hotel? You promised a million, sure. Get out! Sure, I wished I knew. Please, make it quick, fast, and furious. Please, fast and furious. Please help me get out. I am getting my wind back, thank God. Please, please, oh please. You will have to please tell him, you got no case. You get ahead with the dot-dash sys-

The interior of the Palace Chophouse.

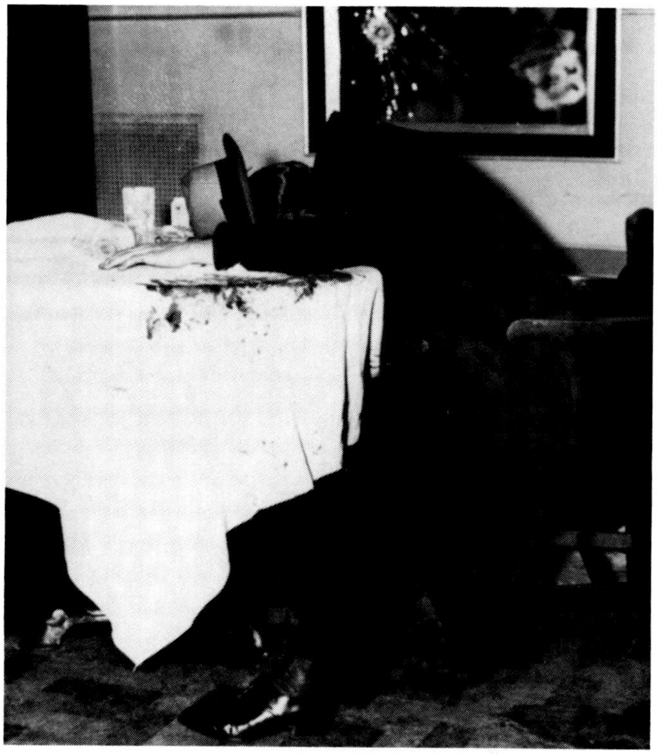

A Schultz gunman, dead in the Palace Chophouse, 1935.

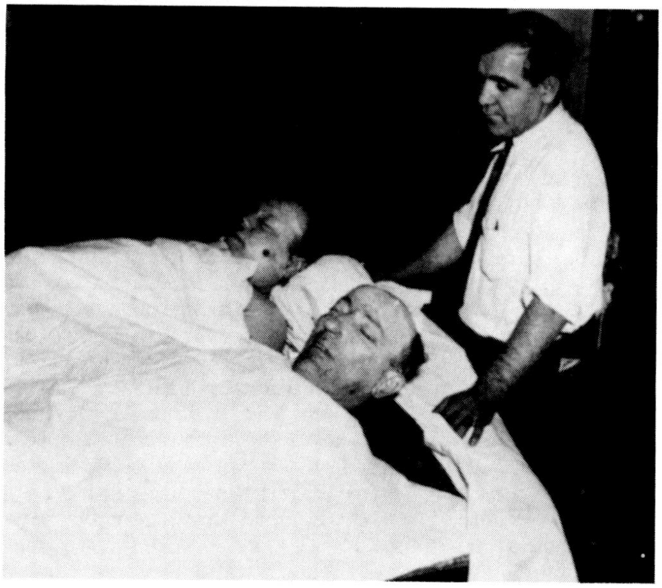

Abbadabba Berman and Abe Landau, dead.

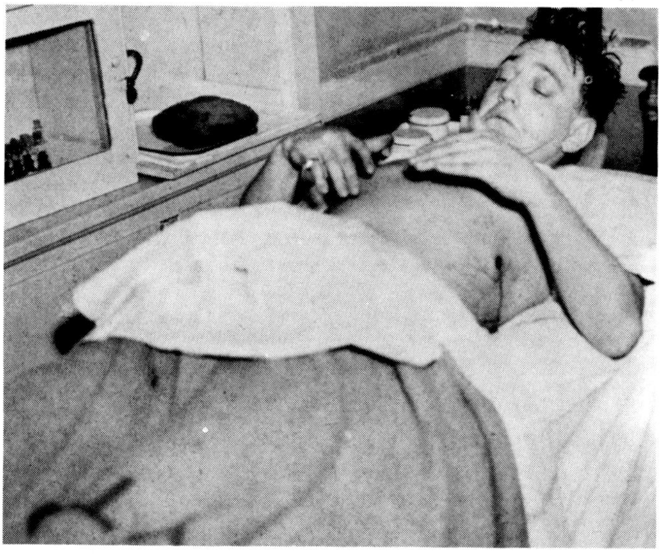

Dutch Schultz inspecting the damage; he is dying.

Schultz's smug killer, at right, Charles "The Bug" Workman, 1935.

tem. Didn't I speak that time last night? Whose number is that in your pocketbook, Phil, 13780. Who was it? Oh, please, please—reserve decision! Police, police, Henry and Frankie. Oh, oh, dog biscuits and when he is happy he doesn't get snappy...please, please, Henry and Frankie, you didn't meet him, you didn't even meet me. The glove will fit what I say..."

At this point Police Sergeant L. Conlon tried to interrogate Schultz in an effort to pinpoint the identity of his killer. "Who shot you?" Conlon asked the crime czar several times.

"The boss himself," replied Schultz.

"He did?"

"Yeah, I dunno."

"What did he shoot you for?"

"I showed him boss. Did you hear me meet him? An appointment. Appeal stuck. All right, mother."

"Was it the boss that shot you?"

"Who shot me? No one."

"We will help you."

"Will you get me up? Okay, I won't be such a big creep. Oh, mama, I can't go through with it. Oh, please, and then he clips me. C'mon, cut that out! We don't owe a nickel. Hold it, instead hold it against him. I am a pretty good pretzler. Winnifred. Department of Justice. I even get it from the department. Sir—please stop. Say, listen—last night!"

"Don't holler," Conlon told the dying gangster.

"I don't want to holler."

"What did they shoot you for?"

"I don't know, sir. Honestly, I don't. I don't even know who was with me, honestly. I went to the toilet. I was in the toilet and when I reach the—the boy came at me."

"The big fellow gave it to you."

"Yes, he gave it to me."

"Do you know who the big fellow was?"

"No." Schultz then slipped back into delirium. "If we wanted to break the ring...I will be checked and double checked and please pull for me. Will you pull? How many good ones and how many bad ones? Please, I had nothing with him. He was a cowboy in one of the seven days a week fight. No business. No hangouts. No friends. Nothing. Just what you pick up and what you need. I don't know who shot me. Don't put anyone near this check...In the olden days they waited and waited. Please give me shot...It is from the factory...I don't want harmony. I want harmony....

"No, no. There are only ten of us. There are ten million fighting somewhere of you, so get your onions up and we will throw up the truce flag...Police are here—Communistic—strike—baloney— honestly, this is a habit I get. Sometimes I give it and sometimes I don't. Oh, I am still in. That settles it. Are you sure? Please let me get in and eat. Let him harness himself to you and then bother you.

"Please don't ask me to go there. I don't want to. I still don't want him in the path. It is no use to stage a riot. The sidewalk was in trouble and the bears were in trouble, and I broke it up. Please put me in that room. Please keep him in control. My gilt-edged stuff and those dirty rats have turned in. Please, mother, don't tear, don't rip! That is something that shouldn't be spoken about. Please get me up, my friends. Please look out. The shooting is a bit wild and that kind of shooting saved a man's life!

"No payrolls, no walls, no coupons. That would be entirely out. Pardon me, I forgot. I forgot that I am plaintiff and not defendant. Look out, look out for him, please! He owes me money; he owes everyone money. Why can't he just pull out and give me control? Please, mother, you pick up now. You know me. No, don't scare me. My friends and I think I do a better job. Police are looking for you all over. Be instrumental in letting us know. They are Englishmen" (here, Schultz may have been referring to Owney "The Killer" Madden, who was born in England). "They are a type and I don't know who is best, they or us. Oh, sir, get the doll a roofing. You can play jacks and girls do that with a soft ball and do tricks with it. It takes all events into consideration. No! No! And it is no! A boy has never wept nor dashed a thousand kim. Did you hear me?"

Conlon was persistent: "Who shot you?"

"I don't know," Schultz said, coming out of the stupor for a few moments.

"The doctor wants you to lie quiet."

"That is what I want to do."

"How many shots were fired?"

"I don't know."

"How many?"

"Two thousand. Come on, get some money in that treasury! Come on, please, get it. I can't tell you to. That is not what you have in the book. Oh, please, warden. What am I going to do for the money? Please put me up on my feet at once! You are a hard-boiled man. Did you hear me? I would hear it, the Circuit Court would hear it and the Supreme Court might hear it. If that ain't the payroll. Please crack down on the Chinaman's" (Charles "Chink" Sherman, a Schultz gang rival) "friends and Hitler's commander. I am sore and I am going up and I am going to give you honey, if I can. Mother is the best bet and don't let Satan draw you too fast."

Conlon doggedly probed Schultz's stupor in an attempt to get the identity of his killer, asking once again: "What did the big fellow shoot you for?"

"Him? John?" (A possible reference to Johnny Torrio). "Over a million, five million dollars."

"You want to get well, don't you?" Conlon asked the gangster.

"Yes."

"Then lie quiet."

"Yes, I will lie quiet."

"John shot you and we will take care of John," Conlon said, trying to draw out the killer's name.

"That is what caused the trouble. Look out! If you do this, you can go and jump right here in the lake. I know who they are. They are French people" (a possible reference to Big Frenchy DeMange, Owney Maddens' partner). "All right, look out, look out! My memory is gone. A work relief. Police. Who gets it? I don't know and I don't want to know, but look out! It can be traced. He changed for the worse. Please look out. My fortunes have changed and come back and went back since that. I was desperate. I am wobbly. You ain't got nothing on him but we got it on his helper."

"Control yourself," Conlon told him.

"But I am dying," Schultz said, staring into the policeman's eyes.

"No, you are not," Conlon lied.

"Come on, mama. All right, dear. You have to get in."

Schultz's wife entered the room and sat next to her dying husband. He barely recognized her, saying: "Then pull me out. I am half crazy. They dyed my shoes. Give me something. I am so sick. Give me water, the only thing that I want. Open this up and break it so that I can touch you."

"This is Frances, Arthur," Schultz's wife said.

He did not recognize her. "Dannie (Iamascia), please let me get into the car!"

Frances left the hospital room weeping. She was told that her husband would most likely die at any time. Schultz sank deeper into his trauma, babbling as if to keep himself alive with the sound of his voice, which tumbled forth distorted memory and image.

"Who shot you?" Conlon started all over again.

"I don't know. I didn't even get a look. I don't know who could have done it. Anybody. Kindly take my shoes off."

"They are off."

"No, there's a handcuff on them. The baron says these things. I know what I am doing here with my collection of papers. It isn't worth a nickel to two guys like you or me, but to a collector it is worth a fortune. It is priceless. I am going to turn it over to...Turn your back to me please. Henry, I am so sick now. The police are getting many complaints. Look out! I want that G-Note. Look out for Jimmy Valentine for he is an old pal of mine.

Come on, come on, Jim. Okay, okay, I am all through. Can't do another thing.

"Look out, mama. Look out for her. You can't beat him. Police, mama, Helen, mother, please, take me out. I will settle the indictment. Shut up! You got a big mouth! Please help me up, Henry. Max, come over here! French-Canadian bean soup. I want to pay. Let them leave me alone!"

These were the last words of Dutch Schultz. He lay in a coma for two more hours, and, at 8:40 p.m., he died. His killer, Charles "The Bug" Workman, was later convicted of his murder and was sent to the New Jersey State Prison to serve a life term. He was paroled some twenty years later. See: **Amberg Brothers; Anastasia, Albert; Buchalter, Louis; Coll, Vincent; Costello, Frank; Dewey, Thomas E.; Diamond, Jack; Genovese, Vito; Kastel, Phillip; LaGuardia, Fiorello; Lansky, Meyer; Long, Huey; Luciano, Charles; Madden, Owen; Maione, Harry; Murder, Inc.; Reles, Abraham; St. Clair, Stephanie; Shapiro Brothers; Strauss, Harry; Syndicate, The.**

REF.: Alexander, *The Pizza Connection;* Campbell, *The Luciano Project; CBA;* Cohen, *Mickey Cohen: In My Own Words;* Cressey, *Theft of the Nation;* Danforth, *The D.A.'s Man;* Eisenberg and Landau, *Meyer Lansky;* Fried, *The Rise and Fall of the Jewish Gangster in America;* Gage, *Mafia, U.S.A.;* ____, *The Mafia is not an Equal Opportunity Employer;* Godwin, *Murder U.S.A.;* Gosch and Hammer, *The Last Testament of Lucky Luciano;* Haskins, *Street Gangs;* Hibbert, *The Roots of Evil;* Hurwood, *Society and the Assassin;* Hynd, *Murder, Mayhem and Mystery;* Katz, *Uncle Frank;* Kobler, *Al Capone;* ____, *Ardent Spirits;* Lait and Mortimer, *Chicago: Confidential;* Maas, *The Valachi Papers;* McClellan, *Crime Without Punishment;* McPhaul, *Johnny Torrio;* Messick, *Lansky;* ____, *Secret File;* ____ and Goldblatt, *The Mobs and the Mafia;* Nash, *Bloodletters and Badmen;* Peterson, *The Mob;* Powers, *Secrecy and Power;* Reuter, *Disorganized Crime;* Sann, *Kill the Dutchman;* Scott, *The Concise Encyclopedia of Crime and Criminals;* Smith, *Syndicate City;* Spiering, *The Man Who Got Capone;* Thompson and Raymond, *Gang Rule in New York;* Whitelaw, *Corpus Delicti;* (FICTION), Wolfert, *Tucker's People;* (FILM), *Force of Evil,* 1948; *Rise and Fall of Legs Diamond,* 1960; *Mad Dog Coll,* 1961; *Portrait of a Mobster,* 1961; *The Cotton Club,* 1984.

Schultz, Raymond T., 1939-77, U.S., suic.-mur. After the suicide death of American Nazi Party (ANP) member Raymond Schultz in a police squad car on May 22, 1977, investigators sifted through a tangled web of evidence found in his Calumet City, Ill., home, including Nazi propaganda, human restraint devices, pornography, and what appeared to be a secret torture chamber.

The bizarre aspects of Schultz's private life became a matter of public concern following the cyanide murder of 63-year-old Sydney Cohen on May 22. The elderly Jewish man was murdered by the fanatical Schultz at Cohen's home in Flossmoor. Cohen's son Jeffrey discovered the body of his father on the floor, and he also found Schultz lying unconscious several feet away. Suburban Flossmoor police arrived on the scene to take Schultz away, but in the squad car the killer sniffed a vial of lethal cyanide and died instantly. An autopsy conducted on Cohen showed that his death was also caused by cyanide poisoning.

Schultz's ties to right-wing hate mongers, and white supremacist groups dated back to 1962 when he was arrested for demonstrating against the showing of Soviet travel films at a Chicago hotel. At the time he listed his address as the ANP headquarters. He remained out of the news for the next fifteen years, but operated two Chicago bookstores that were ANP fronts. It was later learned that Schultz had harassed a number of Chicago-area Jews and prepared what appeared to be a "hit list" of potential murder victims. What puzzled investigators was the source of Schultz's income. The 38-year-old drill press operator owned three buildings and had traveled extensively through Third World countries. There was strong evidence to suggest that Schultz may have been involved in a series of unsolved Detroit child murders. A note found in his residence read: "With the help of God and A.H., I can get it done by July 1." The police believed the "A.H." in question here was Adolf Hitler. REF.: *CBA.*

Schultzenstein, Otto, prom. 1930, Case of, Ger., big. In 1903 Otto Schultzenstein married for the first time. The union lasted until 1923, when the Berlin shoemaker was driven out of the house by his wife, who was persuasively wielding a hatchet at the time. In 1926, Schultzenstein traveled to Leningrad, where he remarried, failing to divorce his first wife. When Schultzenstein returned to Germany with his new bride, he was charged with bigamy by his first wife. The case was dropped by the German court because Germany recognized the civil and criminal laws of Russia, and Soviet law stated that bigamy was not a criminal offense. The case against Schultzenstein was dismissed. REF.: *CBA.*

Schulz, Duane Allan, 1959- , U.S., mur. After he had murdered his girlfriend Teresa Kaminski in a jealous rage, Duane Schulz of Bridgeview, Ill., claimed he felt great remorse. While her body lay in state, Schulz snuck into the funeral home undetected in order to place a rose and a note on the registry. It read: "Very much love to my love Teresa from Duane Allan Schulz."

Schulz strangled Kaminski in his home on Feb. 15, 1981, after the 19-year-old girl expressed her intentions to end their relationship. He then dumped the body in a wooded section of Willow Springs Cemetery, in South Suburban Chicago where it was discovered six days later. The police identified Schulz as the killer through the flower, the note, and a discredited alibi. He claimed to have been involved in a tavern fight the day that Kaminski was killed, but the tavern was not open on the night in question.

On May 19, 1984, Criminal Court Judge James M. Bailey sentenced Schulz to forty years in prison. In his remarks to the court, Judge Bailey described the defendant as "smug" and "remorseless." REF.: *CBA.*

Schuster, Arnold, d.1952, U.S., (unsolv.) mur. Arnold Schuster considered himself an amateur sleuth. When he spotted a man whom he believed to be bank robber Willie "The Actor" Sutton on a New York City subway train, he quickly located a policeman and informed him. Sutton was subsequently arrested. Unfortunately for Schuster, one of the news programs on which he was interviewed after Sutton's arrest was viewed by Albert Anastasia, one of the mob's most ruthless killers. Anastasia had a loathing for informers and, although Schuster had no link to organized crime, ordered his execution. Schuster was murdered on Mar. 8, 1952. See: **Anastasia, Albert; Sutton, William Francis.**

REF.: *CBA;* Gage, *Mafia U.S.A.*

Schutz, Thomas Efford, prom.1904, Brit., asslt. Thomas Schutz worked as an office boy in a London commercial firm. In January 1904, during lunch one day, Schutz suddenly seized a hatchet and, hit the company secretary across the face, apparently without provocation. His alibi that a mysterious stranger had purchased the hatchet and had ordered him to do bodily harm to the secretary was dismissed as the ramblings of a demented child. In February, the 17-year-old was ordered detained at the King's pleasure. REF.: *CBA.*

Schwagel, Anna Maria, d.1775, Ger., witchcraft. The last execution of a woman suspected of witchcraft in Germany occurred in Kempton, Bavaria, on Apr. 11, 1775. The victim was a mentally unbalanced spinster named Anna Maria Schwagel who was convinced that her misfortunes were the result of sexual intercourse with the devil. The Prince-Abbot of Kempton affirmed the verdict handed down by a tribunal of three judges, and Anna Schwagel was duly executed.

The devil was in fact a rakish coachman who promised Schwagel marriage and then jilted her after taking her virginity. Seduced and abandoned, she sought absolution from an Augustinian friar. To her dismay, she discovered that the friar had renounced Catholicism in order to embrace the Protestant faith. In a mad frenzy she wandered about the countryside until a matron named Anna Maria Kuhstaller beat a confession out of her, forcing her to admit to engaging in demonic intercourse.

REF.: *CBA;* Haas, *Die Hexenprozesse: ein cultur-historischer Versuch, nebst Dokumenten;* Lea, *Materials Toward a History of Witchcraft;* Robbins, *The Encyclopedia of Witchcraft and Demonology;* Seth, *Witches and Their*

Craft; Summers, *The Geography of Witchcraft.*

Schwammberger, Josef Franz Leo, 1912- , Ger., war crimes. Josef Franz Leo Schwammberger, the former Nazi commander of a Jewish labor camp in Przemysl, Pol., escaped to Argentina after being arrested in 1947 in Austria. Schwammberger was responsible for the torture and killing of at least 5,000 Jews in Poland. After the Allied Forces' victory in 1945, many Nazis escaped to Argentina, with estimates that thousands fled to South America. A secret group of ex-SS officers, The Odessa, smuggled Nazis out of Europe through a system, known as the "Rat Line", which extended through Italy, Spain, Portugal, Marseilles and France; from those points, they took ships to South American port cities.

Schwammberger was arrested in December 1987, on a farm at his Córdoba retreat; he was seventy-five at the time. Held in a La Plata jail, his extradition to West Germany was approved by Argentinean Judge Vicente Bretal, who ruled against allowing the former Nazi to be tried in Argentina. Although his extradition was approved, Schwammberger's status as an Argentinean citizen made him immune from being sent back. At the time of this writing, Schwammberger is still being held in an Argentinean prison. Another infamous war criminal who found refuge in Argentina, Adolf Eichmann, was kidnapped from there by Israeli Mossad intelligence agents in 1961 and taken to Israel to face trial; he was convicted of crimes against humanity and was hanged. See: **Eichmann, Adolf.** REF.: *CBA.*

Schwart, Emil, prom. 1896, U.S., burg. Emil Schwart was a vagrant who was hired by a Chicago merchant, from whom he stole $15 and a suit of clothes in May 1896. Six months later, the thief turned up on a city street armed with a straight razor. Detectives Clifton P. Wooldridge and Otto Schubert captured Schwart, who was held over for a grand jury hearing, indicted, and arraigned on burglary charges. On July 8, 1896, he was found Guilty of burglary and sentenced to the Joliet Penitentiary for an indeterminate time.

REF.: *CBA;* Wooldridge, *Hands Up.*

Schwartz, Charles Henry (Leon Henry Schwartzhof, AKA: **John Doe Stein, Harold Warren),** 1887-1925, U.S., arson-suic.-mur. For ten emotionally charged days in the summer of 1925 residents of San Francisco followed the progress of a bizarre murder mystery that was eventually solved by reason, logic, and the resources of modern science.

For several months Bay Area newspapers had been providing considerable coverage to the newly formed Pacific Cellulose Company, the brainchild of Charles Henry Schwartz, an Alsatian chemist born Leon Henry Schwartzhof in Colmar, Fr. After attaining his Ph.D. in chemistry from the University of Heidelberg and various other academic honors, Schwartzhof enlisted in the French Army and was detailed to Algiers where he served in the Red Cross. After completing his military service Schwartzhof (who had shortened his name by this time), settled in Derby, England, went to work for a large textile company and married a young widow named Alice Orchard Warren. For medical reasons the couple emigrated to the U.S., choosing the Bay Area as their new home.

In 1921 Schwartz was hired as a chemist for the California Fibre Company of Berkeley, where he was accused of pilfering 1,800 pounds of scrap iron and a bottling machine. After he threatened the life of a fellow employee authorities seized his .25-caliber handgun. Schwartz became a familiar figure at the Berkeley police station, advising Chief August Vollmer about police matters. Although he was dismissed as a harmless eccentric by the police department financial speculators truly believed that he had stumbled on to something when he announced the opening of Pacific Cellulose, a company which would revolutionize the manufacture of artificial silk from wood fibre. Schwartz's imposing two story factory in Walnut Creek was constructed in great haste with money provided by his wife. The founder shunned interviews, and remained out of sight. The only thing he would say about his mysterious process was that he would churn out silk at half the price of other cellulose-spun fabrics. It seemed almost too good to be true.

The inventor's grandiose plans came to an abrubt end on July 30, 1925, when the Walnut Creek factory was rocked by a devastating explosion. By the time the fire department arrived, the building was nearly consumed in flames. Groping firefighters were repelled by a noxious yellow gas as they searched for survivors. The charred remains of a man were pulled from the rubble. Walter Gonzales, an employee of Pacific Cellulose, identified the corpse as that of his employer Mr. Schwartz. "Why, I left him alone here in this room only a little while ago," Gonzales said. "He was working on an experiment and asked me to leave him because he wanted to work alone." Sheriff R.R. Veale of Contra Costa County went through the building and found nothing to suggest that the explosion was anything other than an industrial accident caused by improperly mixed chemicals. After a preliminary investigation Deputy District Attorney James F. Hoey came to a different opinion. The body found in the factory had been lying neatly on a blanket sandwiched between two benches, an unlikely position after a huge explosion. Sheriff Veale learned that Schwartz had insured his life for $185,000 in the event of accidental death. And finally insurance investigators who examined the corpse found that it was three inches taller than the height Schwartz listed on his policy.

Alice Schwartz demanded that the police allow her to bury the remains of her husband, but Veale stalled as he tried to locate experts to establish positive I.D. Dr. Alfred Ruedy, the family physician, positively identified the body as that of Schwartz. In his report the coroner stated that an upper molar was missing from the victim. Schwartz's dentist claimed he had removed the tooth just recently. In light of these contradictions, Veale chose to bring a consulting expert into the case. He hired Berkeley criminologist Edward Oscar Heinrich to conduct an investigation.

Murderer Charles Schwartz.

Heinrich compared hair samples taken from Schwartz's brush with that of the dead man, and determined that they were different. Heinrich examined the cavity in the dead man's mouth and determined the tooth had been knocked out by a chisel, not removed by a dentist. Heinrich determined that the man had been murdered—struck on the back of the head with a blunt instrument. He also deduced that the killer made every effort to have the body identified as that of Schwartz—even to knocking out a tooth that was missing in Schwartz's mouth.

Searching through the debris of the burned-out factory the criminologist found faint reddish blood-stains on the walls. Heinrich determined that the yellow gas was carbon disulfide, a highly flammable chemical that would burn through the lungs of the victim if inhaled for a short period of time. Because there was no trace of this substance in the dead man's lungs Heinrich realized the man was murdered before the explosion. Apparently Schwartz had ignited the fire from the outside. The flames ran toward a pool of liquid surrounding the body. "By tracing the flames on the floor I found that the fire had not started in one place but in five different places," Heinrich said. "There was no evidence of a broken chemical tube which would have suggested the likelihood of an accident." The incendiary liquid had been sprinkled over the outer door in order to permit the murderer to escape. Because of Heinrich's methodical work, a murder indictment was secured by District Attorney A.B. Tinning.

While detectives in Northern California looked for Schwartz, possibly in the company of a manicurist named Elizabeth Adam, Heinrich attempted to identify the victim. Among the items pulled out of the laboratory were several charred newspaper fragments and a portion of a letter. Under strong glasses and with the aid of certain chemical processes Heinrich found these were religious tracts, one a passage from St. John. Cecil Barker, an undertaker from Placerville, Calif., saw an excerpt from the letters in a newspaper and recognized the handwriting instantly as that of Gilbert Warren Barbe, a traveling missionary. Barbe, a self-styled chemistry buff, had answered Schwartz's newspaper placement for a lab assistant and had not been seen or heard from since he answered the ad.

The final piece of the puzzle fell into place on Aug. 10. An Oakland resident named N.B. Edmunds opened his Sunday *Tribune* and saw a remarkable likeness of a man he knew as "Harold Warren." Edmunds excitedly telephoned Berkeley police to advise Captain Clarence Lee that the suspect was living in an apartment building on Forty First Street in Oakland.

Captain Lee, accompanied by building manager C.W. Heywood and Edmunds, battered down the door of the apartment when Warren refused to answer. They found Schwartz lying dead on the floor, clutching a pistol. A suicide note found nearby revealed that Schwartz had killed Barbe in what he described as an act of "self-defense." "He attacked me," Schwartz wrote. "I gave him a blow on his head. He fell. I gave him another. Suddenly I knew he was dead. But I could not make up my mind to go to Bell (his attorney) and tell him." Instead, Schwartz decided to fake his own death and assume a new identity as Harold Warren. Police theorized that Schwartz's creditors were closing in on him and Elizabeth Adam was seeking $50,000 in damages for "alienation of affections." Whatever the actual truth, Schwartz's perfect crime failed and his real motives went to the grave with him.

REF.: Block, *Science vs. Crime;* ____, *The Wizard of Berkeley; CBA;* Gribble, *Adventures in Murder;* ____, *Famous Feats of Detection and Deduction;* Logan, *Great Murder Mysteries;* McGrady, *Crime Scientists;* Nash, *Bloodletters and Badmen;* Rodell, *San Francisco Murders.*

Schwartz, Harry, and **Watt, Newton**, prom. 1886, U.S., (wrong. convict.?) rob.-mur. Kellogg Nichols boarded the Rock Island Express train on the night of Mar. 12, 1886. A messenger for the United States Express Company in Chicago, he carried $22,500 in cash and negotiable securities that were bound for an office in Davenport, Ia.

Between Joliet and Morris, Ill., Newton Watt, an employee of the railroad, reported to his superior that unknown persons had broken into the baggage car and looted the safe. Watt, the brakeman, Harry Schwartz, and the conductor, Fred Wagner, discovered the body of Nichols, who had been beaten and shot to death. An examination of the body indicated Nichols had put up a fight; his hands were bloody and there were bits of skin under his fingernails.

After notifying local authorities of the robbery and murder, Wagner questioned co-worker Watt. Watt said that a masked gunman had held a revolver to the back of his head, but later statements revealed inconsistencies in the story that puzzled the veteran trainman. When detective William A. Pinkerton arrived, he immediately suspected brakeman Schwartz, whose badly scratched hands seemed to have been the result of a recent struggle. Pinkerton called in fellow detective Frank Watt to help solve the case.

Watt posed as a Rock Island employee to learn more about Newton Watt and Schwartz. He soon discovered they were close friends and that Watt was planning to move to Philadelphia. In one of their conversations, Schwartz warned Watt to be careful once in Philadelphia. Schwartz suspected the railroad had put extra detectives on the case and cautioned, "Be careful how you spend your money, Harry. I think they're still onto us and you want to be careful." The investigation zeroed in on Schwartz when he began flashing a large bankroll around Philadelphia. Detective Pinkerton also discovered Schwartz was a bigamist who had a wife in both Chicago and Philadelphia.

Schwartz was arrested on a bigamy charge, and later, on Dec. 3, 1886, was charged with the train robbery. Conversations between Pinkerton and Mrs. Schwartz revealed that her husband had recently come into a large sum of money. He told his wife he had found a brown envelope containing $5,000 under a seat in one of the train cars. In March, the case came to trial. The evidence against Schwartz and his close friend Watt was purely circumstantial, but it was enough to convict them of robbery and murder. Both men were sentenced to life imprisonment. Watt died in the Joliet Penitentiary in March 1889, swearing innocence until his death. Nine years later, Governor John Peter Altgeld pardoned Schwartz amidst a continuing debate about his innocence or guilt.

REF.: *CBA;* Rodell, *Chicago Murders.*

Schwartz, Milton and **Schwartz, Rosalie**, prom. 1955, U.S., abor. In 1955, when 22-year-old Philadelphia heiress and newlywed, Doris Jean Silver Oestreicher discovered that she was pregnant, she turned to her mother, Gertrude Silver, for guidance. The young woman had eloped two months earlier with Earl Oestreicher, a policeman from Miami. After the family doctor who had diagnosed the pregnancy refused to abort the pregnancy, Doris' mother took her daughter to the apartment of Milton and Rosalie Schwartz, who performed abortions. The Schwartzes gave Doris a concoction made of oils, ground-up cinchona, and slippery-elm bard intended to abort the fetus. Instead, the mixture poisoned the girl.

The family initially claimed that her death was due to some sort of freak allergic reaction. When it was discovered that an abortion had been attempted, the Schwartzes and Mrs. Silver were arrested. All three defendants entered pleas of *nolo contendere* (no defense) on Jan. 30, 1956. The following day, Judge Vincent A. Carroll freed 49-year-old Gertrude Silver on a suspended sentence saying that "the memory of this dreadful tragedy (would) be substantial and overwhelming punishment." Rosalie Schwartz was convicted on a charge of abortion resulting in death and was sentenced to an indefinite term in prison. Milton Schwartz received a sentence on the same charge for three to ten years. On Feb. 2, 1956, the same judge reduced the Schwartzes sentences to eleven to twenty-two months, after District Attorney Victor Blanc recommended reconsideration on the grounds that the sentences were more severe than other similar cases. On Dec. 21, 1956, the Schwartzes were granted parole and released from prison. REF.: *CBA.*

Schwartz, Murray Merle, 1931- , U.S., jur. Served on Delaware State Board of Parole from 1971-72. He was appointed to the district court of Delaware by President Richard Nixon in 1974. REF.: *CBA.*

Schwartzbard, Samuel, See: **Petlyura, Symon.**

Schweitzer, Robert, 1943-81, and **Cooper, David**, prom. 1980, U.S., embez.-suic. Robert Schweitzer swindled three Florida-based companies and the University of Miami Hospital out of $1.5 million before killing himself in an Atlantic City, N.J., hotel room.

Schweitzer's criminal career began when he submitted a phony resume to Miami's National Children's Cardiac Hospital in December 1977. He was hired as manager of patient accounts, and gave a job to David Cooper, who acted as the resident attorney responsible for collections. Together they opened a private bank account and began depositing former patient's checks in it. In eighteen months the pair pocketed $750,000. When the hospital officials became suspicious, Schweitzer and Cooper moved on. The next year, they worked for Panelfold Company, a manufacturer of folding doors and partition walls from whom they swindled $120,000. Schweitzer was fired, and an audit of the books showed a number of missing checks.

Cooper and Schweitzer set up at Peninsular Supply Company,

and absconded with $150,000. Then it was on to Anthes, a Miami scaffolding company where they swindled $25,000. In August 1980, Cooper was charged with ninety-six counts of theft, larceny, and racketeering and received a two-year sentence. In October 1980, the state of Florida filed charges against Schweitzer for eighty-three counts of racketeering, theft, and larceny. His court date was set for Mar. 23, 1981. While free on bond, Schweitzer's wife left him, but he met another woman and they planned to marry in January 1981. In his last scam, Schweitzer purchased $70,000 in jewelry on credit from a friend of his fiancée's family. He skipped out on his nuptial obligations and flew to Atlantic City, when he gambled his fortune, and killed himself on Feb. 26, 1981. REF.: *CBA.*

Schweitzer, William (AKA: **James Taylor**), prom. 1928-35, and **Jackson, Florence**, prom. 1935, and **Jackson, Loretta**, prom. 1935, and **Miller, Jean**, 1914- , U.S., mur. Howard Carter Dickinson, on business in Detroit, met four new friends at the Book-Cadillac Hotel in June 1935. One, William Schweitzer, was an ex-convict with a lengthy record of robbery and attempted murder. On June 27, Schweitzer and his three female companions, Jean Miller, Loretta Jackson, and Florence Jackson, met Dickinson at the Detroiter Hotel. Schweitzer drove them around the city, until arriving at Rouge Park, where one of the Jackson sisters asked to be let out. The car continued down Joy Road, when two shots rang out. Schweitzer had killed Dickinson, taking the $125 in his wallet. The four headed to Chicago where Schweitzer spent the money on new clothes for the girls. Police caught up with them in a roadside hotel in Fort Wayne, Ind. Seven weeks after the murder, Schweitzer, the Jackson sisters, and Jean Miller were all sentenced to life imprisonment.

REF.: *CBA;* Rodell, *Detroit Murders.*

Schwindt, Werner, prom. 1975, Ger., mur. Estranged from his daughter since her birth, Werner Schwindt picked up Margret Schwindt in Koellerbach, Ger., on Aug. 25, 1975, and raped her. Then Schwindt panicked and strangled her, leaving the body in a field in Pforzheim, where it was found a short time later. On Sept. 4, he attempted suicide with sleeping pills. He was discovered lying on a park bench and was revived by physicians.

With his confession, Schwindt was found Guilty of murder and was sentenced to life imprisonment.

REF.: *CBA;* Wilson, *Encyclopedia of Modern Murder.*

Scieri, Antoinette, prom. 1916-24, Fr., mur. Antoinette Scieri was born in Italy but moved with her family to France when she was quite young. During WWI she volunteered for duty as a field nurse but far from an "angel of mercy," Nurse Scieri was actually a thief with her own specialized fraud. Scieri obtained the addresses of her patients and then wrote to their friends and relatives for money. Often the soldiers' families obliged and Scieri pocketed the money. After she stole an officer's paybook and requisitioned a 5,000 franc advance she was arrested and imprisoned in 1915.

A year later she married an Italian soldier named Salmon, but the marriage broke up when the man found out about his wife's extra-marital affairs. The ill-fated union produced two children, who lived with Scieri and her next boyfriend, a bully named Joseph Rossignol who beat her frequently. Despite their less than idyllic living arrangements, Rossignol and Scieri remained together and had one child before moving to St. Gilles in southern France in 1920. There, Rossignol took a job in the local vineyards and Scieri resumed working as a nurse.

In the next few years the tranquil country village was plagued by the mysterious deaths of some its leading citizens. An elderly woman named Drouard died on Dec. 11, 1924, while being cared for by Scieri. The doctor's prognosis was heart seizure. Two weeks later when Lachapelle died shortly after consuming a pork sandwich, the cause of death was listed as ptomaine poisoning. Two days later the woman's husband died. Having devised a seemingly foolproof system to deceive the authorities, Scieri decided to kill Rossignol. She served him a meal of poisoned mussels after one of his drunken outbursts and he died several hours later. Without pause, Scieri returned to caring for the sick and the elderly. Sixty-seven-year-old Martin and her sister Madame Doyer were her next victims. "You must not worry about money," the nurse assured them. "My mission is to heal and help the sick. Fees mean nothing to me." Scieri served Marie Martin a glass of poisoned coffee and watched her die. The sister survived only because she threw her coffee down the drain. "It tasted bitter," she said.

The last victim was the sickly wife of a St. Gilles man named Gouan-Criquet. After the 75-year-old woman passed away the husband contacted her physician, Dr. Clauzel, for an opinion. Before signing the death certificate Clauzel called in the police. The detectives searched the house and came up with a bottle containing an odd-looking green solution which chemical analysis showed to be Pyralion or acetate of lead—commonly used as a weed killer. The dosage used on Madame Gouan-Criquet was potent enough to kill 300 persons. When Rossignol's body was exhumed, traces of pyralion were also found in his system. Antoinette Scieri was arrested and charged with murder. She confessed to the crimes, but attempted to shift much of the blame to a neighbor Rosalie Gire. On Apr. 27, 1926, Scieri stood alone in the docket to answer the charges brought against her. "You have been called a monster," the judge said. "But that expression is not strong enough. You are debauched, you are possessed of all the vices. You are also a drunkard, vicious, and a hypocrite, and you have no shame. I do not believe judicial history contains the records of many criminals of your type." Scieri was sentenced to death but the courts later commuted the penalty to life imprisonment.

REF.: *CBA;* Nash, *Look For the Woman.*

Scipio Nasica, Publius Cornelius, prom. 130s B.C., Roman., assass. Served as consul in 138 B.C. and as pontifex maximus. He was vehemently against reforms initiated by Tiberius Gracchus to help peasant farmers, and participated in assassinating him after he tried unconstitutionally to campaign for re-election in 133 B.C. REF.: *CBA.*

Schoolteacher John Scopes, who taught students Darwin's theory of evolution and was taken to court.

Scopes, John Thomas (AKA: **The Monkey Trial**), 1901- , U.S., courts and trials. In March 1925, any teaching about man's evolution contrary to the Bible was outlawed by the Tennessee legislature. Four months later, the first offender, high school teacher John Thomas Scopes, was brought to trial in a small Tennessee town for lecturing about Darwin's theory of evolution. The case pitted three-time presidential candidate, William Jennings Bryan, against the nation's most famous defense attorney, Clarence Darrow, in what became known as "The Monkey Trial."

Scopes, twenty-four, was charged with undermining the peace

and dignity of the state and was brought to trial on July 10, 1925, before Judge John Raulston in Dayton, Tenn. Raulston sat beneath a large banner stating "Read Your Bible." A carnival atmosphere prevailed as traveling hucksters and promoters converged on the town. People carried monkey dolls or wore monkey badges. Fundamentalist preachers bellowed from street corners, attempting to be heard over the countering atheists. Judge Raulston quickly informed the jury of twelve Protestant churchgoers that this was not a test of Darwin's philosophies or the validity of the Bible's teaching, but rather the resolution of a simple question. Had John Thomas Scopes broken an existing law in the state of Tennessee?

To Clarence Darrow, the trial represented an abridgement of Scopes' rights of freedom of speech and religion. In his opening remarks, Darrow stated that the Bible could not be accepted as a literal work. It was really sixty-six books spanning close to 1,000 years, and to accept the words as absolute truths would ignore the sciences of biology, geology, astronomy, and chemistry. To adhere to Biblical beliefs would force one to believe that the earth had existed for a mere 5,000 years. Darrow, an acknowledged agnostic, railed against Fundamentalist belief, blaming religion for war, hatred, and bigotry. To legally interpret the Bible's writings was to make a travesty of justice. If the jury were to find against Scopes, repercussions would be felt by future lecturers, publishers, and writers. A cyclical effect would return mankind to the sixteenth century in which similar renouncers of illogical laws were burned at the stake.

Scopes prosecutor in the "Monkey Trial," William Jennings Bryan.

On the trial's second day, Darrow sought to call expert witnesses to denounce the theory that the story of evolution was contained in the book of *Genesis*. But Judge Raulston denied the testimony, saying that the interpretation would be beyond the jury's comprehension. Darrow refused to call Scopes to the stand, admitting that everything the prosecution had said about him was true. Instead, he called on three high school biology students who denied that Scopes' classes had altered their morals or brought them into a religious confrontation.

Now it was Bryan's turn. The 65-year-old special prosecutor said that the people of the state knew what they were doing when they passed the law and the defense's intent was to demean that effort. To allow contrary teachings was to create discord in fundamentalist households. Children would be returned from the classroom as "skeptical, infidels, agnostics or atheists." The midsummer heat became intolerable and the trial moved outside, the judge on a dais beneath shady tree, while the crowd reassembled on the courthouse lawn. Clarence Darrow asked Judge Raulston for permission to call one more witness for the defense. Raulston complied, only to have Darrow surprise the overheated masses by calling William Jennings Bryan.

Darrow attempted to pin Bryan to accept the Bible's parables as literal. Using Jonah and the whale as an example, Bryan admitted he indeed did believe the story, that he viewed miracles as the act of God and entirely within the realm of possibility. Darrow claimed that if the story of Joshua's making the earth stand still had been true, the planet would have become a molten mass within a short time. One believing the story of Noah would believe the earth's only survivors were the few people and animals on the ark. The interrogation was devastating to Bryan and to the spectators, who were forced to confront traditional teachings. Bryan attempted to belittle Darrow's questioning as a vicious slur against the Bible and hoped to avenge the humiliation by cross-examining him about his agnosticism. But it never happened. Darrow waived his rights to a closing argument, costing Bryan his revenge and an emotional final statement.

On July 21, 1925, the jury was sequestered. Despite the intensity and fervor of the prosecution and defense, the question of John Thomas Scopes' guilt within the narrow confines of the charges was rather simple. He had taught a theory that ran counter to the Bible's teachings. Scopes was found Guilty and fined $100. Later, the Tennessee Supreme Court reversed the decision. The victory was a hollow one for Fundamentalists, who only brought attention to their prejudices and ridicule to the citizens of Dayton. Even Judge Raulston paid tribute to Darrow saying, "It sometimes takes courage to declare a truth or stand for an act that is in contravention to the public sentiment. A man who is big enough to search for the truth and find it and declare it in the face of all opposition is a big man." See: **Darrow, Clarence.**

REF.: Ahlstrom, *A Religious History of the American People;* Allen, *Bryan and Darrow at Dayton: Their Record and Documents of the Bible-Evolution Trial;* Allen, *Only Yesterday;* Bridges, *The God of Fundamentalism and Other Studies;* Bryan, *In His Image;* ____ and Bryan, *The Memoirs of William Jennings Bryan;* Bury, *A History of the Freedom of Thought;* Campbell, *CBA; Records of Rhea;* Cole, *The History of Fundamentalism;* Coletta, *William Jennings Bryan;* Crandall, *The Man from Kinsman;* Curtis, *Fundamentalism vs. Evolution at Dayton;* Daniels, *The Time Between the Wars;* Darrow, *Crime: Its Causes and Treatment;* ____, *The Story of My Life;* Darwin, *The Descent of Man, and Selection in Relation to Sex;* de Camp, *The Great Monkey Trial;* Furniss, *The Fundamentalist Controversy, 1918-1931;* Gatewood, *Preachers, Pedagogues & Politicians;* Ginger, *Six Days or Forever: Tennessee v. John Thomas Scopes;* Glad, *The Trumpet Soundeth;* Grebstein, *Monkey Trial: The State of Tennessee vs. John Thomas Scopes;* Gunn, *Wisdom of Clarence Darrow;* Gurko, *Clarence Darrow;* Haldeman-Julius, *Clarence Darrow's Two Great Trials;* Harrison, *Clarence Darrow;* Hays, *Let Freedom Ring;* Herrick, *The Life of William Jennings Bryan;* Hibben, *The Peerless Leader: William Jennings Bryan;* Hofstadter, *Anti-Intellectualism in America;* Hunter, *A Civic Biology;* ____, *A New Civic Biology;* Keebler, *The Tennessee Evolution Case;* Kemler, *The Irreverent Mr. Mencken;* Kluger, *New Light on the Scopes Trial;* Koenig, *Bryan;* Krutch, *More Lives Than One;* Kurland, *Clarence Darrow;* Levine, *Defender of the Faith: William Jennings Bryan, The Last Decade, 1915-1925;* Lippmann, *American Inquisitors: A Commentary on Dayton and Chicago;* Long, *Bryan, The Great Commoner;* McCann, *God—or Gorilla?;* Manchester, *Disturber of the Peace: The Life of H.L. Menchen;* Mencken, *Heathen Days;* ____, *Prejudices (5th Series);* Milner, *Education of an American Liberal;* Mordell, *Clarence Darrow;* Otto, *Modern Biology;* Peabody, *Biology and Human Welfare;* Potter, *The Preacher and I, An Autobiography;* Price, *The New Geology;* Robinson, *Why Dayton—Of All Places;* Sayer, *Clarence Darrow: Public Advocate;* Scopes and Presley, *Center of the Storm: The Memoirs of John T. Scopes;* Shipley, *The War on Modern Science: A Short History of the Fundamentalist Attack on Evolution and Modernism;* Smallwood, *Natural History and the American Mind;* Stone, *Clarence Darrow for the Defense;* Straton, *The Famous New York Fundamentalist-Modernist Debates;* Stribling, *Teeftallow;* Tierney, *Darrow, A Biography;* Tompkins, *D-Days as Dayton;* Weinberg, *Attorney for the Damned;* ____, *Clarence Darrow, A Sentimental Rebel;* Werner, *Bryan;* Whitehead, *Clarence Darrow—The Big Minority Man;* ____, *Clarence Darrow, Evangelist of Sane Thinking;* Williams, *William Jennings Bryan; The World's Most Famous Court Trial;* (DRAMA), *Inherit the Wind;* (FILM), *Inherit the Wind,* 1960.

Scotland Yard (London Metropolitan Police), 1829- , Brit., law enfor. agen. The London Metropolitan Police Force was consolidated into a single entity by Home Secretary Sir Robert Peel, with the passage of the 1829 Metropolitan Police Act. Prior to this an untrained company of thief catchers known as the Bow Street Runners safeguarded the London streets. The runners worked out of the Bow Street Police Station during much of the eighteenth century. The famous Bow Street patrols were the brainchild of novelist and magistrate Sir Henry Fielding. By the early 1820s, however, the prevalence of crime in the city proved too much for the overtaxed runners, who were also hampered by bribe taking and other forms of corruption in their ranks. Various parliamentary commissions were set up to investigate the situation, one of which resulted in the adoption of the Police Act, which provided for the formation of a 3,000-man force.

The Metropolitan Police, sometimes called "bobbies" or "peelers" after their sponsor, were originally headquartered in Great Scotland Yard and Whitehall Place. The name came from the Scottish noblemen who owned a medieval palace that once occupied the site where they stayed during their visits to the city. The Scotland Yard in Sir Arthur Conan Doyle's Sherlock Holmes adventures was constructed in 1890 and extended from Derby Gate to the bank of the Thames River. This structure was superseded by the New Scotland Yard located at Broadway and Victoria, near Victoria Station, in 1967.

Londoners initially regarded the newly formed police force with mistrust. Sir Richard Mayne, one of the first commissioners of the Metropolitan Force, established the guidelines for his men when he told them that, "The primary object of an efficient police force is the prevention of crime; the next that of detection and punishment of offenders if crime is committed. To these ends all the efforts of police must be directed. The protection of life and property, the preservation of public tranquility, and the absence of crime will alone prove whether those efforts have been successful and whether the objects for which the police were appointed have been attained."

Old Scotland Yard.

In 1842, Scotland Yard detailed its first detective force to gather information on the underworld. These men were referred to contemptuously as "spies" and *agent provocateurs.* In 1878, the Criminal Investigation Division (CID) was created as a special branch of Scotland Yard. At first Superintendent Frederick Williamson and his advisors recruited CID men from outside the force, but this practice was abandoned after 1884, since which time CID officers have been appointed from the ranks of uniformed patrolmen. Over the years the CID has become one of the most efficient crime-fighting agencies in the world. Within the CID are sub-agencies such as criminal records, fingerprint and photography, a detective training school, a tactical mobile flying squad organized immediately after WWI, a forensic laboratory organized in 1934, and a fraud squad created in 1946. The original horse-drawn mobile unit gave way to modern two-way radio cars. The flying squad today is composed of veteran officers who scour the city in search of criminal offenders.

There have been many famous detectives that were members of Scotland Yard, notably Jonathan Whicher, Frederick Cherrill, and Robert Fabian. Cherrill headed up the Fingerprint Bureau for fifteen years in the 1930s and 1940s. He helped convict Frederick Cummins, a latter day "Jack the Ripper," and Bertie Manton, who killed his wife in 1943.

The Metropolitan Police Force is responsible for preventing and detecting crime, the licensing of public vehicles, organizing civil defense, and supervising traffic in Greater London County, Middlesex, parts of Surrey, Kent, Essex, and Hertford, excluding the City of London, which has its own special force. Since 1856, the force has been governed by a commissioner, who is appointed by the royal family upon the recommendation of the home secretary. Reporting to the commissioner are four administrative heads, including a deputy commissioner, and four assistants (or AC's) responsible for traffic and transport, administration, the CID, and recruitment and training. The city proper is further divided into four districts with twenty-three divisions, including the Thames Division (or River Police). The Metropolitan Force provides protection for leading figures within the government, including members of Parliament and out-of-town dignitaries. The Yard maintains an extensive file on criminal offenders active in Great Britain, Ireland, Wales, and Scotland. Nineteenth-century dynamite attacks by the radical Fenians and their splinter groups led to formation of the 400-man Special Branch in 1884; this division of the CID is also concerned with national security matters and the activities of foreign nationals in England. In 1939, following a fresh outbreak of bombing attacks by the Irish Republican Army (IRA), Parliament passed the Prevention of Violence Act. This granted the Special Branch sweeping powers to round up and interrogate suspected Irish terrorists. The Special Branch concerned itself with Nazi saboteurs during WWII.

Scotland Yard serves as the national bureau for British law enforcement agencies seeking access to the International Criminal Police Organization (INTERPOL). Though its jurisdiction covers an area of only 740 square miles, Scotland Yard is frequently called upon to lend assistance to criminal investigations in the outlying counties and in other member nations within the British Commonwealth. See: **Bow Street Runners; Fielding, Sir Henry; Fielding, Sir John; Peel, Sir Robert.**

REF.: Asbury, *The Gangs of New York;* Browne, *The Rise of Scotland Yard;* Burt, *Commander Burt of Scotland Yard; CBA;* Cherrill, *Cherrill of The Yard;* Cobb, *Critical Years at the Yard;* Demaris, *The Director;* Gage, *The Mafia is not an Equal Opportunity Employer;* Lait and Mortimer, *Chicago: Confidential;* Neil, *Manhunters of Scotland Yard;* Ottenberg, *The Federal Investigators;* Savage, *Savage of Scotland Yard;* Scott, *The Concise Encyclopedia of Crime and Criminals;* Smith, *Syndicate City;* Thompson, *The Story of Scotland Yard;* Toledano, *J. Edgar Hoover;* Tullett, *The Scalpel of Scotland Yard;* Unger, *FBI;* Wensley, *Forty Years of Scotland Yard;* Woodhall, *Secrets of Scotland Yard.*

Scott, Andrew George (AKA: **Captain Moonlight**), b.1842, Aus., rob. Andrew George Scott, a parson's son, trained as a priest in Melbourne, then took a £130 a year job as a lay reader. In May 1869, his bank manager handed over £1,000 in notes, gold, and cash at the demand of the young preacher. Authorities refused to believe the manager of the bank when he explained that Scott had made him write a note that said, "Captain Moonlight has struck me up and robbed the bank." The manager was charged with the crime, and Scott was called to be a witness, but soon disappeared and the case was dropped.

Fleeing to Sydney, Scott pretended to be a captain, and bought a yacht with a bad check. He was arrested and served eighteen months in prison. After his release, he was again arrested for the earlier bank robbery, found Guilty, and sentenced to seven years in prison. Escaping once, he seemed to change his ways on his recapture and lectured against crime, leading Bible classes and making appeals to charity as he spoke about the evils of prison. But he soon returned to his old ways. He and a gang took over the Wantabadgery Station on Nov. 16, 1876, and Scott played host to the ensuing feast, urging his hostages to enjoy themselves. One escaped to call the police, and the generous Scott freed the others when he saw that the station was surrounded by officers. In a two-hour battle, one policeman and a gang member were killed. Moonlight and his three remaining cohorts surrendered. All three were found Guilty and hanged. REF.: *CBA*.

Scott, Dred, c.1795-1858, U.S., courts and trials. Launched an unsuccessful lawsuit to gain freedom by reason that he had lived as a slave on free territory for five years, from 1848-57. He was originally the property of a Virginia family named Blow, who moved him to St. Louis, Mo., in 1827. He was sold to Dr. John Emerson, an army surgeon, who brought him to Rock Island, Ill., and Fort Snelling at the Wisconsin territory, both places where he was stationed. When he was returned to the Blow family following Emerson's death, his new owner, Harry Blow, initiated a lawsuit based on Scott's living in Illinois, a free state, and the Wisconsin territory, where slavery was technically banned through the Missouri Compromise in 1820. The suit was defeated in the state supreme court of Missouri, based on the *Strader v. Graham* ruling of 1851, stating that laws where a slave lives determines his status. Because Scott lived in Missouri, he was still a slave.

The civil war in Kansas over the volatile slavery issue reignited hope for Scott's case. He was persuaded to sue John F.A. Sanford, the brother of Emerson's widow, who was now technically his owner, even though he lived in New York. The case reached the U.S. Supreme Court in 1856, but the ruling was stalled until after the presidential election. The decision, issued in February 1857, declared that Scott could not sue anyone because, as a slave, he was not a citizen of the United States. As interpreted by Chief Justice Roger Brooke Taney, the Constitution considered slaves to be property, and made slavery "the duty of the government to protect." The court decision also rejected the Missouri Compromise, calling it an unconstitutional violation of the slave owners' right to due process. The court's response to *Scott v. Sandford* (the owner's name was spelled incorrectly), was widely misconstrued as a declaration of white supremacy, and was one of many elements that precipitated the Civil War. REF.: *CBA*.

Scott, Edward Burke (AKA: **William B. Victor**), prom. 1903, U.S., embez. As a young man, Edward Scott was considered a talented drama critic and manager of top theatrical stars. In 1903 he met and married Kate Condon, a leading star of the Metropolitan Opera. Shortly after their marriage, Scott disappeared, along about $10,000 from his theatrical accounts. During the following years, Condon's career peaked and then plummeted, until nothing was left. Twenty-four years later she received an anonymous letter informing her that a man who was most likely her long-missing husband had committed suicide in New Orleans. She immediately went to that city to identify the corpse.

After leaving Condon for reasons that were never known, Scott had assumed the name William B. Victor and had become a successful and wealthy land speculator. Never revealing his true identity, he had lived a reclusive existence until the day he shot himself in the head at his exclusive club. About $100,000 of Scott's estate was awarded to Kate Condon. REF.: *CBA*.

Scott, Elliot Nathaniel, prom. 1962-72, U.S., fraud. A former beautician, Elliot Nathaniel Scott went into the wig business, soliciting agents to supply him with prospective customers' names. By 1966, Scott went to phone books, mailing tens of thousands of postcards to contact each "Lucky Lady" who had won "an expensive free wig in our annual drawing." Explaining that the wig was worth $89, Scott asked the fortunate winner to pay a minor postal fee of under $3, $1.50 for a plastic head form, and about $7.50 for the two stylings the wig would need. The "winners" received shoddy wigs made of yarn, not the human hair that was advertised. Most of the items were a harsh shade of red, rather than the glamourous colors advertised; they fell apart, sometimes before they were set even once; and some even had bald spots. Over a six month period, Scott cashed about $100,000 worth of money orders. Over several years, he accumulated nearly $1.5 million from about 100,000 customers. By March 1967, Scott had become a common name in newspaper columns as the complaints poured in. Postal Inspector Elbridge M. Hamm, Jr., investigated Scott for several years, and by October 1967, Hamm had a list of hundreds of women eager to testify against him.

Scott was indicted for mail fraud by a grand jury, and was arrested on Oct. 9, 1967. Released on bail, he conducted business as usual until his trial in February 1968. The fourteen-day trial, with a jury comprised of women only, listened to a parade of angry witnesses. On Mar. 13, Scott was found Guilty, and sentenced to a year and a day in prison, followed by four years of probation. Pending execution of his sentence, Scott continued to perpetrate fraud while out on bail, generating another 5,000 complaints and pulling in $160,000. In January 1969, Scott's bail was revoked and he was sent to prison. Released after a year and one day, he returned to his illicit trade before his probation period was over. In June 1972, Scott signed an agreement with the Postal Service's General Counsel agreeing that all mail addressed to his business be returned to senders stamped "Out of Business."

REF.: *CBA; Kahn, Fraud.*

Scott, Francis, 1953- , U.S., rob.-pris. esc. First incarcerated in 1965, when he was twelve years old, Francis Scott was sent to a reformatory in his native Ohio. Over the next few years, Scott reportedly escaped from more prisons than anyone else in the U.S. Explaining his repeated successes in breaking out of jail, Scott pointed to his early experience as a Boy Scout. He explained that he would watch the guards, study them and note the "flaws in the system." His tactics ranged from bolting out of a police car, to posing as a professional counselor, photographer, and a newsman. Convicted of armed robbery and sent to the Chillicothe, Ohio, penitentiary in 1975 for a seven- to twenty-five-year term, Scott escaped. In Chicago, where he was arrested for theft, Scott broke out of Cook County Jail, the first man at that time to do so, by simply going over the fence. Captured by FBI agents, he was charged with assaulting a federal officer and was consequently sent to the Metropolitan Correctional Center in downtown Chicago, from which no one had ever escaped. But Scott escaped again. Prosecutor John Lewis described Scott as "a clever escape artist" and that he was "the best in the country."

On Oct. 30, 1980, after a jury found Scott Guilty of a Sept. 25, 1978, jail break, Cook County Criminal Court Judge Arthur J. Cieslik sentenced the convict to a twelve-year prison term. On Nov. 15, 1980, Scott attempted to break out of the Joliet Correctional Center by sawing his way out of his cell, overpowering a guard, and changing into the guard's uniform before climbing a twelve-foot fence. He was caught as he tried to run for the prison's main wall. See: **Welch, Bernard Charles, Jr.** REF.: *CBA*.

Scott, Sir **Harold Richard**, 1887-1969, Brit., law enfor. off. Sir Harold Scott's lengthy career in public service began in 1911 when he joined the Home Office. After a brief stay in the Foreign Trade Department and the Labor Resettlement Committee, Sir Harold was appointed chairman of His Majesty's Commissioners of Prisons for England and Wales, a position he held from 1932 to 1939. In 1945, he was named commissioner of the London Metropolitan Police, stepping down in 1953. He recounted his experiences in a memoir published in 1963, titled: *Inside Scotland Yard*. Books authored: *German Prisons* (1934), *Belgian Prisons and Reformatory Institutions* (1936), *Scotland Yard* (1954), and *Your Obedient Servant* (1959). REF.: *CBA*.

Scott, Henry (AKA: **Henry Slater, Captain Scott, Captain Brown**), b.c.1846, and **Henry, George Phillip** (AKA: **Henry Slater, Jr.**), b.c.1858, and **Pracey, John**, b.c.1869, and **Davies, Frederick Stanley**, b.c.1862, and **Smith, Cyril Broughton**, b.c.1866, and **Osborn, Albert**, b.c.1865, Brit., consp. When a working mother petitioned for divorce from her husband on the grounds of adultery and cruelty, a large and prosperous detective agency was destroyed. Kate Pollard, a waitress, sent money weekly to her husband, Thomas Pollard, who had not worked for several years and lived with his parents at their seaside home in Plymouth. Pollard stopped her husband's allowance and sued for divorce with evidence of his infidelity. The decree would eventually become final unless some other element was introduced into the case. In

September 1901, a millionaire, Hugh Charles Knowles, walked into Slater's Detective Agency in London. Knowles, an old friend of Mrs. Pollard's, hired the firm to help ensure she got her decree. Owner Henry Scott and staff members, George Phillip Henry, second in command; John Pracey; Frederick Stanley Davies; Cyril Broughton Smith; and the company's lawyer, Albert Osborn, all became in involved in elaborate and costly schemes of fraud, providing false witnesses and manufacturing written testimony, in their concerted efforts to guarantee Pollard's divorce and lighten Knowles' pocketbook. Over the two-year period of gathering "evidence," Knowles paid out almost £5,000 in fees; about £700 of that money went to Osborn.

When several discontented employees moved to another agency, they took reports on the Pollard case. In January 1903, the reports were taken to the King's proctor, and by March 1904, a legal motion was made to intervene in Mrs. Pollard's decree *nisi* being made absolute. Public interest in the case ran high as a special jury tried the matter before the president of the Divorce Court, Sir Francis Jeune, with Sir Edward Clarke, Bargrave Deane, Mr. Barnard, and Mr. Valetta for the petitioner, and Charles Mathews and Guy Stephenson for the King's proctor. After an eleven-day trial, the jury deliberated for five minutes before ruling that the decree *nisi* be rescinded, and Mrs. Pollard be given a judicial separation with custody of their child. On Oct. 21, 1904, Scott, Osborn, Pracey, Davies, Henry, and Smith were brought to trial, charged with conspiring to pervert and obstruct the due course of law and justice. Scott was able to prove himself ignorant of the entire matter. The jury found all of the others Guilty but Osborn, on whose case they could not agree. Justice Darling sentenced Henry to a twelve month jail term; Davies received six months; Pracey received three months; and Smith was given a six month term. Osborn's trial was postponed until the next sessions, when the attorney general dropped charges against him.

REF.: *CBA;* Nicholls, *Crime Within the Square Mile.*

Scott, James (AKA: James Crofts, James Fitzroy), 1649-85, Brit., consp.-treas. Son of Charles II and mistress Lucy Walter and claimant to British throne. Banished in 1679 by James II, he was afforded a safe return to England under the terms of the Exclusion Bill. In 1683, after prominent Whig leaders had been arrested and the Rye House Plot foiled, he was forced to flee. He returned to England in 1685 to claim the crown for himself but was routed in battle by Lord Louis de Durfort at Feversham. He was beheaded on Tower Hill at the behest of his uncle, the king. REF.: *CBA.*

Scott, James (AKA: **James Fitzroy, James Crofts, The Protestant Duke**), 1649-85, Brit., consp. James Scott, the natural son of King Charles II of England, eventually became the Duke of Monmouth, but he had a strong claim to the throne though evidence of his royal birth was suppressed by the jealous Duke of York. Scott earned a reputation as a military leader, distinguishing himself at the naval Battle of Lowestoft when he was sixteen years old. He later commanded four battle campaigns on the Continent and one in Scotland. He gained renown as director of England's internal security and as a military administrator.

Charles II finally acknowledged Scott's birthright in 1663 and exploited his son's talents for his own ends, using his popularity to foil York's ambitions and constantly reminding his scheming brother of the Duke's strength. Scott was made captain general of the king's forces in 1670, when England helped France in their war against the Dutch, and later led troops against the Scots in 1675-79, quelling rebellion with a victory at Bothwell Bridge, where he became still more popular for his clemency. Scott was exiled by Charles II, but later returned to England to champion Protestantism. He became an idol of the people, with republican politician and soldier Colonel Algernon Sidney declaring, "I know of but one general we can have and that is the Duke of Monmouth, whose conduct and integrity I do not doubt."

In 1683, Scott became implicated in the Rye House Plot, a conspiracy to assassinate the king and his brother (who later became James II) on London Road near Rumbold's Rye House in Essex. The plot was exposed and the king's trip cancelled. Coming under suspicion in the plot, Scott, along with Whig leaders Essex, Sidney, and Russell, fled to the Low Countries. When Charles II died later that year from a stroke, Scott arranged to meet a military expedition returning to England. Once it landed, with eighty-two supporters, he claimed his right to the crown over James II. Briefly proclaimed King of Taunton, he then was defeated at Sedgemoor by Churchill and Feversham. When captured, the duke confessed to wrongdoing and offered to become a Roman Catholic but was condemned to die by beheading at Tower Hill. The hangman at that time, Jack Ketch, had become notorious for a recent botched job of executing Lord Russell. On the scaffold Scott handed Ketch six guineas and said, "Pray, do your business well. Don't serve me as you did Lord Russell. I have heard you struck him three or four times." Scott then asked Ketch to hand him the ax. He felt the blade and said, "I fear it is not sharp enough." Scott then gave his servant another purse of guineas to give to the hangman "if he does his work well." Ketch did not earn the extra pay. Apparently disconcerted by the Scott's cool demeanor, he cried out, "I can't do it!" as the duke put his head on the block. The sheriff threatened Ketch who finally took the ax to Scott's neck. After four strokes he still had not succeeded in beheading Scott and was forced to use a knife to finish the job. REF.: *CBA.*

Scott, John, c.1630-96, Brit., ct. mar.-perj. Participated in British capture of New Amsterdam, and was later named president of Long Island. He escaped to the West Indies to avoid arrest for property fraud. He fought the French army at St. Kitts under Lord Francis Willoughby from 1665-67, but was court-martialed and dismissed for cowardice the following year. He was later dismissed for dishonesty from the Dutch army. Any remaining credibility was removed after he appeared as a witness in the Popish Plot and falsely testified against Samuel Pepys, who was later absolved of any wrongdoing. REF.: *CBA.*

Scott, John, See: **Wyatt, Anthony Lewis.**

Scott, Leonard Ewing, prom. 1955, U.S., forg.-mur. In 1949, Leonard Ewing Scott married Evelyn Scott, who had inherited a large amount of money from her four previous husbands. During this marriage, Scott's second, he wrote a handbook for women, *How to Fascinate Men,* a tome that made no money, and for which Scott never paid the printer's bill. On May 16, 1955, his wife sent him out to buy tooth powder; when he returned to their posh Bel Air home, Evelyn Scott was gone. He had not reported the absence because, he explained, his hard-drinking spouse often behaved eccentrically. Friends who asked about the woman were told that she had gone to a sanitarium for treatment. After ten months, police investigators searched the grounds of the Scotts' house, finding metal snaps from a woman's undergarment, false teeth, and eyeglasses buried in a nearby lot; they were identified as Evelyn Scott's. In the ten months since her disappearance, her husband had forged signatures to withdraw money from her bank accounts and safety deposit boxes. Indicted by a Los Angeles jury on thirteen counts of forgery, Scott was arrested in Detroit as he tried to buy a new car. Soon after, his case was reconsidered, and he was indicted for murder. Because there was evidence that the crime had been committed, although neither a murder weapon nor a body was ever found, Scott was found Guilty of murdering his wife in December 1955. Scott was sentenced to life imprisonment.

REF.: *CBA;* Whitehead, *Corpus Delicti.*

Scott, Lindsey, 1958- , U.S., (wrong. convict.) rape-attempt. mur. In October 1983, Marine Corps corporal Lindsey Scott, twenty-five, was convicted of the rape and attempted murder of the wife of a fellow Marine at the Quantico, Va., Marine Base where he was stationed. Scott maintained his innocence throughout the trial, saying that he had been shopping and dining when the crime was committed on Apr. 20. Scott was sentenced to thirty years in the military prison at Fort Leavenworth, Kan.

In July 1987, the U.S. Court of Military Appeals reversed the conviction on the basis that Scott's civilian attorney had fallen "far short of reasonable competence" in not investigating the defendant's alibi. Although Scott had provided his attorney, Ervan E. Kuhnke, with the details of his whereabouts on the evening of Apr. 20, 1983, Kuhnke failed to introduce any mention of them in Scott's defense, saying that he had never expected the case to come to trial. Scott's family and supporters had charged that Scott was convicted in the first trial because he was black and the victim was white. The thirty-year sentence and an $18,000 pay forfeiture imposed on Scott were set aside at the time of the reversal and Scott was released from prison. On Feb. 19, 1988, a jury at Scott's second trial acquitted him of the charges. REF.: *CBA*.

Scott, Paul, 1921- , and **Scott, Don**, 1922- , and **Morris, Earl**, 1920- , U.S., asslt.-rob. In 1951, Earl Morris was captured by police an hour after he robbed the Collinsville, Texas, State Bank. A few weeks later, Paul Scott and his brother, Don Scott, were picked up in Springfield, Ky. In their car, police found $10,000 in cash, stolen from a safe at the Sheppard Air Force Base in Wichita Falls, Texas. All were convicted and sentenced to jail terms at the Texas State Prison. Morris was released after serving two years of a ten-year term, and the Scotts were released after serving three of five years. On Jan. 5, 1957, two Kentucky policemen cruising Fayette County stopped to check a car by the side of the road on Highway 15. Threatened with a machine gun, the officers let Paul Scott and Earl Morris get away, then notified police, who set up roadblocks in the area. The ex-convicts car reached the town of Campton by midnight to meet Don Scott. There, Paul Scott broke into the Farmers and Traders Bank. A night guard, Daniel Boone Stone, shot and wounded Paul Scott. The convicts escaped, after wounding Sheriff George D. Little and stunning Stone with the butt of a machine gun. Briefly eluding state police and a squad of eight FBI agents, headed by Ray L. Faisst of Louisville, the convicts were captured. Don Scott was found in a farmhouse near Pine Ridge, where a couple had given him shelter and food. Paul Scott and Morris were apprehended by Harold Alexander in a cornfield. All three were tried and found Guilty of armed robbery and given thirty-year prison terms. REF.: *CBA*.

Scott, Ronald Allen, 1932- , U.S., mur. Cecelia Arthur, a 50-year-old housewife in East Toledo, Ohio, was a lonely woman who enjoyed socializing with the regulars at the beauty shop and pubs along Starr Avenue. A bartender recalled how Arthur often sat at the bar sipping Diet Coke and conversing about the news of the day with her other customers. Cecelia's husband Terry was an over-the-road truck driver whose work kept him away from home much of the time. During one of his prolonged absences, Arthur met Ronald Allen Scott, an unemployed home-improvements salesman at the neighborhood bar. Scott was well-liked and sociable. Those that knew him recalled that he was a member of the high school football team during its winning days. When Cecilia found out that he had nowhere to stay, she invited him to come and live at her home on Greenwood Avenue.

At first the arrangement worked out fine. Scott seemed to get along with Terry Arthur, and the rent money he paid for his room came in handy. But as time passed, Scott found it increasingly difficult to meet his obligations. After a full day of drinking at the tavern, he returned to the Arthur residence on Mar. 21, 1988. "I was highly intoxicated," Scott later told the police. "Cecelia started in on me about the rent money I owed." Then, according to sworn statements given to the police, Cecelia hit and kicked him. Scott reached for a .25-caliber pistol to "scare her." But she kept on throwing his clothing and other personal items into the back yard. "That's when I raised the gun and shot her," he said.

Terry Arthur was driving his rig through Pennsylvania, and Scott knew that it was only a matter of time before he would be coming home. After brooding about the matter for a day, he decided to dismember the corpse and dispose of it in the Maumee River in Toledo. It took Scott nearly twenty-four hours to complete the gruesome task. On Mar. 24, he carried the body parts, stuffed into plastic trash bags, to an expressway overpass spanning the river. In full view of passing motorists, he dumped them over the side. The bags floated three miles downstream before three teen-age boys found them and notified the police. Scott was taken into custody on Mar. 26 after the owner of the local beauty parlor became concerned when Mrs. Arthur did not answer her phone.

The police were told by the beauty shop owner that the Arthurs were renting a room to a boarder. Scott was grilled by police for two hours before he broke down and confessed. A bloody hacksaw and the .25-caliber handgun used in the murder were recovered from the Arthur home during a police search.

On Sept. 25, 1988, Scott pleaded no contest and was found Guilty of murder and criminal abuse of a corpse in the Lucas County Common Pleas Court. Judge Charles Abood sentenced the defendant to fifteen years to life, for murder and an additional eighteen months for the abuse of the body. REF.: *CBA*.

Scott, Thomas, prom. 1804, Brit., slander. Convicted of slander because he accused Captain Kennah and Kennah's servant of robbery, Thomas Scott was sentenced to stand in the pillory for one hour and to twelve months in jail. The Jan. 28, 1804, *Morning Herald,* reported Scott's woes in the Charing Cross pillory saying he "was greeted by a large mob with a discharge of small shot, such as rotten eggs, filth, and dirt from the streets which was followed up by dead cats, rats, etc." The mob broke the windows of the coach which was taking him to jail and threatened violence.

REF.: Andrews, *Old-Time Punishments; CBA*.

Scott, William (Baron Stowell, Earl of Eldon), 1745-1836, Brit., jur. Became one of England's most noted experts on maritime and international law. He was advocate general for the lord high admiral in 1782, judge of consistory court from 1788-1821, privy councilor in 1798, and judge of the high court of admiralty from 1798-1828. REF.: *CBA*.

Scott, William J., 1927- , U.S., tax evas.-polit. corr. Elected attorney general of Illinois for an unprecedented fourth term, William J. Scott was stripped of his office when convicted of federal income tax fraud. The investigation of his tax returns began in October 1977, sparked by an article in the Chicago *Sun-Times* that revealed the attorney general kept $48,900 cash in safe deposit boxes in 1967. A federal grand jury charged that Scott understated his income by around $50,000 from 1972-75, and kept unclaimed campaign contributions for personal use. The trial lasted forty days, tried before U.S. District Court judge John Powers Crowley, with U.S. Attorney Thomas P. Sullivan for the prosecution, and William A. Barnett heading the defense. During the bitter weeks of testimony, Sullivan accused Scott and his lawyers of withholding evidence, making misleading representations, and behaving improperly throughout the trial. Nearly 150 witnesses testified, and more than 1,000 documents were produced as evidence.

Thirty defense witnesses testified that they gave Scott varying amounts of money with the intention that the attorney general could use the money for any purpose. Prosecutors maintained Scott spent more than 300 days traveling outside the state between 1970-75, most of it financed with cash; defense lawyers labelled this claim as non-evidence, because no documents confirmed the trips. After forty-six hours of deliberation in a six-day period, the jury found Scott Guilty of one count of tax fraud and acquitted him of three others. Scott was the highest ranking Illinois public official to be convicted of a felony. Rejecting a probation plea from Scott's lawyer, Judge Crowley sentenced the former attorney general to one year and one day in prison. He was released from a California federal prison Oct. 8, 1982, after seven months. REF.: *CBA*.

Scott, William Lester, prom. 1931, U.S., mur. On Nov. 9, 1931, engineer Barney McCook and fireman J.E. Bryant, on a passenger train, spotted a stalled car on the tracks near Sasakwa, Okla. Unable to stop, the train smashed into the car. In the crumpled wreckage of the car, they saw the battered body of a young woman, her skin clammy and cold, her limbs set in rigor mortis, and her skull crushed. Local deputy Charles Lyon of Seminole County was called to the scene, along with Jerome Chambers, justice of the peace, and coroner. The car had no license plate, but following the car tracks to an isolated wooded area, investigators found a dental bridge and several teeth which identified the dead woman as Willie Scott, wife of William Lester Scott.

Officers found the young farmer at home the next day at his prosperous establishment. Scott said his wife was visiting her mother and would be back any minute. Lyon found a .38-caliber revolver, and bloodstained pants and shirt in Scott's house. He accused Scott of killing his spouse. The farmer denied the murder, insisting the blood on his trousers came from removing the horns from some steers. He continued to maintain his innocence in the county jail. At a preliminary hearing on Nov. 19, Scott demanded a chemical analysis of the stains on his clothing and gun. When the state chemist ruled that the blood was from an ox, Scott was released on a $15,000 bond. The case was on hold until a newly elected county attorney, Tom Huser, questioned relatives of the Scotts. They admitted that Scott visited them shortly after getting out on bond, and drunk, he responded to a comment that his wife had been killed by a gun saying, "She wasn't killed by a gun. She was killed with a car crank." They told Lyon that Scott then described how he had murdered his spouse. At the trial on Mar. 8, 1933, the jury disagreed over their verdict after lengthy deliberation. Scott was tried a second time on Apr. 16, 1935. After three days of testimony, the jury deliberated for fifteen minutes, finding him Guilty. Sentenced to life imprisonment, Scott entered the state penitentiary at McAlester on Apr. 29, 1935.

REF.: *CBA;* Cohen, *One Hundred True Crime Stories.*

Scotto, Anthony M., 1934- , U.S., org. crime. In 1963, Anthony M. Scotto came into the public eye in New York's longshoremen's union affairs following the death of Anthony "Tough Tony" Anastasio, a relative of Scotto's through marriage. Scotto's father-in-law, also named Anthony Anastasio, was the deceased's nephew. Touted as a "new breed labor leader" Scotto moved in high-level business and political realms, eventually becoming general organizer of the AFL-CIO International Longshoremen's Association as well as president of Local Union 1814 in Brooklyn, one of the three highest positions in the 100,000-member union representing workers from Maine to Texas.

In 1979, federal investigators uncovered a massive cash payoff racket and Scotto was arrested. Anastasio, his father-in-law, was tried with him. Despite a roster of character witnesses that included New York governor Hugh L. Carey and former New York City mayors John V. Lindsay and Robert Wagner, Scotto was convicted of taking more than $200,000 from waterfront businesses. He denied the charge, admitting that he had accepted $75,000 in "political contributions" but had "never taken a cent" for himself. Scotto said he had given the political contributions to New York lieutenant governor Mario M. Cuomo for his unsuccessful 1977 campaign for mayor and to Carey for his victorious 1978 reelection bid.

Both Scotto and his father-in-law were convicted. Saying that he had been "extremely impressed" by letters from political leaders, and businesses and labor figures who pleaded for leniency for Scotto, U.S. District Judge Charles E. Stewart, Jr. bypassed the maximum sentence of a twenty-year jail term and sentenced Scotto to five years in prison and a $75,000 fine. REF.: *CBA.*

Scottoriggio, Joseph R. d.1946, U.S. polit., assass. In 1946, in the 18th Congressional District in New York City, Congressman Vito Marcantonio was fighting for his political life. Marcantonio was a powerful, left-wing Democrat with a reputation of being a Communist and who had possible contact with known criminal elements in East Harlem. He was facing a battle for re-election against a strong Republican opponent.

Just before dawn on election day, Joseph Scottoriggio, the Republican district captain who controlled about 600 swing votes, left his home as his wife watched him walk down the street. She saw four men attack her husband, knocking him to the ground and kicking and beating him senseless. There were more than thirty witnesses to the attack, who saw the killers, but no one got involved. Finally an ambulance was called. Scottoriggio died six days later.

Mayor O'Dwyer and District Attorney Hogan called for an all-out manhunt to apprehend the killers. More than 800 witnesses were questioned, and the thugs and hoodlums who were known to control the district were investigated. Potential witnesses refused to talk in fear of reprisal, other witnesses disappeared, and neither the perpetrators nor those who hired them were ever identified. The main witness, Trigger Mike Coppola's wife, died in childbirth. The political murder of Scottoriggio still remains officially unsolved.

REF.: *CBA;* Danforth, *The D.A.'s Man.*

Scottsboro Case, prom. 1931-37, U.S., rape. The Scottsboro case was a classic civil rights battle that exposed Southern prejudice and involved the alleged rape of two white women, Ruby Bates and Victoria Price, by nine black youths. On the night of Mar. 25, 1931, the nine, who ranged in ages from thirteen to twenty-one, boarded a freight train bound from Tennessee to Huntsville, Ala., to look for work.

Price and Bates were also on board the train, illegally, with seven male companions, all white. According to Price, the nine blacks picked a fight with the white men as the train rumbled through Jackson County, Ala. The blacks threw the white youths off the train, and then gang raped Bates and Price. One of the men who was tossed off the car reported the incident to the sheriff, who promptly organized a posse that intercepted the train at the next stop, Paint Rock, Ala. The nine blacks: Roy Wright, thirteen; his brother Andy, seventeen; Clarence Norris, nineteen; Olin Montgomery, seventeen; Ozzie Powell, sixteen; Haywood Patterson, seventeen; Charles Weems, twenty-one; Willie Robertson, seventeen; and 13-year-old Eugene Williams were taken off the train and jailed in Scottsboro, where they were charged with rape.

A local physician stated that neither of the two women showed any sign of rape, nor did they seem greatly upset. These facts mattered little to hot-headed residents, who organized a lynch party after news of the arrests leaked out. The deputy sheriffs moved the prisoners to separate jails where they were kept in solitary confinement while awaiting trial. They were returned under heavy guard to Scottsboro a week later. The case captured the attention of the national media when deliberations began shortly afterward. One-hundred and two National Guardsmen were positioned outside the courtroom to prevent the many thousands of Southerners from ransacking the building and lynching the prisoners. Judge A.J. Hawkins had difficulty finding a lawyer willing to handle the emotionally charged case. Eight of the nine were found Guilty and sentenced to die. Only because of Roy Wright's young age, was the jury inclined to show mercy in his case.

News of the verdict sparked waves of protest in the more liberal-minded North. A May Day Parade in the Harlem neighborhood of New York attracted 300,000 blacks and whites. The NAACP and various left-wing groups like the International Labor Defense League (ILD) rallied to the cause, popularizing the slogan "the Scottsboro Boys Shall Not Die". The Alabama Supreme Court eventually overturned the conviction of Eugene Williams because he was under the legal age. But it upheld the convictions of the other seven. On Nov. 7, 1932, by a 7-2 margin, the U.S. Supreme Court struck down the ruling of the Alabama Supreme Court on the grounds that the selection of defense lawyers had been insufficient. A new trial was ordered and a change of venue granted, not to Birmingham as the defense had hoped, but to Decatur, in rural Morgan County. Deliberations began on Mar. 27, 1933. This time the defendants were represented by famed Manhattan criminal attorney Samuel A. Liebowitz, whose fees were being paid for by the ILD. This struck a note

The nine Scottsboro Boys surrounded by national guardsmen.

Judge Edward Horton listening to Dr. Bridges testify.

Samuel Leibowitz conferring with his clients in jail.

Clarence Norris leaves Kilby Prison in Montgomery, 1946.

Ruby Bates, testifying.

Victoria Price, testifying.

Andrew Wright, last of the Scottsboro Boys to go free, 1950.

of discord among members of the National Association for the Advancement of Colored People (NAACP), who charged that the group was using the case to promote domestic communism. The NAACP withdrew its support. Liebowitz meanwhile, promised the black community in Harlem that he would "march those Scottsboro boys up Lenox Avenue!"

Price appeared on the witness stand and repeated essentially the same story she had told earlier. However, Ruby Bates shocked and outraged the white community by recanting her earlier testimony. She said the story had been concocted to avoid possible arrest for vagrancy. The Ku Klux Klan, which had been present through much of the proceedings talked of lynching the defendants, and their much-maligned attorney. The sentiment was echoed in more subtle terms by Attorney General Thomas E. Knight, Jr., who demanded that a Guilty verdict be returned. "Show them," he said, "that Alabama justice cannot be bought and sold with Jew money from New York." Judge James E. Horton, a veteran of the bench for nearly twenty-five years was unconvinced. Two months after the trial began Judge Horton ruled that the available evidence did not support a Guilty verdict, because Price's testimony was not only "uncorroborated, but it also bears...indications of improbability and is contradicted by other evidence."

However, the affair was far from over. In December 1932, Haywood Patterson was tried for a third time in the courtroom of Judge William Washington Callahan, who promised to "debunk" the Scottsboro case. (Horton had been pressured into withdrawing from the case.) Ruby Bates was not present for the hearing. She was in a New York hospital at the time, but one of the white men who had ridden on the train that night, Orville Gilley, corroborated Price's story. Patterson was easily convicted. The appeals process reached the U.S. Supreme Court a second time. While reviewing the case of Clarence Norris, the justices on the high court concurred that the convictions should be overturned on the grounds that blacks had been "systematically excluded" from jury duty in the deep South. An angry Governor Bibb Graves expressed his displeasure. "This decision means that we must put the names of Negroes in jury boxes in every county!"

Year five of the Scottsboro affair began on Jan. 20, 1936, when Patterson went to trial a fourth time. After a three-day trial, he was found Guilty and sentenced to seventy-five years in prison. "I'd rather die!" Patterson said. In July of that year Thomas Edmund Knight, Jr., who now served as lieutenant-governor of Alabama, met with Liebowitz at his offices in Manhattan. They proposed a tradeoff. In return for the freedom of four of the defendants, the defense had to agree to plead Guilty to four of the other cases, with Ozzie Powell to be tried separately. In 1937 Clarence Norris was again convicted and sentenced to die. Andy Wright and Charles Weems were likewise found Guilty, and the men received prison terms of ninety-nine and seventy-five years. Powell entered a guilty plea on a stabbing charge and was sentenced to twenty-years. The state in turn, dropped the rape charges against Roy Wright, Williams, Powell, Robertson, and Olin Montgomery.

The coming of WWII temporarily diverted attention from the Scottsboro case. On Jan. 8, 1944, Wright and Clarence Norris were released on probation. Weems was later freed, and Powell's release followed in 1946. Haywood Patterson escaped from prison on July 17, 1948. He settled in the North, but wound up in jail on a murder charge. He died in prison in 1952. The last surviving member of the Scottsboro defendants, Clarence "Willie" Norris, sixty-four, was pardoned by Alabama governor George C. Wallace on Oct. 25, 1976, after having spent the previous six years trying to clear his name. Two days after Norris received his pardon, Ruby L. Bates Schut died of natural causes in Yakima, Wash. At the time of her death she was involved in litigation with the National Broadcasting Corporation, charging libel, slander, and breach of promise for their telecast of a docu-drama titled *Judge Horton and the Scottsboro Boys.* She was sixty-three.

Throughout the ordeal there was strong evidence of double-dealing and fraud in the prosecution's case. In 1950 Haywood Patterson wrote his memoirs, titled *Scottsboro Boy.*

REF.: Carter, *Scottsboro; CBA;* Chalmers, *They Shall Be Free;* Conrad, *Scottsboro Boy;* Crenshaw and Miller, *Scottsboro: The Firebrand of Communism;* Hays, *Trial by Prejudice;* Howe and Coser, *The American Communist Party: A Critical History;* Jordan, *The Unpublished Inside Story of the Infamous Scottsboro Case;* Nolan, *Communism Versus the Negro;* Norris and Washington, *The Last of the Scottsboro Boys;* Reynolds, *Courtroom;* Scott, *The Concise Encyclopedia of Crime and Criminals;* Tindall, *The Emergence of the New South, 1913-1945;* (DRAMA), Wexley, *They Shall Not Die.*

Screaming Mimi, The, 1949, a novel by Fredric Brown. This offbeat work, later made into a film of the same title (directed by Gerd Oswald and starring Anita Ekberg, 1958), profiles a Ripper-like killer who appears to be a neurotic, Junoesque stripper. See: **Jack the Ripper**. REF.: *CBA.*

Scribner, John C., prom. 1900, U.S., hoax. John C. Scribner, an agent for the Wells Fargo Company, perpetrated an innocently intended hoax with far reaching effects when he planted a skull in Marson's Mine, Calaveras County, Calif., around the turn of the century. The skull was "discovered" by Professor James D. Whitney, a California state geologist who then excitedly announced to the scientific community that he had uncovered a genuine artifact of the Pliocene Age.

A battery of paleontologists and anthropologists, including William Henry Holmes, director of the U.S. National Museum, descended on the site to lend their opinion. Holmes declared the skull to be genuine. Scribner kept the secret until he died, when his sister and an Episcopal minister who were privy to the deception revealed the truth of the matter. In 1902, Bret Harte wrote a short story about the affair called "To the Pliocene Skull."

REF.: *CBA;* MacDougall, *Hoaxes.*

Scroggs, Sir William, c.1623-83, Brit., jur. Served as justice of common pleas in 1676, and as England's lord chief justice from 1678-81. He was removed from office without trial for manipulating the Popish Plot trial. REF.: *CBA.*

Scrope, Henry le (Baron Scrope of Masham), c.1376-1415, Brit., consp. Nephew of Richard le Scrope. He served as royal treasurer from 1410-11. He was given authority to help negotiations with foreign countries by Henry IV and Henry V. He was executed by Henry V for conspiring to oust the king. REF.: *CBA.*

Scrope, Richard le, c.1350-1405, Brit., consp. Grandson of Henry le Scrope, noted British jurist, and son of Richard le Scrope, British chancellor and first Baron Scrope of Bolton. He served as bishop of both Coventry and Lichfield in 1386, and as archbishop of York from 1398-1405. He was a co-leader, with Bardolf and Northumberland, of the rebellion beyond Tyne in 1404, for which he was put to death at York. REF.: *CBA.*

Scrope, William le (Earl of Wiltshire), c.1351-99, Brit., polit. corr. Son of British chancellor Richard le Scrope. He served as chamberlain for the royal family of Richard II, as ambassador to Scotland in 1398, and as treasurer of England in 1398. He was executed by order of Henry IV. REF.: *CBA.*

Scrutton, Sir Thomas Edward, 1856-1934, Brit., jur. Served as King's Counsel from 1901-10, and on the High Court, King's Bench from 1910-16, presiding over the trial of George Joseph Smith. In 1916 he joined the Court of Appeal. REF.: *CBA.*

Scurlock, Josiah G. (AKA: Doc), d.1882, U.S., west. gunman. In 1868, in his home state of Tennessee, Josiah G. Scurlock got into a fight with his brother-in-law over a calf. When his brother-in-law tried to push the animal away, Scurlock threatened, "Don't you dare drive that cow beyond my gate. I'll kill you if you do." His brother-in-law persisted and Scurlock emptied both barrels of a shotgun into his body. Fleeing to South America he worked his way back through Mexico toward the U.S., hiring on as a cowhand on John Chisum's sprawling ranch. In 1876, Scurlock was involved in the killing of his friend Mark Harkins, later ruled an accidental death.

After marrying a native of New Mexico, Scurlock secured a small spread of his own but left it to hire on as one of the Mc-

Sween "Regulators" during the Lincoln County War. On Mar. 9, 1878, in Steel Springs, N.M., Scurlock and several other Regulators followed Dick Brewer in a hunt for murder suspects Billy Morton and Frank Baker, whom they captured. An argument about the fugitives on the trip back to Lincoln ended with the posse killing Baker and Morton, with Regulator William McCloskey slain in the gunfire. Scurlock also was present at the Blazer's Mill gunfight in which Dick Brewer and Buckshot Roberts were killed, and he participated in the Regulator raid on a Pecos County cow camp near Black River in Lincoln County. Scurlock, Charlie Bowdre, George Coe, Henry Brown, and three Anglos—one may have been Billy the Kid—along with eleven Mexicans attacked an Indian camp, driving off the herders and taking all the horses, killing two Indians, and wounding two others.

Western gunman Josiah Scurlock.

Tiring of cattle rustling and living as a fugitive, Scurlock rejoined his family, working on Pete Maxwell's ranch in Fort Sumner. By 1882 he was at John Chisum's ranch at Seven Rivers, N.M., and there he began cursing and threatening Fred Roth with a gun. Roth, who was carrying a baby, went inside his house, put down the baby and picked up a rifle, then went back outside and told Scurlock he was ready. Both men fired and Scurlock was hit with two or three slugs. Collapsing, he told Roth, "That's enough. You've got me, Fred. Don't shoot any more." Roth tried to fire again but was stopped by bystander Elias Bly. Scurlock died minutes later. See: **Lincoln County War; Regulator War.**

REF.: Bartholomew, *Jesse Evans;* Brent, *The Complete and Factual Life of Billy the Kid;* Burns, *The Saga of Billy the Kid;* Casey, *The Texas Border; CBA;* Charles, *More Tales of Tularosa;* Coe, *Frontier Fighter;* Coe, *Ranch on the Ruidoso;* Cunningham, *Triggernometry;* Erwin, *The Southwest of John H. Slaughter;* Garrett, *Authentic Life of Billy the Kid;* Hamlin, *The True Story of Billy the Kid;* Hendron, *The Story of Billy the Kid;* Hertzog, *A Directory of New Mexico Desperadoes;* Hunt, *Tragic Days of Billy the Kid;* Keleher, *Violence in Lincoln County;* Klasner, *My Girlhood Among Outlaws;* Lake, *Wyatt Earp;* Lamar, *The Far Southwest;* Mullin, *The Boyhood of Billy the Kid;* ____, *A Chronology of the Lincoln County War;* Nolan, *The Life & Death of John Henry Tunstall;* Nye, *Pistols for Hire;* O'Connor, *Patt Garrett;* Otero, *The Real Billy the Kid;* Raine, *Famous Sheriffs & Western Outlaws;* Rennert, *Western Outlaws;* Siringo, *History of "Billy the Kid";* ____, *Riata and Spurs;* White, *Trigger Fingers.*

Seabury, Samuel, See: **Seabury Investigations.**

Seabury Investigations, 1930-32, U.S., polit. corr. Political maneuvering between rival factions of New York City's powerful Tammany Hall organization and Republican state legislators in Albany led to one of the most sweeping probes into municipal corruption in the twentieth century. For months, rumors circulated that certain politicians in New York City had purchased municipal judgeships. Republican U.S. Attorney Charles Tuttle first drew attention to the shady practice, but Governor Franklin D. Roosevelt was slow to act, for he counted on Tammany Hall to deliver a bundle of votes to his doorstep at election time. Faced with mounting evidence of job-buying, Roosevelt reluctantly ordered an investigation into the affairs of Magistrate George Ewald of the traffic court, who was alleged to have purchased his judgeship for a cool $10,000. When New York County district attorney Charles Crain, a longtime Tammany ally, failed to secure an indictment, the governor was urged to widen the probe.

Lawyer Samuel Seabury, a 57-year-old former state supreme court jurist, was given full authority to conduct a bi-partisan probe into the practices in the lower courts of the Bronx and Manhattan. Seabury's reputation was unassailable. He was regarded as an impartial arbiter who would get to the bottom of the mire.

New York City police were routinely engaging in raids against hundreds of women who had been "shaken down" for bribe money on trumped up morals charges. A number of prominent judges were caught in a web of graft and illegal practices. Magistrate Louis Brodsky was suspended for conducting real estate and stock deals while on the bench. New York's first female magistrate, Jean Hortense Norris, was ousted in July 1931 for judicial malfeasance. The once-esteemed Norris had purchased stock in a bail bonding concern that conducted business in her court. In August, Judge Ewald, who had been the target of the original probe, was forced to resign when it was revealed that he had been selling worthless mining stock by mail. Yet, New York's embattled mayor, James John "Jimmy" Walker, stood by his friends.

Samuel Seabury

In Albany, the legislature voted to launch an even wider investigation encompassing the entire Walker administration, and the levels of corruption that permeated the city, the fifth such inquiry held since 1890. Graft was widespread. The Queens borough president, Maurice Connolly was jailed for "padding" sewer contracts to reap a personal profit. Judge Albert Vitale was removed from office for associating with members of the underworld, and Staten Island's public administrator, James Hennessey, was indicted for a $35,000 deficit in his accounts.

Mayor Walker was forced to explain nearly $246,692 in alleged stock profits he received from men who did business with the city. In his customary flippant manner, the mayor described them as "beneficences." But realizing that his political epitaph had been written, Jimmy Walker resigned on Sept. 1, 1932. He was replaced by 43-year-old Joseph McKee, better known as "Holy Joe" to his constituents. Mayor McKee immediately began shoring up the city's tattered image. He succeeded in cutting municipal spending by nearly $95,747 per day.

REF.: *CBA;* Fried, *The Rise and Fall of the Jewish Gangster in America;* Gosch and Hammer, *The Last Testament of Lucky Luciano;* Levine, *Anatomy of a Gangster;* Logan, *Against the Evidence;* Lynch, *Criminals and Politicians;* Messick, *Secret File;* Mitgang, *The Man Who Rode the Tiger: The Life and Times of Judge Samuel Seabury;* Peterson, *The Mob;* Reppetto, *The Blue Parade;* Reuter, *Disorganized Crime;* Thompson and Raymond, *Gang Rule in New York.*

Seadlund, John Henry (AKA: **Peter Anders**), 1910-38, U.S., kid.-mur. A young Minnesota drifter who wandered the Midwest during the Depression, occasionally trying his hand at minor crime, met up with 22-year-old Kentuckian James Atwood Gray. The pair continued heading South breaking into houses along the way. But in Franklin Park, Ill., they saw a new opportunity. Late in the evening on Sept. 25, 1937, they saw a luxury car being driven by a prosperous-looking old man. Cutting off the car, they abducted the man, Charles S. Ross, a Chicago greeting card manufacturer. His secretary, Florence Freihage, immediately called the police.

Kidnap victim Charles Ross, photographed by Seadlund to prove he was unharmed by his abductors.

During the next several days, as arrangements for the ransom were transmitted through a Wisconsin friend of Ross', J. Edgar Hoover himself came to Chicago to control the FBI search for the kidnap victim. They located a typewriter store where "Peter Anders" had acquired the machine the ransom note was printed on. Anders had left the address he had given, but his fingerprints told them who the kidnapper was. On Oct. 2, an elaborate plan was followed for delivery of $50,000 in ransom, though Ross was not going to be returned until Seadlund had had a chance to use the bills, which he knew would be marked. In fact, the 27-year-old man killed both Ross and Gray and dumped their bodies in a pit near Spooner, Wis.

Smiling kidnapper and murderer John Henry Seadlund.

The ransom bills started turning up all over the country, primarily in relation to race tracks. They knew from the criminal files that Seadlund was a gambler, and they followed the trail of marked bills until they knew he was heading for Santa Anita in Los Angeles. FBI agents manned the betting windows, and when, on Jan. 14, 1938, Seadlund showed up with a marked bill, he was immediately arrested. He readily confessed both to the kidnapping and to the double murder and showed the agents where the bodies were hidden. Most of the money was recovered. Seadlund was found Guilty of kidnapping and murder and was executed in the electric chair within two months.

REF.: Alix, *Ransom Kidnapping in America; CBA;* Messick, *Kidnapping;* Nash, *Almanac of World Crime;* ____, *Bloodletters and Badmen;* Whitehead, *The FBI Story.*

Seager, George, c.1671- , Brit., burg. George Seager ran off to sea and joined the crew of the *Ruby*, a British man-of-war, but he proved a less than trustworthy seaman. For stealing from the captain and his fellow crewmen, he was shackled in chains, keelhauled, and whipped at the mast. When these brutal punishments failed to improve his behavior, the captain put Seager ashore near Plymouth, England. He begged for money along the road, and soon landed in Portsmouth, where he joined the military regiment of Sir John Gibson, a Scottish soldier serving William of Orange.

Assigned to guard duty one night, Seager instead went into town and played cards at the local alehouse. The corporal of the guard found Seager playing a game of all-fours. He was taken to the jail and ordered to run a gauntlet of rope-whips six times, a punishment reserved for hardened criminals.

Seager was sent to Belgium where he robbed a Capuchin friar in the confessional booth. He waited until the friar had received the confession of a young townswoman. "Reverend father," he said. "I perceived the young gentlewoman whom you just now confessed gave you something. But let it be more or less, unless you surrender it to me, for I have most need of it, I will shoot you through the heart, although I was sure to be hanged this very moment for it." The friar handed over two coins. Seager deserted his regiment to return to England, where he committed a number of burglaries around London and Westminster.

George Seager was finally apprehended for stealing items valued at £250 from the house of Lord Cutts. He was hanged at Tyburn on Jan. 27, 1697, for burglary.

REF.: *CBA;* Smith, *Highwaymen.*

Seaman, William (AKA: William Saunders, William King), d.1896, Brit., burg.-mur. While languishing in prison, William Seaman plotted the murder of 77-year-old John Goodman Levy, who swindled Seaman out of £70 in stolen goods before Seaman went to jail. Upon his release, Seaman entered Levy's home on Apr. 4, 1896, finding Levy and his 35-year-old maid, Sarah Gale, alone on the premises. Seaman bludgeoned Gale to death, and then slit Levy's throat. Police arrived minutes after concerned neighbors contacted them.

Seaman found himself trapped on the roof. Rather than surrender to the police, he attempted a perilous forty-foot jump. His fall was broken by a passerby, which, for the time being at least, saved his life. He was arraigned at the Thames Police Court on a charge of murder after he sufficiently recovered from his injuries. The trial was held at the Old Bailey before Justice Hawkins. Seaman was found Guilty, and executed on June 9, 1896. He was one of three murderers hanged at Newgate that day, the last triple execution in Britain.

REF.: Brock, *A Casebook of Crime; CBA;* Dilnot, *Celebrated Crimes;* Logan, *Masters of Crime;* ____, *Wilful Murder;* Stevens, *From Clue to Dock;* Wensley, *Forty Years of Scotland Yard.*

Searcy, Charles J. (AKA: Texas Jack), prom. 1890s, U.S., rob. Richmond, Va., was appalled to its cultivated core in June 1894 when a Chesapeake and Ohio train was held up just outside of the city and $50,000 taken from the Adams Express car. The governor offered $1,000 reward leading to the arrest of the outlaws. Weeks later, Pinkerton detectives surrounded a cabin in the wilds near Cumberland, Md., and flushed out Charles J. "Texas Jack" Searcy and Charles Morganfield, the train robbers. Both men were identified by Adams guards B.F. Crutchfield and H. Murry as the two men who blew the bolted door off the express car with dynamite. Searcy and Morganfield (or "Morgan") confessed and revealed that the money was hidden near Calverton. All but $5,000, which the two men used as traveling funds, was recovered.

Searcy and Morgan were sent to prison for eight years. Their activities were unthinkable by Richmond standards. Train robbing was the lore of the past, something that happened "way out west," not in civilized Richmond, Va. Yet, as the century turned, this sleepy city had its intense, albeit limited, share of riot, murder, and vice.

REF.: *CBA;* Horan, *The Pinkertons.*

Sears, Barnabas Francis (Barney Sears), 1902-85, U.S., crim. law. Despite hundreds of legal triumphs, Chicago's legendary trial attorney Barney Sears was best known for his prosecution of public officials in the 1970s for the raid on a Black Panther apartment during which two members were murdered.

Sears was admitted to the Illinois Bar Association in 1926, and practiced in Chicago from 1942 to 1985. In 1960, he gained prominence as the special prosecutor during the Summerdale police scandal trial in which eight police officers were convicted. The case led to sweeping departmental reform. During the Black Panther case, Sears once again took on corrupt officials but met with more resistance than success. Sears not only lost the case against Cook County state's attorney Edward V. Hanrahan and thirteen others, but also received death threats, wiretaps on his telephone, and legal harassment from the chief criminal court judge of Cook County. Shortly after the Black Panther case, Sears was offered but declined the chance to prosecute the Watergate Scandal. In 1975, for his efforts, his fellow trial lawyers lauded Sears and gave him an award for "Courageous Advocacy." On Nov. 19, 1980, Sears, fell into a wall in his Chicago apartment, and broke his neck. He had earlier suffered a heart attack. See: **Hanrahan, Edward V.** REF.: *CBA*.

Seaton, Terry, c.1952- , U.S., (wrong. convict.) mur. At 5:45 a.m. on May 19, 1971, Grover Beard stopped at the Davis Bakery in Carlsbad, N.M., to visit his friend William L. Davis. The 65-year-old baker lay on the floor of the frying room, his mutilated corpse castrated and covered with hot grease. Several miles away, the bakery's cash register was found in a ditch.

Eddy County chief deputy LeRoy Payne and district attorney investigator Ray Magness had no clues in the case until 24-year-old James Williams told the sheriff's department that he and Terry Seaton had robbed a clothing store in Clovis the night Davis was murdered. Williams continued, explaining that they then drove 110 miles south to Roswell, before continuing another seventy-six miles south to Carlsbad. The times which Williams gave during the trial testimony would have given the alleged bandits only ten minutes to travel the last leg of their journey, requiring a speed of about 426 miles per hour; a fact which Santa Fe public defender Robert Rothstein noted much later, but which officials at the time ignored. It was not until Williams repeated his statement a third time, on May 17, 1972, before Sheriff Tom Granger, that he mentioned the stolen cash register. He repeated his statement to District Attorney Pat Hanagan. During this time, another suspect was being investigated by the Carlsbad police.

Officer Ernie White discovered that Hubert Workman, Jr. had confessed to his sister, Ethel Marie Workman Cook, and girlfriend, Mattie Tweedy Hillman, of having had a dream in which he killed Davis. White also learned from Workman's estranged wife, Karen Mae Workman, that the suspect had threatened to kill the baker for flirting with his wife. Her mother corroborated Workman's hatred of Davis. On Apr. 10, 1972, Workman confessed to Officer White, and even showed the officer where he left the cash register—a spot within fifty yards of where it was found—but he would not consent to a lie-detector test. Not long after Hanagan interviewed Williams, he was killed in a car accident, and with a new district attorney, the case took a new turn.

J. Lee Cathey was appointed district attorney in June 1972, and assistant district attorneys Peter Fleming and Michael McCormick immediately quit. Cathey quickly replaced Magness with Carlsbad Police Chief Carl Hawkins, and by the year's end three more witnesses were found against Seaton. L.D. Bickford and Jerry Burns, fellow inmates of Seaton while he was briefly held in jail on burglary charges, said Seaton told them he killed Davis. Ted Williams, James Williams' brother, claimed he saw Seaton leaving the bakery with the cash register. Seaton turned himself in Dec. 20, 1972, the day the warrant for his arrest was issued. Attorneys Charles Feezer and Leonard May had no idea that their client, Seaton, was not the only suspect. Cathey claimed he was never aware of the investigation into Workman, nor did he know of any file on the man's confession. It was learned later by Rothstein and former Santa Fe public defender director Steven Farber, who joined Rothstein on behalf of Seaton, that information on Workman was in the district attorney's file on Seaton. At the time, McCormick felt Workman was not a viable suspect. On the evidence of prosecution witnesses, Seaton was found Guilty after three days of testimony and thirty-five minutes of jury deliberation in May 1973. He was sentenced to life imprisonment.

Rothstein took up Seaton's case in Fall 1975, after he learned that the wrongly convicted man had already passed a lie-detector test in prison. He also learned that state police officer Larry Allen had investigated the conviction of Seaton in 1973 and 1974, and concluded in October 1974 that "there is no reasonable doubt on whether or not Terry Seaton is guilty...With the evidence they had, I don't see how they convicted the accused." In February 1976, Burns recanted his statement to Rothstein, but disappeared afterwards and did not testify. Bickford followed suit and in March 1978, he recanted his testimony too. At the time Bickford was, and is, serving a 120-year sentence for two murders—one very similar to the Davis murder, with the body found near where the cash register was found (a crime Bickford denies)—and admitted he had fabricated his entire testimony against Seaton. He added that his story had been arranged by police and that he was even given $200 by the district attorney's office.

When Bickford had made his statement against Seaton, he was being held on three felony charges. On July 17, 1972, Cathey allowed Bickford to plead guilty to misdemeanor charges. He was given six months, four of which were suspended, and six months probation. Soon, James Williams also recanted. He told Rothstein and Farber that he had been given the file on the Davis murder and if he agreed to implicate his friend, the charges against him would be dropped. Williams claimed that officers even drove him to where the cash register was found. Cathey, Granger, McCormick, and Payne denied the deals that Williams described.

Eight of his eleven charges had been dropped however, and after he pleaded guilty to the remaining three he was sentenced to one to five years in prison; a sentence which was suspended after five months in jail by District judge D.D. Archer. Although Ted Williams never recanted his testimony, he never appeared against Seaton at the subsequent second trial, for he suffered a mentally induced attack which prevented him from testifying at Seaton's habeas corpus hearing. Seaton was released after six-and-a-half years in prison and he immediately sued for damages. In 1983, the courts awarded $118,000 from Eddy County, the sheriff, and deputy. This verdict was not appealed. Attorneys' fees of $217,500 were also paid by the state. REF.: *CBA*.

Seay, Abraham Jefferson, 1832-1915, U.S., jur. Served as prosecuting attorney in Crawford County, Mo., from 1865-71. He was nominated to the court of the Indian Territory by President Benjamin Harrison in 1890. REF.: *CBA*.

Sebastian, Saint, d.c.288, Roman., her. Participated in armed services under Emperor Carinus and Emperor Diocletian. He was put to death by order of Diocletian for converting others to Christianity despite the emperor's opposition. REF.: *CBA*.

Secret Service Agency, 1865- , U.S., law enfor. agen. A branch of the U.S. Treasury Department, the Secret Service Agency is the most rapidly expanding federal law enforcement unit, and is responsible for the discovery and arrest of counterfeiters, protecting the president of the United States, and guarding the Treasury Department's vaults and buildings.

Formed in 1865, the Secret Service was approved by Abraham Lincoln during his last cabinet meeting to function as the first general law enforcement agency of the federal government. Additional responsibilities, like fighting the Ku Klux Klan, capturing spy rings and opium smugglers, and exposing land frauds and extortion rackets, were added on over the years but soon were transferred to other agencies. In 1901, the protection of the president, which evolved into the Secret Service's primary focus, became all-important after the assassination of President William McKinley. Over the years the Secret Service became responsible for protecting the president-elect, former presidents and their wives, widows, and children under sixteen. In 1968 the agency was made responsible for the safety of major presidential and vice presidential candidates and, in 1971, for the protection of visiting heads of states and foreign dignitaries. When President John F. Kennedy was assassinated in 1963 the agency had a $5.4 million budget and 389 agents. By 1980 the staff had increased to 1,552 agents and a $157 million budget. A large portion of the agency's time is spent checking on possible assassins from a list of about 400 primary suspects, many with a history of mental instability or violence who may be put under twenty-four hour surveillance and require fourteen or fifteen agents when a president visits a city.

Precautions observed when a president travels or appears in public include bulletproof glass shields and heavy armor plating on the floor of his reviewing stand. Bulletproof cars, windows, and tires outfit the presidential vehicle and agents are armed with walkie-talkies, Uzi submachine guns or M-16 rifles, and .357 magnums as helicopters fly overhead to watch for snipers and suspicious aircraft. Psychiatrists drill Secret Service employees on the profiles of potential assassins which, since the 1975 attacks on President Gerald Ford, includes women. Agents, who usually wear sunglasses regardless of the weather, memorize the faces of the "400" suspects. A week before a president's visit they stream into the city to create a "sanitized zone." If the president is expected to be near water, military divers check undersea for bombs, and offshore patrols are provided by the Coast Guard.

The White House protection includes examination of all incoming packages and food, hidden television cameras on the grounds, and seismic sensors on the lawns, as well as a bomb shelter in the East Wing and a tunnel leading to a helicopter for an emergency exit. Rumors that the Secret Service dictates actions to the president have been disproved more than once. When Kennedy was killed there were no agents on top of his automobile at his request, though their presence on top of presidential cars was a standard method of blocking a potential assassin's line of vision. President Calvin Coolidge apparently was extremely entertained for a week by the Secret Service. Once, finding a button on the wall, he pressed it and was quickly surrounded by several agents. Coolidge innocently asked why they were there. Then he pressed the button repeatedly for seven days, forcing his guards to charge in to his office while he kept a poker face. A suspicious agent finally spied on him and saw Coolidge press the alarm. The wires to the button then were cut, and Coolidge was disappointed to find that his trick no longer worked. According to a popular myth in the service this is why "Silent Cal" did not smile again during his presidency.

REF.: Baughman and Robinson, *Secret Service Chief;* Blumenthal, *Last Days of the Sicilians;* Brown and Neal, *The U.S. Secret Service; CBA;* Demaris, *The Director;* Dorman, *The Secret Service Story;* Kobler, *Al Capone;* Ottenberg, *The Federal Investigators;* Scott, *The Concise Encyclopedia of Crime and Criminals;* Toledano, *J. Edgar Hoover;* Unger, *FBI;* Watters and Gillers, *Investigating the FBI;* Whitehead, *The FBI Story.*

Seddon, Frederick Henry, 1871-1912, Brit., mur. Frederick Seddon was an exceptionally vain and greedy individual whose obsession with money led him down a path of ruin in the late summer of 1911. At the time he held down a respectable position with the London and Manchester Industrial Insurance Company, and owned a large, pleasant house at Tollington Park, Islington. Seddon resided there with his wife Margaret Ann, their five children, his aging father, and a servant girl whose mental faculties were suspect. As District Superintendent for Islington, Seddon's income was fairly sizeable. But the bulk of his earnings were rolled over into real estate investments with only the bare minimum reserved for household expenses. Watching his earnings compound seemed to be Seddon's only pleasure in life.

In July 1910, Eliza Mary Barrow, a woman of singularly disagreeable habits presented herself at Seddon's door to inquire about lodgings in the Tollington Park home. Seddon agreed to rent out three unfurnished rooms on the upper floor in return for twelve shillings a week. The 49-year-old Barrow agreed to the arrangement, having just departed the home of her cousin, Frank Ernest Vonderahe, on less-than-amicable terms. Barrow moved in on July 25 with her 8-year-old protegé, Ernie Grant, an orphan boy she had taken under her wing and who referred to her as his "Chickie." Joining them in the attic apartment on Tollington Park were Mr. and Mrs. Hook, who had known Barrow for years and were young Ernie's aunt and uncle. A few weeks after the boarders had settled in, Barrow handed Hook a note, presumably written by Seddon, asking them to pack their things at once and leave. A stormy scene followed in which Hook accused Seddon of trying to lay claim to her estate. "I will defy you and a regiment like you to get it!" Hook thundered as he took leave.

Murderer Frederick Seddon and his wife Margaret on trial at the Old Bailey.

The financial holdings that he was referring to were considerable. The spinsterish Barrow owned £1,600 worth of India Stock, as well as the Buck's Head pub and an adjacent barber shop. In addition, she had £216 deposited in the Finsbury and City of London Savings Bank as well as a sizeable amount of gold and printed notes in her safety deposit box. Eliza Barrow's yearly income was in the neighborhood of £120, and Seddon was fully aware of this when he rented the flat to her.

After the Hooks had departed, the crafty landlord contrived to gain control of Barrow's assets. In October 1910, Seddon persuaded her to assign the India Stock to him in return for his promise that he would pay a life annuity in the amount of £103 and four shillings a year. Three months after this she transferred her leasehold interest in the Buck's Head and the barber shop to Seddon for an additional £1 a week. Barrow closed her account with the Finsbury and City of London Savings Bank for good on June 19, 1911, taking out the entire £216 in gold. His objectives within firm reach, Seddon invited Barrow to accompany the family on a holiday to Southend in early August.

Later that month, Seddon sent his 15-year-old daughter Maggie to a chemist's shop on Crouch Hill to purchase a packet of Mather's Chemical Fly-papers. The label clearly stated that the papers contained arsenic poison, and the buyer was cautioned to beware. On Sept. 1, 1911, Barrow complained of stomach pains and nausea. Dr. Henry George Sworn was attended to the sickly woman, whose ailment was diagnosed as "epidemic diarrhea." For the next two weeks, he administered various medicines and cure-alls, but her condition continued to decline. Early on Sept. 14, Seddon called the doctor to report the death of his tenant.

Burial arrangements were hastily made with a local undertaker friend of Seddon's. The poisoner was awarded a commission of twelve shillings and sixpence for the referral, which was brought up at his trial as an example of the kind of manipulative, insensitive personality Seddon had. Barrow's remains were transported to a common grave and buried before the relatives could intervene. Seddon, his wife, and his father were the only ones to pay their last respects at the Islington Cemetery in East Finchley. Several days later Frank Vonderahe paid a call on his cousin and was surprised to hear from the servant that she was "dead and buried." He returned the next day with his sister-in-law, Mrs. Albert Edward Vonderahe, to inquire into the mystery. Seddon went on the attack, demanding to know why they had not responded to his letter notifying them of Barrow's death. The couple replied that they had received no such correspondence. Seddon pulled out a carbon copy of a letter that he purportedly mailed on Sept. 14 notifying them of what had happened. A second letter addressed to the relatives dated Sept. 21 informed them that Barrow had previously "disposed of her properties and investments" in order to purchase a life annuity, which of course was no good now that she had died. Seddon also shoed Vonderahe a black-edged mourning card, bearing the maudlin inscription: "A dear one is missing and with us no more/ That voice so much loved we hear not again/ Yet we think of you now the same as of yore/ And now you are free from trouble and pain."

Vonderahe demanded to know who the owner of the Buck's Head pub was. "I am, likewise the shop next door," Seddon replied coolly. "I am always open to buy property at a price." When asked about the India Stock, Seddon was elusive. "You will have to write to the governor of the Bank of England and ask him, but everything has been done in a perfectly legal manner through solicitors and stockbrokers. I have nothing to do with it."

Not satisfied with any of this, Vonderahe demanded of the director of public prosecutions that the body be exhumed for a post-mortem. This was done on Nov. 20, and the examination revealed the presence of arsenic in the tissue. Seddon was arrested on Dec. 4, his wife six months later. "Absurd!" the accused murderer screamed. "What a terrible charge—willful murder. It is the first of our family that has ever been charged with such a crime."

The eminent barrister Marshall Hall agreed to defend Seddon, but he was never convinced of his client's innocence. "This is the blackest case I have ever been in!" he said. Margaret Ann Seddon was represented by Gervais Rentoul, who faced the formidable task of trying to convince the jury that his client had not entered into a conspiracy to poison Barrow with arsenic. The prosecution contended that Seddon had diluted the arsenic on the fly-papers in water, then added it to a cup of Valentine's Meat Juice, a prescription administered by Dr. Sworn.

The Seddon's trial opened at the Old Bailey before Justice Bucknill on Mar. 4, 1912. Attorney General Sir Rufus Isaacs established that Maggie Seddon had purchased the fly-papers in question. His key witness was the druggist, Walter Thorley, who recognized the "fair-haired girl." The tactic was roundly criticized by the defense. Marshall Hall told the court that the witness was prejudiced by the pre-trial publicity, including Maggie's photograph appearing in the newspaper. On the eighth day of the trial, the jury retired to consider its verdict. Seddon was found Guilty, but not so much because of the physical evidence against him as for the cool, dispassionate attitude he exhibited on the witness stand. To Filson Young, a courtroom spectator, there was little doubt. "It appeared as if, in fact, Seddon was convicted not because the Crown succeeded in proving his guilt, but because he failed to prove his innocence."

Margaret Seddon was acquitted of murder only because it was shown that her husband kept her in total ignorance of his affairs. Mrs. Seddon was in tears as she was led from the dock. When Justice Bucknill finished passing sentence, Seddon raised his hand and recited words familiar to every member of the Masonic Order. He swore "before the Great Architect of the Universe" that he was innocent of murdering Eliza Barrow. Bucknill, a member of the lodge, was visibly shaken, but was quick-witted enough to say that "our brotherhood does not encourage crime; on the contrary it condemns it. I pray you again to make your peace with the Great Architect of the Universe. Mercy—pray for it. Ask for it." The sentence of death was passed, and on Apr. 18, 1912, Seddon was hanged at Pentonville Prison. A crowd of 7,000 people lingered outside.

REF.: Arthur, *All the Sinners;* Barker, *Lord Darling's Famous Cases;* Bechhofer-Roberts, *Sir Travers Humphreys, His Career and Cases;* Bixley, *The Guilty and the Innocent;* Bowker, *Behind the Bar;* Brock, *A Casebook of Crime;* Browne, *Sir Travers Humphreys;* ____ and Tullett, *The Scalpel of Scotland Yard; CBA;* Cuthbert, *Science and the Detection of Crime;* Eaton, *Famous Poison Trials;* Felstead, *Sir Richard Muir;* Glaister, *The Power of Poison;* Graham, *Fifty Years of Famous Judges;* Hicks, *Not Guilty M'Lord;* Hodge, *The Black Maria;* Humphreys, *A Book of Trials;* ____, *Criminal Days;* Kingston, *Enemies of Society;* Kingston, *A Gallery of Rogues;* Lambton, *Thou Shalt Do No Murder;* Laurence, *A History of Capital Punishment;* Lustgarten, *The Murder and the Trial;* Marjoribanks, *For the Defense, The Life of Sir Edward Marshall Hall; Notable British Trials;* Pearce, *Unsolved Murder Mysteries;* Randall, *The Famous Cases of Sir Bernard Spilsbury;* Reading, *Rufus Isaacs, First Marquess of Reading;* Shew, *A Companion to Murder;* Thompson, *Poisons and Poisoners;* Thomson, *The Story of Scotland Yard;* Thorwald, *The Century of the Detective;* Townsend, *Black Cap, Murder Will Out;* Walker-Smith, *Lord Reading and His Cases;* Wilson, *Encyclopedia of Murder;* Wood, *Survivors' Tales of Famous Crimes;* (DRAMA), Meyerstein, *Heddon.*

Sedley, Bill, b.1786, U.S., rob.-mur. A steady customer of Mother Colby's at the Sure Enuf Hotel, a notorious brothel, and the most ruthless bully in the early river boat days of New Orleans, was a hulking terror named Bill Sedley. Where the legendary Mike Fink of Ohio River lore was mostly fabrication, there was no myth about Sedley. He was an out-and-out killer, a mean-streaked animal of a man who lusted for blood and was unhappy only when he did not have his claw-like hands about the throat of a victim. From Kentucky, Sedley stood six-foot-two, and he was almost as wide as a barrel. He was fond of snarling at would-be victims: "If I'm agin yer, watch out!" And Bill Sedley could be against just about anyone or anything, including a circus.

In Summer 1817, Sedley and about fifty of his flatboat thugs decided that the long-running Gaëtano Circus, located at Rampart and Orleans streets, was ruining business in the Swamp, New Orleans' wide-open vice district. Following a wild drinking bout, Sedley led his goons, all armed with knives, clubs, and a few handguns, to the site of Gaëtano's circus and broke through the barriers and into the main tent. Shrieking like demons, the flatboat men tore apart the tent, destroyed the seats, and battled the squads of constables that had hurried to the scene. The police were badly beaten and their weapons taken from them. Many men in the audience drew sword canes and pistols and engaged the ruffians, but they, too, were knocked down by the score.

Sedley then ordered the cages of the animals opened and, wielding a giant bludgeon, killed the two most dangerous animals in the menagerie as they came racing out. With one blow, he dropped a charging buffalo. Two more whacks from his club, and he split the head of a roaring tiger. Grabbing each animal, Sedley stomped up and down the street outside, dragging the bloody carcasses behind him and idiotically waving to the applauding crowds of prostitutes, pimps and cutthroats. The senseless wrecking of the circus—Gaëtano left New Orleans forever—and the slaying of the beasts bloated the already exaggerated reputation of Sedley, which he knew it would.

This impossible bully ruled the Swamp in New Orleans for another five years until his hysterical fracas with the sleazy managers of the Sure Enuf Hotel, the Contreras brothers, led to his disappearance. Rafe and Juan Contreras had leased the bar and gambling areas of the hotel from Mother Colby in 1822. Shortly thereafter, the Contreras were visited by Bill Sedley, tipsy to the eyeballs, and in the wobbly company of another broad-backed rowdy named Alex Masters. Sedley downed a dozen more drinks in the bar and then wandered alone into the gambling area. He returned within a half hour to the bar and began swearing. Masters asked him what was wrong and Sedley began to curse Rafe Contreras, screaming that he had been cheated and that the gambler had dealt "a card from his sleeve!"

"He ought to be taught manners," Masters counseled, adding that a knife slash across the gambler's mid-section would soon correct the misconduct. Sedley said nothing. After guzzling several glasses of liquor, he again sallied into the gambling section of the Sure Enuf, and moments later a bullet twanged into the bar area. Those at the bar dashed for the door. The other Contreras brother, Juan, who had been tending bar, ran to the door and bolted it shut. Masters began to beat on it from the outside.

Bill Sedley's voice boomed from inside the shabby hotel: "I am the offspring of the snapping turtle!" The battle was on, both Contreras brothers and Sedley attacking one another with knives, pistols, fists, teeth, and feet. The banging and thudding of the fight could be heard a full block away as furniture crashed and broke, and screams pierced the air. For twenty minutes the struggle raged; a crowd of more than 100 river boat men and tarts gathered outside.

Suddenly, the door of the Sure Enuf burst open and, his hands scuffed and his face running blood, Bill Sedley stood triumphant in the entranceway. "Everybody come inside!" he announced, sweeping his hand in the direction of the bar. "The drinks is free!" The mob howled and rushed inside. As the liquor stock was gulped down, Sedley drank from the jagged edges of a broken bottle and waited silently as Masters bound up one arm that had been splinted by a pistol ball. The celebrants finally discovered the Contreras brothers. Beneath a pile of broken tables and chairs, the thugs and whores found Juan Contreras. His throat had been slashed. Also dead, and bent backward over the faro table he had illegally operated, was Rafe Contreras. Sedley's hunting knife was still sticking in his chest; he had been killed by one thrust that had split his heart.

Sedley had no fear of the law; New Orleans constables would never dare to enter the Swamp to arrest him. But the many Mexican friends of the Contreras were another matter and, upon reflection hours later, Sedley thought it prudent to vacate not only the premises of the Sure Enuf, but the city altogether. He slipped into the bayous, crossed Lake Pontchartrain, and was soon working his way up the Natchez Trace where he joined other early pariahs in that outlaw-infested area. He never returned to New Orleans. See: **Sure Enuf Hotel; Swamp, The.**

REF.: Asbury, *The French Quarter;* Anthony, *Paddle Wheels and Pistols;* Baldwin, *The Keelboat Age on Western Waters;* Blair, *Mike Fink, King of the Mississippi Keelboat Men;* Cable, *Old Creole Days;* ____, *Strange True Stories of Louisiana; CBA;* Fremaux, *New Orleans Characters; History of the New Orleans Police Department* (Anon.); Tinker, *Creole City, Its Past and Its People.*

Sedov, Lev Lvuvich (Leon Sedov, AKA: Martin), d.1938, Fr., (unsolv.) mur.? The son of banished Soviet leader Leon Trotsky, Lev Lvuvich Sedov, visited a Paris hospital for an operation on his stomach and died while recuperating on Feb. 18, 1938.

Four days after his operation, attendant physicians said Sedov had considerably improved and his personal nurse was removed. On Feb. 14, he was seen wandering the halls naked and delirious. The surgeon who operated on Sedov was puzzled by the young man's inexplicable death. Although Sedov was officially listed as having died of natural causes, the doctor did not believe that was the case, and even asked Sedov's wife if her husband had suicidal tendencies. Sedov had registered at the hospital under the alias Martin to protect himself. Prior to the death of Sedov, Trotsky had feared that the Soviet GPU would kill his son. This statement followed the murder of Dimitri Navachine on Jan. 21, 1937, and the theft of his own archives dealing with suppressed information of the Russian Revolution. From his exile in Mexico, Trotsky wrote an open letter to magistrate M. Penegal of the Inferior Court, Department of the Seine. In his letter he blatantly denounced and accused the GPU of having murdered his son. He claimed that the secret police had killed sick people in the past by expediting their illnesses, thus killing opponents under the guise of death by natural causes. The GPU organization had previously attempted to kill Sedov, the GPU constantly watched his every move, and the GPU greatly desired the death of Sedov. No proof however, was ever uncovered against the GPU.

REF.: *CBA;* Dewar, *Assassins at Large.*

Seefeld, Adolf, 1879-1936, Ger., mur. Adolf Seefeld, a 29-year-old watchmaker apparently first raped and killed a boy in 1908. As he journeyed through Germany during the next twenty-eight years, he killed at least eleven other boys by feeding them a concoction he made from poisonous toadstools. He was caught in 1935 and executed on May 23, 1936.

REF.: *CBA;* Nash, *Almanac of World Crime;* Wilson, *Encyclopedia of Murder.*

A belly dancer entertaining guests at a scandalous Herbert Barnum Seeley dinner party.

Seeley Dinner Scandal, 1896, U.S., morals. Extravagance among the American rich reached the ridiculous in the mid-1890s. The normally sumptuous feasts and elegant balls society offered up suddenly exploded in cost and attendance, until participants were crowded out of the largest mansions and into the sprawling restaurants. One of the most famous eateries equipped to handle such Belshazzar fêtes, as well as having a reputation for hosting raucous parties for the rich, was Sherry's restaurant in New York. Bachelor dinners, where guests dashed dozens of expensive wine glasses against the wall after each toast, had become a tradition there. (Carpenters built a fake wall at Sherry's to protect the original; so well decorated was this removable wall that patrons could not tell it from the real one. "Otherwise," a society scribe pointed out, "they would have considered themselves cheated out of a share of due enjoyment.")

Sherry's became, on the fateful night of Dec. 19, 1896, the host to yet another bachelor party, an affair that owner Louis Sherry would regret for the remainder of his days. The bash was sponsored by a skittering social upstart named Herbert Barnum Seeley, who quit West Point in favor of establishing his identity within the social ranks. To ingratiate himself with the super rich, Seeley used the considerable fortune (almost $4 million) left to him by his grandfather, showman P.T. Barnum. When Seeley's brother Clinton announced his forthcoming marriage to the desirable Florence Tuttle, Herbert Seeley decided to hold a bachelor dinner to end all bachelor dinners.

At first, Seeley went to Delmonico's, but that august restaurant proved unsuitable for his plans. Sherry's was next selected. Seeley demanded the use of the largest private room on the second floor of the restaurant. Such space was necessary, he explained, to accommodate his special guests; most of the invited were fellow members of the regal Larchmont Yacht Club. Privacy was of great importance, Seeley pointed out to the restaurant manager, M. Flaurand. He intended to provide his guests with something "extraordinarily spicy" in addition to the greatest array of beverages and food ever seen along the banquet circuit.

The spice would come in the way of special entertainment. Dancing girls would perform in the altogether. When the booking agent quoted the price to Seeley, the budding tycoon thundered: "Damn the expense! Go ahead!"

Fifty of New York's most illustrious social lions attended the *affaire Seeley,* including Clarence A. Postley, who was commodore of the Larchmont Yacht Club, and fellow yachtsmen, H.W. Harris and Charles Tobias, the father of the two Seeley brothers. The dancers who were scheduled to cavort on table tops and strip naked before their esteemed patrons consisted of a trio of "artists"—Cora Routt, Minnie Renwood, and a slinky Algerian named Ashea Wabe. The last-named was the star of the show, the very same belly-dancer who had caused hearts to hammer at the Chicago World's Fair of 1893, she being the notorious "Little Egypt."

Police Captain George Chapman, whose ferocious exterminations of vice in the district had earned him the sobriquet "Czar of the Tenderloin," was informed on the night of the stag party that "obscene" dancing was going on at Sherry's. The man who brought the word to "Old Whiskers" Chapman claimed to be the father of one of the dancers and charged that his lovely daughter was being forced to strip against her will before a group of wealthy lechers. (The father was really a disgruntled Broadway agent named Phipps, taking revenge upon Seeley and Sherry's for not engaging his own performers in the affair.)

Captain Chapman led a raid into Sherry's, bounding up the stairs with six detectives panting after him. He broke into Seeley's private party just as the guests were beginning to grow tipsy on their ever-flowing champagne. The dancers were about to go into their "lewd" acts when Chapman burst into their dressing room, mistaking that for the private party room. The screams of the half-dressed girls brought Seeley and his guests on the run, and a swearing match between cop and citizen ensued.

Suddenly Chapman looked about and recognized one distinguished gentleman after another. He abandoned the idea of arresting the entire group and stammered out a lecture on morals to the indignant civic leaders, departing with the shot: "You should all be ashamed of yourselves!" A few minutes after Chapman and his plainclothesmen left, Ashea Wabe did her "Little Egypt" number dressed only in "a Zouave jacket and a pair of lace knickerbockers." She had planned to discard these cumbersome garments with a naked belly-quaking finale, but she and the guests, thoroughly deflated by Chapman's interruption, thought better of it and the party quickly fizzled into mumbled farewells.

The press held the stag dinner all over again in its pages. What was to become the greatest sensation of the era was blared in the New York *World* headline: "FUNNY RAID AT SHERRY'S." The deck beneath declared: "Capt. Chapman and a Squad Invaded a Private Dinner Party; Heard of a Naughty Dance; Report that a Woman Was to Entertain Fifty Revellers in a Shocking Way." The press went wild with the story. Some newspapers reported that "Little Egypt" had worn only a pair of stockings. Others stated that she did her wicked belly dance on top of a table wearing only a diaphanous veil. Still others insisted that she wore nothing at all and, "after drinking a lot of champagne, had executed the same dance for guests individually." The *World* and William Randolph Hearst's *Journal* battled to see which paper could devote more muckraking columns to the affair. (At the time, according to Hearst's biographer, W.A. Swanberg, the newspaper czar himself was escorting about town "two very lovely young sisters, Millicent and Anita Willson," who, as members of the dancing troupe called "The Merry Maidens," were appearing at the Herald Square Theater in *The Girl From Paris,* a risqué show which featured "high kicking dances in which shapely, silk-clad legs emerged from fleecy ruffles.")

Probably the citizen most angered by the Sherry's fiasco was Theodore Roosevelt, who was then police commissioner. He had been accused of being present at the affair. Roosevelt exploded and ordered wholesale raids on every public place which even suggested an exposed ankle. But nothing came of Roosevelt's fulminating. Oddly, some of Seeley's guests, including a family doctor who had been present "in case anyone was overcome with indigestion or nervous shock," preferred "unlawful entry" charges against Captain Chapman. These charges were eventually dismissed, but Chapman's prolonged trial further exploited the Seeley party. Oscar Hammerstein quickly put together a production called *The Silly Dinner,* which audiences thought more licentious than what reportedly went on at the real party. Ashea Wabe capitalized handsomely on the scandal by commanding heavy salaries for years to belly dance before hordes of wide-eyed men. Theater marquees billed her as "Little Egypt, the star of the Awful Seeley Dinner."

Seeley's fête did inspire a few high-hatted flesh-lovers to creative invention. One James L. Breeze, well-to-do bachelor, gave a party in his home on Twenty-third Street. The feature attraction was a centerpiece shaped in the form of a huge pie. Covered by ornate garlands, a hidden trap was at the bottom of the pie. "When the festivities had reached a certain stage," one social historian related, "the trap was wound up, the pie opened, and from it sprang, to dance among the guests, a beautiful girl, described by one who claimed to have been present as 'covered only by the ceiling.'"

REF.: Amony, *Who Killed Society?;* Beebe, *The Big Spenders; CBA;* Crockett, *Peacocks on Parade;* Crowinshield, *Manners for the Metropolis;* Swanberg, *Citizen Hearst;* Wecter, *The Saga of American Society.*

Segee, Robert Dale, 1930- , U.S., arson-mur. Tormented by a recurring nightmare of a scowling woman coming at him out of a fiery grave, Robert Segee confessed to Ohio Fire Marshal Harry Callan that it was he who set fire to a Ringling Brothers and Barnum & Bailey Circus tent in Hartford, Conn., on July 6, 1944—a crime that had puzzled police for nearly six years.

Segee was a pyromaniac and murderer whose crimes dated back to Sept. 5, 1938, when he bludgeoned 9-year-old Barbara Driscoll to death on a river bank near the Portsmouth, N.H., railroad yard. He was only eight at the time, and was not considered a prime suspect because of his age. On Mar. 16, 1943, he killed a night watchman who caught him in the act of setting fire to a warehouse in Portland, Maine. That same year Segee assaulted and killed a small boy on a public beach at Cape Cottage, Maine, who had "talked mean" to him. His fourth murder occurred while he served in Japan with the Army of Occupation in 1949. He strangled a Japanese boy, resulting in his expulsion from the armed forces.

Between 1939 and 1946, the year he moved from Portland, Maine, to Ohio, Segee admitted setting at least twenty-five major fires, including the Hartford blaze, which claimed 169 lives in less than six minutes. As a consequence of the fire, James Haley, vice president of Ringling Brothers, and general manager George Smith were sentenced to prison and forced to settle $2 million in damage claims.

Segee claimed to have been plagued by the same horrible nightmares for several years. The face of a woman appeared in one, but worse yet was the Indian riding bareback on a flaming stallion. The mysterious rider commanded Segee to set the fires and then to flee the premises, according to his later statements to psychiatrists. Unlike the typical arsonist who lingers at the scene of his crime, Segee avoided police detection by quickly returning home. State fire prevention officials were finally alerted to Segee's possible involvement in the circus fire, and a score of lesser alley fires in Circleville, Ohio, by 28-year-old William Graham, who was held for questioning by police. Segee signed a confession on June 30, 1950. He also confessed to murdering Barbara Driscoll and the other three victims.

Psychiatrists and state medical officers examined Segee for six weeks at the state hospital in Lima. He was declared sane and fit to stand trial. After pleading guilty to setting several smaller fires in Circleville, Segee was sentenced to from four to forty years in prison for arson. He was released from parole supervision on May 1, 1959. REF.: *CBA*.

Sehested, Hannibal, 1609-66, Den., embez. Joined court of Christian IV in 1632. He served in the state council from 1640-51, and as stadholder of Norway in 1642. After being accused of embezzlement he lost authority and had his land confiscated by the government. He won back the sovereign's respect after negotiating the Treaty of Copenhagen clearing problems with the Swedes in 1600. In return for his work, he was named lord high treasureer and was again able to serve in the state council. REF.: *CBA*.

Seimsen, John, See: **Dabner, Louis.**

Sejanus, Lucius Aelius, d.31 A.D., Roman., consp.-mur. Named commander of praetorian guard by mentor Emperor Tiberius Caesar in c.15 A.D. He was later put to death by order of Tiberius under suspicion of poisoning Drusus Caesar, the emperor's son, in 23 A.D., and causing the mysterious death of Vipsania Agrippina. REF.: *CBA*.

Selby, Joseph Franklyn, c.1907- , and **Collins, Clarence**, c.1935- , and **Morgan, Maggie**, prom. 1959, and **Bounds, Patra Mae**, prom. 1959, U.S., mur. Accountant Joseph Franklyn Selby lived in the Afton Oaks neighborhood of Houston, Texas, with Wilma Selby, his wife of thirty years. The last five years of the marriage, according to Selby, were not so happy, however, so in the fall of 1958 he decided to have his wife killed.

Selby claimed that his wife's treatment of their daughter Marcia was reprehensible. She would hit her and throw things at her, once even scratching him as Selby tried to break up a fight. He maintained that Mrs. Selby had a quick temper and a violent streak of jealousy. Apparently Mrs. Selby would question his faithfulness quite often, checking his shirt collars for lipstick, following him home from work, or asking him who he had just spoken to on the phone. Once she allegedly told him that if she could not have him, no one would because she would kill him. This allegation coupled with Selby's assertion that his wife told him of threatening phone calls she had received concerning his life, led Selby to conclude that since it was apparent his wife planned to kill him, he would have her killed first. He contacted Pastra Mae Bounds a woman at a massage parlor he frequented, who agreed to put Selby in touch with another woman who would procure him a killer. Selby was introduced to Maggie Morgan and an arrangement was made to have his wife killed, by any means except a knife, for $1,500. Selby gave Morgan a picture of his wife and a key to their house and left the rest up to her.

On Nov. 16, 1959, Selby informed Morgan that he and his wife would be home from dinner about 7:30 p.m.. After dinner Selby and his wife drove home in seperate cars. He made one stop along the way, long enough for Clarence Collins to pull the trigger twice on the .22-caliber pistol and kill Mrs. Selby. Evidence against the four conspirators was almost non existent. But police finally arrested and charged all of them with murder after hours of third-degree grilling. Bounds, who became the prosecution's star witness, was taken by two officers down an isolated dirt road near Humble, Texas. The officers intimidated the woman with death threats, twisted handcuff chains around her fingers, and told her what to say on the witness stand. Collins, unaware of his rights, did not realize that the racially driven officers were breaking the law when they incarcerated him for vagrancy under the name of Joe Smith. He was finally taken to a Texas Ranger station and, exhausted from lack of sleep, confessed. The four were found Guilty; Selby and Morgan received life sentences, Collins was sentenced to ninety-nine years in prison, and Bounds was given a ten-year suspended sentence. Even with the admission by Bounds of torture and the obvious illegalities in the treatment of Collins, attorney William F. Walsh could not convince the state that constitutional rights had been denied. The state's attorney argued that Collins was denied his rights because he did not know what his rights were. His conviction and sentence were upheld.

REF.: *CBA; Wyden, The Hired Killers.*

Selby, Norman (AKA: **Kid McCoy, The Real McCoy**), 1873-1940, U.S., rob.-asslt.-mansl. Norman Selby, a rough and tumble prize-fighter from the bare-knuckle era, left behind an enduring cliche in American slang—"the real McCoy." Although during Prohibition the phrase meant pure unadulterated alcohol, it originated before the turn of the century when Selby was in his heyday. "I'm in a saloon with a charming lady as usual," the fighter recalled. "A drunk is making passes at her. I try to brush him off without too much fuss. 'Beat it,' I says. 'I'm Kid McCoy.' He laughs and says: 'Yeah? We'll I'm George Washington.' I have to clip him a short one and down he goes. He wakes up ten minutes later, rubs his jaw, and says, 'Jeez, it was the real McCoy!'" The oft-told tale was recounted by Damon Runyon and other journalistic lions who wrote of Selby's checkered career in and out of the prize ring.

Ex-boxing champ Norman "The Real McCoy" Selby, convicted of manslaughter in the death of his live-in lover.

Selby, calling himself Kid McCoy, won the middleweight and welterweight championships in 1895 and 1897. Selby flattened the reigning champion, Tommy Ryan, in a grueling fifteen-round affair after bluffing his opponent into thinking he was something less than advertised. Selby had sent a letter to Ryan before the bout begging him to "go easy," and carry him for a few rounds. Ryan eased up on his calisthenics and was wholly unprepared for what was to follow in the ring. "The bastard played possum!" cried Ryan after losing the decision.

Selby retired in 1897 at the age of twenty-four. He was worth half-a-million dollars, part of which was invested in a Broadway cabaret that became the favorite watering hole for celebrities of show business and the sporting world. In 1900 Selby was lured out of retirement for a bout with "Gentleman" Jim Corbett who beat him easily. Within the next two decades Selby married nine different women each one of whom took a sizeable chunk of his assets in the divorce settlement. In 1924, his fortune all but gone, the out-of-shape ex-fighter moved to Los Angeles to work as a Hollywood movie extra. He accepted employment as a security guard in an aircraft factory and became friends with Hub Kittle, a celebrated flyer and a likely suspect in a number of holdups.

Selby began a dangerous affair with Theresa Mors, the wife of Albert Mors, one of Los Angeles' leading art and antique dealers. Mors did not appreciate it when the boozing fighter fell in love with his wife. His rancor only increased when his wife filed for divorce and went to live with the "real McCoy" in an apartment at Hoover and Seventh streets. Happily in love, Selby proposed marriage and Mors readily accepted. Meanwhile, the husband filed a countersuit against his estranged wife naming Selby as corespondent. He advised the U.S. Treasury Department that Theresa Mors was involved in smuggling diamonds. By this time Selby had had enough. He warned Mors to leave her alone. Mors then had the police remove Selby from his home.

The press by now had latched on to the story and everybody had an opinion to offer. Sam Schapps, who owned a millinery store next to the antique dealer, described Selby as a dangerous opportunist bent on securing a $125,000 property settlement bound to come Mrs. Mors' way after her divorce went through. Theresa Mors began to hedge. Albert Mors began acting crazy. He stole from his wife, and then on the night of Aug. 12, 1924, moved out of the family home in the Hollywood Hills to take up residence at the Westgate Hotel. He signed an alias on the guest register.

The room overlooked an alley only a few doors away from the flat Selby and Mrs. Mors had rented. Around midnight the tenant who lived one floor below heard a dull thud coming from Selby's apartment. She then looked out her window and saw a man racing down the stairwell—Albert Mors, there was no denying the fact. Two hours later a drunken Selby appeared in a Hollywood police station asking to see the officer who had forcibly removed him from Mors' home some days earlier. "It's lucky for him he's not here," Selby stammered. "And why was that?" asked one police officer. "Hell, I'll be in the can tomorrow," he said.

The police drove Selby home and told him to sleep it off. At 3 a.m. the following morning Selby appeared at the bedroom window of Jennie Thomas, his sister. Looking haggard and drunk, Selby explained that he had just killed Theresa Mors. He then stumbled from the house and headed toward Mors' antique store where he waited patiently for the owner to arrive. Armed with a .32-caliber pistol, he captured a janitor, Mors, and a clerk, ordering them to sit quietly on one side of the room as the first customers entered. He forced the customers to surrender their cash and valuables and freed only those who appealed to him. Later that morning, Selby shot and wounded a customer who tried to escape. Fleeing from the store, he ran into Sam Schapp and his wife. "My God! What are you doing?" Schapp asked. Before they could make any sense of the situation, Selby turned his gun on them and shot them down.

Selby commandeered a passing car and tried to escape on foot but was brought down by a passing policeman. Investigators later found Theresa Mors lying dead on the floor of her apartment, neatly covered by a bed sheet and a picture of Selby perched at her side. Questioned by Captain Herman Cline of the Los Angeles police, Selby, after he had sobered up, explained that Theresa Mors had committed suicide because of her despondency over her husband's attempt to frame her on smuggling charges. He went on to say that he had struggled with her but the gun had gone off accidentally. Then, believing that he had killed the woman, Selby tried to drink himself to death but had only succeeded in passing out.

Selby was arraigned on murder, armed robbery, and assault charges. The prosecution charged that the defendant had murdered his lover because she had decided not to marry him and planned to return to New York. Defense attorney Jerry Giesler represented Selby. Under cross-examination, he demanded an answer from Mors as to why he had checked into the Westgate Hotel the night of the murder—a perplexing question that went unanswered. Giesler, whose client list would one day be studded with the names of some of Hollywood's biggest celebrities, tried to convince the jury that Theresa Mors stabbed herself with a butcher knife and then inflicted a gunshot wound. However, even he was forced to admit that such a maneuver would be difficult if she had in fact used her left thumb to pull the trigger. The murder charge was reduced to manslaughter and Selby was found Guilty after ninety-nine hours of deliberation. He was sentenced to one to ten years for manslaughter and one to fourteen years on each of the assault charges. Selby served eight years at San Quentin, during which time Governor Al Smith, Sophie Tucker, Douglas MacArthur, and Lionel Barrymore petitioned for his early release. Selby emerged as a tragic but sympathetic figure who had won himself many friends during his incarceration. He was released in 1932 and married for the tenth and last time. In 1940, the year he died, Selby reflected on his times. "It's no fun telling people you're Kid McCoy if they've heard of you before."

REF.: *CBA;* Ellis, *A Nation in Torment;* Nash, *Murder, America;* Wolf, *Fallen Angels.*

Selden, John, 1584-1654, Brit., jur. Served in Long Parliament and assisted impeachment proceedings of William Laud in 1641. He became record keeper at the Tower of London in 1641, and lay member of the Westminister Assembly in 1643. He retired from public life after Charles I was put to death. REF.: *CBA.*

Seldes, Gilbert Vivian, 1893-1970, U.S., writer. Created murder mysteries under pseudonym Foster Johns. He was also a columnist for the New York *Journal* from 1931-37, and professor and dean of the University of Pennsylvania's School of Communications from 1959-63. REF.: *CBA.*

Seleucus I (Nicator), c.358-281 B.C., Mac.-Seleucid Empire, king, assass. Served as Macedonian general for Alexander the Great. He named himself king after defeating Lysimachus in 281 B.C. He was the first of six in the Seleucid dynasty from 306-281 B.C. He expanded the empire to include Syria and Asia Minor by 301 B.C. He was murdered by Ptolemy Ceranus for political reasons, and later was succeeded by Antiochus I Soter, his son. REF.: *CBA.*

Seleucus IV (Philopator), c.217-175 B.C., Seleucid Empire, king, assass. Lost much authority after Romans defeated father Antiochus III. He was assassinated shortly thereafter, and the crown was seized by his brother Antiochus IV. REF.: *CBA.*

Seleucus V, d.125 B.C., Seleucid Empire, king, assass. Murdered by mother, Cleopatra Thea, who was reportedly poisoned by another son, Antiochus VIII, four years later. REF.: *CBA.*

Selfridge, Thomas O., prom. 1806, Case of, U.S., mansl. A scurrilous and highly fictitious report assailing the integrity of Thomas O. Selfridge was circulated throughout Boston by Benjamin Austin, a fellow lawyer, in the Summer of 1806. Enraged, Selfridge demanded that he retract the report at once. Austin refused, claiming that he had nothing to do with it.

On Aug. 4, 1806, Charles Austin, the lawyer's son, struck Selfridge over the head with a cane when the two men encountered each other on State Street. Before he could land a second blow, Selfridge pulled out a small pistol and shot and killed him. He was placed on trial for manslaughter but was acquitted on Dec. 23, 1806. The famous Boston patriot Paul Revere sat on the jury.

REF.: *CBA; A Correct Statement of the Whole Preliminary Controversy Between Tho. O. Selfridge and Benj. Austin; also a Brief Account of the Catastrophe in State Street, Boston, on the 4th August, 1806.*

Selhurst, John, d.1877, Brit., mur. For murdering his wife, John Selhurst was found Guilty and sentenced to death. Before his execution, Selhurst wrote a poetic account of his crime and what motivated him: "With her a fearful life I led,/The drink it did so fly to her head;/On the devil's tipple she used to dote,/But I cured her with a cut on the throat./I wish I could the deed undo,/And so, dear people all, must you." He was hanged in 1877 at Taunton, England.

REF.: *CBA;* Laurence, *A History of Capital Punishment.*

Seligman, Joseph, 1819-80, U.S., law enfor. off. Served on Committee of Seventy group which exposed Tweed Ring. REF.: *CBA.*

Selim I (AKA: **Yavuz, the Grim**), 1467-1520, Turk., geno. Ousted and succeeded father Bajazet II as sultan of Ottoman Empire. He caused the deaths of 40,000 Shiites while attempting to make Sunni Muslims the only members of the Muhammedan faith. REF.: *CBA*.

Selim III, 1761-1808, Turk., sultan, assass. Took control of empire after reign of uncle Abdülhamid I. He instituted reforms based on western society, and signed treaties with Austria in 1791 and Russia in 1792. He was initially allied with forces opposing Napoleon, but later joined with him and declared war against Russia and Great Britain in 1806. His reforms were cancelled by uprisings from the Janissaries in 1805 and the Yamaks in 1807. He was dethroned, jailed, and later strangled in prison by order of his successor, Mustafa IV. REF.: *CBA*.

Seliverstoff, Michael de, d.1890, Fr., gen. assass. On Nov. 18, 1890, General Michael de Seliverstoff, a former chief of the Russian Secret Police, was shot at point-blank range as he sat in a chair in his Paris hotel room. At the foot of the chair, investigators found a bloodstained letter, which they believed was delivered to Seliverstoff by his murderer. The murderer was soon identified as Stanislaus Padlewski, a member of the Russian Nihilists, a movement which advocated the overthrow of the existing social order and the institution of massive revolutionary reforms.

Some time later, a French journalist, Georges deLabruyère, published the account of how he had helped Padlewski to flee the country. Labruyère, who expressed sympathy for Padlewski's political convictions but denied active membership in the Nihilists, claimed to have a duel to fight in the Tyrol, taking a Dr. Wolf with him. Dr. Wolf turned out to be Stanislaus Padlewski, who left Labruyère in Trieste and embarked from there for the U.S. Labruyère served thirteen months in prison for his part in the escape. Padlewski was found dead, an apparent suicide, in a park in San Antonio, Texas, on Oct. 28, 1891. He was known at the time under the alias of Otto Hauser and was only identified as Padlewski in February of the following year.

REF.: *CBA;* Morain, *The Underworld of Paris.*.

Sellers, Sir Frederick Aked, b.1893, Brit., jur. Served as King's Counsel from 1935-46. He was appointed to the High Bench, King's Division in 1946, and presided over the notable murder trials of Walter Graham Rowland and Brian Donald Hume. He was named Lord Justice of Appeal in 1957. REF.: *CBA*.

Sellers, Willie Foster, prom. 1970s, U.S., pris. esc.-rob. On Oct. 12, 1978, Willie Foster Sellers robbed the Chireno, Texas, State Bank. The FBI claimed that the robber had already committed more than 500 bank robberies in the southern U.S.

Prior to Sellers' robbery of the Chireno bank, he had been convicted of bank robberies in North Carolina and South Carolina and sentenced to sixty-five years imprisonment in a federal penitentiary. Sellers had escaped from prison and was still a fugitive from Atlanta authorities when he robbed the Texas bank. Investigators discovered a hair in a ski mask used in the robbery which matched the hair on Sellers' head, and his fingerprints were found on the getaway car as well. This evidence combined with witnesses' testimony led to the robber's conviction exactly one year after the robbery, Oct. 12, 1979. He was sentenced to ninety-nine years in prison. REF.: *CBA*.

Sellis, Joseph (Sellies), d.1810, Brit., (unsolv.) mur. Sellis, a Corsican, was one of three valets to the foul-tempered Duke of Cumberland, King George III's fifth son, who lived in London at St. James's Palace. At about 3 a.m. on May 31, 1810, the duke screamed from his bedroom that he was being murdered. Christopher Neale, the valet who was on duty that night, came running and found the duke bleeding from some wounds on his head. His sword, stained with blood, lay on his bed. A servant went running to Sellis's apartment. Unable to get into the bedroom and hearing grotesque gurgling noises from within, he got help to break down the door. Inside, they found the Corsican lying in his bed, his throat cut.

A coroner's jury met several days later and viewed the scene. They decided that Sellis had wounded his employer and then committed suicide, but they left unexplained knife wounds on Sellis' back. The duke, seriously wounded, gradually recovered. In 1812, and then again in 1832, he successfully sued for libel against writers who thought they solved the mystery. The gossips had theories based on three different sexual combinations of four people: the duke, his wife, Neale, and Sellis, but probably the truth had more to do with Sellis becoming jealous as the younger Neale won the duke's favor.

REF.: Armitage, *Bow Street Runners; CBA;* Pearce, *Unsolved Murder Mysteries.*

Sellman, Edward Leon, c.1943- , and **Simmons, Tommie Bernard**, c.1947- , U.S., kid.-mur. Between Apr. 25, 1971, and Sept. 5, 1972, the bodies of seven young black women were found near the busy interstate highways in Prince Georges and Charles counties in Maryland near Washington, D.C. These murder cases have baffled police for years. The true identity of the "Freeway Phantom" remains unknown.

A year and a half after the last freeway killing, former policemen Edward Sellman and Tommie Simmons were charged with murdering 14-year-old Angela Denise Barnes, the second victim, on July 12, 1971. Unlike the Phantom's six other victims, Barnes had not been molested or strangled. Her death resulted from a gunshot wound.

Sellman had known Simmons since they were boys. They joined the Prince Georges County police department in 1970, and were assigned to patrol duty in the adjacent Fifth and Sixth districts. In fact, Sellman and Simmons did everything together, including murder. Attorney Bruce Harrison characterized their relationship as one of abnormal psychological dependence. Dr. Robert J. Brown, a psychiatry professor, called their relationship a *folie à deux* in which two individuals participate in a crime, but the stronger person influences the weaker. Simmons' actions "were precipitated by Tommie's overwhelming attraction for Eddie Sellman...that was the result of a process of thinking evolving from Tommie's childhood and youth," Harrison said. "He began showing psychological problems in his relation with Eddie Sellman."

Both men were married and had children. Three days after the body of Barnes was found off Route 228 near Waldorf, Md., Sellman's wife saw him bring a handgun into the house in a brown paper bag. He placed it behind a false fireplace. "About the fourth day he took it out of the bag, got a hammer and began to bang on it," Dorothy Sellman said. He removed the remnants of the pistol from the house, and his wife never saw them again. She waited nearly three years before reporting this incident to the FBI office in Annapolis on Mar. 21, 1974.

Simmons was arrested in the parking lot outside his Temple Hills home. At the Maryland State Police Headquarters in Waldorf, he freely confessed to his role in the Barnes slaying. On the night of July 12, 1971, the two men had been driving aimlessly around Southeast Washington in Sellman's 1968 Volkswagen. They spotted Barnes near Wheeler Road SE. "We was talking about rape. Nobody touched the girl. I was, I was scared," Simmons told police, his voice cracking.

As Simmons drove toward Maryland, Sellman warned the girl to keep still. Barnes was in the car only ten minutes before Selman fired the fatal shot. "Nobody executed that girl," Simmons added. "Sellman's not a murderer and neither am I." Simmons described the shooting as "accidental." Both men had resigned their positions on the police force early in 1971 following allegations of misconduct. Sellman went into business as a real estate salesman. Simmons worked for a loan company in Alexandria, Va.

As a result of a tip, police charged the two with murder in Charles County, where Barnes was killed. Simmons testified for the government against Sellman, and was tried separately. Dr. Ronald Dockett, associate professor of psychology at Howard University, said that "excessive stress" may have contributed to Simmons' bizarre behavior. On June 28, 1974, Simmons was found

Guilty of kidnapping, murder, and unlawful possession of a handgun. Judge John Lewis Smith, Jr. sentenced him to twenty years to life for the kidnapping, life for the murder, and one year for illegal possesion of the pistol. Following the trial, he was taken to Oxford, Wis., to begin serving his sentence.

Sellman showed no emotion when a U.S. District Court jury found him Guilty on July 25, 1974. On Aug. 22, Judge Smith imposed the same sentence against Sellman as he did against Simmons, explaining, "This was a senseless killing and there are no mitigating circumstances." Sellman was transferred to Seattle, Wash. Meanwhile, the investigation of the other Freeway Phantom murders continued. Various suspects were detained, but there were no breakthroughs. See: **Freeway Phantom Murders**. REF.: *CBA*.

Selman, John, 1839-96, U.S., west. lawman-gunman. Son of an English schoolteacher, John Selman was raised in Arkansas and moved with his family to Grayson, Texas, in 1858 at age nineteen. During the Civil War he joined the Confederate cavalry and was stationed in Oklahoma, but in 1863 deserted and went to Fort Davis, Texas, with his family. Enlisting in the state militia in 1864, Selman worked for frontier defense and soon was elected lieutenant by his neighbors. Marrying Edna de Graffenreid a year later, they moved to Colfax County, N.M., in 1869, but returned to Texas, near Fort Griffin, after a year. In the 1870s Selman was involved in several conflicts with Indians, allegedly killing several. He was also believed to have murdered a local man named Haulph.

John Selman, schoolteacher turned western lawman.

Selman became a close friend and business partner of John Larn, a gunfighter and rustler who became sheriff of Shackleford County. Selman also became acquainted with western figures Bat Masterson, Doc Holliday, "Killin'" Jim Miller, Jesse Evans, Wyatt Earp, and Pat Garrett. Though he owned a saloon and other property, Selman rustled cattle with Larn. In 1876, he was helping arrest a suspect named Hampton who was unarmed and half deaf. Neither Larn nor Selman were aware of his condition, and after Hampton apparently ignored Larn's command to stop, Selman emptied his gun into him. Larn and Selman subsequently returned to rustling. Texas Rangers were pressured to put an end to their exploits, which resulted in bushwhackings from both sides.

When Larn was arrested and murdered by a mob in early 1878, Selman fled the country. While he was gone his wife, pregnant with their fifth child, died. Selman drifted back into Lincoln County with his brother, Tom Selman later that summer and formed "Selman's Scouts," a gang of outlaws who rustled cattle and robbed stores until pressure from the U.S. Army caused them to disband. Before their break-up, in May 1878 Selman was ambushed by a local farmer enraged at his rustling, and Selman killed the man with his buffalo gun. In September, Selman murdered a gunman named Hart as they competed for leadership of a Lincoln County gang. Selman shot Hart without warning as they waited together in a cabin for a meal. The next month Selman murdered a trouble-making "Selman Scout" in a fight over a poker hand when they were camped out on the Pecos River.

In the next several years Selman drifted around the West, rustling, robbing, and occasionally working in Mexico, Texas, and New Mexico. He married again, lost his second wife, and moved to El Paso in 1888 after being cleared of rustling charges in Texas. After leading several cattle drives he was elected to the post of city constable in 1892. In 1893 he married a sixteen-year-old girl. In 1894 he murdered deputy U.S. Marshal Bass Outlaw who, while drunk, murdered Texas Ranger Joe McKidrict in a brothel. Selman was wounded in the fight and used a cane for the rest of his life.

The next year he killed the famous gunfighter John Wesley Hardin who allegedly had taken money from the body of outlaw Martin Morose, with whose wife he was having an affair, and then reneged on his promise to split the take with Selman. He killed Hardin by shooting him in the back. The murder trial resulted in a hung jury with a retrial scheduled, but Selman was killed before the case again came to court. A heavy drinker by that time, Selman was in a near stupor on April 5, 1896, when fellow lawman George W. Scarborough met him in an El Paso saloon. They stepped into an alley to discuss their fight over money Selman believed Scarborough had gotten from Morose's corpse. Scarborough fired four shots into Selman who never drew his gun. He died the next day. See: **Hardin, John Wesley; Scarborough, George W.**

REF.: Arrinton, *The Lives and Adventures of the Desperadoes of the Southwest;* ____, *The Rangers and Regulators of the Tenaha;* Bartholomew, *The Biographical Album of Western Gunfighters;* ____, *Jesse Evans;* ____, *Kill or be Killed;* ____, *Wyatt Earp;* Breakenridge, *Helldorado;* Bush, *Gringo Doctor;* Casey, *The Texas Border; CBA;* Collison, *Life in the Saddle;* Cunningham, *Triggernometry;* Delony, *Forty Years a Peace Officer;* Douglas, *The Gentlemen in White Hats;* Erwin, *The Southwest of John H. Slaughter;* Farber, *Texans with Guns;* Fulton, *Maurice Garland Fulton's History of the Licoln County War;* Gaylord, *Handgunner's Guide;* Haley, *Jeff Milton;* Hardin, *The Life of John Wesley Hardin;* Hendricks, *The Bad Man of the West;* Holloway, *Texas Gun Lore;* Horan, *The Great American West;* ____ and Sann, *Pictorial History of the Wild West;* House, *Cowton Columnist;* ____, *Oil Field Fury;* Hunter, *The Story of Lottie Deno;* ____ and Rose, *The Album of Gun-Fighters;* Hutchinson and Mullin, *Whiskey Jim;* Jensen, *Texas Ranger's Diary;* King, *Mavericks;* Madison, *The Big Bend Country of Texas;* Mangan, *Bordertown;* Martin, *Border Boss;* Metz, *John Selman;* Middagh, *Frontier Newspaper;* Nolan, *The Life & Death of John Henry Tunstall;* Nordyke, *John Wesley Hardin;* ____, *The Truth About Texas;* Parrish, *Coffins, Cactus and Cowboys;* Penfield, *Western Sheriffs and Marshals;* Plenn and LaRoche, *The Fastest Gun in Texas;* Raine, *Famous Sheriffs & Western Outlaws;* ____, *Guns of the Frontier;* Redmond, *"Four Sixes to Beat";* Rennert, *Western Outlaws;* Ripley, *They Died With Their Boots On;* Rosa, *The Gunfighter, Man of Myth?;* Rye, *The Quirt and the Spur;* Scobee, *Fort Davis, Texas;* ____, *Old Fort Davis;* ____, *The Steer Branded Murder;* Shipman, *Taming the Big Bend;* Siringo, *Riata and Spurs;* Smith, *Frontier's Generation;* Sonnichsen, *I'll Die Before I'll Run;* ____, *Ten Texas Feuds;* Taylor, *Taylor's Thrilling Tales of Texas;* White, *The Autobiography of a Durable Sinner;* ____, *Lead and Likker;* ____, *Out of the Desert;* ____, *Them Was the Days;* ____, *Trigger Fingers.*

Selz, Ralph Jerome Von Braun(AKA: The Laughing Killer), 1909- , U.S., mur. Twenty-seven-year-old Ralph Selz arrived in San Francisco in 1935 and met 58-year-old Ada Franch Rice. Rice, just arrived from Alaska where she had left her husband, the mayor of a small town, and moved to Palo Alto, Calif., with Selz and they took a cottage together. Selz killed Rice and took her body into the Santa Cruz Mountains, where he buried it in a shallow pit.

On Feb. 27, 1936, Selz was arrested for auto theft. When the police discovered that the unemployed man apparently had lots of money, they discovered he had forged Ada Rice's signature on checks. After two weeks of intense interrogation, Selz admitted killing the woman and showed the authorities where she was buried, all the time cracking jokes and laughing, thus acquiring the nickname "The Laughing Killer." He was found Guilty on March 13 and sentenced to life in prison. Serving time in the Chino State Prison, he escaped in 1945 and spent a year as a soldier in the Canadian Army before being captured again. In 1962 he escaped from the San Luis Obispo jail, but was found within three days. He was released from prison in 1966, but was returned about a year later on charges of welfare fraud.

REF.: *CBA;* Nash, *Bloodletters and Badmen.*

Seneca, Lucius Annaeus (Marcus Annaeus Seneca, AKA: Seneca the Elder), c.55 B.C.-39 A.D., Roman., jur. Authored

Controversiae, which presented seventy-four fictional cases of law and methods for arguing them. He was the father of Roman statesman Seneca the Younger. REF.: *CBA.*

Seneca, Lucius Annaeus (AKA: **Seneca the Younger**), c.4 B.C.-65 A.D., Roman., consp.-suic. Served as quaestor from 31 B.C., but was later banished to Corsica for supposedly committing adultery with emperor's niece in 41 A.D. He was called to tutor Domitius, the future Emperor Nero, in 49 A.D., and became praetor in 50 A.D. He enjoyed influence with Nero, and co-sponsored judicial and fiscal reforms in the Senate with Burrus. He later became an enemy of Nero, who eventually charged him with participating in the conspiracy of Piso. As punishment, he was forced by Nero to commit suicide. REF.: *CBA.*

Sennacherib, d.681 B.C., Assyria, king, assass. Succeeded father Sargon II and continued wars, capturing Sidon, many cities of Judah, and destroying Babylon, in 689 B.C. He was killed by his son, or sons. REF.: *CBA.*

Seqenenre II (Seqenenre Tao II), prom. 16th Cent. B.C., Egypt, king, assass. Ruled in seventeenth dynasty. Opposed King Apopi. He was brutally murdered. REF.: *CBA.*

Serafima, prom. 1946, U.S.S.R., mur. Serafima, a beautiful woman with eyes "like the clear summer sky," lived with her mother in a two room Moscow apartment in 1946. Entranced by her beauty and her estate, factory worker Udod gave her 20,000 rubles for the privilege of marrying her and he moved into her apartment. He was not happy, however, when Serafima made him sleep in the second room. After the 20,000 rubles were gone Serafima's mother began to long for the time when she and her daughter could again be alone. One morning, as Udod buckled on his boots, his recent bride smashed him over the head with a sharp piece of iron. After disposing of the body, she repainted the room to hide the bloodstains.

Serafima told her neighbors that her husband was a criminal and had gone into hiding. But police inspector Ivan Kudrin grew suspicious when he discovered that Udod had no prior police record, while Serafima's family had previously engaged in several criminal acts. Observing the recent paint job in the apartment, Kudrin continued to investigate until he turned up Udod's body in the cellar.

In early July the newspaper *Vechernaya Moskva* reported the murder to eager Muscovites who get little in the way of news about crime. Though there was no explicit information about what happened to Serafima, she was consistently mentioned in the past tense, as though she had been executed or imprisoned. REF.: *CBA.*

Sergeant, Jonathan Dickinson, 1746-93, U.S., lawyer. Helped represent New Jersey at Continental Congress from 1776-77. He later served as the attorney general of Pennsylvania, from 1777-80. REF.: *CBA.*

Sergius III, d.911, Italy, mur. Highly corrupt pope in office from 904-11. In 898 he had been driven out of Rome for attempting to snatch the papacy from newly-elected John IX. He ousted the antipope Christopher in 904, and reputedly arranged the death of Christopher and Pope Leo V in 904. His papacy, considered by scholars as one of the worst in the history of the Church, was unduly influenced by Theophylactus, with whose daughter he reportedly conceived a son, later known as Pope John XI. REF.: *CBA.*

Serhant, Robert B., 1939- , U.S., fraud. From late 1980 until September 1982, Robert Serhant, former president of an Oak Brook, Ill., commodities firm, defrauded more than 600 investors out of an estimated $22 million. The former president of Financial Partners Ltd. took money from clients, promising to invest the money in no-risk U.S. Treasury bills and further promising them a return of up to 40 percent. Instead Serhant invested the money in the commodities futures market and lost it all.

On June 28, 1983, Serhant, forty-four, was sentenced to fifteen years in prison, followed by five years probation. The judge hearing Serhant's case insisted that Serhant be taken into custody immediately following the sentencing. REF.: *CBA.*

Sérini, Jean, See: **Capriati, Antoine.**

Serpico, Francisco Vincent (AKA: **Frank**), 1936- , U.S., law enfor. off. A rugged individualist, internationally known New York detective Francisco Vincent Serpico was an honest cop. Born of Italian parents, bred in New York City, and raised in the rough Bedford-Stuyvesant section of the Bronx, he had always wanted to become a policeman. He attended night school at Brooklyn College and later graduated from City College, taking a job as a private investigator until he was ready to join the New York Police Department in 1959. Serpico was single, lived in Greenwich Village, dated a lot, and dressed in "mod" clothes. Fellow cops would compliment him on his "fantastic disguise."

Early in his career Serpico came up against police corruption when his grocer brother was shaken down by a beat policeman in the neighborhood. Complaining to the local police precinct, he was told that the fact that the man being intimidated was his brother made no difference. Further, students at the plainclothes school he attended protested that their thirty-day course took them off the streets making them miss "the nut," or police payoffs. Repeatedly frustrated when police officials ignored his complaints, Serpico began a lonely crusade against corruption and became a persecuted and hated man within the department. He began carrying several guns to protect himself from his co-workers, and often traveled with a tape recording device. Once, while trying to interest officials in investigating a "pad" (an organized system of bribes from numbers operators that was paying crooked cops $800 a month in the South Bronx district where Serpico was assigned) he was told to try to fit in and get along with others. Six months after appearing as the central witness in a perjury trial of a plainclothes officer who denied he had accepted thousands of dollars in graft, Serpico was shot in the face while arresting a narcotics suspect. In the hospital he received a card embossed with the words "With sincere sympathy." Handwritten next to that phrase was, "That you didn't get your brains blown out you rat bastard. Happy relapse."

Finally, Serpico took his story to the New York *Times.* Along with Sergeant David Durk, he charged that officials Jay L. Kriegel, Mayor John V. Lindsay's liaison to the police department, New York City Investigation Commissioner Arnold G. Fraiman, and First Deputy Police Commissioner John F. Walsh had failed on separate occasions to investigate Serpico's report on police accepting bribes in the South Bronx. The first article published in the New York *Times* series, which began on Apr. 25, 1970, created a public furor and resulted in the embarrassed mayor appointing a commission on May 21, 1970. Headed by Whitman Knapp the commission was to investigate corruption in the Manhattan police force. As the sensational and explosive eleven-month Knapp Commission uncovered a massive pattern of corruption in the force, Police Commissioner Howard R. Leary resigned, as did scores of other accused officers. On July 1, 1971, Knapp said that Mayor Lindsay "cannot escape responsibility" for the corruption, and that former Commissioner Leary had "failed to exercise leadership" during his four and a half years as commander of the nation's largest police force.

Included among the moral perversions found by the Knapp Panel Report was that Narcotics Division officers were involved in "extortion, bribery, contradictory court testimony designed to affect the release of a narcotics criminal," and in "the actual sale of narcotics." Payments were regularly made to plainclothes detectives responsible for gambling enforcement, and routine bribes or payments also were taken by officers from prostitution houses. To avoid prosecution of city violations or to insure the cooperation of police in other matters, bars, restaurants, and night clubs made payoffs, as did hotels, trucking companies, and small Spanish groceries. The commission concluded that, as of October 1971, corruption in the Manhattan police force was "an extensive, department-wide phenomenon, indulged in to some degree by a sizable majority of those on the force."

In the fall of 1971, author Peter Maas and Serpico decided

to write a book on the detective's experiences on the force. The story sold millions of copies and was made into a movie starring Al Pacino. Serpico and the actor, who comes from a similar Italian-American New York City background, spent weeks together and became friends as Pacino prepared for his role in the movie "Serpico." Retired on a disability pension in 1974, at the age of thirty-eight, Serpico became a self-exile abroad, eventually living in Switzerland in a small chalet on his $12,000 a year pension from the New York Police Department and on the substantial percentage he received from the Paramount movie based on his life.

As a result of the gunshot wound in his face, Serpico has suffered permanent hearing loss in his left ear and often loses his balance in the dark or becomes disoriented by sounds coming from different directions. Bullet fragments still lodged in his brain, if moved, could cause total paralysis or death. In an interview in *Parade* Magazine, Serpico told a reporter that he made the decision to speak out because, "One day I realized that I had done what was easier for me. Anything else would have been more difficult. I did it for my sanity." Explaining that he was "still being punished for what I did. The more you buck the system, the more they buck you back." Serpico said the reward for his actions was "one's own dignity."

REF.: *CBA;* (FILM), *Serpico,* 1973.

Sertorius, Quintus, c.123-72 B.C., Roman., polit., consp.-assass. Fought against Teutons and Cimbri from 105-02 B.C. He was a life-long supporter of Marius. He became a praetor in 83 B.C. He joined Mithradates VI and Mediterranean pirates in a war against Rome. He was targeted by forces commanded by Pompey and Metallus from 77 B.C., and was murdered for political reasons in a conspiracy headed by Marcus Perperna. REF.: *CBA.*

Servetus, Michael (Miguel Serveto), 1511-33, Spain, her. Escaped custody during trial before Inquisition for publishing *Christianismi Restitutio* in 1533. He was captured in Geneva, and jailed by order of Calvin. He was sentenced to death by burning at the stake. REF.: *CBA.*

Sessions, William Steele, 1930- , U.S., law enfor. off. On Nov. 2, 1987, William Steele Sessions became only the third permanent director of the U.S. Federal Bureau of Investigation since the nation's federal law enforcement agency was designated the FBI.

FBI director William Sessions.

Sessions enlisted in the U.S. Air Force in 1951, and was commissioned and earned his wings the following October. He remained on active duty until October 1955. At Baylor University in Waco, Texas, Sessions received a Bachelor of Arts degree in 1956, and two years later earned an LL.B. (called a Juris Doctor today) degree from the Baylor University School of Law. He entered private practice in Waco following graduation, and was a member of the Haley, Fulbright, Winniford, Sessions, and Bice law firm until 1969 when Sessions was appointed chief of the government operations section, criminal division for the Department of Justice in Washington, D.C. In 1971, he was named U.S. Attorney for the Western District of Texas. On Dec. 11, 1974, President Gerald R. Ford appointed Sessions to the Western District Court of Texas. He served as a judge on that court until February 1980 when he was named the court's chief judge. During this time, Sessions was a member of the Board of the Federal Judicial Center in Washington, D.C., and on committees for the U.S. Judicial Conference and the State Bar of Texas.

Sessions resigned as district judge the day before he was sworn in as FBI director to replace Acting Director John Otto, who had held the position since May 26 of that year. In August 1988, less than a year into Session's ten-year term—a length designed to prevent political interference—Richard Thornburgh was appointed U.S. Attorney General. Early in 1989, the two top law enforcement officials were reported to be on clearly unfriendly terms. By March, Thornburgh had objected twice to having breakfast meetings with Sessions and congressmen. Thornburgh's office denied any rift, citing that the breakfasts were not attended because of proper protocol, in which the attorney general should meet congressmen before Sessions. REF.: *CBA.*

Seton, Miles Charles Cariston, See: **Rutherford, Norman.**

Setrabutra, Panep, d.1886, Thai., (unsolv.) mur. Phya Setrabutra was a trusted and loyal friend of Siam's King Chulalongkorn, the son of King Mongkut, the king who had employed British widow Anna Leonowens to instruct his children, and who became the subject of the musical *The King and I.* Chulalongkorn ordered Setrabutra to journey to the northern province of Chiengmai and act as the area's governor until the princes of the north began to pay proper homage to their king in Bangkok. Setrabutra, the son of Mongkut's chamberlain, made the 700-mile, six-week trek by boat with his new bride Panep Setrabutra.

By the time of the Siamese New Year on Apr. 1, 1886, Setrabutra had reconciled the northern princes to Chulalongkorn, and it was not until he and his wife moved into the governor's home atop Doi Sutep that there was a hint of trouble. The trouble however, was in his own home. His wife had been given more than £10,000 in sterling to secure protection for a large shipment of opium to Bangkok. Mrs. Setrabutra had failed to do anything, and subsequently the shipment was captured thirty miles south of Lampang. Fearing retribution, Setrabutra reinforced the security about his home. But just two weeks later, Chulalongkorn recalled his friend to Bangkok, and Setrabutra felt safe. Only ten days before their departure Mrs. Setrabutra was poisoned to death with morphine. Upon her chest had been placed a white poppy blossom which signified that her death was no accident but an execution carried out by opium dealers. A number of servants were arrested and two were even executed, but the identity of the actual murderer or murderers was never discovered.

REF.: *CBA;* Sparrow, *Vintage Victorian Murder.*

Settembrini, Luigi, 1813-77, Italy, rebel. Jailed for participating in insurgencies against government from 1839-42 and from 1849-58. He escaped from custody and fled to England in 1858, but returned to Naples in 1860. REF.: *CBA.*

Setty, Diane, d.1956, Brit., (unsolv.) sex. asslt.-mur. In 1956, a young girl named Diane Setty of Hertfordshire, England, was seen getting into the car of a man she met at the Crow's Nest Café. The two drove off, and were spotted twenty minutes later by two boys who thought Setty and the man were in a lovers' embrace in the car's back seat. A few minutes later, the car was seen driving away by another passerby, Mrs. Fitzjohn. Fitzjohn described the girl's face as twisted, which led pathologist Dr. Keith Simpson to believe that Setty had already been strangled to death with the scarf she wore about her neck. Before the killer reached the ditch where he dumped the body he was observed again by a farmworker as he drove by. The man dumped Setty's body in a ditch at Leverstock Green, and placed her overcoat over the sexually assaulted and murdered woman. Three more boys saw the man cover the woman up, hop in his car, and drive off. One, who hoped to be a detective one day, even wrote down the license plate number, SUU 138, which turned out to belong to a three-wheeled milk truck. Even with eight people seeing Setty's murderer, the killer was never caught.

REF.: *CBA;* Simpson, *Forty Years of Murder.*

Seventh Passenger, The, 1953, a novel by Paul Capon. Though the author labels his murderer the Rosebud Killer, the slayer is undoubtedly based on Jack the Ripper. See: **Jack the Ripper.** REF.: *CBA.*

Severin, Klosowski, See: **Chapman, George.**

Severus, Lucius Septimius, 146-211, Roman., emp.-jur. Emperor of Rome from 193-211. He restructured the government along military lines and reformed the judicial system. His reign has been called the golden age of jurists, highlighted by the careers of Papinian, Paulus, and Ulpan. REF.: *CBA.*

Sevket Pasa, Mahmud, 1858-1913, Turk., grand vizier, assass. Murdered for political reasons in first year of rule as grand vizier. REF.: *CBA.*

Sewall, Samuel, 1652-1730, U.S., jur. Presided over Salem witchcraft trials and sentenced nineteen people to death in 1692 and 1697. He later confessed to the public his guilt and mistakes for participating in the Salem trials. He served on the superior court of Massachusetts from 1692-1728, as chief justice from 1718. See: **Salem Witchcraft Trials.** REF.: *CBA.*

Seward, William H., See: **Lincoln, Abraham.**

Sewell, Douglas, 1942- , Case of, U.S., mur. Ethel Jean Sewell, a 23-year-old mother, worked as a restaurant hostess at the Dalton Inn where she met 25-year-old William S. Schafner, better known as disc jockey Bill Starr of WTTI radio station in Dalton, Ga. Although she was married and he had a fiancee in nearby Chattanooga, Tenn., the two spent the night together at a Chattanooga motel. After her one-and-a-half-day absence from home, Mrs. Sewell told her 27-year-old husband Douglas Sewell of her affair. Sewell was understandably upset and though he later stated he wanted to save his marriage, he did phone lawyers about a possible divorce and borrowed a .41-caliber double-barreled Derringer.

Sewell and his wife confronted Schafner at the radio station and the disc jockey convinced the couple to join him for dinner and drinks. After dinner Mrs. Sewell left the men alone. After sharing several drinks, Sewell and Schafner returned to the Sewell home and found Mrs. Sewell crying. Schafner persuaded Sewell to leave her alone with him and he would straighten the situation out. The husband returned later and found his wife and the disc jockey embracing. Sewell shot twice, one bullet striking Schafner in the back of the head, the second wounding Mrs. Sewell. He then took his wife to the hospital and left Schafner dying on the floor. Schafner died later that day, Apr. 7, 1970, before being taken to the hospital. At the murder trial six weeks later, the defense argued that Sewell was justified in killing Schafner because the man had seduced his wife. Mrs. Sewell, who had allegedly filed for divorce, was not present at the trial. The jury did not agree with the prosecution that the killing was premeditated, and in less than an hour returned a verdict of Not Guilty and Sewell was released to the delight of a cheering courtroom. REF.: *CBA.*

Sewell, Frederick Joseph, 1932- , Brit., consp.-rob.-attempt. mur.-mur. On Aug. 23, 1971, Frederick Joseph Sewell, thirty-nine; John Patrick Spry, thirty-seven; Dennis George Bond, forty-four; and Thomas Flannigan, forty-three, heisted about £106,000 from a jewelry store on the Strand. The store manager, Joseph Lammond, was able to ring the alarm bell, unnoticed by the thieves. When a fireman walked into the shop, the robbers ran out firing. In the ensuing polise chase, two officers, Carl Walker and Ian Hampson, were wounded. Cornered in an alley, Sewell escaped by firing at Superintendent Gerald Richardson, who died later that day. Sewell turned up on Oct. 7 in Holloway. At the trial, prosecutor Attorney General Sir Peter Rawlinson, said, "Their incompetence as robbers was matched only by their ruthlessness in the use of firearms to evade arrest." Sewell was convicted of murder, attempted murder, conspiracy and robbery. He was sentenced to eighty years in jail. Convicted of manslaughter, Spry was sentenced to twenty-five years in jail. Bond was sentenced to fifteen years for robbery, and Flannigan was given thirteen years for the same charges.

REF.: Borrell, *Crime in Britain Today;* Butler, *Murderers' England; CBA;* Tullett, *Strictly Murder.*

Seye, Blaise Ferrage, 1757-82, Fr., theft-rob.-can.-kid.-rape-mur. Although Blaise Ferrage Seye worked as a mason in Cessan, Fr., not far from Comminges, he was more interested in his amorous affairs than masonry, a hobby which soon led him to flee into the mountains in 1779. From his mountain hideout, he terrorized the local populace. Not only would he steal cattle and poultry, but he also would kidnap young girls, take them back to his lair, rape them, and kill them. He was even known to rape any woman who managed to escape, first shooting her and then committing his assault as she bled to death. Seye soon grew fond of eating his victims, and increased his killings to include men. He was finally captured when police bribed the man who was fencing the stolen property of Seye's victims to point out the hideout. For his many crimes Seye was found Guilty and condemned to death. He was broken on the wheel and executed on Dec. 13, 1782. REF.: *CBA.*

Seymour, Brian, d.1749, Scot., mur. Brian Seymour was born into a military family in Waterford, Ire., and enlisted in the sixth regiment of footguards when he attained the legal age. Seymour first got into trouble with army authorities when he quarreled with a fellow soldier over the services of a prostitute. They settled the matter in a duel, from which Seymour emerged the victor. Because the duel was largely a matter of honor, he was granted a military pardon. In 1745, Seymour was sent to Scotland to fight with the royalists at Culloden Moor against the rebellious Scots. After the battle, his regiment rested at the army's winter headquarters, where the young soldier committed the crime that was to result in his execution.

It was customary for unemployed ministers of the Church of Scotland to perform marriages in public taverns for those who could not afford better. One day Seymour noticed a young couple ready to be married, but the minister had failed to show up. On a whim, Seymour told one of the shopkeepers that if she would provide him a parson's robe, he would perform the service himself. Posing as a clergyman, Seymour conducted the ceremony and then returned to the alehouse and drank himself into a stupor.

On his way back to the barracks, Seymour encountered and insulted a man named Johnson. Johnson slugged him in the face. Seymour drew his sabre and ran Johnson through, and then returned to the barracks. A shoemaker named Young witnessed the murder.

The next morning the cobbler told the lord justice clerk what he had seen. The regiment was lined up on the parade ground, and Young singled out Seymour as the murderer. He was bound over for trial to the local court, and hanged at Edinburgh on Mar. 2, 1749.

REF.: *CBA;* Mitchell, *The Newgate Calendar.*

Seymour, Edward (Earl of Hertford, Duke of Somerset, AKA: The Protector), c.1500-52, Brit., consp. Executed on dubious evidence on charge of participating in conspiracy with Paget and Aurundel to kill Warwick. REF.: *CBA.*

Seymour, Edward (Earl of Hertford, Baron Beauchamp), c.1539-1621, Brit., treas. Denied property and title of Duke of Somerset because of criminal conviction of father Edward Seymour. He was titled by Queen Elizabeth I in 1559. He was fined £15,000 and jailed from 1561-71 for marrying Lady Catherine Grey without royal permission. REF.: *CBA.*

Seymour, Golney (Mac Seymour), 1910- , U.S., rape-mur. In Summer 1931, Henrietta Schmerler, a 23-year-old anthropology student from Columbia University arrived at the White River, Ariz., Apache reservation to study tribal practices. A few weeks after her arrival Schmerler was reported missing. After searching the surrounding area, Schmerler's body was found on July 24 in a nearby ravine. She had been raped, stabbed, beaten, and choked.

Questioning of the Apache population failed to produce any strong suspects. An agent from the Department of Justice posing as a cattleman was called in to gather information in the case. After three months, the agent, J.A. Street, had enough evidence to accuse Golney Seymour, a 21-year-old resident of the reservation. Seymour confessed to the crime saying that Schmerler had suggested that she was willing to have sexual relations with him, but began throwing rocks at him when he approached her. Seymour was charged in the murder and brought to trial in Globe, Ariz. In March 1932, Seymour was sentenced to life in prison for the murder. It was noted in contemporary accounts that the sentence most probably amounted to a death sentence as only one Arizona Apache had ever lasted more than seven years in jail. REF.: *CBA*.

Seymour, Henry Daniel (AKA: **Harvey**), c.1879-1931, Brit., mur. Seymour was a convicted criminal who occasionally used more legitimate jobs, such as selling vacuum cleaners door to door, as a means of learning about places that would be worth robbing. On the Friday of an August holiday weekend in 1931, he showed up at the door of one old customer, a Mrs. Andrews of Oxford, and asked for money to take a bus home. She gave him some, which he used to purchase a hammer and chisel. Then he reappeared at Andrews's house, saying he had missed the last bus. She let him sleep there, but before he left the next morning, she saw his parcel containing the new tools. He then walked to the home of Annie Louisa Kempson, about 54-years-old, where he was seen knocking and entering the house. He attacked the widow with the hammer and chisel and then ransacked the premises, finding a little cash, but missing a box of notes and gold. Kempson was not found until the following Monday, after she failed to show up for an appointment.

Seymour, in the meantime, had returned to the hotel in Aylesbury where he had stayed on the previous Thursday night, but was not allowed to take his suitcase because he could not pay his bill. Opening the luggage, the proprietor found tools similar to those described by newspaper reports. In the hotel room, police found a Brighton address written backward on the blotting pad, checked the address, and discovered Seymour there, living under the name of Harvey. In October 1931, he was tried and was convicted on circumstantial evidence. He was hanged on Dec. 10, 1931, at Oxford Prison.

REF.: Browne and Tullett, *The Scalpel of Scotland Yard; CBA;* Fay, *The Life of Mr. Justice Swift;* Firmin, *Murderers in Our Midst;* Gribble, *Famous Manhunts;* Harrison, *Whitehall 1212: The Story of the Police of London;* Horwell, *Horwell of the Yard;* Lucas, *Laboratory Detectives;* Reynolds, *Murder 'Round the World;* Sanders, *Murder in the Big Cities;* Shew, *A Second Companion to Murder;* Tullett, *Strictly Murder;* Wilson, *Encyclopedia of Murder.*

Seymour, Horatio, 1810-86, U.S., law enfor. off. Served as New York's governor from 1853-55 and from 1863-65. He helped to stave off the draft riots in New York City in 1863 but was charged with sympathizing with the rioters in a speech. He is credited with assisting in removing William Tweed from power in New York City. See: **New York Draft Riots; Tweed, William Marcy.** REF.: *CBA*.

Seymour, Thomas (Baron Seymour of Sudeley), c.1508-49, Brit., treas. Connived to remove brother Edward Seymour from role of protecting youthful King Edward VI and tried to cause Edward to marry Lady Jane Grey. He was seized for agitating opposition to his brother and put to death on a charge of treason. REF.: *CBA*.

Seymour, Dr. **Walter**, 1863-1928, China, (unsolv.) mur. On Apr. 16, 1928, the 65-year-old head of the U.S. Presbyterian Mission Hospital at Tsining, China, Dr. Walter Seymour, was shot and killed by Nationalist soldiers under the command of Marshall Feng Yu-hsiang. The soldiers seized Dr. Seymour on the street just outside the hospital. Seymour broke loose and entered the mission compound, barring the gate after him. The soldiers fired on him through the gate, shooting him through the heart, then entered the compound and robbed him. Dr. Seymour died a short time later.

Although the U.S. Consul General at Shanghai, Edwin S. Cunningham, demanded the arrest and execution of Seymour's murderer, no suspect was ever produced. Cunningham also protested and demanded compensation for the looting of the U.S. mission buildings which followed Seymour's murder. REF.: *CBA*.

Seyss-Inquart, Arthur, 1892-1946, Ger., war crimes. On Oct. 1, 1946, the International Military Tribunal at Nuremberg found Arthur Seyss-Inquart and sixteen other high-ranking Nazis Guilty of war crimes. Seyss-Inquart, the governor of Austria after the Anschluss and the German administrator of the Netherlands was found Not Guilty of conspiring to wage aggressive war, but was found Guilty on three other counts, including crimes against the peace, crimes violating the laws of war, and crimes against humanity.

The French prosecution charged Seyss-Inquart with looting art treasures of the Netherlands and taking them to Germany where they adorned the private homes of high-ranking Nazis. Seyss-Inquart claimed that he had, if without effect, continually tried to stop the Gestapo from shooting Netherlanders without trial, and that Hitler had broken "his promise that Austrian ideals would be maintained as a requisite to a peaceful union with Germany."

Arthur Seyss-Inquart, Nazi war criminal who was hanged at Nuremberg in 1946.

Seyss-Inquart was hanged at Nuremberg prison along with nine of the other convicted Nazis on Oct. 16, 1946. Just before climbing to the gallows, Seyss-Inquart is reported to have said, "I hope this execution is the last act in the tragedy of WWII." REF.: *CBA*.

Seznec, Guillaume, c.1875-1954, Fr., (wrong. convict.) mur. Guillaume Seznec, the owner of a Morlaix, France, sawmill agreed to aid his friend Pierre Quemeneur in selling U.S. Cadillac cars to the Soviet Union. Quemeneur needed money and Seznec had plenty. The two decided that Seznec would provide Quemeneur with $4,000 in gold for his home near Brest. On May 23, 1923, the the sale was made with a waiter at a Brest hotel observing the transaction. The next day both men left in a Cadillac for Paris. Along the way the car continually broke down. According to Seznec, Quemeneur took the train to Paris, while he returned to his sawmill in the rundown car. Quemeneur had still not returned home by June 4, and on June 12, his sister reported him as missing to the police. The next day' she received a telegram apparently signed by Quemeneur in which he stated he would soon be home. He never returned, nor was his body ever found, but young Sûreté inspector Pierre Bony was sure that Quemeneur's companion had killed the missing man.

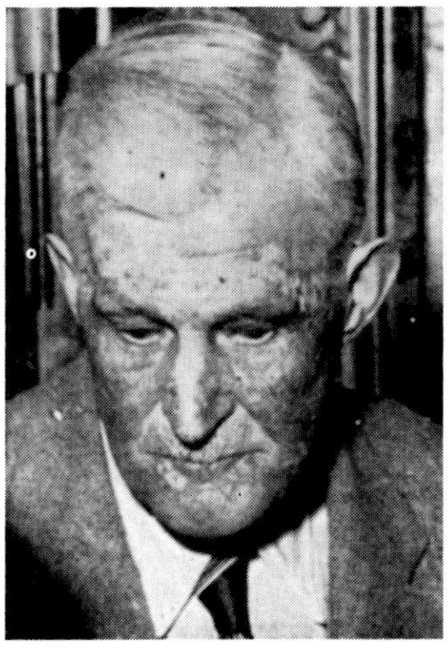

Guillaume Seznec, wrongly convicted of murder in the disappearance of his friend, Pierre Quemeneur.

Commissaire Achille Vidal was in charge of the investigation, but it was Bony who charged Seznec with the murder after all three had journeyed to Houdan, where Quemeneur was last reported seen, and it was Bony who vowed to prove Seznec was the murderer, no matter what. Bony left Houdan and immediately upon his arrival in Le Havre he discovered Quemeneur's luggage, containing the missing man's contract for sale of his home. The inspector claimed that the contract had been typed up after Quemeneur had been killed, and that like the telegram, was forged by Seznec. He even asserted that he would find the typewriter and prove his theory. By this time, Seznec's property had already been searched three times, without a shred of evidence found incriminating him. Shortly after Bony arrived at the sawmill he emerged carrying the typewriter, for the press to photograph with him holding it on July 6. Many wondered why the machine, allegedly purchased on June 12, could look like new and not be covered with dust after sitting in a sawmill for more than two weeks. Not unexpectedly, the size of the typewriter matched the size of a box taken into the sawmill by a police officer before the arrival of Bony. The officer left the building without the box. The only evidence against Seznec was that provided by Bony, or that suppressed by Bony. Seznec's personal lawyer Maitre Bienvenue had remembered that his earlier statement concerning the whereabouts of his client the day he allegedly sent the telegram to Quemeneur's sister was incorrect. He had spent the day with Seznec, and would provide the accused with an alibi. Bony would not let the truth stand in the way of his career, and Bienvenue was not heard from until well after the trial. As for the one man who clearly identified Quemeneur two days after he was murdered, Bony denounced him in court as unreliable. Le Her, a tram conductor had spoken with Quemeneur on May 26, but his testimony, along with only three others, was stacked against over 100 witnesses for the prosecution.

The trial, which was held in the Palais de Justice at Quimper, opened on Oct. 24, 1924, at the Finistère Assizes. Defending Seznec was Maitre Moro-Giafferi, who had earlier defended the murderer Henri Desiré Landru. Before this prestigious advocate could give his closing speech, he left the court to fill his appointment as a minister in the new government in Paris. Junior counsel Marcel Kahn closed the case for the defense, but the trumped up evidence was too much for the younger attorney and Seznec was found Guilty. He was sentenced to penal servitude for life and sent to French Guiana. After his trial, further evidence which Bony had suppressed was made known. A magistrate at Plouviers, M. Hervé, had received a signed statement from five sailors that on the night of May 27-28 a man had been shot on the Brest estate owned by Quemeneur. This information was purposely misplaced by Bony, and after the trial when Hervé fought for Seznec, he was met with stiff police resistance, which resulted in his entering a mental home.

In July 1947, Seznec was released from imprisonment when the penal colony at French Guiana was permanently closed. He lived with his daughter Jeanne Seznec, who had since married Le Her, the man who testified having met Quemeneur. Le Her often beat his wife, and one day Jeanne shot her husband. She was found Not Guilty of manslaughter; a verdict she had fought to obtain for her father. It was not until the death of Bony that the truth was made known. Bony had been a Nazi collaborator during WWII, and seconds before his execution, he informed a priest that he had framed Seznec. He was shot to death at the Mont Valérian fortress. A former colleague of Bony's, Leon Sacré, then corroborated the dying words of the inspector. As for the typewriter, Bony had purchased that himself, and even typed the forged contract in the shop where he bought it. Jeanne, who had always declared her father's innocence, declared that Le Her was the true killer.

REF.: *CBA;* Goodman, *Villainy Unlimited;* Heppenstall, *Bouebeard and After;* Wilson, *Encyclopedia of Murder.*

Sforza, Galeazzo Maria, d.1476, Italy, duke, assass. Under the tyrannical and often violent rule of Galeazzo Maria Sforza, personal liberty was denied to the peasants of the city of Milan, and a series of atrocities were carried out which made his assassination almost inevitable.

Two young scholars, Girolamo Olgiati and Gian Andrea Lampugnani plotted the killing along with Carlo Visconti, whose family had lost the duchy of Milan to the tyrant. On St. Stephen's Day, Dec. 26, 1476, they assassinated the duke when he arrived on the steps of the church to offer his penance. Sforza's bodyguards killed Visconti and Lampugnani, but Olgiati was taken to prison where he was tortured to death. "My death is untimely," he said in his last breath. "My fame is eternal; the memory of my deed will endure forever."

REF.: Bloom, *Money of Their Own; CBA.*

Sforza, Lodovico (Ludovico, Duke of Milan, AKA: Il Moro, The Moor), 1451-1508, Fr., polit. corr. Held title and privileges of Duke of Milan from 1481-99. He served as regent under Gian Galeazzo from 1476-81. He arrogated the bureaucracy in 1481. He allied himself with Italian rulers including Lorenzo de' Medici, and with them successfully removed Charles VIII from Italy in 1495. He was defeated by Louis XII in 1499, and jailed for life in France from 1500. REF.: *CBA.*

Shachori, Ami, d.1972, Brit., polit., (unsolv.) assass. During a one week period in Fall 1972, postal employees around the world—from Buenos Aires, Arg., to Brussels, Belg.; from Montreal, Quebec, to Jerusalem and Tel Aviv, Isr.—detected at least fifty-five explosive devices concealed within letters. One letter bomb that went undetected was a letter addressed to the Israeli embassy in London bearing an Amsterdam postmark. Agricultural attaché Ami Shachori opened the letter. The bomb inside the letter resembled a tea bag making it not as noticeable as other explosives. A detonation system was used by which the charge was ignited when pressure was released from the device. When Shachori broke the seal, the bomb exploded, tearing into his stomach and chest. He died as he staggered from his office.

REF.: *CBA;* Dobson and Payne, *The Terrorists—Their Weapons, Leaders and Tactics;* O'Ballance, *Language of Violence—The Blood Politics of Terrorism.*

Shaddy, Gregory, 1957- , Case of, U.S., mur. On the night of July 24, 1975, 18-year-old Gregory Shaddy returned to his parents' home in a wealthy section of Wichita, Kan., and murdered them with an ax and a knife and stuffed their bodies in a closet. Shaddy, the subject of vicious and repeated beatings from his father and strict discipline from his mother, had left home two months earlier. When arrested, Shaddy confessed to the crime. His first trial resulted in a hung jury. In the second trial, Shaddy was acquitted on grounds of insanity and, as Kansas law dictated, was sent to the state security hospital at Larned, where he was to remain until he was deemed cured by hospital psychiatrists.

In June 1977, hospital officials testified that Shaddy was cured. In addition, doctors at Larned said that they were uncertain if Shaddy had ever been insane. A week after the initial hearing, Shaddy was released. Because he had never been convicted of a felony, it was likely that Shaddy, along with his brother, would inherit the $400,000 estate left by his parents. REF.: *CBA.*

Shadley, Lafe, d.1893, U.S., west. lawman. An Oklahoman law officer, Lafe Shadley, gained fame for his clashes with outlaws during the 1890s. In 1892, in Osage County, Shadley crossed the trail of bank robber and rustler Dan "Dynamite Dick" Clifton. When Shadley tried to take Clifton, a gunfight left Clifton wounded in the neck, but he escaped.

Lawmen around the Ingalls, Okla., area were informed that outlaw Bill Doolin and six of his Oklahombres gang members were tearing up the town. Two wagons of officers headed toward Ingalls. Coming in from the south at around 10 a.m. was Shadley, along with W.C. Roberts, Jim Masterson, Henry Keller, George Cox, Hi Thompson, and H.A. Janson. Their wagon circled Ingalls and stopped by a grove of trees near the residence of Dr. Pickering. At the same time a wagon driven by Dick Speed, accompanied by John W. Hixon, J.S. Burke, Tom Houston, Red Lucas and Ike Steel, rode in from the north. Men from the posse infiltrated the town and shooting began when Speed fired on Bitter Creek Newcomb. Arkansas Tom Jones, who was firing from a hotel window, fatally shot Speed and the injured Newcomb rode out of town. Doolin and four of the Oklahombres began shooting from inside a saloon and the gunfire became so intense that a local boy, Dell Simmons, and a stray horse were both slain.

When Doolin and his gunmen raced to a nearby livery stable Shadley hid behind the dead horse and fired on the front door of the stable. Then Bill Dalton, Tulsa Jack Blake, and Red Buck Weightman came tearing through the door on horseback as Doolin and Dan Clifton rode out the back door. Jones' sniping fire wounded Houston and one of Hixon's bullets clipped Dalton's horse in the jaw. Dalton spurred the wounded animal on but

Shadley dropped the horse with a bullet to its leg. Dalton grabbed some wire cutters and began ripping at a fence which blocked his way out of town. Shadley hid behind a storm cellar, crawled under a fence, and then was spotted by Dalton who pumped three bullets into his body, finished cutting up the fence, jumped up behind Doolin, and sprinted out of Ingalls. Jones surrendered after another hour of gun fire and the battle was over. Shadley and Houston were taken to Stillwater, along with Speed's corpse, and their relatives and friends were called in. Both lawmen died the next morning. See: **Doolin, William.**

REF.: Canton, *Frontier Trails, CBA;* Croy, *Trigger Marshal;* Shirley, *Heck Thomas,* ____, *Six-gun and Silver Star.*

Shadow and the Web, The, (1940), novel by Mary Allerton. In published notes the author admits that her work stems from the exploits of the sinister Wardlaw Sisters, who poisoned several family members for insurance payments (U.S., 1900-09). See: **Wardlaw Sisters**. REF.: *CBA.*

Shadrach, and **Meshach**, and **Abednego**, Biblical, her. In biblical times the Babylonian king Nebuchadnezzar had an image made of gold to honor the gods he worshipped. The figure, built on the Dora plain in Babylon, stood about ninety feet high and nine feet wide. Nebuchadnezzar ordered that all of his followers were to fall down and pray to the idol whenever they heard music. If his people did not obey his command, they would be cast into a burning furnace.

A group of Chaldeans soon accused Shadrach, Meshach, and Abednego—Jews whom Nebuchadnezzar had handling his affairs in Babylon—of not obeying the king's orders. The three men were brought before Nebuchadnezzar and admitted they had not fallen down before the image when music was played. Shadrach, Meshach, and Abednego also professed that their god would save them. Furious, Nebuchadnezzar had the furnace heated seven times hotter than was normal and then had the three heretics bound tightly. According to *Daniel III,* Shadrach, Meshach, and Abednego were then tossed into the fiery pit. The intensity of the flames was so great that the men who threw them in were consumed by the fire. To Nebuchadnezzar's amazement, the three Jews were unhurt by the flames, and apparently the king saw a fourth man among them. He called the three to leave the furnace and they did. The Bible relates how Nebuchadnezzar then cast aside his devotion for his gods and honored the God who had saved Shadrach, Meshach, and Abednego. REF.: *CBA.*

Shaeffer, Daniel, d.1832, U.S., mur. In November 1831, a handyman working at the home of widow Elizabeth Bowers in Lancaster, Penn., raped her and then killed her by suffocating her with a pillow. When she was found some days later, her death was not considered suspicious and she was buried. Several months later, however, Daniel Shaeffer's conscience caused him to confess after he had listened to the sermon given at the hanging of another killer in Frederick, Md. Though the sheriff at first did not believe him, Shaeffer was finally found Guilty and hanged on Apr. 13, 1832.

REF.: *CBA; The Life and Confession of Daniel Shaeffer, Who Was Found Guilty...of the Murder of Elizabeth Bowers;* Nash, *Bloodletters and Badmen.*

Shafer, Russell F., prom. 1960, U.S., mur. On the morning of Apr. 26, 1960, John Muehlenthaler, Jr. discovered the body of 33-year-old Inez Marie Ringgenberg lying in a ditch about a mile north of Ankeny, Iowa. She had been brutally stabbed to death, with at least twenty-two wounds in her neck and chest. Investigators discovered that she had spent the previous evening at the Amvets Club bar with Russell F. Shafer. His white Ford matched the one seen by two men who passed by a parked car at the scene of the murder. Shafer admitted he had been with Ringgenberg the night before and early that morning, and he even confessed to having had an argument with her, but he said she was alive when he left her on the road.

As police still had not found the woman's missing purse or the murder weapon, a search of Shafer's car and home was made. Corwin Johnson, director of the Iowa Forensic-Medical Laboratory discovered no evidence, but did note that the vehicle had recently been thoroughly cleaned.

At first a search of Shafer's house found nothing, but upon searching the premises a second time, a metal bucket containing ashes was unearthed from beneath loose floorboards. Among the ashes was a piece of paper and a cord, both of which were sent to the FBI in Washington, D.C., for analysis. Agents Hilding L. Dahlgreen and Robert E. Duckett learned that the cord was from a plastic purse like that carried by Ringgenberg, and using infrared photography found the charred paper to be the photo of the Riggenberg's niece, 9-year-old Jeanette Doolittle, that the girl's mother, Mrs. Clinton Doolittle, said her sister carried.

With this evidence against Shafer he was charged with second-degree murder. In September, County Attorney Ray Hanrahan and his assistant Lawrence F. Scalise had little trouble convincing the jury of the defendant's guilt—despite efforts by defense lawyer J. Blaine Phipps, who argued that the evidence was circumstantial. Shafer was convicted and sentenced to fifty years in prison. REF.: *CBA.*

Shaffer, Howard, and **Stevens, Charles**, and **Troop, William**, prom. 1926-30, U.S., (wrong. convict.) mur. On Aug. 1, 1926, 67-year-old Mary McMillan was brutally axed to death in her Florida home. Her husband, 68-year-old Malcolm McMillan, said he had been attacked by three men who hit him over the head and chopped at him, before he managed to escape under the house.

At the crime scene, McMillan told officer E.L. Waldron that his assailants had been foreigners; the men who were eventually arrested were not foreigners. Later at the hospital, he told Dr. W.W. Hartman that the men who attacked him wore masks, a statement which he also denied in court. Within a week Howard Shaffer, Charles Stevens, and William Troop were arrested and charged with the crime. During this time, McMillan, while still in the hospital, informed three detectives that he had no idea who committed the crime; statements he denied later in court. No other witnesses saw the men who attacked McMillan. One witness did see Shaffer a few blocks away at the time of the crime, while another once heard Troop mention that Mrs. McMillan deserved a good beating because of her meddling ways.

Other than that, there was only the word, and denials, of McMillan against Shaffer, Stevens, and Troop. The evidence, which favored the defendants at their trial in early 1927, was the well-substantiated testimony of witnesses who had seen or heard McMillan abusing and striking his wife in drunken rages. He even had threatened to kill her with an ax. Despite the lack of evidence and motive, the jury found all three Guilty of first-degree murder.

Judge Daniel T. Simmons immediately threw this decision out and ordered a retrial. Shaffer, Stevens, and Troop once again were found Guilty and sentenced to death in 1928. This decision was appealed to the Florida Supreme Court, which overturned the trial decision because of the inconsistency in McMillan's testimony and the lack of a motive. A new trial was ordered, and on Apr. 30, 1930, after the three had spent three years and eight months in prison, Judge DeWitt T. Gray dropped the charges and Shaffer, Stevens, and Troop were released from custody. REF.: *CBA.*

Shaftesbury, Anthony Ashley Cooper, 1621-83, Brit., polit. corr.-terr. Jailed for opposing closing of Parliament in 1677. He encouraged persecution of Roman Catholics from 1678-80, and caused the death of his foe, William Howard, the Viscount Stafford. He indicted the Duke of York on false charges of high treason in 1681, and later escaped to Holland. REF.: *CBA.*

Shah Shoja (Shah Shuja), c.1780-1842, Afg., king, assass. Began unpopular rule by ousting brother Mahmud, and was in turn ousted by Mahmud in 1810. Dost Mohammed defeated him in battle in 1834, but in 1838 he replaced Dost Mohammed as ruler of Afghanistan with the help of Lord Auckland. He was assassinated in 1842 by Dost Mohammed followers. REF.: *CBA.*

Shah Sultan Husayn, 1668-1726, Per., emp., assass. Hampered by personal weaknesses and Afghan invasion from 1720. He was compelled to yield his powers in 1722. Assassinated in 1726, he was succeeded by Tahmasp II, his son. REF.: *CBA.*

Shaka (Chaka or **Tshaka)**, c.1787-1828, Afr., chief, assass. Originated and headed Zulu Empire in 1816. He developed new military tactics and otherwise improved the army, which succeeded in removing many rival clans and capturing much of southern Africa. He was murdered by his half-brothers shortly after going insane. REF.: *CBA*.

Shannon, R.G., See: **Kelly, George R.**

Shantz, Phyllis, 1946- , U.S., law enfor. off. On Sept. 15, 1970, 24-year-old Phyllis Shantz became the first woman member of the Executive Protection Service, a Secret Service auxiliary formed to help protect the President and his family and foreign diplomats in the Washington, D.C., area. Shantz, a police officer on the Washington, D.C., police force for two years, was selected to be the first of seven women to join the newly created branch of the White House Secret Service. She was assigned to interview juveniles and women who might come under the scrutiny of the Secret Service, and supervise their custody. REF.: *CBA*.

Shapira, M.W., d.1884, Brit.-Palestine, fraud. In 1868, the world was excited by the discovery in Jordan of the Moabite Stone, an engraved stele that confirmed in writing all that was known about the Moab culture from ancient Palestine. M.W. Shapira, a Polish Jew with an antique shop in Palestine, decided to take advantage of the excitement and tried to sell faked Moabite pottery to Prussia for their museums. Charles Clermont-Ganneau, the French archeologist who discovered the stone, exposed the fakes.

On learning of the fake, the British Museum, which was negotiating with Shapira to buy a ninth-century manuscript of the book of Deuteronomy for £1 million, canceled the purchase after Clermont-Ganneau also said the biblical book was fake. Shapira had cut the blank ends off old sheepskin Torahs, made them appear even older, and then created the manuscript. Some years later, Shapira gave up his shop and committed suicide in Rotterdam, Neth. REF.: *CBA*.

Shapiro, Jacob (AKA: **Gurrah**), 1899-1947, U.S., org. crime. One of the most feared gangsters of his time, Jacob "Gurrah" Shapiro was a killer who enjoyed his work. By the late 1920s, he and his partner Louis Lepke were the top industrial racketeers in New York City and possibly in the nation. Shapiro's nickname, Gurrah, came from the fact that he often told people to "Get out of here" and routinely slurred his words so the phrase came out "Gurra dahere." Gurrah and Lepke met as teenagers on the Lower East Side of Manhattan when they were both trying to rob the same pushcart. Their alliance continued for decades, with Lepke functioning as the brains and the short, stocky Shapiro supplying the brawn and brutality.

Ruthless killer Jake Shapiro.

Lepke, along with fledgling criminals Meyer Lansky and Lucky Luciano, eventually came under the tutelage of mastermind Arnold Rothstein, who perceived the great potential in labor racketeering. Taking their cues from Rothstein, Lepke and Shapiro moved in on the garment district's union field. Terrorizing union locals with murders and beatings, they would gain control and set up systems of kickbacks and dues-skimming from members while extorting massive payoffs from garment manufacturers anxious to avoid strikes. The partners started working with Jacob "Little Augie" Orgen, then the key labor racketeer, and provided strikebreaking crews for employers. Orgen was not building his business, but merely going for the quick payoff, and Shapiro and Lepke realized they did not need him. Little Augie formed a new affiliation with the Diamond brothers, Legs and Eddie, for protection. On Oct. 15, 1927, Little Augie and Legs Diamond were on the corner of Delancey and Norfolk streets on the Lower East Side when Lepke drove up. Shapiro jumped out with a gun while Lepke began shooting from inside the car. Diamond was severely wounded but survived. Little Augie did not.

With their rivals out of the way, Lepke and Shapiro muscled in on the big time, extorting from both employers and unions. When the Lansky and Luciano national crime syndicate began to emerge, Lepke joined it and was made the head of Murder, Inc., the execution branch of the association. His right-hand men were Shapiro and Albert Anastasia. Shapiro was a dedicated murderer. Not only did he personally handle many of the hits, he also spent considerable time recruiting new talent for his death squads. Racketeer Dutch Schultz, who was being hounded by the federal government, proposed to the syndicate in 1935 that special government prosecutor Thomas E. Dewey should be eliminated. Although Shapiro and Anastasia eagerly agreed, the other members were strongly against an action that would bring unwanted attention on their organization. When his plan was rejected, Schultz said he would carry it out himself, and soon was murdered. Dewey promptly went after Lepke and Shapiro's labor rackets. Shapiro was sentenced to life imprisonment in 1936, and Lepke was jailed and later electrocuted for a murder he had commissioned.

While Lepke was on trial for murder, Shapiro smuggled a note to his longtime partner reminding him of his vote on Schultz's proposition to murder Dewey. Shapiro concluded, "I told you so." Before dying in jail in 1947, Shapiro said that if he had stayed with his own code of violence he would have remained a free man. See: **Buchalter, Louis; Murder, Inc.**

REF.: Campbell, *The Luciano Project; CBA;* Cohen, *Mickey Coehn: In My Own Words;* Cressey, *Theft of the Nation;* Eisenberg and Landau, *Meyer Lansky;* Fried, *The Rise and Fall of the Jewish Gangster in America;* Gage, *Mafia, U.S.A.;*____, *The Mafia is not an Equal Opportunity Employer;* Gosch and Hammer, *The Last Testament of Lucky luciano;* Katz, *Uncle Frank;* Levine, *Anatomy of a Gangster;* Maas, *The Valachi Papers;* Peterson, *The Mob;* Sann, *Kill the Dutchman;* Thompson and Raymond, *Gang Rule in New York.*

Shapiro Brothers, prom. 1920s-30s, U.S., org. crime. Irving, Meyer, and William Shapiro were three brothers whose street gang controlled a small section of Brooklyn. The Shapiros were deeply involved in the burgeoning garment industry rackets in Williamsburg until they were killed by Louis "Lepke" Buchalter, who moved against them in Summer 1931. Lepke, who backed the rival Amberg brothers, Joseph and Louis, in the battle of Brooklyn, eliminated Irving and Meyer in 1931. The next year he had Bugsy Goldstein and Abe Reles assassinate William Shapiro. Reles recounted the murders of these three Jewish gangsters to District Attorney William O'Dwyer when he turned informant in 1941. Reles' testimony helped send Buchalter to the electric chair. See: **Amberg, Joseph C.; Buchalter, Louis; Murder, Inc.; O'Dwyer, William; Reles, Abraham.**

REF.: *CBA;* Fried, *The Rise and Fall of the Jewish Gangster in America;* Levine, *Anatomy of a Gangster;* Thompson and Raymond, *Gang Rule in New York;* Turkus and Feder, *Murder, Inc.;* Zuckerman, *Vengeance Is Mine.*

Shark Arm Case, See: **Brady, Patrick.**

Sharkey, William J., b.1845, U.S., pris. esc.-mur. Although William J. Sharkey was a prominent ward politician in New York City, he was rumored to be involved with gamblers and pickpockets. It was no surprise therefore in 1872 when he loaned $600 to Bob Dunn, a gambler who wanted to open a faro establishment in Buffalo, N.Y. But when Dunn returned from Buffalo and was unable to produce the money that Sharkey demanded on Sept. 1, Sharkey shot and killed him. Sharkey was convicted of murder and sentenced to death. His execution was to have taken place on Aug. 15, 1873, but a stay was ordered on Aug. 7, until the result of his appeal was final.

During Sharkey's incarceration in the Tombs, his girlfriend, Maggie Jourdan, would visit him everyday. Jourdan visited him as usual on Nov. 19, 1873, and the two talked for hours. At noon another visitor to the prison, Mrs. Wesley Allen, chatted with the couple before visiting her husband. An hour later Jourdan left the prison, presenting the guard the ticket she had been given upon entering. All visitors to the Tombs were handed a ticket when they arrived, and were required to relinquish this ticket upon departure. Shortly after Jourdan's exit, another woman left the prison, presenting her ticket as she did. At 1:55 p.m., Allen passed through the prison gate, but was unable to furnish a ticket when stopped by Kennedy, the jail keeper.

A search of the prison did not turn up the missing ticket, but it did alert officials that Sharkey had escaped. It soon became apparent that Sharkey had been the woman who left after Jourdan, as his clothes and his shaved-off moustache were left behind in his cell. Jourdan and Allen both were held as suspects in his disappearance. Allen was released without a charge filed against her, while Jourdan was charged with aiding in Sharkey's escape. She was found Not Guilty. Sharkey was never recaptured, and what was more of a mystery than his disappearance disguised as a woman, was how he managed to leave his locked cell. REF.: *CBA.*

Sharp, Bartholomew, prom. 1680s, Case of, Brit., pir. As a British sea captain, Bartholomew Sharp was twice removed from his command. As a pirate Sharp was both successful and unsuccessful, even on the same outing. His capture of the Spanish ship *Santa Rosario* in the South Seas would have brought him 400 ingots of rough silver if he had not mistaken the treasure for tin and thrown it overboard. Sharp did manage to save some charts which intricately described islands and waterways already navigated by the Spaniards; these charts later proved to be the far more valuable treasure for Sharp.

After spending two years away from the Caribbean, during which Sharp sailed around Cape Horn, he returned in January 1682. He was chased by a naval frigate near Barbados and was refused permission to land at Antigua, before landing at Nevis. From there, Sharp made his way back to England where he was tried for piracy. Lack of evidence and, more important, the navigational maps, taken from the *Santa Rosario,* which he presented to King Charles II, forced an aquittal. Sharp was also given command of a vessel to arrest pirates and Indians in the Caribbean. Although Sharp was tried twice more for piracy, each time proved as lucky as the first. In 1688, he was appointed "unofficial" governor of Anguilla. REF.: *CBA.*

Sharp, Michael, 1946- , Brit., mansl. In December 1961, 15-year-old Michael Sharp, a sheet-metal worker, was harrassed by four men outside a London tavern one Saturday evening. He pulled out a sheath knife, and in the scuffle, 19-year-old former steeplechase jockey Neville Jenkins ran into the blade. Sharp informed the police of the man's death immediately. He was arrested and brought to trial in February 1962. The boy was found Not Guilty of murder, but Guilty of manslaughter. He was sentenced to three years probation.

REF.: *CBA;* Wilson, *Children Who Kill.*

Sharp, Solomon, See: **Beauchamp, Jereboam O.**

Sharp, Thomas, 1675-1704, Brit., fraud-count.-rob.-mur. By his own estimate, Thomas Sharp had been imprisoned in Newgate Prison at least eighteen times. Between his prison terms, Sharp and his gang of thieves frequented the Vine alehouse at Charing Cross. The owner of the pub was a wealthy old man whose private quarters were upstairs. To get at the secret place where he stashed his money, Sharp lit a small fire in the clubroom. "Fire!" the thief cried. The old man raced upstairs to retrieve his valuables. Sharp followed, and saw for himself the location of the safe. Meanwhile, Sharp's accomplices had extinguished the fire. Sharp and his friends returned the following night with their women. After a sumptuous meal, he quietly removed £500 from the owner's safe.

Sharp was born in Surrey, and earned his living with loaded dice at the gaming tables until he finally grew tired of court fines and the pillory. So Sharp and his robbers turned to counterfeiting. They manufactured Black Dogs, coins resembling shillings, made of cheap pewter. Eventually Sharp was caught and returned to Newgate, while several of his companions went to the gallows.

When Sharp was released, he dabbled in astrology, which proved to be a lucrative fraud. Pretending to understand an Arabic dialect translated by Dutch orientalist Thomas van Erpe, Sharp swindled a printer's daughter out of fifty shillings by predicting her marriage.

In 1704, Sharp added murder to his long list of criminal offenses. Sharp's victim was a shoemaker who owned a small shop facing Great Queen Street. Sharp murdered him for trying to prevent a robbery. Thomas Sharp was captured, convicted, and hanged at Long Acre, Drury Lane, on Sept. 22, 1704.

REF.: *CBA;* Smith, *Highwaymen.*

Sharpe, Violet, 1904-32, U.S., suic. Violet Sharpe, a British immigrant to the U.S. who worked as a maid to the mother of Charles Lindbergh's wife, committed suicide on June 10, 1932. Sharpe had been questioned numerous times in relation to the Mar. 1 kidnapping of the Lindbergh baby, and remained a prime suspect in the crime because she was unable to provide a sound alibi for the night the baby was kidnapped. A few days before her death, Sharpe had identified a photo of taxi driver Ernest Brinkert as the man who accompanied her on a drive the night of the kidnapping. At the time of Sharpe's suicide, Brinker remained a top suspect in the crime as well. Just before Sharpe was to be questioned for the fourth time, she drank cyanide and died soon thereafter. See: **Hauptmann, Bruno Richard.** REF.: *CBA.*

Sharpe, Walter, 1929-50, and **Lannen, George**, 1932- , Brit., mur. A jeweler named Abraham Levine was working in his shop, the Albion Watch Depot, in Leeds, England, when two youths held up his store at 10 a.m. on Nov. 16, 1949. Despite the drawn pistols, the 52-year-old jeweler fought the bandits. He grabbed one, but the other hit Levine over the head with the butt of a revolver. This gunman then fired two shots at Levine and both men ran out the door, shooting wildly as they fled. They escaped through the crowded streets.

Levine was taken to the Leeds General Infirmary, and a massive search using more than 900 police was conducted by Chief Constable J.W. Barnett. The next night Levine gave a brief description of his attackers before dying from his wounds. A bullet recovered from his body proved to have been taken from a Leeds gunsmith during a burglary prior to the murder. On Nov. 18, the murderers were arrested by police in Southport. One of the men, 20-year-old Walter Sharpe, confessed to the shooting. The two criminals then remained silent until they were brought to trial at the Leeds Assizes on Mar. 11, 1950, before Justice Streatfield. At the trial, Sharpe pleaded not guilty, while his co-defendant, 17-year-old George Lannen, pleaded guilty, against the advice of his attorney G.R. Hinchcliffe. Again Sharpe confessed to the shooting. He admitted that he had pulled the trigger while Levine fought with Lannen. But he added that the murder was an accident and that the guns (which he also admitted stealing with Lannen) were only meant to intimidate the jeweller. Regardless of their intent, both men were found Guilty by the jury, which deliberated for only twenty minutes. Lannen was too young to be sentenced to death and was ordered detained for as long as the king desired. Sharpe was sentenced to death and hanged on Mar. 30, 1950, at Armley Jail in Leeds. REF.: *CBA.*

Sharpeville Massacre, prom. 1960, S. Afri., riot-mur. By the beginning of the 1960s, blacks in South Africa had been required to carry passbooks for more than 150 years. But with the advent of the Boer regime of Prime Minister Hendrik Verwoerd, the passbooks become overt tools of racial oppression. Under Verwoerd's rule, blacks were required to carry with them at all times passbooks that showed name, birthplace, tribal affiliation, and arrests. If found without the passbook, the Africans were taken immediately to jail and held there, sometimes for months, without trial. Although black Africans detested the passbook requirement, they complied with it until March 1960, the new and more aggressive Pan-Africanist Congress, headed by 36-year-old Robert Mangaliso Sobukwe, urged black Africans to go to their local police stations without their passbooks and demand to be arrested as a protest to the repressive and discriminatory ordinance.

South Africans turned out in large numbers in response to Sobukwe's call. At Orlando township near Johannesburg, 20,000 blacks gathered at the police station. Fifteen miles further south at Evaton, 70,000 showed up. As urged by Sobukwe, these demonstrations were non-violent and occurred without major incident. But at Langa, near Cape Town, police opened fire on the assembled crowd, killing three and wounding twenty-five. At Sharpeville, twenty-eight miles southwest of Johannesburg, the most violent outburst occurred when police, surrounded by the crowd of 20,000 blacks, opened fire on the crowd with revolvers, rifles, and Sten guns. Between seventy and ninety blacks were killed and more than 200 were wounded. Despite unanimous and universal public outcry against the massacre, Prime Minister Verwoerd refused to back down on his passbook policy, choosing instead to tighten the controls over South African blacks. In the aftermath of the shootings at Sharpeville, Verwoerd placed auxiliary police on call, outlawed outdoor meetings of more than twelve people, and arrested and jailed Robert Sobukwe and eleven of his Pan-African aides. A work boycott by black Africans and a severe drop in gold stocks on the Johannesburg exchange caused the government to ease the passbook requirements, if only temporarily, the following week. REF.: *CBA.*

Sharpeville Six, prom. 1984, S. Afri., mob vio.-mur. In September 1984, in the township of Sharpeville, S. Afri., a black town councilor, Jacob Kuzwayo Dlamini, was killed during rent riots there. Six Sharpeville residents, Francis Mokgesi, twenty-seven, Oupa Moses Diniso, twenty-eight, Reid Mokoena, twenty, Duma Joshua Khumlao, twenty-four, Reginald Sefatsa, twenty-eight, and Theresa Ramashamola, twenty-three, were convicted on murder charges and sentenced to death. No evidence was presented in the trial showing that the six had contributed physically to Dlamini's death. Instead they were convicted under the common purpose doctrine which assigns responsibility to all members of a mob for crimes perpetrated by any of its members.

The severity of the sentences drew worldwide protest; heads of state including President Ronald Reagan, Prime Minister Margaret Thatcher, and Chancellor Helmut Kohl intervened on the behalf of the six. On Nov. 23, 1988, South African president P.W. Botha announced a reprieve. He commuted the death sentences and replaced them with sentences ranging from eighteen to twenty-five years. The six had already spent three years on Death Row when the commutations were granted and had once come within fifteen hours of being hanged. They had also exhausted their last appeal to have the case retried. Botha's reprieve preempted any further applications for clemency. REF.: *CBA.*

Sharswood, George, 1810-83, U.S., jur.. Served as associate justice from 1868-79 and chief justice from 1879-82 on supreme court of Pennsylvania. He also wrote several treatises on the law. REF.: *CBA.*

Shattuck, Jane, prom. 1894-95, Case of, U.S., mur. Truly Shattuck was an attractive girl who had many admirers in her hometown of San Francisco, Calif. One of these admirers was Harry Poole, who stood to inherit $100,000 from his grandfather. The two eventually became intimate. Truly's mother, Jane Shattuck, was not pleased with her daughter's relationship with Poole. On June 4, 1894, she wrote a note to Poole demanding to know of his intentions. The note caused a rift between Truly and her mother. On July 7, Truly returned home in the morning and informed her mother that she had slept with Poole the night before. She claimed that she and Poole were to be married the next day. In response, Shattuck forced Truly to write a letter to Poole, informing him that her mother was dying and wished to see him. The letter said he should come immediately. Poole left home as soon as the message was delivered. At the allegedly dying woman's bedside, Shattuck told Poole that he and Truly had sinned , but confirmed that they were planning to marry the next day. When Truly left the room, Shattuck pulled a revolver out from under her covers and fired a bullet into Poole's temple.

Shattuck was tried for murder before Judge E.A. Belcher, found Guilty, and sentenced to life in prison. Defense counsel argued that Shattuck was insane. Following the murder, she had become hysterical and claimed that she had murdered Poole because he had stolen her daughter from her. A new trial was granted by the Supreme Court. On Dec. 15, 1895, Shattuck was found Not Guilty. REF.: *CBA.*

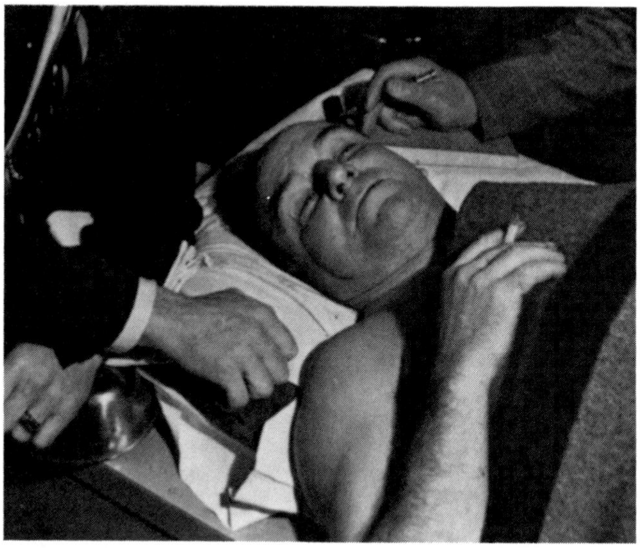

Harry J. Raymond, injured in a car bomb explosion after he got too close to exposing corrupt Los Angeles mayor Frank Shaw.

Shaw, Frank L., 1877-1958, and **Shaw, Joseph,** b.1889, and **Cormack, William H.,** prom. 1930s, and **Kynette, Earle E.,** prom. 1930s, U.S., org. crime. Frank L. Shaw became mayor of Los Angeles in 1933 after promising to clean up the city's rampant vice and racketeering operations. His style of "cleaning up" consisted of making the city more efficient and more profitable—for him.

Shaw appointed his brother Joseph Shaw as his private secretary, a euphemism for bagman. He appointed James E. Davis as chief of police. Davis had a prior reputation; he had allowed much of the graft and vice to thrive during the 1920s as head of the city's police force. Nevertheless, Shaw ran for reelection in 1937, repeating the promise to end graft and vice. He easily won. To make a show of his campaign promise, Shaw empaneled a new grand jury. He filled most of the positions with his friends, but also appointed four genuine reformers. One of these men was Clifford Clinton, who opened and operated the city's first cafeteria, the Cafeteria of the Golden Rule. During the Depression, Clinton had often provided meals to those in need. He now turned from ending hunger to stopping corruption.

Clinton's fight soon turned into a one-man crusade. The district attorney's office denied him funds for an investigation, and he was forced to use his own money for the venture, creating his own task force, Citizens Independent Vice Investigating Committee (CIVIC). He hired former Venice by the Sea and San Diego police chief Harry J. Raymond as his investigator. Raymond had been fired from his post after arresting syndicate members. Clinton and three other jurors eventually issued a "grand jury minority report," which detailed corruption in the district attorney's office, the county sheriff's office, and the city police department. In retaliation, Clinton's restaurant was assessed an additional $6,700 in property taxes, and he was refused a license to open another cafeteria. Stink bombs were set in his kitchen and "customers" complained of food poisoning or fell on his premises and sued Clinton for alleged injuries. Police arrested his grand jury witnesses, beating some and even holding one custody for five days. Clinton's family received threats and he was cited for contempt before the grand jury. On Oct. 27, 1937, a bomb destroyed the first floor and basement of Clinton's home. No one was injured.

Raymond, meanwhile, was uncovering solid proof of the wrongdoings of the mayor and his cohorts. He was also being carefully watched by police who, under the direction of Captain Earle E. Kynette, blatantly trailed the investigator. Finally, Raymond had found enough evidence to incriminate Shaw and Davis. The two public officals realized their predicament and ordered Kynette to stop him. On Jan. 14, Raymond's car exploded when he turned the key in his ignition. Luckily the police had used slow burning black powder for the bomb and Raymond was not killed. He did suffer more than 100 wounds from the explosion that sent him flying from his garage. But the attempt on his life did not stop him from testifying before the grand jury. Special prosecutor Joseph Fainer was appointed to take the case. He accepted the assignment after sending his family (who had been threatened by the mob) to Hawaii.

Fainer subpoenaed Kynette's files and in them found proof of the captain's involvement with the bombing. Kynette and accomplice, Officer Roy Allen, were found Guilty of attempted murder on June 16, 1938, and sentenced to ten years in prison. Joseph Shaw, found Guilty on sixty-three counts of corruption for bribes and sale of patronage positions was sentenced to ten years imprisonment as well. Civil Service commissioner William H. Cormack was found Guilty of the same charges as the mayor's brother on Mar. 23, 1939. Police lieutenant Pete DelGado escaped to Mexico and disappeared. The mayor was defeated in a recall election on Sept. 16, 1938, by a margin of almost two to one. REF.: *CBA*.

Shaw, Joseph, See: **Shaw, Frank L.**

Shaw, Lemuel, 1781-1861, U.S., jur. Prior to his appointment to the Massachusetts Supreme Court, Lemuel Shaw served eighteen years as a member of the state's two legislative bodies. In 1822, he drafted the Boston City Charter. He was elected chief justice in 1830 and held that position until his death. One of the more celebrated criminal cases he ever tried was the 1850 murder trial of Dr. John White Webster, who had killed Professor Parkman of Harvard University. See: **Webster, John White.**

REF.: *CBA;* Scott, *The Concise Encyclopedia of Crime and Criminals.*

Shaw, Tom, prom. 1863, Fr., theft. The Duke of Brunswick had an immense fortune in jewels, estimated at more than £700,000. Popular speculation had it that a great deal of the collector's jewels had been obtained by less than legal means. Therefore, when the duke moved into a large mansion in Paris, he took every precaution possible to guard the collection. On the second floor of his home, he placed a large safe. To enter this room, one had to pass through the duke's study and bedroom. The wrought iron door leading into the third room was blocked by the duke's bed. The safe itself was guarded by an alarm system which sounded if someone tampered with the door. The system also caused one dozen concealed revolvers to fire at the safe. As if that were not enough, the duke employed four detectives to patrol outside his private suite twenty-four hours a day. Unfortunately these precautions did not deter safecracker Tom Shaw from stealing the duke's jewels.

Shaw left Newcastle, England, with forged papers in which he claimed to have been the valet of the Duke of Bedford and Prince Charles of Prussia. Shaw knew the Duke of Brunswick detested both men and would not verify the authenticity of their signatures. Thus he gained employment in the duke's house. After his luggage was searched and he evaded various traps set by the duke—such as not seeming to react to a door ajar in the room that held the safe—Shaw gained the duke's confidence. The thief's several months as a valet paid off when he convinced the duke to have a necklace reset. The duke told Shaw to order a jeweler to stop by the next day at 10 a.m. Shaw then informed the jeweler to come at 10:30. When the duke ordered the safe to be opened for the jeweler, Shaw made his was into the room and stole more than £200,000 worth of jewels. He then slipped out of the house and escaped unnoticed to Boulogne. But Shaw spoiled his own plan of escape when he sent a note to Prince Edward of Wales. The thief believed that a stolen cross rightfully belonged to the queen of England. He wrote that he would return it for 100,000 francs. Scotland Yard turned the letter over to Parisian authorities, who traced the postmark to Boulogne. Shaw was arrested, and although not all of the jewels were recovered, the Duke of Brunswick did not press charges. The thief was still convicted and sentenced to twenty years in prison. REF.: *CBA*.

Shaw, William, d.1721, Scot., (wrong. convict.) mur. Edinburgh, Scot., upholsterer William Shaw did not approve of the man his daughter, Catherine Shaw, had chosen to marry. In fact, he despised John Lawson, calling the man a profligate and ordering his daughter never to see him again. But Catherine continued her liaison with Lawson, and when Shaw discovered her insubordinate behavior, he confined her to her room. He informed her that a man of his choosing, Alexander Robertson, would be her husband. Catherine defied her father's authority, declaring she would sooner die than marry Robertson. One such argument in October 1721 ended with loud screams and protestations heard by another tenant, James Morrison. Shaw locked his daughter in her room and stormed from the building. Not long after his departure, Morrison heard groans coming from the Shaw's apartment and even heard Catherine cry out, "Cruel father, thou art the cause of my death." A constable was sought out and when he entered Catherine's room, he found the woman with her throat slit and the knife lying beside her. Before she died it, witnesses claimed she acknowledged with the nod of her head that her father had stabbed her.

Shaw returned with bloodstains on his shirt and was confronted with the sight of his daughter. Although he claimed that the stains appeared after he removed bandages from an earlier bloodletting, the jury quickly found Shaw Guilty. He was sentenced to death and hanged. Prior to his execution, his last words were, "I am innocent of my daughter's murder." His body was gibbeted at Leith Walk in November 1721 to the delight of a rather large and uproarious crowd. In August 1722, the room that Catherine died in was finally rented out, and the new tenant came across a letter written by Catherine. The letter was a suicide note, which blamed Shaw for her unhappy state of imprisonment. It was proven to be in her handwriting, and an Edinburgh magistrate ordered that the body of Shaw be removed from its chains. Shaw, who had once been a soldier, was given a proper burial, complete with military colors flown over his grave. REF.: *CBA*.

Shawcross, Sir **Hartley William,** 1902- , Brit., atty. gen. Served as barrister of Gray's Inn from 1925 and became King's Counsel in 1939. He was elected to represent St. Helens in Parliament in 1945 and was named attorney general by the same administration. At the Nuremburg trials, he was chief British prosecutor. He also prosecuted John George Haigh. REF.: *CBA*.

Shayk-al-Jabal, See: **Order of the Assassins, The.**

Shays' Rebellion, prom. 1786-87, U.S., mob vio. The post-Revolutionary War depression, combined with high taxes on citizens of Massachusetts to pay off their state's war debt, was hard on local farmers. Mortgages were foreclosed and many farmers were sent to jail or even sold into servitude. In Worcester County alone, there were 4,000 debt suits in 1785-86, with seventy-two of ninety-four prisoners jailed for debt.

Organizing a protest, the farmers followed the pattern established during the war, first holding conventions locally to send grievance petitions to the August 1786 session of the Massachusetts General Court. When the petitions proved ineffectual, the farmers turned to force. Under the leadership of former army officers Daniel Shays and Luke Day, hundreds of western Massachusetts farmers began to force local courts to suspend business. Henry Knox, U.S. secretary of war, persuaded Congress in October to station troops at the Springfield arsenal, supposedly to fight the

Indians, but actually poised to overpower the rebellion. The movement was subdued in the eastern part of the state by November, but Shays' forces continued to control the interior.

Shays sent a message to Day proposing an attack on the Springfield post. On Dec. 26, they shut down the Springfield courts, with Shays' 1,000-member strong army threatening the arsenal commanded by Major General William Shepard. Day sent Shepard a demand that the troops leave their weapons at the public stores with the insurrection's officers and return to their homes. With General Benjamin Lincoln's assistance, Shepard

Farmers fighting against higher taxes followed leader Daniel Shays into a Massachusetts rebellion in 1786.

routed Shays' army. Day did not appear at the confrontation. Shays' army was decimated and with Shepard allowed him to retreat without pursuing the devastated forces. Guerrilla action continued through the winter, but by March the struggle was over. Though several of the leaders of Shays' army were captured, Shays himself was not. The leaders were threatened with execution but released. Shays died thirty years later, in poverty, in New York. REF.: *CBA.*

Shea, Joseph Francis, c.1938- , U.S., (wrong. convict.) mur. Three miles from Miami International Airport, the bullet-ridden body of 23-year-old Mary Meslener was found on Feb. 25, 1959, along the bank of the Miami River. The National Airlines reservationist had last been seen two nights before as she headed toward her car parked at the airport. The bloodstained car was found two weeks later, 250 miles northwest, in Tampa. Not one clue was discovered on the body or car, and it was not until more than a month later that police were informed of a possible suspect.

Joseph Francis Shea, an airman stationed at the West Palm Beach Air Force Base, told colleagues that he had recently harmed a baby but could not remember what he had done. It was later discovered that a woman he was seeing in the Philippines had refused to marry him and run off with their child. A bloodstained shirt found in his possession also could not be explained. Officials at the base notified police of the shirt and of Shea's claim. No children had been reported injured or killed, but the Dade County Homicide Bureau was nonetheless interested. After Detective Philip Thibedeau interviewed Shea, however, he determined that he was not Meslener's killer. A week later, two other detectives returned to the base. The stains on Shea's shirt had been identified as human blood. Detectives questioned Shea a second time, but once again, he did not impress them as a suspect. After this interview, the detectives stopped to talk with two military police officers just outside the room where Shea was held. Shea heard their detailed conversation of the Meslener murder, and when the detectives stepped back into the consultation room, Shea repeated their conversation in the form of a confession. Prior to this "confession," Shea had been examined by a psychiatrist who determined that he was "agitated, depressed, anxious." Two days after his arrest, Shea denied committing the murder; a second confession was made by Shea within a week. This admission came after police told Shea his fingerprints were found on the car—which they were not; that he had failed a lie detector test—which had in actuality proved his innocence; that eyewitnesses identified him—although they were no witnesses; and that the blood on his shirt matched Meslener's—when in fact, it matched his own. In 1959, this confession was used to convict Shea. He was sentenced to life in prison.

Disgruntled by his department's handling of the investigation, Thibedeau quit the police department. Warren D. Holmes, head of the Miami Police polygraph department, felt his superiors' claim that his findings were inaccurate tarnished his record. He resigned. The two men soon joined Miami *Herald* reporter Gene Miller in clearing Shea's name. They discovered that Shea had been on duty eighty miles from the murder scene an hour before the murder. Shea was granted a new trial and with Harry W. Prebish as his lawyer, he was acquitted. In 1967, the Florida state legislature awarded Shea $45,000. That same year, Miller won a Pulitzer Prize for his work on the acquittal of Shea and that of a Louisiana woman wrongly convicted of murder, who Holmes had also worked to clear.

REF.: *CBA;* Raab, *Justice in the Back Room.*

Shearman, Sir Montague, 1857-1930, Brit., jur. Became King's Counsel in 1903 and later served on High Court, King's Bench from 1914-29. He presided over many notable murder trials, including those of Arther Andrew Clement Goslett, Harold Greenwood, Reginald Dunn, Edith Thompson, James Yeldham, Jack Hewett, and Albert Arthur Burrows. REF.: *CBA.*

Sheasby, June, 1950-57, and **Sheasby, Royston**, 1952-57, Brit., (unsolv.) mur. On June 20, 1957, 7-year-old June Sheasby and her 5-year-old brother Royston Sheasby disappeared. The two were last seen at Wickham Glen near an insane asylum, not far from their home in Bristol, England. None of the patients of the hospital were reported missing the day the children disappeared. Numerous ransom letters were received by the parents, asking for £200 and signed "West Indians." The bodies of the children were finally discovered on July 1 under some bushes at the Snuff Mills Beauty Shop, near the same insane asylum where the Sheasby children were last seen. Two hours before this discovery, a letter was posted at Bristol which informed authorities that the bodies had been buried and not cast into the river.

REF.: *CBA;* Furneaux, *Famous Criminal Cases, vol. 5.*

Sheehan, Patrick, and **Mosher, John W.**, prom. 1900, U.S., rob. On July 1, 1900, an elderly man was robbed at a picnic in Sharpshooters' Park in Chicago; officers Patrick Sheehan and John W. Mosher, who were assigned to patrol the park that day, were accused. At 11 p.m., Hugh McDougall had walked into the park and was detained by the policemen who accused him of climbing over the fence. McDougall said he had come in through the gate, but Sheehan and Mosher said there was no gate. Offering to show them, McDougall asked them to follow, and all three headed towards the entrance. Sheehan told the older man he had a gun, and then lifted a spyglass from McDougall's pocket. Mosher took a roll of $160 from the elderly man's vest, saying he would return it at the station. Near the park entrance, the officers attacked McDougall, who grabbed Sheehan's watch chain as he fell. The two officers ran away, and McDougall ran back into the park and relayed the incident to Officer Moore, who did not believe him, but returned to the spot with several other people and found McDougall's hat, two pieces of the watch chain, and a charm.

McDougall later picked out Sheehan and Mosher from a lineup. A first trial resulted in a discharge after the jury failed to reach a verdict. At the second trial, before Judge Horton, the watch charm and the chain were identified as Sheehan's. On May 15, 1901, both Mosher and Sheehan were found Guilty and were sentenced to indefinite terms to be served at the Joliet State Penitentiary. REF.: *CBA.*

Sheen, William, prom. 1827, Case of, Brit., mur. On May 10, 1827, Lydia Beadle returned to her Lambeth, England, home to find the severed head of her 4-month-old son lying in a pool of blood on the table, his body lying at the foot of the bed. When she last saw him alive, he had been lying next his father, William Sheen, who had abused the child since his birth. Sheen was nowhere to be found, and was not arrested until May 17 in Radnorshire.

At the trial, it was a foregone conclusion that Sheen was the murderer. The indictment against him, however, read that Sheen was charged with the willful murder of "his infant son, William Sheen, alias Beadle, on the 10th of May last." Following the prosecution's case, defense counsel pointed out that the baptismal register named the child as Charles William Beadle and not William Sheen. Therefore, the indictment was for the murder of a child who was not named in the charge. Reluctantly, the judge agreed that the wording of the indictment was technically incorrect and instructed the jury to return a verdict of not guilty. Their decision was "Not guilty of killing as laid in the indictment." Sheen was dismissed, but tried again on July 13. The indictment against him this time contained thirteen counts. To avoid any loophole, the crime was described in numerous ways, using variations of the child's name. Sergeant Andrews entered a plea of *autre fois acquit* for Sheen, and it was decided that Sheen had indeed been tried for the same crime, despite the wording of the new indictment. REF.: *CBA*.

Sheldon Gang, prom. 1920s, U.S., org. crime. During Prohibition, Ralph Sheldon of Chicago's Southwest Side formed a gang to supply bootleg liquor to the distribution network of crime boss Al Capone. Competition was fierce and rival gangs fought for the easy money and the territories, which were divided by uneasy truces. Sheldon fought a South Side gang led by Edward "Spike" O'Donnell and in 1925, began battling Joe Saltis, a saloon owner who had formed a gang with Frankie McErlane. Although a Capone supporter, Saltis was suspected of supplying liquor to North Side boss Earl "Hymie" Weiss. The competition turned to bloodshed in April 1926, when Sheldon lost Frank DeLaurentis and John Tucillo, two of his best distributors. In October 1926, a city-wide amnesty was declared by the South Side Capone organization and George "Bugs" Moran's North Side network. But on Dec. 30, 1926, Sheldon Gang member Hillory Clements was shot to death by Saltis rivals. The Sheldons retaliated on Mar. 11, 1927, killing Charlie "Big Hayes" Hubacek and Frank "Lefty" Koncil, who for years had been Saltis' top gunmen. Saltis went to Capone for protection and in exchange for a large stipend, was reassured of peace. By the late 1920s, the Sheldon Gang was also suspected of dealing with the North Side rivals, but as a national crime network began to emerge in the 1930s, the smaller gangs were absorbed and consolidated. The Sheldon Gang ceased to exist in 1932, shortly before the end of Prohibition. See: **Saltis, Joseph**.

Chicago crime boss Ralph Sheldon.

REF.: Asbury, *Gem of the Prairie; CBA;* Kobler, *Al Capone;* Landesco, *Organized Crime in Chicago;* McPhaul, *Johnny Torrio;* Nash, *Bloodletters and Badmen;* ____, *Hustlers and Con Men.*

Shelfo, Rosary, 1920- , U.S., mur. Rosary Shelfo and her husband, Joseph Shelfo, lived in Los Angeles. When she gave birth to their first child, Ross, in February 1943, her attitude began to change. According to Joseph, a 26-year-old employee of the California Shipyards, Rosary had been "moody...with a faraway look in her eye, ever since we brought her home from the hospital a week ago." Because Ross was a quiet baby, Rosary decided he was not normal. "I even had a priest and the doctor over to examine the baby and they assured her he was a perfect child," her husband said. These assurances did not relieve her anxieties.

Shortly before noon on Mar. 8, 1943, Rosary Shelfo fed her 2-week-old son for the last time. As Joseph slept in the adjacent bedroom, she killed the baby with a butcher knife. Awakening her husband, Rosary confessed what she had done. Joe Shelfo called his father, Ross, for whom the infant had been named, and in a few minutes the police arrived.

The case went before Judge Charles W. Fricke of the Los Angeles Superior Court, who found Mrs. Shelfo Guilty of second-degree murder. But after reviewing a psychiatrist's report, the judge ruled her Not Guilty by reason of insanity on May 18. Rosary Shelfo was ordered committed to the Mendocino State Hospital for the Insane on June 19, 1943. She was discharged, after only a year, on July 15, 1944. REF.: *CBA*.

Shell, Terry Lee, 1922-78, U.S., jur. Prosecuting attorney for Arkansas from 1955-60. He was nominated to the district court of Arkansas by President Gerald Ford in 1975. REF.: *CBA*.

Shelton Brothers, prom. 1920s, U.S., boot.-org. crime. Earl, Carl, and Bernie Shelton and their gang bootlegged liquor in Williamson County, Ill., during the 1920s. These homespun moonshiners controlled liquor distribution in the vicinity of East St. Louis and were impervious to the law and rival gangs until Charles Birger arrived from New York. A battle between the Shelton Brothers and Birger's gang commenced in Williamson County, which dragged on for nearly seven years. Before hostilities ceased, both gangs converted trucks into tanks, and at one point, the Sheltons hired airplanes to drop bombs on the Birger stronghold at Egypt, Ill. But in the end, Birger's gang proved stronger and prevailed. See: **Birger, Charles**. REF.: *CBA*.

Shen Kua, 1030-93, China, banish. Joined imperial government service in 1063, and later was named commissioner for prefectural civil and military affairs for Yen-chou province in 1077. He was banished after his troops were defeated by the Khitan tribes in 1081. REF.: *CBA*.

Shephard, Clifford, b.1886, U.S., (wrong. convict.) forg. In 1935 Clifford Shephard was arrested in New Brunswick, N.J., on suspicion of being the "phantom forger" who had been writing bad checks throughout New Jersey. He was soon identified by a number of merchants, and he and girlfriend Betty Lester, were tried for forgery. Although sixteen witnesses testified on their behalf, Shephard and Lester were convicted on the testimony of a liquor dealer, who was positive Shephard was the forger. They were sentenced to nine months imprisonment in the county workhouse.

Following Shephard's release, he was arrested by Newark police for further forgeries committed during the same period as the first conviction. He was found Guilty a second time and sentenced to eighteen months in prison. After serving this sentence, Shephard was once again accused of forgery. However, the grand jury did not indict him for this crime since the forgeries were committed while he was in prison. Months went by before the real "phantom forger"—Edward Sullivan—was arrested. Sullivan was convicted and sentenced to a prison term in Wisconsin. Shephard traveled to Wisconsin where the real criminal wrote a confession stating he had forged the checks Shephard had been convicted of writing. Even with this signed confession, the New Jersey Court of Pardons refused twice to pardon Shephard, who could no longer find worthwhile employment because of his criminal record. Finally, in June 1950, Shephard received a full pardon from New Jersey governor Alfred E. Driscoll. REF.: *CBA*.

Shepherd, Charles, 1887-1928, Case of, U.S., rape-mur. Charles Shepherd, forty-one, was serving a twenty-year sentence for manslaughter at a state prison farm near Parchman, Miss., in 1928 when a white prison guard, J.B. Duvall, allegedly whipped Shepherd, who was black, for some infraction of the prison rules. In retaliation, Shepherd reportedly broke into Duvall's home, attacked Duvall's 18-year-old daughter, slit Duvall's throat with a butcher knife, and stabbed him repeatedly in the head with an ice pick. Shepherd then fled with the woman.

Less than two days later, the woman was found alive in the nearby woods, naked. Shepherd was found shortly thereafter at his brother's home and was turned over to National Guardsmen. Before Shepherd could be returned to the prison, a mob took Shepherd and burned him alive in a huge bonfire reportedly witnessed by many people. When informed of Shepherd's murder, Mississippi governor Theodore G. Bilbo said that no investigation would be made at his instigation. "I have neither the time nor the money to investigate," Bilbo said. A coroner's inquest indicated that Shepherd "came to his death from causes unknown." REF.: *CBA.*

Shepherd, J.C., d.1832, Brit., (unsolv.) mur. In December 1832, a clerk at a London soap factory was found dead in his office by employees arriving at work. He had been beaten to death with an iron poker. A magistrate's officer learned that when Shepherd had gone to Hampstead the previous day on business, someone had seen two "low-looking" types following him. Someone else had seen two similarly "low-looking" men near the Goswell Street factory where Shepherd worked, but they were not located, and the case was turned over to the police.

Superintendent Dixon took over. He found marks indicating that the office safe had been damaged but not broken into, and there were no signs of forced entry into the building. Assuming that Shepherd knew the person he admitted to the building, the police arrested a friend, Samuel Newland, but he had an alibi. Then they arrested two men named Martin and Ainslee, but they were released. Shepherd's murder remained unsolved.

REF.: *CBA;* Cobb, *The First Detectives.*

Shepherd, Oliver, d.1868, U.S., west. outl. During the Civil War Oliver Shepherd battled and robbed with the Missouri guerrillas before joining the James-Younger Gang of outlaws which included Jesse James and Cole, John, James, and Robert Younger. On Feb. 13, 1866, Shepherd and eleven other gang members committed the first daylight bank robbery in the U.S. in Liberty, Mo. Shooting broke out as the robbers were riding out of town with the stolen $57,000. George Wymore, a college student, was caught in the fire and killed.

On Mar. 21, 1868, eight members of the James-Younger Gang, including Shepherd, rode into Russelville, Ky., and robbed the Southern Bank of Kentucky of $14,000. Bank president Nimrod Long was wounded in the head and the gang fled, shooting as they left. An intensive manhunt followed and George Shepherd, Oliver's cousin, was arrested. The gang dispersed with Oliver returning to Missouri trailed by a Kentucky posse. In Jackson County, Mo., he was confronted by another posse and ordered to surrender. Shepherd instead drew his gun and attempted to shoot his way to safety. He was killed, with twenty bullets tearing into his body.

REF.: Breihan, *The Complete and Authentic Life of Jesse James;* ____, *The Day Jesse James Was Killed;* ____, *Younger Brothers;* Castel, *William Clarke Quantrill; CBA;* Crittenden, *The Crittenden Memoirs;* Croy, *Jesse James Was My Neighbor;* ____, *Last of the Great Outlaws;* Edwards, *Noted Guerrillas;* Gardner, *The Old Wild West;* Horan, *Desperate Men;* Hough, *The Story of the Outlaw;* Love, *The Rise and Fall of Jesse James;* Settle, *Jesse James Was His Name;* Wellman, *A Dynasty of Western Outlaws.*

Shepley, George Foster, 1819-78, U.S., jur. Served as U.S. district attorney from 1848-61, and as state representative in Maine from 1866-67. He was nominated to the first circuit court by President Ulysses S. Grant in 1869. REF.: *CBA.*

Sheppard, Jack (John, AKA: Slippery Jack, The Prince of Prison-Breakers), 1702-24, Brit., pris. esc.-rob. When Jack Sheppard, perhaps the most successful prison-break artist of all time, and the only man ever to break out of Newgate Prison twice, was hanged in 1724, the world continued to applaud his memory in verse, in drama, in paintings, and even in sermons. Sheppard, dubbed the "Prince of Prison-Breakers" by Horace Bleackley, was born in Stepney, near London, in 1702. His father, a carpenter, died when Jack was still young. His mother, unable to support her family, sent him to a workhouse in Bishopsgate Street where he remained for a year and a half. When he left the workhouse, he apprenticed under a Mr. Wood as a carpenter. Sheppard proved very adept at his trade, but after he had served six of his seven years of apprenticeship, he met Elizabeth Lyon, also known as "Edgworth Bess." Though Lyon was reportedly married and looked upon by many as a loose woman, Sheppard asked Lyon to move in with him.

A blacksmith removes the iron leggings from Jack Sheppard's feet after his escape from Newgate.

Soon after he began living with Lyon, Sheppard grew impatient with his employment and abusive of his employer. When Sheppard's increasingly hostile behavior caused Wood to suspect him of robbing a neighbor, he barred the young man from his house. However, displaying talents which would later earn him fame, Sheppard broke into his employer's house by picking the locks.

In July 1723, Sheppard broke into the house of a Mr. Braines, on whose home Sheppard was doing some carpentry work, and stole cash and goods in the amount of £21. Braines, discovering that he had been robbed, searched for signs of a break-in, and when he found none he had a woman lodger arrested for the theft. Much later, when Sheppard finally was arrested he confessed to the robbery, explaining he had taken the iron bars from the cellar window and carefully replaced them when he was through.

With only ten months remaining on his apprenticeship, Sheppard left Wood and took up with a group of criminals who included Joseph Blake and James Sykes. On Oct. 23, 1723, again using his trade as a disguise for a robbery, he took a considerable amount of jewelry, silver, and clothing from his fellow boarders. Although he was not arrested or even suspected for this burglary, his brother Thomas, a notorious thief and housebreaker serving time in Newgate Prison, told authorities that Sheppard and Lyon had helped him commit another burglary at the home of William Phillips. Now sought by police, Sheppard met Sykes at Sedgate's, an inn near the Seven Dials. While Sheppard was diverted, Sykes contacted a constable, who arrested Sheppard. Sheppard was confined in the local jail until he could be transferred the next day to Newgate. Within two hours, however, with only a razor and part of a chair, Sheppard broke through the roof and escaped. On May 19, 1724, however, Sheppard was again arrested and locked up at St. Ann's jail in Soho. When Lyon came to visit him the next day, she was also arrested. The various people Sheppard had robbed appeared before Justice Waller to testify against him. Both he and Lyon were sent to the New Prison until they could be transferred to Newgate. The authorities, believing them to be a married couple, allowed them to occupy the same cell, the most secure cell in the jail. Sheppard was also bound with heavy irons. During the four days they remained there, they were allowed visits from their friends, who smuggled in tools to help them escape. After sawing off his chains, Sheppard cut an iron bar from the window, removed a nine-inch-thick solid oak bar, and he and Lyon slid down the twenty-five foot drop on bed linens he had tied together. After landing, Sheppard realized they had escaped from New Prison to Clerkenwell-Bridewell, an adjoining prison. Undaunted, he constructed a scaling ladder. Within ten minutes he and Lyon were over the wall.

Over the next two months, Sheppard carried on his criminal activities with renewed gusto. With a trademark cockiness, Sheppard returned to his old neighborhood on Wych Street and with the help of Anthony Lamb and Charles Grace, planned a burglary. On June 16, the trio broke into the room of a Mr. Burton, who lived in Lamb's employer's home. Grace held a pistol on the sleeping Burton with orders to shoot him in the head if he awoke. The other two rifled the man's belongings. They made off with cash and goods worth up to £300. Sheppard again displayed his lack of fear by having some of the stolen clothing altered and strutting around in public. Grace disappeared after the loot was divided, but Lamb was arrested. Lamb confessed when he was brought before Justice Newton. He received a sentence of transportation.

On July 12, 1724, Sheppard, Joseph Blake, and William Field broke into the house of William Kneebone in the Strand. The trio looted the house for three hours, carrying away a selection of household goods worth £50. On July 19, Sheppard and Blake stopped a coach on the Hampstead road and robbed its occupant. The following night they robbed a Mr. Pargiter. On July 21, they stopped a stage coach and robbed the occupants. Lyon was arrested on July 22 and under interrogation told police where Sheppard was. He was caught the next day at Blake's mother's home and returned to New Prison, where he was confined in the dungeon. The following day he confessed all his most recent robberies to Justice Blackerby, who sent him to Newgate to await trial. He was tried on three separate indictments at the Old Bailey. Although acquitted on two of the counts due to lack of evidence, he was convicted on the third and sentenced to death. He was returned to Newgate, this time to the condemned hole, where he was given tools by other condemned prisoners unable to make their own escape before their execution date. Sheppard broke out of the prison on Aug. 31, 1724, five days before his execution was scheduled. He was again apprehended on Sept. 10, and returned to Newgate, where he was not only put in the condemned hold, but had heavy double chains binding his feet to the floor.

His jailers found escape tools on him on two separate occasions, so they moved him to "the castle," a place located in the body of the jail, where they chained him to two large iron staples imbedded in the floor. On Oct. 15, Sheppard used a crooked nail he found on the floor of his cell to open the padlock fastening his chains to the staple. No longer bound to the floor, Sheppard slowly broke a hole through a chimney, which allowed him to squeeze into a less well-secured room. After making his way through a series of locks and bolts, Sheppard made his way to the street, once again a free man.

With characteristic bravado, Sheppard remained in his old neighborhood, committing robberies and showing himself in public. An ale-house boy recognized him and called the authorities, who arrested him on Oct. 31. On Nov. 10, he was returned to trial and again given a death sentence, with his execution scheduled for six days later. When his execution day arrived, a guard searching him for weapons discovered a penknife with its blade open and pointing up in his shirt pocket. Sheppard admitted his intention to use the knife to cut the ropes binding his hands, then escape into the crowd as he was conveyed to the place of execution. Sheppard's tricks had run out. He was hanged at Tyburn on Nov. 16, 1724, at the age of twenty-two. A sympathetic crowd watched him die painfully. His friends buried him that same evening in St. Martin's churchyard. Sheppard excited people's imagination, and for some time afterward his escapades provided conversation in all ranks of society. Various presses published stories of his life and adventures. A pantomime called *Harlequin Sheppard* presented at the royal theater of Drury Lane depicted his adventures and prison escapes, and a three-act farce called *The Prison Breaker,* or *The Adventures of John Sheppard,* also immortalized him.

REF.: *CBA;* Reppetto, *The Blue Parade;* (FILM), *Where's Jack,* 1969.

Sheppard, Odell, 1948- , U.S., cont./ct.-abduc. During an argument on Sept. 29, 1984, 36-year-old Odell Sheppard beat Norell Sanders, the mother of his 2-year-old daughter. The child, Deborah Lynn Sanders, disappeared after the argument. In August 1986, Sheppard became the first person in Illinois convicted of parental child abduction under a 1985 revision of the law that extended protection to unwed mothers. Sheppard served one year of a three-year sentence. On his release he was returned to court and asked to reveal the whereabouts of his daughter. When he refused, he was sentenced to six months for contempt of court. Despite the judge's intention to continue to cite him for contempt for as long as he refused to return the child, Sheppard repeatedly insisted that he had returned Deborah to her mother in December 1984. At the time of this writing, Sheppard has served three consecutive terms for contempt and still had not revealed his daughter's whereabouts. REF.: *CBA.*

Dr. Sam Sheppard and his wife Marilyn, whom he murdered in 1954.

Sheppard, Samuel, 1924-70, Case of, U.S., mur. Dr. Samuel and Marilyn Sheppard had been high school sweethearts who exchanged passionate love letters when Sam left his eastern Ohio home town to study osteopathic medicine in Indiana and Southern California. Marilyn wrote that life without Sam was impossible and he wrote back that he couldn't wait to see her again. Upon his return in 1945, the couple married and bought a large two-story house on the shores of Lake Erie in the Cleveland suburb of Bay Village. Sam began practicing medicine at a private hospital that he owned with his father and two brothers. The couple's son, Sam Jr., or Chip, was born in 1947. Sam devoted himself to his thriving practice, while Marilyn was involved in school and church activities in the community. But after five years of marriage they began to grow apart. By 1954, Sam's involvement with other women was rumored, including an affair with a laboratory technician at his hospital. No discord was evident on July 3, 1954, when the Sheppards threw an Independence Day party; as people left at midnight, Sam's and Marilyn's friends and neighbors' final memories of the couple would be of mutual affection. Marilyn Sheppard was brutally murdered within four hours.

Shortly before 6 a.m. on July 4, 1954, Mayor J. Spencer Houk, a friend of the Sheppards, received a frantic phone call from Sam, imploring assistance because he thought Marilyn had been murdered. Houk arrived within seven minutes. He found Marilyn Sheppard in a blood-soaked bedroom, her nightgown shredded and her scull crushed with the force of twenty-seven blows from a heavy instrument.

Sheppard told investigators that he had fallen asleep on a downstairs sofa, and been awakened by his wife's screams. Marilyn was four months pregnant and had recently suffered convulsions. Racing up the stairs and entering their bedroom, Sam saw a shadowy figure standing over his wife's bed. As he advanced, he was knocked down from a blow to the back of the neck. Recovering from the blow, he chased someone he described as a bushy-haired figure downstairs, out the door, and along a path adjacent to the lake, where the assailant struck him again, and he lost consciousness on the sandy shore. Awakening two hours later, Sheppard limped back to his house and called his friend.

Dr. Sheppard returning home from the hospital.

Sam's brothers diagnosed him as having suffered a broken neck and placed him in the family's hospital, but he merely had lacerations and a black eye. (A possible spinal injury caused him to wear a leather collar in public.) Investigators were skeptical of Sheppard's account of the fateful night. They determined that it should have taken him less than ten seconds to respond to the screams, though for an assailant to deliver twenty-seven lethal blows would take at least a full minute. Fingerprints had been carefully eliminated from the murder scene, including those normally found in an active household. The violence didn't wake the 6-year-old child or stir the family's dog. And the bloodstained shirt Sheppard was wearing during his pursuit of the attacker had mysteriously disappeared. Sheppard was vehement about his innocence, even offering $10,000 for information regarding the crime. His friend, Mayor Houk, refused to order his arrest, but after a crusade instigated by Louis B. Seltzer, the publisher of the *Cleveland Press,* police arrested Sheppard on July 30, 1954, on the suspicion of murdering his wife.

Sheppard was interrogated by a team of twelve detectives, but he refused to break, finding strength in the Bible. Five days later he was released on a $50,000 bond, but, on Aug. 6, after his involvement with the laboratory technician, Susan Hayes, became known, he was indicted for murder by a Grand Jury.

The longest murder trial in U.S. history commenced in Cleveland on Oct. 18, 1954, at the Cuyahoga County criminal courtroom of Judge Edward Blythin. Sheppard was defended by William Corrigan, an Irish-born criminal lawyer, while the prosecution was presented by John J. Mahon and assisted by Saul S. Danaceau and Thomas Parrino. Thirty-one witnesses appeared before the jury, including Susan Hayes, who detailed her fifteen-month clandestine affair with Sheppard. Mahon's team sought to prove guilt by the time lapsed between the actual crime and the call to Mayor Houk, the missing shirt, and a trail of blood from the murder scene. Corrigan countered that losing a garment was an everyday occurrence, and that the bloodstains were inconclusively matched to Sheppard. Also, as no weapon had been found, there was no forensic evidence to connect Sheppard to the crime. After hearing nine weeks of testimony the jury of five women and seven men retired on Dec. 17. They deliberated for more than 100 hours, discussing 2 million words of testimony and more than 200 exhibits from the Sheppard household. Finally, on Dec. 21, 1954, they announced their verdict that Sheppard was Guilty of second-degree murder, for which Blythin sentenced him to life imprisonment at the Ohio State Prison. Corrigan immediately filed for an appeal. The weight of the trial was devastating to the Sheppard family. Two weeks after the conviction, on Jan. 7, 1955, Sheppard's mother put a gun to her head and committed suicide. Ten days later, the elder Dr. Sheppard succumbed to illness and grief. Sam Sheppard twice stood the public humiliation of attending graveside ceremonies handcuffed to a sheriff.

The defense offered new evidence indicating that the murderer was a left-handed person with the strength of a woman, which would have exonerated the hefty, right-handed Sheppard, but the appeal was rejected three times during the following year. More years passed as Corrigan doggedly pursued the appellate process to higher courts. Corrigan died in 1961, and Sheppard's hopes began to wane, but in 1963 he started corresponding with a wealthy German divorcee, Ariane Tebbenjohanns, and a romance blossomed. His appeal was assumed by F. Lee Bailey, then just six years out of law school. Bailey brought the process to the highest stage when, in the spring of 1966, the final appeal reached the U.S. Supreme Court.

After almost twelve years in prison, Sheppard won a new trial on June 6, 1966, on the grounds that the original conviction had been tainted by prejudicial publicity, the first such opinion in U.S. legal history. The case was again remanded to the Cuyahoga Criminal Court in Cleveland. While he was out on appeal, Sheppard married his girlfriend, Ariane. On Oct. 24, 1966, accompanied by F. Lee Bailey, he reentered the courtroom in Cleveland, now presided over by Judge Francis Talty. Bailey attacked the slipshod police work at the murder scene that possibly ruined fingerprint evidence. Bailey forced coroner Dr. Samuel Gerber to admit that while he had testified that the murder was committed with a surgical instrument, he could not identify its type. But prosecutor John T. Corrigan, (no relation to William Corrigan), countered with testimony from Gerber's assistant, who said she had discovered Sheppard's pocket watch covered with flecks of blood. Bailey persevered, and on Nov. 16, 1966, more than twelve years after the crime was committed, Sheppard was acquitted of his wife's murder.

Life outside of prison brought no relief. Sheppard returned to medical practice in Youngstown, Ohio, but was served with two wrongful death suits. After five years of marriage, the relationship faltered and Ariane filed for divorce, claiming that he had physically threatened her. Moving to Columbus, Ohio, he fought drug addiction and the loss of professional trust. He became a professional wrestler, and married a third time, to the 19-year-old daughter of a fellow grappler. This time the marriage was over within six months, his bride beseeching him to attend to his faltering health. He deteriorated rapidly, and on Apr. 6, 1970, Dr. Sam Sheppard died of natural causes at the age of forty-six.

REF: Bailey, *The Defense Never Rests; CBA;* Holmes, *The Sheppard Murder Case;* Messick, *Syndicate in the Sun;* Nash, *Almanac of World Crime;* Pollack, *Dr. Sam—An American Tragedy;* Rowan, *Famous American Crimes;* Seppard, *Endure and Conquer;* Sheppard, *My Brother's Keeper;* (FILM), *The Lawyer,* 1969.

Sherburne, John Samuel, 1757-1830, U.S., jur. U.S. district attorney from 1789-93, and U.S. congressman from New Hampshire from 1793-97. He was nominated to the district court of New Hampshire by President Thomas Jefferson in 1804. REF.: *CBA.*

Sheridan, Andrew (AKA: **Squint, Andrew Thomas**), 1900-1949, U.S., mur. On Jan. 8, 1947, three men, John M."Cockeye" Dunn, Andrew "Squint" Sheridan, and Daniel Gentile (more commonly known by his former prize ring name of Danny Brooks), ambushed a 43-year-old New York boss stevedore, Anthony Hintz, in the hallway of his Greenwich Village apartment. Hintz, who was in charge of the daily hiring of several hundred longshoremen at New York City's Pier 51, was shot, and died three weeks later of the wounds. When the suspects were tried for the murder, the prosecution contended that the killers were hired by local gangsters who wanted Hintz's position so that they could pick their own men for dock work and collect kickbacks from them.

On Dec. 31, 1947, first-degree murder convictions were returned against all three men. The convictions carried a mandatory sentence of death in the electric chair. The executions were delayed six times in the expectation that Dunn might testify against mob activity on the waterfront in exchange for a commutation of his sentence. Gentile did relent and provided the District Attorney's office with information about waterfront criminal activity. Thirty-six hours after Gentile's sentence was commuted to life imprisonment, Dunn and Sheridan were executed in the electric chair at Sing Sing prison. REF.: *CBA.*

Sheridan, Matthew, 1949- , U.S., mur. On Feb. 28, 1969, a 20-year-old New Jersey man, Matthew Sheridan, was sentenced to life in prison for the murders of 66-year-old Oliver Clarkson and his 64-year-old wife, Ethyl Clarkson. In prison, Sheridan was a model prisoner and earned both a bachelor's degree in political science and a master's degree in education. While in Yardville Prison, Sheridan volunteered to teach remedial reading to young convicts. Following his transfer to a minimum security facility, Sheridan was hired under a work release program to teach and counsel the inmates of the Jamesburg Reformatory for Boys. The $16,690.49 annual salary was held in trust for Sheridan, with deductions being made only for taxes, social security, and $20 per week for his room and board at the prison. Despite taxpayer protest, a spokesperson for the New Jersey Board of Corrections said that Sheridan would stay on the payroll and most likely be offered a job when he was paroled. REF.: *CBA.*

Sheridan, Walter Cartman (AKA: **John Holcom, Charles H. Keene** or **Kean, Charles H. Ralston, Walter Stanton, Walter A. Stewart**), 1838-90, U.S.-Belg., rob.-forg.-fraud. Walter Sheridan, the man behind the great Bank of England forgeries, was one of America's most dexterous swindlers—the nemesis of the Pinkerton Detective Agency for nearly three decades. Sheridan was born in New Orleans to a respectable family and received a liberal education. His foray into crime began while he was still in his teens. In 1858, he was arrested by Missouri authorities for stealing a horse, then a crime often punishable by death. Sheridan was arrested later that same year in Chicago with Joseph Moran, a western outlaw, who helped him plan a bank robbery. This caper resulted in a five-year prison sentence at the Alton Penitentiary.

After his release from Alton, the wily Sheridan, along with Charles Hicks and Philip Pearson, planned a daring holdup of the First National Bank of Springfield, Ill. Hicks and Pearson entered the bank through an open window while Sheridan held the teller at gunpoint. The robbers then removed $35,000 from the vault, and made their way out of the bank without firing a shot. Pearson took his share of the loot and fled to Europe. Hicks was soon arrested and sent to the Joliet Penitentiary. Detective William Pinkerton was assigned to the case by his illustrious father, who at the moment, was in Washington engaged in the war effort. Finding Sheridan proved to be no problem. Holding on to him was another matter.

Pinkerton arrested him in Toledo, Ohio, with $22,000 on his person. He was escorted back to Chicago, but while in transit Sheridan tried to convince the passengers that he was being held hostage by two kidnappers. When this ploy failed, Sheridan offered $10,000 to the second Pinkerton operative assigned to guard him. William Pinkerton sat out the remainder of the train ride with his sidearm poised to shoot Sheridan or his own assistant, if circumstances warranted it. In Chicago, Sheridan spent the bulk of his $20,000 savings to avoid another prison sentence. He forced the courts into granting him a change of venue to Decatur, Ill. Then, armed with the best legal minds available to him, Sheridan won an acquittal from jurors he had allegedly bribed.

Walter Sheridan

In the next few years Sheridan pulled off a series of robberies in the eastern half of the U.S. Following his acquittal in Decatur, Sheridan made off with $120,000 in bonds from the Maryland Fire Insurance Company. He followed this up with the successful holdup of the Merchants' and Mechanics' Bank of Scranton, Penn. With the help of "Little" George Corson, Sheridan looted $37,000 in bonds from the vault. Next came a $40,000 heist of a Cleveland bank. Sheridan got away, but his confederates, Jesse Allen, Joseph Butts, and James Griffin, were captured. Allen and Griffin were convicted and sentenced to the state prison; Butts was discharged.

One of Sheridan's most notorious frauds involved the father of Supreme Court Justice Samuel Milford Blatchford. The elder Blatchford was accosted by Sheridan near Nassau and Liberty streets in Manhattan one day. During their conversation, Blatchford unthinkingly placed his wallet containing $75,000 worth of bonds on an apple stand. In an instant, the billfold was snatched by one of Sheridan's confederates. Several of these bonds were later found in the possession of Horace S. Corp, a brother-in-law of one of the men working for Sheridan.

In 1872, Sheridan and his gang of confidence men, which included the likes of George Wilkes, Andrew J. Roberts, Frank Gleason, Samuel Perry, George McDonald, Austin and Biron Bidwell, and Gottlieb Engels, devised a fabulous scheme to forge notes drawn on the Bank of England. Before the last hand was played out, Sheridan and company precipitated a near-panic on Wall Street that sent dozens of investors to ruin in Summer 1873. The London end of the operation was headed by the Bidwell brothers and McDonald, none of whom could keep the affair to themselves. They spent much of their time drinking and roistering in the pubs in the Argyle and Barnes district of London. When their monies were spent and their criminal intentions revealed, the Bidwells and McDonald crossed the ocean and hid out in New York.

Meanwhile, Sheridan was forced to make adjustments. The remaining members of the gang began forging false bonds made out in the issue of the New York Central Railroad, the Buffalo and Erie Railroad, the Union and Pacific Railroad, New Jersey Central Railroad, Tobo and Neosho Railroad, the California and Oregon Railroad, and the Chicago and Northwestern Railroad. The penman Engels, an artisan in his own right, prepared the bogus securities, whose face value exceeded $2.5 million. Posing as Charles H. Ralston, Sheridan became a member of the New York Produce Exchange and rented an office at 60 Broadway, where he advertised himself as president of the Belgian Stone Company, purveyors of exquisite marble. The forged bonds were placed on the market for astonishingly low prices. A shareholder of the Buffalo and Erie Railroad demanded to know if they were genuine. "Why my dear sir, of course they're genuine," Sheridan replied. "And a surprising bargain at that figure." The man bought $30,000 worth.

Swindler Sheridan being arrested.

The counterfeiters obtained $70,000 from the New York Guarantee and Indemnity Company, giving as collateral $102,000 in forged bonds of the Buffalo and Erie Line. The following day Sheridan secured an additional $30,000 using the same worthless securities. The scheme was revealed in September 1873, by which time Sheridan had already escaped to Europe. Detective Pinkerton traced his movements through Belgium and the continent until Sheridan made the mistake of returning to the U.S. in Fall 1875. The chase continued through Ohio, Nebraska, Colorado, Utah, California, and all over the west until Pinkerton received a tip that Sheridan was returning to New York. At 11 p.m. on the night of Mar. 22, 1876, the con man stepped off a ferry at the foot of Desbrosses Street in Manhattan, into the waiting arms of Robert Pinkerton. "Bob, what's this for?" the startled Sheridan asked. When told that the game was up, he shrugged and accompanied Pinkerton to the Twenty-Seventh Precinct Station. He was arraigned at the Court of the General Sessions the next day on eighty-four counts of forgery. With a staggering amount of evidence against him, Sheridan was convicted and sent to prison for five years.

Upon his release he returned to his former haunts to pick up where he left off, though advancing age and declining health began to take their toll. In January 1890, he was arrested by Canadian police for the robbery at La Banque du Peuple in Montreal. He was sentenced to serve six months in prison, but swore to the judge that he would not live a full week if he were compelled to do hard time. On Jan. 19, Sheridan proved that he was not bluffing when a warder found him dead in his cell. The coroner ruled that the death was brought on by typhoid fever.

REF.: *CBA;* Powers, *Secrecy and Power;* Toledano, *J. Edgar Hoover;* Watters and Gillers, *Investigating the FBI.*

Sheriff, Emma, See: **McGuire, John Francis.**

Sherman, David, prom. 1907-11, U.S., (wrong. convict.) mur. On Nov. 26, 1907, Bob Henderson, Beulah McGhee, and David Sherman were to be hanged for the murder of a Mr. Hix in McGinn County, Tenn. A stay of execution was granted, however, by Governor Malcolm Rice Patterson. The hangings were rescheduled for Jan. 27, 1908. The sentences of Henderson and Sherman were commuted to life imprisonment on Jan. 23.

Prior to execution, McGhee confessed that Sherman had had nothing to do with the murder of Hix. The man just happened to be asleep in the same house as the victim. McGhee repeated his confession to the sheriff while on the scaffold. Based on McGhee's statement and a petition by Attorney General Fletcher, who felt that Sherman was completely innocent of the crime and did not even know a murder had been committed until the next day, Sherman was granted a full pardon by Patterson on Jan. 13, 1911. The board of pardons pointed out to the governor that Sherman's conviction turned out to be "quite a remarkable case of a miscarriage of justice." REF.: *CBA.*

Sherman, James D. (AKA: **Jim Talbot**), d.1896, U.S., west. gunman. James D. Sherman, also known as "Jim Talbot," assisted in trailing a cattle herd from Texas to Caldwell, Kan., in 1881. In Caldwell, Talbot rented a house for his wife and two children. Known as a desperado, he spent several weeks drinking with friends and carousing around town. On Dec. 17, 1881, he and six of his friends, Bob Bigtree, Dick Eddleman, Tom Love, Bub Munson, George Speers, and Jim Martin went on a Friday night drinking binge, became abrasive and threatened to kill a local newspaper editor and Mike Meagher, a former marshal. The next morning Meagher protested to Marshal John Wilson, who soon arrested Love for shooting off his gun. Talbot and his gang jumped Wilson and released Love. When Wilson asked Meagher for help the gang again threatened to murder Meagher.

At 1 p.m. Wilson arrested Martin and fined him for carrying a gun. Deputy Marshal Will Fossett walked down the street with him so Martin could get funds to pay the fine. Talbot, Eddleman, Munson, and Love grabbed Martin and Talbot fired two shots at Wilson, then began running with Meagher and Wilson chasing him. When he reached the Opera House Talbot turned and fired his Winchester, killing Meagher with a bullet through the chest. An angry mob went after the cowboys. Speers was fatally shot and most of Talbot's gang's horses were wounded as the men rode out of town. Pursued several miles into Indian Territory by the irate citizens, the gang hid in a dugout. After they wounded W.E. Campbell their pursuers retreated.

In 1894 Talbot was arrested at his ranch in California, probably for murdering a man in Mendocino County. In 1895 his trial for the murder of Meagher ended in a hung jury and he was acquitted at a second trial. In August 1896 Talbot returned to his Ukiah, Calif., ranch. A concealed assassin—possibly John Meagher avenging his brother's death, but more probably Talbot's wife's lover—fired a shotgun when Talbot was fifty feet from his gate, severing his spinal cord and killing him instantly.

REF.: *CBA;* Drago, *Wild, Woolly and Wicked;* Miller and Snell, *Great Gunfighters of the Kansas Cowtowns.*

Sherman, John, 1823-1900, U.S., lawyer. U.S. congressman and senator whose most notable accomplishment was writing the Sherman Antitrust Act in 1890. REF.: *CBA.*

Sherman, Lydia (AKA: **America's Queen Poisoner**), c.1830-78, U.S., mur. Between 1864 and 1866, Lydia Struck poisoned Edward Struck, her husband of seventeen years who had become a drunkard after being dismissed from the police department, and then she murdered her six children. Although the weapon was arsenic, New York City doctors pronounced the deaths everything but poisonings, and Struck collected insurance on all of them.

Moving to New Haven, Conn., Struck married old Dennis Hurlbut on Nov. 22, 1868. She poisoned him and collected his estate. Then she married Horatio Nelson Sherman of Derby, Conn., who first hired her as a housekeeper in about April 1870. She killed his two children, Frank and Addie, promptly (because they "would be better off," she said later) and then, when he became an alcoholic after their deaths, she poisoned him until he died on May 12, 1871.

The Shermans' physician, Dr. Beardsley, became suspicious and called in other doctors to perform autopsies on the family. Finding poison, they had Lydia Sherman arrested. She confessed to at least eleven murders, though she may have killed as many as fifteen others. Sherman, called "America's Queen Poisoner", was found Guilty of second-degree murder (because all the evidence was circumstantial) and was sentenced to life in prison, where she died on May 16, 1878.

REF.: *CBA;* Dunbar, *Blood in the Parlor;* Nash, *Bloodletters and Bad Men;* ____, *Look for the Woman;* ____, *Murder, America;* Pearson, *Instigation of the Devil; The Poison Fiend! Life, Crimes and Conviction of Lydia Sherman (The Modern Lucretia Borgia); Three Noted Women; Truth Stranger Than Fiction.*

Sherman, Roger, 1721-93, U.S., jur. Served in Connecticut legislature variously between 1755 and 1785. He was a judge on the superior court of Connecticut from 1766-67 and from 1773-88. He served in the Continental Congress from 1774-81, in 1783, and in 1784, and with Oliver Ellsworth he presented the Connecticut Compromise. He served as a U.S. congressman from 1789-91, and as a U.S. senator from 1791-93. He signed the Declaration of Independence, the Articles of Association, the Articles of Confederation, and the U.S. Constitution—the only person to sign all four. REF.: *CBA.*

Shermarke, Abdi Rashid Ali, 1919-69, Somalia, pres., assass. Served as newly-independent Somalia's first prime minister from 1960-64, and as president from 1967 until he was assassinated. REF.: *CBA.*

Sherrington, Charles, prom. 1935, Brit., rob. After the cashier for an Ashton, England, firm left the bank with wages for the company's employees, Charles Sherrington and an accomplice attacked the man, grabbed the money, and drove away. Sherrington was arrested and identified by the cashier and a passer-by. The suspect claimed that he was at a barbershop at the time of the robbery, which three witnesses corroborated.

Fingerprints were discovered on the abandoned getaway car, and Scotland Yard's expert Fred Cherrill was called in to compare them with prints taken from Sherrington. In December 1935 Sherrington was tried at the Birmingham Assizes before Justice du Parcq. At the trial, Cherrill testified that the prints from the car were a perfect match with the defendant's. Sherrington ultimately implicated himself. He stated that he had noticed the time when he entered the barbershop by looking at the clock there. Barber George Bradburn testified that on the day of the robbery there was no clock on the wall, as it had broken the day before. After fifteen minutes deliberation, the jury found Sherrington Guilty. He was sentenced to nine months in prison, and ordered to be given twelve strokes from a cat-of-nine-tails. REF.: *CBA.*

Sherrill, Patrick Henry, d.1986, U.S. suic.-mur. On Aug. 20, 1986, a disgruntled postal worker in Edmond, Okla., entered the local post office armed with semi-automatic sharpshooting pistols and fifty rounds of ammunition. In the shooting spree that followed, Sherrill killed fourteen co-workers and wounded six more before shooting himself. Sherrill had had several run-ins with his superiors at the post office, including one the day before the shootings. Postal inspectors spent six months investigating the shootings. In February 1987, they published a 5,000-page report which found "considerable evidence of premeditation" by Sherrill. REF.: *CBA.*

Sherwood, Ella, prom. 1894, Case of, U.S., mur. On June 5, 1894, Ella Sherwood and Mattie Moore were drinking together in a Chicago saloon, when they began to argue. Sherwood shot and killed Moore with a revolver and then ran into the street where she was apprehended and arrested by Detective Clifton R. Wooldridge. Wooldridge soon learned of the murder and told another officer to take Sherwood to the police station. He did, but took credit for the arrest himself. The "arresting" officer and his partner, unaccustomed to handling murder cases, failed to collect evidence or witnesses and when the case came to trial, it was dismissed.

Earlier that year, Sherwood had allegedly robbed a Kansas rancher of $375 and given the money to a saloon owner for safe keeping. When the owner refused to return the stolen money, she vandalized his saloon. The owner refused to press charges and returned Sherwood's prize. Another victim of Sherwood's refused to testify even though Sherwood had allegedly cut the woman's face from eye to chin for sleeping with her former lover. REF.: *CBA.*

Shevchenko, Taras Hryhorovych (Taras Grigorievich Sevcenko), 1814-61, Rus., exile. Ukranian poet who originated the Brotherhood of Cyril and Methodius organization in 1846 to enact social reforms such as equality and abolition of slavery. The Brotherhood was suppressed by the government and Shevchenko was arrested and exiled the following year for writing poetry critical of Russia. He was later granted a pardon by Czar Alexander II in 1857. REF.: *CBA.*

Sheward, William, 1812-69, Brit., mur. In 1836, an unsuccessful tailor, twenty-four, married his housekeeper, Martha Francis, who was fifteen years his senior. They continually quarreled about their lack of money, and on June 15, 1851, Sheward lost his temper. Grabbing a pair of shears, he slashed his wife's throat, killing her. After leaving the body lay where it fell for a day or so, he hacked it into pieces, placed the pieces in a bag, and over several days distributed the pieces around Norwich. He boiled the head to keep it from smelling worse than it already did, then distributed pieces of it, too. Neighbors believed Martha Sheward had left her husband and gone to New Zealand.

As the body parts were found, they were pieced together by a physician who decided that the corpse was a woman between sixteen and twenty-six. The doctor's description did not match Martha Sheward, a woman in her fifties. Some months later, however, a constable came to the house to find Martha Sheward because she had inherited some money. He believed the tailor when he said Martha Sheward had disappeared and gone to London.

In 1862, Sheward married again. He tried being a publican but became an alcoholic instead. His wife, thinking a change might help, sent him to London to stay with his sister. There he decided to commit suicide and join Martha, but he could not carry out his plan. Instead, on New Year's Day 1869, he walked into the Walworth Station of the Metropolitan Police and confessed. The police did not believe him until the Norwich authorities sent the preserved remains to London for study. Surgeons there pinpointed the age of the body as about fifty-six. Sheward was tried and found Guilty and hanged at Norwich Castle on Apr. 20, 1869.

REF.: *CBA;* Wilson, *Encyclopedia of Murder.*

Shewood, William, See: **Sheward, William**.

Shillitoni, Oresto (Shillitano, AKA: **Paper Box Kid)**, d.1916, U.S., mur. On the evening of May 3, 1913, two New York policemen, Charles Teare and William Heaney, attempted to break up a fight between two men on Mulberry Street. In the course of the scuffle, both police officers and one of the men, a well-known gangster named John Rizzo, were shot and killed. According to eyewitnesses, the man who shot the other three was Oresto Shillitoni. Shillitoni disappeared after the shootings. More than 100 police officers participated in a country-wide search for Shillitoni. In mid-June, an eyewitness to the crime implicated Shillitoni's father in the shootings, and police arrested the elder Shillitoni. Then, to protect his father, Oresto Shillitoni turned himself in.

Shillitoni was found Guilty of the murders and was sentenced to death. A week before his scheduled execution, Shillitoni shot and killed Daniel McCarthy, a guard at Sing Sing, during an escape attempt. His execution was carried out as planned on June 30, 1916. REF.: *CBA*.

Shinburn, Max (AKA: Maximilian Schoenbein, Count Shindle, Henry Edward Moebus, Max Shinborn, Mark Shinburn, Walker Watterson), c.1838-1915, U.S.-Belg., rob. For a time, the king of bank robbers in the U.S. was German-born Max Shinburn, who grew up speaking five languages and soon discovered that he would rather take a bank's money than work in one. Making a thorough study of bank vaults and safe locks by working at the Lilly Safe Company, he invented a mechanism that he could leave, unseen, beneath a combination dial and it would record, over several days, the combination. He retrieved it and then quickly robbed the bank. In 1864, he was arrested and sent to prison for ten years, but he escaped twice, the second time staying at large and continuing his career.

Robber Max Shinburn.

Allan Pinkerton became involved in the hunt for the bank robber after the Lehigh Coal and Navigation Company at White Haven, Pa., was robbed on July 9, 1868. He caught Shinburn and tried to learn the robber's secret, but Shinburn escaped and fled to Belgium. There, he decided he wanted a title, so he returned to the U.S. to get money to buy a title. He robbed the Ocean National Bank of New York on June 27, 1869, of about $1 million, and upon his return to Belgium, he became "Count Shindle."

Fifteen years of high-society living forced him eventually to return to his earlier profession in his new country, but he was soon caught and sentenced to seventeen years in prison in 1883. Less than nine years later he was back in New York, robbing banks, landing in jail, and escaping. Eventually, Shinburn went to a home for reformed convicts in Boston. There he died under the name Henry E. Moebus.

REF.: Asbury, *The Gangs of New York; CBA;* Nash, *Hustlers and Con Men.*

Shinwell, Ernest, c.1918- , Int'l., fraud. Emanuel Shinwell, had been a distinguished member of British Parliament for thirty-five years, making it relatively easy for his son, Ernest, to obtain influence or money. The name of Shinwell however, did not assure him of financial success or being an ethical businessman.

Shinwell's career of financial failure began in 1950 with the purchase of Stone Farm near Crowborough, England, for £3,500. He spent £4,500 in improvements, but government regulated post-war building permits allowed him to spend only £2,250. In February 1951, he was fined £2,000—or faced three months imprisonment—but his father bailed him out. He returned to his farming ventures but declared bankruptcy in June 1953. In 1961, he liquidated a marketing consultant firm after four years of business with debts of £50,000. A travel agency followed this trend, going bankrupt owing £17,000.

Shinwell then looked to Africa. He endeared himself to the governments of Ghana and Nigeria, which aided Shinwell in gaining the trust of lending institutions there. Prince Michael Radziwill, a London businessman, was the chairman of his International Marketing Consultants firm, with his wife Peggy Shinwell, and 11-year-old son E.P. Shinwell rounding out the board of directors. Radziwill introduced Shinwell to William Lowenthal in May 1962. Lowenthal controlled C.H. Perry, which had farms in Rhodesia, and Johore Para, a Malayan rubber company. An agreement was reached where Perry would be purchased for £50,000 and control of Johore Para would cost £72,000. Shinwell intended to use counterfeit F.W. Woolworth shares to raise capital for the deal. At the same time, he was tempting another potential investor with phony Quaker Oats stock. But when the investor, Michael Walker of Walker Aircraft Corporation in New York, became suspicious and found the Quaker Oats stock to be fake, both deals fell through.

During this time, Shinwell and financier Louis Larholt had purchased Overseas Marketing & Advertising (OMA) from Pearl & Dean, by forging the guarantee for a loan and lying to English Transcontinental Bank about the loan's intended use. The loan soon defaulted and Shinwell and Larholt were arrested in November 1963, the same time that Scotland Yard's Fraud Squad Inspector Arthur Slater began investigating Shinwell's phony stock. By February 1964, Shinwell was bankrupt owing £100,000. In May, he and Larholt were tried at the Old Bailey on the charges of false pretenses, conspiracy to defraud English Transcontinental, and convincing Pearl & Dean to sell its OMA shares. Larholt was found Guilty of false pretenses and fined £750 while Shinwell was found Guilty of the last charge and fined £50 by Judge Aarvold. Shinwell claimed he did not know the counterfeit shares were phony, but in February 1965, Aarvold found him Guilty of fraud and sentenced him to three years in prison.

Shinwell entered upon greater schemes after parole. In Ghana, he began a cattle breeding company in December 1967, orchestrating an agreement with the Ghanian government and his Overseas Land Development. The company failed in Summer 1969, causing the bankruptcy of the Earl of Ypres, who had joined Shinwell on the venture. He then enlisted the help of the Mafia, specifically the Angelo Bruno family in Philadelphia, Pa., working directly with Dominic Mantell. Mantell provided Shinwell with counterfeit stock to launder, and Shinwell kept his percentage to back his Agricultural & Industrial Development (AID) company in Panama and the Agricultural & Industrial Marketing (AIM) company in England. Further phony enterprises were begun and Shinwell traveled the world trying to sell his bogus stock. For loan approvals, he employed the signature of a U.S. lawyer named W. Adler, but this fictitious character suddenly died when Scotland Yard wished to question him. As the Panamanian deals began to fail, Shinwell was arrested in Luxembourg in June 1971 for borrowing £62,000 on stolen or forged securities. This fraud was a scheme to place £7 million into Banco Exterior in Panama and £13 million in a Luxembourg bank for the AID venture. Before his trial, Shinwell was charged with conspiracy and theft in Los Angeles concerning £3.2 million worth of stolen securities, but was not tried for the charge. However, on December 1972, he was convicted in Luxembourg and sentenced to four years in prison. While in prison, he was indicted by a New York court for conspiracy to distribute £6.5 million in counterfeit and stolen stock during 1970. Mantell pleaded guilty and was sentenced to three years for this crime. After release from the Luxembourg prison, Shinwell fled to Zambia, but he quickly had to flee to London. He was arrested in March 1975 for buying £70 in clothing on credit while bankrupt. Shinwell was finally tried and convicted for using AIM to defraud a Welsh farmer of £21,000 and a northern England entertainment company of £5,000. He also was guilty of operating a business while bankrupt. At the Old Bailey in June 1976, Judge Lawson sentenced Shinwell to three years in prison. REF.: *CBA*.

Shipman, William Davis, 1818-98, U.S., jur. Served as U.S. district attorney from 1853-60. He was nominated to the district court of Connecticut by President James Buchanan in 1860. REF.: *CBA*.

Shipp, Thomas, 1912-30, Case of, U.S., mur. On the night of Aug. 7, 1930, a young engaged couple were attacked while driving along the highway just outside of Marion, Ind., by three black men. Twenty-three-year-old Claude Deeter was dragged from the car and shot to death. His 19-year-old fiancée, Mary Ball, was attacked by the men, who fled when another car approached. Shortly after the attack, 18-year-old Thomas Shipp was arrested and confessed to the murder and attempted rape, also implicating

Abe Smith and Herbert Cameron. The three men were jailed at Marion awaiting arraignment. By the early evening of Aug. 7, a crowd had formed outside the jail demanding that the prisoners be turned over to them. Eventually, the mob stormed the jail, located Shipp and Smith, dragged them outside, and killed them. The mob hung their bodies in the town square and guarded the suspended bodies throughout the night. Through an error of identification, the third suspect, Herbert Cameron, avoided a similar fate.

In the morning the bodies were cut down. Two companies of Indiana National Guard were ordered to Marion to prevent any further incidents. The sheriff of Marion later said that he was unable to identify a single member of the crowd. A coroner's jury found that Shipp and Smith came to their deaths by being hanged by a mob composed of persons unknown. REF.: *CBA.*

Shippard, Sir Sidney Godolphin Alexander, 1837-1902, S. Afri., jur. Held office in Griqualand West in British Cape Colony as attorney general in 1873 and as high court recorder in 1877. He was a judge on the Cape Supreme Court from 1880-85. REF.: *CBA.*

Shippen, Edward, 1729-1806, U.S., jur. Served as associate justice from 1791-99 and as chief justice from 1799-1805 on supreme court of Pennsylvania. REF.: *CBA.*

Shipper, Lorin F., b.1889, Case of, U.S., theft. Lorin F. Shipper had delivered mail in Water Mill, N.Y., for thirty-three years before his retirement in 1956. During the last few years on his route, Shipper neglected to deliver all of the mail. In 1964, authorities discovered more than two tons of mail in Shipper's garage. According to Postmaster Roy G. Peterson, only ten percent of this mail was first class, most was junk mail. As the five-year statute of limitations on the 75-year-old's crime had run out, no charges were brought against Shipper. Remarkably, not one person had complained of not receiving their mail. REF.: *CBA.*

Shipton, Mother (Ursula Southill or Southiel), c.1486, Brit., witchcraft. Prophesied death of Cardinal Wolsey, London fire of 1666, creation of telegraph and steam engine, and other occurences, according to tradition. She reportedly lived in Yorkshire, England, and may have first appeared in a 1641 tract. She was the subject of a fictional biography authored by Richard Head in 1677, and is mentioned in many chapbooks. REF.: *CBA.*

Shiras, George, 1832-1924, U.S., jur. One of few U.S. Supreme Court justices to be admitted without having prior judicial experience. He practiced law for thirty years in his hometown, Pittsburgh, Pa. He so enjoyed his practice that he rejected a nomination to the U.S. Senate in 1881. His lack of interest in political life changed slightly when he served as a presidential elector in 1888. Four years later, he was nominated to the Supreme Court by President Benjamin Harrison, and he was unanimously confirmed by the Senate in 1892. He retired from the Court in 1903. REF.: *CBA.*

Shirley, Myra Belle, See: **Starr, Belle.**

Shirt Tails, prom. 1820s-50s, U.S., org. crime. The Shirt Tails, so-called because they wore their shirts outside their pants, were one of the meanest and most feared gangs in New York City in the 1820s. Although they did not have the violent appearance of the Plug Uglies, who carried clubs and bludgeons and wore exaggerated high hats, the Shirt Tails never traveled with fewer then three or four weapons concealed under their shirts, which allayed the suspicions of potential victims. Like many other gangs, however, they disappeared not long before the onset of the Civil War, their members, numbered in the low hundreds, joining other criminal organizations. See: **Plug Uglies.**

REF.: Asbury, *The Gangs of New York; CBA;* Haskins, *Street Gangs;* Kobler, *Al Capone;* Nash, *Bloodletters and Badmen;* Peterson, *The Mob.*

Shishekly, Adib (Shishakli, Adib ash-), 1907-64, Braz., brig. gen., (unsolv.) assass. On Sept. 28, 1964, Brigadier General Adib Shishekly was shot to death on a street ir the town of Ceres, Braz. Shishekly, a former president of Syria, was seen walking with a man along a street. After firing six shots at Shishekly, the man escaped in a waiting car.

Although Shishekly's killer was never identified or caught, it was assumed that the shooting was politically motivated. One hypothesis was that Shishekly was assassinated by a Druse who believed Shishekly had persecuted the Druse in Syria. Shishekly first surfaced in Syrian politics in 1949, as one of the leaders of a revolt against the government of President Shukri al-Kuwatly. Shishekly participated in three other coups, the last of which, on Nov. 29, 1951, made him army chief of staff, the sole executive power in Syria, with the resignation of President Hashem al-Atassi. Initially, Shishekly disavowed any interest in being a dictator, but in 1953, he named himself deputy premier and minister of state, and replaced all political parties with his own Arab Liberation Movement. Later in 1953, Shishekly alone ran for president. In February 1954, after Shishekly was ousted by the army, he fled to Paris. In 1955, he was sentenced in absentia to twenty years' imprisonment for torturing a Syrian man to death. In 1957, he was condemned in absentia to life imprisonment on charges of conspiracy and treason and left Paris for Brazil, where he was assassinated. REF.: *CBA.*

Shlyapnikov, Aleksandr Gavrilovich, 1884-1943, U.S.S.R., impris. Served as leader of Metalworkers' Union in 1917 and from 1919-22, and headed Workers' Opposition supporting control of industry by trade unions, from 1920-21. He was removed from the Communist party in 1933 and jailed from 1937-43. REF.: *CBA.*

Shoaf, Mamie Shey, d.1929, U.S., suic.-mur. The day before her desperate act, Mamie Shey Shoaf expressed weariness concerning the financial woes plaguing her husband, Carey Shoaf, and seven children—aged two to seventeen.

On May 24, 1929, Shoaf took three of her children to a cemetery near their home in Lebanon, Ky. In a field she slit the throats of 2-year-old Thomas Shoaf, 7-year-old Ina Shoaf, and 11-year-old Catherine Shoaf. She then cut her own throat. Two boys heard her groans and found her. Just before she died, Shoaf pointed toward the bodies of her dead children. REF.: *CBA.*

Shobek, Michael, 1954-76, Bahamas, mur. In January 1974, 21-year-old, Michael Shobek, a Milwaukee, Wis., native, fatally stabbed Irwin Bornstein of New York, on the island of Nassau in the Bahamas. When arrested, Shobek confessed to stabbing Ohio lawyer Paul Howell, and to strangling 17-year-old Kate Smith, of Detroit, as well as the Bornstein murder. All three victims were tourists in Nassau at the time of the slayings. In his May 1974, trial, Shobek said he "destroyed" his victims because they were "angels of Lucifer."

Shobek was convicted of the Bornstein murder and sentenced to death by hanging. On Sept. 30, 1976, Shobek's last appeal was denied. On Oct. 19, 1976, he was hanged at the Fox Hill prison just outside Nassau. REF.: *CBA.*

Shock Jem, See: **Haseltine, James.**

Shojiro, Goto, See: **Goto Shojiro.**

Shonbrun, Eli, and **Webb, Madeline**, and **Cullen, John**, prom. 1942, U.S., rob.-mur. The gagged, bound body of a middle-aged woman, Susan Reich, was found by a bellboy at the Hotel Sutton on New York's Upper East Side on Mar. 5, 1942. The suite had been rented on Feb. 20 by a couple who registered as "Mr.and Mrs. Ted Leopold" from Miami Beach, Fla. Homicide squad captain Edward Mullins answered a call from an elderly woman who had called repeatedly to talk to her daughter in Room 207, where the murder had taken place. Mullins interviewed 82-year-old Bertha Kolischer and learned that the victim, her daughter, had gone to the hotel to meet her friend, a young actress named Madeline Webb. The actress had invited Reich to meet her new husband, asking her to have lunch with them at the elegant Sutton Hotel. Reich had worn some of her best jewelry to the lunch date, but none of the jewels were found on her dead body. Police discovered Webb had moved from Oklahoma, first to Hollywood and then to New York to pursue an acting career. Meeting with limited success, she had gone into a slow downward spiral, dancing in nightclub revues, posing nude, and drinking as her resources and her youth were depleted. Arrested for disorderly conduct, she was convicted but given a suspended sentence. Not long after that, she became involved with Eli Shonbrun, who left his wife and daughter to live with Webb.

Shonbrun was an unsuccessful singer with a history of petty thefts. He had fallen in love with Webb and encouraged her to invite her wealthy friend to lunch so that they could rob her. Shonbrun's uncle, Murray Hirschl, also known as Harry Hirschl, was picked up by the police after he pawned the mounting from one of the victim's stolen rings. The couple, accompanied by ex-convict John Cullen, had gagged Reich, and she had suffocated. Cullen was arrested and admitted his guilt. Schonbrun and Webb were picked up in a Bronx boarding house, with Reich's diamond hidden in a pillow. Shonbrun's claim that Webb was not present during the murder did not hold up. All four were tried for first-degree murder, with Hirschl receiving a reduced sentence for agreeing to turn state's witness. Assistant District Attorney Jacob Grumet prosecuted, with former State Supreme Court Justice James M. Springer of Oklahoma defending. Webb and Shonbrun put on extravagant displays of emotion at the three-week trial, posing for photographs during recesses. Webb was found Guilty and sentenced to life imprisonment. Shonbrun and Cullen died in the electric chair. REF.: *CBA.*

Shonsey, Mike, prom. 1890s-1900s, U.S., west. gunman. Migrating to Wyoming's cattle country from Ohio, Mike Shonsey started out as a cowboy but soon became ranch foreman. During the infamous Johnson County War he joined forces with powerful cattlemen and hired on as a gunman with the Wyoming Cattle Growers' Association. On Apr. 9, 1892, Shonsey rode into the camp of the Regulators association stating that he had found fourteen rustlers at the DC Ranch. The Regulators spread out before dawn to catch them, with Shonsey and five men posting themselves in a gulch behind the cabin. When the Regulators closed in they only found Nate Champion and Nick Ray along with out-of-work ranch hands Ben Jones and Bill Walker. Jones and Walker came out of the cabin at dawn and were captured. But when Ray walked out shooting erupted and Ray was shot. Champion covered the dying Ray and helped him back inside. In mid-afternoon Jack Flagg, a small-time rancher, came by and was shot at but escaped. Flagg left his wagon behind and the Regulators set it on fire and pushed it against the cabin. Champion came out firing a six-gun and a Winchester and raced for the gulch barefoot. When Shonsey and his five companions opened fire Champion fell, with twenty-eight bullet holes in his body. The Regulators pinned a note to the dead man's shirt which read, "Cattle thieves, beware."

In May 1893 at a cattle camp twenty miles northeast of Lusk, Wyo., Shonsey found Dudley Champion, twin brother of the slain Nate. After a short talk with him Shonsey pulled a gun, shot Champion, and ran from the camp. Champion, struggling with his gun which was jammed with dirt, gasped, "I can't cock it, I can't cock it," before he died without firing a shot. Shonsey went to Lusk where he pleaded self-defense to a murder charge heading to Cheyenne to catch a southbound train. He eventually returned to Wyoming where he died of old age. He was one of the last survivors of the Johnson County War.

REF.: *CBA;* Mercer, *Banditti of the Plains;* Smith, *War on the Powder River.*

Shore, Florence Nightingale, 1865-1920, Brit., (unsolv.) mur. Florence Shore, a 55-year-old nurse, traveled on the London-Hastings train to visit friends in St. Leonards on Jan. 12, 1920. She was in a carriage when someone hit her over the head, probably with the butt of a pistol, and robbed her. At Polegate some railway workers entered the carriage and discovered that she was bleeding. She was taken to East Sussex Hospital where she died four days later.

The woman who had seen Shore off at Victoria Station said that a man about thirty had entered the carriage just before the train left the platform, but no one suspects were ever found the case remained unsolved.

REF.: *CBA;* Goodman, *The Railway Murders;* Nash, *Open Files;* Shew, *A Second Companion to Murder;* Whitbread, *The Railway Policemen.*

Shore, Jane, c.1445-1527, Brit., witchcraft. Manipulated Edward IV with cunning and physical charms. She convinced William Hastings to challenge the assumption of the throne by Richard of Gloucester. She was charged with sorcery by the newly crowned Richard III and forced to show repentance in 1483. She died impoverished.

REF.: Andrews, *Old-Time Punishments; CBA.*

Shores, Cyrus Wells, (AKA: **Doc Wells**), 1844-1934, U.S., west. gunman. Cyrus Wells Shore received both his name and his nickname from the doctor who delivered him. Leaving his hometown near Detroit, Mich., for Montana Territory at the age of twenty-two, Wells worked as a bullwhacker driving ox teams then as a hunter and trapper. He purchased a wagon and hauled ties for the Union Pacific Railroad, brought freight to mining camps, and transported government supplies from Fort Hays to Camp Supply, Okla., for several years. Selling the wagon in 1871, he purchased a herd of cattle which he drove up the Chisholm Trail. Over the next seven years he lived in Kansas selling and buying cattle.

Marrying in 1877, Shores moved with his wife to Gunnison, Colo., and set up a freight company to supply the many local gold camps. In October 1880, he was in his cabin holding his infant son when Jack Smith and Tom Lewis began shooting in the town's streets, injuring a bystander. Shores picked up a Winchester and ran outdoors to chase the ruffians. After exchanging shots he was shkot at by a pursuing posse of fifteen men, but apparently was unharmed. The posse captured Smith and Lewis. In 1884 Shore was elected Gunnison County sheriff, a post he held for eight years, later serving as a U.S. deputy marshal and a Denver and Rio Grande railroad detective. In December 1891, in Crested Butte, Colo., a coal workers' strike of about 250 Italian and Austrian miners prompted Sheriff Shores to gather two dozen deputies and travel into the community to end the conflict. The posse's midnight arrival was met by 150 irate miners who fired on the men. Dashing behind the railroad track bed, the posse started shooting. Shores told his men to aim low and as a result thirty-six miners were wounded, one was seriously hurt. No posse members were shot and the strike soon ended.

In 1915, Shores was appointed Salt Lake City chief of police. During his career Shores associated with Wild Bill Hickok, Jim Clark, and Tom Horn. Perhaps the most notorious fugitive he captured was the American cannibal Alfred Packer. Shores retired in Gunnison and died there at the age of ninety. See: **Packer, Alferd G.**

REF.: *CBA;* Look, *Unforgettable Characters of Western Colorado;* Rockwell, *Memoirs of a Lawman.*

Short, Elizabeth, See: **Black Dahlia, The.**

Short, Luke, 1854-93, U.S., west. gunman. Though a small man, Luke Short was a mean, ruthless, and deceitful gunfighter who earned the nickname of "Undertaker's Friend." For example, a man he once quarrelled with protested when Short put his hand under his coat. Short said, "I'm not trying to pull a gun. I haven't got a gun in there, see!" as he pulled out a gun and murdered the man. Short was part of the Dodge City Gang led by Wyatt Earp and Bat Masterson which controlled a large piece of the vice action in the Plains region.

Short grew up in Texas and became a cowboy at sixteen. At age twenty-two, in 1876, he started a new career as a bootlegger, selling whiskey to the Sioux Indians, which was a federal offense. At least six men died from Short's bullets as he defended his franchise. The U.S. Army finally put him out of business and Short soon turned scout for the U.S. Army, then advanced to gambling in Leadville, Colo. His surefire system was simple. He collected when he won, welshed when he lost, and killed men who owed him money and would not pay. By 1879 Short was in Dodge City, Kan., where he became friends with Earp, following him later to the Arizona Territory and becoming a dealer at the infamous Oriental Saloon where Short continued to garner a reputation as a gunfighter. One day a man named Charley Storms, while playing cards at the Oriental, called Short a cheat and got the drop on him. Masterson broke it up and got Storms to leave, but later that afternoon Storms returned, walked over to Short, and began to trace the outline of Short's mustache with his .45. With incredible speed Short whipped out his Colt and killed Storms with three bullets before the other man fired a shot.

Returning to Dodge City in 1881 Short bought the Long Branch Saloon which he turned into a wildly successful combination bar, casino, and brothel. When a reform movement gripped the town the local government decided to ban women employees in saloons. Since this statute would obviously put a damper on Short's business he fought against it with his gun but he and his backers were soon driven out of town. Short lodged a complaint in Topeka, Kansas' state capital. When the governor did nothing Short started sending telegrams to all his friends. Earp, Doc Holliday, Masterson, Charlie Bassett, Shotgun Collins, Neal Brown, and many more notorious gunmen poured into town, calling themselves the Dodge City Peace Commission. The reformers gave in quickly, inviting Short to reopen his saloon and run it the way he wanted.

Luke Short, western gambler and gunman.

Short later sold the Long Branch and moved on to Fort Worth, Texas, where he opened and ran the White Elephant Saloon and several other gambling saloons and brothels. When gambling was outlawed he became the most successful underground gambling house owner in town. When, in 1887, Longhair Jim Courtright, who had been a Fort Worth city marshal and then headed his own detective agency, came in to shake down saloons for protection payoffs, Short was unimpressed by Courtright's reputation as a top gunslinger. He shot off Courtright's thumb as the ex-marshal tripped back the hammer of his gun, then killed him with three shots as Courtright reached for a second gun. In 1890 saloon owner Charles Wright tried to muscle Short out of business. When Wright came after him Short shot his challenger in the wrist. Short died in 1893 of natural causes at the age of thirty-nine. See: **Oriental Saloon.**

REF.: Archambeau, *Old Tascosa;* Argall, *Outlawry and Justice in Old Arizona;* Bartholomew, *Western Hard-Cases;* Breakenridge, *Helldorado;* Brent, *Great Western Heroes;* Brophy, *Arizona Sketch Book;* Brown and Schmitt, *Trail Driving Days;* Carson, *Doc Middleton;* Casey, *The Texas Border; CBA;* Chafetz, *Play the Devil;* Chrisman, *Fifty Years on the Owl Hoot Trail;* ____, *The Ladder of Rivers;* ____, *Lost Trails of the Cimarron;* Clum, *Apache Agent;* Cox, *Luke Short and His Era;* Cunningham, *Triggernometry;* Dykstra, *The Cattle Towns;* Erwin, *The Southwest of John H. Slaughter;* Faulkner, *Roundup;* Fisher and Holmes, *Gold Rushes and Mining Camps of the Early American West;* Florin, *Ghost Town Album;* Gard, *The Chisholm Trail;* Gardner, *The Old Wild West;* Gaylord, *Handgunner's Guide;* Hendricks, *The Bad Man of the West;* Hertzog, *A Directory of New Mexico Desperadoes;* Holbrook, *Little Annie Oakley & Other Rugged People;* Holloway, *Texas Gun Lore;* Horan, *The Great American West;* ____ and Sann, *Pictorial History of the Wild West;* Hunter and Rose, *The Album of Gun-Fighters;* Jaastad, *Man of the West;* Knight, *Wild Bil Hickok;* Knight, *Fort Worth;* Lake, *Under Cover for Wells Fargo;* Lake, *Wyatt Earp;* McCarty, *The Enchanted West;* McCarty, *The Gunfighters;* Martin, *Border Boss;* Masterson, *Famous Gunfighters of the Western Frontier;* Miller and Snell, *Great Gunfighters of the Kansas Cowtowns;* ____, *Why the West Was Wild;* Myers, *The Last Chance;* O'Connor, *Bat Masterson;* Paddock, *History of Texas;* Parkhill, *The Wildest of the West;* Penfield, *Western Sheriffs and Marshals;* Raine, *Famous Sheriffs & Western Outlaws;* Schoenberger, *Gunfighters;* White, *My Texas 'Tis of Thee;* ____, *Texas, An Informal Biography;* Young, *Dangers on the Trail in 1865.*

Shotgun Man, prom. 1910, U.S., org. crime. Known only by the alias Shotgun Man, this Chicago assassin worked for the Black Hand Society in the Little Italy area on Chicago's West Side. He was suspected of having committed a dozen or more murders around 1910.

REF.: Asbury, *Gem of the Prairie; CBA.*

Shotton, Edward George, 1880-1958, Brit., big.-mur. A lively and flirtatious ex-chorus girl, Mamie Stuart, twenty-six, met marine engineer Edward George Shotton in 1917. They soon married and rented a place in Swansea. In 1919, they moved to a house called Ty-Llanwydd, outside Swansea. One week after the move, Stuart wrote a letter to her parents. They sent a reply but were surprised when their letter was returned, marked "House Closed." They received a Christmas telegram from their daughter, but then heard nothing more. On Mar. 20, 1920, the Grosvenor Hotel manager in Swansea reported to police that a large suitcase had been left at his hotel. Inside this, police found a second smaller suitcase containing shredded dresses and women's shoes cut into pieces. Two weeks later, a cleaning woman at Ty-Llanwydd found Stuart's mildewed leather purse, with her ration card and about £2 in change, behind a wash stand. Stuart's parents were contacted as well as Scotland Yard.

In questioning Shotton, it was discovered that he was married to another woman and living with her and their child a few miles from the Swansea hotel. Admitting he knew Stuart, Shotton denied ever marrying her, and said they had broken up after a fight in December 1919. Shotton was tried at Glamorgan Assizes on a bigamy charge for which he received eighteen months of hard labor. In court he said he had left the large suitcase at the hotel, but maintained that someone else, pretending to be him, had married Stuart.

On Nov. 5, 1961, three Welch fishermen found the skeleton of a woman at the bottom of a long abandoned mine shaft. The body had been cut into three pieces; the physical characteristics and clothing matched those of Stuart. A December 1961 coroner's inquest brought in William Symons, an elderly former-postman, who testified that he had surprised Shotton, who was carrying a heavy sack, outside Ty-Llanwydd. The startled Shotton was relieved to realize he was looking at a postal worker, and said, "Oh, God, for a minute I thought you were a policeman," before driving away. The murder verdict had no effect on Shotton, who had died three years earlier, at the age of seventy-eight. REF.: *CBA.*

Shouse, Minnie, prom. 1890s, U.S., rob. A man and woman robbed farmer Sam Borland of his wallet and revolver as he walked from the Chicago train depot when he arrived in 1893 for the World's Fair. Borland chased the woman. Aiming the gun she had just stolen at Borland's head, she escaped—but not before he had gotten a good look at her.

Borland reported the robbery to the police who arrested Minnie Shouse months later. She escaped from jail but was soon captured and tried. Before her trial a police officer paid Borland $25 of the $42 he had had stolen and informed the man he could return to his home where the remainder of the money would be returned. When the trial date for Shouse was announced, the arresting officer failed to notify Borland. Without a witness, the state's attorney dismissed the case, but with the possibility of reinstating the charge. Borland soon complained that not all of money had been returned. When it was discovered that Borland had not been notified of the trial, the guilty officer was removed from the force and Shouse was ordered apprehended. Shouse was tried before Judge Chetlain on Jan. 21, 1895, found Guilty and sentenced to one year in prison at hard labor. Shouse's police record until then included 300 arrests resulting in thirty-six trials; most of her victims were happy to have the stolen money returned rather than press charges.

REF.: *CBA;* Wooldridge, *Hands Up.*

Showery, Allan, 1946- , U.S., rob.-arson-mur. On Feb. 21, 1977, the body of 48-year-old Teresita Basa, a respiratory therapist, was found under a pile of burning clothes by firemen answering a call to her Chicago apartment. A butcher knife was stuck in her chest. Jose Chua told Chicago detectives that his wife, Remimbas Chua, had gone into a trance several times when the voice of Teresita Basa spoke through her. Jose Chua said that while his wife was in these periods of "possession," she identified Basa's murderer as another hospital employee, Allan Showery. The Chuas worked at Edgewater Hospital, where Showery and Basa also worked.

On the strength of Jose Chua's claims, police questioned Allan Showery, who admitted killing Basa while attempting to rob her. Items of Basa's jewelry described by Basa's "spirit," were found in the possession of Showery's common-law wife. In January 1979, Showery's first trial ended in a hung jury. Although Showery had testified that police had coerced him to confess, in his second trial in February 1979 he pleaded guilty and was sentenced to fourteen years in prison for the murder. He was also sentenced to terms of four years each for armed robbery and arson, sentences which were to run concurrently with the longer sentence. REF.: *CBA.*

Shrimpton, John (AKA: Parker), d.1713, Brit., rob.-mur. As apprentice to a soap-boiler in Ratcliffe Highway, John Shrimpton met a gang of apprentices bent on thievery and committed his first crime in their company. He hid in a tree one day just as a young couple spread out a picnic blanket below him. He then shook the tree so hard that dozens of apples fell onto their heads. The couple fled to a nearby house, leaving behind items valued at £6.

After completing his criminal apprenticeship, Shrimpton took to the highway where he robbed many elegant coaches between London and Oxford. Shrimpton once met a young miller who asked if he could learn the trade firsthand by riding along. The experienced robber obliged, passing on useful information and some details of his successful past crimes. Explaining that he was looking for a particular man carrying a purse of money, Shrimpton told his protégé to ride in the opposite direction to search for their prey. When they reunited at a fork in the road some time later, the apprentice highwayman knocked Shrimpton off his horse with a stick. Shrimpton had apparently told him, "Surely, friend, thou'rt but a young highwayman, or else you would have knocked me down first and have bid me stand afterwards." The miller took four guineas from Shrimpton and warned him to keep silent about the matter or he would reveal to the authorities all he had learned about his past crimes.

Though Shrimpton swore he would never teach another man how to rob on the highway, neither did Shrimpton renounce his criminal ways. One night he was drinking and creating quite a commotion in a brothel in Bristol. He was arrested and led away to the jail on Wine Street. The drunken robber refused to go peacefully, and in a struggle fatally shot the watchman and tossed away the pistol.

The next morning, Shrimpton was taken to Newgate prison in Bristol and held for trial. His pleas for a Queen's pardon were ignored, and he was executed at St. Michael's Hill on Sept. 4, 1713.

REF.: *CBA;* Smith, *Highwaymen.*

Shrimpton, Moses, d.1885, Brit., mur. Moses Shrimpton had spent forty years of his life in and out of British prisons for poaching. In order to escape arrest yet again, Shrimpton killed one of his pursuers. He was convicted and sentenced to death. Shrimpton was hanged at Worcester Jail by executioner James Berry. Berry felt that a drop of nine feet was necessary for a proper hanging. But upon inspection of the body, Berry discovered that Shrimpton's head had been pulled halfway off. The executioner claimed the old man's weak tissue was the cause of the near-beheading rather than an error on his part.

REF.: Atholl, *The Reluctant Hangman; CBA.*

Shriner, Carl Elson, c.1953-84, U.S., rob.-mur. On Oct. 22, 1976, 34-year-old Judith Ann Carter was murdered by a man robbing the Gainesville, Fla., convenience store where she worked.

Carter was killed just twenty-three days after Carl Elson Shriner was released from a Florida prison where he had spent the better part of a five-year sentence for robbery in Miami. After his arrest for Carter's death, Shriner admitted he drove the getaway car, but claimed another man pulled the trigger. Shriner was found Guilty and sentenced to die in the electric chair on Apr. 21, 1982. New lawyers intervened on behalf of Shriner and convinced the 11th Circuit Court of Appeals in Atlanta, Ga., that Shriner's trial counsel had been incompetent. A new execution date was set and the appellate court once again intervened on June 18, 1984. This stay was lifted the next day by the same court, and the case was taken to the U.S. Supreme Court. The Supreme Court deliberated just ninety minutes before upholding the death sentence by a vote of six to two. Shriner was executed at 7:12 a.m. on June 20 at the Florida State Prison in Starke. He became the sixth person in Florida and twentieth person in the U.S. to be executed since the Supreme Court reinstated capital punishment in 1976. REF.: *CBA.*

Shuck, Douglas Paul, c.1968- , U.S., mur. Patricia Sue "Suzy" Toucheck aspired to be a singer and often sang songs into a tape recorder in her Edgewood, Md., home. During the last week of September 1988, the 14-year-old girl recorded the song *If I Close My Eyes Forever* written by Lita Ford whose lyrics speak about death. On Sept. 28, with the discovery of her nude and strangled body on a wooded hillside less than thirty yards from her house, the lyrics rang eerily prophetic.

Five days earlier, on Sept. 23, Suzy had been drinking with a group of friends. The teenager was reported to have had a problem with alcohol as a result of abuse from her stepfather. That night she apparently became very drunk, and needed help in walking. Douglas Paul Shuck, nineteen, who himself had been drinking heavily, offered to walk Suzy home. She was never seen alive again. Later that night, Shuck was observed with bloodstains on his clothing and shoes. Suzy's body, found beneath a beach blanket, had been severely beaten and raped before she was strangled to death. When Shuck was arrested and charged with the murder on Nov. 11, 1988, he became the fourth teenager charged with first-degree murder in less than a year in Harford County. The evidence against the youth was provided by FBI laboratory tests of Shuck's blood and semen samples. His samples matched those taken from the dead girl. The case was the first in Harford County in which a DNA "fingerprint" test was used in linking a suspect to a crime. On June 7, 1989, Shuck entered an Alford plea to the first-degree murder charge, in exchange for the prosecution's dropping the rape charge. Under this plea, Shuck did not admit he committed the crime, but recognized that the state had gathered enough evidence to convict him. In a prepared statement, Shuck told the court he could not "remember what happened on the morning of Sept. 24," and added that "after examining all the evidence, it is clear I must be responsible." Circuit Judge William O. Carr sentenced Shuck to life imprisonment, of which the defendant must serve at least fifteen years before he is eligible for parole. REF.: *CBA.*

Shue, Erasmus Stribling Trout (AKA: Edward Shue, Erastus Shue), 1862-1902, U.S., theft-mur. A state historical marker in Greenbrier County, W. Va., reads:

"Interred in nearby cemetery is Zona Heaster Shue. Her death in 1897 was presumed natural until her spirit appeared to her mother to describe how she was killed by her husband Edward. Autopsy on the exhumed body verified the apparition's account. ...Only known case in which testimony from ghost helped convict a murderer."

Erasmus "Trout" Shue, a blacksmith recently come to the area, said that he planned to have seven wives. He had divorced one wife and the second had died under suspicious circumstances when he married Zona. He had a vicious temper and neglected to mention to Zona that had served time in prison for stealing a horse.

When Zona died on Jan. 23, 1897, three months after she and

Shue got married, she may have been pregnant by another man. Her body was found lying at the bottom of the stairs by a boy who worked for a doctor. He ran to get Shue, who had the body dressed and laid out before the doctor came. The husband's apparent grief prevented the doctor from giving Zona Shue's body much of a thorough examination, though he later told the newspaper that she had died "of an everlasting faint." Rumors concerning Zona's death were flying even before her mother, Mary Jane Robinson Heaster, saw her ghost four nights in a row. And soon, the local prosecutor was forced to investigate.

The prosecutor, John Alfred Preston, and the doctor agreed that an autopsy was needed. On Feb. 22, Zona's body was exhumed and doctors determined that she had indeed, as the ghost had said, died of a broken neck and smashed windpipe. Trout was promptly charged with murder. His trial began on June 23, 1897. The prosecution's circumstantial evidence was met by many defense witnesses testifying to Shue's honesty. He appeared on his own behalf, but he was found Guilty and sentenced to life in prison. He died at age forty of pneumonia within five years.

REF.: *CBA;* Lyle, *The Man Who Wanted Seven Wives.*

Shutt, Barbara Jean, 1946- , U.S., mur. On May 25, 1969, the teenaged children of psychiatrist Dr. Jane Shutt found her body in her office in the basement of their home in Cincinnati, Ohio. She had been shot once in the chest and twice in the head, and then severely beaten on the head with a fireplace poker. The children were not home when the crime occurred, nor, apparently, were the woman's 75-year-old husband—who was almost twice her age—or her 23-year-old adopted daughter, Barbara Jean Shutt.

Shutt and her adoptive father were soon suspected. Lie-detector tests were administered, and after two grueling hours, police were certain that the elder Shutt was telling the truth. But after two polygraph tests of the eldest daughter, police believed she had something to hide. Police also discovered that the riding boots Barbara Shutt had worn that morning had dried blood on them. The part-time school teacher then confessed to killing her mother. She explained that her mother had been seeing another man and planned on leaving her husband. Rather than let the family break up, Barbara decided to kill her mother. As police suspected, she fired into the doctor's chest while she was showering. Barbara said her mother then asked her to call for help, which she said she was doing when the wounded woman attacked her. Following a brief struggle, Dr. Shutt collapsed. Then Barbara dragged her mother by the feet into the basement, accounting for the trail of blood from the bathroom. In the office, she grabbed a pillow, placed it over her mother's head and fired two more bullets from her father's .25-caliber pistol. Still not sure that Dr. Shutt was dead, her daughter battered in the woman's head. The day after this confession, Barbara Shutt recanted, claiming she invented the story to protect her father, whom she felt police suspected.

Despite Shutt's retraction of her confession, she was tried for murder. Melvin Rueger posecuted the case, which opened on Sept. 26 before Judge William Morrissey. Defense Counsel Bernard Gilday disputed the evidence put forth by Rueger and argued that his client had come home early from the Red Fox Stables to find her dead mother, and stained her boots in an attempt to lift the woman. He added that she disposed of the gun in the Ohio River when she realized that her father had probably killed her mother. The jury was given the case, and five hours later they returned a verdict of Guilty of first-degree murder, but with a recommendation for mercy, as the crime carried a mandatory sentence of death. Morrissey sentenced Shutt to life imprisonment. On Oct. 6, the night after the verdict was read, Shutt attempted suicide by swallowing an overdose of sleeping pills she had concealed in her bra. The attempt was discovered and Shutt was saved.

REF.: *CBA;* Gribble, *The Deadly Professionals.*

Siano, Fiore Ernest, 1927- , U.S., drugs. Although Fiore Ernest Siano had been arrested for burglary and federal narcotics law violations dating back to 1948, it was not until late 1954 that he was convicted. Siano was found Guilty of distributing heroin and cocaine in large quantities to interstate drug traffickers, especially those working in New York City. On Nov. 27, 1954, he was sentenced to eight years in prison. The nephew of Joe Valachi, Siano was also known to federal investigators as a hired gun and was implicated in the deaths of Steve Franse and Eugenio Giannini. REF.: *CBA.*

Sibley, Solomon, 1769-1846, U.S., jur. Held office briefly as mayor of Detroit, Mich., in 1806. He also served as U.S. district attorney from 1815-23. He was first appointed to the territorial court of Michigan by President James Monroe in 1824. REF.: *CBA.*

Sibour, Marie-Dominique-Auguste, c.1792-1857, Fr., archbishop, assass. Marie-Dominique-Auguste Sibour had been the Bishop of Digne, Fr., before he became archbishop of Paris in 1848. His predecessor, Archbishop Affre, had been killed by an errant bullet while attempting to stop the fighting during the revolution in June 1848. Sibour had been characterized by his liberal views before and after his appointment. He voted for the restoration of the empire under Louis-Napoleon on Nov. 6, 1852. As his supporters hoped, Sibour continued to oppose the dogma of the Immaculate Conception. But he traveled to Rome after Pope Pius IX announced the dogma's inception on Dec. 8, 1854. Sibour returned reconciled to the new dogma of the Catholic Church, a reconciliation that would result in his death.

On Jan. 3, 1857, Sibour was stabbed to death during a processional for the festival of Saint Genevieve, the patron saint of Paris. His assailant was Jean-Louis Verger, who thrust a large Catalan knife into the archbishop's heart, and then cried out, "No more goddesses! Away with goddesses!" Verger was immediately seized. The 30-year-old man had been banned from the priesthood on Dec. 12, 1856, after a series of failed parish positions dating back to his ordination in 1850. He first came into contact with Sibour in 1844, when he asked the archbishop for help in finding him a new position because his current benefactor, the Abbé Legrand, had made advances toward him. Sibour refused because the charge was groundless. Verger's hostility toward Legrand continued with libelous letters. Disenchanted with Catholicism, Verger appeared at the church of the Madeleine on Feb. 3, 1856, wearing a sign blaming the church for forsaking him. He was arrested, and judged sane, though a police officer was assigned to watch his movements. Verger was appointed priest for the parish of Serris in Seine-et-Marne on Mar. 12, 1856, by Monsignor Allou of Meaux. The Bishop of Meaux removed Verger later that year for his attacks upon the dogma of the Immaculate Conception, and for his work, *Testament,* in which he attacked ecclesiastical discipline, especially clerical celibacy. His attack upon Sibour, Verger claimed, was an attack upon the new dogma.

Verger was tried on Jan. 17, 1857, before the *Cour d'assises* under President Claude-Alphonse Delangle. Verger asked not to be represented, but Delangle appointed attorney Nogent-Saint-Laurens. After the reading of the indictment, Verger stated before the court that his rights were denied because only one of his sixty witnesses was allowed to testify. The court decided that the majority of his witnesses were called only to attack the church and not as his defense. Verger continued to disrupt the trial, and even had to be removed during the prosecutor's closing statement. Nogent explained that his client had acted in a moment of temporary insanity. He introduced Verger's family history as proof, including the fact that his mother and a sibling had each drowned themselves. But the jury took twenty minutes to find Verger Guilty and sentence him to death. His appeal was rejected on Jan. 29, and after the emperor declined to intervene, Verger was guillotined on Jan. 30, 1857, by the executioner Heindreicht before a crowd of 10,000. REF.: *CBA.*

Sica, Joseph, 1911- , U.S., rob.-drugs-org. crime. Born in Newark, N.J., Joseph Sica was arrested for the first time in 1926 when he was only 15-years-old. According to the Senate McClellan Committee, Sica was an important member of the Los Angeles Mafia, associating with such mobsters as Mickey Cohen, Salvatore Iannone, and Thomas DeMayo. His stock in trade was narcotics trafficking, robbery, contract murder, and extortion. In 1950 he was one of fifteen West Coast gangsters indicted in California for conspiring to peddle narcotics. However, the case was thrown out of court after the chief government witness, Abraham Davidian, was shot to death while sleeping at his mother's home in Fresno, Calif.

REF.: *CBA;* Cohen, *Mickey Cohen: In My Own Words;* Demaris, *The Last Mafioso;* Nanvasky, *Kennedy Justice;* Reid, *The Grim Reapers;* Toledano, *J. Edgar Hoover.*

Sickles, Daniel Edgar, 1819-1914, Case of, U.S., mur. By far, the most sensational shooting involving Washington dignitaries in the nineteenth century was the very public slaying of Philip Barton Key by the cuckolded Daniel E. Sickles on Feb. 27, 1859. Sickles, then a Congressman from New York, had been warned anonymously in 1858 that Key, who was district attorney for the District of Columbia, had been regularly seducing his wife, Teresa Bagioli Sickles. The volatile congressman first refused to believe that the son of the author of the national anthem would conduct himself as a libertine. Sickles *did* believe another note he received, which was dated Feb. 24, 1859. It read:

> Dear Sir:
>
> With deep regret I enclose to your address the few lines but an indispensable duty compels me to do so, seeing that you are greatly imposed upon. There is a fellow I may say, for he is not a gentleman, by any means, by the name of Philip Barton Key & I believe the district attorney who rents a house of a Negro man by the name of Jon. A. Gray situated on 15th Street be'twn K & L, Streets, for no other purpose than to meet your wife, Mrs. Sickles. He hangs a string out of the window as a signal to her that he is in and leaves the door unfastened and she walks in and sir, I do assure you. With these few hints I leave the rest for you to imagine.
>
> Your friend, R.P.G.

Sickles, who knew no one with the initials "R.P.G.", found it difficult to accept the fact that his beloved Teresa would be unfaithful. He had known this daughter of a New York music teacher since she was a little girl, and had married her when she was sixteen. Yet the congressman, a suspicious, feisty individual with a volatile nature, wanted to make sure that the wild statements in the letter were false. He asked a friend to investigate, and was soon informed that, indeed, his beautiful 22-year-old wife was visiting Key in secret at the trysting house, that Key was often seen to stand outside and signal with his handkerchief to Mrs. Sickles. The congressman went wild with anger; Key had been his house guest on many occasions over the years and such blatant conduct branded him the worst of villains.

On Feb. 26, Sickles confronted his wife, charging her with adultery. One of the maids heard her cry out, "Oh! I see I am discovered!" The congressman wanted more than his wife's private admission and, after yanking the wedding ring from her finger, Sickles ordered his wife to write out a full confession and then, as punishment, to go sleep on the floor of a guest room, which she did. The confession, which was later published in several journals at Sickles' request, left out nothing. Mrs. Sickles wrote:

> I have been in a house in Fifteenth Street, with Mr. Key. How many times I don't know. I believe the house belongs to a colored man. (The owner was John Gray.) The house is unoccupied. Commenced going there in the latter part of January. Have been alone with Mr. Key. Usually stayed an hour or more. There was a bed in the second story. I did what is usual for a wicked woman to do. The intimacy commenced this winter, when I came from New York, in that house—an intimacy of an improper kind. Have met half a dozen times or more, at different hours of the day. On Monday of this week, and Wednesday also. Would arrange meetings when we met in the street and at parties. Never would speak to him when Mr. Sickles was at home, because he did not like me to speak to him; did not see Mr. Key for some days after I got here. He then told me that he had hired the house as a place where he and I could meet. I agreed to it. Had nothing to eat or drink there. The room is warmed by a wood fire.
>
> Mr. Key generally goes first. Have walked there together say four times—I do not think more; was there on Wednesday last, between two and three. I went there alone. Laura (the Sickles' child) was at Mrs. Hoover's. Mr. Key took and left her there at my request...From there to the milk woman's. Immediately after Mr. Key left Laura at Mrs. Hoover's I met him in Fifteenth Street. Went in by the back gate. Went in the same bedroom, and there an improper interview was had. I undressed myself. Mr. Key undressed also. This occurred on Wednesday, 23rd of February, 1859.
>
> Mr. Key has kissed me in this house (the Sickles' home) a number of times. I do not deny that we have had connection in this house, last spring, a year ago, in the parlor, on the sofa. Mr. Sickles was sometimes out of town and sometimes in the Capitol. I think the intimacy commenced in April or May 1858. I did not think it safe to meet him in this house because there are servants who might suspect something. As a general thing I have worn a white woolen plaid dress, and beaver hat trimmed with black velvet. Have worn a black silk dress there also, also a plaid silk dress, black velvet cloak trimmed with lace, a black velvet shawl trimmed with fringe. On Wednesday I either had on my brown dress or black and white woolen dress, beaver hat and velvet shawl. I arranged with Mr. Key to go in the back way, after leaving Laura at Mrs. Hoover's. He met me at Mr. Douglas'.
>
> The arrangement to go in the back way was either made in the street or Mr. Douglas', as we would be less likely to be seen...Arranged the interview for Wednesday in the street, I think on Monday. I went in the front door, it was open, occupied the same room; undressed myself, and he also; went to bed together. Mr. Key has ridden in Mr. Sickles' carriage and has called at his house without Mr. Sickles' knowledge, and after my being told not to invite him to do so, and against Mr. Sickles' repeated request. (Signed) Teresa Bagioli.
>
> This is a true statement, written by myself without any inducement held out by Mr. Sickles of forgiveness or reward, and without any menace from him. This I have written with my bedroom door open, and my maid and child in the adjoining room, at half-past eight o'clock in the evening.

The cuckolded husband then had two servants sign their names to this admission as witnesses. "Sickles, even in his desolation," wrote one of his biographers, W.A. Swanberg, "was still the lawyer. He wanted written proof and he had it, in his wife's own hand." The congressman, as the next day proved, wanted much more. When Samuel F. Butterworth paid him a friendly visit the following morning, Sickles burst out with the whole sordid story. "I am a dishonored and ruined man," the presidential hopeful blurted between sobs, "and I cannot look you in the face."

While the two men struggled for normal conversation, Sickles moved to the library window. He gasped as he spotted Philip Barton Key standing in Lafayette Square, gesturing toward his house. "That scoundrel is making signals!" yelled Sickles. "My God, this is horrible!"

The friend counseled: "You must be calm and look this matter square in the face. If there is a possibility of keeping the certain knowledge of this crime from the public, you must do nothing to destroy that possibility. You may be mistaken in your belief that it is known to the whole city."

"No, no, my friend," Sickles groaned. "I am not. It is already the town talk."

"If that be so," Butterworth concluded, "there is but one course left for you as a man of honor. You need no advice." (This was later construed to mean that Butterworth was suggesting to Sickles that he kill Key.) With that, Butterworth left and walked across Lafayette Square where he struck up a brief conversation with Key. (Butterworth later strenuously denied that he acted as a decoy to distract Key so that his murderer could approach undetected.)

As the two men stood on Madison Place in full view of the White House, Sickles suddenly appeared. He rushed toward his victim with a drawn pistol and shouted: "Key, you scoundrel! You have dishonored my house! You must die!" Key quickly reached inside his coat pocket but before he could withdraw his hand, Sickles fired. Butterworth, a horrified witness to the whole event, could not tell whether or not this first shot wounded the district attorney, who advanced on Sickles and grabbed him by the collar, attempting to hit him.

Sickles broke free and quickly back-stepped into the middle of the street as a half dozen petrified witnesses looked on. He drew another percussion-cap pistol from his pocket and aimed it at Key who retreated. Key then withdrew a small pair of opera glasses which he had been using to spy on the Sickles house and threw them at his assailant; they bounced harmlessly off the congressman's shoulder. Sickles stalked Key and fired again from a distance of ten feet. Key fell wounded and pleaded loudly: "Don't shoot me!"

Sickles walked over and stood above the injured man, repeating the same line over and over again: "You villain, you have dishonored my house. You must die!" He reloaded his weapon on the spot and fired at the errant lover point blank, killing him. Butterworth then advised Sickles to turn himself over personally to Attorney General Jeremiah Sullivan Black (who would later serve as the defense counsel during the impeachment proceedings against President Johnson).

J.H.W. Bonitz, a White House pageboy who had been one of the startled witnesses to the murder, ran straight to the White House office and reported the killing to President Buchanan. The president was not only Sickles' close friend, but he earlier believed that the flamboyant congressman had every chance to become president. "I was afraid it would happen!" Buchanan stated, and then he told Bonitz to get out of town, that he would be held in jail without bond to testify at the trial if he stayed in Washington, which, of course, was a lie. The president gave the frightened pageboy a large amount of money and a razor as a memento. Bonitz fled the city. Buchanan's actions were obviously designed to help Sickles by removing potentially damning testimony, but neither Bonitz, who conveniently vanished until the affair was back-column history, nor the Washington authorities, ever took steps to charge the president with an apparent criminal act.

After surrendering to Attorney General Black, Sickles was escorted to his house, retrieved some personal items, and was then taken to the District Jail, waiving bond and asking for a speedy trial; he felt sure he would be vindicated. Sickles was given a dungeon-like room in the jail, his bed "black with disease-ridden bugs."

"Don't you have a better room?" Sickles complained to the head keeper.

"No," came the laconic reply. "This is the best place you members of congress have afforded us."

Sympathy was with Sickles from the start of his trial, the universal opinion being that he had acted in the proper fashion, that his was a crime of passion which upheld all the virtues of an honorable man. As one letter-writer to *Harper's Weekly* put it, "...the true doctrine...is that the seducer of a wife, daughter, or sister, forfeits, *ipso facto,* his life; not to the law, but to the outraged husband, father, brother, as the case may be."

Sickles was quickly tried and acquitted. In years to come, Sickles would demonstrate his almost maniacal ability to wage battle, becoming one of the most distinguished Union generals in the Civil War. He would take his wife back, lose a leg at Gettysburg on July 2, 1863, for which he was given the Congressional Medal of Honor, and later go on to be ambassador to Spain. He would die in 1914 a rich and esteemed citizen.

Some days after his release, Sickles was strolling with some friends past the very spot where he had shot Key. He paused for a moment and then said in a pleasant voice: "Of course I intended to kill him. He deserved it."

REF.: *CBA*; Graham, *Opening Speech to the Jury on the Part of the Defense on the Trial of Daniel E. Sickles;* Gribble, *Adventures in Murder;* Moore, *The Works of James Buchanan;* Nash, *Hustlers and Con Men;* Pinchon, *Dan Sickles;* Sanders, *Murder in the Big Cities;* Swanberg, *Sickles the Incredible; The Trial of Hon. Daniel E. Sickles for the Murder of Philip Barton Key; Trial of the Hon. Daniel E. Sickles for Shooting Philip Barton Key;* Van Wyck, *Recollections of an Old New Yorker;* (FICTION), Robertson, *Salute to a Hero.*

Sidky Pasha, Bakir (al-Fariq Barkir Sidqi), 1890-1937, Iraq, dictator, assass. Fought in Turkish army from 1908-18, and in royal army of King Faisal. He assumed power in a coup in 1936 but was killed for political reasons. REF.: *CBA.*

Sidney, Algernon (Sydney), 1622-83, Brit., treas. Considered participating in insurrection with Whig leaders in 1683. He was brought into custody when the Rye House Plot was exposed, and tried under Lord Jeffreys. He was found Guilty of treason and put to death. REF.: *CBA.*

Sidney Street Siege, See: **Siege of Sidney Street.**

Siegel, Benjamin (AKA: **Bugsy, Harry Rosen**), 1906-47, U.S., org. crime. Brooklyn-born Benjamin Siegel was one of five children from hard-working but poor Jewish parents. (He had one brother, Maurice, and three sisters, Ethel, Esther, and Bessie.) He attended public school, but quit at an early age to join a street gang on Lafayette Street in New York's teeming Lower East Side. Siegel developed an athletic body while running through the streets, fleeing from police, after committing one petty theft after another. The blue-eyed, black-haired Siegel was followed everywhere by a diminutive hoodlum, Moe Sedway (Morris Sedwitz), and the pair soon developed a protection racket.

Siegel would stop at a pushcart and fondle some of the seller's cheap merchandise, telling him: "Gimme a dollar."

When the pushcart vender invariably refused payment, Siegel would snarl: "No? Okay, gimme $5!"

The pushcart vender would become enraged, telling the boys to leave him alone. At this point, Siegel would order Sedway: "Okay, pour the stuff on his junk!" Sedway would then splash kerosene from a small container he was carrying onto the merchant's goods and Siegel would light a match, setting the pushcart afire. The two hoodlums would then race from the scene. After several fires of this kind, pushcart merchants on Lafayette Street succumbed to paying Siegel protection money rather than see their carts go up in flames. While still a teenager, Siegel met and befriended Meyer Lansky, who had a penchant for organizing floating crap games and other gambling activities. The pair formed the Bug & Meyer Mob, concentrating on establishing and operating gambling dens and stealing expensive cars, which they remodeled in their own garages and then resold.

Siegel at this time also acted as a for-hire killer. Lansky, head of the gang, loaned him out to other gang bosses whenever an important killing among mob members was called for. In 1926,

Above, police photo of Benjamin "Bugsy" Siegel, 1925, when he was booked for operating an illegal crap game.

Right, Siegel's long-time friend and underworld mentor, Meyer Lansky, who reportedly tried to prevent Siegel's murder in 1947.

Below, Bugsy Siegel in a Los Angeles police photo, arrested for murder; he was acquitted after having been defended by Jerry Giesler.

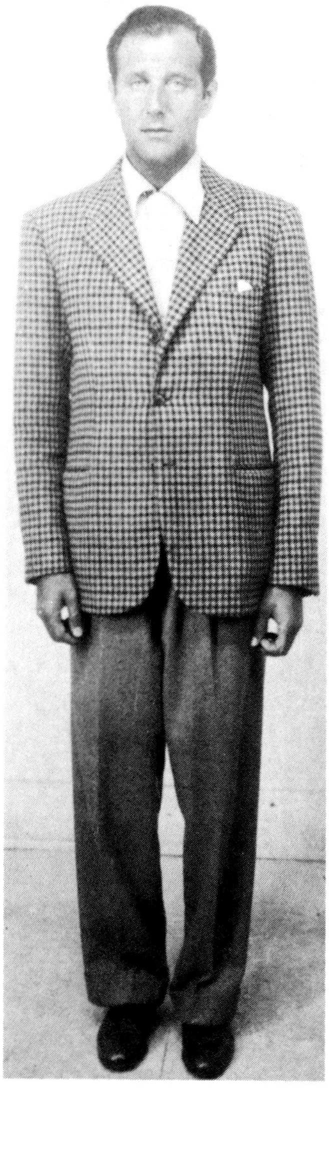

Above, film actress Wendy Barrie was one of Siegel's steady dates in Hollywood when he was not with other steady dates.

Below, Marie "The Body" MacDonald, another one of Siegel's many lady friends in Hollywood.

Above left, Benjamin "Bugsy" Siegel in 1940, when he was beginning his assignment on the West Coast as the top syndicate gangster; he would later control all the rackets in southern California, stealing the thunder of long-time resident gangsters, the Dragna Brothers.

Above right, Virginia Hill, Bugsy Siegel's long-time girlfriend and bag woman for the mob; it was her job to cart enormous amounts of cash to foreign banks.

Below, the Countess Dorothy di Frasso, one of Bugsy Siegel's closest friends on the West Coast; the countess, shown at one of her famous Hollywood lawn parties flanked by Clark Gable and Ramon Novarro, introduced Siegel to the Hollywood elite.

Bugsy Siegel, center, with his lawyer Jerry Giesler, right.

The Flamingo Hotel and Casino in Las Vegas, Siegel's fiasco.

The stately Beverly Hills home of Virginia Hill, mob woman; it was the last thing on earth Bugsy Siegel was to see.

Bugsy Siegel with his life-long friend, actor George Raft.

The end of Bugsy Siegel, shot to death, June 20, 1947.

however, Siegel was arrested and jailed for rape. Lansky's lawyers managed to have Siegel acquitted. The victim was told by Lansky goons that unless she suddenly lost her memory, her face would be scarred forever with acid. In April of that year, Siegel was arrested in Philadelphia for carrying a concealed weapon, but this charge was dismissed. At the time, according to one report, Siegel had been en route to perform a mob murder.

The Bug & Meyer Mob joined the forces of Charles "Lucky" Luciano in 1930, supplying Luciano's men with stolen cars and branching out in Manhattan with new gambling operations and bookmaking establishments. During the Castelammarese War of 1930-31, when the underworld factions of Salvatore Maranzano and Joe "The Boss" Masseria were battling for control of the New York Mafia, Siegel, with Joe Adonis, Albert Anastasia, and Vito Genovese, shot and killed Masseria on Apr. 15, 1931, in Scarpato's Restaurant in Coney Island while Luciano, who worked for Masseria, hid in the men's room. This was a planned execution created by Luciano to appease Maranzano, enhance his own mob standing, and bring the gang war to an end.

The Masseria murder, committed by four mob bosses, established Siegel as a pre-eminent gangster in New York. He went on, under Lansky's supervision, to establish Murder, Inc., a troop of Jewish gangsters who served as killers-for-hire who enforced the newly-born crime syndicate's edicts. Murder, Inc. flourished for more than a decade, later coming under the direction of Louis "Lepke" Buchalter and Albert Anastasia. Siegel, a charming, handsome man who easily ingratiated himself with politicians and important social contacts, was used as a sort of ambassador of the syndicate during the early 1930s, being sent to Philadelphia and Miami to coordinate syndicate takeovers of local mobs and rackets. Those who opposed this arrangement were either killed by Siegel or his troop of Murder, Inc. killers, particularly Siegel's bodyguard, Abe "Kid Twist" Reles.

During this period, Siegel was arrested on minor charges, once in 1932 in Miami, where he was fined $100 for gambling and released, and in the same year in Philadelphia, where he was fined for illegally transporting liquor. At the time, Siegel was accompanying a convoy of trucks carrying bonded whiskey smuggled from Canada and destined for the warehouses of syndicate members in Philadelphia. Siegel was also involved in with a half dozen murders of rival gangsters in the war between New York bootleggers Waxey Gordon and Charles "Chink" Sherman.

One of Gordon's top killers, Francis Anthony Fabrizzo, lowered a bomb down the chimney of the Bug and Meyer Mob headquarters on Grand Street in Manhattan in 1934. The resulting explosion injured Siegel and others. After recovering from his wounds, Siegel tracked down Fabrizzo in southwest Brooklyn and shot him to death. The Bug and Meyer Mob then briefly became aligned with the forces of Dutch Schultz. Siegel, Reles, and others shot and killed Brooklyn loan sharks and rival gangsters, Joseph "Joey" Amberg and Louis "Pretty" Amberg, on Sept. 30, 1935, as a favor to Schultz.

When Luciano siphoned off Schultz's rackets with the help of Abe "Bo" Weinberg, Schultz's top lieutenant, Siegel personally took vengeance on behalf of Schultz by driving Weinberg to Brooklyn one night in 1935 and clubbing him over the head before stabbing him repeatedly in the stomach and killing him. (Siegel stabbed Weinberg in this fashion so that the stomach would not inflate and bring Weinberg's body to the surface after he was dumped into the East River.) This gruesome murder was particularly ironic because Weinberg had been a boyhood friend of Siegel's in Hell's Kitchen, and Siegel had told Weinberg to turn over some of Schultz's rackets to Luciano while Schultz was being tried for income tax evasion in upstate New York, a trial in which the gang bosses expected the Dutchman to be convicted. When Schultz was acquitted, the Weinberg murder was Luciano's way of apologizing to Schultz for prematurely stealing his rackets.

By 1937 Siegel was a much-wanted man, a price put on his head by several rival gangsters for various underworld killings he had committed. The national crime cartel decided that Siegel should move west, allowing him to flee the vengeance of other mobsters, and more importantly, to develop syndicate rackets in southern California. Jack I. Dragna and his brothers controlled most of the gambling operations in that area, and upon Siegel's arrival in Los Angeles, a national wire service was established, hooked up to all of Dragna's gambling dens and bookie parlors. A large portion of the proceeds were funneled back east to syndicate coffers controlled by Lansky, the cartel's banker.

Siegel spent more than $500,000 of syndicate money setting up the national wire service, which was operated by Moses Annenberg, for the mob. But the investment reaped enormous profits. The syndicate, in return for this service, took more than $8 million each year from all West Coast gambling operations. Siegel cut a dashing, handsome figure in the Hollywood scene. He rented a mansion owned by opera singer Lawrence Tibbitt and moved his wife Esther (Krakower) and two daughters, Millicent and Barbara, to the Coast, although Siegel was anything but a faithful husband.

He had many affairs and lady friends in Hollywood, including Ketti Gallion, the French ingenue, and, later Wendy Barrie and Marie "The Body" MacDonald. One of Siegel's boyhood chums, George Raft, who had once been a bootlegger working for Waxey Gordon and for Siegel in New York before going to Hollywood to become a star in gangster films (and who based his movie persona on the slick appearance and traits of New York crime boss Joe Adonis), introduced Siegel to Hollywood high society. Through Raft, Siegel met the social lioness of the era, Countess Dorothy Dendice Taylor di Frasso, who fell madly in love with the rugged gangster. The countess, in turn, introduced Siegel to movie stars Clark Gable, Jean Harlow, Gary Cooper, Norma Shearer, and dozens of others. Siegel also met movie moguls Jack Warner (who was terrified of him), Harry Cohn, and Louis B. Mayer. Siegel later used these movie mogul contacts to extort millions from studios. Through his mobster stooges, Willie Bioff and George Browne, he threatened to close theaters nationwide by calling their syndicate-controlled projectionist union to strike, unless their payoff demands were met.

Then Siegel met a green-eyed, auburn-haired beauty, Virginia Hill, who had run away from her impoverished Alabama home to Chicago as a teenager and who had become a syndicate courier, carrying huge amounts of money from one collection point to another, and even flying regularly to Europe to make staggering deposits in foreign banks where syndicate millions were secreted. The pair developed a deep but tempestuous love affair and aided each other in various rackets. Virginia Hill traveled to Mexico to establish Siegel's first important contacts with hard drug traffickers, and by 1940, Siegel was smuggling millions of dollars worth of heroin and opium into the U.S. from Mexico. The drugs were then distributed throughout the country by syndicate peddlers.

Hill was also a notorious blackmailer who gleaned considerable payoffs from Hollywood stars and magnates to keep their private vices secret. The mob woman lived as richly and extravagantly as did Siegel, buying a mansion in Beverly Hills and entertaining the cream of Hollywood society. Siegel referred to his volatile paramour as "the bait," to his "shark." He had many love affairs, but he always returned to Hill, the only woman ever to dominate his emotions.

Siegel's lifestyle in Hollywood was grandiose. He spent $5,000 an evening entertaining stars and local politicians and twice that much each day betting at Santa Anita racetrack, where his long shot wagers always seemed to pay off. Or, at least, on his income tax forms he reported himself as a "sportsmen," claiming to earn his living from legitimate gambling. Though he had trysts with many women, Siegel oddly held onto his family, which he kept separate from his affairs. He maintained his residence with his wife and daughters, but was often away, living with Virginia Hill or staying with other women. His sexual appetite was reportedly ravenous.

Siegel, for all his show of being an independent sportsmen,

remained a tool of the syndicate. Meyer Lansky informed Siegel that Harry "Big Greenie" Greenberg, a one-time Murder, Inc. member, had fled to the West Coast and was about to turn police informer. In a terse phone call, Lansky ordered Siegel to "take care of this guy." A few nights later, on Nov. 22, 1939, Siegel, accompanied by Frankie Carbo, Whitey Krakower, and Allie Tannenbaum, trapped and killed Greenberg on a Los Angeles street. Krakower returned to the East Coast where he, too, had decided to turn informer, according to later reports by Lansky. Siegel flew to New York and hunted Krakower down on a Brooklyn street, shooting him to death on July 31, 1940.

Siegel was later tried for the Greenberg killing, but was ably defended by Hollywood lawyer Jerry Giesler and was acquitted. At the time of his trial, newspapers publicized the gangster as "Bugsy" Siegel, which infuriated him more than the murder indictment. He hated the name "Bugsy," a nickname from his youth, based upon his bursts of lunatic rage and his recklessness in killing gang rivals. Though he admonished all who used the moniker, the name Bugsy clung to Siegel beyond the grave.

By the mid-1940s, Siegel began to develop an idea for a grand gambling casino in the small desert town of Las Vegas, Nev. Using $1 million of his own funds and about $5 million of syndicate money advanced by Luciano and Lansky, Siegel began construction of the first super gambling casino and hotel, the lavish Flamingo Hotel ("Flamingo" was Siegel's pet name for Virginia Hill). Siegel commuted between Las Vegas and Los Angeles throughout 1946-47 while the construction of his dream casino ensued. More and more Siegel left the day-to-day chores of running syndicate gambling and narcotics operations to his brainless aides, like gun-happy Mickey Cohen. He installed his old friend, Moe Sedway, as manager of the hotel and began spending time in Hollywood watching his friend, George Raft, make movies. Once, while visiting Raft on a movie set, where the star was working, Siegel snorted that he, Benjamin Siegel, could act just as well as Raft before the cameras. In fact, acting had been a lifetime secret ambition of the gangster's. He believed that he could become a movie star if given the right opportunity, but no producer ever stepped forth to offer him a contract.

As Siegel's investment money began to run low, he hurried contractor Del Webb, telling him to finish as soon as possible. Siegel was beginning to feel pressure from Luciano for a return on syndicate money. Webb, on many occasions, overheard Siegel barking orders to have this person "fixed" or that person "taken care of." Noticing the contractor's apprehension one day, Siegel gave Webb his boyish, toothy grin and stated: "Don't worry, Del. We only kill each other," a line that summed up the gangster credo of the U.S.

The opening of the Flamingo did not go well. Most of the Hollywood celebrities Siegel invited to the premiere opening failed to appear, although George Raft and some minor stars were on hand. The public was curious, but failed to appear in the droves Siegel had predicted. He told his eastern syndicate mob bosses that promotion and publicity were needed to establish the reputation of the new gambling center of the U.S. This news angered syndicate bosses in the east, particularly Luciano, who had been deported to his native Italy following WWII, and who had secretly flown to Havana, Cuba, in mid-1947 to confer with his U.S. syndicate associates.

Luciano reportedly called Siegel and demanded that he immediately return the $5 million syndicate loan with substantial interest. Siegel, who no longer thought of himself as a vassal to the eastern bosses, but a crime czar in his own right, an equal to the powerful Luciano, told Luciano to "go to hell!" and that he would pay the loans off in his "own good time." He hung up on Luciano, who then met with Meyer Lansky, Siegel's mentor, telling Lansky that "Ben must be hit and there will be no arguments."

Lansky called Lou Rothkopf, a syndicate chief in Cleveland, and told Rothkopf to contact Mickey Cohen and order Cohen to "stay next to Ben night and day" to guard him against the assassins he knew Luciano would send. Lansky also, according to another account, called Siegel and begged him to make peace with Luciano and try to pay off a portion of the syndicate loans. Siegel ignored the plea.

On the night of June 20, 1947, Siegel went to the Beverly Hills home of Virginia Hill with an associate, Allen Smiley. As the two sat in the elegant living room of the mansion, a Luciano killer aimed a 30.30 rifle through the front window of the mansion and sent three bullets into the handsome head of 41-year-old Benjamin "Bugsy" Siegel, blowing away his left eye, and killing him instantly.

At the time Virginia Hill was conveniently away on a European trip. She did not attend Siegel's funeral, nor did any of his other Hollywood friends, including George Raft, who was suddenly bedridden with an asthma attack. Siegel was buried in an elegant marbled vault reportedly paid for by Meyer Lansky. Siegel's dream of a posh gambling city, Las Vegas, rising out of the desert, became a reality within a decade. See: **Adonis, Joe; Anastasia, Albert; Buchalter, Louis, Carbo, Frank; Cohen, Mickey; Dragna, Jack I.; Genovese, Vito; Gordon, Waxey; Hill, Virginia; Lansky, Meyer; Luciano, Charles; Murder, Inc.; Reles, Abraham; Rothkopf, Louis; Schultz, Dutch.**

REF.: Boar, *The World's Most Infamous Murders;* Bonanno, *A Man of Honor;* Blumenthal, *Last Days of the Sicilians;* Campbell, *The Luciano Project; CBA;* Cohen, *Mickey Cohen: In My Own Words;* Cressey, *Theft of the Nation;* Demaris, *Captive City;* ____, *The Last Mafioso;* Eisenberg and Landau, *Meyer Lansky;* Fried, *The Rise and Fall of the Jewish Gangster in America;* Gage, *Mafia, U.S.A.;* ____, *The Mafia is not an Equal Opportunity Employer;* Godwin, *Murder, U.S.A.;* Gosch and Hammer, *The Last Testament of Lucky Luciano;* Jennings, *We Only Kill Each Other;* Katz, *Uncle Frank;* Kobler, *Al Capone;* Lait and Mortimer, *Chicago: Confidential;* McPhaul, *Johnny Torrio;* Maas, *The Valachi Papers;* Messick, *Kidnapping;* ____, *Lansky;* ____, *Secret File;* ____, *Syndicate in the Sun;* ____ and Goldblatt, *The Mobs and the Mafia;* Morgan, *Prince of Crime;* Nash, *Bloodletters and Badmen;* ____, *Citizen Hoover;* ____, *Look for the Woman;* ____, *Open Files;* Peterson, *The Mob;* Pileggi, *Wiseguy;* Reid, *The Grim Reapers;* Sann, *Kill the Dutchman;* Smith, *Syndicate City;* Thompson and Raymond, *Gang Rule in New York;* Watters and Gillers, *Investigating the FBI;* Wolf, *Fallen Angels;* (DRAMA), Nash, *Last Rites for the Boys* (orig. title, *1947*); (FILM), *Crashing Hollywood,* 1937.

Siegel Trading Company, prom. 1974-80, U.S., fraud. In late 1974, Harold S. Brady, a wealthy Chicago metal dealer, asked Joseph E. Siegel, president of Siegel Trading Company, to provide him with a tax shelter for the $500,000 he had made in capital gains that year. Then, in March 1975, Brady asked Siegel to "shelter" $2 million in capital gains. Brady had ordered Siegel to use his discretion in handling the accounts, but he did not authorize him to make collusive trades with his money. In all, Siegel made twenty-eight fictitious trades between Oct. 17, 1974, and Jan. 27, 1976, for which Brady was charged $91,225. Brady died in 1976, but charges of fraud were still brought against the Siegel Trading Company.

During the five-week trial of Siegel and the company's vice president, Alvin C. Winograd, federal prosecutors Steven Senderowitz and Scott Lasser proved that Siegel had also cheated the government of about $800,000 in 1974 and 1975 by trading on Mexican peso futures on the International Monetary Market (IMM), and that he and Winograd had done this to create a tax loss for Brady. The two men were convicted in February 1980. Siegel was found Guilty on fifteen counts of tax fraud, conspiracy, and rigged commodity trading. Winograd was barred from trading for six months and fined $10,000. At the sentencing of Siegel on Apr. 28, 1980, Senderowitz pleaded with District Judge James B. Moran to send the broker to prison. He pointed out that Siegel's fraud was the largest uncovered by investigators of illegal commodities activities over a three year period. He also said that Siegel, whose net worth was estimated at $4 million, was one of the best-known brokers, and stiff punishment would act as a deterrent. Senderowitz added that a minimum fine of $379,382 should be imposed, as that was the amount of unpaid taxes which could not be recovered from Brady's estate. While the judge did fine Siegel $500,000, Moran claimed a prison term was inappropriate punishment for Siegel, and the judge let him off with a three-year suspended sentence, and barred him from trading for others or himself for one year. Moran said of his lenient punishment that "the legal and illegal are separated by a fairly small degree" in these types of crimes. The defendant told Moran, "I still feel I did nothing wrong." REF.: *CBA*.

Police advance during the battle on Sidney Street.

Siege of Sidney Street, 1911, Brit., burg. Though Winston Churchill would later point to England's finest hours with justifiable pride, his actions during the shootout on Sidney Street on the dank morning of Jan. 3, 1911, were not among them. "The police can hardly be congratulated upon their success in dealing with this formidable conspiracy," exclaimed the *Daily Mail* afterward. Home Secretary Churchill committed a major public relations *faux pas* by appearing in the streets with the police officers—never had it taken so many to bring down so few.

The events leading up to the Sidney Street battle had caused a sensation among conservatives who sought to quell the tide of foreigners with anarchist leanings entering the country. Five Russian and Eastern European nationals attempted to rob a jeweler's store in the Exchange Buildings in Houndsditch, a section of London's East End, on Dec. 16, 1910. The police were summoned by a resident complaining of loud noises in the middle of the night. The burglars were attempting to bore a hole through a wall to reach a jeweler's safe in an adjacent office.

The five robbers were political refugees who had been driven out of their respective countries for subversive activities. The leader of the gang was George Gardstein, otherwise known as Mouremtzov. His accomplices included Max Smoller, a fugitive from the Crimea; Nina Vassileva, Gardstein's mistress, who stood watch outside the store; Jacob Peters, a Communist ideologue, who had been tortured by the czar's secret police; and Yourka Dubof, a locksmith who was to open the jeweler's safe for the gang. Nina alerted Gardstein when the police arrived. The men ceased drilling, as Sergeant Bentley positioned his men around the perimeter of the building. He cautiously approached the door of number eleven and knocked. When Gardstein opened the door, Bentley asked, "Have you been working or knocking about inside?" Gardstein indicated that he understood no English, then disappeared into the rear of the building.

Police officers entered the premises, but it was too dark for them to see. Suddenly, the rear door swung open and a man with a gun opened fire. Bentley was shot in the neck and shoulder and Constable Woodhams was also shot when he tried to assist Bentley. A third man, Officer Tucker, was shot through the chest and died instantly. Gardstein attempted to flee. He pushed past Constable Choat, who was knocked to the ground and shot by Peters and Dubof. One policeman was dead and two others were mortally wounded. Gardstein, who also suffered a serious gunshot wound, escaped with his gang intact. They retreated to the dwelling of Fritz Svaars, a cousin of Peters and an instigator of the aborted robbery, where Gardstein was judged a liability and left to die in his bedroom. The police, meanwhile, launched an intensive manhunt. The field of suspects was quickly narrowed, and the trail of blood left by Gardstein led investigators to Svaars' room. Jacob Peters, Yourka Dubof, and Svaars' mistress, Luba Milstein, were arrested. Smoller disappeared, and Svaars became a fugitive from justice despite having taken no direct part in the robbery-murder. Fearing deportation back to Russia, he took the greatest care not to fall into a police trap.

For the next several weeks, the police focused their efforts on the East End, rousting all suspected anarchists from their known haunts. Detective-Superintendent John Ottaway and Inspector Frederick Wensley were particularly effective in this regard. On New Year's Day 1911, they received a tip that Svaars and a jeweler known as "Joseph" were hiding out at 100 Sidney Street with a woman named Betsy Gershon. Ottaway and Wensley's plan to approach the dwelling with caution was complicated because the building was one of ten four-story abodes, each divided by fireproof walls. A full complement of 200 policemen was deployed throughout the neighborhood to prevent any escapes. Safely removing the other residents of 100 Sidney Street proved to be the most difficult aspect of the operation, and was not accomplished until 4 a.m. The police then tightened their cordon around the tenement building. Inside remained only two men, one of whom was believed to be the notorious Peter the Painter.

The conflict began at 7:30 on the morning of Jan. 3. One of the sergeants from the detail hurled pebbles at the window to draw the attention of the men inside while a second officer pounded on the door. Suddenly, a stream of gunfire came from one of the upper windows. The street scene was chaotic as the police took cover. For the next two hours the police traded shots with the anarchists. Winston Churchill was interrupted in his bath and informed of the situation. He instructed the police to "use whatever force necessary" to bring the situation under control. At 10:15 a.m., a detachment of Scots Guards arrived from the Tower of London. There was furious debate among the officers about the proper way of ending the siege, but nothing was accomplished.

Churchill decided on an impulse to drop by Sidney Street and take charge of the situation. It was a serious breach of protocol that would be severely criticized in the days to come. The home secretary gave the order to bring in field artillery and bring down the house if necessary, but it was decided to storm the building first. Before the Scots Guards could mount their attack, however, an onlooker pointed to a thin wisp of smoke coming from the roof. The house was on fire. The blaze apparently started on the upper floors and worked its way downward. As one of the gunmen poked his head out the window, bullets from the street pierced his head, but neither Churchill nor the police knew that at the time.

The notorious Peter the Painter.

The fire spread quickly inside the bullet-riddled building. The fire brigade arrived on the scene, but Churchill ordered them to stand by and wait before turning their hoses loose. When the upper floors of the tenement collapsed in flames, the firemen quickly moved in. From the massive pile of rubble the police pulled out the charred remains of Fritz Svaars and Jacob Vogel, both of whom worked for Peter the Painter. Vogel had been shot, and Svaars had killed himself in the flames. The Sidney Street shootout became a lively topic of debate in the world press, while the British government struggled with the immigration issue. Ironically, the remaining members of the gang, who had been arrested for the Houndsditch murders, were acquitted for lack of evidence.

REF.: *CBA;* Eddy, *Mystery of Peter the Painter;* Holroyd, *The Gaslight*

Murders; Macnaghten, *Days of My Years;* Nott-Bower, *Fifty-two Years a Policeman;* Reppetto, *The Blue Parade;* Shew, *A Companion to Murder;* Wensley, *Detective Days;* Wilson, *Encyclopedia of Murder;* (FILM), *The Siege of Sidney Street,* 1960.

Siers, David S., c.1944- , U.S., child abuse. As a teacher at Spencer Elementary School in Chicago, David S. Siers would befriend young boys and sexually molest them. The attacks were unknown to school officials or the boys' parents, until one of the children attempted to commit suicide.

The boy, who failed to kill himself, informed police of the sexual assault. The Chicago Police Department, the office of Cook County state's attorney Richard M. Daley, and the police of Forest Park, (where Siers lived), began an investigation. They discovered that at least ten boys aged eight to thirteen had been molested by Siers. At his trial, the former teacher pleaded guilty before Circuit Court Judge Jack A. Welfeld in a Maywood courtroom. His plea saved him from receiving the maximum penalty of thirty years in prison. According to Welfeld, because Siers had "spared the young people the horror and humiliation" of having to testify about their ordeals, the defendant received a sentence of only twenty years in prison on Feb. 26, 1987. REF.: *CBA.*

Sievier, Robert S. (Great Turf Libel Case), prom. 1912-13, Brit., libel. In late 1912, the *Winning Post* newspaper published a series of articles written by the paper's former editor, Robert S. Sievier, who had resigned in 1911. The articles blatantly attacked noted British horse trainer Richard Wooton, claiming that he had fixed races. Wooton charged the paper and Sievier with libel, and the case was brought before a court in July 1913.

Representing Wooton were king's counsel F.E. Smith, Eldon Bankes, and Mr. McCardie. The *Winning Post* was represented by king's counsel Marshall Hall, Bell Hart, and Mr. Schiller. Sievier handled his own defense. A number of eminent figures from the Turf appeared in court, including Lord Derby and Lord Lonsdale. Derby termed that the articles of the newspaper were all "reasonably sensible." The plaintiff and the defense produced a number of witnesses who contradicted each other. For eight days the jury heard testimony which was frequently humorous. One of the jurors had an operation after the fifth day of court precedings and the case proceeded with only eleven jurors. At the trial's completion, the jury said that the articles were not true, but that they were written without malice. Sievier, who contended that he only wrote the articles for the betterment of horse racing and to uncover corruption, was fined one farthing for damages. Darling added the the plaintiff's court costs to this figure.

REF.: Barker, *Lord Darling's Famous Cases; CBA;* Marjoribanks, *For the Defense, The Life of Sir Edward Marshall Hall.*

Sifton, Charles Proctor, 1935- , U.S., jur. Appointed to eastern district court of New York by President Jimmy Carter in 1977. REF.: *CBA.*

Sigebert I, 535-75, Austrasia, king, assass. Youngest son of Chlotar I and Queen Ingund, reigning from 561-75. He defeated the Avars in 562, and again defeated them five years later. He married the manipulative Frankish queen Brunhilde in 567, and was persuaded by her to engage in a civil war against his weaker half-brother Chilperic, who had killed Brunhilde's sister, Galswintha. He was assassinated. REF.: *CBA.*

Sigebert II, 601-13, Gaul, king, assass. First son of Theuderic II, dominated by great-grandmother Brunhilde. She made him Frankish king, but he was never welcomed to the throne. He was presumably murdered by Chlotar II. REF.: *CBA.*

Sighibuldi, Cino dei (AKA: **Cino da Pistoia**), c.1270-c.1337, Italy, jur. Forced into exile from Pistoia for participating in Ghibelline politics from 1303-06. He authored *Lectura in Codicem,* a legal commentary, and taught classes on law at Bologna, Perugia, Naples, and Florence. REF.: *CBA.*

Sigismund, 1368-1437, Hung., consp. Son of Charles IV. He was king of Hungary from 1387-1437 and king of Bohemia from 1419-37, and also reigned as Holy Roman emperor from 1411-37. He engaged in a crusade to defeat the Turks in 1396, but was defeated by Bajaket I in Nicopolis. He supposedly helped arrange the heresy conviction and execution of religious reformer John Huss in 1415. See: **Huss, John.** REF.: *CBA.*

Sigonius, Charles, prom. 1583, Italy, hoax. At Modena, Italy, in 1583, Charles Sigonius announced his discovery of a work by the first century B.C. Roman statesman and orator Marcus Tullius Cicero. The work, entitled "De Consolatione," was an essay in which Cicero consoled himself over the loss of his daughter Tullia. Exactly 200 years later in 1783, a letter written by Sigonius was found by Terabosilii. The letter was a confession by Sigonius that he himself had written the "De Consolatione" by constructing the essay based on a mere fragment he had found.

REF.: *CBA;* MacDougall, *Hoaxes.*

Sigurd II (AKA: **Munnr, Mouth**), 1134-1155, king, assass. Illegitimate son of Harold IV. Held joint rule with half-brothers Ingi and Eystein. He was murdered by backers of Ingi, who also arranged the death of Eystein. REF.: *CBA.*

Sikcles, Daniel, See: **Sickles, Daniel Edgar**.

Silagy, Charles, 1949- , U.S., mur. On Feb. 14, 1980, 31-year-old Vietnam veteran Charles Silagy stabbed and killed his girlfriend, Cheryl Block, with a pocketknife on a road near Danville, Ill. Silagy then went to Block's apartment where he beat and stabbed to death Block's roommate, Anne Waters. Silagy was found Guilty of the murders and sentenced to die in the electric chair on Nov. 7, 1980.

After his execution was postponed, Silagy filed a petition with the Illinois Supreme Court requesting that he be put to death immediately. Claiming that having his execution postponed constituted "cruel and unusual punishment," Silagy asked the court to dismiss his court-appointed attorney and end all proceedings seeking to save him from death. On Nov. 18, 1980, the Supreme Court denied Silagy's requests without specifying reasons for its refusal. Although Illinois courts have handed down the death sentence, final approval for executions must come from the Illinois Supreme Court. The last execution in Illinois took place in 1962. As of October 1989, Silagy still had not been executed. REF.: *CBA.*

Silent Bullet, The, 1912, a novel by Arthur B. Reeve. The protagonist of this fictional work is a "scientific detective," and is based on Dr. Otto H. Schultze. A forensic expert, Schultz worked closely with New York's district attorneys office on important criminal cases at the turn of the century. REF.: *CBA.*

Siler, Eugene Edward, Jr., 1936- , U.S., jur. Nominated to eastern and western district courts of Kentucky by President Gerald Ford in 1975. He also wrote legal articles. REF.: *CBA.*

Silks, Mattie (Martha A. Ready, AKA: **Queen of the Red Lights)**, 1847-1929, U.S., duel-pros. In the early 1880s, Denver, Colo., was the transportation center of the West, and the McGaa Street section was its red light district. Mattie Silks, who took her last name because of her love for fine silk, came to Denver by way of Georgetown, Colo., where she had managed a successful brothel, and made enough money to move to Denver and became the "Queen of the Red Lights" in Denver. Her earliest experience as a brothel owner was in Springfield, Ill. In Georgetown, Silks met Cortese D. Thomson, a gambler and professional foot racer from Texas, who became her lover.

Denver madame Mattie Silks.

Silks dueled with Katie Fulton, a rival madam, over Thomson. Thomson was hit and wounded by Fulton; no one else was hurt. On July 6, 1884, Silks married Thomson and soon moved him out to a horse ranch to provide a home for his orphaned grandchild, Rita. Jack Ready was hired as foreman of the ranch. Thomson continued his ongoing habit of getting involved with other women and, on Mar. 13, 1891, Silks caught him with Lillie Dab, a young prostitute. Silks shot and nearly hit one of Dab's curls before Thomson wrenched the gun from her and beat her with it. Silks sued for divorce the next day, but later reconciled with Thomson. Silks moved to Dawson City in the Yukon in Spring 1898 and made about $38,000 in three months, then returned to Denver and opened up a new brothel on Market Street. In April 1900, Thomson died and Silks legally adopted his granddaughter, and continued her business, installing Jack Ready to serve as her bouncer. Silks bought the property of a rival brothel owner who died, and reclaimed her position as Queen of the Red Lights. Police raids became more frequent, and by 1915, Market Street was a defeated area. Silks married Ready, and in 1929, died at the age of eighty-three. Although more than $1 million passed through her hands, she ended up with only $1,922, after lawyers and public officials had divided up the remains.

REF.: *CBA;* Drago, *Notorious Ladies of the Frontier;* Flanagan, *Out West.*

Silkwood, Karen, 1946-74, U.S., (unsolv.) mur.? "Woman Killed on Way to Secret Meeting." That intriguing Associated Press headline of Nov. 14, 1974, was the tip of an iceberg of corporate greed, union machinations, and nuclear horror. The woman was 28-year-old Karen Silkwood, a laboratory technician at the Cimarron Facility of the Nuclear Division of the Kerr-McGee Corporation, one of the largest employers in Oklahoma. There plutonium was made into fuel rods for use in the new fast-breeder reactor being constructed in Washington State.

Silkwood, originally from Nederland, Texas, was a divorced mother of three, who had left her children with her ex-husband after he married her best friend, knowing that the children would have a mother who could give them all her attention. She went to work at Kerr-McGee as a technician who checked the quality of the plutonium pellets used in making the fuel rods. Soon after she started working in 1972, the Oil, Chemical and Atomic Workers Union went on strike for better pay and greater safety. The strike petered out by mid-January of 1973, but Silkwood, making a name for her outspokenness, soon found herself named to the three-person union bargaining committee.

During the coming months, Silkwood became increasingly aware of the hazards of working with plutonium, though she was not sure most of the employees understood it, or even cared. Several times her radiation-monitoring device indicated that she was "hot" and she had to be thoroughly scrubbed down and had to spend several days taking urine samples before she was determined to be free of contamination. She gradually realized that such events happened regularly to many technicians, but that the company was doing nothing to stop the radiation leaks. When she complained, she was just ordered back to work. When her boyfriend, Drew Stephens, complained about his working situation, he was transferred into a job that made him quit the company.

In September 1974, with employees soon to vote on whether to continue the union in the Cimarron plant, Silkwood; Jack Tice, the head of the union local; and Gerry Brewer flew to Washington to meet with health experts of the OCAW, Steve Wodka and Tony Mazzocchi. There she learned that even the minute exposures to radiation that she and the others frequently received could cause cancer. She left Washington having agreed to get hold of the photomicrographs that would prove her contention that the company was deliberately disguising flaws in the welding of fuel rods so that they did not have to be made over.

In October, union headquarters sent cancer experts to talk with the employees, hoping that fear would convince them to vote the continuance of the union at Kerr-McGee. It worked.

Meanwhile, Silkwood collected information and evidence to turn over to David Burnham, a *New York Times* writer of nuclear issues. On Nov. 5, Silkwood's radiation monitor indicated that she was very hot, and she was required to remove all her clothing and be scrubbed hard enough under a shower to remove a layer of skin. The next day the same thing happened. On the next day, she accidentally spilled a little urine when she was getting the sample she was required to take to the health physicists at the plant. And again she checked out as hot. She was painfully scrubbed down again. Health physicists from the plant then went to the apartment she was now sharing with Sherri Ellis and completely removed every thing from it. The apartment was supposedly sealed, but that night, Silkwood found a back door open and crept in to retrieve an important folder she had hidden inside a wall.

Steve Wodka of union headquarters had come to Oklahoma in preparation for the meeting with Burnham on Nov. 15. He forced the company to send Silkwood, Drew Stephens, and Sherri Ellis to Los Alamos, N.M., to be checked on a special radiation detector at the government research center there. They were examined and analyzed on Nov. 11 and found clean.

After work on Nov. 13, Silkwood delayed her meeting with Burnham for a while to attend a union negotiating session. Morgan Moore, the manager of Cimarron, had suggested to Atomic Energy Commission (AEC) officials that Silkwood had deliberately contaminated herself just to cause trouble. That assertion prevented serious discussion of the union's demand for a health-and-safety committee with authority to make changes in procedures. After the meeting, Silkwood told a fellow employee Kerr-McGee was in for "one big fat surprise."

After that, Silkwood left to meet with the *Times* reporter at a Holiday Inn. She never arrived. Her car was found later in a culvert alongside Highway 74. She was dead, crushed when the left front fender had careened off a concrete wall. Late that night an official of Kerr-McGee went to the garage where her car had been taken and claimed all the papers that had been found in the car.

The union immediately hired road-accident expert A.O. Pipkin, Jr., to investigate. He found that the accident could not have happened the way the local police insisted it had, that some of the dents on the back of the car had to have been caused by another vehicle, instead of the tow truck as the police claimed. Several weeks later, when Pipkin went back to verify his analysis and run actual road tests, he discovered that the highway for several miles on each side of the culvert had been completely reconstructed.

Peter Stockton of Congressman John Dingell's office became interested in the case and went to see AEC officials, who called Karen a "wacko" and a "pervert." Stockton learned that forty-four pounds of plutonium was missing from Kerr-McGee, though no one seemed concerned about that. An investigation ordered by the General Accounting Office used answers provided by Kerr-McGee itself as their own answers and went no further.

After a major radiation spill in December, the Cimarron facility was shut down for a while and all employees who returned were required to pass a security clearance test, which included such questions as "Have you ever talked to Karen Silkwood?... To the media?... Have you ever been involved with anti-company or anti-nuclear activities?" Those who did not pass, especially union members, were fired.

By Spring 1975, the National Organization of Women was involved in the struggle by encouraging people to view Silkwood's death as murder and Kerr-McGee to change their safety practices. Countering the newspaper articles about those activities were others that said she was a drug addict, had deserted her children, and was a "sex-crazed pothead." An organization called Supporters of Silkwood published a poster showing the attractive, dark-haired woman's face and the words: "Dead Because She Knew Too Much?"

On Jan. 1, 1976, Kerr-McGee closed down the Cimarron Facility rather than make the operating changes that the Nuclear Regulatory Commission ordered. There was no way Kerr-McGee could be accused of criminal activities, but fifteen minutes before the two-year deadline on filing civil suits would have been reached, suit was filed in Oklahoma in the name of Karen Silkwood's children, charging the corporation with violating her civil rights, obstructing justice, and depriving her of her right to travel freely on an interstate highway.

The case came to trial in May 1979. While the trial was going on, the meltdown at Three Mile Island nuclear power plant occurred, and the public suddenly became vividly aware of the dangers of radiation. Kerr-McGee attorneys called for a mistrial, but Judge Theis ruled against them. On May 18, the jury determined that Kerr-McGee had been negligent. They granted $550,000 in actual damages plus $10 million in punitive damages. The Court of Appeals later called for a new trial to determine Kerr-McGee's culpability in letting their employees be contaminated. The decision against the firm also called for a number of stringent safety guidelines to be followed by the nuclear industry. In August 1986, the corporation agreed to pay Silkwood's estate $1.38 million.

The day after the original 1979 court decision, a service was held at the site where Karen Silkwood died. One speaker, Sara Nelson, who had been fighting on behalf of Silkwood for almost five years, said, "What (Karen Silkwood) did was something we all could do, something we all should do. She chose to stand for truth instead of deception."

REF.: *CBA;* Kohn, *Who Killed Karen Silkwood?;* (FILM), *Silkwood,* 1983.

Silva, Antônio José da (AKA: **O Judeu**), 1705-39, Port., her. Jailed by Inquisition in 1726 and from 1737-39. He was strangled and his corpse burnt at the stake. He had written several comic plays about classical and mythological figures, and also burlesque productions. REF.: *CBA.*

Silva, Vincente, 1845-95, U.S., west. outlaw. Las Vegas, N.M., in the 1890s, was home to a vicious gang of Latin Americans called Silva's Forty Bandits. The gang's leader, Vincente Silva, was born in Bernalillo County and arrived in Las Vegas in 1875. His gang, which committed all varieties of crime, often met in Silva's Imperial Saloon on Moreno Street. The gang held the area in a virtual stranglehold until 1895, when they decided to hang fellow gang member Pat Maes for an infraction. The gang disintegrated after this and Silva was eventually murdered by former members. He was buried at Campo de los Cadillos on May 19, 1895.

REF.: Baca, *We Fed Them Cactus;* ____, *Vicente Silva and His Forty Bandits;* Callon, *Las Vegas, New Mexico; CBA;* Fergusson, *Murder & Mystery in New Mexico;* Horan and Sann, *Pictorial History of the Wild West;* Jaramillo, *Shadows of the Past;* Otero, *My Life on the Frontier;* Stanley, *Desperadoes of New Mexico;* ____, *The Las Vegas Story;* Thorp, *Story of the Southwestern Cowboy.*

Silva Xavier, Joaquim José da (AKA: **Tiradentes, Toothpuller**), 1748-92, Braz., rebel. Headed first major rebellion protesting Portuguese dominance in Brazil. Revered in Brazilian history, he was captured and beheaded. REF.: *CBA.*

Silvela, Francisco, 1843-1905, Spain, jur. Introduced legislation establishing new criminal and civil laws. He served as minister of justice from 1883-84, and as premier of Spain from 1899-1900 and from 1902-03. REF.: *CBA.*

Silver, Frankie, d.1831, U.S., mur. Mary Surratt of the Lincoln assassination conspiracy is often referred to as the first white woman to be hanged in the U.S., but Frankie Silver was hanged about thirty-five years before Surratt in North Carolina. After hacking her husband to death with an ax while he slept in front of his fireplace, Silver cut his body into small pieces, burned as many of the pieces as she could, and then stuffed the remaining portions into a hollow log.

As she climbed the gallows to be hanged, she showed no remorse, even holding up the execution while she ate a slice of cake, obviously relishing it to the last crumb. REF.: *CBA.*

Silver, Norm, prom. 1920s, U.S., smug. Shortly after William Connors joined Chicago's Prohibition Bureau in November 1927, he and his partner Swanson learned of a large shipment of illegal liquor that would arrive by train from Boston in boxes marked "fish." The prohibition agents followed a truck carrying away the boxes. The agents were in turn tailed by a car that attempted to run them off the road. Instead Connors managed to pull both vehicles over to the roadside and arrest one of gangster Bugs Moran's top lieutenants, Norm Silver, and the truck driver, a man named Egan. Liquor, valued at $50,000, was found inside the truck.

The two men were brought to trial, after failed bribery attempts and intimidating remarks by the assistant U.S. attorney who prosecuted the case. Before the trial started, Swanson had been convinced not to testify. The assistant U.S. attorney asked that the first charge of attempted murder with an automobile be dismissed, which the judge accordingly did. Connors testified to the charge of transporting illegal liquor, although attempts were made to prevent him from doing so. Although his was the only testimony against Silver and Egan, the judge believed the agent, and the smugglers were convicted and each sentenced to two years in prision.

REF.: *CBA;* Kobler, *Ardent Spirits.*

Silvera, Vincent, 1914-53, Jam., mur. Vincent Silvera lived with his wife Martha Silvera in Anchovy, Jam. In 1950, he began an affair with a much younger woman, Princess Campbell. This affair led to a number of fights between husband and wife and in May, Martha Silvera left to live with her mother on the island of St. Elizabeth. She returned in November 1951, and the arguments resumed as Martha Silvera continued to see Campbell. Silvera informed Campbell that his wife would leave him soon, and the two could be together.

On June 15, 1952, Martha Silvera, forty-four, disappeared. Her husband gave friends and neighbors a number of reasons for her departure. He said that her father was ill, she had found employment on St. Elizabeth, she had moved to England, or she had left him. Four days after Martha Silvera's disappearance, a fisherman found a headless, naked body on the cliffs near Anchovy. The next day, clothing was found floating in Bryan's Bay, four miles away. A media campaign to discover the identity of the corpse resulted in the police locating seventy-eight missing women, but not the deceased's name. On June 29, a friend of Martha Silvera's received a letter supposedly from the missing woman, but she did not recognize the handwriting and reported the letter to police. That same day, a Port Antonio dressmaker identified the corpse's clothing as Martha Silvera's. After his arrest on June 30, Silvera claimed that his wife was visiting her sick father on St. Elizabeth. This soon was proved false. Police quickly uncovered enough information to identify the body as Martha Silvera's, and to establish that her husband killed her. The most telling piece of evidence was obtained from photographs of the missing woman. Police enlarged photographs of Martha Silvera and superimposed these upon photographs of the corpse. The photographs matched perfectly. Later, the letter turned into police was proven to be written by Silvera. Also, the head, which was never recovered, had been skillfully removed from the body. A butcher like Silvera would possess the skill to decapitate a body well.

Silvera's trial opened in Kingston on Dec. 5, 1952, and lasted seventeen days. The prosecution called eighty-two witnesses, while the defendant refused to testify or call any witnesses on his behalf. He was convicted and sentenced to death. On Feb. 16, 1953, his appeal was dismissed, and on Mar. 10, he was executed.

REF.: *CBA;* Gribble, *Compelled to Kill;* Jacobs, *Pageant of Murder;* Wilson, *Encyclopedia of Murder.*

Silverius, Saint, d.c.537, Italy, pope, assass. Named pope largely due to authority of Theodat, king of Ostrogoths. He was ousted and replaced by Vigilius to please Empress Theodora in 537, and exiled to Anatolia. He tried but failed to regain the papacy with help from Justinian I and was exiled to Palmaria. He is believed to have been murdered or starved to death. REF.: *CBA.*

Silvers, Rachel, 1954- , Brit., mur. threat. Rachel Silvers may not have read O. Henry's story "The Cop and the Anthem" or even shared the protagonist's motives for committing crime, but she, like Henry's hero, did inevitably obtain her wish: imprisonment.

In "The Cop and the Anthem," Henry, whose real name was William Sydney Porter, told of a vagrant who attempted to get arrested to have a warm place to stay during the cold winter months. He tried to break a window but was given money by the shopkeeper instead and tried to assault a prostitute, who ironically viewed his actions as elevating her to an accepted social level, for which she thanked him. Finally he went to church, found religion, and resolved to go straight. As he left the church the erstwhile criminal was arrested for vagrancy and thrown in prison.

Silvers' real-life adventure is just as wrought with irony as Henry's fictional account. The 25-year-old London woman was so upset by her boyfriend leaving her, that she felt like killing him. To prevent herself from committing murder, Silvers endeavored to get arrested. Her first attempt at crime was to eat at restaurants and refuse to pay the bill. Once, the restaurant staff took up a collection and paid her bill, and another time customers paid her way. Silvers then decided to refuse paying for taxi rides, but, rather than press charges, the drivers merely told her to leave. Her attempt to smash a window with a milk crate failed when the glass did not break. Exasperated, she finally achieved her goal when she ordered a taxi driver to take her to the West End Central Police Station. At the time, Silvers was holding a starting pistol used at the track, with which she forced the driver to call for police. She was found Guilty at the Old Bailey in Novermber 1979 of threatening to murder her former boyfriend and sentenced to one year in prison. See: **Porter, William Sydney**. REF.: *CBA*.

Silver Shirts, The, prom. 1930s, U.S., secret crim. soc. The rise of Adolf Hitler and the Nazi movement in Germany spawned many imitators abroad, not the least of which was William Dudley Pelley of Lynn, Mass. Pelley, the son of a Methodist minister, embarked on a career in journalism. After working for several New England newspapers in the 1920s, Pelley claimed to have received a divine revelation from God. His decision to change careers occurred in 1928 when "he died and went to heaven" for seven minutes. According to Pelley an oracle revealed to him the rise of the Fascist movement in Germany.

With his writing career behind him, William Pelley organized the neo-Nazi Silver Shirt movement in Asheville, N.C., on Jan. 31, 1933. The organization was patterned after the Nazi Brownshirts, and it espoused the same virulent anti-Semitic, anti-Catholic propaganda in the pages of its *Liberation* journal. Within a year, between twenty-seven and forty-six regional chapters sprang up across the U.S. Pelley ran into trouble with the state government in May 1934 when he was charged with fraud and conspiracy after selling worthless shares of stock in Galahad Press, publishers of the Silver Shirt newsletter. He was convicted of violating North Carolina law regulating stock sales but was given a five-year suspended sentence in January 1935 on the condition that he "conduct himself properly" in the future.

The Silver Shirts were investigated by the Dies Committee in April 1940, after government informant Dorothy Waring told congressmen that Pelley was planning a march on Washington, aimed at seizing control of the executive, legislative, and judicial branches. "He told me that he would be dictator of the United States," said Waring. "He said he would put in effect the Hitler program and use the same termite methods here. He told of plans to have seven men in key places around New York who would control the city—utilities, water supplies, and so forth."

Pelley was indicted on eleven counts of sedition against the U.S. in July 1942. He was tried in rural Indiana by a jury comprised of farmers and tradesmen. Defense attorneys argued that Pelley was "an honest critic" of President Franklin Roosevelt and in no way had intended to undermine the Allied war effort. Regarding the charges of anti-Semitism brought against him, Pelley replied that his published works were misinterpreted. "The Jewish people are behind Communism but that is not saying that every Jew is a Communist," he said. On Aug. 12, 1942, the founder of the Silver Shirts was sentenced to serve fifteen-years in prison for aiding the Germans through his speeches and published writings in his newspaper the *Galilean*. The paper was barred from the U.S. mails that same year.

Pelley served only half of his original sentence. He was paroled on Feb. 6, 1950, after seven years. William Pelley emerged from the Terre Haute Penitentiary a forgotten figure whose influence was more illusory than real. He retired to Noblesville, Ind., where he died on July 1, 1965, at the age of seventy-five. See: **Dies Committee Investigation**. REF.: *CBA*.

Silverstein, Thomas, 1952- , and **Gometz, Randy**, 1955- , and **Fountain, Clayton**, c.1955- , U.S., mur. On Oct. 22, 1983, at the federal penitentiary in Marion, Ill., 50-year-old prison guard Merle Clutts, was stabbed forty times with a knife made from a steel bed frame as he led Thomas Silverstein back to his cell. Ten hours later, another guard, 53-year-old Robert Hoffman, Sr., was killed by inmate Clayton Fountain, who attacked Hoffman and two other guards with a homemade knife. On Dec. 1, 1983, a federal grand jury indicted Randy Gometz, along with Silverstein, for Clutts' death, and Fountain for Hoffman's death. Gometz was serving concurrent sentences, two for fifteen years and one for twenty-five years, all for armed bank robberies. He was a difficult prisoner, and earned another year on Apr. 23, 1982, for assault, and a few months later on Sept. 2, 1982, he was sentenced to three more years for assault of a correctional officer. Silverstein had been sentenced to twenty years for the 1978 armed robbery of a California bank. Fountain was serving a life sentence for the 1974 murder of a drill sergeant while he was in the Marine Corps.

On Feb. 9, 1984, Gometz and Silverstein were convicted for the murder of Clutts. Silverstein said he killed the guard in self-defense, but he was sentenced to life imprisonment and transferred to the federal penitentiary at Leavenworth, Kan. On May 24, 1984, Gometz was sentenced to 150 years for Clutts' murder. He was resentenced to life imprisonment on Feb. 6, 1986. On July 8, 1988, Gometz was sentenced to an additional fifteen years for assault with a dangerous weapon and possession of contraband at the Marion Correctional Institution, where he is currently held. Fountain, who had a long and violent criminal history, was sentenced to an additional term of life imprisonment for the murder of Hoffman. REF.: *CBA*.

Silvia, Daniel, 1957- , and **Cordeiro, John**, 1960- , and **Raposo, Victor**, 1961- , and **Vieira, Joseph**, 1956- , U.S., rape. On the evening of Mar. 6, 1983, truck driver Robert Silva passed Big Dan's Tavern in New Bedford, Mass. In the road outside the tavern, a woman wearing only a jacket and one sock flagged him down and told him that she had been raped. The 21-year-old mother of two said she had entered the bar to buy a pack of cigarettes, and had then been stripped and raped repeatedly by several customers, all recently arrived Portuguese immigrants, while others looked on, cheering. Accused of rape were Daniel Silvia, Joseph Vieira, Virgilio Medeiros, Jose Medeiros, Victor Raposo, and John Cordeiro.

Some testimony contradicted the victim's original story. The bartender said the victim had spent a couple of hours in the bar drinking and talking to the men before they raped her, and that she had thrown her arms around one of the men who later attacked her. Two separate jury trials were held. In the first trial, Daniel Silvia, twenty-seven, and Joseph Vieira, twenty-eight, were found Guilty of aggravated rape. Shortly thereafter, a second jury found John Cordeiro, twenty-four, and Victor Raposo, twenty-three, Guilty of the same crime. The jury found Virgilio Medeiros and Jose Medeiros (not related) Not Guilty since, although they had watched the rape, they had not directly participated in the crime. Various women's groups and others outraged by the brutality of the attack felt that the onlookers to the rape should be prosecuted for failing to help the woman, but Virgilio Medeiros and Jose Medeiros were acquitted. On Mar. 26, 1984, Silvia, Raposo, and Cordeiro each received a sentence of nine to twelve years in prison. Vieira was given six to eight years.

The trials divided New Bedford, 60 percent of whose residents are of Portuguese descent. The Portuguese community staged several marches protesting what they saw as a hasty conviction based on ethnic prejudice, although the victim as well as the prosecuting attorney and half the jury were also Portuguese-American. About 100 supporters of the defendants reacted violently to the first jury's verdict, and several, including Joseph Vieira's father, were arrested. The case also drew strong reactions nationwide from supporters of women's rights, who contended that at times it seemed as though the victim, not the defendants, was the one on trial. The Big Dan's incident became the basis for the 1988 film *The Accused,* featuring Jodie Foster, whose portrayal of the rape victim won her that year's Academy Award as Best Actress. REF.: *CBA.*

Simaniuk, George, b.1881, U.S., mur. Two immigrant men who were best of friends vied for the affections of the same woman. The strange affair ended with the murder of Sophie Poleski, a 28-year-old Lithuanian who was thrown into a brick kiln on Manhattan's Lower East Side and roasted alive on Sept. 22, 1925. The story began a few years after John Poleski and his friend, George Simaniuk, emigrated to the U.S. from Romania. Poleski met his future wife, Sophie, in the Lithuanian community where she was considered one of the most desirable women.

Problems arose soon after the two were married. Sophie took a liking to Simaniuk. Hearing of his wife's involvement with his best friend, Poleski moved across the river to New Jersey and went to work for the railroad. In July 1925 Sophie located her husband and asked him to come back to New York. John eventually returned but discovered that Sophie was still seeing Simaniuk. He confronted his friend and they decided to try to share Sophie's affections. The arrangement proved satisfactory to Poleski, but not to Simaniuk who grew impatient and began to make demands on Sophie to leave her husband. "I began to grow tired of handing money over to her," Simaniuk said, "because I knew she was still living with her husband and I fought with her about staying with him. She got very wild about it and a few days ago she threatened to poison me."

Simaniuk was employed in a lumber yard that extended from Lewis Street to the East River, between Fifth and Sixth Streets. There in the early morning hours of Sept. 22, 1925, the Romanian assaulted his lover when she offered port wine he believed was spiked with poison. Simaniuk bludgeoned her over the head with the bottle. He then lifted the woman and threw her into the blazing kiln. Sophie's anguished screams brought Patrolman William Herrick to the kiln house. Simaniuk ran toward the river, but he was quickly apprehended and taken to headquarters for questioning. Meanwhile, Sophie Poleski's charred remains were removed from the smoldering kiln. Dr. Benjamin Schwartz, acting chief medical examiner conducted the autopsy and determined that Sophie died from burns and not from the beating Simaniuk had administered. When the police went to inform John Poleski of his wife's death, they found him lying semi-conscious in his bed. John could not remember who struck him, but the detectives suspected that George and Sophie had tried to kill him and then quarreled. Fearful that Poleski might go to the police, Simaniuk then killed her.

The furnace killer was indicted on a charge of first degree murder by the grand jury on Sept. 25, 1925. He was allowed to plead guilty to a lesser charge of second-degree murder after the state conceded that it did not have enough evidence to prove whether Sophie was actually alive when the body was tossed into the flames. The plea was accepted by Judge Otto Rosalsky on Feb. 16, 1926. He sentenced the defendant to twenty years in prison with the recommendation that the parole board keep him incarcerated for the remainder of his days. George Simaniuk, the vengeful lover, died in the Dannemora prison. REF.: *CBA.*

Simants, Erwin Charles, 1946- , Case of, U.S., rape-mur. On Oct. 18, 1975, 29-year-old Erwin Charles Simants shot and killed six members of the Kellie family, who lived next door to him in the small town of Sutherland, Neb. Simants entered the Kellie home, raped 10-year-old Florence Kellie, shot her, and then shot the other five members of the family as they entered the house in response to Florence's screams. Simants later confessed that he raped Florence again after killing her and attempted to rape the dead body of 57-year-old Audrey Marie Kellie.

Simants was arrested the following day amid massive media attention. Fearing that public disclosure of Simant's confession and the gruesome details of the crimes would undermine a fair trial, a gag order was issued. The press felt that the order was an affront to First Amendment rights, but the gag order was lifted only after Simants' trial had been completed. On Jan. 17, 1976, Simants was found Guilty by the jury on six counts of murder in the first degree and was sentenced to death in the electric chair. Simants received two stays of execution before his conviction was vacated on the grounds that the county sheriff had casually visited with members of the sequestered jury. In a retrial in October 1979, Simants was found Not Guilty by reason of insanity.

REF.: *CBA;* Godwin, *Murder, U.S.A.*

Simececk, James, c.1916- , U.S., mur. In January 1942, lumberjack Joe Holcomb spotted a fire at the farm house of a neighbor near Ellsworth, Wis. Before the roof caved in, he pulled three bodies from the flames. George Petan, ten, was discovered later among the ruins. Investigators discovered that the Petan family had been killed before the house had caught fire. The children, including 6-year-old Neil Petan, and 3-year-old Sylvia Petan, had had their throats slit; their mother, 28-year-old Verna Petan, had been sexually assaulted, stabbed, and shot to death.

A tramp in the area was immediately suspected, as he had once been convicted of rape and had violated his parole. He was cleared by a doctor from Elmswood, Wis., who had given the man a life on the day of the murders. The doctor had noticed a car in the Petans' driveway, however, and police soon learned that the car belonged to James Simececk. Simececk acknowledged having been at the house earlier. He had stopped by to see if Petan wanted any groceries, an offer he usually extended, as the Petans had no car. Petan, according to Simececk, had not desired any groceries, and he had left. Upon further questioning, Holcomb remembered during his resuce attempt, spotting newly purchased groceries on a kitchen chair.

Investigators searched the home of Simececk, whose shirt had already been found to have animal bloodstains, and found a shirt and pants which were heavily covered with human blood. Police also found a .32-caliber revolver, which turned out to be the weapon that had fired the bullet lodged in Petan's body, and a hunting knife. The blond hair caught in Petan's wedding ring matched Simececk's. Confronted with the evidence, Simececk confessed. He said that he shot and stabbed Petan when she refused his advances, and then killed the children, who had run into the house from outside when they heard their mother screaming. The murderer was found sane and tried in March 1942. Simececk was found Guilty on four counts of murder and given four life sentences.

REF.: *CBA;* Wilson, *Encyclopedia of Murder.*

Simenon, Georges (Georges Sim), 1903- , Fr., writer. Created character of Inspector Maigret, hero of detective stories, and wrote many novels under various pen names. REF.: *CBA.*

Simmons, Beoria, 1954- , U.S., mur. As a social worker in Louisville, Ky., 29-year-old Beoria Simmons was disgusted with the immorality and sinful ways of prostitutes, and he felt it was his duty to cleanse the community of these women. He began in 1984 by murdering a teenager whom he believed to be a prostitute, and then proceeding to kill a 29-year-old woman and a 39-year-old woman before his arrest. Simmons showed no signs of insanity. He was found Guilty and sentenced to death. REF.: *CBA.*

Simmons, Ronald Gene, 1941- , U.S., incest-mur. Residents of Cloudcroft, N.M., feared Ronald Simmons. The classmates of his daughter, Loretta, remembered that the retired Air Force master sergeant "had a beer in his hand all the time. He had one little room he would stay in all the time. It was dark and seemed spooky, and it stunk."

In 1981, school officials suspected that Simmons was carrying on an incestuous affair with his 16-year-old daughter, Sheila. School nurse Carol Nix often saw him kissing Sheila good-bye in an illicit and suggestive manner. It was later discovered that Sheila was pregnant with her father's child. Sexual abuse charges were filed against Simmons, whom his wife, Rebecca, described as a violent and abusive father. By this time, the Simmons family had left New Mexico to take up residence in Russellville, Ark., and the charges were dropped when officals were unable to find Simmons. In a safety deposit box at a New Mexico bank, investigators found a five-page letter to Sheila. "You have destroyed me, and you have destroyed my trust in you," Simmons wrote, referring to the allegations of incest that she had made public. He ominously concluded, "I will see you in hell."

Ronald Simmons ruled his large family with an iron fist. His house was described as "fortress-like," and his will was never challenged. For months, his wife considered divorcing him, but she never had the courage. Shortly before Christmas 1987, Simmons decided to kill all fourteen members of his family as a final act of revenge. Prosecuting attorney John Bynum later argued that the decision to murder his family execution style was not the desperate act of a man suddenly possessed by madness. "The family wasn't killed on a sudden impulse," he said. "This was a clear, well-conceived plan."

Simmons purchased a .22-caliber handgun from a local Wal-Mart and shot his wife, forty-six, his seven children, four grandchildren, a son-in-law, and a daughter-in-law on Dec. 23. He strangled one grandchild with a fish stringer and left the body in the trunk of a car. Simmons dug a mass grave behind the mountain home near Dover and soaked the bodies in kerosene. "Why?" Bynum asked rhetorically. "He wanted to keep the smell from coming up out of the ground and attracting animals and people. The top few inches of the ground also had been topped with coils of barbed wire."

Five days later, Simmons drove to Russellville where he shot and killed 24-year-old Kathy Kendrick, who had spurned his romantic overtures, and 33-year-old James D. Chaffin, an employee of a local oil company where Simmons had worked. With a crazed grin on his face, Simmons wounded Roberta Woodley at a mini-mart and Joyce Butts, who had worked with him at Woodline Motors. Both women survived the ordeal and appeared as witnesses in the first of two sensational murder trials, which began in Ozark, but were moved to Clarksville because of publicity. Simmons' murdered family was found by police after the Russellville shootings.

On May 12, 1988, Simmons was convicted of murdering the two Russellville victims after a jury deliberation that lasted an hour-and-a-half. Following the sentencing hearing, the jury handed him a death sentence. "To those who oppose the death penalty (in) my particular case, anything short of death would be cruel and unusual punishment," the convicted man said in a prepared statement.

Simmons went to trial in February 1989 for the mass murder of his family. Before the jury retired, the remorseless killer struck prosecutor Bynum on the chin and then tried to seize a deputy's handgun. This image was fresh in the jurors' minds when they retired on Feb. 10. Four hours passed before they returned a Guilty verdict with a recommendation for death.

As the final plans for Simmons' execution by lethal injection were being made, opponents of capital punishment petitioned Arkansas governor Bill Clinton for a stay and staged a candlelight vigil outside his mansion hours before the execution was to take place on Mar. 16, 1989. Meanwhile, attorney Arthur L. Allen prepared a petition on behalf of another death row inmate, Jonas Hoten Whitmore, II, contending that Arkansas' lack of mandatory appeal made capital punishment "arbitrary and capricious." The written deposition was filed with U.S. Supreme Court Justice Harry Blackmun following the state supreme court's decision not to intervene in the matter. "I felt that our argument was compelling enough that we would receive the stay at some point in the process," Allen said.

At the eleventh hour, the high court granted Simmons a stay of execution. The case could take another six months to a year to be resolved. If the sentence is not overturned, Simmons would become the first Arkansas prisoner executed since 1964. Sheriff Bolin expressed anger and frustration at the decision. "I'm angry that a country such as we live in...can go through this kind of thing," he said. "I had hoped our United States Supreme Court judges would have a little more sense than to listen to some cockeyed death row inmate." REF.: *CBA*.

Simmons, Theodore, 1969- , and **Jones, Milton E.**, 1970- , U.S., rob.-mur. The Reverend A. Joseph Bissonette was deeply involved in the plight of Salvadoran refugees seeking admittance to Canada to begin a new life. The Central American exiles relied on the help of the Buffalo, N.Y., priest whose life was tragically ended on Feb. 23, 1987, by two teenage men he befriended.

Bissonette was pastor of St. Bartholomew's Church on Grider Street in a dangerous inner-city neighborhood of Buffalo. In December 1986 he was named central city vicar of the Diocese of Buffalo, a position created to recruit black men into the priesthood. A former chairman of the Peace and Justice Committee of the Priest's Councils of New York State, Father Bissonette was remembered by his colleagues as a kind, compassionate man. "He didn't care who you were," recalled the city's only black priest. "Color did not mean anything to him. He just wanted to serve people."

Father Bissonette was in his office at the rectory the night of Feb. 23 when 18-year-old Theodore Simmons and his friend Milton Jones, seventeen, dropped by. Simmons explained that he had just been kicked out of his house and needed somewhere to stay. The priest admitted the two young men and told them to sit down while he prepared sandwiches for them. Simmons assaulted Bissonette with a hunting knife in the church kitchen. Then he and Jones bound, gagged their victim and stabbed him repeatedly before escaping the church grounds with $300 removed from the safe. The body was found the next morning by a second priest.

Two weeks later, on Mar. 8, a second Buffalo priest was slain. Seventy-four-year-old Monsignor David P. Herlihy was returning to the rectory of St. Matthew's on Buffalo's East Side when he was assaulted by the same two men. A coroner's autopsy revealed that the priest was stabbed eighteen times. Stymied in their efforts to identify suspects in the Bissonette killing, the police had little trouble the second time. An informant told police he had provided a hiding place for Simmons and Jones and had overheard them planning the murder of a priest "that Teddy knew." The motive in both cases was robbery.

Jones and Simmons hired a Buffalo cabdriver to drive them to Toronto where they planned to pick up prostitutes. However, customs officials at the Peace Bridge linking Canada to the U.S. recognized Jones and arrested him on an earlier delinquency warrant. Simmons, freed on his own recognizance, fled to San Diego, Calif. Buffalo police picked up Jones on Mar. 8. He confessed to the crimes and named Simmons as Bissonette's murderer "because the priest knew Teddy and Teddy told me to stab the priest." The following morning Buffalo police filed extradition papers with San Diego officials. Simmons was arrested and returned to Buffalo to stand trial. On Mar. 18, the defendants entered a plea of not guilty to two charges of murder. Jones and Simmons were tried separately. On Jan. 29, 1988, a Buffalo jury found Milton Jones Guilty of murder and two counts of first-degree robbery. Simmons trial commenced on Sept. 22 and ended in a conviction on one count of felony murder in the death of Father Bissonette. Both men were sentenced to fifty years in prison with no chance of parole by State Supreme Court Justice Frederick Marshall. "Forgiving is one thing," Marshall said, expressing the belief that the priests would be inclined to show compassion for their slayers, "and justice is another." REF.: *CBA*.

Simmons, William Joseph, See: **Ku Klux Klan**.

Simmons, Zachariah, prom. 1870s, U.S., org. crime. Zachariah Simmons was considered by many to be the first organized gambling "policy" king to venture beyond the confines of New York City. He accomplished this feat by first gaining control of policy operators within the city. Simmons formed an alliance with Tammany Hall. To show his power, and that he intended to exact a percentage of their profits, he had the police raid all of the policy shops in Summer 1870. The one-day shutdown of the shops was enough to convince operators to pay Simmons and his three brothers. Within a year of the raid, Simmons had effectively gained control of 75 percent of the policy operations, with the support of the Tweed Ring. He formed the Central Organization to run his empire. Between 1872 and 1875 Simmons' net profits were estimated at $1 million, from twenty different U.S. cities, including Baltimore, Chicago, Philadelphia, Richmond, Va., and Washington, D.C. Simmons was also acclaimed as the man who introduced the policy game to the poor.

Before he emerged as the policy king, the minimum bet in the game was a nickel. In the middle 1870s, he developed "the envelope game" where bets could be as low as a penny. The numbers drawn for the policy game were said to have originated in Louisville and Frankfort, Ky. But it was alleged that Simmons simply chose the numbers himself after learning from operators which numbers had not been picked as often. This allegation was made public by Anthony Comstock, who found two notes initialed by Simmons purporting to arrange the day's numbers.

In 1875, Simmons became one of the managers of the Kentucky State Lottery and the Frankfort Lottery of Kentucky. Ironically, or inevitably, the numbers drawn on Aug. 25, 1879, at Louisville and Frankfort were the exact same numbers drawn in the exact same order. Apparently Simmons would select the numbers in New York and then send a coded telegraph message to Frankfort and Louisville informing the lotteries what numbers to announce as drawn. These numbers were then wired back to New York via Jersey City, N.J., and Cincinnati, Ohio, which was the policy king's Western headquarters. There were reportedly two drawings each day; a morning drawing in Frankfort and an afternoon drawing in Louisville. When Simmons retired from the policy business he was replaced by Albert J. Adams who had started as a policy runner for Simmons.

REF.: *CBA;* Gibson, *The Fine Art of Swindling.*

Master robber, the dapper "Gentleman Harry" Simms, and his band of thieves.

Simms, Henry (AKA: **Gentleman Harry**), d.1746, Brit., burg.-rob. Henry Simms' companions called him "Gentleman Harry" for his spit-and-polish manner and fine dress. He robbed his victims on the open road and wherever else the opportunity presented itself. There soon was a reward on his head, so he signed on as a seaman aboard a privateer. He quickly grew bored with the nautical life, returned to land and enlisted as a foot soldier. At a brothel, he assaulted a prostitute and was sent to the New Prison, but released for lack of evidence. Simms was soon apprehended for burglarizing a baker's shop. He was sentenced to serve time in the Maryland penal colony. When the prison ship dropped anchor in the harbor, he was sold for twelve guineas. Simms soon escaped his indenture and returned to the coast, where he arranged to work his passage back to England aboard a man-of-war.

Returning to England, Simms stole a horse at Whitechapel in order to rob his countrymen on the highway. He quickly squandered the money he gained from these adventures on prostitutes and ale house revels. Deciding that things were too hot for him in London, he fled to Ireland. When he arrived at Harrow-on-the-Hill, he robbed a man named Sleep of his watch and all his money. Simms warned his victim not to report the affair, but he did anyway.

A posse finally overtook Simms near Hockliffe. To prevent his escape, the highwayman was shackled in chains and an iron collar. Simms stood trial at the Old Bailey. There were ten robbery charges against him, but it took only one to send him to the gallows. Henry Simms was hanged on Nov. 16, 1746.

REF.: Bleackley, *Hangmen of England; CBA;* Mitchell, *The Newgate Calendar.*

Simnel, Lambert, c.1475-1535, Brit., fraud. Crowned King Edward VI in Dublin in 1487 while posing as the young Earl of Warwick in a complicated scheme with the support of Margaret, sister of Edward, and an Oxford priest who trained him for the assignment. After he was named king, he traveled to Lancashire with the backing of poorly-supplied Irish levies and Germans. He was beaten at Stoke in 1487. He was granted a pardon, and served as royal falconer thereafter. REF.: *CBA.*

Simon, Saint (AKA: **Simon The Apostle**), prom. 1st Cent. A.D., Egypt, mur.? Reputedly gained following preaching in Egypt, then associated with Saint Judas the apostle in Persia. According to Saint Basil, he met a peaceful death in Edessa, but other accounts claim he was martyred by being cut in half by a saw. REF.: *CBA.*

Simon, Dr. **Carleton**, prom. 1920s-30s, U.S., criminol. Dr. Carleton Simon spent six years, from 1920-26, as a deputy police commissioner for New York City before he began work on a revolutionary identification system that used the patterns of blood vessels in the eye. This approach to identification was suggested by Mount Sinai Hospital opthamologist Dr. Isadore Goldstein. The two men were joined by Allan Broms, who coordinated the charts and graphs for the system.

Like a fingerprint, every person's eyeprint is unique, with the probability of any two being alike fantastically remote. Unlike a fingerprint, however, a criminal would have to lose his sight to alter the pattern. The character of arteries and veins can be changed by disease or age, but the position of these blood vessels would remain constant. Using a Zeiss retinal camera, a person's retina can be photographed straight through the pupil. Veins, rather than arteries, are used as reference points because of their larger size. The main point of reference is the entrance point of the optic nerve. From this point, directions and distances to veins, and forks in veins, are plotted on a graph, and given corresponding coordinates providing a serial number for filing classification and comparison. REF.: *CBA.*

Simon, Sir **John Allsebrook (Viscount Simon)**, 1873-1954, Brit., atty. gen. Served as member of Parliament from 1906-18 and from 1922-40, and as attorney general in 1913. REF.: *CBA.*

Simpson, Charlie, 1948-72, U.S., suic.-mur. Harrisonville, Mo., south of Kansas City, was a quiet farming community on the Kansas border. During the early 1970s, Harrisonville's citizens often complained of the nine long-haired youths who loitered in town. These nine men were natives of Harrisonville, eight of whom received unemployment benefits. Complaints often were filed against the youths, who would sit about daily glaring at passersby. The town council passed an ordinance prohibiting gatherings of three or more people. The nine men claimed police enforced the law only against their group. One night in Spring 1972, the police arrested eight of the nine men. The next day, the ninth, 24-year-old Charlie Simpson, bailed his friends out. He then went on a shooting spree.

Simpson ran through the middle of town firing his M-1 carbine.

He killed two police officers outside the bank, then ran inside and wounded two bank clerks. Back outside, he shot to death a laundry deliveryman, then fired two shots through the sheriff's office window. Sheriff Bill Gough was wounded. Finally, the gunman ran to the steps of the Harrisonville Retirement Home, placed the gun's muzzle in his mouth, and fired one last shot. REF.: *CBA*.

Simpson, Edward (AKA: **Flint Jack**), b.1815, Brit., forg. The science of archeology held a special fascination for Edward Simpson, orphaned son of a Yorkshire sailor. Though he received no formal university training, Simpson was able to deceive specialists with his hand-crafted flint forgeries of native weapons—hence the nickname "Flint Jack." Simpson was raised near the moorlands of Sleights, where there was a wealth of prehistoric material including Stone Age burial grounds. He received some rudimentary training from a local historian named Dr. Young who took him along on fossil-hunting expeditions. By the time he was twenty-five, Simpson was regarded as a local expert and was often called on to classify and clean various prehistoric artifacts. He discovered later that dealers in antiquities would pay top dollar for such items.

In 1843, "Flint Jack" was encouraged to manufacture his own arrowheads. He chipped a perfect facsimile of a flint arrowhead and had no trouble selling it to a collector. In Bridlington he fired up his kiln and began churning out a batch of ancient Roman urns similar to the ones he had seen in Dr. Young's collection. Simpson crafted an assortment of ax heads and other implements which he brought into Whitby where they were sold in one job lot. When asked how he came upon such treasures, Simpson explained that he had discovered them among the "tumuloo" between Kirby Moorside and Stokesley. Laughing about the gullibility of these people years later, Simpson would say, "Nowadays they would be detected at once. They were too thick in the walls, of the wrong material, ornament, shape, and burning. I often laugh at the recollection of the things I used to sell in those days."

After testing the limits of credulity in the village of Whitby, Simpson pushed his wheelbarrow of treasures to other Yorkshire towns. In Malton he passed off a hunk of tin as an authentic Roman breastplate. One day Simpson plucked a stone out of the earth. He carved the fish symbol into the sides with the inscription "IMP CONSTANT EBVR" meaning the "Emperor Constantine, York." A Pickering historian, believing this to be a wonderful find, sent it on to the British Museum which expressed skepticism.

Museum authorities did not declare the stone a fraud but instead wondered what significance it could possibly have. By this time the forger had moved on to Peterborough where he accepted legitimate employment as the paid assistant to Dr. Porter, an esteemed fossil collector. Though he probably enjoyed the work, Simpson could not resist the temptation to filch an extra few dollars out of the unsuspecting. He stole a piece of petrified wood from Dr. Porter and carved the initials "INGULFVS" into a signet ring he had fashioned. To a trained medieval historian the meaning of these letters was perfectly clear. The ring had once belonged to the Abbot of Croyland Abbey. Simpson planted the item in the churchyard where it was found by a laborer. A Peterborough collector paid a handsome sum for the piece.

Moving on to London Simpson flooded the market with a spate of interesting "discoveries." The curators at the British Museum were easily fooled. Fearing that the market would soon be saturated, thereby arousing suspicion, Simpson returned to York where he got himself a job uncovering material in the North Yorkshire moors. Later he went to the Lakes region of England, and then on to Ireland in search of ancient Celtic artifacts to fool the locals. Simpson might have retired a rich man, but this was not to be the case. Alcohol was his downfall. To finance his drinking habits he had to keep moving along, dreaming up new archeological frauds. In 1861, with rumors circulating that Simpson was nothing more than a clever hoaxer, an acquaintance named Professor Tennant confronted him about these allegations. Simpson confessed that it was all true but at the same time added that his buyers had purchased the items through their own gullibility. He had merely presented himself as a humble peddler selling a "few odds and ends." Simpson's career was over, but he was retained by Professor Tennant to demonstrate his forgery skills before a packed house of geologists and archaeologists at the Cavendish Square lecture halls on Jan. 6, 1862. Afterward he drifted into obscurity, selling flint items from a small shop in the Strand and burying his troubles in a bottle. REF.: *CBA*.

Simpson, John Richard, 1932- , U.S., law enfor. off. Born in Boston in 1932, John Richard Simpson attended Loyola College in Montreal, Quebec, and later graduated from the New England Law School in Boston in 1963. He served in the U.S. Army in the mid-1950s. Joining the U.S. Secret Service agency in 1962, he worked in a number of supervisory positions and also was special agent in charge of the Presidential Protection Division and assistant director of Protective Operations. He became Director of the Secret Service in 1981. REF.: *CBA*.

John Richard Simpson

Simpson, Jonathan, 1654-86, Brit., rob. After serving his apprenticeship to a linen-draper in Bristol, Jonathan Simpson opened his own shop and married the daughter of a well-to-do merchant. His new wife, however, soon took a lover, and according to legend, Simpson laid a trap for her. When the cheating couple saw Simpson coming down the lane, the man hid in a large trunk in the bedroom. Simpson ordered his wife from the house and then summoned the wife of the man in the trunk. Simpson seduced her, and then opened the trunk. "Now, come out, brother cuckold!" he ordered, having had the last laugh.

Simpson threw his wife into the streets, closed his shop, and exhausted his savings of £5,000 in little more than a year. To support himself, he took to highway robbery, and was eventually arrested and convicted. As the rope was being fitted around his neck, Simpson received a last-minute reprieve. To the hangman's surprise, however, Simpson said, "I believe I am one of the most unfortunate dogs alive! For both Tyburn and Newgate have this day refused me."

Within six weeks of his release from custody, Simpson committed forty more robberies. Among his many wealthy victims was George Booth, first Baron of Delamere. However, he did not fare so well against heavily armed soldiers from the Second Regiment Footguards. Near Acton he commanded two captains to deliver their loot or face the consequences. But the two burly footguards refused, shooting Simpson in the arms and legs and carrying him off to the magistrate to stand trial for robbery. At Newgate the unhappy robber who considered his whole life a curse received the usual sentence of death for robbery. He was hanged at Tyburn on Sept. 8, 1686.

REF.: *CBA;* Pringle, *Stand and Deliver;* Smith, *Highwaymen.*

Simpson, Sir **Joseph**, 1909-68, Brit., law enfor. off. Sir Joseph Simpson spent thirty-one years as a British peace officer, the last ten as commissioner of the London Metropolitan Police at Scotland Yard. Born in 1909, Simpson graduated from the Manchester University College of Technology before attending the Hendon Police College in 1934. He graduated in 1935 and was retained as a teacher for a year before being admitted to the bar in 1937. But instead of pursuing a career in law, Simpson became the assistant chief constable of Lincolnshire in 1937, remaining until 1943, when he became chief constable of Northumberland. In 1946, Simpson moved to the same position in Surrey, and in 1956, he moved to Scotland Yard as the assistant commissioner. A year later he became deputy commissioner, and in 1958, commissioner of the Metropolitan Police. In this role, Simpson was especially interested in the formation of a cadet corps to insure a progression of qualified recruits. He also fostered the use of police dogs. Simpson served with distinction for ten years until his sudden death on Mar. 20, 1968, at the age of fifty-eight. REF.: *CBA*.

Simpson, Wallis Warfield (Duchess of Windsor), prom. 1946, Brit., (unsolv.) theft. On Oct. 16, 1946, the Duke, Wallis Warfield Simpson, and the Duchess of Windsor, were staying at the Ednam Lodge, lent to them by their friend, the Earl of Dudley, in Sunningdale, when they were robbed of approximately £25,000 worth of jewels. Scotland Yard's Detective-Inspector J.R. Capstick and Detective Sergeant Monk, were called in to investigate by the chief constable of Surrey, Superintendent Currie. The robbery had occurred at around 6 p.m. when the maids were taking a tea break, and it was presumed to be an inside job, since the thief or thieves easily entered Simpson's boudoir, and had no trouble escaping undetected. The case was never solved. REF.: *CBA*.

Simpson, Willie Joe (AKA: **Charlie Smith, Jack Samuels**), 1950-73, U.S., mur. Katherine Cleary lived—and died—on the crime-ridden Upper West Side of Manhattan. She grew up in Holyoke, in northern N.J., a pleasant, middle-class community unlike the teeming sprawl of Manhattan. Cleary had first gone to Newark and then on to New York to teach the deaf. She had a natural rapport with the handicapped because at the age of ten she had developed a serious case of scoliosis that had to be corrected through surgery. For much of her life Cleary bore her physical and emotional scars with quiet dignity. She was well-liked by her students at the St. Joseph's School for the Deaf in the Bronx, a sensitive, giving person genuinely perplexed by the subtle nuances of life, particularly the dilemma of understanding good and evil. Her own childhood experiences in the hospital made her question the Catholic piety of her father, an insurance agent who moved his family out of Brooklyn when their neighborhood deteriorated.

By night Cleary frequented the neighborhood taverns in the vicinity of 72nd Street and West End Avenue. Tweed's, the Copper Hatch, and other establishments she dropped into two or three nights a week were not singles bars. There were no dance floors, blaring disco music, or potted palms to suggest these places were favored by the swinging singles.

On New Year's Day 1973, Cleary left her one-room apartment on the West Side to partake in some holiday cheer at Tweed's Bar on the south side of 72nd Street near West End. At the opposite end of the crowded bar stood Willie Joe Simpson, a blond, blue-eyed hustler from Clay County, Ill. Years earlier Simpson was diagnosed as suffering from "psychological hysteria" resulting from a childhood injury to his foot. The doctors could find nothing wrong with the bones nor was there any evidence of a physical abnormality. His paralysis had been "psychologically induced," according to physicians' reports. Like Cleary, Simpson's physical problems (real or imagined) clouded his outlook on life. He had few boyhood companions and seemed most at ease playing with animals. In 1964, he stole $10.50 from the local Boy's Club, a first brush with the law which earned him a probationary sentence. At sixteen Simpson ran away from home. He took the bus to California, Arizona, Colorado, New Mexico, and then across country to the East Coast, winding up in seamy Times Square. Like other young runaways with no money or job skills, Willie Joe Simpson hustled for a living. He picked up male homosexuals and charged them anywhere from $20 to $50 for an engagement. He preferred the company of women but put aside his natural inclinations to make more money than he had ever seen in his life.

In 1971, Simpson was living in Miami, Fla., where he met the "true love" of his life, 16-year-old Carole Musty. They were married at the Hotel Vagabond, and for a time Simpson was happier than he had ever been. But in a careless moment he stole a car, was arrested, and sentenced to the county stockade for one year. The lax security afforded Simpson a chance to escape one day. With Carole in tow, Simpson caught the first plane out of Miami and returned to New York. In June 1972, he was keeping constant company with his best friend Danny Murray and living less than three blocks from Katherine Cleary.

On New Year's Day Simpson dined with Murray in a restaurant on Columbus Avenue. Afterward he stopped in Tweed's for a quick drink. In the loud din of the crowded bar Simpson met Cleary. In that last year of her life Cleary's friends—those that knew her—recalled a subtle change. According to one West Sider, "All I know was I saw her around the neighborhood. I used to see her in places I wouldn't want to go and she was with men I wouldn't want to be with." Cleary's promiscuous Manhattan lifestyle became the focus of the 1975 motion picture dealing with the tragedy, titled: *Looking for Mr. Goodbar.*

What passed between Cleary and Simpson that night in the bar could only be surmised. But a short time later the 28-year-old teacher took the cowboy drifter back to her apartment. According to sworn statements Simpson provided the police, they engaged in sex. But Cleary became antagonistic and ordered him out of her room when the act was completed. "She went nuts and started pushing me physically to hurry and get dressed and leave," he said. "She was very nasty, a complete reversal of a few moments before. I have problems with my mines (sic) and I often flip out not knowing whether walls, people, etcetera are real. I hear things, I think sometimes I can fly." Simpson seized her by the throat and started choking her. Afterward he grabbed a paring knife and stabbed her eighteen times. Three days later, the horribly mutilated body of Katherine Cleary was found by a concerned co-worker who prevailed upon the landlord to let him in after the woman failed to show up for work. By this time Willie Joe Simpson had flown back to Miami and from there he continued on to Springfield, Ill., where he visited his brother, Fred. New York police were put on the trail of the murderer by Danny Murray, Simpson's friend and former lover. In return for immunity from prosecution, Murray agreed to appear as a witness for the prosecution. Within days of the murder, Simpson was apprehended in Springfield and extradited to New York to answer charges. Simpson told police of his encounter with Cleary, but neglected to add that his sexual impotence may have been the telling factor of the tragedy.

A neurological examination was scheduled for Simpson by physicians at Bellevue Hospital. He was declared fit to stand trial and was awaiting his day in court when prison guards at the Tombs Prison found him hanging from the ceiling bar of his cell on May 4, 1973. On the day that Simpson was interred in the family plot back in Illinois, Carole Musty delivered his stillborn child in Miami.

REF.: *CBA;* Fosburgh, *Closing Time: The True Story of the Goodbar Murder.*

Sims, Loyie, 1923- , U.S., fraud. Loyie Sims, a 60-year-old Wauconda, Ill., man, accused of mail fraud by federal authorities pleaded Guilty on May 24, 1983, to taking more than $400,000 from seventy investors. Sims and two sons, Michael and David Sims, and James R. Wolfe, were accused of falsely promising investors they could get rich by raising and selling earthworms. Investors who paid Sims a minimum of $845 for four tubs of earthworms to raise and sell back to the company were lead to believe that there were more markets for the worms than actually existed. On July 6, Sims received a three-year sentence, a $2,000 fine, and was ordered to repay $243,000 to those who invested in his World Wide Worms company. Later that day, he was sentenced to four years in jail and ordered to pay $185,000 to investors in Vermiculture Laboratories, a marketing agent for World Wide Worms. The prison terms were to be served concurrently. REF.: *CBA*.

Sims, Mitchell Carleton, c.1959- , U.S., rob.-mur. In the early morning of Dec. 3, 1985, an armed robber walked into the Domino's Pizza restaurant in Hanahan, S.C., and leveled a .25-caliber semi-automatic pistol at two 24-year-old employees, Gary Dean Melke and Christopher Leroy Zerr. He tied up the deliverymen with a telephone cord, and after stealing $1,164 from the cash register, shot them. Zerr was shot once in the head and died immediately. Melke was shot four times in the face, head, and neck. After the gunman left the building, Melke stumbled to his car and drove to the police station about 500 yards away. He died two days later in a Charleston hospital. Before he died, he named former Domino's deliveryman Mitchell Carleton Sims as the assailant.

Armed robber and murderer, Mitchell Sims.

Sims had quit his part-time job at Domino's in March after a dispute with his supervisors. Following the shooting in South Carolina, Sims fled with his accomplice and girlfriend, 19-year-old Carolyn Padgett, to California, where he continued his revenge against Domino's. On Dec. 9, the two lured a Glendale deliveryman, 21-year-old John Steven Harrigan, to their motel room by placing a pizza order. Harrigan was robbed and then tortured, bound hand and foot, gagged, and finally drowned in the bathtub. Sims was arrested in Las Vegas on Dec. 25. He and Padgett were tried for the California killing first. Padgett was convicted in February 1986 and sentenced to life in prison without possibility of parole. On May 20, the jury found Sims Guilty of murder, armed robbery, and lying in wait. The verdict and circumstances automatically required a sentence of death or a sentence similar to Padgett's. Pasadena Superior Court Judge Jack B. Tso followed the jury's—which had heard of the South Carolina charges—and Deputy District Attorney Terry A. Green's recommendation, rather than defense attorney Morton P. Borenstein's plea for life. He sentenced Sims to death on Sept. 11, 1987. Sims was extradited to South Carolina in 1988 to face robbery and murder charges there. Authorities had charged Padgett with being an accessory to the murders and armed robbery, but she was not tried.

The May 1989 trial for the Hanahan robbery and murders opened in Berkeley County rather than Aiken County because of extensive pre-trial publicity. Berkeley County public defender Mitchell Lanier and attorney William Runyan, Jr., were appointed by the court to defend Sims before Circuit judge Richard E. Fields. Solicitor Charles M. Condon conducted the case for the prosecution. Ballistics evidence proved that the gun which Sims carried when arrested was the same gun used to kill Melke and Zerr. During the trial, the officer who talked to Melke before his death testified that the dying man informed him that Sims was the killer. Sims' lawyers argued that because Melke did not know he was going to die, the statement made to Hanahan Police Chief George David Pledger should be viewed as only hearsay and not a dying man's last words. On May 9, Fields cleared the jurors from the courtroom to hear Pledger's testimony. Pledger testified that Melke had said he was concerned he would die, and wanted to tell someone who had shot him. The judge declared that this evidence was admissable. Under cross-examination, Charleston County medical examiner Sandra Conradi informed Runyan that it was possible that Melke's mental capacity may have been affected, as he had suffered damage to "thinking functions." Following a brief deliberation, the jury found Sims Guilty on May 11. At his sentencing hearing, Sims' mother, half-brother, and half-sister testified that Sims had been sexually abused by his stepfather. It was alleged that the late Arnold Cranford had forced the children to have sex with him, their mother, and each other. He apparently also forced them to take drugs and drink alcohol. Sims himself pleaded with the jury for mercy. He said, "You have heard what a terrible, dangerous man I am. I am not a nice guy. You know it and I know it. I ask you for your mercy." The jury deliberated seventy minutes and then sentenced Sims to death on May 13. REF.: *CBA*.

Sin, Foo, d.1858, U.S., mur. The first murder committed in the U.S. by Chinese occurred in Jackson, Calif. Five coolies, led by Foo Sin, entered the offices of M.V.B. Griswold, a wealthy businessman. They knew Griswold kept $8,000 in gold in his safe. The Chinese bludgeoned Griswold to death but failed to open the safe. They were quickly apprehended and convicted. All five were hanged at Jackson on Apr. 16, 1858.

REF.: *CBA; Murder of M.V.B. Griswold.*

Sinclair, George (Earl of Caithness), d.1582, Scot., consp. Roman Catholic supporter of Mary, Queen of Scots. He was involved in the strangling death of Lord Darnley and presided over the rigged murder trial of the Earl of Bothswell. REF.: *CBA*.

Sinclair, Harry, See: **Teapot Dome Scandal**.

Sindona, Michele, 1920- , U.S.-Italy, fraud. Michele Sindona, fifty-nine, a one-time financial adviser to the Vatican, was arrested in New York on charges that he had bilked the Franklin National Bank of $45 million, causing its collapse–the biggest bank failure in the nation's history to date. Sindona, who had served as the bank's director and a member of its international executive committee, was found Guilty of sixty-five counts of fraud. He was acquitted of one count of corrupting a former official to help him in a conspiracy. On June 13, 1980, Sindona was sentenced to twenty-five years in prison, was given a $207,000 fine, and was ordered to pay a substantial portion of his own legal costs. Just prior to sentencing, Sindona had attempted to kill himself by taking an overdose of prescription medication.

In 1985, Sindona was sent to Italy to stand trial on fraud charges in connection with the collapse of his *Banca Privata Finanziara*. A court in Milan found him Guilty and sentenced him to twelve years in prison. Sindona was returned to the U.S. to continue serving his prison sentence.

REF.: Blumenthal, *Last Days of the Sicilians; CBA*.

Singh, Boysie, 1908-57, Trinidad, rob.-mur. A Trinidadian of Hindu heritage, Boysie Singh was a tough slum kid who already had a prison record for aggravated robbery by the time he reached adulthood. After murdering the leader of a rival gang and getting away with it, he spent several years at whatever crime came to hand, preparing to take full advantage when the U.S. troops moved into Trinidad during WWII. He ran brothels and other after-hours establishments for servicemen and made his fortune, which he used to buy a fleet of fishing boats. These became his vehicles for smuggling goods into the Venezuelan mainland.

When the Venezuelan coast guard tried to take over Singh's boats, he swore a vendetta, threatening to sink as many of that country's boats as he could. On one occasion when he pretended to need fresh water a Venezuelan boat allowed Singh and his men on board. They killed all eleven on the boat and stole thousands of dollars. He began stopping fishing boats at sea and killing all on board, usually setting the boats on fire and sinking them so no trace remained.

Singh was arrested on Apr. 25, 1950, for the murder of one of his own men, whom Singh believed was an informer. The first trial ended in a hung jury; the second one convicted him and four other men of murder. They were sentenced to hang, but on appeal they were acquitted. While in prison, though, Singh said he had a vision of Jesus, and on his release he became an open-air preacher for several years, speaking to huge crowds. However, when he was fined for driving without a license, his veneer of righteousness thinned. A friend asked his help in disposing of an intrusive mistress, so he killed or helped to dispose of Thelma Haynes. His friend, Boland Ramkisson, could not stand the stress, and he soon accused Singh of killing Thelma. Both men were found Guilty of the murder and sentenced to hang. Singh died on Aug. 20, 1957, at Port-of-Spain. REF.: *CBA*.

Singh, Dalip Lutchmie Persad, d.1955, Trinidad, mur. The son of Hindus who moved to Trinidad as indentured servants, Dalip Singh attended medical school in Scotland, where he acquired a fondness for white women and soon married a beautiful blonde German optician. His appalled parents were barely tolerant of his wife, Inge Singh, when the couple returned to Trinidad to set up practice in the islands. Singh himself became intolerant when his wife turned out to be an alcoholic. His staff would not stay long because she was cruel to them. On Apr. 6, 1954, after Inge returned to Port-of-Spain after one of her regular trips to an office on another island, the two had a major argument, and Singh killed his wife. He bundled her body in a sack filled with sand and drove it out to Godinot Bay, about forty miles from his home, where he sank it. But the sand oozed out of the sack, and the body rose to the surface and was found.

While Dr. Russell Barrow was doing the autopsy, Dr. Singh casually chatted with him, although he and Barrow were not friends. Barrow's autopsy showed that Inge Singh's body had been disemboweled and completely drained of blood, by someone who knew surgery. Singh replied to a police request for a visit by hurrying to headquarters. He readily identified some jewelry as his wife's and said that he had last seen her on Apr. 6. The police questioned Singh's servants and former servants, learning of the distaste they had for her and her abusive drunkenness. Finally, from the houseboy, Kramchand Ramsahaye, they learned of the couple's vicious and loud fight on the evening of Apr. 6, a fight that ended with the sound of blows and Singh's disappearing from the house for many hours.

Dr. Dalip Singh was charged with murdering his wife. He was found Guilty and was hanged on June 28, 1955.

REF.: *CBA;* Gribble, *The Deadly Professionals.*

Singh, Udham, See: **O'Dwyer**, Sir **Michael.**

Singh Sandhu, Suchnam, prom. 1968, Brit., mur. Suchnam Singh Sandhu said he was following an old Sikh tribe custom dealing with family disgrace when he murdered his daughter and sent her dismembered body parts on trains traveling in opposite directions. Then he claimed he didn't do it, but the evidence against the Indian father was overwhelming and a British jury took only ninety minutes to find him Guilty of murder. He was sentenced to life imprisonment.

On Apr. 5, 1968, an abandoned locked olive green suitcase was finally taken off the 10:40 p.m. London train at the Wolverhampton station and opened in hopes of tracing the owner. But the suitcase contained a mutilated upper torso of a woman. Her head, lower torso and legs had been removed. A second suitcase, this one containing the lower torso and legs of a woman, soon was found in the River Roding. British authorities traced the make of the suitcases and the origin of the handmade clothes the woman had been wearing, and examined the victim's remains. They deduced that the body parts found belonged to the same woman, that she was between sixteen and eighteen years old, and of Indian or Pakistani descent. She had been cut with a hacksaw sold near Ilford, England, that was painted blue on one side and yellow on the other. She recently had surgery as evident by suture scars on the inside of one of her legs. Doctors discovered the equivalent of thirty half-grain tablets of phenobarbitone in her stomach but curiously noted that although the woman had ingested a fatal dose, there hadn't been enough time for the poison to take effect before she was murdered. Recently cut pubic hairs suggested that she was Moslem. On May 8, the severed head was discovered in a blue duffel bag in Wanstead Flats. Wrapped around the head was the Mar. 27, 1968, edition of the *Daily Telegraph.* The victim had sustained two extensive blows to the head. After investigating neighborhoods with high Indian and Pakistani populations and women who had recently undergone gynecological procedures, police learned the victim's name: Sarabjit Kaur. Her father, Suchnam Singh Sandhu, explained his motive for the savage killing.

Sandhu said Sarabjit had been his favorite child. On Apr. 4, he confessed to having murdered her. Father and daughter had fought about an already-married man in India whom the girl wished to marry. Sarabjit wanted to kill the man's wife to free him for marriage and her father bitterly objected. Sarabjit then allegedly took the poison, and told her father she was killing herself because he would not allow her to marry the man she chose, and that he would be blamed for her suicide and consequently would hang. He lost his temper, smashed her head with a hammer, rushed out to buy a hacksaw, returned and, while his daughter was still alive, began sawing off her head. He spent the next two days disposing of her body.

Despite Sandhu's graphic confession, he pleaded not guilty at his Old Bailey trial held six weeks after the murder. He was sentenced to life in prison.

REF.: *CBA;* Tullett, *Strictly Murder.*

Sing Lee, prom. 1910, U.S., count. When the Mexican government discovered that the gold coins of that country were becoming lighter in weight, resulting in the loss of thousands of dollars, an investigation revealed that gold was being removed from the inside of the coins and replaced by yellow powder. How the gold had been removed without marring the coins' surfaces was a mystery. Four Chinese eventually were arrested for the tampering but refused to disclose how the gold had been siphoned from the coins. After these men were arrested, another Chinese suspect, Sing Lee, vanished from Mexico and soon resurfaced in New York's Chinatown, where he had formerly lived until a Tong war erupted and endangered his life.

Arriving again in New York, Sing Lee opened a shop on Doyer Street. The U.S. Secret Service put him under surveillance and an agent eventually learned how the gold was removed. Sing Lee had developed a method whereby he drilled a minute hole in the edge of a coin and scraped gold out through the tiny space, refilling it with yellow powder. The only missing part of the scheme was how Sing Lee had covered the hole with real gold. When Treasury agents went to arrest the counterfeiter they found Sing Lee dead, assassinated by one of his Tong enemies, his head split open by a hatchet. REF.: *CBA.*

Singleton, Sir John Edward, 1885-1957, Brit., jur. Named king's counsel in 1922 and elected to represent Lancaster in Parliament in 1922. He served as Judge of Appeal, Isle of Man, from 1928-34, when he was nominated to the High Court, King's Division, presiding over the famed murder trial of Dr. Buck Ruxton. He was named lord justice of Appeal in 1948, serving until his death. REF.: *CBA.*

Singleton, Lawrence, 1928- , U.S., kid.-rape-attempt. mur. On Sept. 29, 1978, Mary Bell Vincent, a 15-year-old runaway from Las Vegas, Nev., who had drifted to San Francisco's Bay

Area earlier that year, hitched a ride from Lawrence Singleton, a middle-aged merchant seaman, in Berkeley, Calif. She fell asleep in the back of his van, and Singleton drove into the desert. He raped her twice and then led her naked down an untraveled road toward a concrete drainpipe where he planned to kill her. Instead, he cut off her forearms with a hatchet. Little did he imagine that Mary Vincent would survive and identify him.

Singleton was arrested, convicted, and sentenced to fourteen years and four months in prison on Apr. 20, 1979, by Superior Court Judge Earl H. Maas, Jr. "If I had it in my power," said Maas, "I would send him to state prison for the rest of his natural life." Under California statutes, however, Singleton would be eligible for parole after nine years and six months.

At the California Men's Colony at San Luis Obispo, Singleton proved to be a model prisoner. On Apr. 25, 1987, he was granted an early release for good behavior and for his active involvement in a special work program. When the media leaked news of his impending parole, however, threats from vigilante groups poured in, and a half-dozen municipalities in California denied Singleton a chance to take up residence. In El Cerrito, locals staged a protest vigil in front of the police station upon learning of his impending arrival. In Rodeo, near San Francisco, a mob of 500 forced police to relocate Singleton under heavy guard to a hotel.

"Understandably no community wants Singleton," said Governor George Deukmejian, "and yet he must be placed somewhere." The only safe place was behind prison walls. Singleton was provided a trailer and a small garden inside the 1,000-acre San Quentin prison compound. He remained in San Quentin until Apr. 19, 1988, when the California Department of Corrections took him to an undisclosed location to complete his last six days on parole. An Azalea, Ore., minister offered him a job, but local opposition forced him to recant the offer.

Compounding Singleton's problems was the civil lawsuit filed on behalf of Mary Vincent. On May 7, 1987, district court Judge Tom Foley had ordered Singleton to pay $1 million in punitive damages, $1 million for pain and suffering, and $430,000 to cover all medical bills. Attorneys conceded that there was little, if any, chance of collecting, however, since Singleton's only income was a $600 monthly social security check.

For Mary Vincent, recovery was long and painful. Ten years after the assault she finally found a man she could be comfortable with and got married. "It's the beginning of a new life, a better one," she said. REF.: *CBA.*

Sinha, Sir Satyendra Prasanno (Baron of Raipur), 1864-1928, India, lawyer. First Indian to be named as Bengal's advocate general, serving from 1907-09 and from 1915-17. He also joined the executive council of the governor general, serving from 1909-10. He represented his country at the Imperial War Conference in 1917, and served as undersecretary of India from 1919-20. REF.: *CBA.*

Sinistrari, Ludovico Maria, 1622-1701, Italy, witchcraft. Ludovico Maria Sinistrari was the last of the demonologists. Known and respected in his native Italy as a scholar, gentleman, linguist, and sophisticated conversationalist, Sinistrari became a Franciscan friar at twenty-five. He later became a professor of theology at Pavia University, a consultant to the Supreme Tribunal of the Inquisition at Rome, and vicar-general to the Archbishop of Avignon. His greatest work, *De Delictis et Poenis (On Crimes and Punishment),* was published in Venice in 1700. The work by which he is most known today, *De Daemonialitate (Demoniality),* wasn't discovered until 1875 in a London book shop. It concentrates on the alleged problems emanating from relations between humans and devils.

REF.: *CBA;* Lea, *Materials Toward a History of Witchcraft;* Robbins, *The Encyclopedia of Witchcraft and Demonology;* Sinistrari, *De Daemonialitate et Incubis et Succubis;* ____, *Demoniality.*

Sinks, Theodore P., 1939- , U.S., mur. Herbert Jacobson, assistant prosecutor for Montgomery County, Ohio, believed that convicted murderer Ted Sinks derived some personal satisfaction out of having buried his wife in a concrete-covered pit where he worked. "Maybe he got his kicks out of having her there," Jacobson theorized. "He could say 'Good morning Judy,' or when he left, 'Goodbye Judy.'"

Theodore Sinks worked as a plumbing, heating, and air conditioning supervisor for Dayton Newspapers, Inc., (DNI). His wife, Judy Sinks, forty-four, was employed by the same company in the circulation department. The couple seemed to have a good marriage, but Judy Sink's co-workers said she was prone to depression, and that Ted Sinks had a "pretty short temper." In September 1986, Judy Sinks tried to kill herself with a gun. Ballistics tests cleared her husband of any involvement in the shooting and Jody Sinks sufficiently recovered to get on with her life—until her husband reported her disappearance on Nov. 24, 1987.

Sinks told police that he had returned home from work at 2:30 p.m., to take her to the doctor. When she didn't return by the next morning, he notified authorities. Judy Sink's purse was found in a mailbox on Main Street, leading police to conclude that she had met with foul play.

Four days earlier, on Nov. 20, Kenneth Rice, a DNI employee who worked for Sinks, helped him load a fifty-five-gallon drum allegedly filled with asbestos from Sink's garage into a pickup truck. Sinks was vague about why he had this material in his garage, but he told Rice that the best way to dispose of it would be to bury the canister in the seventh floor of the DNI building where a water-purifying system was being installed. "It was another way to fill the hole I guess," said Rice. "This way nobody would know and he was the boss. I was just doing what he said."

Rice helped mix the concrete, but Sinks insisted on finishing the job himself. The body of Judy Sinks was buried in the concrete pedestal, and the water filtration unit for the main cooling tower was moved into position over the pit. For the next five months Sinks played the role of the aggrieved husband. When the Dayton *Daily News* offered a $2,000 reward for information about their missing employee, he told them to withdraw the offer and badgered the paper into suppressing news items and follow-up stories about the disappearance. Claiming that his wife had probably taken her own life, he said he feared that continuing publicity would spark a wave of crank phone calls.

The police were stymied in their investigation until they received an anonymous tip on Apr. 26, 1988. With pickaxes and sledgehammers, city workers broke apart the concrete pedestal. The badly decomposed body was exhumed and taken to the Montgomery County Coroner, who ruled that Judy Sinks had been strangled with a nylon-cotton cord, which Sinks had neglected to remove from her throat. Judge Jack Duncan ordered Sinks held at the city-county jail in lieu of a $100,000 bond. The case went to trial on Jan. 4, 1989. Ten days later the jury returned a Guilty verdict, and Sinks was sentenced to fifteen years to life and fined $15,000 by Judge John Kessler of the Montgomery County Common Pleas Court. During the entire proceeding the defendant remained stone cold. "What boils me," said Larry Harmon, a brother of Judy Sinks, "is that all through this, he still didn't show any emotions, and that irritates me. I don't know how anybody can be so damn heartless." REF.: *CBA.*

Sinn Fein, See: **Wilson, Sir Henry Hughes**.

Sioux Indian Massacre, 1862, U.S., kid.-rape-mur. More than 7,000 Sioux Indians were living in abject poverty in the valley of the Minnesota River near Mankato, Minn. With the Civil War occupying the full attention of the government, the Indians decided to reap revenge on white men for taking their lands and livelihood.

Evidence of the Indians' anger first came up in 1857 when a renegade former Sioux chief named Inkpaduta and a small band attacked and slaughtered an entire village and kidnapped and raped four women. A number of similar incidents occurred during the following years. Finally, in 1862, following other incidents of Indian raids and killings, Chief Little Crow, fearing reprisals, decided to attack in force.

A small war ensued in which the Indians engaged in several

major battles as well as sporadic attacks of kidnap, rape, and murder on white settlers. In one attack on a settlement by Lake Shetek, an 11-year-old boy, Mertin Eastlick, saw his parents and two siblings brutally killed by squaws. He carried his baby brother on his back for fifty miles trying to reach safety. Mertin died after delivering his brother into safe hands.

General John Pope, heading troops of cavalry, pursued the attackers and forced the Sioux to return to the reservation. After the hostilities ended, U.S. troops rounded up more than 300 of the worst offenders. This entire group was tried and sentenced to death by a military court. The case was reviewed by President Abraham Lincoln, who selected thirty-eight of the Indians to be hanged as token punishment for all the participants. On Dec. 26, 1862, these thirty-eight Sioux were hanged in a mass execution.

REF.: *CBA;* Duke, *Celebrated Criminal Cases of America;* Mencken, *By the Neck.*

Siple, Frank E., b.1893, U.S., mur. On Jan. 31, 1946, the Reverend Frank Siple, 53-year-old pastor of the Southlawn Church of God in Grand Rapids, Mich., pleaded guilty to poisoning his teenaged daughter seven years earlier.

Dorothy Ann Siple, eighteen, was attending Godwin Heights High School in Grand Rapids when she met her untimely death on July 31, 1939. The school superintendent recalled that she was an exemplary student, active in Drama Club and the Girl's Council, contrary to Reverend Siple's assertion that his daughter was "mentally incompetent" and headed for an insane asylum.

For these reasons, Siple gave Dorothy a capsule laced with potassium cyanide shortly before returning to his church pulpit, where he planned to deliver a sermon. The death certificate listed the cause of death as coronary thrombosis. The facts of the young woman's death did not come to light until January 1946, when Siple was arrested for assaulting Lyle Doan, a church elder. Having attacked Doan with a lead pipe, he then sent him a batch of poisoned fudge—all because of an argument over church policy. The attack occurred shortly before New Year's Eve 1946. When police came to arrest Siple, they found him in the basement, overcome by gas fumes, and near death. He was, however, revived and bound over for trial. While in jail he confessed to murdering his young daughter. The remains were exhumed and a trace of cyanide and arsenic were found. Siple was also suspected in the 1929 death of his wife, Bertie, in Dixon, Ill.

Reverend Siple entered his plea before Circuit Court Judge Leonard D. Verdier on Jan. 31, 1946, and one week later was sentenced to life in prison. "You have sinned not only against the laws of man, but the laws of God," Judge Verdier said in his closing remarks. "Who are you to judge if she was to spend the rest of her days in an asylum?" REF.: *CBA.*

Siqueiros, David Alfaro, 1896-1974, Mex., exile. Imprisoned and exiled frequently for leftist political activities, including organizing unions of workers and artists. A painter, he was deported from the U.S. for including radical ideology in his fresco works on public buildings. See: **Trotsky, Leon**. REF.: *CBA.*

Siragusa, Charles, 1914-82, U.S., law enfor. off. Charles Siragusa fought organized crime for almost forty years and is perhaps best known for his painstaking attempt to convict mobster Charles "Lucky" Luciano. Born and raised in Brooklyn, Siragusa became a federal narcotics agent in 1939 and oversaw the 1944 prosecution of Luciano on a compulsory prostitution charge, only to see the gangster escape his 50-year sentence by being deported to Italy. Italian heroin trafficking increased immediately and Siragusa was restationed in Rome. After eight years of collecting insufficient evidence, Siragusa returned to the U.S., where in 1962 he again built a solid case against Luciano. However, Luciano died before he could be prosecuted. Siragusa retired in 1963 and became the executive director of the Illinois Legislative Investigating Commission. Retiring in 1976, he lived in Florida until his death on Apr. 15, 1982, at the age of sixty-eight.

REF.: Campbell, *The Luciano Project; CBA;* Cressey, *Theft of the Nation;* Demaris, *Captive City;* Eisenberg and Landau, *Meyer Lansky;* Gage, *Mafia, U.S.A.;* Gosch and Hammer, *The Last Testament of Lucky Luciano;* McPhaul, *Johnny Torrio;* Maas, *The Valachi Papers;* Reid, *The Grim Reapers;* (FILM), *Re: Lucky Luciano,* 1974.

Siraj-ud-Dawlah, c.1732-57, India, mur. The young district ruler of Bengal, India, Siraj-ud-Dawlah, led an attack on the British settlement at Calcutta on June 15, 1756. In three days Dawlah's army conquered and looted the city and then broke into Fort Williams. Governor Drake and the garrison commander deserted their posts and boarded the ship *Dodaldy,* while Holwell, who was made leader at Fort Williams, negotiated a surrender with Dawlah, who sought the treasure rumored to be kept in Calcutta vaults by the wealthy East Indian trading company.

Holwell, along with 145 others, including Mary Carey, a 16-year-old Indian girl, were crushed together into the Black Hole Prison, in about eighteen square feet of space with two small barred windows. On a stifling hot, humid night several injured prisoners were trampled to death or suffocated in the first few minutes as they were kicked and pushed through the entrance by guards, Holwell calling to his comrades to stay calm. But panic broke out when a well-meaning elderly guard brought skins of water which the prisoners fought over. Other Indians, delighting in watching the British suffering, brought more water to prolong the panic, holding torches to illuminate the struggles in the hideously cramped prison. When the doors were opened at the order of Dawlah at 6 a.m. twenty-three prisoners had survived the ordeal, among them Carey. In ten hours 123 had perished. Holwell and two other survivors were shackled and forced to march up river in the noon heat to Dawlah's capital, where they were later freed. The heroic Holwell, who later became governor of Bengal, died in 1798. Carey was added to Dawlah's harem.

In 1957, Dawlah was driven out of Calcutta by Robert Clive and Charles Watson. On June 23, 1757, Dawlah hed a large army against Clive, but was defeated by Clive's small force. Dawlah escaped but was captured and executed. REF.: *CBA.*

Sirhan, Sirhan Bishara, See: **Kennedy, Robert Francis.**

Sirikul, Taweeyos, d.1977, U.S., (unsolv.) mur. Sirikul, a university student in Chicago, disappeared on Mar. 4, 1977. Hoping to sell his car, he took a prospective buyer for a demonstration ride and did not return. His body was found three weeks later in a storage locker. He had died of stab wounds. Neither his car nor his killer has ever been found.

REF.: *CBA;* Nash, *Among the Missing.*

Siringo, Charles Angelo, 1855-1928, U.S., det. Considered by many, including outlaw Butch Cassidy, as the finest of the Pinkerton detectives, Charles Angelo Siringo was born in Texas and worked as a cowhand from the time he was thirteen. At twenty-two he went out to join the search for 17-year-old killer Billy the Kid but was forced to give up after he lost all his money gambling. Siringo later worked as a grocer in Kansas for two years. On a visit to Chicago, he went to a blind phrenologist, who "read" the shape of his skull and told him he should be a detective. Siringo joined the Pinkerton Detective Agency and began a twenty-year career, building an enviable record of getting his man.

Pinkerton detective Charles Siringo.

Trailing fugitives through deserts and blizzards, Siringo lived with moonshiners and disguised himself as a wanted criminal to convince Efie Landusky, a member of the Hole in the

Wall Gang, to tell him where infa-mous outlaw Harvey Logan hid out. The detective later barely escaped being killed when he infiltrated a union which was at the center of the Couer d'Alene labor riots of the 1890s. After twenty years with the agency Siringo retired to write about his adventures. One of his pamphlets was called *Two Evil Isms: Pinkertonism and Anarchism.* He published several books but died a poor man in Los Angeles in 1928, solitary to the end. See: **Pinkerton Detective Agency.**

REF.: Appleman, *Charlie Siringo, Cowboy Detective; CBA.*

Sirocco, Jack, prom. 1914, U.S., org. crime-mur. Jack Sirocco and Dopey Benny headed rival gangs on New York's East Side in the pre-WWI years. The two gangs engaged in an ongoing feud and competition for territory, which led to a direct confrontation in November of 1913. Benny and his gang had been hired by a union that was on strike against the Feldman Hat Factory, and Jack Sirocco and his gang were hired to protect strikebreakers. A gunfight broke out, and one of Dopey Benny's cohorts, Max Greenwalt, was killed, probably by Red Murray of the Sirocco gang.

Seeking revenge, Benny arranged to ambush the entire Sirocco gang when they were attending a dance at a local hall. On the night of Jan. 9, 1914, they attacked every Sirocco gang member in sight as they approached the hall. A wild gunfight ensued in which no gang members were even seriously wounded, but an innocent bystander, Frederick Strauss, a much-respected Deputy Clerk of the City Court, was killed. Although "the Dope" was apprehended and questioned, he had not even been on the scene. The rest of the gang had scattered and Strauss' murderer was never apprehended.

REF.: Asbury, *The Gangs of New York; CBA;* Fried, *The Rise and Fall of the Jewish Gangster in America;* Haskins, *Street Gangs;* Logan, *Against the Evidence;* McPhaul, *Johnny Torrio;* Willemse, *Behind the Green Lights.*

Sisk, T. Edward, 1940- , and **Taylor, Charles Frederick,** 1939- , U.S., consp. The presiding judge called it "one of the major corruption cases in the history of the United States" and sentenced T.Edward Sisk, forty-one, and Charles Frederick Taylor, forty-two, to prison for five years.

Sisk, former legal counsel to Tennessee governor Ray Blanton, and Taylor, a former highway patrol lieutenant and member of the governor's security staff, were found Guilty of conspiracy on July 2, 1981. Sisk told Federal District Judge James P. Churchill that he took $10,000 in "loans" to arrange for the release of two Tennessee prisoners. Taylor had been videotaped accepting payoffs for the release of prisoners. He admitted to accepting the bribe but said that he was "induced to commit the crimes by a government officer." Both Sisk and Taylor recieved five-year sentences in exchange for their cooperation in the government's further investigation. REF.: *CBA.*

Sisson, Robert N., and **Sullivan, Maurice J.,** prom. 1922, U.S., (wrong. convict.) asslt.&bat. Although both Robert Sisson and Maurice Sullivan had alibis supported by several people that explained their whereabouts the night of Sept. 20, 1922, they, along with Earle D. Dean, were convicted of assault and battery against two co-workers. Sisson and Dean were sentenced to five years and Sullivan sentenced to seven years at the District of Columbia reformatory at Lorton, Va. A year-and-a-half later, Dean confessed that he and seven other men were guilty of the crime and that Sisson and Sullivan had nothing to do with it. Although seven other men confessed, several were given lighter sentences than either Sisson and Sullivan.

The faulty convictions were based on mistaken identification. The victims, James R. Keeton and Judson L. Powers, who were employed as electricians at the Pullman Company in Washington, D.C., were accosted by seven co-workers because they had failed to comply with a union-organized strike. Keeton and Powers had applied for union membership, but the strike had broken out before they were approved.

Of those seven newly convicted, three received three-year sentences, two others were sentenced to two-and-a-half years, and the others each recieved a year and a half. On July 12, 1924, Sisson and Sullivan were formally pardoned by President Calvin Coolidge. REF.: *CBA.*

Sisson Documents, prom. 1918, U.S., forg. The Sisson documents, first published in the U.S., were the most notable attempt to prove that the Bolsheviks were aligning with Germany during the period following the Russian revolution and before the end of WWI. These documents held such power, in great part, because they were accepted as authentic by Edgar Sisson, then member of George Creel's wartime Committee on Public Information. Sisson accepted the papers as genuine even after Raymond Robins, head of the American Red Cross in Russia, and others had dismissed them as forgeries. In 1918, the documents were proved false by the New York *Evening Post.* The British War Office had already refuted their legitimacy. REF.: *CBA.*

Sitgreaves, John, 1747-1802, U.S., jur. Served as U.S. district attorney for North Carolina from 1789-90. He was appointed to the North Carolina Court by President George Washington in 1790. REF.: *CBA.*

Sitting Bull, U.S., c.1831-90, rebel.-mur. Leader of Indians who mercilessly slaughtered U.S. forces under command of General George Custer at battle of Little Big Horn in 1876. He was later driven back to Canada in 1877 and eventually surrendered in 1881 at Fort Buford. He joined Buffalo Bill's Wild West Show in 1885. Later, however, he resumed life as an agitator but was apprehended and later killed by Indian guards. REF.: *CBA.*

Si Votha (Si Vatha), 1841-92, Cambodia, rebel. Tried in vain to capture throne from half-brother Norodom from 1860-61. He also headed losing revolts against the French in 1876 and 1885. REF.: *CBA.*

Siward (Earl of Northumberland, AKA: The Strong), d.1055, Brit., mur. Killed wife's uncle to become earl of entire Northumberland area in 1041. He also helped establish Malcom Canmore as Malcolm III by launching an invasion of Scotland and killing Macbeth, defeating his army in 1053. REF.: *CBA.*

Sixtus II, prom. 3rd Cent., Roman., pope, assass. Solved troubles between churches of Rome and North Africa. He was put to death on the order of Emperor Valerian. REF.: *CBA.*

Sixtus IV (Francesco Della Rovere), 1414-84, Italy, polit. corr.-consp. Pope who held predominately political papacy from 1471-84. He participated in the conspiracy against Lorenzo dé Medici that sparked war against Florence from 1478-80. He ordered the building of the Sistine Chapel in 1473, and also the Sistine Bridge, but lost much favor due to his extreme nepotism and the stiff taxes assessed to pay for construction. REF.: *CBA.*

Sjahrir, Sutan, 1909-66, Indo., consp.-rebel. Assisted in development of Pendidikan Nasional Indonesia nationalist organization in 1931. Because of his policies he was exiled by Dutch officials from 1934-42, but amassed support of militant nationalists and later returned to serve as prime minister from 1945-47. After originating Partai Sosialis Indonesia, a Socialist political party, he was brought into custody on charges of conspiracy and jailed without trial from 1962-65. REF.: *CBA.*

Skaggs, Elijah, 1810-70, U.S., gamb. A Kentucky native, Elijah Skaggs perfected his card sharping techniques before the age of twenty-one. Skaggs started his career in Nashville, where he had reasonable success. Among his first purchases with the money he made cheating in cards was a true gambler's outfit—black frock coat and pants, black silk vest, white shirt, patent leather boots, and a black stovepipe hat.

Skaggs, who specialized in faro, continued to study the techniques of dishonest dealers. If he couldn't deduce how they pulled a particular cheat, he offered them money; if they refused to divulge the secret, he threatened to expose them. Eventually Skaggs increased the range of his operations to many of the towns along the Mississippi River, including New Orleans and St. Louis. He also hired and trained employees to expand his operation. His efforts were successful—he netted approximately $100,000 a month from his rigged faro games.

By the time Skaggs was thirty-seven, he was a millionaire.

However, amid growing publicity about his crooked operations, Skaggs decided to retire to a plantation in Louisiana. Skaggs invested heavily in Confederate bonds, and when the South lost the war, Skaggs lost his fortune. When Skaggs died in Texas in 1870 at the age of sixty, he was a homeless, penniless drunk.

REF.: *CBA;* Nash, *Bloodletters and Badmen;* ____, *Hustlers and Con Men.*

Chicago gangster Manny Skar, gunned down in 1965 before he could be tried for income tax evasion.

Skar, Manny, d.1965, U.S., (unsolv.) mur. A diminutive hustler and flashy dresser, Manny Skar was a product of the Chicago streets. At the age of seventeen, Manny started his hustling and regular run-ins with the law. No matter what trouble he got into, he was always found Not Guilty or placed on probation.

Avoiding military service during WWII, he got involved in a variety of scams. After the war he dealt in surplus clothing and other war goods. Working closely with the syndicate, he parlayed his business activities into real estate and construction, until he was able to build the Sahara Motel near Midway Airport and the Sahara North near O'Hare International Airport in 1959. Though he claimed the properties were worth millions and that he owned them all, insiders thought he was deeply in debt to the syndicate.

The two Sahara hotels were a continuing source of trouble. They were bombed twice as a warning, and they were used as major drug drops. Manny eventually lost both hotels when his loans were called by the notorious Marshall Savings and Loan Association, controlled by syndicate figure Marshall Caifano. Gene Autry, movie star and real estate magnate, eventually took over the Sahara hotels.

As so often happens with mob-related high-rollers, Manny Skar got in trouble with the Internal Revenue Service. Word was out on the street that he was going to talk. Just before his tax evasion trial was scheduled to start on Oct. 11, 1965, Manny was gunned down behind his Lake Shore Drive residence in Chicago in what was described as a gangland slaying.

REF.: *CBA;* Demaris, *Captive City;* Halper, *The Chicago Crime Book.*

Skene, George, prom. 1812, Brit., forg. In 1812, in the midst of massive riots in Nottingham and throughout the Midlands, a scandal affected the police department when George Skene, the chief clerk at the Queen Square office, who was ranked as the primary officer of the police, was convicted of forgery. Skene was sentenced to death, the standard punishment for that crime at that time.

REF.: Browne, *The Rise of Scotland Yard; CBA.*

Skid Row Slasher, The, See: **Greenwood, Vaughn Orrin**.

Skin for Skin, a novel by Winifred Duke. The murder of Julia Wallace (Brit., 1931), is the basis of this work of fiction. See: **Wallace, William Herbert**. REF.: *CBA.*

Skingle, Arthur, 1946- , and **Sparrow, Peter**, 1943- , Brit., mur. On June 27, 1971, 29-year-old Detective Constable Ian Coward stopped an apparently drunk driver. The two men quarreled when Coward asked for the man's driver's license. In response the passenger in the automobile fired nine bullets into the policeman's body. The two men fled and the officer was rushed to the hospital where he died less than one month later.

Witnesses identified Arthur Skingle, twenty-five, as the gunman and Peter Sparrow, twenty-eight, as the driver of the car. Both men had prior criminal records, and Skingle had been released from prison ten days earlier. Both were convicted and sentenced to life in prison. REF.: *CBA.*

Skinheads, prom. 1980s, Can.-U.S., secret crim. soc. The roots of the Skinhead movement trace back to a style of music and dress that evolved when black Jamaican youths immigrating to England joined forces with working class whites to create ska, a form of music which blended reggae and rock. When escalating unemployment hit England in the later 1970s, racist groups that blamed immigrant labor for the nation's economic woes split the Skinheads into two factions.

When the Skinhead movement traveled to the U.S. the factions polarized still further, with neo-Nazi and other white supremacist factions recruiting from Skinhead ranks and further exacerbating violence and racism. The groups of young people with shaved heads, flight jackets, gaudy tattoos, and black British work boots first appeared in Chicago, Boston, Detroit, San Francisco, Los Angeles, and New York. By the mid-1980s, as racial violence in the U.S. resurfaced during the Reagan years, the violent contingent of Skinheads had increased in numbers and power with disastrous and sometimes lethal results as their hate campaign against blacks, Asians, Jews, and homosexuals escalated. The Skinheads were a factor in the wave of racial violence which reached "epidemic proportions" in the U.S. between 1980 and 1986—a grim account of 121 murders, 301 cross-burnings, and 302 assaults. In San Jose, a gang of Skinheads tried to hang a black woman who attempted to walk into a public park. A Bay Area teenager was thrown through a plate-glass window when he tried to prevent several Skinheads from putting up an anti-Semitic poster. In Chicago, the group was linked to the defamation of an anti-Holocaust memorial. As racist Skinheads began to infiltrate the Pacific Northwest, members of a faction known as the East Side White Pride were charged in the baseball bat-beating murder of a 28-year old Ethiopian bus driver in Portland, Ore., in November 1988. In Spokane, Wash., one Skinhead was charged with attempted murder after he attacked a black man with a knife.

The music of the hate group features white power groups with names like the Final Solution, and recordings like *Nigger, Nigger* and *Prisoner of Peace,* the musical chronicle of Nazi Rudolph Hess. The group's doctrine is based on fear, hatred, and ignorance—according to sociologist William Gibson the "element of warrior fantasy" is a strong motivation of hate groups. A Chicago Skinhead, Clark Reid Martell, twenty-eight, is a long-time racist who became a self-described "born-again Nazi" after reading Hitler's *Mein Kampf.* Martell, with a history of mental problems and trouble with the law, became a Skinhead after quitting the National Socialist People's Party "because they didn't have any women members, and women are vital for ensuring the survival of the white race." In California, former Ku Klux Klan leader Tom Metzger, who now leads the White Aryan Resistance, recruits from among the Skinheads; as of December 1988, Metzger was developing plans to begin recruiting in Seattle, Wash. as well. A national Anti-Defamation League report estimates that the racist Skinheads have about 2,000 members spread out in twenty-one states.

The "anti-racist" Skinheads, which sees its faction as a cultural bonding evolved from the multiracial music of the punk scene and its shared working-class identity, are organizing against the "violent" Skinheads. According to Chicago Skinhead Corky Fields, a member of the Anti-Racist Action (ARA) group, "Real skinheads stand alone. They don't go joining hard-line groups. They respect people for what he or she does and believes in." Members of the Syndicate, a national network struggling to combat the racists, say Nazis are targeting youths who have little education and hard time finding jobs, and that the Skinheads who join up with the neo-Nazis are teens from primarily white areas attracted to their "tough guy" image, and do not personally know any blacks or Hispanics. The anti-racist Skinheads visit high schools to "talk about how racism is used to divide people," says Skinhead member Kieran, and practice "direct action" by beating up Nazi Skinheads. "We're not pacifists," Kieran explained. Some of the anti-racist Skinheads are so angered by the media focusing on the racists that they have considered growing their hair. According to one, "That would be a victory for the Nazis." REF.: *CBA.*

Skinner, Cyrus, d.1864, U.S., west. outl. A California and Idaho saloon owner, Cyrus Skinner was brought to Montana by Sheriff Henry Plummer in the early 1860s to operate a Bannack, Mont., bar. Plummer's gang of outlaws, the Innocents, met at the clapboard saloon run by Skinner. The bar also served as a place to get information about wagon and stagecoach shipments of gold from the mines; keeping a sharp ear Skinner would listen as his customers got drunk and talked too much, later passing the details on to Plummer.

Skinner himself rarely participated in the robberies but one time, when he learned on extremely short notice of a lucrative shipment, he went with Innocent member Bob Zachery to hold up the stagecoach. They murdered the driver and netted a hefty $250,000 in gold. A ruthless opportunist, Skinner was around when an Innocent murdered a friendly Bannack Indian—Skinner lifted the dead man's scalp and hung it above his bar for atmosphere.

After Henry Plummer was hanged by vigilantes on Jan. 10, 1864, his bartender stayed in the area, apparently believing he could brazen it out. The lynchings continued and it became obvious that some of the condemned men would implicate the barkeeper. Nevertheless, Skinner stayed. On Jan. 25, 1864, the vigilantes took Skinner from his porch. Despite his protests that all they had on him were a "heap of suspicions" and no proof, they led him to the gallows that same day. Skinner broke away and ran, pleading with the vigilantes to shoot him instead of subjecting him to the sometimes slow process of hanging. His pleas fell on deaf ears and his captors returned him to the gallows.

REF.: American Guide Series, *Idaho, A Guide in Word and Picture; CBA.*

Skinner, Kenneth, 1934- , U.S., arson. Kenneth Skinner denied setting fire to a San Francisco apartment complex on July 22, 1951, or even being at the scene. But astute police inspectors presented the suspect with incontrovertible evidence. A newspaper photograph clearly showed the 17-year-old substitute newsboy standing among a crowd of curious on-lookers. When shown the photo Skinner freely confessed. He was sentenced to the San Quentin Prison for ten years.

REF.: *CBA;* Nash, *Almanac of World Crime.*

Skipwith, J.K., prom. 1922, Case of, U.S., mur. As a Civil War soldier, Louisiana's J.K. Skipwith fought a losing battle. In 1922, as Exalted Cyclops of the Morehouse, La., chapter of the Ku Klux Klan (KKK), Skipwith fought bootleggers and others who would defy the U.S. establishment. Among his outspoken opponents were Thomas F. Richards, a local garage mechanic, and Watt Daniel, a Louisiana State University graduate. Returning from a Saturday village picnic and baseball game, Richards and Daniel were abducted by Klan members, never to be seen alive again. Skipwith was brought to trial in the case, but since local courts were infiltrated with KKK members, the charges were dismissed. Even after Richards' widow and Louisiana governor John Parker spurred a campaign to bring the Klansmen to trial, and after an explosion in nearby Lake Lafourche exposed two decomposed bodies, the Klan proved too powerful a force to overcome. After two years and fifty prosecution witnesses, the state's charges were dismissed, the alleged murders forgotten and KKK opponents could only view this as Skipwith's first victory.

REF.: *CBA;* Moorehead, *Hostages to Fortune.*

Skobline, Nadine Plevitskaia, prom. 1938, Fr., kid. In mid-December 1938, a Paris court sentenced Nadine Plevitskaia Skobline to twenty years of hard labor and ten subsequent years of exile from Paris as an accomplice in the disappearance of General Eugene Karlovitch de Miller, leader of the Paris colony of the White Russians. More than one year earlier, in September 1937, her husband, General Nicholas Skobline disappeared after he was charged with staging and executing de Miller's kidnapping.

De Miller had been secretly negotiating to send 20,000 men to fight with Spanish Rightists when he left his office for a rendezvous with General Skobline, one of his assistants. De Miller was never seen again, but evidence provided by key witnesses suggested that he had been abducted by the Russians. A note left by de Miller explained that he was going to meet Skobline and ended with the key phrase, "Perhaps this is an ambush."

Witnesses later testified that they saw a coffin-sized box loaded aboard the Soviet freighter *Marya Ulyanova* docked at Le Havre. After the box was loaded aboard, the ship abruptly set sail. It is believed that de Miller's body, dead or alive, was aboard the ship when it left port. REF.: *CBA.*

Skog, John Albert, d.c.1904, Swed.-U.S., count. John Albert Skog's one true passion was making money. In his native Sweden, before 1897, Skog used handmade glass plates to print his own series of Bank of Stockholm 100-Kroner notes and Royal Bank of Copenhagen 50-Kroner notes. He immigrated to the U.S., and was arrested in Chicago for counterfeiting. Skog was sentenced to the state penitentiary in Joliet, Ill., but he escaped. Relocating to Brooklyn, N.Y., he resumed his money-making ventures, printing five-dollar silver certificates and forged foreign notes. In 1904, enough foreign brokers became suspicious of his work and ordered him arrested. Skog fled, and as police officers gained on him, he pulled out a gun and killed himself.

REF.: *CBA;* Smith, *Counterfeiting.*

Skoptzy, prom. 1770-1830, Rus., secret soc. In the late eighteenth century, the extremist Russian religious sect, the Skoptzy, required its male members to be castrated and its female followers to have their breasts and outer genital organs amputated. Far from dissuading would-be members, this required self-mutilation actually intrigued and attracted religious fanatics. A believed reincarnated Jesus Christ, who went by the name Kondrati Selivanov, served as the Skoptzy leader and castrated himself with a red hot iron. He was eventually arrested and confined to a mental health home.

He was released in 1801, at which time he suffered continued mental illness but even greater religious influence. Many of his followers came from the upper classes. Claiming to be Czar Peter the Third, murdered by his wife, Catherine the Great, Selivanov personally castrated and mutilated a hundred men and women. The people were so taken with him that after his death in 1830, they could not accept the fact that he was gone and said that he, like Jesus, had only "withdrawn" from the world but would return one day.

Although Selivanov enjoyed great popularity with his Skoptzy teachings, not everyone adhered to his religious requirements willingly. Frederick Conybeare, an authority on Russian sects, noted that children grew up among the Skoptzy believers knowing that at puberty they would be castrated or otherwise mutilated and that anyone who was caught attempting to run away was killed. REF.: *CBA.*

Skull, Sally (Sarah Jane Newman), b.1813, U.S., mur. Born Sarah Jane Newman in 1813, through a succession of marriages—or liaisons from which she took away yet another name each time—Newman became Sarah Jane "Doe"-Robinson-Skull-Doyle-Watkins-Harsdoff, but she was usually called Sally Skull, a name she kept from one of her many grooms who died mysterious or violent deaths. Coming from Pennsylvania in 1821 with her family, Skull settled in the territory that would later become Texas.

Married for the first time at thirteen to a man whose name is unrecorded, her first husband allegedly went off to fight Indians and never returned. Marrying Jesse Robinson in 1838, Skull was abandoned by him five years later for being a "common scold" and a woman with a violent temper who shot her gun off too close to him.

A few months later she became Sally Skull by marrying a man named George Skull who set her up on a horse ranch near Goliad, Texas. Their profitable business was no doubt enhanced by the sight of blonde Skull with her bullwhip and six-gun. George Skull eventually disappeared—his wife said simply that she did not want to talk about him. In 1852 she married John Doyle. When she was seen in the company of Mexican bandit chief Juan Cortina rumors flew that Doyle, who had taken to drinking, would not be around much longer. Doyle died by allegedly falling into the Nueces River while drunk, but there were whispers that his wife had drowned him in a whiskey barrel.

While the Civil War raged Sally Skull hooked up with a new man named Mr. Watkins, who was not around long enough for locals to learn his first name. On a trip to Corpus Christi Watkins was shot to death by Skull. The debate over whether Watkins was killed because his wife mistook him for an intruder, or whether he died because he woke her up, was never resolved. Skull's story was believed by the authorities and, in 1867, she married William Harsdoff. After a honeymoon and a horse-purchasing trip to Mexico they were never seen or heard from again. Months later the decomposed body of a woman was found on a road the Harsdoffs had traveled down. It was never officially identified as Skull's, and she may have continued her groom-hunting spree in Mexico. REF.: *CBA*.

Skyjacking, See: **Supplements,** Vol. IV.

Slade, Joseph Alfred (AKA: **Jack**), 1824-64, U.S., mur. Gunfighter Jack Slade was known to the famous author and humorist Mark Twain as a kind-hearted individual despite a reputation that suggested otherwise. After encountering Slade in a saloon in 1861, Twain reported that the gunman was "so friendly and so gentle-spoken that I warmed to him in spite of his awful history."

The "awful history" Twain referred to began in 1824 when the future gunfighter was born in the little town of Carlyle, Ill. While still in his youth, Slade headed west to the raw cowtowns of the Southwest. He served in the U.S. Army during the Mexican War and later was hired by the Central Overland California and Pike's Peak Express Company to serve as a line superintendent. His success was closely tied to the safety of stagecoach drivers who covered long stretches of roadway in the Colorado Territory. In 1858, the year that Slade went to work for the Express Company, word came down that a French Canadian named Jules Bene was stealing horses and using the company offices at Julesburg, Colo., to hide fugitive members of his gang.

Western gunfighter Joseph Slade.

Julesburg was as rough and unsavory a place as there ever was. The population never went over 2,000 but with the dawn of each day it was a foregone conclusion that someone would be shot in the streets. Slade arrived in town intent on bringing Bene to justice. Hearing of this, the Frenchman fired five shots into his pursuer. "Bury him," Bene ordered his henchmen. Slade, having miraculously survived the shooting, was about to be lynched when Ben Ficklin, superintendent of the Central Overland Company, suddenly appeared. He persuaded Bene to cut Slade down with the promise that he would leave the state immediately. On his own now, Slade spent some time recovering from his wounds. He returned to work with the Overland company, awaiting the chance to get revenge on Bene. Finally Slade received word that Bene and his associates were holed up near Slade's ranch in Cold Springs, waiting for him to appear.

The hunter quickly became the prey when Jack Slade seized Bene at gunpoint in front of the ranch and strapped him to a post. Slade amused himself by using Bene for target practice. He fired several shots into his legs and arms until he grew tired of it. "To hell with it," he said, stuck the barrel of the pistol into Bene's mouth, and pulled the trigger. For good measure he cut off both of Bene's ears, keeping one of them for a watch fob. The nature of the crime shocked even the most hardened gunfighter. Slade was someone to be reckoned with.

Slade and his wife Virginia pushed on to Virginia City, Mont., in 1861 after he was charged with assaulting a Fort Halleck resident. The couple tried farming but Slade's obsessive drinking habits got him into trouble with the law. He instigated numerous fights, free-for-alls, and mini-riots, which compelled a local vigilante mob to order him from their city for good. Slade complied but for some reason known only to himself he decided to stop by the local watering hole for a last drink on Mar. 10, 1864. He guzzled down a shot and defied the locals to draw on him. The vigilantes rushed into the bar, grabbed him by the arms, and dragged him out to the hanging tree. Then, for the first time in his life, the gunman showed genuine fear. "My God!" he wailed. "Must I die like this? Oh, my poor wife!" Slade was hanged just before his wife arrived to plead for his life. Afterward the body was placed in the street where it was claimed by Virginia.

Mrs. Slade dressed the body down in raw alcohol and prepared to return the corpse to Illinois for burial. She got only as far as Salt Lake City before decomposition set in. Slade was buried in the Mormon Cemetery on July 20, 1864.

REF.: American Guide Series, *Colorado, A Guide to the Highest State;* ____, *The Oregon Trail;* ____, *Utah, A Guide to the State;* Bartholomew, *The Biographical Album of Western Gunfighters;* Beals, *Buffalo Bill;* Bliss, *The Life of Hon. William F. Cody;* Bloss, *Pony Express;* Boar, *The World's Most Infamous Murders;* Brown, *Ghost Towns of the Colorado Rockies;* Bruffey, *Eighty-One Years in the West;* Burke, *Buffalo Bill;* Burton, *The City of the Saints; CBA;* Chapman, *The Pony Express;* Clampitt, *Echoes From the Rocky Mountains;* Clark, *Bonneville County in the Making;* Clemens, *Roughing It;* Collins, *Great Western Rides;* ____, *The Hanging of Bad Jack Slade;* Crawford, *Rekindling Camp Fires;* Croft-Cook and Meadmore, *Buffalo Bill;* Davidson, *Rocky Mountain Tales;* Davis, *Shallow Diggin's;* Dickson, *Covered Wagon Days;* Dobie, *Cow People;* Drago, *Roads to Empire;* El Comancho, *The Old Timer's Tale;* Fisher and Holmes, *Gold Rushes and Mining Camps of the Early American West;* Frederick, *Ben Holladay;* French, *Gray Shadows;* Gray, *Men Who Built the West;* Hendricks, *The Bad Man of the West;* Holloway, *Texas Gun Lore;* Horan, *The Great American West;* ____ and Sann, *Pictorial History of the Wild West;* Hough, *The Story of the Outlaw;* Howard, *Montana Margins;* Hutchens, *One Man's Montana;* Inman, *The Great Salt Lake Trail;* Johnson, *Some Went West;* Kalbfus, *Dr. Kalbfus' Book;* Langford, *Vigilante Days;* Lucia, *The Saga of Ben Holladay;* ____, *Tough Men, Tough Country;* McCarty, *The Enchanted West;* Marsh, *Recollections, 1837-1910;* Michelson, *Mankillers at Close Range;* Mills, *Plains, Peaks and Pioneers;* Monaghan, *The Book of the American West;* Moody, *Stagecoach West;* Mumey, *Hoofs to Wings;* Nash, *Bloodletters and Badmen;* Neider, *The Great West;* O'Reilly, *Fifty Years on the Trail;* Pace, *Golden Gulch;* Parkhill, *The Law Goes West;* Raine, *Guns of the Frontier;* Rosa, *The Gunfighter, Man or Myth?;* ____, *They Called Him Wild Bill;* Russell, *The Lives and Legends of Buffalo Bill;* Sabin, *Wild Men of the West;* Sell and Weybright, *Buffalo Bill and the Wild West;* Shackleford, *Gunfighters of the Old West;* Sherwell, *Old Recollections of an Old Boy;* Skelton, *Riding West on the Pony Express;* Smith, *Brother Van;* Smith, *The Story of the Pony Express;* Stong, *Gold in Them Hills;* Towle, *Vigilante Woman;* Trenholm and Carley, *Wyoming Pageant;* Voorhees, *Personal Recollections of Pioneer Life on the Mountains and Plains of the Great West;* Watrous, *History of Larimer County;* Wheeler, *Buffalo Days;* ____, *The Frontier Trail;* Wilson, *Treasure Ex-*

press; Wilson, *Out of the West;* Winget, *Anecdotes of Buffalo Bill;* (FILM), *Western Union,* 1941; *Jack Slade,* 1953.

Slade, Joshua, d.1827, Brit., rob.-mur. The Reverend J. Waterhouse lived alone in a large rectory in the middle of Little Stukeley, England, until July 2, 1827, the night when Joshua Slade came for a short visit. The reverend was known as a miser who stashed large sums of money in his house. Slade was soon known as a murderer.

On the morning of the day in question, Slade climbed the rectory wall armed with a sword. He entered the house and hid in one of the many rooms, waiting for the perfect opportunity to seize the reverend's riches. Waiting, he grew weary, and in short time, he fell asleep. Slade snored, and Waterhouse, hearing a strange sound, explored until he found the sleeping bandit. Slade awoke and drew his sword on the unarmed man, so the rector asked if he could run and get his gun. Slade denied him this, his final request, and stabbed him to death.

Not long afterward, Slade was apprehended and questioned in the murder, after witnesses said they had seen him loitering near the rectory, and a storekeeper from a nearby inn swore Slade had recently stolen a sword from him. Slade confessed to the murder and graciously accepted his capital punishment. He spent the few days before his execution, on Sept 1., 1927, zealously studying religion.

REF.: Butler, *Murderers' England; CBA.*

Slaney, Sidney, d.1959, Brit., (unsolv.) mur. British police know little about the Jan. 17, 1959, murder of Sidney Slaney, a scrap-metal dealer. His body was found in his Plumstead office. He had been battered to death and police believe the motive was the robbery of the victim's £150. An unnamed woman provided the only real clue in the case when she notified authorities that she had sat next to a man on the bus who had blood on him. The man, who was never identified, had allegedly boarded the vehicle at 10:18 a.m. just a few hundred yards from Slaney's office.

REF.: *CBA;* Furneaux, *Famous Criminal Cases, vol. 6.*

Slánsky, Rudolf Salzmann, 1901-52, Czech., treas. Served as secretary general from 1945-51, and was instrumental in communist domination of Czechoslovakia in 1948. He was convicted of heading a scheme to defeat Communism in Czechoslovakia in 1952, and was hanged. He was cleared of criminal charges after his death. REF.: *CBA.*

Slark, Tom (AKA: **George Western, Thomas Hampson**), d.1929, Brit., burg.-asslt. From 1915-1929, Naval Petty Officer Tom Slark was sentenced to five separate penal servitudes. He served only four. Apparently, the prospect of spending one more year behind bars was less appealing to Slark than death. Facing his fifth sentencing in 1929, the British naval officer smuggled prussic acid into his prison cell with him and committed suicide.

Slark's criminal record began in 1915 when he was sentenced to serve two years for receiving stolen property. He went on, in 1916, to be given a five-year term for being the one to steal the property. In 1922, he was given three years for breaking and entering and in 1925, he was again sentenced to five years after being convicted of burglary, after he nearly killed an elderly woman and assaulting many others. In 1929, Slark once again bothered the police and they arrested him at Putney on Mar. 23.

REF.: *CBA;* Neil, *Manhunters of Scotland Yard.*

Slater, Oscar (Oscar Leschziner, AKA: **A. Anderson, Otto Sando)**, c.1871-1948, Scot., (wrong. convict.) mur. Oscar Slater, a German Jew, left his homeland to avoid being drafted into the military. Slater, whose real name was Leschziner, married May Curtis in 1901, but deserted her in 1905 because she was an alcoholic. He met a prostitute, Andrée Antoine, in London. She became his mistress, and they often traveled together. He earned his living by gambling and selling jewelry. May Curtis Slater badgered him for money, so Slater often used false names.

Slater and his mistress were in Glasgow, Scot., late in 1908. On Dec. 21, he received two letters. One contained a warning from a London friend that May Slater had been asking *him* for money. The second was a business invitation from a previous associate to go to San Francisco. That day, Slater let his servants go, contacted a London bank, went to a billiard room between 6:20 and 6:40 p.m., and ate dinner about 7 p.m.

Marion Gilchrist, an 82-year-old spinster living in Glasgow, spent that same evening reading. She had had extra locks installed on her apartment door and windows because she was worried about her jewelry collection, which was worth about £3,000. At 7 p.m., Gilchrist's maid, 21-year-old Helen Lambie, left the apartment to buy a newspaper, as was her custom. Below the apartment, tenant Arthur Adams heard something "heavy fall and then three sharp knocks." He went upstairs to check on Gilchrist and rang her doorbell three times. When Gilchrist did not answer, Adams went back downstairs to his apartment. There, his sister persuaded him to check again. He went back upstairs and, as he waited at the bell, Lambie returned at about 7:10 p.m. Adams told her he had heard strange sounds, "like sticks breaking," and Lambie thought perhaps pulleys for the clothesline had come down in the kitchen. Adams waited at the door while Lambie entered the apartment. As she started to go into the kitchen, a man walked out of the apartment and rushed out of the building after passing Adams. Gilchrist's body was found by the fireplace, fatally beaten about the head. One crescent diamond brooch, valued at about £50, was gone. Lambie, Adams, and Mary Barrowman, a teenager who said she saw the man running away outside the apartment, gave police conflicting descriptions of the suspect.

Oscar Slater, wrongly convicted of murder.

In the following days, Slater and his mistress continued to make preparations to go the U.S. He pawned a diamond brooch and booked passage for two to New York on the *Lusitania* under the name Mr. and Mrs. Otto Sando. Two days after the murder, John Trench, a police officer investigating the case, talked with a woman named Birrell. She told him that Lambie had told her the name of the killer. On Dec. 25, police learned about the brooch Slater had pawned. They went to question Slater, and found he and his mistress had left a few hours earlier for Liverpool or London. When they learned he was aboard the *Lusitania,* they cabled New York officials to have Slater arrested when the ship arrived. Lambie, Adams, and Barrowman were sent to participate in extradition proceedings in New York, where they identified Slater. He agreed voluntarily to return to Scotland. In the meantime, the brooch Slater had pawned was found to have been his for a long time, and positively did not match Gilchrist's.

Marion Gilchrist, whose savage murder was pinned on Slater.

Slater was brought to trial on May 3, 1909. The trial lasted four days. Information about the brooch and Detective Inspector

Trench's findings were suppressed. No murder weapon was found in Slater's luggage, which had been impounded. The prosecution, undertaken by Alexander Ure, called Lambie, Adams, and Barrowman, who identified Slater, and twelve others who named Slater as a man seen around the Gilchrist apartment building at different times, though the twelve had given conflicting descriptions. The prosecution also attacked Slater's character and sporadic work record and insinuated that he had fled Scotland to escape prosecution. The prosecution also charged that before Slater had seen his name in the newspapers as a suspect before he left for the U.S. and should have come forward, but Slater's name had not actually been printed until about a week later, when Slater was already aboard the ship. Slater, defended by Ewing Speirs, did not take the stand in his own defense. Before the jury was sent out to decide the verdict, the judge, Lord Guthrie, told them, "...a man of that kind has not the presumption of innocence in his favor." The jury of fifteen was out for one hour and ten minutes. One voted not guilty, five did not think the case had been proven, and nine voted guilty. At the time, the U.S. and England already required a unanimous vote for a conviction, but in Scotland only a majority was needed. Slater was judged Guilty and sentenced to be hanged on May 27.

Although Scotland had no means for legal appeal then, 20,000 people signed a petition for a stay of execution. The petition was given to the secretary of state for Scotland on May 17, and eight days later, the undersecretary sent a telegram authorizing a stay of execution. Slater's sentence was commuted to life and he was sent to Peterhead prison on July 8, 1909.

The public continued to lobby for his release. Sir Arthur Conan Doyle, the creator of Sherlock Holmes, wrote *The Case of Oscar Slater,* a leaflet that strongly criticized the verdict in the Slater case, in 1912. When Lieutenant Trench, an officer with an outstanding record, charged that Barrowman and Lambie had lied, a special inquiry was called on Apr. 23, 1914. The two women denied the allegations and Trench lost his job.

In 1925, Slater sent a note to Doyle by placing the note in a pardoned prisoner's mouth. Doyle stirred up controversy, and Lambie, contacted in Pittsburgh, Pa., admitted she knew the killer, who was actually an acquaintance of Gilchrist's. She said when she told police what she knew, they persuaded her to change her story. The suspect's identity was never revealed; he was only called "A.B." After Lambie's admission, Barrowman, too, said she had been influenced by police and had lied in her identification.

Slater was freed in 1927 after eighteen years in prison. During that time, Parliament had established a Court of Criminal Appeal for Scotland in 1926, but because Slater's conviction had occurred before the existence of the court, he could not file an appeal. A special law was enacted on Nov. 30, 1927, to allow his case to be heard before the appeals court. His case came before Lord Alness, Lord Clyde, and three other appeals judges in June 1928. The court overturned the conviction on the grounds that Guthrie had directed the jury inappropriately in a prejudicial speech before the verdict. Slater was awarded £6,000 compensation.

REF.: Birmingham, *Murder Most Foul;* Brome, *Reverse Your Verdict;* Browne and Brock, *Fingerprints; CBA;* Cuthbert, *Science and the Detection of Crime;* Dilnot, *Rogues' March;* Gribble, *Stories of Famous Modern Trials;* Hall, *Sherlock Holmes and His Creator;* Higham, *The Adventures of Conan Doyle;* House, *Square Mile of Murder;* Humphreys, *Criminal Days;* Hunt, *Oscar Slater, The Great Suspect;* Kingston, *A Gallery of Rogues;* ____, *Dramatic Days at the Old Bailey;* Lustgarten, *The Woman in the Case;* Morland, *Pattern of Murder;* Nash, *Almanac of World Crime;* Nordon, *Conan Doyle, A Biography; Notable British Trials;* Park, *The Truth About Oscar Slater;* Roughead, *Classic Crimes;* ____, *The Murderers' Companion;* Shew, *A Second Companion to Murder;* Wilson, *Encyclopedia of Murder;* (FICTION), Muir, *Five to Five.*

Slatin Pasha, Rudolf Anton Karl von (Slatihn Pasha), 1857-1932, Egypt, kid. (vict.) Named governor of Darfur in 1881. He was kidnapped and held by the Mahdi Mohammed Ahmed from 1884-95, but was able to flee to Cairo, where the Khedive appointed him pasha. He also served as British inspector general of the Sudan from 1900-14. REF.: *CBA.*

Slaughter, John Horton (AKA: **Texas John, Don Juan**), 1841-1922, U.S., west. lawman. Born in Louisiana, John Horton Slaughter moved with his family at the age of three months to a land grant in Texas. His family settled near Lockhart and began raising cattle. When the Civil War began, Slaughter fought Indians as a "Minute Man of the Texas Rangers." Slaughter continued battling Indians through the 1870s, and eventually settled in the midst of Apache country.

Cochise County, Ariz., sheriff John Slaughter.

At the close of the war, Slaughter began a ranch of his own in Atascosa and Frio counties. Slaughter married, started a family, and for the next few years acted as trail boss on a number of cattle drives and developed his ranch. Although he was successful, he decided to move to Arizona in 1878. In 1884, Slaughter purchased the 65,000-acre San Bernardino Grant, which extended from Arizona down into Mexico. His operation was large and sophisticated, employing at least twenty cowhands and some thirty families who harvested the crops.

Slaughter was not afraid to use his guns to settle a dispute. He was involved in a number of gun fights over the years, and always emerged unscathed. In 1886, he was elected sheriff of Cochise County with the particular project of checking lawlessness in Tombstone and Galeyville. Slaughter was successful here, too, and was reelected in 1888. The clean-up task was largely accomplished by 1890, and Slaughter retired from law enforcement to tend to his cattle ranch in Arizona and slaughterhouse in Los Angeles.

With a brief period out to serve in the territorial assembly in 1906, Slaughter concentrated on his business, eventually buying a meat market in Charleston and two butcher shops in Bisbee. The wealth he accumulated also turned Slaughter into something of a banker, handling mortgages for many of his neighbors. Slaughter died peacefully at the age of eighty.

REF.: Argall, *Outlawry and Justice in Old Arizona;* Bakarich, *Gun-Smoke;* Bechdolt, *When the West Was Young;* Blythe, *A Pictorial Souvenir and Historical Sketch of Tombstone, Arizona;* Brent, *Great Western Heroes;* Brophy, *Arizona Sketch Book;* Burgess, *Bisbee Not So Long Ago;* Burns, *Tombstone, an Iliad of the Southwest; CBA;* Chisholm, *Brewery Gulch;* Cunningham, *Triggernometry;* Durham, *The Negro Cowboys;* Erwin, *The Southwest of John Slaughter;* Faulk, *Tombstone;* Haley, *Jim East;* ____, *The XIT Ranch of Texas;* Harkey, *Mean As Hell;* Holloway, *Texas Gun Lore;* Hunt, *Cap Mossman;* Hunter and Rose, *The Album of Gun-Fighters;* Jaastad, *Man of the West;* Klasner, *My Girlhood Among Outlaws;* Koller, *The American Gun;* Lake, *Under Cover for Wells Fargo;* Lesure, *Adventures in Arizona;* Liggett, *My Seventy-Five Years Along the Mexican Border;* McDade, *The Annals of Murder;* Martin, *Silver, Sex and Six Guns;* Myers, *Doc Holliday;* ____, *The Last Chance;* Nolan, *The Life & Death of John Henry Tunstall;* Penfield, *Western Sheriffs and Marshals;* Prather, *Texas Pioneer Days;* Raine, *Famous Sheriffs & Western Outlaws;* ____, *Forty-Five Caliber Law;* Rynning, *Gun Notches;* Sloan, *Memories of an Arizona Judge;* Sonnichsen, *Billy King's Tombstone;* Waters, *The Story of Mrs. Virgil Earp;* Way, *Frontier Arizona.*

Slaughterford, Christopher, d.1709, Brit., mur. The son of a miller in Westbury Green, Surrey, Christopher Slaughterford established a malting business in Shalford, where he met Jane Young. Because the locals thought Young was engaged to Slaughterford, he was the first to be suspected when Young's body was found floating in a pond in November 1703.

Young had last been seen on Oct. 5, in the company of Slaughterford. Desiring public vindication, he surrendered to the justice of the peace who believed him to be innocent. Local indignation against Slaughterford ran high, however. Tried at Kingston, he was found Not Guilty, but the villagers, hungry for vengeance, collected enough money to pay for a second trial, and Young's brother filed an appeal. Believing that justice would vindicate him a second time, Slaughterford surrendered to the Court of the Queen's Bench when he could have run away.

Before Lord Chief Justice Holt, witnesses testified that Jane Young was with Slaughterford on the night of her disappearance, and one witness said that Slaughterford told him that he "had put her off," that he had found the perfect way of dealing with women who pressed their claim.

Slaughterford's aunt refuted the testimony. Her nephew was home that night, she said, asleep in his chambers. The jury this time returned a verdict of Guilty and Slaughterford was condemned to die on the gallows July 9, 1709. Had he been pronounced Guilty during the first trial, the king might have intervened. During an appeal, however, there was no legal recourse. Slaughterford went to his hanging quietly protesting his guilt to the very end. More than a few people in England did not doubt him.

REF.: *CBA;* Mitchell, *The Newgate Calendar.*

Slayton, Elmo, prom. 1931, U.S., mur. Witnesses said Elmo Slayton, nephew of Roy Slayton, was drunk when he shot and killed 27-year-old Pitt Bede near Honey Creek, Tenn., on Feb.7, 1931. They said Slayton and another drunken man were fighting when Bede attempted to play the peacemaker. Slayton pulled out his pistol and shot him dead. Slayton was sentenced to the penitentiary where he died shortly after beginning his term. It was said that guards placed him in a water hole and forced him to bail out water with cups to avoid drowning. According to rumor, he came down with pneumonia and died.

REF.: *CBA;* Montell, *Killings.*

Slayton, Roy, b.1873, U.S., mur. Roy Slayton, thirty-four, of the Trunde County Slayton clan, may or may not have had reason to want Cleo Billings, forty-eight, dead. Some people in the small Tennessee town of Honey Creek said Slayton's wife Eula was having an affair with Billings. Others said she just wanted to. Nonetheless, Slayton considered Billings a big enough threat to murder him in 1907 and spend many years in prison.

To stress his angry point, Slayton killed Billings, the middle-aged father of two in the presence of Billings' wife and his own, giving no verbal warning before pulling the trigger of his shotgun. He was convicted and sentenced to the state penitentiary in Nashville. His wife left him and the area and never returned.

REF.: *CBA;* Montell, *Killings.*

Sleeping Clergyman, A, 1933, a play by James Bridie (Osborne Henry Mavor). This drama clearly draws its inspiration, if not complete facts, from the life of accused murderess Madeleine Smith (Scot., 1857). In the play the heroine gives prussic acid to an unwanted lover; the notorious Smith was accused of having administered arsenic to her defaulting lothario. See: **Smith, Madeleine**. REF.: *CBA.*

Sleeping Sphinx, The, 1946, a novel by John Dickson Carr. The murder technique practiced by Dr. Robert Buchanan (U.S., 1892-95) is employed by the fictional killer. The author also weaves several other real life killers into the plot's fabric, including Maria Manning, Kate Webster, George Joseph Smith, Mary Eleanor Pearcey, Henri Desire Landru, Edith Thompson, and Jean Pierre Vaquier. See: **Buchanan, Dr. Robert**; **Landru, Henri Desire**; **Manning, Frederick George**; **Pearcey, Mary Eleanor**; **Smith, George Joseph**; **Thompson, Edith Jessie**; **Vaquier, Jean Pierre**; **Webster, Katherine**. REF.: *CBA.*

Slick, Thomas W., 1869-1959, U.S., jur. Served as prosecutor for St. Joseph County, Ind., from 1896-1900. He was appointed to the northern district court of Indiana by President Calvin Coolidge in 1925. REF.: *CBA.*

Sliwka, Tadeusz, c.1960- , U.S., fraud-mansl. Tadeusz Sliwka began drinking as a 7-year-old boy in his native Poland. After immigrating to the U.S. at eighteen, he began driving. In the next ten years, he was arrested numerous times for doing both at the same time, driving while intoxicated.

On the night of Nov. 9, 1988, Sliwka left a Chicago area pub, pulled south onto the northbound highway without turning on his headlights and plowed head-on into the car driven by Patrick Nalepa, twenty-six. Nalepa was seriously injured, and Sliwka pleaded guilty to felony drunken driving.

In 1984, he had been convicted of reckless homicide and sentenced to three years in prison after crashing his motorcycle into a bicycle ridden by Beth Ann Hayes, twenty-eight, an economics professor at Northwestern University. Sliwka served most of his sentence before being paroled. When he was released, Ginny Siano and her husband, Frank Caringello, Jr., took him into their home and provided him with room and board if he promised not to drink. But on July 15, 1988, Sliwka was found to be riding his motorcycle without the proper license. Later that summer, on Aug. 9, Sliwka was discovered by a highway patrolman, bloodied, lying near his crumpled motorcycle. Hospital tests revealed a broken jaw, and alcohol and cocaine in the driver's blood. On Sept. 2, Sliwka was once again arrested for driving without a license. It was discovered in the course of the investigation that Sliwka had obtained three different invalid Illinois driver's licenses. Judge William D. Black sentenced Sliwka to six years in prison after the Nov. 9, 1988, incident, calling Sliwka a "rampant alcoholic and a sociopath." REF.: *CBA.*

Slocum, Frances, 1773-1847, U.S., kid. (vict.) Raised by Delaware Indians who abducted her at the age of five. She married into the tribe, and decided to maintain her Indian identity after her true background was established and she was introduced to blood relatives. REF.: *CBA.*

Slovik, Edward Donald, 1920-45, U.S., milit. des. There were 40,000 reported cases of U.S. soldiers deserting their outfits during WWII. Of this group, 2,864 were tried before a general courts-martial. Forty-nine were sentenced to death, but only one was executed—Private Eddie Slovik, a 24-year-old man from Hamtramck, Mich. He was shot by a military firing squad at St. Marie aux Mines in the Vosges Mountains of France on the cold, gray morning of Jan. 31, 1945. Slovik was never shown his trial transcript and was marched to his death without being first notified that this was the day of his execution by the military.

Before the war, Slovik worked in a plumbing firm outside Detroit. He was remembered by his employer as an earnest, hard-working, young man who never gave anyone trouble. But between 1932 and 1937, he committed a whole series of petty juvenile offenses which drew the attention of the police. Eddie Slovik, in their view, was someone to watch. On Oct. 1, 1937, Slovik, just two months shy of his eighteenth birthday, was sentenced to prison for six months to ten years for embezzlement. While working as a clerk at the Cunningham Drug store in downtown Detroit, Slovik had taken candy bars, gum, and cigarettes without paying for them. The amount of his thievery was $59.60, a trifling sum which earned him a set of prison stripes at the state penitentiary in Jackson. Slovik was paroled from Jackson on Sept. 9, 1938, having compiled a good-conduct record while in the custody of his warders.

Vowing to go straight, Slovik left the prison to take a job in a grocery store. He promised to report back to his parole officer on a regular basis, but then one night, encouraged by two friends, Slovik stole an automobile and crashed it into a tree. Appearing before the magistrate in recorder's court on Jan. 20, 1939, Slovik pleaded guilty to automobile theft and violation of parole and was sentenced to two-and-a-half to seven-and-a-half years. He began serving his time at Jackson, but was later transferred to Ionia. With the help of Harry Dimmick, a sympathetic prison supervisor, Slovik learned a useful trade. "I trained him to be a wood finisher," Dimmick told author William Bradford Huie, "and me and a couple of the other boys used to travel in the car to the various state-owned institutions to repair and paint the furniture. We'd be gone four or five days at a time. I talked to Eddie a lot. I trusted him. And he never violated a trust, never gave me a minute's trouble."

In April 1942, Slovik was paroled from the Michigan State Reformatory in Ionia. He went to work for the Montella Plumbing Company in suburban Dearborn, where he began courting his future wife, Antoinette Wisniewski. They were married the following November. To earn more money, Slovik went to work at a De Soto plant, where he was paid $1.40 an hour. On Jan. 3, 1944, Slovik was drafted into the army despite having been previously classified 4-F, due to a debilitating condition in his legs.

Slovik was sent to Fort Sheridan, Ill., where he was desperately unhappy. He did not have a soldier's temperament and wanted more than anything to return home. At Camp Wolters, near Mineral Wells, Texas, Slovik wrote to his wife, saying that he felt "like crying" every time he sat down to write a letter. On Aug. 7, 1944, with his basic training behind him, Private Slovik was shipped off to France along with 7,000 other replacements crammed into the hold of the *Aquitania*. Slovik was assigned to the 109th Infantry Regiment of the 28th Division. He was in France less than two weeks when he was accused of deserting his unit for the first time. Actually Slovik and another buck private, John P. Tankey from Detroit, got lost or were separated from their outfit. Slovik and his companion attached themselves to the Canadian 13th Provost Corps, where they remained until Oct. 8, 1944, when they finally caught up with the 109th Infantry. Slovik had been in the camp scarcely a few hours when he decided to make a break for it. The next day, he surrendered to officers of the 28th Division and was thrown into the stockade. Charges were filed against him on Oct. 19. A week later, Lieutenant-Colonel Henry P. Sommer, who was serving as division judge advocate, offered Slovik a deal. He offered to drop the court-martial proceedings in return for Slovik's agreement to go to the front lines, but Slovik declined. On Nov. 11—Armistice Day—Slovik was brought before Colonel Guy M. Williams, who presided over the nine-officer tribunal assigned to review this case. Slovik was defended by Major Edward Woods, who was not formally trained in the law. (The Army did not require the defense counsel to belong to the bar at the time of Slovik's hearing.) The defendant entered a plea of Not Guilty.

The judgement of the court was death by firing squad. "In today's language—well—he could be termed a conscientious objector," Slovik's widow said years later. "I knew he could never kill anyone. He said to me, 'I don't know why they are sending me overseas, because I can't kill.'" On Nov. 27, General Norman D. "Dutch" Cota, a graduate of West Point and a ramrod military officer, approved the death sentence. From his stockade prison in Paris, Slovik wrote to General Dwight Eisenhower pleading for clemency, but the request was denied on Dec. 23. On Jan. 23, 1945, Eisenhower sent through specific orders that Slovik be executed in the 109th Regimental area. The prisoner was transported through a heavy snowstorm to St. Marie aux Mines from Paris, arriving there on Jan. 31.

In the presence of forty-two witnesses, including General Cota, the execution of Private Eddie Slovik—the first man to be put to death for such an offense since 1864—was carried out in all due solemnity. When asked if he had a final wish, Slovik replied that he wanted a glass of water. He was refused on the grounds that there was not enough time.

The body was conveyed to the Oise-Aisne American Cemetery at Fère-en-Tardenois for burial. Slovik, however, was laid to rest in Plot E, reserved for the murderers and rapists who had been put to death by the American military authorities. Back home, Antoinette Slovik did not learn of her husband's fate until 1953, when author William Huie began digging into the facts of the case for a forthcoming book. The army had hushed up the matter. One Pentagon official went so far as to say: "No one had been shot." Mrs. Slovik was simply told that her husband had died in Europe. The government asked her at the time to return his March allotment check. She did so, with bitterness. In June 1945, a package containing Slovik's wallet arrived in the mail. It had been pierced by a bullet.

Antoinette Slovik made numerous appeals to the government for an official correction of the record, and for the $70,000 she believed was due her from a life insurance policy Slovik had taken out shortly before he left for Europe. Despite the sympathetic efforts of members of the media, her plight was ignored by Washington policy-makers. The final indignity came in July 1987, when, after his wife died, Slovik's remains were transported back to the U.S. for re-internment. While in transit, TWA somehow lost the coffin. It finally turned up in San Francisco, but an airline spokesperson passed it off as "just a matter of lost luggage."

REF.: *CBA;* Huie, *The Execution Of Private Slovik.*

Slyter, George B., prom. 1931, (wrong. convict.), U.S., rob. The key witness in a Mar. 18, 1931, Minneapolis, Minn., robbery made a wrong identification, which led to the conviction of George B. Slyter. But the actual robbers committed their same crime the night before Slyter was to be sentenced. The record was quickly corrected and the real thieves were arrested and sentenced.

Two gunmen held up Aaron Oxendale who was working at a Minneapolis garage, and Oxendale later gave police a description of the men. A few days later, Oxendale thought he saw one of the men who had robbed him, and called the police. They arrested Slyter. He was convicted, although he denied knowledge of the crime and said he had been at a St. Patrick's Day party the night of the robbery. Though his mother and sister were able to verify this alibi, they gave different versions of the affair. In addition, Slyter had a prior criminal record, which could have doubled the sentence, turning a five to forty-year term into a ten to eighty-year term.

But the same garage was robbed on Apr. 24. Oxendale was working and recognized the bandits as the same ones who had robbed him earlier. He immediately confessed his error to the court. The following morning, after everyone had gathered for the sentencing, Slyter was set free.

REF.: Borchard, *Convicting the Innocent; CBA.*

Smaldone, Eugene (AKA: **Young Gene**), 1910- , and **Smaldone, Clyde** (AKA: **Flip Flop**), and **Smaldone, Clarence** (AKA: **Chauncey**), prom. 1970s, U.S., gamb.-org.crime. In 1972, Eugene Smaldone and Clyde Smaldone, members of Colorado's best-known crime family, were convicted of federal gambling charges and conspiracy to import cocaine into the U.S. Eugene Smaldone was sentenced to a four-year prison term and fined $4,000 for gambling. He received a ten-year sentence and $10,000 fine for the cocaine charge. He served five years in a federal prison before being paroled in 1978. As of 1982, Eugene Smaldone owed Colorado $10,200 of his original $14,000 in fines, having quit making substantial payments. Clyde Smaldone was fined $10,000 in 1972, of which he still owed half in 1982. At that time, his brother Clarence Smaldone still owed the full $18,000 he was fined by the court in 1976.

Eugene Smaldone's attorney, Peter Ney, says his client is caught in a "Catch-22," maintaining that Smaldone is only able to work at low-paying menial jobs that don't net him enough money to pay off his fines. "You wouldn't want him involved in anything close to what he was doing before. But that limits his earning capacity. I think Mr. Smaldone would have preferred to pay his fines."

In 1986, the Smaldones were among hundreds of convicted criminals who owed the U.S. attorney's office in Denver nearly $3 million in uncollected fines. REF.: *CBA.*

Small, Ambrose Joseph, prom. 1919, Case of, Can., miss. per. The mysterious disappearance of Canadian entertainment impresario Ambrose Small on Dec. 2, 1919, caused a sensation in its day. Despite being a gambler and womanizer (he was suspected to have fixed a horse race on which he realized a $10,000 profit), for the most part the 56-year-old Small's personal life and business life were in good order. He had begun buying theaters after his marriage to wealthy heiress Teresa Small, sixteen years earlier, and sold the entire giant chain of them for $1.7 million just before his disappearance. He seemed to be in good health and good spirits, although he was widely disliked—he cheated on his mistress as well as his wife, he spouted petty prejudices against Catholics and children to whomever would listen, he despised the concept of charity, and took a childish delight in keeping people waiting for appointments. He dined with his longtime mistress Clara Smith the evening before the disappearance, but police cleared her of any knowledge of the case. He was last seen by a news vendor who, because of a blizzard hitting the area from Toronto to New York, was unable to provide Small with his daily copy of the New York *Times,* complete with its early edition racing forms. Small stalked off in a fury of frustration

Small's family and friends thought little of his disappearance at first, assuming he was "shacked up" with a girlfriend. When the disappearance was reported officially, it touched off the largest manhunt in Canadian history. Teresa Small posted a $50,000 reward for information that would lead to finding him.

Ambrose Small

Small's secretary, John Doughty, disappeared that same day. He absconded with $100,000 in negotiable bonds from Small's safety-deposit box, for which he had a key. He was found a year later in Oregon and convicted of the theft of the bonds, but it was determined that he had nothing to do with Small's disappearance.

The manhunt continued with leads pouring in from all over. Legitimate law-enforcement agencies, confidence artists, psychics, and amateur sleuths became involved, and even Arthur Conan Doyle offered his services. But Ambrose J. Small was never found. A Toronto court pronounced him dead in 1923, although investigators dug up the basement of his Grand Opera House in Toronto to look for his remains in 1944.

In 1926, a man called the Toronto *Star* from Albion, Ind. He claimed that he was Small and that he had been held for seven years in an asylum in Wisconsin. At first people believed that Charles E. Morse was Ambrose Small, but he was twenty years younger than Small, and his fingerprints did not match. He was returned to the asylum at Waupan, Wis., where his cell was littered with newspaper clippings about the missing magnate.

REF.: *CBA;* McClement, *The Strange Case of Ambrose Small;* Nash, *Among the Missing;* Smith, *Mysteries of the Missing.*

Small, Frederick L., c.1866-1918, U.S., arson-mur. On Sept. 28, 1916, Frederick Small, a grocer from Lake Ossipee, Mass., made hurried, last-minute arrangements to go with a friend on a combination business-pleasure trip to Boston later that day. As they were leaving Small's residence near Mountainview, N.H., to catch the train, Small made a show of shouting goodbye to his wife, the former Florence Arlene Curry. His companion, Edwin Conner, and the wagon driver, a man named Kennett, did not see or hear any response as they awaited Small in a wagon.

Small's marriage to Arlene, his third, was not happy. He bullied and often beat her. In 1916, he took out substantial insurance policies on both his wife and their house.

Small received a message at his hotel in Boston, informing him that his house was on fire and that he should return immediately. Seemingly grief-stricken, Small returned to the ruins of his home and asked that they be searched for his wife's body. A short time later, informed that his wife's body had been found, he expressed amazement that there were enough remains to be buried.

Investigation proved that Mrs. Small had been bludgeoned on the head, shot, and strangled with a rope from Small's boat. Instead of being burned, her body had fallen through a weakened spot in the floor of the burning house and had fallen into a pool of water in the basement. Small had set a timed incendiary device to go off while he was in Boston. He was found guilty of murder, and hanged on Jan. 15, 1918.

REF.: *CBA;* Jackson, *The Portable Murder Book;* Kobler, *Some Like It Gory;* Nash, *Murder, America;* Pearson, *Five Murders;* Wilson, *Encyclopedia of Murder.*

Small, Kenneth B., prom. 1954, U.S., mur. In May 1954, Kenneth B. Small shot Jules Lack, killing him instantly. At his trial for first-degree murder, Small tearfully said that he had killed Lack, forty-five, because his wife wanted to divorce him and marry Lack. With the aid of his wife's testimony, Small was found Not Guilty by reason of insanity and sentenced to a mental hospital.

Edith Small told Kenneth, a dentist, that she wanted to marry Lack because he made more money. She told Small, "You don't know how to live. You're small. I want to live big now." Small showed up at a rendezvous between his wife and Lack at a party. Bursting through the door, he demanded to know which man was Lack. Lack smiled and extended his hand. "I'm Lack," he said. Small fired two shots and Lack fell. REF.: *CBA.*

Small, Len, 1862-1936, U.S., polit. corr. A farmer from Kankakee, Ill., Len Small became one of the most corrupt governors ever to serve in Illinois. Small functioned as a puppet of Chicago mayor "Big Bill" Thompson, a notoriously dishonest official. Not long after taking office for the first time in 1921, he was indicted for embezzling $600,000 during his previous term as state treasurer. Small was charged with depositing millions of dollars of state funds in a bank controlled by his friend, State Senator E.C. Curtis, and profited by the interest in 1917 when he was serving as state treasurer. Small claimed to have confidence in the jury system, a well-placed sentiment since he was acquitted by a jury in 1922. Small's support behind-the scenes came from Walter Stevens, unofficially known as the dean of Chicago gunmen, "Umbrella Mike" Boyle, a crooked Electrical Workers' Union official, and Jew Ben Newmark, a one-time state's attorney investigator who had branched out into counterfeiting, theft, and extortion. Bribing some jurors and threatening others and their families, they swayed the jury in favor of Small.

Small repaid Stevens, Boyle, and Newmark by later pardoning Boyle and Newmark of charges of jury tampering and Stevens from a murder rap. The governor's record of granting pardons was unequalled in American history. In his first three years in office Small pardoned more than 1,000 felons and freed another 7,000 over the next five years on a cash-and-walk basis. Chicago newsman George Murray described the scam whereby Cook County state's attorney Robert E. Crowe would convict a wrongdoer, Small would sell the convicted man a pardon, and Crowe and Small would split the take. An example of this was the case of Ignatz Potz, who murdered a motorcycle policeman to avoid arrest for running booze. Convicted and condemned to death, Potz had his sentence commuted to life imprisonment in 1922 by Small. Then, in July 1926, Small granted a parole to Potz which stipulated that he be released from prison in 1930.

On July 15, 1927, Governor Small paid $650,000 to the State of Illinois in settlement of the judgment against him from his state treasurer days. By 1928, Small's reign of corruption came to an end. In the infamous Pineapple Primary of 1928—named for the pineapple shaped bombs that were used, along with beatings, threats, and other illegal voting procedures to intimidate voters—the Small-Crowe ticket finally went under, despite the support of mob boss Al Capone. Angry voters turned out in unprecedented numbers to register their protest against corrupt officials and the felon who had reigned as governor of the state for years was voted out of office. See: **Pineapple Primary.**

REF.: Asbury, *Gem of the Prairie; CBA;* Kobler, *Al Capone;* Landesco, *Organized Crime in Chicago;* McPhaul, *Johnny Torrio.*

Smat, Benjamin, prom. 1699, Brit., vagrancy. On Sept. 28, 1699, Benjamin Smat, his wife, and their three children were severely whipped and beaten at Boveney, England, for vagrancy. The homeless family had begged for money, but they were flogged instead.

REF.: Andrews, *Old-Time Punishments; CBA.*

Smerdis (AKA: **Bardiya**), d.c.525 B.C., Per., governor, assass. Son of Cyrus the Great, secretly murdered by brother Cambyses II. REF.: *CBA.*

Smethurst, Dr. **Thomas**, prom. 1859, Case of, Brit., mur. Dr. Thomas Smethurst practiced medicine in England and evidently acquired considerable knowledge. In 1827 he married a wealthy patient, Mary Smethurst, twenty years his senior, and for the next fifteen years, they seemed to have lived a good enough life, enjoying the fruits of his practice and her wealth.

At the time that Smethurst retired, he met Isabella Bankes, a 43-year-old single woman, who moved into the same boarding house where the Smethursts were living. A romantic involvement between the doctor and the new lodger soon became apparent, and she was asked to move. The doctor followed shortly thereafter, and he and Bankes were married bigamously.

In 1859, Bankes became ill with dysentery. After treating her himself for a while, Smethurst called in several other doctors. Although agreeing originally with the diagnosis of dysentery (the doctors did not know that Bankes was two months pregnant), they finally diagnosed that she was suffering from poisoning. They reported their finding to a magistrate and learned that Smethurst was the beneficiary of her recently drawn will. So the authorities were already watching Smethurst when his "wife" died on May 3, 1859.

Smethurst was arrested and a lengthy and controversial trial took place. The autopsy revealed no poison in the body, but the jury still found Smethurst Guilty of murder. However, the Home Secretary intervened, and a prominent physician, Sir Benjamin Brodie, was called in to examine the case. Based on his findings, Smethurst was released on the murder charge, but he was sentenced to a year in prison for bigamy. He was eventually able to claim his bigamous wife's estate.

REF.: Altick, *Victorian Studies in Scarlet;* Ballantine, *Some Experiences of a Barrister's Life;* Bowen-Reynolds, *In the Light of the Law;* Brock, *A Casebook in Crime;* Browne, *Trials for Murder by Poisoning; CBA;* Cobb, *Trials and Errors;* Dewes, *Doctors of Murder;* Dunbar, *Blood in the Parlor;* Furneaux, *The Medical Murderer;* Glaister, *The Power of Poison;* Hardwick, *Doctors on Trial;* Kingston, *Dramatic Days at the Old Bailey;* ____, *Law-Breakers; Notable British Trials;* Parmiter, *Reasonable Doubt;* Parry, *The Drama of the Law;* Parry, *Some Famous Medical Trials;* Pearce, *Unsolved Murder Mysteries;* Thomson, *The Story of Scotland Yard;* Wilson, *Encyclopedia of Murder.*

Smith, Al (Alfred Emanuel Smith), 1873-1944, U.S., law enfor. off. Prominent U.S. Democratic political leader. He served as New York County sheriff from 1915-17, and was governor of New York from 1919-20 and from 1923-28. He lost the U.S. presidential race of 1928 to Republican Herbert Hoover.

REF.: *CBA;* Handlin, *Al Smith and His America;* Josephson, *Al Smith: Hero of the Cities;* Moskowitz, *Alfred E. Smith, An American Career.*

Smith, Alfonso Francis Austin, b.1889, Brit., (Case of) mur. The testimony of one eyewitness was not enough to convict Alfonso Francis Austin Smith of murder in November 1926, though the evidence was against Smith. John Derham had been Smith's best friend, but Smith's wife had been carrying on an affair with Derham and requested a divorce to marry her new love. Devastated, Smith responded with a barrage of tears, pleas, and finally threats.

John Browning Barton witnessed Derham's death as he walked down a Tankerton, England, street on Aug. 12, 1926. Barton glanced into an open window and saw a man, Smith, with his back to the window, and two others, Derham and Kathleen Smith, facing him a few feet away. Barton looked away, heard a shot ring out and looked back in time to see Derham and Mrs. Smith leap towards Smith. Barton saw Derham raise his arm as though striking someone and Mrs. Smith struggle with him. He heard her cry out, "Don't, don't," and then, "Give me the revolver." Derham staggered out into the road with the revolver in his hand, and collapsed.

Smith testified at his trial that he had reached for the pistol in his pant's back pocket to put it down. At that moment he was suddenly struck by Derham, and the revolver fired. Smith said he remembered no more until the police arrived. Smith's attorney suggested to the jury that perhaps Barton had only imagined that the gun went off before the men struggled. Barton denied this but the jury was impressed by the possibility. When the prosecution maintained that the angle at which the bullet entered Derham's body proved that Smith fired the revolver, Smith's attorney went as far as to conduct a mock struggle to prove that the shot could have been an accident.

Smith repeatedly maintained that he had never implied, planned or even considered murdering his wife's lover, and said he was unable to answer the question of whether or not he would have divorced his wife if he had obtained actual evidence of an affair. When Smith held out the revolver at arm's length, he pointed it toward the counsel and said, "No finger of mine ever touched that trigger. That I will swear before God to my dying day." The jury acquitted Smith of murder charges and the judge begrudgingly sentenced him to one year's imprisonment for possessing a firearm with intent to endanger life.

Though he was acquitted, Smith's life remained difficult. His wife carried through the divorce, his young son was killed in a school fire, and Smith spent his final years immersed in debt and litigation. In November 1944, he died in a one-room apartment at Ilfracombe, poor and alone. He had once said that there was no place in the world for a man acquitted of murder.

REF.: Archer, *Killers in the Clear;* Bowker, *Behind the Bar;* Butler, *Murderers' England;* Cannell, *When Fleet Street Calls; CBA;* Gribble, *Strange Crimes of Passion;* Hastings, *The Other Mr. Churchill;* Jackson, *Mr. Justice Avory;* Lang, *Mr. Justice Avory;* Marjoribanks, *For the Defense, The Life of Sir Edward Marshall Hall;* O'Donnell, *The Trials of Mr. Justice Avory;* Shew, *A Companion to Murder;* Symons, *A Reasonable Doubt;* Warden, *His Majesty's Guest;* Warner-Hooke, *Marshall Hall.*

Smith, Andrew M'Laghlin, prom. 1840, Brit., mur. Andrew M'Laghlin Smith was a Scottish gardener with a hot temper. On Apr. 28, 1840, he became so enraged over a produce transaction that the police were forced to take him into custody. He behaved like a caged animal there, and when police officers Dalton, Dawson, and Duke went to check on him, Smith attacked Dawson and Duke with a pruning knife. Duke died twenty minutes later. Several days later, Smith was found Guilty of murder, but insane. Smith boasted that he thought no more of killing men who confronted him than slaughtering cattle.

REF.: Butler, *Murderers' England; CBA.*

Smith, Arthur John, 1946- , Brit., mur. England's Arthur John Smith eventually confessed that on Feb. 23, 1966, he stabbed Phyllis Pearce, forty-eight, six times because she bumped into him and he lost his temper. Smith was sentenced to life imprisonment for what the court superintendent deemed the most meaningless, senseless murder he had ever encountered.

The police interviewed nearly 80,000 people living in the vicinity. In the course of their massive investigation, they discovered that Smith possessed a knife like the murder weapon, and the ominous nickname, "Murder Smith." His father had dumped the knife into Portsmouth Harbor, fearing his son would be suspected in the murder. With that, Smith confessed to the murder and related the tale of his nonsensical attack.

REF.: Butler, *Murderers' England; CBA.*

Smith, Bernard, c.1923- , Case of, U.S., mur. Fourteen-year-old Bernard Smith openly admitted to having shot and killed his 53-year-old father, yet after only a brief deliberation, the jury found the boy Not Guilty of murder.

The jury in this 1937 trial made its astonishing decision shortly after Bernard's attorney told them, "If this boy gets justice, it will be for the first time in his life." Jury members learned during the trial that the youth had been terrorized and beaten by his father since his mother's death while he was still an infant. Jurors heard testimony from child protection authorities who had been called to the Smith residence several times to investigate reports of physical abuse. In his defense, neighbors explained how the distraught boy ran to their home to call a doctor after he shot his father. After jurors acquinted Bernard of his father's murder, he was remanded into the custody of his step-sister.

REF.: *CBA;* Wilson, *Children Who Kill.*

Smith, Bill, d.1902, U.S., west. outl. At the turn of the century, Bill Smith led a gang of train robbers and rustlers in Arizona and Utah. In 1901 the Arizona Rangers were created to bring order to the lawless land. In October of that year, Smith and his cohorts robbed a Union Pacific train in Utah, afterwards stealing a herd of horses to take back to their Arizona hideout at the forks of the Black River. Spotted by three rangers and six cowboys, they were tracked by these men who decided that one of the rangers should go for help while the others kept watch on the outlaws' cabin.

Smith and his brother were outside the cabin at dusk when Rangers Carlos Tefio and Bill Maxwell came after them. Bill Smith ran back into the cabin but his brother pretended to surrender, dragging his rifle on the ground, then abruptly raising it and firing into Tefio's stomach. Mortally wounded, Tefio fired his Winchester and hit two of Smith's gang members. Bill Smith then opened fire on Maxwell, shooting him through the hat before murdering him with a bullet in the eye. The outlaws then fled from their hideout. Later that same year, Smith went into Douglas, Ariz., for the nightlife and was approached by Ranger Dayton Graham and policeman Tom Vaughan in front of a store. When the officers asked Smith what he was doing, he pulled a six-gun and fired, seriously wounding both lawmen, then escaped. Graham recovered and tracked Smith through gambling dens. He finally caught up with him in 1902 at a monte table in a Southern Arizona town. Smith tried to go for his gun but Graham murdered him, firing two bullets into his stomach and one into his head. Found sewn into the lining of Smith's coat were steel hacksaw blades.

REF.: Breihan, *Great Lawmen of the West; CBA;* Hunt, *Cap Mossman.*

Smith, Cathy Evelyn, 1948- , U.S., drugs-mansl. On Mar. 5, 1982, comedian John Belushi, thirty-three, was found dead in a rented $200-a-day, garbage-strewn bungalow at the Chateau Marmont Hotel on Sunset Boulevard in Hollywood. An initial report from Lieutenant Dan Cooke of the Los Angeles Police Department attributed the rotund actor's death to "natural causes." Belushi, who lived in New York City, was in California to work on what would be his last movie project, *Noble Rot,* which was never finished. According to the press, Belushi's physical trainer, William Wallace, found his naked body on a bed shortly after noon. Belushi apparently had been dead for several hours. A woman who drove up to the hotel in a red car owned by Belushi was briefly questioned by police. Cathy Evelyn Smith said she woke Belushi at 8 a.m. when she saw that he was having trouble breathing, and asked him if he was all right. When he said yes and went back to sleep, she left again, returning several hours later to find the police at the Marmont and Belushi dead.

A native of Chicago, Belushi became a major star in the 1970s, first appearing in 1972 in *Lemmings* , a zany off-Broadway rock musical that got rave reviews and ran for ten months in Greenwich Village. He achieved national fame in 1975 on television's wildly successful *Saturday Night Live.* As one of the "Not Ready For Prime Time Players," Belushi performed comic skits, impersonating a host of characters. Born in 1949 of Albanian immigrant parents, Belushi attended several midwestern colleges and married his high school sweetheart, Judith Jacklin, in 1967.

Los Angeles coroner Dr. Thomas T. Noguchi performed the autopsy on Belushi and determined that he had died of an injected overdose of cocaine and heroin, commonly known as a "speedball." Smith meanwhile had returned to her native Canada. But after the *National Enquirer* published an interview with her in June 1982 in which she said that after a night of drug use, she had given Belushi a final "coup de grace"—referring to the cocaine and heroin injection—the Los Angeles district attorney reopened the case. Smith, who had been paid $15,000 for the interview bearing the headline, "I killed John Belushi," said the tabloid had distorted her remarks. A former rock singer, one-time rock groupie, and long-time drug user, she had been arrested for possession of heroin in 1981 and was known as a Hollywood groupie who supplied drugs to celebrities. Days after the article appeared, the Los Angeles *Herald Examiner* revealed that police had never questioned actors Robin Williams and Robert DeNiro, who were seen with Belushi hours before his death. Charged with a cover-up, police lamely explained that the movie stars were hard to contact. On Mar. 18, 1983, one year after Belushi's death, a Los Angeles County grand jury indicted Smith on one charge of murder and thirteen counts of administering a dangerous drug. Accompanied by her lawyer, Smith surrendered to Toronto police on Mar. 19. On Sept. 12, 1984, Judge Stephen Borrins ordered her extradited to Los Angeles to stand trial.

On June 11, 1986, Smith admitted in a Los Angeles Superior Court that she had injected Belushi with the drugs which medical officials said killed him. Pleading no contest to reduced charges of involuntary manslaughter the 39-year-old Smith faced a maximum sentence of eight years and eight months, with prosecuting attorney Elden Fox recommending three years. Her attorney, Howard Weitzman, said, "Cathy's conscience has always been clear...She has denied today and all along that she was responsible for John Belushi's death...That has not changed." The prosecution produced eye-witness testimony that Smith had injected Belushi many times in the final week of his life. His friends Nelson Lyon and Leslie Marks-Moritz testified that Belushi spent his last days searching for drugs, taking drugs, and borrowing money to get drugs. Judge David Horowitz conceded that Belushi was partly responsible for his own death, but ruled that Smith must be punished as "the source of that poison." Weitzman asked for probation rather than a jail term for Smith, noting that she needed treatment at a drug rehabilitation center. Smith had two years earlier published her autobiography, *Chasing the Dragon.* Bob Woodward of The Washington *Post* had put out *Wired,* an extensive account of Belushi's final days.

On Sept. 2, 1986, Judge Horowitz sentenced Smith to a three year prison term. Belushi's sister-in-law, Pamela Jacklin, said it was important to send a message to society about drugs. Jacklin said, "Because victims are willing does not mean you don't do something about it." In sentencing Smith, Horowitz said to her, "You knew how to use the needle. You came into that situation willingly and openly and you injected several people." Smith served eighteen months of her sentence at the California Institution for Women in Frontera, and was released in March 1988. She returned to Canada the day after her release.

REF.: *CBA;* Wolf, *Fallen Angels.*

Smith, Cecil Brown (AKA: **Rev. Thomas Henry Clifford**), prom. 1904, Brit.-Scot., fraud-big. Cecil Brown Smith acted the part of a paralyzed beggar well, taking in more than £6 a week. His con worked until October 1904 when London detective-constable Coney followed him to London Bridge Station where the alleged vagrant treated himself to oysters and ale before ably boarding a train for his lovely home in the London suburb of Norwood. Smith was arrested and charged with fraud.

During his trial, he sobbed, pleaded guilty, claimed he feared for his family's reputation, begged forgiveness, and vowed to straighten out his life if the court showed mercy in their decision. The courtroom audience supported Smith and pitied him until a medical officer proved that Smith was in perfect physical condition. The judge, untouched by Smith's admonitions found him Guilty and sentenced him to three months' at hard labor.

Several years later, Smith discovered religion, and once again found himself in jail. In 1910, while posing as the Reverend Thomas Henry Clifford, Smith preached to congregations and married couples illegally. In addition, he was charged with bigamy. In court, Smith pleaded guilty to all charges except bigamy and was once again found Guilty. He was sentanced to ten months at Hard Labor. REF.: *CBA.*

Smith, Charles, prom. 1894, U.S., rob. Charles Smith was arrested on June 26, 1894 by Chicago Detective Clifton R. Wooldridge who had been staking out an area of the city plagued by high crime rates. Smith was captured after he and an unidentified accomplice ambushed and robbed an elderly victim as he walked down the street. Wooldridge shot one of the robbers in the hip after he tried to attack the officer, while Smith fled, only to be captured by two other officers and a railroad flagman. The wounded robber escaped during the pursuit of Smith. Smith was found Guilty of robbery, fined $100 and placed in the House of Corrections. REF.: *CBA.*

Smith, Charles Manley, prom. 1936, Case of, U.S., consp. In December 1936, the governor of Vermont, Charles Manley Smith, was arrested along with Samuel A. Howard and Bert L. Stafford for failing to report a bookkeeper's $250,000 embezzlement from the Marble Savings Bank of Rutland, Vt. All three men were trustees of the bank. The bookkeeper, John J. Cocklin, was convicted of embezzlement and sent to prison. On Apr. 26, 1937, the charges against the three men were dismissed. REF.: *CBA.*

Smith, Clarice, 1964- , U.S., mur. On May 21, 1987, the mummified corpse of a 3-year-old girl was found in a West Philadelphia housing project apartment. Two workers discovered the body of Sylvia Smith after a resident reported smelling gas and hearing running water coming from the sixteenth-floor apartment, according to West Detective Division officer John Yeakel. The tiny corpse, thirty-eight inches long and weighing only six pounds, was kneeling beside a bed, apparently in the spot where she died three months earlier. Taken into custody after her arrest at the home of a relative was Clarice Smith, twenty-three, the child's mother. Smith initially was charged with the abuse of a corpse, meaning that she knew the child was dead but neglected to report it. After an autopsy, she was charged with murder and endangering the welfare of a child. Acting medical examiner Dr. Robert Catherman listed malnutrition as the cause of death. According to homicide Lieutenant James Hemwood, "The body was mummified, in a sealed-up room, with no air." Sylvia had died around Christmas 1986.

Smith, a cocaine addict, had another daughter, Shantil, six, who had been living with a grandmother for five years. After a three-day non-jury trial at the Common Pleas Court before Judge Michael R. Stiles, Smith was convicted on June 29, 1988, of abuse of a corpse and third-degree murder. Assistant District Attorney James Long and defense attorney Charles Cunningham argued throughout the trial over whether Smith had acted with malice. Long said the defendant had once physically attacked a boyfriend who tried to "show love" to the 3-year-old Sylvia and noted that the doorknob to the bedroom door was found near the body, indicating that the child had tried to escape. Cunningham called the death "a tragic accident" caused by Smith's $1,400-a-week cocaine addiction. After Smith allowed her daughter to starve to death, she abandoned the apartment, fearing that people would think "I was bad person." In September, Stiles sentenced Smith to the maximum ten to twenty years in jail with a concurrent two-year term on the abuse of a corpse charge. Her daughter's death lead to a state welfare department investigation which faulted the city's human services department for inadequately protecting the child, who had come under its supervision in 1984. REF.: *CBA.*

Smith, Edgar Herbert, Jr., 1933- , U.S., mur. In 1957 Victoria Zielinski, a 15-year-old high school cheerleader from Mahwah, N.J., was found bludgeoned with a baseball bat and her skull crushed by a forty-four pound boulder in a gravel pit in Hackensack, N.J. Edgar Herbert Smith, Jr., twenty-three, an acquaintance of Zielinski's, confessed, was tried, and convicted of the crime. Sentenced to die in the electric chair, Smith spent the next fourteen years on death row in a New Jersey prison. Known as "Death Row Smith," he studied the law, and escaped execution nineteen times by appeal. He also became an author, writing *Beyond A Reasonable Doubt* and *Brief Against Death.* He wrote a murder mystery and another book about his experiences as a death row convict fighting charges he repeatedly claimed were false—he claimed police pressured him to confess. The proceeds from his writings helped finance his many appeals. Smith's bestseller, *Brief Against Death,* attracted the attention of journalist William F. Buckley, Jr., who supported his writing and helped him obtain a release from prison.

In 1971, a federal appeals court ruled Smith's confession came from police pressure and ordered a second trial for him, where he was allowed to plead "no defense" to reduced charges of second-degree murder. Sentenced to twenty-five to thirty years in jail, he was given credit for the time he had already served and received seven years off his sentence for good behavior. He was released on parole on Dec. 6, 1971. On his release from prison, Smith was picked up by a limousine to appear on Buckley's television show, "Firing Line," then spent his first night out of prison in a suite at New York City's elegant St. Regis Hotel. His new-found celebrity status resulted in publication of another book, *Getting Out,* and he wrote several articles about the criminal justice system, while meanwhile touring the nation lecturing. Settling in San Diego, Calif., in August 1974, he held a variety of jobs as security guard, public relations consultant, and free-lance writer. He married Paige Diana Heimer, nineteen, in 1974. From March 1976 through October 1976 he was often on welfare.

On Oct. 8, 1976, a warrant was issued for Smith's arrest on charges of kidnapping and attempted murder. Lefteriya Lisa Ozbun, a 33-year-old Chula Vista, Calif., clothing factory employee, was walking toward the plant's parking lot to get a ride home from her husband when Smith leaped from his car, put a knife to her throat, and told her, "Keep your mouth shut or I'm going to cut your throat right here." Throwing her in the front seat of his car, Smith taped her wrists together and drove away. Ozbun fought fiercely, explaining later that she was sure he would kill her. "I'd never seen eyes like that. They were so cold and filled with hate." When she said she kicked out the windshield and grabbed the steering wheel Smith stabbed her with a six-inch butcher knife, missing her heart by a fraction of an inch. The car swerved onto an exit ramp and Ozbun crawled out as Smith raced away. Twelve days later Smith called Buckley from Las Vegas, Nev., leaving his phone and room numbers with Buckley's secretary. Buckley immediately turned Smith in to the FBI. Smith, unarmed and living under an alias, did not resist arrest on Oct. 13. His wife later was arrested on charges of aiding and abetting his flight, and concealing him.

At Smith's San Diego trial in March 1977 he admitted that he had murdered Zielinski and said that his earlier defense—which claimed that police had forced him to confess—was false. He also confessed to all charges of attempted murder, assault, and kidnapping in the Ozbun case. Smith said he decided to reveal his past lies because he had visited the murder victim's grave in Honesdale, Pa., and there "recognized the devil I'd been looking at in the mirror for forty-three years was me..." Superior Court Judge Gilbert Harelson heard the trial without a jury. Smith's sentencing was delayed when he was hospitalized after a beating by prisoners while in a holding cell. In his Apr. 19, 1977, column, Buckley reiterated statements from a Nov. 20, 1976, column, saying, "I believe now that Smith was guilty of the first crime. There is no mechanism as yet perfected that will establish beyond question a person's guilt or innocence. There will be guilty people freed this year and every year." On April 25, 1977, Smith was sentenced to life imprisonment for kidnapping and attempted murder by Judge Harelson, who rejected his request for a new trial and for an examination to determine whether he was a mentally disordered sex offender. Harelson withheld sentencing on three other charges connected with the Ozbun case until Smith completes his sentence.

First becoming eligible for parole in 1982, Smith was turned down five times. Outraged letters, many from New Jersey, poured in to the parole board, urging that he be kept in prison for the rest of his life. Writing to a *Los Angeles Times* reporter, Smith incomprehensibly blamed his prosecutors in New Jersey for his attack on Ozbun and claimed that he himself was also a victim. "Ask those self-righteous public servants why they gave me the opportunity to do it," he wrote, explaining that there are questions "which need answering, which Lisa Ozbun and I need answered." Smith's wife, who divorced him not long after his second crime, said, "Edgar is a master at manipulating the system. He manipulated his way off death row in New Jersey. He conned Bill Buckley. And now he's doing what he's always done. He's working the system, until the odds are in his favor for parole."

REF.: *CBA;* Smith, *Brief Aginst Death;* ____, *Getting Out.*

Smith, Edgar William, b.c.1897, Brit., attempt. mur. In Newark, England, on Jan. 7, 1927, Edgar Smith allegedly assaulted a woman, jumped in his car, and sped away, only to be stopped by off-duty Police Constable Dainty for questioning. Smith identified himself as a commercial traveller and provided Dainty with an alibi for his whereabouts during the evening. When Dainty noticed a black mask and gloves in the back seat of Smith's car, he attempted to take Smith into custody. Smith responded by firing two shots at Dainty at point blank range. As Smith tried to flee, Dainty reached through the open window, grabbed the car's steering wheel, and drove the automobile into a brick wall. The impact knocked the officer off the car and into the road. Smith shot Dainty twice more.

In court, Smith defended himself by explaining that he had every opportunity to kill Dainty if that had been his intention—although he had shot the officer twice in the stomach. Maintaining his innocence, Smith was found Guilty of Attempted Murder and sentanced to Life in Prison. REF.: *CBA.*

Smith, Edward, prom. 1962, Brit., gamb.-drugs. On Oct. 21, 1961, after two horses were drugged at a race at Kelso, Northumberland police visited the stables of Major Bewicke, to check out a report of a suspicious visitor. A French woman, about twenty-five years old, had been to the stables, saying she owned horses in Paris and, since she would soon be bringing them over to England, wanted to inspect the premises. Taking notes as she was told the names of various horses and their boxes, she promised to get in touch with him soon. The stable boy remembered seeing a similar woman with the same quest at a different stable. The woman had visited stables in fifteen British and Scottish counties, sometimes accompanied by a man and once by another woman. The license plate of her car was traced to William Roper, a bookmaker. Police learned they were following Micheline Lugeon, and that Roper had often been her companion. A former stable girl told police her husband and two other men, Bob Herd and Darkie Steward, had been hired to drug horses at £80 a job.

At the races in Brighton, police picked up Edward Smith after he had casually told a couple he just met that he was delivering some drugs to use on the horses in that day's race. Searching his house in Surbiton, police found a large amount of drugs. Smith soon confessed to Chief Inspector Barnett that he was part of a ring that drugged race horses, and that he had been involved in the scheme for the last ten years. At his job with a drug manufacturing firm, Smith had become friendly with one of the pill makers, Richard McGhee, and later met the stable boy, Darkie Steward. Steward contacted McGhee and obtained an effective potion for incapacitating horses. Racing men Joseph Lowry and Edward Dwyer became involved in the syndicate. In approximately 1960, Dwyer brought in Roper, who instructed Smith to get a more powerful drug from McGhee. Dwyer left not long after that and was replaced by Charles Mitchell. All of those involved in the complicated network were tried in Brighton. One hundred and twelve witnesses testified for the prosecution, traveling in from nineteen counties in Ireland, Scotland, and England, as well as from Jersey. All were found Guilty; Lugeon received a one-year term, and the others were given sentences ranging from one to four years in jail. REF.: *CBA.*

Smith, Edmund Munroe, 1854-1926, U.S., jur. Taught comparative jurisprudence and Roman law from 1891-1922 at Columbia University. He was also a Bryce professor of European legal history at Columbia from 1922-24. REF.: *CBA.*

Smith, Ellsworth, prom. 1970s, U.S., rob.-asslt.-mur. Ellsworth Smith, a murderer, bankrobber, mugger, and holdup man, was caught thirty-two times in fourteen years, but spent only five years in prison. Although apprehended repeatedly, he successfully avoided prosecution a number of times by using false identification, jumping parole, or escaping. On occasion, the undeserved lenience of careless judges also worked in his behalf. At one point in the 1970s, Smith was wanted in four states and in Washington, D.C.

Smith was finally apprehended purely by accident when under an alias he went to court in Washington, D.C., to help a girlfriend who was in trouble with the law. A passing detective happened to recognize him and placed him under arrest. Smith was tried and found Guilty of first-degree murder and was sent to prison for life. REF.: *CBA.*

Smith, Evelyn, b.1889, U.S., mur. In August 1935 two Chicago women were convicted of murdering the son-in-law of one of them. Mrs. Evelyn Smith, forty-six, once a burlesque dancer and prostitute, was married at the time of the crime to Harry Jung, a Chinese laundryman, while Mrs. Blanche Dunkel, forty-two, the other woman, was a four-time widow. When Dunkel's former son-in-law, Ervin Lang, planned to remarry not long after his wife's death in December 1934, Dunkel had, she confessed, offered Smith $500 to murder Lang, paying, she claimed, $100 on account with the rest to be paid after the killing. Lang's blanket-wrapped torso later was found in a swamp near the Indiana-Illinois border. His legs, cleanly sawed off with trousers, shoes, and socks still on them, were found about seven miles away in a trunk. Smith and Jung had disappeared. Smith later was arrested in a Manhattan rooming house, while Jung had vanished, seemingly forever.

Rumors surrounding the case ran rampant. Some said Lang was murdered because Dunkel suspected him of murdering her daughter or was angry that he planned to remarry so soon after the death. Testimony revealed that Dunkel herself had an affair with Lang, and speculation arose that she had killed her daughter herself. The press dubbed Smith "The woman without nerves" and "The enigma woman." At first protesting her innocence, Smith soon confessed, saying, "Oh well, I might as well get it over with. Sure, I killed him...Blanche didn't pay me a cent of the $500." She stated she had tried to get her husband to help cut up the body, "but he got sick at the sight of blood." Jung was never found. Dunkel complained that "Evelyn did it all differently than she promised," saying she was supposed to "put Erv to sleep, strangle him, and throw him in the lake."

Smith and Dunkel were convicted and sentenced to 180 years each for murder. Criminal circuit court judge Cornelius J. Harrington stipulated that the two be locked up in solitary confinement once a year on the anniversary of the murder as a reminder of their crime. REF.: *CBA.*

Smith, Francis, b.1775, Brit., mansl. Francis Smith thought he had shot the village ghost. But he discovered that the mysterious phantom that had terrorized the village of Hammersmith, England, for five weeks was a man. The villagers believed their town was possessed by a rambunctious spirit in Winter 1804. A pregnant woman claimed to have been followed home late one night. She said the ghost rose out of a tombstone and frightened her so badly that she collapsed in the road outside her house.

Francis Smith decided to capture the evil spirit. On Jan. 3, 1804, Smith was standing watch in town when he saw a shadowy figure in white. "Damn you, who are you, and what are you? I'll shoot you if you don't speak!" With that, Francis Smith fired his gun, and Thomas Milwood, a bricklayer dressed in the usual white uniform of his trade, lay dead in the road. Milwood's sister heard the shots and rushed to the scene. In a panic, Smith confessed his crime to a wine merchant, John Locke. The night watchman then bound Smith over to the constable for arrest. His murder trial began at the Old Bailey on Jan. 13. The circumstances surrounding Milwood's death divided the jury. The murder was certainly not intentional, but neither did the defendant have the right to fire a gun arbitrarily at anyone, ghost or no ghost. After deliberating the matter for an hour, the jury returned a verdict of Guilty of the lesser charge of manslaughter.

The judge ordered the jurors to reconsider. The verdict must be guilty of murder in the first degree, or acquittal. When the jury returned, they were unanimous in the opinion that Smith had committed murder, and by law should be sentenced to death. Despite the defendant's quiet, trembling manner, the Sessions

The Hammersmith Ghost chasing a village resident.

House was in bedlam. The lord chief baron routinely submitted the trial deposition to the king for review. Shortly before the appointed hour of execution, Smith, twenty-nine, received a royal pardon, conditional on his serving one year in prison. REF.: *CBA.*

Smith, Francis, prom. 1953, U.S., hijack.-org. crime. On Jan. 22, 1953, convict Francis Smith testified before the New York State Crime Commission at the county courthouse in Foley Square in Manhattan to say that Frank Borelli, police chief of the Cliffside, N.J., force for thirty-two years, had helped racketeers hide out from the law in the 1930s. He was brought in from Green Haven Jail where he was serving a seven-to-ten year sentence for hijacking. Smith's account of West Side gunfights detailed how Borelli had protected him and his cohorts in 1935, even letting them know when FBI agents were looking for them. Members of his gang would then hide out in Marlboro, N.Y., until it was safe to come out again for business. Smith said loan sharking, gambling rackets, cargo thefts, assassinations, and murders were as widespread in the mid- to late-1930s as they were later when the infamous Mickey Bowers gang took over control of Local No. 824 of the International Longshoremen's Association.

Smith told the commission how he had set himself up as a pier boss in the mid-1930s after his release from serving a short jail term. With gangsters John Harvey, Thomas Porter (also known as Thomas Protheroe), and George Keeler (also known as George Donovan), Smith decided to move two brothers named Dillon off Pier 59, on the North River, and take control of the pier themselves. The brothers submitted without fighting because, according to Smith, "they knew what would happen." Describing a gang warfare incident in 1935, not long after he had taken over the pier, Smith said he and his partners were cruising along the waterfront when they spied a truck loaded with Russian furs. Keeler spoke to the driver, then returned to his partners to say there was a load worth $100,000 "and he's going to give us the truck." While the four gangsters waited for the truck to pull away from the dock, four other men suddenly hijacked the shipment. Keeler knew where one of the rival hijackers, Sonny Campbell, lived. Smith's gang held him up but he had already informed a gang led by "Charlie the Jew" Yanowski, who was later stabbed to death with an ice pick. Yanowski had hijacked the furs from the original hijackers. The theft triggered a feud that resulted in murders on the waterfront for the next five years, for, though Smith and his gang decided to let the Yanowski gang keep the furs, Campbell's cohorts wanted to revenge his kidnapping by Smith. Protheroe and Donovan were murdered within months, with Protheroe and a female companion shot dead in Long Island City on May 16, 1935. Keeler was shot to death in his bed in Brooklyn.

Then, John "Cockeye" Dunn, later electrocuted, drove up alongside Smith at Pier 72 and shot him nine times. Yanowski's anti-Dunn mob repaid Smith for letting them keep the furs by taking him to a doctor and then sending him to Cliffside Park, N.J., to recover. At that time, Smith explained in his testimony almost twenty years later, Police Chief Borelli promised to give him sanctuary as "long as we didn't do anything." When Borelli told him the FBI was after him, he hid at a Marlboro, N.Y., retreat. Smith later returned to New York City, where he was shot twice more before being arrested and sentenced again for violation of parole. Referring to Smith, Borelli said at the time of the 1953 hearings that he "didn't even know the bum." REF.: *CBA.*

Smith, Frederick D. (AKA: **Curly**), 1908-67, and **Blackstone, David Thomas**, b.1898, and **Oliver, Frank Miles**, 1912- , U.S., mur. When they were boys, Harry Lore and Fred Smith were best friends. They spent hours fishing together in the lakes of the Irish Hill region near Ypsilanti, Mich. In 1927, 19-year-old Fred Smith was arrested for holding up a gas station, and Judge George Sample put him on five years' probation. A year later, on Aug. 25, 1928, Smith was sentenced to five to fifteen years in prison for breaking his parole. Citing a touching letter from Smith's nearly blind mother, Governor Fred Green of Michigan paroled Smith in 1930 after he had served only two years of his sentence. When he was later arrested for the murder of his one-time fishing buddy and three companions, the local press bitterly denounced the decision to release Smith from prison.

On Aug. 11, 1931, Smith left his job at a papermill to meet his two friends, David Blackstone and Frank Oliver, both of whom had a history of petty crime. Blackstone had been released from the Illinois penitentiary a year earlier. They met at Otis Oden's, a saloon near Milan. After drinking whiskey, Smith and Blackstone decided to go out and rob someone. They took Oliver's late-model Pontiac to Peninsula Grove, a popular picnic spot near the County Line Road in Willis, Mich.

As they drove the car slowly through the wooded area and drank, they spotted the car of Thomas Wheatley, a 16-year-old high school student. Smith and Blackstone left their car to "pull the job," according to Frank Oliver. A few minutes later, they returned with $2 and a stolen watch belonging to Anna May Harrison, a 17-year-old guest at the Lore family home. Fearing that Harry Lore would report him to the police, Smith returned to the car and captured its occupants at gunpoint.

Wheatley, Lore, Harrison, and Vivian Gold of Cleveland were driven to Tuttle Hill Road, where they pleaded for their lives. "Yeah," Smith said, "let you go and we'll all go to the jug." Harry Lore struggled with Blackstone, who shot him. Blackstone then shot and killed the other three. Smith first considered burying the victims in a gravel pit near Ypsilanti, but decided that would take too much time. Instead, the killers doused the four bodies with gasoline and placed them in the back seat of Wheatley's car. They set fire to the car and made their way back to Ypsilanti. It was 5:30 a.m.

A farmer in Willis, Mich., soon found the blazing wreck. State police immediately launched an exhaustive manhunt. They took moonshiners Paul Keene and Lawrence Keene into custody, but soon ruled them out as likely suspects.

That morning, David Blackstone drove to Detroit and pawned Anna Harrison's watch for $6. Within seventy-two hours after the discovery of the automobile, Smith, Oliver, and Blackstone were in custody. Blackstone was captured after his gun fell into the hands of an Ypsilanti police informant. Police then traced the weapon to Blackstone.

When news of the shooting spread through Ann Arbor, a crowd

of 10,000 descended on the Washtenaw County courthouse and demanded that the police surrender the killers. State militiamen lined the streets as the Lincoln touring car with the three young men inside made its way through the town. Four deputy sheriffs led Smith and his companions through the hostile mob. Police interviewed the three suspects separately. "We know you did the killing, Blackstone told us all!" screamed one of the deputies to the defiant Fred Smith. After two hours of interrogation, Smith broke down and confessed. He then seized an iron bar from the table and tried to fight his way out of jail, but two deputies quickly overpowered him.

"I don't wonder that the crowd outside is crying for vengeance," exclaimed Judge George Sample. After the full story had been told, the court found each of the defendants Guilty on each of four first-degree murder charges. Judge Sample sentenced them to life imprisonment. Sheriff Henry Bennett was praised for bringing the killers to justice so quickly.

When Smith, Blackstone, and Oliver arrived at the gates of the penitentiary in Jackson, police used tear gas to disperse a crowd of 3,000 spectators. After serving thirty-six years in prison, Frederick Smith died on Feb. 17, 1967. Frank Oliver was paroled on Jan. 16, 1969, and was granted a final discharge from supervision on Jan. 16, 1973. There is no further record of David Blackstone, the man who fired the fatal shots. REF.: *CBA*.

Smith, Frederick Edwin (Earl of Birkenhead), 1872-1930, Brit., atty. gen. Served in Parliament from 1906-18, and as attorney general from 1915-18. His most notable case was the successful prosecution of Sir Roger Casement on charges of treason. He is also credited with sponsoring the Supreme Court of Judicature Act of 1925, and other legal reforms. REF.: *CBA*.

Smith, George, d.1905, Brit., mur. George Smith was sentenced to death in December 1905 for murdering his wife. While awaiting his execution, he threatened executioner John Ellis to such an extent that protection was provided for Ellis on the day of the execution. On that day, however, Smith walked to the gallows calm and collected, easily allowing himself to be pinioned and bound. REF.: *CBA*.

Smith, George, Jr., 1907-45, Brit., mur. Twenty-eight-year-old George E. Smith, Jr., of Pittsburgh, a U.S. Army private stationed in England, was arrested in December 1944, and charged with the murder of retired British diplomat, Sir Eric Teichman. Teichman, who lived on a 3,000-acre estate in Norfolk County, heard shots and went outside to discourage what he assumed were poachers. When he didn't return, his wife searched the grounds. She found her husband dead, shot in the face with a .30-caliber bullet from a U.S. Army carbine. Nearby police found more spent cartridges and wads of chewing gum.

A few days later, Smith was arrested and charged, along with Private Leonard S. Wijpacha. Smith was charged with murder, and Wijpacha, with accessory to murder. On Jan. 12, 1945, Smith was convicted by a U.S. Army court-martial and sentenced to be hanged. General Dwight D. Eisenhower did not reprieve Smith, who was executed on May 8, 1945. REF.: *CBA*.

Smith, George Joseph (AKA: **George Baker, The Brides of the Bath Murderer, John Lloyd, George Oliver Love, Henry Williams**), 1872-1915, Brit., mur. Everything about this turn-of-the-century mass murderer was prim and proper. Though he murdered for profit, Smith nevertheless had the decorum to marry his victims before sending them swiftly to their watery deaths through a method of his own simple but cunning invention.

Born at 92 Roman Road, Bethal Green, London, on Jan. 11, 1872, according to the birth certificate he was using at the time of his arrest, Smith's family was not well off. His father struggled to pay the bills by selling insurance, a then unpopular field of interest, but one, oddly enough, Smith would later recognize as a source of great income, when coupled with his unique brand of murder. Poorly educated and left mostly to the streets, Smith, at the age of nine, stole some fruit from a vendor and was caught by running into the open arms of a London constable. (His other offenses at this time consisted of similar acts of pilferage and the breaking of a street lamp.)

Being of meager means, his parents did not contest a court action which sent the child to a reformatory for eight years, thrusting him into a brutal environment that certainly helped to create the calculating killer who slowly emerged decades later. Reflecting upon Smith's youthful plight, crime writer Colin Wilson later wrote that "George Joseph Smith is one of the most powerful arguments against judicial savagery in criminal history."

"Brides of the Bath Murderer" George Joseph Smith and one of his victims, second wife Alice Burnham.

Smith's evolution as a master criminal lacked lightning and thunder. His way toward the gallows involved a plodding series of criminal acts that almost imperceptively, in deepening shades of gray, led to the ultimate murders he committed. And only toward the end of his horrifying career did he truly earn the reputation given to him by one of his biographers as "the most atrocious English criminal since Palmer." (Dr. William Palmer of Rugeley, England, a nineteenth-century killer, poisoned for profit at least a half dozen persons and was hanged in 1856.) Released from the Borstal institution in 1888, Smith busied himself with small larcenies, was sentenced to a week in jail in 1890 for a petty theft, and six months in prison the following year for stealing a bicycle.

The bicycle was in keeping with Smith's athletically inclined young manhood. Though never proven, he reportedly worked for some time as a gymnasium instructor, and, some time during the early 1890s, enlisted in the army, seeing duty overseas. By 1896, Smith had transformed his once undernourished, bone-thin body into a muscular frame with "unnaturally tough biceps." Also in that year, as he had shed himself of his sickly, unimpressive body, Smith ostensibly did away with George Joseph Smith as a person. Journalist William Bolitho, who studied Smith's life, likened the future killer's transformation to that of "the breaking of the cocoon that frees the full-grown night-moth. The man has separated himself definitely from the caterpillar that was G.J. Smith, to begin a series of lives in other names, each separate in environment, both personal and local, and only joined by the hidden chain of his own identity."

Smith became George Baker, setting himself up in a cheap rooming house in a shabby section of London. He dressed as would any middle-class office worker or government employee, his suits dark and inexpensive, a bowler hat square on his head, the perennial British umbrella hooked on his arm. And there was not only money in his pocket for the first time in his life, but enough for him to start a small savings account. The source of these wondrous new riches were women, several of them, all in love with him, even though he hated all women.

Adorning his hair with gobs of pomade, coating his athletic body with cut-rate cologne, and affecting the manners of a gentleman forced into uncomfortable means, Smith drew the attentions of young, unsophisticated women, mostly domestic servant girls working in the mansions of the rich (which was his plan), who sighed with passion at his slightest nod. Exactly how Smith developed such magnetism is uncertain; perhaps while in the army, or even during his brief stint as a boarding house keeper, imitating the conduct of retired gentlemen in his care. No matter, he was physically handsome in that squarejawed, keen-eyed Victorian tradition made famous by Sidney Paget, who illustrated the first Sherlock Holmes stories for *The Strand* magazine, only a few years before Smith's criminal activities accelerated. Oddly enough, Smith bore a striking resemblance to Holmes as seen by Paget, which may have subconsciously attracted his female admirers. According to Charles Higham, writing in *The Adventures of Conan Doyle,* Paget presented a "sexually attractive, well-fleshed nineties face and figure...His image of Sherlock Holmes had hundreds of thousands of young woman yearn for this fictional character as they might yearn for a stage actor..."

Yet Smith was the antithesis of the great Sherlock. The similarity was only physical; where Holmes struggled to triumph over evil, Smith personified it, commercialized it, made it pay through his bevy of adoring females, a harem he quickly turned into a trained platoon of sneak thieves.

The *modus operandi* of Smith's enterprise was as prosaic as the man himself. Under his directions, these swooning housemaids simply made detailed inventories of the furnishings in the mansions they worked. Smith scrutinized these lists, which catalogued possessions down to the smallest bric-a-brac, then selected the items he thought he might easily sell. The maids then stole the pieces and dutifully returned them to Smith, who in turn sold them. It was during this period that Smith took up the habit of itemizing everything in his life, his true miserly character emerging in exacting ledger books where all income and expenses, down to the last farthing, were detailed, an avaricious trait that led to Smith's downfall years later.

Immediate peril for Smith came in 1896 in the form of jealousy; one of his many working-girl lovers, enraged when he paid too much attention to another, informed on him. Smith was arrested, police finding great quantities of stolen goods in his rooms. He was sent to prison for a year.

Avoiding the London streets, where he figured he might chance upon one of his maidservant cronies, Smith went to Leicester upon his release in 1897, opening a small sweetshop and catering to children. During the day, Smith was the patient and kindly gentleman who peddled penny candies and biscuits to swarms of little ones who had saved for their Saturday spending sprees in his tiny shop. At night, Smith put on his finest linen suit and top hat, and went strolling for bigger commercial game–women. On one of these nocturnal hunts, Smith encountered Caroline Thornhill. Learning that she had a small savings account, he promptly proposed. The couple married in 1898, Smith using the symbolic alias of George Oliver Love. Either out of whimsy or irony, Smith listed his father as a "detective" on the marriage papers. Mr. and Mrs. Love moved into the back rooms of Smith's candy store, which failed a little more each day, until Smith began to eat up his wife's savings. When this meager amount was dissipated, Smith informed his wife that she was useless to him, that he intended to leave her. Caroline Thornhill Love begged Smith to keep her at his side. There must be a way, she pleaded. Well, he admitted, there was–if she was willing to do exactly as he directed. Anything, she agreed. They moved to London.

Mrs. Love's new occupation was one so ably performed by Smith's previous loot-clutching paramours. Her devoted husband meticulously wrote references for her. With these she secured a job as a servant in many handsome homes. Caroline, under Smith's cautious tutorship, became an expert sneak thief, filling Smith's apartment with jewelry, furniture, paintings. Again, Smith made out his niggardly entries into well-kept ledger books, keeping a strict tally on all stolen items received from his wife and their subsequent resales.

With new earnings from his wife's persistent pilferage, Smith suddenly discovered the seaside resorts of England, traveling through the towns of Hove and Hastings, passing himself off as an antique dealer, searching, as would an archeologist for saleable artifacts, more gullible females to woo, win, and rob. It is not known how many women Smith promised to marry, or even married at this time, in order to obtain their savings and dowries, but it is certain that at this time in his life he had decided on bigamy as a living. He did marry a boarding house owner while still the spouse of Caroline Thornhill Love, absconding with the woman's savings, even her wardrobe. When Caroline returned home one day in 1900, hands full of stolen goods, she discovered these feminine articles and flew into a rage. Smith explained that the brief affair with the landlady was only business, but Caroline became so unnerved that she discarded caution and was caught by one of her employers as she attempted to smuggle a suitcase full of stolen candelabras from his house. She immediately informed on Smith who meekly surrendered to bobbies bounding into his tranquil lodgings. Smith received another prison sentence for receiving stolen goods, this time the maximum of two years. When he emerged from prison in 1902, he searched in earnest for his legitimate wife and meal ticket, Caroline, only to learn that she had fled to Canada a few days before his release.

Smith shrugged at the problem; there were thousands of spinster women available. He began marrying and deserting females in record numbers, spinster after spinster, sucking them dry of their worldly goods and money, then leaving them, most of these hapless females being citizens of the seaside resorts. In Brighton, Smith obtained £90 from an elderly woman, his largest amount in the year 1908. With this money, coupled with his ever-increasing inventory in furnishings taken from previously abandoned wives, Smith opened a second-hand shop in Bristol where he met and married Edith Mabel Pegler, who, like most of his other brides, was "a notch above" him, according to Smith's later statements, referring to her social and educational standing.

Pegler, who was soon drained of her savings by Smith, had the distinction of marrying the *real* Mr. Smith, since he used, for whatever odd reason, his own name at the time. Smith purchased a house, his first home, with £240. He reveled in being a property owner, fondling each night his important papers–title deeds, certificates of transfer. This was the heart of Smith's genuine ambitions, property, and possessions. He loathed females in general, a hatred typical of women exploiters, and was inwardly repelled and disgusted by the sexual performances he was obligated, however briefly, to enact. But George Joseph Smith endured it all. His was a hunt for money through the withered fields of middle-class, middle-aged British womanhood. He would have his possessions at any price, even murder.

The precise time of Smith's decision to commit homicide in his marrying and mulcting schemes has never been pinpointed, but it was most probably caused by his marriage to Edith Pegler. He had actually found himself developing affection for this wife, an emotion that undoubtedly troubled Smith, whose business it was to eliminate all emotions, all feelings, in order that he coldly perform his bigamist-bilking chores. In Summer 1910, Smith got rid of Edith in the same fashion he had abandoned his other wives: he took her to a National Gallery showing, excused himself to go to the men's room, and left her forever as she stared at classics on canvas.

Two months later, in August 1910, while strolling through Bristol, Smith met Beatrice Constance Annie ("Bessie") Mundy, a 33-year-old spinster. Not only was the lovesick Bessie easy prey for the much-marrying Smith, but she held the key to his future in that she was also an heiress to £2,500 left to her by her late father, a bank official. After quickly getting Bessie to accept his hand in marriage (while using the alias Henry Williams), Smith's hot dreams of instant riches were dashed against a hard-willed uncle who controlled Bessie's fortune, and who allowed her only £8 a week to live on. The conniving Smith tried wheedling Bessie's dowry from her executor; he wrote in his groveling manner, a plea to the coffer-clutching uncle from Weymouth, where the couple had wed, on Aug. 29, 1910:

Dear Sir,

My wife and self thank you very much for your letter today with kind expressions. In *re* banks, undoubtedly to transact the business there would be rather awkward. Thus we suggest it would be better if you will be good enough to forward a money order instead of checks–however it will suit the circumstances. Any time we change our address we should let you know beforehand. Bessie hopes you will forward as much money as possible at your earliest (by registered letter). Am pleased to say Bessie is in perfect health, and both looking forward to a bright and happy future.

Believe me, yours faithfully,
H. Williams

As a postscript to this missive, Bessie, at the request of her spouse, added in her own hand: "I am very happy indeed. Bessie Williams."

This appeal from Smith was only the first in a month-long series of notes and letters exchanged between him and the uncle; both men employed solicitors to settle the matter of Bessie's inheritance with the result that £138 was sent to Smith. Thinking that these were the only funds he would realize from Bessie's estate, the tight-fisted bigamist turned on the cultured, passive Bessie, and, searching for a way to absent himself from their brief union, accused her of infecting him with a venereal disease as a result of being promiscuous! Such a charge was, of course, absurd since Bessie was a withdrawn, highly moral woman of fine education and propriety, but it served as excuse enough to abandon her.

Smith with another wife, Bessie Constance Mundy.

Smith quickly departed into hazy activities, returning to Mrs. Edith Pegler Smith, resuming his "antique" dealings. He moved secretly about for two years, dragging his docile wife with him from London to Bristol. And it was during this period of sketchy migrations that Smith could very well have begun to murder after marrying his victims, for, by the time he again met the hapless Bessie Mundy, his purpose was clear and his ingenious method for resolving relationships was decidedly lethal, a method Smith had undoubtedly pondered and practiced for some time.

On Mar. 14, 1912, Bessie Mundy, having accepted her miserable lot in life as God's will, left the boarding house of one Mrs. Tuckett in Weston-super-Mare, taking her daily constitutional. She returned at 1 p.m. in a nervous state, telling Mrs. Tuckett that she had accidentally met her errant husband, Henry Williams. "He was looking over the sea," said Bessie with trembling lips. "He turned around, stared into my eyes, and said: 'Ah, Bessie, my dove, it's all been a terrible mistake.'" Two years had elapsed since Smith had deserted Bessie, cursing her as he went for afflicting him with syphilis, yet at the moment of their reunion, she forgot and forgave all. Mrs. Tuckett was not of a similar mind, for she had, on instructions of Bessie's uncle, become the woman's ever-watchful guardian.

When Smith showed up at the boarding house two hours later, Mrs. Tuckett showed him to her drawing room. He sat sipping tea with the landlady and Bessie. Mrs. Tuckett, stiff as a ramrod in her rocker, leaned forward and bluntly asked him: "Why did you leave your wife at Weymouth?"

Smith looked at her with a hurt expression. "Why, I've been looking high and low for Bessie for months in every town in England!"

"What was the point of that? You knew very well, Mr. Williams, the addresses of Bessie's relatives. They could have easily told you where to find your wife."

Without hesitation Smith countered: "Exactly–it was through Bessie's uncle–or was it her brother?–that I learned she was living in this area."

The couple were reconciled within the hour, swearing to live forever with each other, Bessie grateful for the return through Providence of her attractive husband, Smith, who was broke, determined this time to obtain all of Bessie's inheritance, no matter what the cost.

That afternoon the pair, at Smith's insistence, visited Baker & Co., solicitors, where he arranged a loan from his adoring wife in the amount of £150 at 4 percent interest, signing a formal note to that affect, making the transaction legal. Smith then queerly talked about the loan from his wife as being "a wonderful investment for her."

They returned to Mrs. Tuckett's establishment to retrieve Bessie's belongings. Mrs. Tuckett did not like the looks of Smith, and it showed on her face when she greeted them at the door.

"I suppose I may go back to my husband?" asked Bessie, seeking the elderly matron's sanction.

"You are over thirty," snapped Mrs. Tuckett. "I cannot hold you back!"

When Bessie was packed, the couple left the house, Mrs. Tuckett glaring at Smith. "We'll return this evening to say our formal goodbyes," Smith told her in a soft voice. They did not return. Smith realized, however, that Mrs. Tuckett's response to him was that of seething suspicion. He penned a clever letter to allay the landlady's fears concerning his wife's fate, having the missive delivered to Mrs. Tuckett that night. It was a perceptive and telling stroke, this letter, one that summed up the attitudes and fears of the British middle-class of that closeted Edwardian era, displaying an intellectual dimension on Smith's part that put him into that rare class of criminal, one that understood the morality, traditions, and apprehensions of a society that worked against him and his sinister plans. It read:

Dear Madam,

In consequence of the past and the heated argument which possibly would have occurred if wife and self had to face you and your friends this evening, thus, for the sake of peace we decided to stop away and remain together as man and wife should do in the apartments which I have chosen temporarily. Later on I will write a long letter to all Bessie's friends clearly purporting all the circumstances on the whole affair solely with the intention of placing all your minds at rest concerning our welfare. All I propose to state at present beside that which has already been stated by Bessie and myself before the solicitors that it is useless as the law stands and in view of all the circumstances together with the affinity existing between my wife and self for any person to try and part us and dangerous to try and do us harm or endeavor to make our lives miserable. It appears that many people would rather stir up strife than try and make peace. As far as Bessie and I are concerned the past is forgiven and forgotten. Bessie has not only stated that on her oath to the solicitors; but has also given it to me in a letter written by herself to me which I shall always prize. Thus my future object and delight will be to prove myself not only a true husband but a gentleman and finally make my peace step by step with all those who have been kind to Bessie. Then why in the name of heaven and Christianity do people so like to constantly interfere and stir up past troubles? It would be more Christian-like and honorable on their part to do their best to make peace. There is time yet to make amends and if people will only let us alone and with the help of the higher powers which has united us twice, Bessie shall have a comfortable settled home and be happy with me. I trust there is many years of happiness before us. I thank with all my heart all those who have been kind to my wife during my absence.

Yours respectfully,
H. Williams

With that, Smith moved his lost bride to Herne Bay where he rented a house on High Street from a wary Miss Rapley. While making arrangements with the proprietor, Smith, in a pleasing voice, became confidential, telling Miss Rapley that "my wife is a cut above me. Her friends did not at all approve of her marriage. My wife has a private income paid monthly. I have not anything except that I dabble in antiques."

Miss Rapley accepted Smith's volunteered financial confession in lieu of bankers' references, and rented the house to him; her risk was not great since the house itself was rather run-down, and did not even offer an inside public convenience, nor a bath. But that was the exact reason why the sly Mr. Smith so desired to live in it.

Once settled in the house, Smith's waking thoughts concentrated on Bessie's seemingly unattainable inheritance. He knew he would have to move fast; her suspicious in-laws would probably circumvent his move to her money by establishing an annuity with that inheritance. He found his scheming answer in giving over all his worldly possessions to his darling Bessie should he perish, a thoughtful intent echoed by his wife. On July 8, 1912, Smith and Bessie visited a solicitor, lawyer, and parson, the latter a chosen witness to the mutual wills they carefully signed. If Bessie died, her entire estate would be turned over to Smith. If Smith (as Williams) were to die, his estate would be inherited by his wife, which meant she would get absolutely nothing.

The following day, attired in top hat and morning coat, the elegant-looking Smith entered the shop of a man named Hill, an ironmonger by trade. He came to the point abruptly: "The house I have rented with my wife has no bath. She simply will not put up with the lack of such a necessity an hour longer."

Hill showed Smith his iron tubs. The ever-thoughtful husband selected the cheapest model, haggling the ironmonger down to under £2. The bath was delivered on credit that night.

On July 10, the husband and wife paid a surprise call on a Dr. French in Herne Bay, Smith explaining that his cherished one had "suffered some sort of fit." French, thinking Smith meant epilepsy, asked some leading questions, to which Smith, not his wife, replied to the affirmative. "Yes, epileptic fit, that sounds like it," concluded Smith.

Bessie who appeared to Dr. French to be in a drowsy state said: "I don't remember anything so serious. I've always been healthy, but if Mr. Williams says I have had a fit then it must have come and gone outside my consciousness. I *do* remember a headache."

French gave her a bromide and sent the couple home. Two days later, a little past midnight, Smith frantically rang the door to Dr. French's clinic. "My wife has had another fit," Smith told the physician. "Please come at once."

When they reached the William's cottage, Dr. French found Bessie sitting up in bed. It had been a stiffling day. She complained of the heat. She was hot and flushed, that was all. "Keep her quiet," the doctor whispered to Smith. "I can only assume that the intense heat of the day has provoked another epileptic fit." He promised to return later that day, and when he visited Bessie at 3 p.m., Dr. French found Mrs. Williams in astoundingly good health. She felt wonderful, Bessie told him, though she was deeply concerned "about these fits I don't seem to remember." When Dr. French left, Bessie wrote briefly to her uncle a letter, which her dutiful husband was kind enough to get into the mails only minutes after she sealed the envelope. It read in part: "Last Tuesday night I had a bad fit...My whole system is shaken. My husband has provided me with the best medical men, who are...attending me day and night. I have made my will and left all to my husband. That is only natural as I love my husband."

At 7 a.m. on July 13, Smith woke his wife gently from her night's reveries. "I've prepared a nice, hot bath for you, dearest." Bessie rubbed sleep from her eyes with a smile of gratitude. The iron tub, which lacked taps and fittings, and had to be filled and emptied with a bucket, had been placed by Smith in a room without a lock on the door. Bessie entered the room, shed her nightie, and slipped into the tepid water and oblivion. An hour later, Dr. French was handed a note by a schoolboy running an errand for Mr. Williams, who asked in a frantic scrawl: "Can you come at once? I'm afraid my wife is dead."

In minutes, Dr. French was peering down at the naked, cold body of Bessie Mundy Williams, lying on her back in the bathtub, her head submerged, her long legs stretched out stiff, her feet over the end of the tub. In her right hand she clutched a square piece of Castile soap.

French lifted the corpse from the tub, placing it on the floor, trying vainly at artificial respiration. It was no use. The woman was dead. "Where were you, Mr. Williams, when this dreadful thing happened?" quizzed the doctor.

Smith, who had never shown a second's emotion to anyone until that moment, burst into tears, explaining between sobs: "I went out...to fetch some herrings...for our breakfast...When I returned...I found my sweetheart...dead!"

Ordering Smith to sit in the next room and compose himself, Dr. French went for the coroner. A moment later, Smith was himself in the street calling a policeman and a woman neighbor. Through heaving sobs he led the pair into his house and upstairs, pointing at the naked body on the bathroom floor. The policeman thought him temporarily deranged. The woman fainted.

Mrs. Rapley appeared, horrified at the sight. Smith's sorrow was blatantly heaped upon the landlady, though he did manage to murmur: "Lucky thing my wife made her will."

When the coroner arrived, accompanied by Dr. French, the official asked only a few perfunctory questions. He was informed by the doctor that he had treated the poor Mrs.Williams for epilepsy. A hastily convened coroner's jury, acting on Dr. French's statements, so carefully engineered by the plotting Smith, concluded that Bessie's demise was wholly accidental, an epileptic seizure causing her to drown in her bath. Though Herbert Mundy and other family members protested, wagging fingers in Smith's direction, the coroner and his jury refused to be budged. None of the jury members ever asked themselves how such a tall woman could have drowned in such a small bathtub.

Smith haggled with the undertaker, whittling down his price on his cheapest coffin for his dear departed, and ordered the most inexpensive funeral available. He sent only one short note to Bessie's relatives: "Words cannot describe the great shock, and I am naturally too sad to write more." Two hours after burying his bride, Smith appeared in the ironmonger's store, lugging the lethal bathtub. "This thing is no good," he informed Hill. "It killed my wife." He refused to pay for the iron tub, leaving it in the middle of the floor, and going out with a raging slam of the shop door.

Smith immediately began to wage legal war to obtain his wife's estate from her relatives. The Mundy family entered a caveat against the will but when the family lawyer pointed out the decision of the coroner's jury, and Smith's roaring threats to sue the entire family, the Mundys gave in. Smith was given more than £2,000. He then disappeared.

In late August 1912, George Joseph Smith reappeared at the doorstep of Edith Pegler Smith, the wife that thought him a salesman who traveled the world. He explained that he had been in Canada. When she questioned him about the huge amounts of money he was carrying, Smith gave her a benign smile, saying: "Ah, sweet wife. Fortune stroked the back of my neck. I found an ancient jade idol, and made more than £1,000 on the sale of the Chinese statue. It was a beautiful thing. I hated to part with it, but we must live, my dear, we must live."

But Edith Pegler Smith did not share in this newly acquired wealth. Other than some of Bessie Mundy's stolen clothes, she received only a pittance from her husband with which to purchase necessities. Smith thought of himself as a shrewd businessman; he invested Bessie's estate in the purchase of ten small houses in Bristol, dizzying himself in an orgy of deeds, titles, transfer certificates, ledgers, rents, and receipts, attempting to build a great fortune on Bessie Mundy's stolen money. After many months Smith had succceded in losing more than £700. It was time to return to his most rewarding profession. Smith again went carousing among the resort towns, meeting Alice Burnham, a fat 26-year-old nurse in Southsea in late October 1913. His courtly manners and quiet advances soon had the fun-loving nurse crazy for him. Alice took Smith to see her parents in Aston Clinton. He readily accompanied her after learning that, although she herself only possessed £27, her father was holding another £100 for her.

The father, Charles Burnham, a retired coal merchant, took an instant dislike to Smith, later stating that he had "a very evil appearance," and that he "could not sleep while Smith was in the house." Burnham finally asked Smith to leave his home. The distraught Alice went with Smith to the train station on Oct. 31, 1913, feeling her lover persecuted by her family, which was exactly what Smith wanted her to feel. They were married on Nov. 4 in Portsmouth with none of Alice's family members attending. On Dec. 10, Smith and Alice appeared at a boarding house run by a Mrs. Marden in Blackpool, a distant resort. They were shown all the available rooms but Smith, who had married Alice under his real name, sneeringly refused the accomodations. (His confidence had been strengthened by his successful murder of Bessie Mundy; in fact, he was almost blase now about hiding his identity.)

"None of it will do," Smith told Mrs. Marden. "We are civilized people—you have no baths."

The couple finally found rooms with a bath at Mrs. Crossley's boarding house on Regent's Road. Smith had already insured his wife's life for £500, making himself the sole beneficiary. He had also unleashed a torrent of quasi-legal terms and sharp invective, accusing Charles Burnham of "taking refuge in obdurateness, contempt and remorse," and promising that he, Smith, would "take the matter up without delay" through his lawyers. He advised in another letter that "I am keeping all letters that pass for the purpose of justice." In still another letter he boldly threatened: "I do not know your next move, but take my advice and be careful!" Burnham, fearing a protracted and expensive lawsuit, gave in and sent Alice's savings to Smith who had already set in motion the final stage of his "investment scheme" in Alice Burnham Smith.

The ever-solicitous Smith asked Mrs. Crossley if she could recommend a good doctor. "My wife suffers from severe headaches," he told the woman. The landlady suggested they see Dr. George Billing, who examined Alice a short time later. The physician thought he detected slight heart murmurs. He prescribed a mixture of caffeine and heroin. The couple then went on a long walk. That night, at 6 p.m., Mrs. Smith asked Mrs. Crossley to prepare a bath for her.

Two hours later, while the Crossleys sat at the kitchen table, family members looked up to see a huge stain of water on the ceiling which was dripping onto their dinners. "Go and tell Mrs. Smith not to fill the bath so," Mrs. Crossley instructed her oldest daughter.

The girl started to leave the room, then turned, saying: "Oh, mother, they will think we are grumbling already, and they are not two days in the house."

Suddenly Smith appeared at the kitchen, placing a package on the table. "I have brought these eggs for our breakfast." He had earlier insisted that Mrs. Crossley prepare their meals, complaining that his wife was a "terrible cook."

Mrs. Crossley pointed to the stain on the ceiling. Smith rushed out and ran up the stairs to his rooms. In a moment he yelled downstairs to the landlady: "My wife will not speak to me!"

"What is it?"

"Get a doctor—get Dr. Billing! He knows her! Hurry!"

When Billing arrived he found Smith in the bathroom, holding his wife's head above high water which covered the rest of her body. Both men struggled to lift the heavy woman from the bath. Dr. Billing could not revive Alice Smith. He spent only a few minutes examining the body, but noted that no signs of violence were present. (Billing later testified that he could not recall whether Mrs. Smith's head was at the foot or head of the bathtub.) The coroner, who was involved with another death at the time, hurriedly arrived, signing a report that Mrs. Smith had suffered "heart failure in the bath. Accidental drowning."

An hour later, Smith stood speechless in Mrs. Crossley's kitchen. The landlady eyed him coldly. He made no signs of sorrow and this time he did not pretend to weep at the death of this bride. Smith's attitude was one of indifference. Mrs. Crossley became incensed with him.

"How dreadful! What an awful thing this is," she finally said to him, thinking him in shock and attempting to urge his emotions to the surface.

Smith was laconic: "I would not be surprised at anything that might happen now."

"What kind of remark is that with your wife lying dead upstairs?"

The husband merely shrugged.

"Now, Smith," Mrs. Crossley said then, "you cannot stay here tonight."

"Why?"

"Because I'll take good care not to have a callous fellow like you in the house."

Smith slowly headed for his rooms to gather up his single brown suitcase. He stopped in the doorway, turning to Mrs. Crossley. "When they're dead, they're dead," he told her matter-of-factly.

That night, Smith stayed in the house next door, writing long letters to his insurance company, putting in the claim for the £500 on his wife's life.

A coroner's jury rendered a verdict of accidental death in the case of Mrs. Alice Smith. Obtaining the insurance money, Smith left Blackpool, but not before leaving a postcard with Mrs. Crossley on which he had written his new address, a bogus address, of course. Mrs. Crossley kept the card, cryptically writing on it: "Wife died in bath. I shall see him again some day."

Again, the world-weary traveling salesman returned to Edith Pegler Smith in Bristol. Again he explained his new riches as the result of some successful sales in Canada.

Not until the following year, in September 1914, could Smith's insidious activities be again known. In that month he hastily wed one Alice Reavil in Woolwich. He did not bother to go through the motions of his bath routine. After discovering that his spinster bride could not be insured because of ill health, he stole the woman's entire wardrobe, leaving her with only the clothes on her back and returned to his wife in Bristol, to whom he gave the clothes as a not-too-welcome gift.

Three months later, Smith, again rooting through the lovelorn ruins of the resort town of Clifton, encountered Margaret Elizabeth Lofty, thirty-eight, daughter of a clergyman, a companion to the elderly by profession, once engaged, now broken-hearted after learning that her previous lover had been a married man. She was a wounded gazelle to the panther-like Smith, who introduced himself as John Lloyd, a real estate broker from Holloway

Smith's hasty proposal to the love-starved Miss Lofty was clutched as one would a lifeline in a swirling sea. At Smith-Lloyd's suggestion, the couple took a train to Bath, in Bristol–the selection of the town was undoubtedly Smith's grim little private joke–and were married on Dec. 17, 1914, but not before Smith had insured his wife's life for £700 with the Yorkshire Insurance Company in Bristol.

Immediately following the wedding ceremony, the couple withdrew all of Lofty's savings from her Muswell Hill bank, a total of £20. With this paltry sum they took a train to London. This time Smith wasted no time with his new bride; he would dispose of this new "business" in less than forty-eight hours.

On the afternoon of Dec. 17, Smith appeared at a boarding house on Orchard Road, Highgate, London. Miss Lokker, the proprietor, became alarmed by Smith's manner when he insisted on personally inspecting the bathroom in the rooms he had reserved in advance. He got on his knees, spreading his arms to determine the length of the tub. "It's rather small, isn't it?" Smith reproached the landlady. "I guess someone *could* lie down in it."

Returning downstairs to the reception desk, Miss Lokker timidly asked for Smith's references.

"There's a war on," Smith told her, knowing she was of German ancestry and that, since the outbreak of WWI in recent months, Germans, including herself, had been the subject of abuse and threats. "Persons like you shouldn't make demands of loyal British subjects." He perceived the worry on her face, then contemptuously threw down six shillings on the desk. "Here are my references. I'll return shortly."

Before Smith came back, Miss Lokker called a friendly police officer, Detective Sergeant Dennison. Her new roomer acted queerly, made her nervous, she explained to Dennison. He would handle the situation, the policeman assured her. A half hour later Smith appeared.

Dennison shoved the battered brown suitcase Smith had left toward him, at the same time handing him back his deposit. "There are no rooms here. The place is full up."

"What?" roared Smith, his sharp eyes glaring at the plain-clothesman. "I booked these rooms in advance! Explain yourself! I demand a reason for being turned away!"

Dennison began to gently push Smith out the front door. "You are unable to furnish references, and I am acting on behalf of the landlady. That is an end to the matter."

Pathetically, Smith stood at the entranceway, red-faced, clutching his suitcase. "But I have a banker and plenty of money!"

Dennison slammed the door in his face.

Only a few hours later, Smith and his bride showed up at Mrs. Blatch's rooming house at 14 Bismarck Road, where, after Smith made a point of inspecting the bath—"that will do nicely"—the newlyweds rented a sitting room, bedroom, and bath.

Smith's procedure was the same as it had been with his earlier victims. The wife was not well. She asked the landlady if she could suggest a good doctor. A quick trip was made to a Dr. Bates, who found the woman lethargic and "feverish." The husband did all the talking. Perhaps his bride was subject to fits? Perhaps, but Dr. Bates prescribed only a mild sedative. Once again in their rooms, the considerate husband knew just the thing to settle his wife's nerves–a long, hot bath.

Mrs. Blatch drew the bath for Mrs. Lloyd at 7:30 p.m. on Dec. 18, 1914. Minutes later, the landlady heard a faint splashing of water in the tub. Then came the sound of the melodeon in the living room; Mrs. Blatch thought Mr. Lloyd was playing it. Next the front doorbell rang. Mr. Lloyd was outside, explaining that he had forgotten his key. He held up a brown bag. "I've brought some tomatoes for Mrs. Lloyd's dinner." (With Bessie Mundy it had been herrings, with Alice Burnham it was eggs.)

Smith put down the sack of tomatoes, glancing about the living room. "What? My wife isn't down from her bath yet?"

Mrs. Blatch hadn't seen her. Smith suggested that they both fetch her. Going to the bathroom they found the room in darkness. Smith turned on the light. Mrs. Blatch screamed at the sight of Mrs. Lloyd's head submerged under the bath water. Smith yanked the woman out of the tub, pretending to revive her. Of course, it was no use. Dr. Bates was summoned. He quickly concluded that his patient of one day had died "due to asphyxia from drowning. Influenza, together with a hot bath, might have caused an attack of syncope."

Again, missing nothing, Smith called a constable from the streets to view the dead body. The officer was shocked to see the naked body of Mrs. Lloyd exposed on the bathroom floor. "In pity's name," the constable said to Smith, "get something and cover the poor creature. Don't leave her lying like this." Smith shrugged and slowly retrieved a blanket, throwing it over the body. For a bereaved husband, the constable later thought, his lack of outward grief was remarkable.

Following a hasty, cheap funeral, Smith disappeared from the Blatch rooming house, returning to his Bristol wife, Edith Smith. Now there was nothing left to do but collect the £700 of insurance money on Margaret Lofty's death. It was all so simple. Yet, the simplicity of Smith's murder was the very reason for his downfall. Smith had made the mistake most successful criminals make–he had grown comfortable in his *modus operandi. Repetition* would destroy him.

All through the month of January 1915, Smith, through his lawyer, W.T. Davies, badgered the Yorkshire Insurance Company for payment on Margaret's policy. During this time, Charles Burnham, who had never ceased believing Smith was the real cause of his daughter Alice's death, spotted an item published in the popular weekly, *News of the World,* which reported in detail the curious death of Margaret Lloyd, nee Lofty, describing her awkward drowning in a bathtub. Clipping this item to one about his daughter drowning in the same manner the year before, Burnham sent the notices to the police. Joseph Crossley, husband of the suspicious landlady in the Alice Burnham drowning, also noticed the item and sent in two reports of the similar drownings.

Scotland Yard assigned its best man to investigate. Detective Inspector Arthur Fowler Neil, in Kentish Town, was on the case at once. He inspected the bathroom where Margaret Lloyd has died. Measuring the small bathtub, he thought it impossible that a grown person could drown in such a tub. He and his men spread out along the resort towns, piecing together the Burnham and Lofty deaths. When he learned of Bessie Mundy's identical end in Herne Bay, and with descriptions of the three husbands in all the cases, Neil concluded that not only were Williams, Smith, and Lloyd one and the same man but that whomever this man might really be, he had committed murder.

A check of insurance firms revealed that Yorkshire had insured Mrs. Lloyd and was about to settle with Mr. Lloyd's lawyer, W.T. Davies. (Smith had turned over his wife's signed will to Davies only three hours before her death on Dec. 18, 1914.) Neil wasted no time, posting men outside Davies' London offices, watching for a man who had been described in minute detail by three revenge-seeking landladies. Neil had instructed the insurance firm to contact Davies, telling the lawyer they were about ready to pay on Margaret Lloyd's death; the detective knew that Davies would soon be approached by the ubiquitous Mr. Lloyd to collect.

Neil himself, along with two other detectives, was keeping Davies' office under surveillance on Feb. 1, 1915. At 12:30 p.m., Neil spotted a meticulously dressed gentleman walking down the street toward the lawyer's offices. The man hesitated twice, seeming to turn back. Finally, he walked up to the small building and entered. Neil was sure, from the descriptions of Lloyd–the slouching gait, the lean-eyed look, jutting jaw, and peaked nose which seemed to be sniffing for dangerous odors–that he had spotted his man. When the darkly dressed stranger emerged from Davies' offices an hour later, Neil watched him light a cigarette and begin to walk off. Neil and his two men, Page and Reid, moved in on him, crossing the street, and walking along with the man on either side of him. Neil suddenly darted in front of him, blocking his path. The other two men stood so close to him that their coats brushed up against his.

"I am Detective Inspector Neil. Are you John Lloyd?"

Smith's manner was nerveless. "Yes, I am."

"The same John Lloyd whose wife was drowned in a bath on the night of December 18, at Bismarck Road, Highgate?"

"Yes, that's me."

"From my investigation, I have reason to believe you are identical with George Smith, whose wife was found drowned in a bath three weeks after marriage in 1913, at Blackpool. You married Miss Lofty, your last bride, at Bath, Bristol, in the name of Lloyd."

Smith was still unperturbed, giving the detective back his own stare. "Yes, that is so," he said slowly, his large, sensual mouth moving from side to side, "but that doesn't prove that my name is Smith." His normally sallow complexion then seemed to flush red. Suddenly he exploded: "Smith! I don't know the name of Smith! My name's not Smith!"

Neil studied the man for some moments; he later concluded that Smith, from his washed-out appearance, was the "sort of fellow a decent man would at once shun as unlikable." Neil was convinced Smith was a murderer, and even though he had no evidence pointing to that conviction, he was determined not to let this most evasive man slip from his grasp. "Very well," said the detective, "I am going to detain you for making a false attestation on oath to a Registrar."

This minor charge jarred Smith into blurting: "Oh, if that's what you're making all the fuss over, I may as well tell you, I am Smith."

"You admit that fact, then?"

"Certainly! My wife died at Blackpool in 1913. But that's only coincidence. It's a man's bad luck! It's the only charge you can prove against me." Smith gave Neil a thin sneer. "Clever as you think you are, Mr. Neil."

The officer thought he saw a dark menace in the man's eyes. Neil could not resist telling Smith: "Yes! And there may be charges of murder against you!"

"You're bloody well mad! You don't know what you're talking about!"

Neil ordered Smith taken away and locked up on a charge of perjury in giving an alias at his marriage with Margaret Lofty. A short time later, the charge of bigamy was added. The charge of murder was withheld. Neil, with the help of the celebrated pathologist Sir Bernard Spilsbury, attempted to discover exactly how Smith had managed to drown at least three of his victims, making all the deaths appear as accidents. The bodies of Bessie Mundy, Alice Burnham, and Margaret Lofty were exhumed and carefully examined by Spilsbury. He found no signs of violence on any of the corpses, and had to admit that they had all died by drowning.

Had Smith attempted to force any of the women's heads under water there would have been a violent struggle that would have left tell-tale marks on the bodies, Spilsbury and Neil concluded. And the tubs were so small that any other method of murder was inconceivable. G.J. Smith, it appears, *had* baffled the forensic authorities, and would be acquitted for lack of evidence, let alone the absence of any eyewitnesses or confession.

Then Neil had the idea of reenacting the bathtub scenes, using women who were professional swimmers. He positioned these women in several ways inside the very murder tubs, employing females who were the same height and weight as the victims. Yet there seemed to be no way in which he could, without struggle, keep the women submerged. Standing at the foot of the tub, Neil looked over the swimmer sitting in the water which filled the tub to three-quarters. In a flash, the idea came to him. He suddenly grabbed the woman by the ankles, lifting her feet high into the air. She slipped beneath the water, her head wholly submerged. She had been made helpless; the quick lifting of her legs forced her arms, which would have normally gripped the sides of the tub, to slide backward and be rendered useless.

Though the woman had been under water for only a few seconds, when Neil released his hold, the woman remained beneath the water, unconscious. He and Spilsbury quickly lifted her from the bath and, for a terrible half-hour of fright, worked on the swimmer with artificial respiration and restoratives. She finally came around, explaining to the officials that when her legs were lifted into the air and her head slid under the water, her nostrils and mouth were immediately filled with water and she blacked out. This, then, Neil and Spilsbury triumphantly realized, was the method Smith had employed to kill his "Brides of the Bath," as the press later dubbed the victims. The sudden flow of water into mouth and nostrils caused shock and unconsciousness, Spilsbury later explained in court, but how the inventive Mr. Smith stumbled upon this unique murder method is not known to this day.

Smith was charged with murder, though he stoutly denied any guilt. The case against him was circumstantial but overwhelming. Neil and his detectives had taken more than two thousand statements, the most ever known in any criminal case in England to that time. These, plus mounds of documents, including Smith's own copious and incriminating ledgers, were placed on exhibit in a courtroom of the Old Bailey, where Smith was tried for nine days, between June 22 and July 1, 1915.

"Never before had the venerable old structure been so thronged with women," Jurgen Thorwald was to write in *The Century of the Detective*. "They came by the hundreds–the lonely woman, the physically and mentally deprived, the woman hungering for love– women of the type Smith had chosen for his victims."

Smith stood handsome and collected in the dock. Justice Scrutton presided, while Sir Archibald Bodkin prosecuted and Sir Edward Marshall Hall defended. When the judge cautioned the jury that they were about to hear a murder case, Smith exploded, interrupting the judge with a scream that such a charge was "a disgrace to a Christian country!" He then added in a wounded tone: "I may be a bit peculiar but I am certainly no murderer!"

The testimony of 112 witnesses damned Smith day after day, including the angry statements of the landladies in whose houses he had committed his murders. His first wife, the reformed sneak thief Caroline Thornhill, even returned from Canada to testify against him. His wife in Bristol, Edith Pegler Smith, also testified, trying feebly to help her husband, but her statements only brought more suspicion down on Smith, particularly when she recalled her husband warning her against the use of bathtubs! "I should advise you to be careful of those things," Edith remembered Smith saying to her just before the murder of Margaret Lofty, "as it is known that women often lose their lives through weak hearts and fainting in a bath."

Smith said little in his own behalf, merely shaking his head and saying that the three *known* deaths were all "phenomenal coincidences." His defense counsel, Edward Marshall Hall, could offer only thin rebuttal and wild speculation. He reminded the jury of the statements of the doctors who had examined the three women before their deaths, that all had been in seemingly dazed conditions. His theory was that Smith never had to enter the bathrooms and that the brides drowned themselves as a result of being hypnotized by his client! Theories on drugs and poisonous vapors in the tub waters were also put forth.

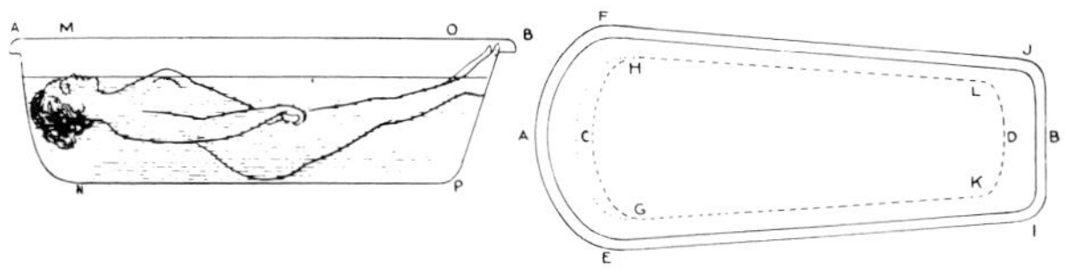

Diagram showing how Smith murdered his wives.

Then Inspector Neil demonstrated before the jury as to the real method used by Smith to kill his wives by simply yanking their legs high into the air. At the end of the demonstration, the jury gasped open-mouthed. Smith clutched the wooden rail of the dock so tightly that his knuckles went white. He yelled in uncontrollable fury: "That man's a villain!" He shook his fist in Neil's direction. "He ought to be in the dock with me now!"

The jury took only twenty-three minutes to return a verdict of Guilty. Smith was sentenced to death. His appeal was denied. In the early hours of Aug. 13, 1915, Smith sat in his cell at Maidstone Jail, listening to a strange hum of human voices. "Outside the wall," wrote Edmund Pearson in *Murder at Smutty Nose,* "a crowd had collected, many of them women–and the loud chatter of women's voices reached the inside of the prison."

At 8 a.m., Smith was taken from his cell. He refused to make any kind of confession. He began to stagger on his walk into the courtyard and toward the gallows. When he saw the scaffold, his legs failed, and he had to be helped up the stairs. His arms were tied, a bag was put about his head, the heavy rope lowered around his neck. A few seconds before the trap was sprung, George Joseph Smith experienced an emotion he had never allowed his "Brides of Bath."

His solemn, low words, heard at the last by the executioner, came from beneath the dark hood: "I am in terror!"

REF.: Arthur, *All the Sinners;* Balchin, *The Anatomy of Villainy;* Barker, *Lord Darling's Famous Cases;* Bechhofer-Roberts, *Sir Travers Humphreys, His Career and Cases;* Boar, *The World's Most Infamous Murders;* Bolitho, *Murder for Profit;* Bowen-Rowlands, *In the Light of the Law;* Bowker, *Behind the Bar;* Brock, *A Casebook of Crime;* Brooke, *Murder in Fact and Fiction;* Brophy, *The Meaning of Murder;* Browne and Tullett, *The Scalpel of Scotland Yard;* ____, *Sir Travers Humphreys;* Butler, *Murderer's England; CBA;* Crew, *The Old Bailey;* Deardon, *Death Under the Microscope;* Dickson, *Murder by Numbers;* Dilnot, *Great Detectives and Their Methods;* Douthwaite, *Mass Murder;* Graham, *Lord Darling and His Famous Trials;* Gribble, *Famous Manhunts;* Gross, *Masterpieces of Murder;* Hicks, *Not Guilty, M'Lord;* Higham, *The Adventures of Conan Doyle;* Hodge, *The Black Maria;* Humphreys, *A Book of Trials;* Hyde, *United in Crime;* Hynd, *Sleuths, Slayers and Swindlers;* Jackson, *The Portable Murder Book;* Keeton, *Guilty But Insane;* Kingston, *Enemies of Society;* Kobler, *Some Like It Gory;* La Bern, *The Life and Death of a Ladykiller;* Lambton, *Thou Shalt Do No Murder;* Lyons, *George Joseph Smith;* Marjoribanks, *For the Defense, The Life of Sir Edward Marshall Holls;* Moiseiwitsch, *Five Famous Trials;* Neil, *Manhunters of Scotland Yard;* Nordon, *Conan Doyle; Notable British Trials;* Randall, *The Famous Cases of Sir Bernard Spilsbury;* Scott, *The Concise Encyclopedia of Crime and Criminals;* Shew, *A Companion to Murder;* Thompson, *The Story of Scotland Yard;* Thorwald, *The Century of the Detective;* Townsend, *Black Cap: Murder Will Out;* Tullett, *Strictly Murder;* Warner-Hooke, *Marshall Hall;* Wensley, *Forty Years of Scotland Yard;* Wilson, *Encyclopedia of Murder;* Wood, *Shades of the Prison House;* Woodhall, *Secrets of Scotland Yard;* (DRAMA), Vosper, *Love from a Stranger;* (FICTION), Berkeley, *Murder in the Basement;* Carr, *The Sleeping Sphinx;* Christie, *Philomel Cottage;* Lowndes, *Jenny Newstead;* (FILM), *Shadow of a Doubt,* 1943.

Smith, George Robert, c.1949- , U.S., mur. The Church of Naturalism, Inc. in Hollywood Hills, Calif., began as a drug counseling center in Chicago in 1965. After alleged troubles with the police, the church moved to Los Angeles. On Nov. 6, 1982, the church's ex-security chief, George Robert Smith, thirty-two, secretly entered the four-and-a-half acre Laurel Canyon compound with his girlfriend, Melinda Gail Faulcon, twenty-five, former secretary of the Naturalism church. Smith wanted to take back some property that he said church founder George Peters, forty-three, and treasurer Patrick James Henneberry, thirty-one, had taken from him. Smith also wanted to confront them about a murder contract he believed they had taken out on his life. When Henneberry and Peters surprised Smith and Faulcon, they were murdered, their heads smashed in with an aluminum baseball bat and shot execution style through the head with a .357-magnum revolver that was church property. Smith and Faulcon then commandeered the church Cadillac limousine and crashed it through the gate to escape.

Although the Church of Naturalism was supposed to be a drug rehabilitation program, prosecutor Harvey Giss said, "in reality they were running a cocaine ring." Smith's work for the organization reportedly included making deliveries of cocaine for the church, which was incorporated for tax purposes. Faulcon was said to have been fired because she refused to have sex with Peters. Smith and Faulcon allegedly admitted the killings to friends the day of the crime. They were arrested about a month later and both pleaded guilty. Defense attorney Earl Hanson said Smith had been brainwashed by Peters and Henneberry and compared the church, which was about four miles from the scene of the 1969 murders by Charles Manson, to the Rev. Jim Jones' People's Temple. Smith was sentenced to two concurrent terms of twenty-seven years to life for first-degree murder. Faulcon was sentenced to two concurrent terms of four years for voluntary manslaughter. See: **Jones, James Warren; Manson, Charles.** REF.: *CBA.*

Smith, Gerrit, 1797-1875, U.S., consp. Agitated for prison reform, prohibition, and abolition of slavery. He also helped violent abolitionist John Brown and is alleged to have had information on his plans to raid Harper's Ferry, Va. REF.: *CBA.*

Smith, Gill, d.1738, Brit., mur. In March 1738, Gill Smith, once a successful English pharmacist, was condemned to die at the Surrey Assizes for killing his wife to collect on a £200 insurance policy. Smith spent his final days satisfying his hungry appetite and cracking jokes for all who would listen. When he learned that two fellow prisoners would be hanged with him, he jocularly noted, "Then there will be room to let here." REF.: *CBA.*

Smith, Grace M., prom. 1945, (wrong. convict.) U.S., mur. On Feb. 20, 1945, the lifeless body of WWII veteran Frank Smith was found in his Harrisonburg, Va., home, suspended from a rope. Blood stains spotted the house, but investigators found no sign of a struggle. By all appearances, Smith had committed suicide, yet the court found his wife, Grace M. Smith, and her alleged lover, Ralph H. Garner, guilty of murder. Grace Smith was sentenced to twenty years in prison. A year and a half later, however, her case was brought back on appeal.

The Virginia Supreme Court of Appeals determined that Grace Smith's original conviction was based on speculation not supported by evidence. This conviction was based on evidence that Grace Smith and her husband fought over her alleged affairs with other men during Frank Smith's absence while serving in the Army. Eventually the Commonwealth of Virginia admitted that Grace Smith alone could not have murdered her husband, dragged him to the basement, and hoisted his heavy body onto the foot stool where it was discovered. The Virginia Supreme Court of Appeals found that together she and Garner may have committed a murder, but that the evidence was in no way conclusive. Furthermore, the Appeals Court ruled that the Lower Court had failed to prove that there was a fight in which Frank Smith was subdued before being carried to the basement. In fact, the only thing that could be proven from the evidence was that Grace Smith was in the house when her husband died. After she had served more than one year of her sentence, her conviction was reversed on Nov. 25, 1946. REF.: *CBA*.

Smith, Henry Sydney, c.1919 Case of, Brit., mur. In court, he was quoted as saying: "I can remember standing up in bed as a child saying, "I will kill that man." On the night of Apr. 22, 1937, Henry Sidney Smith killed his father.

The elder Smith, Sydney Joseph Smith, fifty-six, was a violent alcoholic. When drinking, his evil temper flared and he would abuse his wife. Even as a child, Henry Smith was his mother's constant protector and emotional support. When his father returned home drunk one evening and began yelling obsenities at his mother, threatening to kill her, Henry hit his father over the head with a glass milk bottle and stabbed him with a knife until he was dead.

Jurors reached their verdict after Presiding Justice MacNaghten explained to them that if they were satisfied that Henry had killed his father because he believed his mother's life was in imminent danger, they should find him not guilty. Despite the fact that Smith admitted to the murder and seemed to be glad he had gone through with it, the jury not only found him Not Guilty, but courtroom observers applauded their decision.

REF.: Browne and Tullett, *Sir Bernard Spilsbury: His Life and Cases; CBA;* Shew, *A Second Companion to Murder.*

Smith, Jack, d.1890, U.S., west. gunman. An outlaw who served time in the Colorado penitentiary in 1880, Jack Smith, not long after his release, pistol-whipped a former lawman named Barrett in White Pine, and afterward escaped to Cripple Creek. In late October 1880 near Gunnison, Colo., Tom Lewis and Smith left the White Pine mining camp and began to drink excessively. Meeting lawmen escorting a counterfeiter on the road, Smith and Lewis arbitrarily decided to release the prisoner and hold the officers at gunpoint, after which they rode into town and started shooting randomly in the streets. A passerby was wounded and the two outlaws rode out of town with twenty men chasing them. During a running fight they escaped but were captured the next day in Lake City.

In 1890 in Cripple Creek, Colo., Smith led protestors against authorities in the Bull Hill War, during which there were riots, murders, and the destruction of mines. When one of Smith's men was arrested, Smith marched to the town jail and started shooting at the locks on cells. The city marshal moved in and began firing, mortally wounding Smith.

REF.: *CBA;* Rockwell, *Memoirs of a Lawman.*

Smith, James, See: **Brady, Patrick**.

Smith, James Francis, 1859-1928, U.S., jur. Served as associate justice on supreme court of Philippines from 1901-03, and as governor general of Philippines from 1906-09. He also served as associate justice on the U.S. Court of Customs Appeals from 1910-28. REF.: *CBA*.

Smith, Dr. **James Monroe**, b.c.1886, U.S., embez.-tax evas. James Monroe Smith's friendship with Louisiana governor Huey Long was tragic. Though by all outward appearances it looked as though they were pals in prosperity, they were, in fact, comrades in crime. In November 1930, Long appointed Smith president of Louisiana State University (LSU) in an attempt to get revenge on rival Tulane University for its refusal to award Long an honorary degree when he was elected governor. Together, Long and Smith accomplished this by creating a powerful LSU football team, using scouts instructed to spare no expense in coercing, bribing, and deceiving the country's best high school athletes to play for LSU. Scouts also guaranteed prime recruits university degrees regardless of their academic performance. To compliment their new team, the men assembled the largest college band in the country upon Long's instructions to Smith to count the pieces in the nation's current largest band and add ten to that total.

In 1932, Long was elected to the U.S. Senate and came under investigation for his involvement in a $100 million public building program that he had profited from and failed to mention on income tax returns. The investigation eventually rounded up 149 of Long's cronies and collected $6 million in unpaid taxes. Long himself never served time for the federal violation, as he was assassinated in 1935.

Smith spent the four years following Long's death scrambling for money, and the fifth year explaining his actions. Two special intelligence agents posing as LSU students and investigating the president, learned that he had increased his own salary by writing fictitious minutes from a non-existent board meeting. They also discovered that a $1 million worth of LSU bonds had been stolen from university offices and safety deposit boxes. Smith used the bonds as collateral at brokerage houses for wheat dealings and as collateral at banks for cash loans. The agents learned that he violated Federal income tax statutes after failing to pay taxes on $45,000, the extra padding he had placed around his salary, in 1936.

In June 1939, Smith resigned as president of LSU and fled to Canada with $500,000 of taxpayers' money. He was extradited back to Louisiana where he pleaded guilty to charges of income tax evasion and embezzlement and was sentenced to the Louisiana State Prison in Angela for eight to twenty-four years. See: **Long, Huey**. REF.: *CBA*.

Smith, Jefferson Randolph (AKA: **Soapy Smith**), 1860-98, U.S., fraud. Jefferson Smith, the foremost practitioner of the "soap trick," was a product of the ruined post-Civil War South. Born in Georgia, Smith passed through the difficult Reconstruction period with a firm resolve to escape the ravages of his war-torn homeland. He moved to San Antonio, Texas, where he found work as a cowboy. Moving from town to town Smith ingratiated himself with card sharps, two-bit hustlers, and monte players who plied their trade in the western saloons and concert halls. In the process he earned a reputation as a shrewd, thimble-rigging con-man whose best known fraud was the pea-in-the-shell routine.

Joining a well-known swindler named Taylor, Smith earned himself the famous sobriquet he would take with him to his grave. He would construct a carnival barker's stand in the middle of the town, and then gather the local rubes in a circle. The lure would be soap—lots of it. Inside some of these plain looking cakes of soap, Taylor drawled, was tucked a $20 bill. Smith, posing as the ringer, stepped forward to pick up the only $20 soap brick in the batch. Holding the bill up in the air, Smith would encourage others to share his good fortune. The yokels would obligingly rush forward to buy a bar of soap, devoid of the $20 of course, for a sum of money ten times the normal store price.

Leadville, Colo., was an untamed frontier town dear to "Soapy's" heart. Once he sponsored a foot race between two naked prostitutes who dashed along Main Street for a quart of bonded whiskey. The residents applauded wildly; even more so when Soapy ordered the arrest of a man who had spent the day in prayer and quiet meditation. In 1892, he opened the New Orleans Club in Creede, Colo., providing silver miners with whiskey, girls, and round-the-clock gambling. Those who questioned the honesty of the game—there was little doubt that the outcome was rigged to favor the house—often found themselves staring down the barrel of Smith's gun. The conman ruled with impunity. He owned the local politicians and carried out his business as he saw fit.

When the silver boom played itself out in Colorado, Smith moved on to the Alaska gold fields where he opened a telegraph office for lonesome miners desiring to send messages back home. A telegram cost $5 but few noticed that the roof of the shack was devoid of connecting wires. In Skagway, Smith and his partner, Wilson Mizner, opened Jeff's Place. It stood at the crossroads of the booming gold fields, providing the miners with the only entertainment in the barren wilderness. In time Soapy Smith became the undisputed "King of Skagway," dispensing frontier justice through a band of armed thugs who made sure that a steady flow of cash found its way into the gang's coffers. A local minister who desired to cleanse the town of its sinful ways collected $36,000 from prospectors and other respectable people. The parson explained that Soapy himself backed such an effort.

At day's end the minister had collected his money in three large sacks. Smith's guards took the cumbersome parcels, providing "safekeeping" and gave the minister $1,000. "Thirty-six for one is pretty good odds!" Smith roared. Reform carried with it a price.

The short, spectacular reign of Jefferson Randolph Smith ended in July 1898 at age thirty eight. After leading the annual Skagway Independence Day parade, Smith repaired to his saloon to continue the celebration. A short time later he was met by a vigilante group known as the Committee of 101. They demanded from him some assurance that he was going to reform. When the promise was not forthcoming they shot him down in the saloon. Soapy Smith was buried with honors. Three shells and a pea were placed on the coffin after he was lowered into the ground.

REF.: Allan, *Gold, Men and Dogs;* American Guide Series, *Colorado, A Guide to the Highest State;* Andrews, *The Story of Alaska;* Asbury, *Sucker's Progress;* Bankson, *The Klondike Nugget;* Bartholomew, *The Biographical Album of Western Gunfighters;* ____, *Western Hard-Cases;* Beattie, *Brother, Here's A Man!;* Bennett, *Boom Town Boy in Old Creede, Colorado;* Berton, *Klondike;* _____, *The Klondike Fever;* Black, *You Can't Win;* Breihan, *The Day Jesse James Was Killed;* Buffum, *Smith of Bear City;* Burnham, *Scouting on Two Continents;* Carpenter, *Canada and New Foundland;* Casey, *The Texas Border;* Chafetz, *Play the Devil; CBA;* Clark, *History of Alaska;* Collier and Westrate, *The Reign of Soapy Smith;* Cushman, *The Great North Trail;* Davis, *Sourdough Gold;* ____, *Uncle Sam's Attic;* Davis, *The West From a Car Window;* Denison, *Klondike Mike;* Ellis, *Bonanza Towns;* ____, *Pioneers;* Fetherstonhaugh, *The Royal Canadian Mounted Police;* Fisher and Holmes, *Gold Rushes and Mining Camps;* Florin, *Ghost Town Album;* Frackelton, *Sagebrush Dentist;* Hamlin, *Hamlin's Tombstone Picture Gallery;* Haydon, *The Riders of the Plains;* Hendricks, *The Bad Man of the West;* Hinton and Godsell, *The Yukon;* Hitchcock, *Two Women in the Klondike;* Hunt and Draper, *To Colorado's Restless Ghosts;* Hurd, *Boggsville;* Johnston, *The Legendary Mizners;* Keith, *Sixguns By Keith;* Klein, *Grand Deception;* La Font, *Rugged Life in the Rockies;* Lavigne, *Crimes, Criminals and Detectives;* Longstreth, *The Silent Force;* Lucia, *Klondike Kate;* McKelvie, *The Fenceless Range;* Monroe, *San Juan Silver;* Morgan, *God's Loaded Dice;* Morgan, *Skid Road;* Mumey, *Creede;* Murbarger, *Sovereigns of the Sage;* Nash, *Bloodletters and Badmen;* ____, *Hustlers and Con Men;* Norvell, *Forty Years of Hardward;* O'Connor, *Bat Masterson;* ____, *High Jinks on the Klondike;* Parkhill, *The Wildest of the West;* Powell, *Trailing and Camping in Alaska;* Quiett, *Pay Dirt;* Rickard, *Through the Yukon and Alaska;* Sprague, *Money Mountain;* Steele, *Forty Years in Canada;* Sullivan, *The Fabulous Wilson Mizner;* Tompkins, *Alaska, Promyshlennik and Sourdough;* Trelawney-Ansell, *I Followed Gold;* Walden, *A Dog-Puncher on the Yukon;* Ward, *Bits of Silver;* Warman, *Frontier Stories;* Whiting, *Grit, Grief and Gold;* Williamson, *Far North Country;* Winslow, *Big Pan-Out.*

Smith, Jeremiah, 1759-1842, U.S., jur. Served as U.S. district attorney from 1797-1800. He was appointed to the first circuit court by President John Adams in 1801, and also served as chief justice of the supreme court of New Hampshire from 1802-09, and as New Hampshire governor from 1809-10. He returned to his chief justice post, serving from 1813-16. REF.: *CBA.*

Smith, Jerry Lee, prom. 1977, U.S., obsc.-porn. Individuals distributing obscene material through the U.S. mail are subject to a Federal ban even if the state where they are acting has more permissive standards. The Supreme Court made its decision on May 23, 1977, using Jerry Lee Smith's case. Smith had earlier been sentenced to three years in prison—two and one half of which were suspended—and three years' probation for mailing allegedly obscene films, issues of *Intrigue* magazine, and other pamphlets from Des Moines, Iowa, to Mount Ayr and Guthrie, Iowa. Smith appealed the decision to the U.S. Court of Appeals and finally to the Supreme Court following the Appeals Court decision to uphold his conviction. Supreme Court justice Harry A. Blackmun wrote the majority opinion in the five to four decision. In Federal prosecutions, the court ruled, community standards are matters for the jury, and the fact that the mailings were wholly within a state is irrelevant. Dissenting justices included William J. Brennan, Potter Stewart, Thurgood Marshall and John Paul Stevens. REF.: *CBA.*

Smith, Jerry Paul, 1947- , case of, U.S., riot.-mur. At a Communist Worker's Party "Death to the Klan" rally in the streets of Greensboro, N.C., on Nov. 3, 1979, five party members were killed when the Ku Klux Klan and neo-Nazis opened fire on them. Slain were James Waller, William Sampson, Cesar Vicente Cauce, and Sandra Smith. Dr. Michael Nathan died three days later of gunshot wounds. A sixth victim was confined to a wheelchair after being wounded. Along with several other Klansmen and Nazi supporters, Jerry Paul Smith came to Greensboro from his nearby home in the hills. A fight with sticks between the opposing groups soon escalated into a gun battle. A videotape of the murders showed Smith charging along the street carrying two large-caliber pistols. A club crashed against Cauce's skull, then Smith pumped bullets into the prone body before retreating down the street, covered by other armed Klansmen. Fourteen Klansmen, with an age range of sixteen years to sixty, were charged with murder. All were poorly educated and employed at marginal jobs. Of those murdered, two were medical doctors who had dedicated themselves to radical communist causes rather than to lucrative practices, one was a Harvard Divinity School graduate with a medical degree, another a magnum cum laude graduate of Duke University, and the last a graduate of a prestigious local college.

Charged along with Smith were Roland Wayne Wood, thirty-four, regional commander of the Nazi group, and Rayford Maynard Caudle, thirty-seven, a member of the paramilitary "Storm Troopers," a branch of the American Nazi Party. By the time the case went to trial four Klansmen and two Nazis were charged with the murders. The Klan defendants included Smith, thirty-three, Coleman Blair Pridmore, twenty-seven, Lawrence Gene Morgan, twenty-eight, and David Wayne Matthews, twenty-four. The two Nazi defendants were Jack Wilson Fowler, twenty-seven, and Wood. It was the first time videotapes were admitted as evidence in a North Carolina courtroom. On Nov. 17, 1980, after a ninety-six day trial, the longest in North Carolina history, all six men were acquitted by an all-white jury that had deliberated for seven days. According to defense attorney Robert Cahoon, "It was a case of self defense..." Defendants had said they only meant to "heckle the Communists." Prosecutors said the slayers had come armed and looking for a fight. Communist party members who participated in the rally refused to cooperate with state prosecutors or to testify at the trial, denouncing the proceedings as "a sham."

On Oct. 1, 1981, after a six-month investigation, the Institute for Southern Studies, based in Durham, N.C., determined that an "intimate alliance" had existed between the district attorney's office and police officials in Greensboro and the Klan and Nazi members charged in the slayings. The report criticized local prosecutors for approving jurors reportedly sympathetic to the defense and accused the U.S. Justice Department of inadequately pursuing civil rights violation charges against the assailants. The report stated that local police had been instructed to leave the vicinity when the caravan carrying the Klan and Nazi members moved in on the rally, and that police had "watched and photographed" the formation of the nine-car caravan of Klansmen.

In January 1984 the case was tried again in a Winston-Salem, N.C., courtroom, with District Court Judge Thomas A. Flannery barring the public and press from the proceedings. On April 15 an all-white jury acquitted six Klansmen and three American Nazi party members charged with the murders of the five Communists. Dale Sampson, widow of slain William Sampson, said, "This is a real go-ahead for the Klan and Nazis to kill people." REF.: *CBA.*

Smith, Jim (AKA: **Gipsy**), 1931- , Brit., mur. One thing was certain. Jim Smith, "Gipsy," played an active part in the death of police constable Leslie Meehan. What was not so clear was whether his role constituted murder, manslaughter, or just bad luck. After weeks of legal manuvering, the court found the 29-year-old Smith Guilty of murder on Apr. 7, 1960.

On Mar. 2, 1960, while Smith and George Artus were driving through Woolwich, England, with several stolen scaffolding clips, their car was stopped by Officer Meehan. When Meehan noticed the clips in the back seat of the car, Smith panicked and sped away. Meehan grabbed onto the car, and after being dragged 200 yards, fell off and was killed by a car traveling in the opposite direction. After removing the stolen metal scraps, Smith returned to the place where Meehan had been hit crying, "Is he dead? I know him. I wouldn't do it for the world. I only wanted to shake him off. I didn't mean to kill him."

According to English law at the time, a crime is murder not only when the killing was intended but also when intent to do bodily harm existed. The prosecuting attorney never suggested that Smith intended to kill Meehan, but maintained that Smith meant to cause bodily harm. The vague law was changed during Smith's case and was rewritten to include no distinction between a person who intends to kill and one who does not.

With this ruling, it no longer made any difference whether or not Smith intended to bring harm to Meehan. The fact was, he had, and he was found Guilty of capital murder and sentenced to death. This conviction was set aside upon appeal and replaced with a manslaughter conviction and a sentence of ten years in prison. An appeal to the House of Lords by the director of prosecutions restored the lower court's decision, but the Home Secretary commuted the sentence.

REF.: *CBA;* Furneaux, *Famous Criminal Cases, vol. 7.*

Smith, Jimmy Lee, c.1931- , U.S., drugs-mur. During his adult life, Jimmy Lee Smith has never spent a full year out of police custody. Raised by his great-aunt in Ft. Worth, Texas, Smith grew up during the Depression and in the 1940s moved to Skid Row in Los Angeles where he became a drug addict, shoplifter, and petty thief. While on parole in 1963, Smith joined forces with Gregory Ulas Powell and murdered Los Angeles policeman Ian James Campbell on Mar. 9. Plainclothes officers Campbell and Karl Hettinger were patrolling Hollywood when they chased after the car driven by Powell and Smith. When the officers pulled over the vehicle and approached it, they were confronted with a gun. Powell and Smith disarmed the pair, kidnapped them, and drove to an onion field in Bakersfield. In the field, Campbell was gunned down, but Hettinger managed to escape. The killers were soon apprehended and tried for murder.

Smith and Powell were sentenced to death for Campbell's brutal murder, chillingly recorded in the book *The Onion Field,* written by former police officer Joseph Wambaugh. The sentences were commuted to life in prison when California repealed capital punishment. In 1982, at fifty-one, Smith was paroled.

Four months later, Smith failed a test for drug use and was returned to prison for six months. Upon his release, he moved to Long Beach and worked at a cabinet shop to support the woman he had married while in prison. Smith managed to stay straight for eight more months until he returned to selling drugs. He flunked the routine twice-a-month drug test required of high-risk parolees and was back behind bars. In 1984, shortly after being released from his second sentence for parole violation, counselor Reverend Rex Burns set up a breakfast meeting with Smith and a possible employer. Smith was arrested in the restaurant parking lot for trying to sell drugs to an undercover police officer.

"Every time he's gotten out, he's become involved in some illegal activity and been incarcerated again," complained the judge who sent Smith to prison for five years following the drug arrest. After serving two years and four months, Smith was released in November 1986. His parole was revoked four months later for another six months because he changed his residence without telling authorities and was found carrying a knife. Not long after completing this latest sentence, Smith's parole was revoked for a year for possession of heroin and drug paraphernalia, and for driving under the influence of a drug, and without a license. Several months later, he returned to prison after allegedly making indecent sexual advances to a female co-worker. Those allegations were never proven, but on June 5, 1989, Smith was convicted of possessing heroin and, once again, returned to jail. "My wife and I made a prediction a month ago that he was setting himself up to go home, and 'home' to Jimmy is prison," the Reverend Burns said. REF.: *CBA.*

Smith, Joe, 1924-48, Brit., rob.-mur. The body of 71-year-old William Bissett was discovered in December 1947 lying in a shallow stream near Slough, England. Earlier that evening Bissett had been seen leaving a pub with 23-year-old Joe Smith. The following day, Smith's bloodstained pants were found in a shed lying rolled up in a crate. Buried nearby was a sack containing the dead man's overcoat, jacket and pants. Smith claimed innocence and gave police three conflicting stories that augmented their suspicions. After a medical examination of Bissett found that seven wounds to his head and chest had caused death, Smith was charged with the murder. Smith was found Guilty and, despite the jury's recommendation that he receive mercy from the court on the grounds of his "low mentality," the judge sentenced him to death on Mar. 3, 1948.

REF.: *CBA;* Heppenstall, *The Sex War and Others;* Simpson, *Forty Years of Murder;* Wilson, *Encyclopedia of Murder.*

Smith, John, See: **Beck, Adolph**.

Smith, John, 1580-1631, Brit., abduc. Assisted in development of colony at Jamestown, Va., in 1607, and served on governing council. He had been abducted by Indians and sentenced to die when, according to his own reports, he was saved by Pocahontas in 1607. He was held captive by the French in 1615 en route to a second exploration of the New England coast. REF.: *CBA.*

Smith, John (AKA: **Leicester Boy**), b.c.1602, Brit., witchcraft. Like many other accusers of witches, John Smith, the Leicester Boy, pretended to be bewitched or possessed by demons. His childish pranks accounted for the hanging of nine innocent women.

In 1607, at about the age of five, he charged a number of women with having bewitched him, but no convictions followed. By the time he was thirteen he was responsible for the convictions and hangings of nine women on July 18, 1616. The son of Sir Roger Smith claimed that the women afflicted him through their spirits. His paroxysms included beating himself on the chest and crying out like the animal he claimed was afflicting him.

John's mimicry convicted the women, but his fraud did not go unnoticed. While passing through Leicestershire on Aug. 15, 1616, King James I questioned the boy and grew suspicious of his story. The king had servants of the Archbishop Abbot of Canterbury investigate the matter, and one was on hand for the next trial of women accused by John of witchcraft. Of the six to be tried that October, one had since died in prison, and the remaining five were soon released. King James did not punish the magistrate Sir Humphrey Winch or others involved in the trial, though he did discredit their reputations, and allowed Ben Jonson to poke fun at them in his play *The Devil is an Ass.* REF.: *CBA.*

Smith, John (AKA: **Half-Hanged Smith**), prom. 1700s, Brit., rob. Robber John Smith survived hanging, and then narrowly escaped the gallows two more times. On Dec. 5, 1705, after his first exploit as a housebreaker, Smith was arraigned on four charges, then convicted on two. Although sentenced to death, the robber was confident that he would be reprieved through the influence of his friends. Smith's execution was ordered for Christmas Eve. On that day, he was taken to the execution place at Tyburn where he said his prayers and was hanged. He had been hanging for nearly fifteen minutes when a reprieve came through. He was cut down and soon recovered. Asked often to describe what it was like to be hanged, Smith explained that he had first felt terrible pain, and was intensely aware of his spirits being in a strange turmoil, as if they were pressing upward and forcing their way into his head. He then saw a great blaze of light that seemed to go out of his eyes in a flash, at which point he lost all sense of pain. After he was cut down, the blood rushed throughout his body and caused such pain that he began to wish he had not been rescued. After this bizarre experience, he was nicknamed Half-Hanged Smith.

Smith resumed his thievery, was arrested again, and tried at the Old Bailey for housebreaking. Through some irregularities in the trial, the jury brought in a special verdict. The twelve judges who decided the case ruled in favor of Smith. He was later indicted a third time, and again escaped the law when the

The execution of John Smith.

prosecutor died the day before the trial was to take place. The case against Smith was dropped.

REF.: Atholl, *Shadow of the Gallows; CBA;* Mitchell, *The Newgate Calendar;* Nash, *Almanac of World Crime;* Potter, *The Art of Hanging;* Wren, *Masterstrokes of Crime Detection.*

Smith, John, and **Biggs, Peter,** and **Stokely, John,** prom. 1847, U.S., rob. In 1847, Privates John Smith, John Stokely, and Peter Biggs, while serving with the U.S. Army in the war against Mexico, became the first men in Los Angeles to be tried and convicted for a civil offense under American law.

Smith was the ringleader of the three-member gang and the engineer of the 1847 robbery that ended with their convictions. ON Smith's instructions, Biggs located a trunk containing $640 in the thirty-one-room adobe Avila House, which served as military headquarters where he worked. Smith's plan required that Biggs find the key to unlock the trunk and then leave the room unlocked so he could later sneak in and steal the money. Smith hired Stokely to act as lookout when he entered the room on Aug. 3. The three were arrested two-and-a-half weeks later, on Aug. 20.

At their trial, Biggs testified that Smith had offered him a share of the take if he'd find an officer with money and tell him where it was kept. Biggs swore he didn't partake in the actual robbery, but named Stokely as an accomplice. In a letter, Smith confessed to the crime, begging for leniency, and maintaining that Biggs had initiated the crime by suggesting he could leave the trunk and room unlocked for Smith to later ransack. Stokely reported yet a different account of the incident. He claimed that Smith had Biggs unlock both the trunk and room and that all he had to do was steal the money. Stokely claimed that he never ventured farther than the door of the house because he was afraid of getting caught.

Smith and Stokely were convicted of robbery. Because the court determined that it was his idea, Smith would have been sentenced to five years' and Stokely to two years' imprisonment, except that California had no prison since the territory had yet to be granted statehood. New punishments handed down included dishonorable discharges, forfeiture of all pay and allowances, and five years at hard labor tied to a ball and chain. On Dec. 13, 1847, an explosion in the guard house killed Stokely, who had been chained to a log and was unable to escape. Smith was seriously wounded and rendered physically unable to work at hard labor. He was discharged and freed. Before his release, Biggs was given a public whipping and lived until the early years of the Civil War when a Mexican restaurateur stabbed him to death for advocating the right of any state to secede from the Union.

REF.: *CBA;* Wolf, *Fallen Angels.*

Smith, John Thomas (AKA: **Snowy Rowles**), d.1933, Aust., pris. esc.-mur. George Ritchie spoke to the men who worked for him in the wild Australian bush one night in 1930, quietly detailing the 'perfect murder.' "Supposing I wanted to do you in," he said softly. "I'd kid you into the bush a bit...I'd shoot you dead and burn your body...I'd go through the lot with a sieve, getting out every burnt bone...and toss out the dust for the wind to scatter." Ritchie detailed the gory scenario for the benefit of English novelist Arthur William Upfield, who sought the information for his latest thriller, but John Thomas Smith, alias "Snowy Rowles," was listening the closest; he would need the information for real life. In two years, three of the men huddled together that night would disappear, and one patch of ashes and bones would be discovered.

One morning in 1930, James Ryan, a short and stocky well-sinker, and young Lloyd, who had come from Adelaide looking for work, accompanied Smith to Mount Magnet. Neither Ryan nor Lloyd were ever seen again. By Dec. 31, 1930, police were searching for Louis J. Carron as well. Carron had set off into the outback with Smith in May 1930, telling his friend John Lemon that he would write regularly. After months passed without receiving word from his friend, Lemon convinced authorities to investigate. On Feb. 17, 1931, the search party discovered a well-burned fire, ash, bone, a gold ring, a gold dental band, a copper coin marked "1 cent Hong Kong 1904," and a .32-caliber cartridge case and bullet.

Authorities sought the man who had been calling himself Snowy Rowles only to find John Thomas Smith who was wanted for theft, escaping from prison, and now, murder. A search of his residence turned up two loaded .32-caliber Winchester rifles, three shirts, a wrist watch, a white-handled razor, a watch-chain, a pair of scissors, and a razor-hone. Rowles professed to know nothing of the items, but police were unconvinced. On his way to trial for breaking out of jail, Smith made a startling statement in which he unwittingly admitted his guilt of murder. "What a nice fix I'm in," he said. "I'm not worrying about the escape rap but the murder's a different thing. Anyway I'll never have to do the stretch as they'll fit me with the murder charge and I'll swing because I'll never get a reprieve. If they don't swing me I'll find a way to do it myself." During his trial, the items found in his possession were identified by witnesses as belonging to the missing men. Furthermore, Smith's rifles fired the same type of bullets found among the ashes and bones. On June 13, 1932, John Thomas Smith was hanged for murder.

REF.: *CBA;* Clegg, *Return Your Verdict.*

Smith, Joseph, 1805-44, U.S., mob. vio.-lynch. The history of the Mormon Church begins around the year 1819, when 14-year-old Joseph Smith experienced a religious revelation in the dense woods surrounding his home in Palmyra, N.Y. In 1827 he told of a similar encounter with an angel, who directed him to locate some buried golden plates that allegedly told of the early history of the American Indians—lineal descendants of the ancient Hebrews. According to legend, these Indians had come to the North American continent thousands of years earlier via the Pacific Ocean. Using two spiritual stones known as the Urim and

Thummim, Smith transcribed the *Book of Mormon,* which was published in 1830. The church founded on Apr. 6, 1830 was assailed by skeptics, who believed it to be just a curious blend of polygamy, anti-Masonic demagoguery, and strains of contemporary religious thought tempered by Smith's outlook on life.

The next decade witnessed a remarkable surge of growth in the Mormon Church. Smith attracted hundreds of converts from the eastern states who followed him on a cross-country odyssey to seek spiritual peace. They attempted to settle in Ohio but were driven out in 1832-33 after fearful townsmen burned down their homes and tarred and feathered the pilgrims. The polygamous practices of the Mormons inspired fear and loathing among mainstream Christians during the 1830s and 1840s. The religion was likened to witchcraft in many parts of the U.S., accounting for the acts of violence perpetrated against the Mormons. In 1838 they were driven out of Missouri, where the governor warned his constituents that "the Mormons must be treated as enemies and must be exterminated or driven from the state if necessary, for the public good."

At Haun's Mill on Oct. 30, 1838, eighteen Mormons were savagely killed, an event witnessed and recorded by Brigham Young's elder brother Joseph. A year later, Smith led his flock into western Illinois. They settled in Commerce, which the prophet renamed Nauvoo. With a population of 20,000, Nauvoo was the largest city in Illinois and the Mormons, through sheer strength of numbers, became a force in state politics. The Democrats and Whigs, both equally powerful in Illinois, courted their vote assiduously. As a result Nauvoo was granted a liberal charter by state politicians. "I concocted it," Smith said, "for the salvation of the church and on principles so broad that every honest man might dwell secure under its protective influence." Joseph Smith became the mayor of the burgeoning town, and commander of the Nauvoo Legion, a Mormon military company which was a part of the state militia.

Smith, who claimed to receive his divine inspirations from God himself, announced his candidacy for president in 1844. He was a forceful public speaker who was committed to the notion of "celestial marriage," which allowed his male followers to have many wives. Smith antagonized many of the residents of Nauvoo who did not share his belief in polygamy. Mass meetings were held in the town to protest the prophet's decision to close down the opposition newspaper, the *Expositor,* when it criticized the dictatorial powers Mayor Smith had been given. Smith ordered the *Expositor's* presses and plant destroyed, which led to its publishers swearing out a warrant against Smith on a charge of incitement to riot.

Believing that Nauvoo would soon be torn asunder by the non-believers and anti-Mormon agitators, Smith boldly called out the Nauvoo Legion in June 1844, which his political enemies regarded as a treasonous act. The militia of the village of Carthage, twenty miles from Nauvoo, prepared to do battle with the Legion. With open warfare in Illinois a real possibility, Smith was urged by his counselors to accede to their demands and surrender. Realizing that this meant certain death at the hands of their enemies, Joseph, his brother Hyrum, and a small body of Mormons crossed the Mississippi River and fled into Iowa on the night of June 22. The plan was to flee further West, but Smith's first wife Emma sent word to him, asking that he return and face his accusers. Having received assurances from Governor Thomas Ford that he would not be harmed, Smith decided to go to Carthage with brother Hyrum to stand trial on charges of treason.

They were overtaken on the road by Captain Dunn of the Carthage Greys and escorted back to Nauvoo, where Smith was required to surrender the warehouse of arms stocked by the Legion. This was done peaceably and without incident, after which the prophet and his brother were led back to Carthage. They were jailed in the town lockup on June 24.

The mood outside the jail was emotionally charged. A lynch mob was organized in the center of town. They stormed the jail on the night of June 27 and demanded that the Smith brothers be turned over. Very little was done to safeguard the lives of the two men. Hyrum was shot dead by someone in the crowd. Joseph Smith appeared at the window to appeal to God on high. "Oh Lord, my God, is there no help for the widow's son?" he cried. With that, a rifle bullet tore through his body.

Smith became a martyr to the Mormons, who had known nothing but persecution since the 1830s. They left Illinois for good about a year later. Brigham Young and his band of followers crossed the frozen Mississippi River and migrated to the Great Salt Lake, where they were to sample the first breath of religious freedom.

REF.: Bonney, *Banditti of the Prairies; CBA;* Duke, *Celebrated Criminal Cases of America;* Murdock, *Under the Covenant.*

Smith, Larry Thomas, 1946- , U.S., (wrong. convict.) mur. In 1976, thirty-year-old Larry Thomas Smith was convicted of killing drug dealer Brady Greenlease. With a criminal record that included passing bad checks and attempted breaking and entering, and testimony by the victim's girlfriend, the only eyewitness, that she saw Smith commit the murder.

Five years later, the eyewitness admitted that she had been high on angel dust when the murder was committed and confessed that she did not know what had happened. Other witnesses suddenly were pointing a finger at Larry Noble, who, at the time, was in West Virginia awaiting extradition to Ohio. After he spent five years behind bars, the state of Ohio set Smith free with $230 and an apology. REF.: *CBA.*

Smith, JohnLawrence, See: **Ley, Thomas John.**

Smith, Leonard, c.1947- , Case of, U.S., mur. Technically, Leonard Smith killed a man in cold blood, but legally he was not guilty of murder. Either way, the victim, California Angels outfielder Lyman Bostock, was dead.

Victim and murderer had tenuous, short-lived ties to one another in September 1978. Smith, a former Gary, Ind., steel worker, was estranged from his wife, Barbara Smith, who was a friend of Bostock's uncle. On Sept. 23, Bostock had been visiting Gary, his boyhood home, after a game against the Chicago White Sox in Chicago. He was accompanying his uncle, Thomas Turner, as Turner gave two women, one of whom was Barbara Smith, a ride to their cousin's home. Smith was going to see his wife, but got there just in time to see her climb into the back seat of Turner's car with Bostock. Smith shadowed the car, pulled up alongside it, pulled out a shotgun and killed Bostock. Prosecutors believed he was attempting to kill his wife. Smith testified he could not recall firing the fatal shot.

Smith was found Not Guilty of murdering Bostock by reason of insanity in 1978 and was committed to Logansport, Ind., State Hospital for two ninety-day periods of treatment. In 1980, Smith, thirty-three, was a free man. State prosecutors and mental health experts were livid. According to Ann Hanson, the social worker who directed the unit where Smith was held, he showed no evidence of psychosis while there. Lake County Prosecutor Jack Crawford called the affair a "legal tragedy." The Indiana General Assembly earlier that year had reacted to Leonard's case by changing the state's law concerning criminal insanity. The new law allowed for a defendant judged to have been mentally ill when he committed the crime to be sentenced to prison after receiving psychiatric treatment. Legislators hailed the change as a vast improvement, but know that it came too late to touch Smith, whom Crawford described as a dangerous man prone to violence. REF.: *CBA.*

Smith, Linda, c.1949-61, Brit., (unsolv.) mur. Children's footprints, first short and steady, next long and erratic, weaving back and forth, implied a chase—a chase that ended with the death of 12-year-old Linda Smith. Her body was found on Jan. 20, 1961, four days after her parents last saw her, about eighteen miles from Earls Colne, Essex. She had been strangled. Tire marks around the spot where she was found indicated that a car had been driven to a gap in the brush. A young couple said they had seen a black car reversing down the lane the night before the body was found. Linda's death remains a mystery.

The town baker, Gordon Lankester, was the only suspect. Articles belonging to both victim and accused were examined and both revealed traces of identical, and unusual, materials. Wheat starch grains and two different types of red paint were found on Linda's clothing and Lankester's overcoat and blankets in his car. Further, eight slight impressions around the area where the body was found were similar to marks made by the baker's shoes. Linda was known to go into the bakery quite often and it was believed that she had visited the establishment the day she disappeared. In his own defense, Lankester testified that he had not known the young victim and did not remember speaking with someone of her description that day. In Lankester's defense, people testified having seen Lankester and his wife driving home the day and time the girl disappeared.

Incriminating evidence against Lankester was circumstantial. The jury deliberated only twenty minutes before it returned a verdict of Not Guilty.

REF.: Butler, *Murderers' England; CBA;* Furneaux, *Famous Criminal Cases, vol. 7.*

Smith, Louis Maurice, 1936- , U.S., rape-mur. When nurse Marilyn Kraai of Holland, Mich., took a three-month special course in the treatment of mental patients, she was so interested in the work that she had decided to make it her specialty. One month later, the 20-year-old nurse was brutally murdered by one of her patients.

In 1954, Louis Maurice Smith was an 18-year-old inmate at the Kalamazoo State Hospital where Kraai was assigned to work. Smith had been arrested a year earlier for hitting a young woman from Parchment, Mich., on the head with a mallet. Shortly after the incident, Smith was transferred to the Kalamazoo Hospital as a sex offender. He had previously been arrested for peeping in windows and was once treated at the Neuropsychiatric Institute at Ann Arbor, Mich. A search for Kraai began when she did not show up for a dinner date with three other nurses. Hospital police and attendants searched the grounds and interior of the hospital for three hours. Gerrit Van Noorloos, a member of the hospital police force, noticed scuff marks leading from the linen room to the therapy room in the basement where he discovered Kraai's body concealed between two tubs in the locked therapy room. A brown hospital necktie was knotted around her throat and some of her clothing was ripped away. Police found a letter to a friend in Kraai's purse, which included a notation of the time she stopped writing. Smith was not a suspect until he mentioned that he had seen Kraai writing the letter.

Taken to the Paw Paw State Police station, Smith denied killing the woman until he was confronted with a lie detector test, at which point he broke down abruptly. "I did it," he sobbed, dropping his head into his hands, "I did it and I'm sorry." He explained that he had seen Kraai at her desk and asked her for permission to go down to the basement to get some playing cards he left in the therapy room. When she took him downstairs and unlocked the door, he strangled and then raped her. "I don't know why I did it," Smith said, "It was an impulse, I guess. But she was awful pretty." Smith later used Kraai's master keys to return to his room on the second floor, carefully locking all the doors behind him. He then flushed the keys down a toilet. Three psychiatrists examined Smith and deemed him unfit to stand trial. He was transferred to the Ionia State Hospital for the Criminally Insane, and released in 1979. REF.: *CBA.*

Smith, Madeleine Hamilton (AKA: Mimi), 1836-1928, Case of, Scot., mur. The daughter of James Smith, a prominent Glasgow, Scot., architect, Madeleine Smith was implicated in one of the most sensational murder cases of the Victorian era. She met Pierre Émile L'Angelier in Spring 1855. Although L'Angelier, a 34-year-clerk for a seed company, lacked Smith's social standing, the 19-year-old Smith secretly began corresponding with him, using her maid, Christina Harrison, as the courier. They became lovers in June 1856, and they continued to meet at Smith's country house and at a friend's house. Smith signed her letters "Mimi," a pet name, and called L'Angelier "my beloved husband."

James Smith told his daughter she was not to see the British-born Frenchman and introduced her to William Minnoch, a Glasgow businessman. By January 1857, Smith was cooler toward L'Angelier in person and in her letters, and she asked L'Angelier to give back her letters, writing "I did once love you fondly, but for some time back I have lost much of that." She accepted Minnoch's marriage proposal on Jan. 28, and the wedding date was set for June, although she did not tell L'Angelier. When L'Angelier told her he would show her letters to her father if she stopped seeing him, Smith acted as though she would continue the relationship.

Accused murderer Madeleine Smith during trial.

In the second week of February 1857, Smith sent a servant to the druggist to purchase prussic acid. The servant did not have a prescription, however, and was refused. Three times, in February and on Mar. 5 and Mar. 18, Smith bought rat poison, a mixture of soot and indigo mixed with arsenic. Then Smith met L'Angelier twice more in the basement of the Smith home in Glasgow. After one meeting in February 1857, L'Angelier became sick, reportedly suffering from vomiting and nausea, and was bedridden for a week. In a date book, he wrote "Thurs. 19, Saw Mimi a few moments—was very ill during the night." In another entry, he noted, "Sun. 22. Saw Mimi in drawing-room—Promised me French Bible—Taken very ill." Smith saw L'Angelier for the final time on Mar. 23, 1857. After returning home, the Frenchman became ill again. A doctor summoned by his landlady prescribed laudanum, but L'Angelier died several hours later.

Scene from the movie *Madeleine*, based on Smith's sensational trial and subsequent acquittal.

An autopsy revealed eighty-two grains of arsenic in L'Angelier's stomach. Smith fled in panic, but Minnoch followed her and brought her back home. Smith's letters were found, and she was arrested on Mar. 31. She admitted seeing L'Angelier and deceiving him about her intentions to marry Minnoch, but she said she only wanted to retrieve her letters. Because a defendant was not allowed to testify on her own behalf, Smith prepared a Declaration. Much speculation surrounded the trial; according to the *Morning Advertiser,* "All sorts of rumours are afloat bearing on the character of Miss Smith and the young Frenchman L'Angelier, whom she is accused of having poisoned. It is, of course, out of the question to place any reliance upon these stories, but it is said that the evidence at the trial will be of a very startling nature—so much so indeed that it may be deemed advisable to conduct the case with closed doors." Smith was brought to trial on June 30 at the Edinburgh High Court of Justiciary. Lord Justice-Clerk Hope, Lord Handyside, and Lord Ivory presided over the trial. Smith, who received hundreds of proposals for marriage during the proceedings, was described as calm during the trial, "the only unmoved, cool personage to be seen..." Her fiancee supported her at first, but later changed his mind.

The prosecution, led by Lord Advocate James Moncrieff, charged that Smith, who wanted L'Angelier out of the way because he posed a threat to her marriage plans and reputation, murdered him by giving him a drink of poisoned cocoa. A witness for the prosecution, Mary Perry, testified that L'Angelier had told her that he got sick for the first time after Smith gave him a drink of chocolate. Smith admitted buying arsenic, but claimed she had used it cosmetically (a common practice at the time). Smith's defense lawyer, John Inglis, argued that no proof existed that Smith and L'Angelier had met each time just before L'Angelier became sick. Smith's case was strengthened when L'Angelier's date book, which included notations of their meetings, was not allowed as evidence. Smith's lawyer also suggested that L'Angelier, who had previously threatened to take his life when another woman rejected him, had committed suicide. A toxicologist, Dr. Christison, testified that suicide victims usually ingest large quantities of poison and that L'Angelier had probably taken twice the amount found in his stomach. No soot or indigo were found in L'Angelier's stomach to indicate he had ingested rat poison, and he was also known to have stomach problems and eat arsenic.

On July 9, the jury returned a verdict of Not Proven on two counts and Not Guilty on one count, and Smith was freed. Not satisfied with the verdict, she wrote, "If you ever see Mr. C. Combe (the jury foreman) tell him that the "pannel" was not at all pleased with the verdict. I was delighted with the loud cheer the Court gave." Although most of the townspeople had been sympathetic toward her during the trial, she was afterward shunned by the residents near the Smith's country home. "The feeling in the west," she wrote, "is not so good towards me as you kind Edinburgh people shewed me. I rather think it shall be necessary for me to leave Scotland for a few months, but Mama is so unwell we do not like to fix anything at present." Her parents, who had not been supportive, did not attend the trial, and changed the family name when it ended.

In Fall 1857, Smith and her brother, Jack, traveled to London where she mixed with a group of people involved in the arts and socialism under poet William Morris. She married a member of the group, artist George Wardle on July 4, 1861, and lived with him in the Bloomsbury area of London. She had two children and reportedly began a new fad by setting her dining table with no tablecloth. When her husband died, she stayed in England, but eventually followed her son in 1909 to the U.S., she traveled to the U.S. to be closer to him. In the U.S., she met a man, Sheehy, and they lived together until his death. In her final years, a movie company reportedly attempted to have her appear in a silent movie based on her life, but she declined. U.S. officials also attempted to deport her, but the charges were dismissed. In 1950, a British film based on her life and entitled *Madeleine,* starring Ann Todd and directed and written by David Lean was released.

REF.: Altick, *Victorian Studies in Scarlet;* Atlay, *Famous Trials;* Birmingham, *Murder Most Foul;* Blyth, *Madeleine Smith;* Brophy, *The Meaning of Murder;* Browne, *Rise of Scotland Yard;* Browne, *Trials for Murder by Poisoning;* Boucher, *The Pocket Book of True Crime Stories;* Butler, *Madeleine Smith; CBA;* Curtin, *Noted Murder Mysteries;* Dunbar, *Blood in the Parlor;* Forster, *Studies in Black and Red;* Glaister, *The Power of Poison;* Hartman, *Victorian Murderesses;* House, *Square Mile of Murder;* Hunt, *The Madeleine Smith Affair;* Lambton, *Echoes of Causes Celebres;* Lustgarten, *The Woman in the Case;* Maycock, *Celebrated Crimes and Criminals;* Morland, *That Nice Miss Smith; Notable British Trials;* Pearson, *Instigation of the Devil;* Pearson, *Murder at Smutty Nose;* Roughead, *Classic Crimes;* Rowland, *More Criminal Files;* Thompson, *Poison and Poisoners;* Villiers, *Riddles of Crime;* Williamson, *Annals of Crime;* Wilson, *Encyclopedia of Murder;* Wilson, *Not Proven;* (DRAMA), Barnes, *Dishonored Lady;* Bridie, *A Sleeping Clergyman;* (FICTION), Lowndes, *Letty Lynton;* Lyell, *The House on Queen Anne Street;* Robinson, *Madeleine Graham;* (FILM), *Madeleine,* 1950.

Smith, Mark, 1949- , U.S., rape-mur. Described by his friends as intelligent, witty, and easy-going, Mark Smith, twenty-one, was revealed at his 1970 trial in Chicago as a cold-blooded multiple murderer who raped and killed without remorse. When he was suspected of killing a 17-year-old girl in McHenry County, Ill., Smith had a solid alibi. He later confessed to killing thirteen women. The rapes, mutilations, and beatings began when Smith was stationed in Germany, while serving in the U.S. Army between 1966 and 1969. He confessed to killing nine women in Germany and slaying another, Opal Fay Ash, twenty, in Mountain Home, Ark., in December 1969. Ash was raped, strangled, and stabbed. Smith calmly admitted that he had killed Janice Boylard, twenty-two, in the basement of the chemical plant where they both worked. He also admitted slaying Jean Bianchi, twenty-two, and Jean Lingfelter, seventeen, in McHenry, Ill., his home town. Prior to Smith's trial, he was interviewed by psychologist Joseph Wepman, who found him disturbed but competent to stand trial. Wepman described him as "a rather outspoken psychopath with little or no compassion or feeling" who was "more likely to treat people as objects than as people." At the trial it was brought out that Smith, as a small boy, had once stabbed a playmate twenty times in the back. He was convicted and given a 200-year sentence for the two McHenry country murders, and an additional 50 to 100 years for the murder in Cook County. Smith is serving his time at the Pontiac Correctional Center in Illinois. He will be eligible for parole in July 1990. REF.: *CBA.*

Smith, Mary Eleanor, b.c.1864, and **Mayer, Earl,** 1894-1938, U.S., theft-mur. In 1928, James Eugene Bassett graduated from the U.S. Naval Academy in Annapolis, Md., and traveled to Seattle, Wash., where he was scheduled to depart for an assignment with the Pacific Fleet. When Bassett arrived in Seattle, he placed an advertisement in the newspaper to sell his car. The first person to answer the ad was 63-year-old Mary Eleanor Smith and her physically handicapped son, Earl Mayer. When Bassett went to meet the prospective customers, Mayer hobbled up behind him, hit him over the head with a hammer, and killed him instantly. The mother and son team then cut the body into pieces, burned part of it, buried the rest, and scattered his teeth up and down the road.

Authorities arrested the pair in Oakland, Calif., driving Bassett's car. Their ensuing trial set legal precedent as the first ever to include evidence supplied from a polygraph test and truth serum. Although both confessed to the murder when confronted with the new lie-detecting tests, they recanted their statements. As the prosecution could not find Bassett's body, mother and son were tried and convicted only for auto theft. Mayer was sentenced to life in prison because he was a habitual criminal, and Mrs. Smith received eight years' imprisonment. In an effort to secure a confession from the suspects, authorities placed Mayer in solitary confinement for a year and employed Washington State Patrol Sergeant Joseph McCauley disguised as a clergyman to elicit a confession from Mrs. Smith. But she did not talk until just before her scheduled release in 1938. She said Earl Mayer killed Bassett, as well as three other victims in Montana and Idaho between 1921 and 1923. During his mother's new trial, on Dec. 11, 1938, Earl Mayer strangled himself to death in his cell. Mrs. Smith was found Guilty of murder on Dec. 13, after nineteen minutes' deliberation by the jury, and sentenced to life in prison.

REF.: *CBA;* Nash, *Look For the Woman.*

Smith, Matthew, 1925- , Brit., mur. American soldiers stationed in Great Britain during WWII were there to protect the lives of their allies, not take them recklessly and unnecessarily in a drunken barroom brawl. Nevertheless, in April 1944, 19-year-old U.S. Navy gunner Matthew Smith stabbed to death 29-year-old Englishman Charles Gilbey. The defendant was found Guilty of murder by a U.S. court martial and given a long sentence at Sing Sing Prison.

The tragic night began with revelry, laughing, and a great deal of drinking. The proprietor of London's Railway Tavern, better known as "Charlie Brown's," had emptied his establishment of the drunken mob when a long ebony-handled knife, grasped by a mean hand, thrust thrust through the doorway into the chest of 29-year-old Gilbey. The only clue detectives had to go one was word that the sleeve of the man holding the knife was that of an American soldier.

Detectives had just begun interviewing each of the estimated 4,000 sailors docked in London when a man confided to authorities that he owned a knife fitting the description of the murder weapon and that he had lent it to Matthew Smith, nineteen, the night of the attack. Smith readily admitted to having borrowed the knife and to having stabbed a man, he said, in self defense. The court sentenced him to death in the electric chair, but later reduced his sentence to life imprisonment at Sing Sing, due to his young age.

REF.: *CBA;* Simpson, *Forty Years of Murder.*

Smith, Mattie, prom. 1895, U.S., rob. Mattie Smith made a full confession of robbery to Detective Clifton R. Wooldridge before she had even been arrested for her crime. While Smith gloated with her cohort, Jack Smith, over her successful escape from police custody and her escape from Chicago to Pittsburgh, she didn't realize that Wooldridge was listening to every word from his hiding place in her home. Just as she finished, she slipped from the ladder on which she had been standing and fell into Jack Smith's arms. The embracing couple were then surprised by the bright light and presence of a waiting detective. The woman was tried on Sept. 19, 1895, found Guilty of larceny and sentenced to an indefinite term in the penitentiary by Judge John Barton Payne.

On July 25, Smith had taken in W. Hopkins, ostensibly as a boarder, but with the actual intention of robbing him. While he was in the house, Smith stole $125 from him. When he demanded its return, she concocted a story to try to convince the man, and eventually the authorities, that he had simply misplaced the money. The story didn't work, however, and Smith and her friend in crime, Lillian Belmont, who actually took the money, were arrested. Belmont was sent to jail and Smith was released on a $500 bond, which she readily forfeited by leaving for Pittsburgh. She returned later to secretly collect her belongings and it was then that she unwittingly revealed her crime to the detective and thus landed herself in jail.

REF.: *CBA;* Wooldridge, *Hands Up.*

Smith, Michael (AKA: Mike Atkins, Michael James Cooper, Michael Scott, Dennis Trumbo, Michael Trumbo), 1948- , U.S., rob.-kid.-sod.-rape. A fugitive since January 1988, Michael Smith is wanted as the prime suspect in the rape and robbery at gunpoint of four women. He often identifies himself as a member of the San Francisco 49ers' professional football team. At this writing, Smith is still at large. REF.: *CBA.*

Smith, Michael, 1960- , Case of, asslt.-mur. In October 1981, Michael Smith, the 21-year-old son of a Chicago, Ill., policeman, fatally stabbed his sleeping father. Forty-four-year-old Robert Smith was dozing in bed when Michael came into the room with two butcher knives and began stabbing his father. Michael's mother and younger brother were both injured as they attempted to intervene. The brother finally subdued Michael while his mother called the police.

Michael Smith, who had suffered a mental breakdown the previous year and was under a psychiatrist's care, was tried for murder. On Aug. 12, 1982, he was found Not Guilty by reason of insanity. Smith was ordered to spend a maximum of twenty years in a state mental facility after psychiatrists for both the defense and the prosecution testified that they had diagnosed him as a paranoid schizophrenic who was dangerous to himself and others. The judge stipulated that if at some point psychiatrists felt that Smith could be realeased, that he must first appear before the judge, with whom the final decision would rest. REF.: *CBA.*

Smith, Pearl, prom. 1892, U.S., rob. Pearl Smith used her robbery arrest as an opportunity to see the country. When Detective Clifton R. Wooldridge apprehended her for allegedly robbing a street commission merchant of $320 on Oct. 6, 1892, Smith escaped and ran from her home in Chicago to Kansas City, to Denver, and to Galveston, Texas. After tracking her down via telegrams, police finally rearrested Smith in Hot Springs, Ark. They brought her back to Chicago where she used her money and influence to postpone her trial until Apr. 24, 1893, nearly six months after her indictment. By this time, Smith and her cohort in crime, Mary White, were confident that the merchant they had robbed had forgotten about the whole incident and decided not to prosecute. When they walked in the courtroom that April day and Smith first spied the merchant, she decided her only choice was to run away again. Fleeing out the courtroom door, Smith took off for Michigan, Cincinnati, and Louisville, until Wooldridge caught up with her, this time in Chattanooga, Tenn. Meanwhile, White had been tried, convicted, and sentenced to two years in the penitentiary. Now that the authorities had Smith, they kept a close eye on her. She was tried and found Guilty of larceny on June 19, 1893. She was sentenced to five years in the penitentiary. After her release, she went back to her old ways, and was driven from Chicago by police in 1899. She was later arrested in New York, convicted for robbery, and sentenced to five years in Sing Sing prison.

REF.: *CBA;* Wooldridge, *Hands Up.*

Smith, Perry, See: **Hickock, Richard Eugene.**

Smith, Richard, d.1816, U.S., mur. Richard Smith, a lieutenant in the U.S. Army, fell in love with beautiful Ann Carson in 1812. Her husband, Captain John Carson, away for two years fighting Indians in the West, was missing in action and presumed dead. Smith and Ann Carson married. Four years later, in January 1816, Captain Carson showed up and confronted Smith. An argument and scuffle resulted in which Smith shot and killed Carson.

During Smith's murder trial, his wife attempted to kidnap the governor of Pennsylvania and hold him hostage pending her husband's release. The attempt failed, and Smith was convicted of murder. On Feb. 4, 1816, he was hanged for his crime.

As a weird postscript, Smith's wife embarked on a career of crime. She established a counterfeiting ring, but she and her partners were apprehended and sent to prison in 1823. Smith died in prison in 1835.

REF.: *CBA;* Nash, *Bloodletters and Badmen.*

Smith, Robert Benjamin, 1948- , U.S., mur. Robert Benjamin Smith was an 18-year-old high school senior living in Mesa, Ariz., in 1966. The son of a retired Air Force major, the young man was intelligent and handsome, yet extremely shy. He idolized Jesse James and Napoleon, and when Richard Speck murdered eight nurses in Chicago in Summer 1966, Smith acquired a new hero. He dreamed of mass murder and sadistic torture, of placing plastic bags over his victims' heads and watching them suffocate slowly.

On Nov. 12, 1966, Smith walked two miles from his Mesa home and entered the Rose-Mar College of Beauty, armed with a revolver his father had given him as a birthday present, a knife, lengths of nylon cord, and 200 plastic bags. He fired a shot into a mirror and ordered five woman and two children to lie on the floor. The plastic bags were too small to fit over the women's heads, and in his frustration Smith began shooting. Killed at point-blank range were Glenda Carter, eighteen, Carol Farmer, nineteen, Joyce Sellers, twenty-seven, her 3-year-old daughter, Debbie, and one other woman. Three-month-old Tamara Sellers was saved when her mother cradled the child as she was being fired upon. One other woman also survived the attack. Police arrived at the bloody scene to find a smiling Smith about to leave. He offered no resistance, admitting that "I've just killed all the women in there", as he was placed under arrest. REF.: *CBA.*

Smith, Russell Lee, 1955-75, U.S., suic.-attempt. mur.-mur. A lovers' quarrel turned into assault, mass murder and suicide on May 24, 1975, when Russell Lee Smith, twenty, ended a dispute between himself and his young girlfriend by shooting her in the head. He then wounded two men whom he also had been arguing with before jumping in his car and continuing his rampage.

Smith took his girlfriend's dead body with him, left it at a Dayton, Ohio, hospital ramp and shot and wounded one passerby as he drove away. He shot and wounded the driver of a car on a highway, then drove into a movie theater parking lot. He approached a family of four, shot each one, and critically wounded the couple's 6-year-old daughter. He entered a residential neighborhood and began knocking on doors. He shot and missed one woman, but shot a neighbor through the neck. Smith then kidnapped a girl from a restaurant and drove off. While driving, he noticed a young couple in a car, approached the girl and dragged her into his car. He then killed the first girl and drove the second one to a wooded area where he raped her. It was at this time that police caught up with the killer, but Smith immediately turned the gun on himself and took his own life. Smith had been on probation after being convicted of a 1971 murder. REF.: *CBA.*

Smith, Sir **Sydney Alfred,** 1883-1969, Brit., path. Sir Sydney Alfred Smith turned a childhood pharmacological interest into a life-long career in forensic medicine, and became widely recognized as a scholar and educator as well. He was born in 1883 in the small village of Roxburgh, New Zea. and as a young man, became an assistant to a local pharmacist. After qualifying as a licensed pharmacist, Smith began to study medicine. He moved to Scotland to attend Edinburgh University, where he graduated with first class honors in 1912. Smith became an assistant in the department of forensic medicine, where in 1913 his testimony led to the prosecution of Patrick Higgins, accused of murdering his two young sons.

Smith earned his medical degree in 1914 and returned to New Zealand, where he became a health officer in Dunedin. During WWI, Smith served as a major in the New Zealand Army Corps, moving to Egypt in 1917 to become a lecturer at the School of Medicine in Kasr el-Aini, as well as a medical-legal expert for the government in Cairo. He made numerous innovations in ballistics and firearms research, and in 1924, successfully solved the murder of Sir Lee Stack. In 1925, Smith published the textbook *Forensic Medicine,* which won the Swiney Prize four years later. He returned to Edinburgh in 1928 to teach forensic medicine, and in 1931 became dean of the medical facility. He was also appointed to the General Medical Council and published a second volume, *Recent Advances in Forensic Medicine.* As an expert witness, he began to travel the world, solving cases locally and as far away as Ceylon.

In WWII, he again served as a consultant, and in 1949 was knighted Sir Sydney in recognition of his forensic contributions. Hardly slowing down, he became rector at Edinburgh University in 1954 and a forensic consultant for the World Health Organization in 1956. Smith retired in 1957 to write his memoirs which were published as *Mostly Murder* in 1959, and lived in Edinburgh until his death on May 8, 1969, at the age of eighty-five. Ref.: *CBA.*

Smith, Thomas (AKA: **Bear River Smith**), 1830-70, U.S., west. lawman. A western lawman who became famous for keeping order by using his fists instead of a gun, Thomas Smith was, according to most of his biographers, a policeman in New York City for about six years in the late 1850s or early 1860s and allegedly learned how to fight with his hands on a tough Bowery beat. Smith may have then either fought in the New York Draft Riots of 1863 or moved west before the Civil War. By 1865 he was working for several different freight companies in the Wyoming, Utah, and Colorado territories until 1868, when he became a construction worker at the "end of the track" of the Union Pacific Railroad, in Bear River, Wyoming Territory. Friction between the often rowdy railroad workers and the townspeople resulted in the forming of a vigilance committee. After three railroad workers were captured by the vigilantes who seemed about to hang them, Smith initiated a counterattack, set fire to the jail, and captured most of the vigilantes in a store. Peace was being negotiated when Smith shot a man named Nuckles who may have fired on him first. A battle broke out that left fourteen men dead. Smith was seriously wounded by the time the Fort Brodges U.S. Cavalry arrived. Never tried for his misdeeds, Smith was nicknamed "Bear River" after the fight, and given the post of marshal by the appreciative Union Pacific authorities.

By the time Smith became marshal at Kit Carson in Colorado Territory in 1869, he had stopped using a gun, instead settling fights with his fists. The Abilene, Kan., mayor appointed Smith marshal of that unruly town and Smith's first act was to decree it illegal to carry a gun within city limits. In a few months Abilene had been transformed from a rowdy town to a peaceful place.

New York city policeman-turned-western lawman, Thomas "Bear River" Smith.

But then, as a favor to another sheriff, Smith left Abilene to capture a man named Andrew McConnell on charges of murder. It was an act that doomed him. For, after he found McConnell with his partner, Moses Miles, Smith was cut down with rifle fire as soon as he was in range of the outlaws. As he lay dying, Miles and McConnell almost decapitated him with an ax. Abilene reverted to its turbulent ways until Wild Bill Hickock restored order in 1871. Stories of Smith's exploits have appeared in dime novels and adventure stories, with titles such as *Bear River Smith: Two-Fisted Marshal of Abilene.*

REF.: Bartholomew, *Western Hard-Cases;* Breihan, *Great Lawmen of the West;* Brown and Schmitt, *Trail Driving Days;* Carson, *The Union Pacific; CBA;* Drago, *Great American Cattle Trails;* ____, *Wild, Woolly and Wicked;* Gard, *Frontier Justice;* Gardner, *The Old Wild West;* Hendricks, *The Bad Man of the West;* Hunter and Rose, *The Album of Gun-Fighters;* Hutchinson, *The Life & Personal Writings of Eugene Manlove Rhodes;* Jameson, *Heroes by the Dozen;* ____, *Miracle of the Chisholm Trail;* Johnson, *Famous Lawmen of the Old West;* Miller and Snell, *Great Gunfighters of the Kansas Cowtowns;* Penfield, *Western Sheriffs and Marshals;* Plenn and LaRoche, *The Fastest Gun in Texas;* Raine, *Forty-Five Caliber Law;* ____, *Guns of the Frontier;* Rosa, *The Gunfighter, Man or Myth?;* ____, *They Called Him Wild Bill;* Sandoz, *The Cattlemen;* Schaefer, *Heroes Without Glory;* Shirley, *Buckskin and Spurs;* Steckmesser, *The Western Hero in History and Legend;* Streeter, *Ben Thompson, Man With a Gun;* ____, *Prairie Trails and Cow Towns;* Verckler, *Cowtown-Abilene;* Wellman, *The Trampling Herd;* White, *Texas.*

Smith, Thomas, 1838-1918, U.S., jur. Served as U.S. attorney from 1885-88. He was appointed to the territorial court of New Mexico by President Grover Cleveland in 1893. REF.: *CBA.*

Smith, Thomas, 1919- , U.S., mur. Thomas Smith and Mary Ellen Babcock both eighteen, lived in the same South Buffalo, N.Y., neighborhood. On the night of Feb. 5, 1937, Smith experienced what he described as an "uncontrollable impulse" that led him to beat and brutally murder the young woman.

Mary Ellen Babcock left her family's home in the early evening to attend a wake with a friend. At about 8:20 p.m. she decided to walk home. At noon the next day, two 8-year-old boys, Donald

Hanlon and Edward Murphy, discovered her body in a vacant lot. Medical examiner Rocco N. DeDominicis conducted an autopsy and determined that the girl had not been sexually assaulted. DeDominicis reported that death was the result of a stab wound in the heart, a punctured left lung, fractured skull, and multiple stab wounds in the head and body. A bloodstained four-inch pocket knife with the initials "T.S.," was found beneath the corpse. The only other clue was a small scrap of wool found in the girl's left hand. "She must have put up a terrific fight for her life," said DeDominicis, citing numerous cuts on both her hands and a broken fingernail. Babcock's nose was also broken. Detective Chief John J. Whalen said that blood stains and pieces of Babcock's coat indicated that the body had been dragged across the street and thrown into a slight depression in the field about ten feet from the curb. Although several rewards were offered for information leading to the arrest of the killer, six weeks passed before he was found.

On Mar. 28, 1937, 14-year-old Frances Fitzgerald complained to her mother of a pain in her back. Her mother discovered the five-inch blade of an ice pick embedded under her daughter's left shoulder. Neither the emergency room physician nor the police believed the girl's story that she had tripped on the pick accidentally. She had been seen riding in a car with a man, and she finally admitted to her brother, Pierce Fitzgerald, that she had been picked up by Thomas Smith. Fitzgerald looked up Smith's address in the phone book and went to his house. When the slight 18-year-old Smith answered the door, Fitzgerald recognized him from a high school class and from church. He asked him if he had read about his sister being stabbed. Smith said he had, but denied any involvement at first. He later told Fitzgerald that he had stabbed the girl. Fitzgerald then asked Smith what he knew about the Babcock case, and suggested they go together to the police station. Smith refused, but was willing to talk to a priest. They went to St. Teresa's church nearby and talked with a clergyman. Smith repeated what he had said to Fitzgerald, adding that he had been provoked by an "uncontrollable impulse," and offered to pay Frances Fitzgerald's hospital bill. Pierce Fitzgerald convinced police to pick up Smith for questioning the next day. After asking to see their badges, Smith went quietly with Acting Captain Glenn H. McClellan, Lieutenant William H. Downey, and Detective Patrick J. Hoar to the South Park station.

Smith admitted attacking the Fitzgerald girl, giving extensive details, including the fact that he "would have killed her with an automobile jack but the handle fell off as I chased her...I grabbed her and took her back to the car. I promised to take her home, but warned her not to talk," Smith explained. After his confession, an officer abruptly asked Smith, "What about the Babcock girl? Where did you meet her?" Smith began, "I've got to get this whole thing off my mind," and then went on to confess to this slaying, also. He described how the woman had repeatedly begged for mercy, and how this had provoked him to attack her more fiercely. Smith said the impulse to hurt her left him once she lay still. After the slaying, Smith washed his hands in snow and rubbed snow on his clothing to get rid of the bloodstains. Once home, he washed the blood out of his jacket and shirt at a sink in the cellar. Lieutenant Downey, who was present at the confession, said Smith had read all the newspaper stories about the case, but was not worried because he knew the police did not suspect him. Police commissioner James W. Higgins said Smith, "told us that sometimes something seemed to 'click' in his brain. When that happened, he would want to attack and maim." Besides the Babcock murder, Smith admitted attacking another South Buffalo girl, and attempting to lure 8-year-old Marjorie Galvin into his car.

District Attorney Walter C. Newcomb filed a first-degree murder charge against Smith on Mar. 31, 1937. During the trial, Smith wept in court when his attorney described him as being on the verge of dementia. Newcomb told the jury it did not make "much difference if he was an imbecile or an idiot," as far as their duty was concerned. On June 16, 1937, the jury returned from deliberation to find Smith Guilty of murder and recommended life imprisonment. REF.: *CBA.*

Smith, Thomas L. (AKA: **Pegleg Smith**), 1801-66, U.S., fraud-rob. One of the old West's infamous mountain men, Thomas L. Smith had a career that included theft, slavery, rustling, and perpetrating a variety of cons, including touting fictitious gold mines to gullible searchers. Born in Crab Orchard, Ky., on Oct. 10, 1801, Smith was a teenager when he ran away to flatboat on the Mississippi, later heading for St. Louis, Mo., where he worked for a fur merchant and met mountaineers and trappers like Kit Carson, Jim Bridger, and Milton Sublette. Smith went along on Alexandre Le Grand's first expedition to Santa Fe, N.M., and learned several Indian dialects. When an Indian shot him below his right knee Smith got both a wooden leg and his nickname. During the 1830s he became a successful trapper, maintaining his equilibrium on a horse despite his handicap.

By the late 1830s animal pelts were severely devalued and Smith switched to kidnapping Indian children to sell to rich Mexicans looking for slaves. Knowing that enraged Indians were on the lookout for him, Smith moved to California where, for about a decade, he stole horses, one time leading 150 Utah Indians across the Sierra Nevada into California to steal several hundred of them. In partnership with scouts Bill Williams and Jim Beckwourth, Smith was part of the biggest horse-stealing ring that ever existed in that state. With pressure from the law increasing the gang disbanded and Smith cashed in on the gold fever. Saying that he had found abundant samples of gold bearing quartz in the Chocolate Mountains, or the Santa Rosa Mountains, or the Borego Badlands, but was forced to flee angry Indians, Smith sold maps of the alleged mines or was staked by gullible gold seekers. After Smith's death in 1866 at a hospital in San Francisco, eager fortune-seekers continued to look for the Lost Pegleg Mine, which is still sought by some even to this day. REF.: *CBA.*

Smith, Tom, d.1893, U.S., west. lawman. Born in Texas, Tom Smith became a law enforcement officer in Texas and Oklahoma. He also served as a deputy U.S. marshal in the 1870s. A decade later Smith worked for the powerful Wyoming Stock Growers' Association, which sought to drive out homesteaders seeking to settle the grazing lands of the Western plains.

Smith faithfully served the interests of the wealthy cattle barons. At Powder River on Nov. 1, 1891, the association ordered Smith and detectives Joe Elliott, Fred Coates, and Frank Canton to rid the territory of accused rustler Nate Champion. In the early morning, Smith and his men congregated outside a cabin owned by Ross Gilbertson on the Powder River. As the men approached the building one of their guns accidentally discharged, touching off a panic. They rushed the cabin with guns blazing. Champion attempted to defend himself but was cut down by Smith's bullets. The governor and two U.S. senators intervened on behalf of the Stock Growers' Association and helped Smith gain back his freedom.

In Spring 1892, Smith was sent into Texas to hire gunfighters for the Johnson County War which raged in Wyoming. Smith found twenty-six men willing to work for $5 dollars a day and they were promised an additional $50 for every homesteader they shot down. These "Regulators" were given a list of seventy men targeted for murder. However, the plan collapsed and most of the gunfighters were driven out of town or arrested. Smith was taken into custody and held until Summer 1893. Following his release, he returned to Gainesville, Texas, but was shot down by a man in a quarrel on board a train.

REF.: Canton, *Frontier Trails; CBA;* Mercer, *Banditti of the Plains;* Smith, *War on the Powder River.*

Smith, William, d.1753, Brit., mur. William Smith was a prosperous Yorkshire farmer. His mother had remarried Thomas Harper of Ingleby Manor, who had several children. Smith decided to rid himself of these intruders who might come between him and his late father's estate. Apparently Smith had been considering different methods of murder for some time when he went to a druggist to buy medicine for his horses. He asked the pharmacist for some arsenic to kill the rats in his barn, and left with two pennies' worth of the poison. On Good Friday in 1753, a large cake was being prepared for a holiday party with the neighbors. Smith mixed some arsenic in with the flour. The neighbors couldn't attend, but the lethal dessert was eaten by Thomas Harper and two of his children, William and Anne. As soon as Smith saw that the poison had taken effect, he left for Liverpool. His recently acquired relatives died in great pain within a day.

Once in Liverpool, Smith's conscience began to bother him. When he returned to the scene of the crime, he was immediately apprehended and confessed. He was tried in York before Sergeant Eyre. To Smith's own confession were added the testimonies of the pharmacist and a servant who had seen him doctor the cake flour. Smith was quickly found Guilty and condemned to death. He was hanged on Aug. 14, 1753. Smith's body was delivered to the surgeons for dissection.

REF.: *CBA;* Mitchell, *The Newgate Calendar.*

Smith, William, 1697-1769, U.S., jur. Helped successfully defend German printer John Peter Zenger on charges of seditious libel in 1735. He also served as associate justice on the supreme court of New York from 1763-69. REF.: *CBA.*

Smith, William, 1728-93. U.S.-Can., jur. Chief justice of New York in 1780. He fled the country after declining to swear allegiance to the American revolutionary government. He later served as chief justice of Canada from 1786-93. REF.: *CBA.*

Smith, Dr. **William**, prom. 1853, Case of, Scot., mur. A Scottish physician, Dr. William Smith, took out several insurance policies on the life of William M'Donald, a 29-year-old farmhand who lived with his family about two miles west of Kirkton. In October 1852, the doctor took out a policy for £999 and nineteen shillings for five years; in November 1852, Smith took out a policy for £499 for five years, and he purchased another policy for £500. All of the policies included a clause which stated that the policy was still valid even in the event of suicide. On Nov. 19, 1853, William M'Donald left his home to keep a meeting with the doctor at his St. Fergus house at about 6 p.m. The farmhand's body was found later by his brother, Robert M'Donald, shot in the head with a pistol nearby. Not long afterward, the doctor arrived on the scene, and called the death a suicide. Smith was put on trial at Edinburgh in the spring of 1854. During the trial, witnesses testified that Dr. Smith had purchased a pistol and gunpowder, which Smith claimed was used in ointment. Smith further maintained that he bought the insurance policies on M'Donald's life for William Milne, his deceased uncle and that he did not know he was the beneficiary. At the trial's end, Lord Justice Clerk advised the jury that there was not enough evidence to either find Smith guilty of murder or even know for certain there was a murder case. The jury returned a verdict of Not Proven.

REF.: *CBA;* Parry, *Some Famous Medical Trials;* Poynter, *Forgotten Crimes;* Roughead, *Tales of the Criminous;* Turner, *The Inhumanists.*

Smith, William, prom. 1895, U.S., theft-rob. In April 1895, a Chicago policeman, Clifton R. Wooldridge, saw William Smith emerge from a railway box-car and carry away a bag of coal. Smith was arrested by Woolridge but escaped. Following a chase, the officer located Smith in a garbage bin and after another tussle, rearrested the alleged thief. As Wooldridge took took his prisoner to the station house, August Frank recognized the thief and accused Smith and an accomplice of robbing him of a watch and $13 a few days earlier. Smith was tried, convicted, sent to prison, and fined $50.

REF.: *CBA;* Wooldridge, *Hands Up.*

Smith, William Francis, 1903-68, U.S., jur. Served as U.S. attorney from 1940-41. He was appointed to the district court of New Jersey by President Franklin D. Roosevelt in 1941, and to the third circuit court by President John F. Kennedy in 1961. REF.: *CBA.*

Smith, William French, 1917- , U.S., atty. gen. Appointed U.S. attorney general by President Ronald Reagan, serving from 1981-85. REF.: *CBA.*

Smolianoff, Solomon (AKA: **Sali Smolianoff**), b.1897, Ger., count. Born in Poltava, Russia, in 1897, Solomon Smolianoff was sent to art school in Odessa in 1913 when he was sixteen years old. One of his professors was Eugen Zotow, an engraver and artist, who also was known as Ivan Miassojedov and Ivan Vernitchy and who had served a two-year sentence for counterfeiting. Also an arsonist, Zotow was once caught starting to set fire to the house of a widow, and tried to explain that he was a convert to Hinduism and was practicing "suttee," the "Hindu practice of widow burning." Smolianoff fled from Russia in 1925, lived in Constantinople for a year, then moved to Vienna and Berlin. In Germany he met Zotow, who was now calling himself "Professor Ivan Vernitchy" and was counterfeiting British pounds and other currencies. Smolianoff is believed to have assisted him, smoothing out rough areas on the plates. By the summer of 1928, Smolianoff was living in Amsterdam and passing off counterfeit £50 notes. Arrested on June 12, 1928, he was convicted and served a two-and-a-half-year prison term.

REF.: Bllom, *Money of Their Own; CBA;* Whitehead, *Journey into Crime.*

Smollett, Tobias George, 1721-71, Brit., writer. Harassed and jailed for supporting unpopular Earl of Bute John Stuart. Books authored: *Ferdinand Count Fathom* in 1753, an early model for later horror and mystery stories, as well as several political satires, novels, and historical works. REF.: *CBA.*

Snaith, Paul, prom. 1930, Case of, U.S., fraud. In the late 1920s, Paul Snaith, who lived with his wife in Iowa, took out a life insurance policy on himself, making his wife the beneficiary. On Feb. 3, 1931, Snaith, a chemical expert, attempted to fake his death by placing a dead body in a car and setting fire to it. Six weeks later, while his wife was still grieving for her husband, Smith married a 20-year-old woman and settled in Kansas. Investigators, however, found that the charred corpse taken from the car had already been embalmed before it was destroyed. Doctors confirmed that the remains were not those of Snaith.

About three months later, a farmhand found Snaith tied up and gagged beside a road. Snaith told authorities that he had been kidnapped, confined in a cellar for three months, and then thrown in a ditch. When doctors declared Snaith insane, no charges were filed against him and he was sent to an institution for the mentally ill.

REF.: *CBA;* Whitelaw, *Corpus Delicti.*

Snell, Ivan Edward, 1884-1958, Brit., jur. Accepted to Bar by Inner Temple in 1909, practicing on South-Eastern, East and West Kent, and North London Circuits, and serving as junior counsel in murder trial of Edith Thompson. He was later named metropolitan police magistrate in 1925, and worked mostly on the Marylebone Police Court. REF.: *CBA.*

Snider, Paul, d.1980, U.S., mur. Snider was a Vancouver, B.C., street punk and pimp who transformed himself into a Los Angeles hustler. In 1977, Snider returned to Vancouver, telling his friends that he was going straight. That summer he met the beautiful 18-year-old Dorothy Ruth Hoogstraten, a clerk in a Dairy Queen. Snider quickly overwhelmed the girl, who had no ambitions beyond becoming a secretary. Snider told her she was beautiful and suggested that she could be the twenty-fifth anniversary Playmate for Playboy magazine.

After gaining her mother's permission, Snider took Dorothy to Los Angeles for photographic tests. She lost out as the special anniversary Playmate but was named August 1979 "Playmate of the Month" as Dorothy Stratten. On June 1, before the magazine appeared on the stands, Dorothy and Paul Snider were married. He immediately set about procuring small TV and film roles for his wife. Stratten had considerable natural talent for acting, and when Playboy named her the 1980 "Playmate of the Year", bigger studios began to look at her as a potential star.

When Stratten began meeting other men who were more sophisticated than Paul Snider, he resented being left behind.

Dorothy left Snider and went to New York to appear in a Peter Bogdanovich film. Bogdanovich and Stratten became romantically involved. On her return to Hollywood, Dorothy asked Snider for a divorce and moved in with Bogdanovich.

On Aug. 12, 1980, Snider telephoned his wife and asked her to meet him at his home to finalize details of their divorce. The next day he bought a 12-gauge shotgun. On Aug. 14, when Dorothy came to his home, he shot her and then himself. Later that afternoon, Snider's most recent protegée found the bodies. Peter Bogdanovich later noted: "Dorothy looked at the world with love, and believed that all people were good down deep. She was mistaken, but it is among the most generous and noble errors we can make."

REF.: Bogdanovich, *The Killing of the Unicorn; CBA;* Nash, *Murder*
e r
Among the Mighty; (FILM), *Star 80,* 1983.

Snook, James Howard, 1884-1930, U.S., mur. Before he went to the electric chair for the murder of his 24-year-old sweetheart, Professor James Howard Snook asked permission to invite his most intimate friends to join him in a "last supper" at the Ohio Penitentiary. The warden, sympathetic, acquiesced. Four chefs were brought in to prepare a sumptuous feast for Dr. Snook, his long-suffering wife, and two dinner companions. The warden drew the line, however, when Snook asked if he might be permitted to wear his tuxedo for the occasion.

Dr. Snook was a professor of Veterinary Medicine at Ohio State University. He was a distinguished-looking middle-aged man who had participated in the pistol-shooting competition at the 1920 Olympics. He was also a very private man who kept his peccadillos to himself. The professor had a secretary named Theora Hix, who was working her way through medical school on a meager $600 a year allowance from her parents. Hix was the daughter of a retired university professor who lived in Bradenton, Fla. She kept occasional company with William Miller, a 35-year-old instructor from the College of Agriculture, but the relationship was not going anywhere. The one true love of her life was Dr. Snook, the 49-year-old professor she once described as the "nicest man I know!"

Snook conducted his affair with the student with the utmost discretion. He rented a room in downtown Columbus from Margaret Smalley, using the alias "Howard Snook." The professor explained that he was a demonstrator for a salt company, and that his "wife" would be sharing the quarters from time to time. For nearly three years the two led a double life. Snook was revered by family and was the soul of conformity. They lived in a spacious home on the edge of the campus. Theora Hix was perceived by her classmates to be a demure but earnest student with little time to spare for leisure-time activity. Beneath the facade was an iron-will resolve to control the men in her life, and a strong dependency on cocaine. She forced Dr. Snook to sterilize her so that their lovemaking might continue without complication. At times Hix would diabolically pit Snook against Miller, heightening their anxiety with taunting remarks.

On the night of June 14, 1929, Snook decided to take Hix for an automobile ride. They parked near a local golf course but a tournament was going on and Hix was apprehensive that they might get caught by the police. Snook steered his late model coupé to the nearby New York Central rifle range on the outskirts of Columbus. He killed the engine and went about his lovemaking with Hix. According to Dr. Snook's statements to police, Hix complained about the cramped confines of his car and made allusions to Miller's superiority as a lover. They quarreled bitterly and Hix struck him in the groin. Snook seized an automobile hammer and inflicted a series of savage wounds to her face and head. After beating her to a bloody pulp he bent over and cut her jugular vein with a pen knife. The prostrate body of the coed was found lying in the weeds shortly after sunrise by two small boys. Coroner Joseph Murphy examined the corpse and determined that the killer had inflicted seventeen separate blows. The corpse was taken to a funeral parlor and it was identified by friends.

The police had little to work with in the way of clues, but had received reports that Hix was riding around with a stockily built man driving a blue Ford coupé. The description did not fit William Miller, who was considered a suspect. The search for the blue car led to the doorstep of the retiring Dr. Snook who told police that the woman had been his mistress for three years. "Neither of us wanted to marry each other," he said. "She was a good companion in a different way than my wife." Questioned simultaneously by police, Miller proved to be the weaker of the two. He was ill-at-ease and his answers to probing questions carefully measured. Dr. Snook explained that Miller had also been carrying on an affair with Hix and there was much personal jealousy between the two. The missing pieces were supplied by
b y
the landlady Margaret Smalley and an anonymous tipster. Mrs. Smalley readily identified Snook as her tenant and a little brown hat with a rolled brim that Hix had been wearing. A caller who refused to leave a name suggested to the police that they closely examine a suit of clothes Snook had recently taken in for dry-cleaning. The garment was impounded and given to the city chemist for analysis. Bloodstains were found on the knees. Confronted with this evidence Dr. Snook broke down and confessed to the crime. He said Hix had warned him not to go out of town for the weekend with his wife and daughter as he had originally planned. "She threatened that if I did go she would take the life of my wife and baby," he sobbed. Dr. Snook was indicted for first-degree murder. The trial, which ended on Aug. 14, 1929, was punctuated by sensational details of the adulterous affair, spelled out in graphic detail in a series of lurid letters written by Snook that bordered on the pornographic. Throughout the trial, Helen Snook maintained a stoic attitude. She supported her husband up to the moment he walked into the execution chamber on Feb. 28, 1930.

REF.: *CBA;* Gribble, *The Deadly Professionals;* Radin, *Crimes of Passion.*

Snorri Sturluson, 1179-1241, Ice., jur.-consp., assass. Served as president of high court of Iceland from 1215-18 and from 1222-32. He frequently conspired with and against Haakon IV, king of Norway, who later ordered his assassination. REF.: *CBA.*

Snow, Lorenzo, 1814-1901, U.S., poly. Named apostle of Morman church one year after arriving at Salt Lake City with Brigham Young in 1849, and became leader of Mormon colony in Brigham City, Utah, in 1853. He was found Guilty of unlawful cohabitation in 1886, four years after the passage of the Edmunds Act prohibiting polygamy. The ruling against him was reversed by the U.S. Supreme Court in 1887. REF.: *CBA.*

Snow, William (**AKA: Skitch**), d.1789, Brit., rob. A highway robber, William Snow, was condemned to be executed. In 1789, he was taken to Exeter, England, where a noose was secured around Snow's neck. When the executioner tried to hang Snow, the rope came off the scaffold and he dropped to the ground. While Snow was waiting for the hangman to fasten the rope again, he reportedly said the crowd, "Good people, be not hurried; I am not hurried; I can wait a little." The highwayman was hanged properly the second time.

REF.: Atholl, *Shadow of the Gallows;* Bishop, *Executions; CBA.*

Snow, Zerubbabel, 1809-88, U.S., jur. Served as prosecuting attorney in Salt Lake City, Utah, and as prosecuting attorney for county of Salt Lake from 1876-84. He earlier was appointed to the territorial court of Utah by President Millard Fillmore in 1850. REF.: *CBA.*

Snyder, A. Cecil, 1907-59, U.S., jur. Served as U.S. attorney for Puerto Rico from 1933-42. He was appointed to the supreme court of the territory of Puerto Rico by President Franklin D. Roosevelt in 1941. REF.: *CBA.*

Snyder, Donald, 1927-53, U.S., mur. In June 1952, after escaping from the New York prison at Stormville, 25-year-old Donald Snyder walked into the home of Marvin and Dorothy Arnold in nearby Lake Mahopac. He told Arnold that he was an escaped convict, and that he would kill her children if she did not let him in. Inside the house, he held 9-year-old Betty Jean

Arnold hostage with a butcher knife while police surrounded the house. Later, he led Mrs. Arnold and the child out to the family car. He instructed Mrs. Arnold to get behind the wheel while he took the girl and got into the back seat. A police officer entered the garage and tried to convince Snyder to surrender. When he refused, the officer shot Snyder. Before Snyder was subdued, however, he stabbed the child in the abdomen.

Betty Jean Arnold died shortly after being stabbed. Snyder was wounded but recovered and was placed on trial for the girl's murder. He was convicted on Sept. 15, 1952, and was executed in the electric chair at Sing Sing during the week of July 13, 1953. REF.: *CBA.*

Snyder, Edward, 1856-80, U.S., lynch.-mur. Edward Snyder was twenty-four when he murdered his landlords, Jacob and Annie Geogle, in their bed. Snyder lived with the Geogles at their home, three miles north of Bethlehem, Pa. During the day he worked alongside of Jacob at the local ore mine. By night he entertained lustful thoughts for Geogle's young daughter Alice, who never reciprocated Snyder's affections. Deciding that he had to possess this woman at all costs, he crept into Geogle's bedroom on the night of Dec. 27, 1880. Armed with an ax, Snyder rained blow after blow upon the hapless couple who he believed stood in the way of his plans. The bodies were found by one of the Geogle children shortly afterward.

Snyder blamed an intruder for the murders, but Alice believed otherwise. She informed her neighbors about the horrible crime and summoned police. Before the lawmen could arrive the German residents of the neighborhood seized Snyder and lynched him from the highest limb. They feared he might cheat the hangman and escape conviction if he were brought into court.

REF.: *CBA; The Murder of Geogles and Lynching of the Fiend Snyder, By the Otherwise Peaceable and Law-abiding Citizens of Bethlehem, Pa.*

Snyder, Dr. **LeMoyne,** prom. 1944, U.S., law enf. off. In May 1944, Dr. LeMoyne Snyder, the medico-legal chief for the Michigan State Police, published *Homicide Investigation,* a work that outlined effective methods for conducting murder and suicide investigations. In the publication, Snyder argued that the first fifteen minutes of an investigation are the most crucial, that the scene should be thoroughly photographed and sketched, and that distances should be measured and fingerprints taken. Snyder addressed several fallacies concerning murder cases. They included the beliefs that quicklime destroys bodies, the victim's expression will remain fixed, the killer always returns to the scene of the crime, and a bullet in the heart is always fatal. In addition, Snyder discussed different types of poisons, including bichloride of mercury, morphine, strychnine (which can kill in as little as fifteen minutes), and arsenic. The latter two are both easily traced in the body. Snyder also detailed differences between murders and suicides, saying that suicides often hang themselves and try several times to shoot themselves. Snyder also discussed lie detector tests, methods for extracting specks of gunpowder from a victim's hand, and detecting lead by X-ray. In addition, the medico-legal expert warned against making snap assumptions, such as assuming that a body discovered in water had been drowned. REF.: *CBA.*

Snyder, Leroy, 1932- , U.S., mur. In July 1970, 38-year-old Leroy Snyder, a former Camden, N.J., junkyard worker, confessed to murdering six women and a man in an eight-month period in 1969. Snyder claimed that robbery was his motive in six of the slayings, but he could not remember why he had committed the seventh. Two of the women had been raped.

Snyder pleaded no defense to the seven murder charges in his 1970 trial. Under New Jersey law, the death sentence could not be imposed on a self-confessed murderer. Snyder was sentenced on July 16, 1970 to three consecutive life prison terms, making him eligible for parole in 2014, at the age of 82. REF.: *CBA.*

Snyder, Ruth May Brown, 1896-1928, and **Gray, Henry Judd,** 1893-1928, U.S., mur. By 1927, Ruth May Brown Snyder was a tall, overage flapper with bobbed blond hair, a voluptuous body, and a ravenous appetite for men of all kinds and sizes. She had an icy stare and a jutting jaw, and she looked upon any male who entered her life as her sexual prey, from doorstep salesmen to delivery boys. The fact that she was married meant little or nothing. Ruth Snyder, in fact, despised her husband and, according to later testimony, had attempted to murder Albert Snyder several times.

Albert and Ruth Snyder lived comfortably in a large three-story house in Long Island, N.Y., on Snyder's $115-a-week salary. He was the art editor of *Motor Boating* magazine and had a power boat of his own. The couple had a 9-year-old daughter, Lorraine, whom Ruth felt was a burden. Forty-four-year-old Albert Snyder busied himself with hunting, fishing, and boating. There was little room for domestic frolic. Ruth Snyder's "dream marriage" had turned into a dull, unpromising routine. She intended to change all that by murdering her husband, whom she had insured for $100,000.

Ruth was born into poverty. By age thirteen she left school to work as a night telephone operator. She studied shorthand and bookkeeping during the day. She later worked as a secretary and, in 1915, met and married the successful Snyder. Within a year, Ruth was referring to her husband as "the old crab." Snyder did little to make his wife happy. He antagonized her by referring to his former lover, Jessie Guishard, as "the finest woman I have ever known." Worse, Snyder placed a picture of Guishard, his first fianceé, above their bed, as a way of honoring her memory; the woman had been dead for ten years by that time.

Ignored by her husband, Ruth Snyder began to have brief affairs with many men. The peroxide blonde dressed as a flapper, wearing short skirts and high heels. Telling her husband she was seeing female friends, she went to dances alone, performing wild *Charleston* dances and picking up men to go to hotels for a few hours of "sexual ecstacy," as one reporter later put it. According to another account, the aggressive Ruth even preyed upon delivery boys who came to her home. At these times, Lorraine was in school and Snyder was busy drawing sketches of motorboats in his Manhattan offices.

One day in June 1925, Ruth and a lady friend went to lunch in Manhattan. The friend introduced the buxom flapper to 33-year-old Henry Judd Gray. Gray was short and myopic and wore thick-lensed glasses. He was nevertheless dapper and wore stylish clothes. Gray was addicted to homburg hats, handmade gloves, tight-fitting three-piece suits, and spats. Gray lived in Orange, N.J., was married and had an 11-year-old daughter. He worked for the Bien Jolie Corset Company, selling corsets. When Ruth heard this news, she excitedly told Gray that she was in Manhattan that day to buy a corset. How ironic. Could he show her some of his merchandise? Gray was delighted and took Ruth to his office after sending Ruth's friend on her way.

Said Gray later: "She removed her dress and tried on a garment to see if it was the right size. She was very badly sunburned and I offered to get some lotion to fix her shoulders." This was the beginning of the Snyder-Gray sex relationship, one which would lead to murder in less than two years. The couple met clandestinely in Manhattan hotels, usually the Waldorf Astoria. On these occasions, Lorraine Snyder would accompany her mother to the hotel and be left in the lobby to read books and while away the hours while her mother and Gray indulged in sexual exploits in a room upstairs. To Ruth Snyder, this was her great romance, this tawdry affair in which she addressed Gray as "Lover Boy," or "Bud." He called her "Momsie," or "Mommie," and was decidedly the weaker of the pair, submitting wholly to the dominant Snyder. The couple baby-talked to each other and sent each other the kind of little love notes usually written by high school sophomores. But beyond this secret affair, Ruth Snyder thought about a future without the hindrance of her cuckolded husband.

In late 1926 she took out the $100,000 life insurance policy on Albert Snyder and began making plans to murder him. According to later statements made by Gray, Ruth Snyder made seven attempts in 1926 to kill her husband by gas, by poison, and

Ruth Snyder, sash-weight killer.

Albert Snyder, murdered.

The Snyder home in Queen's Village, Long Island.

Above, Judd Gray, corset salesman gone wrong, shown awaiting trial with his mother.

Below left, Gray being booked for the murder of Arthur Snyder.

Below center, Ruth Snyder, going to the death house in Sing Sing.

Below right, Ruth Snyder being electrocuted; a news photographer smuggled a small camera into the death chamber strapped to his leg and took this sensational shot.

even by drowning on one occasion when Ruth "accidentally" bumped her husband overboard from the boat in which they were motoring. Snyder did not grow suspicious, however, blaming the attempts on his life on his wife's "clumsiness, her big-boned awkwardness." Meanwhile, ladies' man Gray began to drink to excess. As Albert Snyder's scheming spouse made each new attempt on her husband's life, Gray became more agitated. Ruth told him that she needed his help to murder Albert, but the corset salesman shook his head and went on another bender. At one point, after Snyder had been haranguing the corset salesman to aid her in her lethal efforts, Gray turned to her and asked: "Do you realize what it would mean in the eyes of God?"

Ruth Snyder by then had nothing to do with such thoughts. She wanted her husband dead and she was impatient for his demise. She cajoled, pleaded and finally ordered Gray to help her kill Albert. On the night of Mar. 19, 1927, Gray appeared in Long Island. According to his later claim, he had agreed to murder Albert Snyder but he kept busy on Mar. 19, hoping that somehow none of this would happen. On the morning of Mar. 19, Gray was selling corsets in Syracuse. That afternoon he took the train to Long Island and arriving at dusk, his two overcoat pockets stuffed with two large bottles of Mountain Dew whiskey. He wandered about the area where the Snyders lived, stopping beneath lampposts to pull out a bottle and take long swigs of the rotgut bootleg liquor. It appeared as if he was seeking to be arrested as a common drunk or for violating the Volstead Act. Neither happened.

Finally, Gray went to the Snyder home and entered it through a back door Ruth had left unlocked. The family was out, attending a party at a neighbor's house. Gray went to the guest room, following a map of the house Ruth had drawn for him. He looked at the bed, on which his lover had placed the tools for him to commit the murder: A bottle of chloroform, rubber gloves, and a heavy iron sash weight. Gray sat down on the floor, drinking from his bottles, draining one and then going to work on the other.

A little after 2 a.m. the door opened. Ruth Snyder stood in the dimly lit hallway whispering into the dark room: "Are you there, Bud, dear?"

"I'm here, Momsie," Gray replied.

Ruth closed the door and returned a few minutes later wearing only a slip. She and Gray then had sex for more than an hour. Ruth told her half-drunk lover to pick up the sash weight and follow her. He obeyed meekly. Ruth led him into her bedroom, where her husband lay sleeping. She pushed Gray forward and then left the room, standing in the hallway. Gray closed his eyes and then brought the heavy sash weight down on Snyder's head with all his strength. Albert Snyder roared with pain and bolted upright to a sitting position in bed. He reached upward and grabbed the terrified Gray. The corset salesman screamed: "Momsie, Momsie, for God's sake help!"

Ruth Snyder was there within seconds, standing on the other side of the bed. She grabbed the sash weight from Gray's hand as he struggled with Albert Snyder and then brought this down on her husband's head with a powerful blow, knocking her spouse unconscious. As Albert fell, Ruth grabbed the picture of her husband's former fiancée and unwound the wire behind it, looping this around Albert's neck. She twisted it so tightly that the wire became imbedded in the flesh. At the same time, she ordered the quaking Gray to retrieve the bottle of chloroform. Slipping on the rubber gloves, Gray soaked a rag with the chloroform and placed this over Albert Snyder's face, splashing so much onto the rag that it burned the victim's flesh.

Five hours later, at 7:30 a.m., Ruth Snyder, bound and gagged, wiggled her way into her daughter's bedroom, nudging her child awake. The frightened girl removed the gag from her mother's mouth. Ruth told her to run to the neighbors and call the police. Instead the girl brought over the neighbors, who reached down to untie Ruth Snyder. "No, no," she told them. "Leave me be. The police will take care of that. Call them immediately." Her plan, of course, was fixed in her mind and she would not deviate from it; the police, not the neighbors, were to find her bound. When police did arrive, they untied Ruth, but instantly realized that she was so loosely bound that she could have easily freed herself.

The story Ruth Snyder told police that morning was as ridiculous as a plot from a silent film. Snyder said that a burglar wearing a fake mustache like that worn by Bartolomeo Vanzetti, of the Sacco and Vanzetti case, which was much in the news at the time, had barged into her bedroom, tied her and her husband up, and killed her beloved spouse before robbing the place and fleeing.

A medical examiner from the coroner's office, Dr. Howard Neail, looked over the corpse of Albert Snyder in the bedroom. The body was bound loosely with small ropes. There was a picture wire tied around his neck. His head had been crushed on one side and he had been chloroformed. A revolver was found on the bed and three unspent cartridges were on the floor. Dr. Neail determined that Snyder had died of asphyxiation killed by strangulation from the wire.

Police were suspicious of Ruth Snyder from the beginning. She claimed that she too had been knocked unconscious, but Dr. Neail found no evidence of any kind of blow to her head or anything that would render her unconscious for five hours. The house had been ransacked and the money from Albert Snyder's wallet was missing. Ruth said that the burglar had also taken her jewelry. She also stated that all the doors of the house had been locked before she and her family retired that morning, yet police found no signs of forcible entry.

Detectives searched the house and found Ruth's jewelry stuffed inside of a mattress. She suddenly remembered: "Of course, how silly of me. I put it there for safekeeping some nights ago when I thought I heard a burglar prowling outside the house." The detectives went on searching, by this time believing that they were dealing with a killer named Ruth Snyder. After a few hours they were rewarded with the discovery of a bloody sash weight, which had been placed in a tool box in the basement. A bloody pillow slip, which had been used to wipe the blood from the killer's hands, was found in the bathroom laundry hamper. The murderers had been sloppy, indeed. (Broadway columnist and wit Damon Runyon would later term this killing "The Dumb-bell Murder," because, in his words, "it was so dumb."

Detective Arthur Carey continued to lead the investigation over the next few days. In the bedroom he found a tie clasp with the initials "JG" on it. Inside Ruth's desk he found a cancelled check made out to "H. Judd Gray." Gray's name and address, with his phone number heavily circled in red ink was found in Ruth Snyder's address book, along with the names and addresses of twenty-eight other men whose names were either underscored or circled in red ink. Some of the names had exclamation marks after them.

Two days later, Detective Carey discovered a bank safe deposit box registered under Snyder's maiden name, Ruth Brown. In the box was a $100,000 life insurance policy on her husband; the sole beneficiary was Ruth Brown Snyder.

Judd Gray was tracked to a Syracuse, N.Y., hotel room. When accused of murdering Albert Snyder, the little corset salesman became indignant at such an accusation. "My word, gentlemen," he said with a tone of injured pride, "when you know me better you'll see how ridiculous it is for a man like me to be in the clutches of the law. Why, I've never even been given a ticket for speeding." He was handcuffed and put aboard a train heading for New York City. Detectives grilled him during the trip and Gray finally broke down and confessed to the murder. But he emphasized that he had weakened at the last minute and Snyder had actually murdered her husband.

Snyder was then separately confronted. She was told that Gray had confessed and was already behind bars. Ruth Snyder lifted her lantern jaw and said: "Poor Judd, I promised not to tell." With that she admitted being present when her husband was killed but insisted it was the ruthless Judd Gray who had performed the awful deed. She went on to state that Gray had proposed the murder all along so that he could be with her. She painted herself as one of the most alluring sex goddesses of the age, intimating that her bedroom techniques drove men wild. She could not help it, shrugged Ruth Snyder. It was her animal magnetism.

The pair went to trial in Queens County on Apr. 27, 1927. The defendants were represented by separate lawyers. It was apparent from the beginning that they would each plead cases that incriminated the other. The press dubbed the trial the "Ruth Versus Judd" case. It was a celebrity affair, drawing such distinguished citizens to the spectator gallery as Mary Roberts Rinehart, David Belasco, D.W. Griffith, Peggy Hopkins Joyce, Will Durant, and even evangelists Aimee Semple McPherson and Billy Sunday. McPherson represented the sensation-seeking tabloid, the New York *Evening Graphic*, having received a substantial fee to write about this sordid murder case. To that end, Sister Aimee interviewed several persons outside the courthouse and quoted one young man as saying: "I want to have a wife like mother, not a red-hot cutie."

Edgar F. Hazleton, who represented Snyder, harped on the fact that Albert Snyder "drove love from out that house," by carrying the torch for a fiancée who had been dead a decade, and that it was Judd Gray who had arranged for the insurance policy on Albert Snyder. Thundered Hazleton: "We will prove to you that Ruth Snyder is not the demimondaine that Gray would like to paint her, but that she is a real loving wife, a good wife, and it was not her fault that brought about the condition in that house." Hazleton then put his client on the stand. The 120 reporters present described her every step toward the witness chair, women reporters later stating that she wore a simple black dress that was "not chic but decorous." A black rosary and crucifix hung conspicuously about her neck.

Ruth Snyder acted out the part of the discarded wife, the wronged woman. She said her husband ignored her and never "took me out," except to see an occasional movie. She pointed out that she read the Bible to her daughter Lorraine and took her to Sunday school and church, functions her uncaring husband never attended.

Hundreds of spectators who could not get into the jammed courtroom stood in the corridors and listened to Snyder talk through a microphone clamped to the witness chair. Hazleton then lightly touched upon the Snyder-Gray affair as if it had been only a few brief encounters and not a relationship that had stretched over two years. Snyder said of Gray from the witness stand: "He was in about the same boat I was. He said he was not happy at home." She pointed out that Gray was a hopeless, irresponsible drunk when she met him and that she spent most of her nights going to such hot spots as the Frivolity Club and the Monte Carlo, where she watched Gray drink himself into stupors. Added Snyder: "I rarely took a drink with him and never, ever smoked!"

Snyder went on to claim that Judd Gray urged her to take out the insurance policy and, after the policy had been issued, "he sent me poison and told me to give it to my husband." All of the seamy machinations of the affair and the murder plans, all of the attempts on the life of her husband, said Ruth, were the doing of Henry Judd Gray, the evil genius in her confused, sad life. She was a misdirected pawn in the hands of a ruthless killer. That was all there was to it. *She* was the victim.

Sam Miller, Gray's lawyer, attacked Snyder's statements with heroic bombast and then told the jury: "The tale of my client is the most tragic story that ever gripped the human heart." He described how his client had been almost force-fed twenty shots of whiskey to steel his nerves on the night of murder and to bolster his resolve just to enter the bedroom where Albert Snyder snored away the last few minutes of his life. Gray was a law-abiding citizen until he met the scheming Snyder, said Miller. "He was dominated by a cold, heartless, calculating mastermind and master will," said Miller. "He was a helpless mendicant of a designing, deadly, conscienceless, abnormal woman, a human serpent, a human fiend in the guise of a woman. He became inveigled and drawn into this hopeless chasm when reason was gone, when mind was gone, when manhood was gone, and when his mind was weakened by lust and passion."

Gray next took the witness chair. He was dressed in a well-tailored double-breasted business suit. He wore his glasses and adjusted these as he spoke in a quiet, unassuming voice. He played the love slave to the hilt, describing in detail the many attempts Snyder had made upon her husband's life. "She put poison in his prune whip once," intoned Gray, pretending shock. Then she tried to gas him to death, he added. "I told her I thought she was crazy." He then said that Ruth had given Albert Snyder poison on another occasion when he had the hiccups. "I said to her that was a helluva way to cure the hiccups! I criticized her sorely." Gray then said that Ruth had tried to murder her husband with sleeping powders, but that this had not worked. It was Ruth who thought up and arranged for the insurance policy, said Gray, and he emphasized that it was his ex-lover who had strangled Snyder with the picture wire, describing how powerful she was and that she possessed great upper body strength.

At that moment Ruth Snyder sobbed loudly in court and Judd Gray glanced at her briefly, but for the most part Gray continued to stare ahead during his testimony, his eyes fixed on his mother, who sat nodding at him in the spectator gallery. Next to Mrs. Gray sat the actress and singer Nora Bayes. Gray went on to claim that he had been "hypnotized" by Snyder and was not in his right mind on the night of the murder. He had acted as if he had been sleepwalking, he said.

On May 9, 1927, the trial came to an end. The "Putty Man," and the "Granite Woman" (or "Bloody Blonde" or "Marble Woman") as the press had dubbed the defendants, heard a jury—after only ninety-eight minutes of deliberation—convict them of premeditated murder in the first degree. Both were sentenced to death. While awaiting execution, both Ruth Snyder and Henry Judd Gray wrote their hurried autobiographies, each portraying the other as evil and themselves as good but hapless victims. Snyder wrote a poem which was later published in one of the tabloids, one which attacked the press for painting a dark picture of her. It read:

> You've blackened and besmeared a mother,
> Once a man's plaything—a toy—
> What have you gained by all you've said?
> And has it—brought you joy?
>
> And the hours when 'Babe needed my love,
> You've seen fit to send me away—
> I'm going to God's home in heaven,
> Ne'er more my feet to stray.
>
> Someday—we'll meet together,
> Happy and smiling again,
> Far above this earthly span
> Everlastingly in His reign.

On the cold, wintry night of Jan. 12, 1928, the two ex-lovers were executed at Sing Sing Prison. Judd Gray was the first to go. Warden Lewis E. Lawes found Gray in his Death Row cell smiling. He had received a letter at the last minute from his wife, who had forgiven him, not for killing Albert Snyder, but for sleeping with Ruth. "I am ready to go," Gray told Lawes. "I have nothing to fear." Minutes later Gray sat down calmly in the electric chair. He made no further comments and when the lethal current was sent through his body, Ruth Snyder, still in her death cell, looked up to see the lights dim, indicating that "Lover Boy" was gone.

The "Marble Woman" was next. She had already uttered her last words to Warden Lawes, saying that she knew "God has forgiven me and I hope the world will." She walked steadily into the death chamber and was strapped into the electric chair. A black hood was placed over her head and some reporters later claimed to hear her sobbing, some said praying. All cameras had been long banned from the room in which the electric chair was located but Thomas Howard, an enterprising cameraman for the New York *Daily News*, had strapped a small camera to his ankle under his trouser leg. Just as the current surged into Ruth Snyder, propelling her body against the head, arm, chest, waist and ankle straps of the chair, Howard, sitting in the first row, crossed his leg, lifted his trouser leg, and squeezed a plunger attached to a cord that ran inside his clothes to the camera. The photo that caught Ruth Snyder at the moment of death took up the entire front page of the morning edition of the *Daily News*. (Because of Howard's crafty photo-taking, all witnesses thereafter were completely searched before entering the execution chamber.) This photo is considered to be the most horrifying in the annals of execution and illustrates the desperate measures taken by yellow journalists in the tabloid era of the 1920s. That photo also gave Ruth Snyder black, undying fame, which outlasted her mawkish memoirs and silly sonnets.

REF.: Bechhofer-Roberts, *Famous American Trials;* Bishop, *Executions;* Brophy, *The Meaning of Murder;* Carey, *Memoirs of a Murder Man;* Carey, *On the Track of Murder; CBA;* Cook, *The Girl in the Death Cell;* Corder, *Murder My Love;* Dilnot, *Rogues' March;* Elliott, *Agent of Death;* Furneaux, *Courtroom USA;* Gribble, *Adventures in Murder;* Jacobs, *Pageant of Murder;* Kobler, *Some Like It Gory;* ____, *The Trial of Ruth Snyder and Judd Gray;* Logan, *Great Murder Mysteries;* Mackaye, *Dramatic Trials of 1927;* Morland, *Background to Murder;* Nash, *Bloodletters and Badmen;* ____, *Look For the Woman;* Roberts, *The New World of Crime: Famous American Trials;* Rowland, *More Criminal Files;* Russell, *Best Murder Cases;* Scott, *The Concise Encyclopedia of Crime and Criminals;* Sheridan, *I Killed for the Law;* Wilson, *Encyclopedia of Murder;* (DRAMA), *Machinal;* (FICTION), Cain, *Double Indemnity;* ____, *The Postman Always Rings Twice;* Matthews, *To the Gallows I Must Go;* (FILM), *State's Attorney,* 1932; *Criminal Lawyer,* 1937; *Double Indemnity,* 1944.

Charles Sobhraj en route to court for his murder trial.

Sobhraj, Gurmukh Charles (AKA: **Alain Gautier**), 1944- , India, theft-rob.-pris. esc-drugs-mur. As a young child Charles Sobhraj alternately lived with his father in Vietnam and in Paris with his mother as a young child. After several years of small crimes, he stole a car in France and was sentenced to six months in prison where he practiced karate and meditation. In 1968, he married a woman, Chantal, in France, and soon afterward stole a check from his sister's checkbook, forging it for 6,000 francs. His sister registered a complaint which she later withdrew. In 1970, Sobhraj and his wife went to Bombay, India, where he stole Americans' passports, smuggled diamonds, and sold luxury items he bought with bad checks. After he was involved in a botched jewel robbery in Delhi, he was arrested. When he was granted bail, he and Chantal escaped to Kabul, Afg., where they were put in jail on charges of stealing a car, not paying a hotel bill, and trying to cross the border illegally. However, Sobhraj once again escaped, by drugging his guards. During his escape, he seized a taxi driver, and after drugging him, put the driver in the trunk of the car where he suffocated to death. The body was tossed into a river.

From 1972 to 1975, Sobhraj stole throughout Tehran, Iran, where he was imprisoned for another year for carrying numerous forged passports. Officials also suspected him of involvement against the Shah. Meanwhile, his wife also was jailed for six months, and after her release, she went back to France and divorced Sobhraj. In November 1973, Sobhraj worked with his younger brother, Guy, robbing tourists in Istanbul, Turk., by first drugging them. When one Lebanese businessman recognized the two at an airport, they were arrested, but Sobhraj escaped. Then he went to Delhi where he met a Canadian, Marie-Andrée Leclerc, who became his girlfriend and with whom he later lived in Bangkok. There, he ran a heroin business, used hippies as couriers, and then allegedly killed them and several tourists. Beginning in October 1975, he reportedly killed Teresa Knowlton, Vitali Hakim, Stephanie Parry, Cornelia Hemker, Henricus Bitanja, Connie Jo Bronzich, and Laurent Carrière. They were drugged, strangled, and some of the bodies were doused in gas and burned.

Another associate, Allen Aren Jacobs, was found dead in his bed in northern India. When the Thai police raided Sobhraj's apartment in Bangkok, they found stacks of passports, but Sobhraj was permitted to leave the city. Local citizens suspected Sobhraj had bribed authorities. In Bombay in 1976, Sobhraj drugged and killed tourist Luke Solomon. He also passed out vomit-inducing drugs to a group of about sixty French engineering students in Agra, India. Finally, Sobhraj was arrested. He was tried for Solomon's murder, convicted and sentenced to ten years in prison for murder with an additional two years for drugging the students. In 1982, Sobhraj and his girlfriend Leclerc were tried at Varanasi, India, for the murder of Allen Jacobs. both were convicted and given life terms. Facing more charges in other countries, Sobhraj was returned to Agra, India, where charges were dismissed.

REF.: *CBA;* Thompson, *Serpentine;* Wilson, *Encyclopedia of Modern Murder.*

Socco the Bracer, See: **Gayles, Joseph**.

Société Générale Robbery, See: **Spaggiari, Albert**.

Society for the Recovery of Stolen Horses and Bringing Thieves to Justice, prom. 1799, U.S., vigil. In 1799, to put a stop to horse thefts, a group of residents in Montgomery County, Pa., established a posse called the Society for the Recovery of Stolen Horses and Bringing Thieves to Justice. Participants were paid six cents per mile, $25 for recovery of a horse, and $60 for catching both thief and horse. The group pursued thieves and after catching one, put a noose around his neck, and placed him on the stolen horse. The culprit was hanged as the horse galloped from underneath him.

REF.: *CBA;* Robinson, *Science Catches the Criminal.*

Socley, Gabriel, b.c.1906, Fr., asslt.-kid.-mur. On Good Friday 1935, Gabriel Socley kidnapped and murdered a little girl, Nicole Marescot, in Chaumont, Fr., located in northeastern France. Socley, reputedly a transvestite, was convicted and sent to a prison at Château Thierry, which housed special cases. In 1960, Socley was freed, but on July 27, 1971, he grabbed another girl by the shoulders in Dijon. He was then sent to the Sarreguemines psychiatric hospital for life. Socley briefly escaped from the hospital in March 1971.

REF.: *CBA;* Heppenstall, *Bluebeard and Others;* ____, *The Sex War and Others.*

Socrates, c.470-399 B.C., Gr., suic. Athenian philosopher whose unconventional lifestyle engendered many foes and, eventually, charges of being degenerate and of corrupting youth. He ridiculed his judges in a speech given in self-defense, and was convicted. He drank hemlock in jail in the presence of his students in 399 B.C. REF.: *CBA*.

Sodeman, Arnold Karl, 1900-36, Aus., mur. Arnold Sodeman was a quiet man who kept to himself. But after a few drinks, he would experience an uncontrollable need to kill. On Nov. 9, 1930, Sodeman had several drinks at the Orrong Hotel in Armadale, Aus., and decided to go for a walk. Passing through Fawkner Park in Melbourne's inner suburb of South Yarra, Sodeman came across a group of young girls playing. Overcome by one of his disastrous moods, he asked 12-year-old Mena Griffiths to run an errand for him, and went with her, later suggesting that they go on a short trip. They took a tram and then a bus, ending up near an abandoned house on Wheatley Road. By Sodeman's own later confession, "I took her in there...as soon as we got in I seized her by the throat. I then let her go and she fell to the ground. Looking back down on her my memory came back and I said: 'My God, she's dead. I have killed her.'" Sodeman stood wondering what to do, then remembered having read or heard something about "tying people up." He stripped, bound, and gagged the body with the girl's own clothing and left it in a bathroom. Though Sodeman claimed not to have "interfered" with the girl, Coroner Surgeon Dr. Crawford Mollison said that Griffiths had had sexual intercourse on the day she died.

After murdering Griffiths, Sodeman returned to his wife and their 2-year-old daughter, Joan. Police arrested a young man in the Griffiths murder, but released him because he had a perfect alibi. About two months later, on Jan. 9, 1931, Sodeman killed his second victim in the suburb of Ormond. The body of 16-year-old Hazel Wilson was discovered by her brother in a vacant lot in Oakleigh Road. She had been on her way to a dance. The similarities in the crimes led police to intensify their investigation, but they found no clues. Sodeman moved his family to Gippsland in eastern Victoria. It was another four years before he killed again. On New Year's Day 1935, after Sodeman had been drinking, he met 12-year-old Ethel Belshaw at a picnic on the beach at Inverloch. According to Sodeman, Belshaw asked if she could walk with him. He first refused, but then changed his mind. On a back road, he strangled the girl, and left her body bound and gagged as he had his other victims. Police questioned many picnickers, including Sodeman, but did not suspect him. He later attended Bradshaw's funeral. Less than a year later, on Dec. 1, 1935, Sodeman, then working at a road camp near Dumbalk, strangled 6-year-old Jane Rushmer, a friend of his daughter. Rushmer had asked the apparently gentle man to give her a ride on his bike. Sodeman, who had been drinking, took the child to a deserted area and killed her. Returning to his camp after the murder, Sodeman became angry when a coworker joked about the slaying. Police knew that the child had been seen with a man on a bike, and the coworker facetiously remarked that Sodeman had been riding his bike the night of the murder. The worker contacted the police the next day and Sodeman immediately confessed.

Sodeman's trial took place at the Melbourne Open Court, beginning on Feb. 17, 1936, with Justice Gavan Duffy presiding. Sodeman pleaded insanity, explaining that he knew that he had a mania of some kind. His family had a long history of insanity. Two prison doctors and a psychiatrist testified that he was insane when he killed. Government medical officer Dr. Albert Philpott explained that Sodeman was not conscious of what he was doing when he murdered. Philpott testified that Sodeman's condition was, "an obsessional impulse which is there all the time but which does not affect him when he has no liquor." The jury found Sodeman Guilty of murder and Justice Duffy sentenced him to death. He was hanged at Pentridge on June 1, 1936. A post-mortem examination revealed that Sodeman suffered from leptomeningitis, a disease of the brain.

REF.: *CBA;* Godwin, *Killers Unknown;* Gurr, *Famous Australasian Crimes.*

Soderburg, Erland H., prom. 1907, U.S., mur. A San Francisco pile driver, Erland Soderburg, was living with his elderly mother in Oakland, Calif., in 1907. On Mar. 23, he returned home drunk and angry, grabbed a butcher knife, stabbed his mother to death, and stuffed her into a closet. Then he cleaned the kitchen floor, burned the bloody rags, and the next morning, went to work as usual. Later in the day, neighbors noticed the old woman's cat crying, and when one woman went over to feed it, she saw the burned rags and the freshly washed floor. Police were notified and Soderburg confessed soon after. He was tried, convicted, and, on May 17, 1907, he was given a life sentence in the California state prison.

REF.: *CBA;* Duke, *Celebrated Criminal Cases of America.*

Sodini, Raymond, c.1928- , U.S., brib. A Cook County circuit court judge since 1971, Raymond Sodini, fifty-nine, was one of fifty-five people indicted in the Operation Greylord judicial investigation in Chicago. Sodini, who formerly presided over Gambling Court, a misdemeanor branch, was charged in 1985 with accepting bribes from lawyers in exchange for letting them solicit unrepresented defendants in his courtroom. He was also accused of receiving bribes of more than $1,000 monthly for three years, beginning in 1980. Prosecuted by U.S. Attorneys Anton Valukas, James Schweitzer, and Jeffrey Rogers, Sodini pleaded guilty in the middle of his trial on Jan. 20, 1987, admitting that he had accepted thousands of dollars in bribes. He was the second circuit court judge to plead guilty in the Greylord investigation. Sodini also pleaded guilty to one count of racketeering conspiracy and one count of filing a false income tax return in 1980. He agreed to pay the Internal Revenue Service $40,000 in unpaid income taxes and penalties.

In sentencing him, U.S. District Judge James Holderman called Sodini's courtroom a "cesspool of corruption," and also sentenced an attorney, Howard Brandstein, fifty-seven, who practiced there, and former deputy sheriff, Frank Mirabella, sixty-four, who was assigned to Sodini's court. Holderman sentenced Sodini to eight years in jail, and ordered him to perform 750 hours of community service during a five-year probation period. Brandstein was sentenced to a year and a day in prison, and Mirabella was given a seven-month jail term. Sodini's defense attorneys, Patrick Tuite and Cynthia Giacchetti, said of their client, "He knows what he did was wrong. He knows that he will be punished. He accepts that punishment." See: **Greylord Judicial Investigation.** REF.: *CBA.*

Soeder, Leon (AKA: **Leon Seter**), prom. 1900s, U.S., rob.-mur. In 1882, a German cook emigrated from Germany to the U.S. He was soon arrested for a burglary in Alameda County, Calif., convicted, and in October 1884, received a three-year sentence in San Quentin. Leon Soeder was arrested again on Jan. 29, 1894, in connection with the burglary of a San Francisco restaurant. He was convicted and sent to San Quentin for another three years. In approximately 1901, the criminal married Pilar Mirander and while they were living in Tesla, Calif., Soeder poisoned several dogs. In December 1902, the couple settled in Petaluma, Calif. After insuring his wife's life for $2,000, she soon died. In 1904, he traveled to Germany where he persuaded his brother-in-law, Jos Blaise, to return to the U.S. with him. On Dec. 23, Soeder tried to take out a $10,000 life insurance policy on Blaise but because of his criminal record was only allowed to take out a $3,000 policy. He then tried to purchase a $10,000 policy from another company,

Murderer Leon Soeder.

but the agent did not think Soeder would be able to make the payments, and sold him a second $3,000 policy. On Jan. 11, 1904, Soeder attacked Blaise. The body was found at the bottom of a cliff. The next day, he told his landlady Blaise had not returned home and reported to police that his brother-in-law was missing. He identified the body at the morgue, but when police discovered the insurance policies and a knife bearing human blood in Soeder's possession, he was arrested. In jail, Soeder told a cell mate, John Cooper, where he had killed Blaise, drawing a diagram which was later used as evidence. When confronted with Cooper's testimony, Soeder confessed to killing Blaise with a shovel and also to killing his wife. He was tried on May 23, 1904, convicted, and sentenced to death. Soeder was hanged on Mar. 29, 1907.

REF.: *CBA;* Duke, *Celebrated Criminal Cases of America.*

So Evil My Love, 1947, a novel by Joseph Shearing (British title: *For Her to See*). The sensational Bravo poisoning case (Brit., 1876), is the basis for this fictional whodunit. A film by the same title was made in England in 1948, directed by Lewis Allen and starring Ray Milland and Ann Todd. See: **Bravo, Florence Ricardo**. REF.: *CBA.*

Sofocleus, See: **Harding,** Sir **John**.

Soga Iruka, d.645, Japan, imperial minister, assass. Named imperial minister by his father, he ordered the assassination of Prince Yamashire Oe, the likely heir to the throne, in 643. Soga himself was assassinated by Prince Nakano Oe, the future Emperor Tenchi, and Kamatari Fugiwara. REF.: *CBA.*

Soga Umako, d.626, Japan, polit. corr.-mur. Destroyed Mononobe clan and seized supreme power for Sogas in 587. He planted Sushun as his personal choice for emperor in 587, but later arranged his murder. He put up his neice, Suiko, as empress, and her brother, Shotoku Taishi, as regent in 592. REF.: *CBA.*

Sogdianus, See: **Xerxes II.**

Sohappy, David, b.c.1926, U.S., consp. In 1855, the Yakima Indians ceded nine million acres of land to the U.S. government, but the Indians reserved the right to catch salmon for personal and ceremonial use. An elder of the Wanapum band, David Sohappy, explained that the tribe believes, "If you catch all those fish," they'll come back a thousandfold. But if we stopped fishing, they wouldn't come back." Federal officials did not have the same view. For fourteen months, an undercover agent of the National Marine Fisheries Service, Rich Severtson, bought 6,100 fish from tribe members for $150,000, including 317 salmon from Sohappy for $9,685. Federal officials also accused Sohappy of buying fish from other fishermen and reselling them. In Spring 1982, federal agents raided and arrested the Indians on charges of conspiring to catch and sell fifty-three tons of salmon illegally and interstate trafficking. Although most of the charges were dismissed against the Yakimas, Sohappy was convicted and sentenced to prison for five years. REF.: *CBA.*

Sokolnikov, Grigori Yakovlevich, b.1888, Rus., consp. Brought into custody in 1907, and exiled to Siberia in 1909 for Bolshevik activity. He fled custody and lived abroad for eight years. He served as ambassador to Britain from 1929-32, and worked in the timber industry as assistant commissar until he was arrested as a Trotskyist in 1937. He received a ten-year jail sentence. REF.: *CBA.*

Sokoloff, Alexander Konstantinovich, See: **Alexander II**.

Solanis, Valeria, 1940- , U.S., attempt. mur. Actress-writer Valeria Solanis emerged as a heroine to the militant wing of the National Organization of Women (NOW) following her ill-fated attempt on the life of pop artist Andy Warhol at his studio on Union Square West, New York City, on June 3, 1968. Solanis was described by her attorney as "one of the most important spokeswomen of the feminist movement." The daughter of a Syracuse, N.Y., lawyer, Solanis starred in the Warhol production of *I, A Man,* in which she played a lesbian.

She had recently presented Warhol with a play she had written concerning a man-hating vagrant. When the underground filmmaker failed to register enthusiasm for the production, Solanis, armed with .32-caliber automatic pistol, went his sixth floor loft on Union Square West. Warhol was on the telephone speaking with actress Susan Hoffmann when the elevator door suddenly opened and Solanis appeared. After exchanging a few words with writer Mario Amayo, the frustrated young playwright began firing. Bullets struck Warhol in the abdomen and left and right side. He was rushed to Columbus Hospital in critical condition and for a time wavered between life and death. Amayo suffered only superficial wounds.

Solanis fled from the building. That night she voluntarily surrendered to New York City patrolman William Schemalix in Times Square. "The police are looking for me. They want me," she said, adding that Warhol had "too much control" of her life. Solanis lived a Bohemian lifestyle, mingling with the artistic and literary clientele at the Chelsea Hotel, which Warhol immortalized in one of his avant-garde films. In 1967, Valeria Solanis organized a radical feminist movement called "SCUM" the "Society for Cutting Up Men." The aims of her organization were two-fold, the overthrow of the U.S. government and the elimination of the male sex. Her attorney Florynce Kennedy was quick to point out that violence was never intended. "I think she means that men control society and look what a mess they have made," Kennedy said.

The actress was booked on charges of felonious assault and possession of a deadly weapon. Appearing before State Supreme Court Justice Joseph A. Brust on Aug. 16, 1968, Solanis was declared incompetent to stand trial and ordered to the Mattewan State Mental Hospital. She remained there until Dec. 16 when doctors submitted a report stating that she was fit to stand trial. On Feb. 25, 1969, Solanis entered a plea of guilty to first-degree assault charges before Justice Gerald P. Culkin. She was sentenced to three years in prison on June 9 after waiving the right to appeal the sanity ruling handed down by Elmhurst Hospital psychiatrists. "I believe myself fully competent," she said. "This is my first offense. I've been locked up for a year. People have been convicted of homicide who had records and got less." Andy Warhol recovered from the shooting attack and resumed his career. REF.: *CBA.*

Solano, Vincent (AKA: **Vincent Rizzo, Vincent Innocence**), b.1919, U.S., org. crime. Vincent Solano began his criminal career as a chauffeur in the Chicago syndicate and rose to the number two post in the city. Solano allegedly served as a bodyguard and chauffeur to Chicago boss Ross Prio, who died in 1972, and he also headed the Chicago Local 1 of the Laborers International Union as president beginning in 1956. Solano reputedly gained control of all North Side Chicago operations, including gambling, loan sharking, extortion, and prostitution. He later stepped into the second highest ranking position, succeeding John Cerone, who was sent to prison. Solano's name was also linked to an assassination attempt on the life of Ken Eto. Eto, one of Solano's former lieutenants who was under indictment on gambling charges, claimed that Solano ordered him murdered in January 1983 and on Feb. 10, 1983. After the bungled second attempt in which Eto was to meet with Solano for dinner, two of Solano's henchman, Jasper Campise and John Gattuso, were charged with attempted murder and in July 1983 were both killed in a gangland-style slaying. Eto later became a government informer and said that Solano wanted him murdered to keep him from talking. REF.: *CBA.*

Soleilland, Albert, b.c.1881, Fr., rape-mur. After living off the proceeds of a prostitute during the 1800s, Albert Soleilland eventually married the woman. He had been convicted of acquiring money fraudulently and sentenced to an eight-month prison term by default. In March 1910, Soleilland allegedly tried to rape his 22-year-old sister-in-law, Julia Bremard. When she came up to his room, he pushed her to the floor and threatened her with an awl. While he was momentarily distracted, she escaped. Earlier, on Jan. 31, 1907, 26-year-old Soleilland saw a woman who had previously worked for his family as a housekeeper and asked if her daughter, 11-year-old Marthe Erbelding, would like to go to a concert with his wife. The mother at first declined, but then gave her consent, and Soleilland walked back to his Paris apartment with the child. There, he threatened her with a knife, raped her, and when she screamed, he strangled and stabbed her. Then he covered the body with canvas and put it in the Gare de l'Est, a train station. Calmly, he returned at 5 p.m. to the mother's house, asking if Marthe had come back home. Alarmed, she checked the theater and then reported the missing child to the police. They arrested Soleilland on Feb. 3. A witness was found who saw the killer with the child at the time she was supposed to have been at the concert and Soleilland confessed. His trial began on July 2, 1907, and he was convicted and sentenced to death, but the sentence was later commuted to a prison term by Pres. Clément Fallières.

REF.: *CBA;* Morain, *The Underworld of Paris.*

Soli, Salvatore and **Maleno, Steven,** prom. 1975, U.S., rob.-mur. Salvatore Soli and his companions in crime, Isais Felix Melendez and Steven Maleno, were vicious criminals, especially Soli, who was a known drug-peddler, car thief, and armed robber. He was once accused of attempted murder. Maleno, a homosexual, often robbed his male lovers. The youngest of the trio, Melendez, was a homosexual prostitute. All three, along with others, comprised a murderous gang that entrapped and robbed wealthy homosexuals.

John S. Knight III, heir apparent to the Knight-Ridder newspaper fortune, well-known socialite, a graduate of top schools, and a rising star in the Knight-Ridder newspaper chain, was also a homosexual. Unknown to most of his close associates and friends, he indulged in nefarious and pornographic activities.

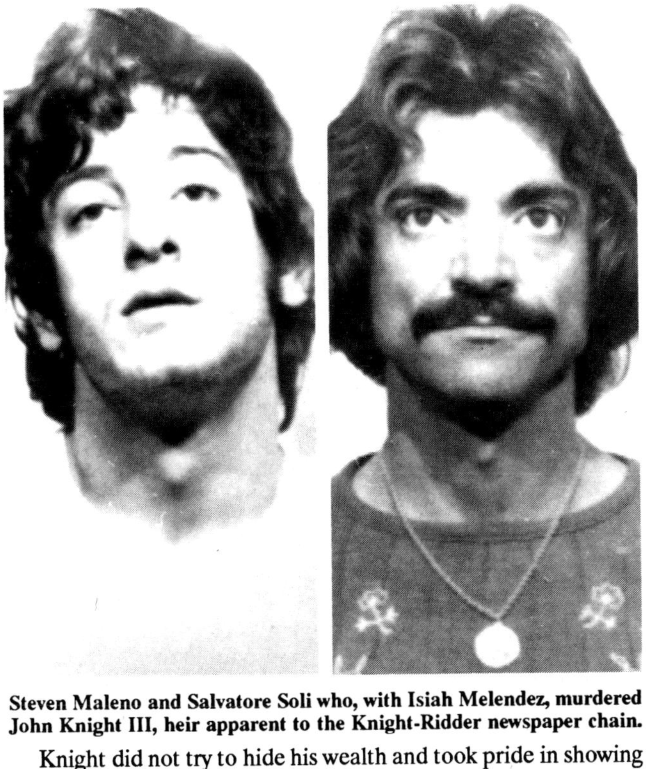

Steven Maleno and Salvatore Soli who, with Isiah Melendez, murdered John Knight III, heir apparent to the Knight-Ridder newspaper chain.

Knight did not try to hide his wealth and took pride in showing off his penthouse and collections of art, books, and erotica to his lovers. He was known as a free-spender who paid his lovers well. In doing so, he set himself up for a hit by the Salvatore Soli gang.

On the night of Dec. 7, 1975, Knight entertained guests for dinner at his penthouse. Later, all guests left except for a doctor and his wife, who were spending the night. At about 4 a.m., loud noises were heard from the apartment and the doctor's wife was awakened by an intruder demanding money and jewelry.

The woman was threatened, treated roughly by the three intruders, and then tied up. After the apartment was thoroughly ransacked, two of the thugs left. The one remaining, a young man who was high on drugs, untied the woman, who rushed back to her bedroom to awaken her husband.

The doctor confronted the young invader and, after a brief struggle, was knocked to the floor as the young man fled the apartment. Rushing to Knight's bedroom, the doctor found his friend unconscious, badly beaten, with a dozen or more neckties tied around his head and neck, and firmly bound. He was not breathing and no pulse was found. After attempting CPR, the doctor gave up. Knight had been stabbed to death. In the meantime, the doctor's wife called the police.

Knight's penthouse, ransacked by his murderers on the night of his death.

During the subsequent investigation, the police found extensive lists of Knight's homosexual contacts and a trunk of related photographs, videos, and paraphernalia. They proceeded to track down the people named on the list and eventually issued warrants for the arrests of Soli, Melendez, and Maleno.

Maleno turned himself in almost immediately, and Melendez's body was found a few days later in New Jersey. He had been murdered. A few days later, Linda Mary Wells, an associate of Soli's, contacted police in Miami, Fla., stating she knew about the murders in Philadelphia. She became the main witness against the gang, providing information leading to the apprehension of Salvatore Soli and implicating Maleno and Melendez. Soli and Maleno were brought to trial, and Maleno confessed to the slayings of both Knight and Melendez. Maleno received two consecutive life sentences. Soli, the leader of the gang, was convicted and, after losing an appeal, was sentenced to life in prison.

REF.: Bell, *Kings Don't Mean a Thing; CBA;* Godwin, *Murder, U.S.A.;* Nash, *Murder Among the Mighty.*

Solis, Magdalena, and **Solis, Eleazor,** and **Hernandez, Santos,** and **Hernandez, Cayetano,** prom. 1963, Mex., mur. In early 1963, two Mexican brothers convinced the villagers of Yerba Buena, Mex., that Inca gods would reward followers with treasure if they sacrificed money and sexual favors. Everyone except for Jesus Rubio was duped by the story, so he was bribed with some of the income. The cult continued for several months, but when no riches appeared, the villagers began to balk. So Santos Hernandez and Cayetano Hernandez went to Monterey, Calif., where they induced a brother and sister, actually a pimp and prostitute, to impersonate the two chief Inca gods. Eleazor Solis and Magdalena Solis agreed and returned to the village where they appeared to the villagers amid a cloud of smoke. Later, when the villagers were still not showered with treasure, two of the doubters were beaten to death. Followers then mixed the victims' blood with chicken blood and drank the mixture.

Six more distrustful villagers were killed during the next two months. Around that time, one teenager, Celina Salvana, Magdalena Solis' personal favorite, began having sex with a male cult member. Solis ordered the girl tied to a cross on May 28, 1963, and the former prostitute knocked her unconscious. Then the other followers attacked her, beat her to death, and burned her body. An awestruck 14-year-old Sebastian Gurrero witnessed the sacrifice and murder of another "unbeliever." The youth ran to police in Villa Gran where a policeman, Luis Martinez, was assigned to go with the boy to investigate the report. Both were slain and police and soldiers arrived at the village where the cult members were hiding in a cave. Three policeman and Santos Hernandez were killed in the shootout and the rest of the cult members were arrested. Cayetano Hernandez had disappeared, and Rubio later admitted to killing him because he planned to take his place as high priest. On June 13, 1963, the Solis brother and sister, along with twelve other cult members, were tried, convicted, and given thirty-year jail terms.

REF.: *CBA;* Wilson, *Encyclopedia of Modern Murder.*

Sollazzo, Salvatore (AKA: **Tarto**), and **Goldsmith, Jack**, and **Rivlin, William**, and **Lamont, Daniel**, and **Serota, Joseph**, and **Klukofsky, Eli** (AKA: **Eli Kaye**), and **Gard, Eddie**, prom. 1940s-50s, U.S., brib.-gamb. During the late 1940s and early 1950s, gamblers contacted star basketball players of New York City colleges, bribing them to fix games. Frequently, the gamblers first induced induced the players to control the win-loss point spread of games, and then later, to throw games. Corrupt athletes also were encouraged to recruit other players to the scheme. During a two-and-a-half year investigation that began in 1950, authorities uncovered evidence concerning basketball seasons played from 1947 to 1951, in which ninety of the games were discussed and forty-nine were actually altered. Thirty-three players from six major colleges were implicated and twenty-one were indicted. The primary gambling "fixers" included Salvatore Sollazzo, who furnished bribe money and used Eddie Gard, formerly a star for Long Island University, as his agent. Other gamblers were Jack Goldsmith, bookmaker William Rivlin, Joseph Serota, financial backer and gambler Daniel Lamont, and bookmaker Eli Klukofsky.

During the investigation, officials confronted Gard and other players, who all cooperated and in exchange for pleading guilty to misdemeanors, most receiving suspended sentences. Gard was given an indeterminate prison term, and three other players received prison terms because, in addition to accepting bribes, they had recruited others. Goldsmith was convicted on bribery charges and received a two-and-a-half-year sentence, Rivlin was convicted and sent to prison for one year, and Serota and Lamont were convicted, each sentenced to six months in prison. Additionally, in July 1951, Sollazzo was convicted of conspiracy and twenty-seven felony counts, receiving an eight-to-sixteen-year prison term. Investigators also found that Sollazzo used his wedding ring business as a disguise for smuggling and illegally selling $5,000 worth of gold per year. Sollazzo was convicted of tax evasion and illegal sales of gold, and in March 1953, he was fined $12,000 and sentenced to two years in prison. Still under indictment, Klukofsky died in August 1952.

REF.: *CBA;* Danforth, *The D.A.'s Man.*

Solomon, Alfred (AKA: **Alfie**), prom. 1924, Brit., mansl. In 1923, Barnett "Barney" Blitz, a prize boxer and member of a racing gang, was held by police on a racing charge. Blitz believed Edward Emmanuel had tipped police off and confronted him with the accusation one night in September 1924 in the Eden Club in London. Blitz began arguing with Emmanuel, who was accompanied by Alfred Solomon and Mr. Mansfield, and a fight ensued. During the brawl, Blitz grabbed a broken glass and shattered it in Emmanuel's face. The manager intervened and forced the men outside. As they started to leave, the fight erupted again, and Solomon pulled a carving knife and struck the boxer on the head. Blitz was taken to the hospital where he later died; and Solomon was arrested and held on murder charges.

Solomon's friends came to his aid, collecting money for his defense and then in a steady stream, Solomon's racing associates each visited the prominent lawyer Sir Edward Marshall Hall and pleaded with him to take the case. Hall agreed to take the case, entering a plea of self-defense. During the November 1924 trial, the attorney dramatically took a glass and broke it as an example of what the boxer had first used in his attack, and went on to describe the environment that night in which even a wrong word could lead to a fight. The jury found Solomon Guilty of manslaughter and sentenced him to three years in prison.

REF.: Bowker, *Behind the Bar; CBA;* Marjoribanks, *For the Defense, The Life of Sir Edward Marshall Hall;* Shew, *A Second Companion to Murder.*

Solomon, Charles (AKA: **King**), d.1933, U.S., org. crime. Charles "King" Solomon was the rackets boss of New England during the Prohibition era. He was one of several dozen Mafia kingpins present at the first major gangster "conference" held at Atlantic City in May 1929, which was convened to settle territorial disputes and establish a working national policy. Solomon returned to rule his gambling and prohibition empire until rival gunmen assassinated him at south Boston's Cotton Club on Jan. 24, 1933. See: **Atlantic City Conference.**

REF.: *CBA;* Eisenberg and Landau, *Meyer Lansky;* Fried, *The Rise and Fall of the Jewish Gangster in America;* Gage, *The Mafia is not an Equal Opportunity Employer;* Gosch and Hammer, *The Last Testament of Lucky Luciano;* Katz, *Uncle Frank;* McPhaul, *Johnny Torrio;* Messick, *Lansky;* ____, *Secret File;* ____ and Goldblatt, *The Mobs and the Mafia;* Peterson, *The Mob;* Thompson and Raymond, *Gang Rule in New York.*

Solovyof, Mr., See: **Alexander II.**

Soltysik, Patricia, See: **Weathermen, The.**

Somers, Baron **John (Sommers)**, 1651-1716. Brit., lawyer. Served successfully as junior counsel in defense of William Sancroft and six other bishops together charged with seditious libel. He also headed the committee that wrote the Declaration of Rights, served as attorney general in 1692, and held the office of chief minister under William III from 1696-1700. REF.: *CBA.*

Sommer, Gerhard Martin, b.c.1915, Ger., war crimes-mur. During WWII, an SS guardsman, Gerhard Sommer, was stationed at Buchenwald concentration camp, located in a forest near Weimar, Thüringia, in central Germany. There, Sommer tortured prisoners as overseer of the punishment cellblock between 1938 and 1943. He was later accused of beating inmates with a stout stick on a whipping block, making his victims count each lash. If a prisoner lost count, he was forced to start counting over again. Sommer also hanged prisoners by their wrists to trees in what was dubbed the "singing forest" because of the screaming victims. The torturer allegedly beat one minister, hanging him outside, and after throwing buckets of water on the man, left him to freeze to death.

In addition, Sommer had a personal cache of torture equipment, including needles to inject air and carbolic acid, which he kept hidden in the floor under his desk. He also reputedly put bodies under his bed at night. Sommer's brutality appalled even his Nazi superiors, who transferred him to the war front where he lost an arm and a leg. After the war, West German officials at first found Sommer unfit for trial. But after the former SS officer married in 1956, had a child, and requested an increase in his veterans' pension, West German officials decided to press charges. A psychiatrist found him sane but sadistic. When the trial opened, the prosecutor charged him with fifty-three murders, saying Sommer was responsible for "probably the most hideous group of sadistic atrocities unearthed since the war." Onlookers called out, "Beast" and "Monster" when he was wheeled into the courtroom. To limit the trial length, all of the charges except twenty-three murders by injection were eventually dismissed. In July 1958, Sommer was found Guilty in the Bayreuth Circuit Court and sentenced to a life term, the maximum punishment allowable under West German law. REF.: *CBA.*

Sommerhalder, Richard (AKA: **Blue**), prom. 1976, U.S., mur. During the 1970s, Richard Sommerhalder operated a store that sold drug paraphernalia in Rio Del Mar. In 1976, the bodies of Mary Gorman and Vickie Bezore were found naked and bludgeoned to death in the mountainous region of Santa Cruz, Calif. Sommerhalder was arrested and charged with their murders. He was convicted and sentenced to two life terms.

REF.: *CBA;* Godwin, *Murder, U.S.A.*

Somodevilla y Bengoechea, Zenón de (Marqués de la Ensenada), 1702-81, Spain, her.-exile. Served as prime minister from 1743-54, promoting education and improving army and navy. His anti-British policies caused him to be exiled to Granada from 1754-59. He was able to resume government work after the coronation coronation of Charles III in 1759, but was again exiled in 1766 for espousing pro-Jesuit beliefs. REF.: *CBA.*

Songgram, Philbul, prom. 1940s-50s, Siam, war crimes. Japanese-controlled Marshal Philbul Songgram took over the leadership of Siam (later Thailand) during WWII. When the war ended in 1945 another Thai national, Nai Pridi, threw Songgram out of office and invited 19-year-old King Ananda II, who had weathered the war in Switzerland, to resume his throne. On June 9, 1946, Ananda was assassinated in his bedroom. On Nov. 8, 1947, Songgram again seized power in a bloodless coup, vowing vowing to find and kill the king's murderers. Songgram used this popular cause as an excuse for a manhunt in which he purged the country of his enemies. The purge ended finally in 1955. REF.: *CBA.*

Son of Sam, See: **Berkowitz, David.**

Brothers in crime George and John Sontag.

Sontag Brothers, prom. 1880s-90s, U.S., rob.-mur. George and John Sontag were born in Minnesota in the 1860s. The boys were three years apart in age, living with their mother and her second husband in Mankato. George, the younger of the two, went to work as a train brakeman and then later as a grocery clerk in Nebraska. He embezzled money from his employer and was sentenced to the state prison. After serving about a year George escaped with another convict. He later returned to jail on his own volition to complete the original sentence, which ended in 1887.

Meanwhile, John Sontag had moved to Los Angeles in 1878 where he went to work on the Southern Pacific Railroad as a brakeman. He was badly injured in an industrial accident and continued to harbor deep resentment against his employers during his convalescence. Short of cash, Sontag found employment with a Visalia, Calif., farmer named Chris Evans, who also had an intense dislike for the railroad. Together these men decided to avenge themselves.

On Jan. 21, 1889, they boarded a train at Goshen, Calif., and robbed the express car clerk of $600. A month and a day later they repeated the same crime at Pixley, only this time the take was $5,000. Having escaped detection John Sontag returned to Mankato in May 1891. He confessed to his brother George all he had done. John Sontag returned to California a month later to sample the pickings. Reunited with Evans, they attempted to rob the Southern Pacific but were driven off by Detective Len Harris. Having failed, John headed back to Minnesota where he enlisted George to the cause. After carefully considering the matter the Sontag brothers decided that the most likely plum would be train No. 3 out of Chicago, which stopped at Western Union Junction, Wis., on the evening of Nov. 5, 1891. The robbery went off like clockwork, and the brothers rejoined their relatives in Racine, $9,800 richer.

After this the Sontags traveled west to rendezvous with Evans. The three held up a passenger train at Collis Station, in Fresno, Calif., on Aug. 1, 1892, making off with three sacks of money. Later, George Sontag boarded the same train in the suburbs of Fresno where he joined in the conversation with the excited passengers who recounted the robbery minute by minute. His actions aroused the suspicion of the local authorities. Detective Smith and Deputy Sheriff Witty ordered George Sontag to appear at headquarters and answer a few questions. How was it, they wanted to know, that Sontag happened to be on the same train right after the robbery? Meanwhile, Smith and several deputies went back to Evans' home to question him at length. The daughter told the men that her father was not home, whereby they pushed aside a portiere and found John Sontag. He leveled a shotgun at the officers who attempted to flee. Evans drew his own weapon and fired upon Witty who fell to the floor dead.

John Sontag and his friend Chris Evans were now fugitives. Meanwhile, George was quietly arrested and placed on trial for the Fresno train robbery on Oct. 25, 1892. On Nov. 3, after a Guilty verdict had been returned, he was sentenced to life imprisonment at Folsom. His brother and Chris Evans were given help by the villagers northeast of Visalia, frustrating efforts to arrest the pair. But Evans, who along with Sontag had been wounded in an earlier gunfight, was trapped in a straw shack outside Visalia. Barely able to walk, he was taken into custody. John Sontag was captured soon after.

Meanwhile, George Sontag plotted his escape from Folsom Prison. He ingratiated himself with a fellow convict named William Fredericks who had been imprisoned for holding up the Mariposa stage. On June 27, 1893, the two, armed with smuggled weapons, seized the lieutenant of the guards. Using the man as a shield, Sontag, Williams, and four other hard cases marched through the gates under the watchful gaze of the tower guards who trained a Gatling gun on them. As they approached the brink of a deep gulch the lieutenant managed to extricate himself from his captors. At the precise moment he leaped over the cliff the Gatling gun opened fire. George Sontag was badly wounded in the affray, but miraculously survived. On July 3, 1893, his brother John succumbed to his own gunshot wounds and died in the Fresno jail. It was a hard blow for his brother. Chris Evans went on trial for murder on Nov. 28, 1893. George Sontag volunteered to give evidence against his former associate after explaining that Mrs. Evans had mistreated his mother when she had come to

Posse that captured John Sontag.

California to nurse John. Based on his testimony, the jury returned a Guilty verdict against Evans who was sentenced to life imprisonment. Evans made a bid for freedom on Dec. 28, 1893. He seized a knife and held it to the throat of jailer Ben Scott, who opened the door and let him out. The desperado, having recovered sufficiently from his wounds, made his way back to the ranch in Visalia. He remained there until Feb. 19, 1894, when a posse surrounded the house and took him prisoner. Evans surrendered and was returned to the state prison to serve out a life sentence. George Sontag was pardoned on Mar. 21, 1908. He went to work at Tim McGrath's gambling resort on Pacific Street in San Francisco before settling down to write his memoirs.

REF.: Block, *Great Train Robberies of the West;* Botkin and Harlow, *A Treasury of Railroad Folklore;* Burt, *American Murder Ballads; CBA;* Conger, *Texas Rangers;* Dillon, *Wells Fargo Detective;* Doctor, *Shotguns on Sunday;* Duke, *Celebrated Criminal Cases in America;* Glasscock, *Bandits of the Southern Pacific;* Haley, *Jeff Milton;* Harlow, *Old Waybills;* Holbrook, *The Story of American Railroads;* Horan and Swiggett, *The Pinkerton Story;* ____ and Sann, *Pictorial History of the Wild West;* Hunter and Rose, *The Album of Gun-Fighters;* King, *Main Line;* Koller, *The American Gun;* Lewis, *High Sierra Country;* Menefee and Dodge, *History of Tulare and Kings Counties California;* Morrel, *The Twenty-Fifth Man;* Nash, *Bloodletters and Badmen;* Small and Smith, *History of Tulare County, California;* Smith, *Garden of the Sun;* ____, *Prodigal Sons;* Torchiana and van Coenen, *California Gringos;* Vandor, *History of Fresno County, California;* Warner, *A Pardoned Lifer;* White, *Lead and Likker;* Wilson and Taylor, *Southern Pacific;* Woods, *Lights and Shadows of Life on the Pacific Coast.*

Soper, Daniel E., and **Scotford, James O.**, and **Covert, Adolphe B.**, and **Scoby, Alpheus**, prom. 1907, Case of, U.S., fraud. During the early 1900s, a Detroit gang manufactured fake antiques, buried them near a town, and then "discovered" the items, selling them as authentic. They disposed of articles such as copper battle axes, bronze tables, spearheads, and Indian tools. The fraud was detected by a Wisconsin collector, H.P. Hamilton, and although no laws existed at the time that could be used to prosecute the swindlers, a newspaper crusade begun by the Detroit *Daily News* helped put an end to the scheme for a time.

REF.: *CBA;* MacDougall, *Hoaxes.*

Sophia Alekseevna (Sofya Alexseyevna), 1657-1704, Rus., consp.-mur. Prompted rebellion by household troops after brother Czar Fyodor III died without an heir in 1682. The uprising caused the murders of many backers of her half-brother, the future Peter I, and she was able to plant another brother, Ivan V, as co-ruler with Peter. She served as regent for her siblings and became the de facto ruler of Russia from 1682-89, when Peter placed her in a Moscow convent against her will. She was jailed from 1698 on unproven charges of trying once more to spark insurrection. REF.: *CBA.*

Sophia Dorothea (Sophie Dorothea, Princess of Ahlden), 1666-1726, and **Königsmark, Philipp Christoph**, 1665-94, Brit., adult. In 1682, Sophia Dorothea married the Crown Prince of Hanover, who later became King George I of England. Their marriage was not harmonious, and with the help of Count Philipp Christoph Königsmark, she unsuccessfully tried to escape from Hanover once or twice. Although it is unclear whether Königsmark was Sophia's lover, they were accused of an illicit relationship and on July 1, 1694, Königsmark disappeared. He was probably assassinated. Sophia was arrested, tried, and convicted, and after her marriage was annulled, she was confined in the Castle of Ahlden for thirty-two years, where she was known as the Princess of Ahlden.

REF.: *CBA;* Lambton, *Echoes of Causes Celebres.*

Sorel, Agnes (Dame de Beauté), c.1422-50, Fr., mur.? Lived in estate at Beauté-sur-Marne given to her by paramour Charles VII of France. She amassed many foes in her lifetime, and was believed by some to have been murdered by poisoning.

REF.: Bullough, *An Illustrated History of Prostitution; CBA.*

Sotades, prom. 3rd Cent. B.C., Gr., libel. Gained reputation for producing salacious writings. He was executed by being placed in a sealed chest of lead and thrown into the sea for writing satirical verse about Ptolemey II Philadelphus. REF.: *CBA.*

Soto, Erno, 1939- , Case of, U.S., burg.-drugs-mur. A patient at a mental institution, Erno Soto, had previously spent about eleven years in jail for burglary and narcotics offenses and was a suspect in several New York murder cases. He was an outpatient at the Dunlap-Manhattan Psychiatric Center in 1972 and on Wards Island in 1973. In early March 1972, a boy was sexually mutilated and murdered, and several days later, Soto was admitted to the psychiatric facility for becoming "violent with grandiose religious delusions." Soto left the grounds and on Apr. 20, 1972, and another child was similarly mutilated, but survived. Soto went back to the hospital and was discharged on Apr. 23, 1972. Two more boys were molested and killed on Oct. 23, 1972, and on Mar. 6, 1973.

In April 1973, Soto was placed back in the institution because he had "an uncontrollable violent outburst." On Aug. 7, 1973, the patient was given a weekend pass. Soon after, the mutilated body of 7-year-old Steven Cropper was found on the roof of a tenement building. Soto was discharged from the facility on Aug. 31, and nine months later, he was arrested on charges of child molestation and was later charged with the Cropper murder. During his trial, one psychiatrist said the defendant assaulted for "ritualistic" and "religious" reasons. In November 1976, Soto was acquitted of the Cropper murder on the grounds of insanity and was readmitted to the mental hospital. REF.: *CBA.*

Soto, Juan (AKA: The Human Wildcat), d.1871, U.S., west. outl. The notoriety that earned Juan Soto a place in the history of the U.S. West came at the end of his life. Soto was of mixed Indian and Mexican heritage and became notorious in California as a thief and murderer. Soto and two other men robbed a store in Sunol, Calif., on Jan. 10, 1871, killing a clerk and shooting a number of rounds into the living quarters of the store owners.

The "Human Wildcat" Juan Soto.

Soto and his men were then tracked by Sheriff Harry Morse. The lawmen followed the outlaws into the Sausalito Valley about fifty miles outside the town of Gilroy. Morse and a deputy found Soto and a dozen of his followers. Soto drew on the sheriff when told he was under arrest. After a skirmish, Morse broke free and pursued Soto outside. There Soto had attempted to mount a horse but the animal spooked and ran away. Soto ran 150 yards before Morse was able to draw a bead on him. Even at this distance the sheriff hit Soto. As Soto ran back toward the sheriff, Morse fired again, this time hitting Soto in the head and killing him.

REF.: Baker, *Past and Present of Alameda County, California;* Bancroft, *Works of Hubert Howe Bancroft; CBA;* Dana and Harrington, *The Blonde Ranchero;* Duke, *Celebrated Criminal Cases of America;* Erwin, *The Southwest of John H. Slaughter;* Fisher and Holmes, *Gold Rushes and Mining Camps;* Shinn, *Pacific Coast Outlaws.*

Soulakiotis, Mariam, prom. 1940s-50s, Gr., fraud-embez.-mur. In the early 1920s, a Greek monk, Father Matthew, established a religious sect called the Calendarists and built a convent about thirty miles southeast of Athens, near Keratea. He was aided by a former factory worker, Mariam Soulakiotis, who began to take control of the convent during WWII when Father Matthew was in his eighties. She began sending monks and nuns to recruit wealthy converts, and as they arrived, they were required to confess, fast, go without sleep, pray, maintain silence, and turn over their estates. New converts who did not adhere to these policies were beaten and other members were regularly punished.

In about 1949, local villagers began to gossip about screams coming from the convent and in early 1950, the daughter of one convert contacted the Athens prosecutor, and charged that Soulakiotis had forced her mother to sign over her estate. After investigating, the prosecutor discovered that about 500 recruits had left their estates to the convent and then died.

In December 1950, Soulakiotis was arrested and in September 1951, she was tried on charges of unlawfully confining a girl in the convent for twelve years. The child, placed in the convent in 1938, had been told she was an orphan and her father had been told that she had died. Soulakiotis was convicted, and sentenced to twenty-six months in prison. A nun was also convicted as an accomplice and was sentenced to four months in prison. About a year later, in 1952, Soulakiotis, eight nuns, and a phony bishop were tried on charges of withholding food and medical treatment from a monk and three nuns, causing their deaths and obtaining their estates by fraud. On Feb. 6, 1953, Soulakiotis was sentenced to ten years in prison, a nun received a ten-year sentence, another nun was given a three-year sentence, and the fake bishop received a year in prison. Soulakiotis was again brought to trial on charges of embezzlement, fraud, and illegal detention and abuse of a convent member. On Nov. 18, 1953, she was given another four-year term, to be served concurrently with the prior sentence.

REF.: *CBA;* Rowan, *Famous European Crimes.*

Soulder, Frank, and **Swolley, Gale E.,** prom. 1930s, U.S., kid. During the 1930s, a Chicago gambler, James J. Hackett, operated slot machines throughout southern Cook County, Ill. He refused to give local gangsters a share of the proceeds, although he was threatened. On Mar. 2, 1931, a bomb that failed to explode was discovered near Hackett's gambling den. On May 1, 1931, the 57-year-old Hackett was playing golf with his 20-year-old son, George, at the Navajo Country Club. At gunpoint, kidnappers ordered Hackett to go with them. They held him in an Aurora house and demanded $150,000 ransom. Meanwhile, Hackett's wife liquidated jewels and securities, and took out a mortgage on their home. After she paid the ransom, Hackett was put blindfolded in his own car on May 3, 1931, told to wait five minutes, and then he drove home unharmed. The gambler was kidnapped again on May 27, 1933, and $1,500 of a $10,000 ransom was turned over to the abductors. Frank Soulder a Benton, Ill., gambler and bootlegger, and Gale E. Swolley, a saloonkeeper in Peoria, Ill., were arrested and charged in connection with the kidnappings. They were convicted on Jan. 22, 1934. Each received a life term. REF.: *CBA.*

Soursas, Simone, 1913- , Fr., mansl. In 1952, 39-year-old Simone Soursas was preparing to leave Paris to join her husband in the French Sudan when she met 32-year-old Pierre Clair. The two, who were both shy and unattractive, immediately became lovers and Clair would beat the older woman during lovemaking sessions. After Soursas flew to the Sudan to join her husband, the lovesick Clair inundated her with letters, begging her to come back. She agreed, but after two months of beatings, she again returned to the Sudan.

Clair persisted with his love letters, although he had found another girlfriend. Only after he threatened suicide did Soursas fly back to Paris, and in December 1954, she became pregnant with his child. In May 1955, Soursas attempted suicide by swallowing poison, but was saved by her landlady. It was after her recovery that she discovered a photograph of Clair's other lover in his coat pocket. On May 18, Soursas, seven months pregnant, stood outside Clair's hotel. When he emerged, Soursas shot him four times in the chest. She was arrested, and while in custody, she gave birth to a daughter, Christine. Soursas was tried, convicted of manslaughter with extenuating circumstances, and given a five-year suspended sentence.

REF.: *CBA;* Goodman, *Crime of Passion;* Heppenstall, *The Sex War and Others.*

Southampton, Henry Wriothesley, 1573-1624, Brit., consp. Helped persuade Robert Devereux to scheme to remove counselors of Elizabeth I. He attempted to win support for the plot by launching a revival of *Richard II,* Shakespeare's tale of ousting the king. The conspiracy failed, and he received a death sentence in 1601, but he was released from prison by newly crowned James I in 1603. REF.: *CBA.*

Southard, Lydia, b.1892, U.S., pris. esc.-mur. Lydia Southard lost four husbands to "typhoid": Robert Dooley, William Gordon McHavie, Harlan C. Lewis, and Edward Meyer. She collected sizeable amounts of insurance after each death. Southard was on her honeymoon in Honolulu with her fifth husband, Paul Vincent Southard, when she was arrested and extradited to Twin Falls, Idaho, where she was tried in 1921, accused of extracting arsenic from flypaper and poisoning fourth husband Meyer. Southard was convicted and sentenced to ten years to life in the Idaho State Penitentiary. After serving ten years, Southard charmed her way out of the facility. She persuaded a prison blacksmith to make her a ladder and she coaxed a guard to bury it in the prison yard. In May 1931, Southard dug up the ladder, climbed the wall, and escaped in a waiting car that prison officials believed was driven by recent probationer, David Minton. Southard fled to Denver where she was hired by Harry Whitlock as a housekeeper. She married Whitlock, but when she read in the newspaper that Minton was being questioned by police, she fled to Topeka, Kan., where she was arrested. Whitlock annulled the marriage, and Southard was incarcerated again. Ten years later, in October 1941, the 49-year-old Southard was paroled into her sister's custody for a six-month probationary period. REF.: *CBA.*

Southern Michigan State Prison Riot, 1952, U.S., riot. In April 1952, inmates at the Southern Michigan State Prison rioted for five days, setting fires and destroying property. Nine people were injured, one prisoner was killed, and $2.5 million worth of property was damaged. Inmate leaders Jack Hyatt and Earl Ward negotiated terms, demanding the firing of cruel guards, the creation of a more lenient prison system, and a guarantee that inmates would suffer no punishment for rioting. Prison administrators agreed to the terms, promising the prisoners that they would not be disciplined, but admitting that inmates might face penalties from other law enforcement organizations. REF.: *CBA.*

Southern Tenant Farmers' Union, prom. 1935, U.S., mob vio. During President Franklin D. Roosevelt's New Deal administration in the 1930s, the main solution to the U.S. Depression crisis in agriculture was to cut down production by supplementing government subsidies to cooperating farmers. Though the tactic successfully raised agricultural prices, it devastated tenant farmers, laborers, and sharecroppers in the South, as landlords grabbed acreage reduction benefits intended for the tenant farmers and even dispossessed sharecroppers and tenants who then became disenfranchised laborers and went on relief. Blacks and whites together reacted by organizing tenants' unions, not for the first time. An earlier Alabama Sharecroppers Union in the Depression years was violently broken up by the authorities.

The most effective new organization was formed in Arkansas. Socialists H.L. Mitchell and Clay East, advised and backed by Norman Thomas and the Socialist Party, formed the Southern Tenant Farmers' Union. Earlier efforts in Arkansas had been quickly repelled by violence, and in 1919 a Phillips County union of blacks was massacred. But by 1935, the new interracial movement included Socialists and ministers, with 10,000 members in eighty local branches. The group focused on peaceful action, but was met with massive mob violence, with local whites and absentee corporations trying to break the union through harassment, threats, beatings, and murder. Despite all this, the Union endured, struggling unsuccessfully against great odds to change the economic structure of the area. A reign of violence in March 1935 continued for about two and a half months as terrorist tactics against the union prevailed in northeastern Arkansas, with meetings broken up and members falsely accused, jailed and convicted on fraudulent charges. Relief was cut off and member were evicted by the hundreds as vigilante bands patrolled the highways. Organizers were beaten, mobbed, tortured, and slain.

Incidents in a ten-day period of this terrorism included the attempted lynching of a 70-year-old black minister, Reverend A.B. Brookins, a member of the Southern Tenant Farmers' Union National Executive Council. After four unsuccessful attempts on his life, Brookins' home was riddled with bullets one night by a mob. His daughter was shot through the head and his wife escaped only by lying prone on the floor. W.H. Stultz, president of the union, received a note warning him to leave Poinsett County within twenty-four hours. After nightriders tried to blow up his home, he and his family were moved to Memphis by the union. A black preacher and union organizer, Reverend T.A. Allen, was found in the Coldwater River near Hernando, Miss., shot through the heart, his body weighted down with chains. The local sheriff told a United Press reporter that Allen had probably been slain by angry planters and that there would not be an investigation into the murder.

Mary Green, the wife of a Mississippi County union member, died of shock when armed vigilantes went to her home to kill her husband, a union organizer. Mob violence continued when a group of black men and women, returning from church near Marked Tree, were viciously beaten with flashlights and pistols as scores of children were trampled. On Norman Thomas' return to New York, he began a nationwide radio broadcast with a denunciation of what he had seen: "There is a reign of terror in the cotton country of eastern Arkansas. It will end either in the establishment of complete and slavish submission to the vilest exploitation in America or in bloodshed, or in both...The plantation system involves the most stark serfdom and exploitation that is left in the Western world." REF.: *CBA.*

Southgate, Susan, 1875-1958, Brit., (unsolv.) mur. On Apr. 17, 1958, the home of Susan Southgate, near Chelmsford, Essex, was burgled. The 83-year-old woman was found bound and gagged on Apr. 18, after police received a telephone call from an unidentified man saying, "There's been a break-in at a Mill House near Colchester and we've tied up an old lady. You had better get along and release her." When policemen arrived, Southgate was dead and officers later discovered £5,000 that the intruder had missed.

REF.: *CBA;* Furneaux, *Famous Criminal Cases, vol. 5, vol. 6.*

South Korean Riots, 1987-88, S. Kor., riot. In 1980, Chun Doo Hwan took control of South Korea after a bloody coup overthrew the previous regime. President Chun promised that the new military dictatorship would be a transition government and that a democracy with free elections would later be established. In April 1987, Chun halted discussions of a new constitution and proposed an election in favor of Chun supporter, Roh Tae Woo. Frustrated by the lack of change, although not ideologically opposed to the regime, students began rioting in June 1987, demanding democracy, freedom of the press, and freedom of speech. Riots erupted at seventy-eight colleges and in fourteen cities, led primarily by students and joined by middle-class Korean citizens. Although riot police were called to quell the disturbances, they were ordered not to shoot and the military was not deployed. Seven days later, the chaos had claimed only one life. Rioters in Taejon seized a bus and drove the vehicle through a line of police officers, killing one.

A year later, South Korea was experiencing solid economic growth and more lenient political policies, leading to a resurgence of nationalism throughout the country. Roh was installed as the new president and freedom of the press was granted. Students incited another riot in June 1988, calling for reunification with North Korea and for the expulsion of the U.S. REF.: *CBA.*

South Moluccan Kidnappers, prom. 1977, Neth., kid.-terr. On May 23, 1977, nine South Moluccan terrorists hijacked a train at Glimmen, north of Assen in the Netherlands, holding more than fifty passengers captive for nineteen days. Later that same day four South Moluccans seized a school at Bovensmilde, nearby, taking more than 100 children, between the ages of six and twelve, hostage along with five teachers. The South Moluccan Kidnappers demanded that the Dutch Government help them to obtain independence for their homeland, once known as the Spice Islands, which had been annexed to Indonesia. About 40,000 Moluccans lived in the Netherlands in a strained relationship with the Dutch people. Alienated Moluccan youths remained isolated in Dutch society.

An earlier act of terrorism, in December 1975, involved the hijacking of a Dutch train and the seizure of the Indonesian consulate in Amsterdam. Three passengers were executed and a fourth hostage fell from a consulate window to his death during the fifteen-day siege. The South Moluccan kidnappers demanded the release of twenty-four of their group held in jail for terrorist actions, and a Boeing 747 to fly them and the current terrorists to an unspecified country, saying the hostages would be "in serious danger" if demands were not met by 2 p.m. on May 26. Andreas van Agt, Dutch minister of justice, appeared on television to say that the children must be released before the government would consider the kidnappers' demands. On May 25 the terrorists made two shows of force. In one, they shoved a couple from the train onto the tracks, blindfolded, handcuffed, and with nooses around their necks. In another, holding the children hostage, they forced several youngsters to stand at an open window chanting, "We want to live, we want to live." A 2 p.m. deadline the next day passed without incident. By May 27, several children came down with stomach infections, and the kidnappers freed all 105 of them within two days.

On May 29, the South Moluccans in Glimmen refused to release the remaining fifty-six hostages, including a woman seven months pregnant. By May 31 their demands were weakening, with no more mention of releasing the imprisoned Moluccans, and no insistence on taking the hostages with them. On June 2 an outbreak of shooting when the hijackers fired at some television masts soon after asking that they be removed. No one was hurt in the incident. On June 11, about 2,000 commando marines, sharpshooters, and armored military police units surrounded the train and the school. Marines began firing submachine guns as jets from the Royal Netherlands Air Force dropped smoke bombs to cover the troops. In a 5 a.m. attack, six terrorists' and two hostages were slain, with one terrorist, two marines, and nine prisoners wounded.

Prime Minster Joop Den Udyl pleaded with Netherlands citizens not to take revenge on the Moluccan community for the terrorists actions stating, "The Moluccan problem is not a color problem. It is a problem of history and ideals." On Sept. 22, 1977, seven South Moluccans were given prison terms ranging from six to nine years for the kidnappings in northern Holland, with an eighth given a one-year jail sentence for supplying ammunition and a weapon. On Aug. 31, 1978, the Netherlands government agreed to name a commission of South Moluccans to study ways the minority group could be integrated into Dutch society.

REF.: *CBA;* Clutterbuck, *Kidnap and Ransom.*

South Sea Bubble, The, 1710-20, Brit., fraud. The South Sea Company (or The Governor and Company of Merchants of Great Britain trading to the South Seas and other parts of America) was founded in 1710 to defer responsibility for Britain's fast-growing national debt from the government to private enterprise. The idea (originated by author Daniel Defoe and championed by Chancellor of the Exchequer Robert Harley) was to set up a trading company that would exploit the American colonies and independent areas in the new world, issue stock in the new company, and use the dividends to pay off investors who had purchased government bonds, thereby paying off the national debt. The inducement of easy money in the form of colonial slave trading or hypothetical gold mines in unexplored territories inspired many to put money into the scheme, which was legal, if not entirely ethical. The company found no gold mines, but it was lucrative and prestigious.

The scheme first went afoul of the law in 1719, with the appearance of South Sea board member John Blount (or Blunt), who took the idea of the watered stock several steps further. He approached Parliament with the idea of taking on the responsibility for the national debt on condition that £100 of South Sea stock be issued for every £100 of debt incurred—a generous offer on the surface, since the real value of South Sea stock had increased to £128 for each £100 face value. But Blount's proposal to Parliament included these implications: "Suppose that shares were forced up to £300. That would mean that in order to convert £1,200 of government stock the company need only issue four shares of £300 each, not twelve at £100. That will leave eight surplus shares over, which, by selling them, would provide a profit of £2,400." Blount had discovered a way to manufacture money out of thin air; all it took was a government desperately in debt enough to let him get away with it.

Blount found it necessary to bribe members of Parliament to secure approval for the issuing of the stock. During the debates on the subject, the face value of the stock was inflated by "very artificial engines and secret springs." In the spirit of skullduggery infecting the venture, false rumors were voiced about Peruvian lands soon to be acquired by the company. This bloated the value of the stock, demand for which quickly grew out of proportion to its true value—the initial issue upon Parliament's approval was £2.25 million of stock at £300 per share of £100 face value stock. Royal Assent for this issue was received on Apr. 7, 1711, and by Apr. 28, the company declared a 10 percent dividend and issued a further £1.5 million of stock, this time at £400 per share for £100 face value. The three weeks in which a little over £1.1 million true value of stock was sold for £3.75 million was not enough time for a single ship to be outfitted and sail to the new world.

The public was especially impressed by the pedigree of some of the scheme's backers. King George I himself was persuaded by his two mistresses, Baroness von Kielmansegge and Madame Schulenburg, to accept an appointment as governor of the company, and the Earl of Sunderland, who was serving as first lord of the Treasury, was enthusiastic in supporting Blount's proposals. The high hopes Blount generated in the government and among investors led to a sort of mania among the public, many of whom wanted in on the deal. This led to any number of lesser swindles, as people who could not acquire South Sea stock invested in any similar deal that came along. A phony insurance company was set up to insure marriages against divorce, a fake research and development scheme promised "the making of a wheel of perpetual motion," and £2,000 were spent on worthless stock offered by an enterprising con man who advertised "an undertaking of Great Advantage, but no one to know what it is."

The directors of South Sea itself moved to put their even more dishonest competitors out of business, using the technicality that, as partnerships without a government-approved charter of incorporation, they were not legally entitled to issued securities at all. South Sea brought action against four of these fly-by-night operations in August 1720, and Parliament passed an act banning such companies. However, with the competitors forced out of business, the artificially high stock prices readjusted themselves in the marketplace, independent of directorial control. By the end of September, South Sea shares formerly valued at £1,000 had fallen to £190. By the end of October, they had fallen to £135. At least three investors committed suicide. The House of Commons formed an investigative committee which levied fines against Blount and other board members, but the Earl of Sunderland and the king's mistresses were allowed to keep the profits they had made.

REF.: Carswell, *The South Sea Bubble; CBA;* Nash, *Hustlers and Con Men;* Scott, *The Concise Encyclopedia of Crime and Criminals.*

Southwell, Robert, 1561-95, Brit., fraud. Lived as fugitive in the home of Mary Howard, the countess of Arundel, after officials discovered he was a native-born Roman Catholic Jesuit. He was jailed and tortured from 1592-95, and was finally put to death. REF.: *CBA.*

Southworth, John, c.1582-1654, Brit., her. Although Catholic priests were prohibited in England at the time, John Southworth secretly ministered there for eight years during the rule of King James I. Southworth was arrested in Lancaster and placed in the custody of the French ambassador. But Southworth continued to work as a priest in England for another twenty years until he was arrested again. Although the custom of hanging priests had begun to ebb and French and Spanish ambassadors urged mercy, Oliver Cromwell demanded the execution of the 72-year-old priest. On June 28, 1654, Southworth was hanged and quartered.

REF.: *CBA;* Potter, *The Art of Hanging.*

Sovereign, Henry, d.1832, Can., mur. In 1828, Henry Sovereign was convicted of shooting and killing a horse. He was sentenced to death, which was the mandatory sentence for this offense. Judge James Buchanan Macaulay recommended executive clemency, and eventually Sovereign was freed. Four years later, the same judge presided over Sovereign's murder trial.

In 1832, Sovereign, his wife, and their ten children were living in Ontario, Canada. On Jan. 22, with three of the children not at home, Sovereign stabbed and hacked his wife and seven of his children to death. Covered in blood, he ran to a neighbor's house, claiming that two assailants had wounded him. Returning to the house with help, the bodies were found. But Constable John Massacer became suspicious, believing Sovereign was responsible when he found white hairs similar to Sovereign's in his dead wife's clenched fist. A knife and a maul, a tool used to split wood, were discovered to be the murder weapons, and Sovereign was arrested. He was jailed in London where he spent seven months in prison awaiting trial. On Aug. 8, he was convicted, and sentenced to death a second time by Judge Macaulay. Sovereign, Ontario's first mass murderer, was hanged on Aug. 13.

REF.: *CBA;* Miller, *Twenty Mortal Murders.*

Sowden, Mr., See: **Bodmin Jail Riot**.

Sower, Christopher, 1721-84, U.S., treas. Published second and third editions of Germantown or Sower Bible in 1763 and 1776. He was charged with treason in 1778, jailed, and robbed of his property. REF.: *CBA.*

Sowrey, Alfred, d.1887, Brit, mur. The case of the conviction and hanging of Alfred Sowrey is not noteworthy in itself, but the effect it had on his hangman is. Sowrey had killed his sweetheart and then, in attempting suicide, failed and was thus saved for the gallows. Sowrey's fear and agony at the thought of hanging was so great that he not only suffered great mental anguish in the days leading up to the event but struggled with four or five warders up to the very moment the lever was pulled. The hangman, James Berry, who had participated in the execution of more than 200 people, was so affected by Sowrey's reaction to hanging that from that time on he opposed capital punishment.

REF.: Atholl, *The Reluctant Hangman;* ____, *Shadow of the Gallows; CBA.*

Spada, André, d.1935, Fr., mur. Corsica's infamous bandit, André Spada, built his reputation on murder and extortion. Famous for squeezing money from the rich, he was loved by the poor on the French island, located off the western coast of Italy. Spada, a name meaning "sword," shot two police officers in 1922, killing one. When a young man stole his lover, Spada killed the rival's uncle and cousin in retaliation. Spada also kept a careful watch over the highway connecting Ajaccio and Sopigna, collecting money from travelers. In 1931, the outlaw closed the road for two months after Depression-era travelers petitioned him to decrease the charge. Spada reportedly earned money from blackmail and extortion, and secured political influence with fixed elections. In 1931, the French government vowed to catch the desperado, dead or alive, and sent supplies and men to Corsica. General Fournier led the manhunt with 800 soldiers and 200 armed reporters. The mission turned up only a few small-time bandits.

In May 1933, Spada arrived in Coggia, haggard and incoherent. He wore a crown of twigs on his head and a cross around his neck. Villagers recognized the unkempt man as Spada and told the outlaw to hide, but he was later arrested. In March 1935, he was tried at Bastia, Corsica, on fourteen counts of murder. André Spada was guillotined at Bastia in June 1935. REF.: *CBA.*

Spafields Riot, 1816, Brit., riot. In 1816, pamphlets urging revolt were spread throughout London, drawing thousands of ruffians to the Spafields area. On Dec. 2, 1816, a rebel, Mr. Watson, gave a speech before a crowd, criticizing social conditions. The speech incited a riot in Spafields, which spread to central London. The mob broke into gun shops, arming themselves for assaults on taverns, stores, and the Royal Exchange. No one was killed and the disturbance was quelled by the military.

REF.: Bleackley, *Hangmen of England; CBA.*

Spaggiari, Albert, 1932- , Fr., rob. The mastermind of "le fric-frac-du siecle" (the heist of the century) was a fast-living adventurer named Albert Spaggiari, who, by his own claim, loved women and animals. "All kinds of animals," Spaggiari explained, "but mostly the ones that are hunted because we share the same fate." Albert Spaggiari had served as a paratrooper in French IndoChina, then later as a hired gun for the outlawed Organisation Armée Secrète (OAS), a right-wing cabal composed of former military officers dedicated to preserving Algeria as a French colony. "I couldn't help it because I'm a wolf," Spaggiari wrote. "I got fed up with all those Communists and their crybaby demonstrations." He was, without saying, firmly to the right in his political thinking.

Master robber Albert Spaggiari.

In early Spring 1976, Spaggiari ran a photo supply store in Nice and tried to decide what avenues to pursue in life. "I travel and I dream," he said, "I've spent my life dreaming. For me a dream is the reality you have just before the big problems start." In this case the *attainable* dream seemed to be the Société Générale Bank, situated on the Rue Deloye and the Rue L'Hôtel-des-Postes in Nice, Fr. It was an imposing structure enclosed by heavy grillwork and stone masonry. The vault, as Spaggiari soon learned, was ancient. It had been constructed in the early 1900s.

Spaggiari spent weeks drawing maps and floor plans based on his visits to the teller windows and anteroom of the bank. He devised a foolproof plan to gain after-hour admittance to the vault, which housed millions of francs in gold ingots, negotiable securities, and cash, tucked neatly into safe-deposit boxes. Much of this wealth was hidden from tax officials and therefore uninsured. It was a rich plum for an enterprising burglar. During one of his many reconnaissance trips to the bank he took note of a city work crew entering a sewer manhole on the Rue Deloye. "My heart skipped a beat," he recalled. "According to the maps—I knew them by heart—the vault was located right in line with the manhole." If he could tunnel through the underground masonry of the bank building it stood to reason that the safe-deposit boxes could be looted with relative ease and escape would be a certainty.

The job could not be completed alone so Spaggiari recruited a number of his former associates, men living on the fringe, like Gaby Anglade, who had attempted to assassinate Charles DeGaulle in 1962. Jean Kay was another Spaggiari henchman lured into the plot. Kay was wanted by the police for bilking Marcel Dassault, an aerospace industrialist, out of eight million francs. In May 1976, the thieves entered the manhole to begin tunneling operations. For the next two months they labored tirelessly to construct a twenty-five-foot tunnel leading from an adjacent parking garage to the bank. A half-mile section of cable connected to a fluorescent light illuminated their way. While this was going on the bank thieves were plied with generous amount of food by Spaggiari—catered into the tunnel.

The operation was brought off faultlessly on July 20, 1976, the Independence Holiday in France. The gang entered the vault and removed assets totaling sixty million francs from the locked boxes. The total haul far exceeded the notorious 1974 Purolator Robbery in Chicago, still fresh in everyone's mind. It was Europe's biggest theft, and the thieves were careful to cover their tracks. They welded the vaults shut, leaving behind a cryptic message, "Without weapons, without hate, and without violence." The theft was discovered the following Monday. Bank officials spent the next few weeks tallying their losses and placating anxious depositors whose uninsured fortunes were lost overnight. Spaggiari and his associates knocked over the Paris branch of the Société-Générale just a few weeks later.

In October, French police received their first clue. A garage owner was apprehended for selling bonds traced to the Nice theft. The investigation plodded along until October 1976 when eleven suspects were arrested and charged with complicity in the burglary. Albert Spaggiari was picked up on Oct. 27 after making the "grand tour" of New York, Hong Kong, and Bangkok. "Rule number one for the critical situations: rise to the occasion," the thief wrote in his memoir. "Don't allow circumstances to alter your plans, your appearance, or your habits." Unfortunately for Spaggiari his best-laid plans backfired. He was arrested on the Rue de Marseille three days after landing at the Nice Côte d'Azur Airport.

Spaggiari remained a prisoner exactly four months. Facing a likely fifteen to twenty-year sentence, he set his dreams aside and formulated a brilliant plan of escape. The courtroom in which he was tried overlooked the street. A large window fastened to the sill with just one little clip was all that stood between him and freedom. On Mar. 10, 1977, Spaggiari leaped to his feet, unfastened the window, and climbed out on the ledge. "No, not that!" screamed his lawyer, Jacques Peyrat, but it was already too late. The prisoner jumped from the ledge, bouncing harmlessly off the roof of a parked Renault automobile, and onto the back seat of an awaiting motorbike whose rider had come to pick him up. He gestured obscenely to the gaping attorneys and police officers who could only stand by and watch, and then roared off to freedom.

In 1978, two reporters from Paris *Match,* Hubert Lassier and Arnaud Hamelin, located Spaggiari in Madrid, Spain. Their interview with the fugitive (who continued on to Argentina where he lived among the right-wing exiles of the Hitler era) formed the basis of Spaggiari's book, appropriately titled *Fric-Frac.* "Farewell native land," he said. "I'll be back in twenty years or twenty centuries."

REF.: *CBA;* Nash, *Almanac of World Crime;* Spaggiari, *Fric-Frac: The Great Riviera Bank Robbery.*

Spanish, Johnny (Joseph Weyler), 1890-1919, U.S., org. crime. Spanish, one of the most feared holdup men in Manhattan, murdered his first man in 1907 at seventeen. A brooding, lone-wolf gunman and a Spanish Jew, he claimed to be related to General Weyler, the cruel Spanish dictator of Cuba prior to the Spanish-American War—thus his sobriquet, Johnny Spanish. Although he operated on occasion with the Five Points Gang under the direction of Johnny Torrio and later worked as a lieutenant for crime boss Paul Kelly, Spanish preferred to conduct his criminal business alone. He specialized in holding up underworld saloons and crap games or stuss operations.

When Spanish walked into the street, he was a moving arsenal. He always wore two guns in his waistband and two more in his pockets. He carried at least two knives, matching sets of brass knuckles, and a blackjack stuffed into a back pocket. To establish a fearless reputation Spanish devised a highly publicized robbery that served as his calling card. He selected the toughest saloon keeper in his territory, Mersher the Strong Arm, who operated a bar on Norfolk Street. A messenger arrived to tell Mersher that Spanish would appear at his saloon the next night at 8 and that Spanish intended to take every dime from Mersher's till. Mersher laughed at such bravado but Spanish appeared at the doorway of the saloon precisely at 8 p.m. He was a small, slight man, wearing a porkpie hat low over his eyes. In each hand he held a gun and behind him stood another man, also holding two guns. The man did not enter the saloon but served only as a street lookout and backup to Spanish. After firing a single shot that shattered the expensive mirror behind the bar, the youthful gangster strode boldly into the bar, shoved the behemoth Mersher aside, and emptied the till. He then took every dime from Mersher's dozen customers at the bar and left without exchanging a word with his victims.

Spanish fell in love with a young girl in 1911 and resolved to obtain a fortune so he could support her in style. He began raiding the crap and stuss games on the East Side, selecting expensive operations ruled by the equally fierce Kid Jigger. He then decided that he would merely rake off 50 percent of Jigger's nightly gross and confronted the Kid with this less-than-attractive proposition. "An' why do I give youse half my stuss graft?" the Kid smirkingly asked Spanish.

"Because if youse don't," snarled Spanish while he glared at Kid Jigger, "I'll bump youse off and take it all!"

Kid Jigger roared with laughter at that and dismissed the young gangster as a lunatic.

Spanish kept his stare fixed on Jigger, however, and said: "Okay, Kid, I'll bump youse off tomorrow night."

The next night Spanish waited for Kid Jigger to emerge from his stuss operation on Forsyth Street, between Hester and Grand. When the Kid stepped into the street, Spanish began shooting at him. He missed the gambler but hit an 8-year-old girl playing nearby, killing her. The gangster fled the city and remained in hiding for several months. When he returned he was told that Kid Jigger had thought better of his proposal and was willing to share his proceeds with Spanish. The effort was misdirected, however, in that the woman for whom Spanish had taken the risk had taken up with rising hoodlum Nathan "Kid Dropper" Kaplan, who would go on to become one of the ruling gang bosses of New York in the early 1920s.

The gangster went berserk with jealousy, and he abducted the woman some nights later. He took her to Maspeth, Long Island, where he tied her to a tree and then shot her four times in the abdomen. Incredibly, she lived to deliver the child she was carrying, a baby born with three of its fingers shot off and fathered by none other than Johnny Spanish. The gangster was later caught by police, convicted of a robbery, and sent to Sing Sing for seven years. His rival, Kaplan, ironically, was also charged with robbery about the same time, received an identical sentence, and was sent to Sing Sing to serve time. In prison, the two men vowed to kill each other—Kaplan would later make good this promise.

Both were released in 1917 and immediately set up rival gangs, vying for control of the garment district unions. About thirty gunmen in each of their gangs made up their forces, not formidable when comparing the hundreds of gangsters belonging to such feared organizations as the Gophers. The Spanish and Kaplan gangsters, however, were all top gunmen—ruthless killers who stopped at nothing to achieve the ends of their bosses. Of the two gangs, Kaplan's was more successful, working its way into the union hierarchy and gleaning 50 percent of dues, along with enormous thefts of goods. In 1919, Spanish made an all-out effort to eliminate Kaplan but Kid Dropper moved faster. He and two others waited outside a restaurant at 19 Second Avenue on the steamy night of July 29, 1919. Inside, dining alone, was Johnny Spanish. As Spanish emerged, picking his teeth, Kaplan and two henchmen stepped behind the gang chief and emptied their guns into him.

When police found the body of Johnny Spanish (he was carrying more than $3,000 in cash in his pockets, along with his four guns), a call went out to arrest his arch enemy, Kaplan. But Kid Dropper had an alibi; he had several friends state that he was attending a party at the time Johnny Spanish met his gun-blasting fate. A waiter in the restaurant where Spanish had eaten, had been looking out the window at the time of the killing and had initially described Kaplan as one of the killers. He later changed his mind, saying he had been "mistaken." With the death of Johnny Spanish, Kaplan became the most powerful gangster in New York. See: **Kaplan, Nathan**; **Kelly, Paul**.

REF.: Asbury, *The Gangs of New York; CBA;* Fried, *The Rise and Fall of the Jewish Gangster in America;* Harlow, *Old Bowery Days;* Levine, *Anatomy of a Gangster;* Lewis, *The Apaches of New York;* Nash, *Bloodletters and Badmen;* Nevins, *The Greater City—New York, 1898-1948;* Willemse, *Behind the Green Lights.*

Spann, Enoch F., and **Eberhardt, Susan**, d.1872, U.S., mur. In 1872, Enoch Spann and his wife lived on a farm near Preston, Ga. With the aid of his servant, Susan Eberhardt, Spann engineered a plan to murder his wife. First they tried to drown Mrs. Spann during a ride to church by startling their horse, causing the woman to be thown into a stream. On May 4, while Mrs. Spann slept, Eberhardt placed a handkerchief in the victim's mouth and Enoch Spann strangled his wife with a rope. The two then disappeared, and the body was discovered the next morning by a farm worker. The fugitives were arrested six weeks later in Alabama where they worked on a plantation. They were sent back to Georgia for trial. Both Spann and Eberhardt were convicted, sentenced to death, and hanged.

REF.: *CBA;* Cohen, *One Hundred True Crime Stories.*

Spara, Hieronyma (La Spara), d.1659, Italy, mur. Hieronyma Spara, or "La Spara," in seventeenth-century Rome started an unusual version of an early woman's movement. Women met at her home each evening, they performed rites to the goddess Diana, and then, if they had the money, they purchased her expensive poison with which they could eliminate their husbands or lovers. Early in 1659, Roman clergymen began to whisper together about receiving confessions of murder from a number of respectable women. They went to Pope Alexander VII, who put a female spy among the group. When the spy reported back that she was able to purchase poison and was even encouraged to kill her husband, La Spara was arrested. Under torture she revealed the names of more than thirty women who attended her gatherings. La Spara, her assistant La Gratiosa, and three other women were hanged for murder. The others were all driven through the streets by whips.

REF.: *CBA;* Glaister, *The Power of Poison;* Nash, *Look For the Woman.*

Sparrow, William, and **Maggs, William**, and **Hurd, William**, prom. 1852, Case of, Brit., rape-mur. In the town of Frome, England, on Sept. 24, 1852, Mr. and Mrs. Watts returned home from the store around 4 p.m. to find their kitchen splattered with blood. In the dairy, they found their 14-year-old daughter, Sarah, murdered. She had been raped and suffocated and her face was badly bruised. A watch was missing, but no cash was taken. After the whey tub was emptied, blood was found at the bottom, indicating that the girl had been hit on the head and then held face down in the tub. Three men, William Sparrow, William Hurd, and William Maggs, had been seen together at a pub that day, and Sparrow and Maggs were later seen walking toward the cottage. All three were seen still later that day in the store wearing different clothes, and one was heard to say to another, "A watch, but no tin." On Sept. 29, at a county fair, Sparrow told a woman he had seen Sarah Watts lying face down in the tub, and that one man had killed her, but he would not say who it was. All three men were arrested and charged, and a wound on Sparrow's hand, when examined, proved to have been made around the time of the assault, although he claimed it was much more recent. The evidence against the men proved inadequate, however, and after fifteen minutes of deliberation, the jury acquitted them all. REF.: *CBA.*

Spartacus, d.71 B.C., Rome, rebel. Became slave after being apprehended for leaving army without authorization. He headed the slave rebellion known as the Gladiatorial War from 73-71 B.C., but was eventually defeated by Marcus Crassus and killed.

REF.: *CBA;* (FILM), *Spartacus,* 1960.

Spatchett, Walter, See: **Furnace, Samuel James**.

Speakman, Howard, 1892-1952, U.S., jur. Superior court justice of Maricopa County, Ariz. He presided over the celebrated murder trial of Winnie Ruth Judd, who was found Guilty of killing two women and sending their bodies to Los Angeles in a trunk in 1932. Seven years later, he disqualified himself from the double murder trial of Robert M. Burgunder. REF.: *CBA.*

Special Branch, 1800s-1900s, Brit., law enf. agency. Special Branch (SB)" is a division of England's Scotland Yard that was created in 1884 to combat Irish attacks on British targets. The department, primarily an investigative unit, is concerned with cases of treason, violations of the Official Secrets Act, riots, and sedition, and has infiltrated several extremist organizations. Just before WWII, the bureau detected a sabotage plan masterminded by the Irish Republican Army (IRA), which resulted in the Prevention of Violence Act, giving the Special Branch the authority to arrest IRA suspects. REF.: *CBA.*

Speck, Richard Franklin (AKA: **B. Brian, Richard Franklin Lindbergh, Richard Benjamin Speck**), 1941- , U.S., rape-mur. When he was nineteen, mass-murderer Richard Speck emblazoned a tattoo into his left forearm which accurately summed up his emotional and mental state at the time. It read: "Born to Raise Hell." Years later, Speck burned the tattoo off using the ember of a lit cigar. From his cell in the Stateville Penitentiary at Joliet, Ill., he dreams of the day he will be paroled. By his own admission though, the convicted killer of eight student nurses believes that the chances are not good. "If he was ever freed on parole, I'd probably take up arms myself," explained John Wilkening, father of one of the slain women. "I have a lot of friends and so I would probably have to wait in line."

Richard Franklin Speck was born in Kirkwood, Ill. He was one of eight children belonging to Margaret and Benjamin Speck. In 1947, the family moved to Dallas, Texas, where Speck completed junior high school. It was the only formal education the young man received before he left home. By the time he was twenty, Speck had been arrested ten times on charges ranging from criminal trespass to burglary. He had tallied thirty-seven arrests by Spring 1966, when he returned to Chicago to find work as a merchant seaman. The semi-literate drifter spent his waking hours reading comic books and drinking to excess. He was a habitual pill-popper with a distorted view of reality, evidenced by his total lack of recall concerning his movements the night of July 13, 1966.

Speck shipped out on the cargo vessel the *Randall,* owned and operated by the Inland Steel Company. He was discharged in June 1966 for insubordination and fighting with a superior officer. His sister in Chicago, Martha Thornton, provided him with pocket money and drove him to the National Maritime Union hall, where Speck hoped to find work on a cargo ship heading to New Orleans. But there were no berths available to him on July 10, 1966, the day he made his application. Speck brooded about this for the next three days. He drank heavily in the taverns and skid row dives that dotted the west side of Chicago, plotting ways to earn enough money to pay for his trip to New Orleans. On the night of July 13, the besotted Speck injected a narcotic into his veins and headed to the South Side to see what he could come up with.

Speck wandered up to a two-story townhouse belonging to the South Chicago Community Hospital on East 100th Street around 11 p.m. He dug into his pockets and pulled out a handgun and a knife. He rapped on the door, and after a few seconds had passed, 23-year-old student nurse Corazon Amurao appeared. "I'm not going to hurt you," he said. "I'm only going to tie you up. I need your money to go to New Orleans." Amurao and two of her companions were directed to the upstairs bedroom where three of their other roommates were sleeping. At gunpoint, the nurses were ordered to lie flat on the floor. The young women complied with Speck's directive. He bound their hands and feet with strips torn from the bed sheets and then waited. At 11:30 p.m., Gloria Davy returned home from a date. Speck seized her at the door and led her upstairs. Then at midnight, Suzanne Farris and Mary Ann Jordan arrived home. Jordan did not live at the address; it was her tragic luck to be Farris' overnight guest.

After Speck had assembled all nine of the women, he demanded their money. He reiterated his peaceable intentions. "Don't be afraid, I'm not going to kill you," he said. A few more minutes passed. Speck chatted with Merlita Gargullo, who was born in the Philippines. "Do you know karate?" he asked. According to the statements of Amurao—the only survivor that night—Speck became increasingly agitated. He led 20-year-old Pamela Wilkening into the adjacent bedroom and stabbed her with his knife. Her muffled scream was stifled when Speck twisted her neck with a strip of sheet. The killer was apparently sexually excited by this and decided to continue killing. Speck returned moments later for Mary Ann Jordan and Suzanne Farris. The two of them were repeatedly slashed in the face, neck, and chest. Farris, the daughter of a Chicago Transit Authority employee, fought him, but was stabbed eighteen times. Afterward, Speck calmly went into the washroom, where he rinsed the blood off his hands. The next victim was 24-year-old Nina Schmale from suburban Wheaton. He stabbed the woman in the neck and then strangled her to death. The remaining student nurses attempted to hide under beds, but Speck tracked them all down but one: Corazon Amurao, who succeeded in pushing herself under the bed and out of the killer's view. Paralyzed with fear, she heard the death cries of her two friends from the Philippines: Valentina Passion and Merlita Gargullo who were stabbed from the next room. Twenty-year-old Patricia Matusek, a former swimming champion, was carried to the bathroom. She begged Speck to untie her ankles before he killed her. He kicked her in the stomach and then strangled her to death. This left Gloria Davy, the only one of the eight that Speck sexually molested.

Amurao remained underneath the bed for hours, fearful that Speck would find her if she attempted to escape. Not until 5 p.m. the next day did she venture out. She stepped out onto a narrow ledge outside her bedroom and called for help. Her cries were heard by two local residents. The police arrived minutes later. What they found shocked and sickened them: eight student nurses, savagely mutilated, were lying dead. Detectives found thirty fingerprints and a man's T-shirt was found beside Davy's body. Police artist Otis Rathel sketched a composite drawing of the suspect from a description provided by Amurao. The Chicago dailies ran the likeness the next day. As it turned out, Rathel's sketch bore an amazing likeness to the killer.

Speck's identity was established when a gas station attendant recognized the suspect from the police sketch. This man told the attendant that he was looking for work at the National Maritime Union. The union retrieved Speck's application from a wastepaper basket. Fingerprints taken at the murder scene were matched to a set of Speck's prints on file with the Dallas police. With a name and a description of their suspect, police prepared to search for Speck. As it turned out, the killer made himself easy to locate.

After the murder spree, Speck had returned to his ninety-cent room at the Starr Hotel on West Madison Street to crash for the night. On July 16, the gaunt, thin-faced killer slashed his right wrist and left arm with a blade. As the blood poured out. Speck called to the man in the next bunk. Failing to elicit sympathy, Speck stumbled into the hall. A police ambulance was summoned and he was taken to the Cook County Hospital emergency room and attended to by Dr. LeRoy Smith. "What's your name?" Smith asked. He answered, "Richard. Richard Speck."

It took a Cook County jury only forty-nine minutes to convict Richard Franklin Speck of the crime of murder. On June 15, 1967, he was sentenced to die in the electric chair. After the U.S. Supreme Court set aside the death penalty, Speck was re-sentenced on Nov. 22, 1972, to 400 to 1,200 years at the Stateville Penitentiary—the longest jail term ever given, up to that time. Nevertheless, Speck became eligible for parole in 1976. In 1977 and again in 1981, the convicted killer sent a tersely worded note to the state parole board saying that he was not interested in an early release. He was content to remain behind bars, where he happily pursued his hobby of oil painting. "Why don't you give parole to some of those young guys in here?" he complained. "They don't need to be in here in the first place." In August 1987, Speck had a change of heart and asked that the Illinois Prison Review Board consider granting his application for early release. There was little chance of that occurring, however. The memory of Speck's crime was still fresh in the public's mind. According to Joseph Matusek, Patricia's father: "We can't let this go. We'll be there to oppose it."

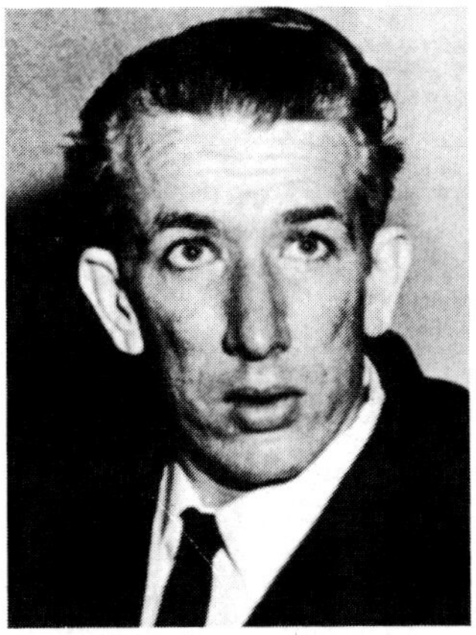
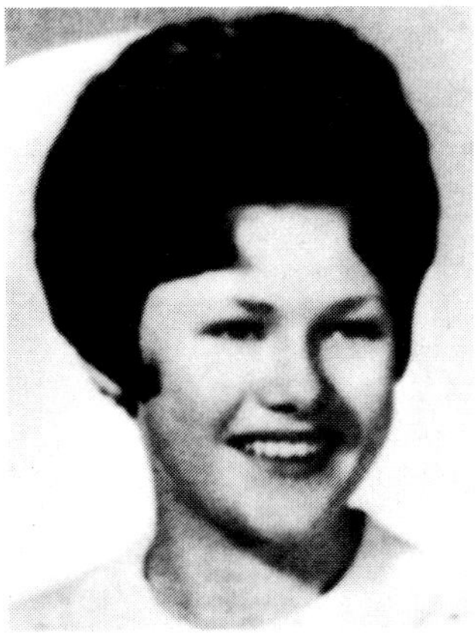
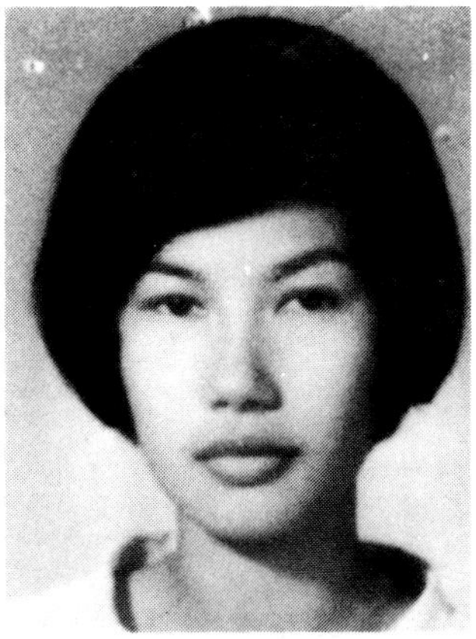
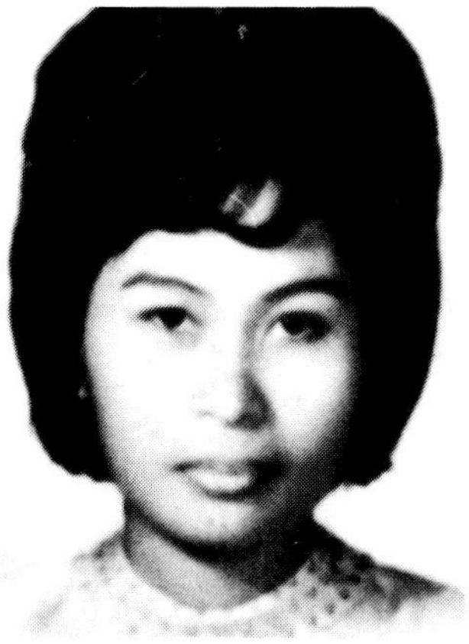

Richard Speck, mass killer, and his victims, left to right, Mary Ann Jordan, Marlita Gargullo, Valentine Passion.

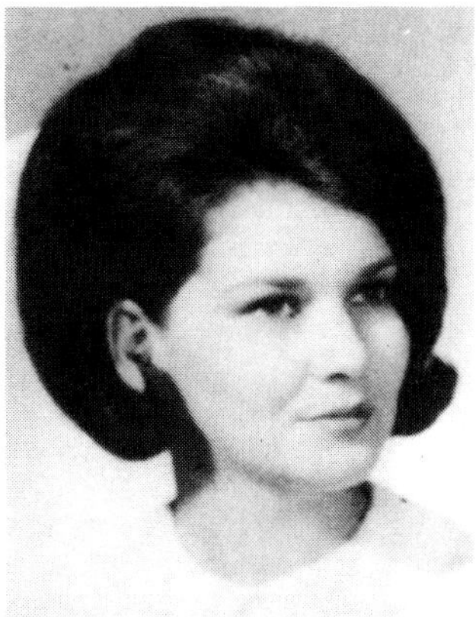
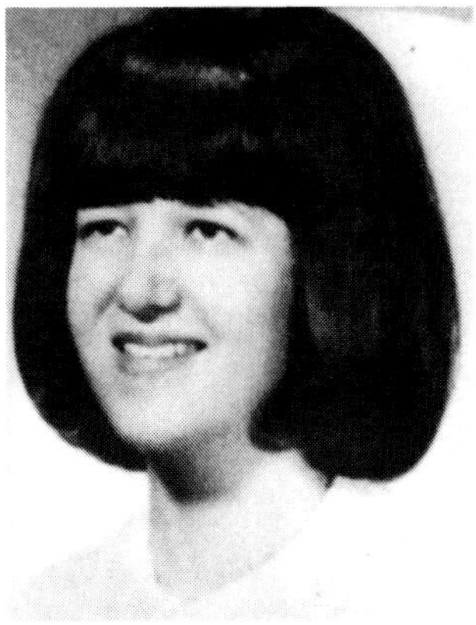

More of Speck's murder victims: left to right, Pamela Wilkening, Gloria Davy, Nina Schmale, Patricia Matuse.

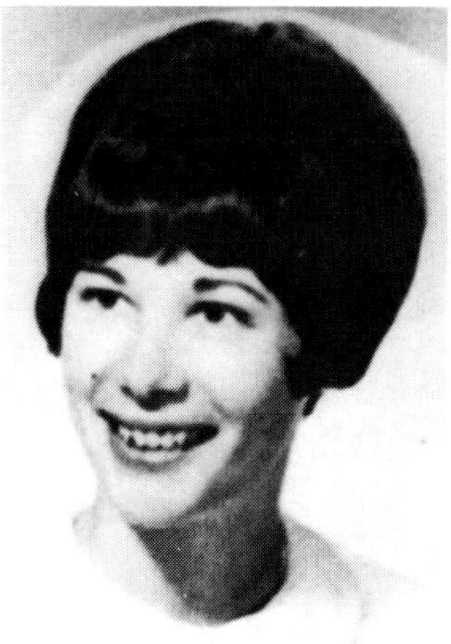

Another victim, Suzanne Farris, and survivor Corazon Amurao.

Two views of the seedy flophouse where Richard Speck spent his last moments of freedom bleeding from self-inflicted wounds.

REF.: Altman, *Born to Raise Hell; CBA;* Fox, *Mass Murder;* Godwin, *Murder, U.S.A.;* Gribble, *Compelled to Kill;* Henderson, *The Super Sleuths;* Nash, *Almanac of World Crime;* ____, *Bloodletters and Badmen;* Presley and Getty, *Public Defender;* Wilson, *Encyclopedia of Modern Murder.*

Spee, Friedrich von, 1591-1635, Ger., writer. A German theologian and philosopher, Friedrich von Spee was appalled at the persecution of individuals as witches and one of his influential works, *Cautio Criminalis,* helped to halt the zealots. Spee was educated at the Jesuit College at Cologne and he later studied philosophy at Würzburg and theology at Mainz, two locations that were focal points for the witch trials. In 1627, Spee became a professor at Würzburg, where he also listened to confessions from accused witches. In 1626 and 1628, he observed the furor that followed two failed harvests. In 1631, *Cautio Criminalis,* meaning Precautions for Prosecutors, was published anonymously because many judges and princes supported the Jesuits and their activities. The publication attacked the prosecutors, saying they aggravated the witch hunts because they considered losing a case humiliating. Spee charged that the suspects usually were not advised of the specific charges and were denied counsel. He further criticized the system, saying that the accused who immediately confessed were burned, and the rest were tortured until they confessed and were then executed. All behavior was accounted for as the devil's work. Spee's rational arguments were translated into German, Dutch, French, and Polish during the latter half of the 1600s, effectively helping to brake the fervor of the witch hunts.

REF.: Barbe, *Histoire du couvent de Saint-Louis de Louviers;* Burr, *Translations ans Reprints, University of Pennsylvania;* Cardauns, *Frankfurter zeitgemasse Broschüren; CBA;* Cornelis von Stockum, *Friedrich von Spee in de Heksen processen;* Duhr, *Die Stellung der Jesuiten in den deutschen Hexenprozessen;* Ebner, *Friedrich von Spee und die Hexenprozesse seiner Zeit; A Jesuit Philanthropist;* Lea, *Materials Toward a History of Witchcraft;* Leitschuh, *Beiträge zue Geschichte des Hexenwesens in Franken;* Reilly, *Freidrich von Spee's Belief in Witchcraft;* Robbins, *The Encyclopedia of Witchcraft and Demonology;* Rüttenauer, *Freidrich von Spee: ein lebender Märtyrer;* Schwickerath, *The Attitude of the Jesuits in Trials for Witchcraft;* Spee, *Cautio Criminalis;* ____, *Advis aux Criminalistes sur les abus qui se glissent aux procès de sorcellerie;* Stone, *The German Witches and Their Apostle;* Thomasius, *Kurze Lehr-Sätze von dem Laster der Zauberei;* Williams, *Witchcraft;* Zwetsloot, *Friedrich Spee und die Hexenprozesse.*

Speed, James, 1812-87, U.S., atty. gen. Served in Kentucky senate from 1861-63, and was named U.S. attorney general by President Abraham Lincoln in 1864. As attorney general he supported black voting rights and backed the Fourteenth Amendment. He resigned as attorney general in 1866 after a policy disagreement with President Andrew Johnson, and resumed his law practice. REF.: *CBA.*

Speer, Albert, prom. 1940s, Ger., war crimes. During WWII, Albert Speer served as the director of war production in charge of munitions for Germany. At Nuremberg, Ger., during the trials of Nazi war criminals, prosecutors charged that Speer tried to increase cruel SS measures, pressuring prisoners to work faster. In 1946, Speer was convicted and sentenced to twenty years in prison. REF.: *CBA.*

Speer, Elliott, 1882-1934, U.S., (unsolv.) mur. In 1934, Dean Thomas Edwin Elder borrowed a book, *The Public School Murder,* from the headmaster, Elliott Speer, of Mount Hermon School for Boys at Northfield, Mass. In the novel, the victim is killed by a bullet shot through his window and the murderer hides the weapon in a pond. On Sept. 14, 1934, while Speer was reading in his study, a bullet was fired through the study window, killing him. No gun was found in the pond on Speer's property. Elder, 52-years-old, resigned five months after the incident, and moved to Alton, N.H., to raise poultry. In 1937, the former dean was charged with, and acquitted of, assault with intent to murder and assault with intent to frighten. See: **Elder, Thomas Edwin**. REF.: *CBA.*

Speer, Emory, 1848-1918, U.S., jur. U.S. congressman from Georgia from 1879-83, and U.S. district attorney from 1883-85. He was appointed to the southern district court of Georgia by President Chester A. Arthur in 1885. REF.: *CBA.*

Spehl, Eric, See: **Hindenburg Disaster**.

Spellbound, 1927, a play by Frank Vosper. The Thompson-Bywaters murder case (Brit., 1922) provides the basis for this drama. The Vosper play is not to be confused with the Hitchcock film of the same title (which takes its story from *The House of Dr. Edwardes* by Francis Beeding). See: **Thompson, Edith**. REF.: *CBA.*

Spence, Gerald L., 1929- , U.S., atty. Outside the courtroom Gerry Spence resembles a millionaire cattle rancher, but inside the courtroom Spence has become recognized as one of the most tenacious defenders of those who fight for survival against huge corporations.

Spence, born in Wyoming in 1929, graduated magna cum laude from the University of Wyoming law school in 1952. After two years in private practice, Spence became a public prosecutor in Fremont County and retired in 1962 to run (unsuccessfully) as a Republican candidate for Congress. After the loss, he entered private practice, representing insurance companies against personal injury claims.

In 1970, Spence abruptly severed all corporate ties and began arguing for the opposite side—personal individuals vs. corporations. He became known for his meticulous pre-trial preparation and the adroit methods of cross-examination. In 1979, Spence won $10.5 million in damages for the Karen Silkwood estate in a suit against the Kerr-McGee Corporation. Silkwood had died in a mysterious auto accident five years earlier, while on her way to meet a newspaper reporter with information of alleged radioactive contamination. Spence also won a $26.5 million libel suit against *Penthouse* magazine for his client, a former Miss Wyoming. Spence has also chronicled his successes in many books, including, *Gunning for Justice* (1982), *Of Murder and Madness* (1983), and *Trial by Fire* (1986). REF.: *CBA.*

Spencer, Al, d.1923, U.S., rob. Al Spencer, a native of the Cookson Hills in Oklahoma, learned bank robbing from Henry Starr. After leaving Starr's gang, Spencer formed a gang in the early 1920s that included Frank "Jelly" Nash, Ray Terrill, and Earl Thayer. His gang's robberies were thoroughly planned and well-executed. Spencer continued to use automobiles in his jobs, Starr's innovation, but went a step further, and "souped up" the cars for speedier getaways.

Spencer's gang operated between 1920-23 robbing as many as two or three banks per week. On Aug. 21, 1923, they halted the Katy Limited of the Missouri, Kansas & Texas Railroad outside Okesa, Okla. After robbing the train of $20,000 in Liberty Bonds and cash, the gang members each drove to a separate hideout. Spencer ended up in Coffeyville, Kan., where an informant spotted him. He was killed by police as he tried to escape. Nash, Thayer, and other members of the gang were caught and given long prison sentences in Leavenworth. Terrill escaped and joined first with the Kimes Brothers and later with Herman Barker. In 1931, he was killed by police. See: **Kimes-Terrill Gang; Nash, Frank**

REF.: *CBA;* Cooper, *Ten Thousand Public Enemies;* Edge, *Run the Cat Roads;* Nash, *Bloodletters and Badmen;* Wellman, *A Dynasty of Western Heroes.*

Spencer, Ambrose, 1765-1848, U.S., jur. Served as chief justice of the supreme court of New York from 1819-23. REF.: *CBA.*

Spencer, Anthony, 1962- , U.S., rob.-mur. On June 15 and June 25, 1979, Anthony Spencer committed two robberies, for which he was convicted, and received two six-year sentences. Released on bond, he attacked a Canadian family, Dr. John Ng-Lun, his wife, and children, on Aug. 2, 1979, in Chicago as the family searched for a cab after visiting a Chinatown restaurant. Spencer and an accomplice grabbed a pocketbook containing $50 from Valerie Ng-Lun, the doctor's 21-year-old daughter, fatally shot the doctor, and then fled. Spencer, 18-years-old, was convicted of murder and sentenced on Sept. 8, 1980, to a forty-year prison term. REF.: *CBA.*

Spencer, Barbara, d.1721, Brit., count. A quarrelsome child who enjoyed watching condemned men die on the gallows at Tyburn, Barbara Spencer of St. Giles, England, was apprenticed to a weaver by her parents. She proved so unruly and incorrigible that her employer sent her home. Unable to live under the same roof with her mother, Barbara ran off to London where she joined a band of counterfeiters. She was quickly arrested and placed on trial at the Old Bailey with Alice Hall and Elizabeth Bray in May 1721. Hall and Bray were eventually acquitted, but Spencer was convicted of treason. (Counterfeiting and coining were considered treasonous acts at the time, since the offender had altered sacred images of royalty on the coin.) The condemned woman was taken to Tyburn and hanged on July 5, 1721. A large, unruly throng of spectators threw stones and dirt at Barbara, preventing her from giving penance before God. According to Reverend Villette, the Ordinary of Newgate, "She was very desirous of praying and complained of the dirt and stones thrown by the mob behind her which prevented her from thinking sedately on futurity. One time she was quite beat down by them." Afterward, her body was burned to ashes.

REF.: *CBA;* O'Donnell, *Should Women Hang?;* Mitchell, *The Newgate Calendar;* Potter, *The Art of Hanging.*

Spencer, Bertram G., prom. 1910, U.S., rob.-mur. In the early months of 1910, the residents of Springfield, Mass., were troubled by the presence of a housebreaker in the community. Armed with the usual assortment of burglar's tools, the thief would sneak into a victim's house late at night and hide under the bed until the occupants were asleep. With the greatest stealth he would emerge some time later to pilfer jewelry boxes and other valuables lying about. He was not a clever thief. Often his movements would be detected by one or more family members. In such a case, the burglar was forced to escape at the point of a gun. One Christmas Eve he held a mother and her children at bay while looking over the Christmas presents. After hearing the woman's anguished appeal he finally departed, leaving the gifts for the children.

Murderer Bertram Spencer, 1910.

The burglar left behind only one incriminating piece of evidence. While attempting to flee from a Springfield house he had just burgled, he accidentally dropped a locket in the yard. The locket bore the initials "BGS". For the next six months he kept a low profile, fearful that the police would connect him with the locket. Finally, "BGS" ventured out again. He entered the home of Harriet Dow, who was working a picture puzzle with two of her guests. The thief brazenly stepped into the parlor demanding their money. Martha Blackstone, one of the houseguests, screamed. The gunman fired two shots. One struck Blackstone, a schoolteacher, through the heart, and another grazed Dow in the head. He then turned and fled.

The police figured out that BGS was 29-year-old Bertram G. Spencer. The murder he committed in March 1910 put an end to his nocturnal forays into the homes of Springfield's law-abiding citizens. Spencer was taken into custody. His only defense was insanity and to this end he proved to be a capable actor. Spencer cheated the hangman for nearly a year as psychiatrists deliberated the issue of his sanity at the state hospital. Satisfied that he was merely feigning mental illness to save his neck, the courts ruled him fit to stand trial. Bertram was tried, found Guilty, and executed in the electric chair.

REF.: Briggs, *The Manner of Man That Kills; CBA;* Pearson, *More Studies in Murder.*

Spencer, Brenda, 1963- , U.S., mur. In 1979, a 16-year-old high school student opened fire at an elementary school in San Diego, Calif., killing two and injuring several others. The sniper, Brenda Spencer, was a problem child and the product of a broken home. She lived with her father after her parents' divorce several years earlier. Spencer was frequently absent from school, abused drugs, and committed petty thefts. She enjoyed watching violent programs on television and shooting birds. She once used a BB gun to shoot out the windows of Cleveland Elementary School, located across the street from her home. For Christmas 1978, Spencer's father gave her a semi-automatic .22-caliber rifle and about 500 rounds of ammunition.

In early January 1979, apparently preparing for an attack, Spencer moved her weapons to the garage and dug a tunnel as a hideout in her backyard. During the week of Jan. 22, she announced that she planned to "do something big to get on TV." On Monday morning, Jan. 29, she watched the principal of Cleveland Elementary School approach the school's gate. As Principal Burton Wragg opened the gate to the waiting school children, Brenda opened fire. She killed Wragg and janitor Michael Suchar. One of the first police officers to arrive on the scene, 30-year-old Robert Robb, was wounded in the neck as he helped a victim. Nine children from age six to twelve were wounded during the twenty-minute shooting spree, including two 9-year-olds, Christy Burell and Monica Selvig.

For the next several hours, Spencer hid in her house. Talking with police and reporters by telephone, she explained, "I just started shooting. That's it. I just did it for the fun of it. I just don't like Mondays...I did this because it's a way to cheer up the day. Nobody likes Mondays." Six hours after the shooting, Brenda walked out of her house, laid down her rifle, and surrendered to police.

After a change of venue, Spencer was tried in Santa Ana, Calif., and convicted of two counts of murder and one count of assault. She received two concurrent sentences, a twenty-five-year to life term for murder and a forty-eight-year term for assault with a deadly weapon. Spencer's Monday morning shooting spree prompted the song, "I Don't Like Mondays," by the British rock group The Boomtown Rats.

REF.: *CBA;* Godwin, *Murder, U.S.A.*

Spencer, Brenda, and **Smith, Lucille**, and **Willock, Essie Mae**, prom. 1974, U.S., pris. esc.-rob.-mur. In 1974, three female convicts, at the Kentucky Correctional Institution located near Louisville, escaped from the facility after beating a guard with a broomstick and spraying another with Mace. Brenda Spencer, Lucille Smith, and Essie Mae Willock, then hijacked a pickup truck and burgled a house where they stole two pistols and a change of clothing. They drove to Brinkley, Ark., where they robbed a small grocery store of cash and all the beer in stock. After the robbery, policeman Morris Greenwalt pulled their speeding truck over and Spencer shot him once before getting out of the truck and firing seven more bullets into his body with the officer's service revolver. Following the murder, the escapees forced their way into a farmhouse where they held the family hostage. Police officers surrounded the house, but retreated when the women threatened to kill the family. Later that night, after drinking all of the stolen beer, Spencer, Smith, and Willock surrendered. Spencer and Smith were tried, convicted, and sentenced to life terms for the murder of the police officer. Willock received an eleven-year sentence. REF.: *CBA.*

Spencer, Charles, 1674-1722, Brit., polit. corr.-fraud. Member of powerful Junto group of five Whigs exerting control over British government from 1708-10. He successfully conspired with James Stanhope to expedite the removal of Charles Townshend over a dispute regarding policy towards France, and caused Robert Walpole to resign. He also was forced to resign, in 1721, after he was charged with accepting a £50,000 bribe while publicizing the South Sea Bubble. He was a son of Henry Spencer, the first Earl of Sutherland. REF.: *CBA.*

Spencer, Henry, 1880-1914, U.S., rob.-mur. In June 1914,

Henry Spencer arrived in Wheaton, Ill., a Chicago suburb. He made friends quickly and soon he met Allison Rexroat, an unmarried woman ten years older than he. The two became romantically involved and Spencer talked of marriage.

During their courtship, Rexroat told Spencer she had some substantial savings, and arranged for him to have access to the funds. One summer day, Spencer proposed a picnic in the countryside surrounding Wheaton. As Rexroat reclined on a blanket spread on the ground, Spencer approached her from behind and bludgeoned her with a hammer. After killing her, he dug a shallow grave with a shovel. He went back to Wheaton, where he visited the bank and withdrew her savings. Spencer then waited for the next train. As the train arrived, the Wheaton sheriff, who had been alerted to Spencer's sudden withdrawal of Rexroat's funds by the bank president, arrested Spencer.

Illinois murderer Henry Spencer, in shirt sleeves, eating breakfast.

Initially, Spencer denied any wrongdoing and claimed he did not know where Rexroat was. However, her grave was discovered after a farmer reported having seen them picnicking on his land. Shortly thereafter, the murder weapon was found and Spencer confessed to the murder.

Spencer was brought to trial, convicted, and sentenced to hang. While awaiting his execution, he was visited by a brother and sister evangelist team, the MacAuslins. By the time Chicago journalists Wallace Smith and Ben Hecht arrived to cover the execution for the Chicago papers, Spencer claimed to have converted and said he was prepared to die without remorse. Smith and Hecht were cynical and bet between themselves on whether or not the convicted murderer could maintain his new salvation in the face of the hangman's noose. On the August day when Spencer was to be hanged, a large crowd gathered. When Spencer reached the top of the gallows he spoke glowingly of his new faith. In his final moments, Spencer's religious facade dropped and he yelled at the crowd.

REF.: *CBA;* Nash, *Bloodletters and Badmen.*

Spencer, Timothy Wilson, 1962- , U.S., rape-mur. On Sept. 22, 1989, the Virginia Supreme Court upheld the murder convictions of Timothy Wilson Spencer. The landmark decision marked the first time an appeal had been upheld by a higher court solely on the strength of DNA evidence. In handing down its decision the court expressed its confidence in the DNA test results introduced into evidence at two of Spencer's trials. "The record is replete with uncontradicted expert testimony about the reliability of DNA fingerprinting," the court explained.

With three juvenile and three adult convictions for burglary already behind him, Timothy Spencer was paroled to a Richmond, Va., halfway house in September 1987. In the three months following Spencer raped and murdered four women in Arlington County and Richmond. On Sept. 19, 1987, the young black man described by psychiatrists as having a mother fixation entered the Richmond apartment of Debbie Dudley Davis, thirty-five. Davis was bound, raped, and strangled with a sock. Victim number two, Dr. Susan Elizabeth Hellams-Slag, lived only a short distance away from Davis. Hellams, a neurosurgery resident at the Medical College of Virginia, was strangled with a belt on Oct. 3, 1987. Her body was found stuffed into a closet by her husband Marcel when he returned home later that night.

Timothy Spencer

The third slaying, that of 15-year-old Diane Cho on Nov. 22, established a definite pattern in the minds of police investigators. Cho, like Davis and Hellams, was of medium height and stockily built. The teen-age girl was found strangled to death in her family's apartment in Chesterfield County. Duct tape was affixed over her mouth, and for the third time, the killer attempted to conceal the dead body on the premises. Spencer committed his fourth and final rape-murder a few days after Thanksgiving 1987. The victim was identified as 44-year-old Susan M. Tucker of Arlington. Her body was found on Dec. 2 in the bedroom of her townhouse.

With a pattern established, Arlington Police detective Joseph Horgas went to work on a series of earlier rape cases dating to 1983 in which the assailant had used a rope and burglary tools to gain admittance to homes. Horgas recalled an arson fire set in the mid-1970s in which a 10-year-old boy named Timmy had been implicated. His recollection put him on the trail of Timothy Spencer, who was picked up in January 1988. However, DNA tests commonly called "genetic fingerprinting" conclusively proved that the same man was involved in the Davis, Hellams, and Tucker slayings. DNA (deoxyribonucleic acid) is the basic genetic material found in all human cells. With the exception of identical twins, DNA makeup is different in every person. Using this sophisticated procedure police and forensic investigators compared blood and semen samples taken from a victim with that of a suspect. Genetic testing of this sort analyzes hair roots, blood, semen, and various other body fluids for DNA. In the case of Spencer, his blood and that found on the victim matched only thirteen percent of the population. The scientific odds against such a match in black North Americans were one in 705 million, according to DNA experts.

Timothy Spencer, dubbed the "South Side Strangler" by the media, was convicted in July 1988 in Arlington County for the rape-murder of Susan Tucker. The case against Spencer rested primarily on DNA fingerprinting evidence submitted by Dr. Michael Baird, forensics laboratory director at Lifecodes Corporation of Valhalla, N.Y., who matched semen samples found in Tucker's bedroom. "This is a major point in the case," explained Commonwealth Attorney Helen Fahey. "The judge found (DNA testing) reliable and that it is supported by the scientific community." On July 16, 1988, Spencer was sentenced to death by an eight-woman, four-man jury who deliberated for an hour.

On Nov. 2, 1988, Spencer received a second death sentence for the rape-strangulation murder of Debbie Davis. The defendant's conviction resulted from a DNA pattern found in his blood. "This whole case, the identification of Timothy Spencer, relies strictly on that," explained defense counsel Jeffery L. Everhart who pointed out that Britain's Home Office had stopped using DNA fingerprinting to identify paternity in immigration cases. Everhart would later take his case before the State Supreme Court, arguing unsuccessfully that DNA evidence "is not now ready to be used in a capital murder case." In passing sentence Judge James B. Wilkinson noted with sadness: "I can think of no murder case...in twenty-eight years in this business where the facts are as outrageous as the facts are in this case."

Spencer was convicted by a South Richmond jury of murdering Dr. Hellams in January 1989. For the third time the jury recommended the electric chair on the grounds that the defendant posed a serious threat to society. On Mar. 27, Judge Wilkinson imposed the death sentence and two life terms plus twenty years. After hearing the decision, Spencer accused Detective Horgas and the Commonwealth attorneys of "setting him up." The fourth and final murder trial took place in Chesterfield County in May 1989. Prosecutors Warren Von Schuch and William Davenport pointed to the similarities in the three earlier murders with that of Diane Cho. The evidence they submitted included a more sophisticated genetic typing method called amplified PCR DNA. The tests matched body fluid stains found at the murder scene with samples taken from Spencer. On May 12, 1989, the jury returned a Guilty verdict, sentencing Spencer to death on capital murder charges, life imprisonment for rape, and twenty years for burglary.

The conviction of Timothy Spencer had far-reaching implications, not only in future murder trials involving DNA fingerprinting but also for an Arlington man convicted of raping and murdering Washington lawyer Carolyn Hamm in January 1984. A 41-year-old fast food employee named David Vasquez was sent to prison for the Hamm murder on Feb. 6, 1984. The similarities between the Tucker murder and that of Hamm were striking. In each case the victim had been bound and gagged without apparent signs of struggle. Attorney Fahey petitioned the governor to pardon Vasquez, described as a semi-literate "incapable of understanding his Miranda rights." On Dec. 31, 1988, Virginia Governor Gerald L. Baliles granted Vasquez a full and unconditional pardon. Timothy Spencer, meanwhile, remains on death row pending the outcome of more appeals. REF.: *CBA*.

Spencer, Verlin, 1902- , U.S., mur. Verlin Spencer, a 38-year-old principal at South Pasadena Junior High School in Pasadena, Calif., had been at the school for seven years. He had served as vice-principal for five years until he was appointed principal in 1938. His perfectionism and intense ambition made him an abrasive and critical leader. Spencer's superiors insisted in 1939 that he take a three-week leave of absence. One year later, in Spring 1940, Spencer was again in conflict with his staff. He disagreed with Ruth Barnett Sturgeon, a long-time teacher, and Verner V. Vanderlip, head of the mechanical arts department. Following an investigation, George C. Bush, superintendent of the South Pasadena city schools, John E. Alman, principal of South Pasadena High School, and Will R. Speer, business manager of the South Pasadena-San Marino School District, decided not to rehire Spencer. Bush informed Spencer of the decision in a letter; Spencer demanded a hearing. The meeting was to be held at 3 p.m. on May 6, 1940.

On that day, Spencer arrived at the school just as the students were leaving for the day. He joined Bush, Alman, and Speer in Bush's second-floor office. Within a few minutes, Spencer's angry voice was heard from the hallway. Then five shots rang out in rapid succession, followed by a short silence, and then another shot. Spencer had shot Alman and Speer in the heart, killing them both instantly. Although Spencer missed Bush's heart, the 62-year-old superintendent died twenty minutes later. Spencer then moved across the hall to find Dorothea Talbert, Bush's secretary, who had heard the shots but remained at her desk. As Spencer aimed his .22-caliber automatic pistol at her, Talbert ducked and was hit in the shoulder. Spencer fled. Police later timed the first murders at 2:55 p.m.

Spencer drove to the art department of the school, parked his car, and went inside to search for Ruth Sturgeon. He found her alone in the department, and then shot and killed her. Spencer hurried out of the building and reloaded his gun. He found Vanderlip, his next victim, in the schoolyard. Witnesses gave different versions of this encounter. Some said that the two men spoke briefly, then walked together toward the machine shop. Others said Spencer forced Vanderlip to go with him at gunpoint. Inside the machine shop, police found evidence of an intense struggle and chase. Vanderlip apparently fought for his life, and lost to Spencer. Vanderlip's body was found an hour later by two schoolgirls searching for their missing teacher.

Spencer then headed back toward his car, but as he crossed the schoolyard, he noticed that he was being watched. He ran through the cafeteria in an attempt to reach the street. As he entered the building, police officers Clarence Sexton, Clyde Rohyback, and Ray Broadstone, all armed with shotguns, cornered him. As one of the officers took aim, Spencer pressed his own gun against his right side and fired twice, critically wounding himself. He was rushed to Huntington Hospital, where two of his victims lay dead and another was dying. Police found a note from Spencer to his wife, Polly, telling her that he was sane. He left his property to her with the stipulation that she spend no more than $200 on hospital care or funeral expenses for him.

The disgruntled ex-principal survived his wounds and was tried for murder. He pleaded Guilty to all charges and was given five consecutive life terms. He was discharged by California's Department of Corrections in 1977, at the age of seventy-five. REF.: *CBA*.

Spendle, Robert Courtney Fraser (AKA: **Luang Art, Daeng**), and **Nai Krit**, prom. 1940s, Siam, theft-kid. Robert Spendle was born in Siam, the son of the British advisor to the police in Bangkok. After the birth of his son, the elder Spendle returned to England and the boy was raised by the Prince of Ratburi. Spendle later became a police officer and a successful lawyer during the Japanese occupation of Siam in the 1940s. As a hobby, he raced horses, and in 1947 he won the Siamese Derby after he and friend Nai Krit stole the favorite, Golden Shower, from the stable of owner, Phya Rada. Spendle's horse, Beautiful Dawn, easily won the Gold Cup and the large purse awarded the winner. Golden Shower was later found unharmed on a Bangkok golf course.

Spendle and Nai Krit then turned to kidnapping, abducting the infant son of a wealthy Chinese entrepreneur, Nai Rert. They returned the child after receiving a ransom of 100,000 baht in unmarked bills. After this first success, he kidnapped the baby of Chow Fa Depsadit Depsawongse, the king's uncle, from his palace at Dhonburi. Spendle was paid 1 million baht for the child's safe return, but was arrested one week later after two accomplices identified him as the ring leader. Spendle was convicted and sentenced to life in prison, where he died.

REF.: *CBA*; Sparrow, *The Great Abductors*.

Spenkelink, John A., 1949-79, U.S., mur. In 1973, 24-year-old John Spenkelink, an escapee from a California prison, picked up a hitchhiker, 43-year-old Joseph Syzmanklewicz of Detroit. Syzmanklewicz, an Ohio parole violator, traveled with Spenkelink for about two weeks, assaulting, sodomizing, and robbing the younger convict. Later, Syzmanklewicz was found dead in a motel in Tallahassee, Fla. He had been shot twice.

Spenkelink and another man, Frank Brumm, were arrested for the murder, but Brumm was acquitted. Spenkelink claimed that he and Syzmanklewicz had agreed to part company and Spenkelink had told Brumm, "If you hear a shot, come to room twelve." Spenkelink claimed he retrieved Syzmanklewicz' gun from the car and returned to the hotel room to give it back to him. There, Spenkelink said Syzmanklewicz tried to assault him and he shot him in self defense. He told the jury that his earlier statement to Brumm meant that if gunfire were heard, Brumm should rush to help him. The jury interpreted Spenkelink's statement as premeditation to murder, convicted him in 1974, and he was sentenced to be executed.

Spenkelink's case aroused the indignation of anti-capital punishment groups and his defence lawyer doubted that his guilt had been established beyond a reasonable doubt, but on May 18, 1979, Florida governor Robert Graham signed Spenkelink's death warrant. Six appeals by Spenkelink to the U.S. Supreme Court were unsuccessful. On May 22, about 400 convicts at the Florida State Prison at Starke, Fla., where Spenkelink was held, refused to eat their breakfast to demonstrate their objection to the scheduled executions of Spenkelink and another inmate, Willie Jasper Darden, Jr. On May 25, 1979, yelling, "This is murder! This is murder!," Spenkelink was electrocuted at the Florida prison, the first inmate to be executed in the U.S. since the execution of Gary Gilmore in January 1977. REF.: *CBA.*

Spenser, Edmund, c.1552-99, Brit., law. enfor. off. Major English poet who served as sheriff of Cork in 1598. His youngest child was killed, and some of his literary work lost, when the Kilcolman castle was destroyed by Irish insurrectionists in 1598. REF.: *CBA.*

Sperati, Giovanni de (AKA: **Jean de Sperati**), b.1884, Brit., count. In the early 1900s, Giovanni de Sperati, his wife, and his sister-in-law joined a stamp counterfeiting ring operating out of Pisa, Italy. In 1911, Sperati's first phony stamps surfaced in Berlin. For the next forty years, his masterful works threatened to devalue the international stamp business.

An expert in inks, printing, plating, gums, and perforations, he eventually created 538 types of stamps that, if authentic, would have been worth more than $5 million. He printed all except one of his copies from nineteenth century signets, primarily faking stamps from the U.S., France, Italy, Germany, Switzerland, Spain, Colombia, and Argentina. In the 1920s, his wife and sister-in-law sold the fakes as genuine and he eluded detection because dealers who had been duped often resold the stamps themselves to cover their own losses.

When Sperati sent stamps to Lisbon, Port., censors discovered the forgeries and he was arrested on charges of exporting capital worth $7,500. Because counterfeiting stamps was a much smaller violation than exporting capital, Sperati declared he had made the stamps. Sperati, his wife, and sister-in-law, Anna Corne, were tried on fraud charges. Sperati was sentenced to a one-year suspended term and ordered to pay 300,000 francs to the stamp dealers' association. The women each received a four-month suspended sentence. When Sperati appealed, a new court affirmed the verdicts in 1952 and increased Sperati's sentence with a two-year suspended prison term, a fine of 500,000 francs (about $1,400) payable to the dealers, an additional fine of 120,000 francs, and 30,000 francs in court costs.

In February 1954, officials of the British Philatelic Association finalized negotiations with the counterfeiter to purchase all of his equipment for $15,000 in exchange for his promise not to make any more stamps.

REF.: Bloom, *Money of Their Own; CBA.*

Spicer, Edward A., 1951- , and **Good, Earl,** 1947- , U.S., rob.-mur. On Nov. 15, 1975, the Leading Food Store in Clayton, Mo., near East St. Louis was robbed and employees Ben Siegel, sixty-four, of Creve Coeur, Mo., and Emanuel Ukman, fifty-nine, of Clayton were murdered. Two Chicago men, Edward A. Spicer, twenty-five, and Earl Good, twenty-eight, were charged and given separate trials in Chester, Ill., in April 1976. A tape-recording activated in the store as part of the alarm system and a recording of Siegel and Ukman's screams as they were slain were the Chicagoans' downfall. The seven-minute tape began with sounds of the store's safe being opened and of drawers being pulled out, followed by a voice ordering the two men to "Lie down, spread 'em out," and then another voice pleading, "Don't kill me, don't shoot." The next sounds were five shots and then a voice screaming, "My God, I'm shot, I'm shot. Oh, I'm shot. Police, help me, I'm shot..." A nationwide hunt resulted in Spicer's arrest three days later. The jury deliberated for ninety minutes before finding him Guilty on two counts of murder and one of armed robbery.

On June 11, 1976, County Circuit Court Judge Alvin Maeys, Jr. sentenced Good, who had been convicted after Spicer, to two ninety to 180-year terms to run concurrently. Earlier in the week Spicer was sentenced to 410 to 830 years for two counts of murder. REF.: *CBA.*

William Spiggot being tortured with the press to induce a confession.

Spiggot, William, 1693-1720, and **Phillips, Thomas,** d.1720, Brit., rob. William Spiggot and Thomas Phillips refused to plead guilty to the charge of robbery. They had been accused of robbing Charles Sybbald on Finchley Common, England. Another cohort, Burroughs, turned out to be a patient who had escaped from a mental institution. After his evidence caused Spiggot and Phillips to be arrested, he was returned to the famous mental hospital, Bedlam.

Spiggot and Phillips refused to plead until the effects taken from them when they were arrested were returned. According to King William and Queen Mary's "Act for Encouraging the Apprehending of Highwaymen," this was not possible. The court informed the robbers that they could either plead or accept the legal punishment: weighting with iron or stone until death. The obstinate robbers chose the punishment and were taken to Newgate Jail to be pressed to death. At the sight of the torture room, Phillips changed his mind and opted to plea. Spiggot was put under the press. He endured a half hour with 350 pounds on his body. When another fifty pounds was added, he changed his mind as well. Both men were indicted, convicted, and condemned to death. They were hanged at Tyburn on Feb. 8, 1720. Spiggot was twenty-seven years old.

REF.: Atholl, *Shadow of the Gallows; CBA;* Mitchell, *The Newgate Calendar;* Pringle, *Stand and Deliver.*

Spilotro, Anthony (AKA: **Tony the Ant, The Little Guy, Little Tony**), 1938-86, U.S., org. crime-(unsolv.) mur. Learning his trade from established mob terrorist Felix Alderisio, Anthony Spilotro began his criminal career burgling homes on the Northwest Side of Chicago, eventually becoming the head of mob operations in Las Vegas, Nev., for the Chicago mafia. As a young man, Spilotro stole cars to go joyriding and was first arrested in January 1955 for stealing a shirt in River Forest, Ill. He was fined $10. Later, he became a juice collector, collecting money from loans with high interest rates for Sam DeStefano, a Chicago mobster. In the early 1970s, the Oak Park, Ill., native first set up a boutique in Las Vegas, entrenching himself in mob activity, and his boyhood friend, Frank Cullotta, soon joined him as his chief lieutenant. Under investigation, Spilotro was acquitted in 1975 on charges of involvement in a scheme to swindle $1.4 million from a Teamsters pension fund. He was investigated again in 1976 on suspicions that he misused funds from another pension fund. In January 1980, Spilotro's power grew after reported negotiations between Chicago and East Coast mobsters. The East Coast families handed over complete control of Las Vegas to Chicago gangsters, and in return, the Chicago syndicate agreed to stay out of gambling operations in Atlantic City, N.J. Any East Coast operatives involved in bookmaking, the juice rackets (high interest loans), or narcotics traffic, were directed to report to Spilotro and hand over a portion of their profits. Internal Revenue Agents confirmed the reports, saying Spilotro received a percentage of illegal Las Vegas profits and that a stream of transplanted Chicago hoodlums were meeting with Spilotro.

Gangster Anthony Spilotro, murdered in 1986.

In 1981, facing an indictment with three others for conspiracy, racketeering, wire fraud, and receiving stolen property at his Gold Rush, Ltd., jewelry store, Spilotro planned to kill the entire grand jury and an informant, Sam Romano, by poisoning their catered food, according to Cullotta, who became a government informant in April 1982. Meanwhile, during the investigation Spilotro muscled in on unattended territory in southern California, after several mobsters had been convicted. Spilotro took over their loansharking and bookmaking operations.

In January 1983, after Meyer Lansky, head of the southern Florida crime syndicate died, Spilotro reportedly had been chosen to take over the operation, an appealing prospect because the Las Vegas economy was declining and the gangster wanted to avoid further publicity caused by the 1981 investigation. Several weeks later Spilotro was indicted on charges in connection with a 1962 double murder, which reportedly cinched Spilotro's foothold into the mob. Spilotro ordered the murders of the "M & M boys," William McCarthy and James Miraglia, who were slain because the two burglars had killed three people in Elmwood Park, an off-limits area since many mob leaders lived there. The indictment came as a result of Cullotta's testimony. Because of the new indictments, a successor, Joseph Cusamano, Spilotro's chief lieutenant, was chosen to take over the Las Vegas operation. More testimony by Cullotta threatened a new indictment when the informant said Spilotro had ordered him to kill Sherwin Lisner in 1979 because Lisner had become a government informant.

On Jan. 27, 1983, Spilotro was jailed on fugitive charges and about a month later agreed to return to Chicago. In 1985, the gangster stood trial with seven other top Chicago mobsters for skimming—taking money before the funds are reported for taxes—from a casino in Las Vegas. In April 1986, the trial of the nine bosses ended in a hung jury and a week afterward, contracts were reportedly issued for 48-year-old Spilotro and his brother, 41-year-old Michael Spilotro, because the mob discovered that Anthony had skimmed money for himself before he turned over the funds to the others. Spilotro also was reputedly trying to muscle in on some of the Chicago crime syndicate's territory. On June 14, 1986, the two Spilotro brothers left the home of Michael Spilotro and did not return. Michael Spilotro's wife notified police. On June 21, a farmer tilling his cornfield in northwest Indiana, located about a mile-and-a-half from a farm owned by Joseph Auippa, found the bodies of the two brothers, wearing only underwear.

REF.: *CBA;* Demaris, *The Last Mafioso;* Fried, *The Rise and Fall of the Jewish Gangster in America;* Reid, *The Grim Reapers;* Zuckerman, *Vengeance is Mine.*

Spilotro, Victor, 1935- , U.S., gamb.-fraud-extor. Victor Spilotro, the brother of former mafia boss Anthony Spilotro, was convicted in 1980 on gambling and tax fraud charges in connection with an illegal bookmaking operation disguised as a racetrack messenger service. Spilotro, of Riverwoods, Ill., was sentenced to eighteen months in January 1980 and released after serving thirteen months. In June 1986, his two brothers, Anthony and Michael, were found dead in an Indiana cornfield, bringing attention to the Spilotro family name. In 1987 he was tried on fraud and extortion charges, accused of accepting $40,000 in protection money between 1981 and 1984 from the National Credit Service, an illegal credit card company that processed payments made to prostitutes. The firm actually was set up by the Federal Bureau of Investigation in a probe of vice in suburban Chicago. Spilotro, fifty-two, was found Guilty but received a light penalty from a judge who commented, "It is a troublesome case. If your name wasn't Spilotro, you wouldn't be here." On July 17, 1987, Judge James B. Moran sentenced the defendant to six months of work-release, five years' probation, and restitution costs.

REF.: *CBA;* Demaris, *The Last Mafioso;* Fried, *The Rise and Fall of the Jewish Gangster in America;* Reid, *The Grim Reapers;* Zuckerman, *Vengeance Is Mine.*

Famous medical pathologist Sir Bernard Spilsbury.

Spilsbury, Sir Bernard Henry, 1877-1947, Brit., pathol. Britain's esteemed criminal investigator who integrated the science of pathology with modern police work was the eldest son of James Spilsbury, a chemist. Sir Bernard Spilsbury was educated at Magdalen College, Oxford, where he finished second in his class in the field of physiology in 1899. Upon graduation he was admitted to the medical school of St. Mary's Hospital in Paddington where he was greatly influenced by three masters of forensic medicine, Arthur Pearson Luff, Augustus Joseph Pepper, and William Willcox, who helped shape his thinking. In 1905, Spilsbury was appointed assistant demonstrator at St. Mary's where he displayed remarkable skills as a lecturer and educator. He later served as president of the Medico-Legal Society.

Spilsbury's reputation in academic circles continued to grow but it was not until 1910, during the trial of Dr. Hawley Harvey Crippen that he began to make his mark as one of Britain's most analytical investigators in the realm of law enforcement. On the witness stand Spilsbury demonstrated remarkable aplomb as defense lawyers cross-examined him about a piece of forensic evidence submitted by his colleagues from St. Mary's. "I am responsible for my own opinion which has been formed on my own scientific knowledge," he said in a detached, self-confident manner. His findings showed that Crippen had poisoned Belle Elmore, a dance hall singer. Her murderer went to the gallows as a result. Shortly afterward Spilsbury was named junior honorary pathologist to the Home Office where he was reunited with his mentor William Willcox.

For the next thirty-five years Spilsbury dominated British pathology like no other individual before or since, specializing in murder cases seemingly devoid of workable clues. In this sense he was the worthy incarnation of the fictional Sherlock Holmes. His learned opinions based upon methodical investigation and dispassionate calculation convicted dozens of murderers in many celebrated cases. In 1915, Spilsbury appeared as witness for the Crown in the infamous "Brides of the Bath Case." The post-mortem evidence he provided the prosecution helped convict George Joseph Smith as the murderer. The mysterious death of Katherine Mary Armstrong, the wife of a former military officer in February 1921, was another sensational murder Spilsbury helped solve after the police had exhausted the possibilities. The remains of Mrs. Armstrong were exhumed by court order. Applying the skills he had learned from Willcox, Pepper, and Luff, Spilsbury uncovered the presence of arsenic in the system which resulted in the arrest and conviction of the woman's husband.

In 1923, Spilsbury achieved his highest accolade when he was knighted. Shortly afterward he left St. Mary's to accept a similar position at St. Bartholomew's Hospital. In 1924, Spilsbury achieved national acclaim when he conducted the first post-mortem on a convicted murderer, Patrick Herbert Mahon, a soda fountain worker executed for decapitating his paramour, Emily Kaye. His research led to gradual improvements in the manner of execution.

The case of Norman Thorne, a poultry farmer from Crowborough, Sussex, accused of murdering his girlfriend, Elsie Cameron in 1925, presented Spilsbury with his greatest challenge. Thorne claimed Cameron's death was a suicide, a view supported by eight medical men. The woman was found hanging by the neck from a beam in one of Norman Thorne's huts in what seemed to be an obvious suicide, but Spilsbury refuted the earlier testimony. The jury chose to believe the pathologist. Thorne was duly convicted which prompted considerable debate among professionals in the legal field concerning Spilsbury's fallibility as a witness. "The verdict of a jury on a question of pathology is valueless," exclaimed the *Law Journal*. "Thorne is entitled to feel that he has been condemned by a tribunal which was not capable of forming a first-hand judgment, but followed the man with the biggest name."

Unquestionably, Spilsbury was the biggest name of his era, though he never claimed to be infallible. He was, in the words of one source, a "professional cross-examinee" who spoke about pathological matters from the perspective of experience, not emotion. In 1932, Spilsbury was called on to give evidence against Elvira Barney, a London society woman who was accused of murdering her sweetheart Scott Stephen in Knightsbridge. Spilsbury upheld the view of Scotland Yard that Mrs. Barney had shot the young man to death. On the witness stand, though, defense counsel Sir Patrick Hastings subsequently demonstrated that Stephen's death was in fact a suicide. Barney was freed, but a shadow of doubt about Spilsbury's methods and ready acceptance of Scotland Yard's investigative abilities remained. British crime writer Edgar Lustgarten later wrote, "To the man in the street he stood for pathology as Hobbs stood for cricket or Dempsey for boxing or Capablanca for chess. His pronouncements were invested with the force of dogma and it was blasphemy to hint that he might conceivably be wrong." When he died his files were found to contain some 25,000 entries from every single post-mortem investigation he had conducted.

At all times Spilsbury carried with him a "murder bag," containing the tools of his trade, the rubber gloves necessary to examine a corpse and the medical compass. Sir Bernard retired from the Home Office in 1934 but continued on as an "honorary pathologist," assisting in numerous murder cases. In 1940, Spilsbury suffered a minor stroke. In the next few years he lost two sons and a sister, tragedies that brought on a period of despondency. An intensely private man who did not appreciate being touched by other people, Spilsbury became somewhat of a recluse in his final years. In failing health, Sir Bernard turned on the gas in his laboratory at the University College in London, Dec. 17, 1947. For more than an hour doctors tried unsuccessfully to revive him through artificial respiration. Of Spilsbury, a literary wag once remarked, "When arsenic has closed your eyes, This certain hope your corpse may rest in—Sir B. will kindly analyze the contents of your large intestine." See: **Armstrong, Herbert Rowse; Crippen, Dr. Hawley Harvey; Fox, Sidney Harry; Mahon, Patrick Herbert; Mancini, Tony; Rouse, Alfred Arthur; Seddon, Frederick Henry; Smith, George Joseph.**

REF.: Browne and Tullett, *The Scalpel of Scotland Yard; CBA;* Hyde, *United in Crime;* Shew, *A Companion to Murder.*

Spinelli, Evelita Juanita (AKA: **The Duchess**), 1889-1941, U.S., mur. More than three hundred convicts at San Quentin in California petitioned to the governor to prevent the hanging of Juanita Spinelli, more popularly known as "The Duchess." The petition stated that, "After establishing a worthy and universally commendable record, a 100-year record, of never executing a woman, the State should not break that record. If that is done the world at large would declare, in sad disillusionment, that deterioration and retrogression had entered the world's most golden State."

Spinelli was a San Francisco widow who decided when she found herself alone in middle age to go in for crime. She led her new common-law husband, Mike Simeone, in gathering a gang that would follow her commands. She planned the robberies, and she distributed the loot afterwards. On nights when there was no robbery planned, her men were expected to roll drunks.

When the gang held up a barbecue stand and ended up shooting the owner, Leland Cash, Spinelli, Simeone, and three others fled to Sacramento. But when 19-year-old gang member Robert Sherrard showed an inclination to turn himself in to the police, the gang's leader slipped him some chloral hydrate, and the other men took him to the Freeport-Clarksburg Bridge and threw him into the Sacramento River. Another gang member, Albert Ives, arrested for some other deed, turned informer. Spinelli, Simeone, and Gordon Hawkins were all found Guilty and sentenced to death. Ives himself was later found to be insane.

Spinelli's execution was reprieved several times, once in response to the convicts' petition, but on Nov. 21, 1941, in front of sixty-six witnesses and with pictures of her children and a grandson strapped under her clothing, the middle-aged crime kingpin became the first woman to be officially executed in California

REF.: *CBA;* Godwin, *Murder, U.S.A.;* Nash, *Look For the Woman.*

Spinelli, William, 1879-1940, U.S., mur. William Spinelli married Rose in 1909. At the time of her murder, they had been married for twenty-nine years and had five children. She had supported the family with her work as a maid in Beverly Hills for ten years while her husband remained unemployed. In the basement of the Spinelli's Los Angeles home, police found a can containing $900 in cash which Spinelli said he had saved out of his wife's wages. The household was apparently not a happy one. Spinelli's parents were both alcoholics, and he became one himself. Psychiatric tests following his arrest revealed that he had had incestuous relations with two of his three daughters over a number of years, and may have fathered one of his own grandchildren. When asked if he thought his wife was aware of the incest, he replied, "We had fights about it, although she never caught me in the act." He was diagnosed as a schizoid personality.

At the request of one of Spinelli's daughters, Helen Angieli, homicide bureau detectives broke into the home on Dec. 20, 1938, and found the bedroom and bathroom heavily stained with blood. Spinelli claimed he had cut his head and hands, adding that his wife had run away with another man on Dec. 12. He showed detectives a letter, supposedly signed by Rose Spinelli, that said she was "eloping to South America." Spinelli and his son, William Spinelli, Jr., were booked on suspicion of murder. The son admitted he suspected that his father killed his mother, but said his father threatened to kill him in his sleep if he did not keep quiet. The son first claimed that his father forced him to forge the letter from his mother, but police later learned that a gas station operator wrote the letter. Police chemist Ray Pinker examined the blood-stained rooms and concluded that no one could lose that much blood and survive. Detective Lieutenants D.R. Patton, Lloyd Hurst, and Aldo Corsini searched the home and ground after learning from neighbors that, on the day Mrs. Spinelli disappeared, her husband had a fire burning in the incinerator for five hours. They discovered bone fragments and a gold ring in the driveway of the home. In the backyard, they found a piece of charred cloth, a purse, and a blood-stained hatchet hidden in a box.

The Spinelli son explained that he had come home around 10 p.m. on Dec. 12 to find his father in the backyard with a fire in the incinerator. "I thought it was funny, but he had threatened me several times so I didn't say anything." Two large suitcases were also missing, the son explained. Neighbors reported seeing the elder Spinelli leave the house several times with packages. Police officers questioned Spinelli for almost seventy-two hours before he confessed. Spinelli explained that, after an angry exchange between the couple, "I laid down on the bed and she hit me. I threw up my hands and grabbed for a hatchet, and I kicked her in the stomach and she fell down, and I got up and hit her two times in the head." After going to the hospital "to get my face fixed up," he wrote a note to the family and left it at the house. The note, supposedly written by his wife, explained to her children that she was going away. Spinelli then went out to a restaurant for supper, and returned home later to dismember his wife's body with a saw, wrap the pieces, and burn them in the backyard incinerator. When his son came home and asked what he was burning, the father replied, "I am burning some trash."

Spinelli was tried and convicted in Los Angeles in December 1938. He was executed in the gas chamber at San Quentin on May 17, 1940. REF.: *CBA*.

Spink, Mary Isabella, See: **Chapman, George**.

Spires, John, 1955- , U.S., rape. First convicted of rape in 1978, John Spires of Chicago pleaded guilty to raping a 16-year-old girl and to taking an 11-year-old girl and a 12-year-old boy into an abandoned building where he tied up the boy and forced him to watch as he raped the girl. Spires was twenty-one at the time. Judge Fred Suria sentenced him to six years in jail in February 1978. Spires began serving his sentence in March 1978 and was paroled in August 1979. In the following year and a half he committed another four rapes.

On Sept. 5, 1980, Spires grabbed a 12-year-old girl, threatened to murder her, drove her away, and raped her in his car. Nineteen days later, he broke into a home on North Kenneth Avenue, let in a 13-year-old girl who was selling candy, and assaulted and raped her. On Dec. 8, 1980, he told a 12-year-old girl walking in her schoolyard that his cat was trapped in a basement and asked for her help. Leading her to an abandoned basement on Rosemont Avenue, he said he would kill her if she did not do what he said, then he raped her. Finally on Jan. 9, 1981, Spires grabbed a 13-year-old girl on her way to school and raped her in an alley behind North Rutherford Avenue. She escaped to a gas station and hid in a back room until an attendant finally persuaded her to come out and call her parents.

Before police suspected Spires of the rapes, he went to psychiatrist Andrew Pundy to ask for a lobotomy "to stop his compulsion to rape." Spires also asked his family to stop him from leaving the house alone. Tried in October 1985, Spires, thirty, was sentenced by Criminal Court Judge Thomas Hett to the maximum sentence for each charge, totalling 240 years in jail. Spires will not be eligible for parole for about 120 years. Spires admitted to the four rapes he had committed after being paroled and apologized for his crimes. He had been physically abused as a child and made the first of many suicide attempts at the age of seven. An insanity defense was rejected by Hett who, on Oct. 18, found Spires Guilty but mentally ill.

Talking to a reporter in 1989 Spires said, "I feel like an animal. I feel like I should be taken out in the morning and shot." As his four victims testified in court, Spires wondered what he had done to their lives and said he was comfortable in the Menard prison psychiatric unit "because I know I can't hurt nobody." REF.: *CBA*.

Spirito, François (AKA: **Le Grand Lydro, Al Capone of Marseilles, Charles-Henri Faccia**), c.1900- , and **Carbone, Paul**, (AKA: **Venture**), d.1941, and **de Lussatz, Gaetan** (AKA: **The Baron**), prom. 1930s, Fr., org. crime. An Italian family, the Spiritos, moved from Naples, Italy to Marseilles, Fr., during the 1890s and the eldest son, François Spirito, eventually became one of the most powerful gangsters in Marseilles. As a young man he committed petty thefts before joining Antoine la Rocca, the leader of a prostitution ring in Marseilles. Under la Rocca, Spirito committed robberies and reputedly was responsible for several murders. In the 1930s, Spirito began vying for power with Paul Carbone, but after several members of each gang had been killed, the two decided to combine forces and together established an extremely profitable international drug trade. Once, at the end of 1930 in Cairo, Egypt, police found Spirito during a raid on a brothel and deported the gangster back to France. Later, in Marseilles, Spirito, Carbone, and Gaetan de Lussatz were arrested by Inspector Bony for the murder of Councillor Prince. Reportedly Bony was told to arrest someone for the killing and he asked his criminal associates to present themselves, knowing they wielded enough power to be released. A month later in Dijon, a judge ruled that there was not enough evidence against them and the three were freed.

Also in the 1930s the two leaders began to import gangsters from Corsica, primarily as hired guns. Two of these, Jean-Paul Stefani and Ange Foata, were used as enforcers for the Spirito-Carbone drug traffic in Marseilles and later were put in charge of the Marseille operations while the two kingpins went to Paris. The two Corsicans began a feud that became known as the "Vendetta" that claimed at least fifty lives. The two leaders returned to Marseilles, briefly putting a stop to the slayings, and the Spirito-Carbone enterprise continued until the German occupation in 1940s, which disrupted, but did not destroy the drug supply lines they had created.

In 1941 Carbone died in a train accident and, in 1948, Spirito, then about forty-eight, traveled to the U.S. where he pawned his sister's jewels and bought a small amount of heroin. He was arrested trying to sell the drugs, then tried, convicted, and sentenced to two years in jail. Meanwhile, in France Spirito had been given the death penalty in absentia for collaboration with the Germans and was wanted on armed robbery and blackmail charges. On Christmas Eve 1953, after the French gangster had been released from the Atlanta Penitentiary, he was arrested by French agents and sent back to France, arriving on Feb. 7, 1954. He was tried on the old charges and sentenced to life in prison. REF.: *CBA;* Goodman, *Villainy Unlimited.*

Splett, Norbert, 1952- , and **Schumacher, Petra**, 1954- , Ger., mur. In June 1972 Kurt Rheiners' wife and 10-year-old son vacationed in the Tyrol, Aust. Left alone in his house in Hanover, Ger., Rheiners, a 36-year-old plumber, invited some friends to go to the Ant Tavern on June 20. He drank beer with Norbert Splett, a 20-year-old apprentice pastry cook, and Splett's girlfriend, 18-year-old Petra Schumacher. They downed more than forty glasses of beer by midnight and left together, tipsy, the girl clinging to both men. They went to Rheiners' house where the host suggested they play strip poker and all agreed, continuing with the game until all were naked by 2 a.m. At this point, Splett later said, he had to go to the bathroom to vomit and when he returned he saw Rheiners on top of his girlfriend. Splett said he thought the woman was struggling and that Rheiners was raping her. Splett grabbed Rheiners' homemade wooden spear, stabbed the man in the back, and then left with his girlfriend.

Rheiners was found the next morning about 9:30 by Hardy Bruggemann, who was at first arrested for the crime. Later that day Splett arrived at the police station to confess. He was charged with murder and Schumacher was charged as an accessory after the fact. Splett's confession, however, did not match the forensic evidence, which indicated that Rheiners had been participating in unforced sex at the time of his death and his body did not bear any marks from a fighting woman. Additionally, police could find no evidence of vomit in the bathroom and when Rheiners' wife returned she said 1,300 marks were missing. On May 22, 1973, Splett was convicted of murder with extenuating circumstances and received a ten-year sentence. Charges against Schumacher were dismissed.

REF.: *CBA;* Dunning, *The Arbor House Treasury of True Crime.*

Spooner, Bathsheba, 1748-78, U.S., mur. The trial of Bathsheba Spooner in 1778 marked the first time an American court sat in judgement on its own, without the encumbrances of the British legal system. The irony of the affair was that the accused murderer had been a Royalist sympathizer during the Revolutionary War. Bathsheba was the daughter of General Timothy Ruggles, a staunch Tory landowner from Worcester, Mass. The general imparted his own political views upon his favorite daughter and fervently hoped that her future would be a secure one. When she was eighteen, he arranged her marriage to Joshua Spooner, a grandfatherly type, with a large home and a full complement of servants.

Bathsheba entertained a long line of lovers during her marriage. Joshua Spooner did not seem to notice, nor did he show concern. During the war for independence Mrs. Spooner frequently invited hungry soldiers who tramped by her home to stop in for food, shelter, and frivolity. It did not matter if they were fought on the side of the British or Continental armies. Her husband Joshua, who supported the colonial cause, was away most of the time. Ezra Ross was one of many stragglers to cross her threshold. Barely past his sixteenth birthday, Ross and his three brothers had fought at Bunker Hill and numerous other engagements with the British regulars.

Bathsheba fed the emaciated youth and tenderly nursed him back to health. Joshua Spooner treated Ross with kindness, never suspecting he was dallying with his wife. Ross and others like him provided Bathsheba with the inner resolve to kill her husband, whose advanced age prevented him from fulfilling all of his marital obligations. Equally repugnant to the fiery young woman was his sympathy for the patriot cause. After sometime had passed Bathsheba inveigled Ross to kill her husband. On a business trip to Princetown which Ross was invited by her husband to attend, she handed Ross a bottle of aquafortis, advising the boy to slip a few drops into Spooner's ale. "Do it," she said. "It will make a man out of you." But Ross did not have the stomach for murder. He returned with Spooner, having failed in his mission.

Her prayers were answered on Feb. 8, 1778, when two bedraggled British soldiers stopped at her home. Bathsheba ordered her manservant Alexander Cummings to fetch them into the house. The two men, 30-year-old James Buchanan and William Brooks, twenty-seven, had escaped from a prison camp in Rutland, Mass., and were on their way to the Canadian border. They wanted no further part of the king's war. "My husband is away on business," Mrs. Spooner told them. "You are welcome to stay until he returns." Grateful for the opportunity to sleep in a warm bed and eat home cooking again, the men agreed. Bathsheba correctly sized them up as n'er-do-wells and after two days she enlisted them to her scheme. She promised them $1,000 if they would kill Mr. Spooner.

Upon his return Spooner ordered the troopers out of his house. Ross, a mere boy, was perfectly acceptable but these two had to go. "The old man fears you think to rob him," said Reuben Olds, a neighbor. "You must leave." Buchanan fumed. "It won't be healthy for him for I would put him in the well for two coppers!" he said. Ross, Buchanan, and Brooks were plied with strong drink and additional encouragement from Bathsheba. Finally on Mar. 1, 1778, the conspirators carried out the murder. The old man returned late that night from Cooley's Tavern. As he prepared to step into his home, Brooks knocked him to the ground. Ross seized the man's pocketwatch and gave it to Buchanan. He then helped Brooks carry Spooner to the well, dumping him in head first. "Before they carried him away, I, Buchanan, pulled off his shoes. I was instantly struck with horror of conscience as well I might..." the soldier later recalled.

Bathsheba awarded her three assistants with $243, promising more later. The murderers rode off to Worcester taking with them Spooner's personal belongings. The next morning Bathsheba dispatched her servant Cummings to town to see if Mr. Spooner was there or not. "Get a horse. Ride to the tavern and inquire as to the whereabouts of my husband!" Hearing of his disappearance Ephraim Cooley, proprietor, commenced an immediate search. A hat belonging to Spooner was found in the snow. Cooley reached the well where he noticed blood spots on the rim. He raced back to town to summon authorities. Brooks, Buchanan and Ross were arrested at Brown's Tavern in Worcester. Curiously, they were wearing the dead man's clothes at the time. All three confessed. Bathsheba was brought before the body of her deceased husband and made to touch the skin. A widespread belief held that the skin would turn red after being touched by the guilty murderer. In this case there was no discoloration.

Spooner and the other three conspirators were tried for murder on Apr. 1, 1778. Robert Treat Paine, a signer of the Declaration of Independence, prosecuted, specifically charging Spooner with being "an accessory before the fact and that she invited, moved, abetted, counselled, and procured" the murder. Levi Lincoln, who was to become distinguished in his own right as U.S. attorney general under Thomas Jefferson, represented the defense. He knew there was not much chance to save the soldiers but concentrated on an acquittal for young Ross. He pointed to the boy's exemplary record in the war, but the jury was not swayed.

In the case of Bathsheba Spooner, Lincoln attempted to show that the woman was insane at the time of the murder. All four were found Guilty and ordered to hang on June 4, 1778. Before the sentence could be carried out, Spooner boldly announced that she was pregnant. A jury of matrons, headed by the volatile patriot Elizabeth Rice, informed the court that in the opinion of the examining midwives Spooner was not with child. Political sentiment may have influenced her decision in this regard. The condemned woman loudly protested the decision, but the plea fell on deaf ears. On July 2, 1778, Spooner, Brooks, Ross, and Buchanan were hanged outside of the Worcester jail before 5,000 spectators—the last public hanging in the Commonwealth. A team of surgeons, complying with Mrs. Spooner's last request, performed an examination. A five-month old fetus was removed from her womb.

REF.: *CBA; The Dying Declaration of James Buchanan, Ezra Ross and William Brooks Who Were Executed at Worcester;* Mccarty, *The Guilt of Innocent Blood Put Away;* ____, *Account of the Behavior of Mrs. Spooner After Her Commitment and Condemnation for Being Accessary in the Murder of Her Husband; The Lives, Last Words and Dying Speech of Ezra Ross, James Buchanan and William Brooks;* Nash, *Bloodletters and Badmen;* ____, *Look for the Woman;* ____, *Murder, America;* Pearson, *Instigation of the Devil.*

Sportsmen's Hall, prom. 1845-70, U.S., org. crime. The three-story frame building on Water Street in New York City's Fourth Ward, commonly known as Sportsmen's Hall, provided entertainment to some of city's most notorious criminals. From approximately 1845 until it was torn down in 1870, Sportsmen's Hall was the scene of various atrocities regarded by the clientele as sporting events. On the hall's first floor, terriers and large rats were pitted against one another in life or death battles.

Among the hall's well known patrons, Jack the Rat also provided entertainment of a unique nature. For a dime, Jack would chew the head off of a live mouse; for a quarter, he would perform the same feat with a live rat. Gallus Mag, the hall's bouncer was a ferocious six-foot-tall woman whose trademark was biting off the ears of overly boisterous patrons. They were then pickled and kept in a jar behind the bar.

The roughest New York gangs of that era—including the Daybreak Boys, Border Gang, Patsy Conroys, Shirt Tails, Hookers, Buckoos, Swamp Angels, and Slaughter Housers—frequented Sportsmen's Hall. Murders were not uncommon—seven people were killed there in a two-month period in 1845. Known murderers like Slobbery Jim and Patsy the Barber actually roamed its hall looking for victims. When Sportsmen's Hall was torn down in 1870 as part of a redevelopment program, the thugs and murderers moved to the Five Points section where they continued their many criminal activities.

REF.: Asbury, *The Gangs of New York; CBA;* Nash, *Bloodletters and Badmen.*

Sposato, Frank, prom. 1901, Case of, U.S., mur. On Mar. 3, 1901, Frank Sposato went to a Denver bar and two men, Frank Lotito and Lolito's brother-in-law, John Brindisi, entered, sitting down on either side of Sposato. After Brindisi crowded against Sposato and Lotito seized his shoulder, Sposato punched both men and the three were told by the bartender to go outside. There, the two friends hit Sposato, who returned the swings, and the two left. A short distance away, Lotito shot at Sposato and he shot back twice, killing Lotito. Lotito's wife came to the scene, taking her husband's gun back to her home. A policeman arrived and Sposato admitted that he shot the man, but in self-defense. Police found Sposato's gun but did not find a gun on Brindisi or near the corpse, and Sposato was charged with murder.

Sposato asked a friend, Horace N. Hawkins, to represent him. During the investigation, the lawyer was contacted by a gypsy who showed him a confession Brindisi had written, saying that Lotito's wife had taken his gun home after the shooting. With three lawyers present, but hidden, the gypsy induced Brindisi to write and sign another confession, which he later admitted to in court. Sposato was acquitted. REF.: *CBA.*

Spradley, A. John, 1853-1940, U.S., west. lawman. Born into a Simpson County, Miss., farming family, A. John Spradley was the oldest of nine children and lived with his family until 1871, when he was eighteen. Previously he had fought with a local boy, Jack Hayes, and was confronted by Hayes and his brother Bill Hayes. Spradley's own brother, Bill Spradley, was with him. When the Hayes brothers pulled derringers and began to fire, John Spradley brought out an old cap and ball pistol and shot them both. The Hayes' died that night and Spradley fled to Texas, where he worked at the Nacogdoches farm of an uncle and then at a mill. He was appointed deputy sheriff of Nacogdoches County in 1880, becoming sheriff one year later, a post he held for thirty years, followed by two years as a U.S. deputy marshall. Spradley often wore a steel shirt under his clothes for protection.

In the summer of 1884, Spradley arrested Bill Rogers, and was taking him to jail when Whig Rogers, Bill's drunken brother, stopped him and went for his gun. Spradley released Bill, warning Whig not to shoot. Bill Rogers fired twice at the deputy, and one of the bullets tore through Spradley's back. Though he was not expected to live, a silk kerchief pulled through the wound healed it. Three years later Spradley was confronted by a young man with a gun who had a grudge against him, and Spradley narrowly missed being killed when the youth fired. The assailant escaped but was arrested in the street and later sent to jail. On July 16, 1893, in Longsport, La., Spradley was waylaid by saloon keeper Joel Goodwin, who had nursed a two-year grudge against Spradley for arresting him for murdering an employee. Informed that Goodwin was after him, Spradley armed himself with a shotgun as well as his usual revolver. Goodwin waited at the depot and began firing his Winchester at Spradley as his train pulled in. Spradley fired his shotgun, instantly killing Goodwin. Goodwin's distraught wife began firing at Spradley, and the train pulled out before anyone else was injured. It returned briefly when the engineer came back to pick up the mail, forgotten in the fray.

During his years as a deputy, Spradley owned part interest in a Nacogdoches saloon, but sold out after one of his nearly fatal gunfights, and afterward became an ardent prohibitionist. When he retired from his job as a lawman, Spradley became a farmer and was involved in politics until he died in 1940.

REF.: *CBA;* Fuller, *A Texas Sheriff.*

Sprengtporten, Jakob Magnus, 1727-86, Fin., consp. Designed and headed coup giving Gustav III absolute rule in 1772. His work led to a promotion to lieutenant general. REF.: *CBA.*

Spreull, John, prom. 1681, Case of, Scot., rebel-treas. Amid religious dissension, a group of Scottish rebels assassinated the archbishop of St. Andrews, Mr. Sharp, the chief of the Episcopal Church. Then the insurgents tried to revolt against the king but the royal military conquered them at Bothwell Brigg. In 1681, John Spreull, a druggist, was charged with treason and rebellion in Edinburgh, Scot. Though Spreull at first confessed to taking part in the uprising, he later refused to admit to the crime under torture—torture that was called into question because those who administered it had not had proper authority. But since Spreull had previously acknowledged involvement with the revolutionaries, he was tried. He was acquitted but prosecutors were not content with the verdict. Later in 1681 the defendant was at a hearing of the Scottish Privy Council where he made no statement regarding any connection to the rebels, so the council fined him 9,000 marks and confined him on the Isle of Bass until he paid the money. He was freed six years later by permission of the king.

REF.: *CBA;* Parry, *Some Famous Medical Trials.*

Springer, James, 1958-79, U.S., suic.-mur. On June 8, 1979, 21-year-old James Springer apparently stabbed his grandparents to death in Skokie, Ill., a northern suburb of Chicago. After murdering 84-year-old Gust Bergmark and his wife, Annette, about eighty-two, Springer, from Morton Grove, Ill., went into their garage where he started a car and died from carbon monoxide poisoning. Springer's mother later found the bodies about 5 p.m. A friend said that for several months before the slayings, Springer had been acting strangely. REF.: *CBA.*

Springfield (Ill.) Race Riot, 1908, U.S., mob vio. In 1908 in Springfield, Ill., a white woman claimed she had been raped by George Richardson, a black man. Whites rioted and 4,200 militiamen were called in to quell the violence. Richardson was quickly taken out of town to prevent a lynching. In two days of rioting, Aug. 14 and 15, two blacks were lynched, six others were killed, and more than seventy blacks and whites were badly wounded. Several people were arrested and indicted, but no one who instigated the riot ever was punished.

Richardson was freed when the woman who accused him admitted that she had been raped by a white man, whom she refused to name. The riot in Springfield resulted in a racially mixed group, including Jane Addams, W.E.B. Du Bois, and William Dean Howells, meeting in New York City the next year and founding the National Association for the Advancement of Colored People (NAACP). REF.: *CBA.*

Sprinkle, Jacob, and **Sprinkle, Nancy,** prom. 1840s-60s, Case of, U.S., count. During the mid-1800s a Kentucky couple set up a counterfeiting operation in the northeast part of the state. Jacob Sprinkle and his wife, Nancy Sprinkle, owned two log cabins located five miles southeast of Vanceburg, Ky. An underground tunnel connecting the two buildings was used to store their minting equipment and the Sprinkles made silver dollars from ore mined in the county. Their counterfeit coins were extremely popular with county residents and others who lived in Ohio because the silver content was higher than U.S. government-minted dollars.

In 1840, the Lewis County prosecutor brought the couple to trial on counterfeiting charges. Before the proceeding started, Judge Walker Reed displayed some of the Sprinkle coins, declaring, "I defy the United States to produce from their mints dollars as good as these I hold in my hand." The trial resulted in a hung jury and before the next trial, the Sprinkles moved to California and directed their lawyer to submit their death certificates to the Kentucky court. The two counterfeiters later died in California in the 1860s.

REF.: Bloom, *Money of Their Own; CBA.*

Spruzheim, John Casper, 1776-1832, U.S., criminol. John Casper Spruzheim wrote treatises on the pseudo-science of phrenology. Phrenology, which enjoyed acceptance in various scientific circles through the 1920s, maintained that measurement and study of physical shapes and proportions, mainly the human head, could predict intelligence and behavior. The theory was particularly popular in the field of criminology where it was applied to the detection of criminal "types." Spruzheim, along with co-worker George Combe, divided the scalp into regions, naming the sections after moral and religious characteristics such as secretiveness, self-esteem, benevolence, individuality, and ideality. REF.: *CBA.*

Squatters' Riots, 1850, U.S., mob vio. Speculators bought large tracts of land in California from Mexicans in the 1840s. When gold seekers rushed to California soon after, legal titles were largely ignored, with newcomers settling almost anywhere. Some landowners managed legally to remove the squatters, but by 1850 the squatters had banded together to challenge the existing titles and oppose absentee ownership. Squatter John F. Madden, in May 1850, was sued successfully. The court ordered his eviction. The Squatters' Association denounced the order, and though armed members of the association came to guard Madden's home, the sheriff dispossessed him and arrested several of the squatters. The Squatters' Riots resulted when, on Aug. 14, an armed and organized group of squatters tried to retake Madden's property.

The Sacramento *Daily Times* of Aug. 15 and 16, 1850, said forty squatters came to the levee at 2 p.m. Mayor Hardin Biglow had asked citizens to help suppress the threatened uprising, and many armed local people were on the streets. Meeting the squatters, Biglow demanded that they turn over their arms and disperse. The squatters responded by firing at him, and Biglow fell from his horse and was taken to his home, seriously wounded. J.W. Woodland, who stood next to Biglow, was shot in the groin and died soon afterwards. Jess Morgan, who was alleged to have shot Biglow, was soon fatally shot himself, and James Harper was seriously wounded while supporting the sheriff. Maloney, the mounted leader of the squatters, was killed and Dr. Robinson was wounded. Both Robinson and Henry A. Caulfield were arrested later in the afternoon for shooting at Biglow.

A citizens' meeting was held and groups went out to track down the squatters. Brigadier General A.M. Winn declared martial law and ordered citizens to form into volunteer companies. By night the city was quiet. A police force of 500 men was brought in for duty, but during the night, Sheriff Joseph McKinney was killed, as were several squatters. A man named Allen, who had fired on McKinney, was wounded but escaped. REF.: *CBA.*

Squillante, James (AKA: **Jerome**), d.1960, U.S., org. crime. Known as the boss of the garbage collection racket in New York City, James "Jerome" Squillante was a ruthless killer. Squillante was named by Mafia informer Joe Valachi as one of the hit men who murdered Frank "Don Cheech" Scalise, crime lord Albert Anastasia's underboss and a longtime ally of Lucky Luciano, on June 17, 1957. Scalise was selecting some fruit at a stand in the Bronx when Squillante and another thug shot four bullets into his neck and the back of his head.

After the murder, Scalise's brother, Joe Scalise, publicly declared he would get revenge, probably believing Anastasia would support him. When Anastasia remained silent, Joe Scalise disappeared, surfacing several months later when he heard he had been forgiven. Valachi testified that Joe Scalise accepted an invitation to a party on Sept. 7 at Squillante's house, where Squillante personally cut his throat. Then he and several other party-goers armed with butcher knives cut Scalise's corpse into pieces to be taken away by one of Squillante's garbage trucks.

Three years later, Squillante was indicted on extortion charges and disappeared. When word went around that he would not hold up under the pressures of the courtroom and jail, it was decided that he should be "put out of his misery." After he was shot in the head, Squillante's body was loaded into the trunk of a car which was put through a crusher that reduced the auto to a small scrap cube to be melted down in a blast furnace. REF.: *CBA.*

Squire, Edward, See: **Elizabeth I.**

Squires, Sir Richard Anderson, 1880-1940, Can., polit. corr. Served as attorney general and as minister of justice from 1914-17. His terms as prime minister of Newfoundland, from 1919-23 and from 1928-32, saw much corruption and extravagance. REF.: *CBA.*

S.S. Athenia Sinking, 1939, Ger., war crimes. Just ten hours after the British entered WWII, the Nazis torpedoed the first unarmed passenger ship. When the *S.S. Athenia,* a 13,581-ton cruise ship departed Glasgow en route to Montreal, 1,450 people were on board. On Sept. 3, 1939, two-hundred miles west of the Hebrides, a torpedo fired from a German U-Boat ripped apart the hull of the *Athenia,* sinking it within an hour. At least 100 people died in the maritime tragedy. Winston Churchill, first Lord of the Admiralty, denounced the incident as inhumane and in violation of international law. The Swedish tycoon Axel Leonard Wenner-Gren rescued 200 survivors and transported them back to Ireland on board his luxury yacht, ahead of the Norwegian freighter *Knute Nelson* which picked up 800 more passengers in the water. The remaining surviviors were rescued by British naval vessels.

In response to Churchill's angry denunciations, the German propaganda office in Berlin claimed that the *Athenia* had struck a British mine. These charges were dismissed by the British. REF.: *CBA.*

Ssu, Li, See: **Li Ssu.**

Stabile, Joseph, 1938- , U.S., perj. Special FBI agent Joseph Stabile, from Commack, Long Island, who was assigned to the agency's Queens, N.Y., branch office and had been with the bureau since 1962, was convicted of committing perjury in September 1978 in an attempt to cover up his acceptance of payoffs from gambling figure John Caputo. A federal grand jury in New York City charged Stabile just before the five-year statute of limitations for prosecution expired.

Stabile was charged with lying under oath when he denied receiving a $15,000 payment from Caputo after he falsely represented to the gambler that the payment would result in the dismissal of a gambling indictment against him. FBI agent George Moresco told the grand jury about several talks with Stabile in which the agent told him of receiving $10,000 from Caputo on one occasion and $5,000 on another. Assistant Attorney General Phillip Heymann of the FBI's criminal division said his agency had fully cooperated with the Justice Department in the investigation. In February 1979, Stabile surrendered to begin serving a year and one day in jail.

REF.: *CBA;* Pileggi, *Wiseguy.*

Stacey, Robert, and **Stacey, Rebecca**, and **Hatcher, Edward**, and **Jordon, Josiah**, and **George, John**, and **Smith, Thomas**, and **Connolly, Ann**, prom. 1788, U.S., rob.-mur. Edward Hatcher, who worked sporadically as a ship's carpenter, knew that a captain who had arrived in Charleston Harbor from the Netherlands carried florin and guilders, valuable Dutch currency. On the evening of Mar. 12, 1788, Captain Marston was robbed of cash, a watch, and the Dutch money. A short time later Nicholas John Wightman was fatally shot in the chest. Police rounded up a gang, including Edward Hatcher, Robert Stacey, Josiah Jordon, John George, Thomas Smith, Ann Connolly, and Rebecca Stacey. Hatcher claimed Stacey shot Wightman, though Stacey denied it. They were tried and all except Rebecca Stacey were found Guilty and hanged. REF.: *CBA.*

Stacher, Joseph (AKA: **Doc**), d.1977, U.S., org. crime. When three Israeli journalists wrote a book about crime boss Meyer Lansky, their main source of information was former mobster Joseph Stacher, who had emigrated to Israel in 1965. Stacher, an intimate friend of mobsters Bugsy Siegel, Frank Costello, and Lucky Luciano as well as Lansky, had become wealthy because of his associations in organized crime, and was loyal to Lansky.

Coming to Newark, N.J., when he was ten years old, Stacher rapidly moved from juvenile thief to working for the Lansky and Siegel gang. By the 1920s, he was running bootleg liquor and assisting "Longy" Zwillman, a New Jersey syndicate leader, in gambling rackets.

By 1931, Stacher, under Lansky's orders, became the main organizer of a meeting of all New York Jewish gangsters at the Franconia Hotel, where it was decided that the Jewish and Italian mobsters would merge to create a national crime syndicate. Lansky made Stacher his payoff man in Las Vegas, as well as his bribe paymaster to Cuba's dictator, Fulgencio Batista, who permitted the syndicate to set up and run extravagant casinos.

In the 1960s, the Internal Revenue Service charged Stacher with income tax evasion. To escape a five-year jail term, he made an arrangement and was allowed to emigrate to Israel under that country's "Law of Return" for Jews. Anxious to get Israeli citizenship, Stacher allegedly had his long-time friend, singer Frank Sinatra, intervene on his behalf with an Orthodox member of parliament. Stacher donated $100,000 to an Orthodox charity and was enraged when the parliament member used the funds to build a kosher hotel in Jerusalem. Stacher sued, and was the focus of many headlines and jokes. Eventually he got his money back.

Stacher's emigration set a trend, with scores of other Jewish mobsters moving to Israel. When Lansky tried to emigrate in 1971, public outrage and pressure on the Israeli government by U.S. officials caused his expulsion from Israel. Stacher died of cancer in 1977.

REF.: *CBA;* Demaris, *The Last Mafioso;* Eisenberg and Landau, *Meyer Lansky;* Fried, *The Rise and Fall of the Jewish Gangster in America;* Messick, *Lansky;* ____, *Secret Files;* ____ and Goldblatt, *The Mobs and the Mafia;* Nash, *Bloodletters and Badmen;* Ottenberg, *The Federal Investigators;* Peterson, *The Mob;* Reid, *The Grim Reapers.*

Stack, Sir **Lee Oliver Fitzmaurice**, 1868-1924, Egypt, assass. The assassination of Major General Sir Lee Stack, governor-general of the Anglo-Egyptian Sudan and Sudar, by Egyptian nationalists on Nov. 19, 1924, brought into sharp focus the problems confronting England as it tried to govern its burgeoning colonial territories.

Stack and his entourage had just arrived at the capitol building in Cairo when seven Egyptian students garbed in traditional effendi dress surrounded his auto and began firing. Bullets struck Stack in the stomach, hand, and foot, and he died from shock and hemorrhage the next day. Captain Patrick K. Campbell, his aide, and chauffeur Fred Marsh were wounded in the attack carried out by members of the "Society of Vengeance." The attack against British colonials was not the first. In London the press denounced this latest atrocity on the part of Egyptian separatists. "Apologies and honorary satisfaction will of course be demanded and will of course be forthcoming," the *Times* editorialized. "But something more is required in our interests and in the interests of Egypt."

Egyptian king Faud met with Viscount Allenby, assuring the full cooperation of his government in catching the assassins. At the same time his government balked at several of the sanctions imposed by the Crown, including a removal of all native officers from the troubled region of the Sudan. Stack had favored a policy of integrating tribal chieftains into the government of the state. King Faud agreed to pay £500,000 restitution demanded by the British Parliament, however. The police conducted a relentless door-to-door search, and they enlisted the help of a spy, Neguib Helbawi, a former nationalist imprisoned in 1914 for complicity in a plot to assassinate the prime minister. For a payment of $49,400, Helbawi agreed to infiltrate the separatist movement. He pointed the police in the direction of a young law student named Abdullah Fattah Enayat and his brother Abdullah Hami. Following instructions, Helbawi told the brothers that the police were about to make an arrest and the best course of action was to flee the country. He advised them to take a train to Tripoli which criss-crossed through the arid desert regions making their escape all but impossible.

The Enayats boarded a train at Alexandria on Jan. 31, 1925. That afternoon they were arrested. Four automatic pistols and some ammunition was discovered in a basket of fruit. Forensic tests performed on the cartridge cases showed the bullets to be identical to the ones fired into the Stack's body. The brothers' confession led to the arrest of six other men, including rebel ringleader Shafik Mansour and Mahmoud Rachid. The conspirators were tried for murder in May 1925. All eight were found Guilty on June 7 and hung two months later. The eighth had his sentence commuted because he had assisted the investigators in the capture of the other seven.

REF.: *CBA;* Smith, *Mostly Murder.*

Stack, Richard, 1956- , U.S., mur. A Southwest Side Chicago man was charged on Mother's Day, May 12, 1980, with murdering his wife and their infant son. Richard Stack, twenty-four, was arrested at Holy Cross Hospital where he was being treated for cuts on his hands and head. Police were called to the scene by neighbors who said Stack had been leaning out a window he had broken, shouting. Family members told officers the Stacks were high school sweethearts who had married in 1978. The victims, Carol Ann Stack, twenty-two, and the infant, Richard Stack, Jr., thirteen months, suffered multiple stab wounds from a broken pool cue.

Tried in April 1982 in a Chicago criminal court before Judge James M. Bailey, Stack had been an unemployed laborer at the time of the murders. Defense attorney Geary Kull presented the testimony of two court-appointed psychiatrists who said Stack was insane when he murdered his wife and child to rid them of demons. Assistant state's attorneys Ernest DiBenedetto and Michael Goggin charged that Stack slashed and stabbed both victims, throwing his child against the wall and cracking the baby's skull. DiBenedetto also said Stack had asked psychiatrists at the Chester Mental Health Center to explain the criteria for being judged insane shortly after he was evaluated as mentally competent to stand trial. On Mar. 30, the jury ruled that Stack was not insane. Calling the murders "brutal and heinous," Bailey sentenced Stack to life imprisonment on Apr. 26, 1982. REF.: *CBA.*

Stafford, Annie, b.1838, U.S., pros. Known as "Gentle Annie" in her youth, Annie Stafford was the leading combatant in Chicago's 1857 "Whore War." Representing the forces of The Sands, a downtown vice district, against an assault by State Street madams soliciting new talent for their brothels, Stafford, at that time a 50-cent prostitute at Anna Wilson's house, was the main fighter for the Sands. Tiring of not making more profit from her endeavors, Stafford determined to become a madam herself and by the early 1860s ran what she referred to as "a classy place with thirty boarders."

Stafford's long-term affair with Chicago gambler Cap Hyman ended in marriage after she stormed into his house in September 1866 carrying a rawhide whip with which she chased him out of the house and along the street until he proposed. Hyman's wedding gift to his bride was a tavern in Sunnyside, just outside the city limits, which was turned into "a high-toned roadhouse."

Sunnyside's opening night was a festive occasion, with visitors from city and county governments as well as young businessmen and sports figures, reporters, and big-time gamblers. Three other important madams were invited, while about twenty-four of Stafford's prostitutes greeted the guests. After several cases of champagne had been drunk, Cap Hyman shot out the lights, Gentle Annie yelled at the other madams for soliciting business, and several of the whores had set up free-lance business in upstairs rooms.

Although Sunnyside was hailed as a success, it died as a business enterprise because, Stafford explained, gentlemen would not travel that far even for high-class hookers. The Hymans returned to Chicago. Cap Hyman collapsed in 1875, both mentally and physically, and died the next year with his wife beside him. Stafford ran her brothel until around 1880, when she disappeared. See: **Sands, The.** REF.: *CBA.*

Stafford, Edward (Third Duke of Buckingham), 1478-1521, Brit., treas. Served as privy councilor in 1509. He was castigated and put to death on allegations of being disloyal to Henry VIII. REF.: *CBA.*

Stafford, Henry (Second Duke of Buckingham), c.1454-83, Brit., consp. Proclaimed sentence of George Clarence, who was found Guilty of using necromancy to assassinate the king in 1478. He was put to death at Salisbury for gathering troops to fight Richard III. REF.: *CBA.*

Stafford, Humphrey (Earl of Devon), 1439-69, Brit., nobleman, assass. Held post of privy councilor in 1469, among other positions. On order of Edward IV he battled Robin of Redesdale, a Yorkshire rebel. He argued with the Duke of Pembroke and withdrew his troops, for which he was executed. REF.: *CBA.*

Highwayman Philip Stafford robbing one of many coaches.

Stafford, Philip, prom.1640s, Brit., rob. When a British civil war broke out in the early 1640s, 20-year-old Philip Stafford left his home in Newbury to join the fight. After the war, Captain Stafford, like many veterans, became a highwayman. He was not fond of nonconformist preachers and once stole forty guineas from a minister. Stafford, who was later ordained as a pastor, absolved himself before his parishioners but later stole some linen and the sacramental plate. After robbing a farmer of £33, Stafford was tried at the Reading Assizes, convicted, and sentenced to death. He tried to escape before his execution at Reading but was thwarted and hanged.

REF.: *CBA;* Pringle, *Stand and Deliver.*

Stafford, Roger Dale, 1951- , U.S., mur. Arrested in a North Side Chicago YMCA without incident on Mar. 13, 1979, was Roger Dale Stafford, twenty-seven, implicated by his estranged wife, Vera Stafford, in the slayings of at least nine people.

Stafford was the prime suspect in the first-degree murder of six employees of the Sirloin Stockade Steakhouse in Oklahoma City, Okla., on July 16, 1978, during a robbery that netted $1,300. The body of Terri M. Horst, fifteen, was found in the walk-in freezer. Also murdered were Anthony Tew, seventeen; David Lindsey, seventeen; David Salsman, fifteen; Issac Freeman, fifty-six; and Louis Zacharias, forty-three. Stafford's brother, Harry Stafford, also a suspect in the murders, was killed in a motorcycle accident in Tulsa, Okla., not long afterward. Stafford was also the main suspect in the killings of air force sergeant Melvin Lorenz, thirty-eight, of San Antonio, Texas; his wife, Linda Lorenz, thirty-one; and their 12-year-old son, Richard. The bodies of the Lorenz' were discovered along Interstate 35 on June 22, 1978, near Purcell, Okla.

Found Guilty in an Oklahoma City courtroom of the shootings of the six steakhouse employees, Stafford was sentenced on Oct. 24, 1979, by Judge Charles Owens to be executed by lethal injection. Stafford proclaimed his innocence, saying, "I wish to God the police department would quit harassing me and find the people who did it." According to Oklahoma law, executions must be carried out by injections of lethal barbiturates. As of this writing, he is still awaiting execution. REF.: *CBA.*

Stafford, Wendell Philips, b.1861, U.S., jur. Reported decisions of Vermont Supreme Court from 1896-1900. He became a judge on the court, serving from 1900-04. He also served as associate justice on the supreme court of the District of Columbia from 1904-31. REF.: *CBA.*

Stahl, David, 1920-70, U.S., jur. Attorney general of Pennsylvania until 1968, when appointed to third circuit court by President Lyndon B. Johnson. REF.: *CBA.*

Stain, David L., and Cromwell, Oliver, prom. 1887, U.S., (wrong. convict.) mur. On Feb. 22, 1878, a bank cashier, John Wilson Barron, was found about 7 p.m. lying in a bank vault in Dexter, Maine. The unconscious man, hands tied behind his back, had been gagged with a bucket handle and had bruises and cuts on his head. Some townspeople claimed he was murdered, while others thought he committed suicide because some money recently had been missing from the bank. No suspects were arrested until ten years later.

In 1887, Charles Francis Stain was jailed and his father refused him $25 for bail. In jail, Stain told authorities that his father, David L. Stain, and Oliver Cromwell had killed Barron, claiming his father confessed to him one night not long after the killing. Stain and Cromwell were arrested and their trial began in March 1888. Convicted, both were sentenced to a life term in prison. However, their attorney continued to fight the case and produced witnesses collaborating their alibi that they had been in their hometown of Medfield, Mass., the day of the murder. The lawyer also proved that witnesses who identified his clients were shown pictures of the two and the younger Stain's credibility was destroyed when evidence showed that earlier he had confessed to a robbery he did not commit. On Jan. 1, 1901, after serving thirteen years in prison, Stain and Cromwell were granted full pardons.

REF.: Borchard, *Convicting the Innocent; CBA.*

Stainback, Ingram Macklin, 1883-1961, U.S., jur. Served as U.S. Attorney for Hawaii from 1934-40, and as U.S. district judge in Hawaii from 1940-42. REF.: *CBA.*

Stalin, Joseph (Iosif Vissarionovich Dzhugashvili), 1879-1953, U.S.S.R., mur. Joseph Stalin, the son of a cobbler who became a mass murderer, grew up in Gori, a small town in Georgia, then a Russian colony, in the western Asian Caucasus. He studied for the priesthood at Tiflis Theological Seminary in the Georgian capital, but was soon reading Karl Marx and other revolutionary theorists. He worked briefly as a clerk in the Tiflis Observatory, the only known time he ever held a nonpolitical job. He joined an underground organization in 1900 and encouraged strikes and labor unrest throughout the Caucasus. He became a Bolshevik in 1903 and was arrested for revolutionary activity seven times between April 1902 and March 1913. He masterminded a June 25, 1907, holdup that netted money to finance revolutionary activities. Nevertheless, party leaders virtually ignored him until Nikolai Lenin gave him his first big promotion, to serve on the first Central Committee of the Bolshevik party in 1912. About this time, he adopted the revolutionary code name "Stalin," from the Russian word for steel, *stal.*

After editing *Pravda* for a short time, Stalin went into internal exile in Siberia from July 1913 to March 1917. When he returned, he resumed his editorial activities, advocating cooperation with the moderates who took over the reins of government after the czar was dethroned, but he quickly became more militant at Lenin's behest. At the urging of Lenin, Stalin, and Stalin's rival, Leon Trotsky, and armed insurrectionists seized control in 1917.

Lenin appointed Stalin secretary-general of the party's Central Committee in 1922, a position he held until his death. He was also a member of the Politburo. He used leverage from these positions to outmaneuver theorists like Trotsky, Grigory Zinoviev, and other members of Lenin's inner circle. Lenin fell ill in about

1921 and never fully regained his health before his death in 1924; Stalin's increasingly hard line and his independence from Lenin's more moderate policies led Lenin to write his famous testament, warning the new Soviet leadership to remove Stalin from power. In January 1924, Lenin died and rumors of poisoning by Stalin's agents surrounded his death. Even so, Stalin exploited Lenin's memory, and a pervasive cult of Lenin, including unquestionable dogma forged from his heavily edited writings, was used to consolidate Stalin's status as a mythic figure.

In the years that followed, Stalin began to liquidate all his rivals. Trotsky was expelled from the Soviet Union in 1929. Zinoviev, Nikolai Bukharin, Lev Kamenev, Alexei Rykov, and others disappeared in the Soviet judicial system, languishing in jail until their executions.

Other policies Stalin instituted in his early years in power included forced industrialization under his five-year plans and forced collectivization of all farmland. The latter particularly evoked resistance, which caused Stalin to have millions of peasant farmers shot, exiled, or jailed in his newly established rural forced-labor prison camps. (Much of the credit Stalin took for bringing the Soviet Union into the industrialized twentieth century is due to the slave-like conditions of these camps.) Despite a major famine in the Ukraine, Stalin continued to export grain. Altogether, an estimated 10 million peasants were starved, murdered, or worked to death. When the five-year plans for industrialization did not work, Stalin placed the blame firmly on his subordinates, staging trials of factory managers and bureaucrats, who were tortured into making absurd confessions.

But the atrocities were just beginning. The Stalinist purges began in late 1934, shortly after the Dec. 1 assassination of potential rival Sergei Kirov in Leningrad. Those in the Politburo who posed a threat to Stalin were rounded up and accused of treason. Kamenev and Zinoviev were forced to read public "confessions" before they were shot in August 1936. Hundreds of lesser party members were treated similarly, and in June 1937, the pre-eminent Soviet military figure, Marshal Mikhail Tukhachevsky, and several other generals were tried on charges of treason and executed. Meanwhile, Lavrenti Pavlovich Beria, the head of Stalin's secret police who was in charge of jailing, torturing, and butchering the accused, also produced forged papers in 1935 that purportedly demonstrated that Stalin was more important than Lenin in formulating the 1917 revolution.

Once started, the purges snowballed. Everyone who confessed implicated others. Independent thinkers were liquidated, then anyone whose loyalty was slightly suspect, then Stalinist apparatchiks to whom no suspicion could be justifiably attached, then agents of Stalin's own secret police. The ranks of political, military, industrial, and agrarian leaders, along with diplomats, academics, artists, engineers, and lawyers, were all drastically and randomly reduced. Left unprepared for WWII, Stalin tried to compensate by approaching the western powers to try to forge an alliance against Germany and its allies in August 1939. When that plan did not work, he appeased Adolf Hitler with a mutual nonaggression pact, which prompted the German dictator to invade Poland. To shore up his eastern boundaries, Stalin annexed the Baltic republics and parts of Poland and Romania. Still, Soviet unpreparedness allowed Hitler to invade deep into Russia, enslaving the Soviet peoples in occupied territory to a degree that rivaled their treatment at Stalin's hands. Following the war, famine hit the Ukraine, and once again millions starved.

After the war the purges continued. The motivation this time was the defection of Josip Broz Tito, Communist dictator of Yugoslavia, who rejected Soviet influence in 1948 in favor of independence for his country. This slap caused the paranoid Stalin once again to liquidate those who could challenge his power, and once again his chief henchman was "Beria the Butcher." By the early 1950s, however, Stalin felt he could no longer trust Beria. He had the secret police chief arrested in 1951 and charged with being an imperialist agent for the West.

Stalin made his final accusation of conspiracy against Beria in January 1953. He claimed that the doctors who treated top Soviet leaders in the Kremlin had been responsible for murdering certain patients. The stage was set for another wave of show trials, with the "Doctor's Plot" as a pretext, but then, on Mar. 5, 1953, Stalin died. Whether or not foul play was involved, the Soviet people were rid of their greatest oppressor. Change was slow, however and three years passed after Stalin's death before his successor, Nikita Khrushchev, criticized Stalin's "cult of personality." However, Stalin's policy of brutally suppressing individual liberty remained for decades. Although precise figures for the number of deaths Stalin caused are difficult to pinpoint, estimates range in the tens of millions. Some historians set the figure as high as 70 million, a number that, if correct, makes him one of the most prolific mass murderers in history. See: **Beria, Lavrenti Pavlovich; Hitler, Adolf; Lenin, Vladimir Ilich; Trotsky, Leon.**

REF: Bialer, *Stalin and His Generals;* Bornstein, *The Politics of Murder; CBA;* Clutterbuck, *Guerrillas and Terrorists;* Demaris, *Brothers in Blood: The International Terrorist Network;* ____, *The Director;* Deutscher, *Stalin: A Political Biography;* Djilas, *Conversations with Stalin;* Dobson and Payne, *The Terrorists—Their Weapons, Leaders and Tactics;* Fischer, *The Life and Death of Stalin;* Hacker, *Crusaders, Criminals, Crazies: Terror and Terrorism in Our Time;* Hurwood, *Society and the Assassin;* McClellan and Avery, *The Voices of Guns;* McNeal, *Lenin, Stalin and Khurshchev: Voices of Bolshevism;* Morgan, *Prince of Crime;* Paine, *The Assassins' World;* Powers, *Secrecy and Power;* Schreiber, *The Ultimate Weapon—Terrorists and World Order;* Toledano, *J. Edgar Hoover;* Tolstoy, *Stalin's Secret War;* Wolfe, *Three Who Made a Revolution;* (FILM), *The Great Citizen,* 1939; *Mission to Moscow,* 1943; *The Girl in the Kremlin,* 1957.

Stalinist Guards, See: **Berneri, Camillo.**

Stamboliyski, Aleksandur, 1879-1923, Bul., prime minister, rebel.-assass. Led Agrarian Union or Peasant party. He was jailed from 1915-18 for favoring the Allied Powers over King Ferdinand during WWI. Upon his release he headed a revolution which ousted the king and formed a new but short-lived, republic. He reorganized the judicial system while prime minister. He was deposed and put to death by a military coup. REF.: *CBA.*

Stambolov, Stefan, 1855-95, Bul., premier, assass. Oppressive ruler noted for establishing cordial relations with Turkey and for antagonism toward Russia. He was assassinated. REF.: *CBA.*

Stamp Act Riot, 1765, U.S., mob vio. Just as gambling, deadly fights, and opium smoking were spawned in Boston's taverns, so too was the American Revolution. The pubs were the perfect gathering spots for political radicals who, when properly in their cups, encouraged themselves to acts of patriotic gore. (It would be an established but little accepted fact, that most of those who "fired the shot heard 'round the world" at Lexington and Concord had been kept up all night in their local drinking spas by Samuel Adams and other ardent revolutionaries, plied with stinging booze and oratory, and then led teetering and red-eyed at dawn to the greens and revolution.)

The despised Stamp Act, signed into law on Aug. 15, 1765, by Arthur Oliver, the king's stamp distributor, was the cause of one of Boston's most destructive riots. (Riots also occurred in a half dozen other cities but none rivaled Boston's.) Drinking for hours in The Bunch of Grapes and the Royal Exchange, mobs became, in the words of one historian, "cruel, cowardly and dedicated to loot and insult more emphatically than ever it was concerned for the cause of liberty or other high aspirations."

The mobs were led by a heavyset rabble-rouser named Ebenezer Mackintosh, a shoemaker by trade, but a mob organizer by instinct and a very effective one at that, particularly when in the pay of those who wanted bloody demonstrations to better undermine the British rule of the colonies. Though Mackintosh was clearly recognized by authorities as the ringleader of the Boston Stamp Act Riot, he was never punished for the wholesale destruction he caused. It was feared that should the popular Mackintosh be jailed, the fierce mobs would rise up again and burn down half the city.

Scores of drunken patriots poured out of Boston pubs on the night of Aug. 26 and headed for Admirality Court, torches and weapons in hand, oaths and curses on lips. The homes of Chief Justice Thomas Hutchinson and the comptroller of currency were quickly looted and set afire. Swinging about in its fury, the mob raced to the home of Arthur Oliver which was situated on the summit of Fort Hill. Terrified, Oliver gathered his family about him and left by his back door. His son, last to leave, heard one of the mob leaders, as the front door was broken down, shout to his companions: "Damn him! He's upstairs! We'll have him!"

Rioters outraged over the Stamp Act.

The rioters, however, were greeted by an empty house. This seemed to further enrage them, and they proceeded to destroy a historic landmark. Oliver hid in a neighbor's house and received from friends an almost minute-by-minute account of the devastation. He later wrote: "Not content with tearing off the wainscot and hangings, and splitting the doors to pieces, they beat down the partition walls; and though that alone cost them near two hours, they cut down the cupola or lanthorn, and they began to take up the boards and slate from the roof, and were prevented only by the approaching daylight from a total demolition of the building. The garden house was laid flat and all my trees, etc., broke down to the ground.

"Such ruin was never seen in America. Besides my plate and family pictures, household furniture of every kind, my own children's and servants' apparel, they carried off about £900 of money, and emptied the house of everything whatsoever, except a part of the kitchen furniture, not leaving a single book or paper in it, and have scattered and destroyed all the manuscripts and other papers I have been collecting for thirty years together, besides a great number of public papers in my custody."

It is a wonder that in all this rioting only one person was hurt. The lone, injured rioter was too drunk to move fast enough to escape a falling brick wall of one of the destroyed houses.

REF.: Brown, *Strain of Violence; CBA;* Gipson, *The Coming of the Revolution, 1762-1775;* Haskins, *Street Gangs;* Headley, *The Great Riots of New York, 1712-1873;* Heaps, *Riots, U.S.A., 1765-1970;* Jennings, *Boston, Cradle of Liberty;* Labree, *The Road to Independence, 1763-1776;* Miller and Morgan, *The Stamp Act Crisis;* Zobel, *The Boston Massacre.*

Stanbery, Henry, 1803-81, U.S., atty. gen. Appointed U.S. attorney general by President Andrew Johnson in 1866, broadly interpreting Reconstruction legislation. He resigned in 1868 to successfully represent Johnson in impeachment proceedings. Johnson again appointed him as attorney general near the end of the impeachment trial, but the Senate voted against him. He resumed his law practice in Cincinnati, Ohio. REF.: *CBA.*

Stanciel, Elijah, c.1961- , and **Burgos, Violeta**, c.1964- , U.S., mur. A blind couple living on the North Side of Chicago murdered the woman's child and received relatively light sentences because of their handicaps and lack of previous criminal records. In 1984, Eleticia Asbury was born to Violeta Burgos and Andre Asbury. Then the parents separated, Burgos caring for the child. In December 1984, the infant was taken from the mother by the Illinois Department of Children and Family Services because her boyfriend, Elijah Stanciel, allegedly broke the child's arm. The state organization directed Burgos to attend parenting classes, obtain counseling, and avoid Stanciel. Eleticia was reunited with her mother in October 1985. For several months before the toddler's death on Apr. 19, 1986, she was tortured. An autopsy revealed 130 wounds on the body, some of them bites.

The sightless pair stood trial and were convicted. During sentencing, their lawyers pleaded for leniency from Cook County Criminal Court judge James Bailey, claiming a prison sentence would be a difficult ordeal for the killers because they were blind. Stanciel's attorney Sam Adam asserted, "you have before you an individual who has no prior convictions for anything at all...A severely handicapped individual, a man who is legally blind." Judge Bailey sentenced the pair to sixty years in prison each, though the prosecution had argued for the death penalty. Relatives of the child were outraged, including the child's natural father, who contended that blindness should not be used to justify a murder. The child's uncle, William Asbury, commented, "I don't see any more than they do. They didn't have to see to kill her...These are two individuals that took the life of a child. Sixty years is awful light for taking a life." REF.: *CBA.*

Standard, Jess, 1854-1935, U.S., west. gunman. Working as a cowboy for Pink Higgins in Texas during the 1870s, Jess Standard participated in the violent and bloody Horrell-Higgins feud in Lampasas County.

Western gunman Jess Standard.

On Mar. 26, 1877, several members of the Higgins gang ambushed brothers Sam and Mart Horrell as they rode to court in Lampasas. When Sam was thrown from his horse, Mart charged his assailants, firing. The Higgins men fled. On June 14, 1877, the feud ignited in the Lampasas streets when Frank Mitchell was slain and Bill Wren was wounded, but none of the Horrell men were hit. In July 1877, in Lampasas County, Standard and thirteen others followed Higgins to the headquarters of Horrell, pinning them inside the bunk and ranch houses and wounding two of their men. After a two-day siege, ammunition ran low and the Higgins faction left the ranch.

Standard eventually moved his family to Tuscola, Texas, where he farmed and worked as a carpenter.

REF.: *CBA;* Gillett, *Six Years With the Texas Rangers;* Webb, *Texas Rangers.*

Stangl, Franz, c.1908-71, Ger., war crimes. A young Austrian apprentice weaver, Franz Stangl, abandoned his craft and eventually supervised two concentration camps during WWII for the Nazis. During the 1930s, 23-year-old Stangl joined the Austrian police force and once received recognition for detecting Nazi weapons that had been smuggled into Austria. When the Germans arrived in Austria, Stangl feared he might be punished for his earlier deed, so the 32-year-old accepted an offer to serve as police superintendent of the Euthanasia Institute, a facility for killing "inferior" Austrians and Germans. He later became the commandant of the Treblinka and Sobibor concentration camps in Poland, overseeing the shooting and gassing of approximately 1.2 million men, women, and children in one year. Nazi hunter Simon Wiesenthal later found an inventory of goods taken from Treblinka victims, signed by Stangl, which included huge amounts of cash, gems, jewelry, clothing, drugs, and women's hair. After the war, Stangl was arrested as an SS agent and put in prison by U.S. officials who did not realize his position. When the Austrian government learned that the prisoner had been employed at Castle Hartheim, the Nazi school specializing in the science of human extermination, they started proceedings to try him. On May 30, 1948, Stangl escaped to Rome and then to the Middle East.

Ten years later, in 1959, Wiesenthal heard that Stangl was in Damascus, Syria, but Stangl bolted soon afterward because Adolf Eichmann had been extradited from Argentina to Israel. In 1964, Wiesenthal picked up Stangl's trail again after getting a tip from the cousin of Stangl's wife and information from a former Gestapo official, who told the Nazi hunter that Stangl was working in São Paulo, Braz., for Volkswagen as a safety officer. In February 1967, Brazilian authorities arrested the former concentration camp chief and sent him back to Germany where he was tried and convicted for killing 400,000 people. He received a life term and died in confinement in Düsseldorf on June 28, 1971. REF.: *CBA.*

Staniak, Lucian (AKA: **The Red Spider**), 1941- , Pol., rape-mur. A young man who traveled throughout Poland in his work translating for publishing companies, 26-year-old Lucian Staniak murdered about twenty girls, also raping some of them. During the killings and mutilations, which occurred between 1964 and 1967, Staniak sent letters to the Polish press penned in red spider-like writing. When police investigated Staniak they became more suspicious when they saw his paintings, dominantly red and created with a knife. One of the works portrayed a woman with a slit stomach and flowers growing out of the wound. Staniak was arrested and readily confessed, claiming that the killings began after his sister and parents were killed by a girl in a hit-and-run accident and the girl had not been punished. He said his first victim resembled the girl. Staniak was convicted and sentenced to confinement for life in a facility for mentally ill patients at Katowice. REF.: *CBA.*

Stanley, Arthur Cromwell, d.1923, S. Afri., mur. Former WWI soldier and hopeful diamond digger in the city of Kimberley, Arthur Stanley was unable to provide for his family. Having decided to turn to crime, he learned that William James Thompson, a diamond buyer, would be making a circuit of various mines the next day, carrying cash to buy stones. Early on Mar. 7, 1923, Thompson's chauffeur picked up the buyer. At a gateway into a farm, two men appeared and at first seemed about to open the gate for the car. Instead, they turned and fired. A bullet went through Thompson's head and five more bullets injured the driver. Stanley and his partner took the money and left, thinking that both men had been killed.

As Stanley and his companion were burying most of the money, investigators were learning Stanley's identity, because the chauffeur, regaining consciousness, named Arthur Stanley as one of the assailants. The killer set off by cab to go to Schmidt's Drift Road where his family was waiting, but the cab drivers already knew that Stanley was wanted by police. Stanley was met at Schmidt's Drift by a policeman and arrested. He was tried and found Guilty. The judge ignored a recommendation of mercy, and Stanley was hanged on June 11, 1923.

REF.: *CBA;* Melville, *Famous Duels and Assassinations.*

Stanley, Edwin Monroe, 1909-71, U.S., jur. Served as judge in Greensboro, N.C. (1951-54), and as U.S. attorney (1954-57). He was appointed by President Dwight D. Eisenhower to the middle district court of North Carolina in 1957. REF.: *CBA.*

Stanley, Henry (Lord Strange), c.1531-93, Ire., jur. Participated on commission convicting Mary, Queen of Scots of conspiring with Anthonly Babington and others to kill Queen Elizabeth I. REF.: *CBA.*

Stannard, Albert, and **Strong, John Patrick**, prom. 1935, Case of, Aus., mur. Two men, Albert Stannard and John Patrick Strong, were tried for murder in connection with the so called "Shark Arm Case." On Apr. 8, 1935, James Smith disappeared, and on Apr. 25, 1935, a shark in an aquarium in Coogee, a suburb of Sydney, Aus., vomited up Smith's arm. A boat builder, Reginald Holmes, said that a launch owner, Patrick Brady, was the person who Smith went to meet on Apr. 8, and that Brady was blackmailing he and Smith. On June 12, the day before the Smith inquest, Holmes was murdered. With the primary witness dead, Brady was acquitted of Smith's murder. However, at his trial he mentioned another man, Albert Stannard, a launch owner whom he had seen at the cottage with Smith the day Smith disappeared. Stannard and laborer John Patrick Strong were tried for the murder of Reginald Holmes, but both were acquitted. See: **Brady, Patrick.**

REF.: *CBA;* Godwin, *Killers Unknown.*

Stannard, Mary, See: **Hayden, Herbert H.**

Stano, Gerald Eugene, 1951- , U.S., mur. In 1981, Gerald Eugene Stano was sentenced to three life terms in a Florida prison for strangling and stabbing three women in Florida's Volusia County. Arrested in April 1980 in Daytona Beach, Fla., after slashing a prostitute, Stano was initially saved from the death penalty in a plea agreement that left him ineligible for parole until he is 103 years old. He confessed to three other murders, including those of Susan Bickrest, twenty-four, and Cathy Muldoon, twenty-three. By mid-August 1982, Stano had confessed to eleven slayings, by October, thirty-three. He may be responsible for as many as forty, a record number for an American murderer this century, an infamous position formerly held by Chicago's John Wayne Gacy, who was convicted of slaying thirty-three boys and young men.

All of Stano's victims were women. Most were stabbed or shot with a .22-caliber pistol. Most lived in Tampa or in the central Florida area, and many frequented the bars along Tampa's Dale Mabry Highway. According to Stano's confessions, he also killed two women in New Jersey and "four to six" in Pennsylvania. Almost all of the victims had had to rely on someone else for transportation on the day they were killed, and all were either single, divorced, or separated. Many of the victims were hitchhikers or prostitutes, ranging in age from twelve to the mid-fifties. The victims willingly got into Stano's car after he had charmed them with small talk and offered them beer or marijuana and a relaxing ride.

Stano worked at semiskilled jobs—cleaning windshields or working as a short-order cook. The bodies of his victims were dumped in desolate areas of Pasco County, with most of the murders occurring in 1976 and 1977.

The killings began in 1973, the year Stano moved from New Jersey to Florida with his adoptive parents. Stano said he killed the women because they argued and "I can't stand a bitchy chick." A psychological profile by Dr. Ann McMillan classified Stano as a multiple killer of the type who "simply enjoys killing." McMillan described Stano as a man who hated women and could probably only obtain sexual release after murdering and mutilating them. Stano frequently mentioned "seeing red" when he described attacking his victims, and often killed women who wore blue, a color he apparently connected with a younger brother on whom he wanted to take revenge. Coming from a background of extreme abuse and neglect, Stano became a juvenile delinquent, damaging property and setting fires. Alcohol triggered his lethal rages. Apparently he never committed murder until he had drank beer or whiskey. He kept his prized treasure, his car, spotless, scrubbing all bloodstains and evidence of the murders off the seats and upholstery.

By December 1982, authorities had come up with no physical

evidence or witnesses to link Stano to the additional murders he claimed to have committed. He had not directed law-enforcement officers to any bodies that had not already been found, according to Florida Department of Law Enforcement agent Ed Williams, who coordinated the investigation for several counties. Sergeant Paul Crow, a Daytona Beach police detective, was the person to whom Stano confessed many of the murders.

In January 1984, Stano was sentenced to death for murder. He was under three death sentences and was serving seven life sentences for ten murders committed in Florida. On May 18, 1988, the eve of his fourth appointment with the electric chair, Stano won an indefinite stay of execution from the Atlanta Circuit Court of Appeals. Stano still resides on Death Row in a Florida state prison as of this writing.

REF.: *CBA;* Fox, *Mass Murder.*

Stansfield, Philip (Standsfield), d.c.1687, Scot., mur. A son who thought he was ill-treated by his father committed parricide. On Nov. 21, 1687, Sir James Stansfield returned to his house in New Milns, close to Dumfries, with the Reverend John Bell. The two arrived home late, reputedly because Stansfield wanted to avoid his son, Philip Stansfield, a heavy drinker whom he had removed from his will. That night the son, accompanied by a servant, James Thompson, and a prostitute, Janet Johnston, strangled the elder Stansfield and dumped his body into a garden pond. The next morning the son asked the reverend, who had heard noises during the night and attributed them to spirits, where his father was, but the clergyman did not know. The younger Stansfield said he was going to search for his father.

The body was discovered in the pond, and as the son helped to carry it out of the water, the cadaver began bleeding, soiling the son's hands. The incident was more proof to observers of the son's guilt because at the time people believed a murdered person's body would bleed if the killer touched it. Later, two children testified that they overheard the culprits discussing the murder after it was completed. Philip Stansfield was convicted at Edinburgh, given the death penalty, and also sentenced to have his tongue cut off because he had cursed his father. At his execution the rope knot did not hold and Stansfield dropped to his knees, forcing the hangman to strangle him. The body was later displayed in chains.

REF.: *CBA;* Laurence, *A History of Capital Punishment;* Wilson, *Encyclopedia of Murder.*

Stapirius, Michael, prom. 1628, Ger., witchcraft. Reverend Michael Stapirius served as a pastor of Paderborn, located in north central West Germany. There he listened to the confessions of people convicted as witches in the Westphalian trials, horrified when many told him that they had admitted guilt and denounced others as witches only because they had been tortured. In around 1628, the clergyman wrote *Brillentractat,* a work that described and criticized the proceedings. See: **Spee, Friedrich von**.

REF.: *CBA;* Gibbons, *Some Rhenish Foes of Credulity and Cruelty;* Robbins, *The Encyclopedia of Witchcraft and Demonology.*

Starchfield, Willie, 1906-14, Brit., (unsolv.) mur. Eight-year-old Willie Starchfield was sent on an errand by his mother about 1 p.m. on Jan. 8, 1914. He was not seen again until his body was found stuffed under the seat of the Chalk Farm to Broad Street train late that afternoon. The blond, curly haired boy was strangled. The cord was still around his neck. The murder brought Willie's father, John Starchfield, before the public for the second time. Starchfield was a newspaper vendor who had single-handedly captured killer Stephen Titus, a tailor who had gone crazy and killed hotel manager Esther May Towers fifteen months before. Starchfield had been awarded £50 from the government and a small pension by the Carnegie Heroes Fund as compensation for the wounds he had received in his struggle with Titus.

This time Starchfield was in the news as a grieving father. Weeks later, he was indicted for his son's murder. Officials surmised that Willie was killed elsewhere and the body smuggled onto the train in a large suitcase. Witnesses claimed to have seen Willie with his father not long before he was killed, but no other evidence existed against Starchfield. By the second day of the trial, prosecutors clearly had no case. Justice Atkin apologized to Starchfield, dismissed him, and reprimanded the coroner's jury for hasty action. Willie's killer never was found.

REF.: Adam, *Murder By Persons Unkown;* Brock, *A Casebook of Crime;* Browne and Tullett, *The Scalpel of Scotland Yard; CBA;* Goodman, *The Railway Murders;* Lambton, *Thou Shalt Do No Murder;* Nash, *Open Files;* Shew, *A Companion to Murder;* Whitbread, *The Railway Policemen.*

Starkie, Dr. **Richard**, prom. 1921, Brit., drugs. During the early 1900s a former police surgeon, Dr. Richard Starkie, began performing abortions, which were illegal at the time. On July 17, 1921, he was arrested and charged with administering toxins with the intent of performing an abortion on a married woman and with performing illegal operations on four unwed women. The doctor was acquitted on charges of performing the abortions, but convicted and sentenced to nine months in prison for administering drugs. Reportedly when he was released from Wormwood Scrubs Prison, he was greeted by six hundred of his patients.

REF.: Browne and Tullett, *The Scalpel of Scotland Yard; CBA.*

Starkweather, Albert L., 1841-66, U.S., mur. On Aug. 1, 1865, the bodies of Harriett Starkweather and her daughter Ella were found in the burned ruins of their house in Oakland, Conn. As well as being burned, their heads had been crushed and their bodies repeatedly stabbed. The police became suspicious of Starkweather's son Albert, who appeared at the crime scene with a bump on his forehead, claiming to be an attack victim as well. He was subsequently arrested and charged with the murders of his mother and sister.

Albert Starkweather was romantically involved with a woman named Emerett Campbell. He sought to convince her to marry him by presenting her with a deed to a homestead which his mother had given him, as well as the proceeds from the sale of a prized bloodmare. Mrs. Starkweather balked at Albert's generosity and threatened to nullify the sale.

Albert was arraigned by a grand jury and ordered to stand trial in December 1865. Knowing that a conviction was likely, Starkweather attempted to bribe his way out of jail, first by offering his attorney, Apollos Fenn, his entire fortune, and later an inmate trusty, John Leonard, a reward for his complicity. Leonard informed the warden, and Starkweather remained incarcerated until his December trial in the Connecticut Superior Courtroom of Justice William White. Starkweather was found Guilty and sentenced to death and on Aug. 17, 1866, he was hanged from the gallows in Hartford, Conn.

REF.: *CBA; The Manchester Homicide.*

Starkweather, Charles (AKA: Little Red), 1940-59, and **Fugate, Caril Ann**, 1945- , U.S., rob.-mur. Diminutive Charles Starkweather, also known as Little Red, committed the first of eleven murders at seventeen and died in Nebraska's electric chair two years later. He and his girlfriend, Caril Ann Fugate, terrorized the plains states for a week in 1958 when they went on a murder rampage.

Charlie Starkweather wanted to be like James Dean. He followed the charismatic actor's career in films like *Rebel Without a Cause* while working as a garbage man. In keeping with the rebel image, he took up with a much younger girl. Where girls Starkweather's age were put off by his five-foot, two-inch stature, fourteen-year-old Caril Ann Fugate was flattered by his attentions. She was well-developed for her age, rebellious in school, and at home.

On Dec. 1, 1957, Starkweather robbed a service station. He pulled a gun on attendant Robert Colvert, took his money, drove him to a remote spot outside Lincoln, and shot him in the head. Starkweather was seventeen at the time, Colvert twenty-one.

In late January 1958, Starkweather called on Fugate at the home she shared with her mother and stepfather, Marion Bartlett. Fugate was not yet home from school, so Starkweather passed the time quarreling with Fugate's mother, Velda Bartlett. Starkweath-

Caril Fugate and Charles Starkweather before the murders.

Mr. and Mrs. Bartlett, victims.

Carol King, victim.

Betty Jean Bartlett, victim.

Robert Jensen, victim.

August Meyer, victim.

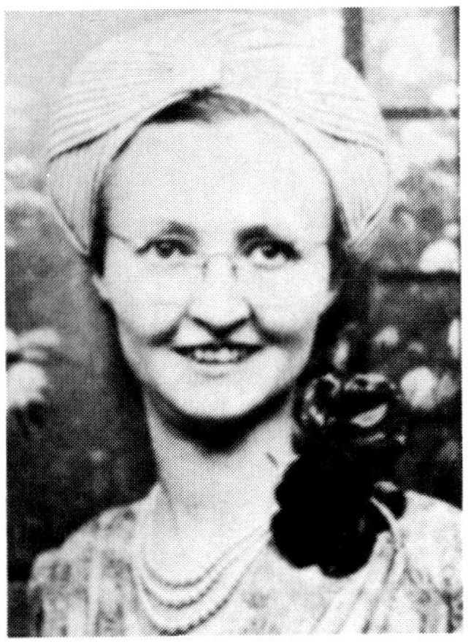

Lillian Fencl, victim.

Mrs. Ward, victim.

C. Lauer Ward

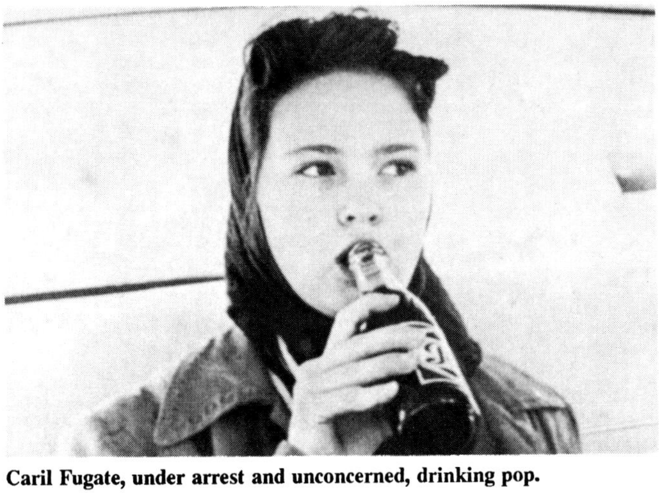

Caril Fugate, under arrest and unconcerned, drinking pop.

Charles Starkweather, condemned to death, unconcerned.

er had his prize possession, a hunting rifle, with him—he was rarely without it. One thing led to another, and soon Mr. and Mrs. Bartlett were dead. Starkweather later related what happened. "They said they were tired of me hanging around. I told Mrs. Bartlett off and she got so mad that she slapped me. When I hit her back, her husband started to come at me, so I had to let both of them have it with my rifle." In his mind, it was the victims' fault for arguing with him.

Starkweather knew Fugate did not like her parents, so he was not surprised that she did not interfere. She did not stop him when he murdered her sister, either, choking two-year-old Betty Jean Bartlett by shoving the gun barrel down her throat. He hid the baby's body in a cardboard box, put Marion Bartlett's body in a chicken coop behind the house and wrapped it in rags and newspapers, then disposed of Mrs. Bartlett in an abandoned outhouse, covering her with newspapers, too. The two then ate sandwiches and watched TV. To keep away unwanted visitors, Fugate insisted Starkweather put a note on the front door: "Stay Away. Every Body is Sick With the Flu."

The note failed to deter Fugate's older sister when she came to call. She knocked anyway, and Fugate warned her to stay away. The sister told her husband that Caril Ann had refused to let her in. Both of them thought her behavior strange, so they called the police. They, too, were refused entrance. The police went away unsatisfied and were called again two days later when Fugate turned away her grandmother. Assistant police chief Eugene Masters sent two officers with the grandmother to check on the Bartlett house. They ignored the warning sign and entered to find the house empty except for the bodies. Police surmised that the couple had made more sandwiches, packed them in Starkweather's car, and left. They swore out arrest warrants and the search began. A short time later, a gas station attendant in nearby Bennet, Neb., told police that the fugitives had been by to fix a flat, fill their tank, and buy shotgun and rifle ammunition.

Starkweather's next victim was farmer August Meyer. Police received a tip that Starkweather's car was parked outside Meyer's farmhouse. Sheriff Merle Karnopp and his men surrounded the house and called through a bullhorn for Starkweather's surrender. When no answer came, police entered the building to find Meyer dead, his head torn apart by a shotgun blast.

Farmer Evert Broening found two bodies in an storm cellar near Meyer's farm. Seventeen-year-old Robert Jensen and 16-year-old Carol King were shot in their heads. Jensen's car was missing, and King had been raped before being killed. The posse seeking Starkweather and Fugate swelled to 200 police officers.

The next victims died at the home of businessman C. Lauer Ward. A car was parked in Ward's driveway, and his own 1956 Packard was gone, although Ward had not come to work. There was no answer when officers knocked on the Ward's door. When they entered the house, police found Ward, forty-seven, dead in the foyer, shot in the head like the other victims. His wife, Clara, and their maid, Lillian Fenci, were bound and gagged in a bedroom. The women had been stabbed to death and mutilated. To aid in the manhunt the National Guard was called.

Starkweather and Fugate headed west, getting as far as Douglas, Wyo. As they neared Douglas, they noticed a car parked by the side of the road, where shoe salesman Merle Collison was napping. Starkweather woke him up with a gunshot, then fired nine bullets into him as he got out of the car on Starkweather's command. When Starkweather could not release the emergency brake, he flagged Joseph Sprinkle and ordered him to help him with the brake. Sprinkle saw Collison's body and realized that his only chance was to grab Starkweather's rifle as he maneuvered around the brake.

As the two struggled for the firearm, a police car arrived. Fugate ran toward Deputy Sheriff William Rohmer's car. "Help!" she yelled. "It's Starkweather! He's going to kill me! He's crazy! Arrest him!"

Sprinkle wrested the gun away from Starkweather, who took off in Collison's car at 115 miles per hour. In the ensuing chase, the rear window of Starkweather's getaway car was shot out. He suddenly stopped the car and staggered out, complaining of a superficial cut on his ear from broken glass.

"You're a real tough guy, aren't you?" one of the officers asked the murderer.

Fugate claimed at her trial that she had been an innocent hostage all along. Starkweather was willing to support this until her testimony labeled him a killer. He turned on her and painted a picture of a less-than-innocent hostage. "One time," Starkweather claimed, "she said that some hamburgers were lousy and we ought to go back and shoot all them people in the restaurant."

In Fugate's defense, the warning sign on the Bartlett household's front door was brought out. Her attorney claimed that she refused to let her sister or the police enter to avoid further bloodshed. The jury did not believe it.

Caril Ann Fugate was sentenced to life imprisonment but was paroled in 1981. Charles Starkweather was electrocuted in the Nebraska State Penitentiary at midnight, June 24, 1959. True to his character, he rejected the request that he donate his eyes for transplant after his death, saying, "Hell, no! No one ever did anything for me! Why the hell should I do anything for anyone else?"

REF: Allen, *Starkweather: The Story of a Mass Murderer; CBA;* Beaver, Ripley and Trese, *Caril;* Boucher, *The Quality of Murder;* Fox, *Mass Murder;* Nash, *Almanac of World Crime;* ____, *Bloodletters and Badmen;* ____, *Murder, America;* Reinhardt, *The Murderous Trial of Charles Starkweather;* (FILM), *Badlands,* 1974; *The Boys Next Door,* 1985.

The infamous Belle Starr.

Starr, Belle (Myra Belle Shirley), 1848-89, U.S., rob. Born in Carthage, Mo., the notorious Belle Starr moved with her family at the age of sixteen to Scyene, Texas, just outside of Dallas. In

1880, Starr became involved with bank robber Cole Younger, Jesse James' partner. The couple spent several months together in a small cabin on the Oklahoma Strip while Younger was hiding out from the law after robbing the Liberty bank in Missouri. After Younger rejoined the James gang, Starr gave birth to a daughter, Pearl, who was thought to be Younger's child. Starr's next romance was with another bank robber, Jim Reed. Along with Reed and two other criminals in 1869, Starr robbed a California prospector suspected of having hit a rich vein. The four tortured the prospector until he told them where his gold was hidden, and they got away with $30,000.

After Reed was shot in a gun fight in 1874, Starr and an Indian outlaw named Blue Duck organized a horse-and-cattle rustling ring. Starr then married a Cherokee Indian named Sam Starr and continued stealing livestock. Belle and Sam Starr were arrested in 1883 and sentenced to six months in jail. After their release, they immediately returned to rustling and were arrested again in 1886. Although they appeared before "hanging" Judge Isaac Parker at Fort Smith, they were released for lack of evidence.

Sam Starr was shot and killed in a barroom brawl in December 1886. Starr's last lover was a Creek Indian named Jim July. On Feb. 3, 1889, after riding part of the way to Fort Smith with July, Starr turned back to her home in Younger's Bend. A gunman apparently lying in wait shot her off her horse. She was found by a passing traveller who took her home to her daughter. When she died, Pearl had her tombstone engraved with the following inscription:

> "Shed not for her the bitter tear,
> Nor give the heart to vain regret,
> 'Tis but the casket that lies here,
> The gem that fills it sparkles yet."

REF.: Aikman, *Calamity Jane and the Lady Wildcats;* Appell, *Belle's Castle;* Bartholomew, *The Biographical Album of Gunfighters;* ____, *Some Western Gunfighters;* Beebe, *The American West;* Beverly, *Hobo of the Rangeland;* Booker, *Wildcats in Petticoats;* Botkin, *A Treasury of Western Folklore;* Breihan, *The Complete and Authentic Life of Jesse James;* ____, *Great Gunfighters of the West;* ____, *Younger Brothers;* Brown, *The Gentle Tamers, Women of the Old West; CBA;* Chrisman, *Fifty Years on the Owl Hoot Trail;* Crawford, *The West of the Texas Kid, 1881-1910;* Croy, *He Hanged Them High;* ____, *Last of the Great Outlaws;* Dale, *Adventures and Exploits of the Younger Brothers;* Dalton, *Under the Black Flag;* Douglas, *The Everglades;* Drago, *Great American Cattle Trails;* ____, *Notorious Ladies of the Frontier;* ____, *Outlaws on Horseback;* ____, *Red River Valley;* Eaton, *Pistol Pete;* Edge, *Run the Cat Roads;* Elman, *Fired in Anger;* Emery, *Court of the Damned;* Farber, *Those Texans;* Gard, *Frontier Justice;* Gardner, *The Old Wild West;* Glasscock, *Then Came Oil;* Godwin, *Murder, U.S.A.;* Gradet, *Images Du Far-West;* Hagan, *Indian Police and Judges;* Harman, *Belle Starr;* Harrington, *Hanging Judge;* Harris, *This Is Three Forks Country;* Harrison, *Hell Holes and Hangings;* Henderson, *100 Years in Montague County;* Hendricks, *The Bad Man of the West;* Hicks, *Belle Starr and Her Pearl;* Holloway, *Texas Gun Lore;* Horan, *Desperate Men;* ____, *Desperate Women;* ____, *The Great American West;* ____ and Sann, *Pictorial History of the Wild West;* House, *Cowtown Columnist;* Howe, *Timberleg of the Diamond Trail;* Hunt, *A Dictionary of Rogues;* Hunter and Rose, *The Album of Gun-Fighters;* Hutto, *The Dallas Story;* James, *My Experience With Indians;* Kane, *100 Years Ago With the Law and the Outlaw;* Kelley, *Jesse James;* Kingston, *Remarkable Rogues;* Koller, *The American Gun;* Lavender, *The American Hertiage History of the Great West;* Lemley, *The Old West, 1849-1929;* Lieberson, *The Columbia Records Legacy Collection;* Lindquist, *Jesse Sweeten;* Logue, *Tumble Weeds and Barb Wire Fences;* Lyon, *The Wild, Wild West;* McKennon, *Iron Men;* Mapes, *Old Fort Smith;* Masterson, *The Katy Railroad and the Last Frontier;* Miller, *Shady Ladies of the West;* Monaghan, *The Book of the American West;* Nash, *Bloodletters and Badmen;* ____, *Look For the Woman;* Neville, *The History of Lamar County;* ____, *The Red River Valley;* Newsom, *The Life and Practice of the Wild and Modern Indian;* Osborn, *Let Freedom Ring;* Parkhill, *The Wildest of the West;* Plenn, *Saddle in the Sky;* Preece, *The Dalton Gang;* Randolph, *Who Blowed Up the Church House?;* Rascoe, *Bell Starr;* Rayburn, *Ozark Country;* Rogers, *Gallant Ladies;* Rogers, *The Lusty Texans of Dallas;* Sabin, *Wild Men of the Wild West;* Santerre, *Dallas' First Hundred Years, 1856-1956;* Schmitt and Brown, *The Settler's West;* Schrantz, *Jasper County;* Scott, *Belle Starr in Velvet;* Shackleford, *Belle Starr;* Shirley, *Buckskin and Spurs;* ____, *Henry Starr;* ____, *Law West of Fort Smith;* ____, *Outlaw Queen;* Shoemaker, *Missouri Day By Day;* Sonnichsen, *Cowboys and Cattle Kings;* Webb, *The Handbook of Texas;* Wellman, *A Dynasty of Western Outlaws;* White, *Lead and Likker;* Williams and Pepper, *The Mysterious West;* Wilson, *Encyclopedia of Murder;* (FILM), *Belle Starr,* 1941; *Belle Starr's Daughter,* 1947; *Montana Belle,* 1952; *Son of Belle Starr,* 1953; *The Outlaws Is Coming,* 1965; *The Long Riders,* 1980.

Starr, Henry (AKA: **The Bearcat**), 1873-1921, U.S., rob. As a teenager on the Oklahoma Strip, Henry Starr, alleged nephew of notorious robber and livestock rustler Belle Starr, received initiation as a livestock rustler. In the late 1890s, Starr, who was part Cherokee Indian, organized a gang that specialized in robbing small banks throughout Oklahoma, Texas, and Arkansas.

Bank robber Henry Starr.

Starr shot and killed Floyd Wilson, a deputy of Judge Isaac Parker, in 1903. Although he was convicted and sentenced to death, he managed to appeal his case successfully and was released. Parker persisted, and Starr was retried for the same crime, convicted again, but was saved a second time by a pardon from President Teddy Roosevelt. Only a month later, Starr, Kid Wilson, and three other men robbed a bank in Bentonville, Ark., of $11,000. Starr and Wilson were captured in Colorado Springs, Colo., in July 1903. After serving a five-year term in prison, Starr was released and immediately returned to robbing banks. In 1914, Starr earned himself a "first" in the history of crime by using an automobile to escape from the scenes of his crimes. Starr's innovation stood him in good stead for the next six years until the police also began using cars. While escaping from a successful bank robbery in Harrison, Ark., in 1921, Starr's car broke down, and he was overtaken by a motor-driven posse. He was shot and killed in the ensuing gun battle.

REF.: American Guide Series, *Tulsa, A Guide to the Oil Capital;* Anderson, *A Quarter Inch of Rain;* Bartholomew, *The Biographical Album of Gunfighters;* ____, *Some Western Gunfighters;* Benedict, *Muskogee and Northeastern Oklahoma;* Breihan, *Great Gunfighters of the West;* Bristow, *Lost on Grand River;* Bristow, *Tales of Old Fort Gibson; CBA;* Chrisman, *Fifty Years on the Owl Hoot Trail;* Cooper, *High Country;* Crawford, *The West of the Texas Kid, 1881-1910;* Douglas, *The History of Tulsa, Oklahoma;* Drago, *Red River Valley;* ____, *Road Agents and Train Robbers;* Elman, *Fired in Anger;* Emery, *Court of the Damned;* Gibson, *Fabulous Empire;* Glasscock, *Then Came Oil;* Gordon, *I Arrested Pearl Starr;* Graves, *Oklahoma Outlaws;* Harman, *Cherokee Bill;* Hendricks, *The Bad Man of the West;* Horan, *The Great American West;* ____ and Sann, *Pictorial History of the Wild West;* Houts, *From Gun to Gavel;* Houts, *From Gun to Gavel;* Howe, *Timberleg of the Diamond Trail;* Hunter and Rose, *The Album of Gun-Fighters;* Lavigne, *Crimes, Criminals and Detectives;* McCarty, *The Enchanted West;* McKennon, *Iron Men;* Mapes, *Old Fort Smith;* Miller, *Bill Tilghman;* Nash, *Bloodletters and Badmen;* Neville, *The Red River Valley;* Newsom, *The Life and Practice of the Wild and Modern Indian;* Nix, *Oklahombres;* Osborn, *Let Freedom Ring;* Preece, *Lone Star Man;* Rascoe, *Belle Starr;* Rayburn, *The Eureka Springs Story;*

____, *Ozark Country;* Rea, *Boone County and Its People;* Russell, *Behind These Ozark Hills;* Scott, *Belle Starr in Velvet;* Shirley, *Buckskin and Spurs;* ____, *Heck Thomas;* ____, *Henry Starr;* ____, *Law West of Fort Smith;* Sutton, *Hands Up!;* Taylor, *Colorado, South of the Border;* Tilghman, *Marshal of the Last Frontier;* ____, *Outlaw Days;* Watson, *A Century of Gunmen;* Wellman, *A Dynasty of Western Outlaws.*

Starr, Pearl (AKA: Pearl Younger, Rosa P. Reed, Queen of the Row), 1867-1925, pros. In 1867 in Texas, the notorious Belle Starr gave birth to an illegitimate child fathered by outlaw Cole Younger, whom she named Pearl Younger. When 19-year-old Pearl and a young man asked her mother for permission to marry, Belle Starr refused and sent Pearl to Chickalah, Ark., where the woman learned she was pregnant. Pearl gave birth to a girl, Flossie, in April 1887 and later gave the child up for adoption. After Belle Starr was shot to death on Feb. 3, 1889, and her brother was sent to prison on a bootlegging charge, Pearl, calling herself Rosa Reed, became a prostitute, ostensibly to raise money to help her brother. She went to work in a Van Buren, Ark., brothel run by Madame Van where she became the most sought-after prostitute in the town. Saving enough money to open her own establishment across the Arkansas River, Pearl Starr rented a house in Fort Smith, Ark., in November 1891. Publicizing herself as Pearl Starr, daughter of Belle Starr, she was welcomed by other madames and built a prosperous business working as both madame and prostitute. Though Fort Smith had passed ordinances against prostitution, the madames were able to operate by paying a weekly tax, but when more ordinances prohibiting prostitution were approved, Pearl Starr defiantly affixed a gaudy red and white electric sign in the shape of a star on her house.

During her career in Fort Smith, she gave birth to three more children, Ruth Reed on June 29, 1894, Arthur E. Erbach in August 1898, and Jennette Andrews on Nov. 8, 1902. Pearl Starr's business came to an end in 1916 when she broke her agreement not to operate a house of prostitution out of another house she bought. She was arrested in February, and the charges were dropped only when she promised to leave the town. Pearl Starr died on July 6, 1925, in a hotel in Douglas, Ariz., where her daughters buried her as Rosa Reed to avoid publicity.

REF.: *CBA;* Drago, *Notorious Ladies of the Frontier.*

Starr, Raymond W., 1888-1968, U.S., jur. Served as attorney general of Michigan from 1936-38, and as justice of Michigan Supreme Court from 1941-46. He was appointed to the western district court of Michigan by President Harry Truman in 1946. REF.: *CBA.*

Starr, Tom, 1813-90, U.S., west. outl. An extremely violent character, even for the Wild West, Tom Starr, a full-blooded Cherokee Indian, fathered a vicious clan of eight sons and two daughters who, along with their children, nephews, and cousins, made up the notorious Starr clan gang.

Born in Tennessee, Starr was brought to the Oklahoma territory by his parents. By the time he was twenty, Starr was six feet seven inches tall and accomplished with a bowie knife. After killing David Buffington, a rival tribesman, Starr went unpunished. In 1843, with no apparent motivation, he burned an entire family to death. Leading groups of half-breeds, whites, and Indians on horse-rustling raids, Starr became hated and feared. His enemies attacked his homestead in 1845, killing his father and his brother, Buck Starr, twelve. Starr postponed his horse stealing long enough to get revenge and was alleged to have slain all thirty-two raiders, torturing them slowly before they died.

After the mass murders, Starr returned to thievery and rustling. Jim Reed was a member of the Starr gang. His young lover would come to be known as Belle Starr when she later married "Uncle" Tom's son, Sam. Before his retirement in the 1880s, Starr's territory, now part of Adair County, Okla., was known as the most dangerous in the region. Starr, who was alleged to have murdered more than 100 men, also traveled into Texas on his crime sprees. After his death in 1890, clan members apparently decided to rewrite history, telling journalists that Uncle Tom Starr was a charming man "full of fun and eager to josh folks." REF.: *CBA.*

Starrett, Vincent (Charles Vincent Emerson Starrett), b.1886, U.S., writer. Creator of detective novels. Books authored: *Estrays, Banners in the Dawn, The Great Hotel Murder,* and others. REF.: *CBA.*

Start, Charlie, See: **Hadley, Charles B.**

Starzynski, Stefan, 1893-c.1940, Pol., mayor, assass. Planned and executed protection of Warsaw from invading German army in 1939. He was captured by the Nazis and placed in a concentration camp the same year. He was shot to death shortly thereafter. REF.: *CBA.*

Stas, Jeane Servais, 1813-91, Fr., pathol. French-chemist Jeane Stas was born and educated in Louvain. With his quick mind and keen appreciation of science, he soon absorbed everything that the professors of chemistry and medicine could teach him. Stas set up an attic laboratory in his parents' home, in which he discovered phlorizin, a glucoside found in the bark of fruit tree roots. His work drew the attention of the famed Swedish chemist Jöns Jacob Berzelius, who foretold great things for Stas.

In 1835, Stas continued his chemistry studies in Paris. Five years later, he was appointed to fill a vacancy as a chemistry professor at Brussels. Stas became such a well-recognized expert in his field that he could refuse offers of higher pay and better equipped laboratories from the German chemist Justus Liebig. Instead, he set up his own laboratory in a tiny house on the Rue de Joncour in Saint-Gilles.

In November 1850, Stas made a startling breakthrough in the field of criminal investigation. He discovered a process by which traces of vegetable poisons could be detected in the remains of a murder victim. The French police had prevailed upon Stas to investigate the death of Gustave Fougnies, whom they believed was killed by sulfuric acid. Stas ruled this out because he smelled vinegar on the remains. The chemist learned that the body had been washed in vinegar, thereby covering up the effects of other poisons. The discovery that Fougnies had been poisoned with nicotine helped reveal the identity of the killer, Hippolyte de Bocarmé, who was convicted and guillotined for murder on July 19, 1851. Stas went on to become internationally famous. See: **Bocarmé,** Comte **Hippolyte de** REF.: *CBA.*

Stasia, prom. 1970s-80s, Ger., secret pol. The Stasia is a plainclothes secret police organization in East Germany which serves the Communist hierarchy, its agents functioning as internal spies. Agents are assigned jobs in all important places of business and industry, with the purpose of reporting any and all conversation and activities that could be considered counter-revolutionary. Members of the Stasia are undoubtedly the most hated members of the Communist dictatorship in East Germany, preying upon their neighbors and relatives in order to betray their political beliefs. These agents are invariably recruited from diehard German Communist families and receive special training in Moscow. REF.: *CBA.*

Staten Island Murder, See: **Bodine, Mary.**

Staunton, Louis, See: **Staunton Family.**

Staunton Family, prom. 1876, Brit., mur. In 1875 an auctioneer's clerk who had very little money, 23-year-old Louis Staunton, proposed marriage to a mentally retarded girl about thirty, Harriet Richardson. Her mother opposed the marriage and unsuccessfully tried to have her daughter committed to an asylum. After the wedding, Staunton refused to let his mother-in-law visit the couple in their Brixton home. The couple then moved to Norwood where the wife had a child, who was sent to be cared for by Staunton's brother, Patrick Staunton, and his wife, who lived

Louis Staunton with mistress Alice Rhodes.

in Cudham. Shortly afterward, Louis Staunton fell in love with his sister-in-law's sister, Alice Rhodes, so he paid his brother to take care of his wife at his home in Cudham while Louis Staunton and Alice Rhodes also moved into a house together in Cudham as husband and wife. Staunton induced Harriet to sign over control of her money. Afterward, she was kept prisoner at Patrick Staunton's house and slowly starved to death. Her baby died in April 1877 and on Apr. 12 the four captors took the incapacitated Harriet Staunton to Penge where they rented a room for her and called for a doctor. On Apr. 13, Harriet Staunton died about 1:30 p.m., and a doctor signed a death certificate which stated that the cause of death was cerebral disease and apoplexy.

However, when one of the Stauntons when to a post office to ask where to register a death certificate, the clerk, who was the dead woman's brother-in-law, grew suspicious and called the doctor and identified the body. The body was examined and other doctors agreed that Harriet Staunton had died from starvation and neglect. The three Stauntons and Alice Rhodes were arrested on murder charges and the trial was moved to the Old Bailey because local popular sentiment was against the Stauntons. At the Old Bailey, the two men and two women were convicted on Sept. 26, 1877, and condemned to death. However, the death penalty was commuted a month later and Rhodes pardoned. Patrick Staunton died in prison, his wife served several years of her term before she was freed, and Louis Staunton served twenty years in prison. One of the defense lawyers for the Stauntons, Sir Edward Clarke, also offered Staunton £2 per week for two years or £100 to start a business with a relative and Staunton chose the £100.

Harriett Staunton

REF.: Altick, *Victorian Studies in Scarlet;* Bowen-Rolands, *In the Light of the Law;* Brock, *A Casebook of Crime;* Browne and Tullett, *The Scalpel of Scotland Yard;* Burnaby, *Memories of Famous Trials; CBA;* Clarke, *The Story of My Life;* Deardon, *Some Cases of Sir Bernard Spilsbury and Others;* Hodge, *The Black Maria;* Humphreys, *Criminal Days;* Kingston, *A Gallery of Rogues;* Kobler, *Some Like It Gory;* Lustgarten, *The Murder and the Trial;* ____, *The Woman in the Case; Notable British Trials;* Thomson, *The Criminal;* Walker-Smith and Clarke, *The Life and Famous Cases of Sir Edward Clarke;* Williams, *Leaves of a Life;* Wilson, *Encyclopedia of Murder;* (FICTION), Jenkins, *Harriet.*

Stavisky, Serge Alexandre (AKA: Sacha), c.1886-1934, Fr., fraud. A colossal swindle perpetrated by Serge Stavisky brought scandal and ruin down on the heads of some of France's most esteemed government leaders in the years preceding the outbreak of WWII. "L'Affaire Stavisky" filled reams of official court transcript as prosecutors attempted to sift through conflicting evidence to learn how it was possible for a Russian-born swindler operating out of a government-supervised pawn shop to cause so much chaos in the marketplace. As the court pondered, hordes of angry citizens standing outside the Chamber of Deputies chanted, "Assassins! Thieves! Staviskys!" A new word had entered the French lexicon of popular slang. Who was this character who seemed to anticipate the techniques of the notorious American swindler Charles Ponzi?

Serge Stavisky was born in Kiev to Russian-Jewish parents. Nicknamed "Sacha," his first encounter with the law occurred in 1908 with his arrest for fraud. After a short stretch in prison he resumed his career on the streets. In 1912, Stavisky was arrested a second time, and the disgrace brought on his family contributed to his father's suicide. Shortly before WWI, Stavisky left his home to settle in Paris where he acquired residential status. Stavisky carved out a living trafficking in drugs and women, small-time stuff when weighed against the skill and dexterity he later showed in passing stolen bonds and securities. Serge spent the war years and the early 1920s running a casting bureau and a medical clinic where he promised women an accurate diagnosis of pregnancy. He called his bogus examining device a "matrascope." The clinic brought Stavisky into close personal contact with the wives of leading political figures of the Republic—invaluable contacts he was quick to exploit. Stavisky became a wealthy man overnight. For a time he spied for the Sûreté Générale, informing on the riff-raff of the French underworld. During the 1920s, Sacha was often seen in the company of some of France's most glamourous women. He later married Arlette Simon, a dress model for the house of Chanel after promising her he would "go straight."

Serge Stavisky

In 1926, the arch-swindler was imprisoned for bilking two clients out of seven million francs in a crooked stock deal. He was housed in the Santé Prison in Paris for eighteen months, awaiting a trial that never came. In 1927, Stavisky was given his freedom by shame-faced French authorities who were unable to sort out the tangled network he had so carefully built. One reason for Sacha's early release was his business dealings with men in public life who did not wish to be embarrassed by revelations of wrongdoing. The chief prosecutor of Paris, Georges Pressard, a brother-in-law of Premier Camille Chautemps, obstructed and postponed Stavisky's trial nineteen times. Joseph Garat, the mayor of Bayonne and a deputy of France, helped the con man set up the municipal pawnshop in his town which became a "clearing house" for a gigantic swindle that bilked the country out of millions of francs.

Stavisky paid out in excess of $3 million in bribes to French business leaders and politicians over a six-year period. Their names were entered into a ledger listing the monies paid as "stock dividends." Sacha then had himself named as the agent for the municipal bonds floated by several French cities, his collateral was a cache of stolen jewels. The bonds would then be discounted at a well-known bank and the money in turn would be invested in one of the swindler's companies.

Premier Chautemps, leader of the left-wing coalition, approved of the government's investment in pawnshop securities. (The pawnbrokers had been carefully regulated by the state dating to the time of King Louis XVI. A Crédit Municipal, or local council as it was known, could not be organized without the assent of the premier.) Using the fake jewelry as backing for the Bayonne pawnshop, Stavisky and Mayor Garat issued fraudulent bonds in the sum of 239 million francs. The swindle went unde-

Arletta Stavisky.

tected until Christmas Eve, 1933, when police—those not on Serge's payroll—arrested a party to the scheme who told all. Warrants were issued for the arrest of the members of the ring including two chamber deputies and editors Albert Dubarry of the right-wing *La Volanté* newspaper and Camille Aymard of *Liberté,* a leftist journal. DuBarry acted as intermediary between Stavisky and the corrupt politicians, passing on 1,000 franc notes as bribe money. (Stavisky cleverly cultivated the support of both of France's political factions to ensure the success of his scheme.)

The newspaper *L'Action Française* exposed Albert Dalimier, France's Minister of Colonies, as the party responsible for persuading the insurance companies to invest in the worthless municipal bonds issued out of Bayonne. Dalimier was forced to resign from the cabinet. The full-blown scandal came to a head on Jan. 8, 1934, when police found Stavisky lying dead in a mountain cottage at Chamonix. They listed his death as a suicide, but a pistol was found in his left hand when there were entry wounds above the right temple. The mystery deepened when Appellate Judge Albert Prince was murdered a day before his scheduled appearance before the Parliamentary Committee investigating the scandal. Prince was lured to the Dijon railroad station one night in February 1934, and tied to the railroad track by his assailant. Railway police found his mangled body several hours later. When questioned about the matter, two eyewitnesses swore that they had seen Stavisky's former secretary, Gilbert Romanigo, lurking about Prince's apartment several days before his murder.

The public outcry was immediate and far-reaching. Suspecting a sinister government cover-up, Royalist sympathizers took to the streets against the embattled leftists. The country teetered nervously near civil war as the most serious rioting since the 1871 Commune was reported in the neighborhoods of Paris. Unable to hold the government together, Premier Chautemps turned over the reins to Gaston Doumergue, brought out of retirement from his home in Southern France. To pacify the mobs the new premier forged a bipartisan cabinet and promised sweeping reforms. The remains of Stavisky were exhumed from his mountain grave and an official inquiry was launched. It was conceded that the shooting had been "somewhat forced," an ambiguous explanation that failed to placate hard-liners who believed his execution was carried out by the French Secret Police.

Twenty people, including Arlette Stavisky, were tried at the Palace of Justice in November 1935 for the swindle that looted French coffers of $18 million. "To be able to go away and forget all this by migrating with my children to America!" Arlette cried. "To bring up my children to love me and respect the memory of their father! That is all I ask!" The eleven-week trial ended with the conviction of just nine of the original defendants. Seven-year prison sentences were doled out to Gustave Tissier, Stavisky's right-hand man and manager of the Municipal Pawnshop in Bayonne, and to Henri Hayotte, erudite manager of the Empire Theatre of Paris where in former days the arrogant Stavisky was known to entertain lavishly. Editor Dubarry and the grieving widow were acquitted, but three other defendants received lesser sentences, including: General Joseph Bardi de Fourtou (two years), whose name appeared on the phony stock prospectus, and Deputy Gaston Bonnaure, who was sent to for one year.

REF.: *CBA;* Goodman, *Villainy Unlimited;* Heppenstall, *Bluebeard and Others;* MacDougall, *Hoaxes;* Nash, *Hustlers and Con Men;* Scott, *The Concise Encyclopedia of Crime and Criminals;* (FILM), *Stolen Holiday,* 1937; *Stavisky,* 1974.

Stavsky, Abraham, See: **Arlosoroff, Dr. Chaim.**

Stead, William Thomas, 1849-1912, Brit., asslt.-drugs-abduc. In 1885, Bramwell Booth, chief of staff of the Salvation Army, invited William Thomas Stead, editor of London's *Pall Mall Gazette,* to talk with several teenagers who had been forced into prostitution before they were rescued by the Salvation Army. At the time, the age of consent was thirteen and a child under thirteen had to testify that she understood what giving evidence under oath meant, so usually offenders were extremely difficult to prosecute. In June 1885, Stead talked with Rebecca Jarrett, a former prostitute, who agreed to help him obtain a young virgin, and he assigned reporter Sampson Mussabini to the story. With the consent of the mother of 13-year-old Eliza Armstrong, Jarrett purchased the girl for about £3, then Jarrett and midwife Irena Mourez rented a room and Stead entered briefly. Afterward the girl was taken to a doctor, who certified that she was still a virgin. Following this experiment, Stead continued to investigate child prostitution, horrified by his discoveries.

On July 6, 1885, the first of a series of articles appeared, "The Maiden Tribute of Modern Babylon...A child of thirteen bought for £5," which described the atrocities of child prostitution and called for reform, including the passage of the Criminal Law Amendment Bill. The articles, which were reprinted in New York City and Chicago, caused an immense public outcry and were lauded by reformers and clergymen. At the end of the week, on June 10, the bill was hastily passed. The age of consent became sixteen, and the law requiring children to understand the meaning of giving testimony under oath was abolished. Obtaining girls and women under age twenty-one for prostitution or persuading them to leave home to live in brothels became crimes. Additionally, parents were forbidden to sell their children into prostitution and the bill outlawed using threats or drugs to coerce a girl into prostitution.

William Stead

Ironically, Stead and his associates were charged with kidnapping, administering drugs, and assault in connection with the mock procurement of Eliza Armstrong. Stead, Mussabini, Jarrett, and Mourez were convicted on abduction, drug, and assault charges, while Booth was acquitted of abduction and not tried on the other charges. Stead was sentenced to three months in prison, Mourez received a six-month sentence with hard labor, Jarrett was given a six-month sentence, and Mussabini was sent to prison for one month. Stead served only about two months of the sentence and later died in the 1912 *Titanic* tragedy.

REF.: Asbury, *Gem of the Prairie; CBA;* McPhaul, *Johnny Torrio;* Morgan, *Prince of Crime;* Reppetto, *The Blue Parade;* Schults, *Crusader in Babylon: W.T. Stead and the Pall Mall Gazette;* Scott, *The Life and Death of a Newspaper;* ____, *The Story of the Pall Mall Gazette;* Smith, *Syndicate City;* Stead, *My Father: Personal and Spiritual Reminiscences;* White, *The Life of W.T. Stead.*

Steamboat Squad, prom. 1870s-80s, U.S., law enfor. agen. River pirates terrorized the Hudson and East rivers off Manhattan until the mid-1870s, looting cargo crafts at piers, robbing riverfront businesses and homes, and boarding boats on the river to rob passengers.

The New York City police organized the Steamboat Squad in 1876, starting out with one craft, the *Seneca,* and soon adding several others to patrol the rivers. Police hidden in the cabin would row out after gangs of pirates, or police boats would be boarded by unsuspecting gangsters who would be suddenly surrounded by two dozen officers holding clubs. Steam launches were eventually added to the fleet. These teams of harbor police developed into the New York Marine and Aviation Division, recognized as one of the most effective branches of the city's law enforcement department. During the early years of the Steamboat Squad, New York officers often traveled to other cities to teach their techniques. Within a few years, the piracy that had crippled the waterfront since colonial days was ended. REF.: *CBA.*

Stedul, Nikola, 1937- , Scot., polit., attempt. assass. On Oct. 19, 1988, a postal agent noticed an unfamiliar black car parked in a neighborhood in Kirkcaldy, a coastal town of Scotland. The postal worker wrote down the car's license number, thinking the car might belong to a prowling burglar. The next day, Oct. 20, 51-year-old Nikola Stedul, president of the Croatian Movement for Statehood, left his home in Kirkcaldy to walk his dog and was shot three times in the face, neck, and thigh by 49-year-old Vinko Sindicic. Though the injuries were nearly fatal, Stedul survived and the would-be killer was arrested.

Sindicic, of Rijeka, Yug., was recognized by a former Yugoslavian secret service agent who had defected to the West in 1984, and the agent identified him as a member of the military department of the secret police in Yugoslavia, responsible for carrying out missions in foreign countries. Sindicic allegedly had assassinated other Croatian exiles. During his trial, the defendant accused Stedul of blackmailing him to force him to assassinate King Alexander. Sindicic was convicted of attempted murder, possession of guns, and using a false passport. He was sentenced to fifteen years in prison. REF.: *CBA.*

Steele, Ann, c.1902-56, Scot., (unsolv.) mur. In January 1956, in Glasgow, Scot., Ann Steele, fifty-three, was found murdered in her apartment in Aberfoyle Street, Dennistown. Her killer left his fingerprints behind but never was found. Steele had received severe head injuries. The night she was mortally wounded a youth with a bloody face, wearing the jacket of a Teddy Boy, a popular gang in England during the 1950s, was seen running through Glasgow's East End streets.

REF.: *CBA;* Furneaux, *Famous Criminal Cases,* vol. 4.

Steele, Louisa Maud, d.1931, Brit., (unsolv.) mur. A servant in the home of Kathleen Andrews, Louisa Maud Steele went out to run brief errands on the evening of Jan. 23, 1931. When she had not returned from the library and pharmacy by 11 p.m., Andrews called the Lewisham police. Steele was found the next morning, lying dead in Blackheath Woods. She had been strangled and apparently the killer had violently kicked her several times. Bite marks on her neck led to the rumor that a vampire was loose. The police were unable to solve the murder.

REF.: Adam, *Murder Most Mysterious; CBA;* Nash, *Open Files;* Shew, *A Companion to Murder.*

Steelman, William, See: **Gretzler, Douglas.**

Stefani, Jean-Paul (AKA: **Capitaine des Corses**), d.c.1938, Case of, Fr., mur. In the 1930s, two Corsicans, Jean-Paul Stefani and Ange Foata, were brought from their native island and employed by François Spirito and Paul Carbone, leaders of organized crime in Marseilles. Stefani and Foata worked as enforcers for the Spirito-Carbone drug trafficking business and later were put in charge of the Marseilles operations while the two kingpins went to Paris. Then Stefani and Foata began a feud that became known as "The Vendetta," claiming at least fifty lives. Stefani had started to neglect the drug trade and began establishing pimping operations, and Foata, left in charge, cheated Stefani. When Stefani discovered Foata had betrayed him, Stefani banned Foata from the gang. Angry, Foata threatened to kill Stefani. On Dec. 22, 1934, Foata was drinking in a bar with his mistress and 7-year-old son, François, when Stefani burst in and began shooting, killing Foata's son. Two hours later, Stefani's brother, Etienne Stefani, was shot dead.

In 1936, Stefani was tried for the murder of Foata's son but was acquitted on insufficient evidence. After Stefani was freed he visited the grave of his wife, who had died while he was waiting for trial. There, Foata opened fire on his rival, missing Stefani but injuring Stefani's bodyguard, Dominique Paoleschi. Foata was tried, convicted, and sentenced to seven years in prison for assaulting the bodyguard. Stefani next chose a girl, Zizi, as his mistress, but the girl's pimp, André Maguin, retaliated by fatally shooting Stefani. Alarmed at the killings, the two gang leaders, Spirito and Carbone, returned to Marseilles, briefly putting a stop to the slayings. However, the Vendetta continued when Maguin was fatally shot on July 9, 1938, at Cannes. See: **Spirito, François.**

REF.: *CBA;* Goodman, *Villainy Unlimited.*

Steger, William Merritt, 1920- , U.S., jur. U.S. Attorney in Tyler, Texas from 1953-59. He was appointed to the eastern district court of Texas by President Richard Nixon in 1970. REF.: *CBA.*

Steiger, Schultheiss Niklaus Friedrich von, 1729-99, Switz., consp. Served as chief magistrate of Bern from 1787-98 and enjoyed political dominance during waning years of Swiss Confederation. After the Bernese were defeated by the French, he escaped to Bavaria in 1798. He tried but failed in numerous bids to remove the French-supported Helvetian Republic. REF.: *CBA.*

Stein, David, 1935- , Fr.-U.S., theft-fraud. A Frenchman, David Stein, served in the military in Algeria where he tried painting frescoes. When he returned to France, he painted a copy of Cocteau's work, selling it as an authentic Cocteau for $100. Using primarily watercolors, crayons, or gouache, and aging paper with cold tea, Stein created at least 400 pieces, mimicking Picasso, Modigliani, Klee, Chagall, Van Gogh, Manet, Dufy, Cézanne, Matisse, Van Dongen, Laurencin, and Renoir. Moving to New York, Stein peddled forty imitation Cocteaus within four hours, charging $100 for each painting, and sold one fake Chagall, "Quelle Vie, Quel Plaisir," ("What a life, What Fun") for $4,000. After establishing the Gallery Trianon in 1965, Stein continued his profitable trade selling real and copied works, earning about $1 million by January 1967.

Stein's downfall came in 1966 when he sold three fake Chagalls for $10,000, giving forged certificates of authenticity to art dealer Irving Ysmet. When the dealer met with artist Marc Chagall a few hours later, Chagall detected the fake works and Stein barely escaped arrest, fleeing down his back stairs with a drink in his hand. He next moved to San Francisco where he sold three more phony Cocteaus, but art dealer Ysmet happened to be in San Francisco and alerted police. On Jan. 20, 1967, Stein was arrested, transferred to New York, and confined for eight months in prison because he was unable to raise $50,000 bail. In January 1969, the forger was tried on ninety-seven counts of fraud and grand larceny and given a three-year sentence in Sing Sing. During his term, Stein helped the New York Police Department establish an art forgery division. Freed in February 1970, Stein went back to France where he faced more charges and was sentenced to two-and-a-half years imprisonment. He was held in confinement until March 1972 and, upon release, the imposter began lecturing on forged works.

REF.: *CBA;* Rose, *The World's Greatest Rip-offs.*

Stein, Edith (AKA: **Teresa Benedicta of the Cross**), 1891-1942, Ger., mur. (vict.) Religious philosopher converted and baptized into Roman Catholicism from Judaism in 1922, becoming a Carmelite in 1934. Because of her Jewish background, she was seized by the Nazis and killed in the Auschwitz gas chamber. REF.: *CBA.*

Stein, Harry, and **Wissner, Nathan**, and **Cooper, Calmen**, d.1955, U.S., mur. A messenger was killed on Apr. 3, 1950, in the offices of *Reader's Digest* near Pleasantville, N.Y. Two months later, three ex-convicts, Harry Stein, Calmen Cooper, and Nathan Wissner, were arrested for the murder, convicted, and sentenced to die in February 1951, but through nine stays of execution, they stayed alive more than four years. However, in July 1955, their luck ran out. After three Supreme Court justices and the governor of New York rejected their last-minute pleas, the three convicts went to the electric chair in Sing Sing Prison. REF.: *CBA.*

Steinbach, Emil, 1846-1907, Aust., jur. Joined ministry of justice in 1874 and became head of department in 1887. He was appointed president of the supreme court of justice in 1904. REF.: *CBA.*

Steinberg, Joel B., 1941- , U.S., mansl. For more than a decade Joel B. Steinberg, a disbarred lawyer, battered his live-in girlfriend of twelve years and finally beat his illegally adopted daughter to death. In 1976, Hedda Nussbaum, an editor of children's books, met Steinberg and began living with him the same year. Beginning in 1977, Steinberg continually struck and browbeat his lover, and the woman suffered from broken ribs, nose fractures, and chipped teeth. According to Nussbaum, her companion used drugs, humiliation, brainwashing methods, and only allowed her to eat with his permission to coerce her into believing that she was "a worthless person who could be saved only through his wisdom and special powers." If she ate without his consent, she alleged, he made her take an ice-water bath. Countless times neighbors called police to investigate screams coming from the Manhattan, N.Y., apartment, but nothing was found. In 1979, Nussbaum began using drugs, including cocaine and heroin, and Steinberg convinced his lover that many of their friends were cult members attempting to hypnotize him and that she had been involved in sex with numerous people.

The couple illegally adopted two children, Elizabeth (Lisa) in 1981, and Mitchell in 1986. By 1987, Lisa wore dirty clothes, her hair was tangled, and she had no toys. She also had no bed and slept on the couch. Several weeks before her death in November 1987, Steinberg reputedly seized Lisa, shook her, and threw her to the floor. On Oct. 23, 1987, according to one of Steinberg's clients, Mr. Scannapieco, he was driving with Steinberg and Lisa when the father hit the sleeping child on the side of the face for "...staring, just staring," telling his client that Lisa could put herself into a trance. Steinberg then ordered Lisa to smile and blink to stay awake and she obeyed. Steinberg also complained to Nussbaum several weeks before Lisa's death that the child continually stared at him. Said Nussbaum, "He thought the staring was dramatic and important."

On Nov. 1, 1987, Lisa's father struck her three times with his fist at about 6:30 p.m. and left her lying on the bathroom floor. Later, he carried the first-grader out of the bathroom and placed her in Nussbaum's arms, claiming the unconscious child had been "staring at him," and telling Nussbaum to "Relax—go with her. Stay in harmony with her." Steinberg then left to go out to dinner with a friend and Nussbaum considered calling for help but she later explained, "Joel said he would take care of her, he'd get her up when he got back. I didn't want to show disloyalty or distrust for him, so I didn't call. I expected him to get Lisa up because I thought he was a healer." Later that evening, when Steinberg returned, the couple smoked cocaine and Steinberg admitted to Nussbaum that he had hit the child. At 6:35 a.m. the next morning Nussbaum called for emergency help. When officials arrived, they found the unconscious Lisa and 16-month-old Mitchell tied to his playpen and covered with excrement. Police also found burglary tools, drugs, handcuffs, chains, and a gun amid urine and rotting food in the Manhattan apartment. Lisa was taken to the hospital where she was declared brain-dead and died three days later on Nov. 5., one of approximately 1,200 children who died from neglect or abuse in the U.S. in 1987. An autopsy revealed that she had died from a brain hemorrhage as a result of a blow to the head.

Originally both Nussbaum and Steinberg were arrested and charged with murder in November 1987, and the same month their son, Mitchell, was returned to his mother. On Oct. 26, 1988, charges against 46-year-old Nussbaum were dismissed and she became the primary witness against 47-year-old Steinberg. Tapes of Nussbaum, taken about the time of arrest, showed missing hair, open wounds, bruises, and an ulcerated left leg. She also had a broken nose, fractured ribs, a cut lip, and a black eye when she was arrested. In November 1988, Nussbaum filed a $3 million civil suit against her former lover for the violence he had inflicted on her. Steinberg's trial began in late 1988 and, during the proceedings, he contended that the child had vomited, choked, and, after becoming unconscious, she had hit her head and her bruises had been caused by his trying to rescue the child. Steinberg was convicted on Jan. 30, 1989, of first-degree manslaughter and sentenced in March 1989 to eight-and-one-third to twenty-five years' imprisonment.

The case prompted new child abuse laws in New York, the "Lisa Steinberg laws," because though Lisa's injuries had been noticed by teachers and friends of the family, no one had alerted authorities. The laws stipulated that those who notice child abuse but do not report it are subject to criminal prosecution. REF.: *CBA.*

Steinberg, Louis, c.1923- , and **Freedman, Leonard**, and **Santowski, Donald**, and **Baum, Frank**, prom. 1971, U.S., fraud. In 1953, Louis Steinberg and Frank Baum opened an account at the Cosmopolitan National Bank in Chicago for their discount chain, Steinberg-Baum. Allegedly ninety-four checks were written when the firm had no money to cover the checks. Donald Santowski, former vice president and bookkeeper of the Cosmopolitan Bank, admitted he held the Steinberg-Baum company's checks several times, and seventy-seven checks had been covered. However, funds were never deposited to cover the other seventeen, which totaled $6.8 million. In February 1971, bank officials discovered that the $6.8 million in overdrafts had never been recorded.

In April 1971, four men were indicted on charges of mail fraud and conspiracy for their involvement in the scheme, which was, at the time, called the biggest bank fraud in U.S. history. Those indicted included President Baum, Vice President Steinberg, the firm's general manager Leonard Freedman, and Santowski. Baum, Freedman, and Santowski stood trial and were convicted and sentenced. Steinberg, however, fled to Rhodesia, which did not have an extradition treaty with the U.S., and set up a successful auction business in Salisbury. In 1978, he turned himself in to U.S. marshals in Johannesburg, S. Afri. In June 1978, Steinberg's wife and 3-year-old child returned to the U.S. from Rhodesia, settling in Boston. On July 16, 1978, Steinberg arrived in Chicago, and at his trial he explained, "I love this country...and I had to come back because I am getting on (in age)...my plan now is to get settled and start again." On Feb. 7, 1979, Steinberg was convicted on twenty-two counts of bank and mail fraud and on Feb. 23 was sentenced to a ten-year prison term and fined $20,000. REF.: *CBA.*

Steiner, Renate, See: **Reiss, Ignace**.

Steinhagen, Ruth, 1930- , U.S., attempt. mur. Teen-ager Ruth Steinhagen saw Chicago Cubs first basemen Eddie Waitkus play baseball for the first time in 1946 in Wrigley Field in Chicago. She had a crush on the ballplayer for the next several years. During that time, she took a job as a typist at an insurance company and her hero was traded from the Cubs to the Philadelphia Phillies. Steinhagen continued to worship him, writing in her diary, "Phils are losing. I bet it's none of Eddie's fault...I'll be glad when you're dead, you rascal you." Her parents sent her to a psychiatrist for one visit and then the girl moved out of the family house in January 1949. In June 1949, she bought a 22.-caliber rifle at a pawn shop, withdrew $85, her entire savings, from the bank, and reserved a room at the Edgewater Beach Hotel in Chicago for three days, the same hotel where the Phillies players were staying. Then the 19-year-old checked in, ordered two whiskey sours and a daiquiri, and wrote a note to Waitkus, "It's extremely important that I see you...We're not acquainted...my name is Ruth Anne Burns and I'm in Room 1297-A...Please, come soon. I won't take up much of your time, I promise." Then she gave a bellhop $5 to deliver the note to her idol and he called her back about 11:20 p.m., saying he had just returned to the hotel and that he would come down. When he arrived, Steinhagen tried to stab him with a paring knife, but the ballplayer walked past her and sat in a chair. She went to a closet and got the rifle, saying, "I have a surprise for you. For two years you've been bothering me and now you're going to die." Then she shot him in the chest and picked up the telephone, calling the operator to say she had just shot a man. Waitkus later recovered. On June 30, 1949, Steinhagen was found insane and committed to the Kankakee State Hospital. At the end of the proceedings, Steinhagen commented, "I felt rather weak after seeing Waitkus this morning." REF.: *CBA.*

Steinheil, Jeanne-Marguerite (Jeanne-Marguerite Japy), 1869-

1954, Case of, Fr., mur. It was at the time a murder fraught with passion, intrigue, and mystery. The accused killer was Jeanne-Marguerite Steinheil, former mistress of French president Félix Fauré, who suffered a heart attack on Feb. 16, 1899, while making love. Fauré fell to the floor clutching a lock of her hair. Steinheil, naked and screaming hysterically, had to be taken away from the dying man by the servants. She ran through the garden, leaving behind her corset which an obliging civil servant retrieved as a souvenir. But it was not the death of the aging French president that brought Steinheil, described by one bemused reporter as the "Sarah Bernhardt of the Assize," before the courts. Rather, it was the dual murders of a cuckolded husband and a disapproving mother that led the police to her door.

Steinheil lived on the Impasse Ronsin in Paris, one of four pampered children born to a prosperous businessman in Beaucourt. She was courted by dozens of suitors before settling on Adolphe Steinheil, an unpleasant-looking portrait painter, as her husband. As an artist Steinheil was second-rate but his ambitious wife hoped that one day he might become a great master. To this end she took on a series of lovers, requiring each to purchase a painting from her struggling husband. President Fauré commissioned the artist to prepare a portrait, one that was bought and paid for at state expense. Steinheil was knighted for his efforts and named to the Legion of Honor. Jeanne-Marguerite had fulfilled her husband's greatest dream.

On the morning of June 1, 1908, her exciting, glamorous life fell apart. At 6 a.m. a servant named Couillard was alarmed by a scream coming from Madame Steinheil's upstairs bedroom. He ran into the room and found his mistress tied to her bed. Nearby the body of her husband lay in the open doorway, a cord wrapped around his neck. The assailant, whoever he was, had strangled not only the artist but Jeanne-Marguerite's mother, Madame Japy, as well. Octave Hamard, chief of the Sûreté, arrived with the examining magistrate Auguste Leydet, who was another in a long line of lovers who had been welcomed to Jeanne-Marguerite's bed.

Steinheil claimed that three men and a red-headed woman had invaded her bedroom shortly after midnight, demanding money and jewels. She refused to tell the location of the valuables whereby one of the assailants beat her across the face and head. An inventory of the missing items was taken. Steinheil determined that 6,000 francs and several valuable items of jewelry were missing. Coincidentally, the artist was in debt for the same amount at the time of his death.

At first the police accepted her story. A theatrical agent reported that three costumes that closely matched the descriptions given by Madame Steinheil were stolen from his agency. A man and a woman were picked up by the police, but they had a concrete alibi. Nevertheless Steinheil positively identified them as her assailants. Next she accused Couillard of masterminding the murders. By this time her credibility had worn thin. It was completely shattered when the police learned that Steinheil had sent her maid, Mariette Wolff, to a small villa in Bellevue to retrieve a jewel box containing a number of the items claimed to have been taken from her room the night of the murder. The missing jewels were then taken to a specialty shop for alteration. The jeweler, in turn, notified the police. Steinheil was arrested and charged with obstructing justice and lying to the police. She was incarcerated in the Saint Lazare Prison while a murder indictment was drawn up.

The remains of the victims were exhumed but no traces of poison could be found. It was later determined that a swab of cotton wool found at the bedside had not been touched by human hands; this was the same wool that Steinheil said was used to gag her during the assault. The trial was an emotional ordeal for all concerned. Steinheil frequently became hysterical, which greatly taxed the patience of the court. The high point of the trial was reached when a young man named Jean Lefèvre appeared to confess to his role in the murder. Lefèvre said he had disguised himself as the red-headed woman, but his statements were discounted by the president of the court who saw through the ruse. Lefèvre was hopelessly in love with Madame Steinheil and wanted to help her any way he could. The young man was led away to be charged with vagrancy.

To the charge that she had repeatedly lied to the police and the courts, Steinheil said she had only done so to save herself. The lies were, after all, proof-positive that she was innocent, she said. The jury, seeing no other recourse in the matter, acquitted her of murder charges. Steinheil left France for good. She moved to England, married into the British aristocracy, and died as Lady Abinger in Brighton in 1954. See: **Faure, Felix François.**

REF.: Brophy, *The Meaning of Murder; CBA.*

Steinman, Jacob, prom. 1906, Case of, U.S., mur. On Apr. 19, 1906, during the San Francisco earthquake and fire disaster, a National Guardsman, Jacob Steinman, was patrolling to help keep order. At about 9 p.m., Steinman and another man, Mr. Bush, saw Joseph Meyers, superintendent of the city's children's playgrounds. Bush and Meyers began arguing and the superintendent said to Steinman, standing several feet away, "You know me." Steinman responded, "No, I don't know you and don't want to." Bush and Meyers began fighting and Steinman pulled out his revolver, fatally shooting Meyers. On May 2 Steinman was arrested and during his trial, a witness swore that Meyers had acted as if he were going for a gun. On Sept. 13, Steinman was acquitted.

REF.: *CBA;* Duke, *Celebrated Criminal Cases of America.*

Steinman, Moe, c.1917- , U.S., tax evas. A middleman who wielded considerable clout in the U.S. meat industry, Moe Steinman, was investigated by federal officials on suspicion of bribery and tax evasion.

Steinman, whose official title was vice president of labor relations for the Daitch-Shopwell supermarket chain, reputedly hobnobbed with mobster John Dioguardi, negotiated labor disputes, and made investments with labor union leaders. He also was a broker for the meat industry, buying meat from packing houses, from which he received an exorbitant commission. Using part of the proceeds from the commissions, Steinman paid off supermarket administrators and their relatives to buy the meat through him. The bribes allegedly totalled about $100,000 a year to each manager. Other parts of the commission reportedly went to pay off the butchers' union, the Amalgamated Meat Cutters and Retail Clerks union, and to foster labor relations or "labor peace."

Steinman, along with supermarket executives and union officials, was indicted for the kickback scheme and after cooperating with the government Steinman, fifty-eight years old, was sentenced in early May 1975 to two concurrent one-year prison terms on tax-evasion charges and fined $5,000. Two supermarket executives involved in the kickback scheme, George George and Jules Tantleff, were convicted. George was convicted on perjury charges and fined $500 and Tantleff was convicted of criminal contempt and received a sentence of four months in prison.

REF.: *CBA;* Moffitt, *Swindled.*

Stelescu, Michael, d.1936, Rom., assass. Among the many fascist groups to emerge in Romania during the 1930s were the Brothers of the Cross, founded by a young right-wing idealogue, Michael Stelescu. His order joined forces with Cornelius Codreanu's fanatical anti-Semitic Iron Guard, which used terror methods similar to those employed by the Brown Shirts in Germany, and Benito Mussolini's Italian Black Shirts. Codreanu's forces gained an immense following in the 1930s, as they ruthlessly moved against the moderate regime of Prime Minister Jon Duca, who recognized the threat posed by the Iron Guard. In December 1933 Duca banned the wearing of the traditional green shirts favored by Codreanu's followers and the Iron Guard was considered an outlaw organization. Their response was immediate and deadly. On Dec. 30, 1933, as Duca stood on a train platform in Carpathia, he was assassinated by five members of the Iron Guard.

He was not the only political figure to fall victim to Codreanu's brand of terror. Michael Stelescu shared many of Codreanu's objectives, but they differed on one fundamental issue. Stelescu was anti-German and could not sanction an alliance with the Nazis. By 1936, Stelescu realized his position was unpopular with Iron Guard leaders. Fearing assassination, he ordered the publisher of his Brothers of the Cross newspaper to publish the names of the eight men he believed to be hand-picked for the task.

On July 16, 1936, Stelescu recuperated in the hospital after an appendectomy. The Iron Guard hit team visited him in his room, pumping thirty-eight shots into him. See: **Codreanu, Cornelius Zelea; Duca, Jon.** REF.: *CBA.*

Stemp, Jeanie Tremayne and Peggy, See: **Collins, James Thomas.**

Sten Sture (AKA: **The Elder**), c.1440-1503, Swed., jur. Named regent after death of Charles VIII in 1470, holding post from 1470-97 and from 1501-03. He worked to fortify Swedish legal institutions during his tenure. REF.: *CBA.*

Stephen, Saint, d.c.36 A.D., Roman., her. First Christian martyr, stoned to death after being charged with blaspheming Jewish law. REF.: *CBA.*

Stephen, c.1097-1154, Brit., kid. (vict.) Nephew of Henry I who reneged on promise to recognize Henry's daughter Matilda and her son Henry of Anjou as heirs to throne. He was crowned king in Westminster in 1135 but was kidnapped by supporters of Matilda in 1141. Regaining the throne only six months later, he was forced to finally proclaim Henry of Anjou as the heir to the throne after the death of his own son Eustace. REF.: *CBA.*

Stephen VI (VII), d.897, Italy, pope, assass. Coaxed by Emperor Lambert to convene Cadaver Synod, or Synodus Horrenda, in which the late Pope Formosus' corpse was dug up, charged, convicted of several crimes, and thrown into the Tiber River to discredit his reign. Later, he was ousted by a rebellion, jailed, and strangled in prison. REF.: *CBA.*

Stephen, Sir **James Fitzjames**, 1829-94, Brit., jur. James Fitzjames Stephen passed his bar examinations in 1854, and because his practice was small, supplemented his income by writing articles. In 1863, he wrote *General Review of the Criminal Law,* which was well-received, and in 1868 he became a judge. In 1869 he traveled to India, where he practiced law and was involved in codifying and creating new laws, until he went back to England in 1872.

In 1877, he wrote *Digest of Criminal Law,* an authoritative work, and in 1876 authored *Digest of the Laws of Evidence,* also a definitive work. In early 1879, Stephen was appointed to the Bench of the High Court, where he became known for sentencing convicted defendants to long prison terms, once saying, "It is morally right to hate the criminal."

Stephen presided over the murder trial of Florence Maybrick and during his final summary made so many mistakes that the public questioned her guilt. Stephen fumbled again, sentencing a man convicted of a petty assault to seven years in prison, a sentence that exceeded the maximum allowed by law. He later became sick and retired from his judicial duties when he was sixty-two years old. See: **Maybrick, Florence Elizabeth.**

REF.: *CBA;* Hibbert, *The Roots of Evil;* Scott, *The Concise Encyclopedia of Crime and Criminals.*

Stephen, William Thomas Scott, See: **Barney, Elvira Dolores.**

Stephens, Carol, c.1952-59, Brit., (unsolv.) mur. Carol Stephens, six years old, disappeared from her home in Cardiff, Wales, on Apr. 7, 1959. No one witnessed her abduction, though one person told the police of seeing her getting out of a car about a week earlier. Three weeks after Carol disappeared, her body was found by a surveyor in a deep ravine sixty miles from her home in the Carmarthenshire village of Horeb. She had been suffocated. After many months and few leads, police were unable to solve her murder.

REF.: *CBA;* Furneaux, *Famous Criminal Cases, vol. 6.*

Stephens, John S. (AKA: **John Cyphus**), d.1859, U.S., mur. In about 1859, John S. Stephens began to pursue a woman who was the girlfriend of another man, King. The two men fought, Stephens killing King. Stephens was tried, convicted, and sentenced to death in a Baltimore, Md., court. He was hanged on Apr. 8, 1859. REF.: *CBA.*

Stephenson, David Curtis, b.1891, U.S., kid.-mur. A member of the Ku Klux Klan, David C. Stephenson, became the Grand Dragon of the Realm of Indiana, often taking a percentage of enrollment fees from new members.

In 1923, Stephenson broke from the Klan and went into politics. In January 1924, he was tried, convicted, and thrown out of the Klan for committing indecencies in several states. In January 1925, he met Madge Oberholtzer, of Irvington, an employee of the Indiana State Department of Public Instruction. They had dinner several times and on Mar. 15, 1924, Stephenson phoned and asked her to come to his house. Drunk, he told the woman, "I love you more than any woman I have ever known," and forced her to drink a liquid that made her sleepy.

Ku Klux Klansman David Stephenson.

Armed, Stephenson and two other men, Earl Klinck and Earl Gentry, took her to a train station. Aboard the train, Stephenson brutally assaulted the woman, undressed her, repeatedly bit her, and attempted to rape her. The three men disembarked with Oberholtzer at Hamilton and checked into a hotel. With Oberholtzer in extreme pain, Gentry helped dress her wounds. One of the men then took her, at her request, to a drugstore where she purchased bichloride of mercury, and later ingested six pills to try to commit suicide. On Mar. 17, the men drove the sick woman back to her parent's home, telling them that their daughter had been in a car accident. On Apr. 14, 1925, Oberholtzer died from poisoning. Stephenson, Gentry, and Klinck were tried on murder charges and the prosecution fought to establish that Oberholtzer had committed suicide as a direct result of her mental condition after the vicious attack. Stephenson was convicted and received a life term in prison while the other two men were acquitted.

REF.: Busch, *Guilty or Not Guilty; CBA;* (FICTION), Dudley, *King Cobra.*

Stern, Abraham, 1907-42, Isr., terr. Born in Poland, Abraham Stern traveled through several wars and revolutions to reach Israel in 1922. He was fifteen years old at the time. Enrolling in the Hebrew University, he joined an underground military organization called Haganah. The illegally-armed secret home guard protected Israeli settlers from Arab raiders when the British would not. Although forceful, the Haganah did not believe in reprisals. Stern won a scholarship that took him to Florence when he was twenty-one. He came to admire Benito Mussolini, and returned to Israel to form a group known as the Revisionists. They eventually evolved into the Stern Gang, an organization that believed in reprisals and in aggressive action. The Revisionists were part of the National Military Organization Irgun Zwei Leumi. By 1939, after spending time in Poland procuring guns and training for Irgun officers, Stern returned to Israel and launched an all-out attack on both British and Arab factions. He was shot and killed by a British police officer in February 1942. See: **Mussolini, Benito Amilcare Andrea.**

REF.: *CBA;* Demaris, *Brothers in Blood: The International Terrorist Network;* Hurwood, *Society and the Assassin;* Hyams, *Killing No Murder;* Laquer, *Terrorism;* O'Ballance, *Language of Violence—The Blood Politics of Terrorism;* Paine, *The Assassins' World.*

Stern, Herbert Jay, 1936- , U.S., jur. U.S. Attorney in Newark, N.J., from 1971-73. He was appointed to the district court of New Jersey by President Richard Nixon in 1973. REF.: *CBA.*

Sterndale, Sir William Pickford, 1849-1923, Brit., jur. Accepted to Bar by Inner Temple in 1874 and practiced primarily on Northern Circuit. He was named Queen's Counsel in 1893, and appointed to the High Court, King's Division in 1907. He presided over the murder trial of Cornelius Howard. REF.: *CBA.*

Stesel, Anatoli Mikhailovich, 1848-1915, Rus., ct. mar. Led garrison at Port Arthur in 1904 that was defeated by Yasukata Oku, and surrendered to General Nogi in 1905. He was court-martialed in 1906 and received the death penalty. In 1908, his sentence was commuted to ten years, and he was pardoned in 1909. REF.: *CBA.*

Steunenberg, Frank R., d.1905, U.S., assass. On Dec. 30, 1905, former two-term Idaho governor Frank Steunenberg was killed in a bomb blast as he walked toward his residence in Caldwell. The dynamite explosion had been triggered by Industrial Workers of the World (IWW) member Harry Orchard, who allegedly was acting under orders from William D. "Big Bill" Haywood, the fiery leader of the IWW "Wobblies". Steunenberg, who worked in a local bank at the time of his death, became a union target after he had called in federal troops to suppress IWW rioters during his administration. See: **Haywood, William Dudley; Orchard, Harry.**

REF.: *CBA;* Duke, *Celebrated Criminal Cases of America;* Horan, *The Pinkertons;* Laquer, *Terrorism;* Paine, *The Assassins' World;* Reppetto, *The Blue Parade.*

Stevens, Dallas Ray, 1953- , U.S., rape-mur. Known to the Edwards children, Nichole Lynae, five, Stacy, eight, and Desiree, four, as "Uncle Dallas," Dallas Ray Stevens had been a frequent visitor at their home, and was related to the children by marriage. His sister-in-law, Coleen Edwards, had driven with her four children to Creswell, Ore., on the evening of Feb. 26, 1988. Stevens joined them in another car, according to Lane County Sheriff David Burks, after dropping off the youngest child with friends. The three girls then rode with Edwards and Stevens in one car to get a part for Stevens' car. Returning to Creswell to pick up the youngest sibling, the three girls decided to ride with Stevens back to their home in Cottage Grove, while their mother drove ahead with her youngest child. When Edwards stopped along the road to buy cigarettes, the other car pulled in behind her. But when she came out of the store, it was gone. Edwards drove home, and was alarmed to find neither her children nor Stevens there. After searching with a friend for about five hours, she reported her daughters missing at 3 a.m.

Around 6 a.m. on Feb. 27, Linn County deputies arrived at Hector MacPherson's Bannockburn Farms Dairy. In a small house where Stevens had been living since he began working on the farm a week earlier, they found the bodies of Stacy and Desiree. They spotted Stevens shortly after, milking cows, but he fled when he saw the officers. After a three-hour search with a tracking dog, they found Stevens hiding behind a tree near the dairy. After questioning Stevens, officers located the body of Nicole in the attic of the house. The 5-year-old had been strangled with a sock, stabbed, then stuffed into a plastic bag. She had been sexually abused, as had both of her sisters. Stevens admitted to the killings, but said it all seemed to be part of a "bad dream," and that he was high on injections of amphetamines at the time.

Stevens was charged with three counts of aggravated murder, four counts of first-degree kidnapping, two counts of first-degree sexual abuse, one count of rape, and two counts of second-degree assault. Stevens had choked both of the surviving sisters with a dog chain and had hit one of them over the head. Stevens' defense attorneys argued for reduced charges, saying that their client was not capable of "intending" to murder the child. Kathryn Wood, Stevens' attorney, argued during the trial that her client, who had a long history of drug abuse, was in a "dreamlike state" when he committed the crimes. Wood also moved for a mistrial because the psychiatrist's report did not include in-depth personality tests. Circuit court judge William O. Lewis denied the motion. Several witnesses for the prosecution testified that Stevens had a long history of sexual violence, often involving children. Co-prosecutor Daniel Murphy referred to him as a "dangerous and insidious predator" and a "thrill seeker" who had victimized women and children for eighteen years. On Nov. 9, 1988, after six-and-a-half-hours of deliberation, a jury found Stevens Guilty of the aggravated murder of Nicole Edwards and Guilty of all other counts as well.

On Nov. 21, the same jury, after seven hours of deliberation, returned with a unanimous decision to give Stevens the death sentence, judging that the murder was provoked, deliberate, and that the slayer would continue to commit violent crimes if allowed to live. Noting that the conviction and the death sentence could possibly be overturned in the automatic appeal required by the state's capital punishment law, Judge Lewis added a total of 100 years in prison sentences for Stevens' nine other felony counts. All of the sentences are to begin after Stevens serves a fifteen-year sentence for a previous sodomy conviction. Stevens is the fifteenth inmate on the penitentiary's death row, now filled to capacity. There have been no executions under Oregon's capital punishment law. REF.: *CBA.*

Stevens, James, b.1882, Brit., mur. In 1905, James Stevens lived with his mother in a barren cottage in Wadhurst, Sussex, in southeast England. The 23-year-old son insured his mother's life, making himself the beneficiary, shortly before her death in December when her throat was slit. On Dec. 11, Stevens, a wood-chopper, left work to check on his mother, and when he returned to work in a few minutes he told another worker, "Somebody had been in and killed her." When the insurance policy was discovered, Stevens was arrested. In February 1906, he was tried, convicted, and sentenced to death, though little evidence connected him with the crime. He was later reprieved.

REF.: *CBA;* Shew, *A Second Companion to Murder.*

Stevens, John, prom. 1851, Brit., asslt. After two days without food, the wife of John Stevens asked her husband for a meal. In response, he hit her with a picking rod—a weaver's implement with spikes. Stevens was convicted for repeated assault and sentenced to six months of hard labor in prison.

REF.: *CBA;* Thomson, *The Story of Scotland Yard.*

Stevens, John Paul, 1920- , U.S., jur. U.S. Supreme Court justice. After graduating as valedictorian of the Northwestern University Law School class of 1947, he worked one year as a law clerk for Supreme Court justice Wiley Rutledge, then practiced law in Chicago. He quickly developed expertise in antitrust law. He was appointed to the U.S. Seventh Circuit Court of Appeals by President Richard Nixon in 1970. Five years later, he was appointed associate justice to the U.S. Supreme Court by President Gerald Ford. In *Jurek v. Texas* in 1976, he wrote the majority opinion stating that the death penalty does not constitute "cruel and unusual punishment," and that, more specifically, Texas sentencing procedures were within the scope of the Constitution. He wrote the majority opinion again in *Roberts v. Louisiana* in 1976, arguing that there are certain crimes which cannot be classified as capital offenses. In *Nebraska Press Asssociation v. Stuart* that same year, he voted with the majority, holding that judges could place restraints, or gag orders, on press coverage of criminal trials only if such barriers were necessary to ensure a fair trial. REF.: *CBA.*

Stevens, Peter, 1923- , and **Harding, Arthur**, 1921- , and **Roberts, Luke**, 1923- , Brit., theft-mansl. Late one day in November 1938, five boys stole an Austin and went joyriding. When the car ran out of gas, they stole a Ford and took a second drive in London. They pulled up near two police officers, Haines and Armstrong, and two of the youths got out of the car. Then 15-year-old Peter Stevens drove off, racing down a hill, and braked quickly. Haines began talking with the two boys at the top of the hill as Armstrong walked toward the car. Stevens next put the car in reverse and backed up the incline, almost running into Armstrong. Armstrong fell to the pavement, jumped up, and started ran to the car. Haines jumped on the running board, yelling at Stevens to halt, and the car careened down the hill again past Armstrong. It lurched erratically up on a curb and crashed into a bus going up the hill. Haines, who was caught between the two vehicles, died soon after the accident.

Three boys, including Stevens, 17-year-old Arthur Harding, and 15-year-old Luke Roberts, were charged in connection with the incident. Stevens, the driver of the car, was charged with manslaughter and found Guilty. The charge against the other two teenagers was reduced from theft to taking a car without the owner's permission and they were also found Guilty. Stevens was sentenced to be held in custody for three years, Roberts was sent to a special school, and Harding was released on probation.

REF.: *CBA;* Wilson, *Children Who Kill.*

Stevens, Thaddeus, 1792-1868, U.S., lawyer. Served as U.S. congressman from 1849-53 and from 1859-67, staunchly opposing slavery. As an instrumental force in developing the Radical Republicans' strategy for reconstruction, he initiated the impeachment proceedings against President Andrew Johnson, and was the chief manager at his trial. REF.: *CBA.*

Stevens, Walter, 1877-1939, U.S., org. crime. Walter Stevens was an enigma. A ruthless gunman known to have killed at least sixty men, he was also a loving husband to an invalid wife and father to three adopted children. He never drank and preferred to read classical literature, especially the novels of Jack London and Robert Louis Stevenson, as well as the poetry of Robert Burns.

Stevens was a free-lance gunman and enforcer with strong ties to Chicago mobsters Al Capone and Johnny Torrio. As a young man, he straddled the line between labor and management, working for Maurice "Mossy" Enright as hired "muscle" during labor disputes. Without scruple, Stevens would kill a man from either side for $50 or give him a solid beating for half that amount. Along with Enright, Stevens was responsible for the 1919 murder of notorious gunman Pete Gentleman. Stevens had become politically well-connected years earlier. After bribing and strong-arming jurors, he won an acquittal for Illinois State Treasurer Len Small, accused of embezzling $600,000. The favor was repaid later, when Stevens was convicted for the murder of a police officer in Aurora, Ill., and pardoned by Small, who had been elected governor.

After Enright was killed in 1920, Stevens offered his talents to the Chicago mob, then in the midst of early bootlegging wars, following the institution of the Volstead Act. While working for Capone, he killed five members of Spike O'Donnell's South Side gang. Stevens became known as the "dean of Chicago gunmen," reciting poems and passages of his favorite works to his illiterate peers. Working as an intermediary, he won political favors for Capone from the still-grateful Governor Small. He slowed down a bit in the 1930s, when mob life was less mercurial following the repeal of Prohibition. He died of natural causes in 1939, at the age of sixty-two.

REF.: Asbury, *Gem of the Prairie; CBA;* Kobler, *Al Capone;* Lindberg, *Chicago Ragtime: Another Look At Chicago 1880-1920;* McPhaul, *Johnny Torrio;* Nash, *Bloodletters and Badmen.*

Stewart, Alexander (Earl of Mar), c.1375-1435, Scot., mur. Murdered first husband of Isabel, Countess of Mar, and forced her to marry him in attempt to inherit Douglas family property. REF.: *CBA.*

Stewart, Alexander (Duke of Albany, Earl of March), c.1454-85, Scot., consp. Schemed in 1482 with supporter, England's Edward IV, to usurp Scottish throne from elder brother James III. He had James jailed and then went to England, where his sovereignty was acknowledged by Edward. He was indicted and branded as a criminal after Edward died in 1483. REF.: *CBA.*

Stewart, Alfred Walter (AKA: **John Jervis Connington**), b.1880, Ire., writer. Wrote detective fiction such as *Dangerfield Talisman, Murder in the Maze,* and others under Connington pseudonym. REF.: *CBA.*

Stewart, Andrew, prom. 1548-98, Brit., consp. Participated in uprising led by Moray protesting marriage of Mary, Queen of Scots and Henry Stewart in 1565, and helped cause death of David Rizzio. REF.: *CBA.*

Stewart, David (Duke of Rothesay), c.1378-1402, Scot., nobleman, assass.? Most likely starved to death in Falkland by Robert Stewart, the Duke of Albany, who was given custody of him by his father, Robert III. REF.: *CBA.*

Stewart, Mrs. **Francis**, 1831-74, Brit., mur. For an unknown reason, Mrs. Francis Stewart killed her newborn grandchild. When she was hanged at Newgate Prison in 1874, she became the first woman in England to be identified as a grandmother who had killed her grandchild.

REF.: *CBA;* Nash, *Look For the Woman;* O'Donnell, *Should Women Hang?*

Stewart, Frederick, c.1900-28, Brit., burg.-mur. On Feb. 9, 1928, Frederick Stewart, a professional burglar, went from house to house "sounding the drum"—or knocking on doors—in the Baywater area of London to determine which residents were at home. At one home, a woman answered and he told her he was from the Warwick Garage, a fictitious business. Moving on, he broke into the home of Alfred Charles Bertram Webb, an accountant and hotel owner. As Stewart rifled the apartment, Webb returned home with his son and a friend. When Webb noticed glass from his door had been broken, he told the other two to go for help and as Webb looked into his apartment, Stewart pulled out his revolver and fired at him. Stewart fled, having fatally wounded Webb.

Police searched the neighborhood, questioning the woman whom Stewart had approached as a representative of Warwick Garage. A police officer recalled Stewart, a burglar who frequented Warwick Mews, and located him at a dog track in Southend. The thief confessed to burglarizing the apartment and shooting Webb, but said the gun had accidentally fired. In April 1928, Stewart was tried at the Old Bailey, convicted on murder charges, and received the death penalty. On June 6, he was hanged at Pentonville Prison.

REF.: *CBA;* Gribble, *Clues That Spelled Guilty;* Hastings, *The Other Mr. Hastings;* Horwell, *Horwell of the Yard;* Hoskins, *They Almost Escaped;* Shew, *A Companion to Murder.*

Stewart, Dr. **Glen Gold** (AKA: **Glen Campbell, Dave Burrows, Robert Fennel**), prom. 1970, Can., mur. In 1956, Glen Gold Stewart finished his medical studies at the University of Alberta in Canada and sought a position as a surgeon. After several non-medical jobs, he took a post in Smithers, British Columbia, and there became friendly with Sheila Haupt, the wife of a Canadian soldier serving in Germany. The two appeared in public together, Stewart introducing her as his sister.

In April 1969, Haupt and her child vanished at about the same time Stewart left his current position. Police looked for Stewart to question him about the disappearance. A year later, traveling up and down the Canadian-U.S. coast in the *Gypsy* with an Italian woman, he anchored twice near the Shantyman's Christian Association Bible Camp, located on the west coast of Vancouver Island in British Columbia, where he was charged with stealing a dingy. Stewart also applied for a post as caretaker of the Bible camp, but the post had already been filled by a 24-year-old art student, Gordon Adrian Kralt.

Sometime during the first days of November 1970, Stewart visited Kralt, shot him, stabbed him, crushed his skull with an ax, and apparently carved out Kralt's right lung. Then the murderer dragged the body about half a mile into the woods and stole the young man's car. Authorities in Canada and the U.S. searched for the couple as they zigzagged back and forth between the two countries, finally locating them in a San Francisco hippie community. When police arrived, Stewart refused to let them in and turned on the gas from a stove, but police broke in and saved the couple. Stewart was sent back to Canada and, with the woman's help, police located Stewart's gun, which he had thrown into water off a ferry dock. The woman, who was not involved in the murder, became a witness for the prosecution and on Mar. 19, 1971, Stewart was found Guilty of the Kralt murder and sentenced to life in prison.

REF.: *CBA;* Gribble, *The Deadly Professionals.*

Stewart, James (Stuart, Earl of Mar, Earl of Moray), c.1531-70, nobleman, assass. Fought with half-sister Mary, Queen of Scots over joining Reformers in 1556, but became de facto prime minister after she reassumed throne. He fled to England in protest against Mary's marriage to Lord Darnley in 1565, but returned after the murder of David Rizzio in 1566. He renewed peace with Mary, but then left for France following the murder of Darnley in 1567. He was asked back into the regency after Mary abdicated the throne in 1567, and avoided efforts to prosecute Darnley's assassins. He defeated Mary and a following of 6,000 at Langside in 1568, and recommended her imprisonment to Queen Elizabeth I. He was assassinated in Linlithgow by James Hamilton, who sought to avenge Mary. REF.: *CBA*.

Stewart, James (Stuart, Earl of Moray), d.1592, Brit., nobleman, assass. Killed on orders of James VI by the Earl of Huntly's men, probably because of his association with the queen. His body was left unburied for a lengthy time, as depicted in popular ballads. REF.: *CBA*.

Stewart, James (Earl of Arran), d.1596, Brit., assass. Served as missionary in the Netherlands in 1581, and as privy counselor. After his cousin James Hamilton was declared insane, he gained the title of Earl of Arran and the leadership of the Hamiltons. He lost his post during Ruthven's plot against James VI in 1582, but two years later served as an aggressive lord chancellor. He was exiled after Queen Elizabeth I blamed him for the slaying of Lord Russell in 1585, and later was assassinated by Sir James Douglas. REF.: *CBA*.

Stewart, James, c.1702-52, Scot., (wrong. convict.?) mur. During the eighteen century, two rival Scottish clans, the Stewarts and the Campbells, clashed over land. The Hanover government seized the lands of Charles Stewart of Ardsheal after he fled to France and Colin Campbell of Glenure, the "Red Fox," was appointed to oversee and collect rents for the region. Campbell chose James Stewart of the Glen to help him, but in spring 1951 Stewart was ordered off the land and all the Stewart tenants were directed to vacate their homes by May 15, 1752.

On their behalf, Stewart went to Edinburgh and secured a Bill of Suspension on Apr. 18, 1752, and returned home to organize a protest. Campbell also traveled to Edinburgh and influenced Lord Haining to strike down the bill Stewart had won. On May 14, 1952, Campbell was riding home with a servant, Mackenzie, a sheriff, and his nephew, Mungo Campbell, a lawyer. During the ride, Campbell was shot dead in the Wood of Lettermore. Mungo Campbell later altered his description of the murderer to fit Allan Breck Stewart, the foster son of James Stewart, and James Stewart was incriminated as a conspirator. A short time later in the day, James Stewart remarked when he heard the news, "Well, whoever did the deed, I am the man they will hang for it."

During the proceedings, Allan Stewart was in France and the trial of James Stewart was presided over by a Campbell clan leader and decided by a jury composed of eleven Campbell members. Stewart was convicted and, still protesting his innocence, hanged. According to Stewart legend, the actual murderer was Donald Stewart. REF.: *CBA*.

Stewart, John (Earl of Atholl), d.1578, Brit., consp.-assass.? Schemed with Huntly to capture Edinburgh to favor papists. After Huntly lost power, he headed the Catholic nobles of Scotland. Although he served as Mary, Queen of Scots' chief counselor after she married Henry Stewart, known as Lord Darnley, he did not participate in the conspiracies to murder either Darnley or David Rizzio. He fought against James VI to return Mary to favor in 1570. Eight years later, he fought Morton alongside Argyll, and was named chancellor. He and Morton eventually conciliated. He died under mysterious circumstances and may have been poisoned. REF.: *CBA*.

Stewart, Matthew (Earl of Lennox), 1516-1571, Scot., polit. corr.-abduc. Succeeded as heir of Scotland Stuart family after death of James V. In Edinburgh in 1543, he abducted Mary of Guise and Princess Mary in a desperate attempt to marry the former. He took sides with Henry VIII after making unpatriotic agreements, and married his niece, Lady Margaret Douglas. He served briefly as governor of Scotland in 1544 but was branded a criminal and lost his post the next year. Upon his return, in 1564, he regained his title and property, and devised the marriage of Mary, Queen of Scots to his oldest son, Henry Stewart. He helped arrange the imprisonment of Mary at Loch Leven following Henry's death in 1565, and served as provisional regent for his baby grandson, the future James VI. After his regency was made official in 1570, he battled Huntly, the Hamiltons, and other supporters of the queen, and was soon seized at Stirling, where he sustained mortal wounds. REF.: *CBA*.

Stewart, Patrick (Earl of Orkney), d.1614, Brit., polit. corr. Son of Robert Stewart who served as powerful leader of Orkney Islands and Zetland. His power lasted until he was barred from the justiciary and jailed for tyranny and cruelty. REF.: *CBA*.

Stewart, Potter, 1915-85, U.S., jur. U.S. Supreme Court associate justice. Although he had supported his friend Senator Robert A. Taft for president, the then vice-mayor of Cincinnati, Ohio, actively campaigned for presidential nominee Dwight D. Eisenhower in 1952 and was well-awarded. Two years later, he received a presidential nomination to the sixth circuit court of appeals, where he served from 1954-58. He was nominated associate justice of the U.S. Supreme Court by President Eisenhower in 1958 and, despite some opposition by southern Democrats who feared his support of civil rights, he was confirmed by the Senate in 1959. As justice, he focused mostly on criminal procedure cases, usually with the philosophy that suspects are protected by the Bill of Rights only after they are formally indicted or arraigned. In *Elkins v. United States* in 1960, he wrote the majority opinion stating that illegally obtained evidence was inadmissible in federal criminal trials. He supported the majority in *Gideon v. Wainwright* in 1963, and supported the defendant's right to a lawyer in *Massiah v. U.S.* in 1964. He dissented, however, in *Escobedo v. Illinois* in 1964 and *Miranda v. Arizona* in 1966, two landmark cases that expanded the rights of criminal defendants. He and a majority of the justices on the court further limited the scope of police searches in *Coolidge v. New Hampshire* in 1971, declaring that police needed to obtain a warrant before making a search after the time of arrest. He retired from the court in 1981. REF.: *CBA*.

Stewart, Robert (Earl of Orkney), d.1592, Scot., consp. Son of James V who served as abbot of Holyrood in 1539. He reportedly told Henry Stewart of a plot against him, but was jailed by Morton for allegedly attempting to give the Orkneys to Denmark in 1575. He helped lead the conspiracy that ended Morton's career in 1581. REF.: *CBA*.

Stewart, William, d.1848, Ire., mur. On May 9, 1928, Captain William Stewart, commander of the *Mary Russell,* set sail from Barbados to Cork, Ire., with six crew members, three apprentices, and four passengers. The captain began acting strangely and about midway through the journey called his crew together and announced that he knew the men were plotting a mutiny and he was prepared to resist them. When the surprised crew denied the accusations, the captain seemed appeased.

Within a few days, however, he suspected a passenger, Raynes, former chief mate of another ship, and an apprentice of trying to commandeer the vessel, so he threw all charts and navigation instruments overboard, tore up his logbook, and armed himself with several weapons, including an ax and harpoon. The following day, the captain borrowed some guns from another ship and tied up one of the crew, whom he denounced as the leader, and then, ordering the apprentices to help him, he tied up six more men. Two of the crew, Howes and Murley, resisted but later agreed to be bound.

The next morning, Stewart began fixing nooses around the men's necks when he found that Howes had partly untied himself. When Howes would not allow the apprentices to bind him again, Stewart fired his gun at Howes and the injured Howes pretended to be dead. Later, the captain saw Howes moving, so he shot him again in the thigh and Howes ran for cover where he was later discovered by the apprentices and beaten with an ax. The same afternoon, the captain attacked the seven other bound men with a crowbar, killing all except for Smith, and then Stewart tried to harpoon Howes. Smith joined Howes, who armed himself with a pistol and ax.

Not long after the slaughter, the *Mary Stubbs,* whose captain was a friend of Stewart's, arrived and the two boats continued to Cork together. After Stewart jumped over the side of his ship and was saved, he was taken to the other ship where he jumped overboard again as the vessels came close to the harbor. After swimming to another boat, Stewart jumped off the third boat, swimming to a fishing boat. He was turned over to the Coast Guard and the police and then tried at the Cork Assizes. Stewart was declared insane and indefinitely confined in an institution for the mentally ill. He died twenty years later.

REF.: Brock, *A Casebook of Crime; CBA.*

Stewart, William Morris, 1827-1909, U.S., lawyer. Served as California attorney general in 1854. He practiced law in Virginia City and Carson City, Nev., and represented Nevada in the U.S. Senate from 1864-75. He wrote the version of the Fifteenth Amendment that was formally adopted into the U.S. Constitution. REF.: *CBA.*

Stewart, William Rhinelander, 1852-1929, U.S., social reformer. Millionaire philanthropist who served on seventy-member committee investigating Tammany Hall in 1894. REF.: *CBA.*

Stewart-Canning Duel, 1809, Brit., duel. Robert Stewart, Viscount Castlereagh served as war secretary from 1805-09. During the same administration, undersecretary George Canning, Stewart's political rival, made plans to seize the Danish fleet. Stewart disagreed with the strategy and the two men duelled over the issue in 1809. Although Canning was slightly wounded, he later outmaneuvered Stewart, replacing him as foreign secretary. Stewart committed suicide in 1822.

REF.: *CBA;* Melville, *Famous Duels and Assassinations.*

Steyn, Marthinus Theunis, 1857-1916, S. Afri., jur. Served on high court from 1889-96 and as president of Orange Free State from 1896-1900. A staunch supporter of apartheid, he led guerilla troops during the South African War from 1900-12, after which he opposed Louis Botha's reconciliatory plans. REF.: *CBA.*

Stielow, Charles F., b.c.1878, and **Green, Nelson**, b.c.1896, U.S. (wrong. convict.) rob.-mur. In 1915, Charles B. Phelps, in his seventies, and his housekeeper, Margaret Wolcott, lived in the western part of New York state, about one mile south of West Shelby, N.Y., in Orleans County. During the night of Mar. 21, 1915, Erwin King and Clarence O'Connell broke into the farmhouse, shooting the housekeeper and Phelps, and looting the house. The dying housekeeper struggled to a tenant house and collapsed on the doorstep in the snow.

Several hours later, at 5 a.m., a farmhand, Charles Stielow, rose to begin his chores and found the dead housekeeper outside his house. Investigating, he discovered the unconscious Phelps on the kitchen floor. Phelps was rushed to the hospital where he later died from three bullet wounds.

During the police investigation, officials brought a dog to track the killer and it followed a scent to a stream. Police also found that money had been taken and that the victims had both been killed with a .22 caliber revolver. Though Stielow had a .22-caliber revolver that had not been fired in years and a rifle in the house, his wife and mother-in-law urged him to move them. He took them to the barn, and then gave them to his brother-in-law, Raymond Green. Authorities later found the guns in Green's possession and determined that the bullets that killed Phelps and the housekeeper had been fired from Stielow's handgun.

On Apr. 21, 1915, Stielow, about 37-years-old, and Nelson Green, about 19-years-old, another brother-in-law, were arrested on murder charges and on Apr. 23, officials procured an alleged confession from Stielow, which he steadfastly refused to sign.

Stielow's trial at Albion began on July 11, 1915, and he was convicted, primarily on the strength of the unsigned testimony, which Judge Cuthbert W. Pound allowed, saying that both sides could testify regarding the methods used to secure the admission. Pound sentenced Stielow to be executed in early September. Green was then tried, and, pleading guilty to save his life, he was convicted and sentenced to twenty years to life in prison at Auburn Penitentiary.

On Feb. 22, 1916, Stielow's conviction was affirmed. Appealing to prison officials, Stielow continued to protest his innocence and a New York lawyer, Grace Humiston, as well as the Humanitarian Cult, became active in trying to win his release. A motion for a new trial was refused on July 16, 1916. Stielow received his second stay of execution a mere forty minutes before he was to be sent to the electric chair on July 29, 1916.

Stielow became more hopeful a month later when a peddler, Erwin King, who had been arrested on another charge, confessed on Aug. 11, 1916, to two killings at the Phelps farm. Two days later, when King was transported back to Albion, he was accompanied by Detective George Newton, the same official who had acquired Stielow's admission. King withdrew his confession and another motion for a new trial was struck down. Then the case was presented to New York governor Whitman, who agreed to hear it on Nov. 28, 1916. On Dec. 4, the governor commuted Stielow's sentence to a life term, stating that he thought the prisoner was guilty, but evidence existed that made his guilt questionable.

After another month, King began writing letters from a Buffalo jail to friends, which were published by a newspaper, and the governor had King questioned. Satisfied that King was more probably the culprit, the governor secured $25,000 for additional investigation. George H. Bond, a former district attorney, conducted the new inquiry. At first assuming Stielow to be guilty, he later found evidence to the contrary. Bond found recordings of Stielow's conversations that contained no comments implicating him in the crime. Ballistics experts were hired whose tests proved conclusively that the bullets that killed the victims had not been fired from Stielow's gun and that the prisoner's gun had not been used in years. Bond further reasoned that the housekeeper would not have run for protection to a killer's house. This report was further strengthened when King made another voluntary confession in December 1917.

That month, a grand jury hearing was held in which Bond presented his findings. However, an indictment was not returned against King, possibly because popular opinion and the newspapers continued to denounce Stielow. When Governor Whitman read Bond's report, and because Bond had changed his opinion about the case, the governor believed both Stielow, forty, and Green, twenty-two, were innocent. He commuted Stielow's sentence and on Apr. 16, 1918, directed that he be freed. Green's sentence also was commuted and he was freed. Neither received financial restitution for their three years in prison.

REF.: *CBA;* Robinson, *Science Catches the Criminal;* Thorwald, *The Century of the Detective.*

Stigand, d.1072, Brit., polit. corr. Served as chief adviser to Queen Emma following the 1035 death of King Canute, under whom he had been chaplain. He became the bishop of Elmham in 1038 and also the bishop of Winchester in 1047. After he was named archbishop of Canterbury in 1052, he went unacknowledged by all in the papacy, with the exception of Benedict X, who supported him briefly. He acquiesced to William I in 1066. He was eventually ousted and jailed for life by the papal legates under charges of plurality and usurpation. REF.: *CBA.*

Stiles, William Larkin (AKA: **William Larkin**), d.1908, U.S., west. outl.-gunman-lawman. Gunman William Stiles, who allegedly killed his father when he was twelve, became notorious around the turn of the century in the Southwest. After assisting lawman Jeff Milton, Stiles was hired by Willcox, Ariz., marshal Burt Alvord. Together they formed a gang of train robbers which included George and Louis Owens, Jack Dunlap, Bravo Juan Yoas, and Bob Brown. On Apr. 8, 1900, Stiles, recently released from jail, visited Alvord and other gang members at the Cochise County courthouse. While being guided from the cell by jailer

George Bravin, Stiles pulled a gun and demanded Bravin's keys. Stiles shot Bravin in the leg and released the prisoners.

William Stiles

In January 1908, in Nevada, Stiles, then deputy sheriff, shot a man to death while arresting him. The victim's 12-year-old son then shot and killed Stiles.

REF.: American Guide Series, *Arizona, A State Guide;* Axford, *Around Western Campfires;* Bakarich, *Gun-Smoke;* ____ and Bennett, *There's Treasure in Our Hills;* Bartholomew, *Kill or be Killed;* Breihan, *Great Lawmen of the West; CBA;* Chisholm, *Brewery Gulch;* Chrisman, *Fifty Years on the Owl Hoot Trail;* Coolidge, *Fighting Men of the West;* Erwin, *The Southwest of John H. Slaughter;* Gregory, *True Wild West Stories;* Haley, *Jeff Milton;* Hendricks, *The Bad Man of the West;* Hertzog, *A Directory of New Mexico Desperadoes;* Holloway, *Texas Gun Lore;* Horan and Sann, *Pictorial History of the Wild West;* Hughes, *South From Tombstone;* Hunt, *Cap Mossman;* Hunter and Rose, *The Album of Gun-Fighters;* Johnson, *Famous Lawmen of the Old West;* Love, *The Rise and Fall of Jesse James;* Martin, *Tombstone's Epitaph;* Miller, *The Arizona Story;* Penfield, *Dig Here!;* Rynning, *Gun Notches;* Schultz, *Southwestern Town;* Shirley, *Buckskin and Spurs;* Small, *The Best of the True West;* Sonnichsen, *Billy King's Tombstone;* Waltrip, *Cowboys and Cattlemen.*

Stilicho, Flavius, c.365-408, Roman., treas. Served as commander in chief of Emperor Theodosius' army, and as chief minister under Emperor Flavius Honorius. He was deserted by his soldiers, and later ordered put to death by Honorius after being suspected of scheming against the emperor. REF.: *CBA.*

Stillwell, Thomas, See: **Woodhouse, Joan Mary**.

Stiltz, Moses S. (AKA: **Bud**), prom. 1959, Case of, U.S., mur. The famous child actor Carl W. Switzer, better known as the character Alfalfa, appeared between 1935 and 1942 in *Our Gang* movie shorts. These films were made into a television series in 1955 called *The Little Rascals.* Though the program netted huge profits, none of the actors received residuals from reruns. During the 1950s, Switzer desperately sought acting roles to support himself. He also picked up odd jobs, including guiding hunters.

In the late 1950s, Switzer borrowed a hunting dog from his friend, Moses Stiltz, a welder. Switzer lost the dog, infuriating Stiltz. Switzer then offered a $35 reward for the dog and a man later found and returned the dog to Switzer at a bar where he worked. There, the grateful Switzer bought the finder $15 worth of drinks.

After giving the dog back to Stiltz, Switzer badgered the dog owner for the $50 he had spent to recover the dog, but Stiltz refused. On Jan. 22, 1959, sulking and drinking with photographer Jack Piott, Switzer became more convinced that the welder owed him the $50. Later that night, the two men went to Stiltz's house in Mission Hills, Calif. When Stiltz answered the door, Piott showed him a fake police badge and they forced their way inside. Switzer demanded the money and Stilz responded, "I don't owe you any fifty. You lost the dog, you pay." Switzer then seized a clock and hit the dog owner on the face with it. Stiltz retreated to his bedroom and pulled a .38-caliber revolver from his closet, still trailed by Switzer, who tried to grab the gun. Switzer pushed Stiltz into the closet, set the handgun on a dresser, and took out a switchblade, opening it as Stiltz came out of the closet and grabbed the gun. When Switzer threatened Stiltz with the knife, Stiltz shot Switzer in the stomach. The former actor died on the way to the hospital. Stiltz was exonerated by a coroner's inquest, which decided the shooting was justifiable homicide.

REF.: *CBA;* Wolf, *Fallen Angels.*

Stilwell, Frank C., c.1857-1882, U.S., west. gunman. Frank C. Stilwell, younger brother of noted lawyer and army scout, S.E. "Comanche Jack" Stilwell, was born circa 1857 in the border area between Kansas and Missouri. He arrived in Arizona in 1878 and went to work as a miner and teamster in Mohave County. After his initial stint of legitimate employment, Stilwell signed on with N.H. Clanton and his gang of cattle rustlers in Tombstone.

Stilwell apparently kept his rustling activities a secret since he was also appointed deputy sheriff of Cochise County (of which Tombstone was the county seat). Even during his tenure as a law enforcement officer, Stilwell involved himself in a stage-robbing partnership with Pete Spence. Stilwell's criminal activities came to light when he and Spence robbed the Tombstone-Bisbee stage of $3,000 and were arrested. The pair went to trial and were acquitted. However, Wyatt Earp, making a reputation for himself as a tough law enforcement officer, brought them back for a second trial. Again they were acquitted. Stilwell was considered a prime suspect in the wounding of Virgil Earp on Dec. 28, 1881, and of Morgan Earp's murder on Mar. 18, 1882. Two days after Morgan Earp's murder, Wyatt Earp and several of his men encountered Stilwell and Ike Clanton, who was believed to be behind the murders of the two Earp brothers. Clanton and Stilwell split up. Stilwell's bullet-riddled body was discovered later.

REF.: Bartholomew, *The Biographical Album of Western Gunfighters;* Bartlett, *History of Wyoming;* Bechdolt, *When the West Was Young;* Blythe, *A Pictorial Souvenir and Historical Sketch of Tombstone, Arizona;* Boyer, *An Illustrated Life of Doc Holliday;* Breakenridge, *Helldorado;* Breihan, *Great Lawmen of the West;* Brent, *Great Western Heroes;* Brophy, *Arizona Sketch Book;* Burns, *Tombstone; CBA;* Chisholm, *Brewery Gulch;* Clum, *It All Happened in Tombstone;* Cox, *Luke Short and His Era;* Cunningham, *Triggernometry;* Donoho, *Circle Dot;* Erwin, *The Southwest of John H. Slaughter;* Gardner, *The Old Wild West;* Hall-Quest, *Wyatt Earp;* Hendricks, *The Bad Man of the West;* Hertzog, *A Directory of New Mexico Desperadoes;* Hogan, *The Life and Death of Johnny Ringo;* Holloway, *Texas Gun Lore;* Horan and Sann, *Pictorial History of the Wild West;* Jaastad, *Man of the West;* Jahns, *The Frontier World of Doc Holliday;* Johnson, *Famous Lawmen of the Old West;* King, *Wranglin' the Past;* Lake, *Under Cover for Wells Fargo;* Lake, *Wyatt Earp;* Martin, *The Earps of Tombstone;* ____, *Tombstone's Epitaph;* Masterson, *Famous Gunfighters of the Western Frontier;* Miller, *The Arizona Story;* Myers, *Doc Holliday;* ____, *The Last Chance;* O'Connor, *Bat Masterson;* Penfield, *Western Sheriffs and Marshals;* Raine, *Famous Sheriffs & Western Outlaws;* Rosa, *The Gunfighter, Man or Myth?;* Sterling, *Famous Western Outlaw-Sheriff Battles;* Waters, *Earp Brothers of Tombstone;* Way, *The Tombstone Story;* Wellman, *Glory, God and Gold;* ____, *The Trampling Herd;* White, *The Autobiography of a Durable Sinner;* Wilson, *Out of the West.*

Stimson, Ann, b.1768, and **Bosworth, Mary**, b.1769, and **Male, Mary**, b.1770, Case of, Brit., mur. In 1778, three children, 10-year-old Ann Stimson, 9-year-old Mary Bosworth, and 8-year-old Mary Male, attached three pins to a stick and struck 3-year-old Sarah Bright with the weapon, sexually mutilating the baby. The toddler died several days later. The three girls were brought to trial on murder charges at the Huntingdon Lent Assizes in

England where they were found *non capex doli,* meaning they unable to understand the nature of the act, and they were acquitted. REF.: *CBA;* Wilson, *Children Who Kill.*

Stimson, Frederic Jesup (AKA: **J.S. of Dale**), 1855-1943, U.S., writer. Attorney in Boston, Mass., and professor at Harvard University from 1903-14. He wrote many novels under the Dale pseudonym, such as *The Crime of Henry Vane* in 1884, as well as several treatises on the law. REF.: *CBA.*

Stinney, George Junius, Jr., 1929-44, U.S., mur. George Stinney met 11-year-old Betty June Binnicker and 8-year-old Mary Emma Thames on Mar. 24, 1944, as they were picking flowers near the Alderman Lumber Company's plant in Alcolu, S.C. When the girls did not return home that evening, their parents notified the police. A search party of 200 looked all night for the children and found their battered bodies in a water-filled ditch at 7:30 the next morning. Thames' skull was fractured and she had five head wounds. Binnicker's head was crushed in several places. Within a few hours, police had arrested Stinney, the 14-year-old son of a sawmill worker. He confessed to Deputy Sheriff H.S. Newman and S.J. Pratt of the governor's office that he killed the girls when Binnicker resisted his advances, beating them to death and hiding their bodies in the ditch. He led police to the spot where he had thrown away the murder weapon, a foot-long railroad spike. Stinney was hidden away to protect him from a lynch mob.

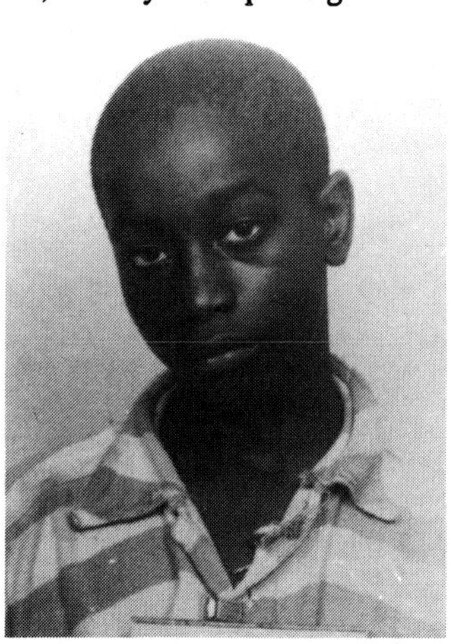

George Stinney, executed at the age of 14 for killing an 11-year-old girl.

Stinney was returned to Clarendon County for trial on Apr. 24, 1944, exactly one month after the murders. A special court session had been called to try him, and a local lawyer, Charles Plowden, was appointed his defense counsel. Stinney admitted his guilt, and Plowden, who had reluctantly accepted the appointment as counsel and who was preparing to run for elective office, saw no defense. He also decided there was no need for a psychiatric examination of his client. The Clarendon Courthouse was filled to several times its capacity. A crowd of 1,500 spilled over into the hallway, staircases, and grounds. Plowden never asked to move the trial to another county. Testimony started at 2:30 p.m., and the defense had finished presenting its case about an hour and a half later. Stinney's confession was the main evidence. The last evidence presented was his birth certificate, entered to prove that he had attained the traditionally accepted age of responsibility—fourteen. The jury left the courtroom at 4:55 p.m. and returned ten minutes later to pronounce Stinney Guilty as charged with no recommendation of leniency. The 14-year-old bit his finger while facing the judge for sentencing, and showed no response to the verdict. If Plowden had then filed a one-sentence, routine notice of appeal, and then appealed Stinney's case to the state supreme court, the execution would have been automatically delayed for a year. The attorney informed neither Stinney nor his family of his right to appeal, nor did he ever see his client again after that afternoon. The only possibility of delay, in the absence of an appeal, was an order of clemency from South Carolina governor, Olin D. Johnston.

Although Stinney's case received little coverage in South Carolina, and none outside of the state, as the execution date neared, Governor Johnston began to receive letters and telegrams from the NAACP, labor unions, and clergymen, most of them in support of clemency. Johnston, who would also be running for elective office in a few months, apparently never considered a stay of execution. He visited Stinney on June 14 in his small cell a few feet from the death chamber. The day before, prison officials had interviewed Stinney, who repeated his confession and said that he had been finishing the seventh grade when arrested. According to a newspaper report of Johnston's visit, Stinney told the governor that "his mind sometimes went blank." The next day, Johnston announced that he would not grant clemency. On June 16, 1944, thirty witnesses gathered at the Clarendon County State Prison to watch the execution. Stinney told Sheriff Gamble that he was sorry for committing the crime and hoped God and his parents would forgive him. He walked into the death chamber carrying a bible. The Associated Press reported that "the guards had difficulty strapping the boy's slight form into the wooden chair built for adults," and said that he was so small, "it was difficult to attach the electrode to his right leg." The death mask slipped off after the first 2,400 volt shock, and remained that way as two additional shocks followed. Stinney was the youngest person executed in the U.S. this century.

Most of the countries that still use capital punishment require a minimum age of eighteen. The controversy over executing young people resurfaced recently when Charles F. Rumbaugh was executed in Texas on Sept. 11, 1985, for a murder committed during a robbery when he was seventeen. Prior to Rumbaugh's death by lethal injection, there had been no executions of juveniles since 1964. REF.: *CBA.*

Stinson, Joe, 1838-1902, U.S., west. gunman. After migrating to the California gold fields in the 1850s, Joe Stinson joined the California Column during the Civil War and marched with them into New Mexico. After the war ended, Stinson stayed in New Mexico where he was miner. Although not overly successful, he gathered together enough money to open a saloon in Elizabethtown, N.M. In October 1871, Stinson shot and killed a belligerent drunk, Wall Henderson, who threatened to burn down Stinson's saloon. After killing Henderson, Stinson moved his business to Santa Fe, where he was involved in several other shootings, none of them fatal. On June 24, 1886, after drinking all night with Reddy McCann, the pair argued and Stinson threw McCann out. When McCann returned to resume the argument, Stinson pulled a gun and fired point-blank into his face. Surprisingly McCann survived, although missing the base of his nose. By 1890, Stinson was enfeebled by alcoholism. For several years he lived on a $10-a-month veteran's pension. In 1895, he was admitted to the National Home for Disabled Soldiers near Los Angeles where he died in 1902. REF.: *CBA.*

Stirling, David, Jr., 1931- , and **Stirling, William G.**, 1938- , and **Yanowitch, Harold M.**, 1920- , and **Schulz, Edwin J.**, 1934- , and **Phillips, Rubel L.**, 1925- , U.S., fraud. Two Canadian brothers, David Stirling, Jr. and William G. Stirling, were raised in New York and established Stirling Homex Corporation, a company producing modular housing assembled at home-sites. Beginning in 1969 company officers inflated income and profit figures by disclosing large land sales made to shell companies that had no assets to pay for the land. In 1970 and 1971, the firm's stock was sold publicly at prices as high as $55 per share, but the stock plummeted when the company declared bankruptcy in July 1972.

On July 27, 1976, five men were indicted on charges of conspiracy, fraud, and faking U.S. Security and Exchange Comission registration documents. On Jan. 29, 1977, four of the company's officer's were convicted, including 45-year-old David Stirling, Jr., chairman of the board, 38-year-old William Stirling, president, 56-year-old Harold M. Yanowitch, executive vice president, and 42-year-old Edwin J. Schulz. A lawyer, 51-year-old Rubel L. Phillips, of Jackson, Miss., also was convicted. All of the defendants were sentenced on Mar. 11, 1977. David Stirling, Jr., received a one-year term and was fined $10,000. William Stirling received a six-month sentence and was fined $5,000. Yanowitch was given a one-year prison term and fined $2,000. Schulz received a suspended sentence and was fined $2,500. Phillips was sentenced to a ten-month term and fined $5,000. REF.: *CBA.*

Stockport Riots, 1863, Brit., mob. vio. In June 1863, riots were instigated in Stockport, England, when a group of Roman Catholics assaulted a Protestant school and the Protestants retaliated, wrecking an alehouse favored by the Catholics. The riot raged for three days as Protestants destroyed Catholic churches, burning sacred icons and furniture. The riot claimed one life and sixty-seven others were injured, and the fray finally had to be crushed by the military.

REF.: *CBA;* Thomson, *The Story of Scotland Yard.*

Stockton, Port 1854-81, U.S., west. lawman-gunman. Texans Port Stockton and his brother, Ike, both showed an early inclination toward wildness. When 17-year-old Port was charged with attempted murder, Ike helped him escape. Port then drifted for a few years, spent some time in Dodge City, and finally settled in Lincoln County, N.M., where Ike had opened a saloon. In 1876, after marrying, Port moved to Trinidad, Colo., with Ike. In October 1876, in Cimarron, N.M., after shooting and killing an unarmed man, Juan Gonzales, in Lambert's Saloon, Port was arrested. Once again, Ike helped him escape and the pair returned to Trinidad where Port, two months later, shot and killed another unarmed man. Ike came to the rescue and saved Port from the posse that had arrested him.

The Stocktons moved to Animas City, Colo., where Port was appointed city marshal. However, enraged citizens ran him out of town after he shot at a barber who had nicked him with a razor. After a brief stint as marshal in Rico, Colo., a job he lost when his reputation caught up with him, Port and his family moved to a shack near Farmington, N.M. In Farmington, Port joined suspected rustlers Harge Eskridge and James Garret. On Jan. 10, 1881, ten days after the three shot up a New Year's Eve Party, Alf Graves , a rancher who had fought with Port, rode past Stocktons' home with Frank Coe and several other friends. Stockton grabbed a Winchester and demanded that Graves come back and settle the argument. Graves walked back, they spoke briefly, and Graves pulled out a gun, and killed him. Not long after Port's death an outbreak of rustling in the area caused Governor Lew Wallace to issue a reward for Ike Stockton's arrest. In September 1881, in Durango, Colo., Ike was shot in the leg. His leg was amputated and he died shortly thereafter.

REF.: Brown, *An Empire of Silver; CBA;* Coe, *Frontier Fighter.*

Stockton, Richard, 1730-81, U.S., jur. Associate justice on supreme court of New Jersey from 1774-76. He also participated in the Continental Congress in 1776, and signed the Declaration of Independence. REF.: *CBA.*

Stockwell, John Frederick (AKA: **Johnny, Jack Barnard, J.F. Smith**), 1915-34, Brit., rob.-mur. Early on the morning of Aug. 7, 1934, a theater attendant, John Frederick Stockwell, battered the owner of the Eastern Palace Cinema, Dudley Hoard, with an ax. Then 19-year-old Stockwell stole £90 from the building's safe and fled, stashing the stolen money at the Aldgate East Station.

Meanwhile, the victim staggered out of his apartment over the theater and into the cinema where cleaners found him later that morning. By this time Stockwell was traveling by train to Lowestoft. Thinking police would connect him with the cinema murder, he sent a letter back to London, stating he had fled. Next, Stockwell laid some of his clothing and belongings on a beach, articles which were picked up and found, before he sent a note to a post office which explained his intent to commit suicide and asked the postal inspector to give thirty shillings from his post office savings account to his girlfriend.

Stockwell's scheme was uncovered when he checked into the Metropole Hotel in Great Yarmouth and gave his address as Luton, Hertfordshire. The hotel manager, suspicious of the youth, thought it strange that, as a resident of Luton, he did not know that the town was in Bedfordshire. The manager alerted police and Stockwell was arrested. He was tried and convicted at the Old Bailey. He received the death penalty and on Nov. 14, 1934, was executed.

REF.: *CBA;* Shew, *A Second Companion to Murder.*

Stoddard, William Osborn, 1835-1925, U.S., law. enfor. off. U.S. marshal of Arkansas from 1864-66. Originally employed as coeditor of the central Illinois *Gazette,* he had earlier endorsed Abraham Lincoln for U.S. president, and served as Lincoln's private secretary from 1861-64. He later authored several books on Lincoln. Books authored: *Abraham Lincoln, Inside the White House in War Times,* and *The Table Talk of Lincoln.* REF.: *CBA.*

Stokes, Edward S., See: **Fisk, James, Jr.**

Stokoe, John, prom. 1818, Brit., ct. mar. After Emperor Napoléon Bonaparte's defeat at Waterloo in 1815, the British took extraordinary precautions to insure that their prisoner would not escape. He was kept captive under heavy guard on St. Helena, a remote island off the west coast of Africa.

Naval surgeon John Stokoe examined Napoléon during his incarceration. Stokoe was subsequently denounced for failing ot comply with the rules of Sir Hudson Lowe, the British offical in charge of the emperor's imprisonment. Stokoe was accused of relaying information to Napoléon from letters, books, and documents sent to Napoleon from Europe. The doctor was also charged with accepting notes from French inmates and replying to them. Additionally, Stokoe wrote an apparently false health report which stated Napoléon's life was in grave danger and that medical treatment was not readily available. He was accused of insinuating that British authorities were trying to kill Napoléon. Stokoe was also charged with not returning from his call on Napoléon at a specified time, disobeying his superior officer's orders. Because of British public sentiment at the time, the incident was considered very serious and the surgeon was tried by a court-martial in 1818 aboard the British ship, *Conqueror,* found Guilty, and discharged from the military at half his pay.

REF.: *CBA;* Parry, *Some Famous Medical Trials.*

Stolarz, John, b.1895, U.S., mansl. On Aug. 10, 1981, John Stolarz, an elderly Hammond, Ind., resident, met with his lawyer because the retired carpenter and musician wanted to divorce his 70-year-old wife, Helen, and remove her from his will. His attorney advised him that he would have to pay his wife a large amount of alimony. Angry, Stolarz returned to his home where his wife and 33-year-old daughter, Sharon, sat watching television. There, Stolarz shot his wife and then pointed the gun at his daughter, later saying he did not shoot her because "she was too young. She could still have babies." Then he drove to the police station and confessed to the crime.

On Jan. 29, 1982, 87-year-old Stolarz, who at the time was the oldest person ever tried for murder in Indiana, was found Guilty but mentally ill. On Feb. 18, 1982, he was sentenced by Judge James Clement to a six-year prison term at Westville Correctional Institute. Protesting the sentence, the defendant said, "Do you expect me to live that long? I don't want to. I want to die right now. You give me the chair now." Then Stolarz, who played the clarinet, accordion, organ, saxophone, and piano, asked the judge if he would be allowed to play his musical instruments in prison and the judge replied affirmatively. Stolarz was paroled in 1984. REF.: *CBA.*

Stoll, Alice Speed, See: **Robinson, Thomas H., Jr.**

Stoll, Willy Peter, See: **Baader-Meinhof Gang.**

Stompanato, Johnny, See: **Crane, Cheryl.**

Stone, Debra, 1957-87, U.S., (unsolv.) mur. On Mar. 10, 1987, 10-year-old Christopher Stone went to sleep about 10 p.m. in his home in northeast Dallas, Texas. Later that night the boy heard a knock on the apartment door which his mother, 30-year-old Debra Stone, answered. Soundlessly, Stone, the former wife of rock musician band leader Gary Stone, was kidnapped and her car taken from the apartment complex parking lot.

Christopher called his mother's employer the next day when she had not come home by 5 p.m. and Debra Stone's mother reported her missing to police. Early on the morning of Mar. 12, Stone's body was spotted not far from Greenville, Texas by a motorist on his way to work. Stone, a model and promoter for a company that sold resorts, had been raped and strangled and her body was discovered on a barbed wire fence about ten yards from a highway. Police were unable to solve the murder and her former husband, who had been on tour in Florida with his band, Vince Vance and the Valiants, passed a lie detector test. REF.: *CBA*.

Stone, Ellen Maria, 1846-1927, Bul., kid. (vict.) Kidnapped by bandits along with associate while doing missionary work in 1901. She was released in 1902 upon a ransom payment approximating $66,000. After returning home, she gave lectures on her experiences and also on the benefits of temperance. REF.: *CBA*.

Stone, Elton M., 1905-36, U.S., rape-mur. On Nov. 24, 1935, 30-year-old Elton Stone, a paroled ex-convict, murdered 14-year-old Mary Louise Stammer, daughter of Walter Stammer, a prominent Fresno, Calif., lawyer, after waiting outside the family home in the exclusive Fig Garden section of Fresno for three nights to get "one of the Stammers." That night, Stammer's wife drove him to catch an evening train for a business trip to San Bernardino. Daughter Virginia, twelve, went with them, while Mary Louise stayed home with the two youngest children, Joan, seven, and Walter, Jr. When Stammer's wife returned home, she found Mary Louise in an upstairs bedroom, fatally shot through the head. The investigation later indicated that the killer knew the family and the layout of their home, and that he had shot the girl through a window into the room where she sat alone. Police found no shells from the gun, only a single thumb print on a shattered fragment of glass from the back door, which had been broken.

On Jan. 22, 1936, after a two-month investigation, Sheriff George Overholt and a squad of deputies arrested Stone in North Fork, some fifty miles east of Fresno. He was taken to Fresno, where he confessed, then was immediately moved to Sacramento to prevent his being lynched. Having followed a lead on a paroled convict who had lived briefly with his parents a quarter of a mile from the Stammer's, Overholt discovered that Stone had disappeared. He compared Stone's thumb print with that on the glass fragment, found a perfect fit, and found Stone still working as a garage mechanic for the people to whom he had been paroled. He submitted without struggle. "I didn't much care which one of the Stammers I got," Stone told police, "and I don't care what rap I have to take for this. I'd do the same thing again." "That's my business," he added when asked what his grievance against the family was. Stone wore gloves to commit his crime, removing one to shoot at Mary Louise when he saw her reading alone in the music room. He held his hand over the breach to catch the shell, which he later chewed up before throwing away. When Mary Louise collapsed, Stone smashed the glass in the back door and unlatched it from inside, forgetting to replace his glove. He picked up Mary Louise, carried her into the bedroom, pulled down the shades, and beat and raped her. Then he fled through the back door upon hearing the front doorbell. Stammer's wife had forgotten her keys.

Because of the consistent methods, Stone was a suspect in four other rape murders, two of them in San Diego: Virginia Brooks, whose mutilated body was found on a mesa on Feb. 11, 1931; Bertha Bragg, who was raped and murdered in July 1934; Sarah Jean Kelly, seven, who was raped and strangled on Oct. 6, 1935; and Louise Teuber, found hanging from a tree on Black Mountain on Apr. 30, 1931.

Stone's criminal record dated back to 1924, with charges for petty and grand theft, and burglary. In July 1931, he was sent to San Quentin for stealing a car, and on July 7, 1934, was paroled. Convicted of Stammer's murder, Stone was hanged on June 12, 1936. His only regret was having left the finger print that led to his capture. See: **Teuber, Louise**. REF.: *CBA*.

Stone, Harlan Fiske, 1872-1946, U.S., atty. gen.-jur. Associate justice and chief justice of U.S. Supreme Court. He is credited with expanding the role of the U.S. attorney general while serving in that capacity in the administration of Calvin Coolidge, taking direct command of several significant cases. He was appointed to the U.S Supreme Court by Coolidge in 1925, and was named chief justice by President Franklin D. Roosevelt in 1941. His early years as justice were mainly concerned with New Deal programs, which he generally supported despite a basic belief in judicial restraint. He expanded the role of the Bill of Rights in court decisions in *U.S. v. Carolene Products Co.* in 1938, a case concerning federal regulation of milk products. His tenure as chief justice was notable for marked dissention and disagreement among the court's members. He was stricken while on the bench and died the same day.

REF.: *CBA;* Lowenthal, *The Federal Bureau of Investigation;* Nash, *Citizen Hoover;* Mason, *Harlan Fiske Stone: Pillar of the Law;* Overstreet, *The FBI in Our Open Society;* Toledano, *J. Edgar Hoover;* Watters and Gillers, *Investigating the FBI;* Whitehead, *The FBI Story*.

Stone, James Madison Wyatt, d.1880, U.S., mur. The last public hanging of note in Washington, D.C., was one of the most gruesome on record. That James Madison Wyatt Stone was partly educated and almost completely unbalanced was never in contention. Yet this overweight restaurant owner was sent to his death on the scaffold on Apr. 2, 1880, without too much concern on the part of his executioners.

Stone was a self-made man. He had begun working in Washington, D.C., as a messenger and saved enough money to open a small restaurant near the Baltimore and Ohio Station. In 1874, the eatery owner wedded one Alberta Pitcher but the marriage was a disaster from the start. Arguments and sometimes out-and-out brawls became daily rituals for the couple.

Alberta finally left and moved in with her sister Lavinia, a scheming shrike, Stone said, who had caused all of his domestic problems. Lavinia was a vicious prune of a woman, childless, loveless, whose sole ambition had been achieved—the wrecking of his marriage.

Brooding upon this, Stone decided to end his frustration with murder. On the night of Oct. 5, 1878, the seething restaurant owner rammed his 200-pound frame against the front door of Lavinia's home, bursting inside with a bellow and a flashing razor, which he circled in the air like a dervish about to make the kill. He caught the sister on the main floor and with a vicious swipe, slashed her throat. Before Stone could make another pass with the razor, Lavinia broke free and ran outside screaming. Hearing the commotion, Alberta raced downstairs and right into the arms of her estranged husband who, without a word, gashed the woman's throat so deeply that the one movement severed her jugular vein and windpipe and all but beheaded her.

Neighbors hearing the uproar cornered and captured Stone as he ran raving into the street. Quickly convicted and sentenced to hang for the murder of his wife, Stone became as meek and manageable as a puppy in prison. He projected a childlike attitude toward the gallows as workers hammered it into existence in the prison yard. Whenever his skeptical lawyer trudged into his cell, Stone would lead him to the window and point through the bars at the platform and trap, saying almost in gleeful anticipation: "There's where I'll stand and I'll fall through that."

Religion ran deep through Stone's last days. Stone wrote several ministers he knew telling them that he was positive the Lord would allow him into Heaven. In one missive he stated: "I now close and pray that we meet in Paradise. Fare you well." During his last night on earth, Stone found it difficult to sleep, waking up several times to recite fervent prayers. At 8:30 in the morning, Stone gobbled down a huge breakfast. Some time later a guard asked Stone if he enjoyed his meal and he replied: "Why, I took that," and pointed to a quart cup, "full of coffee with a whole chicken fried and potatoes and other trimmings."

A few minutes before it became time for Stone to take his last walk, he launched into a zestful rendition of "I Am Going Home to Jesus Tonight." The other prisoners in the same tier joined in, some breaking into sobs, as the condemned man was well liked. Stone, on the other hand, remained calm, almost blissful, and led the prisoners with a booming voice in singing "Wash Me and I Shall Be Whiter Than Snow." He was still humming the hymn as he sauntered into the prison yard.

Stone made no speech before the hundreds assembled in front of the gallows. He took quiet goodbyes with his lawyer and priest and then stood patiently as the executioner adjusted the rope around his neck and pulled a black cap over his face. The trap was sprung at a little after 1 p.m. Suddenly, the spectators gasped, many shouting: "My God, the rope has broken!"

The overweight body of James Stone plummeted to earth landing on its back, while the head remained in the noose. One physician explained later that the prisoner was so fat that the muscular tissues had become weakened and the slipping rope, after it broke the skin, was accelerated by the fat, reaching and snapping the spinal column. The scene was horrifying. The few women in the yard fainted at the sight of the blood spurting in a stream from the neck, splashing onto the shoes of guards at the base of the gallows, causing several to vomit. The head momentarily remained in the noose, swinging crazily about, and then dropped, bouncing along the ground a few feet from the body and spattering the gallows and witnesses with awful gore.

According to the Washington *Evening Star,* "Some of the physicians immediately went to the body and while the blood was spurting from the neck felt for the pulsations of the heart and they stated that there was a muscular movement for about two minutes. Dr. Crook picked up the head, the black cap having fallen off, and as he did so he noticed that the lips moved and the features appeared calm."

An undertaker named Wright who had brought along a handsome imitation rosewood coffin with polished handles and trimming was beside himself. The casket had a glass panel through which friends and relatives could get a last glimpse of the deceased before it was covered at his grave side, a funeral custom in those days. Wright was alarmed that the decapitation made the glass panel impractical. He solved his problem, after complaining long and loud to an embarrassed executioner, by affixing Stone's head to his body in a makeshift manner and then painting the glass panel black.

REF.: *CBA;* Mencken, *By the Neck.*

Stone, John, 1806-40, U.S., mur. The first man to be legally executed in Chicago, John Stone arrived in that city in 1838. He brought with him a record of prison sentences in his native Canada for murder and robbery and in New York for stealing horses. In 1839, the *Chicago American* newspaper warned "suspicious loafers about the city" that they "had better...make themselves scarce, or the city watch will be at their heels." Stone, who sometimes worked chopping wood, spent most of his time at liquor stores or at a billiard hall.

About a year after the thinly veiled newspaper warning, Stone was arrested on charges of raping and murdering Lucretia Thompson, wife of a Cook County farmer. Evidence against him included a piece of his flannel shirt found near the victim's body, and the murder weapon, a club that had Thompson's hair on it. Stone also burned the clothes he had worn the day of Thompson's disappearance, and a witness claimed Stone threatened Thompson with sexual assault. Stone, who pleaded innocent, was found Guilty, and sentenced to hang. On July 10, 1840, the handcuffed, chained Stone, escorted by 260 men, was taken in a wagon to a spot on the lake shore about three miles from the courthouse. Colonel Seth Johnson presided over the hanging. Stone protested his innocence to the last, claiming two men were involved in the murder but refusing to name them. Finally, Stone was hanged. REF.: *CBA.*

Stone, John T., c.1933- , U.S., fraud. From 1961 to 1970, John T. Stone worked as an officer of the Janeff Credit Corporation in Madison, Wis. During the next three years, he kept his ties to the financial firm and also set up his own companies. By late 1973, Stone had consolidated many of his businesses under the corporate name Recreation International. To finance his companies, Stone obtained nearly limitless credit. When banks refused him further backing, Stone's shady financing methods caused one Wisconsin bank, Algoma Bank, to collapse—the first Wisconsin bank to fold in twenty-eight years.

Stone was brought to trial before a federal court in Wisconsin, charged with securities fraud, bank kickbacks, filing fraudulent financial statements, and failing to register stock. Convicted in July 1976, he was sentenced to one year and one day in prison and fined $50,000. The same month Stone published an autobiography, *Going for Broke, How I Built an Empire from Scratch and Lost $20 Million,* with a percentage of the royalties earmarked to repay some of his bank debts. William O'Connor, the president of Algoma bank who arranged for Stone's two lines of credit, both for $1 million, was convicted for involvement in a kickback scheme with Stone and sentenced to ninety days in prison. REF.: *CBA.*

Stone, Lawrence Clinton, 1910- , U.S., mur. Lawrence Stone, a 24-year-old emergency relief worker, had been drinking on the afternoon of Oct. 14, 1934. A powerfully built man, he was working on a street-widening project on Third Avenue in Mount Vernon, N.Y., in front of the exclusive Pelhutchinson apartments, where he had formerly been employed. In the apartment lobby and on the terrace, 5-year-old Nancy Jean Costigan, who was visiting her aunt, Mrs. Russell Newhouse, played with a rubber ball. Building superintendent Cyril Gildon and hallmen Carl Hutchinson and James Nash saw her playing there as late as 4:30 that afternoon. At 5 p.m., however, Hutchinson was on his way down to the basement to regulate the furnace when he found his usual entrance locked. He took the elevator down to find a small pool of blood on the floor, then followed a trail of blood to the ping-pong room, where he saw a rubber ball. The trail continued down a metal staircase to a subbasement and the furnace, in front of which was a large bloodstain. On his way out to call the police, Hutchinson glimpsed a figure in the shadowy recesses of the room.

Less than a block from the apartment building, the patrol car answering the call collided with another car. As the injured policemen were climbing into the ambulance, Stone, intoxicated, climbed in, saying he had been injured. Although his shirt and trousers were covered with blood, physicians found no injuries. At Mount Vernon police headquarters, Stone was charged with murder. Although he admitted to having seen the little girl that afternoon, he protested his innocence. A tenant at the apartment building, however, later identified Stone as the man she saw playing with Nancy at about 4 p.m. Police found Nancy's charred body in the oil-burning furnace, burned beyond recognition. She was identified by a small gold ring, her wristwatch, and fragments of clothing. Her purse was found near the basement entrance where she had apparently struggled and dropped it.

Stone pleaded guilty, was convicted of second-degree murder, and sentenced to fifty years to life in prison at Sing Sing by New York Supreme Court justice William F. Bleakley. He was later transferred to a state hospital. REF.: *CBA.*

Stone, Leslie George, 1913-37, Brit., mur. During the early 1900s, Ruby Keen, a factory worker, and George Leslie Stone, a sandpit laborer, were lovers until Stone left Leighton Buzzard, England, to join the army. When he returned to his hometown during the week of Apr. 5, 1937, on a medical discharge from the service, the 24-year-old Stone found that his sweetheart was engaged to a police constable.

On Apr. 11, he put on a new suit and went out with 23-year-old Keen to a pub where observers later said that he begged the girl to leave her fiancé. After an evening of drinking, the two went for a walk along The Firs, a lover's lane in the town. There they began arguing and the angered Stone strangled the woman with her scarf. Her body was found the next morning and Scotland Yard was immediately asked for assistance. Stone voluntarily came to police to admit he had been with the girl the previous night, but said he dropped her off at home. Police took casts of impressions made in the soil by knees and later examined Stone's new suit. They found soil samples that matched the sandy earth at the murder scene and a silk fiber similar to the dead girl's dress was also found on the suit. Stone was tried in June, convicted of murder, and sentenced to death. On Aug. 13 he was hanged at Pentonville Prison.

REF.: Browne and Tullett, *The Scalpel of Scotland Yard; CBA;* Cohen, *One Hundred True Crime Stories;* Cuthbert, *Science and the Detection of Crime;* Shew, *A Companion to Murder;* Tullett, *Strictly Murder.*

Stone, Loy Dean, and **Stone, Louise**, prom. 1977, Case of, U.S., witchcraft-mur. Just before Halloween 1977 a television interview featured Loy Dean Stone, forty-nine, and his wife, Louise Stone, forty-nine, both self-proclaimed witches. After seeing the program, teenagers in the small Panhandle town of Dimmitt, Texas, rode out to the Stones' farm on Halloween night. The sheriff came out once to chase away the carloads of teenagers. After the officer left, a pickup truck carrying five youths pulled into the Stones' driveway and was turning around when shots rang out. Fifteen-year-old Roxanne Casas, of Dimmitt's Chicano community, was wounded and died in the hospital an hour later. Two other passengers were slightly wounded. The driver and another passenger were unharmed. The sheriff returned to the Stones' home where he found "no evidence of foul play." The Stones said they had heard no shots.

Later that night, the sheriff found a shotgun in the Stones' house that had been recently fired. On Nov. 3, 1977, the Stones were arrested and charged with one count each of murder and two counts each of aggravated assault. They pleaded innocent to all charges. The Stones' trial, which began on Jan. 7, 1980, was moved to Plainview, forty-three miles from Dimmitt, because of hostility in Dimmitt's Chicano community. On Feb. 1, 1980, the Stones were acquitted of criminal charges. A wrongful death civil suit brought against them by Raul and Karen Casas, parents of the slain girl, was settled out of court on May 13, 1980. The suit was dismissed by Dimmitt District Judge Van Stovall. Though the terms were not revealed, the family had sought damages of $77,556.71. REF.: *CBA*.

Stone, O.M., and **Turner, J.W.**, prom. 1900, U.S., fraud. During the early 1900s a swindler skilled in telegraphy and electricity set up an illicit operation in Chicago. Using the guise of a pool room, wiretappers O.M. Stone and an accomplice, J.W. Turner set up their instruments and tapped into the lines of the Western Union Telegraph Co. to collect racing results. The crooks, pretending to scoop all other news sources, sold the information. They were detected by Detective Clifton Wooldridge, who arrested Stone on Jan. 3, 1900.

On July 22, 1900, Stone was tried on charges of running a phony pool room, and received a heavy fine from Judge Baker. Soon after his release, Stone established another wiretapping business and when Wooldridge discovered the cheat he ordered Stone to cut all of his illegal wires and personally supervised him doing so.

REF.: *CBA;* Wooldridge, *Hands Up*.

Stone, Scott C., b.1866, U.S., rape-mur. On Aug. 23, 1924, in Baldwin Hills, Calif., sisters May Martin, twelve, and Nina Martin, nine, went to visit their grandmother, Carrie Lovelace, whose house was a short walk from their home. At 6 p.m., they were seen along the route home, laughing and talking. For the next two weeks, about 300 police officers, detectives, deputy sheriffs, Boy Scouts, and concerned neighbors, combed a three-square-mile area and found nothing. May and Nina's mother, Mrs. Paul Buus, searched daily for almost six months, repeatedly telling friends, "I know my children need me—*I must find them.*" Then, on Feb. 5, 1925, rancher Leo B. Saulque seeded one side of his field and was about to start the other when he noticed a small depression amid high grass and discovered the girls' bodies in a stream bed.

The decomposing bodies lay close together in a ditch, hidden from the road by weeds and brush. The only discernible mark of violence was May's broken ankle. Their clothing was torn, and, from the condition of their jaws and the positions of their bodies, it was obvious that they had been strangled. They had also been sexually assaulted. Scott C. Stone, a night watchman, was tried and convicted of killing the girls. Having lured them into his car with the promise of candy, he raped and murdered them in the nearby field. Stone initially faced the death penalty on two counts of murder, but, after losing his appeal to the Supreme Court, California Governor C.C. Young commuted his sentence to life in prison in response to the urgings of District Attorney Asa Keyes and the deputies who prosecuted the case. For undisclosed reasons, Keyes asked for commutation because of the circumstantial nature of the evidence that convicted Stone. REF.: *CBA*.

Stone, Thaddeus, prom. 1914, U.S., embez. By 1914, Thaddeus Stone of Dumont, N.J., had worked as a cashier for Moore & Terry brokerage firm in New York for twenty years. But then he became obsessed with gambling and he absconded with $10,500 from his firm to finance his bets. He later said he took the money right to a crap game on Broadway, and every penny was gone within twenty minutes. The appalled would-be gambler went into hiding at his New Jersey house, where detectives found him several weeks later. Stone was found Guilty of robbery and sent to prison for five years.

REF.: *CBA;* Nash, *Among the Missing*.

Stone, William, c.1603-60, U.S., rebel. Named governor of Maryland by Lord Baltimore in 1648 but was compelled to resign by English puritan parlimentary commission in 1654. Upon the command of Baltimore, he gathered supporters and engaged the puritans at the battle of Severn in 1655. After being wounded, defeated and seized, he was prosecuted and received the death sentence. He was permitted to live, however, and served on the governor's council in 1657. REF.: *CBA*.

Stone, William Joel (AKA: **Gum-Shoe Bill**), 1848-1918, U.S., polit. corr. Dominated Democratic party of Missouri as U.S. congressman from 1885-91, governor from 1893-97, and as U.S. senator from 1903-18. He earned the "Gum Shoe" moniker for eluding formal charges of political corruption from 1902-03. REF.: *CBA*.

Stonehouse, John Thomas (AKA: **Joseph Arthur Markham, Donald Mildoon**), 1925- , and **Buckley, Sheila**, 1951- , Brit., theft-forg.-fraud. A member of Parliament, John Thomas Stonehouse, desired to become prime minister of England after joining the House of Commons in 1957. When his party fell from power in 1970, Stonehouse became a businessman.

In the next five years he established twenty unsuccessful companies, which he propped up by pumping money from one to another. Eventually he sunk more than £1 million into debt, was hounded by banks and credit card firms for £375,000, and was responsible for personally guaranteeing £729,000. In 1973, Stonehouse, forty-eight, decided to engineer his disappearance with the help of his mistress and secretary, 22-year-old Sheila Buckley. Stonehouse created two new identities for himself, Markham and Mildoon, and set up nine new bank accounts in Switzerland and Australia under the new names.

On Nov. 16, 1973, the businessman pretended to drown in Miami, Fla., and after flying to San Francisco he arrived in Melbourne, Aus., on Nov. 27. There, his charade was detected by a bank clerk, 22-year-old Bryan King. On Nov. 28, King opened a new account of $21,500 (Australian) at the Bank of New Zealand for Stonehouse, alias Donald Mildoon, who said he was emigrating to New Zealand. After lunch that same day, King noticed Stonehouse leaving another bank and depositing more money at the bank where he worked. King alerted his superior, who called the other bank where officials said they had no customer named Mildoon, but a recent British resident, Markham, had been withdrawing large amounts of money.

King's bank called the Victoria State Police who immediately began trailing Stonehouse. One officer noticed that the suspect regularly bought the London paper and the officer saw two articles about missing people, Stonehouse and Lord Lucan. Victoria police requested pictures of Lucan and Stonehouse and, on Dec. 25, 1973, arrested Stonehouse and found a letter from his mistress in his pocket.

Before his arrest, Stonehouse had called his wife and persuaded her to bring his lover to Australia, which she did. In the phone conversation, which was being taped by police, he explained how he had faked his death and was now living under another name. The two women arrived, and after a confrontation, his wife left. Buckley and Stonehouse were sent back to England and their trial at Old Bailey began in April 1976. On Aug. 6, 1976, Stonehouse was convicted on fourteen charges of theft, forgery, and fraud charges and sentenced to seven years in prison. Buckley was convicted on charges of aiding Stonehouse and received a two-year suspended sentence. After serving three years of his sentence, Stonehouse was released and he and Buckley married in February 1981. REF.: *CBA*.

Stoneley, John William, 1943- , and **Sykes, George Ernest** (AKA: **Bill**), 1941- , Brit., mur. In October 1964, between about 10 p.m. and 11 p.m., two Southampton men robbing a taxi driver beat him to death with an iron pipe. A 21-year-old unemployed cable maker, John William Stoneley, and a 23-year-old dairy worker, George Ernest Sykes, left the cabbie, 60-year-old George Newbery, dying close to a road about seven miles north of Southampton.

Soon after the murder Stoneley used the victim's postal savings account book to withdraw £3 from the post office at Woolston, and the criminal left a distinctive fingerprint on the withdrawal form. When Stoneley was later caught burglarizing a garage, police matched his fingerprints to the print found on the savings book. Stoneley implicated Sykes and though both admitted robbery each blamed the other for the killing. They were tried and Stoneley was convicted of capital murder and sentenced to death, but the sentence was later commuted to a life term in prison. Sykes also was found Guilty, and sentenced to life imprisonment.

REF.: Butler, *Murderers' England; CBA;* Simpson, *Forty Years of Murder.*

Stone of Destiny, See: **Hamilton, Ian**.

Stoner, George, See: **Rattenbury, Alma Victoria**.

Stoner, J.B., 1922- , U.S., consp.-bomb. On June 29, 1958, dynamite exploded near the Bethel Baptist Church in a mostly black neighborhood in the Birmington, Ala., area. The blast smashed the windows of the church, a meeting place for civil rights activists, and windows of surrounding homes. White supremacist J.B. Stoner of Marietta, Ga., was indicted in 1977 and arrested as a conspirator in the case. Stoner, who claimed he was "proud to be a white racist," was convicted on May 14, 1980, as a conspirator in the bombing and sentenced to a ten-year prison term. REF.: *CBA*.

Wanda Stopa and lover Yeremya Kenley Smith.

Stopa, Wanda (AKA: **Glaskoff**), 1899-1925, U.S., suic.-mur. Wanda Stopa, of Chicago's Little Poland section, became an assistant district attorney right out of college. But then Stopa, who had always thought she had the soul of a poet, discovered the Jazz Age and the Bohemian lifestyle. She met an art-minded Russian émigré, Vladimir Glaskoff, whom she quickly married. When reality did not meet Stopa's expectations, she turned her attention to Yeremya Kenley Smith, an advertising executive who enjoyed having the awestruck young woman at his feet while he talked philosophy. While she fell in love, she also became a morphine addict.

Smith gave Stopa money to live in Greenwich Village. But when Smith's payments stopped, she held a party for all her new friends and announced that she was leaving for Chicago "to kill a woman—perhaps a man...I'll probably kill myself afterwards." Her appreciative audience thought she was joking, but she arrived in Chicago on Apr. 24, 1924, and immediately took a cab to Smith's Palos Park country estate. She walked into the house and confronted Mrs. Smith, who just called her "ridiculous." Henry Manning, a gardener who had seen Stopa enter, heard her shoot at Mrs. Smith and miss. His employer leaped from her sick bed, flew out the window, and ran to a neighbor's house while Stopa continued to fire after her. One of her bullets hit the old gardener. Stopa laid down the gun and left the house, going right to a train station.

Two days later, a man passing through the lobby of the Hotel Statler in Detroit recognized Wanda Stopa from newspaper photographs. The police found her at the hotel, registered under the name Glaskoff. As they reached her room, she was near death after having taken poison. She died soon afterward.

REF.: *CBA;* Nash, *Look For the Woman;* ____, *Murder, America.*

Stopes, Marie, prom. 1923, Brit., libel. Marie Stopes was a Quaker woman who authored an exposition on birth control, titled *Married Love and Radiant Motherhood.* Stopes, somewhat ahead of her time, argued that joyful sex was encumbered by the constant dread of unwanted children. She advocated artificial birth control and opened a clinic in the London slums to dispense rubber diaphragms and literature on conception to poor working-class women. Dr. H.G. Sutherland, a Catholic, opposed Stopes on moral and religious grounds. In his own book, *Birth Control,* he referred to Stopes' work as a "monstrous campaign of birth control."

Stopes filed a libel suit against Sutherland but the judge's prejudicial attitudes influenced the jury to return a verdict against her. However, the decision was reversed on appeal. The House of Lords considered the matter and restored the original verdict. The case had dragged on for two and a half years. The great irony of the *Stopes vs. Sutherland* affair came years later. Posing as a poor charwoman, Marie Stopes was fitted for a contraceptive device by the same gynecologist who had criticized her views on birth control at the trial. REF.: *CBA*.

Storeyville, 1897-1917, U.S., pros. The officially designated Red Light District of New Orleans from 1897 to 1917, Storeyville took its name from Sidney Storey, a city committeeman who mapped out the district in 1896. This legendary area became the core of unrestricted prostitution and also boasted a wide reputation for being the hub of jazz. New Orleans, by the early 1890s, had become infamous as *the* center of American prostitution and, in fact, was referred to as the "Queen of Prostitution" throughout the U.S. The city's clergy, enraged at this image, mounted a strenuous campaign to obliterate prostitution.

One prime mover in the movement to reform the image of New Orleans as the capital of vice was Methodist minister Reverend E.A. Clay, who, on Oct. 30, 1892, mounted his church pulpit and declared war on the scarlet ladies, fulminating: "I am going to speak of those houses of darkness and death and blackness and despair, of those human slaughterhouses, of the gravest things of all the pitfalls in the way of virtue in this great city...There are over five hundred of those dark places scattered throughout this city from Carrollton to the barracks, and they run the gamut of condition from the palatial palaces of velvet and gilt down to the veriest stinking and reeking pesthold of four bags and noiseomeness. Fifteen hundred angels of death and damnation inhabit these places. They affect and imperil the virtue and honor of every girl in the city."

Supporting the clergy were several aldermen unusually not on the payroll of the assignation houses, chief of whom was Sidney Storey, who drew up a plan in 1896 to contain the spreading red light districts. His ordinance was amended and ratified on July 6, 1897. The new law restricted the red light district to a thirty-eight block area adjoining Canal Street. The boundaries were St. Louis, Basin, Robertson, and Customhouse streets. Much to the eternal disgust of the lofty-minded alderman who sponsored this law, the district was popularly and forever known as Storeyville.

The new red light district became the headquarters of not only the most accomplished tarts in the country, but the hub of gamblers, pimps, homosexuals, footpads, burglars, bank robbers, and the earliest jazz musicians. In fact, the giants of jazz got their first jobs playing in the sporting houses. These were distinguished from the whorehouses where strict sex was the business. Brothels were singularly noted for their richly stocked bars as well as their amply endowed ladies.

It was in the sporting houses where small black bands entertained wealthy whites and their tantalizing trollops. The very kings of jazz were found inside the ornate parlors—Louis Armstrong, whose first flame, a red light girl named Daisy Parker, played dozens of sporting houses. (Daisy favored greeting Armstrong with a brickbat if he came home too late.) The great horn player would never forget the alluring strumpets "standing in their doorways nightly in their fine and beautiful negligees—faintly calling to the boys as they passed their cribs—lot of the prostitutes lived in different sections of the city and would come down to Storeyville just like they had a job...There were different shifts for them...Sometimes two prostitutes would share the rent in the same crib together...One would work in the day and the other would beat out the night shift...And business was so good in those days with the fleet of sailors and the crews from those big ships that come in the Mississippi River from all over the world—kept them very, very busy."

Danny Parker, Alphone Sicou, Jelly Roll Morton, Spencer Williams, and the immortal Bunk Johnson all played their jazz for the likes of Lulu White in her famed Mahogany Hall or the gilded sporting house of Countess Willie Piazza, or the seemingly endless houses operated by Tom Anderson who was surely the uncrowned king of Storeyville.

Anderson ran so many bordellos, saloons, and gambling dens that he had a hard time keeping track of the roster of whores in his employ. In his runaway ledgers he wrote their monikers and weekly earning ability. Their curiously appropriate names linger still: Meathouse Mary, Bang Zang, Birdy Nora, Smoke Stack, Boogers, Pupsy, Lily the Crip, Miss Thing, Boxcar Shorty, Coke Eye Laura, Buck Tooth Rena, Cold Blooded Carrie, Big Piggy, Nakes Mouf, Bodidily, Linker-Top, Tee Nome, Raw Head, Big Boo Boo, Roody Doody, Yellow Gal, Steel Arm, Knock on the Wall, Bull Frog Sonny, Tenderloin Thelma. There was no end to them and to the boom of the sex palaces that Storeyville enjoyed for more than two decades.

Thomas C. Anderson began as a saloon owner and later became the boss of the Fourth Ward. The Real Thing on Rampart Street, the Stag on Gravier Street, and the Arlington on Rampart, were Anderson saloons. The boss held court each day in the Annex, his headquarters, where he issued his daily decrees. Writing for *Collier's Weekly* in 1908, one-time con man Will Irwin stated: "No large city in the United States gets such poor returns for the public money expended as New Orleans. It is ill-paved, ill-policed, behind in municipal improvements; the public money is needed for a thousand and one sinecure jobs. By the same token, no other city of the country runs vice of every kind so wide open. Tom Anderson has been a great help. Highly prosperous himself, he has not failed to divide up with the power which enabled him to be prosperous; and he has helped to make the saloon-keepers, the gamblers and the brothel-keepers generous."

Anderson lived to prove that there were unlimited opportunities in vice. He died in 1931 with a depleted estate of $120,000. There might have been more, but it was never located. Such was Anderson's aversion to banks that he kept his ill-gotten loot in old tin cans, hoes, and rolled-up newspapers. Much of this was thrown out as junk upon his death.

The boss pimp was noted for his love of jazz men and can be credited with hiring the first officially recognized jazz band in the city to entertain the guests of a brothel in which he had a generous interest. The Spasm Band was composed of Emile "Stalebread Charles" Lacomb, who played a fiddle made from a cigar box, harmonicist Willie "Cajun" Bussey, Charley Stien, who played bells, cow horns, and jiggled pebbles, and whistle players who also doubled on homemade horns, Emile "Whiskey" Benrod, Frank "Monk" Bussey, and an ubiquitous fellow named Warm Gravy. Chinee played a makeshift bull fiddle and the singer of the group was Harry Gregson. The crooner could not afford a real megaphone so he sang into a piece of gas pipe. It was the hooting, hollering Spasm Band which first introduced the "hi-de-hi" and "hi-de-ho" to white jazz enthusiasts. This weird conglomerate of sound was called the "Razzy Dazzy Spasm Band."

When another band in 1900, imitators of the successful original, was engaged by Jack Robinson of the Haymarket on Customhouse Street, they billed themselves exactly as the original band. Customers revolted, hurling raw eggs and fruit, along with more lethal bricks. Hurriedly, the management made up a new sign advertising the "Razzy Dazzy Jazzy Band," and thus, out of commercial desperation, jazz as a word was born.

For seventeen years, Storeyville went full blast, beginning at the turn of the century. The scores of brothels and their hundreds of inmates were freely and widely advertised in such risqué publications as the *Blue Book,* the *Mascot,* and the *Sunday Sun.* Any visitor to New Orleans could find his sexual pleasure by merely purchasing any of these periodicals and thus locate the harlot haven of his tastes. (These publications are now so rare that collectors pay as high as $500 per copy.)

The news items on the various madams and courtesans bordered on the ridiculous and really served as ads for the brothels and their inhabitants. From the *Mascot:* "Miss Bessie Lamothe, 9 South Franklin Street, wishes for friends to understand that she did not announce that she received in a pink dress on New Years, but she desires it to be understood that she receives every night in a robe, blanc de nuit." Another of the same period from the same publication: "Miss Carrie Freeman has favored us with a recent photograph of herself taken since she adopted her new diet of spaghetti. Carrie no longer sees ghosts but she, at times, sees spirits."

Most brazen of the scandal sheets was the *Sunday Sun,* which featured bold ads for saloons, gambling dens and, of course, bordellos. The four-page weekly featured a running column of whoredom gossip called Scarlet World. Some excerpts of 1904:

"Miss Josie Arlington is suffering with a bad cold but she is on deck all the same attending to business...Tillie Thurman or Carlisle, who keeps a joint on Basin Street, near the corner of Conti, next to Pelican Four's truck house, is certainly a pelican of the first water. Boys, if you are out looking for a good time and wish to save a doctor's bill we sincerely advise you to give the above establishment all the room possible. When it comes down to the real thing in the way of low-down tarts, then this is the house you are looking for...Clara Henderson is now occupying the beautiful cottage at 1554 Conti Street and has living with her Cleona Miller, a lovely blonde who is in the 20 karate class. Clara is well-known by the founders and is a thorough good fellow.

"Lou Raymond, better known as Kackling Lou, ought to attend to her own business and quit poking her nose into her neighbor's affairs. The way Kackling Lou has put the devil in a couple of young girls who were doing nicely with a neighbor of hers, was a caution. Such conduct on the part of a woman as old as Kackling Lou is most horrifying. Now, will you be good, you ugly old girl and attend to your own business?...Alda Dugaot, one of Lulu White's finest, has a good one on her staff. Alda is now wearing a pair of $600 diamond earrings. Alda, they are very becoming...Stella Clements, who now calls herself Stella Moore, has taken the name of a performer in Haverly's Minstrels. Are you going to do the Couche, Couche Stella?

"Jessie Brown is expecting two girls from Atlanta, Ga....Last Tuesday, George S. Roddy, advance agent of King Dodo, which is now playing at the Tulane Theater, was out in the Tenderloin acting anything but a gentleman. He went into Maestri's row of low prostitutes, bilking them. One of the women grabbed his hat and had it not been for the officer on the beat, Mr. Roddy could have fared badly. This is the recognized 50 cents colony. George, that is below the standard; did you want it cheaper?...Truxie Leroy is the latest arrival in Fanny Lambert's. Truxie comes from Evansville, Ind. She has been named the Little Casino of the house.

"Bertha Golden, the landlady who presides at 213 Basin Avenue, is one of the best-looking women on that thoroughfare. Bertha conducts a swell house and is known all over the country. She is surrounded by a bevy of choice girls and it goes without saying that they are beauts, entertainers, dancers, etc....Estelle, who occupies rooms at 305 Losin Ave., near Bienville, has an idea of business. Estelle is a pronounced brunette and a genuine Parisian, a buxom and very pretty woman. Estelle has many friends who admire her for the many good qualities she possesses. She is an entertainer, speaks several languages, and is a thorough good fellow. A visit to her will not be regretted...There is a drugstore at the corner of Customhouse and Marais Streets that is selling certain drugs that are prohibited by law except when ordered by a physician. It is not lawful to sell cocaine but it is sold here just the same."

The *Blue Book* was to the residents of Storeyville what the first "400" listing was to the elite of New York. Reportedly backed by the multi-talented Tom Anderson, the *Blue Book* was printed on blue-tinted paper and was an annual directory of the bordellos which sold for 25¢. Everyone in the city seemed to be selling it from 1902 on, from bartenders to bellhops, from steamboat stewards to train conductors. Containing a complete list of every whore in Storeyville, with addresses and descriptions of their physical and lascivious character, the *Blue Book* became the bible of the bagnios.

Only the finest assignation houses were profiled in detail within the *Blue Book,* its publishers careful to print upon its cover the warning that "this book must not be mailed," in order to avoid breaking postal regulations. Some of the stars featured in the *Blue Book* included (from its pages): "Eunice Deering, at the corner of Basin and Conti Streets. Known as the idol of the society and club boys. Aside from the grandeur of her establishment, she has a score of beautiful women...Margaret Bradford who resides at 1559 Iberville Street. Pretty women, good time and sociability has been adopted as the counter sign of Miss Bradford's new and costly home...The Cairo at 320 North Franklin. Run by Snooks Randella. Snooks has the distinction of keeping one of the liveliest and most elaborately furnished establishments in the city, where an array of beautiful women and good times reign supreme."

Of Martha Clark, who operated a house at 227 North Basin, the *Blue Book* commented: "Her women are known for their cleverness and beauty. Also, in being able to entertain the most fastidious of mankind." There was Diane and Norma who received at 213-15 North Basin and whose "names have become known on both continents, because everything goes as it will, and those that cannot be satisfied must surely be of a queer nature." At 1310 Conti Street, one could find Madame Louise Dreyfus: "She has some of the most beautiful and select girls in the District—one of whom is Chiquita, the Spanish Beauty." There was the celebrated House of All Nations, officially known as The Studio, at 331-33 North Basin where Emma Johnson reigned. "Everything goes here. Pleasure is the watchword. Remember the name Johnson."

The delights offered by Countess Willie V. Piazza at 317 North Basin were guaranteed to banish depression. It was "one place in the Tenderloin district you can't very well afford to miss. The Countess Piazza has made it a study to try to make everyone jovial who visits her house. If you have the blues, the Countess and her girls can cure them. She has, without doubt, the most handsome and intelligent octoroons in the United States. You should see them; they are all entertainers. The Countess wishes it to be known that while her mansion is peerless in every respect, she only serves the 'amber fluid.'"

The rich rake could discover the pleasure-dome of Alice Williams "who has a lot of jolly good girls as guests who are the 'goods' as one would term them. Don't overlook Alice." And, not last but apt, there was Lizette Smith who ran a sex emporium at 217 North Basin. Lizette also "has some of the most beautiful and select girls in the district, who know how to do things as you like 'em."

A few of the sporting houses, especially the most expensive, published brochures of their own, selling them as souvenir booklets for as much as $1. Perhaps the most lavish of these advertised the New Mahogany Hall, "a picture of which appears on the cover of this souvenir, which was erected specially for Miss Lulu White at a cost of $40,000. The house is built of marble and is four story; containing five parlors, all handsomely furnished, and fifteen bedrooms. Each room has a bath with hot and cold water and extension closets.

"The elevator, which was built for two, is the latest style. The entire house is steam heated and is the handsomest house of its kind. It is the only one where you can get three shots for your money—

The shot upstairs,
The shot downstairs,
And the shot in the room.

"This famous West Indian octoroon first saw the light of day thirty-one years ago. Arriving in the country at a rather tender age, and having been fortunately gifted with a good education it did not take long for her to find out what the other sex was in search of.

"In describing Miss Lulu, as she is most familiarly called, it would not amiss to say that besides possessing an elegant form she has beautiful black hair and blue eyes, which has justly gained for her the title of the 'Queen of the Demi-Monde'...She has made a feature of boarding none but the fairest of girls—those gifted with nature's best charms, and would, under no circumstances, have any but that class in her house.

"As an entertainer, Miss Lulu stands foremost, having made a life-long study of music and literature. She is well read and one that can interest anybody and make a visit to her place a continued round of pleasure."

In 1916, the mounting number of reformers began to demand that New Orleans leaders close down the now legendary Storeyville, stating that the vice district made New Orleans a national disgrace. New Orleans had, because of Storeyville's international reputation, become a "city of whores, gamblers and ruffians," according to one civic leader. Storeyville must go, demanded the reformers. Petitions were gathered, endless sermons were preached in church pulpits, and a large number of voters began to threaten politicians with removal at the polls if the vice district was not shut down.

First the city council attempted to mollify the crusaders by segregating black prostitutes from white bordellos, but this blatantly racist move caused only more protest. Finally, Mayor Martin Behrman (1904-20) bowed to public pressure and, on Oct. 2, 1917, introduced an ordinance to the city council that would abolish Storeyville as the official vice district of New Orleans. On Nov. 12, 1917, the district was legally closed and it became unlawful for brothels to operate within the city limits.

Thousands of prostitutes and pimps streamed out of the area, leaving the city for points north and west, seeking better opportunities in the skin trade. Some diehards remained, including Gertrude Dix, a madam who actually attempted to legally fight the ordinance, attempting to preserve her bordello by trying to obtain a restraining order. This move failed, and Madam Dix and her five ladies were arrested two days after the ordinance went into effect. The red lights were turned off throughout the district, and Storeyville was no more. See: **Arlington, Josie**.

REF.: Asbury, *The French Quarter;* Berendt, *Jazz, a Photo History;* Cable, *Old Creole Days;* Carter, *The Past as Prelude; CBA;* Fremaux, *New Orleans Characters;* Huber, *New Orleans;* Keepnews and Grauer, *A Pictorial History of Jazz;* Laughlin, *New Orleans and Its Living Past;* Longstreet, *Sportin' House;* McGinty, *A History of the Great Reform Movement in New Orleans;* Ripley, *Social Life in Old New Orleans;* Rose, *News Orleans Jazz;* Stearns, *The Story of Jazz;* Szarkowski, *Storeyville Portraits;* Tinker, *Creole City.*

Storm, Theodor (Hans Theodor Woldsen Storm), 1817-88, Ger., lawyer. Served as magistrate in Heiligenstadt from 1856-64, and held other various judicial positions in Helsum from 1864-80. REF.: *CBA.*

Storms, Charles, d.1881, U.S., west. gunman. As a professional gunfighter, Charles Storms was envious of the reputation of gunslingers such as Bat Masterson and Wild Bill Hickok. When Jack McCall walked into Carl Mann's Saloon in Deadwood, Ariz., on Aug. 2, 1876, and shot Hickok in the back of the head, Storms, sitting nearby, grabbed one of Hickok's pearl-handled pistols for a souvenir.

However, Storms' career as a gunfighter never blossomed. He lived through several gunfights in Deadwood, but his career ended in Tombstone, Ariz., on Feb. 21, 1881. After drinking whiskey, Storms argued with Luke Short, a professional gambler, and eventually slapped him. Bat Masterson interceded and separated the two men before any shots were fired. An hour later Storms reappeared and grabbed Short as though he intended to pull him into the street. As Storms was attempting to draw his pistol, Short quickly drew his and shot Storms in the chest killing him instantly. Short was found Not Guilty on grounds of self defense and released.

REF.: *CBA;* Nash, *Bloodletters and Badmen.*

Storrs, George Henry (AKA: Mystery of Gorse Hall), prom. 1909, Brit., (unsolv.) mur. The curious behavior of 49-year-old mill owner George Storrs of Dukinfeld, Cheshire, began on Sept. 10, 1909. He and his wife and niece were sitting at dinner when a bullet crashed through the window. Leaping up, he saw a dark figure running into the darkness. When the police came, Storrs hesitated before saying he did not know who shot at him. But he promptly installed an alarm on the roof. Six weeks later, on Oct. 31, the alarm rang, and the police guard, who was on the last day of his assignment there, came flying. The red-faced Storrs apologized and said he was just testing the bell. The next day, guard gone, a man got into the house through the scullery window. Storrs came from the dining room, and the intruder stabbed the mill owner about fifteen times and escaped through the scullery window. Storrs died by the time the police arrived.

The police arrested Storrs's cousin, Cornelius Howard, on the basis of his wife's and niece's description. Howard, however, was in jail at the time of the murder and was acquitted. Mark Wilde, a man who was staying nearby, was then arrested. But he, too, was acquitted. The matter rested there.

REF.: Brock, *A Casebook of Crime;* Butler, *Murderers' England; CBA;* Nash, *Open Files;* Symons, *A Reasonable Doubt.*

Story, John, c. 1510-71, Brit., kid.-treas. Lecturer at Oxford on civil law in 1535, and first regius professor in 1544. He was banished in 1548, presumably for being against the Act of Uniformity, while serving in Parliament. He prosecuted loyal Protestants for Queen Mary upon his return to England in 1553, and served under the Duke of Alba in setting up the Netherlands' Inquisition in 1565. He was seized by the British and put to death for committing high treason. REF.: *CBA.*

Story, John Huntington, 1926- , U.S., rape. In the small town of Lovell, Wyo., Dr. John Huntington Story was quiet family man, founder of the Bible Church, and a physician there for twenty-six years. Story was also a rapist and child molester who gave "thorough" pelvic exams to patients who came to see him for minor illnesses such as colds and sore throats. His known victims, numbered between 150 to "over a thousand," ranged in age from ten to sixty-eight. Story selected his victims from his most vulnerable patients, including children, women whose marriages were in trouble, single women, and elderly women. Many were Chicanos and Mormons, women sheltered from sex, or those too young or inexperienced to understand what the doctor was doing. Many victims rejected their suspicions and blamed themselves for having "sick" minds. Others were afraid to tell, fearing excommunication or that they had instigated the attack.

Police Sergeant Judi Cashel, of Casper, Wyo., helped build the case, and three Mormons, a mother and her daughters, led the fight to prosecute the doctor. The charges against Story divided the town. Story's defenders raised thousands of dollars for his defense, and shunned the accusers, even boycotting their businesses. They also located a psychiatrist who, without meeting the victims, diagnosed them as "hysterical" and "sexually disturbed." Witnesses testified that religious and civil leaders did nothing, although repeatedly informed of Story's rapes and improprieties. The women were told to "drop it."

When Story finally was convicted on two counts of forcible rape and three counts of assault and battery with intent to rape, the National Organization for Women called for a grand jury investigation of public officials who had hindered "the discovery or prosecution of a crime." The county attorney declined. In the book *"Doc," The Rape of the Town of Lovell,* author Jack Olsen suggested that Story was drawn to Lovell by the reputation of its former physician, Dr. William Watts Horsley, who was banned from the hospital for "perversion," but continued for years to molest boys in his private office. REF.: *CBA.*

Story, Joseph, 1779-1845, U.S., jur. Youngest U.S. Supreme Court justice, who began public career in Massachusetts legislature. He served briefly as a U.S. congressman from 1808-09. At the age of thirty-two he was appointed associate justice to the Supreme Court by President James Madison. As justice he spoke for the court on two important cases regarding the legal domain for prosecuting slaves, *United States v. Schooner Amistad* in 1841, and *Prigg v. Pennsylvania* in 1842. He amassed an international reputation and was instrumental in establishing school policies at Harvard Law School, where he was a professor from 1829-45. In that time, he wrote a highly respected series of legal textbooks. He remained on the court until his death. REF.: *CBA.*

Story of Mary Surratt, The, 1947, a play by John Patrick. This drama is based on the mother of John Surratt, one of the leading conspirators in the plot to assassinate President Abraham Lincoln (U.S., 1865). See: **Lincoln, Abraham**. REF.: *CBA.*

Stössel, Anatoly Mikhaylovich, 1848-1915, Rus., ct. mar. Unsuccessfully led troops at Port Arthur in 1904, and later surrendered to Japanese in 1905. He was court-martialed in 1906 and sentenced to a ten-year term, but was pardoned after three years. REF.: *CBA.*

Stoudenmire, Dallas, 1843-82, U.S., law enfor. off. Dallas Stoudenmire's career as the marshal of El Paso, Texas, was short but distinguished. Beginning with the day of his appointment, Apr. 11, 1881, his presence had a calming influence on a violent town, as he repeatedly showed himself able to outdraw and outshoot anyone looking for trouble. He was the typical western lawman, even carrying his two six-guns in his belt because he found holsters too cumbersome in a gunfight. During his year in office, however, a feud developed between Stoudenmire and the wealthy Manning brothers. Stoudenmire and his deputy, Doc Cummings, believed that the Mannings had hired gunmen to assassinate them, beginning with shots fired at Stoudenmire in the dark just six days after he took office. The attempts continued on Stoudenmire's and Cummings' lives for a year, until Stoudenmire left town briefly to marry Isabella Sherrington. During Stoudenmire's absence, the Mannings killed Cummings in the Coliseum Saloon (the Mannings owned the Coliseum, along with part interests in most of the other saloons in town, and one of the biggest cattle ranches in Texas). A hearing determined that the Mannings acted in self defense.

Stoudenmire began drinking heavily. Although he had signed a truce with George, Frank, and James Manning, he repeatedly threatened to kill them when he was drunk. By Autumn 1882, he was asked to resign from the marshal's office by the El Paso Vigilance Committee.

Stoudenmire was drunk on the night of Sept. 18. He sought out George "Doc" Manning at his saloon to pick a fight with him.

An employee of Manning's, Walter Jones, tried unsuccessfully to intercede. Doc Manning drew first, but his shot was stopped by pocketful of letters Stoudenmire was carrying in his shirt. After Stoudenmire wounded Manning in the arm, he caught Stoudenmire in a bear hug to prevent him from firing again. Their wrestling carried them out the front door just as James Manning arrived. James killed Stoudenmire with a shot to the head, but George picked up one of Stoudenmire's guns and vented his rage by pistol-whipping the corpse.

El Paso marshal Dallas Stoudenmire.

At their trial for Stoudenmire's murder, James and George Manning were again ruled to have killed in self-defense.

REF: Bartholomew, *The Biographical Album of Western Gunfighters;* _____, *Kill or be Killed;* Bronson, *Red Blooded;* Casey, *The Texas Border; CBA;* Cox, *Luke Short and His Era;* Cunningham, *Triggernometry;* Dils, *Horny Toad Man;* Foster-Harris, *The Look of the Old West;* Hendricks, *The Bad Man of the West;* Holloway, *Texas Gun Lore;* Hunter and Rose, *The Album of Gun-Fighters;* Mangan, *Bordertown;* Martin, *Border Boss;* Metz, *Dallas Stoudenmire;* Middagh, *Frontier Newspaper;* Mills, *Forty Years at El Paso, 1858-1898;* Nash, *Bloodletters and Badmen;* Parrish, *Coffins, Cactus and Cowboys;* Raine, *Famous Sheriffs & Western Outlaws;* _____, *Guns of the Frontier;* Rosa, *The Gunfighter, Man or Myth?;* Sonnichsen, *Pass of the North;* Watson, *A Century of Gunmen;* White, *The Autobiography of a Durable Sinner;* _____, *Out of the Desert;* _____, *Texas;* _____, *Them Was the Days;* _____, *Trigger Fingers.*

Stoughton, William, c.1630-1701, U.S., jur. Served on Massachusetts council as assistant from 1671-86, and as lieutenant governor from 1692-1701. He was one of the judges at the Salem witchcraft trials. REF.: *CBA.*

Stourton, Lord Charles, d.1557, Brit., asslt.-mur. In 1548 Lord William Stourton died, leaving all his personal property to his mistress, Agnes Ryce. Stourton's son, Charles Stourton, was furious with her and her supporters, including William Hartgill, who had managed the elder Stourton's estates.

Disputes arose between the younger Stourton and Hartgill when the son asked Hartgill to help induce his widowed mother to sign a document stating that she would not remarry. When Hartgill insisted that the son allot some of the money to support his mother, the young man refused. Angered, Hartgill told Stourton that he planned to see that Agnes Ryce received the property left to her.

Stourton was also suspicious that Hartgill was cheating him of rents and land, so he rode to the Kilmington Church one Sunday in the late 1540s. There, he and his confederates forced Hartgill, his wife, and servants to take cover in the church tower while Hartgill's son, John Hartgill, fought off the assailants. John Hartgill then rode for help and during the several days while he was gone Stourton kept the elderly couple and servants captive in the tower. The high sheriff of Wiltshire, Sir Thomas Speake, arrived to free the prisoners and arrest Stourton. Stourton was held in the Fleet prison for a short time.

After his release, Stourton began looting Hartgill's land and the Hartgills appealed to Mary I in 1553 and a council seemingly settled the quarrel between the two families. But shortly afterward John Hartgill was attacked by six of Stourton's accomplices. Stourton was imprisoned again in Fleet Prison but released when he agreed to pay £2,000 bail to the Hartgills. On Jan. 11, 1557, Stourton rode to the Kilmington Church with about sixty of his supporters, ostensibly to pay Hartgill the money. However, John and William Hartgill were seized, clubbed, and their throats were cut. The bodies were buried beneath the Stourton house.

Stourton and four servants were arrested and brought to trial on Feb. 26, 1557, in Westminster Hall. Stourton refused to plead, and at the time, if a defendant would not enter a plea the proceedings could not continue. So the court threatened to apply torture, *peine forte et dure,* in which a board is fastened onto a captive and weights are slowly and continuously added. Faced with this threat, Stourton pleaded guilty, was convicted. On Mar. 2, he was hanged as a nobleman, with a silk noose, at Sarum. The other four accomplices were also found Guilty and hanged in chains at Mere, near Bath.

REF.: *CBA;* Lambton, *Echoes of Causes Celebres;* Postgate, *Murder, Piracy and Treason.*

Stout, Marion Ira, d.1858, and **Littles, Sarah Stout**, prom. 1858, U.S., mur. Sarah Stout's father and a brother were criminals who were often in prison in New York. Once, when they were both jailed, Stout met Charles W. Littles of Rochester who fell in love with her. She confessed the truth about her criminal relatives, still the pair was married.

When Sarah Littles' brother, Marion Stout, was released, Sarah admitted to him that she was finding life with Littles boring. So they entered Littles' bedroom on the night on Dec. 19, 1857, and killed him with a hammer. The police had little difficulty determining who murdered Littles. The two were arrested and tried for murder. Found Guilty, Sarah Littles was sent to prison while her brother was hanged on Oct. 22, 1858, in Rochester, N.Y.

REF.: *CBA;* Nash, *Bloodletters and Badmen.*

Stout, Peter, d.1803, U.S., mur. A Dover, N.J., youth became annoyed by a mild insult given him by a 14-year-old acquaintance, Thomas Williams. When Stout saw Williams a few days later, he walked with him along the street and then suddenly bashed his ax into the youth's head. Stout then dropped his ax and plunged his hands into the blood pouring from Williams' skull. After wiping his hands on his clothing, he sat down and waited for a police officer to arrive. Stout was hanged on May 13, 1803.

REF.: *CBA;* Nash, *Bloodletters and Badmen.*

Stout, Rex (Rex Todhunter Stout), 1886-1975, U.S., det. writer. Wrote fictional detective adventures centered around character sleuth Nero Wolfe. Books authored: *Fer-de-Lance, Black Orchids, Gambit, A Doorbell Rang, A Family Affair,* and others. REF.: *CBA.*

Stout, Sir **Robert**, 1844-1930, New Zea., atty. gen.-jur. Held office as attorney general from 1878-79, and other governmental posts later. He also served as chief justice of New Zealand from 1899-1926, and served on the legislative council from 1926-30. REF.: *CBA.*

Stout, Samuel, prom. 1882, Case of, U.S., mur. Banker Henry Mead ran Mead's Exchange Bank in Waupaca, Wis. On Oct. 7, 1882, Mead, an older bachelor, made his usual round of the neighborhood after banking hours. The next morning, when he failed to appear at the restaurant where he always had breakfast, two waitresses went to the bank where they found him murdered. Suspects included Charles W. "Tab" Prior, the night watchman, E.C. Bronson, a local merchant who owed Mead payments on a loan, and Samuel Stout and Kenny Sherman. A drifter was tried, but freed for lack of evidence. Years later, Kenny Sherman, arrested for burglary, admitted that Prior and Stout had come to a livery barn where he worked on the night of Mead's murder to wash their hands, and had paid him to get rid of a bundle of clothing. Prior was arrested and held, but then Sherman refused to testify. In 1891, a $2,000 reward was offered for Mead's killer or killers, and Sheriff E.O. Williams and his brother, Andrew Williams, began gathering evidence against suspects. In March 1892, a grand jury was called.

On Apr. 8, Stout, Alfred Poll, and saloon keeper David Holmes were arrested. The sheriff told former Mayor A.R. "Fred" Lea to go before Judge Webb in Stevens Point. Prior and E.C. Bronson were also indicted. The trial began in June 1893. Faced with only circumstantial evidence, the defense charged prejudice and suggested that the decade-old murder be forgotten. Many witnesses "forgot" testimony they had given to the grand jury. James Collier testified that, in 1885, Sam Stout asked him if he wanted to join him in robbing Mead. When Collier refused, the drunken Stout told him he had no nerve, and that he, Lea, and Prior would do the job. The jury took fifteen minutes to decide that Stout, Prior, and Bronson were not guilty. The prosecutor said that "never in his career as an attorney had he presented a plainer case in any county, and then lost it." In 1907, one of the three men tried for Mead's murder was dying and confessed. His identity was not revealed. Another defendant's daughter corroborated the story. Seven men had gone to rob Mead; six had been indicted or implicated. They had intended to keep Mead unconscious, but when he revived, they killed him. No one was ever convicted for the crime. REF.: *CBA.*

Stowe, Louis Richard (AKA: **Robert Stratton**), c.1940s, U.S., mur. Louis Stowe, a heavyset salesman working as a buyer for a grocery store chain under the name Robert Stratton, became involved with Phyllis Blaine. On a night when Blaine's daughter, Ida, had gone to a movie, Stowe, apparently laughing the whole time, came to the house, killed Blaine with an ax and then put three bullets into her head. Taking the body to his car, he drove onto the highway, where he dropped it alongside the road near a farm. A woman at the farm saw him and came running, so Stowe shot her, too. At the noise, the woman's husband appeared, and he also died.

Stowe took off at high speed, driving with his gun in his right hand. Passing a car with four young people in it, he took aim at the driver, Thomas Allen. Viola Burns, sitting next to him, took the wheel and slowed slow the car to safety as Allen beside her was bleeding to death.

Phyllis Blaine's body was seen by people in a passing car. They went to the nearest farm, where young Jean Clay came out, and discovered that both her parents were lying dead in the darkness. Phyllis Blaine was eventually identified, and her daughter, Ida Blaine, described the man she knew as Robert Stratton, who, she said, had been acting weird lately. Although Stratton was not at home, the police found a bloodstained suit. They located Stratton at a restaurant, where they were able to capture him.

Stratton, quickly identified as Stowe, was tried and found Guilty but insane. His weird behavior was caused by a brain tumor.

REF.: *CBA;* Cohen, *One Hundred True Crime Stories.*

Straffen, John Thomas, b.1930, Brit., mur. At seventeen, John Straffen had the mind of an 8-year-old. The youth, who had grown up in a school for mentally retarded children, assaulted a 13-year-old girl and the courts sent him to an institution. Released at age twenty-one, he lived in Bath until he strangled two girls, as he said, to annoy the police because he hated them. At his trial at the Taunton Assizes in October 1951, he was found unfit to plead and was committed to Broadmoor Asylum.

Six months later he escaped. He was at large for only a few hours, but in that time he murdered another girl, Linda Bowyer. He told police without being asked, "I did not kill the little girl on the bicycle." His mental condition brought up several questions of how mentally incompetent defendants should be tried in capital cases. In his July 1952 trial for the third murder, he was found Guilty, but his death sentence was commuted to life imprisonment.

REF.: Adamson, *A Man of Quality;* _____, *The Great Detective;* Butler, *Murderers' England; CBA;* Eddy, *Scarlet and Ermine;* Harrison, *Criminal Calendar;* Keeton, *Guilty But Insane;* Lucas, *The Child Killers;* Neustatter, *The Mind of the Murderer; Notable British Trials;* Roberts, *Law and Life;* Rowland, *Unfit to Plead.*

Strafford, Sir Thomas Wentworth, See: **Wentworth, Thomas.**

Stralla, Anthony Cornero, See: **Cornero, Anthony.**

Strang, James Jesse (Jesse James Strang, AKA: **King James)**, 1813-56, U.S., religious leader, assass. Converted to Mormon religion by founder Joseph Smith in Illinois, and consecrated as Mormon elder in 1844. He was ousted from the church for trying to use deceptive means to succeed Smith after his death in 1844. He formed the Strangite sect from dissident Mormons he brought to Voree, Wis., then led the 5,000-member group to Beaver Island, Mich., in 1847, where he proclaimed himself King James I, and established the City of St. James. He was charged but acquitted of counterfeiting and robbing the mails in 1851, and served as a Democrat in the Michigan legislature from 1852-54. He was shot by former sect member Alexander Wentworth. He had refused to name a successor and his sect perished with his death. REF.: *CBA.*

Strang, Jesse (AKA: **Joseph Orton**), d.1827, U.S., mur. In 1825, Jesse Strang abandoned his family, moving to Albany, N.Y. Under the name Joseph Orton, he found a job working on the estate of John Whipple. Whipple's promiscuous wife seduced Strang and persuaded him to help her get rid of her husband. Strang purchased large amounts of arsenic, but soon gave up on this idea and spent long weeks practicing to make a distance shot with a fancy rifle Elsie Whipple gave him. On May 7, 1827, Strang shot through the window of the Whipple house and killed Elsie's husband as he was preparing for bed.

The coroner's jury, on which Strang served, believed Elsie's tale of a passing drunk firing at random. Then officials learned that Elsie Whipple and Strang were romantically involved. After they were arrested, Strang confessed to the minister of a local church. During his trial, the two lovers turned on one another, with Whipple testifying against Strang. Thinking that if Whipple were convicted, too, his chances of commutation would be tied to hers, Strang offered to testify against Whipple, but was not permitted to do so. Strang was hanged on Aug. 24, 1827. Whipple was acquitted.

REF.: *CBA;* Nash, *Bloodletters and Badmen.*

Strange Case of Dr. Jekyll and Mr. Hyde, The, 1886, a novel by Robert Louis Stevenson. In this gripping thriller a dual personality is explored with devastating perception. The twin nature, one good and one evil, was largely drawn from the split personality of Deacon William Brodie, a pillar of Scottish society by day, but at night an arch criminal (Scot., 1788). See: **Brodie, William.** REF.: *CBA.*

Strange Case of Lucile Clery, The, 1932, a novel by Joseph Shearing (British title: *Forget-Me-Not*). The brutish wife murder by the Duke de Praslin (Fr., 1848), is the inspiration for this work of fiction. See: **de Praslin, Duke**. REF.: *CBA.*

Strathclyde, Lord Alexander Ure, 1853-1928, Scot., jur. Elected Liberal member of Parliament, representing Linlithgow, from 1895. He was named solicitor general for Scotland in 1905, and later was promoted to Lord Advocate in 1909. In this post he prosecuted Oscar Slater for murder in a case marred by many irregularities and a wrong conviction. Four years later, he was designated lord president of the court of session and lord justice general of Scotland, serving from 1913-20. REF.: *CBA.*

Stratten, Dorothy, See: **Snider, Paul.**

Stratton, Albert, 1885-1905 and **Stratton, Alfred**, 1883-1905, Brit., rob.-mur. Of all the brutal robbery-murders committed in London over the years, the murders of Thomas and Ann Farrow have earned a prominent place in the annals of crime. It was in this case that a murderer was first convicted on the strength of a fingerprint found at the scene of the crime. The Farrows, an elderly couple, managed a paint shop at 34 High Street in Deptford in southeast London and lived in an apartment over the store. On the morning of Mar. 27, 1905, a young boy who worked as an apprentice in the paint shop arrived, and found the front door locked. Normally, Farrow would have the shop open by the time the boy arrived to accommodate painters who needed supplies for their work. When his knocking failed to raise his employer, the boy climbed over the wall of the next door property and made his way around to the back of the paint store. Peering through a rear window, he saw his employer lying in a pool of blood, his head bashed in.

Detective Inspector Fox and several other policemen arrived on the scene within twenty minutes, followed shortly by Melville Macnaghten, an expert in the new science of dactyloscopy, or fingerprinting. Every piece of furniture was overturned in the small room behind the shop and there was blood everywhere. The body lay on the floor with his head resting near the fireplace. He was still dressed in his nightshirt, with trousers and a jacket pulled on over it, which suggested to the police that he had come downstairs to open the shop for someone he probably assumed was an early customer. There was also a trail of blood leading part way up the stairs that led to the Farrows' apartment. Thomas Farrow had apparently tried to prevent the intruders from reaching his wife in the apartment above. Upstairs, the police found Ann Farrow lying on the floor, badly injured but still breathing. The assailant seemed to have used the same metal tool to beat both of the elderly people. Mrs. Farrow was taken to the hospital, where she died four days later without ever regaining consciousness.

The police investigation uncovered several pieces of evidence. First, the milkman told them that he had seen two men rush out of the paint shop at 7:15 that morning, leaving the door open behind them. Police theorized that the mortally injured Farrow must have locked the door after the assailants fled, out of fear that they would return. In the kitchen of the apartment, the police found two masks fashioned out of women's stockings, which turned out to belong to Mrs. Farrow. The police reasoned that the intruders had fashioned them to protect their identities in case Mrs. Farrow regained consciousness while they were rifling the tiny apartment for valuables. They were uncertain what loot the intruders might have found until they discovered a small metal cash box lying under the bed. The box had been broken into and was empty except for an overlooked sixpence piece and a tally that indicated that the box had contained £9.

Macnaghten immediately examined the box for fingerprints and found what he believed to be a clear imprint. After ascertaining that one of the policemen involved in the investigation had touched the box, Macnaghten carefully wrapped it up and had it transported to the fingerprinting division for testing. He took the fingerprints of the officer who had touched the box and those of the apprentice as well. He also took fingerprints from the Farrows—the first time fingerprints had ever been taken from a corpse in London. The following morning Chief Inspector Collins of the fingerprint division reported with the results. The mark on the cash box was, in fact, a fingerprint. No match had been found for it among the 80,000 prints on file, and none of the prints taken from the Farrows or the others matched it either.

A house-to-house search of the neighborhood was launched for the killer or killers. One of the detectives overheard conversation in a pub that mentioned two brothers, Albert and Alfred Stratton as being "capable of it." Although the two had no existing criminal records (they were twenty and twenty-two years old, respectively), they were generally considered good-for-nothings who, if they had not yet committed a crime, had only failed to do so from lack of initiative. Inspector Fox learned that Alfred Stratton had a mistress, Hannah Cromarty, who lived on Brookmill Road. When Fox located the woman, she showed signs of a recent beating. Fox determined that Stratton had administered it. With a little encouragement, Cromarty supplied Fox with information regarding Stratton's whereabouts on the night of the Farrow murders. According to Cromarty, Stratton had been with her on the night of Mar. 26. Late in the evening, a man had come, had a conversation with him, and then departed. Toward morning, there had been a knock at the window and Alfred had dressed and left. When Cromarty awoke it was daylight. Stratton was back in the room. He instructed her to tell anyone who asked that he had spent the entire night with her and had not left until after 9 a.m. the next morning. Cromarty also told Fox that Stratton had not had his overcoat since that night and, without explanation, had also dyed his brown shoes black.

Acting on Cromarty's information, Macnaghten issued orders for the Stratton brothers's arrest. Alfred was captured in a pub the following Sunday, and Albert was picked up the next day. Although the evidence against them was circumstantial, the police magistrate agreed to hold them for a week and have them fingerprinted. When the tests revealed that the thumbprint found on the cash box corresponded in eleven of a possible sixteen points to the print of Alfred Stratton's right thumb, the two men were charged with the murders.

Due to the insubstantial nature of the other evidence, the case against the Strattons rested on the prosecutor's ability to convince the jury that dactyloscopy was an exact science. To that end, the prosecutor, Richard Muir, went to Scotland Yard, where Macnaghten and Collins educated him in the forensic technology of fingerprinting.

The trial began on May 5 at the Old Bailey. Judge Channell, who presided, had no experience with dactyloscopy. He cautioned the jury that in his opinion fingerprint evidence should be accepted only with considerable reservations. The defense, carried out by Curtis Bennett and Harold Morris, focused their attempts on discrediting fingerprinting as a reliable source of evidence as singularly as the prosecution did on trying to vindicate it. When the defense pointed out discrepancies in the photographs of the fingerprints Inspector Collins had submitted as evidence, Muir seized the opportunity for a dramatic demonstration. Collins took the thumbprints of the jurymen several times in succession and then showed them that the prints contained discrepancies like those to which the defense had objected. The entire jury had the opportunity to observe directly that the "discrepancies" had nothing to do with the characteristic patterns that made their own prints uniquely identifiable.

After two hours of deliberation, the jury returned a Guilty verdict for both defendants. Judge Channell sentenced both men to death by hanging. The two brothers went to their deaths, each blaming the other for the murders.

REF.: Boar, *The World's Most Infamous Murders;* Brock, *A Casebook of Crime;* Browne, *The Rise of Scotland Yard;* Browne and Brock, *Fingerprints; CBA;* Cherrill, *Cherrill of the Yard;* Cuthbert, *Science and the Detection of Crime;* Dilnot, *Triumphs in Detection;* Felstead, *Shades of Scotland Yard;* Hibbert, *The Roots of Evil;* Jacobs, *Aspects of Murder;* McConnell, *The Detectives;* Shew, *A Second Companion to Murder;*

Thorwald, *The Century of the Detective;* Tullett, *Strictly Murder;* Tyler, *Gallows Parade;* Wilson, *Encyclopedia of Murder.*

Stratton, Richard L., 1946- , U.S., drugs. An aspiring writer, 37-year-old Richard L. Stratton was tried in federal district court in the Portland, Maine, on charges of conspiracy to smuggle marijuana and hashish. Stratton claimed he became involved with drug traffickers while researching the drug trade for seven years for a book, *Drug War,* but had never imported or sold drugs.

At Stratton's trial, which began on March 7, 1983, the prosecution's key witness, Michael J. Sanborn, serving a five-year jail term for his role in the same drug case, testified that Stratton was his chief in a smuggling operation that ended when $1.5 million worth of hashish and marijuana was seized in Springvale, Maine, in March 1982. Stratton and Sanford were among fifteen people indicted in the case. The prosecution detailed how Stratton had purchased a small plane and traveled extensively. Witnesses testified that Stratton had used his plane to carry drugs and that he had claimed to be the boss of a drug operation. Writer Doris Kearns Goodwin said Stratton had chosen drug-smuggling as a likely subject, which, "had now become a way of life for him." Author Norman Mailer, a friend of Stratton's, testified that he had no knowledge of Stratton being involved in dealing or smuggling drugs. During the trial, two Canadian drug agents conspicuously talked with prosecutor Richard S. Cohen, and afterward, Stratton decided not to take the stand in his own defense. A warrant for Stratton's arrest had previously been issued by Canadian authorities. On Mar. 25, the jury returned a Guilty verdict. On Apr. 28, 1983, Stratton was sentenced to a maximum of fifteen years in jail, calling him a "major actor" in the international drug ring. Stratton began serving his term in September 1982. REF.: *CBA.*

Strauss, Harry (AKA: **Pittsburgh Phil**), 1908-41, U.S., org. crime. Born in 1908 in the Williamsburg section of Brooklyn, Harry Strauss became one of the most prolific and sadistic killers in the history of organized crime. Known as "Pittsburgh Phil" (although he had no connection to that city), Strauss relished killing in different and innovative ways. He was on the payroll of Murder, Inc., the strong-arm organization founded in the early 1930s when the national crime syndicate came into being. A dapper dresser during the Depression and a well-known womanizer, Strauss carried on a long affair with Evelyn Mittleman, known as the "Kiss of Death Girl." Strauss would make trips to other cities to dispose of his victims and quickly returned to his home in a luxurious hotel.

Murder Inc.'s Harry Strauss.

To be a killer for Murder, Inc., one had to be adroit with a variety of weapons and killing techniques. Strauss was equally adept with a gun, ice pick, or a length of rope. He was fearless, often cornering a victim in a public place and carrying out his deed while bystanders watched in horror. During the 1930s, he was known to have killed at least 100 people, although some estimates are five times that number.

By 1934, Strauss had been arrested seventeen times in New York City on assorted charges including homicide, assault, larceny, and narcotics possession. But each time he escaped conviction. This infuriated Police Commissioner Lewis Joseph Valentine, who said after Strauss eluded a murder conviction, "This man is a paid assassin. When you meet such men draw quickly and shoot accurately." Valentine's outburst drew sharp rebuffs from constitutional scholars, who felt Strauss was in danger of losing his rights to a fair trial. A short time later he was arrested for the eighteenth time, and after two days in jail, he was acquitted in the Brooklyn Homicide Court for lack of evidence.

In 1937, Strauss and Harry "Happy" Maione were dispatched to Detroit to kill a man named Harry Millman. Finding Millman in a crowded restaurant the two assassins calmly walked down an aisle, opened fire, and killed Millman while wounding five other diners. That same year Strauss, along with Gangy Cohen, Jack Drucker, and Abraham Levine, were sent to Pittsburgh to kill Walter Sage, who was suspected of skimming the mob's gambling profits. Taking Sage for a ride, they grabbed him from behind and stabbed him to death with an ice pick. The body was tied to a pinball machine and deposited in a nearby lake. But intestinal gases bloated the corpse and in time it worked free of its restraints and floated to the surface. In the future, Strauss made a point of puncturing the stomachs of all victims given a burial at sea.

In 1940, Murder Inc. member Abraham Reles turned informant, and Strauss was indicted for the murder of Puggy Feinstein. With five additional homicide indictments pending, Strauss' only recourse was to appear insane. He entered the courtroom dirty and unshaven, and chewed constantly on a leather strap. The jurors were not swayed and found him Guilty of first-degree murder, and he was sentenced to death. Strauss continued the insane act on death row, hoping the governor would commute his sentence. But in the late evening of June 12, 1941, Strauss died in the electric chair. See: **Murder, Inc.; Reles, Abraham.**

REF.: *CBA;* Eisenberg and Landau, *Meyer Lansky;* Fried, *The Rise and Fall of the Jewish Gangster in America;* Gosch and Hammer, *The Last Testament of Lucky Luciano;* McPhaul, *Johnny Torrio;* Peterson, *The Mob;* Pileggi, *Wiseguy;* Reid, *The Grim Reapers;* Sann, *Kill the Dutchman.*

Strawhim, Samuel (Strawan), 1845-69, U.S., west. gunman. Known in Hays City, Kan., as a vicious killer and gunfighter, Samuel Strawhim ignored vigilantes that ordered him to leave town, and pistol-whipped one of their leaders, Alonzo B. Webster. However, when "Wild Bill" Hickok became sheriff in August 1869, Strawhim left town. On Sept. 27, he returned with eighteen cowboys. The gang took over John Bitter's Leavenworth Beer Saloon where Strawan declared he was going to "kill someone tonight just for luck." Strawhim, who threatened to break every glass in the saloon, was challenged and shot dead by Hickok. Some reports say Hickok turned his back on Strawhim, saw the gunman drawing on him in a mirror, turned, and fired first. Others claim Hickok simply drew faster. See: **Hickok, James Butler.**

REF.: *CBA;* Miller and Snell, *Great Gunfighters of the Kansas Cowtown;* Nash, *Bloodletters and Badmen.*

Street, Cecil John Charles (AKA: **John Rhode**), b.1884, Brit., writer. Using Rhode as a pseudonym, he wrote detective stories centered on fictional sleuth Dr. Priestley. REF.: *CBA.*

Streicher, Julius, 1885-1946, Ger., war crimes. German journalist and politician Julius Streicher, a notorious anti-Semite, began his campaign against Jews in 1919. He joined the Nazis, and took part in Adolf Hitler's 1923 Munich Putsch. As managing editor of *Der Stürmer* from 1923-45, Streicher became known as the foremost "Jew-baiter" in Europe for his vicious anti-Semitic writings. In April 1946, he was brought to trial in Nuremberg, Ger., where officials charged that he had turned his own local anti-Semitic society over to the Nazis. Streicher said, "I'm proud of it," explaining that it became "a bridge" for spreading the National Socialist doctrine to northern Germany. While waiting his turn at the gallows in Octo-

Nazi Julius Streicher.

ber 1946 with nine other war criminals, Streicher yelled "Heil Hitler" and "Purim Festival 1946," referring to a Jewish festival held to commemorate the hanging of Haman, a fifth century "Jew-baiter." REF.: *CBA*.

Stretz, Vera, prom. 1935, Case of, U.S., mur. On a sea cruise in 1934, German Dr. Fritz Gebhardt met and wooed American Vera Stretz. Within the year, Stretz and Gebhardt were living on different floors of the Beekman Hotel in New York City. On Nov. 25, 1935, the doctor called Stretz and asked her to come to his apartment claiming he was sick. When she arrived, Gebhardt propositioned her. When Stretz refused, Gebhardt threatened her with a gun. During a struggle, she wrested the gun from him and shot him.

Pre-trial publicity in the press ran heavily against Stretz, who was labeled the "Icy Blonde" and heralded with headlines such as "With Such A Lady—Be Careful." Stretz's lawyer, Samuel Leibowitz, developed a case in which he railed against German philosopher Friedrich Wilhelm Nietzsche, whose "Superman" philosophy was expounded by the Nazis and Field Marshal of the Third Reich Hermann Goering, with whom Gebhardt had served in WWI. Leibowitz effectively used Gebhardt's nationality to get his client acquitted, playing off anti-Nazi and anti-German sentiments. The choice presented to the jury was that they could vote for "the supermen of the German master race, or for American womanhood." Stretz was found Not Guilty. REF.: *CBA*.

Strickland, Carl Willis, 1933- , U.S., mur. Twenty-six-year-old Irene Marion Conole joined the Navy in September 1952. The pretty, dark-haired WAVE was assigned to the Patuxent Naval Air Station in St. Mary's County, Md. In Spring 1954, Conole eagerly looked forward to her impending wedding with a sailor based out of San Diego, Calif., when tragedy struck. On the morning of May 29, 1954, the partly submerged body of Conole was found floating a few yards off of a beach near Point Lookout, Md. in Chesapeake Bay. She had been beaten over the head with a soft-drink bottle that was found lying in the sand nearby. Death had occurred as a result of drowning, according to police investigators.

Later that afternoon Lieutenant Paul C. Zimmerman of the Rocky Mount, N.C., police ordered the arrest of Carl Willis Strickland, a 21-year-old Navy airman attached to the Patuxent Base. The sailor was picked up at his father's home and taken to the Leonardstown, Md., jail where he was held without bond while police spent hours attempting to crack his alibi. The young airman explained that he had gone night-clubbing with Conole the night before, and while driving her home she had noticed a hitchhiker standing on to the side of the road and suggested that they give him a ride. He stopped the car and offered the man a lift. The hitchhiker told Strickland that he wanted to be taken to Hays Beach, near Point Lookout.

Strickland said that he left Conole and the stranger at the beach at their request and then decided to head home to Lexington Park. Noticing that Irene had left her purse in his car, Strickland doubled back to Point Lookout. He got out of his car but could find no trace of the couple—only the blanket from his back seat which he had loaned them. Strickland refused to waiver from this story, even after detectives escorted him to the funeral parlor to view the remains of the murder victim. Meanwhile, dozens of sailors were organized into search parties to track down the missing items of clothing Strickland claimed to have discarded. On June 1, blood-soaked trousers, underwear, and socks were found by sheriff's deputies in St. Mary's County. It was sufficient evidence to merit a second-degree murder indictment. Strickland was found Guilty and sentenced to eighteen years in prison, the maximum penalty under Maryland law for this type of crime. He was paroled on June 24, 1963. REF.: *CBA*.

Strickland, Obed F., 1833- , U.S., jur. Served as attorney general in Salt Lake City, Utah Territory. He was appointed to the territorial court of Utah by President Ulysses S. Grant in 1869. REF.: *CBA*.

Stride, Herbert William, b.1857, and **Millard, Frederick William**, b.1864, Brit., theft. In December 1907, at a Chelmsford Assizes Court, Herbert William Stride, fifty, and Frederick William Millard, forty-three, were tried before Justice Grantham on the charge of stealing about 1,000 pheasant eggs from Sir Walter Gilbey. Attorneys for Stride were Marshall Hall and Mr. Valetta. R.D. Muir and Graham-Campbell defended Millard, and E.E. Wild and Claughton Scott prosecuted. Until July 1907, Stride had been gamekeeper on Sir Gilbey's Elsenham estate. He had also maintained a 272-acre tenant farm of his own, called Little Henham-Hall, about three miles from Elsenham. Millard was the editor of the *Gamekeeper*, a local trade newspaper, and the secretary of the Gamekeeper's Association of the United Kingdom. Stride initially said he had kept some of Gilbey's pheasants in a separate pen on his own farm. He denied the theft of the eggs, and said all the eggs he sent to Millard were properly accounted for. He later admitted that his testimony about the separate pens was false. On Dec. 7, 1907, both men were found Guilty by the jury, with a recommendation of mercy for Stride. Judge Grantham sentenced both Millard and Stride to a year in jail with hard labor. REF.: *CBA*.

Strode, William, c.1599-1645, Brit., treas. Served in Parliament from 1624 during reign of Charles I. He was jailed from 1629-40 for joining others in using mild force against John Finch, speaker of the House of Commons, to obtain passage of Sir John Eliot's resolutions criticizing the king's economic program and religious views. He participated in the king's Short Parliment in 1640, and in the Long Parliament he successfully sought the impeachments of William Laud and Sir Thomas Wentworth, the king's prized advisers. He and four others were later impeached by the king on charges of high treason in 1642. REF.: *CBA*.

Strodtman, Herman, c.1682-1701, Brit., mur. In 1694, Herman Strodtman and his friend, Peter Wolter, were sent together by their parents from their homes in Lisland, Ger., to London, where they were apprenticed to the Dutch firm of Stein and Dorien. The young men were the best of friends until Wolter's sister married into the Dorien family. Wolter then began acting superior toward Strodtman, talking about him behind his back. Strodtman began to hate him. He mixed some white mercury with a powder Wolter took for scurvy but, realizing it might be months before Wolter would need the remedy, Strodtman considered stabbing as an alternative. As Wolter's taunting escalated, Strodtman grew frightened of losing control and killing Wolter in front of his employers, so he pleaded with one of the maids to suggest to his masters that they send him to the West Indies. No answer was forthcoming.

On Good Friday, Strodtman was sent out on an errand, but took off on his own to plot Wolter's demise. He planned the crime for Saturday, but decided to wait until after Sunday, not wanting to deprive his victim of the Easter sacrament. Strodtman was fired and then took rooms at an alehouse in Queen Street. He had a key to his master's house, which he had secretly made for his own use, and let himself in about 8 p.m. the next Saturday. He sneaked up the stairs into the room where he used to sleep, lit a candle, and went up another flight to the room adjoining Wolter's. Hearing footsteps, he put out his candle and then fell asleep. Awaking around midnight, he went downstairs, stole some checks and cash from the business office, then went back upstairs, carrying with him a large piece of wood. He entered Wolter's room, hit him in the head about six times, and then held a pillow over his mouth to make sure he had finished the job. Strodtman had brought along pistols to shoot Wolter in case other methods failed. He then left a candle on a chair near the curtains and another on a dresser, hoping the house would burn down and conceal his crime.

A few days later, while trying to cash the stolen checks, Strodtman was found out and later questioned by his employer, Mr. Stein. Strodtman denied his guilt, but was found to have a £20 stolen check in his pocket. When Stein then promised that if Strodtman confessed, he would keep him safe from the law by arranging to have him sent overseas, Strodtman confessed, and was taken to Newgate, tried, and found Guilty. Despite his employer's promises, he was hanged at Tyburn on June 18, 1701, at the age of eighteen.

REF.: *CBA;* Mitchell, *The Newgate Calendar;* Smith, *Highwaymen.*

Strollo, Anthony C. (AKA: **Tony Bender, Tony Benda**), 1899-1962, U.S., org. crime. Anthony Strollo was a New York mobster for about forty years, serving as a high-ranking member of three Mafia families, beginning in the early 1920s. Born on June 18, 1899, Strollo worked as a murderer, thug, and bootlegger during Prohibition. In 1931, Strollo became the crime boss of New York's Greenwich Village, running gambling operations and serving as a lieutenant of Charles "Lucky" Luciano. Fearing competition, he directed Joseph Valachi and Peter Mione to eliminate Michael "Little Apples" Reggione, who was killed with three gunshots to the head on Nov. 25, 1932. Following Luciano's deportation, Strollo became an underboss for Frank Costello, running a string of Village nightclubs prior to WWII, including the Black Cat, the Hollywood, the 19th Hole, and the Village Inn. When Costello was expunged from the mob, Strollo oversaw the mob's Manhattan drug-trafficking operations for Vito Genovese, who had just returned from Italy after seven years in exile. On Sept. 20, 1952, Eugenio Giannini was shot to death by Joseph and Pasquale Pagano, Fiore Siano, and Joseph Valachi, under orders by Strollo. On June 19, 1953, suspected informant Steven Franse was strangled to death at Valachi's Lido nightclub in Greenwich Village. Strollo ran the operations for another nine years until he disappeared from his Fort Lee, N.J., home on the night of April 8, 1962, never to be seen again. Valachi later testified that Strollo was the victim of a Mafia "hit" and that his body had been destroyed. Strollo may have been slain on Genovese's orders.

REF.: *CBA;* Eisenberg and Landau, *Meyer Lansky;* Gage, *Mafia U.S.A.;* _____, *The Mafia is not an Equal Opportunity Employer;* Gosch and Hammer, *The Last Testament of Lucky Luciano;* Katz, *Uncle Frank;* McClellan, *Crime Without Punishment;* Maas, *The Valachi Papers;* Martin, *Revolt int he Mafia;* Messick, *Lansky;* Nash, *Bloodletters and Badmen;* Peterson, *The Mob;* Reid, *The Grim Reapers.*

Strom, J. Preston, prom. 1957, U.S., law enfor. off. South Carolina Law Enforcement head, J. Preston Strom was responsible for reversing the murder conviction of a wrongly convicted man. In June 1956, a 38-year-old Gainesville, Ga., house painter, James Foster, was accused of murdering 57-year-old Charles Drake. Foster, who protested his innocence throughout his trial, was nonetheless convicted and sentenced to death. A year after the conviction, Strom received information from another convict, William Patterson that Foster was indeed innocent. With this information, the real killers were located and brought to trial. On Aug. 14, 1958, A.D. Allen and Charles Paul Rothschild were convicted of the murder and sentenced to life in prison. Foster was subsequently released from prison. REF.: *CBA.*

Strong, William, 1808-95, U.S., jur. U.S. Supreme Court justice. He first entered public life as a U.S. congressman from Pennsylvania from 1847-51. He later joined the supreme court of Pennsylvania, serving from 1857-68. He was considered as a candidate to the Supreme Court following the death of Chief Justice Roger B. Taney in 1864, but Salmon P. Chase was selected by President Abraham Lincoln instead. He appeared to have once again lost a court seat after President Ulysses S. Grant picked former secretary of war Edwin M. Stanton to fill the next vacancy, but was eventually appointed when Stanton died just four days after being confirmed. His ten-year tenure was marked by two important cases regarding the Fourteenth Amendment: *Strauder v. West Virginia* in 1880 and *Ex parte Virginia* the same year. After retiring from the court in 1880, he taught law at Columbian University, later named George Washington University. REF.: *CBA.*

Stroud, Robert Franklin (AKA: **The Birdman of Alcatraz**), 1887-1963, U.S., mur. Robert Stroud committed his first murder in Alaska at the age of nineteen, killing a bartender who would not pay $10 for Kitty O'Brien, one of Stroud's prostitutes. He was sentenced to twelve years for manslaughter, time he divided between the federal penitentiary on McNeil Island in Puget Sound in the Pacific northwest and Leavenworth Prison in Kansas. He had a reputation for being quiet and aloof, and the other prisoners found him repulsive.

Stroud had almost served his time when he killed again on Mar. 26, 1916. His victim was Andrew F. Turner, a guard he attacked with a knife in the Leavenworth mess hall. Stroud told another convict, "The guard took sick and died all of a sudden. He died of heart trouble. I guess you would call it a puncture of the heart. Anyhow, there was a knife hole in the guard's heart. I never have given any reason for doing it, so they won't have much to work on; only that I killed him, and that won't do much good. I admit that much."

The "Birdman of Alcatraz," Robert Stroud.

The gallows on which Stroud was sentenced to die were located in the Leavenworth exercise yard less than 200 feet from his cell, but his mother petitioned President Woodrow Wilson and his wife, Elizabeth Bolling Wilson in 1920, just before the execution was scheduled to take place (Wilson had had a heart attack, so his wife was exercising most of the duties of his office). Elizabeth Stroud impressed the president's wife with her son's studies in ornithology—he had become fascinated with canaries, and his knowledge of how to treat their diseases may already have been the most extensive in the U.S. at the time—so his sentenced was commuted to life in solitary confinement eight days before he was to hang.

Prison officials accommodated him with a double cell, tearing down the wall between two standard-sized cells so he would have more room to keep birds for his experiments. In 1943, he published the *Digest of Bird Diseases,* and he wrote an unpublished treatise on prison reform entitled *Looking Outward,* criticizing the U.S. penal system. He was later transferred to Alcatraz, where he died of natural causes in 1963.

REF: *CBA;* Nash, *Bloodletters and Badmen;* Gaddis, *Birdman of Alcatraz;* (FILM), *Birdman of Alcatraz,* 1962.

Stroud, William, prom. 18th Cent., Brit., fraud. William Stroud was an extremely fashionable man who took lodgings in Bond Street and dressed like a wealthy gentleman. Stroud lived extravagantly, supported several expensive courtesans, and was soon reduced to indigency. He managed to get credit from a tailor for several elegant suits, rented a house and servants, and posed as a man of wealth. He then obtained a large credit allowance from several tradesmen. When the merchants tried to collect his debts, he sold his furniture, left the house, and rented a new one in Bloomsbury. There he set himself up as the steward to a nobleman. Later, he took a house in Westminster and hired an agent who ordered goods for the false nobleman. The tradesmen were told to leave their bills with the steward. As soon as the items were delivered, Stroud sold them off and later, of course, moved on to set up shop somewhere else.

Stroud took summer vacations in the countryside. Familiar with the best London stores, he met their supply wagons outside the city and signed for the merchandise as a representative of the merchant. In his career as a swindler, Stroud duped jewelers, watchmakers, tailors, drapers, upholsterers, silversmiths, and lacemakers. When he was apprehended and committed to Gatehouse Jail in Westminster, he was charged, among other things, with the theft of a golden coach, velvet suits trimmed with gold, cabinets, and at least £100 worth of rings. Crowds of witnesses came to testify against him, and he was soon found Guilty. Stroud was sentenced to six months' hard labor at Bridewell Prison, during which time he was publicly whipped in the streets six times.

REF.: *CBA;* Mitchell, *The Newgate Calendar.*

Strozzi, Giovanni Battista (AKA: **Filippo II**), 1488-1538, Italy, consp.-suic. Engaged in plots against powerful Medici family. He was captured and jailed after failed attempts to attack Florence, and killed himself in prison. REF.: *CBA.*

Struck, Ira G., prom. 1886, Case of, U.S., mur. Ira Struck, a businessman from New Albany, Ind., read a gossipy item in the newspaper concerning his wife, a church organist, and Charles V. Hoover, the soloist with the church choir. Struck later saw Hoover in a store and took a shot at him, but the singer ducked. Struck went to Florida on business, but was forced to return to answer a charge of assault. On July 27, 1886, Struck saw Hoover and his father on the courthouse steps and fired again, killing Hoover and wounding the father. Ira Struck was tried but acquitted on the grounds of insanity.

REF.: *CBA;* Nash, *Almanac of World Crime.*

Struck, Lydia, 1833-79, U.S., mur. Lydia Struck was married for seventeen years to sometime New York City policeman Edward Struck, a drunk who frequently beat her. After one beating, he threatened to kill himself. His wife purchased some arsenic to use as rat poison and Struck soon was dead. Neighbors and police agreed that Struck, in a fit of remorse, had committed suicide. Lydia Struck collected a $5,000 insurance policy. She moved to Connecticut, where she murdered her four children one by one because they reminded her of her spouse. Because no insurance claims were filed and because Struck was new to the state, no investigations were made. Before long, Struck married a 75-year old widower, Dennis Hurlbut, who promised to leave her his entire estate. Hurlbut was dead within fourteen months after they married, allegedly from natural causes but actually from arsenic. She married her next husband, Horatio Sherman of Derby, Conn., in the mistaken belief that he was wealthy. In fact, Sherman married her for her money. Sherman's two children from a previous marriage were the first to die, followed by Sherman. Police, suspicious about the Sherman deaths, exhumed Sherman's body and found arsenic. Meanwhile, Struck was considering marriage to an apple farmer when police tracked her down. Struck confessed to eight murders, but probably committed three more. She insisted that Hurlbut had taken arsenic "accidentally." Sentenced to life imprisonment, she served six years at the Connecticut State Prison at Wethersfield, and died of cancer in 1879. REF.: *CBA.*

Struensee, Johann Friedrich, c.1749-1808, Den., treas. King Christian VII of Denmark was a neglected child, raised by a vicious, depraved tutor named Reventlow. The cruelty he underwent in his childhood was later reflected in King Christian's character as an adult. He ascended to the throne of Denmark at seventeen and, that same year, married Caroline Matilda, the 15-year-old sister of King George III of England.

The marriage soon soured, as Christian blamed Caroline for his political troubles. In 1768, the king planned to visit France and England. His erratic behavior worried diplomats, so a doctor, Johann Friedrich Struensee of Altona, was hired to keep an eye on him. Struensee was a socially ambitious libertine whom women, including Caroline, found irresistible.

Struensee began an affair with Caroline and gained considerable influence over the governement and the Danish military, who resented him as a foreign interloper. On Jan. 16, 1772, the doctor's enemies struck. The dowager queen, Juliane Marie, awakened King Christian in the middle of the night and told him that Struensee was preparing to commit high treason, and that Caroline had been his willing accomplice all along. Struensee was beheaded and the king was granted a divorce. Caroline Matilda was exiled to Hanover, and died there three years later. Christian VII ruled until 1808, when his insanity forced him to relinquish his throne to Crown Prince Fredrick. REF.: *CBA.*

Strumm, Franz Felix, b.1847- , Brit., forg. In 1870 a German baker, Napoleon Stanger, and his wife, Elizabeth, opened a business in England. Stranger hired one of his German friends, Franz Strumm, who began having an affair with Stranger's wife, reputedly a heavy drinker who often attacked her husband. On Nov. 12, 1881, a journeyman baker, Zentler, passed the bakery and saw his employer, 38-year-old Stanger, talking in the doorway with 34-year-old Strumm and two other men. Stanger was not seen after that night and two weeks later Strumm moved in with Stanger's 31-year-old wife and put his name on the bakery.

In April 1882, neighbors collected £50 and offered a reward for information leading to the discovery of Stanger's whereabouts. Crowds gathered outside the shop every day until Elizabeth Stanger could no longer stand the commotion and went to live with Strumm's wife. Several months later the trustees in charge of Stanger's will found that Strumm and Mrs. Stanger had forged a check and Strumm and the woman were arrested. Charges against Mrs. Stanger were dropped, but Strumm was tried, convicted of forgery, and sentenced to ten years in prison. After his release he went back to Germany, accompanied by his wife and Mrs. Stanger.

REF.: Brock, *A Casebook of Crime; CBA;* Whitelaw, *Corpus Delicti.*

Stuart, Lady Arabella (Stewart), 1575-1615, Brit., consp.-polit. corr. Utilized in conspiracies to oust first cousin James VI, whom she followed as second in line of succession to thrones of England and Scotland. She was heavily watched by Queen Elizabeth I, but managed to secretly marry William Seymour, also in line for the throne, in 1610. She was jailed in the Tower of London, where she died, insane. She was the granddaughter of John Stewart. REF.: *CBA.*

Stuart, Esmé (Stewart, Duke of Lennox, Earl of Darnley), c.1542-83, Brit., consp. Titled by James VI, whom he befriended while on assignment to Scotland to re-establish Roman Catholicism. He and the king obtained the execution of James Douglas on false charges of being an accomplice in the death of Lord Darnley in 1581. He was later ousted from Scotland for his part in plans for an invasion of England by the Spanish army in 1582. REF.: *CBA.*

Stuart, James, d.1851, U.S., asslt.-rob. During the California gold rush the population of San Francisco swelled, quickly outnumbering a small police force. On Feb. 19, 1851, two men robbed a store owned by C.J. Jansen of $2,000, and nearly murdered Jansen. Two suspects, Thomas Burdeu and Mr. Windred, were arrested and tried by an informal citizens' court where they were acquitted. Several months later, the real culprit, James Stuart, was arrested and confessed to the Jansen robbery and other crimes. On July 11, at another citizens' court, Stuart was convicted. The onlooking crowds sentenced him to execution, and he was hanged.

REF.: *CBA;* Duke, *Celebrated Criminal Cases of America.*

Stuart, Sir **James**, 1780-1853, Can., jur. Served as solicitor general of Lower Canada in 1801, and in House of Assembly as representative from Montreal from 1808-17 and from 1825-31. He also held office as chief justice of Lower Canada from 1838-41, and as chief justice of Canada from 1841 following the passage of the Act of Union, which he authored. REF.: *CBA.*

Stuart, Mamie, 1891-1920, Brit., (unsolv.?) mur. The true facts surrounding the disappearance of Mamie Stuart remained shrouded in mystery for forty years. The glamourous 26-year-old chorus girl became somewhat of a local legend among residents living near the windswept coast of South Wales. Where had she gone? Or more correctly, what fiend had ended the woman's life?

In July 1917, Stuart fell in love with Everard George Shotton, who worked as a marine surveyor in Cardiff. On Mar. 25 of the following year, they were married in a civil ceremony in Cardiff. Afterward, the young woman took her bridegroom home to Sunderland to meet her parents. Then, in February 1919, they decided to move to Swansea, South Wales. They rented a modest suite of rooms on Trafalgar Terrace from a couple named Hearn.

There they remained until July 19 when business concerns took Shotton away. Mamie decided to visit her parents' home in Sunderland while her husband was out of the area. She took the train back to Swansea on Nov. 5, 1919, and was met by her husband at the station. They proceeded not to the Hearn residence as Mamie expected but instead to a rented house overlooking the majestic Swansea Bay, on a desolate cliff. The house was called "Ty-Llanwydd," which translates to "the abode of peace." A week later the Stuart family received word from their daughter that she had arrived safely and had settled into the new living quarters. They sent back a reply which came back to them a few days later marked "House Closed."

At Christmastime Mamie's uneasy parents received a card wishing them "the compliments of the season." But this did not alleviate their worry. Nothing more was heard from Swansea until March 1920 when the manager of the Grosvenor Hotel notified police that he had found an unopened piece of luggage in one of the guest rooms. Inside the police found several items of jewelry and women's clothing which had been shredded. A piece of paper with the Sunderland address scrawled on it established the identity of the owner: Mamie Stuart. The hotel manager said that to the best of his recollection the portmanteau was left by a man who was traveling alone. Several weeks later a mildewed handbag with a sugar-ration card made out to Mamie Stuart was found by a cleaning woman behind a washstand. Chief Inspector William Draper of Scotland Yard was brought into the case at this point. He determined that George Shotton, far from being a dutiful husband and son-in-law, was a bigamist. He had a wife and a child in Caswell Bay, a mile from Ty-Llanwydd.

Shotton denied being married to Mamie Stuart. He said they had lived together for a time but had parted on or about Dec. 5. Mrs. Hearn filled in some of the missing details. She told of Shotton's excessive jealousy and violent temper. On one occasion Mamie had confided to her, "If I am ever missing, do your utmost to find me, won't you?" A letter written by Stuart to her parents repeated the same concern. "If you don't hear from me, please wire to Mrs. Hearn and see if she knows anything about me. The man is not all there. I don't think I will live with him very long. I am very much afraid of him. My life is not worth living."

Convinced that Shotton was their man, the police conducted a searching investigation but turned up nothing. The only thing they could hold Shotton on was a charge of bigamy. In his defense, Shotton argued feebly that someone using his name impersonated him during the wedding ceremony. He was sentenced to eighteen months at hard labor in June 1920. The matter might have ended there had it not been for a chance discovery by three men named John Gerke, Colin MacNamara, and Graham Jones, who were exploring an abandoned lead mine airshaft on Nov. 5, 1961—the exact anniversary of Mamie's disappearance forty-one years earlier. At the bottom of the arid shaft in a dimly lit, bat-infested cavern, they found a collection of human bones in a tattered cloth sack. The bundle was hidden behind a pile of rocks. Lying nearby they found a butterfly comb with a tuft of hair still entwined in its teeth.

The bones were removed to the Forensic Science Laboratory at Cardiff for examination. There two pathologists, Dr. William Reginald James and Dr. John Lewis Griffiths, determined that the killer had severed the body into three pieces. The skull was superimposed over a stage photograph of Mamie taken during her vaudeville days. All that was left to do was find someone still alive to provide corroborative evidence. A retired mail carrier, Bill Symons, provided the missing piece. He recalled Shotton struggling with a large, bulky sack. Symons asked whether Shotton needed any help. "Oh God, for a minute I thought you were a policeman!" Shotton exclaimed. He declined the offer and continued on in the direction of Brandy Cove where the parcel would remain undetected for the next forty years.

The authorities attempted to track down George Shotton, but he had died penniless in Bristol's Southmead Hospital on Apr. 30, 1958. He was buried in Arno Vale Cemetery in an unmarked grave. His landlady recalled that Mr. Shotton "was such a perfect gentleman."

REF.: *CBA;* Furneaux, *Famous Criminal Cases, vol. 7;* Picton, *Murder, Suicide or Accident.*

Stuart, Rupert Max, 1931- , Aus., rape-mur. On Dec. 19, 1958, the Fun Land Carnival arrived in Ceduna, South Australia. The next day three children went to play on a local beach, including 9-year-old Mary Olive Hattam. Two of the youngsters wandered off and while they were gone Mary was attacked by an aborigine carnival worker, 27-year-old Rupert Max Stuart. He raped the girl, beat her head with a stone, and left her body in a nearby cave. Mary's friends, unable to find her, told her father, who called police.

After trackers identified footprints as aborigine, police questioned several migrants, including Stuart, who had previously been arrested for drinking. (At the time, aborigines were not allowed to drink alcohol.) Stuart confessed—saying he was drunk when he committed the crime—and was tried on murder charges at Adelaide. He was convicted and received the death penalty, but the sentence was later commuted to a life term in prison.

REF.: *CBA;* Chamberlain, *The Stuart Affair;* Inglis, *The Stuart Case.*

Stuart-Boswell Duel, 1822, Scot., duel-mur. On Dec. 26, 1821, an anonymous song was published in the *Sentinel*, a newspaper in Glasgow, Scot. When James Stuart read the piece he was offended because he thought the song implied that he was a coward. He found out the song was written by Sir Alexander Boswell. Confronting Boswell, Stuart asked if Boswell authored the song, but Boswell refused to answer. Representatives for the two men arranged for a duel on the continent two weeks later. Stuart's emissary then told the other intermediary that Stuart would consider the song a bad joke if Boswell would state that the song was not meant as a criticism of Stuart's courage. Boswell's envoy said he was sure Boswell would not agree to the proposal.

Later the dueling place was changed to Auchtertool, near Balmuto, England. The rivals met on Mar. 26, 1822. Stuart's shot hit Boswell's shoulder blade and lodged in his spine, leaving him paralyzed. Boswell died the following day. On June 10, Stuart was tried on murder charges at Edinburgh, where the jury heard evidence about his conduct during the duel, his lack of malice, and his regret about the matter. Stuart was acquitted.

REF.: *CBA;* Melville, *Famous Duels and Assassinations.*

Stubb, Peter (AKA: **Stubbe, Stump, Stumpf, Stube**), d.1589, Ger., lycanthropy-mur. After a large number of wolf attacks around Cologne, Ger., in about 1589, hunters and dogs were sent to hunt the animal. Stalking the wolf, they nearly caught it one day, but it disappeared and the hunters spotted Peter Stubb, who was walking toward Cologne. Stubb was arrested as a werewolf and after undergoing torture admitted to incest with his daughter and sister, to killing and raping numerous victims over a twenty-five year period, and to changing himself into a werewolf by means of a magic belt given to him by the devil. Though Stubb told officials where the belt could be found, they could not locate it, so they reasoned that the devil had taken it. Stubb, his daughter, and his mistress, Katherine Trompin, were tried in 1589 near Cologne and sentenced on Oct. 28, 1589. The daughter and mistress were ordered to be burned. Stubb was sentenced to be broken on the wheel, have the skin pulled off his bones with red-hot pincers, his head cut off, and his remains burned. The executions took place on Oct. 31, 1589.

REF.: *CBA;* Del Rio, *Les controverses et recherches magiques de Martin Delrio;* Robbins, *The Encyclopedia of Witchcraft and Demonology;* Summers, *The Werewolf; A True Discourse, Declaring the Damnable Life and Death of One Stubbe Peter;* Wilson, *Witches.*

Stubbs, John (Stubbes), c.1543-91, Brit., libel. Punished along with his printer by having hands chopped off for writing *The Discoverie of a Gapin Gulf* in 1579, a pamphlet criticizing Queen Elizabeth I's plans to marry the Duke of Anjou. REF.: *CBA.*

Stubbs, William Morley, d.1821, Brit., rob. William Stubbs was highwayman who was sentenced to death and hanged on Apr. 21,

1821, at the York Jail. The executioner, Jack Ketch, was drunk and had trouble getting the noose around Stubb's head. Finally a jailer and a sheriff's officer helped Ketch complete the job.

REF.: *CBA;* Poynter, *Forgotten Crimes.*

Stucley, Thomas, 1525-78, Brit., count.-pir. Early in his career, Thomas Stucley, rumored to be an illegitimate son of Henry VIII, served in the military in Europe and reputedly was recruited as a French spy. He returned to England, falsly alerting authorities of a French plot, and when his allegiance to the French was discovered, was put in prison in the Tower of London for a time. After his release he served with the British forces in Europe. He again alerted British officials of a French plot and in return received protection from his creditors. However, he later was arrested on counterfeiting charges. After an escape, Stucley turned to piracy, but abandoned the seas after he married a rich Irish woman. When her money was exhausted, Stucley became a privateer, raiding French, Spanish, and Portuguese ships for about two years before the British arrested him off the Irish coast. He was taken back to England, but was later freed. He died during an assault on Morocco.

REF.: *CBA;* Hunt, *A Dictionary of Rogues.*

Study in Terror, A, 1966, a British film directed by James Hill in which the immortal Sherlock (John Neville) is on the trail of Jack the Ripper (Brit., 1888). The Ripper is determined to be an educated physician in this production, which captures with rich flavor the murky and sullen Whitechapel of London's 1880s. See: **Jack the Ripper**. REF.: *CBA.*

Stüllgens, Robert Wilhelm, 1950- , Ger., rape-mur. Robert Wilhelm Stüllgens was imprisoned on charges of attacking a young mother and her child, raping the woman, and trying to rape the child. After his release from prison in Spring 1980, he spotted Margret Deck in the basement of a Düsseldorf, Ger., apartment complex on June 10. Stüllgens, thirty, waited for Deck's husband, Wilhelm Deck, to return and asked him to help him move some furniture. Deck accompanied the ex-convict to his apartment, where Stüllgens stabbed the man. Then, taking Deck's keys, he went back to the Deck apartment, opened the door, and waited for Margret Deck. When she returned with her two children, 2-year-old Thomas and 6-week-old Christian, Stüllgens ordered her to take off her clothes and perform oral sex. Then he stabbed the woman and her children to death.

On June 12, 1980, concerned neighbors called police, who found the bodies of Margret Deck and the children. Several days later they found Deck's body in Stüllgen's apartment and Stüllgens was arrested in Essen, Ger. He admitted to the crime, was tried, convicted, and sentenced to a life term in prison.

REF.: *CBA;* Wilson, *Encyclopedia of Modern Murder.*

Stürgkh, Karl von, 1859-1916, Aust., prime minister, assass. As prime minister of Austria, Count Karl Strugkh sought to prolong WWI, abolished the legislature, made major diplomatic concessions to Hungary, arranged death sentences for soldiers for minor infractions, and imposed censorship so severe that Austrians could not obtain foreign newspapers from allied countries, let alone enemies. As he garnered more dictatorial power, dissident Austrians became alarmed; when he refused to meet with the Social Democratic parliamentary delegation, even to receive a message of support, his arrogance shocked even his severest critics.

One of these was Dr. Friedrich "Fritz" Adler, a scholarly physicist and secretary of the Austrian Social Democratic Party, whose father had founded the Social Democrats. In Vienna on Oct. 21, 1916, Adler dined at the Hotel Meissl & Schadn, the restaurant where Strugkh always ate. At 2:30 p.m., Adler left his table, walked past the prime minister's seat, then turned and fired three shots into the back of his head. Adler cried, "Down with tyranny! We want peace!" before being wrestled to the floor.

Adler was tried for murder and sentenced to death, but the sentence was never carried out. On Oct. 31, 1918, he was included in a general amnesty of all Austrian political prisoners.

REF.: *CBA;* Florence, *Fritz;* ____, *The Story of a Political Assassin;* Laquer, *Terrorism.*

Sturla, Theressa (AKA: Madeline, Teresa Sterling), b.1861, U.S., pros.-mansl. Charles Stiles was a "sporting man" from the West, an itinerant gambler of fine manners and comportment whose pursuit of the ponies took him from town to town in search of the fast buck. In 1875, Stiles temporarily abandoned the racing game to open a faro bank in Philadelphia. The city fathers looked forward to the gala Centennial Celebration a year hence, and Stiles was eager to stake his claim.

The gambler was no stranger to the opulent bordellos of the East Coast. During one visit to Madame Fay's establishment in Baltimore in 1875, he met 15-year-old Theressa Sturla, an Italian immigrant woman with flashing dark eyes and a natural musical talent. She played opera music on the piano with the skill of a master. Sturla said her one-time suitor Galvenio had forsaken her. Seizing upon her misfortune, Stiles curried her favor. He said that such musical talent should be nurtured and what better place than in Chicago. After quarreling with Galvenio one last time, Sturla allowed Stiles to move into her apartment. She did not have the slightest inkling of his true character even after he had filched $200 of her money and pawned all her jewelry to cover his wagers at the track.

When the racing season was ended Stiles returned to Chicago but remained in communication with Sturla through the mail. Lured by promises of a stage career, the young woman took the money she had saved by working at Madame Fay's resort and went to Chicago. There she was joined by Stiles, who put her up in an elegant suite in the Palmer House. Stiles, whose family lived in Dixon, Ill., a rural farming community south of Chicago, was ashamed to tell his mother of his living arrangements. When the gambler returned home to be with his aging mother, Sturla remained in Chicago, amusing herself with two little children who lived down the hall. Her new life in Chicago was far from the romantic picture Stiles had painted for her in Baltimore. He became an abusive lover who demeaned her scarlet past. "And how he used to talk to me!" she recalled. "In the old days he used to tell his friends, 'I've got an Italian woman who will stab me to death one of these days unless I kill her first.' Men believed him until they saw how he treated me, and then they knew that I was not to blame."

Longing for a home of her own, Sturla turned over $600 of her money to Stiles to furnish a flat on Wabash Avenue. For a time she accepted male boarders there. Stiles' father was a frequent visitor, and he encouraged Sturla to be patient. "Charlie hasn't treated you right but one of these days he will marry you," he told her. Then we will all go east and live there together." But her future happiness was dashed when the old man died of heart disease—in the arms of his future daughter-in-law. "Then it was I lost my only friend, for after the funeral the relatives ordered me to leave the flat that had been bought with my own money."

No longer able to tolerate Stiles or his intemperate ways, Sturla entered the Clark Street resort of Carrie Watson, one of Chicago's most famous brothel madames, on Sept. 2, 1881. Watson's resort in the Custom House Levee was a showplace during the Gaslight era and Theressa Sturla became one of its most sought-after "demimondes." "Well," she sighed, "I could sing and play and I knew how to make myself agreeable. I could entertain visitors and I attended to business. A great many men on the board of trade knew me. Charlie constantly visited me. He spent my money and I never tried to keep it from him." Sturla, now known as "Madeline Stiles," prospered in her new setting. For a time her common-law husband approved of the arrangement, but on other occasions he was seized by jealousy and would burst in on Madame Watson's establishment and forcibly remove Sturla, to her great embarrassment.

After a time the woman would invariably wind up back at Carrie Watson's resort. Sturla would straggle through the door in a wretched condition, her jewels and fine clothing sold or pawned at Stiles' discretion. On four occasions she was forced to take refuge in the Clark Street bagnio. Carrie Watson noted with alarm a gradual deterioration of her sanity. One time Sturla purchased a bottle-green dress, only to take it to a commercial artist who painted a skull and cross-bone pattern on the fabric.

In April 1882, Sturla again was reunited with Stiles. They set up housekeeping in a Wabash Avenue apartment where they lived for a time as man and wife. The landlord remembered Theressa as a kindhearted woman of simple tastes. "She never had any gentlemen callers and when Mr. Stiles was out of town, as he generally was from Friday until Monday, being at his home at Dixon, she never went out of the house. At those times she cooked her meals on an oilstove and contented herself indoors."

Their days together passed without incident until the night of July 9, 1882. Her landlady, Mrs. Harvey, received a hand-written note from Stiles directing her to inform "Effie" (his pet name for Sturla) that he could no longer provide for her as he should. Stiles called off the relationship with a curt apology. Later that day he appeared in the hallway of the apartment building. "Now my dear," he said to Sturla, "get on your things and we will take a ride." They left the building together and took a buggy ride out into the country for dinner. While on the way to Downing's eatery, Stiles used the opportunity to ask her for some money, but she had none to give. They quarreled bitterly until reaching their destination, outside Batavia. Nothing further was said until they had finished dinner. Stiles lit up a cigar and excused himself. A few anxious minutes passed before a messenger appeared at her table to say that Mr. Stiles had left the establishment—and, as it turned out, with an unpaid dinner bill. Sturla sobbed uncontrollably. Outside rain had begun to fall in torrents. With no other recourse, the heartbroken young woman walked through the rain back to downtown Chicago—a distance of about eight miles.

In her wet clothing, Sturla reached the Palmer House Hotel the following morning, July 10. She marched up to the room her husband was accustomed to staying in, demanding an explanation. "What made you leave me out at Downing's last night?" she asked. Stiles ordered her out of the room, whereby Sturla vowed to return to Carrie Watson's. "You ain't going back to Carrie's!" Stiles grabbed her by the throat but Sturla pulled out a small pistol and pointed it toward him. The gun fired twice and Stiles fell to the floor dying. The manager and several guests of the hotel entered the room. "If he brought me home last night this would not have happened." she said.

Theressa Sturla was taken to the Armory Police Station and booked on a murder charge. A steady parade of Levee girls visited her in the jail. Carrie Watson pledged her financial support and that of her "sisters" in the red-light district. On the morning of Dec. 15, 1882, a compromise verdict was reached by the jury after considerable debate between defense attorneys. Theresa Sturla was found Not Guilty of murder, but Guilty of manslaughter. A recommendation for a one-year prison sentence was attached to the decision. Judge Gardner accepted the jury's findings, adding, "I cannot in fact conceive of a stronger defense than that imposed by your able and eloquent counsel. This will be seen from the result. Your term is the lowest known to the law."

REF.: *CBA; Sturla-Stiles Tragedy.*

Sturm, Beate, See: **Baader-Meinhof Gang.**

Sturmer, Boris Vladimirovich, 1848-1917, Rus., consp. Held offices of premier, minister of foreign affairs, and minister of interior and was blamed for Russia's difficulties in WWI, being suspected of having surreptitious contacts with Germany. Following the Russian Revolution, he was taken into custody, and died as a prisoner shortly thereafter. REF.: *CBA.*

Sturtivant, William E., 1850-75, U.S., mur. On Feb. 16, 1874, the battered bodies of brothers Simeon and Thomas Sturtevant and their housekeeper, Mary Buckley, were found on their homestead in Halifax, Mass. The house had been ransacked. It was well known that, due to a distrust of banks, the family kept large sums of money in their home. The following day the police arrested William Sturtivant, a 24-year-old grand-nephew of the brothers, when they discovered bloodstained clothing and stolen financial securities in his possession. The younger Sturtivant was arraigned in the East Bridgewater, Mass., courtroom of Justice W.H. Osborne, pleaded not guilty, and was ordered to stand trial on June 29, 1874. He was found Guilty of the triple murder and sentenced to death. He was hanged on the gallows in Plymouth, Mass., on May 7, 1875.

REF.: *CBA; Trial of William E. Sturtivant for the murder of Simeon Sturtevant in Halifax, Mass.*

Styles, Sylvia, c.1922-48, Brit., (unsolv.) mur. On Jan. 27, 1948, a woman was overheard arguing with a man in Lovers' Lane close to Syon Park, Isleworth. The next morning, the body of Sylvia Styles, a 26-year-old A.R.P. warden during WWII, was found strangled. Police were only able to learn that she had planned to meet a sailor named Dan that evening and the murder remained unsolved.

REF.: *CBA;* Harrison, *Criminal Calendar.*

Suarez, Don Pedro, prom. 1900s, Case of, Brit., fraud. A native of Bolivia, Colonel Don Pedro Suarez served as the military attaché and chargé d'affaires at the Bolivian Legation in London in 1905 and continued to live in London afterward as a Bolivian minister.

Suarez had a brother, Francisco Suarez, who died in England in 1897, and after his death Don Pedro Suarez offered to become the trustee of his brother's estate.

During the next several years he apparently collected about £250,000 on behalf of the estate but allegedly did not add the money to the estate, instead keeping it for himself. When a nephew of the two brothers, Nicolas Suarez, asked where the money had gone, he did not receive a complete answer so he filed a complaint in 1914. A warrant was issued for the arrest of Don Pedro Suarez, charging him with fraudulent conversion. He was not arrested because he had diplomatic immunity, but after he was fired from his position in England he went back to Bolivia where he was trailed by British police. The British were unable to force him to return to England and he remained free.

REF.: *CBA;* Nicholls, *Crime Within the Square Mile.*

Suárez Gómez, Roberto, Sr. (AKA: **Papito**), 1932- , Bol., drugs-org. crime. Roberto Suárez Gómez, Sr., the leading Bolivian cocaine trafficker known by the local peasants as the "Little Father," lives like a feudal prince in Santa Ana de Yacuma, Bol. Suárez Gómez and his family are major suppliers of cocaine base to the Medellin cartel od Colombia and the Guadalajara cartel of Mexico. The U.S. State Department estimated in 1986 that 100,000 acres of coca were being cultivated in the foothills of the Bolivian Andes.

The refining and distribution of the coca paste is controlled by the Santa Cruz Mafia, named after the town where the cartel originated. Suárez Gómez rejected his family's cattle business to build the first drug laboratories in the Beni Department, the lowlands east of Cochabamba. In 1980, a military coup in Bolivia brought General Luis Garcia Meza to power. The coup was allegedly financed and planned by the Santa Cruz Mafia and it was believed several Nazis, including Klaus Barbie, advised Bolivian security forces. Due to the Bolivian government's apparent ties to cocaine traffickers, the U.S. suspended all military and economic assistance.

The right-wing regime of Garcia Meza was toppled in September 1981, and the succeeding military junta allowed the election of a civilian president, Hernán Siles Zuazo, who vowed to clean up the drug problem, following his inauguration on Oct. 10, 1982. However, the corruption continued and Suárez Gómez produced coca at a record pace until his semi-retirement in 1985, two years after his son, Robert Suárez Levy, was acquitted of drug trafficking in Miami, Fla. A nephew of Suárez Gómez, Jorge Roca Suárez, took over the business. The efforts of the DEA to penetrate the empire have been thwarted by unstable governments, internal corruption, and the attitude of the local populace. In 1986, after the arrival of U.S. troops to eradicate the coca industry, Bolivian peasants demonstrated in front of the U.S. embassy, chanting, "Long live coca!"

REF.: *CBA;* Shannon, *Desperados.*

Subway Slasher, See: **Ford, James.**

Sucre, Antonio José de, 1795-1830, Bol., pres., assass. Served under Simon Bolivar as chief lieutenant in drive against Spanish army in Quito in 1821. They won important battles in 1822 and defeated the Spanish at Junin in 1824. A Venezuelian, he served as the first president of Bolivia, from 1826-28, resigning at the request of Bolivians wanting a natural-born president. He was murdered in Columbia, near the region of Pasto. REF.: *CBA.*

Sudbury, Simon of (AKA: Simon Theobald, Thebaud, Tybald), d.1381, Brit., polit. corr. Served as bishop of London in 1361 and was named archbishop of Canterbury in 1375. He presided at Lambeth over John Wycliffe's second trial for heresy in 1378. He was appointed chancellor of England in 1380 and levied a hefty poll tax, partially inciting the Peasants' Revolt of 1381. He was put to death by a band of Wat Tyler's supporters, who dragged him from the Tower of London and beheaded him. REF.: *CBA.*

Suffragettes, prom. 1906-18, Brit., bomb. When the women's suffrage movement appeared stalled, many of its supporters decided that radical means were justified to bring attention to their cause. In 1905 Christabel Pankhurst and Annie Kenney of the Women's Social and Political Union were ousted from a Liberal meeting in Manchester when they tried to speak. When they then spoke in front of a crowd gathered outside, they were arrested for obstruction. Instead of paying the fine, as had been their policy in the past, the two chose to go to jail.

In 1908, when Pankhurst was arrested for inciting a crowd in Trafalgar Square, she got cabinet ministers David Lloyd George and Herbert Gladstone as witnesses in court, and there displayed the inconsistency of their anti-suffrage position. Soon, numerous suffragettes were going to prison, where a new means of gaining attention was discovered in hunger strikes. In 1910, Winston Churchill, then the home secretary, introduced the policy of force-feeding the women hunger strikers. Prison guards held a woman prisoner down, forced a tube down her throat, and poured nourishment directly into her stomach. When the public became enraged at the tactic, Churchill instituted the "Prisoners (Temporary Discharge for Ill-Health) Act" (nicknamed the "Cat and Mouse" Act), under the terms of which hunger strikers were released from prison. As soon as the protestors regained their strength, they were imprisoned again.

In 1913, a more radical contingent of women turned to bombs to make their point. In February, Lloyd George's house at Walton-on-the-Hill was slightly damaged by an explosion of five pounds of gunpowder. In May an electrical firing device was used to try to set off a charge under the Bishop's Throne at St. Paul's Cathedral in London, but it failed to function. The next month such a device placed under the Coronation Chair at Westminster Abbey exploded, causing slight damage. In December an attempt to blow a hole in the wall of Holloway Prison where several suffragettes were being held also failed.

The following year, WWI started and the women's suffrage movement was overshadowed by the war effort. In 1918, Parliament gave older property owners and wives the right to vote. Ten years later, Parliament enlarged the franchise to include all women. REF.: *CBA.*

Sugarman Gang, prom. 1910, Brit., consp.-burg.-fenc. A ring known as "The Sugarman Gang," which operated in London and Leeds, was broken up by Detective Ernest Nicholls in 1910. Stolen goods were funneled from William Mallinson, who posed as a jewelry auctioneer, to Samuel Sugarman, who ran a remnant business. Sugarman actually was a fence who sold stolen goods, including jewelry, watches, drapes, clothing, and clocks. Nicholls arrested Sugarman and recognized the criminal as a man who had previously tried to report a fake burglary.

Sugarman was charged with conspiracy, fraud, and receiving stolen goods. He was tried at the Old Bailey, convicted, and sentenced to an eighteen-month term in prison with hard labor. Two others in the gang, Mallinson and Harold Jenkins, escaped and were never caught, but a fourth, Harry Jacobson, was arrested. Jacobson, freed on bond, defrauded his mother of £600, telling her he intended to use the money to compensate the burglary victims, but instead fled with the money.

REF.: *CBA;* Nicholls, *Crime Within the Square Mile.*

Sukarno (Kusnasosro), 1901-70, Indo., polit. corr.-rebel. Ardently nationalist politician jailed from 1929-31 and banished from 1933-42 by Dutch colonial rulers. He declared the independence of Indonesia in 1945 and finally acquired formal independence from the Netherlands in 1949. He served as Indonesia's president from 1949-67, making improvements in health care and education. His reign grew steadily more authoritarian and corrupt and he lost much influence following General Sunarto's coup in 1966, losing office in 1967. He was in custody for the rest of his life. REF.: *CBA.*

Sukhomlinov, Vladimir Aleksandrovich, 1848-1926, Rus., treas. Served as chief of general staff in 1908, and as minister of war in 1909. He was blamed for the Russian army's lack of readiness for WWI. He was found Guilty of treason in 1917, and was given a life sentence by the provisional government. He was granted amnesty by the Soviet government, however, in 1918, and moved to Germany. REF.: *CBA.*

Suleiman Pasha, 1840-92, Turk., treas. Participated in removal of Sultan Abdul-Aziz in 1876 after revolt. He commanded troops in Bulgaria during a war with Russia from 1877-78, and was driven back to Constantinople. He was jailed on charges of treason in 1878, but was later pardoned. REF.: *CBA.*

Sullivan, Alexander Martin, 1871-1959, Brit.-Ire., lawyer. Served as Irish King's Counsel from 1908, and as English King's Counsel from 1919. He defended Sir Roger Casement, charged with treason, and Samuel Dashwood, found Guilty of murder. He practiced law exclusively in Ireland after the new republic was founded in 1949. REF.: *CBA.*

Sullivan, Howard, d.1884, U.S., necro.-mur. Howard Sullivan, a black youth, strangled and raped Ella Watson in Yorktown, N.J., on Aug. 18, 1884. Armed with a cane, Sullivan murdered the 15-year-old girl and took from her the money she had earned selling poultry and eggs in town. Afterward Sullivan engaged in sex with the corpse. A Pinkerton detective disguised as a prison inmate was placed in the cell with the accused man to wring a confession out of him. The ruse succeeded, and Sullivan was convicted of first-degree murder in Salem County in October 1884. He was hanged on Dec. 1.

REF.: *CBA; The Yorketown Tragedy; Ella Waatson's Tragic Death.*

Sullivan, Jeanette, 1921-61, U.S., (unsolv.) mur. Charles Boothroyd, fifty-five, Jeanette Sullivan, forty, and her daughter Denise, fourteen, were sightseeing in their Volkswagon at Dead Horse Point when they came across a man claiming to have car trouble. The stranger asked to borrow their flashlight as he had "generator trouble." He then pulled out a rifle and demanded they give him their money. Boothroyd threw his wallet on the ground but an angry Sullivan grabbed the wallet and turned to walk away. The stranger shot her in the back of the head and turned the rifle on Boothroyd, shooting him twice in the face. Denise attempted to drive their car away but the stranger, using his car, ran her off the road and abducted her. An oil rigger found Boothroyd holding his head, Jeanette Sullivan, fatally wounded, lying nearby, and their crumpled Volkswagon in the ditch. FBI agents caught up with the murderer within a week, but he killed himself before he could be identified. Denise Sullivan, dead or alive, was never found. REF.: *CBA.*

Sullivan, John, 1740-95, U.S., jur. Served as delegate to Continental Congress from 1780-81, and held office of attorney general of New Hampshire from 1782-86. He was appointed to the district court of New Hampshire by President George Washington in 1789. REF.: *CBA.*

Sullivan, Percy B., prom. 1896, U.S., (wrong. convict.) count. Late in the summer of 1896 a well-dressed crook named Tyler passed counterfeit money in Evansville, Vincennes, and Terre Haute, Ind. About the same time Percy B. Sullivan, an insurance agent from a prominent Bowling Green, Ky., family, made calls in those towns. Police tracked Sullivan and he was arrested in St.

Louis by a U.S. Marshal and sent back to Indianapolis. After several Evansville residents were shown Sullivan's photograph, he was identified as the culprit and a grand jury indicted him on Nov. 12, 1896. He was tried and convicted on Dec. 8, 1896, received a four-year sentence, and was fined $100. He began serving his term at the South Prison at Jeffersonville, but then was transferred to the Michigan City prison.

Later the real criminal, Tyler, was arrested and confessed to passing counterfeit notes in the three Indiana towns. Authorities showed Tyler and Sullivan's pictures, which were not labeled, to victims, who identified Tyler as the counterfeiter. Tyler was then tried, convicted, and sentenced. On May 12, 1898, President William McKinley granted a full pardon to Sullivan and he was freed. REF.: *CBA*.

Sullivan, Robert Austin, 1947-83, U.S., mur. Robert Austin Sullivan, manager of a Homestead, Fla., motel, was charged in August 1972 with stealing from the motel. He pleaded guilty, and was sentenced to five years probation and ordered to repay $6,000. On April 3, 1973, Sullivan and Reid McLaughlin robbed the motel after binding and gagging Donald Schmidt, the assistant manager. They then drove Schmidt to the Everglades where they killed him. Later, Sullivan maintained he was innocent, but McLaughlin testified against him in return for a reduced sentence. Sentenced to death and imprisoned in Starke, Fla., Sullivan's struggle against execution eventually was supported by Pope John Paul II. On death row for ten years before Florida state governor Bob Graham gave final approval, Sullivan told a reporter, "The hardest thing about all of this is that my life is totally out of my own control...I certainly don't like it. But I haven't much choice." Sullivan was executed on Nov. 30, 1983, the ninth man to be executed since the Supreme Court lifted a ban on capital punishment in 1976. REF.: *CBA*.

Sullivan, Ronald Joseph, See: **Waddingham, Dorothea Nancy.**

Sullivan, Steven, See: **Scanlan, John.**

Sullivan, Timothy (AKA: Big Tim, The Big Feller), 1863-1916, U.S., polit. corr. For most of the nineteenth century, the political fortunes of New York City were in the hands of a puissant ethnic-Irish cabal that came to be known as Tammany Hall. Through the usual blend of charity and patronage dispensed through the wards by the district leaders, the Tammany "Democracy," as corrupt and venal as it was, became an invincible political machine. It reached the height of its power around 1901, when "Big" Tim Sullivan, the swaggering boss of the Lower East Side, installed Tom Foley as the Tammany leader of the rebellious second district. To ensure the victory of this saloon keeper against the respected incumbent Paddy Divver, Sullivan brought in members of Paul Kelly's Five Points Gang to form a human chain around the polling places. Kelly's gang was composed mostly of Italians. The Irish residents of the fourth ward organized their own gang to do battle, but the heavily armed Italians drove them away from the polls, while Police Chief William Devery and his men passively stood by. Devery was Sullivan's erstwhile "business" partner, who regulated (as opposed to suppressing) gambling and vice in the city.

Tim Sullivan ran the show his own way for nearly twenty-five years. Born in the gang-infested Five Points tenement in 1863, Sullivan passed his formative years in the company of the Whyos, then one of New York's most formidable street gangs. He drifted into politics, a natural segue in those days for an ambitious young man with connections. In time, Sullivan became a trusted Tammany lieutenant, and later a state senator. In 1889, New York police inspector Thomas Byrnes attempted to push through the Albany legislature a bill that would permit his men to arrest known criminals on sight. Sullivan spoke against it, and continued to do so for his entire term of office in the assembly. Byrnes denounced Big Tim as an associate of criminals, which wasn't far from the truth.

In 1911, Big Tim succeeded in passing his own modified piece of crime legislation, which became known as the "Sullivan Law." The bill made it a crime to carry a concealed weapon, and any hoodlum caught doing so faced a mandatory term of seven years in prison. The enforcement of this measure depended solely on the policeman's willingness to enforce it. And as every New Yorker of that era knew and understood, Sullivan controlled the police, who in turn cut their own separate deals with the underworld. The police chiefs were mere figureheads, placed in office to do the bidding of the Tammany district leaders.

Tammany Hall crime boss "Big Tim" Sullivan.

Sullivan earned the respect and admiration of the voters in his district by distributing free shoes to the needy and touting the interests of the non-Irish, whose numbers had grown appreciably since the 1850s. He worked closely with Italian gang leaders like Paul Kelly, (real name Paolo Vaccarelli) who emerged as a major player in the International Longshoreman's Association. Tim Sullivan would later boast to a meeting of Tammanyites in the Bowery district that he had saved Kelly from a twenty-year stretch in prison for the murder of a man named Harrington in 1905. Edward "Monk" Eastman, whose Tenderloin dives also enjoyed the protection of Sullivan and his crowd. In 1912 Eastman was jailed for the second time, this time for drug dealing. After WWI, he received a pardon from Governor Al Smith, whose political career was launched by Tom Foley, who ran him for the state assembly years earlier.

Big Tim's headquarters was the elegantly appointed Hesper Club, where the East Side riff-raff would gather every St. Patrick's Day to celebrate the achievements of the Irish, and to drink to the continued prosperity of the organization. According to one observer present at Hesper's:

> The streets of the Tenderloin lie vacant of its women; the eyes of the city detective force are focused on the great dancing hall—stuffed to the doors with painted women and lean faced men. In the center box...sits the "Big Feller."...Around him the gathering of his business and political lieutenants...he leads through the happy mazes of the grand march a thousand pimps and prostitutes to the blatant cry of the band "Sullivan, Sullivan, a damn fine Irish man!"

The downfall of Tim Sullivan came in 1912. A case of unchecked paresis slowly eroded his mind, forcing him to spend the better part of his waking hours confined to a bed. The dissolute Sullivan could do little to hold together his organization as former protegés like the corrupt police lieutenant Charles Becker (who along with gambler Herman "Beansie" Rosenthal owned a piece of the Hesper Club) grabbed for power. These two men became the principal players in what was to become one of New York's most serious police scandals. Tim's health meanwhile, continued to decline. He failed to win re-election to the

State Senate in 1912, but settled instead for a seat in Congress (in the view of the Tammany regulars, it was a lesser role). Boss Sullivan never made it to Washington. He was committed to an insane asylum, where he remained until 1916. He escaped from the institution, was run over by a train, only to be rescued at the point of death. Tim Sullivan was removed to New York's Bellevue Hospital, where he died ten days later. A policeman who recognized the fallen king ran through the wards screaming "It's Big Tim! Lord God, it's Big Tim!" What was left of Sullivan's organization in lower Manhattan was divided between Tom Foley and Arnold Rothstein, who attended to matters down in the Tenderloin. See: **Becker, Charles; Tammany Hall; Eastman, Edward; Rothstein, Arnold.**

REF.: Asbury, *The Gangs of New York; CBA;* Eisenberg and Landau, *Meyer Lansky;* Fried, *The Rise and Fall of the Jewish Gangster in America;* Logan, *Against the Evidence;* Peterson, *The Mob;* Reppetto, *The Blue Parade;* Thompson and Raymond, *Gang Rule in New York.*

Sulpicius Rufus, Publius, c.124-88 B.C., Roman., treas. Caused other tribunes to lose power by promoting reforms contrary to Senate views. He was captured by Lucius Sulla and put to death for supporting Gaius Marius in the clash between the two politicians. REF.: *CBA.*

Sulpicius, Rufus, Servius, c.106-43 B.C., Roman., jur. Explored rhetorical methods with Cicero and served as consul in 51 B.C. and proconsul of Achaia. He wrote many treatise on law, all now lost. REF.: *CBA.*

Summerdale Police (Chicago), See: **Morrison, Richard.**

Summers, Montague (Alphonsus Joseph-Mary Augustus Montague), 1880-1948, Brit., writer. Man of letters and expert on demonology and witchcraft. Books authored: *History of Witchcraft and Demonology, Horrid Mysteries, The Vampire, His Kith and Kin, The Werewolf, The Black Mass,* and *A Popular History of Witchcraft.* REF.: *CBA.*

Summit House Mystery; or, The Earthly Purgatory, 1905, a novel by Lily Dougal. Lizzie Borden, one of the most popular accused murderesses in U.S. history, is the inspiration for this work. See: **Borden, Lizzie.** REF.: *CBA.*

Sumner, Charles, See: **Brooks, Preston.**

Sundance Kid, The (Harry Longabaugh), c.1863-1908, U.S., west. outl. Born and raised in Mont Clare, Pa., Harry Longabaugh moved to Wyoming in his youth, becoming a horse thief while still in his teens. He was apprehended, and from August 1887 until February 1889, he served a sentence in the Sundance jail, and henceforth was known as The Sundance Kid. Returning to a life of crime, Longabaugh robbed banks and trains, and rustled cattle, becoming a frequent user of the craggy Robber's Roost in the western Rocky Mountain Hole-in-the-Wall area. In 1892, with Harry Bass, Bert Charter, and Bill Madden, Longabaugh was captured following a failed train robbery near Malta, Mont., but he escaped, and a short time later he met Butch Cassidy for the first time. Years later their paths crossed again while they both worked at a Wyoming ranch. Soon thereafter, Cassidy formed the Wild Bunch gang.

Harry Longabaugh, the Sundance Kid.

The Wild Bunch robbed a bank in Belle Fourche, S.D., in 1897, but Longabaugh and three others were arrested. Escaping from a jail in Deadwood, S.D., Longabaugh participated in crime for the next five years, living a lavish life that included frequent vacations in New Orleans and Denver. He also began to consort with Etta Place, a former schoolteacher. Longabaugh escaped a posse led by Sheriff Joe Hazen on June 5, 1899, after robbing a train at Wilcox Siding, Wyo., with "Flat Nose" George Curry and Harvey Logan. Logan killed Hazen during the shootout.

Accompanied by Etta Place, Longabaugh fled to Argentina in 1902, where he met Cassidy and became his partner in a cattle ranch. The trio migrated to Bolivia, where, in 1905, Longabaugh was caught in a bedroom with the wife of a neighboring rancher, and forced to shoot the irate husband in the shoulder. In 1907, Longabaugh and Place returned to the U.S. for a vacation. After visiting New York, the pair journeyed to Denver, where Place was hospitalized for appendicitis. While waiting for her release, Longabaugh encountered a few old friends, and after becoming quite drunk, wounded a bartender during a saloon shootout.

Upon returning to Bolivia, Longabaugh and Cassidy went to work for a mining company, supplementing their income with occasional bank robberies. In 1908, the pair robbed a mule train near San Vicente, Bol. Two days later they were recognized in the plaza at San Vicente and surrounded by police and a cavalry troop. Despite overwhelming odds, Longabaugh shot the cavalry commander, seized his ammunition belt, and retreated with Cassidy into the safety of a nearby restaurant. After dark, while still hopelessly surrounded, Longabaugh attempted to sneak across the plaza to reach a cache of arms. He was cut down by a barrage of bullets, but Cassidy dragged him to safety. With Longabaugh seriously wounded and unable to seek medical attention, Cassidy ended his friend's life with a gunshot to the head before escaping under cover of darkness. See: **Cassidy, Butch; Wild Bunch, The.**

REF.: Baker, *Wild Bunch*; *CBA*; Horan and Sann, *Pictorial History of the Wild West*; Pointer, *Butch Cassidy;* Repetto, *The Blue Parade;* (FILM), *Return of the Badmen,* 1948; *Butch Cassidy and the Sundance Kid,* 1969.

Sung Chiao-jen, 1882-1913, China, polit., assass. Relocated to Tokyo after revolutionary activities caused expulsion from school in 1904. He joined the T'ung-meng-hui revolutionary party originated by Sun Yat-sen in 1905, quickly becoming a leading member. He served for a short time in the cabinet of provisional president Yüan Shih-k'ai in 1912, and then started the Kuomintang, or Nationalist, party. He was killed shortly thereafter. REF.: *CBA.*

Sung Djang Djing, d.1919, Brit., mur. On June 23, 1919, the body of Wu Zee Ming, a Chinese factory worker, was discovered in a wooded area near the Warwickshire-Worcestershire border in England. His head was crushed, his jaw shattered, and two ribs and his breastbone were broken. The next day, another Chinese man brought the dead man's post office savings book to the West Kensington branch and tried to draw cash, but was refused.

A month later, on July 25, 1919, an intruder attacked Dsou Kuo Doung with a hammer as he slept in his room in London. Dsou survived, and told police he could not tell if his assailant was Chinese or English, as he wore a handkerchief over his face. The burglar stole £7 and a watch and chain. Police found a bloody hammer, a cap, and a loose button at the site. Dsou told them that Sung Djang Djing, who had lodged at the house some weeks earlier, had written him asking for money. When Dsou refused, Sung wrote another letter, this one abusive and threatening. Dsou reported that Sung now worked in a foundry in Birmingham, near the scene of Wu Zee Ming's murder.

Scotland Yard notified Birmingham authorities, who detained Sung. The physical evidence from Dsou's room matched his belongings, and he was tried for murder, attempted murder, and burglary. He first claimed that another Chinese worker had murdered Wu over an old debt from China and that he had merely witnessed the killing along with several others. But each of the men Sung named produced a provable alibi. Post office employees also identified Sung as the man who tried to draw on Wu's savings. Sung was convicted of murder on Oct. 22, 1919, sentenced to death, and executed.

REF.: *CBA; Savage, Savage of the Yard;* Shew, *A Second Companion to Murder.*

Sun in Capricorn, 1942, a novel by Hamilton Basso. This work of fiction is a thinly disguised biography of the rabble-rousing

Huey Long of Louisiana and depicts his gruesome assassination (U.S., 1935). See: **Long, Huey Pierce**. REF.: *CBA*.

Sunset Slayer, See: Clark, Douglas Daniel.

Sun Yat-sen (Sun Wen, Chung Shan), 1866-1925, China, rebel.-kid. (vict.) Sun Yat-sen was suspected of participating in a secret revolution in Canton in 1895 and, when the revolution was defeated, was compelled to leave, traveling to various locations such as England, Hawaii, the U.S., and Japan, from 1895-1911. Shortly into his exile, in 1896, he was kidnapped by Chinese members of a legation in London and held for ten days. He returned to China and planned the revolution that overthrew the Manchus and gave rise to the new Chinese Republic. He is remembered as the "father of the Revolution."

Sun Yat-sen, father of modern-day China.

REF.: *CBA;* Laquer, *Terrorism;* (FILM), *Dr. Sun Yatsen*, 1987; *The Story of Dr. Sun Yat-Sen*, 1987.

Supayalat, prom. 1878-85, Burma, banish. Enjoyed much influence over husband, King Thibaw, urging him to defy British authorities. She and Thibaw were banished to India after losing the Third Burmese War. REF.: *CBA*.

Sure Enuf Hotel, 1820s-50s, U.S., gamb.-pros. One of the wicked establishments in the Swamp, the vice district of old New Orleans, was the foul-smelling Sure Enuf Hotel, a two-story structure of unsound construction operated by a portly hag named Mother Colby. The main floor held a rough bar and a large gambling area where roulette and faro were played around the clock. A small kitchen and sleeping quarters, separated by a thin wall, functioned as Mother Colby's room. Another area made up half the downstairs and consisted of cubicles with shabby, torn curtains blocking the cramped interiors from view. Whores on Mother Colby's penny-ante payroll strolled in from the street and, for a few pennies, sold their bodies to the Sure Enuf's customers, occupying the cubicles for no more than ten minutes.

Riots and fights were commonplace at the Sure Enuf, one of the more spectacular outbursts occurring in Spring 1845 when four gangsters squared off in front of Mother Colby's dilapidated hotel, using only their hands and teeth. Jim Rider and Bob McBride accused Bill Curry and Jim Rogers of cheating at cards and also added that their women were cheats, too. The four flew at one another. The accusers quickly lost the battle. McBride was blinded forever when Rogers dug his thumbs into his eyes and gouged them out, holding them up to the applause of blood-lusting supporters. Jim Rider, McBride's buddy, fared no better. Curry leaped upon him and gnawed away at him as would a starved rat, chewing off part of his jaw and both his ears. The victors carried these grisly trophies about with them for years, to show to disbelieving friends.

The Sure Enuf was the scene of another bloody occurrence in 1855, probably the most bizarre murder in the city's history. The new owner of the hotel, Frederick "Crazy Bill" Krause, who had bought out Mother Colby, met a spectacular end. Krause had double-crossed his prostitute sweetheart and had taken up with another tart. The rejected slattern presented her one-time lover with a brand new money belt as a parting gift. Krause was deeply moved and promised to wear it forever. He put it around his waist. The whore smiled and lit a match, applying it to a short fuse sticking out from one of the pouches on the belt which was lined with brimstone and powder. In a few seconds, "Crazy Bill" exploded, pieces of him flying in all directions up and down Girod Street. See: **Swamp, The**.

REF.: Asbury, *The French Quarter;* Buel, *Metropolitan Life Unveiled; CBA;* Fremaux, *New Orleans Characters;* Huber, *New Orleans;* Laughlin, *New Orleans and Its Living Past;* Tinker, *Creole City: Its Past and Its People.*

Sûreté-Nationale, 1800s- , Fr., law enfor. agen. Four major policing agencies are responsible for maintaining law and order in France: the Paris Prefecture of Police, with jurisdiction in the capital city and the department of the Seine; the Gendarmerie, a military body accountable to the minister of war but responsible for conditions in the rural hinterland; the municipal police forces of provincial France; and the Sûreté-Nationale, a state police headquartered in the Rue des Saussaies in Paris but under the aegis of the minister of the interior. Its criminal investigation division, known as the Police Judiciare, is similar in many ways to the CID of Scotland Yard. The Sûreté, however, is a civilian agency that operates throughout France. Police power is vested in prefects, appointed civil servants who head up the ninety departments within the country. The local prefect is vested with policing powers and is responsible for conditions in his locale. In municipalities with a population of 10,000 or more, the Sûreté-Nationale shares its responsibilities with the local police. In smaller, rural districts the municipal police and the Gendarmerie carry on these duties.

The agency is further divided into four important sub-divisions: (1) Counter-espionage, which is similar to the FBI in the U.S. Agents assigned to this division investigate incidents of treason and foreign subversion within France. (2) The Criminal Investigation Division, which leads the fight against crime, be it robbery, murder, narcotics trafficking, forgery, arson, terrorism, or counterfeiting. (3) The Special Branch, an advisory body to the minister of interior and the departmental prefect. This agency assesses the potential impact of domestic disputes such as labor strikes, public demonstrations, etc. The Special Branch also maintains jurisdiction over public gambling, airports, railways, and seaports. (4) Public Security, the uniform branch usually found in cities of 10,000 or more. The director of public security provides coordination and general management but does not exercise central administrative control over this branch, a task left to the commissaire of police. However, the director functions as the head of the Republican Security Companies (CRS), sixty uniformed branches deployed over the entire country. In the event of a civil emergency, the prefect of a department is empowered to recruit the CRS after first obtaining the approval of the minister of the interior.

Over the years the Sûreté-Nationale has employed some of the greatest detective minds in Europe. Eugene François Vidocq became the head of the agency in 1811. A former convict, Vidocq pioneered modern criminal investigation and did much to place the Sûreté at the forefront of the world's premier policing agencies. Gustave Macé took over the agency in 1879. He believed that there was no substitute for practical field experience. Ten years earlier, Macé conducted the Voirbo murder investigation, a case which helped established his reputation on the continent. Marie-François Goron was another brilliant investigator who took over the reins of the Sûreté in 1887. His method of wringing a confession out of a suspect became known as "Goron's Cookshop." In the twentieth century Commissioner Jean Belin arrested Henri Landru, the notorious "French Bluebeard" who poisoned his victims and then strangled them with a thin wire. In 1913, members of the Sûreté broke up the Bonnot gang, led by Jules Joseph Bonnot who was described by the French prime minister as the "most dangerous criminal of the century." Bonnot, a former race car driver turned bank robber, terrorized France for nearly fifteen months being trapped in his hideout in March 1913. See: **Bonnot Gang; Vidocq, Eugène-François**.

REF.: Belin, *Secrets of the Sureté; CBA;* Morain, *The Underworld of Paris;* Reppetto, *The Blue Parade;* Scott, *The Concise Encyclopedia of Crime and Criminals.*

Surfleet Stockade Escapes, prom. 1830, Brit., riot. A general unrest pervaded most European countries in 1830. The year saw an unusually large number of riots in England. King George IV had just died, there was widespread dissatisfaction with the conditions in industrial operations, and the economy was depressed. Sympathy with their continental colleagues only made English workers more likely to revolt. On Oct. 9, police placed several youths in the stockades. A crowd gathered, gave them tankards of ale, and when everyone was drunk, broke the stockades and released the youths. REF.: *CBA*.

Surrey Pubs Bombings, 1974, Brit., bomb. The Irish Republican Army (IRA) staged several terrorist attacks in the London area throughout Summer and Fall 1974. The most serious incidents occurred on Oct. 4, when IRA men carrying shopping bags containing explosives entered two pubs in Guildford, Surrey, the Horse and Groom, and the Seven Stars. Both pubs catered to young WRAC (Women's Royal Air Corps) and Guards at Pirbright recruits. The bombs exploded, killing five people and injuring sixty-eight others. Christopher Rowe, assistant chief constable of Surrey, and Detective Superintendent Walter Simmons of the CID photographed the 400 people known to have been in either of the pubs that night. The CID eventually traced the bombers through composite sketches completed with the help of photographs and a minute-by-minute reconstruction of the events leading up to the blast. REF.: *CBA*.

Susanna (Susannah), prom. c.590 B.C., Case of, Babylonia, adult. Subject of Apocryphal book, falsely charged with adultery by Jewish elders. The wife of Joachim, she was exonerated by Daniel during the Hebrews' captivity in Babylonia. Her accusers, who had lusted after her, were put to death. REF.: *CBA*.

Suspect, 1940, a play by Edward Percy (pseudonym for Reginald Denham). This drama is based upon the celebrated Borden case (U.S., 1892). See: **Borden, Lizzie**. REF.: *CBA*.

Suspect, The, 1944, a film based upon the wife murderer Dr. Hawley Harvey Crippen (Brit., 1910), taken from the James Ronald novel, *This Way Out*. Charles Laughton is wonderful as the henpecked husband whose shrewish wife drives him to homicidal action. Stanley Ridges does an admirable job as the Scotland Yard sleuth who is based upon the dogged Inspector Walter Dew, who tracked Crippen across an ocean to make his arrest. See: **Crippen, Dr. Hawley Harvey**. REF.: *CBA*.

Sutcliffe, George M., prom. 1923, U.S., fraud-mansl. In 1923, George M. Sutcliffe was arrested on charges of manslaughter in the death of Albert C. Hoody. Hoody, a mechanic in Unionville, Conn., was taken to Sutcliffe after he got a finger caught in a stamping machine while at work. Sutcliffe strapped Hoody to the table, stating that he needed to amputate the finger. During the procedure, Sutcliffe had Hoody's friend, who had brought him to the office, administer more than three cans of ether to the patient. Hoody died from inhaling the ether fumes.

When Sutcliffe was apprehended, he revealed to authorities that he was a former news photographer and had bought a high school certificate and an M.D. degree at the St. Louis College of Physicians and Surgeons, and a license to practice in Connecticut from the Eclectic Medical Examining Board of Connecticut. During Sutcliffe's ten months of practice, he signed seven death certificates. When arrested, Sutcliffe agreed to cooperate with authorities and supplied them with information about how such diploma "mills" operated. According to Sutcliffe's testimony, students who had attended only six classes were awarded diplomas showing that they had completed four years of work. The cost of a diploma was usually $250. Sutcliffe's arrest and subsequent testimony lead to a lengthy investigation of licensing practices in various states. The licenses of over two hundred "graduates" of the various diploma mills were called into question in the wake of the investigation. Sutcliffe pleaded *nolo contendere* to the charge of manslaughter and was sentenced to six months in jail. REF.: *CBA*.

Sutcliffe, Peter William (AKA: **Peter Williams, The Yorkshire Ripper**), 1946- , Brit., rape-asslt.-mur. The hunt for the "Yorkshire Ripper" lasted five years and nearly cost Assistant Chief Constable George Oldfield, a man obsessed with capturing the fiend, his life. Oldfield worked around the clock trying to piece together fragmented clues that might bring the killer to justice. Thirteen women were brutally murdered between 1975 and 1980, most of them prostitutes. The British press portrayed this hulking night-stalker as a 1970s reincarnation of Jack the Ripper, who had murdered several London street-walkers in the late 1880s. Before this latter-day Ripper was apprehended, the British police had questioned 200,000 people. They searched 30,000 houses and checked the registration on some 180,000 motor vehicles. It was without doubt the widest manhunt in British history. But then, the Yorkshire Ripper was the worst mass-murderer in twentieth-century England.

The first attack attributed to the Ripper occurred on July 5, 1975, when Anna Rogulskyj was assaulted by a man wielding a hammer. Six weeks later, on Aug. 15, Olive Smelt was struck from behind in a similar manner. Both women recovered after surgery. Not so lucky was Wilma McCann, a 28-year-old Scotswoman who had reverted to prostitution to take care of her four children. McCann was canvassing the pubs of Leeds on the night of Oct. 29-30 in search of customers when the Ripper pounced on her from behind. Struck on the head with a ball-headed hammer, the woman was dragged into an empty field and viciously assaulted with a knife. Her mutilated body was found the next day. The random murder of a prostitute carried little weight in the media. One of the dead woman's neighbors expressed the opinion that "Hotpants" McCann was "no better than she ought to have been."

No one knew at the time that the McCann murder would set into motion a series of these crimes, the next one occurring on Jan. 20, 1976, when 42-year-old Emily Jackson was battered over the head and stabbed to death in a Chapeltown alley in Leeds. Jackson was married to a roofing specialist who did not know that his wife was supplementing the family income by turning "tricks" on the side, By this time the CID and the press were aware that a serial killer might be loose. Chief Superintendent Dennis Hoban expressed concern. "I can't stress strongly enough that it is vital we catch this brutal killer before he brings tragedy to another family." The killer was dubbed the "Yorkshire Ripper" by writer George Hill, who covered the murder for the *Daily Express*.

The Ripper kept a low profile for the next year, re-surfacing on Feb. 5, 1977, when he stabbed 28-year-old Irene Richardson to death in Roundhay Park in Leeds. The murder site was scarcely a mile away from Chapeltown, the notorious red-light district where the Ripper cruised for his victims. Richardson, like Emily Jackson before her, was nominally connected to the trade. She had taken to the streets after separating from her husband. The murder count climbed to four on Apr. 23, when Bradford prostitute Patricia Atkinson, thirty-two, was found bludgeoned to death in her apartment on Lumb Lane. This time the killer left behind an important clue: a bloody footprint identical to one found at the scene of the Jackson murder. The scarcity of eyewitnesses however, hampered the investigation.

Sixteen-year-old Jayne MacDonald was certainly no prostitute. She was a fun-loving teenager who had been dancing the night away at the Hofbrauhaus in Leeds. On June 26, 1977, she was grabbed by the Yorkshire Ripper near Roundhay Park and stabbed to death, possibly because he mistook her for a street-walker. The girl lived only a few doors down the lane from Wilma McCann. Maureen Long narrowly avoided a similar fate on July 27. While walking through Bradford, she was accosted by the Ripper and dragged unconscious to a darkened street nearby. Before he could inflict the final fatal blows, something caused him to flee. Long was removed to a local hospital. She provided police with a sketchy description of the suspect and his car, which was proven to be inaccurate when the real killer was arrested several years later.

In the next two years, six more women were murdered, beginning with 21-year-old prostitute Jean Bernadette Jordan on Oct. 1, 1977, in Manchester, and followed by Yvonne Pearson, twenty-two, on Jan. 21, 1978, in Bradford. On Feb. 1, the body of 18-year-old Helen Rytka was found under a railroad viaduct in Huddersfield, West Yorkshire. Next came Vera Millward, a 41-year-old prostitute from Manchester, on May 16, 1978. She was murdered on the grounds of the Manchester Royal Academy. This was followed by the bludgeoning death of Josephine Whitaker, a 19-year-old building society clerk from Halifax, Yorkshire, the night of Apr. 4, 1979.

Following this latest outrage, the Ripper communicated for the first time with the police. On June 26, Constable Oldfield played back a tape-recording he had received from the killer to members of the press. In a slow, recognizable Geordie accent, the killer taunted his pursuers. "I'm Jack," the voice said. "I see you are still having no luck catching me. I have the greatest respect for you, George, but, Lord, you are no nearer catching me than four years ago when I started. I reckon your boys are letting you down, George. You can't be much good, can ya? The only time they came near catching me was a few months back in Chapeltown when I was disturbed. Even then it was a uniform copper, not a detective." The message closed with a chilling warning: "Well, I'll keep on going for quite a while yet. I can't see myself being nicked just yet. Even if you do get near I'll probably top myself first. Well, it's been nice chatting to you, George. Yours, Jack the Ripper."

The next month the emotionally spent constable suffered a heart attack and was forced to temporarily withdraw from the investigation. He was replaced by veteran Leeds detective James Hobson, who seemed to have no better luck than his predecessor. A toll-free number for citizens wanting to hear the voice of the Ripper was provided by the phone company, but after thousands of calls the police were no closer to identifying a suspect.

Even during this major barrage of publicity, the Ripper was able to kill again. On Sept. 1, 1979, Barbara Leach, twenty, a student at Bradford University, told some friends she was with that evening that she was going to get some fresh air before going home. She walked away from the Mannville Arms pub and was never seen alive again. Her body was found the following afternoon beside a back-alley dustbin, covered with old carpets. The wounds showed unmistakably mark of the Yorkshire Ripper: Leach had been stabbed with the same rusty screwdriver used in the Whitaker killing.

Now that the police investigation was becoming so intense, the Ripper laid low for almost a year before his next attack. On Aug. 20, 1980, a 47-year-old civil servant from the Department of Education in Pudsey named Marguerite Walls was assaulted and strangled while on her way home to her apartment in Farsley. After two more unsuccessful attacks against women in Leeds and Huddersfield, the Ripper claimed his final victim, 20-year-old Jacqueline Hill, a literature student at Leeds University. She was taking a bus back to her dormitory on Nov. 17, 1980, when she was assaulted in the "triangle of terror," the familiar stretch of ground that included Leeds, Bradford, and West Yorkshire—the killer's favorite haunt. Hill was the madman's thirteenth victim.

On Nov. 25, West Yorkshire Chief Constable Ronald Gregory announced the formation of a special squad to deal with the Ripper case. Hobson, who superseded Oldfield as the head of the investigation, echoed the words of the killer when he predicted that the fiend would be eventually be captured by the men on patrol. His prophecy was realized on Jan. 2, 1981, when Sergeant Robert Ring and PC Robert Hydes pulled their squad car next to a Rover V-8 parked in an office complex in Sheffield. There they found Peter William Sutcliffe, an over-the-road truck driver from Heaton, engaged in a sex act with a black prostitute named Olivia Rievers. The driver of the car told the officers that his named was Peter Williams, but a quick check of the registration tags showed that they did not belong to the Rover. While the police were deciding what to do with Sutcliffe and Rievers, Sutcliffe asked if he could relieve himself. The officers consented, and he wandered over to some nearby bushes. It would be two days before Sergeant Ring, realizing that the man they had picked up could be the Ripper, would return to the bushes where Sutcliffe had stood and would find the hammer and knife used in several of the murders.

Sutcliffe and Rievers were taken to the police station for further questioning. Again, Sutcliffe asked to go to the bathroom, and again, he unloaded another murder weapon: a knife, which he deposited in a cistern in the bathroom. When asked to empty his pockets, the suspect pulled out a length of clothesline. On Jan. 4, during an interview with Sergeant Des O'Boyle, the officer produced the hammer and knife found where Sutcliffe had been arrested. "I think you're in trouble," O'Boyle told Sutcliffe, "serious trouble." Sutcliffe then admitted that he was the Ripper. He confessed to committing eleven murders, but the police charged him with thirteen, and had strong suspicions that he may have killed Joan Harrison, whose body was found in Preston, Lancashire.

Sutcliffe's motive for murdering prostitutes was tied to an unfortunate incident that occurred in 1969, when he was twenty-two years old. Sutcliffe picked up a streetwalker one night, but was unable to perform. The woman kept the £10 note he handed her, refusing to return the £5 he had coming in change. He ran into her at the same pub several weeks later, and, when asked about the £5, she laughed and rebuked him. "I developed and played up a hatred for prostitutes," Sutcliffe told the West Yorkshire Police in a confession that took seventeen hours to record. He said that he had deliberately arranged the clothes of his victims so that they "would be known for what they were."

In 1974, Peter married Sonia Szurma, a Czech national he had been dating off and on again for seven years. The immigrant girl had been previously diagnosed as a schizophrenic, a condition of the mind that contributed to many violent arguments in the next few years. While Sonia took teacher-training courses in London, Peter prowled the red-light districts in search of fresh-faced girls who sold themselves on the street.

For the residents of Yorkshire, the long nightmare was over. Peter Sutcliffe went on trial at the Old Bailey on May 5, 1981, amidst the jeers of a thousand angry spectators who lined the streets outside chanting "Hang him! Hang him!" He pleaded not guilty to the charge of murder on the grounds of diminished responsibility. He told the court about "his mission from God," but a jailer overheard the prisoner tell his wife that he would be let off with a ten-year sentence if he could convince the jurors that he was a prime candidate for the "looney bin." Consequently, the jury found him Guilty of thirteen murders, and seven other assaults. On May 22, 1981, the Yorkshire Ripper was sentenced to life imprisonment with no chance for parole for thirty years by Justice Leslie Boreham. See: **Jack the Ripper.**

REF.: Boar, *The World's Most Infamous Murders; CBA;* Wilson, *Encyclopedia of Modern Murder.*

Sutherland, George, 1862-1942, U.S., jur. President of the American Bar Association from 1916-17. In 1922 he was appointed associate justice to the U.S. Supreme Court by President Warren G. Harding and served in that capacity for 16 years. REF.: *CBA.*

Sutherland, John, d.1809, Brit., mur. One of the last seamen executed at Executioner's Dock, Captain John Sutherland, was hanged for murdering his black male servant while drunk. On his journey to the gallows on June 29, 1809, Sutherland pleaded that in his drunken stupor he had not meant to hit the servant as hard as he had. His execution, performed by William Brunskill, enraged many other sea captains who felt that killing a black servant was of no consequence.

REF.: Bleackley, *Hangmen of England; CBA;* Laurence, *A History of Punishment;* Potter, *The Art of Hanging.*

Sutherland, Thomas, 1932- , Leb., abduc. Thomas Sutherland, acting dean of agriculture at the American University in Beirut, was abducted by Muslim extremists on June 9, 1985, and is still being held. See: **Lebanon Hostage Situation.** REF.: *CBA.*

Suttey, Winifred, 1920-1956, Brit., (unsolv.) mur. On Sept. 7, 1956, three boys saw a man drop a body into some bushes and drive away. They described him as wearing a blue pinstriped suit, horn-rimmed glasses, and kid gloves. The police identified the victim as Winifred Suttey, a 36-year-old nurse. She had been strangled with her own scarf and bitten on the neck. Though they traced her movements after she got off work and circulated plaster casts made of the teeth marks from her body among dentists, the police never tracked down the murderer.

REF.: Butler, *Murderers' England; CBA.*

Sutton, Beatrice Vilna, See: **Field, Frederick Herbert Charles.**

Sutton, Michael, 1922- , U.S., burg. A career burglar who spent most of his seventeen-year career behind bars, Michael Sutton was known by prison authorities for keeping notebooks containing ideas and future plans for committing crimes.

Sutton got an early start as a criminal. He spent two years in reformatory school, starting when he was eleven, though he ran away eight or nine times. First arrested on Apr. 4, 1931, in Patterson, N.J., for automobile theft, he received subsequent prison sentences for burglary in 1933, 1936, 1939, 1945, and 1947. Sutton inevitably burglarized a house within two months following each parole. He would then be arrested, convicted, and sentenced to prison. Also inevitably, prison authorities released him after two to three years for good behavior. During his seventeen years in and out of prison, Sutton was a free man for only ten months. He was last arrested for burglary in 1949.

REF.: *CBA;* McKelway, *The Big Little Man from Brooklyn.*

Sutton, William E. See: **Sutton-Taylor Feud.**

Sutton, William Francis (AKA: **Willie, Willie the Actor, Edward Lynch**), 1901-80, U.S., rob. No American bank robber ever employed the dramatic techniques and the inventiveness displayed by William Francis Sutton, better known as "Willie the Actor." Born in Brooklyn, N.Y., the son of a blacksmith, Sutton, like many before and after him, quit school at an early age and earned his living by shoplifting and, in his late teens, burglary. He preferred to operate alone, although he often took in a partner or two when robbing banks, which became his specialty in the late 1920s. Sutton was not only a student of other people—their mannerisms, quirks, facial expressions—but a student of his own face and body.

While working for a munitions plant in New York during WWI, Sutton made good money and purchased a handsome wardrobe. He then began hanging around clubs off Broadway, befriending actors. He was intrigued with the theater and was soon backstage, where he watched avidly as performers made up their faces. An old trooper gave him his used make-up box and Sutton cherished this gift, keeping it all his life. What came out of that make-up box were as many faces and characters as Lon Chaney, Sr., ever created (Chaney being the silent film star who was called "The Man of a Thousand Faces."

Sutton would use his make-up to create a different face for every robbery he committed. He would insert cork into his nostrils to make his nose appear wider, powder his hair to make himself appear older, and, just as often, use different dyes to color his hair, changing it from its natural black. Sutton would insert pads into his cheeks to broaden his face and use gum arabic to create longer earlobes or to fill in the bridge of his nose or add more chin and jowls to his face.

In 1920, Sutton fell in love with Bessie Hurley, daughter of a Brooklyn shipyard magnate. At the time Sutton was helping to build ships in the Brooklyn Navy Yard. He also helped himself to $16,000 of Hurley's money in the paymaster's office and ran off with Bessie. The couple was tracked down to a Poughkeepsie, N.Y., hotel a short time later and Sutton was arrested. Bessie's father interceded on Sutton's behalf and saved him from serving a jail term.

Sutton then went to Jack "Legs" Diamond and was hired as a collector for various rackets Diamond was operating. He continued to work in this capacity for such bootlegging crime czars as Dutch Schultz and Arnold Rothstein. By 1922, Sutton met and became the willing pupil of Edward "Doc" Tate, one of the foremost safecrackers in the U.S. Tate approached safes as if giving a solo performance before royalty. He never used an acetylene torch or nitroglycerin, preferring to work exclusively with his fingers, "feeling out" the quirks of a safe's tumblers.

Tate gave Sutton a set of golden rules by which Sutton was to live as a professional thief and burglar. "Plan every detail in advance," Tate told his pupil. "Always use ordinary tools and leave them behind you when you finish a job, except for your jimmy. Keep that with you until you are clear. Never overlook the possibility of locked doors barring your escape."

On their first night together, Tate took Sutton along to four different shops, where they broke into safes and went away with more than $10,000. Tate, in a typical gesture of bow-taking, left his jimmy on the window sill of a police station. Sutton worked with Tate for four years and was never caught, but his first solo safecracking job in 1925 was a disaster. He forgot Tate's advice and got trapped in a locked hallway and was apprehended. He drew a four-year sentence in Sing Sing. Upon his release, Sutton teamed up with Jack Bassett and, in 1930, went into bank robbery.

Sutton appeared at the bank in Jamaica, L.I., at 8 a.m. A guard answered his knock and opened the door to see Sutton dressed as a Western Union messenger, wearing the complete uniform. Sutton informed the guard that he had a telegram for the bank president. The guard began to sign for the telegram when Sutton jammed a gun into the guard's stomach and said: "Now be a good boy and you won't get hurt." He backed the guard into the bank, with Bassett slipping in behind them and locking the door.

The president of the bank was summoned and Sutton, his face made up to look much younger than his twenty-eight years, ordered him to open the vault. He did, and Sutton scooped up $48,000. As he and Bassett were about to depart, Sutton said: "We're leaving now. But I have a third man outside. If anyone goes through this door in the next five minutes, he will be shot." Sutton and Bassett slipped outside only a few minutes before the bank was scheduled to open. There was no third man waiting outside but Sutton correctly figured that the bank employees would believe him and wait several minutes before giving the alarm, just enough time for Sutton and Bassett to blend in with the heavy crowds on the street.

Sutton had planned this robbery well, obtaining a Western Union uniform and then sending a telegram to himself. He steamed open the envelope and substituted a telegram he had typed himself on Western Union stationery, one showing the bank president's name. He then resealed the envelope and was ready to rob the bank. At the time, Sutton was married. He explained to his wife that the $24,000 he brought home was an inheritance from a rich uncle who had just died in Ireland. A few days later Sutton and Bassett used the same Western Union ruse to gain entrance to the Rosenthal Jewelry store on Broadway in Manhattan. The manager was so terrified that he completely forgot the combination to the safe that held the company jewels. A janitor was forced at gunpoint to call the firm's owner to get the combination. Sutton and Bassett took more than $130,000 in rare gems from the Rosenthal store. In all, Sutton and Bassett robbed thirteen banks and jewelry stores within a few weeks. Their take was staggering.

Bassett's wife, however, was jealous over her husband's mistress and informed police that her husband and Sutton were the bandits they were seeking. Both men were arrested. Sutton withstood five days of rubber-hosing from the police without confessing. Witnesses from his robberies were brought forth, but they failed to recognize him. One witness told police that Sutton was "far from the man you want." One victim said: "No, no, the man who robbed my place had a flat nose and puffy cheeks." Another stated: "The robber was taller and heavyset. This guy is puny." Of course Sutton, when robbing this last man, had worn elevator shoes and had padded his stomach.

Only the porter made a positive identification of Sutton as the man who robbed the Rosenthal store. Sutton was sent back to Sing Sing for thirty years. In less than two years he was again outside. In December 1932, Sutton picked four locks in Sing Sing's "escape-proof" block house, used a rope ladder of his own making to get over the wall, and fled in a car which had been left near the prison by an associate. He returned to robbery immediately.

Within weeks, Sutton by himself had robbed a number of banks and jewelry stores, using various disguises in each robbery. At one bank where he got away with more than $18,000, Sutton was dressed as a policeman, spoke with a thick Irish accent, and wore a red wig. He turned up at an exclusive Fifth Avenue jewelers dressed as a fireman and carrying city credentials. He informed the jewelers that he was there to check on possible fire code violations, so he was allowed to inspect every corner of the place freely. When he was inside the vault, Sutton held up the owners, taking jewels worth hundreds of thousands of dollars. At a Manhattan bank a few days later, Sutton appeared outside the locked door dressed as a postman carrying a large package that was too big to slip through the mail slot. The guard opened the door to take the package, and Sutton backed him into the bank at the point of a gun. Sutton looted this bank of more than $130,000.

Though he was rich, Sutton was also one of the most wanted men in the East. He could not go near his wife, who had given birth to a daughter, because he knew police would be watching her residence. He flitted from hideout to hideout, paying enormous amounts of money for these havens, but he was told to "keep moving" because he was "too hot to stay in one spot" for any length of time. He lived a lonely, furtive life. His only enjoyment was reading books. By 1934, Sutton realized just how alone he was. One of his partners, Johnny Eagan, was killed by gangsters in New York for not turning in part of his loot from a burglary. Another partner, Eddie Wilson, was trapped inside a store and was blinded for life by a police bullet. Jack Bassett was captured and sent to prison for fifty years. Then Sutton's mentor, Doc Tate, was sent to prison, where he died of lung problems.

Sutton did not remain inactive. He and Joseph Pelango robbed a bank in Philadelphia. Sutton used his policeman's routine to gain entrance to the bank and, within minutes, had taken more than $160,000 out of the vault. But Pelango was arrested and he informed on Sutton, who was arrested at his small apartment by a half dozen policemen wielding Thompson submachine guns.

On Feb. 4, 1934, Sutton, following a conviction for bank robbery, entered Eastern State Penitentiary to serve twenty to fifty years. This was a maximum security prison, one of the toughest in the U.S., and its administrators prided themselves on its thick steel doors, double teams of guards, and an informer system whereby convicts were rewarded with substantial time off for turning in other convicts who were about to escape. Sutton's reputation preceded him. He was placed in solitary confinement for the first eighteen months of his stay at Eastern. Guards told him that he would never be able to escape from Eastern like he had from Sing Sing.

When Sutton was placed in a regular cell, he carefully planned his escape. During an exercise period, he slipped into the prison's 200-foot underground drainage system. He crawled along until he reached a second tunnel, which was filled with water. Stripping, Sutton swam under water for several feet until he reached an underwater iron door. He dove repeatedly downward in an attempt to find the handle to the door but realized, almost too late, that the door was controlled by an automatic device. His lungs nearly bursting, Sutton barely managed to get to the surface and returned to the first conduit. He put on his clothes and returned to his cell only a few minutes before roll call.

For two years Sutton collected materials, piecing together a plaster of Paris head which was almost a perfect likeness of himself. He painted the skin area a sallow flesh tone and pasted hair from his own head onto the skull eyebrows, using the cuttings from the prison barber shop. Then he made a plaster of Paris arm. On a winter night, he positioned the fake head and arm in his bunk so that he appeared to be sleeping. By then Sutton had also acquired a rope, a hacksaw blade, and a grappling hook. He sawed through the bars of his cell window, then worked himself through the opening and onto a ledge of the cell block. He flung the grappling hook attached to the rope to the outer wall and was about to swing out to it, where it would be a simple matter to let himself down the other side and escape. At that moment, however, prison alarms went off. Another group of convicts were making an escape attempt in another part of the prison. Sutton, realizing his ridiculous position, crawled back into his cell. A short time later, the severed bars and fake head and arm were discovered and he was sent to the isolation block for two years. Sutton decided to settle into prison life, serve his time, and work toward an early release as a model prisoner.

He learned shorthand and was made assistant to the prison psychiatrist. After ten years, however, Sutton realized there was little hope for parole. He and twelve other inmates began digging a tunnel at the end of 1945. Within six months the convicts had dug ninety-seven feet and broken the earth on the other side of the prison wall. The convicts leaped from the hole and ran in all directions. As Sutton arrived at ground level he found himself looking into the muzzle of a policeman's revolver. He was sent back to the isolation ward, another ten to twenty years added to his sentence.

In August 1946, Sutton was transferred to Holmesburg County Prison outside of Philadelphia. On Feb. 9, 1947, Sutton and other inmates, using a smuggled .38-caliber revolver and a hacksaw, worked their way out of their cells and into a guardhouse. They marched the guards to the fire house, where they obtained two ladders. Sutton and the others, using the guards as hostages, carried the ladders into the yard, placing them against the wall. It was snowing heavily, and the convicts hoped that the swirling snow would hide them from the guards in the towers.

One of the tower guards, however, fired a shot at the group. A quick-thinking convict shouted up to the tower guard: "Stop that! Can't you see we're guards?" The guard ceased firing and the convicts raced up the ladders and dropped to freedom on the other side of the wall. They commandeered a milk truck and drove it to Philadelphia.

Sutton was free after thirteen years in prison. All of the other convicts went to underworld gathering spots and were soon caught, but the wily Sutton found the perfect hiding spot. He took a low-paying job as a hospital porter at Farm Colony, a home for retired persons operated by the City of New York. Giving the name Edward Lynch, Sutton was hired at $20 a week and was also given room and board. The City of New York had provided him with a hideout and walk-about money as well! Sutton worked hard, minded the rules, and lived quietly. He planned to spend the rest of his days working at Farm Colony, but in August 1949, one of the nurses showed him a picture of himself in a newspaper, saying that he looked enough like Willie Sutton the bankrobber to be Willie Sutton.

"If I were Willie Sutton," said Sutton, "I wouldn't be working here for $80 a month." The nurse and Sutton laughed at the joke, but Sutton, shaken by the experience, decided to quit. Some days later Sutton entered the Manufacturer's Trust Company bank in Sunnyside, N.Y., a suburb of New York City. He longed to rob it, but according to his later claims, he resisted the temptation that had for years compelled him to steal (years earlier, Sutton admitted in his memoirs, he once robbed a bank even though he had more than $40,000 in his pockets; the temptation was too strong to resist). Sutton further claimed that he passed information around the Sunnyside bank to some bank robbers he knew, and the bank was robbed of $64,000 some weeks later. The thieves used Sutton's techniques so well that he was blamed for the robbery (if, indeed, he did not commit it).

While riding the subway on Feb. 18, 1952, Sutton was identified by 24-year-old clothing salesman Arnold Schuster. The young man followed Sutton off the subway at the Bergen Avenue station and trailed him to a garage. He then went to the nearest precinct station and told officers that he believed he had recognized one of the most wanted men in the country, Willie "The Actor" Sutton,

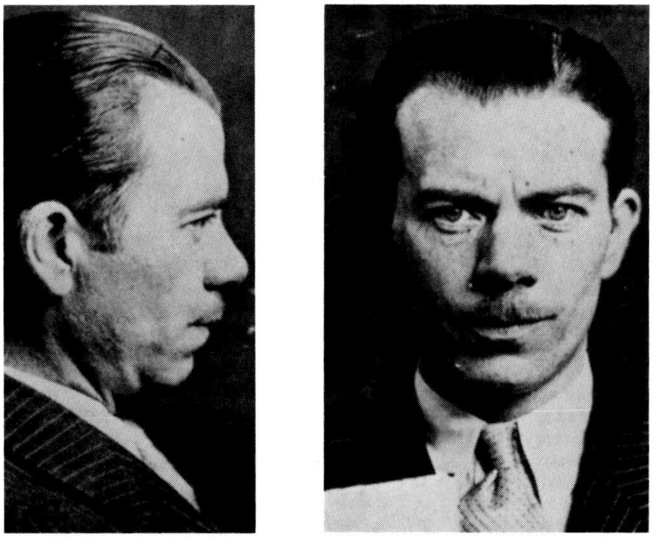

Police photos of Willie Sutton, 1930.

Willie Sutton, center, under arrest again.

Willie "The Actor" Sutton, explaining his techniques.

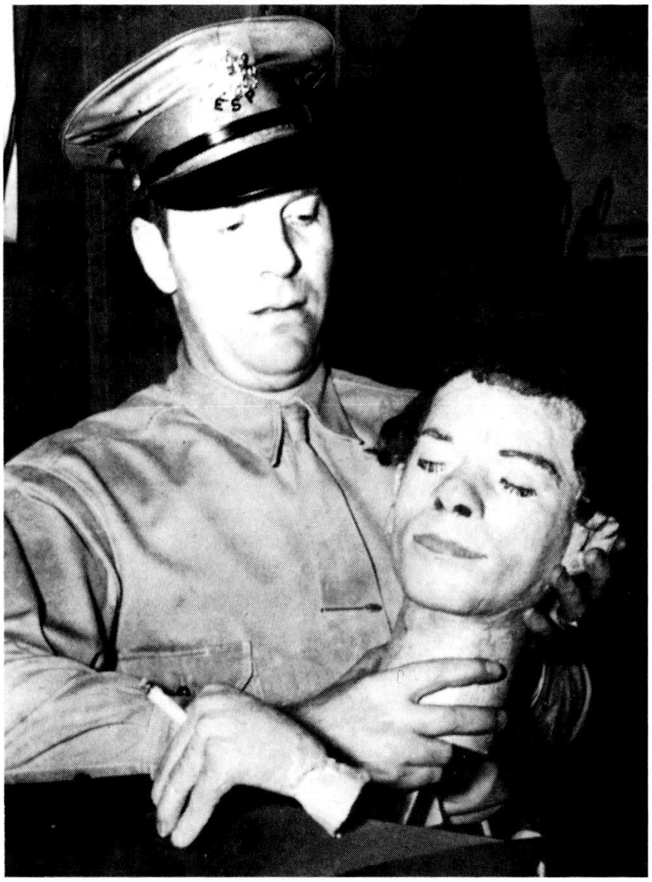

The dummy head Sutton left behind during a prison escape.

Sutton, center, examining nails.

Sutton, free of prison with license.

Author Jay Robert Nash interviewing Willie Sutton, 1979.

saying that the man he had followed looked just like a photo of Sutton on a wanted poster he had recently seen.

Two uniformed officers investigated, finding Sutton tinkering on an old car in his garage. They asked to see his driver's license and he politely showed them a license with the name Edward Lynch on it. The officers left but returned with a detective minutes later. "You better come along with us to the station," the detective told him. "You look too much like Sutton to be wandering about loose." At first Sutton insisted that it was merely a case of mistaken identity, but when his fingerprints were taken and checked, he knew the game was over. "I might as well be dead now," sighed Sutton, tired of running from the law. "You can shoot and kill me for all I care."

Schuster was hailed as a hero. He was given a reward and he was interviewed on television, lauded for his civic action in bringing a desperate criminal to justice. Watching the TV program was one of the worst killers in New York, Albert Anastasia. The New York gang chief jumped to his feet and shouted to several of his goons: "I hate squealers. Hit that guy!" On Mar. 9, 1952, a gunman shot and killed Schuster as he was walking home. A bullet was sent into each eye of the victim, the ritualistic shooting of an informer.

Sutton claimed for the rest of his life, emphasizing in a 1979 interview that, "I had nothing to do with that. I didn't even know Anastasia or the man he sent out to kill Schuster. He was a nice boy and he thought he was doing his duty as a citizen. I don't blame him and what was done to him was terrible, awful. It was that maniac Anastasia. He would kill anyone he didn't like. If he hadn't liked my looks he would have killed me! That's the kind of nut he was."

Sutton was tried for the robbery of the Sunnyside bank, and witnesses swore that he was the man who led the bank raid. Sutton argued that they had looked at so many photos of him in newspapers and mug shots of him from files that these witnesses had been "conditioned" to recognize him. He was nevertheless convicted and sent back to prison to serve an additional thirty years. The irony of all this, according to Sutton, was that he was convicted of the one crime he had not committed.

At the time of his arrest, more than $7,000 was taken out of Sutton's pocket. He explained that this money was his life savings. He was asked why he had not placed the money in a bank. Sutton replied: "It's never safe in a bank!" Sutton spent several more years in prison but was finally paroled. He wrote his autobiography and earned enough money to move to a retirement village in Spring Hill, Fla., where he died peacefully in bed of natural causes on Nov. 7, 1980. See: **Anastasia, Albert.**

REF.: *CBA;* Cohen, *Mickey Cohen: In My Own Words;* Gage, *Mafia, U.S.A.;* Gosch and Hammer, *The Last Testament of Lucky Luciano;* Horan, *The Pinkertons;* Hurwood, *Society and the Assassin;* Katz, *Uncle Frank;* Maas, *The Valachi Papers;* Nash, *Bloodletters and Badmen;* Rowan, *Famous American Crimes;* Scott, *The Concise Encyclopedia of Crime and Criminals;* Sutton, *Where the Money Was;* ____ and Reynolds, *I, Willie Sutton;* Wade, *Great Hoaxes and Famous Imposters.*

Sutton-Taylor Feud, 1840s-70s, U.S., mur. The Sutton-Taylor feud began in the late 1840s in South Carolina where the Sutton and Taylor families were neighbors. After the Civil War, William E. Sutton, and his family moved to Clinton, Texas. Coincidentally, so did the Taylor family. A truce existed between the two families until Mar. 25, 1868, when William Sutton, then deputy sheriff of Bastrop, Texas, shot and killed Charley Taylor on suspicion of stock theft. Later that year, on Dec. 24, when Sutton shot and killed Buck Taylor in a saloon in Clinton, the feud began with renewed vigor. Each family recruited gangs of about 200 members. On Sutton's side were lawman Jack Helm, cattleman Shanghai Pierce, and Indian fighter Old Joe Tumlinson. Fighting with the Taylors were the hostile Clements brothers and an East Texas cousin, John Wesley Hardin.

On Aug. 26, 1870, an ambush at the home of Henry Kelly, related to the Taylors by marriage, resulted in the shooting deaths of Kelly and his brother, William Kelly. Jack Helm, a Texas State Police captain, who had come with Doc White and John Meador to arrest Henry Kelly, was fired for his part in the killings. James "Jim" Taylor, son of murdered Pitkin Taylor, first tracked Bill Sutton down on Apr. 1, 1873, in Cuero, Texas. In Cuero, Taylor and his friends badly wounded Sutton. Then on Mar. 11, 1874, when Sutton and his young wife and child had just boarded a steamboat in Indianola, Texas, bound for New Orleans, Jim and William "Bill" Taylor appeared and shot and killed Sutton and Sutton's friend, Gabe Slaughter. Although the Taylors escaped, they were ambushed and killed the following year by Sutton supporters. The feud, virtually over, claimed about forty lives. See: **Hardin, John Wesley; Taylor, James; Taylor, William.**

REF.: Artrip, *Memoirs of Daniel Foe (Jim) Chisholm;* Bartholomew, *Kill or be Killed;* Casey, *The Texas Border; CBA;* Day, *The Sutton-Taylor Feud;* Delony, *40 Years a Peace Officer;* Douglas, *Famous Texas Feuds;* Emmett, *Shanghai Pierce;* Farrow, *Troublesome Times in Texas;* Feder, *Longhorns;* Fisher and Dykes, *King Fisher, His Life and Times;* French, *Indianola Scrap Book;* Gard, *Frontier Justice;* Hardin, *The Life of John Wesley Hardin;* Horan and Sann, *Pictorial History of the Wild West;* Huson, *Refugio;* King, *Ghost Towns of Texas;* Monaghan, *The Book of the American West;* Morris, *Pictorial History of Victoria and Victoria County;* Nordyke, *John Wesley Hardin;* Penfield, *Western Sheriffs and Marshals;* Plenn and LaRoche, *The Fastest Gun in Texas;* Raine, *Guns of the Frontier;* Raymond, *Captain Lee Hall of Texas;* Ripley, *They Died With Their Boots On;* Russell, *Grandpa's Autobiography;* Sonnichsen, *I'll Die Before I'll Run;* Sutton, *Sutton-Taylor Feud;* Sweet and Knox, *On a Mexican Mustang Through Texas;* Webb, *Handbook of Texas;* ____, *Texas Ranger.*

Svaars, Fritz, See: **Houndsditch Murders.**

Sverdlov, Yakov Mikhaylovich, 1885-1919, Rus., rebel.-assass. Secretary of Bolshevik Central Committee and served as chairman of the Central Executive Committee from 1917, controlling state party and bureaucracy. He ordered the assassinations of Czar Nicholas and family in 1918. REF.: *CBA.*

Sverre (Swerro, Sverre Sigurdsson), c.1152-1202, Nor., rob.-rebel. The leader of a robber gang with aspirations to rule, he battled King Magnus V Erlingsson from 1179-84. He eventually defeated him in a conflict at Norefjord, where Magnus was slain in combat. He was crowned after the victory, and during his eighteen-year reign became very popular among the peasantry through his anti-aristocrat policies. REF.: *CBA.*

Svinhufvud, Pehr Evind, 1861-1944, Fin., consp.-rebel. Served as speaker in legislature from 1907-12, then was ousted by ruling Russian government and sent to Siberia from 1914-17. He later headed efforts in the Civil War and eventually helped obtain independence from Russia in 1918. He served briefly on the supreme court in 1919, became Finnish premier in 1930, and served as president from 1931-37. REF.: *CBA.*

Svorskov, Col. **Gregory**, and **Grunspavnin**, Count **Nikolas**, prom. 1940s, Brit., fraud. Alfred Pybus, a poultry dealer, amassed £10,000 in savings, two large chicken farms, and numerous shops by 1945. Shortly thereafter, Pybus was introduced by Mr. Weiner, a man who owed him money, to two Russians, Colonel Gregory Svorskov and Count Nikolas Grunspavnin, who offered to sell him a shipment of platinum. Pybus agreed to pay £12,272 for a chest of the ore, supposed to be worth £17,000. He also agreed not to resell the goods for six months, so not until four months later when he examined the contents of the box did he discover bars of stainless steel.

Police found an address on the box which the culprits had tried to file off, and they used it to trace the Russians. The two were arrested, tried, and convicted. Svorskov, who had previously been found Guilty of theft in 1933 and deported, received a five-year sentence. Grunspavnin was sentenced to a three-year term, and Weiner was acquitted of conspiracy charges. REF.: *CBA.*

Swamp, The, 1800-40s, U.S., pros. One of the most notorious vice districts in old New Orleans was called The Swamp, an area awash with all manner of crime and criminals, which local authorities took little or no pains to eradicate for more than four decades. Swaggering along the vice-ridden area known as the

Swamp, the boatmen would bellow out this song:

I'm looking for the bully,
The bully of the town;
I'm looking for the bully,
But the bully can't be found;
I'm looking for the bully of the town.
And when I walk this levee round,
I'm looking for the bully of the town.

The Swamp was roughly a six-block area of jumbled, broken-down structures that resembled decrepit shanties, far from the stately buildings with filigree ironwork for which New Orleans later became known. Saloons, gambling dens, brothels, dance halls, and dingy hotels took up the squalid space of the Swamp. Here, the bars were crude, often nothing more than a board resting on two barrels.

Boatmen swarmed into the area, noting the bordellos from the red lanterns that swung from their entrances. These harlot havens also functioned as hotels, and for about 5¢ a swarthy worker of the Mississippi could have a drink, a woman, and a bed for the night. Chances were, at best, that he would be robbed in his sleep by the whore or clubbed unconscious by her pimp and then stripped of everything, including his underwear. Usually, the boatman was murdered; it was more convenient. An average of a dozen murders a week took place in the Swamp.

Bodies were normally dumped into the river or the swamp areas and forgotten. If the killers were lazy, the corpses would be piled up in the street and left to rot. Police never entered the Swamp, so no official investigations ever took place for any of these rampant homicides.

REF.: Anthony, *Paddle Wheels and Pistols;* Asbury, *The French Quarter;* Cable, *Strange True Stories of Louisiana; CBA;* Green, *Gambling Exposed;* Huber, *New Orleans;* Spear, *Ancient and Modern New Orleans.*

Swan, Edith Emily, b.1890, Brit., libel. In May 1920, Edith Swan filed a complaint against her neighbor with the police in Littlehampton, England. Prior to this, Swan had filed a complaint with the National Society for the Prevention of Cruelty to Children accusing her neighbor, Rose Emma Gooding, of abusing her sister's illegitimate child, who was frequently in Gooding's care. Since the time of that complaint, Swan told police, Gooding would not leave her alone. She had pushed obscene notes under Swan's door and had threatened her. Upon the suggestion of the police, Swan retained a lawyer and prosecuted Gooding, who was convicted on Dec. 13, 1920. She received a fourteen-day prison sentence.

Gooding was released from prison on Dec. 22. The libels recommenced almost at once. With her own lawyer, Swan again prosecuted Gooding and on Mar. 3, 1921, Gooding was convicted. Mr. Justice Avory gave the defendant a stiffer sentence of twelve months in prison. This time, however, more of the libelous notes were sent while Gooding was in prison. Police investigations revealed that the blotting paper in the Gooding household did not resemble that used in the notes. Swan's blotting paper, however, was the same as that upon which the notes were written, and the word "local" on Swan's paper appeared in exactly the same handwriting as that on the libelous letters. By way of explanation, Swan claimed Gooding borrowed her blotting paper. Police began to follow Swan's movements. On Sept. 17, policewoman Moss observed Swan dropping a document in front of her own door. Moss retrieved the document, which this time libeled the wife of a police officer. Swan was indicted for libel and placed on trial Dec. 9, 1921. She was acquitted on the recommendation of the judge who felt the jury would never convict a soft-spoken woman who pursued two libel suits against another woman.

Two years later, Littlehampton townspeople once again began receiving obscene and libelous postcards and letters. A watch was placed on Swan. With the help of the postmaster, who caught two letters Swan attempted to post, Swan was apprehended on July 19, 1923, and charged with attempting to post libelous letters. The jury convicted her after only ten minutes of deliberation and Mr. Justice Avory, stating he could not believe Swan was of sound mind, sentenced her to twelve months in prison.

REF.: *CBA;* Humphreys, *Criminal Days.*

Swan, Robert, prom. 1853, Case of, U.S., mur. One day in January 1852, William O. Sprigg of Cumberland, Md., spit in the face of Robert Swan. This impulsive act of rancor triggered a chain of events in which Swan sought to assuage his honor and Sprigg tried not to appear completely acquiescent. The two disagreed over published accounts of the feud and over different versions of their stated apologies to each other, until Feb. 11, 1852, when Swan met Sprigg at a Cumberland hotel. After a hostile exchange, he shot Sprigg to death, after which he turned himself over to the police. He was imprisoned and brought to trial in July 1853 at the Circuit Court for Washington County in Hagarstown, Md. On Oct. 5, 1853, after months of testimony (in which character witnesses attested to Sprigg's volatile nature, contrasting with the now-docile mien of the defendant), the jury found Swan Not Guilty for the deliberate shooting of William Sprigg.

REF.: *CBA; Trial of Robert Swan Charged With the Murder of William O. Sprigg.*

Swancutt, Beaufort George, 1913-44, U.S., suic.-mur. Thirty-one-year-old Lieutenant Beaufort George Swancutt was drinking beer and playing cards at the Camp Anza Officer's Club in Louisiana on Mar. 5, 1944, with Second Lieutenant Harry J. Light, 19-year-old Dorothy Douglas, and 18-year-old Lourdine Livermore. The couples had just returned from dinner in Riverside. It was about 10:30 p.m. Earlier in the evening, Swancutt had excused himself to change his shirt. When he returned, no one noticed that he was wearing his .45-caliber pistol. Suddenly, Swancutt stood up, pulled out the pistol and shot Douglas, Livermore, and Light. He then turned the weapon on Lieutenant Aldace Minard, who was passing by. Swancutt ran over to the officers' quarters and awakened Captain Aubrey G. Serfling, his superior officer, and asked for an additional gun clip because he had lost his own. When Serfling refused and began to question him, Swancutt shouted: "I've killed four others already tonight, and I won't be alive by morning. I see no reason why you should be, either." He shot Serfling in the stomach, then grabbed another gun clip and rushed outside, where he wounded Corporal Robert Sampson, who was walking by.

In the parking area, Swancutt pressed a gun into the side of Sergeant John E. Roberts and told him to drive a staff car to nearby Arlington. There, Swancutt ordered Roberts to pull up on the wrong side of the street, about 200 feet from the Arlington substation of the Riverside Police Department. Ray Schlegel, traveling with his wife, their 8-month-old son, and Euel Atchley, a university student, was forced to stop when the army car blocked his way. Swancutt commanded Schlegel's wife to drive him and, when Atchley protested that the woman could not drive, forced Schlegel to take the wheel instead. Radio patrolmen Arthur Simpson and Ernest Cole were coming out of the substation when they noticed the car on the wrong side of the street and went to investigate. When Mrs. Schlegel called out to them, "The officer has a gun," Cole opened the door and pulled Schlegel out of the army car. Simpson ran up holding his gun in his hand, and Swancutt shot and fatally wounded him. Cole fired at Swancutt and hit him twice. Schlegel received a flesh wound, but Simpson died minutes later. Military police had arrived on the scene, and took Swancutt to Camp Anza Hospital.

Swancutt was charged with murder and tried in a military court. Wounded in the rampage, he heard the verdict from a wheelchair. He was sentenced to hang for the four murders. The trial revealed that Swancutt, who was from LaCrosse, Wis., was a father of two boys, and had divorced and remarried his wife. He had a long police record in his hometown, with charges of attempted suicide, drunk and disorderly conduct, and larceny, and had been serving a ninety-day sentence for vagrancy when he was drafted. The police released him to join the army, and he graduated from the Ft. Benning, Ga., Officer's Candidate School. While stationed in Wilmington, Del., Swancutt was again arrested, on July 18, 1943, for battery and disorderly conduct. He had molested a young woman in a bar and then assaulted two officers. The case was dismissed because Swancutt was about to ship out for Europe. The defense tried to prove him insane, but army psychiatrists ruled that he was not and the court martial accepted their judgment. Swancutt had apparently murdered Douglas and set off on the later killing spree because she would not marry him.

On July 7, 1944, the wardmaster discovered Swancutt's body at the Army's Letterman General Hospital. The lieutenant had torn up a bed sheet and hanged himself with it from the ceiling radiator in his room. REF.: *CBA.*

Swann, Emily, 1861-1903, and **Gallagher, John,** 1874-1903, Brit, mur. One of few women executed in England, Emily Swann and her lover were hanged for murdering her husband in 1903. A 42-year-old mother of six from Wombwell in Yorkshire, Swann gained a reputation for frequenting the local inns after completing her housework. During one of her trysts, she started an ongoing affair with John Gallagher, thirteen years her junior.

The two lovers decided to kill Swann's husband. Gallagher performed the task, though he had to return a second time with a hatchet to finish the job. Suspicion immediately fell on the couple and Gallagher fled Wombwell. Authorities arrested him in Middlesbrough and returned him to face trial with Swann. The court convicted both of murder and sentenced them to death. When taken to the gallows on Dec. 29, Swann said to her lover who was waiting there, "Good morning, John" to which he replied, "Good morning, love." As the noose slipped around her neck, Emily Swann cried out, "Good-bye. God bless you!"

REF.: *CBA;* Laurence, *A History of Capital Punishment;* O'Donnell, *Should Women Hang?*

Swanson, Carolyn (Carolyn MacLeon, AKA: Scotty Suffrin), 1967- , and **Swanson, Scott (AKA: Michael James),** 1965- , Case of, U.S., miss. per. Carolyn MacLeon and Scott Swanson, students at Wheaton College in Wheaton, Ill., had been dating each other less than a year when they inexplicably vanished. When MacLeon's car was found in an alley in downtown Chicago on Apr. 2, 1988, along with the couple's credit and identification cards, police and the couple's family feared they had been kidnapped and possibly murdered. The disappearance received extensive media coverage and captured much public attention.

When, early in the investigation, police discovered that the couple had been secretly married on Mar. 26, they abandoned their original theory of foul play in favor of the idea that Swanson and MacLeon had run away together. Although the couple did not fit the standard profile for runaways—both were apparently well adjusted college students from affluent families—the bits of evidence that began to accumulate suggested that this was the case. Police found a journal in which MacLeon had talked about selling her sports car and running away to a foreign country. Friends of the couple also told police that they were aware that the couple had been saving money for a special trip. There was also evidence that Swanson had begun to have second thoughts about the military career to which he had committed through his college ROTC program.

Four months after their disappearance, the couple simultaneously alerted both sets of parents that they were alive, well, and living in San Diego, Calif. In their letters, they explained that they had run away to escape the materialism they felt surrounded their lives, and to find "perfect love." MacLeon and Swanson supported themselves working in fast food restaurants and had become disillusioned with the difficulty of their styles of living when they contacted their parents. The police estimated that they had spent $28,000 to locate the couple. Although public opinion seemed strongly in favor of holding the couple responsible for the cost of the investigation, no charges were filed against them. REF.: *CBA.*

Swapp, Addam, 1961- , U.S., poly.-mansl. In Marion, Utah, in 1979, police shot 47-year-old John Singer to death when he allegedly pulled a gun on them. An avowed white supremacist, Singer had lived in Germany and had been involved in the Hitler Youth Movement before settling in Utah. The Singer clan saga began in 1963 when John Singer married Vickie Lemon, twelve years his junior and the high school homecoming queen. Singer and his wife, residents of the small town of Kamas, Utah, observed a rigid interpretation of Mormon beliefs, including polygamy, a tenet long ago rejected by the church. In 1973, Singer withdrew his seven children from public school in protest over a history text that ranked Martin Luther King, Jr. with George Washington. The Singers spent the next several years fighting with the courts and law officers to keep their children out of a school system they felt would bring them in contact with racial intermixing, drug abuse, and sexual promiscuity. It was during this stand-off that police shot and killed Singer.

Nine years later, 27-year-old Addam Swapp, who had married two of the Singers' daughters, Heidi and Charlotte Singer, and later married their mother, John Singer's widow, led the clan in a thirteen-day siege that ended when a police officer was killed and Swapp was wounded.

On Jan. 16, 1988, a bomb exploded at the Mormon church where John and Vickie Singer had been excommunicated. Adam Swapp and his clan came under suspicion and admitted the bombings to friends, claiming that they were acting on direct orders from God. The family believed a violent confrontation with police would result in John Singer's resurrection and the return of Jesus Christ, who would aid them in their battles. Heidi Swapp, twenty-three, Charlotte Swapp, nineteen, and Vickie Singer, forty-four, along with six children under the age of six and several older children, barricaded themselves in a fortified log farmhouse in the Wasatch Mountains waiting for Singer's return. Police moved in to surround the family after Swapp sent the governor a letter stating that they had formed their own nation and would shoot any trespassers.

The thirteen-day stand-off ended just before dawn on Jan. 28, when a gun battle erupted while police tried to sneak into the compound. Lieutenant Fred House of the Utah Corrections Department, who joined an FBI team in the effort to arrest the Swapps, was shot and killed by wheelchair-bound John Timothy Singer, twenty-two.

On Dec. 22, 1988, a jury deliberated for twenty-five-and-a-half hours at the Third Circuit Court in Coalville, Utah, before finding Addam Swapp and his brother-in-law John Singer Guilty of manslaughter. Addam's brother, 21-year-old Jonathan Swapp, was found Guilty of negligent homicide. All three men had been charged with second-degree murder. Judge Michael Murphy sentenced Addam Swapp and John Timothy Singer to one to fifteen years in jail and gave Jonathan Swapp a one-year sentence. Vickie Singer, who, along with the three men, had been found Guilty in May 1988 of federal violations in the bombing and stand-off, was sentenced to five years in jail. REF.: *CBA.*

Swart, Marthinus Erich, b.1893, S.Afri., mur. A 44-year-old woodworker and father of three, Marthinus Swart was an alcoholic whose mood swings grew violent when he was drunk. He severely beat his wife and abused his children, threatening to kill them several times. On one occasion, he threw their 5-year-old daughter across the room, crippling her. On another occasion, a neighbor stopped him from shoving potatoes and pumpkins down his infant's throat. Swart made a few attempts at reform but returned to drinking and beating his family.

It was Swart pressing a man he had met on a recent trip to live at his house that triggered a series of events leading to the murder of the three Swart children. Swart began accusing the man and his wife of having an affair. At one point, he kicked her out of the house. When she asked to take the children, he refused, claiming he would never part with them. Two days later, on Aug. 28, 1937, he borrowed a gun from a friend, took the children to a garbage dump, and shot them. Swart then escorted his wife to the dump where they found one child dead and the two others bleeding and unconscious; both died soon after. Police arrested

Swart and charged him with murder.

Psychological evaluations proved that Swart suffered from *psychasthenia,* a "compulsion neurosis" marked by addictive behavior, obsessions, fear, and anxiety. It manifests itself in an uncontrollable urge to kill. With a vote of eight to one the jury found Swart Guilty of murder but with extenuating circumstances. The judge sentenced him to ten years' imprisonment. He was released two years early, since , deprived of alcohol, he had behaved well in prison. Upon his release a woman employed him on her farm. One evening he attacked her and attempted to set her son's nightclothes on fire. She fled as Swart burned down the farmhouse. Police found his burned body in the ruins.

REF.: Bennett, *Genius for the Defense; CBA.*

Swart, Stephen, 1890-1927, S. Afri., suic.?-mur. In the early 1900s, Stephen Swart operated a farm in South Africa. Over time, he alienated his neighbors and harbored grudges against numerous people. He was annoyed when he lost a civil case and he continually filed petty grievances in court which were dismissed. In 1922, the 32-year-old Swart married a wealthy 58-year-old woman, promptly beating and berating her, and going out with other women. Swart was further irritated when a sexual offense charge was lodged against him in early 1927. Fearing that his wife and farm manager, A.J.C. Visser, would testify against him, in March 1927 he allegedly locked them in a room and threatened to shoot them unless they agreed not to testify.

On Mar. 11, the two hurriedly left the farm, his wife going to live in Charleston, a village on the border of Natal province. During the following weeks, Swart became convinced that at the upcoming trial he would be sent to prison for life and the distraught man did not sleep and scarcely ate. On May 3, 1927, he visited a neighbor's house and shot at the farm manager, but missed his mark. He then went back home. Police issued a warrant for his arrest and on May 5, Swart declared that any trespassers would be shot on sight. That night, Swart summoned his lawyer, dictating a twenty-eight page statement detailing complaints against numerous people and describing how he had set his car on fire on May 3 to prevent any enemies from getting it if he died.

At 4:30 a.m. on May 6, twelve policemen, led by Captain Ashman, set out to capture Swart, arriving at the farm about 6 a.m. They met one of Swart's hands who told them the farmer knew of the planned raid and had armed several of his workers. In the fog, Swart murdered five policemen, including officers Crossman, Mitchell, Grove, van Wyk, and Captain Ashman. Another policeman, Feucht, was injured and sent to the hospital.

Swart then rode to a farm owned by neighbor S.J.M. Swanepoel, asked for some coffee, told of the slayings, and said he planned to go to Charleston. Afterward, Swart rode off, and along the road killed Knight, a woman who had previously testified against him, her companion, Roets, and, later, a native. Riding into Charleston, he located the home of the van Vuurens, where his wife was staying. The family had evacuated the house, but Mrs. Swart remained inside. Swart entered the house, shooting his wife dead, and then he rode off again and tried to commandeer a car. When the first car sped by, he shot at the occupants, injuring the driver and the passenger, but the driver managed to drive away.

Meanwhile, policemen and local townspeople were hunting for the murderer when a railway foreman, Mr. Kriel, spotted Swart, and two more men joined Kriel. They followed Swart along a road, firing at him. A group of policeman soon pulled up and found Swart's body. He had been shot through the head, either by his own hand or by one of the posse.

REF.: Bennett, *Up for Murder; CBA.*

Swayne, Noah Haynes, 1804-84, U.S., jur. Appointed to U.S. Supreme Court without any judicial experience. He replaced his friend, the late Justice John McLean, who had favored him to be his successor. His nomination was also backed by Ohio Governor William Dennison and many state legislators, based on his displayed ability as U.S. attorney, district of Ohio, where he served from 1830-38. His selection, by President Abraham Lincoln, was confirmed by the Senate in 1862. Before his retirement in 1881, his most notable criminal case concerned military justice. In *Ex parte Milligan* in 1866, he joined the five to four majority in ruling that Lambdin P. Milligan, who was found Guilty of treason, should be freed because President Lincoln had sent his case to a military tribunal even though a federal court in Indiana was available. Milligan's death sentence was later commuted to life. REF.: *CBA.*

Swearingen, George, d.1829, U.S., mur. As sheriff of Washington County, Md., George Swearingen had tried to run off prostitute Rachel Cunningham, but in the process, he fell for her himself. He was soon neglecting his wife and his work. None of his friends' warnings could dissuade the wealthy landowner. One day in early 1829, Swearingen invited his wife on a horseback ride, but instead of giving her renewed attention, he killed her. He claimed that she had fallen from her horse, and his word was accepted until his relationship with Cunningham became apparent.

The pair fled to New Orleans, where they were arrested and extradited to Maryland. Swearingen was found Guilty of murder and was hanged on Oct. 2, 1829.

REF.: *CBA;* Nash, *Bloodletters and Badmen.*

Swedish Dynamiters Case, The, See: **Kreuger, Alexander.**

Sweeney, Dennis, prom. 1980, U.S., mur. At the heart of the political foment and change in the U.S. during the 1960s was Allard Lowenstein, a liberal activist and assistant dean of men at Stanford University in Palo Alto, Calif. Dennis Sweeney, who attended Stanford, idolized Lowenstein, who picked the working-class scholarship student from Portland, Ore., as one of his protégés. Lowenstein got Sweeney to volunteer to work in Mississippi for the Student Nonviolent Coordinating Committee, but the SNCC became militant. Lowenstein withdrew his support, but Sweeney became more involved, readily taking to violent action before he was thrown out of the organization by black-power advocates.

Later, Lowenstein was elected to Congress, while Sweeney turned to drugs. In 1973, Sweeney was admitted to an Oregon mental hospital, but he stayed only a few days, despite his growing belief that he was being controlled by aliens who planted ideas into his head by invisible wires. "I am fairly certain that I have software I wasn't born with," he wrote one friend. He even tore the fillings out of his teeth because he was afraid that CIA could reach his brain through the metal. In 1975, he called Lowenstein on the phone to accuse him of putting people on his trail.

At the beginning of 1980, Sweeney was living in New London, Conn., working as a carpenter. When he returned from Portland after his stepfather's funeral, he began mumbling that Lowenstein had killed his stepfather. He purchased a .380 semiautomatic pistol, lying on the application about whether he had been in a mental hospital. He made an appointment to see Lowenstein on Mar. 14 at his Layton & Sherman office in New York City. The two of them talked for a few minutes, then Sweeney said, "Al, we've got to put an end to this obsession." He pulled out his gun, killed his mentor, returned to the lobby, and sat waiting for police. He told them, "He's been controlling my life for years. Now I've put an end to it."

Sweeney pleaded guilty and was sent to a mental institution for life.

REF.: *CBA;* Nash, *Murder Among the Mighty.*

Sweeney, George Clinton, 1895-1966, U.S., jur. U.S. attorney for Boston, Mass., from 1933-35. He was appointed to the district court of Massachusetts by President Franklin D. Roosevelt in 1935. REF.: *CBA.*

Sweeney, James, prom. 1926, U.S., (wrong. convict.) rob.-mur. On the morning of Oct. 14, 1926, a mail truck was transporting $300,000 in registered mail from the Federal Reserve Bank in New York to the Elizabethport National Bank. The truck was driven by John Enz, who was accompanied by Patrick S. Quinn. Police officer Jacob Christman, followed on motorcycle. Suddenly, a sedan rounded a corner, driving toward the truck, causing it to swerve onto a side street and collide with a parked car. Another car hit the police officer and a shotgun blast was fired at him. Meanwhile, Enz was cut down in machine gun fire, and as Quinn jumped from the vehicle, he fired twice before he himself was shot in the arms, hands, and left leg. A bystander was also wounded. Gang members then forced open the truck door, taking $151,300 in mail and drove off, running over the dead truckdriver and his injured helper. Later the gang members drove to a Newark apartment where they divided the haul. The robbers included James Cuniffe, William Crowley, Frank Kiekart (alias Charles Miller), William Fanning, Charles Neary, Daniel Grosso, and Benjamin Haas.

The public was outraged and authorities started an intense investigation which included giving state troopers orders to "shoot on sight and shoot to kill," as well as top post office department detectives. During the investigation, one of the gang, Haas, was questioned and police found a business card for James Sweeney, listed as "making books on crap games." Sweeney was arrested and put on trial on Apr. 11, 1927. Sweeney, an ex-convict who had twice been convicted, had one conviction for attempted grand larceny. He was positively identified by two eyewitnesses to the robbery, and the prosecutor cast doubts on Sweeney's alibi. Sweeney was found Guilty and given a life term in prison.

Later, however, Sweeney's lawyer learned that one witness had not even been present at the scene of the crime. Two of the actual gang members, Haas and Kiekart, were arrested and soon confessed, clearing Sweeney. Sweeney was released in November 1928. Of the other six robbers, Cuniffe was murdered in Detroit, Crowley was killed in Detroit when he resisted arrest, and Fanning, Neary, and Grosso were electrocuted on Apr. 10, 1931. REF.: *CBA.*

Sweeny, Peter Barr, 1825-1911, U.S., polit. corr. Served as district attorney of New York in 1857, and later as member of William Tweed's Tammany Hall. When Tweed lost power, he escaped to Canada in 1871, and then fled to France. He handed $400,000 in state funds back to New York to avoid prosecution. REF.: *CBA.*

Sweet, Willis, 1856-1925, U.S., jur. Served as attorney general for territory of Idaho from 1885-87, and was appointed to the territorial court of Idaho by President Benjamin Harrison in 1889. He also held office as attoiney general of Puerto Rico from 1903-05. REF.: *CBA.*

Sweeting, Whiting, prom. 1791, U.S., mur. Whiting Sweeting murdered Darius Quimby who had come to arrest him on a charge of theft the night of Jan. 3, 1791, in Stephantown, N.Y. When Sweeting attempted to run away, Quimby wrestled him to the ground. During the struggle Sweeting plunged a dagger into his opponent. The murderer was apprehended and placed on trial in Albany County. Incensed by the killing, the local judge instructed the jury to disregard any notions it had about a manslaughter conviction. "If a man resists an officer before he is taken, and death ensues, it is murder," he said. Sweeting was executed and his body delivered to a surgeon for dissection.

REF.: *CBA; The Narrative of Whiting Sweeting.*

Swendsen, Kurt, prom. 1702, Brit., consp.-kid.-fraud. In 1702, Danish businessman Kurt Swendsen dealt in timber and spent his free time drinking, gambling, and visiting prostitutes. He was soon short of cash, so he decided to marry into money.

Kurt Swendsen first persuaded an acquaintance in London, Stott, to help him kidnap her wealthy neighbor, Pleasant Rawlins. One day in March, Stott offered Rawlins and her governess a ride. The carriage was stopped by two men posing as bailiffs. The impostors charged Rawlins not paying her debts and trying to flee London, then they took her to a private room where they told her she would go to prison if she did not pay the debts and that the Lord Chief Justice would shortly arrive to settle the matter. When the imposter judge came into the room, he was attended by Swendsen, who offered to marry the young lady, saying he would cover her debts so she would save face. Rawlins agreed and a marriage ceremony was performed.

That night Swendsen went to bed drunk and the next morning his new wife sent notes to her friends and trustees, who immediately came to her aid. Swendsen was arrested and faced charges of conspiracy, kidnapping, and fraud. He was tried, convicted, sentenced to death, and hanged about a year after the kidnapping. Rawlins later married a country squire.

REF.: *CBA;* Sparrow, *The Great Assassins.*

Swett, Jane, b.1805, U.S., mur. The wife of Baptist minister Charles Swett of Kennebunk, Maine, endured her husband's alcoholism for most of their thirty-year marriage. However, Jane Swett reached her limit on Sept. 23, 1866. Charles Swett died after drinking a glass of whiskey to which his wife had added a large dose of morphine. Jane Swett was convicted and sent to prison for six years.

REF.: *CBA;* Nash, *Look For the Woman.*

Swift, Janie Tremayne, See: **Collins, James Thomas.**

Swift, Sir Rigby Philip Watson, 1874-1937, Brit., jur. Served as King's Counsel from 1912 and defended Lieutenant Colonel Norman Cecil Rutherford, found Guilty of murder. He also held office as a Conservative member of Parliament from 1910-18. He was named to the High Court, King's Division in 1920, where he served until death. He presided over the celebrated murder trials of Alexander Campbell Mason, Madame Fahmy, Charles Houghton, and John Robinson. REF.: *CBA.*

Swope, Edwin B., 1888-1955, U.S., law enfor. off. A native of New Mexico, Edwin B. Swope became warden of the New Mexico State Prison in 1934, overseeing the facility for four years. Swope then joined the federal penitentiary system as a prison warden at McNeil Island, Wash. He later was warden at the Terre Haute, Ind., prison, and also the Federal Correctional Institute at Englewood, Colo. On Apr. 20, 1948, Swope was appointed the second warden of Alcatraz Prison in San Francisco Bay, succeeding James A. Johnston. He began his duties on Apr. 30, 1948, and served until January 1955, when he retired from the federal prison system and took a job as warden of the prison at Sante Fe, N.M. Swope died at the age of sixty-seven during a vacation in San Francisco. REF.: *CBA.*

Edwin Swope

Sydney Ducks, prom. 1850s, U.S., org. crime. Of the many criminals who arrived in San Francisco after the discovery of gold in 1849, the most notorious were the former inmates of Australia's penal colony. The section of town where they settled, known as Sydney-Town, was described by the *San Francisco Herald* as "little better than the Five Points of New York or St. Giles of London." The newspaper further told how unsuspecting miners and sailors were trapped, lured into dens, and fed liquor or drugs to make them easy victims. Almost all vicious crimes in San Francisco were attributed to the Sydney-Town residents with the saying, "The Sydney ducks are cackling in the pond." More than 100 murders were attributed to them between 1849 and 1851. They were also known to set fires all over the city and then loot nearby sections as citizens and authorities struggled to extinguish the flames. In 1851, citizens took action. In the first of San Francisco's vigilante movements, Duck leaders James Stuart, also known as English John, John Jenkins, Robert McKenzie, and Samuel Whittaker were hanged. The hangings caused panic in Sydney-Town. While many Ducks left town, those who remained operated their dens and brothels with great caution. REF.: *CBA.*

Sykes, Troisville (AKA: **Bill Sykes**), prom. 1883, Case of, U.S., mur. During the late 1800s, Troisville Sykes and Kate Townsend lived in the same house in New Orleans, and the two became lovers for the next twenty-five years. In 1866, when Townsend opened a brothel in Basin Street, Sykes moved in with her. There, Townsend's business flourished and the house was the most opulent on the street. But Townsend apparently beat Sykes, who was known as a mild-mannered man.

A depiction of the Townsend Tragedy.

In early November 1883, Townsend had been having one of her ugly drinking bouts and on Nov. 3, when she summoned housekeeper, the brothel owner was holding a Bowie knife with a nine-inch blade. Remarking that she had been cutting off corns, Townsend asked for her morning coffee and said she wanted to see Sykes. When he arrived, she apparently hit him on the head with a goblet. When the housekeeper brought the coffee, the door was locked. Townsend then tried to attack Sykes with the Bowie knife, but he dislodged it and she grabbed a pair of pruning shears and stabbed him, cutting a deep gash in his thigh. Then, as he later claimed, he went blank, stabbing his lover with the knife. When he came to, he was crouched over her body, still holding the knife. He tossed the weapons out the window, and called for help.

When the police arrived, he confessed. On Jan. 29, 1884, his trial began and, after changing his plea from not guilty to self-defense, he was acquitted. Though he was to receive Townsend's estate of about $100,000, legal difficulties reduced his share to $340 from concubinage laws; $34,000 went to the government, and lawyers' fees amounted to about $65,000.

REF.: *CBA;* Tallant, *Ready to Hang;* Wilson, *Encyclopedia of Murder.*

Sylvester, David Joseph, 1945- , and **Ford, Jessie**, and **Davis, Nelson Grant**, and **Davis, Clarence**, prom. 1976, U.S., mur. At approximately 6 p.m. on July 20, 1976, 17-year-old Paulette Royal and 30-year-old Eddie Smith, key witnesses in an important drug case were slain in a New Orleans, La., motel. Pillows were placed over the victims' faces and bullets fired through the pillows into their heads. The lone survivor, Samuel Williams, told police that three men were responsible for the murders. Smith and Royal were in protective custody awaiting the trial of New Orleans drug czar, David Sylvester, which was to have started just two days later. However, the night before the murders, Royal and Smith had been wandering the French Quarter unprotected.

Thirty-one-year-old Sylvester was the biggest heroin dealer in the area and had a long record of drug trafficking. He was also thought of as a "Robin Hood" by the poorer residents of the New Orleans ghetto. He had been charged with possession with intent to distribute cocaine, and was probably headed for prison for life. Smith, a male prostitute and female impersonator, and Royal, also a prostitute, had both worked for Sylvester as runners and had agreed to testify against him at the upcoming trial. Samuel Williams, twenty-two, was a friend looking for a job in New Orleans and had happened to be at the hotel when the murders occurred.

Five-time Medal of Merit recipient Detective John Dillman was put in charge of the case. He went undercover in the seamier side of New Orleans to hunt down the killers and eventually learned that two local hoodlums, Clarence and Nelson Davis, had committed the murders. Female impersonator Jessie Ford, a friend of the witnesses, helped the killers enter the room and drove the car. Ford and Clarence Davis were caught, but Nelson Davis remained at large.

The trial began on Nov. 11, 1976, in the courtroom of Judge Charles Ward, without Nelson Davis. Prosecutor Harry Connick, was able to prove that Sylvester knew the location of the witnesses. Jessie Ford testified that he had taken the killers to the room and let them in. David Sylvester was found Guilty of two counts of murder and one of attempted murder, and sentenced to life in prison. The other parties to the killings, Jessie Ford and Clarence Davis, were also found Guilty and given lesser sentences. Nelson Davis was apprehended later in an unrelated crime, and in a separate trial, was also found Guilty of the two murders and sent to prison. REF.: *CBA.*

Symbionese Liberation Army, prom. 1973-77, U.S., terr.-kid.-rob.-mur. Within a four-month period, the public image of Patricia Campbell Hearst, granddaughter of the wealthy and powerful newspaper publisher William Randolph Hearst, went from tragic kidnap victim to leftist sympathizer to bank robber, and finally to "armed and dangerous fugitive." Hearst was the most prominent victim of a group of university intellectuals and hard-core criminals called the Symbionese Liberation Army, or SLA.

The SLA was founded by Donald David DeFreeze, who had escaped from prison in March 1973 after being sentenced four years earlier for possession of a bomb. In prison DeFreeze learned both the rhetoric and strategy of revolutionary action. He called himself Field Marshal Cinque and advocated equality and the abolition of capitalism. The group shot Marcus A. Foster, the school superintendent of Oakland on Nov. 6, 1973, because Foster endorsed the use of mandatory student identification cards to control juvenile crime.

Two months later, on Jan. 10, a policeman stopped a van in Concord, Calif. The van's occupants, Russell Little and Joseph Remiro, pulled guns. Little was apprehended. Remiro got away but was caught later. When the SLA headquarters was set on fire that night, police found records listing names of members, and a written entry alluding to Patricia Hearst.

On Feb. 4, 1974, Steven Weed, Patricia Hearst's fiancé answered a knock at the door of their shared townhouse. As a woman engaged Weed in conversation, two men appeared and pushed the door open. Weed was beaten on the head and 19-year-old Hearst, dressed in a bathrobe, was carried screaming to a waiting car. Three days after Hearst's abduction, authorities received word that the SLA was demanding the donation of millions of dollars worth of food to the poor of California. In a tape recording delivered to a radio station, Hearst said, "These people aren't just a bunch of nuts. They're perfectly willing to die for what they're doing."

Randolph Hearst, Patricia's father, organized a quick giveaway of packaged foods, but the SLA said the shipment was inadequate. Another tape on which Patricia criticized her father's lack of generosity caused speculation that the kidnapping had been planned by Patricia Hearst and her friends. Although Hearst gave away more food totaling another $2 million the SLA did not release his daughter. DeFreeze then made a statement that she would be held until Remiro and Little were released.

In Patricia Hearst's own version of the kidnapping, told seven years later, she said that she spent the first fifty-seven days of her captivity in a closet, blindfolded and bound. She was raped repeatedly and gradually brainwashed into believing that the SLA members were the only people who cared about her. Just as her parents believed that she was about to be released, they received

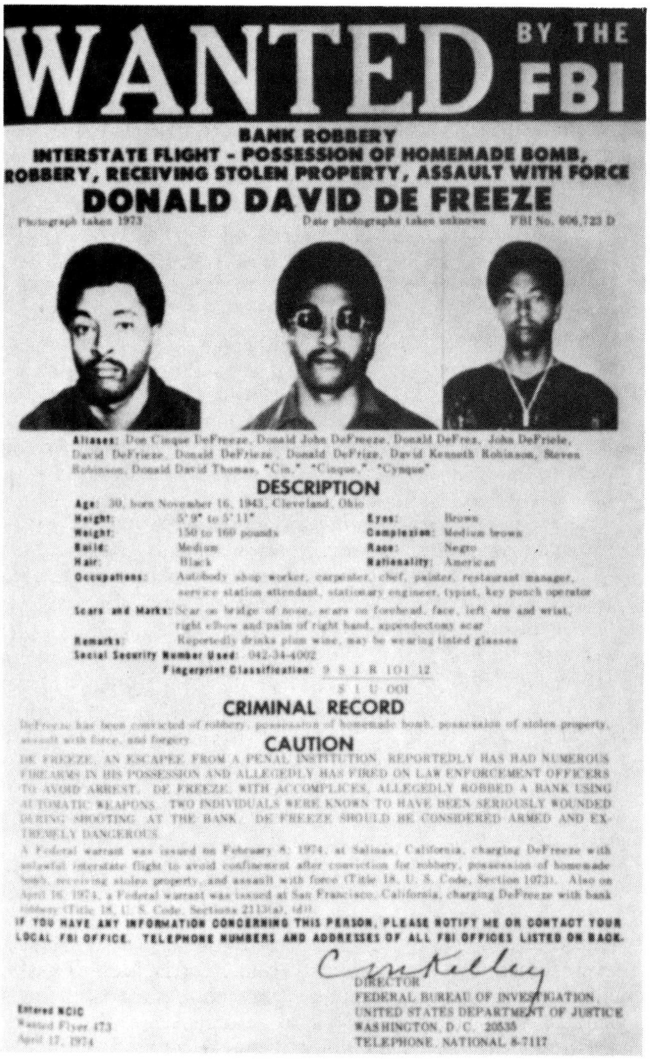
WANTED BY THE FBI

BANK ROBBERY
INTERSTATE FLIGHT - POSSESSION OF HOMEMADE BOMB, ROBBERY, RECEIVING STOLEN PROPERTY, ASSAULT WITH FORCE

DONALD DAVID DE FREEZE

Photograph taken 1973 Date photographs taken unknown FBI No. 606,723 D

Aliases: Don Cinque DeFreeze, Donald John DeFreeze, Donald DeFrez, John DeFriele, David DeFrieze, Donald DeFrieze, Donald DeFrize, David Kenneth Robinson, Steven Robinson, Donald David Thomas, "Cin," "Cinque," "Cynque"

DESCRIPTION

Age: 30, born November 16, 1943, Cleveland, Ohio

Height:	5'9" to 5'11"	Eyes:	Brown
Weight:	150 to 160 pounds	Complexion:	Medium brown
Build:	Medium	Race:	Negro
Hair:	Black	Nationality:	American

Occupations: Autobody shop worker, carpenter, chef, painter, restaurant manager, service station attendant, stationary engineer, typist, key punch operator

Scars and Marks: Scar on bridge of nose, scars on forehead, face, left arm and wrist, right elbow and palm of right hand, appendectomy scar

Remarks: Reportedly drinks plum wine, may be wearing tinted glasses

Social Security Number Used: 042-34-4002

Fingerprint Classification: 9 S 1 R 101 12 / S 1 U 001

CRIMINAL RECORD

DeFreeze has been convicted of robbery, possession of homemade bomb, possession of stolen property, assault with force, and forgery.

CAUTION

DE FREEZE, AN ESCAPEE FROM A PENAL INSTITUTION, REPORTEDLY HAS HAD NUMEROUS FIREARMS IN HIS POSSESSION AND ALLEGEDLY HAS FIRED ON LAW ENFORCEMENT OFFICERS TO AVOID ARREST. DE FREEZE, WITH ACCOMPLICES, ALLEGEDLY ROBBED A BANK USING AUTOMATIC WEAPONS. TWO INDIVIDUALS WERE KNOWN TO HAVE BEEN SERIOUSLY WOUNDED DURING SHOOTING AT THE BANK. DE FREEZE SHOULD BE CONSIDERED ARMED AND EXTREMELY DANGEROUS.

A Federal warrant was issued on February 8, 1974, at Salinas, California, charging DeFreeze with unlawful interstate flight to avoid confinement after conviction for robbery, possession of homemade bomb, receiving stolen property, and assault with force (Title 18, U. S. Code, Section 1073). Also on April 16, 1974, a Federal warrant was issued at San Francisco, California, charging DeFreeze with bank robbery (Title 18, U. S. Code, Sections 2113(a), (d)).

IF YOU HAVE ANY INFORMATION CONCERNING THIS PERSON, PLEASE NOTIFY ME OR CONTACT YOUR LOCAL FBI OFFICE. TELEPHONE NUMBERS AND ADDRESSES OF ALL FBI OFFICES LISTED ON BACK.

C M Kelley
DIRECTOR
FEDERAL BUREAU OF INVESTIGATION
UNITED STATES DEPARTMENT OF JUSTICE
WASHINGTON, D. C. 20535
TELEPHONE, NATIONAL 8-7117

Entered NCIC
Wanted Flyer 473
April 17, 1974

FBI wanted poster for Donald David De Freeze, leader of the SLA.

Patricia Soltysik, SLA.

Angela Atwood, SLA.

William Wolfe, SLA.

Nancy Ling Perry, SLA.

SLA symbol, hydra-headed cobra.

Camilla Hall, SLA.

Los Angeles SLA hideout in flames where five died, 1974.

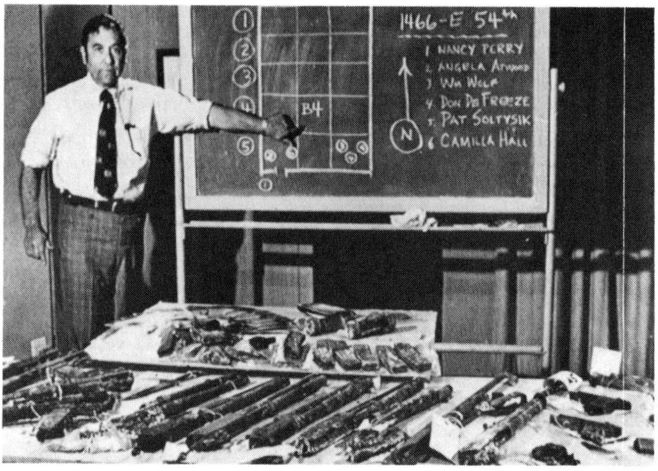

LAPD sergeant Charles Loust, before SLA chart and arsenal, 1974.

another tape in which she said, "I have never been forced to say anything on any tape. Nor have I been brainwashed, tortured, hypnotized or in any way confused....My love has...grown into an unselfish love for my comrades here, in prison and on the streets. A love that comes from the knowledge that 'no one is free until we all are free.'...I have been given the choice of (1) being released in a safe area, or (2) joining the forces of the Symbionese Liberation Army...I have chosen to stay and fight."

While the public continued to believe that Patricia Hearst was being coerced, the SLA robbed a branch of the Hibernia Bank of more than $10,000. Hidden cameras in the bank showed "Tania," as Hearst was called by SLA members, holding a semi-automatic carbine and apparently giving orders.

On May 17, police discovered the Los Angeles hideout of the SLA and attacked it with 150 policemen, as television cameras watched. The members inside chose to fight, and somehow, the building was set on fire while more than 6,000 shots were fired. The next day, the bodies of four women and two men were found in the ruins. The dead were identified as DeFreeze and William Wolfe, purported to be Hearst's lover, Camilla Hall, Nancy Ling Perry, and Patricia Soltysik. At the time of the shootout, Hearst was with William and Emily Harris in Las Vegas. They went East and tried to keep the SLA going even when its original leaders were dead. At first Patricia Hearst was still a captive, but gradually she was given freedom to do as she chose. She chose to stay.

In 1975, the remaining SLA members robbed a bank in Carmichael, Calif. Emily Harris killed a woman in the robbery. On a third attempt to bomb a police station on Sept. 18, 1975, Patricia Hearst and Wendy Yoshimura were caught by the police. The rest of the group were apprehended within a few days.

Patricia Hearst was tried and found Guilty of armed robbery. She was sentenced to seven years in prison, but her sentence was commuted by President Jimmy Carter after two years. The Harrises, jailed for kidnapping, were paroled in 1983. In June 1977, Michael Remiro and Russell Little were sentenced to life in prison for the killing of Marcus Foster, and six months to twenty years for the attempted murder of Robert Blackburn, Foster's deputy, who was wounded at the time of Foster's murder. See: **Hearst, Patricia Campbell.**

REF.: Alexander, *Anyone's Daughter;* Alix, *Ransom Kidnapping in America;* Baker, *Exclusive! The Inside Story of Patricia Hearst and the SLA;* Bell, *Assassin; CBA;* Clutterbuck, *Guerrillas nad Terrorists;* ____, *Kidnap and Ransom;* Cohen, *Mickey Cohen: In My Own Words;* Dobson and Payne, *Counterattack—The West's Battle Against the Terrorists;* ____, *The Terrorists—Their Weapons, Leaders and Tactics;* Godwin, *Murder, U.S.A.;* Hacker, *Crusaders, Criminals, Crazies: Terror and Terror in Our Time;* Laquer, *Terrorism;* Liston, *Terrorism;* McClellan and Avery, *The Voices of Guns;* Messick, *Kidnapping;* Moscow, *Every Secret Thing;* Payne and Findley, *The Life and Death of the SLA;* Schreiber, *The Ultimate Weapon—Terrorists and World Order;* Unger, *FBI;* Wilson, *Encyclopedia of Modern Murder.*

Symes, J. Foster, 1878-1951, U.S., jur. District attorney in Colorado from 1921-22. He was appointed to the district court of Colorado by President Warren G. Harding in 1922. REF.: *CBA.*

Symmachus, Quintus Aurelius Memmius, d.524, Rome, consul, treas. Made consul in 485. He was executed without trial on the orders of Theodoric, for supporting his son-in-law Anicius Boethius against charges of treason. Boethius was executed at his side. REF.: *CBA.*

Sympson, Thomas (AKA: **Old Mobb**), d.1690, Brit., rob. Thomas Sympson, as dangerous a highwayman as ever lived, successfully practiced his villainy for nearly forty-five years before he was apprehended in Westminster. Sympson, who traversed the public roads using the moniker "Old Mobb," was born in Romsey, Hampshire. He had a wife, five children, and several grandchildren at the time of his death.

Sympson became a legend in his own time for the many famous characters he targeted for robbery. John Gadbury, the famous Puritan astrologer, was relieved of £9 in gold and silver on the road between Winchester and London. When he raised a voice in protest, Sympson silenced him with a stern rebuke. "No, no, you must not sham poverty to me, who knows as good things as yourself," the highwayman preached. "Therefore if you do not instantly deliver your money this pistol shall prove as fatal to you as that raging star which threatens our climate with death and disease in the Dog days."

Louise de Kerouaille, the mistress of King Charles II, was another who did not escape the scathing verbal taunts of Sympson. He encountered Louise, the Duchess of Portsmouth, outside New Market one day, asking her what she carried in her basket. It was grain, she replied. Sympson demanded she hand it over. "Deliver," he said, "for as you have no commodity about you but what is French, I may answer by law, the seizure of that prohibited by an Act of Parliament." Without a whimper of protest, the duchess retreated to her carriage where she handed over £300 in currency, an expensive brocaded necklace, a gold watch, and some diamonds.

When Sympson accosted Baron George Jeffreys, chief justice of England, he reminded him of their previous encounter. "Yes sir, I know you well enough and ought to charge you with a constable, for I'm sure you once put me in a great danger of my life at Hertford assizes," he said. "Wherefore I'm resolved to be even with you now." He took fifty-six guineas. The luck of the resourceful highwayman did not hold, however. He was arrested on Tothill Street in Westminster and remanded to the jailer at Newgate. Indicted for thirty-six robberies, Sympson was found Guilty and hanged at Tyburn on May 30, 1690. REF.: *CBA.*

Syndicate, The, prom. 1930- , U.S., org. crime. Created to eliminate gang warfare, facilitate communication, and maximize profit among several mobs, the Syndicate was established as a nationally organized directorship in 1934. It had its roots in the extensive bloodshed of the Roaring Twenties, which inspired such legendary killers as Al Capone, Johnny Torrio, and Charles "Lucky" Luciano to turn to negotiation to settle their differences. Several times in the late twenties Luciano, Torrio, Meyer Lansky, and other criminal kingpins had attempted to unite the various gangs across the country under a single organizational structure, with clearly defined boundaries and responsibilities for each.

With Luciano, Lansky, and Torrio in the lead, the 1934 conclave also brought Dutch Schultz, Louis "Lepke" Buchalter, Frank Costello, Vito Genovese, Thomas Lucchesi, Abner "Longy" Zwillman, and Jacob "Gurrah" Shapiro together to work out guidelines and protocol for the new organization. Together they worked out territories, rules and regulations, and the command hierarchy.

The Syndicate was also a method of resolving conflicts based on the gangs' ethnic lines, with the powerful Irish and Jewish gangs of the twenties taking part commensurately with their strength. As time went on, however, the Syndicate became almost wholly controlled by the Mafia.

The Syndicate is known for being absolutely dogmatic in its devotion to discipline. Any infraction of rules or disregard of orders from a superior is severely punished, regardless of rank, circumstances, or previous service. This was established early on when Dutch Schultz, a founding member and holder of a seat on the national board of directors, was murdered for ignoring a board directive in 1935. Since that time, standards of discipline have never wavered.

Neither the methods nor the interests of the Syndicate have changed much in almost sixty years. The main business ventures of the thirties included gambling, vice, union racketeering, and narcotics—the recent repeal of Prohibition had just put the mobsters out of the bootlegging business. Its biggest money makers today remain narcotics and gambling. See: **Black Hand, Mafia.**

REF: *CBA;* de Leeuw, *Underworld Story; The Kefauver Committee Report on Organized Crime;* Kennedy, *The Enemy Within;* Lait and Mortimer, *Chicago: Confidential;* McPhaul, *Johnny Torrio;* Mooney, *Crime*

Incorporated; Nash, *Bloodletters and Badmen; The Rise of Organized Crime and Vice Rackets in the U.S.A.;* Reckless, *The Crime Problem;* Scott, *The Concise Encyclopedia of Crime and Criminals.*

Szálasi, Ferenc, 1897-1946, Hung., treas. Originated anti-Semitic National Will political party in 1935. He was frequently jailed by the government, but eventually became the leader of the fascist Arrow Cross, and rose to become head of the government in 1944. He accepted all demands by the German occupation during the war, and later fled the country along with the Germans in 1945. He was arrested, sent back to Hungary, and executed. REF.: *CBA.*

T

Tabinshwehti, 1512-50, Burma, king, assass. Succeeded father Minkyinyo. He unified Burma, first by overpowering the Mon kingdom of Pegu in 1539, and by capturing most of Lower Burma and Prome in 1542. He adopted Pegu as his capital in 1546. He led a failed attack on Ayutthaya, the capital of Siam and was assassinated in 1550. REF.: *CBA*.

Taborsky, Joseph, 1923-60, U.S., mur. On Oct. 7, 1955, Joseph Taborsky was released from the Connecticut State Prison's Death Row, where he had been sent in 1951 for murdering Louis Wolfson while robbing his liquor store with his brother, Albert Taborsky. Albert received a life sentence for turning state's evidence. Joseph declared his innocence and called his brother crazy. Granted another trial after Albert's transfer to a state hospital for displaying bizarre behavior, the state was left without a case and Taborsky was released.

Within a year, a wave of murders swept through Connecticut which police called the "Chinese Executions" because all the victims had been kneeling when shot from behind. The slayings began on Dec. 15, 1956, when a 67-year-old Hartford, Conn., tailor was found robbed and shot in the back of the neck. Thirty minutes later, gas station operator Ed Kurpiewski was robbed and forced into the restroom where his murderer shot him through the back of the head. Daniel Janowski, who drove up to the gas station when Kurpiewski was shot, was next. He was found in the storeroom, also shot through the back of the head. Samuel Cohn, a liquor store owner, was similarly killed eleven days later and ten days after that, in North Haven, Bernard Speyer and his wife were killed as they walked into a shoe store. The shoe store owner, who had been knocked unconscious, told police that two men had robbed the store and fatally shot the couple.

Investigations led to the arrest of Arthur Culombe and Joseph Taborsky. The shoe store owner positively identified Taborsky as the killer of the husband and wife. Taborsky confessed to those slayings, as well as to the murder of Louis Wolfson, the murder for which he was initially imprisoned in 1955. Convicted of murder, he was executed in 1960. REF.: *CBA*.

Taby, Arpad, prom. 1940's, Hung., rebel.-pris. esc. Hungarian lieutenant Arpad Taby, a highly decorated WWI hero, passionately opposed Communism. When a Communist government controlled Hungary briefly in 1919, Taby organized an anti-Communist movement near his former garrison at Eger. The movement failed, but so did the government, replaced with the old monarchy. Taby joined the Hungarian gendarmerie and rose to the rank of major. In 1939, he was elected to Hungary's parliament. When the Red Army approached Hungary during WWII, Taby enlisted to fight the Soviets. After the war, the Soviets arrested Taby and imprisoned him in Budapest.

The Hungarian Communists could not find witnesses to testify against Taby. On the fifth day of his trial, the judge withdrew without explanation and without a verdict. Taby demanded acquittal but was ordered to be retried. The new trial, held under heavy secrecy, lasted fifteen minutes, and Taby was sentenced to eight years forced labor. During an appeal, a Communist judge hoped to convert the resolute Taby and released him from prison when he agreed to plead guilty.

Although a free man, Taby was constantly harassed and his friends were forced to avoid him. For seven years, he barely subsisted by hauling coal. In October 1954, Taby again was arrested for resisting the party. Weak and ill from malnutrition, he was sentenced to fifteen years hard labor. During the uprising of 1956, he was released by rebels who overcame the prison guards. Although still ill, Taby joined the anti-Communist forces. When the Red Army put down the Hungarian uprising, Taby crossed the border into Austria and lived as a political exile.

REF.: *CBA;* Whitehead, *Journey Into Crime*.

Tacitus, Marcus Claudius, c.200-76, Roman., emp., assass. Became emperor following assassination of Emperor Aurelian. He defeated the Goths in battle in Asia Minor. He also initiated reforms during his brief reign. He was murdered by his own soldiers and succeeded by Florianus, his half-brother. REF.: *CBA*.

Tacklyn, Larry Winfield, and **Burrows, Erskine Durrant**, prom. 1972, Berm., mur. On Sept. 9, 1972, George Duckett, police commissioner of Bermuda, was shot to death in his home. Despite an offer of a $24,000 reward, local people would not talk. On Mar. 10, 1973, Sir Richard Sharples, governor and commander-in-chief of Bermuda, and Captain Hugh Sayers of the Welsh Guards were murdered on the terrace of the Government House, shot at close range during a dinner party. Two men were seen directly after the shooting, but no one could identify them. On Apr. 6, store owners Victor Rego and Mark Doe became the next victims. The police were certain the five victims were killed by the same man and increased the reward to $3 million. Soon, suspect Larry Winfield Tacklyn was identified and arrested.

The arrest set off a violent retaliation by the drug traffickers of Bermuda's underworld. On May 5, a motorcycle gunman shot out the windows of police headquarters. The incident reoccurred shortly after, and then a series of armed robberies and shooting incidents occurred near the headquarters. On Sept. 25, 1973, the Bank of Bermuda was robbed by a lone gunman, who was identified as Erskine Durrant Burrows. Burrows was apprehended on Oct. 18. Police found the guns of both Tacklyn and Burrows, and ballistics proved them to be the murder weapons. Burrows was charged with the murder of George Duckett, and both men were charged with the four subsequent killings. They were sentenced to death and hanged.

REF.: *CBA;* Tullett, *Strictly Murder*.

Taewon-gun (AKA: **Yi Ha-ung**), 1821-98, Korea, kid. Held office as regent under son King Kojong from 1864-73. He enacted reforms to centralize the government and improved the army by increasing troop levels and modernizing weaponry. Resisting all concessions to the West and Japan, he led an anti-Japanese revolt in 1882. He was kidnapped and held captive in China from 1882-85 and lost his power when he returned. REF.: *CBA*.

Taft, Alphonso, 1810-91, U.S., atty. gen.-jur. Practiced law in Cincinnati, Ohio, and was named judge of Cincinnati Superior Court in 1865, serving until 1872. He served two months as U.S. secretary of war under President Ulysses S. Grant in 1876, then accepted a presidential appointment to serve as attorney general until 1877, the end of Grant's term. As attorney general he helped set up the commission that settled the controversial 1876 presidential election returns. He was appointed U.S. minister to Austria-Hungary in 1882, and held the same post in Russia from 1884-85. He was the father of William Howard Taft, U.S. president and Supreme Court chief justice. REF.: *CBA*.

Taft, Henry Waters, 1859-1945, U.S., lawyer. Brother of U.S. president and Supreme Court chief justice William Howard Taft, and son of U.S. attorney general Alphonso Taft. He practiced law in New York City. He helped investigate and prosecute the Tobacco Trust as special assistant to the U.S. attorney general. REF.: *CBA*.

Taft, William Howard, 1857-1930, U.S., jur. Only U.S. president to also serve as U.S. Supreme Court chief justice. After graduating from the University of Cincinnati Law School, he quickly became involved in Ohio Republican politics, and served in various positions until 1890, when he was named U.S. solicitor general. After displaying his skills to President Benjamin Harrison, he was appointed to the sixth circuit court, serving from 1892-1900, when he was appointed by President William McKinley to head the Philippine Commission. He was appointed civilian governor of the islands within one year, and held that office until he was selected to serve as U.S. secretary of war under President Theodore Roosevelt in 1904. He became such a major political figure that he was nominated for president after Roosevelt declared he would not seek reelection, and was elected in 1908.

As president, Taft nominated six justices to the Supreme Court, including Edward Douglas White, whom he would later replace as chief justice; Charles Evans Hughes, who would later replace

Taft; Horace Lurton, Willis Van Devanter, Mahlon Pitney, and Joseph Lamar. He was renominated by his party in 1912, but faced both the Democrats' Woodrow Wilson and Roosevelt, running on the Bull Moose ticket, and was defeated. Once returned to private life, the former president headed the American Bar Association, tried to defeat liberal Louis Brandeis' nomination to the Supreme Court, and taught constitutional law as a Kent Professor at Yale University Law School. He reached his ultimate goal in 1921, when he was confirmed as chief justice of the Supreme Court, having been nominated by President Warren G. Harding. As chief justice, he effectively used his experience as solicitor general to reorganize the federal judiciary system, which was becoming overwhelmed by a backload of cases.

The Judiciary Act of 1922, which he helped draft, gave federal judges the authority to revise court procedures. He also shaped the direction of the Supreme Court by helping create the Judiciary Act of 1925. In judging criminal cases, he generally supported warrantless searches when accompanied by reasonable suspicion that a crime had occurred. In *Carroll v. United States* in 1925, he spoke for the court in supporting automobile searches made by federal authorities who had reasonable grounds to believe a crime was being committed. That same year he had the opportunity to support his Oval Office successors with *Ex parte Grossman,* in which the Court backed the concept of presidential pardons. In *Olmstead v. United States* in 1928, he ruled that police wiretaps were constitutional, as they did not physically violate the subject's property. Due to poor health, he left the court in 1930 and died shortly thereafter.

William Howard Taft

REF.: *CBA;* Mason, *William Howard Taft, Chief Justice;* Pringle, *The Life and Times of William Howard Taft.*

Tait, Sydney D., prom. 1930, U.S., perj. In 1930, certain members of the New York City police department vice squad were allegedly setting up prostitutes to be arrested and then extorting money from them. They would hire a stooge to proposition the woman. The police would wait ten minutes after the couple returned to a prostitute's apartment and then enter, finding the couple in a compromising position. In April 1929, vice squad members Sydney Tait and Eugene Baccaglini arrested Icie Sands. She was convicted of vagrancy, and given a thirty-day sentence. When many such arrests occurred, the Appellate Division of the New York Supreme Court began an investigation into the practices of the vice squad. Before a grand jury, Chile Mapocho Acuña confessed that he made his living framing these women. Acuña had been involved in the arrest of Icie Sands, and said he worked for Officer Tait. Tait denied the charge, stating he had previously employed Acuña, but not in this instance.

On Jan. 10, 1931, the grand jury returned an indictment for perjury against Sydney Tait. In March, in the Court of General Sessions before Judge Morris Koenig, a jury found Tait Guilty, and sentenced him to two-and-a-half to five years in Sing Sing. Prior to the trial, on Dec. 22, 1930, New York governor Franklin D. Roosevelt pardoned six women who were serving sentences as a result of perjured testimony. REF.: *CBA.*

Taksin (Phraya Taksin or Phya Taksin), 1734-82, Thai., king, assass. Served as provincial governor in 1764 with administrative title *phraya.* As king, he lifted the Burmese suppression of Ayutthaya in 1768, formed one kingdom from the five feudal Thai realms, established Thon Buri as the new capital, and regained the western provinces from Cambodia. However, he estranged himself from his people by commanding them to worship him, and was ousted and put to death by Chao Phraya Chakki, who also succeeded him as king. REF.: *CBA.*

Tal, Schlomo, prom. 1977, and **Balabin, Pinhas,** 1949- , U.S., mur. Million-dollar deals are sealed with a handshake and the Yiddish blessing "mazel un brucha" on New York City's Forty-seventh Street between Fifth Avenue and the Avenue of the Americas. This midtown block is the center of the world's diamond industry. Its more than 200 diamond brokers account for more than $1 billion in annual sales. Negotiation is intense, with a profit margin of only 1 or 2 percent. But the area is considered so safe that many brokers conduct their business without insurance. Robbery is extremely rare and murder virtually unheard of.

In late September 1977, the body of 25-year-old diamond cutter Pinchos Jaroslawicz, who had been missing since Sept. 20, was found bound and stuffed into a small box in the 47th Street office of another diamond cutter, Schlomo Tal. Jaroslawicz had died of head injuries and asphyxiation after a plastic bag was put over his head. The $1 million in gems he had been carrying in his wallet were missing. Earlier in the week, Tal's wife reported him missing, but he was found sleeping in his wife's car in Queens. Tal said two masked men entered the office and robbed and killed Jaroslawicz, and that he hid the body and did not report the murder for fear of reprisal. Tal said the two men then returned, abducted him, and drove him around Nassau County for three days, finally abandoning him after drugging him. Upon waking, he was found by the police and arrested as a material witness.

The Jaroslawicz case bore a similarity to the unsolved murders of four other diamond merchants. Leo Dershowitz and Howard Block were murdered in Puerto Rico in 1974. In 1977, Abraham Shafizadeh was also murdered in Puerto Rico, and Haskell Kronenberg was murdered in Florida. More than $1.5 million in gems were taken from the four victims. The police questioned Tal's shaky alibi, and when they learned that he had a criminal record in Israel, they arrested him and another diamond cutter, 29-year-old Pinhas Balabin, on Mar. 30, 1978, for the murder of Pinchos Jaroslawicz. Both men were convicted of murder and sentenced to twenty-five years to life in prison. REF.: *CBA.*

Tal, Wasfi, 1920-1971, Egypt, premier, assass. On Nov. 28, 1971, three gunmen assassinated 51-year-old Jordanian premier Wasfi Tal in a Cairo hotel, also wounding Jordanian foreign minister Abdullah Salah and a Cairo police officer. The killers, members of the Palestinian Black September movement, were Monzer Soleiman Khalifa, twenty-seven; Gowad Khalid Boghdady, twenty-three; and Izzat Ahmed Rabah, also twenty-three. They had entered Egypt using Syrian passports. Two of the gunmen were captured near the hotel and the other was found in a nearby apartment. A fourth man, 26-year-old Zeyad Mahmond Badran, was arrested later. Tal, an outspoken critic of the Palestinian movement, was in Cairo to for a meeting of the Arab League's Joint Defense Council.

Tal entered government service in 1949, and was premier and defense minister of Jordan twice during the early 1960's. He also served as chief of King Hussein's cabinet.

REF.: *CBA;* Demaris, *Brothers in Blood: The International Terrorist Network;* Dobson and Payne, *The Terrorists—Their Weapons, Leaders and Tactics;* Laquer, *Terrorism;* O'Ballance, *Language of Violence—The Blood Politics of Terrorism;* Paine, *The Assassins' World.*

Talat Pasha, Mehmed (Mehmet Talaat Pasha, AKA: Talaat Bey), 1872-1921, Turk., polit., rebel.-assass. Jailed on charges of dissident political activity from 1893-95, and led Young Turks after 1908 Turkish revolution. He served twice as the minister of the interior and also as postmaster general between terms. In 1917, he became grand vizier, succeeding Said Halim Pasa. He was forced to retire after twenty months and later was assassinated by an Armenian. REF.: *CBA.*

Talbot, Sir George John, 1861-1938, Brit., jur. King's Counsel from 1906, specializing in ecclesiastical matters. He succeeded the late Lord Darling on the High Court, King's Bench, in 1923, and served there for fourteen years, presiding over the notable murder trials of Alfred Arthur Rouse and Stanley Eric Hobday. He retired from the bench in 1937. REF.: *CBA*.

Talbot, Julie, prom. 1937, Case of, U.S., mur. Julie Rowan and Rosie Slayton lived in impoverished Appalachia. Rowan married Len Talbot, whose brothers were involved in a fight with the Baylanch clan.

Although married, Len Talbot continued to see Slayton and lived with both Slayton and his wife Julie. On May 26, 1937, the women confronted each other as they traveled on a road, and Slayton, armed with a .22, threatened to kill Julie Talbot. Talbot charged underneath the gun and fatally stabbed Slayton in the throat before Slayton could fire. No charges were ever brought against Julie Talbot.

REF.: *CBA;* Montell, *Killings.*

Talbot, Lug, prom. 1930, U.S., mur. In 1930, a bordello was set up at a sawmill camp in Hemp Hollow, near Brownsville, Ky. On Oct. 4, three men from Brownsville and three men from Rutherford, Ky., visited the brothel. The two groups fought over who would receive the women's services first, and an ensuing brawl ended in a double killing. Oren Baylanch shot and killed Ben Talbot and was then shot to death by Ben's brother, Lug Talbot. Lug was eventually arrested and turned over to Brake County officials. Lug Talbot pleaded guilty to voluntary manslaughter and was sentenced to fifteen years at the Kentucky state penitentiary. After his release, he moved to Owenton County, and in a fit of depression, he committed suicide by hanging himself.

REF.: *CBA;* Montell, *Killings.*

Talbott, Charles E., and **Talbott, Albert**, d.1881, U.S., mur. Charles Talbott and his brother, Albert, found their father's frequent beatings impossible to withstand any longer, so they schemed to kill him. One night, while the senior Talbot was preparing to go to sleep, Charles entered his bedroom and fatally shot him. The brothers were found Guilty and executed by hanging.

REF.: *CBA;* Nash, *Bloodletters and Badmen.*

Talfourd, Sir **Thomas Noon**, 1795-1854, Brit., jur. Served as sergeant-at-law in 1833. He was a member of Parliament in 1835, and judge of the common pleas in 1849. He was unsuccessfully prosecuted for publishing Shelley's *Queen Mab*. REF.: *CBA*.

Talizin, General, See: **Paul I**.

Tallien, Jean Lambert, 1767-1820, Fr., polit. corr. Served as secretary of Commune of Paris in 1792, and member of both the National Convention in 1792 and the Committee of Public Safety. He was sent by the Convention to Bordeaux, where he stepped up convictions and executions in 1793 during the Reign of Terror. He helped lead the Revolution of Ninth Thermidor that removed Robespierre in 1794. After the Reign of Terror ended with Robespierre's execution, he adopted more moderate political beliefs, becoming a leader of the Thermidorians. He repressed the Jacobins and the Revolutionary Tribunal, and later joined the Council of Five Hundred, where he served from 1795-98. REF.: *CBA*.

Talmadge, T. DeWitt, prom. 1870s, U.S., reformer. The Rev. T. DeWitt Talmadge, pastor of the Brooklyn Tabernacle during the 1870s, battled mightily against widespread corruption and vice in New York, waging war particularly against its low dives, brothels, and gambling dens. In one of his rousing fire-and-brimstone sermons, Talmadge aptly labeled New York as "the modern Gomorrah." His zeal propelled him into the streets and hell-holes of Manhattan where he would lecture the drunken denizens and common streetwalkers on their sinful ways. Few of these dedicated gamblers, thieves, and prostitutes were ever reformed.

In 1878, Talmadge made headlines by storming into the wicked dives of Satan's Circus, an area between Twenty-fourth and Fortieth streets and Fifth and Seventh avenues, teeming with brothels, gambling halls, saloons, and all-night dance halls. Talmadge was hooted, jeered, and mocked by the gangsters, gamblers and whores he tried to reform. He realized his utter failure to alter the lifestyles of these profligates and retreated back to his pulpit where he continued to thunder his damnation of such creatures. Talmadge and other reformers such as Henry Ward Beecher of the Plymouth Church in Brooklyn, compelled Mayor Peter Cooper to close many of the dives in Satan's Circus. But this was merely a gesture on the part of a corrupt political administration that profitted greatly from the existence of such places.

Reformer T. DeWitt Talmadge being mocked by whores in The Strand during one of his invasions to save souls in Satan's Circus.

Most of those dives, like The Strand, were soon back in operation after the reformers discontinued their visits to Satan's Circus, which resumed its illicit activities without further hindrance. Satan's Circus flourished for twenty-five years, a period in which, according to one historian, "the criminal classes revelled in an orgy of vice and crime."

REF.: Asbury, *The Gangs of New York;* Brace, *The Dangerous Classes of New York;* Byrnes, *Professional Criminals of America; CBA;* Costello, *Our Police Protectors;* Lewis, *The Apaches of New York;* Mott, *The New York of Yesterday;* Parkhurst, *My Forty Years in New York; The Volcano Under the City;* Walling, *Recollections of a New York Chief of Police.*

Talwell, John, See: **Tawell, John**.

Tamerlane the Great (Tamburlaine, Timur i Leng), 1336-1405, Mongolia, mur. A descendant of Genghis Khan, Tamerlane (from "Timur the Lame") set about retaking all the territory that the great Khan had originally held, and he made no effort to do so in gentle fashion. Taking the throne at Samarkand at age thirty-three, he built an army that helped him usurp the thrones of rivals and then roared across the plains all the way to Mesopotamia. As he took cities, he made no attempt to pacify the citizenry. Instead, his troops would kill everyone in sight. Then they would delight their leader by building huge pyramids of heads that would rot to mountains of shiny skulls.

Before reaching a country, he sent his agents on ahead to corrupt the officials into preparing the way for him. Then, when he reached the capital, he quickly got his revenge on any who opposed him. Twice he had his men herd people into a massive building, then quickly brick up the windows and doors so that they slowly starved to death inside while he sat outside laughing. He rarely took prisoners, preferring instead to toss them over cliffs or run them over with horses.

As an old man, Tamerlane renewed his earlier goal of conquering distant China. He and his troops were on the way there, camped beside the Syr Darya river in February 1405, when he became ill and died. REF.: *CBA.*

Tamm, Edward Allen, 1906- , U.S., jur. Deputy director of the FBI from 1930-48. He was appointed to the district court of Washington, D.C. by President Harry Truman in 1949 and to the circuit court of Washington, D.C. by President Lyndon Johnson in 1965. REF.: *CBA.*

Tammany Hall, prom. 1789- , U.S., polit. corr. Tammany is a name that has become synonymous with big city "bossism" and political corruption. It remains, however, a viable political organization that has controlled New York City politics in one form or another since the time of the founding fathers. Named after Delaware Indian chief Tammanend, the society was founded in 1789 to oppose the policies of the conservative Federalist party, which failed to represent the interests of the less affluent residents of New York. In 1805, Tammany was incorporated as a fraternal society, closely affiliated with the emerging Democratic party. With the arrival of the first wave of Irish "famine" immigrants, the nature of the society changed markedly. The Irish pushed aside the nativist factions to seize control, and henceforth Tammany Hall was guided by powerful Irish politicians while claiming to represent the interests of various other ethnic and religious minorities in Manhattan.

Tammany Hall in 1926.

The strength of the organization rested in its ability to elect candidates to the state legislature in Albany and to the board of aldermen in New York City. Tammany approached the zenith of its political power in the 1860s, when William Marcy Tweed took over as head of Tammany's General Committee. In 1868, he became a state senator while holding down various influential city posts, including chairmanship of the board of supervisors. The 1870 city charter that Tweed pushed through the legislature granted Tammany Hall the means to control the city treasury without interference. The "Tweed Ring," as they came to be known, plundered the city of millions of dollars through bid-rigging schemes, padded bills, and overpriced goods and services provided by Tammany henchmen. Largely through a public campaign spearheaded by civic reformers, whose efforts were reinforced by the famed newspaper cartoonist Thomas Nast, the rapacious Tweed Ring was finally smashed.

There were other unsavory characters to take Tweed's place, however. Richard "Boss" Croker held the reins of leadership from 1886 until he retired to Ireland with his fortune in 1903. "Big" Tim Sullivan, proprietor of the lavish Hesper Club, a famous Lower East Side gambling den and gathering place for the New York underworld, guided the destiny of Tammany for the next ten years or so. Sullivan continued the policies of Tweed, Croker, and others by protecting vice elements and delivering the Democratic vote at election time. The "Tammany Tiger" was impervious to the demands of the reformers during these years.

Tammany Hall's power was curbed in 1932, when Franklin Roosevelt reduced to a county organization after the political sachems in Manhattan refused to support his candidacy for president. That same year, Mayor James "Jimmy" Walker resigned from office after the Seabury Investigations uncovered layers of municipal graft in every city agency. Tammany continued its decline during the administrations of reform mayors Fiorello H. LaGuardia (1933-45) and John V. Lindsay (1966-73). See: **Becker, Charles; Croker, Richard; Seabury Investigations; Sullivan, Timothy; Tweed, William Marcy; Walker, James J.**

REF.: Asbury, *The Gangs of New York; CBA;* Eisenberg and Landau, *Meyer Lansky;* Godwin, *Murder U.S.A.;* Haskins, *Street Gangs;* Kobler, *Al Capone;* Logan, *Against the Evidence;* Lynch, *Boss Tweed;* McPhaul, *Johnny Torrio;* Parkhurst, *Our Fight with Tammany; Tammany, A Patriotic History;* Riordon, *Plunkett of Tammany Hall;* Werner, *Tammany Hall.*

Tanaka Kakuei, 1918- , Japan, polit. corr. On Aug. 16, 1976, former Japanese prime minister Tanaka Kakuei and fifteen other government and business leaders were indicted for accepting $2.1 million from Lockheed Corporation to influence Japanese airlines to buy the company's planes. Tanaka was also charged with violating foreign exchange laws. The trial lasted seven years, causing mass demonstrations by anti-Tanaka forces who sought to oust him as the leader of the Liberal Democratic Party. Tanaka denied accepting bribes, but in October 1981, Mieko Enomoto, the ex-wife of Tanaka's secretary, testified that her ex-husband handled overseen the $2.1 million in bribes on Tanaka's behalf. Tanaka was previously forced to resign from office in 1974 when accused of questionable financial and real estate practices.

On Oct. 11, 1983, a three-judge panel in the Tokyo District Court found the 65-year-old Tanaka Guilty of accepting bribes, sentenced him to four years in prison, and ordered him to repay the money at the current exchange rate. Toshio Enomoto, his former secretary, was sentenced to one year in prison for acting as a courier. Hiro Hayama, former chairman of Marubeni Corporation, was sentenced to two-and-a-half years. Two managing directors of Marubeni, Toshiharu Okubo and Hiroshi Ito, received two-year sentences. Ten other defendants were previously found Guilty and were appealing or serving suspended sentences. The last defendant's trial was postponed due to his illness. The convictions rekindled the protest forces, and more than 350,000 people took to the streets demanding that Tanaka resign from the party leadership. But he refused to do so pending his appeal, which could take up to ten years. REF.: *CBA.*

Taney, Roger Brooke, 1777-1864, U.S., atty. gen.-jur. Began practicing law in Frederick, Md., in 1801, and was elected state senator fifteen years later. After his five-year term ended, he moved to Baltimore, from where he was appointed state attorney general in 1827. He was appointed U.S. attorney general in 1831 by President Andrew Jackson, whom he had served as an adviser. Jackson nominated him as chief justice of the U.S. Supreme Court, and he was confirmed in 1836.

Roger Brooke Taney, U.S. Supreme Court justice.

Taney presided over the famous Dred Scott case, *Scott v. Sandford,* ruling in 1857 that Scott, a slave, could not sue in a federal court because slaves were defined as property in the Constitution and thus were not U.S. citizens. He went on to reject the Missouri Compromise as an unconstitutional violation of slave-owners' Fifth Amendment right to due process. This decision created a firestorm of controversy. He later confronted President Abraham Lincoln in *Ex parte Merryman* in 1861, arguing that military justice which usurped the judicial and legislative branches effectively placed citizens under the whim of local military officers. Although Lincoln never responded to his argument, the chief justice was posthumously vindicated in *Ex parte Milligan* in 1866, in which the Court ruled that such military actions, which Lincoln supported during the Civil War, were unconstitutional. See: **Scott, Dredd.** REF.: *CBA.*

Tanner, John, b.1780, Case of, U.S., mur. John Tanner was kidnapped by a Shawnee Indian when he was nine. He grew up as an Indian, forgot how to speak English, married two Shawnee women, and fathered several children. He returned to his white culture thirty years later, relearned his language, and located relatives in Kentucky and Ohio. Tanner decided to live in Michigan though he could persuade only two of his daughters and his second wife to live with him. He chose Mackinac and later Sault Ste. Marie, where he worked as an interpreter for U.S. Indian agent James Schoolcraft in 1828.

Tanner became an outcast in both the white and Indian worlds. Indians regarded him as a renegade while whites grew suspicious of him, accusing him of every unsolved crime in the area. His wife eventually returned to her tribe and his eldest daughter was taken away from him by legislative order. He then married a white woman, but, labeling him violent and his living habits intolerable, she soon left him. Then, in 1846, Tanner's boss, Schoolcraft, was found murdered. Tanner immediately became the prime suspect and fled town to escape the vigilantes and troops scouring the countryside for him. According to one rumor, the vigilantes captured and killed him to resolve the "white-Indian" problem. Another claimed he went back to live with the Indians. An army officer confessed to Schoolcraft's murder several years later. REF.: *CBA*.

Tansey, John, prom. 1907, U.S., mur. In May 1907, a labor strike shut down the entire San Francisco street-car system. By Sept. 2, Labor Day, no settlement had been reached, but non-union employees kept the system running. Early the following morning, police officers P.J. Mitchell and Edward McCartney heard a ruckus at a nearby saloon. Four men were leaving as the officers approached. Two fled, but the police confronted the other two, shoved them, and warned them that they might be locked up. One of the men drew a gun and shot Officer McCartney in the neck, killing him instantly. During the ensuing manhunt, a railroad inspector stated that the man described was John Tansey, a striking carman. Tansey was arrested when the surviving officer identified him. Tansey's partner, a man named Bell, was apprehended, and also stated that Tansey was the murderer. Tansey countered that Bell had pulled the trigger. But it was Tansey who was convicted of manslaughter and sentenced to ten years in prison. He was paroled on May 10, 1909, because he had consumption.

REF.: *CBA;* Duke, *Celebrated Criminal Cases of America.*

Tanuma Okitsugu, 1719-88, Japan, polit. corr. Overpowered central government as highest minister under shogun Tokugawa Ieharu from 1772-86, becoming widely hated. He restored the Japanese economy by instituting banks and promoting industry but was accused of corruption. He was ousted from his positions and lost much of his sizeable fief in Kazusa following Ieharu's death in 1786. REF.: *CBA*.

Taoka Kazuo (AKA: The Bear), 1913-81, Japan, org. crime. Taoka Kazuo, the Japanese yakuza's "boss of bosses," was born in 1913 on the island of Shikoku. After being orphaned, Taoka was sent to work in a Kobe shipyard, where, at age fourteen, he became involved with a small gang headed by Yamaguchi Noburu. Taoka apprenticed with the gang for the next nine years. During that time he earned a reputation for being a rough fighter and the nickname "the Bear." In 1936, he became a blood member of the group and was sent to prison for the slashing murder of a rival gang member.

Taoka returned to the gang after leaving prison in 1943. In October 1946, Yamaguchi died, and Taoka, then thirty-three, stepped in to lead the gang. Despite the decline of the gang both in size and power as a result of the war, Taoka used his ferocity and his tremendous ability to organize the remaining members. He returned to the Kobe docks where he founded the *Yamaguchi-gumi* Construction Company. Simultaneously he took a larger share of the local gambling and extortion rackets. Starting in the 1940s, Taoka's gang began a systematic expansion into the territory of other gangs. The local *Honda-kai* were absorbed, as were the *Meiyu-kai* and their territory in Osaka, and the *Miyamoto-gumi.*

In addition to absorbing other gangs and their territories and shares of the rackets, Taoka expanded into the entertainment field, with a talent agency that pushed Osaka-area performers and a touring group called the Home Run Hit Parade. Despite his expansion, the heart of his business remained in the Kobe docks, where, by the mid-1960s, the Yamaguchi syndicate controlled almost 80 percent of all cargo loading.

Japanese crime boss Taoka Kazuo.

At the zenith of Taoka's thirty-five-year career as the godfather of Japanese syndicates, he controlled hundreds of gangs and some 13,000 yakuza. Attracted by the power of his organization, right-wing politicians, including the powerful Kodama Yoshii, backed his operations. In return, Taoka, like other yakuza bosses, lent his troops in support of the anti-Communist agenda of the right-wing faction. Through Kodama, Taoka was introduced to, and eventually became a blood brother with, Machii Hisayuki, Korean boss of Tokyo's *Tosei-kai.* Through this new alliance, the *Yamaguchi-gumi* expanded into Tokyo as well. By the time Taoka died of a heart attack in 1981, his organization was grossing over $460 million annually. Taoka's greatest contribution as a yakuza boss was in opening doors into Japan's rapidly expanding economy for the Japanese underworld. In addition to the standard underworld pursuits of gambling, prostitution, and extortion, Taoka was singlehandedly responsible for introducing the mob into professional sports and entertainment, including the lucrative film industry. See: **Inagawa Kakuji; Jirocho Shimizu no; Kimura Tokutaru; Kishi Nobusuke; Kodama Yoshio; Machii Hisayuki; Nakasone Yasuhiro; Ogawa Kaoru; Osano Kenji; Sasakawa Ryoichi; Toyama Mitsuru; Yakuza.**

REF.: *CBA;* Kaplan and Dubro, *Yakuza.*

Tapner, Benjamin, and **Cobby, John**, and **Hammond, John**, and **Carter, William**, and **Mills, Richard, Jr.**, and **Mills, Richard, Sr.**, and **Jackson, William**, d.1749, Brit., mur. Benjamin Tapner and his gang of smugglers lived in and around Sussex. On Jan. 16, 1749, all seven men were indicted for the murders of William Galley and Daniel Chater, two custom-house officers sent to arrest the robbers of the king's warehouse in Poole.

The king's revenue collectors were always unpopular, and when Chater and Galley arrived at the White Hart tavern in Rowland's Castle on Feb. 14, 1748, the innkeeper alerted the smugglers to their presence. William Jackson and William Carter spoke at length with the two officers to determine what their business was, and soon a quarrel broke out. Galley decided it would be best if he and Chater moved on. But the smugglers were anxious to read a letter directing Chater to apprehend a robbery suspect named Diamond and tried to ply the two revenue agents with rum.

Galley and Chater got drunk and passed out. When the smugglers examined the letter, they discovered the agents' true identities. Diamond was a friend of the smugglers, and they took revenge against his two pursuers. William Steele suggested dropping them in a well. Someone suggested sending them to France, but this idea was rejected because they might come back.

While the two revenue men slept, Jackson horsewhipped them in their beds. Richard Mills, Jr. suggested tying a long string to the trigger of a rifle so that all would share equally in the murders. However, this was considered too merciful a way for the agents to die. The smugglers divided into two groups, each taking a revenue agent. Chater was led to a deep well in Harris' Wood and dropped over the side with his head in a noose. The rope was cut and Daniel Chater crashed to the bottom where he died in agonizing pain. Meanwhile, Tapner cut and slashed Galley with a clasp-knife. His remains were placed in an unmarked grave.

The perpetrators of these brutal murders were soon captured. They were indicted and brought before Sir Michael Foster, who issued a sober warning: "Christian charity obliges me to tell you that your time in this world may be very short." William Jackson died in prison. The six other smugglers were hanged at Chichester on Jan. 18, 1749. Their bodies were placed in a pit near the place of execution. A marker was placed on top, which read: "As a memorial to posterity, and a warning to this and succeeding generations, this stone is erected A.D. 1749."

REF.: *CBA;* Mitchell, *The Newgate Calendar.*

Tarafa (Tarafah), prom. 500s, Arabia, executed. Poet put to death on command of King 'Amr ibn Hind for writing satirical poems about sovereign life. REF.: *CBA.*

Tarnower, Dr. **Herman**, See: **Harris, Jean Struven.**

Tarnowska, Countess, See: **Naumoff, Nicolas.**

Tarquinius, Sextus, c.510 B.C., Roman., rape. According to legend, the rape of Lucretia led to the formation of the Roman Republic. In about 510 B.C., Collatinus and other warriors at the front speculated about the fidelity of their wives. Wagers were made, and Collatinus and Sextus Tarquinius, the son of the Tarquin king, went home to settle the argument. Tarquinius' wife was having a splendid banquet in his absence, while Lucretia, Collatinus' wife, was found working alone in her home. Tarquinius paid Collatinus, but felt himself attracted to Lucretia.

After Collatinus returned to the war, Tarquinius called on Lucretia, who, according to custom, welcomed him to her home. That night, he demanded at knife point that she sleep with him, but she refused. When he threatened to kill her and a male slave and leave their bodies together to look like Lucretia committed adultery, she was forced to comply. Lucretia yielded, but the next morning she reported the deed to her husband and her father before stabbing herself to death. Her body was carried to the Roman forum, and Tarquinius' crime led to a rebellion against the Tarquin king and the establishment of the Roman Republic. REF.: *CBA.*

Tarter-Coffelt Feud, prom. 1933-84, Case of, U.S., mur. The Tarters of Kentucky were a hill family whose moonshining tradition dated from the 1920s. Bing Tarter, the family patriarch was arrested at various times for adultery, interfering with the election process, and shooting at people with the intent to kill. On Jan. 24, 1933, he was gunned down by deputy Cleo Parks.

The Tarters later intermarried with the Coffelt family. On Sept. 4, 1975, Bing's son, Alvis Tarter, and Alvis' son were visiting Alvis' sister when her husband, Winford Coffelt, came home intending to kill her. As Alvis intervened, Coffelt wounded him. Alvis and his son both returned fire, and which one killed Coffelt is not clear. The local sheriff held Alvis Tarter for one night in jail and released him. On June 24, 1984, Sammy Tarter, another of Bing's sons, shot and killed Bertram Coffelt, the brother of Winford, and Bertram's son Curtis. While fleeing from the police, Sammy died of a gunshot wound to the head, which a jury later ruled was self-inflicted. Like Alvis and Winford, Sammy and Bertram were brothers-in-law.

REF.: *CBA;* Montell, *Killings.*

Taschereau, Sir Henri Elzear, 1836-1911, Can., jur. Judge on Superior Court from 1871-78 and on Supreme Court from 1878-1906, serving as chief justice from 1902-06. He wrote several important works on criminal and civil law in Canada. REF.: *CBA.*

Taschereau, Sir Henri Thomas, 1841-1909, Can., jur. Served as judge on Quebec's Superior Court from 1878-1907 and as chief justice of the King's Bench from 1907-09. REF.: *CBA.*

Tate, Albert, Jr., 1920- , U.S., jur. Appointed to fifth circuit court by President Jimmy Carter in 1979. From 1954-60, he had served on the Louisiana First Circuit Court of Appeals and from 1960-70, he was presiding judge over the Louisiana Third Circuit Court of Appeals. He served as associate justice on the Louisiana Supreme Court from 1970-79. REF.: *CBA.*

Taudien, Hugo, prom. 1933, Japan, pir.-mur. In 1933, Captain Hugo Taudien, a German seaman, organized a gang of hoodlums. On June 26, 1933, Taudien and his four thugs boarded a Chinese cargo steamer in the port of Tientsin. Taudien, an old friend of the ship's captain, received a warm welcome. But 200 miles out to sea, Taudien and his men murdered the captain and nine members of his crew. They renamed the ship and headed for California. While stopping in the Japanese port of Dairen, the ship ran aground. Taudien sent a man to shore for help, but he did not return. When Taudien left the ship, he was arrested on suspicion of smuggling sugar. The Japanese found no sugar on the ship, but they did find the remaining captives from the Chinese crew, who related the tale of the pirates.

There was no Japanese law covering piracy, so the five men were tried for entering the ship illegally. But, because of the brutality, and to avoid setting a bad example, the Japanese penalized the men for the full extent of their crimes. Hugo Taudien, Butcher Westermann, Arthur Gautschi, and Walter Müller were all sentenced to death. Only George Schroeder, whose protestations of innocence moved the court, was spared, and was given a sentence of ten years imprisonment. REF.: *CBA.*

Taunton, William, d.1769, Brit., mur. Born in Gloucestershire, William Taunton worked in Tewkesbury as a stableman before drifting to London, where he took up with Mrs. Phipps, a widowed innkeeper who lived with her children at the Lamb Inn in Colnbrook.

Years passed and the relationship began to deteriorate. Taunton considered suicide as a way out, but one night instead begged Phipps to do him in with a kitchen poker. "You must knock my brains out," he said. "If you will not knock my brains out, I will knock yours out." Phipps said she would never hurt a hair on his head, so Taunton bashed her head in. A doctor dressed her wounds, but five days later, on Aug. 4, 1769, Taunton decided to finish what he had started and killed her.

At the Old Bailey sessions, Will Taunton tried without success to gain acquittal through insanity. He was convicted on Sept. 9, 1769, and executed at Tyburn two days later. Afterward, the body was given over to the college of surgeons for dissection.

REF.: *CBA;* Mitchell, *The Newgate Calendar.*

Tausand, Franz, prom. 1924-31, Ger., fraud. As a young man, Franz Tausand was obsessed with chemistry. In 1922, he published in Munich a tract of non-proven alchemical theories, hoping to attract investors for his method of reproducing gold. In 1924, he saw an ad offering financial backing for a chemical business. The financier, Rudolf Reinhardt, thought the production of gold would solidify the post-war economy and sought the cooperation of German president Hinderberg. His lobbying attempt was derided, but a war veteran, General Ehrich von Ludendorff, seeking to regain his former power, formed "Society 164," named after the number for gold in the Periodic System.

Tausand promised that his process would produce forty pounds of gold daily. Indeed, he was able to produce a nugget on demand, and eager investors happily financed the venture. However, the large quantities promised were not forthcoming, as Tausand had produced the occasional nugget through sleight-of-hand. In 1927, Ludendorff backed out, taking almost all of the investors money with him. Tausand, still promising a fortune in gold, organized a new scam; gold vouchers issued by the Tausand Chemical Research Company. In 1929, investors who had bought two factories for the anticipated production of gold, were understandably restless.

Tausand went on a driving trip around the German countryside. But he was arrested when he knocked down a pedestrian and drove away. As he was awaiting trial for the traffic violation, the financial deception caught up with him. He was accused of defrauding investors of more than £75,000, and spent twenty months in jail as the fraud case was prepared against him. In 1931, Tausand was found Guilty of fraud and sentenced to three years. After his release, he returned to fraud, and was jailed again in 1938. He died in prison in 1939. REF.: *CBA.*

Tavannes, Seigneur de (Gaspard de Sauix), 1509-73, Fr., consp.-mur. Earned reputation as skillful soldier at Metz in 1552, Calais in 1558, and at other battles. He served as marshal of France in 1570. He was a leader in the Massacre of St. Bartholomew in 1572. REF.: *CBA.*

Tavernier, Jean Baptiste (Baron d'Aubonne), prom. 1665, Burma, rob. While visiting the city of Pagan, Burma, world traveler Jean Baptiste Tavernier first saw the 279-carat blue diamond, later to known as the Hope Diamond. Tavernier's host, the Great Mogul of Pagan, allowed him to hold the spectacular gem which generally served as the center eye of a statue of the god Rama-Sita in a Pagan temple. Tavernier became determined to steal the diamond and take it to King Louis XIV of France. Several nights into his visit he went to the temple and stole the diamond.

Tavernier immediately left Pagan and returned to France. King Louis was equally fascinated with the unique gem and purchased it from Tavernier for money and a title. Tavernier, who had been warned in Burma that possession of the stone by anyone other than its rightful owner was bad luck, was later killed by wild dogs. Louis eventually had the diamond cut down to a 65-carats gem. The stone was passed on to subsequent members of French Royalty in the following years. All experienced some degree of misfortune. Whether the bad luck was attributable to possession of the diamond variously known as "The French Blue," the "Diamond of Death," or the "Hope Diamond," or to some other cause, is impossible to determine. REF.: *CBA.*

Tawell, John, d.1845, Brit., forg.- mur. As a young man, John Tawell was convicted of forgery and sent to serve out his sentence in Australia. On completion of his sentence, he returned to his previous career as a druggist. Tawell eventually became a successful businessman and adopted the Quaker faith. He returned to England as a man of wealth. After settling in Southwork, Tawell married and began a family. After his wife died, Tawell began an affair with a young servant girl, Sarah Hadler. When Hadler became pregnant, he moved her to a house of her own and maintained her there to avoid scandal. Hadler subsequently gave birth to a second child fathered by Tawell. In 1845, Tawell decided to marry a young heiress and at the same time suffered some financial reverses. Apparently this combination of events made him decide to kill Hadler.

On New Year's Day in 1845, Tawell visited Sarah and shared a glass of ale with her. Suddenly she convulsed and fell to the floor screaming. A neighbor, responding to the screams, saw Tawell leaving hurriedly and called a doctor who diagnosed poisoning. The police deduced that Tawell had probably taken the train to London and, using the newly invented telegraph, wired ahead to London. Tawell was apprehended as he stepped off the train. He became, in fact, the first criminal ever apprehended through the use of the telegraph. When it was proved that Tawell had purchased the poison, he was charged with the murder. Tawell was brought to trial on Apr. 12, 1845. he was convicted and on Mar. 28, 1845, was hanged. On the night before his execution, he confessed to the murder and to an earlier, unsuccessful attempt.

REF.: Altick, *Victorian Studies in Scarlet;* Brock, *A Casebook in Crime;* Browne, *Trials for Murder by Poisoning;* Butler, *Murderers' England; CBA;* Kobler, *Some Like It Gory;* Logan, *Rope, Knife and Chair;* Robinson, *Science Catches the Criminal;* Thompson, *Poison and Poisoners;* Thomson, *The Story of Scotland Yard;* Whitbread, *The Railway Policemen;* Wilson, *Encyclopedia of Murder.*

Tayler, Robert Walker, 1852-1910, U.S., jur. Appointed to northern district court of Ohio by President Theodore Roosevelt in 1905. He had been the prosecuting attorney for Columbiana County, Ohio, from 1880-94, and he served in Congress from 1894-1902. REF.: *CBA.*

Taylor, Anna Katherine Johnston Diggs, 1932- , U.S., jur. Appointed to eastern district court of Michigan by President Jimmy Carter in 1979. REF.: *CBA.*

Taylor, Arthur, and **Bredell, Baldwin S.**, prom. 1890's, U.S., count. In the late nineteenth century, the U.S. cigar business was highly competitive. Over 14,000 firms produced cigars, often with a very slight profit margin. Most of the price of the cigars went for federal tax, which was indicated on the cigar box by an ornate tax stamp. If a manufacturer could reproduce this stamp, their increase in profits would be enormous. One Philadelphia firm, owned by Jacobs and Kendig, hired master engravers Arthur Taylor and Baldwin Bredell to reproduce the stamp. Their work went undetected, and the firm made great profits. The two owners speculated that the engravers would be equally adept at counterfeiting money. The scheme involved printing $10 million in counterfeit notes, and with the collusion of a Treasury Department employee, converting them into certificates of deposit negotiable anywhere in the world. Each engraver was to receive $1.5 million. The bills were reproduced almost flawlessly, and were detected only because of a faded seal and slightly thick paper. When a bill was placed in hot water, the paper separated, and the hoax was uncovered.

The Secret Service quietly investigated all Philadelphia engravers. It was obvious that Taylor and Bredell were living more luxuriously than their peers. They were placed under surveillance, and soon led federal agents to Jacobs' cigar factory. Inspection of the company's cigar boxes in a Chicago warehouse revealed the counterfeit stamps. On Apr. 18, 1899, federal agents confronted Taylor and Bredell about the Jacobs-Kendig operation. Both engravers confessed. The trial opened on Oct. 9, 1899. Kendig and Jacobs were found Guilty, sentenced to twelve years in prison, and fined $5,000. Meanwhile, Taylor and Bredell were detained but not sentenced. They plotted to continue their operation while in prison. Under difficult conditions, they imported the necessary engraving equipment and chemicals into their cells. They shipped the prepared plates back to outside conspirators who printed phony $20 bills. On May 28, 1902, Taylor and Bredell were finally sentenced to seven years, with the three years already served deducted from the sentence. On July 1, 1905, Kendig and Jacobs, after a petition drive, received a pardon from President Theodore Roosevelt. Taylor and Bredell were also released in 1905. Taylor lived a quiet life, occasionally working for his old partner Bredell, and died in the mid-1920's. Bredell opened his own engraving shop, and was suspected when counterfeit notes turned up in the Philadelphia area. He died in a state hospital in 1956.

REF.: Bloom, *Money of Their Own; CBA.*

Taylor, Courtney Townsend, 1908- , U.S., theft-forg.-fraud. Courtney Taylor turned an innocuous childhood lie into one of the most prolific careers in check-forging history, culminating in a novel method of obtaining any corporate bank check. Taylor was born in Connecticutt in 1908, and turned to crime early in life. After putting down five dollars on a clock for his mother's birthday, he stated on the credit application that he had been working at his present job for six months, when in fact he had been there less than two weeks. The credit manager discovered the lie and refused to give Taylor the clock or return his deposit. Taylor got even by cashing more than $600 in fraudulent checks with the same credit manager. At sixteen, he was convicted of breaking and entering and was committed to a reformatory. Released at age twenty, he forged his first check after steaming open a neighbor's letter and copying the enclosed check. In January 1929, Taylor was arrested for auto theft and sentenced to a reformatory in Mansfield, Ohio. For the next ten years, Taylor was in and out of prison on mail theft and forgery charges.

In January 1943, Courtney Taylor became a specialist. While in prison, he read every available book on printing. By obtaining a corporate logo, he was able to print a bogus check from virtually any corporation in the country. For the next eighteen months, Taylor cashed checks in twenty-eight states before he was apprehended in June 1944 in Seattle. He admitted passing more than $55,000 worth of checks during that time, and in fact had 172 checks worth $16,000 in his possession. He was sentenced to two years' imprisonment in October 1944. He was released after four months, but was shuttled through the legal systems of other states, and remained incarcerated until Apr. 14, 1950.

Six days out of prison, Taylor embarked on a new career using a voucher system, and hired commercial printers. But the process was cumbersome and the payoff low, so he returned to check forging within two months. For the next eight months, Taylor circled the country and cashed hundreds of dollars in fake checks each day. The end came on Feb. 16, 1951, in Mobile, Ala. A jewelry clerk had seen an FBI bulletin warning merchants of Taylor's ploy and called police, who apprehended Taylor. He was returned to Providence, R.I., to face charges there, and then remanded to federal jurisdiction in New York. Between April 1950 and February 1951, Taylor reportedly had passed 734 fraudulent checks. He pleaded guilty to 225 separate counts of federal violations and was sentenced to fifteen years in prison. Seven states placed detainers against him after he completed the original sentence. He was last sentenced on Apr. 22, 1964, to eight years for the transportation of forged securities.

REF.: *CBA;* McGuire, *The Forgers.*

Taylor, Edwina, See: **Edwardson, Derrick.**

Taylor, Elizabeth, See: **Chapman, George.**

Taylor, Ernest, 1950-77, U.S., kid. On May 28, 1977, in Detroit, Ernest Taylor took seven members of his family hostage at gunpoint, including his estranged wife and two of his own children, and escaped in a car. The police, in a dozen cars and two helicopters, chased Taylor for twenty miles until his car blew a tire, stranding him in an expressway median. Three of the hostages scrambled from the car, while Taylor trained a sawed-off shotgun on the remaining four. Police surrounded him and when he refused to surrender, a police marksman shot him in the forehead. None of the hostages were harmed. REF.: *CBA.*

Taylor, Gary Addison (AKA: **Phantom Sniper**), 1936- , U.S., rape-mur. "He is unreasonably hostile toward women and this makes it very possible that he might very well kill a person," said a court psychiatrist of Gary Addison Taylor. Before anyone heeded his words, however, Taylor had raped, robbed, and murdered his way across three states. By the time he was apprehended, he was suspected of killing at least twenty persons in Michigan, Colorado, Texas, and Washington.

At the age of eighteen, Taylor allegedly assaulted a woman at a St. Petersburg, Fla., bus stop with a monkey wrench. He was acquitted. Three years later, in 1957, he drove through the Detroit suburbs randomly firing at female passersby. Known as the "phantom sniper" of Royal Oak, Taylor was ruled insane and sent to the Michigan Ionia Hospital. Three years later, he was transferred to the Lafayette Clinic in Detroit.

Granted a special pass to attend a welding class, Taylor instead walked into a Detroit home and robbed and raped the woman inside. A year later, he threatened a rooming house manager and her young daughter at knife point while on a second pass. Taylor did not stand trial for either crime but was instead sent back to Ionia.

In 1972, Taylor was released from the Michigan Center for Forensic Psychiatry in Ypsilanti because state law then required that a defendant acquitted by reason of insanity could not be confined for indefinite periods without additional certification. Having examined Taylor, Dr. James Robey concluded that although he was afflicted by an untreatable character disorder, he would not be a danger to society if he took his medicine and refrained from drinking alcohol.

During a convalescent leave from court-ordered therapy in 1973, Taylor disappeared. He married a Michigan woman and moved to Seattle. In December 1974, the couple separated and Taylor moved to Houston, where he raped and killed 21-year-old Susan Kay Jackson, a cocktail waitress. He was never charged with this killing, but confessed to four other murders on May 24, 1975. In June 1975, the 39-year-old former mental patient was indicted on three counts of sexual abuse, one count of aggravated rape, and the rape of a pregnant Houston teenager.

In San Diego, Taylor's ex-wife, Helen Taylor, told police that her ex-husband once told of burying four bodies in their backyard in Onsted, Mich. "He would get drunk and say, 'Hey, you know those people? I killed them and buried them outside our house in Michigan.'" Fearing for her safety, she withheld this information from the police until she found out that Taylor was safely behind bars in Houston.

Alerted to these new developments, police officials in Onsted, forty-five miles southwest of Detroit, began digging and found the remains of two young women from Toledo: Lee Fletcher, a 25-year-old prostitute, and Deborah Heneman, twenty-three.

Reports filtered in from across the nation about other murders Taylor might have committed. Police in Vail, Colo., believed that 26-year-old ski instructor Julie Cunningham may have been one of his victims because psychiatric reports from Michigan indicated that Taylor had fantasized about murdering a skier. In Enumclaw, Wash., the worst fears of police were realized when a body was found buried in the backyard of Taylor's former residence. Lenawee County Sheriff Richard Germond linked Taylor to at least six Seattle murders.

On Apr. 30, 1976, in Seattle, Taylor was sentenced to life in prison for the 1974 murder of Vonnie Stuth. Taylor met Stuth, nineteen, when he moved in across the street from her in the Seattle suburb of Burien. When she refused his sexual advances, he killed her and buried her beneath twenty inches of topsoil near a creek behind his home.

The Washington State Parole Board sentenced Taylor to a minimum of eighty years behind bars. "He might be eligible for parole if he lives to be 100," said King County assistant prosecutor Philip Kallien. "He's iced now, for good." REF.: *CBA.*

Taylor, George William, and **Stuart, Norman**, prom. 1923, Brit., blk. In November 1923, a man known only as "the Captain" came to London. At a theater, he met a young musician named Norman Stuart. Stuart invited the Captain to his apartment for a drink and the Captain agreed. While in the flat, George William Taylor, pretending to be Stuart's brother, accused the Captain of homosexual behavior with his brother. Taylor demanded £50 for his silence. The Captain proclaimed his innocence, but paid the money. Within a short time, Taylor had appeared many times at the Captain's home and extorted additional money. The Captain complied because he felt that the police wouldn't believe him, and he couldn't deny making the previous payments.

In July 1925, a man named Maples visited the Captain, claiming to be Norman Stuart's father. For £200, he would send his son to Australia, where he would be no further trouble to the Captain. Next, a man named Tanner, claiming to be a police detective, extracted £1,000 in hush money. Tanner returned with two letters, threatening to send them to high officials, and left with another £2,000. Finally, the Captain paid a man named Brown, who claimed to be a Scotland Yard detective specializing in blackmail, £1,400 to pursue the blackmailers.

At last, the Captain hired a lawyer and the case was brought to the police. Six men were apprehended and found Guilty of blackmail. George William Taylor was sentenced to life imprisonment, Maples to fifteen years, Norman Stuart to twelve years, Leonard and Tanner to ten years each, and Brown to eight years.

REF.: *CBA;* Humphreys, *A Book of Trials.*

Taylor, Jack Hays, d.1869, U.S., west. gunman-outl. A feud between the Suttons and Taylors in Texas broke out in 1867 and became the bloodiest in the state's history. Many of the Sutton faction were lawmen while the Taylors were an anti-Reconstruction southern Texas family. Jack Hays Taylor, the son of Texas ranger Creed Taylor, was an expert shot with a pistol and cold-blooded as well. In November 1867, he and his brother, Phillip "Doboy" Taylor, were in Mason, Texas, when soldiers from Fort Mason harassed them. One soldier knocked Hays' hat to the ground, and Hays calmly drew his pistol then shot him. More soldiers poured in and demanded that the murderer be handed over to them. A gunfight ensued, during which the Taylor brothers shot and killed an army sergeant and fled town. Now with the excuse of hunting the fugitives, the Suttons stepped up the feud. On Aug. 23, 1869, a posse of Sutton Regulators led by

Jack Helm ambushed the Taylor residence and fired on Creed. Phillip, though wounded, escaped. Hays Taylor rode into the midst of the posse firing his gun and wounded five Regulators. The Regulators then opened fire and killed Jack Hays Taylor.

REF.: Artrip, *Memoirs of Daniel Foe (Jim) Chisholm;* Bartholomew, *Kill or be Killed;* Casey, *The Texas Border; CBA;* Day, *The Sutton-Taylor Feud;* Delony, *40 Years a Peace Officer;* Douglas, *Famous Texas Feuds;* Emmett, *Shanghai Pierce;* Farrow, *Troublesome Times in Texas;* Feder, *Longhorns;* Fisher and Dykes, *King Fisher, His Life and Times;* French, *Indianola Scrap Book;* Gard, *Frontier Justice;* Hardin, *The Life of John Wesley Hardin;* Horan and Sann, *Pictorial History of the Wild West;* Huson, *Refugio;* King, *Ghost Towns of Texas;* Monaghan, *The Book of the American West;* Morris, *Pictorial History of Victoria and Victoria County;* Nordyke, *John Wesley Hardin;* Penfield, *Western Sheriffs and Marshals;* Plenn and LaRoche, *The Fastest Gun in Texas;* Raine, *Guns of the Frontier;* Raymond, *Captain Lee Hall of Texas;* Ripley, *They Died With Their Boots On;* Russell, *Grandpa's Autobiography;* Sonnichsen, *I'll Die Before I'll Run;* Sutton, *Sutton-Taylor Feud;* Sweet and Knox, *On a Mexican Mustang Through Texas;* Webb, *Texas Handbook, II.*

Taylor, Jack S., prom. 1970, U.S., mur. On Feb. 16, 1970, the badly decomposed body of a woman was found in a swampy area near Palm Beach, Fla. A finger had been severed from the body and there was a gaping wound under its left eye. Fingerprints were taken, and the FBI identified the corpse as Judy Ann Vukich of Clarksville, Tenn. Her parents said she had moved to Florida and was living with a man named Jack Taylor. A warrant was issued and he was arrested two weeks later in Oklahoma City. He had killed Vukich for hiding liquor from him. Taylor was tried and convicted for manslaughter and sentenced to twenty years in the Florida State Penitentiary. REF.: *CBA.*

Taylor, Jim, 1852-75, U.S., west. gunman. Jim Taylor became the Taylor leader during a feud between the Suttons and Taylors. Jim's father, Pitkin Taylor, was ambushed by the Suttons in 1872. He died six months after the ambush and Jim, with his brother Bill Taylor, swore revenge on the Sutton faction leader, Bill Sutton. In the following months, the Taylors killed three Sutton men. The Sutton-Taylor feud began in 1867 and ended with the death of Jim Taylor in 1875.

On Apr. 1, 1873, a band of Taylor men led by Jim opened fire on Bill Sutton in a pool room. Sutton, though critically wounded, recovered. In June, Jim and several friends gunned down Sutton man Jim Cox and a companion. The following month, Jim and a relative, John Wesley "Wes" Hardin, the West's most feared gunman, were in Albuquerque, Texas, when they spied Jack Helm, a Sutton leader, in the company of six friends. Hardin aimed his shotgun at Helm and shot him through the chest while Taylor pumped several bullets into his head. Then on Mar. 11, 1874, Hardin informed Jim that Bill Sutton and his family were sailing from Indianola on a steamer. Jim and Bill Taylor rushed to the ship and spotted the Sutton family gathered on the deck. A gunfight followed and Jim killed Sutton while Bill shot Gabe Slaughter in the head. The Suttons retaliated by lynching Scrape Taylor, Jim White, and Kute Tuggle on June 20. In turn, the Taylors assassinated the new Sutton leader, Rube Brown, who was also the Cuero town marshal.

On Dec. 27, 1875, Jim Taylor and a few friends rode into Clinton, Texas. They had left their horses with Martin King when a Sutton posse charged into town and began firing. King released the animals and Taylor and two friends found themselves cut off. Dashing through King's house, the three were stopped by Sutton man Kit Hunter who shot Jim in the arm. The Sutton posse surrounded the Taylor men, opened fire, and killed them. With the death of the Taylor faction's young and aggressive leader, the feud quickly ended.

REF.: Artrip, *Memoirs of Daniel Foe (Jim) Chisholm;* Bartholomew, *Kill or be Killed;* Casey, *The Texas Border; CBA;* Day, *The Sutton-Taylor Feud;* Delony, *40 Years a Peace Officer;* Douglas, *Famous Texas Feuds;* Emmett, *Shanghai Pierce;* Farrow, *Troublesome Times in Texas;* Feder, *Longhorns;* Fisher and Dykes, *King Fisher, His Life and Times;* French, *Indianola Scrap Book;* Gard, *Frontier Justice;* Hardin, *The Life of John Wesley Hardin;* Hendricks, *The Bad Man of the West;* Holloway, *Texas Gun Lore;* Horan and Sann, *Pictorial History of the Wild West;* Huson, *Refugio;* King, *Ghost Towns of Texas;* Monaghan, *The Book of the American West;* Morris, *Pictorial History of Victoria and Victoria County;* Nordyke, *John Wesley Hardin;* Penfield, *Western Sheriffs and Marshals;* Plenn and LaRoche, *The Fastest Gun in Texas;* Raine, *Guns of the Frontier;* Raymond, *Captain Lee Hall of Texas;* Ripley, *They Died With Their Boots On;* Russell, *Grandpa's Autobiography;* Sonnichsen, *I'll Die Before I'll Run;* Sutton, *Sutton-Taylor Feud;* Sweet and Knox, *On a Mexican Mustang Through Texas;* Webb, *Texas Handbook;* White, *Trigger Fingers.*

Taylor, John, prom. 1720, Brit., pir. In 1720, a fierce battle was fought in the waters off Madagascar between an English East India merchant vessel the *Cassandra,* captained by James Macrae, and two pirate ships, *Fancy,* captained by Edward English, and *Victory,* captained by John Taylor. The pirates slaughtered the *Cassandra*'s crew and looted the ship of £75,000 in valuables. Then the two pirate captains disagreed over the disposal of Captain Macrae. Macrae was turned loose in a badly damaged pirate boat and arrived in India a month and a half later. He eventually became the governor of Madras. A year later, Taylor committed one of the largest pirate heists in history.

On Apr. 26, 1721, Taylor sailed the *Cassandra* toward the island of Bourbon in the Mauritius Islands. He looted a Portuguese vessel the *Nossa Senhora do Cabo,* of priceless silks, porcelain and gems easily worth over £1 million. Some of the pirates settled in Madagascar with their new-found wealth. Others received a pardon from France and settled on the island of Bourbon. The remaining crew sailed to Jamaica with Taylor, seeking a pardon from England. When they were refused, they sailed to Panama, and were pardoned by the Spanish in recognition for their huge spending power in the local economy. Taylor was never brought to justice.

REF.: Botting, *The Pirates; CBA.*

Taylor, John (AKA: **Bartholomew Browne**), prom. 1800, Case of, Brit., count. John Taylor, who spent a career putting the wrong names on documents, was saved by someone else putting a wrong name on a document. In 1800, at the Essex Assizes in England, Taylor was found Guilty of forgery and sentenced to death. However, due to a clerical error, the indictment had been entered in the name of an alias, Bartholomew Browne. The judge had no choice but to release Taylor.

REF.: *CBA;* Potter, *The Art of Hanging.*

Taylor, John, 1808-87, U.S., poly. Moved with Brigham Young to Utah following death of Joseph Smith. He was named president of the Mormon Church in 1880, three years after Young died. He was compelled to leave the U.S. to avoid arrest for polygamy in 1884, but was able to continue his administrative duties. REF.: *CBA.*

Taylor, Linda, 1927- , U.S., fraud. On Aug. 8, 1974, Linda Taylor reported that $14,000 in cash, jewelry and furs had been stolen from her home on Chicago's South Side. Suspicious of the report, detectives investigated the theft and instead uncovered one of the nation's largest cases of welfare fraud. Within four months, five state and federal agencies had opened investigations into Taylor's fraudulent practices. The FBI claimed she was receiving several Social Security checks, including one which had arrived every month for twenty-eight years. The U.S. Department of Agriculture said Taylor received food stamps, though she owned two luxury cars. Postal authorities questioned her use of the mails to receive Social Security and welfare checks under as many as eighty names. The FHA claimed that Taylor had purchased three federally insured homes on which she collected rent. The Illinois Legislative Advisory Committee on Public Aid said that, within a year, she had accrued $154,000 in welfare payments by using fourteen aliases.

Taylor was arrested in November 1974, but remained free on bond until early 1977. On Mar. 17, 1977, she was found Guilty of theft and perjury for fraudulently collecting about $8,000 in public aid payments by using two phony names. She was sentenced to two to six years, and began serving her sentence in

May 1977 at the Dwight, Ill., Correctional Center. REF.: *CBA*.

Taylor, Louisa Jane, 1846-83, Brit., mur. Seeking someone to care for his 82-year-old ailing wife, William Tregillis invited Louisa Jane Taylor, widow of a friend of his, to live with them and care for his wife in return for room and board. Shortly after Taylor's arrival, the 85-year-old Tregillis began to notice that valuable items were missing from the house from time to time. He also became concerned when Taylor began receiving nocturnal visits from a male friend during which Taylor left the elderly Tregillis to look after his wife.

Mary Ann Tregillis' health deteriorated steadily under Taylor's care. At one point Taylor suggested to Tregillis they abandon his wife and elope. Soon thereafter, Taylor began to ask Mrs. Tregellis's doctor for lead acetate to use as a beauty preparation. Dr. Smith provided Taylor with large quantities of the chemical, which she then used to systematically poison Mrs. Tregillis.

Taylor became increasingly bold in her larceny. After living in the Tregillis home for several months, Taylor talked the old man out of £10 pension money. Tregillis became upset and called the police. When Dr. Smith heard of the problem, he began to suspect Taylor of foul play. On Oct. 6, 1882, he finally realized that his patient was being poisoned with a chemical that he himself had provided. On her deathbed, the old lady said that she had watched her caretaker prepare her daily, poisoned medicines. She died on Oct. 23.

Taylor stood to gain very little from Tregillis' death. Therefore it seemed that she had poisoned her charge out of sheer malice. Louisa Jane Taylor was arrested, tried, and convicted. She was hanged at the Maidstone Prison on Jan. 2, 1883.

REF.: *CBA;* Marjoribanks, *For the Defense, The Life of Sir Edward Marshall Hall;* Nash, *Look For the Woman;* Rowland, *Poisoner in the Dock;* Smith-Hughes, *Eight Studies in Justice;* Wilson, *Encyclopedia of Murder.*

Taylor, Perry Alexander, 1967- , U.S., mur. On Oct. 24, 1988, 38-year-old Geraldine Birch was choked and beaten to death on a Tampa, Fla., baseball field by 22-year-old Perry Alexander Taylor. Taylor admitted his guilt, but claimed that he had been provoked. His trial began on May 10, 1989, in the Tampa courtroom of Judge M. William Graybill. Taylor testified that he had paid the woman to have sex with him, and that she injured him during the act, prompting him to choke her and kick her repeatedly. The prosecution countered that Taylor was a habitual criminal. When he was sixteen, he had been convicted of raping a 12-year-old. The prosecution also said that his latest victim had died a slow, agonizing death. The jury agreed, and on May 12, 1989, convicted Taylor of first-degree murder and sexual battery and sentenced him to die in the electric chair. REF.: *CBA*.

Taylor, Phillip (AKA: **Doboy**), d.1871, U.S., west. gunman-outl. The son of Texas Ranger Creed Taylor and the younger brother of Jack Hays Taylor, Phillip "Doboy" Taylor became another of the casualties of the Sutton-Taylor feud, the bloodiest in Texas history. Following a gunfight in Mason, Texas, in which Hays and Doboy killed two soldiers, the two were declared "wanted" by Reconstruction authorities. Becoming fugitives, the brothers were aggressively pursued by the Suttons, many of whom were law-enforcement officials. A posse of Sutton Regulators ambushed the Taylor home on Aug. 23, 1869, killing Hays and wounding Doboy in the arm. Doboy next was attacked by Sutton Regulators on Sept. 7 in William Connor's house near Pennington, Texas, in the company of two friends named Kelleson and Cook. Kelleson was killed, but Doboy and Cook escaped. In November 1871, Sim Holstein and Doboy quarreled about a job Doboy wanted. Doboy drew his pistol, fired, and missed. Holstein grabbed the gun and shot him three times. Doboy Taylor died six hours later.

REF.: Artrip, *Memoirs of Daniel Foe (Jim) Chisholm;* Bartholomew, *Kill or be Killed;* Casey, *The Texas Border; CBA;* Day, *The Sutton-Taylor Feud;* Delony, *40 Years a Peace Officer;* Douglas, *Famous Texas Feuds;* Emmett, *Shanghai Pierce;* Farrow, *Troublesome Times in Texas;* Feder, *Longhorns;* Fisher and Dykes, *King Fisher, His Life and Times;* French, *Indianola Scrap Book;* Gard, *Frontier Justice;* Hardin, *The Life of John Wesley Hardin;* Horan and Sann, *Pictorial History of the Wild West;* Huson, *Refugio;* King, *Ghost Towns of Texas;* Monaghan, *The Book of the American West;* Morris, *Pictorial History of Victoria and Victoria County;* Nordyke, *John Wesley Hardin;* Penfield, *Western Sheriffs and Marshals;* Plenn and LaRoche, *The Fastest Gun in Texas;* Raine, *Guns of the Frontier;* Raymond, *Captain Lee Hall of Texas;* Ripley, *They Died With Their Boots On;* Russell, *Grandpa's Autobiography;* Sonnichsen, *I'll Die Before I'll Run;* Sutton, *Sutton-Taylor Feud;* Sweet and Knox, *On a Mexican Mustang Through Texas;* Webb, *Texas Handbook.*

Taylor, Phoebe Atwood (AKA: **Alice Tilton**), 1909- , U.S., writer. Wrote detective novels such as *Cold Steal* in 1939, and *Left Leg* in 1940, featuring character detective Leonidas Witherall, and *Deadly Sunshade* in 1940, featuring character detective Asey Mayo. REF.: *CBA.*

Taylor, Rowland, d.1555, Brit., her. Protestant burnt at stake for heresy. He opposed the restoration of the mass and also supported Lady Jane Grey. He was named chaplain to Thomas Cranmer in 1540 and became archdeacon of Exeter in 1552. REF.: *CBA.*

Taylor, Tom, 1662-91, Brit., arson-rob. During his eight-year career as a gambler, pickpocket and housebreaker, Tom Taylor confined his criminal activities to Colchester in Essex, the town of his birth.

One day, at Guildford in Surrey, Taylor placed himself in the public pillory and entertained the spectators while his cohorts moved through the crowd, picking pockets. Among the victims was the keeper of the pillory, who stood idly by laughing at Taylor. "I hope you cannot lay anything to my charge if ye have suffered any loss," he told the crowd before he was released. "For ye are sensible I was in no capacity to do it." As he disappeared down the road, his victims discovered that their pockets had been picked clean.

One night at the Drury Lane Theatre, Taylor purchased a ticket in the pit so that he could sit beside the man he had victimized only a day before. Wise to Taylor's tricks, however, the man had lined his pockets with fish hooks, and when Taylor's hand was caught, led him outside and turned him over to a mob of vigilantes, who dunked him in a horse pond and broke one of his legs.

During a fourteen-month period, Taylor committed some sixty burglaries. He was finally captured after setting fire to a barn between Brentford and Osterley. When the owners ran out from their farmhouse to extinguish the flames, Taylor sneaked inside and rifled the contents of a trunk. He made off with £140 and some silver plate before being taken at Hammersmith and charged with burglary. Tom Taylor hanged at Tyburn on Dec. 18, 1691, the customary punishment for thieves of the period.

REF.: *CBA;* Smith, *Highwaymen.*

Taylor, William prom. 1872-75, U.S., west. gunman. William "Bill" Taylor, the brother of Jim Taylor and the son of Pitkin Taylor, involved himself in the famous Sutton-Taylor feud after he and Jim swore to avenge their father's killing by Sutton Regulators. The brothers got their revenge on Mar. 11, 1874, in the presence of Sutton's wife and child, when Jim killed Bill Sutton and Bill shot Gabe Slaughter in the head. The Taylors escaped but Bill later was arrested and jailed in Indianola. On Sept. 15, 1875, in the midst of a fierce tropical storm that battered the coast of Texas, Bill escaped from jail but helped rescue several people from the flooding waters. Later imprisoned in 1877, he shared the Austin jail with his relative Wes Hardin. The following year, Bill Taylor was arrested again and charged with horse theft, forgery, and assault, but was not imprisoned. He left Texas after 1881 and moved to Indian Territory, where, according to family members, he became a lawman and, ironically, was killed by a criminal. See: **Hardin, John Wesley; Sutton-Taylor Feud.**

REF.: Artrip, *Memoirs of Daniel Foe (Jim) Chisholm;* Bartholomew, *Kill or be Killed;* Casey, *The Texas Border; CBA;* Day, *The Sutton-Taylor Feud;* Delony, *40 Years a Peace Officer;* Douglas, *Famous Texas Feuds;* Emmett, *Shanghai Pierce;* Farrow, *Troublesome Times in Texas;* Feder, *Longhorns;* Fisher and Dykes, *King Fisher, His Life and Times;* French, *Indianola Scrap Book;* Gard, *Frontier Justice;* Gray, *Pioneering in Southwest*

Texas; Hardin, *The Life of John Wesley Hardin;* Horan and Sann, *Pictorial History of the Wild West;* Huson, *Refugio;* King, *Ghost Towns of Texas;* Monaghan, *The Book of the American West;* Morris, *Pictorial History of Victoria and Victoria County;* Nordyke, *John Wesley Hardin;* Penfield, *Western Sheriffs and Marshals;* Plenn and LaRoche, *The Fastest Gun in Texas;* Raine, *Guns of the Frontier;* Raymond, *Captain Lee Hall of Texas;* Ripley, *They Died With Their Boots On;* Russell, *Grandpa's Autobiography;* Sonnichsen, *I'll Die Before I'll Run;* Sutton, *Sutton-Taylor Feud;* Sweet and Knox, *On a Mexican Mustang Through Texas;* Webb, *Texas Handbook, II.*

Taylor, William Desmond (William Cunningham Deane-Tanner), 1877-1922, U.S., (unsolv.) mur. The killing of Hollywood director William Desmond Taylor in 1922 has remained one of filmdom's greatest unsolved crimes, one that has baffled investigators, criminal historians, and armchair detectives for almost seventy years. The tall, ruggedly handsome 45-year-old film director was considered one of the most cultured men in Hollywood, the envy of matinee idols and the love object of a bevy of Hollywood vamps and ingenues.

Born in Mallow, County Cork, Ire., Taylor's original name was William Cunningham Deane-Tanner. He was the oldest son of a wealthy landowner who had been a colonel in the British army. His grandfather had been a member of the British parliament. Taylor, who had been trained from childhood to become an officer in the British army, graduated from Clinton College in 1895, but instead of joining the army, shocked his family by becoming a member of a theatrical group in Manchester, England. He took the stage name of William Desmond Taylor, one that he would use thereafter as his legal name.

Taylor's acting career stalled and he immigrated to Canada. He worked briefly as an engineer and then moved to the Klondike during the gold rush. He failed to find gold and moved to New York, where he met his younger brother, Dennis Deane-Tanner. The brothers opened an antique store but saw little profit due to Taylor's expensive tastes and habits. He was addicted to custom-made clothes and the cuisine of expensive restaurants. He was also a blatant opportunist, so when he met Ethel Harrison, a member of the Floradora Sextet and niece of real estate tycoon Daniel J. Braker, he quickly proposed. The couple married a short time later, Taylor's wife knowing him only as William Dean-Tanner.

Meanwhile, Taylor's brother, who had been living meagerly and wearing threadbare suits because of Taylor's wastrel habits, was left to run the antique shop alone. Taylor continued to spend money lavishly, borrowing heavily from his wife's uncle. The ne'er-do-well actor told his drinking companions that he expected to inherit Braker's vast estate. The millionaire died in 1908, but Taylor was shocked to learn that all that was left him was the money Taylor had already borrowed. Taylor, desperate for cash, took $600 from the antique shop till, all the cash his brother had on hand, pocketed $100, and sent the balance to his wife before deserting her. He left no forwarding address.

In 1912, Ethel Tanner was granted a divorce on charges of adultery. She claimed that shortly before her husband abandoned her and their small daughter Daisy, he had had an affair with a Broadway showgirl, taking this woman to an Adirondacks retreat where he used the name Townsend. Dennis Tanner (neither brother was using the full name Deane-Tanner by this time) then sold his antique shop and, imitating his brother's actions, he, too, abandoned his wife and child.

Nothing was heard of either brother until 1914, when relatives of Tanner's ex-wife attended a movie and were stunned to see the missing man on the screen dashing about as a cowboy hero. The missing Dennis Tanner also had a minor role in the film. The film credits revealed no William Cunningham Deane-Tanner, however. The man playing the hero in the film was called William Desmond Taylor. The relatives rushed to reveal their discovery to the ex-Mrs. Tanner, but she was unconcerned with this news. She was already remarried to the millionaire owner of Delmonico's, one of New York's finest restaurants.

Taylor's daughter Daisy, however, wrote to her father. Taylor wrote back from Hollywood, telling her he was delighted to hear from her. When he joined the Canadian air force to fight in WWI, Taylor sent his daughter a photo of himself wearing a captain's uniform of the Royal Canadian Air Force. He cut quite a dashing figure, wearing jodpurs and boots, and carrying a walking stick. This was Taylor's favorite photo of himself and he had dozens of copies made, giving this autographed photo to his many female admirers over the years.

After deserting his wife in New York, Taylor took bit parts in Hollywood movies to survive, but his striking, sharp features and charming manners soon earned him bigger parts. By 1917, he was given leading roles. A few years later Taylor began directing one-reelers, then features. He was appointed the chief director for Famous Players-Lasky, a subsidiary of Paramount Studios, in 1922, working under studio manager Charles Eyton. Both Eyton and Paramount chief Adolph Zukor considered Taylor one of the most gifted directors in Hollywood. They paid him a salary of $50,000 a year, then a staggering amount, he was given hefty bonuses for bringing his pictures in on schedule, and his expense account was almost equal to his salary.

The director lived stylishly in a bungalow court on Alvarado Street. The interior of his house was adorned by tapestries and original paintings, along with thousands of books. Taylor exuded the air of the refined, urbane middle-aged gentleman. Nothing in his life outwardly reflected an excessive lifestyle, which was then the hallmark of Hollywood. Other homes of Hollywood celebrities were adorned with bearskin or tigerskin rugs, sexually suggestive paintings and sculpture, and full bars where all manner of illegal liquor was available to guests. In some homes, like that of actress Barbara Lamarr, guests were invited to help themselves to trays laden with cocaine and opium. All this William Desmond Taylor disdained. He was the epitome of good taste and noble living, or so everyone thought. Secretly, Taylor was carrying on a half-dozen affairs with some of Hollywood's greatest silent film stars, including Mabel Normand, one of the most popular comediennes in the business, and ingenue Mary Miles Minter, who looked no more than fifteen but was thirty during her tempestuous affair with Taylor in 1922. The director, who had an enormous sexual appetite, was also seeing actress Claire Windsor, along with a number of other Hollywood personalities, from extras to stars.

Much in Taylor's life remained a mystery, however, even to his Hollywood intimates. He seldom spoke about his background, and when he did he described his past in vague, contradictory terms, his stories varying widely. At the time, Taylor also employed a truculent chauffeur named Edward F. Sands, a man who avoided cameras whenever his employer's photo was taken. Henry Peavey, Taylor's butler, was as eccentric as Sands. He was discernibly homosexual, walking in mincing steps, employing feminine gestures in an exaggerated manner—flopping limp wrists, swaying his hips, speaking in a high falsetto voice that turned to a screech when he was excited.

In early 1922, Taylor took a European vacation. Upon his return, he called one of his paramours, Mabel Normand, to invite her to his house on the evening of Feb. 1, 1922. The two dined together, eating a supper prepared by the fussy Peavey. That night Taylor told Normand that his chauffeur, Sands, had all but destroyed him financially, explaining that Sands, who had disappeared just before Taylor returned from Europe, had stolen his jewelry, damaged the director's two expensive cars while drunk, run up bills on his charge accounts, forged checks against Taylor's bank account, and even taken a good portion of his employer's wardrobe with him.

Taylor showed Normand his desk, which was littered with cancelled checks, bills, and receipts. He explained that while he was completing his income tax forms he had discovered his chauffeur's thefts. "That contemptible Sands has almost undone me," he told Normand. "Nearly every one of those checks is forged. He did such a good job that I can't tell which are my signatures and which are his. I've been going over them all day and it's driving me mad."

"What are you going to do about him?" Normand asked.

"I'll do plenty if they ever find Sands," Taylor said in a voice full of threat and anger.

Normand left the Taylor home at 7:45 p.m. Through the opened window of her limousine, Taylor handed her two books he wanted her to read. The comedienne gave him an affectionate kiss on the cheek and was driven home. Shortly after 8 p.m., actor Douglas McLean and his wife Faith, along with others living in the bungalow court, heard what they thought was the sound of a car's backfire. They later stated that these sounds could have been shots being fired. Faith McLean looked out her front window at the time and saw a man leaving the Taylor house. "I suppose it was a man," she later told police. "It was dressed like a man, but you know, funny-looking. It was dressed in a heavy coat with a muffler around the chin and a cap pulled down over the eyes. But it walked like a woman—quick little steps, with broad hips and short legs."

Edna Purviance, who had been Charlie Chaplin's first female costar and who occupied one of the bungalows in the court, saw lights go on in the Taylor house a few hours later and she went and knocked on Taylor's front door. There was no answer. Purviance thought Taylor was entertaining another one of his female friends, so she returned to her bungalow.

A short time later, Howard Fellows, Taylor's new chauffeur, knocked on the front door but got no answer. He had been instructed by his employer to park the Taylor limousine if no one answered the door and then go home, which he did. At 7:30 the next morning, Henry Peavey, the butler, who lived elsewhere, arrived at the backdoor of the Taylor house. He picked up the morning milk bottle and, using his key, entered the bungalow. He walked into the living room and saw Taylor lying face-up on the floor. A chair rested on top of his legs. The director was fully dressed. His arms were at his sides and his legs were close together. His position was later described as "lying at attention."

A small trickle of blood had crusted about Taylor's mouth. Peavey leaned down and saw that the director was not breathing. He jumped up, raced out the backdoor, and ran through the court and down the sidewalk screaming: "Massa Taylor's dead!" (according to one Los Angeles newspaper).

Peavey was like a man possessed. He shook and twitched and jerked his body about in his frenzied flight from the murder scene, screeching in his falsetto voice as he ran down Alvarado Boulevard. Douglas McLean and Edna Purviance were the first to answer his cries. They went into the Taylor house through the unlocked back door and Purviance spotted the director lying dead on the floor. She ran back to her own house and called Mabel Normand, not the police. Normand called Charles Eyton, Taylor's superior, and Eyton called Paramount mogul Adolph Zukor. Purviance, who knew about the director's many affairs, then called Mary Miles Minter. The ingenue was not available but her protective mother, Charlotte Shelby, took the call and seemed indifferent to the news of Taylor's death.

While Purviance was making her Hollywood calls, McLean phoned a doctor, who arrived shortly to examine Taylor. He felt for a pulse and found none. He listened for a heartbeat and heard none. "This man's dead," announced the physician.

"Of what?" McLean asked.

"He died of gastric hemorrhage," said the doctor who then called the coroner's office to report Taylor's death. A few minutes later Charles Eyton and his aides arrived. Edna Purviance went back to the Taylor bungalow to see Adolph Zukor, one of the most powerful men in Hollywood, arrive. By then Eyton and his aides were tidying up the bungalow. Eyton found some bottles of liquor and almost threw them at McLean, barking: "Get rid of this booze, quick!" Zukor walked up to the body of his top director, studied it for a moment, and then turned to Eyton and said: "Find anything that might damage the studio's reputation and destroy it!"

Paramount had suffered major scandals in the recent past, including the horrendous rape-murder case against its stellar comedian, Roscoe "Fatty" Arbuckle, and Zukor did not want his studio to undergo another publicity disaster. Eyton and his men dashed around the bungalow, gathering female garments that were tucked into desk and bureau drawers, along with piles of love letters sent to the director from many of Hollywood's top female stars. A fire was started in the fireplace and Zukor, Eyton, and other studio executives began burning everything and anything that might incriminate Paramount in Taylor's untimely death.

Mabel Normand then arrived and raced into the bedroom where she began a desperate search for many of her own love letters to the philandering Taylor. As the Paramount executives and Normand were ransacking Taylor's home, Peavey, the butler, continued his hysterical screaming and gyrations up and down Alvarado Boulevard. Neighbors finally called police and Peavey, who had to be subdued, babbled out the fact that his employer was dead.

A coroner's assistant arrived and looked down on Taylor's corpse, saying: "He looks too neat lying there like that."

"Yeah," another person in the living room said, "like someone had laid him out."

Eyton stopped burning papers for a minute to glance over to the body and then he nervously shouted: "Turn him over! Turn him over!" The body was turned over and all in the living room gaped at the two bullet holes that had punctured the back of William Desmond Taylor. "Murder," gasped Eyton. A minute or so later Mabel Normand departed the Taylor house. Zukor then left, telling Eyton to remain behind and "handle this awful mess."

When detectives arrived to inspect the body, they concluded that Taylor had not been shot where his body was found. The holes in his suitcoat did not line up with the holes in his back, so they propped the body up at his desk chair and hiked up the suitcoat so that the holes lined up. Taylor had been seated at his desk, working, they theorized, when his killer crept up behind him and shot him twice. Then the killer laid out the body on the floor, perhaps to rifle Taylor's pockets, which the detectives found were empty.

At the backdoor of the house were a number of cigarette butts, indicating that the killer had waited there the previous evening, until Normand and Peavey had left for the night. Edna Purviance again called Charlotte Shelby, mother of Mary Miles Minter, to tell her that Taylor had been shot to death. Shelby drove to her mother's home, where her daughter Mary had been living. Mother and daughter had been arguing for several months, mostly about Mary's clandestine affair with Taylor, and Mary had moved out of her mother's house, going to live with her grandmother, Julia Branch Miles. Shelby went to the Miles home and confronted her daughter, shouting through a locked door: "Mr. Taylor was found murdered this morning!"

Mary Miles Minter quickly grabbed the keys to her car and began to leave the house when her mother grabbed her, ordering her to stay in her room. Mary struggled free, ran to the car, and drove at high speed to the Taylor residence. Police were swarming over the place and refused to let her in. Minter then went to see Mabel Normand and stayed with her for several hours. Whatever these two movie stars had to say about their dead paramour was never revealed.

The worst they anticipated came about when detectives unearthed their gushing love letters to Taylor. The press soon acquired these and published the intimate thoughts of both Normand and Minter. Police also found, beneath a stack of film scripts, dozens of pornographic photos showing Taylor with several film actresses.

The scandal heightened when it was learned that Mabel Normand was an opium addict. A note found in the director's home from Taylor to Normand chastised her for continuing this "filthy, beastly habit." So incensed had Taylor been about Normand's drug problem that he had conducted his own investigation of drug dealers in Los Angeles' Chinatown. He had turned

William Desmond Taylor, 1921.

Taylor in *Captain Alvarez.*

Taylor as an officer in the Canadian army, a prop.

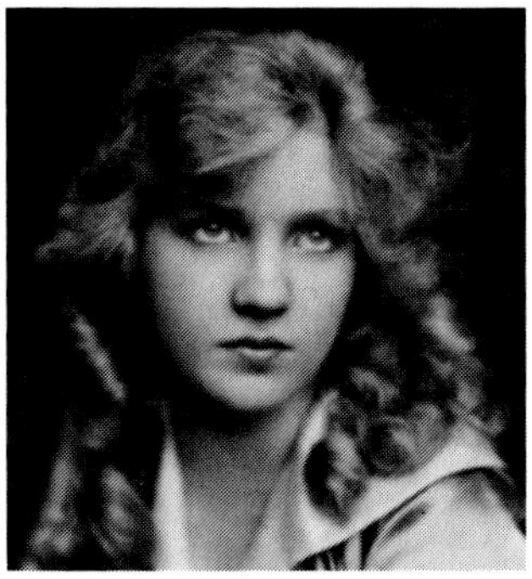

Mary Miles Minter, 1920.

Mabel Normand, 1920.

Claire Windsor, 1921.

Taylor with his mysterious chauffeur, Edward Sands.

Dennis Deane Tanner

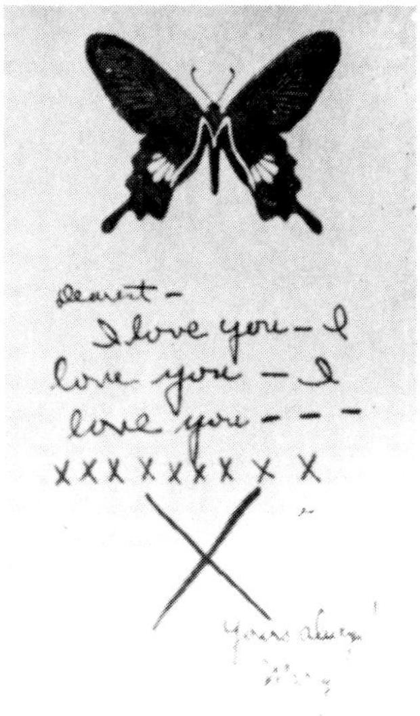

Minter's gushing love note.

over his findings to the district attorney, leading to speculate that Taylor might have been murdered by drug traffickers for revenge.

Even Mary Pickford, the greatest film star of the era, was drawn into the case. She had merely given Taylor an autographed picture of herself, but because he had kept this on his bedstand, it was suggested that even the pristine Pickford was having an affair with the director. When asked about her relationship with Taylor, Pickford replied that she did not heed Hollywood gossip. "I will pray," was her final comment as she closed her door to reporters.

A strong suspect in the case was the missing chauffeur, Edward Sands, who turned out to be none other than Taylor's brother, Dennis Deane-Tanner. Detectives pursued the theory that Sands-Tanner had looted his brother's checking account, wardrobe, and jewelry box in retaliation for Taylor's bankrupting him in New York and later using him as a lowly servant in Hollywood. This so rankled the younger brother, one account had it, that Tanner went to the bungalow on the night of Feb. 1-2, 1922, and shot his brother dead.

Charlotte Shelby also became a prime suspect. Taylor had been shot with a .38-caliber revolver, and Shelby was known to possess just such a weapon. In fact, she was seen practice-firing this weapon only a short time before the director was murdered. Her motive, it was said, had nothing to do with protecting her daughter's image, but that Shelby herself had been having an affair with Taylor and murdered him in revenge being rejected in favor of her daughter. It was Shelby, some said, who left the Taylor home that night disguised as a man.

The valet-butler Henry Peavey was a suspect briefly. Peavey had been arrested a few weeks before the murder on a morals charge, for attempting to seduce a young boy in a Hollywood park. Taylor had used his influence to save his butler from a jail term and paid his fine for him. Peavey, instead of appreciating Taylor's kindness, it was claimed, resented his employer's knowing about his perversions and killed him for that knowledge. Peavey later went insane and died of paresis in a Napa mental institution in 1931.

Taylor's killer was never identified. He was buried as the victim of an unsolved murder case, one that has caused amateur sleuths to sift through the slim evidence in the case over the years and produce wild conjecture and impossible theories. Taylor's murder and the resulting publicity ended the careers of Mabel Normand and Mary Miles Minter. Normand was branded a dope fiend and found it almost impossible to obtain movie roles. Her life was further complicated in 1923 when her chauffeur, Horace A. Greer, shot and almost killed millionaire Courtland S. Dines as the Denver oil tycoon was about to enter Normand's limousine for a night on the town with the star. Both chauffeur and tycoon had been battling over Normand's sexual favors. This scandal, hot on the heels of the Taylor murder, utterly destroyed her career. She married actor Lew Cody in 1926. A few years later she contracted tuberculosis and died in a sanitarium on Feb. 22, 1930, at age thirty-three.

Mary Miles Minter fared better. She separated from her domineering mother, later battling Shelby in court for control of her own estate. Mary invested her savings wisely in real estate and lived out her life in comfort. To the end of her days, Mary Miles Minter kept an autographed portrait of Taylor in her bedroom. He was her one great love and her one great mistake. See: **Arbuckle, Roscoe Conkling**.

REF.: *CBA;* Kirkpatrick, *A Cast of Killers;* Nash, *Almanac of World Crime;* ____, *Open Files;* Purvis, *Great Unsolved Mysteries;* Rodell, *Los Angeles Murders;* Sutherland, *Ten Real Murder Mysteries;* (FILM), *Affairs of a Gentleman,* 1934; *Hollywood Story,* 1951.

Taylor, William G., d.1893, U.S., mur. William G. Taylor, condemned for killing a fellow inmate at Auburn Prison, was the second person in the U.S. to be executed by electrocution. Technical flaws in the electrocution process, however, turned his execution into a horror.

On Aug. 27, 1893, Taylor was strapped into the chair, and the current was turned on. His corpse contorted from the electric shocks, and his legs pulled loose from the restraining straps. The current was turned off and the chair was reinforced. When the switch was thrown again, there was no current because a generator had burned out.

Taylor, who was unconscious but still alive, was placed on a cot and given drugs for his pain. Before prison officials could restore the power Taylor died. However, because the law required that Taylor be electrocuted, his body was strapped back into the chair, and the current was sent charging through it once again. This done, the warden announced, "Gentlemen, justice has been done."

REF.: *CBA;* Nash, *Open Files.*

Tazewell, Henry, 1753-99, U.S., jur. Virginia Supreme Court justice from 1785-93, serving as chief justice from 1789-93. He served on the Virginia Court of Appeals in 1793 and was a member of the U.S. Senate from 1794-99. REF.: *CBA.*

Tbilisi Opera and Ballet Fire, 1973, U.S.S.R., arson. On May 9, 1973, a fire caused extensive damage to the Tbilisi Opera and Ballet Theater in Soviet Georgia. Arson was suspected, and six theater employees were arrested. In May 1975, Tengiz Rukhadze, the nephew of Vakhtang M. Chabukiani, who had been dismissed as the theater director shortly before the fire, was also arrested. Rukhadze allegedly had paid the six employees 50,000 rubles to burn the building. When the KGB stepped into the investigation, the original six confessed their guilt, but could not produce the money. The confessions implicated Chabukiani, who held three Orders of Lenin for his contributions to Russian ballet, and was credited with developing the Georgian theater. He had been dismissed because he refused to choreograph a ballet to music composed by the Georgian Minister of Culture.

The trial opened on Nov. 15, 1976, before Judge Shalva Makharadze, and the six defendants immediately repudiated their confessions, claiming that they were beaten with rubber truncheons until they confessed. On Jan. 24, 1977, the judge found all of the defendants Guilty and sentenced them to terms of from five to eight years, but halved the sentences immediately as a gesture of amnesty to war veterans. Rukhadze, who had already served twenty months since his 1975 arrest, received a commutation of the rest of his sentence. The incident left great bitterness among Georgian intellectuals, who thought that the trial was an overt attempt to ruin the reputation of Chabukiani. REF.: *CBA.*

Teach, Edward (AKA: **Blackbeard**), d.1718, Int'l., pir.-mur. Between 1715 and 1718 Englishman Edward Teach established himself as the most fearsome buccaneer in history. He operated out of Ocracoke Inlet in North Carolina. He was killed in a sword fight and his head hung from the bowsprit of the ship of the man who killed him. See: **Blackbeard**. REF.: *CBA.*

Teamsters Union (International Brotherhood of Teamsters, Chauffeurs, Warehousemen and Helpers of America), 1899- , U.S., org. crime. Founded in 1899 as the Team Drivers International Union, the Teamsters numbered 40,000 by 1907. Growing steadily, they became the nation's largest union by 1940, with membership passing 1 million ten years later. The Teamsters were headed by Daniel J. Tobin between 1907-55. Two years later they were expelled from the AFL-CIO for corruption among their executives, and they came under federal investigation for illegal use of union funds. Within the next three decades, three incumbent Teamster presidents were sent to prison.

David Beck was elected president of the Teamsters in 1952. He quickly provided himself with a rent-free Seattle estate, with a guarantee of life-long occupancy. Robert Kennedy, investigating Beck's personal finances for the Senate's McClellan Committee, alleged that the union leader was skimming a fortune from the union. Brought before the committee, Beck said he had nothing to fear, yet he took the Fifth Amendment more than 200 times. He was subsequently found Guilty of income tax evasion and sent to prison.

James R. Hoffa became Teamsters president in 1958, and immediately attracted the attention of Robert Kennedy. Unable to bring Hoffa to trial while working as chief counsel for McClellan, Kennedy continued the investigation after he was appointed attorney general. In 1962, Hoffa was indicted for extortion, but escaped conviction with a hung jury. Kennedy, however, proved Hoffa had attempted to bribe a juror, and the union leader was convicted and sentenced to eight years in prison. In 1964, Hoffa was given another sentence for misappropriating $1.7 million in union monies. After exhausting appeal efforts, Hoffa served about five years in prison before he received a pardon in 1971 by President Richard Nixon on the condition that he distance himself from the union. But Hoffa attempted to regain his previous seat, and after an abortive attempt to oust union president Frank Fitzsimmons, Hoffa was seen for the last time on July 30, 1975.

In 1982, Roy L. Williams became the third Teamster president to be convicted following a federal investigation. A year after assuming union leadership, Williams was found Guilty of bribing Nevada senator Howard Cannon in an attempt to manipulate legislation concerning the trucking industry. He testified from a wheel chair, wearing a respirator for his emphysema and heart ailment, and after exhausting appeal, he served three years of his ten-year sentence at the U.S. Medical Center for Prisoners in Springfield, Mo. See: **Beck, David; Hoffa, James Riddle; Williams, Roy Lee.** REF.: *CBA.*

Teapot Dome Scandal, 1922-29, U.S., polit. corr. Warren Gamaliel Harding (1865-1923) became president at the dawn of the Roaring Twenties, which ushered in Prohibition, bootleg hootch, and organized crime, and let loose the wildest, gaudiest spree in American history. Although it would be years before the whole truth came out, Harding took full advantage of his office or, more to the point, sank delightedly into its tub of pleasures, while his political cronies leisurely looted the land in what later became known as the Teapot Dome Scandal.

The twenty-ninth president of the U.S. (1921-1923) had not aggressively sought the office of chief executive. Born in a small farmhouse outside of Blooming Grove, Ohio, on Nov. 2, 1865, Harding was raised in poor surroundings but managed to work his way through Ohio Central College (now defunct) and was lucky enough to meet and marry Florence Kling, an ambitious young woman whose father was the richest man in Marion, Ohio. The couple wed on July 8, 1891. Three years later, Warren Harding was the editor and publisher of the Marion *Star*, a small daily paper purchased with his wife's money.

The tall, handsome Harding loved the newspaper business and would have been content to spend the rest of his days tinkering with ink-smeared hot type in the composing room of his newspaper. But his wife, Florence, who longed for high social position, had other ideas. She encouraged Harding to enter politics. He responded that he knew nothing of politics and that he would fail miserably as a public servant.

A short while later, a local lawyer named Harry Micajah Daugherty encountered the publisher of the Marion *Star* as he waited for Harding to finish having his shoes shined. (Another story has it that the two men met on a path between an outhouse and a Marion brothel, both being frequent guests at the place.) As Daugherty liked to remember it, he introduced himself and began to work on Harding's considerable ego, telling the publisher that he had the makings of a top-flight politician and that he, Daugherty, who had influence in the dizzy stratas of Republican state politics, could manage his career. (Although it was never proved, Daugherty may have acted on the encouragement provided by Florence Kling Harding, who knew the lawyer through her wheeler-dealer, millionaire father.)

After Harding yielded his seat on the shoeshine stand to Daugherty, he lingered to listen further as the oily-tongued lawyer spewed forth slippery dreams of easy glory. From that moment on, Warren Harding was Daugherty's man—political tool, really. The lawyer engineered Harding into a state senate seat in 1900 and then to the position of the Ohio lieutenant governorship in 1904.

Daugherty, along with what would later be labeled the "Ohio Gang", shunted Harding into the U.S. Senate in 1915, where he was called "The Roman Idol," because of his magnificent bearing, aquiline nose, and leonine head of white hair. He had a kindly, mobile face, friendly, with a constant hint of a smile playing upon wide lips, but the firm jaw and piercing eyes of a man who wore a constant look of thoughtful earnestness. It was Harding's looks alone that moved Daugherty to remark to a crony only hours after having met him some twenty years earlier: "Gee, what a president he'd make!" (Political editor for the *New Republic* in the twenties, Bruce Bliven, was struck with Harding's overwhelming physical makeup when they first met: "...this man, who talked like somebody invented by Sinclair Lewis, looked more like a president than any president who ever lived, with the possible exception of George Washington.")

But with Harding, it was all veneer. As a politician, he was hopelessly ineffective, voting in the Senate exactly the way his political sponsors from Ohio, chiefly Daugherty, told him to vote. It was also Daugherty who more or less ordered Harding to set up headquarters in Chicago prior to the Republican National Convention in 1920, as a standby candidate for the office of president. It was only a smoke screen, Daugherty told Harding. His prestige had begun to slip in Ohio, and such a move would bring him into the national limelight. Of course, Daugherty had other ideas.

Other than the Ohio Gang, no one believed that Harding had a chance; however, Daugherty knew that General Leonard Wood and Frank O. Lowden, the party favorites, did not have enough convention votes to swing the candidacy. He and other Republican bigwigs let them slug it out on the floor to a stalemate. Then Daugherty let it be known that Harding would be the man of the hour the following day. Newspapermen, sniffing a "dark horse," surrounded crafty Daugherty. Piped one: "You don't really think Harding has a chance, do you?"

"I'll tell you what I think," responded the lawyer in his quick banter. "After the other candidates have failed, we'll get together in some hotel room, oh, about 2:11 in the morning, and some fifteen men, bleary-eyed with lack of sleep, will sit down around a big table. When that time comes, Senator Harding will be selected."

That very night, in room 401 of Chicago's Blackstone Hotel—the legendary smoke-filled room—a group of the party elders decided that Harding, indeed, could easily beat any candidate the Democrats put up. He had one of the most undistinguished records in the U.S. Senate, and the elders reasoned that opponents could not fault him for making any serious senatorial mistakes. To their knowledge, Harding was simply a small-town hick with an untainted record and, most importantly, a man who would take orders.

Harding had no idea that Daugherty was attempting to shove him into the White House, and when he answered a 2 a.m. summons to appear before his political mentors at the Blackstone, he originally thought that they would be asking him to throw his votes to either Wood or Lowden. He was shocked when he was told that he was their choice for president. Then Colonel George B. M. Harvey, who had defected from the Democrat ranks, bluntly stated: "Senator, we want to put a question to you. Is there in your life or background any element which might embarrass the Republican party if we nominate you for President?" Stunned, Harding stood silent before the Republican patriarchs. Daugherty asked him if he would like to go into an adjoining room to think over the question before answering, and Harding nodded and left. He returned inside of ten minutes and said to the men: "No."

The next day, Harding was nominated and chosen as the Republican standard bearer. He appeared to be in shock. The members of the press were also amazed and crowded about the candidate, asking for an explanation. Harding replied with the parlance of a poker player, a game he played endlessly with his Ohio Gang cronies: "We drew to a pair of deuces, and filled."

Harding had little or no platform to run on; he wanted to avoid any real issues and problems. Not too strangely, this was the basic attitude of the entire U.S. electorate at the time. The citizens of the U.S. had had a bellyful of war and deep involvement in international politics and intrigue. Following WWI, the U.S. turned its back on its own image as the industrial and social leader of the world. Harding spoke for the single-mindedness of the country at the time, reflecting a prevailing attitude of isolationism.

"What is the greatest thing in life, my countrymen?" he asked a crowd assembled before his front porch in Marion at the dawn of his aimless campaign. "Happiness. And there is more happiness in the American village than in any other place on the face of the earth." He was selling Gay Nineties nostalgia. He did not want to look forward. A short time later, reporters asked the candidate what he planned to do in his campaign.

Replied Harding, who liked to coin words: "I like to go out into the country and bloviate." *Bloviate* meant to talk endlessly in alliterative cliches to small-town people who politely applauded while never for a moment understanding his gobbledygook.

The do-nothing candidate coined his own campaign slogan on May 4, 1920, when addressing members of the Home Market Club in Boston. In his best rhetoric, Harding thundered: "America's present need is not heroics but healing, not nostrums but *normalcy,* not revolution but restoration, not agitation but adjustment, not surgery but serenity, not the dramatic but the dispassionate, not experiment but equipoise, not submergence in internationality but sustainment in triumphant nationality." The word, *normalcy,* never existed until this moment, but it struck a responsive chord in the press and "Back to Normalcy" was soon Harding's campaign slogan, which really meant back to the past, a standstill philosophy where the status quo was venerated and social stagnancy admired.

The Democrats, sadly, had little to offer against Harding. Their presidential hopeful, Ohio governor James M. Cox, was even more lackluster than Harding, although his running mate, Franklin Delano Roosevelt, showed exceptional charisma and charm. Senator Frank Brandegee of Connecticut, who was later to become a member of Harding's notorious "Poker Cabinet," flaunted the power of the Republican bosses to elect and control their candidate by publicly stating: "Harding is no world-beater but he is the best of the second-raters."

Harding went on bloviating through the campaign months, saying very little of consequence. On one occasion, while sitting in his Senate Office Building suite, Harding complained to one interviewing journalist that Americans were living beyond their means. By way of illustration, he swung out of his large swivel chair, walked to the door of his chamber and opened it, revealing an attractive young woman sitting at a desk some twenty feet away in the outer office. He pointed to her and said: "That girl owns a five-hundred-dollar fur coat. That's twice as much, by George, as I can afford to spend on a coat for Mrs. Harding."

The young woman in Harding's outer offices was Nan Britton and the fur coat she owned had been paid for by none other than Harding himself. She was, as Britton would later reveal in a sensational book, Harding's mistress. Britton and Harding had been having a torrid, secret affair for a decade. So comfortable with this extramarital arrangement was Harding that he utterly failed to mention it after pondering his background in that Chicago hotel room. The political sachems to whom Harding gave that fateful "no" were concerned, he undoubtedly believed, with any political "taint" in his life, not his private sexual relationships.

The future president did have his misgivings about his impending election but seldom voiced them. On one occasion, Harding grumbled that the upcoming November showdown was like a poker game, full of surprises. "I feel like a man who goes in with a pair of eights and comes out with aces full," he said. His power-fascinated wife, Florence, who would be known as "The Duchess" in Washington—Harding called her Flossie—suddenly pulled back from her White House dreams. She was having last-minute nightmares after undoubtedly reviewing the real nature of her manipulated spouse. "I can see but one word written above his head if they make him president," she prophetically sighed in a rare, unguarded moment, "and that word is *tragedy.*"

The November election signalled no such fate. Harding and his running mate, Calvin Coolidge, received 16 million votes, a landslide over the 9 million votes gleaned by Cox and Roosevelt. With the most overwhelming majority ever given to a candidate, Harding was swept into office and with him the most corrupt administration in American history, the Ohio Gang, which happily embraced the spoils of their victory. Shortly after assuming the reins of government in 1921, Harding began to complain about his role as president. "I am a man of limited talents from a small town," he murmured to aides. "I don't seem to grasp that I am president." He later stated: "I am not fit for this office and never should have been here." He undoubtedly knew that his political mentors intended to loot the country's coffers and lamely sought refuge in religion and prayer.

"Talk to God about me every day by name and ask Him somehow to give me strength for my great task," Harding asked a Washington bishop. To those audiences who came to hear the president provide more bloviation, Harding pleaded: "It will help if we have a revival of religion...I don't think any government can be just if it does not have somehow a contact with Omnipotent God."

Privately, Harding sat back and let the Ohio Gang take over the federal government. His manager, Harry Daugherty, was appointed attorney general. Charles R. Forbes took over the Veteran's Bureau. Harding originally thought to name as secretary of state a blustering New Mexico rancher named Albert B. Fall, whom the president had known and admired in his Senate days, but Fall, his larcenous instincts already formulating big-time boodle, asked to be named secretary of the interior. Harding handed him the appointment. Dozens more of these incredibly opportunistic types were given government posts and went to work speedily, stealing with both hands.

Harding knew these men to be venal to the core, but ignored their avaricious ways except on rare occasions, when he grumbled over the blatant boondoggling on the part of his political cronies. To journalist William Allen White, Harding once blurted, "My God, this is a hell of a job. I have no trouble with my enemies. I can take care of them all right. But my damn friends, White, they're the ones that keep me walking the floor nights."

This was all a front, of course. Harding lost no sleep over the wholesale corruption flourishing beyond the Oval Office. He was more interested in his own pleasures—poker, booze, and women, other than his wife, an attitude that permeated the federal government at the time. Despite the fact that the 18th Amendment banned the selling of alcohol, political leaders followed Harding's lead and went on a delirious bender.

When Prohibition was young, congressmen openly imbibed illegal hooch, their bootleggers displaying their wares and selling from smart leather cases carried down the corridors of every federal building. The use of liquor was so blatant on the part of the lawmakers that Representative Upshaw of Georgia rose indignantly in the House in December 1922 and shouted: "Too many of these officials are striking a grandiose posture and calling upon the people with tears in their eyes to respect and honor the laws of our nation, and then going out the back way and buying blind-tiger bootleg liquor for their personal consumption! Is the law of our land to be so twisted as to make this a rich man's prohibition—so as to allow the wealthy and the office-holder to shield his hip pocket with ready cash, a pious hand, and an oily tongue?"

The outcry caused the bootleggers to disappear from the halls of Congress for a few weeks, but after the sporadic tirades subsided, it was business as usual, with society bootleggers like Raymond "Razor" Gray and Ronald Hendley Irvine, both only twenty-eight, becoming millionaires through their exclusive service of providing bonded booze to powerful Washingtonians. Following the arrest of these men in a rare raid, some of the city's most prominent lawyers quickly appeared at the station house to post bond for them. There was even a scuffle between several thirsty barristers over which one would be lucky enough to post bail.

President Harding and his wife, 1922.

U.S. oil reserves were near Teapot Dome, Wyo.

At right, U.S. attorney general Harry Daugherty.

Albert M. Fall and E.L. Doheny, partners in crime.

Edwin N. Denby

Charles R. Forbes

Gaston Bullock Means

Nan Britton

While bootlegging flourished beneath the capital dome, graft and corruption inside of Harding's cabinet mushroomed. To be sure, there were honest and upright men serving with the president's inner circle—Mellon, Hughes, and Hoover—but they were not privy to the real workings of the Harding administration. The president and his close cronies made all the top level decisions on the second floor of the White House where Harding would meet almost every night with Daugherty, Forbes, and other hustlers of high finance, occasionally joined by newspaper publisher Edward B. McLean and Mort Mortimer, personal bootlegger to the White House. It was this "poker cabinet," as the group later came to be known, that decided the issues of the day and planned strategy in scooping up enormous spoils.

Harding was content to play president; Daugherty did all the real thinking and the real wheeling and dealing. Publicly, Harding encouraged the image of outdoorsman, taking up ping-pong and golf, setting a presidential standard for his club-swinging successors. He told newsmen that he occupied his evening hours with bridge, but he invariably returned to the poker table and the Ohio Gang.

Alice Roosevelt Longworth was visiting Mrs. Harding one night and took a wrong turn into a room where Harding and Daugherty were presiding over their usual poker game. Mrs. Longworth fled the scene to later report in shock: "No rumor could have exceeded the reality; the study was filled with cronies...the air heavy with tobacco smoke, trays with bottles containing every imaginable brand of whiskey stood about, cards and poker chips ready at hand—a general atmosphere of waistcoat unbuttoned, feet on desk, and spittoons alongside."

This description was tame compared to events that took place at 1625 K Street, later to be called the "Little Green House." Daugherty rented this hideaway through his friend, the shadowy Jess Smith, who had taken an office close to the attorney general in the Department of Justice Building. Smith's position and duties were never specified, but he served as Daugherty's liaison between government officials and businessmen eager to lease oil-rich government lands.

The house on K Street was used by Daugherty and Smith for all manner of pleasures, including drunken parties for money-doling lobbyists and millionaires seeking political favors. Booze, gambling, expensive Washington prostitutes, even hard drugs such as opium and heroin, were all made conveniently available to any and all guests. Harding not only knew of the infamous Little Green House but, through Edward McLean, his friend and publisher of the Washington *Post,* rented a similar place on H Street, a trysting place, really, for himself and his flighty mistress, Nan Britton. Daugherty, the evil genius behind the entire, corrupt administration, encouraged Harding at this time to make secret investments in Wall Street. The president plunged and lost $180,000, his debts covered by his friend Daugherty, who also knew about the president's mistress, Nan Britton, information that undoubtedly helped him control the president in important matters where the Ohio Gang stood to profit enormously.

Nan Britton was not the product of an overnight affair. She had known Harding as early as 1910, when she was fourteen and he forty-five. At the time, Nan hero-worshipped Harding and kept one of his early-day campaign posters over her bed. Her father, a prominent physician in Marion, knew Harding and his wife and thought his daughter's fascination with the then newspaper publisher was nothing more than a girlish crush. Nan's obsession with the older man remained constant, however, and she wrote to him in 1916 from New York, where she was completing a secretarial course, asking Harding, then in the U.S. Senate, for his advice about her business career. The dashing senator wrote back, stating that he remembered her and suggested a meeting.

They met and continued to meet in various New York hotels. At first, according to Britton's later claims, Harding assumed the role of surrogate father, obtaining a $16-a-week secretarial job for her through his powerful friend, Judge Elbert H. Gary, who was chairman of U.S. Steel. While counseling her on her future, Harding became amorous, fondling and kissing his 21-year-old protegée in their secret meeting places. She became "his bride," in her own words, on the night of July 30, 1917, in a Manhattan hotel room on Seventh Avenue.

The sexual liaison continued without interruption through Harding's White House years. Prior to his election as president, Harding traveled around Ohio campaigning with Nan at his side; she was introduced to inquisitive sorts as his niece. Mrs. Harding, at these times, remained in the background. As far as she was concerned, Nan Britton was nothing more than a hero-worshipping girl who performed occasional secretarial work for her husband. This was to be Mrs. Harding's public posture throughout the torrid affair between her husband and Nan Britton, but insiders felt that Mrs. Harding knew of the relationship and finally took terrible vengeance upon her husband.

Harding gushed out his love to Nan in massive missives, one love letter running, according to Nan, more than sixty pages. All the while Harding was a U.S. Senator, he met with his paramour in New York hotel rooms; when Nan visited Washington, she stayed with Harding at the Ebbitt House or in apartments the senator borrowed from friends. Nan even visited Harding in his Senate office, where they made love on his leather couch.

According to Nan, she became pregnant in early 1919 and gave birth to a daughter on Oct. 22 in Asbury Park, N.J. She named the girl Elizabeth Ann Christian; the male secretary to Harding at the time was named George Christian. Although the 54-year-old Harding never saw the girl, he cherished reports of her growth, according to Nan. Moreover, he gave Nan a good deal of money, sending her between $100 and $150 every week for support. On other occasions, he bestowed lump sums of up to $500 on her. After Harding's election, Nan continued to see him, visiting him secretly in the White House where he would give her more money from his desk in the Oval Office. On other occasions, a Secret Service agent whom Nan called "Tim Slade," a pseudonym, delivered amounts of money to her for Elizabeth's upkeep.

While the childless Mrs. Harding slept in an upstairs White House bedroom, Nan Britton often slipped into the home of the president. "He introduced me to the one place where, he said, we might share kisses in safety," Nan later claimed. "This was a closet in the anteroom, evidently a place for hats and coats...we repaired there many times in the course of my visits to the White House, and in the darkness of a space no more than five feet square the President and his adoring sweetheart made love."

On other occasions, Harding boldly went arm-and-arm with Nan to the house on H Street. Those grafters working out of Daugherty's pleasure den on K Street would convince wealthy lobbyists that they could accomplish any transaction for them by simply taking them to the H Street house to watch Harding, Daugherty, and Nan Britton arrive arm-in-arm, wave casually to the grafter and thereby convince the lobbyist that the "fix was in."

The philandering and filching went on until mid-1923 when Harding embarked upon a tedious cross-country trip to Alaska, ostensibly a pilgrimage to mend political fences. His wife Florence was at his side, not Nan Britton. Left to their own devious wiles in Washington, Daugherty, Fall, and others went into high gear in courting illegal deals to enrich themselves. Oil men Edward L. Doheny and Harry Sinclair vied with each other in plying Fall with enormous bribes to allow them to tap, through secret contract without bidding, the oil reserves in Wyoming. (The words "Teapot Dome" came from a curious rock formation near the oil deposits which was shaped like a teapot, and the geological word "dome" indicated an earth strata curved upward and then down again which brought oil to the surface.) Doheny gave Fall $100,000 as a "loan." Sinclair gave Fall $304,000 in cash and Liberty Bonds. The deal brought the oil men more than $600 million from their illegal drilling on government lands, with the government receiving only 16 percent of the profits. All of it was done in secret and it was not until the late 1920s that the entire, sordid deal was revealed through the efforts of such corruption ferrets as "Fighting" Bob LaFollette, the senator from Wisconsin, and Senator

Thomas J. Walsh of Montana.

By then Harding was dead, following his arduous Alaskan trip. His train had been boarded en route by mysterious figures, all carrying arcane messages. Harding's trip to Alaska, although much publicized, was meaningless. He was actually evading Washington sleuths hot on the graft-strewn trail of his cronies Daugherty and Fall. As reports of impending exposés reached him, Harding's nerves splintered. His hands shook. He played endless, mindless bridge. Just as his train neared San Francisco on the melancholy return trip to Washington, the president was stricken by what doctors loosely termed "ptomaine poisoning." Later the problem was diagnosed alternatively as pneumonia, apoplexy, and coronary occlusion. No matter, Harding died on Aug. 2, 1923, as his wife read to him and his own troubles perished with him. (Nan Britton later insisted that she was enjoying a European vacation—an all-expenses-paid tour funded by her lover Harding—when he died in San Francisco.) The redoubtable Gaston B. Means, a discredited Bureau of Investigation agent and a henchman of Jess Smith who later coached Nan Britton in the writing of her book, authored a scandalous best-seller, *The Strange Death of President Harding*, in which Means claimed that Mrs. Harding murdered her husband with poison to protect him against inevitable imprisonment and/or in retaliation over his secret affair with Nan Britton. Bizarre as this implication might have been, a great many persons believed it.

There would be no such convenient ends for Harry Daugherty and Albert B. Fall. Daugherty was tried for accepting $400,000 in bribes. He had, it was proved, burned Ohio bank ledger books which would have revealed his illegal deposits. However, Daugherty implied that he burned these books and other important documents because they might have implicated someone "higher up." The inference was clear—the dead president had participated in the massive frauds, yet no one ever mentioned Harding's name in this connection. Daugherty was acquitted, but it was reported that some members of his jury may have accepted bribes.

Albert B. Fall did not escape. The New Mexico rancher who had coveted the Department of the Interior and swaggered about Washington wearing a broad-rimmed hat, had, it was proved at his trial in October 1929, pocketed almost $500,000 in bribes from Doheny and Sinclair. Doheny later smugly stated that his bribe to Fall was nothing more than "a bagatelle to me...no more than $25 or $50 to the ordinary individual."

Fall was convicted, fined $100,000, and given a year in prison. This was the first time that a cabinet-level member of the government was convicted as a criminal and put behind bars. The former secretary of the interior declared bankruptcy and went to the New Mexico State Penitentiary after his doctors insisted he had tuberculosis and the air in New Mexico could alleviate his condition. Fall was carried to his cell on a stretcher, served his year while constantly complaining that he was at "death's door," and was released to enjoy the luxury of his sprawling New Mexico ranch, living for more than a decade, dying in 1944. (Fall had really brought about the initial investigation into the Teapot Dome Scandals. He had convinced the simple-minded Edwin N. Denby, secretary of the navy, to turn over the Wyoming lands and other oil-rich reserves in California to his office, secretly leased these off, and resigned his cabinet post in 1922 after lining his pockets with bribes. Retiring to his New Mexico ranch, he began to spend money lavishly on improvements, arousing suspicions and triggering investigations into his financial affairs by agents of the U.S. Secret Service.)

Other Ohio Gang cronies were exposed. Charles R. Forbes, who headed the Veterans' Bureau, cheated taxpayers out of $200 million and was sent to jail. His assistant, Charles F. Cramer, committed suicide, although no charges were officially brought against him. Ironically, Cramer had purchased the Washington house from the president, a house Harding had lived in when a senator. It was in this house that Cramer blew out his brains.

Thomas W. Miller, the Alien Property custodian, who worked directly under Daugherty, was found guilty of returning $7 million to a German metal firm and had received kickbacks for the favor. He was sent to prison. Daugherty's secretive minion, Jess Smith, who was accused of taking a $50,000 bribe, did not wait for trial; he, like Cramer, blew out his brains. Gaston B. Means was also convicted of bribery and went to jail. He died in 1938 after fleecing Evalyn Walsh McLean, the wife of Harding's poker-playing crony, out of $100,000 in a zany, bogus scheme to recover the missing Lindbergh child.

Means' pointing finger wagged like that of a ghost rustling an empty sleeve for years. Many came to believe that Harding, indeed, had either been murdered by his wife Florence for his unfaithfulness with Nan Britton, or had himself taken poison to escape the impending scandals brought about by his mentors. John Truslow Adams was to state in "The March of Democracy": "Without accepting the most sensational of the stories of his death, it must be admitted that the mystery of it has never been cleared up." J. Hampden Jackson, world-respected British historian, was to write: "Before these scandals came to light, Harding died with suspicious suddenness." Frederick Lewis Allen, writing in *Only Yesterday*, commented: "Both the suicide theory and the Means story are very plausible."

Nan Britton's story did not appear until 1927 with the publication of her notorious book, *The President's Daughter*. The book, in the words of chronicler Mark Sullivan, "made Harding's memory almost a rag in the gutter." Nan told all, but was unable to produce any of the love letters that had passed between her and Harding, later stating that she and Harding had burned them, agreeing that they would hurt the feelings of others if ever published. The book was produced by "Elizabeth Ann Guild, Inc.," an amorphous firm named after Nan's daughter. Nan was the real publisher, abetted, it was said, by the ubiquitous Mr. Means. (The same firm published Means' accusatory book.)

Many publications refused advertisements submitted for the Britton book and most of the book reviewers in the country side-stepped reviewing the work. It nevertheless became a much-sought piece of literary contraband, being kept on shelves beneath counters and sold in hurried and whispered transactions, more than 90,000 copies of it at $5 each over the summer of 1927. Libraries across the country, however, refused to offer the book, and those who did reported hundreds of people on their waiting lists.

The book made Nan rich, but she insisted that she had not published her sexual memoirs of Harding for anything so base as money. She explained in her preface that she had undertaken the publication to advance the cause of illegitimate children, that the Elizabeth Ann Guild was founded so that "the name of the father be correctly registered in the public records" in all births of illegitimate children. This was her crusade; the book was incidental, said the author. Her dedication summed up her lofty purposes:

THIS BOOK IS DEDICATED
WITH UNDERSTANDING AND LOVE
TO ALL UNWEDDED MOTHERS,
AND TO THEIR INNOCENT CHILDREN
WHOSE FATHERS ARE NOT USUALLY
KNOWN TO THE WORLD...
NAN BRITTON

Nan went on to state, in her kiss-by-kiss memoirs, that after the president's death she married a Swedish ship captain but soon separated from him. She next approached the Harding family to see if the deceased president had made any provisions for his child in his will. Nan said she went to Abigail "Daisy" Harding and Mrs. Herbert Votaw, the president's sisters, and that Daisy gave her a few hundred dollars. This proved insufficient, and Nan asked the family for a $50,000 settlement for her daughter. Doctor George Harding, the president's brother, met with her once, note pad on knee, pen at the ready, and wrote down her answers to his questions: "When was that?" "Where did the meeting take place?" "Do you have the letters?" Nan provided only a few innocuous notes Harding had written to her. In the end, Nan received nothing more from the family. Daisy Harding was incensed with the publication of the Britton book, telling reporters: "The author tells of her great love for my brother. If she loved him as she says she did, would she have written such a book about him after his death?"

Florence Harding never had to face the incredible and profitable scandal spread by Britton. She died in 1924 without ever commenting on the affair that had flourished under her own nose. Ironically, Nan Britton's book appeared almost to the month when Warren and Florence Harding were laid to rest side-by-side in a new expensive memorial in Marion, Ohio, where the citizens stubbornly continued to think of the Hardings as common folk who had gone to Washington to be injured and defamed, a case of small-town people crushed beneath the weighty evils of big government and the sinful ways of the metropolis. See: **Means, Gaston Bullock.**

REF.: Adams, *Incredible Era, The Life and Times of Warren Gamaliel Harding;* Allen, *Only Yesterday;* Allsop, *The Bootleggers;* Bagby, *The Road to Normalcy, The Presidential Campaign of 1920;* Britton, *The President's Daughter;* Butterfield, *The American Past; CBA;* Chapple, *Life and Times of Warren G. Harding;* Coffey, *The Long Thirst;* Cox, *Journey Through My Years;* Daugherty, *The Inside Story of the Harding Tragedy;* Giglio, *Harry M. Daugherty and the Politics of Expediency;* Gilbert, *The Mirrors of Washington;* Hoover, *Forty-two Years in the White House;* ____, *The Memoirs of Herbert Hoover: The Cabinet and the Presidency, 1920-1933;* Hynd, *Murder, Mayham and Mystery;* Israel, *The Chief Executive;* Johnson and Walker, *The Dynamics of the American Presidency;* Kohlsaat, *From McKinley to Harding, Personal Recollections of Our Presidents;* Leighton, *The Aspirin Age,* 1919-1941; Longworth, *Crowded Hours;* Lorant, *The Glorious Burden;* Lott, *The President's Speak;* Lowry, *Washington Close-ups;* Lustgarten, *The Story of Crime;* McLean, *Father Struck it Rich;* Means, *The Strange Death of President Harding;* Mee, *The Ohio Gang;* Messick, *Sceret File;* Nash, *Citizen Hoover;* ____, *Hustlers and Con Men;* Noggle, *Teapot Dome: Oil and Politics in the 1920s;* Powers, *Secrecy and Power;* Russell, *The Shadow of Blooming Grove, Warren G. Harding and His Times;* Scott, *The Concise Encyclopedia of Crime and Criminals;* Schriftgiesser, *This Was Normalcy;* Sinclair, *The Available Man: The Life Behind the Masks of Warren G. Harding;* Starling, *Starling in the White House;* Stoddard, *As I Knew Them;* Sullivan, *Our Times* (Vol VI); Unger, *FBI;* Werner, *Privileged Characters;* White, *The Autobiography of William Allen White;* Whitehead, *The FBI Story;* (FICTION) Sinclair, *Oil!.*

Teasdale, William, prom. 1938, Brit., mur. Police constable William Teasdale was engaged to be married, though he already had a wife and daughter. On Mar. 3, 1938, while at the theater with his fiancée enjoying *Me and My Girl,* the couple came face-to-face with his wife. He denied being married and claimed that the woman who said she was his wife was crazy. The next day, Ruby Jeannie May Teasdale was found strangled to death, and William Teasdale was arrested in Sunderland, England. He claimed that she struck him in the face and that he retaliated by holding her head down on a bed until she was unconscious. On Apr. 28, 1938, in the Old Bailey courtroom of Justice Goddard, Teasdale was found Guilty of murder and sentenced to death. He was reprieved on May 13, 1938.

REF.: *CBA;* Shew, *A Companion to Murder.*

Teashop in Limehouse, A, 1931, a short story collection by Thomas Burke. The collection offers a tale entitled "The Hands of Mr. Ottermole," which is clearly drawn from two serial killers, Dr. Thomas Neill Cream (U.S.-Brit., 1881-92), and Jack the Ripper (Brit., 1888), although the murderer in the story is a strangler, not a poisoner or slasher. (British title: *The Pleasantries of Old Quong.*) See: **Cream, Dr. Thomas Neill; Jack the Ripper.** REF.: *CBA.*

Tebbitt, William, b.1882, Brit., attempt. mur. On Mar. 4, 1912, Leopold de Rothschild, of the famed Rothschild banking family, was driving home from work when, without warning, William Tebbitt shot several rounds at close range into Rothschild's car.

The 67-year-old millionaire was unharmed. When Tebbitt, thirty, was arrested, police discovered he had known Rothschild since he was a boy. Tebbitt was pronounced insane and committed to the Broadmoor Criminal Lunatic Asylum.

REF.: *CBA;* Nicholls, *Crime Within the Square Mile.*

Tegart, Sir Charles Augustus, b.1881, Brit., law enfor. off. Officer on Indian police force from 1901-31. He served on the council of India from 1932-36, and spent the following year in Palestine helping the government organize its police force. He constructed "Tegart's Wall," the electrical wire barrier along the border of Palestine and Syria. REF.: *CBA.*

Tegh Bahadur c.1621-75, India, her. Sikh Guru charged by Emperor 'Alamgir I with assisting Hindus. He was put to death for resisting religious conversion to Islam, making him the second martyr of the Sikhs. REF.: *CBA.*

Teissier, Lazare, prom. 1924, Fr., mansl. Lazare Teissier was a Parisian concierge who also served as an illegal bookmaker. In May 1924, when he was being pressed by some his many creditors, Teissier was approached by 70-year-old Louis Boulay, whom he had long known as Pere Louis, to place some bets. He did so, and his client won. When Boulay came to collect on May 30, Teissier had decided to keep Boulay's winnings for himself. He took Boulay down into the dark cellar of the building which he managed and bashed him over the head, killing him.

Teissier hid the body in a small, dark, coal-storage cellar beyond the regular cellar. Before dawn on June 8, he wrapped it as a package and dumped it in the Bois de Boulogne, where it was found several hours later by a bicyclist. The victim was identified as Boulay through the missing persons file. Marks of coal dust were on the clothing, and further investigation by forensic scientist Edmond Bayle also revealed sand, sawdust, stone, and almost invisible particles of cardboard, and minute dead insects on Boulay's clothing. Teissier became a suspect and after many months, Bayle's innovative research proved to a jury that Boulay's body had been hidden in Teissier's coalbin. On Dec. 13, 1925, Lazare Teissier was found Guilty and sentenced to ten years in prison for manslaughter.

REF.: *CBA;* Thorwald, *Crime and Science.*

Teitelbaum, Hubert Irving, 1915- , U.S., jur. Appointed to western district court of Pennsylvania by President Richard Nixon in 1970. He was a FBI special agent from 1940-1943 and served as U.S. attorney from 1955-61. REF.: *CBA.*

Te Kooti Rikirangi, c.1830-93, New Zea., rebel. Founded Ringatu religious sect while jailed on Chatham Islands in 1867. He escaped the following year and headed a group of insurgents. He was absolved in 1883. REF.: *CBA.*

Tell, William, See: **Gessler.**

Telles, Felix, prom. 1927, Arg., mur. Augustin Martelletti was a partner in the firm of Cores, Martelletti, Hermanosa Cia, one of Argentina's oldest and wealthiest firms. During the night of Jan. 17, 1927, he and his wife were murdered in their apartment above the corporate offices. The two had been beaten unconscious with a blunt instrument and then stabbed. The next morning, employees discovered the gruesome scene, and began a manhunt. The break in the case came on Feb. 12, when the owner of a cleaning establishment notified police that he had received a pair of bloodstained trousers. The owner of the trousers was identified as Felix Telles. Telles was apprehended, and when confronted with the murder weapons, he broke down and confessed. He was a former employee who knew where valuables were hidden. Attempting to burgle the office, he was surprised by the couple. They recognized him, so he killed them. In one of Argentina's speediest trials, the judges unanimously found Telles Guilty and sentenced him to twenty years of hard labor on an island penal colony.

REF.: *CBA;* Cohen, *One Hundred True Crime Stories.*

Tellez, Hector, prom. 1986, U.S., consp. Hector Tellez, a resident of Oak Forest, Ill., plotted to lead a coup against the government of Surinam, formerly a Dutch colony on the northern coast of South America. Through *Soldier of Fortune* magazine and advertisements for mercenaries, he met Tommy Lee Denley, who was looking for someone to lead a military operation. Denley, a 45-year-old former U.S. Customs Service patrol officer, planned to oust Lieutenant Colonel Desi Bouterse as ruler of Surinam, and set up an international bank for laundering money. Tellez and Denley met several times in the Chicago area to coordinate plans to recruit sixteen men to overthrow Bouterse, pay them $500 a week, and a $1 million bonus after the overthrow.

Tellez contacted a military paraphernalia distributor in Chicago to purchase several machine guns, mines, and rockets. The wary distributor informed the FBI, which sent three agents to meet him. One of the agents was Tony Dunbar, who, through the distributor, met Tellez and told him that he was a munitions supplier who could outfit him. Tellez then took Dunbar to New Orleans to meet Denley and others involved in the coup plot, and disclosed the entire scheme to Dunbar: They would pose as potential buyers of a Surinam bank, and, while meeting with Bouterse and his top aides, take the country's leader hostage.

The plot came to a halt on July 28, 1986, when Tellez and thirteen others arrived at a small airport in New Orleans where they thought a DC-3, full of munitions, was ready to fly them to South America. Approaching the hanger, they were met by three FBI SWAT teams who arrested the entire group, with the exception of Dunbar.

Tellez pleaded guilty to federal charges of violating the neutrality act in November 1986 and was sentenced to eighteen months in prison, winning release in September 1987. The others pleaded guilty or no contest. During the investigation, Dunbar discovered that Denley planned to assassinate Tellez as he thought Tellez boasted too much and thus threatened the operation. REF.: *CBA*.

Telling, Michael, prom. 1983, Brit., mansl. Michael Telling was a wealthy young man. Rejected by his mother and alcoholic father, he spent his early life in boarding schools, and was drinking and smoking heavily by the age of nine. He was transferred to a special school for the maladjusted, and eventually to a mental institution. In 1978, Telling married an 18-year-old Australian girl, but the marriage quickly failed. Two years later he met Monika Zumsteg, who became his second wife in 1981. The marriage was a disaster. Monika's days were filled with alcohol, drugs, and infidelity. She publicly belittled him and admitted that she was only after his money.

On Mar. 29, 1983, as Monika berated him, Telling took a rifle and shot her to death, hitting her in the throat and the chest. He put her body on a bed, and left it there for two days, often kissing and talking to the corpse. He moved the body to the sauna, were it remained for five months. Teller returned to his normal routine, claiming that his wife had left him and gone to the U.S. In September, Telling decided to bury his wife, but to avoid identification he severed and kept her head. Two days later, the body was found and, through clothing, identified. Detectives found her skull in Telling's possession, and arrested him.

Telling was tried at Exeter Crown Court in June 1984. His defense rested on his state of mind, as nobody denied his guilt. After the lurid details of his life and marriage were splashed across the front pages of the British tabloids, the jury found Telling Guilty of manslaughter, not murder, and sentenced him to life in prison. REF.: *CBA*.

Telvi, Abraham, 1933-56, U.S., org. crime. Abraham Telvi, hit man for labor racketeer Johnny Dio in 1956, was recruited by Dio to blind Victor Riesel, a pro-labor newspaper columnist, with acid. One morning at 3 a.m., as Riesel walked out of New York City's Lindy's restaurant on Broadway, Telvi threw sulfuric acid, a chemical used in explosives, in his face, permanently blinding him. Dio and his conspirators paid Telvi $1,175 for the hit. The attack brought public pressure on the mob. Federal investigators persuaded two conspirators, one of them Gondolfo Miranti, to identify Dio as the plot's mastermind. Death threats from the mob, however, dissuaded Miranti and the other conspirator from testifying. In consideration of the extensive investigation, Telvi felt he deserved more for the hit, and, in anger, demanded more money. Dio and the other conspirators promised him a larger payoff within two weeks. On July 28, exactly two weeks later, on New York's Lower East Side, Telvi was murdered gangland style. REF.: *CBA*.

Temme, Jodocus Donatus Hubertus (AKA: **Heinrich Stahl**), 1798-1881, Case of, Ger., treas. Served as judge in Prussia from 1839-49. He was dismissed from the judiciary on a charge of treason, stemming from his liberal activities, but was acquitted. He also wrote many crime stories. REF.: *CBA*.

Templar, Henry George, 1904- , U.S., jur. Republican nominated to district court of Kansas by President John F. Kennedy in 1962. He earlier served as U.S. district attorney for Kansas from 1953-54. REF.: *CBA*.

Temür Khan (AKA: **Ch'eng Tsung**), 1267-1307, China, law enfor. Grandson and successor of Emperor Kublai Khan. He ruled China from 1295-1307, during which time he tried to eradicate political corruption and successfully quelled revolts in Korea and South China. REF.: *CBA*.

Tenderloin, 1870-90s, U.S., vice district. The "Tenderloin District" refers to the area of any major U.S. city where crime and vice flourish. The term originated in the late 1800s and referred to the district of New York City between Twenty-fourth and Fortieth streets and from Fifth to Seventh avenues. In the 1860s-70s, New York City was only the island of Manhattan. Estimates at the time calculated more than 20,000 full-time prostitutes and an equal number of part-timers operated in Manhattan, approximately one prostitute for every twenty persons. The island was home for 5,000 brothels. While Manhattan witnessed more crime and vice during the post-Civil War days than nearly all other U.S. cities combined, the Tenderloin itself teamed with prostitutes, pimps, footpads, madams, holdup men, live sex shows, pickpockets, swindlers, burglars, and murderers. For twenty blocks along Sixth Avenue, gin mills, dance halls, and brothels averaged ten per block, and it was once estimated that half the buildings in that area housed some form of vice. Competition in the Tenderloin for live sex shows grew so fierce that ticket prices dropped from $5 to fifty cents per person. Observing the immoral activity on Sixth Avenue, a Brooklyn minister called the place "Satan's Circus."

Part of the 29th Police District, the Tenderloin gave birth to the most far-reaching political corruption and police graft of its time. In 1876, Captain Alexander "Clubber" Williams organized police graft on a level it never achieved before nor since. He gave the district its name when he told a friend, "I've had nothing but chuck for a long time, and now I'm going to get the tenderloin." The Tenderloin survived from the 1860s until the 1890s when reformers, including police Commissioner Theodore Roosevelt, pressured the city for tighter control of vice and corruption. See: **Williams, Alexander S.**

REF.: Asbury, *The Gangs of New York*; *CBA*; Fried, *The Rise and Fall of the Jewish Gangster in America*; Lait and Mortimer, *Chicago: Confidential*; Logan, *Against the Evidence*.

Ten Most Wanted List, 1950- , U.S., law enfor. A casual request from a wire service reporter in 1949 led to the creation of the FBI's Ten Most Wanted List. The list included descriptions of the ten toughest fugitives the bureau would like to capture. The early 1930's was an age of spectacular gangsters: John Dillinger, Pretty Boy Floyd, Baby Face Nelson, Machine Gun Kelly, and Bonnie and Clyde. The Ten Most Wanted List replaced the occasional "Wanted" posters and the misunderstood "Public Enemy Number One." The "list" considers all entries to be of equal rank and occasionally expands to accommodate more people, if warranted by a particular crime spree. The list is used as an internal incentive for agents. Its history reveals the nature and evolution of crime. In the 1950s, bank robbers and murderers dominated the list, while today, terrorists and organized crime figures are included. REF.: *CBA*.

Tengler, Ulric, prom. 1509, Ger., witchcraft. When suspected witches were brought to trial in the early sixteenth century, they were prosecuted according to the book of Ulric Tengler. In 1509,

Tengler wrote *Layenspiegel Mirror for Layman,* the all-inclusive manual of witch prosecution. The book covered topics such as encouraging informers, prescribing tortures, and developing a line of questioning to determine the degree of demonic possession. The book, derived from the earlier *Malleus Maleficarum,* remained a popular witchcraft manual for the following 200 years.

REF.: *CBA;* Hansen, *Quellen und Untersuchungen zur Geschichte des Hexenwahns und der Hexenverfolgung im Mittelalter;* Lea, *Materials Toward a History of Witchcraft;* Robbins, *The Encyclopedia of Witchcraft and Demonology;* Tengler, *Layenspiegel;* ____, *Der neu Layenspiegel.*

Tennes, Jacob (AKA: Mont), 1874-1941, U.S., gamb. When Mike McDonald's Chicago gambling empire began to crumble, his protégé Jacob "Mont" Tennes was there to pick up the pieces. Though only a bit player in the Chicago underworld of 1897, Tennes was destined for major success in the next two decades. Tennes was born in Chicago on Jan. 16, 1874. He acquired his famous nickname from his mother; not from the famous card game, as popular legend would have it. Tennes' first job was as a bartender, and in 1898 he purchased a North Side saloon and billiard parlor, which eventually became a favored spot of the city's horse players and card sharpers.

By the turn of the century, Tennes was making his move to become the "king" of the North Side handbooks and poolrooms. Gambling interests south of Madison Street were dominated by James O'Leary, and to the west, by the Bud White-Harry Perry Syndicate. These men fought for control of the gambling territories in a more refined manner than their successors would during Prohibition. When Tennes wanted to move against his rivals, he called out the private constable force, headed by Dickie Dean to harass them. The Dean constables, a private agency who could legally arrest and incarcerate criminal offenders after receiving a proper warrant, got those warrants from Tennes. In 1907, a major gambling war broke out in Chicago between Tennes, South Side boss John O'Malley, and the White-Perry combine. At stake were the right of the White-Perry syndicate to keep the *City of Traverse* gambling ship afloat, and control of the "racing wire," a service which dispensed racetrack results from across the country to subscribing poolrooms. Tennes' monopoly on this service was being challenged by O'Malley, O'Leary, and the combine. Although the war dragged on through Summer and Fall 1907 and thirty-two bombs were thrown at the various poolrooms and handbooks were scattered across the city, there were no casualties.

Alderman Michael "Hinky Dink" Kenna was finally called in to arbitrate the dispute, and through his intervention, Tennes was dealt the winning hand. The *City of Traverse* was eventually closed down, and the White-Perry group ceased to operate in Chicago. Tennes claimed the spoils, and was soon recognized as the most powerful and influential gambler in Chicago since Mike McDonald. In 1910, Tennes founded the General News Bureau to compete with Payne. To eliminate Payne as competition, he bombed their Cincinnati headquarters. Afterward, the poolrooms of Chicago and other major cities had little choice but to fall in line.

Mont Tennes remained the gambling czar of Chicago until 1927 when he sold his majority interest in the racing wire to Moses Annenberg, one-time newspaper slugger. During Tennes' long career, he was never arrested or jailed. In 1916, Judge Kenesaw Mountain Landis presided over an inquiry into organized gambling in the city, but Tennes escaped censure. On Mar. 27, 1922, he was indicted for operating a horse betting parlor, but the case was not prosecuted after the state failed to establish a clear-cut conspiracy. After selling out to Annenberg and two of his own nephews, Tennes pursued other business interests. He died on Aug. 6, 1941. See: **Annenberg, Moses L.; Landis, Kenesaw Mountain; McDonald, Michael Cassius.**

REF.: Asbury, *Gem of the Prairie; CBA;* Demaris, *Captive City;* Kobler, *Al Capone;* Lait and Mortimer, *Chicago: Confidential;* Landesco, *Organized Crime in Chicago;* Lindberg, *Chicago Ragtime;* Nash, *Bloodletters and Badmen;* Reppetto, *The Blue Parade;* Reuter, *Disorganized Crime;* Smith, *Syndicate City.*

Tenth Avenue Gang, prom. 1860s-70s, U.S., org. crime. The Tenth Avenue Gang committed the first train robbery in Manhattan. Led by Ike Marsh, burglars and holdup men formed the gang in 1860. In 1868, two years after the Reno Gang committed the first U.S. train robbery, the Tenth Avenue Gang decided to rob a train because they were "as good as those cowboys." At Spuyten Duyvil in Upper Manhattan, Marsh and several other gang members boarded a Hudson River Railroad train, forced their way into the mail car, bound and gagged the guard, and threw a box containing $5,000 in cash and bonds over the side. The gang thus gained notoriety with the railroad and fame in the underground. Extensive investigations, however, by the railroad forced the Tenth Avenue Gang to merge with a larger, more powerful criminal organization, Hell's Kitchen Gang.

REF.: Asbury, *The Gangs of New York; CBA.*

Tenuto, Frederick J. (AKA: The Angel), prom. 1952, U.S., org. crime. Frederick "The Angel" Tenuto, was a diminutive thug whose greatest claim to fame was a crime for which he was never convicted. Tenuto escaped from the Philadelphia County Prison on Feb. 10, 1947, with four other inmates, including notorious bank robber Willie "The Actor" Sutton. In early 1952, Sutton was identified on a New York subway train by Arnold Schuster of Brooklyn. On Mar. 8, 1952, Schuster was killed after telling his story on television. The suspected murderer was Frederick Tenuto. Tenuto had been on the FBI's Ten Most Wanted list since May 24, 1950. He remained on the list until Mar. 9, 1964, when he was dropped because of rumors that he had died and had been secretly buried. Tenuto's name was on the list longer than any other, nearly fourteen years. REF.: *CBA.*

Frederick J. Tenuto, one of the FBI's "Most Wanted."

Tepes, Vlad, See: **Vlad Dracul.**

Tepic Prison Riot, 1988, Mex., pris. riot. On Dec. 22, 1988, inmates at the prison in Tepic, Mex., rioted after they were denied Christmas pardons. Twenty-four people, including the warden, were killed and six more injured during the two-day siege. A group of inmates held fourteen prison employees and thirty-two visiting relatives hostage until 130 commandos flown in from Mexico City quelled the disturbance in a fierce fifteen-minute gun battle. Four inmates and three prison guards were arrested for complicity in the uprising. REF.: *CBA.*

Teresa, c.1070-1130, Port., exile. Daughter of King Alfonso VI. She became regent in 1112 after the death of her husband, Henry of Burgundy. She was forced into exile in 1128 by the followers of her son, the future Afonso I, after refusing to release her powers to him. REF.: *CBA.*

Teresa, Vincent Charles (AKA: Fat Vinnie), 1930- , U.S., org. crime. The No. 3 man in the New England Mafia by his own admission, Vincent Teresa was considered the highest-ranking organized crime figure to become a federal witness. As such, Teresa differed from Joe Valachi, a government witness whose testimony a decade earlier was inconsistent and limited. Teresa claimed that Valachi was not close to the real power in the Mafia. With Jimmy "the Weasel" Fratianno, Teresa produced more convictions, solutions to murders, and leads on criminals than Valachi. When he started "singing" for the government, the mob placed a $500,000 price tag on his head, compared to Valachi's price of $100,000. Teresa turned witness while in prison, claiming the Mafia stole his money, refused to help his wife while he was locked up, and threatened one of his children. Teresa's knowledge of Mafia rackets and operations ranged from New England to Europe and the Bahamas. His testimony about casino operations, stock thefts, fixed horse races, numbers rackets, and gang wars led to the convictions of fifty Mafiosi. In court, he even testified against Meyer Lansky—something no other informer dared to do.

During his twenty-eight-year career as a Mafioso, $150 million poured into Mafia coffers through his efforts. For himself, Teresa made $10 million as a Mafia boss. During his time as a federal witness, he wrote a book, *My Life in the Mafia,* with Thomas C. Renner. After testifying, the government sheltered Teresa under the Federal Witness Protection Program. He assumed the name Charles Cantino, whose address was listed as Maple Valley, Wash. In December 1984, the government blew his cover after he allegedly smuggled endangered animals into the country. A grand jury indicted Teresa and five family members that December. See: **Fratianno, Jimmy; Lansky, Meyer; Valachi, Joseph Michael.**

REF.: Bonanno, *A Man of Honor; CBA;* Davis, *Mafia Kingfish;* Eisenberg and Landau, *Meyer Lansky;* Fried, *The Rise and Fall of the Jewish Gnagster in America;* Kirby and Renner, *Mafia Enforcer;* Peterson, *The Mob.*

Terig, Duncan (AKA: **Duncan Clerk**), and **Macdonald, Alexander Bain**, prom. 1749, Case of, Scot., mur. Arthur Davis served as a sergeant in the British army and commanded an eight-man regiment in the Scottish Highland area of Dubrach, near Braemer. He was known as an officer of tact and moderation, who had married the widow of a former comrade. On Sept. 28, 1749, Davis left his home early in the morning, never to return. He was last seen climbing a hill to shoot a deer—behavior his men found strange, as he rarely ventured out alone. He was reported missing the following day. A search party was organized, but abandoned after four days.

Nine months later, in June 1750, Donald Farquharson, who had been Davis' landlord, received a message from Alexander McPherson, who said he had been visited by the ghost of Davis. The ghost insisted that the bones of the deceased be buried and directed him to the exact location of the body. When asked who killed the sergeant, the ghost disappeared. McPherson led Farquharson to the body, and the two men buried the remains. The ghost story became legend throughout the area, as well as a rumor that the ghost had named two young Inverey men, Duncan Terig, alias Clerk, and Alexander Bain Macdonald as the murderers. Their guilt was speculated about for almost four years, until they were arrested and held at the castle of Braemer in September 1753.

The trial of Terig and Macdonald began on June 10, 1754, at the High Court of Justiciary in Edinburgh, before Lord Justice-Clerk Alva. McPherson testified of his ghostly encounters with the dead sergeant, while others testified that Terig's wife was seen wearing a ring that had belonged to the deceased. In addition, an eyewitness said he saw the two men shooting Davis. Two days later, after twenty-one consecutive hours of testimony, the defendants were found Not Guilty and released.

REF.: *CBA;* de la Torre, *Villainy Detected;* Gribble, *Murders Most Strange.*

Terpening, Oliver, Jr. (AKA: **Jacobowsky**), 1930- , U.S., mur. Wondering what it would be like to watch someone die, 16-year-old farm boy Oliver Terpening, Jr., shot his 14-year-old friend, Stanley Smith, while the two boys were searching for crows outside Imlay City, Mich., on May 26, 1947.

Terpening shot Stanley with his father's .22-caliber rifle as he rested beneath a tree. Then, when Stanley's three sisters arrived on the scene, he shot them, too. "I thought the best thing to do was kill them all," he said. The bodies of Barbara Smith, sixteen, Gladys Smith, twelve, and Janet Smith, two, were found several hours later by their sister, Ella Mae Smith, roughly 100 yards from where their brother had been killed. Wildflowers were found in their hands. Terpening went home and ate his dinner, but it "went down pretty hard," as he later recalled. Realizing that the authorities were probably onto him, Terpening stole the family car and drove to Port Huron, Mich., where he abandoned it.

Without a dime in his pocket, Terpening hitchhiked through Detroit and camped out for the night in a filling station on U.S. Highway 24 near the Ohio state line. Concerned for his son's safety, Oliver Terpening, Sr., notified the Michigan State Police, who issued a physical description of the boy on all the local radio stations.

Terpening was spotted by a farmer from Erie, Mich., as he stood on the side of the road, with his thumb out. The farmer's son, Norman Dombrosky, Jr., recognized the hitchhiker from the radio accounts. When asked where he wanted to go, Terpening said: "Any place." "I told him my name was Jacobowsky," he said later, "and that I lived on Flager Street in Toledo. I'd seen that street name in Port Huron and it was the first that came to mind." The elder Dombrosky was suspicious, so he drove to the outskirts of the city and the offices of Justice R.O. Stevens, who had Terpening arrested by local constables.

Terpening was taken back to Erie, where he was questioned about the four murders. "I've always kinda wondered what it would be like to kill somebody," he said in a matter-of-fact way. "I'll tell the truth. I did it. I just wanted to see someone die." Terpening added that he didn't get the kind of thrill he was looking for when he originally decided to murder his friend.

Terpening's father told police that his son had always been a problem child. After he dropped out of the eleventh grade, he ran away to Louisiana because he could not get along with his stepmother. There were times, said the younger Terpening, when he wanted to kill her. His discouraged father sent him $25 for a train ticket when his money ran out.

Circuit Court Judge Albert Perkins signed the warrant accusing Terpening of murder. On June 10, 1947, however, Terpening was declared by three psychiatrists to be mentally unbalanced. At this writing, he remains confined in the G. Robert Cotton correctional facility in Jackson, Mich. REF.: *CBA.*

Ter-Petrosyan, Semyon (AKA: **Kamo**), 1882-1922, U.S.S.R, (unsolv.) mur. An Armenian, Semyon Ter-Petrosyan, under the pseudonym Kamo, committed robberies on orders from Joseph Stalin to help finance the Bolshevik Revolution. He was infamous for the robbery of a post office coach in Tbilisi, Georgia, in 1907. Once the Soviets came to power, the crimes became an embarrassment, and Ter-Petrosyan and others died by mysterious means. Ter-Petrosyan was eulogized in July 1922 as a loyal party member. But with his death, the details of the pillaging of Transcaucasia will never be known.

REF.: *CBA;* Chalidze, *Criminal Russia.*

Terranova, Ciro (AKA: **Artichoke King**), 1881-1938, U.S., org. crime. Operating under the Morello Family and Ignazio Saietta, Ciro Terranova was Dutch Schultz's junior partner and an underboss for Joe "the Boss" Masseria. He was also the most overrated Mafioso boss. For a time he ran a racket in artichokes, a staple of Italians, and the newspapers called him "Artichoke King." According to mob informant Joe Valachi, Terranova cornered the market on artichokes coming into New York City and then named his price.

He gained fame as a killer who ordered and committed several murders. Yet Terranova felt more comfortable leaning on the strength of the Morello family, playing a dynamic secondary role without accepting the responsibility of leadership. Thus Mafia bosses grew to consider him a coward and a weakling. When Saietta and others of the Morello family passed the torch of leadership in the 1920s, Terranova passed up the opportunity to claim control of New York's Mafioso, and Masseria became the dominant New York boss. Later, in 1930-31, during the Maranzano-Masseria war, Terranova showed no initiative, allowing Charles "Lucky" Luciano to demonstrate leadership and gain prominence. Terranova became merely a Morello gang appendage, overshadowed by younger, more dynamic crime bosses.

Luciano and Vito Genovese grew to hate Terranova and began to strip him of his power. Their contempt for him was rooted in an incident when Terranova was to be the get-away driver for Masseria's murderers. After Genovese, Albert Anastasia, Joe Adonis, and Benjamin "Bugsy" Siegel shot Masseria dead in a restaurant, they walked outside to find Terranova trembling so hard he could not put the car into gear. Siegel shoved him aside and drove away. When Luciano ordered the murder of Dutch Schultz, he also retired Terranova, who was attempting to take control of the Harlem numbers racket. Although a mob boss forcibly retired was usually executed to avoid his going to war to retain power, Luciano spared Terranova because he correctly predicted that Terranova would do nothing. Terranova died three years later, his death considered by the mob to be the final death of the Morello gang. See: **Adonis, Joe; Anastasia, Albert; Genovese, Vito; Luciano, Charles; Masseria, Joe; Saietta, Ignazio; Schultz, Dutch; Siegel, Benjamin; Valachi, Joseph Michael.**

New York crime boss Ciro Terranova.

REF.: *CBA;* Cressey, *Theft of the Nation;* Eisenberg and Landau, *Meyer Lansky;* Gage, *Mafia, U.S.A.;* Gosch and Hammer, *The Last Testament of Lucky Luciano;* Katz, *Uncle Frank;* Kobler, *Al Capone;* Lait and Mortimer, *Chicago: Confidential;* Levine, *Anatomy of a Gangster;* Lynch, *Criminals and Politicians;* Maas, *The Valachi Papers;* Messick, *Secret File;* Nash, *Bloodletters and Badmen;* Peterson, *The Mob;* Reid, *The Grim Reapers;* Sann, *Kill the Dutchman;* Thompson, *Gang Rule in New York.*

Terrell, William, prom. 1840s, U.S., mur. The first "officially recorded" homicide of Atlanta, Ga., was the stabbing of James McWilliams by William Terrell on the night of Sept. 14, 1848. Young men from wealthy families, they had been at odds for months over political issues. While drumming up votes, they accidentally met in front of the house of John Kile, Jr., and began to scuffle. McWilliams knocked Terrell down and then jumped on him. Terrell managed to free a hand, withdraw a six-inch knife, and plunge it into the cursing McWilliams.

Terrell then fled as doctors tried to save McWilliams' life. It was no use. McWilliams died the next day. Apprehended in Alabama, Terrell was returned to Atlanta where he was found Guilty of voluntary homicide and given a four-year prison term. REF.: *CBA.*

Terrill, Ray, See: **Kimes-Terrill Gang.**

Terror on Broadway, 1954, a novel by David Alexander. Jack the Ripper visits Times Square and begins his horrific murders all over again. See: **Jack the Ripper**. REF.: *CBA.*

Terrorism, See: **Supplements,** Vol. IV.

Terry, David S., See: **Neagle, David.**

Terry, David Smith, 1823-89, U.S., duel-asslt. David Terry was a bombastic, posturing soldier-politician whose celebrated pistol duel with Senator David C. Broderick foreshadowed his own demise thirty years later. Terry was born in Todd County, Ky., but moved with his family to Texas in 1833. At age thirteen he fought on the side of the Texans at the battle of San Jacinto. Admitted to the bar in 1843, he took time out from his legal work to enlist in the U.S. Army, then engaged in a war with Mexico for control of the Texas territory. The California Gold Rush lured Terry westward in 1849. After staking his claim in Calavaras County he retired to private law practice in Stockton. In September 1855, he was elected chief justice of the California Supreme Court on the Know-Nothing ticket. By this time he was in the public limelight and carried tremendous responsibilities.

These weighty matters did not deter Terry from lashing out against those individuals to whom he took offense, however. On June 20, 1856, the San Francisco Vigilance Committee arrested him for assaulting one of their members, Sterling A. Hopkins, with a knife while Hopkins endeavored to arrest Reuben Maloney. During his period in jail, Terry, a strident foe of the Vigilantes, was befriended by David Broderick, a power in state politics who did what he could to secure his release.

At the Lecompton Convention of 1859 Broderick was in control of the state delegation and Terry desired renomination. For practical reasons the senator decided not to nominate Terry, who then went out and delivered an incendiary reply to Sacramento legislators accusing them of cowardice. Two days later Broderick sat discussing the matter over breakfast at the International Hotel in San Francisco with D.W. Perley, Terry's former law partner. The senator referred to his former friend as a "damned miserable ingrate." Taking offense, Perley challenged Broderick to a duel in Terry's name, but with an impending election the senator deferred action until after Sept. 7 when the campaign would be over. Broderick lost his re-election bid and found himself in the unenviable position of having to face the hotheaded Terry on the field of honor.

Calhoun Benham, former district attorney of San Francisco, was designated to handle the arrangements for the duel which took place at sunrise on Sept. 11, 1859, near Lake Merced in San Mateo County. In respect to his office, Judge Terry deemed it prudent to step down. Detectives I.W. Lees and H.H. Ellis issued warrants for their arrest. After the distances had been marked, Terry and Broderick were taken into custody, but their cases were obligingly dismissed by Judge Coon on Sept. 12. The next day the combatants met again. They agreed that the signal to fire would be at the count of three. However, Broderick's pistol discharged prematurely, the bullet landing harmlessly at Terry's feet. At the count of two Terry coldly took aim and fired. The ball pierced Broderick in the chest and he fell to the ground mortally wounded.

David Broderick, killed by David Terry in 1859.

Broderick died five days later and an arrest warrant charging the judge with murder was sworn out. Terry surrendered in Oakland after receiving a promise from the courts for a change of venue. The case was dismissed in Marin County by Judge James Hardy, but Terry subsequently was indicted by the grand jury of San Mateo County. After considerable legal wrangling he was acquitted but was ostracized by the community at large. He went into self-imposed exile in Virginia City for a short time, then returned to Stockton to resume his law practice. The Civil War found him in the service of the Confederacy as a brigadier general. When the war ended Terry remained behind in Texas where he worked in the cotton and wool industries. Failing at these endeavors, he returned to Stockton to practice law. In the 1870s, Terry regained a measure of his former political power. He was elected a delegate to the state constitutional convention in 1878 and a presidential elector two years later. But complications set in following the death of his wife, Cornelia Runnels, on Dec. 24, 1884.

A year later Terry became interested in a property dispute between Sarah Althea Hill, a Missouri woman who had come to California in 1870, and U.S. senator William Sharon, the man she claimed entered into a marriage contract with her on Aug. 25,

1880. Sharon, who owned a hotel in Nevada and was a millionaire twice over, arranged through his attorneys to have the contract declared null and void. Terry took charge of the case after Hill created a sensation by pointing a gun at Judge O.P. Evans during the hearing. "I am not going to shoot you now unless you would like to be shot and think you deserve it!" she said. Such a woman was ideally suited to the temperament of a man like Terry. On Jan. 7, 1886, he married the 38-year-old Hill and at the same time renewed his fight for part of Senator Sharon's estate. On Sept. 24, 1888, Sarah's hopes were shattered when Stephen Field, then a U.S. Supreme Court justice denied her petition. "How much money did you get for that decision?" the woman screamed. U.S. Marshal Franks dragged Mrs. Terry from the courtroom. Terry drew out a Bowie knife and advanced toward Franks but was pulled aside before he could inflict a serious injury. He was sentenced to six months in the Alameda County Jail for this outburst and his wife to thirty days for hers.

Terry, making no secret of his displeasure with Justice Field's decision, swore he would have his revenge as soon as he was out of jail. Hearing of this, Field appointed Deputy U.S. Marshal David Neagle to serve as his bodyguard. Neagle, a western gunfighter of stature, had served for a time as the city marshal of Tombstone, Ariz. Once when one of his deputies was killed in a gunfight with a Mexican desperado, Neagle rode off into the hills to track his man down. He returned the next day with the body of the dead Mexican slung over the saddle. On Aug. 13, 1889, Field and Neagle left Los Angeles for San Francisco by train. In Fresno the Terrys boarded the same train but did not run into Field or his hired gun until the next morning. The train rumbled into Lathrop at 8:15 a.m. The conductor advised the passengers that there was time to have breakfast in the dining room of the depot. Terry spied his antagonist across the room, whereby Sarah exited the depot in a hurry. The headwaiter, T.W. Stackpole, asked Terry if he contemplated an act of violence in his restaurant. Terry mumbled an incoherent statement and walked over to Justice Field's table. He slapped him in the face, which brought Neagle to his feet. Showing no fear, Terry reached for Field a second time. Neagle stuck the gun in Terry's chest and fired.

Judge David S. Terry.

David Neagle shooting David Terry in 1889.

The hysterical widow swore out an arrest warrant for Justice Field charging him with complicity to murder. The circuit court dismissed the charges against Field on Aug. 27, 1889. Neagle's case was thrown out on Sept, 16, 1889. The grateful Field presented him with a gold watch and chain as a token of esteem. Mrs. Terry, meanwhile, had to be committed to the Stockton Insane Asylum. See: **San Francisco Vigilance Committee.**

REF.: Buchanan, *David S. Terry of California; CBA;* Duke, *Celebrated Criminal Cases of America.*

Terry, John Victor, 1940-c.1961, Brit., mur. On Nov. 10, 1960, 20-year-old John Victor Terry, upon hearing of the execution of his friend Francis "Flossie" Forsyth, claimed he had become the reincarnation of U.S. gangster "Legs" Diamond. He then walked into a bank in Sussex, England, and shot a bank guard in the head. When apprehended, he defended his actions by saying, "When a person dies his mind leaves him and goes into another body. My mind was from Legs Diamond." The hallucination may have been caused by Terry's drug use. He was found Guilty of the murder, and in the end, he emulated not Legs Diamond, but Flossie Forsyth, when he hanged from the same gallows at Wandsworth Prison. REF.: *CBA.*

Tessnov, Ludwig, d.1904, Ger., mur. At the turn of the century, a German chemist named Paul Uhlenhuth, experimenting with human and animal blood, discovered that if the two samples were mixed together the blood serum of the human would not react in any way to that of the animal's. Uhlenhuth determined that a rabbit injected with a specimen of human blood would develop a natural resistance to it. His research with bloodstains proved invaluable to criminologists and members of the legal profession attempting to use this material as evidence during important murder trials.

The first practical application of Uhlenhuth's theories to a crime involved an itinerant German carpenter named Ludwig Tessnov, implicated in the sex-murders of four German children between 1898 and June 1901. At the same time a farmer in Göhren reported the slaughter of six or seven sheep. The entrails of the animals were scattered across a wide plain. The similarities between the mutilation of the animals and that of the children were so remarkable the prosecutor of Greifswald asked Uhlenhuth to conduct an analysis. "If we prove the presence of sheep blood, that, along with identification by the shepherd, should make it clear that Tessnov is the killer of the sheep. And considering the way his clothing is spattered, some of it must be human blood, too." Uhlenhuth received two bundles of Tessnov's clothing on July 29, 1901. The scientific community anxiously awaited the results.

The tragedy of the children began in the village of Lechtingen, outside Osnabrück, on Sept. 9, 1898, when two girls, Hannelore Heidemann and Else Langemier, failed to return home from school. A search party that evening found the girls lying dead in a patch of bushes in the surrounding woods, their bodies hacked to pieces. A journeyman carpenter, identified by local authorities as Ludwig Tessnov of Baabe on the island of Rügen, explained that the red spatter marks on his work clothes were wood stains. Unable to conduct a chemical blood analysis, police released Tessnov and the murders entered the books as officially unsolved.

The shocking crime was repeated almost exactly on July 1, 1901, on the Baltic island of Rügen, when Hermann Stubbe, eight, and his brother Peter, six, failed to show up for their evening meal. The boy's father, joined by a policeman and several villagers, searched the adjacent woods with little success. The next morning a neighbor found the mangled bodies in a thicket. The arms and legs had been hacked off and their organs scattered through the woods. Nearby investigators found a bloodstained rock that presumably had been used by the murderer. A local fruit peddler reported to police on July 2 that she observed Tessnov talking to the children shortly before their disappearance.

Tessnov was arrested on suspicion. He claimed that the spots on his hat were cattle blood and other stains resulted from varnish he used in his work. Dr. Uhlenhuth, aided by an assistant, examined nearly 100 stains. He demonstrated through sophisticated blood analysis that there were definite traces of human blood in six areas of Tessnov's trousers, vest, and jacket. Uhlenhuth's evidence not only helped convict Tessnov, but his work with bloodstains greatly advanced forensic science. Tessnov was executed at Greifswald Prison in 1904.

REF.: *CBA;* Thorwald, *The Century of the Detective;* ____, *Dead Men Tell Tales.*

Testa, Philip (AKA: Chicken Man), 1924-81, U.S., org. crime. When Philadelphia mob boss Angelo Bruno was assassinated in 1980 by New York's crime families, Philip Testa assumed control of the Philadelphia Mafia. Unlike the New York families, the Philadelphia Mafia was homogeneous and had experienced two decades of peace under Bruno's leadership. Bruno most likely was killed so that the New York families could move into Atlantic City to control the lucrative, newly legal gambling casinos. The underboss in Bruno's regime, Testa, was the most violent person in the organization and a tough leader who would fight for what the Philadelphia Mafia considered to be its own: Atlantic City's crime concessions. Using a chicken shop as cover, Testa controlled the organized crime of Philadelphia for nearly a year. The city, which once regarded its Mafia with a fond tolerance, watched Testa's short career with enthusiasm. A restaurant called Cous' Little Italy added the Testa Burger to its menu, promoting it with such phrases as, "If you didn't eat it, you'd get your fingers broken." An astrologer predicted Testa's future, "...no matter what's going on, Testa will come out in a better position than he started." This prediction, however, was proved wrong when in March 1981, less than a year after Bruno's assassination, a remote-control bomb filled with shrapnel was planted under Testa's porch, killing him when he returned to home in the middle of the night. Crime analysts speculated that either the New York mobs struck again, or that Philadelphia's mob was no longer was cohesive and someone in his own organization killed him. Cous' Little Italy stopped serving the Testa Burger the night after he was blown up. REF.: *CBA.*

Testa, Salvatore, 1956-84, U.S., org. crime. Salvatore Testa aspired to be a Mafia Don like his father, Philip Testa, who was killed in 1981. He became a capo, or lieutenant, under Philadelphia's new boss, Nickodemo Scarfo, less than a year after his father's death. While still in his twenties, Testa survived two attempts on his life and gained a reputation as "unkillable." The first attempt occurred while Testa sat eating clams outside a South Philadelphia pizza parlor. Two men approached his table and blasted him out of his chair with shotguns. Though hit in eight places, he survived. The executioners were caught by police and identified as soldiers for rival Mafia boss Harry Riccobene. The second attempt made on Testa's life occurred while he and three bodyguards drove through a warehouse district. A car with four Riccobene enforcers cut them off and opened fire. Testa emerged unharmed. From then on, he considered his opponents incompetent.

Testa's complacency made him careless and he thought he needed no protection. He left his house alone on Sept. 14, 1984, dressed in tennis whites for an afternoon of sports. At 10:23 p.m., his body was found twenty miles southeast of Philadelphia along a country road. He had been shot twice in the back of the head with a small caliber gun at close range, making him the twenty-third casualty since the 1981 murder of Philadelphia boss Angelo Bruno. REF.: *CBA.*

Tester, William, See: **Great Gold Robbery.**

Testro, Angelina, prom. 1912, U.S., mur. During Franklin D. Roosevelt's tenure as governor of New York from 1929 to 1933, he pardoned Angelina Testro, who had served eighteen years of a life sentence at Auburn Prison for murdering her intended on their wedding day.

Testro, a 43-year-old widow, ran a rooming house in the Bronx. A young tenant, Arturo Costello, known throughout the neighborhood as "the Dude," began to pay her attention, which she returned. She also lent him small sums of money to purchase a stylish wardrobe. The widow begged Costello to marry her, and they procured the marriage license. With Testro in her wedding dress and a priest waiting, a friend of Costello entered the home and said that Costello would not go through with the marriage unless he received $400. That evening, she met her lover at a nearby railway bridge. He was found shortly thereafter with a knife protruding from his chest, gasping his last few breaths.

Angelina Testro confessed to the crime, saying, "I killed him because he made a fool of me." She was found Guilty of murder in the first degree and sentenced to death at Sing Sing. But Governor Whitman commuted the sentence to life, and she served eighteen years before being given a full pardon by Governor Roosevelt. REF.: *CBA.*

Tetzner, Kurt Erich (AKA: Stranelli), 1903-31, Ger., fraud, asslt.-mur. Kurt Erich Tetzner, a young German businessman, was convicted of killing an unidentified man as part of an insurance fraud. In an earlier insurance fraud, Tetzner convinced his mother-in-law to postpone an operation for cancer so that he could insure her life. She subsequently underwent an operation and died.

Successful in his first effort, he and his wife decided to find another victim. After failing once to entrap a victim, on Nov. 25, 1929, he picked up a hitchhiker, murdered him, crashed his car into a tree, and then set it on fire with the victim at the wheel. Tetzner's wife claimed that the victim was her husband and attempted to claim the death benefit on Tetzner's accident policies.

However, physical discrepancies between the victim and Tetzner caused suspicion. Using recently developed forensic medicine techniques, officials determined by the condition of the victim's lungs that he had been dead before the fire.

Tetzner, meanwhile, had hidden in Strasbourg, Fr., using the assumed name of Stranelli. Apprehended there by police, he readily confessed. He was tried in March 1931, found Guilty, and put to death at Regensburg on May 2, 1931.

REF.: Boar, *The World's Most Infamous Murders;* Brophy, *The Meaning of Murder; CBA;* Thorwald, *The Century of the Detective;* ____, *Dead Men Tell Tales;* Wilson, *Encyclopedia of Murder.*

Teuber, Louise, 1914-31, U.S., (unsolv.) mur. In the early 1930s, San Diego was plagued by a rash of unsolved murders. One victim, Virginia Brooks, was found on a deserted mesa on Feb. 11, 1931. Then, just two months later on Apr. 19, 12-year-old Fred Chase told police about a woman he saw tied and gagged in the back seat of a blue Dodge sedan at the foot of Black Mountain.

Police investigating the site found nothing until picnickers discovered a young woman hanging naked from the limb of a stunted oak tree, six miles east of La Mesa, Calif. Clothing, an army blanket, and the addresses of school friends were found nearby. The body was identified as that of 17-year-old Louise Teuber, a dime store clerk. With little evidence to go on except the sailor's knot the killer had used to tie the noose, police surmised that the murderer was a seaman or merchant marine. A wound at the base of the skull indicated that Teuber had been bludgeoned before she was hanged.

Police tried to reconstruct Teuber's movements after she quit her job at the dime store. With her last paycheck, she purchased clothing from a local store and was seen leaving the store with a young man. That was the last anyone saw of her.

Teuber's diary was made public, and an image of Louise as a fun-loving party girl with many boyfriends began to emerge. Allegations that she was secretly married or planning to elope were later discounted. "Louise was never married," explained Mrs. J.A. Prouty, Teuber's sister. "She was having too much fun."

Local cafes and restaurants were searched when a chemist's report indicated that Teuber had eaten shortly before her death. Although this knowledge established the approximate time of the murder, it provided no new clues to the killer's identity. The mystery was never solved, though some police investigators believed there was a definite link to Elton M. Stone, who confessed to killing Mary Louise Stammar in Fresno in November 1935. Stone, however, had never been at sea and would not have been able to tie the kind of knot used to hang Louise Teuber. See: **Stone, Elton M.** REF.: *CBA.*

Teufel, Albert, prom. 1866, U.S., mur. The body of James Wiley, the captain of the *Ohio,* was discovered beside a canal near

Narrowsville, Penn., on Nov. 25, 1866. An apparent robbery victim, he had also been brutally beaten, his mouth was stuffed with cloth, and a noose was around his neck. Wiley had been accompanied on the voyage by crewmen Harman Rick and Albert Teufel. On Feb. 6, 1867, after testimony by Rick, Teufel was indicted for Wiley's murder. Teufel was brought to trial the following day in the Bucks County Courtroom of Justice Chapman, and on Feb. 12, 1867, was found Guilty of first-degree murder. Teufel denied his guilt and said the actual murderers were his father, Christian Teufel, and Rick. However, the jury abided by their initial conviction and Teufel was sentenced to death by hanging.

REF.: *CBA; Life, Adventures and Confessions of Albert Teufel, Convicted of the Murder of James Wiley.*

Tevendale, Brian, 1945- , and **Garvie, Sheila W.**, c.1934- , Scot., mur. Maxwell Garvie married Sheila Watson in 1955 and during the next nine years, the couple had three children. In 1967, Sheila Watson Garvie began an affair with 22-year-old Brian Tevendale, while her husband became attracted to Tevendale's married sister, Trudy Birse. The foursome cavorted until May 14, 1968, when Maxwell Garvie left on a trip from which he was not to return. Five days later, he was reported missing and a search began. Mrs. Garvie admitted to her mother that she killed her husband, and her mother went to the police. In mid-August the body of Garvie, bludgeoned and shot through the neck, was found in an underground tunnel. On Aug. 17, Mrs. Garvie, Tevendale, and another friend, Alan Peters, were charged with the murder. In November, Mrs. Garvie and Tevendale were found Guilty of murder and sentenced to life. Peters was released when the court found his participation in the crime Not Proven.

REF.: *CBA;* Harris, *The Garvie Trial;* Heppenstall, *The Sex War and Others;* Wilson, *Encyclopedia of Modern Murder.*

Pirate Thomas Tew, left, regaling Governor Benjamin Fletcher with his escapades.

Tew, Thomas, prom. 1694, U.S., pir. Piracy and profiting from piracy were common in the American colonies at the end of the seventeenth century. Pirates were welcomed to the colonial markets, where they sold their goods at high prices. The pirate Thomas Tew made frequent journeys to the Red Sea area, where he plundered Arab merchant ships of their cargo. On one voyage, Tew returned to Boston with a large cargo of ivory tusks, gold, and silver. The spoils were divided per previous agreement between the ship's backers and the pirates. Open consorting with pirates and backing of their voyages became commonplace. Governor Benjamin Fletcher of Pennsylvania was so flagrant with his involvement with piracy that he finally lost his position and was returned to England. Tew was eventually killed in the Red Sea by a cannon shot from an enemy ship.

REF.: *CBA;* Mitchell, *Pirates;* Rankin, *The Golden Age of Piracy.*

Tewksbury, Edwin, d.1904, U.S., west. gunman-lawman. John D. Tewksbury and his Indian wife had three sons, Edwin, James, and John, Jr. In 1880 the family moved to Pleasant Valley, Ariz., and began raising sheep. A feud broke out in 1887, when the Tewksburys opposed the Hash Knife cowboys and the Grahams, a ranching family. The Grahams and the cowboys, who believed sheep ruined the grazing land for cattle, ambushed the Tewksbury clan twice. In the first ambush, the Tewksburys were at a hideout when Edwin Tewksbury, posted as a lookout, spied a cowboy crawling toward the camp. He called to his brother, Jim, who shot and killed the cowboy, allowing the Tewksburys to escape. Then, on Sept. 2, the Grahams ambushed and killed John Tewksbury and Bill Jacobs. The surviving Tewksburys, trapped in a cabin, fended off a day-long assault before escaping. The feud ended shortly thereafter. Nearly five years later, John Graham, the leader of the Graham faction, was ambushed and fatally wounded while driving a load of grain into Tempe, Ariz. Before he died, he named Edwin Tewksbury and John Rhodes as his murderers. The two were arrested and spent two and a half years in jail before they were acquitted in 1896. Edwin Tewksbury served as constable of Globe, Ariz., and deputy of Gila County until his death in 1904. See: **Tewksbury, Jim.**

REF.: *CBA;* Coolidge, *Fighting Men of the West;* Drago, *Great Range Wars;* Forrest, *Arizona's Dark and Bloody Ground;* Raine, *Famous Sheriffs and Western Outlaws.*

Tewksbury, Jim, d.1888, U.S., west. gunman. Jim Tewksbury was a violent member of the Tewksbury family, who began raising sheep in Pleasant Valley, Ariz., angering the Hash Knife cowboys and the Grahams, a ranching family. Graham offered a $500 reward for the death of one of the sheepherders and $1000 for the clan leader John Tewksbury, Sr. Outnumbered, the Tewksburys were forced to move their herds from camp to camp. Jim, alerted by his brother, Edwin, killed one of the Hash Knife cowboys when they attempted to ambush the sheepherders. The other cowboys were afraid to move, and their injured companion bled to death. On Aug. 10, 1887, eight cowboys led by Tom Tucker rode to Jim's cabin, hoping to fight. A shootout ensued in which Jim and his friends killed Hampton Blevins and John Paine, and wounded Tucker, Bob Gillespie, and Bob Carrington. Two weeks after John, Sr., and Bill Jacobs were killed in ambush, the Tewksburys were attacked at dawn by several cowboys. Jim Tewksbury and Jim Roberts, firing from their blankets, killed Harry Middleton and wounded Joe Underwood before driving off the others. Jim Tewksbury died in his cabin in 1888 of consumption. See: **Tewksbury, Edwin.**

REF.: *CBA;* Coolidge, *Fighting Men of the West;* Drago, *Great Range Wars;* Forrest, *Arizona's Dark and Bloody Ground;* Raine, *Famous Sheriffs and Western Outlaws.*

Texarkana (Texas) Slayings, 1946, U.S., (unsolv.) rape-mur. For three terror-filled weeks in Winter and Spring 1946, the residents of Texarkana, Texas, spoke of little else but the five heinous murders committed by an unknown madman in "lover's lane." Dozens of suspects were arrested and questioned, but all were cleared of the murders, which began on a moonlit night in late February 1946. Lou Denton and his girlfriend, Irma Black, were parked off Morris Lane, a mile west of Texarkana. They were listening to the radio and necking when suddenly a masked assailant crept up from behind and struck Denton over the head with the butt of a revolver. The gunman seized Black and threw her to the ground. After beating and raping her, the man rifled Black's purse and Denton's wallet for money. Then he disappeared.

Denton and Black later described the rapist to Sheriff W.H. Presley and Deputy Zeke Hensley as a man who stood six feet tall and weighed 185 pounds. A set of tire tracks found near the scene of the crime suggested that the gunman was driving a compact car. A check of local automotive dealerships was made to see if any tires matching the tire tracks had been sold in recent weeks. In the days that followed dozens of tips from anxious citizens poured in, but police had little tangible evidence.

A month later, on Mar. 24, Richard Griffin, twenty-four, and his 19-year-old girlfriend, Polly Ann Moore, parked their car on North Park Road, less than a mile from where Black and Denton were assaulted. Lurking in the shadows fifty feet away was the lover's lane rapist. Armed with a small-caliber handgun he advanced on the couple. The next morning a café worker named Charles Walters noticed a parked car in the patch of woods. Then he recoiled in horror at what he saw. Lying 200 yards away was the body of Moore. She had been raped and shot to death. Griffin was less than a few yards away. "I'd say the chap was killed at least two hours or more before the young woman was," the examining physician concluded. "The murderer held his gun very close to the victims. Powder burns are evident around the wounds on both bodies." Six suspects were questioned. A detachment of Texas Rangers conducted a house-to-house search for a vehicle that matched the tire tracks found nearby. "It's not probable that two criminals are driving cars with identical tires," Sheriff Presley said.

Tragedy struck for a third time on Apr. 13, 1946, when 15-year-old Betty Jo Booker and her boyfriend, Paul Martin, seventeen, were slaughtered on the North Park Road after leaving a VFW dance in Texarkana. The pair had parked their car in the same area as the recent murders. At 9 a.m. the next day, an insurance salesman, G.H. Weaver, slowed his car. "Look!" he cried to his wife. "There's a man lying on the ground over there. He's a mess of blood; I'm sure he's dead. We'd better notify the sheriff." Martin had been shot in the back three times. Booker was found lying several yards away, her stomach and abdomen slashed open. A friend of the couple reported that Booker had left the dance carrying a saxophone. Police from the adjoining states of Texas, Arkansas, and Louisiana were advised to be on the lookout for such an instrument.

The madman finished his reign of terror on May 3, 1946, at the home of Virgil Starks, ten miles northeast of Texarkana. Starks had just sat down to read his evening paper when a bullet pierced the front window. Starks fell to the floor with a fatal wound in his neck and head. His wife, who was attending to household chores upstairs, rushed to her husband's side. Two more shots rang out, hitting her in the face. Despite the severity of her wounds, Mrs. Starks did not lose consciousness. She staggered out of the house and made her way toward the home of a neighbor, A.V. Prater. The farmer helped her and then went out with his hunting rifle to look for the gunman. Minutes later Sheriff W.E. Davis from the Arkansas side arrived on the scene. Outside the living room window he found two spent .22-caliber-Long Rifle cartridges. The lock on the back door had been broken and bloody footprints were left in the living room. "The slayer must have broken in before he knew that Starks' wife had escaped," Davis said. "It was only by the grace of God that Mrs. Starks got away. Otherwise there's no doubt but that she would have received the same treatment as those other women got at the hands of the sex fiend."

The killer never was heard from again. Life in Texarkana returned to normal but a feeling of dread persisted for months. The investigation continued. Military authorities at nearby Barksdale Field in Shreveport, La., permitted the police to question personnel, but nothing new turned up. At least six men in five different cities confessed to the Texarkana Lover's Lane murders, but they were dismissed as crackpots and lunatics. On May 7, 1946, four days after the Starks murder, a drifter matching the physical description of the rapist stepped in front of a moving train outside Texarkana, Ark. There was no wallet or piece of identification to suggest who this man was, though he did not appear to be a homeless vagabond. At the same time an automobile was burned beyond recognition in a heavily wooded area not far away. The tires were completely gone, making identification of the tread marks nearly impossible. Investigators could not determine whether the fire was started by the killer before he ended his life.

REF.: *CBA;* Nash, *Open Files;* Wilson, *Encyclopedia of Murder.*

Texas Property Wars, 1840s, U.S., feud. A feud in rural Texas in the early 1840s, became so violent that the intercession of Texas president Sam Houston was required. Two factions of Shelby County, the Regulators and the Moderators, became embroiled over issues ranging from cattle stealing to law and order to property rights. Poor recordkeeping by earlier Mexican authorities and fraud perpetrated by crooked land speculators caused one of the bloodiest wars in Texas history. Houston recognized that Shelby County was in a state of anarchy and commanded all citizens to lay down their arms and return to their homes. An uneasy peace existed until the Mexican War, when both sides vented their frustrations on a common enemy.

REF.: *CBA;* Hurwood, *Society and the Assassin.*

Texas Rangers, 1826- , U.S., law enfor. agen. The Texas Rangers were formed in 1826 at the urging of Governor Steven Austin, who wanted twenty to thirty rangers in the field at all times. The rangers, an independent law enforcement agency, became the most controversial, as well as the most fabled, lawmen in the U.S. According to legend, they always got their man, yet they had a penchant for pursuing outlaws and fugitives across state and country borders, frequently into Mexico. The pre-Civil War rangers of the Wild West were as much villains as heroes, however. Heroes such as Ben McCulloch, Big Foot Wallace, Frank Jones, John Coffee Hays, and Leander McNelly are remembered with such rangers-turned-villains as Bass Outlaw, Ben Thompson, and Scott Cooley. For a short period, they were disbanded, then re-established in 1873 and they captured several notorious outlaws including King Fisher, Sam Bass, and Wes Hardin. The twentieth century rangers came under sharp criticism for anti-black, anti-Chicano, and anti-labor views. A state legislative committee found that they consistently ignored civil rights, killed criminals without provocation, and frequently murdered their prisoners. In one incident during WWI, nine rangers shot and killed fifteen Mexicans in cold blood. The nine were dismissed, but no criminal charges were ever brought against them.

When Ma Ferguson was elected governor, she fired the entire ranger force because they openly supported her opponent. The only ranger she did not fire was Frank Hamer, the ranger on special assignment who was one of the lawmen, who killed Clyde Barrow and Bonnie Parker in 1935. Ferguson appointed her own people as replacements. The Ferguson Rangers, as the group came to be called, was one of the most corrupt law enforcement agencies ever formed, made up of thieving murderers. Ferguson's successor disbanded the agency and reformed it under the Department of Public Safety. The Texas AFL-CIO, in 1967, called for their disbandment, claiming they were used as tax-paid strikebreakers. The state Supreme Court ruled against the rangers, claiming they used excessive force in breaking up a United Farm Workers strike. In the 1970s, a candidate for governor ran a very strong, albeit unsuccessful, campaign calling for the abolition of the rangers. Their status at present is unresolved.

REF.: *CBA;* Reppetto, *The Blue Parade;* Webb, *The Texas Rangers;* Wellman, *A Dynasty of Wetsern Outlaws;* (FILM), *Hello Trouble,* 1932; *The Return of the Rangers,* 1943; *Gunsmoke Mesa,* 1944; *Enemy of the Law,* 1945; *Flaming Bullets,* 1945; *Marked for Murder,* 1945.

Texas Slave Insurrection, 1860, U.S., mob vio. The so-called

Texas Slave Insurrection began on July 8, 1860, when most of the business section of Dallas burned to the ground. Seven other Texas towns suffered fires in the following days, including Henderson, which was destroyed by a fire that burned down forty-three buildings. Rumors circulated that the fires were set as part of a Northern abolitionist plot to kill whites and free slaves. Yet in all likelihood, insurrection was not plotted. Vigilante committees formed, slaves were tortured, and lists were compiled of suspected abolitionists and blacks to be immediately hanged. That summer, between seventy-five to 100 men were lynched, mostly blacks, though a few Northern whites were also lynched. The violent reaction was probably rooted in the long-standing Southern fear of widespread slave revolution. The Harper Ferry raid in 1859 and the presidential elections of 1856 and 1860 heightened Southern anxieties, making rumors of a plot to free all slaves easy to believe. REF.: *CBA.*

Texas Strangler, prom. 1968-71, U.S., mur. The series of rape-murders that occurred on opposite ends of Texas—Dallas and Odessa—between October 1968 and August 1971, remain unsolved. The murderer who came to be called the "Texas Strangler" claimed his first victim in Odessa. Linda Lee Cougot, a 24-year-old barmaid, was abducted after leaving a laundromat. Her body was found almost two months later in the desert twelve miles from the city. She had been tied up, raped, and strangled.

Two of the strangler's victims were related to the police. Investigation indicates that this was coincidental. Because the Strangler seemed to watch laundromats, a 23-year-old with a record of attacking women in Amarillo laundromats was approached for questioning by the police. The suspect pulled out a shotgun and killed himself. Everyone hoped his death would end the attacks, but it did not.

The last woman whose death could be positively linked to the Texas Strangler was Carolyn Montgomery, also a barmaid. A note found by her body said, "Got wrong one—sorry." Although police had no theory about what would make a "right one," perhaps it was that mistake which ended the killings.

REF.: *CBA;* Nash, *Open Files.*

Thacher, Thomas Day, 1881-1950, U.S., jur. Judge of southern district court of New York from 1925-30, and of New York State Court of Appeals from 1943. He also served as U.S. solicitor general from 1930-33. REF.: *CBA.*

Thacker, William J., d.1903, U.S., mur.-lynch. William Thacker killed John Gordon and was convicted three times: twice in a court of law, and a third and final time by a vigilante mob. In 1900 Thacker, a man in his early forties, lived in the small hamlet of Noah, in northeastern Kentucky. He owned a general store and doubled as the postmaster. A burly man who liked to drink, Thacker's true passion in life was the Republican Party. The more he drank, the more stoic he became about his party, which had been dominated by the Democrats since the Civil War.

On July 30, 1900, Thacker, accompanied by his 16-year-old son, Robert, left his home on a hunting expedition—not for animals—but for Democrats. He bought a few bottles of liquor, announcing his intended targets to the shopkeeper. Outside the store, he encountered Gordon, a man in his early twenties, who worked at a local sawmill. Asking Gordon if he knew of any local Democrats, Gordon admitted to being one. Thacker goaded Gordon into fighting him with a knife. As Gordon advanced, Thacker drew his gun and shot Gordon in the head. He covered Gordon with brush and left him to die. Thacker was convinced to surrender and he and his son were taken to the Flemingsburg jail. Robert Thacker was later released.

In January 1901, Thacker was convicted of the murder and sentenced to life imprisonment. He appealed, and received the same sentence exactly one year later. He appealed again, but before the third trial, an angry mob gathered outside the Flemingsburg jail. After midnight on July 15, 1903, the mob stormed the jail, and dragged the screaming Thacker from his cell. Shortly after, his clothes shredded and his face gashed by rocks, he was hanged from a honey locust tree. No action was taken against the lynchers. The jury at the coroner's inquest returned a verdict of death by persons unknown.

REF.: *CBA;* Seagle, *Acquitted of Murder.*

Thälmann, Ernst, b.1886, Ger., impris. Served in Reichstag in 1924, and as first leader of communist Red Front group in 1925. He was jailed by the Nazis in 1933. He also ran unsuccessfully for the German presidency in 1925 and 1932. REF.: *CBA.*

Thames Police, founded 1798, Brit., law enfor. agency. In the 1700s the docks along London's river Thames were the shipping crossroads of the world. But perhaps only one-half of all the cargo ever reached these warehouses because crime was so rampant. A Scotsman, Patrick Colquhoun, became a London magistrate in 1789 and began to advance the idea of a river policing force. Accordingly, the Marine Police Institution was founded in 1798 to patrol the fifty miles from the estuary of the Thames to Staines Bridge in Middlesex. Forty years later, after Scotland Yard had been in existence for ten years, the specialized police force became the Thames Division of the Metropolitan Police.

Using three-person launches instead of police cars, the contemporary river police enforce shipping laws, deal with stowaways, and handle the accidents and legalities of an increasing amount of pleasure-boating on the river. The river police also deal with a large number of suicide cases. A special Underwater Search Unit, which is expert on the river below the surface, does everything from retrieving bodies to hunting for guns thrown into the river.

In recent years, a new task was given to the river police. In 1954, Antoni Klimowicz, a Polish sailor aboard the *Jaroslaw Dabrowski,* sought political asylum in Britain. The captain of his ship found out and imprisoned him in a cabin, planning to sail him out of the country and back home. As the ship left its dock and sailed down the river, a fleet of Thames Division launches formed a line, preventing its passage. If the ship had reached the estuary, it would have found a waiting British Navy destroyer, but the captain gave up to the river police and released his captive. REF.: *CBA.*

Tharme, Lilian, d.1960, Brit., (unsolv.) rape-mur. The last time Lilian Tharme was seen alive was 1:30 a.m. on Jan. 17, 1960. She was on her way home from a dance in the town of Poole, England. Her body was found in a ditch next to a small green car, her clothing scattered about the road. She had been raped and killed, and then run over with a stolen car to make it appear she was an accident victim. However, the car lost control and ended up next to her in the ditch. The police searched for a man between seventeen and twenty who had been seen near the murder site, but a suspect was never found.

REF.: *CBA;* Furneaux, *Famous Criminal Cases, vol. 6.*

Thaw, Harry Kendall (AKA: **John Smith**), 1872-1947, U.S., mur. Few murders among America's social elite and super rich rivaled the sensational 1906 murder of architect Stanford White by the demented millionaire Harry K. Thaw. The slaying of White was a public affair, committed in front of hundreds of horrified spectators. Thaw performed this deed with arrogance and disdain, as if dismissing an annoying servant or an unwanted party guest. Harry Thaw was used to having his own way since childhood, and as far as he was concerned, his killing of Stanford White, ostensibly over an affair with Thaw's beautiful wife, Evelyn, was merely a nasty chore he was compelled to perform.

The pampered Thaw was the son of a Pittsburgh magnate who had cornered the coke market in a short time and had accumulated a then staggering fortune of $40 million. Harry Thaw was the profligate heir to this fortune. Terribly spoiled by an over-indulgent mother, Thaw's education was a shambles although he was sent to the finest schools, including Harvard, where he ignored his studies and spent most of his time conducting high-stake poker games in his suite of rooms off campus. He was finally dismissed for gambling activities. Thaw's father was so vexed at his son's wastrel ways he reduced his allowance to $2,000 a year. Harry wined and carped until his mother awarded him an additional $8,000 a year. Still the headstrong Thaw complained that this was only pin money for a man of his esteem and standing.

Taking a lavish suite of rooms in Manhattan, Thaw attempted to buy his way into several prominent men's clubs, but he was barred because of his eccentricities. Incensed, Thaw rented a horse and tried to ride it into these clubs, knocking down doormen and porters. He was arrested and escorted home. His mother paid his fine. A short time later, Thaw participated in a marathon poker game with New York sharpers and lost $40,000. His mother paid the gambling debt. To vent his wild rages and satiate his sexual perversions, Thaw took another apartment inside of one of New York's fanciest bordellos. There he brought young, gullible women, promising them careers on Broadway or, at least, in the chorus lines of important musicals. After Thaw inveigled the women to his brothel apartment, he fiendishly attacked them, raping them and beating them with sticks and whips.

The bordello madam, Susan Merrill, later stated that she heard a woman screaming in Thaw's apartment and when she could bear it no longer, forced her way inside. She later testified: "I rushed into his rooms. He had tied the girl to the bed, naked, and was whipping her. She was covered with welts. Thaw's eyes protruded and he looked mad."

Merrill ordered Thaw out of the house, and when he refused, she called the police. The millionaire playboy was escorted from the brothel despite his protests that he had paid rent a year in advance. He was barred from the brothel and Madam Merrill was happy to repay him his advance rent. A short time later, Thaw was ejected from one of the finer Fifth Avenue shops. The sales manager refused to have his models show the latest gowns to a bevy of Broadway tarts Thaw paraded into the shop. At this point Thaw had what was later described as a "sort of fit. His eyes bulged and rolled, and he screamed like a child having a tantrum." Police escorted the playboy outside and sent him home; the whores were locked up. In retaliation, Thaw rented a car the next day and drove it through the shop's display window, almost running over the gaping manager. Thaw was again arrested and fined.

Mrs. Thaw advised her son to leave Manhattan and take a European vacation. Thaw sailed for Paris where he scandalized a city that was weaned on scandal. He rented an entire floor of the Georges V Hotel and invited the city's leading prostitutes to a party that lasted several days and cost him $50,000. He was finally asked to leave the hotel after he was discovered whipping naked women down the hotel corridors.

Another product of Pittsburgh at that time was a 16-year-old sultry brunette, Evelyn Nesbit. She came from poverty and had little formal education, but she had singing and dancing talent and, after being a photographer's model for a short period of time, soon won a spot in the prestigious Floradora Sextette. While performing in the Floradora chorus, she caught the lecherous eye of Stanford White, the most distinguished architect in New York. White, who was tall and heavyset, weighing some 250 pounds, wore a sweeping handlebar mustache and was always sartorially dressed, glittering with a diamond stickpin, gold watch chain, an expensive jewel-encrusted watch fob, and rings.

White was many times a millionaire, having made a fortune designing the resplendent Fifth Avenue mansions of New York's wealthiest movers and shakers. He was a high society architect who catered exclusively to the super rich, although he was known widely for having designed the elegant Washington Square Arch and the Hall of Fame at New York University. He had also designed Madison Square Garden, including its restaurant, arcade, fashionable shops, the amphitheater where prizefights and horse shows were held, and the magnificent roof garden where musicals were performed for open-air audiences who dined while watching the shows.

The tower of Madison Square Garden was reserved by White for himself. There he maintained a lavish home-away-from-home (he was married but seldom saw his wife). This apartment featured a red velvet swing which hung from the ceiling of the tower. According to Evelyn Nesbit's later statements, White was in the habit of bringing his mistresses and one-night stand show girls to the tower where he would swing them high so that he could lasciviously look beneath their billowing skirts. (The portrait of White as a lewd and lustful old man was painted by Nesbit at her husband's trial, certainly a colored, prejudiced view which was designed to vindicate Thaw's murderous actions, although White's skirt-chasing habits were certainly well known long before he ever met Nesbit.)

For three years, Nesbit carried on a relationship with White. He lavished gowns and jewels on her, paid for her stylish apartment and chauffeured limousine, and took endless photos of her in seductive poses. When he tired of her, he sent her away to a finishing school.

Harry Thaw had also seen Evelyn Nesbit on the stage briefly and knew that she was White's pampered mistress. While she was in boarding school, he contrived to meet her and then pursued her slavishly until she accepted his marriage proposal. Thaw, however, after the nuptials on Apr. 4, 1905, was more concerned with White than he was with his own wife, persecuting Nesbit for her relationship with the architect. He insisted that she refer to White as "The Beast" or "The Bastard." When she refused, he told her that she must, at least employ the letter "B" whenever she mentioned White. This Nesbit did.

Thaw took his 19-year-old bride to Europe, but it turned out to be a nightmarish honeymoon. Aboard the luxury liner carrying the couple to France, Nesbit later claimed, Thaw tied her to a bed and whipped and beat her until her body was coated with red welts. She finally told her unhinged husband what he wanted to hear—or all she could imagine that was vile and rotten about Stanford White. She told Thaw that White had tricked her into going to The Madison Square Tower apartment on the promise of marriage, but once there, he stripped and raped her, and then forced her to mount the red velvet swing naked while he took obscene photos of her. This story, of course, drove Thaw into blind rages and he forced his wife to repeat this story often so that he could work himself into a frenzy about White, vowing terrible revenge against "The Beast."

On the warm night of June 25, 1906, Harry Thaw took his berserk revenge on Stanford White. Harry and Evelyn Thaw were dining in Rector's with two of Thaw's friends, when White and a party of people left one of the private dining areas. Thaw stiffened as Evelyn passed him a hand-written note which read "The B. is here." She had followed his instructions of informing Thaw any time she saw White in public. Thaw crumpled the note and pocketed it, then patted his wife's hand and said: "Yes dear, I know he's here. I saw him. Thank you for telling me."

A few hours later White was sitting at the best table on the Madison Square Garden rooftop to witness a new, frothy musical, *Mamzelle Champagne*. White was interested in one of the chorus girls to whom the manager promised to introduce him following the performance. Harry, Evelyn, and two of their friends also arrived at the Madison Square Garden rooftop.

Evelyn saw White sitting alone watching the show and early-on, asked Thaw to take her home, noticing the agitated state he was in. She told her husband that the show bored her and he got up and began to escort her and their friends to the elevator. Suddenly, he was gone. Minutes later he stood glaring down at Stanford White. The architect looked up at Thaw, whom he knew and disliked. "Yes, Thaw, what is it?" White reportedly asked the staring young man. Without a word, Thaw reached into his pocket and withdrew a revolver, pointing it only a few feet from White's head. He fired one shot and then two more. White, his face a mass of blood, collapsed on the table, then fell sideways, taking the table with him. He sprawled dead on the floor with a bullet in his head and two more in his shoulder.

At first there was a horrible silence. The show stopped completely, performers frozen on the stage. The band did not play a note. The hundreds of customers present stared at the bizarre scene of Thaw standing over the fallen White and then piercing screams came from the women and everyone made a mad dash

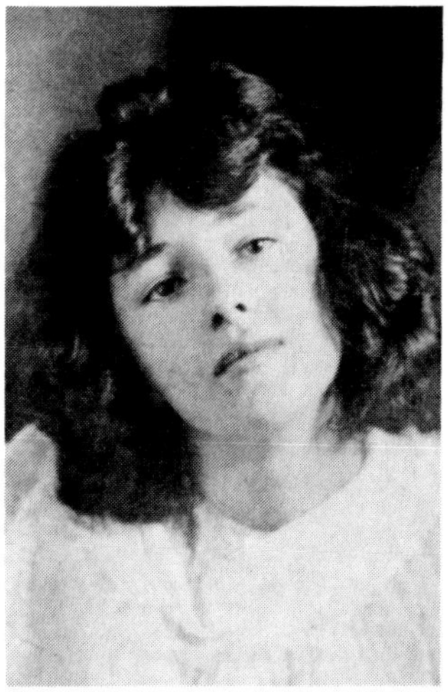

Top and middle rows: Evelyn Nesbit in various exotic poses, photographed by Stanford White's private photographer; she became White's mistress at age sixteen after briefly appearing in the Floradora Chorus in New York; she would later meet mad millionaire Harry K. Thaw, who would commit the sensational murder of White in 1906.

Evelyn Nesbit performing her ballet act with a hired partner.

Harry K. Thaw, 1905.

Stanford White, 1895.

for the exits, knocking over tables and chairs in a panic to escape what they thought was a madman on the loose. Thaw, according to some witnesses standing near him, raised the revolver over his head and emptied the remaining three live cartridges from the weapon which fell to the floor. He said something that was later interpreted to mean: "I did it because this man ruined my wife." Some claimed that Thaw said: "This man ruined my life."

Within seconds, Thaw, still holding the weapon above his head, made his way to the elevator where Nesbit and his friends waited in shock. "My God, Harry," Nesbit said. "What have you done?"

The roof garden was by then in pandemonium with women screaming and men shouting for police officers. The manager leaped upon a table and shouted to the band: "Go on playing!" To the stage manager he cried: "Bring on the chorus!" At this moment, a doctor was leaning over White and saw part of White's face blown away, his entire head was blackened by powder burns from bullets fired at close range. The physician pronounced White dead.

In the elevator lobby, Thaw, still clutching the weapon, was confronted by an off-duty fireman who said: "You'd better let me have that gun." Thaw meekly turned it over. A policeman then arrived and Thaw submitted to arrest. He was marched to the Center Street Station where he said his name was John Smith and was a student living at 18 Lafayette Place, New York City. He was searched and his own identification papers quickly revealed his true identity—Harry Kendall Thaw, the millionaire.

"Why did you do this?" a sergeant asked Thaw.

Thaw stared blankly at the policeman for some moments, then replied: "I can't say." He refused to make any more statements until his lawyer arrived. Thaw was charged with murder and placed in a cell in the New York Tombs to await trial. Fifteen months passed before Thaw was brought into court, a stalling tactic designed by Thaw's brilliant defense attorney, California criminal attorney Delphin Delmas, who had defended hundreds of clients in murder trials and claimed never to have lost a case. Delmas was called "the little Napoleon of the West Coast bar." Hired for an estimated $100,000 by Thaw's mother (the figure was never substantiated), Delmas told the elderly Mrs. Thaw that because her son chose to execute his victim in public, the best they could hope for would be to keep him out of the electric chair. To that end, Delmas mounted a crusade to blacken the name of the victim, a shameless and brazen technique to win Thaw any kind of sympathy.

Press agent Ben Atwell was hired by Mrs. Thaw to destroy the image of Stanford White and a short time later stories appeared in New York newspapers which detailed White's profligate ways. One story dealt with 15-year-old model, Susan Johnson, who was inveigled to White's Madison Square Tower apartment, which the *Evening Journal* described as being "furnished in Oriental splendor." The tale was told how Susan Johnson was plied with liquor, seduced, and soon afterward abandoned by the heartless White to make her way penniless through life. The vilification campaign against White went on day after day, month after month, until, it seemed Stanford White had seduced half the female population in New York City.

Mrs. Thaw made no excuses for unleashing the dogs of slander and libel against the dead Stanford White. "I am prepared to spend $1 million to save my son's life," she had announced. The publicity campaign and legal fees for her son's defense, it was later estimated, cost Mrs. Thaw more than $2 million.

Thaw himself was not spared negative publicity. His sordid exploits with prostitutes and his wife were .eaked to the press by the prosecution which was headed by the famous William Travers Jerome, New York's district attorney. Said Jerome before the trial: "With all his millions, Thaw is a fiend! No matter how rich a man is, he cannot get away with murder, not in New York!" Jerome's aides unearthed a lawsuit filed against Thaw in 1902 that had been filed by Ethel Thomas. Her story was almost identical to the one later told by Evelyn Nesbit. After meeting Thaw, Thomas had been swept off her feet by Thaw who oozed affection and respect. He had given her flowers, jewels, and clothes. "One day," Thomas stated in her deposition, "I met him by appointment and we were walking toward his apartment at the Bedford, and he stopped at a store and bought a dog whip. I asked him what that was for and he replied laughingly: 'That's for you, dear.' I thought he was joking but no sooner were we in his apartment and the door locked than his entire demeanor changed. A wild expression came into his eyes and he seized me and with his whip beat me until my clothes hung in tatters."

The most bizarre ploys were used by the defense to create hatred for White and glean sympathy for the "befuddled" Thaw. One story related how a medium had conducted a seance on July 5, 1906, and that a "spirit from beyond appeared to insist that he, a long-departed soul named Johnson, had guided Harry Thaw's hand" and the spirit was the true killer of Stanford White, not Thaw!

Finally, on Jan. 21, 1907, Thaw was brought to trial. Thaw himself took the stand to appear penitent and remorseful, saying: "I never wanted to shoot that man. I never wanted to kill him...Providence took charge of the situation." Apparently Thaw had read the account of the seance and was now pinning the blame on the spirits. Delmas and his battery of lawyers insisted Thaw was not in his right mind when he killed White, that he suffered from "dementia Americana," a neurosis that was singularly American; wherein American males believed that every man's wife was sacred and if she were violated, he would become unbalanced, striking out in a murderous rage.

District Attorney Jerome fought back against this psychological gobbledygook, cross-examining Evelyn Nesbit with dogmatic persistence. He asked about the character of her husband and her replies were so explicit that she insisted on whispering her answers to him. Her responses were later whispered for the court reporter recording the trial transcript and then her sordid stories were shown in printed form to the jury members. By then, however, the jury believed that Stanford White was a beast in human form and deserved to die, that he had ruined the lives of dozens of young women and that Thaw, who was unhinged at the time of the shooting, was merely doing what any noble-minded American male would do, taking vengeance for wronged women all over the U.S.

The jury, on Apr. 11, 1907, could not agree, seven holding for conviction, five others insisting on a not guilty vote. Thaw was tried again, and, on Feb. 1, 1908, he was found Not Guilty "by reason of insanity." This was the verdict Delmas had sought. His client would not face the electric chair. Thaw was sent to the New York State Asylum for the Criminally Insane at Matteawan, N.Y. He was to remain here for life, despite efforts by his mother to free him.

When Mrs. Thaw's millions could not move the courts, she reportedly financed her son's escape on Aug. 17, 1913. Thaw was escorted through unlocked doors to freedom where a limousine was waiting for him. He was driven to Canada and a luxury apartment. The U.S. State Department brought heavy pressure against Canadian officials to have Thaw returned to the U.S. and he was finally turned over, but he was placed in a Concord, N.H., jail where, as had been the case in the New York Tombs while he awaited trial, Thaw dined on catered meals and was offered every convenience and comfort. His lawyers battled extradition to New York until December 1914 when they secured another trial for the murderer.

In the third trial, the same evidence and testimony was examined, but the jury, on July 16, 1915, returned a verdict of Not Guilty and also stated that Thaw was no longer insane and urged his release. He was set free. In 1916, Thaw was back in the news, accused of kidnapping, beating, and sexually molesting 19-year-old Frederick B. Gump. He was arrested, jailed, and went through another trial where he was declared insane. Another hearing was held and Thaw was declared sane and the charges were dropped. It was reported that Thaw's mother had bestowed more than $500,000 on the Gump family to convince them to drop

The rooftop theater at Madison Square Garden, site of Thaw's public execution of Stanford White on June 25, 1906.

Thaw dining in the jail cell.

Thaw at time of trial.

Mrs. Thaw, Harry's mother.

Evelyn on the witness stand whispering answers to William Travers Jerome.

Thaw with his mother following his conviction.

Evelyn performing years later.

Thaw's attorney, Delphin Delmas.

Evelyn writing her memoirs.

the charges. Thaw then resumed his eccentric lifestyle, buying his way through life. He died in February 1947 of a heart attack, a wizened, shrunken creature of seventy-six.

Evelyn Nesbit had her moment of glory and infamy during the Thaw trial and for some years afterward. She was abandoned by the Thaw family, who reportedly bought her off. She later appeared as a vaudeville attraction, billed as "the girl in the red velvet swing." In 1915, though she had long been divorced by the irresponsible Thaw, Nesbit insisted that her newly born son was Thaw's child, that she had bribed guards at Matteawan to allow her into Thaw's rooms for a night of bliss. Thaw angrily denied this and his parentage. His lawyers reportedly paid her off.

REF.: Bechhofer-Roberts, *Famous American Trials;* Boucher, *The Quality of Murder;* Brophy, *The Meaning of Murder; CBA;* Churchill, *The Pictorial History of American Crime;* Corder, *Murder My Love;* Dilnot, *Rogues' March;* Duke, *Celebrated Criminal Cases of America; Famous Trials;* Furneaux, *The Quality of Murder;* Gribble, *Stories of Famous Modern Trials;* ____, *Strange Crimes of Passion;* Lait and Mortimer, *Chicago: Confidential;* Langford, *The Murder of Stanford White;* Lebrun, *It's Time to Tell;* Lustgarten, *The Story of Crime;* Mooney, *Evelyn Nesbit and Stanford White: Love and Death in the Gilded Age;* Nash, *Bloodletters and Badmen;* ____, *Murder Among the Mighty;* Nesbit, *Evelyn, The Untold Story;* Roberts, *Famous American Trials;* Samuels, *The Girl in the Red Velvet Swing;* Sanders, *Murder in the Big Cities;* Sann, *Kill the Dutchman;* ____, *The Lawless Decade;* Scott, *The Concise Encyclopedia of Crime and Criminals;* Thaw, *The Traitor;* (FILM), *The Girl in the Red Velvet Swing,* 1955; *Ragtime,* 1981.

Thayer, Earl, prom. 1920s, U.S., rob. Earl Thayer joined Al Spencer's gang of bank robbers in the early 1920s. With George "Whitey" Curtis, Grover Durrill, Curtis Kelly, Frank Nash, Wilbur Underhill, and Spencer, Thayer was involved in at least twenty-five bank robberies before the end of 1923. The gang enacted its most spectacular exploit on Aug. 20, 1923, when they halted a luxury passenger train, the Katy Limited, near Bartlesville, Okla., and stole $20,000 in Liberty Bonds from the mail car. Curtis, Durrill, Nash, and Thayer were apprehended and sentenced to twenty-five years in Leavenworth, while Spencer was killed in a shootout with authorities.

Frank Nash escaped from Leavenworth on Oct. 19, 1930, and returned to a life of crime. Seeking to reunite the old Spencer gang, Nash smuggled guns to his former cohorts in Leavenworth and on Dec. 11, 1931, Thayer, Curtis, Durrill, as well as Charles Berta, Stanley Brown, William Green, and Tom Underwood, walked out the prison's front gates, taking Warden Tom White hostage. They commandeered a car, only to careen into a ditch from the rain-slicked road. After another vehicle failed, the group split in two, with Curtis, Durrill, Green, and Thayer driving off, leaving the others with their hostage. The four holed up at a nearby farmhouse, which was quickly surrounded by a posse of prison guards, augmented by a national guard troop. They rained bullets and tear gas on the hopelessly besieged escapees. Green shot Curtis and Durrill to death, before turning his gun on himself. Only Thayer managed to escape amidst the chaos, but he was caught the next day, cold and hungry, roaming in a farmer's field. Thayer was returned to Leavenworth. When an additional twenty-five years were added to his sentence, he said, "You might as well make it a thousand, I'll never live to serve it out." He died a few years later in his prison cell. REF.: *CBA.*

Thayer, James Bradley, 1831-1902, U.S., lawyer. Respected expert on constitutional law and law of evidence. He helped develop the case method of teaching law. He taught as a law professor at Harvard University from 1874-1902. REF.: *CBA.*

Thayer, Webster, 1857-1933, U.S., jur. Though Webster Thayer led a long and notable career on the Superior Court bench, he will be remembered primarily for the seven-year trial—from 1921 to 1927—of Nicola Sacco and Bartolomeo Vanzetti. Thayer had been admitted to the Bar in 1882 and elevated to the Superior Court in 1900. He had been universally regarded as an able and conscientious judge—until the Sacco-Vanzetti case. During the case he was vilified by liberals and accused of extreme prejudice by Supreme Court Justice Felix Frankfurter. Later scrutiny of the courtroom transcripts exonerated Thayer of the accusations of prejudice. Even the defense concurred. Yet, because of an unsubstantiated conversation in a golf course locker room, Thayer's reputation was irrevocably blemished. While presiding over the trial, Thayer reportedly commented, "I am going to hang those anarchist s.o.b.'s!" Protest against the verbal exchange probably led to the 1932 bombing of Thayer's house, injuring his wife and a servant, which necessitated a constant police guard until his death, by natural causes on Apr. 18, 1933. See: **Sacco, Nicola and Vanzetti, Bartolomeo.**

REF.: *CBA;* Scott, *The Concise Encyclopedia of Crime and Criminals.*

Themistocles, c.527-c.460 B.C., Gr., treas. Led successful campaign to make Athens major naval post instead of military post as Aristides desired. He defeated the Persians at Salamis with support from Aristides in 480 B.C. He was blackballed for continued attempts to strengthen Athens against attack, and eventually was exiled on charges of being an accomplice to the treachery of General Pausanias. He lived out his days in Persia, supported by King Artaxerxes I. REF.: *CBA.*

Theodahad (Theodat), d.536, Tuscany, mur.-assass. The nephew of Ostrogoth King Theodoric, Theodahad served as joint ruler with Theodoric's daughter, Queen Amalasuntha, after 534. Amalasuntha favored friendly relations with the Byzantine emperor and opposed the Ostrogothic nationalism that Theodahad endorsed. Theodahad arranged to have Amalasuntha strangled in her bath on an island in Lake Bolsena. Eastern Roman emperor Justinian I used Amalasuntha's murder as a pretext to invade Tuscany, and the Byzantine armies laid waste to Theodahad's lands. Theodahad himself was assassinated soon thereafter. See: **Amalasuntha.**

REF.: *CBA;* Diehl, *Cambridge Medieval History;* Seville, *History of the Kings of the Goths.*

Theodora, Empress **(Augusta),** 500-48, Byzantium, pros. The daughter of a circus bear keeper, Theodora became a prostitute, offering her body for sodomy as a child. She later became an adept actress and comedienne who attracted men by her lewd dancing and stripteases. She went to North Africa as one man's mistress, but soon left him and returned to Constantinople where she attracted Justinian. He was able to influence his uncle, Emperor Justin, to repeal a law that forbade upper-class citizens from marrying prostitutes and actresses. The pair married, and Justinian, also called August, soon became the emperor of Byzantium, or the Eastern Roman Empire.

Theodora, who was called Augusta when she was crowned empress, had an unexpected political wisdom, and her husband frequently followed her advice. On her own, she developed a home for aging prostitutes and those who wanted to get out of the profession and was credited with rehabilitating many of them.

REF.: *CBA;* Henriques, *Prostitution;* Nash, *Almanac of World Crime.*

Theodore II, d.897, Italy, pope, assass.? Verified pontificate of Stephen VI's foe Formosus, and respectfully oversaw Formosus' internment. He died suspiciously within weeks of assuming the papacy. REF.: *CBA.*

Theodore Studites (Theodore of Studius), 759-826, Roman., exile. Abbot of monastery who refused to support Constantine VI's second marriage on grounds of adultery, and was exiled from 796-97. He brought his parish to Constantinople in 799 and lived in the monastery of Studius. He was again exiled, from 816-20, for rebuking Iconoclasm. REF.: *CBA.*

Theodoric II, 426-466, Italy, king, mur.-assass. Murdered and succeeded brother King Thorismond. Once he assumed the throne, he attacked Spain and won some battles on the Iberian Penninsula. He was murdered and succeeded by his brother Euric. REF.: *CBA.*

Theodosius, d.376, Roman., consp. Stifled revolt in Mauretania in 370. He was executed on a charge of conspiracy brought by Emperor Valens. REF.: *CBA.*

Theophanes, Saint **(AKA: The Confessor),** c.752-818, Gr., banish. Banished to island of Samothrace for resisting policies of Eastern Roman Emperor Leo V, and died in exile. He founded the Great Field monastery near Cyzicus. REF.: *CBA.*

Theophilus, d.412, Gr., reform. Served as patriarch of Alexandria from 385-412, and demolished temples of Mithra, Dionysius, Sarapis, and other pagan shrines in North Africa. He avidly fought followers of Origenism, and severely punished monks of that sect. He and Empress Eudoxia arranged the exile of John Chrysostom. He was canonized by the Egyptian Coptic church. REF.: *CBA.*

Theramenes, d.404 B.C., Gr., treas. Athenian general who led Council of Four Hundred in 411 B.C. and replaced it with Committee of the Five Thousand in 411. He helped destroy the Spartan fleet based near Cyzicus in 410, and arbitrated the conceding of Athens to Lysander in 405. He was appointed one of the Thirty Tyrants assigned to govern Athens in 404, but he was forced to drink hemlock after Critias charged him with treason. REF.: *CBA.*

Theroigne de Mericourt (AKA: **Anne Joseph Terwagne, Amazon of Liberty**), 1762-1817, Fr., rebel. Led 1789 attack on Bastille prison, and later led mob protests. REF.: *CBA.*

Therrien, Armand R., prom. 1975, U.S., mur. In 1975, Chin Enterprises was a four-man partnership which owned the popular Hawaiian Garden restaurant in Seabrook, N.H. The corporation sought to borrow $166,000 from a Boston bank to open another restaurant in Marietta, Ga. Three of the four partners were oriental, but the fourth, referred to as Uncle Harry, was a former New Hampshire state policeman named Armand R. Therrien. As a policeman, he specialized in cases involving embezzlement. In 1973, he resigned to become an insurance agent. He had severe financial difficulties after he divorced and began doing odd jobs at the Hawaiian Garden, eventually becoming secretary-treasurer of Chin Enterprises. In January 1975, Therrien left Boston to supervise the construction of the Marietta restaurant.

On Feb. 11, 1975, in the Boston suburb of Westwood, two patrolmen, William Sheehan and Robert P. O'Donnell, approached a car with its emergency lights flashing. The driver appeared to be slumped in his seat. A man exited a passenger-side door and approached the officers, assuring them that the driver was ill but not in need of help. But the officers, suspecting a drunk driver, looked in the drivers window and saw blood. As they turned to confront the passenger, Therrien, he shot them with a .38-caliber snub-nosed pistol. Sheehan died of a bullet wound to his head. O'Donnell survived with two minor wounds, and was able to return fire and wound Therrien. The driver of the car, John Oi, one of Therrien's partners, had been killed before the officers arrived.

Authorities speculated that Therrien, supporting two households since his recent divorce, was financially strapped. A bank loan secured by Chin Enterprises stipulated that corporate officers were limited to annual salaries of $15,000. Chin Enterprises had insurance policies on all partners, which would pay the corporation $200,000, or more than enough to pay back the loan and return a handsome amount to each partner, thus solving Therrien's cash flow problem. Therrien was arraigned and brought to trial at Dedham, Mass. The jury found him Guilty of first-degree murder in the deaths of Oi and Sheehan and sentenced him to two consecutive life terms at the Massachusetts Correctional Institution at Walpole.

REF.: *CBA;* Trillin, *Killings.*

Therrien, Joseph W., 1925- , and **St. James, George L.,** 1930- , U.S., mur. Police in Bristol, Conn., received a phone call on Christmas night, 1948, telling them about the body of a woman lying in the snow. The caller identified herself as Rose Lombardi, who said she had stumbled over the body on her way to the garbage bin. "Who is she?" Police Chief Edmund S. Crowley wanted to know. The distraught Lombardi, whose Christmas celebration was upset by the tragedy replied, "I never saw her before. I have no idea how she got here—or why." Medical Examiner Fred T. Tirella examined the corpse and determined the woman had been strangled a few hours earlier.

The police searched the immediate vicinity. Entering a locked barn they found a late-model automobile containing a tube of lipstick, a twenty-dollar bill, and several long strands of hair trapped in the screw socket of the rear window frame. The vehicle had been rented to a neighbor who had an unshakable alibi. But the car was somehow linked to the slaying. That much seemed certain when detectives found a woman's handbag lying in the snow near the barn. Inside the purse was a small slip of paper with the word "rich" scrawled in pencil.

No further action was taken and the investigation was stymied until a mortician from Plainville notified police that he knew of a family named Rich in his community. Digging further, the police learned the body was that of Lillian Rich, estranged wife of Harold Brackett. The Plainville police reported that Rich, in her forties, had been evicted from a local café with two young men half her age. The three had been drinking and carousing loudly. One of the youths was identified as 23-year-old Joseph W. Therrien, who had been previously arrested for burglary and car theft. Therrien had served six months in prison, but had recently taken up residence at the home of Rose Lombardi in Bristol. When asked about this by Chief Crowley, Lombardi said that she had not seen Therrien for several days. The police obtained a search warrant.

In the Lombardi basement they found a damp, mud-stained dress. A charred, half-burned Social Security card bearing the name of Lillian Rich Brackett was found inside the furnace. "What a Christmas!" wailed Lombardi. "Now you won't believe a word I say!" She went on to say that Therrien, his friend George St. James, and a drunken woman had stumbled into her kitchen on Dec. 24. The young men, chased out of the house, took Brackett to the garage where they raped her in the neighbor's car, and then strangled her to death. A hole was dug in the ground and the body buried. Then they told Lombardi what had happened. Fearing her boarders had buried the woman alive she told them to dig up Brackett and bring her to the kitchen. There they carefully scrubbed the body and changed the clothing, using one of Lombardi's housedresses. It was a snug fit, but she decided it would pass. The corpse was next placed in the snow to make it look like an accident. "But why on earth did you protect these killers?" Crowley asked. "I had to," Lombardi replied. "Therrien is engaged to my daughter and I didn't want anything to happen to postpone the marriage."

Lombardi's hopes for her daughter's marriage were dashed when Therrien and St. James were committed to the state prison for life. As an accessory to murder, Lombardi received three years.

REF.: *CBA;* Nash, *Murder, America;* Reynolds, *Murder 'Round the World.*

Thesiger, Frederick (Baron of Chelmsford), 1794-1878, Brit., lawyer. Appointed solicitor general in 1844, attorney general in 1845 and 1852, and served as lord chancellor from 1858-59 and from 1866-68. REF.: *CBA.*

They Shall Not Die, 1934, a play by John Wexley. The sensational Scottsboro rape case (U.S., 1931), is the basis for this drama. See: **Scottsboro Case.** REF.: *CBA.*

They Won't Forget, 1937, a film directed by the socially conscious Mervyn LeRoy. The tragic and innocent lynch victim, Leo Frank, who was murdered by a Georgia mob for supposedly murdering 14-year-old Mary Phagan (U.S., 1913-15), is the basis of this gripping motion picture, which was based on Ward Greene's novel, *Death in the Deep South.* LeRoy centers his action on the trial, in which a ruthless Claude Rains prosecutes Edward Norris (enacting a fictionalized Frank) although he knows the defendant is innocent. This powerful but rarely shown film aptly portrays the lethal racial prejudice which long clutched at segments of the American South.

The film was extremely controversial when released. Followers of racist newspaper publisher and populist political leader Tom Watson were still very much in evidence in 1937, and many theaters in Georgia refused to show it. Watson was the real power behind the railroading of Leo Frank. It was Watson who decided Frank's guilt long before the man's trial. When he was told that the little girl was most likely murdered by a black janitor who worked for Frank, Watson snapped: "We can lynch a nigger any time but when do we get to hang a Yankee Jew?" LeRoy knew of Watson's attitude, as faithfully reflected in Greene's novel, and postures Rains, in the re-creation of the bigoted Watson, as a vicious racist. At one point, Rains almost duplicates Watson's racist remark by stating: "Anyone can convict a Negro in the South," realizing that Norris (Frank) is bigger game to be legally slaughtered. Lana Turner made her film debut in this film as the murder victim, although she was two years older (or more) than the actual victim, Mary Phagan. See: **Frank, Leo**. REF.: *CBA*.

Thick, Edwin Claude, prom. 1931, Brit., mur. Edwin and Ivy Thick were married in 1928 and within two years had one child. In late 1930, Edwin gave the child to his parents, saying that Ivy had run off with a Frenchman and that he was going after her. Seven months later, the anxious parents of Ivy Thick reported the disappearance to the police, who searched the couple's house. The dismembered remains of Mrs. Thick were found in a wall cavity. She had been beaten to death with five blows to the head, after attempted strangulation. Edwin Thick admitted that he must have killed his wife, but could not remember how. In July 1931, at the Birmingham Assizes, he was found Guilty of his wife's murder and was remanded to an insane asylum rather than prison.

REF.: Brock, *A Casebook of Crime; CBA.*

Thief-Takers, 1692-1825, Brit., law enfor. agency. Thief-taking, as practiced in England prior to the establishment of the Metropolitan Police system, often encouraged the crimes it was designed to suppress. In 1692, an Act For Encouraging the Apprehending of Highwaymen was passed by Parliament. Until this time law enforcement was left to private entrepreneurs who recovered stolen property and brought wanted felons to justice for a financial reward. The system relied on paid informants and the deterrent effect of capital punishment to maintain the peace. The act offered a reward of £40 for the arrest and successful prosecution of a highwayman. The "thief-taker" was also entitled to the highwayman's private property, including his horse, weapons, money, and any other items not taken during the commission of a robbery. The first thief-takers were invariably former highwaymen and thieves who realized it was safer to betray an accomplice for the reward money. But while more dangerous felons were arrested and prosecuted, the act fostered criminality. Highway robbery, and other forms of lawlessness continued to increase. Thus, a sliding fee scale was established for various types of criminals. The professional thief-taker was required to share his reward money with the parish constable or other civic-minded individuals if their services were needed. Conversely, the reward money was paid to the thief-taker's family, if he were to be killed while taking the felon into custody. It was a dangerous profession reserved for adventurers, knaves, and those on the fringe of the underworld. Often, a gullible young man was lured into committing a crime by a thief-taker, who then betrayed him for the reward.

Jonathan Wild, perhaps the most famous of all British thief-takers, sent at least 100 footpads and highwaymen to the gallows before joining them on the scaffold himself in 1725. In 1749, Sir Henry Fielding founded the Bow Street Runners, essentially a group of thief-takers organized under the auspices of the police magistrate. This system of crime detection came under attack in 1754, when Stephen McDaniel, a Marshalsea bailiff and private thief-taker, conspired with two other men to "fake" a robbery and frame two innocent youths of the crime. The victim was James Salmon, who claimed to have been robbed near Deptford. The stolen goods were sold to a fence named Egan. Salmon identified two young men named Kelly and Ellis as the ones responsible for the crime. As it turned out, Salmon, McDaniel, and Thomas Blee had hatched the conspiracy. Joseph Cox, High Constable of Blackheath, dug into the facts of the case. He turned up the names of at least sixteen people arrested on trumped-up charges. Egan and Salmon were pilloried and stoned to death by angry Londoners.

There was an immediate public outcry against the high-handed antics of the Bow Street Runners, but the system did not change for years. In fact, the total reward money paid out continued to escalate to a rate of £18,000 a year by 1815. In 1825, when yet another scandal involving Runners who dipped their hands into the blood money rocked London, a bill was passed authorizing the creation of the Metropolitan Police, with Robert Peel at the helm. See: **Bow Street Runners; Fielding,** Sir **Henry; Peel,** Sir **Robert; Wild, Jonathan.**

REF.: *CBA;* Scott, *The Concise Encyclopedia of Crime and Criminals.*

Thiel, Alexander (AKA: **Mr. X**), 1890-1956, U.S., forg. Known as the most accomplished U.S. forger, Alexander Thiel netted between $600,000 and $1 million before police apprehended him in 1945. Born in Chicago in 1890, Thiel was the son of a successful architect who lost all his money in the bank crash of 1904. Thiel later claimed, "Right then and there I decided banks and bankers were all a bunch of no-goods and someday I was going to get even with them." Thiel, a multi-talented criminal known as "Mr. X," forged an extraordinary number of checks, causing police to believe he was the leader of a gang. He could imitate any signature from memory, and was an expert second-story burglar. Thiel frequently broke into business offices, stole blank checks, and stamped the check stubs "Defective Checks. Removed by Printer." As he had no accomplices who could implicate him, Thiel avoided detection for nearly twenty-five years.

Thiel's career began while he worked as a card dealer in an illegal gambling casino where he discovered his talent for forgery by accident. When a gambler committed suicide, Thiel quickly wrote out an IOU for $2,500, using the form the gambler had recently shown him. His employers at the casino thought the gambler killed himself over an unpayable gambling debt and cashed the IOU without questioning its authenticity. Thiel quit his dealing job and decided to swindle banks.

In his largest and first major forgery operation, Thiel stole blank checks belonging to multi-millionaire Messmore Kendall. He pilfered Kendall's account of $162,000 without the millionaire learning of the theft for three weeks. For the following twenty years, Thiel cashed numerous smaller checks from $5,000 to $15,000. He commenced living the high life, frequenting nightclubs and speakeasies in New York City. He was finally tripped up by a drug habit that forced him to write several thousand dollars worth of forged checks a year.

By the late 1930s, Thiel had signed $4,160 worth of checks under the name George Workmaster. His face was remembered and police began searching for a "John Barrymore look-alike." However, another man, Bertram Campbell, was apprehended, identified by five witnesses, and sentenced to five to ten years in prison. Thiel wrote to District Attorney Thomas E. Dewey, who prosecuted Campbell, and then to several newspapers, telling them that an innocent man had been imprisoned. The forgeries continued, reinforcing the police's theory that Campbell was only one member of a criminal gang.

Then, in 1945, two detectives came to the U.S. Hospital at Lexington, Ky., searching for check forgers among patients being treated for drug abuse. Spying a John Barrymore look-alike among patient photos, the officers recalled Campbell's case, arrested Thiel, and brought him back to New York where he was identified. Thiel confessed. Campbell, who had spent eight years in prison, won a pardon. Thiel was sentenced to nine years in prison, and was freed when he was in his mid-sixties. He forged one last check for $100 and was caught in 1956. When the authorities came to arrest him, he was near death and said, "Give me a pen and a blank check and I'll square my bill with the undertaker now." REF.: *CBA*.

Thiers, Louis Adolphe, 1797-1877, Fr., polit.-writer. Noted political leader and historian. He held a number of offices, including that of president of the Third Republic from 1871-73. Books authored: ten-volume *Histoire de la Révolution Française,* nineteen-volume *Histoire du Consulat et de l' Empire*. REF.: *CBA*.

Thierschwald, Otto, See: **Matteotti, Giacomo.**

Thieves' Exchange, prom. 1860s-1890s, U.S., crime district. Just as New York City was once home to the nation's largest area of vice and corruption, the Tenderloin, the city also sheltered the Thieves' Exchange, a section in the Eighth Ward near Broadway and Houston Street where thieves found their "fences"—buyers of stolen goods.

During the latter third of the 1800s, the Thieves' Exchange boasted the most open and blatant fencing operations in the country. Fences and thieves met in public places over drinks each night to haggle over the price of stolen goods, discuss financial backing for future jobs, and solicit funds in exchange for first option on future loot. The Thieves' Exchange existed because the important fences paid bribes to the police, and commissions of a fence's gross business were given to major politicians and high-ranking police officers. The fences finally moved out of the Thieves' Exchange during the police reform movements of the 1880s and 1890s. REF.: *CBA*.

Thiri Thu Dhamma, prom. 1634, Arakan, mur. Thiri Thu Dhamma, the Buddhist king of Arakan since 1622 had a goal: conquest of the world. His court was filled with sages and mystics, one of whom delayed his coronation for twelve years, saying the ascendancy would cause instant death. Another stated that for world conquest, the king had to drink the blood of the hearts of 2,000 white doves, 4,000 white cows and 6,000 people. While the advice contradicted Buddhist pacifism, Thiri determined this to be a small price for omnipotent power. The hearts of the doves and cows were procured, but the people resisted. After the deaths of a few vagrants, word traveled quickly, and people barricaded themselves in their homes. But Thiri persisted, and 6,000 people, including some police, were impaled alive. At last the monarch had his elixir, which he drank with great ceremony. He died three years later. REF.: *CBA*.

Thirteen Men, 1930, a novel by Tiffany Thayer. This work of fiction is based on the mass killer Earle Nelson (U.S., 1920s). See: **Nelson, Earle Leonard**. REF.: *CBA*.

Thistlewood, Arthur, and **Ings, James**, and **Brunt, John**, and **Tidd, Richard**, and **Davidson, William** (AKA: **Cato Street Conspirators**), d.1820, Brit., treas.-mur. "I have now but a few moments to live and I hope the world will think that I was at least sincere in my endeavors," said Arthur Thistlewood, leader of a group of radicals who conspired to kill the entire British cabinet, as he was about to be hanged and decapitated. Thistlewood was an ex-soldier who blamed England for the loss of his fortune, which disappeared in the Napoleonic economic troubles. First he was involved in 1802 in a conspiracy to kill the king. In 1816, he was tried on charges of treason with Dr. James Watson but was acquitted. Finally, in 1820, he learned that the entire cabinet of the king's advisors was going to dine at the home of the Earl of Harrowly (or Harrowby) on the evening of February 23. He organized a conspiracy to kill them all, with particular attention to be paid to Lord Castlereagh, the prime minister.

He found twenty-five men who were interested in helping in the assassination. They assembled an arsenal in a room above a stable on Cato Street, so they went down in history as the Cato Street Conspirators. One of the twenty-five was a government spy, so, as the men gathered in the Cato Street stable, they were watched from across the street by Bow Street Runners, who attacked when they were all together. Thistlewood himself killed Smithers, the leader of the Runners, running him through with a longsword. Many of the conspirators got away, including Thistlewood, though he was captured the following day.

All eleven men were sentenced to death, but six had their death sentences commuted to transportation for life. Thistlewood, James Ings, John Brunt, Richard Tidd, and William Davidson were executed in public in the clearing before Newgate Prison on May 1, and, as decreed for traitors, their heads were cut off and exhibited to the crowds. Schoolboys from all over the London area were given the day off to attend the execution.

REF.: Armitage, *Bow Street Runners;* Atholl, *Shadow of the Gallows;* Bleackley, *Hangmen of England;* Browne, *The Rise of Scotland Yard; CBA;* Cooper, *Lesson of the Scaffold;* Hibbert, *The Roots of Evil;* Laurence, *A History of Capital Punishment;* Mencken, *By the Neck;* Postgate, *Murder, Piracy and Treason;* Potter, *The Art of Hanging;* Sparrow, *Vintage Victorian Murder;* Thomson, *The Story of Scotland Yard;* Woodhall, *Secrets of Scotland Yard.*

This Way Out, 1939, a novel by James Ronald. This work is based on the sad life and gruesome wife murder by mild killer Dr. Hawley Harvey Crippen (Brit., 1910), with a film, *The Suspect* (1944), based upon it. See: **Crippen, Dr. Hawley Harvey**. REF.: *CBA*.

Thoman, J. Clarence, prom. 1932, U.S., extor. In the midst of the frantic 1932 search for the Lindbergh baby, ominous letters demanding money began appearing at the homes of families in Bloomsberg, Pa. On Apr. 14, 1932, a wealthy carpet manufacturer, Harry Magee, received a letter threatening the abduction and murder of his wife and daughter unless he was paid $15,000. He contacted the police, and a week later, a second letter arrived reiterating the demand. Subsequent letters detailed a scheme in which the money should be dropped from an airplane over a wooded area. On June 3, a duffle bag containing the money was indeed dropped over the specified location. Amazingly, the extortionist eluded the large posse, but made off with only forty dollars, the rest was blank paper placed between the two $20 bills.

On June 16, 1932, one of the marked twenties turned up at a local bank. The bill was traced to a gas station, which in turn had the licence number of the man who had remitted it. The motorist, J. Clarence Thoman, was questioned, but denied any knowledge of the threats. But the bills had been treated with silver nitrate, a substance found on Thoman's hands. Thoman then admitted his guilt, stating he had acted alone. He was sentenced to eighteen years in prison and fined $6,000. He was released by a governor's parole on Oct. 23, 1938, after serving six years.

REF.: *CBA;* Cohen, *One Hundred True Crime Stories.*

Thomas, Alfred Delavan, 1837-96, U.S., jur. Appointed to district court of North Dakota by President Benjamin Harrison in 1890. He had served as district attorney of Walsworth Co., Wis., during the 1860's. REF.: *CBA*.

Thomas, Alice, prom. 1672, Brit., pros. One of the first known brothel madams in the American colonies, Alice Thomas was found guilty in 1672 of "giving frequent secret and unseasonable entertainment," and of giving both men and women "opportunity to commit carnal wickedness." As a whorehouse keeper, she was sentenced to be whipped as she was paraded through the streets of Boston.

REF.: *CBA;* Nash, *Almanac of World Crime.*

Thomas, Annie, See: **Hearn, Sarah Ann.**

Thomas, Alvin Clarence (AKA: **Titanic Thompson**), prom. 1910s-20s, U.S., fraud. Alvin Thompson, an expert con artist, was on board the *Titanic* to fleece passengers when the luxury liner made its ill-fated voyage in April 1912. When the ship struck the iceberg, Thompson, and his fellow hustlers, the Hashhouse Kid, Hoosier Harry, and Indiana Harry got into lifeboats. The con men survived and arrived in New York a day or two later. Thompson and his associates immediately filed exorbitant claims for reimbursement of lost luggage and valuables—not only for themselves, but for items belonging to the many hundreds of passengers who died.

Gambler Alvin Clarence Thomas, better known as Titanic Thompson.

In the 1920s "Titanic" Thompson, as he was popularly known, associated with New York gambler Arnold "Big Bankroll" Rothstein. He sat in on the last poker game Rothstein played before he was gunned down in 1928. Thompson also defrauded people on the golf course, where he swindled dozens of amateur players. He reportedly collected $250,000 annually in bets with wealthy golfers. His victims thought he was strictly second rate, but actually Thompson hit well left- and right-handed. After trouncing his opponent while playing right-handed, he would offer his partner a chance to recoup his losses by playing left-handed. Thompson then doubled his earnings, for he was a natural lefty. See: **Rothstein, Arnold.**

REF.: *CBA*; Nash, *Hustlers and Con Men;* (FICTION), Wilstach, *Under Cover Man.*

Thomas, Arthur Alan, prom. 1970, N. Zea., mur. Jeanette and Harvey Crewe were a New Zealand couple, living on a farm near the village of Pukekwa. One day in June 1970, Jeanette's father stopped by the farm and found the couple's 18-month-old child, apparently abandoned. Bloodstains were found, and the police, aided by the army, mounted a massive search. On Aug. 16, the body of Jeanette Crewe was found in the Waikato River, wrapped in a sheet. She had been shot in the head with a .22-caliber bullet and bound with wire. Exactly one month later, the body of Harvey Crewe, killed by a bullet of the same caliber and weighted down by a car axle, was found in the same river. Test firings of all .22-caliber weapons in the area led police to suspect Arthur Alan Thomas, a neighboring farmer. Officials later learned that Thomas had once courted Jeanette Crewe. In November 1970, he was charged with the double murder. In February 1971, in the Auckland Supreme Court, Arthur Thomas was found Guilty of the murders and sentenced to life imprisonment.

REF.: Bell, *Bitter Hill; CBA;* (FILM), *Beyond Reasonable Doubt,* 1980.

Thomas, Donald George, c.1925- , Brit., mur. Police constable Nathaniel Edgar stopped a suspicious-looking character while patrolling a crime-ridden area of London on Feb. 13, 1948. People nearby heard three shots, saw a man running from the scene, and found that an officer had been gunned down. The mortally wounded officer had obtained his assailant's name and address and had them written in his notebook—Donald Thomas, 247 Cambridge Road, Enfield.

Thomas was an army deserter who had been on the military's wanted list for many months. The police tracked Thomas down and arrested him as he was trying to hide the gun that had killed Edgar. Police also found rounds of ammunition, a rubber truncheon, and a book on handgun shooting. Furthermore, he had confessed the crime to his landlady.

In April, Thomas was tried, found Guilty of murder, and sentenced to death. The sentence was commuted to life in prison because the courts enacted a temporary suspension of the death penalty.

REF.: Beveridge, *Inside the CID; CBA;* Harrison, *Criminal Calendar;* Heppenstall, *The Sex War and Others;* O'Donnell, *The Old Bailey and Its Trials;* Scott, *Scotland Yard;* Shew, *A Companion to Murder;* Wilson, *Encyclopedia of Murder;* Wyles, *A Woman at Scotland Yard.*

Thomas, Earl of Lancaster (Earl of Leicester, Derby, Lincoln, and Salisbury), c.1277-1323, Brit., treas. Grandson of King Henry III and son of Edmund, the Earl of Lancaster. He controlled baronial opposition to King Edward II, and successfully forced the king to relinquish his powers to a baronial committee comprised of twenty-one lords ordainers in 1311. He was also instrumental in arranging the banishment in 1308 and eventual execution in 1312 of the king's beloved adviser, Piers Gaveston. He temporarily seized all of the king's powers following the British defeat in Bannockburn in 1314, but was soon rendered ineffective. He was seized by Edward's soldiers after a failed reconciliation following the 1318 Treaty of Leake, and was beheaded. REF.: *CBA.*

Thomas, Edward, prom. 1941, U.S., mur. On Apr. 22, 1941, 73-year-old Addie Gilman was found dead on the floor of her Brooklyn home, an apparent suicide. Gas jets had been left on and there were no signs of a violent struggle. Also, she had been depressed by the departure of her daughter, who had moved upstate. However, no suicide note was found, and upon further examination of the corpse, officials determined she had been strangled.

The murderer had left no clues, but a note indicated that the woman had recently had financial troubles with the upstairs tenant, Jerry Croft. A search of her diary entries uncovered the name of Croft's brother-in-law, Edward Thomas. Also, a friend of Gilman's had stopped by for a visit just before her murder. Gilman was expecting another visitor soon, and mistakenly called out "Hello, Eddie" when he arrived. The friend, however, did not see Gilman's other visitor. This, plus the diary entries, led detectives to Edward Thomas. Thomas, a 21-year-old airport mechanic, was greeted by detectives Harry G. Lavin and William Brennan when he returned home from work. He admitted he had been in the Gilman home, but only to negotiate a settlement of his relative's back rent. Detective Lavin continued to question Thomas, finally accusing him of choking Gilman. The suspect then blurted out information only the killer would have known. Realizing his error, Thomas confessed. On June 3, 1941, Edward Thomas pleaded guilty to first-degree manslaughter, and three weeks later was sentenced to a term of ten-to-twenty years in Sing Sing.

REF.: *CBA;* Radin, *Twelve Against the Law.*

Thomas, Elizabeth, 1875-1953, Brit., (unsolv.) mur. On Jan. 10, 1953, 78-year-old Elizabeth Thomas was found beaten and stabbed in her home in the British village of Laugharne, in Carmarthenshire. She was found by a neighbor who heard her screams. She died the following day. A local man, George Roberts, deaf and dumb since birth, had been seen near the victim's cottage. He was arrested, but the police could not communicate with the illiterate man. Police found no bloodstains on his clothing, nor did they find his fingerprints in the cottage. He was still brought to trial in Cardiff, but was found Not Guilty. The murder of Elizabeth Thomas remains unsolved.

REF.: *CBA;* Furneaux, *Famous Criminal Cases, vol. 1.*

Thomas, Frederick Jerome, 1959- , and **McAdoo, Anthony LaQuin,** 1961- , U.S., rob.-mur. On Nov. 12, 1980, Sarai Ribicoff, the niece of former Connecticut senator Abraham Ribicoff, was having dinner with a friend in Venice, Calif. Upon leaving the restaurant, two young men, Frederick Jerome Thomas and Anthony LaQuin McAdoo, accosted the pair. Thomas, brandishing a 9-mm. automatic weapon, demanded the couple's jewelry. During an ensuing struggle, Thomas put the barrel of the pistol to Sarai Ribicoff's back and pulled the trigger. The bullet went straight threw her, piercing both lungs as well as her heart, killing her. But police found evidence of two different blood types on the sidewalk, and a check of hospital emergency rooms turned up Frederick Thomas on the same date. He had been shot by the same bullet.

Robber and killer Frederick Jerome Thomas.

Thomas and McAdoo were arrested and charged with the murder. During the trial, Thomas was hostile and unrepentant. He avoided the death penalty by a narrow margin and was sentenced to life imprisonment with no possibility of parole. McAdoo turned state's evidence, and thus was sentenced to only twenty-five years in prison with the possibility of parole after seventeen years. REF.: *CBA.*

Thomas, Henry (AKA: Thomas Dean, James Mitchell), 1815-46, U.S., mur. Born in the heart of the Midwest, Henry Thomas was an accomplished burglar by his mid-twenties. His criminal career came to an abrupt halt on Nov. 20, 1844, in Bourneville, Ohio. Thomas and a henchman, Leroy J. Maxon, were attempting to rob a store owned by Frederick Edwards when the proprietor happened on the scene. Thomas brandished a knife and stabbed Edwards repeatedly until he fell to the floor dead. The murderer was tried and convicted of first-degree murder at Chillicothe, Ohio, in December 1845. His partner traded state's evidence in return for a lesser conviction on a charge of theft. Thomas was hanged on Mar. 6, 1846, in Chillicothe. Eyewitnesses reported that the condemned man met his death with "unexampled fortitude" and not a single nerve or muscle in his body quivered as he was led to the gallows.

REF.: *CBA; The Life and Adventures of Henry Thomas, the Western Burglar and Murderer;* Nash, *Bloodletters and Badmen.*

Thomas, Henry Andrew (AKA: **Heck**), 1850-1912, U.S., west. lawman. One of the Wild West's most effective lawmen, Henry Andrew Thomas, apprehended many notorious outlaws including members of the Doolin gang, the Dalton Gang, and the Sam Bass Gang. A native of Athens, Ga., Thomas was a courier in the Civil War when he was twelve. He joined the Atlanta police force after the war and gained fame as a fearless fighter after being wounded in one of the city's race riots. He and his wife moved to Texas in 1875 where he worked as a guard for the Texas Express Company. He was promoted to detective in 1876 after preventing a train robbery by hiding the money in an unlit stove. As detective, he led posses that captured several members of the Sam Bass Gang. Thomas turned to bounty hunting in 1885, capturing two murderers, brothers Jim and Pink Lee. Pursuing the brothers another time, Thomas gave them the chance to surrender as was his custom. The brothers declined and fired on Thomas, who killed them in the shootout.

Lawman Heck Thomas.

Thomas was appointed deputy U.S. marshal later that year and moved to Fort Smith, Ark. Under the jurisdiction of "Hanging Judge" Isaac Parker, Thomas pursued outlaws and fugitives in the Indian Territory. During his tenure, fifteen Indian Territory officers were killed while Thomas, often singlehandedly, brought in numerous outlaws. On his first excursion, for example, he apprehended eight murderers, a bootlegger, a horse thief, and seven other outlaws. Another time, while riding alone, he brought in four murderers. His wife divorced him by 1888, and by 1891, he and Chris Madsen, another deputy U.S. marshal, were trailing the Dalton and Doolin gangs. The Daltons, desperate to avoid the two lawmen, attempted to simultaneously rob two banks in Coffeyville, Kan., to get enough money to go to South America. Most of the gang was slaughtered during the attempt, Thomas and Madsen arriving shortly after the gunfire ceased.

Thomas and Madsen, joined by William Tilghman, tracked the Doolin Gang, and Thomas captured and killed several members. In 1893, the three lawmen, later known as the "Three Guardsmen," were assigned to tame Perry, a town in Oklahoma Territory, and within three years, they arrested more than 300 wanted men. In 1896, Thomas collected the reward for killing William Doolin. According to one story, he led a posse to Doolin's cabin at night and engaged the outlaw in a shootout. Another story told of how Thomas found Doolin dead of consumption, blasted the corpse twice with his shotgun, took the body in, and gave the $5,000 reward money to Doolin's widow. The lawman moved to Lawton, in the Oklahoma Territory, in 1902, and served for seven years as the town's chief of police. He retired in 1909 after a heart attack and died on Aug. 15, 1912. See: **Dalton Brothers; Doolin, William M.; Tilghman, William.**

REF.: American Guide Series, *Oklahoma, A Guide to the Sooner State;* Bartholomew, *The Biographical Album of Western Gunfighters;* Breihan, *Badmen of Frontier Days;* ____, *Great Gunfighters of the West;* ____, *Outlaws of the Old West;* Bryant, *Great American Guns and Frontier Fighters;* Canton, *Frontier Trails; CBA;* Croy, *He Hanged Them High;* ____, *Trigger Marshal;* Denton, *A Two-Gun Cyclone;* Douglas, *The History of Tulsa, Oklahoma;* ____, *Territory Tales;* Drago, *Outlaws on Horseback;* ____, *Red River Valley;* ____, *Road Agents and Train Robbers;* Elman, *Fired in Anger;* Gardner, *The Old Wild West;* Glasscock, *Then Came Oil;* Graves, *Oklahoma Outlaws;* Hall, *The Beginnings of Tulsa;* Hanes, *Bill Doolin;* Harrinton, *Hanging Judge;* Hendricks, *The Bad Man of the West;* Hicks, *Belle Starr and Her Pearl;* Holloway, *Texas Gun Lore;* Horan and Sann, *Pictorial History of the Wild West;* Hunter and Rose, *The Album of Gun-Fighters;* Hutchinson, *The Life & Personal Writings of Eugene Manlove Rhodes;* Lake, *Under Cover for Wells Fargo;* McKennon, *Iron Men;* Miller, *Hail to Yesterday;* Newsom, *The Life and Practice of the Wild and Modern Indian;* Nix, *Oklahombres;* Preece, *The Dalton Gang;* Raine, *Guns of the Frontier;* Sabin, *Wild Men of the Wild West;* Shirley, *Heck Thomas;* ____, *Henry Starr;* ____, *Law West of Fort Smith;* ____, *Six-Gun and Silver Star;* Sterling, *Famous Western Outlaw-Sheriff Battles;* Sutton, *Hands Up!;* Tilghman, *Marshal of the Last Frontier;* ____, *Outlaw Days;* Wellman, *A Dynasty of Western Outlaws*

Thomas, John Robert, 1846-1914, U.S., jur. Appointed to territorial court of Indian Territory by President William McKinley in 1897. He served as Illinois state's attorney from 1871-74, and as a U.S. congressman from 1879-89. REF.: *CBA.*

Thomas, Leonard Jack, 1903- , Brit., mur. In London on Mar. 13, 1949, Leonard Jack Thomas stabbed his estranged wife, Florence Ethel Lavinia, thirteen times with a jackknife. She survived and on May 2, Thomas was sentenced at the Old Bailey to seven years in prison for attempted murder. Then his wife died of her injuries, and Thomas was ordered to be retried for murder. On July 13, the defense moved for dismissal, as Thomas was already serving time for the same attack, and no man could be put in peril twice for the same offense. However, the plea was rejected and Thomas stood trial for murder. He then pleaded temporary insanity stating he and his wife had had an argument over dancing lessons, but that he had blacked out, only to find himself standing with a knife over his wounded wife. The jury was unsympathetic and sentenced him to death. However, more than 12,000 people signed an appeal, begging for mercy, which was sent to the home secretary. The king, on the advice of the secretary, commuted the death sentence.

REF.: *CBA;* Harrison, *Criminal Calendar;* O'Donnell, *The Old Bailey and its Trials;* Shew, *A Second Companion to Murder.*

Thomas, Roma, 1889-1918, Aus., (unsolv.) mur. On Aug. 31, 1918, the body of 29-year-old Roma Thomas was found in her home in the slums of Melbourne, Australia. Her death was the final step of the gradual downfall of the woman, who at one time seemed destined for a prominant and prosperous stage career. As an 18-year-old in 1907, Roma was a trim, vivacious, and popular show girl. She had inumerable suitors and her life was filled with champaign suppers. However, the lifestyle took its toll and she lost her job at the theater. She became a hotel barmaid, and her drinking problem worsened. In 1914, she married a sailor, Peter Samuel Smith, but he quickly tired of her promiscuous ways. She next lived with a postal worker, Thomas Norman Violet, and their life together degenerated into a series of drunken rows. WWI forced hotel closings, and Roma was suddenly out of a job. She supported herself as prostitute until she was stabbed to death. Her murder was never solved.

REF.: *CBA;* Gurr, *Famous Australasian Crimes.*

Thomas, Sarah Harriet, 1832-49, Brit., mur. In early 1849 in Bristol, England, 61-year-old Elizabeth Jefferies was murdered by her maidservant, 17-year-old Sarah Harriet Thomas. The young woman had been treated shamelessly, and was often kept near starvation by Jeffries. Thomas retaliated by sneaking into Jeffries' bedroom and beating her on the head with a stone until she died. Because the attack had obviously been premeditated, it was impossible to reduce the charge from murder to manslaughter, and Sarah Thomas was sentenced to death. In a heart-rending scene, eliciting pity from even the executioner, William Calcraft, she was hanged at Bristol on Apr. 20, 1849.

REF.: Altick, *Victorian Studies in Scarlet;* Bleackley, *Hangmen of England; CBA;* Potter, *The Art of Hanging.*

Thomas, William, See: **Beck, Adolph**.

Thomas, William F. (AKA: **Podmore**), prom. 1928, Brit., theft-mur. In September 1928, Mr. Vivian Messiter was appointed manager of an oil company in Southhampton, England. On Oct. 30, he left his home to meet a client, and was never seen alive again. His landlord reported his absence to the police, but a search revealed no clues. On Jan. 10, 1929, Messiter's replacement at the oil company found the corpse of his predecessor on the floor of a locked company garage. The body was badly decomposed, hindering the medical investigation, but it was determined that the death was caused from blows to the head with a blunt instrument.

The investigation was stymied until police found a note signed by Messiter to W.F. Thomas, stating he had adjusted the time of an appointment on the day that Messiter disappeared. As the police searched for Thomas, they learned that he had also robbed a Downton man of £143. Further, Thomas and his wife had fled from Birmingham when news releases stated that Messiter's body had been found. Thomas was found living under the alias of Podmore in a London hotel.

The police in England were not able to detain a man merely for the purpose of interrogating him, so, Thomas was charged with the theft of an automobile and sentenced to six months at Manchester. Upon release from Manchester, he was transferred to Winchester, and found Guilty on the theft charge. During his second prison term, he admitted to fellow inmates that he had killed Messiter. While in Winchester, he was found Guilty of the murder, sentenced to death, and executed Apr. 22, 1929.

REF.: *CBA;* Thomson, *The Story of Scotland Yard.*

Thomas, William King, prom. 1875, Ger., bomb.-suic. On Dec. 11, 1875, in Bremerhaven, Germany, an explosion occurred on a horse-drawn wagon approaching a ship, killing more than 100 people. The owner of the wagon, William King Thomas, was already aboard the ship when the blast destroyed his wares. He committed suicide, but not before admitting that the explosion was intentional. He had planted a barrel of powder amidst his goods and a fusing mechanism was timed to explode when the ship was far out to sea, Thomas himself had disembarked in Southhampton, and if his plan had been successful, he would have collected a large sum of insurance money.

REF.: *CBA;* Thorwald, *Crime and Science.*

Thomasius, Christian (Thomas), 1655-1728, Ger., jur. Taught at University of Halle from 1694, credited with enhancing its excellent academic reputation. Books authored: *Institutiones Jurisprudentiae Divinae, Fundament Juris Naturae ac Gentium,* and others. REF.: *CBA.*

Thomas of Woodstock (AKA: **Duke of Gloucester, Earl of Buckingham**), 1355-97, Brit., consp. Seventh and youngest son of King Edward III. He participated in the defeat at Dover of the French and Spanish in 1380, and helped quell the revolt by Essex peasants in 1381. He was named duke in 1385, headed the opposition against his nephew King Richard II, and participated in the removals of two of Richard's aides, Michael de la Pole, also known as the Earl of Suffolk, in 1386, and Robert de Vere, in 1387. He justly earned a reputation for seeking barbaric vengeance while serving as head of the lords appellant in the Wonderful Parliament in 1388. He lost much of his power when Richard II took control of the government in 1389, but was selected lieutenant of Ireland in 1392. He was seized by Richard II on a charge of conspiracy in 1397, and killed in Calais, presumably on the king's orders. REF.: *CBA.*

Thompson, Anne E., 1934- , U.S., jur. Appointed to district court of New Jersey by President Jimmy Carter in 1979. Earlier, she served as New Jersey public defender from 1967-70, as judge in the municipal court of Trenton, N.J., from 1972-75, and as county prosecutor of Mercer County, N.J., from 1975-79. REF.: *CBA.*

Thompson, Ben, 1842-84, U.S., west. gunman. Born in Knottingly, Yorkshire, England on Nov. 11, 1842, western gambler and gunfighter Ben Thompson immigrated to Austin, Texas, with his family in 1849. He had his first gunfight in 1858, when he shot another teen-ager in the back with a load of buckshot as the other boy turned and fled. After finishing his schooling, Thompson went to work as a printer. In 1860, he moved to New Orleans, where he worked in the related field of book binding. While pursuing these conventional occupations, Thompson got into more fights, showing the tendency toward violence that would later dominate his life.

Ben Thompson, the deadly western gunman.

When the Civil War began, Thompson joined the Confederate Army and served in Texas, New Mexico, and Louisiana. Various accounts indicate that Thompson split his attention during those years between soldiering and other activities such as gambling and smuggling whiskey. He was wounded and mustered out of the army in 1863 and married soon after. He got into a shootout in Austin in 1865, was arrested and jailed, and bribed the two men guarding him to let him escape. He made his way to Mexico with the two former jailers and serviced with distinction as a mercenary soldier in the employ of Emperor Maximilian.

For the next fifteen years, Thompson divided his time between Texas and Kansas and was involved in several shootings. He saved the life of a judge in Austin in 1867, but the following year he shot his brother-in-law in the side (he claimed he just meant to scare him) for beating up Thompson's wife. Thompson turned himself in but got into an argument with a magistrate, whose life he threatened and who sentenced him to four years as a result. Thompson served two years of the sentence. In 1869, in a saloon in Ogallalie, Kan., he shot the gun out of the hand of a man who was causing trouble by pointing it at the other men at the bar as a joke. He said afterward, "I just wanted to slow him down a bit before he got himself into real trouble." Thompson later owned and operated the Bull's Head Saloon in Abilene, Kan., with an old friend, Phil Coe but sold out and moved to Ellsworth, Kan., in 1873. There he got into the most famous gunfight of his career when his brother, Billy Thompson, shot and killed the popular sheriff C.B. Whitney. He told Billy to get out of town, saying, "You've shot Whitney, our best friend." After Billy left, Thompson stayed to face the angry crowd alone. Ben finally surrendered to deputy sheriff Ed Hogue, although Sheriff Wyatt Earp claimed for years to come that he had captured Thompson. Whitney exonerated Billy on his deathbed, acknowledging that the shooting was accidental; when Billy was tried in 1877, he was acquitted.

In 1881, Thompson was elected marshal of Austin, Texas. He was a highly effective lawman but gave the job up the following year after killing Jack Harris, the owner of the Variety Theater in Austin. On Mar. 11, 1884, fourteen months after he was acquitted of Harris' murder, Thompson and his friend, John "King" Fisher, were watching a show at the Vaudeville Theater in San Antonio when Jack Harris' two partners, Joe Foster and William Sims, started a gunfight in which Thompson was killed and Foster and Fisher were mortally wounded. See: **Earp, Wyatt Berry Stapp; Fisher, John King.**

REF.: American Guide Series, *Texas, A Guide to the Lone Star State;* Barkley, *History of Travis County and Austin;* Bartholomew, *The Biographical Album of Western Gunfighters;* ____, *Wyatt Earp, 1848 to 1880;* Breihan, *Badmen of Frontier Days;* ____, *Great Gunfighters of the West;* ____, *Great Lawmen of the West;* ____, *Outlaws of the Old West;* Brent, *Great Western Heroes;* Brown and Schmitt, *Trail Driving Days;* Bushick, *Glamorous Days;* Casey, *The Texas Border; CBA;* Chapel, *Guns of the Old West;* Chilton, *The Book of the West;* Clark, *Then Came the Railroads;* Connelley, *Wild Bill and His Era;* Cook, *Fifty Years on the Old Frontier;* ____, *Longhorn Cowboy;* Corner, *San Antonio de Bexar;* Cunningham, *Triggernometry;* Curtis, *Fabulous San Antonio;* Davis, *The West From a Car Window;* Dobie, *A Vaquero of the Brush Country;* Drago, *Great American Cattle Trails;* ____, *Wild, Woolly & Wicked;* Durham, *Taming the Neuces Strip;* Dykstra, *The Cattle Towns;* Elman, *Fired in Anger;* Emmett, *Shanghai Pierce;* Farber, *Texans With Guns;* Fergusson, *Rio Grande;* Fisher and Dykes, *King Fisher;* Fitzpatrick, *This Is New Mexico;* Foster-Harris, *The Look of the Old West;* Frantz and Choate, *The American Cowboy;* Gard, *The Chisholm Trail;* ____, *Frontier Justice;* ____, *Rawhide Texas;* Gaylord, *Hangunner's Guide;* Grey, *Seeking a Fortune in America;* Hall-Quest, *Wyatt Earp;* Hardy, *Wild Bill Hickok;* Hart, *Old Forts of the Southwest;* Hendricks, *The Bad Man of the West;* Holloway, *Texas Gun Lore;* Horan, *Authentic Wild West;* ____, *The Great American West;* ____ and Sann, *Pictorial History of the Wild West;* Hough, *The Story of the Outlaw;* House, *City of Flaming Adventure;* ____, *Cowtown Columnist;* Hudson, *Andy Adams;* Hunter and Rose, *The Album of Gun-Fighters;* Huson, *Refugio;* Hutchinson, *The Life & Personal Writings of Eugene Manlove Rhodes;* Jameson, *Heroes by the Dozen;* Jelinek, *Ellsworth, Kansas, 1867-1947;* ____, *90 Years of Ellsworth and Ellsworth County History;* Jennings, *A Texas Ranger;* Johnson, *Famous Lawmen of the Old West;* Knight, *Wild Bill Hickok;* Knowles, *Gentlemen, Scholars and Scoundrels;* Lake, *Under Cover for Wells Fargo;* Lake, *Wyatt Earp;* Leakey, *The West That Was;* Lieberson, *The Columbia Records Legacy Collection;* McCarty, *The Enchanted West;* McCarty, *The Gunfighters;* Marshall, *Swinging Doors;* Masterson, *Famous Gunfighters of the Western Frontier;* Miller and Cooper, *Footloose Fiddler;* Miller and Snell, *Why the West Was Wild;* Monaghan, *The Book of the American West;* Myers, *Doc Holliday;* ____, *The Last Chance;* Nash, *Bloodletters and Badmen;* Nordyke, *John Wesley Hardin;* O'Connor, *Bat Masterson;* ____, *Wild Bill Hickok;* O'Neal, *They Die But Once;* Orman, *A Room For the Night;* Paddock, *History of Texas;* Paine, *Texas Ben Thompson;* Parkhill, *The Wildest of the West;* Penfield, *Western Sheriffs and Marshals;* Peyton, *San Antonio;* Plenn, *Texas Hellion;* ____ and LaRoche, *The Fastest Gun in Texas;* Preece, *The Dalton Gang;* ____, *Lone Star Man;* Raine, *Famous Sheriffs & Western Outlaws;* ____, *Guns of the Frontier;* Rascoe, *Belle Starr;* Rath, *Early Ford County;* Raymond, *Captain Lee Hall of Texas;* Ripley, *They Died With Their Boots On;* Roberts, *Springs From Parched Ground;* Rosa, *The Gunfighter, Man or Myth?;* ____, *They Called Him Wild Bill;* Sabin, *Wild Men of the Wild West;* Sandoz, *The Cattle Men;* Schoenberger, *Gunfighters;* Scott, *Such Outlaws as Jesse James;* Siringo, *Riata and Spurs;* Small, *The Best of True West;* Snell, *Painted Ladies of the Cowtown Frontier;* Stanley, *Dave Rudabaugh;* Steckmesser, *The Western Hero in History and Legend;* Steen, *The Texas News;* Streeter, *Ben Thompson;* ____, *The Kaw;* ____, *Prairie Trails & Cow Towns;* ____, *Tragedies of a Kansas Cow Town;* Sutton, *Hands Up!;* Tilghman, *Marshal of the Last Frontier;* Triplett, *History, Romance and Philosophy of Great American Crimes and Criminals;* Waters, *The Story of Mrs. Virgil Earp;* White, *Texas;* Williams, *Texas Trails;* Wilson, *Out of the West;* Young, *True Stories of Old Houston and Houstonians.*

Thompson, Edith Jessie (Edie), d.1923, Brit., mur. Edith Thompson and Frederick Bywaters became lovers during Summer 1921. Bywaters, a sailor, was a family friend of Thompson and her husband, Percy, and in June had accompanied the couple on a vacation at the Isle of Wight. The Thompsons began to experience marital discord, and by September Thompson was secretly meeting Bywaters during his extended leaves from sea. The affair continued into the following year until late in the evening of Oct. 4, 1922, when Percy Thompson was stabbed to death by an assailant as he and his wife were returning to their London home. Police encountered an hysterical Edith Thompson, who proclaimed that she had done everything within her power to save her husband's life. Authorities might have believed her, but a neighbor stepped forward and told of the relationship with Bywaters.

Edith Thompson, murderess.

Frederick Bywaters, Edith and Percy Thompson, 1922, shortly before Bywaters and Edith killed Perry Thompson.

Searching Bywaters' quarters, police discovered sixty-two letters from Edith proclaiming her love and detailing aborted attempts to poison her husband. The couple was arrested, and Bywaters was charged with the Percy Thompson murder, Edith Thompson charged with being an accessory. They were brought to trial on Dec. 6, 1922, in the Old Bailey courtroom of Justice Shearman. Sir Henry Curtis-Bennett, defending Thompson, and Cecil Whiteley, defending Bywaters, attempted to have the letters dismissed as evidence, but Prosecutor Sir Thomas Inskip successfully won their inclusion. Bywaters confessed to the attack but said it was in self-defense and in no way premeditated. He further absolved Edith Thompson of any complicity. But Thompson took the stand and, under intense interrogation, admitted the details of the affair and conversations with Bywaters about eliminating her husband. The jury of eleven men and one woman deliberated for two hours before finding both defendants guilty of murder. Amidst pleas of innocence, both were sentenced to death. They appealed, were denied, and at 9 a.m. on Jan. 9, 1923, Edith Thompson swung from the prison gallows at Holloway, while Bywaters met a similar fate a short distance away at Pentonville.

REF: Bowker, *Behind the Bar;* Broad, *The Innocence of Edith Thompson;* Brophy, *The Meaning of Murder;* Browne, *Sir Travers Humphreys;* ____ and Tullett, *The Scalpel of Scotland Yard; CBA;* Cuthbert, *Science and the Detection of Crime;* Deans, *Notable Trails, Difficult Cases;* Dearden, *Some Cases of Sir Bernard Spilsbury and Others;* Dilnot, *Rogues' March;* Dudley, *Bywaters and Mrs. Thompson;* Goodman, *Posts-Mortem—The Correspondence of Murder;* Gribble, *Adventures in Murder;* Grice, *Great Cases of Sir Henry Curtis Bennett KC;* Humphreys, *A Book of Trials;* Hyde, *United in Crime;* Lambton, *Thou Shalt Do No Murder;* Lustgarten, *The Murder and the Trial;* ____, *Verdict in Dispute;* Morland, *Hangman's Clutch;* Neil, *Manhunters of Scotland Yard;* Nicholls, *Crime Within the Square Mile; Notable British Trials;* O'Donnell, *Should Women Hang?;* Parmiter, *Reasonable Doubt;* Potter, *The Art of Hanging;* Randall, *The Famous Cases of Sir Bernard Spilsbury;* Shew, *A Second Companion to Murder;* Speer, *The Secret History of Great Crimes;* Thomson, *The Story of Scotland Yard;* Townsend, *Black Cap, Murder Will Out;* Wensley, *Forty Years of Scotland Yard;* Whiteley, *Brief Life;* Wilson, *Encyclopedia oj Murder;* (DRAMA), Vosper, *Spellbound;* (FICTION), Iles, *As for the Woman;* Jesse, *A Pin to See the Peep Show;*

Thompson, Elizabeth, and **Fromant, Kenneth Joseph**, prom. 1971, Brit., mur. On Nov. 5, 1971, the body of 35-year-old Peter Stanswood was found in a parked car on a road near Portsmouth, England. Stanswood, a local businessman, had been stabbed seven times with a Japanese paper knife. The ensuing investigation revealed that Stanswood, a married man with two children, had been involved in an extraordinary number of extramarital affairs. Two of the women bore his children, while a third woman was pregnant. A prime suspect would have been his wife, but it was revealed that Heather Stanswood had had about two dozen lovers of her own. The most recent was Kenneth Fromant, a 39-year-old gas company worker, who had a criminal record. It was further revealed that Peter Stanswood was involved with Elizabeth Thompson, the wife of his business partner.

Nine months after the murder, a Scottish woman stated that her boyfriend had been at the crime scene with Kenneth Fromant. On July 17, 1972, Fromant was interrogated and stated that he had spent the night with Elizabeth Thompson. However, his blood matched the sample taken from the victim's car, and soil samples from Fromant's car tires matched similar samples on the other car. The police waited almost three years, until May 19, 1975, to arraign Fromant and Heather Stanswood on the charge of murder. Stanswood was soon released, and Thompson arrested instead. Thompson stated that she had met Stanswood but they had been surprised by Fromant. A fight ensued and Fromant killed Stanswood. Thompson was formally arrested on Aug. 5, and ordered to stand trial with Fromant.

At the trial on Oct. 21, 1975, at the Winchester Crown courtroom of Justice Talbot, Fromant admitted to being at the murder scene but stated that the killer was Elizabeth Thompson. The jury sentenced them both to life imprisonment.

REF.: *CBA;* Dunning, *The Arbor House Treasury of True Crime.*

Thompson, George, 1804-78, Brit.-U.S., exile. British abolitionist who worked with John Greenleaf Whittier and William Lloyd Garrison in U.S. anti-slavery movement from 1834-35. He was censured and forced to leave the U.S. by President Andrew Jackson. REF.: *CBA.*

Thompson, George (AKA: **Buck Jones**), d.1962, S. Afri., mur. Dillie and Koos Scholtz, a happily married young couple, had good jobs, a nice home, and were quite content in Greenways, a suburb of Cape Town, S. Afri. On July 3, 1961, Koos left for work at about 8 a.m. and Dillie twenty minutes later. When Dillie Scholtz failed to arrive at work, the police were called. Soon it became apparent that Dillie Scholtz had disappeared within a few minutes of leaving the house that morning. Her car was still parked in the garage.

When the police arrived, Koos described his wife's usual routine, and they explored the grounds. While they were in the alley, they were greeted by George "Buck Jones" Thompson, a local handyman who was known to the police as an occasional informant. Buck, apparently somewhat drunk, said he had not seen the woman.

On July 9, while excavating a compost heap a short distance from the garage, the police discovered Dillie Scholtz's body, buried with her purse, keys, a coat, and some work she had been taking to her office. The body, which was burned, was in a sack and had a necktie tied around the throat. One of the constables assigned to the case recognized the necktie as belonging to George Thompson. Investigation determined that on the morning of the murder Thompson was seen by one of his friends standing by a fire near the garage. He had told his friend to wait for him and that he would buy him a drink. He showed up a short while later with a shopping bag and plenty of money.

Thompson was charged with murder. During his trial, he tried to implicate another person, but the chain of evidence was too strong and he was found Guilty of premeditated murder. He was hanged on Mar. 29, 1962.

REF.: Bennett, *Murder Will Speak; CBA.*

Thompson, George, and **Weipert, Lee**, prom. 1932, U.S., rob.-mur. In December 1932 in Council Grove, Kan., four men robbed a local cafe. During the robbery, an unsuspecting citizen, O.T. Winters, walked in, surprising the bandits, and was shot dead from point-blank range. The police suspected George Thompson, who was an accomplice in an earlier robbery in Pilsen, Kan., for which Charles Smith already had been sentenced. Thompson was traced to a Kansas City hotel and two men, Lee Weipert and Harry Styles, were found drunk in his room. Thompson was found in a nightclub a short distance away and was arrested.

George Thompson and Lee Weipert were identified by eyewitnesses as the the killers of O.T. Winters. In the courtroom of Judge C.M. Clark, they both pleaded guilty and were sentenced to life imprisonment.

REF.: *CBA;* Cohen, *One Hundred True Crime Stories.*

Thompson, Gerald, 1910-35, U.S., rape-mur. Gerald Thompson was a mild-mannered young man who lived with his grandmother and had a good work record as a toolmaker for the Caterpillar Tractor Company in Peoria, Ill. Yet this most unlikely rapist/murderer had once bragged to an ex-friend that he had raped more than fifty-two women in the previous year.

Rapist-murderer Gerald Thompson, 1935.

His *modus operandi* included picking up unsuspecting young women and driving them to a secluded spot. To prevent them from escaping he had wired the door handles of his car to the battery so a woman trying to open the door would receive an electric shock. He would then use a pair of scissors to methodically cut away his victim's clothes and proceed to rape them. Many times, after the rape was completed, he would turn on the headlights of his car and force his victim to perform additional sex acts with him in the bright lights while an automatic camera photographed them in action.

But on June 18, 1935, he finally met one victim who resisted his efforts violently. In the struggle, Thompson killed Mildred Hallmark, the daughter of one of his fellow workers. During the battle between them, Hallmark scratched and fought back with all her strength, drawing blood with her fingernails. Thompson went berserk and started to beat her wildly. Hallmark still fought back, striking him repeatedly with a fountain pen until she fell back, unconscious, and died. He dumped her body in a nearby ravine and went home to bed. He later claimed to have had a good night's sleep.

On a tip, Thompson was picked up by the police six days later and, after hours of grilling, confessed. In addition to his confession, they had Thompson's bloodstained clothes, a bloodstained car cushion, and his diary which contained the names and addresses of many of his rape victims. Police also found numerous obscene photos that he had taken following the rapes.

Gerald Thompson's career as a rapist and murderer ended when he was electrocuted at Joliet Penitentiary on Oct. 15, 1935.

REF.: Boucher, *The Quality of Murder; CBA;* Holmes, *Serial Murder;* Nash, *Bloodletters and Badmen.*

Thompson, Sir John Sparrow David, 1844-94, Can., jur. Served as Canada's minister of justice in 1885, supporting hanging of Louis Riel for treason. He also held the office of prime minister from 1892-94, and helped settle the Bering Sea Controversy in 1893. REF.: *CBA.*

Thompson, John Taliaferro, 1860-1940, U.S., firearms. Invented various airplane devices and firearms, most notably Thompson submachine gun (patented 1920), developed with assistance of U.S. naval commander John N. Blish. REF.: *CBA.*

Thompson, Lydia, c.1898-1945, U.S., (unsolv.) mur. The murderer of Lydia Thompson, wife of a wealthy Detroit businessman, had tortured her and mutilated her body before discarding it in a swamp. Her headless body was found on Oct. 13, 1945, near Pontiac, Mich.

Lydia Thompson, whose 1945 murder was never solved.

British-born Lydia and Victor Louis Thompson had immigrated to the Detroit area, where they began a business that provided them with a beautiful home. But Lydia did not enjoy the lavish social life Louis enjoyed, and as time went on they grew apart.

In early 1945, Lydia learned her husband was seeing other women, and she hired detectives. Discovered, Louis Thompson begged forgiveness and they reconciled. In May 1945, Lydia was informed by one of her detectives that her husband was in Miami with his secretary, Helen Budnik, and Lydia followed them to confront them both at their motel. They returned to Detroit, and the affair continued, with Louis eventually moving out of his wife's home.

Lydia, who had told friends that she feared for her life, was seen on Oct. 11, talking with an unidentified man and a woman outside her suburban home. No one saw her after that. Louis Thompson reported that she had substantial sums of money available to her and seemed puzzled as to what had happened to all of it. Some people thought it went to pay for detectives. Others thought she was planning to have a professional killer murder Budnik.

Helen Budnik and Louis were married only four months after Lydia's death. On Mar. 23, 1947, they were indicted for conspiracy to commit murder and murder. Fewer than two months later the accused were released for lack of evidence. The case of the murder of Lydia Thompson is still open and unsolved.

REF.: Asbury, *Gem of the Prairie; CBA;* Nash, *Open Files;* Rodell, *Detroit Murders.*

Thompson, Monroe (AKA: **Chick Monroe**), prom. 1895, Case of, U.S., rob. On Oct. 6, 1895, Monroe Thompson allegedly robbed a man of $36 on the near South Side of Chicago. The following day he was arrested by Detective Clifton R. Wooldridge and brought to trial. The prisoner attempted to escape through a crowd, but was apprehended by the agile detective. Thompson was next sent to a grand jury under an $800 bond. The case was dropped when the robbery victim refused to testify.

REF.: *CBA;* Wooldridge, *Hands Up.*

Thompson, Phil B., Jr., prom. 1883, Case of, U.S., mur. On Apr. 27, 1883, the congressman from the Eighth Congressional District of Kentucky, Phil B. Thompson, Jr., killed Walter Davis as Davis was entering a train near Harrodsburg, Ky. In December 1882, Davis allegedly coerced Thompson's wife to commit adultery in a Cincinnati hotel room after he had persuaded her to get drunk. In a trial that began May 8, Judge Charles A. Hardin drew a broad guideline for the jury, stressing that they should consider Thompson's mental health at the time of the shooting, considering the alleged actions of Davis. The sympathetic jury found that under the judge's broader definition of murder, Phil Thompson was Not Guilty.

REF.: *CBA;* Johnson, *Famous Kentucky Tragedies and Trials.*

Thompson, Robert J., 1909- , Mex., rape-rob.-mur. On Aug. 23, 1958, a Philadelphia woman, while on vaction in Mexico, met a man claiming to be an American engineer. She agreed to accompany him to a local village, but while in the car, she took a drink from a bottle and passed out. She awoke the next morning, naked, having been raped, beaten, and robbed. On Sept. 18, a New York woman escaped when a group of men appeared as the "American engineer" was about to attack her. Two more victims were not so lucky. A retired school teacher from Chicago was found dead by a road on Sept. 19. An autopsy revealed that her stomach contained a large quantity of chloral hydrate, or "knock-out drops." The fifth and final victim was a 52-year-old interior decorator who was also robbed, raped, and beaten on Sept. 23 and left on the side of a road near Pueblo. She died of her injuries two weeks later.

The final victim had taken two photographs of her attacker, which were found by a hotel bellman. The man was identified by Interpol as Robert J. Thompson, an itinerant engineer, mechanic, aviator, and mining prospector. He had several current warrants for robbery and assault against him. The photograph was widely distributed, and in late October Thompson was apprehended in the bar of a Mexico City hotel. The surviving victims identified him as the attacker, and in November 1958, Robert Thompson was sentenced to life imprisonment. REF.: *CBA.*

Thompson, Smith, 1768-1843, U.S., jur. Anti-federalist with presidential aspirations, beginning political career in New York state legislature in 1800. He was named associate justice of the state supreme court two years later. In 1814 he succeeded his family friend James Kent as chief justice of the court. He served five years as U.S. secretary of the navy, from 1819-23, when he was nominated to the U.S. Supreme Court by President John Tyler. He was critized five years into his tenure for staying on the court while he ran for governor of New York. He lost the election to family friend Martin Van Buren, and remained on the court as a staunch supporter of states' rights. In *Groves v. Slaughter* in 1841, he agreed with the majority in declaring the sale of slaves in Mississippi legitimate despite the state constitution. He strayed from his usual line in *Prigg v. Pennsylvania* in 1842, arguing that the Fugitive Slave Act constitutionally usurped state laws. REF.: *CBA.*

Thompson, Titanic, See: **Thomas, Alvin Clarence**.

Thompson, Tilmer Eugene, and **Mastrian, Norman**, and **Anderson, Dick**, prom. 1963, U.S., mur. St. Paul, Minn., attorney Tilmer Thompson and his wife Carol, the parents of four children, had met while attending Macalester College together in the late 1940s. On Mar. 6, 1963, Carol Thompson was attacked in her home, stabbed twenty-five times in the head and face, and clubbed with a blunt object. She died in the hospital after collapsing on a neighbor's doorstep. Cartridges from a luger pistol that had evidently misfired were found on the floor of the victim's home.

A few days after his wife's murder, Tilmer Thompson was seen in a local nightclub with an attractive woman. Investigators also discovered a dozen insurance policies on his wife's life, worth more than $1 million, naming him as the sole beneficiary. And his wife was sole heir to her parents' million-dollar fortune. Three extension phones had recently been removed from the Thompson house, and the family's pet dog, which had served as protection for the family, had been given away.

On Apr. 9, Minneapolis salesman Wayne F. Brandt reported to police that a luger pistol had been stolen from him on Feb. 14. On Apr. 17, two small-time hoods arrested for an attempted holdup of a St. Paul bar admitted stealing the luger from Brandt's apartment. They gave the gun to Norman Mastrian, who in turn was seen handing it to Dick Anderson. Mastrian, a 39-year-old ex-boxer, had been suspected of a 1961 murder, but was released. He was also a college classmate of the Thompsons. On Apr. 19, he was arrested for his involvement in the Thompson murder and police began to search for Anderson, whom they arrested shortly in a Phoenix motel. Anderson tried to plea bargain, hoping to reduce the first-degree murder charge. On June 20, he confessed to murder, saying that Mastrian had hired him to kill the woman in a manner that made her death seem accidental.

Tilmer Eugene Thompson was arrested and charged with first-degree murder on June 25, 1963, by the Ramsey County Grand Jury. On Dec. 6, 1963, before Judge Donald Odden, Thompson was found Guilty of instigating the murder plot and sentenced to life imprisonment "at hard labor." Dick Anderson and Norman Mastrian were also found Guilty and sentenced to life. REF.: *CBA.*

Thompson, William (AKA: **Texas Billy**), c.1845-88, U.S., west. gunman. The younger brother of the notorious western gunman Ben Thompson, William "Billy" Thompson continually needed his brother's protection. A less accurate gunman than Ben, he was more cold-blooded. When he was very young, his parents emigrated from Yorkshire, England, to Austin, Texas. The brothers enlisted in the Texas Mounted Rifles during the Civil War. Billy killed a fellow soldier and, with his brother's help, deserted and escaped to the Indian Territory, where he turned to gambling. After the war, he followed his brother to Ellsworth, Kan. One night in August 1873, Billy got drunk and in a rage shot and killed Sheriff C.B. Whitney. Ben helped his brother get out of town to sleep off his drunkenness. Billy returned to Ellsworth for a few days before fleeing to Buena Vista, Colo., where the outlaws made him mayor of the town. Three years later, he was captured by Texas Rangers and extradited to Kansas, where he was eventually acquitted of murder. Allegedly, his brother used threats and bribes to clear Billy.

Gunfighter Billy Thompson.

Billy returned briefly to Austin before following his brother to Dodge City, Kan. He then wandered into Nebraska, found employment, and supposedly shot off Texan Jim Thompson's finger. The rancher shot Billy in the back, and Bat Masterson helped him escape from Ogallala. Drifting down to Texas, by coincidence he was in San Antonio and saw his brother and King Fisher gunned down by a hidden marksman in 1884. Unarmed, Billy did not take revenge, but merely cried over the body of his protector. He wandered around the streets of San Antonio for a few days and then left town. After that, little is known of the younger Thompson brother. After reportedly hiding out in El Paso for a few months after committing murder in Corpus Christi, Texas, rumors persist that Billy Thompson was killed in Laredo, Texas, in 1888. See: **Thompson, Ben; Masterson, Bat.**

REF.: Bartholomew, *The Biographical Album of Western Gunfighters;* ____, *Wyatt Earp, 1848 to 1880;* Breihan, *Great Gunfighters of the West;* ____, *Great Lawmen of the West;* Brent, *Great Western Heroes;* Brown and Schmitt, *Trail Driving Days; CBA;* Chilton, *The Book of the West;* Drago, *Great American Cattle Trails;* ____, *Wild, Woolly & Wicked;* Dykstra, *The Cattle Towns;* Eisele, *The Real Wild Bill Hickok;* Flannery, *John Hunton's Diary;* Gard, *The Chisholm Trail;* ____, *Frontier Justice;* Hall-Quest, *Wyatt Earp;* Hart, *Old Forts of the Southwest;* Hendricks, *The Bad Man of the West;* Holloway, *Texas Gun Lore;* Horan, *The Great American West;* ____ and Sann, *Pictorial History of the Wild West;* Hough, *The Story of the Outlaw;* Hunter and Rose, *The Album of Gun-Fighters;* Huson, *Refugio;* Jelinek, *Ellsworth, Kansas, 1867-1947;* ____, *90 Years of Ellsworth and Ellsworth County History;* Jennings, *A Texas Ranger;* Johnson, *Famous Lawmen of the Old West;* Lake, *Under Cover for Wells Fargo;* Lake, *Wyatt Earp;* Metz, *Dallas Stoudenmire;* Miller and Snell, *Great Gunfighters of the Kansas Cowtowns;* Nelson, *Land of the Dacotahs;* O'Connor, *Bat Masterson;* Orman, *A Room for the Night;* Paine, *Texas Ben Thompson;* Parkhill, *The Wildest of the West;* Penfield, *Western Sheriffs and Marshals;* Plenn, *Texas Hellion;* ____ and LaRoche, *The Fastest Gun in Texas;* Preece, *The Dalton Gang;* ____, *Lone Star Man;* Raine, *Famous Sheriffs & Western Outlaws;* ____, *Guns of the Frontier;* Rascoe, *Belle Starr;* Raymond, *Captain Lee Hall of Texas;* Rosa, *The Gunfighter, Man or Myth?;* ____, *They Called Him Wild Bill;* Sandoz, *The Cattlemen;* Schoenberger, *Gunfighters;* Snell, *Painted Ladies of the Cowtown Frontier;* Steckmesser, *The Western Hero in History and Legend;* Streeter, *Ben Thompson;* ____, *The Kaw;* ____, *Prairie Trails & Cow Towns;* ____, *Tragedies of a Kansas Cow Town;* Wellman, *A Dynasty of Western Outlaws;* ____, *The Trampling Herd;* White, *Bat Masterson;* White, *Lead and Likker;* ____, *Texas;* Wilson, *Out of the West;* Young, *True Stories of Old Houston and Houstonians.*

Thompson, William, prom. 1853, Brit., mur. In 1853, the body of Lorenzo Beha, a watchmaker, was found on a lane connecting the English villages of Wellingham and Tittershall. His head had been nearly severed with a hatchet. A witness saw a local laborer, William Thompson, standing near the body. Thompson's cottage was searched and a large quantity of jewelry was found. Thompson claimed that he had seen a stranger commit the crime, and had then been forced to keep possession of the stolen gems or face an immediate death. The jury found him Guilty anyway, and sentenced him to the immediate death he had feared.

REF.: Butler, *Murderers' England; CBA.*

Thompson, William George, 1830-1911, U.S., jur. Appointed to territorial court of Idaho by President Rutherford B. Hayes in 1879. He served as prosecuting attorney of Linn County, Iowa, from 1854-56, and as a state senator from 1856-60, as well as serving in numerous other governmental positions. REF.: *CBA.*

Thompson, William Hale, 1867-1944, U.S., polit. corr. "Big Bill" Thompson was the mayor of Chicago for twelve stormy years. His liberal policies earned Chicago a reputation in the 1920s as a lawless, dangerous place where gunmen, thieves, resort keepers, and crooked politicians got away with the crimes they committed. Through it all, Thompson railed against his foes for alleged acts of treachery while cloaking his own misdeeds in a wash of civic boosterism. "Throw away your hammer!" he chortled. "Get a horn and blow loud for Chicago!"

The future mayor was part of a wealthy New England family, one of whose ancestors had arrived in the U.S. in 1700. His father was a successful real estate mogul who was elected to the New Hampshire state legislature on the Republican ticket in 1877. Thompson attended the Charles Fessenden Preparatory School in Chicago. Following the completion of his studies in Chicago, young Bill was seized by the compulsion to head West and sample life on the plains. In 1888, the senior Thompson bought his son a sprawling 3,800 acre ranch in Nebraska, which showed a tidy $30,000 profit after three years. In 1891, following his father's death, Thompson returned to Chicago to manage the family holdings.

In 1899, a friend convinced him to enter the political field. Thompson was narrowly elected as the reform candidate for alderman of the second ward. Politics held little interest for him at this stage of his career, a fact to which his less than impressive record in the city council attests. Thompson nevertheless was an attractive candidate to Republican party boss William Lorimer who sponsored him for a seat on the Cook County Board of Commissioners in 1902. He completed his term in 1904 and returned to private life unscathed. Thompson's considerable athletic prowess and his proven abilities in the sport of yacht racing garnered much favorable newspaper publicity in the next few years. With the help of Fred "the Poor Swede" Lundin, the first-rate political manipulator who succeeded Lorimer, Thompson was persuaded to re-enter the political fold, this time as a mayoral candidate in the 1915 general election. Lundin's behind-the-scenes machinations carried the day for Thompson who won by the largest plurality ever given a Republican candidate in the city.

Chicago's corrupt mayor William Hale Thompson, the tool of Al Capone.

Thompson's first eight years in office were marked by one scandal after another. The police department was thoroughly corrupt, and a serious racial problem was allowed to erupt into a full-blown riot in July 1919, before Thompson acted. The Chicago *Tribune* led the crusade for the mayor's ouster and sued Thompson for conspiring to defraud the city out of $2,000,000 in expert fees. (The mayor in turn, sued the *Tribune* for unrelated matters but was turned back in court.) On the eve of the 1923 election, Fred Lundin and twenty-two other administration hacks were indicted in a kickback scheme that defrauded the school treasury of over $1,000,000 through false bids and padded supply bills. Against his will, Thompson was forced to temporarily withdraw from politics. His retreat permitted a Democratic reformer, William Dever, to take office. The mayor traced his larger failures back to Fred Lundin and the two men became bitter enemies in the next few years.

In 1927, Thompson won his third term as mayor. He easily defeated Democratic candidate William Dever using a blend of demagoguery and assorted half-truths. School superintendent William McAndrew became a favorite scapegoat of "America First" Thompson, who accused the public official of "propagandizing" the textbooks with pro-British material. The voters guffawed when Thompson promised to punch the King of England in the "snoot" if he came to Chicago. Nevertheless, he was returned to city hall by a wide margin, thanks in part to the strong-arm support received from Al Capone and the other bootleg gangsters who counted on Thompson to "open up" the town again, as he had in 1915. Chicago careened out of control between 1927 and 1931 when Thompson left office for the final time. The city was in the hands of the gangsters, and all the civic works projects the mayor had introduced did little to compensate for the sorry record of the city police and the administration which controlled them. Having had enough of Thompson's buffoonery, Chicago voters went to the polls in 1931 and elected Anton Cermak, a Democrat who promised—and delivered—decisive action against the crime syndicate.

In 1936, Thompson ran for governor; in 1939 he tried for the Republican mayoral slot. He was soundly defeated both times, marking an anti-climatic end to his political career. Thompson lived reclusively until his death from heart disease in 1944. See: **Capone, Alphonse; Cermak, Anton Joseph.**

REF.: Asbury, *Gem of the Prairie;* Bright, *Hizzoner Big Bill Thompson; CBA;* Eisenberg and Landau, *Meyer Lansky;* Faris, *Chicago Sociology, 1920-32;* Kobler, *Al Capone;* Lait and Mortimer, *Chicago: Confidential;* Landesco, *Organized Crime in Chicago;* Levine, *Anatomy of a Gangster;* Lewis and Smith, *Chicago, A History of Its Reputation;* Lindberg, *To Serve and Collect: Chicago Politics and Police Corruption;* Linn, *James Keely, Newspaperman;* Lynch, *Criminals and Politicians;* Merriam, *Chicago, A More Intimate View of Urban Politics;* Morgan, *Prince of Crime;* Nash, *People to See;* Smith, *Syndicate City;* Spiering, *The Man Who Got Capone;* Thompson, *Eight Years of Progress;* Wendt and Kogan, *Big Bill;* (FILM), *Little Caesar,* 1931.

Thompson, William Paul (AKA: **Bud**), 1938-89, U.S., mur. William Paul "Bud" Thompson spent 28 of his 51 years in prisons or reform schools on various charges, including breaking and entering, counterfeiting, forgery, and murder. In April 1984, Thompson killed a 28-year-old transient, Randy Waldron, in Reno and was sentenced to die by lethal injection. After that sentence, he was also convicted of the murders of two brothers near an Auburn, Calif., campsite. Thompson confessed that he had killed three others and stated that if freed he would likely kill again. On June 18, 1989, the 300-pound Thompson was given a last supper of four double bacon cheeseburgers, two large orders of fries, and a large cola. At 2:01 the following morning, at the Nevada State Penitentiary in Carson City, he was given a lethal injection, and he died eight minutes later. REF.: *CBA.*

Thomson, Sir Basil Home, 1861-1939, Brit., law enfor. off.-writer. Governor of Darmoor Prison to 1907. He served as head of Scotland Yard's Criminal Investigation Department from 1913, and as director of Scotland Yard Intelligence from 1919-21. Books authored: *The Story of Dartmoor Prison, Mr. Pepper, Investigator, The Story of Scotland Yard,* and others. REF.: *CBA.*

Thoravensen, Bjarni Vigfusson, 1786-1841, Ice., jur. Served on Iceland's Supreme Court as deputy justice from 1811-17, and as justice from 1817-33. REF.: *CBA.*

Thoresen, Louise, 1937- , Case of, U.S., mur. On Apr. 26, 1967, 30-year-old William Thoresen III, heir to a Chicago steel fortune, was arrested in San Francisco for illegally possessing fully automatic weapons. His wife, Louise, was also arrested and 35,000 pounds of guns and ammunition were seized. A month later, Louise Thoresen, was ordered to undergo psychiatric testing for her penchant for collecting machine guns after she was arrested for the fourth time. On June 28, the couple was formally indicted by a federal grand jury on twenty-two counts for possessing seventy-seven tons of illegal weapons, including guns actively used by the army. The two pleaded not guilty before Judge Albert C. Wollenberg in the San Francisco U.S. District Court, but they were found Guilty, and on Apr. 3, 1969, William Thoresen III was sentenced to six months in prison, fined $4,000, and placed on probation for nine and one-half years. Louise Thoresen was fined $4,000 and placed on three years' probation for aiding and abetting her husband. Soon after, Louise filed for divorce.

On June 10, 1970, William Thoresen III died of multiple gunshot wounds to the chest after being shot by his estranged wife during a quarrel. Louise was arrested and charged with first-degree murder. She claimed, however, that she had killed her husband in self-defense because he had tried to force her to take a lethal dose of drugs and on Nov. 21, 1970, was acquitted. Four days later, she attempted to be appointed executor of his million-dollar estate. REF.: *CBA.*

Thorismond (Thorismund), d.453, Roman., king, assass. Son of Theodoric I, also king of Visigoths. He brought his own forces to assist his father's armies in a decisive victory over Attila the Hun at Catalaunian Plains in 451. He was murdered by his brother Theodoric II. REF.: *CBA.*

Thorn, Martin George (Martin Torzewski), 1868-97, U.S., mur. On June 26, 1897, in Manhattan, a man's torso with a tattoo of

WILLIE GULDENSEPPE: THE MAN WHO WENT TO PIECES

Willie Guldensuppe; his remains were scattered about New York.

Part of Willie's body being discovered in a drainage area.

MURDERER OF GULDENSUPPE, MARTIN THORN, WILL PAY THE PENALTY AND BE KILLED TO-DAY.

Condemned Murderer Is Calm, Says He Has No Fear, and Is Sure of Forgiveness.

Mrs. Nack and Thorn on the Staten Island ferry, depositing remains.

Mrs. Nack shown pulling Martin Thorn into the electric chair.

a naked woman on the chest was found, wrapped in oilcloth, floating in the East River. The torso had been cut cleanly away from the rest of the body just above the diaphragm. The precision with which the mutilation was accomplished indicated some degree of surgical knowledge. The next day, the lower torso was discovered in a wooded area approximately eight miles from where the first discovery was made. Shortly thereafter the corpse's legs, wrapped in the same oilcloth, were fished out of the river.

Police were stymied, with no clue as to the corpse's identity, the motive for the murder or knowledge of possible suspects. A tip from a New York *World* reporter, who coincidentally overheard two masseuses at the Murray Hill Baths talking about a missing co-worker, Willie Guldensuppe, gave police their first lead. One of the co-workers, Frank Gartner, went to the morgue and immediately identified the body as Willie Guldensuppe. Further physical identification was made by Dr. J.S. Cosby who had done minor surgery on Guldensuppe's finger. From a scar on the dead man' finger, Cosby also positively identified him as Guldensuppe.

The police went to Guldensuppe's address on Ninth Avenue and found that it was a boarding house owned by a German immigrant, Augusta Nack, who also practiced midwifery. Shortly after this discovery, a New York *Journal* reporter found a hardware merchant in Queens who claimed to have sold red and gold oilcloth like that in which Guldensuppe's body was wrapped, to a woman fitting Nack's description. Nack was taken into custody and questioned by police, who reportedly tried to shock her into confessing by thrusting the now badly decomposed legs in front of her and asking, "Are those Willie's?" Nack's reported reply was, "I would not know as I never saw the gentleman naked."

Nack denied having known her former tenant intimately, but neighbors testified that she and Guldensuppe had been lovers for years until a new tenant, Martin George Thorn, had taken his place about ten months earlier. The neighbors claimed that the two men argued over Nack until Guldensuppe began to date another woman. Either because Nack felt slighted by Guldensuppe's adjustment to the situation or because Thorn bore a grudge against him for a beating he had suffered at Guldensuppe's hands, the two apparently conspired to do away with Guldensuppe.

According to testimony given by a barber named John Gotha, Thorn, also a barber, had confided in him that he and Nack had lured Guldensuppe to a small farm Nack had rented in a Woodside, a suburb of Queens. Nack allegedly had told Guldensuppe that she wanted to start a legitimate midwife's practice and wanted his opinion on the building she was considering buying. Guldensuppe complied and appeared at the farm. Nack encouraged him to take a thorough look around the house and then make his appraisal. Meanwhile Thorn, armed with a knife and a pistol, hid in one of the closets. Finally, Guldensuppe worked his way around to this closet and, as he opened its door, Thorn jumped out and attacked him. Nack appeared after Guldensuppe was dead and helped to haul his body into the bathtub. Thorn had specifically told his fellow barber that Guldensuppe was still breathing when he cut off his head with a razor. The couple covered the head in plaster of paris to weight it down and threw it in the river. Then Thorn carved the rest of the body, and Nack wrapped the parts in oilcloth. Nack and Thorn then deposited the grisly parcels in the various locales where they were later found.

Thorn was arrested on the strength of this detailed and convincing statement. The police questioned him extensively and he finally told them he had gone to the Long Island house on June 25 to discover that Nack had already killed Guldensuppe. Thorn claimed that his only part in the crime had been in helping to dispose of the body parts. Nack was also arrested. Soon thereafter police investigating a Long Island farmer's claim that his white ducks had turned pink, found that a drainage pool near Nack's cottage had turned red with human blood. Inside the cottage they found evidence of the murder and mutilation, including a saw and butcher knife still caked with human blood and flesh. John Gotha appeared as a witness for the prosecution and testified that Thorn had bragged about the murders. The next day, Nack unexpectedly stood up in court and accused Thorn of doing the whole job himself. Her description was so explicit that several members of the jury fainted, causing a mistrial to be declared. In the second trial, Thorn turned on Nack and claimed she had appeared one day in his room announcing that she had just killed Guldensuppe.

Thorn's attorney, Big Bill Howe, took an aggressive stance on his client's behalf. Nack's attorney, Emmanuel "Manny" Friend, used a more subtle defense. The jury, though they convicted Nack of murder, found her sympathetic and sentenced her to twenty years in jail. Thorn was less fortunate and got the electric chair, being executed at Sing Sing on Aug. 1,1898. Nack served ten years of her sentence.

REF.: Carey, *Memoirs of a Murder Man; CBA;* Corder, *Murder My Love;* Duke, *Celebrated Criminal Cases of America;* Gross, *Masterpieces of Murder;* Kobler, *Some Like It Gory;* Nash, *Bloodletters and Badmen;* Pearson, *More Studies in Murder;* Russell, *Best Murder Cases.*

Thornberry, William Homer, 1909- , U.S., jur. Appointed to western district court of Texas by President John F. Kennedy in 1963, and to fifth circuit court by President Lyndon Johnson in 1965. He served as district attorney of Travis County, Texas, from 1941-42. REF.: *CBA.*

Thorne, Graeme, See: **Bradley, Stephen Leslie.**

Thorne, John Norman Holmes, d.1925, Brit., mur. Elsie Cameron, a plain, rather thin, neurotic young secretary fell in love with young John Thorne. Although Thorne, a Sunday school teacher and boys' club supporter, was a most unlikely choice, being a less-than-successful chicken farmer who lived in a shack on his squalid little farm in Sussex, Elsie still wanted him. In November 1924, after a lengthy correspondence in which she falsely claimed she was pregnant, Elsie kept insisting on coming to see him and that they get married. Thorne, in response, informed her that he was involved with another woman and was not interested.

In spite of her erstwhile lover's protestations, Elsie packed her bag and left London to confront John face-to-face on Dec. 5. Six days later Elsie's father sent John Thorne a telegram asking of Elsie's whereabouts. John replied that although he had expected her she had not arrived in Sussex.

John informed the police that he had not seen Elsie, but witnesses came forward to say that they had definitely seen her going to the farm. The police then returned to the farm to dig up the chicken yard and discovered her dismembered body.

Thorne claimed that while he was out of the house, Elsie had hanged herself. In a panic, he had tried to dispose of the body. However, an autopsy revealed that she had been beaten to death. He was charged with murder and tried at Lewes Assizes in March 1925. He was found Guilty of murder and was executed at Wandsworth on Apr. 22, 1925.

REF.: Adamson, *A Man of Quality;* Arthur, *All the Sinners;* Browne and Tullett, *The Scalpel of Scotland Yard;* Butler, *Murderers' England;* Cannell, *When Fleet Street Calls; CBA;* Cuthbert, *Science and the Detection of Crime;* Dearden, *Death Under the Microscope;* ____, *Some Cases of Sir Bernard Spilsbury and Others;* Duff, *A New Handbook on Hanging; Famous Trials;* Grice, *Great Cases of Sir Henry Curtis Bennett;* Hastier, *Dead Men Tell Tales;* Hastings, *The Other Mr. Hastings;* Hoskins, *The Sound of Murder;* Jackson, *A Case for the Prosecution;* Jacobs, *Aspects of Murder;* Jowitt, *Some Were Spies;* Knowles, *Court of Drama;* Logan, *The Murder and the Trial;* ____, *Verdict and Sentence;* Lustgarten, *Verdict in Dispute;* Randall, *The Famous Cases of Sir Bernard Spilsbury;* Shew, *A Second Companion to Murder;* Thorwald, *The Century of the Detective;* Townsend, *Black Cap, Murder Will Out;* Twyman, *The Best Laid Schemes;* Wensley, *Forty Years of Scotland Yard;* Wilson, *Encyclopedia of Murder.*

Thorne, Thomas Harold, b.1896, Brit., asslt.-bat.-mur. In early 1921, Harry Blackmore, a 61-year-old man from Hampstead, England, was found dead from twenty stab wounds to the head. His assailant, 25-year-old Thomas Thorn was apprehended, but found insane, and sentenced to a mental institution in Broadmoor. In 1937, Thorn was released with tragic results. After working briefly as a tobacconist in Chester, he attacked a woman Alice Hannah Johnson, who barely survived. Before Justice Singleton at the Chester Assizes, Thorne was sentenced to fifteen years in prison.

REF.: Browne and Tullett, *The Scalpel of Scotland Yard; CBA.*

Thornhill, Hillary, 1915- , and **McCain, Willie B.**, 1930- , and **Robertson, Eugene**, 1928- , U.S., mur. In 1960, Hillary "Hill" Thornhill was the bootlegging kingpin of rural Columbia, Miss. A local sheriff, J.V. Polk, had recently declared war after years of casual enforcement, and Thornhill brought in two men, Willie McCain and Eugene Robertson, to eliminate the problem. The two men made two unsuccessful attempts on Polk's life, before Robertson withdrew. But on Apr. 22, 1960, McCain succeeded, killing Sheriff Polk with a 12-gauge shotgun at a distance of seventy-five feet. All three conspirators were arrested and all confessed to the plot. Thornhill and McCain were sentenced to life imprisonment, while Robertson was sentenced to ten years.

REF.: *CBA;* Wyden, *The Hired Killers.*

Thornton, Abraham, prom. 1817, Case of, Brit., mur. The case of death by drowning of 20-year-old Mary Ashford was sensational, not only because of the death itself, but because of two major points of law. The Ashford girl and a friend, Hannah Cox, had gone to a dance on May 27, 1817. While there, young Abraham Thornton commanded most of her time. Later that night Mary was found drowned in a pond.

Having confided to a friend earlier in the evening that he "would have her" that night, Abraham Thornton left the dance with Mary around midnight. The girl returned to her friend's house at 4 a.m., and changed from her dancing frock back into her regular clothes, then left for her own home carrying her dress-up clothes under her arm. Later that morning Mary's bonnet, dance dress, and shoes were found at the edge of a pond or pit, which the authorities dragged, recovering her body. She was fully clothed and there were no marks of violence on her body.

Being the last person seen with the victim, Thornton was charged with murder and brought to trial. He readily admitted being with Mary and that, while seducing her, he had discovered that she was a virgin, which explained the large amount of blood found on her neatly folded dance clothes. Thornton maintained that he was innocent—that the girl had submitted to his advances willingly and that he had not murdered her.

Witnesses said they saw Thornton walking home several miles from the pond at about the time Mary drowned. There was no evidence to connect him with her death. After a six-minute deliberation the jury found him Not Guilty.

Mary's brother appealed the case and asked for another trial, this being the practice at that time because proscription of "double jeopardy" was not yet in effect. Brought to trial for a second time, Thornton proclaimed his innocence and, using an old law called the Appeal of Murder—the principle that one could prove his innocence in combat—threw down a glove challenge young Ashford to a duel. Ashford, a much smaller man than Thornton, was prevented from responding to the challenge, and Thornton was again found Not Guilty. Soon afterward, both double jeopardy and the Appeal of Murder were abolished under British law.

REF.: Altick, *Victorian Studies in Scarlet;* Butler, *Murderers' England; CBA;* Culpin, *The Newgate Noose;* Nash, *Almanac of World Crime;* Pearce, *Unsolved Murder Mysteries.*

Thornton, Beryl Lilian, See: **Kopsch, Alfred Arthur**.

Thornton, Lonzo, and **Ivory, James**, prom. 1926, U.S., rob. On Oct. 6, 1926, in Middletown, Ohio, a recent immigrant, Louie Parkalab was accosted on the street by two men, and robbed of twenty dollars and an insurance policy. A police officer observed the incident and after a short chase, apprehended one of the men. James Ivory, was locked up and the next morning received a visitor. The police wondered if the second man could be the second assailant, and brought Louie Parkalab to the station. Parkalab quickly concurred that the other man, Lonzo Thornton, had also attacked him. On Feb. 15, 1927, in the Butler County courtroom of Judge Clarence Murphy, Thornton and Ivory were found Guilty and sentenced to the Ohio penitentiary for ten to twenty-five years. Less than a year after they were imprisoned, Simon "Babe Ruth" Williams confessed that he was the second man who, with Ivory, robbed Parkalab. Williams resembled Thornton, and had such convincing information regarding collateral evidence that Thornton received a pardon. Williams was charged, then convicted. REF.: *CBA.*

Thornton, Mark, 1679-1717, Brit., rob.-mur. Mark Thornton received a university education at Cambridge, but squandered his annual allowance of £100 at local brothels and gaming houses. After repeated warnings, he was expelled by the schoolmasters.

When his father died, Thornton left with his inheritance for London, where he lived comfortably for nearly three years. When the money was gone, he took to highway robbery, victimizing such prominent English noblemen as Lord Grey of Wark, one of the Rye House plotters who escaped execution only by paying £40,000 to the Crown. Thornton caught up with him at Hounslow Heath.

"How dare you, sir, have the impudence to stop a nobleman?" Lord Grey demanded. "Let me come out of my coach and mount one of my servant's horses and I'll fight you at pistol." Reminding Lord Grey of how he'd sold out to James Scott, the Duke of Monmouth, during the Rye House trial, Thornton said he did not trust him to be fair in a duel. "I'm a gentleman bred and born," Thornton said. "And you see I now live by my sword and pistol, too, one of which you shall instantly have through your head and the other in your guts." Lord Grey handed over £100.

Sir John Germain, son of William of Orange, was Thornton's next victim, near Banstead Downs. When Germain reminded Thornton that in England robbery was a capital offense, Thornton retorted that the law "authorizes me as much to steal your money from you as it does you to steal the Duke of Norfolk's wife from him and live in adultery." Germain reluctantly surrendered a diamond ring, a sum of guineas, and a gold watch.

That same day, Lady Mary Mordaunt, former wife of the aforementioned Duke of Norfolk, drove by. "What do you think your gallant Monsieur Germain, whom I've also robbed but two or three hours ago will say if I let you pass by unmolested?" Thornton asked, having pulled over her coach. "Truly he'll swear I don't do fair to make fish of one and flesh of the other." He took twenty guineas, a gold watch, and a diamond before sending her home to her lordship.

Apprehended near Lynn after robbing and murdering a Norwich weaver, Thornton was tried and condemned at the Lent Assizes at Norwich in 1717 and hanged at Thetford shortly thereafter.

REF.: *CBA;* Smith, *Highwaymen.*

Thornton, Thomas Patrick, b.1898, U.S., jur. Appointed to eastern district court of Michigan by President Harry Truman in 1949. He earlier served as assistant U.S. attorney from 1937-44, as chief assistant attorney from 1944-47, and as U.S. attorney from 1947-49. REF.: *CBA.*

Thorvik, Louis, and **Hughes, George**, prom. 1921, U.S., rob. On July 23, 1921, the Farmers State Bank of Almelund, Minn., was robbed by four men who escaped in a green car. A posse was organized, but the robbers were not apprehended. In October, in St. Paul, George Hughes, who fit the description of one of the robbers, was arrested for auto theft. Witnesses to the bank robbery identified Hughes. In the courtroom of Judge J.N. Searle, Hughes was convicted of the robbery and sentenced to life imprisonment at Stillwater. In May 1922, a deputy sheriff in Chisago County, testified that Louis Thorvik had confessed to taking part in the robbery. The robbery witnesses identified Thorvik as a second bandit. On Aug. 22, 1922, Thorvik was also sentenced to life imprisonment at Stillwater. The remaining two robbers were never caught. REF.: *CBA.*

Thrane, Marcus Moller, 1817-90, Nor., sedition. Socialist founder and head of movement bearing his name. He was jailed for sedition from 1851-55, and upon his release moved to the U.S., where he became a Chicago publisher of Socialist newspapers written in the Norwegian language. REF.: *CBA*.

Thrasea Paetus, Publius Clodius, d.66 A.D., Roman., polit., assass. Served as Roman consul in 56 A.D. He left political life in protest against the dissolute Emperor Nero in 63, and was put to death at the emperor's orders three years later. REF.: *CBA*.

Thrash, Marshall, 1950- , U.S., asslt.&bat. On Apr. 19, 1980, in an incident of apparently random racial violence, three members of the Ku Klux Klan drove through a black neighborhood in Chattanooga, Tenn., one of them shooting at four black women as the women walked from a tavern. While the women lay wounded on the sidewalk, shot in the legs and hips, police pursued the three men, Bill Church, imperial wizard of the Justice Knights of the Ku Klux Klan, and Klan members, Larry Payne, and Marshall Thrash. When police stopped the car fifteen minutes later after an auto chase, two shotguns and used and unused shells fell out of the car.

All three men were charged with felonious assault with intent to commit murder in the shootings of Opal Lee Jackson, forty-six, Viola Ellison, sixty-three, Lila May Evans, sixty-five, and Kathleen Johnson, forty-eight. During the trial, Thrash, identified as the gunman, claimed he was shooting the gun to call attention to two crosses set ablaze a short distance away. On July 22, 1980, an all-white jury acquitted Church and Payne. Thrash was convicted on two counts of assault and battery and one count of simple assault, resulting in a fine of $225, two workhouse sentences of nine months each, and another of two months. All four women recovered from their wounds. REF.: *CBA*.

Thrasybulus, d.388 B.C., Gr., banish. Fought successfully in Peloponesian War, helping Alcibiades defeat Spartans. He was banished from Athens by the Thirty Tyrants in 404 B.C., but returned the following year and played an essential role in restoring Athenian democracy. He persuaded Athens to enter the Theban League to help maintain the battle with Sparta, and led a fleet against Spartan forces in 389 B.C. REF.: *CBA*.

Three Men Die, 1934, a novel by Sarah Gertrude Millin. Murderess Daisy de Melker (S. Afr., 1932), serves as the role model for the female protagonist in this fictional work. See: **de Melker, Daisy**. REF.: *CBA*.

Three Waxworks, **The**, See: ***Waxworks***.

3-X Slayer, 1930, U.S., (unsolv.) mur. The killer claimed to belong to a secret international society whose mission was to procure a set of papers, and, if he failed, fourteen persons and possibly more would meet an untimely death. A series of cryptic letters written to the New York *Evening-Journal* identified the writer as "3-X," who in Summer 1930 precipitated a panic in the borough of Queens, as police commenced the widest manhunt in city history up to that time.

The first 3-X murder occurred on the night of June 11, 1930, when Joseph Moyzynsky, a College Point grocer, was shot and killed in the presence of his 19-year-old girlfriend Catherine May. They were parked in an automobile in Whitestone, Queens, when the killer advanced from behind. He fired a revolver through the open window of the vehicle, killing Moyzynsky instantly. May was dragged from the car and taken to the main road where the killer put her on the first bus. When questioned by police, May identified one Albert Lombardo, a gangster from the Lower East Side, as the assailant. However, Lombardo had an unshakable alibi and was discharged. May was held as a material witness. Six days later, on June 17, 26-year-old Noel Sowley was killed in a similar fashion in a secluded spot in Creedmore, Queens, a short distance from the state hospital.

Sowley, who worked as a mechanic for the Cable Radio Tube Corp. in Brooklyn, was in the company of 20-year-old Elizabeth Ring when a lone gunman crept up from behind and fired two shots into his head. "You're going to get what Joe got!" the killer said an instant before pulling the trigger. Turning to the girl he mumbled something under his breath about killing thirteen men and one woman as he rifled through Sowley's pockets. Ring described the man as a foreigner, five-feet-six-inches in height. Police later found several news clippings about the Moyzynsky murder stuffed into the dead man's coat pockets with the notation "here's how" scrawled in pencil. The killer released Ring unhurt. She caught a bus on Rocky Hill Road.

The police were convinced that the assassin was an escaped inmate from the state hospital at Creedmore. His letter to the police threatened the life of an unnamed third victim, prompting Police Commissioner Edward Mulrooney to deploy 2,000 uniformed patrolmen across the less traveled roads of Queens. "I am the agent of a secret international order and when I met Moyzynski that night it was to get from him certain documents, but unfortunately they were not in his possession at the time," the killer wrote, adding, "We always get them through their women." Several suspects were taken in to be identified, but Ring could not say that any of them were the man. The next day Inspector John Gallagher received two more threatening notes from "3-X" written on cheap notepaper in blue ink. "Thirteen more men and one woman will go if they do not make peace with us and stop bleeding us to death," the note read.

The killer's next correspondence originated in Philadelphia on June 20 and was sent to Joseph Moyzynsky's brother John, who worked as a plumber. "You must have those papers, they're mine," the note read. "Give them to me by putting them in a newspaper and leaving it back door entrance to men's room Broad Street Station, Sat. af. If you don't have them, leave word who has. No foolin and keep the gumshoe squad off." Moyzynsky told Philadelphia police he had no idea what the killer was talking about, nor what he wanted. The ninth letter in the 3-X series was sent to a Brooklyn man named Meyer Newmark who was threatened with death unless he handed over document "U.J. 4-3-44." Meanwhile, detectives in Coatesville, Pa., questioned a former soldier named Dewey Ede, who said he spoke with a man who told him of being selected for a secret mission by the Red Diamond of Russia. "Now that the papers have been returned, I can return to my country," the man had said.

The bizarre case took on added dimensions on June 25, when a 35-year-old Brooklyn woman named Rebecca Hirsch told of a nocturnal visit by the 3-X killer. According to the hysterical woman's testimony, a man entered her room and tied her to the bedpost. He then set fire to her clothing before fleeing out the window. A note left behind was signed "Maniac" with a drawing of the moon accompanied by two X's. The letters and phone calls continued and still the New York City police were no closer to establishing the true identity of 3-X. On June 28, the private secretary to George U. Harvey, president of the borough of Queens, received the second of two threatening phone calls. "This is 3-X," the caller said. "You put the cops after me and I'm going to get you next!" The police traced the call to a pay phone in a cigar store at Lexington Avenue and 12th Street, but the caller had disappeared by the time the officers arrived. Inspector Thomas Mullarkey of the Fifteenth Inspection District detective force summed up the frustration of his colleagues when he said, "The man responsible for these murders was a man with a delusion that certain conditions needed reforming. He has either come to the conclusion that he has succeeded in doing what he set out to do or he has been scared away by the vigilance of the hunt we are making for him."

The investigation was hampered by a series of anonymous calls made to the police by a private investigator who said that he could furnish clues leading to the arrest and conviction of 3-X in return for a cash reward. The caller turned out to be Aaron Blattman, a 33-year-old fingerprint expert who worked for the Bronx magistrates court. During the Hall-Mills murder trial, Blattman was scheduled to appear as a defense witness, but was never summoned. He later sued Mrs. Edward Hall for $56,000 in lost wages from a series of articles he was hired to write for a newspaper syndicate. Blattman was found Guilty of conduct unbecoming a court officer for the phone calls he had made to the police.

Then in early August a third man was found murdered. However, the police were convinced that the slaying of Prudential insurance agent Hector Avalone was committed by a 3-X copycat. Ballistics experts determined that the bullets removed from the body did not correspond with those found in Moyzynsky's or Sowley's bodies. Police Commissioner Mulrooney quietly withdrew the police guard assigned to the backroads of Queens, believing 3-X had left the area for good. Mulrooney's theory was given credence nearly a year later when Chief Inspector John O'Brien received a letter postmarked from Pittsburgh, threatening a renewed round of violence. "Ha! Ha! In my own little efficient way I have removed another undesirable from this world," the note read. "A Pittsburgh girl between eighteen and twenty-five is next. Tell Pittsburgh police to watch out for me and try to catch me."

O'Brien alerted Detective Inspector Frank R. Boyd of the Pittsburgh police. On June 1, 1936, a suspect was arrested in Elizabethtown, N.Y., and identified as the likely 3-X murderer. Twenty-nine-year-old Frank Engel was picked up in a public garage by state troopers Walter Rockburn and Elmer Salisbury after the officers had noted his "queer actions." Engel, who was a member of the College Point Volunteer Life Saving Corps, freely confessed to the 1930 murders after the troopers had arrested him on a disorderly conduct charge. Catherine May and Elizabeth Ring, the only eyewitnesses to the tragedy, were taken to the district attorney's office to provide positive identification. "No, he is not the man," Ring told Charles Sullivan, the district attorney, "The man you want was older in 1930 than this man is today." May agreed with her. Engel was declared an incompetent and committed to the state hospital on June 11, 1936, by order of State Supreme Court Justice George E. Brower. See: **Hall-Mills Murders**.

REF.: *CBA;* Nash, *Open Files.*

Thrift the hangman, shown in terror at those he had executed.

Thrift, John, d.1752, Brit., mur. John Thrift, the Crown's official executioner from 1735-52, beheaded nine rebel followers of Bonnie Prince Charlie and earned himself the eternal hatred of the remaining Jacobites. In Spring 1750, a group of angry, jeering Jacobites surrounded Thrift's house. Thrift appeared and, himself angry after years of being harassed and defiled by the public, ran at the crowd waving a sword. In the ensuing riot, David Farris was killed, and witnesses blamed his murder on Thrift. Thrift was brought to trial, found Guilty, and sentenced to death. He was, however, released so that he could continue his work as executioner.

Thrift, who performed in his official capacity for the first time on March 11, 1735, had more than his share of difficulty in plying his trade. In his first public hanging, he forgot to adjust all the white caps on the thirteen victim's heads before letting them drop. Their purple, contorted faces were revealed to the crowd who were deeply offended by Thrift's ineptitude. Thrift died of natural causes in 1752, just eighteen months after his release from prison.

REF.: Bleackley, *Hangmen of England; CBA;* Laurence, *A History of Capital Punishment;* Potter, *The Art of Hanging.*

Throckmorton, Francis (Throgmorton), 1554-84, Brit., consp. Tortured until he confessed to planning to oust Queen Elizabeth I with the help of French and Spanish conspirators, in 1583. He was put to death. He was the nephew of Sir Nicholas Throckmorton. REF.: *CBA.*

Throckmorton, Sir Nicholas (Throgmorton), 1515-71, Brit., consp. Served in Parliament from 1545-67, as ambassador to France from 1559-64, and as ambassador to Scotland from 1565-67, in which post he maintained friendship with Mary, Queen of Scots. He was jailed on charges of participating in a plot to help Mary in 1569.

REF.: *CBA;* (FILM), *Mary of Scotland,* 1936; *Mary, Queen of Scots,* 1971.

Throgmorton, William, 1668-1719, Brit., rob. William Throgmorton's father was an oil merchant who hoped that his son might become a classical scholar, or at the very least a clerk's apprentice. When Throgmorton balked at learning, writing and arithmetic, the elder Throgmorton took him into the family business. The father soon died, however, leaving his estate to his son who gambled it away and was forced to close the shop.

In London, Throgmorton perpetrated many frauds and ran up debts, so when his actions made the city too dangerous, he joined Colonel Colt's regiment headquartered at Portsmouth. The detachment was split up, and Throgmorton was assigned to duty on one of the vessels commanded by Lord Cutts. Before the flotilla shipped off for the West Indies, however, Throgmorton engineered a near mutiny when it became apparent that Lord Cutts was not going to pay the crew what was due them until after the cruise.

Ordered arrested, Throgmorton was held for court-martial, but the other men rose to his defense and Lord Cutts was held prisoner until the governor and mayor of Plymouth could raise the necessary £2,500 to pay the crewmen. Considered a brave hero by his mates, Throgmorton was actually a slippery thief who waited for the precise moment to make his break. Just before the fleet set sail, he broke into the captain's quarters and stole 800 guineas from a trunk while pretending to be on sentry duty.

He wrapped the money up in his clothes and lowered himself over the side. Throgmorton swam to shore and made his way to Bristol where he temporarily took up residence. After robbing his lodging house of £30, he then fled to the country, though he committed a series of highway robberies en route to London. Back in the city, he lived the life of a gentleman, attending concerts, plays, and balls. Always alert to the possibilities, Throgmorton more often than not left his host's home a few dollars richer.

When he wasn't dipping into people's pockets he cheated them at cards and dice. His favored rendezvous was at the widow Burton's house on Harding Street. It was only a matter of time, of course, before his good fortune ran out. Near Blandford in Dorsetshire he attempted to rob a man riding a prized gelding. Protected by his servants, the nobleman was unwilling to surrender his valuables to a highwayman. Throgmorton's horse was shot out from under him, and he was carried off to the Dorchester jail. He was condemned for his crimes and sentenced to die. He was hanged on Apr. 18, 1719.

REF.: *CBA;* Smith, *Highwaymen.*

Thrower, Allan E., 1949- , U.S., (wrong. convict.) mur. On July 12, 1973, 24-year-old Allan E. Thrower of Cleveland, was convicted of first-degree murder in the August 1972 ambush death of Columbus police officer Joseph Edwards. Thrower was convicted in spite of his own claims of innocence, a lack of motive, and the testimony of three alibi witnesses who swore that Thrower was in Detroit on the night of the murder. The only evidence against Thrower was the testimony of Edwards' partner, Charles W. McFadden. Throwers' conviction was affirmed on appeal and after serving five years of his sentence, an internal police investigation revealed that McFadden had perjured himself when testifying against Thrower.

When McFadden's perjury and that of a police detective, who had falsely testified at the trial that he heard two of the alibi witnesses plotting to perjure themselves, was discovered, a new trial was ordered and Thrower was released. In 1979, all charges against Thrower were dropped. REF.: *CBA.*

Thuggee, c.700-1900s?, India, secret crim. soc. The mystic and murderous killer cult of Thuggee (pronounced "Tugee") plagued India for twelve centuries, a religion within religions that insisted upon human sacrifice to its gory goddess, Kali (Bhowani or Bhawani). Its fanatical followers were known in southern India as Phansigars, stemming from the Hindustani term *Phansi,* meaning noose; these killers employed strangling cords or nooses and were known as "noose operators." In northern India, the same sect of killers were commonly called Thugs (pronounced "Tugs"), after the Sanskrit word *othag,* meaning to conceal, or *othaga,* one who cheated. To the rest of the world, when the existence of this cult was recognized in shock by western civilization, Thugs were known as the most sinister of human creatures, clandestine, bizarre, utterly unconscionable. They took lives, tens of thousands a decade, to edify their blood lusting goddess and to enrich themselves with spoils taken from their unsuspecting victims.

Operating in strict secrecy, Thugs were known to Indian civilization as early as 700 or earlier, but they conducted their cabalistic rites with such controlled stealth that local chiefs and sultans had no real idea of the sect's widespread influence or so it was claimed, though some historians insist that many Indian leaders protected the Thugs in order to receive part of the spoils from their murder raids. Further assuring the murder cult's anonymity was the rigidly enforced rule of death to any who revealed its secret rites and practices. Uniting all the bands of Thugs throughout India was its totemic goddess, Kali, who, through its high priests, established strict codes that dictated the murder methods of its worshippers.

In mythology, Kali, the wife of the God Shiva (or Siva), is the Hindu goddess of Destruction and Death. She was also known as a deity of war and to the Thugs, Kali was worshipped as "the divine mother." Surviving images of Kali present a frightful picture of a black-skinned goddess with three glaring eyes, many arms, and an open mouth displaying long teeth, blood-soaked lips, and an extended, drooling tongue coated with human gore. (Only when appearing alone does Kali transform into her true and hideous nature; when appearing with Shiva the goddess is beautiful and fair.)

Kali, according to myth, first appeared on the banks of the Hooghli River, a site now called Kali Ghat (whence Calcutta) where her most venerated shrine stood for eons. The goddess encouraged its earliest apostles to go forth and destroy unbelievers; with each murder the killer Thug would thus attain a higher status in the hereafter. Moreover, the goddess was obligingly protective of her killers, disposing of the bodies of their victims so they could go on undetected. Legend has it that after depositing several bodies at the foot of Kali's statue, a band of Thugs retreated, turning their backs to Kali, forbidden, according to tradition, to cast eyes upon the goddess and witness how she destroyed the human remains. An apprentice Thug, however, unable to control his curiosity, turned to see Kali eating the body.

Her grisly custom exposed, the goddess thereafter refused to hide the evidence of the cult's murders and would consume no more corpses. The high priests pleaded for forgiveness and aid. Kali responded by spitting out one of her teeth which took the form of a pickax. One of her ribs became a long knife and from the hem of her sari she provided a noose. All these items became sacred in the tradition of Thuggee. The noose was the instrument of death, to be employed as a strangling cord. The knife was to dismember the limbs of victims and the pickax, the most sacred of all these lethal instruments, was to be used to gouge out the eyes of the murdered victims and dig their unhallowed graves.

Ironically, the eternal rifts between Muslim and Hindu were put aside in that both religious sects joined the Thugs, worshipping a Hindu goddess and putting her before all other gods, although members went on practicing their separate religions. Even stranger was the fact that before its wholesale eradication by the British, the sect was predominately Muslim, followers risking everything to pay homage to this ancient Hindu image. Initiates were brought into the Thuggee fold from their own families or by older Thugs who had taken young boys, usually under ten, in a raid, and raised them to become Thugs, not unlike the methods of Hitler and Mussolini in the twentieth century when these dictators began training their legions almost from the cradle to follow fascism to the grave.

Initiates into the cult were brought together in a row, stretching from the towering image of the goddess in a hidden temple, usually in a remote mountainous area. They faced veteran Thugs, kneeling before them. As the veterans chanted out an oath to preserve the customs of Kali, the initiates repeated the vow. From their waists the veterans unwound their *rumals,* long handkerchiefs, holding these forth. The initiates would take the strangling cords, accepting these as instruments of death. Each was then given a pickax, which was held aloft, announced to be sacred as the burial tool used to dig the graves of victims. A long knife was handed to each and these were then used to slaughter small animals, especially sheep. The initiates dipped their hands into the gore and, one by one, stepped up to the goddess, smearing the blood on its figure. (The statue of Kali, often towering twenty feet, usually had a large base which, after each initiation ceremony, was given another coat of gore, so that this dried gore was often several feet thick over the eons; often enough, the blood preserved from the bodies of recently killed victims was used instead of the animal blood on such occasions.)

A similar ritual was enacted before every raid by a band of Thugs. A party of between ten and twenty Thugs would gather before Kali and seek the goddess' approval. Fresh fruit, cakes, and wine would be placed before the statue, along with flowers. The Thug priest would then have a sheep brought before the image and order its head to be cut off. The right forefoot of the decapitated sheep would be placed in its mouth and a lighted lantern placed upon the disembodied head. Oil that had been blessed by the priest would then be poured down onto the head of the sheep while the priest chanted his invocation, asking Kali to approve of the band's murder mission. If the nostrils and mouth of the sheep's head gave any sign of movement, usually a convulsive, nerve-ending quiver, it was seen as a sign from Kali that she had given her consent to launch another murder attack. Seldom, if ever, would Kali withhold her approval and the body of Thugs would then leave their local village under cover of darkness and gather in a lonely spot, then travel to a well-used trade route where they would lay in wait for caravans of merchants or, most desired, rich princes en route from one palace to another.

The absence of the Thugs from their villages was, of course, noticed, but family members knew full well the purpose of their spouses and other male members. Wives had no voice in the sinister pursuits of their husbands, nor had any other member of the family. All knew that if one of their number was ever exposed, the entire family would suffer. Moreover, the local chieftains of the villages said nothing when residents vanished for long periods of time, knowing they were off on a murder raid for Kali and also knowing that when these killers returned to resume normal law-abiding existences, they, the chieftains, would be enriched with part of their spoils. The Thugs only practiced their murderous religion during the winter months in India, so that during the rest of the year they were at home in their villages, toiling as honest laborers and craftsmen. Many of them were pillars of their communities, holding minor offices, observing and enforcing the local laws, appearing to be upright citizens. On the road, looking for sacrificial quarry, however, they were the worst kind of lethal cutthroats in the history of murder.

The long success enjoyed by the Thugs was due to their clever deceits, practiced with care. They cunningly convinced any gullible traveler that they were themselves seeking protection against the marauding bands of Dacoits, nomadic tribes who practiced armed robbery but not necessarily murder. Ten of the twenty Thugs would position themselves along a trade route and plead with some passing merchant prince that they be allowed to join his party for protection. The other ten Thugs would be miles distant, already digging the graves of the intended victim. When the merchant's party would stop to make camp for the evening, at a spot invariably suggested by one of the accompanying Thugs, the band would wait until the merchants were asleep and then, with those members laying in wait outside the campfires, leap upon their victims, strangling them to death. (The victim could only be murdered with the *rumal,* not the knife or pickax, to meet the religious requirements of Kali.)

Once all the victims had been slain, some of the Thugs would dismember the bodies and disembowel them so no gasses or odors would be forthcoming from the shallow graves into which they would be placed. It was necessary that no wild animals, jackals and other scavengers, seek out the graves and accidentally reveal the hiding place of Thug corpses. Sometimes young boys of ten were taken to these murder scenes and forced to watch their elders kill, dismember, and bury their victims so they would acquaint themselves with the methods of their teachers, be indoctrinated into the looting of the victims, and share the responsibility of the act.

The Thugs earned their reputation as sly deceivers. If a party traveling on the road inadvertently came upon a group of Thugs kneeling next to their victims the Thugs would instantly send up a mournful chant, pretending to mourn the loss of one of their own tribesmen who had suddenly taken ill and died. In carrying out their gruesome rituals, the Thugs doggedly maintained strict rules. No robbery could occur unless the victim was murdered, and no goods or money could be taken unless the victim was murdered in the proper fashion.

Even the way in which the Thugs strangled their victims had to follow an exact code. According to one report "two *Phansigars* are considered to be indispensably necessary to effect the murder of one man, and commonly three are engaged. While traveling along, one of the *Phansigars* suddenly puts the cloth round the neck of the person they mean to kill, and retains hold of one end, while the other end is seized by an accomplice; the instrument crossed behind the neck is drawn tight, the two *Phansigars* pressing the head forwards; at the same time the third villain, in readiness behind the traveler, seizes his legs, and he is thrown forward upon the ground. In this situation he can make little resistance. The man holding the legs of the miserable sufferer, now kicks him in those parts of the body endowed with most sensibility (the scrotum), and he is quickly dispatched."

Just *who* the Thugs would kill was also a matter of strict regulation. Their selection of victims was rife with superstition and mixed with the laws of their separate religions, along with their worship of the dreadful Kali. Since their murder goddess was a woman, the Thugs killed no women and allowed any caravan with women in it to pass unmolested. They never killed male children under the age of ten, taking these as hostages to their cult. Also spared from their strangling cords were any craftsmen who worked with gold, brass, and iron. Carpenters, smiths, stonecutters, dancing masters, shoemakers, pot makers, and washer men also went unharmed.

It was also forbidden to molest any infirm person, particularly the blind or anyone who had suffered mutilation. No herder leading cows or female goats were ever molested by Thugs. Lepers were never approached as was the case with pariahs. It was often told in the campfires of the Thugs how one band of their cult had attacked a caravan carrying a beautiful princess and how the twenty some Thugs, after slaughtering her retainers, had each raped the woman before strangling her to death. Kali's fortunes no longer smiled on this band, the story went, and each member shortly thereafter fell upon hard times, each of them dying premature and painful deaths, their families destroyed.

It was also important for any band of Thugs to operate at least one hundred miles from their native village. Once the decision had been made to attack a traveling party, it was mandatory that all in the party, except those exempted, must be killed. As each band set out to perform its ritual murders, its members were ever mindful of the images that surrounded their demanding Kali, that of the lizard and the snake. If the members heard a lizard chirping while en route to kill it meant that the raid would be a success. If a snake crossed the road in front of them it meant that the attack would fail or bad luck would ensue. Crows and partridges cawing to each other from either side of the road meant good luck.

The most fortuitous sign any Thug band could encounter was the sight of a tiger. This wild beast reflected in the eyes of the Thugs their own way of life and survival, cunning and savagery without remorse. There were bad omens that included the sight of an ass braying, a hare crossing the road, a lone jackal howling, an owl screeching, a crow sitting on the back of another animal cawing, and, the very worst, a dog shaking its head. If three or more of these signs were present on a murder raid, the superstitious Thugs would invariably turn back or take another road.

All of this ritualistic murder, as high as a million victims a century, according to one account, went on in India without detection by the western world, a thousand years of mass slayings in a country that could apparently afford to lose ten million souls in ten centuries without giving pause to look for the vanished. In the teeming subcontinent of India such numbers of missing persons meant little or nothing, but to the western mind the loss of life is staggering, unthinkable. And when the presence of the Thugs and their sweeping activities were first revealed to Europeans, the mere concept, let alone the reality of such mass murder, was thought to be nothing more than a dark fantasy.

Shortly after the turn of the nineteenth century, as Britain flexed her military muscles in support of its East India Company to capture the commerce of India, the new authorities were brought reports by its soldiers and officials that gave vague but terrifying descriptions of bands of stranglers operating throughout the country. British troops were sent out to investigate and returned with more reports of missing travelers, mostly merchants. At first it all seemed confusing and as unreal as the mystical people who had come under British domination, but then more than 100 Thugs were rounded up near Bangalore. They wore long *rumals* and carried knives with ornate handles carved with the images of snakes and lizards, along with pickaxes. These men refused to speak, admitting to nothing. In 1810, near Jumna, bodies were discovered at the bottom of wells, more than thirty of them, all mangled and disfigured, limbs torn out, eyes gouged. Though the British authorities suspected that the bodies and a strange strangling sect were one and the same, it proved almost impossible to develop anything but a loose and unbelievable theory. Their first breakthrough followed six years later in Madras.

Dr. Richard Sherwood, stationed at Fort St. George, interrogated several Thugs who had been picked up on suspicion and managed to isolate in their number some who were willing to talk. Exactly how Dr. Sherwood convinced the Thugs to break their oath of silence is not recorded by Sherwood, but later reports had it that he threatened several with execution unless they revealed the nature of their secret society. Sherwood had discovered a

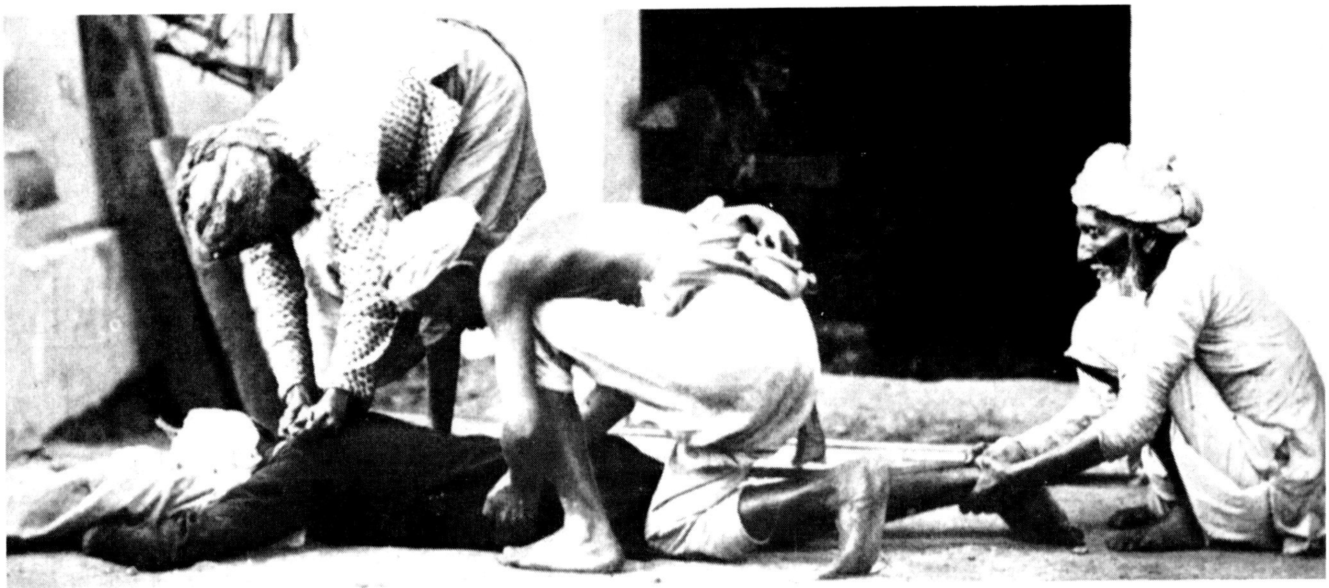

Captured thugs demonstrating to visiting British dignitaries the killer cult's method of strangling victims.

A thug distracting a rich traveler about to be strangled.

Thugs pulling a wealthy traveler from his horse.

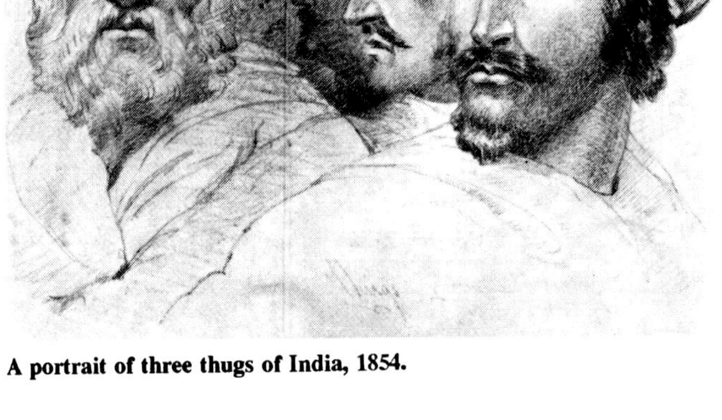

A portrait of three thugs of India, 1854.

Thugs mutilating their victims before the ritual burial.

pickax with strange markings on it, one that the Thugs treated as a holy relic. When he asked one Thug its use, the cultist shrugged. Sherwood told him that he would be hanged immediately unless he revealed the true nature of his cult. The Thug was then shown a large tree where ropes with nooses had been tied to high limbs. He shrank back in fear and, trembling, began to talk, explaining that the pickax was the most sacred tool of his faith, Thuggee, and that "it could fly into the hands of its user" when necessary. Slowly he and a few others began to detail the cult of Kali. Every ritual was outlined, every murder freely admitted without any sense of guilt displayed. Sherwood carried on his investigation for months and subsequently wrote a shocking paper entitled *Of the Murderers Called Phansigars.*

Sherwood not only pinpointed the oaths, the superstitions, and the murder procedures of Thuggee, but he even provided a brief lexicon exclusively used by the cultist killers. The secret language included such phrases as "Sweep the place" ("See that no one is about"), "Bring firewood" ("Take up your positions"), "Eat betel" ("Kill him"), "Look after the straw" ("Bury the corpse and watch for strangers"), "Descendants of bhowani?" ("Are you also Phansigars?"). There were numerous secret signs that provided warnings to other Thugs. According to Sherwood "drawing the back of the hand along the chin, from the throat outward, implies that caution is requisite—that some stranger is approaching. Putting the open hand over the mouth and drawing it gently down implies that there is no longer cause for alarm." The sacred knife was called *cathini,* the revered pickax was called *mahi.*

The Thugs interviewed by Sherwood reported the killing of their victims without expressing any regret, and the numbers of victims were staggering. One killer "stopped counting when he reached the thousand." Sherwood's western morality was numbed by the admissions of the Thugs: "What constitutes the most odious feature in the character of these murderers is, that prodigal as they are of human life, they can rarely claim the benefit of even the palliating circumstance of strong pecuniary temptation. They are equally strangers to compassion and remorse–they are never restrained from the commission of crimes by commiseration for the unfortunate traveler–and they are exempted from the compunctious visits of conscience, which usually follow, sooner or later, the steps of guilt." *Phansigari,* Sherwood went on to explain "is their *business.*" (In the latter part of the same nineteenth century the Mafia would excuse its ceaseless murders with the same word, *business.*) They were not, the Thugs patiently told Sherwood, the cause of countless deaths. These murders were ordained by Kali, the blameless goddess of destruction. The Thugs were merely the instruments of a goddess that could only survive through killing.

A young British officer in the Bengal army, William Sleeman, read Sherwood's paper with obsessive interest. He had already learned four Indian dialects and was much interested in the country's natives. At Sleeman's request, he was transferred to civil service in 1818, continuing his own investigation of Thuggee, which the military authorities still considered an infrequent problem occurring in the most remote areas of India. High officials refused to accept Sherwood's evaluation of the killer cult, believing that the surgeon had exaggerated the extent of the sect. Sleeman's own discoveries not only enforced Sherwood's evaluation of the secret society as a massive and controlled menace, but they pinpointed the areas, mostly the well-traveled trade routes, where the Thugs operated with abandon. Now the killer band had discarded much of Kali's traditions, killing women and children, motivated by the promise of loot. Their numbers increased so that the marauding bands often exceeded 150 to 200 armed men.

When Sleeman was given control over the entire Nerbudda Valley in 1822, he increased his probes into the mysteries of Thuggee, preparing exhaustive reports on Thug activities. In 1826, he was ordered to explore the possibility of Thuggee being an organized murder cult throughout India. In 1830, Sleeman was able to convince his immediate superior, Lord William Bentinck, governor general, that Thuggee was a nation-wide secret society that wielded vast power and influence. After reading Sleeman's reports, Bentinck became convinced that Thuggee was real and a national threat. He gave Sleeman his orders: Wipe out the Thugs. This was no easy task, despite the number of men put under Sleeman's command. As had been the case for centuries, the Thugs operated under the guise of marauding Dacoits when Sleeman's men arrested them and invariably most were released since the bodies of their victims were seldom discovered. No local police system then existed in India, other than that newly established by the British, and these poorly organized constabularies operated in only a few districts that were under strict British control. Sleeman carefully selected his own men, both British and Indian, trusting only to these specially trained paramilitary sleuths to ferret out Thugs. When suspected Thugs were arrested, Sleeman's force was hampered by local courts who balked at trying Thugs accused of murders in far flung areas.

To understand the motivations and methods of this secret murder sect, Sleeman learned from imprisoned Thugs the language of Thuggee, called *Ramasi.* Further, Sleeman recorded the history of this astounding killer cult, tracing its existence as far back as 700, according to some reports from informing members. Feringheea, a Thug priest who confessed his membership to Sleeman under pain of execution, boasted of the long and distinguished history of Thuggee, saying that its activities were accurately recorded in the cave drawings and carvings discovered at Ellora; these early etchings and sculptures could be dated back to the early eighth century. Said Feringheea: "In one place (of the cave drawings) you see men strangling; in another burying the bodies, in another carrying them off to the graves. There is not an operation in Thuggee that is not exhibited in the caves of Ellora." Sleeman believed that the sect may have developed as early as four centuries before the gruesome artistry of the Ellora caves when discovering in Herodotus reports of the tribe of Sagartii, Persian nomads known for their horsemanship, who Herodotus depicted as using a dagger and a noose of twisted leather to dispatch their enemies.

Much that Sleeman found in his own history of Thuggee pointed to the strong possibility that the religious murder sect was an offshoot of the dreaded Order of the Assassins, founded in the late eleventh century by Hasan Sabbah, a clever Persian who fused Muhammadanism with political murder as a way of wielding enormous power. This sect was developed in its most fanatical period by a bloodthirsty elder of Sabbah's sect known simply to western Crusaders in the twelfth century as The Old Man of the Mountains. A century later more than 1,000 Thugs were captured after a pitched battle near Delhi, according to one historian, but the local sultan released them, either through bribery or believing their plea that their group had nothing to do with the invading army that had been defeated. The Thugs were set free and shortly thereafter this formidable band spread murder and terror throughout Bengal. The existence of the Thugs in succeeding centuries became known to local and even European historians who erratically recorded their presence in India.

Sleeman learned that though the orthodox Hindus regarded Kali as a goddess that licked the blood from wounds they received in battle, the Thugs believed that the deity had grown tired epochs earlier of giving succor to a mankind persecuted by demons and had made two men from her own person, instructing these creations to murder the demons with handkerchiefs, shedding no blood in the act of murder so that she would no longer have to consume the blood. Thus sprang forth the cult of Thuggee, bloodless, methodical killers believing that they were killing not humans, but the reincarnation of ancient demons, anyone, actually, who did not follow Thuggee. This, of course, was but a cold-blooded rationale, according to other historians, to excuse murder for profit, irrespective of the fact that Thugs paid offhand homage to Kali by placing in the hands of her priests some portion of the loot they took from their victims.

By Sleeman's time, it was evident that Thuggee was no longer the "pure" murder sect of ancient times. It was basically a murder-for-profit organization that briefly nodded in Kali's direction before its avaricious followers killed and got rich. The number of members in each murder raid, by the 1830s, was no longer strictly controlled. Instead of ten to twenty Thugs carefully planning their ambushes, the bands were bloated to several hundred, all eager to enrich themselves under the religious umbrella of Kali. Decorum and protocol were ignored by priests demanding a share of the spoils and the sect, perhaps numbering as high as 500,000 in 1830, was populated by known criminals who later informed on Thug operations to save themselves from the hangman's noose. The devout Thug was quickly intimidated into cooperation with Sleeman and his men when told that he would not only be hanged if he did not confess his crimes and point out other Thugs, but that his corpse would be left to dangle from a tree limb and would be covered with the sacred blood of cows or pigs, depending upon whether the Thug was Hindu or Muslim, thereby assuring eternal damnation for his soul.

Muslim members of the sect puzzled Sleeman, especially since Thuggee was more Muslim than Hindu in numbers. He confronted one Muslim Thug, telling the accused murderer that he was disloyal to his own religion by worshipping a Hindu goddess. The Muslim shrugged and said that Kali was the twin of Fatima, daughter of Muhammad, and therefore a Muslim deity as well. To the Thugs, Sleeman was the embodiment of the avenger of their transgressions, as foretold by their own priests. The Thugs had long believed that because they had murdered the *wrong* people, from sweepers to tradesmen, and because they had ignored or misinterpreted Kali's dictates, the Europeans would be the cause of their destruction. Sleeman was thought to be the avenger and so well versed in Thug language and custom had he become that he was recognized by the Thugs as one who possessed as much knowledge of their secret society as the most respected of their high priests.

William Sleeman, to his prey, was not a foreign demon but a European guru seemingly gifted with the ability to look into the heart and soul of a Thug and know his secrets. By the time Sleeman began to round up Thugs in great numbers, thanks to his countless informers from their sect, the sect believed that their days were ending, that Kali had abandoned them for breaking her taboos. Sleeman and his men compelled informers to reveal hundreds of murder sites, known as *beles,* where thousands of bodies were unearthed along trade routes that criss-crossed North India for thousands of miles. For a decade Sleeman's men counted corpses and skeletons, then estimated that within the last hundred years the Thugs had murdered more than a million travelers.

The Thugs truly believed that their mass murders were not immoral and that they had committed no real offenses, except to Kali, when breaking her sacred rites. Buhram, one of the most notorious Thugs captured, freely admitted to murdering 931 people, saying, as did most of the Thugs interrogated, that he was merely following the fate decreed by Kali. She had thrown the travelers into his hands, commanding him to kill them. Had he refused, his family and friends would have suffered want and misery for the rest of eternity. Buhram went stoically to the gallows in 1840, convinced that he was being executed not for his wholesale slaughter of fellow humans whom he still considered demons, but because he had displeased Kali in the manner of his murder. Nasir, another Thug extensively interrogated by Sleeman, endorsed Buhram's rigid perspective, stating: "I have a hundred times heard my father and other old and wise men say when we had killed a sweeper and otherwise infringed their rules, that we should be some day punished for it; that the European rulers would be made the instruments to chastise us for our disregard of omens and neglect of the rules laid down for our guidance."

Sleeman learned from another Thug that the pickax, once consecrated in a temple of Kali, was so sacred that no Thug could swear a falsehood when touching it. He employed the pickax with great effect thereafter, bringing Thugs to him and having them place their hands on their own pickax, then demanding they tell him what he wanted to know. When a Thug shrank back from the pickax, holding his hands behind him, this was tantamount to a confession that he was a practicing Thug. But most Thugs were so obsessed with their own ritual that, once placing their hands on the pickax, unblinkingly admitted their countless murders, pointing out the graves of their victims and quickly identifying their fellow members in village after village. Next to Kali herself, the pickax was the most worshipped symbol of Thuggee.

Every bizarre ceremony conducted by the Thugs was recorded by Sleeman as he pried revelations from Thug informers. From Feringheea he learned of the ritual murder feast, *Tuponee.* Following the mass slayings of travelers in a caravan, a band of Thugs would erect a ten-foot tent so as to shield themselves from other travelers and inside gather in a circle and pass *goor* from hand to hand, this being lumpy pieces of coarse sugar. Each Thug who had committed a murder that night licked and consumed a portion of the *goor.* If any of this substance fell accidentally to the ground, it had to be buried immediately with the murder victims in their nearby graves. Only Thugs who had performed the murders were permitted to partake of the *goor,* and if a novice Thug ate any of this sacred substance, he was ordered to immediately go forth and strangle a victim so as to be worthy of consuming the *goor.* As the Thugs licked and swallowed this substance they would chant to Kali, asking her to provide more demon travelers for them, so they could share in more loot, a moaning prayer for gain repeated over and over again. As often as not, this murder feast was performed directly upon the graves of the victims killed only hours earlier. Some historians have likened this ritual to that of communion where bread and wine are consumed.

The pickax was ever present, placed on a sheet. Sitting next to the pickax was the Thug leader of the band, always facing west, with other elders ringed about him, leading the prayer to Kali, placing some silver next to the pickax, this was meant to be an offering to Kali, part of treasures stolen that day from the murder victims. The leader would then sprinkle holy water on the pickax and silver, still chanting, pleading with Kali to provide more victims, more treasure, and to present good omens the next day which would assure them of success. Other Thugs of lower rank and accomplishment sat in several circles about the inner circle of elders, repeating the prayer to Kali.

Such rituals made a indelible impression on any novitiate. To the younger untried Thugs this murder feast bonded them to the older men and to Thuggee itself. Said Feringheea: "We all feel pity sometimes, but the *goor* of the *Tuponee* changes our nature. It would change the nature of a horse. Let any man once taste of that *goor,* and he will be a Thug though he know all the trades and have all the wealth in the world. I never wanted food; my mother's family was opulent, her relations high in office. I have been high in office myself and become so great a favorite wherever I went that I was sure of promotion. Yet I was always miserable when absent from my gang, and obliged to return to Thuggee. My father made me taste of that fatal *goor* when I was a mere boy, and if I were to live a thousand years I would never be able to follow any other trade."

Sleeman discovered that dozens of leading Thugs were also leaders in their local communities, men who were respected for their upstanding and law-abiding ways, such as Makeen Lodhi, who had murdered innumerable travelers. As one of his aides put it, Lodhi considered his victims fair game, an attitude any hunter had for his prey, one shared by all Thugs: "They all look upon travelers as a sportsman looks upon hares and pheasants; and they recollect their best sporting grounds, and talk of them, when they can, with the same kind of glee!" It was this kind of gregarious talk, bragging of their kills, that led many Thugs into Sleeman's traps. He had a small army at his command by the mid-1830s, which he used in sweeping wide areas of India. So well briefed were Sleeman's men that they easily ferreted out the Thugs from villages and towns. Sleeman had prepared precise charts and genealogical maps that documented Thug families, from grandfathers to babes in arms. Using regular British troops, European volunteers, and loyal Sepoy soldiers, Sleeman was able to arrest thousands of Thugs.

The British government allowed him a free hand, and Sleeman's kangaroo courts quickly convicted and condemned hundreds of Thugs. Those who cooperated with Sleeman–they were called "Approvers"– were spared. They were given minor government jobs and were reeducated, along with their children–Sleeman's army of bureaucrats teaching these reformed Thugs new trades, new concepts of morality. Feringheea proved to be the most informative of Sleeman's captured Thugs and he was spared the gallows, despite the fact that he had murdered more than 100 people by January 1831 when he was arrested. Even the older Thugs, most dedicated to Kali's teachings, refuted the blood goddess in the end, accepting the ways of the Europeans, attending schools established for them where they, along with their children, learned bricklaying and the art of weaving. Some of these Thugs, mass killers all, became the most accomplished carpet weavers in the world, and one of their products was later given to Queen Victoria, a massive two-ton, 40-foot-wide, 80-foot-long carpet which later decorated the mammoth dining hall in the Waterloo Chamber at Windsor Castle.

Further aiding Sleeman in breaking up the Thug gangs was the rapid expansion of British-controlled commerce. No longer did the followers of Kali find easy prey in unprotected caravans. British and Sepoy troops accompanied these merchants, guarding against the Thug techniques. Groups of Thugs begging to join a caravan to seek protection were invited to do so but that night British soldiers would round up the stranglers and put them under arrest to prevent their wholesale slaughter of the caravan. This protective system, coupled with later improvements in communication and travel, particularly the coming of the railroad to India, made the murder methods of Thuggee obsolete. In the late 1830s, Thugs by the hundreds were tried and quickly convicted of murder. By 1840, about 3,700 Thugs, most of them cult leaders and the worst mass murderers, had been tried. About 500 were hanged and these were public executions where the body was defiled so that such executions served as effective propaganda, implanting real fear into the hearts of other still unexposed Thugs.

To those witnessing their public executions, the condemned Thugs showed no concern for their own horrible fate, stoically accepting their fate with what appeared to be a normal destiny. One eyewitness to a public execution of twenty-five Thugs in 1831, a friend of Sleeman's, Mrs. Fanny Parks, later wrote: "It would be impossible to find in any county a set of men who meet death with more indifference than these wretches; and had it been in a better cause, they would have excited universal sympathy. As it was, there was something dreadful in the thought that men, who had so often imbrued their hands in blood, should meet their death with such carelessness. I believe that they had previously requested to be allowed to fasten the cord about their necks with their own hands; certain it is that each individual as soon as he had adjusted the noose, jumped off the beam and launched himself into eternity; and those who first mounted the ladder selected their ropes, rejecting such as did not please them. One of them who had leaped off the beam and had been hanging for more than three seconds put his hands up and pulled his cap over his face."

Fifty-six Thugs, some of them mass murderers, were spared execution because they had turned informer. These "Approvers" survived only because they allowed Sleeman to unearth thousands more of active members. Sleeman found himself battling for the lives of these Approvers since the British government insisted upon executing them. In the end, Sleeman had his way, explaining that without his informers he would never have been able to break Thuggee's strangle-hold on Indian commerce. The rest of the leading Thugs were sent to prison for life, or, as was the case with half of them, were transported to other countries where they were sentenced to penal servitude for life. By 1848, another 650 Thugs were tried, half of these being executed, the remainder imprisoned for life. By then the religion of Thuggee as a practicing murder cult was all but finished.

By the 1870s, the cult of Thuggee held interest to British dignitaries visiting India only as a curiosity. Ancient stranglers who had been imprisoned for forty years were brought from their miserable jails to amuse British royalty by reenacting their strangling methods. This then was the residue of the most feared murder sect in ten centuries, skeletal creatures with long white beards, holding up anachronistic *rumals* and pickaxes while chanting dead prayers to the fallen idol of now bloodless Kali. This secret criminal society, however, did not completely die out for there were isolated reports that Thuggee was still being practiced in remote northern regions of India as late as the early 1900s, but these tales went unsubstantiated. Thuggee is thought to be, mercifully, at this writing a defunct sect, its nightmare rites and horrible murders buried long ago with its sacrificial victims. See: **Order of the Assassins, The**.

REF.: Becher, *Personal Reminiscences in India and Europe, 1830-88;* Bruce, *The Stranglers, The Cult of Thuggee and its Overthrow in British India; CBA;* Chunder, *Travels of a Hindu;* Churcher, *Some Reminiscences of Three Quarters of a Century in India;* Collier, *The Great Indian Mutiny;* Cust, *Pictures of Indian Life;* De Watteville, *The British Soldier;* Dewar, *In the Days of the Company;* ____, *Bygone Days in India;* Dubois, *Hindu Manners and Customs;* Dutt, *India in the Victorian Age;* Foster, *John Company;* Franzius, *History of the Order of Assassins;* Hurwood, *Society and the Assassin;* Hutton, *A Popular Account of the Thugs and Dacoits, The Hereditary Garroters and Gang Robbers of India;* Judd, *The Victorian Empire;* Kaye, *Peregrine Pulteney;* Kinsley, *The Sword and the Flute: Kali and Krasna;* Laquer, *Terrorism;* Lang, *Wanderings in India;* Lawrence, *Forty Years' Service in India;* Lewin, *The Government of the East India Company and Its Monopolies;* Ludlow, *British India, Its Races and Its History;* MacKenzie, *Secret Societies;* MacMunn, *Religions and Hidden Cults in India;* Milne, *The Indian Criminal;* Hilton, *A Popular Account of the Thugs and Dacoits, The Hereditary Gang Robbers and Garroters of India;* Mottram, *Trader's Dream, The Romance of the East India Company;* Nash, *Almanac of World Crime;* Pinkerton, *Murder in All Ages;* Russell, *Tribes and Castes of the Central Provinces of India;* Scott, *The Concise Encyclopedia of Crime and Criminals;* Seaton, *From Cadet to Colonel;* Sleeman, *Thug;* Sleeman, *A Journey Through the Land of Oude;* ____, *Ramaseeana, or a Vocabulary of the Peculiar Language Used by the Thugs;* ____, *Rambles and Recollections;* ____, *Report on Budhuk, Alias Bagee, Dacoits and Other Gang Robbers by Hereditary Profession;* ____, *Report on the Depredations Committed by the Thug Gangs of Upper and Central India;* ____, *The Thugs or Phansigars of India, Comprising a History of the Rise and Progress of that Extraordinary Fraternity of Assassins;* Smith, *The Oxford History of India;* Spear, *A History of India;* Temple, *In the Century Before the Mutiny;* Tuker, *The Yellow Scarf, The Story of the Life of Thuggee Sleeman;* Webster, *Secret Societies and Subversive Movements;* Williams, *Religious Thought and Life in India;* Woodruff, *The Men Who Ruled India;* (FICTION), Giroux, *The Rishi;* Masters, *The Deceivers;* (FILM), *Gunga Din*, 1939; *Indiana Jones and the Temple of Doom*, 1984.

Thuna, Max, prom. 1910, U.S., wh. slav. In 1910, in Seattle, a crackdown on vice netted a white slaver by the name of Max Thuna. Thuna was arrested on charges of white slavery and convicted largely on the testimony of immigration officials who had confiscated correspondence written by Thuna which detailed how he earned $150 a week from a woman identified only as Lottie. In addition to the observation that Lottie was the most profitable woman he ever owned, Thuna also said enough to indicate that he and the intended recipients of the letters were engaged in an extensive and profitable white slave business.

REF.: *CBA;* Roe, *The Great War on White Slavery.*

Thunderbolt, Captain, See: **Ward, Frederick.**

Thurlow, Edward (Baron Thurlow), 1731-1806, Brit., atty. gen-jur. Served as solicitor general in 1770, as attorney general in 1771, and as lord chancellor from 1778-83 and from 1783-92. Thurlow presided over the corruption trial of Warren Hastings in 1788, until he was removed on the orders of William Pitt. REF.: *CBA.*

Thurmond, Thomas Harold, 1909-33, and **Holmes, John Maurice**, d.1933, U.S., kid.-lynch.-mur. On Nov. 9, 1933, Thomas Thurmond and a friend, John Maurice Holmes, kidnapped and killed 22-year-old Brooke Hart, son of a San Jose, Calif., department store owner. That day, as Hart left his job at the department store, Thurmond and Holmes followed him. After forcing his car to the side of the road, they drove Hart in his car to the San Mateo-Hayward Bridge, which spans San Francisco Bay. There they bludgeoned him with a brick, fastened cement blocks to his body, and threw him into the bay. When Hart regained consciousness and started yelling, Thurmond shot at him. The cries ceased, and Hart sank beneath the water.

Shortly thereafter Thurmond telephoned Hart's father and demanded $40,000, warning him not to contact the police. Hart disregarded the instruction and immediately called the police, who initially considered it a prank and did nothing. Eventually, however, it became clear to police that the kidnaping was genuine.

Kidnapper Thomas Harold Thurman, lynched in 1933.

After several complications in delivering the ransom, Hart was able to keep Thurmond on the telephone long enough for the police to trace the call. Captured in a phone booth, Thurmond confessed but placed most of the blame on Holmes. When Holmes was apprehended, he too confessed, and likewise claimed Thurmond was the mastermind.

About a week later, Brooke Hart's body was found on the shore by several hunters. The entire community, especially the students at San Jose College, went wild upon hearing the news. A crowd numbering in the thousands gathered in front of the Santa Clara County Jail where the kidnappers were being held. Sheriff William Emig, realizing he had a potential lynch mob on his hands, called in all available manpower to protect the jail and his charges. His request that California governor James Rolfe send the National Guard was refused.

At about 9:00 p.m. on Nov. 24, the crowd had increased to around 15,000 and was going wild. They stormed the building, and police held them off for two hours using high-powered hoses and tear gas. Finally, a group of young ringleaders led a mass charge and entered the jail. They located both Thurmond and Holmes, beat them unmercifully, and dragged them from the jail. Despite their pleas, they were then taken across the street to a park and hanged. No one was ever indicted for these killings, and, even more remarkably, governor Rolfe commended the lynch mob for their actions.

REF.: Alix, *Ransom Kidnapping in America;* Boar, *The World's Most Infamous Murders;* Boucher, *The Quality of Murder; CBA;* Logan, *Rope, Knife and Chair;* Messick, *Kidnapping;* Moorehead, *Hostages to Fortune;* Nash, *Bloodletters and Badmen;* Postgate, *Murder, Piracy and Treason;* Whitelaw, *Corpus Delicti;* Wilson, *Encyclopedia of Murder;* (FICTION), DeFord, *Homecoming;* (FILM), *Fury,* 1935.

Thurston, Lorrin Andrews, 1858-1931, Hawaii, rebel. Headed revolutionary movement in 1887 and was named minister of interior in newly created government. He took a major role in the revolution in 1893, removing Queen Lilinokalani after two years on the throne, and helped draft the constitution for the Republic of Hawaii in 1894. REF.: *CBA.*

Thurtell, John, d.1824, Brit, mur. There is said to be no honor among thieves. In this case the axiom proved to be true about gamblers. John Thurtell, who loved gambling, drinking, and women, was at best an unlucky gambler. Losing heavily to a crooked bookmaker named William Weare, Thurtell decided to get even. Thurtell suggested that Weare join two of his friends from the pubs and gaming houses of London, Joseph Hunt and William Probert, on a trip to the country for a weekend of shooting at Probert's cottage. The target would be William Weare.

Three British killers, William Probert, Joseph Hunt, and John Thurtell.

The four set out for the country on Oct. 24, 1823, with Hunt and Probert going ahead in one gig and Thurtell and Weare following in another. As Thurtell and Weare reached an isolated spot on the road near Probert's cottage, Thurtell pulled out a pistol and shot Weare in the face. Only wounded, Weare tried to escape, but Thurtell followed him, cut him with a knife, and then crashed his heavy pistol into the man's skull.

Thurtell and friends disposing of Weare's body.

Thurtell hid the body and joined his companions at the cottage for dinner. Afterwards they took Weare's body and dumped it in a nearby pond. They searched for the gun and knife which Thurtell had mislaid in the excitement but could not find them. The bloody weapons were found the next day by two laborers who had watched the guilty pair searching.

The hanging of Thurtell in 1824.

The local authorities sought the help of several Bow Street Runners from London. They found the body and on Oct. 29

placed Thurtell and Hunt under arrest. Hunt confessed and pointed to Thurtell as the killer. Thurtell was found Guilty and hanged in 1824. Hunt was transported to the penal colony at Botany Bay in Australia. Charges against Probert were dropped in a deal to get his wife to testify.

REF.: *CBA;* Wilson, *Encyclopedia of Murder.*

Thyng, Rosalie A., prom. 1876, Case of, U.S., mur. George A. Thyng of Fall River, Mass., died of a huge dose of poison on July 9, 1876. His wife, Rosalie Thyng, was accused of the murder because she was the only person who could have given him the poison. However, Mrs. Thyng's lawyers won an acquittal because the prosecution was unable to show how Mrs. Thyng had purchased the poison.

REF.: *CBA;* Nash, *Almanac of World Crime.*

Thynn, Thomas (AKA: **Tom of Ten Thousand**), d.1682, Brit., assass. In the latter part of the seventeenth century when a yearly income of £5,000 was considered a fortune, the £10,000 that Thomas Thynn received made him the richest commoner of his day. An income of these proportions made associations with royalty and participation in politics natural activities for Thynn. Although Thynn had ended up on the bad side of James II, he was befriended by the Duke of Monmouth and was regarded highly enough by Dryden that the poet characterized him as the "wise Issachar" in *Absalom and Achitophel.* In 1681, Thynn married Lady Ogle, the 14-year-old daughter of Lord Northumberland and the widow of Lord Ogle. For reasons that are not entirely clear, Thynn's new wife left England almost immediately after the wedding.

On the night of Feb. 12, 1682, with his bride out of the country, Thynn was shot while riding in his coach in London. Three men, Charles George Borosky, John Stern, and Christopher Vratz were arrested for the crime. Borosky admitted killing Thynn, but claimed that he had done so at the request of Count Charles John von Konigsmark. The Swedish-born von Konigsmark, an aristocrat with an impressive military record, had previously visited England, and it was on this earlier visit that he had met, and attempted to court Lady Ogle. Borosky claimed that von Konigsmark had hired him to shoot Thynn to settle an earlier argument. Because of Borosky's accusations and the suspicion of a motive of romantic jealousy, von Konigsmark was charged as an accessory before the fact. Von Konigsmark denied the allegations and was acquitted. The three defendants were found Guilty and were hanged in Pall Mall in March 1683. The body of Borosky, who had actually fired the gun, was suspended in chains near Mile End until it decayed. An elaborate white marble tomb depicting the assassination scene was erected in Westminster Abbey.

REF.: *CBA;* Lambton, *Echoes of Causes Celebres;* Sparrow, *The Great Assassins.*

Tibbs, Delbert, 1939- , U.S., (wrong. convict.) rape-mur. In 1974, Delbert Tibbs, thirty-four, a black divinity student and aspiring writer, was hitchhiking through the South gathering material for a novel. Police in Daytona Beach, Fla., picked Tibbs up for hitchhiking and photographed him. When police in Fort Myers began searching for a black man who had raped a 16-year-old white girl and murdered her male companion, the Daytona police sent Tibbs' pictures. The Fort Myers police improperly showed the rape victim pictures of Tibbs before having her attempt an identification of her attacker in a line-up. The girl, Cynthia Nadeau, a runaway who later admitted to being high on marijuana at the time of the crime, identified Tibbs as her assailant from the subsequent line-up, causing Tibbs to be charged with both crimes.

Tibbs claimed never to have been in Fort Myers and only Nadeau's testimony placed him within even 200 miles of the crime. An all-white jury found Tibbs Guilty of rape and first-degree murder after only ninety minutes of deliberation. Tibbs was subsequently sentenced to die in the electric chair and spent two years on death row before the Florida State Supreme Court reversed his conviction on the grounds that it was not supported by "weight of the evidence." Tibbs was released on bail in 1977, and later discovered that despite semantic similarities, "weight of evidence" does not mean "insufficient evidence." In 1982, the U.S. Supreme Court ruled that Tibbs could be retried for the crimes on the same evidence used in the first trial because a reversal on "weight of evidence" does not mean acquittal is the only proper verdict. Joseph D'Alessandro, Lee County state's attorney, announced plans to exercise the newly elucidated option to retry Tibbs, but when James Long, who prosecuted Tibbs in 1974 announced that he would testify in Tibbs' behalf, D'Alessandro decided not to reopen the case. REF.: *CBA.*

Tiberius (Tiberius Claudius Nero Caesar Augustus), 42 B.C.-37 A.D., Roman., tort.-mur. Tiberius, the second Roman emperor, came to power as a result of the kind of political intrigue that characterized Rome during these difficult and bloody years. His father, Tiberius Claudius Nero, was a high-ranking court priest and magistrate; his mother the scheming Livia Drusilla who became the mistress of Emperor Augustus in 39 B.C. Augustus forced the elder Tiberius to surrender Livia and upon divorcing his own wife they married. Young Tiberius and his brother Drusus eventually were adopted by the emperor.

Tiberius passed through his young adulthood in the service of the Roman army, commanding a military expedition to Armenia in 20 B.C. and to Germany thirteen years later and winning great military victories on behalf of the empire. At home, Livia plotted against all those who stood in the way of her son. She poisoned Marcellus, the husband of Augustus' daughter Julia, and her two sons, which made it possible for Tiberius to accede to the throne in September 14 A.D., following the death of his stepfather. The first years of the second emperor's rule were a textbook of efficiency and clean government. He ended bureaucratic waste and strengthened the navy. But Tiberius provided a clue as to what was to follow when he exiled the entire Jewish community from Rome after four Jews were accused of stealing a woman's belongings. The emperor's sexual mores were perverse. Open debauchery throughout the empire was encouraged as Tiberius entertained a legion of small boys which he called his "minnows." There is evidence that he was a voyeur with a sadistic bent. According to the historian Suetonius, the incense carriers at the Roman temples were often raped and sodomized by Tiberius. Those who refused to submit willingly had their legs broken.

Roman Emperor Tiberius.

In 23 A.D., Tiberius' son Drusus was poisoned, and the grieved emperor increasingly turned away from affairs of state to lead a more self-indulgent lifestyle. Before this, however, he had fallen under the evil spell of his minister Sejanus, whose political ambition far exceeded that of even Livia. Sejanus convinced Tiberius of eminent plots against the throne. Blinded to the treachery of this man, the emperor sanctioned an "inquisition." Dozens of accused conspirators were tortured or executed, including entire families. Sejanus saw himself as the future emperor of Rome, and to this end he was prepared to go to any length. At his insistence Tiberius' son Germanicus was arrested as a conspirator and poisoned to death with the approval of his father.

Sejanus then arranged the death of Drusus in order to marry his wife Livilla, who was a party to her husband's murder. In 31 A.D., Sejanus was at the height of his power. That year Tiberius was elected consul of Rome for the fifth time, and Sejanus the co-consul. Now Sejanus was one of the most powerful figures in Rome and Tiberius began to have second thoughts about his trustworthiness. The emperor had a letter delivered to an assembly of Roman senators in which Sejanus was denounced for his political treachery and treason. The letter effectively discredited Sejanus who was taken off to a dungeon and strangled, the corpse taken to the banks of the Tiber River and left to rot in the sun. After that, Tiberius' only concern was the naming of a worthy successor. He selected the great-grandson of Augustus; Gaius Caesar, better known to history as Caligula. "I am nursing a viper in Rome's bosom," Tiberius once remarked. After his murder in Spring 37 A.D., by the Praetorian commander Macro, the world would soon find out how prophetic those words were. See: **Caligula**.

REF.: Africa, *Rome of the Caesars;* Balsdon, *The Romans;* Carcopino, *Daily Life in Ancient Rome;* Gibbon, *The Decline and Fall of the Roman Empire;* Grant, *The World of Rome;* Grimal, *Hellenism and the Rise of Rome;* Johnson, *Famous Assassinations in History;* Robinson, *History of Rome;* Rogers, *Studies in the Reign of Tiberius;* Suetonius, *The Twelve Caesars;* (FILM) *The Robe*, 1953; *Ben Hur*, 1959.

Tiberius III Apsimar, d.705, E. Roman., emp., assass. Defeated Leontius in 698 and assumed control over Eastern Roman Empire, ruling from 698. He was abducted and put to death after Justinian II returned to the empire. REF.: *CBA*.

Tichborne, Roger Charles Doughty, See: **Orton, Arthur.**

Tidal Basin Scandal, 1974, U.S., morals. Political permissiveness and promiscuity on a wholesale basis was never more flagrant in Washington, D.C., than in the 1970s. At that time, entertaining mistresses and prostitutes, and having extra-marital affairs were thought to be as natural as a congressman's right to abuse his franking privileges. The first headliner in these low-life follies was the relationship between venerable Congressman Wilbur Daigh Mills, a 65-year-old democrat from Arkansas, overlord of the Ways and Means Committee for seventeen years, and 38-year-old Annabella Battistella, a sultry, raven-haired Washington stripper who billed herself as "Fanne Foxe, the Argentine Firecracker." This unlikely couple—Mills, married for forty years to Polly Mills, a former postmaster from Kenset, Ark., and Battistella, the divorced mother of three—were actually neighbors, but no one knew it or cared until the night of Oct. 14, 1974.

At about 2 a.m. that day, two park policemen spotted a blue Lincoln Continental racing toward the Jefferson Memorial with headlights off. They gave chase and, when abreast of the Continental, motioned the driver to pull over next to the Tidal Basin. Five persons were inside the car and all of them emerged unsteadily at the orders of the police. One of the two men was the driver, Albert Gapacini, thirty-nine. The women included 56-year-old Gloria Sanchez, an Argentinean, and a 27-year-old who gave the name of Liliane Kassar. The last two persons to get out of the car looked as if they had been fighting. An elderly man stood with scratches on his face and was bleeding from the nose. His speech was incoherent and he blinked confusedly at the officers' questions. Next to him stood a tall, blonde woman who seemed to have two black eyes. She was hysterical. As one of the officers approached her, she quickly spun about on a spike heel and made a dash for the Tidal Basin, jumping into the murky backwaters of the Potomac. The officer raced after her, pulling her from the inky waters to the shore. The woman was taken to the hospital and arrangements were made to have everyone else driven home. No names were to be used in the report of this bizarre incident, and the players may never have been identified had it not been for a freakish incident.

A TV film crew, on a routine assignment to chronicle the work of Washington's park police, showed up just at the moment when an officer was leading away the elderly man with the scratches and nosebleed. The cop was overheard by the TV crew to say to the elderly man who had to be held upright: "Come on, Mr. Congressman. You don't need this bad publicity."

He nevertheless got it, the crew seizing upon the occurrence to film the old man as he staggered into the night. Two days later, he was identified, to the shock and horror of Washington, as Congressman Wilbur Mills, a satrap of Congress and, after thirty-six years of Washington service, one of the most powerful men on Capitol Hill.

The woman who had tried to evade police by leaping into the Tidal Basin was no blonde at all, but voluptuous stripper Fanne Foxe (she had been wearing a wig that night, it was reported), real name Annabella Battistella, "just a good friend," she said when the storm first broke. She lived in the Crystal Towers Apartments in Arlington, Va., as did Mills and his wife, Polly.

Born in a small village 175 miles west of Buenos Aires, Annabella Villagra began dancing in South American nightclubs after marrying piano player Eduardo Battistella at age twenty. When the act began to slide, the alluring Battistella began to strip for a living and continued being an ecdysiast when she and her husband immigrated to the U.S. in the early 1960s. They moved to Washington where, in 1973, they met and befriended Polly and Wilbur Mills, both hard drinkers who liked to nightclub with Annabella and her husband. In October 1974, the Battistellas divorced, with Annabella's three children, ages fifteen through nineteen, staying with their strip-teasing mother.

Mills tried to shrug off the Tidal Basin episode, saying that he, Battistella, and the others in his Continental were merely having a bon-voyage party for Battistella's cousin, and fellow Argentinean, Gloria Sanchez, before she returned to her native country. The congressman was asked why his wife had not been with him. She had a broken foot at the time, replied Mills, and was confined to their home. He then admitted that the group had been celebrating at the Junkanoo, a Caribbean nightclub, but had left at 9 p.m., then went to another "public place." He added that "after a few refreshments," Battistella became ill and the party left to take her home. In the car, the stripper unexpectedly became a little crazy and attempted to leave the car while it was moving. Mills tried to restrain her. "In the ensuing struggle," Mills explained, "her elbow hit my glasses and broke them, resulting in a number of small cuts around my nose."

He insisted that his relationship with Battistella was strictly platonic. News hounds dug deeper and discovered that Mills, sometimes accompanied by his heavy-drinking wife, frequently visited the Silver Slipper, a Washington strip joint. The congressman and his wife often argued loudly in the club but were tolerated because of his political position and, chiefly, because he was a big spender, sometimes throwing out hundreds of dollars to buy drinks and watch Fanne Foxe strip to her G-string. On one occasion, Mills, according to the club's employees, squandered $1,700 on magnums of champagne for his friends.

It was soon learned that Mills was a regular nocturnal visitor to all the sleazy, girlie places in Washington and other cities. He was known in such hard-porn areas as Pershing Square in Los Angeles and Times Square in New York. Once, while frolicking at the Body Shop in L.A., Mills drunkenly climbed upon a stage to cavort wildly with a pulchritudinous stripper.

Public reaction was mixed. Wilbur Mills obviously had a problem, said many of his political opponents, and he was slipping. "He doesn't have the grip on things as he used to," one associate reluctantly admitted. Mills scoffed at his Tidal Basin critics and promptly returned to Arkansas, where he campaigned for his next term. His wife, Polly, was on his arm as he made his rounds.

"Was there anything between you and the young lady?" a reporter asked the political sachem at one campaign stop.

Mills gave him his best, benign smile and said: "No. I ought to be flattered at my age of sixty-five for anybody to ask me such a question."

At a gathering of the Jaycees, members took a jocular view of an elderly man running about tipsy with a steamy stripper. They laughed and shouted: "Good for you, Wilbur!"

Good old boy Wilbur responded with: "I was one of those who went out one night and did something I shouldn't have done." He said he should never have drunk champagne. "It goes to my head. I apologize to you, my friends, for any embarrassment I have caused. Don't go out with foreigners who drink champagne." Such down-home xenophobia appealed and edified Mills' grassroots supporters. He won handily against his opponent, Judy Petty.

While Mills was wooing his trusting constituents in Arkansas, success exploded over the head of the sexy Annabella Battistella. The 38-year-old stripper, whose career had been at ebb before the Tidal Basin incident, was suddenly in great demand. Following two decades of obscurity, of snaking and grinding and bumping her body up ramps and down runways, Battistella was all at once offered enormous amounts of money to take her clothes off in several cities. She accepted a reported $3,000-a-week job as headline stripper at Boston's Pilgrim Theater, which was in the heart of the Combat Zone, a two-and-a-half block slice of the city's downtown, a seedy, dangerous area, designated by the city fathers as a containment area to house hard-core pornography of every description, prostitutes and pimps of every stripe.

The stripper's introduction to her almost all-male audiences was elaborate compared with the usual burst of sensual music. An announcer boomed, following a fanfare: "You've read about her and here she is–in person–The Tidal Basin Bombshell!" Then, through the curtains bounced Fanne Foxe, going into her disrobing act. After the first show, reporters gathered backstage to interview the perspiring, half-naked dancer. Great things were in the making, she gushed. Big money was beckoning to her from New York, Ohio, Florida, and North Carolina. Suddenly she was a star. Why, even a toy company was planning to mass market a Fanne Foxe doll. And she had been cloaked in respectability by the Harvard Republican Club, which bestowed upon Foxe its award for "the political newcomer of the year." Of course, she would accept the title, oblivious of its sardonic nature.

The publicity generated by Foxe no doubt reached the eyes and ears of her good friend Wilbur Mills who had just won re-election to his House seat. He had triumphed over scandal. But Wilbur Mills was drawn back to the voluptuous Foxe, an apparently irresistible force compelling him to see the woman once again. He persuaded Fanne's former husband, Eduardo, to accompany him to Boston—just to show those who might ask that he was merely a family friend—chartering a Lear jet at $800 for the trip.

When Mills arrived in Boston, he claimed he felt sick and that his heart was skipping beats. A local doctor gave him a vitamin injection. That night, Mills stood in the balcony shadows of the Pilgrim Theater to watch Fanne Foxe strip. He had to get closer. Mills moved downstairs to the back of the orchestra, then, almost row by row, worked his way to a front-row seat.

Foxe played to him, wiggling and heaving in his direction, discarding garments until she wore only a tiny, black G-string and a red wig. She bounced offstage to mediocre applause, then returned, as would a diva to take her roses, in a see-through, pink peignoir. Beaming before her audience of balding men, Foxe sauntered to the footlights and said to the audience in her soft voice: "I'd like you to meet somebody." She turned to the wings and called sweetly: "Mr. Mills! Mr. Mills! Where are you?"

From the wings came Congressman Wilbur Mills, who clasped Foxe's outstretched hand, and gave her a fleeting hug. He blinked into the hot footlights at an audience he could not see, nor one that would award his strange and unfamiliar presence on stage with applause. In embarrassed silence, after perhaps no more than five seconds upon the stage, Mills was led like a small boy by Fanne Foxe into the wings, hurrying a bit so that the scheduled hard-core pornographic film could begin.

Mills' stage debut was brief, but a disaster for him in that a Hearst newspaper photographer, either by accident or design, was on hand to take a photo of a smiling Mills and a grinning Fanne Foxe, clasping hands on stage. The photograph, taken by Gene Dixon for the Boston *Herald American,* appeared in newspapers across the country the following day, amusing the public at large and horrifying the U.S. Congress. (The author hereof was later told by a staff member of the Boston *Herald-Examiner* that "we got a tip that he *might* be there (at the Pilgrim Theater) that night.") Whether or not that tip came from Foxe, who certainly knew how to exploit her relationship with Mills, is not known.

That night, Mills and Foxe celebrated their friendship at a striptease club, where Mills admiringly patted the behind of Lilly Pagan, the resident stripper, before merrily going off with the Tidal Basin Bombshell. Reporters caught up to him the next morning as he escorted Foxe from her four-room suite at the Howard Johnson hotel (Mills was not a registered guest). Once again Mills was found later that day in the wings of the Pilgrim, ogling Foxe disrobing on stage and following her to her dressing room. He appeared wobbly legged and had to quickly sit down, explaining that he was taking sedatives for his heart and that they "make me drunk."

With the kind of autocratic disdain for the press he had shown while ruling the powerful House Ways and Means Committee, Mills laughed at reporters who suggested that he and Fanne Foxe were lovers. No, just good friends. Foxe, he said, was "my little ole Argentine hillbilly." Why had he come to Boston and appeared on the stage of a striptease and pornographic film theater? To be seen, answered Mills indignantly, and to quiet a lot of stupid gossip.

Someone asked if he thought such conduct on the part of one of Congress' leading figures might not be politically harmful.

Sneered Mills: "This won't ruin me. *Nothing* can ruin me!"

He was dead wrong. The photo showing Mills and Foxe on stage together galvanized even his most ardent supporters to pronounce his demise on the American political scene. Upon his return to Washington, his close friend, House Speaker Carl Albert, asked him to his face: "Wilbur, are you sick?" Mills sighed, then collapsed in a chair in the cloakroom, answering: "Yes, Mr. Speaker, I am."

A Democratic caucus quickly took away all of Mills' powers, and Albert announced that Mills would not be Ways and Means chairman when the 94th Congress convened in January. Mills, at the urging of friends, went to the medical center in Bethesda, Md., where examinations revealed he was an alcoholic. (As a matter of fact, the announcement was no revelation to him; he knew that he had been a drunk for years and would later admit that he turned his devoted wife Polly into a drunk.) Mills later insisted that he had no memory whatsoever of the sultry stripper, Fanne Foxe. The Tidal Basin incident and the stage frolic with her in Boston were blurry and undefinable memories. He had simply blacked out, he claimed. All of it was a blackout. His career in Washington, after forty years, was then blacked out.

For Fanne Foxe, the Mills friendship was not milked out. She was suddenly propelled into a limelight she had sought all her life. News hounds descended upon her and she gave out one interview after another. To Sally Quinn she coyly said: "What if Wilbur Mills told people he was going to leave his wife and marry me? How would people react?" To Barbara Davidson of *Newsweek,* the Tidal Basin Bombshell intimated a closer liaison to Mills than mere friendship, quipping that he was "a young man in an old body."

It would be several years before all of the story behind Mills' madcap escapades with Foxe was revealed. In 1977, Polly Mills, two years older than her spouse, admitted that she knew about her husband's affair with the Argentinean stripper and, in mid-1973, had packed her bags and left him, mulling over divorce. She decided to stay with him. "Being an alcoholic myself, I knew what he was going through, how sick he was," she told Michael Satchell of *Parade* Magazine. Mills was out of Congress by 1978, working as a tax expert for a Washington law firm. He also became one of the guiding lights of Alcoholics Anonymous, taking the pledge and, whenever possible, giving speeches about drinking. To this day, he claims to remember nothing of his affair with Fanne Foxe.

Battistella remembered well. She later claimed that Wilbur Mills had impregnated her but that she had aborted the child since it might further ruin Mills' reputation. She went on to small film roles, one for a cable firm for which she received $10,000 and one made for $5,000 in Argentina, where she was thought of as a curiosity. She later tried to commit suicide, taking a handful of sleeping pills, and wound up in a psychiatric ward. In 1982, the retired stripper was reportedly working on a gothic novel about an Argentinean woman who was executed in the early 1800s with her lover, a priest. The book is about the only thing concerning Fanne Foxe that remains unpublished. REF.: *CBA.*

Tieri, Frank (AKA: Funzi, Funzola, The Old Man), 1904-1981, U.S., rob.-rack.-consp.-fraud-org. crime. Despite numerous indictments and allegations, Cosa Nostra boss Frank Tieri had only one conviction on his record (a robbery in 1922) when he was brought to trial in 1980. Tieri was indicted on federal racketeering charges that named him "boss of one of the five New York City 'families' of La Cosa Nostra." It was the first time that the racketeering laws, generally used in regard to unions or businesses, were employed to prosecute the head of a crime family. Their use against Tieri implied that federal agents had compiled substantial evidence tying Tieri not only to specific crimes but also to his primary position within the Cosa Nostra as head of the Genovese "family".

New York Mafia boss Frank Tieri.

Tieri, known simply as "the Old Man," came to the U.S. from Naples in 1911. He was denied U.S. citizenship twice and lived as a resident alien in a modest home in Brooklyn. Throughout his life, Tieri claimed to be an employee of a sportswear manufacturer, rather than a well-positioned member of the Genovese "family". Federal prosecutors maintained that he was head of the largest crime family in the U.S. and received proceeds from extortion, gambling, fraud, narcotics, and murder. Tieri was specifically charged with racketeering, racketeering conspiracy, fraud conspiracy, and tax evasion. Additional evidence presented during the trial linked Tieri to an alleged murder scheme. The 76-year-old Tieri was convicted on Nov. 21, 1980, and sentenced to ten years in prison on Jan. 23, 1981. He died of natural causes on Mar. 31, 1981, at Mount Sinai Hospital in New York.

REF.: *CBA;* Demaris, *The Last Mafioso;* Zuckerman, *Vengeance Is Mine.*

Tiernan, Helen, 1911- , U.S., asslt.-mur. Helen Tiernan, a divorced mother of two, loved George Christodulas, a poor Greek immigrant, but she could not marry him—until her children were out of the way. She lived in a two-room tenement flat on West Forty-seventh Street in New York City. Described as quiet and reserved, Tiernan supported her children by working as a stitcher at an Eighth Avenue embroidery firm. The money her boyfriend earned as a steward at the Foltis-Fischer restaurant on Seventh Avenue was not enough to move the four of them into larger quarters. Deciding that the love of this man was more important to her than the lives of her children, Tiernan took her 7-year-old daughter Helen and 3-year-old son James down to the Pennsylvania Railroad Station on May 15, 1937, where she boarded a train bound for Brookhaven.

She told them they were going on a picnic in the woods. But in her suitcase she carried the murder weapons: a carving knife, hatchet, scissors, and a bottle of gasoline. In a dense thicket near busy Yaphank Road, Tiernan cut Helen's throat and then poured gasoline on her. The girl fell to the ground as her mother lit a match. She struck James with the hatchet, but he ran off before the fire could be started. When the 3-year-old was found later that afternoon by Warren Brady and May Savage of Long Island, all he could say was "Mommy! Mommy!" A hundred feet away, Helen's body was found.

The next day, Tiernan told Christodulas at Jones Beach that the final impediment to their marriage had been removed. The children had been turned over to relatives. Emma McGowan of the West Side Nursery School was notified that her services would no longer be needed, but the woman took note of Tiernan's uneasiness. Later she noticed a picture in the paper of a badly injured boy who had been found in the Long Island woods. Irene Roggeveen, a social worker who listened to Helen Tiernan's story, called Detective Frank Naughton at the West Forty-seventh Street police station. Within minutes he arrived on the scene to take the distraught mother into custody. Tiernan changed her story several times. At first she denied any prior knowledge of her children's disappearance, but then admitted that there had been an attack. A strange man attacked them in the brush, she explained. There was little else to do except run away. But Tiernan did not adequately explain why she had failed to notify the police of this.

Homicide charges were filed, and the prisoner was transported to Suffolk County Jail in Riverhead. George Christodulas was held as a material witness, but was later cleared of involvement in the child murders.

Tiernan, whose own mother died in a state sanitarium, was sentenced to twenty years to life by Justice James Hallinan of the Suffolk County Supreme Court on June 21, 1937. Before she was led away, she asked to see her son, who had been placed in the care of the New York City Child Welfare Board. The request was denied pending approval of the social welfare department.

Tiernan served fourteen years in prison before being paroled on Aug. 27, 1951. A final discharge from jurisdiction was granted in 1964. REF.: *CBA.*

Tierney, George, 1761-1830, Brit., duel. Member of Parliament and opponent of British statesman William Pitt. He and Pitt fought a duel, but neither was injured. REF.: *CBA.*

Tierney, Nora Patricia, b.1920, Brit., mur. Mrs. Basil Ward left her 3-year-old daughter to play with a neighborhood friend, Stephanie Tierney, while she went to the store. When she returned, her child was missing. Three days later the child's body was found in a nearby bombed-out house with her head crushed. The only clue to the murderer's identity was the imprint of a woman's shoe found near the body.

The playmate's mother, Nora Tierney, was uncooperative while being questioned. Tierney told Scotland Yard inspector James Jamieson she knew nothing about the child's disappearance. Jamieson took several pairs of Tierney's shoes for examination. When he asked for cuttings from her fingernails, she broke down and told Jamieson that her husband had murdered the child with a hammer.

The police soon discovered that James Tierney was elsewhere at the time of the killing. Nora Tierney was charged with the murder and was tried at the Old Bailey in October 1949. She was convicted and condemned to death, but the sentence was commuted to confinement in Broadmoor Criminal Lunatic Asylum.

Nora Patricia Tierney, murderess.

REF.: *CBA;* Cuthbert, *Science and the Detection of Crime;* Nash, *Look For the Woman;* Reynolds, *Murder 'Round the World;* Wilson, *Encyclopedia of Murder.*

Tigellinus, Ofonius, d.69 A.D., Roman., consp.-suic. Served under Nero as chief adviser from 62-68 A.D., and made prefect of praetorian guard in 62 A.D. Later, he promoted Nero's bloody purge of the empire following the plot by Piso. He was forced by Marcus Otho to kill himself.

REF.: *CBA;* (FILM), *The Sign of the Cross,* 1932; *Quo Vadis,* 1951.

Tikhon (Vasily Ivanovich Belavin), 1865-1925, Rus., impris. Bishop of Orthodox church in North America from 1898-1907, and later head of Russian Orthodox church and patriarch of Moscow, elected in 1917. Opposed to the Bolshevik revolution, he was jailed from 1922-23, a victim of communist persecution. REF.: *CBA.*

Tilak, Bal Gangadhar, 1856-1920, India, consp. Indian nationalist jailed in 1897 and from 1908-14 by British for pro-independence activities. REF.: *CBA.*

Tilden, Samuel Jones, 1814-86, U.S., lawyer. Leader in fight against corrupt Tweed Ring in New York City, and served briefly as New York governor, from 1875-76. As the Democratic presidential candidate in the controversial race of 1876, he accepted defeat by Republican challenger Rutherford B. Hayes to keep the peace, even though he received a majority of the popular vote and insisted throughout his life that he had won. REF.: *CBA.*

Tilden, William Tatum, II (Big Bill), 1893-1953, U.S., morals. Tennis has always been considered the sport of gentlemen and gentle ladies, the sport of the sophisticated and the wealthy, snooty to some in that many of its star athletes have proven to be haughty prima donnas, egomaniacs, and vainglorious creatures living only for the limelight. One such individual, considered by many as the greatest tennis champion ever, was William Tatum "Big Bill" Tilden, II. Tilden was the great powerhouse of the courts and its most superlative champion from 1920 to 1925. His cannonball serve and incredibly intuitive playing skills brought him the amateur national championship seven times (1920-25, 1930). He was the first American to win the men's championship at Wimbledon in 1920 and then took that crown again in 1921 and in 1930. Playing singles, doubles, and mixed doubles, the lanky Tilden—he stood almost six-foot-two—won thirty-one national titles. Indoors and outdoors, he was ranked as the number one player of the U.S. for ten years, 1920-29. In addition to being a paragon singles player, Tilden's performance as a doubles contestant was equally astonishing; he lost only one match in doubles in a total of twenty-two cup matches.

Tennis champ Big Bill Tilden, convicted of morals charges.

No player in the world, from 1920 to 1925, stood a chance against Tilden who, for decades, was considered to be *the* ace of Davis Cup teams. Born in Germantown, Pa., on Feb. 10, 1893, Tilden was taught the game of tennis before he turned ten, and it became his whole life. Big Bill quit the amateur ranks in 1930 when he went into motion pictures, making a series of shorts about tennis. He later turned professional in the 1930s. On Feb. 3, 1950, Tilden was named by members of the Associated Press as the greatest tennis player of the first half of the twentieth century, receiving 310 votes with Jack Kramer, placing second, getting thirty-two votes. At the time Tilden stated that he was "grateful" for the honor, but disagreed with the choices of runners-up selected, a typically disdainful view by this autocrat of the courts. Also by then, Tilden had fallen from the good graces of public opinion, in fact, he had committed the seemingly unforgivable act of molesting a child.

The titan of the tennis courts, as the world discovered in early 1947, was a homosexual, a secret he had managed to keep private or almost private for thirty years. Tilden had lured a 14-year-old boy to his Los Angeles apartment, and the boy's screams had brought neighbors and, subsequently, police to the scene. He was arrested and charged in juvenile court with contributing to the delinquency of a minor.

When the tennis star appeared in court on Jan. 16, 1947, he looked up at the judge to state: "I regret this incident very much. It has taught me a tough lesson." Then he pleaded guilty.

The judge responded with: "You have been the idol of youngsters all over the world. It has been a great shock to sports fans to read about your troubles. I am going to make this an object lesson." Then Tilden was sentenced to one year in prison, a term that was suspended moments later when the judge put him on probation for five years, the first nine months to be served in the Los Angeles County Jail. There Tilden waited on tables, scoured pots and pans in the kitchen, and was later made storekeeper which he said, sarcastically, was "a very responsible position." He was released seven and a half months later. He then busied himself for many months writing his memoirs, *My Story,* in which he recounted his spectacular career on the tennis court but made no mention of the morals charge that had ruined his reputation.

Tilden's self-centeredness was apparent throughout the book, capped with the line: "I can stand crowds only when I am working in front of them, and then I love them!" He went on to demean most of the world's tennis champions, giving grudging kudos to Frenchmen Rene Lacote and Jean Borotra. Don Budge, according to Tilden at the time, had been a graceless player who exemplified pure power only, and it was the inventive, flamboyant Bobby Riggs, later to become a comedic sexist in the 1970s in his challenges of Billie Jean King, that Tilden picked as the greatest all-around player of 1948.

The book sold poorly, due to Tilden's morals conviction, yet the Hollywood elite graciously accepted him back into their fold, thinking that he had, indeed, learned that "tough lesson" from his mistake. He made good money giving private tennis lessons to the Joseph Cottons, David Selznick and his wife Jennifer Jones, and Mrs. Charles (Oona O'Neill) Chaplin.

It appeared that Tilden had put his life in order. Then, in 1949, Tilden slipped back into disaster. He had failed to report to his probation officer and detectives going to his apartment found Tilden with a 16-year-old youth, both of them naked in bed. This was a severe violation of Tilden's 1947 probation in that it had been decreed that he must never be in the company of a minor without the presence of parents. Tilden had also violated his probation by failing to seek psychiatric help.

On Feb. 10, 1949, Tilden faced Superior Judge A.A. Scott who found him Guilty of violating his probation and contributing to the delinquency of a minor, his second such conviction. Judge Scott sent Tilden to jail to serve another year, telling the once-great champion: "I hope sincerely you'll learn your lesson this time."

A year later Tilden emerged from jail gray, stoop-shouldered, his face withered. He was shunned this time by almost all of his old friends, including the Hollywood bigwigs who once thought him rehabilitated. Tilden moved downward on the social scale until he was living in a cheap hotel room, alone and penniless. Only a few weeks before his death of a heart attack at age sixty on June 5, 1953, Tilden had pawned his last three trophies for $45 in a Hollywood hockshop.

There were some loyal in death; Ellsworth Vines and John Doeg, both former national champions, attended the funeral services, but for the most part Big Bill Tilden was ignored as he was buried as a national hero turned national disgrace. REF.: *CBA.*

Tildy, Zoltan, 1889-1961, Hung., impris. Member of parliament in 1936, premier of Hungary in 1945, and first president of Hungarian Republic from 1946 until compelled to resign by Soviets in 1948. He served for barely more than one month as minister of state in the revolutionary cabinet of Imre Nagy in 1956, then was jailed by the Soviets until 1959. REF.: *CBA.*

Tilghman, Edward J., 1934- , U.S., law enfor. off. Edward J. Tilghman began his career with the Baltimore, Md., police department on Mar. 21, 1957. In August 1975, he was appointed to the position of district commander, and in December 1981, after promotion to the rank of major, Tilghman was placed in charge of Patrol Area III. From 1983 to August 1984, Tilghman held the ranks of lieutenant colonel, colonel, and deputy commissioner of the administrative bureau and in April 1987, he was appointed police commissioner. Tilghman graduated from the FBI National Academy, and was a former president of the Maryland chapter of the National Organization of Black Law Enforcement Executives. He was also a member of many professional organizations, including the Maryland Chiefs of Police Association, the International Association of Chiefs of Police, The Governor's Commission on Black and Minority Health, and the Governor's Council on Child Abuse and Neglect. REF.: *CBA.*

Baltimore police commissioner Edward J. Tilghman.

Tilghman, John, 1828-51, U.S., mur. John Tilghman of Lenoir County, S.C., was madly in love with his uncle Joseph's young wife Susan. For nearly a year Tilghman had been seeing Susan without Joseph Tilghman's knowing. In Summer 1850, Susan became restless. She wanted to legitimize her relationship with John but at the same time was reluctant to let go of her husband's considerable fortune. Susan persuaded John to murder his uncle and then they would claim the estate and marry.

Failing in their initial attempt to poison Joseph with arsenic, Tilghman and Susan next decided to shoot him. The two men confronted each other on Aug. 5, 1850. Joseph admonished his nephew for all the "cockcrowing" going on behind his back. He made a grab for the rifle in John's hands but the weapon discharged and Joseph Tilghman was shot above the right eye. The murder trial of John Tilghman was conducted in Craven County in October 1850. Susan betrayed her lover by insisting that she never had an affair with him. She was never implicated in the shooting death of her husband, and had little to say when John was hanged on June 3, 1851. Rumors began to circulate through Lenoir County that John did not actually die on the gallows. According to one account, his father resuscitated him while conveying the body from Craven to Lenoir.

REF.: *CBA; A True Story of Real Life: Seduction, Murder, and a Violent and Premature Death.*

Tilghman, William Matthew, Jr., 1854-1924, U.S., west. lawman. A lawman who held several positions in Dodge City, Kan., Lincoln County, Oklahoma Territory, and Oklahoma City, Okla., Bill Tilghman was credited with bringing in several outlaws, including Bill Raidler, Kid Donnor, John Braya, and Bill Doolin. At the age of twenty-three, Tilghman was a deputy under Dodge City sheriff Charlie Bassett. Tilghman was appointed city marshal of Dodge City in 1884, serving two years, and he, not Wyatt Earp, established and enforced the no-guns-in-Dodge rule. In 1892, Tilghman accepted an appointment as deputy U.S. marshal and brought in several Kansas outlaws alive. In 1893, Tilghman, Chris Madsen, and Henry "Heck" Thomas brought law to the town of Perry, where the three became known as the "Three Guardsmen." Tilghman also tangled with Jennie "Little Britches" Stevens and "Cattle" Annie McDougal. The Three Guardsmen tracked the Doolin gang, capturing several members.

Tilghman earned a reputation for never killing unnecessarily. In one instance, on Sept. 6, 1895, he shot and severely wounded Doolin gang member Bill Raider, but nursed him back to health so he could travel. Tilghman also captured Bill Doolin in Eureka Springs, Ark., and locked him up in the wooden jailhouse in Guthrie, Oklahoma Territory. Doolin escaped, and was later apprehended by Henry Thomas. Tilghman served as sheriff of Lincoln County, Oklahoma Territory, in 1900, and eleven years later as chief of police of Oklahoma City, retiring three years later at the age of sixty. He was persuaded to come out of retirement in 1924 and clean up Cromwell, Okla. There, a shady and very drunk prohibition officer, Wiley Lynn, shot and killed the 70-year-old Tilghman as he led Lynn to jail. See: **Doolin, William M.; Thomas, Henry.**

Lawman Bill Tilghman.

REF.: Bartholomew, *The Biographical Album of Western Gunfighters;* ____, *Wyatt Earp, 1848 to 1880;* Benedict, *The Roundup;* Breihan, *Great Lawmen of the West;* Brent, *Great Western Heroes;* Bryant, *Great American Guns and Frontier Fighters; CBA;* Chilton, *The Book of the West;* Chrisman, *The Ladder of Rivers;* Clark, *Then Came the Railroads;* Cox, *Luke Short and His Era;* Croy, *Trigger Marshal;* Davis, *The Arkansas;* Drago, *Great American Cattle Trails;* ____, *Outlaws on Horseback;* ____, *Road Agents and Train Robbers;* ____, *Wild, Woolly & Wicked;* Elman, *Fired in Anger;* Gard, *Frontier Justice;* ____, *The Great Buffalo Hunt;* Gardner, *The Old Wild West;* Gaylord, *Handgunner's Guide;* Gradet, *Images du Far-West;* Graves, *Oklahoma Outlaws;* Hanes, *Bill Doolin;* Hendricks, *The Bad Man of the West;* Holloway, *Texas Gun Lore;* Horan, *Across the Cimarron;* ____, *Desperate Women;* ____, *The Great American West;* ____ and Sann, *Pictorial History of the Wild West;* Howard, *This Is the West;* Howe, *Timberleg of the Diamond Trail;* Hunter and Rose, *The Album of Gun-Fighters;* Hutchinson, *A Notebook of the Old West;* Johnson, *Famous Lawmen of the Old West;* Knight, *Wild Bill Hickok;* Koller, *The American Gun;* Lake, *Wyatt Earp;* Lavender, *The American Heritage History of the Great West;* McCarty, *The Enchanted West;* McKennon, *Iron Men;* McRill, *And Satan Came Also;* Masterson, *Famous Gunfighters;* Miller, *Bill Tilghman;* Miller, *Hail to Yesterday;* Miller and Snell, *Great Gunfighters of the Kansas Cowtowns;* Miller and Snell, *Why the West Was Wild;* Monaghan, *The Book of the American West;* Myers, *Doc Holliday;* ____, *The Last Chance;* Newsom, *The Life and Pratice of the Wild and Modern Indian;* Nix, *Oklahombres;* O'Connor, *Bat Masterson;* Osborn, *Let Freedom Ring;* Parkhill, *The Wildest of the West;* Penfield, *Western Sheriffs and Marshals;* Preece, *The Dalton Gang;* Raine, *Famous Sheriffs & Western Outlaws;* ____, *Forty-Five Caliber Law;* ____, *Guns of the Frontier;* Rascoe, *Belle Starr;* Rath, *Early Ford County;* Ray, *Wily Women of the West;* Rayburn, *The Eureka Springs Story;* Rickards, *Mysterious Dave Mathers;* Ridings, *The Chisholm Trail;* Rosa, *The Gunfighter, Man or Myth?;* ____, *They Call Him Wild Bill;* Sabin, *Wild Men of the Wild West;* Schoenberger, *Gunfighters;* Shirley, *Henry Starr;* ____, *Law West of Fort Smith;* ____, *Six-gun and Silver Star;* Small, *The Best of True West;* Sterling, *Famous Western Outlaw-Sheriff Battles;* Sutton, *Hands Up!;* Tilghman, *Marshal of the Last Frontier;* ____, *Outlaw Days;* Vestal, *Short Grass Country;* Watson, *A Century of Gunmen;* Wellman, *A Dynasty of Western Outlaws;* ____, *The Trampling Herd;* White, *Bat Masterson;* Wilson, *Out of the West.*

Tillman, Emil, 1918-58, Ger., kid.-mur. In Stuttgart, Ger., in April 1958, 40-year-old gardener Emil Tillman kidnapped 7-year-old Joachim Goehner. Although Goehner's motive for the kidnapping was to ransom the child for enough money to marry his girlfriend, he strangled the boy shortly after abducting him. After hiding Joachim's body in a wooded area he contacted the boy's father, demanding 15,000 marks. When Tillman complied with the father's request to call him back, the police recorded Tillman's voice on the phone.

Although the body was discovered before the ransom was paid, the elder Goehner continued to negotiate with Tillman in hopes of apprehending the murderer. When Tillman discovered the body missing, and stopped trying to contact the father, police broadcast the tape recording of the kidnapper's voice over the radio. Several days later, Marguerite Helmut called police to identify the voice as that of a man who had worked for her as a gardener. When police brought Tillman in for questioning, he denied knowledge of the crime. The similarity between his voice and the voice on the tape recording, however, was great enough that the police persisted in their interrogation, and Tillman eventually confessed to the murder. Tillman never stood trial for the crimes, however, as he committed suicide in his jail cell by hanging himself with a sheet on May 26, 1958.

REF.: *CBA;* Heppenstall, *The Sex War and Others;* Wilson, *Encyclopedia of Murder.*

Tilton, Theodore, 1835-1907, U.S., adult. Unsuccessfully sued pastor Henry Ward Beecher for committing adultery with his wife, Elizabeth Tilton, in 1875 in celebrated case. He eventually moved to France. Previously, he had been employed as an editor on the Congregational journal, the *Independent,* from 1856-71. REF.: *CBA.*

Timagenes, prom. 1st Cent. B.C., Rome, kid. (vict.) Raised in Alexandria, kidnapped and enslaved in Rome. He started a Roman school of rhetoric after he was freed, and befriended EmperorAugustus. REF.: *CBA.*

Timarchus, d.c.160 B.C., Babylonia, king, assass. Named satrap by Antiochus IV, shortly thereafter declaring himself king. He was removed and put to death by Demetrius I of Syria. REF.: *CBA.*

Time After Time, 1979, a British film directed by Nicholas Meyer. This picture employs H.G. Wells, played by Malcolm MacDowell, and his time machine which goes forward from gas-lit London to modern San Francisco. But the machine also allows Jack the Ripper (Brit., 1888), played by David Warner, to similarly escape his time and the police pursuing him to wreak havoc and murder in the City by the Bay. See: **Jack the Ripper**. REF.: *CBA.*

Timmons, Ronald, 1958- , U.S. rob.-burg.-asslt. On Oct. 26, 1976, 19-year-old Ronald Timmons and 22-year-old Zachary Shannon beat and robbed 82-year-old Adelaide Fleming in her Bronx, N.Y., apartment. The police, responding to calls from Fleming's neighbors, arrived and arrested the two men following a struggle. Timmons, free on bail, fled to Baltimore where he was apprehended by FBI agents who discovered that he had an extensive juvenile record consisting of sixty-seven different court appearances, many for attacks on elderly people.

Timmons pleaded guilty to a seven-count indictment charging him with robbery, burglary, assault, and possession of a weapon. On May, 2, 1977, he was sentenced to the maximum term of eight-and-a-half to twenty-five years in prison. REF.: *CBA.*

Timoleon, d.c.336 B.C., Gr., exile. Reluctantly agreed to execution of brother Timophanes in c.364 B.C. He was exiled by his family after Timophanes' death. REF.: *CBA.*

Timotheus, d.354 B.C., Gr., milit. misconduct. Athenian general sued by Chares for failing to attack enemy ships because of adverse weather, while both men and Iphicrates co-commanded fleet of ships in Social War from 357-55 B.C. He was found Guilty and was heavily fined, but was unable to pay and left Athens. REF.: *CBA.*

Tinker, Edward, d.1811, U.S., fraud-mur. The captain of a schooner, Edward Tinker was the first U.S. captain to attempt insurance fraud by sinking his ship. Tinker sold off his ship's cargo and scuttled the schooner off Roanoke Island, N.C. Three of the ship's crew, Durand, Potts, and Edwards, conspired with Tinker. Durand and Potts supported the fraud, while Edwards grew wary. The captain, fearing Edwards' betrayal, took him to the country on the pretense of duck hunting and murdered him, tied rocks to his body, and threw him into the sea. Edwards' body washed ashore, however, and Tinker was arrested, since he was the last person seen with Edwards. The captain wrote a letter to Durand to persuade him to implicate Potts in Edwards' murder, but Durand gave the letter to the authorities. Tinker was found Guilty and hanged at Cateret, N.C., in September 1811.

REF.: *CBA; Trial of Edward Tinker, Mariner, for the Willful Murder of a Youth, Called Edward, at Carteret Superior Court, September Term, 1811.*

Tinné, Alexandrine-Pieternella-Françoise, 1839-69, Neth., mur. (vict.) Explored Nile to Gondorko, from 1861-62, and Upper Nile up to northeastern section of Congo. He was killed by Tuareg tribesmen at the start of a new journey. REF.: *CBA.*

Tinning, Marybeth Roe, 1943- , U.S., mur. Marybeth Tinning and her husband Joseph had lived their entire married life in Schenectady County, N.Y., moving from one two-flat apartment to another. Joseph Tinning worked as a foreman at the General Electric plant in Schenectady. The Tinnings were a nice couple who freely gave of themselves and their time, according to neighbors. But there was something odd behind this facade. In a period of just less than fourteen years, nine of the Tinnings' children died. All died before the age of five.

The daughter of Ruth and Alton L. Roe, Sr., Marybeth Tinning grew up in Duanesburg, a community fourteen miles outside Schenectady. Tinning was the elder of two children and throughout her childhood and adolescence she claimed to have suffered from isolation and her parents' neglect and mistreatment. At twenty-three, she married Mr. Tinning, who, unlike his high-strung and outgoing wife, was overly timid. Together, the Tinnings had eight children of their own and had almost adopted a ninth.

The first of the Tinning children to die was Jennifer Lewis, their third child. Born on the day after Christmas 1971, Jennifer died just eight days later, on Jan. 3, 1972, from respiratory failure and a brain abscess. Her death was the only one attributal to natural causes. On Jan. 20, 2-year-old Joseph "Joey" Tinning, Jr. died. Only days before, Tinning had taken him to Ellis Hospital where she told the pediatrician that her son had choked on his own vomit. The doctors could find nothing wrong with the boy and discharged him to his mother's care a few days later. A few hours later Tinning brought him back to the emergency room dead. She explained that she had put him in the crib for a nap and had found him a little while later lying dead, twisted up in the sheets. She claimed Joey had had convulsive fits.

Four-year-old Barbara Ann, the Tinnings' first child and the child who lived the longest of any of the Tinning children, became the third fatality. A hospital autopsy concluded that Barbara had died of Reye's syndrome, partly basing this conclusion on information provided by Tinning. Although no autopsy had been performed on Joey, it was reasoned that he, too, had died of the disease.

The next child born to the Tinnings was also the next to die. Timothy, born on Nov. 21, 1973, died on Dec. 10 of that year. His death and those of the next two children—5-month-old Nathan on Sept. 2, 1975, and 3-month-old Mary Frances on Feb. 22, 1979—were attributed to Sudden Infant Death Syndrome (SIDS). This malady would later be erroneously ascribed to the Tinning's last three children. As the years passed, Tinnings' memories of her two sons Timothy and Nathan became blurred.

There were suspicions about Marybeth Tinning, primarily among the nurses at Ellis Hospital who by 1979, when Mary Frances was born, were more attuned to the signs of child abuse than they had been seven years earlier when the first suspicious death occurred. Although people noted that Tinning failed to display normal emotions in the face of these appalling events, no one called for an investigation into the children's deaths. The circumstances surrounding the death of Jonathan D. Tinning, on Mar. 24, 1980 were markedly similar to those surrounding Mary

Frances' death. The boy was taken to St. Clare's suffering from a lack of oxygen. A genetic consultant had the boy moved to Boston Children's Hospital where he ordered a battery of tests. The test results revealed that Jonathan's birth defects were unrelated to the present difficulty. Before Jonathan was discharged, a Boston physician described him "as wiggly and active a child as you can imagine." He was returned to Tinning with an apnea monitor. Three days later the baby was back in the emergency room having suffered permanent brain damage, a sequence of events almost identical to Mary Frances' last few days.

With six children already dead, the Tinnings applied to the state adoption service. They were in the process of adopting 31-month-old Michael, when, on Mar. 2, 1981, while adoption officials reviewed the Tinnings' petition, the boy died of viral pneumonia. Dr. Robert Sullivan, Schenectady's medical examiner, concurred that the cause of Michael's death, "showed acute Pneumonia," but added, "the family history is bizarre."

On Dec. 20, 1985, another Tinning child, Tami Lynne, died. This last death went beyond the point of coincidence, even for those who still found it difficult to point an accusatory finger at a woman who had suffered so much. An investigation was begun in earnest. No longer were the children's deaths viewed one at a time by investigators. Dr. Thomas F.D. Oram took into account the deaths of all nine children, along with the information supplied by Tinning and medical personnel, and concluded that only Jennifer had died of natural causes. Oram also concluded that the remaining children could very likely have died from suffocation. When Oram called a colleague, who was an expert on SIDS, he was told, "There's only one explanation for all this, and it has to be smothering."

It was not until February 1987, however, that Tinning admitted killing Tami Lynne. In her thirty-six page confession to police she also admitted murdering Nathan and Timothy, but denied having killed any of the others. With regard to Tami Lynne, Tinning told police, "I did not mean to hurt her. I just wanted her to stop crying." Of the three she admitted killing, Tinning said, "I smothered them each with a pillow because I'm not a good mother. I'm not a good mother because of what happened to the other children."

At Tinning's trial, which began in June 1987 in the Schenectady County Court before Judge Clifford T. Harrigan, her attorney Paul M. Callahan claimed that the police had coerced a confession out of Tinning, and argued that his client's civil rights had been violated through "trickery and deception." Forensic pathologist Dr. Jack Davies testified that in his view Tami Lynne had died as a result of a rare genetic disorder known as Werdnig-Hoffmann syndrome, akin to amyotrophic lateral sclerosis, or Lou Gehrig's disease. Although mention was made of Tinning's confession to killing Nathan and Timothy, the jury was not allowed to know of the five other suspect deaths. Mr. Tinning was not charged, as it was apparent he knew nothing of his wife's actions. On July 17, 1987, the six-week trial ended with a verdict of Guilty returned against Tinning for committing second-degree murder with a "depraved indifference to human life." Judge Harrigan sentenced her on Oct. 1, 1987, to a term of twenty years to life in prison.

REF.: *CBA;* Egginton, *From Cradle to Grave.*

Tinsley, James, prom. 1915, Brit., mansl. Near the Scottish-English border on the morning of May 16, 1915, a multiple-train accident claimed the lives of 240 people. The crash, involving a troop train carrying more than 500 Scottish soldiers and two passenger trains was caused by human negligence. The crash occurred shortly after James Tinsley had relieved another railroad employee named Meakin as the duty signal man. Tinsley was scheduled to begin his shift at 6 a.m., but in order to hitch a ride on an incoming train, and thereby avoid a long walk between his home and the switching station, he delayed his arrival until 6:30 a.m. Meakin cooperated with his fellow worker by listing movements after 6 a.m. on a separate piece of paper so that Tinsley could record them in his own writing in the official log when he arrived.

About a half mile from the station where the men worked were loops where slower moving trains could be shunted while express trains were allowed to pass through. When a northbound local arrived on the morning of May 22, both the northbound and the southbound loops were already filled. Meakin instructed the local to move onto the main southbound tracks, another procedure that was fairly common. The appropriate signals, indicating to southbound traffic that there was a train already on their tracks, was to be set by the local's fireman. The fireman failed to comply with this procedure, thinking it redundant on this occasion because everyone concerned was already notified—Meakin had just called with the instruction, and Tinsley was aboard the local with him.

When Tinsley arrived at the station, a series of matters claimed his attention. For the most part, he was concerned with completing his log so his superiors would not become aware of his habit of arriving after the start of his shift. Tinsley forgot that a train was sitting on the southbound track, and when permission was requested for a troop train to pass through, he gave clearance. The troop train, traveling at approximately seventy miles per hour, slammed into the rear of the waiting local. Following a tremem-dous explosion, Tinsley and Meakin realized what had happened. Tinsley also realized that a northbound express was due at any moment and the northbound tracks were still shunted into the southbound side. Before he could switch them back, the express plowed into the other end of the already devastated local train. Soldiers injured and trapped on the troop train in the first crash were burned to death when munitions and flammable supplies caught fire.

Both Meakin and Tinsley were arrested a week after the accident. The only excuse Tinsley could offer to officials was that he had simply forgotten that he had a train on the southbound tracks. Both were charged and brought to trial. Tinsley was sentenced to three years in prison and Meakin to eighteen months.

REF.: Canning, *Fifty True Tales of Terror; CBA.*

Tinsley, Mona Lilian, See: **Nodder, Frederick**.

Tiplitz, William, prom. 1949, gamb.-consp.-org. crime. Early in 1949, in the course of a routine investigation of gambler Tony Bender, one of the major underworld figures of the East, the FBI discovered what appeared to be a mob-run lottery in some way based on the numbers racket. A court-ordered wire tap yielded a series of short, cryptic conversations placed at almost exactly the same time each day, in which callers always mentioned three digits. After reading hundreds of daily newspapers, agents learned that the first two digits were taken from the daily noon bond sales, and the third digit came from figures released daily by a stock clearinghouse in Cincinnati. The FBI discovered that the mob obtained the first two digits from newspaper employees who called them in before they were printed in the paper and from William Tiplitz. Tiplitz called the figures into a mob-operated policy bank just after noon each day from the customers' room of a Newark brokerage house. Knowing what the first two digits of the winning number would be for that day, the clerks tallied the day's bets to determine which third digit would have the lowest play—and therefore require the lowest payout—for the day.

When the preferred third digit had been determined, Tiplitz called again to get it. Then, at 12:45 p.m. each day, Tiplitz passed his information along to a man named Kane. Kane telephoned the Cincinnati brokerage house and spoke to a man named Bill who was able to alter the figures for what had cleared through the banks on a given day. If the correct daily figure was $38,000,000, and the mob wanted the number "6" to appear, Bill would change the figure to $36,000,000.

On July 26, 1949, the FBI and the police staged simultaneous arrests in New Jersey, New York, and Cincinnati. Nine people were arrested and indicted on charges of conspiracy to rig a lottery. In January 1950, eight of the nine, including William Tiplitz, were fined and sent to jail for sentences ranging from six months to two years.

REF.: *CBA;* Danforth, *The D.A.'s Man.*

Tiptoft, John (Earl of Worcester), c.1427-70, Brit., mur. Named earl in 1449 and served as lord high constable from 1462-67 and in 1470. In this post he executed Lancastarians, the Earl of Oxford, and others, quickly developing a loathsome reputation. He also served briefly as Edward IV's de facto prime minister in 1470, but was seized and put to death after the king temporarily lost power. REF.: *CBA*.

Tipu Sahib (Fateh Ali Tipu), c.1749-99, India, tort.-mur. Claiming he received his directions from the prophet of Islam, Tipu Sahib, the Sultan of Mysore, India, mistreated, tortured, and killed thousands of Hindus and Europeans during his reign from 1782 to 1799. He captured European children, and occasionally with the help of two Abyssinian slaves, subjected them to sadistic tortures, rapes, and slayings. He imprisoned many and made them submit to acts of sexual abuse and torture. In one instance, he forcibly circumcised thousands of Hindu men and compelled them to eat beef—forbidden by their religion. Another time, Tipu Sahib had twenty English drummer boys castrated and trained as singers and dancers. The Sultan himself often participated in sexual orgies with men, women, and animals. His reign ended in 1799 when he was killed in action during the Fourth Mysore War. REF.: *CBA*.

Tirel, Walter, See: **William II.**

Tiridates II (AKA: Khosrow the Great), d.c.238, Armenia, king, assass. Held throne from 217-c.238 after Romans unsuccessfully attempted to overrun Armenia. He withstood pressures from the Sasanian Persians, but was eventually murdered by a Persian agent. REF.: *CBA*.

Tirrell, Albert John, prom. 1840s, Case of, U.S., mur. The murdering of prostitutes in Boston was a rare occurrence, but Albert John Tirrell proved that one could not only slay one's sex partner with alacrity but, with unusual legal arguments, live to enjoy his notoriety. Tirrell's exploits were both sensational and macabre, and the acts of this strangest of throat-slitters certainly rivals the diabolical wanderings of London's Jack the Ripper.

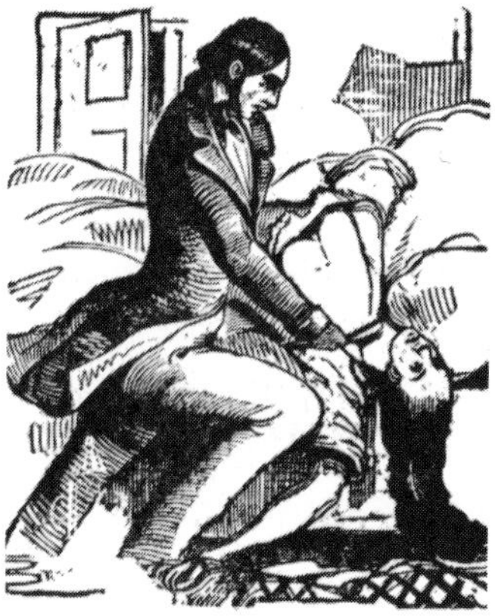

Albert Tirrell murdering Maria Bickford.

In early 1845, Tirrell met the beautiful harlot Maria Ann Bickford, a statuesque, bosomy creature who, no doubt, could not be called a common whore by today's standards but be classified a party girl or call girl. She lived stylishly and wore the finest clothes. She had a maid and selected only a few lovers, men of wealth, to keep her in fashion. Tirrell was not of this caste but a middle class man with a wife. Tirrell fell in love with Bickford and soon grew jealous of the time she spent with those who kept her.

On the night of Oct. 27, 1845, Tirrell found himself in Bickford's bedroom. A male visitor had just departed and the impassioned Tirrell, clutching a razor, was enraged at the sight of his sultry beloved sprawled before him in dishabille, her parted nightgown exposing her considerable charms.

Tirrell leaned forward wordlessly and pinned Bickford to the bed with one arm and then brought forth his razor-wielding hand in a quick slash across her lovely throat. The murderer withdrew, leaving his paramour draped across her love bed, her head dangling over the side, held to the trunk only by a few strands of flesh, blood welling up in a dark pool beneath. The maid and some others saw the killer leave the premises after he set several fires in the building. Tirrell was identified. He fled the city, first losing himself in Manhattan and then journeying to New Orleans. Authorities arrested him on Dec. 6 just as he was entering his stateroom on the paddle wheeler *Sultana* as it pulled away from the New Orleans dockside. He was returned to Boston and held for trial.

Fortunately for the killer, he managed to acquire the services of the colorful and unorthodox lawyer Rufus Choate. In March 1846, Choate the spellbinder, somehow managed to convince an enraptured jury that his client was not guilty of cutting the throat of Bickford. Yes, *someone* by the name of Albert John Tirrell may have slashed her to death, he pointed out, but not the man seen conscious before them in court. No, that man and the killer were not one in the same. Indeed, it was a perplexing argument.

Choate went on to explain that his client was a victim of somnambulism; his habit of sleepwalking caused him to travel the many blocks between his own home and that of Bickford on that murderous night. Moreover, the hardworking Tirrell, a normally loyal spouse when awake, suffered from a dreaded malady, a diabolical disease of the mind that clawed its way to the surface only when Tirrell was in his helpless slumber. Choate termed this mental affliction an "insanity of sleep." In that ignorant era before Freud, the awestruck jury members seemed to instantly embrace a new found wisdom of the inexplicable darkness in the human mind. They found Tirrell Not Guilty. The murderer, grinning, left the court room a free man.

For some odd reason, Tirrell traveled to New York and contacted that writer of the demoniacal, Edgar Allan Poe. He had avidly read Poe's works, paying particular attention to his story, "The Mystery of Marie Roget," a tale Poe constructed from the celebrated murder of Mary Cecilia Rogers, the "beautiful cigar girl" who was found murdered in New York in 1842, her killer never apprehended. Tirrell begged and then demanded that Poe publish a newspaper devoted to his (Tirrell's) exploits. The author of the sinister took one shivering look at the gaunt-faced Tirrell and ordered him from his quarters, sending him to a pamphleteer named Estabrook who delighted in publishing a scandalous broadside entitled "The Life and Death of Mrs. Maria Bickford, A Beautiful Female, Who was Inhumanly Murdered in the Moral and Religious City of Boston, etc."

In January 1847, Tirrell was again arrested and charged with arson, based on his attempt to burn down Bickford's house after murdering her. That charge was also eliminated by the deft Rufus Choate who once more elaborated upon Tirrell's singularly strange disease of "insanity of sleep" and quickly won the murder's acquittal. Albert John Tirrell lived to read the works of Poe long into his own senility, feeling casually slighted that his favorite writer lacked the fecund perception to include him in his literary chamber of horrors. See: **Robinson, Richard; Rogers, Mary Cecilia.**

REF.: *The Authentic Life of Mrs. Mary Ann Bickford; CBA; Eccentricities and Anecdotes of Albert John Tirrell, the Reputed Murderer of the Beautiful Maria Bickford; The Life and Death of Mrs. Maria Bickford,* A Beautiful Female, Who was Inhumanly Murdered in the Moral and Religious City of Boston; Pearson, *Instigation of the Devil;* Rodell, *Boston Murders; Tirrell's Trial!; The Trial of Albert J. Tirrell;* Weeks, *Trial of Albert John Tirrell.*

Tirrell, Betsy Frances, See: **Hersey, George Canning.**

Tissaphernes (Chithrafarna), d.395 B.C., Asia Minor, satrap, assass. Ruled Lydia and Caria but was displaced by Darius. He favored Artaxerxers II over Cyrus the Younger, and was later named chief ruler in western Asia by Artaxerxes. In Syria, he lost to King Agesilaus in 395 B.C., and was put to death on Agesilaus' command. REF.: *CBA*.

Tisza, István, 1861-1918, Hung., prime minister, assass. Opposed changes regarding relationship with Austria as prime minister from 1903-05 and from 1913-17. He was later blamed for supporting ties with Germany in WWI that proved detrimental to the country. He was assassinated shortly after leaving office. He was the son of Kálmán Tisza. REF.: *CBA*.

Titan, The, 1914, a novel by Theodore Dreiser. Charles Yerkes, Chicago tycoon and stock swindler, served as the inspiration for this work. See: **Yerkes, Charles Tyson, Jr.** REF.: *CBA*.

Titley, George Eric, c.1950, Brit., embez. George Eric Titley, a chartered accountant, took advantage of client transactions to make himself a little extra money. In one instance, he embezzled approximately £30,000 when a road haulage company which he represented was nationalized. On another occasion, Titley embezzled £2,900 when he sold a leather company for the widow of the late owner. Scotland Yard's Fraud Squad, a special unit credited with solving numerous cases of fraud, discovered his crimes despite Titley's skilled efforts at covering them up. Titley was captured in Queensland and extradited to England to stand trial. He was sentenced to seven years' imprisonment.

REF.: *CBA;* Scott, *Scotland Yard.*

Titley, Thomas, prom. 1880, Brit., abor. In 1880, pharmacist Thomas Titley was reported to local police for dispensing abortifacients to his female customers. One of Titley's former assistants substantiated the reports of wrongdoing but was unable to offer any hard evidence, and the case was turned over to the Director of Criminal Investigations, Howard Vincent.

Vincent hired a woman to approach Titley requesting drugs to end her daughter's pregnancy. The attempt failed when the pharmacist required a meeting with the pregnant girl before dispensing the medication. Vincent eventually employed an undercover police officer to pose as the child's father and Titley handed over the drugs. The officer noted that although he made it clear that he had plenty of money, the pharmacist took no more in payment than the value of the drugs.

Titley was arrested after an analysis of the drugs confirmed that they were abortifacients. On his arrest, Titley told police that he had only been trying to help people in distress. Titley's attorneys presented a strong defense at his trial, emphasizing that the impersonation that made the charges against Titley possible had been conceived of and authorized by high-ranking police officials. Titley was found Guilty and sentenced to eighteen months at hard labor. The judge, however, delivered a stiff reprimand to the police officers involved for their deceptive methods.

REF.: *CBA;* Cobb, *Critical Years at the Yard.*

Titus, Stephen, See: **Starchfield, Willie.**

Tjoflat, Gerald Bard, 1929- , U.S., jur. Appointed to middle district court of Florida by President Richard Nixon in 1970, and to the fifth circuit court (known as the eleventh circuit court since 1981) by President Gerald Ford in 1975. He served as circuit judge of the fourth judicial circuit court of Florida from 1968-70. REF.: *CBA.*

Toal, Gerard, 1909-28, Ire., mur. Eighteen-year-old Gerard Toal worked as a chauffeur for Father James McKeown. It was a commonly known fact that Toal disliked Mary Callan, McKeown's housekeeper. Questioned about Callan's disappearance on May 16, 1927, Toal denied any knowledge of the woman's whereabouts. No progress was made in the case until months later when a new housekeeper discovered dismantled parts of a woman's bicycle in Toal's room. When confronted, he insisted that he had stolen them. Police continued to be suspicious that the parts belonged to Callan's bicycle which had disappeared on the same day she had.

In April 1928, Toal was dismissed by McKeown. Toal claimed to be headed for Canada but was arrested ten days later for theft in the town of Dundalk. A closer investigation of the priest's home yielded more bicycle parts and women's clothing. When Callan's decomposed body was found in a water-filled quarry nearby, Toal was arrested and charged with murder.

Toal was tried in Dublin in July 1928. The judged advised against a verdict of manslaughter and Toal was found Guilty of murder and hanged on Aug. 29, 1928.

REF.: *CBA;* Deale, *Beyond Any Reasonable Doubt.*

Toba II (AKA: **Go-Toba**), 1180-1239, Japan, consp. Made emperor by Minamotos and held throne from 1183-98. He abdicated in order to be succeeded by his son, but maintained power by creating a covert government he later used to provoke an uprising against Hojo Yoshitoki to restore full command to the imperial house. The plan failed within a month, and he was banished from the country. REF.: *CBA.*

Tobin, Sir Alfred Aspinall, 1855-1939, Brit., jur. Began legal career practicing on Northern Circuit. He was made king's counsel in 1903, in which post he defended celebrated killer Dr. Hawley Harvey Crippen. He was elected to represent Preston in the House of Commons in 1910, but resigned his seat in 1915 to accept an appointment as country court judge presiding over Herefordshire and Shropshire cases. Nine years later, he was transferred to the court of Westminister County, where he remained until retiring in 1935. See: **Crippen, Dr. Hawley Harvey.** REF.: *CBA.*

Tobin, Wayne, c.1934- , Case of, U.S., med. mal. On Christmas Eve 1977, 12-year-old Becky Vadala awoke complaining of headaches and nausea. When the symptoms persisted, her mother Betty Vadala, rushed her to the emergency room of Baptist Hospital in Miami, Fla., where she was treated for a migraine headache and released. At Vadala's request, the hospital referred Vadala to a local neurologist, Dr. Wayne Tobin. On Dec. 28, one of Tobin's associates, Dr. Michael Aptman, examined the girl and prescribed medication for a migraine headache, instructing Vadala to bring Becky back if the headaches did not subside. The medication worked. However, on the afternoon of June 25, 1978, the headaches returned. Two days later, Becky was in extreme pain. Vadala claimed that she called Tobin's office at 9 a.m. and waited all day for a return phone call from one of the doctors. After dinner, Becky suffered a severe seizure and the Vadalas rushed her to Baptist Hospital.

Tobin, who had never examined Becky before, arrived at the hospital after the girl had been admitted. While he was examining her, she had a second seizure, a decerebrate fit, indicating that her life was endangered. Fearing meningitis, Tobin performed an emergency spinal tap. While Tobin was out of the room, Becky went into cardiac and pulmonary arrest and died shortly afterwards.

When the explanations given by Tobin and another of his associates for her daughter's death failed to satisfy her, Vadala enrolled in a practical nursing program. She graduated in November 1979, and one month later she was hired by Baptist Hospital. While reading a textbook on surgical nursing, Vadala came across what she considered to be proof that Tobin had made a serious mistake that had cost her daughter's life. Armed with this information, Vadala filed a medical malpractice suit against Tobin and Aptman eight days before the statute of limitations on such a case was to run out.

Tobin resolutely maintained his innocence in the case, remarking that Vadala had been neglectful in not bringing the child to the hospital earlier. He added that there was no record of Vadala's alleged phone call to his office. Tobin and his insurance company settled out of court with the Vadalas for $350,000. Tobin claimed that he was forced to do so by his insurance company, which felt they could pay up to $2 million if the case went to trial and was resolved in Vadala's favor. After receiving the settlement, Vadala vowed to continue to publicize the case "to damage Tobin's reputation." In fact, she contacted reporters and even accepted $10,000 from *Good Housekeeping* magazine to publish her story. REF.: *CBA.*

Tocco, Albert Caesar, 1929- , U.S., org. crime. Reputed Chicago mob kingpin Albert Tocco has been described by government informants as a vicious murderer who violates rules of Mafia procedure. "Usually you don't hurt the (informants') families," explained Charles "Guy" Bills, a former street collector for Tocco in Chicago's south suburbs. "But he would throw it (a family) out a window if it was up to him—the wife, the family, (and) their cats and dogs. Whatever it took. He was very vicious." Tocco's estranged wife Betty called him a sociopath.

Government officials considered Tocco to be the reigning mob boss for the territory south of 95th Street. Prior to his racketeering conviction in November 1989, he collected "street taxes" from the proprietors of stolen car "chop-shops," houses of ill-repute, and gambling operations in the southern corridor of Cook County. His base of operations was Chicago Heights. From there he commanded an army of extortionists and street assassins who imposed his will and maintained "discipline." Those who betray mob secrets to the government face certain, violent death. Among the gangland hits attributed to Tocco were those of William and Charlotte Dauber, who were slain a few miles outside the Will County Courthouse in July 1980. "Mr. Tocco told me to stay away from him (Dauber), that he was no good," Bills explained. After the couple were ambushed by Mafia gunmen on a rural road in Will County, Tocco came back to Bills to express his dismay with their sell-out: "Can you believe he (Dauber) was informing for the government?" The government has never confirmed nor denied such allegations, but Tocco considered Dauber a traitor to the organization.

The Greek-American mob boss has also been linked to the 1975 murder of Milwaukee, Wis., gangster August Maniaci and the 1978 shooting of Dino Valente, who owned a vending machine company. Valente was punished for his attempt to "muscle in" on Tocco's territory. Albert Tocco was a fugitive at the time he was arrested in Greece in August 1988. He was returned to Chicago in January 1989 and charged with extortion, conspiracy to commit racketeering, and other federal offenses. See: **Dauber, William E.** REF.: *CBA*.

Tocqueville, Alexis-Charles-Henri Clérel de, 1805-59, Fr., writer. Studied prisons in U.S. for nine months with Gustave de Beaumont in 1831-32, and coauthored with him *Du système pénitentiaire aux États-Unis et de son application en France,* in 1833. He also served in the Legislative Assembly in 1849, and held the office of minister of foreign affairs the same year. He was jailed briefly for resisting the coup directed by Louis-Napoléon in 1851. He is most well-known to Americans for his two-volume *La Démocratie en Amérique*. REF.: *CBA*.

Todd, Thelma (AKA: **The Ice Cream Blonde, Blonde Venus**), 1906-35, U.S., (unsolv.) mur.? Beautiful Thelma Todd was a gifted comedienne who lived on the wild side, corrupted, as so many stars were, by celebrity fame. Todd, the "Ice Cream Blonde" and "Blonde Venus," died in her garage above the Will Rogers Beach on Dec. 15, 1935. Publicists at the Hal Roach studio expressed their regrets over the unfortunate death of their brightest star. It was their belief that Todd fell asleep or passed out at the steering wheel of her car and was asphyxiated by carbon monoxide fumes. Others were not so sure. The whole thing hinted at a coverup engineered by Hollywood insiders to protect the interests of the studio. A nasty murder investigation would sully the reputation of key industry figures in the public limelight. No one, least of all Hal Roach or Joe Schenck, founder of 20th Century Fox, wanted that to happen.

Todd was born in Lawrence, Mass., the daughter of a local politician named John Shaw Todd. While still in her teens she won the crown of Miss Massachusetts. The blonde-tressed glamour girl never aspired to a career in show business. The ambitions of others, coupled with incredible happenstance, made her a star of the silver screen almost overnight. A theater manager in Lawrence who was on friendly terms with her father sent Todd's photograph to Jesse Lasky of Paramount Studios in Hollywood, urging the mogul to give the girl a chance. Todd, who was teaching sixth grade at the time, had no prior knowledge of this. Lasky was impressed with her natural beauty and offered her the opportunity to learn acting at the Paramount school in Astoria, Queens. There she was taught the finer points of etiquette, makeup, dancing, and other necessary skills needed for a successful screen career. After six months she was one of sixteen candidates awarded a one-year contract by Paramount. They appeared together as a group in *Fascinating Youth,* a box-office hit in 1926.

Todd displayed a natural talent for light comedy. Within a year she had taken Hollywood by storm. The studio loaned her to Hal Roach where she starred in seventeen two-reelers with her best friend ZaSu Pitts. By the early 1930s she had appeared alongside Buster Keaton in *Speak Easily,* and Stan Laurel and Oliver Hardy in *The Bohemian Girl*. Todd had a beautiful speaking voice and easily made the transition to talkies in 1927. However, she wanted desperately to perform in serious drama and went so far as to change her name to "Alison Lloyd" "so that no taint of comedy would cling to her skirts." In 1930, director Roland West starred her opposite Chester Morris in *Corsair,* a gangster drama that became an immediate sensation. She appeared in several other dramas but went back to being Thelma Todd after Roach threatened to change her name to "Susie Dinkleberry. So that no taint of drama would cling to her skirts," he said half-seriously.

In July 1932, Todd eloped with Pasquale "Pat" DeCicco, a talent agent. The marriage ended disastrously in March 1934 after Todd charged her husband with physical and mental cruelty. During this time Todd acquired a taste for liquor, fast cars, and handsome leading men. She had affairs with actor Ronald Colman, band leader Abe Lyman, and the mercurial director Roland West who achieved critical acclaim with *The Bat Whispers,* and *Corsair,* before his career stagnated. On Jan. 23, 1933, Todd slammed her car into a palm tree on Hollywood Boulevard, suffering severe internal injuries. Upon her recovery Roach hired a private chauffeur, Ernest Peters, to drive her to her numerous parties and social engagements.

Peters was behind the wheel the night of Dec. 14, 1935, when Todd was the guest of honor at the opulent Trocadero nightclub on Sunset Strip. The party was thrown by Stanley Lupino whose daughter Ida was on the brink of stardom. DiCicco demanded inclusion on the guest list, only to show up with two glamorous starlets hanging on each arm. Ida Lupino later recalled the anger in Todd's voice as she upbraided her husband for his callous and manipulative conduct. The evening ended on that sour note, as Todd left the party. Turning to her many admirers at the nightclub, she waved before leaving.

Todd told Peters to drive her back to her "Sidewalk Café" on Posetano Road, below where she lived with her current lover and business partner West. She urged the chauffeur to drive fast, for she believed that there were gangsters following close behind. Arriving at the cafe, Todd told Peters to go home. "Don't you want me to walk you up to your apartment?" he asked. "That won't be necessary," she replied. "Go home Ernest." It was the last time anyone saw Thelma Todd alive.

At 10:30 a.m. on Dec. 16, Todd's private maid, May Whitehead, arrived at the Roadside Rest with a load of packages. As was her usual custom, she opened the garage door to pull the 1933 Lincoln phaeton sedan into the driveway in order to leave her own car in its place. Approaching the Lincoln from the passenger side the maid noticed her employer slumped over the wheel, dressed in the same outfit she had worn to the Trocadero two nights before. Roused from his bed, West stumbled down to the garage after being informed of the tragedy by Whitehead. The police found traces of blood on the seat and running board, yet there was no evidence of an open wound on the body, just a facial laceration that was believed to have been caused when the actress fell forward into the steering wheel. The police theorized that Todd, discovering that she was locked out of the apartment, decided to sleep in her car. Since it was a cold, windswept night she started the motor to keep warm. Her death by asphyxiation was called a terrible accident. It was a tidy explanation that nervous studio officials accepted at face value despite evidence from an autopsy that showed a bruise inside her throat, the kind that a bottle might make if forced into her mouth.

A coroner's jury returned a verdict of death by carbon monoxide poisoning. The case was closed by police but nagging questions remained. Why were her silk slippers not scuffed? If indeed Todd had trudged up 271 stairs from the restaurant to the garage as the police thought, the slippers would have bore definite marks of wear. To further confuse matters, Todd was reportedly seen alive some time after the estimated time of death. Mrs. Wallace Ford insisted that she had received a phone call from Todd on Sunday afternoon in which the actress confirmed her acceptance of an invitation to a cocktail party that night. "And when you see

Actress Thelma Todd, and in a cheesecake pose.

Thelma Tood's Roadhouse on the Pacific Highway.

Thelma Todd, as a brunette in the film *Kismet*.

Dining with friends; Thelma Todd liked to party and was found dead after having been out all night.

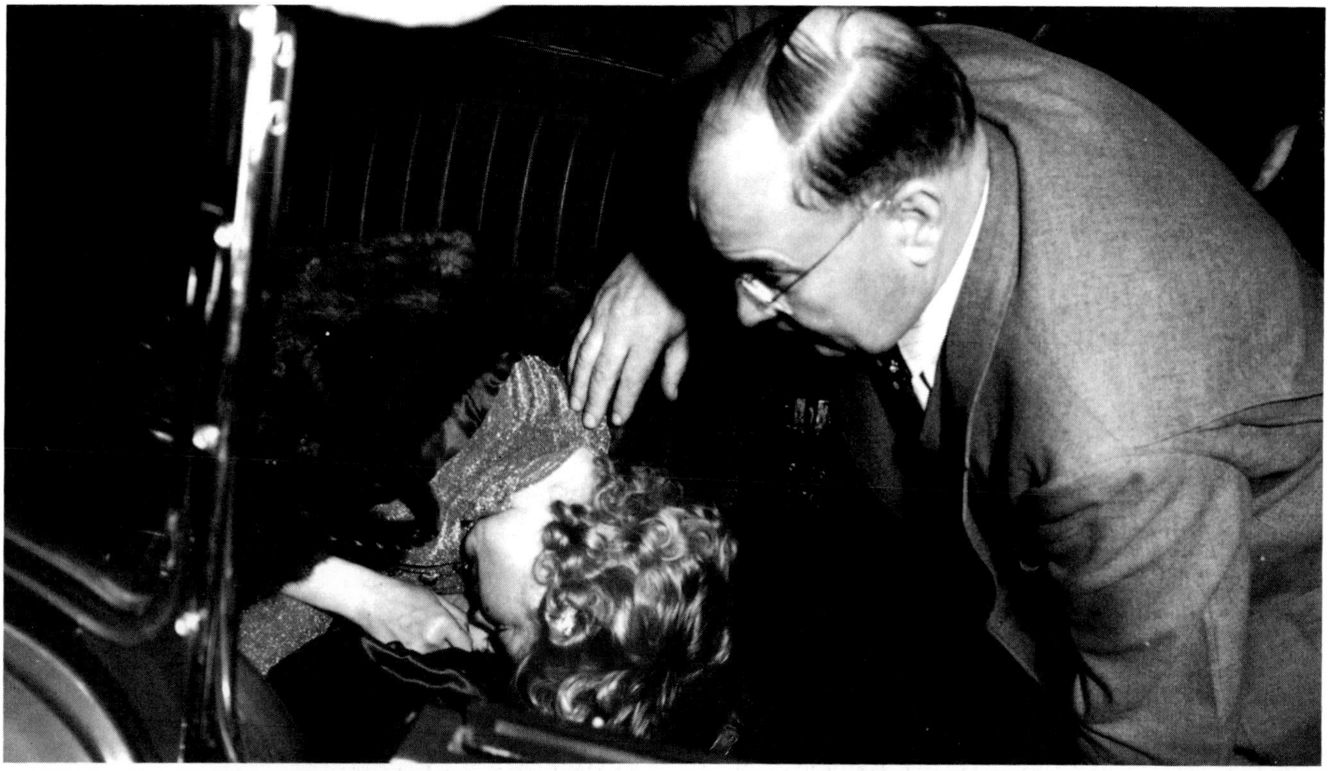

Police captain Bert Wallis, examining Thelma Todd's body, found her car inside a closed garage.

The exterior to the Todd garage only minutes after the body was found.

Director Roland West, left, being questioned by a detective.

Pat DiCicco, Thelma's former husband, a suspect.

who's coming with me you'll drop dead," Todd said. Jewel Carmen, the estranged wife of Todd's live-in lover Roland West, testified that she had seen her on the street with an unknown male companion. This person was never found. Deputy District Attorney George Johnson dismissed the accidental death theory as preposterous. "It seems too difficult to believe Miss Todd went to that garage and started the motor of her car to keep warm," he said.

But who then actually murdered the movie actress? There were several likely suspects. New York mob boss Charles "Lucky" Luciano had demanded of Todd the right to locate a gambling casino on the upper floor of her café. When she refused, veiled threats were made against her life. Pat DeCicco, the erstwhile booking agent, was embittered by the pending divorce action and reportedly would stop at nothing to exact revenge. The most likely suspect was Roland West. On Dec. 17, 1935, three deputies from the Los Angeles County Sheriff's office allegedly had told Hal Roach that West confessed to killing Todd. "West was very possessive, very controlling," Roach admitted years later. "He told Thelma she was to be back by 2 a.m. She said she'd come and go as she well pleased. They had a little argument about it and then Thelma left for the party. When Sid Grauman called West, about 2:30, to tell him Thelma was leaving, West went into her apartment and locked her out. He was going to teach her a lesson." Then, according to one version, West followed her back to the garage and locked her inside with the engine running. "He wasn't thinking about carbon monoxide, just about teaching her a lesson about who was the boss. So he left and went back to bed," Roach added. The story was quickly suppressed by Roach to protect the integrity of his studio. Todd was still a married woman and the details of her adulterous affair with West could result in a scandal not unlike the Roscoe "Fatty" Arbuckle debacle of 1921, still fresh in everyone's mind. Such a scandal could prove ruinous for business at a time when Will Hays exerted tremendous influence over the moral climate in Hollywood. West also had friends in high places. Eugene Biscailuz, formerly of the California Highway Patrol, was the sheriff at the time. West was a 32nd Degree Mason and an esteemed lodge brother of Biscailuz. The oath-bound Masons were pledged to help each other whenever the need arose. Members of the Los Angeles Police Department were equally culpable. Under the iron-fist rule of Mayor Frank Shaw, political corruption filtered downward through the ranks. For the good of the city, as well as the movie studio, it was deemed advisable to put the wraps on the story, though Detective Chief Thad Brown had the "goods" on West. No indictments were returned against any of the suspects. Roland West died in 1951 after he reportedly confessed his guilt to his close friend Chester Morris. Morris then later told director Alex Gordon. An ironic footnote to the tragedy can be found in a cryptic scene from one of Todd's movies with the Marx Brothers, entitled *Monkey Business*. In it, comedian Groucho Marx seizes Todd's arm and says, "Now be a good girlie or I'll lock you in the garage!"

REF.: *CBA;* Nash, *Murder Among the Mighty;* ____, *Open Files;* Wolf, *Fallen Angels.*

Todd, Thomas, 1765-1826, U.S., jur. Judge on court of appeals of Kentucky from 1801-06. He was appointed associate justice of the U.S. Supreme Court, and served from 1807-26. He presided over the newly formed western circuit containing Ohio, Kentucky, and Tennessee. REF.; *CBA.*

Toffania, La, 1653-1723, Italy, mur. La Toffania was a mass poisoner, who sold her poisonous concoctions to women in Naples, Italy, who wanted to get rid of their husbands. The poison was thought to be a mixture of arsenic and a harmless herb, cymbalaria. When finally accused as the supplier of the poisonous mixture being used to murder hundreds of men, La Toffania fled to a nearby convent seeking sanctuary. When the police sought to remove her the nuns would not permit it. Soldiers were finally sent to forcefully remove her.

Although the local archbishop threatened to excommunicate the authorities responsible and the entire community as well, the police refused to release La Toffania, and even threatened the archbishop if he did not withdraw his threat of excommunication.

La Toffania was tortured and finally confessed to responsibility for the deaths of more than 600 people. Although many prominent women were identified as her clients, none was prosecuted. The Viceroy of Naples ordered La Toffania strangled to death and her body tossed over the convent wall.

REF.: *CBA;* Glaister, *The Power of Poison;* Nash, *Look For the Woman;* Smith, *Famous American Poison Mysteries;* Thompson, *Poison and Poisoners.*

Tojo Hideki (AKA: **The Razor**), 1884-1948, Japan, war crimes. Tojo Hideki, the Japanese prime minister during WWII, was born in Tokyo on Dec. 30, 1884. After graduating from the Imperial Military Academy and the Military Staff College, Tojo advanced quickly in his military career, becoming a chief of staff serving in Manchuria by 1937. Tojo served as vice minister of war, 1938-39 and minister of war, 1940-41. He was appointed prime minister on Oct. 16, 1941.

Japanese war criminal Tojo Hideki.

Prime Minister Tojo led the Japanese forces following the bombing of Pearl Harbor and was credited with the spectacular Japanese successes early in the war. When the tide of the war turned, however, and Japan began to suffer equally impressive defeats, Tojo received the blame and resigned under pressure. At the close of the war, Tojo was arrested and put on trial with twenty-seven other high-ranking Japanese officials for war crimes. While in custody, Tojo made an attempt to kill himself with a pistol but failed. The Allies sought to prove that Tojo was culpable of participating in a conspiracy against peace and humanity. The trial, held before the International Military Tribunal for the Far East, lasted two-and-a-half years and cost $9 million. The proceedings ended in November 1948 when Tojo and six codefendants were sentenced to death. Sixteen other defendants were given life sentences. Tojo Hideki was hanged on Dec. 23, 1948.

REF.: Bergamini, *Japan's Imperial Conspiracy;* Byas, *Government by Assassination; CBA;* McNelly, *Politics and Government in Japan;* Manchester, *American Caesar: Douglas MacArthur, 1880-1964;* Morton, *Japan: Its History and Culture;* Mosley, *Hirohito: Emperor of Japan;* Reischauer, *Japan: The Story of a Nation;* ____, *The United States and Japan;* Scalapino, *Democracy and the Party Movement in Prewar Japan;* Toland, *The Rising Sun.*

Tokuda Hisakichi (AKA: **Mad Doctor**), prom. 1940s, Japan, war crimes. Called the "mad doctor" of Shinagawa Prison during WWII, Tokuda Hisakichi was tried in a military court in Yokohama, Japan, for performing cruel experiments on prisoners of war, causing at least four known deaths. According to witnesses, the doctor found amusement in injecting soybean protein directly into prisoners' veins. One of his victims, British merchant mariner William Holland, died screaming, his legs convulsing. In January 1948, Tokuda was found Guilty. On Oct. 8, 1949, General Douglas MacArthur approved the death penalty for the doctor, and he was hanged. REF.: *CBA.*

Tokugawa Hidetada, 1579-1632. Japan, geno. Held shogun title from 1605-23, but wielded little power until father Tokugawa Ieyasu died in 1616. The following year he initiated a policy of removing Christianity from the country, proceeding to execute missionaries en masse. REF.: *CBA.*

Tokugawa Iemitsu, 1604-51, Japan, geno. Strived to achieve goal of father Tokugawa Hidetada to rid Japan of Christianity. He arranged murders of Christians at Shimabara Peninsula in 1638, and forced all Japanese to register themselves with Buddhist temples. REF.: *CBA.*

Tokugawa Ieyasu (Matsudaira Takechiyo), 1543-1616, Japan, terr.-mur. Established Tokugawa shogunate in 1603, and maintained full control after abdicating in support of son Tokugawa Hidetada in 1605. He caused Toyotomi Hideyori to commit suicide and killed the lingering supporters of Toyotomi Hideyoshi in attacking Toyotomi castle in Osaka, from 1614-15. REF.: *CBA*.

Tokugawa Tsunayoshi (AKA: **Dog Shogun**), 1646-1709, Japan, polit. corr. Served first half of shogunate from 1680-1709 as champion of peace. Later he issued a proclamation giving the death penalty to anyone found injuring or otherwise harming dogs. His love of canines also led him to keep more than 50,000 dogs, which he cared for with funds from the treasury. He was the brother of Tokugawa Ietsuna, whom he succeeded. REF.: *CBA*.

Tokugawa Yoshimune, 1684-1751, Japan, jur. Held shogunate from 1716-45, instituting programs to defeat corruption. He also assisted in drafting a new legal code, known as the Kansei Code, completed and enacted after his death. REF.: *CBA*.

Tokutaro, Kimura, See: **Kimura Tokutaro**.

Tolbert, William Richard, Jr., 1913-80, Liberia, pres., assass. Vice-president of Liberian republic from 1951-71, then president from 1971-80. He was murdered following the coup headed by Samuel Doe. REF.: *CBA*.

Toledo, Francisco de, 1515-84, Peru, polit. corr.-mur. Viceroy of Peru from 1569-81. He ordered the abduction and beheading of Inca Chief Tupac Amarú in 1572, and brought the Inquisition to Peru. REF.: *CBA*.

Tolin, Ernest Allen, 1904-61, U.S., jur. Appointed to southern district court of California by President Harry Truman in 1951. He served as assistant U.S. attorney from 1943-46, and in other governmental positions. REF.: *CBA*.

Tolliver-Martin Feud, 1884-87, U.S., feud. The events and battles of the Tolliver-Martin feud, which took place in Rowan County, Ky., between August 1884 and June 1887, read like an account of a war in miniature. On several occasions, the government deployed the military to enforce the peace, but the confrontations resumed once the soldiers were withdrwn. Even the state legislature deemed the feud serious enough to merit their attention. In 1887 a joint resolution was passed by the House and Senate to investigate lawless Rowan County.

The investigation determined that the feud began in August 1884, when Republican W. Cook Humphreys was elected county sheriff. On election day, a dispute between two men named William Trumbo and Price led to a fistfight. During the fight, John Martin had a tooth knocked out. Martin claimed that it was John Day and Floyd Tolliver who hit him. He responded by drawing his pistol and firing at the two men, who drew their guns as well. When the smoke cleared, Solomon Bradley, an innocent bystander, had been shot dead. At first, the feud had the shadings of a political fight—Bradley had been a Republican, as were the Martins who had supported the new Republican sheriff, while the Tollivers were Democrats. It became apparent before long that the political nature of the feud was secondary to the more basic motive of revenge. On Dec. 2, 1884, Floyd Tolliver was killed by John Martin in a barroom brawl. On Dec. 10, Martin was murdered after five men used a forged release order to return him to Rowan.

Between August 1884 and June 1887, twenty people were murdered and sixteen more were wounded in Rowan County. On June 22, 1887, a private citizen, Boone Logan whose family had been drawn into the feud, and Hiram Pigman, with the cooperation of the current sheriff, recruited a posse of 113 men. On June 22, 1887, with arrest warrants in hand they surrounded the town of Morehead where the Tollivers were gathered. Following a two-and-a-half-hour battle in which about 2,000 shots were fired, the long feud was ended. Several of the Tollivers and their supporters escaped, but four were dead. The four were: Hirim Cooper, Craig, Bud and Jay Tolliver.

REF.: *CBA;* Johnson, *Famous Kentucky Tragedies and Trials.*

Tolomelli, Lucia, prom. 1665, Case of, Italy, mur. In Spring 1665, Elisabetta Sirani, a noted Bolognese painter, began to experience severe stomach pains. Over the following months, her health eroded, and in August, the pains intensified. Her physician, Dr. Gallerati, declined to prescribe any medication because "the Sun was in Leo" and, in his opinion, "the pain was due to a little catarrh." Sirani, twenty-six, died on Aug. 28.

An autopsy, performed at her father's request, found perforations in her stomach and concluded that they were caused by a "corrosive poison." A servant in the Sirani household claimed that another maid, Lucia Tolomelli, had put a suspicious substance in some of Sirani's food. Tolomelli was arrested on Sept. 1, 1665, and charged with murder. After a long trial, the evidence against Tolomelli was declared insufficient and she was released.

REF.: *CBA;* Thompson, *Poison and Poisoners.*

Tolson, Clyde A., 1900-75, U.S., law enfor. off. Clyde A. Tolson joined the FBI in 1928, having previously served as the confidential secretary to three secretaries of war. He was J. Edgar Hoover's longtime assistant, and was eventually named associate director of the FBI. Hoover and Tolson were virtually inseparable, lunching and going to the horse races together. Hoover died in 1972 and left Tolson his entire estate of $551,500. Tolson resigned from the FBI two days later. See: **Hoover, J. Edgar.**

REF.: *CBA;* Demaris, *The Director;* Nash, *Citizen Hoover;* Powers, *Secrecy and Power;* Sullivan, *The Bureau;* Toledano, *J. Edgar Hoover;* Unger, *FBI;* Watters and Gillers, *Investigating the FBI;* Whitehead, *The FBI Story.*

The original Tombs in New York.

Tombs, The, 1883- , U.S., pris. With the increase of New York's criminal element, New York's old British style jails became hopelessly inadequate. Debtors, as well as felons, crowded the small prisons. In 1816 there were 729 persons locked up in cells for debts of less than $25. by 1829, New York's Common Council had selected the site for its new, sprawling jail at Lafayette, Leonard, Franklin, and Center Streets. Its original name was Halls of Justice but most New Yorkers never called it anything other than the Tombs. The architect of that foreboding structure had lifted the design from an ancient Egyptian mausoleum illustrated and detailed in *Steven's Travels.*

Completed on June 15, 1838, the Tombs began to fill rapidly with miscreants of the city, chiefly shoplifters, drunks, and prostitutes (the first booked being Catherine Hagerman who was sentenced to six months for vagrancy). One of the first luminaries brought raging into the towering prison was Tom Hyer, bare-knuckle fighter and butcher by trade. A Tammany tough, Hyer was jailed for slicing off the nose of one of his political opponents. He proved truculent, and before he could be placed in a cell, he almost killed a jailer named Coggeshall by repeatedly slamming his head against a wall.

The first murderer booked at the Tombs was the gigantic Five Points gang leader Edward Coleman. Described as "a ragged Negro," Coleman admitted murdering his wife, one of the "hot corn girls" who inhabited Paradise Square. These women, many considered quite ravishing, would carry cedar buckets containing hot, roasted ears of corn and hawk their wares with the plaintive:

Hot Corn! Hot Corn!
Here's your lily white corn.
All you that's got money—
Poor me that's got none—
Come buy my lily hot corn
And let me go home.

One of the prettiest of the hot corn girls attracted Coleman's eye, and it became his habit to walk along with her as she sold her corn, battling off other thugs who made advances. It was only a short while later that he married the woman and only days after that, in a jealous rage, he murdered her in broad daylight. On the bright, warm morning of July 28, 1838, Coleman slipped up behind his wife as she stood in front of Jolie's Music Shop on Broadway and Walker. Grabbing her from behind, Coleman pulled her head hard against his chest and then drew his other arm, which contained a long, glistening razor, across her throat. He almost decapitated the poor woman and as she sagged to the ground, Coleman lamely threw the razor into the mud. He then waited in a daze for the watch to arrive. At the first appearance of the police he told them: "I done it."

The New York *Sun* was to state of the gruesome killing: "It appears that the horrible deed resulted from Coleman's belief in her infidelity and if the statements of their acquaintances are correct his belief was not without cause." Such sympathetic editorializing failed to aid the murderer, and Coleman became the first person to be executed in the Tombs, hanged on Jan. 12, 1839.

Many of the inmates of the Tombs were jailed for minor offenses. Visiting sailors were rounded up in huge lots each night and charged with wrecking several bordellos. Typical of those locked up overnight were George Fredericks and Augustus Hutchens. They were charged with spitting tobacco juice all over the expensive carpets in Maria Adams' brothel. They were both fined $10 and Judge Osborne gave them a severe lecture about "ruining the property of respectable citizens."

Runaway bond servants, drunks, and petty thieves were carted in groups to the Tombs each night, police acting more like dogcatchers than law officers, but the territories of the criminal in New York were so vast that officers were compelled to conduct massive nightly sweeps. Hundreds occupied the cells in the old Tombs. The more difficult prisoners were thrown into a block house in the Tombs' yard which was called "the Hole." It was exactly that.

If a prisoner could not afford to buy his way out of this foul pit, he was usually forgotten. One drunk, William Kitcherman, booked for being intoxicated on Oct. 17, 1839, was completely forgotten, and it was four months before lantern-carrying jailers, making one of their irregular checks of the "Black Hole," shrank back in horror. In one dark alcove were the remains of Kitcherman. Still scurrying and gnawing over his body were packs of huge rats who had eaten him alive.

Graft was rampant. Guards and wardens alike charged prisoners for the most essential supplies, material that should have been free. A blanket cost a dollar a week. Food averaged seventy-five cents a day. If one had no money one slept cold and waited for trial with an empty belly. It was also the custom in that period to lock up witnesses to serious crimes. Many times, an innocent bystander who had seen a murderer slay his victim was incarcerated next to the very man against whom he was to testify. And just as many times these poor souls were threatened and cowed into forgetting their stories; sometimes they met with "accidents" that guaranteed their silence. New Yorkers learned early not to "get involved."

Wealthy prisoners received special treatment for a price. In the grafting days of Warden Malachi Fallon, almost any convenience was made available once the head jailer's palm had been filled. Fallon allowed his paying customers to have fancy paper on the walls of their cells, carpets on the floors, and food catered from hotel restaurants. Some were even allowed to have singing canaries in their cells. The warden was an "animal lover". He maintained carrier pigeons on the jail roof and trained fighting cocks and pit dogs in the prison yard.

Showman Phineas T. Barnum came to Warden Fallon with an unusual request. He had already amazed New York when he put on display at William Niblo's Saloon in 1835 an alleged 161-year-old ex-slave named Joyce Heath. Barnum insisted that the Heath woman had been George Washington's nurse but nobody cared. The claim was preposterous enough to assure the showman sellout crowds at his new museum on lower Broadway. (Perhaps Barnum's most outlandish trick was emptying his place of customers reluctant to leave by standing at unmarked exit doors and hollering: "This way to the egress, folks! The greatest egress in the world!") Now Barnum wanted the exclusive right to have death masks made of murderers, pirates, and highwaymen awaiting execution in the Tombs. These masks would be put on display in his museum, he informed Warden Fallon. Help yourself, Fallon jovially responded, and a price was set for each moulage.

Fallon loved dignitaries and accompanied with an absurd grin any celebrity who wished to visit the Tombs. One such person was the eccentric (or perhaps mad) actor, Junius Brutus Booth, father of Edwin and John Wilkes. The hammy thespian usually arrived at the Tombs at dusk, and he was usually close to being in an alcoholic stupor. As usual, he would be conducted along the gloomy tier of cells known as "Murderers' Row."

Booth particularly enjoyed the company of a killer who was known simply as Dave Babe. This convicted murderer, reputed to be the errant son of an Episcopal bishop, had slit the throat of the mate of the *Sarah Lavinia* in 1843. He had been convicted of piracy and murder but had been spared the gallows seven times.

It was Booth's habit to stagger into Babe's cell, with several guards looking on in amusement, and point derisively at the shackles attached to the man's feet at one end and a large stone in the floor at the other. "Strike the fetters from that unfortunate creature!" Booth would boom. As torrents of tears coursed his cheeks, the actor would then implore the jailers to "secure me in his place!"

Guards would then soothe the emotionally upset Booth but not before he slipped the killer a dozen expensive cigars rolled in a lace handkerchief. He would then stagger, half supported by the keepers, down Murderers' Row. On one occasion, he withdrew a twenty-dollar bill from his vest pocket and handed it to a black prisoner who had been convicted of strangling his wife.

Warden Fallon's eyes popped at the sight of such magnanimity, and he tried to swipe the bill out of the strangler's hand. The killer was quicker and jammed the bill into his mouth, hastily attempting to swallow the money rather than turn it over to Fallon. The warden, however, was a determined man. Flinging wide the cell door, he rushed inside and began to choke the prisoner who, preferring to breathe, coughed up the bill into Fallon's cupped hand.

Fallon eventually tired of the actor's hysterics and when Booth subsequently visited the Tombs, the warden had him locked in a cell in Murderers' Row. This was grist for Booth's ever-grinding mill of drama and on such occasions the Shakespearian actor would moan out long soliloquies as he theatrically rattled the bars, shook chains, and made such a nuisance of himself that even his friends, the killers in the adjoining cells, cursed him. Booth would wear himself out with these tirades and eventually fall into a deep alcoholic sleep on the cell cot provided for him. Shortly before he was due at the theater for the evening's performance, two of Fallon's guards would rouse Booth from his torpor and literally carry him to the theater. The burly guards would stand by as the actor applied his make-up and dressed, and then support him on either side through the wings until he emerged on stage to surprisingly render a superb Richard III.

The famous British novelist, Charles Dickens, visited the Tombs in 1842. This was at a time when the prison was less than four years and yet it had turned into a rank and scabrous place that gave the author a decidedly clammy feeling. "What is this dismal-fronted pile of Bastard Egyptian," he wrote later, "like an enchanter's palace in a melodrama!—a famous prison called the Tombs. Shall we go in?

"So. A long narrow lofty building, stove-headed as usual, with four galleries, one above the other, going round it, and communicating by stairs. Between the two sides of each gallery, and in its center, a bridge, for the greater convenience of crossing. On each of these bridges sits a man: dozing or reading, or talking to an idle companion. On each tier, are two opposite rows of small iron doors. They look like furnace-doors, but are cold and black, as though the fires within had all gone out. Some two or three are open, and women, with drooping heads bent down, are talking to the inmates."

The author asked one of the jailers if he would open a door. "All, if you like," the jailer responded. He was amused and flattered by the distinguished guest. With a great show and rattle of keys, the jailer opened one cell and the fascinated writer peered inside. "A small bare cell, into which the light enters through a high chink in the wall. There is a rude means of washing, a table, and a bedstead. Upon the latter, sits a man of sixty, reading. He looks up for a moment; gives an impatient dogged shake; and fixes his eyes upon his book again. As we withdrew our heads, the door closes on him and is fastened as before. This man has murdered his wife, and will probably be hanged."

As he was led down the gallery, Dickens suddenly stopped and inquired: "Pray, why do they call this place the Tombs?"

"Well, it's the cant name," replied the guard.

"I know it is. Why?"

Whether to appear knowledgeable or important, the guard immediately lied to Dickens, saying: "Some suicides happened here, when it was first built. I expect it comes from that."

When Dickens asked why there were no hooks in the cells for prisoners to hang their clothes upon, the guard further compounded his lie by stating: "Why, I say that's just it. When they had hooks they *would* hang themselves, so they're taken out of every cell, and there's only the marks left where they used to be!"

This, of course, was nonsense. The marks on the walls were from old water pipes that had been removed. They had been rerouted along the ceilings and one prisoner, Frederick Smith, a horse thief condemned to the gallows, had used his handkerchief to hang himself from one of these pipes on the ceiling. Smith's self-inflicted demise was merely an unsavory hors d'oeuvre before the Tombs served up the entree of John C. Colt whose sensational suicide in prison jarred the entire city. Facts carelessly assembled subsequent to Colt's reported death only increased the suspicion of the community that this self-admitted murderer may not have died in the Tombs after all and may have effected a permanent escape.

Throughout six murdering decades, the original Tombs did a land office business with more than 500,000 men and women passing through its foreboding gates on criminal charges. The original Tombs was torn down in 1897. Days before demolition began, singer Lillian Russell visited Murderers' Row dressed in ermine and lamb. Her perfume drove the prisoners wild. After singing a few ditties for the murderer, she was greeted with a thunderous noise from the women's quarters which she mistook for applause. The raging female prisoners banged tin basins against the bars of their cells. The new Tombs officially opened at the new site on Sept. 29, 1902. Escapes from this less formidable jail became more frequent.

Murderer and holdup artist Reynold Forsbrey wiggled through a ventilation shaft from his solitary confinement cell and dropped down into the carpenter's shop on Sept. 2, 1912. From the shop, the killer broke into the yard and climbed the wall to freedom by using a nail-studded joist. He was caught some months later in the Bronx rooms of his sweetheart Mary Ryan. She helped Forsbrey to subsequently escape from Clinton and Auburn prisons, but he was always returned to his cell. Police invariably knew where to find Forsbrey. He would be with the woman for whom he had committed his first robbery, Mary Ryan. "All I ever wanted to do was get enough cash to buy her a fancy ring," the stickup man moaned.

In 1926, three tough cons—Robert Berg, a member of Chicago's Whittemore gang, Michael McKenna, and Hyman Amberg—made a bloody breakout attempt from the Tombs that took several lives. Armed with pistols smuggled to them, the trio hid behind a coal pile in the yard and began a wild shoot-out. Two guards, Dan O'Connor and Jeremiah Murphy, charged them with their guns blasting. The prisoners shot them dead in their tracks. Warden Peter J. Mallon became enraged at the sight of his men being mowed down and led another charge. He was felled with a bullet in the lung and later died of the wound. The gun battle went on for several hours with police rushing more and more reinforcements to the Tombs. By the time hundreds of detectives and patrolmen advanced, spraying the area with machine gun bullets, the three prisoners were already dead. They had turned their pistols on themselves.

In the free-and-easy days of Gentleman Jimmy Walker, the Tombs became quite comfortable for those who had the money to buy extra privileges. The worst felons and murderers in the jail were allowed out of their cells after the warden left so that they could play poker. Several inmates paid guards $100 two nights a week to be allowed the pleasure of female company in their cells. Guards sold heroin to prisoners for hefty sums; the narcotics were originally allotted to addicts who were supposed to receive a ration of four-and-one-eighths grains to keep them from going berserk. Other convicts bought their drugs and the addicts went crazy. The guards used cotton plugs to drown out their screams. Such was the second Tombs before the third and final building was erected in 1941. See: **Appo, Quimby**; **Colt, John Caldwell**; **Hicks, Albert E.**

REF.: Asbury, *The Gangs of New York;* Barnum, *The Life of P.T. Barnum; CBA;* Dickens, *American Notes;* Haskins, *Street Gangs;* Kimmel, *The Mad Booths of Maryland;* Martin, *Secrets of the Great City;* Robinson, *Hot Corn;* Skinner, *Mad Folk of the Theatre;* Sutton, *The New York Tombs, Its Secrets and Mysteries.*

Tomlinson, Richard, prom. 1833, Brit., mur. In December 1833, Richard Tomlinson and his 20-year-old girlfriend, Mary Evans, were traveling to High Ercall, England, to consult with a psychic in hopes of locating some of Evan's missing belongings. Before reaching High Ercall, Tomlinson became ill and the couple turned back toward Ranton. Along the road they quarrelled and Evans accused Tomlinson of stealing her belongings. Tomlinson later alleged that she had also insulted his parents. When Evans refused to be silent, he knocked her into a roadside ditch and beat her.

Evans' body was found on Dec. 16, her face badly lacerated. Tomlinson had been arrested and confessed to the murder within two hours. Although Tomlinson claimed he killed her by jumping on her head, a bloodstained stone found nearby was considered to be the murder weapon. Tomlinson was found Guilty of murder and was executed.

REF.: Butler, *Murderers' England; CBA.*

Tompkins Square Police Riot, 1874, U.S., mob vio. During the depression of 1873, unemployed workers formed labor groups and asked the government to assist in creating new jobs, particularly in public works. The Committee of Safety was one such group formed that year in New York City. The Committee asked city officials to meet with them, and when they were denied, planned a march from Tompkins Square to city hall. When police refused them a marching permit, the Committee organized a demonstration in Tompkins Square. The night before the demonstration, police decided to prevent it, but did not inform the organizers. At 10:30 a.m. on a day in January 1874, more than 7,000 workers, mostly immigrants and their families, gathered in the square. Police surrounded the park and advanced upon a group of men carrying a labor banner, clubbing them. Next, mounted police charged the crowd, indiscriminately trampling and beating demonstrators. Police Commissioner Abram Duryee and the press were pleased with the efficiency with which the police dispersed the crowd, and advocated total suppression of any "communistic" elements. Thereafter, the unemployed were reluctant to organize. REF.: *CBA.*

Toney, Donald, 1956- , and **Toney, Leonard**, 1959- , U.S., rape. On the evening of Aug. 20, 1979, an 18-year-old woman and two male companions from Tennessee got lost after leaving the Stevenson Expressway on Chicago's South Side. They stopped to ask directions from a group of eight young men on South Federal Avenue, but before the trio could leave, the group attacked the car, and abducted the young woman. She was taken to a nearby building and raped.

Donald Toney, twenty-three, and his 20-year-old brother, Leonard Toney, were arrested and charged with rape, deviant sexual assault, and aggravated kidnapping. Following a bench trial, the two were convicted of the charges on Apr. 2, 1980. Although neither of the brothers had previous convictions, on Apr. 23, Criminal Court judge William Cousins, Jr., gave them both the maximum sentence of thirty years. The rape victim returned to Chicago twice to testify in the case. Her testimony was considered instrumental in obtaining the convictions. The earliest possible parole date for the Toneys is 1995. REF.: *CBA.*

Tongs, The (AKA: **Highbinders**), prom. 1860s- , U.S., secret crim. soc. The influx of thousands of poor Chinese immigrants into California in the 1840s-50s gave rise to a secret society organized to protect and defend the members of this community from the terror tactics of marauding white hoodlums. Many of the Chinese worked as section hands on the railroad—"coolie labor" to some—and in the gold fields. The resentment against the Chinese on the part of the Anglo-Americans was profound. The "tong gangs"—unheard of in China—were prominent in the railroad construction camps. Gradually they expanded to the larger urban centers, notably San Francisco. There along the Barbary Coast the Hop Sings and Suey Sings gained control of the gambling rackets and opium trade within the highly insulated Chinese community.

Opium, a by-product of British colonialism, became a staple product of the narcotics traffic practiced by the tong gangs in the U.S. The Hop Sings, Suey Sings, and to a lesser extent, the Kwong Ducks, also engaged in the importation of Chinese women. The restrictive policies of U.S. immigration authorities limited the number of women entering the U.S., and so the tongs smuggled them in and then sold them to the highest bidders. Often the women were forced to share a wretched cellar apartment or "crib house" with twenty other illegals. By the 1880s, the tong gangs of San Francisco's Chinatown were virtually above the law. Much like the Italian Black Hand, the tongs for the most part victimized their own people. Each gang had its share of assassins or "hatchet men" ready to split open the head of an adversary or anyone unwilling to bow to the organized extortion. For years the reigning hatchet man on the West Coast was Fung Jing Toy, better known as "Little Pete." As the leader of the Sum Yops, Little Pete was responsible for the deaths of at least twelve rivals, though he had nothing to do with the murder of Low Sing in 1875, a crime illustrative of the kind of gang war in San Francisco's Chinatown at that time.

Low Sing was a member of the Suey Sing Tong who had claimed a slave girl named Kim Kum Ho for his own. This did not sit well with Ming Long, who split open his rival's head with a razor-sharp hatchet. Low Sing identified his killer moments before his death, resulting in a bloody showdown between the most skilled hatchet men from the two opposing tongs. It was conceded that the Suey Sings prevailed that night, because they had succeeded in injuring the greatest number of rival gang members. Ming Long was ejected from his gang and driven out of the country.

The 1906 earthquake reduced Chinatown and the Barbary Coast to rubble, the cesspools of vice and the secret dens of the Tong Gangs for the most part eliminated. Not until much later in the century did the tong gangs re-emerge in great numbers. Every major city in the U.S. has experienced tong warfare over the years. In New York the most powerful tong leader was Mock Duck, whose Hip Sing gang was in constant warfare with the rival On Leong. Mock Duck squared off against his enemies in the street, shooting at random until they fell before his blazing guns.

The New York tong war of 1909 that was to claim fifty lives was ended in the courts by Judge Warren W. Foster, who arbitrated a peace settlement. Hostilities resumed in the 1920s, with periodic outbreaks. The Flying Dragons and Ghost Shadows currently vie for control of New York's chinatown extortion, gambling, and drug rackets. The story is much the same in Chicago where the Gray Shadows, Ghost Shadows, and Black Ghost Shadows have succeeded the established On Leong and Hip Sings for criminal preeminence in the South Side Chinatown. Today, the On Leong Tong operates a cultural center and social club in the heart of the Chinatown retail district, where from time to time, the police stage gambling raids. See: **Bow Kum; Mock Duck.**

REF.: *CBA;* Godwin, *Murder U.S.A.;* Nash, *Almanac of World Crime;* (FILM), *Tongs—A Chinatown Story,* 1986.

Tong Wars, prom. 1860-1930s, U.S., org. crime. Once meaning parlor, the word "Tong," during the late 1800s and early 1900s, stood for feuding Chinese organizations in the U.S. For 2,000 years, tongs were rebel or bandit organizations. With the immigration of several thousand Chinese to the U.S., tongs became organizations of mutual aid and protection. Tong members, composed of laundrymen, restaurateurs, servants, and merchants, paid dues and gained financial support and physical protection from competitors and from Chinese and white authorities. As tongs were occasionally involved in drugs, prostitution, and gambling, gangs of hired assassins called "highbinder societies" were formed. A tong employed these strong-arm gangs to eliminate competition. The press called these assassins hatchet men, after their favorite weapon. To the Chinese, they were *boo how doy.* In the early 1900s, an average price to assassinate a tong leader was $10,000, while a hit on a servant was $500.

In the 1930s, there were fifteen tongs nationwide, compared to more than thirty on the West Coast alone in the 1860s. From the 1860s to 1930, wars were fought among the tongs for various reasons. White law enforcement officials were ineffective in stopping them, and as the Tong Wars affected only the Chinatown districts in major U.S. cities such as San Francisco, Chicago, Baltimore, Pittsburgh, Boston, and New York, the U.S. public were mostly unconcerned.

The 1897 war between the Sum Yops and the Sue Yops in San Francisco was resolved by a peace treaty, drafted with the help of Chinese statesman Li Hung Chang after a group of white U.S. citizens appealed to the emperor of China, Kwang Hsu. Chang reported, "I have cast into prison all relatives of the Sue Yops in China, and have cabled to California that their heads will be chopped off if another Sum Yop is killed in San Francisco." In New York's Chinatown, the murder of one-time slave girl Bow Kum in 1909 started the war between the Hip Sings and On Leongs, which continued intermittently until 1925. The war left more than 350 Chinese dead nationwide. A peace was reached after immigration and health officials threatened to deport more than 200 Chinese if the killings continued. See: **Bow Kum.**

REF.: Asbury, *The Gangs of New York; CBA;* Livingston, *The Murdered and the Missing.*

Tonner, Francis Ian (AKA: **Dr. Speedo, The Wizard**), 1929- , U.S., drugs. In November 1988, 59-year-old Francis Ian Tonner was arrested in Virginia for possession and manufacture of an illegal drug—methamphetamine. When police raided his illegal laboratory, Tonner attempted to kill himself by taking cyanide. A companion, Andrew McConaghy, succeeded in his suicide attempt. Tonner, a research chemist, built his first drug laboratory at thirteen. During the 1960s, Tonner used psychedelic drugs with Timothy Leary and others at Harvard University. Since the early 1970s, he has been charged with drug violations in Massachusetts, Scotland, and Canada.

During his 1989 trial, Tonner informed U.S. district judge John

A. MacKenzie that his illegal lab was to be used to manufacture a legal substitute for "crack" cocaine. He also professed an interest in producing a drug to fight Parkinson's disease without detrimental side effects. On May 4, 1989, Tonner was sentenced in federal court to sixteen years in prison for the manufacture of an illegal drug. Five days later, he was sentenced to an additional ten years in state prison for drug possession. Tonner will serve the state sentence before serving the federal term. REF.: *CBA.*

TonTons Macoutes, prom. 1970s-80s, Haiti, secret crim. soc. Closely aligned with the regimes of Haiti's presidents, Francois "Papa Doc" Duvalier and his successor son Jean-Claude "Baby Doc" Duvalier, the Tontons Macoutes protected the regime's political, social, and religious interests. Uniformed in blue denim accented with a red neckerchief, the Macoutes used random violence and voodoo fear tactics to enforce the Duvaliers' wishes for more than thirty years. The Macoutes were largely illiterate blacks recruited from Haiti's slums and small villages who unsentimentally exercised their sizeable power, often against members of the class from which they themselves came. They were present in every institution from government offices to local service industries.

The Macoutes, whose name is Creole for "bogeyman," were patterned after Hitler's SS troops. They killed with impunity on election days, often leaving corpses on display to insure victories for the Duvalier candidates. The Macoutes as well as the Duvaliers were deeply influenced by voodoo, and frequently decisions and penalties were determined by its ancient rites. When a traitorous Macoute was alleged to have turned himself into a dog to escape punishment, Duvalier ordered the mass execution of dogs.

The TonTons Macoutes lived above the law. They commandeered land and automobiles without paying, rode free in taxis and buses,and took food when hungry. Through their random reign of terror, the TonTons Macoutes perpetuated the despotism of the Duvaliers over one of the most desperately poor countries of the world for more than three decades. REF.: *CBA.*

Toohey, Michael, prom. 1818, and **Toohey, Martin,** d.1819, U.S., mur. Michael and Martin Toohey murdered Attorney James W. Gadsden in Charleston, S.C., on Dec. 21, 1818. The brothers were returning home from an Irish Volunteers Meeting when Michael Toohey and Gadsden scuffled on Market Street. Martin crept up from behind and plunged a bayonet in Gadsden's back. The brothers were quickly arrested and tried for murder at the Charleston Courthouse in January 1819. No provocation could be found for their actions other than the fact that Michael was drunk. Michael was convicted on a manslaughter charge, while Martin, adjudged to be sober at the time, was found Guilty of first-degree murder.

Michael was branded with an upside-down "M" on the bulb of his left thumb by the hangman. Martin, who was ordered to die on the gallows, escaped from prison before the sentence could be carried out. He reached the outskirts of the county where he was gunned down by Edward Morris.

REF.: *CBA; A Report of the Trial of Michael & Martin Toohey, on an Indictment for the Murder of James W. Gadsden, Esq.*

Tooke, Horne (John Horne), 1736-1812, Case of, Brit., treas. Ordained minister who founded Constitutional Society to protest for sovereignty of American colonies and to institute reforms in Parliament. In 1794, he was charged with treason for backing William Pitt, but was acquitted. He was elected to Parliament in 1801, but was not allowed to take his seat because of a special act prohibiting clergymen. REF.: *CBA.*

Toolan, Sean, 1938-81, U.S., (unsolv.) mur. ABC reporter and former Chicago newsman Sean Toolan was murdered in Beirut, Leb., on July 14, 1981. He was stabbed four times and shot in the spine with a 9-mm. pistol. Nothing was stolen from his person. According to a witness, Toolan was shot while walking toward his home after leaving Beirut's Commodore Hotel at 1:55 a.m. where he had been drinking with several other journalists. Investigators could not determine whether the killing was politically or criminally motivated. Toolan, born in England, had worked several years as a correspondent in Beirut and in the U.S., where he hoped to become a naturalized citizen. REF.: *CBA.*

Toole, Gerald, 1838-62, U.S., arson-mur. Not long after he arrived in Connecticut from his native Ireland Gerald Toole was imprisoned for setting fire to his saloon with the intention of collecting insurance money. While languishing in prison Toole was savagely beaten with a cat-o'-nine-tails by Warden Daniel Webster for failing to complete his allotment of twelve boots a day. On Mar. 27, 1862, Toole stabbed the warden to death with a cobbler's knife. Prison officials starved and tortured the 24-year-old man up to the moment of his trial. Toole was convicted of first-degree murder at the Hartford courthouse in May and hanged in that city on Sept. 19, 1862.

REF.: *An Autobiography of Gerald Toole; CBA.*

Toplis, Percy, d.1920, Case of, Brit., mur. On the morning of Apr. 25, a farm laborer discovered the body of taxi driver George Spicer beside a road near Andover, Hampshire. He had been shot in the head with a service revolver and his taxi had been stolen. Soldiers from Bulford, a nearby British military base, told police that they had ridden with Spicer the night before. When Spicer stopped for gas, a serviceman approached the driver and asked him for a lift. Spicer agreed to return for the unidentified man when he had delivered his current passengers to their destination. Soon after the discovery of Spicer's body, a policeman in a nearby community spotted Spicer's cab parked by the side of the road with two men in military uniforms inside. A few days later, a soldier named Harry Fallows admitted to having been in the cab with Percy Toplis, but maintained his innocence. According to Fallows, Toplis had come to the base looking for him and asked him to accompany him while he sold Spicer's cab.

One month later, reports of a stranger living in an abandoned hut near the village of Tomintoul, lead police to military deserter Toplis. When they confronted him, Toplis opened fired, killed one policeman, seriously injured another, and escaped. In June, he was spotted by another police constable near Carlisle. When Toplis threatened him, the constable went in search of reinforcements. A squad of police found Toplis within an hour. When Toplis drew his gun, the police shot and killed him.

REF.: *CBA;* Gribble, *Famous Manhunts;* Wilson, *Encyclopedia of Murder;* Woodhall, *Secrets of Scotland Yard.*

Toppan, Jane (Nora Kelley), 1854-1938, U.S., mur. Born Nora Kelley in Boston in 1854, mass murderer Jane Toppan may have had a genetic claim to insanity. Toppan's mother died when she was an infant, and her father cared for her and her siblings until he too went insane. He was found one day trying to sew his eyelids shut and was sent to an insane asylum. The children went first to live with their grandmother but were later sent to an orphanage. Jane was adopted by Mr. and Mrs. Abner Toppan in 1859. She grew up to be an attractive, apparently normal, and bright young lady. However, when she was jilted by her fiance she was devastated, and she tried twice to kill herself. She ended a several-year period of seclusion by attending a Cambridge, Mass., nursing school.

When a patient who was in Jane's care and not seriously ill, suddenly died, she was questioned about the incident and although no report was made, she was discharged from the hospital staff. Without ever finishing her training, Toppan became a private nurse in dozens of New England homes, gaining the confidence of those she cared for.

In 1901, one of Toppan's patients, Mattie Davis, died. Three other members of her family died shortly thereafter. The trusting family insisted each time that she stay to tend the remaining members. However, when Captain Gibbs, a Davis family relative, returned from a sea voyage to find his wife dead, he became suspicious. The police were called, and several autopsies were performed. In each case, it was determined that the death had been caused by morphine poisoning.

Jane was traced to New Hampshire, but not before she had murdered another Davis relative. Protesting her innocence, she was returned to Massachusetts and charged with murder. As the investigation of her past began, dozens of the bodies of people she had cared for were exhumed and it was discovered that all had died of morphine and atropine poisoning. The atropine counteracted the constriction of the victims pupils so that morphine poisoning would not be suspected. It was also discovered that Toppan had obtained large quantities of the drugs over the years using forged prescriptions.

While Toppan was in jail, a psychologist, Dr. Stedman, visited her. Eventually she told him she had killed over thirty of her patients. (The actual number is probably closer to 100.) On June 25, 1902, Jane Toppan went on trial. When Dr. Stedman testified that she was suffering from an incurable form of insanity, Jane denied his diagnosis, claiming she was completely sane and always knew what she was doing. She was sent to the Taunton State Asylum for the Criminally Insane where she died in 1938 at age eighty-four.

REF.: *CBA;* Gross, *Masterpieces of Murder;* Nash, *Look For the Woman;* Rodell, *Boston Murders.*

Torello, James Vincent (AKA: **Turk Torello**), 1930-79, U.S., org. crime. James Vincent Torello was born in Chicago in December 1930. Torello's first arrest in 1945 was followed by numerous others for auto theft, armed robbery, burglary, and hijacking. He was convicted of a violation of the firearms act and sentenced to two years in a federal penitentiary. Torello was the alleged successor to Fiore "Fifi" Buccieri, the chief enforcer for the Chicago mafia, on Buccieri's death in 1973. In addition to the crimes for which he was arrested, Torello was also involved in loan sharking, gambling, and pornography. He died of cancer in April 1979 at Northwestern Memorial Hospital in Chicago. See: **Buccieri, Fiore**. REF.: *CBA.*

Toreno, Conde de (José Maria Queipo de Llano y Ruiz de Sarabia), 1786-1843, Spain, banish. Took part in Spanish revolution in 1808 and later served in Cortes as deputy from 1811-14 and from 1820-23. His years as deputy were interrupted when he was banished twice, from 1814-20 and from 1823-32. He eventually held office as prime minister in 1834 while Maria Christina was in power. REF.: *CBA.*

Torquemada, Tomás de, 1420-98, Spain, jur. In November 1478, Pope Sixtus IV issued his edict to combat the "problem" of apostate former Jews and Muslims in Spain, thus beginning the Spanish Inquisition. He drew upon the papal Inquisition instituted in 1231 by Pope Gregory IX to deal with the large scale heresies that had threatened the church in the eleventh and twelfth centuries. The procedure as laid out by Pope Gregory allowed the accused heretic to admit his crime and absolve himself. If the accused did not confess, he was interrogated by an appointed inquisitor and tried with the benefit of testimony of witnesses. The use of torture to elicit confessions and denunciations of other heretics was not part of the original procedure, but was added by Pope Innocent IV in 1252.

Sixtus IV authorized the Spanish Inquisition at the request of King Ferdinand V and Queen Isabella I of Spain, who had determined to create political and religious unity in their country. The Spanish Inquisition got underway in Seville with such ferocity that the pope attempted to curtail its authority. However, the monarchs, realizing the power of the tool they now possessed, refused to allow him to institute any limitations. In August 1483, they compelled him to appoint a grand inquisitor for Castile. The man selected for the job, Tomás de Torquemada, was a Dominican friar who had served as the prior of the Santa Cruz Monastery in Segovia between 1452 and 1474. He was selected for the post by Ferdinand and Isabella because of his belief that various groups within Spain—the Marranos (Jewish converts), the Moriscos (Islamic converts), the Jews, and the Moors—might harm the welfare of the country.

Two months after his appointment, his territory was extended to include Aragon, Catalonia, Valencia, and Majorca. He established tribunals at Seville, Ciudad Real, Córdoba, Jaén, and Zaragoza. In 1484, he drew up twenty-eight articles to help judge crimes of heresy, usury, witchcraft, apostasy, blasphemy, and bigamy. The articles, which became known as the "Code of Terror," authorized the use of torture to obtain evidence when the accused would not confess. Under Torquemada's ruthless supervision, the accused were subjected to various tortures including the rack, the hoist, and water torture—in which a piece of cloth placed over the victim's mouth was filled gradually with water so the victim slowly suffocated. Those judged by Torquemada's standards as "violent" offenders were burned at the stake, a method that claimed approximately 2,000 lives during Torquemada's tenure.

In 1492, Torquemada, who was himself of Jewish descent, induced Ferdinand and Isabella to expel all Jews who refused baptism into the Catholic faith. As a result, 170,000 Jews were forced to leave Spain. Torquemada's reign of terror continued undiminished until June 1494 when, because of his advanced age and failing health, as well as numerous criticisms about the brutality of his reign, Pope Alexander VI displaced Torquemada by appointing four assistant inquisitors with power equal to his own who took their direction from the pope. With his power thus diluted, Torquemada's version of the Spanish Inquisition drew to a close. He died in 1498 at age seventy-eight in the monastery of St. Thomas at Avila, which he had built during his reign of terror. REF.: *CBA.*

Torres, Florentino, 1844-1927, U.S., jur. Appointed to district court of Philippine Islands by President Theodore Roosevelt in 1902. He earlier served as prosecuting attorney in Madrid for the government of Spain from 1871-73, and held other Spanish posts. From 1899-1901 he served as attorney general for the military government of the Philippines. He represented the Philippines at the Peace Council held in 1901 at the end of the Philippine-U.S. hostilities. REF.: *CBA.*

Torres, Pedro, 1948- , U.S., (wrong. convict.) mur. Thirty-seven-year-old Mexican citizen Pedro Torres was arrested for drinking beer in the parking lot of a Dallas convenience store. When police ran his name through their computer, they discovered that Torres was wanted for the murder of 18-year-old Manuel Ortega on Apr. 17, 1983. Torres, who was in the U.S. illegally, was arrested, tried, and convicted despite his claim that he was 250 miles from the crime when the murder was committed. He was sentenced to seventy-five years in prison. Three months later, the trial judge received information that Torres' alibi might be sound. He had Torres' original attorney, Carlos Garcia, file a motion for a new trial. When Torres' work records, which for some reason Garcia had neglected to introduce as evidence in the first trial, were examined, it became clear that the wrong Pedro Torres had been arrested and sent to jail. In April 1985, the conviction was reversed and Torres was released. REF.: *CBA.*

Torrey, Charles Turner, 1813-46, U.S., impris. Tried and sentenced in 1844 to six years in Maryland State penitentiary for helping slaves escape. He died in prison. REF.: *CBA.*

Torrio, John (Johnny, AKA: Frank Langley, J.T. McCarthy), 1882-1957, U.S., org. crime. Born in Osara, Italy, in February 1882, Johnny Torrio immigrated to New York with his mother in 1884. Torrio's father, Thomas Torrio, was a common laborer who slaved in Italian vineyards for twenty years and saved his earnings so he could some day take his family to the U.S. He died only a short time before his wife and little boy sailed for the U.S. The 2-year-old son Thomas Torrio sent to the U.S. grew to be one of the craftiest killers in organized crime, and a crime lord who more than anyone else, laid the foundation of the national crime syndicate formed by Charles "Lucky" Luciano and others in the early 1930s.

The five-foot-six-inch, brown-eyed, stocky Torrio began his career in U.S. crime as a street thug and, thanks to his organizational genius, rose to gang boss in New York, then crime overlord in Chicago, and, eventually, to the position of elder statesman of organized crime in the U.S. Torrio was responsible for establishing billion-dollar rackets and, over a fifty-year period, caused the deaths of hundreds of rival gangsters and gamblers. To his nefarious credit, Torrio could take sinister pride in never having been arrested for any major offense.

Secrecy was at the core of the cunning Torrio's character. From the time Torrio was a boy, he kept out of the limelight and the police showups by convincing others to commit the crimes he masterminded. As a teenager, Torrio established his credo among the youths and later the adult gangsters who obeyed his orders: "No one is *ever* to mention my name. No one!" Others took the risks and received the prison sentences if caught. Torrio provided the police and legal protection and counted the money.

Though he would die a millionaire, Torrio's arrival in the U.S. was inauspicious. In fact, he appeared a bit ridiculous as he toddled down the gangplank of the ship that brought him to Ellis Island in New York Harbor. He wore a little girl's tattered dress, the only garment his impoverished mother could afford. Upon it was pinned a piece of paper, reading: "John Torrio."

Torrio's hardworking mother, Maria Carlucci Torrio, immediately went to work in New York as a seamstress to support herself and her infant son. Torrio was left alone in a crib much of the day with neighbors occasionally checking on him. His home was a single room of spartan furniture in the disease-ridden Lower East Side of New York. In 1886, Maria Torrio married Salvatore Caputo, the owner of a small grocery store on James Street. Caputo operated an illegal bar behind the grocery store and while a teenager, Johnny Torrio went to work as a swamper, cleaning the floors of the saloon.

Although Torrio joined the James Street Gang at an early age, this was more a matter of self-protection than an actively sought role. To avoid being beaten up regularly by gang members, the diminutive Torrio became one of the gang. He avoided committing crimes with other gang members, preferring to perform his thefts and burglaries alone. He reasoned that in this way, he could never be turned in by other gang members seeking to avoid a conviction. Thus, no police arrests of Torrio were ever made during this time.

In 1904, using money accumulated from his various robberies and burglaries, Torrio, using the alias of J.T. McCarthy, opened a large saloon at James and Walker streets. He rented the upper floors of the building and the building next door where he installed about twenty prostitutes. This was Torrio's first bordello. He was to go on making money from prostitutes until his forced retirement from the rackets in 1925. To protect the saloon and brothel operations, Torrio hired a dozen of the toughest gunmen from the old James Street Gang. He expanded his rackets to include several gambling dens. As he prospered, Torrio also came to the attention of other established gangsters, chiefly Paul Kelly (Paolo Vaccarelli), then the most powerful gang lord in New York. Kelly persuaded Torrio to join him in his Manhattan rackets, and by 1905, Torrio was Kelly's top lieutenant in the Five Points Gang.

While Torrio looked after Kelly's brothels in Manhattan he found time to act the part of Fagin by teaching youngsters the black arts of pickpocketing and burglary. These youthful thieves, some as young as ten, brought their stolen items to Torrio who fenced them, keeping the lion's share for himself. Several graduates of this gang, such as Frankie Yale and Al Capone (who became a Torrio-trained thief at the age of nine), later joined the adult Five Points Gang as labor sluggers assigned to break up picketing strikers.

By the time he reached his early twenties, Torrio was a wealthy man. He dressed in conservative three-piece suits, wore a derby and disdained anything garish. His ties were always black and the only bit of color in his daily ensemble was a blood red handkerchief poking from the breast pocket of his suit coat. In his attire, Torrio aped his boss, Paul Kelly. He also imitated Kelly's mannerisms. He spoke slowly and softly and forced himself to discard the stereotypical Italian habit of gesturing with the hands to emphasize what he said.

In 1908, a bloody gang war broke out between the factions headed by Kelly and Edward "Monk" Eastman. Political pressure to end this war came from the ruling powers at Tammany Hall. Rather than incur the enmity of political sachems, Torrio bowed out of the Kelly operations, retreating to Brooklyn where he and Frankie Yale opened a large saloon called the Harvard Inn. This sawdust strewn saloon served as the headquarters of the Torrio-Yale gang which concentrated on Black Hand rackets, preying upon Italian immigrants in Brooklyn. Torrio also continued to expand his brothel operations so that by the end of 1908, he controlled two dozen brothels and realized about $5,000 a week in profits.

In 1909, Torrio received a letter from Chicago crime lord, James "Big Jim" Colosimo, asking him to come to the Windy City and become his right-hand man in charge of all brothel and gambling operations. Colosimo had married a Chicago brothel madam, Victoria Moresco, who was Torrio's aunt. The offer came at a propitious moment, in that Torrio's relationship with Kelly had soured and he was receiving considerable pressure from the police to kick back a larger share of the spoils from his Brooklyn whorehouse operations. Selling his share in the Harvard Inn to Frankie Yale, Torrio packed his bags and took the next train to Chicago. At the time, Chicago was a wide-open city, its red light district, the Levee, operating around the clock. This area and points north and west were controlled by aldermen James "Hinky Dink" Kenna and John "Bathhouse John" Coughlin, who were Colosimo's front men, political protectors, and partners in crime. Kenna and Coughlin had grown rich receiving payoffs and kickbacks from the myriad brothels and gambling halls operated by Colosimo.

Colosimo had also grown enormously rich but was being preyed upon by Black Handers who threatened to beat up his prostitutes and customers, as well as burn down his gambling dens and saloons unless they were given a large portion of Colosimo's weekly take. When Torrio arrived he was immediately given the chore of ridding Colosimo of these costly extortionists. Torrio first took over Colosimo's flagship brothel, the Saratoga, acting as a male madam. Next, he collected the best of Colosimo's gunmen and went after the Black Handers. Torrio arranged a meeting with three of the top extortionists, telling them that he would personally give them the first installment of the $50,000-a-week they were demanding. The boss Black Hander in Chicago at that time was James "Sunny Jim" Cosmano and it was Cosmano who had been behind the extortion of Colosimo. Cosmano sent his three top lieutenants to collect from Torrio at the appointed meeting which was to be held beneath the elevated train tracks near Grand Avenue.

Instead of delivering money, however, Torrio and his men pulled guns and shot the three Black Handers dead. Torrio then sent word to Cosmano that if Colosimo ever received another Black Hand demand from *anybody*, he, Torrio, would personally kill Cosmano. Cosmano quickly went into retirement. The triple killing performed by the New York gangster quickly established Torrio as a fierce, unyielding gangster, one who would protect Colosimo's rackets with bullets. Torrio's dark star rose over Chicago. Colosimo's crime empire embraced, for the most part, scores of brothels and gambling dens, and Torrio was made the manager of these nefarious enterprises. His job was to make sure that Colosimo bagmen collected the correct amount of money in kickbacks and percentages from each and every operation, including such prestigious brothels as the Everleigh Club, operated by the celebrated sisters, Ada and Minna Everleigh, who later retired to New York with millions.

By 1912, Torrio married Anna Jacobs, a Jewish woman, and leased an expensive apartment on Chicago's South Side. He also established his own headquarters at 2222 South Wabash, called The Four Deuces. This establishment was not far from Colosimo's Cafe, a famous nightclub and restaurant which drew celebrities from around the world. Colosimo, an opera lover, counted among his friends Enrico Caruso, the famous tenor, and other singing stars of the day.

Torrio's headquarters at the Four Deuces consisted of a cheap bar on the main floor and a bordello in the two floors above. The

Earliest known photo of Johnny Torrio, the heavyset young man at right, shown with Big Jim Colosimo, left, and Colosimo's father, center, in 1911.

Torrio in January 1925, shortly after his recovery from gunshot wounds following an attack on his life by North Side gangsters; the scarf around his neck hides an ugly bullet wound.

Anna Torrio, fear written on her face, only hours after her husband was shot and almost killed on Jan. 24, 1925.

Al Capone, Torrio's successor to a multimillion-dollar bootleg empire.

Torrio in 1956, a year before his death at age seventy-five.

George "Bugs" Moran, who came close to executing Torrio in 1925.

Torrio in 1936 when arrested for income tax evasion; he is flanked by federal agents who took him into custody in White Plains, N.Y.

gang leader had a small office in the rear of the bar from which he managed Colosimo's many rackets, as well as his legitimate operations. For several years, Torrio faced little or no opposition from rival gangsters as he expanded Colosimo's brothel and gambling operations north and south in the city. In late 1918, Torrio learned that one of his own bodyguards had been paid to kill him. He personally murdered this thug and then sent for one of his New York protégés, the hulking Al Capone, his erstwhile sneak-thief student. Capone arrived in Chicago in 1919 and received orders to protect Johnny Torrio at all times. He slavishly followed Torrio about, wearing two guns beneath his cheap suit coat.

Capone had been anxious to flee New York. When he received Torrio's offer, he was suspected of murdering one of Torrio's Brooklyn prostitutes after a dispute concerning the money she made, and was also about to be charged in the murder of a rival gangster. Although he began as a $35-a-week bouncer in the Four Deuces, within a year Capone had become Torrio's top enforcer and manager of the Colosimo brothel empire. He was a shrewd, street-smart thug, who instantly saw the possibilities of a million-dollar racket through bootlegging when the Volstead Act went into effect on Jan. 16, 1920. Prohibition offered enormous opportunities as Torrio also knew. But Big Jim Colosimo, who had grown fat and lazy with success, wanted nothing to do with this new racket. "Stick to the girls and the gambling," he told Torrio after his lieutenant urged him to throw his entire operation into bootlegging.

Torrio however realized that the smaller Chicago gangs would seize the Colosimo territory which encompassed much of the Loop and the South Side as their own bootlegging fiefdoms if he did not act promptly. On May 11, 1920, Colosimo was contacted by a liquor distributor who promised to deliver a truckload of bonded whiskey to his cafe so that he would have plenty of stock for his customers during Prohibition which Colosimo thought was only an "experiment" and would not last but a few months. With $10,000 in his pockets and wearing $50,000 in diamonds (on his cufflinks, rings, stickpin, and belt buckle), Colosimo went to his cafe which was not open for business. Only a few employees were about and none in the foyer where the crime boss waited for the liquor delivery.

Colosimo was looking out the small window of the front door when his killer crept up behind him. The killer placed a .38-caliber revolver to Colosimo's head, pulled the trigger and blew away part of his skull, instantly killing the crime lord, who crashed heavily to the floor. The killer, Capone by all reliable reports, then rifled Colosimo's pockets, took his money and stripped him of some of his diamonds before fleeing through the front door.

Following Colosimo's death, Torrio took over Colosimo's empire and Capone became his right-hand man. Torrio carved up the city, taking the South Side for himself, allocating the North Side to Charles Dion O'Bannion and his powerful gang. Many mobs worked under Torrio's command. Ragen's Colts and Ralph Sheldon's gang on the South Side distributed Torrio beer at $45 a barrel to saloons. This beer was made by federally closed breweries that operated clandestinely for Torrio, the largest of which was the Stenson Brewery. A series of breweries across the state line in northern Indiana also provided brew for Torrio distributors. By the end of 1922, Torrio and Capone had built up a network of hundreds of small breweries which produced beer at a cost of $5 a barrel.

Many satellite gangs received Torrio's beer and homemade liquor, including Claude Maddox of the Circus Gang, the Marty Guifoyle gang and the Druggan-Lake mob known as the Valley Gang. But several truculent Chicago gangsters bristled at being told by Torrio in which territories they could operate. The first gang to rise against Torrio was the South Side O'Donnell mob led by Edward "Spike" O'Donnell. From 1923 to 1925, Torrio's gunmen, directed by Capone, battled the O'Donnells. Capone killers Frank "Sunny" Dunn; Walter Stevens, assisted by Frank McErlane of the Saltis-McErlane Gang; Jack "Machine Gun Jack" McGurn; Sam "Golf Bag" Hunt, who carried a shotgun in a golf bag; and William "Three-Fingered Jack" White blasted the O'Donnell gang to pieces, killing a dozen of their number before Spike O'Donnell quit the rackets.

Trouble was also stirring in Torrio's own ranks, or, at least, in the ranks of gangs who had sworn loyalty to him, particularly the unruly Genna Brothers, who controlled the near West Side and Little Italy. In the heart of this unpoliced area, the Gennas, six brothers whose lethal guns spat out death at the slightest provocation, reigned supreme. The Gennas, Sicilian to the core, controlled the Unione Siciliane, a brotherhood linked to the rackets in the U.S. The Gennas also operated thousands of stills which produced a raw, rotgut alcohol that passed for liquor of all kinds, from whiskey to gin. None of it was comparable to bonded whiskey produced by legitimate distilleries, but the demand for liquor was so intense that whatever the Gennas produced, Torrio's distributors had no trouble selling to thousands of saloons and thirsty customers.

The Gennas constantly demanded additional territory for their own bootlegging racket, particularly the lucrative North Side, but Torrio knew that to grant this expansion into O'Bannion's territory would mean total gang warfare. Also, the West Side O'Donnell Brothers gang, unrelated to the South Side O'Donnells, informed Torrio that their territory was too confining, and they, too, demanded more space in which to peddle their booze. The worst of Torrio's problems came from the North Side and the unpredictable O'Bannion.

Although O'Bannion, who controlled several north side breweries, had a better supply of beer than any bootlegger in Chicago, his men regularly hijacked bonded Canadian whiskey being shipped to Torrio from the Purple Gang in Detroit. In 1923, O'Bannion expanded his bootlegging operations into Cicero, a western suburb which Torrio and Capone had already selected as their new headquarters during the reign of reform mayor, William E. Dever. To assure an easy takeover of Cicero, Sheriff Peter Hoffman of Cook County, who was on Torrio's payroll, unleashed massive raids against the local gang operations in Cicero, gathering up hundreds of slot machines and closing down brothels and bookie parlors. The local gangs submitted to Torrio's rule immediately.

Meanwhile, Capone consistently urged Torrio to eliminate the pesky North Siders, especially O'Bannion and his top lieutenants, George "Bugs" Moran, Early "Hymie" Weiss, and Vincent "The Schemer" Drucci. Torrio, however, prided himself on his diplomatic skills and, instead of instituting gang warfare, called meeting after meeting with O'Bannion and his men. At these meetings, the wily O'Bannion always promised to abide by earlier agreements in which he and his gang would remain within the provinces assigned to them. But after each of these conferences, O'Bannion would sneer at Torrio's edicts and order his men to continue encroaching upon Torrio-Capone territories.

O'Bannion challenged the Genna Brothers, labeling them "spaghetti benders." Angelo Genna went to Torrio and begged him to allow the Gennas to murder O'Bannion. Torrio told him to wait. O'Bannion then insulted Capone, calling him a "dago pimp" and had several of Capone's top gunmen killed. Capone insisted that O'Bannion be murdered, but Torrio said no, for that would lead to a bloody war. In May 1924, O'Bannion came to Torrio with a proposition. He, Torrio, and Capone had joint ownership in a huge gambling resort called The Ship. O'Bannion wanted to sell his interest in the operation to Torrio. Moreover, he offered to sell Torrio his ownership of the finest brewery on the North Side, Sieben's Mid-City Brewery.

"I'm gonna retire, Johnny," O'Bannion told Torrio. "The rackets are wearing me out. The Gennas are invading my territory and the bodies are piling up. I'm gonna buy some nice ranch land near Louis Alterie's spread in Colorado and live out a life of ease. No more guns, no more street fights. I want to unload The Ship and Sieben's."

The ever distrustful Capone snorted: "Just like that?"

"Yeah, Al," O'Bannion said, smiling and snapping his fingers. "Just like that."

Despite Capone's insistence that O'Bannion could not be trusted, Torrio agreed to the deal, reportedly delivering $500,000 in cash to the Irish gang leader a few days later. On May 19, 1924, Torrio arrived at Sieben's to inspect his new property. O'Bannion and his most devoted follower, Earl "Hymie" Weiss, were there to greet him and showed him through the sprawling brewery. Suddenly, they heard two loud buzzing noises.

"What's that?" Torrio asked.

O'Bannion turned to Weiss with a smile on his face. "How many you count, Hymie?"

"Two." Weiss had a wide grin on his long face.

"My count's the same." O'Bannion turned to Torrio and said with a wide smile: "You know something, J.T. When you have two, that's the cops."

In a second Torrio knew that he had been set up by O'Bannion. He reached for a telephone and then said to the party at the other end: "Mid-City. A pinch."

Within a few minutes the place was swarming with gun-poking policemen. The raid was personally led by Morgan A. Collins, Mayor Dever's new chief of police. O'Bannion, Weiss, and Torrio were promptly arrested and taken to police headquarters. This was the first time O'Bannion and Weiss had been arrested for violating the Volstead Act, which meant a fine. Torrio, however, had been arrested in June 1923 for violating the Prohibition law, and a second arrest, as O'Bannion well knew, meant a prison term for Torrio.

A bond of $7,500 was set for each man. Ike Roderick appeared to post bond for Torrio, but the South Side mob boss refused to provide bond for O'Bannion and Weiss. He stormed out of the holding cell, listening to O'Bannion and Weiss laugh at his departure. The North Siders were bailed out a short time later by their own bondsman, William Skidmore.

Torrio seethed at being set up. Then Capone repeated a remark to Torrio supposedly passed by the gloating O'Bannion upon his release: "I clipped the pimp for $500,000 and then dumped him in the can." Torrio decided to act. He enlisted the aid of the Gennas, who provided two men O'Bannion did not know, Albert Anselmi and John Scalise, professional killers who dipped their bullets in garlic, mistakenly believing that if the wounds they inflicted were not fatal the garlic would infect the victim and cause death. A third man, Frankie Yale, Torrio's old Brooklyn partner, was brought from New York, and the three visited O'Bannion's North State Street flower shop on Nov. 10, 1924.

Mike Merlo, president of the Unione Siciliane, had recently died of natural causes and his funeral was to be a big event. All the Italian mobs ordered their floral wreaths from O'Bannion, including Torrio and Capone. Yale called O'Bannion a few hours before his visit to the shop to see when Torrio's wreath would be ready. O'Bannion told him at noon. Shortly before that time Yale, Anselmi, and Scalise arrived at the shop, and while Yale held O'Bannion's hand in a vise-like grip, Anselmi and Scalise shot the Irish gang leader to death. O'Bannion never got the chance to reach for one of the three guns he was carrying under his linen duster at the time. This attack was known as the "Handshake Murder." The killers fled and were never brought to justice, although their identities were well known.

Torrio had had his revenge but at a cost he knew in advance he would have to pay. The O'Bannion killing touched off the bloodiest gang war in Chicago history. A short time later Torrio received a $2,500 fine and a nine-month prison sentence as a result of the Mid-Century raid. While his lawyers appealed, Torrio began to collect his bootleg millions, depositing enormous amounts of money in New York and European banks. On Jan. 24, 1925, after returning from a Loop shopping trip, Torrio and his wife Anna got out of their chauffeur-driven limousine in front of their South Shore apartment building. Torrio, loaded with packages, was following his wife into the building when a black Cadillac with four men inside pulled to the curb across the street.

Moran and Weiss, armed with automatics, leaped from the car and ran across the street firing at Torrio. One bullet struck him in the chest, another in the neck. He fell to the pavement as his chauffeur, Robert Barton, pulled a gun and fired at the attackers. The other two men in the Cadillac, Drucci and Frank Gusenberg, began to fire at Barton with shotguns. Barton was struck in the leg with a load of buckshot and slipped down on the seat of the limousine.

George "Bugs" Moran stood over the fallen Torrio. He leaned close to the gang leader, placing his automatic next to Torrio's head and said: "This is for Deanie O'Bannion, you dago bastard!" He pulled the trigger and nothing happened. The automatic was empty. Frantically, Moran started to load another clip into the weapon but Drucci, behind the wheel of the Cadillac began to beep the horn wildly, the signal that police were arriving. Cursing his luck, Moran, accompanied by Weiss, ran back to the Cadillac, and jumped inside. The car roared away.

Torrio began crawling toward the entrance to the apartment house, leaving a long trail of blood behind him. His wife ran from the building, hysterically calling for help as she dragged her wounded husband inside the building's foyer. A police ambulance arrived a short time later and rushed the little gangster to Jackson Park Hospital. En route, Torrio, believing his attackers had dipped their bullets in garlic as did his own killers, screamed to hospital attendants: "Cauterize it! Cauterize it!"

After a lengthy operation, Torrio miraculously survived, although the bullet wound in his neck left a permanent scar. Torrio met the press some days later, a scarf drawn around his neck. "Sure, I know all four men," he told newspaper reporters. "I'll never tell their names."

On Feb. 9, 1925, Torrio stood before federal Judge Adam Cliffe and was officially sentenced to serve nine months in the Waukegan County Jail, a site requested by Torrio's lawyers, who explained that Torrio's wounds would require a jail where he could receive proper medical attention. The real reason for requesting the Waukegan jail was that the warden was friendly to Torrio's organization and that Capone's gunman would be better able to protect the boss.

The warden of Waukegan Jail, Sheriff Edwin Ahlstrom, fitted the windows of Torrio's cell with bullet-proof plating. Extra deputies guarded the cell and the corridors day and night. Stuffed chairs, throw rugs, and a large bed were placed in the largest cell in the jail. Torrio spent his nine months in considerable comfort, dining on catered meals in his cell and on home cooking from the Sheriff's home outside the jail. He spent long hours sitting on Ahlstrom's front porch.

Torrio had much to think of during this period. He could look back to his days in New York and how he had survived gang wars as a member of the James Street Gang and the Five Points Gang. He had survived the early gang wars of Chicago and even his execution at the hands of Moran and Weiss. Through his organizational abilities he had established the largest and most lucrative bootlegging empire in the U.S., accumulating a personal fortune estimated to be $75 million. Torrio, always practical, came to the realization that the North Siders had marked him for death. They would stop at nothing now to avenge their fallen leader, O'Bannion. Torrio had no stomach for such gang vendettas. He called Capone, who arrived in Waukegan with lawyers the next day.

The gang overlord startled his 25-year-old protégé by telling him that he was quitting the rackets and turning over everything—the gambling dens, the hundreds of brothels and saloons, the bootlegging enterprises, the dozens of legitimate businesses he had insisted upon buying as fronts for the mob and sources of considerable revenues—to Capone. "I'm through," he told Capone. "It's all yours, Al. I'm going back to Italy...if I can get out of this city alive."

"I'll see to that," promised Capone, jubilant that he was now the supreme gang lord in Chicago and inheritor of a $100 million-a-year crime empire. Only the brutal Capone would embrace this opportunity that went hand-in-hand with a five-year bloodbath that claimed the lives of 1,000 gangsters and innocent people. He not only inherited Torrio's crime kingdom but all the liabilities that attended it.

Upon release from jail, Torrio and his wife were escorted to safety by Capone in his armor-plated limousine, which took the retired gang lord to an Indiana train station and an eastbound train. A caravan of cars jammed with armed men accompanied the Torrios and Capone. Two dozen additional Capone gangsters patrolled the Gary, Ind., depot, marching up and down on the platform with submachine guns cradled in their arms as the Torrios waited for their train. When the Twentieth Century Ltd. pulled into the station, Capone escorted Torrio and his wife to their stateroom, placing his best bodyguards in compartments on either side. "Nobody bothers the boss," Capone told his men. Then he turned to Torrio and embraced him, saying: "So long, Johnny Papa. You come back when you feel better."

"Me?" replied Torrio. "I'll *never* be back here again!" Torrio kept his word. Though little evidence supports the claim, some reports allege that the attack on Torrio by the North Side gangsters was arranged by Al Capone to rid himself of his boss, in the same manner as Torrio rid himself of Big Jim Colosimo. Torrio's movements in Chicago were always shrouded in secrecy, and on the day he was gunned down on the street, only Al Capone knew that Torrio would be taking a shopping trip into the Loop and when he would be returning home, details that Capone reportedly passed along through a third party to Weiss and Moran. Torrio's subsequent behavior in turning over a fabulously lucrative crime empire to the youthful Capone could only mean that he at least suspected his protégé of arranging for his execution and to remain in Chicago would invite certain death at the hands of his ostensibly loyal lieutenant.

When arriving in New York, the Torrios immediately took a train to Florida, but Weiss' gunmen trailed them and they booked passage to Italy, sailing to Naples, where they rented a luxurious villa and lived for three years. Bored, Torrio longed for the U.S. and something to do. He and his wife sailed for New York, where they moved into a luxury apartment. The self-exiled gang leader made the city his permanent home.

Torrio had another reason for leaving Italy in 1928. The country's dictator, Benito Mussolini, who had been waging war with the Mafia in Sicily, had publicly threatened Italian-American gangsters who had returned to Italy, either to avoid prosecution for crimes in the U.S. or to establish new rackets in Italy. Mussolini had boldly stated that he intended to sweep Italy clean of such "vermin," and after his state police had collected all of these U.S. gangsters, he would have them placed in cages and paraded through the streets of Rome. This policy, more than anything else, caused Torrio to depart his native land and return to the U.S.

In New York, Torrio spent large amounts of money buying real estate, apartment and office buildings. He also formed a partnership with Charles "Lucky" Luciano, Abner "Longy" Zwillman, and Meyer Lansky establishing a liquor distribution system that stretched from New York to Florida. Torrio supervised warehousing of all liquor and maintenance of inventory. He saw that shipments were made on time, proper records were kept, and that all the bills were paid. This proved to be a multi-million dollar business that later served as a front.

Moreover, Torrio was accorded great respect by the eastern gangsters who formed the national crime cartel in the early 1930s, acting as an adviser to the board members of the crime syndicate begun by Luciano, Lansky, Joe Adonis, Frank Costello, Louis Buchalter, and others. Torrio prospered in the real estate business and when Repeal went into effect, his liquor distribution operations became even more successful. The authorities had not overlooked Johnny Torrio. On Apr. 22, 1936, he was arrested for income tax evasion. His bail was set at $100,000. Anna Torrio appeared hours later, and to the amazement of federal officials, delivered the bail in crisp $1,000 bills that were wrapped in a newspaper. Following a lengthy trial, conviction, and many appeals, Torrio finally paid $86,000 in back taxes and received a two-and-a-half year sentence, that he began serving in 1939 in the Leavenworth federal penitentiary.

Paroled on Apr. 14, 1941, Torrio went into semi-retirement. He busied his days with long walks and he and his wife, childless, spent their time in their apartment, occasionally dining out. The former gang lord read newspapers and books most of the day and was seldom seen with other gangsters. Though gang wars in New York raged about him, Johnny Torrio remained aloof and remote. On Apr. 16, 1957, Torrio entered a New York barbershop, as he had each day for years. A hot towel was placed about his bullet-scarred neck. He suddenly twitched in the chair and moaned, then slipped downward, the victim of a heart attack. He died six hours later in Cumberland Hospital, his wife at his side.

Thus passed the U.S.'s first modern gang lord and one of the architects of the national crime syndicate. His funeral, unlike many of his friends' and enemies' in Chicago, was unspectacular. Only a dozen or so people attended his funeral in Greenwood Cemetery. Even in death, Torrio's credo of silence was observed. His widow made no public announcement of Torrio's passing, and the press did not discover his death until three weeks after his burial. His death did not create headlines, even in the Chicago papers where one veteran newsman wrote of him: "He could dish it out but he couldn't take it." See: **Adonis, Joe; Anselmi, Albert; Black Hand; Buchalter, Louis; Capone, Alphonse; Circus Gang; Colosimo, James; Costello, Frank; Coughlin, John; Drucci, Vincent; Druggan-Lake Gang; Eastman, Edward; Everleigh Sisters; Five Points Gang; Genna Brothers; Kelly, Paul; Kenna, Michael; Luciano, Charles; McErlane, Frank; McGurn, Jack; Maddox, Claude; Moran, George; O'Bannion, Charles Dion; O'Donnell Brothers; Purple Gang; Stevens, Walter; Tammany Hall; Unione Siciliane; Weiss, Earl; Yale, Frank; Zwillman, Abner.**

REF.: Alsopp, *The Bootleggers;* Asbury, *Gem of the Prairie;* ____, *The Gangs of New York;* Bennett, *Chicago Gangland;* Berger, *The 8 Million;* Bonanno, *A Man of Honor;* Bullough, *The History of Prostitution;* Burns, *The One-Way Ride; CBA;* Chafetz, *Play the Devil;* Cook, *Secret Rulers;* ____, *A Two-Dollar Bet Means Murder;* Cooper, *Ten Thousand Public Enemies;* Crane, *Sins of New York;* Cressey, *Theft of the Nation;* Danforth and Horan, *The D.A.'s Man;* Dedmon, *Fabulous Chicago;* Demaris, *Captive City;* Eisenberg and Landau, *Meyer Lansky;* Feder and Joestein, *The Luciano Story;* Fried, *The Rise and Fall of the Jewish Gangster in America;* Gosch and Hammer, *The Last Testament of Lucky Luciano;* Harrison, *Stormy Years;* Hibbert, *The Roots of Evil;* Irey, *The Tax Dodgers;* Johnson, *Carter Henry Harrison;* Katz, *Uncle Frank;* Kobler, *Al Capone;* Lait and Mortimer, *Chicago: Confidential;* Landesco, *Organized Crime in Chicago;* Levine, *Anatomy of a Gangster;* Lewis and Smith, *Chicago: The History of Its Reputation;* Lundberg, *Imperial Hearst;* Lyle, *The Dry and Lawless Years;* Lynch, *Criminals and Politicians;* McPhaul, *Johnny Torrio;* Messick, *Lansky;* ____, *Secret File;* ____ and Goldblatt, *The Mobs and the Mafia;* Mezzrow and Wolfe, *Really the Blues;* Morgan, *Prince of Crime;* Murray, *The Legacy of Al Capone;* Nash, *Bloodletters and Badmen;* ____, *Citizen Hoover;* ____, *People to See;* Pasley, *Al Capone;* ____, *Muscling In;* Peterson, *The Mob;* Pileggi, *Wiseguy;* Prall and Mockridge, *This is Costello;* Reid, *The Grim Reapers;* Reppetto, *The Blue Parade;* Sann, *Kill the Dutchman;* Servadio, *Mafioso;* Sinclair, *Era of Excess;* Smith, *Syndicate City;* Spiering, *The Man Who Got Capone;* Starr, *The Purveyor;* Stead, *If Christ Came to Chicago;* Sullivan, *Chicago Surrenders;* ____, *Rattling the Cup on Chicago Crime;* Thompson, *Gang Rule in New York;* Washburn, *Come Into My Parlor;* Wendt and Kogan, *Big Bill;* ____, *Lords of the Levee;* Whitehead, *The FBI Story;* (FILM), *Scarface*, 1932; *Al Capone*, 1959; *Capone*, 1975.

Torsney, Robert, prom. 1976, Case of, U.S., mur. In Brooklyn on Thanksgiving Day 1976, police officer Robert Torsney shot and killed an unarmed black youth without provocation and then walked away. Torsney was tried for the murder and found Not Guilty by reason of insanity. His mental condition at the time of the murder was attributed to a form of epilepsy. After his acquittal, Torsney became the charge of the Mental Hygiene De-

partment which soon found that he was not sick and petitioned for his release. At first a judge agreed, but the initial decision to release Torsney was overturned by an appellate court. Torsney remained hospitalized until midsummer 1979, tended to by doctors who would not treat him because they believed him to be healthy.
REF.: *CBA;* Lubin, *Good Guys, Bad Guys.*

Toth, Andrew, b.1849, and **Rusnok, George**, prom. 1890, and **Sabol, Michael**, prom. 1890, U.S., (wrong. convict.) mur. The murder on New Year's Day 1890 of Michael Quinn, a furnace boss at the Edgar Thompson Steel Works in Braddock, Pa., provided some insight into the lives of many immigrants who worked in the steel mills. Quinn, along with four hundred men, had decided to work on New Year's Day. A group of immigrant Hungarian workers, angry over low wages, poor working conditions, and seven-day work weeks, and fueled with alcohol consumed in celebration of the new year, became indignant with the workers who had willingly sacrificed their holiday. The two hundred Hungarians, armed with clubs, ax handles, and shovels, assaulted the men at work. Many were badly beaten before the workers drove the Hungarians back. Quinn was among the badly injured and died five days after the attack.

Fifty-four men were arrested within several days of the attacks. Although it was unclear who had killed Quinn, police charged three of the Hungarians, Andrew Toth, Michael Sabol, and George Rusnok, with the crime on Feb. 4, 1891. A jury returned a verdict of first-degree murder against all three defendants and sentenced them to death by hanging. The Supreme Court of Pennsylvania reviewed the case and on June 5, 1891, affirmed the judgment of the trial court.

In contrast to pre-trial public sentiment, which ran strongly against the Hungarians, a movement with influential advocates such as Andrew Carnegie and Charles M. Schwab began to form. Arguing that the Hungarians, with their slight knowledge of English, had not received as impartial a trial as three Americans would have received, they requested that the governor commute the three men's sentences to life imprisonment. The request was granted on Feb. 25, 1892. By September 1897, Sabol and Rusnok had been pardoned. Because there had been direct testimony against Toth, the governor refused to grant him any further clemency. A second application for a pardon, filed in 1902 by Toth's son, was refused. In 1911, a rumored deathbed confession to the murder by a man named Steve Toth rekindled the fight to gain freedom for Andrew Toth. A review of the evidence revealed that it was highly unlikely that Andrew Toth had been Michael Quinn's attacker. Toth received a full pardon on Mar. 17, 1911. He was immediately released from prison after having served nearly twenty years. When a petition to the state requesting financial compensation for Toth was turned down, Andrew Carnegie, Toth's employer in the steel mills, arranged for Toth to receive $40 a month for the rest of his life.
REF.: *CBA;* Cohen, *One Hundred True Crime Stories.*

Toth, Robert W., 1932- , U.S., Case of, mur. In September 1952, while stationed at an Air Force bomb dump in Taegu, South Korea, sergeant of the guard Robert Toth was involved in the death of a Korean civilian, Bang Soon Kil. Kil, apparently drunk, had wandered into a restricted area. He did not stop when called to by Airman Thomas L. Kinder, the guard on duty. Kinder tried to get an attack dog to stop Kil, but the dog wouldn't attack. Kinder then fired two shots, waking Toth, who joined him in his efforts to stop Kil. The two soldiers soon caught Bang Soon Kil and put him in a jeep. According to Toth, Kil then tried to take his pistol, and Toth hit Kil. When they arrived at the office of the guard, Toth told the officer in charge what had happened. The officer, Lieutenant George Schreiber, told the men to take Kil out and shoot him. Toth claimed that he wanted nothing to do with the killing, so he left. The man who killed Kil was Kinder, who took Kil to a secluded place and shot him to death.

Toth was given an honorable discharge from the army in March 1953. He returned to the States and began work at the Jones and Laughlin steel mill in Pittsburgh. In May, air police arrested him for his part in the slaying and returned him to Taegu, where he was held for a trial by court-martial on a charge of murder. In August 1953, an Air Force court-martial in Korea sentenced Schreiber to life imprisonment. At the same time, Kinder's sentence was reduced to two years. There was no question about Schreiber's or Kinder's trials or sentences as both were still in the military, Toth, however, as a civilian, presented a different case. Although still under a murder charge and still in Air Force custody, Toth was allowed to return to the U.S. in August 1953.

Toth's case, which was not resolved until November 1955, highlighted the issue of the constitutionality of Article 3a of the 1950 Uniform Code of Military Justice, which stated that former servicemen who committed major crimes while in military service should face a trial by courts-martial regardless of their military status. The legal dilemma the Toth case clarified was that if Article 3a was found unconstitutional, Toth would probably never stand trial, since the case was clearly outside the jurisdiction of any civil court. On the other hand, if the article were upheld it would mean that anyone who had become a veteran since the act became effective (over 3 million in 1955) could be held for court-martial even years after his or her discharge. In November 1955, in a 6-to-3 decision, the Supreme Court found Article 3a unconstitutional. REF.: *CBA.*

To the Gallows I Must Go, 1931, a novel by T.S. Matthews. The notorious Snyder-Gray murder case (U.S., 1927), serves as the basis of this arresting work of fiction. See: **Snyder, Ruth May Brown**. REF.: *CBA.*

Totterman, Emil, b.c.1875, U.S., mur. Born in Finland and decorated for heroism at the Battle of Santiago during the Spanish-American War, Emil Totterman was convicted of the December 1903 murder of Sarah Martin and spent the next twenty-five years in prison. There was some doubt that Totterman, a sailor at the time, committed the slashing murder, but he was convicted and sentenced to the electric chair on Mar. 2, 1904, because his luggage was found in the dead woman's room. His death sentence was commuted to life imprisonment on July 25, 1905.

Except for an escape from a work farm on Aug. 20, 1916, Totterman was a model prisoner. In his years at Sing Sing, he enthusiastically involved himself in the mechanical trades and iron-working, and was designated the official steeplejack, painting the high chimney whenever needed and placing the flag on a high pole on holidays. On Dec. 24, 1929, Totterman received a Christmas pardon from Governor Franklin Roosevelt. Through the cooperation of the Finnish consulate, he was able to relocate and reestablish himself in his native land. REF.: *CBA.*

Toto, Fran, 1945- , U.S., attempt. mur. Fran Toto, a native of Brooklyn, married her childhood sweetheart, Tony Toto. Things went smoothly enough until Tony began working from twelve to sixteen hours a day and going out with other women—sometimes calling them in the presence of his wife.

That Toto was having serious trouble with his family was attested to by the seven attempts made on his life by various family members or people acting on their behalf. The final series of attempts began in August 1982 when 14-year-old John Kotch, a friend of one of Toto's sons, waited for him in the bushes outside the Toto residence in Allentown, Pa., with a baseball bat. When Toto came out, the boy got the bat tangled in the bushes, panicked, and ran. Two months later, Toto's daughter's boyfriend, Donald Erney, ran a wire from the distributor of Toto's car to the gas tank, intending for the car to blow up with Toto in it. Nothing happened. Then, in January 1983, when Tony stayed home sick from work, 21-year-old Anthony Bruno, Toto's daughter Elizabeth's new boyfriend, entered the bedroom and shot Tony in the head. The bullet lodged in Toto's skull, only stunning him. Bruno was too upset to try again but recommended two cousins, Donald and Ronald Barlip to finish the job. Two days later, the Barlips showed up to shoot Toto in the heart—for a purported fee of $500 from Fran. The bullet missed by an inch. Fran, Elizabeth, and the Barlips were sitting around talking about how to dispose of the body when Toto managed to get out of bed and walk to the doorway, all the while dripping blood, to ask what was going on. At this point Fran allegedly fed her husband chicken soup laced with barbiturates to finish him off, but the barbiturates only retarded the bleeding. Police came to the Toto home two days later and found Toto semiconscious.

Fran was arrested and charged with solicitation to commit murder. She pleaded guilty and was sent to prison. In the meantime, Toto made a recovery that his doctors termed miraculous. While he was recovering, he thought about the error of his ways and came to believe that perhaps he deserved what Fran had tried to give him. He made a vow to be a model husband and posted bail for Fran. Fran served four years of her sentence and was released from prison in February 1989. REF.: *CBA*.

Toucey, Isaac, 1796-1869, U.S., atty. gen. Practiced law in Hartford, Conn., from 1818, and later served as Hartford County state attorney from 1822-35. A Democrat, he was also elected twice to the U.S. House of Representatives, where he held office from 1835-39, but lost his third congressional campaign. He again served as state attorney, from 1842-44, and was governor of Connecticut from 1846-47. In 1848 he was sworn in as U.S. attorney general under President James Polk, and held that post until 1849. He was the acting U.S. secretary of state from 1849-50, and entered the Connecticut senate in 1850. In 1852 he served briefly in the Connecticut state House of Representatives, but resigned to take a seat in the U.S. Senate, where he served from 1852-57. He also served as U.S. secretary of the navy under President James Buchanan from 1857-61. REF.: *CBA*.

Touhy, Roger (AKA: **The Terrible**), 1898-1959, U.S., org. crime. Roger Touhy was a prominent bootlegger who operated with a small gang in the northern suburbs of Chicago during the 1920s. Born in Chicago, the son of a policeman, Touhy's large family (two sisters and five brothers) moved from Chicago to the suburb of Downer's Grove, Ill., in 1908 after a kitchen stove blew up and killed his mother. Touhy's childhood was normal and crime free. He attended St. Joseph's Grade School in Downer's Grove and graduated in 1911. Touhy was an altar boy in the local Catholic church and went to work as a Western Union messenger in his early teens. He later became a telegraph operator and manager of a small Western Union office, a job he kept until 1915 when he was fired for union activities.

Moving to Colorado, Touhy continued to be a telegraph operator, working for the Denver & Rio Grande Railroad. During WWI, Touhy enlisted in the Navy and in 1918 taught morse code to Navy officers at Harvard. When mustered out of service, Touhy sought adventure by traveling to the boom towns of Oklahoma where he worked as an oil rigger and engineer. He bought and sold oil leases and built up a nest egg of $25,000 before returning to Chicago in 1922.

Following his marriage, Touhy purchased several trucks and began a trucking firm with his brother Tommy. By 1926, Touhy, Tommy, and their brother Eddie began distributing illegal beer and liquor, controlling most of Chicago's northwestern suburbs. Touhy hired a top chemist to establish a brewery. He and his partner, Matt Kolb, produced what was considered the best Prohibition beer in the Midwest at a cost of $4.50 a barrel, which they sold for $55 a barrel. Touhy paid off police in Des Plaines and other suburbs with barrels of beer or cases of bottled beer (he had his own bottling plant at the time).

In late 1926 Touhy and Kolb began installing slot machines in suburban saloons until hundreds of these one-armed bandits were producing thousands of dollars each week. So famous was Touhy's ybeer that Al Capone began ordering hundreds of barrels from him. One order brought a Capone payment of $30,000. At the time Touhy's headquarters were located in The Arch, a road house in Schiller Park. Capone, coveting the northern territories controlled by Touhy, sent two representatives, Frank Rio and Willie Heeney, to negotiate a Capone takeover of this area.

Touhy had no real gang at the time. He was a middle-class brewer who had a long list of saloon clients. He met with Heeney and Rio while a parade of farmers and off-duty policemen, all friends of Touhy's, marched through Touhy's offices brandishing submachine guns and shotguns, play-acting as gangsters. The show of force unnerved Capone's men who reported back to Scarface that the "Touhy mob is tough and big. He must have a hundred guys up there, all killers. Touhy spent most of the time on the phone giving orders to have guys bumped off."

The phone conversations were also part of Touhy's play-acting. Aside from a few truck drivers, Touhy had no gang at all. Yet Capone believed he was up against a powerful organization and he continued to play a cat-and-mouse routine with Touhy, sending more and more emissaries to see Touhy but getting no results. Touhy rebuffed all attempts by Capone to install whorehouses and gambling dens in the northern suburbs. At one point Touhy told Capone gunmen that he had "two hundred guys out here from every penitentiary in the United States and from Canada." He then invited the gunmen to attend a party the following Saturday night, asking they bring Capone along. "Most of my guys will be here," Touhy said.

On Saturday night Touhy closed The Arch down. Several squads of police arrived to raid the place only to find it locked up. As he suspected, Capone had contacted his stooge, Cook County sheriff Peter Hoffman, ordering him to raid the Touhy headquarters and arrest his entire gang, thus putting his competitor out of business. There was, however, no one to arrest. Capone, nevertheless continued to send representatives to Touhy. Two of these included Murray "The Camel" Humphreys and James "Red" Fawcett. When Humphreys got tough with Touhy, the bootlegger went to a wall rack containing several submachine guns and began fingering one of these weapons. Humphreys panicked, thinking he was about to be killed. He offered Touhy his new $16,000 roadster, saying: "If you drive me back inside the Chicago city limits, I'll give you the car. I want to get home alive."

"Go on back to Chicago, both of you," Touhy told them. "You won't get hurt."

Both men left hurriedly. A few minutes later, Fawcett returned and told Touhy that the cowardly Humphreys disgusted him. "Listen, Touhy," Fawcett said. "For five grand I'll kill that s.o.b. Humphreys on the way back to the city, and for another five thousand I'll go to Cicero and knock off Frank Nitti (Capone's top enforcer). What do you say?"

Touhy declined the offer. The frustrated Capone, angered at having to pay Touhy $37.50 a barrel for beer had Touhy's partner Matt Kolb kidnapped and ransomed for $50,000. Capone called Touhy to tell him that he had learned of Kolb's kidnapping and that he would act as a go-between to bring about Kolb's release. Touhy personally delivered the $50,000 to Capone, boldly marching through an army of bodyguards stationed in Capone's Chicago headquarters in the Metropole Hotel. He threw the money onto Capone's desk and demanded to know where Kolb was. Capone nervously counted the money and replied: "Now, Rog. I want you to know that I had nothing to do with this. I like Matt. I'm trying to help him." Within the hour Kolb was released from a Capone hideout a few blocks away. Capone went on buying beer from Touhy but resented having to pay a premium price. In 1931 his gangsters once more kidnapped Matt Kolb but asked for no ransom. They merely shot Kolb to death and dumped his body in a ditch.

In 1933, Touhy, who had now been dubbed by the press: Roger "The Terrible" Touhy, stemming from the horror stories told about him by Capone men, was arrested by Melvin Purvis of the FBI and wrongly charged with kidnapping millionaire St. Paul brewer William A. Hamm, a crime that actually had been committed by the Barker Brothers. Touhy and three others were found Not Guilty. Shortly thereafter they were charged with kidnapping Jake "The Barber" Factor, a known Capone associate. Factor set himself up for a kidnapping which was really performed by Capone gunmen so that Touhy would be wrongly convicted and sent to prison, thus allowing Capone to take over the northern suburbs.

Touhy and three others were convicted with testimony that was

Roger Touhy, bootlegger, on trial for kidnapping Jake Factor.

Jake Factor, protected by bodyguards to bolster fake kidnapping.

Touhy, second from right, and gang, at trial for kidnapping, 1934.

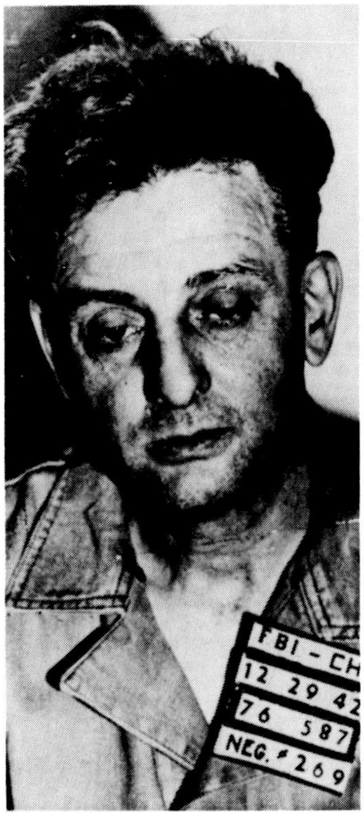

Touhy after recapture, 1942.

Touhy in prison, 1958.

Roger Touhy, paroled, 1959.

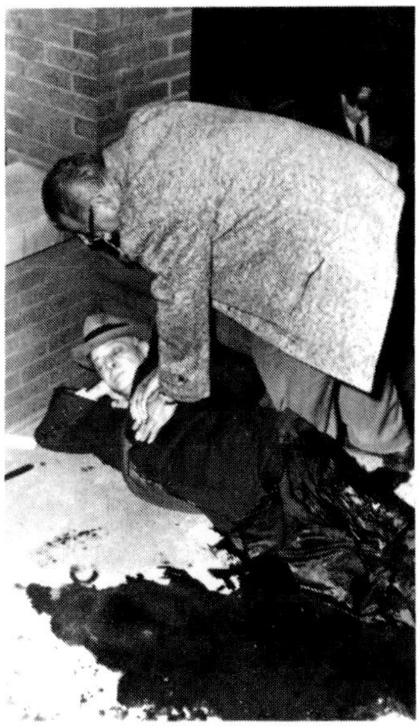

Touhy dying, killed by Capone men.

later determined to be perjured. He was sent to Joliet Prison to serve 199 years. For almost a decade Touhy tried to prove his innocence in the Factor kidnapping, spending his bootleg fortune on expensive lawyers. He was a model prisoner but after some time he believed he would never be released. A short time later he agreed to join a prison break which included six other veteran convicts: Basil "The Owl" Banghart, Eugene O'Connor, Edward Darlak, Martlick Nelson, Edward Stewart, and St. Clair McInerney.

On Oct. 9, 1942, Touhy and the other six men escaped Joliet. Using a makeshift rope ladder, the seven men scaled a wall to a guard's tower and then slipped over it to freedom. Touhy and the others became Public Enemies on the FBI's Most Wanted List. Bureau agents cornered the escaped convicts in a Chicago boarding house in December 1942. McInerney and O'Connor chose to shoot it out with agents and were killed in a wild gun battle. Touhy and the others were returned to Stateville.

Touhy persisted in attempting to prove his innocence in the Factor kidnapping, and his lawyers successfully argued his case before federal Judge John P. Barnes, who declared the Factor kidnapping "a hoax." The wrongly convicted Touhy was released from prison on Nov. 25, 1959. By then he was broke and in ill health. He returned to Chicago to live with a sister. As he was entering his sister's home on the night of Dec. 17, 1959, Touhy was met with several shotgun blasts which almost tore his body in half.

While being rushed to a hospital, Touhy told newsmen riding in the ambulance: "I've been expecting it. The bastards never forget!" According to best reports, Touhy's execution had been ordered by his old enemy, Murray "The Camel" Humphreys. Humphreys had never forgiven Touhy for frightening him half to death in 1931, and for the demeaning remarks Touhy had made about him in his book, *The Stolen Years*, published only a short time before Roger "The Terrible" Touhy was released from prison. See: **Banghart, Basil; Capone, Alphonse; Humphreys, Murray; Nitti, Frank.**

REF.: *CBA;* Demaris, *Captive City;* Gribble, *Clue That Spelled Guilty;* Halper, *The Chicago Crime Book;* McPhaul, *Johnny Torrio;* Messick, *Kidnapping;* Moorehead, *Hostages to Fortune;* Morgan, *Prince of Crime;* Nash, *Bloodletters and Badmen;* ____, *Citizen Hoover;* Nicholls, *Crime Within the Square Mile;* Powers, *Secrecy and Power;* (FILM), *Roger Touhy, Gangster!,* 1944.

Tourbillon, Robert Arthur (AKA: **Rat, Dapper Dan Collins**), b.1885, U.S., fraud. Robert Tourbillon was as smooth a con man as ever lived. His talents were recognized by at least one member of the federal bench. In passing sentence on Tourbillon for the June 15, 1911, robbery of the Hotel Roy in midtown Manhattan, Judge Edward Swann noted, "He is as smooth a rascal as ever came before me...He is a real Raffles. I consider this man a very dangerous character, for he is a smooth talker and such a fine dresser." It was the highest compliment anyone could ever pay Bobby Tourbillon, the man the Broadway crowd liked to call the "Rat" from the initials of his name.

Confidence man Robert Arthur Tourbillon.

Born in Atlanta, Ga., Tourbillon began his career as a circus performer. His specialty was the "Circle of Death" in which he rode a bicycle down a chute and past a cage filled with hungry lions. Traveling with an itinerant Southern circus was not the glamorous life he first imagined. So by his twenty-third birthday Tourbillon found himself in New York associating with underworld characters at their favorite haunt, Curly Bennett's pool hall. Within a month of his arrival in 1908, Tourbillon was arrested for burglary but the charges were dropped. During this time his reputation as a "fancy dan," and silver-tongued con man began to spread. His pretentious behavior and stylish manner of dressing belied his true criminal nature. In 1915, having completed his first tour in a U.S. prison, Tourbillon hooked up with a gang of thieves who pilfered telephone coin boxes. The ring was broken by New York City detectives and Tourbillon was handed over to federal authorities on a charge of interstate white-slave blackmail. In 1916, he was sentenced to two years in the Atlanta federal penitentiary.

Following his release, Tourbillon attempted to swindle New York property owner Julius Scholtz, who allegedly kept $20,000 hidden in a trunk on his farm. Posing as an IRS agent, Tourbillon flashed a badge. "Mr. Scholtz, we are compelled to search your farm," he said. The farmer protested that he had nothing. Tourbillon proceeded with the investigation anyway but was dismayed to find that the only items in the trunk were German-language magazines. Tourbillon apologized and bade farewell. "Goodbye Julius," he said. The suspicious farmer thought it peculiar that the agent should know his first name. Tourbillon was arrested for impersonating a federal officer but won an acquittal through a brilliant defense conducted by his attorney William Fallon, known as the "Great Mouthpiece." However, Tourbillon was convicted of robbing an American Express guard of $5,000 in 1920. Fallon secured bail for his client but Tourbillon decided not to test the patience of the legal system. He jumped bail and remained out of sight until May 15, 1921, when he shot John H. Reid of New York, over the affections of Mrs. Hazel D. Warner.

The Roaring Twenties were particularly good years for Tourbillon. Like many other crooks of the era who saw the intrinsic value of Prohibition, the Rat quickly diversified. In 1921, he purchased a deluxe yacht called the *Nomad* which he used to smuggle Canadian liquor into U.S. coastal waters. The *Nomad* was allegedly financed in part by Tourbillon's good friend Arnold Rothstein. In the first four years of Prohibition, Bobby Tourbillon was one of the most important rumrunners along the eastern seaboard. But when things began to get hot for him and the government went through with an indictment on a charge of grand larceny, Tourbillon fled to France. Operating under the alias of "Harry Hussey," the dapper swindler posed as Victor "The Count" Lustig's "ministerial secretary" when he was attempting to peddle the Eiffel Tower to a scrap-metal merchant. It was a neat trick, but doomed to failure. Tourbillon's real specialty was rich, lonely American women. Mrs. Helen Petterson in particular fell victim to his charm. She supplied him with a generous amount of money and even some pieces from her jewelry collection in an effort to win his affections. Tourbillon rewarded her generosity by pushing her off the third-floor balcony of the Hotel Majestic one New Year's Eve. When he was thrown into prison for debt, Mrs. Petterson visited him each day. "We are going to be married," she gushed to reporters.

In 1924, two detectives from the New York City Police Department arrived in Paris to extradite a burglar named Mourey back to the U.S. While touring the Sante Prison the men were startled to run across their old adversary. After exchanging formalities the detectives arranged extradition for Tourbillon aboard the liner *S.S. France.* On his arrival in New York the swindler was confronted with reporters eager to hear about his latest adventures. "I suppose every milk bottle and door mat stolen since I went away will be attributed to me," he said sarcastically. Actually, the robbery charges that resulted in his extradition failed to stick and he walked away a free man—temporarily.

Tourbillon's last hurrah was at the expense of a New Jersey apple farmer named Thomas Weber from whom he swindled $30,000. For this he was sentenced to sixteen months at the New Jersey State Prison in Trenton. "This was an excellent prison," he told reporters when his hitch was up in August 1930. "I recommend it as a wonderful vacation spot." When asked about his future plans, Tourbillon said he was going back to Paris—without the lovesick Mrs. Petterson at his side. He was never heard from again. See: **Lustig, Victor**.

REF.: *CBA;* Nash, *Bloodletters and Badmen;* ____, *Hustlers and Con Men;* Thompson, *Gang Rule in New York;* (FICTION), Wilstach, *Under Cover Man.*

Toussaint-Louverture (François Dominique Toussaint), 1743-1803, Haiti, consp.-rebel. Freed from slavery in 1777 and helped direct an insurrection by slaves from 1791-93. As the leader of the French republicans, he drove the British from the island in 1798, and defeated the mulattoes led by Rigaud in civil war in 1799. He freed more slaves in Santo Domingo in 1801, and became the ruler of the island. He was able to withstand pressures by Louis-Napoléon to reintroduce slavery, but was defeated by French General Charles Leclerc in 1802. He was imprisoned in France on charges of conspiracy, and died a prisoner.

REF.: Aptheker, *American Negro Slave Revolts;* CBA.

Towerly, William, 1870-87, U.S., west. outl. A horse thief in Indian Territory, William Towerly killed two lawmen. On Nov. 29, 1887, Towerly camped on the Arkansas River with Dave Smith, another horse thief, Lee Dixon, and Dixon's wife. Lawmen Frank Dalton and James Cole approached the camp on horseback, carrying warrants for Smith's arrest. Smith shot Dalton in the chest, and as the Dixons joined the firing at Cole, Towerly ran up to Dalton and shot him through the mouth and then through the head. Cole killed Smith and the Dixons, and Towerly fled to his family's home near Atoka in Indian Territory. In December, lawmen Ed Stokley and Bill Moody learned of his whereabouts and set up an ambush. One morning as Towerly emerged from his house, Stokley shouted, "Hands up!" Towerly went for his gun and both officers fired at the same time, hitting him in the shoulder and leg. Towerly dropped his gun and collapsed to the ground. As Stokley approached, Towerly grabbed his gun and shot the lawman in the groin and heart. While the outlaw was trying to reload, Towerly's sister and mother jumped Moody and dragged him into the house. Moody finally shook them free, walked outside, and killed Towerly.

REF.: *CBA;* Shirley, *Heck Thomas.*

Tower of London, 1078- , Brit., pris. The Tower of London is the product of centuries of additions and deletions to the original fortifications built on the north bank of the Thames River during the time of William the Conqueror. Constructed upon the foundations of an ancient Roman fort, the imposing structure controlled access to the Pool of London prior to the building of the docks further down the river in the nineteenth century. According to William Shakespeare's *Richard III,* the original inspiration for a Tower of this sort came from Julius Caesar himself, a notion which has been advanced by various other writers and historians over the years. The main portion of the fortress, known as the White Tower, was designed by Gundulf, bishop of Rochester, and built with quarried limestone in the year 1078. In the twelfth and thirteenth centuries the military fortifications were extended beyond the city wall, around which all future construction was arranged in concentric circles.

The inside portion of the Tower of London contains thirteen towers. The most famous of these are the Bloody Tower, Wakefield Tower, and Beauchamp Tower. The outer wall, with six towers and two bastions, was surrounded by a moat that connected with the Thames River until 1843, when it was drained.

The infamous Tower of London served as a prison from Norman times until the nineteenth century. In the thirteenth century, when the Tower still functioned as a state prison, the Traitor's Gate, then called the Water Gate, swung open to receive a long line of high-born prisoners. Much of the Tower's historical importance comes from its many famous prisoners, including Sir Thomas More, Ann Boleyn, Katherine Howard, Lady Jane Grey, the Duke of Monmouth, and Sir Walter Raleigh. Lady Jane and Anne Boleyn were put to death on Tower Green, though many other executions were performed on Tower Hill, outside the privacy of the fortress' walls. There have been few successful escapes from inside the heavily fortified tower over the years. Perhaps the most famous occurred in February 1716 when Lady Nithsdale disguised her husband as a woman and successfully conveyed him past the guards. In 1483, Edward V, the 13-year-old king who had been crowned when his father died in April of that year, disappeared with his brother inside the walls of the Tower. It has been alleged that Richard III ordered their executions after assuming the throne. Another theory proposes that the murders were committed by Henry Stafford, the duke of Buckingham, while others maintain it was done by King Henry VII, the first of the Tudor kings, who succeeded Richard. In 1674 two skeletons were found buried in the Tower, perhaps those of the martyred king and his brother.

The Tower of London served as the official residence of the royal family well into the seventeenth century. In those days, it also housed the Royal Mint, the public records, an ordinance store, and the Royal Menagerie in Lion Tower. The Crown Jewels are still housed in an underground chamber known as the Jewel House. Today the Tower of London is primarily a tourist site, though a military garrison is maintained on the grounds. See: **Boleyn, Ann; Grey, Jane; Henry VII; Nithsdale, Earl of; Raleigh, Sir Walter**. REF.: *CBA.*

Towers, Esther May, See: **Starchfield, Willie.**

Towneley, Francis, and **Deacon, Thomas**, and **Dawson, Jimmy**, prom. 1746, Brit., treas. In 1746, the British ended the practice of decapitation, but not before hangman John Thrift staged one of the country's most elaborate executions. Since he had been appointed in 1735, most of Thrift's work was done with an ax. But in the aftermath of the Jacobite rebellion of 1745, Thrift was ordered to execute nine revolutionaries for the crime of high treason. On July 30, 1746, the condemned men were brought from the jail at Southwark to Kennington Common, where the gallows stood. Among the victims were Francis Towneley, Thomas Deacon, and Jimmy Dawson.

The orders from King George II included a request that the traitors be drawn, hanged, beheaded, and quartered. Underneath the gallows was a pile of wood which was ignited after Thrift had secured the nine prisoners on the crossbeam. After dangling at the end of a rope for five minutes, Thrift cut down the semi-conscious Towneley and removed his head with a meat cleaver. After detaching Towneley's head, Thrift disembowelled the corpse and tossed the heart and entrails into the bonfire. The hangman repeated the procedure eight more times. When he was finished, Thrift, a bloody mess, stood up and declared "God Save King George!" Thrift, who retired in 1752, was the last executioner to work with an ax.

REF: *CBA;* Potter, *The Art of Hanging.*

Townley, George, 1838-65, Brit., mur. George Townley, a merchant's son, became engaged to 16-year-old Bessie Goodwin in 1859. When Townley became a clerk in a mercantile firm, Goodwin's family told her to terminate the engagement, feeling that she could make a more prosperous match. By way of enforcing the separation, Bessie's family sent her to live with an 82-year-old relative, Captain Goodwin. Despite the distance, the affair continued and the couple became engaged again in 1862. However, when a young clergyman came to stay with Captain Goodwin, Bessie's relatives once again saw the possibility of a better match and instructed her to terminate the engagement. On Aug. 12, 1863, Bessie obediently wrote to Townley asking to be released. On Aug. 21, Townley went to the Captain's home and made one last attempt to persuade Bessie to marry him. When she refused, he cut her throat with a knife. Captain Goodwin then offered Townley tea while waiting for the police to arrive.

Townley was tried at Derby on Dec. 11, 1863, found Guilty, and sentenced to death. His sentence was later amended to reflect insanity and he was imprisoned at Pentonville prison where, on Feb. 12, 1865, he committed suicide by jumping over a staircase onto a stone floor below.

REF.: Butler, *Murderers' England; CBA;* Wilson, *Encyclopedia of Murder.*

Townsend, Harry (AKA: **Mr. Fay, Mr.Collier, Mr. Collins**), prom. 1926, U.S., mur. In 1921, Harry Townsend, a native of Nova Scotia, murdered his sister. Her body was found in a closet in the tenement house they shared in New York City. Police learned that Townshend had been a bargeman and always had a great love for the sea. Believing that he would at some time return to sea, the investigators spread a description of Townsend around in nearly every port along the U.S. eastern seaboard.

In 1926, nearly five years after the crime, police were alerted that a man who fit Townsend's description was working on a coal barge in Philadelphia under the name of Collier. The search for Collier led police to New York where they finally located him, working under the name of Collins. When police confronted him with the crime, he admitted to killing his sister. He pleaded guilty and was sentenced to life in prison.

REF.: Carey, *Memoirs of a Murder Man; CBA.*

Townsend, Jean, 1933-54, Brit., (unsolv.) attempt. rape-mur. A 21-year-old English woman, walking home late on the evening of Sept. 15, 1954, in the English town of Ruislip, was murdered. The body of Jean Townsend was found by police the next day, fully clothed except for shoes and stockings and an unspecified article of underwear. The killer had strangled her with her own silk scarf and had tried to rape her.

During the course of a police investigation, several women admitted that they had been accosted in this same area under similar conditions. The attacks were always at night after the street lights had been turned off, and in at least one instance, the assailant attempted to strangle his victim. In all cases, the man was described as being in his late twenties, about five feet six inches tall, with thick, black, wavy hair, and a high forehead. Additionally, he spoke in an identifiably American accent. After Townsend's murder on Oct. 9, another woman returning home by herself late at night was attacked about two-and-a-half miles from the Townsend murder scene. The woman escaped and was able to give police a description of her assailant identical to previous victims' descriptions. Despite the extensive description supplied by witnesses and victims, no suspect was ever arrested in the Townsend murder.

REF.: *CBA;* Furneaux, *Famous Criminal Cases, vol. 2.*

Townsend, William, prom. 1854, Case of, Can., rob.-mur. Late in 1854, a gang of criminals embarked on a spree of burglaries, highway robberies and murders in the Niagara Peninsula of Ontario, Can. Suspicion, in particular for the robbery and murder of John Hamilton Nelles on Oct. 18, fell upon William Townsend, a resident of the area and the alleged leader of a gang bearing his name. Although Townsend was a man noted for his cleverness in the use of disguises and dialects and he initially eluded pursuers, his companions, John Blowes, William Bryson, and a man by the name of King, were captured and, in Spring 1855, were tried for the Nelles murder. Although all three testified that it was Townsend who had shot Nelles, they were found Guilty. Blowes and King were later hanged, but Bryson, who had turned Queen's evidence, was sentenced to life imprisonment.

Townsend came out of hiding and resumed his criminal activity as early as November 1854. Crimes ranging from robbery to murder are attributed to him for the period between late 1854 and his arrest in 1857. John Iles, a Cleveland boarding house proprietor and former London constable who had known Townsend for eight or nine years, recognized him as he ate dinner in a saloon. Townsend was arrested and charged with the murder of John Nelles. His trial began on Sept. 27, 1857. Although Townsend did not say who he was, he insisted that he was not William Townsend. Large numbers of witnesses on either side took the stand to either affirm or deny the identity of the man standing trial. The jury, unable to reach a verdict, was discharged. On Mar. 26, 1858, Townsend was brought to trial again, this time for the murder of a constable, Charles Ritchie. Once again the question of identity dominated the trial. The most persuasive piece of evidence presented by the defense was that Townsend was known to have large, misshapen feet, whereas the man standing trial in Ritchie's murder—who by now claimed to be a Scottish emigre named Robert J. McHenry—was shown to have small well-formed feet. On Apr. 6, the jury announced that they believed the defendant to be Robert J. McHenry and therefore, Not Guilty.

REF.: *CBA;* Miller, *Twenty Mortal Murders.*

Toxicology, See: Supplements, Vol. IV.

Toyama Mitsuru, 1855-1944, Japan, org. crime. Born in Fukuoka in 1855, Toyama Mitsuru forever altered the course of organized crime and politics in Japan. Toyama, born to a family of obscure samurai rank, grew up as a tough street kid who idolized the samurai tradition. Toyama's political career began in his early twenties. He joined one of several samurai uprisings for which he was sentenced to three years in jail. When released, he joined an ultra-nationalist group, the *Kyoshisha,* and soon thereafter began to attract his own following. The discipline and organization provided by Toyama transformed his streetwise recruits into both a work force and a fighting force which he employed to quell labor unrest in the area's coal mines.

Toyama Mitsuru, founder of Japan's dreaded Black Dragon Society, which practiced assassination and controlled organized crime in Japan for sixty years.

In 1881, Toyama founded *Genyosha* (Black Dragon Society, or Dark Ocean Society), a federation of previously existing nationalist societies which was to become the forerunner of Japan's modern secret societies and patriotic groups. Through his fascination with the samurai tradition, Toyama recognized the tremendous potential in such an organization for tapping the strong sentiment among the ex-samurai for expansion abroad and authoritarian rule at home. As the Black Dragon Society grew in size and power, its members went to work as bodyguards for government officials, as "muscle" for local political bosses, and also in legitimate jobs in unions associated with the society. They saw all of their activities, regardless of criminal nature, in the light of the righteous highly-patriotic politics espoused by Toyama.

In addition to lending the Black Dragon Society as aid in breaking strikes and other right-wing activities, Toyama also actively pursued his own agenda of creating a new social order. To this end, *Genyosha* activists were responsible for numerous attacks on, and assassinations of, moderate or liberal political figures. The *Genyosha*'s mobilization in Japan's national election of 1892—the first large-scale cooperation between rightists and the underworld—turned it into the bloodiest election in Japanese history. The *Genyosha,* whose agenda included expansion into Korea and China, were also responsible for the assassination in 1895 of the Korean queen, an event which marked the beginning of half a century of Japanese occupation of Korea.

Literally hundreds of secret societies sprang up in the mold of the Black Dragon Society, all with the same right-wing agenda. Though some of these societies were financed by wealthy patrons, others supported their activities through prostitution, gambling, and other standard criminal activities, traditionally the province of the yakuza or criminal gangs. The political interests of the gangsters were similar to those of the rightists—any political movement toward the left jeopardized their authority. As the rightists became more involved in criminal activities and the gangsters became more invested in rightist politics, the lines between the two continued to blur.

In 1919, Toyama formed the first national federation of gangsters—*Dai Nippon Kokusui-kai,* or the Great National Essence Society. The *Kokusui-kai,* a force of 60,000 gangsters, laborers, and ultra-nationalists, though billed as an organization to promote ancient Japanese values, actually functioned as a massive strikebreaking force. The *Kokusui-kai,* with Toyama acting as chief advisor, operated much like their Fascist contemporaries in Italy, and enjoyed the support of the Home Ministry, the police, and some high-ranking military officials. Eventually the *Kokusui-kai* evolved into the paramilitary arm of the *Seiyukai,* one of the two major political parties. Throughout the 1920s, Toyama's political power continued to grow despite a trend in Japanese politics toward the left. Toyama acquired even more power and prestige in the 1930s as democracy faded entirely from view in Japan. The ruthless militarism that overtook Japan in this era did so even as the Nazis took over in Germany and the Fascists came to power in Italy. Toyama died in 1944 at the age of eighty-nine, having seen Japan conquer much of Asia and the Pacific. See: **Black Dragon Society; Inagawa Kakuji; Jirocho Shimizu no; Kimura Tokutaru; Kishi Nobusuke; Kodama Yoshio; Machii Hisayuki; Nakasone Yasuhiro; Ogawa Kaoru; Osano Kenji; Sasakawa Ryoichi; Taoka Kazuo; Yakuza.**

REF.: Abend, *Chaos in Asia;* ____, *My Life in China;* Bergamini, *Japan's Imperial Conspiracy;* Byas, *Government by Assassination;* ____, *The Japanese Enemy; CBA;* Craigie, *Behind the Japanese Mask;* Grew, *Ten Years in Japan;* ____, *Turbulent Era;* Kajima, *Emergence of Japan as a World Power;* Kaplan and Dubron, *Yakuza;* Kennedy, *A History of Japan;* Mosley, *Hirohito;* Murofushi, *Nihon no Terorisuto;* Sansom, *A History of Japan;* Scalapino, *Democracy and the Party Movement in Prewar Japan;* Tsurumi, *Nihon no hyakunen;* Vaughn, *Under the Japanese Mask;* Young, *Imperial Japan;* ____, *Japan in Recent Times.*

Toyotomi Hidetsugo, 1537-98, Japan, banish.-suic. Named chief warrior, or *kampaku,* following retirement of his uncle and adopted father, Toyotomi Hideyoshi, in 1582. Although he was a courageous fighter, he was an incompetent leader and was eventually banished by Hideyoshi and forcibly compelled to kill himself. REF.: *CBA.*

Tracey, Frank J. (AKA: **George Salvage**), prom. 1916, U.S., rob.-mur. Early in the twentieth century, certain immigrant groups discovered that junk was the gold in the streets of America. Junkmen bought anything they could resell at a profit, making deals on the spot. In Boston, Morris Taitel was one such junkman. The deal he made with two men offering to sell copper boilers, however, was nearly his last. Taitel had gone to a Boston boarding house to make a deal with Frank J. Tracey and Joe Rogers. After establishing that Taitel had enough money in his pocket to pay for the boilers, the two men robbed Taitel and locked him in a closet with the promise that they would return shortly to kill him.

After a while, Tracey and Rogers returned with another junkman. Taitel watched through a crack in the door as the scene was replayed. This time, after robbing their victim, they shot him in the head. While the murderers were out of the room, disposing of the body, Taitel broke through the door and jumped through a window to the sidewalk below.

Police were skeptical of Taitel's story until they returned to the boarding house with him and found the victim's body, buried in the coal pile. Taitel identified Tracey from police photos and the police sent out circulars on the two men. Almost immediately, Boston police received a reply on Rogers. He had served eight years in prison in Trenton, N.J. Police found Rogers at his mother's home in Jersey City and arrested him. Tracey was a little harder to find. Finally, in February 1916, a warden at the Iowa State Penitentiary noticed a distinctive mole on an incoming prisoner's cheek. Remembering a circular he had received some months earlier, he identified the man, now operating under the name of George Salvage, as Frank Tracey. Tracey and Rogers were brought to trial for murder. They were both found Guilty and sentenced to life imprisonment.

REF.: *CBA;* Cohen, *One HUndred True Crime Stories.*

Tracey, Walter, 1596-1634, Brit., rob. The handsome and debonair Walter Tracey was born in Norfolk and educated at King's College, Cambridge. The yearly stipend of £120 his father sent him was not enough to satisfy his expensive tastes or those of the young women he entertained in the village. Tracey began robbing people on the highway, and when things became too hot for him, he left the university to settle in Cheshire.

He lived with a sheepherder for a while, but spent the better part of his time seducing the young women of the countryside. Tracey fancied himself a poet, and his musical abilities charmed the local women. He put his lyrical abilities to good use after fleeing to London to escape the drudgery of country life. He met the famous poet and playwright Ben Jonson on the road to Buckinghamshire. Tracey commanded him to "stand and deliver." "Fly villain hence," Jonson replied, "or by thy coat of steel I'll make thy heart my leaden bullet feel." Tracey appreciated the lyrical reply and, with disguised amusement in his voice, answered:

"Art thou great Ben? Or the revived ghost
Of famous Shakespeare? Or some drunken host?
Who, being tipsy with thy muddy beer,
Dost think thy rhymes will daunt my soul with fear?
Nay, know, base slave, that I am one of those
Can take a purse as well in verse as prose,
And when thou art dead, write this upon thy hearse:
Here lies a poet who was robbed in verse.

Not knowing how to reply to this artful poetry, Jonson was compelled to hand over ten gold coins. Tracey continued to rob the highways for many years until he was captured and hanged at Westminster in 1634 for robbing the Duke of Buckingham.

REF.: *CBA;* Pringle, *Stand and Deliver;* Smith, *Highwaymen.*

Trackenburg, Max (AKA: **Israel Trackenburg, Max Burks**), prom. 1910, U.S., wh. slav. On Jan. 17, 1910, Max Trackenburg was convicted in Philadelphia of white slavery and was sentenced to one year in the county prison. Trackenburg was accused by a young woman named Flora who alleged that Trackenburg induced her to leave her home and become a prostitute. She further testified that Trackenburg had controlled her existence as a prostitute and collected a percentage of her earnings.

REF.: *CBA;* Roe, *The Great War on White Slavery.*

Tracy, Ann Gibson, 1935- , U.S., mur. On Nov. 14, 1960, cocktail waitress Ann Tracy could no longer stand the infidelities, lies, and torment of her lover, Amos Stricker.

Stricker was a wealthy building contractor who had carried on an affair with Tracy for several years. However, he still saw other women and taunted her with stories of his other affairs. As they were lying in bed together, she shot him dead.

Tracy confessed and was tried and convicted of second-degree murder. Sentenced for life to the Corona Woman's Prison, she still protested that she loved him.

REF.: *CBA;* Godwin, *Murder U.S.A.;* Nash, *Bloodletters and Badmen;* ____, *Look For the Woman.*

Tracy, Benjamin Franklin, 1830-1915, U.S., lawyer. Represented Pastor Henry Ward Beecher, who was acquitted of adultery in suit initiated by Theodore Tilton in 1875. He also served on the New York Court of Appeals from 1881-82, and as U.S. secretary of the navy from 1889-93. REF.: *CBA.*

Tracy, Harry, 1877-1902, U.S., rob.-mur. By the end of his criminal career, Harry Tracy had earned himself a reputation as one of the U.S.' most violent outlaws. He demonstrated no criminal tendencies until the age of fifteen, when he met another 15-year-old Vancouver, Wash., resident, David Merrill. Although Merrill was the instigator of their joint criminal activities, Tracy soon exceeded him.

Outlaw Harry Tracy.

David Merrill

Tracy's and Merrill's first prison sentence—twenty days for stealing geese from a farmer—did not discourage them. After practicing shooting pistols at a local barracks until they became expert shots, the two started off on a run of petty offenses that ended with Tracy's arrest for house-breaking in Provo, Utah, for which he was sentenced on July 10, 1897 to a year in prison. On Oct. 8, Tracy and three other prisoners working on a labor gang outside the prison walls escaped. Tracy traveled to Colorado, where he joined the "Robbers Roost" gang, whose members included Merrill, Dave Lent, Pat Johnson, and John Bennett.

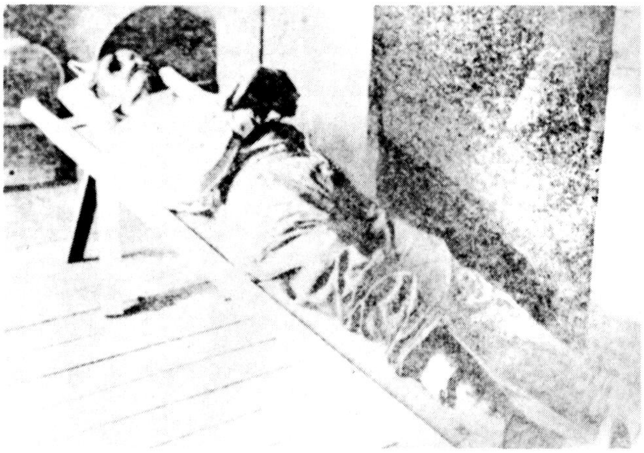

Harry Tracy's body on display.

When the gang murdered a young man named William Strang, a posse set out after them, catching up with them on Mar. 1, 1898, outside Craig, Colo. During the ensuing gun battle, a deputy sheriff was killed. Although the gang escaped, they were tracked down again on Mar. 4 by another posse that captured Lent, Tracy, Johnson and Bennett. Johnson, accused of the Strang murder, was extradited to Wyoming, where he was tried and acquitted due to a lack of a evidence. Bennett was lynched by a mob, and Tracy and Lent escaped from jail but were recaptured the next day. They escaped again and this time Tracy rejoined Merrill.

Tracy and Merrill returned to Portland, Ore., where they set about terrorizing the citizenry with a series of robberies and holdups. Merrill was arrested on Feb. 6, 1899, and Tracy was arrested the following day. Both men were found Guilty of robbery and were sentenced to the Salem prison on Mar. 22, Tracy for twenty years and Merrill for fifteen. On June 9, 1902, after having a rifle smuggled in to them, Tracy and Merrill broke out of prison. An intensive manhunt ensued. The two men eluded authorities, mostly by breaking into private citizens' homes, and forcing them to provide food, weapons, and supplies, and occasionally taking hostages to assure that their demands were met. On June 28, Merrill and Tracy had a falling out. Tracy said later that their argument proved Merrill was faint of heart. They agreed to a duel in which they stood back to back and started to count off ten paces. At the eighth step, Tracy turned and shot his partner in the back.

Tracy remained at large until Aug. 6, 1902, when a posse surprised him on a ranch near Creston, Wash. Tracy managed to dash into an adjoining wheat field. The posse fired volleys of shots into the field but heard Tracy fire only one shot in return. The following morning, Sheriff Gardner of Lincoln County and his posse searched the field, where they found Tracy dead, a suicide. One of his legs had been shattered by two of the rifle balls fired by the posse. He had attempted to stop the flow of blood with a bandage, but when it became obvious he could not escape, Tracy apparently decided to make good on his promise that he would never be caught alive, and shot himself in the head. His body was returned to Salem prison for identification and was displayed to the inmates as an object lesson in the rewards of a life of crime. The men who finally stopped Harry Tracy received a reward of $4,100—the same as it would have been if he'd been captured alive.

REF.: Bartholomew, *The Biographical Album of Western Gunfighters;* ____, *Western Hard-Cases;* Botkin, *A Treasury of Western Folklore;* Breihan, *Badmen of Frontier Days;* ____, *Outlaws of the Old West;* Burroughs, *Where the Old West Stayed Young;* Carter, *Harry Tracy, the Desperate Outlaw; CBA;* Duke, *Celebrated Criminal Cases in America;* Duncan, *Over the Wall;* Dunham, *Our Strip of Land;* Fultz, *Famous Northwest Manhunts;* Hawkeye, *Tracy, the Outlaw, King of Bandits;* Hemphill, *Down the Mother Lode;* Henderson, *Keys to Crookdom;* Hennessy, *Tracy, the Bandit;* Holbrook, *Promised Land;* Holloway, *Texas Gun Lore;* Horan, *Authentic Wild West;* ____, *Desperate Men;* ____, *Desperate Women;* ____ and Sann, *Pictorial History of the Wild West;* ____, *The Wild Bunch;* Howard, *This Is the West;* Hunter and Rose, *The Album of Gun-Fighters;* Kelley, *Thirteen Years in the Oregon Penitentiary;* Kelly, *The Outlaw Trail;* Leckenby, *The Tread of the Pioneers;* Lucia, *Tough Men, Tough Country;* Lyons, *Thrills and Spills of a Cowboy Rancher;* Raine, *Famous Sheriffs & Western Outlaws;* Ray, *Harry Tracy;* Rennert, *Western Outlaws;* Rockwell, *Sunset Slope;* Rosa, *The Gunfighter, Man or Myth?;* Sonney, *The American Outlaw;* Urquhart, *Roll Call;* Ward, *Harry Tracy;*

Martha Tracy robbing a victim.

Tracy, Martha, d.1745, Brit., rob. Martha Tracy worked as a servant in a rooming house in London. Because she was very attractive to the male lodgers, she got more than her share of attention. One man bought her a wardrobe of new clothes with the hope of seducing her. When the keeper of the lodging house saw Martha in her new finery, she became suspicious. The next day she fired Martha for carrying on a romance with one of the guests.

The lodger, still anxious to keep her as his mistress, found another room in the city. Martha Tracy lived there for a few months, believing that the man would marry her someday, but this was never his intention. When he found out that she was pregnant, the man stopped paying her rent and abandoned her. The baby was taken away, and she was forced to pawn her clothes. With no other recourse, Tracy became a prostitute. She also learned how to pick pockets and rob. In January 1745, her gang of thieves accosted an older gentleman named Mr. Humphreys on the King's Highway in the Strand. After knocking the man down, Tracy took a guinea from his pocket and hid the coin in her mouth as her cohorts fled the scene. Humphreys struggled with his assailant, and held her until the constable arrived. At the watchhouse, the guinea was pulled from her mouth, and was submitted as evidence at the Old Bailey sessions. For the crime of highway robbery, Martha Tracy was found Guilty, and condemned to die according to English law. She was hanged at Tyburn on Feb. 16, 1745.

REF.: *CBA;* Mitchell, *The Newgate Calendar;* O'Donnell, *Should Women Hang?.*

Trafficante, Santo, Sr., 1886-1954, U.S., org. crime. Succeeding Ignacio Antinori as Florida's Mafia chief, Santo Trafficante, Sr. controlled the Tampa, Fla., narcotics and gambling empire. He formed alliances with the New York Mafia bosses, especially Charles "Lucky" Luciano, as well as the bosses of Kansas City and St. Louis. Born in Sicily, Trafficante moved to Tampa by the age of eighteen. By 1920, he had gained prominence in the Tampa Mafia, and when Antinori was murdered in 1940, Trafficante was already godfather. He gradually took control of the gambling concessions of Charles Wall, an independent operator, and forced Wall into several Mafia business ventures and partnerships. During that time, three attempts were made to kill Wall, who thought the only thing keeping him alive was a document detailing his involvement with Trafficante.

Mafia boss Santo Trafficante.

Trafficante tried to establish gambling operations on the east coast of Florida, but top syndicate boss Meyer Lansky had already claimed the territory and tolerated no competition. In 1946, Trafficante sent his son, Santo Trafficante, Jr., to Havana, Cuba, to establish a casino. But Lansky had claimed Cuba as well, and Trafficante remained a junior partner. Trafficante died in 1954, and that same year, Wall was found dead in his home, his throat slashed. See: **Lansky, Meyer; Luciano, Charles; Trafficante, Santo, Jr.**

REF.: Blumenthal, *Last Days of the Sicilians; CBA;* Davis, *Mafia Kingfish;* Demaris, *The Last Mafioso;* Eisenberg and Landau, *Meyer Lansky;* Gosch and Hammer, *The Last Testament of Lucky Luciano;* Martin, *Revolt in the Mafia;* Messick, *Lansky;* Peterson, *The Mob;* Reid, *The Grim Reapers;* Zuckerman, *Vengeance Is Mine.*

Trafficante, Santo, Jr., 1914-87, U.S., org. crime. A U.S.-born godfather, Santo Trafficante, Jr. was one of the few sons to succeed his father as chief of an organized crime family. Santo Trafficante, Sr. bequeathed his empire to Santo, Jr. in 1954. The son, through guile, violence, and determination, became one of the most powerful crime bosses in the U.S. He operated many of the same rackets as his father had, including gambling, loan sharking, and, most profitably, narcotics.

Santo went to Cuba in 1946 to open a casino in Havana. Fidel Castro jailed Trafficante, and ousted the Mafia when he took control in 1959, but Trafficante was soon released and allowed to leave the country with all his money. He was later involved in the CIA plot to assassinate Castro, and according to his testimony before a Congressional committee in 1975, recruited several other members of the underworld for this purpose in the early 1960s, including Johnny Roselli. Roselli, Chicago boss Sam Giancana, and some lawmen thought Trafficante sold out to Castro. They believed Trafficante never intended to assassinate Castro, that he destroyed the poisons made by the CIA, and that he kept the money provided to finance the operation. Questions were raised concerning his release from the Cuban jail. Trafficante was called before a House committee in 1978 to answer questions about a sworn statement by Jose Aleman that Trafficante told him "Kennedy's gonna get hit." However, Trafficante emerged unscathed. He died of heart failure in 1987. REF.: *CBA.*

Train, Arthur, 1875-1945, U.S., lawyer-writer. Assistant district attorney of New York County from 1901-08, and held other New York posts. He created Ephraim Tutt, a fictional attorney featured in several novels, and wrote many other books concerning courts and the law. Among books authored: *The Prisoner at the Bar, True Stories of Crime, By Advice of Counsel, The Strange Attacks on Herbert Hoover, Manhattan Murder, From the District Attorney's Office.*

REF.: *CBA;* Logan, *Against the Evidence.*

Trapia, Francisco, prom. 1926, U.S., mutil. When he woke and found the dead body of his wife, Brooklyn longshoreman Francisco Trapia, assumed he had killed her the night before in a drunken stupor. Trapia panicked when he considered being caught for the crime. His solution was to carve off the head, arms, and legs, thinking it would be easier to dispose of her body. While dumping a package containing the arms and legs in the river, Trapia was spotted by police and questioned. When they searched his apartment, they found the rest of the body and arrested Trapia on a charge of murder.

When the chief medical examiner saw the woman's head, he commented cryptically that there was no cause of death. What he referred to was the bright red color of the face—a fact that indicated the victim had died of carbon monoxide poisoning. An autopsy substantiated the examiner's conjecture. Apparently, after Trapia and his wife had both fallen asleep, full of alcohol, a heater in the apartment had malfunctioned, filling the place with noxious fumes. For some unclear reason, Mr. Trapia survived while his wife succumbed to the gas. Trapia was tried on a charge of mutilating a corpse and carrying it through the streets without a permit. He was convicted and served several years in prison.

REF.: *CBA;* Martin, *The Doctor Looks at Murder.*

Trapnell, Garrett Brock, 1938- , U.S., skyjack. Before Garrett Trapnell, a Boston native, was convicted the 1972 skyjacking of a plane en route from Los Angeles to New York, he was arrested several times and charged with serious crimes ranging from armed robbery to skyjacking. Each time he convinced the courts and the psychiatrists that he was insane when he committed the crime but was no longer insane by the time of the trial.

Trapnell, who detailed his life as a con man and criminal in a book entitled *The Fox Is Crazy, Too* , was found Guilty in the 1972 skyjacking and sentenced to life imprisonment in the nation's toughest federal prison, in Marion, Ill. Trapnell, who once told a federal judge that any man sentenced to life "has an inherent right to escape" was identified at his trial by a prison official as "an extreme escape risk." In May 1978, 43-year-old Barbara Oswald, a woman who had read his book and somehow got on his approved visitors list, attempted to break him out of the Marion penitentiary. She rented a helicopter saying she wanted to look over some property along the Mississippi River but once in the air, she drew a pistol and ordered the pilot to fly to the prison. In a struggle for the gun, Oswald was shot and killed. The pilot managed to land the helicopter safely outside the prison.

Just before Christmas 1978, Oswald's 17-year-old daughter, Robyn Oswald, hijacked a TWA DC-9 with 87 passengers on board in another attempt to free Trapnell. Robyn surrendered to FBI agents about ten hours after the plane had been diverted to an airport near the prison.

REF.: *CBA;* Godwin, *Murder U.S.A.*

Trapnell, John Graham, 1876-1949, Brit., jur. Practiced law on western circuit and named king's counsel in 1931. He served as judge-advocate of the fleet from 1933-43, when he was made official referee to the Supreme Court. He participated in the murder trials of William Walter Burton and Reginald Woolmington. REF.: *CBA.*

Trapped, 1928, a play by Samuel Shipman. This drama is based on the kidnapper-murderer William Edward Hickman (U.S., 1927). Actor Edward Woods, later to distinguish himself as James Cagney's gangster pal in the film, *Public Enemy*, enacted the role of Hickman with chilling accuracy. The actor bore an amazing resemblance to the real-life killer. See: **Hickman, William Edward.** REF.: *CBA.*

Trash Bag Murderer, The, See: **Kearny, Patrick Wayne.**

Traveling Mike Grady Gang, prom. 1880s, U.S., org. crime. One of the better known New York City gangs of sneak thieves in the 1880s was Traveling Mike Grady's Gang. Beside Grady, the gang included Greedy Jake Rand, Boston Pete Anderson, Hod Ennis, and Eddie Pettengill. Despite earlier successes, the gang surpassed themselves on Mar. 7, 1866. Having targeted wealthy Wall Street financier Rufus L. Lord for a robbery, the gang went to his office at 38 Exchange Place. Grady entered the office first and distracted Lord, who worked alone, by inquiring about a loan and intimating broadly that he was willing to pay interest of up to 20 percent. While Grady had their target thus engaged, Pettengill and Anderson slipped into the office unobserved and took a tin money box from the open safe. The thieves discovered that the box contained $1.9 million in cash and negotiable securities. All gang members except Grady retired after this windfall. Grady himself continued stealing and fencing for years to come. REF.: *CBA.*

Travers, George, prom. 1814, U.S., mur. George Travers, a Navy man assigned to the base at Charlestown, Mass., picked a fight with a fellow serviceman named Stocker on Nov. 26, 1814. In a moment of agitation he began throwing brickbats and snowballs with stones in them at Seaman Stocker, who retaliated with his fists. The fight was broken up by one Sergeant Geary. The next morning, Geary, accompanied by Sergeants McKim and Hasey, appeared in Travers' room to get to the bottom of the incident.

George Travers, perhaps fearing that he would be severely reprimanded for the altercation, picked up his musket just as the men entered the room. Geary deflected the muzzle away from himself, but the gun discharged and the bullet plowed through Sergeant McKim's breast and into Hasey who was standing right behind. Both men died from their wounds.

Travers was tried for murder at the Charlestown Navy Yard on Nov. 27, 1814. He was found Guilty of manslaughter due to his "ungovernable temper and violent passions." Lucky to escape with his life, he was sentenced to three years in prison and a $1,000 fine for each conviction.

REF.: *CBA; Trial of George Travers.*

Traxler, Roy (AKA: Pete), prom. 1937, U.S., pris. esc.-kid.-mur. Roy "Pete" Traxler killed a Pauls Valley, Okla., police officer and was sent to McAlester Penitentiary. He escaped twice, but was recaptured and extradited to Texas, where he was sentenced to ninety-nine years in an Eastham, Texas, prison camp for robbing a store in Lipscomb. On July 9, 1937, Traxler and eight other convicts, including Fred Tindol and Charles Chapman, escaped from the prison camp. One escapee was killed and a guard was seriously injured. Traxler was wounded in the left arm and Chapman was shot in his left shoulder.

Traxler, Tindol, and Chapman headed for Oklahoma, abducting a Texas rancher and stealing two cars along the way. In Ada, Okla., on July 15, they kidnapped Baird H. Markham, Jr., the son of a New York oil executive, but released him unharmed the same day. Chapman left the group while Traxler and Tindol drove to Verden, Okla., and picked up Nell Tingley, Traxler's wife. Spotted by police, the escapees and Tingley fled in the car, but were trapped by police in a secluded area. In the ensuing gunfight, the car was shot full of holes. Tingley was found inside the car and arrested by police. Traxler and Tindol, however, escaped and fled through the woods. On July 21, they stumbled upon J.E. Denton's vacation home early in the morning, kidnapped Denton, and took his car. They sped for seventy miles until they ran out of gas near Frank Trimmer's farm. They broke into Trimmer's house, abducted the farmer, and changed cars. The car broke down fifteen miles later, and the escapees, exhausted from their flight, fell asleep. Five minutes later, Denton and Trimmer overpowered their abductors. Denton later said, "I grabbed the gun and shot Tindol under the left armpit, then I turned to the front of the car and fired at Traxler, then to make sure of the job, I turned back and let Tindol have it again." Though seriously wounded, Traxler tried to jump from the car but stopped when Denton pointed the gun at him and told him "not to act foolish." Traxler was treated in the hospital for gunshot wounds and sent back to prison. REF.: *CBA.*

Treadaway, Jonathan C., 1954- , U.S., (wrong. convict.) sod.-mur. In 1975, 21-year-old Jonathan C. Treadaway was convicted and sentenced to death for sodomizing and then suffocating 6-year-old Brett Jordan in the Jordan home in Phoenix. Two county medical examiners who performed an autopsy on the Jordan boy determined the cause of death as suffocation, and found evidence of sodomy. The prosecution used a partial palm print on the window sill and hair samples found on the boy's body as evidence that Treadaway was the killer.

Treadaway spent three years on death row before his conviction was reversed because evidence of a prior criminal act by Treadaway had been improperly introduced in the original trial. During the retrial, pathologists from five other states testified that on the basis of their examination of tissue slides and photographs of the Jordan boy's body, there had been no sodomy and the boy had died of either pneumonia or bronchitis. The county medical examiners who had performed the Jordan autopsy testified that they did not conduct microscopic examinations of body tissues before reaching their conclusions. Jurors meeting with attorneys after the retrial said they had voted to free Treadaway because the prosecutors had failed to provide sufficient evidence that Treadaway was even in the Jordan home. Treadaway was freed immediately after the acquittal. REF.: *CBA.*

Trease, Edward, and **Cox, Frank,** prom. 1921, U.S., rob.-attempt. mur. On Apr. 9, 1921, two servicemen in Monterey, Calif., engaged Lorenzo Selaya, a local taxi driver, to drive them to the nearby town of Salinas. Sometime later police received an anonymous report that there had been gunfire on the highway just outside of Salinas and several persons appeared to be wounded. When police arrived, they found Selaya lying on the ground near the cab, bleeding profusely from head wounds. One of the servicemen, Frank Cox, had been shot in the neck and was unconscious. The other serviceman, Edward J. Trease, had been shot in the leg. Cox died without regaining consciousness. When interrogated by police, the two survivors baffled police by rendering contradictory accounts of what had happened. Trease claimed that Selaya had attacked them when they objected to the exorbitant fare he intended to charge, while Selaya insisted that the two men had attempted to rob and murder him.

Evidence indicated that Trease and Cox had intended to desert from the military and police suspected that they had intended to kill Selaya and escape in his cab. However, not until a noted criminologist by the name of Heinrich was asked to assist in the investigation were they able to confirm their suspicions. From several hairs imbedded in the surface of a blackjack found at the crime scene, Heinrich established that Selaya had indeed been the victim. Trease was charged with robbery and attempted murder and brought to trial on May 23, 1921. Trease was found Guilty and was sentenced to serve an indeterminate term of from one to fourteen years in San Quentin Penitentiary.

REF.: Block, *Wizard of Berkeley; CBA.*

Trébert, Guy, prom. 1959, Fr., mur. Guy Trébert worked as a paint sprayer at a garage in Paris. On the evening of Mar. 15, 1959, he met a young woman by the name of Arlette at a movie theater. Arlette was not particularly interested in Trébert, and when she went to the country on Mar. 26 to visit her two children, she did not inform Trébert of her departure. On her return she found a number of notes from Trébert demanding that she call him immediately. They met once more and Arlette drove with Trébert to the forest of St. Germain. On Apr. 5, her body was found strangled and mutilated.

Trébert was brought to trial for the murder of Arlette in November 1962. Three women testified that Trébert had taken them to the forest at St. Germain also. He had attacked one of the women with a metal tool, and had attempted to strangle two of them while having intercourse with them. Trébert was convicted of murder and sentenced to life imprisonment. REF.: *CBA*.

Trebonius, Gaius, d.43 B.C., Rome, consp.-assass. Roman general who participated in assassination of Julius Caesar in 44 B.C. For this he was given the governorship of Asia. He was assassinated by Dolabella at Smyrna. REF.: *CBA*.

Trefethen, James, prom. 1891, U.S., mur. Delteena Davis, a young woman from East Cambridge, Mass., had been missing for several days when her body was found floating in the Mystic River. The girl's mother accused Delteena's suitor, James Trefethen, and his cousin, William H. Smith, of throwing her off the Wellington Bridge and into the icy waters on Dec. 23, 1891. Trefethen disavowed any responsibility, claiming that she had committed suicide.

Trefethen had been courting Davis for years. In July 1891, the young woman announced that she was pregnant with his child. James Trefethen had lost interest and sought to end the relationship. He began ignoring Davis and treating her coldly. On the night of her disappearance the jilted young woman was to confront him in town to discuss the matter. Trefethen and his cousin were placed on trial for the murder of Davis in February 1892 at the courthouse in East Cambridge. Smith was acquitted but Trefethen was found Guilty. In September 1893, he was granted a retrial and was acquitted on all murder charges.

REF.: *CBA; A Condensed Report of the Trial of James Albert Trefethen and William H. Smith for the Murder of Deltena J. Davis, in the Superior Court of Massachusetts.*

Treffene, Phillip John, d.1926, Aus., mur. In the early part of the twentieth century, stealing gold was prevalent enough on the Kalgoorlie goldfields of western Australia to warrant the formation of a special police squad to combat it. In May 1926, two members of the Goldfields Detection Force, John Joseph Walsh and Alexander Henry Pitman set out on bicycles to investigate reports of an illegal gold treatment plant. The Force acted independently and it wasn't unusual for them to be out of touch on an investigation for days at a time. When Walsh and Pitman did not return by May 10, however, searchers were sent out after them.

On a tip from two Kalgoorlie men, the mutilated bodies of the two police officers were found at the bottom of a mine shaft. Along with the bodies, which had been burned, were a bloody saw, parts of an old gold treatment plant, gold scales, and parts of a furnace. Also in the mine shaft were a pair of specially tailored trousers which had been made in Perth for a Phillip John Treffene. After an intensive investigation, police linked Treffene and two other men, William Coulter and a man named Clarke to the brutal murders of Walsh and Pitman. As police suspected, Pitman and Walsh had come upon the plant where Coulter and Treffene processed stolen gold ore. Rather than sacrifice a highly lucrative enterprise, the two shot the officers. Clarke, who owned the bar where Treffene occasionally worked, aided the pair in covering up the crime and disposing of the bodies. Treffene and Coulter were tried on Aug. 16, 1926, and found Guilty of murder. They both were hanged two months later in Fremantle Jail. Clarke, who had cooperated with the police, was not tried despite a formal statement from the jury in the Treffene-Coulter trial deploring the fact that Clarke did not also stand trial.

REF.: *CBA;* Clegg, *Return Your Verdict;* Gurr, *Famous Australasian Crimes.*

Tregoff, Carole, See: **Finch**, Dr. **Raymond Bernard**.

Treloar, James Gray (Buster Treloar), prom. 1958, Case of, U.S., mansl. Woodrow Wilson Daniel, a 37-year-old black man living in Water Valley, Miss., made his living delivering groceries and bootlegging. The local sheriff, James Treloar, elected on a strong prohibition platform, had been keeping an eye on Daniel since he had been acquitted a few months earlier on a bootlegging charge. When Treloar caught Daniel with some bottles of bootlegged liquor in June 1958, he arrested him and took him to jail. Sometime during that night, Daniel sustained head injuries that resulted in his death nine days later.

When a grand jury indicted Treloar for manslaughter, white citizens of the area organized to prevent the black population from hiring a lawyer from the NAACP, and to ensure that a white attorney acted as the district attorney's special prosecutor. Witnesses testified during the trial that they had seen Sheriff Treloar hit Daniel with a club. In explanation, Treloar said he "had to tap (Daniel) on the head." The all-white jury deliberated for twenty-six minutes before finding Treloar Not Guilty. Underscoring the racist nature of the proceedings, Treloar was quoted as saying before the leaving the court room, "Now, by God, I can get back to rounding up bootleggers and niggers." REF.: *CBA*.

Tremamunno, Donato, prom. 1962, Italy, suic.-mur. Donato Tremamunno and Antonio Ragone were boyhood friends who parted ways when they became adults. Tremamunno traveled the world with the French Foreign Legion, and Ragone settled in Torrazza, Italy, with his wife and two daughters to work as a foreman at a Genoa factory. In 1961, Tremamunno, tired of travel, married a young woman and moved to Torrazza, where Ragone put the couple and their child up in a small cottage. But Tremamunno was unable to find work and feeling pressured for rent by Ragone, grew depressed.

On Aug. 24, 1962, Tremamunno and Ragone went for a walk. Later the same day, Tremamunno appeared on Ragone's doorstep without Ragone and told Ragone's 13-year-old daughter, Vita, that her father needed help in the orchard. That night, Ragone's wife and older daughter found Ragone's body in the orchard. He had been shot with a 7.65-millimeter pistol through the back of the head. Police later found the bodies of Tremamunno's wife Sebastiana and her infant son, Emilio, in the cottage. Sebastiana had been shot and her throat slit, and the child had been shot in the head.

More than 500 police officers and volunteers combed the countryside looking for the murderer. Late one afternoon, they found the two bodies. Vita Ragone was naked and had been savagely attacked and strangled. Next to her lay the body of Donato Tremamunno, dead from a gunshot wound to the mouth, the gun—a 7.5-millimeter pistol, standard issue for the French Foreign Legion—till clenched in his hand.

"I write this with a calm mind," read the note found in his cottage. "I have grown tired of the struggle for existence in this insane world, and I curse my parents for bringing me into it. I do not want to live anymore. I shall welcome death with open arms." REF.: *CBA*.

Trenchard, Lord **Hugh Montague**, 1873-1956, Brit., law enfor. off. Served as commissioner of the Metropolitan Police Force from 1931-36. Prior to this, Trenchard had served in the military for thirty-eight years, during which time he was named marshal of Britain's Royal Air Force. REF.: *CBA*.

Trenck, Baron **Franz von der**, 1711-49, Aust., war crimes. Court-martialed and sentenced to die in 1746 for joining regiment of Croatian peasants infamous for atrocities and pillage. His sentence was commuted to imprisonment. REF.: *CBA*.

Trent, Lindbergh (AKA: **Lindbergh Heist**), 1924- , U.S., rape-mur. The day after Lindbergh Trent brutally stabbed Shirley Ann Woodburn to death, he sold more than 100 copies of the Cincinnati *Post* at Eighth and Vine. A front-page extra containing all the details of a lurid murder translated into brisk newsstand sales. "Six-year-old girl found slain!" he yelled, without displaying the slightest guilt or remorse.

The 14-year-old youth was an enigma. The other newsboys thought him rather strange. "He seemed sort of dead," said Eugene Snow. His own mother could not say with certainty just how old he was. When asked about his peculiar name, Betty Lou Trent explained that there was no connection to the famous aviator Charles Lindbergh. "I guess I am just an unusual person," she said. After Lindbergh's father died, the widow's second husband gave his last name to the boy. Lindbergh was both a Heist and a Trent, according to Betty Lou.

Shirley Woodburn was a shy, withdrawn girl who was afraid of strangers. When she disappeared on May 29, 1938, after going out to play, her worried mother began a door-to-door search. "I put a clean brown dress on her and told her to come back soon because we were going out for a walk," Catherine Woodburn said.

The neighbors told her that Shirley had been playing on a wooded hillside near the two-story frame building on McMicken Avenue where the Woodburns lived. For the moment, Mrs. Woodburn was relieved, thinking that her daughter had probably gone to a friend's house in the neighborhood. When she did not return by nightfall, the police were summoned.

Major Gustave Lorenz organized a search party numbering 100 policemen and Boy Scouts. They combed the surrounding neighborhood for traces of the missing girl. Five-year-old Arthur Rahn tipped police about a stranger "who didn't have a beard like my daddy." The man, according to little Arthur, took Shirley to the hillside to show her a rabbit. The girl's nude and battered body was found in a wild cucumber bush 200 feet up the hillside. A coroner's autopsy reported that the victim had been stabbed twenty-eight times by a dull, blunted object. The killer had attempted to conceal the remains in a muddy quagmire.

Police first suspected Lindbergh Trent after a streetcar operator named Matthew O'Leary told them that he had seen a boy washing his mud-caked clothing in a public fountain near the Main Street car terminal. "How'd you get so dirty, buddy?" O'Leary inquired. "I fell down a hill hunting rabbits," he said.

The motorman went to the police, and within an hour Lindbergh Trent was in custody. "I must have been crazy if I did it," he sobbed. "But I don't remember doing it." Trent admitted that he had smoked a cigarette given to him earlier in the afternoon by a stranger. He believed it was "muggles"—a rolled marijuana cigarette.

In his statement to police, Trent admitted that he chased the girl up the hill and assaulted her with a piece of tin. The stab wounds, however, closely matched the pocket knife found in his possession.

In August 1938, Lindbergh Trent went on trial in Hamilton County for the rape and murder of Shirley Ann Woodburn. A panel of three judges considered the evidence, and sentenced Trent to life in prison at the Ohio State Penitentiary. He was paroled on Mar. 5, 1970, and granted a final release from supervision on Mar. 25, 1975. REF.: *CBA*.

Trenton Prison Riots, prom. 1952, U.S., pris. riot. In 1952, the state prison at Trenton, N.J., was dangerously overcrowded. Thirteen hundred prisoners were squeezed into quarters built to house 1,100. Lack of work kept 300 able-bodied men in their cells for up to twenty hours a day, neither able to reduce their sentences for "work faithfully performed" nor able to earn the prison wage of ten cents an hour.

On Mar. 30, 1952, dozens of prisoners barricaded themselves into the segregation wing of the prison, but they were starved into surrendering two days later. On Apr. 18, 1952, sixty-nine inmates led by August Doak and William Dickens seized four hostages and barricaded themselves in the prison print shop. They made no attempt to escape, demanding only better food and an investigation into prison-guard brutality. Three days later, the siege ended when Trenton officials agreed to an investigation by the Osborne Association, which specialized in prison reform.

Meanwhile, 231 convicts at the nearby Rahway State Prison Farm took nine guards hostage. Demanding a new parole board and an end to brutality, they wrote their grievances on bed sheets and hung them from the prison windows. The resistance ended when food and water ran out and the men were forced to drink water from a rusty radiator and a fire hose.

News of the New Jersey uprisings increased tension in prisons across the country, including Jackson, Mich., where one convict was killed and eight others were wounded when four hostages were taken and prison buildings were burned.

On May 2, 1952, a New Jersey commission acknowledged the overcrowded conditions of the Trenton prison, calling them medieval and the prison itself a firetrap. In mid-July fourteen ringleaders of the spring riots were transferred to other penal institutions, but, on Oct. 12, the third outbreak in eight months occurred shortly after dinner when twenty prisoners took control of a prison wing containing 350 inmates and three guards. An hour later, however, the rebellion leaders were disarmed by guards crashing into the cell block with machine guns. Two prisoners were injured during the brief exchange. REF.: *CBA*.

Trepoff, General Dmitri Feodorovich (Trepov), 1855-1906, Rus., attempt. assass. On Jan. 24, 1878, a young Russian woman, Vera Ivanovna Zasulich (Sassoulich or Zasulitch), entered the office of General Dmitri Feodorovich Trepoff, the chief of police and governor of St. Petersburg. The 26-year-old Zasulich mingled with a group of people who had come to the governor's office with petitions and requests. She waited until she was able to approach the general without arousing suspicion. When she finally stood near him, she drew a pistol and shot him at point-blank range.

The assassination of General Trepoff by Vera Zasulich.

Although seriously wounded, Trepoff survived the attack. Zasulich was taken into custody and it was discovered that she was one of a group of student revolutionaries enraged over Trepoff's treatment of a condemned prisoner in one of the St. Petersburg prisons. According to reports, Trepoff was visiting the prison on July 25, 1877, and saw some prisoners talking with each other in the inner court. When Trepoff queried the prisoners about what he considered an infraction of prison rules, a prisoner named Bogoluboff replied that because he was already condemned, he was not breaking a rule by talking with another prisoner charged in a wholly different crime. Trepoff found his response impertinent and ordered him to a cell for disciplinary punishment. When the two men happened to pass each other in the hall later, Bogoluboff failed to remove his cap. Trepoff, angered by this display of disrespect, raised his hand to knock the hat from the prisoner's head. Although it was unclear whether Trepoff actually hit Bogoluboff, his hat fell to the ground. Trepoff then ordered Bogoluboff flogged

Word of the flogging spread among the prisoners and then to the general populace. Even people unsympathetic to the revolutionary cause were incensed by Trepoff's actions, so that when Zasulich acted, she did so with public sympathy if not outright support. Zasulich, who had spent the majority of her life since age seventeen either in prison or under police surveillance for her revolutionary activities, was tried in April in Russia's only jury trial of a political prisoner. She pleaded that she had shot Trepoff to call the country's attention to his continuing brutality toward the students. When Zasulich, despite her admission that she had shot the general, was found Not Guilty, the verdict was greeted with wild applause from the onlookers. It was generally taken as a public reprimand to a high-placed official who had arbitrarily overstepped the limits of his authority.

Trepoff's reputation for being tough with revolutionaries earned him the position of governor general of Moscow following the assassination of Grand Duke Sergius in 1905. His ruthless measures succeeded in quelling the subsequent student rebellion, and in June 1905, he was appointed assistant minister of the Interior. In this position he was responsible for bringing back the Third Section, the hated political police. After a brief period of moderate reform, Trepoff was once again called in to suppress popular uprisings. Late in 1905, he convinced the czar that he was his only hope of personal safety and the czar named him master of the Palace at Tsarskoe-Selo. Despite seven attempts made on his life throughout his career—some by his own family members—Trepoff died of natural causes on Sept. 15, 1906.

REF.: Bell, *Assassin; CBA.*

Tresca, Carlo, 1879-1943, U.S., (unsolv.) mur. A controversial figure in life, the fiery Italian socialist editor Carlo Tresca was even more so in death. Born in Sulmona, Abruzzi, Italy, Tresca was the fourth son of a wealthy landowner whose financial speculations resulted in forfeiture of his property holdings. Unable to fund his university education the younger Tresca became increasingly embittered against the capitalist system and what he perceived to be the greed of the bourgeoisie. He joined a socialist club in the 1890s but quickly became bored with the Marxist-tinted dogma. However, Tresca truly enjoyed confrontational politics and soon joined a movement to organize the peasant classes in the village. In 1904, he published a scathing criticism of the Catholic church in the pages of the radical journal *Il Germe.* Convicted on a libel charge, Tresca decided to flee to the U.S. rather than go to jail for six months, which the courts had decreed.

In Philadelphia Tresca got caught up in the left-wing movement, joining the Italian Socialist Federation and editing its news organ, *Il Proletario.* After putting up with two years of vicious infighting among the Marxist editors who Tresca differed with on philosophical points, he started his own weekly, *La Plebe,* through the help of Enrico Malatesta, a leader of the anarchist movement. In 1909 Tresca was convicted of libel after accusing a Roman Catholic priest in Pittsburgh of having an affair with his maid. The U.S. Post Office retaliated by revoking the mailing privileges of *La Plebe.* Moving on to New Kensington, Pa., he founded *L'Avvenire,* which, like its predecessor, championed the cause of the Italian immigrant. Gradually Tresca shifted his involvement in labor issues beyond the scope of the Italian community to embrace the cause of the International Workers of the World (IWW). He led the free-speech movement in Lawrence, Mass., in 1912, and in Paterson, N.J., a year later. Rightwingers targeted him for assassination on at least two occasions. One ill-fated attempt left a permanent knife scar on the left side of his face. In 1914, Tresca's long-suffering wife filed for divorce, naming Elizabeth Gurley Flynn, a left-wing activist, as correspondent.

With the coming of WWI Tresca found himself in trouble with the government. He was arrested for violations of the wartime Espionage Act, but the case never went to trial. *L'Avvenire,* however, was banned by the postal system. The mainstream labor movement in the U.S. considered Tresca too far afield for their tastes. In the 1920s, prominent union leaders distanced themselves from Tresca, who increasingly became associated with the Bolshevik movement. In the 1930s, the horrors of the Stalinist purges caused the Italian editor to change his thinking. He joined a commission headed by Professor John Dewey to investigate the circumstances surrounding the murder of Leon Trotsky, and afterward published daring exposés of the infamous Moscow treason trials.

Carlo Tresca, killed by parties unknown in 1943.

In 1938, Tresca accused the Soviets of kidnapping Juliet Stuart Poyntz, a disillusioned member of the Communist Party who was thought to be a spy, and dragging her off to Russia for execution. This only served to further alienate his few remaining supporters on the extreme left. In the pages of *Il Martello* (The Hammer), a mainstream Italian newspaper he had purchased after WWI, Tresca launched a broadside against the Fascist regime in Italy. In 1923, the federal government indicted him on a charge of using the mails to send obscene material. A four-line advertisement in the newspaper advocating birth control resulted in his conviction, though many believed the charge was politically motivated. Italian ambassador Don Gelasio Caetini strenuously objected to Tresca's repeated attacks against his government and demanded of Washington that something be done to silence him.

After President Calvin Coolidge commuted his prison sentence to four months, Tresca stepped up his attacks against the Fascists. During WWII he joined the Mazzini Society and helped organize the Italian-American Victory Council, designed to influence American public opinion toward liberating Italy at the earliest possible moment. Tresca's fifty-year career in left-wing circles came to a sudden, unexpected end in the streets of Manhattan the night of Jan. 11, 1943. Accompanied by his friend Giuseppe Callabi, Tresca emerged from the offices of *Il Martello* on West Fifteenth Street as a late-model sedan pulled up curbside. A lone gunman jumped out of the car and pumped three bullets at close range into the editor's head before speeding off. Tresca collapsed into the gutter, dead. Captain David Winthrop of the West Twentieth Street Station deployed two emergency squads through the neighborhood. They found a .38-caliber Colt revolver—standard police issue—100 feet from the body, concealed by ash cans. The police were not sure whether the gun belonged to the assassin or to Tresca. The editor had carried a weapon like this in 1931 when the Italian Fascists marked him for death.

There were those who accused the Communists of carrying out the assassination. Others blamed it on the Fascists. The Socialist leader Norman Thomas, no doubt convinced that right-wing elements had marked Tresca for death, kept the investigation open for another ten years. But the murder has never been officially solved though there are those who believe that an up-and-coming Mafia hood named Carmine Galante was the actual assassin. See: **Galante, Carmine.**

REF.: Campbell, *The Luciano Project; CBA;* Dewar, *Assassins at Large;* Gage, *Mafia, U.S.A.;* Gosch and Hammer, *The Last Testament of Lucky Luciano;* Katz, *Uncle Frank;* McCellan, *Crime Without Punishment;* Martin, *Revolt in the Mafia;* Nash, *Among the Missing;* Peterson, *The Mob;* Reid, *The Grim Reapers.*

Tresham, Francis, c.1567-1605, Brit., consp. Exposed Gunpowder Plot to brother-in-law William Parker, the fourth Baron Monteagle, after being brought into the conspiracy. REF.: *CBA.*

Treves Witch Trials, prom. 1581-99, Fr., witchcraft. By the late 1500s, much of Europe was in the midst of hunting for witches at the behest of the Roman Catholic Church. In Alsace, the witch hunts started in 1570, and the religious persecution had spread to Luxembourg by 1580. Remy, a witch judge, claimed to have executed about 900 people from 1581-95. The witchcraft trials in Treves started around 1581 under the auspices of Prince-Archbishop Johann von Schönenburg, Bishop Peter Binsfield, Governor Johann Zandt and notary Peter Ormsdorf. Overseeing the witch trials was Dietrich Flade, who was frequently accused by Zandt of being too lenient with suspects. Zandt later charged Flade with witchcraft and saw to it that after a lengthy trial, Flade was executed.

While there were a number of people who believed that Flade was unjustly prosecuted, attempts to exonerate him were discouraged. Cornelius Loos tried to publish a book that examined the procedures used by the church during the trials, but the Papal Nuncio ordered the book destroyed and Father Loos exiled to Brussels. In the meantime, Binsfield wrote *Tractatus,* backing the Catholic's purge of witches. The bishop blamed the spread of witchcraft on a lenient legal system and ignorant clergymen. As with most witch trials, nearly all individuals who were accused ended up being convicted. The executioner in Treves was kept very busy and the possessions were seized of those tried and convicted, while the families were banished. A witch register discovered outside the city walls at the Benedictine Abbey of St. Maximin revealed detailed court records showed that more than 300 people had been accused of being witches from 1587-94. The accused in turn had named some 1,500 people as witches.

REF: Burr, *Translations and Reprints, University of Pennsylvania; CBA;* Hennen, *Ein Hexenprozess aus der Umgegend von Trier aus dem Jahre 1572;* Liel, "Der Verfolgung der Zauberer und Hexen in dem Kurfürstenhume Trier"; Robbins, *The Encyclopedia of Witchcraft and Demonology;* Ruland, "Zwei Hexenprozesse zu Trier".

Trevor, Harold Darien, 1879-1942, Brit., fraud-rob.-mur. Swindler and robber Harold Trevor spent most of his adulthood in jail. In 1941, the 62-year-old Trevor, known to the police as "The Monocle Man," answered an advertisement for an apartment to rent in Kensington. On Oct. 14, Theodora Greenhill agreed to rent it to him. She was sitting at a desk writing out a receipt when Trevor hit her over the head with a beer bottle. Then he strangled the woman and ransacked the apartment.

Greenhill's daughter found her mother dead that afternoon. The name of Trevor was on the partially written receipt, and Trevor's fingerprints were found on some of the broken glass from the beer bottle. He was arrested at Rhyl, Wales, and returned to the Old Bailey for trial. He was found Guilty and, saying, "If my life can be of any satisfaction to them (Greenhill's daughters), take it," he was hanged.

REF.: Browne and Tullett, *The Scalpel of Scotland Yard; CBA;* Cherill, *Cherrill of the Yard;* Shew, *A Second Companion to Murder;* Tullett, *Strictly Murder.*

Triad Society (AKA: Dagger Society, Heaven & Earth Society, Hung Society, Red Society), 1674- , China, secret crim. soc. The Triads of China and greater Southeast Asia pose as great a threat to law and order in their corner of the world as the U.S. Mafia. The Triads date back to the late seventeenth century, the time of the Ch'ing dynasty. By comparison the Cosa Nostra is a newcomer to the world stage.

The sects were organized to overthrow the oppressive yoke of the Ch'ing emperors who had come out of Manchuria to conquer and subjugate the Ming dynasty. The Chinese in the southern provinces regarded the Ch'ings, and their emperor K'ang-Hsi, as foreign invaders. They took refuge at the Siu Lam monastery in the Fukien Province, where the Buddhist monks aided and abetted the military uprising fomented by the Mings. The monastery, according to popular legend, was surrounded by the Ch'ing army and blown up. There were only eighteen survivors, of which thirteen eventually died from starvation and powder burns. The remaining five crossed the Yangtze River, managing to stay one step ahead of the pursuing Ch'ing armies. The fugitives of the Siu Lam monastery were henceforth known as the "First Five Ancestors," a story that is more allegory than fact. Continuing on to Muk Yeung in the Fukien Province, they hooked up with five other loyal supporters of the cause—the "Second Five Ancestors" who established the city as a home base of operations for the fledgling "Triad Society." The Triad, symbolizing heaven, earth, and man, was divided into five lodges in five provinces of China, each under a separate banner.

The initial aim of the Triad movement was to overthrow the brutally oppressive Manchus. Their motto was "Overthrow Ch'ing; Restore Ming." But in 1736, the society was suppressed and driven into exile throughout the provinces. In the next sixty years there were a series of bloody insurrections, notably by the Eight Diagrams and Nine Mansions Sects in 1786-88, the Heaven and Earth Society in 1786-89, and the White Lotus sect in 1794 that dragged on for eight years. The influential White Lotus was a religious sect that took up arms only in times of extreme persecution. Such was the case in 1794. According to a Chinese imperial decree published in 1813, the White Lotus "was engaged in daily worship...and reading scripture, claiming thereby to make its members invulnerable to weapons, fire or drowning; but in times of famine and disorder they might plot for the Great Enterprise." Future Triads—the Big Swords, Red Spears, Yellow Beards, Small Daggers, Dragon Flower Sacred Religious—were organized on this principle.

The power of the Triads continued to grow and in 1851 the great Taiping Rebellion nearly toppled the government of the Manchus. With the popular support of villagers in the southern provinces, the Taipings, led by Hung Hsiu-Chu'an, scored a series of impressive military victories over the Manchu armies. In 1853, Hung seized Nanking where he declared himself emperor. The Triads conquered Shanghai, Amoy, and several other important cities in a ten-year rebellion that cost 20,000 lives and decimated some of the richest land in the country. In 1864, Hung Hsiu-Ch'uan committed suicide after his military forces were crushed by the combined forces of the British and Chinese statesman Li Hung-Chang.

The focus of the secret societies began to shift in the next fifty years as the Manchu base of power was eroded by the foreign interventionists. The Boxer rebellion, or the *I Ho Chuan,* meaning "The Fists of Righteous Harmony," began in Shantung in 1898 and was aimed at the final expulsion of European and American interests which had encroached on the economic and social life of the nation. The Boxers' reliance on mysticism and the power of the supernatural did them little good, for the mainland of China was soon back in Western hands following the capture of Peking on Aug. 14, 1900.

In 1911, the Manchus were deposed and the Triads were recognized by Dr. Sun Yat-Sen, himself a former member. The Republican Revolution provided them with a degree of legitimacy previously unheard of in China. Bureaucrats and politicians scrambled to join the secret societies in order to enhance their prestige and reputation in the government. Triad influence was soon felt in Hong Kong, Malaya, and Singapore. In 1925, a power struggle in Malaya resulted in a five-way split between the 18, 24, 36, 108, and Independent Groups. (The five groups honored the five founding monks. Eighteen and thirty-six are the number of monks who escaped the massacre at the monastery, and the number 108 corresponds to the number at Shaolin).

From its revolutionary beginnings the Triads segued into organized crime, extortion, drug trafficking, and vice. Following the 1949 Communist takeover, British Hong Kong became the center of the criminal activity in Southeast Asia. Seven Triad groups masquerading under the guise of trade guilds and fraternal societies vied for the control of the criminal rackets. Before 1941 only 8 percent of the population in Hong Kong belonged to Triad societies. This figure grew to a staggering 15 percent by 1958. After the 1949 Communist Revolution, the Green Pang Triad, made up of political refugees from the mainland who had fought with the Nationalists, dominated the prostitution, labor unions, and the narcotics trade on a large scale. The Green Pang was one of the oldest established Triads whose members belonged to the higher socio-economic classes. By the mid-1950s, the 14K Association, originally organized to do battle with the Communists, had become Hong Kong's second-most powerful criminal gang. Conservative estimates placed total membership in the area of 80,000 by 1954. The threat posed by the 14K Association compelled the other Triads to bolster their memberships. To be admitted into a Triad carried with it a heavy obligation, the penalty of death for violating the tenets of the secret oath-bound brotherhood. There are thirty-six such oaths a new member must swear. Those who refused to join the Triads were branded as pro-Communist, a tactic encouraged by the Nationalist government led by Generalissimo Chiang Kai-Shek.

The growth of the Triads during this period led to serious incidents of rioting and gang wars in 1956, forcing the Hong Kong police to enact stern measures to deal with the problem. The Triads pillaged more than $25 million worth of goods during the civil disturbance. There were 900 murders in Hong Kong in 1958, most of them attributed to the Triad societies. An example of the ferocious bloodletting that went on in Hong Kong during those troubled times involved a prosperous merchant named Ko Sun Wei, who lived in the city of Kowloon. Wei, two daughters, one son, and his wife were found dead in their home. The women were raped repeatedly and then tortured to death with knives. The Ko Sun Wei family were but five of the 350 murder victims entered into the police records for September 1958. Today the Triads control the bulk of the drug trade and street prostitution in Hong Kong and Singapore. Though they were outlawed by the British colonial government as far back as 1845, the Triads continue to operate with impunity. In Singapore alone, there are at least 9,000 active members belonging to six different groups. Despite the thrust of technology and profound Western influence, the Triads endure as a formidable criminal network. See: **Boxers, The; White Lotus Society, The.**

REF.: *CBA;* Mackenzie, *Secret Societies;* Scott, *The Concise Encyclopedia of Crime and Criminals;* Whitehead, *Journey into Crime.*

Tribonian, d. 545, E. Roman., jur. Chief legal minister, serving under Emperor Justinian. He joined nine other commissioners in producing the collection of imperial constitutions known as *Codex,* and was named by the emperor to head other commissions that produced the *Institutes,* the *Digesta,* and other works. He also served as quaestor from 530-32 and from 534-45. REF.: *CBA.*

Trieber, Jacob, 1853-1927, U.S., jur. Appointed to eastern district court of Arkansas by President William McKinley in 1900. He earlier served as U.S. attorney in the eastern district of Arizona from 1897. REF.: *CBA.*

Trimble, Robert, 1777-1828, U.S., jur. Judge on Kentucky Court of Appeals from 1807-09 and later became Kentucky's U.S. district attorney. He was appointed to the district court of Kentucky by President James Madison in 1817, where he served until he was appointed to the U.S. Supreme Court by President John Quincy Adams. REF.: *CBA.*

Trimble, William, b.1797, U.S., jur. U.S. district attorney and judge on first judicial district court from 1819-20, both in Arkansas territory. He was also a magistrate on the county court of Hamstead County from 1823-24. He was appointed to the territorial court of Arkansas by President James Monroe in 1824. REF.: *CBA.*

Tripp, Glenn Kurt, 1963-83, U.S., skyjack. When Glenn Kurt Tripp hijacked his first plane in July 1980, a friend told police that Tripp often spoke of hijackings and planes as part of a fantasy life. Tripp attempted to hijack a Northwest Airlines Boeing 727 at the Seattle, Wash., airport by claiming he had a bomb in the briefcase he carried. Tripp managed to hold the plane for ten hours until FBI agents delivered a $100,000 ransom he had demanded. However, when Tripp tried to dash from the plane to a getaway car he had also demanded, FBI agents captured him.

Tripp was charged with and pleaded guilty to first-degree kidnapping and first-degree extortion and was sentenced to twenty years in prison. Tripp's sentence was rescinded in favor of his attendance at a vocational training institute on the recommendation of probation officers and the county prosecutor because of Tripp's diminished mental faculties. He was described during the sentencing procedures as "mentally retarded."

In January 1983, Tripp boarded a Northwest Orient jetliner, claiming to have a bomb in a small carton. FBI agents sent on board to stop the hijacking were not aware of Tripp's identity and shot him to death. REF.: *CBA.*

Tripp, Grace, 1691-1710, Brit., rob.-mur. Grace Tripp was Lord Torrington's housekeeper in London when she took up with a man named Peters who engineered a plan to rob the Torrington estate while the owners were away on vacation. Grace was apprehensive, but Peters was a charming young suitor, and he promised to marry her after the crime.

Late one night, Grace Tripp admitted Peters to the house. Just as they were about to make off with the silver, a house maid came downstairs to see what all the commotion was about. Peters grabbed the girl and cut her throat from ear to ear, while Grace stood helplessly by holding a candle. Peters took thirty guineas from the dead girl's pocket and he and Tripp fled through the back door.

They were arrested a few days later. To save his own neck, Peters turned evidence for the crown against Grace Tripp. Peters avoided the death sentence by betraying Grace. Her protests fell on deaf ears. The housekeeper went to the gallows at Tyburn on Mar. 17, 1710.

REF.: *CBA;* Mitchell, *The Newgate Calendar;* Nash, *Look For the Woman;* O'Donnell, *Should Women Hang?*

Trippet, Robert S., c.1919- , U.S., fraud. By 1974, the Home-Stake Production Company of Tulsa, Okla., an oil-drilling tax-shelter concern, had raised $100 million by promising its investors a 400 percent return on their money. When the returns failed to appear and after the Internal Revenue Service determined that the investment money had not been used for drilling and was therefore taxable, disgruntled investors, including Walter Matthau, Alan Alda, and singer David Cassidy, initiated a class-action suit.

Con man Robert S. Trippett.

Having gone public in 1964, Home-Stake attracted increasing investment money every year until 1971, when investments declined. The company was founded by Robert Trippet, a Tulsa lawyer, who was discovered to be running a "Ponzi scheme" in which small amounts of money collected from investors are returned to them as interest, while the bulk of the money, ostensibly being used to produce a product, is pocketed by the schemer. In the case of Home-Stake, $14 million of the $18 million collected could not be accounted for. In Autumn 1973, the Securities and Exchange Commission suspended trading in Home-Stake stock, filed suit for fraud, and declared the company insolvent. Trippet, who had recently resigned as chairman, and the new managers sued each other for mismanagement. Trippet agreed to an injunction against violations of federal security laws without admitting or denying he had committed any violations.

In Los Angeles in December 1975, Trippet and twelve others were indicted and charged with forty-five counts of conspiracy, tax fraud, securities fraud, and mail fraud. One man pleaded guilty and the case against three others was dropped in early 1976, but on Dec. 21, 1976, in the Tulsa courtroom of U.S. District Court Judge Allen Barrow, Trippet and former vice president Frank Sims pleaded no contest to one count of conspiracy and nine counts of mail fraud. Another former vice president, Harry Fitzgerald, pleaded no contest to two counts of selling unregistered securities. Trippet was sentenced to three years' probation, fined $19,000, and ordered to remit $100,000 to the widows and orphans of Home-Stake investors. Sims received a year of probation and was ordered to place $5,000 in the widows and orphans fund. Fitzgerald was given a year of unsupervised probation. The case was closed in 1977 when charges against Kent M. Klineman, a New York tax lawyer and the final defendant, were dropped. REF.: *CBA.*

Tri-State Gang, prom. 1930s, U.S., org. crime. The Tri-State Gang was formed in 1930 in Philadelphia and led by Robert Mais, Walter Legenza, and Anthony Cugino. The gang was notorious for killing its own members. Cugino had been imprisoned for fifteen years for a 1919 jewel robbery. Upon his release, he formed the Tri-State Gang along with Mais, Legenza, Salvatore Serpa, Eddie Wallace, John Zurkorsky, and others. After robbing a plant of its payroll and killing a police officer, Cugino and Serpa suspected their partners, Wallace and Zurkorsky, might go to the police. The two drove Wallace and Zurkorsky outside the city and shot them. Zurkorsky lived, but Cugino and Serpa allegedly killed his and Wallace's girlfriends, Florence Miller and Ethel Greentree, whose bodies were found in a shallow grave outside Downington, Pa. Cugino shot gangster Johnny Horn and later stabbed Serpa. His loyalty lay only with Mais and Legenza.

While they were jailed in Richmond, Va., awaiting execution for murdering a guard during a mail-truck robbery, Cugino sent Mais and Legenza two pistols hidden in a baked turkey. The pair killed a guard, escaped, and joined Cugino in stealing $48,000 from an electric company. But the two escapees were informed on by other gang members, and they were returned to Richmond and electrocuted. Cugino moved to New York, where he recruited new members and controlled the Tri-State Gang from a distance. When Cugino killed Anthony Zanghi over the split in a counterfeit operation, Philadelphia gangsters became disturbed and informed police where he could be found. Cugino was arrested on Sept. 8, 1935, and questioned by police for fifteen hours straight. He revealed some facts about the murder of James J. Garvey, a New York police detective, and then hanged himself in his jail cell that night. The Tri-State Gang disintegrated after his death. REF.: *CBA.*

Trolia, John, 1944- , U.S., mur. According to court testimony, on Sept. 1, 1974, John Trolia, a 30-year-old man from Burbank, Ill., and Paula Popik, a 21-year-old cocktail waitress, were seen leaving a South Side Chicago lounge in her car. Later that morning, Popik's car was found burning. Five days later, her body was discovered floating in the Des Plaines River. She had been shot, and her body had been in the river two or three days.

An initial grand jury investigation and hearing implicated no one, then several friends of Trolia said they lied during the hearing and changed their stories. Linda Szilagyi said she saw Trolia and Popik together on Sept. 1. Richard Maskas testified that, on Aug. 30, Trolia borrowed a pistol from him and returned it several days later telling him it could be "hot." Two of Trolia's friends, Thomas O'Neill and Robert Holwell, initially arrested for the murder, testified that Trolia confessed to Popik's murder. After hearing this testimony, the jury convicted Trolia of murder and Justice Louis B. Garippo sentenced him to twenty-five to seventy-five years in prison.

After the trial, a police report surfaced that included a statement by Rebecca Lavin that she had seen Popik on Sept. 3, two days after she was reportedly killed. An appellate court ruled that the new evidence negated the Guilty verdict. After serving five years in prison, Trolia won a new trial. In August 1980, Trolia was again convicted of murder, and Judge Frank Machala sentenced him to twenty-five to seventy-five years in prison. REF.: *CBA.*

Trolle, Gustav Eriksson, 1488-1535, Swed., mur. Archbishop of Sweden and head of council of state from 1514. His regency was briefly lost to Sten Sture the Younger in 1517, inciting civil war, but was returned in 1518. Shortly thereafter, in 1520, he convinced King Christian II to put eighty-two nobles to death in a massacre known as the Stockholm Bloodbath, after which he was forced to escape to Denmark. He was seized at the battle of Oxnebjerg in 1535. REF.: *CBA.*

Tronolone, John (AKA: **Peanuts**), c.1910- , U.S., org. crime. In November 1985, John Tronolone ascended to the head of the Cleveland mob upon the death of James T. Licavoli, eighty-one, who died while serving a seventeen-year sentence at the federal prison in Oxford, Wis. After Licavoli's initial sentencing, Angelo A. Lonardo became boss, but became a protected federal witness against his former Mafia family members after he was convicted on a drug charge in 1983.

Tronolone, born in Buffalo, N.Y., was arrested three times for gambling before his twenty-first birthday. In 1975, he was convicted of running a $1 million-a-week bookmaking operation, sentenced to two years in prison, and fined $2,000. Although active in the Cleveland mob, Tronolone lived in Miami, where he operated the Peter Pan Travel Agency. On Mar. 21, 1985, in New York City, Tronolone and fourteen other organized-crime figures were indicted on federal racketeering charges and charged with conspiring to defraud the Teamsters Union by influencing and controlling the selection of Roy Lee Williams as president of the union in 1981. The twenty-nine-count indictment included accusations of conspiracy to commit murder, labor racketeering, gambling, and bid rigging in the construction and food industries. On May 4, 1985, the mobsters were acquitted on all charges. Tronolone was expected to move back to Cleveland and revive the sagging mob by inducting new recruits. REF.: *CBA.*

Troppmann, Jean-Baptiste, 1849-70, Fr. fraud-theft-mur. It was rumored that the diabolical murders of Jean Kinck, his wife, and six children by the fiend Jean Troppmann was engineered by Otto von Bismarck, Germany's "Iron Chancellor," to undermine the government of Napoléon III. Troppmann was the agent provocateur, according to one account, paid to do away with Kinck, a Prussian spy who had become an embarrassment to Bismarck. The story was dismissed out of hand when the true facts of the case came to light in Fall 1869.

Troppmann was born in Cernay (Haut-Rhin), west of Mulhouse. As a boy he was apprenticed to his father's manufacturing company, Troppmann et Kambly. In December 1868, the firm sold some heavy equipment to a Paris businessman and the son was sent to the city to supervise its installation. The young man made a good accounting of himself and was greatly admired for his thrift and ambition. After the project was complete Troppmann continued on to Roubaix where he made the acquaintance of Jean Kinck, an Alsatian businessman who had risen from the status of common laborer to private entrepreneur engaged in the manufacture of spindles and looms. The enterprising Kinck desired to resettle in Alsace, his ancestral home. He owned a house in Bühl but had so far been unable to persuade his wife, a native of Roubaix, to agree to move. Troppmann exploited this gnawing ambition in Kinck, a man thirty years his senior. In time the two became fast friends, discussing at length their ambitions to grow wealthy together in Alsace.

Jean Troppmann convinced Kinck to map out a journey with him to Bollwiller, Alsace, where presumably they would set into motion their grandiose plans. On Aug. 24, 1869, Kinck left Roubaix, having told his wife that he would "be home between ten and eleven on the morning of September 2nd." He carried in his valise a number of blank checks issued by a bank in Roubaix. At the train station Kinck was greeted by Troppmann who escorted him to the village of Guebwiller by carriage. From there the trusting businessman fully expected to be taken to Wattwiller to meet some family members. But he was never seen again, at least by those family members who expected him for a visit.

Jean-Baptiste Troppmann, mass murderer.

Troppmann appeared in Cernay, about a dozen miles from Bollwiller, on the twenty-fifth. He told of an important business contact he had made and of an impending transaction involving large amounts of money and bank-notes. Meanwhile, back in Roubaix the anxious wife awaited some news of her husband. On Aug. 27 she received a curious letter in Troppman's handwriting. Kinck explained that he had met with an accident and was unable to hold a pen, but his young friend Troppmann was taking down his instructions. Hortense Kinck was directed to cash an enclosed check in the amount of 5,500 francs and remit the cash to her husband in Alsace. The money arrived at Guebwiller on the thirty-first, and, using Kinck's identification papers, Troppmann attempted to claim the money. The skeptical postmaster, however, refused to turn it over.

Troppmann devised a new strategy. He returned to Roubaix and presented a letter to Hortense, allegedly dictated to him by Kinck. "You must all of you come to Paris for two or three days. Don't fear the expense as Troppmann has given me a half a million. I insist on your coming. You, Gustave, must go at once to Guebwiller to draw out the money." The next day Hortense received power of attorney and 500 francs as promised in the letter. The check, however, was in Troppmann's handwriting. The wife barely concealed her uneasiness about her husband's continuing disability which prevented him from writing in his own hand, but she trusted Troppmann and followed his instructions to the letter.

He kept insisting that the family join him at the Hôtel du Chemin de Fer du Nord in Paris, and to bring money. Troppmann's parents received several dispatches from their son alluding to a fabulous business transaction that was to make them all rich for the rest of their days. Puzzled, they simply waited. On Sept. 17 Gustave Kinck met Troppmann at the railway station in Paris. Two days later Hortense and her five children left Roubaix with trepidation they hoped would be diminished once they were reunited with Jean Kinck. When at last Troppmann made his rendezvous with the Kinck family, he told them that they must go with him by carriage to Pantin. Troppmann directed the driver to continue on past the farms and fields to a secluded spot off the main road. When the cab stopped, Troppmann, Madame Kinck, and the two youngest children made their way down a winding path toward a dark and silent building that stood nearby. The other three youngsters remained behind, prattling happily with the driver. Half an hour later, and under the cover of darkness, Troppmann returned alone. "We have decided to stay the night here, children," he said. Thinking nothing more of it, the cabman received his fare and drove off. The following Monday morning Troppmann returned to Paris to change into clean clothing in preparation for his journey to Le Havre, where he planned to set sail for America. His bloodstained clothes were carelessly left behind in the hotel. This mistake was to cost Troppmann once his identity had been established by the Sûreté.

Troppman victims Jean Kinck, center, with his wife and oldest son.

The bodies of Hortense Kinck and her five children, Emile, Henri, Alfred, Achille, and Marie, were unearthed on Sept. 20 by a farmer named Langlois who reported his discovery to the police. Each of the victims had been bludgeoned over the head and there was evidence that the younger ones had been buried alive. The identity of Hortense Kinck and her children was quickly established by clothing labels identified by the innkeeper who had recognized them as belonging to his guests. In Le Havre the police quickly became suspicious of a young man shopping for immigration papers. The suspect was arrested and taken into custody after registering at two different hotels on successive nights. The man claimed to speak only Bavarian, but he was overheard conversing in French.

Placed under intense questioning, Troppmann said he was merely an accessory. Jean Kinck and his son Gustave had plotted the murders of Hortense and the five children. On Sept. 26 a seventh body was pulled out of the Langlois field, that of Gustave Kinck who had been stabbed through the throat. When shown the grisly remains Troppmann was indignant. "The swine! He has now killed his remaining son." The police continued to hammer away at Troppmann until they at last forced a confession out of him. "I murdered the father," he said, "to get possession of the money which he said he had in the bank and which would have been paid out to his order. That order I proposed to forge by copying his signature. Having murdered him it was almost a matter of necessity to me to kill all the rest of the family, since they all knew that Kinck had gone with me to my home." On Nov. 25 what was left of Jean Kinck was found in a wooded glade outside the castle of Herinfluch, north of Cernay. Troppmann explained that he had poisoned Kinck in Alsace using prussic acid poured into a wine flask.

Following the discovery of the eighth and final body an indictment charging Troppmann with theft, fraud, and murder was returned by the courts. The trial commenced at the Assize of the Seine on Dec. 28, 1869. The gallery was packed with spectators from all strata of French society including politicians, artisans, and nobles. It was in many respects the gala social event of the year as people finagled for scarce tickets. Troppmann was represented by the notable attorney Charles-Alexandre Lachaud, who attempted to portray his client as a weak, innocent knave who suffered from a diseased mind. Lachaud was a highly respected advocate, well thought of by leading political figures in the government. But the task before him proved too great. For his part, Troppmann persisted in his assertion that he had accomplices, which gave rise to the theory that Prussian agents were behind all of this. Invasion of France was imminent, some said. Left-wing sympathizers accused the emperor of paying Troppmann to murder the Kinck family to divert public attention away from the sagging fortunes of the Second Empire. Both theories were baseless conjecture.

Jean Troppmann was adjudged Guilty and executed on the Place de la Roquette the morning of Jan. 19, 1870, amidst solemn fanfare. The event was witnessed by a score of celebrities including the Russian writer Ivan Turgenev, who wrote about Troppmann in one of his novels. Observing the curious solemnity of the day, Turgenev quoted a remark made by one of his friends: "It seemed to me as though we were in 1794 instead of 1870, as though we were not ordinary citizens escorting to the scaffold a common assassin but Jacobins hurrying to his execution a ci-devant marquis."

REF.: Bertrand, *Etude médico-légale au sujet de Troppmann;* Bolitho, *Murder for Profit;* Bouchardon, *Troppmann;* Brophy, *The Meaning of Murder; CBA;* Douthwaite, *Mass Murder;* Hessling, *Trois monstres;* Irving, *Studies of French Criminals in the Nineteenth Century;* Logan, *Masters of Crime;* Metternich, *Souvenirs d'enfance et de jeunesse;* Williams, *Manners and Murders in the World of Louis-Napoleon;* Wilson, *Encyclopedia of Murder;* (DRAMA), Percy, *The Last Straw.*

Trotsky, Leon (Lev Davidovich Bronstein), 1879-1940, Rus.-Mex., assass. Had Leon Trotsky won his power struggle with Joseph Stalin following the death of Vladimir Lenin in January 1924, the history of the Soviet Union would probably have been quite different. Trotsky, the intellectual light of the Bolshevik Revolution, often disagreed with Lenin. He was an early advocate of the Menshevik position, the liberal democratic alternative to Bolshevism. His theory of a "permanent revolution" dependent on the class revolt that would inevitably occur in all capitalist democracies contradicted the views of Stalin, his formidable adversary after 1917.

Trotsky compromised the liberal ideal in 1917 when he joined the Bolshevik faction, thereby subordinating himself to Lenin's will. During the early months of the Civil War (1918-20), as commander of the Soviet troops, Trotsky effectively crushed the White armies and thwarted the counteroffensive launched by Alexsandr Kerensky at Petrograd. In 1918 he finalized the Brest-Litovsk treaty, which gave the Germans considerable lands in exchange for Soviet withdrawal from WWI. Trotsky then resigned his post as foreign commissar in order to assume the task of building the Red Army from what remained of the Czarist forces. By 1920 he was clearly established as the number two man in the Soviet hierarchy behind Lenin. Trotsky, one of the five members of the Politburo from its birth in 1919, antagonized many of his peers in the government with his intellectual arrogance and the preferred status he enjoyed within Lenin's inner circle. His acceptance of Lenin's ideological compromise of communism in favor of the "New Economic Policy" cost him a significant amount of political influence at the Tenth Party Congress in March 1921.

In May 1922, Lenin suffered a cerebral hemorrhage. When a second attack resulted in his death in January 1924, the issue of succession dominated the subsequent Politburo meetings. Trotsky, Lev Kamenev, and Grigory Zinovyev, who had formed an uneasy alliance at the Fourteenth Party Congress in 1926, opposed Stalin and his supporters who had drifted away from the party philosophy of worldwide revolution. By October 1926, Stalin had consolidated his base of support and succeeded in purging Trotsky from the Politburo. A year later Trotsky was also dropped from the Central Committee. In January 1928, Stalin drove Trotsky and several of his key followers into exile in Alma-Ata in remote Central Asia. A year later, Trotsky was forced to leave the country. He settled in Turkey, then France, and then Norway. In 1935, he attacked Stalin in his book, *The Revolution Betrayed.* In 1936, the Norwegian government yielded to pressure from Stalin and expelled Trotsky, who now appealed to Mexican President Lázaro Cárdenas for political asylum. By this time Russia was in the midst of the notorious treason trials, which resulted in the capture and execution of dozens of top ranking party officials. Trotsky was convicted *in absentia* as a Red "heretic." Stalin's dreaded secret police, the GPU, were ordered to track exiled political opponents, and various Trotskyite leaders such as Rudolf Klement in Paris were hunted down and murdered.

Trotsky, meanwhile, was welcomed as a true revolutionary hero by factions of the Mexican government. He was invited to live with the renowned painter Diego Rivera, who had championed the peasant class struggles through his own artwork. In 1939, a rift, attributed to a flirtation between Trotsky and Rivera's wife, the artist, Frieda Kahlo, developed, and Trotsky and his wife, Natalya, moved out of Rivera's house and took up residence in Coyoacan, a suburb of Mexico City. Rivera later insisted he had asked Trotsky to leave to facilitate the demise of an enemy of the revolution.

Fearing for his safety, Trotsky moved into a heavily fortified compound with a watchtower and a barricaded gate. The estate was patrolled around the clock by ten Mexican policemen and several Americans Trotskyites. Trotsky took these elaborate precautions after learning of Klement's fate and the demise of the doomed Fourth International in Paris. Following the Stalinist dictates, the Mexican revolutionaries condemned Trotsky as the revolution's "Judas," and sentenced him to death. On May 24, 1940, the painter David Alfaro Siqueiros and a gang of Marxist ideologues, artists, soldiers, and a group of mine workers descended on Trotsky's compound. The police guards were lured away from their posts by two women posing as prostitutes, leaving only a few guards, including the American Robert Sheldon Harte. Siqueiros and his lieutenant, an artisan named Pujol, were dressed in military uniforms. They loaded their vehicle up with rope ladders, a rotary saw, incendiary bombs, several revolvers and a machine gun, and drove to the villa where they were met by Harte, who admitted them without question.

As Trotsky and his wife slept, the raiding party of twenty heavily armed men entered the courtyard. Trotsky's guards were captured and held prisoner in the guard house while Siqueiros and

Leon Trotsky in Russia, 1920.

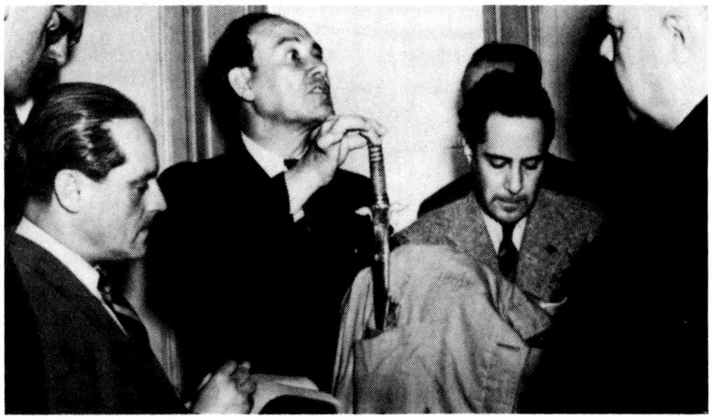

Police chief Jose Nunez shows Monard's dagger.

Trotsky's funeral procession in Mexico City, 1940.

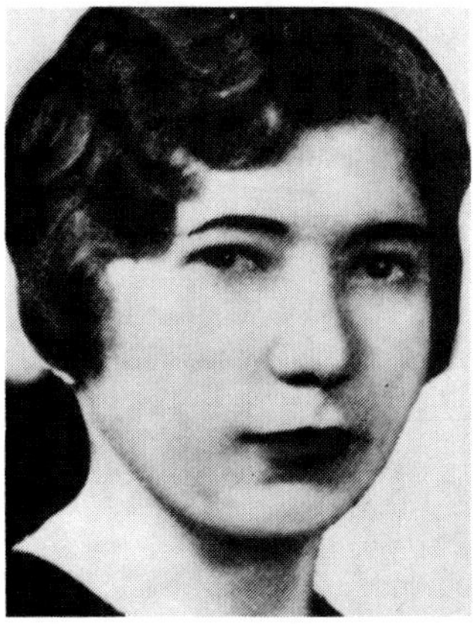

Sylvia Ageloof, Mornard's mistress.

Trotsky's study where Mornard attacked him.

David Siqueiros, would-be assassin.

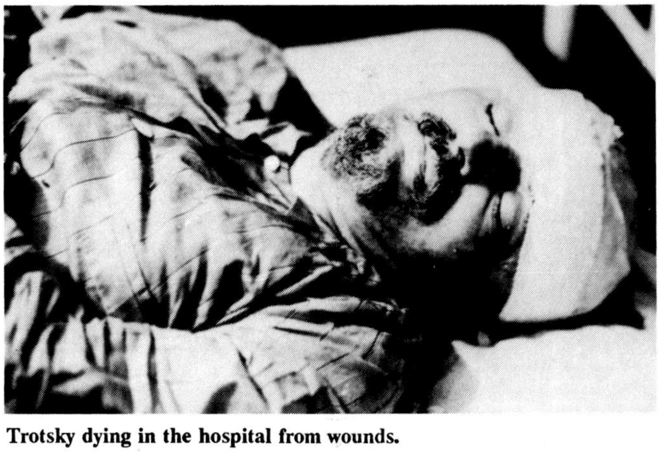

Trotsky dying in the hospital from wounds.

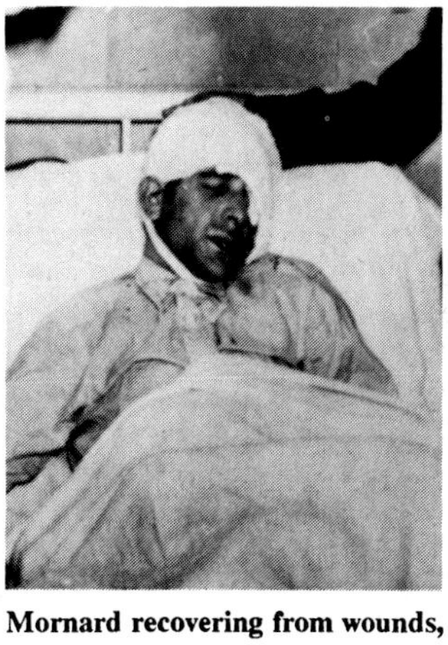

Mornard recovering from wounds, and later in prison.

several of his men positioned the machine gun outside the Trotskys' bedroom. When the machine gunners opened fire, Trotsky and his wife hurled themselves to the floor and hid under the bed. Two incendiary bombs were thrown, one of which struck the door of Trotsky's grandson Seva. Miraculously, no one was killed or seriously injured, though the house was in shambles.

Having failed in their first attempt, the extremists in the Mexican Communist Party regrouped. When the body of Robert Harte, who had been taken away by the raiders, was found buried in a pit of quicklime near a remote farmhouse, the police began a search for his murderer and the gunmen went into temporary hiding. In 1942 Siqueiros was permitted to leave Mexico and eventually wound up in Chile, having suffered no reprisals for his botched attempt on Trotsky. He was alternately described as an "uncontrolled element considered half mad," and as a romantic revolutionary who had served with distinction in the Spanish Republican Army.

In Coyoacan, Trotsky ordered construction of a new watchtower and had an elaborate alarm system installed in the house. In the summer of 1940, a Trotsky sympathizer who went by the name of Frank Jacson, began cultivating Trotsky's friendship. Four days after the Siqueiros assassination attempt, he paid a social call on Trotsky and, over the next four weeks, made a point of visiting him on a regular basis. He expressed profound admiration for Trotsky's work, particularly the ill-fated Fourth International. Having ingratiated himself with Trotsky, Jacson left for New York in June.

What Trotsky did not know was that Jacson was really Jaime Ramón Mercader del Rio Hernandez, the son of a Spanish businessman and a Cuban mother with communist sympathies. Mercader joined the Republican army during the Spanish Civil War, and was ultimately recruited for work in the GPU (the State Political Bureau which had replaced the Cheka) by Leonid Eitigon, one of his mother's lovers. In Paris, posing as Jacques Mornard, a French journalist, Mercader seduced Sylvia Agelof, an American social worker whose sister had once worked as Trotsky's secretary. Mercader was introduced to Sylvia during the Fourth International conference by Ruby Weill and within months they had become lovers. When Sylvia returned to the U.S. she took Mornard with her. He used a Canadian passport and the alias of Frank Jacson to gain admission to the U.S. This same passport also got him into Mexico.

Returning to New York, Mercader received his orders from the Gaik Ovakinian, the head of GPU operations in the U.S., to kill Trotsky. Mercader returned to his hotel room in Mexico City, and considered how to carry out the assassination. He continued, as before, visiting the aging revolutionary at his home to discuss the issues of the day. In August, Mercader asked Trotsky if he would consider looking over an essay he had written. His host agreed and invited him back on the twentieth to go over the document. On Aug. 20, he returned, armed with a thirteen-inch dagger, a pistol, and an Alpine ice ax, concealed by a top coat draped over his arm. After greeting him, Trotsky sat down at the desk in his study and began to read Mercader's manuscript.

Mercader had decided to use the ice ax because it was both deadly and silent, and if all worked well, he might be able to murder Trotsky and then slip away unnoticed by the guards. As Trotsky perused the document, Mercader stood up and plunged the ax into his mentor's skull. The blow was not strong enough to render Trotsky unconscious, however, and he cried out in pain, bringing the American bodyguards, Joseph Hansen and Jake Cooper into the room. Hansen and Cooper wrestled Mercader to the ground and beat him senseless. Trotsky prevented them from killing him, saying that Mercader would have "a story to tell."

Trotsky lived another next twenty-five hours. Before lapsing into a coma, he dictated a statement to Hansen: "I am close to death from the blow of a political assassin who struck me in my room... Please say to our friends: I am sure of victory of the Fourth International. Go forward!"

Once in custody, Mercader claimed that he had killed Trotsky in defense of Sylvia Agelof's honor, a contention Agelof vehemently denied. On Apr. 17, 1943, Mercader, tried under the name of Mornard, was convicted of murder. Mercader insisted throughout the trial that he was not a Soviet agent and that his name really was Mornard. For the next seventeen years he was a model prisoner in the Juarez penitentiary in Mexico City. The longer he stuck to this story, the greater the doubt in the authorities' minds. However, in 1950 Dr. Alfonso Quiroz compared a set of fingerprints taken from the man believed to be Mercader with prints taken from Mercader by the Madrid Police in Barcelona in 1935. They were found to be identical and the question of Mercader's identity was finally laid to rest.

Mercader was released on May 6, 1960. He moved to Prague where he became a journalist, and subsequently returned to Moscow where he spent the next fifteen years. The Soviets gave him the "Order of the Soviet Union." In published interviews, however, Mercader persisted in calling himself Mornard. Mornard-Mercader established his final residence in Cuba where he died in 1978. See: **Lenin, Vladimir Ilich; Stalin, Josef.**

REF.: Bell, *Assassin;* Bloom, *Money of Their Own;* Bornstein, *The Politics of Murder; CBA;* Demaris, *Brothers in Blood: The International Terrorist Network;* _____, *The Director;* Dewar, *Assassins at Large;* Hurwood, *Society and the Assassin;* Laquer, *Terrorism;* McClellan and Avery, *The Voices of Guns;* Nash, *Almanac of World Crime;* Paine, *The Assassins' World;* Powers, *Secrecy and Power;* Schreiber, *The Ultimate Weapon—Terrorists and World Order;* Sparrow, *The Great Assassins;* Toledano, *J. Edgar Hoover;* (FILM), *The Assassination of Trotsky,* 1972; *Zina,* 1985.

Trotter, Clarence, 1958- , U.S., rape-mur. In July 1986, Clarence Trotter and two other men abducted 40-year-old Betty Howard as she left her apartment on Chicago's southeast side with her 2-year-old son. Howard was taking the boy to a birthday party when the three men abducted them and took them to a vacant apartment. After locking the boy in a bathroom, the men tied Howard to a radiator and raped her. She was then stabbed several times, including once in the heart. She was also shot once in the forehead.

Trotter, who maintained his innocence throughout the trial, was convicted of the crimes in November 1988. He was sentenced a month later to life in prison without parole, the maximum sentence for his crimes. Michael Tillman, twenty-two, the janitor of the building in which the rape and murder occurred, was sentenced to life in prison for the murder. A third man was acquitted. REF.: *CBA.*

Trousseau Murderer, The, See: **Boyce, Arthur Robert.**

Trowbridge, Edmund, 1709-93, U.S., jur. Attorney general of Massachusetts from 1749-67, and also served as judge on superior court of Massachusetts from 1767-75. In this post he presided over the Boston Massacre trial. REF.: *CBA.*

Truber, Manfred, 1957- , and **Filipovitz, Peter**, 1957- , and **Wallner, Walter**, 1955- , Aust., rob.-asslt.-rape-mur. In June 1974, three Viennese juveniles began a two-month crime spree that included two murders, two rapes and twenty-three assaults and robberies. In many instances, the crimes showed a particularly sadistic touch and in most cases, the victims were elderly or women. One man, Johann Kuehn was beaten and kicked as he lay on the ground. In another attack, the three boys knocked down a 70-year-old woman, kicked her unconscious and ripped off her underwear.

The trio, 17-year-old Peter Filipovitz, 19-year-old Walter Wallner, and 17-year-old Manfred Truber, were frequently described to police by the victims as neat and well-dressed—"nice" boys. On Aug. 30, the "nice" boys selected their last victim. As a 68-year-old woman walked down a darkened alleyway in the late afternoon, the three stepped from a doorway and one of them punched her on the side of the head. Enraged, the woman swung her handbag into his face, knocking him to the ground, then kicked him hard in the throat. She kneed another boy in the groin and hit the third in the face. When the boy on the ground tried to get up she kicked him in the face.

Police arrived shortly and arrested the three. The boy on the ground turned out to be the gang's leader, Truber. Truber carried a carving knife which laboratory tests proved was the murder weapon in the second slaying. All three were charged in the crimes and brought to trial. Although they were all found Guilty, they received only short prison sentences because they were underage criminals. REF.: *CBA.*

True, Nellie Grace, See: **Greenwood, David.**

True, Ronald, 1891-1951, Brit., mur. Ronald True had difficulty handling reality, and thus indulged in a strong fantasy life. His wealthy Bedfordshire family supported him in his many attempts—becoming a sheep farmer, joining the Royal Canadian Mounted Police, learning to fly. True became a drug addict, divorcing him even further from reality. While living in New York City, he convinced an actress he was a WWI pilot so she would marry him. He eventually left her to run a flying school, though he had never actually learned to fly. Returning to Europe, his family arranged for him to go to Africa for a mining job, but he did not last any longer in that than he had in any other attempt.

True spent the next several years in and out of nursing homes for his addiction. When he was out of them, he frequented questionable nightspots in London. In early 1922, he began to hunt for "the other Ronald True," whom he blamed for the bad things he did, like writing bad checks and stealing money from friends. On Mar. 5, "the other Ronald True" spent the night with a prostitute he had known before, Olive Young (real name: Gertrude Yates). When they rose in the morning, he killed her with a rolling pin. He dragged Young's body into the bathroom, nodded politely to the cleaning lady when she arrived, and left.

Murderer Ronald True.

Young's body was found immediately, and the cleaning lady was able to identify True to the police. True pawned Young's jewelry and then dressed to spend an evening at the theater. He was arrested in his box at the Hammersmith Palace. True was found Guilty and sentenced to death, but the home secretary had him examined by psychiatrists and commuted his sentence to life at Broadmoor. He lived another twenty-eight years in that institution.

REF.: Bowen-Rowland, *In the Light of the Law; CBA;* Clegg, *Return Your Verdict;* Eddy, *Scarlet and Ermine;* Grice, *Great Cases of Sir Henry Curtis Bennett;* Hodge, *The Black Maria;* Hyde, *United in Crime;* Jacobs, *Pageant of Murder;* Lambton, *Thou Shalt Do No Murder;* Lustgarten, *The Story of Crime; Notable British Trials;* Oswald, *Memoirs of a London County Coroner;* Pearson, *Instigation of the Devil;* Pollock, *Mr. Justice McCardie;* Rowland, *Unfit to Plead;* Shew, *A Second Companion to Murder;* Wilson, *Encyclopedia of Murder.*

Trujillo Molina, Rafael Leonidas, 1891-1961, Dom., dictator, assass. One of eleven children of a postal clerk, Rafael Trujillo rose to power through the military, one of the few ways available to him. He entered the military in 1918 and survived in part by serving as a "gofer" for American soldiers stationed in the Dominican Republic during the occupation of 1916-24. In 1930, as head of the army, Trujillo led the ouster of President Horacio Vasquez and declared himself president. He served officially in that capacity from 1930-38 and again from 1942-52, and remained the power behind the presidency whenever he was out of office. By solidifying his position through nepotism and political murder, Trujillo maintained his dictatorship of the island nation for thirty years, often using torture and mass detention.

Trujillo achieved peace for his people, but deprived them of their civil liberties. After a hurricane destroyed 70 percent of the capital, Trujillo rebuilt it by imposing rigid economic measures. Business prospered under his guidance, and the Dominican Republic achieved as high a standard of living as the rest of Latin America, with, however, a disproportionate amount of the wealth going to Trujillo's family. He paid off foreign debts most observers were certain would be defaulted on, only by levying crushing taxes. Good roads were built but were dotted with military checkpoints. In 1937, when he still felt it necessary to demonstrate his power, he had 15,000 Haitian men, women, and children, who had taken up residence along the border, killed in a thirty-six-hour period.

As is often the case with dictators, Trujillo's downfall was rooted in his own efforts to suppress dissent. On Feb. 27, 1956, (Dominican Independence Day) a Spanish scholar named Jesus Galindez presented his doctoral dissertation on "The Trujillo Era" at Columbia University in Manhattan. Galindez had lived in the Dominican Republic and was passionately opposed to Trujillo's rule, but his study was surprisingly balanced, giving Trujillo credit for his accomplishments as well as blasting his extensive civil rights abuses. Trujillo's highly efficient secret service, which had carried out kidnappings in New York City and Havana in his name, informed Trujillo of Galindez's presentation. Only two weeks later, on Mar. 12, Galindez was kidnapped and flown to the Dominican Republic, where he was murdered on Trujillo's orders. Gerald Murphy, the American pilot of the plane bragged about the kidnapping to other Americans in Miami. Murphy was killed on Dec. 3, 1956, and his Dominican co-pilot, Octavio de la Maza, was arrested for his murder.

It was a common practice for loyal Trujillistas to confess to crimes they had not committed if the government requested that they do so. Those who cooperated and confessed were rewarded for their loyalty. De la Maza, however, did not comply. He refused to confess to Murphy's murder and offered evidence of his innocence. When he was hanged in his cell on Jan. 7, 1957, his death was ruled a suicide.

By December 1958, Trujillo's excesses became such an embarrassment to his supporters in the U.S. government that the CIA was offering foreign aid to dissident Dominicans who wanted to assassinate him. Six months after the communist takeover of Cuba, an invasion of Dominican emigres left Havana for Ciudad Trujillo. Though the attempted overthrow failed, the domestic resistance movement took a new name from the date of the invasion, June 14, 1959--"El Catorce de Junio," or 1J4. The following January, hundreds of 1J4 members were arrested and tortured by the Dominican secret service. General Juan Tomas Diaz, a lifelong Trujillista, was appalled by the way Trujillo and his son, Rafael Leonidas "Ramfis" Trujillo, ordered him to treat the emigre prisoners of war, and secretly changed his political loyalties accordingly.

The following June, Trujillo was ostracized by other Latin American leaders for attempting to have his agents assassinate Venezuelan president Romulo Betancourt. It was one of many foolish actions the dictator took in his declining years. He also wasted millions of dollars on projects that came to nothing, spent $50 million on arms in two years, and attacked the Roman Catholic church in a predominantly Catholic country. He became increasingly irritable in his later years, gaining a reputation for cuffing puppet president Joachin Balaguer in a rage, spitting on subordinates, and kicking palace aides in the groin. In the aftermath of the attempt on Betancourt's life, the Organization of American States voted to sever ties with the Dominican Republic, and to impose economic sanctions.

In 1960, relatives of General Diaz were implicated in a political plot to supplant Generalissimo Trujillo. From the position of disgrace this brought upon his family, Diaz joined together with Antonio de la Maza, the brother of the co-pilot murdered in the Murphy case, to put together a plot to kill the Dominican strongman.

On May 30, 1961, Trujillo was travelling by car to meet with

Rafael Trujillo, dictator of the Dominican Republic.

Dictator Trujillo with his playboy son, Rafael Trujillo, Jr.

Zsa Zsa Gabor with new Mercedes-Benz, a gift from Trujillo, Jr.

Actress Kim Novak with Rafael Trujillo, Jr.

The bullet-ridden Chevrolet in which Rafael Trujillo, Sr., was slain.

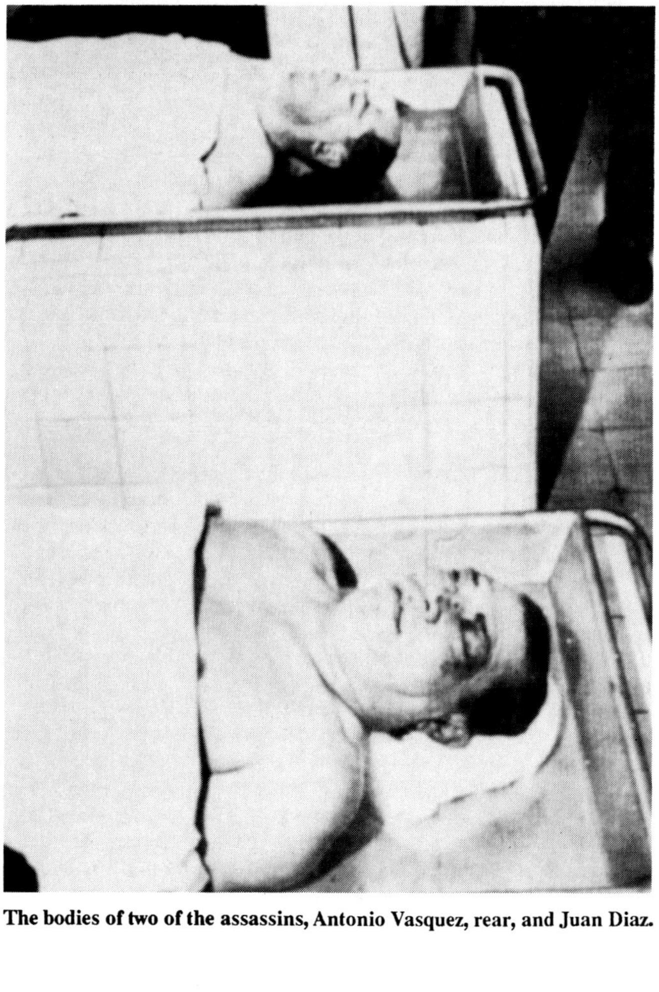

The bodies of two of the assassins, Antonio Vasquez, rear, and Juan Diaz.

one of his many mistresses when another car with at least ten men in it pulled alongside. The men opened fire and Trujillo was wounded, but insisted that his chauffeur stop so they could fight back. The 69-year-old dictator jumped from the car with six-guns blazing, despite the fact that he was bleeding severely from his wounds. The chauffeur said later, "I heard machine gun fire behind us. I swerved our car to get away. The generalissimo jumped out, firing his revolver. Blood spurted from his back..."

Trujillo died as the chauffeur fired a machine gun at the other car. His body, riddled by twenty-seven bullets, was thrown into the trunk of a car abandoned by the side of the road. The killing had not been planned for that day; the conspirators took the opportunity to kill Trujillo when it presented itself.

The aftermath of the assassination was quiet. Diaz was an aristocrat rather than a revolutionary and merely wanted revenge for the wrongs he believed he had suffered. Trujillo's son, Rafael, succeeded him and immediately arrested Diaz and his son. Diaz's wife was tortured and he and his son were executed. Pedro Cedeño and Lieutenant Amado Garcia were arrested and executed for their parts in the assassination. Within months, the young Trujillo was ousted by Balaguer and a coalition government.

REF: *CBA;* Diederich, *Trujillo: The Death of the Goat;* Hacker, *Crusaders, Criminals, and Crazies: Terror and Terrorism in Our Time;* Nash, *Almanac of World Crime;* Paine, *The Assassins' World.*

Oscar Collazo, would-be assassin of President Harry Truman, lies wounded at the steps of Blair House in Washington, Nov. 1, 1950.

Truman, Harry S., 1884-1972, U.S., pres., attempt. assass. On Nov. 1, 1950, two Puerto Rican nationals, Oscar Collazo and Griselio Torresola, made an attempt on the life of the thirty-third president of the U.S., Harry S. Truman. In November 1950, the White House was undergoing redecorating, and consequently the president was staying across the street at Blair House. Blair House, separated from Pennsylvania Avenue by only a narrow strip of grass, was a secret service man's nightmare. Had the two would-be assassins been better prepared, the day might have a different outcome.

Oscar Collazo was born in Puerto Rico in 1914 and automatically became a U.S. citizen when he was three under the Jones Act. He went to New York at the age of seventeen, where he worked at a number of unskilled jobs. There he also experienced firsthand the prejudice against Puerto Ricans and gradually became more active in the Puerto Rican independence movement. He married Rosa Mercado and lived in the Bronx with her and two of her daughters from a previous marriage. Collazo became a leader in the nationalist movement as well as a union leader in the factory where he worked as a metal polisher. He was a thoughtful man who was liked by his fellow employees and his employers.

Less is known about Griselio Torresola. Born in Puerto Rico in 1925, Torresola came to New York in 1948. He also lived in the Bronx. Some accounts claim that Collazo and Torresola were friends, while others say that the two men met only two weeks before the attempt on Truman's life. But they were drawn together by a shared desire for Puerto Rican independence.

On the morning of Nov. 1, Collazo and Torresola made their way toward Blair House armed with guns which Torresola had obtained. They separated when they neared the house and from opposite directions, each approached the front entrance. White House policeman Donald Birdzell was guarding the entrance to Blair House, standing just at the bottom of the stairs leading to the front door. When he heard a faint click, he turned to see a man—Collazo—aiming a Walther P-38 automatic pistol at him. The gun discharged, hitting Birdzell in the leg, as he made a grab for his own pistol. Birdzell ran out into Pennsylvania Avenue. As Collazo dashed up the stairs, two other agents, Joe Davidson and Floyd Boring, began shooting from the street, as did Birdzell. Collazo was injured slightly as he ducked on the staircase. Torresola approached from the other direction. He shot Leslie Coffelt, a guard stationed in a sentry booth just outside the building, and another guard. Although fatally injured, Coffelt shot Torresola in the head, killing him instantly. Coffelt died three and a half hours later. Meanwhile, Collazo was shot once in the chest. Twenty-seven bullets were fired during the three minute gun battle.

President Truman, who had been upstairs at Blair House taking a nap, stuck his head out the window just after the last shots were fired. After dressing hurriedly, he went downstairs to confer with aides who had been called to the scene following the shooting. He decided to keep his scheduled appointment to dedicate a monument to Field Marshall Sir John Dill at Arlington Cemetery and left via a rear entrance. In the meantime, Collazo and the other injured men were taken to a hospital. A search through Torresola's clothing uncovered a letter addressed to him from Pedro Albizu Campos, leader of the Puerto Rican Nationalist Party, talking about the possibility of Torresola assuming the leadership of that organization in the U.S. At the hospital Collazo freely confessed they wanted to draw attention to the Puerto Rican cause. As Collazo confessed, police learned how ill-planned the plot had been. He admitted that neither he nor Collazo knew if the president was home. He also admitted that they had not checked a newspaper to try to track his movements—had they done so, they would have known of Truman's visit to Arlington and could far more easily have killed him either as he left Blair House or at the cemetery where he would have been out in the open for a prolonged period.

Collazo was arrested and indicted on three charges, including the murder of Coffelt, assault with intent to kill two guards, and intent to kill the president. Rosa Collazo was also arrested and charged with complicity but was released later. During his trial Collazo spoke with emotion about how the U.S. had taken advantage of Puerto Rico economically and manipulated its government. He was found Guilty of Coffelt's murder in March 1951 and was sentenced to die in the electric chair on Aug. 1, 1952. Although he declined his right to plead for clemency, on July 24, 1952, just a few days before he was to be executed, President Truman commuted his sentence to life imprisonment. Latin Americans worldwide and New York Puerto Ricans gathered thousands of names on petitions and resolutions demanding clemency for Collazo. The U.S. State Department advised Truman that following through with Collazo's execution could seriously jeopardize U.S. relations with Latin America. Truman's announcement came just one day before Puerto Rico became a "free commonwealth." In September 1979, President Jimmy Carter granted clemency, for "humanitarian" reasons, to Collazo and three other Puerto Ricans convicted of an armed attack on the U.S. House of Representatives in 1954.

REF.: *CBA;* Deamris, *Brothers in Blood: The International Terrorist Network;* Dorman, *Secret Service;* Lester, *Crime of Passion;* Paine, *The Assassins' World;* Pearl, *The Dangerous Assassins;* Truman, *Memoirs.*

Trupiano, Matthew M., Jr. c.1938- , U.S., org. crime. Matthew (Mike) Trupiano ascended to the leadership of the St. Louis mob in 1980 after the death of his uncle, Anthony Giordano. Trupiano was also the president and international representative of Laborers Local 110 of the Laborers' International Union. The local mob's fortunes had been waning in the 1970s and the St. Louis faction was increasingly dominated by the large and powerful Chicago underworld. Then, in November 1982, the FBI conducted an investigation into suspected labor racketeering, loan sharking, extortion, narcotics, and gambling surrounding the St. Louis mob, and implicated fifteen underworld figures, including Trupiano.

In July 1984, Mike Trupiano and four mob associates—Frank Parrino, fifty-three; Fred Garozzo, fifty-three; Eugene Pisani, forty-nine; and Thomas Williams, fifty-five—were indicted for conducting, financing, managing, and supervising an illegal gambling business that netted over $1 million a year. Trupiano was also charged with neglecting to secure a gambling-tax stamp and neglecting to file excise-tax returns on the gross amounts of the bets. In October 1984, Trupiano and 44-year-old ex-convict Anthony Virgil Daly were purported to be the central figures in a $1 million-a-year fencing operation. The operation dealt with shoplifters who were paid up to 50 percent for easily disposable items such as liquor and cigarettes. On Nov. 1, 1985, Trupiano and East St. Louis mob boss, 73-year-old Arthur J. Berne, were indicted in the U.S. district court in St. Louis for conspiracy to extort money and racketeering. Accused of planning to bomb nightclubs to extort protection money from the owners, both pleaded Not Guilty and were released on $100,000 bond.

The gambling trial resulting from the 1985 indictments began on Feb. 17, 1986, in the U.S. district courtroom of Judge John F. Nangle. On Mar. 4, Trupiano and Parrino were found Guilty, and on Mar. 21, Garozzo, Pisani, and Williams were found Guilty as well. On May 23, 1986, Trupiano was sentenced to four years in federal prison and fined $30,000. REF.: *CBA.*

Truscott, Steven Murray, 1945- , Can., mur. On summer evenings, large groups of children regularly gathered on the school playground of the Canadian Air Force Station at Clinton, Ontario. On June 9, 1959, 12-year-old Lynne Harper left her home in the non-commissioned officers area after dinner to join some of her friends at the playground. Witnesses who saw Lynne there later told police that she left soon after arriving, riding on the crossbar of the bicycle of 14-year-old Stephen Truscott. Truscott, the son of a non-commissioned officer stationed at the base, reportedly returned approximately an hour after leaving with Lynne. No one who saw him was able to recall anything unusual in his appearance or demeanor. When asked by one of the other children about Lynne, Stephen said that he had taken her, at her request, to a nearby highway where she had accepted a ride in a 1959 grey Chevrolet with yellow license plates. Stephen said that Lynne had told him that she intended to visit a "white house where there were some ponies."

Harper's body was found in a nearby wooded area two days later. She had been raped and strangled. Truscott, described as an amiable, well-adjusted boy with no previous record, was interrogated closely in connection with the murder. A small sore or abrasion on Truscott's genitals, discovered in the course of a physical examination, strengthened the case against him and he was arrested, charged with murder and ordered to stand trial as an adult. The trial, which began on Sept. 16 and lasted for two weeks, included testimony from child witnesses. Both the prosecution and the defense alleged deliberate perjury by the children. Despite obvious omissions and errors in Truscott's defense, the boy was found Guilty and sentenced to death on Sept. 30, 1959. A subsequent appeal was denied but Truscott did receive a reprieve from execution. Truscott remained under the care of the Ontario Department of Reform Institutions until his eighteenth birthday when he was transferred to a prison.

REF.: *CBA;* Helpern, *Autopsy;* Lebourdais, *The Trial of Steven Truscott;* Simpson, *Forty Years of Murder;* Wilson, *Children Who Kill.*

Tsafendas, Demitrios, See: **Verwoerd**, Dr. **Hendrik Frensch.**

Tse-ne-gat (Everett Hatch), prom. 1915, Case of, U.S., mur. Tse-ne-gat, a Ute Indian born in southeastern Utah shortly after 1887, found himself in 1915 at the heart of the only legal case in U.S. history whose outcome meant either war or peace for the U.S. Tse-ne-gat, whose name means "Cry Baby" in English, was accused in 1915 of the murder of Juan Chacon, a Mexican sheepherder living near Bluff, Utah. The young Indian admitted spending part of the evening with Chacon and another sheepherder. He further admitted attempting to interest them in gambling their money, horses or other possessions against his horse and rifle. He claimed, however, that he was far away by the time the murder was actually committed.

In July 1915, when Tse-ne-gat was taken to Denver to stand trial in federal court, his father, Old Polk, whose English name was Billy Hatch, warned that if his son were found guilty of Chacon's murder, he and his gang of rebel Indians would declare war against the U.S. Chacon's murder had sparked skirmishes between whites and Ute Indians, who had, until recently, been at war over land rights in Utah. It was widely held at the time of the trial that the faction of whites who pronounced against Tse-ne-gat and favored a guilty verdict for him did so to encourage prejudice against the Indians and ultimately have them removed from the land. When an expert witness refuted the evidence placing Tse-ne-gat at the scene of the crime, the jury returned a verdict of Not Guilty, Tse-ne-gat was released, and war was averted.

REF.: *CBA;* Rodell, *Denver Murders.*

Tsumaki, Matsukichi, 1900- , Japan, burg. Matsukichi Tsumaki, known as a *sekkyo goto* or preaching bandit, began his criminal career at the age of eighteen when he stole money and sandals from his boss. After a ten-year hiatus, Tsumaki began robbing houses. But he was softhearted, leaving a home in the midst of a burglary if a baby cried. Tsumaki even lectured his victims about the lack of security in their homes.

Tsumaki was apprehended and sent to prison in 1929. He served eighteen years. Returning to Tokyo after his release in 1947, he commented on the devastation brought about by WWII: "When I walk down the streets of Tokyo and see the ashes and rubble of what once were fine houses, I think of how I used to enter them at night, and I feel sorry for the people who used to live there and whom I used to rob." REF.: *CBA.*

Tubman, William Vacanarat Shadrach, 1895-1971, Liberia, jur. Associate justice of supreme court of Liberia from 1937-44, starting his career in law as a trial judge and as public prosecutor. He went on to serve as president of Liberia from 1944-71. REF.: *CBA.*

Tuck, Mark, prom. 1872, Brit., disorderly conduct. For the crime of drunkenness and disorderly conduct, British officials in Newbury sentenced a man to the stocks in 1872. Mark Tuck, a dealer of rags and bones, who had previously spent time in Reading jail, was seated on a stool as officials clamped his legs in the wooden stocks. For the first time in twenty-six years, the stocks were hauled into the Butter and Poultry Market and Tuck was imprisoned for four hours as the crowd laughed at him.

REF: Andrews, *Old-Time Punishments; CBA.*

Tucker, Charles Louis, c.1880-1906, U.S., rape-rob.-mur. At age twenty-four, Charles Tucker was a widower and unemployed. While out walking on Mar. 31, 1904, the Auburndale, Mass., man ran into a friend, Arthur Woodward, who drove a fishwagon. On board the wagon was Mabel Walker, a visitor from Damariscotta, Maine. Tucker rode a while, chatting, then invited Walker to go watch trapshooting with him. After an hour, he left her, and went to the home of Mabel Page, a 41-year-old spinster. He apparently told her that her brother had been in an accident. She wrote a note and was preparing to leave when Tucker attacked and raped her. Then he stabbed her and cut her throat with a blade about five inches long. He took $14 from the absent housekeeper's purse.

The dead woman's elderly father, Edward Page, found her later that afternoon. Police began to interview every man the family knew, including Charles Tucker, who had purchased a dog from them several years before. When Tucker's friend from the fishwagon, Woodward, saw him mentioned in the newspaper, he recalled finding a leather sheath for a five-inch blade in his wagon after Tucker had left. The leather had tooth marks on it that were matched to Tucker's teeth, and the police found a broken, bloodstained knife blade in one of Tucker's jacket pockets. His trial began on Jan. 2, 1905, and he was found Guilty on Jan. 24, and was hanged on June 12, 1906.

REF.: *CBA;* Gross, *Masterpieces of Murder;* Nash, *Murder, America;* Pearson, *Studies in Murder.*

Tucker, Felix, d.1943, U.S., mur. When his wife admitted to having an affair with another man, Felix Tucker flew into a rage and began to choke and beat her. Minnie Margaret Tucker and her husband separated for a couple of weeks, but got back together again. In May 1942, Minnie had exhausted all possible chances for reconciliation and told her husband that she was leaving him to live with Charley Brenner and was taking the couple's 11-month-old baby with her. Tucker beat her up again. The same evening, Tucker ran out of his house screaming for neighbors to call the police because his wife had been murdered.

Tucker said he returned home at 6:10 p.m. to find his wife dead on the bedroom floor. Tucker first told police that his wife had quarrelled with Brenner. Brenner admitted that he was in love with Minnie and the couple were planning to marry, and said he did not kill her. Only Tucker's fingerprints were found on the crime scene, and authorities found that a footprint left in the soggy grass matched Tucker's. Under intense questioning, Tucker admitted to murdering his wife. He said he would have stabbed her more than twice if the knife had not gotten stuck in her body. Rather than face the pain of losing his wife to another man, he had killed her, Tucker told police. He was electrocuted on July 15, 1943.

REF: *CBA;* Rice, *Forty-five Murderers.*

Tucker, Henry St. George, 1780-1848, U.S., jur. U.S. congressman from 1815-19, later serving as judge on superior courts of chancery of Virginia from 1824-31. He was president of the state supreme court of appeals from 1831-41. He also wrote the two-volume *Commentaries on the Laws of Virginia,* and other books on law. He was a son of jurist St. George Tucker, and the father of Nathaniel Beverley Tucker, who was incorrectly implicated in the conspiracy to assassinate Lincoln. REF.: *CBA.*

Tucker, St. George, 1752-1827, U.S., jur. Judge on general court of Virginia from 1788-1803. He produced and published a five-volume annotated edition of *Blackstone's Commentaries* in 1803. He later served on the supreme court of appeals from 1803-11, and on the district court of Virginia from 1813-27. REF.: *CBA.*

Tucker, Tom, prom. 1880s-1908, U.S., west. gunman-lawman. A cowboy who occasionally hired himself out to feuding factions, Tom Tucker rode with the Hash Knife Gang in Arizona and with Oliver Lee in New Mexico. On Aug. 10, 1887, while riding with the Hash Knife Gang, who were feuding with the Tewksburys, Tucker led seven cowboys to the cabin of Jim Tewksbury. A shootout ensued, during which John Paine and Hampton Blevins were killed, and Bob Gillespie and Bob Carrington were wounded. Tucker was shot and seriously wounded. He crawled to Bob Sigsby's cabin, where he slowly recovered. Tucker later rode with Lee while he was feuding with the Good family. Tucker killed several Chinese during a shootout at Silver City, N.M., in 1889, and was later tried and acquitted on the grounds of self-defense. In 1908, Tucker became an undersheriff in Santa Fe, N.M., and helped Dee Harkey corner the outlaw band led by Jim Nite. Tucker died in Texas. See: **Tewksbury, Jim.**

REF.: *CBA;* Drago, *Great Range Wars;* Gibson, *Colonel Albert Jennings Fountain;* Harkey, *Mean as Hell;* Raine, *Famous Sheriffs and Western Outlaws;* Sonnichsen, *Tularosa;* Stanley, *The Shakespeare.*

Tucker Prison Farm, prom. 1967, U.S., penal scandal. During a routine check of the prison records, Tom Murton, the new superintendent of the Tucker Prison Farm in Arkansas discovered that nearly 200 inmates were listed as escapees. As he continued to investigate, Murton was told by many prisoners that the prison might contain more than 100 bodies. These were men, the inmates said, who had antagonized previous wardens.

Murton ordered a patch of sunken ground to be overturned. Murton discovered three human skeletons that had been buried in makeshift wooden coffins. For weeks, the prison scandal captured the attention of the country, but authorities halted digging on the premises and fired Murton, thus diverting attention from Arkansas prison. REF: *CBA.*

Tuckett-Brudenell Duel, 1840, Brit., duel-asslt. After reading a series of derogatory letters insulting his character in the *Morning Chronicle,* the Earl of Cardigan, James Thomas Brudenell, issued a challenge to Captain Harvey Garnett Phipps Tuckett, whom he believed had written the letters. Brudenell said that he would call off the duel if the Captain would apologize. Tuckett promised to retract his statements if Brudenell would deny the charges. Brudenell admitted that some of the accusations were true, but most were lies and he refused to apologize.

As the two men selected pistols and marked off twelve yards between them, the first volley of shots rang out. Both Tuckett and Brudenell misfired, but on the second round Brudenell shot Tuckett just below the ribs. Brudenell was arrested following the duel and ultimately charged with intent to murder, intent to maim and disable, and intent to do grievous bodily harm. Tuckett survived the shooting, and Brudenell's attorneys argued that if Tuckett had been killed the charges would have been less severe. His defense also questioned Tuckett's true identity. In the end, Brudenell was absolved of all charges.

REF: *CBA;* Melville, *Famous Duels and Assassinations.*

Tudor, Owen, c.1400-61, Brit., consp. Began Tudor dynasty in England. He had four children by Catherine of Valois, the widow of Henry V, who secretly became his wife in 1429. He fought for the Lancastrians at Mortimer's Cross, and was seized and beheaded by the Yorkists. REF.: *CBA.*

Tuer, William Franklin, 1940-73, Can., mur. On Jan. 23, 1974, after weeks of searching, Canadian police discovered the body of Angus McDougall Tuer in a well on his farm just outside of Stratford, Ontario. Tuer had been shot in the head, wrapped in a heavy chain, and dropped down the well weighted with an old truck transmission housing.

Three days after Tuer's body was discovered, the police arrested William Franklin Tuer and charged him with the murder of his younger brother. Tuer's trial began in October 1974, and the prosecution maintained that Tuer had murdered his brother to gain his money. The trial lasted thirteen days, and the jury returned a verdict of Guilty. Tuer was sentenced to life imprisonment.

REF: *CBA;* Miller, *Twenty Mortal Murders.*

Tufts, Henry, 1748-1831, U.S., rob. Although highwaymen such as Michael Martin, known as "Captain Lightfoot," and murderers such as John Billington (who arrived with the original intrepid band of Pilgrims on the *Mayflower*) had provided the Boston citizenry with eons of anecdotes, perhaps no other criminal offered such amusing escapades than the fabulous Henry Tufts, a horse thief extraordinary. (Tufts wrote the first American criminal autobiography in 1807.)

Born in New Hampshire on June 24, 1748, Tufts delighted in assuming respectable disguises. Like thousands of other rogues of this period, Tufts fought in the Revolutionary War, taking part in some of the battles around Boston, and it was even rumored that he was one of those who participated in the Boston Tea Party in 1773. When constables got too hot on his trail, Tufts merely re-enlisted in the Continental Army and lost himself in the ragged ranks. He would then pop up in a New England community, chiefly in Boston or a neighboring town, assuming the role of businessman or military officer. He once donned the robes of a visiting preacher and delivered a fiery sermon to a spellbound congregation only an hour before he stole almost every horse in town.

After Tufts' sermon, the resident pastor gratefully exclaimed to his flock that the visiting clergyman was, indeed, a most inspired man. "Never was a sermon preached so loud to my soul!" the pastor intoned. Turning to the straight-faced Tufts, he said:

"You are a saint, sir, a heaven-born saint!"

Tufts bowed humbly and then sat down. An attractive woman in the first pew stood up, anger streaking her face. "*He* a saint!" she shouted. "Then so is the devil! I have no belief in his pretended sanctity, let him profess what he will."

"I'm sure you can explain yourself," the startled pastor responded.

"If I must explain myself further, permit me to say that my opinion of this man is derived from his conduct. On his entrance into the meeting, he first surveyed my face, then my feet, then my whole person, in such a carnal way and manner that I perceived he had the devil in his heart."

The pastor and congregation members tut-tutted the young woman and Tufts was sent on his way with heartfelt gratitude. As the meeting continued, the horse thief rounded up every available horse in town and led them away on ropes he had been careful enough to bring along for that purpose. Of his attractive denouncer, Tufts later stated: "This accusation was literally true, though I could not but admire at the intuitive sagacity of the young gypsy who was able to hit off, so adroitly, my real character."

One Massachusetts gentleman of means who owned a prized horse suspected Tufts of being a thief when the two met. Tufts looked over the well-groomed steed under the pretense of purchasing the animal. To the horse thief's surprise, the owner then announced: "This horse I keep closely locked up, and guarded by sentries every night. So, if you can make out to steal him, you shall be extremely welcome, and never be called to account for so doing."

Before Tufts could protest, the owner further stated that he had purchased the animal from a thief and expected the previous owner to return in the dead of night and steal back the animal, hence his precaution. Tufts was later to write: "Feeling somewhat nettled, as a gentleman of my profession would, at being bantered thus, I resolved to execute some stratagem for the attainment of the horse."

"I went away, and procuring a quart bottle of rum, and adding a suitable quantity of opium (used as a knock-out ingredient), tarried till late in the evening; I then drew near the stable, where I knew the courser must be. Here I was hailed by a couple of servant men, who demanded my motives for traveling at that season of the night.

"I told them that the object of my pursuit was a thief, named *Henry Tufts,* who had stolen my horse; but that I believed I had gotten already in advance of him. They said they had frequently heard of that gentleman, and that he was accounted the greatest knave and most arrant horse thief in all that country.

"Our dialogue growing familiar, I finally concluded to make a half in this place, that Tufts might arrive. Meantime, I expressed a desire to purchase a little rum to cheer my spirits that cold evening; but being told that none could be attained in that quarter, without more ceremony I took out my bottle, and tasting of the contents, offered it to my new acquaintances, who received the gratuity with cordiality. Upon the whole, I could but admire at its sudden effects, which were such that immediately my pot-companions were both stretched on the ground, encircled in the arms of Morpheus. By searching their pockets I found the key of the stable, which I unlocked and directly had the pleasure of fixing myself on the back of a very fine horse.

"Avoiding the glare of day, I rode him a night or two, till being out of harm's way, I exchanged him for another horse, and received as boot, thirty-five dollars in ready cash. This last horse I sold for forty-dollars more; and, with the property, made a speedy decampment."

With this loot, a considerable sum during Revolutionary days, Tufts outfitted himself with not only a new and dazzling wardrobe but equipped his depleted rucksack with a complete set of burglar tools, as well as "a variety of false and spring keys, so constructed as to open almost any sort of lock." Tufts also purchased a wide assortment of paints ("by means of which I could so alter the looks of any horse that the owner must be puzzled to know him again while the disguise lasted, which was usually a week or more, unless the paint were sooner displaced by hard riding or rainy weather"). Tufts possessed a mobile blacksmith shop, carrying with him various saws, blades, locks, and horseshoes, several sets being cork shoes covered with sole leather which he employed when wanting to muffle the sound of his horse. "I also furnished myself with vitriol, aqua fortis, and other corrosive ingredients to soften or eat away iron. Those liquids I sometimes carried in a phial, tied up in the club of my hair; while the blades of my compass-saws were frequently concealed between the soles of my shoes. A number of articles above enumerated I confided to the keeping of confidential friends of whom I had now a connected string reaching from New York to the District of Main, and from thence through Vermont to the Canada line."

Tufts was then a charter member of the first organized crime syndicate in America, in existence at a time when George Washington had no horses for his ragged army. According to the first of the so-called reformed gambler, Jonathin F. Green, who published an empirical exposé of crime in the U.S. in 1847, there existed as early as 1798 a "secret band of brothers" numbering upwards of 2,000 men who controlled wholesale theft throughout the Continental States of America. Henry Tufts, who died in 1831 at the age of eighty-three, was, no doubt, an early member of this criminal federation.

REF.: *CBA;* Green, *Secret Band of Brothers;* Hamilton, *Men of the Underworld;* Tufts, *Autobiography of a Criminal.*

Tufverson, Agnes Colonia, See: **Poderjay, Ivan.**

Tukhachevski, Marshal, d.1937, U.S.S.R., treas. The reign of terror under which Joseph Stalin guided the Soviet Union reached new heights in June of 1937 when nine Red Army leaders, including Marshal Tukhachevski, were executed. As Nazi Germany and the Soviet Union jockeyed for position prior to WWII, Stalin set the military leaders up for a fall. Stalin gave the president of Czechoslavakia information that Tukhachevski and his associates were negotiating with the Nazis. The Czech president dutifully returned the information to Moscow and soon officials in London and Paris received word that Tukhachevski's treasonous activities had been discovered by the Czechs. The Soviet government issued a statement accusing the nine men of conspiring to undermine the Red Army. Soviet officials said Tukhachevski and his accomplices were tried and convicted, but evidence that a trial did indeed take place is sketchy, due to the death of those who supposedly served on the court. Subsequently, many of the army's senior staff officers were murdered.

REF: Bornstein, *The Politics of Murder; CBA.*

Tuller, Charles A., 1926- , **Tuller, Bryce**, 1953- , and **Tuller, Jonathan**, 1955- , U.S., rob.-skyjack.-kid.-mur. In 1972 Charles A. Tuller, a government employee with a history of mental problems, led his two sons and a fourth man in a bank robbery attempt. Tuller, who fancied himself a revolutionary, hoped to fund his fight against capitalism with the proceeds from the bank robbery. Tuller and his two sons, 19-year-old Bryce and 17-year-old Jonathan, killed a bank teller and a policeman at the Arlington, Va., bank before escaping without a cent. The inept trio then accidentally killed an Eastern Airlines ticket agent in Houston and hijacked a jetliner to Cuba.

After three years of exile, the Tuller family decided to return to the U.S. and did so with ease in Miami. With forged drivers' licenses, they slipped back into the country and sent Bryce to rob a store in North Carolina. Bryce was disarmed by the store owner and arrested by police. Within three days, the two remaining Tullers had surrendered to the FBI. Each was sentenced to more than 100 years in prison after being convicted of felonious assault, attempted robbery, double murder, air piracy, and kidnapping. In court, one psychiatrist called the elder Tuller "a unique thinker" and praised his social conscience. Two other psychiatrists diagnosed the three men as having "schizoid personalities."

REF: *CBA;* Godwin, *Murder U.S.A.*

Tully, Samuel (AKA: **R. Heathcote**), d.1812, U.S., pir.-mur.

Sam Tully left his native England to become a sailor after allegedly killing his father. Tully assumed the name of R. Heathcoate and took a job on the *George Washington*. On Jan. 21, 1812, the ship's captain was ashore at Cape Verde. Tully and a companion, John Dalton, decided to seize the ship. They sailed to the West Indies where they sank the vessel. When crew member George Cummings objected to their plan, they killed him. Tully and Dalton were captured and taken to Boston where they were tried and found Guilty. Although they were both sentenced to hang, Dalton was reprieved at the last moment and sent to prison. Tully was hanged in South Boston on Dec. 10, 1812, while a huge crowd watched.

REF.: *CBA;* Nash, *Bloodletters and Badmen.*

Tully, Thomas Alton, c.1911- , U.S., rape. Thomas Tully, son of novelist Jim Tully, was in and out of prison five times on criminal assault charges before his twenty-fifth birthday. After three convictions, Tully was found Guilty for the fourth time on Mar. 15, 1934, for the Dec. 4, 1933, attempted assault of 24-year-old Violet Robey. Before Superior Court Judge William Tell Aggeler in Los Angeles, Tully was sentenced to one to fifteen years in San Quentin. He was paroled, however, within a year, only to attack with a wrench and twice rape 16-year-old Juanita Sheppard while working in a lumber camp in September 1935. On Sept. 23, 1935, in Susanville, Calif., Tully pleaded guilty to the charge of statutory rape and was sentenced to one to fifty years in San Quentin. Tully's well-known father commented that his son was "suffering from a terrifying disease, for which he must wear the stripes of a felon." REF.: *CBA.*

Tulsa Bludgeonings, 1942-48, U.S., (unsolv.) rape-mur. The North Side of Tulsa, Okla., provided the setting for five grisly murders committed over a six-year period during the 1940s. A black man was arrested and sent to jail for a murder he never committed but in the end Tulsa police were no closer to identifying the sex killer than they were on a smoldering day in July 1942 when the tragedy first began to unfold.

Helen Brown, a 20-year-old expectant mother, said goodbye to her husband Bill, who went off to work on the morning of July 10, 1942. The attacker entered the couple's home on Main Street through an open window a short time later. The unknown assailant struck the woman across the face repeatedly and then strangled her to unconsciousness. Brown was rushed to St. John's Hospital later that morning but efforts to save her life and that of the unborn child were doomed to failure. Examining physicians told police that the bruise marks on her stomach suggested that the killer had trampled her to death. William C. Brown, a fruit-truck driver, was subjected to five hours of intense questioning and dismissed as a suspect by Tulsa police. He said that his wife did not have an enemy in the world. County Attorney Dixie Gilmer was unable to establish any kind of motive for the senseless crime, nor did the clues shed any light on the identity of the killer.

The Brown murder was still fresh in everyone's mind when Attorney J.B. Underwood notified police that one of his employees had been slaughtered in a similar fashion on Jan. 14, 1943. Thirty-one-year-old Georgia Green was employed as a stenographer by Underwood. When she failed to report for work he called her residence several times but received no answer. Underwood decided to stop by after dinner. After several minutes had passed and Green failed to answer the door of the three-story duplex, the lawyer summoned a tenant from the building, who let him inside. There he found Georgia and her mother, Mrs. Clara Luzila Stewart, lying in a bloody mess in their bed. They had been bludgeoned with an ax and raped. Chief of Police George Blaine took charge of the investigation before county authorities could intervene. He expressed the opinion that the women had not been criminally assaulted, which was later disproven by Dr. J. Jeff Billington, who concluded that the rape had been committed after the women were murdered. Seven eggshells were found in the kitchen sink, and the residue of scrambled eggs remained in the frying pan, suggesting that the killer sat down to a hearty breakfast after assaulting the women with his ax. The hatchet was found several blocks away by schoolchildren. It had been stolen from the garage of a local man who said he used it for carpentry.

Two years passed before the killer was heard from again. Then, on May 15, 1945, Mrs. Panta Lou "Pat" Liles, a 20-year-old factory worker at the Douglas Aircraft company, was found sprawled on her blood-soaked bed. The killer had administered repeated blows to her head using a heavy, blunt instrument before raping her. The murder bore a striking similarity to the Brown-Green-Stewart slayings, except this time the killer was conversant with Liles' roommate, Irma Seburn, who worked as a night nurse for a Tulsa manufacturing company. Seburn telephoned Pat Liles at 5 a.m. the following morning to awaken her. She allowed the phone to ring upwards of five minutes before someone picked up the receiver. A voice that sounded "gruff" according to Seburn's recollections answered. "Pat?" she asked. The masculine voice on the other end mumbled an inaudible response which sounded like "Yes." The conversation broke off a few minutes later, with Seburn unsure of whether she had spoken with her roommate or not. She called back at 5:10 to ask if Pat was going to work with "Edith" or not. The voice answered in the affirmative, only no "Edith" existed. Irma Seburn called the police.

On June 7, Tulsa police arrested and charged 33-year-old Leroy Benton with murder. The black man surrendered voluntarily after hearing that a warrant had been issued for his arrest. Benton, who was convicted of rape in 1927, worked as a porter at several Tulsa cafes and department stores following his release from prison in 1929. "The only thing I can say is that Benton has a guilty knowledge of the crime," said Captain Phil Hoyt of the Kansas City, Mo., police department. "He either saw it committed or committed the crime himself." Benton was given a lie detector test in Kansas City and subjected to round-the-clock interrogation. "I confessed," he told news reporters, "because I thought I might get a life sentence and because I thought while I was serving my time the real murderer might be found and I would be released." He later denied entering Liles' apartment and indicated his willingness to undergo additional lie-detector tests to support this claim. On the strength of FBI lab reports linking him to the crime, Benton was convicted of murder after a five day trial and handed a life sentence at the state penitentiary in McAlester. He began serving his sentence on Nov. 24, 1945, while awaiting the outcome of his appeals. The state criminal court overturned the conviction on the grounds that his confession was coerced and that the police had denied him right to legal counsel. Benton was released to the sheriff of Tulsa County on Mar. 3, 1948. He immediately moved to Hammond, Ind.

The final chapter of the Tulsa saga was written on July 2, 1948, when the assassin invaded the apartments of Ruth Norton, a 45-year-old building service employee, and Mrs. J.B. (Alsey) Cole who lived in the same building on North Cheyenne Avenue. Norton was raped and beaten to death in her apartment, which showed no visible signs of struggle. A billfold containing $33 in cash was found at her bedside indicating that robbery was not the motive. The police came to the unavoidable conclusion that the same man who assaulted Clara Stewart and Georgia Green was responsible for this latest tragedy. The wounds on each of the three women were inflicted with the same weapon.

Earlier that same night the assailant entered the apartment of Mrs. Cole, where he inflicted multiple head wounds to the 38-year-old woman, her daughter Doris, thirteen, and a neighbor girl, LeVon Gabbard, fourteen. The three women were criminally assaulted in their beds as they slept. They were rushed to Hillcrest Hospital in critical condition. Appeals were made to Tulsans to disclose any information they might have—"no matter how ridiculous it may sound"—but the suspects in the case, including 25-year-old Sam McCutcheon, Gabbard's brother-in-law, were eventually cleared for lack of evidence. The chilling Tulsa murders ended on that note. For the panic-stricken residents of the North Side there was little comfort in knowing that the fiend was still on the loose. REF.: *CBA.*

Tulsa Jack, See: **Blake, John.**

Tulsa Race Riot, 1921, U.S., mob vio. Rumors of a lynching touched off one of the worst race riots in U.S. history. On May 31, 1921, Dick Rowland, a black man arrested for raping an orphaned white girl, was jailed in the court house in Tulsa, Okla. Shortly after his arrest, rumors circulated that whites intended to lynch Rowland. Within a few hours, a group of armed black men arrived at the court house to defend Rowland. Police and groups of white men appeared at the court house, and the groups began shouting and threatening each other. The shooting began when police shot and killed an armed black man who reportedly resisted arrest. White men began firing at the black men, who returned their fire and then quickly retreated to the black ghetto. The governor called in the National Guard, who quickly dispersed the mob while deputy sheriffs removed Rowland from the jail. By this time, however, a small group of whites led by American Legionnaires surrounded the ghetto, a densely populated district about one square mile. Whites began burning buildings and shooting people as they fled. Nearly the entire ghetto, thirty city blocks, was burned to the ground, and fugitives were housed in detention centers. Eighty-five people died, sixty blacks and twenty-five whites. But the head of the Salvation Army, O.T. Johnson, placed the number of dead at 150, claiming that many more people were caught inside burning buildings. Police chief Daly later raised the number of fatalities to 175. REF.: *CBA.*

Tung Cho, d.192, China, gen., assass. General of China who burned capital of Lo-yang in 190 and brought the emperor to Ch'ang-an, the ancient capital city, where Tung's cruel and dictatorial approach divided the empire into separate satrapies that were ruled by feuding generals. He was assassinated in 192. REF.: *CBA.*

Tupac Amarú, d.1572, Peru, chieftain, assass. Incan leader who made no effort to fight Spaniards. He was seized and beheaded at Cuzco on the order of Viceroy Francisco de Toledo. He was the youngest and last surving son of Manco Inca. REF.: *CBA.*

Tupac Amarú (José Gabriel Condorcanqui), 1742-81, Peru, rebel. In 1771, assumed name of Inca chief to whom he was related and instigated an Indian rebellion against the Spanish government in 1780, obtaining control of large portions of Peru, Bolivia, and Argentina. Within one year, however, he was seized, tortured, and eventually put to death. He was acknowledged as the legal heir of the Incas by the Spanish, and was referred to as "the last of the Incas." REF.: *CBA.*

Tupamaros, The, prom. 1963-73, Urug., kid.-terr. From 1903-53, the South American country of Uruguay was a thriving democracy. By 1953, the country was sliding into a recession and exports of meat, hides, and wool had been decreased drastically. The Uruguayan currency was devalued, and by the 1960s inflation was rampant and the government was crumbling under the weight of depression and unrest. Out of this turmoil came a group of young workers from the northern provinces who called themselves The Tupamaros. Named in honor of Tupac Amarús, a rebel Inca leader who led an unsuccessful 18th Century revolt in Peru, the group was formed in 1963. Under the leadership of Raúl Sendic, the urban guerrillas spent nearly five years studying the teachings of Che Guevera and formulating plans to help the country's impoverished citizens.

A popular force when they emerged on the streets of Montevideo, the Tupamaros attempted to establish their own government, complete with medical facilities, military outposts, and jails for prisoners. They earned populist respect stealing food and distributing the goods in the poor sections of the city. They would often warn innocent people prior to an attack and were known to pay cab drivers after commandeering a vehicle. A favorite ploy for the guerrillas was to steal incriminating documents that proved government corruption and send the stolen papers to various courts.

In August 1968, the Tupamaros kidnapped Ulysses Pereira Reverbel, the head of the government-owned power and telephone company and a close friend of President Jorge Pacheco Areco. Although Reverbel was released after four days, the revolutionaries sent a message that the safety of government officials would be in jeopardy. In the next five years, the Tupamaros kidnapped more than twenty government officials, diplomats, and industrialists. In return for the safe release of the prisoners, the group demanded cash payments be made to labor organizations or that political prisoners be released.

In October 1969, fifty Tupamaros seized nearly 18,000 pesos, weapons, and police uniforms in a raid on the town of Pando. But as the revolutionaries made their escape, their car broke down and three men were killed and sixteen were captured by the government. This action prompted the military to declare the entire country unsafe and to forbid people from calling the group the Tupamaros. In newspapers they were called "the nameless ones." In August 1970, the kidnapping of Dan A. Mitrione, an advisor to the Uruguayan police, touched off a war that threatened the Tupamaros' reign of populist terror in the country. The group said they would kill Mitrione unless the government released 150 political prisoners, but officials held fast to their policy of not releasing political captives.

Eleven days after he was kidnapped, Uruguayan police found Mitrione's body in a car on a Montevideo street, and the government declared martial law. Sendic and Raoul Bidegain Greissing, two top Tupumaro leaders, were arrested after a massive police search. But the Marxist guerrillas, who numbered between 2,000 and 3,000, responded by abducting British Ambassador Geoffrey Jackson. The Tupamaros held Jackson as well as Claude L. Fly, an American agronomist and Aloysio Dias Gomide, a Brazilian government official. Gomide was released in 1971 after his wife paid nearly $250,000 in ransom, and Fly, after suffering a heart attack, was left on the steps of a hospital, the results of two electrocardiograms lying beside his body. The Tupamaros released Jackson after holding him for eight months in a three-foot by six-foot cell. A week earlier, the guerrillas had managed to free more than 100 jailed comrades—including Sendic—by digging an escape tunnel underneath and into Punta Carretas prison.

A 1971 election brought to power Juan Maria Bordaberry, who immediately gave increased power to the country's military. Within months more than 2,400 suspected Tupamaros were arrested. Amodio Perez, a former chief aide to Sendic, defected to the government's side and identified many guerrillas. With the country in chaos, the military gained more power and reigned over the population with "death squads," who broke down the Tupamaros and instilled the fear of death in the rest of the population. In June 1973, Bordaberry dissolved the Uruguayan Parliament and installed a military dictatorship.

REF: *CBA;* Clutterbuck, *Guerrillas and Terrorists;* ____, *Ransom and Kidnap;* Demaris, *Brothers in Blood: The International Terrorist Network;* Dobson and Payne, *The Terrorists—Their Weapons, Leaders and Captives;* Hacker, *Crusaders, Criminals, Crazies: Terror and Terrorism in Our Time;* Laquer, *Terrorism;* McClellan and Avery, *The Voices of Guns;* Moorehead, *Hostages to Fortune;* O'Ballance, *Language of Violence—The Blood Politics of Terrorism;* Schreiber, *The Ultimate Weapon—Terrorists and World Order.*

Turan-Shah, d.1250, Egypt, sultan, assass. Served for one year as sultan in Ayyubid dynasty. He was assassinated by a group of soldiers on order of Baybars I. His death precipitated the Mamluk dynasty. REF.: *CBA.*

Turgenev, Nikolay Ivanovich, 1789-1871, Rus., consp. Helped create Northern Society that schemed the Decembrist Plot against Czar Nicholas I in 1825. After this, Turgenev fled to Paris. REF.: *CBA.*

Turkus, Burton B., prom. 1940, U.S., lawyer. In Spring 1940, assistant district attorney for New York City, Burton B. Turkus, received a message from an inmate at Rikers Island prison, purporting to have information about a murder. Such messages were commonplace in the attorney's office, as prisoners used whatever leverage possible to gain a reduced or commuted sentence. Turkus went to the prison and met a man who called himself "Harry Rudolph." Rudolph spoke of the 1933 murder of his 19-year-old friend Red Albert and named the assailants as three Brownsville hoodlums: Buggsy Goldstein, Dukey Maffetore, and Abe "Kid Twist" Reles. The three were known members of Murder, Inc., the strong-armed wing of the national crime syndicate. Turkus was skeptical of Rudolph's story and demanded some proof of the story's validity. Rudolph pulled up his shirt, revealing a gruesome scar where he had been shot during the same exchange of gunfire. Turkus was thus convinced and immediately issued warrants on the three alleged killers, who were soon brought into custody.

Reles suspected that he had been betrayed by someone within the criminal organization and offered to turn state's evidence in return for protection and immunity from prosecution. Turkus soon learned of the murder network hierarchy run under Louis "Lepke" Buchalter and Jacob "Gurrah" Shapiro. Reles further revealed the gangs ruthless methodology and admitted that the Brownsville gang had been responsible for as many as 1,000 murders during the past decade. When it was learned that Reles was talking to the authorities, several members of the syndicate put out a contract on him. But Reles was kept under heavy security at the Half-Moon Hotel near Coney Island. Eighteen police officers were assigned for the sole purpose of giving Reles around-the-clock protection, and at least six officers were always in his room at any time.

Crusading New York Assistant D.A. Burton B. Turkus, who smashed Murder, Inc.

On Nov. 12, 1941, Turkus received a call that Reles had jumped out of a sixth-floor window to his death. It was never discovered whether Reles had jumped or was pushed, but his body was discovered twenty feet further from the building than gravity would have taken it. While the New York crime bosses breathed a sigh of relief, Turkus still had enough of Reles' testimony to indict several leading crime figures. Indictments were issued for Frankie Abbandando, Lepke Buchalter, Louis Capone, Happy Maione, Harry Strauss, and Mendy Weiss. All were convicted of murder, and within two years, all had died in the electric chair. See: **Murder, Inc.**; **Reles, Abraham.**

REF.: *CBA;* Gage, *The Mafia is not an Equal Opportunity Employer;* Messick and Goldblatt, *The Mobs and the Mafia;* Peterson, *The Mob;* Reuter, *Disorganized Crime;* Sann, *Kill the Dutchman;* Turkus and Feder, *Murder, Inc.;* (FILM), *The Enforcer,* 1951.

Turley, Preston, d.1858, U.S., mur. Preston S. Turley was a minister of the Baptist church in Charleston, Va., now West Virginia. In the late 1850s, the Baptist church expelled Preston for drinking. Then, in 1858, he and his wife, Mary Susan Preston, returned home very drunk. In the presence of his children, Turley began quoting scripture and then strangled his wife. He threw the body in a nearby river, and evidently expected his children to say nothing. The children did talk, and Preston was arrested, convicted of murder, and sentenced to be executed. Given the opportunity to make a final statement on the scaffold, Turley preached to the crowd for three hours about the wages of sin and the evils of alcohol. His children did not go to his hanging, even after he wrote them a letter in which he asked, "Don't you want to go and see Pa hung?"

REF.: *CBA;* Nash, *Bloodletters and Badmen.*

Turlis, Thomas (AKA: **Mr. Tullis, Mr. Tollis**), d. 1771, Brit., execut.-theft. Thomas Turlis was public executioner at Tyburn in 1752. During his twenty years of service, Turlis hanged such notable English criminals as Archibald Cameron, Theodore Gardelle, John Ayliffe, and John Rice.

In 1763, Turlis was arrested for stealing coal from a neighbor's basement. Admitting guilt and saying he needed the money, the Sheriffs of London managed to obtain a pardon for the hangman, and in order to help him with his financial difficulties, they appointed Turlis public whipper. On several occasions, Turlis suffered abuse from crowds gathered for the public hangings, but he rarely failed to finish his work. Turlis died in 1771.

British executioner Turlis hanging a condemned man at Smithfield, 1761.

REF: Bleackley, *Hangmen of England; CBA;* Laurence, *A History of Capital Punishment;* Potter, *The Art of Hanging.*

Turner, Aaron (AKA: **Treetop**), 1919- , Case of, U.S., mur. Over a ten-year period, Aaron Turner was tried five times for the same murders, and in spite of being convicted by a jury on each occasion, Turner walked out of prison a free man. In June 1946, Turner was arrested after Clarence Lofton implicated him in the 1945 slaying of two men in a Philadelphia broom factory. The 26-year-old Turner had a lengthy arrest record and was taken to the station without an arrest warrant. After four days of persistent questioning, Turner confessed to the crimes, as did Lofton and Jasper Johnson. Turner said that he planned to burgle the factory, but ended up killing proprietor Charles Simmons and an employee, Frank Endres, with a window-sash weight wrapped in newspaper.

The three men were put on trial for the murders, and Lofton, who had turned state's evidence, was found Guilty and sentenced to life imprisonment. Johnson and Turner were also found Guilty of first-degree murder and sentenced to death. If not for the industrious and untiring work of attorney Edwin P. Rome, Turner might not have weathered his decade-long legal storm. The young lawyer took an initial appeal to the U.S. Supreme Court and won a retrial for his client on grounds that Turner had been arrested without a warrant and had been unlawfully detained for five days.

Three more trials resulted in convictions, but the verdict was overturned each time on appeal. As the legal battle became more drawn out, Lofton tired of testifying and recanted his testimony against Turner prior to "Treetop's" fifth trial. Lofton said that both he and Turner were innocent. The 1954 trial featured Lofton as a hostile witness for the prosecution. Lofton's refusal to testify for the state shifted the brunt of evidence to a conversation two policeman overheard while in a cell next to Turner. Despite a weakened case, Turner was still convicted, but for the first time he was sentenced to life imprisonment instead of death. Three years later, the Supreme Court of Pennsylvania overturned the conviction on the grounds that in allowing Lofton to testify as a hostile witness, the judge had erred. The district attorney agreed to *nol-pros* the case in 1957, thus freeing Turner after more than ten years in prison.

REF: *CBA;* Seagle, *Acquitted of Murder.*

Turner, Ben, d.1873, U.S., west. gunman. Cowboy Ben Turner worked for the Horrell brothers during the Horrell-Higgins feud in Lampasas, Texas. On Mar. 19, 1873, state police officers came to Lampasas to arrest Clint Barkley, a member of the Horrell faction. Turner, with Barkley, and Mart, Tom, and Sam Horrell, killed three officers as they entered Jerry Scott's saloon. Turner later helped Mart Horrell and Scott break out of jail in Georgetown, Texas. In December 1873, Ben Horrell was killed by Mexicans in Lincoln County, N.M. In revenge, his brothers began indiscriminately killing local Mexicans. A group of angry Mexicans shot and killed Turner in a gunfight.

REF.: Askins, *Texans, Guns & History; CBA;* Gillett, *Six Years with the Texas Rangers;* Webb, *Texas Rangers.*

Turner, Ellen, See: **Wakefield, Edward Gibson**.

Turner, Ezekiel B., 1825-88, U.S., jur. Appointed to northern district court of Texas by President Rutherford B. Hayes in 1879, and to western district court of Texas by Hayes in 1880. From 1850, he had served as prosecuting attorney for St. Joseph County, Mich. He was a U.S. attorney for the western district of Texas from 1867, and became Texas attorney general that year. In 1871, he became judge of the thirty-second district court, and became judge of the sixteenth district court four years later. REF.: *CBA.*

Turner, Glenn W., c.1934- , U.S., fraud. Glenn Turner, an Orlando, Fla., businessman, took advantage of relaxed security regulations in the late 1960s to amass a personal fortune through alleged fraudulent securities schemes. He was suspected of operating pyramid schemes through two endeavors: Koscot Interplanetary Inc. and Dare To Be Great. With Koscot, Turner sold distributorships for selling mink-oil cosmetics at $5,000 apiece, but did not reinvest the money to produce the product. Accused since 1969 for the business impropriety, Turner was formally charged in 1972 with sixty-five counts of violating Florida's security law by selling unregistered securities and by failing to register as a dealer. The Federal Trade Commission estimated that as many as 70,000 investors had lost $44 million. Turner countered that he had paid $110 million in commissions, that less than 1 percent of the investors were dissatisfied, and that anyone who had lost money simply had done a poor job selling the product.

Turner was tried in October 1972, but the case ended in a hung jury. Retried on Jan. 12, 1973, in the Pinellas County circuit courtroom of Judge David Patterson, Turner pleaded no contest to five misdemeanor charges, was fined $2,500, and was placed on five years' probation. A codefendant, 25-year-old David Baumann of St. Petersburg, Fla., also pleaded no contest for three misdemeanors and was fined $1,500. In 1974, his $3-million dream house unfinished, $700,000 in debt, and a possible $182 million in liabilities, Glenn Turner sought a Florida Senate seat as a Democrat and lost. REF.: *CBA.*

Turner, John Virgil, d.1930, U.S., (unsolv.) mur. The father of actress Lana Turner was a copper miner who neglected his family in favor of gambling. Her mother, Mildred Turner, took Julia Jean Mildred Frances Turner, the future Lana, to a foster home in Modesto, Calif. John Turner made his way from Idaho to San Francisco, where he was playing craps on Dec. 15, 1930. Apparently one of the big winners, he walked away from the game only to be beaten to death with a blackjack in an alley. The murderer was never found.

REF.: *CBA;* Nash, *Murder Among the Mighty.*

Turner, Joyce 1928- , and **Noakes, Audrey**, and **Gay, Clestell**, prom. 1956, U.S., mur. The operator of a Columbia, S.C., day-care and mother of six often chatted with Clestell Gay and Audrey Noakes, swearing that some day she was going to kill her bartender husband, Alonzo. In June 1956, Gay asked "Well, are you going to do it or not?" Turner grabbed a .22-caliber pistol gun from Gay, ran to her home, and shot her sleeping husband.

Turner told police that an intruder had killed her husband and complained at his funeral that he saw other women. When the police checked, they found that the man was too lazy even for affairs. They also found out that the gun belonged to Gay. All three women pleaded guilty in separate trials and were sent to prison for life.

REF.: *CBA;* Nash, *Look For the Woman;* Wilson, *Encyclopedia of Murder.*

Turner, Lana, See: **Crane, Cheryl; Turner, John Virgil**.

Turner, Maurice T., Jr., 1935- , U.S., law enfor. off. Maurice Turner joined the metropolitan police department of Washington, D.C., on July 29, 1957, after serving three years in the U.S. Marine Corps, and retired thirty-two years later after serving eight years as chief of police. In 1965, after eight years as a patrolman, Turner was promoted to supervisory sergeant, and in 1969, to lieutenant. In 1970, after spending six weeks in Tokyo and Hong Kong learning prevention methods, he was transferred to the Special Operations Division, specializing in presidential security details and crowd control during riots, demonstrations, and protests. Turner moved up quickly. He was promoted to captain in 1971, to inspector in 1974, to deputy chief in 1976, and to assistant chief in 1978. On July 1, 1981, Turner was appointed the twenty-fourth police chief of the District of Columbia, a position he held until his retirement in August 1989. REF.: *CBA.*

Turner, Nat, 1800-31, U.S., slave revolt-mur. Nat Turner, a black American slave, rallied a band of followers to stage the most important slave revolt in U.S. history. Nat Turner's rebellion also took more white lives than any other slave uprising.

Turner was born in 1800 on a small plantation in Southampton County, in the southeastern part of Virginia. His mother was a native African who did not conceal her hatred of slavery from her son. After learning to read from one of his master's sons, Turner immersed himself in the Bible. He took readily to religious thought and soon became a spiritual leader among the slaves. In his Bible readings, Turner discovered an anti-slavery message which inspired him to think about leading his own people from slavery. Turner was sold in the early 1820s to a neighboring farm. In the next ten years, Turner, known to his fellow slaves as "the Prophet," became more and more involved in his religious convictions, and by 1828 had become convinced that he had a mission to lead a rebellion against the white oppressors. In Turner's own words, he "heard a loud noise in the heavens, and the Spirit instantly appeared to me and said that the Serpent was loosened, and Christ had laid down the yoke he had borne for the sins of men, and that I should take it on and fight against the Serpent, for the time was fast approaching when the first should be last and the last should be first."

He was sold again in late 1830 or early 1831, to Joseph Travis, a craftsman. On Feb. 12, 1831, a solar eclipse occurred. Turner interpreted this as a sign from God that he should start the rebellion. Turner spent the next six months recruiting his fellow slaves and developing a plan for the revolt. The plan was to capture the armory at the county seat, Jerusalem, before moving on to the Dismal Swamp, some thirty miles further east. There, he reasoned, he and his band could hide from the whites who would inevitably pursue them.

On the night of Aug. 21, Turner and seven other slaves began their rampage. Stealthily entering the Travis family home, they murdered its five occupants in their beds. The chilling determination with which Turner approached his mission is evident in the confession he gave before his execution: "It was then observed that I must spill the first blood. On which, armed with a hatchet, and accompanied by Will, I entered my master's chamber. It being dark, I could not give a death blow, the hatchet glanced from his head, he sprang from the bed and called his wife, it was his last word; Will laid him dead, with a blow of his axe, and Mrs. Travis shared the same fate, as she lay in bed. The murder of this family, five in number, was the work of a moment, not one of them awoke; there was a little infant sleeping in a cradle, that was forgotten, until we had left the house and gone some distance, when Henry and Will returned and killed it..."

After murdering the Travis family, Turner ran his recruits through a series of quasi-military maneuvers before marching them in file to a neighboring property owned by Salathul Francis. Two of Turner's men knocked on the door, and told Francis they had come to deliver a letter. When he opened the door, the two men pulled him out and killed him by beating him on the head. At the next property, the band entered the house as its occupants slept and killed the owner, Mrs. Reese, in her bed. When her son awoke, they killed him also. At each stop, the band recruited more slaves, swelling their ranks to about fifty or sixty. Slaves who resisted joining or tried to protect their masters were killed as well. The rebel slaves also took arms and ammunition from each property they invaded.

Toward the end of the second day, the band reached the property of James W. Parker. Turner had information that Parker himself was not present and so he declined to go down the road to the house, but a large number of his group wanted to liberate family members who were slaves on the property. Leaving Turner at the gate, they went on to the house. According to some accounts, the group who went to the house found the wine cellar and got drunk. Turner, growing impatient, had to go get them. As the reunited band returned to the main road, they encountered a group of eighteen white men who had discovered the rebels' work and followed their trail. Turner's men stood their ground and fired at the whites. About half of the whites retreated after the first round of fire, and more retreated as the rebels rushed them. However, as Turner's band cleared the top of a small hill, they discovered two other parties of whites following the first.

As word of the massacre spread, white posses formed. In all, 2,000 members of the local militia and 800 federal soldiers joined in the search for the band of renegades. As the posses combed the countryside, they killed between 100 and 200 blacks. In some instances, those killed had participated in the uprising, while others had sympathized or assisted in it. Still others were innocent victims of the hysterical rage that gripped the white populace in the wake of the massacre. Mutilated black bodies were displayed along the roads and in other prominent places as a grisly warning against future slave insurrections. When their advance was finally stopped, Turner and his men had gotten within a few miles of the county seat. Turner himself remained at large for six weeks before being captured by a white posse. Of the participants in the rebellion, fifty-five were captured. Turner was hanged after making his articulate and chillingly detailed confession. Of the others, seventeen more were hanged, twelve others were "transported," and twenty were found Not Guilty. The other five died before they could go to trial, of wounds suffered in their capture.

Now that white Southerners could no longer believe in the myth that black slaves were content to remain without freedom, the treatment of slaves became more oppressive. Turner's rebellion inspired a wave of legislation designed to curtail what few freedoms slaves had, and thereby eliminate the possibility of any future insurrection. However, for the slaves, the rebellion, commonly referred to as "Old Nat's War" or "Nat's Fray," became a watershed in their history of oppression.

REF.: Aptheker, *Nat Turner's Revolt, The Environment, The Event, The Effects;* ____, *American Negro Slave Revolts;* ____, *Negro Slave Revolts in the United States, 1526-1680;* Carroll, *Slave Insurrections in the United States, 1800-1865; CBA;* Coffin, *An Account of Some of the Principal Slave Insurrections;* Drewry, *Slave Insurrections in Virginia, 1830-1865;* Halasz, *The Rattling Chains: Slave Unrest and Revolt in the Antebellum South;* James, *A History of Negro Revolt;* Johnson, *The Nat Turner Slave Insurrection;* McClellan and Avery, *The Voices of Guns;* Nash, *Bloodletters and Badmen;* Turner, *The Confessions of Nat Turner.*

Turner, Richard, d.1976, rob.-rape-suic.-mur. At the age of twenty-three, Richard Turner was sentenced to prison for the rape of two teenaged girls. He pleaded guilty to the charges, telling the judge he was drunk at the time of the attack and did not know what he was doing. In prison at Cañon City, Colo., Turner was classified as extremely dangerous and was denied parole on three occasions. While in prison, Turner witnessed a stabbing and testified against the assailant. For fear of reprisal, he asked to be transferred to another facility.

When Turner was moved to Fremont County Jail, a minimum security facility, his records and parole board hearing reports never accompanied the convicted rapist. While incarcerated in Fremont, Turner was reunited with John Hardin, a part-time prison guard from Cañon City. The prisoner had managed to convince Hardin that his rape "victims" had been willing participants. Hardin talked the sheriff into allowing Turner out on work release. On Aug. 26, 1976, Hardin and his wife, another couple, and Turner went to Gab's Lounge in Penrose. As the evening wore on, Turner became drunk and obnoxious, grabbing women in the bar and trying to start fights with many of the male patrons.

Hardin managed to get the drunken prisoner into his van, but later he and his wife were found dead in their carport. Hardin's two daughters and three-year-old son had also been beaten to death. The three females had been raped. The state mounted a massive search for Hardin's stolen yellow pickup truck and his gun collection. Police were too late to prevent the rape of a 13-year-old girl near Willard, but they found the disabled truck on the side of the road. As authorities approached the vehicle they encountered a farmer with his head under the truck's hood. They yelled for the man to get out of the way and they heard a gunshot in the truck. Turner was slumped across the steering wheel when officers found him, dead from a self-inflicted wound.

REF: *CBA;* Godwin, *Murder U.S.A.*

Turow, Scott, c.1949- , U.S., law enfor. off. Scott Turow, the author of the best-selling novel *Presumed Innocent,* about a prosecutor falsely accused of murder, was accused of obstructing justice during a criminal investigation. It was alleged that while working as an assistant U.S. attorney in 1983, Turow used attorney Marvin Glass as an informant against his client, Ronald Ofshe, who was arraigned on drug charges in Florida. Turow authorized Glass, who turned informer in an attempt to lessen his own criminal culpability, to record conversations with Ofshe with a hidden wire, but warned him about divulging attorney-client conversations. Glass was subsequently sentenced to eight years for drug offenses in Texas and Florida.

In June 1987, the U.S. Court of Appeals for the 11th Circuit in Atlanta refused to dismiss the case against Ronald Ofshe. On Aug. 6, 1987, while filing a motion in the Atlanta courtroom, Turow's attorney, John Powers Crowley, denied that his client violated ethical guidelines, and sought to withdraw the disciplinary recommendation against him. On Apr. 29, 1988, Turow was exonerated of any wrongdoing by the acting criminal division chief of the Justice Department, John Keeney, who stated that Turow "did not hinder or obstruct the administration of justice in any way" and that "the conduct in question was proper and necessary for effective law enforcement." REF.: *CBA.*

Legendary highwayman Dick Turpin, shown torturing an old woman to learn the whereabouts of her treasure.

Turpin, Richard, (AKA: **Dick Turpin, Dick Palmer, John Palmer, Tom Palmer**), 1706-39, and **King, Tom**, d.c.1737, Brit., theft-rob. Richard "Dick" Turpin was a British highwayman whose exploits became legendary. He was reportedly born in "The Crown Inn," the son of John Turpin, an Essex innkeeper. Turpin served an apprenticeship under a Whitechapel butcher and set up his own business by the time he was twenty-one. Accused of stealing livestock, Turpin left the area. In Essex, he became a member of a smuggling gang and then joined a gang that stole live deer, primarily in Epping Forest. When the group began committing robberies, Turpin became the leader.

The robbers' first target was a Mr. Strype, who ran a Watford chandler's store. They robbed Strype's house of money, but did not harm him. They next broke into the home of a Loughton woman, blindfolding her and her maid. When the woman refused to tell the robbers where she kept her money, they allegedly tortured her by putting her over a fire until she told them. They got more than £400. At a farm in the Barking area, the gang tied up the farmer, his son-in-law, wife, and maid, and stole more than £700. The thieves' next target was the house of Mr. Mason, an official in charge of Epping Forest. Turpin, however, had gone to London, gotten drunk, and apparently forgotten about their plans. The gang went ahead without him. They broke in, kicked and hit Mason, and vandalized the house. After finding 120 guineas, they left and went to London, where they found Turpin and gave him some of the loot.

On Jan. 11, 1735, they raided a farmer's house at Charlton, Kent, interrupting a card game. They forced the farmer, Mr. Saunders, to take them through the house, where they found more than £100. They also allegedly ate mince pie and drank wine before leaving with threats to return if the robbery were reported too quickly. The gang attacked the Surrey home of Mr. Sheldon on Jan. 18, tied up Sheldon's coachman in the stable, captured Sheldon, and robbed his home of jewelry, eleven guineas, and other valuables. On Feb. 4, the bandits burst into the home of Mr. Lawrence of Edgware, Middlesex, and stole money, silver, and other valuables, Before leaving one of the gang members also raped the maid. After the Lawrence robbery the king was notified, and a reward of fifty guineas was offered for their arrest and conviction.

The gang set out to rob a farmer's house in the Marylebone region on Feb. 7. They tied up two servants and the farmer, Mr. Francis, in the stable. In the house, they tied up and beat the farmer's daughter, wife, and maid before making off with jewelry, money, and other valuables. After this attack, the reward for their capture was increased to 100 guineas. Two of the leaders were arrested, tried, convicted, and hanged in chains, effectively discouraging the rest of the gang. The group disbanded, so Turpin decided to become a highway robber.

Turpin met Tom King, a notorious highwayman, on Cambridge Road in February 1735. Turpin reportedly did not recognize King and ordered him to hand over his valuables. When King identified himself, the two agreed to begin robbing together. They were successful in robbing many travellers, and were thought to have operated from a cave in Epping Forest. On May 4, 1737, Turpin shot and killed Thomas Morris, a servant who intended to capture him for a reward. After that incident, additional reward money was offered for Turpin, who was described as "...about thirty...marked with the small-pox, his cheek-bones broad, his face thinner towards the bottom...." Turpin and King continued their robberies, however.

Close to the Green Man in Epping Forest one evening, they caught up with another traveler, Mr. Major. Turpin's horse was exhausted, so he took Major's horse. Major reported the theft to authorities, who learned that a similar horse had been spotted at the Red Lion in Whitechapel. A constable went to investigate and when he attempted to question King, the highwayman pulled out his pistol, which misfired. King shouted to Turpin, who was approaching, telling him to shoot the lawman. Turpin's shot missed the constable and instead fatally wounded King, who died a week later. While he lingered, he told officials about likely places to find Turpin, and huntsmen and bloodhounds searched the region guided by this information.

Turpin fled to Long Sutton, Lincolnshire, and then traveled to Welton, Yorkshire, where he assumed the name John Palmer. He made repeated trips to Lincolnshire, stole horses, and brought them back to Yorkshire to trade or sell. He was arrested and confined in York Castle on suspicion of stealing horses in early February 1739. He allegedly was identified as Richard Turpin after he sent a letter to his brother in Essex that was seen by his former teacher, Mr. Smith, who traveled to York and identified Palmer as Turpin. On Mar. 22, 1738, Turpin was brought to trial at the York Assizes with Sir William Chapple presiding. The highwayman was convicted of stealing a foal and a mare at Welton and given the death penalty. He admitted to a few robberies and to one murder. Turpin reportedly bought some new clothes while awaiting execution and hired five men as mourners. When he was hanged at York on Apr. 7, 1739, he reportedly spoke with the hangman for about half an hour and then jumped off the ladder. He was buried at the cemetery of St. George's church, but the body was later found in the garden of a city surgeon. A crowd carried it back to St. George's, where it was reinterred.

Richard Turpin was immortalized in the novel, *Rookwood,* published in 1834 by William Harrison Ainsworth (1805-82). Ainsworth, who primarily wrote historical novels, was fascinated by highway robbers, especially Turpin. In the preface to *Rookwood,* he stated "I had always had a strange passion for highwaymen and have listened by the hour to their exploits, as narrated to me by my father, and especially to those of 'Dauntless Dick', that 'chief minion of the moon'...Turpin was the hero of my boyhood."

REF.: *CBA;* Culpin, *The Newgate Noose;* Gollomb, *Master Highwaymen;* Hibbert, *Highwaymen;* Hunt, *A Dictionary of Rogues;* Mitchell, *The Newgate Calendar;* Potter, *The Art of Hanging;* Pringle, *Stand and Deliver;* Reppetto, *The Blue Parade;* Scott, *The Concise Encyclopedia of Crime and Criminals;* Stevens, *From Clue to Dock;* Turner, *The Inhumanists;* Woodhall, *Secrets of Scotland Yard;* (FILM), *Dick Turpin,* 1933.

Turtletaub, Sam (AKA: **Sam Green, "Big Greenie"**), prom. 1930s, org. crime-mur. Big Sam Green was a gunman for Louis "Lepke" Buchalter, the mobster who controlled the garment district of New York City in the 1930s. The district attorney's office was fully aware of Big Greenie's role whenever Lepke wanted someone hit, so when some of Lepke's men broke up a meeting of the Needle Workers' Union in April 1933, they were able to find witnesses to identify him as the man who shot Manny Burdy and Harry Gottlieb, the two main men who had been encouraging the union to stand up against Lepke. Sam Green was arrested and charged with assault and inciting a riot, but he was out on bail in almost no time and had disappeared by the time the two men died of their wounds.

When Thomas E. Dewey took over the district attorney's office in 1935, the investigation he started of Lepke's activities included finding Sam Green. It took until 1940 to find a key to locating him. An investigator moved into a room in the same boarding house where a former girlfriend of Green lived. They became friendly, as she believed that he, too, was in the rackets. He learned from her that Green was in Cincinnati, where other investigators discovered that he was using the name Baker and that he had a new car. Checking its registration led them to his address, but Green was warned and had left by the time they reached his hotel room.

Green's trail led from Ohio all over the Southwest. He was finally arrested in Tucson, Ariz., on the basis of a wanted flyer that had been distributed nationwide. He was returned to New York, found Guilty of murder, and sent to prison for life.

REF.: *CBA;* Danforth, *The D.A.'s Man.*

Tussaud, Marie (AKA: **Madame Tussaud**), 1760-1850, Switz.-Brit., wax museum curator. Originated Madame Tussaud's exhibition of wax models of tyrants and victims of French revolution. In 1802, she had moved her wax figures to London from Switzerland, eventually locating on Baker Street in 1833, where she added a Chamber of Horrors, comprised of torture devices and criminals made of wax. REF.: *CBA.*

Tutt, David, See: **Hickok, James Butler.**

Tuttle, Arthur J., 1868-1944, U.S., jur. Appointed to eastern district court of Michigan by President William Howard Taft in 1912. He served as prosecuting attorney for Ingham County, Mich., from 1899-1902, and as district attorney for the eastern district from 1911-12. He also served as a state senator, representing the fourteenth district from 1907-11. REF.: *CBA*.

Tweed, William Marcy, 1823-78, U.S., polit. corr. Heading the wheeling and dealing activities of the inner council of New York's Tammany Hall was an obese, squinty-eyed, scraggly-bearded politician named William Marcy Tweed. From 1840 until his arrest in 1871, Tweed was a corrupt colossus scooping up booty in the name of New York. Born on Cherry Street in 1823, this first of the great "bosses" was the great-grandson of a Scottish blacksmith whose ancestors took their name from the Tweed River which snaked through the lowlands southeast of Edinburgh. Tweed's father, Richard, became a successful chair maker in New York, but his two sons, William and Richard, managed to drain in useless schemes every penny of his $200,000 fortune. The old man was forced to come out of his retirement and again take up chair making to make ends meet. He never forgave his sons or spoke to them again. He fell dead in a fit of apoplexy while at work.

Tweed did not mourn. He had no emotion whatever, or, at least, displayed none. As a youth he took particular delight in beating up all the smaller children in his neighborhood, one of whom was a sickly child named Thomas Nast. Through bullying and threats, Tweed became the foreman of the Americus or Big Six fire engine company after being on the force for a mere six months. He was then 270 pounds and he was described as "a tall overgrown man, full of animal spirits with a swaggering gait, free-and-easy manners, the constant use of slang, and he displayed a coarse humor greatly in vogue among his firemen associates. He talked much and with a sputtering volubility that made it hard to understand him." In those early years, Tweed drank himself into insensibility and whored with such abandon that he was soon afflicted with venereal disease.

This brutish, bullying boss was elected an alderman in the rigged election of 1851 and served on the council for two years. It was Boss Tweed who led the money-grubbing "Forty Thieves" in their looting exercises. A year before his death in 1878, Tweed boasted to a *Herald* reporter that "there never was a time when you couldn't buy the Board of Aldermen." Naturally, he included himself. After serving a stint as a U.S. congressman (1853-55), Tweed was elected to the Board of Education and immediately instituted two-handed graft in his office. In a later investigation, it was revealed how Tweed compelled teachers to kick back thick slices of their annual salary to get their appointments. One lame woman, a teacher who had to walk on crutches, was "taxed" by Tweed $75 of her annual $300 salary to keep her position.

It was during his reign of the Board of Supervisors, to which he was elected in 1857, holding the post until 1870, that Boss Tweed flourished as a super high-binder, developing the notorious Tweed Ring. Tweed controlled the six democrats on the board and paid one of the six opposing Republicans, Peter P. Voorhis, $2,500, to stay away from meetings in which appointments and appropriations were decided. Naturally, he had things his own way when Voorhis sent word that he had gotten sick. Voorhis was always sick at times most advantageous for Tweed.

The boss' most able assistants in pilfering public funds and establishing payoffs and bribes were John R. Briggs and Walter Roche. Later such Machiavellian types as Richard Connolly, Abraham Oakey Hall, and Peter B. "Brains" Sweeney, joined Tweed in the plundering of the city. Hall was elected mayor of New York with Tweed's backing in 1864. City Hall then did the boss' bidding without question.

Hall fancied himself a playwright and while in office he produced his own epics. The stagestruck mayor even acted in a few of these literary abortions. His masterpieces of folderol included *Loyalina, Brigadier General Fortunio and His Seven Gifted Aides-de-Camp, Humpty Dumpty* (a burletta), and *Let Me Kiss Him for His Mother.* While A. Oakley Hall was cavorting on the boards, Boss Tweed and his cronies, with the mayor's blessing, sacked the city treasury.

The judiciary of New York, with Judge George G. Barnard at its scurrilous head, did Tweed's bidding day and night. Barnard, a one-time "stool-pigeon" in a gambling house, minstrel performer, and pimp, was elevated by the boss to the state supreme court, despite a warning from Barnard's brother that "George knows about as much law as a yellow dog."

In court, Barnard would sleep through most of the testimony of cases he was hearing. He would sometimes whittle absent-mindedly. One of the courtroom attendants who often swept up his shavings was Richard Croker, who would become the infamous Boss Croker, another Tammany tiger. Judge Barnard drank heavily in court and would become animated to the point where he would interrupt proceedings to tell obscene jokes. He made lewd remarks to the women on the stand and in the spectator's area, but mostly he slept. Judge Barnard was a tired man. Tweed usually kept him up half the night playing poker. (Tweed always won.) It was Barnard who, through his ramrod judgments, enabled the robber barons Jay Gould and Big Jim Fisk, Tweed's personal friends, to perpetrate their gigantic stock frauds and become multimillionaires.

In one astounding examination, Judge Barnard questioned Daniel Breezy, asking: "If you had a claim for a client of $50,000 against the city, what would be the first step you would take to recover it?"

"I would go and see Bill Tweed," Breezy replied.

Barnard beamed his approval: "You will make your mark as a corporation lawyer."

There were dozens of judges in Boss Tweed's pocket. Albert Cardoza, whose son Benjamin became a U.S. Supreme Court justice, was another Tweed-ruled judge. Cardoza was once described by an opponent as having "the eyes of a serpent looking from the face of a corpse."

To control the elections of the late 1860s, Tweed and his fellows took over the naturalization of immigrants who made up almost half of New York's population. Tammany members sold naturalization papers to those who would vote the Tammany ticket. These papers were genuine and were issued by Tweed's controlled courts. A man named Rosenberg sold thousands of these papers to immigrants before being arrested by U.S. marshal Robert Murray, who posed as a foreigner without papers. Said Rosenberg before he was promptly set free by Tweed's hirelings: "Mr. Murray, every certificate that you have purchased from me is genuine, and came out of the courtroom. I am at work for the democratic party, and paid for this thing, I get but very little of the $2 that is paid for these certificates."

Millions of dollars flowed unceasingly into the pockets of the Tweed Ring, the boss taking the largest share; Tweed gleaned $133,187 in two days of furious political appointments. Not until July 1871, after Tweed had controlled the city and state of New York for a generation, was the corruption fully exposed, beginning with attacks by the New York *Times* and *Harper's Weekly.* Reformers such as Samuel Tilden, who was then governor, and State Attorney General Charles Fairchild brought charges against Tweed, who was promised his freedom if he agreed to talk. Tweed told the whole grim history of his stealing public funds. Fairchild backed off from his promise to free Tweed after the boss testified. Tweed was thrown into jail and his bail was set at $6 million. The boss sent his family abroad with what money he had transferred into accounts for his wife and daughter and then settled into prison life.

One of the men who helped put Tweed behind bars was the one-time victim of the boss' childhood beatings, Thomas Nast, whose acerbic cartoons had flayed the Tweed Ring and aroused the public to the point of riot. One of Tweed's close associates, a banker, visited with Nast at the time the political cartoonist was in the middle of his crusade against the boss. The banker, over breakfast, said to the genius of the drawing board: "I hear that you have been made an offer to go abroad for art study?"

"Yes, but I can't go. I haven't time," Nast replied.

"But they will pay you for your time," the banker said, alluding to Tweed and this boys. "I have reason to believe that you could get $100,000 for the trip."

Boss William Marcy Tweed during his heyday.

"WHO STOLE THE PEOPLE'S MONEY?"—DO TELL. N.Y.TIMES. 'TWAS HIM.

The famous Tweed Ring cartoon, accusing the next fellow.

Mayor Fernando Wood of New York.

Tweed's arch foe, newsman Horace Greeley.

"CAN THE LAW REACH HIM?—THE DWARF AND THE GIANT THIEF"

One of Thomas Nast's cartoons showing Tweed as unreachable.

TWEED-LE-DEE AND TILDEN-DUM.

A Nast cartoon showing Boss Tweed in prison stripes.

Nast's eyes lit up and he threw back the bait: "Do you think that I could get $200,000?"

The banker squirmed a bit. "Well, possibly. I believe that from what I have heard in the bank that you might get it. You have great talent but you need study and you need rest. Besides, this Ring business will get you into trouble. They own all the judges and jurors and can get you locked up for libel. My advice is to take the money and get away."

The cartoonist then asked with a subtle goad, "Do you think I could get $500,000 to make the trip?"

"You can," the banker said emphatically.

"Well, I don't think I'll do it!" Nast went back to his drawing board and Tweed went to jail, where he died on Apr. 12, 1878. A few days before he died, Boss Tweed told a friend, "This is a moral for the world. They will be preaching sermons about me, saying, 'Look at the record of this evildoer!'" See: **Fisk, James; Gould, Jay; Nast, Thomas; Tammany Hall.**

REF.: Alexander, *The Political History of the State of New York;* Asbury, *Gem of the Prairie;* Barrett, *The Old Merchants of New York City;* Beecher, *A Biography of Henry Ward Beecher;* Berger, *The Story of the New York Times;* Bigelow, *The Life of Samuel J. Tilden;* Blake, *History of the Tammany Society from Its Organization to the Present Time;* Booth, *History of the City of New York;* Bowen, *The Elegant Oakey;* Brace, *The Dangerous Classes of New York;* Breen, *Thirty Years of New York Politics;* Browne, *The Great Metropolis; CBA;* Cook, *The Life and Public Services of of Hon. Samuel J. Tilden;* Crapsey, *The Nether Side of New York;* Foster, *New York by Gaslight;* Fried, *The Rise and Fall of the Jewish Gangster in America;* Greeley, *Recollections of a Busy Life;* Halstead and Beale, *Life of Jay Gould, How He Made His Millions;* Hennessey, *What's the Matter with New York;* Hershkowitz, *Tweed's New York;* Hopkins, *A History of Political Parties in the United States;* Hudson, *Journalism in the United States;* Ivin, *Machine Politics and Money in Elections in New York City;* Jones, *The Life of James Fisk, Jr.;* Katz, *Uncle Frank;* Kilroe, *Saint Tammany and the Origin of the Society of Tammany or Columbian Order in the City of New York;* Lee, *History of American Journalism;* Lewis, *The Apaches of New York;* ____, *The Boss and How He Came to Rule New York;* Logan, *Against the Evidence;* Lynch, *Boss Tweed: The Story of a Grim Generation;* Lynch, *Criminals and Politicians;* McAlpine, *The Life and Times of Col. James Fisk, Jr.;* Mehling, *Scandalous Scamps;* Moss, *The American Metropolis;* Munro, *Personality in Politics, Reformers, Bosses and Leaders, What They Do and How They Do It;* Myers, *The History of Tammany Hall;* Nash, *Hustlers and Con Men;* Orth, *The Boss and the Machine;* Paine, *Thomas Nast: His Period and His Pictures;* Parton, *The Life of Horace Greeley;* Peterson, *The Mob;* Reppetto, *The Blue Parade;* Sann, *Kill the Dutchman;* Scott, *The Concise Encyclopedia of Crime and Criminals;* Smith, *Political Parties and Their Places of Meeting in New York City;* Stafford, *A Life of James Fisk, Jr.;* Stevens, *The Shame of the Cities;* Stone, *History of New York City;* Thompson, *Gang Rule in New York;* Tilden, *The New York City Ring;* Townsend, *New York in Bondage;* Tweed Ring Investigation *(Report of the Special Committee of the Board of Aldermen Appointed to Investigate the "Ring" Frauds, Together with the Testimony Elicited During the Investigation);* Volunteer Special, *The Volcano Under the City;* Walling, *Recollections of a New York Chief of Police;* Werner, *Tammany Hall;* White, *The Wizard of Wall Street;* (FICTION), Twain, *The Gilded Age.*

Twelfth Street, Kansas City, Mo., prom. 1870s-1950s, U.S. gamb.-pros. This red light district flourished in Kansas City, Mo., for seven decades. Here could be found, by anyone seeking pleasures of the flesh or gaming excitement, all manner of illegal operations. The area was spawned by the state's first important political boss, James Pendergast, a puddler who had bet all his savings on a race horse, Climax, which came in first and returned a small fortune. Pendergast quit his job at the Jarboe Keystone iron foundry and purchased a saloon-inn in an area known as the West Bottoms, located on St. Louis Avenue and Twelfth Street.

Pendergast first called his place The American House, then changed it to Pendergast House. Around this establishment mushroomed gambling dens, brothels, and all manner of illegal operations, protected in later years by Jim and Tom Pendergast, who became the most powerful political satraps in the Midwest at the time. One of the earliest and most popular theaters in this district was the burlesque house run by Joe Donegan, a Pendergast ally who also helped to deliver the Democratic vote. In addition to the Century Burlesque Theatre, Donegan also ran the Edward Cabaret, where bets on all sporting events were liberally taken.

Whores, pimps, racetrack touts, gamblers, and assorted miscreants peopled the Century Theatre and, during the early 1900s, Frank James, bandit brother of the notorious Jesse, worked as a bouncer in the theater, manhandling some of the more rowdy denizens. In later years, such types were personified by Oscar Benson, the Terrible Swede, and Solly "The Terrible" Weissman.

As the Twelfth Street area flourished, Tom Pendergast bought and operated three saloons and had his hand in many other operations with Donegan, including the Free and Easy and the Jefferson Cabaret, which was to feature an enterprising singer named Tommy Lyman, who in the 1910s became America's first "crooner." It was Lyman who first sang "My Melancholy Baby," composed by Ernie Burnett, in the Edward Cabaret, where Burnett was the musical director, and it was Lyman who coined the words "torch song" while crooning through the Pendergast-controlled joints. "The Twelfth Street Rag," composed by Euday Bowman, also emerged in this period and symbolized the wide-open vice district of the day, where anything but murder was tolerated by a corrupt police force and a venal political machine.

Police Chief John L. Miles was typical of the do-nothing attitude regarding this vice area. During Miles' long term in office, he prudently restricted his raids to black jazz joints, which he insisted were the real gambling and prostitution centers along Twelfth Street. A grandstander who loved publicity, Miles would personally lead these ax-wielding raids at the head of half the force, arrest scores of people, and never get one conviction. One place catering strictly to jazz, the East Side Musicians Club on Twelfth Street, was designated by Miles as the center of his wrath. He raided the place ninety-nine times and arrested everyone in the place, including the disgusted musicians. To commemorate the 100th raid, proprietor Doc Fojo had the band play "I Can't Give You Anything But Love" when Miles and his minions burst through the door.

Directly protecting Twelfth Street and all other Pendergast operations in K.C. was the boss' front man, City Manager H.F. McElroy. For thirteen years, 1926-37, McElroy made sure that none of the real gambling and vice resorts on Twelfth Street were ever bothered by the limelight-lusting Chief Miles. McElroy's daughter Mary was a close friend to many of the young hoodlums who worked for Pendergast enforcer Johnny Lazia (murdered by a rival faction in 1934), and would later figure in a sensational kidnapping where she would fall in love with her kidnapper.

The Twelfth Street area was besieged for decades by reformers who attempted unsuccessfully to clean up the area, from temperance leaders to religious zealots who led torchlight marches up and down the notorious street without police or political support. Until the 1950s, when the area died of old age, the denizens merely shrugged at such reform activities and would step to the street applauding the exhortations of clergymen and do-gooders, often paying the Twelfth Street bands considerable money to serenade the reformers as they marched past. See: **Audett, James Henry; Lazia, John; McElroy, Mary; Pendergast Machine.**

REF.: *CBA;* Dorsett, *The Pendergast Machine;* Redding, *Tom's Town.*

Twentieth Century Sporting Club, prom. 1940s, U.S., org. crime. A 1947 investigation by the New York district attorney's office uncovered a number of abuses in the sport of boxing. Crime syndicate figures were guiding fighters through Mafia-controlled managers listed with the State Athletic Commission. The mob bosses were maneuvering fighters through mismatches and fixed fights, and then pinching more than the standard one-third fee from a fighter's purse. Mike Jacobs, the head of the Twentieth Century Sporting Club, which operated out of Madison Square Garden, and matchmaker Nat Roberts came under fire.

Because of the grand jury recommendation, the New York State Legislature made it a misdemeanor for unlicensed managers to guide a fighter's career. They also fingerprinted all licensed managers and trainers. In hopes that the State Athletic Commission would impose strict punishment on unlicensed individuals, the grand jury minutes were released to the S.A.C. in June 1947. The Commission fined the club $2,500 but never held formal hearings into the grand jury findings. REF: *CBA.*

***Twenty-one Clues,* The**, 1941, a novel by J.J. Connington. This work is based on the sensational Hall-Mills murder case (U.S., 1922). See: **Hall-Mills Case**. REF.: *CBA.*

.22 -Caliber Killings, The, 1978, U.S., (unsolv.) mur. One month after police in Columbus, Ohio, found the bodies of three murder victims, they arrested Claudia Yasko. She waived her right to an attorney and confessed that she and two male accomplices had perpetrated the brutal slaying of nightclub owner Robert McCann, his mother, and his girlfriend. The trio was indicted on first-degree murder charges and faced the death penalty. Attorney Lewis William Dye defended Yasko and found that ballistics experts had determined the gun used to kill McCann had been used to commit other crimes during the time his client was incarcerated. The McCann murder weapon had never been found, but police were reasonably confident that the same .22-caliber Luger was involved in as many as nine murders.

The 27-year-old Yasko, who worked as a waitress and sometimes as a topless dancer, had been undergoing therapy and had spent almost half of her life in mental institutions over several stays. Yasko also had a penchant for confessing to crimes that she could not have committed or had never occurred. Despite a lack of evidence and a confession from an unstable woman, Franklin County prosecutor George Smith and chief prosecuting attorney James O'Grady proceeded with the case.

Before her trial, Yasko could not recall confessing to the crime. She explained that her psychic powers had taken her to the scene mentally, not physically. With no more than circumstantial evidence, the prosecution dropped charges against Yasko and her accomplices. The case remains unsolved. REF: *CBA.*

Twiss, Sir Travers, 1809-97, Brit., jur. Oxford University law professor from 1855-70, and author of *The Law of Nations.* He was forced to retire from public service in 1872 due to a sensational libel incident. In 1884 he wrote the constitution of the Congo Free State for the king of Belgium. REF.: *CBA.*

Twist, Kid, See: **Reles, Abraham; Zwerbach, Max.**

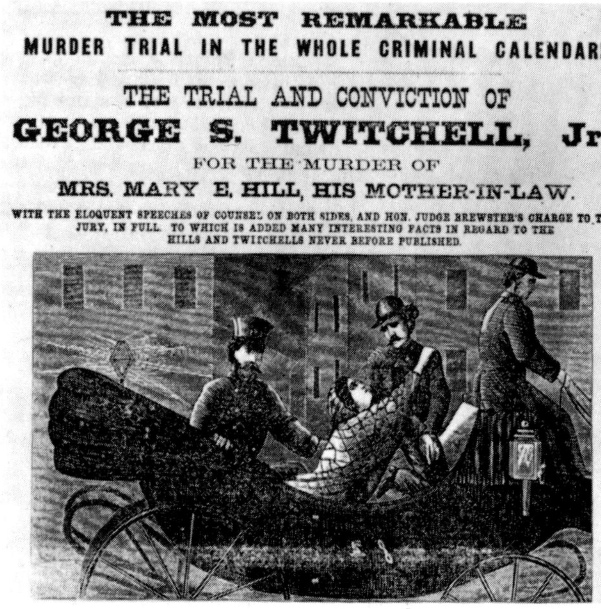

THE MOST REMARKABLE
MURDER TRIAL IN THE WHOLE CRIMINAL CALENDAR!
THE TRIAL AND CONVICTION OF
GEORGE S. TWITCHELL, Jr.,
FOR THE MURDER OF
MRS. MARY E. HILL, HIS MOTHER-IN-LAW.
WITH THE ELOQUENT SPEECHES OF COUNSEL ON BOTH SIDES, AND HON. JUDGE BREWSTER'S CHARGE TO THE JURY, IN FULL. TO WHICH IS ADDED MANY INTERESTING FACTS IN REGARD TO THE HILLS AND TWITCHELLS NEVER BEFORE PUBLISHED.

A broadsheet relating the crimes of murderer George Twitchell.

Twitchell, George S., 1827-69, U.S., mur. Upon returning to the Twitchell household in November 1868, servant Sarah Campbell found George S. Twitchell asking for his mother-in-law, Mrs. Hill. Campbell told Twitchell she had not seen her, but minutes later she discovered her dead, in the backyard of their Philadelphia home. Twitchell's wife said that her mother must have jumped out the second-floor window, but blood on the stairs and a second-floor windowsill suggested otherwise. She told police that her mother always carried a couple thousand dollars in her bosom and that a burglar had committed the murder. After discovering that the Twitchells stood to profit from Hill's death and wondering why the dogs had remained silent throughout the alleged attack, police charged the Twitchell couple with murder.

George Twitchell went on trial first and was found Guilty and sentenced to death. After an appeal was denied, Twitchell told police that his wife had killed her mother and that he had helped her cover up the murder. The judge disbelieved Twitchell's testimony and days later the convicted murderer poisoned himself. Mrs. Twitchell was never brought to trial and ultimately was released.

REF: *CBA; A Full and Complete History of the Hill Homicide;* Hubbell, *The Commonwealth of Pennsylvania versus George S. Twitchell, Jr. and Camilla E. Twitchell;* Pearson, *Instigation of the Devil; The Trial and Conviction of George S. Twitchell, Jr. for the Murder of Mrs. Mary E. Hill; The Twitchell Tragedy;* Wilson, *Encyclopedia of Murder.*

Twysden, Sir **Roger**, 1597-1672, Brit., polit. corr. Member of Parliament from 1625-26, and justice of peace in 1636 and 1660. For his anti-parliamentary actions he was imprisoned in 1642 and from 1643-47. He also authored *The Laws of Henry I* in 1645. REF.: *CBA.*

Tyburn Tree (AKA: **Deadly Never Green**), Brit., executions. The gallows at Middlesex were known as the Tyburn Tree. From the time the first man was hanged there in 1196 until the last man met his end in 1783, the site was a major source of entertainment for the British. Established around 1690, "Tyburn Fair" happened every six weeks or so. A public holiday was declared and local businesses were closed. Hundreds of people would line the three-mile stretch of road from the Newgate Jail to Tyburn Tree. For the condemned criminals it was a merciless last ride. They had to endure the public's scorn while contemplating their demise. At one time, drivers would often stop at St. Giles Hospital, where the condemned man would receive a last drink, but a number of drunken hangings put an end to that practice.

At the hanging site, wealthy people were seated in stands that were known as Mother Proctor's Pews, or would rent houses where they could dine and view the execution. The hangman attached the noose to the scaffolding while a horse waited patiently for orders to pull away. Frequently, a short drop failed to kill a victim and considerate friends and relatives would pull his legs to finish the job. The popular "Tyburn Fair" was abolished in 1783 and the site was moved because the area was starting to attract more residents.

REF: *CBA;* O'Donnell, *Should Women Hang?;* Scott, *The Concise Encyclopedia of Crime and Criminals.*

Tyburski, Leonard, 1944- , U.S., mur. On Oct. 2, 1985, Leonard Tyburski reported the disappearance of his 37-year-old wife to Canton Township police. Tyburski, the head of the attendance department at Detroit's Mackenzie High School, told police that Dorothy Tyburski had been very depressed ever since the death of her sister in 1984. He speculated that she may have left because of emotional problems, and police treated the incident as a missing persons case for more than two years, until they dropped the case due to a lack of progress. For 20-year-old Kelly Tyburski, the disappearance of her mother was manifesting itself in recurring nightmares. Kelly, a student at Michigan State University, could not shake the vision of her mother locked up or tied up somewhere in the family's home in suburban Detroit.

On Jan. 2, 1989, Kelly managed to pry the lock of a basement freezer open and discovered her mother's body. She had been bludgeoned to death. Two days later, Leonard Tyburski was arraigned on murder charges in District Court at Plymouth. The courtroom drama began to unfold in June, when Craig Albright, Kelly's live-in boyfriend, told the courtroom he had been enticed into having sex with Mrs. Tyburski on two occasions. On Sept. 28, 1985, Albright said that he refused the woman's advances. On that same day, Tyburski would testify, Dorothy told her husband of her affair with the teenager and called her husband a "wimp." In a fit of rage, Tyburski attacked his wife, who in trying to defend herself stabbed him with a steak knife. At first, Tyburski told the court his wife had fallen into the freezer, then he admitted he had thrown her into the unit. Subsequently he said he had gone berserk over her confession and smashed her head against a basement beam before depositing her in the freezer. Tyburski testified that even while his wife was wounded in the freezer, she called him a "wimp" and a "punk" and called out for Albright.

In defense of her client, attorney Carole Stanyar portrayed Tyburski as a man emasculated by his wife's taunts and constant humiliation. It was in self-defense that Tyburski acted, Stanyar told the courtroom. Assistant Wayne County Prosecutor Glenn Page argued that Tyburski's story had changed so frequently that the truth might not have been told. Page questioned how Tyburski, in good conscience, could have lied about his wife's whereabouts, filed for divorce, and entertained in his home while Dorothy's body was in the basement. On June 26, it took a jury less than two hours to decide that Tyburski was Guilty of second-degree murder charges. In July, Wayne County Circuit Judge Richard Hathaway sentenced Tyburski to twenty to forty years in prison. REF: *CBA*.

Tylenol Murders, 1982, U.S. (unsolv.) mur. On Sept. 29, 1982, 12-year-old Mary Kellerman woke up feeling sick. She took an Extra-Strength Tylenol capsule and died on the bathroom floor at her Elk Grove Village, Ill., home. Kellerman was the first of seven people in the Chicago area poisoned to death by the cyanide-laced capsules before Tylenol recalled the product.

Adam Janus, twenty-seven, of Arlington Heights, was the second victim. He went into a coma and died at 3:15 p.m. the same day after swallowing several capsules. His brother, 25-year-old Stanley Janus, and Stanley's 19-year-old wife, Theresa Janus, would be victims four and five, after each took capsules later that evening from the same tainted bottle while grieving over Adam's death. The third victim was 27-year-old Mary Reiner of Winfield, who died, also on Sept. 29, after slipping into a coma in her living room. Mary McFarland, a 31-year-old mother of two, swallowed a capsule after lunch on Sept. 29 and died at 3:15 a.m. on Sept. 30. Victim number seven was 35-year-old flight attendant Paula Prince, who died in her Chicago apartment after she took a capsule Wednesday night, Sept. 29.

After the deaths, seven stores removed the capsules from shelves. Three more contaminated bottles were found. The search for the killer began. Illinois attorney general Ty Fahner, Illinois Department of Law Enforcement Director James Zagel, and FBI Chicago bureau chief Edward Hagerty employed more than 120 investigators in the search, followed more than 2,000 leads, compiled more than sixty volumes of information, and spent almost $3 million, but were still unable to identify the murderer. One of the many suspects was Roger Arnold, a loading dock worker for Jewel, the food chain where Kellerman's mother and Janus purchased their bottles of Tylenol. Coincidentally, he knew the father of a victim, and owned a book describing ways to commit murder. After three days, Arnold was released from custody, but publicity surrounding him caused considerable depression. Not long after his release he got drunk, and shot and killed 46-year-old John Stanisha, for which he was convicted of murder and sentenced to thirty years in prison. Stanisha was said to resemble the man Arnold believed implicated him in the poisonings.

The most likely suspect, according to investigators, is James Lewis, the man who attempted to extort Johnson & Johnson, the manufacturer of Tylenol. A week after the killings, Johnson & Johnson received a letter demanding that $1 million be placed in a north suburban bank account or the killings would continue. The account belonged to a businessman who identified Lewis as a disgruntled ex-employee. The FBI traced the letter to Lewis, who lived in Kansas City, Mo. As a tax accountant and real estate salesman there, Lewis was already suspected of defrauding an elderly client of his property. He also had been charged with the 1978 murder and dismemberment of another elderly man, but the charge was dropped because the evidence had been illegally obtained. Lewis also had reportedly threatened his adoptive parents with an ax. Lewis was arrested for extortion in December 1982, and was convicted the following October. He admitted writing the extortion letter, but claimed it was a joke, not to be taken seriously. He was sentenced to ten years' imprisonment on June 14, 1984. Though Lewis could have obtained his information from news accounts of the killings, and no direct link has been made between him and the murders, his statements, theories, and past history lead investigators to believe the killer is behind bars, but for the wrong crime.

James Lewis

Lewis claimed he was not in Chicago during the time when the tainted bottles were placed on the shelves, but witnesses claim to have seen him. According to investigators, he was once placed in a mental institution for aggressive physical behavior, but Lewis stated he committed himself to escape the draft during the Vietnam War. Dr. James Cavanaugh, who also testified in the trial of murderer John Wayne Gacy, told investigators that Lewis' psychological profile matched that of the poisoner being sought. Lewis would not submit to a lie-detector test, which he called "voodoo electronics."

In statements made after his arrest, Lewis speculated in detail about how the crime was committed. The poisoned capsules contained different amounts of cyanide. Lewis told investigator Jeremy Margolis in 1983 that the killer may have inserted empty halves of Tylenol capsules into holes pre-drilled into a bread board so that when the powdered poison was drawn over the capsules by a knife—so that the killer would not touch the substance—different amounts would be allotted because less would reach the capsules further from the poison.

Johnson & Johnson's chairman, James E. Burke, led the company's campaign to regain the public's confidence in Tylenol. The company spent over $100 million to recall and destroy all available capsules, set up a telephone pool to handle inquiries, and offered free replacements for bottles of Tylenol consumers had thrown away. They also led the way in designing tamper-proof packaging now featured by many over-the-counter products.

REF.: *CBA;* Fox, *Mass Murder.*

Tyler, Jesse, d.1900, U.S., west. lawman. Utah lawman Jesse Tyler brought in stolen cattle and rustlers, and frequently pursued Butch Cassidy's Wild Bunch. He was bested by a group of rustlers in February 1899 in the San Rafael Valley, and another time was sued by the wife of a horse thief for retrieving stolen horses from her corral. On May 16, 1900, Tyler led a posse after cattle rustlers near Thompson, Utah. Thinking they were riding up to an Indian camp, Tyler and deputy Sam Jenkins dismounted, left their horses, and approached unarmed. The camp turned out to be that of the band of rustlers led by Harvey Logan. The lawmen turned to run and Logan opened fire, shooting both men in the back. The rest of the posse fled, abandoning the bodies of Tyler and Jenkins for two days. See: **Logan, Harvey.**

REF.: Baker, *Wild Bunch; CBA.*

Tyler, John, 1747-1813, U.S., jur. Virginia General Court judge from 1789-1808. He was one of the first justices to sustain the judiciary's overruling power. He was elected governor of Virginia, serving from 1808-11, and was appointed to the district court of Virginia by President James Madison in 1811. His son John Tyler became the tenth president of the U.S. REF.: *CBA.*

Tyler, John, prom. 1851, Brit., attempt. rob. In June 1851, British police were alerted to the presence of ex-convict John Tyler and a partner in the vicinity of Westminster Bank in St. James' Square. Police alerted bank officials and they placed most of their reserves in a secured vault and left marked bills in the cashbox in the manager's office. Six weeks later, Tyler and his accomplice were apprehended as they tried to carry the box out of the bank. The two men were sentenced to be deported for seven years.

REF: *CBA;* Thomson, *The Story of Scotland Yard.*

Tyler, Lindsay, 1942- , and **Tyler, Stephanie**, prom. 1976, and **Tyler, Robert** 1968- , and **Tyler, Sarah**, 1971- , Eth., (unsolv.) kid. In May 1976, a British family of four was kidnapped by an Ethiopian guerrilla organization, the Tigre Liberation Front, and held for $1 million in ransom. The family, 34-year-old veterinary surgeon Lindsay Tyler, his wife Stephanie, and their children, 8-year-old Robert and 5-year-old Sarah, were kept in the desert, living under a bush and sleeping on the ground, and were given two meals a day. Tyler was working on an aid project in Ethiopia when kidnapped. On Jan. 7, 1977, the family was released without harm in Port Sudan, and they arrived in Khartoum three days later. REF.: *CBA.*

Tyler, Wat (Walter), d.1381, Brit., rebel.-mur. vict. Led Peasants' revolt protesting economic difficulties, statute of laborers, and new poll tax, in 1381. He was murdered by Sir William Walworth while listing his demands to Richard II. One day earlier, he had demanded an end to serfdom, amnesty for rebels, and termination of various trade and labor restrictions. REF.: *CBA.*

Tyler, William Frederick, See: **Hefeld, Paul.**

Tyndale, William (Tindal, Tindale), c.1494-1536, Brit., her. Finished printing translation of New Testament in 1526 and was later able to avoid capture ordered by Thomas Wolsey. At Antwerp in 1531 he was again arrested. He criticized Roman Catholicism and Henry VIII's divorce from Catherine of Aragon in *The Practyse of Prelates,* in 1536, causing him to lose the king's support and bringing a sentence of death for the crime of heresy. He was strangled and burned at the stake. REF.: *CBA.*

Tyner, Hugh Leon, Jr., 1940-80, U.S., abduc.-mur.-suic. In northwest Harris County, Texas, Hugh Leon Tyner, Jr. killed his wife and father following a quarrel in early August 1980. After killing them, Tyner went to the home of his son-in-law, murdered him, and abducted his 15-year-old stepdaughter. After unsuccessfully trying to rape the teenager, Tyner put the .25-caliber pistol to his head and killed himself. REF: *CBA.*

Tyrell, Walter, See: **William Rufus**, King.

Tyrrel, Sir James, d.1502, Brit., consp. In 1502, James Tyrrel was ordered arrested by King Henry VII. Tyrrel was accused of helping the Earl of Suffolk, a nephew of Edward IV and an heir to the throne, escape to Germany. Stationed in France at the time of his arrest, Tyrrel was returned to Britain and held in the Tower of London and shortly thereafter beheaded without a trial. In the same year, Tyrrel was murdered, Henry's journalist Polydore Vergil released the first official account of the 1486 death of Elizabeth Woodville, queen to Edward IV, and her children. Vergil's version of the events named Tyrrel as the murderer of Elizabeth's children and said he acted on orders from Richard III. In fact, it was Henry VII who had proclaimed that Edward IV's children were illegitimate heirs to the British throne and had systemically tried to eliminate them.

REF: *CBA;* Williamson, *Historical Whodunits.*

Tyrrell, John F., 1861-1955, U.S., graphologist. Handwriting expert John F. Tyrrell helped convict several murderers, forgers, and kidnappers. He also identified papers and inks with uncanny accuracy, and he could identify the type on a document, trace it to a specific machine, and then identify the typist by the way the keys were struck. Tyrrell grew up in Milwaukee and started work at an insurance company. He detected forgeries on medical forms and helped end many common insurance frauds. Tyrrell wrote for William Kinsley's *Penman's Art Journal,* and won one of the two prizes the magazine awarded. Albert S. Osborn of Rochester, N.Y., who later became another handwriting expert, won the other prize. Osborn and Tyrrell were two of the founders of the American Society of Questioned Document Examiners.

In the early 1900s, Tyrrell distinguished the handwriting of identical twins Lloyd and Leon Longley. One of the Longley brothers would write a bogus check while the other created an alibi across town. Tyrrell established the existence of the two brothers, exposing their forgery operation. Tyrrell also testified in the murder trial of Roland B. Molineux in 1899, in which he proved that Molineux addressed a package containing poisoned seltzer. In the trial of Albert T. Patrick, charged with murdering millionaire William M. Rice and forging documents to receive the estate, Tyrrell showed that Rice's signature on each document was identical and therefore traced. Tyrrell's testimony about a typewriter convinced Clarence Darrow to change the plea of Leopold and Loeb to guilty, and Tyrrell gave the most convincing testimony during the Lindbergh baby kidnapping trial. REF.: *CBA.*

Tytler, Alexander Fraser (Lord Woodhouselee), 1747-1813, Scot., jur. Judge advocate of Scotland in 1790. He also served as judge of the court of session. He was the son of William Tytler. REF.: *CBA.*

Tytler, William, 1711-92, Scot.-U.S., writer. Historian who vindicated his subject in *Inquiry into the Evidence against Mary Queen of Scots,* published in 1760. He also wrote verses and dabbled in science. His *The Historical Register* resulted in a move to Salem, Mass., to avoid arrest. REF.: *CBA.*

Tz'u-Hsi (AKA: **Hsiao-Ch'in, Dowager Empress of China**), 1835-1908, mur.? Tz'u-Hsi, the daughter of a Manchu official, was sent to the Imperial Court of China at age sixteen to become a concubine to the 20-year-old emperor, Hsien-Feng. There was little chance that she would have been noticed among the 3,000 others like her, except that the emperor's wife proved to be barren. Having curried favor with the empress, Tz'u-Hsi was called by the emperor for a single night of abandon. She delivered a son exactly nine months later. The child, Tung-Cheh, was the emperor's only son. Tz'u-Hsi quickly discovered the joys of having power over people, especially over her weak-willed lord, who cared little for the activities of government. When Europeans invaded the Forbidden City, it was she who gave the order that all captives should be beheaded.

The young emperor died of his excesses in 1861, leaving Tz'u-Hsi and Empress Niuhuru as regents for Tung-Cheh, who was raised in complete debauchery. The empress did not care about running the government, and Tz'u-Hsi never let go of her power for the remaining forty-seven years of her life. Nor did she let go of the money that came her way, a great deal of which came in the form of confiscated estates and ever-increasing taxes on the people.

Tung Cheh ostensibly took control of the country on his majority, but he died three years later at age nineteen of venereal disease and smallpox. Tz'u-Hsi made her nephew, 3-year-old Kuang-hsu, the new emperor, in preference to the unborn child of Tung Cheh's wife, who committed suicide. Kuang-hsu's age gave his aunt many years in which to manipulate her continuance in power. As he grew, he feared his aunt and ran to Empress Niuhuru for protection. Niuhuru died suddenly after a visit from Tz'u-Hsi, who had brought a present of rice cakes.

When Kuang-hsu became emperor in 1887, he befriended the European nations, which was abhorrent to Tz'u-Hsi. Learning that the emperor was about to have her imprisoned, the aging woman took him prisoner and kept him in solitary confinement for many years, with no one to oppose her renewed regency. When the anti-foreign Boxer Rebellion began in the late 1890s, the Dowager Empress supported the movement, but as foreign armies poured into Peking to protect their nationals, Tz'u-Hsi and the emperor had to flee the capital. They lived in exile until a peace treaty was signed in 1901. She spent her last few years reluctantly letting European influence build in China, and even had the history of her regency rewritten to expunge any record of her support for the Boxers. She suffered a stroke in 1907 and progressively worsened during the following year. Her nephew, too, was dying, although of what the doctors were not certain. He had kidney disease, but the final symptoms that killed him seemed more like poison than natural causes. He died writing a curse on Tz'u-Hsi on Nov. 14, 1908. His powerful, hated aunt died the next day. The 267-year-old Manchu Dynasty lasted only four more years, with Kuang-hsu's infant nephew, Py'i, the new emperor, and the infant's father as regent. REF.: *CBA*.

Uale, Frank, See: **Yale, Frank.**

Ubaldini, Ruggiero, prom. 1276, Italy, mur. Served as Archbishop of Pison and was imprisoned in 1288. He starved Ugolino della Gherardesca, his two sons, and his two grandsons. REF.: *CBA.*

Uckele, John Joseph, and **Matysek, Stanley**, prom. 1945, U.S., rob. Thurston M. Patterson and Victor H. Lohn left the Hollywood State Bank with more than $111,000 in the back seat of an Oldsmobile. The two messengers were to take the money to Lockheed Aircraft Corporation to cash payroll checks on July 30, 1945. As they navigated a back road on their way to Burbank, Calif., a man in an army MP's uniform halted the car. The MP then pointed a gun at Patterson. As the messengers moved toward their guns on the seat, a second gunman appeared and forced Lohn and Patterson into the rear of the car. The robbers drove into the hills and bound and blindfolded the guards.

When questioned by police, Lohn and Patterson told authorities that one of the men wore a Lockheed employee badge on his shirt. While officials worked on the Lockheed lead, they also found the stolen car the thieves had used and discovered in it a printed address. The address turned out to be a garage that had been rented by two men. Inside the building, police discovered six bags of silver coins, an army uniform, a gun belonging to the messengers and a Lockheed identification badge. FBI scientists identified John Joseph Uckele as the original owner of the ID badge. Lockheed officials identified Uckele and Stanley Matysek as good friends and former company employees.

In the University of California, Los Angeles (UCLA) dormitory room that Uckele and Matysek shared, police found burglary equipment, a bayonet and a twelve-page short story by Uckele in which a hitchhiking soldier murders an insurance salesman. Within days, Uckele and Matysek were arrested and charged with armed robbery. They would not reveal where the stolen money was hidden, and blamed the whole incident on someone named "Nate." Officials finally found the money in Sawtelle Veterans' Facility Cemetery, near the UCLA campus. When informed of the discovery, Uckele finally was given a chance to confess, but he tried to escape. Upon his recapture, Uckele admitted his involvement in the robbery. Matysek also confessed and was sentenced to twenty-one years in prison. Uckele received a twenty-year sentence. REF: *CBA.*

U'dall, John (Uvedale), c.1560-92, Brit., her. Preached Puritan philosophy and was supposedly involved with *Martin Marprelate* leaflets. He was put in prison in 1590 for his criticism of the episcopacy, and in 1591 he was sentenced to death. He was later pardoned. REF.: *CBA.*

Udderzook, William E., d.1874, U.S., fraud-mur. In what has become a common form of insurance fraud, William Udderzook was foiled when his supposed fire victim threatened to expose him. In 1873, Udderzook and his brother-in-law, Winfield S. Goss, both residents of a town near Baltimore, schemed to burn Goss' house and make it appear that Goss had been killed in the blaze. They took out a large insurance policy on Goss and stole a dead body, which they planted in the house before setting it on fire. After the fire, Mrs. Goss filed a claim for her husband's death in the fire, but the insurance company refused to pay. Mrs. Goss then sued, and a jury awarded her the insurance. The insurance company appealed the decision because they were convinced that Goss was still alive and continued to look for him.

Udderzook had kept Goss well hidden, but with the insurance investigators hot on their trail, Udderzook panicked and killed him. Goss' body was found along with other evidence which led to Udderzook's apprehension. He was found Guilty and hanged in November 1874.

REF.: *CBA;* Nash, *Bloodletters and Badmen;* ____, *Hustlers and Con Men;* Pearson, *Murder at Smutty Nose.*

Ulasewicz, Anthony T., prom. 1972-77, U.S., tax evas. In 1973, former New York City policeman Anthony T. Ulasewicz told a congressional committee that he paid more than $200,000 to men involved in the break-in of Democratic National Headquarters in Washington, D.C. A confidential investigator for former President Richard M. Nixon, Ulasewicz distributed the Watergate hush money and pocketed $45,000 for himself.

In February 1977, Ulasewicz was tried for falsifying his income tax returns for 1971 and 1972. The government accused Ulasewicz of receiving cash payments totaling $45,000 and only reporting $5,000 as income. In his defense, the retired policeman said he intended to claim the income in 1972, but when the Watergate scandal broke, he became frightened. In July 1973, Ulasewicz had filed an amended income tax return and paid penalties and interest on the tax. Ulasewicz was found Guilty, but sentenced to only one year of unsupervised probation. See: **Watergate Scandal.** REF: *CBA.*

Ulbricht, Walter, 1893-1973, Ger., exile. Joined the Communist Party in 1919 and entered the Reichstag in 1928. He was exiled during the Nazi years, during which time he relentlessly persecuted followers of Trotsky and others who did not adhere to the party line. After WWII he became the party chairman in East Germany. He ruled his own country with an iron fist but obediently followed orders from the Kremlin. He erected the Berlin Wall in 1961. REF.: *CBA.*

Ullathorne, William Bernard, 1806-89, Brit., penal reform. Catholic priest and vicar general in Australian penal colony from 1832-42. He wrote *Horrors of Transportation Briefly Unfolded* in 1836, and testified about penal conditions in Australia. In 1857, his testimony helped end the practice of sending British felons to Australia. REF.: *CBA.*

Ullo, Joseph Spencer, 1929- , U.S., org. crime. Once a New York hoodlum, Joseph Ullo was suspected by police of two gangland-style murders. Ullo moved to California in the early 1960s and allegedly began a loansharking enterprise. He was arrested in September 1977 on loan-sharking charges while prosecutors attempted to link him to the slaying of Jack Molinas, a 43-year-old pornography distributor and gambler, and Vincent Calderazzo, a soldier in the New York Mafia. Molinas apparently owed Ullo money. Both men were shot with a .22-caliber pistol, and were only two victims of the Mafia-controlled " .22-caliber hitters." Police also hoped to connect Ullo to the murder of Michael Ariola, a Los Angeles massage parlor operator, fatally wounded with a .22-caliber gun during a Mafia takeover of his establishment. Even with the testimony of car thief Eugene Connor, who claimed he drove the getaway car in one of the murders, Ullo was not convicted.

Apparently the Mafia elected to kill Ullo for refusing to pay a loan. When crime boss Frank Tieri was indicted on racketeering and conspiracy charges in 1980, the indictment charged he had voted for the murder of Joseph Ullo in September 1976. Ullo eluded these attempts on his life. However, he did spend six years and one day in prison on a charge of making false statements to federal agents. He was released from prison on Jan. 21, 1983. REF.: *CBA.*

Ulpian (Domitius Ulpianus), c.170-228, Roman., jur. Served as council member under Emperor Lucius Septimius Severus. Heliogabalus banished him from Rome, but Alexander Severus later summoned him back, making him chief adviser to the emperor. REF.: *CBA.*

Ulrich, Charles, b.c.1825, U.S., forg.-count.-fraud. While serving a fifteen-year prison sentence in the Ohio Penitentiary in Columbus for counterfeiting, Charles Ulrich made good use of his engraving skills. He engraved a likeness of Governor William Allen and asked the prison warden to present it to him. Flattered by the metal etching, Allen soon arranged for Ulrich to be paroled. For a few years after his release, Ulrich operated an engraving shop in Columbus. William Burns, the teenaged son of a local tailor, often stopped in to hear Ulrich's tales of war and prison. The two men went their separate ways around 1875 and met again some twenty years later.

After running a pottery business, Ulrich returned to counterfeiting and soon was arrested and sentenced to fifteen years in a New Jersey prison. After his family pleaded with the judge, and he promised to leave the country, Ulrich was released. He returned to his native Germany but was jailed for possession of stolen goods. Ulrich's wife and children returned to Columbus in 1887. In the meantime, Burns was making quite a name for himself, first as a private detective and then, after 1891, with the U.S. Secret Service. When Burns heard that Ulrich had been released and was headed for the U.S., he volunteered to shadow him.

Burns picked up the trail in Columbus and tracked Ulrich to New York where he was meeting with a group of counterfeiters headed by William "Long Bill" Brockway. Two Secret Service agents escorted Ulrich from the train station to a hotel where the con man became reacquainted with Burns. After much talk, Ulrich agreed to serve as an informant and infiltrate the Brockway gang. Within months, the federal agents had gathered enough information to break up the counterfeiting ring. Ulrich, who turned out to be the star prosecution witness, testified under the threat of death. Brockway was convicted and sentenced to ten years in prison with his associates receiving lesser sentences.

REF: Caesar, *Incredible Detective; CBA.*

Umar I (Umar ibn al-Khattab), c.586-644, Arabia, caliph, assass. Helped Abu Bakr expand Islamic empire. He was assassinated in Medina by a Persian slave. REF.: *CBA.*

Umbert I, See: **Humbert I.**

Uncas, See: **Miantonomo.**

Unden, Bo Osten, 1886-1974, Swed., jur. Delegate to League of Nations Assembly from 1921-39. He served as minister of foreign affairs from 1924-26 and also authored legal writings about Swedish and international law. He was a delegate to the United Nations from 1946 to 1961. REF.: *CBA.*

Under Cover Man, 1931, a novel by John Wilstach. This fictional work is loaded with *romans a clef* entries. Included are famous 1920s New York criminal attorney William Fallon, the dapper crook Nicky Arnstein, who was Fannie Brice's paramour, con men Titanic Thompson (Alvin Clarence Thomas) and Dapper Dan Collins, and New York police commissioner Grover Whalen. See: **Arnstein, Jules W.; Collins, Dan; Fallon, William Joseph; Thomas, Alvin Clarence; Whalen, Grover**. REF.: *CBA.*

Underhill, Wilbur (AKA: The Tri-State Terror), 1897-1934, U.S., rob. Wilbur Underhill earned his nickname by robbing small town banks in Arkansas, Oklahoma, and Kansas in the late 1920s. He served a sentence in Kansas State Penitentiary at Lansing but escaped with two inmates, Bob Brady and Jim Clark, in September 1933. They hid out in the Cookson Hills until Underhill joined the Fred Bradshaw Gang and left his two companions. In Fall 1933, Underhill, Bradshaw, and others robbed banks in Coalgate, Okla.; Helena, Kan.; Okmulgee, Okla.; and Stuttgart, Ark.

Wilbur Underhill, the Tri-State Terror.

Underhill married in 1933, and he was on a honeymoon in Shawnee, Okla., when R.H. Calvin arrived with a team of federal agents on Jan. 1, 1934. Underhill held them off in a half-hour gun battle before running out into the street and right through the police cordon, dressed only in long underwear. He tried to take refuge in a furniture store and dove through its plate glass window, but he passed out once inside. Underhill died of bullet wounds five days later in McAlester, Okla.

REF.: American Guide Series, *Oklahoma, A Guide to the Sooner State; CBA;* Cooper, *Ten Thousand Public Enemies;* Edge, *Run the Cat Roads;* Nash, *Bloodletters and Badmen;* Wellman, *A Dynasty of Western Outlaws.*

Unger, Dr. **August M.**, prom. 1900, U.S., fraud. In a bizarre plot to bilk ten insurance companies out of $70,000, Dr. August M. Unger convinced Chicago model Marie Defenbach to fake her own death. Defenbach insured herself for $70,000 and moved to a boardinghouse using another name. Unger told her he would administer a drug to induce a death-like sleep, sign her death certificate, and substitute another body for cremation. Unger and two accomplices promised her half the insurance money upon her revival, at which time she would take a tour of Europe.

On Aug. 25, 1900, the trusting Defenbach drank the "medicine" and died fifteen minutes later. Unger signed the death certificate and the three conspirators collected the insurance money. An uncle of Defenbach, with the help of private detectives investigating her disappearance, uncovered the plot to defraud the insurance companies. One of Unger's accomplices turned state's evidence. The state could not prove murder, but Unger and his other accomplice, Frank Brown, were convicted of fraud and sentenced to five years in prison. REF.: *CBA.*

Ungern-Sternberg, Roman Nikolaus von, 1885-1921, Rus., rebel. General who fought against Bolsheviks before they took power in 1917. Later, he continued to fight in eastern Siberia. The Bolsheviks caught him and he was executed. REF.: *CBA.*

Unified Anti-Re-election Command, prom. 1970, Dom., kid. On Mar. 24, 1970, Lieutenant Colonel Donald J. Crowley became the third U.S. official kidnapped in Latin America in six months. Ambassador C. Burke Elbrick was abducted in Rio De Janeiro and later released in exchange for fifteen political prisoners. Sean Holly, a U.S. government employee, was kidnapped in Guatemala City and freed following the release of three prisoners. A U.S. air attaché in Santo Domingo, Dom., Crowley was exercising polo ponies when five gunmen wearing military uniforms abducted him.

Calling themselves the Unified Anti-Re-election Command, the kidnappers demanded that President Joaquin Balaguer release twenty-one political prisoners or they would kill Crowley. Among the prisoners was Maximiliano Gomez, who fought in the 1965 Civil War in the Dominican Republic, and was a leader of the pro-Cuban revolutionary movement. The terrorist organization wanted to block the re-election of Balaguer, whom they believed had escalated violence and torture in the country. After two days of negotiations, the kidnappers agreed to free Crowley in exchange for the release of twenty prisoners who would then be flown to Mexico. Crowley was released unharmed in Santo Domingo shortly after the political prisoners boarded the airplane that would take them to freedom. REF: *CBA.*

Unione Siciliane, prom. 1920s, U.S., org. crime. The Unione Siciliane started as a fraternal organization in the 1880s to provide insurance and social gatherings for Sicilian immigrants in New York City. As it grew in influence, the votes cast by its members were enough to affect elections in several city wards. Headquartered in Harlem, the Unione's influence soon reached into cities across the country.

By the time WWI began, the Unione had changed drastically. Ignazio Saietta murdered and intimidated his way to the group's presidency and used its power to establish Sicilian primacy in racketeering, prostitution, extortion, kidnapping, and murder for profit. He had installed in his office meathooks, from which to hang victims, and he burned at least six victims alive in the basement furnace. He went to prison in 1918 and passed the reins of leadership to Frankie Yale, an equally violent character, but one with vision to broaden the interests of the organization. Yale was killed by Al Capone ten years later.

Capone tried to muscle in on the Unione leadership, but, as a Neapolitan, he was regarded as an outsider. Capone was also a Chicagoan, not a New Yorker. In the early 1920s, the Unione's Chicago branch was run by a Capone ally, Mike Merlo, but his death in 1924, the year the name was changed to Italo-American National Union, led to a bloodbath as various factions competed for domination of the Unione (Merlo was, in fact, the only Unione president in the 1920s to die of natural causes). "Bloody Angelo" Genna proclaimed himself president of the Unione but was murdered the following year under the auspices of the North Side mob; the order for the hit probably came from Vincent Drucci, Bugs Moran, or Earl "Hymie" Weiss. Samuzzo "Samoots" Amatuna became the new president, but before 1925 ended, Drucci killed Amatuna in a barber shop. Capone had garnered enough power by this time to be able to appoint the next president. He chose Anthony Lombardo. With Capone's backing, Lombardo lasted three years. He exercised tremendous power as a negotiator between Black Hand kidnappers and their victims' families. Lombardo was killed on Sept. 7, 1928, along with bodyguard Joseph Ferraro, as they turned the corner onto State and Madison in Chicago. Two gunmen shot them down but missed another bodyguard, Joseph Lolardo. Lolardo gave chase, but, ironically, a passing patrolman mistook him for one of the killers and arrested him.

The next president was Lolardo's brother, Pasqualino "Patsy" Lolardo, who lasted about four months until his murder on Jan. 8, 1929. Patsy invited his friends Joseph Aiello and his two brothers to his house on North Avenue. His wife served them sandwiches, pastries, and wine and then left them alone. The four men joked for an hour in Patsy's den before the three guests offered a toast. When Patsy raised the glass to drink to his own health, the three brothers fired eleven bullets into him. Joseph Aiello assumed the presidency the next day and held the position for more than a year and a half, until Capone had him killed on Oct. 23, 1930.

By this time, candidates for the Unione presidency were becoming skeptical of the value of the office. After so many had been killed, few of the survivors were interested in the job. As the 1930s Depression began to take its toll, the Unione faded quietly out of existence. See: **Aiello, Joseph; Amatuna, Samuel Samuzzo; Black Hand; Capone, Alphonse; Drucci, Vincent; Lombardo, Antonio; Mafia, The; Moran, George; Saietta, Ignazio; Syndicate, The; Weiss, Earl; Yale, Frank.**

REF.: Asbury, *Gem of the Prairie; CBA;* Cressey, *Theft of the Nation;* Fried, *The Rise and Fall of the Jewish Gangster in America;* Gosch and Hammer, *The Last Testament of Lucky Luciano;* Hamilton, *Men of the Underworld;* Katz, *Uncle Frank;* Kobler, *Al Capone;* Lait and Mortimer, *Chicago: Confidential;* Lynch, *Criminals and Politicians;* McPhaul, *Johnny Torrio;* Morgan, *Prince of Crime;* Nash, *Bloodletters and Badmen;* Peterson, *The Mob;* Sann, *Kill the Dutchman;* Smith, *Syndicate City;* Spiering, *The Man Who Got Capone;* Thompson, *Gang Rule in New York.*

Union Station Massacre, See: **Kansas City Massacre.**

Unruh, Howard, 1921- , U.S. mur. Born and raised in Camden, N.J., Howard Unruh had a normal, uneventful childhood. He was a good student and graduated high school during the early stages of WW II. Unruh was drafted into the army and served with an armored division. In basic training he became a sharpshooter and his fellow GIs noticed that he had a fascination for weapons. He would spend hours each night sitting on his bunk taking apart his rifle and putting it back together again. Unruh never took advantage of weekend passes and was never seen in the company of women. He preferred to remain within the confines of his barracks and occupy himself reading his Bible or cleaning his rifle.

Religion had been deeply rooted in Unruh since childhood. He had attended church regularly, gone to Bible class and read the Bible each day at home. Unruh continued to carry his Bible with him through battle after battle as his armored unit fought its way up the boot of Italy in 1943. Unruh by this time was a machine gunner in a tank turret. In the following year, Unruh's unit, part of General George Patton's Third Army, helped to liberate Bastogne in the bloody Battle of the Bulge. Throughout these war years, Unruh kept a diary in which he wrote daily his private thoughts. A fellow GI, who later became a New York policeman, sneaked a look at Unruh's diary and was horrified to view its contents. Unruh had recorded the death of every German soldier he had killed, the hour and the place he had killed them and how they appeared in death after he had shot them.

Yet the Army looked up Unruh as a hero and before receiving his honorable discharge at war's end, he was awarded several commendations for his heroic service during battle. There was no hero's welcome for Howard Unruh when he returned to Camden. He was just another soldier, among millions, returning to civilian life. Unruh announced to his parents that he intended to become a pharmacist and, to that end, he took some refresher high school courses and then enrolled at Temple University in Philadelphia. Unruh continued his Bible classes and here met the only girl he ever dated. The relationship was only a mild flirtation and quickly ended.

Mass murderer Howard Unruh, under arrest.

This brief affair left Unruh embittered. By 1949, he was considered the neighborhood recluse. He became more withdrawn and seldom spoke to his parents, keeping to his room. The only preoccupation that made him joyful was maintaining his collection of weapons which he had begun after his military discharge. Unruh set up targets in the basement of his parents' home and practiced his marksmanship each day.

Unruh then began to take offense at off-handed comments made by neighbors. These became in his mind terrible insults and he suffered what doctors later termed accute paranoia and schizophrenia. He started another diary, or a hate list, wherein he jotted down every imagined and real insult made by neighbors and friends. No grievance was too small to record. This diary was no less exact than the one he had kept in service where his compiled in gruesome detail the German soldiers who had died at his hands.

The next-door neighbors, the Cohens, were particularly annoying to Unruh. Once, while taking a short-cut through the Cohen backyard, Mrs. Cohen had yelled at him: "Hey, you! Do you have to go through our yard?" The Cohens gave their 12-year-old son a bugle which he practiced daily and Unruh looked upon this as a personal offense against him, as if the neighbors had purposely awarded their son this noisy instrument to annoy him. The list of names and those who offended Unruh grew and grew and after each offense, Unruh wrote the abbreviation "retal," meaning "retaliate."

At first Unruh tried to shut off the world that offended him, rather than attack it. He built a high wooden fence around the tiny Unruh back yard. With his father's help, he built a huge gate that was locked against the intrusions of the world. Unruh's room was another haven where he took refuge from offensive neighbors. Here the young man kept a 9mm German Luger which he had purchased for $40, several pistols, a large quantity of ammunition, a knife and a machete, both kept razor sharp by their owner.

Unruh's shaky world collapsed on Sept. 9, 1949. He came home at 3 a.m. that morning to find that someone had stolen the massive gate he and his father had labored so long to erect. Local pranksters had done the deed but to Unruh, everyone living was responsible for this unforgivable insult. Unruh was up all night, staring at the ceiling of his room, seething with hatred. He decided to take revenge. At 8 a.m. he sat down to a breakfast prepared by his mother. He stared at her strangely and later admitted that she was to be his first victim. He had to kill her to spare her the grief he would bring upon the family through his homicidal plans. Unruh went to the basement, then returned, eyes glaring at her, walking toward her menacingly. His mother ran from the house and to a neighbor's where she blurted her fears about her unstable son.

Going to his room, Unruh loaded his Luger and another pistol, pocketing these weapons, along with a knife. He gathered up several clips of ammunition for both guns and filled his pockets. He walked outside and scrambled over the fence instead of going through the gaping area where the gate had been. At 9:20 a.m., Unruh stood in the doorway of a small shoemaker's shop owned by John Pilarchik. The cobbler, who had just recently finished paying off the mortgage for his shop, was busy working on childrens' shoes. Pilarchik looked up to see Unruh, someone he had known since boyhood. He stared in disbelief as Unruh pulled out the Luger and fired two bullets into his head. Pilarchik pitched forward dead onto his work bench.

Unruh then stepped next door, into the barbarshop owned by Clark Hoover who had been cutting Unruh's hair since he was a little boy. Sitting on a small plastic horse in the shop was 6-year-old Edward Smith, whose mother and 11-year-old daughter stood nearby. Without a word, Unruh raised his Luger and shot the boy dead and then pumped two more bullets into the startled Clark. He ignored the screams of Mrs. Smith and her daughter who rushed forward to cradle the dead child. Unruh looked at both of them but strangely did not fire his Luger. With a vacant stare, he wheeled about and headed for the corner drugstore which was owned by the Cohen family, the people he most hated.

James Hutton, Unruh's insurance agent, stepped from the drugstore. "Hello, Howard," he said affably.

"Excuse me," Unruh said in a monotone. He leveled the Luger at Hutton and fired twice. The insurance agent toppled dead to the sidewalk. Cohen, who saw Unruh shoot Hutton through the window of his shop, raced upstairs to warn other members of his family. Unruh entered the drugstore, inserting another clip into the Luger and then plodding up the stairs after his mortal enemy. Upstairs, Unruh saw no one about. He suspected that the Cohens were hiding and when he heard a noise in a closet he fired a bullet through the closet door. He opened this to see Mrs. Cohen sagging to the floor. He sent another bullet into her head. Cohen and his son slipped out a window and walked along the second-storey ledge of the building, scrambling to a nearby roof.

Unruh went into another room of the Cohen apartment and saw Cohen's elderly mother desperately calling police on a phone. He fired twice, killing her. Then he spotted Cohen and his son scrambling across a sloping roof and he leaned calmly from a window and fired a bullet that slammed into Cohen's back, causing him to slide off the roof and crash to the pavement below. Unruh carefully leaned further out the window and fired straight down at Cohen, sending another bullet into his back, although the man was already dead. The Cohen boy had by this time slid down to the edge of the roof and was clinging to its edge, screaming. Unruh glanced at him but did not shoot him. He walked back downstairs and went outside.

He found Alvin Day, a passerby, kneeling at the body of James Hutton, trying to help a man who was already dead. Day looked up to see the muzzle of Unruh's Luger poking into his face. Unruh fired twice, killing Day, a man he had never met before this moment. Reloading the Luger, Unruh began to leisurely stroll across the street. A car was idling at the corner, its driver waiting for the light to change. Unruh walked up to the car and stuck the Luger through the window, shooting the female driver dead. He then fired at and killed the woman's mother who was in the back seat of the car, along with her young son.

Unruh then began walking down the street. He spotted a truck driver getting out of the cab of his truck a black away. Taking careful aim, Unruh shot him in the leg. By then panic had gripped the entire area. The maniac in the streets was shooting anyone he encoutered. The manager of a supermarket quickly locked the front doors and told his customers to lie down on the floor. So did the manager of a bar which Unruh approached. As bar customers huddled on the floor, Unruh tried the door and found it locked. He fired twice, trying to blow away the lock but it held. He moved on, seemingly unconcerned.

Going into the tailor's shop next door, Unruh found the place empty. Tom Fegrino, the proprietor, was not present but Unruh heard a noise in the back room. He pushed back a drape to see Mrs. Fegrino cringing behind a chair. "Oh, my God, please don"t," she pleaded. Unruh said nothing as he sent two bullets into her, killing her instantly. Stepping outside, Unruh looked about at the now empty street. The only persons present were those whom he had already killed. Neighbors and passersby had rushed into houses and shops and had locked themselves inside against the random rage of the lunatic. Unruh looked up to see 3-year-old Tommy Hamilton staring down at him. He fired once, killing the boy.

Walking to a nearby house, Unruh entered it by the back door which he found unlocked. Inside the kitchen, he found Mrs. Madeleine Harris and her two sons. The older son, a courageous youth, saw the gun in Unruh's hand and dashed forward, driving his shoulder into the body of the tall killer. Unruh fired twice, wounding the youth and his mother. He then stood over these two fallen victims who squirmed in pain. He leveled the Luger at them but, oddly, decided not to end their lives. He turned on his heel and walked once more outside.

Police sirens wailing from squad cars could be heard in the distance. Unruh increased his pace as he walked back to his home where he went to his second-storey room, barricading the door and reloading his Luger. He waited patiently as police surrounded his house. He looked out his window at them without firing. His identity was by then known and had been reported to Phillip Buxton, editor of the Camden *Courier Post*. Buxton obtained Unruh's listed phone number and took a chance, calling the killer.

Unruh picked up the phone and one of the strangest phone conversations in the annals of murder then occured.

"Hello," Unruh said in a calm voice.

"Is this Howard?" Buxton inquired.

"Yes, this is Howard," Unruh replied. "What is the last name of the party you want?"

"Unruh."

"Who are you and what do you want?" Unruh asked politely.

Buxton was diplomatic: "I am a friend and I want to know what they are doing to you."

"Well, they haven't done anything to me yet," Unruh said in an even voice, as if he were chatting with an old friend. "But I am doing plenty to them."

"How many have you killed?"

"I don't know yet—I haven't counted them, but it looks like a pretty good score." (Thirteen persons had been shot to death by Howard Unruh within twelve minutes.)

"Why are you killing people, Howard," Buxton asked, trying to control his own passions while writing down the murderer's every word.

He was greeted by silence. After some moments, Unruh replied in a low voice: "I don't know. I can't answer that yet—I'm too busy. I'll have to talk to you later." He hung up.

At that moment tear gas cannisters fired by police outside

smashed through the glass of the bedroom windows and exploded inside, filling the room with eye-searing gas. These were followed by fusilades of bullets that smacked into the walls of Unruh's room, chipping the plaster. After a few minutes, Unruh took down the barricade in front of his door and walked downstairs and outside. He put his hands slowly into the air at a command barked by a police officer. Dozens of guns were trained upon him.

Detectives rushed forward, manhandling him, manacling his large hands. Detective Vince Connelly, sickened at the sight of the bodies in the street nearby, stared at Unruh and said: "What's the matter with you? Are you a psycho?"

Howard Unruh lifted his head indignantly and snapped: "I am no psycho! I have a good mind!"

More than twenty psychiatrists who examined Howard Unruh disagreed. They believed him to be hopelessly and criminally insane. The mass killer was never brought to trial but sent to the New Jersey State Mental Hospital for life. He had no remorse for his brutal, unthinking murders. In one interview with a psychiatrist, Unruh stated: "I'd have killed a thousand if I'd had bullets enough."

REF.: *CBA;* Nash, *Bloodletters and Badmen*. (NOTE: Add ref. from biblio ref and other sources.)

Untouchables, See: **Ness, Eliot**.

Upfield, Arthur William, 1888-1964, Aus., writer. Born in Britain and traveled to Australia in 1911. He created Inspector Napoleon Bonaparte, a half-Aboriginal character who appeared in more than thirty books. Books authored: *The Barrakee Mystery, Murder Down Under, The Widows of Broome,* and others. REF.: *CBA.*

Urabi Pasha (Arabi Pasha, Ahmad Urabi Pasha al-Misri), 1839-1911, Egypt, rebel. Nationalist who served in Egyptian army in war against Ethiopia from 1875-76, and who participated in officers' rebellion against Ismail Pasha in 1879. He opposed Turkish and Circassian officers' power in the Egyptian army and headed a rebellion against them in 1881. He became the minister of war in 1882, opposing British and French influence. After the British victory at at-Tall al-Kabir in 1882, he was condemned to death, but was instead exiled to Ceylon from 1882-1901. REF.: *CBA.*

Urich, Dr. **Heinz Karl Gunther** (AKA: **Dr. Henri Urich**), prom. 1960, Mor., suic.-mur. A high-ranking official of the SS in Nazi Germany, Dr. Heinz Karl Gunther Urich, was captured by the French near the end of the war. While serving time in a French prison, Urich was offered the chance of joining the French Foreign Legion in North Africa with the rank of medical major and serving out his sentence. The fact that he would be a commissioned officer in the French forces eliminated the possibility of his being tried for war crimes committed in France. Within months after he arrived in Morocco, Urich managed to get a discharge from the Foreign Legion and became the director of a local hospital owned by a mining company. By the time he married Rose Ascensio in 1948, the doctor had changed his name to Henri Urich. Through the marriage, Urich gained a teenage stepdaughter named Liliane with whom he fell in love.

On June 28, 1960, Police Commissioner Ali Mamoud read an obituary notice in the newspaper concerning the death of 22-year-old Liliane Urich. She had died, the notice read, in Hannover, Ger., following an operation. The commissioner was aware of Mrs. Urich having health problems, but the death of his daughter Liliane caught him by surprise. Upon investigation of the doctor's house, police found that Urich had left town three days ago and requested a three-month leave of absence from the hospital. In investigating the disappearance, police questioned Liliane's boyfriend who said that Urich did not approve of him and discouraged the girl from seeing him. In conversation with a neighbor of the Urichs', police found postcards and a letter from the doctor, detailing his daughter's demise. She had a brain tumor, the doctor wrote, and died almost immediately following surgery. The neighbor said that she was surprised that Urich had written to her because usually Mrs. Urich did the writing.

Police inquiries to Germany revealed that Liliane had never been admitted to the Hannover hospital and there was no death certificate on file. Unexpectedly, Urich returned to his Moroccan home on July 8 and repeated the story about the tragic tumor for the police. Ali Mamoud also asked him about the houseboy, who had not been seen in a few weeks. The doctor said he had been fired. The Moroccan police received further information from German authorities that contradicted the doctor's story. On Aug. 10, officials sought to question Urich again, but found him dead in a chair. He had shot himself in the head. On a table was a note dated July 15 saying goodbye to his wife and his daughter Monique. Upon further investigation of the house, police discovered the bodies of Mrs. Urich, Liliane and Monique underneath the garage floor. Police found the houseboy, who said he had been paid by the doctor to keep quiet. He had witnessed the murders, he told police. The shootings occurred after the doctor argued with Liliane, who refused to stop seeing her boyfriend.

REF: *CBA;* Gribble, *The Deadly Professionals.*

Urschel, Charles F., See: **Kelly, George R.**

Ursins, Marie-Anne de La Trémoille des, 1642-1722, Spain, consp. Noblewoman born in France. She was influential in arranging the marriage of Philip V of Spain and Maria Luisa of Savoy, then became the principal lady of the bedchamber for Maria Luisa in 1701. She gained power over policy because she influenced Maria Luisa, who controlled Philip. Later, she arranged Philip's second marriage. His new wife, Isabella Farnese, had been alerted to her maneuverings and she was banished from Spain. REF.: *CBA.*

Ursinus, d.c.385, Roman., exile. Served as Antipope from 366-367, and became Roman deacon. He and Damasus I were elected to replace Liberius as pope. He was exiled to Gaul when disputes arose between opposing groups, but in 367 Emperor Valentinian I permitted him to return. He and his supporters were exiled from Rome again when violence broke out in 368. He lived in Milan until a Roman religious council forced him into exile in Germany in 378. REF.: *CBA.*

Ursinus, Sophie, 1760-1836, Ger., attempt. mur.-mur. Although guilty of at least three murders, Sophie Weingarten Ursinus lived in luxury even after being sentenced to prison for life. She was apprehended by the police when her servant, Benjamin Klein, reported that she was trying to poison him.

Along with this accusation, Klein informed the police that Sophie had also killed her elderly husband, a lover named Rogay, and her aunt, Christina Regina Witte. She was sentenced to life imprisonment for the murder of her aunt, the only one proven in court. However, her great wealth (which she inherited from the aunt she murdered) and her high social status led the prison authorities to allow her every privilege and to live out her days in prison in luxury. She died on Apr. 4, 1836, and was treated to a grand funeral at which her generosity was extolled and in which there was no mention that she killed anyone or that she died in prison.

REF.: *CBA;* Nash, *Look For the Woman.*

Ursula, Saint, d.c.451, Ger., martyr. According to legend, she headed a pilgrimage to Rome accompanied by more than 11,000 virgins. They were all slain by Huns near Cologne, Ger. REF.: *CBA.*

Ursuline Convent Riot, 1834, U.S., mob vio. The most terrifying riots are those involving mobs that strike out of bigotry and racial hatred. The most awesome of these in the nineteenth century was the rabid Boston mob that attacked the Ursuline convent in Charlestown in 1834. The path to the door of this convent had been well-worn by propaganda, rumor, and slanderous lies.

Boston was awash with calumnious anti-Catholic propaganda; the swelling Irish population had alarmed the comfortable descendants of the Puritans. The town was inundated with publications from abroad such as *Jesuit Juggling, Master Key to Popery, Forty Popish Frauds Detected and Disclosed,* and the most libelous of the lot, *Female Convents, Secrets of Nunneries Disclosed,* the work of a former priest named Scipio de Ricci. (Published works of pornography, it is interesting to note, were also passionately sought by many Massachusetts citizens. As early as 1786, Isaiah Thomas of Worcester attempted to obtain copies of *Fanny Hill.* Thomas Evans, a London bookseller, wrote Thomas: "If you must have the *Memoirs of a Woman of Pleasure,* I must beg you will apply to some of the Captains coming here, as it is an article I do not send to my customers if I can possibly avoid it." (Thomas was successful in getting this pornographic work and it appears that he might have intended publishing Cleland's infamous book since several volumes of *Fanny,* bound in marbled-over sheets, were found in his library upon his death. These were sent by heirs to the American Antiquarian Society of Worcester.)

The de Ricci publication incensed the hosts of virulent anti-Catholics with its depictions of debauchery between nuns and priests and the even more provocative horror stories of infant bodies found in heaps in secret basement vaults of European convents. There had been a number of anti-Catholic riots in Boston preceding the 1834 mania, the most serious being the Nativist gangs who invaded the Irish districts in 1829 and burned and looted scores of houses.

Catalyst of the violent eruption of mob hate in 1834 was a lethargic young woman, Rebecca Theresa Reed, who worked as a kitchen helper in the Ursuline convent in Charlestown. Judged by today's standards of intelligence, Reed would, no doubt, be labeled a *non compos mentis,* yet her wild tales of lasciviousness, ungodly sex, outright murder, and secret burials of unwanted progeny produced by fornicating nuns and priests (later published as a book entitled *Six Months in a Convent,* a group effort on the part of the more literary anti-Catholics in Boston) inexplicably convinced hundreds that the Ursuline order in Charlestown was a den of vile creatures.

Tiring of her kitchen chores, Reed had asked the convent's Sister Mary Edward St. George, the mother superior, if she could become a nun (this, it was speculated, to escape her rigorous chores). Refused, Reed fled the nunnery, her mind overflowing with six months of stored-up imaginings of the convent's "terrible" secrets. Though stupid, Reed was intuitive and canny enough to go directly to the leaders of the anti-Catholic legions in Boston, seeking out immediately the followers of the anti-papist Puritan, the Reverend Dr. Lyman Beecher, the father of Harriet Beecher Stowe. Beecher, a hell-and-brimstone orator, often thundered from the pulpit his pet phrase "the Devil and the Pope of Rome" to incite the more bigoted of his flock.

The Beecherites cried openly that Reed was "an escaped nun," and that she had revealed to them how "forced conversions," perverted penances, and other dark doings were perpetrated by the mother superior and the Catholic bishop of Boston, the Right Reverend Benedict J. Fenwick. (Three years later, a pregnant New York woman named Maria Monk would cause similar uproar and much persecution of Catholics by claiming that she had been abducted by six priests, one of whom was the father of her child, and had been held captive in a Catholic asylum.)

Reed submitted totally to her anti-Catholic mentors, taxing her mind to exhaustion in reviling the convent. She was to say (the words carefully rewritten for her): "I was particularly hurt in witnessing the austerities put on a religieuse named Sister Mary Magdalene, who came from Ireland. Once, while reciting the office, she by accident or losing breath, spoke in a lower key than she should. At a signal from the superior (Mother St. George), she fell prostrate before her desk, and remained so for an hour, until the office was finished and she had permission to rise.

"She (the mother superior) seemed determined to know my thoughts, and put many questions to me that were hard to answer. I complained of my strength's failing and of my diet, and she immediately imposed the following penances: to make the sign of the cross on the floor with my tongue, and to eat a crust of bread in the morning for my portion.

"On one of the Holy Days the bishop (Bishop Fenwick) came in, and after playing on his flute, addressed the superior, styling (calling) her mademoiselle, and wished to know if Mary Magdalene wanted to go to her long home. The sister (mother superior) beckoned to her (Sister Magdalene) to come to them and she approached on her knees. The bishop asked her if she felt prepared to die. She requested that she be anointed before death. The bishop said: 'Before I grant your request, I have one to make; that is, that you will implore the Almighty to send down a bushel of gold for the purpose of establishing a college for young men on Bunker Hill...'" Reed added that after Sister Magdalene had made the pledge, she slavishly knelt before the bishop, who had removed his shoes, and kissed his feet. In addition, the one-time scullery worker hinted darkly (taking a leaf from de Ricci) that there were many secret vaults beneath the convent, and these crypts, the most naive and hateful easily concluded from her remarks, contained the skeletons of children born out of wedlock to nuns and priests, infants who were murdered and hidden from the righteous wrath of those who properly opposed the Roman church. Bishop Fenwick, whom Reed labeled "the monster," was behind it all.

These tales were scandal-mongered through the household of Boston and Charlestown overnight, inflaming thousands of anti-Catholics. City leaders did nothing to suppress the libel. Town fathers traditionally condemned such conduct. As early as 1829, before the main convent was built on the twenty-seven acres purchased by Bishop Fenwick, a Charlestown selectman had openly threatened to gather forty men and burn down the farmhouse in which the nuns dwelled while their convent was being constructed.

Rebecca Reed's noxious chatter was but wind to an already smoldering flame. Posters appeared plastered suddenly all over the streets of Boston and Charleston. One of the more popular read:

> Go Ahead! To Arms! To Arms! Ye brave and free the avenging Sword unshield: Leave not one stone upon another of that curst Nunnery that prostitutes females virtue and liberty under garb of holy Religion. When Bonaparte opened the Nunneries in Europe he founds cords of Infant skulls!!!!!

Coupled to this inflammatory public display was the fact a that a real nun, Elizabeth Harrison, known as Sister Mary John, did leave the convent, appearing in her nightgown on the night of July 28 at the home of Edward Cutter, whose daughters had once been among her students. Sister Mary John was not fleeing "an evil den" as later claimed; she was suffering a nervous breakdown as a result of teaching fourteen music lessons a day in preparation for an exhibition.

This nun's departure, however, was widely heralded as an escape and new posters shortly appeared, all reading:

> The Selectmen of Charlestown! Gentlemen—It is currently reported that a mysterious affair has recently happened at the Nunnery in Charlestown. It is your duty gentlemen to have this affair investigated immediately; if not, the truckmen of Boston will demolish the Nunnery Thursday night—August 14.

Though Sister Mary John had returned to the convent, apologizing to Bishop Fenwick and Mother St. George for creating further trouble for them, selectmen from Boston and Charlestown appeared at the nunnery. They explained to an irate Mother St. George that they were only following the placarded demands of their constituency and would she be kind enough to allow them to inspect their premises. She would not, replied the offended mother superior. One historian reported the selectmen less polite, stating that they showed up at the Charlestown convent in the company of a "number of evil-dispossessed men of the dregs of society," who shouted "Down with the convent! Down with the nuns!" One of the selectmen then demanded that they have access to the "dungeons and cells of iniquity."

Mother St. George, another account insists, heard out the more reasonable selectmen who assured her that their visit was peaceful, its conclusion meant to convey an all's-well message to their aroused citizens. The mother superior agreed to allow one of the selectmen to tour the premises, but, reports writer J.P. Chaplin, "as he approached the gaping pitch-black entrance he lost courage and departed in company with his fellow selectmen."

The failure of the selectmen to settle the matter became tacit approval for hundreds of Boston truckmen to gather on the peaceful grounds of the convent at 8:30 p.m. on Aug. 11. Inside, the nuns and their students were at their prayers, just about to retire. A scream from outside pierced their tranquility. Mobs of wildly gesturing, shouting men approached the convent. "Down with the convent!" they shouted. "Release your prisoners!"

An angry mother superior met them at the front door. She was adamant in her refusal to allow anyone inside to inspect the building and, in a voice close to a shout, admonished the hundreds of torch-carrying truckmen (there may have been several thousand) to stop annoying the nuns and to let the children go to sleep. A stern authoritarian, she ordered the grumbling truckmen off the convent grounds but then suggested that they return in the form of a small delegation during a proper daylight hour. They could then make their inspection of the nunnery. This conciliatory gesture seemed to quiet the mob and many began to edge away from the convent. Apparently, they did not move fast enough for Sister St. George. According to unfriendly reports, she suddenly bellowed in near raging anger: "Disperse immediately, for if you don't the bishop has twenty thousand Irishmen at his command in Boston, and they will ship you all into the sea!"

This ignited the mob's fuse and they responded to the tongue lashing by unleashing a curtain of stones that smashed through windows and thudded dangerously close to the mother superior who instantly retreated inside, bolting the heavy door behind her. The rioters proceeded to set fire to several tar barrels in a nearby field. The glow from this blaze was lurid upon the faces in the mob, distorted as they were with growling hatred.

As the fire blazed up, hundreds more rioters arrived, as if the fire had been a prearranged signal. More than 4,000 persons arraigned themselves before the convent, hooting, throwing rocks and clubs. About fifty ringleaders, all dressed in women's clothes to disguise themselves, ordered barrels of rum to be opened. Fortified with great gulps of rum, the rioters then proceeded to taunt the terrified nuns inside the convent, yelling out obscenities and vile descriptions of the building's alleged crypts.

Almost everyone in the mob was drunk by midnight. Some of the more besotted rioters lurched against the heavy front door of the convent. Mother St. George threw it open and tried to reason with the rioters. Someone in the crowd fired off a musket and the shot barely missed the nun who again slammed the door. Scores then began to batter at the barrier. Sister St. George scurried to the children's quarters, gathered up her charges, and led the girls and the other nuns out a back door and into a garden, going unnoticed by the mob.

It was only a matter of minutes before the front door was smashed down and, howling like Indians, some rioters raced inside, gleefully beginning their looting while guzzling more and more rum. First they scoured the cellars, the object of their suspicion and imaginative fears. They found nothing that interested them so they joined the throngs on the upper floors. Anything that would burn—books, manuscripts, bedding, furniture, even Bibles and crucifixes—was collected in the reception hall on the main floor and torched.

Many of the ringleaders went out the front door ahead of the flames with their pockets bulging with money looted from the mother superior's office and the student's personal belongings, from silverware to timepieces. "What a scene must this midnight conflagration have exhibited," The Boston *Evening Transcript* later stated, "lighting up the inflamed countenances of an infuriated mob of demons attacking a convent of women, a seminary for the instruction of young females, turning them out of their beds, half naked in the hurry of their flight, and half dead with confusion and terror. And this drama, too, to be enacted on the very soil that afforded one of the earliest places of refuge to the Puritan fathers of New England."

Nuns and students in the garden watched in horror as the convent blazed up. They heard the roaring approval from the crowd. Men from several Catholic families found the tiny cluster of refugees before the rioters discovered their whereabouts and spirited them away to friendly homes.

Their lust of destruction sparked, the rioters turned their fury upon the bishop's lodge and hundreds broke into this building, dragging outside entire shelves of books from the man's celebrated library. A bonfire was quickly built and a youth named Marvin Marcy began to auction off the volumes in mock transactions with drunken members of the mob. He then read the titles of the books, giving them new titles of either a profane or obscene nature. He was cheered and applauded as he hawked out each vile title. As he spoke, Marcy tore the cover from each book and threw is ceremoniously into the fire.

Several fire companies arrived in answer to the dozens of fire bells that tolled chillingly from all points of Boston, Charlestown, and Cambridge. But nothing was done to put out the raging fires in the three-story convent or the bishop's lodge. One company of firemen conscientiously attempted to go forward and put out the flames, but hundreds of rioters blocked the way and cut the hoses on their horse-drawn wagon. The other firemen merely stood within the ranks of the crowd and watched the flames consume the buildings. One fire wagon returned to Boston festooned with drapes pilfered from the convent and other repugnant mementos of the fire, its firemen riders as drunk as the crowd that straggled home down the road after them. But that was not until dawn when the mobs tired of their burning and looting.

Just before sunrise, the more devilish of the rioters tore down the small fence surrounding the consecrated graveyard near the convent, broke into tombs and dug up graves. Skeletons and bodies were played with as if they were dolls. Many were hanged from trees, other arrayed in obscene positions. Silver nameplates were torn from markers and entire marble tombstones were carted away.

One man who had helped to loot and set fire to the chapel in the convent suddenly displayed the consecrated bread he had stolen from the altar. He took the wafers to one of the all night Boston dives and derisively handed them out to prostitutes. This man, the story goes, in a depressed state some days later, climbed upon a table in the same tavern and, in full view of his fellow denizens, announced his shame, and then committed suicide by instantly slitting his throat.

There was never any compensation for the loss of the $50,000 convent, though many promises were made. The Reverend Beecher delivered three rousing sermons deploring the riot and burning. More than 100 men were arrested for the riot, but only thirteen were indicted. Only one, the 17-year-old Marvin Marcy, was convicted and sent to prison for seven months. Ironically, he was pardoned from a full year's term on the strength of the petition signed by Bishop Fenwick, the Ursuline sisters, who remained homeless since their convent was never rebuilt, and 6,000 Boston Catholics.

The rage against the Catholics continued in Boston for three more decades, flagrant acts of bigotry and religious violence finally drowned out in the sea of blood that flowed from the Civil War. See: **Monk, Maria.**

REF.: *An Answer to 'Six Months in A Convent'*; Archer, *Riot! A History of Mob Action in the United States;* Beecher, *The Works of the Reverend Lyman Beecher;* Billington, *The Protestant Crusade, 1800-1860;* Block, *Vio-*

lence in America; Brown, *Strain of Violence; CBA;* Chaplin, *Rumor, Fear and the Madness of Crowds;* Frothingham, *The Convent's Doom: A Tale of Charleston in 1834;* Leahy, *The Catholic Church in New England;* Marden, *Minorities in American Society;* Myers, *History of Bigotry in the United States;* Reed, *Six Months in a Convent;* Ricci, *Female Convents: The Secrets of Nunneries Disclosed;* Shea, *History of the Catholic Church in the United States;* Spofford, *New England Legends;* Whitney, *The Burning of the Convent.*

U Saw, See: **Aung San**.

U.S. Embassy Bombing, 1983, Leb., bomb. A bomb set by a fanatic pro-Iranian Moslem group exploded in the U.S. Embassy in Beirut, Leb., on Apr. 18, 1983. Sixty-three people were killed, their mutilated bodies found buried in the rubble. The bomb was inside a van, allegedly driven by a suicide driver, that drove past Lebanese guards and through the front door of the embassy during lunch hour. It blew apart the front wall of the central section of the embassy from ground level to the top floor and caused severe damage in the visa section on the ground floor of the northern wing.

Robert S. Dillon, the U.S. ambassador to Lebanon, was sitting in his office when the bomb exploded. The office collapsed under him, burying him in the rubble. Freed by rescuers, he climbed out a window and down to the ground unscathed. Robert C. Ames, a senior CIA analyst, was killed in the blast along with twenty-three other Americans, including several U.S. Marines. The remaining dead were Lebanese citizens, many of whom worked in the embassy or were applying for visas.

The pro-Iranian group, Islamic Jihad (Muslim Holy War), Lebanese Shiite Muslims, first claimed responsibility but were quickly followed by two other radical organizations claiming to have detonated the bomb. REF.: *CBA.*

Usher, Cornelius, prom. 1902-04, U.S., (wrong. convict.), burg. When a Lynn, Mass., police officer walked out of a local pawn shop, he saw Cornelius Usher walk in with a large bundle. The recent robbery of a shoe factory made him suspicious of what Usher was pawning and it turned out to be a stolen pair of lasting pincers. Usher was arrested and charged with burglary although he told police that he was innocent and did not know the tools had been stolen. Usher said he met a man named Coughlin in a bar and he was given the tools after Coughlin himself was unable to pawn them. Despite his pleas of innocence, Usher was sentenced to from three to five years in prison.

Nearly two years later, John H. Coughlin was arrested in Salem, Mass. When news of the arrest was made public, a man stepped forward and told police that he was there when Coughlin gave the tools to Usher. Judge John W. Berry recalled Usher from prison and initiated proceedings to secure a pardon for the wronged man. On May 20, 1904, Coughlin pleaded guilty to robbing the shoe factory and was sentenced to eighteen months in prison. Five days later, Usher was granted a pardon by the governor and later received $1,000 in restitution for his wrongful imprisonment. REF: *CBA.*

Uskoks, prom. 1600s, Italy, pir. Based in the Adriatic seaport of Segna, near Fiume, Italy, the Uskoks were a small but substantial group of about 500 pirates. They fought in the name of Christianity, battling the Turks, and any ships that were thought to carry Muslim goods and cargo. The Uskok society ostracized those men who refused to join the pillaging. The pirates raided almost any ship that came within their sights. After planting Muslim goods on the ship, the Uskoks would claim the vessel as part of their crusade.

The Uskoks became the bane of the Italian government. Captured Uskoks were executed and beheaded and their heads were publicly displayed in St. Mark's Square. The pirates would attack vessels with a number of medium-sized galleys and usually overwhelm their much larger opposition. While the government condemned the pirates as part of the Devil's pact, they failed to recognize that Uskok spies had infiltrated the government.

REF.: *CBA;* Mitchell, *Pirates.*

U.S. Steel Strike, 1919, U.S., mob vio. Labor unions began a vigorous drive to organize workers after WWI. In 1919, they targeted U.S. Steel, whose head, Judge Elbert Gary, had repeatedly resisted unionization. On Sept. 22, 1919, more than 250,000 U.S. Steel workers walked off their jobs and began picketing the company's plants. The company responded by surrounding its sites with armed guards and deploying tough special "deputies" to patrol the Monongahela River between Clairton, Pa., and Pittsburgh, breaking up strike meetings. Picketers and strikers were run down by mounted police. One striker was killed and twenty injured in Farrell, Pa., during mob violence touched off when the steel company brought in strikebreakers, and two men were killed in Donora, Pa., when steelworkers and strikebreakers fought.

In Gary, Ind., eleven companies of state militia, 500 police, and 300 deputies were needed to quell two days of rioting as strikers attacked the strike breakers. Martial law was declared and, playing on anti-Bolshevik revolution sentiments, General Leonard Wood swore to round up "the Red element." The strikers were defeated when public support lessened due to the media's insistence that the violence was "an attempt at revolution, not a strike." Steelworkers were not unionized until the Congress of Industrial Organizations became prominent in the 1930s. REF.: *CBA.*

Ustacha, The (Ustache or **Ustasa** or **Ustachi)**, Yugo., sec. soc. Established in 1929 by Croatian leader Dr. Ante Pavelic, Ustacha was a secret terrorist society dedicated to the establishment of Croatian dominance of the newly established Yugoslavian state. Yugoslavia, which had been created following WWI, had absorbed Croatia-Slovenia, Serbia, Montenegro, Bosnia, and Herzegovina. Ruler of this heterogeneous country was Alexander I of the Karageorgevic dynasty, a sovereign who consistently sided with Serbian policies and particularly ignored the customs, habits, and national desires of the Croats. When several Croatian leaders were executed in a wild shoot-out in the Yugoslavian Parliament in 1928, Ante Pavelic organized a paramilitary organization named Ustacha. The aims of this terrorist group was to spread fear among Croatia's enemies and assassinate anyone suppressing Croatian political ties to the Fascist governments of Germany and Italy who secretly supplied funds and, in the case of Hungary and Italy, training sites inside their borders.

Recruits to Ustacha were required to swear the following oath: "I swear to God and by everything sacred to me to fight in the ranks of the Ustachi for the creation of a free and independent Croatia. I swear to obey at all times our supreme leader, execute every order and guard faithfully the secrets with which I will be entrusted. If I fail this oath, I shall be punished by death. So help me God." The leader of the group, Pavelic, demanded much of the Ustacha. He expected members to lay down their lives according to his dictates, and there were an ample number of willing volunteers.

Alexander I became the object of Pavelic's determined hate. The Ustacha leader, called the Poglavnik, marked the sovereign for death just as he had been designated for the hangman by Alexander's police. In 1929, Alexander abolished the democratic constitution of Yugoslavia, disbanded the Parliament, and ordered the arrest of all members of Ustacha, particularly that of Dr. Pavelic. A wave of oppression swept through Croatia-Slovenia. Hundreds of suspected Ustacha members were arrested and jailed without trial, and dozens were murdered. Pavelic unleashed his own terror raids into Serbia, which proved to be equally bloody and murderous. A truce was reached in the early 1930s. A titular Yugoslavian senate was established with Pavelic as its president, but this too was abolished by Alexander, who chose to rule as a supreme military monarch, siding with France and Czechoslovakia and against Germany and Italy, the two countries with whom Ustacha felt it shared most common ground.

Pavelic decided that the best course of action for Croatia and Ustacha was to rid Yugoslavia once and for all of Alexander I. He ordered the king assassinated in 1933, but those assigned to the task of blowing up the monarch backed out at the last minute and never hurled their bombs. Pavelic gathered his most loyal and fanatical followers in the following year and sent a team of killers to France to kill Alexander when he landed in Marseilles on a state visit. One of the Ustacha killers, a man known as Velitchko or Chernozamsky (both names were aliases; his real name was never learned), managed to jump on board the king's touring car while it made its way through the Marseilles streets on Oct. 9, 1934, and fire two bullets into Alexander, killing him. The assassin also shot and killed French foreign minister Jean Louis Barthou, a purposeful killing in that Barthou, a dedicated foe of fascism, had also been marked for death by Nazi supporters of Ustacha.

Ustacha members, led by Pavelic and others, acted as an effective fifth column in helping the Nazis take over Yugoslavia in 1941. As a reward, Pavelic was named head of a so-called autonomous state of Croatia. The state, however, was supervised by authorities in Berlin and Rome, and Pavelic was never anything more than a cruel puppet dictator who unleashed pogroms and persecutions against his own people for several years. When the Balkans fell to the Russian armies in 1945, Pavelic fled, escaping to South America. Ustacha as a secret criminal society of terrorists ceased to exist at this time. See: **Alexander I (Karageorgevic)**; **Pavelic**, Dr. **Ante.**

REF.: Bornstein, *The Politics of Murder; CBA.*

Utter, Earl Ray, 1955- , U.S., sex. asslt.-kid. In 1980, a 25-year-old former psychiatric patient abducted and molested three children on the South Side of Chicago. Earl Ray Utter, who had a history of mental and emotional problems, was neglected and sexually abused as a child. In 1977, he was charged with theft and given six months' parole. That same year another arrest, for child molesting, led to his conviction in 1979 and parole in October 1980 as he had served more than two years in psychiatric hospitals while awaiting trial.

On Oct. 31, 1980, less than a month after his hospital release, Utter kidnapped and molested Felicia Murray, a 6-year-old Bridgeport girl. The kidnapping took place within two blocks of her home. Police implementing an extensive search by using dogs and door-to-door interviews, found the girl two days later under a viaduct two miles from her home, naked, lying face-down, bound with shoestrings, and gagged with her underwear. Felicia gave a description of Utter as six feet tall with a thin build, fair complexion, and sandy hair.

Two weeks later, on Nov. 14, a 7-year-old boy and his 5-year-old sister were abducted in front of a grocery store where they had been sent by their mother to buy sugar. Utter told them he could buy cheaper sugar if they came with him, and they did, taking a bus to an abandoned building on 43rd Street on Chicago's South Side. There Utter forced them into a bathroom, stuck several knives into the door frame, told them he had killed another boy and girl, and then punched the boy in the stomach, saying that he would kill one of them if the other screamed. Then he sexually molested the two children, bound them with tape, and said he would return with a partner.

The quick-witted boy chewed through his tape and freed his sister by using one of the knives in the door frame. A police car subsequently took them to a hospital where they were treated and released after providing a description of Utter that matched Felicia's. Meanwhile, a woman had called in an accurate description of Utter, whom she had seen leave the grocery with the two children.

Police arrested Utter the following day and a grand jury indicted him on three counts each of aggravated kidnapping and taking indecent liberties, and two counts of armed violence and deviant sexual assault. Bond was set at $750,000, which Utter could not pay. While in jail the sex offender attempted and failed to commit suicide by cutting his wrists with a piece of plastic. At his trial he pleaded guilty, and on May 4, 1981, received a seventy-five-year prison sentence. REF.: *CBA.*

Vaccarelli, Paulo Antonio, See: **Kelly, Paul.**

Vaccarizi, Raymond, prom. 1984, Spain, org. crime. A Mafia gang leader, Raymond Vaccarizi, thirty-four, was being held in a jail in Barcelona, Spain. Every evening his wife would come to talk with him for about half an hour, calling out to him from the street below his cell so that he would lean out the window to speak with her. Prison authorities were aware of the couple's arrangement and saw no harm in allowing it to continue. But the Mafia was also aware of the nightly chats. Anxious that Vaccarizi might talk too much to the authorities after his anticipated extradition to France to face charges of murder, robbery, and weapons smuggling, the Mafia was present one July evening when his wife visited. As Vaccarizi leaned out of his cell window, two shots from a high-powered rifle hit him in the face and heart, killing him. REF.: *CBA.*

Vaccaro, John, prom. 1960, U.S., drugs. On Aug. 7, 1960, customs agent Fred Rody, Jr. received information that an American was in Nuevo Laredo's red light district, on the Texas-Mexico border, trying to buy twenty pounds of marijuana. The buyer, John Vaccaro, had been convicted earlier of a marijuana violation in New Orleans. Agents watched as someone put a suitcase on the front seat of Vaccaro's car, and Vaccaro, with his wife and 14-year-old daughter, entered soon after. As they drove down San Bernardo Avenue and on to U.S. Highway 59, three customs agents followed; in heavy traffic, they hedged in the Vaccaro's car on three sides. Agent T.S. Simpson identified himself, telling Vaccaro to stop. In response, Vaccaro feigned a stop, then accelerated and roared away, with agents tailing him at 110 miles an hour. Agent Grady Grazner began to catch up to his quarry when Vaccaro, his wife and daughter screaming in the back seat, increased his speed. Grazner fired warning shots, then finally pulled alongside the drug smuggler's car. Vaccaro swerved, sending knocking the agent's car off the road. Only Grazner's safey belt saved his life as the car rolled six times.

Police set up a roadblock in Ferret, Texas, where Vaccaro was finally stopped. Although only fragments of marijuana were found in his car, a suitcase, filled with the drug and marked with Vaccaro's fingerprints, was spotted by helicopter where he had thrown it from his speeding car. Vaccaro was convicted of smuggling drugs and was sentenced to a twenty-five-year jail term.

REF.: *CBA;* Whitehead, *Border Guard.*

Vachell, Charles Francis, 1854-1935, Brit., lawyer. A prosecuting attorney in England's superior court, Charles Francis Vachell was noted for his wit and style. Vachell's reedy, light voice had a pedantic tone, but his clever remarks and sometimes malicious humor were well received. Although he worked both the Oxford Circuit and London, his success never measured up to his abilities, which may have been due to his apparent boredom with cases that did not interest him. One of Vachell's most famous cases was the Crown versus Herbert Rowse Armstrong. Vachell was eighty-two when he died on Nov. 5, 1935. See: **Armstrong, Herbert Rowse.** REF.: *CBA.*

Vacher, Joseph (AKA: **The French Ripper**), c.1869-98, Fr., mur. A lust for killing which he ascribed to the bite of a mad dog turned this frustrated army corporal into a serial murderer. Between 1894 and 1897 Joseph Vacher is known to have murdered at least eleven people, though some estimates place the number much higher. The famed criminologist Professor A. Lacassagne, (author of a book on the case, titled *Vacher l'Eventreur et les Crimes Sadique*), believed that the madman was responsible for at least fifteen murders and five rapes between June 1888 and July 1897.

Vacher was the fifteenth and final child born to a respectable working class family in Beaufort, Fr. According to Lacassagne, except for Vacher, there was no hint of aberrant behavior in the family until his sister went insane after Vacher's death. At the age of eight Vacher was bitten by a rabid dog and was treated by a local magician who compelled him to drink a strange potion, an event Vacher, at least, credited for his future criminal nature.

In 1888, Vacher attempted to rape a male servant employed by the Marist brothers, who had educated him. In November 1890 he was drafted into the 60th Infantry Regiment at Besançon. Vacher seemed to enjoy the military life and desperately wanted to advance through the ranks. When his promotion to full corporal failed to come through he attempted suicide by cutting his throat with a razor. Hearing of this incident, the colonel of the regiment authorized the promotion at once, and Vacher recovered. His persecution complex however, was soon apparent in other ways. Vacher's roommates went to bed each night holding their bayonets out of fear that the unstable corporal might attack them.

In May 1893, Vacher was granted a sick leave. He traveled to Baume-les-Dames in June where he met a young woman named Louise. When she spurned his advances, Vacher fired three shots at her, none of which, however, caused serious injury. He then turned the pistol on himself and fired a bullet into his face. The bullet pierced his right eye, paralyzing the right side of his face. The courts found Vacher insane and committed him to the asylum at Saint-Ylle on July 7, 1893. In the asylum Vacher behaved like an unredeemable madman. However, when Vacher was transferred to a hospital in Saint-Rober in December his mad behavior suddenly stopped, and he began behaving normally. On Apr. 1, 1894, the director of the institute approved his discharge papers.

French killer Joseph Vacher.

Six weeks later, on May 20, the body of Eugénie Delhomme, a 21-year-old factory worker, was found on a country road near Vienne. She had been raped, knifed to death, and disemboweled. She was the first of Vacher's confirmed victims, most of whom were rural farm workers he met while he roamed from town to town begging for food and shelter. "A sort of frenzy drove me blindly forward to commit my crimes," he said. "Never did I look for victims: chance meetings decided their fates. The poor creatures need not be pitied. None of them suffered longer than ten minutes."

The second victim was 13-year-old Louise Marcel, whose mutilated remains were found in a stable near Blais. On May 12, 1895, Adèle Mortureux, seventeen, was strangled and disemboweled in the Bois de Chêne. In August, the murderer, known as the Ripper, attacked a 60-year-old widow, Mme. Morand, killed her, and then raped the corpse. A week later Vacher crept up on Victor Portalier, a youthful shepherd in Onglas, and stabbed him to death. The Portalier murder was the one for which Vacher ultimately would be held accountable. The killings continued for another two years and four months before Vacher was apprehended. The police had little to go on except a sketchy physical description supplied by various villagers. A vagrant with a black beard and a scarred face had been observed in the vicinity of the murders.

On Aug. 4, 1897, Vacher encountered Marie-Eugénie Plantier in the countryside near Bois des Pelleries. Plantier was picking pine cones with her husband and children and had been separated from them. When Vacher grabbed her from behind, she fought fiercely and called for help. Plantier's husband appeared and struggled with Vacher until a peasant farm hand named Henri Nodin arrived and helped the husband subdue Vacher. Vacher was tried before the Tribunal Correctionel of Tournon. Subsequent interrogation, and the testimony of a score of eyewitnesses who had seen Vacher, convinced the defendant that further resistance was useless. He confessed to his crimes, but blamed his psychological malady on the dog bite he received at age eight.

A five month inquiry into the state of his mind began on Dec. 16, 1897. The three psychiatrists, led by Professor Lacassagne, concluded that Vacher was only pretending to be mad. His fantasy about the mad dog was dismissed as "puerile." Vacher was found Guilty of murder on Oct. 28, 1898, at the Assizes of Ain, and was guillotined on Dec. 31, 1898.

REF.: *CBA;* Kershaw, *Murder in France;* Logan *Great Murder Mysteries;* Nash, *Almanac of World Crime;* Wilson, *Encyclopedia of Murder.*

Vacko, Pavel, prom. 1941, Ger., rob.-mur. On Oct. 29, 1941, Adolph Stephan, sixty, an accountant for the Mitropa Restaurant, was found slain in his office at the Stettiner Railroad Station in Berlin. Forensic pathologist Franz Joseph Holzer identified Stephan's blood as Group A, identifying MN factors in the sample as well. Pavel Vacko, a 19-year-old silver polisher at Mitropa, was arrested for murder a few days later. Bloodstains were found on his clothes, particularly the right leg of his pants, and on a brass clock weight in his room. Holzer identified the blood as matching Stephan's type; his work was facilitated by the freshness of the stains. Vacko eventually confessed, explaining how he had used the heavy clock weight to murder Stephan, and had later put it in his pants pocket.

REF.: *CBA;* Thorwald, *Crime and Science.*

Vaillant, Auguste, 1861-93, Fr., terr.-bomb. A 32-year-old militant anarchist, Auguste Vaillant returned to France from Argentina with the intention of avenging himself on society for his lack of success in life. Studying chemistry and explosives, Vaillant made a bomb out of an iron box, gunpowder, and about sixty nails. He decided to throw it in the Chamber of Deputies to protest that body's indifference to social ills. Vaillant made two tries before he was able to get admitted to the Chamber. On Dec. 9, 1893, he threw the bomb at the ministerial bench, but it hit the shoulder of a woman next to him and exploded in mid-air, wounding about fifty people; no one was seriously hurt. Tried at the Cour d'Assises in Paris on Jan. 11, 1894, Vaillant was prosecuted by Bertrand, who painted the accused man as a vain egotist, and defended by Labori, who said the defendant had tried to avoid killing anyone by putting nails instead of bullets inside his bomb. The jury found Vaillant Guilty. He was guillotined on Feb. 4, 1894.

REF.: *CBA;* Irving, *Studies of French Criminals;* Morain, *The Underworld of Paris.*

Valachi, Joseph Michael (AKA: **Joe Cargo, Joe Cago, Anthony Sorge, Michael Valachi, Joe Kato, Joe Siano**), 1904-71, U.S., org. crime. Joseph Valachi gave the U.S. public its first insider's view of the Mafia when he took the stand before a Senate Investigations subcommittee in 1962. He told about the pervasive network through which the Mafia operated. The stories of murder, blood bonds, and corruption shocked the American public although they revealed little more about the inner workings of U.S. organized crime than was already known by law enforcement officials.

Mafia informer Joseph Valachi.

Valachi took the Cosa Nostra oath in 1930 from Salvatore Maranzano who was then engaged in warfare with then-Mafia chief, Joe "the Boss" Masseria. Valachi worked as a muscle man for the more than thirty years he was in the mob. He was involved with numbers running, narcotics, and trading in stolen ration stamps during WWII. Valachi's luck ran out when Vito Genovese took control of the mob. Genovese disliked and distrusted Valachi for his previous association with other Cosa Nostra members. Valachi knew his life was in jeopardy and decided to talk to federal agents to buy himself protection. Once Valachi had betrayed the Cosa Nostra, Genovese offered a reward of $100,000 to anyone who could gain access to him. After he had told his story, Valachi was sent to La Tuna Federal Prison in Texas where he died of a heart attack in 1971.

REF.: Blumenthal, *Last Days of the Sicilians;* Bonanno, *A Man of Honor; CBA;* Cohen, *Mickey Cohen: In My Own Words;* Cressey, *Theft of the Nation;* Davis, *Mafia Kingfish;* Demaris, *The Director;* ____, *The Last Mafioso;* Gage, *Mafia, U.S.A.;* ____, *The Mafia is not an Equal Opportunity Employer;* Gosch and Hammer, *The Last Testament of Lucky Luciano;* Katz, *Uncle Frank;* Kirby and Renner, *Mafia Enforcer;* Kobler, *Al Capone;* Maas, *The Valachi Papers;* McPhaul, *Johnny Torrio;* Messick, *Lansky;* ____, *Syndicate in the Sun;* ____ and Goldblatt, *The Mobs and the Mafia;* Nash, *Citizen Hoover;* Navasky, *Kennedy Justice;* Overstreet, *The FBI in our Open Society;* Peterson, *The Mob;* Pileggi, *Wiseguy;* Powers, *Secrecy and Power;* Reid, *The Grim Reapers;* Reuter, *Disorganized Crime;* Sann, *Kill the Dutchman;* Servadio, *Mafioso;* Toledano, *J. Edgar Hoover;* Unger, *FBI;* Watters and Gillers, *Investigating the FBI;* Zuckerman, *Vengeance Is Mine.*

Val-de-Grâce, Jean Baptiste du Cloots (Anacharsis Cloots), 1755-94, Fr., rebel. Member of Jacobin club in 1789 and member of National Convention in 1792. He urged freedom through revolution and supported Hébert. He was guillotined along with other Hébertists. REF.: *CBA.*

Valdemar II, 1170-1241, Den., impris. Succeeded brother Canute VI as king and ruled from 1202-41. He successfully invaded Estonia in 1219 and set up two diocese of bishops. Count Heinrich of Schwerin put him in prison from 1223-25, but he was freed when he gave up control of most of the Eastern area. REF.: *CBA.*

Valdemaras, Augustine, prom. 1926, Lithuania, prime minister, attempt. assass. The limousine of Professor Augustine Valdemaras, Lithuanian prime minster and minister of foreign affairs, as well as dictator of that country since 1926, drove to the State Theater of Kovno in May 1929. Valdemaras, his wife, his aide-de-camp, Lieutenant Gudinas, and his young grand-nephew stepped into an enclosed garden. Suddenly, two grenades fell beside the car; when they failed to explode, a series of rapid gunfire burst out from the shadows. Shielding Valdemaras, Gudinas was fatally wounded. The young nephew was shot in the stomach and a passerby was hit in the leg. The attackers, rumored to be Polish nationals, left behind only empty cartridge shells. Unhurt, Valdemaras carried his wounded grand-nephew into the theater lobby, then stayed with the dying boy all night. The next day, Valdemaras returned to his post at the Foreign Office. REF.: *CBA.*

Valdès (Pierre Valdès, Pierre Valdo, Peter Waldo Valdès, Petrus Valdesius, Waldenses), d.c.1218, Fr., banish. Began preaching in Lyons, Fr., in the 1170s. He took a vow of poverty in 1179 and was confirmed by Pope Alexander III, but the pope instructed him not to preach. In 1184, he and his adherents, variously termed the Paupers, Pauperes Spiritu, or Pauperes de Lugduno, were excommunicated, banished from Lyons, and subjected to harsh persecution. REF.: *CBA.*

Valenti, Rocco, d.1922, U.S., org. crime. Erroneously known as the best shot in the underworld, Rocco Valenti was a seasoned Mafia boss who reportedly killed twenty people. In the early 1920s when the New York crime organizations struggled for control over the rackets, Valenti and Peter Morello, head of what remained of the old Morello family, aligned themselves against Joe Masseria, each believing they were the superior in the alliance.

On Aug. 9, 1922, without consulting his partner, Valenti set out to kill Masseria. On Second Avenue he found his quarry in the company of two bodyguards, whom Valenti shot and killed, then calmly reloaded his gun as Masseria, unarmed, ran into a millinery shop. Valenti approached his victim, aimed, and, just as he fired, Masseria jumped aside. Valenti shot again and missed as Masseria ducked. Valenti then fled, leaving Masseria untouched except for two bullet holes in his new straw boater. Following this weird incident, and until his assassination, Masseria became known as "the man who can dodge bullets."

Morello and Valenti decided to make peace with Masseria and called for a meeting at a restaurant on Twelfth Street. Three of Masseria's men met Valenti, accompanied by three anti-Masseria men outside the restaurant. They all spoke for a while until Valenti realized that neither Morello nor Masseria were in the restaurant. Valenti turned and ran firing as Masseria's men drew their guns. The assassins returned his fire, and two of their bullets accidentally wounded a street cleaner and an 8-year-old girl. The third assassin calmly aimed his weapon and fired as Valenti, still shooting, jumped on the running board of a taxi. The mobster's bullet was well placed and Valenti fell to the pavement, dead. His killer was a young hoodlum named Salvatore Luciana, later known as "Lucky Luciano," one of the three assassins who would before long murder Joe Masseria. REF.: *CBA.*

Valentine, Jimmy, fictional character created by O. Henry in his short story, "A Retrieved Reformation" (in the collection, *Roads of Destiny,* 1909). This supposedly greatest of all safecrackers is based on Jimmy Connors, a convict in the Ohio State Penitentiary where the author, a fellow inmate, met him. See: **Porter, William Sydney**.

REF.: *CBA;* (FILM), *The Return of Jimmy Valentine,* 1936.

Valentine, Lewis Joseph, 1882-1946, U.S., law enfor. off. A highly influential figure in New York's police force, Lewis Joseph Valentine had a reputation as an honest cop, and spent forty-two years as a police officer, eleven of them as commissioner of New York City's police force, the largest in the world. Born in Brooklyn, Valentine was twenty-one and bored with business when he took entrance examinations for both the fire and police departments. An $800-a-year probationary patrolman job came through first, and Valentine joined the force in 1903 as a rookie cop in Flatbush and Manhattan. His refusal to compromise his honesty and integrity in a city that was then in the grip of a strong, corrupt political machine caused Valentine to be repeatedly passed up for promotions, and he was frequently exiled to remote districts. Ten years passed before he became a sergeant. While serving at that post and as lieutenant, Valentine supervised the work of a confidential squad established by Dan Costigan, also known as "Honest Dan," helping to rout grafters, and so acquired his reputation as a "straight cop" who could not be bribed or swayed. Making political enemies among Tammany Hall powers, Valentine only reached the rank of captain in 1926, when George V. McLaughlin was appointed police commissioner. Rapidly promoting Valentine again, McLaughlin made him a deputy inspector and gave him instructions to drive gamblers out of the city. In 1928, when Grover Whalen was appointed commissioner, Valentine's assiduous work at getting rid of gambling got him demoted to captain; Whalen sent him across the river as punishment.

New York police official Lewis J. Valentine.

When Judge Samuel Seabury was appointed by a New York State committee to investigate corruption in city government, the Tammany political machine was dealt its death blow, with Mayor James Walker falling along with the machine. Valentine testified before the committee in 1931. When Fiorello La Guardia was elected mayor of the city on the Reform ticket in 1933, he appointed Valentine as chief inspector. Within a year, Valentine was given the post of police commissioner, which he held for eleven years—the longest term in New York history.

A colorful figure, Valentine was often in the news. He was outspoken and memorable in his directives and comments, once ordering his detectives not to coddle gangsters and thugs, but to "mark 'em and muss 'em up." His philosophy of the policeman's vocation was populist and simple. According to his standards, "The police must, above all else, be human...They must be intelligent citizens, ready to protect, direct, and advise the rest of the community." Under his leadership, the 18,000-man police force was regenerated, racketeers, and gamblers were driven out or sent undercover. *Time* magazine estimated that Valentine "fired some three hundred men, officially rebuked three thousand," and "was even harder on the crooks." Valentine resigned in September 1945, when he was sixty-three, and announced that he had accepted an offer to appear on a weekly radio crime show, *Gangbusters,* which dramatized crime investigations.

In 1946, General Douglas MacArthur asked Valentine to help reorganize the police, prison, and fire systems in Japan and South Korea. Valentine agreed, flew east, and submitted a report to MacArthur, who called it sound and comprehensive. On his return to New York, Valentine resumed his *Gangbusters* appearances, making cameo appearances on other programs, appeared in a series of movie shorts on crime, reviewed crime stories for a publisher, and served on the editorial board of *True Police Cases* magazine. In 1946 he accepted the post of chief investigator for the New York State Fraud Bureau. Valentine died on Dec. 16, 1946.

REF.: *CBA;* Eisenberg and Landau, *Meyer Lansky;* Gosch and Hammer, *The Last Testament of Lucky Luciano;* Katz, *Uncle Frank;* Limpus, *Honest Cop: Lewis J. Valentine;* Lowenthal, *The Federal Bureau of Investigation;* McPhaul, *Johnny Torrio;* Nash, *Citizen Hoover;* Peterson, *The Mob;* Reppetto, *The Blue Parade;* Sann, *Kill the Dutchman;* Thompson, *Gang Rule in New York;* Valentine, *Nightstick;* (FILM), *Muss 'Em Up,* 1936.

Valentinian III (Flavius Valentinianus), 419-455, Roman., emp., assass. Raised to power by Theodosius II but dominated by his mother's regency from 425-437. After her rule, his general Aëtius was given primary control of the government. In 454, he killed Aëtius, but vengeful supporters of Aëtius killed him. See: **Aetius, Flavius.** REF.: *CBA.*

Valentino, Rudolph (Rudolpho Guglielmi, AKA: Rudolpho Di Vanentina), 1895-1926, Case of, U.S., wh. slav. Hollywood's Great Lover, Rudolph Valentino, died on Aug. 23, 1926. Valentino's life, as it was later unraveled, proved to be brimming with sordid secrets, almost from the first moment he arrived in New York in 1913 as an impoverished Italian youth from Castellaneta, enriched only with the noble name of Rudolpho Alfonzo Raffaeli Pierre Filibert di Valentina d'Antonguolla, or so said the press releases flooding from movie studios seven years later. Actually, his name was Rudolpho Guglielmi, a peasant boy who arrived in America with a single dollar sewn into the lining of his coat and the names of two families from his home town living in New York.

The 18-year-old youth picked up menial jobs—working as a busboy, messenger, janitor's helper—while he learned English. He later became a landscape gardener on the estate of Cornelius Bliss on Long Island where he watched from afar the courtly manners of the rich as they strolled across lawns he had mowed and rode down bridle paths he had shoveled clean of horse droppings. He was fired when caught hiding behind some shrubbery, mimicking the gestures and movements of wealthy guests who were playing tennis.

Valentino moved back to Manhattan, got himself a $2-a-week room, and began frequenting the cafes and bistros in mid-town where he learned to perform the fashionable dances of the day, from the Hesitation to the Castle Walk, made famous by Vernon and Irene Castle. He became more than proficient at the tango and was soon the most desired male escort dancer—sneering males called them gigolos—among the socially elite women coming alone to such posh clubs as Delmonico's, the Ritz Grill, and Bustanoby's.

Silent screen lover Rudolph Valentino, who was arrested in 1916 for white slavery.

The Italian youth wore formal wear and lavished polished manners and precise but heavily accented English upon his partners. He made them all look good on the dance floor, and they, in return, paid him off with expensive silk shirts, men's toiletries, and cash bonuses. Valentino became the rage at Maxim's where he appeared exclusively, earning top wages and dancing only with celebrities like silent film star Mae Murray and successful Broadway dancer Bonnie Glass, who hired him as her dancing partner for $50 a week. By 1915, he was making double that but had changed his partner to Jean Sawyer after Bonnie Glass married a millionaire. (Glass never spoke to him again when he boldly asked her if her future husband had any unwed sisters.) At the height of his popularity as a tango dancer, the future sheik was then known as Rudolpho Di Vanentina, (later changed to Valentino) and he spent most of his spare time secretly pitching wood to Bianca De Saulles, the wife of a wealthy socialite who had grown bored with her.

Valentino's sexual activities at this time were profuse, to say the least. He busied himself in strange ways with Georgia Thym, who operated a small but elegant brothel out of an apartment on Seventh Avenue between 57th and 58th streets. He apparently acted as a high-class pimp, inveigling political sachems and business tycoons to the apartment for assignations with young immigrant women who had been shanghaied into the nefarious services of the mysterious Thym.

The Thym operation was really a part of the white slave traffic then rampant in New York. Thym, Valentino, and cohorts, using captive immigrant girls, compromised successful businessmen, then blackmailed them for their silence. One New York merchant balked, however, and complained to the police. On Sept. 5, 1916, detectives raided Thym's bordello. With Assistant District Attorney James E. Smith leading the way, the police pounded on the madam's door, shouting that they were there to serve a subpoena which Thym had long evaded. "Don't try to escape!" shouted Detective McGlynn. "The entire building is surrounded."

The policemen listened for a moment and then heard several locks on the door turn over and bolts slide back. The door opened a bit and a well-dressed young man with pomaded hair stood peering out at them coldly with large, dark eyes. "What's all this fuss about?" asked the young man.

"Where's Mrs. Thym?" demanded a detective.

"Out of town. She's been gone for three weeks."

"You're lying. Clear out of the way!"

The dark young man was defiant, saying: "If you don't clear out I'll call the police."

Detective Duffy held up his badge. "We *are* the police."

Smith, who was standing in the shadows of the hallway, then moved to the door, recognizing with some surprise the young man at the door. "Rudolpho, what are you doing here?"

The young man slipped behind the door, snorting: "Rudolpho hasn't been here since last May. Now beat it!" He tried to close the door but the officers threw it open and ran inside. Thym was quickly located in a back closet where she had been hiding. Both she and Rudolpho Valentino were arrested, taken to a police station, and booked for white slavery, graft, and blackmail.

All the way to the station, Valentino begged Smith to let him go. The assistant district attorney, who had met the gigolo in his rounds of the better cafés, remained stonily unresponsive to this request. At the station, Valentino and Thym threatened the officers with terrible retribution from high-placed city officials unless they were immediately released. The threats were dutifully recorded by Smith who secretly questioned the pair, then told newsmen as the couple was being booked (Valentino under his real name Guglielmi) that the dancer "is a bogus count or marquis, and he had made statements which, if true, are of immense importance in this investigation. He is a handsome fellow, about twenty years old, and wears corsets and a wristwatch. (A wristwatch in 1916 was a mark of effeminacy.) He was often seen dancing in well-known hotels and tango parlors with Joan Sawyer and Bonnie Glass."

Valentino as the lustful sheik in a silent film.

Valentino was then ushered in front of newsmen but refused to make any statements. He was told that he could make one phone call before being locked up pending a hearing. The gigolo raced to the wall phone and called Deputy Commissioner Frank Lord, who had apparently shown considerable interest in Joan Sawyer in the past. "I'm in bad, Frank," begged Valentino on the phone. "I wish you'd come down and help me out."

Lord spoke for a few minutes, then hung up. Valentino, in a rage, turned to Smith and told him that Lord certainly knew who he was, that the commissioner had spent three weeks in Philadelphia lusting after Joan Sawyer and that he, Rudolpho Guglielmi, had dined with him at the Café L'Aiglon in that city.

Reporters dashed off to the offices of Frank Lord who huffily denied everything, saying: "I would find it quite difficult to remain away from New York for three weeks, as this fellow charges...My acquaintances are not made up of liars and fake nobles...This afternoon he called me on the telephone and said he was Rudolpho. I didn't know him until he finally added that he was Miss Sawyer's dancing companion. Then I remembered who he was.

I told him I was unable to help him."

As material witnesses to a white slavery investigation, both Thym and the dancer were put in jail, lacking the $10,000 bail set for them. The bail was forthcoming from a source unknown to this day, and the couple was set free after having served three days behind bars. A week later, Valentino appeared at the divorce proceedings of Bianca De Saulles against her playboy husband.

The dancer blithely told the court how he had taken his partner, Joan Sawyer, to the De Saulles home for an apparent assignation. He testified that he saw Sawyer and Jack De Saulles at the Narragansett Hotel in Providence together and that they had been in the same overnight train compartment when traveling. The wife was quickly awarded her divorce. (The following year, on Aug. 3, 1917, she shot and killed her wandering former husband and was acquitted of murder.) Valentino, his career wrecked in New York, such as it was, joined a small musical company as a chorus dancer and traveled west. His police file to this day remains gutted and no record of disposition toward the case is available; all documents are missing from it, and it is impossible to tell if Rudolph Valentino was ever found guilty of white slavery or not. The newspaper accounts remain, even though Valentino, when he became America's greatest silent film star, desperately tried to have the New York *Times* index referring to the arrest destroyed.

After drifting about California, Valentino moved to Los Angeles where he picked up bit parts, then some supporting roles playing South American villains. Jean Mathis, the top script writer for Metro, spotted Valentino in a movie and recommended him for the role of Julio in the forthcoming epic *The Four Horsemen of the Apocalypse* which she adapted for the screen. The film was a smash hit and shot Valentino to stardom.

The one-time gigolo enjoyed enormous fortunes from successful films such as *The Sheik, Blood and Sand, Monsieur Beaucaire, The Eagle,* and others. A superb dancer, Rudolph Valentino (he had dropped the "o" when he was a movie extra) became a master horseman, had his clothes tailor made on Saville Row in London, and bought an elegant estate, Falcon Lair, in Hollywood. Valentino's acting ability was that of an excellent pantomimist, a talent really learned while he stood behind bushes on the Bliss estate and mimicked the mannerisms of the rich. Moreover, his dashing figure, flashing eyes, and quick embraces of Agnes Ayres and Vilma Banky electrified American women who idolized their beloved "Rudy."

Paradoxically, the Great Lover's love life was a bust. His first wife, Jean Acker, a rising starlet he met when down and out in Hollywood, locked him out of the bridal chamber on the first night of their marriage, a union that was never consummated and was later annulled. His second wife, Natacha Rambova, attempted to run his life and was, undoubtedly like her mentor, the actress Nazimova, a lesbian.

Although he was linked romantically with the actress-vampires of the day—Nita Naldi and Pola Negri, Valentino lived an almost celibate life unknown to the millions of female fans who swooned at the very mention of his name. He was generally disliked by males, hated by some. A Chicago *Tribune* reporter interviewing the great "sheik" one day stepped into Valentino's hotel bathroom to find pink talcum powder, along with delicate imported colognes. These unmanly items caused the reporter to write a scathing piece on the Great Lover in which he profiled his subject as effeminate.

Valentino, after finishing *The Son of the Sheik,* was so enraged by the story that he challenged the offending reporter to a duel, either with swords or fists. The newsman declined.

Then the impossible happened. While seeing friends in New York in mid-August 1926, Valentino collapsed and was rushed to a hospital where physicians operated on him to remove an inflamed appendix. The doctors found that the star had two perforated gastric ulcers. His condition worsened into pneumonia and peritonitis. He was dead by Aug. 23 at the age of thirty-one.

When the news broke, pandemonium burst forth. Hysterical women across the country went into paroxysms of pain and grief. Several committed suicide, jumping from high buildings or sticking their heads into gas stoves. The hysteria was still tumultuous days later when the Great Lover lay in state at Campbell's Funeral Home on Broadway. Through the dark halls and main reception room of this somber place tramped more than 30,000 women and some men to gape at the dead actor.

When it appeared as if the chapel might close its doors before all could view the corpse, a riot ensued and dozens of mounted policemen had to ride into the crowds swinging clubs, supported by 100 beat cops slicing away with nightsticks. More than 100 persons were injured seriously enough to seek medical attention.

Harry C. Klemfuss, a zany press agent hired by Campbell's to whip up interest in the funeral, posted guards dressed in Fascist black shirts around Valentino's coffin and had a large wreath placed nearby which read: "From Benito." When Mussolini heard of this in far-off Italy, he wired a denial that he had ever sent an honor guard and flowers to the funeral of "a cheap actor."

Natacha Rambova remained silent about the death of her husband, but Pola Negri bought $3,000 worth of mourning clothes and displayed great grief at the funeral, telling one and all that Valentino was her one true love and that, had he lived, they would have been married. At this juncture of bathos in the private ceremony, Ziegfeld *Follies'* Marion Kay Brenda bolted upright, screaming: "That's a lie! He was going to marry *me!*

The grieving went on long after Valentino's body was shipped west to be entombed in Hollywood Memorial Park where for decades a dark-veiled woman visited his grave to lay flowers on the anniversary of his death, a mystery woman whose identity was never revealed. REF.: *CBA.*

Valenzuela, Delfina Gonzalez, See: **Gonzalez Valenzuela, Delfina.**

Valerio, Colonel, See: **Mussolini, Benito Amilcare Andrea.**

Valis, Adolfo, d.1976, Arg., terr.-assass. On Nov. 9, 1976, Argentinean gunmen assassinated retired air force Major Adolfo Valis, an executive in an industrial company, as he left his Buenos Aires home for work. That same night two bombs exploded in the Buenos Aires Province police headquarters while officers conducted promotion examinations. Twelve men were wounded, including assistant police chief Colonel Ernesto Tortz, who lost an arm. The government blamed the bombings on "subversive delinquents," the term used to describe left-wing guerrillas. On Nov. 10, nineteen people believed to be leftist guerrillas were killed by security forces as they tried to escape from the police's search for the bombers of the La Plata headquarters. Four of those slain died in a gun battle at a roadblock in a Buenos Aires suburb; four were killed after they resisted turning over papers to police at a La Plata railroad station; eight more were killed at a La Plata roadblock. By Nov. 13, the Argentine government had killed more than 100 suspected guerrillas in a two week period, and nearly 1,230 since the beginning of that year. Hundreds more people considered subversive had been abducted or had disappeared. Commander of the navy, Admiral Emilio Massers, announced that anyone who proposed pacts to try to settle the conflict by peaceful means would be considered guilty of treason. REF.: *CBA.*

Vallandigham, Clement Laird, 1820-71, U.S., rebel. U.S. congressman from 1858-63. Beginning in 1862 he headed a group in the northwest called the Peace Democrats, or the "Copperheads", who were strongly against policies that brought about the Civil War. He disregarded orders from General Burnside stating that no one was permitted to publicly oppose the war or side with the enemy. He was arrested in 1863, convicted, and banished to the Confederacy. He returned in 1864. REF.: *CBA.*

Vallanzasca, Renato, 1950- , Italy, rob.-kid.-mur. Renato Vallanzasca was serving an eight-year sentence for a $60,000 supermarket robbery in 1972, when he broke out of an Italian jail in July 1976. After his breakout, Vallanzasca acquired a Skorpion machine gun and began a crime spree that earned him the title of "Italy's Dillinger." The Italian press avidly followed the exploits of the hard-bitten young mobster with the good looks of an actor. In March 1977, a Milan weekly paper published a survey in which 900 out of 1,000 women polled said that they loved Vallanzasca. According to police, he and his gang had robbed at least two banks, with Vallanzasca functioning as the trigger man in the murders of a policeman, two Carbinieri militiamen, and a bank teller. In November 1976, he told a magazine reporter that he slept with a grenade under his pillow, saying, "They'll never take me alive."

Vallanzasca's sudden rise to popular attention came after he abducted Emanuela Trapani, the dark-haired, attractive 16-year-old daughter of a cosmetics magnate. Released in January 1977 after 41 days as a hostage, Trapani told reporters she had drunk champagne with Renato and spent time as a captive in a room with a Louis XV bed. Rumors spread that Emanuela and Renato had been seen dancing in a nightclub, shopping arm in arm, and drinking many bottles of champagne together. Trapani denied the gossip. "I was not fascinated by him. I was scared of him. I was trying to get a grip on myself," she said. One paper transformed Trapani's statements into, "Yes, Renato, I smiled at you. And I drank with you when you offered me champagne...But in my heart I was afraid." And the usually staid *Corriere della Sera* newspaper was even bolder, asking: "Did or did not Emanuela make love with her jailer?"

Vallanzasca hid out with a wide variety of weapons and explosives in the Rome apartment of an absent model until police captured him in a pre-dawn raid. According to police officer Antonio Cornacchia, the fugitive at first threatened to blow the place up with a hand grenade, but started begging for mercy when police hurled tear gas bombs. Surrendering without a fight, Vallanzasca was allowed to appear at a televised news conference. When reporters asked him if he considered himself a victim of society or a political prisoner, he said: "Don't be stupid...I'm no victim. I like money, that's all." When asked if he felt like a monster Vallanzasca replied, "You made me into one. You need monsters on the front pages because the public craves that sort of thing—and you know how to provide it." On Mar. 25, 1977, Vallanzasca was imprisoned for twenty-one years for kidnapping. Three years later, on Apr. 29, 1980, Vallanzasca and terrorist leader Corrado Alunni, of the Front Line group, allegedly connected with the Red Brigades terrorists, attempted to escape from the Milan prison where they were serving time, taking sixteen other convicts with them. Both men were wounded in a shootout with police, and were returned to jail.

REF.: *CBA;* Moorehead, *Hostages to Fortune.*

Valletutti, John, prom. 1946-48, U.S., (wrong. convict.) mur. In the early morning of Oct. 11, 1945, Leo Conlon, thirty, attempted to stop a robbery in a Coney Island bar and was shot and killed by the robber. William Cronholm, eighteen, was found sleeping in a stolen car; with him were two revolvers; three more were found in a garage he rented near his Brooklyn home. Cronholm confessed to killing Conlon, claiming at first to have tried to rob the bar alone, and he later signed a confession naming three accomplices. At his trial, however, he reverted to his original story. Cronholm was convicted and sentenced to life in prison.

Investigating detectives learned that John Valletutti, twenty, was a friend of Cronholm. Valletutti had been sentenced to jail for stealing a car; he was out on parole the night Conlon was killed. Within a month of the slaying, Valletutti was returned to prison due to a parole violation. Released from Coxsackie Prison on Dec. 7, he was taken to Brooklyn to be questioned about the Conlon killing. About thirty hours after Valletutti was taken into custody, his confession was recorded by a stenographer and an assistant district attorney. Since no one recognized him from the bar, or could place him in the vicinity, or saw him with Cronholm that night, the confession was the only evidence against him in his trial at King's County Court on June 2, 1947. Valletutti protested his innocence, saying he had confessed only after he was beaten for several hours. Witnesses supported his claim that he had been playing shuffleboard several miles away from the bar the night of the slaying. A routine physician's report made when the defendant entered jail recorded several bruises on Valletutti's lower chest and scalp. Although Cronholm was brought in from jail to testify that Valletutti had not been with him and that he had acted alone, Valletutti was found Guilty of first-degree murder by the jury, which recommended mercy, indicating a sentence of life imprisonment. Assistant District Attorney James McGough said that he offered Valletutti the chance to plead guilty to second-degree manslaughter, which had a maximum sentence of fifteen years in prison; Valletutti refused, saying he was innocent. On June 17, Judge Louis Goldstein disregarded the jury's recommendation; referring to Valletutti, as a vicious killer, he sentenced him to death in the electric chair.

A mandatory appeal, according to New York State law, resulted in a majority opinion reversing the conviction and ordering a new trial, with Judge Desmond pointing out that Valletutti had not been arraigned in court until about forty-eight hours after he was taken into custody, and that he had been held without being allowed to talk to a lawyer, friends, or relatives. Returned to Brooklyn for a new trial, Valletutti was brought before Judge Goldstein again. The prosecution admitted that the defendant's confession was the only evidence against him, and agreed to dismiss the case; the judge said he wanted to study the case further. On Sept. 28, 1948, the district attorney dismissed the indictment. Valletutti was released after spending two years in jail. REF.: *CBA.*

Valley Gang, prom. 1920s, U.S., org. crime. Allied with Alphonse Capone, the Valley Gang was the most flamboyant and affected Chicago gang of the 1920s. Each gang member, for example, no matter how low in the hierarchy, rode around in a Rolls-Royce.

This tough Irish street gang of simple thugs, burglars, pickpockets, and killers for hire was formed in the 1890s. Under the leadership of Frankie Lake and Terry Druggan, the Valleys became bootleggers and rumrunners, and later acquired a string of breweries in 1920. Their members became exceedingly wealthy and were the favorites of politicians and police through bribes and payoffs. In 1924, Lake and Druggan disregarded an injunction against one of their bootlegging fronts and were jailed for contempt. Yet through the persistence of aldermen who did not want the source of their graft inconvenienced by jail, and with the help of $20,000 in bribes given by the Valley leaders to various jail officials, Lake and Druggan stayed only occasionally in jail and enjoyed dining in fine restaurants, golfing, shopping, and attending the theater. Druggan spent most of his jail sentence at his luxury duplex with his wife, being driven there in his chauffeur-driven limousine. Lake frequently visited his mistress.

The *Chicago American* wrote a major exposé about the Valley Gang leaders' liberties when a newspaper reporter attempted to interview the two in jail and was told that both were downtown but would be back after dinner. Capone admired the style of the Valleys and eventually absorbed the gang en masse into his empire, where they became his staunchest and most faithful corps of soldiers. When Druggan, the last of the Valley Gang, died in the 1950s, he died a millionaire. See: **Druggan-Lake Gang.**

REF.: Asbury, *Gem of the Prarie; CBA;* Kobler, *Al Capone;* Landesco, *Organized Crime in Chicago;* Smith, *Syndicate City.*

Vallint, Miles, c.1948-59, Brit., (unsolv.) mur. The body of an 11-year-old boy, Miles Vallint, of Croydon, England, was discovered on Aug. 28, 1959. He had been strangled. Police believed he might have been lured into a car after he left a bicycle store on Aug. 27. Witnesses questioned by police mentioned they had seen a boy who could have been Miles, talking to a man outside the store that day, but this information never led to an arrest.

REF.: *CBA;* Furneaux, *Famous Criminal Cases, vol. 6.*

Vallisi, Patrizia, 1955- , Italy, (unsolv.) kid. Twenty-two-year-old Patrizia Vallisi was held for fifteen days in Milan by kidnappers who demanded a $10 million ransom for her return. Police were able to trace the gang during negotiations and Vallisi was rescued unharmed, and with no ransom paid.

REF.: *CBA;* Clutterbuck, *Kidnap and Ransom.*

Valois, Charles de (Duc d'Angoulême), 1573-1650, Fr., consp. Served in French military in cavalry commanded by Henry IV fighting Catholic League. Although he was involved in Marshal de Biron's conspiracy, he was pardoned in 1601. In 1605 he was put in prison for involvement in a Spanish conspiracy, but was freed later. REF.: *CBA.*

Vanartsdalen, Donald West, 1919- , U.S., jur. Served as district attorney of Bucks County, Pa., from 1954-58. He was nominated to the eastern district court of Pennsylvania by President Richard Nixon in 1970. REF.: *CBA.*

Van Bever, Maurice, and **Van Bever, Julia**, and **Hart, Mollie**, and **Hart, Mike**, and **Tyler, Dick**, and **Garfinkle, David**, prom. 1900s-10s, U.S., wh. slav.-org. crime. In its heyday around the turn of the century, the 22nd Street Levee on Chicago's South Side was a haven for thieves, gunmen, and white slave traders whose criminal activities ultimately led to the passage of the Mann Act in 1910. Before WWI there were three identifiable vice rings operating in the Levee with the cooperation of the police and local politicians. The worst of the Levee panderers were Maurice Van Bever, a French pimp who immigrated to Chicago around 1905, and his wife, Julia Van Bever. Their Paris Resort and White City Saloon on South Armour Avenue was both saloon and brothel. Though prostitution was never legal in Chicago, the "resort" keepers had an understanding with city officials that it would be allowed within the "segregated" Levee district, as long as the names of the women, their ages, and former occupations were listed in a police log book. Regular payoffs to aldermen, police inspectors, and ward committeemen kept the system running.

Maurice Van Bever, who maintained that he closely adhered to the letter of the law, "recruited" his prostitutes from throughout the Midwest through deception, and in some cases, abduction. While the Van Bevers went to the theatre, the opera, and took leisurely carriage rides along the shore of Lake Michigan, they left the dirty work to Mike Hart and Dick Tyler who worked as bartenders at the White City Saloon and procured women for the brothel.

Tyler and Hart often traveled to Danville and Rock Island, Ill., or St. Louis, Mo., where they selected underage victims based on looks, poise, and naiveté. The two men lured the girls to a quiet hotel in East St. Louis where they described the excellent job opportunities in Chicago. If swayed by the men's promises, victims were placed on a train and sent to a suburb south of Chicago where they were greeted by Julia Van Bever or Mollie Hart, a former white slave victim who lured friends and acquaintances from St. Louis to the Paris resort.

The ring was broken on Oct. 13, 1909, when federal detectives arrested Maurice Van Bever in downtown Chicago on the complaint of Sarah Joseph, a 19-year-old St. Louis woman brought to Chicago by Mike Hart. In November 1909, the Van Bevers were sentenced to one year in jail and assessed $2,000 in fines by Judge Edwin Walker. David Garfinkle, their St. Louis connection, was given six months and a $300 fine for aiding and abetting the white slave traffic. Dick Tyler forfeited his bond and became a fugitive. Mike Hart was ordered to jail for ten months, and fined $300. Mollie Hart received six months. This did not put an end to the Van Bevers' operations. Maurice Van Bever was back on the streets the following year only to be re-arrested in November on a charge of abducting a St. Louis woman named Pearl Sypher. By this time the Mann Act, barring the transport of women across state lines for immoral purposes, had become law. It was introduced by Congressman James Mann of Chicago, and signed into law on June 26, 1910, by President William Howard Taft. The bill effectively curtailed a growing menace to the safety and welfare of young women making their way into America's large urban centers.

REF.: *CBA;* Lindberg, *Chicago Ragtime: Another Look At Chicago 1880-1920;* Roe, *The Great War on White Slavery.*

Van Buuren, Clarence Gordon, prom. 1956, S. Afri., mur. On Oct. 2, 1956, Myrna Joy Aken, eighteen, vanished from her home in Durban, S. Afri. A friend reported that she had seen Aken getting into a light-colored car; she had been observed in the company of a man who had come to see her at her office. When the car was traced to a radio shop, the owner of the auto said it had been used by one of his salesmen, Clarence Gordon Van Buuren, thirty-three, who returned it to him the day after Aken vanished, and then disappeared himself. When a search for Aken turned up no clues, her distraught family hired a medium, Nelson Palmer, who went into a trance and said the woman's body would be found sixty miles away, in a drain under the road. Palmer went with the family to the spot he had described, just north of the village of Umtwalumi; the naked corpse was found there. Aken had been raped and shot.

Nine days after the slaying Van Buuren was picked up near Pinetown. His criminal record dated back to when he was seventeen, with charges of theft, forgery, escaping from custody, and passing bad checks. He claimed to have asked Aken out for a drink; she refused, and he went into a bar alone. Returning an hour later, he explained, he found the car parked fifty yards away, and opened the door to find the young woman with blood on her face. Panicking, he got rid of the corpse by throwing it in the culvert, he said. Tried in February 1957, Van Buuren maintained his innocence. But the fact that he had a large supply of .22-caliber ammunition—the type used to kill Aken—weighed against him, as did the fact that he was the last person to be seen with her. He was found Guilty, and hanged at Pretoria Central Prison on June 10, 1957.

REF.: Bennett, *Murder Will Speak; CBA;* Wilson, *Encyclopedia of Murder.*

van de Corput, Piet (AKA: **John Hendricks**), prom. 1915-16, U.S., mur. In Autumn 1915, Barbara Wright, a widow, was walking with her son from the club where she worked in New York City, heading toward the rooming house where she lived. A man sprang out from behind a car and drove a long-handled dagger into her chest. He ran away as terrified onlookers watched. The detective assigned to the case interviewed the eyewitnesses and other roomers at the boarding house, and became convinced that the killer was John Hendricks, a Dutch man who also lived at the house and had attempted to assault Wright three months earlier. At that time he was arrested and found to be carrying a long-handled dagger. He claimed he was drunk at the time and did not know what he was doing. Convicted and sent to the workhouse, he wrote several letters to Wright while there, attemping to force himself on her again a few days before she was slain.

Thousands of flyers picturing the suspect's face were circulated throughout New York and all major cities in the world, but turned up nothing. A detective went to a home for Dutch sailors in Hoboken, N.J., and learned from a man there that "Hendricks" was really Piet van de Corput, from the town of Breda near the Belgian border. It was about a year after the killing when van de Corput was finally arrested in New York City. Not only had he been in New York the entire time, he had been robbed while on a drunk in the Bowery, and made a complaint against his assailants, later going before a grand jury and testifying in court.

Eyewitnesses to the Wright murder picked van de Corput out of a line-up easily. Prosecuted by Assistant District Attorney William Edwards, and defended by Bob Moore, who tried to prove that van de Corput's confession was inadmissable because third-degree methods were used to obtain it, van de Corput himself overruled his defense. When Moore said that the line-up was not fair to the defendant, van de Corput himself announced to the court, "They treated me fairly." The jury deliberated only a few minutes before finding him Guilty; he was sentenced to death. While awaiting execution at Sing Sing Prison, van de Corput obtained a picture of the woman he killed, which he carried with him to the electric chair, saying he would "meet Barbara in heaven."

REF.: *CBA;* Willemse, *Behind the Green Lights.*

Vandendreschd, Jacques Mornard, See: **Trotsky, Leon.**

Vanderbourg, Charles, prom. 1782, Fr., hoax. In 1782, Joseph Etienne, the Marquis de Surville, discovered in the family archives the poems of Clothilde, a supposed poetess in the time of Charles VII, and an elaborate hoax of literature perpetrated by Charles Vanderbourg. Clothilde's real name was Marguérite Eléonore Clotilde. The themes of her poetry included the victory of Fornovo by Charles VII in 1495, and the battle of Orleans, led by Joan of Arc, in 1429. Many of her poems were said to have been lost during the Revolution, but the surviving copies allegedly had been kept and given to Vanderbourg by Etienne's widow. Vanderbourg's hoax began to unravel when critics found allusions to events that occurred outside of Clothilde's time, including a quotation from Lucretius, who was unknown in France until fifty years after Clothilde's "death." An allusion to the seven satellites of Saturn also destroyed the illusion of the poetess, since the satellites had been discovered between 1655 and 1789. REF.: *CBA.*

Van der Lubbe, Marinus, See: **Reichstag Fire.**

van der Merwe, Dorothea, and **Swatz, Hermanus Lambertus**, prom. 1920, S. Afri., mur. In 1920, a convict named Gibson, also known as Dr. Gibson, who had been employed in a South African prison hospital since the 1918 influenza epidemic, attended a patient named Hermanus Lambertus Swatz. Swatz, who had been convicted of theft and was serving time at the Pretoria Central Prison, confided in Gibson, asking him about the way a body stayed preserved both in and out of a coffin, and what the chances were of fatal wounds being diagnosed after some years. Thinking that this information might lead to a remission of his own sentence, Gibson informed the head warder of their conversations. The body of Louis Tumpowski, a Polish Jew on the Treurfontein farm in the Lichtenburg district of Transvaal, was unearthed. When Tumpowski had disappeared, it was assumed that he had only left the district. Dorothea van der Merwe and Swatz had brutally murdered Tumpowski together. With Gibson's evidence against Swatz, the killers were convicted and hanged.

REF.: Bennett, *Genius for the Defense; CBA.*

Van Devanter, Willis, 1859-1941, U.S., jur. In his twenty-seven years as a Supreme Court justice, Willis Van Devanter held a reputation as an extreme conservative. Born in Indiana, Van Devanter followed his father's career by becoming a lawyer. Admitted to the bar in 1881, he established his own practice in Cheyenne, Wyo., in 1884, and served there as city attorney. He was elected to the territorial legislature in 1888, a year in which he also received a presidential appointment to become chief justice of the territorial supreme court. An active Republican politician, Van Devanter became assistant U.S. attorney general in 1897, and was named judge for the U.S. Court of Appeals for the 8th Circuit in 1903.

President William Howard Taft appointed Van Devanter to the U.S. Supreme Court in 1910. During his long term, Van Devanter advocated extreme conservatism, dissenting in *Bunting v. Oregon* (1917), which upheld regulation of working hours, and upholding rent control laws in the Rent Law Cases of 1921. Van Devanter wrote the *Evans v. Gore* (1920) controversial majority opinion, which stated that federal judges' salaries could not be subject to income tax. In the 1931 argument over "The Newspaper Gag Law" Van Devanter debated whether the suppression of defamatory or obscene periodicals violated the 1st and 14th Amendments. Devanter also wrote the majority opinion in the case of *New York Central v. Winfield* (1917), which overturned state support for workers who had been disabled in railroad accidents. Planning to retire from his position in 1932, Van Devanter changed his mind when Franklin D. Roosevelt was elected President in 1932, deciding that his conservative viewpoint was needed on the Supreme Court. Remaining on the bench until 1937, Van Devanter died four years after his retirement. REF.: *CBA.*

Van Dine, Harvey, d.1904, and **Marx, Gustave**, d.1904, and **Neidemeyer, Peter**, d.1904, and **Roeski, Emil**, prom. 1901-03, U.S., rob.-mur. A gang of four young thugs held Chicagoans in a state of fear during the months of July and August 1903. Of the four gang members, three participated in the initial theft that brought them together. Peter Neidemeyer, Harvey Van Dine, and

Chicago bandits and killers Harvey Van Dine and Gus Marx.

Gustave Marx stole some lead pipe from Chicago's Audubon School; they were sent to prison for three-month terms as a result. Beginning on July 3, 1903, the gang began a two-month spree of robbing and shooting. On July 3, Neidemeyer and Roeski held up L.W. Lathrop and Martin Doherty at the Clybourn Junction Station of the Chicago and Northwestern Railroad, shooting Lathrop and robbing him of $70. Six days later, Harvey Van Dine and Emil Roeski held up a North Ashland Street saloon, slaying customer Otto Bauder as he tried to escape, by shooting him in the back. The take for the evening was less than $50. The next night, Van Dine and Roeski robbed another saloon, taking $25. Two nights after that, the same duo robbed a Sheffield Avenue saloon, then held up a Milwaukee Avenue establishment eight days later. On Aug. 1, Van Dine and Neidemeyer invaded a North Avenue bar, opening fire without provocation, wounding several men, and murdering proprietor Benjamin La Cross and Adolph Jennsen as they played cards. The night's haul was $64. On Aug. 30, Neidemeyer joined Marx and Van Dine to rob the Chicago Street Railroad Company, killing employees William Edmund and J. Johnson in the process. They later divided up the $2,250.

Van Dine gang members Emil Roeski and Peter Neidemeyer.

When Assistant Chief Schuettler heard that Marx was spending money in West Side bars, he and detectives John Quinn and William Blaul arranged to capture him at Greenberg's saloon. On the night of Nov. 21, 1903, Quinn and Blaul entered simultaneously from different entrances. Marx saw them and shot Quinn, killing him. He wounded Blaul, who overpowered him and took him to jail, where he made a full confession to Schuettler. Van Dine, Roeski, and Neidemeyer took a train to Indiana and hid in an abandoned cellar. Going to a country store on Thanksgiving Day for supplies, a school teacher who had seen their pictures in the newspaper recognized them and called the police. A posse chased them in the snow to an old dugout and cornered Neidemeyer and Van Dine. Detective Joseph Driscoll was slain by the killers in an exchange of gunfire. Roeski, wounded, took off on his own, while Van Dine and Neidemeyer climbed into a railroad car, killing brakeman L. Scovia and forcing Engineer Coffey to take them for a ride. A party of hunters tracked the criminals, shooting Van Dine in the face, after which both he and Neidemeyer surrendered. Roeski gave up without a struggle. Van Dine, Neidemeyer, and Marx were found Guilty of the murders of Johnson and Stewart, and hanged on Apr. 22, 1904. Roeski was tried for Bauder's murder, was found Guilty, and was sentenced to life imprisonment at the Joliet Jail.

REF.: *CBA;* Duke, *Celebrated Criminal Cases of America.*

Van Dine, S. S., See: **Wright, Willard Huntington.**

Van Doren, Charles, prom. 1958-59, U.S., fraud. American television networks brought in the enormously successful formula of quiz shows beginning in 1955. Ratings soared and contestants' progress toward the big prizes was followed closely, as the public created national stars and heroes-of-the-moment out of the winners. Charles Van Doren, a Columbia University professor in New York, was one of these winners, winning $129,000 in 1958 on NBC's *Twenty-One,* and gaining a $50,000 consulting position as a result of his television fame. By November 1959, Van Doren stood before a House Special Committee on Legislative Oversight and confessed that the program had been rigged. Van Doren's spectacular win had been carefully structured from the beginning. He had received all the answers in advance of the programs. The man who came in second, winning $49,500, had known from the first that he was the fall guy. The quiz show scandal was top news as contestant after contestant told of lists of answers, and detailed instructions on facial expressions, brow-mopping, and shrugs to give the shows the appearance of honesty. Dan Enright, producer of *Twenty-One,* admitted that the program had been corrupt for years, along with all of the other quiz shows. Van Doren and nine other winners were tried for perjury in a New York City Court; all were given suspended sentences. Van Doren resigned from his teaching post. CBS took all their quiz programs off the air, and fired their network president, while NBC put in a supervision system, eventually dropping their quiz shows altogether. REF.: *CBA.*

Vane, Charles (AKA: **Charles of Vaughan**) d.c.1719, Int'l., pir. Pirate captain Charles Vane plundered the seas around Jamaica and Barbados in the early eighteenth century. Around 1717, in New Providence, an island in the Bahamas, he and many other pirates were granted conditional amnesty by Governor Woodes Rodgers. Vane refused, firing at one of the governor's man-of-war ships as he sailed away. Two days later, Vane and company captured a ship headed to Barbados, appropriating the vessel and adding its twenty-five pirate sailors and quartermaster, Yeats, to the crew. In the Spring of 1718, they captured sloops from Cuba, Puerto Rico, and New Providence, and through the summer and into the fall looted ships from Antigua and Guinea. Eventually the pirates had two ships, one commanded by Yeats, the other by Vane.

Yeats, however, soon disgusted with how Vane treated him and the men, decided to defect. One evening he set sail with his own boat. When Yeats neared Charleston, S.C., he sent a message to the governor requesting amnesty for himself and his men if they surrendered. The governor granted his request, so Yeats in return turned over several stolen slaves and much of his loot.

Vane set sail, hoping to catch Yeats; instead, he captured two ships from Charleston bound for England, eluding capture forces commissioned by the governor of South Carolina. In late November, Vane's ship was struck by a French man-of-war. Vane wanted to flee, but some of his crew and his quartermaster, John Rackham, wanted to board the ship and fight it out. Vane said it was "too rash and desperate an enterprise, the man-of-war appearing to be twice their force." Robert Deal, the first mate, seconded Vane, but the rest sided with Rackham. The captain, however, insisted on flight and they sailed away from the French ship. But the crew branded Vane a coward and relieved him of his command the next day, sending him and his supporters off in a small sloop with provisions and ammunition. Rackham was voted captain, and Vane's main ship sailed without him for the Caribbean.

Vane's sailed toward Honduras. In Febuary 1719, a typhoon destroyed his ship and drowned most of his men, stranding him on a small uninhabited island near the Bay of Honduras. He survived for several weeks on fish and turtles until a Jamaican ship landed to replenish its water supplies. Holford, the ship's captain, refused, however, to transport Vane. "Charles," he said, "I shan't trust you aboard my ship unless I carry you a prisoner; for I shall have you caballing with my men, knock me on the head, and run away with my ship a-pirating." Captain Holford said he'd be back in a month and, if he found Vane again would take him to Jamaica and see him hang. Soon after Holford's departure, however, another ship landed and took Vane on board as a crewman. This captain did not recognize him.

Pirate Charles Vane, executed circa 1719.

Some weeks later Holford met up with this same ship, was invited to dine by the captain, and noticed Vane hard at work down in the hold. Holford told the captain who Vane was and volunteered to take him prisoner and surrender him to authorities in Jamaica. Vane was tried, convicted, and executed soon after.

REF.: Botting, *The Pirates; CBA;* Rankin, *The Golden Age of Piracy.*

Vane, Sir Henry (Harry Vane), 1613-62, Brit., treas. Member of Parliament in 1640. He opposed Pride's Purge in 1648 and was a member of the council of state in 1649. After criticizing Cromwell's Protectorate, he was put in prison in 1656. In 1660, he was put in prison for two years, and then tried for treason and executed. REF.: *CBA.*

Van Fleet, William Cary, 1852-1923, U.S., jur. Served as assistant district attorney in California from 1878-79, as judge on superior court of California from 1884-92, and as justice on state supreme court of California from 1894-99. He also served as prison director in the California Bureau of Prisons from 1883-84. He was nominated to the northern district court of California by President Theodore Roosevelt in 1907. REF.: *CBA.*

van Heerden, Cornelius Johannes Petrus, c.1909-1931, S. Afri., suic.-mur. A 22-year-old railway worker who lost his job because of frequent, unexplained absences, Cornelius Johannes Petrus van Heerden lived with his parents in Bethlehem, S. Afri., about one hundred miles from Charleston. On Nov. 4, 1931, van Heerden had his first run-in with the law. Charged on six counts of theft by conversion, his father was the defrauded party who brought charges against him. Although he was found Guilty, the magistrate gave him a suspended sentence, taking his youth and, most probably, his first-time offender status, into consideration. Another charge, that of negligent driving, was still pending. Had van Heerden been found guilty of this offense, his maximum sentence would have been a moderate fine. He had not been arrested, but only summoned to appear n court. But, to avoid another appearance in any court, van Heerden decided to commit suicide, taking several people with him. On Nov. 25, the unemployed man went to Bethlehem, stayed overnight there, and purchased fifty rounds of rifle ammunition and several revolver cartridges the next day. Looking up T.S. Lessing, an acquaintance, van Heerden informed him he would "be damned if" he would appear in court, and brought a handful of cartridges out of his pocket, warning, "You watch, there is going to be bloodshed..." Returning home to pick up his father's rifle, he told his brother he was going out for "a bit of shooting." During that day, or the night before, van Heerden wrote several letters, including ones to the police, his father, and his girlfriend. He told the police that "though you now contemplate prosecuting me, you will probably have to prosecute my corpse."

Van Heerden's first victim was J.E. Darby, a commercial traveler whom he shot through the head when Darby pulled up on the road. Taking his car, the killer pushed Darby's body down on the seat beside him, and continued on. Coming upon a native woman, he shot at her, continuing on to fire on a railway gang as he looked for his father's group, presumably with the intention of murdering his father. Not finding him, the killer threw a wallet with his farewell letters into the road. An Anglo-Boer war veteran, A.M. Prisloo, a well-known local citizen, was the next of van Heerden's rampage victims; he was slain along with two of his native servants. Van Heerden killed five people and wounded six others, before he turned the gun on himself.

REF.: Bennett, *Up For Murder*; *CBA*.

van Meegeren, Han (Henricus Antonius van Meegeren), 1889-1947, Neth., fraud. Hailed as the greatest art forger of all time, Han van Meegeren was born in Deventer, Neth. His father, Henricus van Meegeren, was a schoolmaster who did not encourage his son's ambitions to become a painter. When van Meegeren was twelve his severe parents looked over his sketches and then tore them to shreds, telling their disheartened son he had no artistic abilities whatever. Van Meegeren was allowed, however, to enter the Delft University to study architecture. He failed his examinations and left the university. Van Meegeren, against the wishes of his father and discouraged by other relatives and friends, stubbornly embarked on a career as a painter. He exhibited his work for the first time in 1916 and was well-received by the critics and the public alike. Success in his chosen profession seemed assured.

Throughout the early 1920s, van Meegeren enjoyed continued success. His shows were largely organized and promoted by his wife, Anna. At one show, however, the artist met Johanna Oerlemans, the beautiful and sophisticated wife of a leading art critic. She became his mistress. This affair caused van Meegeren's divorce in 1923. He continued his affair with Oerlemans, who, in turn, was also divorced. They married in 1929. By then van Meegeren's career began a downslide, his popularity dropping off and critics becoming disinterested in his work. He was in financial difficulties in the early 1930s, and angered at being ignored as an artist, decided to mock the critics and make an enormous amount of money by faking works by long-dead masters.

This was not an original idea. Van Meegeren's friend Theo Wijngaarden another painter who had suffered due to Holland's greatest critic, Dr. Abraham Bredius, took his vengeance by faking a work of Rembrandt. Wijngaarden had discovered a painting he believed to be a genuine Frans Hals. It was pronounced authentic by the art critic de Groot, but when Dr. Bredius inspected the work, he called it a fake. To embarrass Bredius, Wijngaarden painted a work that he brought to the art critic, claiming it to be a Rembrandt. The pompous Bredius inspected it carefully, then pronounced it genuine. At that moment, Wijngaarden produced a long knife and slashed the canvas to pieces as Bredius and others stepped back in shock and horror. Wijngaarden announced that he had painted the work and that Bredius was a fool.

Van Meegeren resolved to perform the same feat, but go even further, creating fake de Hooths and Vermeers and collecting enormous sums for these "discoveries." He would then tear up the check in front of those whom he intended to dupe.

Van Meegeren spent more than four years seeking to duplicate works of Jan Vermeer, a noted sixteenth-century painter with whom he was familiar, having paid particular attention to Vermeer in his art studies as a youth. For years van Meegeren worked with pigments and other materials. The painter baked his canvases so that they would appear to have aged by hundreds of years, and he ground earth and stone by hand into his pigments to provide the proper irregular look to them. Thus, if experts examined them under a microscope, they would be convinced the paintings had been produced by ancient methods rather than pigments produced mechanically.

To authenticate the age of his fake paintings further, van Meegeren discovered that he could strip down a canvas that was three hundred years old and the "crackle," the tiny cracks that appeared over the decades when the oil dried on the canvas, would remain. When he painted over these canvases the crackle of the first layer of paint still appeared on the newly painted canvas, thus making the new painting appear ancient. Living on the Riviera, van Meegeren supported himself by painting portraits of tourists while continuing his research.

He bought chairs, pots, and other items of the seventeenth century so these trappings would appear as genuine in his fake Vermeers. But it was with the oil paint that van Meegeren took the most care. Vermeer had been famous for his ultramarine blue, but van Meegeren found this almost impossible to duplicate. The oldest available paint coming close to this color had a different chemical make-up, one which was not created until 1802, 127 years after Vermeer's death. Van Meegeren solved this problem by locating a firm that produced powdered lapis lazuli, which is what Vermeer used to create his ultramarine blue. Van Meegeren bought all the powdered lapis lazuli the firm had on hand.

Van Meegeren then mixed his oil paints with lilac oil and phenol resin, which produced the proper viscosity and drying properties. However, van Meegeren also knew that the oil paints used by the old masters often took decades to dry thoroughly, so he sped up the drying process by baking his canvases in an electric oven at 105° centigrade for about two hours. He then coated the canvas with a light coat of varnish and, when the crackles broke through to the new surface of paint, brushed india ink over it. Next, he wiped away the ink, which rode inside the crackles, making it appear that three centuries of dirt clung to the canvas. A final coat of yellow-colored varnish was lightly added to the entire canvas to give it a natural yellowing look, the result of aging. He would then roll the canvas to create a few more crackles. As a final touch, van Meegeren would purposely damage a small portion of the canvas and then "restore" this portion.

The human figures van Meegeren chose for his subjects were based on those appearing in genuine Vermeers. He used live models but carefully selected persons who bore a resemblance to Vermeer's subjects. Since Vermeer's work was mostly of a religious nature, van Meegeren opted for the same genre. His first fake Vermeer, produced in 1936 or 1937, he titled *Christ at Emmaus*. He used himself as the model for Christ, painting him-

Hans Van Meegeren, master art forger, stands before one of his own creations, a huge painting entitled *The Young Christ.*

A Vermeer showing Christ with apostles.

Van Meegeren's *Christ at Emmaus.*

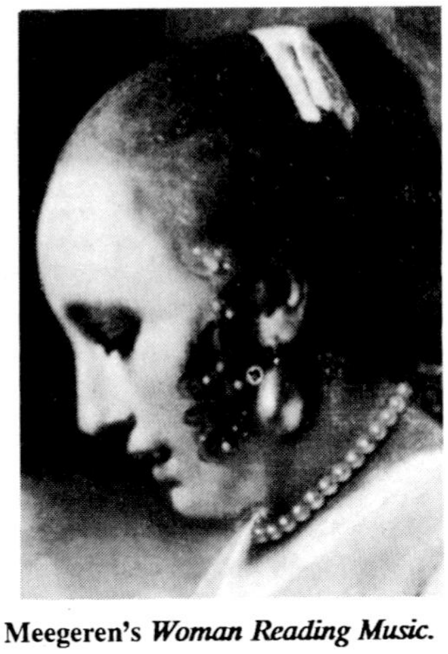

Vermeer's *Woman in Blue* and Van Meegeren's *Woman Reading Music.*

Hans Van Meegeren on trial for art forgery; he was convicted.

self as reflected in a full-length mirror. When he finished, van Meegeren called a lawyer from Amsterdam, telling him that he had acquired the painting and other items from a noble French family that had fallen on hard times and did not wish their identities known. The lawyer saw the signature of Vermeer and took the painting to the art critic Bredius, who excitedly pronounced the work genuine. The painting was then purchased by Dr. D.G. van Beuningen for about $450,000. Dr. van Beuningen then presented the work to the Boymans Museum in Rotterdam, where it was accepted as an authentic Vermeer.

Van Meegeren painted more fake Vermeers, including *Isaac Blessing Jacob*, *The Last Supper*, *The Washing of Christ's Feet*, and *Christ and the Adulteress*. He also passed off a fake de Hoogh titled *Interior with Drinkers*. These paintings, completed between 1937 and 1943, brought millions in payment and were marketed by Dutch art dealer Rienstra van Strijvesande. Van Meegeren grew rich, buying a large house in Holland, then more and more properties. He frequented nightclubs and even bought one of these clubs. Many beautiful women became his mistresses and he indulged himself in heavy doses of morphine until he was addicted to the drug. To explain his new-found riches, van Meegeren claimed that he had inherited a small fortune from a distant relative. He then claimed that he had won a lottery, then two more lotteries.

Van Meegeren's masterful forgeries might never have been discovered had it not been for the treasure-acquiring habits of Nazi Field Marshal Hermann Goering. Following the war, van Meegeren's *Christ and the Adulteress* was discovered in a salt mine near Salzburg, Aust., part of the art treasures hidden by Goering at the close of the war. Dutch authorities learned that Goering had paid $1.25 million for this painting, acquiring it from Aloys Miedel, a German banker. Miedel had gotten the painting from a Dr. Hofer, who had secured hundreds of art treasures for leading Nazis during the war. Hofer, in turn, had acquired the fake Vermeer from the Dutch art dealer Strijvesande, who told Dutch authorities that he had gotten the painting from van Meegeren.

Van Meegeren was visited by police and he claimed that the Vermeer had been obtained through "an old Italian family." This was a mistake. Dutch officials believed that van Meegeren had been acquiring art treasures from the Italian fascists and selling them through his contacts to the Nazis. He was arrested and charged with selling national art treasures and being a collaborator. He was interrogated for several weeks, but he refused to identify the source of the painting. Finally, exhausted, he finally blurted: "You are fools like the rest of them! I sold no great national treasure! I painted it myself!" To prove his claim, van Meegeren said that if he were allowed to return to his studio and left undisturbed (provided he was given enough morphine), he could create another Vermeer.

The court agreed. The painter went to work on another brilliant fake, which he completed within two months while two members of the Dutch security police watched his every move. The charges of collaboration were dropped, but new charges of forgery and fraud were substituted. Eight faked Vermeers and de Hooths were studied by the best art experts in the Netherlands and finally proclaimed bogus after being subjected to x-ray examinations. Van Meegeren was found Guilty and sentenced to one year in prison, but he was by then ill and was confined in a hospital. His lawyers appealed to Queen Wilhelmina to grant a pardon, and after prosecutors agreed to this, the painter was granted his freedom. It was too late. Han van Meegeren, master art forger, died on Dec. 29, 1947, in Amsterdam's Valerium Clinic. Following his death, several more fake Vermeers created by van Meegeren appeared in the art world, but these works, ironically, though known as fakes, brought enormous prices from collectors who finally appreciated the brilliant van Meegeren.

REF.: Block, *Science vs. Crime; CBA;* Cole, *Counterfeit;* Coremans, *Van Meegeren's Faked Vermeers and de Hooghs: A Scientific Study;* Kilbracken, *Van Meegeren: Master Forger;* MacDougall, *Hoaxes;* McGuire, *The Forgers;* Rose, *The World's Greatest Rip-offs;* Scott, *Concise Encyclopedia of Crime and Criminals;* Symons, *A Pictorial History of Crime;* Wade, *Great Hoaxes and Famous Imposters.*

Van Meter, Homer, See: **Dillinger, John.**

Van Niekerk, Andries, 1891-1926, and **Markus, Edward**, 1901-26, S. Afri., rob.-mur. On Dec. 1, 1925, ex-convicts Andries Van Niekerk, thirty-four, and Edward Markus, twenty-four, arrived at the Waterval Farm in South Africa's Transvaal. Manager of the farm, Bill Nelson, sixty, and his companion, Tom Denton, fifty-five, an ex-soldier who ran a store for native laborers, were impressed with the men's hard-time stories, and they were given shelter and work. On the night of Dec. 2, shots were heard at the farm, and several of the buildings were set on fire. The corpses of Nelson and Denton were found in the ruins; both had been shot through the head. Police closed in on Van Niekerk and Markus. Van Niekerk struggled violently upon his arrest, while Markus was passive, and quick to confess to the murders. They were tried together at Pretoria in February 1926, with Markus claiming to be a reluctant accomplice of Van Niekerk, who purported to be mentally unbalanced. Both men were found Guilty; both were hanged on Apr. 14, 1926. REF.: *CBA.*

Van Orsdel, Josiah Alexander, 1860-1937, U.S., jur. Served as county and prosecuting attorney for Laramie County, Wyo., from 1892, and as attorney general for Wyoming from 1898-1905. He also served as a judge on the Wyoming Supreme Court from 1905-06. He was nominated to the circuit court of Washington, D.C., by President Theodore Roosevelt in 1907. REF.: *CBA.*

van Rem, Mathijis, 1945- , Neth., vandal. On Apr. 25, 1978, a Dutch painter, 33-year-old Mathijis van Rem, slashed a self-portrait by Vincent van Gogh in the Amsterdam Van Gogh Museum. Tried in an Amsterdam court, van Rem was acquitted on the grounds of temporary insanity, and was released after spending four months in prison. The court's decision was based on a psychiatric report that said the painter was not responsible for his actions when he tore at the masterpiece. The report also said that van Rem appeared to have recovered from his lapse of sanity. REF.: *CBA.*

van Rensburg, Smartryk Johannes Jacobus Jansen, and **Gordon-Lennox, Ellen**, prom. 1923, S. Afri., mur. Arriving in Upington, S. Afri., in January 1921, handsome and flirtatious Barend van Rensburg was popular with the women. He had an affair with Ellen Gordon-Lennox, daughter of George St. Leger Gordon-Lennox, better known as Scotty Smith, the uncrowned "King of the Kalahari" in the late 1870s. When Lennox became pregnant, van Rensberg obtained some pills that terminated her pregnancy.

At the same time, van Rensburg was involved with Rachel de Kock, who also became pregnant. When de Kock revealed her condition to her father, and hinted that van Rensburg had offered to marry her, the seducer reluctantly became a bridegroom, even though he had already arranged a date to marry Lennox later that year. On Apr. 25, 1922, de Kock and van Rensburg married. A child was born three months later. Unhappy with his marriage, van Rensburg soon resumed his relationship with Lennox, and began asking Solomon Gilinsky, an Upington merchant, what grounds were sufficient for divorce. Lennox wrote love letters to van Rensburg, and he was often called in at night to go to "work," meeting Lennox for clandestine evenings. Their love affair became common knowledge, and soon reached Mr. de Kock, who came to complain. His son-in-law denied anything but friendship with Lennox.

Soon after Christmas, van Rensburg obtained some strychnine and added it to one of his wife's headache powders. On Jan. 4, 1923, when Rachael complained of a headache, her husband brought in the box of various powders and she chose one to put in her coffee. She was soon reeling in pain, and Dr. W.M. Brocherds was called in. A neighbor who arrived on the scene, Lena Wylbach, was told by the gasping woman that her husband had given her a headache powder, and that she was sure it contained poison. The doctor arrived to find van Rensburg with his arms around his spouse's neck, begging her to withdraw her accusation. Her last words to him were, "Kiss me. I'm dying."

Through the incriminating evidence of love letters between Lennox and van Rensburg, both were arrested for the murder, and tried together on Apr. 18, 1923, in Upington. Justice H.S. van Zyl presided, with E. Wingfield prosecuting along with A.J. Pienaar, and C.G. Hall for the defense. Van Rensburg claimed his wife had lied about his giving her a powder. Lennox, pregnant again, was found Guilty along with her lover. Van Rensberg was executed on May 26, 1923. Lennox had her baby in jail, and was released in 1931 after seven years as a model prisoner.

REF.: Bennett, *Too Late for Tears; CBA.*

Van Valkenburgh, Arba Seymour, 1862-1944, U.S., jur. Assistant U.S. Attorney for western district of Missouri from 1898-1905, and as U.S. Attorney from 1905-10. He was nominated to the western district court by President William Howard Taft in 1910, and to the eighth circuit court by President Calvin Coolidge in 1925. REF.: *CBA.*

Van Valkenburgh, Elizabeth, 1799-1846, U.S., mur. Elizabeth Van Valkenburgh of Fulton, N.Y., claimed in court that she was trying to cure both her husbands of alcoholism when she served them tea laced with arsenic. She was executed by hanging on Jan. 24, 1846.

REF.: *CBA;* Nash, *Bloodletters and Badmen;* ____, *Look For the Woman.*

Van Wie, Francis, prom. 1945-52, U.S., big. Called "The Ding-Dong Daddy" by the newspapers because he was once a streetcar conductor, Van Wie was newsworthy because of his sixteen known marriages. He claimed that it all started because life on the road was lonely when he was a lion-tamer in a circus. He also claimed that he never married for money but only for love. "I know how to make a woman feel as though she's the only woman in the world—and I the only man," he said.

He was first brought to trial in 1945 after it was discovered he had taken twelve wives to the alter. He served only sixteen months in prison and was back in court in 1949, at which time there were three more wives. He was in court again in 1952, at which time he had reached a grand total of sixteen wives. REF.: *CBA.*

Van Wyk, Stephanus Louis, d.1931, S. Afri., fraud-mur. Stephanus Louis Van Wyk was arrested in Bloemfontein, S. Afri., on charges of fraud and was taken to Johannesburg for trial. Before he was arrested, Van Wyk gave about £850 to his nephew, John Frederick Moller, a 28-year-old Bloemfontein Supreme Court clerk. Van Wyk was tried for fraud and swindle, found Guilty, and sentenced to eighteen months in jail. While serving his time, Van Wyk became convinced that his nephew had tried to swindle him out of a few pounds and heard also that Moller had supplied details of his transgressions to the police.

Developing an intense hatred of his relative, Van Wyk went to see him just days after he was released from prison. On July 12, he visited his nephew, and the two took a trip to Waterval in Moller's car, with a borrowed pick and shovel in the back seat. That night, a woman who lived close to Waterval was awakened when Van Wyk came to ask for a torch, telling her his car was stuck. He refused lodging and disappeared.

On July 19, the police search for the missing Moller ended when his corpse was discovered in a jackal pit, buried face down. His head was smashed and there was a severe injury at the base of his spine. The pick and shovel were found nearby, as well as a pair of socks with the initials "S van W." Van Wyk was arrested. He claimed that he and Moller had gone out to look for £3,000 that had been buried after a 1929 robbery. He had accidentally hit his nephew with the pick, and Moller had fallen into the jackal pit, hurting his head as he fell. Van Wyk panicked and buried the body on the spot. At the trial, which began on Oct. 21, 1930, before Judge-President Sir Etienne de Villiers, with Crown prosecutors W.G. Hoal and A.V. Dickenson, and defense attorneys F.P. de Wet and N.J. Grobler, Van Wyk was acquitted, and delivered an impassioned newspaper interview bemoaning the "suffering, mental, physical, and spiritual," that he had endured during the course of the trial.

In January 1931, the virtually penniless Van Wyk offered farmer Cyril Grigg Tucker £4,500 for his land and farm, "Appeldoorn." The plan was for Tucker and Van Wyk to travel together to Pretoria to conclude their deal there. On Feb. 3, the two men set out together; that night, Van Wyk battered in the farmer's skull, then buried the body in a field. He took over the farm briefly, but was arrested on unrelated charges when he tried to pass off a spurious coin as genuine. He concocted a complicated story of how he and Tucker had argued over a woman, and, when the farmer came at him, he struck out in self defense, then panicked and buried the body. Van Wyk was tried in Pretoria on May 4, 1931, and found Guilty, despite an attempt at an insanity plea. While awaiting execution he confessed to killing Moller. Van Wyk was executed, leaving behind a wife and two children, on June 12, 1931.

REF.: Bennett, *Up For Murder; CBA.*

Vaquier, Jean Pierre (Vacquier, AKA: J. Wanker), c.1878-1924, Brit., mur. An impassioned French hotel clerk, a British matron on the verge of a nervous breakdown, and a drunken husband who managed an inn in Surrey comprised an unusual love triangle that culminated in murder in early Spring 1924. Jean Pierre Vaquier had served as a telephone operator in the French Army during WWI. After the war his skills with a wireless won him a job at the Hotel Victoria in Biarritz, demonstrating the entertainment potential of the radio to curious vacationers staying at the hotel. Using his own receiver Vaquier beamed musical concerts directly into the hotel salon.

British killer Jean Pierre Vaquier.

In January, Mabel Theresa Jones registered at the Victoria to recover from the emotional shock of a serious business reversal which had left her nearly bankrupt. Jones was attracted to the middle-aged Vaquier and after a week they had begun an affair. Jones was only mildly drawn to Vaquier, and when her husband, Alfred George Poynter Jones, sent a telegram urging her to come home, Mabel broke off her relationship with Vaquier. Although Vaquier begged her not to go she remained firm on her resolve. She did permit Vaquier to accompany her to Paris but from there continued to Surrey alone.

The next day after parting with Jones in Paris, Vaquier headed for London. He dispatched a telegram to Jones from the Russell Hotel in Bloomsbury. "Arrived from Paris on business. Shall be very pleased to see you and to meet Mr. Jones. Perhaps you will inform me which evening." Without waiting for a reply Vaquier turned up at the Jones' Blue Anchor Inn at Byfleet, Surrey, on Feb. 14, 1924. Although Jones paid his hotel bill and attempted to make him comfortable, it became evident to Vaquier that her ardor had cooled. When Jones refused to go away with him, Vaquier became increasingly desperate and finally decided to kill his rival, in the misguided hope of regaining Jones' affection.

On Mar. 1, Vaquier called on an apothecary on Southampton Row, London. Vaquier told the clerk in French, that he required two grains of strychnine—enough poison to kill four healthy men—for a wireless experiment he was conducting. After completing the purchase, Vaquier signed the register under the alias, "J. Wanker." Back in Byfleet he waited for the right moment to administer the poison to the unsuspecting Mr. Jones. The opportunity came on the evening of Mar. 28 when the innkeeper threw a big party.

Guessing that Mr. Jones, an inveterate drunk, would probably wake up with a terrible hangover, Vaquier laced the hotel bar's bromo salts with strychnine. The next morning Mr. Jones did wake up with a hangover and as Vaquier had anticipated, took some of the medicine. Vaquier was actually present at the bar as Mr. Jones took the salts and complained they were bitter. His wife immediately examined the blue bottle and found they had been tampered with. Vaquier obligingly helped carry Mr. Jones up to his bedroom, but the innkeeper was dying. When Dr. Frederick Carle arrived, he was unable to help Mr. Jones who died minutes later. Although Vaquier had removed the bottle, Carle noticed several crystals lying on the floor near the bar. A chemical analysis revealed the presence of strychnine.

Vaquier remained at the Blue Anchor for a few more days. He was about to move to the Railway Hotel when Jones confronted him with her suspicions. The Frenchman moved to Woking on Apr. 4. When a picture of Vaquier was printed in the paper, the Southampton chemist who sold Vaquier the poison, recognized it and notified Scotland Yard. Vaquier was arrested at the Railway Hotel on Apr. 19, and tried at the Guildford Assizes the following July before Justice Horace Avory. He was found Guilty of murder and hanged at Wandsworth Prison on Aug. 12, 1924.

REF.: Ashton-Wolfe, *The Underworld;* Bowker, *Behind the Bar;* Brock, *A Casebook of Crime;* Brophy, *The Meaning of Murder;* Browne and Tullett, *The Scalpel of Scotland Yard;* Butler, *Murderers' England; CBA;* Glaister, *The Power of Poison;* Gribble, *Adventures in Murder;* Heppenstall, *Bluebeard and After;* Lambton, *Thou Shalt Do No Murder;* Marjoribanks, *For the Defense, The Life of Sir Edward Marshall Hall;* Shew, *A Companion to Murder;* Thompson, *Poison and Poisoners;* Townsend, *Black Cap, Murder Will Out;* Wilson, *Encyclopedia of Murder;* (FICTION), Carr, *The Sleeping Sphinx.*

Varain, Leland, See: **Alterie, Louis.**

Varecha, James (AKA: Iggy Varecha, Iggy the Bad 'Un), 1915- , U.S., rape-mur. Nicknamed by Chicago police "Iggy the Bad 'Un," 17-year-old James Varecha went on a two-day spree of robbery, rape, and murder in 1932. Lillian Henry, former Police Commissioner John Alcock's 20-year-old neice, and Frank Jordan, a 38-year-old widower, were out for a ride in Jordan's car when Varecha stopped them, robbed them and held them for five hours. He then murdered Jordan and repeatedly raped Henry, eventually releasing her. Commissioner Alcock, lieutenants Michael Alcock and Patrick Alcock—Henry's uncles—and Sergeant Thomas Alcock—Henry's cousin—led the search for Varecha. Police raided the suspect's family home, taking his older brother, Frank Varecha to the Chicago Lawn station for questioning.

Frank told officers that his brother, "Iggy," had been in trouble since the age of thirteen. Charges of truancy, larceny, and assault with intent to kill led him to become a ward of the juvenile court. Sent to a foster home, he ran away and was caught in a robbery, committed to a juvenile detention home, released, but then arrested a few months later for attacking a schoolmate with a crowbar, fracturing his skull. According to Frank, doctors who examined James at that time said "he was wrong in his head." Judge Mary Batelme sent Varecha to the state school for epileptics in Dixon, Ill., but in August 1931 he escaped. "We would search him every time he entered the house," Frank said of his brother's visits home, and on his last visit he had a gun. When his mother begged him to return to Dixon, Frank continued, "he pulled it out and was going to fire when the rest of us jumped on him. We called the police and he was booked for assault with intent to commit murder." Varecha was sent back to the institution and escaped three weeks later with three other inmates. The family had heard nothing from him since, except for a post card from Mexico.

After a three-day, city-wide, search Varecha was apprehended at a burlesque theater on South State Street. "I'm the guy they're looking for in the South Side killing, and I've got two guns on me now," he had bragged to Jay Andrews, a fellow patron. Andrews told the doorman, who called police. Varecha at first insisted that his name was Daniel Minski, but a note in his pocket exposed him: "In case of accident to James Varecha, notify Father Patrick Maloney of St. Peter's Church, Polk and Clark Streets."

"I wouldn't kill anybody," he protested to Deputy Alcock. "And I didn't kill that man. If I did, you don't think I'd let a couple of cops get me so easy, do you? I'd have shot them—no, I don't mean that. Anyways, the doctors all say I'm crazy." Varecha later smilingly confessed to a multitude of killings, shootings, kidnappings, and rapes, many of which had taken place within forty-eight hours. He admitted he was the "lone wolf bandit" who had attacked couples parked in cars for the past several months and gave details of over twenty such assaults. He said he had held up so many couples and stores on the South Side that he could not remember them all.

On Dec. 16, 1932, Varecha was sentenced to die in the electric chair. REF.: *CBA.*

Varenhorst, Gerritt Hendrick, prom. 1917, Brit., attempt. mur. Early one March morning in 1917, Mrs. de Leerch woke feeling sick and having trouble breathing. She smelled gas, and heard a hissing noise coming from an empty back room. Her spouse woke when he heard sounds like someone moving furniture. Attempting to open the front hall door of their Tottenham Court home, he found it blocked. Mr. de Leerch locked the door, while his wife screamed for help. Forensic investigator Bernard Spilsbury arrived at the house at 4 a.m. Examining the de Leerchs' rooms he found that a back door had been forced open, and that another door had a hole pierced through it, with a seven-foot length of rubber hose connecting to a gas main squeezed into the door. The would-be killer had been caught when the hissing noise of the forced gas awakened Mrs. de Leerch. He obviously intended to return after his victims were dead. The perpetrator was Gerrit Hendrick Varenhorst, who lived in a basement just down the street from the de Leerchs. Found in his possession was a key to their front door, tubing which fitted the length of their back room, and wood chips from the hole cut in the door. Tried and convicted, Varenhorst was sentenced to penal servitude.

REF.: Browne and Tullett, *The Scalpel of Scotland Yard; CBA.*

Varesanin, Marijan, prom. 1911, Yug., gen., attempt. assass. In the volatile atmosphere of revolt by Serbian nationalists in the early 1900s, individuals began to strike blows for the freedom of their country. On June 3, 1911, Bogdan Zerajdic, twenty-three, the son of a peasant, borrowed a gun from a student. He had decided to murder Emperor Franz Joseph, who was visiting Sarajevo. Instead, on June 15, he shot General Marijan Varesanin, governor of two provinces, five times, and then turned the gun on himself. Before committing suicide, Zerajdic said, "I leave my revenge to Serbdom." He was buried in an unmarked grave. Varesanin survived. See: **Joseph, Franz.**

REF.: Bell, *Assassin; CBA.*

Varga, Mariea, See: **Fazekas, Suzanne.**

Vargas, Anastacio, prom. 1926-29, U.S., (wrong. convict.) mur. In 1925, Anastacio Vargas of Austin, Texas, was convicted of murder and was sentenced to life in prison. The conviction was reversed on appeal and Vargas was tried again, with another conviction and a sentence of death. In the final stages of preparation for execution—his head had been shaved and he had been served his last meal—and with four hours left to live, a lookalike killer confessed to the crime. A judge investigated the case and commuted Vargas' sentence to life imprisonment. In 1929, the wrongly convicted man was granted a full pardon, and released after four years in the Boexer County Jail. He sued the state for damages and was given an award of $20,000 in 1965. Although the state appealed, the award was affirmed. REF.: *CBA.*

Vargas, Getulio, 1883-1954, Braz., suic. The president of Brazil in 1954, Getulio Vargas had once been a popular public figure; he had survived coups, revolutions, and even one 1939 uprising started by the Nazis. By 1954, however, the dictator and revolutionary president was being attacked in the media. Both Vargas and Brazil had benefited from U.S. defense expenditures during WWII; by the 1950s, the rampant corruption was severely criticized from many sectors of the Brazilian populace and media.

Carlos Lacerda, a voluble critic of Vargas' administration, was attacked by assassins. Although Lacerda was not seriously injured, an air force major was murdered. Believing that the assassination attempt was directed against them, the armed services, once loyal to President Vargas, demanded an investigation, and the government agreed. The search led straight to officials close to Vargas, especially the commander of Vargas' guard corps. Surrounded by an atmosphere of national outrage, Vargas committed suicide as his New State, touted as Brazil's Third Republic in 1937, collapsed in ruins.

REF.: *CBA;* Paine, *The Assassins' World.*

Vasil, George T., 1959- , U.S., mur. In Fort Pierce, Fla., George Vasil, a slight boy of fourteen, tried to rape 12-year-old Pamela Vasser on Sept. 19, 1974. Physically unable to commit the act, Vasil crushed Vasser's skull with a rock, sexually assaulted her with a branch, and hid her corpse in the grass. Because of the "brutal and vicious" nature of the crime, Vasil was tried as an adult in a local circuit court three months later. He was found Guilty by a jury and, on Dec. 12, 1974, was sentenced to death in the electric chair. He had just turned fifteen. On Oct. 10, 1979, Vasil's sentence was changed to life in prison.

REF. *CBA;* Godwin, *Murder U.S.A.*

Vasily I (Vasily Dmitriyevich), 1371-1425, Rus., kid. (vict.) Ruled as grand prince of Moscow from 1339-1425. In 1383, he went to see Tatar khan Tokhtamysh to obtain authorization for his father to become prince of Vladimir and control Russian lands. Instead, he was held hostage from 1383-86. REF.: *CBA.*

Vasily Shuysky, 1552-1612, Rus., rebel. Ruled as czar of Russia from 1606-10. In 1591, he inquired into the death of Dmitry Ivanovich, who was to succeed Czar Fyodor I. He then began to support the first False Dmitry, but later denounced him as an impostor, for which he was exiled. He initiated a plot with Russian aristocrats against the False Dmitry, assassinated him, and took power as czar in 1606. He was deposed by Muscovites in 1610. REF.: *CBA.*

Vasquez, David, 1947- , U.S., (wrong. convict.) rape-mur. Carol Hamm, a 32-year-old Washington, D.C., lawyer, was found murdered in her Arlington, Va., home. Hamm had been assaulted, raped, and hanged with a piece of rope from a water pipe in her garage on Jan. 25, 1984. Investigations led police to David Vasquez, a man who had lived in the Arlington neighborhood for several years, and who would later be described in court as having "borderline retarded/low normal" intelligence. A neighbor had seen Vasquez walking near Hamm's house around the time of the murder, and another had observed him two days later, on the same day police found the body. Vasquez maintained that he was home or with a friend the night of the killing.

Arrested at the McDonald's where he worked cleaning tables, Vasquez was taken to the Manassas police station. He was not read the Miranda warning by detectives William Shelton and Robert Carrig. Henry E. Hudson, who prosecuted in the Vasquez case, said the warning was unnecessary because Vasquez was then considered a potential witness, not a suspect. However, in this first ninety-minute session with the extremely frightened man, who was described as acting like a child by those who knew him, the detectives told him they found his fingerprints at the scene of the crime, which was not true, according to later testimony. They told him dozens of details about the murder, and encouraged him to repeat them. Vasquez repeatedly cried for his mother. Later, the detectives took him to the Arlington station, where they read him the Miranda warning, which he signed, and then asked him to repeat the crime details. Later in the session Vasquez went into a sort of trance, and told of "a horrible dream," going into a rambling monologue in a deep voice, repeating the details of the case as he had learned them from the detectives. That day he was arrested and charged with rape, capital murder, burglary, and robbery. Carrig and Shelton questioned him a third time, with Shelton suggesting, "think about your dreams." Vasquez again recounted the story he had heard; this version was admitted as evidence.

Vasquez waited in jail a year before he was tried, after a court-appointed psychiatrist judged him competent to stand trial. Although forensic tests proved that the blood type in stains found at the scene of the crime did not match Vasquez's, his court-appointed attorneys, Richard J. McCue and Martin Bangs, did not know how to explain Vasquez's "confessions." On the advice of his attorneys, Vasquez used the "Alford plea", which allows a defendant to maintain his innocence while recognizing that the evidence probably will result in a guilty verdict. The Alford plea is essentially a guilty plea. By choosing it, a defendant forfeits his right to a jury trial and to an appeal. Prosecutors reduced the capital murder charge to second-degree murder. Prosecutor Hudson said he believed Vasquez had not acted alone. On Feb. 4, 1985, Judge Winston found the defendant Guilty and sentenced him to thirty-five years in prison, stipulating that he receive psychological treatment. On Aug. 15, Vasquez entered the Buckingham Correctional Center in Dillwyn, Va., where he was repeatedly sexually assaulted and where he saw a psychiatrist only infrequently.

From September to November 1987, four rape-murders that fitted the pattern in the Hamm slaying occurred. Timonthy W. Spencer, a 27-year-old man who had grown up in the Arlington neighborhood, was later identified as the perpetrator. Detective Joseph Horgas noticed the similarities and pieced together the circumstantial evidence that implicated Spencer in the Hamm case as well as the others. On Jan. 4, Vasquez's attorney informed him that he had received a full pardon. He was released from prison, after serving five years for a crime he did not commit. See: **Spencer, Timothy Wilson.** REF.: *CBA.*

Vásquez, Tiburcio, c.1838-75, U.S., west. outl. A criminal by the time he was in his teens, Tiburcio Vásquez quickly went on to bigger things. Vásquez, half Indian, was born and raised in California. He was barely eighteen years old when he engaged in his first gunfight. In about 1856, Vásquez abducted the daughter of a wealthy Mexican rancher who lived in the Livermore Valley. The rancher followed them and demanded the return of his daughter. When Vásquez refused the rancher pulled out a gun and fired a shot into the young desperado's arm, shattering the bone. With that Vásquez rode away alone. In about 1855, Vásquez stabbed to death a Monterey man, but evaded the authorities and was never charged.

Vásquez specialized in horse stealing and cattle rustling and was arrested and sent to prison for five years at San Quentin in 1857. After an escape in 1859 and subsequent recapture on theft charges, Vásquez was freed from jail on Aug. 13, 1863. Following his third conviction, this time for armed robbery, Vásquez was returned to jail. He was released on June 4, 1870, only to begin a new career robbing the stagecoach lines.

Bandit Tiburcio Vásquez.

Vásquez and his band gained a reputation up and down the California coast as notorious outlaws. In Summer 1872 the bandits held up a stage near Arroyo Cantua in the northern part of the state. While en route to their hideout they were confronted by a posse led by Alameda County sheriff Harry Morse, the constable of Santa Cruz, and the San Benito County sheriff. In the gunfight that followed, Vásquez was shot in the chest. Bandit Francisco Barcenas was killed, and a third man, Garcia Rodriguez was badly injured. Rodríguez was tracked down by the posse two days later and died not long afterward, but Vásquez escaped to the mountains where he nursed himself back to health.

The Mexican bandit resumed his outlawry on Aug. 26, 1873,

when he and six accomplices looted the town of Tres Piños, Calif., murdering sheepherder William Redford, an old man known as Davidson, and teamster James Riley. While this was going on, José Chavez hit a small boy over the head with a club, rendering him unconscious. This cold-blooded act of violence was typical of the outlaw gang. The Tres Piños shootout sufficiently aroused the ire of the community. Posses were quickly formed, and an $8,000 reward was offered by the state for the capture of the fearsome Vásquez.

Tiburcio Vásquez and his gang robbed a Kingston hotel and some stage coaches before they were finally overtaken by one of the posses on their home ground in Alison Canyon, Los Angeles County in December 1874. The bandit was hiding out in an adobe shack owned by "Greek" George Allen when the posse broke through the doors. George Beers injured Vásquez, who attempted to make a break for freedom through the back window. Beers took aim and brought down Vásquez with a volley of buckshot. The bandit survived his wounds and was taken back to stand trial for the murders of the three Tres Piños men. Vásquez was convicted, and sentenced to death. On Mar. 19, 1875, he was hanged at San Jose, Calif. REF.: *CBA*.

REF.: American Guide Series, *California, A Guide to the Golden State;* Ayers, *Gold and Sunshine;* Bancroft, *Works of Hubert Howe Bancroft;* Bartholomew, *The Biographical Album of Western Gunfighters;* Beers, *Vasquez;* Belden, *Life of David Belden;* Benefield, *For the Good of the Country;* Block, *Great Stagecoach Robbers of the West;* Brown, *History of Kings County;* Burnham, *Scouting on Two Continents;* Carr, *Los Angeles, City of Dreams;* ____, *The West Is Still Wild;* Caruthers, *Loafing Along Death Valley Trails; CBA;* Cleland, *The Cattle on a Thousand Hills;* Cole, *Memoirs of Cornelius Cole;* Corle, *The Royal Highway;* Dane, *Ghost Town;* Dillon, *California Trail Herd;* Drago, *Road Agents and Train Robbers;* Drury, *California, An Intimate Guide;* Duke, *Celebrated Criminal Cases in America;* Finger, *Foot-Loose in the West;* Fisher, *The Salinas;* Fisher and Holmes, *Gold Rushes and Mining Camps;* Gay, *Calle de Alvarado;* Greenwood, *The California Outlaw;* Guinn, *Historical and Biographical Record of Southern California;* Henderson, *Keys to Crookdom;* Hendricks, *The Bad Man of the West;* Hoover, *Historic Spots in California;* Horan and Sann, *Pictorial History of the Wild West;* Hunt and Van De Grift, *A Short History of California;* Hunter and Rose, *The Album of Gun-Fighters;* Hutchinson, *Another Notebook of the Old West;* Jackson, *Bad Company;* James and McMurray, *History of San Jose, California;* Kirsch and Murphy, *West of the West;* McGroarty, *The Pioneer;* Miner, *Outdoor Southland of California;* Morgan, *History of Kern County;* Mott, *Legends and Lore of Long Ago;* Mylar, *Early Days at the Mission San Juan Bautista;* Nadeau, *City-Makers;* Nash, *Bloodletters and Badmen;* Newmark, *Sixty Years in Southern California;* Norris, *Golden Empire;* Older, *Love Stories of Old California;* Page, *Pasadena, Its Early Years;* Palmer, *History of Hollywood;* Peirson, *Kern's Desert;* Phillips, *History of Santa Barbara County;* Powers, *Old Monterey;* Rambo, *Trailing the California Bandit Tiburcio Vásquez, 1835-1875;* Rensch, *Historic Spots in California, The Southern Counties;* ____, *Historic Spots in California, Valley and Sierra Counties;* Ridge, *Life and Adventures of Joaquin Murieta;* Robinson, *Panorama;* Rojas, *California Vaquero;* Sabin, *Wild Men of the Wild West;* Saunders, *The Southern Sierras of California;* Sawyer, *The Life and Career of Tiburcio Vásquez;* Sheridan, *History of Ventura County;* Shinn, *Graphic Description of Pacific Coast Outlaws;* Shippey, *It's an Old California Custom;* Smith, *Garden of the Sun;* Spaulding, *History and Reminiscences, Los Angeles;* Vandor, *History Fresno County;* Walter, *The Great Understander;* Winchell, *History of Fresno County;* Winther, *Via Western Express & Stagecoach;* Wolf, *Fallen Angels;* Wood, *California's Agua Fria;* Workman, *Boyle Workman's the City That Grew;* Wynn, *Desert Bonanza.*

Vaudreuil, Pierre Cavagnial de Rigaud, Marquis de, 1698-1778, Fr.-U.S., polit. corr. The Marquis de Vaudreuil, for all his elegant balls and lavish fetes in his much publicized ardor to duplicate the grace and refinements of Versailles and the salons of Paris, was the first great crook of New Orleans, serving as the French governor of Louisiana (1742-53). The marquis was a man of intense personal tastes, and to pay for his pleasures he simply used his powerful position to enrich himself.

First came a host of the governor's relatives and those of his wife, who were put on the city's payroll. These nepotistic and inept officials kicked back part of their inflated city salaries to their illustrious relative. Next, Vaudreuil sold off trade monopolies to the highest bidder eager to foist a huge premium into the marquis's outstretched hands. Moreover, the governor received a handsome percentage of all profits taken in by traders.

In 1751, the condition of the French soldiery was a lamentable mess; although enormous supplies had been sent to the colony from France, the average grenadier was starving. The marquis was confiscating half of the food supplies, selling them to citizens and pocketing the profits. He sold the Indians and bands of felons arms and ammunition intended for his own soldiers and reaped huge sums of money. The troops were issued inferior goods to replace the stolen stores—blankets with great holes in them, meat coated with maggots, muskets that usually would not fire and if they did would likely blow up in the user's hands.

The enterprising marquis was not without enemies who had influence at court in France. One, Michel de la Rouvillière, who held the important post of intendant-commissary in New Orleans, was forever sending off juicy missives to his king in which the foppish marquis was castigated for his wholesale graft and governmental corruption. One read: "No justice is to be expected from M. de Vaudreuil; he is too lazy, too negligent; his wife is too malicious, too passionate, and has too strong interests in all the settlements, and in the town of New Orleans, not to prevail upon him to keep on fair; and with others...

"There is no discipline; the most indulgent toleration is granted to the soldiers, provided they drink their money at the licensed liquor-shop (from each, the marquis was given a share of the daily profits), where they are given drugs which ruin their health; for several months there has never been less than a hundred of them at the hospital...The soldiers are allowed to do as they please, provided they drink at the liquor-shop designated for them; and they carry out of it wine and spirits which they sell to the Negroes and to the Indians...What is positive is that M. de Vaudreuil as Governor has drawn upon the treasury for ten thousand livres of his salary...and it is with these funds that the supplies of the liquor-shop have been bought...

"Moreover, Madame de Vaudreuil is capable of carrying on a still baser sort of trade. She deals here with everybody, and she forces merchants and other individuals to take charge of her merchandise and to sell it at the price which she fixes. She keeps in her house every sort of drugs, which are sold by her steward, and in his absence she does not scruple herself to descend to the occupation of measurement and to betake herself to the hell (taverns, et al). The husband is not ignorant of this. He draws from it a handsome revenue, which is his sole wish and aim."

Such indictments failed to remove the dissolute marquis from office. He went blithely on with his plundering, his regime marked by fabulous drunken brawls and bloody duels. Vaudreuil encouraged loose morality and happily tolerated the fact that most of his officers kept mistresses who were received in the governor's mansion and, in most instances, seated at formal dinners so as to overshadow the legitimate wives of the officers.

During this reign of depravity, New Orleans became a hotbed of cutthroats, unemployed drifters, whores, and gamblers. Brothels, gambling dens, taverns, and drug dens became so numerous that the few respectable families in the city feared to step outside their homes. The river front area was the worst and was soon recognized as the first criminal section of the city. All types of vice and crime were practiced here and without any interference from authorities.

To further increase his own purse, the marquis secretly had counterfeit currency circulated throughout the city and territory. When the fake bills were discovered, the governor feigned shock and had the counterfeiters, his own men, arrested. He allowed the three white men in the ring to escape but ordered that the free black, still in custody, a man named Joseph, be branded and whipped. Joseph was then sold back into slavery and shipped to Martinique (one report had it that his tongue was cut out so that he could not tattle on the marquis).

Much to his chagrin, the marquis soon realized that the blatant flooding of the city with counterfeit notes had brought down an at-large reform movement among the citizens who feared that New Orleans was fast becoming another Sodom. Public outrage compelled the graft-bloated governor to institute new strict laws in February 1751, which signaled the first attempt by city authorities to crush (at least, within reason) vice and crime in New Orleans.

Among the thirty articles of law, it was decreed that any free blacks living in the city who harbored escaped slaves or induced them to plunder their master's stores or "lead a scandalous life, shall lose their freedom and become the slaves of the King." Any Frenchman encouraging the blacks or Indians to steal or become prostitutes was to be whipped before the entire population and then sent to work for life as a galley slave. Liquor could not be kept or drunk in any private home in the city. No tavern keeper could sell liquor to Indians, blacks, or soldiers, except two officially designated pubs which were to provide the troops with spirits. All grog shops were to be closed during holidays, Sundays, and each night at 9. Those who had left their own lands and had taken up degenerate ways of life were given eight days to either return to their farms or be driven at the point of a bayonet from the city.

Vaudreuil privately smarted under the new laws, but he winked at his officers-of-the-guard and soon the taverns, gambling dens, and whorehouses were again operating around the clock. By the time the fun-loving Vaudreuil turned over his duties to his successor, Louis Billouart de Kerlerec, and assumed the governorship of Canada (1755-60), the marquis had become a millionaire many times over. He had made corruption in high office a fine art. Yet, there was justice in his case; for his inept handling of Canada and for capitulating to the British in 1760, Vaudreuil returned to France in shame and was immediately imprisoned for two years.

REF.: Asbury, *The French Quarter;* Carter, *The Past as Prelude, New Orleans, 1718-1968;* Castellanos, *New Orleans as It Was; CBA;* Gayarre and Howe, *Municipal History of New Orleans;* Rightor, *Standard History of New Orleans;* Ripley, *Life in Old New Orleans;* Saxon, *Fabulous New Orleans;* Southward, *Beauty and Booty, the Watchword of New Orleans;* Spear, *Ancient and Modern New Orleans.*

Vaughan, George, prom. 1816, Brit., consp.-rob. A member of the Foot Patrol in Britain's famous Bow Street Runners, George Vaughan was himself arrested for planning robberies and then arresting the thieves who carried them out. Vaughan and two other Bow Street runners were tried and convicted in July 1816 of inducing several 13-year-old boys to commit burglary; then arresting them to collect £40. All three of the men were found Guilty and were given five-year jail terms. During the same court session, Vaughan was charged with committing a robbery. For this offense, he and his cohort in the crime were hanged. See: **Bow Street Runners**.

REF.: Armitage, *Bow Street Runners;* Browne, *The Rise of Scotland Yard; CBA;* Thomson, *The Story of Scotland Yard.*

Vaughan, James Clayton, Jr., See: **Franklin, Joseph Paul.**

Vaughan, Jerry, prom. 1980, U.S., theft. In a one-year shoplifting spree in and around the Arroyo, Calif., area Jerry Vaughan stole at least $30,000 in merchandise between Los Angeles and Modesto, Calif., before he was arrested in February 1980. Included in the massive haul were three kitchen sinks, a 250-pound radial arm-table saw, a coin-operated bubble gum machine, various kitchen appliances, and piles of expensive clothing.

Investigator John Tooley explained that a flatbed truck and a skip-loader had to be used to haul the goods from Vaughan's house. An unemployed former prison guard and ex-reserve police officer in Guadalupe, Vaughan usually stole with his wife, Noemi Vaughan, twenty-five, and their 4-year-old child, using a covered baby carriage to hide property. Sometimes Vaughan simply backed his van up to the door and loaded items in. He also stole security tape from check-out counters, stuck it to large items, and walked out.

A Sears store clerk in San Luis Obispo became suspicious when Vaughan tried to carry out a microwave oven. He was arrested in another Sears store in Carson, Calif., a Los Angeles suburb, when he again tried to take a microwave oven. Both Vaughan and his spouse pleaded guilty to possession of stolen goods. Vaughan was sentenced to a two-year jail term; his wife was fined $350, ordered to contribute 200 hours of community service, and placed on five years of probation.

The Vaughans peddled clothing, much of it worn only once, at weekend flea markets. Tooley said that "about $5,000 worth of stuff had to be returned to Vaughan because we couldn't prove he had stolen it." Another $15,000 worth of goods was returned to the stores. REF.: *CBA.*

Vaughan, Richard William, d.1758, Brit., forg. Forgery became punishable by death in England in 1634. The first forger at the Bank of England was Richard William Vaughan, a cloth maker from Stafford. Using artists to help him copy bank notes, Vaughan was caught when he gave a few samples to the young woman he was engaged to marry. She attempted to cash them, and Vaughan was arrested. He was hanged for the crime at Tyburn in 1758.

REF.: *CBA;* Nicholls, *Crime Within the Square Mile.*

Vaughan, Thomas, prom. 1710, Brit., extor. In his youth, Thomas Vaughan served as a page to a lady. He married and began work in a milliner's shop in Pall Mall but soon turned to extortion and prostitution in the piazzas in Covent Garden. Vaughan worked as a "Molly," a thief who worked bars and restaurants known as "Molly Clubs" while dressed in women's clothing to solicit and then extort victims. Vaughan was not caught until he and a criminal cohort tried to blackmail an elderly druggist.

Vaughan and his friend visited the druggist in his shop by the maypole in the Strand, and told him that they had private business with him. Expecting the two young men to ask about venereal disease, he took them into his private chambers, but Vaughan instead charged him with picking him up a few nights earlier and giving him a guinea to commit sodomy on him in a public bathroom. Vaughan then demanded fifty guineas to keep him from going to the police. The druggist promised to raise the cash in two hours, and Vaughan and his friend went to a local pub to wait. The apothecary conferred with friends and decided to get a warrant to arrest the blackmailers. When the two men returned for the money, the police were waiting with a warrant for their arrest.

Imprisoned at Newgate, both were tried and sentenced to be whipped in the streets from Temple Bar to Charing Cross, and to pay fines of £10 each. Vaughan's friend paid his fine and was released, but the penniless Vaughan spent three years at Newgate before he could come up with the funds to get his fine remitted. See: **Margrove, Stephen**.

REF.: *CBA;* Smith, *Highwaymen.*

Vaught, Millard, b.c.1885, and **Stiles, Will**, b.c.1877, and **Bates, W.L.**, b.c.1867, Case of, U.S., mur. In Fall 1907, a human skeleton was found about four miles from the Bates sawmill. J.W. Terry, a man in his early twenties, who had worked at the sawmill as a lumber checker had been missing since August 1907. His aunt and his friends made an extensive search for him and, finding no trace, the aunt was paid on his insurance policy.

In November 1909, Sam Swider, another worker at the Bates sawmill, was convicted of larceny and sentenced to five years at the Oklahoma State Penitentiary. Two years later, Swider told the warden he wanted to tell what he knew about Terry's disappearance, and then explained that he had seen Millard Vaught, W.L. Bates, and Will Stiles, fellow workers at the sawmill, murder Terry during a fight in August 1907. Louis McKibben, another worker at the sawmill, corroborated his confession. Vaught, Bates, and Stiles were charged with the murder on Nov. 18, 1911, and were tried at a sensational and extensive trial before Judge W.H.

Brown beginning May 7, 1912. The discovered skeleton was brought into court, and positively identified by Julia Knotts, Terry's aunt, who noted a front tooth with a gold filling, and an ankle bone scar from a childhood accident. Swider explained in detail how the three men murdered Terry after Vaughan accused him of lying about Vaughan's wife; Vaughan smashed his skull with a two-by-four and Bates and Stiles encouraged, then participated in the fray. Swider and McKibben said they were warned to keep quiet or they, too, would be slain. The defendants denied the charges, claiming that since Terry's health was poor he had headed South, saying goodbye to Vaughan and McKibben before leaving.

The statute of limitations made it impossible to try them for manslaughter, so they were tried for murder. The jury deliberated forty-eight hours, but could not agree, and the judge declared a mistrial.

The defendants were released from jail on bond. Stiles was tried alone, and acquitted. The jury ruled that Vaughan, Bates, and Stiles killed Terry, but that the crime was manslaughter, so they could not bring in a guilty verdict. The defendants, enraged at their loss of reputation, searched for Terry for five years. He was finally located in the Los Angeles County Hospital, confirming he had left Oklahoma because of his health. Confronted, Swider and McKibben pleaded guilty to perjury and were convicted, each given twenty-five year sentences. REF.: *CBA.*

Vaux, James Hardy, 1782-c.1851, Brit., theft-rob. An English thief, James Hardy Vaux, was transported three times to Australia for his crimes. His published memoirs give a record of the English underworld and of the conditions of penal life in the colonies. Vaux described the convict ships carrying prisoners in double irons as "a scene of misery." In Australia, Vaux, like other literate convicts, was able to improve the quality of his life by doing clerical service. He authored a vocabulary of convict's slang, called *Flash Language.*

REF.: *CBA;* Hunt, *A Dictionary of Rogues.*

Vaux, Roberts, 1786-1836, U.S., penal reformer. Philanthropist involved with prison reform who also was influential in setting up shelters and services for juvenile delinquents in 1826. REF.: *CBA.*

Vegnaduzzi, Andre, prom. 1960, Fr., rob.-mur. Angry at his parents for their rejection of the girl he wanted to marry, whom they considered too good for him, Andre Vegnaduzzi of Nancy, Fr., murdered them both with an iron and several other heavy objects. He then robbed the house and cleaned off his fingerprints. He was apprehended in Strasbourg, tried, and sent to prison. REF.: *CBA.*

Vehme, prom. 1919-24, Ger., war crimes. Designed to mimic medieval secret tribunals whose self-appointed judges claimed it was their right and duty to assassinate alleged traitors, the German Vehme organization was a training school for German nationalists who became officials in the Nazi party. The Vehme's first "official" murders were those of Rosa Luxembourg and Karl Liebknecht in 1919. The Vehme said they killed them for promoting a Communist revolution in Germany, but they were murdered because they denounced German war guilt and made strong appeals to abolish militarism.

Army officers and high officials of the new republic publicly condoned the Vehme murders, and often covered them up. Wilhelm Frick, chief of the Bavarian police administration, supported the Vehme and was later made Minister of the Interior by Adolf Hitler. After the war he was one of the war criminals tried, convicted, and hanged at Nuremberg. Many Vehme defenders surfaced later as leaders of the SS or SA, Nazi military organizations; many were made chiefs of police in Germany's largest cities. Between 1919-24, hundreds of people opposed to German militarism and nationalism were slain as "traitors forfeited to the Vehme."

By the second half of the 1920s, the reactionary German Supreme Court, the Reichsgericht in Leipzig, virtually took over the functions of the Vehme. Laws intended to protect the republic against national conspiracies were used to protect secret preparations for war, including major rearmament. Reporting on these activities was considered treason, and pacifist journalists and writers were tried and sentenced to prison terms, and often even killed. Carl von Ossietzky, awarded the Nobel Prize for his fight against the Nazis, was tortured and murdered in the concentration camps by the Reichsgericht. Also murdered under Vehme auspices was Rudolf Formis, who fled to Czechoslovakia in 1934 to broadcast anti-Nazi radio programs from a secret hideout in a hotel. See: **Formis, Rudolf; Frick, Wilhelm; Hitler, Adolf; Nuremberg Trials.**

REF.: Bornstein, *The Politics of Murder; CBA.*

Vela, Filemon Bartolome, 1935- , U.S., jur. Served as attorney to 107th district court in Cameron-Willacy County, Texas, from 1975-80. He was nominated to the southern district court of Texas by President Jimmy Carter in 1980. He also served as a law instructor at Texas Southmost College and as a criminal law instructor at Rio Grande Valley Police Academy from 1972. REF.: *CBA.*

Velasco Alvarado, Juan, 1910-77, Peru, rebel. Served as soldier and in 1965 commanded a division as general. He took over power as president from 1968-75, after ousting President Belaunde Terry. His government was later forced out of power by a military coup. REF.: *CBA.*

Velez, Luis S., 1949- , U.S., mur. On the night of Sept. 16, 1975, Manhattan police officers Sergeant Frederick Reddy and Andrew Glover were checking a car parked in front of one of the tenement buildings on East Fifth Street between avenues A and B. Luis S. Velez pulled out a loaded revolver and shot both officers before they could draw their guns. He later said that he was afraid they would arrest him on bank robbery charges. Manhattan district attorney Robert Morgenthau recommended that Velez be allowed to plead to lesser charges of second-degree murder, rather than face the death penalty if convicted. In requesting that Judge Burton B. Roberts of the State Supreme Court accept the plea, Assistant District Attorney Robert J. Lehner cited a June 1976 U.S. Supreme Court ruling which raised questions about the constitutionality of the mandatory statute in New York which demands execution in cases of the murder of prison guards or police officers.

At a two-hour hearing, during which Velez repeatedly laughed whenever the crime was mentioned, Justice Roberts explained, "..It is in the public's interest to accept the plea." The prosecutor feared that the state's new death penalty law might be invalid or that a first-degree murder conviction would have resulted in a costly retrial. Velez remained standing with his arms folded throughout most of the hearing and told Roberts he shot the officers after they called him racist names. Criticism of the reduced charges plea came from the officers widows and from state Senator James Buckley who called it "an affront to every policeman, every wife of a policeman, and every widow of an officer slain in the line of duty." On Nov. 22, 1976, Justice Roberts sentenced Velez to a 25-year-to-life jail term. When Velez told Roberts in court, "I have no regrets," Roberts called the convicted man a "lying, despicable, cowardly, brutal, thieving human being." Velez maintained that he had been the victim of the inequitable rules of a "police state," adding, "If I don't get dignity, I take it." District Attorney Morgenthau recommended that Velez never be granted parole.

REF.: *CBA;* Godwin, *Murder U.S.A.*

Velgo, Marie Havlick, See: **Cerny, Wenzel.**

Vella, Joseph, prom. 1782-96, Si., hoax. Visiting the monks at Palermo, Si., in 1782, the chaplain of the Knights of Malta, Joseph Vella, expressed his hope to some day discover Arabic writings that would complete the history of their order. Seven years later, Vella published six volumes of *The Diplomatic Code of Sicily Concerning the Governance of Arabia, Published Under the Studied Guidance of Alfonso Airoldi.* The books, purporting to be an Arabic translation of seventeen of Livy's last books, contained a complex history of Sicily. Visiting Sicily, a German orientalist named Hager looked at the books and declared them phony. Vella was exonerated by memorizing a few passages from his Italian translation of the supposed Arabic tomes, and reciting them before a commission. His ruse succeeded because the listeners did not speak Arabic. A later group of Arabic scholars examined his work and announced that the story they contained was the tale of Muhammad, not Sicily's history. Vella confessed in 1796 and was sentenced to fifteen years in prison for his hoax. REF.: *CBA;* MacDougall, *Hoaxes.*

Velleff, Randy, 1959- , and **Cecconi, Patrick**, 1944- , U.S., pris. esc.-rob. On New Year's Eve 1982, two convicts threw a 40-foot rope of knotted bed sheets over a wall and escaped from the Stateville Correctional Center in Joliet, Ill. Randy Velleff, twenty-seven, and Patrick Cecconi, thirty-nine, were the first escapees from the maximum security prison since 1941. Both were missing from the 9 p.m. bed check on Dec. 31, 1982, and prison investigators believed they had hidden inside a prison wall before making their escape at around 12:20 a.m. on Jan. 1, 1983. Velleff had been sentenced to seven to twenty years in prison for armed robbery, and a fifteen-year sentence for a robbery in Nevada. Cecconi had been sentenced to a forty-year-term in October 1981 for armed robbery, with an upcoming release in April 2001. Five people were charged with aiding Velleff and Cecconi in their escape.

The Apprehension Squad, a relatively unknown branch of the Illinois Department of Corrections, tracked the men down in two months. Tracing Velleff's family tree, investigators flew to the home of a distant relative of his in Dallas, Texas, and found a receipt issued to Velleff by the Bartender's Academy of Texas, where he had been studying for two weeks. Apprehension Squad supervisor Michael Kraft said the fugitive "was caught completely off guard in a bartender's classroom."

Cecconi was flushed out of hiding in a woods near Charlotte, N.C., after the squad learned that the convict was receiving funds wired to him in Charlotte. About twelve FBI agents and local police officers surrounded Cecconi at a Western Union office, but he broke away and escaped in a car. After he abandoned the vehicle in the woods, he was hunted down by bloodhounds. REF.: *CBA.*

Venegas, Juan, 1950- , U.S., (wrong. convict.) mur. Convicted in California of first-degree murder, Juan Venegas received a life sentence. In December 1971, Venegas left Colorado to visit Lawrence Reyes, a childhood friend. Reyes committed the murder in another house while Venegas was asleep. Both men were arrested and charged with the murder. Although Reyes exonerated Venegas of the murder, a bartender, who later said police told him to lie, testified that both men had been in his bar shortly before the slaying. Venegas spent two and a half years in jail. In 1974, the state supreme court reversed Venegas' conviction because the evidence against him was not sufficient to sustain the conviction. He was released and prosecutors made no attempt at a retrial.

In 1980, Venegas won a $1 million suit against Long Beach City for false imprisonment, on the grounds that his conviction was secured partially through false testimony resulting from police misconduct. Presiding Los Angeles County Court judge Ronald E. Swearinger explained, "I think the jury was horrified at what happened to this man." The jurors, in voting unanimously for the judgement, "wanted to show there was no doubt that Mr. Venegas wasn't involved in the murder." Venegas hugged the jurors in the emotional moments following the verdict. The judgment was reversed later on the grounds of governmental immunity, but in 1986 Venegas was awarded a judgment of more than $2 million for his false conviction. REF.: *CBA.*

Venizelos, Eleutherios, 1864-1936, Gr., rebel. Held position as premier from 1910-15, in 1924, from 1928-32, and in 1933. Beginning in 1933, he headed the opposition to the government, and in 1935 he initiated an unsuccessful navy and military rebellion. He was exiled, court-martialed, and sentenced to death. Later in 1935 when King George II returned to power, he was pardoned. REF.: *CBA.*

Vera Gerard Case, The, 1937, a novel by Joseph Cottin Cooke. The unsolved murder of New York call girl Vivian Gordon (U.S., 1931). See: **Greenberg, Sam.** REF.: *CBA.*

Vera Serafin, Aldo, c.1932-76, P.R., polit., (unsolv.) assass. On the night of Oct. 25, 1976, Cuban Aldo Vera Serafin was shot and killed while walking along a suburban street in San Juan, P.R. His companion, José Rodriquez Gómez, was wounded by the shots fired from a passing car. Two of the bullets fired struck Vera Serafin, killing him instantly. Since both men were prominent exiles from Cuba, the murder most likely was politically motivated.

In 1958, Vera Serafin became a member of Fidel Castro's Twenty-sixth of July Movement which overthrew the dictatorship of Fulgencio Batista. When Castro came into power in January 1959, he appointed Vera Serafin head of the Cuban police technical investigations department. Due to Castro's increasingly socialist doctrines, however, the two parted ways and Vera Serafin eventually fled the country in the early 1960s. In Puerto Rico, the exiled Vera Serafin diligently fought Castro and was involved in the Fourth Republic, an organization with links to Orlando Bosch. REF.: *CBA.*

Vercingetorix, d.46 B.C., Roman., rebel. Gallic leader of Arverni who headed the revolt that led to Gallic War. REF.: *CBA.*

Verdung, Michel, and **Mentot, Philibert**, and **Bourgot, Pierre** (AKA: **Big Peter**), d.1521, Fr., witchcraft. At a French witchcraft trial, Michel Verdung, Philibert Mentot, and Pierre Bourgot were tried together in December 1521 by the Dominican friar, Jean Boin, who was also the Inquisitor General of Besançon. A man traveling through the Poligny district claimed he had been attacked by a wolf, and found that the wounded animal's trail led to a hut where Verdung's wife was tending to her husband's wounds. Verdung confessed that he had been involved in Bourgot's pact with the devil. Bourgot said that in 1502, a storm had scattered his flock, and that he had met three black horsemen while searching for the sheep. One of these horsemen, named "Moyset", said that if Bourgot would serve him as his master, he would help him. Pierre said yes, and found his sheep. Soon after, he discovered that the stranger was a minion of the devil. Two years later, when Bourgot returned to Christianity, another servant of the devil—this time it was Verdung—made Bourgot honor his pact with the devil. Verdung gave Bourgot a magic ointment, and Bourgot became a wolf.

Under torture, Bourgot confessed to assaulting a 7-year-old boy, eating a 4-year-old girl, and breaking the neck of a 9-year-old girl before devouring her. All three men said they had mated with wolves and enjoyed it. All three men were burned as witches. REF.: *CBA.*

Vere, Robert de (Earl of Oxford, Duke of Ireland), 1362-92, Ire., treas. Close friend of Richard II. He was accused of treason by Thomas of Woodstock while Richard was temporarily out of power, but Vere was able to escape punishment with Richard's help. REF.: *CBA.*

Vereneseneckockockhoff, Albert Frederick George (AKA: **Hoff**), prom. 1897, U.S., mur. Albert Frederick George Vereneseneckockockhoff, known as Hoff, was called by Mary Clute to help her lay some carpet in her new home, which she decided to move into on Dec. 12, 1897. Buying the carpeting, by the upholsterer told Clute that he would not sell her the lining unless she gave him the work of laying the carpet. Clute agreed, and told Hoff the next morning, when he came to work, that she was sorry to inconvenience him; she asked him to return the next morning, on Dec. 15, to help her hang her pictures. When Hoff showed up the next day, Clute was not in. Hoff rang her downstairs neighbor, L.A. Legg, and asked her if she knew where Clute may have gone.

Hoff then went to Page Street and met Clute at her former home in the late afternoon. She said she was very sorry, and asked him to come the next day. Clute announced to a neighbor, in Hoff's presence, that she was going to her new house, and then left the handyman to talk with the neighbor about some other possible work. Hoff then left again to see Clute.

At around 4 p.m., Legg saw Hoff ring Clute's bell and go up. Soon after, sounds were heard coming from the upstairs apartment, and Legg and her father-in-law watched Hoff come out, brush by them without responding to a question, and walk away with his bag of tools. Clute's mutilated body was found upstairs. All her jewelry and other valuables were untouched. Reading about the crime the next day, Hoff turned himself in to Chief Lees, explaining that he had been there but knew nothing about a murder. He was tried on Mar. 15, 1898, found Guilty on Apr. 2, and was sentenced to hang. Attorney William Schooler appealed the case on a technicality. Hoff was granted a new trial before Judge Carroll Cook on Dec. 3, 1900, and was again found Guilty of murder. He was sentenced to life in prison. REF.: *CBA.*

Verger, Jean-Louis, 1826-57, Fr., mur. Jean-Louis Verger, a priest who had a family history of insanity, was at odds with his superiors. He denied the Immaculate Conception and accused at least one superior of homosexual advances. The purity of Verger's celibacy was questionable.

Finally, after removal from the priesthood, Verger sought revenge. On Jan. 3, 1857, Verger stabbed and killed 65-year-old Marie-Dominique-Auguste Sibour, archbishop of Paris, while he was conducting mass. At his trial, Verger continually disrupted the proceedings and had to be removed. He was brought to trial on Jan. 17, found Guilty, and sent to the guillotine on Jan. 31, 1857.

REF.: *CBA;* Constant, *La Clef des grands mystères;* Fouquier, *Causes célèbres de tous les peuples;* Heppenstall, *The Sex War and Others;* Kershaw, *Murder in France;* Poujoulat, *Vie de Mgr. Sibour;* Verger, *Réfexions impartiales d'un auditeur aux débats de la cour d'assises de Seine-et-Marne, séant à Melun le 15 novembre 1856;* Vervost, *Autographe de Louis Verger, rectifiant quelques assertions et justifiant le clergé;* Williams, *Manners and Murders in the World of Louis-Napoleon.*

Vergniaud, Pierre Victurnien, 1753-93, Fr., treas. Politician who advocated revolution. He was one of the leaders of the Girondists and a member of the National Convention. He was guillotined. REF.: *CBA.*

Vermilye, Claudius I., 1931- , U.S., porn.-pros. An Episcopal priest, the Reverend Claudius I. Vermilye established the Tennessee Boys Farm in 1971, ostensibly as a sheltering environment. The establishment in Alton, Tenn., operated for five years, selling young boys, some as young as eleven, through photographs, slide shows, and films, to a network of "sponsors" throughout the nation. Vermilye, who had served as pastor of the Alto parish from 1958-62, operated one of the largest homosexual pornography rings in the nation.

Tried in June 1977, Vermilye took the stand in his own defense, denying that he had committed homosexual acts with the boys, or that he had them pose for pornographic pictures. The prosecution produced close to 2,000 photographs and thirteen letters which were written to a Delaware sponsor in 1976, offering $25 slide sets and advertising the skills of two 15-year-old farm residents. The priest then admitted, on June 3, that he had taken nude photographs of the boys, including his own son, but claimed he had not had sexual relations with any of them. The divorced father of five explained that he sent the photographs to members of his ministry in order to help them abandon their homosexuality. The prosecution's case, headed by District Attorney General Bill Pope, produced farm residents who testified that Vermilye seduced boys as young as eleven, and brought in sponsors from Florida to Michigan who testified that their tax-free contributions gained them pornography and even orgies which Vermilye arranged for them.

Vermilye, who liked to boast of coming from a wealthy New York family, could not post his $20,000 bond. The jury deliberated for slightly more than an hour, and found Vermilye Guilty of seven counts in five indictments which charged him with committing homosexual acts with the boys and with aiding and abetting crimes against nature by filming them. In pronouncing sentence, Circuit Court judge Thomas Greer explained that he had considered the fact that the crimes occurred over a four-year period, and that profit was one of the motivations in the case. Greer consolidated the twelve sentences, which totalled 105 to 165 years, into three groups, running twenty-five to forty years. County Juvenile judge Roy Tripps, who took custody of several of the youths in November 1976, said he felt that justice had been done by the jury. Judge Greer said, "The disturbing part to me is the mess we're left with. These boys are wrecked for life." REF.: *CBA.*

Verney, Sir **Francis**, prom. 1600s, Alg., pir. Francis Verney was forced into a childhood marriage by his stepmother and was tricked out of his inheritance. Entering the Foreign Legion of Muley Sidan, pretender to the throne of Morocco, Verney reportedly became a pirate in Algiers after Sidan death in 1607, and plundered English merchant ships "from Plymouth and Poole." The gentleman adventurer was captured by a corsair from Sicily and spent two years as a galley slave before he escaped with the help of an English Jesuit. Verney died at thirty-one in a hospital after enlisting in the Sicilian army.

REF.: *CBA;* Mitchell, *Pirates.*

Vernon, Hazel, See: **De Vere, Pearl.**

Vernon, Roger (Robert, AKA: **Charles Lacroix, Georges Lacroix)**, prom. 1936-37, Brit.-Fr., mur. On Jan. 24, 1936, the body of 56-year-old Max Kassel, also known as Red Maxie or Scarface, was discovered by a carpenter riding his bicycle outside St. Albans, Hertfordshire. The maker's labels had been removed from his clothing and, although no money was in his pockets, an expensive ring remained on his finger. Marks on his knuckles and face indicated that he had struggled for his life. Scotland Yard Inspector Sharpe obtained a photograph and fingerprints of the man. He had been both a pimp and a white slave trader in earlier years, and owned a small jewelry shop which served as a front for his fencing. Under the alias of "Allard", Kassel had pretended to be a French Canadian. Scotland Yard was soon on the trail of Roger Vernon, an ex-convict who had some business dealings with Kassel. The two had fought about the debt on the Jan. 23, 1936. Vernon's girlfriend, Suzanne Bertron, a prostitute, was implicated in the crime; it was later deduced that the murder had taken place in her London apartment in the Soho district. Vernon and Bertron were arrested at a Paris Hotel, where they had gone after they fled Great Newport Street. Both were tried in Paris, because of a French law which prohibited their extradition. On Apr. 29, the Paris jury deliberated for forty minutes before finding Vernon Guilty of premeditated murder but with extenuating circumstances. He was sentenced to ten years hard labor. Bertron was acquitted on charges of being an accessory.

REF.: *CBA;* Sanders, *Murder Behind the Bright Lights;* Shew, *A Companion to Murder.*

***Veronica* Mutineers**, prom. 1902, Brit., mut.-mur. In October 1902, the barque *Veronica* set sail on a voyage filled with mutiny and murder. Under the command of Captain Alexander Shaw, the *Veronica,* with a crew of twelve, set sail from Ship Island in the Gulf of Mexico for Montevideo. The captain and his officers were known as rough taskmasters of the old school. The remainder of the crew included Gustav Rau and Otto Monsson, the ringleaders of the impending mutiny. Their intentions were clear when they both brought guns on board. Another rough character, Willem Smith and 19-year-old Harry Flohr, eventually joined the Germans in the mutiny.

Although it definitely was not a happy ship, things went well until they were becalmed in the Atlantic off Brazil. On Dec. 8, 1902, after a minor altercation, First Officer Alexander MacLeod was beaten and thrown overboard. After holding the captain and second mate hostage for several days, the men killed them and put the other four seamen overboard. That left Rau, Monsson, Smith, Flohr and the ship's cook. After setting the ship afire, they set sail in a lifeboat and were picked up by a passing ship which took them to a Brazilian port. From there they boarded a British ship, and on the way back to England Harry Flohr and the ship's cook confessed. The remaining three mutineers were tried for mutiny and found Guilty. Monsson was let off because of his youth, but Rau and Smith were hanged at Liverpool's Walton Prison on June 2, 1903.

REF.: *CBA;* Shew, *A Second Companion to Murder.*

Verres, Gaius, d.43 B.C., Roman., polit. corr. Held positions in Sicily as Roman magistrate in 74 B.C. and as governor from 73-71 B.C. He plundered and unfairly taxed citizens and subjected them to extortion. He was tried in 70 B.C. but fled into exile. He was later killed on the command of Mark Antony. REF.: *CBA.*

South African prime minister Hendrik Verwoerd and his assassin Dimitri Stifianos.

Verwoerd, Dr. **Hendrik Frensch**, 1901-66, S. Afri., prime minister, assass. Prime minister of South Africa since 1951, Dr. Hendrik Frensch Verwoerd designed the system of apartheid—literally, "apartness"—that separated the country's 3.2 million whites from the 12 million blacks. Early in his reign, Verwoerd had been considered an extremist who was leading South Africa into disaster with his policy of white supremacy. But by the time he was murdered on Sept. 6, 1966, Verwoerd had convinced many that his racist policies were visionary, and he was considered reasonable and even moderate in his views.

An attempt was made on Verwoerd's life in 1960, when South Africa was in a state of emergency following riots in Sharpeville, where police killed sixty-seven blacks. Verwoerd dismissed the incident as "a periodic phenomenon." Verwoerd, fifty-eight at the time, was in Johannesburg attending a prize cattle show on Apr. 9, 1960, honoring the fiftieth anniversary of South Africa's nationhood. He had just given a speech when David Pratt, a 54-year-old white farmer, raced up to the podium and fired twice with a .32-caliber automatic. Pratt, who had no involvement in politics, was seized by guards as Verwoerd was rushed to the hospital for emergency surgery. As racial tensions, already high, reignited in the wake of the attempted assassination of the National Party leader, Foreign Minister Eric Louw announced to a radio interviewer, "We will not hand over control of South Africa to a native majority. South Africa has gotten used to being slandered in the past fourteen years."

On Sept. 26, 1960, Pratt was declared mentally unfit to stand trial on attempted murder charges. A state-appointed psychiatrist testified in Supreme Court in Pretoria that Pratt's mental condition had deteriorated as the result of epilepsy; the court ruled that Pratt would be detained in jail until Governor Charles R. Swart ordered him committed to an institution. On Oct. 2, 1961, Pratt was found dead, hanging from a twisted bed sheet in his cell at the Bloemfontein mental hospital where he had resided since September.

In 1962, a reporter asked Verwoerd if he was afraid of another attack. The prime minister said he was not, saying he did not believe anyone wanted to kill him, adding, "If someone really wants to kill you, it's not a very hard job." On Sept. 6, 1966, just after 2:00 p.m., as the prime champion of apartheid sat on a bench in the South African Parliament, Dimitri Stifianos, a 45-year-old white South African, stabbed him to death. A temporary messenger, Stifianos had complained to co-workers that Verwoerd was doing too much for non-whites and not enough for "poor whites." Stifianos, later judged insane, did not stand trial.

REF.: Bell, *Assassin; CBA.*

Verzeni, Vincent, prom. 1867-71, Italy, mur. During the period of 1867-71 in Italy, Vincent Verzeni committed vampiric assaults on a number of women and attempted to murder several others. His first victim was Johanna Motta, a 14-year-old girl who left for a neighboring village one morning and never returned. Her corpse was discovered near her village in a field, naked and mutilated, torn by her slayer's teeth. Eight months after Motta's murder, a 28-year-old woman named Frigeni was found by her husband, who searched for her when she did not return by nightfall from working in the fields. Frigeni's naked and mutilated body showed marks on the neck where she had been strangled by a thong; her flesh was torn by her killer's teeth.

When Maria Previtali, Verzeni's 19-year-old cousin, went into the fields the day after Frigeni's death, she noticed Verzeni following her, and was afraid, knowing that he had been in trouble several times for trying to choke women. She managed to fight him off when he attacked her, and she immediately reported the incident. After long questioning, Verzeni, twenty-two, made a detailed confession. He explained that he received sexual satisfaction from choking his victims, grasping them by the throat, biting their necks, and sucking their blood. He had often allowed victims to live, but in both cases of murder, his sexual reaction was delayed and he continued to strangle the women until they died. Verzeni described feeling satisfied and remorseless after his acts. At twelve he first became aware of experiencing sexual pleasure from inflicting pain when he was wringing the necks of chickens. Recognizing that he would repeat his offenses if released, he was in agreement with the court's verdict that he should be imprisoned for life.

REF.: *CBA;* Masters, *Perverse Crimes in History.*

Vesalius, Andreas, 1514-64, Belg., anatomist. Contradicting Galenic tradition, one of the first to dissect a human body for anatomical study. The Inquisition sentenced him to death for his dissections, but he was allowed to make a pilgrimage to commute the sentence. He wrote *De Humani Corporis Fabrica* in 1543. REF.: *CBA.*

Vesco, Robert Lee, 1935- , U.S., fraud. Until the Wall Street insider trading scandals broke in the 1980s, revealing a new generation of white-collar con men, Robert Lee Vesco was considered by many to be the top financial swindler of modern times. Vesco's ties extended from the board rooms of corporate America to the Nixon White House. Even while in exile, this former "boy wonder" of international finance seemed to enjoy the protection of the government at the very highest levels.

Vesco, the son of a Detroit auto worker, dropped out of high school at sixteen to work as an apprentice in an auto body shop. Later in his career, while working as an automotive engineer, Vesco designed the one-piece aluminum grille, an innovation roundly criticized by consumers and insurance adjustors, because, according to its inventor, "You had to pull the whole damn thing out to put in a whole new one and it ran you three times as much money!" In 1957, Vesco left Detroit to accept a position as an administrative assistant in a New York-based engineering and chemical company. Vesco gained a toehold in the investment world when he bought up two New Jersey manufacturing companies in the early 1960s. By the middle of the decade he had merged them into a major consortium known as International Controls Corporation (ICC). Vesco's October 1967 buy out of Fairfield Aviation was the first of many mergers and acquisitions that established ICC as a major player in world markets. Within three years, company profits climbed from $1.3 million to more than $100 million.

In 1971, Vesco assumed control of Investor's Overseas Services Ltd. (IOS Ltd.), a Geneva-based international mutual fund empire headed up by the enigmatic Bernard Cornfield, himself the target of a Securities and Exchange Commission (SEC) probe. Vesco's tactics also left him open to scrutiny from the SEC. As early as 1971, White House counsel John Dean warned President Richard Nixon about the "potential embarrassments" it might cause the administration if the press were to make an issue about the fact that the president's nephew, Donald, was employed by Vesco. Dean's concerns were not unfounded. In 1971 Vesco and two associates were jailed in Switzerland after misusing an IOS Ltd. shareholder's stock. Vesco's people contacted attorney Harry Sears, New Jersey State Senate majority leader, and chairman of the local committee to reelect Nixon. Sears got in touch with Attorney General John Mitchell, who placed a discreet call to the U.S. embassy in Berne. Richard Vine of the diplomatic corps worked through a CIA operative in Berne who negotiated with Swiss intelligence officers to do something on Vesco's behalf. The prisoner was released on a $125,000 bail and left Geneva the next day. The grateful Vesco paid Sears a $10,000 "legal fee" and then offered $500,000 in up-front money to Maurice H. Stans, the chief fundraiser for Nixon's 1972 reelection campaign. Stans accepted only $250,000, part of which went to the Watergate "plumbers" as payment for their covert raid on Democratic campaign headquarters in June 1972. Stans and Mitchell were indicted in New York for their role in the affair but were acquitted in 1974.

Meanwhile, Vesco had further legal problems to contend with. In November 1972, the SEC charged him with embezzling $224 million in cash from the overseas mutual funds belonging to investors of IOS Ltd. On the heels of the SEC investigation, the Justice Department indicted Vesco for making illegal campaign contributions to Stans and the Committee to Re-elect, as a form of bribery in order to influence a favorable outcome of the government probe into his financial affairs. Facing the possibility of a lengthy jail sentence, Vesco fled the country. He settled in San Jose, Costa Rica, where he remained a fugitive from justice for the next five years, despite persistent State Department efforts to have him extradited.

Super swindler Robert Lee Vesco.

A month before Vesco was scheduled to become eligible for citizenship, a Costa Rican national named Gerardo Wenceslao Villalobos positioned himself in front of the millionaire's posh suburban home and randomly fired a clip of bullets through the windows. "You do not pay taxes, you are corrupting my country!" he screamed. Vesco survived the attack, but a week later on June 9, 1977, President Daniel Oduber ordered him to leave the country. The fugitive financier headed for the Bahamas where he was reportedly reunited with a vast secret fortune estimated at $50 million. While traveling abroad Robert Vesco has been rumored to be involved in a number of lucrative ventures, and has accrued a secondary fortune through the sales of international arms to third world countries, including Libya. At present he resides in Cuba at a lavishly appointed home complete with private yacht and airplane.

REF.: *CBA;* Fried, *The Rise and Fall of the Jewish Gangster in America;* Herzog, *Vesco;* Unger, *FBI.*

Vesey Uprising, 1822, U.S., (wrong. convict.) consp. On June 21, 1822, Denmark Vesey, a free black man, was arrested and charged with plotting a slave insurrection in Charleston, S.C. The preemptory arrest was made after a local Charleston slave, Devany Prioleau, warned his owner in late May that another slave, William Paul, told him of a supposed slave insurrection scheduled for June 16. Both Prioleau and Paul were arrested and Paul implicated several others in the plot, all of whom also were arrested. On June 14 one of the arrested men corroborated Paul's story. A hastily convened court met and heard secret testimony from those detained. Vesey, along with five others, was convicted of "crimes of the blackest hue," and summarily hanged on July 2, each proclaiming their innocence.

The court hearings and the hangings sent all of Charleston into a panic. All blacks became potential assassins, while blacks themselves feared vigilante reprisals. More slaves and free blacks were arrested, and the court grew fanatic in its pursuit of revolutionaries, ordering the hanging of twenty-two supposed insurrectionists in one day. It also ordered the arrest of more than 100 persons and the hanging of thirty-seven slaves and free blacks without a trial by jury. Men were found Guilty without a shred of evidence except forced confessions through torture and the testimony of secret witnesses. One witness, Pharo, who turned state's evidence to save his life, was executed along with other alleged conspirators. Then a canny slave owner brought two slaves to the court from outside Charleston. When they dressed in simple country cloths, the court decided they were not insurrectionists and released them. The owner then washed and dressed the two in finer clothes and again presented them to the court. This time secret witnesses identified the two, and the court convicted them of conspiracy. The owner thereupon exposed the court's false witnesses and the witchhunt was over. More than 100 slaves convicted of conspiracy were released from jail, though the court ordered the deportation of thirty-seven of them. Many scholars who have studied the events in 1822 doubt that an insurrection ever existed. The court justified its actions to the governor by writing, "The terror of example we thought would be sufficiently operative by the number of criminals sentenced to death."

REF.: Aptheker, *American Negro Slave Revolts;* ____, *Negro Slave Revolts in the United States, 1526-1860;* Carroll, *Slave Insurrections in the United States, 1800-1865; CBA;* Coffin, *An Account of Some of the Principal Slave Insurrections;* Halasz, *The Rattling Chains: Slave Unrest and Revolt in the Antebellum South;* Hamilton, *Negro Plot;* James, *A History of Negro Revolt;* Kennedy and Parker, *An Official Report of the Trials of Sundry Negroes Charged with an Attempt to Raise an Insurrection in the State of South Carolina;* Lofton, *Insurrection in South Carolina: The Turbulent World of Denmark Vesey.*

Vétsera, Marie, See: **Rudolph, Archduke.**

Veza, Daniel T., 1917- , U.S., law enfor. off. An officer in Indianapolis, Ind., Daniel T. Veza first joined that force in September 1942, serving for a year and two months, until he was detailed to the armed services in November 1943. After receiving an honorable discharge, Veza was reassigned to active duty in November 1945, and was promoted to acting detective sergeant in March 1948. A full detective sergeant by May 1953, Veza continued to advance, going from lieutenant to captain, and becoming an inspector in December 1958. He received several commendations for initiative, courage, bravery, and alertness from Chief Robert E. Reilly and Acting Chief Carl C. Schmidt. In April 1963, Veza was appointed acting deputy chief in charge of Direction and Management of the Uniformed Division. Promoted to acting chief of police on Jan. 5, 1967, by Mayor John J. Barton, Veza became chief of police on Jan. 17, 1967, and was demoted one year later, on Feb. 25, 1968, to captain of police. Veza retired from the Indianapolis Police Department on Apr. 2, 1968. REF.: *CBA.*

Viau, Théophile de, 1590-1626, Fr., banish. Helped write *Parnasse Satirique* in 1622, for which he was sentenced to death. The sentence was commuted and he was banished. REF.: *CBA.*

Vicars, Henry Edward (AKA: **Flannelfoot, Henry Williams**), 1888-1942, Brit., burg. England's greatest burglar, Henry Edward Vicars is believed to have committed over a thousand burglaries. He never used violence or did damage to the houses he was burglarizing. He was a meticulous and highly skilled craftsman, obviously the master of his trade, and did not associate with known criminals.

Although he was first arrested in 1911, Vicars did not fully start his career in crime until after WWI. He developed a technique of targeting neighborhoods and homes on the outskirts of London. Usually on weekends, he would travel by bicycle, tram, or subway to and from his destinations. He would enter a number of different homes in one neighborhood, never leaving fingerprints. Sometimes he wore heavy socks or cloth over his shoes so as to not leave tracks and to muffle his footsteps. This practice earned him the nickname of "Flannelfoot."

Scotland Yard worked for years trying to track Vicars down. Finally on a tip concerning a woman he was living with (he was using the alias Henry Williams at the time), they determined that he was their man. Using an elaborate plan of constant surveillance, the police were finally able to apprehend him in 1937 as he left the scene of what was to be his last burglary. He pleaded guilty to a number of specific burglaries and was sentenced to five years in prison. He died shortly after his release in 1942.

British burglar Henry Edward "Flannelfoot" Vicars.

REF.: *CBA;* Scott, *The Concise Encyclopedia of Crime and Criminals;* ____, *Scotland Yard.*

Vicars, John, d.1750, Brit., mur. The son of a farmer, John Vicars was born in Dodington in the Isle of Ely. At fourteen he was apprenticed to the Earl of Leicester's gardener. He completed his apprenticeship and was working as a journeyman, but quit after getting involved with a married woman whose husband swore revenge. Vicars then worked for another gardener at Kensington, and then enlisted as a sailor on the naval warship *Exeter.* After his brief naval career, he hooked up with a gang of smugglers from Sussex, was arrested, sent to Newark Prison, tried, and acquitted. After his release, he worked as a gardener for a botanist named Millar, leaving that job because of his suspected involvement with another woman. Vicars then returned to his birthplace and married. Living unhappily with his chronically ill wife, he left to serve briefly again as a soldier; within a year of his return his wife died. The following year he remarried, but his wife, Mary Hainsworth, tired of their fights, soon returned to her mother's home.

One day soon after, Vicars visited his wife, offering fruit as a token of affection. His wife, however, heeding her mother, went after her husband with a knife. Vicars escaped, but the two women swore out a warrant for his arrest. Before Vicars could sell his possessions and leave town, he saw her again. Approaching her, apparently to embrace her, he cut her throat. When she cried out, he said, "Molly, 'tis now too late, you should have been ruled in time." Vicars ran back into the street, shouting for someone to arrest him, threatening that he might cause more harm if they did not. A man named Thomas Boone took his arm and Vicars at once surrendered. In prison he claimed that, although he loved his wife, she provoked him so that he could not let her live, nor could he live without her. He said he had intended to kill himself as well, and would do it all over again. Vicars was executed at Ely on Nov. 7, 1750.

REF.: *CBA;* Mitchell, *The Newgate Calendar.*

Viccei, Valerio, 1956- , Brit., rob. Valerio Viccei, thirty-four, was a folk hero of sorts in his hometown of Ascoli, Italy, south of Bologna. He began his criminal career there at sixteen; by twenty years of age, the charming and intelligent Viccei was known as a local godfather, a ruthless manipulator who rarely took part in robberies himself, but made others carry out his plans. Viccei fled Italy in 1985 when he was temporarily released after robbery and arms offense convictions. In London, he lived life in the fast lane with numerous parties, women, and expensive cars. When Italian police informed Scotland Yard that they believed Viccei was in London, an attempt was made to arrest him. Stopped by officers, Viccei went back to his own car—to turn off his car telephone, he explained—climbed out another door, and fled.

Viccei, who said he wanted to be the best in the business, partnered with Parvez Latif in Spring 1987. Heavily in debt, Latif was unable to repay any of the loans he had obtained from friends and family to open his business, a safety deposit box center in Knightbridge. Viccei offered a solution. Latif raised his insurance from £1 to £3.5. On July 17, 1987, Latif was the only staff member on duty when Viccei and an accomplice arrived. Pretending to be customers, they brought out guns and overpowered the guards while Latif acted out his part as victim. After the security guards were locked away, Latif helped the robbers empty 120 boxes. The haul was estimated by Viccei to have been about £40 million, while police valued it at £30 million.

Scotland Yard's "Operation Crest" investigation found a single fingerprint inside a vault and traced it to Viccei, who they tracked down at the Whites Hotel in Bayswater. Viccei was preparing to fly to Columbia, but had delayed his departure in order to ship his new £85,000 Ferrari with him. Police rammed the car as Viccei tried to escape. Inside the black Ferrari they found about £2 million in jewelry. Viccei told the Scotland Yard officers, "It's only a game. You have won." Viccei and his accomplices were found Guilty of robbery on Jan. 30, 1989. In sentencing Viccei, Judge Lymbery told him, "I have seen in this court a man of charm, courtesy, and substantial ability. However, these and other qualities serve to make you a dangerous man." Viccei was sentenced to twenty-two years in jail. Latif was sentenced to an eighteen-year term, and Poole was given sixteen years in jail. On May 19, 1989, Viccei was sentenced for raids on five London banks; all had occurred prior to the Knightsbridge safe deposit theft. In confessing to the bank raids, Viccei reiterated his philosophy. "I think life is a game. Once you realize you have lost it is silly to give aggravation to the winners. It is better for me to clarify all my responsibilities for what I have done in this country." According to prosecuting attorney Nigel Sweeney, Viccei and an accomplice stole about £292,000 in the five robberies. An additional seventeen years were added to the sentence Viccei was already serving for the Knightsbridge heist. REF.: *CBA.*

Vicksburg Gamblers, 1835, U.S., mob vio. In the 1830s, citizens of Mississippi River towns were anxious to rid their towns of faro dealers and other gamblers. In July 1935, the angry citizens of Vicksburg, Miss., posted public notices ordering all gamblers to leave town within twenty-four hours or face the consequences. Five gamblers braved it out, but more than 100 citizens surrounded their house. A brief but deadly gunfight followed in which one of the brazen gamblers was wounded and Dr. Hugh S. Bodley, a Vicksburg citizen, was killed. The incensed townspeople then stormed the house, seized the gamblers, and promptly hanged them from the town scaffold. By such legal and illegal means gamblers likewise were ousted from New Orleans, La.; Clinton, Iowa; Natchez, Miss.; Louisville, Ky.; Cincinnati, Ohio; and Chicago. REF.: *CBA.*

Vicksburg Race Riot, 1874, U.S., mob vio. During the Reconstruction period after the Civil War many acts of civil violence were suffered by blacks and their supporters. The first major riot occurred in Memphis, Tenn., in May 1866. With permission of the state authorities, blacks then formed a militia and other less structured groups to defend themselves, which prompted further violence from whites.

The 1874 race riot in Vicksburg, Miss., was one instance of black resistance and white retaliation. The white citizens of

Vicksburg forced the black Republican sheriff Peter Crosby to resign at gunpoint. Crosby gathered blacks in his defense and on Dec. 7, 125 blacks, most of them armed, marched into the city. A look-out spotted the men as they approached, and the city was placed under martial law with an experienced Confederate officer, Colonel Horace H. Miller, in command. Miller immediately identified Crosby as the leader of the blacks and arrested him. Miller then drove all blacks off the city's streets with extreme brutality. Then, with 100 well-armed men, Miller confronted the group of black men, whose leader, Andrew Owens, said the march was in response to an order from Sheriff Crosby. Owens won permission to visit Crosby in his jail cell, during which the former sheriff told Owens and the marchers to go home. Owens returned to the group of blacks and persuaded them to disperse. As they left Vicksburg, white soldiers on horses opened fire, killing eight or nine blacks. The whites looted in the black sections of town, then spilled into the countryside and killed blacks indiscriminately. Two whites, Brown and Vaughn, were killed in the riot, and several blacks were lynched in retaliation. Not counting the number of blacks missing or lynched outside the city, twenty-nine blacks were murdered in Vicksburg. REF.: *CBA.*

Victor, Claude (Claude Victor Perrin), 1766-1841, Fr., milit. Soldier and commander of army forces in Spain in Peninsular War. During the Hundred Days, he supported the Bourbons. When officers were tried for treason during the Hundred Days, he was the presiding officer and he voted to sentence Michel Ney to death. REF.: *CBA.*

Victor, Sara M., b.1827, U.S., mur. Born in southern Ohio, 39-year-old Sara Victor was a divorcee with an unsavory reputation. Living with her brother, William Parquet, in Cleveland following her divorce, Victor, in January 1866, began administering liberal doses of arsenic to his food and drink, hoping to kill him and collect on a sizeable life insurance policy. On Feb. 4, 1867, Parquet died. An autopsy revealed that the man had ingested ten grams of arsenic.

Victor's trial on charges of premeditated murder began in Cleveland in May 1868. When the verdict of Guilty was handed down and the death sentence read, Victor collapsed. During the entire ordeal she had lost seventy pounds and had suffered from extreme mental fatigue. She was diagnosed insane and ordered confined to the Cleveland Asylum for several months before being transferred to the state penitentiary. Victor's death sentence was commuted to life in prison, and in 1887, after serving nineteen years, Victor was granted an official pardon by Governor Joseph Benson Foraker who believed that her conviction had been obtained on circumstantial evidence. REF.: *CBA.*

Edward Oxford firing at Queen Victoria and Prince Albert, near Constitution Hill, June 10, 1840.

Victoria (Alexandrina Victoria), 1819-1901, Brit., queen, attempt. assass. The long and successful reign of Queen Victoria, the last of the Hanoverians, who became synonymous with an age remembered for its elegance and style, was disrupted by six failed assassination attempts. The first of these occurred on June 10, 1840, when the queen, four months pregnant at the time, and her husband, Albert, the Prince Consort, exited Buckingham Palace for their customary drive through Constitution Hill. Their phaeton had only traveled a few hundred feet when a man crept out of the shadows of the Green Park fence to take aim on the monarch. He fired two shots in quick succession, neither of which struck the queen or her husband. Victoria, who was looking in the other direction, was unaware of the first shot fired. By the time the assailant fired his second shot, the prince had pushed Victoria down in the carriage and had ordered the phaeton to proceed quickly. When they arrived at Hyde Park, they decided to take a second drive through the area to let the public know that the queen was unharmed. Crowds of spectators who had heard about the attempt on her life gathered to cheer the royalty.

The assailant was seized by the crowd outside the palace and was carted away to the Gardner's Lane Police Station. There he was identified as Edward Oxford, an 18-year-old drifter who most recently worked as a barman at the Hog in the Pond pub on Molton Street. Oxford was charged with high treason and committed for trial on July 9 at the Central Criminal Court. It was shown in court that Oxford had purchased two pistols on May 4 and had spent much of his time since then engaged in target practice. A collection of papers and secret codes were found in his residence, suggesting that Oxford had organized a society bent on anarchy. There was no evidence to suggest, however, that his "Young England" movement was anything more than the paranoid delusions of a lunatic. Oxford was found Not Guilty on grounds of insanity, but a year later the law was amended and the verdict was revised to read: Guilty, but Insane. Oxford was confined to the Bedlan institution. He was released in September 1867 and allowed to emigrate from England.

No doubt inspired by the demented Oxford, John Francis positioned himself along the palace wall to await the arrival of the queen's carriage on May 30, 1842. As the driver guided the phaeton toward the gates of Buckingham Palace, Francis stepped into the middle of the road and fired a shot on behalf of the unemployed British masses. The shot missed the mark, and a constable wrestled the gun away from Francis before he could get a second shot off. Francis was examined by the Privy Council, according to custom. He was condemned to death, but the queen herself expressed remorse. "The feeling that he is to be executed is very painful to me," she wrote. The government feared that Francis might become a martyr to the underclass if he were to be executed, and therefore commuted his sentence to "transportation" for life on July 1.

A third attempt on the queen's life was made just two days later, when a hunchbacked boy named John William Bean pointed a pistol at the queen as she was riding to Chapel Royal in St. James. The gun exploded, but there was no bullet in the chamber. Bean had loaded the muzzle with a wad of paper and tobacco. He was arrested a few days later, after the London constables rounded up all of the known hunchbacked men in the city for questioning. Following the attempt made by John Francis, Sir Robert Peel proposed to the home secretary that a separate detective department within Scotland Yard be established. On June 20, the permission to establish such an agency was granted. Peel hired two detective inspectors who were paid £200 a year, and eight sergeants who worked directly under them.

On May 19, 1849, an Irishman from Adare named William Hamilton borrowed his landlady's pistol for the sole purpose of scaring the queen during her ride through Constitution Hill. For days Hamilton had tinkered with a piece of wood, attempting to whittle a reasonable facsimile of a gun, but he had not done so to his satisfaction and had given up. When the police arrested Hamilton, they found that his pistol was not loaded. Nevertheless, he was transported for seven years under the tough new laws championed by Peel seven years earlier.

A retired army lieutenant from the 10th Hussars named Robert Pate assaulted the queen in the garden of Cambridge House on July 27, 1850. Pate, armed with a truncheon, advanced on her carriage as it entered the grounds of the estate. He struck the queen violently above the eye, causing her to pass out momentarily. Lieutenant Pate was surrounded by the throng of the queen's well-wishers and beaten to a bloody pulp. By this time, Victoria had lost all of her patience and sympathy for the type of men who would plot such fiendish assaults against a woman. "Certainly it is very hard and very horrid that I, a woman—a defenseless young woman and surrounded by my children, should be exposed to insults of this kind, and be unable to go out quietly for a drive," she wrote in her journal. Pate was sentenced to seven years' transportation.

Rumors of an Irish-Fenian plot against the queen's life circulated through London in the fall of 1867, compelling the authorities to take added steps to insure her security. On Nov. 23, three of the accused conspirators were hanged in Manchester for their alleged intrigues against the government. The Irish, Victoria noted, "had never become reconciled to the English rule, which they hate! So different from the Scotch, who are so loyal."

Then came perhaps the most serious assassination attempt to date. On Mar. 2, 1882, another mentally unbalanced Englishman fired on the royal carriage, this time outside the Windsor station. The gunman was Roderick McLean, who was subdued by two young Eton men who pummeled him with their umbrellas. At the time the queen did not fully comprehend the gravity of the situation; she did not imagine that the bullet was meant for her. Prime Minister William Ewart Gladstone commented with a touch of wry wit that foreign assassins carry out their treacherous deeds in the name of politics, but in England they were all imbeciles.

Queen Victoria displayed uncommon bravery on each occasion. She refused to vary her daily routines because of the possibility of being struck by a madman's bullet. She ruled England and Ireland for nearly sixty-four years before her death on Jan. 22, 1901. See: **Fenians; Peel,** Sir **Robert**.

REF.: Browne, *The Rise of Scotland Yard;* Buckle, *The Letters of Queen Victoria; CBA;* Goodman, *The Correspondence of Murder;* Keeton, *Guilty But Insane;* Longford, *Queen Victoria;* Paine, *The Assassins' World.*

Vidal, Ginette, 1931- , Fr., mur. Although Gerard Osselin had signed a contract giving his lover the right to kill him if he was unfaithful, the contract did not keep her from being tried for murder in a court of law. Osselin and a somewhat older neighbor, Ginette Vidal, fell in love and left their families to set up housekeeping together. The pair entered into a contract which provided that if either of them was unfaithful, the aggrieved party could kill the guilty party.

In November 1972, Ginette found evidence that Osselin was seeing his former wife. In keeping with the terms of the contract, she picked up a gun and shot him to death as he slept. After staying alone with the corpse for a number of days, acting as if he were still alive, the police, alerted by the Osselin family, broke in and arrested Vidal. Vidal proudly displayed the contract which she believed was complete justification for her actions. The French courts did not agree. She was convicted and sent to prison. REF.: *CBA.*

Vidocq, Eugène-Francois, 1775-1857, Fr., law enfor. off. Eugène-Francois Vidocq was a firm believer in that oft-repeated line: "It takes a thief to catch a thief." He was not actually a thief or a crook at the beginning of his career, as most believe. Vidocq began as a professional soldier, fighting under the banner of Napoléon Bonaparte. In 1797, the young Vidocq, who was quite the ladies' man, learned that one of his female friends had been seduced by a rival suitor, whom he beat up. He was convicted and sent to prison for disturbing the peace and assault. Once in prison, the freedom-craving Vidocq planned an escape. He managed to slip outside the prison but was recaptured. Several more escapes followed, and each time Vidocq was recaptured more years were added to his original sentence. As an habitual escapee, Vidocq was sent to the galleys for eight years.

In 1799, Vidocq made good his escape. Returning to Paris, he set himself up as a used clothes dealer, running a shop for a number of years. The underworld of Paris, however, knew well that Vidocq was a fugitive. He was blackmailed by dozens of the worst criminals of the city. He paid and paid until he could no longer bear the extortion. In 1809, Vidocq went to the police and made them an ingenius proposal. If the charges and prison sentence against him were dropped, said Vidocq, he would become an informer on the most vicious criminals in Paris, providing police with enough evidence to send these felons to prison. His offer was accepted, and for the next year Vidocq used his knowledge of the Paris underworld to send more than 800 felons to prison.

Police officials were so impressed with Vidocq that they appointed him chief of the *Sûreté*. It was Vidocq's contention that major crimes and criminals were best handled by criminals themselves and he quickly hired about twenty ex-convicts he had known in prison. These men, with Vidocq at their head, formed the basis of the newly established French Criminal Investigation Department. Vidocq then arrested his own men on bogus charges and sent them to prison, where they served as spies, gathering information on crimes and criminals in and outside prison. When they had collected enough useful information, Vidocq arranged for his men to escape prison, or he had them feign their own deaths. They were carted from prison in coffins, only to rise again to serve the *Sûreté* once more.

Vidocq's undercover men, though former convicts and felons themselves, were loyal to Vidocq unto death. They were also grateful to this greatest of detectives in that Vidocq had old charges and prison sentences pending many of against them dismissed. He later wrote: "During the twenty years I spent at the head of the *Sûreté*, I hardly employed any but ex-convicts, often even escaped prisoners. I preferred to choose men whose bad record had given them a certain celebrity status. I often gave these men the most delicate missions. They had considerable sums to deliver to the police or prison offices. They took part in operations in which they could easily have laid hands on large amounts. But not one of them, not a single one, betrayed my trust."

Eugène-Francois Vidocq, France's greatest detective.

This informant system was so effective that Vidocq was able to sweep Paris and other cities in France clean of major criminals. Moreover, his attention to detail, his exacting records of criminals he arrested and his painstaking sleuthing soon earned him the reputation as the greatest detective in France. Vidocq, among his many talents, was also a master at disguise. On one occasion he appeared as a white-haired, misshapen old man, hobbling around on a cane, looking for a young wife he said had run away with a younger man. He described the scoundrel who had stolen his wife to one shopkeeper after another.

Finally, a tailoress listened to Vidocq croak out his tale and nodded. She knew the man and the woman and gave him the address. Vidocq next appeared at the address in the disguise of a coalman, his arms and face blackened with soot. He labored outside the house until nightfall, when the man he was looking for, a notorious jewel thief named Fossard who had stolen a fortune in gems, appeared and went into the house. A short time later, accompanied by a squad of heavily armed gendarmes, Vidocq burst through the door of the house and arrested the culprit, recovering 18,000 francs, along with the stolen jewels.

Another spectacular coup performed by the indefatigable Vidocq concerned an outwardly respectable music teacher named Madame Noel. She gave piano lessons to upper-class children and claimed she was the widow of a man who had been guillotined during the French Revolution, implying her departed spouse had been of the unmentionable noble class. In truth she was the mother of one of the most notorious criminals in Paris, Noel of the Spectacles, who was currently imprisoned. Noel, however, had a large house and a network of hide-outs where she hid fugitives and escaped prisoners from the galleys. Vidocq resolved to snare the clever harborer of criminals and those she shielded from the law.

Vidocq thought long and hard to create a disguise that would convince the clever Noel that he was a friend of her imprisoned son. He finally remembered Captain Germain, a man with whom he had once served time in prison who was also friendly with Noel's son. Germain was about the same height and weight as Vidocq but his hair was black, he wore a beard, and he had a long, narrow nose. Vidocq blackened his hair with dye, grew a beard, and used gum arabic to lengthen his nose. He then rubbed his wrists and ankles with abrasive materials to create the kind of blisters convicts acquired when wearing shackles. Vidocq was detailed in his disguise that he obtained a sack of lice and slept near it until he was covered with the vermin, as were most escaped convicts. He then obtained prison garb marked with the telltale letters G.A.L. (meaning galley prisoner). He appeared at Noel's home claiming to be Germain and begging to be taken in and hidden from the police he claimed were searching for him.

Vidocq rounding up escaped felons at a Madame Noel hideout.

Madame Noel examined Vidocq carefully, noting the marked prison clothes, the marks and blisters on his hands and feet, even the lice he had supposedly carried from his prison cell. She pronounced him a genuine escaped convict and sent him into her system of hideouts. After learning the addresses of the places which housed scores of escaped convicts, Vidocq summoned his police squads and arrested Noel and several hundred wanted felons. Once again, Vidocq's attention to detail and his dedication had resulted in success. Though thousands of men and women were sent to prison because of his astounding detective work, Vidocq himself was never threatened with assassination by any of those he caused to be imprisoned. He was not only respected by the great criminal classes but feared as one who seemed to know every trick, every move they might make. Said one master thief of the great detective: "No one can escape Vidocq. His ears and eyes are everywhere." The underworld dubbed him "the Wolf."

One of Vidocq's most astounding cases involved a butcher named Fontaine who was robbed on a lonely road near Milly in Fall 1821 by two well-dressed gentlemen who stabbed him twenty-eight times and left him for dead. The burly butcher was taken to a hospital where he recovered and described his assailants to Vidocq. The detective was given a single clue, a torn scrap of paper with a partial address written on it.

Vidocq studied the address for hours and then, employing one of the most remarkable memories in the annals of detective work, recalled a shop at an address that came close to what appeared on the scrap of paper. It was owned by a wine merchant named Clair Raoul, who was also a thief and a fence. Vidocq and some of his men kept Raoul's shop under surveillance. A man was seen to visit the wine merchant at night. Vidocq trailed the man to a Paris apartment. He fit the description provided by the stricken Fontaine and Vidocq recognized him as an ex-convict named Court whom he had previously arrested and sent to prison.

After obtaining a warrant, Vidocq arrested Court and charged him with the robbery and attempted murder of Fontaine. Court quickly confessed and implicated Raoul as a cohort. Vidocq wanted more evidence before he arrested the wily Raoul. Vidocq went to the wine merchant's shop on the pretext of looking for subversive political propaganda. Raoul told Vidocq that he had no political inclinations and when Vidocq found no political pamphlets, he asked Raoul if he would permit a search of his Montmartre apartment. The cool-headed Raoul shrugged and agreed. Both men, accompanied by some of Vidocq's men, went to Montmartre where the detective methodically searched the apartment. In a desk he found a torn piece of paper which matched the one found at the scene of the Fontaine attack and robbery.

Realizing he had been discovered as one of the thieves, Raoul leaped for a pair of pistols on a shelf. Vidocq and his men were quicker and blocked the thief's path. Raoul was taken into custody and later admitted his part in attacking Fontaine. In a suspenseful moment before a magistrate, the burly Raoul, examining a knife taken from his apartment and supposedly used in the robbery and leaned forward, saying: "We fell on him with our cudgels. It would have done for an ox but the butcher was only knocked out. To settle him, I brought out my knife—this knife!" With that Raoul seized the knife and the magistrate fell backward, as did the police officers next to him. Vidocq held his ground.

"Gentlemen," soothed the unruffled Vidocq, "Raoul isn't capable of abusing your confidence. He only picked up the knife to show you how he used it on the butcher." Then Vidocq turned to the heavily breathing Raoul and said: "Isn't that so?"

Raoul stood holding the knife with the point aimed at Vidocq's heart. Unarmed, Vidocq slowly walked toward it, smiling at Raoul who finally said: "Yes, I only wanted to show the gentlemen so they could judge the movement." He placed the knife on the exhibit table and sat down. Both Court and Raoul were identified by Fontaine from his hospital bed. The were tried, found Guilty, and condemned to death. While they awaited the guillotine, the ever-convivial Vidocq visited them in prison, having both men brought into the warden's office where Vidocq had ordered a fine meal to be served.

As the *Sûreté* chief sat down to dine with the two condemned men, a guard nervously asked Vidocq: "Shall I lay knives?"

"Of course," boomed Vidocq. "How else do you expect these gentlemen to cut their meat." While the three dined, Vidocq engaged the convicts in nostalgic conversation and they were soon confiding to him many of their past crimes. Vidocq asked them if they had ever attacked a poultry dealer and they nodded, adding that they had had an accomplice named Michel Pons-Gerard, a towering brute of a man who had committed many robberies with them. Raoul and Court gave Vidocq the address of Pons-Gerard who lived in a small village near Hirson on the Belgium frontier. (The cagey detective had arranged the dinner to specifically learn the identity of Pons-Gerard.) Before returning to their cells, Raoul and Court warned Vidocq that Pons-Gerard was a dangerous man, a giant who would not hesitate to kill the detective if he learned his true identity. The genuine concern the convicts had for Vidocq's safety was part of the detective's strange mystique; he had the power or talent to inspire even the men he arrested to feel friendship and affection for him.

Disguised as a horse cobbler, Vidocq and a few of his men traveled to the village where Pons-Gerard lived. They found him working as a supervisor of a road gang and Vidocq immediately sauntered up to the large man and gave him a friendly greeting.

"I do not know you," growled Pons-Gerard, glaring down at the portly detective.

"I am a friend of Raoul and Court," Vidocq whispered conspiratorially.

Pons-Gerard nodded and then took Vidocq to a pub in Hirson. Pons-Gerard sat across from the man he thought to be a horse cobbler and a fellow criminal, waiting to hear news from Paris and, perhaps, plans for another robbery. Instead Vidocq told Pons-Gerard that their friends Raoul and Court had been arrested, imprisoned, and sentenced to death.

"Who arrested them?" snarled the vicius Pons-Gerard.

"Vidocq," the detective told him.

Pons-Gerard took a long drink of wine and then said: "If ever he comes my way, I'll give it to him!"

"No you won't," Vidocq said quietly. "You'll do like the others. You'll say nothing and be the first to give him a drink."

"I'll give him a knife!" hissed the giant, swigging down more wine. "I'll kill him!"

"You'll give him a drink," Vidocq said, holding out his glass, "and good wine, too."

Pons-Gerard filled Vidocq's glass and said: "I'd die a thousand times over first."

"Die when you're ready," said the detective. "I am Vidocq, and I arrest you."

The giant sat with popping eyes and gaping mouth for some moments. Two of Vidocq's men came forward and grabbed his powerful arms but this was not necessary. Pons-Gerard offered no resistance. He was in shock at being confronted by the legendary detective. He was easily led away and was later given a life sentence.

Raoul and Court went to the guillotine. Vidocq accompanied the men to the executioner. Fontaine, one of their many surviving victims, had fully recovered from his wounds and was on hand to witness the beheadings. He marched up to the two condemned men, taunting them with their impending, dreadful fate. He gloated over their terrible end. Vidocq turned to Fontaine and said: "This is no way to act toward men who are about to die." He ordered Fontaine removed from the area. Both Raoul and Court thanked the detective for this consideration and then, oddly, embraced him, the very man who had brought them to their fate. Then they mounted the steps to the scaffold. The guillotine's slashing blade took their lives moments later.

The display of kinship between criminal and detective would be repeated many times over. Vidocq's successor, Pierre Allard, evoked the same kind of strange affection from the murderer Pierre Lacenaire. The friendship between lawman and outlaw in the American West would see amiability and comradeship between a killer like Billy the Kid and lawman Pat Garrett, the man who eventually shot the Kid to death. Much of this had to do with the intense emotional experience shared by the criminal and captor while the hunt ensued, producing an inexplicable bonding, an intimacy difficult for outsiders to understand. Since Vidocq was likely the greatest tracker of men the world has ever seen, his quarry, always bested by him, respected and admired him for his courage and dedication to the law that was equal to their dedication to crime.

In 1827, Vidocq resigned his post as head of the *Sûreté*, stating that old wounds and injuries from his prison life had enfeebled him. He was arthritic and decidedly overweight when he left office. Yet, in 1832, the government asked him to assume his old post, which he did for only a few months while crushing a political revolt. Again he resigned but the pull of law enforcement was too strong for him. Vidocq established a private detective agency, the first of its kind, and was instrumental in establishing protective measures for tradesmen and merchants who had been victimized by myriad swindles and sharpers. He also undertook private cases, leading his counterparts in the *Sûreté* to resent his successes. He was accused of wrongdoing but vindicated himself in court at great expense.

Vidocq spent his later years writing several books, one dealing with the history of the criminal class, another about the rehabilitation of criminals and two huge novels based upon his detective experiences. His oft-quoted *Memoirs* suffered at the hands of many translators and Vidocq was critical of those who cavalierly misrepresented his exploits and statements. Balzac, who was Vidocq's lifelong friend, depicted the detective as the character Vautrin in his *Comédie Humaine*. Vidocq died at the age of seventy-seven, hailed as "an honest man" who was truly the first great detective in the world, one whose pioneer exploits were more factual than fictional, which made this remarkable person all the more legendary, all the more heroic. See: **Billy the Kid; Lacenaire, Pierre**.

REF.: *CBA;* Edwards, *The Vidocq Dossier;* Froment, *Histoire de Vidocq;* Griffiths, *Mysteries of Police and Crime;* Hamre, *Vidocq, Maitre du Crime;* Hibbert, *The Roots of Evil; Histoire Complète de Vidocq* (Anon.)*;* Hodgetts, *Vidocq: A Master of Crime;* Jagot, *Vidocq;* Kingston, *Dramamtic Days at the Old Bailey;* Ledru, *La Vie de Vidocq;* Maurice, *Vidocq;* Morain, *The Underworld of Paris;* Reppetto, *The Blue Parade;* Savant, *La Vie Fabuleuse et Authentique de Vidocq;* Scott, *The Concise Encyclopedia of Crime and Criminals;* Stead, *Vidocq: Picaroon of Crime; Vie et Adventures de Vidocq* (Anon.)*;* Vidocq, *Mémoires;* ____, *La Paravoleur;* ____, *Les Chauffeurs du Nord;* ____, *Les Voleurs;* ____, *Les Vrais Mystères de Paris;* (FICTION), Balzac, *A Harlot's Progress;* (FILM), *A Scandal in Paris,* 1946.

Viger, Denis Benjamin, 1774-1861, Can., sedition. Politician who served as member of Lower Canada legislature from 1808-30. In 1828 and 1830, he went to Britain to express complaints of French Canadians. He was put in prison in Canada for writing seditious works from 1838-40. He later held positions in the Canadian government. REF.: *CBA*.

Vigilantes' Executive Committee, prom. 1864, U.S., vigil. In the wake of the Montana Gold Rush of 1861, gangs of murderers and thieves organized themselves to start preying on miners, ranchers, and the stagecoaches that transported the gold from the area. They became known in the Montana Territory as road agents, and were a serious threat in the unsettled country. After one of the most notorious agents, George Ives, robbed and murdered Nicholas Tbalt, a twenty-five-citizen committee was formed to bring him to justice. He was tried, convicted, and hanged on Dec. 21, 1863. Within days, Vigilante Committees, modeled after those founded in California and other mining areas, were formed. A Virginia City, Mont., Vigilantes Executive Committee met on Jan. 13, 1864, and voted to hang five local road agents: Boone Helm, Jack Gallagher, Frank Parish, Haze Lyons, and George Lane (also known as Club-Foot George Lane). All exits out of town were blocked, and the five men were captured. All insisted they were innocent but the Vigilantes decided to hang them after a brief hearing. They were marched to the gallows in front of the Virginia Hotel. While the ropes were prepared, Gallagher swore and joked, Club-Foot George begged for character references from an associate, and Parish was serious and fearful. After hanging for about two hours, the bodies were cut down and put in the street in front of the house, where friends came to take them away for burial. See: **Ives, George.**

REF.: *CBA;* Mencken, *By the Neck.*

Vigilantes of Montana, prom. 1860s, U.S., lynch. The most effective and notable outbreak of vigilantism in U.S. history occurred in Montana between 1863 and 1864, focusing on a gang of outlaws led by Sheriff Henry Plummer, known as the Innocents.

The Innocents were known as killers and cutthroats, and at one time claimed more than 100 members. So blatant were their activities that several members of the gang were publicly identified, with Plummer exposed as their leader.

The vigilante movement became a formal organization under a covenant each of the members signed on Dec. 23, 1863, stating that the organization would arrest thieves and murderers, never violate a right, never reveal a secret, and uphold justice. The vigilantes of Montana did not wear masks or confine their activities to nighttime. They reportedly allowed an intended victim the chance to prove his innocence, and gave targeted lynch victims the opportunity to flee the territory by posting a paper with the numbers 3-7-77 on their doors. Beginning in late 1863, the vigilantes hanged about twenty-six Innocents, including Sheriff Plummer. They killed several other outlaws, but reportedly not a single innocent citizen. The historian of the vigilantes, an English professor who graduated from Oxford University, Thomas J. Dimsdale, wrote an impassioned book supporting lynch law entitled *Vigilantes of Montana.* The Montana vigilantes claimed in their membership the "best" people of Montana, including Nathaniel Pitt Langford, founder of Yellowstone Park, Colonel Wilbur Fisk Sanders, a U.S. senator, and Nelson Story, a successful businessman and rancher. They were rarely criticized during their time, and some writers claim that the vigilante justice made the creation of courts and law-enforcement agencies much easier as territorial government was set up in Montana.

REF.: American Guide Series, *Montana, A State Guide Book;* Ayers, *Life in the Wilds of America;* Bailey, *River of No Return;* Ballou, *Early Klickitat Valley Days;* Bancroft, *Works of Hubert Howe Bancroft,* Vol. XXXI; Barrows, *The United States of Yesterday and Tomorrow;* Barsness, *Gold Camp;* Berry, *The Whoop-Up Trail;* Birney, *Vigilantes;* Blankenship, *And Then There Were Men;* Briggs, *Frontiers of the Northwest;* Brosnan, *History of the State of Idaho;* Brown, *Before Barbed Wire;* Bruffey, *Eighty-One Years in the West;* Buffum, *On Two Frontiers;* Burdick, *Life and Exploits of John Goodall;* ____, *Tales From Buffalo Land;* Burdick, *Jim Johnson, Pioneer;* Burlingame, *The Montana Frontier; CBA;* Mencken, *By the Neck.*

Vigilantes of San Francisco, 1850s, U.S., lynch. Justice in California first took the form of miners' courts and vigilance committees in larger communities. During this time, crime overran San Francisco, giving rise to one of the toughest vigilante committees ever formed on the West Coast. Samuel Brannan, a former Morman elder, organized the first San Francisco Committee of Vigilance in 1851, a committee unique in that it gave each accused person "a fair and reasonable trial" before hanging him. The first criminal to be hanged by the committee was an Australian highwayman caught in the act of robbing a safe. The crowd that gathered to see him lynched roared with approval when vigilantes pushed aside the chief of police who attempted to rescue the condemned man. The committee lynched three of the city's leading criminals before disbanding.

The committee reformed in 1855 when corrupt city officials virtually turned the city over to criminals. Claiming prominent citizens among its ranks, such as William T. Coleman and Leland Stanford, who later became governor and later a U.S. senator, it hanged several men before again disbanding with the election of an honest city administration. Their first lynching victims were two men who killed a U.S. marshal. Later they hanged New York hoodlum Philander Brace and Englishman Joseph Hetherington. Before dissolving, the committee staged a jubilant parade with 5,000 marchers through San Francisco's streets. The London *Times* reported that it was seldom did "self-constituted authorities retire with grace and dignity, but it is due to the vigilante committee to say that they have done so."

REF.: *CBA;* Coblentz, *Villains and Vigilantes;* Mencken, *By the Neck;* Myers, *San Francisco's Reign of Terror;* Stewart, *Committee of Vigilance: Revolution in San Francisco, 1851.*

Vignon, Henri, prom. 1949, Fr., org. crime-(unsolv.) assass. One of the many victims of the bloody Corsican Vendetta, a bitter gangland-style battle between the rival Corsican families in Paris and Marseilles, Henri Vignon was riding in the car of underworld leader Ange Salicetti as the funeral procession for Mathieu Costa headed from the Sancio Antonio Church in Paris to the Pantin Cemetery. Suddenly, a black Citröen with a Thompson machine gun sticking out of its rear window swerved toward the Salicetti car and opened fire. Incredibly, Salicetti was the only person unharmed. Wanted gangster Robert Regent was slain, and Vignon was rushed into an emergency operation at the Marmottan Hospital, but died a few hours later. See: **Corsican Vendetta, The.**

REF.: *CBA;* Goodman, *Villainy Unlimited.*

Vilas, William Freeman, 1840-1908, U.S., lawyer. Taught law at University of Wisconsin from 1868-85, and from 1889-92. REF.: *CBA.*

Villa, Pancho (Doroteo Arango, AKA: Francisco Villa, The Centaur), 1878-1923, Mex. bandit and rebel, assass. Pancho Villa was born Doroteo Arango in a squalid hut in Rio Grande, Durango, Mex. He was a *mestizo* with some Negro blood. Raised without an education and sent at an early age to work in the fields of a large landowner, a *hacendado*, Villa had little hope for any other life in an era when dictator Porfirio Diaz ruled Mexico. At the age of sixteen he killed the *hacendado's* son, and raped his daughter, and fled into the hills to join a bandit gang, later becoming its leader. He was savage, uncouth, and unremorseful for any of his many crimes. He took the name Francisco Villa and then opted for the first name of Pancho which he liked better, thinking it to be a manly name.

Heavyset, bowlegged, and pigeon-toed, Villa was a master horseman and a crack shot. His temper was legendary and mercurial. He had a killer's instinct and a butcher's habit of shooting his prisoners. Mercy was unknown to him, yet he was capable of maudlin displays of tenderness with the poor he often championed. He was known, long before his defiance to Diaz, as a sort of Mexican Robin Hood, raiding the estates of the rich landowners, and sharing his food and booty with the starving peons. Americans, as well as Mexicans, learned of Villa's exploits through dime novels whose authors had little idea of what Villa was really like.

When Francesco Madero was denied a free election by the Diaz regime and proclaimed open revolution against the dictator and his regime, Pancho Villa was one of the first join Madero. He gathered a force of 500 in northern Mexico and began to take small towns away from Diaz commanders. In the southern state of Morelos, Emiliano Zapata, Villa's counterpart, attacked the forces of Diaz. Within two years of revolution, the Diaz regime collapsed and the dictator fled to Spain.

Madero became president and his most devoted follower, Villa, was almost executed for disobeying orders. Victoriano Huerta, a brutal, former Diaz officer who had gone over to Madero, gave orders to have the insubordinate Villa shot by a firing squad on June 4, 1912. Villa, knowing that Madero would never issue any such orders, stalled for time while his representatives raced to Madero. Villa actually was placed before a firing squad and he literally cajoled, begged and pleaded for his life. Villa offered the money in his pockets, his horse, and his gold watch to Captain Hernández if he would only postpone the execution. At the last minute, he was saved when Rául Madero, the president's brother, appeared with a reprieve in hand, one that had been hastily penned by Madero. Villa was jailed pending an investigation. He was later released and sent back to his northern retreat.

Meanwhile, Madero proved to be an ineffective president, his every move blocked by Huerta and other Diaz regime officials. He insisted that his program for returning the land to the peons and dismantling the great estates be put into effect. Madero's land reforms were never instituted. Huerta ordered his assassination and then seized power.

Once again Villa, Zapata and other revolutionaries gathered their forces and confronted Huerta who was also defeated, after a prolonged civil war which saw endless atrocities and slaughter on both sides. Villa and Zapata both hanged all prisoners, believ-

Top, Pancho Villa, center, on horseback, leading his *División del Norte* into battle against the forces of Victoriano Huerta, 1913; Villa's military strategy was summed up by the centaur with a simple phrase: "I hit the enemy with one terrific blow!"

Far left, Pancho Villa in 1916, at the height of his military power in Mexico.

Left, Francisco I. Madero, Villa's mentor and father-figure, whose assassination in 1913 left Villa devastated and filled him with a ruthless vengeance for his murderers.

The brutal, scheming Victoriano Huerta.

Villa, in throne chair, and Emiliano Zapata, right, in the National Palace, 1914.

ing that "they are not worth bullets." Villa and Zapata met and drank a glass of cognac together to celebrate their victory, although Villa admitted to Zapata: "I accept this drink solely for the pleasure of joining you, for the truth is I never drink liquor." Together, on Dec. 6, 1914, Villa and Zapata assumed joint leadership. Villa was briefly the nominal president of the country, a position he quickly abdicated. At the time, Mexico was split into many factions with Villa and Zapata representing the Conventionists (which advocated the reforms of Madero) and Venustiano Carranza and Alvaro Obregón heading the constitutionalists.

The revolution went on, until Carranza was installed as president, later usurped by Obregón. Zapata was assassinated in 1919 and Villa, the old warrior, retired to his ranch in Canutillo in 1920. He was provided with considerable funds by the federal government, then in the control of Obregón, to remain on his large estate where he improved the land and made a model ranch out of what was once a broken down farm. Villa bought American farm machinery and began to till the land. He used peon labor to construct a road from his ranch to the town of Parral. Yet, consistent with his contradictory nature, Villa had a modern school built for his peon workers and bodyguards. He specified that the windows be placed high on the walls for proper ventilation and to make sure that the children did not stare out of the window but concentrated on their studies.

Villa, by then a millionaire, sent many peon's sons across the border to business schools in El Paso, Texas. He gave interviews to the American press but grew short-tempered with their abusive questions. Once, when a reporter dared to ask him to perform some cowboy tricks with his lasso, Villa reached for his guns and almost shot the man. He later requested that an American salesman who was sending farm equipment also send him two large portraits of George Washington and Abraham Lincoln to hang in the school he sponsored.

The once-feared leader of the Division of the North, grew fat and indulged himself with rich food, stuffing himself on imported canned sardines and peanut brittle. He bought several American cars and had many mistresses, although he remained married to the same woman. He knew that he had many enemies, especially in the nearby town of Parral where he owned a hotel. When he visited the town he was accompanied by two dozen heavily armed bodyguards. Machine guns were mounted on the cars that preceded and followed Villa's large touring car. One of Villa's most dedicated enemies was Jesús Salas Barraza, who organized a group of middle-class merchants and businessmen in a plot to murder the Centaur, as Villa was called by his loyal followers. Barraza, a member of the Durango state legislature, raised $50,000 from those who had suffered at Villa's hands during the revolutionary years. He bought guns and ammunition and hired eight killers to murder Villa.

As Villa drove into Parral, Barraza studied the speed of his car and noted that the auto always slowed down to turn a corner where a large house jutted into the street. Barraza rented the house and positioned his hired killers here. On July 10, 1923, the eight gunmen positioned themselves at the window of the house, but when Villa's large Dodge touring car turned the corner, the killers held their fire, lest they accidentally shoot a group of children who were leaving a nearby school. When Villa left the town that day, his car turned the corner too quickly for the gunmen to take aim.

On July 19, 1923, Villa arrived in Parral to attend the christening of of one of his workers' sons. Villa stayed overnight in his hotel and then set off for his ranch early the next morning in the 1919 Dodge. Villa himself sat behind the wheel. His secretary, Colonel Miguel Trillo, sat next to him. Two bodyguards sat in the back seat and two more rode on the running boards of the large car.

The eight killers waited at the windows of the rented house. They had taken precautions this time, employing a pumpkin seed vendor to stand in the street and signal them when Villa's car approached. He was to remove his hat when Villa's car neared, shouting "Viva Villa" once if the Centaur was behind the wheel, twice if he was in the back seat. All of the men in the car wore pistols and carried rifles.

It was 8 a.m., July 20, 1923. Villa was driving the car at what was then considered to be high speed. "General," Trillo said to Villa, "did you ever dream some day that you would be traveling at forty-five miles an hour in a machine?"

"Never!" replied Villa. "Impossible!" He laughed as he drove the car through the small town.

At the windows of the house, the killers waited for the orders of their leader, Melitón Losoya. The Canutillo estate where Villa lived had once been part of his family's lands. As a member of the landed gentry, Losoya had nursed a seething hatred for Villa, who had killed many of his family and looted his father's estates. He had vowed to murder the Centaur at the first opportunity, and when Barraza looked for recruits to murder Villa, Losoya was the first to enlist. Urging on Losoya was none other than Alvaro Obregón, who pretended friendship toward Villa but secretly feared him, believing that until Villa was dead there would be no peace in Mexico. He also knew that Villa was the only leader left from the revolution who could muster an army against him and his plans for a presidential dictatorship.

As Villa's car approached the house on the corner, the vendor suddenly shouted: "Viva Villa!" He waved his sombrero. The Dodge roared to the front of the house and Losoya carefully aimed his rifle and sent a bullet through its windshield into the broad chest of Pancho Villa who slumped forward on the wheel. The Dodge slammed into a pole as Losoya's gunmen poured a terrific fusillade into the car. Trillo and the others reached for their guns. Trillo stood up in the car, but a half dozen bullets ripped into him, sending him toppling backward over the door of the car, his body hanging there grotesquely.

Medrano, another bodyguard, crashed out of the car, a bullet in his head. Losoya and his men, all his relatives, screamed with joy as they continued to pump a hailstorm of bullets into the car, hitting Hurtado, another bodyguard, in the chest several times, killing him. Ramón Contraras, a large man and last of the bodyguards, jumped from the running board of the car and began to return fire with his rifle. A bullet struck him in the arm and he retreated down the street, firing his Winchester as he moved, finally disappearing down a side street. He was the only survivor of Villa's party.

Villa lay slumped against Trillo's body, seven bullets in him. Trillo had been shot nine times. The big Dodge was riddled with more than 100 bullets. The eight assassins slowly advanced on the car. Ramón Guerra was the first to reach the car. He looked down at the bullet-ridden body of Pancho Villa. He turned to Losoya and shouted: "The dirty pig! We taught him!" As he glanced back into the car, Guerra's face went white with fear. Though he was shot to pieces, Villa's hand moved upward with a large revolver clutched in it. He fired one shot which tore into Guerra's face and killed him. More bullets were quickly pumped into Villa until his assassins were sure that he was dead. His bleeding body was carried, along with the others, to Villa's hotel where it was photographed. Losoya insisted on these photos to prove to Villa's superstitious followers that the Centaur was, indeed, dead.

The legendary bandit and revolutionary leader was not taken to the expensive, elegant mausoleum he had purchased in Chihuahua City for his last resting place. His body was instead buried in a common grave at Parral. Ghouls dug up Villa's body in 1926 and severed his head, stealing this grisly trophy which was never recovered.

Barraza later admitted organizing Losoya and his men, and he was placed on trial. Found Guilty, Barraza was sentenced to twenty years in prison, but Obregón reduced the sentence to six months, a brazen act that all but served as an admission on Obregón's part that he, too, was behind Villa's assassination. Moreover, Obregón made Barraza a colonel in the army. In 1951, on his deathbed, Barraza shouted to a priest: "I am not a mur-

Villa, left, in a rare photo, facing his firing squad, 1912; he talked his way out of the execution.

Emiliano Zapata, patriot.

Alvaro Obregón, Pancho Villa, General John Pershing, peace conference.

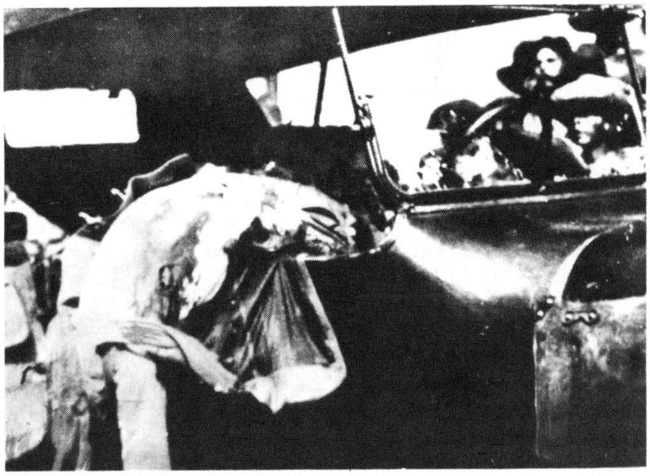

The ambush: Villa's shot-up car and bodyguard; Parral, Mex., 1923.

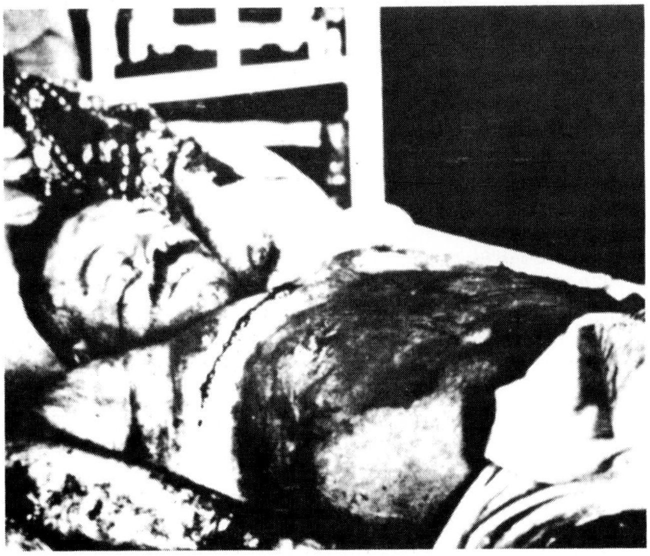

Pancho Villa in death, shot to pieces by his enemies, July 20, 1923.

Alvaro Obregón, Villa's foe.

The wife of Pancho Villa.

derer! I rid humanity of a monster!" See: **Carranza, Venustiano; Madero, Francisco; Obregón, Alvaro; Zapata, Emiliano.**

REF.: Alba, *The Mexicans;* Alessio, *Historia Politica de la Revolución;* Atkin, *Revolution!;* Baerlein, *Mexico, The Land of Unrest;* Baker, *Woodrow Wilson, Life and Letters;* Barrera, *Villa Contra Todos;* ____, *Villa Contra Todo y Contra Todos;* Beals, *Porfirio Diaz: Dictator of Mexico;* Bell, *The Political Shame of Mexico;* Blasco Ibañez, *Mexico in Revolution;* Blum, *Woodrow Wilson and the Politics of Morality;* Braddy, *Cock of the Walk: The Legend of Pancho Villa;* ____, *Pancho Villa at Columbus;* Brand, *Mexico: Land of Sunshine and Shadow;* Breceda, *México Revolucionario, 1913-1917;* Brenner and Leighton, *The Wind That Swept Mexico;* Bulnes, *The Whole Truth About Mexico;* Bush, *Gringo Doctor;* Calcott, *Liberalism in Mexico, 1857-1919;* Callahan, *American Foreign Policy in Mexican Relations;* Calvert, *The Mexican Revolution, 1910-1914;* Campobello, *Apuntes Sobre la Vida Militar de Francisco Villa;* Camreon, *Mexico in Revolution;* Casasolka, *Historia Gráfica de la Revolución; CBA;* Cervantes, *Francisco Villa y la Revolución;* Clendesen, *The United States and Pancho Villa;* Cline, *The United States and Mexico;* Creel, *The People Next Door;* Creelman, *Diaz: Master of Mexico;* Cumberland, *Mexican Revolution: Genesis Under Madero;* De la Huerta, *Memorias;* Dillon, *Mexico on the Verge;* Dromundo, *Francisco Villa y la Adelita;* ____, *Vida de Emiliano Zapata;* Dulles, *Yesterday in Mexico;* Dunn, *The Crimson Jester: Zapata of Mexico;* Estol, *Realidad y Leyenda de Pancho Villa;* Estrada, *La Revolución y Francisco Madero;* Evans, *Letters from Mexico;* Flandrau, *Viva Mexico;* Foix, *Pancho Villa;* Frances, *Vida y Aventuras de Pancho Villa;* Fyfe, *The Real Mexico;* George, *Woodrow Wilson and Colonel House;* González, *Contra Villa: Relatos de la Compaña de 1914-1915;* Grayson, *Woodrow Wilson;* Grieb, *The United States and Huerta;* Gruening, *Mexico and Its Heritage;* Guzmán, *The Eagle and the Serpent;* ____, *Memoirs of Pancho Villa;* Haley, *Revolution and Intervention: The Diplomacy of Taft and Wilson with Mexico, 1910-1917;* Harris, *Pancho Villa and the Columbus Raid;* Hendrick, *Life and Letters of Walter H. Page;* Herrera, *Francisco Villa, Ante La Historia;* Inman, *Intervention in Mexico;* Johnson, *Heroic Mexico;* ____, *Mexico;* King, *Tempest Over Mexico: A Personal Chronicle;* Lara Pardo, *De Porfirio Diaz á Francisco Madero;* Liceaga, *Félix Diaz;* Link, *Wilson the Diplomatist;* Lord, *The Good Years;* Magaña and Guerrero, *Emiliano Zapata y el Agrarismo en México;* Márquez, *Los Ultimos Dias del Presidente Madero;* Meyer, *Huerta: A Political Portrait;* Moats, *Thunder in Their Veins;* Moore, *The Legend of Pancho Villa;* Muñoz, *Pancho Villa: Rayo y Azote;* Nash, *Almanac of World Crime;* Obregón, *Partes Oficiales de las Batallas de Celaya;* O'Hea, *Reminiscences of the Mexican Revolution;* O'Shaughnessy, *A Diplomat's Wife in Mexico;* ____, *Intimate Pages of Mexican History;* Palacios, *Emiliano Zapata;* Parkes, *A History of Mexico;* Pinchon, *Viva Villa!;* ____, *Zapata the Unconquerable;* Plenn, *Mexico Marches;* Puente, *Pascual Orozco y la Revuelta de Chihuahua;* ____, *Vida de Francisco Villa;* ____, *Villa En Pie;* Reed, *Insurgent Mexico;* Regler, *A Land Bewitched;* Reyes, *A History of Mexico;* Reyes, *Cabalgando Con Villa;* Rippy, *The United States and Mexico;* Robinson, *The Foreign Policty of Woodrow Wilson;* Robleto, *La Mascota de Pancho Villa;* Roscoe, *The Treasure Album of Pancho Villa;* Ross, *Francisco I. Madero: Apostle of Mexican Democracy;* Schuster, *Pancho Villa's Shadow;* Sherman, *Victoriano Huerta, A Reappraisal;* Simpson, *Many Mexicos;* Smith, *Benighted Mexico;* Stevens, *Here Comes Pancho Villa;* Strode, *Timeless Mexico;* Tannenbaum, *Peace by Revolution;* ____, *Mexico: The Struggle for Peace and Bread;* Taracena, *Madero, Vida del Hombre y del Politico;* Tompkins, *Chasing Villa;* Torres, *La Cabeze de Villa;* ____, *Veinte Vibrante Episodos de la Vida de Villa;* Turner, *Barbarous Mexico;* Turner, *Bullets, Bottles and Gardenias;* Tweedie, *Mexico: From Diaz to the Kaiser;* ____, *Porfirio Diaz;* ____, *Mexico As I Saw It;* Wagner, *Bullion to Books;* Walworth, *Woodrow Wilson;* Wilson, *Diplomatic Episodes in Mexico, Belgium, and Chile;* Wise, *Woodrow Wilson, Disciple of Revolution;* Womack, *Zapata and the Mexican Revolution;* Zayas, *The Case of Mexico and the Policy of President Wilson;* (FILM), *Viva Villa!*, 1934; *Pancho Villa Returns*, 1950; *Villa!*, 1958; *Villa Rides*, 1968; *Pancho Villa*, 1975.

Villagran, Dovie Beams, prom. 1987, U.S., fraud. After Ferdinand Marcos left the Philippines in February 1986, the Presidential Commission on Good Government, with the responsibility of trying to regain the wealth allegedly taken by the ex-president and his associates, filed $100 billion in lawsuits against Marcos and his cohorts. A Nashville actress who was Marcos' mistress from 1968-70, Dovie Beams Villagran and her husband Sergio Villagran were charged by a Los Angeles federal grand jury of forty-two counts of bankruptcy fraud, bank fraud, and making false statements on their loan applications. The total amount they obtained from savings institutions and banks in southern California was estimated to be $18 million. On Nov. 10, 1987, Dovie Villagran was found Guilty and sentenced to eight years in prison. See: **Marcos, Ferdinand**; **Marcos, Imelda Romualdez.** REF.: *CBA.*

Villa Madeira Murder, See: **Rattenbury, Alma Victoria.**

Villamor, Ignacio, 1863-1933, Phil., jur. Served as attorney general in Philippine Islands from 1907-13. He was also nominated to the supreme court of the Philippine Islands by President Woodrow Wilson in 1920. REF.: *CBA.*

Villard, Jacques, prom. 1921, U.S., (unsolv.) kid. An advertisement in Chicago newspapers for an editor at the salary of $10,000, a princely sum in 1920, attracted many applicants. On Dec. 10, 1920, Jacques Villard, the editor of *New Age* Magazine and owner of a St. Louis correspondence school, came to Chicago with his wife seeking an editor. After several weeks of running the ad and many responses, Villard had not found the right person. He urged his wife to return to St. Louis. She did so with some concern, for Villard was a double amputee.

Concerned when she did not hear from her husband for several days, Mrs. Villard called the Chicago hotel where he had been staying and was told that he had left the hotel with a man who had paid his bill and driven off with him and his luggage. Because of his obvious wealth and the cash and valuables Villard carried, it appeared to be a case of kidnapping.

An intensive nationwide search yielded no clues until finally, on Jan. 7, 1921, Villard was found on a Chicago street, asking for help. Villard told police he had been kidnapped from his hotel room by a Polish man and held captive in a shack. His captor tortured him and threatened to kill him. He also had Villard write letters requesting that his wife pay a large ransom. However, none of the letters was ever mailed. The kidnappers evidently became disenchanted with their plan and, afraid of being caught, dumped him on the street where he later was found.

REF.: *CBA;* Nash, *Among the Missing.*

Villareal, Antonio, 1880-1944, Phil., jur.-atty. gen. Served as auxiliary judge of First Instance from 1916-20, district judge from 1920-21, and attorney general from 1921-25 for Philippine Islands. He also taught law at the University of the Philippines and other schools from 1925-41. REF.: *CBA.*

Villiers, George (Duke of Buckingham), 1592-1628, Brit., duke, assass. When George Villiers, the First Duke of Buckingham, arrived at the court of James I, his rise was due mostly to his social standing. He ascended in power, becoming Master of the Horse in 1616, and later Viscount, followed by Baron of Waddon. He gained the position of Lord High Admiral and leadership of the Navy. Villiers' ambitions then became highly political. He was arguably the strongest influence over King Charles I; some considered Charles I a tool in the manipulating clutches of Villiers, for whose warlike schemes Charles I repeatedly demanded supplies from a disgruntled Parliament. Tension between the English and French courts increased, and by early 1627, the condition was open war. Parliament had impeached Villiers for accepting bribes and selling honors, and public feeling ran strong against him.

A young officer, John Felton, wounded and almost starving in his London garret, was owed back pay and had been denied a promotion he felt he strongly deserved. His anger and frustration focused on Villiers, who had twice denied his application for promotion. Felton bought a long knife and sewed the sheath into the inside pocket of his coat in order to hide it. Into his hat he stitched two pieces of paper carrying the messages, "Let no man condemn me," and that a man "afraid to sacrifice his life for the honor of God, his King, and Country," was not worthy of the name of a gentleman and a soldier.

Felton traveled to Portsmouth and found out where Villiers

lived. Early the next morning, on Aug. 23, as the restless and anxious duke (whose death had been predicted by a psychic) walked down a shadowy corridor in his High Street household, he was murdered by Felton. Caught almost immediately, Felton surrendered. He confessed that he had acted alone in assassinating Villiers, and was spared the torture of the rack. Tried at the King's Bar Bench on Nov. 27, he was condemned to death and was hanged at Tyburn two days later. The majority of the populace acclaimed him as a martyr and a patriot, but Felton went to his death saying he had been guilty of a great crime. His body was hanged in chains for public viewing after his demise.

REF.: *CBA;* Melville, *Famous Duels and Assassinations.*

Villiers, Harry, prom. 1898, Brit., theft. A petty thief who had come to London from Paris, Harry Villiers took a trip to Brighton and there became involved with a young, wealthy widow. He pretended that he had large estates in France and England but that his possessions were temporarily tied up by lawyers. After he had received about a thousand pounds from the woman, to whom he had become engaged, she found some letters he left lying around and became angry over the suspicion that he might have duped her. Confronting him to insist that he return her money, she was herself confronted with Villiers' temper—he fired at her with a revolver. Unharmed but hysterical, the widow had Villiers arrested, then had a change of heart and bailed him out. He apologized and said that he would clear up the misunderstanding the next day. He was going to board a train en route to Paris when he saw a small group of wealthy people. Watching a maid protecting a leather case, Villiers managed to steal it from her, and found himself with a cache of extremely valuable jewelry belonging to the Duchess of Sutherland. Villiers broke many of the gems from their settings, returned to his fiancée, and claimed that he had retrieved some of his vast family wealth from the bankers.

The woman, having read the newspapers, became suspicious and reported him to the French police. Because she spoke French poorly, they had little interest in her claims. A detective was sent to Villiers' apartment for a routine check, made formal inquiries, and left. Scotland Yard searched for the jewels, but to no avail. It was not until Villiers came to London and continued the profligate spending he had begun to indulge in—buying champagne for all of the patrons of a sleazy nightclub to impress the pretty wife of a pickpocket—that the police heard of his suspect behavior and extravagant unaccountable funds. Villiers was arrested in his South Kensington apartment by Detective-Inspector Dinnie. Readily admitting his guilt, Villiers told Dinnie, "You would not have got me if it had not been for the women and drink. I was a fool." Tried at the Clerkenwell Sessions, he pleaded guilty, but refused to tell where most of the jewelry had gone. Villiers was sentenced to seven years in prison.

REF.: *CBA;* Dilnot, *Great Detectives and Their Methods.*

Vincent, Saint, d.304, Roman., her. On the orders of Diocletian, who persecuted Christians, he was tortured and executed at Valencia, Spain. REF.: *CBA.*

Vincent, Gaius Tom, and **Dawson, Frank Albert**, prom. 1910, Brit., fraud. Two "businessmen" whose entire operation consisted of mailing out fraudulent circulars and collecting money from "investors" were arrested in April 1910 in London. Gaius Tom Vincent and Frank Albert Dawson worked together as two separate companies that were businesses in name only.

Their circulars explained how simple it was to turn £5 into £40. Readers who invested £5 based on the brochure were then written to and congratulated on the profit they had made with their initial investment. None of the money was sent to the clients, but they were told that an additional £20 would increase their profits still more. The letter of congratulations came from "McPherson, Brady & Co.," which was Vincent's mythical company. By the next morning, the lucky investors would receive a pamphlet from Dawson's "Bruce Desmond & Co.," organization, an equally fictitious business which sent out pamphlets titled, "How to make money hand over fist." The detective who raided Vincent and Dawson's shared office found only rubber signature stamps, and a hard working but ill-informed typist. Each week, about 11,000 circulars were mailed out. About £12,255 had come in to the entrepreneurs from all over England by the time of their arrest. Both Vincent and Dawson were found Guilty, and sent to jail.

REF.: *CBA;* Nicholls, *Crime Within the Square Mile.*

Vincent, Sir Howard (Charles Edward Howard), 1849-1908, Brit., law enfor. off. First director of criminal investigation for Scotland Yard, from 1878-84. Book authored: *Police Code and Manual of Criminal Law.*

REF.: *CBA;* Jeyes, *The Life of Sir Howard Vincent.*

Vincentello d'Istria, 1380-1434, Istria, rebel. Instigated revolt with Alfonso V of Aragon against Genoese in Corsica, circa 1414. He was later caught and executed by the Genoese. REF.: *CBA.*

Vindiola, Bernard, prom. 1977, U.S., (wrong. convict.) mur. Shortly after midnight on July 22, 1976, T.J. McCoy, a security guard at the Peek-A-Boo Bar in Fowler, Calif., was shot to death while trying to break up a fight at the bar. Two brothers, Bernard and Eddie Vindiola, were involved, along with their sisters and several friends. Four witnesses in the dimly lit bar said they thought Bernard Vindiola had killed McCoy. Christina Vindiola told officers that night that Eddie had shot McCoy, but later said she implicated Eddie only because she was angry with him.

Bernard was convicted of second-degree murder, and was sentenced to five years to life. But the conviction was reversed on appeal, on the grounds that only hearsay evidence identified Bernard, rather than Eddie, as the murderer, and because the judge excluded evidence of Eddie's prior felony convictions, which might have impeached his testimony. Eddie been arrested for a parole violation only that day, and was known to be carrying a gun. His girlfriend had been involved in the brawl that McCoy was trying to break up when he was shot. The higher court also questioned the reliability of the eyewitness account. When a prosecution witness admitted that she had earlier told police that Bernard had not committed the crime, the prosecution dropped the charges, and Bernard Vindiola was released. REF.: *CBA.*

Viner, Charles, 1678-1756, Brit., jur. Wrote twenty-three volume *Abridgement of Law and Equity,* published from 1742-53. REF.: *CBA.*

Vineyard, James R., prom. 1842, Case of, U.S., mur. In 1842, the Council of the Territory of Wisconsin was hotly debating the appointment of a sheriff for Grant County. While Governor Doty appointed nominee Enos S. Baker as his choice, the post was also sought by both Councillor James R. Vineyard and his brother. Baker's petition had 430 signatures; while the petition for Councillor Vineyard's brother had 811. The total number of signatures (1,241) was far greater than the number of legal voters in the county. On Feb. 5, 1842, the council set aside time to debate Baker's nomination, and the discrepancy in the number of signatures was discussed. The Honorable Charles Coatsworth Pinckney Arndt was unrestrained in his criticism of the petitions and he railed against the situation. Vineyard was extremely unhappy about Arndt's diatribe. The matter was repeatedly tabled unitl Feb. 11, when Vineyard openly accused Arndt of being a liar. The council adjourned, and Arndt asked Vineyard if he had accused him of lying. Vineyard said yes, Arndt tried to strike Vineyard, who pulled out a gun and shot him to death. According to the Madison *Enquirer,* Vineyard later said he was sorry Arndt was dead, but that it could not be helped. When Vineyard wrote a letter of resignation to the council, it was rejected; the council voted to expel him instead.

Although the inquest clearly stated that Arndt had been murdered, almost a year went by before Vineyard was tried. Defense lawyers called witnesses who testified to seeing Arndt and Vineyard standing near the fireplace "with their arms around each other's necks" just minutes before the shooting. Attorneys for the defense, Alexander P. Field, Moses Strong, and William Hamilton, secured a writ of *habeas corpus* and a bail of $20,000 for their client. The case was debated in both the Milwaukee and Madison press at great length, assiduously argued back and forth in editorials. In Oct. 1843, Vineyard was tried and acquitted. Author Charles Dickens made note of the affair in his *American Notes,* using it to bolster his argument about the connection between slavery and brutalization. Following his acquittal, Vineyard left Wisconsin to search for gold in California.

REF.: *CBA;* Derleth, *Wisconsin Murders.*

Vinocur, Barry Allan, prom. 1980, U.S., fraud. Pretending to be a physician for four years, Barry Allan Vinocur specialized in the care of newborn infants at Mt. Zion Hospital and the University of California Medical Center in San Francisco. Vinocur won national recognition in 1978 for helping to discover a rare and fatal infant disease. In July 1980, the 32-year-old was brought before Municipal Court Judge Frank Hart. In the ten-minute proceeding, Vinocur pleaded no contest to misdemeanor charges of claiming to be a doctor when he had no license, and practicing without a license. Hart gave Vinocur a ninety-day suspended sentence, put him on probation for eighteen months, fined him $200, and ordered him to perform 100 hours of community service. Vinocur had used the credentials of his cousin, who had the same surname and was almost the same age, to obtain a medical license. A reviewing committee discovered the fraud in April 1980. REF.: *CBA.*

Vinogradoff, Sir Paul Gavrilovitch, 1854-1925, Brit., jur. Russian-born historian of medieval Britain and expert on customs and laws of early Britain. He taught jurisprudence at Oxford from 1903-25. Books authored: *Villainage in England* in 1892, and an uncompleted work, *Historical Jurisprudence.* REF.: *CBA.*

Vinson, Frederick Moore, 1890-1953, U.S., jur. Born in Louisa, Ky., Frederick Moore Vinson was the son of a county jailer. Vinson earned a law degree in 1911, and set up private practice in his hometown. Appointed city attorney in 1913, Vinson was active in local Democratic politics. After serving in WWI, he resumed his practice and was soon appointed commonwealth attorney for the 32nd Kentucky judicial district, a position he held for two years until being elected to congress in 1924. Vinson became a specialist in economic matters in the House of Representatives and was active on the House and Ways Means Committee where he supported a reform of federal tax codes. Defeated in 1928, he returned to the House two years later and was reelected for another three terms.

Vinson resigned from the House in 1938 to accept a presidential appointment as U.S. Court of Appeals Judge for the District of Columbia. In 1946, he was appointed by President Harry S. Truman to be chief justice of the U.S. Supreme Court, a position he held for seven years. Vinson became a defender of federal intervention in social and economic matters. In 1947, he upheld the contempt convictions of union leader John L. Lewis, who had refused to call off a strike by miners despite a court order. Vinson argued in favor of the president's constitutional authority to nationalize the steel industry during a national emergency (the Korean War), and viewed government loyalty oaths and investigations of subversive groups during the Cold War years as a legitimate concern of national security. One of Vinson's last controversial opinions was in the case of Julius and Ethel Rosenberg, who were convicted of selling nuclear secrets to the U.S.S.R., and were sentenced to death. When Associate Justice William O. Douglas granted a last-minute stay of execution, Vinson called a special session of the Supreme Court to lift the stay, on the grounds that legal objections to the death sentence in this case were not adequate to justify further litigation. The Rosenbergs were executed later that same day. Vinson died in 1953 in Washington, D.C. See: **Douglas, William O(rville).** REF.: *CBA.*

Vintenon, François, d.1946, Fr., (unsolv.) mur. An introverted, sensitive man, François Vintenon was tall and thin, and had a face that his friends described as that of a "perverse angel." From a prosperous family, Vintenon joined the French surrealists of the Left Bank, wrote incoherent poetry, lived by stealing, and frequented Paris' exotic Latin Quarter. After the German invasion, his merchant father became a collaborator to save his business; he persuaded his son to become a writer for a Nazi publishing company for 10,000 francs monthly. After eight months, Vintenon quit and joined the Resistance, where he carried messages and distributed underground pamphlets. Liberation left him at loose ends, and he turned to a morphine derivative called eubine to enliven his existence. He used the drug at first on weekends, when he would see his girlfriend, Jeanne. He found it increased his sexual prowess. Vintenon was soon addicted, and began forging prescriptions to supply his ever-increasing needs. Police tracked him for eight months, and captured him while he slept on a bench after drugging himself with sleeping pills when he could not get eubine.

Criminal charges were delayed while he tried to cure himself of his addiction, but Vintenon soon dropped the program and sought aid from friend and doctor Pierre Roumeguere. Roumeguere practiced medicine only briefly while in the navy, preferring to study for years, amassing numerous diplomas and degrees. He had escaped from the Nazis after being sentenced to death on three different occasions. Roumeguere had a beard, dark eyes, and a long nose; features that inspired the moniker "Dr. Satan." Roumeguere had once been a pupil of Jean-Paul Sartre, the creator of Existentialist philosophy. Later, Roumeguere branched off into his own studies of "psychophysiological" aesthetic principles. Dr. Satan kept a hut, used for romantic and erotic liaisons, in a wooded area near Gif-sur-Yvette; he called his hut "the House of the Good God." Vintenon and Roumeguere visited the hut one Saturday night together. The next day Vintenon's girlfriend joined him there, and Roumeguere left. On Sunday, Vintenon returned to Paris with Jeanne, then went back to the hut alone, after stopping at a village tavern to eat a meal and swallow several pills. The next weekend, Roumeguere discovered what he believed to be the body of a very large black man in the hut. It was Vintenon's corpse, bloated, black, and gleaming. Both sides of the torso, from groin to rib, had apparently been burned by a very strong chemical.

When held for investigation by police, Roumeguere, the primary suspect, fasted to sharpen his thoughts. When an irate interrogator yelled and asked him why he knew such crazy people, Roumeguere responded, "I am a psychiatrist. It is my business to know crazy people. But how about the people you associate with? Aren't most of them criminals?" The psychiatrist-philosopher was soon released. Farmers had seen a painter near the hut, and Existentialist artist Georges Patrix was questioned, but was also cleared. A Nazi document in the hut told of a painter, Claude Lormeau, who had fought with the Germans against the Russians. A Lormeau original in the hut of a black, white-eyed face, looked grotesquely like the face of Vintenon's corpse. But the painting had been done months before the murder, and Lormeau was also cleared. The bizarre circumstances of Vintenon's death have never been accounted for. Details of the case were used in the 1947 movie *The Two Mrs. Carrolls.*

REF.: *CBA;* (FILM), *The Two Mrs. Carrolls.*

Viola, Mr., See: **Matteotti, Giacomo.**

Visconti, Gian Galeazzo (Giangaleazzo, Giovanni Galeazzo), 1351-1402, Italy, mur.? Member of influential Lombard family of Milan. He and his uncle, Bernabo, held power as joint rulers from 1378-85. On his orders his uncle was put in prison and may have been murdered. REF.: *CBA.*

Visconti, Gianmaria (Giovanni Maria), 1389-1412, Italy, duke, assass. Son of Gian Galeazzo Visconti and ruler of Italy from 1402-12. He was assassinated. REF.: *CBA.*

Visconti, Girolamo (Hieronymous Vicecomes), prom. 1448-77, Italy, witchcraft. The manuscript *Little Book on Witches,* published about 1460 by Girolamo Visconti, was one of the earliest diatribes to spread the delusion of witchcraft. Professor of Logic at the University of Milan from 1448 and Lombardy's Dominican provincial from 1465 until his death in 1477, Visconti's writings purported to distinguish between the reality and the heresy of witchcraft. Visconti were believed to be the inquisitor at Como whose massive burnings of witches were admired in the *Malleus Maleficarum.*

REF.: *CBA;* Hansen, *Quellen und Untersuchungen zur Geschichte des Hexenwahns und der Hexenverfolg im Mittelalter;* Lea, *Materials Toward a History of Witchcraft;* Robbins, *The Encyclopedia of Witchcraft and Demonology;* Visconti, *Lamiurum sive Striarum Opusculum.*

Vitale, John Joseph (AKA: **Johnny V., John Vitali**), 1909- , U.S., drugs-org. crime. Born in St. Louis, John Vitale's criminal record dates back to when he was eleven and includes arrests for armed robbery, forgery, carrying a concealed weapon, receiving stolen property, murder, and violation of Federal narcotic laws. He was a member of the Mafia's midwestern narcotics trafficking organization, which supplied pure heroin to New York and other U.S. cities.

REF.: Alexander, *The Pizza Connection; CBA;* McClellan, *Crime Without Punishment.*

Vitalis, Leon, and **Boyer, Marie**, prom. 1877, Fr., mur. When retired merchant Boyer died in May 1874, his only child, Marie Boyer, was enrolled in a Marseilles convent and his wife was having an affair with Leon Vitalis, a 21-year-old bookseller's assistant. Boyer had left his fortune, about 100,000 francs, to his daughter, appointing his wife as her legal guardian until Marie came of age. Realizing that the money would go to the church if Marie took religious vows, Madame Boyer removed 15-year-old Marie from the convent. She also gave Vitalis enough money to buy a bookstore, where he sold pornographic books and photographs while working as an illegal moneylender. When Marie returned home, Vitalis began a campaign to win her affections. Her mother became jealous and reenrolled her daughter in a convent in Lyons. The widow Boyer and Vitalis then moved to a country house in Montpellier.

In the winter of 1875, Boyer and Vitalis gave up their country house and moved to a Montpellier suburb. In January 1876, security bonds valued at about 11,000 francs were stolen from Boyer's home. Soon afterwards, Vitalis left for Paris on business and Boyer was convinced that he had taken the bonds. During his abscence, Vitalis frequently wrote Marie, and when Madame Boyer became seriously ill in January 1877, he and Marie became lovers. Boyer then became repentant, decided to renounce her paramour, and recover her power of attorney from him. When she recovered from her illness, Boyer turned on Vitalis, accused him of swindling her, and ordered him to leave the house.

The young couple, who had often wished that Boyer would die, decided to murder her. On Mar. 19, Vitalis struck Boyer when she returned from church. As Marie banged cupboard doors and kitchen drawers to cover her mother's cries, the slight and clumsy Vitalis tried first to strangle his former lover. When that failed, he asked Marie to give him a cheese knife (he had dropped a kitchen knife during the struggle), and he stabbed Boyer to death. The couple then dismembered the body, carried it out of the house in parcels, and dumped them into a ditch. An inquisitive neighbor reported their actions to police who recovered the parcels and arrested the couple. Tried at the Aix Assizes on July 2, 1877, Vitalis was sentenced to death, and executed on Aug. 17. Marie was given penal servitude for life; her exemplary behavior in jail earned her an early release in 1892.

REF.: *CBA;* Irving, *A Book of Remarkable Criminals;* Pearce, *Unsolved Murder Mysteries.*

Vittorio, Emanuele III, 1869-1947, Italy, king, attempt. assass. In late April 1928, it was time for Milan's annual Sample Fair. Italy's king Vittorio Emanuele III was to officially open the proceedings with a royal procession through town. Thousands of Italians lined the streets to catch a glimpse of the man who had ruled the country since the turn of the century. As Vittorio's car moved slowly through Milan, a thunderous explosion ripped through the Square of Julius Caesar. Some ten minutes later, the king drove past the grisly scene in which the streets were still slick with blood. After officially opening the Sample Fair, the king rushed to the hospital where many of the victims were being treated. Eighteen people were killed in the bombing. See: **Mussolini, Benito.** REF.: *CBA.*

Vizzini, Calògero (AKA: **Don Calò**), 1877-1947, Si., org. crime. From his domain in the mountains of western Sicily, Don Calògero Vizzini, an unkempt peasant's son, commanded more respect than all the politicians in Rome. For Vizzini was the acknowledged ruler of the Sicilian Mafia—known as the "Honored Society" to the fearful inhabitants of the feudal, backward town of Villalba which he called home for his entire life.

Early on, Vizzini abandoned the spiritual teachings of his parents for the traditional agnosticism of the admired local mafiosi. At seventeen he was arrested for assault, after beating up the suitor of a girl that Vizzini liked. His uncle got the charges dismissed but the following year Vizzini joined up with the bandit king Paolo Varsalona. The Varsalona bandits, with Vizzini riding among them, terrorized the villages of Sicily for many years.

Sicilian Mafia don Calògero Vizzini.

Vizzini remained a trusted sidekick of Varsalona through WWI. During this time he was admitted to the Honored Society and given the title of *Zu,* meaning uncle, or trusted friend. The prefix *Don,* the highest honor afforded a Mafioso would come later. Vizzini had become, in Mafia parlance, a "man of respect" and was recognized as the head of the Cosa Nostra in the Province of Caltanissetta. Before Benito Mussolini came to power in 1922 and curbed the growing power of the Mafia, Vizzini ruthlessly displaced a number of the feudal barons of the region. After seeing to it that there were no other bidders present he bought uncultivated land from the Suora Marchesa estate at minimal cost. Vizzini and other Mafia chieftains continued to purchase feudal lands despite the protestations of the largely powerless aristocracy. Those who attempted to organize armed vigilante groups for their own protection found their grapevines cut down and their livestock slaughtered.

Vizzini's funeral in Villalba, Si., 1954.

The clash between Mussolini and the Mafia deprived Vizzini of some of his newly won privileges. Under the leadership of Cesare Mori—the Duce's "incarnation of the pure white flame of Fascist justice"—powerful and long-standing Mafia leaders like Don Vito Cascio Ferro were imprisoned. When Ferro died in prison Vizzini rose to the top rung of the Mafia hierarchy. When the war came, Vizzini and his henchmen cooperated with the allies as a way of ending the Mori terror. After U.S. forces liberated Sicily, the aging Mafia don was named an honorary colonel in the army, days after being elected the mayor of Villalba. His political influence and connections were immense. The exiled U.S. crime boss Vito Genovese worked through Vizzini, helping to supply him with all the blackmarket gasoline he required. Vizzini was permitted to sit in on sensitive political discussions among the allied governments about the future of Sicily. He argued for moderates who favored a union with the British or Americans.

The growing spectre of trade unionism and domestic communism was the thing Vizzini feared the most under the post-war democratic government of Italy. In characteristic fashion, he took steps to assure that the unbending power of the Mafia would not be challenged by the left-wing Popular Front, or other contemporary socialist coalitions. On Sept. 16, 1944, the leaders of the Popular Front staged a political rally in the public square of Villalba. Vizzini permitted the left-wing politician Girolamo Li Causi to deliver an address to the villagers, but stipulated that he would not be permitted to raise the issue of agrarian reform. When Li Causi began speaking about the forbidden subject, Vizzini's private army fired on the crowd. The socialist politician and thirteen other persons were wounded. Those responsible for the massacre at Villalba were not apprehended for another fourteen years. The gunmen were eventually found Guilty, but were given general amnesty because of the vagaries of the Sicilian legal system and the pervasive influence of the Mafia.

Because of Vizzini's influence, western Sicily was spared much of the wartime devastation suffered by the Italian mainland. Though he did not succeed in his post-war goal of unifying Sicily with the U.S. (as the forty-ninth state), the Mafia leader was revered in death. A funeral notice posted on the church door proclaimed that his virtues were acknowledged by "friend and foe alike." See: **Black Hand; Mafia, The.**

REF.: *CBA;* Lewis, *The Honored Society;* Moorehead, *Hostages to Fortune;* Peterson, *The Mob;* Servadio, *Mafioso.*

Vlad Dracul (Basarab), prom. 1436-47, mur. Vlad Dracul of the Basarab dynasty, ruled Walachia, later Romania. His barbarousness and cruelty resulted in the legend of Dracula. Dracul, meaning devil or the terrible one, was noted for ordering mass killings for his amusement. Another legend contends that Vlad Dracul bathed in the blood of his victims. REF.: *CBA.*

Vladimirescu, Tudor, c.1780-1821, Gr., consp. Served in Russian army as officer before joining Greek rebel group Philiki Etairia. He instigated a rebellion in 1821 in Walachia in opposition to the Greek-Turkish administration. He was thought to have conspired with the Turks and was put to death at the command of the rebels. REF.: *CBA.*

Vlad Tepes (Basarab, AKA: **Vlad the Impaler)**, prom. 1456-62, 1476-77, mur. Vlad Tepes rivaled his father, Vlad Dracul, in practicing extreme cruelty in his kingdom of Walachia (later Romania). Vlad Tepes' castle, high in the Carpathian Mountains of Transylvania, later inspired novelist Bram Stoker for the location of the castle of his infamous fictional monster, Dracula. Stoker drew from the lives of both Vlad Dracul and Vlad Tepes to create his frightening character, but most of his research is based on Vlad Tepes, also known as Vlad the Impaler.

Vlad Tepes, bloodthirsty ruler of Walachia (Romania), on whom the Dracula legend is based.

Vlad Tepes impaled his enemies on high spikes, reportedly murdering 50,000 victims in this fashion. He became a sadistic monster who dined amidst victims impaled on spikes. It was also said that he drank the blood of these hapless persons, thus giving rise to Stoker's tale of a blood-drinking vampire, who survived on the blood of the living. Vlad Tepes was a hopeless pervert who enjoyed the pain of others, reserving his special wrath for Saxon invaders and Turkish merchants. He impaled the Saxons and tortured the Turks by having their turbans nailed to their heads.

Though feared as a bloodlusting maniac by foreigners, Vlad Tepes was considered a hero by his own people—a great warrior who finally rid Walachia of foreign invaders. Historically he is remembered, thanks to novelist Stoker, as an inhuman beast whose lethal reputation conjured images of undead spirits and bloodsucking vampire bats.

REF.: *CBA;* (FILM), *Dracula,* 1931; *Son of Dracula,* 1933; *Dracula's Daughter,* 1936; *The Return of the Vampire,* 1944; *House of Dracula,* 1945; *The Horror of Dracula,* 1958; *The Return of Dracula,* 1958; *Dracula—Prince of Darkness,* 1966; *The Naked World of Harrison Marks,* 1967; *Dracula Has Risen From His Grave,* 1968; *Dracula (The Dirty Old Man),* 1969; *Guess What Happened to Count Dracula,* 1970; *The Scars of Dracula,* 1970; *Taste the Blood of Dracula,* 1970; *Dracula A.D. 1972,* 1972; *Dracula Versus Frankenstein,* 1972; *Dracula's Great Love,* 1972; *Lake of Dracula,* 1973; *The Lady Dracula,* 1974; *Son of Dracula,* 1974; *Old Dracula,* 1975; *The Saga of Dracula,* 1975; *Dracula and Son,* 1976; *Dracula and the Seven Golden Vampires,* 1978; *Dracula's Dog,* 1978; *Dracula,* 1979; *Fracchia Contro Dracula,* 1985; *Transylvania 6-5000,* 1985.

Vogel, Amsel, and **Smilovics, Jankel**, and **Herschko, David**, and **Gross, Martin**, and **Klein, Ignatz**, prom. 1882, Case of, Aust.-Hung., mur. On Apr. 1, 1882, Esther Solymossy, a 14-year-old maid, left her mistress' house in the small town of Tisza-Eszlár, Hung., to go shopping. Solymossy never returned. A search of the area, directed by Security Commissioner Recsky, revealed nothing. By May, grotesque rumors of Solymossy being murdered in a "Jewish blood ritual" began to circulate. The district to which Tisza-Eslár belonged was represented in Parliament by Deputy Onody, a malicious anti-Semite, known for spreading slander against the Jews. The son of Joseph Scharf, a rabbi's assistant, allegedly told of his father and the butcher slaughtering Solymossy in the synagogue. He and his brother Moritz has seen "the blood being caught in a plate." Onody encouraged several local families to bribe the Scharf children into making accusatory statements. Examining Magistrate Bary came with his clerk, Piczely, and security commissioners Recsky and Pay, along with several policemen, to investigate. A tool of Onody, Bary turned Moritz Scharf over to his clerks with instructions to get "some kind of usable confession." Locking the boy in a stable, and then beating him brutally, the clerks got their confession, then kept Scharf in complete isolation. Joseph Scharf's well-corroborated statements regarding his whereabouts the day of the alleged murder were ignored by Bary, who received many letters from anti-Semites which reinforced his idea of a ritual murder.

On June 18, 1882, the field keeper of the village discovered the corpse of a young girl in the river. In its hand was a cloth in which vitriol crystals were wrapped; Solymossy had purchased crystals the day she disappeared. Bary rushed to the scene, and brought in the bereaved mother who confirmed the fact that the dead girl was wearing a dress that looked like one of Esther's. With no explanation, she maintained that the corpse was not her daughter. Two local physicians concluded that the deceased was at least eighteen years old, had been dead for ten days at most, had died of anemia, had had frequent intercourse, and had belonged to a wealthy class, based on her smooth hands and feet. None of these observations applied to Solymossy. Bary decided the dead girl was linked with Solymossy, and was dressed up in her clothing as a decoy, to save the defendants from murder charges. An anonymous letter from a writer who made the same conclusion accused two rivermen, Jankel Smilovics and David Herschko, of participating in the "plot," and said Amsel Vogel had masterminded it. All three were tortured and made to confess.

The case became the focus of Parliamentary debates in Vienna and Budapest. Prosecutor Szeiffert was assigned to the case by the Chief Prosecutor's Office in Budapest, with noted defense lawyer Parliamentary Deputy Karl von Eötvös volunteering to represent the defense. Eötvös brought in three pathologists, Johannes Belki, thirty-two, of Budapest, and two older pathologists for support. Bary refused the request for exhumation of the body, but State Prosecutor Szeiffert supported the motion, and the body was exhumed on Dec. 3, 1882. The report, made on Jan. 8, stated that the girl was fourteen or fifteen, could easily have been in the water for several months, was a virgin, had probably often walked barefoot, and that the first examiners were in complete ignorance of the changes that occur in the skin of someone who drowns. They concluded that the corpse was Solymossy. Bary refused to enter their verdict in the record, so Eötvös called in Professor Eduard von Hoffman, the highest Austrian authority on forensic medicine, in June 1883. Hoffman gave Eötvös a statement that became the cornerstone of the attorney's seven-hour speech. Since the trial had begun on June 13, Bary's methods had been exposed and Piczely, his clerk, revealed as a murderer and ex-convict. On Aug. 3, 1883, all the defendants were pronounced innocent.

REF.: *CBA;* Thorwald, *The Century of the Detective.*

Vogt, Milo F., 1899- , U.S., brib. A contractor in downstate Illinois, Milo F. Vogt pleaded guilty to bribery in June 1975 in a Springfield federal court. He had participated in a scheme in which bribes were paid to former Secretary of State Paul Powell so that Vogt's plumbing and heating company would be awarded a $1.5 million contract for work on the State Capitol. Vogt was given an $11,000 fine and a three month jail sentence, which he did not serve because of a heart condition. When the semi-retired Vogt, seventy-three at the time, was indicted in 1975, contractor Ralph Vancil was also charged; it was established that Vogt and Vancil met and agreed that Vogt would submit a lower bid for the capitol work. Vancil also pleaded guilty, and was given a two-year sentence. He died serving his time at the federal penitentiary in Marion, Ill. REF.: *CBA.*

Voight, Wilhelm, d.1914, Ger., fraud. Uniforms represent the law of the land, and the commands of a uniformed officer are to be obeyed. Playing on the substantial power of military uniforms, Wilhelm Voight, a petty criminal turned shoemaker, had a field day with the people in the town of Kopenick, Ger. On Oct. 16, 1906, Voight, dressed in a newly purchased and very impressive uniform of a Prussian captain, commandeered a small detachment of German soldiers in the town of Kopenick. He led them to the town hall where he placed the town's burgomaster, Dr. Langerhans, and its treasurer under arrest. He informed them that he had to take them to Berlin to discuss irregularities in the town's finances.

German imposter Wilhelm Voight.

Voight leaving prison, 1908, after serving twenty months for his outrageous impersonation of a Prussian officer.

Local police officials came into the city hall while this was going on and were also impressed into the captain's service. 1After relieving the treasurer of all of the cash in the town's vault, Voight marched his troops and prisoners to Berlin, where he left them and disappeared.

After much confusion as to why the Kopenick officials were in Berlin, the incident was determined to have been a hoax. When the news of the incident got out, the newspapers ridiculed the town of Kopenick for their inordinate respect for a uniform. Nine days later, Voight was apprehended and placed under arrest. The bogus captain served only twenty months in jail, after which he spent a lucrative few years on the American vaudeville circuit telling the story of his adventure in uniform.

REF.: *CBA;* MacDougall, *Hoaxes;* Nash, *Zanies;* (FILM), *Captain from Koepenick,* 1933; *The Captain from Koepenick,* 1956.

Voirbo, Pierre, c.1838-69, Fr., suic.-mur. The apprehension of Pierre Voirbo was a brilliant piece of detective work on the part of Gustave Macé, a renowned French sleuth. Voirbo, the illegitimate son of an executioner's assistant, worked as a tailor in Paris. While his wife he was serving time in prison, Voirbo became involved with Adélia Rémondé, a young woman who was studying to become a nun. Adélia gave up her vows to marry Voirbo, but the tailor first needed to obtain a divorce. Voirbo approached his friend Désiré Bodasse for a loan of 10,000 francs to complete the legal work. When the 72-year-old Bodasse refused to hand over the money, Voirbo decided to lure the old man up to his room on Mazarine Street to murder him.

On Dec. 13, 1868, as Bodasse entered the room, Voirbo dealt him a single blow with a blunt iron rod, killing him immediately. Voirbo hacked the body to pieces and threw the head into the Seine River from the Concorde Bridge. The smaller body parts were disposed of in a similar manner. Voirbo then sewed Bodasse's legs into black calico bags and dropped them into a well behind Lampon's Eating House on Princesse Street. Satisfied that he had adequately covered his tracks, Voirbo moved to new quarters on Lamartine Street. In January 1869, he married Adélia Rémondé.

When the water in his well began tasting bad, the owner of Lampon's cleaned out the interior. On Jan. 26, he removed Voirbo's bloody parcel. The horrifying discovery was reported to Detective Macé who launched an investigation. The fine sewing and the embroidered letter "B" on the bundle was obviously done by a professional. Macé interviewed numerous people in the district, including a tailoress who lived above the restaurant. She told the detective that Voirbo was a frequent visitor, and had often fetched water from the well for her. She knew Désiré Bodasse as well. Pierre Voirbo and the retired craftsman were good friends, it seemed.

Bodasse's aunt identified the stocking on the disembodied leg as belonging to her nephew. When asked about his friend's disappearance, Voirbo displayed characteristic glibness. Unimpressed, Macé commenced a thorough search of Voirbo's rooms. He found a tin box containing Bodasse's personal belongings. Although the room had been scrubbed clean following the murder, Macé lifted the floor tiles and found specimens of dried blood on the underside. Voirbo confessed to the murder and was arrested the day before he was scheduled to sail for the U.S. Failing in his escape attempt the tailor smuggled a straight razor concealed in a loaf of bread into his prison cell and used it to cut his throat.

REF.: Brock, *A Casebook of Crime; CBA;* Cohen, *One Hundred True Crime Stories;* Dilnot, *Great Detectives and Their Methods;* Gribble, *Famous Feats of Detection and Deduction;* Hibbert, *The Roots of Evil;* Kingston, *A Dictionary of Remarkable Rogues;* Lambton, *Echoes of Causes Celebres;* Logan, *Rope, Knife and Chair;* Whitelaw, *Corpus Delicti;* Wilson, *Encyclopedia of Murder;* Wren, *Masterstrokes of Murder.*

Voisin, La, See: **Deshayes, Catherine.**

Voisin, Louis Marie Joseph (Louis Voison, AKA: The Soho Butcher), c.1875-1918, and **Roche, Berthe**, d.1919, Brit., mur. Louis Voisin was a French butcher who lived and worked in the Soho district of London during WWI. Voisin had two mistresses, neither of whom knew of the other. In the midst of an air raid attack from the German Zeppelins on Oct. 31, 1917, one of Voisin's mistresses, 32-year-old Émilienne Gérard, disappeared. Gérard lived in a flat on Munster Square near Regent's Park and on Nov. 2, a street sweeper making the rounds of Regent Square in Bloomsbury found two curious looking meat sacks wrapped in a sheet. The man opened the packages and found the torso and arms of Émilienne Gérard. A piece of brown paper bore the inscription "Blodie Belgiam."

Detective Frederick Wensley of Scotland Yard undertook the investigation. Through a laundry mark found on the sheet, he established the identity of the victim and then searched her apartment for clues. A portrait of Voisin and a £50 IOU put him on the butcher's trail. Wensley found Voisin and Berthe Roche, his other girlfriend, in his building on Charlotte Street. Voisin denied any knowledge of the murder.

A search of Voisin's basement turned up Gérard's head and hands in a covered cask. Confronted with this evidence, Voisin claimed that he had stopped by her place on Nov. 1 and found body parts scattered around the flat. Fearing that someone was trying to "set him up," Voisin said he decided to dispose of the remains in the streets. The police deduced that Gérard had paid an unexpected call on Voisin during the air raid instead of seeking shelter in the subway and had found him with Roche. A violent quarrel ensued and Gérard was killed. Pathologist Bernard Spilsbury testified that the dead woman had been beaten over the head repeatedly.

Charged with murder, Louis Voisin and Berthe Roche appeared before Justice Charles Darling at the Old Bailey in January 1918. Voisin repeated his original alibi and was found Guilty of murder. He was subsequently hanged at Pentonville Prison. Roche was charged as an accessory after the fact and was held over until the next session. She was eventually sentenced to seven years in prison by Justice Horace Avory. After another year had passed Berthe Roche was certified insane. She was transferred to the institution at Highgate where she died on May 22, 1919. See: **Wensley, Frederick.**

REF.: Barker, *Lord Darling's Famous Cases;* Brock, *A Casebook of Crime;* Browne and Tullett, *The Scalpel of Scotland Yard; CBA;* Dearden, *Some Cases of Sir Bernard Spilsbury and Others;* Dilnot, *The Real Detective;* Heppenstall, *Bluebeard and After;* Jacobs, *Aspects of Murder;* Kingston, *Dramatic Days at the Old Bailey;* Laurence, *A History of Capital Punishment;* Shew, *A Second Companion to Murder;* Speer, *The Secret History of Great Crimes;* Thomson, *The Story of Scotland Yard;* Townsend, *Black Cap, Murder Will Out;* Tullett, *Strictly Murder;* Wensley, *Forty Years of Scotland Yard;* Whitelaw, *Corpus Delicti;* Wilson, *Encyclopedia of Murder;* Woodhall, *Secrets of Scotland Yard.*

Voiss, Peter, b.1862, Case of, U.S., mur. Peter Voiss, seventy-four, prospected for gold in the hills of the Sierra Nevadas, and charged tourists fifty cents to take his picture. Dr. Jasper Gattucio met Peter Voiss in late March or early April 1936. With camera in hand, he asked to take a photograph of the old prospector; Voiss posed next to his trademark wooden two-wheeled cart and his three burros. After taking the photograph, Gattucio thanked the man, then climbed back into his car, and resumed his journey. Voiss, expecting his usual fifty cents, angrily scribbled down the dentist's license plate number, vowing to collect on the debt. Three weeks later, on Apr. 23, the two men met by chance near San Jose, Calif.

Pleased to have another chance to take Voiss' picture, Gattucio readied his camera. Voiss grabbed a gun from the back of his cart, and shot Gattucio to death as he tried to jump into his car. In the three-week trial of the "Camera Killer," the defense pleaded that the murder was justifiable homicide. Voiss testified that he had drawn his gun to frighten Gattucio but that it had fired accidentally. A witness for the prosecution explained that two weeks before Gattucio's murder, she had photographed Voiss, and he had afterwards threatened her with the same gun he later used to kill the dentist. On July 2, 1936, having concluded the murder was an accident, the jury found Voiss Not Guilty. REF.: *CBA.*

Vojkov, Peter Lazarevitch, prom. 1927, Pol., polit., assass. On his way back to Moscow on a train from Berlin in mid-June 1927 A.P. Rosengolz, the expelled Soviet *chargé d'affaires* to Britain, was welcomed by Peter Lazarevitch Vojkov, the Soviet minister to Poland, when the train stopped at the Warsaw Central Station. As the comrades paced the platform, talking, 19-year-old Boris Kovemnko, a Vilna high school student, approached and asked Vojkov if he would please help him obtain a passport to Russia, beginning to explain in detail how he had been refused. When Rosengolz and Vojkov ignored Kovemnko, he pulled out a revolver and fired at Vojkov, emptying his gun into the prone body. Rosengolz was wounded before he could fire in defense. At a Special Tribunal which heard his case soon after, Kovemnko explained, "I killed M. Vojkov, but I did not kill him as a person. I killed him because of what the Bolshevists have done in Russia." Taking into consideration that Kovemnko, an anti-Communist, had once served in the Soviet army, and that his character was vouched for as "entirely honorable," the court sentenced the assassin to life imprisonment, recommending that it be commuted to fifteen years. REF.: *CBA.*

Voldemaras, Augustinas, b.1883, Lithuania, polit. corr. Tyrannical ruler who held power as premier in 1918 and from 1926-29, when he was ousted. After he tried to force his way back into power in 1934, he was arrested and sentenced to twelve years at hard labor. REF.: *CBA.*

Voliva, Wilbur Glenn, 1870-1942, U.S., hoax. In 1895, John Alexander Dowie settled in Zion, Ill., where he founded the Christian Apostolic Church. A fierce, uncompromising Scotsman, Dowie proclaimed himself "General Overseer" of Zion and ruled the community with an iron fist until he was removed from office by his religious associate, Wilbur Glenn Voliva, in 1905. Voliva was an even sterner taskmaster. He made it a criminal offense to smoke or drink in Zion, and a violation of the curfew laws to stay outdoors after 10 p.m.

Zion, about forty miles north of Chicago, was ruled like a dictatorship by Voliva. Provocative attire for women, such as short skirts, swim suits, and high heels were strictly forbidden. Voliva was a proponent of the flat earth theory, and argued that the North Pole was at the center of the earth. Wilbur Voliva offered $5,000 to anyone who could prove him wrong. He claimed to be an authority in all subjects and once bragged, "I can lick to smithereens any man in the world in a mental battle. I have never met any professor or student who knew a millionth as much on any subject as I do." And when challenged in court once, Voliva screamed: "Every man who fights me goes under. Mark what I say! The graveyard is full of fellows who tried to down Voliva!"

Voliva predicted the end of the world for 1923, and revised his prediction often until his disillusioned followers finally abandoned him. Voliva vowed to live until he was 120, but died at the age of seventy-two, on Oct. 11, 1942. REF.: *CBA.*

Volk, Adam, prom. 1890, U.S., mur. Adam Volk, a saloon keeper, lived in Plain, Wis., a rough pioneer settlement where rival families frequently feuded. After Sunday Mass on July 6, 1890, several young village men crowded into Volk's saloon. Danny Ahern, a carpenter from Chicago who was visiting his fiancée, insulted Volk. Ahern continued his harangue by returning several times throughout the day growing more and more drunk, until he finally left at 4 p.m. Volk left the bar at 6 p.m. en route to the store to buy matches, when he was accosted by Ahern who challenged him to shoot it out. Volk accepted and returned to his bar to get his Winchester. When his wife, in advanced stages of pregnancy with their seventh child, tried to stop him, he pushed her away with such force that she knocked over a table and chairs in her fall; the baby was stillborn. Ahern and Volk shot it out, with Ahern the loser, dying thirty minutes later. On July 8, District Attorney R.D. Evans and Sheriff W.O. Canon arrived in Plains and arrested Volk, who claimed he had killed Ahern in self defense. The case was apparently connected with a feud between the Helkers family and the Volks, and Ahern's alleged purpose of visiting Plain to see his fiancée seemed suspicious, since he did not spend time with her. Besides, Ahern was aggressively determined to provoke Volk, whom he had never before met. Still, Volk was found Guilty and sentenced by Judge Stevens to fourteen years in Waupun Prison. After serving just three months of his term, Volk died in prison on July 6, 1891, of Bright's disease.

REF.: *CBA;* Derleth, *Wisconsin Murders.*

Vollaro, Luigi, 1938- , Italy, org. crime-mur. Part of Neapolitan folklore for years, Luigi Vollaro was one of Naples' most feared godfathers. Vollaro was captured by police in a fortress-like bunker of his luxury villa in the town of San Sebastiano on the slopes of Mt. Vesuvius. With him were his twelve "wives" and his twenty-seven children. Two dozen Carbinieri were sent to arrest the legendary figure. Police had visited Vollaro before, but were surrounded by Vollaro's harem in the garden; the godfather slipped through a trap door and escaped into the bunker where he hid until the police left. In March 1982, officers again visited the villa, refusing to leave until Vollaro went with them. Vollaro said he would kill himself by exploding a package of dynamite, "just like Hitler," but Vollaro's comrades convinced him to surrender.

Vollaro was tried and convicted of murdering his former lieutenant Giuseppe Mutillo after Mutillo left Vollaro's clan to join Raffaele Cutolo, another Neapolitan mafioso boss. With the assistance of his 22-year-old son, Raffaele Vollaro, the gangster incinerated Mutillo's body in a car. The Vollaro son was given a twenty-seven year sentence for the crime. On the day of the elder Vollaro's sentencing, his twelve consorts clung to him, weeping at the prospect of losing their lover, as Vollaro also sobbed. Legally wed to only one of the women, Vollaro also was accused of murdering one of his lovers, Giuseppina Vellota, forty-two, in a fit of rage. He allegedly used a butcher knife to cut up the corpse of the mother of three of his children, and had thrown her body parts into a smoldering Mt. Vesuvius volcanic crater. Vollaro claimed Vellota ran away to live with relatives in the U.S. In another murder charge, Vollaro was said to have slain Antonio Scuotto, a garage attendant who coveted Concetta, one of the godfather's wives. Residents of San Sebastiano said Vollaro was more concerned about the honor of his women—from whom he demanded absolute fidelity—than about taking care of business, and that this proved to be his downfall. REF.: *CBA.*

Vollman, John Jacob, 1938- , Can., mur. On May 13, 1958, 16-year-old Gaetane Bouchard of Edmundston, New Brunswick, failed to return home after a shopping trip. Her father, Wilfrid Bouchard, contacted his daughter's 20-year-old boyfriend John Vollman. Vollman said he had broken off their relationship, and planned to marry someone else. After notifying police of his daughter's disappearance, Bouchard and his 15-year-old son, Jean Guy Bouchard, went down to the local lover's retreat area, a gravel pit on the outskirts of town. They found a suede slipper, and then the body of the murdered girl. She had been stabbed and her body dragged over the ground. Plaster casts were made of automobile tire tracks found near the pit, and two miniscule chips of green paint were discovered.

A farmer remembered seeing Bouchard and a friend get into a green Pontiac with Maine license plates, and two other witnesses recalled seeing Bouchard sitting next to the driver in the same car. One of Bouchard's schoolmates later claimed that Vollman had a reputation for wanting to "go too far." Questioned by officers, Vollman denied any involvement, but the paint chips found at the scene fit spots on his car, and a strand of his hair was found clutched in Bouchard's fist. Tried on Nov. 4, 1958, in Edmundston, before Judge Arthur L. Anglin, Vollman pleaded not guilty. He was defended by attorney J.A. Pichette. Albany M. Robichaud handled the prosecution. Vollman later claimed a loss of memory resulting from psychic shock as explanation for why he could not remember the events of the day of the girl's death. The jury found him Guilty of murder and he was sentenced to death. On Feb. 14, 1959, the sentence was commuted to life imprisonment.

REF.: *CBA;* Thorwald, *Crime and Science.*

Vollmer, August, 1876-1955, U.S., law enfor. off. One of America's most influential and farsighted police chiefs, August Vollmer was the chief of police in Berkeley, Calif., from 1905 to 1932. He served in the U.S. Army as a Philippine scout and delivered mail in Berkeley before joining the police force. As a police officer, his advancement culminated with the command of a force of merely thirty officers. Since he had so few officers, he could "be fussy" in recruitment, choosing candidates who had some college education and an exposure to science.

Vollmer apprised himself of the latest scientific advances and actively sought means of implementing them in police investigations. Before the introduction of the radio, seeking a means for police to quickly respond to emergencies, he installed flashing lights connected to police headquarters in all major intersections of the city. When an officer saw a light flashing in his area, he called headquarters and received instructions. Interested also in experiments conducted in the area of lie detection, Vollmer asked a colleague, John A. Larson, to construct a lie-detecting device. He then recruited Leonard Keeler, a brilliant student at the University of California, to perfect the device which ultimately became the Keeler Polygraph.

Vollmer was well-read in police sciences. He once solved a case involving an arsonist without leaving his office by telling investigating officers to search door-to-door for a feeble-minded youth who had recently moved into the area. The officers found such a youth who readily confessed to setting the fires. When asked how he knew who to look for, Vollmer pointed to Hans Gross' work *Criminal Psychology,* where, in a chapter on nostalgia, Gross wrote that when feeble-minded people are moved to strange places they become homesick, and alleviate this feeling by starting fires.

Perhaps the most indicative measure of his effectiveness as a police chief was manifest after his retirement in 1932. By the 1940s, twenty-five former Berkeley officers under Vollmer had become police chiefs in other cities. REF.: *CBA.*

Volpi, Albino, See: **Matteotti, Giacomo.**

Volstead, Andrew John, 1860-1947, U.S., lawyer. Served in U.S. House of Representatives from 1903-23. He was the author of the Volstead Act in 1919, designed to enforce Prohibition. REF.: *CBA.*

Voltaire (AKA: **François Marie Arouet**), 1694-1778, Fr., consp. When the acerbic wit of the sharp-tongued French playwright and philosopher Voltaire offended nobleman Chevalier de Rohan, Voltaire found himself under attack. Eating dinner with a duke, Voltaire was called to the door to speak with someone, only to be dragged out by thugs who beat him up while the Chevalier cheered them on. The enraged Voltaire took fencing lessons and prepared for his revenge. His plan was cut short when the Chevalier told a royal minster of the playwright's plans. Voltaire was thrown into the infamous Bastille and released only on the condition that he leave France.

In 1761, thirty-six years later, Voltaire became involved in another case of injustice by correcting the mistaken conviction of Jean Calas, who had been found Guilty and hanged for murdering his son, Marc Antoine Calas, a young man who had actually committed suicide. Voltaire launched a one-man campaign to clear the Calas family name and to restore the property of the bereaved mother and daughters. In March 1765, the Parliament of Toulouse decided that Calas had been wrongfully executed. Voltaire called his success at vindicating the Calas name "the finest fifth act the theatre can give us." See: **Calas, Jean.** REF.: *CBA.*

Vom Rath, Ernst, d.1938, Fr., assass. The assassination of a Nazi diplomat in Paris on Nov. 7, 1938, by a German-Jewish refugee touched off a campaign of state-sponsored terror which exultant leaders of the Third Reich dubbed the *Kristallnacht* (Crystal Night). The widespread destruction and looting of Jewish businesses, homes, and synagogues deep inside German was the most serious act of terrorism perpetrated against the Jews to date. The spontaneous attacks were ordered by Propaganda Minister Dr. Joseph Goebbels and carried out by Reinhard Heydrich, number two in the S.S. hierarchy behind Heinrich Himmler. The

Nazis justified their barbarous actions of Nov. 10 as a "political demonstration" aimed against curbing Jewish terror at home and abroad.

The assassin's victim was Ernst vom Rath, third secretary of the German Embassy in Paris. Ironically, Vom Rath was the target of an internal investigation by the Gestapo who questioned his dedication to the party philosophy. Vom Rath did not share the xenophobia of his colleagues towards the Jewish race. He became a target only after the assassin, Herschel Grynszpan, could not get in to see Ambassador Count Johannes von Welczeck on Nov. 7. Grynszpan's father was one of 10,000 Jews recently deported to Poland. His decision to kill a high-ranking German official in Paris was motivated by his desire to avenge the indignities suffered by his people at the hands of the Nazis.

Young Grynszpan was arrested and held by the French government. His defense fund was raised by Dorothy Thompson, the American-born wife of author Sinclair Lewis. The money she raised by private subscription was used to pay the legal fees of France's most famous criminal lawyer of that time, Vincent de Moro-Giafferri, who gained early fame for his celebrated defense of the "French Bluebeard," Henri Désiré Landru. Grynszpan was sentenced to twenty years' imprisonment by a French court "under German supervision." See: **Heydrich, Reinhard Tristan Eugen; Himmler, Heinrich**. REF.: *CBA*.

Claus von Bülow at his trial, accused of lethal injections.

von Bülow, Claus Cecil (Claus Cecil Borberg), 1926- , Case of, U.S., asslt. Claus von Bülow's social rank as a son of the German aristocracy, his wealth, and his privileged place in J. Paul Getty's oil empire permitted him to maintain an extravagant lifestyle. Life was easy for him until July 6, 1981, when a Newport County, R.I., grand jury indicted him for attempting to murder his wife, the former Martha "Sunny" Crawford.

Von Bülow was on a business trip for Getty in 1960 when he met Martha Crawford, the wife of Alfred von Auersperg, an Austrian prince. Though titled, Martha's husband was not wealthy, and in contrast to the self-assured von Bülow, Martha considered him pompous and stodgy.

Martha met von Bülow again in 1964, by which time she had left her husband. Two years later, she and von Bülow married. "I've finally found the right girl," he said. With Martha's inherited fortune to depend on, von Bülow quit his job with Getty and set up housekeeping in a well-appointed Manhattan co-op. Martha also spent a fortune on Clarendon Court, a nineteenth-century Newport, R.I., estate, that appealed to her husband's societal pretensions. For the next thirteen years, the von Bülows lived in New York and Rhode Island and were an ideally suited couple.

In 1979, von Bülow began complaining that his wife refused to have sex with him, and had withdrawn into a world of books, television, and sweets. But her maid of many years, Maria Schrallhammer, claimed that it was Claus who seemed to be having a nervous breakdown. Von Bülow was actually having an affair. He backed Broadway productions so he could linger in New York with 33-year-old actress Alexandra Isles, whom he met in 1978. Isles loved von Bülow, but in 1979 she imposed a deadline for him to divorce his wife.

The thought of losing Alexandra played havoc on von Bülow's mind during the Christmas holiday of 1979. Then, on Dec. 27, Martha lapsed into unconsciousness, which von Bülow attributed to a case of the flu, aggravated by too much eggnog. At the maid's insistence, von Bülow finally summoned Dr. Janis Gailitis of Newport Hospital, who revived Martha and diagnosed her illness as hypoglycemia. But Maria Schrallhammer suspected von Bülow.

For the next few months, Martha von Bülow was lethargic and depressed. Claus insisted that she had a drinking problem and took barbiturates. In April 1980, tests at New York's Columbia-Presbyterian Hospital confirmed that Martha indeed suffered from hypoglycemia. On Thanksgiving Day, Schrallhammer found a bottle marked "insulin" and several other containers of drugs in a black bag in von Bülow's closet. She gave the bag to Dr. Richard Stock, Martha's personal physician, for chemical analysis. He determined that an odd-looking paste found in the bag would not have been prepared by any legitimate druggist.

Martha von Bülow lapsed into a second coma on Dec. 21, 1980, in the New York apartment. She was rushed to the hospital, where tests showed low blood sugar but a high insulin count. Martha was placed on a life support system. Von Bülow suggested that she be allowed to die. On Jan. 23, 1981, Schrallhammer turned the black bag over to Newport police, who found traces of Diazepam, Amobarbital, and insulin on a syringe. On July 6, Claus von Bülow was indicted on two counts of assault with intent to murder.

His trial began in Newport on Feb. 1, 1982. Von Bülow pleaded not guilty before Judge Thomas Needham in a courtroom packed with journalists. The prosecution based its case on the testimony of Maria Schrallhammer. The thirty-one-day trial ended on Mar. 16, 1982, when von Bülow was found Guilty. He was sentenced to thirty years in prison, but was released on $1 million bail pending appeal. Outside the courtroom, a throng of spectators chanted, "Free Claus! Free Claus!" But a year would pass before any further action.

During that time, the defense a filed 100-page brief seeking a reversal of the conviction, and on Apr. 27, 1984, the judgment of the lower court was reversed. After the U.S. Supreme Court refused a request from Rhode Island attorney general Dennis J. Roberts to review the case, the state announced plans to retry Von Bülow. The second trial began in Providence on Apr. 25, 1985, and ended in a final acquittal on June 10. Claus von Bülow was at last a free man. There were allegations that he had been "framed" by his step-children, Prince Alexander von Auersperg and Princess Annie Laurie Kneissl. Another theory held that von Bülow and his mistress drove Martha to attempt suicide by taking insulin. At this writing, Martha von Bülow remains on a life support system.

REF.: *CBA;* Dershowitz, *Reversal of Fortune;* Nash, *Murder Among the Mighty;* Wright, *The Von Bülow Affair.*

Vonck, Jean-François, 1743-92, Belg., exile. Started Pro Aris et Focis, a clandestine group organized to elicit support for representative government. He and Henri Van der Noot founded the United Belgian States in 1789, but Van der Noot forced him into exile in 1790. REF.: *CBA.*

Von Cosel, Karl Tanzler, 1869-1952, U.S., grave rob. Karl Von Cosel was sixty when he fell in love with 22-year-old Elena Milagro Hoyos Mesa. Mesa was terminally ill when they met. She died in 1931, but Von Cosel lived with and slept beside his beloved until 1940.

A native of Dresden, Ger., and a graduate of Leipzig University with nine degrees in electrical engineering, medicine, and chemistry, Von Cosel was an x-ray technician at the Marine Hospital in Key West, Fla., when he fell in love with Elena Mesa. Explaining in court, years later, that she reminded him of a vision from his early youth, Von Cosel claimed Mesa had promised to marry him. He also said that on Oct. 31, 1931, the day before she died, he told her that "no matter what happened to her, I would take care of her in life and death."

Six months after Mesa died, he could no longer bear that she was underground. With permission from her sister, Von Cosel built with his own hands an elaborate monument to his beloved, and disinterred and relocated her body. He visited the vault daily, even connecting a telephone from the mausoleum to his house so "I could talk with her on rainy days," he said. Believing he could bring her back to life, Von Cosel secretly removed her corpse to Marine Hospital to experiment with tissue restoration, using electrodes in an effort to reanimate the body, and feeding her special formulas. Von Cosel later removed her body from the hospital, in a broken airplane chassis, to the abandoned garage where he lived. He planned to rebuild the plane and fly away with Mesa when he brought her back to life.

Nine years later, Mesa's sister, Mrs. Mario Medina, began to suspect that her sister's body was not in its tomb. On Oct. 9, 1940, Medina visited Von Cosel and recognized an old family double bed that Mesa had occupied when she was ill. Peering through netting, Medina saw the image of her sister. She went to Enrique Esquinaldo, justice of the peace, and had a warrant issued for Von Cosel's arrest. Hours later police broke into Von Cosel's shack. Sculpted masks of Elena hung on the walls, and in the room's only bed they found what was left of her corpse. The elderly man was charged with grave robbery and taken to jail. Mesa's skeletal remains, which had been preserved and artificially restored with papier-mâché and wax, were put on display at the Lopez Funeral Home in Key West. In three days, 6,000 people viewed her remains.

Von Cosel was charged with "willfully removing a tombstone," and "wantonly and maliciously destroying the contents of a grave." He was released on bond while awaiting trial; by the time the trial came up the judge ruled that the statute of limitations had run out and dismissed the case. Von Cosel took steps to bring the case to court, arguing that he deserved to reclaim the body. His request was denied. Shortly after, Medina, her husband, an undertaker, and a sexton buried the body in the middle of the night at a secret location where Von Cosel would not find it. The destitute man was evicted from the shack, which was torn down, and went to live with a sister in Zephyrhills, Fla. A few days after his departure, Mesa's empty crypt was destroyed by an explosion. Twelve years later, in 1952, Von Cosel's body was found in his home in northern Florida, with newspaper clippings and photographs of the trial thrown about the living room. A life-size replica of Mesa was propped up in a corner of the room. Von Cosel was eighty-two. REF.: *CBA*.

Von der Heydt, James Arnold, 1919- , U.S., jur. Judge of superior court of state of Alaska from 1959-66. He was nominated to the district court of Alaska by President Lyndon B. Johnson in 1966. REF.: *CBA*.

von Holleben, Ehrenfried, 1909- , Braz., kid. In mid-June 1970, the West German ambassador to Brazil, Ehrenfried von Hollenben, sixty-one, was abducted by gunmen who murdered his security guard. Von Hollenben had been provided with a police escort, but it was ambushed during the kidnapping. Left-wing Latin American kidnappers demanded the release of forty political prisoners in exchange for von Hollenben. Walter Scheel, West German foreign minister, promised to use all "conventional and unconventional" means to save the ambassador, and the Brazilian government agreed to release the jailed political prisoners, many of whom allegedly were guilty of terrorist crimes against Brazil's right-wing, dictatorial, government, which was run by the military. The released prisoners were flown to Algeria, and von Hollenben was released unharmed. REF.: *CBA*.

von Manstein, Fritz Erich, 1887-1973, Ger., war crimes. Tried in Hamburg, W. Ger., in August 1949, Field Marshall Fritz Erich von Manstein, sixty-two, was the last of the defendants in the WWII war crimes trials. Von Manstein was charged in a 17-point indictment of permitting atrocities in areas under his command, after having been been held for four years in British custody without being tried. Brought before the military tribunal in August 1949, von Manstein was charged with condoning the drowning, gassing and shooting of Gypsies, Jews, and other minorities; the execution of civilians, political commissars and Russian soldiers; and deporting Russians to Germany for slave labor. He denied knowledge of atrocities, but admitted to condoning the execution of Russian partisan fighter's wives in retaliation for attacks on German soldiers. He said that Russian civilians "used every form of illegal warfare possible—shooting in the back, wearing German uniforms, employing women and children as spies and poisoning the water supply." In December 1949, von Manstein was found Guilty on nine counts regarding maltreatment and execution of Russian civilians and soldiers. He was sentenced to eighteen years in prison. Released on a medical parole for a cataract operation in August 1952, von Manstein received notice that a remission board order had terminated his sentence. He died in 1973. REF.: *CBA*.

von Neurath, Konstantin, 1873-1956, Ger., war crimes. Former foreign minister of the Nazi Third Reich, Baron Konstantin von Neurath was one of twenty-one defendants who were tried at Nuremberg, Ger., for war crimes. In an individual case presented by the British government, documents were presented to show how von Neurath, the one-time protector of Czechoslovakia, had participated in a conspiracy to break international treaties. The prosecutor explained that the Nazi official's policy was to "break only one treaty at a time." Von Neurath had helped realize Hitler's policies of violating the military clauses of the Versailles Treaty by re-establishing mandatory military training, torpedoing the disarmament conference, rearming German forces, and fortifying the Rhineland. In early October 1946, von Neurath was sentenced to fifteen years in prison. He was released from prison in 1954 and died two years later. REF.: *CBA*.

Vonones I, d.19 A.D., Parthia, (unsolv.) kid. Ruled as king of ancient Parthia, located in northeast part of modern Iran, from c.7-11 A.D. He was kidnapped and held hostage in Rome. REF.: *CBA*.

von Papen, Franz, 1879-1969, Ger., war crimes. A German diplomat and a spy during WWI, Franz von Papen functioned as the vice chancellor of Germany under Adolf Hitler from 1933-34, and served as ambassador to both Austria and Turkey for the Third Reich. At the Nuremberg Trials, the British charged von Papen with acting to attain Hitler's goals and objectives. Although it was proved that von Papen worked to strengthen the Nazi Party in Austria by participating in intrigue and bullying, his participation in active aggression to promote war was not established. The Tribunal found him Not Guilty; he was acquitted and released. Von Papen died in 1969. REF.: *CBA*.

von Schirach, Baldur, 1907-74, Ger., war crimes. At the Nuremberg Trials, Baldur von Schirach, the 39-year-old head of the Hitler Youth Organization, was called the "poisoner of a generation." Joining the Nazi party in 1927, von Schirach formed the Nazi Students League in 1928 and became director of the Hitler Youth movement in 1933. Found Guilty of crimes against humanity, von Schirach was given a twenty-year jail sentence. REF.: *CBA*.

von Stauffenberg, Count Klaus Schenck, See: **Hitler, Adolf.**

von Sydow, Frederick, prom. 1932, Swed., suic.-mur. On Mar. 4, 1932, a triple murder was committed on the small resort island of Mortnas, off the Swedish coast near Stockholm. The victims, Mr. and Mrs. Zetterberger, and Mrs. Zetterberger's sister, were beaten to death with a piece of iron pipe. Their house had been ransacked and the contents of their safe stolen. Chief Police Inspector Thour soon learned that Zetterberger had loaned money recently, and that several of his investments were failing. A bank guard and a cab driver informed the police inspector that Zetterberger had visited the home of Swedish aristocrat Baron Hjalmar von Sydow not long before he was killed. Von Sydow contributed no new information, but Thour observed that he seemed overwrought and unnerved. A new twist in the case developed when von Sydow was found dead, killed with his housekeeper and a maid. There was evidence of an intense struggle, and a crushed piece of silk from a woman's slip was found under the murdered man's body. The murder weapon, an iron rod, was found in the manager's office of the Tanger restaurant. A cab driver recalled picking up an attractive young couple and taking them to von Sydow's address, where they told him to wait, reappearing a half hour later and ordering him to drive them to the Tanger. Baron von Sydow's son, Frederick von Sydow, a student at Upsala University, came to Stockholm, and talked to police, but was unable to add anything to the investigation.

Inspector Thour went to Commissioner Gustavason and said he believed he knew the identity of the murderers and would need to use the baron's son to capture them. Gustavason agreed, with misgivings, to the plan of having the son stay at the baron's apartment. At 10 p.m., Thour and Gustavason walked to the door of von Sydow's apartment and heard a stifled scream from inside. Thour lunged for the door, broke it open, and watched a young woman felled by a gunshot. Rushing towards the door where the gunfire had come from, Thour was stopped by Frederick von Sydow, who told him he was too late, then turned his gun on himself and fired. With his wife as an accomplice, von Sydow had committed all of the murders. The couple, who had been heavy drinkers and lived wildly in the two years since they met and wed, had turned to Zetterberger to borrow money when the baron, disgusted with their lifestyle, had finally refused to finance them any longer. When Zetterberger went directly to the baron to demand payment, he told the money lender to have his son arrested for the debt. Rejecting the idea of jail, the son had chosen murder, and suicide, as his way out.

REF.: *CBA;* Rice, *Forty-five Murderers.*

Vontsteen, Franciscus Wynand, prom. 1971, S. Afri., mur. A real estate agent in Pretoria, South Africa, Franciscus Wynand Vontsteen met Sonjia Raffanti in 1967, and became her lover. Vontsteen was jealous and possessive of Raffanti, who married police officer François Swanepoel two days after meeting Vontsteen. When her husband was posted to official duties on the northern border of South Africa, Vontsteen and Raffanti moved in together, and she became pregnant with his child. When the child was born, Swanepoel accepted it as his own, and Vontsteen became increasingly jealous.

On July 3, 1971, the Swanepoels came back to their house to discover that they had been robbed, and a pistol stolen. Four days later, Raffanti claimed she had been accosted on the street by a native who carried her husband's gun, and threatened to shoot her. On the night of Aug. 2, she was heard shouting that there was a native in the house, just before her husband was found dead from gunshot wounds. A local man soon came forward to say that Vontsteen had asked him to help murder Swanepoel. Told that Sonjia had confessed, Vontsteen admitted stealing the pistol and firing two shots into Swanepoel's head while his wife lay beside him in bed. They were tried together for murder in Pretoria in 1971, a trial that resulted in Sonjia receiving a fifteen-year prison sentence and Vontsteen hanging for his crime in October 1971. REF.: *CBA.*

Von Veltheim, Franz (AKA: **Karl Ludwig Kurtze, Kismet, Franz Ludwig Kurtz Von Veltheim**), b.1857, Brit., rob.-blk.-big.-mur. Born in 1857 to a lower-class German family, Karl Ludwig Kurtze became Franz von Veltheim in 1880. Serving as a sailor in the German army, he deserted right after stealing a gold watch which belonged to his captain. Taking it to a pawnbroker, he assured him that he was von Veltheim and the property belonged to him. From that time on, he lived as von Veltheim, using his appearance and his glib tongue to commit bigamy, blackmail, and homicide. Leaving Europe, von Veltheim traveled to Australia and married a girl from a wealthy family; she believed he was the son of a baron and would inherit vast estates. Not long after their wedding, von Veltheim left his spouse to go to South Africa, later attempting to blackmail an English man who became friendly with his wife. He was appointed U.S. Consul at Santa Marta, leaving the post after stealing funds from his employer. He fled to London, and married again, disappearing from there with police of several countries looking for him. In South Africa, von Veltheim joined the police force. His legal wife, whom he had deserted in London identified a drowned body as her husband's. When the publicity regarding the case reached South Africa, he was identified as a criminal and thrown out of the police force.

By 1898, when South Africa was in turmoil politically, von Veltheim had been hired by wealthy diamond merchant Woolf Joel, the leader of a group of millionaires who opposed the policies of statesman Paul Kruger. When Joel argued with von Veltheim and decided to break off relations, von Veltheim shot and killed him. The prosecution contended that the defendant had killed Joel in cold blood when the merchant refused his blackmail demands, but the jury ruled that von Veltheim had killed in self-defense.

Deported the day after the murder trial was resolved, von Veltheim was later arrested for vagrancy in Delagoa Bay and was deported to England, which he rapidly left, having too many wives and victims to watch out for there. Returning to South Africa, he was imprisoned for violation of his expulsion order, but was soon rescued by British troops who apparently presumed he was a political offender. Von Veltheim often posed as a secret service agent, and continued to marry after talking his way into society repeatedly. After another botched blackmail attempt, von Veltheim was arrested at his Paris hotel, and spent several weeks in jail before being extradited to England in 1908 to stand trial at the Old Bailey. Forgetting that there was a record of his evidence at the Joel trial in Johannesburg, von Veltheim perjured himself during his cross examination by Sir Charles Gill. Found Guilty of blackmail, he was sentenced to twenty years of penal servitude by Justice Phillimore. The home secretary reduced the term to fifteen years, and von Veltheim was transferred to an internment camp in 1918. He was later deported to his native Germany. But in April 1923, he was in trouble with the law in South Africa again for infringing immigration laws, and was yet again returned to Germany.

REF.: Bennett, *Murder Is My Business;* Brock, *A Casebook of Crime; CBA;* Kingston, *Dramatic Days at the Old Bailey;* Lambton, *Thou Shalt Do No Murder.*

Votyak Tribe Murders, 1895, Case of, Russia, mur. A decapitated human body, with portions of the chest removed, was found near the village of Stary Multan in Russia's Vyatka province in 1895. A group of Votyak villagers were tried for practicing human sacrifice, with the district police officer getting peasants to confess by forcing them to take an oath in front of a stuffed bear, an animal spiritually venerated by the tribe. Two of the villagers were convicted in the local court, but the sentences were suspended by a Senate Appeals Division on the grounds that there had been violation of due process. A retrial ended in acquittal. REF.: *CBA.*

Voyer, Marc-Rene (Marquis d'Argenson, Marquis de Paulmy), 1652-1721, Fr., law enfor. off. Served as lieutenant general of police of Paris from 1697-1718. REF.: *CBA.*

Voynich, Wilfrid Michael, 1865-1930, Pol., rebel. Participated in Polish national movement and was put in prison from 1885-90. REF.: *CBA.*

Vratz, Christopher, 1644-82, Brit., rob.-mur. Christopher Vratz, the youngest son of a gentleman in Pomerania, a region in Poland, took to highway robbery to make his living. He often attempted robbery when he was outnumbered. Unlike most highwaymen, however, Vratz saved his money, amassing enough to buy a captain's commission in the German army. There he befriended Count Konigsmarck, with whom he went to England.

In England, Konigsmarck fell in love with a young woman. The woman, however, secretly married a man named Thomas Thynn. This so enraged Konigsmarck that he challenged Thynn. Thynn ignored him, so the count challenged him a second time. Thynn ignored this as well, so Konigsmarck ordered Vratz to hire two assassins. On Feb. 12, 1681, John Stern and George Borosky shot Thynn on the road in his coach.

Because of Thynn's high station and the fact that his 15-year-old bride was heiress to the earl of Northumberland, the assassins were apprehended the next day. Vratz, Stern, and Borosky were questioned by the king. Konigsmarck was captured about a week later at Gravesend while boarding a ship bound for Sweden and was arrested as an accessory. Because of Konigsmarck's influence, however, he was acquitted by a dishonest jury. Vratz, Borosky, and Stern were imprisoned at Newgate, tried at the Old Bailey on Feb. 28, 1682, and sentenced to death.

Vratz remained passive to the end, denying all of Stern and Borosky's testimony against him but refusing to defend himself. He had confessed his sins to God, he said, and was not bound to answer to anyone else. On Mar. 10, 1682, Vratz, then thirty-eight, was executed at Pall Mall with Stern and Borosky.

REF.: Bierstadt, *Curious Trials and Criminal Cases; CBA;* Smith, *Highwaymen.*

Vucetic, Slobodan, 1944- , and **Simic, Slobodan**, 1949- , and **Potkonjac, Vjekoslav**, 1942- , Ger., mur. At the very beginning of 1971, Werner Schmidt and his wife were driving home from a New Year's celebration in Hennef, Ger. To avoid the drunks on the autobahn, the Schmidts took a seldom-used country road that led through the villages of Neunkirchen, Wohlfahrt, and Much. It was a cold, blustery night with temperatures near zero.

Suddenly a naked man appeared before them in the roadway, waving frantically. Mrs. Schmidt, who had been dozing, did not see the figure in the snow and encouraged her husband to keep driving.

At 5 a.m., Hans-Dieter Mueller drove down the same road on his way to work. Although Mueller saw a man lying beside the road, he did not stop. When he later reported the incident to Constable Gunther Weber in Wohlfahrt, police investigated and found the body of a young man dressed in only a pair of briefs with his feet tied together with baling wire.

The victim was 18-year-old Ulrich Nacken, an electrician who had failed to come home the night before after celebrating the new year at the Toeff-Toeff Discotheque in Cologne. His parents told police that he had left his home in the 1966 gray Ford automobile he had purchased a month earlier. It was determined that death was caused by freezing, not by the blows to the face which Nacken had suffered. A trail led 200 yards back into the woods from where the body was found. The evidence indicated that the victim had been tied to a tree, but had managed to extricate himself and hop to the side of the road. A bulletin was issued in the surrounding area for the gray Ford. Two junior patrolmen, Arnold Klein and Leopold Brettweiler, spotted the vehicle between Wohlfahrt and Neunkirchen.

The driver attempted to escape from the pursuing officers, but was trapped on a dead-end road. The operator of the vehicle was a Yugoslav national named Slobodan Vucetic. A quick search of the car uncovered Ulrich Nacken's driver's license in the glove compartment. It was apparent that one or more accomplices had escaped just before the police arrived. Police dog patrols easily tracked down the second man who was identified as Slobodan Simic. Vucetic immediately accused Simic of killing Nacken.

By the time they had reached the police station, a third man, 29-year-old Vjekoslav Potkonjac, was also implicated in the murder. According to the confessions of the three men, they were drinking beer at the Toeff-Toeff when Nacken stopped by. On the spur of the moment they decided to abduct Nacken and steal his car. They forced him to the car at knifepoint, bound him with wire they found in the car, and put him in trunk. After visiting Simic's girlfriend in Siegburg, they stripped Nacken, beat him, and tied him to a tree in the woods. The three Yugoslavians might have slipped through the police dragnet and returned to Yugoslavia undetected, but they became curious and were returning to the scene of the crime when they were spotted by the two officers.

On Nov. 30, 1971, Vucetic, Simic, and Potkonjac were found Guilty of premeditated murder and sentenced to life imprisonment. Werner Schmidt received six months for failing to assist a person in danger, a serious crime under German law.

REF.: *CBA;* Dunning, *The Arbor House Treasury of True Crime.*

Vucetich, Juan (John), 1858-1925, Arg., criminol. Sir Edward Henry and Francis Galton of Great Britain have long been recognized as the forefathers of modern fingerprinting, which for nearly a century has been the accepted method of prisoner classification. Juan Vucetich, a Croatian-born criminologist, is no less important to the field than his illustrious contemporaries. The prevailing attitudes of his own people have doomed him to relative obscurity, however. Shortly before he died in 1925, Vucetich wrote to his friend Edward Lomax, saying: "My work is destroyed and perhaps will be forgotten...nobody will ever remember me."

Vucetich was born on the island of Lesina, near the coast of Dalmatia in 1858. Lesina was then a part of the Austro-Hungarian empire, but it was to remain free of the kind of political turbulence that swept through the Balkans while Vucetich was growing up. After completing his studies at the university school in Spalato, Vucetich entered the local police force, but found the work dull and unrewarding. A restless young man with intense nationalistic leanings, Vucetich emigrated to Argentina in 1884 rather than live on an island under the political thumb of the Austrian colonial government. He settled in the bustling city of La Plata, where he quickly assimilated into the local culture, even to the point of changing his name from "John" to the Spanish "Juan."

Criminologist Juan Vucetich.

Vucetich went to work for the Central Police Department, where he greatly impressed his superiors with his energy, enthusiasm, and willingness to take on whatever tasks came his way. By 1891 he was the head of the Statistical Bureau and was given the responsibility of organizing the Department of Identity. French criminologist Alphonse Bertillon's anthropometric method of prisoner classification had recently come into vogue in the police agencies on the European continent and in the U.S. *bertillonage* implemented a series of criminal suspects' body measurements, which could be easily identified and catalogued. It was up to Vucetich to implement *bertillonage* in La Plata. In order to familiarize Vucetich with the Frenchman's work, Chief Nuñez of La Plata provided his subordinate with a file folder of articles and instructions. Among the relevant publications contained was a French journal known as the *Revue Scienifique.* An article by Henri de Varigny describing the recent work of British criminologists Francis Galton and Edward Henry caught Vucetich's eye.

To Juan Vucetich, the Galton-Henry fingerprinting system was going to revolutionize police work. Unlike *bertillonage,* which allowed for a margin of error, a suspect's fingerprint was entirely unique. Vucetich went ahead and introduced *bertillonage* to the La Plata police force, but he harbored grave doubts about its long-term effectiveness. In the next twelve months, Vucetich closely followed the progress of Henry Faulds and Sir William Herschel of the Indian Civil Service, who proved that fingerprints rarely change over the course of time.

By September 1891, Vucetich had come up with his own system of ten-finger classification, in which he identified four common traits: arches, prints with a triangle pattern on the right side, those with a triangle on the left side, and prints with triangles on both sides. Vucetich categorized these under the first four letters of the alphabet. The system became known as "dactiloscopia," but it would take several more years to catch on. Vucetich encountered stiff resistance among his reactionary superiors in the La Plata police force. In Summer 1892, Vucetich was given his first opportunity to demonstrate the practical usages of dactiloscopia. In Necochea, a coastal town 200 miles south of La Plata, there occurred a particularly heinous murder. Francisca Rohas, a 25-year-old mother of two, informed the police that a man named Velasquez from a neighboring village had battered her children to death in a jealous rage. Velasquez admitted that he loved Rohas very much, but categorically denied killing her young ones. The La Plata police tried to beat a confession out of him, even though he had an indisputable alibi that showed he could not have committed the murders. In the end, it was Vucetich's disregarded fingerprint system that established the true identity of the actual killer.

Inspector Carlos Alvarez went back to the murder scene to take a second look. He found a bloody thumbprint on the door. Alvarez carefully cut out the piece of wood and brought it back to the station where a comparison was made with the right thumb of Mrs. Rojas. It was clearly shown that they were identical. Under questioning, the woman confessed that she had murdered her own children and framed Velasquez in order to please a secret lover who objected to the presence of two children. She was tried for murder and convicted, but, more importantly, Vucetich gained widespread credibility throughout South America for his work in this case. In 1894, he published his classic study of criminal identification methods entitled *Dactiliscopia Comparada*. That year, the police chief of Buenos Aires province adopted the Vucetich system. Thus, Argentina became the first nation in the world to discard *bertillonage* in favor of fingerprinting. As might be expected, Alphonse Bertillon and his followers did not react well to Vucetich. There was a great enmity and professional rivalry between the two men, which was apparent in 1913 in Paris when Bertillon publicly snubbed Juan Vucetich at the moment of his greatest triumph.

On July 18, 1916, the Argentine parliament passed into law a controversial bill requiring that every man, woman, and child be fingerprinted and catalogued in central police files. Vucetich was appointed to oversee the project, but no one, certainly not the head of the Statistical Bureau himself, foresaw the great public outcry this policy engendered. There were riots in the streets as young and old alike protested this perceived violation of their rights. The General Registry building was stormed and the windows smashed before order was restored. Within days, Juan Vucetich had gone from hero to scapegoat. He was banished from the city, and in May 1917 many of his files were destroyed. Bitter and disillusioned by all this, Vucetich retired to the country estate of his friend Edward Lomax. He lived out his final years in quiet contemplation before passing away from stomach cancer in 1925. See: **Bertillon, Alphonse; Galton, Francis; Henry,** Sir **Edward Richard; Herschel,** Sir **William John.**

REF.: *CBA;* Scott, *The Concise Encyclopedia of Crime and Criminals;* Symons, *A Pictorial History of Crime.*

Vuong, Phung (Vough), 1963- , Case of, U.S., burg.-asslt. & bat.-mur. Phung Voung is wanted by the Federal Bureau of Investigation in connection with the shooting deaths of two men and the robbery of several others during a home invasion. The five-foot-five-inch Vietmnamese native Vuong is believed to to be traveling across the U.S. with fellow fugitive Hung Huu Nguyen. At last report, the two men were sighted in Wichita, Kan. REF.: *CBA.*

Vyshinsky, Andrey Yanuaryevich, 1883-1954, U.S.S.R., lawyer. Served Soviet government as public prosecutor beginning in 1920, as deputy in 1933, and as chief prosecutor in 1935. He became well-known internationally when he prosecuted cases in the Great Purge trials from 1934-38. REF.: *CBA.*

Wable, John Wesley, 1929-55, U.S., rob.-mur. On July 25, 1953, Harry Franklin Pitts, a 39-year-old truck driver from Bowling Green, Va., was shot in the head as he slept in his tractor-trailer along the Pennsylvania Turnpike. Three days earlier another driver, 39-year-old Lester B. Woodward of Duncannon, Pa., had been found dead in the cab of his parked truck. Both men were killed by bullet shots through the head. Woodward's wallet had been emptied of about $75; Pitts had not been robbed. By the time a third shooting had occurred—34-year-old John K. Shepperd, was shot in the head with a .32-caliber bullet as he slept by the side of the road just fifteen miles from the western end of the Pennsylvania Turnpike—combined rewards of $11,000 were being offered by the Pennsylvania trucking industry for the capture of the "Phantom of the Turnpike." Shepperd survived and provided police with clues to the assailant. Following the third shooting, the Pennsylvania Motor Truck Association and American Federation of Labor Teamsters Union president Edward Crumbock ordered that no truckers were to sleep beside the highways and that when trucks broke down, passing trucks must stop until the trouble was fixed and then proceed in convoy.

On Oct. 12, 1953, John Wesley Wable, twenty-four, of Ohiopyle, Pa., was arrested in Albuquerque, N.M., after pawning a watch that had belonged to one of the turnpike victims. Picked up along with Wable were Marvin H. Parsons, twenty, and J.D. Francis, seventeen. Both had hitched a ride with Wable after their car broke down in the Mohave Desert, and both were identified as having been with Wable when he robbed a New Mexico service station. Charged with the July murders of Pitts and Woodward, Wable protested his innocence and threatened to commit suicide. "I didn't kill nobody," he said. "But I think I know who did, and I've got friends who will take care of him."

On Mar. 13, 1954, a Greensburg, Pa., jury convicted Wable of murdering Pitts and Woodward and of shooting Shepperd. Judge Edward G. Bauer ended the two-week trial with a three and one-half hour charge before the jury's four-hour deliberation. Wable was sent to the death house at Rockview State Penitentiary in Bellefonte, Pa. On Sept. 26, 1955, he was electrocuted after losing two last-minute appeals. He was twenty-five years old. REF.: *CBA*.

Waddell, Reed, 1859-95, U.S., fraud. Operating in the U.S. and Europe, Reed Waddell was a successful swindler at two schemes which netted him more than a quarter of a million dollars between 1880 and 1890. As a young man, he rejected the Springfield, Ill., family business, preferring the company of gamblers and con men, concentrating on the green goods and gold brick swindles.

Waddell first used the gold brick swindle in New York in 1880, a con game he was credited with creating though Wyatt Earp and Mysterious Dave Mather pulled a similar swindle by selling gold bricks to cowboys in 1878 in Mobeetie, Texas. Waddell's gold bricks consisted of a lead bar covered with three plates of gold and a gold slug in the middle. Posing as a penniless miner, he would find a potential customer and tell him he hated to part with the gold was forced to sell it in order to return to his Colorado mine. He asked for cash. Waddell then directed the buyer to an "assayer" who declared it pure gold. His first gold brick swindle in New York netted $4,000. At times, Waddell got twice that price, and the least he ever netted was $3,500. Waddell preferred this swindle as there was a long time lag before the victim realized the swindle.

The other fraud Waddell pulled was the green goods swindle in which he would show a victim a substantial amount of real cash, tell the person it was counterfeit, and offer to sell a quantity of it at a discount price. When the victim agreed to make a large buy, Waddell again showed them real cash, but just as the transaction was completed, he would substitute blank strips of green paper for the cash. He took his games to Europe and was successful until March 1895, when he was shot and killed in Paris by another confidence man, Tom O'Brien, over disputed spoils.

REF.: Asbury, *Gem of the Prairie*; ____, *The Gangs of New York*; *CBA*; Nash, *Bloodletters and Badmen*; ____, *Hustlers and Con Men*.

Waddill, Edmund, Jr., 1855-1931, U.S., jur. Edmund Waddill, Jr., served as judge of Henrico County, Va., from 1880-83, and as U.S. attorney in Washington, D.C., from 1883-85. Waddill also served as a U.S. congressman from 1890-91. He was nominated to the eastern district court of Virginia by President William McKinley in 1898, and was later nominated to preside over the fourth district court by President Warren G. Harding in 1921. REF.: *CBA*.

Waddingham, Dorothea Nancy, 1899-36, Brit., mur. Dorothea Waddingham ran an unlicensed nursing home in Nottingham, England, the setting for one of Britain's most celebrated murders in the 1930s. She entered the health care profession later in life. As a young woman she had worked in a factory, and then as a ward-orderly at the Burton-on-Trent Workhouse Infirmary. Her criminal record was fairly extensive. It contained several convictions for a string of petty thefts and frauds. While nursing her elderly husband, Thomas Willoughby Leech, through the final stages of throat cancer, she decided to take in the sick and elderly as a way of providing for the needs of her five children, who ranged in age from eighteen months to nine years. She was assisted by her lover, 39-year-old Ronald Joseph Sullivan, who took on a greater role following the death of the infirm Thomas Leech. They opened their nursing home on Devon Drive in Nottingham in 1935.

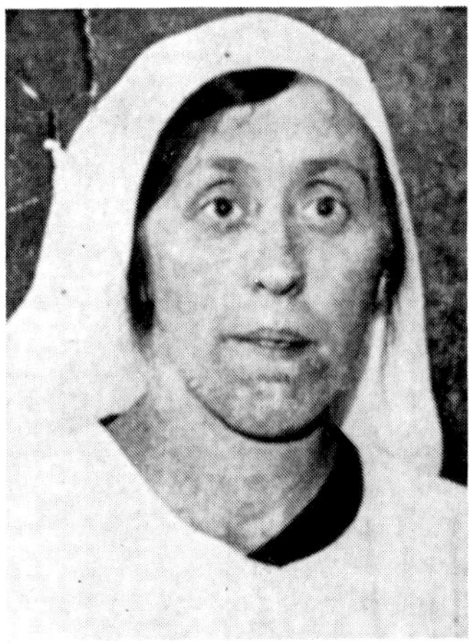

Dorothea Waddingham, the lethal British nurse.

Neither Waddingham nor Sullivan were licensed to care for the sick or the elderly, but this did not dissuade them from operating an increasingly lucrative business. The small, out-of-the-way home received accreditation from the County Nursing Association, which sent them two patients in January 1935: 89-year-old Mrs. Baguley, and her 50-year-old daughter Ada Louisa. Baguley was bedridden and Ada Baguley suffered from creeping paralysis, which had rendered her virtually helpless. The two patients required constant care—more care apparently than Waddingham and Sullivan had anticipated, for they allegedly complained of how little they were paid in return for the care they were required to give the two women. On May 6, 1935, Ada Baguley rewrote her will, leaving her entire estate of £1,600 to Waddingham on the condition that the nurse would care for both her and her mother until their deaths. No one was particularly shocked when the elderly Baguley died on May 12, 1935. Her death was officially attributed to old age. Four months later, however, on Sept. 11, 1935, Ada Baguley also died. The cause of death cited on the death certificate, cerebral hemorrhage, was derived from Waddingham's descriptions rather than from an actual examination of the body. Waddingham allegedly told the doctor that the old woman had consumed too many of the chocolates given to her by her friend, Mrs. Briggs. A coroner's autopsy was not ordered. There was no concrete evidence at this point to link Baguley's death to Nurse Waddingham.

Immediately following Ada Baguely's death, Waddingham produced a letter dated Aug. 29, 1935. It was purportedly written by the deceased woman and said, "I desire to be cremated at my death, for health's sake. And it is my wish to remain with Nurse and my last wish is my relatives shall not know of my death." In keeping with the law, Waddingham forwarded this letter to Dr.Cyril Banks, the Nottingham medical officer with a request to to be allowed to proceed with the cremation. Waddingham's eagerness aroused Dr. Banks' suspicions and he ordered an autopsy. According to Dr. Roche Lynch, who performed the autopsy, there was no evidence that death had been caused by cerebral hemorrhage, as shown on the death certificate. Instead, he found more than three grains of morphine in the corpse, a sufficient amount to suggest morphine poisoning as the cause of death. Because of the results of this autopsy, Mrs. Baguley's remains were exhumed and autopsied. Again, a sufficient amount of morphine was found in the corpse to convince the doctor that she too had been poisoned.

Dorothea Waddingham and Joseph Sullivan were jointly charged in Ada Baguley's murder. Their trial began on Feb. 24, 1936, at the Nottingham Assizes before Justice Rayner Goddard. Goddard quickly ruled that because of insufficient evidence, a verdict of Not Guilty should be returned against Joseph Sullivan. This decision left Waddingham to face the murder charges alone. When confronted with the coroner's evidence regarding the amounts of morphine found in the dead women's bodies, Waddingham admitted giving morphine to the Baguleys, but claimed that she had done so on Dr. H.H. Manfield's orders. Manfield denied prescribing morphine for either of the Baguleys but told the court that he had prescribed it for a Mrs. Kemp, another of Nurse Waddingham's patients, who had died at the nursing home in February 1935. He suggested that it was this morphine that Waddingham had given to the Baguleys.

The evidence against Waddingham continued to mount, despite the fact that Ada Baguley was directed to the Waddingham home by the County Nursing Association, and was not coerced by either Waddingham or Sullivan. Dr. Jacob, the long-time family physician, testified that he had visited Ada Baguley just two weeks before she died. She showed no outward signs of approaching death, and her paralysis, in its present form, would have taken several more years to become fatal. Additional evidence introduced during the trial showed that on the day before Baguley's death, Waddingham fed her two rather large meals. "Can you as men of common sense," Justice Goddard asked, "think that anybody in their senses would give a woman suffering from such sharp abdominal pains that morphia had to be given her three nights, two helpings of pork, baked potatoes and fruit pie?"

Nurse Waddingham was found Guilty and hanged at Winson Green Prison in Birmingham on Apr. 16, 1936, despite the jury's urgent plea for mercy. Justice Goddard was less inclined to be charitable because of her sex. "I see no reason why a woman convicted of murder should not hang," he told the royal commission on capital punishment afterward. Nurse Waddingham had the dubious distinction of becoming one of the few women executed in Britain during the twentieth century.

REF.: Bowker, *Behind the Bar;* Bresler, *Lord Goddard; CBA;* Glaister, *The Power of Poison;* Gribble, *When Killers Err;* Huggett, *Daughters of Cain;* Jacobs, *Pageant of Murder;* Nash, *Look For the Woman;* O'Donnell, *Should Women Hang?;* Rowland, *Poisoner in the Dock;* Shew, *A Companion to Murder;* Smith, *Lord Goddard;* Wilson, *Encyclopedia of Murder;* Wilson, *Murderess.*

Wagenfeld, Frederick, prom. 1840, Ger., hoax. Dr. Heinrich Friedrich Gesenius was Germany's foremost biblical scholar during the 1830s. His research into the ancient Hebrew languages earned him the acclaim of his contemporaries, yet Gesenius was easily duped by one of his students, Frederick Wagenfeld, who produced what he claimed to be a fragment of the writings of the first century Greek scholar Philo Byblius. The ancient text was a translated history of Phoenicia, originally written by Sanchuniathon in the thirteenth century B.C. The fragment was a poor forgery, yet Gesenius and another noted scholar, Georg Grotefend, authenticated the discovery. Grotefend went so far as to write an introduction to the German translation.

REF.: *CBA;* MacDougall, *Hoaxes.*

Waggles Case, 1949, Brit., fraud. In October 1949, an anonymous letter informed Scotland Yard of a deception perpetrated by the owner of a prized racing greyhound named Red Wind. The owner of the dog, according to the letter, had substituted, in Red Wind's place, an Irish greyhound named Waggles, who had previously won a number of important races. The real Red Wind had fared poorly in his first time trials.

The Fraud Squad of Scotland Yard found that Waggles had been sold to a man in Edgware. The new owner and his brother were found Guilty of fraud at the Central Criminal Court, and were each sentenced to two years and eighteen months in prison. REF.: *CBA.*

Waggoner, Charles Delos, prom. 1929, U.S., fraud. With the onset of the Great Depression, the Bank of Telluride, Colo., was failing. The mining industry that fueled the economy of this small town 200 miles from Denver had floundered and deposits in the Bank of Telluride had dropped by eighty percent. The embattled bank president, Charles Waggoner, was determined to stave off bankruptcy by whatever means necessary.

On Aug. 31, 1929, six New York banks received telegrams from Colorado requesting that they transfer more than half a million dollars to the Chase Manhattan Bank, to the credit of the Bank of Telluride. That so large a sum of money was to be transferred on credit for a tiny bank in the rural mining district of Colorado did not strike anyone as unusual at the time. The following week, Waggoner appeared in the offices of Chase Manhattan asking that bank officials certify some $270,000 worth of checks drawn on the Telluride Bank. Waggoner then went to the Central Hanover Bank where he discharged $215,000 in debts using money drawn from the Chase account.

Through a complicated series of bank transfers, involving nineteen institutions in New York, Colorado, and various other states, Waggoner succeeded in paying old debts and re-establishing his credit at the same time. By the time nervous bank officials sifted through the seemingly indecipherable maze of transactions and concluded that they had been the victim of a massive fraud, Waggoner had disappeared.

The Bank of Telluride was debt free, but the state of Colorado had closed it down, pending further investigation. Waggoner was arrested in New Castle, Wyo., and charged with fraud. He was described as a modern day "Robin Hood" who had robbed the wealthy New York bankers to keep a small, impoverished Colorado bank afloat. "It was a matter of protecting my depositors, people of Telluride whom I knew and did not want to suffer," Waggoner told the New York judge hearing the case. A plea of guilty was entered and Judge Coleman sentenced him to fifteen years in prison. Waggoner petitioned the judge to allow him to withdraw his guilty plea, and asked for a jury trial. Judge Coleman softened, and reduced the penalty to ten years, with parole eligibility coming after five. Waggoner was transported to the Atlanta Penitentiary.

REF.: *CBA;* Roberts, *Famous American Trials.*

Wagner, Charles, d.1890, Brit., (unsolv.) mur. Charles Wagner was one of several children who mysteriously disappeared in West Ham near Ramsgate, England in 1890. The boy's body was found a short time after he was missed near the Ramsgate Cliffs. The cause of death was undetermined and the body showed no marks or bruises.

REF.: *CBA;* Nash, *Among the Missing.*

Wagner, Clair C., prom. 1963, U.S., fraud. Clair Wagner capitalized on the public's seemingly insatiable demand for large, spacious, backyard pools in a franchising scheme that landed him in jail. In 1963, Wagner's shady scheme came to the attention of Postal Inspector Doyle C. Marshall, who received complaints from two Oklahoma plumbers who had been sold the rights to a nonexistent franchise.

Wagner's licensing company was known by several names: Bermuda Pools, Cinderella Pool Corporation, and Town and Country Pools, none of which were legitimate. Wagner would lure his victims from the Denver telephone book. Most were connected with the construction business in some way and had the necessary skills to dig pool foundations. The intended victims were flown to Denver at Wagner's expense and were given a preview of the swimming pools they could expect to build. The carrot that Wagner dangled in front of them was a free "display" pool built for their backyard to show potential customers.

The victim was told to begin excavating his yard immediately, with the arrival of the standard materials guaranteed for a later date. By the time the gaping hole was dug, the pool liner, basic plumbing, and filtration system would arrive COD for $3,000. The dealer who was led to believe that all this material was to be provided at no cost, was given a take it or leave it option. By this time, though, there was very little choice. Wagner was indicted, found Guilty, and sentenced to prison for mail fraud. The dealers were left with their own pool, but little else for their trouble. REF.: *CBA.*

Wagner, Franz, 1874-1938, Ger., mur. On the night of Sept. 3, 1913, Franz Wagner went on a maniacal rampage, killing six members of his family and nine townspeople. He also set fire to houses and barns and shot at cattle and horses as they fled. There was no apparent provocation for the murders.

Wagner, a teacher, had said that his five children were unwanted as far as he was concerned and he became obsessed with the thought of suicide. When his rampage ended with his arrest, Wagner demanded that he be executed, but he was placed in an institution for the insane, where he died in 1938.

REF.: *CBA;* Nash, *Almanac of World Crime.*

Wagner, Gustav Franz, 1911-80, Ger., suic.-war crimes. During a fifteen-month period between 1942-43, more than 250,000 Jews and Poles perished at the Sobibor extermination camp in Poland. Unlike other concentration camps which required the inmates to perform various menial tasks, the Sobibor Camp in Poland was a killing "factory" in which victims were herded from the train directly into a gas chamber. The room was connected to a Soviet tank engine that funneled noxious carbon monoxide fumes inside. It was built by the Nazis to expedite the killing process, and the day-to-day operation was supervised by Gustav Wagner, an Austrian.

By posing as a humble motorcyclist, Wagner evaded allied capture in 1945. He slipped out of the country in 1950, to resettle in Atibaia, a mountain resort fifty miles outside of Sao Paulo, Braz. His true identity was discovered in 1978, and extradition proceedings were begun by the governments of West Germany, Austria, Poland, and Israel. Four times between 1978 and 1980 the former Nazi attempted to commit suicide. Wagner finally succeeded on Oct. 3, 1980, when he plunged a dagger through his heart. REF.: *CBA.*

Wagner, John F., 1893-1905, U.S., embez.-suic. A lifelong resident of Cecil, Pa., John Wagner embezzled $1.125 million from the First National Bank of Cecil where he worked as a cashier. When examiners arrived at the bank on a Monday morning in 1950, they found Wagner stretched out on the floor in front of the vault, dead from a bullet in his head, the victim of suicide. Investigators were puzzled over the motivation for this trusted employee's embezzling such a large sum, for Wagner did not gamble, drink, or lead a high life. Examining his effects, they found a note in his handwriting that read, "The reason for the shortage was because of paying checks that were not good." A list of bank customers who defaulted on loans was attached to the note. Apparently, Wagner had allowed his friends' checks to clear even if their accounts were overdrawn, and had paid off their loans using the bank's funds. The authorities attempted to exact payment from those named on Wagner's list. Wagner had paid his own debt with his life. REF.: *CBA.*

Wagner, Louis, 1845-75, U.S., mur. Out of work and penniless, German immigrant Louis Wagner had been heard saying he needed money badly enough to kill for it. Wagner had worked as a fisherman in Portsmouth, N.H., and had lived with the Hontvet family on Smutty Nose Island in the Isles of Shoals.

On the evening of Mar. 5, 1873, Wagner saw the Hontvet brothers, all the men in the family, in Portsmouth and learned that they would not be returning home that night. Wagner stole a boat and rowed the twenty miles to the island, arriving around midnight. Entering the Hontvet home, he first encountered Karen Christensen and killed her. Her sister-in-law, Anethe Christensen, rushed into the room and struggled with the intruder, calling his name. Karen's sister, Maren Hontvet, fled the house as Wagner killed Anethe. After searching for Maren, who was hiding on the island, Wagner rowed back to the mainland. In the morning, neighbors found Maren and notified the authorities. They found the Hontvet home ransacked and the two women dead. Wagner was immediately apprehended at his rooming house. Maren identified him, and police found a bloody shirt in his room. Wagner had gained only $20 from his crimes. Tried and found Guilty of murder, Wagner was executed at Thomaston Penitentiary on June 25, 1875.

REF.: Boucher, *The Pocket Book of True Crime Stories* ("A Memorable Murder" by Celia Thaxter, originally published in 1875); *CBA;* Dempewolff, *Famous Old New England Murders;* Jackson, *The Portable Murder Book;* Pearson, *Instigation of the Devil;* ____, *Murder at Smutty Nose;* Wilson, *Encyclopedia of Murder.*

Wagner, Wilhelm, 1906- , Ger., war crimes. A Nuremberg court convicted former Nazi Wilhelm Wagner of murder on Dec. 20, 1982, sentencing him to life in prison. Wagner was accused of killing two women and one man in the Polish village of Wieliczka in 1942. After the war, Wagner had returned to Germany, resuming his former occupation as a policeman. During the seven-month trial, the defendant steadfastly denied his guilt. REF.: *CBA.*

Wagstaff, William, prom. 1928, Brit., burg. A series of nocturnal warehouse-office robberies in the vicinity of Manchester puzzled British police for several months in 1928. The suspicion that the same person was responsible for the break-ins was born out when fragments of glass were examined for fingerprints. It was determined that they belonged to William Wagstaff, a common housebreaker who was thought to be living in London on strict parole.

Wagstaff had traveled by rail to Manchester at night, committed his burglary, and then returned to London the following morning to keep his parole appointment at the Greenwich police station. The fingerprint evidence was convincing, despite the suspect's seemingly airtight alibi. Wagstaff was sentenced to eighteen months of hard labor.

REF.: *CBA;* Cherrill, *Cherrill of the Yard.*

Wagstaffe, John, 1633-77, Brit., witchcraft. In the seventeenth century the Oxford-educated writer John Wagstaffe tried to dispel the belief in of witchcraft. In 1677, *The Question of Witchcraft Debated* was translated into German. It was a compassionate and human document that spoke out against the horrors of the satanic inquisitions. He believed that such stories of possession were "partly founded in mistaken interpretation of Scripture, partly in the knavish and gainful impostures of some men, partly in the vain foolish credulity of other men." Wagstaffe's influence was not a lasting one. He died on Sept. 2, 1677, from the ravages of alcoholism, leaving behind this one volume on witchcraft.

REF.: *CBA; Doctrine of Devils;* Robinson, *The Encyclopedia of Witchcraft and Demonology;* Wagstaffe, *Gründliche Ausgeführte Materie von der Hexerei;* Wagstaffe, *The Question of Witchcraft.*

Waightman (Weightman), George (AKA: Red Buck), d.1895, U.S., west. outl. George Waightman was a member of the egregious Bill Doolin gang of bank robbers, active in the Southwest during the 1880s and 1890s. Born in the Lone Star State of Texas, Waightman was a horse thief, bank robber, and cold-blooded killer who would shoot a man down at the slightest provocation. In 1889 he was arrested by Heck Thomas in Oklahoma for horse stealing, a serious offense in those days. Waightman was sentenced to spend three years in jail. After completing his sentence, the gunman joined up with Bill Doolin.

There was a streak of meanness in Waightman that even Doolin—who was never shy with a gun himself—found appalling. After robbing a train outside Dover, Okla., on Apr. 3, 1895, the Doolin mob found themselves encircled by a local posse. Tulsa Jack Blake was killed in the ensuing gunfight, and Waightman's horse was shot out from under him. He jumped on Bitter Creek Newcomb's mount and made a getaway with the remnants of the gang.

Doolin and his men passed a farm where several horses were grazing in the pasture. Waightman jumped off his horse and scaled the farmer's fence. Just as he was about to ride off with one of the unattended horses, the owner suddenly burst out of the house and demanded that Waightman leave at once. Without a word Red Buck turned and fired on the hapless preacher. Later that day, Doolin discussed the matter with Bill Dalton, his second in command. It was agreed that Waightman should be drummed out of the gang. They broke camp, leaving Red Buck behind. Without the gang's protection, the peace officers soon caught up with the murderer. In Arapaho, Okla., on Oct. 2, 1895, a posse of lawmen surrounded Waightman's hideout and demanded he surrender. Waightman tried to shoot his way to freedom, but was cut down instantly. See: **Doolin, William M.**

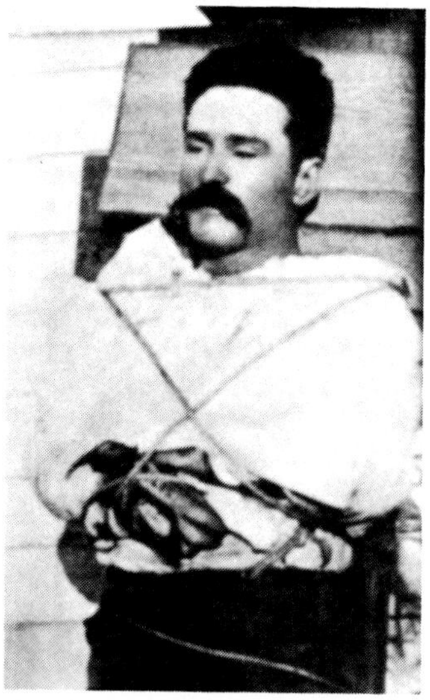

Oklahoma bandit George "Red Buck" Waightman, dead, 1895.

REF.: Bartholomew, *The Biographical Album of Western Gunfighters;* Breihan, *Badmen of the Frontier Days;* ____, *Great Gunfighters of the West;* Bryant, *Great American Guns and Frontier Fighters;* Canton, *Frontier Trails; CBA;* Croy, *Trigger Marshal;* Drago, *Outlaws on Horseback;* ____, *Road Agents and Train Robbers;* Eisele, *History of Noble County, Oklahoma;* Graves, *Oklahoma Outlaws;* Hanes, *Bill Doolin;* Holloway, *Texas Gun Lore;* Horan and Sann, *Pictorial History of the Wild West;* Hunter and Rose, *The Album of Gun-Fighters;* James, *They Had Their Hour;* Miller, *Bill Tilghman;* Newsom, *The Life and Practice of the Wild and Modern Indian;* Nix, *Oklahombres;* Osborn, *Let Freedom Ring;* Preece, *The Dalton Gang;* Raine, *Famous Sheriffs & Western Outlaws;* Sabin, *Wild Men of the Wild West;* Shirley, *Heck Thomas;* ____, *Six-Gun and Silver Star;* ____, *Toughest of Them All;* Sutton, *Hands Up!;* Tilghman, *Marshal of the Last Frontier;* Wellman, *A Dynasty of Western Outlaws;* (FILM), *Cattle Annie and Little Britches,* 1981.

Wainewright, Thomas Griffiths (AKA: **Janus Weathercock**), 1794-1852, Brit., forg.-mur. As a young man, Thomas Wainewright was a promising artist, but financial difficulties arose that caused him, without the slightest regard for the morality of his actions, or their likely consequences, to embark on a criminal career that ended in murder.

Born in Chiswick, London in 1794, the future artist was raised by his grandfather, who edited *The Monthly Review,* and received his early training at the Academy of Charles Burney. He worked for the renowned painter Thomas Phillips before purchasing a military commission in the guards; it was Wainewright who said that no soldier should ever agree to serve unless he was permitted to design his own uniform. Perhaps it was for this reason that Wainewright decided against pursuing a soldier's life, though he gave "pronounced hypochondria and other neurotic symptoms" as reasons to resign his commission. Wainewright returned to the art world, where he struck up friendships with some of England's shining literary lights of the day, including the critic Charles Lamb, essayist William Hazlitt, biographer John Forster, actor William Macready, and poet William Wordsworth.

In 1821, Thomas Wainewright married Frances Ward. She was a poor girl with only "her looks and good nature." Within a few short years Wainewright found himself in a financial bind. Despite having exhibited his work in the Royal Academy for the years 1822, 1824, and 1825, he found it necessary to petition his trustees to grant him power of attorney to free up £2,250 in inheritance money held by the Bank of England. When the lawyers refused, Wainewright forged four signatures, which were accepted by the bank's officers.

But it seemed that no amount of money could satisfy the extravagant young artist, whom contemporaries described as "a somewhat overdressed young man whose white hands were bespangled with regal rings." By 1829 he had squandered the entire sum, and thus found himself hard pressed for additional cash. In 1828 Wainewright and his wife were invited to stay with their bachelor uncle, George Edward Griffiths, at his Linden House in Turnham Green, London. The old gentleman became ill shortly after their arrival and soon died. It was later charged that Wainewright had produced some deadly strychnine, which caused Griffiths to die in a convulsive fit. The property and the bulk of the estate fell into Wainewright's hands, but the upkeep was beyond his means to pay. Complicating matters was the announcement from his mother-in-law, Mrs. Abercrombie, that she had decided to move in with the Wainewrights in their hour of grief. She brought her two daughters, Helen and Madeleine.

Thomas Wainewright agreed to the arrangement, though he knew he could not possibly support the entire lot of them in his present circumstances. In August 1830 he poisoned Abercrombie and then insured the life of 20-year-old Helen for £18,000. In December 1830 the young woman abruptly became ill following a theater party. Helen died eight days later at Wainewright's overnight lodgings on Conduit Street. Her death was a terrible one. The doctor and nurse who attended her were repelled by the screams of pain. Her symptoms were not unlike Abercrombie's. Wainewright said later he had poisoned Helen because her thick ankles had offended him.

Wainewright was turned away from the offices of the various insurance companies when he tried to claim the money on Helen's life, as there was sufficient evidence to suggest that the woman had been murdered. Outraged, Wainewright filed a lawsuit against one of them, the Imperial, for the sum of £5,000, but he fled to northern France before hearing of the outcome of the case. Having abandoned his wife and all the money, Wainewright took up with a young French woman in 1831. He persuaded her father to insure his life for the sum of £3,000 with the Pelican Insurance Company, then slipped strychnine crystals into the man's coffee. He collected the money from this latest murder and continued on to Paris, where he worked as a painter for several more years.

After running through all of his money, the poisoner returned to London in 1837, where he lived at a hotel in Covent Garden. He was recognized by one of the Bow Street Runners, who arrested him on an 11-year-old forgery warrant. "Wainewright the Poisoner" was brought before a justice at the Old Bailey on July 5 on a charge of "intending to defraud the Governor and company of the Bank of England." Fortunately for him, no mention was made of the trail of poisoning murders in England and France. Wainewright entered a guilty plea and was sentenced to transportation for life. While waiting for his ship to sail, Wainewright received visits in his cell at Newgate from Charles Dickens and his other friends from the literary world. They could not imagine him in such a "horrendous condition and company." To an agent of an insurance company who came to settle accounts with him in his cell, Wainewright was haughty and aloof: "You city men enter on your speculations and some succeed and some fail. Mine happen to have failed, yours to have succeeded. That is the only difference, sir, between you and me. I have always been a gentleman throughout my life, and still am. It is the custom here for the inmates of a cell to take their morning's turn in sweeping it out. When my turn comes, my companions here never even offer me the broom!"

Wainewright was exiled to Tasmania, where he died of apoplexy in 1852. Oscar Wilde would later describe him as "one of the most subtle and secret poisoners of this or any age."

REF.: Altick, *Victorian Studies in Scarlet;* Boucher, *The Pocket Book of True Crime Book Stories; CBA;* Hunt, *A Dictionary of Rogues;* Kingston, *A Gallery of Rogues;* Norman, Pearce, *Unsolved Murder Mysteries;* Scott, *The Concise Encyclopedia of Crime and Criminals;* Secombe, *Twelve Bad Men;* Wilson, *Encyclopedia of Murder;* (FICTION), Dickens, *The Hunted.*

Wainwright, Henry (AKA: **George Willams**), c.1836-75, and **Wainwright, Thomas**, b.1846, Brit., mur. With £11,000 left to him by his late father, Henry Wainwright of London opened a brush manufacturing concern in the city's East End. The business flourishing, Wainwright took advantage of his new-found status in the community to indulge his interests in the theater. He hobnobbed with stage actors who appeared at the Pavilion Theatre in Whitechapel, for it was considered an honor to take supper with the wealthy Mr. Wainwright. When Arthur Orton, a notorious Tichborne claimant, appeared at the theater, it was Wainwright who saved him from serious bodily harm at the hands of an angry throng. Life was good for Wainwright, his wife, and his four children in those years until Harriet Louisa Lane, an attractive milliner from Waltham Abbey, entered the picture in 1871.

Henry Wainwright, businessman and killer.

Wainwright, the blustering executive about to enter his middle years, was enchanted with the 20-year-old woman and adopted the alias of "George William" to cover his affair. In 1872, a notice was placed in a Chelsea paper announcing the betrothal of Harriet Lane to "Perry King." King, of course, was Wainwright and the marriage never took place as it was a well-timed guise on the part of Wainwright to dispel ugly rumors. In the next year he put his lover up in a house on Sidney Square, with a £5-a-week allowance. During this time only one person was privy to the double life Wainwright lead, Harriet's best friend Ellen Wilmore who also worked as a milliner.

In May 1874, Wainwright found himself in a precarious position. Unexpected business reversals compelled his brother William to dissolve their partnership. Hard-pressed, Wainwright found it difficult to provide for his own family let alone a mistress. Out of desperation Wainwright decided to kill Harriet Lane. On Sept. 10, 1874, he purchased fifty pounds of chloride of lime and sent it to the shop on Whitechapel Road. That same day he sent £15 to Harriet to help clear her debts. On Mar. 11 she packed a valise with clothing, telling Wilmore that she was going to keep an appointment with Wainwright. Shortly afterward she disappeared.

It was commonly believed that the killer fired three shots into Lane while her back was turned, then the killer removed the floorboards in the paint room, fashioned a shallow grave, and buried the corpse in the lime. When Lane did not appear at her lodging after three days Ellen Wilmore made discreet inquiries. Wainwright said she had gone to Brighton to buy a new outfit. He revised this story after Wilmore expressed skepticism. Two days later a letter postmarked from the Charing Cross Hotel arrived at Wilmore's residence from an Edward Frieake who spoke of his love for Harriet and their plans to elope, adding, "I dare you or anyone else to interfere, as I intend to marry her." The handwriting was later proven to be that of another Wainwright brother, Thomas.

When the real Edward Frieake was located Wainwright was forced to modify his story again. He said that the man who ran off with Lane was one "Teddy Frieake." No further action was taken by Wilmore and Wainwright congratulated himself on a fine piece of deception. Business problems continued to plague him, however. The shop on Whitechapel Road mysteriously burned down but the insurance company refused to pay £3,000 in claims. In July 1875 the mortgage company seized the property after Wainwright petitioned for bankruptcy. Fearing that someone would accidentally come across the body buried under the floor, Wainwright decided to take precautions. A year to the day of Lane's disappearance he hired a man named Stokes to help haul away several bundles.

The parcels were heavy and awkward to carry. "For God's sake don't drop it or else you will break it!" Wainwright said at one point. When they reached the Whitechapel Church Stokes was told to remain with the packages while Wainwright flagged down a hansom cab. Stokes later claimed that an "inner voice" commanded him to open a bundle. What he found inside sickened him. He stared at what had once been a human hand. Stokes retied the bundle and loaded it into the cab when Wainwright returned. The same voice then ordered Stokes to follow the cab. On Commercial Road the cab slowed down to pick up a woman, Alice Day, an actress Wainwright lately had been seeing. Stokes followed the rig on foot to the London Bridge. He reported the incident to the police and within hours the murderer was under arrest. For his part, Stokes received a reward of £30. Thomas Wainwright, who helped dig the trench to hide Lane's body, was arrested and charged as an accessory after the fact. The trial convened at the Old Bailey in November 1875 before Lord Chief Justice Sir Alexander James Cockburn. The defense attempted to show that the body was not that of Harriet Lane but some other woman who may have killed herself. Cockburn sarcastically asked why a suicide victim would first dig her own grave. There was no answer.

The jury convicted both defendants after fifty-three minutes of deliberation. Thomas was spared a rendezvous with the hangman after a conversation between the two brothers was overheard by a warder at the Newgate Prison. Henry was hanged on Dec. 21, 1875. Before he went to his death Wainwright stared contemptuously at the assembled spectators and said, "Come to see a man die, have you curs?" They had, indeed. See: **Cockburn,** Sir **Alexander, James Edmund; Orton, Arthur.**

REF.: Altick, *Victorian Studies in Scarlet;* Bleackley, *Hangmen of England;* Boar, *The World's Most Infamous Murders;* Bowen-Reynolds, *Seventy-two Years at the Bar;* Brock, *A Casebook of Crime;* Burnaby, *Memories of Famous Trials; CBA;* Curling, *Janus Weathercock: The Life of Thomas Griffiths Wainewright;* Dilnot, *Celebrated Crimes;* Hodge, *The Black Maria;* Kingston, *A Gallery of Rogues;* ____, *Dramatic Days at the Old Bailey;* ____, *Law-Breakers;* Lindsey, *Suburban Gentleman;* Norman, *The Genteel Murderer; Notable British Trials;* Pearce, *Unsolved Murder Mysteries;* Whitelaw, *Corpus Delicti;* Wood, *Tales of Famous Crimes.*

Wait, Frederick T. (AKA: **Dash Wait, or Waite**), 1853-95, U.S., west. gunman. Frederick Wait, a cowboy and a quarter Cherokee Indian, married an Indian woman and moved to Lincoln County, N.M., where he found a job as a Regulator under John Tunstall, an English rancher. When the Lincoln County War broke out, Wait rode with Billy the Kid. On Apr. 1, 1878, Wait, "the Kid," Henry Brown, John Middleton, and Jim French ambushed Sheriff William Brady and four other lawmen on the streets of Lincoln. The five rose from concealment behind an adobe wall and opened fire, killing Brady and another lawmen. Wait and the Kid ran toward the two bodies to seize their rifles and received grazing wounds from Deputy Billy Matthews, who had run for cover when the shooting began. The ambushers then rode out of Lincoln.

Along with three other Regulators, Wait encountered Buckshot Roberts at Blazer's Mill on Apr. 4. In the ensuing gunfight, Dick Brewer, the Regulator's leader, was shot and killed. The others rode off, leaving Roberts fatally wounded.

Wait followed Billy the Kid into the Texas Panhandle when the outlaw prudently decided to leave New Mexico. There, a posse captured him, but he escaped. When Tom O'Folliard and Billy the Kid returned to New Mexico, Wait moved back to the Cherokee Nation in Indian Territory and became a tax collector. He died at the age of forty-two in 1895. See: **Billy the Kid.**

REF.: Bartholomew, *Jesse Evans;* Breihan, *Badmen of Frontier Days;*

Brent, *The Complete and Factual Life of Billy the Kid;* Burns, *The Saga of Billy the Kid; CBA;* Coe, *Frontier Fighter;* Fulton, *Lincoln County War;* Fulton, *Roswell in Its Early Years;* Garrett, *Pat F. Garrett's Authentic Life of Billy the Kid;* Hamlin, *The True Story of Billy the Kid;* Hendricks, *The Bad Man of the West;* Holloway, *Texas Gun Lore;* Hough, *The Story of the Outlaw;* Hunt, *The Tragic Days of Billy the Kid;* Keleher, *Violence in Lincoln County, 1869-1881;* King, *Pioneer Western Empire Builders;* Moore, *The West;* O'Connor, *Pat Garrett;* Otero, *The Real Billy the Kid;* Rickards, *Blazer's Mill;* Siringo, *Riata and Spurs;* Wellman, *The Trampling Herd.*

Waite, Arthur Warren (AKA: **Dr. Walters**), 1889-1917, U.S., perj.-mur. It was hard not to like the personable Dr. Arthur Waite. While it was true that he had committed two fiendishly calculated murders and felt no apparent regrets, the jurors, impressed with his charm, were barely able to stifle their laughter after listening to him tick off one humorous anecdote after another. Dr. Waite was something of anomaly: a physician sworn to uphold the Hippocratic oath, yet scornful of all it stood for, at least in regard to his in-laws.

Arthur Warren Waite was born and raised in Grand Rapids, Mich., his parents were struggling farmers who could not provide for their son the life he envisioned for himself. Realizing that his future would be inextricably tied to the soil unless he did something about it, Waite set his eyes on Clara Peck, the pampered daughter of lumber baron John E. Peck, one of the wealthiest men in town. Much attention was given to their courtship, which Clara's father opposed.

Waite attended the University of Michigan before completing his studies at the University of Glasgow in Scotland. He sent back glowing reports to his parents and his thoroughly captivated girlfriend in Grand Rapids, neglecting to mention that he had cheated his way through medical school and had forged false credentials.

With his fresh degree in dentistry, Waite accepted a position with a mining firm in South Africa. While serving as the company's chief dentist, the social-climbing Waite attempted to marry a wealthy young heiress but was thwarted by the woman's father. He was released from his duties before the contract with the mining firm expired, returning to Michigan $20,000 richer and ready to plot new strategy. Clara, happy now that the conquering hero was coming home, decided to make him her husband. On Christmas Day 1914 she proposed against the stern admonishments of 76-year-old John Peck. Nevertheless they were married on Sept. 9, 1915.

As a gesture of reconciliation the elderly Peck gave them a rent-free apartment on Manhattan's fashionable Riverside Drive and a generous allowance of $300 a month. Waite opened a dental practice, but found the work tedious and dull. He spent most of his time on the tennis courts, a throwback to his days in Scotland where he was a reigning court pro. To her concerned parents, Clara wrote, "He's Metropolitan Champion. Isn't that wonderful?"

During these idle times, Waite met a glamorous socialite named Margaret Weaver Horton, wife of an aeronautical engineer of some renown. They began an affair, a costly one no doubt, since Mrs. Horton expected only the best. Their suite at the Plaza Hotel cost Waite a small fortune. The $300 allowance from his father-in-law did not go far enough to meet his mounting expenses. "I expected $50,000 outright!" he thundered to his wife, who received fewer and fewer kind words from him each day. Seeing no other way out of his difficulties, Waite concocted a harebrained scheme to murder his in-laws and his wife and seize control of the family estate.

He waited until Jan. 10, 1916, when his mother-in-law arrived for a short visit, to put his plan into action. "I started poisoning her from the very first meal after she arrived," Waite would later tell the court. "I gave her six assorted tubes of pneumonia, diphtheria, and influenza germs in her food. When she finally became ill and took to her bed I ground up twelve five-grain veronal tablets and gave her that, too, last thing at night." During her short, unexpected illness, Warren doted on his mother-in-law, bringing her flowers and footwarmers. When she died on Jan. 20 Waite suggested that the only correct thing to do under the circumstances would be to cremate the woman. It was her last wish, he explained.

Peck arrived in town to console himself the first week of February. Within days the old man began feeling ill. As Waite later explained, "I used to insert tubes of typhoid, pneumonia, and diphtheria in his soups and rice pudding. Once I gave him a nasal spray filled with tuberculosis bacteria." Peck was a robust, healthy individual for his age. His system resisted the deadly germs in a way that mystified Waite. "Still nothing happened," he said. I tried to give him pneumonia by putting water in his Wellingtons, damping his sheets, opening his bedroom window and wetting the seat of the automobile before taking him out for a drive." Waite then administered eighteen grains of arsenic, which debilitated the old man but still failed to kill him. Waite ended the ordeal by smothering him with a pillow on Mar. 12.

Waite consoled his wife as best as he could, again suggesting that the body be cremated to spare the family needless torment. Percy Peck, Clara's older brother, drew the line. He insisted that his father be returned to Grand Rapids for proper burial. Warren acquiesced but chose to remain behind in New York while the family went to Michigan. Percy Peck received a telegram from a friend, Mrs. Hardwicke, which confirmed his own suspicions about his brother-in-law. "Don't allow cremation until an autopsy as been carried out," it read. The embalmed remains were examined and arsenic and chloroform were found. Advised of these developments, Clara still refused to believe her husband was a murderer. Catherine Peck, Clara's aunt, supported Waite. "I like him so well I gave him a $3,000 wedding present," she added. It was later learned that Aunt Catherine was also on Waite's murder list.

Meanwhile, the New York Police located an atomizer belonging to Waite that contained typhoid and anthrax germs. It was clear by now who the murderer was. The police questioned Oliver Eugene Kane, the embalmer who prepared Peck's body for burial. He told the officers that Waite offered him a $9,000 bribe to inject arsenic in the embalming fluid.

Kane accepted the offer but later reneged and kept the money anyway. "I was so scared I buried it (the arsenic) out in the sand at Orient Point on the tip of Long Island," he said. Waite tried to kill himself with sleeping pills but, having failing badly, blamed the attempt on insanity. "A bad man from Egypt dwells in my body," he said. "He makes me do things! He struggles for possession of my soul."

Waite broke down and confessed the whole sordid affair to the police. He told of his early experiences in the university and how he had forged his postgraduate certificate at Glasgow, as well as the sterling newspaper accounts of his achievements in Europe and South Africa. He secured the deadly poisons and bacteria slides while working at Flower Hospital in New York. "In November 1915, to test my knowledge and to test the effect of germs, I inoculated myself with cultures of anthrax, typhoid, and pneumonia. By the time Mrs. Peck arrived in January 1916 I was ready for her," he told police.

Waite said that he planned to kill his wife because "she was not my equal in anything and I meant to find a more beautiful wife." Experts in psychiatry attempted to show that anyone who killed with such cheerful abandon must be truly crazy. The jury, which had enjoyed listening to the light-hearted antics of the young dentist, nevertheless returned a verdict of Guilty.

Arthur Warren Waite was put to death in the electric chair on May 24, 1917. As his execution time loomed near, the doctor showed remarkable composure. In the hours before his execution, he read passages from the Bible and a selected verse from John Keats.

REF.: *CBA;* Hughes, *The Complete Detective;* Laurence, *Extraordinary Crimes;* Laurence, *A History of Capital Punishment;* Nash, *Murder, America;* Reynolds, *Murder 'Round the World;* Smith, *Famous American Poison Mysteries;* Wilson, *Encyclopedia of Murder.*

Defiant dentist Dr. Warren Waite used poison on his victims.

Waite's father-in-law, John E. Peck, murdered.

A host of germs unleashed by Waite killed Mrs. Peck.

Mrs. Margaret Weaver Horton

Mrs. Peck and Mrs. Warren Waite.

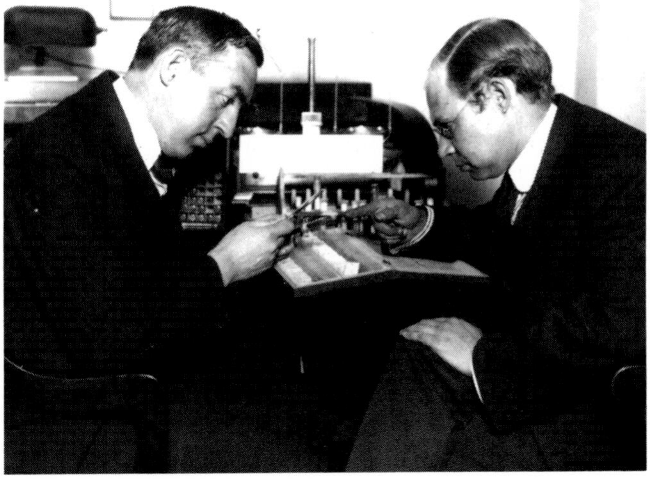

Experts examining Waite's germ lab.

Waite, Morrison Remick, 1816-88, U.S., jur. Born to a prominent New England family, Morrison Waite later moved to western Ohio, where he studied law. Waite was admitted to the bar in 1839, practicing in Maumee City for the next eleven years. He entered public life in 1850, becoming a member of the Ohio House of Representatives. In 1863 he was offered a seat on the Ohio Supreme Court, but declined. Eight years later, Waite became a national figure by virtue of his work with the Geneva Arbitration, empaneled to seek compensation from Great Britain, which had allowed Confederate naval vessels to be outfitted in their ports during the Civil War. Waite helped win a $15.5 million settlement for the U.S., and returned home to accept President Ulysses Grant's nomination for chief justice of the Supreme Court, which was approved by Congress on Jan. 21, 1874.

His fourteen-year term on the bench reflected the growing conservatism within the country. Civil Rights advances were largely negated by several controversial measures passed in the 1870s. Waite wrote the majority opinion in *United States vs. Reese*, 1876, which overturned two sections of the 1870 Civil Rights Act on the grounds that they were unauthorized by the Fifteenth Amendment. Throughout his term, Justice Waite upheld his long-standing view that Federal intervention in Southern racial issues was an infringement of states' rights. In 1875 he wrote the majority opinion in *Minor vs. Happersett* which upheld a state law denying women's suffrage.

Justice Waite remained on the bench until his death in 1888. He was succeeded by Melville W. Fuller who was nominated by President Grover Cleveland. REF.: *CBA*.

Wakefield, Edward Gibbon, 1796-1862, and **Wakefield, William Hay**, 1803-48, and **Wakefield, Frances**, prom. 1826, Brit., consp.-kid. Edward Wakefield, born into a distinguished Quaker family in England, eloped with a wealthy young heiress named Eliza Pattle, who died before her twenty-first birthday. Consequently, Edward Wakefield was denied a sizeable inheritance which would have taken care of his needs for life.

In 1825, Edward's stepmother, Frances, suggested that the handsome young widower marry Ellen Turner, the 15-year-old daughter of the high sheriff of Cheshire. Ellen stood to inherit not only her father's estates but her brother's as well. Edward and his brother William then decided to kidnap the young girl with the connivance of Mrs. Wakefield. Until the passage of the "Offenses Against the Person Act" in 1861, which outlawed marital abductions, this practice was not uncommon. By compromising a respectable woman's chastity, the fortune-seeking rogue virtually assured himself of a marriage, and lifelong income from the victim's family.

On Mar. 7, 1826, Wakefield's servant appeared at the offices of a boarding school near Liverpool where Ellen was staying. He explained to the head mistress that her mother was afflicted with a serious illness, and that Ellen's presence was requested immediately. Outside, the carriage of Edward Wakefield was waiting.

The young lawyer introduced himself, and explained that her father had been financially ruined, and the only way out of the dilemma was for them to immediately marry. Wakefield was convincing. The three-day "prank" ended in Calais, Fr., after Wakefield and Ellen exchanged their vows in Gretna Green. When he learned of the marriage, Turner's father secured a letter from the Foreign Secretary to the British Legation in Paris requesting the repatriation of his daughter. Two of Ellen's uncles, accompanied by Grimsditch, a lawyer, and a policeman were sent to France to bring the girl back.

Wakefield meekly surrendered his "bride" saying that he had not violated her in any way. In Dover, William Wakefield was arrested by the authorities. Frances and her two stepsons were charged with conspiracy and found Guilty in a trial that attracted great public interest. Edward and William were each sentenced to three years in prison. Frances was released after the Turners decided not to press charges. Two years after his release, Edward Wakefield recounted his experiences in a best-selling book titled, *Facts Relating to the Punishment of Death In the Metropolis*. He later went on to complete a career in the foreign service.

REF.: Bierstadt, *Curious Trials and Criminal Cases; CBA;* Cooper, *Lesson of the Scaffold;* Franklin, *Woman in the Case.*

Wakeman, Sir **George**, prom. 1685, Case of, Brit., treas. Sir George Wakeman was created a Baronet by King Charles II in 1661, and was appointed to serve as Queen Catherine's personal physician in 1670, largely because he was reputed to be a most capable Roman Catholic doctor.

Wakeman was indicted for high treason on July 18, 1679, for allegedly conspiring to poison King Charles. The accusations were brought against him by Titus Oates and Dr. Israel Tonge, rector of St. Michael's Wood Street church. They claimed that Wakeman had been offered a large sum of money to murder the king and the Duke of York in order to establish the Catholic religion in England. The charges were unfounded, and absurd, given the king's proclivity toward Catholicism.

Oates claimed that Wakeman had initially refused an offer of £10,000 to poison the king, saying that it was not enough. Accordingly, the stakes were supposed to have been raised in order to accommodate Wakeman who desired an appointment as physician-general. The case was tried before Lord Chief Justice William Scroggs, who found Wakeman Not Guilty. See: **Oates, Titus**.

REF.: *CBA;* Parry, *Some Famous Medical Trials.*

Wala, d.836, Fr., rebel. Served as adviser to Charlemagne and escaped when Louis I came to power. He tutored Louis' son, Lothair I, and later incited the revolts of Lothair in 829 and Pepin I in 830 against Louis. Louis exiled him to Italy with Lothair in 834. REF.: *CBA*.

Walafrid Strabo, c.808-49, Swabia, banish. Made abbot of Reichenau in 838. He was banished in 839 because he supported Lothair I's revolt against his father, Louis I. He was reinstalled in 842. REF.: *CBA*.

Walcott, Thomas, and **Rouse, John**, and **Hone, William**, d.1683, Brit., consp. Thomas Walcott, John Rouse, and William Howe were three of the conspirators hanged for their role in the infamous "Rye House Plot," in which agents of Anthony Cooper, the 1st Earl of Shaftesbury, planned to murder King Charles II and the Duke of York in the Spring of 1683. The plot was detected before it could be carried out, and Captain Walcott and his two associates were hanged and quartered at Tyburn on July 14. Afterward, their heads were severed and placed on poles for public display. See: **Rye House Plot**.

REF.: *CBA;* Potter, *The Art of Hanging.*

Waldeck-Rousseau, Pierre Marie René, 1846-1904, Fr., lawyer. Defended Ferdinand de Lesseps, president of French company that began construction of Panama Canal and who was tried for misappropriation of funds. He served as senator from 1894-1904, and as premier of France from 1899-1902. He also pardoned Alfred Dreyfus in 1899. REF.: *CBA*.

Walden, Bernard Hugh, d.1959, Brit., mur. "I am not as other men," Bernard Walden told the court at his 1959 murder trial. "I am a cripple and must be armed to put me on fair terms with others...I have an absolute right to kill." His chilling statements were without compassion, yet the jury recommended mercy.

Walden was a lecturer at Rotherham Technical College. Convicted of a homosexual offense in 1949, the dowdy teacher became infatuated with a woman on campus. When she spurned his advances, Walden shot and killed both the girl and her boyfriend. He was diagnosed as suffering from chronic paranoid development, but despite the unsoundness of mind, Walden was hanged at Leeds in August 1959. His execution was controversial in light of the recently enacted Homicide Act which generally limited the death sentence to individuals who killed while in pursuit of criminal activities.

REF.: *CBA;* Hibbert, *The Roots of Evil.*

Walder, Arnold (AKA: **The Bottle Imp**), b.1857, Fr., (unsolv.) rob.-mur. Each year, on the anniversary of his crime, Arnold Walder would send to the Paris Police a note that reminded them that he was still at large. Each message sent would be carefully wrapped inside a perfume bottle, hence his nickname the "Bottle Imp." Arnold Walder was a 22-year-old chemist's assistant who worked in Pierre Legrange's apothecary shop in Paris. At various times during his checkered career he had been a bellhop, a barber, and a weaver. Walder had high ambitions but no money. He began stealing perfume bottles from his employer and reselling them at half-price.

Realizing that he needed more money, Walder chose another method of obtaining it. On Oct. 5, 1879, he bludgeoned his employer and the servant girl Zélie Gaillot in the cellar of the pharmacy. In the afternoon Walder cheerfully minded the store, pocketing all the money taken in for perfume and prescriptions. Then, after the shop closed at eight, Walder took the midnight train to Havre. The police traced him to Paris, where he sent the first of a long series of messages to the police. In his first note, the Bottle Imp told of his plans to commit suicide. "I have committed suicide. Better that, than the terror of the guillotine." But Walder had a change of heart, when he realized that it was possible to avoid the police. For many years they searched for the elusive Imp, but the trail simply vanished.

REF.: Birmingham, *Murder Most Foul; CBA;* Wilson, *Encyclopedia of Murder.*

Waldis, Burkard, c.1490-c.1556, Ger., her. Became adherent of Lutheranism in 1524. He was put in prison during the religious persecutions between 1536-40. REF.: *CBA.*

Waldmann, Hans, c.1435-89, Switz, assass. Accumulated wealth and ruled as near-dictator after selling Swiss mercenary troops to several rulers. After trying to extend his power, he was arrested and executed by an opposing group in Zürich. REF.: *CBA.*

Waldo, Henry Linn, 1844-1915, U.S., jur. Served as attorney general in territorial government of New Mexico from 1878-80. He was nominated to the territorial court of New Mexico by President Ulysses S. Grant in 1876. REF.: *CBA.*

Waldo, Rhinelander, b.1877, U.S., law enfor. off. Rhinelander Waldo, a graduate of West Point and a member of New York's social register, was made deputy police commissioner by Mayor William J. Gaynor in 1911. Waldo was naive and knew little about police procedures, and his approach to law enforcement was based on his own code of military tactics. To clean up the rampant vice and gambling in Manhattan, Waldo established several "strong-arm" squads which, without warrants, barged into gambling dens and brothels, arrested everybody in sight, and destroyed the establishments with axes as Waldo ordered. Waldo's policies slowed down gambling and bordello operations somewhat, but his record of arrests collapsed in courts which threw them out for lack of proper procedures.

Worse, one of Waldo's handpicked men leading a strong-arm squad was none other than Charles Becker who was secretly in league with New York gamblers and was boss of the Tenderloin district underworld. When Becker was finally exposed and convicted of ordering the death of gambler Herman "Beansie" Rosenthal (Rosenthal was executed at Sing Sing in 1915), Waldo's reputation was severely damaged. The deputy police commissioner had been made a laughingstock by the press, which had pictured him in cartoons dressed in a Boy Scout uniform, blindly leading his men into dense woods on childish expeditions. The portrait drawn of Waldo in the so-called "fact novel," *Ragtime,* was a complete fabrication, as was the case of a revolutionary black dealing with Waldo in this questionable piece of fiction. See: **Becker, Charles.**

REF: Logan, *Against the Evidence;* Peterson, *The Mob;* Reppetto, *The Blue Parade.*

Waldron, Sir **John Lovegrove**, 1909-75, Brit., law enfor. off. Sir John Waldron joined the London Metropolitan Police in 1934. He served as deputy inspector-general of the CID from 1944-47, and assistant commissioner from 1959-66, and again from 1966-68. In 1968, he was named to the post of commissioner of police, which he held until 1972. REF.: *CBA.*

Waldron, William Henry, Jr. (AKA: **Robert Coleman Johnson**), prom. 1950s-60s, U.S., embez.-mur. After embezzling $7,000 from a local bank, successful attorney William Henry Waldron, Jr., left his wife and family in West Virginia and disappeared without a trace. He did communicate once with his wife, deeding the family home to her. Once his wife had repaid the bank, the charges of embezzlement against Waldron were dropped. Waldron, now called Robert Johnson, settled in Madeira Beach, Fla., worked at various menial jobs, and found a new wife. On Aug. 21, 1966, he beat his wife, Phyllis Johnson, to death. Waldron was arrested and sentenced on Feb. 2, 1967, to twenty years in prison for second-degree murder.

REF.: *CBA;* Nash, *Among the Missing.*

Kidnapper Harman Waley in custody, 1935.

Waley, Harmon, and **Waley, Margaret**, and **Dainard, William J.**, prom. 1935, U.S., kid. Nine days after his grandfather passed away, 9-year-old George Weyerhaeuser of Tacoma, Wash., was abducted on his way home from school. The kidnappers, who had read about the death of the millionaire lumber tycoon, demanded $200,000 for the boy's safe return. The May 24, 1935, abduction of the Weyerhaeuser boy was described as the "biggest kidnapping case the Pacific Northwest has seen."

The Weyerhaeuser family paid the ransom demand and their boy was released unharmed on June 1. The marked bills soon began appearing in various towns scattered across the U.S. This led to the arrest of Harmon Waley and his wife Margaret in Salt Lake City on June 9. The couple stood trial in Tacoma for kidnapping under the terms of the Lindbergh Law. Fearing a possible death sentence, the Waleys entered a plea of guilty. Harmon was sentenced to forty-five years in prison; his wife was sentenced to twenty. The third party to the crime, William Mahan, was arrested and tried in Tacoma. He received two concurrent sentences of sixty years each. See: **Dainard, William J.**

REF.: Alix, *Ransom Kidnapping in America; CBA.*

Walker, Charles, 1941- , U.S., rob.-mur. Starting his criminal career when he was still a boy, Charles Walker was sentenced to death at age thirty-three for the double murder of a downstate Illinois couple. The product of a broken home, he began drinking heavily and committed burglaries in his pre-teens to buy alcohol. After dropping out of high school at age fifteen, he was repeatedly imprisoned for burglary, and then, in 1969, he engaged a police officer in a shoot-out in which he lost his right eye. He served more than a decade in prison, and three years later after his release, found work on a maintenance crew at Scott Air Force Base.

On June 18, 1983, Walker was fishing for catfish at Silver Creek. He had drank a couple of six packs of beer and half a pint of vodka and wanted to buy more beer but did not have enough money. Kevin Paule, a 21-year-old janitor, and his fiancée Sharon Winker, a 23-year-old preschool teacher from Mascoutah, Ill., sat fishing nearby. Walker struck up a conversation with them and then pulled a .25-caliber pistol from his pocket, robbing them of $40 and tying them to a tree, facing each other. Paule then said, "I know you; you're Charles Walker." Walker shot and killed the couple, later claiming, "I just wanted to get away. I didn't want to go back to prison."

In 1984, Walker was convicted of first-degree murder and sentenced to be executed. Illinois had not executed a criminal since 1962, and Walker's case was continually appealed to the Illinois Supreme Court. In January 1988, from death row, Walker told a group of reporters he did not want his sentence appealed again and said he wanted the state to execute him. "A lot of people fear death. I don't," he said. Regardless, anti-death sentence groups appealed his sentence again in 1989 but the appeal was denied by the 7th Circuit U.S. Court of Appeals because they "lacked standing" to represent Walker. At the time of this writing, Walker continues his long wait on Death Row. REF.: *CBA.*

Walker, Daniel, 1922- , U.S., fraud. Dan Walker was elected governor of Illinois in 1972 on a platform that called for political reform and an end to corrupt practices. To illustrate his independence from the Democratic political machine of Chicago Mayor Richard J. Daley, Walker hiked the length and breadth of Illinois, canvassing for the kind of grassroots support sorely needed to claim the statehouse. Prior to the 1972 gubernatorial campaign, Walker had become a popular figure among Illinois liberals for his work on the committee appointed to investigate the 1968 Democratic Convention disorders. The *Walker Report: Rights in Conflict,* laid much of the blame for the August riot with the Chicago police and Mayor Daley.

Walker was elected governor of the state but his unwillingness to negotiate with Democratic party regulars cost him a chance at a second term in 1977. Walker then joined the private sector as chairman of the Oakbrook-based First American Savings and Loan Association, which he owned jointly with his wife. In 1986 regulators took over the business after First American was declared insolvent by the Federal Home Loan Bank Board. A federal grand jury determined that the former governor had engaged in insider trading and high risk commercial lending. In August, Walker pleaded guilty to three counts of bank fraud. He was accused of misapplying $280,000 from First American, concealing information from U.S. banking officials, and filing a false financial statement in order to borrow an additional $1.1 million from five lending institutions.

He was found Guilty of the charges and sentenced to seven-years at a federal prison camp on Nov. 19, 1988, by U.S. District judge Ann Williams. Dan Walker served a year-and-a-half at a minimum security camp in Duluth, Minn., before Judge Williams reduced the sentence to "time served" on June 21, 1989, in consideration of his declining health. REF.: *CBA.*

Walker, Ernest Albert, 1905- , Brit., mur. When Ernest Walker of London lost his mother, he appears to have also lost his mind. This was the only explanation he could give for murdering 14-year-old Raymond Charles Davis one night in April 1922. At the time, Walker worked for Colonel Charles Trotter as a personal footman. One night when Trotter was out, Walker summoned a courier from the Sloane Street offices of the District Messenger Company. According to a carefully prepared thirteen-point agenda Walker had prepared, he would torture and murder whomever the company sent over. The unfortunate victim was Davis.

When the vicious act was carried out, Walker fled the house and boarded a train at the Charing Cross station, bound for Kent. There, he cornered a policeman and confessed to what he had done. A court-appointed physician determined that Walker suffered from epileptic automatism, and was not able to fully comprehend what he had done. Consequently, the 17-year-old boy was found Guilty, but insane. He was sent to the Broadmoor Institution. Walker was ordered released in 1937, after the authorities determined that he no longer posed a threat to society.

REF.: *CBA;* Oddie, *Inquest;* Shew, *A Second Companion to Murder.*

Walker, Isobel, b.1716, Scot., mur. Isobel Walker, daughter of William Walker, lived with her mother and older sister Helen in a run-down cottage in Cluden, Kirkcudbrightshire, Scot. Her father died while she was in her teens, and she and her sister worked as day laborers to make ends meet. In 1736, a youth named Waugh seduced Isobel and then deserted her when he discovered she was pregnant. The desperate young woman killed her newborn, but the body was found in the nearby river where she had thrown it. Confronted with the body, Isobel denied the child was hers, but she was nevertheless convicted of infanticide and condemned to be hanged.

Her sister Helen, who was about five years older, testified that her sister was innocent of the crime of which she stood accused and got up a petition signed by hundreds of neighbors, begging the authorities to commute Isobel's sentence to transportation to America. When officials ignored Helen's pleas, she set out on foot to walk to London to plea for royal intercession. Her epic walk, a tremendous hardship of hundreds of miles, later inspired Sir Walter Scott to make her the heroine of his opus, *The Heart of the Midlothian.* Helen did arrive in London, as the story goes, and managed to meet with the Duke of Argyll who went to the king with her petition which was allegedly granted. Records reveal that Isobel Walker's date of execution was several times postponed while a petition begging for transportation in lieu of execution was considered. This was eventually granted in 1738, and she ostensibly left for America within four months of being released, according to a court order that also stipulated that if she ever stepped foot in England she would be immediately executed.

Yet records also indicate that Isobel Walker apparently re-entered England years later and married Waugh, the young man who had contributed to her problems, and settled in Whitehaven. Her heroic sister never married, working as a seamstress until her death in 1791 at the age of eighty-one.

REF.: *CBA;* Crockett, *The Scott Originals;* (FICTION), Scott, *The Heart of the Midlothian.*

Walker, James John, 1881-1946, U.S., polit. corr. Fun- loving, freewheeling Jimmy Walker loved everything about New York City, including the "Gay White Way" of Broadway, the roar of spectators cheering Babe Ruth at Yankee Stadium, and all-night parties at the Central Park Casino, where he danced till dawn with his mistress, former show girl Betty Compton. Above all else, Jimmy Walker enjoyed being mayor of the biggest, grandest city in the country.

Walker was the son of Irish immigrants who raised him in the narrow boundaries of Greenwich Village. Following his graduation from the New York Law School in 1904, Walker began frequenting the swanky bistros and theaters uptown. In 1912 he married a musical comedy singer, and was admitted to the New York State bar. Politics always held a special fascination for Walker. It was the perfect stage to showcase his oratorical skills and easy-going manner, which the voters of New York found irresistible.

Walker finagled his way into Tammany Hall, thanks to the nurturing assistance provided by his mentor, Alfred E. Smith, future governor of New York and Democratic presidential aspirant. In 1909 Walker was elected to the Assembly. Five years later he became a member of the State Senate. The Tammany organization touted the enthusiastic Walker for mayor in 1925, and the voters responded. During his first term in office, Mayor Walker pushed through many notable civic projects, including the formation of New York's Department of Sanitation. He unified the city's public hospitals, improved its park system, and got the Board of Transportation to approve construction contracts for a revamped subway system.

Dapper James J. Walker and wife, the former Betty Compton.

Re-elected by a wide plurality in 1929, Walker encountered greater obstacles in his second term. Rumors of rampant municipal corruption spurred an investigation into the city's affairs that began in 1931. Judge Samuel Seabury, counsel for the Hofstadter Committee, called on Walker to explain his connection with Russell T. Sherwood, a low-ranking accountant who mysteriously accumulated a fortune of $700,225 and then disappeared. Seabury accused Sherwood of "fronting" for Walker, a charge vigorously denied by the mayor. But it was conclusively shown that on the eve of a cruise Walker took to Europe, Sherwood withdrew $263,838 from the bank for his boss. Battered by Seabury's intimidating questions, Walker admitted to having banked $432,677 in just four years. He claimed that much of it came from financial speculation with members of the Wall Street community, although he could not produce records of the transactions. Most of the money was spent before the investigation started, Walker acknowledged.

Walker was but one of many New York public officials whom the relentless Seabury caught with their hands in the till. The maze of corruption stretched from Gracie Mansion to the police department to the city inspectors. As the most visible public figure in the state other than Governor Franklin D. Roosevelt, Walker had to be made an example by the politicians. After reviewing the fifteen charges Judge Seabury brought against the mayor, Roosevelt demanded Walker give a satisfactory explanation. Realizing that the next step was removal from office, Walker quietly submitted his resignation on Sept. 1, 1932, a protest, he said, against the "unfairness" of the hearings. Joseph McKee, the president of the Board of Aldermen, was named interim mayor. Shortly afterward, Jimmy Walker and Betty Compton sailed for Europe, where they remained until the controversy died down. Returning to New York in 1935, Walker was appointed by Mayor Fiorello LaGuardia to head up the mammoth National Cloak and Suit Industry in 1940. See: **Seabury Investigations**.

REF.: *CBA;* Fowler, *Beau James: The Life and Times of Jimmy Walker;* (FILM), *The Night Mayor,* 1932; *Beau James,* 1957.

Walker, Jesse, 1899-1920, U.S., mur. In 1919, at the encouragement of an acquaintance, Henry Rauth, Jesse Walker, twenty, and fellow seaman Guy Nichols, decided to rob a small candy shop in Brooklyn, N.Y. According to Rauth, the owner of the shop, Samuel Wolchak, kept large amounts of cash in a drawer under the counter. While Rauth stood guard outside, Walker and Nichols entered the store. Walker approached the counter and pointed his gun at Wolchak. Instead of surrendering, the shopowner threw a punch at Walker. Without hesitation, Walker shot Wolchak at point blank range, rupturing an artery in Wolchak's chest.

Walker found a two dollar bill in Wolchak's pocket and four more dollars in the cash drawer. In the search for the money, however, Walker managed to get blood on the two dollar bill and on his shirt collar. With the paltry rewards from the crime, the three men left. Walker discarded the blood stained collar and washed off the two dollar bill in a room the three men had previously rented. At a nearby clothing store Walker used the $2 bill to purchase a new collar. Although the officer assigned to investigate Wolchak's murder got as far as finding the blood-stained collar and tracing Walker to the haberdasher's where he got a reasonable description of the murderer, the trail went cold and the case was set aside as one that would most likely remain unsolved.

Walker's crime to this point had little about it of distinction. However, Walker, who was evidently of below average intelligence, had begun keeping a careful diary several years before. Walker's impetus for this effort was a story he had read in the newspapers about a suspect in a murder case who was cleared of the crime because of the discovery of a diary in which he had carefully recorded his activities on the date of the crime. The man in the account that Walker had read was exonerated when the alibi his diary showed checked out. In the simplistic belief that the keeping of the diary was some sort of magic token, Walker from this point on carefully recorded his every activity—including criminal ones. Some months after the Wolchak murder, the Brooklyn police were notified by police in Matoon, Ill., that they had apprehended a man in the theft of a fur coat in whose possession they found a diary which detailed a number of crimes in the New York area. Among the entries for the first week in November was the Wolchak shooting, with all the details of the crime including the names of Walker's accomplices. Carefully inscribed on the inside cover of the diary was the name, Jesse Walker. Walker was returned to New York where he, Nichols and Rauth were tried for first-degree murder. Rauth was acquitted when it was determined that he had remained outside during the commission of the crime. Nichols and Walker, however, were found Guilty. Both men were executed in the electric chair some time later. REF.: *CBA.*

Walker, Joe, 1850-98, U.S., west. outl. Joe Walker never knew his father, a Texas rancher who died when Walker was an infant. After her husband's death, Walker's mother turned their ranch property over to the management of her brother, Dr. Whitmore, who merged his herds with theirs. Whitmore subsequently moved to a ranch in northern Arizona and later was killed in a skirmish with Indians. His widow, along with her two sons, George and Tobe, sold the Arizona ranch and moved to Carbon County, Utah, eventually becoming a prominent ranching and banking family. After the death of his mother, Walker traveled to Utah to make a property settlement with the Whitmores, who denied their relationship to him as well as his claim to a portion of their property. The cowboy took jobs in ranches and at a sawmill, privately awaiting a chance for revenge.

Walker hounded the Whitmores for some time. In 1895, he became a wanted man for shooting up the town of Price, Utah, where he caused considerable property damage. Then he joined a band of outlaws at Robbers Roost. Stealing horses and rustling cattle, he frequently took Whitmore stock. In 1896 a posse intercepted him, and after a running gunfight and a fifteen-mile chase, the rustler escaped to Robbers Roost. In 1897, Walker quarrelled with fellow rustler C.L. Maxwell after stealing some Whitmore horses, and Maxwell informed sheriffs C.W. Allred and Azariah Tuttle of Walker's whereabouts which allowed them to catch Walker by surprise. Walker scaled a canyon wall, then wounded Tuttle as Allred raced for help. The outlaw and the wounded lawman held each other at bay for several hours until nightfall when Walker brought Tuttle a bucket of water and then escaped.

Walker threw in with the Wild Bunch and Butch Cassidy a few months later, and on Apr. 21, aided the gang in the Castle Gate payroll robbery by cutting the telegraph wires. The robbery netted $8,000. Walker returned to raiding Whitmore cattle. In May 1898, he and another cowboy, Johnny Herring, were again rustling Whitmore cattle. They were camped near Thompson, Utah, when a nine-man posse caught up with them one night. The posse thought Herring was Butch Cassidy and at dawn, just as Walker stirred awake, the posse opened fire and slaughtered the two men in their bedrolls. See: **Cassidy, Butch.**

REF.: Baker, *The Wild Bunch at Robbers Roost; CBA.*

Walker, John, and **Sharp, Mark,** prom. 1632, Brit., mur. John Walker was a yeoman farmer living in the village of Great Lumley, in Durham. His house was tended to by a young woman named Anne Walker, whom he was distantly related to. Eventually Anne became pregnant with his child, and to avoid a scandal, Walker sent Anne to stay with her aunt Dame Carr, who lived two miles away.

Shortly after her arrival, a friend of John Walker's, Mark Sharp, paid a visit. He led Anne out of the house and into the countryside. She was never seen alive again. About two weeks later, a miller named James Graham who lived nearby reported seeing a ghostly apparition in the moonlight. According to his sworn testimony, Anne Walker implored him to notify the constable that she had been murdered with a pick-axe by Mark Sharp, and had been buried in a coal pit.

Graham told his story to the magistrate on Dec. 20, 1632. A search of the moor was ordered. The corpse of Anne was located, and the two murderers were brought to trial at the Durham Assizes. Walker and Sharp were found Guilty and hanged. The story was later told in Dr. John Webster's book *Witchcraft and the Supernatural.*

REF.: *CBA;* Lambton, *Thou Shalt Do No Murder;* Whitelaw, *Corpus Delicti.*

Walker, Jonathan, prom. 1844, U.S., rob. From the 1600s-1844 the branding of criminals was a common practice in the U.S. The last man branded by a court for a crime was Jonathan Walker, accused of stealing slaves. He helped a slave escape to the Bahamas, and had the initials "SS" for "Slave Stealer" were burned into his palm. The abolitionist poem "The Man with the Branded Hand," written by John Greenleaf Whittier, was inspired by Walker's plight. REF.: *CBA.*

Walker, Lee Dell, 1913- , U.S., (wrong. convict.) mur. On the night of Feb. 17, 1954, two gunmen entered a small grocery store in Detroit, which was owned by John Drousiotis. The gunmen brandished pistols and demanded the cash in the till. The outraged owner lunged at the first robber, and wrestled him to the floor. However, the bandit broke free and fired two shots, killing the store owner.

Six days later a petty thief named Lee Walker was arrested by Detroit police in connection with an unrelated mugging attempt. According to Walker, he was detained by police for four days and tortured into confessing to a murder he knew nothing about. At one point, police officers placed a gun in his mouth and threatened to fire unless he admitted to killing Drousiotis. At the same time, Bill Johnson, the man who was alleged to have been Walker's partner in the robbery attempt was killed by police in a second stick-up. Johnson and Walker were linked together by virtue of a gun that was later found in an abandoned automobile. The police theorized that Walker had hidden the gun under the hood. The suspect denied the charge, maintaining that his car had been stolen by the probable murderer, and through an unfortunate set of circumstances he had been wrongfully implicated. Walker said he was visiting a girlfriend in Inkster at the time of the shooting.

The murder trial began on June 21, 1954. It lasted one week before a Guilty verdict was returned. Walker had renounced his earlier confession, but the court concluded that it had been given "voluntarily." The defendant was sentenced to life imprisonment and his appeals were denied. In February 1965, Recorder's Court judge John Ricca ruled that the original confession was voluntary. By 1971, Walker had become a model prisoner, who assisted fellow convicts in their legal work. A reporter named Howard Kohn from the Detroit *Free Press* became interested in Walker's plight, and initiated an investigation into the case late in 1971. He concluded that the system had wrongly convicted Lee Walker. Through Kohn's efforts, a new trial was granted. The prosecution entered a motion of nolle prosequi, and Walker was set free after eighteen years in prison. An indemnity bill which would have granted him a $25,000 judgment failed to clear the state senate. REF.: *CBA.*

Walker, Moses, prom. 1906, U.S., (wrong. convict.) attempt. mur. Moses Walker, a poor black farmer from Lauderdale County, Miss., was arrested and charged with attempted murder in the autumn of 1906. He was accused of firing bullets into the home of a white farmer named Harrington. A load of metal slugs was found embedded in the wall. Taking Harrington at his word, Walker was taken into custody and charged with felonious assault with intention to kill.

The trial began in the Circuit Court on Jan. 18, 1907. Walker was found Guilty as charged, and ordered to serve ten years at hard labor in the state penitentiary. An appeal to the state Supreme Court was denied. Five years later, after Harrington had died, his widow explained that the shooting had been a "frame-up" against the black man, whom her husband deeply resented. Walker was granted a pardon from the governor. The state awarded him $500 as compensation. REF.: *CBA.*

Walker, Nathaniel, 1942- , U.S., (wrong. convict.) abduc.-sod.-rape. Ten years after he went to jail for abducting and raping an Elizabeth, N.J., woman, 44-year-old Nathaniel Walker was freed by Judge Alfred Wolin when new forensic evidence came to light. The crime for which he was charged occurred on the night of Oct. 19, 1974, when the woman was abducted near her home, and forced to drive with her assailant to a parking lot outside a public housing project in Newark. There she was assaulted and raped.

Police chief Richard D. Walker.

In February 1975, the victim picked Walker out of a police lineup. He was convicted in a jury trial and received a life sentence in June 1976 despite testimony from co-workers that he was driven home shortly after completing his shift at 11:30 p.m. at the Phelps Dodge Plant. In 1978, the conviction was overturned on appeal, and Walker was freed on bail. Then, just a year later, the New Jersey Supreme Court reinstated the conviction. Walker fled to Los Angeles where he was eventually arrested and returned to New Jersey to finish out his sentence.

In July 1985, James McCloskey, a graduate of Princeton Theological Seminary, became interested in the case. Laboratory tests were conducted at the Elizabeth General Hospital on vaginal fluids taken from the victim at the time she was brought in. McCloskey demonstrated that the actual rapist had B antigens in the red blood cells, but Walker and the victim both had A antigens. The case was reopened, and Nathaniel Walker was granted his freedom on Nov. 5, 1986, after nearly a decade in prison. REF.: *CBA.*

Walker, Richard D., prom. 1955- , U.S., law enfor. off. Richard Walker's career in law enforcement began in 1955 when he joined the Portland (Ore.) Bureau of Police. In the next thirty years, he advanced steadily through the ranks—as detective, sergeant, lieutenant, captain, and then as deputy chief. He also served as an instructor at Portland State University in the Administration of Justice Department. On Apr. 7, 1987, he was named chief of police in Portland. REF.: *CBA.*

Walker, Thomas Ray, Jr., 1944-80, U.S., mur. Thomas Walker placed a call to Dallas television station KDFW from outside a grocery store. He told the switchboard operator on Dec. 1, 1980, that "he had a good story to tell," Walker went on to say that he had shot and killed his wife Linda while she showered, and then called in his four children one by one to murder them. The children, ranging in age from eight to thirteen had been taken out of school for the day. Walker cited emotional despondency and the gnawing fear that his family could not get along without him in the event of his suicide.

The police were able to trace the location of the phone booth after Walker placed a second call to the station. As he stepped from the phone booth, he called to police, "Shoot me! Shoot me!" Walker ran from the scene, but was cut down by police gunfire. At the family home in southeast Dallas, police found the bodies of Linda Walker and her children—Tracie, thirteen; Tammy, eleven; Tommy, nine; and Nicholas, eight—exactly where he said they would be. REF.: *CBA.*

Walker, William, 1824-60, Nic., rebel. William Walker was a U.S. citizen who led a group to Nicaragua, joining forces with revolutionaries in 1855. They conquered Grenada and he became the commander in chief of the army for the new administration. Walker was elected president in 1856 and his administration was recognized by the U.S. When he began capturing the ships of Cornelius Vanderbilt, Vanderbilt successfully lobbied a coalition of Central American countries to expell him. He escaped to a U.S. battle ship in 1857. Although Walker tried to go back to Nicaragua several times, he was arrested and taken back to the U.S. He was again arrested in 1860 by an officer of the British navy in Honduras, and was handed over to Honduran authorities. Walker was court-martialed, condemned, and shot to death. REF.: *CBA.*

Walker, William, d.1889, U.S., rob.-mur. William Walker and his father, David Walker, were leaders of a wild outlaw band that terrorized Christian County, Mo., in the late 1890s. They reportedly had as many as 400 members in their gang at one time and were known as the Bald Knobbers. Those who dared to testify against Walker and his clan were summarily executed by gang members. In 1888, five witnesses came forward to describe a robbery and several murders committed by Walker and his Knobbers, but these men were lynched by Walker and his men before they could testify in court. All five witnesses were mutilated, a large gash made on the forehead of each as a symbol of the informant. William and David Walker, along with John Matthews, one of their men, were captured and convicted of killing Charles Green and Charles Edins. All three were sentenced to be hanged at Ozark, Mo., on May 10, 1889.

Missouri bandit and killer William Walker, hanged in 1889.

The three men were taken to a scaffold and, before a large crowd, were forced at gunpoint to jump off a crude gallows. The ropes around their necks were too long, and William Walker's rope ripped his neck, causing blood to spurt. He was dragged back to the top of the scaffold and forced to wait until his father and Matthews, their knees on the ground, had slowly strangled to death. As William Walker screamed in agony, causing the crowd to look away, another rope was affixed around his neck and the bandit was once again hanged. He was pushed off the scaffold and dangled for fifteen minutes before he too strangled to death.

REF.: Bartholomew, *The Biographical Album of Western Gunfighters; CBA.*

Walker, William L., 1950- , Case of, U.S., mur. Exonerated of murder by the Brooklyn Supreme Court, police officer William L. Walker was dismissed from the New York Police Department on Mar. 22, 1977, for causing the "wrongful death" of 22-year-old John Brabham.

The victim was a student at Kingsborough Community College in New York City. He was shot by Officer Walker on Apr. 7, 1973, following a car chase that ended in the Bedford-Stuyvesant section of Brooklyn. Brabham attempted to flee, but was shot down by Walker, who "planted" a toy gun on the body to make it look as if the shooting were in self defense. The facts of the shooting were covered up by Walker and his partner, Officer Emanuel Pepitone. Three policemen assigned to the 81st Precinct in Brooklyn were told to keep quiet about the matter. Officer Jesse Murden finally came forward with the facts of the case, resulting in a 1974 grand jury indictment. Patrolman Pepitone later admitted that he had lied under oath.

In February 1977, Walker was acquitted of murder charges, but was later brought before a Police Trial Board. The seven-year veteran was found Guilty of filing a false report, and making it appear as if he had fired in self defense. Walker was dismissed from the force and deprived of his pension. REF.: *CBA.*

Wall, Joseph, 1737-1802, Brit.-Goree, mur. Joseph Wall, son of a well-to-do Irish farmer, joined the British army in 1760. Aside from being an adventurer, Wall also displayed signs of a violent nature, as evidenced by his proclivity for dueling. When he killed a relative during a duel in Ireland, Wall fled to England. There he ingratiated himself with members of society and secured an appointment as the governor of a small island then called Goree off the coast of Africa near Cape Verde.

Wall was not a popular governor, certainly in part because of his tendency to hand out excessively severe punishments, and after two years, planned a trip to England to recover from the tribulations of his time on Goree. When word reached the troops that Wall and the paymaster were planning to leave the island, they became concerned that their supplies, which were often late in arriving, should reach them before Wall's departure. To that end, a group of approximately twelve soldiers led by Sergeant Benjamin Armstrong went to talk with the paymaster. Wall intercepted the committee and turned them away. Two hours later, Armstrong headed up a second party whom Wall also intercepted and ordered back to their quarters.

Charging that the men had been unruly, Wall had Armstrong arrested for mutiny. Without a court martial or trial of any sort, Wall sentenced Armstrong to be flogged in front of the entire company. The 800 lashes which Wall stipulated as the punishment was excessive, but not uncommon at that time; however, Wall's insistence that the flogging be administered with a rope rather that the traditional cat of nine tails, was seen as both severe and dangerous within the contemporary context. Underscoring the cruelty of the punishment, Wall urged on the men administering the punishment by crying out "Cut him to the liver, cut him to the heart." Armstrong died a few hours after the flogging.

Wall left for England two days later. Several complaints were made against him regarding the flogging, but most of the witnesses were then thought to have been lost at sea and the matter was dropped. The lost witnesses, however, finally arrived and a warrant was issued for Wall's arrest. He was arrested at Bath but managed to escape. A £200 reward was issued for his capture on Mar. 8, 1784, but by this time, Wall had safely escaped to the Continent.

After living for a number of years in France and Italy, Wall and his wife returned to England in 1797 where they lived quietly for some time under the assumed name of Thompson. In 1801,

Wall, apparently assuming that most of the witnesses in the case would be dead and wanting to clear his name, wrote to the Home Secretary and identified himself as the fugitive Joseph Wall. He was arrested and brought to trial at the Old Bailey on Jan. 20, 1802. Wall was defended by Newman Knowlys and the case was heard by Judge McDonald. The trial lasted only fourteen hours. Wall was found Guilty and sentenced to hang. Despite numerous attempts to gain a reprieve, Wall was subsequently hanged at Newgate.

REF.: Atholl, *Shadow of the Gallows;* Bleackley, *Hangmen of England;* Brookes, *Murder in Fact and Fiction; CBA;* Turner, *The Inhumanists.*

Wall, Tessie, 1869-1932, U.S., pros. Once described as a "flamboyant, well-upholstered blonde," Tessie Wall was San Francisco's best-known madam from 1900 to 1917. Her most famous brothel, on O'Farrell Street, sported only blonde, slightly plump women. She charged $20 for an assignation, an incredible price for the early 1900s. The services were said to be worth it, however. Clothes were pressed and shoes shined for patrons spending the night. Others who might need to return to Oakland the same evening would be interrupted by Wall and told the last ferry would be leaving shortly.

Wall could drink an incredible amount and once out drank boxer John L. Sullivan. She gave generous donations to the police ball, usually starting the event on the arm of Mayor Sunny Jim Rolph. Her husband, Frank Daroux, a gambler who owned several brothels, bought her a home in the country in the hope that she would move there with him. She told him, "I'd rather be an electric light pole on Powell Street than own all the land in the sticks." Eventually he divorced her and Wall unsuccessfully pleaded with him to return to her. Wall vowed that if she could not have him, no woman would have him. In Summer 1916, she shot Sullivan three times with a .22-caliber revolver, and when police arrived confessed, "I shot him because I love him—damn him!" He survived and refused to testify against her.

Tessie Wall retired as a madam the following year due to civic reforms that wiped out all vice on the Barbary Coast and in the Upper Tenderloin, which was home to San Francisco's best theaters and restaurants. She moved into a small comfortable flat on Eighteenth Street as she had not saved much from her years of wild and extravagant living. She died in April 1932. A needlepoint motto hung on her wall that read: "If every man was as true to his country as he is to his wife—God help the U.S.A." REF.: *CBA.*

Wallace, Ernest, prom. 1917, U.S., (wrong. convict.) mur. Ernest Wallace was convicted of murdering Jacob Levine, a Chicago saloonkeeper, on the night of June 16, 1916. An eyewitness to the shooting identified Wallace as the gunman, but three other persons present at the time said that the robbers all wore masks. Wallace was sentenced to die on the gallows, but through the efforts of Attorney O.J. Wray and five concerned Chicagoans the condemned was granted a second trial by the Illinois State Supreme Court on June 21, 1917. Wray had worked tirelessly to exonerate his client without receiving a salary. Wallace's conviction was later overturned because of insufficient evidence. REF.: *CBA.*

Wallace, George Corley, 1919- , U.S., att. assass. George Wallace was sworn in as the forty-seventh governor of Alabama on Jan. 14, 1963. The election of this farmer's son to the state's highest office was viewed as a clear-cut victory for segregationists and state's rights advocates who sought to preserve the racial status quo still prevalent in the South. In his first year of office Wallace justified the confidence of his constituency by attempting to prevent the desegregation of Alabama public schools. In a celebrated incident emblematic of the civil rights struggle in the South, Wallace barred the path of James A. Hood and Vivian J. Malone, two black students attempting to enroll at the University of Alabama on June 11, 1963. Wallace defied the directive of Deputy U.S. Attorney General Nicholas Katzenbach who demanded that he comply with federally mandated orders which called for the peaceful desegregation of public schools. "My action is a call for strict adherence to the Constitution of the United States as it was written," Wallace argued. The governor was forced to back down only after President John F. Kennedy issued an order federalizing the Alabama National Guard. Wallace stood aside as the black students registered for classes without further incident.

Governor George Wallace seated, out of sight, is shot by Arthur Herman Bremer, wearing dark glasses at right, May 15, 1972.

The school integration crisis soon spread to other Alabama municipalities. Before the year was out Kennedy was forced to mobilize the National Guard to uphold the federal directives. Wallace, a loser in his fight against the administration, emerged as a national figure and champion of the far right-wing. "Segregation now, segregation tomorrow, segregation forever!" became the familiar battle cry from this churlish ex-prizefighter from Barbour County. His folksy, down-home style of campaigning appealed to white voters fed up with the so-called "welfare loafers, lenient judges, pseudo intellectuals, and pointy-head liberals." In 1968 Wallace entered the race for president, cheered on by a broad spectrum of people representing the extremes of the political right. His words were particularly encouraging to Southern Klansmen and white Northerners troubled by the issue of forced busing and the presence of youthful agitators on the nation's campuses. Wallace promised to deal with sit-down demonstrators who would dare to block the path of his car. "It'll be the last car he'll ever lie down in front of!" the governor vowed. He won five Southern primaries in 1968, an impressive total for the maverick Democrat. The message was much the same in 1972 when Wallace entered a generally weak field of presidential contenders. His slogan, "Send them a message," was clear enough to voters in Florida who carried him to victory in the state primary over frontrunners Edmund Muskie, Hubert Humphrey, and George McGovern. Wallace rolled on to victory in five primaries and finished second in six others before taking the campaign to Maryland in May.

It was a foray into unfamiliar territory. Not everyone in this "border" state shared Wallace's extreme views toward race, the Vietnam War, or federally funded welfare programs. That much was evident at a rally in Frederick when someone hurled a brick at him. In Hagerstown a group of students jeered him relentlessly until the police had to be called in. "Somebody's going to get killed before this primary's over," Wallace told an aide. "And I hope it's not me." The governor wrapped up his Maryland campaign on May 15, 1972, with a scheduled appearance at the Laurel shopping center, where he was greeted by 2,000 residents who gathered around a podium in the parking lot. As usual, the specially constructed 600-pound podium was in place. Country and western singer Billy Grammer warmed up the crowd with renditions of *Detroit City* and *Gotta Travel On,* while Wallace made his way to the platform. His speech was met with derision, especially by several collegians standing in the rear. "Go back to Alabama. You don't even know where you are!" one said, referring to Wallace's remark mistakenly calling Prince George County "Princess George County."

After nearly an hour of hot rhetoric aimed at "social schemers" and "ultra-false liberals," Wallace stepped down from behind the barricade. A woman outfitted in Wallace regalia called to him. "Over here, George. Over here!" The candidate unbuttoned his jacket and moved toward the woman. At that moment a squat, blond-haired man wearing sun-glasses pushed his arm through the throng of onlookers and fired five shots from a snub-nosed revolver in quick succession. Secret Service agents pounced on the would-be assassin even as the gun continued to fire. Four bullets struck the governor, who collapsed to the hot asphalt. Three other persons were injured including Captain E.C. Dothard of the Alabama Highway Patrol, Secret Service Agent Nicholas Zarvos, and a volunteer Wallace campaign worker, Dora Thompson, who was shot in the knee.

Wallace was taken to Holy Cross Hospital in Silver Spring, where he underwent emergency surgery. Two bullets were removed during the operation, and hemorrhaging was quickly brought under control. A third bullet, lodged near the spinal column, caused far more serious damage. Governor Wallace would never walk again. The gunman, identified by the Secret Service as 21-year-old Arthur Herman Bremer, was taken into custody. Born and raised on the South Side of Milwaukee, Wis., Bremer fit the mold of the urban political assassin who typified the 1960s. Described as a "withdrawn," "incredibly defensive" individual, Bremer left home in 1971 to study photography at the Milwaukee Area Technical College, supporting himself by working half-days as a bus boy at the Milwaukee Athletic Club and as a janitor at the Story Elementary School. On Nov. 18, 1971, he was arrested for carrying a concealed weapon in his parked car. A court-appointed psychiatrist described him as "dull" but sane. He was released after paying a $38.50 fine.

On the same day that George Wallace declared his intentions to run for president, Bremer purchased a five-shot, snub-nosed revolver from a Milwaukee gun shop. A month later, on Feb. 16, he quit his jobs to embark on a patchwork quilt odyssey that led him to the shopping center in Laurel, Md. Bremer began following the candidates on Apr. 7, 1972, when he was seen at a dinner given for Hubert Humphrey at New York's Waldorf-Astoria Hotel. He turned up at the New Carrollton, Md., Sheraton Motor Inn on Apr. 15-18, at a Wallace rally at Cadillac, Mich., on May 10, and at another one held at the Reid Hotel in Kalamazoo on May 12-13. How it was possible for this unemployed bus boy to finance an eighteen-week trip of this nature has never been explained. Certainly his parents, who barely lived above the poverty line, could not have funded the bizarre expedition. Conservative estimates of his travel expenses were placed at $5,000. Yet Bremer would claim that his net worth was only $300. It was reported by *Life* magazine that Bremer had "companions" whom he kept company with shortly before the assassination attempt. One of these mysterious friends was identified as Dennis Cassini, who was found dead in the trunk of his car in Milwaukee, the victim of an apparent heroin overdose.

While stalking President Richard Nixon and George Wallace, Bremer kept a diary which may clear up some of the mystery and place him beyond the pale of the conspiracy theorists. One excerpt read:

> "I've decided Wallace will have the honor of—what would you call it? Like a novelist who knows not how his book will end—I have written this journal...You know, my biggest failure may well be when I kill Wallace. I hope everyone screams and hollers and everything!! I hope the rally goes mad!! One thing for sure my diet is too soft. Weakens my posture, maybe affects my insides too. I am one sick assassin. Pun! Pun! Is there anything else to say? My cry upon firing will be, a penny for your thoughts."

The theory that Bremer was hired by powerful interests who wanted Wallace out of the way is unsupported. It was rumored at various times that Charles Colson of the White House staff ordered E. Howard Hunt to enter Bremer's apartment right after the shooting and "plant" several left-wing journals for the police to find. At the time, Wallace posed the biggest threat to President Richard Nixon's bid for a second term of office. Interviewed by Barbara Walters on the *Today* Show, Governor Wallace said, "So I just wondered if that were the case. How did anyone know where he lived within an hour after I was shot? I myself didn't know who shot me until several days later, but of course I wouldn't know because I was in a condition not to know." Bremer was found Guilty of attempted assassination and sentenced to sixty-three years in prison.

REF.: Bremer, *An Assassin's Diary; CBA;* Greenhaw, *Watch Out for George Wallace.*

Wallace, Lewis (Lew Wallace), 1827-1905, U.S., lawyer. Became major general in 1862. He presided as president of the court that tried and condemned Henry Wirz, commandant of Andersonville Prison. He also served on the court-martial that tried the conspirators involved in the assassination of President Abraham Lincoln. REF.: *CBA.*

Wallace, Michael Shaw Stewart, b.1812, and **Wallace, Patrick Maxwell Stewart**, b.1816, Brit., fraud. The Wallaces were the principal owners of a small 204-ton merchant ship known as the *Dryad.* The vessel was engaged in commercial trade with the British colonial possessions in the West Indies, and was heavily insured with a number of London-based firms. On Sept. 7, 1839, the brig set sail from Liverpool bound for Santa Cruz, near the island of Cuba. The captain signed a bill of landing that listed a cargo of durable goods bound for the North American continent, when in fact the hold was empty. In the event of a disaster, the Wallaces stood to claim £6,466 in insurance money.

On Nov. 10, 1839, the ship struck a reef at Cape Cruz, a calamity that could have easily been avoided. The carpenter on board the *Dryad* said that the reef was visible to the crew, but no attempt was made to alter the course. The ship sank and, remarkably, no one died. The Wallaces attempt to collect the insurance money led to criminal prosecution against them.

The trial was conducted at the Old Bailey in March 1841 before Chief Justice Nicholas Tindal and Sir John Bosanquet. The defendants were found Guilty two days later and sentenced to penal transportation for life.

REF.: *CBA;* Poynter, *Forgotten Crimes.*

Wallace, Sir William (Walays, Wallensis, AKA: The Hammer and Scourge of England), c.1272-1305, Scot., rebel. Engaged in continuous fights with the British. He became the warden of Scotland but was conquered by Edward I of England in 1298. After requesting help from France, Norway, and Pope Boniface VIII from 1299-1302, he was declared an outlaw by Edward in 1304. Betrayed at Glasgow, Scot., in 1305, he stood trial in Westminster Hall in London, where he was condemned. He was hanged and drawn and quartered. REF.: *CBA.*

Wallace, William Herbert, 1878-1933, Case of, Brit., mur. William Herbert Wallace, an insurance salesman and amateur chess player, was scheduled to play in the Second Class Championship at the Liverpool Central Chess Club on Jan. 19, 1931, the night before his wife was murdered. Julia Wallace, like her husband, was mild-mannered and refined. They had met in Manchester in 1911 after he had returned from the orient, where he had done bureaucratic work in China and India while studying western stoic philosophy. The two were intellectual, sharing an interest in music and philosophy. They were married in 1913. Wallace recorded eighteen years of peaceful, happy married life in his diary.

On the night of the chess championship, club manager Samuel Beattie took a telephone message for Wallace. A man who identified himself only as R.M. Qualtrough requested Wallace meet him at 7:30 the next night at 25 Menlove Gardens East. Although the name Qualtrough is fairly common in Liverpool, the caller spelled out his name for Beattie to make sure he got it. When Wallace, fifty-two, arrived late at the club and received the message, he remarked that he did not know anyone by that name.

The victim, Mrs. Julia Wallace.

Assuming the matter concerned insurance, Wallace went to meet Qualtrough but the address proved to be fictitious. When Wallace returned to his Liverpool home about 8:45 p.m. he was apparently unable to get in. The front and back doors were bolted from the inside and his wife did not answer. His neighbors, John and Florence Johnston, were leaving their house then, and he spoke to them about his house being locked. Then he tried the door again and was able to open it.

Upstairs, Wallace found 50-year-old Julia Wallace dead. She had been bludgeoned eleven times, although the police pathologist later testified that the first blow almost certainly killed her. Wallace ran back downstairs, calling out to the Johnstons, "Come and see. She has been killed."

Qualtrough was never found. Wallace told police that he had been home between "about 6:05 and 6:45 on the night of the murder. A 14-year-old milk delivery boy said he saw Julia Wallace take in the milk at 6:30, and the evening paper was delivered at 6:35. The paper was found spread on the kitchen table. The pathologist, Professor John Edward MacFall, set the time of death at 6:10. When a locksmith was asked to check the locks on the doors, he found them inadequate. The strongest evidence against William Wallace was his stoicism, by which he had resolved years before to live his life. Police thought he was behaving too calmly. He was arrested on Feb. 2 and went to trial on Apr. 22.

The locked rear entrance of the Wallace home.

The prosecution suggested that Wallace made the "Qualtrough" call himself to avert suspicion. Beattie said the voice on the phone was "gruff but ordinary"; surely Beattie would have recognized Wallace's voice. Wallace had no apparent motive for killing his wife and no murder weapon was found. Justice Wright instructed the jurors that all the evidence against Wallace was circumstantial, strongly suggesting that he considered the case not proven. The jury nevertheless found Wallace Guilty of murder. Wright reluctantly sentenced Wallace to death.

The Court of Criminal Appeal overturned Wallace's conviction four weeks later, and Wallace was set free. A bizarre backlash of public opinion occurred; during the trial, Liverpool residents seemed to believe that Wallace had been horribly wronged, but afterward he was harassed by people who believed he had gotten away with murder. His insurance company considerately transferred him out of the field to a desk job, but his former chess playing partners refused to associate with him, and children taunted him by calling rhymes they made up about the murder.

The suspect, William Herbert Wallace; he was released after appealing his murder conviction.

Wallace had had recurring stomach troubles and they returned full force in December 1932. By Feb. 9, the pain was so severe he needed to be hospitalized, and he died of kidney disease on Feb. 26, 1933.

REF.: Adam, *Murder Most Mysterious;* Bennett, *Why Did They Do It?;* Bridges, *Two Studies in Crime;* Brophy, *The Meaning of Murder;* Butler, *Murderers' England; CBA;* Cobb, *Trials and Errors;* Dilnot, *Rogues' March;* Duke, *Six Trials;* Goodman, *The Killing of Julia Wallace;* Hussey, *Murderer Scot-Free;* Jackson, *The Portable Murder Book;* Jones, *Unsolved Classic True Murder Cases;* Kobler, *Some Like It Gory;* Logan, *Great Murder Mysteries;* Lustgarten, *The Murder and the Trial;* Moiseiwitsch, *Five Famous Trials;* Morland, *Background to Murder;* Nash, *Open Files;* Rice, *Forty-five Murderers;* Rowland, *More Criminal Files;* ____, *The Wallace Case;* Russell, *Best Murder Cases;* Sayers, *The Anatomy of Murder;* Shew, *A Second Companion to Murder;* Simpson, *The Anatomy of Murder;* Wilson, *Encyclopedia of Murder;* Wyndham, *Consider Your Verdict;* Wyndham-Brown, *The Trial of William Herbert Wallace;* (FICTION), Duke, *Skin for Skin.*

Wallenstein, Albrecht Eusebius Wenzel von (Duke of Friedland and Mecklenburg, Prince of Sagan), 1583-1634, Aust., gen., assass. Led successful military campaigns from 1625-27. After failing in several missions, the Diet of Regensburg discharged him in 1630. He was involved in a conspiracy with Gustav II Adolphus before he was returned to command. After he tried to stage a rebellion with his loyal generals in 1634, he was again withdrawn from his post and assassinated by Scottish and Irish officers. REF.: *CBA.*

Waller, Edmund, 1606-87, Brit., consp. Presided at impeachment of Sir Francis Crawley in 1641. He was a participant in Waller's Plot, a conspiracy to take control of London for Charles I, but his involvement was discovered in 1643. Escaping execution by revealing his confederates, he was ejected from the House of Commons, fined £10,000, and banished, in 1644. Later, he was allowed to return. REF.: *CBA.*

Waller, John (AKA: **John Trevor**), d.1732, Brit., perj.-rob. Although John Waller was convicted for the highway robbery of John Edglin, his testimony itself, later found to be false, was what caused his death. During Waller's trial it emerged that Waller, using the name John Trevor, attended hearings and trials as often as many judges and attorneys, testifying falsely against the accused to obtain the reward money.

Sentenced to two years in prison and required to pay a fine, Waller also had to undergo the indignity of the pillory. On June 13, 1732, Waller, locked in the pillory bareheaded with his crime

Thief John Waller, is pelted to death in 1732.

advertised in large letters, was pelted to death by an angry crowd. The next day the coroner's statement read: "Wilful murder by persons unknown."

REF.: Bleackley, *Hangmen of England; CBA;* Mitchell, *The Newgate Calendar.*

Walling, George W., See: **Nathan, Benjamin.**

Walling, Robert Alfred John, b.1869, Brit., writer. Wrote mysteries and invented detective character Mr. Tolefree. REF.: *CBA.*

Wallis, Dorothy Edith (AKA: **Daisy Wallace**), 1913-49, Brit., (unsolv.) mur. Dorothy Wallis, the 36-year-old proprietress of the Adelphi Secretarial Agency, was murdered in her Drury Lane office in High Holborn on Aug. 15, 1949. A neighbor in an adjacent apartment heard the victim cry "Murder!" but was unable to identify the assailant. A man described as having a swarthy complexion was seen fleeing from the agency about the time of the killing, but no one could identify him.

A detailed diary left behind by the victim listed the names of dozens of business clients and social friends, but none could shed light on the Holborn murder mystery. Wallis was active in theater, a film club, and had no known enemies. A pathologist concluded the wounds were inflicted by a man. A matching set of fingerprints found at the scene of the crime did not exist at the Criminal Record Office. The case file was closed on Oct. 27, with a verdict of homicide by person or persons unknown.

REF.: *CBA;* Firmin, *Murderers in Our Midst;* Harrison, *Criminal Calendar II.*

Walls, Samuel Cornelius, 1939- , U.S., rape-mur. A paroled ex-convict and substance abuser with a long record of murder, rape, and kidnapping, was charged with the strangulation murder of a young housewife at an Oceanside, N.J., motel on Aug. 24, 1988. Cornelius Walls, forty-nine, was arrested and charged with killing 29-year-old Mary Jean DeOliviera, an alcoholic young mother he met in a chance encounter outside the Hempstead courthouse. According to police, DeOliviera agreed to accompany him to the Oceanside Motel, an $18 a day fleabag where patrons normally do not sign their correct names on the guest register.

Six days later the badly decomposing corpse of Mary DeOliviera was found underneath a platform bed in the room after customers complained about the foul stench. Police arrested Walls on Sept. 1 in Garden City. In the back seat of his 1981 Buick they found a 27-year-old woman bound and gagged. She had been abducted and raped just hours after he had left the Oceanside Motel. Walls was easily traced after motel employees identified a man with a severely disfigured face. As a teenager Cornelius Walls sustained serious injuries when another youth threw lye in his face during a street fight.

He was arraigned on second-degree murder charges at the First District Court in Hempstead. It was the second time in his criminal career he had been accused of murder. In 1959 he was convicted in the beating death of Bernard Rogue, a 38-year-old salesman he had robbed in Hempstead Village. Walls served fifteen years of a twenty-year sentence before earning parole in 1974. In the next fifteen years following his release, Walls was arrested eight times on various charges, and was returned to prison four different times for parole violations. Walls was found Guilty of second-degree murder in June 1989 and sentenced to twenty-five years in prison. REF.: *CBA.*

Wall Street Bombing, 1920, U.S., (unsolv.) bomb.-mur. Minutes before the noonday lunch break, a drayman eased his wagon to the side of the curb directly in front of the U.S. Assay Building at Broad and Wall streets in the heart of New York City's financial district. It was a clear, Indian Summer day, Sept. 16, 1920. Few if any paid attention to the nondescript peddler and his wagon. That much was evident when New York police questioned eyewitnesses later. He was clean-shaven, some said. Others would claim that he had a dark, flowing mustache and was foreign-born. No one was even sure whether the driver had made a run for it, after the explosion or had sat calmly on top of his wagon waiting for the end to come.

Whichever the case a powerful fragmentary bomb containing 500 pounds of window weights hacked into tiny fragments exploded at precisely 11:59 a.m., a minute before the lunch break sent 100,000 employees of the brokerage houses streaming into the streets. The blast was heard ten miles away. A vaporous cloud of gas smothered the district and a torrent of deadly metal chips rained down on the unfortunate victims who happened to stand in the way. The police deduced that the bomber had labored for months to construct this bomb, packing the sash

The carnage of the Wall Street Bombing, 1920.

weights carefully into the interior. The streets were filled with a sea of broken glass. Every window within 100 feet of the blast had been blown out. When it was over a crowd of onlookers gathered around a pool of blood that had been a horse. The wagon it was pulling was completely obliterated. Curiously though, the statue of George Washington standing in front of the nearby Subtreasury Building was not even scratched.

Across the street from the blast area stood the J.P. Morgan Company, the imposing monument to laissez-faire capitalism all but destroyed and the firm's chief clerk, Thomas Joyce, one of the thirty-eight reported casualties. The immense power of this bomb conceivably could have taken many more lives. It was impossible to say with certainty, because all that remained were body fragments. An additional 300 people were seriously injured by flying glass and shrapnel. The police were never able to bring a suspect into custody. Forensic experts analyzed the blood samples taken from the few scattered remains of the horse and determined that the animal had digested grass shortly before. The grass they said, came from a remote location in the country. A check of stables failed to yield any possible clues.

The offices of J.P. Morgan and Company, wrecked by the explosion.

Reward money totalling $100,000 was offered for the bomber, but it remained unclaimed. Many theories were put forward. A Communist, a Black Hander, a former broker whose business had fallen off, or a Wobblie had done it—it could have been any of them, or none. William J. Flynn, chief of the Justice Department's Bureau of Investigation, attributed the bombing to Italian terrorists, which remains an unsupported theory to this day. See: **Hoover, J. Edgar; Palmer, A. Mitchell; Red Raids.**

REF.: Carey, *Memoirs of a Murder Man; CBA;* Lowenthal, *The Federal Bureau of Investigation;* Nash, *Almanac of World Crime;* ____, *Open Files.*

Wall Street Mail Robbery, See: **Chapman, Gerald**.

Walmsley, Martha, 18th Cent., Brit., theft. Martha Walmsley was convicted of stealing clothing valued at £3 and ten shillings from the residence of Henry Grinling. The crime was punishable by death, but in an effort to obtain leniency for the woman, the judge whispered to the prosecutor: "If you can fix the value under forty shillings you will save this person's life." The counsel for the plaintiff readily agreed. Walmsley was found Guilty for the amount of eight shillings.

REF.: *CBA;* Potter, *The Art of Hanging.*

Walpole, Horace (Earl of Orford), 1717-97, Brit., hoax.-forg. The noted author, parliamentarian, and eighteenth-century cynic perpetrated several well-publicized deceptions during his career. He forged a letter written from the King of Prussia to the philosopher Rousseau as an authentic document, and in his best known hoax, he published a Gothic romance titled *The Castle of Otranto* in 1764. The title-page attributed authorship to Onuphrio Muralto, with an English translation supplied by William Marshal. The first edition sold well, forcing Walpole to drop all pretenses and admit that it was his own work in the second edition.

REF.: *CBA;* MacDougall, *Hoaxes.*

Walsh, Bill, 1910- , Brit., rob. On Apr. 29, 1947, three masked robbers held up Jay's Jewelry Store in London. As the gang attempted to escape, a motorcyclist named Alec de Antiquis blocked their path. His gallant attempt to thwart the robbery cost him his life. One of the gunmen shot him through the head. The identity of the robbers puzzled police for a long time. Sir Bernard Spilsbury and Robert Churchill the foremost experts in pathology and forensic science were called in to investigate.

Police were put on the trail of two youthful felons: Harry Jenkins and Christopher Geraghty. Brought in for questioning, Jenkins implicated Bill Walsh as the likely gunman. Walsh was out on parole at the time, having served his time for an earlier robbery. The 37-year-old was arrested in Plumstead, but denied having taken part in the robbery at Jay's. Walsh admitted to committing an earlier jewelry store robbery with Jenkins.

After the robbery, Walsh had gone to Southend with the loot. Having cut his partner out of the take, Jenkins was understandably angry. It was only then that he decided to frame Walsh for the De Antiquis murder. Walsh and a second man, Michael Joseph Gillam, were cleared of murder, but were tried for robbery and sentenced to five years each at the Central Criminal Court. See: **Geraghty, Christopher James**. REF.: *CBA.*

Walsh, Daniel, prom. 1869, U.S., mur. Daniel Walsh left his wife, Rose Weldon, just hours after they were married on Feb. 6, 1869, in Chicago. The distraught bride and her family searched diligently but could find no trace of the missing husband. Finally, they learned that Walsh already had a wife and child in Buffalo, N.Y., whom he had left some years before.

Weldon immediately obtained an annulment. Walsh's employers, upon learning of the decree, fired him. Walsh obtained a revolver and shot Weldon. He was immediately apprehended, and when Weldon died ten days later, he was tried and convicted of murder. Although sentenced to be hanged on Dec. 10, 1869, Walsh's sentence was commuted when many of his friends interceded with the governor on his behalf. Walsh died in prison.

REF.: *CBA;* Nash, *Murder, America.*

Walsh, James, d.1932, Brit., suic.-mur. With his love affair collapsing, and his prospects for employment none too good, former London policeman James Walsh committed suicide in February 1932. Before he turned the gun on himself, he shot and killed his lover, Gladys Isobel Luff, who had taken a new lover. Walsh,a former policeman was discharged from his job after contracting tuberculosis. He shot Luff in her apartment, then returned to his room and shot himself in the head. Walsh died in the hospital a few days later.

REF.: *CBA;* Nicholls, *Crime Within the Square Mile.*

Walsh, Johnny (AKA: **Johnny the Mick**), d.1883, U.S., org. crime. The leader of a New York Bowery gang known as the Walshers, Johnny Walsh—usually called Johnny the Mick—was a vicious gangster who would kill without hesitation. Very protective of what he considered his turf, he would kill any criminal who dared attempt to operate in it. He and the Walshers had a long-standing feud with the Dutch Mob led by Johnny Irving as the two gangs battled for supremacy over the Bowery, and on at least three occasions Walsh and Irving engaged in knife fights that caused neither harm. The police did not interfere and the chief of police once stated that only good could come out of their bad blood. Late in 1883, in Shang Draper's saloon on Sixth Avenue, Irving and a friend, Billy Porter, bumped into Walsh. As the two gangsters glared at each other, Walsh pulled out a revolver and killed Irving. Porter then drew a gun and shot Walsh dead. Drawing his gun, Draper shot Porter. Porter survived and neither he nor Draper were brought up on charges, each claiming to have been simply keeping the peace. With both gang leaders dead, the police were satisfied with the story. REF.: *CBA.*

Walsingham, Sir **Francis**, c.1532-90, Brit., law enfor. off. Responsible for establishing capable secret intelligence organization, primarily with own funds, to uncover plots against Queen Elizabeth I. He uncovered the Throckmorton plot in 1583 and Anthony Babington's plot in 1586. His efforts brought about the conviction and execution of Mary, Queen of Scots in 1587, and he alerted Elizabeth about activities of the Spanish Armada. REF.: *CBA.*

Walter, Albert, Jr., c.1908-36, U.S., mur. Albert Walter, Jr., traveled to San Francisco from his home in the fashionable Back Bay section of Boston, because, as he explained, he was afraid he might kill his wife Angela. Instead, he murdered a young college student named Blanche Cousins, whom he met on the transcontinental bus after the driver had stopped in Salt Lake City to pick up passengers. Cousins had worked as a bookkeeper at the Latter Day Saints Hospital in Idaho Falls, Idaho, for seven years before striking out for the big city. She was, according to her friend

Dorothy Edmonds, "the most lonely person in the world. She always believed that a big city would give her the happiness other people had," Edmonds recalled. "She loved the theater and other things she couldn't get in Idaho Falls." In San Francisco Walter took the woman to an apartment he had rented the night of June 16, 1936. He strangled her after she refused his sexual advances. "I became highly inflamed but she stopped me at a certain point as she had done on previous occasions," he said. "Then I began to hate her. I have hated all women for years and all the hate I felt for women rose up in me right there." The next day he disposed of all his personal belongings before walking into the Bureau of Inspectors at police headquarters where he freely confessed his crime.

Walter explained that at the age of fourteen he had become permanently embittered against women following an unfortunate affair with an older woman who gave him syphilis. "I've tried to lead a normal life, but this hatred and bitterness keeps cropping up in spite of me. I left my wife in New York because I was afraid I'd kill her," he said, adding that his only wish was to be hanged and forgotten.

Angela Walter was located and together with her father-in-law they journeyed west. They told of Albert's erratic life, which included stints in the military, the legal profession, and sales. His fixation against women and his past history of sudden, unprovoked psychotic episodes culminated in murder. Despite his protestations, the defense entered an insanity plea, but state-appointed psychiatrists contended he was sane. Albert Walter was found Guilty of murder. He was executed on the gallows of San Quentin, Dec. 4, 1936.

REF.: *CBA;* Cohen, *One Hundred True Crime Stories.*

Walter, Clarence, b.1893, U.S., mur. On Feb. 5, 1934, in Los Angeles radio station KHJ's largest studio, cooking expert Mona Van Dyke was on the air, leading her audience through a recipe—"then add half a cup of sugar, stir well, and let it come to a boil,"—when a scream went out over the air waves. Van Dyke raised her voice and continued her broadcast, but it was not enough to block the screams that followed, a man's curses, the thud of a body falling to the ground, or the general sounds of a scuffle. Over all, station manager C.E. Wylie was heard calling out: "Tell everyone we're just rehearsing a dramatic act for a broadcast tomorrow!" Meanwhile, 21-year-old Edwin Wolverton lay dying from knife wounds to his head.

According to a police reports, 41-year-old Montana rancher Clarence Walter initially approached KHJ receptionist Grace Kane and, pointing to the studio, said, "You have a job waiting for me in there." When Kane asked for his name, Walter pulled a knife. "Never mind my name!" he shouted. You've got a job for me in there!" He raised the knife, but Wolverton, a vacationing announcer from KFXJ in Grand Junction, Colo., and newsman Warren Fehlman rushed in to disarm him. Walter stabbed Wolverton in the head, however, before being subdued by more than twelve men. "I never saw him before in my life," Wolverton said as he lapsed into unconsciousness, never to recover.

"I've been listening to that station," Walter said later, telling what led to the slaying. "I wanted them to let me work there. I wrote them letters asking for work. They answered me in a song they broadcast—('There's a Ring Around the Moon'). I recognized the message telling me to come to work every time I heard the song."

Walter, was found Not Guilty by Judge Frank G. Swain after three psychiatrists agreed he was insane at the time of the killing. Committed to Mendocino State Hospital, he appeared again before Judge Swain in June 1935, to seek release on the grounds that he had recovered his sanity. The court ordered Walter to be removed from Mendocino State to a state mental institution in Montana. REF.: *CBA.*

Walters, Ann Carol, 1940- , and **Walters, Wayne**, 1947- , and **Bean, Harold Walter**, 1940- , and **Bryon, Robert**, 1949- , and **Egan, Robert Danny**, prom. 1982, U.S., consp.-mur. For Dorothy and George Polulach, an elderly couple from Chicago's Southwest Side Polish neighborhood, their 1969 marriage was only the beginning of what they hoped to be the "golden years" of retirement. A dozen years later it ended tragically in suicide and murder.

Dorothy, a newspaper fashion artist, married George Polulach after his first wife had filed for divorce on the grounds of adultery. The daughter from the first marriage, Ann Carol Walters, harbored deep resentments against her stepmother for many years. At stake was a lavish inheritance and control of the family estate. George Polulach was a prosperous small businessman who owned several retail concerns. Ann Walters later contended that Dorothy had "tricked" her natural mother Frances into signing away the Chicago home, valued at $100,000. In 1979, George Polulach committed suicide. He was in failing health and despondent because of his advancing age. The widow continued to live a comfortable life in the Southwest Side bungalow, while Walters languished in comparative poverty with her husband Wayne and invalid mother in Florida. The tension continued to grow, until Ann hired an ex-convict and mobster named Harold Bean to murder Dorothy for $7,500.

Dorothy Polulach, now eighty-one, expressed a feeling of growing apprehension to church officials and close friends. Three days later on Feb. 18, 1981, a man dressed as a priest entered the Polulach home. Dorothy Polulach was tied up and shot through the head twice by Bean. Robert Byron, thirty-three, and Robert Danny Egan, who had been recruited by Bean, rifled through the house overturning furniture and ransacking every room.

Chicago police traced the conspirators through phone company records, which showed a number of long distance calls between the Florida home of Walters, and a female accomplice of Bean in Chicago. Confronted by this evidence, Carol Ann tearfully confessed her role, and that of her husband. Harold Bean and Robert Byron were both convicted of murder and sentenced to death. Wayne Walters received a seven-year prison sentence for conspiracy. In return for his guilty plea on an armed violence charge, Robert Egan was sentenced to seven years. He had driven the getaway car. Ann Walters was handed a twenty-five year prison term on Jan. 18, 1982, by Judge James Bailey in the criminal court. She asked the judge for an early parole in order to care for her infirmed mother in Florida but was denied. REF.: *CBA.*

Walters, Annie, See: **Sach, Amelia**.

Walters, Catherine (AKA: **Skittles**), b.1839, Brit., pros. Born in 1839, the same year that Queen Victoria ascended to the throne of England, Catherine Walters attained royal notoriety of a different sort. One of the most famous British nineteenth-century prostitutes, Walters entertained a number of dignitaries, including Queen Victoria's son, the Prince of Wales. Walters acquired her nickname while working in the Black Jack Tavern, where the game of "skittles", a variation of nine-pins, was popular with the local gentry.

By the 1860s, Walters had risen to prominence, and was celebrated in both London and Paris. At age forty, she met Gerald Saumeraz, a man half her age. The two became lovers and stayed together until the day she died. Throughout her career, to be seen in her company, either professionally or socially, was deemed a great honor.

REF.: Bullough, *An Illustrated History of Prostitution; CBA.*

Walters, Henry (AKA: **Will Osborne, Sidney Montague**), and **Murray, Edwin**, and **Kurr, William**, prom. 1873, Case of, Brit., fraud.-asslt. The speed with which horse racing fraud rings worked caused London detectives the greatest amount of trouble. In 1873, seventy-one con men were sent to jail by the investigative unit, headed by Chief-Inspector Clarke, assigned to flush out the "philanthropic societies" organized to help a gambler offset his losses.

Using names like "The Systematic Investment Society," the swindlers acted as an insurance company for racetrack bettors who sustained heavy losses. Customers would send in a premium payment, and would receive a receipt and little else. After a few weeks had passed, inquiries would be placed, but invariably the culprits had long since moved on. One such operation was headed by Henry Walters and William Kurr, a well-known criminal who helped him promote the "The General Society for Insurance Against Losses on the Turf." Newspaper ads appearing in various European countries brought in patrons from all over the continent.

The ring was broken up by Scotland Yard when a man named Daniel Portch identified the four ring leaders as the same men who had assaulted him. Walters was well known to the police, and based on descriptions provided, he was picked up along with Edwin Murray. Upon hearing the news that a warrant was out, William Kurr immediately fled. The charge of assault against the two men was dismissed by the magistrates. As Murray and Walters left the courthouse they were re-arrested and charged with conspiracy to defraud by Chief-Inspector Clarke. While out on bail, the swindlers fled to America.

REF.: *CBA;* Cobb, *Critical Years at the Yard.*

Walters, Norby, and **Bloom, Lloyd,** prom. 1980s, U.S., rack. Norby Walters and his business partner, Lloyd Bloom were sports agents linked to the Mafia who capitalized on the spiraling salaries of sports figures in the 1980s. They violated NCAA college eligibility rules and threatened strongarm practices against athletes who refused to allow Walters to represent them. Athletes who fraudulently accepted scholarships while under professional contract with Walters and Lloyd were granted immunity from federal prosecution in return for testimony against the pair. Basketball and football players allegedly intimidated included Brad Sellers of the Chicago Bulls, Ron Morris of the Chicago Bears, Terrance Flagler of the San Francisco 49ers, Cris Carter of the Philadelphia Eagles, Garland Rivers of the Detroit Lions, Kenny Flowers of the Atlanta Falcons, Bob Perryman of the New England Patriots, and Tony Woods of the Seattle Seahawks. REF.: *CBA.*

Walters, Ted (AKA: **Huron Ted Walters**), 1913-71, U.S., pris. esc.-rob.-kid. As part of the Hamilton gang, Huron Ted Walters terrorized the Southwest in the 1930s. With brothers Raymond and Floyd Hamilton and the infamous Bonnie Parker and Clyde Barrow, he committed numerous armed robberies, earning him the label of the "Tri-State Terror of the Southwest." In 1938, FBI director J. Edgar Hoover added Walters to the most wanted public enemies list.

Walters and Floyd Hamilton, the last living members of the gang, were caught in 1938. Walters spent more than twenty years in the prisons at Alcatraz and Leavenworth. While at Alcatraz, he made one of the rare escape attempts from that prison. Guards shot him in the back as he scaled the wall. He still jumped into San Francisco Bay, and he was recaptured just about the time he became paralyzed by the icy waters. He was returned to the prison, from which he was paroled in May 1971.

Walters had his last collision with the law on Oct. 13, 1971. A police car in Euless, Texas, made a routine stop of the car Walters was driving. Walters jumped out of the car firing a shotgun, but did not hit anyone. Although slightly wounded by a police bullet, he managed to escape. The following morning, 49-year-old Hoyt Houston, a resident of nearby Bedford, found Walters lying in a boat in the boat house in back of his property. Houston took Walters into the house, where Houston's wife, seeing that he was wounded, offered to clean his wounds. The couple's 15-year-old daughter, Pamela, slipped out a bedroom window and went to a neighbor's house to call police.

When the police arrived, Walters instructed the Houstons to tell them that all was well. Despite the Houstons' assurances, the police were suspicious and refused to leave. At this, Walters forced the Houston's and their 5-year-old daughter, Jana, into the family car. Walters got into the back seat, with the Houstons in the front, and kept his shotgun trained on Hoyt Houston's head. Police halted the car on a nearby bridge and attempted for twenty minutes to talk Walters into letting the family go. Walters refused to give up his hostages, so Texas Ranger Tom Arnold took aim with a rifle and, while Walters was momentarily distracted, shot him in the head. The first shot was most likely fatal, but other Rangers fired four more pistol shots into him from closer range. Huron Ted Walters, who had told reporters in the 1940s that: "I'd rather be shot down like a mad dog than have the cops take me," was finally dead. The Houston family escaped uninjured. See: **Barrow, Clyde Champion; Hamilton, Ray**. REF.: *CBA.*

Walters, William E. (AKA: **Bill Anderson, Billy Brown, Bronco Billy**), b.1869, U.S., west. outl. William E. Walters, born at Fort Sill, Indian Territory, worked as a cowboy and later as a section hand for the Santa Fe Railroad. Walters turned gunman and bandit in Arizona during the late 1890s, at one point joining the Black Jack Ketchum gang. He was credited with shooting several men and committing a number of robberies with his own gang after leaving Ketchum. Walters and others attempted to rob a train at Grants Station, N.M., but lawmen drove them off with heavy gunfire. Walters was tracked down by a posse led by Jeff Milton, who shot Walters in a duel. Walters was convicted of train robbery and sent to prison for life. He was released in 1917 and moved to Hachita, N.M., where he worked as a wrangler for the Diamond A Cattle Company. Walters was killed when he fell from a windmill tower he was repairing.

Outlaw William E. Walters.

REF.: Bell, *On the Old West Coast; CBA;* Hunter and Rose, *The Album of Gunfighters;* Rascoe, *Some Western Treasures;* Walters, *Tombstone's Yesterdays.*

Waltham Blacks, prom. 1723, Brit., rob.-mur. In the early 1720s, a group in Hampshire, England, formed a secret outlaw society which became known as the Waltham Blacks. Part of the name came from the black tar used to disguise their faces when perpetrating what seemed to be their main crime: poaching deer. The first half came from a confrontation in Waltham-Chase when the Bishop of Winchester's gamekeeper caught the group poaching. He was murdered. Seven of the Blacks were soon apprehended and were executed at Tyburn on Dec. 4, 1723. They were: Edward Elliot, Robert Kingshell, Henry Marshall, John Pink, James Ansel, Edward Pink, and Richard Parvin.

A 1722 statute enacted to control the poachers became known as the Waltham Black Act. It made poaching and over 350 petty crimes capital offenses, and gave judges the widest latitude in sentencing offenders. A clause in the statute also mandated that every person found Guilty of violating the Black Act would be hanged without benefit of clergy. Dozens of persons were executed in the country by an over-zealous court system. The statute stayed on the books, with deadly results, until 1823.

REF.: *CBA;* Potter, *The Art of Hanging;* Sparrow, *The Great Assassins.*

Waltheof (Waldevus, Guallevus), d.1076, Brit., consp. Involved in Earl of Norfolk's plot opposing the king but was forgiven. However, he was condemned for his part in the Danish plot to attack Britain in 1076 and was decapitated. REF.: *CBA.*

Walther, Fritz, prom. 1946, Ger., sab. Railroad switchman Fritz Walther served three German leaders during his twenty-four year career: presidents Friedrich Ebert and Paul von Hindenburg of the Weimar Republic, and Chancellor Adolph Hitler of the Third Reich. In January 1946, Walther deliberately threw the wrong switch which sent a passenger train into a parked freight train containing Soviet Red Army troops and supplies. Eighteen men were killed and thirty-two injured. The ex-Nazi was sentenced to be shot at dawn by a Russian military tribunal. REF.: *CBA.*

Walton, Charles, c.1870-1945, Brit., (unsolv.) mur. The gruesome slaying of Charles Walton on Feb. 14, 1945, near Stratford-upon-Avon, England, had all the elements of a ritualistic murder. Walton, a 74-year-old gardener and landscaper, was found dead, a pitchfork driven through his body, and his throat slashed in the sign of a cross.

Although Scotland Yard investigated the case for months and interviewed several thousand people, no witnesses or clues were found. It was determined that other ritualistic murders had occurred in the area through the years and that in this case the victim had been slain in the ancient manner used to kill witches. The case has never been solved.

REF.: Butler, *Murderers' England; CBA;* Fabian, *Fabian of the Yard;* Nash, *Open Files;* Shew, *A Second Companion to Murder;* Wilson, *Encyclopedia of Murder;* ____, *Witches.*

Walton, George, 1741-1804, U.S., jur. Presided as chief justice of Georgia from 1783-89, and as judge of the Georgia Superior Court from 1790-92, 1793-95, and from 1799-1804. REF.: *CBA.*

Walton, Valentine, d.c.1661, Brit., jur. One of sixty-seven judges presiding over trial of Charles I, who was charged with being a tyrant and an enemy of the nation. The judge was also one of the signers of the condemned king's death warrant in 1649. He was the brother-in-law of Oliver Cromwell, and later escaped to Germany in 1660. REF.: *CBA.*

Waluch, Mr., See: **Konovalec, Evhen.**

Walworth, Sir William, d.1385, Brit., law enfor. off.-mur. Served as London sheriff in 1370 and as lord mayor in 1374 and afterward. He protected London Bridge against an attack during the Peasants' Revolt in 1381. Later, at Smithfield, with Richard II present, he murdered Wat Tyler, the leader of the rebellion. REF.: *CBA.*

Wampanoag Indian War, prom. 1676, U.S., rebel. In 1676, Meracomet, the tribal leader of the Wampanoag Indians of Rhode Island, attempted to settle long standing grievances with the deputy governor and the white settlers of the colony. Meracomet, called "King Philip" by the English settlers, had presented a list of problems that he asked be resolved. The tavern owners had been plying his men with alcoholic beverages and then swindling them of their property, in some cases inciting them to commit a crime. Then, if found guilty by the colonial magistrate, the Indian prisoners could be legally remanded over to the custody of the New England slave traders who would sell them to plantation owners in the West Indies.

Meracomet asked that these objectionable practices immediately cease, but the deputy governor was intransigent. Angered, Meracomet ordered his people to war. It was the most destructive armed conflict since the founding of the settlement. Before the Wampanoag Indians and their allies the Narragansett were eventually vanquished by superior firepower, thirteen white settlements had been laid to ruin and an entire harvest was lost. Meracomet was captured and beheaded. For the next twenty-five years his head was displayed on a pole in Plymouth. His wife and children were sold into slavery.

REF.: *CBA;* Kobler, *Ardent Spirits.*

Wanderer, Carl Otto, 1887-1921, U.S., mur. Chicago has had many classic murder cases but one of its most remarkable murders involved a war hero and two colorful newspapermen, Ben Hecht and Charles MacArthur, whose canny sleuthing solved the Ragged Stranger case. The culprit, Carl Otto Wanderer, appeared to be anything but a murderer clever enough to fool the police department and the press in two sensational killings. Born and raised in Chicago, Wanderer attended public schools and, upon graduation from eighth grade, began an apprenticeship as a butcher. His frugal German parents had raised him to be thrifty and law-abiding and nurtured in him a deep love of America. After opening a successful butcher shop in partnership with his father, Wanderer became obsessed with the exploits of Mexican bandit Pancho Villa, incessantly reading about the bloody raids Villa led into Texas border towns.

When volunteers were summoned to fill the ranks of the First Illinois Cavalry in 1916, Wanderer, a patriot to the core, gladly enlisted, telling his startled parents that he was off to fight Villa. He served under General John J. "Black Jack" Pershing and proved to be such an excellent leader of men that Wanderer, at the outbreak of WWI the following year, was promoted to the rank of lieutenant. Wanderer went to France and fought in all the major battles involving American troops. In 1919, he returned a hero, his chest covered with citations. The five-foot-ten-inch, brown-eyed Wanderer, his brown hair thinning, was given a celebrity welcome in Chicago, the press lauding his overseas heroics. In the fall of that year, Wanderer met and married Ruth Johnson, an attractive 20-year-old. The war veteran and his wife moved into a small apartment with her parents. A few months later Ruth Wanderer proudly announced to her husband that she was pregnant and that the baby was expected the following year.

War hero Carl Wanderer signing his confession of murder.

Unlike most expectant fathers, Carl Otto Wanderer was not delighted by the news. He became withdrawn and moody. He argued with his wife and in-laws constantly and whenever the unborn child was mentioned, he became enraged, slamming his powerful fists against walls before storming out of the apartment. Wanderer spent less time with his wife and was gone from his apartment for long periods of time. Some time later, his spirits seemed to lift and he asked his wife to go to the movies on the night of June 21, 1920. Upon returning to the apartment that night, the couple entered the small vestibule of the building where they lived. The light in this area was off and Ruth Wanderer ran her hand along the wall, groping for the switch. According to Wanderer's later statement, he heard a voice say: "'Don't turn on the light!' I reached for my gun."

It was not then unusual for men to carry weapons. Chicago laws were lax about such conduct, and in the few years immediately following the war, it was the habit of many former soldiers to carry their service automatics. Wanderer said that the strange man in the dark foyer shouted obscenities at him and his wife and then fired a shot at them. More shots followed and Wanderer returned fire from his Colt .45-caliber automatic, emptying the clip in the direction of the intruder. Fourteen shots were fired by both men, all within a minute's time.

The noisy gunfire brought Ruth Wanderer's mother running. She entered the vestibule, switched on the light, and saw to her horror that her daughter was on the floor, mortally wounded with two bullets in her. Kneeling next to a man dressed in rags, also shot several times and in a dying condition, was Carl Wanderer. Possessed of rage, he was slamming his empty Colt against the dead man's head, screaming: "You've killed my wife, you bastard! You've killed my wife!"

Ruth Wanderer lived for only a few minutes, moaning to her mother: "My baby...my baby is dead." She died en route to the hospital.

The man dressed in shabby clothes, the Ragged Stranger as the press later dubbed him since his identity was unknown, was taken to Ravenswood Hospital. He never came out of a coma and died within a few hours. Police found only $3.80 in his pockets.

The public was shocked to learn of this heinous crime. Carl Otto Wanderer, an admirable war hero, had lost his lovely wife and unborn child to the maniacal whim of a savage killer and thief who struck in the darkness of Wanderer's own home. The war hero was again praised for courageously battling the ruthless murderer, again risking his life to save his pregnant wife. Newspapermen flocked to Wanderer, writing down his every word.

These were few. His grief was hard and long and he had little to say after telling police about the attempted robbery and his gun battle with the would-be thief. Chicago newspapers gave front page coverage to the story for many days. Photos of Wanderer, his wife, and relatives stared back at stunned readers. Every aspect of the case was examined, and even the two big .45-caliber automatics, Wanderer's and that of the Ragged Stranger, were photographed side by side.

This photo disturbed Ben Hecht, a veteran crime reporter on the staff of the Chicago *Daily News*. Hecht studied the photo, shaking his head. The Ragged Stranger, he knew, had less than $4 to his name. Why then would he not pawn the automatic he was carrying for $15 or $20, rather than risking a random holdup, particularly one involving Wanderer who was known to carry a gun, and take the chance of being shot? None of it made any sense. Hecht thought about the *type* of weapons both men possessed. Wanderer had held on to his service automatic as a matter of habit. Hecht thought it odd that the Ragged Stranger possessed the same kind of weapon. Perhaps this unknown killer had also been a WWI veteran.

The great writing team of Charles MacArthur, at typewriter, and Ben Hecht; they solved the Wanderer case in 1920 when both were working as Chicago reporters.

Hecht talked with his good friend Charles MacArthur, a reporter for the Chicago *Herald-Examiner*, who also agreed that the fact that Wanderer and the thief owned the same kind of weapon was odd, perhaps suspicious. MacArthur checked with the Colt Arms Manufacturing Company and learned that the Ragged Stranger's weapon had been sold for the first time in 1913 to a Chicago sporting goods firm. By checking the records of this store, MacArthur discovered that the automatic was sold to a Peter Hoffman, a Chicago telephone repairman.

MacArthur interviewed Hoffman and learned that the repairman had sold the automatic to a mailman some years earlier, one Fred Wanderer, a cousin of Carl Wanderer. MacArthur asked him if he still had the weapon. No, said Fred Wanderer. He had loaned the automatic to Carl on the very day of the shooting. Fred Wanderer believed that the weapon he had given his cousin was the one Carl Wanderer had used to defend himself. When he was told by MacArthur that this was the weapon the Ragged Stranger had fired, Fred Wanderer bolted to his feet, bug-eyed. He fainted dead away.

Hecht and MacArthur compared notes, and before going to the police with the information about the automatic, decided to give Wanderer the benefit of the doubt. The automatics might have gotten mixed up and Wanderer's weapon wrongly identified as that of the Ragged Stranger. Hecht decided to confront Wanderer. He went to the war hero's apartment, entering by the back porch. He stood for a moment, and through the screen door, heard Wanderer humming and whistling happily. He peered into the kitchen to see Wanderer pressing a pair of pants. The war hero stood barechested performing this domestic chore with the carefree abandon of a man who had miraculously been stripped of grief while his wife and unborn child had been buried only days earlier.

Hecht knocked on the door and asked to come inside. Wanderer cheerfully welcomed him. After a few minutes of idle chatter, Hecht asked to use Wanderer's washroom. Inside the bathroom, Hecht noticed Wanderer's bathrobe hanging on a door hook. A strange object dangled from its pocket. Hecht pulled out a woman's silk stocking. Then he pulled another stocking from the pocket. In the other pocket, he discovered lipstick, mascara, and rouge. From the breast pocket of the bathrobe, the snooping Hecht pulled several letters Wanderer had written, love letters. These had been written to a man. The reporter quickly realized that the virile veteran of a dozen bloody battles on the Western Front was homosexual.

The reporter stepped from the tiny bathroom, quickly explaining to Wanderer that he was working against a deadline and had to rush back to his newspaper. Hecht rushed to join MacArthur and explained his discovery. MacArthur told Hecht that he had checked on the guns and that Wanderer's weapon was, indeed, his service automatic and that the other weapon was the one Fred Wanderer had loaned to Carl. Both men then went to the police. MacArthur explained the discrepancy of the automatic and how the Ragged Stranger's gun belonged to a Wanderer relative. Hecht then told detectives how Wanderer had been acting that morning and how he suspected the war hero of being homosexual. This, Hecht theorized, was the motive for Wanderer's killing *both* the Ragged Stranger and his wife. Ruth Johnson Wanderer was pregnant with Wanderer's child and his homosexuality had so rebelled against the idea of heterosexual love producing a child that he could not bear the thought of it. He had arranged the murder of his wife rather than go on living a sexual double life.

Police Lieutenant Mike Loftus listened and nodded. He ordered Wanderer picked up and when the war hero arrived, Loftus interrogated him, pointing out that the automatic used by the Ragged Stranger was the property of Fred Wanderer. "This is some mistake," Wanderer said. He began a long-winded story about how the automatics had been a part of a large shipment of weapons sent to several training camps during the war and that the weapon used by the Ragged Stranger could not have been his cousin's weapon. He said he did not remember borrowing Fred Wanderer's weapon.

Meanwhile, Hecht checked the bank accounts of Wanderer and his dead wife Ruth. He learned that on the day of her death Ruth Wanderer had withdrawn her life savings of $1,500 from the Second Security Bank. The bold Hecht searched Wanderer's apartment and found $1,500 in bills taped behind a bureau. He took the money to police headquarters and then was allowed to confront Wanderer. He told the war hero that he knew about his love for a man named James, saying that he had read the love letters Wanderer had written but not mailed to James. Hecht decided to bluff his way along, telling Wanderer: "James is coming to see you, Carl. I just talked with him."

The tough-looking war hero began to tremble. "No, not here! Don't let him come here," pleaded Wanderer. "Oh, my God!" Wanderer turned to Lieutenant Loftus and admitted that he was a homosexual and had married Ruth Johnson for her money, even though he hated her. He hated all women, Wanderer said. "The thought that she was going to have my child was repulsive," he said. He said he feared that once the child was born, his affair with James would collapse. He had killed his wife and the Ragged

Stranger, he said, to preserve his secret relationship with another man. It had been simple, explained Wanderer. He had spent several nights in skid row bars until he met an ex-Canadian soldier who said his name was Al Watson.

Down on his luck, Watson was looking for a job. Wanderer told him he had an idea that would make Watson some quick money. He explained to Watson that because of his effeminate manners, his wife had doubted his record as a war hero and that he wanted to reaffirm his heroic image. Watson was to stage a fake holdup of the pair when they returned from the movies on June 21, 1920. Watson would wait in the vestibule, and when Wanderer appeared with his wife Watson was to pretend to rob them. Wanderer would hand Watson a gun in the dark and when his wife switched on the light, Watson would point the weapon at the pair and demand their money. Wanderer would then fake throwing a powerful punch that would knock Watson down who would then scramble to his feet and flee. Wanderer would thus become a hero in his wife's eyes.

This was the scenario Wanderer created for Watson, except that when the couple arrived home on the night of the killings, Wanderer did not hand Watson the gun. He fired both automatics at the same time, emptying their clips, firing at his wife and at Watson simultaneously, eliminating a wife he did not want and creating a dead scapegoat for her murder. He knew that Mrs. Johnson would rush to the vestibule once she heard the firing, and to convince her that he had been defending Ruth, he placed one of the automatics in the hand of the fatally wounded Watson and then leaped upon his victim, striking him in his pretended rage at Watson's ostensible murder of his wife.

Wanderer went through two lengthy trials and was convicted of killing both Ruth Johnson Wanderer and Al Watson. He was sentenced to death. While awaiting execution, Wanderer was visited many times by the very men who had unearthed the evidence that convicted him. They became friends, playing poker together in the Cook County Jail's holding cell. At one point, the penniless Wanderer (his wife's money had been returned to the family), was loaned $5 by MacArthur, an act of kindness that caused Wanderer to ask MacArthur if he could do *him* a favor. MacArthur thought for a moment and then said, yes, there was something the condemned man could do. "Just before you step off the platform, you'll be asked if you have any last words," MacArthur said. "Let me write out a speech for you."

"I'm not good at memorizing," Wanderer said.

"It's okay," MacArthur told him. "You can read it."

MacArthur, with Hecht's help, wrote a long tirade against the editors of both the *Herald-Examiner* and the *Daily News*, the bosses of Hecht and MacArthur. On the day of Wanderer's execution, Mar. 19, 1921, MacArthur gave the speech to the condemned man, who was taken into the courtyard of the old Criminal Courts Building where a high gallows stood. Wanderer mounted the scaffold, with dozens of witnesses standing in the courtyard, including Hecht and MacArthur. He clutched the speech the two scribes had deligned in writing but he never got a chance to read it. The reporters had forgotten that condemned prisoners about to be hanged were tied hand and foot. Wanderer could only look down at the typewritten sheets rolled up in his hand which was pinioned to his side. He shrugged, and as a way of compensating his friend MacArthur, sang an old ballad, "Dear Old Pal of Mine," as the rope was placed around his neck. A black hood was placed over Wanderer's head, but he sang on in a smooth voice until the trapdoor sprang open and Wanderer's singing was cut off by the jerking rope.

The cynical MacArthur turned to his friend Hecht, with whom he would later write the hit play, *The Front Page*, and said: "You know, Ben, that son-of-a-bitch should have been a song plugger!" See: **Hecht, Ben.**

REF.: *CBA;* Fetherling, *The Five Lives of Ben Hecht;* Hecht, *Charlie;* _____, *A Child of the Century;* ____, *Gaily, Gaily;* Nash, *Bloodletters and Badmen;* Robbins, *Front Page Marriage.*

Wang, Stephen Sui-Kuan, Jr., 1964- , U.S., fraud. The second largest insider-trading scandal in U.S. history came to light in June 1988 when the Securities and Exchange Commission (SEC) filed charges against 24-year-old Stephen Wang, Jr., a trainee in the New York-based investment firm of Morgan Stanley. Wang was accused of giving illegal information to Fred C. Lee, a Taiwanese businessman who reaped a $15.5 million profit before leaving the company. The advance information he received between July 1987 and April 1988 was used to buy stock in fourteen different companies about to merge or be taken over by competitors. The SEC recovered $12.6 million from an account Lee maintained in the New York branch of the London-based firm, Standard Chartered Bank.

The SEC filed a lawsuit seeking return of the illegal profits plus triple damages which would have totalled $76 million. Two years earlier, the SEC recovered $100 million from Wall Street mogul Ivan Boesky in the largest insider-trading scandal to date. Boesky was sentenced to three years in prison. Unlike his more successful counterpart, Stephen Wang of Buffalo Grove, Ill., appeared before U.S. district judge Kevin Duffy virtually penniless. "He's disgraced his family and hurt the firm that trusted him," said defense counsel Ira Sorkin, who tried to obtain leniency for his client. "If a message is to be sent, Stephen Wang's situation today is that message."

Judge Duffy sentenced Wang to three years in prison on Oct. 26, 1988, but did not impose a monetary fine. "You're worth zero," Duffy said. "And a quarter of zero is zero." REF.: *CBA.*

Wang Canwen, 1921- , China, embez. Wang Canwen, a Chinese politician convicted of embezzling $14,000 from a Shanghai institute in 1952, was elected to a seat in the provincial assembly in February 1980. Wang, fifty-nine, had served seven years of an original life sentence and was freed in 1959 for good conduct. "It is the Communist Party that gives me a second life," he was quoted as saying. The transformation of criminals into productive members of society was a long-standing policy of the Peking government, according to official news sources. REF.: *CBA.*

Wang Ching-wei (Wang Chao-ming), 1883-1944, China, attempt. assass. Revolutionary who tried to assassinate the prince regent in 1910. He was sentenced to life in prison, but after the republic was founded he was freed in 1911. He became a supporter of Chiang Kai-sheck and held the position of president of the administrative council from 1932-35. He was shot and almost killed in 1935. After shifting his loyalties several times, he became a supporter of the Japanese and was installed by the Japanese military as a puppet ruler of China in 1939. Another assassination attempt was made on his life in 1939. REF.: *CBA.*

Wang Mang (AKA: The Usurper), 33 B.C.-23 A.D., China, emp., assass. Ruled as regent for two child emperors from 1-8 A.D. before usurping throne and ruling from 9-23 A.D. He instigated numerous reforms that affected prices, taxes, and land ownership. He also faced a populace agitated by the calamity caused when the Yellow River abruptly changed its course. Rebellion resulted and he was assassinated by members of the rebel Red Eyebrows group. REF.: *CBA.*

Wanka, Alfred, 1927-61, S. Afri., pris. esc.-mur. While training to become a miner at the Crown Mines in Johannesburg in 1953, Alfred Wanka, a Czechoslovakian, shot and killed a night watchman who caught him and three of his friends stealing peaches. Wanka later claimed the guard was killed because he had uncovered a bootlegging ring Wanka was operating at the time. The South African courts sentenced him to twelve years, but released Wanka after two. Wanka remained in South Africa, and in the 1950s, joined up with a gang of ex-convicts who committed a string of robberies and thefts in different parts of the country.

While attempting to flee from the police, Alfred Wanka shot and killed Detective Constable Phillipus Johannes Jordaan. The policeman had recognized Wanka on a Durban street on July 26, 1960, and was trying to arrest him when Wanka fled. Before Wanka could flee, he was arrested in Capetown Aug. 2.

He was found Guilty of murder on Oct. 17, 1960, and was sentenced to die on the gallows, despite protests from his lawyer that he was mentally unsound. On Mar. 25, 1961, he attempted to escape from the Pretoria Central Prison. He shot and wounded a prison guard but was executed a short time later.

REF.: Bennett, *Murder Will Speak; CBA.*

Wan Zian Sung, prom. 1926, U.S., (wrong. convict.?) mur. Five years after narrowly escaping the hangman, a student named Wan Zian Sung was given his final release from custody on June 16, 1926. He had served seven years for the Jan. 29, 1919, murders of Dr. Ben Sen Wu, under-secretary of the Chinese Educational Mission of New York; Dr. T.T. Wong; and Dr. Chang H. Hsie. The murder of the three academics was attributed to a forged check in the amount of $5,000 that Wan's brother Tsong Ing Van allegedly tried to cash.

The conviction of Wan was based solely on a "third-degree" confession taken by a New York City police officer. Found Guilty and sentenced to die on the gallows, Wan's sentence was commuted to life imprisonment several days before the execution date. Former Democratic presidential aspirant John W. Davis agreed to act as voluntary counsel for the defendant during his Supreme Court appeal. The high court granted Wan a new trial, and both subsequent juries refused to convict him. Attorney Peyton Gordon asked that the original judgment against Wan be dropped since the prosecution could uncover no new evidence to support a conviction. Forgery charges against Tsong were not prosecuted at Gordon's request. REF.: *CBA.*

Wapner, Joseph A., 1919- , U.S., jur. Each afternoon, twenty million television viewers in the U.S. tune in *The People's Court* to watch simulated courtroom drama involving actual lawsuits filed in the Los Angeles area. The cases are selected on the basis of human interest and drama, and represent a cross-section of the suits filed each day in the California Small Claims Court.

The People's Court premiered in 1981, and has a legion of fans, including Supreme Court justice Thurgood Marshall and actor Dustin Hoffman, whose character in the movie *Rainman* planned his entire day around Judge Wapner. Prior to sitting on *The People's Court* bench, Joseph A. Wapner was presiding judge of the Los Angeles Superior Court for twenty years, retiring in 1979. A decorated infantry officer during WWII, he returned home to begin a successful career in law.

After a case is selected for airing, the respective parties must sign an agreement allowing Wapner to arbitrate the matter. The plaintive and defendant are each paid a $50 honorarium. The show pays any damages assessed the defendant. If Judge Wapner rules for the defendant, both sides agree to split $500. In 1988, Judge Wapner's memoir of electronic jurisprudence, titled *A View From the Bench,* was published by Simon & Schuster. REF.: *CBA.*

Warbeck, Perkin, 1474-99, Brit., fraud. The servant of a silk dealer in Ireland, Perkin Warbeck had a penchant for impersonation. In 1492, he claimed to be Richard, the Duke of York, the son of Edward IV. His pretense was accepted by Edward's sister Margaret, the dowager Duchess of Burgundy, and the earls of Desmond and Kildare also believed his charade. He also duped Charles VIII of France into thinking he was Richard IV, and he was given funds by Emperor Maximilian I for attacks that failed. Arriving in Cornwall in 1499, the charlatan announced that he was king. He was taken into custody and admitted his fraud. Held prisoner in the Tower of London, he was hanged after an escape attempt. REF.: *CBA.*

Warboys Witches, prom. 1589, Brit., witchcraft. The hysterical testimony of three children doomed to death on the gallows in April 1593 an old woman, her husband, and daughter. The unfounded charges of witchcraft were brought against 76-year-old Alice Samuel of Warboys, in Huntingdon by the three precocious daughters of Robert Throckmorton. On Nov. 10, 1589, 10-year-old Jane Throckmorton developed the symptoms of what appeared to be influenza. Mrs. Samuel stopped by to pay her respects, and it was not long afterward that the other girls became similarly afflicted.

Jane's accusations of witchcraft were given credence by Dr. Philip Barrow of Cambridge University, who examined the children. Then, in September 1590, the wife of Sir Henry Cromwell, grandfather of the Protector (Oliver), encountered Alice Samuel. She died ten months later after describing "bad dreams" and physical suffering she had endured. These afflictions were blamed on Samuel, who was indicted for witchcraft along with her husband and daughter. The three were tried at Huntingdon and found Guilty after five hours' deliberation. They were hanged forthwith. An account of the trial was later published in pamphlet form. It was titled *The Most Strange and Admirable Discovery of the Three Witches of Warboys* (1593).

REF.: Boulton, *A Complete History of Magic; CBA;* Davies, *Four Centuries of Witch Beliefs;* Ewen, *Witchcraft and Demoniasm;* Harrison, *Elizabethan Journal 1591-94;* Kittredge, *Witchcraft in Old and New England; The Most Strange and Admirable Discovery of the Three Witches of Warboys;* Naylor, *Four Sermons Preached at All Saints Church, Huntingdon, on the 25th Day of March, 1792-3-4-5: The Inanity and Mischief of Vulgar Superstitions;* Notestein, *History of Witchcraft in England from 1558 to 1718;* Robbins, *The Complete Encyclopedia of Witchcraft and Demonology.*

Ward, Benjamin, 1926- , U.S., law enfor. off. Benjamin Ward was appointed New York City's thirty-fourth police commissioner on Nov. 7, 1983, by Mayor Ed Koch. He became the first black to hold the office.

It had been a long hard climb for Ward, who grew up in the tough Bedford-Stuyvesant neighborhood of Brooklyn. In June 1951, he took the police examination and finished third among 78,000 applicants. He was initially assigned to direct traffic on First Avenue, but was soon transferred to Crown Heights in Brooklyn, where he walked a beat in the racially polarized Irish community. He accepted the intolerant attitudes of the community—and his fellow officers—with grim resignation.

He advanced steadily through the ranks. In 1975, he was appointed the state of New York's first black commissioner of correctional services, working under Governor Hugh Carey. The state prison system was still reeling from the costly Attica prison riot in 1971. Ward took special steps to ease racial disharmony and unsuccessfully fought to prohibit Ku Klux Klan membership among prison employees. In 1978, he petitioned for a transfer back to the city police force.

As police commissioner, Ward was faced with racial problems plaguing the police force. Complaints from various minority groups were rampant. He introduced several community programs aimed at "giving the streets back to the people." The "Total Patrol Concept" emphasized the "cop on the beat" concept rather than the over-reliance on 911 emergency calls. See: **Attica Prison Riot**. REF.: *CBA.*

Ward, Charles William, Jr., 1909-28, Brit., mur. Charles Ward of Ackworth, England, thought he had established a foolproof alibi for murder. After plunging a pick-ax through the skull of his father shortly after their midday meal on Mar. 28, 1928, young Ward left the house for a business appointment in Barnsley. When the body of his father was found in the easy chair, Charles Ward would simply say that he was in Barnsley at the time of the murder and could not possibly have known about it. Unfortunately for Ward, he had not counted on the wonders of forensic science.

A team of pathologists headed up by the eminent Sir Bernard Spilsbury conducted an autopsy on the remains, and concluded that the elder Ward had died within an hour of completing his meal. This evidence pointed to Charles Ward, the only person who had been present in the cottage at that time. He was convicted at the Leeds Assizes, and was sentenced to die on the gallows by Justice Travers Humphreys. REF.: *CBA.*

Ward, Christopher, b.1842, Can., mur. Mary Mayne arrived in Canada in early 1876. She went to live in Toronto with her uncle, who worked as a gardener in one of the government buildings. The arrangement was temporary, because Mary was engaged to be married.

During her journey to North America, Mary Mayne had a shipboard romance with a wealthy Ontario cattleman named Christopher Ward, thirty-four, who owned a farm thirty miles outside of Toronto. In February 1876, they were married. Mary moved into the grand house in the township of Caledon. The marriage was not a happy one, however, for Ward was mentally ill.

One day there was a great fire in the house, and Ward was severely burned. He said he tried to save Mary, but could not. Detective Murray, however, was suspicious. The marital problems between the couple were common knowledge in the village. After the fire was put out and the ruins cooled down, a search for the remains began. A twisted butcher's knife was found near the severed torso, suggesting that the body had been dismembered. A barrel of fiery tallow had been used to melt down pieces of the body. Murray's evidence was submitted to Professor Henry Holmes Croft at the School of Practical Science for confirmation. Based on these findings, Ward was indicted for murder and placed on trial at the Brampton Assizes on May 11, 1876.

A Guilty verdict was returned quickly despite the contention of the defense that Ward was insane and therefore not responsible for his actions. He was sentenced to life imprisonment at the Kingston Penitentiary, but his erratic behavior compelled the prison officials to move him to Rockwood Asylum, where he died.

REF.: Campbell, *A Century of Crime; CBA.*

Ward, Frederick (AKA: **Captain Thunderbolt**), 1836-70, Aus., rob.-mur. Frederick Ward was jailed for the first time in 1863 for horse theft. He was sent to Australia's Cockatoo Island, from which he escaped a short time later. With a fellow convict he swam to the mainland where he donned some women's clothing to effect an escape. To his utter dismay, Ward discovered that the love of his life had died in an asylum during his period of incarceration. Embittered by this dreadful turn of events, Frederick Ward stole a horse and turned to highway robbery as a full-time vocation.

He dubbed himself "Captain Thunderbolt," and set upon the highway robbing and bushranging. From a half-caste girl named Yellow Long, he learned the words to a song that he would adopt as his theme: "Her Bright Smile Haunts Me Still". Ward would whistle this tune while he stole from his robbery victims. After Yellow Long died in June 1868, the twice-grieved robber vanished for a short time, but soon reappeared with a vengeance. The law caught up with him on May 25, 1870, at a hotel in Uralla. He was turned in by a robbery victim to whom he had shown mercy—a peddler Ward allowed to escape who ran straight to the police. The bushranger was chased by pursuing police and shot down. Captain Thunderbolt died without revealing the whereabouts of his estimated £20,000 loot. REF.: *CBA.*

Ward, John (AKA: **Captain Ward**), prom. 1603-15, Brit.-Tunisia, pir. Finding that his prospects for financial gain as a humble fisherman in Faversham, Kent, were minimal, John Ward drifted into Plymouth, and then Portsmouth, where he incited a gang of adventurous seamen to join him as pirates under his direction.

Ward and his band of buccaneers seized a twenty-five-ton bark bound for Havre with only minimal resistance, and outfitted it for pirate duty. They sailed down the English Channel until they encountered a rich prize: a French merchantman, which they promptly boarded. The vessel was rechristened the *Little John,* and it set sail for the open waters of the Mediterranean.

Ward made friends with the Turks and flew the Tunisian flag from his mast. He plundered the vessels of the Venetians, and built a substantial fleet of ten ships. Tunis became Ward's home port, and he built a lavish home there constructed of marble and alabaster. Captain Ward plundered French, Flemish, and Portuguese ships at random. In later years, it was rumored that Ward had settled in Villefranche under the protection of the Duke of Savoy. His exploits survived in a popular ballad of the day titled *Captain Ward and the Rainbow.*

REF.: *CBA;* Mitchell, *Pirates.*

Ward, John (Jerome Levigne), d.1868, U.S., mur. On Aug. 28, 1865, John Ward and his friend Walter Moore murdered Mrs. Ephraim Griswold in the town of Williston, Vt. Ward, a hired assassin brought in from New York, also burglarized the home of the man who had hired them to do the job—Mrs. Griswold's son-in-law Charles H. Potter. She was a surly old woman who had a good deal of money and property that Potter hoped to inherit. Seeing no other way to gain control of the estate, he hired Ward and Moore to kill her. They beat her over the head with a billy club and then severed her jugular vein with a knife.

After the killing, Ward and Moore returned to New York to await payment from Potter. When the money failed to arrive Ward returned to Vermont, where he was arrested. Potter and Ward were tried for murder at the Chittenden County Court in April 1866. Walter Moore was never tried, and Potter was acquitted by the jury. John Ward, having been found Guilty of murder, was hanged in Windsor, Vt., on Mar. 20, 1868. REF.: *CBA.*

Ward, Joseph (AKA: **Winston**), prom. 1895, U.S., (wrong. convict.) rob. On Feb. 19, 1895, James Mahoney was arrested by Boston police and charged with pickpocketing May Ivers. She had $3 and small change on her at the time. A second man involved in the crime had escaped. Mahoney was released on bail, and the police resumed their search for the accomplice.

Through the description provided by two female store detectives and a witness to the crime, an ex-convict named Joseph Ward was arrested. Ward was found Guilty of robbery and sentenced to five years in the state prison. During the trial he refused to testify on his own behalf because he feared that his past criminal record would influence the jury to return an even harsher sentence.

Later, Mahoney told police that his partner had not been Ward, but a New Yorker named Dooley. The resemblance between the innocent man and Dooley was a strong one, which resulted in Ward's wrongful conviction. On Jan. 30, 1896, the governor of Massachusetts granted Ward a formal pardon in what had been a case of simple mistaken identity. REF.: *CBA.*

Ward, Joshua, 1685-1761, Brit., fraud. Britain's most famous quack doctor of the later eighteenth century began his career in politics. Joshua Ward was elected to Parliament in 1716, but his name was erased by the House of Commons when it was learned that he had not received a single vote. Ward fled to France where he promoted a quack medicine known as "White Drop of Ward and the Pill," which, if used in excess, caused permanent liver damage. Ward advertised this noxious medicine as a cure for all diseases. He was spared imprisonment in the Bastille by his friend John Page, and traveled back to England to market the drop and the pill to the public.

British quack Joshua Ward.

King George II became his most devoted patron after he succeeded in "curing" His Majesty's dislocated thumb. George granted him his own apartment in the almonry office. Ward purchased three lavish country houses, and converted them to hospitals for his poor patients, an act of charity inconsistent with the dubious nature of his business. On Nov. 28, 1734, an item appeared in the *Daily Courant* which charged Ward with plotting to introduce "popery" into Protestant England through the dissemination of his drop and pill. There were other attacks against the harmful side effects of the nostrums, but Ward continued marketing his products until the day he died. REF.: *CBA.*

Ward, Judith, 1949- , Brit., terr.-bomb. Judith Ward, a 25-year-old member of the Irish Republican Army (IRA), was responsible for one of the worst terrorist acts in Britain to date. On Feb. 4, 1974, she planted a bomb in the luggage compartment of a bus that traveled from Manchester to Yorkshire. It exploded at Birkenshaw, Yorkshire, killing twelve people returning to their military base following a weekend leave.

Soon afterward, Ward exploded a twenty-pound gelignite bomb in the National Defense College at Latimer, Buckinghamshire, which injured ten people. Ward was identified and arrested. She was tried and found Guilty of murder at the Wakefield Crown Court six months later. It was revealed that she had been responsible for a third bombing at the Euston railway station a year earlier. She received a life sentence for the bus murders, twenty years for causing the explosion, an additional ten years for the school bombing, and five years for the attack on Euston Station. "These offenses are so heinous that no figure could be put on what would be appropriate to their gravity," commented Justice Waller.

REF.: Borrell, *Crime in Britain Today; CBA.*

Ward, Margaret, d.1588, Brit., her.-pris. esc. Margaret Ward and four accomplices were executed in August 1588 for helping a priest escape from prison by supplying a rope that he could lower from the window. Ward was accused of heresy and conducting unauthorized religious services in defiance of a court order that she leave the country.

REF.: *CBA;* O'Donnell, *Should Women Hang?*

Ward, Matthew F., and **Ward, Robert J.**, prom. 1853, Case of, U.S., mur. William Ward attended the Louisville High School. He and his brother Matthew were the sons of the wealthiest man in the state, Robert J. Ward. On Nov. 1, 1853, young William was scolded by his teacher William H. Butler for arguing about chestnuts during a class session, a deliberate defiance of school rules. The schoolmaster administered a whipping to William because he believed that the student had lied. This angered not only the defiant high schooler, but his older brothers Robert and Matthew.

All three of the Ward boys confronted Butler in the school building, demanding a retraction for inferring that Matt was a liar when he said that he had not eaten any chestnuts. There were angry words and a gunshot. Mr. Butler fell to the floor mortally wounded. He was carried to a neighbor's home by the other students, where he died a short time later. Robert and Matthew Ward were charged with premeditated murder after it was learned that the brothers had purchased a pistol from a gunsmith in Louisville. Because of the intense excitement and press reaction brought on by the shooting, a change of venue to Hardin County was granted. The trial commenced on Apr. 18, 1854, in Circuit Court. The defense team included eighteen lawyers, including John J. Crittenden, recently elected to the U.S. Senate. The prosecution was headed by Alfred Allen of Breckinridge, who was assisted by three lawyers.

Crittenden secured an acquittal amidst charges that the Ward money had saved Matt from the gallows. Crittenden introduced seventy witnesses, and spoke out against the premeditated malice Matt and Robert Ward may have harbored against the deceased. The defendants were discharged, but the matter did not end there. The outraged citizens of Louisville organized a public protest, censuring Crittenden for what they perceived to be a miscarriage of justice. The home of Robert Ward, Sr. was surrounded, and pelted with stones. In the end, four jurors who had found the Wards Not Guilty ended up being indicted for perjury. Senator Crittenden went on to complete his third term in the U.S. Senate, despite a public demand for his resignation.

REF.: *CBA;* Johnson, *Famous Kentucky Tragedies and Trials.*

Ward, Return J.M., d.1857, U.S., mur. Described as a "hulking lout," Return Ward was left by his wife because he regularly abused her. After much persuasion, Olive Ward returned to him in 1857, against the advice of her friends and family. When she had not been seen for twenty-four hours, a throng of neighbors descended on Ward's house, demanding to see Olive, and accusing Ward of killing her, but then they left after conducting a fruitless search for her. Unfortunately, they had not looked under the couple's bed where Ward had stashed her body on hearing the approach of the neighbors. When they finally left he dragged the corpse into the kitchen, cut it into small pieces, and burned the pieces in the fireplace, cleaning the ashes out in the morning and placing them outside his house. Ward was arrested for murder after neighbors, who were keeping watch, discovered Olive's jawbone in the ashes. Return Ward was brought to trial in Sylvania, Ohio, where throngs of people gathered, hoping to see a hanging. The jury convicted him before hearing his entire testimony. After Ward told the court he killed his wife by accident, and cut up her body in a panic, then continued into detailed descriptions of the burning, the jury decided it had heard enough and pronounced him Guilty, sentencing him to death. Ward's hanging was the best-attended execution in pre-Civil War Ohio. Legal scholars used the Ward case as an example of a "legal lynching" obtained from an illegal verdict.

REF.: *CBA;* Nash, *Bloodletters and Badmen.*

Ward, Stephen, See: **Profumo Scandal**.

Ward, Tommy, and **Fontenot, Karl**, prom. 1984, U.S., theft-kid.-mur. On Saturday night, Apr. 28, 1984, shortly after 8:00 p.m., in Ada, Okla., Donna Denice Haraway was seen leaving a convenience store where she worked accompanied by two men in an old, nondescript pickup truck. Several customers who were about to enter the store saw them leave, and when they found no one tending the store and the cash register open and empty, they called the police. Haraway's purse with identification was found at the scene.

Because of sloppy handling at the crime scene, some evidence and possible fingerprints were destroyed. However, composite drawings of the suspects were published in the local newspapers and broadcast on television. After weeks of investigation, police narrowed their search to two young men, Tommy Ward and Karl Fontenot. Despite the fact that neither man had a bad record—Karl Fontenot, for example, had never been arrested—they came "from the wrong side of the tracks" and were considered part of Ada's hard-drinking, drug-oriented subculture.

Taken into custody, the men told conflicting stories and were caught in numerous lies. Each finally confessed to the abduction, rape, and murder of Haraway and implicated a third party, Odell Titsworth. Lengthy videotaped confessions were obtained from each suspect. Some people claim that the Ada police department and the Oklahoma State Bureau of Investigation used some unethical techniques in obtaining these confessions.

Both suspects later repudiated their confessions, each telling convoluted stories of what might have happened. Tommy Ward even claimed that what he had confessed to had all been a dream. Odell Titsworth was released when it was proved that at the time of the abduction he had been elsewhere and that he was just recovering from a broken arm that would have made it impossible for him to commit the acts of which he was accused.

For the next six months, the authorities tried to find the missing victim. No trace was found. But the state proceeded to charge Ward and Fontenot with theft, kidnapping, rape, and first-degree murder.

Following a long and arduous trial, both of the accused were found Guilty of all charges except rape. Ward and Fontenot were sentenced to die on Jan. 21, 1986. In the course of the appeals, the date was set aside and the two young men sat on Death Row in the Oklahoma State Penitentiary.

On the date originally set for their execution, Haraway's body was found. It was determined that she had been shot in the head, and a gun had never been mentioned in either confession. This laid the case wide open and provided valid reasons for further appeals. No positive evidence of the stabbings described in the confessions was found on the body. Attorneys appointed by the court to represent Ward and Fontenot are still trying to overturn the convictions based on the new evidence and the contention that their clients had been denied due process of law by "official police misconduct." At this writing, the case is still under appeal.

REF.: *CBA;* Mayer, *The Dreams of Ada.*

Ward, Walter S., prom. 1923, Case of, U.S., mur. Rather than submit to a blackmail scheme, Walter S. Ward, heir to a New York-based baking fortune, confronted the felon on the morning of May 16, 1922. Two days later, the blackmailer's body, found on the Chappaqua Road in White Plains, was identified as Clarence Peters, who had been recently rejected by the Marines when he had tried to enlist at Paris Island, S.C.

Ward voluntarily surrendered to the authorities and claimed that he shot Peters in self-defense after the man gave him the choice of surrendering money or facing death. On June 15, the Westchester County grand jury indicted Ward for murder, but the indictment was dismissed on Jan. 2, after the county failed to bring him to trial in reasonable time. On Mar. 27, 1923, Governor Alfred Smith of New York ordered a special investigation of the shooting. Ward was portrayed as a wealthy man's son who might have harbored sinister feelings for Peters. The investigation resulted in the Attorney General obtaining a second indictment.

The case went to trial on Sept. 12, and after two weeks of deliberation a Not Guilty verdict was returned. REF.: *CBA.*

Ward, William, 1697-1719, Brit., rob. Born in Norfolk County, England, William Ward studied and worked as a millwright, moved to London, and married before he began to steal for a living. Particularly adept at robbing tradesmen, Ward and a cohort once fooled a linen draper into thinking they were making a major purchase from him by inviting him into their coach to discuss prices. While Ward's partner finalized the deal, Ward convinced the man's apprentice, in the shop, to give him several expensive bolts of material. When the linen draper returned to his shop, Ward and his companion were already selling the material from their coach on the street. Ward also made a practice of stealing trunks from hackney coaches, but was caught in the act of removing one from a coach parked at the Four Swans Inn in Bishopsgate Street, arrested, imprisoned at Newgate, and tried at the Old Bailey in October 1718. Found Guilty of only one felony, he was sentenced to be transported. During his confinement, however, he was convicted of two other charges: breaking into the house of Thomas Lane and stealing ten pounds of tea on Apr. 12, 1717; and stealing about £40 of silver plate on July 24, 1717, from the house of Julian Bayley, with a man named Samuel Lynn. Because of these additional indictments, Ward was sentenced to hang. On Feb. 16, 1719, he was executed at Tyburn, at the age of twenty-two.

REF.: *CBA;* Mitchell, *The Newgate Calendar.*

British boxer William Ward beating Edwin Swain to death, 1789.

Ward, William, prom. 18th Cent., mansl. Boxer William Ward set out by stagecoach on the seventy-mile trip from London to Stilton to attend a fight between two boxers. Stopping at Enfield to change horses, Ward was challenged by a local blacksmith, Edwin Swain. Ward accepted the challenge, but though they seemed physically well matched, the amateur could not hit the trained professional. Swain soon conceded, but Ward followed him, catching him off guard and beating him to death. He then hired a coach to London but was chased, arrested, and jailed.

The sixteen jurors were split: seven judged Ward's offense as "wilful murder," and nine judged it "manslaughter." Arraigned at the Old Bailey on June 5, 1789, Ward was found Guilty of manslaughter by Justice Ashurst, fined one shilling, and sentenced to three months in prison—a lenient sentence because Swain had provoked the contest. There was thus no evidence of actual malice.

REF.: *CBA;* Mitchell, *The Newgate Calendar.*

Wardas, Roman, and **Ganev, Gantscho**, prom. 1978, Switz., grave rob.-extor. Intending to extort $600,000 from the Chaplin family, Roman Wardas, a 25-year-old Polish refugee, conceived a plot to steal the body of actor Charlie Chaplin. At night on Mar. 1, 1978, with Gantscho Ganev, his 39-year-old Bulgarian accomplice, Wardas disinterred Chaplin's 300-pound oak coffin from its grave in Corsier-sur-Vevey, the Swiss village where the actor had lived for twenty-five years before he died on Christmas day, 1977, at the age of eighty-eight. Wardas initially planned not to steal the coffin but rather to bury it deeper in the grave. But this proved too time-consuming, so the grave robbers removed the coffin and reburied it in a cornfield. Police arrested Wardas on May 16 in a phone booth while he was making one of twenty-seven phone calls to the Chaplin estate attempting to collect a ransom, initially set at $600,000. Police found Chaplin's coffin in the cornfield the following day, his body untouched. Charlie Chaplin's body was returned to the cemetery at Corsier-sur-Vevey, where it was placed in a protective vault. Convicted of attempted extortion and disturbing the peace of the dead on Dec. 14, a Swiss court sentenced Wardas to four-and-a-half years in prison, and gave Gantscho an eighteen-month suspended sentence. REF.: *CBA.*

Wardell, Robert, 1936- , U.S., jur. Creede, Colo. (population 400), is a quiet silver-mining town surrounded by 900 square miles of wilderness. Robert Wardell, who obtained neither a college diploma nor a law degree, has served as the town's only judge since 1964. Since that time, he has tried 10,000 cases, but only two were appealed; both were denied. Judge Wardell does not permit lawyers in his courtrooms. He prefers to arbitrate the problems of Mineral County himself. Since the most serious offense he considers only carries a one-year maximum sentence, most people feel there is no need for lawyers.

His common sense approach to the law has developed from a lifetime spent pumping gas. Wardell owns a filling station in town and can often be seen filling up a tank or two in his judicial robe. REF.: *CBA.*

Warder, Alfred William, d.1866, Brit., suic.-mur. Alfred Warder, a medical doctor, was a well-respected expert on poisons. Dr. Warder married three times. His first wife died in 1863, his second in 1865, and his third wife died soon after their marriage in 1866. Experts on poisons were brought in and determined that the death of the third Mrs. Warder was probably caused by poisoning with aconite under circumstances similar to the death of the other wives. Even though the evidence was inconclusive and a jury would probably have found Warder Not Guilty, he took a fatal dose of prussic acid and died before going to trial.

REF.: *CBA;* Furneaux, *The Medical Murderer;* Kingston, *Dramatic Days at the Old Bailey;* Nash, *Almanac of World Crime;* Parry, *Some Famous Medical Trials;* Wilson, *Encyclopedia of Murder.*

Warder, Frank H., prom. 1931, U.S., brib. Frank Warder, former New York State Superintendent of Banks, entered Sing Sing Prison in January 1931, to begin serving a five- to ten-year sentence for accepting a $10,000 bribe to stave off an audit of the books belonging to the City Trust Company. The bank failed in 1929, and Warder vainly tried to conceal the evidence of mismanagement. When the court of appeals upheld his conviction, it ended Warder's fourteen-month legal fight to stay out of jail. REF.: *CBA.*

Warder (Idaho) Bombing, 1899, U.S., bomb. A decade of tension between the labor unions and management in the Idaho mining regions culminated in the sabotage of the Bunker-Hill-Sullivan Mine near Warder, Idaho, in April 1899. The destruction of the mine by militant union men prompted Governor Frank Steunenberg to call in federal troops to suppress the disturbance. Eight hundred suspects were rounded up and placed in a stockade pending their court appearances. Eventually, ten prisoners were convicted of willfully destroying the property of the mine owners. They were each sentenced to twenty-two years in prison. The miners' imprisonment only heightened the resentment felt by the labor men, and in the aftermath of the Bunker-Hill bombing, there were terrible reprisals. Governor Steunenberg was himself the victim of a bomb thrown by Harry Orchard. See: **Orchard, Harry**. REF.: *CBA.*

Virginia Wardlaw, left, and her sister Caroline Wardlaw Martin, right.

Wardlaw Sisters, prom. 1900-13, U.S., mur. The three "Sisters in Black," born into a prominent Southern family, chose to lead a weird life of seclusion, regularly moving from town to town. They always dressed in funereal black. The leader of this strange trio was Virginia Wardlaw, a graduate of Wellesley College who became a respected educator. Her sisters, Caroline Wardlaw Martin and Mary Wardlaw Snead, went to live with Virginia after leaving their husbands.

The sisters collected $12,000 insurance on Mary's son, John Snead, when he burned to death. Sister Caroline, after being reunited with her husband, a Colonel John Martin, moved to New York. There, the colonel died from causes never determined, probably poison, and Caroline collected $10,000 insurance. Caroline, along with her daughter Oscey, joined her two sisters in Tennessee, where Virginia had become the head of Soule College in Murfreesboro.

Mary Wardlaw Snead, murderess.

An insurance policy was taken out on Oscey, who was pregnant after being married and separated from her husband. While living with the three sisters, she too became ill and died, apparently starved and ultimately drowned in a bathtub. When the sisters tried to collect on the insurance policy, they were arrested and charged with the murder of Oscey. Virginia starved herself to death in jail. Caroline was convicted of the murder of her daughter, certified insane, and died in 1913. Mary was acquitted.

REF.: *CBA;* Nash, *Bloodletters and Badmen;* Zierold, *Three Sisters in Black;* (FICTION), Allerton, *The Shadow and the Web.*

Ware, Ashur, 1782-1873, U.S., jur. Served as first secretary of state of Maine, from 1820-22. He was also district court judge in Maine from 1822-66, and he was considered an authority on U.S. maritime law. REF.: *CBA.*

Ware, David John, prom. 1947-51, Brit., (attempt.) mur. After Walter Rowland was sentenced to death for the murder of Olive Balchin at the Manchester Assizes in October 1946, David Ware confessed to the crime. Ware's statements were not allowed to be given, on the grounds that he had been in prison between Oct. 23, 1946, and Jan. 15, 1947, which would have given him ample opportunity to familiarize himself with the facts of the case through the newspapers.

It was further shown that Ware's confession, though containing elements of truth, was essentially a false one. Four years after Rowland went to the gallows, David Ware was arrested for attempting to murder a girl, whom he attacked brutally. He was found Guilty, but insane, and was committed to the Broadmoor Asylum. See: **Rowland, Walter Graham.**

REF.: Bowker, *Behind the Bar; CBA;* Duff, *A New Handbook on Hanging;* Hibbert, *The Roots of Evil.*

Warehouse Brothel, prom. 1850s, U.S., pros. The most infamous brothel in Chicago, the Warehouse, located on South Water Street on the second floor of a plain brick warehouse. Home for a huge population of resident prostitutes, the Warehouse also contained a series of cubicles rented to transient streetwalkers. Since it was the target of continual police raids, the many prostitutes learned to flee the premises quickly. This training proved advantageous on Oct. 19, 1857, when a drunken prostitute accidentally started a fire when she kicked over a lamp. The fire spread quickly and consumed the warehouse as well as surrounding property. Twenty-three persons were killed and half a million dollars of property was destroyed. The dead all were male brothel customers and residents of communities nearby. None of the prostitutes died. Rumors of prostitute lynchings circulated throughout Chicago following the fire but waned several days later. After the Great Chicago Fire of 1871, the Warehouse tragedy was labeled the "Little Chicago Fire." REF.: *CBA.*

Wareru (AKA: Mogado, Chao Fa Rua), prom. 1300, Burma, mur. Joined forces with Mon prince Tarabya and expelled Burmese forces from Irawaddy delta. He murdered Tarabya, taking control as king, and set up the Hanthawaddy dynasty, headquartered at Martaban, Burma. He prepared *Dharmasastra,* or *Dhammathat,* the first Burmese code of laws. REF.: *CBA.*

Waring, John U., prom. 1835. Case of, U.S., mur. In the 1830s, John Waring became one of the most powerful men in the Commonwealth of Kentucky, inheriting the bulk of his father's estate, including a prosperous steamship company.

Waring's real estate business in Kentucky frequently brought him into contact with the lawyer Samuel Q. Richardson. Richardson became involved in some unproductive business transactions with Waring involving large areas of land in Ohio. The lawyer was forced to mortgage all of his property in order to satisfy the large debt he had incurred at the hands of Waring, reputed to be a violent and dangerous man.

On Feb. 8, 1835, Richardson and Waring met each other on the steps of the Mansion House, one of Frankfort's most opulent hotels. As Richardson ascended a flight of stairs, Waring accosted him with a small pistol. He was restrained by several men, but later produced a pistol of larger caliber. He re-emerged in the hall and fatally shot Richardson at point blank range.

Waring was arrested and tried in Franklin County for murder. A request for a change of venue by the defendant was denied, and the first of four trials began in March 1835, three of which produced the verdict of Guilty. In March 1837, Waring was tried for the fourth time and found Not Guilty. Eyewitnesses speaking on Waring's behalf stated that Richardson had been planning his creditor's death all along, and had reached for his pistol on the stairway. The jury accepted this argument. Waring lived another ten years until he was shot and killed in Versailles, Ky., by a 16-year-old youth named Shelton who had courted Waring's daughter.

REF.: *CBA;* Johnson, *Famous Kentucky Tragedies and Trials.*

Warner, Albert S. (AKA: **George Johnson**), and **Hardy, Joseph M.**, and **Blake, H.G.**, prom. 1890s, U.S., kid. While consulting with a lawyer for his defense in a blackmail case in New York City, Albert Warner mentioned his plan to go into kidnapping as a commercial venture. Though his statement was dismissed, Warner proceeded with his plan.

On the morning of Aug. 16, 1897, Albert Warner offered candy to Johnny Conway, the child of Michael J. Conway, an Albany train dispatcher. Johnny accompanied the stranger to a wagon heading out of Albany. A short time later Mrs. Conway received a ransom note demanding that $3,000 be delivered to a specified location that same evening.

The kidnapper's letter was given only a cursory examination by police, and interviews with the neighbors yielded no tangible clues. The Albany newspapers conducted an independent investigation, discovering that Joseph Hardy, a brother-in-law of Michael Conway, had previously attempted to extort money from the father.

A close friend of Hardy's, H.G. Blake, was located and brought in for questioning. With the promise of bribe money, Blake took reporters directly to the kidnap gang. On Aug. 18, the party arrived at a campfire deep in the woods where young Conway was being held.

In the confusion, Conway slipped away. He returned to his parents the next day. Hardy was arrested almost immediately. Blake was captured in Schenectady on Aug. 19, and after a long, exhaustive search, Albert Warner was arrested in Riley, Kan., where he was working as a field hand under the name of George Johnson. He was extradited to Albany, where he was sentenced to fifteen years in prison. Hardy and Blake each received fourteen-and-a-half years in the Dannemora State Penitentiary for their part in the abduction. REF.: *CBA.*

Warner, Alonzo M., See: **Christianson, Willard Erastus**.

Warner, Charles, prom. 1913, Case of, Brit., mur. On Nov. 3, 1912, in response to anxious queries from the neighbors, police battered down the door of Elmgrove House, in Broughty Ferry, Scot., where a 65-year-old spinster named Jean Milne lived. The woman was the daughter of a wealthy tobacco manufacturer and lived comfortably on £1,000 a year. Milne was found at the foot of the stairs, bound, gagged, and beaten to death. Detective-Lieutenant Trench of the Glasgow City Police ascertained that Jean Milne had been murdered on Oct. 15, and that robbery was definitely not the motive. Valuable diamonds and rings had been left behind by the intruders.

Police thought they had a likely suspect in Charles Warner, a Toronto man who had been traveling through the British isles on a holiday. Six London witnesses identified Warner as a companion of Milne, claiming to have seen them together at two fashionable hotels. In his defense, Warner claimed to have been in Antwerp at the time, and recalled pawning a waistcoat for a franc. Detective Trench traced his steps, Warner's story held up, and the charges were dropped by the Crown Office on Jan. 6, 1913. See: **Milne, Jean**.

REF.: *CBA;* Roughead, *Tales of the Criminous.*

Warner, Matt, See: **Christianson, Willard Erastus**.

Warnock, Stephen, 1946- , Brit., mur. Fifteen-year-old Stephen Warnock was apprenticed to a baker, and attended bakery classes at a technical school in the London suburbs. One day in 1961, two classmates named Gray and Robbins tormented Warnock, teasing and kicking him until a fight broke out in class. Later, Robbins let the air out of Warnock's bicycle tires.

When Warnock saw what had been done, he rushed back into the school building and stabbed Robbins to death with a pastry knife. He was allowed to plead not guilty to murder, but guilty to manslaughter on the grounds that he had been provoked. Various character witnesses appeared on Warnock's behalf to attest to his otherwise good behavior and fine manner. The judge sentenced the boy to three years' probation.

REF.: *CBA;* Wilson, *Children Who Kill.*

Warr, Carl (AKA: **Alfred Henry Davis, John Sanders**), b.1878, U.S., bomb. A "believer in the working classes" who felt that "the human race is degenerating through hardship coming from unjust treatment to the working man," Carl Warr in an attempt to "better the workman's condition on the Pacific Electric," created a bomb powerful enough to decimate a city block.

On Nov. 19, 1912, at 11 p.m., the German-born Warr, then thirty-four, walked into the Los Angeles' central police station wearing a grotesque face mask and carrying an accordion-shaped box. There, in the offices of Chief of Police Sebastian, he demanded to see Paul Shoup, president of the Pacific Electric Railway. What he wanted from Shoup, he explained, was a promise to increase his employees' wages and improve their working conditions. If Shoup would not see him, Warr continued, he would blow up the building. Sergeant Hilf, Secretary Snively, E.L. Onley, and Tom Graham laughed at him, so Warr took a stick of nitroglycerine out of his pocket and warned that any attempts to stop him would result in his blowing up the building. Warr again demanded that Shoup be brought to him.

Chief Sebastian sent officers to evacuate the building. Justices adjourned all court sessions. Lieutenant Butler of the traffic squad roped off an area from First Street to Broadway and Hill. As news of the bomber spread, a crowd of 5,000 gathered in less than half an hour. Reporters and police moved through Chief Sebastian's office in a futile attempt to talk Warr into surrendering. Only once, however, did Warr lose his cool, when he realized his picture was being taken: "No more pictures," he demanded. "The next one that is taken will mean the end of everything, for I'll turn this thing loose."

Police considered starving him out, overpowering him with an ammonia ball, even shooting him. Then detectives Hosick, Fitzgerald, and Browne suggested that the three of them might overpower Warr if one sneaked up behind him while the other two grabbed the bomb. Sebastian approved it, but ordered all the buildings on the block vacated in case the plan failed. With a blackjack hidden in his hand, Hosick entered the reception room followed closely by Browne and Fitzgerald.

Warr, still seated with Hilf and Snively, turned to see the blackjack being brought down on his forehead. As Warr fell forward, Fitzgerald grabbed the bomb, releasing the trigger. The fuse spluttered. Hosick hit Warr a second time, and knocked him unconscious as six men leaped to grab him. Browne picked up the box, and ran from the room, extinguishing the fuse with his fingers before throwing it into the street. There it broke into a dozen pieces, scattering fifty-three sticks of dynamite and the crowd in all directions.

In the hospital, where Warr was treated for injuries, he gave his name as Alfred Henry Davis, and repeatedly asked that someone shoot him. He later gave his real name and the address of the small one-story house where he had manufactured the bomb after two years of experimenting. The machine was his own invention, he said, and he did not want a description of it to get into the newspapers "for fear others will steal my idea." Found to be sane, Warr was charged with and convicted of malicious handling of explosives. He served twelve years of a twenty-year sentence in San Quentin.

Twenty-five years later, in March 1938, Warr was again arrested in Los Angeles, this time under the name John Sanders. Having become a drifter, he was given a five-day suspended sentence for evading railroad fare. When Warr revealed his true identity, the press asked him about the bomb. "It was a bluff," said Warr. "I had the machine fixed so it wouldn't go off...I guess Los Angeles never will forget me." REF.: *CBA.*

Warren, Charles, b.1868, U.S., lawyer-writer. Served as assistant attorney general of U.S. from 1914-18. Books authored: *History of the American Bar, The Supreme Court in United States History, Congress, the Constitution and the Supreme Court.* He won the Pulitzer prize for the latter work, published in three volumes in 1922. REF.: *CBA.*

Warren, Sir **Charles,** 1840-1927, Brit., law enfor. off. General Charles Warren was a graduate of Sandhurst, the celebrated British military academy and training center for the Royal Officer Corps. Warren's long military career was interrupted in 1886 when Queen Victoria appointed him commissioner of the London Metropolitan Police. Warren had the bad luck to be commissioner at the time Jack the Ripper terrorized the East End of London in 1888. Warren later received considerable criticism for his handling of the case, and when he seemed powerless to stop the bloody Ripper murders, he even drew harsh remarks from Queen Victoria.

Sir Charles Warren

The techniques Warren proposed to catch the Ripper were old-fashioned and a bit ridiculous. He rented two bloodhounds named Barnaby and Burgho, who, on their first outing, not only failed to sniff out the Ripper's trail, but promptly got lost in a London fog and had to be tracked down by a large search party. Warren then proposed that the soles of the shoes of his constables be replaced. The standard hobnailed boots that clattered loudly on cobblestones would be replaced with rubber-soled shoes, thus enabling policemen to "quietly sneak up" on the Ripper.

Moreover, Warren's actions were odd and contradictory when it came to the Ripper. More than once he destroyed evidence in the case, notably the wiping out of a message the Ripper had reportedly written on the wall of building on Goulston Street following one of the killings, one that read:

> The Juwes are not the
> men that will be blamed
> for nothing.

City detective Daniel Halse remained at the scene to guard the wall and sent a message to C.I.D. Inspector James MacWilliams that he would wait at the spot until dawn when a photograph of the message could be taken. Warren, however, arrived shortly before daylight and ordered the entire message rubbed out. Halse tried to persuade Warren to preserve the message until there was enough light for it to be photographed. Warren adamantly insisted on wiping out the message. He later explained in a letter to the home secretary that he feared that if the message was seen by anti-Semites—and there were thousands in the East End—riots would ensue, Jewish shops and merchants would be persecuted, and great damage to lives and property would occur.

Halse then argued that the message could be covered up until it was photographed. Warren rejected this notion. Then Halse said that perhaps only the top line should be rubbed out. Superintendent Arnold, Warren's own man, then argued that perhaps they could wipe out only the word "Juwes" and preserve the rest of the handwriting so that it might be later examined and compared with that of suspects in the Ripper slayings (the writing on the wall was described as a "good schoolboy hand"). Warren rejected this proposal, too. He then took a dry sponge that he had ordered an inspector to bring to the spot earlier and personally wiped away the message.

Some Ripperologists later claimed, stretching a point considerably, that Warren's real reason for wiping out the message was to protect the Masons. Warren was a high-ranking Mason and he immediately recognized the strange writing of the message, some claim, as a cryptic Masonic statement, that the oddly spelled word "Juwes," related to an archaic Masonic spelling of the word "Jews."

Some later claimed in Warren's defense that he was hamstrung on many occasions during the complex Ripper investigation. Forces he could not control, chiefly the C.I.D. and the Home Office, constantly demanded results in the case, but gave Warren no useful aid. For his part, Warren had a considerable force in handling the case, more than 600 officers assigned night and day to the Whitechapel killings. Because of his failure to solve the Ripper killings, Warren resigned from his post as commissioner of the Metropolitan Police. He was later assigned to various military commands. Toward the end of his life, although he never made his opinions public, Warren intimated to friends that he believed the Ripper was an Irish maniac. According to another story, he believed Montague Druitt, one of the primary suspects in the killings who drowned himself in the Thames, was the real Jack the Ripper. See: **Abberline, Frederick George; Jack the Ripper.**

REF.: Anderson, *Criminals and Crime;* ____, *The Lighter Side of My Official Life;* Barnard, *The Harlot Killer;* Besant, *East London;* Browne, *The Rise of Scotland Yard: A History of the Metropolitan Police; CBA;* Cullen, *When London Walked in Terror;* Dilnot, *The Story of Scotland Yard;* Griffiths, *Mysteries of the Police and Crime;* Jones and Lloyd, *The Ripper File;* Knight, *Jack the Ripper;* Leeson, *Lost London;* McCormick, *The Identity of Jack the Ripper;* Macnaughten, *Days of My Years;* Matters, *The Mystery of Jack the Ripper;* Moylan, *Scotland Yard and the Metropolitan Police;* Prothero, *The History of the C.I.D. at Scotland Yard;* Rumbelow, *The Complete Jack the Ripper;* Sims, *The Mysteries of Modern London;* Sinclair, *East London;* Spiering, *Prince Jack;* Stewart, *Jack the Ripper;* Thomson, *The Story of Scotland Yard;* Whittington-Egan, *A Casebook on Jack the Ripper;* Williams, *The Life of Sir Charles Warren;* Woodhall, *Jack the Ripper.*

Warren, Earl, 1891-1974, U.S., jur. Chief Justice Earl Warren reflected the shift to liberal thinking sweeping the country during the 1950s and 1960s. He was nominated to replace Chief Justice Fred Vinson on the Supreme Court Sept. 30, 1953, by President Dwight Eisenhower. After a long career in public service, including four years as California attorney general (1939-43), and a decade as state governor (1943-53), Earl Warren had emerged as a national leader in Republican politics, and a staunch Eisenhower supporter at the 1952 nominating convention. His work in California helped deliver the state's crucial electoral votes in that presidential election. As a reward for faithful service, Eisenhower was said to have promised the Governor a seat on the high court when the first vacancy opened.

For the first two years of his term on the bench, the chief justice remained in the political center on controversial issues. The first indication of Justice Warren's liberal philosophy occurred on Mar. 17, 1954, when he wrote the majority opinion for the landmark case of *Brown v. the Board of Education*, which outlawed school segregation in the South. Justice Brown argued that racial segregation deprived children of equal educational opportunity. The *Brown* decision effectively ended sixty years of legal segregation in the South, and paved the way for the era of civil rights, giving blacks the impetus to knock down other long-standing barriers to racial equality.

In the 1960s, the Warren Court continued to champion the rights of blacks. Justice Warren and his colleagues ruled that "lunch counter" segregation on state owned property was illegal. In December 1964, the Court sustained the key provisions of the Civil Rights Act, and three years later declared that state laws banning miscegenation were unconstitutional. It was one of the last legal barriers to full racial equality in the U.S.

In the realm of criminal law, Justice Warren liberalized the interpretation of a suspect's rights. Speaking for a five-man majority in the case of *Miranda v. Arizona,* 1966, Warren overturned the defendant's rape conviction on the grounds that he had not been apprised of his legal protections under the Constitution prior to arrest. Henceforth, every law enforcement officer in the

U.S. was required to inform a suspect that he had the right to remain silent, and to have an attorney present.

In 1963, Justice Warren accepted an invitation from President Lyndon B. Johnson to chair a special commission to investigate the circumstances surrounding the assassination of President John F. Kennedy. The massive *Warren Report* upheld the single assassin theory, declaring that Lee Harvey Oswald had acted alone in his intention to murder the president.

Chief Justice Earl Warren

After sixteen years on the bench, Justice Warren announced his resignation from the Supreme Court in 1969. He was replaced by Chief Justice Warren Burger, a jurist of a more conservative political bent. Earl Warren presided over the Supreme Court during a period of profound social change in the U.S. His contributions during this time were far-reaching, and did much to change the quality of life for thousands of Americans. According to Archibald Cox, the Warren Court gave "creative and enduring impetus to the responsibility of government for equality among men, the openness of American society to change and reform, and the decency of the administration of criminal justice." See: **Burger, Warren Earl; Kennedy, John Fitzgerald.**

REF.: *CBA;* Katcher, *Earl Warren, A Political Biography;* Overstreet, *The FBI in our Open Society;* Peterson, *The Mob;* Powers, *Secrecy and Power;* Weaver, *Warren: The Man, The Court, The Era.*

Warren, Robert Willis, 1925- , U.S., jur. Served as district attorney of Brown County, Wis., from 1961-65, and as attorney general of Wisconsin from 1969-74. He was nominated to the eastern district court of Wisconsin by President Richard Nixon in 1974. REF.: *CBA.*

Warriston, Lord **Archibald Johnston**, 1611-63, Scot., her. Prepared Scots National Covenant in 1638 with Alexander Henderson, which supported Presbyterianism during the period when Charles I tried to establish episcopacy in Scotland. In 1641 he presided as judge, or lord, of session. He continued to oppose Charles and he was eventually tried by the parliament of Scotland, condemned, and hanged. REF.: *CBA.*

Washam, Norman, and **Beck, Robert**, prom. 1925, U.S., mur. On Dec. 11, 1925, in eastern Kentucky, Norman Washam and Robert Beck were drinking whiskey together. Afterward, both went to Beck's grocery store. There, Beck mentioned a debt that Washam still owed at the store. Washam drew his knife and slashed Beck, who grabbed a gun from behind the counter. Beck shot Washam to death and later died from the knife wounds.

REF.: *CBA;* Montell, *Killings.*

Washam-Bede Feud, prom. 1880s, U.S., feud. A feud that probably began during the Civil War was continued for decades by the Washam and Bede families, who lived near the Kentucky-Tennessee border. The fighting ended with an 1888 shootout between Jes, Sherrod, and Pole Bede and Duck, Mart, and Marion Washam. See: **Bede Gang**.

REF.: *CBA;* Montell, *Killings.*

Washington, Aaron, 1954-82, U.S., rob.-mur. Aaron Washington was on probation for grand larceny and auto theft when he robbed a South Side Chicago grocery store on Sept. 27, 1982. The 28-year-old Washington stole $130.84 and a jar of honey from Southtown Health Foods before fleeing from the store pursued by owner Emil Mahler. He shot Mahler before driving seven blocks north to a shopping center where he abandoned his car. After running several more blocks, Washington forced his way into a house and demanded that 30-year-old Kathleen Frantz give him the keys to her car. When she refused, Washington entered the bathroom where she was hiding and shot her in the shoulder. Frantz ran from her home with Washington following. Outside, the two were intercepted by Chicago police officer Martin E. Darcy, Jr. Washington shot the 52-year-old officer three times in the chest, fatally wounding him, then stole his service revolver, and ran into an alley, where he was cornered by other policemen. There a gun battle ensued. Washington injured 42-year-old policeman Jerry Johnson before officers fired two bullets into his stomach and heart, killing him instantly. REF.: *CBA.*

Washington, Allen, 1948- , U.S., child abuse-mansl.-mur. In 1969, when 3-year-old Elisa Handy died, her father Allen Washington was a suspect in the case, but the coroner's inquest ruled the death accidental, caused after the child fell off a table. In 1970, Washington, a Chicago garbage collector, beat his 23-month-old daughter, Angela, to death. He was tried in 1971, convicted of involuntary manslaughter, and sentenced to ten years in prison, only to be released after serving two and a half years of the term. On Sept. 7, 1978, Washington hit his 3-year-old son James E. Smith with his hand and left the child lying on the bathroom floor. The next day, he reported his son missing and hired a private detective to search for his son, explaining to the private investigator that he had struck James for wetting his pants and then the boy hit his head on the bathtub. Three weeks later, police officers found the toddler's battered and burned body in a garbage dump. On June 26, 1980, Washington, thirty-two, was convicted of murdering his son, and on July 30 he was sentenced to forty years in prison. REF.: *CBA.*

Washington, Bushrod, 1762-1829, U.S., jur. A native of Virginia and the nephew of George Washington, Bushrod Washington took part in the Revolutionary War and later studied law. Washington was elected to the Virginia House of Delegates in 1787, and in 1788 to the Virginia convention, where he argued for ratification of the federal Constitution. On Dec. 19, 1798, President John Adams nominated Washington as associate justice to the U.S. Supreme Court, and he served from 1798 to 1829. During his tenure, his opinions closely coincided with those of Chief Justice John Marshall. However, in *Mason v. Haile* in 1827, Washington disagreed with the majority, contending that a state cannot invalidate a prison term for debt retroactively. After George Washington died in 1799, the childless president left Mount Vernon to his nephew, who lived there until he died. REF.: *CBA.*

Washington, Jeffrey, c.1957- , U.S., rape-mur. On Christmas Day, 1987, 73-year-old Alice Carcieri entertained relatives and a friend in her Mount Pleasant, R.I., apartment. Meanwhile, Jeffrey Washington, her handyman, hid in the basement for approximately six hours, eating canned food and smoking crack cocaine. About midnight, Washington went up to Carcieri's bedroom while she slept. He placed a bedspread over her head so she could not identify him, tied her wrists to the bed posts, and raped her. Carcieri, who had had both legs amputated several years before, tried to resist before she died of a heart attack. Carcieri's partially nude body was found by her sister.

The following morning Washington fled the state, but police arrested him three days later in Riverhead, N.Y., for robbing an elderly man. While in custody, Washington told police that he was wanted for murder in Providence and in January 1988, he wrote letters of apology to the Carcieri family. Washington explained the crime, saying, "I loved her. I thought I was doing something good for her because she felt bad" that she had never had a sexual experience.

On May 8, 1989, Washington was convicted of first-degree murder and, in a separate ruling, the jury also found him Guilty of committing the crime with aggravating circumstances. On June 27, he was sentenced to life imprisonment without parole by Superior Court judge Thomas J. Caldarone, Jr., who received petitions signed by 600 residents of Rhode Island calling for a life sentence. The judge exercised an option under a 1984 Rhode

Island law permitting a life term with no parole for crimes involving aggravated battery or torture. Washington was only the fourth defendant convicted under the law. REF.: *CBA.*

Washington, Leon, 1946- , U.S., mur. Leon Washington, owner of a downtown Chicago executive recruiting firm, left his home on June 6, 1981, dressed in cowboy boots and hat and armed with a semi-automatic handgun and a hunting knife. During the afternoon, the 35-year-old ex-Davenport, Iowa, police officer drank excessively and accompanied friends to the Marina City bar, where he continued to drink.

First deputy police superintendent James J. Riordan and his date were going to dinner when they met Alice and Martin O'Brien. The O'Briens invited Riordan and his date to Marina City for a drink. There Alice O'Brien apparently told the noisy Washington to "shut up," and Washington walked over to her husband, explaining to him that he would allow him to remain in the bar if O'Brien would buy him a drink. Alice and the bartender both claimed that Washington then held an unloaded gun to her head and pulled the trigger three times. Riordan told the O'Briens to go to the back of the bar while he quieted Washington. Washington walked into a coat check room and loaded his gun. When he returned to the bar, both he and Riordan walked outside, where Washington shot Riordan three times. Riordan died en route to the hospital.

Pleading self-defense, Washington was tried and convicted on Oct. 30, on murder charges, and on Dec. 2, 1981, he was sentenced to thirty-five years in prison. The death penalty was not invoked because Riordan was off-duty when he was killed. In January 1982, Washington's mother, Hazel Washington, filed a $500,000 suit against two businesses for serving alcohol to her son. REF.: *CBA.*

Washington, Thomas George, 1941- , U.S., skyjack. An unemployed Philadelphia chemist and former teacher, Thomas George Washington picked up his 2-year-old daughter, Denise, from his estranged wife on Dec. 19, 1968. Then he and the child, who had been placed in her mother's custody, boarded an Eastern Airlines flight bound from Philadelphia to Miami. Flashing a toy gun, Washington hijacked the plane to Cuba, where he and Denise lived for about a year. On Nov. 2, 1969, they and five other U.S. citizens who had hijacked jets to Cuba voluntarily returned to the U.S. They arrived in Montreal aboard a Cuban freighter and were met by immigration officials, who escorted them to the U.S. border. The six men were taken to Plattsburgh, N.Y., and 4-year-old Denise was returned to her mother. In 1970, Washington, twenty-nine, was tried on a charge of interfering with the crew of an airliner, convicted, and sentenced to two years in prison. But his lawyer won Wasington immediate parole because of his otherwise clean record. REF.: *CBA.*

Watchman, Louis, and **Watchman, Philip**, prom. 1910, U.S., wh. slav. During the early 1900s, two brothers set up a phony employment agency in East St. Louis, Ill., to lure young girls into prostitution. Louis and Philip Watchman, who claimed they were Russians, planned to send the girls to Chicago. However, before the scheme was completely established, they were arrested and tried on charges of involvement in white slave traffic. They were convicted, sentenced to six months in prison, and fined $500. Before their release on Nov. 15, 1910, they filed documents stating they were paupers, in order to avoid paying their fines. But before they had left the prison, they were rearrested and authorities began deportation proceedings. REF.: *CBA.*

Waterbury, Ward, prom. 1892, Case of, U.S., kid. In the late 1800s, there were few ransom kidnappings. One of the rare ones occurred in late January 1892, when 8-year-old Ward Waterbury of Longridge, N.Y., while walking to school on a Monday morning, was approached by two men in a church shed who persuaded him to help them look for an ax. One man was short, stout, and wore a black beard and moustache. The second man wore a moustache and goatee. The strangers led Ward through the woods to a white house, where they gave him food and picture books to read. The boy slept in the house that night with one of the men, fully clothed except for his overcoat and hat. When he asked to go home, the men promised to return him when "the old woman found the horse." At night, the man with the goatee moved Ward to a cave where they met the stout man, and the two kidnappers then dropped the boy off at a farmer's house. The farmer, Louis Close of Sandwich, took him home that evening. In the meantime, Ward's father had received a ransom note for $6,000, which he brought to the scheduled place for the ransom payment, but the kidnappers did not appear.

The nephew of Ward's father, Charles E. Waterbury, and two accomplices were arrested in early February. Searching Waterbury's home, police found the remains of a false beard in the stove. One of the accomplices, John McCann, was arrested before Charles Waterbury and confessed to the judge at his arraignment. The other accused kidnapper, Samuel Sutherland, claimed he had nothing to do with the abduction. Charles and McCann confessed how they, with Sutherland, thought up the plan to kidnap a child from reading a dime-store novel about another kidnapping—that of Charley Ross. They initially intended to kidnap the child of a wealthy Greenwich man named Hanford Lockwood, but abandoned the scheme as too dangerous. The kidnappers intended to open a "dive" in Greenwich, Conn., with the ransom money. Charles Waterbury and McCann were identified as the two men who took Ward to the house, and the court sentenced them to four years' imprisonment. For his part of the plot, Sutherland received a two-year sentence.

REF.: Alix, *Ransom Kidnapping in America; CBA.*

Waterford, Jack (Frances Warren, AKA: **Millionaire Streetwalker)**, b.1840, U.S., pros. Described as "a pug-nosed, ugly-looking little critter," Jack Waterford was a hard-working streetwalker turned business manager for a bevy of streetwalkers. Waterford, born Frances Warren, claimed she paraded along Chicago's streets every night for ten years, servicing five to twenty-five clients a night at prices ranging from $1 to $10. A very industrious lady, she came to be known as the "Millionaire Streetwalker."

She organized a number of prostitutes into a structured unit, renting working and living space on the top floors of office buildings. Jack became their business agent, also making sure they kept themselves clean and attractive. Each day at "shape up" time she designated the areas of town they were to operate in—the preferred women being assigned to hotels and railroad stations. At the end of each night the women would hand over the money they had made and Jack would give them a spending allowance, pay for legal costs and police protection, take a small cut herself, and place the remaining money in trust for the women. She never stole from her stable of women, many of whom opened brothels after leaving Waterford's organization.

Waterford told a newspaper reporter she did not wish to open a brothel, but rather intended to retire upon saving $30,000. Apparently she succeeded, for she faded from the public eye in 1880. REF.: *CBA.*

Watergate Scandal, 1972-75, U.S., polit. corr. Although the political crisis which culminated with the resignation of a U.S. president and jail terms for some of the highest-ranking members of the administration did not become public until June 1972, the scandal had its beginnings in May 1971, when Pentagon employee Daniel Ellsberg released a classified document to the New York *Times.* The report, which became known as the "Pentagon Papers," outlined various U.S. miscalculations made during the Vietnam War, and offered a gloomy assessment for the prospects of military success in that war. President Richard M. Nixon authorized the formation of a special covert unit to "plug" future news leaks, and to pick up any worthwhile information that might be used against Ellsberg in his upcoming trial for illegal possession of classified documents. This squad was known as the "White House Plumbers."

White House employee Egil "Bud" Krogh hired E(verette). Howard Hunt, Jr. and G(eorge). Gordon Liddy to run the secret unit. Hunt had been a CIA agent for twenty years and was the author of forty-two spy novels; Liddy was once a government prosecutor from Poughkeepsie, N.Y., and later acted as general counsel to Nixon's re-election committee. The first task facing these two was to discredit Ellsberg. On Aug. 25, 1971, Hunt and Liddy broke into the Beverly Hills, Calif., office of Ellsberg's psychiatrist, Dr. Lewis J. Fielding, for reconnaissance purposes. Hunt and Liddy returned on Sept. 4 with three others, but were unable to retrieve Ellsberg's files. A few months later the plumbing operation was disbanded. (A federal judge dismissed the charges against Ellsberg in 1973 because of government mischief.) Hunt and Liddy were reassigned to the Committee to Re-Elect the President (CREEP), as attention shifted to the upcoming 1972 campaign.

CREEP was headed at the time by an ambitious White House aide named Jeb Stuart Magruder, whose budget included monies allotted for intelligence work. Liddy was given about $200,000 from a secret slush fund of unreported contributions to CREEP. Magruder entrusted Hunt and Liddy with the task of planting listening devices in Democratic National Committee headquarters at the Watergate, a Washington, D.C., apartment, hotel, and office complex. Specifically, they were to install wiretaps on telephones belonging to Democratic national chairman Lawrence F. O'Brien and R. Spencer Oliver, O'Brien's deputy. James W. McCord, Jr., former FBI man and CIA security agent, was assigned by Hunt and Liddy to lead the wiretapping missions. The "bugs" were surreptitiously planted during the first of two break-ins at the Watergate on May 28, 1972. Four men from Miami worked under McCord.

The Cubans—the label the press gave the men for their anti-Castro sentiments—were Bernard L. Barker, Virgilio R. Gonzalez, Eugenio R. Martinez, and Frank A. Sturgis. The monitoring was done by Alfred Baldwin, III at a Howard Johnson's motel directly across Virginia Avenue from the Watergate, but the bug in O'Brien's phone malfunctioned. The White House Plumbers were ordered to return to the Watergate during the early morning hours of June 17 to replace the defective wiretap. Prior to the break-in, McCord had placed tape over locks on the doors leading to the Democrats' offices. This tape was removed twice by a night watchman, who alerted police when the tape was noticed a third time. According to Hunt, McCord's carelessness blew the operation. "The last man in was supposed to remove the tape, and that was McCord," Hunt said later. All five burglars were arrested at the Watergate. Hunt and Liddy were picked up later, as was Baldwin, who became chief witness for the prosecution. The five burglars, Hunt, and Liddy were indicted on Sept. 15, 1972, and placed on trial before U.S. District Court judge John J. Sirica on Jan. 10, 1973.

Immediately following the bungled break-in, a massive cover up was enacted in an attempt to distance President Nixon from involvement with the political espionage. The actions of the Watergate burglars was described by White House press secretary Ronald L. Ziegler as a "third-rate burglary." Nixon, who was elected in November 1972 to a second term in a landslide victory despite rumors of his involvement, denied that anyone in his administration participated in the Watergate break-in. His denials were subsequently proven to be falsehoods by two enterprising reporters from the Washington *Post,* Bob Woodward and Carl Bernstein. The two journalists were supplied with sensitive information on an ongoing basis from a secret informant who came to be known in the media as "Deep Throat." The identity of this person was never revealed by either Woodward or Bernstein, but according to Samuel Dash, chief counsel for the Senate Watergate committee, he was probably an amalgam. "I don't believe there was a Deep Throat as such," Dash explained. "From what I know of the evidence the information couldn't have been uniquely known by one person."

White House counsel John Wesley Dean was appointed by Nixon to head a special investigation into allegations of possible administration involvement in the growing scandal. On June 23, 1972, Nixon apparently ordered the CIA, through Dean, to put an end to the FBI's investigation of White House involvement. Dean later refused to release a proposed fictitious report which denied a cover up, and eventually told federal investigators of White House participation in Watergate. However, in the months which preceded the Watergate burglars' trial, Nixon and his aides managed to stave off investigators.

The trial of the Watergate break-in conspirators lasted just under three weeks. Although it was apparent that people higher up at the White House were behind the break-in, no evidence or testimony shed much light on just who was involved. Their testimony gave the impression that the break-in was engineered by Liddy alone. Even Magruder—then deputy to former attorney general John Newton Mitchell, who had taken over as CREEP chairman—denied knowledge of the covert activities, though he himself had authorized payment to Liddy. Hunt, Barker, Martinez, Sturgis, and Gonzalez pleaded guilty on all counts. McCord and Liddy were convicted by a jury on Jan. 30, 1973.

On the day of sentencing, Mar. 23, 1973, Judge Sirica read aloud a letter from McCord in which he accused the Nixon White House of attempting to cover-up its role in the break-in. He went on to say that the burglars were pressured into entering guilty pleas and were ordered to remain silent about the matter during their testimony. McCord added that perjured testimony had been given, and that the burglary was not a CIA operation as some, even the Cubans, had been led to believe. (Barker and Martinez were both contract employees for the CIA during the botched Bay of Pigs Operation in 1961.) During the trial, McCord had been warned by Dean through John J. Caulfield to keep silent and avoid "fouling up the game plan." McCord was told to plead guilty like the others, accept a light prison sentence, and then receive presidential clemency. Caulfield told McCord that these directives came from "the very highest levels of the White House."

The sentences, except for Liddy's, handed down by Sirica were provisional and dependent upon the outcome of ongoing investigations by the Senate and a federal grand jury. Liddy was sentenced to serve from six years and eight months to twenty years in prison and fined $40,000. His sentence was reduced to eight years by President James Earl Carter on Apr. 12, 1977, and he was paroled later that year. The remaining defendants were given maximum sentences of thirty-five to forty years in prison. In November 1973, final sentences were imposed by Sirica. Hunt was given thirty months to eight years, and served thirty-one and one-half months. McCord received one to five years. Barker was sentenced to eighteen months to six years; and Gonzalez, Martinez, and Sturgis were each given terms of one to four years in prison. Of the last five, none served more than fourteen months.

After sentencing the burglars and before the grand jury investigating the Watergate break-in was reconvened, Magruder, who had earlier said the break-in was not approved by the committee, abruptly changed his story. He accused Mitchell, his superior at CREEP, and Dean of ordering him to commit perjury. There was then no doubt that the White House was implicated in the Watergate burglary.

To distance himself from the Watergate scandal, Nixon announced on Apr. 17, 1973, that he had ordered a new investigation to clear matters up. His press secretary, Ziegler, also noted that previous statements made by the White House concerning Watergate were "inoperative." On Apr. 30, Nixon said he took full responsibility for the actions of his subordinates, and announced at the same time the resignations of U.S. chief of staff H(arry). R(obbins). "Bob" Haldeman, presidential domestic advisor John D(aniel). Ehrlichman, Attorney General Richard G. Kleindienst, and Dean. The president assured the American public that he had no prior knowledge of the break-in, nor had he sanctioned campaign espionage against the Democrats or a coverup of the break-in.

The same day the resignations were announced, Secretary of Defense Elliot L. Richardson was appointed attorney general. His confirmation by the Senate hinged on the condition that Richardson appoint an independent special prosecutor to handle the Watergate investigation and any other executive branch indiscretions. Richardson selected Harvard law professor Archibald Cox to head the Watergate Special Prosecution Force, and he and Cox were sworn in together on May 25.

Meanwhile, the Senate Select Committee on Presidential Campaign Activities, established on Feb. 7, 1973, and chaired by North Carolina senator Sam J. Ervin, Jr., continued to press its investigation. The biggest break in the case, and the one which eventually led to Nixon's political demise, was provided by Dean, who began testifying before the Watergate committee on June 25, 1973. In five days of testimony, Dean explained how he, at Nixon's bidding, had handled the cover-up as early as Sept. 15, 1972, and that during a secret meeting on Mar. 21, 1973, when Dean warned Nixon of "a cancer on the presidency," the president apparently approved of paying the Watergate burglars to remain silent. He added that Ehrlichman had authorized White House special counsel Charles W. Colson to silence Hunt with a promise of executive clemency. Dean also revealed information concerning the burglary of Dr. Fielding's Beverly Hills office to discredit Ellsberg.

The American public, which watched the Senate investigation on television, continued to be shocked by Dean's revelations. On July 13, 1973, former presidential aide Alexander P. Butterfield revealed to the committee for the first time that most of Nixon's private conversations with his top advisors dating back to Spring 1971 had been secretly tape-recorded.

Special prosecutor Cox subpoenaed the tapes on July 26, after earlier requests to the White House failed. Citing executive privilege and national security, Nixon refused to hand over the tapes. Judge Sirica, who was presiding over the Watergate grand jury, intervened in the matter on Aug. 29 when he ordered the president to give him the tapes in order to determine whether they should be released to the grand jury. His decision was upheld in the U.S. Court of Appeals on Oct. 12. Nixon came back with a compromise measure. He offered to provide a summary of the tapes to be given to Sirica and the committee members.

The compromise became known as the "Stennis compromise," for Nixon chose John Stennis, Democratic senator from Mississippi, to verify that the tape transcripts were correct. Alexander Haig, Nixon's new chief of staff, met with Attorney General Richardson to convince Cox to accept the compromise. Cox accepted, but with the provision that the special prosecutor's office aid Stennis in his verification. Cox's proposal was ignored and Richardson could not convince him to accept the compromise. On Oct. 20, Haig ordered Richardson to fire Cox for his refusal of the Stennis compromise. Richardson resigned rather than break his promise to the Senate of non-interference. Deputy Attorney General William D. Ruckelshaus followed suit—though Ruckelshaus was fired before his resignation reached the White House—and the firing of Cox was left to Solicitor General Robert H. Bork, who became acting attorney general. Nixon abolished the office of special prosecutor as well.

The events of Oct. 20, 1973, became known as the "Saturday Night Massacre." Afterward Cox said, "whether we shall continue to be a government of laws and not of men is now for Congress and ultimately the American people to decide."

By firing the special prosecutor, Nixon had incensed the American people. Public opinion polls showed Nixon's approval rating at 27 percent, a new low for the man who less than a year before had won election by a landslide. On Oct. 23, in an attempt to silence his critics, Nixon notified Sirica that he would relinquish transcripts of the tapes as ordered. It was then noted, however, that only seven of the nine tapes existed. This revelation led the House Judiciary Committee to investigate whether Nixon had committed an impeachable offense. Facing congressional pressure, on Nov. 1, Nixon nominated Ohio senator William B. Saxbe to replace Richardson as attorney general. That same day, Acting Attorney General Bork stated that Leon Jaworski of Houston had accepted the post of special prosecutor and would have even greater power than Cox.

On Nov. 21, yet another glaring White House cover-up attempt was made public. Nixon's special counsel, J. Fred Buzhardt, informed the grand jury that the tape of June 20, 1972, in which Nixon discussed the Watergate break-in with Haldeman, contained an eighteen-minute, fifteen-second "gap." Prior to his statement before the grand jury, Buzhardt told Judge Sirica that "it doesn't appear from what we know at this point that it could have been accidental." The White House, however, claimed that the erasure was an accident caused by Nixon's secretary Rose Mary Woods, presidential aide Stephen Bull, or possibly the president himself. Knowledge of the tape's erased portion had been discovered Nov. 14 by the Senate committee, who, like the grand jury concluded that the erasure could not have been an accident.

The addition of the White House tapes as evidence before the Watergate cover-up grand jury greatly improved the prosecution's already unbeatable case. Prior to release of the tapes, four key figures in the cover-up had pleaded guilty. Frederick C. LaRue, a former aide to Mitchell who delivered "hush money" to Hunt, pleaded guilty to conspiracy to obstruct justice on June 28, 1973. LaRue was sentenced to one to three years in prison, but served only four-and-a-half months. That summer Magruder, who earlier admitted he committed perjury during the break-in trial, pleaded guilty on Aug. 16. Magruder was given a ten-month to four-year prison term. The day before the "Saturday Night Massacre," Oct. 19, 1973, Dean pleaded guilty to conspiracy to obstruct justice and defraud the U.S. Dean's lawyer, Charles Shaffer, noted that the former White House counsel was no longer afraid of becoming "the Watergate scapegoat." On Aug. 2, 1974, Dean was sentenced to serve from one to four years in prison. In Fall 1973, Krogh, the former aide in charge of the White House Plumbers, pleaded guilty to violating the civil rights of Ellsberg's psychiatrist, Dr. Fielding. Krogh was sentenced to two to six years in prison, of which all but six months was suspended. He served four and a half months.

On Feb. 25, 1974, Nixon's personal attorney, Herbert W. Kalmbach, pleaded guilty to illegally raising funds for Republican election campaigns. Kalmbach was fined $10,000 and sentenced to six to eighteen months in prison. In January 1975, Judge Sirica reduced the sentences of Kalmbach, Dean, and Magruder to time served. The same day Kalmbach pleaded, the grand jury, following Jaworski's recommendation, unanimously named Nixon as an unindicted co-conspirator in the Watergate cover-up trial.

At the end of the week, Mar. 1, 1974, the grand jury indicted Mitchell, Ehrlichman, Haldeman, Colson, Kenneth W. Parkinson, Gordon C. Strachan, and Robert C. Mardian. The first conviction in the Watergate cover-up case came on Apr. 5, when Nixon's former appointments secretary Dwight L. Chapin was found Guilty on charges of perjury. He was sentenced to ten to thirty months in prison, but served only six months. Colson agreed to plead guilty on May 31 to obstructing justice and was sentenced to one to three years, though he served just seven months in prison.

Colson's plea was made the same day the U.S. Supreme Court agreed to accept prosecutor Jaworski's demand for sixty-four additional White House tapes. On July 24, the Supreme Court justices voted eight to zero in favor of Jaworski's petition. The judgment was viewed as an express message to Nixon that he could no longer hide behind executive privilege. Chief Justice Warren Burger said, in reading the court's decision, that "neither the doctrine of separation of powers nor the need for confidentiality...can sustain an absolute, unqualified presidential privilege from judicial process under all circumstances...the legitimate needs of the judicial process may outweigh presidential privilege."

Earlier, Burger noted that Nixon had overstepped the bounds of the executive branch, citing a passage from *Marbury v. Madison*. "It is emphatically the province and the duty of the judicial department to say what the law is."

Not only was Nixon losing his legal battle with the Watergate grand jury and the judicial branch, but the legislative branch was also leveling accusations at the president. The Senate Select Committee had already been investigating Nixon's "dirty tricks" tactics since January 1973, when, on Oct. 23 and 24, 1973, the House Judiciary Committee began hearing evidence to support impeachment proceedings. On July 27, 1974, by a vote of twenty-seven to eleven, the committee approved the first article of impeachment. This first article accused Nixon of using his office in regard to the Watergate break-in "to delay, impede, and obstruct investigations of such unlawful entry...to cover up, conceal, and protect those responsible and conceal the existence and scope of other unlawful covert activities." Article two calling for the president's impeachment regarded Nixon's abuse of presidential powers for political purposes. Such abuse included the break-in at the office of Ellsberg's psychiatrist. The third article of impeachment dealt with Nixon's contempt of Congress in relation to his failure to abide by the committee's subpoenas. The last two articles were approved by votes of twenty-eight to ten and twenty-one to seventeen respectively. Two other articles of impeachment were rejected.

Following the House Judiciary Committee's vote for impeachment, Nixon's closest advisors—Haig, Buzhardt, and, James St. Clair—began to formulate the president's resignation, as it was apparent Nixon would soon be forced to face a trial before the Senate. The subpoena for the transcripts of the June 23, 1972, tape left St. Clair, Haig, and Buzhardt with little choice. On the tape, Nixon contradicts all previous statements in which he denied knowledge of the Watergate cover-up until Spring 1973; for in a discussion with Haldeman, the president tells his chief of staff to use the CIA to steer the FBI away from the White House staff during its investigation. On Aug. 5, 1974, Nixon released the transcripts of June 23. The insurmountable evidence involving Nixon in the cover-up, combined with the likelihood of impeachment—as twenty senators, at most, still supported the president—led Nixon on Aug. 8, to announce his resignation from office effective the following day. Gerald R. Ford, who was sworn in as vice president on Dec. 6, 1974, replacing Spiro T. Agnew, succeeded Nixon to the presidency. It marked the first time in U.S. history that the president had not been elected either as president or vice president. On Sept. 8, Ford granted Nixon "a full, free, and absolute pardon...for all offenses against the United States which he...committed, or may have committed." This decision, which was greatly criticized by the media and the American public, made it impossible to prosecute the former president for his apparent criminal activities.

The scandal came to an end on Jan. 1, 1975, when the Watergate cover-up trial jury returned its verdicts for the five remaining defendants. Parkinson, an attorney for CREEP, was acquitted, while Mardian, Ehrlichman, Haldeman, and Mitchell were found Guilty of conspiring to obstruct justice. The latter three were also found Guilty of obstruction of justice. Ehrlichman and Mitchell were convicted of committing perjury before the Watergate grand jury; and Haldeman and Mitchell were convicted of committing perjury before the Senate Select Committee. On Feb. 21, Judge Sirica sentenced Ehrlichman, Haldeman, and Mitchell to terms of thirty months to eight years in prison. He sentenced Mardian, an assistant attorney general under Mitchell, to ten months to three years in prison. On appeal, Mardian won a new trial and the charges against him were subsequently dropped, as were the charges against Strachan, a former aide to Ehrlichman whose case had earlier been severed from that of the last five defendants. Ehrlichman served only eighteen months before his release in April 1978. Haldeman also spent just eighteen months in prison, being released in December 1978. Mitchell was released on Jan. 19, 1979, after serving nineteen months of his sentence.

Others were also convicted in connection with Watergate. Attorney Donald H. Segretti, sometimes referred to as the "dirty trickster" for distributing illegal campaign literature, was found Guilty and sentenced to six months in prison. Segretti's accomplice, accountant George A. Hearing, was given a one-year term. Maurice H. Stans, who headed Nixon's campaign finances, was fined $5,000 for accepting illegal contributions and violating financial reporting requirements. Former Attorney General Kleindienst was given suspended sentences of thirty days in prison and a $100 fine for refusing to answer Senate Select Committee questions. Thomas V. Jones, Northrop Corporation chairman, and George M. Steinbrenner III, American Ship Building Company chairman, were fined for making illegal campaign contributions. Jones was fined $5,000 and Steinbrenner $15,000. See: **Agnew, Spiro; Mitchell, John Newton; Nixon, Richard Milhous.**

REF.: Barber, *The Presidential Character;* Ben-Veniste and Frampton, *Stonewall: The Legal Case Against the Watergate Conspirators;* Bernstein and Woodward, *All the President's Men;* ____ and ____, *The Final Days; CBA;* Dean, *Blind Ambition: The White House Years;* Demaris, *The Director;* Doyle, *Not Above the Law: The Battle of Watergate Prosecutors Cox and Jaworski;* Eisenstadt, Hoogenboom, and Trefousse, *Before Watergate;* Ervin, *The Whole Truth: The Watergate Conspiracy;* Fields, *High Crimes and Misdemeanors;* Gold, *The Watergate Tapes;* Horowitz, *The White House Transcripts;* Hunt, *Undercover;* Kornitzer, *The Real Nixon;* Mazo, *Richard Nixon: A Political and Personal Portrait;* Messick, *The Politics of Prosecution;* Nixon, *RN: The Memoirs of Richard Nixon;* ____, *Six Crises;* Powers, *Secrecy and Power;* Sirica, *To Set the Record Straight: The Break-in, the Tapes, the Conspirators, the Pardon;* Unger, *FBI;* Velie, *Desperate Bargain: Why Jimmy Hoffa Had to Die;* Wills, *Nixon Agonistes;* (FILM), *All the President's Men,* 1976; *Nasty Habits,* 1986.

Waterhouse, Lily, See: **Calvert, Mrs. Louie**.

Waterloo Road Mystery, See: **Grimwood, Eliza**.

Waters, Bridget, 1908- , U.S., mansl. Bridget Waters married her husband Frank, a 36-year-old U.S. serviceman she met in Ireland during WWII. Their marriage faltered after several months, and Frank Waters was transferred to France on Oct. 13, 1944. Before leaving Ireland, Waters wrote a letter to his mother explaining that he had tried to reconcile with his wife, but had been unsuccessful. By the time Waters returned to the U.S., in late 1945, his wife had a child, and in December 1945, he filed for divorce in Las Vegas. On Apr. 15, 1946, Bridget and her baby arrived in the U.S. and Waters rented a house for her. During a preliminary divorce hearing, the jury found in her favor and she was granted a maintenance of $100 per month. She next apparently tried to repair her marriage and she claimed that Waters had proposed to pay her $4,000 if she would give up the child and agree to a divorce. She said she refused. On Sept. 2, when Waters and his mother drove over the his wife's house to pick up the baby, Bridget shot and killed her husband with a borrowed gun. Her trial began in October 1946, and on Nov. 6, 1946, she was convicted of involuntary manslaughter. On Nov. 7, she received a one-to-five-year sentence.

REF.: *CBA;* Rice, *Forty-five Murderers.*

Waters, Tom, 1665-91, Brit., rob. Tom Waters was raised by an uncle who apprenticed him to a notary public at the Royal Exchange. Waters ran away from his employer and joined the Earl of Dover's troop of guards, but he quickly grew tired of service and took up highway robbery to support his extravagant habits. In one of his first exploits, Waters robbed an entire gang of gypsies. Seeing about twenty to thirty members of a tribe leaving a barn one morning near Bromley in Kent, Waters ordered them at gunpoint to deliver their valuables, threatening to shoot half a dozen if they did not. The gypsies begged for mercy, and wailed loudly. Waters robbed them of about £60 in silver spoons, mugs, and gold rings, probably stolen from others. The gypsies' commotion brought several farmers wielding clubs and pitchforks to investigate. Waters explained that the gypsies had picked his pocket when they told his fortune, and that he had only retrieved his property. The farmers commended Waters, and he rode off with his haul.

On his way to London, Waters met a stable groom who had once betrayed him in an inn in Yorkshire. When the highwayman robbed him of about £40, the groom complained that he was ruined. Waters replied, "Where was your tender heart when you once went to betray me to be hanged?" He shot the groom's horse from under him and rode away. Waters also bantered with Sir Ralph Deavall, a distinguished vice admiral in the navy, about nautical terms before robbing him of about ninety guineas and a gold watch. Later that day, Waters met on the road a famous hermaphrodite dressed in women's clothes who begged the thief to "not so much unman himself as to rob a single woman." Waters countered that he could not lose face in the situation because "thou'rt both man and woman," and, "I rob two persons in taking your money."

Waters was apprehended and sent to Newgate for robbing John Hosey of £1,000 in money and silver on Hounslow Heath. He was condemned for that crime and executed at Tyburn on July 17, 1691, at twenty-six years of age.

REF.: *CBA;* Smith, *Highwaymen.*

Watkins, Jesse, 1903- , U.S., mur. On Aug. 21, 1927, at the Presidio Army Base in San Francisco, Henry Chambers was bludgeoned to death. Jesse Watkins, a stable hand who had just been fired, had vowed revenge on Chambers, according to a soldier who overheard an argument between the two men.

That night, Chambers, awakened by Watkins breaking into his quarters, fired several shots at the intruder. Watkins, took a bullet in his cheek, but pistol-whipped Chambers to death, took some valuables, and returned home. He cleaned himself of bloodstains and washed his bloody shirt. Later his roommate, believing that Watkins had been attacked by robbers, removed the bullet from his cheek.

Watkins was arrested and charged with murder. Criminologist Edward O. Heinrich proved that the bullet that wounded Watkins had been fired from Chamber's gun, that ultraviolet rays detected specks of Chambers' blood on Watkins' shirt, and that a bloody heel print at the murder scene was made by Watkins' boot. Watkins, tried and found Guilty, was sentenced to life imprisonment.

REF.: Block, *Science vs. Crime;* ____, *The Wizard of Berkeley; CBA;* Cooper, *Ten Thousand Public Enemies;* Nash, *Bloodletters and Badmen.*

An old print depicts Oliver Watkins strangling his wife.

Watkins, Oliver, d.1831, U.S., mur. Oliver Watkins of Sterling, Conn., murdered his wife so that he could marry widow Waity Burgess. Even Burgess' father threw her and her five children out when her behavior with the men of the town became intolerable.

During March 1829, Waity wandered the streets, uttering predictions of impending death. On Mar. 21, after his wife Roxana was asleep, Watkins strangled her with a whip. Because she appeared to have been strangled by her own necklace, her death was called accidental by the coroner's jury. But the state's attorney disagreed and arrested Watkins. He was tried and found Guilty and was executed on Aug. 2, 1831.

REF.: *CBA;* Dempewolff, *Famous Old New England Murders;* Nash, *Murder, America.*

Watkins, Thomas, 1705-64, Brit., rob.-mur. On Feb. 4, 1764, a robber broke into the house of the elderly Hammersley sisters, and stole their purses from under their pillows without waking them. The two awoke only when they heard sounds of a struggle. They called for their maid but got no answer. They found the woman brutally murdered, a handkerchief stuffed in her mouth, a rope around her neck, and her body tied to the bedstead with her head forced between her legs. When a reward of £50 was offered for the arrest and conviction of the murderer, Thomas Watkins, a gardener, was brought in on suspicion and taken to Reading Jail. At his trial, which lasted eight hours, he adamantly maintained his innocence and, although all of the evidence against him was circumstantial, he was found Guilty of the robbery and murder and sentenced to be hanged.

On his way from Reading to the execution place at Windsor, Watkins told a spectator, "I had no design to do it, but she refused to be familiar with me." He then explained in detail how he had choked the woman for refusing his advances and then raped her after she was dead. On Mar. 7, 1764, Watkins was hanged at the age of fifty-nine. His body was then displayed in chains.

REF.: *CBA;* Mitchell, *The Newgate Calendar.*

Watrous, John Charles, 1801-74, U.S., atty. gen.-jur. Attorney general for Republic of Texas from 1836-39. He was nominated to the Texas District Court by President James Polk in 1846. REF.: *CBA.*

Watson, Caroline Victoria (Carrie), b.1850, U.S., pros. Caroline Victoria "Carrie" Watson came to Chicago in 1866 as a teenager to learn the brothel trade, apprenticing at the notorious Mansion run by Lou Harper. She went into business for herself in 1868, at the age of eighteen, by assuming the lease of a brothel at 441 S. Clark Street when the previous madam, Annie Stewart, killed a policeman and had to leave town. Watson later bought the property with the help of saloonkeeper Al Smith.

Watson brought in new decor, including expensive paintings and tapestries, plush rugs, and damask upholstered furniture. The three-story mansion featured five parlors, a score of bedrooms, and a billiard room. Champagne was poured from silver buckets into golden goblets while a three-piece orchestra serenaded the waiting customers. The women, all newly hired by Watson herself, numbered twenty to thirty, numbers that doubled during the World's Fair. Business was conducted discreetly—Watson hung no red lights or red curtains, and soliciting from windows was strictly forbidden. The brothel's only advertisement was a parrot kept out front that said, "Carrie Watson. Come in, gentlemen."

The brothel remained open for a quarter century, during which time Watson became renowned for showing off her expensive clothes and her diamonds. She traveled the Levee in a white carriage pulled by black horses. She also contributed heavily to charity, particularly the two houses of worship in the neighborhood. The Catholic church across the street from her establishment benefitted greatly from her generosity, and she was rumored to pay the entire rent for the Jewish synagogue nearby. See: **Custom House Place; Everleigh Sisters.**

REF.: *CBA;* Dedmon, *Fabulous Chicago;* Lindberg, *Chicago Ragtime: Another Look At Chicago 1880-1920;* Nash, *People To See.*

Watson, Clarence Edward, Jr., 1934- , U.S., rape-mur. Washington, D.C., police had questioned hundreds of suspects in their efforts to solve the July 4, 1953, murder of National Science Foundation secretary Alyce O. Taggart in her all women's residence hotel. Believing that the killer was familiar with the 21st and O Street NW neighborhood, police suspected Clarence Edward Watson, Jr., nineteen. Watson had been arrested on Jan. 9, 1953, when two neighborhood women returned to their car and found him lying in the back seat with a knife. An off-duty policeman heard screams and arrested Watson who was fingerprinted and fined $25. Also, an airline hostess who had been raped and robbed in the same area on May 1, 1953, gave a description of her assailant that applied to Watson. Police arrested Watson in his rented room eight blocks from where Taggart was murdered. According to Deputy Police Chief Edgar E. Scott, Watson, when apprehended, said, "If you are arresting me for the murder on O Street on July 6, I took a trip."

Police questioned Watson for eight hours. He admitted raping the airline hostess, robbing an elderly woman of $75, gagging and robbing another woman in her house, and killing and raping Taggart. Watson said he had been watching the Fourth of July fireworks at the Washington Monument when he decided to break into the residence hotel, entering through the rear door. Finding

Taggart's door open, and the woman asleep, he ransacked her dresser, then, as she began to stir, took a souvenir duckpin from her dresser and hit her with it five times. When she fell to the floor, Watson raped her. In his re-enactment of the crime at the hotel, Watson referred to an overstuffed chair which was no longer in the room, and to positions of the dresser and bed which had been changed since the night of the crime. In a police line-up, two residents of the hotel said Watson resembled the man they saw on the night of the murder, but they could not identify him positively. Police also took Watson to the home of the airline stewardess, where he re-enacted the robbery and rape.

His employer at the Pentagon Shoe Repair Shop, William J. Thomas, said Watson was absent from work between July 6 and 13. Watson was charged before Municipal Judge George D. Neilson with felonious murder and the rape of the airline hostess. Court-appointed attorney Thomas A. Wadden asked for a continuance on the murder case, and said his client would plead not guilty to the rape charge. Watson was convicted of raping the stewardess and sentenced to forty years in prison. He was also convicted of the murder of Alyce Taggart, but the D.C. Court of Appeals overturned the conviction, invalidating his confession because police questioned him for too long after his arrest without his lawyer present. The district government declined to retry Watson for the murder, and he was paroled from his sentence for the rape charge on Sept. 13, 1971.

REF.: *CBA;* Seagle, *Acquitted of Murder.*

Watson, Edward Minor, 1874-1938, U.S., jur. Nominated to supreme court of territory of Hawaii by President Woodrow Wilson in 1914. He was also twice nominated to the first circuit court of Hawaii, initially by President Calvin Coolidge in 1928 and then by President Franklin D. Roosevelt in 1933. Roosevelt later nominated him to the district court of Hawaii, in 1935. REF.: *CBA.*

Watson, Ella See: **Averill, James.**

Watson, Jack, d.1890, U.S., west. gunman-lawman. Shot in the instep while fighting in the Confederate army, Jack Watson suffered a pronounced limp throughout the remainder of his life following the Civil War. He worked as a cowboy for years, enlisted for a brief time with the Texas Rangers, and frequently was hired by Texas ranchers to track down rustlers. On one occasion in 1880 some cattlemen hired him to capture a horsethief. Watson followed the outlaw for nearly a week before overtaking him one morning as he was cooking breakfast over an open fire. Watson killed the rustler and ate the dead man's breakfast.

Four years later, on Feb. 7, 1884, the local marshal of Montrose, Colo., arrested Watson for drunkenness and a judge fined him all the money he possessed, $85. Watson was furious. When he mounted his horse he began searching for the marshal and judge. When he found them, he opened fire, hitting and wounding the lawman in the arm and the judge in the side. Then he exchanged fire with some citizens and rode out of town. A price of $600 was placed on his head. Watson later was arrested by Sheriff C.W. Shores of Gunnison County, a one-time fellow cowboy of the fugitive, for knifing a man at Crystal mining camp. After Watson won acquittal of the charge, Shore offered him a position as deputy sheriff. Watson accepted and served faithfully as a lawman until his assassination in 1890. Watson had been working undercover in Price, Utah, and had made many local enemies. These men hired a gunman named Ward to kill Watson. One evening as Watson stumbled drunk out of a saloon in Price, Ward shot him from behind a hay wagon. He then was killed with Ward's second volley as he crawled back into the saloon to retrieve his gun.

REF.: *CBA;* Rockwell, *Memoirs of a Lawman.*

Watson, Dr. **James** (AKA: **John Watson, Thomas Watson**), d.1838, and **Thistlewood, Arthur**, 1770-1820, Case of, Brit., treas. Following Napoleon's defeat at Waterloo, British citizens faced unemployment and a depressed economy. Reformers Dr. James Watson and Arthur Thistlewood called for revolutionary measures. In November 1816, Watson organized a demonstration in support of social reform. On Dec. 2, 1816, Watson delivered a fiery speech at London's Spafields, an open field, that led the agitated crowd to riot. They looted shops and destroyed property until soldiers quieted the mob. Thistlewood, Watson, and Watson's son fled to Northampton, where Watson was arrested. During the arrest, he stabbed one of the officers with a cane sword, so in January 1817, he was indicted at the Old Bailey on charges of cutting and maiming, but he was found Not Guilty. In June 1817, both Thistlewood and Watson were tried for treason. Both were acquitted. See: **Spafields Riot**. REF.: *CBA.*

Watson, James P. (AKA: **Joseph Gillam, Laurence Harris**), c.1879-1939, U.S., big.-mur. James P. Watson, a traveling salesman, admitted to marrying twenty-five women for money and murdering many of them. Watson, a native of Eureka Springs, Ark., was first married to a 16-year-old girl in about 1896 when he was seventeen. After their divorce, Watson traveled throughout the nation, placing personal advertisements in newspapers, and after marriage, he persuaded his new wife to make him the beneficiary in her will.

He explained his long absences from home by saying that he worked for the U.S. Secret Service. At one time, he was married to four Tacoma, Wash., women, and another time he fled to Canada after he was charged with mail fraud. His final wife, Katharine Wombacker, began to doubt her husband's honesty when he transferred her Liberty Bonds into his name. She hired a private detective and police soon arrested Watson.

After his arrest, Watson led police to the grave of Nina Lee Deloney, whose body he had buried near El Centro, Calif., and he confessed to murdering sixteen wives, among them, Elizabeth Prior, whom Watson said he hit with a hammer near Spokane, Wash. Watson was tried for the Deloney murder, and in 1920 was sentenced to life in San Quentin.

In 1930, still in prison, he apparently convinced Wycliffe A. Hill, a Hollywood script writer, that most of the money stolen from his dead wives was secretly buried. Hill searched for five years and later sued the prisoner, although he received no compensation. Watson, about sixty years old, died in 1939, and left a letter directing the warden to a safe hidden in his cell. The safe, however, contained nothing of value.

REF.: *CBA;* Holmes, *Serial Murder;* Rice, *Forty-five Murderers.*

Watson, John Selby, 1804-84, Brit., mur. The Reverend John Selby Watson was educated in Ireland, where he met his wife to be, Anne Armstrong. But they were unable to marry for twenty years because Watson had no money and very little income.

He finally obtained a post as headmaster that paid him enough to support a family. He married Armstrong, continued teaching, and wrote many scholarly works. However, he was treated unkindly by the school owners and was discharged without a pension at age sixty-four. Watson became depressed and on Oct. 8, 1871, killed his wife and attempted suicide. Unfortunately for him, he recovered, only to be tried at the Old Bailey on Jan. 10, 1872, and found Guilty. Watson spent the rest of his life in prison, where he died in 1884.

REF.: Altick, *Victorian Studies in Scarlet; CBA;* Gribble, *The Deadly Professionals;* Gross, *Masterpieces of Murder;* Lambert, *When Justice Faltered;* Pearce, *Unsolved Murder Mysteries;* Pearson, *Instigation of the Devil;* Wilson, *Encyclopedia of Murder;* Wyndham, *Famous Trials Retold.*

Watson, Lionel Rupert Nathan, c.1910-41, Brit., big.-mur. Lionel Rupert Nathan Watson committed bigamy when he married his second wife, Phyllis Elizabeth Crocker, and later fathered a daughter with the woman. On May 19, 1941, Watson poisoned Phyllis and their 18-month-old daughter, Eileen Alice, with prussic acid. He buried their bodies in the garden in back of their home in Greenford, Middlesex. On May 26, 1941, his digging was noticed and reported to police. In June, the bodies were exhumed and in September, Watson was tried at the Old Bailey where he claimed that he had found his wife and child dead, but was afraid to call for help because he had bigamously married the woman. Watson was convicted, and he was hanged at Pentonville prison on Nov. 12, 1941.

REF.: Browne and Tullett, *The Scalpel of Scotland Yard;* Butler, *Murderers' England; CBA;* Shew, *A Companion to Murder.*

Watson, Robert J., d.1932, and **Afong, Abram Henry, Jr.** (AKA: **Harold Harvey**), prom. 1928, U.S., mansl. Two soldiers stationed at Fort Moultrie on Sullivan's Island, S.C., met with Ham Fetter on Oct. 28, 1928, to pick up a load of green corn whiskey. Fetter, Private Robert J. Watson, and Corporal Harold Harvey stashed the bootleg liquor on the Isle of Palms, S.C., near a sand dune. The alcohol began disappearing; Harvey and Fetter accused Watson of taking it with him on his two leaves of absence, but Watson claimed innocence. On Dec. 26, 1928, Harvey and Watson went to a party at Fetter's, both armed with pistols, and the three left to check on their cache and to possibly catch the thief. Watson later said that all of the whiskey was missing and Fetter started accusing him of taking the alcohol and threatening to kill him. Watson claimed that Fetter shot at him and as Fetter was still advancing, Watson fired back. Watson said that Harvey joined him then and Watson took Harvey's gun and then shot at Fetter again. Fetter's body, shot in the leg, left side, and head, was hidden beneath underbrush. Afterward, Harvey returned to the Fetter party and Watson turned himself in to the military guard house.

The trial began on June 6, 1929, with the prosecution maintaining that Harvey, whose real name was Abram Henry Afong, Jr., had loaded the two guns at Fetter's party, and that he had used Watson as a tool to kill the unarmed Fetter. The jury acquitted Harvey, but Watson was convicted on a charge of manslaughter. Watson was sentenced to ten years in prison with hard labor. He was later granted a leave of absence that was extended when he apparently tried to poison himself with bichloride mercury twice. On Oct. 12, 1931, Watson's sentence was suspended by the governor for good behavior. He later was rearrested for trespassing and received a suspended sentence. On Jan. 30, 1932, he was found dead in a Jacksonville boarding house after apparently shooting himself. After Watson's murder trial, Harvey was court-martialed on charges of theft, desertion, carrying concealed weapons, false enlistment, and leaving his post without correct relief. Harvey was found Guilty of four charges and sentenced to six years and three months in prison. The sentence was later commuted to fifteen months' imprisonment, and after serving ten months of his term, he was released in June 1930.

REF.: *CBA;* Rodell, *Charleston Murders.*

Watson, William, c.1559-1603, Brit., consp.-treas. Became Roman Catholic priest in France in 1586, and worked in Britain as missionary from 1586-1603. He opposed the Jesuits and was put in prison and tortured several times. Jesuits exposed his failed plan to kidnap James I and coerce him into allowing toleration of Catholicism. As a result he was executed for treason. REF.: *CBA.*

Watt, Hugh, d.1921, Brit., consp. A member of Parliament, Hugh Watt also built a substantial shipping business, but frittered away his wealth in unsuccessful investments. Near bankruptcy, Watt decided to murder his wife to gain her marriage settlement of approximately £60,000. He offered to pay two hoodlums £20 each to kill his wife; when they hesitated, he gave them ten sovereigns. Realizing that the men might blackmail him in the future, Watt consulted a private detective, a former agent of Scotland Yard. However, Watt did not think the detective was handling the matter quickly enough, and one day he went into the investigator's office where he was meeting with a Scotland Yard chief inspector. Watt launched into a tirade and also told about how he had hired men to kill his wife. Unable to ignore the confession, the Scotland Yard official had Watt arrested. During his trial, the defendant entered a plea of insanity, but the jury convicted him and sentenced him to five years' imprisonment.

REF.: *CBA;* Kingston, *A Gallery of Rogues.*

Watt, Miriam, c.1949- , U.S., mur. On Jan. 5, 1987, Sandra Ferguson entered a hospital to give birth and left her children, Andrea and Jasmine, with their paternal grandmother, Miriam Watt in Harvey, Ill. On May 3, 1987, 2-year-old Jasmine Ferguson was taken from her grandmother, suffering from head injuries and a large burn and peeling skin on her buttocks caused from immersion in scalding water. The grandmother claimed she thought Jasmine had severe diaper rash and had not taken the child to a doctor because she could not locate a "green card," a state card authorizing the holder to receive free medical care. Two days later, Jasmine was declared brain dead. Her grandmother went on trial for murder in late 1988. On Dec. 15, 1988, Watt was found Guilty of murder and on Jan. 9, 1989, she was sentenced to life in prison with no possibility of parole. REF.: *CBA.*

Watt, Newton, d.1889, U.S., rob.-mur. In Chicago, on Mar. 12, 1886, a messenger for United States Express Company, Kellogg Nichols got on board the Rock Island Express train headed for Davenport, Iowa carrying a satchel containing over $22,000. Somewhere between Joliet and Morris, Ill., a train employee, Newton Watt, who had been recruited at the last minute to fill in as baggagemaster, gave the alarm that someone had held him at gunpoint and robbed the train's safe. Members of the train's crew entered the mail car where Nichols had been riding and where the safe was located. The safe had indeed been broken into and Nichols was found dead, shot through the shoulder with a small caliber gun and then brutally beaten on the head with a fire poker that the killer had then fastidiously returned to its hook on the wall.

Because of the gravity of the crime, the Pinkerton Agency was called in to investigate. William Pinkerton, son of the Agency's founder, personally took the case on. The baggagemaster, Newton Watt and the train's brakeman, Fred Schwartz soon came under suspicion. The only evidence that Pinkerton was able to uncover, however, was highly circumstantial: Nichols had bits of skin under his fingernails indicating that he had scratched his murderer and Schwartz had deep scratches on the backs of his hands a few days after the crime. Both Watt and Schwartz were reported as spending money freely soon after the murder. Pinkerton was unable to get anything concrete on either of the two men until Schwartz met and married a young woman by the name of Ella Washam. Pinkerton who had come to know a great deal about Schwartz, knew that Schwartz had failed to obtain a divorce from his previous wife. Pinkerton immediately had Schwartz arrested on a charge of bigamy. Once Schwartz was in jail, his wife confided in Pinkerton that Schwartz had "found" a large sum of money on the train. When confronted, Schwartz said that he had found an envelope containing $5,000 under a seat on the train. Both Watt and Schwartz were brought to trial on charges of robbery and murder. They were found Guilty and sentenced to life in prison. Watt died in prison in March 1889. Nine years later, Schwartz's sentence was reduced to twenty years and then further shortened for "exemplary conduct," permitting him to leave prison a free man in 1898.

REF.: *CBA;* Rodell, *Chicago Murders.*

Watts, Coral Eugene, 1953- , U.S., burg.-mur. Coral Eugene Watts, who killed an estimated forty women, felt that all women were deceitful and unfaithful. In 1974, Watts attended Western Michigan University in Kalamazoo, Mich. There, he attempted to strangle a woman but was arrested before he killed her, a "mistake" he did not make again for eight years. Watts was jailed for a few days before the court released him on bond. Six days following the attempt on the woman's life, Watts stalked Gloria Steele, a student at the university. She was found the next morning in her apartment, stabbed thirty-three times, with many jagged incisions made after her death. The police suspected Watts but could not link him to the crime. He was convicted of assault for the earlier attack and sentenced to one year in prison. Upon his release in 1975, he moved to Ann Arbor, Mich.

Watts eventually became a bus mechanic, working during the week and traveling on weekends. During this time, several young women were attacked and killed in Ann Arbor, the victims of multiple stabbings. Many of the bodies were severely mutilated—several with jagged postmortem wounds. Police suspected

Watts as the so-called "Sunday Morning Slasher." At that time, Watts was also allegedly killing women in Detroit and Windsor, Canada, as well. Not all of his associations with women were violent and fatal, however. In 1980, he married, but his wife found him peculiar and left him within two months. He had a relationship with another woman who gave birth to his child.

In 1981, Watts lost his bus mechanic job and moved to Houston, Texas. There he worked regularly and attended a local Pentecostal church. The Ann Arbor police sent Houston law enforcement officials their suspicions of Watts, and Houston police placed surveillance on him over the weekends for about sixty days. Not finding anything peculiar about his behavior, they discontinued the survey.

Mass murderer Coral Eugene Watts.

In January 1982, two women were killed. Phyllis Tam, a 27-year-old advertising art director was hanged with her own clothes in a secluded area near Rice University where she jogged every morning. Two weeks later, police found the body of an architecture student stuffed in the trunk of her car. On Jan. 18, student Margaret Fossi had been sideswiped on the road while driving. When she stopped, Watts had pulled her from her car and beaten her to death. In each of the attacks, Watts left no physical evidence and made sure his victims were dead.

On May 23, Watts attacked 20-year-old Lori Ann Lister in her apartment. He twisted a coat hanger around her wrists and throttled her before attempting to drown her in the bathtub. A neighbor called police after rescuing her from the bathtub. Police arrested Watts and charged him with attempted murder, aggravated kidnapping, and burglary. The mass murderer arranged a plea bargain in which he would give the police information on several murders and, in exchange, he would be charged with merely first-degree burglary. In the ensuing months, he took police to the burial sites of many of his victims. He cleared up twenty-two killings in three states and two countries. After reinvestigating other unsolved murders, police concluded that Watts murdered at least forty women. When asked why he killed so many women, Watts replied that women were evil.

The district attorney could not definitely link Watts to any of the murders and proceeded with the plea-bargained charge of first-degree burglary. Facing a sixty-year prison sentence, Judge Doug Shaver sentenced him to the maximum sentence, sixty years in prison. Because the judge ruled that the water-filled bathtub was a deadly weapon, Watts must serve at least twenty years of his sentence before he can become eligible for parole. Shaver asked that the Texas Department of Corrections and the state legislature make sure he completed the entire sentence without a chance for parole. At the sentencing on Sept. 3, 1982, Shaver said to Watts, "I hope you serve each and every minute of the sixty years."

REF.: Cartell, *Serial Mass Murder; CBA.*

Watts, John Sebrie, 1816-76, U.S., jur. Served as prosecuting attorney for county court of Monroe County, Ind., from 1839-43. He was also appointed to the territorial court of New Mexico by President Millard Fillmore in 1851 and by President Andrew Johnson in 1868. REF.: *CBA.*

Watts, Walter, c.1817-50, Brit., theft. Walter Watts was not satisfied with his £230 per year income as a clerk at the Globe Insurance Company. He began altering company accounts in 1844, first changing a £876 payment to the company to a £7 payment, then altering the company books, changing a £7 disbursement to £867. Watts pocketed £860. By the summer of 1844, Watts had bought two mansions and during the next six years, he poured money into two unsuccessful theaters and gambled away more money. By 1849, the first theater folded after losing £18,000, but he bought another house and in about 1849, Watts bought the second theater. His wealthy friends assumed that he was an international financier.

In 1850, Watts' sham was discovered and his employer confronted the 33-year-old, estimating the company's loss at £70,000. At his trial for theft, Watts maintained that because he owned a few shares in the company, which he had inherited from his father, he was one of the owners, and therefore could not steal what was his. He argued that if some of the stolen funds belonged to other shareholders, he would settle with them. The judge changed the charge to theft, stealing a piece of paper worth one penny, which was a check Watts had made out for £1,600. Watts was convicted, but the judge waited to sentence the swindler until a court of appeals ruled that Watts, as a shareholder of a firm, could be convicted of stealing from the same business. On July 12, 1850, the judge sentenced Watts to ten years in prison. Placed in an infirmary, Watts hanged himself later that night.

Walter Watts in the prison cell where he later hanged himself.

REF.: *CBA;* Ellis, *Black Fame;* Kingston, *Dramatic Days at the Old Bailey.*

Watts, William (AKA: **John Ramsey**), and **Lustig, Victor**, prom. 1935, U.S., count. In 1934, a major counterfeiting ring began flooding the U.S. with high quality bogus hundred-dollar bills—up to $250,000 a month. The Secret Service got its first break in the case when it was determined that the new bills resembled those made by William Watts a known counterfeiter. They knew little about Watts or his whereabouts, but they did have the name of one of his known criminal contacts—Victor Lustig.

Lustig, a known con man, was tracked down through Hanna Smith, operator of a call-girl operation in New York. The police staked out Smith's place of business, until Lustig appeared. Lustig eventually admitted knowing Watts and offered his help. He claimed he could get the plates, but denied knowing Watts' whereabouts. Lustig did turn over some plates and some bogus money to the Secret Service, but they were not the plates producing the high-quality counterfeit currency. Lustig was charged with conspiracy and possession of counterfeit plates and money.

Lustig managed to escape from the federal detention center where he was being held but was soon captured. An exhaustive search finally led the authorities to Watts' apartment in Union City, where they found the set of near-perfect plates and a quantity of the $100 bills.

Watts and Lustig were partners; Watts manufactured and Lustig distributed them. On Dec. 5, 1935, the pair went to trial and were found Guilty. Together they had distributed over $1.3 million in counterfeit bills. See: **Lustig, Victor.**

REF.: *CBA;* Humphreys, *Criminal Days.*

Watts Race Riots, 1965, U.S., riot. In August 1965 the southeast Los Angeles neighborhood of Watts exploded in racial violence. Thirty-four people died and 1,032 were injured in the six days of rioting which caused an estimated $46 million in damages to 744 buildings in the predominantly black section of the city. Two alleged incidents of police brutality on that day sparked the initial outburst. Witnesses said police used excessive force while arresting a black man who was driving while drunk, and that police had clubbed a pregnant black woman. Relationships between the police and the citizens of Watts grew increasingly tense, with blacks calling all police officers prejudiced. Chief of Police William Parker refrained from sending in riot squads when the trouble first broke out, yet he saw the riots worsen.

They began on Aug. 12, with fifty to seventy-five black youths throwing stones at automobiles, police cars, and white passersby. Police sent to the area were nothing but a menacing presence, neither firing their weapons nor making arrests. The stone-throwing crowd dispersed upon the arrival of the police, but returned when they withdrew. They broke windows in buildings, threw bricks, and burned automobiles. Groups of black youths took control of the rioting, citing as their enemy "The Man." The following evening, rioters burned and looted white-owned stores. As buildings were set on fire, the police refused the fire department entry into the area for the safety of the firefighters. Violence escalated until riot police and the National Guard were called in. Up to that point there were no fatalities. But when 14,000 guards invaded Watts, rioters began to die. The soldiers gunned down a black woman charging at a National Guard blockade, and shot dead an 18-year-old man caught looting. In all, more than 3,400 adults and 500 juveniles were arrested. Many of those arrested—more than 3,000—faced felony charges of arson, looting, armed burglary, and murder. The number of black rioters was estimated at between 7,000 to 10,000 persons.

In the 1960s, Watts experienced soaring unemployment and lack of federal, state, and city relief. Thirty-four percent of Los Angeles' black youth and thirty percent of its black men were jobless. Los Angles mayor Sam Yorty received blame for ignoring the legitimate needs of the black residents of the city. Such examples as the lack of representation of "the poor" on the city's anti-poverty board, along with the U.S. government's well-publicized withholding of $20 million in aid which would have helped create job opportunities for blacks, were pointed to as probable incitements of the rioting. The riot's youth leaders spoke of their enemy as "The Man," a term which could refer to the white cop, the shopkeeper, the successful and assimilated black, the politician—anyone symbolizing the deprivation of blacks. One woman who participated in the riots claimed, "This wasn't no race riot. It was a riot between the unemployed and the employed. We are tired of being shelved and told we don't want to work."

Civil rights leaders gave varying responses to the riots. Dr. Martin Luther King, Jr. called the riot a "lashing out" and a "temper tantrum" of poor people at the edge of despair. Baynard Rustin said of the youths who became riot leaders, "They have rejected their elders. These elders are not people of achievement. Their fathers are out of work. Their mothers are on relief. And the established civil rights leadership is out of touch with them... They can't look to their fathers and they can't look to us." In 1980 Ted Watkins, a resident of the community for thirty-five years, told a reporter, "It's a worse hovel now than it was in 1965—drugs, crime, too much alcohol, anything you can name. Children born here don't have a chance."

REF.: *CBA;* Hofstader and Wallace, *American Violence: A Documentary History;* Watters and Gillers, *Investigating the FBI.*

Watzl, Ernest (AKA: **Johann Flassak**), d.1930, Aust., fraud-suic. On Mar. 24, 1930, a double suicide occurred in a hotel in Vienna, Aust., ending a worldwide search for a pair of tragic lovers. Dr. Ernest Watzl, a world-renowned chemist and his secretary/lover, Mary Horvath MacGranahan, killed themselves rather than face their families.

Watzl, brilliant chemist and successful businessman, had left his wife and family in Cleveland, Ohio, faked a suicide, and had run away with his beautiful secretary. After traveling around the world, they ended up in his birthplace, Vienna. Unable to pay insurance premiums on a policy to support his wife and children, Watzl and MacGranahan decided to commit suicide.

REF.: *CBA;* Nash, *Among the Missing.*

Waxworks (alternate title, *The Three Waxworks*), 1924, German silent film directed by Paul Leni that featured Werner Krauss as Jack the Ripper (Brit., 1888). See: **Jack the Ripper**. REF.: *CBA.*

Waye, Alton, 1955-89, U.S., rape-mur. An army veteran and former textile worker, Alton Waye, attacked a woman in her Kenbridge, Va., home on Oct. 14, 1977. Waye raped and murdered 61-year-old Lavergne Marshall, stabbing her forty-two times. He placed her naked body in her bathtub and poured bleach over the corpse. After the attack, Waye returned to his home, about two miles from the Marshall house, and immediately confessed to his father. Then he confessed to police the same day and took police to the scene of the crime. Waye was convicted in 1978 and sentenced to death. The 34-year-old criminal was executed in the electric chair at the Virginia State Penitentiary at Richmond on Aug. 30, 1989. REF.: *CBA.*

Wayne, James Moore, 1790-1867, U.S., jur. James Moore Wayne served in various legislative positions before taking a seat on the U.S. Supreme Court. Wayne served in the Georgia House of Representatives from 1815 to 1816, and as mayor of Savannah, from 1817 to 1819. He then became judge of the Savannah Court of Common Pleas, 1820-22, then judge of the Georgia superior court, 1822-28, and later, a member of the U.S. House of Representatives, 1829-35. On Jan. 7, 1835, President Andrew Jackson nominated Wayne as an associate justice to the U.S. Supreme Court; he served on the court from 1835 until 1867. While on the Supreme Court, Wayne supported a consolidated country, keeping his seat with the court even when his state seceded from the Union. In several important cases, Wayne concurred with the majority, including *Scott v. Sanford,* 1857, (the Dred Scott case), and *Ex parte Milligan,* 1866, in which the court ruled that the president cannot refuse to protect the civil liberties of U.S. citizens who had never lived in a state that was trying to revolt and who were not serving in the military. He died at age seventy-seven from typhoid. REF.: *CBA.*

Weaker Sex, The, 1901, a novel by Frederick J. Stimson. The confusing manslaughter case of Frank Lewis, one of the true legal oddities in U.S. jurisprudence, in which one man was convicted of killing a man who killed himself, is the basis for this work of fiction. See: **Lewis, Frank.** REF.: *CBA.*

Weallans, Clifford Alexander, prom. 1949, Brit., arson. Clifford Weallans, a former British soldier who had served in Palestine said he "hated the Jews." In 1949, as a policeman in London, he had no other explanation when he set fire to a number of Jewish-owned shops in London's East End. Weallans was sentenced to five years in prison.

REF.: *CBA;* Nash, *Almanac of World Crime.*

Weare, Meshech, 1713-86, U.S., jur. Judge of New Hampshire Superior Court from 1747-75, chief justice from 1776-82. He was also the first president of New Hampshire, under the old constitution, from 1784-85. REF.: *CBA.*

Weart, James Brennan, Jr., 1935- , U.S., burg. In October 1960, commercial pilot James Weart decided to rob the People's National Bank of Washington, in Seattle, and began methodically digging a tunnel toward the bank, a new section each night. By the end of October, Weart had completed a shaft eighteen feet long. He began to dig upward, gaining access to the furnace room, which was next too the bank's vault. Then he asked a tool shop clerk how to drill through an eighteen inch concrete foundation. Later that night, he returned to the hardware store, and stole a power hammer and drills. Next, he bought some nitroglycerin, drilled holes in the bank's foundation, and set off the explosives. Bank employees began complaining about plaster dust, and after a search upstairs, they attributed the debris to a large paper cutter and jets flying over the building. On Feb. 17, Weart placed more nitroglycerin below the bank and detonated the explosive about 1:40 a.m., blowing open a hole in the middle of the vault without triggering any burglar alarms. At approximately midnight the next night, Weart returned to the bank, carrying away more than $45,000 and burying most of the money. Bank employees did not discover the theft until Feb. 20, and because of the elaborate preparation, police suspected professional burglars. Weart was caught as soon as he began spending the money, buying a station wagon for $1,000 cash, making house payments, and opening a savings account. Alert to all large cash transactions in the area, police matched serial numbers from bills that Weart used to pay for the car with those on the stolen money. Weart was arrested, tried, convicted, and sentenced to twenty years in prison. REF.: *CBA.*

Weatherall, Florence Jean, c.1927-51, Brit., (unsolv.) mur. Florence Jean Weatherall, a woman who had recently given birth to twins, disappeared on Feb. 2, 1951, after she left home to go shopping; her husband, Edward Christopher Weatherall, alerted police. Her partially nude body was found on Feb. 23, 1951. Florence, who had allegedly been promiscuous before her marriage, had been partially asphyxiated and strangled. Her corpse was then dumped in a ditch along an isolated country road about nine miles outside of Nottingham. During a police investigation, authorities were unable to locate her companion, but they theorized that she had been unintentionally killed. At a coroner's inquest, the jury ruled Florence had been found dead, rather than murdered or killed by manslaughter.
REF.: *CBA;* Harrison, *Criminal Calendar II.*

Weatherill, Miles, prom. 1868, Brit., mur. In 1868, a weaver fell in love with a servant girl in the village of Todmorden, located between Burnley and Halifax. When the girl's employer, Reverend Plow, learned of the romance, he sent the girl back home. The annoyed lover, Miles Weatherill, began disturbing Plow so much that the cleric hired a night guard. On the night of Mar. 2, 1868, Weatherill, armed with a gun and ax, began pounding on the rector's back door, and when Plow opened the door, the weaver shot at him once, missing, and then struck Plow with the ax. Next, Weatherill seized a servant girl, almost cutting off one hand before he shot her to death. Finally, Weatherill ran into Plow's bedroom where the clergyman's wife was sleeping and beat her to death with a poker. When the assailant was arrested, he commented, "I've done all I wanted to do. I'm only sorry the pistols didn't go off better." Weatherill was tried, convicted, and hanged by William Calcraft at New Bailey Prison in Salford before a crowd of 20,000 people.
REF.: Butler, *Murderer's England; CBA.*

Weather Underground Organization (AKA: **Weathermen**), prom. 1968-70s, U.S., rebel.-terr. A radical U.S. revolutionary group, the Weathermen was a splinter group of the Students for a Democratic Society (SDS) who broke with its parent group to avoid police infiltration. Taking its name from a line in a Bob Dylan song—"You don't need a weatherman to know which way the wind blows"—the Weathermen renamed the organization the Weather Underground, because fifteen of its thirty-seven members were women. The group was comprised mainly of college-educated white women and men, many of whose parents were wealthy or politically powerful. The Weathermen provided the leadership for several of the better known radical protests in the late 1960s and early 1970s such as the student occupation of five buildings at Columbia University in 1968 and the 1969 "Days of Rage" riot in Chicago, a four-day rampage involving several hundred radicals. The last known revolutionary activity of the Weather Underground was the bombing a New York bank in 1975. Its prominent members included Bernardine Dohrn, Mark Rudd, Jeff Jones, Bill Ayers, Jim Mellen, Terry Robbins, and John Jacobs.

The Weathermen set off more than 4,000 bombs in 1969 and 1970, with no loss of life except for members of its own ranks. The radical organization set the normally precise and well-timed bombings to detonate in the early morning hours and warned police so that no one would be killed in the explosions. In their Greenwich Village, N.Y., bomb factory, three Weathermen were accidentally killed. In seven years of terrorist activities, the group planted bombs in twenty-five "symbols of American imperialism" including the Pentagon and the Capitol building. They were continually forced to dodge the FBI, but were never caught. A booklet and magazine titled *Prairie Fire* was printed by the Weathermen promoting its ideology of revolution and freedom. Five members, Kathy Boudin, Dohrn, Cathy Wilkerson, Ayers, and Jones, appeared in the movie *Underground* by director Emile de Antonio.

According to later reports, the group used sex to fuse its membership into one mind. Monogamy among members was abolished and mass orgies were held which later included homosexual sex. Pleasure was not the purpose of the mixed couplings. Rather, sex was always bleak and coerced, necessarily so, according to the Weathermen, to level the bourgeouis conceit surrounding pleasure and power. Dohrn, however, remained aloof from the orgies. According to some members of the group, Dohrn used sex as the ultimate political tool, as a means of bringing people together in one mind and purpose.

It was Dohrn who broke up the Weathermen in January 1977 by issuing a manifesto accusing the other four Weather Underground leaders of sins against ideological purity. That year, several members turned themselves in. Mark Rudd, one of the most notorious of the Weather Underground, who in 1968 led the Columbia University student sit-in, surfaced in New York City in September. He appeared in a Manhattan and a Chicago court facing a total of eight misdemeanor charges including criminal trespassing, unlawful assembly, criminal solicitation, obstructing government administration, and jumping bail. He did not give interviews, refused to tell the court of his time underground, pleaded guilty, and was later given an unconditional discharge. Weather Underground members Phoebe Hirsch, thirty-one, and Robert Roth, twenty-seven, appeared around the same time and were given probation for their participation in the "Days of Rage." See: **Dohrn, Bernardine Rae.**

REF.: *CBA;* Clutterbuck, *Kidnap and Ransom;* Demaris, *The Director;* Godwin, *Murder, U.S.A.;* Sullivan, *The Bureau;* Tully, *Inside the FBI;* Watters and Gilllers, *Investigating the FBI.*

Weaver, Joseph, prom. 1920s, U.S., (wrong. convict.) mur. A night guard for Midland Steel Products Co., in Ohio, Jasper Russell, was murdered on Mar. 13, 1927, by Alex Maynor. After Maynor was arrested, he implicated Joseph Weaver and the two were put on trial in 1927. Maynor was convicted of manslaughter and received a life sentence. Weaver was convicted of murder and sentenced to die. For two years, Weaver's lawyers fought to keep him from going to the electric chair. After his conviction was upheld by an appeals court, authorities planned to execute Weaver in 1929. Days before the execution, Maynor came forward, withdrawing his accusation against Weaver. Three days later, the Ohio Supreme Court ordered a retrial, stating that inadmissible hearsay evidence had been presented at the first trial. During the retrial, on Apr. 5, 1929, Judge W.R. White, directed the jury to acquit Weaver on the grounds that the government had not proven Weaver's guilt at the first trial. Freed, Weaver left the Cuyahoga County jail, declining to shake Maynor's hand, saying, "Why should I shake his hand? He's luckier than I am...I should have been free these last two years. He lied me into prison and saved his own life in the bargain." REF.: *CBA.*

Webb, Alfred Charles Bertram, See: **Stewart, Frederick.**

Webb, Edwin Yates, b.1872, U.S., jur. U.S. congressman from 1903-19. He was a co-sponsor of the Webb-Kenyon Act in 1913, a law that outlawed interstate transportation of intoxicating liquor. REF.: *CBA.*

Webb, George W., prom. 1914, U.S. , kid.-rape. George Webb, a janitor at Public School No. 7 in the Bronx, had been drinking heavily on Aug. 7, 1914. He abducted 13-year-old Katherine Larkin, raped her, and placed her bound and gagged body in a small enclosed space beneath the boys' lavatory at the school. Police and dozens of her classmates and friends began a search as soon as it was determined that the girl was missing. Four days later, police decided to search the school and found the girl.

Katherine told her story of the abduction and rape and Webb was arrested. He insisted he was innocent, but the belt, necktie, and a handkerchief with which he had tied the girl were identified as his. He was the only person other than the school superintendent who had a key to the space in which Katherine had been confined. Webb was convicted of kidnapping and sentenced to forty years in Sing Sing.

REF.: *CBA;* Nash, *Among the Missing.*

Webb, John Joshua (AKA: **Samuel King**), 1847-82, U.S., west. lawman-gunman. Serving most of his adult life as a lawman, John Joshua Webb was a also a hunter, a teamster, surveyor, hired gun, and member of the notorious Dodge City Gang in Las Vegas, N.M. Born on Feb. 13, 1847, in Iowa, Webb traveled west in 1871, becoming a buffalo hunter and then a surveyor in Colorado. He drifted from Deadwood to Cheyenne, Wyo., to Dodge City, Kan. He found work as a lawman in Dodge City in the late 1870s, and later became a deputy sheriff of Ford County. When the Santa Fe and the Denver & Rio Grande railroad disputed over the right-of-way through the Grand Canyon of the Arkansas River, Webb hired out his gun to smooth the struggle. He also became close friends with Dave Rudabaugh, a train robber he arrested in 1878.

In 1880, Webb accepted the position of city marshal of Las Vegas, N.M. While marshal, he joined the Dodge City Gang led by Justice of the Peace Hyman Neill, known as "Hoodoo Brown." On Mar. 2, 1880, Webb shot and killed Michael Kelliher after a fight. Regardless of his status as a marshal, Webb was convicted of murder and sentenced to hang. Rudabaugh attempted and failed to break him out of jail on Apr. 30. Webb's sentence was appealed and commuted to life in prison. Rudabaugh landed in prison with Webb, and, along with two other prisoners, they attempted to escaped on Sept. 19, 1881, and one of their party, Thomas Duffy was killed. Then on Dec. 3, along with five other convicts, Webb and Rudabaugh escaped after digging their way out with a knife and a pickax. They raced to Texas and then to Mexico, where Rudabaugh was later killed. Webb returned to Kansas, took the name "Samuel King," and worked in Kansas and Nebraska as a teamster. He died in 1882 in Arkansas of smallpox.

REF.: Bartholomew, *Wyatt Earp, 1848 to 1880;* ____, *Wyatt Earp, 1879 to 1882;* Beck, *New Mexico; CBA;* Holloway, *Texas Gun Lore;* Keleher, *Violence in Lincoln County;* Lake, *Wyatt Earp;* Miller and Snell, *Great Gunfighters of the Kansas Cowtowns;* Stanley, *Desperadoes of New Mexico;* ____, *The Lamy;* Thompson, *Bat Masterson;* Vestal, *Queen of Cowtowns, Dodge City;* White, *Bat Masterson.*

Webb, Nathan, 1825-1902, U.S., jur. U.S. district attorney from 1870-78, and nominated to district court of Maine by President Chester A. Arthur in 1882. REF.: *CBA.*

Weber, Adolph, c.1884-1906, U.S., rob.-mur. On May 26, 1904, Adolph Weber, robbed the Bank of Placer County in Auburn, Calif. Dropping his gun during the robbery, 20-year-old Weber absconded with $5,000 and buried a five-pound can filled with $20 gold pieces in the back yard of his family's home. As evidence began to mount against Adolf, his father, Julius Weber, secured an out-of-court agreement to prevent the young man's prosecution. In July 1904, the young Weber bought another pistol in a San Francisco pawn shop. On Nov. 10, Weber murdered his father, his mother, his 18-year-old sister, Bertha, and used the butt of his gun to beat his 8-year-old invalid brother Earl on the head. Then he set fire to the house about 7 p.m., bought a new pair of pants, and returned to the burning home where he tossed his old pair of pants into the flames. A neighbor, George Ruth, noticed the fire and he discovered the two women dead in a room that the blaze had not yet engulfed. The unconscious child later died from head injuries. On Nov. 12, Weber was arrested, and on Nov. 21, the pistol used to kill the family was discovered underneath the flooring in the Weber barn. On Nov. 23, authorities found the buried money from the bank robbery, and Weber was put on trial on Feb. 6, 1905, for the murder of his mother. On Feb. 22, Weber was convicted and sentenced to death. He was hanged on Sept. 27, 1906.

Adolph Weber, robber and mass murderer.

REF.: *CBA;* Duke, *Celebrated Criminal Cases of America.*

Weber, Jeanne (AKA: **Madame Moulinet, Madame Bouchery**), 1875-1910, Fr., mur. After committing at least eight and perhaps as many as twenty child murders, Jeanne Weber, a Parisian housewife, was caught in the act of strangling her last victim one night in 1908. She had earlier been accused and tried twice for the deaths of children in her care but was acquitted each time.

On Mar. 2, 1905, two children were left in Weber's care, and one of them died. She was not suspected, though there were bruises on the child's neck. Within less than a month, three more children, including Weber's own son, died of strange congestive or convulsive maladies, all with marks on their throats.

A few weeks later, while relatives were visiting, Weber's 10-year-old nephew, Maurice, died. The boy's mother, Weber's sister-in-law, accused her of murder and called the police. The case attracted great attention, and public opinion demanded that she be found Guilty. A brilliant lawyer and some of the best forensic scientists and doctors in France convinced the jury that the children died from various medical problem, not at the hands of Jeanne Weber. She was freed amid great public outcry.

Deserted by her husband and still vilified by many of her neighbors, Weber made an unsuccessful suicide attempt and then left Paris. She next surfaced as Madame Moulinet, living with a man named Bavouzet as his housekeeper and mistress. Bavouzet's son Auguste was found dead in the same manner as the previous victims. Although the police were called in, no charges were brought. Some days later, Auguste's older sister, searching through Moulinet's belongings, found some newspaper clippings about Jeanne Weber and the earlier murder cases. The police were called again. The attending physician attributed Auguste Bavouzet's death to murder by strangulation. Her identity revealed, Jeanne Weber again was brought to trial for murder. The same defense team who got her off in the previous case again got her acquitted.

The director of the Society for Protection of Children, then hired Weber to care for some children. Seen strangling a child, she was fired immediately, but the director made no public charges because of the bad publicity that would result.

Weber returned to Paris, and even confessed to the original murders when she was picked up for vagrancy. After being sent to an asylum, Weber recanted her confession, but a psychiatrist declared her sane and released her. She then became known as Madame Bouchery, and told her landlady that her husband was beating her and asked if one of the landlady's children could sleep with her to keep her husband away. That night, loud noises came from her room. Another guest in the house rushed in to find Weber strangling the boy. This time, Weber was arrested, tried, and found Guilty.

On Oct. 25, 1908, Weber was found insane and sent to a hospital. In 1910, after many months of insane ravings, Jeanne Weber strangled herself to death.

REF.: *CBA;* Nash, *Look for the Woman;* Thorwald, *The Century of the Detective;* Wilson, *Encyclopedia of Murder.*

Weber, Randolph Henry, 1909-61, U.S., jur. Served as prosecuting attorney in Butler County, Mo. He was nominated to the eastern district court of Missouri by President Dwight D. Eisenhower in 1957. REF.: *CBA.*

Webster, Daniel, 1782-1852, U.S., lawyer. Served as member of U.S. House of Representatives from 1813-17 and from 1823-27. The notable Dartmouth College case in 1818 brought him national fame for his legal assistance to Dartmouth College trustees. He was also a U.S. senator from 1827-41, gaining fame as an orator, especially in speeches opposing John C. Calhoun. He served as U.S. secretary of state (1841-43), in the Senate (1845-50), and again served as secretary of state (1850-52). REF.: *CBA.*

Webster, Daniel R., 1926-1977, U.S., suic.-mur. In October 1977, Daniel R. Webster was tried and convicted in a North Carolina court for murdering his wife. During the proceedings, he begged the jury to give him the death sentence, saying, "You're looking at a cold-blooded murderer and if I had it to do over again I would probably do the same thing and I don't think I would think any more about killing you than I did her." Webster was sentenced to die in the gas chamber, but on Nov. 6, while on death row, the 51-year-old Webster committed suicide by slashing his neck and arm. REF.: *CBA.*

Webster, John, 1610-82, Brit., witchcraft. An evangelical preacher and teacher from Yorkshire, John Webster wrote *The Displaying of Supposed Witchcraft,* 1677, a satire of those who believed in witches.

REF.: Camfield, *A Theological Discourse of Angels and Their Ministries; CBA;* Glanvill, *Saducismus Triumphatus;* Robbins, *The Complete Encyclopedia of Witchcraft and Demonology;* Webster, *The Displaying of Supposed Witchcraft;* Webster, *Untersuchung der vermeinten und sogenannten Hexeryen.*

Webster, John Stanley, 1877-1962, U.S., jur. Served as prosecuting attorney in Harrison County, Ky., from 1902-06, and as chief deputy prosecuting attorney in Spokane County, Wash., from 1907-09. As a judge, he served on the Spokane County Superior Court from 1909-16, and on the state supreme court from 1916-18. He also represented the fifth district of the state of Washington in the U.S. House of Representatives. He was nominated twice to the eastern district court of Washington, once by President Warren G. Harding in 1923, and once by President Calvin Coolidge in 1924. REF.: *CBA.*

Webster, Dr. **John White**, d.1850, U.S., mur. Dr. John White Webster, who earned his medical degree from Harvard and was a professor of chemistry and mineralogy at the Massachusetts Medical College in the 1840s. His office was directly below that of Oliver Wendell Holmes, Sr., who would later offer testimony in this most sensational nineteenth century murder case. The murder of Dr. George Parkman was a heinous crime in a gentler age; one that filled the pages of the national press for months.

Webster apparently was forced to borrow money from various sources to cover the debts he had incurred from his high living. Far from a reclusive bookworm, the Cambridge physician enjoyed entertaining the cream of the literary set. Henry Wadsworth Longfellow was a frequent guest at Webster's table. To remain in good standing with the scions of Boston society, it required a tremendous cash outlay. With an annual salary of $1,200, Webster could ill afford such extravagance. He soon found himself borrowing large sums of money from his closest friends.

Parkman, a colleague of Webster's who donated the land upon which the Massachusetts Medical School was constructed, lent him $400. But when the debt had not been repaid by 1849, Parkman began harassing Webster. Parkman's tactics bordered on the ludicrous. At first he would take his place in the front row of the lecture hall where Webster tutored his students. He would sit on the bench, silently glaring at his adversary. Then one day he appeared before Webster's students in an outlandish stovepipe hat and a long frock coat. He heckled Webster unmercifully while he attempted to deliver a lecture. On Nov. 23, 1849, Parkman reached the limit of his tolerance. In a mad fury he went to visit Webster at the college. "Have you got the money?" Parkman demanded. "No, I have not," came the reply. In near-hysteria, Parkman reminded him of his obligations. "I got you your professorship and I'll get you out of it!" he cried.

This comment so incensed Webster that he picked up a large piece of kindling wood from the fireplace and hit Parkman on the head. Webster tried to revive him with spirits of ammonia, but the telling blow had smashed poor Parkman's skull and killed him. Reflecting on Parkman's angry denunciations months later, Webster wrote: "I was excited by them to the highest degree of passion." Fearful of the consequences, Webster decided to use his medical skills to dispose of the body. After locking the office doors, he hauled the body into his washroom and cut it into pieces. The college janitor, Empraim Littlefield, had witnessed an earlier argument between the two men and had seen Parkman arrive earlier that afternoon, obviously angry. The door to Webster's office and the door to an adjoining office were locked. Littlefield touched the wall that backed Webster's assay furnace and found it hot. Even as Littlefield stood wondering what Webster was doing, the doctor burned Parkman's severed head.

Webster disposed of most of the body parts, stashing a few bones with specimens he kept for teaching and research. Three days after the argument and Parkman's murder, a $3,000 reward was offered for his safe return by his brother-in-law, Robert Gould Shaw. Rumors to the effect that the good doctor had been abducted by a kidnapping gang and was to be held for ransom circulated through town. Spurred on by the promise of a sizeable reward, nearly the entire city of Boston turned out to search for the missing man. The tenement districts were invaded by search parties, and every suspicious character and drunkard was taken in for questioning. An Irish immigrant who was found with $20 in his pocket emerged as a suspect. But this instance was more of a case of anti-Gaelic prejudice on the part of the local authorities than anything else. Littlefield, as it turned out, had the inside track all along. He tried to gain access to Webster's dissection vault, but found that the chamber was securely locked. The janitor spent the next two days tearing apart the wall that covered up Webster's bloody deed. Finally, Littlefield broke into the locked vault. He found a bloody pelvis and parts of a leg, and immediately contacted the police.

An investigation uncovered more of Parkman's body parts and Webster was arrested and charged with the murder. When en route to jail he tried to commit suicide by taking strychnine, but vomited the poison before it had any effect. Webster had a very weak stomach and could not hold the vile substance down. The trial received tremendous public attention. By not allowing any of the spectators to sit in the gallery longer than five minutes, more than 60,000 spectators witnessed the trial. Many of them had come from as far as New Orleans. Webster, who pleaded that he had not intended to commit the murder, but was only acting from uncontrolled anger, was convicted and sentenced to death. The jury was convinced of his guilt because he had dissected the body, and then tried to conceal it from view. Webster was hanged in August 1850. A letter written shortly after Webster's execution reveals the extent of the horror that was felt by the residents of this genteel New England community.

> "...the terrible Cambridge tragedy still seems to darken our sky—though it is a great comfort to know the poor doctor seemed to die penitent. He wrote a letter to Dr. Parkhurst (the Reverend) entreating that some softer feelings might at least be recovered towards his family, that his wife and children were wholly innocent, and that she had often expressed her gratitude to him for his (the Reverend's) help in her spiritual culture. I hear she is tranquil, but what their plans are I know not."

The Parkman tragedy remained a lively topic of discussion for years, much to the embarrassment and chagrin of his socially connected family. Twenty years after the murder the celebrated British novelist Charles Dickens visited the city. When asked which tourist attraction he most wanted to see, Dickens replied: "The room where Dr. Parkman was murdered."

REF.: Bechhofer-Roberts, *Famous American Trials;* Birmingham, *Murder Most Foul;* Boucher, *The Pocket Book of True Crime Stories;* Brock, *A Casebook of Crime; CBA;* Dempewolff, *Famous Old New England Murders;* Duke, *Celebrated Criminal Cases of America;* Dunbar, *Blood in the Parlor; Famous Trials;* Furneaux, *The Medical Murderers;* Gribble, *Hallmark of Horror;* Gross, *Masterpieces of Murder;* Irving, *A Book of Remarkable Criminals;* Kingston, *Rogues and Adventuresses;* Mencken, *By the Neck;* Morris, *Fair Trial;* Nash, *Almanac of World Crime;* ____, *Bloodletters and Badmen;* Parry, *Some Famous Medical Trials;* Pearce,

Dr. George Parkman, a stern money lender.

The Massachusetts Medical College in Boston.

Professor Webster murdering Dr. Parkman over a loan.

Professor John White Webster of Massachusetts Medical College.

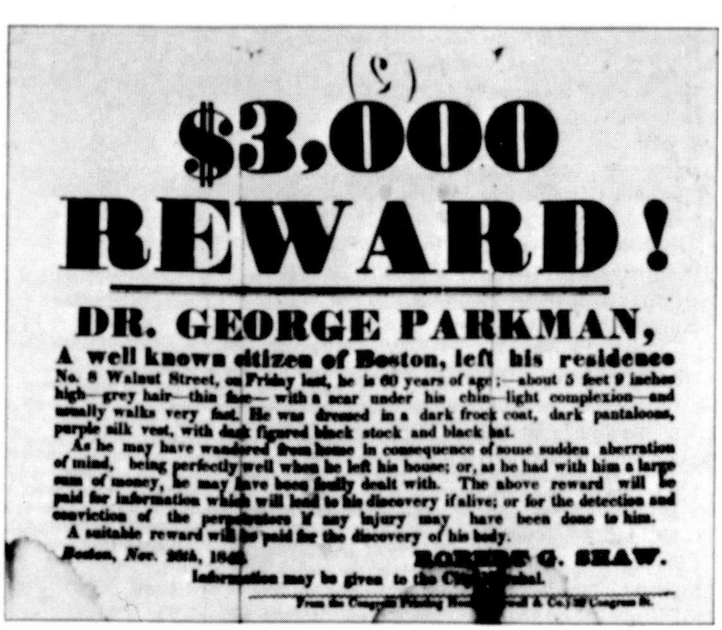

(2)

$3,000 REWARD!

DR. GEORGE PARKMAN,

A well known citizen of Boston, left his residence No. 8 Walnut Street, on Friday last, he is 60 years of age;—about 5 feet 9 inches high—grey hair—thin face—with a scar under his chin—light complexion—and usually walks very fast. He was dressed in a dark frock coat, dark pantaloons, purple silk vest, with dark figured black stock and black hat.

As he may have wandered from home in consequence of some sudden aberration of mind, being perfectly well when he left his house; or, as he had with him a large sum of money, he may have been foully dealt with. The above reward will be paid for information which will lead to his discovery if alive; or for the detection and conviction of the perpetrators if any injury may have been done to him.

A suitable reward will be paid for the discovery of his body.

Boston, Nov. [illegible] **[illegible] G. SHAW.**

Information may be given to the City [illegible].

From the [illegible] Printing [illegible] & Co. [illegible] Congress St.

A reward for the missing Parkman before the murder was known.

Unsolved Murder Mysteries; Pearson, *Instigation of the Devil;* Pearson, *Parkman;* Thomson, *Murder at Harvard;* Whitelaw, *Corpus Delicti;* Wilson, *Encyclopedia of Murder.*

Webster, Kate, 1849-79, Brit., rob.-mur. Kate Webster was born in County Wexford, Ire., in 1849. Her criminal nature was evident in childhood when she was caught stealing lace and inexpensive jewelry. When confronted with her loot, young Webster would be repentant. She would cry and beg forgiveness of her accusers in such a way that deeply touched the injured parties. While still in her teens Kate Webster sailed to Liverpool, having paid her passage with stolen funds. In the city she lived by her wits, filching coins from the pockets of businessmen. More often than not, however, her thievery was detected by the constables. When she was eighteen, Webster was sentenced to four years in prison. After securing her freedom she ventured to London, where she took a job as a charwoman. On the side she picked up extra cash by prostitution. She gave birth to a son while living on Kingston-on-Thames. The father was never identified.

Webster supported herself and the boy by robbing lodging houses and selling the loot to London pawnbrokers. Within a few years Kate Webster's arrest record listed thirty-six counts of larceny. In January 1879, she took her boy to Richmond where she lived off the charity of a Mrs. Crease, who secured a job for her as the governess to Julia Martha Thomas. The arrangement worked well up to a point. The boy stayed with Mrs. Crease while Webster performed her domestic tasks at the cottage on Park Road. But soon she reverted to her loathesome habits, idling time away at the Hole-In-the-Wall Pub in town. On May 2, 1879, Thomas reluctantly informed Webster that she was being dismissed. Webster hurled a stream of angry epitaphs at Thomas as she went off to church. Later that day, after Thomas returned home, Webster attacked her with a hatchet. Thomas fended off her attacker as best she could, but Webster was much younger and stronger. After a brief but intense struggle, the maid split open her employer's head.

Webster went to the Hole-In-the-Wall pub where she drank herself into a near stupor. Returning home, Webster hacked up the body and threw the remains into a large copper vat and boiled them. When the nauseating task was completed, she packed the remains into cloth bags lined with brown paper. The residence was scrubbed clean and some of Mrs. Thomas personal belongings, including items of clothing and a set of gold bridgework, were sold to a pawnbroker for six shillings. Pub owner Mrs. Hayhoe would later describe two jars of animal fat—or so it was advertised to the patrons of the tavern—that Webster tried to sell. The murky-looking substance was made from Thomas' parts.

Kate Webster, thief and killer.

Kate Webster assumed control of her employer's estate. To a resident of nearby Hammersmith named Henry Porter, Webster offered several fine pieces of furniture. While he was not personally interested, Porter put her in touch with John Church, a dealer in used furniture. Accompanied by Porter and his son Robert, Webster went to see Church. On the way home she excused herself for a moment, explaining that she had a parcel to deliver to the other side of the Hammersmith Bridge. The package contained the skull of Mrs. Thomas, and it found its way to the bottom of the river. Later that day Robert Porter was called on to help Kate Webster transport a large black box to the middle of the bridge. "Leave me with it in the middle of the bridge," she said. "You go back the way we came and I'll catch up after I've talked to my friend." The box surfaced in the river the next day. Several fishermen pulled it out of the water and turned it over to the police who commenced an immediate investigation.

Kate Webster, hatchet in hand, is about to attack her horrified employer, Julia Thomas.

When John Church appeared at the Thomas home to claim the furniture on Mar. 18, a neighbor named Miss Ives became suspicious and notified the police. The constables arrived at the home and initiated a search, but Kate Webster had already fled to her childhood home in Killane, Ire. It was not difficult for the police to trace her. She was arrested by the Royal Irish Constabulary in Killane on Mar. 28, 1879, and returned to England to stand trial, outfitted in the deceased woman's clothes and jewelry. When she was brought face-to-face with John Church, Webster pointed an accusing finger. "Here's your murderer!" she cried. But Church had a solid alibi. The trial of Kate Webster began on July 2, 1879. "I never done it!" she screamed, pointing an accusing finger at Henry Porter and John Church. When this tack failed to sway the jury, and a Guilty verdict was returned, Webster then claimed she was pregnant. A jury of women was summoned but they could find no evidence to support her claim. Kate Webster was executed at Wandsworth Prison on July 29, 1879.

REF.: Altick, *Victorian Studies in Scarlet;* Atholl, *The Reluctant Hangman;* Birmingham, *Murder Most Foul;* Bleackley, *Hangmen of England;* Brock, *A Casebook of Crime;* Browne, *The Rise of Scotland Yard; CBA;* Cobb, *Critical Years at the Yard;* Forster, *Studies in Black and Red;* Gross, *Masterpieces of Murder;* Kingston, *A Gallery of Rogues;* Lambton, *Thou Shalt Do No Murder;* Laurence, *A History of Capital Punishment;* Lewis, *Trunk Crimes Past and Present;* Logan, *Masters of Crime;* Logan, *Wilful Murder;* Morland, *Background to Murder;* Nash, *Look For the Woman; Notabel British Trials;* O'Donnell, *Should Women Hang?;* Pearce, *Unsolved Murder Mysteries;* Whitelaw, *Corpus Delicti;* Wilson, *Encyclopedia of Murder;* (Wood, *Survivors' Tales of Famous Crimes;* FICTION), Carr, *The Sleeping Sphinx.*

Webster, Robert, 1922- , U.S., rape-mur. On July 1, 1946, Robert Webster raped and strangled Carrie Delores Bendel, a 19-year-old waitress in Belmont Shore, Calif., leaving her body ina Eucalyptus grove. He assaulted another woman, Alice Sullivan, on Aug. 10, 1946, before police arrested him on Sept. 18, identifying him by fingerprints on Bendel's purse. He was convicted of rape and murder and sentenced to life at San Quentin Prison.

The prison paroled Webster less then nine years later and he took a job as an oil worker. In August 1963, he met 38-year-old divorcée Diane Jane Harley. On Sept. 3, Webster and Harley were drinking at a Long Beach, Calif., bar until 11 p.m. At 8:30 a.m. the following day, Harley's partly clothed body was found in the back of her apartment, beaten and strangled. The police investigation lasted seventeen hours, and found that Harley had been at a bar drinking with a man named Bob. They arrested Webster in his apartment at 1 a.m., and after five hours of interrogation he confessed. He was convicted of murder and sentenced to life imprisonment. Upon appeal, he was granted a new trial. On May 5, 1968, he was again convicted and sentenced, on July 2, to life imprisonment. REF.: *CBA.*

Webster, William Hedgcock, 1924- , U.S., law enfor. off. A native of St. Louis, Mo., William H. Webster earned his law degree in 1949, and served in WWII and the Korean War as a U.S. Navy lieutenant. While in the military, he defended a seaman charged with theft who had not been advised of his right to counsel. He instructed the seaman not to testify. Although Webster's directions angered officials, his action was later added to the Uniform Code of Military Justice.

FBI director William H. Webster.

Returning to Missouri as a civilian, Webster practiced law in St. Louis, from 1949-59 before becoming the U.S. Attorney for the Eastern District of Missouri, serving from 1960-61. After resigning in early 1961, he practiced law again, and he was a defense counsel for Mobil Oil Corporation. From 1964-69, he held a position on the Missouri Board of Law Examiners. Webster was appointed in 1970 as judge for the U.S. District Court for the Eastern District of Missouri, where he helped institute reforms at the St. Louis County jail. In July 1973, he became judge of the U.S. Court of Appeals for the Eighth Circuit, frequently refusing to strike down verdicts on the basis of legal violations he considered relatively insignificant. For instance, he once opposed granting a new trial on the grounds that the defendant had not been advised of his rights, because during the trial, substantial evidence had proved a man guilty of kidnapping, raping, and murdering a 10-year-old girl. While Webster presided as a judge, he was chairman of the Judiciary Conference Advisory Committee on the Criminal Rules.

On Feb. 23, 1978, Webster became the third permanent director of the Federal Bureau of Investigation, appointed to a ten-year term. During his tenure, he tried to repair the FBI's public image, update equipment, expand an anti-terrorist program at the FBI Academy, and renew staff morale. Webster was recognized on numerous occasions for his professional and law enforcement service, including a 1981 Riot Relief Fund Award in New York City, and the 1985 First Annual Patrick V. Murphy Award from the Police Foundation, Washington, D.C., for distinguished service in law enforcement.

REF.: *CBA;* Tully, *Inside the FBI.*

Wecksler, Irving, See: **Gordon, Waxey.**

Wedderburn, Alexander (Baron Loughborough, Earl of Rosslyn), 1733-1805, Brit., jur. Alexander Wedderburn was a member of Parliament from 1761-80 and attorney general from 1778-80. Wedderburn presided as chief justice of the court of common pleas from 1780-93 and as lord chancellor from 1793-1801. REF.: *CBA.*

Wedderburne-Stanhope Duel, 1821, Brit., duel. On Apr. 21, 1821, Charles Stanhope, Fourth Earl of Harrington, and T. Webster Wedderburne engaged in a duel prompted by a newspaper article in which Stanhope believed Wedderborne had insulted his character. The men met at Coombe Wood, near Kingston at 3 p.m. After Stanhope and Wedderburne each fired one shot and missed, they decided the matter had been settled. REF.: *CBA.*

Wedtech Scandal, prom. 1980s, U.S., tax evas.-rack.-extor. John Mariotta, the son of Puerto Rican immigrants, founded Welbilt, a small tool and die company, in 1965 with $3,000 and operated from a plant in the impoverished South Bronx area of New York. Five years later, with the business struggling, Mariotta took on as a partner Fred Neuberger, who had fled Eastern Europe as a child. The partners discovered that they were eligible for certain government contracts reserved for minority-owned businesses. By the time the company changed its name to Wedtech in 1983, 95 percent of its multimillion-dollar yearly sales came from "set-aside" military supply contracts. As the stakes grew, Wedtech began bribing government officials who influenced the awarding of those contracts. But in its new quarters near Yankee Stadium, the company employed more than 1,000 largely minority workers, leading President Ronald Reagan to call Mariotta one of the "heroes of the 80s."

Wedtech's connections ranged from local officials like Bronx Borough president Stanley Simon to Reagan presidential aide Lyn Nofziger and Attorney General Edwin Meese. In violation of government ethics laws, Nofziger lobbied for Wedtech only months after his January 1982 departure from the White House. Simon, in return for $50,000 in political contributions and other considerations, helped Wedtech win a lease from New York City on a waterfront lot. In 1984, with annual revenues of more than $70 million, almost all in military contracts, Wedtech went public. Stock sales brought Mariotta, Neuberger, and other company officials a fortune, but it also meant that Mariotta was no longer the principle stockholder, and thus Wedtech was no longer a minority-owned business. The company turned to the law firm of Richard Biaggi, son of U.S. Congressman Mario Biaggi of the South Bronx. The lawyers arranged for Mariotta to retain nominal ownership of most of Wedtech's stock, and the Small Business Administration allowed Wedtech to retain its preferred status. But in 1986, after management quarrels led to Mariotta's ouster, Wedtech was finally forced to surrender its claim of minority ownership. The price of Wedtech stock plummeted, and within the year the company had filed for bankruptcy. The ensuing investigation uncovered years of bribery and corruption and led to criminal indictments.

After convictions earlier in the year, on Nov. 19, 1988, five Wedtech conspirators were sentenced in federal district court in Manhattan. Representative Mario Biaggi was sentenced to eight years in prison and a $242,000 fine for fifteen felony convictions ranging from racketeering to obstruction of justice and bribery. His term was to be served concurrently with an earlier two-and-a-half-year sentence for accepting gratuities. Richard Biaggi, convicted of receiving bribes and mail fraud, received two years in prison and a fine of $71,000. For racketeering, fraud, conspiracy, tax evasion and bribery, John Mariotta received an eight-year sentence and a fine of $291,550. Stanley Simon received five years and a $70,000 fine for racketeering, conspiracy, tax evasion, extortion, and perjury. Peter Neglia, formerly with the Small Business Administration, was sentenced to three years and fined $30,000 for helping Wedtech bypass government regulations. REF.: *CBA.*

Weeks, Levi, prom. 1799, Case of, U.S., mur. A domestic murder brought together two famous attorneys, Alexander Hamilton and Aaron Burr, in the first great New York City murder mystery. In 1799 the Ring family operated a boarding house in New York City's Greenwich Village. Two young cousins from England, Hope Sands, her sister Gulielma Elmore (Elma) Sands, and a number of boarders lived in the house. Among the boarders were two young men, Levi Weeks and Richard David Croucher. Weeks and Croucher competed for the attention of the young women living in the house. Although Elma Sands rebuffed Croucher's approaches, she became interested in Levi Weeks, and their affair progressed rapidly. Croucher greatly resented Weeks' success with great Sands.

On Dec. 22, 1799, Elma Sands failed to return to the boarding house. When she had not returned after several days, Mrs. Ring began to question her boarders, especially Levi. He denied having any knowledge of her whereabouts. On Jan. 2, 1800, the neighborhood conducted a search of the area. Elias Ring discovered Elma Sands's body in an abandoned well. The death was first considered to be a suicide but before long Levi Weeks was arrested for murder.

Although a number of witnesses testified on both sides when Weeks was brought to trial, little hard evidence was produced. His fellow boarder, Richard Croucher, spoke vehemently against him. Weeks' uncle retained the two famous attorneys, Hamilton and Burr, to defend his nephew. After a month, the judge ordered a verdict of Not Guilty for lack of evidence. The case remained officially unsolved. Sometime later Croucher was convicted and jailed on a rape charge. He was indicted for fraud in Virginia, and, finally, was hanged in England for an unknown offense.

REF.: *American State Trials; A Brief Narrative of the Trial for the Bloody and Mysterious Murder of the Unfortunate Young Woman in the Famous Manhattan Well; CBA;* Coleman, *Report on the Trial of Levi Weeks;* Crouse, *Murder Won't Out;* Guttmacher, *The Mind of the Murderer;* Hardie, *An Impartial Account of the Trial of Mr. Levi Weeks;* Nash, *Open Files;* Pearson, *Instigation of the Devil;* (FICTION), Fay, *Norman Leslie.*

Weger, Chester, 1939- , U.S., mur. On Mar. 14, 1960, Chester Weger, a dishwasher at the Starved Rock Lodge located in Starved Rock Park near Ottawa, Ill., went into the woods, planning to steal purses when he encountered three middle-aged women from the Chicago suburb of Riverside. As Mildred Lindquist, Lillian Oetting, and Frances Murphy, the wives of prominent Chicago businessmen, hiked through the park, Weger threatened them with a broken tree limb and ordered them to lie on the ground. He bound two of them with string that he had stolen from the lodge's kitchen and as he tied up the third woman, one of the others freed herself and hit Weger with a pair of binoculars. Weger then struck the fighting woman with the tree bough, knocked her unconscious, and pulled her into a nearby cave. When the other women struggled Weger hit them, and also dragged them into the cave. Then he pulled up their clothing to make the attack appear to be a sex crime. The three bodies were found two days later on Mar. 16, by a group of boys.

Leading the investigation, La Salle County State's Attorney Harland D. Warren, learned that the string used to tie up the women was the same as that used in the kitchen of the Starved Rock Lodge. Initially, Weger passed two polygraph tests and bloodstains found on his jacket were determined to be animal blood. Later, however, Weger failed two additional lie detector tests and a Federal Bureau of Investigation laboratory determined that the blood on his coat was human. Weger confessed several times, but when he was tried, he retracted his statements. He was convicted on his twenty-second birthday, Mar. 4, 1961, and sentenced to life in prison. REF.: *CBA.*

Wehde, Albert, prom. 1917, U.S., fing. ident.-rebel. In 1917, engraver Albert Wehde, was convicted of attempting to furnish East Indian insurgents with guns in connection with a plot he was allegedly leading in Illinois to topple the British government. Wehde was sentenced to three years in prison, but a court of appeals added several more years to his sentence. During his imprisonment, Wehde worked in Leavenworth's prison laboratory where he performed experiments with fingerprints and in 1921 Wehde lifted a fingerprint for police from a whisky flask from which train robbers had taken drinks. Several months later, H.A. Murphy, a private investigator, brought a photograph of the fingerprint taken from the flask to the Leavenworth lab where Murphy altered it in an attempt to claim a $35,000 reward that had been offered for the conviction of the train robbers. Observing Murphy's actions, Wehde proved that police could potentially use fingerprints to convict innocent men. In 1922, Wehde was pardoned by President Woodrow Wilson and released from prison. REF.: *CBA.*

Wei Chung-hsien (AKA: **Li Chin-chung**), 1568-1627, China, polit. corr.-suic. Eunuch member of imperial court who served mother of future Chinese ruler Chu Yu-cho. Holding substantial leverage, he was given control of the government when Chu became emperor in 1620. He persecuted Confucian reformers and scholars, and furthered corruption within the government. When Chu died in 1627, Wei Chang-hsien lost power and committed suicide so that he would not have to stand trial. REF.: *CBA.*

Weick, Charles, b.1899, U.S., jur. Nominated to northern district court of Ohio in 1956 and to the sixth circuit court in 1959, both times by President Dwight D. Eisenhower. REF.: *CBA.*

Weidmann, Eugen, d.1939, and **Blanc, Jean**, prom. 1937-39, and **Million, Roger**, prom. 1937-39, Fr., kid.-mur. In great anticipation, Jean De Koven, a professional dancer from Brooklyn, N.Y., crossed the Atlantic to begin a vacation in the "City of Lights," Paris. De Koven was chaperoned by her aunt Ida Sackheim, who accompanied her to the usual tourist attractions, the Louvre, the Eiffel Tower, and the Café de la Paix. It was an idyllic summer. The looming war was but an echo on the continent. It was a time for lovers, and Jean De Koven was no exception. On the boulevards of Paris she met a handsome German named Eugen Weidmann, who seemed perfect in every way. He spoke French, English, and Portuguese fluently, and was a ral charmer to women.

American dancer Jean De Koven.

Ida Sackheim had no inkling that her niece was with this man—an ex-convict who had spent five years in German prisons for larceny—when she disappeared from Le Studio Hotel on July 23, 1937. Jean had returned from a day of sightseeing, changed her clothes, and told the elevator operator at the hotel that she expected to be back by 8 p.m. "I have no time to leave her (Sackheim) a note," she said. "Somebody is waiting for me." When she failed to turn up the worried aunt notified the American Embassy and the French police. The law enforcement officers told Sackheim not to worry because young women frequently got caught up in romantic intrigues. A ransom note was delivered to the hotel demanding $500 or "we will stop all negotiations and she will be taken for a ride. You know how the gangsters of Chicago operate." The police insisted it was a publicity stunt until $240 in American Express travelers' checks belonging to Jean De Koven turned up in Paris. The missing woman's young brother Henry arrived from New York to post a 10,000 franc reward. New York governor Herbert Lehman placed the local FBI office at the disposal of the Sûreté, but the investigation was already in the hands of Detective Primborgne, whose work on this case was remarkable for its thoroughness. In September the body of Josef Couffy, a chauffeur, was found lying in a ditch south of Paris. The police surmised that the man had been shot in the back of the neck while driving his client to the Riviera. The car had been stolen. On Oct. 16 Roger Leblond, a young press agent was found slumped over in his abandoned car in Neuilly, a Paris suburb. He, too, had been shot in the back of the neck. A month passed before another shooting murder was reported to police. On Nov. 22, real estate agent Raymond Lesobre was found lying on the stairs of an empty house in Saint Cloud, a suburb not far from Neuilly. A business card belonging to Arthur Schott was found in Lesobre's office.

Schott was a German businessman who provided a detailed

account of his movements before, during, and after the murder. He was ruled out as a suspect but his client list was examined for possible clues. Schott told the Sûreté that he was concerned about one of the names on the list, a German exile named Fritz

The house at La Voulzie where Jean De Koven was murdered.

Frommer who had fled his native land after Adolph Hitler came to power. The police called on Frommer at his Paris hotel but found out from the concierge that he had left the premises on Nov. 22 and had not returned. From his uncle, an Alsatian named Hugo Weber, they learned that Frommer had recently been keeping company with Siegfried Sauerbrey, a former political prisoner in Germany. Sauerbrey had changed his name to Karrer, and Weber believed this man was somehow connected to the murder of Lesobre.

The detectives went to a house Karrer had rented on the outskirts of the Saint Cloud forest. The outer gates were locked and the house looked deserted until suddenly a French-speaking man with a foreign accent inquired of the detectives their reason for coming. "Are you Monsieur Karrer, because if you are we would like to have a word with you about your tax payments," a detective replied. Karrer asked for further identification. The detective produced his badge and one look told Karrer he had been duped. He turned his back on the men, pulled out a Mauser pistol, began firing wildly. A fight began that was ended by the detectives only after they had clubbed Karrer over the head with a hammer. When he came to at police headquarters, Karrer

Eugen Weidmann, with bandaged head, confessing his crimes to police.

issued a statement. "My name is neither Sauerbrey nor Karrer as you may think," he said. "But my real name is Eugen Weidmann. Now I'll tell you a story that you won't believe, but every word I am going to tell you is true." Weidmann went on to say that he had rented the villa at La Voulzie with two petty criminals named Roger Million and Jean Blanc for the purpose of extorting money out of the friends and relatives of kidnap victims. "Now I am going to tell you something that will absolutely horrify you. I killed Jean De Koven," he said with an air of diffidence.

Weidmann explained that murder was never in his plans. He merely intended to extort some money out of her but was seized by a sudden, uncontrollable impulse. "Darling Jean, how sweet she was...she was gentle and unsuspecting," he added with regret. "I enjoyed speaking English to her, which I learned in Canada. When I reached for her throat she went down like a doll." The body was buried at the doorstep of the villa La Voulzie. Detectives found several items of women's clothing. which turned out to be those of Weidmann's fifth victim, 30-year-old Jeannine Keller of Strasbourg, Fr., who answered an ad in a Paris newspaper. Weidmann told the woman he was seeking the services of a "nurse-companion." She was murdered in the caves at Forest of Fontainebleau near Barbizon.

Weidmann's accomplices, including Reneé Tricot, mistress of Jean Blanc, were quickly arrested and charged with murder. The four were tried at the Assize Court at Versailles. In attendance during much of the deliberations was the famous French writer of the pleasures and pains of love, Sidonie-Gabrielle Colette, who covered the case for her newspaper. "Weidmann was a romantic," she wrote. "He loved flowers and was cultivating roses. He also loved nature. It was not merely the necessity of the professional killer that made him choose the forests for his murders..." After three weeks Weidmann, Million, and Blanc were found Guilty. Tricot was acquitted on all charges. A death sentence for Roger Million was commuted to life imprisonment by the president of the Republic, while Blanc received twenty months. On June 17, 1939, Weidmann the romantic was guillotined. He was the last man in France to be publicly executed with the guillotine, and his ordeal was cause for a great public celebration.

REF.: Belin, *My Work at the Surete; CBA;* Greenwall, *They Were Murdered in France;* Grierson, *Famous French Crimes;* Heppenstall, *Bluebeard and After;* Jesse, *Comments on Cain;* Nash, *Among the Missing.*

Weightman, George, See: **Waightman, George.**

Weil, Joseph (AKA: **Yellow Kid, King Con**), 1875-1976, U.S., fraud. No other confidence man in the U.S. ever approached the audacity and ingenuity of Joseph "Yellow Kid" Weil. Weil lived for 101 years and was known in his chosen field of crime as "King Con," the most successful confidence man of the twentieth century U.S. He claimed to have swindled more than $12 million from greedy, wealthy suckers, but his take was more likely $8 to $10 million. He live like a rajah, headquartering in Chicago, owning hotels and racetracks, and having myriad mistresses. Yet, he died in a nursing home and was buried in a pauper's grave.

He was born on June 30, 1875, in Chicago. His parents were immigrants, his mother French, his father German. Joseph Weil operated a saloon in the vice-ridden First Ward, known as the Levee and later managed "The French Village," an exhibit at the 1893 world's fair in Chicago. During the 1890s, Joseph Weil sold patent medicines and shilled for racetrack touts. He later graduated to the sale of fake stocks, rigged horse races, and the "salting" of worthless mines. Always inventive, Weil developed many unique confidence games of his own.

He traveled through rural areas of the Midwest, selling a patent medicine of his own creation, Meriwether's Elixir, one he claimed would kill tapeworms. He also worked the spectacles-and-magazine short con. He had several pages of a magazine reset in large type and inserted them in the publication. When stopping at a farm where the proprietor had poor eyesight, Weil sold him the Elixir and then asked if the farmer had lost an expensive pair of spectacles. As he talked, Weil turned the pages of the magazine and encouraged the farmer to try on the glasses. Just as the farmer put on the spectacles, Weil turned to the pages of enlarged type and the farmer thought his vision suddenly had been been vastly improved by the glasses. The glasses, which had gold rims, appeared expensive, but the rims were actually painted. The farmer gladly paid $3 or $4 for the spectacles, promising to return them to the owner if he encountered him. The glasses cost Weil no more than fifteen cents each and he bought them by the gross.

"I never cheated an honest man, only rascals," Weil was fond of saying. Of his victims he stated: "They may have been respectable, but they were never any good. They wanted something for nothing. I gave them nothing for something." Weil not only fleeced his customers, he convinced them that *they* were cheating *him*. Weil appeared to be a wealthy dandy. His attire was sartorial, complete with spats, white winged collars, silk cravats, diamond stickpin, and tailored, three-piece suits. By the 1890s, he had acquired his fanciful sobriquet. While lounging in the Chicago saloon owned by Alderman John "Bathhouse John" Coughlin, he discovered a cartoon strip drawn by Ocault, one that featured a character named "The Yellow Kid," an adventurous ne'er-do-well.

Coughlin noticed Weil chuckling over the antics of this character and boomed: "You know, Joe, you're just like that character in that cartoon strip you're always reading, just like that guy, always pulling capers on people. That's you all over, just like the Yellow Kid. That's what I'm calling you from now on, the Yellow Kid." The name stuck and became part of Weil's image as a conniving, cunning con man who never really met his match, although there were some artful swindlers who occasionally worked as his partners, such as Fred "The Deacon" Buckminster.

The meeting of these men was classic. At the turn of the century, Buckminster was a member of the Chicago Police Department, a detective working in the bunco squad. He trailed Weil about for a few days and saw him work some short cons. He arrested Weil on State Street, telling him he was going to run him in for practicing confidence games. The two men strolled toward a precinct station. At the corner, Weil reached into his pocket and pulled out a wad of money, all in large bills. Without a word he placed the money into Buckminster's hand.

"What's this?" Buckminster asked, staring incredulously at about $8,000.

"That?" asked Weil. "That's just walkabout money. I made that in two hours this morning."

"In two hours?"

"Yes, and so can you. I can use a guy like you, one who knows the ropes. Put that in your pocket." Weil stood staring straight ahead as he talked to Buckminster. "Go ahead, it's chicken feed to me. You can see that kind of dough every day if you throw in with me."

Buckminster clutched the money, then took his badge from his vest and looked at both the money and the badge. He pocketed both and shook Weil's hand. He quit the police force then and there and joined Weil.

Weil and Buckminster worked the pedigree dog swindle with alacrity and for tens of thousands of dollars each year. Selecting a wealthy bar owner, Weil would saunter into a saloon, dressed elegantly and walking a finely groomed, richly-scented dog that pranced at the end of an expensive-looking leash. Weil would tie the dog to the bar rail and then order a drink.

In the course of his conversation with the bar owner, Weil proudly showed pedigree papers for the hound, along with several blue ribbon prizes the dog had won. He would then take out his solid gold watch and then exclaim: "Great Scott! I'm late for an urgent business meeting!" He would then tell the bar owner: "I can't take Rex into the bank where I have my meeting. Will you be kind enough to watch my dog until my meeting is over?" Weil would slip a $10 bill on the bar, an unheard of tip, cautioning the bar owner: "This dog is priceless so please watch him closely." He would then dash from the bar to keep his appointment.

A few minutes after Weil's departure, Fred Buckminster appeared in the bar. He stood next to the dog, ordered a drink, and then looked at the animal. He spit out some beer in excitement and sputtered: "Oh, my Lord! I've been looking for this breed of dog for five years!" He quickly rummaged through his wallet and took out $50, shoving the money toward the bar owner, begging him to sell the dog to him.

"I can't do that, sir," came the usual response. "This dog belongs to a fellow who only left him until his meeting is over. He'll be back in an hour."

"Okay, okay," Buckminster would say, "so you want more. Just say so. The animal is worth more. I'll make it $100!" He then placed $100 on the bar, offering the money to the owner.

"I told you, sir, the animal is not mine to sell."

"All right, no more bickering. I'll make it three hundred!" He then pulled out more money, but the startled bartender would refuse, again telling Buckminster that the animal was not his to sell. Buckminster would not be denied. He put $50 on the bar and told the owner the name of the hotel where he was staying, adding: "Call me as soon as you can persuade the owner to sell. I'll have the other two hundred and fifty waiting for you." Buckminster then gave a maudlin display of affection for the animal and departed.

A half hour elapsed before Weil reappeared. His demeanor was completely changed. He was no longer the confident, ebullient boulevardier. He was crestfallen as he slowly walked to the bar, almost oblivious to the dog.

"What's the matter, sir?" the solicitous bar owner asked, "you look like you've lost your best friend."

Weil shook his head sadly and then explained that his business deal had collapsed and that he was facing financial ruin. "I've been wiped out, emptied, nearly destroyed."

The bar owner seized the opportunity, offering to buy the dog for $200. Weil pretended shock: "Sell Rex, the grand champion for only $200!"

After doing some quick mathematics, the bar owner invariably raised the offer by $25 or $50. He thought that since he already had Weil's $10 tip and Buckminster's $50 down payment, he would clear between $110 and $135 once the dog was delivered and Buckminster paid him the balance of $250. Weil reluctantly took the purchase price from the bar owner and weeping, took his leave of the dog.

When the bar owner appeared at the hotel where Buckminster was to be contacted, dog in hand, he quickly learned that no such person was registered. Buckminster and Weil then pocketed between $165 and $190 for an investment of $60. They then returned to their own kennel, where dogs from the street or from pounds were being groomed for the next sucker. On a good day, Weil and Buckminster sold ten dogs, making as much as $5,000 a week.

Many of Weil's other schemes, such as his use of an empty bank building in Muncie, Ind., were much more elaborate. After reading that the Merchants National Bank of Muncie was moving to a new location, Weil went to Muncie and rented the old bank building. With Buckminster handling the details, the old bank building underwent quick renovations. In the lease Weil stipulated that all the tellers' cages and other banking accouterments remain intact. Weil then secretly established his own bank. He printed deposit and withdrawal slips and put them into desk slots in the foyer. Streetcar conductors were hired as bank guards and tellers and other bank officials were culled from the ranks of some of Chicago's most notorious cofidence men and women.

All of the preparations were done for a single day's business: the bank operation was only a ruse to inveigle a multimillionaire sucker into another scheme. When all was ready, a Chicago investor worth millions was escorted by train to Muncie where he was met by a chauffeur-driven car and taken to Weil's "bank". Buckminister acted as the shill. He had groomed the sucker for months by telling him that the president of the bogus bank, Weil, was one of the shrewdest money men in the Midwest and that when most other banks were having difficulties in this Depression period, his bank was thriving. Buckminister had told the sucker that the bank president had gained control of rich government lands that could be purchased for a quarter of their value and that buyers were waiting to pay twice that much to obtain the federal lands.

Joseph "Yellow Kid" Weil, the greatest confidence man in America, 1924.

Weil, second from left, in court on fraud charges, 1956.

Fred Buckminster and Joe Weil, covering up, 1936.

The Yellow Kid, testifying on the techniques of confidence men, 1963.

Fred "The Deacon" Buckminster

The Yellow Kid, 1949.

Author Jay Robert Nash and "Yellow Kid" Weil, 1976.

The president of the bank, Buckminister stated, would only deal in cash, however. The sucker arrived in Muncie with a large briefcase filled with money, an estimated $500,000. When he entered the bank he was amazed to see the furious business the bank was doing. The place was packed with customers lined up at tellers' cages, thrusting wads of greenbacks at tellers as deposits. Bank officials were dragging sacks of money into a huge vault that appeared to be brimming with money. The customers were all prostitutes, racetrack touts, and gamblers whom Buckminster and Weil had hired for the day. The sucker was overwhelmed by the booming success of the Muncie bank.

He was kept waiting for almost an hour so he could witness the bustling business. He heard clerks complaining to superiors that they could not handle the traffic and that more guards had to be added to protect the burgeoning millions the bank was storing. Then the sucker was finally shown into Weil's offices and was met by Weil, who acted the part of a disinterested tycoon. Yes, he admitted, he had federal land leases in Indiana and out West where oil was in great abundance. He showed bogus leases and oil surveys that supported his claims. The sucker opened his briefcase, prepared to buy all the land he could obtain. The nerveless, cool-headed Weil then offered the sucker the *convincer*, telling him he could not have all of the lands promised to him by Buckminster.

"I've got a lot of friends here in Indiana to take care of," Weil explained. "You're an outsider and if it weren't for my good friend Harry here," Weil said, motioning to Buckminster, "I wouldn't be talking to you at all." At this point, the sucker's greed, which Weil was an expert at manipulating, got the better of him. He began to argue with Weil for all that Buckminster had promised him. But Weil was adamant, even while calmly glancing at the stacks of money in the open briefcase, telling the sucker that he could not have all he expected. Weil reportedly took only $400,000 from the sucker in the land deal and watched with steel nerves as the briefcase closed on the remaining $100,000. "Never be greedier than the mark," was Weil's lifelong credo and in this instance, he proved his words. By allowing the mark to retain a portion of his money, Weil knew, the sucker would be absolutely convinced that he had participated in a crooked deal and that he had gotten the best deal possible for himself.

After the sucker had been given signed deeds to lands that did not exist, he was driven to the depot and escorted to Chicago by Buckminister. By the time the train left the depot, Weil had paid his army of swindlers and closed the bank. The whole operation cost him $50,000 and he and Buckminster had made $350,000 on the deal. This kind of money was average for Joe Weil, who spent lavishly and lived high. He bought a small hotel on the North Side of Chicago and then a string of race horses. He preferred to keep company with tall, voluptuous blondes selected from the chorus lines of Chicago nightclubs and he showered furs and jewels upon these women.

Weil squandered great sums on gambling, bad investments, and women. Moreover, every time he was sent to prison—he served about ten years in prison out of 101 years of life—his brother, a Chicago bailiff, seized his property. Each time Weil was released, he had to start building his fortune again. The few times he ventured away from the world of confidence games, he ran afoul of the law. In 1924, Weil agreed to fence some of the money taken in the Roundout Mail Robbery that had occurred north of Chicago. He was caught exchanging the "hot" money and sent to the federal penitentiary at Leavenworth to serve six years.

During his term at Leavenworth, Weil met such arch criminals as Frank Nash, Earl Thayer, Thomas Holden, Francis Keating, and George "Machine Gun" Kelly, bankrobbers all. At one point, while walking in the exercise yard, Kelly approached Weil and said: "You know, Kid, I've been thinking about you. I just don't understand how a guy like you operates. I mean, you go right up to people, make friends with them, and take them for their money. You spend a lot of time with them and they know who you are and they can bring the law right to your doorstep."

"Really, George," Weil replied. "Well, if you knew anything about the con, you'd know that the sucker can't bring the law to my doorstep because they would also have to admit to the police that he was involved in a shady deal, too. I only do shady deals, George, so the sucker is convinced that he is going to make a ton of money, more than he would make in a legitimate operation. You, on the other hand, George, go into banks armed to the teeth, shoot up the place and maybe clip some poor people who have no business being hurt and then run like crazy with police shooting at you. What kind of a criminal are you anyway?"

"I'm not a sap who pals around with my victims like you," snorted Kelly.

"You're not a sap, huh?" Weil smirked. "How much time are you doing here, George?"

"Twenty years."

"For what?

"Bank robbery."

"And how much did you get out of the bank?"

"About three thousand."

"Three thousand and twenty years," Weil hummed. "Well, I'm finishing up a six-year stretch. I'm going out next month with time off for good behavior. Five years for a caper that netted me almost a quarter of a million. And you'll still be in this tank doing fourteen more years for three thousand. Who's the sap, George?"

When Weil got out, he embarked on a new series of confidence games he had concocted while serving his time in Leavenworth. He sold fake copper mine stock and pills that he claimed would turn water into gasoline. He even took a trip to Italy where he convinced dictator Benito Mussolini that he was a U.S. mining engineer and government official, selling Il Duce the rights to rich mining lands in Colorado. By the time Mussolini's secret police uncovered this scam, the elusive Weil had already sailed with a reported $2 million in cash from Mussolini's coffers.

Returning to his old haunts in Chicago, Weil began to suffer one setback after another. Fred Buckminister was arrested for a federal offense and sent to prison. Many of Weil's other associates were also sent to jail and he found his reputation preceded him wherever he went. On Feb. 3, 1934, Weil was arrested in a Peoria, Ill., hotel room. Police had heard that he was in town and about to put across another swindle. They found two suitcases in his room filled with newspaper cut to the size of money, banded together in piles and marked "$200,000." Since the arrest was premature, Peoria Police Chief Walter Williams could only hold Weil for a short time. "I know you're up to something, Kid," Williams told Weil.

"Give me proof that I've broken the law," Weil challenged Williams.

"I can't," said the disgusted police chief, "so I have to turn you loose. You get on a train and get out of town. If you ever come back to Peoria, we'll thrown you in jail on suspicion."

Weil left town, realizing that his infamy was his undoing. He went into semi-retirement. He lived off his swindled fortunes for some years and then wrote his memoirs in 1948. Still, Weil pulled a short con or two in his dotage merely to keep busy. The author met Weil in the early 1960s, when Weil was in his eighties and knew him until his death in 1976 at the age of 101. At one point the author spotted Weil standing at a corner on the North Side of Chicago. He was not wearing his customary elegant attire, but was startlingly dressed in threadbare clothes that verged on being rags. He was unshaven and dirty.

Weil staunchly declined an offer of money to see him through this period of financial reversal, and after continuously asking the author to "get out of here," he became angry and finally blurted: "Go away, dammit, can't you see I'm *working*!" He had been interrupted during one of his short cons while awaiting the arrival of the traditional sucker. Weil finally retired to a North Side nursing home where the author regularly visited him. At one point he was asked: "If you could get out of that wheel chair and get to the street, would you attempt to pull off another scam?"

Joseph "Yellow Kid" Weil did not hesitate for a moment, replying: "Does a hungry dog like food?" He died a few days later and was buried in Archer Woods on the South Side of Chicago, interred in a pauper's grave.

REF.: *CBA;* Hamilton, *Men of the Underworld;* Hynd, *Murder, Mayhem and Mystery;* Klein, *The Double Dealers: Adventures in Grand Deception;* Nash, *Almanac of World Crime;* ____, *Bloodletters and Badmen;* ____, *Hustlers and Con Men;* ____, *The Innovators;* Scott, *The Concise Encyclopedia of Crime and Criminals;* Weil, *Yellow Kid Weil.*

Weil, Levi, d.1771, Brit., mur. Levi Weil practiced medicine in London but decided crime was more lucrative. He wrote to a brother and several friends in Amsterdam, inviting them to England, where money could be made by thieving. The group included Asher Weil, Levi's brother; Jacob Lazarus; Marcus Hartagh; Daniel Issacs; Solomon Porter; Lazarus Harry; and Abraham Linevill. With Levi Weil as the leader, they planned to choose likely houses during the day and return to rob them at night.

One Saturday evening in King's Road, Chelsea, a wealthy farmer's widow, Mrs. Hutchings, after putting her children to bed, went to the kitchen to talk with her female servants. When they answered a knock at the door, Weil's gang forced their way into the house. The gang went upstairs to search the house, fortunately not waking Hutchings' two sons, and bypassing her daughter's room. When they got to the attic they found John Slow and William Stone, two farmers who worked for the widow, asleep. Levi Weil struck Stone, intending to kill him, but only stunned the man. As Slow rose up in bed, the other gang members yelled, "Shoot him! Shoot him!" Weil fired a pistol, fatally wounding Slow. Stone, recovering consciousness, jumped out of bed and escaped to the roof through the window. The robbers stole silver and other valuables from the house, brutally beat Hutchings, and took her watch and a purse containing sixty-four guineas. The thieves escaped, and Slow staggered downstairs to say to Hutchings—"How are you, madam? For I am dying"—before falling to the floor.

The gang was at large for a long time until Daniel Issacs, eager for the reward money offered by the Secretary of State's Office and the City of London, went to Mr. Myers, treasurer of a synagogue, and confessed all. Myers took Issacs to the office of Sir John Fielding, where Isaacs gave evidence against his accomplices. The court indicted the Weil brothers, Hartagh, Lazarus, Porter, and Harry on charges of robbery and murder. Linevill, was also indicted, but escaped. The Weil brothers, Lazarus, and Porter were convicted of capital crimes, while Hartagh and Harry were acquitted. The convicted were taken to Tyburn, where a large crowd watched them hanged on Dec. 9, 1771. After the bodies had hanged for the customary time, they were taken to Surgeon's Hall for dissection.

REF.: Browne, *The Rise of Scotland Yard; CBA;* Kingston, *Dramatic Days at the Old Bailey;* Parry, *Some Famous Medical Trials.*

Wein, Edward Simon, 1924- , U.S., rape-kid. At a Long Beach, Calif., cocktail party on Nov. 10, 1956, a slight man wearing glasses accidentally stepped on another man's foot. The guest's date took one look at the man's face and immediately identified the man to her escort as the rapist who had assaulted her at knife point. She told another guest, an off-duty policeman, about the rapist, saying, "I'd never forget what he looked like." The policeman held Edward Wein for Long Beach officers. By 4:30 a.m., the 32-year-old painting contractor was under arrest. By Nov. 12, seven victims, all housewives, had positively identified him as their attacker. Detectives J.B. Close and W.R. Schottmiller said the method in all of the attacks was the same. The rapist knocked on the door of a private home, in answer to a newspaper ad for a rental or an article for sale. While talking to the woman of the house, he pretended to lose his watch stem and asked her to help him look for it. As the woman began to search, he grabbed her arms, tied them behind her back, then forced her into a bedroom, and raped her. The attacks occurred in Burbank, Alhambra, the San Fernando Valley, south Los Angeles, and Hollywood. Wein, booked on suspicion of kidnapping as well as the rape charges, denied everything. He told police that his real failing was gambling, and that he had lost "a quarter of a million dollars."

By Nov. 14, a 14-year-old girl became the eighth victim to identify Wein. She said he attacked her in her parents' home at knife point on Aug. 6, 1956. She had admitted him when he told her that her father had sent him to make an estimate on a tile job. The girl sobbed as she explained, "He threatened to kill me and my little brothers and sister if I didn't do what he told me to." By Dec. 11, Wein had been charged with twenty-three felony counts. Under Section 209 of the California Penal Code, commonly known as the Little Lindbergh Law, five of the charges carried the death penalty. The Little Lindbergh Law allows death in the gas chamber for kidnapping for the purpose of robbery when the victim suffers bodily harm. Nearly twenty witnesses told stories of robbery, kidnapping, sex offenses, and assaults by Wein.

Wein was tried by jury under Superior Court judge Leroy Dawson. Prosecutor J. Miller Leavy produced a check written by Wein and left behind at the home of one of his victims, and his fingerprints found on a drinking glass at another woman's home. Attorney Rexford Eagan defended Wein. After a three-week trial, the jury deliberated for eight hours before returning on May 11, 1957, with Guilty verdicts on twenty-two felony counts. The judgment included five death verdicts. Wein claimed he had been convicted before he ever came to trial because of negative newspaper stories. Eagan requested a new trial because Prosecutor Leavy, in his final argument to the jury called Wein "worse than (Caryl) Chessman," who had been sentenced to die eight years earlier and was still appealing for clemency. Dawson rejected Eagan's argument before imposing sentence.

On May 23, 1957, Wein was sent to San Quentin's Death Row to await execution. The first date set was for Sept. 19, 1958. The California Supreme Court, on Sept. 3, rejected a request to delay the execution. After the State Supreme Court affirmed the death penalty, Judge Watson scheduled the execution for Dec. 5. On Oct. 20, the Supreme Court denied Wein's appeal of his kidnapping conviction, the crime that carried the death penalty. He claimed that he had only forced his victims to move from two to seventy-five feet within their homes. Wein also pleaded that he had been denied due process of law since he had been detained for five days after his arrest before he was arraigned. On Nov. 17, the Supreme Court refused to grant a rehearing of the case. On Dec. 2, 1958, Wein's lawyer Russell E. Parsons reiterated the claim that his client's constitutional rights had been violated by the arraignment. A year and a half later, California governor Edmund G. Brown granted an executive clemency hearing to Wein and, on June 4, commuted his sentence to life in prison without possibility of parole. Brown said the death penalty should not be imposed for the kidnapping charges because Wein had only moved his victims within their homes. Three years later, in August 1961, Wein, contending that he was denied due process of law and that he had ineffective counsel at his trial, made a bid for complete freedom. Superior Court Judge Richard M. Sims denied him a writ of habeas corpus. As of October 1989, Wein is serving his sentence at the California Men's Colony in San Luis Obispo, Calif. REF.: *CBA.*

Weinbaum, Dr. Sidney, b.1898, U.S., perj. After working as a theoretical scientist at Bendix Aviation, Dr. Sidney Weinbaum, was employed in 1946 as a senior research engineer in the top secret jet propulsion laboratory at the California Institute of Technology located in Pasadena. Beginning in 1949, the Russian-born Weinbaum held a research position at the university until the Army Intelligence revoked his clearance to work on classified government projects after learning that Weinbaum had formerly belonged to the Communist Party. When his affiliation was disclosed, Weinbaum was charged with perjury and fraud for lying on job applications. In a Los Angeles court in September 1950, Weinbaum was convicted on a perjury charge and on Sept. 12, 1950, the 52-year-old scientist received a four-year sentence. REF.: *CBA.*

Weinberg, Dr. **Joseph W.**, 1917- , Case of, U.S., perj. During WWII, Dr. Joseph W. Weinberg was employed at the University of California radiation laboratories. In 1943, atomic security agents became suspicious of the physicist when they discovered that Weinberg had been meeting with Steve Nelson, a reputed Communist leader. In 1949, when Weinberg was teaching at the University of Minnesota, the House Un-American Activities Committee charged him with giving atomic secrets to Nelson during the war. He was indicted on three counts of perjury, including denial that he was a Communist, denial that he had been present at several Communist meetings, and denial that he was acquainted with Nelson. The 36-year-old Weinberg was tried in federal court in Washington, D.C., in 1953. Prosecutors dismissed one charge and the court dismissed another. In March, Weinberg was acquitted on the first perjury charge. Judge Alexander Holtzoff told the jury he was certain they had carefully considered the case, but he commented, "The court does not approve of your verdict." REF.: *CBA.*

Weiner, Bertha, prom. 1901, Brit., burg. A German woman, Bertha Weiner, ran a highly organized burglary ring that regularly stripped goods from large suburban London homes. Weiner directed a gang of twelve men, most of whom were German, including her lover, Mr. Rebork, and her brother, Ludwig Weiner. She planned the burglaries in minute detail; a group of four or five men carried them out. In early 1901, police noticed some of the gang members loitering and began surveillance. Plans were made to raid the gang's home after the next burglary. On Oct. 29, 1901, the gang struck again. The raid took place two days later and property stolen on Oct. 29, was recovered. All the gang members were tried and convicted at the Old Bailey. Bertha Weiner was sentenced to seven years in prison, eleven men were each given a five-year prison sentence, and a younger Weiner relative received a one-year term.

REF.: *CBA;* Wensley, *Forty Years of Scotland Yard.*

Weinger, Mitchell, 1948- , U.S., mur. Twenty-five-year-old drug dealer Mark Demetrius called 28-year-old Mitchell Weinger on May 2, 1976, requesting that Weinger stop by Demetrius' girlfriend's Chicago apartment to buy cocaine. When Weinger arrived, Demetrius' 23-year-old girlfriend, Marigray Jobes, an aspiring actress, was also present. While the two men discussed the price, Weinger stabbed Demetrius and his girlfriend to death. In 1980, Weinger, vice president of Midland Industries, Inc., a family-owned business, stood trial. In May 1980, he was convicted on murder charges, and on July 2, 1980, Weinger received a sentence of thirty to forty years in prison. REF.: *CBA.*

Weir, Thomas, c.1600-70, and **Weir, Jane**, c.1610-70, Scot., witchcraft. Thomas Weir had served as a major in command of troops protecting Edinburgh, and also had participated in evangelical Protestant prayer meetings until 1670, when the 70-year-old man suddenly denounced himself for crimes of witchcraft, incest, adultery, and bestiality. He also incriminated his sister, Jane Weir. Thomas Weir's trial began on Apr. 9, 1670, charged with adultery, bestiality, incest with his sister, Jane, and his stepdaughter, as well as the attempted rape of his sister when she was ten. Jane Weir was also tried on charges of sorcery, incest, and consulting with devils, witches, and necromancers. Both Weirs were convicted and sentenced to be strangled and burned to death. Weir was executed on Apr. 11, 1670 between Leith and Edinburgh and his sister was executed the next day at the Grass Market in Edinburgh.

REF.: *CBA;* Hickes, *Ravillac Redivivus;* Robbins, *The Encyclopedia of Witchcraft and Demonology;* Sharpe, *Historical Account of the Belief in Witchcraft in Scotland;* Sinclair, *Satan's Invisible World Discovered;* Summers, *The Geogrpahy of Witchcraft.*

Weiss, André, 1858-1928, Fr., jur. Member of Hague Tribunal in 1920 and judge of Permanent Court of International Justice in 1922. REF.: *CBA.*

Weiss, Carl Austin, See: **Long, Huey Pierce**.

Weiss, Earl (Earl Wajcieckowski, AKA: Hymie, Perfume Burglar), 1898-1926, U.S., org. crime. Earl "Hymie" Weiss, a gangland rival of Al Capone, preferred to settle territorial disputes with a gun. On two occasions he unsuccessfully tried to murder Capone. Al was not about to become a moving target for a third time.

Born in Chicago to Polish Catholic parents, Weiss' criminal record dated to 1908 when he was arrested for the first time on a burglary charge. He was dubbed the "Perfume Burglar" by the Chicago press corps after the police caught him in the act of robbing an apothecary store. "Are you some sort of a pansy, fella?" one of the police asked, after catching a whiff of the spilled perfume on Weiss' clothing. The insinuation stung him very deeply. Weiss was a devout church goer who regularly attended the Holy Name Cathedral. Here he met Dion O'Bannion, a former alter boy. O'Bannion like Weiss, was a strong-arm burglar who enjoyed virtual immunity from arrest due to his political connections on the North Side. On one occasion the police lifted a set of fingerprints that belonged to Weiss and O'Bannion from a safe at the Parkway Tea Room. The two burglars were arrested and charged, but a bribed jury returned a Not Guilty verdict. Outside the courtroom O'Bannion joked with reporters. "It was an oversight. Hymie was supposed to wipe off the prints and he forgot."

Chicago gang chief Earl "Hymie" Weiss.

With the onset of Prohibition, O'Bannion and Weiss decided bootlegging was far less risky than burglary, and the profit potential was much greater. Together with George "Bugs" Moran, Frank and Peter Gusenberg, and Vincent "Schemer" Drucci, they took over the North Side, supplying bootleg alcohol to hundreds of cabarets in the 42nd and 43rd Wards near the Chicago lake front. Hymie enjoyed looking the part of a flashy gangster. He always carried a thick role of cash, usually $10,000. "Ain't you afraid of a heist?" Drucci asked. "Naw," Weiss replied, "you never can tell when you'll need dough quick. Besides I got the roscoe (an automatic pistol) with me." Weiss never shied from using a gun. In July 1921, killed Steve Wisniewski, who had commandeered an O'Bannion beer truck. "That jerk needs a lesson," Weiss said. Wisniewski was lured into Weiss' car, and shot to death in a remote spot outside the city limits. Thus Weiss is credited with inventing the "one-way ride."

Inevitable warfare developed between the Capone faction and Weiss. In 1924 territorial agreements were broken by the Capone mob when triggerman Frank McErlane shot Walter O'Donnell and Jerry O'Connor, occasional allies of the O'Bannions. Weiss was full of rage. "You can tell Capone this for me," he said to one of Al's henchmen. "If he ever pulls anything like that on us, I'm going to get him if I have to kill everybody in front of him to do it." Weiss proved that this was no idle threat following the Capone-ordered assassination of his friend, Dion O'Bannion, on Nov. 10, 1924, at the State Street flower shop he maintained as a business front.

Weiss struck with a vengeance on Jan. 12, 1925. With Moran and Drucci as triggermen, Weiss swept by a South Side eatery at State and Fifty-fifth and sprayed Capone's car with bullets. Chauffeur Sylvester Barton was injured, but Capone escaped unhurt. On Jan. 20, the same tandem cornered Johnny Torrio outside his South Side home and seriously wounded him with a fusillade of bullets. Capone's long-time mentor survived, but the attack was enough to drive him out of Chicago for good. Angelo Genna, nominally affiliated with the Capone organization, was the next to fall. Weiss' men murdered him on June 13, 1925. The Northsiders were exacting a heavy toll. Fearing for his life, Capone ordered construction of a $26,000 armored car. Realizing the car would not be enough to stop Weiss, Capone struck back. South Side gunmen twice attempted to kill Weiss in broad daylight on Michigan Avenue, but both times they missed.

Capone only succeeded in antagonizing his rival. On Sept. 20, 1926, a caravan of cars cruised by Capone's Cicero headquarters at the Hawthorne Hotel. Numerous pedestrians clogged the streets as Weiss, the Gusenberg Brothers, and Drucci pumped 1,000 machine gun bullets into the hotel lobby. Al Capone, who was thrown to the floor by his bodyguard, again escaped. The highly publicized attack compelled Capone to attempt to make peace with Weiss. Through Tony Lombardo, president of the Unione Siciliane, Weiss made it known that he wanted Albert Anselmi and John Scalise, two imported gunmen that many believed killed O'Bannion. "I wouldn't do that to a yellow dog!" Capone yelled. The terms were unacceptable.

With no other options, Capone dispatched Frank Nitti, Frank Diamond, Scalise, and Anselmi to the North Side to kill Weiss. The gangsters rented several rooms across the street from Holy Name Cathedral and adjacent to O'Bannion's flower shop on State Street. For several days the Capone men maintained a vigil. On Oct. 11, 1926, Weiss, his bodyguards Benny Jacobs, Sam Peller, Paddy Murray, and lawyer William W. O'Brien pulled up in their car, and prepared to enter the church. As the men crossed the street, the shots rang out from the second-story windows opposite Holy Name. Murray and Weiss were killed immediately. Peller, O'Brien, and Jacobs sustained wounds. The hail of bullets flew into the flagstone of the church, partially obliterating an inscription from St. Paul's Epistle to the Philippians, 2:10, which read, "At the name of Jesus every knee should bow in heaven and on earth." All that was left were six words, "every knee should...heaven and...earth."

Interviewed only hours after the double slaying, Al Capone expressed his profound regrets. "That was butchery. Hymie was a good kid. He could have got out long ago and taken his and been alive today." But did Capone kill Weiss, the reporters wanted to know. "I knew I'd be blamed for it...Why should I kill Weiss?" Chief of Detectives William Schoemaker disagreed. "Capone knows why and so does everybody else," he said. "He had Hymie killed...and all those others." See: **Capone, Alphonse; Drucci, Vincent; Moran, George; O'Bannion, Charles Dion.**

REF.: *CBA;* Demaris, *Captive City;* Fried, *The Rise and Fall of the Jewish Gangster in America;* Gosch and Hammer, *The Last Testament of Lucky Luciano;* Kobler, *Al Capone;* Landesco, *Organized Crime in Chicago;* Lindberg, *To Serve and Collect: Chicago Politics and Police Corruption;* Lyle, *The Dry and Lawless Years;* Lynch, *Criminals and Politicians;* Messick and Goldblatt, *The Mobs and the Mafia;* Morgan, *Prince of Crime;* Nash, *Bloodletters and Badmen;* Smith, *Syndicate City.*

Weiss, Emmanuel (AKA: Mendy), prom. 1930s, U.S., org. crime. Emmanuel "Mendy" Weiss was one of the most ruthless paid assassins in Louis "Lepke" Buchalter's Murder, Inc., and served as Buchalter's bodyguard during the 1930's. In 1935, New York mobster Dutch Schultz organized a plot to kill U.S. Prosecutor Thomas E. Dewey. Realizing the repercussions of such an act, crime bosses Charles "Lucky" Luciano and Meyer Lansky turned to Buchalter for assistance. On Oct. 23, 1935, Weiss and Charles "The Bug" Workman traveled to Schultz's hangout, the Palace Chop House in Newark, N.J. Shortly after 10 p.m., as Shultz's henchmen sat around a table counting the day receipts, the two gunmen opened fire, killing all three gangsters. Schultz was killed by Workman in a nearby washroom, while Weiss left the restaurant. Weiss' departure caused discord between the two assassins, and Buchalter had to work out a peaceful settlement.

On Sept. 13, 1936, Weiss, with James Ferraco and Harry Strauss, murdered Brownsville candy store owner Joseph Rosen. They escaped detection until 1941, when Abe "Kid Twist" Reles, turned informant and listed the many deeds perpetrated by Murder, Inc. Weiss fled to Kansas City where he posed as a mining company executive, but he was apprehended and returned to New York. Tried for Rosen's murder, he was convicted and sentenced to death. Weiss died in the electric chair at Sing Sing on Mar. 4, 1944. See: **Buchalter, Louis; Murder, Inc.**

REF: *CBA;* Fried, *The Rise and Fall of the Jewish Gangster in America;* Messick, *Lansky;* Sann, *Kill the Dutchman;* Smith, *Syndicate City;* Turks and Feder, *Murder, Inc.*

Husband killer Jeanne Weiss, taking strychnine in her prison cell.

Weiss, Jeanne Daniloff, 1868-91, Alg., mur. Felix Roques, a handsome young Frenchman, became enamored of Jeanne Weiss, a young French woman married to an army lieutenant stationed in Algeria. Weiss fell in love with Roques and became pregnant with his child. She continued to live with her husband, who assumed the child was his own. Finally the guilty pair decided to poison the husband.

Jeanne Weiss began giving her husband doses of arsenic and, although Lieutenant Weiss became quite ill, he did not die. Meanwhile, Jeanne and Felix carried on a poorly conceived correspondence which was detected by the post-mistress in Ain-Fezza, Alg., where the Weiss' were living. The post-mistress told one of the Weiss' friends who instigated an investigation of Lieutenant Weiss' illness. When the post-mistress intercepted a final letter containing complete evidence and admission of the crime, she and the Weiss' friend turned it over to the police.

When the police arrested Jeanne, they found a large amount of poison in the house. Jeanne tried to take some of the poison, but failed to consume enough to kill herself. Roques, arrested a few days later, was more successful: he grabbed a guard's gun and shot himself.

During Jeanne Weiss' trial, Lieutenant Weiss condemned and rejected his wife in a carefully worded statement. On May 29, 1891, Jeanne Weiss was found Guilty and sentenced to twenty years in prison. The next day, May 30, Weiss bit through the hem of her handkerchief in which she had concealed strychnine, and died.

REF.: *CBA;* Gribble, *The Dead End Killers;* Irving, *Studies of French Criminals;* Kingston, *Remarkable Rogues;* Morain, *The Underworld of Paris;* Nash, *Look For the Woman;* Stevens, *From Clue to Dock.*

Weiss, Joseph J., b.c.1899, and **Gross, Martin**, b.c.1891, and **Messman**, Dr. **Hirsch L.**, b.c.1888, U.S., fraud. In December 1933, three shady New York professionals concocted a plan to defraud insurance companies. Joseph Weiss, a 34-year-old disability lawyer had a client who carried heavy life insurance with permanent disability provisos. After suffering a heart attack, Weiss' client began receiving $500 per month and was not required to pay any more premium costs. Weiss presented his plan to 42-year-old Martin Gross, a salesman for The Maccabees, an insurance company, and 45-year-old Dr. Hirsch Messman. Weiss suggested that Gross locate customers who held large policies containing the permanent disability clause, but who were having trouble meeting premium payments, and persuade them to participate in the scheme. The doctor advised the other two that he could help fake heart attack symptoms by administering digitalis, a drug used to stimulate the heart, to fool the electrocardiograph. The three then agreed to skim a third of the insurance companies' payments to the clients and that portion would be split among the three.

In January 1934, Messman instructed 42-year-old Jake Harrison about heart attack symptoms, and the swindlers began collecting insurance money. By December 1934, the three had completed eighteen similar frauds, and by Spring 1936, the originators were raking in about $7,000 each, and they had recruited a few more doctors, six more lawyers, and a total of 106 insurance customers. In January 1937, Mr. Phipps an actuary who calculated risks for an insurance company, found fifty-eight coronary cases on Long Island and in the Bronx, all Weiss' cases, in which none of the patients died. Checking with other companies, Phipps found that other companies also had heart cases handled by Weiss, and not one client had died, contrary to medical and actuarial statistics. After an investigation, Weiss, Gross, Messman, thirty-six insurance policy holders, and thirteen co-conspirators were arrested on May 18, 1937. Messman became a witness against Weiss and Gross, who were convicted, each receiving a three-year sentence. Messman was convicted and given a suspended sentence. Two others, doctors Goldstein and George Krupp, were each sentenced to one year and one day. Some of the insurance customers were convicted and sentenced to light or suspended terms.

REF.: *CBA;* Hynd, *Murder, Mayhem and Mystery.*

Weiss, Mandy, See: **Buchalter, Louis**.

Weiss, Morris, 1922- , Case of, U.S., asslt. When a group of fifty persons ransacked and burned a Nazi bookstore in San Francisco, Auschwitz survivor Morris Weiss, fifty-five, was arrested for assault with a deadly weapon and resisting arrest. His son, Allen Weiss, twenty-four, was arrested for malicious mischief. The store, located in the city's Sunset district, stood directly across the street from the Temple B'nai Emunah in whose congregation consisted primarily of German Jews, many of whom had survived the holocaust. Operated by the National Socialist-White People's party, a small group of uniformed Nazis opened the store with a ceremony on Mar. 28, 1977, by painting a swastika on the store's window. Several Jewish leaders interpreted the action as inflammatory, and the building's owner, Nathan Green, an Auschwitz survivor, served the group an eviction notice, requiring them to move out by Apr. 5. On Apr. 2, the night before Passover, while 150 people looked on, fifty persons smashed down the door of the bookstore, overturned shelves, shredded and burned tracts and banners, and set fire to Nazi literature. The fire department and ten police cars arrived shortly after and were jeered by the crowd. Police arrested only Weiss and his son. Three Nazis wearing storm-trooper uniforms, escaped. Shortly after midnight, pro-Nazi demonstrators threw rocks and bottles at the Jewish temple, breaking five stained-glass windows.

Because of the spontaneous nature of the incident and the fact that "the bookstore was provocative and inciting" according to District Attorney Joseph Freitas, the felony charges against Morris Weiss and the misdemeanor charges against his son were dropped a week later. On June 13, the U.S. Attorney's office formally declined to press charges against the group that vandalized the store. REF.: *CBA.*

Weiss Club, prom. 1900s-20s, U.S., pros. The Weiss Club, operated by Ed and Aimee Weiss, stood next door to the Everleigh Club, Chicago's extravagant and lavish brothel run by the Everleigh sisters. Modelled after the Everleigh, the club possessed a certain anonymity and was the Everleigh's only true competition. Aimee, one of the Everleigh's most beautiful courtesans, purchased the vacant building from its former owner, Madam Julia Hartrauft, after Hartrauft was robbed of $3,000 and sold the brothel at a low price to recoup her losses.

Renamed the Weiss Club, Aimee decorated the building with luxurious furnishings, and procured women who were as attractive as the Everleigh courtesans. Her husband Ed secured customers to pay the Weiss' high prices with shrewd payoffs to area cab drivers. When a cabbie picked up a fare who asked to be taken to the Everleigh—but was too drunk to know where he was actually going—the driver would bring him to the Weiss Club. As the atmosphere and service were comparable, the patron would never know the difference.

The Weiss Club was closed, along with the Everleigh, in 1911 when Mayor Carter Harrison, Jr. ordered a crackdown on the city's vice districts. Ed Weiss later attempted to buy the Everleigh in 1913, by agreeing to pay $25,000 a year for police protection, but the deal was never finalized. Weiss worked as a player in Al Capone's brothel empire in the 1920s, but never opened another Weiss Club. REF.: *CBA.*

Weissman, William (AKA: Solly), 1895-1930, U.S., org. crime. Weissman was a product of the venal Pendergast political machine of Kansas City, Mo., a hulking 300-pound slugger who bullied voters into casting ballots for Tom Pendergast's hand-picked candidates. In the 1920s, Weissman, with the sanction of Johnny Lazia, crime overlord of Kansas City and Pendergast's enforcer, opened a gaudy gambling den on Thirteenth and Baltimore streets. He was soon closed down when three bettors, all winners, were shot on Weissman's premises, one of these gamblers later dying.

Police arrested the giant thug but realized that not much of a case could be made against him, although many witnesses initially stated that he was the triggerman. As detectives expected, the witnesses to the shooting either vanished or lost their memories. It was an old story for Weissman, whose criminal career trailed back to his early teen-age years when he busied himself by rolling drunks, particularly farmers, wandering into Kansas City for a night on the town. His specialty was administering knock-out drops to these rural revelers, carrying them to their dilapidated cars outside and emptying their pockets en route.

Weissman, before 1929, had established a long police record, a rap sheet that recorded twenty-nine arrests and a conviction which symbolized his extravagant and braggadocio manner. Weissman encountered a thief on the street one night, a pilferer who trembled before a large, menacing crowd, which, with one voice, stated it would beat the man senseless for gathering delicacies from iceboxes opening upon back porches.

The lumbering Weissman broke through the crowd and shielded the apprentice thief with his massive body, then turned to the irate citizens and announced confidently that he would handle the matter, adding that he was a plainclothes detective. He sent the jittery thief on his way when the crowd dispersed but someone reported the actions of this "fat flatfoot," and Weissman was later arrested and convicted for impersonating the very kind of person he hated most—a police officer. He was compelled to pay a $500 fine for his good deed, vowing he would never again play the good Samaritan, even for crooks.

As one of Lazia's high-ranking strong-arm men, Weissman's fortunes soared in the late 1920s. He adorned his corpulent figure in expensive suits, zipped about the streets in a flashy sportscar, and tried to emulate the manners of movie stars he admired, especially comedian Harold Lloyd. He learned that the horn-rimmed glasses Lloyd wore in films were without glass and bought a pair, wearing them night and day because he thought they gave him "that classy look." By then, Weissman was operating another gambling den on Thirteenth Street, next door to Convention Hall where he was seen regularly attending the boxing and wrestling matches.

Another public obsession of the day was dance marathons, and Weissman capitalized on these strange events by betting on couples he figured would win with his help. In 1928, a huge dance marathon was held at Convention Hall and Weissman attended, exploding at the judges when his hand-picked couple was eliminated. Weissman and his goons stormed the judges' stand and had the dance stopped until the Weissman hoofers were reinstated. Following the marathon dance, the event's promoters suddenly disappeared, along with the prize money. Weissman and his boys had taken the sharpers for "a ride," the story goes, killing them and pocketing the proceeds.

Kansas City ganster William "Solly" Weissman.

The portly Weissman's prestige was increased mightily when crime kingpin Lazia invited him to become his partner in a posh dog-racing enterprise on the north side of Kansas City. The track lined the fat gangster's pockets with unexpected profits. Now the one-time strong-arm thug came to believe that he was truly a big shot, worthy of ranking with Lazia. He began to envision himself as an underworld czar and schemed night and day to make millions from his Lazia-endorsed position.

One of his brainstorms was tapping the wire of the national syndicate which reported the daily racetrack results, learning the results seconds before they reached the betting parlors and laying off last-minute big-time bets that would make him an overnight millionaire. One man, however, stood in his way, Hard Luck Charley Haughton, who ran the wire service in Kansas City. Haughton earned his nickname after suffering massive betting reversals a decade earlier, when his many betting parlors lost huge amounts of money to lucky winners and he insisted on paying them off. Haughton was known up and down the Twelfth Street vice district in Kansas City as an honest man, and he lived up to this reputation by telling Weissman that he would never allow a tap on the syndicate wires.

Weissman's reaction was to explode, threatening the little Haughton with a beating so severe he would be hospitalized for months. Haughton only sneered at the obese gangster. Then Weissman, who is credited with first practicing the "one-way ride" in Kansas City, suggested that his boys might drop by to pick up Haughton in one of their roadsters one night. Again, Haughton waved off the threat with a contemptuous gesture. Vowing he would return, the stymied Weissman left Haughton's second floor office above Rayen's Turf Betting Agency. But Weissman's attentions were diverted from Haughton when he tried to muscle in on some of Lazia's other gambling enterprises. Since he was a part owner of the Riverside Dog Track Operation, called "Pendergast's Track" by the sharpers of Kansas City, he felt that other Lazia enterprises, such as the high society gambling spas, The Green Hills Club, and Cuban Gardens, needed his "protection."

Johnny Lazia, a cool, collected, and subtle gangster who always sought a low profile, had paid Weissman off for his long years of labor as a slugger by giving him a piece of the dog track. But he had no intention of sharing the enormous spoils flowing from his swanky gambling country clubs where the cream of Kansas City society spent fortunes each night at roulette and blackjack while sipping imported champagne.

"I can't have a monkey like Weissman smelling up my best places," he told his aide, Michael James "Jimmy Needles" LaCapra (who was later to become a nervous but willing police informant following the bloody Union Station massacre in Kansas City in 1933). Lazia gave orders to local police, most of the force being on his payroll, to pressure Weissman out of town. Police Chief John L. Miles knew Weissman controlled much of the liquor distribution for Lazia in the notorious Twelfth Street district, and his officers, working with Prohibition agents in this constitutionally dry period, put together a hastily constructed liquor conspiracy charge.

Before he was about to be picked up by police, Weissman received a call from his boss, Lazia, telling him that officers were on the way to arrest him. The behemoth gangster burst into sweat, thanked Lazia (the man who had set up the whole thing), blubbered some hasty orders to his minions, and left town immediately—exactly what Lazia wanted. Fat Solly Weissman went to Chicago where he was given a less-than-hearty welcome by the Capone mob, Lazia having put the word out along the criminal grapevine that Weissman was not a man to be trusted.

Weissman inquired about the possibility of entering the Chicago rackets, but he was met with indifference. He moved about from one Chicago hotel to another, brooding about his fall from power in Kansas City. He concluded that it was all the fault of Hard Luck Charley Haughton for turning down his wiretapping scheme. The heavyset gangster packed his bags and took the next train back to Kansas City.

Upon his arrival, Solly Weissman checked his bags in Union Station and took a cab to Haughton's office. It was Oct. 28, 1930, the last day of Solly Weissman's life. He barged into Haughton's office, knocking aside the racetrack cronies there. Haughton was behind a large desk, watching the massive gangster approach. Weissman's heavy jowls waggled and a froth came out of his mouth as he cursed the little gambler. His gargantuan frame went over the desk and huge arms bent downward, fat fingers spread as they sought Haughton's throat.

Haughton leaned back in his chair just out of Weissman's long reach and pulled out a pistol, aiming it upward, he fired one shot. The bullet went straight through Weissman's throat, killing him. His giant body crashed down onto the desk, tipping it sideways to the floor, going over with the falling gangster.

Haughton later surrendered to police who believed his story of self-defense. Hard Luck Charley was acquitted of murder and, in fact, became a local hero, applauded for ridding Twelfth Street of a murderous monster who aspired to high society status and more criminal power than he knew how to handle. See: **Audett, James Henry**; **Cuban Gardens**; **Green Hills Club, The**; **Kansas City Massacre**; **Lazia, John.**

REF.: *CBA;* Dorsett, *The Pendergast Machine;* Eisenberg and Landau, *Meyer Lansky;* Fried, *The Rise and Fall of the Jewish Gangster in America;* Louderback, *The Bad Ones;* Milligan, *The Inside Story of the Pendergast Machine and the Man Who Smashed It;* Reddig, *Tom's Town;* (FILM) *G-Men,* 1935.

Weissman-Bessarabo, See: **Myrtal, Héra**.

Wei Tao-Ming, b.1899, China, lawyer. Practiced law in Shanghai. He also served as minister of justice from 1928, and as secretary-general of the Executive Yuan from 1937-41. REF.: *CBA.*

Weitzman, Irving, prom. 1934, Case of, U.S., mur. During the strain of the Great Depression, Louis J. Weitzman loaned $108,000 to Eli Daiches, the owner of The Thomas M. Bowers Agency, a Chicago advertising firm. As collateral, Weitzman, a relative of Daiches' wife, received stock in the company and he became the chairman of the board of directors and the actual owner of the firm. Daiches transferred life insurance policies worth $317,000 at the same time, designating his company as the beneficiary.

On Mar. 3, 1934, as Daiches was driven from his apartment in a limousine, another car pulled up, and a young man, armed with a double-barreled sawed-off shotgun, got out of his car. He walked toward the limousine and fatally shot Daiches in the chest and head. Then the killer returned to his car and drove away in the morning rush hour. A local reporter, Harry Read, discovered the connection between the loan and the insurance policy and he also learned that Weitzman had two cousins with police records, and two brothers, Irving and Leon, who operated a bakery in Chicago. Irving Weitzman was implicated in the murder plot along with Jerry Pilot and a Mr. Toner. Pilot was suspected as the killer and Toner as Pilot's assistant. In early April 1934, Pilot was murdered and Toner was killed as he went home from Pilot's funeral, both shot to death with the same gun responsible in the Daiches murder. Irving Weitzman was tried, and on Feb. 23, 1935, he was found Guilty and sentenced to a life term, however, after an appeal and a retrial, he was acquitted.

REF.: *CBA;* Rice, *Forty-five Murderers.*

Welch, Albert, 1903-47, Brit., (unsolv.) mur. Two schoolboys in search of lost golf balls at the Potters Bar Course in Middlesex, England, pulled out of the water what seemed to be a strange object—a human torso as it turned out. Not knowing what to do with the putrefied remains, the boys buried it under the brush. Several days later, two other boys discovered a severed human hand and forearm along the banks. The police were summoned by a group of golfers alerted to the possibility of a murder on their grounds.

The Thames Police dragged the pond for additional body parts and eventually all the remains were located, but because of their decomposed condition of the remains, it was difficult to identify the victim. The thick cracks between the bones on the skull indicated to pathologists that the victim was well past his thirty-fourth birthday since the sutures are wide at birth, but knit together with advancing age. The skull had been battered with a heavy, blunt object, with death occurring as a result of injuries to the brain. The body had been hacked to pieces and tossed into the pond at least six months prior to discovery. Superintendent Colin MacDougall of Scotland Yard poured over a ream of missing person's reports going back twelve months to May 1947 to see if that would shed any light on the identity of the victim. By comparing the measurement of the left and right clavicles and scapulae, experts had been able to determine that the subject was left-handed, and two persons on the list were found to be left-handed.

Helped by that, the police determined that the victim was Albert Welch, a 44-year-old railway worker reported missing by his wife the previous October. Welch had lived in Potter's Bar, and was known to have a deformed finger on his left hand. So, too, did the severed hand of the victim. To confirm their findings MacDougall located a dentist who had performed work on Welch. The doctor recalled the time when he had removed Welch's lower teeth and had fitted him for a denture. The lower jaw on the skull corresponded with these findings. There were no teeth.

Pathologists meticulously reconstructed the lower jaw, which was placed in the correct anatomical position by using dental articulators. A photograph was taken and superimposed over a life-size image of the rebuilt skull. The findings were carefully assembled and brought before Hendon coroner Dr. Cogswell. A jury was hastily summoned and a verdict was returned stating that these were the remains of Albert Welch, though the grieved widow refused to accept these findings. While this was a victory for forensic science, the police were unable to establish a motive nor could they locate a probable suspect.

REF.: *CBA;* Cuthbert, *Science and the Detection of Crime;* Hibbert, *The Roots of Evil;* Nash, *Open Files;* Scott, *Scotland Yard;* Shew, *A Second Companion to Murder.*

Welch, Bernard Charles, Jr., 1940- , U.S., burg.-mur. The fifteen-year crime career of Bernard Welch ended in 1980 with his arrest and murder conviction in the death of Washington, D.C., resident Dr. Michael J. Halberstam. Welch began burglarizing luxury homes in 1965 at the age of twenty-five, specializing in the theft of furs, silverware, art objects, and rare coins. He worked alone, making it difficult for law enforcement officials to capture him. Furthermore, he melted down most of the precious metal he stole. However, he was arrested twenty-five times, but managed to avoid imprisonment either by jumping bail or escaping from prison. It was estimated that between 1965 and 1980, Welch netted between $10 and $20 million.

In 1974, Welch escaped from Dannemora Prison in New York by hiding out on the grounds after a softball game, then scaling a twenty-five-foot-high fence. He became one of the FBI's most-sought-after criminals, and 15,000 circulars with his description and *modus operandi* were distributed to police. After his escape, Welch paid $245,000 cash for a home in Falls Church, Va. He made $750,000 in improvements on the home and lived there with his common law wife and three children. He told neighbors he was a very successful stockbroker, and frequently invited them over to see his private art collection, indoor swimming pool, and environment room. He further equipped his home with an elaborate security system that monitored the grounds with a host of remote control cameras and closed-circuit televisions.

Dr. Michael J. Halberstam, left, and Bernard Charles Welch, right.

After burglarizing four homes on Dec. 5, 1980, Welch broke into Dr. Halberstam's home. Halberstam, a well-known cardiologist and author, surprised the burglar, and Welch shot him. Halberstam did not die immediately and managed to escape from the house and get into his car. Outside, he saw Welch and ran him over with the auto. Halberstam died on the operating table. With Welch in custody, investigators searched his Virginia home. They found fifty boxes of stolen goods belonging to nearly 2,000 burglary victims who were called to reclaim their property. Welch was sentenced to nine consecutive life terms in prison, making him eligible for parole in 143 years. REF.: *CBA.*

Welch, Bobby, See: **Great Train Robbery, The.**

Welch, Ed, c.1865-1912, U.S., west. outl. A member of the Wild Bunch, or Hole-in-the-Wall Gang, Ed Welch was killed during a train robbery. After many successful robberies with Butch Cassidy and the Wild Bunch, Welch was jailed in Atlanta, Ga. His cell mate was the "Tall Texan," fellow Wild Bunch member Ben Kilpatrick. The two were released on June 11, 1911, and began their search to reunite the Wild Bunch. By the time they got to Texas, they learned that both the Wild Bunch and "Black Jack" Ketchum's gang had disbanded. Kilpatrick reluctantly allowed Welch to be his partner, and the two men robbed a couple of banks.

In 1912, Kilpatrick and Welch attempted to rob a Southern Pacific train in Dryden, Texas. They stopped the train by claiming to be railroad detectives, and then entered the express car. As Welch was loading up the money, Kilpatrick became momentarily distracted and the guard in the express car hit Kilpatrick a fatal blow to the head with a mallet. The guard then turned to Welch and shot him dead. REF.: *CBA.*

Welch, James, See: **Jones, Thomas.**

Welch, Joseph Nye, 1890-1960, U.S., lawyer. Legal counsel for U.S. Army during 1954 U.S. Senate subcommittee hearings led by Senator Joseph R. McCarthy. REF.: *CBA.*

Welfare Island Prison Scandal, 1934, U.S., polit. corr. One of the first duties of Austin H. MacCormick after being appointed corrections commissioner by New York City mayor Fiorello H. La Guardia was to expose the wretched conditions of Welfare Island Prison. MacCormick initiated investigations after the murder of inmate George Holsoe, better known as "Horseshoes." Holsoe was the leader of one of two inmate gangs seeking to control the narcotics trade in the prison. Warden Joseph A. McCann scheduled a summit to mediate the dispute between Holsoe's faction and the rival gang led by Joie Rao. But before the meeting, Rao's gang allegedly stabbed Holsoe with knives manufactured in the prison machine shop. Pandemonium broke out as rival gangs attacked each other. Police airplanes and fireboats encircled the facility as 200 riot police stormed Welfare Island. Eventually, the outburst was brought under control.

The prison was a study in mob-controlled territory. The new leaders of the prison gangs, Joie Rao and Ed Cleary, along with their henchmen, lived in luxury in the prison hospital where they ate the best available food cooked by personal chefs. Rao owned several suits, had a personal barber, and when he chose to, he left the prison to take his wife out to dinner in Manhattan. The rest of the prison was virtually unfit for human habitation. Inmates received little food and almost no heat during the winter. They had to pay steep prices to the cell block bagmen for meat and the electricity to run a stove. But for $75 a week, any inmate could stay in the hospital wing with Rao and his henchmen.

One of the largest rackets in the prison was the sale of meat. The guards, who took orders from the top mobsters, received kickbacks on the deal. Prison guards received 250 pounds of meat each day—with the understanding that prisoners would eat all the leftovers. Another racket was the sale of lingerie and accessories for the gay prison population. Furthermore, one could reduce his sentence at the cost of $100 for a month reduction.

MacCormick initiated Operation Shakedown on Jan. 24, 1934. On a ruse, McCann was called to the commissioner's office. He was quietly escorted to a waiting car, part of a convoy of vehicles containing thirty policemen and twenty-five keepers from other prisons. Operation Shakedown officers uncovered Rao and Cleary's activities and confiscated knives, meat cleavers, rugs, lead pipes, table lamps, surgeon scalpels, electric grills, dozens of loaves of bread, large hunks of uncooked meat, razors, canned goods, and several walking sticks. Warden McCann was immediately discharged, and Welfare Island was demolished in 1935 with the completion of Rikers Island penitentiary.

REF.: *CBA;* (FILM) *Blackwell's Island, 1939.*

Welham, Edward George, c.1907-31, Brit., (unsolv.) mur. British entrepreneur Thomas Hathaway enjoyed hunting dogs, so in 1929, he built Coverdale Kennels in Dorset County, located in southwestern England. Several months later, his trainer and manager, William Steer, was found shot to death; the incident was ruled an accident.

Twenty-four-year-old Edward Welham was then hired for the position. On Oct. 1, 1931, Welham visited the kennels before breakfast and about 8 a.m., went back to the Hathaway home where he was boarding. During Welham's absence, someone slipped into his office and stole his 16-bore gun. Welham returned to his office and asked his assistant, Frederick Deamen to locate a dog. The assistant left and several minutes later, Welham was shot by someone using his stolen gun. The murderer placed the gun near the body and took £9 from Welham's wallet.

When Deamen returned, he found Welham's body and ran to the Hathaway home to call Thomas Hathaway. Hathaway and his two children went to the office with Deamen and waited until police arrived. Later, Hathaway told police that he had removed a stick that had a string attached to the gun's trigger, implying that Welham had committed suicide. However, pathologists determined the stick and string apparatus could not have been used to discharge the gun, and the assistant, Deamen, did not remember seeing any such device. Pathologists also determined that the trainer had been shot in the back, while leaning over or kneeling, and from a distance of about twelve feet. Although police had a suspect, they did not have enough evidence to bring charges.

REF.: Browne and Tullett, *The Scalpel of Scotland Yard; CBA.*

Wellesley–Finch-Hatton Duel, 1828, Brit., duel. In January 1828, Arthur Wellesley, the First Duke of Wellington, became the prime minister of England. As a staunch adversary of Catholic emancipation, a party of Protestants counted on his support to oppose measures in favor of Catholics. However, as the Catholic Association grew in power, Robert Peel and Wellesley believed that the Catholics should be emancipated to prevent a civil war. In 1829, the ministry under Wellesley initiated the Catholic relief bill. During the dispute over the Catholic issue, George William Finch-Hatton, the Earl of Winchelsea, harshly criticized Wellesley for his change of view and Finch-Hatton sent a letter to the *Standard* newspaper expressing his opinion. The prime minister demanded an apology. Finch-Hatton refused, so Wellesley challenged him to a duel in 1828. The two men met in Battersea Fields, now Battersea Park, in London. Wellesley fired the first shot and then Finch-Hatton shot harmlessly into the air. Wellesley then accepted a written statement from Finch-Hatton after Finch-Hatton added the word "apology" to the document.

REF.: *CBA;* Melville, *Famous Duels and Assassinations.*

Wellman, Edward John (AKA: **Aleck Kerr, Alex Kerr, John Matson**), b.1894, and **Koslov, Walter**, prom. 1930s-1940s, and **Greenwald, Emil** (AKA: **Alecksander Rosen**, prom. 1930s-1940s, and **Raamat, Elmar** (AKA: **Walter Stone**), prom. 1930s-1940s, U.S., count. Four Russian nationals, all from the northwestern republic of Estonia, met in the U.S. in 1933. Two of them, Edward Wellman and Walter Koslov, went into the counterfeiting business together not long after they met. When they had difficulties with a plating process, they asked a countryman, electrical engineer Emil Greenwald, for help and offered him a share of the enterprise. Wellman perfected his silver plating skills by 1938, so he decided to establish his own business. The other men each went into business alone, but all remained on friendly terms.

In April 1941, Wellman was arrested in New York for passing counterfeit half dollar coins and officials discovered about 1,000 in his possession. Out on bail, Wellman fled to an apartment where he ran his operations with Elmar Raamat. The two divided the equipment and coins and Wellman set up a new operation at a different location in New York, later moving to Miami. On Dec. 30, 1941, Wellman, was arrested at a Florida racetrack. But on Jan. 25, 1942, Wellman and another prisoner unlocked their cell using a spring from an alarm clock and the 48-year-old Wellman escaped to New York. Meanwhile, police were trailing Wellman's former associates, eventually arresting Koslov, Greenwald, and Raamat, and seizing counterfeiting equipment and fake coins. On Oct. 8, 1942, Wellman was arrested again.

On Mar. 8, 1942, Koslov, Greenwald, and Raamat pleaded guilty. Koslov and Greenwald were each sentenced to five years in prison and Raamat received a three-year sentence. On Nov. 13, 1942, Wellman pleaded guilty and he was given an eight-year sentence.

REF.: *CBA;* Gibson, *The Fine Art of Swindling;* Smith, *Counterfeiting.*

Wellman, William Mason, prom. 1940s, U.S., (wrong. convict.) rape. After an elderly white woman was raped in Iredell County, N.C., on Feb. 11, 1941, she identified her attacker as William Mason Wellman, a black man. At the time of the rape, however, Wellman was working for a construction firm at Fort Belvoir, Va., nearly 350 miles from the crime scene. He collected his pay about midday and signed a payroll receipt, which was not available at his trial. In August 1942, Wellman was convicted and sentenced to death. The morning that Wellman was supposed to be executed, the North Carolina governor learned that another man had admitted to the crime and the governor granted a reprieve, which arrived just after Wellman had taken a seat in the electric chair. Following an investigation by the State Parole Commission, the board found the original payroll records, verified Wellman's signature, and located two witnesses who stated that Wellman was present at work that day. Wellman was granted a full pardon by Governor Joseph Broughton on Apr. 15, 1943, and freed that afternoon; the first man under the death penalty ever released by the state of North Carolina. REF.: *CBA.*

Wells, Alfred, d.1942, U.S., mur. The 1941 murder spree of Alfred Wells shocked the citizens of San Bernadino and communities throughout Southern California. The search for Wells, paroled from San Quentin in 1939, touched off a five-county manhunt.

Until the Spring 1941, the hunchbacked Wells had been involved in an incestuous relationship with his half-sister, 24-year-old Violet Wells who, on Apr. 26, decided to leave him and return home to her parents. That day, Violet's brother, David Raymond Wells, and his wife, Jean Wells, drove her to her parents' home in Escondido. Upon learning of her disappearance, Alfred Wells threatened David and Jean with bodily injury if they did not tell him where Violet was. The young couple said they knew nothing, but Wells was not convinced.

On May 7, 1941, Wells again arrived at David and Jean's San Bernadino home and convinced Jean and her friend, Rose Destree, to drive him to the desert to a chicken ranch where he had just gotten a job. Jean put her 13-month-old baby, Hester, into the car, and she and Rose drove Alfred Wells to the desert.

After traveling several miles, Wells ordered Jean to pull to the side of the road, and once again accused her of keeping Violet from him. Brandishing a gun, he forced her to write a note to her husband explaining that she, Rose, and the baby were being held hostage until David provided him with Violet's whereabouts.

Wells then shot Jean twice in the chest at close range, killing her instantly. He turned on Rose Destree and shot her twice as well. He laid baby Hester in her mother's arms. Once he had gone, Destree began an arduous crawl toward the road that ended four hours later when her calls for help were answered. Rescuers found Destree slumped in the desert scrub grass and Hester clinging to her mother's dead body.

By the time Destree reached the hospital, Wells had returned to town and had lured David from work with the note. David drove Alfred within two miles of the murder site. There Alfred shot him in the back of the head. David's body was found four days later in a desolate canyon near Cajon Pass in the San Bernadino foothills.

After news of Wells' spree reached the San Bernadino Sheriff's Department, several of his relatives throughout Southern California were taken into protective custody until Wells was apprehended.

Alfred Wells was convicted of the murders of 24-year-old David Wells, 18-year-old Jean Wells, and 17-year-old Rose Destree, who died of her injuries. Wells was sentenced of death.

On Dec. 4, 1942, he was taken to the San Quentin gas chamber that he had helped construct five years before while serving a sentence for robbery. Ten minutes after being strapped into one of the chamber's chairs, Wells was pronounced dead. REF.: *CBA*.

Wells, Carolyn, 1862-1942, U.S., writer. Wrote detective fiction, novels, and short stories. Books authored: *The Maxwell Mystery, Spooky Hollow, The Killer,* and others. REF.: *CBA*.

Wells, Charles (AKA: C.E., Charles Hill Wells, de Ville Wells, Lucien Rivier, Monte Carlo Wells), 1841-1926, Brit., fraud. A gambler and inventor, 44-year-old Charles Wells began defrauding wealthy victims in the middle 1880s. During the next several years, Wells took out provisional patents and by 1889, he had taken out at least 192 applications. Then he placed advertisements in newspapers, offering a high return on an investment. Wells' victims included William Crosby Trench and Catherine Mary Phillimore. When one of the victims filed a civil suit to try to recover his loses, he won the case and Wells fled aboard his yacht the same day. In 1892, he gained notoriety after breaking the Monte Carlo bank by winning increasingly larger sums, until he finally won £16,000. He became known as "the man who broke the bank at Monte Carlo," and a ballad was later written about him.

Pursued by creditors, Wells left the gambling tables and went to Havre, Fr., where he was arrested on his boat in December 1892. Extradited to England, Wells faced twenty-four warrants and was charged with fraudulently acquiring £29,800. He was convicted and sentenced to eight years in prison. Several years after his release from Dartmoor, Wells teamed up with a man named Moyle. Together the two sold a life-saving device, which they claimed could revive the dead. Wells and Moyle were tried and convicted of fraud. Wells received a three-year sentence and Moyle was given an eighteen-month prison term. When Wells was free again, he went to Paris where he opened a bank in 1910, attracting customers with a high interest rate. With Jeannette Burns, he stashed hundreds of pounds in England. He was arrested in January 1912 on a yacht with Burns. British and French authorities fought over custody, and finally Wells was handed over to the French.

REF.: *CBA;* Nicholls, *Crime Within the Square Mile.*

Wells, Edmund William, 1846-1938, U.S., jur. Edmund William Wells served as Arizona attorney general from 1902-04. Previously, Wells had presided over the territorial court of Arizona, a position to which he was nominated in 1891 by President Benjamin Harrison. REF.: *CBA*.

Wells, Harry, prom. 1930s, U.S., hijack.-rob.-attempt. mur. Harry Wells walked into the Citizens State Bank in Luling, Texas, on Mar. 5, 1934, and left with $2,482 in stolen cash. He escaped, and on Mar. 12, he shot at two policemen near Beeville and stole their car. Other officers engaged in a chase that ended when Wells abandoned the squad car after having a flat tire. Fleeing from the car, he fired at approaching police officers and commandeered another vehicle, taking the owner hostage. Wells escaped and drove to East Bernard, where he stopped for gasoline and released his hostage.

On Mar. 15, officials surrounded a shack on the edge of Gladwater and flushed the fugitive out with tear gas. Wells surrendered, was arrested, and was appeared in court to face charges of hijacking, assault with intent to kill, and robbery. In April, he was convicted and sentenced to ninety-nine years in prison for the first two charges and given a ninety-year prison sentence for the Luling bank robbery.

REF.: *CBA;* Cohen, *One Hundred True Crime Stories.*

Wells, Ida Bell (Ida Wells-Barnett), 1862-1931, U.S., writer. From 1891-92, Ida Bell Wells edited the Memphis *Free Speech,* of which she was part owner. Wells used the publication to speak out against mob violence and lynching, but ironically a mob opposing her viewpoints forced her out of Memphis. In 1895, she published a work titled *Red Record,* which examined the lynching phenomenon. REF.: *CBA*.

Wells, Ira Kent, b.1871, U.S., jur. Ira Kent Wells served as U.S. Attorney from 1921-24, and as assistant U.S. attorney general from 1924-25. Wells was nominated twice to the district court of the territory of Puerto Rico. His first nomination came from President Calvin Coolidge in 1925, and again in 1929 from President Herbert Hoover. REF.: *CBA*.

Wells, Nicholas, 1684-1712, Brit., rob.-mur. Nicholas Wells began his first adulterous affair with a woman in Lambeth. The affair was short but fatal to his marriage, and launched him on a career of thievery when he ended the liaison by stealing a gold watch, several diamond rings, and 250 guineas from his mistress.

Soon thereafter, Wells began robbing travelers as they rode through the English countryside. He stole twenty guineas from General Robert Fielding, whom he met on Putney Heath. He knocked Fielding from his horse and bound his hands and feet while he rifled through his pockets. After he stole thirty guineas, a silver watch, and several silver pieces from a butcher near Epsom, Wells was apprehended and confined to Marshalsea Prison in Southwark.

On Mar. 28, 1712, Wells was led to the gallows at Kingston-on-Thames. Once the rope was secured around his neck, Wells confessed to the murder-for-hire of a prosecutor who had sentenced fellow thief Elizabeth Harman to death. Before her death, Harman told Wells that her soul could not rest in peace if her prosecutor lived. For three guineas, Wells agreed to murder the man. After stalking him for several days, Wells stabbed him with a rapier. Following this confession, the 28-year-old Wells was hanged.

REF.: *CBA;* Smith, *Highwaymen.*

Wells, Robert William, 1795-1864, U.S., jur. Robert William Wells served as Missouri attorney general from 1826-36. Wells was nominated to the district court of Missouri by President Andrew Jackson in 1836 and was assigned to the western district court in 1857. REF.: *CBA.*

Wells, Thomas, 1850-68, Brit., mur. During the 1860s, England outlawed public executions. In 1868, Thomas Wells murdered Mr. Walsh, the station master at Dover. Wells, an 18-year-old railway porter, was condemned to die, and he was hanged by William Calcraft at Maidstone on Aug. 13, 1868, the first English convict executed in private.

REF.: Andrews, *Old-Time Punishments;* Bleackley, *Hangmen of England; CBA;* Cooper, *The Lesson of the Scaffold;* Potter, *The Art of Hanging.*

Wells Street, Chicago, prom. 1830s, U.S., pros. Chicago's Wells Street, between First and Jackson, was one of the nation's largest red-light districts in the 1800s. Although the city attempted to curb vice activity, small, shabby dives were in open operation during the 1830s. The district surrounding Wells Street grew so bad that the aldermen renamed the street Fifth Avenue so as not to blemish the name of Captain Billy Wells, the famous Indian fighter after whom the street was named. With the wave of reform at the turn of the century, Fifth Avenue improved and it was renamed Wells Street. REF.: *CBA.*

Welsh, Leila, 1921-41, U.S., (unsolv.) mur. Twenty-year-old Leila Welsh was killed around 3 a.m. on Mar. 9, 1941, in Kansas City, Mo. She was stabbed repeatedly with a sharp knife, and her skull was crushed with a blunt instrument. The only clues police found were those deliberately left by the murderer to throw investigators off his trail. A pair of pants found at the scene led police to an unidentified well-known citizen who had the pants thrown in the garbage by his servant. A pair of gloves, apparently used by the murderer, were later found to have been soaked with blood after Welsh was dead. A butcher knife with a man's fingerprints was found but was dismissed as the murder weapon. Another potential weapon, a stonemason's mallet, was also thrown out as evidence. The killer had also littered the scene with fifty cigarette butts collected from around the city. The final clue, a phone number inside a book of matches led investigators to yet another innocent person. Kansas City police eventually arrested and charged a man with the murder, but he was acquitted.

REF.: *CBA;* Nash, *Open Files.*

Wenham, Jane, d.1730, Brit., witchcraft. The residents of Walkerne, England, were afraid of Jane Wenham, who was thought to be a "wise woman." Once, in 1712, the elderly woman reportedly asked Matthew Gilson, a farmhand, for some straw. When he refused to sell her any, she allegedly cast a spell on him which caused him to fill his shirt with manure and to request straw from everyone he met. Gilson told the story to his employer, who denounced Wenham as a witch. Offended, Wenham filed a warrant for defamation of character, but the judge urged her to settle the disagreement out of court before Mr. Gardiner, the local pastor. Gardiner, who believed in witches, told Wenham to live with her neighbors without arguments and Gilson's employer paid a one-shilling fine for the insult.

Jane Wenham, the last person tried for witchcraft in England.

Not long afterward, the minister's servant, Anne Thorne, claimed that Wenham had caused her to suffer from a "running spell." Thorne, who had a dislocated knee, said she had been able to run until she met Wenham, and that she told Wenham she was going to Cromer to collect sticks for a fire. Thorne explained that Wenham told her to get sticks from a nearby oak tree, take off her dress and apron in order to carry the sticks, and then the woman pinned the material together to secure the load. Thorne then rushed home to the minister, screaming: "I am ruined and undone!"

Wenham was arrested, placed in jail for several days, and searched for marks of the devil. In 1712, she stood trial, accused of "conversing familiarly with the devil in the form of a cat," and reportedly, some "magic salve" and "magic cakes" were found in her home. After sixteen people testified against her, Wenham was convicted and she received the death penalty. Judge Powell, however, was able to secure a reprieve and a pardon for Wenham, the last person tried on charges of witchcraft in England.

REF.: Bragge, *A Defense of the Proceedings Against Jane Wenham;* _____, *A Full and Impartial Account of the Sorcery and Witchcraft Practiced by Jane Wenham;* _____, *Witchcraft Further Displayed; The Case of the Hertfordshire Witchcraft Considered; CBA; A Full Confutation of Witchcraft; The Impossibility of Witchcraft Plainly Proving...That There Never Was a Witch.*

Wensley, Frederick, d.1949, Brit., law enfor. off. Called "the greatest detective of all time" by Crown prosecutor Sir Richard Muir, Chief Constable Frederick Wensley handled more important murder cases for Scotland Yard than any other investigator at the time of his retirement in 1929. Wensley, an inspiration for the character Sherlock Holmes, was called "the Weasel" in London's underground and gained a reputation as a man who never gave up a case. Wensley often "cracked" cases by gathering clues while posing as a vagrant or petty thief. Famous crimes that Wensley was involved in include the Thompson Bywaters murder; the pursuit of Peter the Painter, the leader of a band of anarchists; the Gerard murder case, which Wensley solved with only two clues; the "S" case, in which Wensley tracked down and apprehended the notorious alleged murderer Stein Morrison.

Chief Constable Wensley began his forty-two year career as a patrolman in London's East End, where he gained an understanding of the East End gangs and their activities. He was promoted to detective within two years, and walked the Spitalfields slum shortly after Jack the Ripper ended his murders and mutilations in the same area. Wensley rose in the ranks and founded the "Big Five,"—the organization of senior detectives of Scotland Yard's Criminal Investigation Department (CID). He was named Chief Constable in 1924, the highest position in the CID, specifically developed for him in deference to his superior work as a detective. He retired in 1929, and died Dec. 4, 1949, at his home in London. See: **Morrison, Stein.**

REF.: *CBA;* Wensley, *40 Years of Scotland Yard.*

Wentworth, Asa, and **Wentworth, Horace**, and **Wentworth, Henry T.**, prom. 1845-50, Case of, U.S., mur. James L. Parker, the tax collector of Manchester, N.H., was murdered on Mar. 26, 1845. At the time of his death, Parker was carrying several thousand dollars in cash received from the sale of real estate. His corpse was found on a back street. He had been brutally mutilated with a razor and butcher's knife, the head severed from the body and most of the cash stolen. It took five years before three Wentworth brothers, Henry T., Asa, and Horace, were formally accused of Parker's murder. In May 1850 they were placed on trial but acquitted, much to the chagrin of the villagers in Manchester who took note of the fact that the brothers had come into a considerable amount of money following Parker's death. REF.: *CBA.*

Wentworth, Thomas (Earl of Strafford), 1593-1641, Brit., treas. Thomas Wentworth, the Earl of Strafford, served under England's King Charles I as the lord deputy of Ireland. From 1632-41 Wentworth carried out the king's policies and earned large profits for both King Charles and himself. In 1640, he commanded the royal forces against Scotland and was defeated. Later that year, John Pym, a parliamentary leader, started impeachment proceedings against both Wentworth and the Archbishop of Canterbury. Wentworth, accused of treason, faced multiple charges implementing martial law during peacetime, unlawfully evicting men from their estates, extorting taxes, and handing out illegal fines and imprisonment. Wentworth also was denounced for trying to cause a rift between Scotland and England.

When Wentworth's trial began in 1641, he faced three new charges; withdrawing £40,000 from the Exchequer in Ireland for his personal use, supporting military posts in Ireland at England's expense, and helping to place papists in the Church of Ireland. Although he denied most of the charges, and King Charles proclaimed that he had no reason to be persecuted, he was convicted and condemned. While Wentworth was confined in the Tower of London, King Charles planned a rescue attempt, which was discovered and reported to the Commons. Wentworth was hanged on May 12, 1641.

REF.: Earl of Birkenhead, *Famous Trials of History; CBA.*

Wentz, Arthur Philip, 1919- , U.S., (unsolv.) kid. On the afternoon of July 29, 1919, Elsie Wentz parked her baby carriage in front of a department store on crowded Third Avenue in New York City. Lying inside the carriage was her 7-week-old son Arthur. When the woman returned five minutes later, the infant was gone. The police interviewed a score of pedestrians who had passed by the store, but they could only provide sketchy details. The officers filed this report back at the station house: "The boy was stolen from his carriage by an unknown white woman, about nineteen years of age, blonde, dressed in white middy blouse, white skirt, no hat." Arthur Philip Wentz was never found. REF.: *CBA.*

Wentzel, Gerald C., prom. 1946, U.S., (wrong. convict.) mur. In December 1946, Miriam Greene, a 27-year-old divorcée was strangled with a scarf in her Pottstown, Pa., apartment. When she did not report for work her landlady opened the apartment on Dec. 9, and found the body. During the police investigation, officials questioned her former husband, George Greene, and her married lover, Gerald Wentzel. Wentzel initially claimed he only knew the murdered woman, but later admitted to having an affair with her and to finding her body on Sunday night, Dec. 8. He did not notify police, he said, because he was married and did not want to get involved. Wentzel also gave police an alibi, saying that he was hunting from Dec. 5, until the evening of Dec. 8, with fifteen other men several hundred miles away. Each of the hunting partners independently verified his alibi.

When Wentzel was brought to trial, pathology experts gave conflicting testimony about the time of death. The jury found Wentzel Guilty and he was sentenced to a ten- to- twenty-year term at the Pennsylvania Penitentiary. After Wentzel's conviction, Greene's mother and sister announced that they believed Wentzel was innocent, and offered a substantial reward for information leading to the true killer's arrest.

After Wetzel's conviction, medico-legal expert Dr. LeMoyne Snyder determined that the time of death was the evening of Dec. 7, while Wentzel was still on the hunting trip. This information was sent to the Board of Pardons and Paroles of Pennsylvania and in the early 1950s, Governor John S. Fine commuted Wentzel's original sentence to a term for the time already served, an action that automatically prevented Wentzel from obtaining compensation. See: **Snyder, Dr. LeMoyne**. REF.: *CBA.*

Werboczi, Istvan, c.1458-1542, Hung.-Turk., chancellor, assass. Hungarian jurist who prepared codified Hungarian law in *Tripartitum* in 1514. He was an advocate of János Zápolya, and served as chancellor. He began working for the government of Turkey in 1541, but was poisoned by the pasha of Buda. REF.: *CBA.*

Werewolf of Paris, The, 1933, a novel by Guy Endore. Francois Bertrand, a sergeant in the French army who was tried for robbing graves and defiling bodies (Fr., 1849), is the role model upon which Endore based his horrific story. See: **Bertrand, Francois**. REF.: *CBA.*

Werner, Karl, 1950- , U.S., mur. As a youth, Karl Werner, a newspaper boy in Marlboro, Mass., had threatened a young housewife with a knife, so police admitted the boy to the children's mental ward of a state hospital for evaluation. There, psychiatrists determined that Werner experienced, "epileptic-like attacks, marked by violence and outrage." His father soon took the family to San Jose, Calif. There, Werner spent time building mechanical devices in the basement of his parents' home.

On Aug. 3, 1969, Werner went for a walk in the park where he met two high school girls from his neighborhood, Debra Gaye Furlong, fourteen, and Kathy Snoozy, fifteen. After talking with them for a few minutes, Werner later said, "This loud bang went off in my head," and he pulled out a pocket knife, first stabbing Kathy, then Debra. He continued to stab one and then the other, knifing Kathy more than 200 times and Debra about 100 times. All of the injuries were above the waist, primarily on the midsection of the bodies, and neither was raped. A motorcyclist found their bodies that evening about 8 p.m. On Apr. 11, 1970, Easter Sunday, Werner attacked 18-year-old Kathy Bilek, while she was reading a book at Villa Montalvo park in Saratoga. Werner stabbed her forty-nine times, leaving knife marks in a pattern similar to those found on the other dead girls. Police appealed to the public for help, and a 23-year-old woman told police that two weeks prior to Bilek's murder she had been approached by a youth named Karl. The woman said she thought he was going to kill her, and she became even more alarmed when he told her he had lost his keys in the woods and asked her to help him search. She told him her legs were tired and left the trail. A ranger at the Villa Montalvo park also said he had spoken with a youth named Karl and on the day of Bilek's murder, and had written down the young man's licence plate number. On Apr. 29, police arrested Werner, a 19-year-old engineering student at San Jose City College. Werner confessed to the murders, reenacted the crimes, and led police to the murder weapons. During his trial, he pleaded guilty to all three murders, and on Sept. 29, Werner was sentenced to life in prison. REF.: *CBA.*

Wertham, Frederic, 1895-1981, U.S., psychiatrist-writer. Frederic Wertham, a noted Freudian psychiatrist and neurologist born and educated in Germany, advanced the thesis that violent crime would be greatly curtailed if psychiatry was used by law enforcement agencies. Dr. Wertham argued this point convincingly in his 1949 book *The Show of Violence,* which presented eight case histories in which he himself appeared as an expert witness. Wertham points out that the wrong diagnosis concerning the mental health of a criminal was a contributing factor to future crimes the subject might commit. Commenting on one of the doctor's later works in the New York *Times Book Review,* Abraham Kardiner of Columbia University noted: "It is Dr. Wertham's thesis that murder can be prevented, that society can be protected from the murderer and the murderer from himself."

Wertham emigrated to the U.S. in 1927. He joined the staff of Johns Hopkins University, serving as chief resident in psychiatry and assistant in charge of outpatients of the Mental Hygiene Clinic. During this time he befriended Clarence Darrow, the famed defense attorney, who was finding it difficult to get members of the psychiatry profession to appear in court cases as expert witnesses. Wertham harbored no such prejudices and often assisted Darrow in his cases. In 1932, largely through the efforts of Dr. Menas Gregory, Wertham helped organize the psychiatric clinic affiliated with the Court of the General Sessions in New York City, recognized as the first clinic of its kind to administer a psychiatric examination of a convicted felon with the final report then passed on to the court.

In 1941, while holding the title of senior psychiatrist for the New York City Department of Hospitals, Wertham published a chilling case study of a teenage murderer that in many ways mimicked Shakespeare's *Hamlet.* The book, *Dark Legend: A Study In Murder,* concerned an Italian immigrant boy who stabbed his widowed mother to death after she had married his uncle. The Oedipus complex was evident in the young man, whose name was Gino. Matricidal impulses in men are fairly common, according to Wertham's hypothesis, except that they are rooted deep in the subconscious. Such neuroses are manifest in obsessive handwashing and a fear of knives, among other things. Gino had murdered his mother as a safety valve to preserve his rapidly slipping sanity, according to Wertham. "Today he is a normal young man in his twenties," the author happily stated. Gino was declared sane and was released from custody in September 1941.

In later years Wertham led the crusade against horror films and children's comic books which he believed "overstimulated the children's fantasy in the direction of violence and cheap sexiness." In 1948 he organized a symposium in which he displayed a collection of graphically detailed comic books that played up the sex and violence themes. An article in the *Saturday Review of Literature* followed, titled: "The Comics...Very Funny!" REF.: *CBA.*

Wessel, Horst, 1907-30, Ger., mur. Horst Wessel, the son of a Protestant minister, joined Hitler's Brown Shirts, the SA, in 1926, abandoning his music studies and family in Berlin. He went to live with a prostitute, Erna Jaenecke, whom he had taken away from another Nazi, Ali Hoehler. Wessel made most of his money pimping for Jaenecke. On the strength of his mistress' sexual favors to Nazi superiors, Wessel was named a group leader of the SA in Berlin. He was foiled, however, by the man from whom he had stolen Jaenecke. Seeking revenge, Hoehler went to Jaenecke's former landlady, Frau Salm and got the address where Wessel and Jaenecke were living. He broke into their Berlin apartment on Jan. 14, 1930, shot Wessel in the mouth, then grabbed Jaenecke and fled.

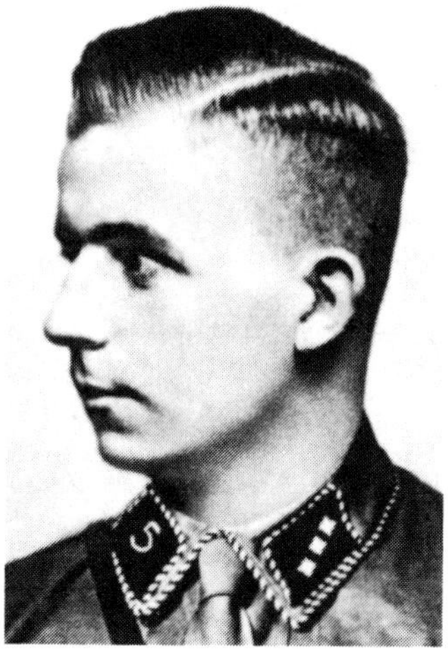

Pimp and thug Horst Wessel who was promoted as a Nazi martyr.

When Nazi propaganda chief Paul Josef Goebbels learned of this party scandal, he adroitly turned it into a heroic Nazi myth. He immediately covered up the facts and informed the German public that Wessel had courageously battled a gang of bloodthirsty communists, and, outnumbered, had been fatally wounded. Meanwhile, SA leader Ernst Roehm had his Brown Shirt thugs track down Erna Jaenecke, Ali Hoehler, and Frau Salm. They were all murdered, their bodies secretly buried so that Goebbels' myth about the martyred Horst Wessel would not be challenged.

Wessel stayed alive long enough to see himself transformed from thug to martyr, reading about his legendary and fabricated exploits in the pages of *Der Angriff*. After Wessel died on Feb. 23, 1930, Goebbels, rummaging through Wessel's effects, came across several songs Wessel had written and chose one of these to promote. The maudlin "Horst Wessel Song," which plaintively cried out the glories of the Nazi struggle and promised eventual political victory ("For the last time the rifle is loaded...Soon Hitler banners will wave over the barricades.") was just the thing to inspire Hitler youth, Goebbels concluded. Hitler himself decreed that the song was to be sung by National Socialist members at the close of all meetings and it soon became the Nazi anthem, adding to the mystical rituals of the Nazis and Adolf Hitler. See: **Goebbels, Paul Joseph; Hitler, Adolf.**

REF.: *CBA;* Fest, *Hitler;* Heiden, *Der Fuehrer;* Payne, *The Life and Death of Adolf Hitler;* Shirer, *The Rise and Fall of the Third Reich;* Vogt, *The Burden of Guilt.*

Wesson, Daniel Baird, 1825-1906, U.S., firearms. Created new repeating mechanism for rifles and pistols in 1854 while in partnership with Horace Smith. In 1857, he established the Smith & Wesson Company, which produced the new guns. REF.: *CBA.*

West, Dr. Eugene, prom. 1893, Case of, U.S., mur. Addie Gilmour, a Colusa, Calif., milliner, traveled to San Francisco in August 1893 to purchase hats. To acquaint herself with the latest fashions, she took a job at the F. Toplitz millinery on Market Street. She lived in rooms at the Elmer House on Bush Street. When her partner, Laura Allen, arrived in San Francisco on Sept. 1, she was told that Gilmour had left both her job and her lodgings without notice. Allen returned immediately to Colusa, and when Gilmour wasn't there she grew concerned.

Gilmour's twin sister received a letter from Addie dated Sept. 4, explaining that Addie was about to undergo surgery, to be performed by Dr. Eugene West. With this information, investigators learned that Gilmour had moved to Dr. West's address on Turk Street on Sept. 1. West later told police that he completed the operation on Sept. 4, but that Gilmour died on Sept. 9, at which time he gave the body over to dissection. Several days later, on Sept. 12, fishermen pulled Gilmour's head from the San Francisco Bay. After that, her torso and several other body parts were found in the bay. On Sept. 28, an oil can floating in an Oakland creek was found to contain two arms, a foot, and Gilmour's purse. Dr. West was arrested, which came as no surprise to the medical community, which held him in very low esteem. Annie Staley, his assistant, was thought to know damaging information about West, but she kept silent, and even married him on Sept. 28 so that she could not be called to testify against him, and so that she could visit him in jail.

A co-worker of Gilmour's who went to Dr. West's office after hearing about the note found May Howard there, who claimed to have met Gilmour three times—twice in West's office, and once on the Oakland ferry, where Gilmour was reportedly despondent and considering suicide. Howard told of Gilmour entering the ladies' room and never coming out, and of finding the window there open. But before West's trial began, Howard recanted, saying that the story about the ferry was completely fictional, and that Dr. West had persuaded her to tell it.

West's trial began on Feb. 5, 1894, before Judge Wallace. On Feb. 16, he was found Guilty of second-degree murder, and several days later was sentenced to twenty-five years in prison. But on appeal to the Supreme Court, he won a second trial, which began in December 1895. This time West claimed that he inherited Gilmour's case from a colleague, Dr. W.A. Harvey, whose previous malpractice had already doomed her. West said he gave Gilmour's body to Dr. Tuchler, and that he had refrained from identifying the two men in his previous trial because they were his friends and he wished to protect them. The jury, after an hour's deliberation, finally acquitted Dr. Eugene West.

REF.: *CBA;* Duke, *Celebrated Criminal Cases of America.*

West, Richard (AKA: Little Dick), d.1898, U.S., west. outl. After William Doolin was killed in 1896, the last surviving member of his gang, Richard "Little Dick" West tried to form another gang, recruiting novices. West named his outfit the Al Jennings Gang, after the leader of the group he had fallen in with, but Jennings, his brothers, and their friends the O'Malley brothers looked to West to guide them in robbing trains.

Outlaw "Little Dick" West, shown dead, 1898.

The gang's first attempted train robbery occurred near Oklahoma City on Aug. 16, 1897, at Edmond. While they looked at the door of an express car they had just stopped, a conductor asked them what they were doing. The outlaws panicked and ran for their horses. West had no choice but to follow.

West set up another train robbery near Muskogee, Okla., but his gang failed him again. They refused to attempt a bank job because they saw armed guards inside. They waylaid a Rock Island train in Indian Territory under the control of the Chickasaw

Nation, but used all the dynamite they had by mistake in their first attempt to blow the train's safe. The car containing the safe was blown apart, but the safe was unharmed, so they robbed the passengers, from whom they collected $300 in cash, some whiskey, and a stalk of bananas. During the holdup, Al Jennings' mask fell from his face. Someone who recognized him alerted lawman William Matthew Tilghman.

West took his share of the robbery and headed on alone. Tilghman hunted him down in a stable near Guthrie, Okla. On Apr. 7, 1898, West was currying his horse when Tilghman ordered him to surrender. West fired on Tilghman and tried to get away on foot, but the lawman killed him with one shot.

Jennings and his gang were later caught. Jennings was given a long sentence, of which he served less than five years. See: **Doolin, William; Tilghman, William.**

REF.: Breihan, *Badmen of Frontier Days;* ____, *Great Lawmen of the West; CBA;* Croy, *Trigger Marshal;* Graves, *Oklahoma Outlaws;* Hanes, *Bill Doolin;* Horan and Sann, *Pictorial History of the Wild West;* Hunter and Rose, *The Album of Gun-Fighters;* Hutchinson, *The Life & Personal Writings of Eugene Manlove Rhodes;* Jennings, *Beating Back;* Miller, *Bill Tilghman;* Newsom, *The Life and Practice of the Wild and Modern Indian;* Nix, *Oklahombres;* Raht, *The Romance of Davis Mountains;* Rouse, *A History of Cowboy Flat;* Sabin, *Wild Men of the Wild West;* Shirley, *Six-Gun and Silver Star;* Sutton, *Hands Up!;* Tilghman, *Marshal of the Last Frontier;* ____, *Outlaw Days;* Wellman, *A Dynasty of Western Outlaws;*

West, Ronald Eugene, 1961- , U.S., theft-rob.-sod.-kid.-rape-mur. On Mar. 30, 1988, Ronald Eugene West, a 27-year-old unemployed Washington, D.C., security guard, raped and robbed a Georgetown woman in the parking garage of an apartment building where he was once employed. On Apr. 19, West robbed another victim at gunpoint, and on May 8, he robbed and raped a woman in downtown Washington. On May 19, West attacked a second Georgetown woman in the same parking garage. He sexually assaulted 27-year-old Dawn Denise Fest and shot her twice in the head on May 19. The next morning, Fest, three months pregnant, was found partially clothed in the trunk of her abandoned car. When police televised a picture shot by a surveillance camera at an automated teller, a viewer recognized the suspect as West, and he was arrested two days later.

On June 16, 1989, West was convicted on nineteen charges following an eight-day trial. In connection with the Fest case, West was convicted of first-degree murder, kidnapping, armed robbery, and theft, but he was acquitted of rape. In the other cases, West was found Guilty of two weapons charges, three counts of theft, three counts of armed robbery, one count of sodomy, two counts of kidnapping, and two counts of rape. On Sept. 7, 1989, West was sentenced to life plus an additional 183 years in prison. REF.: *CBA.*

West, Samuel H., 1872-1938, U.S., jur. Served as prosecuting attorney for Logan County, Ohio from 1893-1900. He was nominated to the northern district court of Ohio in 1928 by President Calvin Coolidge. REF.: *CBA.*

West, Thomas (Baron De La Warre), 1577-1618, Neth.-Ire., rebel. British soldier in service to the Earl of Essex in campaigns in Ireland and the Netherlands. He was put in prison in 1601 for his involvement in the rebellions led by Essex. REF.: *CBA.*

West, Velma, prom. 1928, U.S., mur. In December 1928, Thomas Edward West and his wife, Velma, were invited to a dinner and bridge party. While the Perry, Ohio, couple discussed the matter, Velma West stood on a chair, fixing a broken curtain rod with a hammer, nails, and twine. Her 30-year-old husband did not want to go to the affair because he did not enjoy parties, bridge, or the company of the hostess, Mabel Young. Annoyed, Mrs. West beat her husband on the head with the hammer, put a pillow over his head, and hit him again with a chair leg. To keep her already dead husband from following her to the party in Cleveland, she bound his hands and legs with the twine. Afterward, she dressed, went to the party, played bridge, and danced.

Mrs. West was arrested, and dubbed the "Split-Mind Flapper Slayer" by the newspapers because she had been dropped on her head as a child. She was tried, convicted, and sentenced to a life term in prison. REF.: *CBA.*

West, Willie, and **West, William**, prom. 1903, U.S., fing. ident. Correctional facilities across the U.S. switched to the fingerprinting system of identification after the case of two look-alike brothers—Willie and William West. In 1903, the most common method of identification used by law enforcement agencies was that developed by French criminologist Alphose Bertillon in the 1880s. Bertillon's identification system called for measurements to be taken of specific physical features of an individual and worked on the assumption that each person possessed a unique set of measurements. Though a fingerprinting system had been developed by 1903, few were in current use.

That year, Willie West was sentenced to a prison term at the federal correctional facility in Leavenworth, Kan. Normal processing included taking a photograph of the new inmate and recording his Bertillon measurements. The prison clerk who performed these tasks believed that Willie West was William West, a current Leavenworth inmate. He decided that it was unnecessary to take the new inmate's measurements, only doing so after Willie had protested that he had never before been to prison. Willie's measurements proved to be identical to those of William. Prison officials hired a fingerprint expert who took both men's prints and found them to be completely different. Within a year, several correctional facilities, including New York's Sing Sing Prison and the St. Louis corrections system, switched from the Bertillon identification system to fingerprinting. The War Department began fingerprinting military personnel in 1905. See: **Bertillon, Alphonse.**

REF.: *CBA;* Cooper, *Ten Thousand Public Enemies.*

Westenhaver, David C., 1865-1938, U.S., jur. Served as prosecuting attorney for Berkeley County, W. Va., from 1886-87. He was nominated to the northern district court of Ohio by President Woodrow Wilson in 1917. REF.: *CBA.*

Westermann, François Joseph, 1751-94, Fr., consp. Arrested with revolutionary leader George Jacques Danton and guillotined. REF.: *CBA.*

Westervelt, William, b.1831, U.S., kid.-mur. On July 1, 1874, two men abducted four-year-old Charley Ross, the son of a Germantown, Pa., grocer, as he played in front of his home. A note demanding $20,000 ransom was delivered to the family. The boy's father, Christian Ross, attempted to comply with the terms set out in the note, but was unable to deliver the ransom, and the boy was never seen again. The Ross' friends and neighbors told police that a stranger, later identified as former New York City police officer William Westervelt, had been asking questions about the finances of the Ross family. Handwriting analysts identified Westervelt's brother-in-law William Mosher, a habitual burglar, as the author of the ransom note. On Dec. 14, 1874, Mosher and Joseph Douglas were shot while resisting arrest during the burglary of a Brooklyn home. In his dying breath, Mosher adnitted that he and Douglas had abducted Charley Ross. Westervelt was brought to trial for the kidnapping, convicted, and sentenced to seven years of solitary confinement. Reports circulated that Westervelt had brought the boy to New York, but had panicked when the search for the boy intensified and drowned him in the East River. See: **Ross, Charles B.** REF.: *CBA.*

Westlake, John, 1828-1913, Brit., lawyer. Helped establish Institut de Droit International in 1873 and served as member of Parliament from 1885-86. He taught international law as a at Cambridge from 1888-1908, and was considered an authority on private international law. REF.: *CBA.*

Weston, George (AKA: **William Johnson**), c.1752-82, and **Weston, Joseph** (AKA: **Samuel Watson**), c.1758-82, Brit., asslt.-forg.-rob. Brothers George and Joseph Weston left their parents' Staffordshire home for London, where George became a merchant's clerk, and after he allegedly altered the company's books, absconded with about £2,000. The Westons fled to the Netherlands, where they lived for a time before returning to Manchester,

England. In Manchester, George became a teacher and was appointed high constable. The brothers supplemented this income by stealing horses, committing forgery, running confidence games, and smuggling. When George was caught blackmailing innkeepers, he and his brother fled, turning to highway robbery.

On Jan. 29, 1781, they ambushed a royal mail coach traveling from Maidenhead to London, robbing it of £15,000. A £200 reward was offered for the capture of either man, and the Westons sought refuge in Winchelsea, posing as William Johnson and Samuel Watson, and living with two prostitutes who acted as their wives.

Embezzler George Weston.

By December 1781, they had rented a large house, lavishly furnished on credit, and they moved in local high society circles. The Westons still had not paid for the furniture by April 1782, and the owners of the furniture store reported the two men to the police. On Apr. 15, the creditors and a sheriff's officer confronted the Westons, but when the officer tried to arrest George, he hit him with a riding whip, and the Westons fled again, this time to London.

On Apr. 17, after being chased by police, the Westons were arrested and confined in Newgate. With the help of their female companions, the brothers escaped, but were soon recaptured. In July 1782, they were tried and acquitted on robbery charges in connection with the mail theft. They were immediately arrested again and tried the same day for forging endorsements on the bills they had allegedly stolen. George Weston was convicted and sentenced to death. Joseph Weston was acquitted, but tried again the same day on charges of shooting and wounding a porter during his escape attempt from Newgate. He was then convicted and received the death penalty. On Sept. 3, 1782, the Westons were hanged at Tyburn.

REF.: Armitage, *Bow Street Runners; CBA;* Pringle, *Stand and Deliver.*

Westwood, Billy (William), 1948-65, U.S., mur. Although he died not long after his seventeenth birthday, Billy Westwood, who never allowed anyone to call him William, was known throughout the Ozarks of Arkansas as a "bad seed."

At sixteen, Westwood was charged with the death of a classmate, Chad Wilson. Friends of the two claimed Westwood shot Wilson because Wilson called Westwood by his given name. The charges were dropped on Dec. 17, 1964, due to lack of evidence. Two days later, Westwood was in a barbershop in Franklin County, Ark., when another classmate kidded Westwood about his disdain for his first name. Five minutes later, four men were dead and one man seriuosly wounded by gunfire from Westwood's six-gun. For five weeks, a massive hunt was conducted by police for Westwood, who escaped to the mountains. On Jan. 29, 1965, police found Westwood's body in a ravine. A note was found next to the body which claimed Westwood had been shot by a vigilante who felt justice was best handled with a shotgun. REF.: *CBA.*

Westwood, Sarah, 1801-44, Brit., mur. In 1843, 42-year-old Sarah Westwood, wife and mother of five children in Burntwood Green, England, had been having an affair with Samuel Phillips, a man renting a room in her home. Westwood asked her lover's mother, considered a "wise woman," if she knew of a remedy to "cure the itch." The women purchased the necessary items from a druggist, who combined the ingredients at the pharmacy. Westwood returned to the drugstore later and coaxed the druggist to sell her arsenic alone.

In November 1843, Westwood poisoned her 40-year-old husband John Westwood. A medical examination revealed large amounts of arsenic in the man's body and Westwood was charged with murder, for which she was convicted and condemned to death. She pleaded for a stay of execution on the grounds of pregnancy, but authorities determined she was not pregnant, and in January 1844, Westwood was executed at Stafford.

REF.: Butler, *Murderers' England; CBA.*

Westwood, William John (AKA: **Jackey Jackey**), 1821-46, Aus., forg.-rob.-riot-mur. Nicknamed "Jackey Jackey" after an Indian chief, William John Westwood was convicted of forgery in England and transported to Australia when he was sixteen. The son of a Kent farmer, Westwood escaped from the penal colony in 1841 and joined Paddy Curran. Together, they reportedly abducted an overseer and flogged him fifty times with his own whip. After he and Curran parted, Westwood joined forces with a man named Riery. They traveled throughout New South Wales during the following seven months.

Westwood was recognized and re-arrested in August 1841 near Berrima. He was given another prison term and after several failed escape attempts, he was sent to the strictest prison camp in Tasmania. After another failed attempt to flee, he was transferred to Norfolk Island, where he instigated an inmate uprising in 1846, killing two guards with an ax. Another group of prisoners killed two more guards, and the chaos continued until 300 troops quelled the disturbance. Westwood was sentenced to death for the incident, and with eleven others, the 25-year-old was hanged in October 1846. REF.: *CBA.*

Wet, Christiaan Rudolf de, 1854-1922, S.Afri., treas. Directed Orange Free State military in Boer War in 1900 and headed guerilla resistance against British. He instigated an unsuccessful revolt of Afrikaners that was stopped by Louis Botha in 1914. Condemned for treason, he was imprisoned in 1915. REF.: *CBA.*

We the People, 1933, a play by Elmer Rice. The Sacco-Vanzetti robbery-murder case (U.S., 1920) provides the basis for this polemic drama. See: **Sacco, Nicola**. REF.: *CBA.*

Wexler, Irving, See: **Gordon, Waxey**.

Weyer, Johan, 1515-88, Ger., witchcraft. Johan Weyer, a doctor who attended Duke William of Cleves, was one of the first to object to Germany's unbridled persecution of witches. Weyer, who believed in Satan, made a delineation between women who might have an agreement with the devil but did not perform magic, and women who worked actively for the devil. In particular, Weyer protested against torture used to extract confessions. Although his outspokenness endangered his life, he was protected by Duke William, and Weyer's ideas helped to temper the furor of the time. His works, *De Praestigiis* (On Magic), 1563, and *De Lamiis* (On Witches), 1577, reflected his views on witchcraft.

REF.: Axenfeld, *Jean Wier et la sorecellerie;* Binz, *Doctor Johann Weyer; CBA;* Eschbach, "Dr. med. Johannes Wier...Ein Beitrag zur Geschichte der Hexenprozesse"; Lea, *Materials Toward a History of Witchcraft;* Robbins, *The Encyclopedia of Witchcraft and Demonology;* Singer, *Studies in the History and Method of Science;* Weyer, *De l'imposture et tromperie des diables;* ____, *De Praestigiis Daemonum et Incantationibus ac Veneficiis;* ____, *Histoires, disputes et discours des illusions et impostures de diables;* ____, *Von Teufelsgespenst, Zauberern und Giftbereytern;* Zilboorg, *The Medical Man and the Witch During the Renaissance.*

Weyerhauser, George, See: **Dainard, William J.**

Weyler, Joseph, See: **Spanish, Johnny**.

Weyman, Stanley Clifford (AKA: **Stephen Jacob Weinberg, Ethan Allen Weinberg**), 1890-1960, U.S., fraud. Con man Stanley Clifford Weyman, who engaged in deceptions for most of his life, was proficient in his many impersonations. In 1921 Weyman introduced himself to Princess Fatima of Afghanistan as a naval officer representing the U.S. State Department. While escorting her around New York, he bilked the princess out of $10,000. He was imprisoned the following year for impersonating a hospital administrator who took patients' money. His sentence was lengthened by two years for defrauding Princess Fatima.

Many of Weyman's activities were for fun rather than for profit. He masqueraded as an authority on prison reform at Sing Sing. Following the death of Rudolph Valentino, he posed as a physician and arranged to attend to grief-stricken actress Pola Negri. When reporters discovered he was a fraud, the actress defended him and no charges were brought. Once, posing as the consul general to Algiers, he invited a number of illustrious people to dinner at the Brooklyn's St. George Hotel. Although the party was a huge success, he was subsequently unmasked and his father had to pay the $400 bill and bail him out of jail.

While clerking at a hotel in Yonkers, N.Y., Weyman struggled with robbers to keep them from getting the hotel's cash box. He succeeded, but he was killed.

REF.: *CBA;* McKelway, *The Little Man from Brooklyn;* Nash, *Hustlers and Con Men.*

Whale, Anne, c.1730-52, and **Pledge, Sarah**, d.1752, Brit., mur. After John and Anne Whale were married, they moved into Sarah Pledge's boarding house. Pledge and Whale had several arguments and John Whale forbade Pledge from entering his apartment. Following a reconciliation, the women, for unknown reasons, conspired to kill John.

Anne and Pledge concocted a scheme to poison John. Inexperienced in poisoning, they believed that putting roasted spiders in his beer would cause death. When this attempt failed, Pledge opted for a more direct approach. She bought a vial of poison from a pharmacy. Anne mixed it into her husband's supper and he died the following day.

A coroner's autopsy revealed poison in the young man's system, and a subsequent investigation resulted in murder charges against the two women. Although Pledge attempted to reduce her punishment by testifying against Whale, the two women were convicted of murder and sentenced to death.

On Aug. 14, 1752, Sarah Pledge was hanged for her part in the conspiracy, while Anne Whale was tied, strangled, and burned at the stake, the punishment required by Saxon law for a woman who murders her husband.

REF.: *CBA;* Mitchell, *The Newgate Calendar.*

Whale Barroom, prom. 1870s-80s. In San Francisco in the late 1800s, the Whale Barroom, run by Johnny McNear, was one of the city's most notorious saloons, frequented by numerous criminals traveling the Barbary Coast. Fugitives felt secure at the Whale, because few policemen dared enter without a large backup force. Suspected criminals were rarely taken from the Whale without a gunfight.

During its heyday, 1870-80, regulars at the Whale included Cod Wilcox, a prominent San Francisco Bay "pirate" later imprisoned in San Quentin Prison, and Tip Thornton, known as one of the deadliest fighters along the Barbary Coast. Thornton, a Whale mainstay, always carried a long knife with a razor-sharp, narrow blade.

During a fight, Thornton would attempt to cut off his opponent's nose, and if that proved futile, he would slice off an ear. Other Whale regulars kept count of the number of noses and ears that Thornton had removed, but they lost count after forty. Thornton was eventually arrested by the only police officer who would enter the Whale alone, Officer Jack Cleary. Cleary had to fend off about six other customers before he dragged Thornton away in handcuffs. The Whale never regained the same notoriety after Thornton was sent to San Quentin. REF.: *CBA.*

Whalen, Grover Michael Aloysius, 1886-1962, U.S., law enfor. off. Grover Whalen, named after President Grover Cleveland because he was born on the president's wedding day, held a variety of municipal jobs in New York City, and was best known as the city's official welcomer who first employed the tickertape parade. On Dec. 18, 1928, Mayor James J. Walker, a friend of Whalen's, appointed him police commissioner. Whalen took office amid public criticism over handling of the unsolved shooting of Arnold Rothstein and for what was described as a decline in morale of police ranks.

His first act as commissioner was to appoint a new chief of detectives in charge of the Rothstein case. Whalen next eliminated the current homicide squad, retired the squad leader, and instituted new homicide squads in each borough. He dismantled the internal investigation division, transferring the leader to Long Island. He also ordered a squad of large, burly officers to comb the city looking for gangsters to harass with nightsticks. In addition, Whalen armed officers with axes and crowbars, ordering them to demolish all the speakeasies they raided; he arranged for undercover officers to infiltrate Communist groups; and he would frequently arrive at police quarters for unannounced, early-morning inspections. On May 21, 1930, Whalen was succeeded by Edward P. Mulrooney.

NYPD commissioner Grover Whalen.

REF.: *CBA;* Levine, *Anatomy of a Gangster;* Lynch, *Criminals and Politicians;* Peterson, *The Mob;* Thompson, *Gang Rule in New York;* Whalen, *Mr. New York: The Autobiography of Grover Whalen;* (FICTION), Wilstach, *Under Cover Man.*

Whalen, Lawrence E., 1937- , U.S., law enfor. off. After serving three years in the U.S. Marine Corps, Lawrence Whalen began training for the Cincinnati Police Division in November 1958. Whalen began his career as a beat officer, followed by district investigator, field supervisor, internal investigator, district commander, S.W.A.T. commander, and operations chief before becoming the chief of police.

Whalen also graduated from the 92nd Federal Bureau of Investigation National Academy Class and he is a member of the International Association of Chiefs of Police and the Police Executive Research Forum. REF.: *CBA.*

Whaley, Edward, d.c.1674, Brit., jur. One of sixty-seven judges at trial of King Charles I and signed Charles' death warrant in 1649. REF.: *CBA.*

Wharton, Elizabeth, prom. 1870, Case of, U.S., mur. A Baltimore, Md., widow who was running short of money, Elizabeth Wharton borrowed $2,600 from General William Scott Ketchum. In June 1870, Ketchum left his home in Washington, D.C., to collect the debt. After arriving, the general became extremely sick, and for the next several days, Wharton gave him alcoholic beverages. During that week, Wharton purchased some tartar emetic, which she later said was for her own use. During his illness, Ketchum reportedly claimed that Wharton had poisoned his lemonade, and another guest, a banker named Van Ness, who was aware of Wharton's financial situation, was given a glass of beer which was said to have been laced with a tartar emetic containing antimony. The tartar emetic was also allegedly found in Ketchum's milk punch.

Ketchum died at the end of the week, and Wharton was arrested. Her trial was held in Annapolis. During the proceedings, she swore that she had repaid Ketchum, and that, in fact, he owed her $4,000. Although several druggists testified that traces of antimony were found in Ketchum's body, Wharton was acquitted.

REF.: *CBA;* Gross, *Masterpieces of Murder;* Morse, *Famous Trials;* Pearson, *Instigation of the Devil; Trial of Mrs. Elizabeth G. Wharton.*

Wharton, Francis, 1820-89, U.S., lawyer. Practiced law in Philadelphia. He worked for the U.S. Department of State from 1885-89 and wrote several legal works. He was also a clergyman. REF.: *CBA.*

Whatman, John, c.1872-1946, Brit., (unsolv.) mur. In early March 1946, robbers looted the home of wealthy cattle dealer John Whatman. The thieves forced open the safe in his Hollington, England, home, and fatally shot Whatman twice, leaving him to die in the yard. Police were never able to solve the murder.

REF.: *CBA;* Simpson, *Forty Years of Murder.*

What Really Happened, 1932, a novel by Marie Belloc Lowndes.

This work of fiction is based on the sensational Florence Bravo poisoning case (Brit., 1876). See: **Bravo, Florence Ricardo.** REF.: *CBA.*

Wheat, Clarence, d.1980, U.S., suic.-mur. In 1979, Clarence Wheat was sentenced to five years in prison at the Mississippi State Penitentiary at Parchman for the shooting death of a Mississippi police officer during a family disturbance. After serving only eight months of his sentence, Wheat, suffering from diabetes, heart disease, and terminal cancer, was pardoned by the governor of Mississippi so that he could return to his home and die there.

Six months later, in June 1980, the ex-convict shot and killed his wife and son before turning the gun on himself. His daughter and her three children escaped. John Watkins, the state corrections commissioner, said that releasing terminally ill convicts was routine practice, and added that it was "...terrible to die in prison." REF.: *CBA.*

Wheat, Thomas, and **Stocks, Maria**, prom. 1920, Brit., big. Simply believing that one is divorced without written proof of that divorce is not a defense to a charge of bigamy. This was the decision of five learned judges of the British high courts in the case of *Rex vs. Wheat and Stocks,* which began innocently enough at the Assize of Lincoln in 1920.

Thomas Wheat was married for the first time in 1911. He fathered two children before joining the army in 1914 to fight in WWI. While he was gone, his wife left him for another man. When his hitch in the army was up in 1918, Wheat returned home to discover that his wife had moved in with this man and had given birth to two children. He filed for divorce and went to live with Maria Stocks, who provided a home for Wheat and his children.

While the lawyers took their time finalizing the divorce action, Stocks announced that she would soon give birth to Wheat's child. This unexpected development necessitated swift action on the part of the courts. The solicitor sent back a letter that the couple mistakenly believed to be confirmation of the divorce. Wheat told a friend about it, expressing his complete satisfaction. "Thank God my divorce has gone through!" he said happily. Three weeks later, Wheat and Stocks were married, not knowing that the solicitor's letter was merely an acknowledgment of receipt and not an official divorce.

A charge of bigamy was brought against Wheat. Maria Stocks was charged with aiding and abetting. The trial was conducted at the Derby Assizes later that year. Justice John Sankey directed the jury to return a verdict of Guilty against both parties, although the jury found "both prisoners in good faith and on reasonable grounds believed that Wheat had been divorced." Sankey therupon ordered the prisoner to serve one day in prison, which was tantamount to an immediate release. Believing that a standing conviction was an affront to the defendants' excellent reputations, however, the instructing solicitor, Norman Birkett, entered an appeal on their behalf. The case by this time attracted a great deal of attention and was adjourned to the full court, where the attorney general was empowered to represent the crown.

The court consisted of Justices Reginald Bray, Horace Avory, Arthur Salter, Montague Shearman, and Arthur Greer. Norman Birkett led for the defense, arguing that the mistake was, in fact, not law. He cited what he believed to be a precedent: a case where an entire family had thought that a marriage was invalid simply because the wedding ring was made of brass and not gold. In the end, the court upheld the judgment of Justice Sankey and dismissed the defense's appeal. Thomas Wheat and Maria Stocks did not bother to appear at the hearing in which they figured so prominently.

REF.: Bowker, *Behind the Bar; CBA.*

Wheatland Riot, 1913, U.S., mob vio. In 1913, a large group of California migrant workers were defeated when they attempted to organize themselves into an agricultural workers union. E.B. Durst, a hops grower near Wheatland, Calif., hired 2,800 men, women, and children to harvest his crop. He needed fewer than half that number of workers to complete the job and provided inadequate facilities for all those employed. Available housing accommodated barely 1,400 persons, they had to walk more than one mile for drinking water, and Durst withheld 10 cents from every dollar in wages. His intent was to pay back these funds to the worker at the end of the season, but because many of his employees left before the end of the harvest, the withheld wages were money in his pocket.

A small group of Industrial Workers of the World (IWW) members organized Durst's pickers, formed a committee, and elected Blackie Ford leader of the resistance. When the committee met with Durst and confronted him with the unbearable living conditions of his employees, Durst slapped Ford and fired the members of the committee. A constable attempted to arrest Ford, but he was prevented from doing so by other workers. The workers held another mass meeting on Aug. 3, 1913, and the constable arrived with the sheriff, his deputies, and the district attorney. The constable ordered the meeting broken up, and the sheriff attempted to arrest Ford. Several workers turned on the sheriff and assaulted him, and a deputy fired a shot in the air. A gunfight between members of both factions erupted. A deputy, two workers, and the district attorney were killed in the exchange of gunfire.

Five companies of state militia and a posse of several hundred armed men were called in. Many workers fled, while others were arrested. Police and private detectives—hired to augment police forces—beat and starved several of those taken prisoner. Ford and two other migrant workers were arrested and convicted of second-degree murder on the basis that their activities stirred up resentment, and this charge led to the ensuing violent riot. REF.: *CBA.*

Wheaton, Henry, 1785-1848, U.S., jur. Practiced law in Providence, R.I., from 1806-12, and worked as a reporter for the U.S. Supreme Court from 1816-27. He wrote several legal works. REF.: *CBA.*

Wheeldon, Alice, and **Mason, Alfred**, and **Mason, Winnie**, prom. 1917, Brit., consp. The war in Europe had dragged on for nearly three years. The loss of life was staggering, and there was considerable agitation to bring the conflict to a close. Three British subjects who blamed Prime Minister David Lloyd George for the hardships brought on by WWI entered into a conspiracy in 1917 to assassinate him. Alice Wheeldon conceived the idea of approaching Lloyd George during a public rally, and stabbing him with a needle swabbed in curare. The plot was foiled when Winnie Mason discussed it with a friend, who tipped off the authorities. Winnie Mason, her husband Alfred, and Alice Wheeldon each were sentenced to long prison terms at their trial at the Central Criminal Court on Mar. 10, 1917. REF.: *CBA.*

Wheeler, Ben, See: **Robertson, Ben F.**

Wheeler, Bernard, 1947- , Brit., mur. A middle-aged man who lived in a bungalow on the edge of Oxford, England, was shot to death with a shotgun in early 1970. Police charged four men, 22-year-old Bernard Wheeler and his three 21-year-old accomplices, with the murder. The four defendants were convicted, with Wheeler sentenced to a life term and the others receiving lighter sentences.

REF.: *CBA;* Tullett, *Strictly Murder.*

Wheeler, George, d.1884, U.S., mur. George Wheeler married in Massachusetts in 1869. By 1875, he was having an affair with his wife's sister, who had been living with the couple. When Della Tillson became pregnant by Wheeler and lost her baby, all threemoved to San Francisco and then to Cisco, in Placer County, where Wheeler found a job. In Cisco, Tillson met George Peckham and began dating him. When Wheeler learned that Tillson had been "unfaithful," he made her promise to stop seeing Peckham and move to San Francisco with him, where they rented an apartment as husband and wife. Meanwhile, Tillson kept in contact with Peckham, and through Peckham, Wheeler's wife learned her husband's address. In September 1880, she moved to San Francisco and lived with the couple as a sister-in-law. On the evening of Oct. 20, 1880, the 21-year-old Tillson told Wheeler that she had been in touch with Peckham and that she planned to marry him. Wheeler strangled the young woman in his fury and stuffed her body into a trunk. Later that evening, he walked into a police station and confessed to the crime.

Strangler George Wheeler.

Wheeler stood trial four times before he was finally convicted and sentenced to death. He was hanged on Jan. 23, 1884.

REF.: *CBA;* Duke, *Celebrated Criminal Cases of America.*

Wheeler, Grant, d.1895, U.S., west. outl. Grant Wheeler was a train and bank robber who raided through California, Arizona, and New Mexico during the mid-1890s. Wheeler along with Joe George, another western desperado, stopped a Southern Pacific train near Cochise, Ariz., on Jan. 3, 1895. They forced their way into the express car at gunpoint and set a charge of dynamite next to the express car safe. The bandits used too much dynamite and the resulting explosion sent a shipment of Mexican silver dollars sky high. Wheeler and Grant spent several hours collecting the coins, gathering about $1,000, before they gave up the exhausting work. For years thereafter tourists and prospectors collected the silver dollars in an area of several blocks. Wheeler and George fled to California where George attempted a lone holdup and was shot to death.

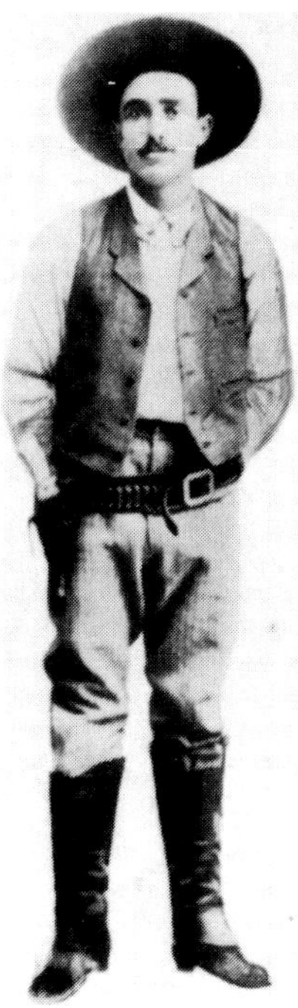
Outlaw Grant Wheeler.

Some weeks later Wheeler appeared in a saloon in Deming, N.M., where he got into an argument over a bar girl. He was wounded in the resulting gunfight. Recovering from his wound, Wheeler learned that he was being tracked by several posses for his robbery of the Southern Pacific train. Former sheriff of Tombstone, Ariz., and railroad detective William Breakenridge trailed Wheeler to Mancos, Colo. There, on Apr. 25, 1895, Breakenridge and Wheeler shot it out and Wheeler was wounded. The embattled outlaw, however, refused to surrender, continuing to exchange shots with Breakenridge while dodging behind rocks. Wheeler soon exhausted all of his ammunition, except for his last bullet, with which he shot himself in the head, committing suicide.

REF.: Axford, *Around Western Campfires;* Bartholomew, *The Biographical Album of Western Gunfighters;* Breakenridge, *Helldorado; CBA;* Chisholm, *Brewery Gulch;* Erwin, *The Southwest of John H. Slaughter;* Franke, *The Ploughed Up Hell in Old Cochise;* Hendricks, *The Bad Man of the West;* Hunter and Rose, *The Album of Gunfighters;* King, *Main Line;* Walters, *Tombstone's Yesterdays;* Wilson, *An Unwritten History.*

Wheeler, Harry, d.1925, U.S., west. lawman. The son of an army officer, Harry Wheeler served as an army scout, Arizona Ranger, sheriff, and army captain. Under the command of Nelson A. Miles, Wheeler was a scout in the Spanish-American War and during the military campaign against Indian chief Geronimo. Wheeler joined the Arizona Rangers in 1902, and killed a robber named Bostwick while the man had a group of saloon patrons lined up against the wall. When Wheeler burst into the bar, he and Bostwick exchanged fire. Wheeler shot Bostwick in the chest, killing him.

Wheeler was appointed captain of the Rangers two years later, replacing Thomas Rynning. In February 1907, in Benson, Ariz., the Ranger captain fatally wounded J.A. Tracy, a man who was threatening a couple boarding a train. Apparently Tracy was infatuated with the man's female companion. Following a gun battle in which Wheeler was shot twice and Tracy was shot four times, both men shook hands and wished each other a quick recovery. Tracy died shortly afterwards on the train before reaching Tucson.

Lawman Harry Wheeler.

In 1909, the Arizona Rangers disbanded and Wheeler was later elected sheriff of Cochise County. He led the group responsible for the 1917 "Bisbee Deportation" in which 1,200 striking laborers were forcibly removed from the town. After serving as captain in the army during WWI, Wheeler was defeated in a re-election bid for the position of sheriff of Cochise County.

REF.: *CBA;* Coolidge, *Fighting Men of the West;* Hunt, *Cap Mossman;* Liggett, *My Seventy-Five Years Along the Mexican Border;* Wagoner, *Arizona Territory.*

Wheeler, John, c.1686-1719, Brit. burg. During his long burglary career, John Wheeler burglarized over 100 homes and stole property valued at several hundred pounds. Wheeler specialized in night burglaries, but was often careless and frequently broke in while the occupants were awake and at home. On one evening, he entered the home of Thomas Cree. Cree was away, but his wife and children were sleeping when Wheeler broke in. He ransacked the home and stole as many of Cree's tailoring tools as he could carry.

In 1719, Wheeler was apprehended during his final burglary. He was held in Newgate Prison, tried, and convicted on two counts of burglary, and sentenced to death. On May 25, 1719, the 32-year-old Wheeler was hanged before a large crowd at the Tyburn gallows.

REF.: *CBA;* Smith, *Highwaymen.*

Wheeler, Mary Eleanor (AKA: **Mary Pearcey**), prom. 1866-90, Brit., mur. During the late 1880s, Frank Hogg was dating two women at the same time when one, Phoebe Styles, became pregnant. Hogg thought of fleeing, but his second lover, Mary Eleanor Wheeler, who went by the name Mary Pearcey, borrowing the surname from a man she had lived with, convinced him to stay and marry Styles. The newlyweds lived in Kentish Town, and Wheeler befriended the couple, nursing Phoebe Hogg through her second pregnancy and subsequent miscarriage.

On Oct. 24, 1890, Wheeler invited Phoebe and her child for a visit. During their visit, they apparently argued, and at about 4 p.m., neighbors heard screaming and breaking dishes. Later that evening, a neighbor testified that she saw Wheeler leaving her home with a baby carriage. Phoebe's body was found that night, her skull smashed. Soon afterwards, her 18-month-old toddler was also found dead.

When the murder was reported, the newspaper mentioned that the dead woman had the initials P.H. embroidered on her underwear and Phoebe's sister-in-law, Clara Hogg, recognized the initials and accompanied Wheeler to identify the body. At the mortuary, when Wheeler claimed the body was not Phoebe Hogg's and tried to stop Clara Hogg from seeing the body, police became suspicious. They questioned Wheeler, and after a search of her home, they found traces of blood and a carving knife and fireplace poker covered with blood. Officials also discovered that Wheeler was wearing two wedding rings.

Wheeler, twenty-four, was arrested and tried at the Old Bailey in December 1890. She was convicted and condemned to death. Before her execution, she directed her lawyer to place an advertisement to appear in the Madrid newspapers on Dec. 23, 1890, the day that she was hanged, reading: "M.E.C.P. Last wish of M.E.W. Have not betrayed." The identity of "M.E.C.P." was never discovered. REF.: *CBA.*

Wheeler, Mavis, prom. 1954, Brit., asslt. Lord Vivian and his mistress, Mavis Wheeler, began living together in London around Christmas 1953. On July 30, 1954, the couple went to a cottage at Potterne. They went to a pub from about 6 p.m. to 9:45 p.m. Returning to the cottage, they could not find the key, so they entered through a window and Wheeler said she was going to fix a meal. Her companion went back to the pub. When he returned home, Lord Vivian climbed through the window because he could not find his keys. He was shot in the wrist and abdomen as he came through the window. Wheeler owned the U.S. Army Colt automatic that wounded Lord Vivian.

Later she said that her lover had come back in through the window holding the gun. She said he pointed it at her, said, "Hands up," and she took it away. As he came through the window, the gun fired. In a different version, Wheeler said she took the gun, fired it inside the house twice, and as Lord Vivian reached to take the gun, it discharged. Lord Vivian testified that after he returned from the pub, he started to crawl through the window and a gunshot fired near him. The police found the gun and three cases inside the cottage. Wheeler was acquitted on a charge of shooting with intent to murder and shooting with intent to cause grievous bodily harm. She was convicted of unlawful and malicious wounding, and unlawful possession of a firearm. Wheeler was sentenced to six months in prison and was released on Feb. 2, 1955, greeted by Lord Vivian.

REF.: *CBA;* Furneaux, *Famous Criminal Cases.*

Wheeler, Wayne Bidwell, 1869-1927, U.S., lawyer. General counsel and superintendent of Anti-Saloon League of America from 1898-1915, then became national superintendent from 1915-27. He was a primary force in the struggle to pass the Eighteenth Amendment to the U.S. Constitution in 1919, which ushered in Prohibition. He also claimed to have written the Volstead Act. REF.: *CBA.*

Wheeler, William Almon, 1819-87, U.S., lawyer. Served as member of U.S. House of Representatives from 1861-63 and from 1869-77, and as U.S. vice president in the administration of President Rutherford B. Hayes from 1877-81. REF.: *CBA.*

Wheelock, Norman, 1911-40, U.S., attempt. asslt.-mur. Norman Wheelock's criminal life began in the early 1930s when, at the age of twenty-three, he was arrested for the attempted assault of a 24-year-old woman. He was sentenced to two-and-a-half years at New York's Attica State Prison in April 1934. Paroled shortly thereafter, Wheelock returned to his hometown of Prattsburgh, N.Y., where he worked as a telephone repairman for the family-owned Prattsburgh Home Telephone Company.

On Sept. 19, 1939, 13-year-old Evelyn Reed hurriedly left her Penn Yan, N.Y., middle school. It was her mother's birthday, and she wanted to surprise her with a freshly baked cake. When a man in a truck stopped her on Elm Street and offered her a ride, she was glad to accept. They drove past Alene Hallock's fruit stand, where Evelyn's mother often stopped, and Evelyn waved at the woman.

When Evelyn did not come home from school, her mother began to worry. At dusk, thirty miles south of Penn Yan, a local woman heard a young girl's scream from a wooded knoll near her home.

A massive search for the missing girl began the next day. Three days after Evelyn disappeared, Clifford Van Gelder was flying his plane low over an area south of Branchport, N.Y., when he noticed a man running from a wooded hill, through a field, and into another wooded area. Soon afterward, a fisherman saw the same man come out of the nearby woods, get into a car parked next to the highway, and drive away. Their sightings were dismissed as insignificant, but the man they had seen was Norman Wheelock, Evelyn Reed's murderer.

On Sept. 25, two members of the search party working south of Branchport found Reed's body. Her semi-nude corpse was leaning against a moss-covered stump in a wooded area west of Lake Keuka. The body was badly bruised, and the skull had been fractured. She had died from a puncture wound to the left temple. The only clue left at the site was a set of footprints. They led from the knoll through a nearby field, into another wooded area, out into a gulley, and finally ended when the owner of the footprints at the highway.

Hallock described the Prattsburgh Home Telephone repair truck in which she had seen Evelyn riding. Norman Wheelock, on parole from Attica Prison, where he had been serving a sentence for a previous assault, was the prime suspect.

Less than twenty-four hours after Reed's body was discovered, police sergeant Harry M. DeHollander and Trooper Michael Fort arrived at Wheelock's Prattsburgh home to question him. He refused to cooperate, and struggled to free himself from the officers' grasp as they took him into custody. During questioning, Wheelock gave a full confession, explaining to them how he had enticed the girl into his truck and attacked her that evening in the woods near the lake.

Norman Wheelock was convicted of first-degree murder and sentenced to death in the electric chair. On Aug. 1, 1940, Wheelock was executed at Sing Sing Prison. REF.: *CBA.*

Wheelwright, John, c.1592-1679, U.S., her. Clergyman born in Britain, traveling to America in 1636. He supported his sister-in-law, Anne Hutchinson, who was banished for slandering ministers. Embroiled in the Antinomian dispute, he was arrested, tried on charge of sedition and contempt of civil authority, and convicted in 1637. He was sentenced to disenfranchisement and banishment from Massachusetts. He sentence was revoked in 1644 after he voiced regret for his participation in the matter. REF.: *CBA.*

Whelan, Francis C., b.1907, U.S., jur. Served as U.S. Attorney in San Diego, Calif., from 1961-64. He was nominated to the central district court of California by President Lyndon B. Johnson in 1964. REF.: *CBA.*

Whelan, John, See: **Brown, John Whelan**.

Whelan, John (AKA: **Rocky**), d.1855, Aus., rob.-mur. Born in Ireland, John Whelan was transported to the British penal colony in Australia after fomenting an unsuccessful revolt against the government. After serving his time quietly, Whelan was released. He did not stay out of trouble for long, however. He was arrested for sheep stealing and sent to Norfolk Island, and then Van Dieman's Land, a harsh, uncompromising prison that fostered in Whelan a mad desire for revenge. In 1855, he retreated to the bush country, where he commenced a crime spree that did not end until he was finally hunted down by vigilantes and dragged to the gallows.

Whelan believed that the only way to get away with crime was to leave no witnesses. He usually shot and killed his victims after taking their valuables. Whelan never varied from this routine until he met with a man named Taylor on the road. The man pleaded with Whelan to spare his life, promising that he would not go to the police with his story. But that is exactly what he did the second he was free of the bushranger.

In June 1855, Whelan murdered a police magistrate named James Dunn, and made off with his expensive, custom-made Wellington boots. Whelan loved these boots and wore them every day until he had worn through the sole. He took them to a bootmaker for resoling, but failed to erase the name "Dunn" which had been etched into the side. The cobbler reported this to the police, and after a desperate shootout with the bandit, Whelan was captured and brought to justice. Before the rope was placed around his neck, Whelan said of Taylor, "My only regret is that I didn't put a bullet through his head." REF.: *CBA.*

Whelpton, George, 1916-c.1947, Brit., mur. In 1936, 20-year-old George Whelpton suffered a head injury from a motorcycle accident and afterward, relatives said that the young man sometimes acted peculiarly. Just before going off to war in 1939, Whelpton married. He served in North Africa, and after the war found a job as a bus driver in Doncaster, England. He and his wife had separated when he met Alison Parkin, a widow, in 1947. She lived with her two children, 23-year-old Joyce Parkin and 15-year-old Maurice Parkin.

On Oct. 9, 1947, Whelpton and Parkin went out to a pub together and later the couple went back to Parkin's home, arriving about 11:15 p.m. Parkin's daughter arrived home shortly afterward. After an apparent argument, Whelpton strangled the widow, her daughter, and her son. When a neighbor discovered the bodies the next day, the mother and daughter were naked and all three had been sexually mutilated, their bodies bearing marks similar to those made by North African desert tribesman. Whelpton soon was arrested and he said he remembered a fight with Parkin after she asked for money. Whelpton said he struck the widow, her daughter, and her son. Although Whelpton pleaded insanity at his trial, he was still convicted, sentenced to death, and hanged.

REF.: *CBA;* Gribble, *Compelled to Kill.*

Where the Sidwalk Ends, 1950, a film directed by Otto Preminger. Written by veteran crime reporter and Hollywood screenwriter Ben Hecht, this story is taken from the novel *Night Cry* by Frank Rosenberg. Rosenberg based the story of the hard-boiled cop who hits thugs too hard on the corrupt NYPD lieutenant Charles Becker. In the film, Dana Andrews, in a superb portrayal of the tough cop who has already been reprimanded for beating up hoodlums, hits a suspect too hard and kills him, then spends most of the movie covering up his crime, planting false clues, and creating for himself an even deeper dilemma. This was exactly the case with Charles Becker who, in 1896, shot and killed an innocent man and tried to pass the body off as that of a notorious burglar. See: **Becker, Charles**. REF.: *CBA.*

Whipple, Lawrence Aloysius, 1910- , U.S., jur. Served as acting magistrate for Jersey City, N.J., from 1949-51. He also served as deputy attorney general in Hudson County, N.J., from 1957-58, and as prosecutor for Hudson County, N.J., from 1958-62. He was nominated to the district court of New Jersey by President Lyndon B. Johnson in 1966. REF.: *CBA.*

Whiskey Rebellion, 1794, U.S., mob vio. In March 1791, the U.S. Congress passed the Excise Act, a federal tax on distilled whiskey, requested by secretary of the treasury Alexander Hamilton. Western Pennsylvania frontiersmen were most effected by the tax, since distilling whiskey was the most profitable industry in the region. The frontier distilleries also provided the easiest and most economical method of transporting and selling grain raised by Pennsylvania farmers. Deep resentments developed when profits diminished and tax offenders had to travel several hundred miles to Philadelphia to appear in court.

On May 13, 1794, thirty-seven subpoenas were issued by the Philadelphia federal court against distillers in western Pennsylvania. Federal Marshal David Lenox and excise inspector John Neville, instructed to deliver the subpoenas, were forcibly prevented from carrying out their task by a group of distillers. Afterwards, the insurrection grew steadily, beginning with the terrorizing of excise collectors traveling in western Pennsylvania. Frontiersmen refused to appear in court and robbed mail stages. On July 17, an armed mob of 500 surrounded Neville's home and demanded that he resign as excise collector. Led by James McFarlane, the mob attacked the inspector's house, but were initially rebuffed by eleven federal soldiers. When told by the soldiers that Neville was not home, McFarlane demanded that they be allowed to search the home. A battle ensued, and the insurrectionists burned Neville's home to the ground. McFarlane was killed in the melee.

On June 6, an amendment added to the Excise Act permitted state courts to hear federal tax cases, and on Aug. 7, President George Washington ordered the distillers to comply with the law. When they refused, Washington, Henry Lee, and Alexander

Pennsylvania farmers tar and feather a tax collector during the Whiskey Rebellion of 1794.

Hamilton led an army of 12,900 men into western Pennsylvania. Upon sight of the army, the insurrectionists dispersed. Twenty persons were arrested and two were found Guilty of high treason; both were later pardoned by President Washington. The tax was repealed in 1802. REF.: *CBA.*

Whispering Smith, 1906, a western novel by Frank H. Spearman. Based on the legendary Joe LeFors, one of the most feared lawmen in the Old West. While Smith is LeFors, the novel's sinister gunslinger, Harvey Dushayne, is based on the fierce Wild Bunch killer, Harvey Logan, better known as Kid Curry. See: **Lefors, Joseph; Logan, Harvey.** REF.: *CBA.*

Whistlecraft, George (AKA: **Joe**), prom. 1929-30, Case of, Brit., mur. On Dec. 8, 1929, gamekeeper Charles Ernest Cornwell was shot to death in the woods in Suffolk, England. Police found a large number of .410-caliber shells near the body. Footprints found at the crime scene led to George Whistlecraft's house, and castings taken at the murder scene matched Whistlecraft's footprints. Police also found a .410-caliber single-barreled folding gun in his house.

Whistlecraft, a farm laborer in his late fifties, conducted his own defense during the preliminary proceedings, but was advised by legal counsel when put on trial at the Suffolk Assizes at Ipswich. Robert Churchill, a ballistics expert, testified that the casings found in the woods had been fired by a gun with a blunt hammer. Whistlecrafts' gun had a pointed hammer. He was acquitted in January 1930.

REF.: *CBA;* Hastings, *The Other Mr. Churchill.*

Whistler, James Abbott McNeill, 1834-1903, U.S., libel. Fame in the art world came slowly to James Whistler. His recognition as a reigning genius of American impressionism was stunted, due in part to his disagreeable temperament and quirks of personality. In 1855 Whistler settled in Paris and London, where he produced such classics of the art world as *Valparaiso* (1866), *Artist In His Studio* (1867-68) and his seminal work *Arrangement In Grey and Black, No. 1: Portrait of the Artist's Mother* (1872).

But it was his celebrated lawsuit brought against the London critic John Ruskin in 1878 that brought Whistler into the public limelight. Ruskin, a strong traditionalist, viewed eight paintings of Whistler's, including *Black and Gold, the Falling Rocket* at the Grosvenor gallery in 1877. He remarked that, "For Mr. Whistler's own sake no less than for the protection of the purchaser, Sir Coutts Lindsay ought not to have admitted works into the gallery in which the ill-educated conceit of the artist so nearly approached the aspect of the willful imposture. I have seen and heard much of Cockney impudence before now, but never expected to hear a coxcomb ask two hundred guineas for flinging a pot of paint in the public face."

Whistler filed a libel suit against the celebrated critic in November 1878. Ruskin refused to retract his criticisms. He was convinced that Whistler's work was a vulgar expression that flew in the face of the sentimental "subject" picture favored by the traditionalists of the London art world. In this sense Whistler was well ahead of his time, but it would take another quarter-century before the artist would be recognized as a master.

The critic Ruskin declared that he would retire forever from writing criticism if he lost. The jury found in favor of the plaintiff, but Whistler's vindication was short-lived. The court awarded the artist the nominal sum of one farthing. John Ruskin gave up his Oxford professorship and lived out the remainder of his life in seclusion. Before he died he bequeathed his considerable fortune to philanthropic causes. Whistler, meanwhile, was forced to sell his home and many of his personal belongings to satisfy his considerable legal fees. In 1890 he came out with a memoir of the famous trial titled: *The Gentle Art of Making Enemies*. REF.: *CBA*.

Whitby, Roy, 1948-77, U.S., suic.-mur. In May 1976, a married Chicago area couple separated. Shirley Whitby kept their two children, not allowing her husband to see them. In February 1977, Roy Whitby lost his job as a parking lot attendant in downtown Chicago and went to live with his brother. On Mar. 10, the divorce was made final. On the morning of Mar. 22, 1977, 29-year-old Roy Whitby told his brother he was upset because he wanted to see the children, and he thought his ex-wife was dating other men. He blamed one of his wife's co-workers, 25-year-old Tamera Clarke, for the breakup, believing she told his wife to divorce him. After talking with his brother, he went to the securities brokerage company where his 28-year-old ex-wife worked as a clerk. He fatally shot her and Clarke with a .22-caliber handgun and then turned the gun on himself. REF.: *CBA*.

White, Alexander, 1762-84, U.S., pir.-mur. Boston seaman Alexander White lacked sufficient money to marry the girl he loved. White's solution was to rob the captain of the boat on which he worked. During the robbery, White killed the captain. Realizing that a passenger had seen him commit the crime, White tried to attack the witness with a knife. The passenger dived overboard and swam to shore. When White returned to shore, the harbor authorities arrested him immediately. Convicted of piracy and murder, he was hanged on Nov. 18, 1784.

REF.: *CBA;* Nash, *Bloodletters and Badmen.*

White, Alice, c.1921- , Case of, U.S., mur. During the late 1940s, a U.S. serviceman met and married a British woman. Sergeant Andrew White and his wife Alice, along with her son from a previous marriage, moved to Germany in December 1949. But in September 1951, just after the birth of their first child together, they separated and Alice White returned to Preston, England, with the children. White was then transferred to Las Vegas, Nev., and in about November 1952, the couple resolved their differences and Mrs. White joined her husband in the U.S.

Several weeks later, she announced that she was pregnant again, expecting her third child in August 1953. White believed the child was not his, and he allegedly threatened his wife with a carving knife. The serviceman drank heavily and by May 9, 1953, he had been drinking for eight days straight. His wife, six months pregnant, said that on that day, White visited a military club, and when he came home, he directed one of the children to get his gun. He reportedly beat his wife and pulled her hair. That evening, Mrs. White claimed, her husband walked from room to room, holding the gun, while she bathed her children. White went to bed, the gun lying beside him, and when his wife went to bed, he allegedly took the gun and told her to go into the living room where they argued over bills and White's drinking for the next four hours. Then they went to bed. About an hour and a half later, Mrs. White took the shotgun and fatally shot her husband. At about 3:45 a.m., she ran to her neighbor's door, saying that she had just shot and killed her husband.

Mrs. White was arrested, but released into the sheriff's custody and then placed into the custody of friends until after her child was born. Her trial began Sept. 14, 1953, and she pleaded self-defense, claiming her husband bought the gun to kill his family, that he treated her and the children cruelly, and that she murdered him to save herself and her children. Several days later, Alice White was acquitted. REF.: *CBA*.

White, Bob, d.1941, Case of, U.S., rape. In about 1938, the wife of Texan W.S. Cochran was allegedly raped by a black man, Bob White. He was tried, convicted of rape, and sentenced. After an appeal, the Texas Court of Criminal Appeals overturned the conviction. White was tried and convicted again, although he claimed police beat him to make him confess. The U.S. Supreme Court struck down the decision and ordered a new trial. During jury selection for the third trial in June 1941, Cochran walked into the courtroom and fatally shot White in the head. Cochran gave his gun to the prosecutor, turned himself over to authorities, and a week later, after deliberating ten minutes, a jury acquitted him of murdering White. REF.: *CBA*.

White, Bouck, b.1874, U.S., rebel. Member of American Congregational clergy expelled for socialist ideals. He then became a pastor of the Church of the Social Revolution in New York City in 1913. He was sentenced to prison in 1914, 1916, and 1917 for inciting political unrest. REF.: *CBA*.

White, Byron Raymond (AKA: **Whizzer**), 1917- , U.S., jur. U.S. Supreme Court justice Byron Raymond White offered the court sterling credentials, including outstanding scholastic, athletic, and military achievements. A native of Colorado, White excelled at his studies and at sports, especially football, at the University of Colorado, where he was dubbed "Whizzer." After graduation, White played for the Pittsburgh Pirates, now Steelers, during the 1938 season for $15,800, the highest salary in the National Football League at the time. In 1939, he was a Rhodes scholar at Oxford University, but returned to the U.S. after war broke out. During 1940 and 1941, White studied at Yale University Law School and played professional football for the Detroit Lions. He interrupted his studies in 1942 to join the U.S. Navy, later receiving his law degree from Yale in November 1946. In 1947, White worked as a clerk under U.S. Supreme Court Justice Fred Vinson and then practiced law in Denver for the next fourteen years. White supported John F. Kennedy's bid for the presidency in 1960, managing his pre-convention campaign in Colorado. In 1961, Kennedy appointed him deputy attorney general, and on Mar. 30, 1962, Kennedy nominated White as an associate justice to the U.S. Supreme Court. White was confirmed on Apr. 11, 1962.

U.S. Supreme Court justice Byron R. "Whizzer" White.

While on the Supreme Court, White took a special interest in the jury's role in criminal proceedings. In *Duncan v. Louisiana* in 1968, White wrote the majority opinion, which ruled that a clause in the Fourteenth Amendment allows defendants facing serious crimes in state courts to be tried by jury. He wrote majority opinions in *Williams v. Florida* in 1970, in which the court affirmed that a six-person jury in state criminal cases was constitutional, and in *Taylor v. Louisiana* in 1975, in which the court decided that a state jury selection barring women from jury duty was unconstitutional.

In *Malloy v. Hogan* in 1964, White disagreed with the court, which gave criminal defendants in state courts the privilege against self-incrimination. He was in the minority in important cases concerning criminal defendants' rights, including *Escobedo v. Illinois* in 1964, and *Miranda v. Arizona* in 1966. In *Camara v. Municipal Court of San Francisco* in 1967, White wrote the majority decision in which the court ruled that a routine city housing inspection of a private residence could not be carried out without a warrant. In *Terry v. Ohio* in 1968, White supported the police "stop and frisk" policies, and in *Chimel v. California* in 1969, White condoned searches without warrants if the search was reasonable. Concerning capital punishment, White ruled that the death penalty violated the Eighth Amendment, which outlawed cruel and unusual punishment, in *Furman v. Georgia* in 1972. But in *Gregg v. Georgia* in 1976, White supported the death penalty for murder cases in which recent state laws made the death penalty mandatory for murder or set limits for the judge or jury in sentencing. As of this writing, he is still serving on the Supreme Court.

REF.: *CBA;* Nash, *Citizen Hoover;* Navasky, *Kennedy Justice;* Unger, *FBI.*

White, Charles Thomas, 1804-27, Brit., arson. A successful Holborn bookseller, Charles Thomas White burned down his house during the early 1800s to defraud an insurance company. White was tried, convicted, and sentenced to death. On Jan. 2, 1827, the 23-year-old was taken to the scaffold in the Press Yard where hangman James Foxen stood. There, White's hands were tied, but as Foxen went down to pull the bolt, White freed his hands. The prisoner's hands were bound again. When the bolt was pulled, White tried to jump on the platform, and, one foot kicking, and one foot supported by the platform, he tried to loosen the noose with a hand he had freed. The hangman, Foxen, shoved White off the scaffold and he grabbed the prisoner's legs, hanging on until White was dead.

REF.: Atholl, *Shadow of the Gallows;* Bleackley, *Hangmen of England; CBA;* Potter, *The Art of Hanging.*

White, Daniel James, 1946-85, U.S., mansl.-suic. Daniel White gave up his job with the San Francisco fire department to run for the post of supervisor, which he won. White ran on a strongly anti-gay platform, committed "to the confrontation which can no longer be avoided by those who care." In 1978, Supervisor White earned half the salary he had made as a fireman. His wife opened an arcade food stand in the tourist section, which helped financially, but added to other pressures. White began eating junk foods, but the binges solved nothing and ultimately compounded his depression.

San Francisco supervisor Dan White, killer.

On Nov. 10, 1978, White offered his resignation to Mayor George R. Moscone. Supervisor Harvey Milk, the U.S.'s first openly gay elected official, got Moscone's promise to appoint a replacement for White who would support the gay community. White's resignation would change the balance of power in the city council.

Then White's family and friends began to pressure him to recant his resignation and ask Moscone to reinstate him as supervisor. White met with Moscone on Nov. 14 and the mayor agreed to return White's letter of resignation. The next morning, both men announced the news to the press, but Moscone also said they needed to check the legalities of the move and possibly reappoint White instead of just canceling the resignation. However, during the next two days, Moscone was advised that if he renamed White, he would not be re-elected for a second term as mayor.

Supervisor Harvey Milk and Mayor George Moscone, both killed by White.

During the next few days, newspapers speculated about White's replacement. But the story was overshadowed by news of the deaths at Jim Jones' People's Temple in Guyana as most of the victims were former San Franciscans. Dan White clipped each article concerning his status and read and reread them. On Nov. 27, he heard that Moscone had avoided accepting petitions from more than 1,000 White supporters.

Dan White dressed neatly, put a loaded five-bullet gun in his pocket, and went to City Hall. He waited in Moscone's outer office until the mayor could see him. Moscone took White back to his private office and told him that he would not be reappointing him to the supervisor's position. White pulled his gun and fired at the mayor. When Moscone fell to the floor, White emptied the other four bullets into his back and head. White ran down the hall, reloading the gun, grabbed a key to the back door of the supervisors' office, and went to Harvey Milk's office. White fired five bullets into Milk, then ran down the stairs and out of the building past policemen arriving in response to Moscone's secretary's phone call. White called his wife and they met at St. Mary's Cathedral, then walked to the local police station where White turned himself in.

Dan White went on trial on May 1, 1979, before Judge Calcagno. His attorney, Douglas Schmidt, concentrated his defense on the periodic depressions White had suffered most of his life. In what came to be known as "the twinkie defense," the testifying psychiatrist, Dr. Donald Lunde, pointed out that a change in eating habits is an important sign of clinical depression. He also said that White had been so depressed that he was incapable of formulating a plan for murder, and thus the killings were not premeditated.

On May 21, 1979, the jury brought in a verdict of Guilty of voluntary manslaughter. Thousands of people, mostly gay, rioted in San Francisco in protest of the lenient verdict. More than 100 people were injured and $1 million in damage was done to City Hall and other public property.

White served five years, one month, and nine days at the Soledad State Prison in California. He was released on Jan. 6, 1984, with a probation requirement that he remain in the Los Angeles area for a year. After his parole expired, he returned to his home in San Francisco. On Oct. 21, 1985, White, reportedly devastated by the trouble he had caused his family and himself, used a rubber hose to pipe exhaust fumes into an automobile in his garage and died of carbon monoxide poisoning.

REF.: *CBA;* Nash, *Murder Among the Mighty.*

White, Edward Douglass, 1845-1921, U.S., jur. Served as U.S. Supreme Court justice from 1894-1921, and as chief justice from 1910-21. He was born in Louisiana and served in the Confederate army from 1861-63. He was a U.S. senator from 1891-94 and was nominated to the High Court by President Grover Cleveland. He became chief justice during the administration of President William Howard Taft. He is noted for his "rule of reason" used to interpret and apply to antitrust laws. REF.: *CBA.*

White, Edward Douglass, Jr., 1845-1921, U.S., jur. Raised on his family's Louisiana sugar plantation, Edward Douglass White, Jr. served in the Confederate army until his capture in 1863. After he was freed, White studied law, passed the bar in 1868, and practiced law in New Orleans. In 1874, White was elected to the state senate and in 1878, the 33-year-old was appointed by Governor Francis T. Nicholls as an associate justice on the Louisiana Supreme Court. When the governor lost a re-election bid, the new governor pushed through a new state constitution in 1880 that contained an age requirement for state judges, and White had to resign. However, when Nicholls won back the governor's post, White was elected by the Louisiana state legislature to the U.S. Senate, where he served from 1891-94.

On Feb. 19, 1894, President Grover Cleveland nominated White as an associate justice to the U.S. Supreme Court and he was confirmed by the Senate on the same day. White later was nominated as chief justice to the court on Dec. 12, 1910, by President William H. Taft and confirmed on the same day. White was the first associate justice of the court to be confirmed as chief justice and he served in the post until his death. During his tenure on the court, White handled several cases dealing with the extent of businesses' power. In *Standard Oil Co. v. United States* in 1911, White wrote the majority opinion in which he created the "rule of reason," which was used to determine the unlawfulness of trusts in the business world. He interpreted unlawful trusts as only those that unreasonably restricted trade. In another case, *United States v. American Tobacco Co.* in 1911, White presented similar arguments, and the case resulted in a reorganization, not elimination, of the trust. REF.: *CBA.*

White, Henry (AKA: **Henry Devonport**), b.1869, and **Freeman, Morris** (AKA: **Wyndham, Wendham**), b.1862, and **Gibbons, Thomas** (AKA: **Fitts, Fitsey**), b.1857, Brit., forg. At the turn of the century, a gang of counterfeiters attempted to flood England, Europe, and South Africa with forged £5 notes. The band was traced by the police, arrested, and brought to trial. Bookmaker Alfred Hurley was acquitted, while the ringleaders were sentenced to long prison terms. Henry White, a 33-year-old fish curer who gave the court the name of Henry Devonport, Morris Freeman, a 40-year-old civil servant, and Thomas Gibbons, a 45-year-old plasterer, pleaded guilty before Justice Ridley and were sentenced to fourteen years penal servitude. Police arrested them with 200 forged £5 notes in their possession. Lesser gang members included William Wells and Joseph Southgate, who each received three year prison sentences. Friedman Levey received a sentence of eighteen months in prison.

REF.: *CBA;* Nicholls, *Crime Within the Square Mile.*

White, Hugh Lawson, 1773-1840, U.S., jur. Judge of Tennessee Supreme Court of Errors and Appeals from 1809-15. He was a U.S. senator from 1825-40, and unsuccessful candidate for U.S. president in 1836, losing to Martin Van Buren. REF.: *CBA.*

White, Isaac (AKA: **Ike**), 1864-1943, U.S., writer. Known by many as one of the greatest crime reporters in the country, Isaac White solved crimes in his New York *World* newspaper columns while the police were just beginning an investigation. He was a part-time writer and part-time detective. He solved many mysteries on his own including learning the identity of the "bearded stranger," who planted a bomb in an 1891 attack on financier Russell Sage.

He also brought to justice Dr. Robert Buchanan. Perhaps most interesting was the murder of Melody Brown. Arriving at the scene before the police, White found Melody hanging from a rafter. The police arrived and began formulating a suicide theory. White, however, spoke with the building superintendent and learned the woman's boyfriend, George, worked in a building nearby as a janitor. He approached the boyfriend while he was conversing with neighbors and said, "It's no good, George, you didn't do a good enough job hanging Melody. We revived her and she told us everything." Silence hung in the air until George responded, "Thank God. I must have been crazy to go that wild. I don't really hate her...I'm sorry." White wrote a column about the murder, quoting George's confession, while the police still called the death a suicide. Upon his death in 1943, an obituary claimed White was the greatest crime writer in the history of American journalism. REF.: *CBA.*

White, John Duncan (AKA: **Charles Marchant**), and **Curtis, Winslow** (AKA: **Sylvester Colson**), d.1826, U.S., rob.-mut.-mur. John White, wanted for robbery in New England, changed his name to Marchant, and with his partner, Sylvester Colson (actually Winslow Curtis), signed on to work aboard a merchant ship called the *Fairy* in 1826. The two mutinied, killing Captain Edward Selfridge and first mate Tom Jenkins. They turned back toward Nova Scotia, where they sank the ship. White and Curtis were caught and tried in Boston. They were both sentenced to hang, but White hanged himself. Curtis was hanged by the court.

REF.: *CBA;* Nash, *Bloodletters and Badmen.*

White, Captain **Joseph**, See: **Crowinshield, Richard.**

White, Louise (AKA: **Mary Hooker, Mrs. King**), prom. 1865, U.S., theft. A gypsy queen became the talk of the Clarksville, Tenn., area during the last days of the Civil War. Young people went to her to have their fortunes told. Elizabeth Redford went to see Mary Hooker, the alias of Louise White. Elizabeth told her father about the visit, and announced that she knew he had bags of gold hidden in his attic. Redford, horrified that anyone should know his secret, went to see the gypsy. He returned home having committed himself to letting her double his gold before his eyes.

Following the gypsy's instructions, Redford brought his $15,000 in gold coins to the living room. They gypsy brought a bag of her own, supposedly containing $1,000 that she wanted to double. The bags of coins sat in front of White, Redford, and his daughter all afternoon, while White crooned an incantation. The chanting went on until dusk, when the gypsy ordered Redford to put the bags back where he had hidden them and to leave them there one day for each additional $1,000 he wanted to appear in the bag. At the end of two weeks, she would come for her bag of coins. However, after fourteen days passed, Redford heard that the gypsies had left the area. He ran to check his gold coins and found bags filled with metal slugs, rivets, and scraps.

Elizabeth Redford took the case to detective Allan Pinkerton. Through his gypsy connections, he learned that White's tribe was likely to split into three parts, and he sent an agent to infiltrate each of the three sections. One agent learned that they replenished their supply of gold coins from a certain wagon. They moved on to meet another group at New Harmony, Ind., where the Pinkerton agent discovered two bags containing approximately $15,000 in gold coins in the room of a man named Zed, whom he promptly arrested.

Louise White, meanwhile, had not reached New Harmony because she was swindling Ezra Allen. When at dusk her fellow swindler waiting outside the window changed the gold for base metal, he was grabbed by a Pinkerton agent. Louise White and three cohorts were convicted of theft and sent to prison.

REF.: *CBA;* Rowan, *The Pinkertons.*

White, Mary, prom. 1736, Brit., perj. In 1736, Mary White accused hangman John Thrift of breaking into her house on May 24, 1736, and robbing her of some money. When her allegations were found to be false, Thrift was released and White was convicted on a charge of malicious prosecution and sent to prison.

REF.: Bleackley, *Hangmen of England; CBA.*

White, May, See: **Churchill, May Vivienne.**

White, Roy, 1933- , Brit., attempt. mur.-mur. Twenty-five-year-old Roy White of Chale, England, worked as a farm laborer for the Phillips family at Brighstone. White became fond of 14-year-old Christine Phillips, and was soon asked by her parents to stop bothering her. However, on Mar. 16, 1958, Mrs. Phillips told her husband that White was causing trouble again, so the laborer was immediately fired. White drove off on his motorcycle, but later returned armed with a shotgun. The family was inside the house and when the farmer answered the door, White shot at Phillips, injuring him. Phillips put the children into the cellar and called to his wife. White then killed Mrs. Phillips as the farmer rushed back from the cellar and took White's gun. Phillips collapsed and White fled. The next day, White surrendered and was charged with murder and attempted murder. He was found Guilty but insane on both charges and was sent to Broadmoor.

REF.: Butler, *Murderers' England; CBA.*

White, Stanford, See: **Thaw, Harry Kendall.**

White, William Jack (AKA: **Three Finger**), prom. 1920s, U.S., org. crime. William White was a minor figure in the Al Capone Gang of the 1920s. He earned his famous nickname from a freak accident he suffered as a boy, when a brick fell off a construction project and smashed his right hand. White was embarrassed about his deformity and wore a white glove in public, stuffing the empty fingers with cotton.

Capone gunman William "Three Finger" White.

White was included on the Chicago Crime Commission's first published list of public enemies, or those persons "who are constantly in conflict with the law." The listing, which appeared in 1923, also included such underworld luminaries as James "Mad Bomber" Balcastro, Al Capone, Jake Guzik, and Edward "Spike" O'Donnell. A feared gunman, White was indicted for the murder of a policeman in 1924, convicted, freed on appeal, and then re-sentenced.

REF.: *CBA;* Kobler, *Capone;* Nash, *Bloodletters and Badmen.*

White Caps, 1880s, U.S., vigil. A vigilante movement known as the White Caps, with connections to the first Ku Klux Klan, began in Indiana in the 1880s. Gaining a great deal of popularity in the rural sections of the country, the White Caps persecuted undesirable "white trash," though certain elements displayed anti-Black and anti-Mexican sentiment. REF.: *CBA.*

White Caps, Mexican (***Gorras Blancas***), prom. 1880s, U.S., vigil. In an attempt to fight against the encroaching Anglos moving into the Mexican Territory, Juan Jose Herrera formed a Mexican vigilante group called *Gorras Blancas* or White Caps. (This vigilance organization should not be confused with other White Cap groups whose activities resembled those of the Ku Klux Klan.) An educated English-speaker, Herrera had lived in the Anglo culture and had observed the tactics that labor groups had used when attempting to gain reforms and concessions from railroad and mining companies in Colorado. Herrera enjoined his fellow Mexicans to use these tactics, which included sabotage, assault, and murder, against the Anglo population which was stealing land and illegally fencing out the indigenous farmers. By 1888, the White Caps numbered 1,500 members and they terrorized Anglos by cutting fences and destroying railroad property. The White Caps were charged with murder, assault, and other violent activities. White Cap membership deteriorated when spies began infiltrating the structure and the leaders decided to shift the focus of the organization to polits. REF.: *CBA.*

Whitechapel Murder, 1927, a novel by F. Allen, based on Jack the Ripper. See: **Jack the Ripper**. REF.: *CBA.*

***White Cloud* Arson**, 1849, U.S., arson. On May 17, 1849, a small fire was set by a sailor angry over being denied work aboard the *White Cloud,* one of many wooden ships moored in the St. Louis, Mo., harbor. The fire quickly spread to the other ships, destroying twenty-five steamships, and then to the harbor, the crowded wharves, and fifteen square blocks of residential St. Louis. The resultant housing shortage led to overcrowded and unsanitary conditions, which caused a cholera epidemic. Together, the fire and the epidemic claimed at least 4,000 lives.

REF.: *CBA;* Nash, *Almanac of World Crime.*

White Devil or Vittoria Corombona, The, c.1610, a play by John Webster, based on the murder of Vittoria Accoramboni (Italy, 1587). See: **Accoramboni, Vittoria**. REF.: *CBA.*

White Family, prom. 1890s-1920s, U.S., org. crime. Also known as the Weiss gang, the White Family was a large familial organization of Chicago criminals. Two daughters and six sons of the widow Margaret Weiss began the White Family when they married into the Renich family's ten daughters and two sons in the 1860s. Through intermarriages and the addition of cousins and other relatives, the gang grew to 100 individuals by the turn of the century. According to authorities, each family member was a criminal, and at any time twenty family members were in jail.

In the 1890s, the gang was ruled by Eva Gussler, known as "Eva the Cow." It was her task to assign certain crimes to each family member. Reputedly one of the best pickpockets and shoplifters in Chicago, Eva supervised the schooling of all the children in the family, teaching them the techniques of theft by the time they learned to walk. One White Family member, Mary Boston and her 5-year-old niece were arrested for shoplifting. Apparently Boston knocked items from the shelves, and her niece who walked inside the folds of Boston's dress, picked them off of the floor, and placed them inside hidden pockets under her aunt's dress. In the early years of WWI, police were still arresting gang members, and several White Family members were involved with bootlegging operations during Prohibition. REF.: *CBA.*

Whitefield, John, d.1771, Brit., rob. Criminal John Whitefield was hanged in 1771 in Cumberland, England. Afterward, his body was hung in chains. But Whitefield revived after swinging in the chains for an hour. He was taken down and pardoned.

REF.: *CBA;* Nash, *Almanac of World Crime.*

Whitefoord, Dr. Caleb C., prom. 1880, Brit., forg. Just before Charles Shurety was to be hanged at Newgate in 1880, officials received a written reprieve. Because the reprieve's wording varied from the usual statement and the signature did not seem to match the Home Secretary's, officials decided the document was a forgery and hanged their prisoner. A few months later, Dr. Caleb Whitefoord was arrested for forgery and attempting to obstruct judgment in connection with the phony reprieve. Whitefoord, who apparently did not know Shurety, was convicted of both charges, sentenced to a two month prison term, and fined £50.

REF.: Atholl, *The Reluctant Hangman; CBA.*

Whitefriars; or, The Days of King Charles the Second, 1844, a novel by Emma Robinson, based on the unsolved murder of Sir Edmund Godfrey (Brit., 1678), later dramatized by Thompson Townsend. See: **Godfrey, Sir Edmund Berry.** REF.: *CBA.*

White Front Cigar Store, prom. 1920s-30s, U.S., org. crime. Operated by Richard T. Galatas, the White Front Cigar Store in Hot Springs, Ark., was a safe haven for criminals, similar to Murder, Inc.'s candy store. Hot Springs was called "Bubbles," and known as a "safe city" in the underworld. Galatas functioned as a liaison between the visiting hoodlums and the local chief of detectives, Dutch Akers. Upon meeting the most recently arrived hoodlum, Akers would welcome him to the city and ensure his safety as long as he did not attempt to move in on local vice operations. Akers collected payoffs from every prostitute in town, shared the numbers racket with Galatas, and sold police guns to White Front hoodlums with the provision they use the guns outside of Hot Springs. Visiting hoods included Lucky Luciano, Alvin Karpis, most of the Barker Family, the Purple Gang, Frank Nash, Owney Madden, and the elite of Al Capone's gang.

The FBI considered the Hot Springs police force not only lax, but the most untrustworthy in the country. On June 16, 1933, FBI agents apprehended Frank Nash in a Hot Springs horse parlor. When Galatas notified Akers of the federal snatch, he put out an all-points bulletin stating that a man had been "taken for a ride" by unknown persons. The agents escaped Akers' police dragnet but were gunned down, along with Nash, in what later came to be known as the Kansas City Massacre. Galatas was forced to leave Hot Springs, and the White Front Cigar Store closed its doors. Galatas was caught in 1934 and sent to Alcatraz for harboring Nash, a prison escapee. REF.: *CBA.*

White Glove Gang, See: **Great Mail Robbery.**

White Hand Gang, prom. 1900s-20s, U.S., org. crime. The Irish gangs surrounding the waterfront district of Brooklyn, N.Y., banded together to form the White Hand Gang, so named because they claimed to be fighting the Italian "Black Hand." The White Hand battled the growing Italian mafioso between 1900 and 1925, in a bloody war for control over the lucrative waterfront rackets. With a tight control of the Brooklyn Bridge-Red Hook section, White Handers forced barge and wharf owners to pay tribute. For the right to work, longshoremen gave the Irish gangsters a daily commission. Those who did not pay were beaten up, their barges and wharfs looted, burned, and wrecked. Other longshoremen paid the commission because they were Irish and believed that the White Hand would keep the waterfront free of Italians.

The White Hand Gang continued in the tradition of nineteenth century Irish gangs in that they would kill one of their own if there was a profit in it. Following the murder of Dinny Meehan, the first leader of the White Hand, Wild Bill Lovett took control of the waterfront war. Known as a crafty killer, Lovett was able to gain the upper hand on the Italian gangsters, and extended his gang's influence. But in 1923, Lovett was assassinated by the Sicilian murder expert Dui Cuteddi with a meat cleaver. Following Lovett's assassination, the Italian mafia, under the direction of Vince Mangano, Albert Anastasia, and Joe Adonis moved in to claim the waterfront rackets.

The leadership of the White Hand was taken by Richard "Peg Leg" Lonergan, a killer whose leg was dismembered by a train during a railway looting expedition. Lonergan was credited with killing at least twenty people. He himself was killed on Christmas 1925 when he led a group of White Handers to the Adonis Social Club, a mafia-controlled speakeasy. Seeing two Irish women dancing with Italian men, Lonergan told the women to "get back with the white men." The lights were suddenly turned off, and machine gun fire killed the Irish leader and two of his top aids. Police claim that Al Capone, who was visiting his childhood neighborhood that Christmas, pulled the trigger, though they could not gather enough evidence to prosecute. With their last strong leader killed, the White Hand Gang fell apart within three years, leaving the waterfront open for the Italian mafia.

REF.: Asbury, *The Gangs of New York;* ____, *Gem of the Prairie; CBA;* Kobler, *Al Capone;* Landesco, *Organized Crime in Chicago;* McPhaul, *Johnny Torrio;* Nash, *Bloodletters and Badmen.*

White Hand Society, 1907-13, U.S., vigil. In Chicago in 1907, a group of Italian businessmen, professionals, Italian newspapers, several Italian fraternal orders, and the Italian Chamber of Commerce formed the White Hand Society to fight the Black Hand gangsters. The White Hand was a rare organization formed to fight criminals in their own ethnic group. Black Hand gangs were prominent in the "Little Italys" of every major city, extorting money from businesses and threatening death or maiming if they were not paid. Many Black Hand extortionists were mafioso connected, though an equal number only pretended to be Mafia-Camorra. In Chicago alone, murder victims of the Black Hand reached as many as fifty in one year.

The White Hand assisted police in their investigations of Black Hand murderers by translating witness statements and providing evidence needed for convictions. The vigilance organization also provided money for the prosecution of men arrested due to their efforts. Though the White Hand helped drive from Chicago ten of the most dangerous extortionists, lax judges and apathetic police allowed several Black Handers to return to the streets where they merely escalated the violence surrounding their extortion rackets. Most disheartening for the White Hand was their inability to bring to justice a hired Black Hand killer known as "Shotgun Man."

The White Hand disbanded in 1913 due to their lack of success as well as the growing sentiment among Italian-Americans that the White Hand's efforts to expose Italian crime had created a backlash against all Italians. With the White Hand no longer a factor, the Black Hand gangsters continued to extort money from the Italian community. See: **Black Hand.**

REF.: Asbury, *The Gangs of New York;* ____, *Gem of the Prairie; CBA;* Kobler, *Al Capone;* Landesco, *Organized Crime in Chicago;* McPhaul, *Johnny Torrio.*

Whitehead, Philip, d.1811, Brit., forg. In 1811, Philip Whitehead worked as a clerk in the chief cashier's office at the Bank of England in London. The young man began living beyond his means, and bank officials tried to persuade him to be less extravagant. Angered, Whitehead resigned and began gambling, falling deeper in debt. Whitehead then drew a forged bill on the bank. He was arrested, convicted, and condemned. In November 1811, Whitehead was executed at Newgate. His sister, 19-year-old Sarah Whitehead, who had kept house for her brother and doted on him, was not told of her brother's arrest. When she learned of his execution, she reportedly visited the bank for the next twenty-five years, asking for her brother, and became known as the Old Lady of Threadneedle Street.

REF.: *CBA;* Nicholls, *Crime Within the Square Mile.*

Whiteley, George Cecil, 1875-1942, Brit., jur. After George Whiteley was called to the bar in 1900, he practiced law on circuit, at the Old Bailey, and at the Surrey and London Sessions. Whiteley served as a junior counsel to the Treasury, 1912 to 1921, participating in several murder trials, including those of George Smith, John Williams, Jeannie Baxter, and the Jack Alfred Field and William Gray case. Whiteley became a judge in 1921 and later served as chairman of the County of London Sessions in 1931-32, as judge of the Mayor's and City of London Court from 1932-34, and as Common Serjeant of the City of London from 1934-42. He died on Oct. 15, 1942. See: **Baxter, Jeannie; Field, Jack Alfred; Smith, George Joseph.** REF.: *CBA.*

Whitelocke, Bulstrode, 1605-75, Brit., lawyer. Directed committee in charge of prosecuting Thomas Wentworth, the Earl of Strafford. He served as commissioner of the Great Seal under Commonwealth in 1648, in 1649, and from 1654-55. However, he was discharged after he disputed the alterations in the courts of chancery that were made by Oliver Cromwell. REF.: *CBA.*

White Lotus Society (AKA: **Incense Smelling Sect, White Yang Sect**), prom. 376-1900s, China, secret soc. Buddhist followers of the deposed Sung Dynasty organized the White Lotus Society as a religious sect in 376. The mystical origins of the group were rooted in ancient Buddhist thought. The early leaders invoked the name of Amitabha Buddha of the "Pure Land" as the means of gaining entrance through spiritual devotion. The T'ang emperors brutally suppressed the White Lotus Society, which may have contributed to the group's eventual transformation to a broad-based political movement aimed at driving the foreign invaders out of China.

In 1344, Han Shan-Tung lured thousands of new members to the sect after he proclaimed the coming of Maitreya, the "Buddha of the Future." The discovery of a religious relic—the image of a one-eyed man cast in stone found on the banks of the Yellow River—was interpreted to be a favorable omen, indicating that the downfall of the Mongol Dynasty was at hand.

The White Lotus rebellion spread across China, fueled by the exhortations of four prominent leaders. Han Shan-Tung was killed but with the help of the famous sea captain, Fang Kuo-Chen, who was aided by the former Buddhist monk Chu Yuan-Chang, the Mongol hordes were at last driven out of China. Chu Yuan-Chang became the emperor of the Ming dynasty, given its name by the White Lotus Society. With the objectives achieved, the

White Lotus receded into the background during much of the time the Mings held sway. Not until 1644, when the Manchus (or Ch'ing Dynasty) seized control were the White Lotus heard from again.

For the next 250 years the White Lotus attempted to throw off the yoke of Manchu oppression. They were aided in the struggle by the newly formed Triads which came to prominence during this time, including the Eight Diagrams, the Nine Mansions Sect, and the Heaven and Earth Society. There were White Lotus rebellions in 1774 and 1794, the latter uprising lasting eight years before it was put down by the Manchus. See: **Triad Society.**

REF.: *CBA;* Mackenzie, *Secret Societies.*

Christine Reed and Barbara Songhurst, murdered by Whiteway in 1953.

Whiteway, Alfred Charles, 1931-53, Brit., rob.-rape-mur. On May 31, 1953, 18-year-old Barbara Songhurst and 16-year-old Christine Reed spent the day bicycling along the towpath of the Thames River. That evening, they chatted with three campers and then left before 11 p.m. They ran into 22-year-old laborer Alfred Whiteway near Teddington Lock. He wounded them both with an ax and a knife, then raped the still-living Songhurst and the now-dead Reed. Then he threw both bodies in the river.

Songhurst's body was found near Richmond the next morning, but Reed's did not appear for another five days. Police interviewed more than 7,000 people in 4,000 homes. In late June, Whiteway was arrested for attacks on a 14-year-old girl and a 56-year-old woman on Oxshott Heath. Somehow Whiteway hid his ax under the seat of the police car. The next day, a policeman found it, took it home, and used it to chop wood. When Whiteway was questioned about Songhurst and Reed, he said that he had been with his wife the night of the murders.

When, in mid-July, the embarrassed policeman returned the ax, it was found to fit exactly the wounds in the heads of the victims, though there was no dried blood found on it. Whiteway was charged with Barbara Songhurst's murder in August and went on trial in October. He was found Guilty and was hanged on Dec. 22, 1953.

REF.: *CBA;* Furneaux, *Famous Criminal Crimes, vol. 1;* Heppenstall, *The Sex War and Others;* Jacobs, *Aspects of Murder;* Lucas, *The Sex Killers;* Lustgarten, *The Story of Crime;* Traini, *Murder for Sex;* Webb, *Deadline for Crime;* Wilson, *Encyclopedia of Murder.*

Whitfield, John, prom. 1777, Brit., rob. John Whitfield of Coathill, England, was well known as a thief and murderer. One day in 1777, he killed a horseman near Barrock. He was identified by an eyewitness, and a button from his coat was found at the scene. Whitfield was hanged.

REF.: Andrews, *Old-Time Punishments; CBA.*

Whitfield, John Leonard (AKA: **Sam DeCaro**), prom. 1923, U.S., theft-pris. esc.-mur. On May 11, 1923, Cleveland police visited the home of John Leonard Whitfield, a spark-plug salesman. Whitfield was suspected of stealing plugs from the company warehouse and selling them directly to his clients. He initially tried to bribe the officers, Dennis Griffin and Henry Hughes, but finally agreed to accompany them to the station. Whitfield drove his roadster, accompanied by Officer Griffin, while Hughes followed in the squad car. Before reaching the station, the squad car had a flat tire, and Griffin and Whitfield continued alone. They never reached the station. Three days later, Griffin's body was found in a shallow grave. He had been hit on the side of the head with a pistol butt and shot at point-blank range with a .45-caliber revolver. Whitfield's photograph was published in newspapers and displayed on posters, nationwide.

On June 25, 1923, Whitfield was arrested while working at a Detroit lumber company, under the alias Sam DeCaro. He was tried on July 23, in the Cleveland courtroom of Judge Frank C. Phillip. The prosecution sought the death sentence, but on Aug. 8, the jury found the defendant Guilty but recommended mercy. The judge was forced to sentence Whitfield to life imprisonment. Five years later, on Mar. 9, 1928, after bribing prison guard Oren Hill, Whitfield escaped from prison. He was later found hiding in Hill's home, and after a brief skirmish in which he stabbed a policeman, Whitfield was shot to death.

REF.: *CBA;* Cohen, *One Hundred True Crime Stories;* Rodell, *Cleveland Murders.*

Whitla, Willie, See: **Bogle, James H.**

Whitley, Richard Lee, 1946-87, U.S., mur. Richard Lee Whitley had a long history of sex offenses. He raped his mother, sexually molested his 10-year-old daughter, and sodomized a male hitchhiker before committing one of the most shocking murders in the history of Fairfax County, Va.

Born in Chicago, Ill., 34-year-old Whitley lived in the middle-class Washington D.C., suburb of Pimmet Hills, Va. On the evening of July 25, 1980, Whitley went to the home of his 63-year-old neighbor, Phoebe Parsons, to use her telephone. He had been on a drinking binge for several days, and his wife had left him two weeks earlier. Parsons knew Whitley well, and had often employed him to do repairs around her home. Whitley later told police that he went to Parson's house a second time to use the phone. During their visit, Whitley explained, he and Parsons stood talking in her living room. "We just stood around and talked about my wife and going to church and everything, and the next thing I know she was dead," said Whitley.

The next day, Parsons' bloody, mutilated body was found on her bed, covered by clothes and boxes from her bedroom closet. A rope was tied around her neck and she had been stabbed in the throat with a small knife. Once dead, the murderer laid her body on the bed, stripped it naked, and sexually abused it. Whitley was arrested in Tampa, Fla., after he had fled Virginia in Parsons' Volkswagen. He told Tampa Detective Jerry Feltman that Parsons had been praying as he stabbed her with his plastic-handled Boy Scout knife, and that he stabbed Parsons in the jugular vein because "they die quicker when you cut them there." Whitley was returned to Fairfax County and immediately charged with the murder.

He was brought to trial before Circuit Court Judge F. Bruce Bach. After hearing the sordid details of Whitley's violent past and police testimony about his confession, the jury retired to make their decision. On May 13, 1981, after only thirty-two minutes of deliberation, the jury returned a Guilty verdict and recommended the death penalty. Two weeks after the trial, Judge Bach sentenced Whitley to death in the electric chair.

After more than five years of appeals, and an Amnesty International plea for a stay of execution to the governor of Virginia, and a U.S. Supreme Court denial for a stay of execution, Whitley was electrocuted on July 6, 1987, at 11 p.m. REF.: *CBA.*

Whitman, Charles Joseph, 1941-66, U.S., mur. Once an altar boy, Eagle scout, and U.S. Marine, Charles J. Whitman of Lake Worth, Fla., committed one of the most ruthless murder rampages

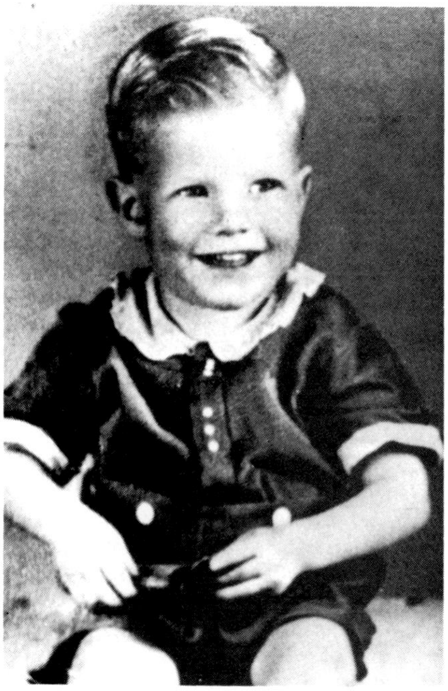

Mass killer Charles Whitman shown, left to right, as a happy 2-year-old child, with his younger brothers Patrick and John, and at the age of twenty-four.

Whitman asleep, a day before his murder spree in Austin.

Whitman's murderous gunfire wounds a man, left, and drives a girl to cover, right.

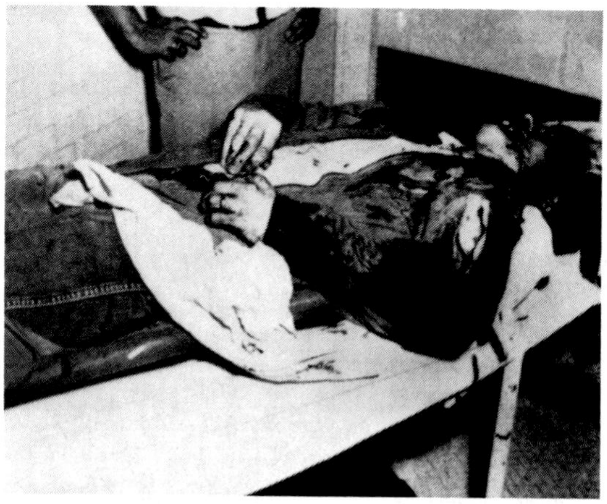

Above, the end of Charles Whitman, shot to pieces, Aug. 1, 1966; right, Austin police officer Ramirio Martinez, who shot and killed sniper Whitman by inching around a wall on the twenty-seven-story University of Texas Tower and firing six bullets into the berserk Whitman, who traded shots with him; far right, the Texas Tower which haunted Whitman, who, as a student on the Austin campus, stared at it for long periods of time. He later told his psychiatrist that he thought of going to the top and shooting people from it.

in U.S. history. In July 1966, Whitman, twenty-five, was enrolled as a junior for the summer semester at the University of Texas in Austin. A student in architectural engineering, Whitman was taking an unusually heavy class load of fourteen credit hours. In the early morning hours of Aug. 1, 1966, Whitman stabbed his 24-year-old wife, Kathleen Leissner Whitman, to death in his Austin apartment, then shot and killed his mother, Mrs. C.A. Whitman. Nothing indicated that the attacks were provoked. Whitman left three cryptic notes in his apartment. The first, addressed to "Roy" read: "My mother's ill and won't be at work today." The two remaining notes were addressed "To whom it may concern." In one, Whitman professed love for his wife and mother, but confusion about why they had to die, except to "save them the embarrassment" of the action he had planned. Whitman expressed contempt for his father, a plumbing contractor from Lake Worth. He said he hated him "with a mortal passion."

Whitman spent the remainder of the morning assembling an arsenal of weapons and gathering provisions. A mail carrier, Chester Arrington, watched as Whitman retooled his shotgun in the family garage. "I talked to Whitman for about twenty-five minutes on the day he did it," Arrington recalled years later. "I saw him sawing off the shotgun, and I knew that was illegal." Arrington did not call police. "All I had to do was pick up the phone and report him. It could have stopped him. I've always blamed myself." When Whitman was finished with his preparations, his foot locker resembled an arsenal. It contained a 6-mm. rifle with a telescopic sight, a Remington .35-caliber pump rifle, a .357 magnum pistol, a 9-mm. Luger pistol, a 30.06 reconditioned army carbine, a 12-gauge sawed off shotgun, and a large Bowie knife. The locker was well stocked with food and two bottles of water.

Whitman carried the locker to the tallest building in Austin, a twenty-seven story tower on the university campus. The granite tower housed the university library and administration offices with an observation deck on the top level. In 1966, the deck was open to the public, commanding an expansive view of the entire campus and a significant portion of Austin. Whitman entered the tower, shot and killed the woman at the visitor's registration desk, and proceeded to the elevator. He next killed a mother and her two children who were spending the day sightseeing. Just before noon, Whitman reached the observation deck, and with his cache of weapons he began shooting at random. An office worker on the eighteenth floor of the tower, Ruth Kiykendall, heard gunshots and called a friend in a nearby building. "Somebody's up there shooting the tower," she said. "There is blood all over the place!" The campus was thrown into an uproar as students, faculty, and visitors scurried for cover. Whitman fired his shots with unerring accuracy. He killed a student riding his bicycle near the Texas Union Building and a police officer standing behind a wood fence. Whitman fired on a small boy and a pregnant woman, Mrs. Claire Wilson, who was taken to a hospital where she gave birth to a stillborn baby.

Police sectioned off the campus, and tried frantically to keep 10,000 students and curiosity seekers out of the line of fire. A police airplane flew over the tower in an attempt to shoot the sniper. Armored cars were called in to rescue the wounded, several of whom lay bleeding in the 98 degree heat for more than an hour.

Whitman sprayed Guadalupe Street with bullets for a eighty minutes. Police officers Romero Martinez, Houston McCoy, Jerry Jay, and George Sheppard rode up the tower elevator with civilian Allen Crum to subdue the sniper. Martinez and Crum slowly moved around the observation wall while the others covered exit doorways. Whitman spotted Martinez and fired once at him. Martinez fired six rapid shots while McCoy kicked in a door and emptied his shotgun. Martinez waved a green flag from the top of the tower signaling the all clear. Whitman lay dead on the observation deck, his head covered with blood. "The sniper was on the northwest corner of the roof," Crum told reporters. "We rushed through the door and spread out." Whitman's body was carried out of the tower at 1:40 p.m. Later that day, administration officials allowed reporters up to the tower for a look. A pile of bloody rags was found lying in the corner. The glass face on the massive clock overlooking the campus grounds was chipped and fragmented with three bullet holes. The ex-Marine's murder spree left sixteen dead and thirty-one wounded. School officials expressed shock over Whitman's actions. They were unable to uncover a motive. According to graduate faculty advisor Leonardt F. Kreisle, Whitman "seemed to be more mature than most people his age." University Chancellor Harry Ransom released Whitman's student records, which showed that he had never been treated at the university for a psychiatric disorder, and was a "B" student. He had received an honorable discharge from the Marine Corps on Dec., 4, 1964, but had gone through court martial proceedings on one occasion for providing gambling loans. Hugo Ley, the owner of a Needville drug store remembered Whitman as a fine young man. "I loved Charlie," he said. "He was the kind of boy you would want for a son."

The residents of Austin were badly shaken by the slayings. Texas governor John Connally cut short a diplomatic visit to Rio de Janeiro to return home to launch a "complete and thorough investigation" into the sniper killings. Connally said that he hoped some good would result, and the inquiry would "shed light on the background and causes and give us some clues on preventing future occurrences of this nature." In 1975, a made-for-television movie adaptation called *The Deadly Tower* starring Kurt Russell and John Forsythe aired on NBC. Martinez sued the network for $1 million, in a breach-of-contract suit, claiming the movie invaded his privacy and misrepresented his character by showing him as a radical. The same year, the University of Texas closed the observation deck, which had also been the site of several suicide attempts. As of this writing, it has not been reopened.

REF.: Boar and Blundell, *The World's Most Infamous Murders; CBA;* Fox, *Mass Murder;* Godwin, *Murder, U.S.A.;* Lester, *Crime of Passion;* Nash, *Bloodletters and Badmen;* Steiger, *Mass Murderer;* Wilson, *Encyclopedia of Modern Murder;* (FILM), *Targets,* 1968.

Whitman, John Lorin, 1862-1926, U.S., penol. Called the "Boy Guard" by the inmates of Cook County Jail, John Lorin Whitman first became a jail guard in Chicago when he was twenty-eight. A very slender and young-looking guard, he was thought of as a boy by inmates at the jail, and they grew fond and protective of him. As a result, he experienced few problems during his duty shifts, and was able to develop a kind, compassionate attitude toward the prisoners. His superiors took notice, and promoted him to jailer. As jailer, and later as superintendent of the House of Correction in Chicago, he initiated reforms and programs noted today for their humane nature. As a consequence of these reforms and programs, the correctional institution had fewer inmate problems than any other in the country. Whitman died in 1926, still referred to as the "Boy Guard." REF.: *CBA.*

Whitney, Chauncey Belden (**AKA: Cap**), 1842-73, U.S., west. lawman. One of the first settlers of Ellsworth, Kan., in 1867, Chauncey Whitney was the town's first sheriff. He built the Ellsworth Jail, and in 1868, fought in the Battle of Beecher Island, in which several armed "scouts" killed attacking Indians who were armed with only spears and arrows. He later served as city marshal, deputy sheriff, and county sheriff. On Aug. 15, 1873, when he was thirty-one, Whitney was killed when Billy Thompson, brother of Ben Thompson, accidentally shot the lawman in the shoulder and breast. The bullet fragments pierced a lung before becoming embedded in his spine.

Lawman Chauncey B. Whitney.

Whitney lingered in agony for three days before he died. See: **Thompson, Ben.**

REF.: Bartholomew, *Wyatt Earp, 1848 to 1880;* Breihan, *Great Gunfighters of the West;* Brent, *Great Western Heroes; CBA;* Drago, *Wild, Woolly & Wicked;* Hall-Quest, *Wyatt Earp;* Horan and Sann, *Pictorial History of the Wild West;* Jelinek, *Ellsworth, Kansas, 1867-1947;* ____, *Ninety Years of Ellsworth and Ellsworth County History;* Johnson, *Famous Lawmen of the Old West;* Lake, *Wyatt Earp;* Miller and Snell, *Great Gunfighters of the Kansas Cowtowns;* Rosa, *The Gunfighter, Man or Myth?;* Snell, *Painted Ladies of the Cowtown Frontier;* Streeter, *Prairie Trails and Cow Towns;* ____, *Tragedies of a Kansas Cow Town;* Wilson, *Out of the West.*

Whitney, James, d.1693, Brit., rob. One-time thief James Whitney bought an inn, the stopping place of a number of highwaymen. Whitney was charmed by the robbers' tales and gave up his inn to join them. In the fashion of the "good thief," he often shared his spoils with those in need. Whitney was arrested and sent to Newgate Prison. Although he escaped, he visited a brothel whose madam betrayed him to the authorities. He was scheduled to die with twenty other highwaymen in January 1693, but received a reprieve at the last moment with the rope already around his neck. However, Whitney's luck ran out and he was executed the following week.

REF.: *CBA;* Potter, *The Art of Hanging;* Pringle, *Stand and Deliver.*

Whitney, Richard, 1889-1974, U.S., embez. Richard Whitney was no grass roots hustler. He was deeply rooted in the American past, and he looked like it, a tall, ruddy-faced (thanks to his fondness for bonded whiskey), lantern-jawed man who dressed and spoke impeccably, a man of wealth and tradition who was thought to be the very image of America's super rich and super intelligent businessman. In reality he was, after two decades of the most horrendous frauds and swindles, discovered to be as crooked as the cheapest mugger absconding with a bag lady's purse. Yet even when he went behind bars he insisted upon the courtesies extended to any high-born gentleman.

Whitney's ancestors were easily traced back to Plymouth Rock, coming from England on the *Arabelle* in 1630, in the wake of the *Mayflower.* Born in 1889, the son of a Boston banker, Whitney attended Groton, an exclusive boy's preparatory school, where he established himself as a resolute leader, becoming captain of the football and baseball teams. At Harvard, where he became an important man on campus, he was an oarsman helping to triumph over other ivy-league boat racers in 1909. He exemplified the well-dressed, well-groomed, well-educated Bostonian who could be counted on to become a captain of finance. His brother George, who attended the same schools, however, was nothing like his outgoing, limelight-loving brother Richard, a serious and stellar student who spent his time in the library and not on the gridiron or pursuing popular college activities. George Whitney would die a multi-millionaire partner in the omnipotent firm of J.P. Morgan, while his dashing and suave brother would end up struggling to pay his laundry bills.

At twenty-seven Richard decided to marry well, wedding Mrs. Gertrude Sheldon Sands in 1916. She was a widow of one of the Vanderbilts. Also in that year, Richard placed himself on the New York Stock Exchange, buying a seat with money loaned to him by a relative. Through his father-in-law, George Sheldon, who was head of the Union League Club and treasurer of the Republican National Committee, Whitney came to meet what few members of New York's 400 he had not already met through his own family connections. These could not only be well-paying customers with staggering commissions, but, later on, individuals from whom Richard Whitney would borrow hundreds of thousands of dollars.

As a broker, Whitney soon earned a reputation as a hard-driving, keen-minded businessman of short words and an occasional acid tongue which could whiplash any subordinate into frenzied duties. He was equally short with his peers who respected but never as a whole liked the man. He was a good organizer, so good that he was soon a member of the governing committee at the exchange, becoming its chairman. He sat in judgment of members accused of misconduct, an ironic role considering Whitney's later transgressions. Whitney's rise was meteoric at the exchange. He was 39-years-old in 1928 when he was elected vice-president and forty-one in 1930 when he became the exchange's president, the youngest man to hold that post in the history of the securities exchange.

In addition to the prestige these Olympian positions brought Whitney, he became *the* Morgan broker. Orders placed by J.P. Morgan and Company earned Whitney more than $50,000 in commissions alone from this account each year. (The Morgan orders actually came through Whitney's brother George who was a high-ranking company official and later a Morgan partner.) Yet these handsome profits proved to be inadequate for Whitney whose tastes ran to the sublimely expensive.

Whitney and his wife maintained a 495-acre estate at Far Hills, N.J., and a Manhattan townhouse. He owned a fleet of eight expensive cars and a yacht. An army of servants slaved to meet his needs–butlers, maids, cooks, and at the country estate gardeners, herdsmen for his dogs and foxes (he rode with the hounds regularly), and jockeys for his private stable of horses, which cost him thousands each month. His wardrobe was vast with over fifty newly tailored suits hanging in his closets. His wine cellar was always stocked with magnums of champagne and vintage imported wines. He also maintained elegant, fifteen-room offices on Broad Street.

All of these enormous costs caused Richard Whitney to look about frantically for capital. He began borrowing from his brother George—during the mid-1920s, as much as $575,000—to purchase fertilizer and mineral stocks which proved worthless. The man who was thought to be the most astute securities analyst in the country knew nothing about stocks and repeatedly plunged into foolhardy, even bizarre investments that spiraled his debts into the millions. Whitney used as collateral more than $100,000 in stocks which belonged to the account of his dead father-in-law to cover one loan from the Corn Exchange Bank, where he was director and later president—the first of his criminal acts of embezzlement and fraud.

He continued plunging in useless stocks for which he became the chief purchaser and using securities and stocks of others he was holding as collateral for loans that soared into the millions, loans so large that he could not even afford to pay the interest on them, a maddening, round-robin routine that would have caused any normal man to crack, but Richard Whitney was a nerveless type and raced forward in his wild schemes, confident that he would eventually make a killing that would pay off all his debts. A great deal of his courage undoubtedly stemmed from his knowledge that his brother George was always available for a vital bailout.

For a brief moment in the Great Crash of 1929, this misfit of finance became a hero in the eyes of the world. On Oct. 24, 1929, Black Thursday, when stocks were crashing downward across the board, Whitney, who was then vice-president of the exchange and the ranking officer present (with exchange president Edward H.H. Simon in Europe) went to the rescue of the market. Actually, he had been selected to represent J.P. Morgan and Company and the pool of great investors Morgan had gathered to shore up the sinking stock market.

As panic gripped the floor of the exchange and brokers burst blood vessels in desperation to sell off stock, Whitney, calm and stoic, appeared at 1:30 p.m. The hundreds of fear-frenzied men on the floor became, in the instant of his appearance, a stone-silent crowd, staring at him as he moved resolutely to Post Two. He said in a loud clear voice which he obviously intended the entire floor to hear, (directing his question to Oliver Bridgeman): "What was the last bid you received for Steel?"

"One-ninety-five," replied Bridgeman.

In an even louder voice, like that of a rescuing god, Richard Whitney boomed: "Ten thousand at two hundred and five!" This was ten points above the last bid and the price of the last sale. In that second he had tossed more than $2 million of the Morgan pool into the market to stem the downward tide. The act was electric and caused the brokers to shout out roaring cheers. Whitney, the hero of the hour, his finest moment in life, in fact, then marched like an avenging angel against fear and panic, to several more posts placing upward of $30 million in purchase orders of fifteen or twenty important stocks in blocks of 10,000 shares.

As the Morgan people estimated, the clear movement by their moneyed clan to back up the market caused a brisk rally that sent the stock market upward again, dizzily so. But the downward trend had been gnawing away at the underpinnings of the synthetic market for many months, and the move by Whitney, representing Morgan and his people, really came too late. The selling panic resumed the next day and the following week, on Black Tuesday, Oct. 29, 1929, the market all but collapsed. The pandemonium was ear-shattering as supposedly solid stocks fell $40, $50, even $60 a share, more than sixteen million shares being sold. It was, as the New York *World* termed it, "a financial nightmare, comparable to nothing ever before experienced in Wall Street."

Bedlam ruled the exchange floor that day. Said one stock exchange guard who witnessed the financial collapse: "They (the brokers) roared like a lot of lions and tigers. They hollered and screamed, they clawed at one another's collars. It was like a bunch of crazy men. Every once in a while, when Radio or Steel or Auburn would take another tumble, you'd see some poor devil collapse and fall to the floor."

Wall Street embezzler Richard Whitney, testifying.

Whitney did not appear on the floor that fatal day. He had made his bold play the week before and Morgan's people, seeing that their millions had not stemmed the tide, refused to pour more millions down the drain. Whitney and other high-ranking exchange members sat in a smoking room beneath the floor puffing on cigarettes, helpless. Whitney later remembered how the "panic was raging overhead on the floor. Every few minutes the latest prices were announced, with quotations moving swiftly and irresistibly downward. The feeling of those present was revealed by their habit of continually lighting cigarettes, taking a puff or two, putting them out and lighting new one–a practice that soon made the narrow room blue with smoke and extremely stuffy."

When many of his ruined peers later blew out their brains or stuffed their heads into gas stoves or leaped from high office windows, Whitney merely shrugged. He would survive and did, but his methods had nothing to do with the business practices his exchange committee insisted be followed. In Summer 1930, Whitney was given charge of the New York Yacht Club's securities, worth more than $100,000; he was then president of the club. Whitney, instead of locking these in his vault, used them to negotiate personal loans at thirteen separate banks. Moreover, he walked into the Corn Exchange Bank, where he was a director, and demanded and got, without any securities, another $300,000 loan. When another nervous director asked timidly what the dynamic stock exchange president (he would serve four terms in that lofty office) was putting up as collateral, Whitney replied archly with his favorite line: "I am taking the loan on my face."

By 1934, Whitney's incredible loans, which totaled in the millions, cost him $250,000 a year in interest, and to cover this, he took out more loans using as collateral more securities belonging to others and entrusted to his care. He shamelessly borrowed $2 million from his brother George, but this gave him only momentary relief from his debts. (George Whitney was never repaid for the many enormous loans made to his brother, and these amounts later became nothing more than very costly gifts.)

When Prohibition was repealed, Whitney thought that the shrewdest investment he could make would be to buy the controlling stock in Distilled Liquors Corporation which was about to turn out millions of gallons of alcoholic applejack. First he bought 15,000 shares at $15 each and was pleased to see the stock shoot to $45. He did not, however, sell out and take his handsome profits which would have helped to set his ledgers right. He stayed with the stock which began to plunge when consumers opted for beer and wine and hard liquor. Still, he continued to buy more and more of DLC stock, pouring hundreds of thousands of dollars into the losing proposition, good money after bad, again and again. He took out more loans, borrowed more money. He never had enough.

In 1937, another windfall presented itself to the drowning broker. The stock exchange entrusted to his care its Gratuity Fund of more than $2 million in cash and bonds, sums taxed from exchange members and intended for widow and orphans of deceased members. Whitney promptly used the bonds a collateral for new loans and used the cash to pay off interest on old loans.

At a meeting of trustees for the fund it was voted that $175,000 in bonds be sold and that these bonds be turned back by Whitney. He was asked politely five times by George W. Lutes, clerk of the trustees group, to return the bonds for sale but Whitney stalled him. Finally the trustees gave Whitney a deadline to return the bonds.

The casual broker was unruffled. He went to millionaire Bernard Smith, a powerful stockbroker he barely knew and boldly asked Smith to loan him $250,000.

"On what collateral?" asked Smith.

"On my face," replied Whitney with his favorite line.

"I don't like your face," snorted Smith and closed the discussion.

Whitney went back to brother George who, along with other Morgan partners, agreed to cover the losses to save the face of J.P. Morgan and Company. But the self-destructive, money-hungry Richard went on as before and within the next twelve months took out staggering loans that exceeded $27 million. There was really no hope of ever even paying off the interest on this amount, let alone the principal. Finally, after being compelled to submit to the exchange a routine financial statement, it was obvious to executive board members that Whitney's firm existed only on paper and had been gutted by its director. He was asked to withdraw from the exchange, despite pleas he made to Averell Harriman, a partner in Brown Brothers, Harriman and Company, to bail him out.

Brother George could no longer help. Other Morgan partners felt that they could no longer spend millions to support Richard Whitney's wastrel ways. When the broker's firm was removed from the exchange it became apparent that he had at least mismanaged funds, and this brought about an investigation into his incredible affairs by New York's energetic District Attorney Thomas E. Dewey.

All of Whitney's many years of fraud were slowly revealed, and he was arrested and charged with embezzling his father-in-law's estate. His trial was brief and he was quickly convicted, sentenced to five years in Sing Sing. When Richard Whitney went to prison, his conduct was as formal as if he were entering one of his private clubs. He was more than $6 million in personal debt, not including the almost $3 million his brother had given him. His townhouse and country estates, his horses, cars, and even his wardrobe had been sold to pay creditors.

Yet the stolid, gray-faced man insisted upon personal dignity and was strangely accorded high respect by fellow convicts in Sing Sing—they tipped their hats to him—even the guards. When he first arrived in prison, a turnkey stated: "All men who came in Saturday and Mr. Whitney please step out of their cells." He was addressed as "Mr. Whitney" by convicts and guards alike through his three-year stay at Sing Sing, being paroled in 1941.

The fact that Whitney had stolen millions and had only received a minimum five-year sentence rankled many citizens, and, in particular, a St. Louis judge. The judge was to sentence a youth who had stole $2 from a gas station. One report stated: "Taking pencil and paper, he made elaborate computations and then announced his decision. 'Richard Whitney got five years for stealing $225,000,' he said. 'That would be $45,000 a year, $120 a day, $5 an hour. You stole $2. That would be twenty-four minutes and that is your sentence!'"

When Whitney emerged from prison, he returned to his heavily mortgaged estate and his wife Gertrude. His brother George saw to it that Richard could live out his life in the comfort to which he was accustomed, irrespective of the blatant corruption with which he had stained the Whitney name. On Dec. 5, 1974, Richard Whitney died in comfort at the age of eighty-six.

Whitney is not remembered with ill will by members of the New York Stock Exchange. He is not remembered at all. In the elegant Board of Governors room at the exchange hang huge oil paintings of past presidents of the exchange, all except one—Whitney.

REF.: Adams, *Dictionary of American History;* Allen, *The Great Pierpont Morgan;* Allen, *Lords of Creation;* ____, *Only Yesterday;* ____, *Since Yesterday;* Amory, *Who Killed Society?;* Beebe, *The Big Spenders;* Bendiner, *Just Around the Corner;* Brooks, *Once in Golconda;* Butterfield, *The American Past; CBA;* Conger, *The Thirties, A Time to Remember;* Crane, *The Roosevelt Era;* Ellis, *A Nation in Torment, The Great American Depression, 1929-1939;* Galbraith, *The Great Crash, 1929;* Horan, *The Desperate Years;* Hoyt, *The House of Morgan;* Jenkins, *The Stock Exchange Story;* Leighton, *The Aspirin Age, 1919-1941;* Lundberg, *AMerica's Sixty Families;* Lundberg, *The Rich and the Super Rich;* Mayer, *Wall Street: Men and Money;* Mayer, *Wall Street–The Inside Story of American Finance;* Mehling, *The Scandalous Scamps;* Mitchell, *Depression Decade, 1929-1941;* Morris, *What a Year!–The Colorful Story of 1929;* Myers, *The Ending of Hereditary American Fortunes;* Patterson, *The Great Boom and Panic;* Pecora, *Wall Street Under Oath;* Powers, *Secrecy and Power;* Rees, *The Great Slump;* Robbins, *The Great Depression;* Rogers, *I Remember Distinctly;* Sann, *The Lawless Decade;* Schlesinger, *The Crisis of the Old Order, 1919-1933;* Seldes, *The Years of the Locust: America, 1929-32;* Shannon, *The Great Depression;* Simon, *As We Saw the Thirties;* Sobel, *The Big Board: A History of the New York Stock Market;* ____, *Panic on Wall Street: A History of America's Financial Disasters;* Soule, *Prosperity Decade, 1919-1929;* Sparling, *Mystery Men of Wall Street;* Studenski, *Financial History of the United States;* Tanner, *All the Things We Were;* Thomas, *The Plungers and the Peacocks;* Thomas and Morgan-Witts, *The Day the Bubble Burst, A Social History of the Wall Street Crash of 1929;* Thorndike, *The Very Rich;* Tully, *Era of Elegance;* Warshow, *The Story of Wall Street;* Wechter, *The Age of the Great Depression;* Weingarten, *The Sky is Falling;* Whitney and Perkins, *Selling Short–For and Against.*

Whittaker, Charles Evans, 1901-73, U.S., jur. Charles Evans Whittaker rose from humble beginnings on an eastern Kansas farm to attain a five-year tenure as a U.S. Supreme Court justice. Born on Feb. 22, 1901, Whittaker quit school at age sixteen after his mother's death, but with private tutoring he was able to enter the University of Kansas Law School four years later. After graduating in 1924, Whittaker joined the private law firm of Watson, Gage & Ess, and within two years was named senior partner. Whittaker served as president of the Missouri Bar Association from 1953-1954. He was appointed to the bench for the first time in 1954 when he became a judge of the U.S. District Court for the Western District. Two years later, he was appointed to the U.S. Court of Appeals for the Eighth Circuit.

On Mar. 19, 1957, President Dwight Eisenhower nominated Whittaker to the U.S. Supreme Court, replacing Justice Stanley Reed. Whittaker, a Republican, became a conservative voice on a number of important issues, including civil liberties. He voted to uphold the imposition of multiple sentences for a single narcotics conviction; he agreed that passports should be withheld from those refusing to sign an affidavit denying membership in the Communist Party; he disagreed that racial segregation on interstate bus routes violated the Interstate Commerce Act; he voted to strike down a state redistricting law which effectively denied voting rights to blacks; he agreed that the due process rights of the defendant had been violated if he was incapable of representing himself and had been denied legal counsel; and finally, he wrote the majority opinion which stated that the warrantless search of a defendant's apartment violated the Fourth Amendment, even if police had the consent of the landlord.

Whittaker was forced to retire from the court in 1962 after suffering a long-term illness. He was replaced by Justice Byron R. White. In his retirement, Whittaker served on the legal staff at General Motors and later helped the Senate Committee on Standards and Conduct devise a code for senatorial ethics. Whittaker died on Nov. 26, 1973, in Kansas City, Mo. REF.: *CBA.*

Whittaker, Samuel, 1875-1937, U.S., mur. In 1937, 62-year-old musician Samuel Whittaker was convicted of first-degree murder in the death of his wife, who was killed during a phony robbery that Whittaker arranged to bilk $18,000 from his insurance company. Whittaker, a Los Angeles theatre organist, enlisted the help of 24-year-old James Culver, who later turned state's evidence.

During his trial, Whittaker maintained his innocence and dramatically proclaimed to the court, "May God may strike me dead before I get to my cell if I am guilty of this horrible crime." Whittaker was found Guilty of murder, and upon his arrival at California's San Quentin prison, he complained of chest pains and was immediately transferred into the custody of the prison physician. Whittaker died of a heart attack in the prison infirmary before receiving his cell assignment. REF.: *CBA.*

Whittemore, Richard Reese, d.1926, U.S., mur. A delinquent from the age of ten, Richard Whittemore killed a guard while serving his second prison term for armed robbery. Born into an old Maryland family with a reputation for honesty, Whittemore was initially sent to reform school for truancy. He repeatedly ran away from the school and began robbing stores before his teens. He had several conflicts with police, and when WWI broke out, he attempted to enlist in the army, and then the Coast Guard.

In October 1921, Whittemore robbed a Baltimore home of property worth $377 and was sent to the Maryland Penitentiary for fifteen years. Upon his release, he formed a gang of his reformatory and prison companions that "shook down" saloons in Baltimore and Philadelphia while posing as IRS agents. Whittemore was captured in January 1925, convicted of robbery, and sentenced to fifteen years and three months in prison. After being locked up less than a month, he escaped from prison on Feb. 20, killing guard Robert Holtman in the process. He hit Holtman over the head with a pipe because he was convinced the guard would shoot him.

Whittemore escaped to New York where his gang began operations that netted $750,000 in stolen jewelry within a year. He was arrested in connection with a Buffalo, N.Y., bank robbery in which two bank messengers were killed. He was acquitted of those murders but immediately sent to Baltimore where he was tried and convicted of first-degree murder in the slaying of the Holtman. He was sentenced to hang. The governor of Maryland denied a stay of execution and U.S. Supreme Court Justice Oliver Wendell Holmes denied a last minute writ of error. On Aug. 13, 1926, Richard Whittemore was hanged in the Maryland State Penitentiary. His last words were, "I wish to say good-bye. That's the best I can wish to any one."

REF.: *CBA;* Kobler, *Ardent Spirits.*

Whittington, Richard, c.1358-1423, Brit., pris. reform. Richard Whittington served as Lord Mayor of London four times between the years 1393 and 1420. His tenure was marked by great reform and generosity, including the restoration of Westminster Abbey, the building of Greyfriars Library, and acquiring Leadenbull for the city. A man who built a large fortune before his public service, Whittington generously loaned large sums of money to both Henry IV and Henry V. In 1421, he burned a £60,000 note owed him by Henry V.

Whittington was particularly appalled by prison conditions during his first term as mayor, and immediately improved the living conditions of the incarcerated. In 1420, his last year as mayor, Whittington ordered the reconstruction of Newgate prison. He died in 1423, bequeathing his entire fortune to charity and public purposes. Executors spent the money to repair St. Bartholomew's Hospital and to build St. Michael's college.

REF.: *CBA;* Nicholls, *Crime Within the Square Mile.*

Whittle, William, d.1766, Brit., mur. In 1766, Europe's religious conflicts led Englishman William Whittle to murder his wife and two children. Whittle believed God wanted his family dead because his Protestant wife was a "heretic" and his children had been to the "church of the heretic." Whittle said the death of his children would save their souls from eternal damnation. Whittle was found Guilty of the murders and was executed at Lancaster Moor on Apr. 5, 1766, after which his body was hanged in chains.

REF.: *CBA;* Mitchell, *The Newgate Calendar.*

Whitty, Dennis, 1940-63, and **Pascoe, Russell,** d.1963, Brit., mur. William Garfield Rowe was an eccentric 64-year-old WWI deserter who lived on his family's farm near Falmouth, England. By 1963, all of Rowe's family members had either died or moved away, and he lived a reclusive life. On Aug. 15, 1963, a cattle dealer named Henry Pascoe found Rowe's body lying on the floor of his farmhouse. Rowe had been beaten and stabbed to death. Police interviewed known criminals in the area including Russell Pascoe (no relation to Henry Pascoe), who was living with three girls and another man named Dennis Whitty. Rowe's brand of cigarettes were found in the house, and one of the girl's told police that they knew Rowe had recently been stabbed although this information had not been made public. Implicated in the crime, the two men admitted to being on Rowe's property and accused each other of the murder. However, it was proven that Rowe had been stabbed and beaten simultaneously, and both men were convicted of the murder. They were executed in December 1963.

REF.: Butler, *Murderers' England; CBA.*

Whitty, Ken, 1940-84, Gr., polit., (unsolv.) assass. Ken Whitty, a 44-year-old British cultural representative, was assassinated on an Athens street on Mar. 28, 1984. Whitty and a Greek woman, Artemis Economidou, were riding together in a car when they were flagged down by an Arab man in his late twenties. When Whitty rolled down the window, the man killed him with three shots to the head from a 9-mm. pistol. Economidou was shot once in the neck and was considered clinically dead upon arrival at a hospital. REF.: *CBA.*

Whyos, The, prom. 1860s-90s, U.S., org. crime. Without a doubt, the Whyos were the most vicious street gang active in Manhattan in the latter nineteenth century. This unsavory collection of pickpockets, second story men and mercenary killers did not confine their activities to a single city block, or neighborhood. Indeed they claimed the whole of Manhattan as their turf, defying anyone to take it away from them.

The gang came into prominence after the Civil War, and remained a force in organized crime until the turn of the century when Paul Kelly and Edward "Monk" Eastman organized their own gang. The origin of their peculiar name is shrouded in mystery. It has been suggested that the moniker was borrowed from a strange howl known only to the gangsters. The Whyos evolved from the earlier Chicester Gang. The dominated the Fourth Ward of the Lower East Side, an impoverished Irish ethnic ghetto that spawned crime. Gang headquarters was in the back of a grimy saloon appropriately named the Morgue. It was the scene of at least 100 grisly murders over the years. Gang fights at the Morgue occurred with alarming regularity. Sometimes the guns would blaze for hours on end.

Among the disreputable members of the Whyos who earned a dubious notoriety in the 1880s-90s were the dregs of the underworld: Red Rocks Farrell, Slops Connolly, Big Josh Hines, Hoggy Walsh, Piker Ryan, Dorsey Doyle, Mike Lloyd, Bull Hurley, Fig McGerald, and Googy Corcoran. It was Big Josh Hines who perfected the shakedown technique that was copied by other gang members. Each night he would drop by the faro dens and dice parlors demanding a cut of the take. Hines sported a pair of pistols in his belt—fair warning to those who would be so foolish as to think they could get off with not paying. To a police detective who expressed concern that the operators of the faro bank were getting upset with these shakedowns, Hines replied: "Them guys must be nuts! Don't I always leave 'em somethin? All I want is me fair share."

Mike McGloin commanded the Whyos Gang in the early 1880s. He established one simple membership requirement for anyone seeking admission to the gang: the apprentice would have to murder a foe. "A guy ain't tough until he has knocked his man out!" McGloin was quoted as saying in 1883. McGloin lived up to his own word and was hanged in the Tombs prison on Mar. 8, 1883 for the murder of saloon keeper Louis Hanier.

The police were afforded a rare glimpse into the day to day operations of the street gang in 1884, when they arrested Piker Ryan and found in his pocket a checklist of "services" offered and the corresponding fees:

Punching	$2
Both eyes blackened	4
Nose and jaw broken	10
Jacked out (beaten with a truncheon)	15
Ear chawed off	15
Leg or arm broken	19
Shot in leg	25
Stab	25
Doing the big job (murder)	100 and up.

Danny Lyons and Danny Driscoll jointly ruled the Whyos in 1887. Driscoll was hanged on Jan. 23, 1888 after accidentally shooting a prostitute named Beezy Garrity during a saloon row with John McCarthy. Lyons accompanied Driscoll in death on Aug. 21, 1888 when he was hanged for the murder of Joseph Quinn, who was shot to death in a gun battle in the Five Points on July 5, 1887. The dispute occurred as a result of a quarrel over the favors of a streetwalker named Pretty Kitty McGown.

Dandy John Dolan was another Whyo gangster of some note. He invented a copper eye gouger worn on the thumb. He put this insidious device to use in the Summer of 1875 during a robbery at Noe's jewelry store. The proprietor of the establishment, James H. Noe, attempted to block the path of the murderous Dolan but was battered over the head with an iron crow bar. For good measure the gangster gouged out his eyeballs and carried them around in his vest pocket to show off to his pals. Police Detective Joseph M. Dorcy found them in his possession during the interrogation phase. Dolan was convicted of murder, and was hanged on Apr. 21, 1876. See: **Eastman, Edward; Kelly, Paul.**

REF.: Asbury, *The Gangs of New York; CBA;* Godwin, *Murder, U.S.A.;* Kobler, *Al Capone;* Nash, *Bloodletters and Badmen;* Peterson, *The Mob;* Reppetto, *The Blue Parade.*

Wicked Lady, The, See: **Ferrers, Katherine.**

Wickersham, George Woodward, 1858-1936, U.S., atty. gen. Born in Pittsburgh on Sept. 19, 1858, George Woodward Wickersham practiced law in Philadelphia for two years before moving to New York in 1882 to become managing clerk in the law firm of Strong and Cadwallader. He became a full partner in the firm in 1887, and on Mar. 5, 1909, Wickersham was named U.S. Attorney General by President William Taft. Wickersham's most notable contributions included initiating many suits against the monopolistic practices of corporations; proposing a regulatory body similar to the Interstate Commerce Commission; drawing the original draft of the Mann-Elkins Railroad Act; and assisting with the corporation tax provision in the Payne-Aldrich Tariff Act. Returning to private practice, Wickersham became the floor leader at the New York Constitutional Convention in 1915; commissioner of the War Trade Board to Cuba, in Summer 1918; a special correspondent for the New York *Tribune,* during the Paris Peace Conference in 1919; a member of the League of Nations committee to codify international law; the president of the American Law Institute; and in 1929, he was appointed head of the National Commission on Law Observance and Enforcement by President Herbert Hoover. Wickersham died in New York City on Jan. 26, 1936. REF.: *CBA.*

Wickersham Commission, prom. 1929, U.S., law enfor. agen. President Herbert Hoover appointed the National Commission on Law Observance and Enforcement in 1929. Headed by former attorney general George W. Wickersham, the commission examined law enforcement costs, police practices, juvenile delinquency, Prohibition, and the common belief that most crimes were committed by immigrants. The Wickersham Commission, as it came to be known, concluded that law enforcement was utterly inadequate and that it cost more than $1 billion a year. The commission also found Prohibition to be a disaster and recommended its repeal. Wickersham was one of four members who wished to continue testing Prohibition, but in 1932, he changed his position and advocated the sale of alcoholic beverages, with government regulation. Wickersham's decision was said to be the death blow to Prohibition.

REF.: *CBA;* Lowenthal, *The Federal Bureau of Investigation;* Lynch, *Criminals and Politicians;* Reppetto, *The Blue Parade;* Thrasher, *The Gang.*

Wicks, Edward, c.1684-1713, Brit., rob. Edward Wicks, known as Ned, served his first jail term at Marshalsea Prison in Southwark after being apprehended for his third robbery. But before finishing his sentence, he escaped with the help of fellow thieves. Wicks joined forces with highwayman Joe Johnson. Their partnership ended in 1704 when Johnson was shot during a robbery as Wicks fled the scene. Johnson was easily captured, and he was hanged at Tyburn on Feb. 7, 1704.

One of Wicks' most daring robberies was his ambush of the royal coach of Lord Charles, Baron of Mohun. Wicks engaged the Baron in a swearing duel in which each man wagered fifty guineas that he could out-swear the other. Wicks eventually won the duel, judged by the baron's coachman, and rode off with the baron's money.

Wicks was apprehended shortly thereafter in London and charged with a robbery in Warwickshire. He was sent to Newgate, where he unsuccessfully attempted to escape. He was then transferred to Warwick, and condemned to death. His wealthy parents pleaded for his life, but on Aug. 29, 1713, he was hanged.

REF.: *CBA;* Smith, *Highwaymen.*

Wienchowski, Joseph, prom. 1935, U.S., mur. Joseph Wienchowski lived with his wife and their 17-year-old son Gregory on a farm in northern Michigan. The teenager was headstrong and frequently argued with his parents. In March 1935, Gregory Wienchowski's mutilated body was found in a forest near the farm. While the elder Wienchowski appeared grief stricken, police became suspicious when they discovered bloodstains in the barn. When they found a life insurance policy on Gregory's life which would more than pay for the farm, and a gardening fork whose prongs matched the wounds in the boy's body, they arrested Wienchowski. He confessed that he had killed his son, but only after Gregory had attacked him with a hammer. Wienchowski was convicted of murder and sentenced to life at the state prison in Jackson.

REF.: *CBA;* Whitelaw, *Corpus Delicti.*

Wierzbiki, Edward F., 1941- , U.S., mur. On June 4, 1979, Edward Wierzbiki was convicted of the 1978 murder of a 5-year-old Chicago child, and was sentenced to 80 years in prison by Judge R. Eugene Pincham. In 1978, Wierzbiki had lured Patrick Chavez, Jr. from the child's backyard, and strangled him in an apartment on the city's North Side. The judge ordered that a minimum of forty years be served, leaving Wierzbiki eligible for parole at age seventy-eight. REF.: *CBA.*

Wiesenthal, Simon, 1908- , Ger., Nazi hunter. Eighty-nine members of Simon Wiesenthal's family perished in the Holocaust during the long, grim years of the Third Reich. When the ordeal was over and the continent of Europe freed from Nazi tyranny, Wiesenthal dedicated the remainder of his life to tracking down and bringing to justice those persons responsible for the extermination of six million Jews. "You can forgive crimes against you personally, but no one is authorized to forgive crimes against others," Wiesenthal said. "I want to build a memento for murderers who may yet be born. I have a warning, that the murderers of tomorrow will never have any rest."

Simon Wiesenthal was trained as an architectural engineer. He received his degree from the Technical University of Prague in 1932 before settling in Lvov, Pol., on the eve of WWII. After the Russian army seized the city in 1939 Wiesenthal was forced to close down his architectural firm in the name of state socialism. He narrowly avoided deportation to Siberia by bribing a commissar of the Soviet secret police (NKVD). The Red Army was driven out of Lvov by the invading German Wehrmacht in 1941. Wiesenthal was arrested by the Gestapo and interred in the Mauthausen concentration camp in Poland. In a desperate moment the future Nazi-hunter attempted suicide by slashing his wrists, but recovered in a hospital. "I'll look at the scars on my wrists and think:, 'Was this really so?'" he said. He made it through the war and was reunited with his wife who had passed herself off as a Polish national to escape the death camp. After sufficiently recovering his health, Wiesenthal answered his calling. He began the monumental task of collecting and collating information on Nazi fugitives, those who took part in Adolph Hitler's "final solution." In 1947, Wiesenthal and thirty volunteers opened the Documentation Centre on the Fate of Jews and Their Persecutors in Linz, Aust. His early work was of particular value to the War Crimes Tribunal convened at Nürnberg to review the cases of former Nazis arrested in the waning days of the conflict.

There was a mindset in Western Europe and the U.S. that the majority of Nazi war criminals had already been tried before Allied courts, and there was little else left to do. Indeed, between 1951 and 1958 there was no systematic prosecution of ex-Nazis, while public officials on both sides of divided Germany showed extreme reluctance to ferret out former SS men. "The East Germans don't even answer letters," Wiesenthal told an interviewer in 1976. "It's in their own interest. It's part of their propaganda to let the world know that thousands of Nazis are free in West Germany." The Cold war proved to be the greatest detriment to the Wiesenthal organization

In 1954, the Linz office was closed due to apathy and a lack of funding. The massive index file was transferred to offices in Israel for safekeeping where it remained until 1961. Wiesenthal continued his work on a "free-lance" basis. Still at large were Adolf Eichmann, overseer of Hitler's extermination policies, and Dr. Josef Mengele, the sadist who conducted genetic experiments on concentration camp inmates. In 1959, Israeli agents traced agents traced Eichmann to Buenos Aires, but establishing his identity was another matter. Wiesenthal sent a team of photographers to South America to cover the funeral of the former Nazi's father. The developed photos proved that this was indeed the same Eichmann. The aging Nazi was seized on the streets of Buenos Aires in May 1960, and transported back to Israel where he was placed on trial. He was executed in 1961 for crimes against humanity. The capture of Eichmann was a personal triumph for Wiesenthal whose work helped focus world attention back to the plight of the forgotten victims of the Holocaust. In 1961 he opened the Jewish Documentation Center in Vienna, which has provided the necessary evidence to arrest more than 1,000 Nazi war criminals since its implementation. In a two-room office on a site formerly occupied by the Hotel Metropol—Gestapo headquarters during the war—Wiesenthal stores his files and maintains contacts with a worldwide network of informants. Some of his most substantial leads have come from individuals with information to share. One such tip led to the capture of Franz Stangl in 1967. During the war Stangl was the SS commandant of the Treblinka and Sobibor death camps where at least 400,000 Jews were killed. Stangl slipped away from an allied internment camp on May 30, 1948, and made his way to Sao Paulo, Braz., through contacts within the shadowy network.

Organized by a clique of opportunistic SS officers during the closing months of WWII, ODESSA was bankrolled with large deposits of gold sequestered in foreign bank accounts. The money helped defray the travel expenses of top-ranking Nazis, providing them with new identities and forged papers to get them started in Spain, Argentina, Brazil, and the Middle East. Stangl was spirited away to a new life in Brazil, where he worked as a safety officer in a Volkswagen plant in Sao Paulo. Ironically it was a former Gestapo man that tipped Wiesenthal off about Stangl. "Because of men like him we little fellows have had nothing but trouble since the end of the war," the man said. "The big men, the Eichmanns, the Stangls—they had all the help they needed. False papers, money, new jobs. But look at me. No one will give me a job because I've been in the Gestapo." The man asked for and received $7,000 as his price for Stangl.

In February 1967, the Brazilian police arrested the former death camp commandant and extradited him back to West Germany to stand trial. Charged with the deaths of 400,000 men, women, and children, Stangl was convicted by the courts and sentenced to life imprisonment. He died at the Düsseldorf prison on June 28, 1971. Eichmann and Stangl were major finds, but it was the arrest of a relatively obscure former SS officer that Wiesenthal considers his most significant achievement. For years there were a handful of pro-Nazi sympathizers who considered the haunting story of Anne Frank a piece of Jewish fiction. The war time diaries detailing Frank's experiences living in hiding with her family in Holland were published several years after she had perished in the Belsen concentration camp. It was a poignant expression of man's inhumanity, eloquently told by an adolescent girl whose innocence belied the horrors of war. Thanks to Wiesenthal, the arresting SS officer, Karl Silberbauer, was captured and brought to justice. Anne Frank, one of the Nazi hunter's "six million clients," was at last vindicated.

There were, of course, some major disappointments and setbacks. In 1975 nine defendants were placed on trial in Düsseldorf and charged with complicity in the murders of 200,000 men, women, and children at the Majdanek camp near Lublin, Pol. The Soviet army liberated the camp in July 1944. By this time most of the inmates were either dead or evacuated to other camps. Not until 1965 were West German officials able to locate the staff rosters of Majdanek. "We had the names and were able to pass them on to Düsseldorf," said Adalbert Rueckerl, state's attorney. "But we had to establish a connection between the names and the crimes."

With the help of Wiesenthal's task force, SS guards Arnold Strippel and Hermine Braunsteiner were tracked down after twenty-one years and brought to trial. Braunsteiner had married an American serviceman named Russell Ryan and had fled in exile to the U.S. She was extradited to Germany and sentenced to life in prison following a trial that dragged on for more than five years. Strippel received only three and a half years. Six others received lesser sentences and one was acquitted. "For me, the sentences are the best sign of the devaluation of human life," Wiesenthal said ruefully. "If you give three years for help in murdering a large number of people, the value of life certainly has depreciated." The presiding judge in the trial, Guenter Bogen, pointed to contradicting evidence and the failing memories of eyewitnesses. "After such a lapse of time there is only a limited possibility of clarifying the events at Majdanek by evidence of witnesses," the judge said. For Wiesenthal the task continues. "When you know your office is the last office," he said, "and that you are the last man who knows the job, then you cannot close down the office and stop." See: **Barbie, Klaus; Eichmann, Karl Adolf.** REF.: *CBA.*

Wigmore, John Henry, 1863-1943, U.S., lawyer. Practiced law in Boston from 1887-89. He was dean of the faculty of law at Northwestern University from 1901-29. He also wrote several legal works. REF.: *CBA.*

Wigwam Murder, See: **Sangret, August.**

Wilber, Lewis, 1816-39, U.S., mur. Lewis Wilber, a boatman aboard a river boat on the Erie Canal, struck up an acquaintance with a passenger, Robert Barber. The other passengers overheard the two men chatting about Barber's forthcoming wedding and other subjects. The next morning, Aug. 30, 1837, when the boat picked up supplies at New Boston, the two men got off the boat. For an unknown reason, Wilber killed Barber in the woods and cut his body into pieces. Then Wilber walked back and again boarded the boat four miles from where he and Barber had gotten off. He explained Barber's absence by saying Barber had decided to walk to Syracuse.

CONFESSION
OF
LEWIS WILBER,
WHO WAS EXECUTED AT MORRISVILLE, N. Y. OCTOBER 3, 1839
FOR THE MURDER OF
ROBERT BARBER,

A contemporary pamphlet describing murderer Wilber Lewis.

When Barber's corpse was found eight months later, passengers aboard the boat the day Barber disappeared were located. They told police that they remembered Wilber going off with Barber. Wilber was found in Ohio and returned to New York for trial. Found Guilty, he was hanged on Oct. 3, 1839.

REF.: *CBA;* Nash, *Bloodletters and Badmen.*

Wilbur, Curtis Dwight, 1867-1954, U.S., jur. Presided as judge of ninth U.S. Circuit Court of Appeals, beginning in 1929, and as senior circuit judge beginning in 1931. REF.: *CBA.*

Wilby, Ralph Marshall (AKA: **James W. Ralston, Alexander Douglas Hume**), prom. 1939, U.S., embez.-forg. Ralph Marshall Wilby was one of the more clever embezzlers of the 1930s and 40s, who when convicted was usually deported to his native Canada rather than imprisoned. As a young man, he worked as a Toronto bookkeeper. Using an alias, he paid himself thousands of dollars in dividends by putting himself on the company books as a stockholder. He was arrested, convicted, and spent a short time in a reformatory. Upon his release, he moved to the U.S., married an American woman, and lived happily until he was found Guilty of embezzlement in Norfolk, Va., in 1935. Wilby was deported and the marriage was annulled.

In 1939, Wilby worked under the name of James W. Ralston and was caught diverting thousands of dollars into a personal account while employed as an accountant at a San Francisco auto agency. While awaiting prosecution, it was also found that Wilby had fleeced a San Diego agency of $800 cash while posing as an auditor. The two cases were merged, but Wilby received a suspended sentence and ten years of probation. He was again deported, and his second marriage was annulled.

Three months later, using the alias Alexander Douglas Hume, Wilby, again recently married, was working in New York as an auditor. Within two years, he stole nearly $400,000. In early 1944, he told the company treasurer he was taking a short vacation, but he never returned. A company audit quickly uncovered the breadth of Wilby's crime. A warrant was issued, and Wilby finally was traced to western Canada. While in a hotel lobby in Victoria, B.C., a society reporter ordered a photographer to snap a picture of a beautiful woman staying at the hotel. The picture ran nationwide, and authorities in Toronto recognized her as Wilby's wife. Wilby was arrested in March 1944, but not extradited, as Canadian law required extensive proof of the crime. Finally, after months of preparing the case at a cost of thousands of dollars, Wilby was extradited to New York. On Feb. 1, 1945, he was found Guilty of embezzlement, sentenced to five-to-seven years in Sing Sing, and his third wife filed for divorce.

Embezzler-forger Ralph Wilby.

REF.: *CBA;* McKelway, *True Tales;* Nash, *Hustlers and Con Men.*

Wild, Sir **Ernest Edward,** 1869-1934, Brit., jur. Ernest Edward Wild, born in 1869, was admitted to the bar in 1893 and practiced on the South-Eastern Circuit in England. He became known for his forensic gifts, most notably in his defense of William Gardiner in 1902. Named a judge in 1912, Wild was elected to the House of Commons in 1918. He was knighted the same year. In 1921, he was elected Recorder of the City of London, and retired from his seat in Parliament. As a jurist, Wild was known as a compassionate man, punishing only one type of criminal with severity: blackmailers. He considered the crime to be "murder of the soul." In failing health during his later years, Wild died at age sixty-five on Sept. 13, 1934. REF.: *CBA.*

Wild, Jonathan, 1682-1725, Brit., fenc.-rob.-law enfor. off. Jonathon Wild was the first great criminal mastermind in England, a man who lived an incredible double life. Before a police force was organized in London, Wild was a famous thief-taker who appeared to be the law enforcement champion of the law-abiding. He was also the boss of the criminal underworld in London, where his word was supreme. Wild came to this powerful position late in life.

Born in Wolverhampton, Wild lived a docile life until he went to London in 1707 where he ran up so many debts that he was sent to prison to serve a four-year term. In debtor's prison, Wild met a prostitute, Mary Milliner, and when both were released, she introduced Wild to London's leading thieves. Wild lived with Milliner for some time while she plied her trade in the streets. He, in turn, became a receiver of stolen goods, fencing the items his new friends brought to him. Charles Hitchin, the corrupt city marshal of London approached Wild, and instead of arresting him, made a deal with him.

Jonathan Wild, the thief-taker general of London and the city's criminal mastermind.

Hitchen proposed that Wild share the spoils with him from his fencing operations, explaining that he, Hitchen, combined thief-taking with kickbacks from the same thieves he arrested and then let go on some pretext. Hitchen and Wild entered into a shaky partnership that ended two years later after they argued about spoils. Wild then disassociated himself from Hitchen, publicly announcing to robbery victims that he was in the business of thief-taking, a sort of an early-day private detective. Wild said he would capture thieves who had looted warehouses, shops, and houses, and he would retrieve stolen goods for a handsome price, of course.

Hundreds of London merchants and private citizens enlisted as subscribers to Wild's thief-taking operation, and he began to produce results almost immediately. Unlike Hitchen, who had worked a simple payoff scheme with London's criminals, Wild organized the criminals, planning robberies and burglaries for them. He then received the stolen goods and sold them back to the victims. Within a year, he became the criminal mastermind of the city with the entire underworld at his command. No important theft in London occurred without his sanction. A great organizer, Wild separated the city of London into districts and established gangs for each area, naming gang leaders and lieutenants who carried out his orders. He punished those who invaded territories not assigned to them by arresting them and sending them to prison.

Wild was utterly ruthless in dealing with London's felons. When he desired the woman of one arch thief and was rebuffed, he presented evidence to the court that caused the thief's conviction and execution. Then Wild took the thief's woman. Few thieves dared to challenge Wild's authority. If one did, Wild presented trumped up evidence to bring the thief into court, charged with a felony. The law prohibited a thief charged with a felony from giving evidence against anyone else, so whatever the thief said to damn Wild was dismissed as remarks of vengeance against the man who had brought him to justice.

Thus assured of no retaliation for his actions, Wild exercised his power in the underworld. He assumed grand airs and soon moved his headquarters near the Old Bailey. He advertised himself in the press and in flyers as the "Thief-Taker General of Great Britain and Ireland." Wild assumed the role of the great detective and law enforcement officer by walking about with a large staff that had a gold crown, his symbol of self-styled authority. The public and most government officials believed Wild was acting for the common good, but one government official, Sir William Thompson, recorder of London, saw through Wild's ruses, and after conducting his own private investigation into Wild's fencing operations, took action to confound Wild's schemes. When becoming solicitor general in 1717, Thompson introduced a bill in Parliament that made it a capital offense to receive payment for the return of stolen goods while conspiring with those who committed the theft.

Wild sidestepped this trap by pushing through a bill that allowed him sanctions in thief-taking and ostensibly prevented anyone from challenging his operations. He grew even richer, buying a mansion staffed with servants and warehouses in which to store the stolen goods. He also bought a sloop that he used to convey stolen goods to France and other countries where the goods were sold at handsome profits. He paid his minions well, sharing generously with them all the spoils brought to him. However, those who complained about their cut were convicted of felonies framed by Wild and hanged.

In 1723, Wild petitioned the lord mayor of London to give him the authority to arrest anyone at will, under a Freedom of the City act. Wild pointed out in his petition that he had acted as a public benefactor by sending sixty felons to the gallows. When the act was passed, Wild's power became enormous, but he was almost foiled in 1724 when a thief named Joseph Blake, also called "Blueskin," slit Wild's throat just before the thief-taker was to give evidence against him at the Old Bailey. Blake had been one of Wild's most enterprising thieves and when he realized that Wild was about to sacrifice him, he drew a knife in the courtyard of the Old Bailey and cut Wild's throat almost ear-to-ear. Fortunately for Wild, doctors were present who stopped the flow of blood and saved his life. Blake was hanged on schedule.

Wild shown capturing a thief who had been hiding beneath a barrel.

Sir William Thompson, Wild's avowed enemy, however, won the day against the cunning thief-taker. Wild was caught red-handed by city marshals with a shipment of stolen lace. He had already told the owner of the lace that he had no idea where the stolen goods were, but thought he could track down the criminal and return the goods. He had been paid a handsome sum, but before he returned the lace, he was discovered in possession of it, thus breaking the law Thompson had earlier concocted. Worse, Thompson was the magistrate in his case. When Wild was brought before him, he tried to evade the scaffold by offering Thompson the identities of more than 100 London thieves, promising to deliver the culprits to justice in a short time if charges against him were dropped. Thompson ignored his plea and found Wild guilty. The thief-taker general was placed in an open wooden cart on May 24, 1725, and driven to Tyburn. Thousands lined his death route and both honest citizens and criminals hurled stones and rotten food at him, and showered him with obscenities. The great criminal mastermind was completely humiliated before he was hanged before a cheering throng estimated to be more than 5,000. See: ***Beggar's Opera, The;*** **Blake, Joseph; Burnworth, Edward;** ***Children of Darkness;*** **Doyle**, Sir **Arthur Conan; Holmes, Sherlock**.

REF.: Bleackley, *Hangmen of England; CBA;* Culpin, *The Newgate Noose;* Gollomb, *Master Highwaymen;* Hibbert, *Highwaymen;* ____, *The Roots of Evil;* Howson, *The Thief-Taker General: The Rise and Fall of Jonathan Wild;* Hunt, *A Dictionary of Rogues;* Mitchell, *The Newgate Calendar;* Postgate, *Murder, Piracy and Treason;* Potter, *The Art of Hanging;* Pringle, *Stand and Deliver;* Reppetto, *The Blue Parade;* Scott, *The Concise Encyclopedia of Crime and Criminals;* Thorwald, *The Century of the Detective;* Turner, *The Inhumanists;* (DRAMA), Gay, *The Beggar's Opera;* Mayer, *Children of Darkness.*

Wild, William, b.1821, Brit., mur. A farmhand at Castle Broughton in Derbyshire, England, William Wild had been employed by Joshua Smith to round up cows and perform other small tasks. But the 13-year-old boy did not like farm work. In May 1835, after working about a month on the farm, he ran away to his home, but his mother sent him back to the Smiths. A few days after his return, Ann Smith, the farmer's wife, asked Wild to get her three children, John, seven, Elizabeth, three, and Martha, eighteen months, from a neighbor's house. Wild returned alone and told the mother that the girls would not come with him and that she needed to bring them back herself. She started toward the neighbor's house and passed a deep pit filled with water. Floating on the surface were the bodies of Elizabeth and Martha Smith. Wild was sent for the doctor, but returned to tell the Smiths that the doctor refused to come. Joshua Smith returned with the doctor, who had not seen Wild and pronounced the girls dead from drowning. Wild tried to flee, but the town constable arrested him. On July 30, 1835, Wild was tried for the murder of Martha and Elizabeth Smith. He told several versions of the events of May 22, and eventually confessed to pushing the girls into the pit. When asked why he did it, Wild replied, "You shouldn't have fetched me after I ran away." The jury found the boy Guilty of murder, and the judge sentenced Wild to be hanged. The sentence was later commuted to transportation for life.

REF.: *CBA;* Wilson, *Children Who Kill.*

Wild Animal Hoax, 1874, U.S., hoax. On Nov. 9, 1874, readers of the New York *Herald* awoke to the startling news of a mass escape of animals from the Central Park Zoo. Forty-nine people were said to be dead, while more than 200 were injured, many of them seriously. Twelve animals were still at large, and prominent New Yorkers were taking part in an animal hunt. It was only in the last paragraph that the story was revealed to be a hoax. It had been written to draw attention to the zoo's problems, but many people never reached the final paragraph. One staff member appeared in the office with two revolvers, ready to join the search, while the editor of the rival New York *Times* berated officials at police headquarters for giving the *Herald* an exclusive story.

REF.: *CBA;* MacDougall, *Hoaxes.*

Wild Bill Hickok, See: **Hickok, James Butler.**

Wild Bunch, prom. 1880s-90s, U.S., west. outl. In the late 1880s and through the 1890s, when the West was being tamed in dozens of frontier towns, the last bastion of the outlaw was Hole-in-the-Wall, a seemingly impenetrable fortress of towering cliffs, deep gorges and mountainous retreats. This was the hideout of the last of the great outlaw bands, The Wild Bunch. The shelter was located where the state lines of Utah, Colorado, and Wyoming now meet and only those who belonged to the infamous band knew the treacherous path to the high mountain hideout. Another less celebrated hideout for Wild Bunch members was Robber's Roost in Southeastern Utah.

The hundreds of members of the Wild Bunch were part of a loose federation of mostly cowboys who had turned outlaw following the disastrous blizzards of 1888. After the blizzards drastically reduced the great herds of cattle in the West and caused the collapse of thousands of small ranches, many owners and their hands turned to other means to survive. Many turned to crime, rustling cattle, robbing banks and trains, drifting to Hole-in-the-Wall when the great posses led by Joe LeFors, William Breakenridge, and others hunted them across the plains.

Living in huts and small cabins built on a small plateau, Wild Bunch members worked together or continued their lone banditry, occasionally joining larger bands of outlaws from the Wild Bunch community. The most notorious Wild Bunch members were the McCarty Brothers, George "Flat Nose" Curry, Butch Cassidy, the Sundance Kid, Ben "The Tall" Texan Kilpatrick, Harvey Logan, William Carver, Ellsworth Lay, O.C. Hanks, and Harry Tracy, but scores more, who occasionally rode with the infamous members, continued to inhabit Hole-in-the-Wall in the early 1900s. Beyond the super star bandits, the most notable of the many outlaws who rode in and out of Hole-in-the-Wall for twenty years and were classified as members of the Wild Bunch were:

Dave Atkins, a ranch hand who turned to train robbery and murder while in his mid-twenties. He was fast on the draw, but backed down twice from pulling his gun on Harry Longbaugh (or Longabaugh), who was called The Sundance Kid. On one occasion Atkins made fun of the Kid because of his preference for Ralston's cereal food. Sundance finished his bowl of cereal, stood up, and gave a speech about its "healthy properties." He

The famous Wild Bunch photo of Butch Cassidy and friends.

William Cruzan, robber.

O.C. Hanks, robber.

Elza Lay, robber.

Ben Kilpatrick, robber.

Above, Dave Land, outlaw.
Right, Tom O'Day, thief.

James Lowe, thief.

Bob Lee, train robber.

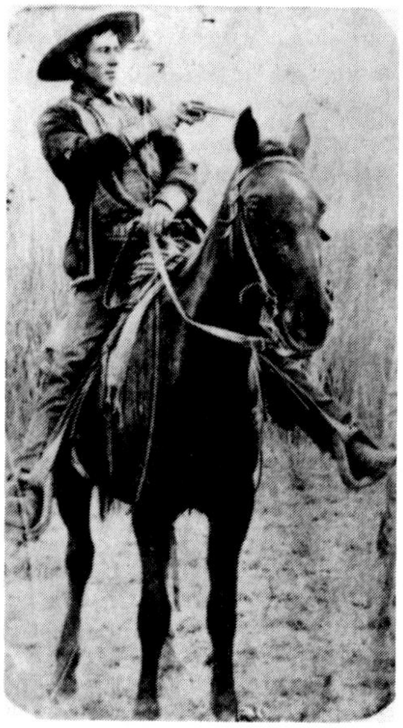

Will Roberts, rustler.

Jesse Linsley, horse thief.

Dave Atkins, train robber.

Frank Elliott, robber.

then invited Atkins, while resting his hands on his two holstered six-guns, to have a bowl. Atkins reluctantly sat down, ate some of the cereal, and then quickly agreed with the Kid that it was the best tasting food he had ever eaten.

Jack Bennett, a freightman who brought the Wild Bunch supplies to Hole-in-the-Wall and occasionally rode with some of its members in various holdups. In March 1898, a posse caught Bennett and lynched him from the crossbars of a Wyoming ranch.

Sam "Laughing Sam" Carey, who received his ironic name because he never smiled and displayed a mean streak that was often lethal. Carey, one of the first to use Hole-in-the-Wall as a hideout, began robbing trains and banks in the late 1880s with the Taylor Brothers, Bud Denslow, and H. Wilcox. Carey operated throughout Wyoming, Montana, and South Dakota. Carey's gang was shot to pieces by citizens in Spearfish, S.D., and he alone survived, riding back to Hole-in-the-Wall where another Wild Bunch member pried three bullets from his body. Carey rested for a week, then rode out to rob another bank.

Joseph Chancellor, born in Texas, made his reputation as a gunfighter in Oklahoma. He was caught rustling cattle and was sent to the penitentiary in Santa Fe. He was released on Jan. 28, 1897. The 37-year-old Chancellor drifted into Hole-in-the-Wall as late as 1904. He was so addicted to cigarettes that his fingers were completely stained yellow and he got up several times each night to smoke a dozen or so cigarettes before going back to sleep.

William Cruzan, who was thirty-three in 1901 when he arrived at Hole-in-the-Wall after serving several years in prison for rustling and robbery. He preferred to commit robberies alone, but he occasionally and was shot to death in 1905 while trying to rob a train single-handedly.

Frank "Peg-Leg" Elliot was twenty-one when he reached Hole-in-the-Wall, where he met Robert Eldredge, another cowboy turned horse and cattle thief. These two rode out to rob a train in October 1891, and were trapped by a posse and shot to death.

Swede Johnson, a pathological murderer, rode into Hole-in-the-Wall in 1898 and befriended Harry Tracy and Dave Lant where were as trigger-happy as Johnson. Willie Strang, a witless 17-year-old, dumped a pitcher of water on Johnson and Johnson went crazy, emptying his six-gun into Strang. For this murder Johnson was tracked down and sent to the Wyoming State Prison for life.

Bob Lee, cousin of Harvey and Lonnie Logan, was one of the first outlaws to ride into Hole-in-the-Wall. He later brought the Logans, and Harvey Logan became one of the most feared members of the Wild Bunch and its worst six-gun killer. Lee participated in several robberies and was later sent to prison.

Jesse Linsley, horse thief, ex-convict, rode into Hole-in-the-Wall about 1899. He committed some minor robberies, but he did not have the stomach for the kind of train robberies committed by Butch Cassidy and others, especially since they used dynamite to blow open locked express cars. Linsley vanished in 1901.

James Lowe, a 32-year-old train robber when he arrived in Hole-in-the-Wall in 1903, led many raids against trains and banks and was killed by lawmen in 1910.

Tom O'Day, a hardcase cowboy from Wyoming, joined the Wild Bunch in 1899 and participated in several bank robberies. Occasionally he rode with Butch Cassidy, but usually he operated as a lone bandit, which pleased other Wild Bunch members since O'Day seldom bathed and reportedly "smelled like a skunk" most of the time. O'Day attempted to rob the bank in Casper, Wyo., was arrested, and sent to prison to serve a long term.

Will Roberts, cowboy turned gunman and outlaw, used the alias "Dixon." He robbed many banks and trains before he was captured and sent to prison. He was one of the last important members of the Wild Bunch, which ceased to exist after 1910.

Matt Warner, one of the original inhabitants of Hole-in-the-Wall, participated in several holdups but retired early from outlawry. However, he maintained a sort of general store and hotel in Hole-in-the-Wall, selling supplies to the outlaws and offering them necessities. He later wrote a fine account of the Wild Bunch that stands as a classic in the western field.

Little remains of the old Hole-in-the-Wall hideout used by the Wild Bunch except the skeletal remains of a few shacks. Little is left to prove that the worst criminals in the U.S. ever inhabited this barren mountainous area. When they were present, however, no lawman or posse dared to enter Hole-in-the-Wall. Peace officers of the day estimated that as many as 100 to 200 outlaws were hidden in its rocky recesses at one time, an army of ruthless killers no sheriff thought to capture at one time. See: **Bullion, Laura; Briant, Elijah S.; Carver, William; Cassidy, Butch; Christianson, William Erastus; Curry, George; Hanks, Orlando Camillo; Ketchum, Thomas E.; Kilpatrick, Benjamin; Lay, William Ellsworth; Logan, Harvey; McCarty Brothers; Sundance Kid, The; Tracy, Harry.**

REF.: *CBA;* Coblentz, *Villains and Vigilantes;* Coburn, *Stirrup High;* Coolidge, *Fighting Men of the West;* Crawford, *The West of the Texas Kid;* Cunningham, *Triggernometry;* Dunham, *Our Strip of Land;* French, *Some Recollections of a Western Ranchman;* Horan, *Desperate Man;* ____, and Sann, *Pictorial History of the Wild West;* Johnson, *Famous Lawmen of the Old West;* Lavigne, *Crimes, Criminals and Detectives;* Mazzulla, *Outlaw Album;* Morgan, *The Humboldt Highroad of the West;* Pence and Homsher, *The Ghost Towns of Wyoming;* Rosa, *The Gunfighter;* Sims, *Gun-toters I Have Known;* Smith, *You Can Escape;* Stanley, *The Alma (New Mexico) Story;* Swallow, *The Wild Bunch;* Warner, *The Last of the Bandit Riders;* Wolle, *Montana Pay Dirt.*

Wilde, Lady **Jane (Jane Francesca Elgee, AKA: Speranza)**, Brit., libel. In Ireland in 1845, Jane Francesca Elgee began publishing poems in *The Nation,* using the pen name Speranza. Her verses, which passionately urged the young men of Ireland to take up arms, were printed for the next three years, until the editor of *The Nation* was arrested for sedition. He was acquitted after she shouted, "I alone am the culprit. I wrote the offending articles."

Shortly after the trial, Elgee met Sir William Wilde, a Dublin ophthalmologist and surgeon. The two married in 1851 and had two sons, one of whom was Oscar Wilde. William Wilde was known as a philanderer, and when he met Elgee, he jilted a previous consort named Moll Travers. One day when Wilde was lecturing, small boys distributed a pamphlet entitled "Florence Boyle Price," which told a tale of a "Dr. Quilp," who had taken the virginity of an unconscious young woman. The pamphlet was written by "Speranza" but of course the actual author was Moll Travers.

The Wilde's ignored the document as it became the talk of Dublin. However, when Lady Wilde found the book for sale in her own hallway, she snatched the offending copies. Moll Travers immediately sued the couple for nonpayment. Jane Wilde then wrote an angry letter to the girl's father about the conduct of his daughter, for which Moll Travers added a writ of libel to the earlier suit, claiming damages of £200. While the letter was not libelous, William Wilde refused to appear as a witness to rebut charges. The jury awarded Travers a farthing in damages and determined that Lady Wilde should pay several thousand pounds in court costs. As for the initial suit, Sir William Wilde slapped a penny in front of Moll Travers and said, "There's the price of your virtue. Now give me my change." REF.: *CBA.*

Wilde, Leonard, prom. 1975, Brit., rob. In what is thought to be the largest bank robbery in British history, an unlikely group of robbers broke into the Mayfair branch of the Bank of America in West London on Apr. 24, 1975. The gang, who wore hoods, held bank employees at gunpoint and tied them up. They then drilled into a safe where they collected all the available cash before breaking into a number of private safety deposit boxes. Initial estimates of the losses were placed at £300,000 but soon rose to £8 million, and then £10 million.

In all, eleven men and one woman were arrested and charged in the robbery. They included two greengrocers, a carpenter, two electricians, a former bookmaker, a launderette operator, a car dealer, and a company director. After a three-month trial, three of the defendants were found Not Guilty. Convicted on charges ranging from conspiracy and robbery to handling stolen money and jewels were Leonard Wilde, fifty-three, Peter Colson, thirty-two, Michael Anthony Gervaise, forty-four, Henry Taylor, thirty-seven, William Gear, forty-four, James O'Loughlin, thirty-eight, Henry Jeffrey, fifty, Edward Gerty, thirty-five, and John O'Connell, forty-two.

At the time of sentencing in November 1976, only about £500,000 of the stolen money and jewels had been recovered, roughly the cost of the robbers' trial. The judge in the case assigned sentences with the idea of preventing the convicted robbers from ever benefitting from the spoils of their crime. Judge King-Hamilton was quoted as saying to the convicted men at the time of sentencing, "It would be a sad day for this country if robberies of this magnitude came to be regarded as normal. It is the duty of the court to try to ensure that the defendants will not be allowed to enjoy any part of this vast sum for a great many years." The judge then assigned the following sentences: Leonard Wilde, twelve years for an abortive plot to rob the same bank in 1974 to run concurrently with a twenty-three year sentence for the successful 1975 robbery; Peter Colson, twenty-one years; William Gear, eighteen years; James O'Loughlin, seventeen years; Henry Jeffery, twelve years; Henry Taylor, three years; Edward Gerty, two years; Michael Gervaise, eighteen months. John O'Connell, the last defendant in the case was shot on his way to court. An unknown assailant shot O'Connell in the back of the legs with a sawed-off shotgun in June 1976. O'Connell lost his left leg due to the shooting. When he returned to court for sentencing in December 1977, the judge gave him a suspended sentence. In March 1978, the Court of Appeal reduced the convicted robbers' sentences as follows: Wilde, Colson, Gear, and O'Loughlin, by three years each. Henry Jeffery's sentence was reduced by four years, Harry Taylor's by one year. Michael Gervaise, who had already served his eighteen month sentence was refused leave to challenge his conviction. REF.: *CBA.*

Wilde, Mark, See: **Howard, Cornelius.**

Wilde, Oscar (Fingal O'Flahertie Wills), 1854-1900, Brit., morals. Poet, playwright, lecturer, and celebrated "bon vivant," Oscar Wilde encountered more than his share of misfortune at the hands of the British judicial system. In an age defined by its rigid social mores and an unbending adherence to the tenets of conservative Christian theology, Oscar Wilde was an anomaly. He was the son of Sir William Wilde, a distinguished surgeon, and Jane Francesca Elgee, an essayist who advanced the cause of Irish nationalism. After leaving Trinity College in Dublin, Wilde quickly established himself as one of Ireland's leading men of letters, whose sharp wit and caustic flamboyance placed him at the forefront of the Aesthetic movement, which was then sweeping England. Wilde achieved critical success as a dramatist in 1892 with *Lady Windermere's Fan,* which he followed up with *A Woman of No importance* (1893); *The Importance of Being Earnest,* (1895); and *An Ideal Husband,* (1895).

Wilde's private affairs left him open for public ridicule and censure by the British establishment which disdained his foppish behavior and effete mannerisms. Though he was joined in marriage to Constance Lloyd of Dublin in 1884, there was little doubt of his homosexuality, which he often flaunted. While vacationing in Chelsea during Summer 1892, Wilde was introduced to Lord Alfred Douglas, the 22-year-old son of the eighth Marquis of Queensbury. The marquis was an eccentric in his own right, though he stood at the opposite end of the spectrum from Wilde. Lord Alfred's father was not one to write sonnet verse in his spare time. Here was a man of noble birth whose boorish manner and raging temper had scandalized his entire family. On one occasion he attacked the British prime minister with a horse whip. The idea of his own son engaged in a homosexual dalliance with Oscar Wilde was loathsome. He vowed to take whatever steps possible to end the disgrace—short of murder.

On the night of Feb. 14, 1895, *The Importance of Being Earnest* debuted in London. The marquis contrived to disrupt the play by making a public announcement about Wilde to members of the audience, but was prevented from doing so by the police who had learned of the scheme before hand. Four days later, the marquis left a calling card for Wilde at the Albemarle Club in London bearing the inscription: "To Oscar Wilde posing as a somdomite." The marquis had unintentionally misspelled the word sodomite, but there was little doubt about the content. Wilde was forced into a position where he had to file a libel suit to protect his good name. The marquis had counted on it from the very beginning. He hoped to expose the playwright once and for all as a debauched roué. Hearing of his father's actions, Lord Alfred sent a telegram to him. "What a funny little man you are," he tittered.

The marquis was arrested on Mar. 2, 1895, and was charged with criminal libel. The trial began amidst great fanfare on Apr. 3 at the Old Bailey. During the month leading up to the opening session, the marquis had employed a battery of detectives to hunt down Wilde's homosexual companions in London. Unaware that this was happening, the playwright relaxed in the resort towns in the south of France with his constant companion—"Bosie" Douglas. When he returned, Wilde was apprised of the seriousness of the situation. If he were to lose the libel case, it was likely that the authorities would arrest him for public indecency. His friends in the literary community, notably George Bernard Shaw and Frank Harris, urged him to leave the country at once and drop the prosecution.

Poet Oscar Wilde at the time of his conviction for indecency.

Wilde did not flinch. He chose to remain in London to appear as a witness in the libel trial. His courtroom repartee with the prosecutor Edward Carson was both brilliant and amusing; a true reflection of the spirit of the artist. When Carson suggested that Wilde's only published novel, *The Picture of Dorian Gray* was a "hymn to homosexuality," the author replied: "that could only be to brutes and illiterates. The views of Philistines on art are incalculably stupid." Carson moved on to another line of questioning. He produced a sonnet that Wilde had written to Lord Alfred some months earlier. The letter was addressed to "My own boy." "Suppose a man who was not an artist had written that letter, would you say it was a proper letter?" Carson demanded. "A man who was not an artist could not have written it," Wilde replied. "He certainly could not write the language unless he were a man of letters."

Carson saved his trump card for the last. At the opportune moment, he ticked off the names of the men that Oscar Wilde had been intimately acquainted with in London. All had been introduced to Wilde through a homosexual ponce who went by the name Alfred Taylor. The details of these encounters—some of them involving boys as young as sixteen—increasingly put Wilde on the defensive. On the third day of the trial, Sir Edward Clarke, who was representing Wilde, advised his client to withdraw the prosecution. By doing so, he would be admitting that the libel was in effect true, but to continue the trial at this point could result in Wilde's imprisonment.

The day after the Not Guilty verdict was entered into the record, Lord Queensbury filed a warrant against Wilde and Alfred Taylor, charging them with twenty-five counts of indecency. On Apr. 26, the two of them appeared before Justice Charles at the Old Bailey. One by one, the prosecution called its witnesses who related their experiences with the decadent Wilde. To the charges of impropriety brought against him, he replied: "The love that dare not speak its name in this century is such a great affection of an elder for a younger man as there was between David and Jonathan, such as Plato made the very basis of his philosophy and such as you find in the sonnets of Michelangelo and Shakespeare." The jury was unable to agree on a verdict on seventeen of the original twenty-five counts, so Wilde was ordered released on a £5,000 bail pending a new trial, which began on May 22.

The defendants were tried separately the second time around. Weary from his long ordeal, Wilde appeared haggard on the stand, and was seemed unable to respond with clear, crisp replies to the questions put forth by the prosecution. The trial lasted five days, after which the jury retired to consider its verdict. This time the defendants were found Guilty and were sentenced to two years in prison at hard labor. Wilde was ordered to serve his time at the Wandsworth Prison, but after six months he was transferred to Reading. While in jail Wilde was still haunted by his relentless adversary. The vengeful and unforgiving marquis sued the estate for the costs of the libel trial. Before it ended, Wilde's creditors had seized his home, and all his assets. On May 19, 1897, the playwright emerged from prison a free, but broken man. He went into permanent exile in France using the alias of Sebastien Melmoth. In 1898 he published *The Ballad of Reading Jail,* which dealt with inhumane conditions at the British penal institutions. It was his last creative effort. Wilde died in Paris on Nov. 30, 1900, from cerebral meningitis.

REF.: Asbury, *Gem of the Prairie;* ____, *The Gangs of New York;* Beer, *The Mauve Decade;* Bendz, *Oscar Wilde;* Benson, *As We Were: A Victorian Peep Show;* Birnbaum, *Oscar Wilde:* Fragments and Memories; Brasol, *Oscar Wilde: The Man, The Artist, The Martyr;* Braybrooke, *Oscar Wilde, A Study;* Brémont, *Oscar Wilde and His Mother; CBA;* Crew, *The Old Bailey;* Davray, *Oscar Wilde: La Tragédie Finale;* Douglas, *City of the Soul;* ____, *My Friendship with Oscar Wilde, Being the Autobiography of Lord Alfred Douglas;* ____, *Without Apology;* Douglas, *Oscar Wilde and the Black Douglas;* Gide, *Oscar Wilde: A Study;* Harris, *Oscar Wilde: His Life and Confessions;* Hopkins, *Oscar Wilde: A Study of the Man and His Work;* Humphreys, *A Book of Trials;* Hyde, *The Trials of Oscar Wilde;* Ingleby, *Oscar Wilde: Some Reminiscences;* Jullian, *Oscar Wilde;* Kenilworth, *A Study of Oscar Wilde;* Lewis and Smith, *Oscar Wilde Discovers America;* Nash, *Hustlers and Con Men;* ____, *People to See;* O'Sullivan, *Aspects of Wilde;* Pacq, *Procès d'Oscar Wilde;* Pearson, *The Life of Oscar Wilde;* Ransome, *Oscar Wilde: A Critical Study;* Raymond, *Portraits of the Nineties;* Renier, *Oscar Wilde;* Scott, *The Concise Encyclopedia of Crime and Criminals;* Sherard, *Life of Oscar Wilde;* ____, *Oscar Wilde: The Story of an Unhappy Friendship;* ____, *The Real Oscar Wilde;* Symons, *A Study of Oscar Wilde;* Tobin and Gertz, *Frank Harris: A Study in Black and White;* Winterich, *Twenty-Three Books and the Stories Behind Them;* Winwar, *Oscar Wilde and the Yellow Nineties;* Zanco, *Oscar Wilde;* (DRAMA) Stokes, *Oscar Wilde;* (FILM), *The Man With the Green Carnation,* 1960; *Oscar Wilde,* 1960.

Wilde, Thomas (Baron Truro), 1782-1855, Brit., jur. Held positions as solicitor general in 1839, as attorney general in 1841 and 1846, and as chief justice of common pleas from 1846-50. REF.: *CBA.*

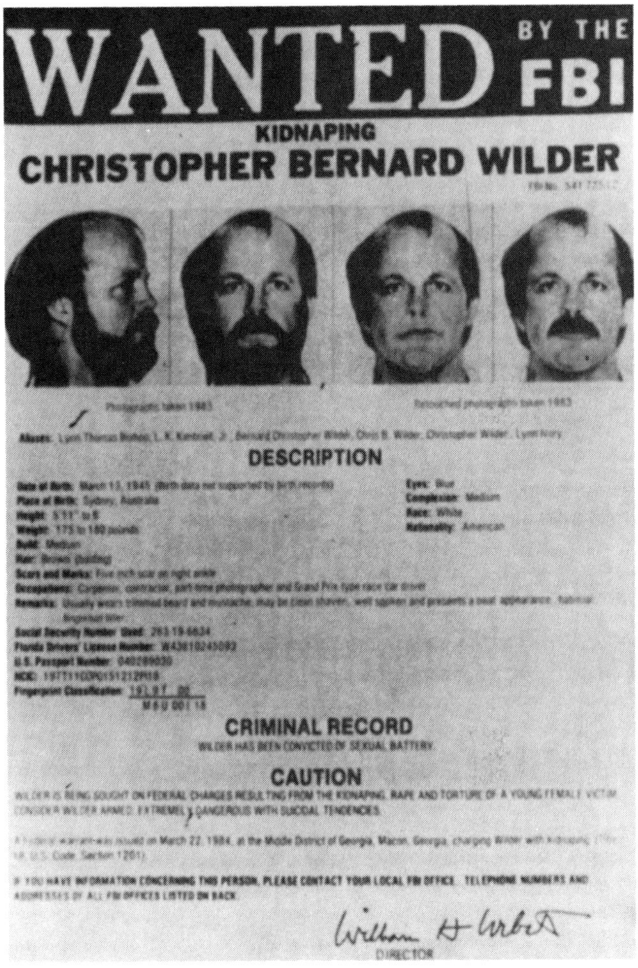

FBI poster on rapist-murderer Christopher Wilder.

Wilder, Christopher Bernard, 1946-84, U.S., kid.-rape-mur. Five hundred FBI agents trailed an elusive killer believed responsible for the murders of at least nine young women between Feb. 26 and Apr. 12, 1984. Christopher Wilder was a wealthy playboy whose lifestyle and easy manner women found attractive. His technique was not unlike that of Ted Bundy, who raped and killed thirty-six women in the 1970s before being captured. Unlike Bundy, however, Wilder's trail of death ended abruptly in Colebrook, N.H., on Apr. 13, 1984. The state trooper who bagged the killer was not sure at the time who he was dealing with. "Hold on, we want to talk to you," ordered Detective Leo C. Jellison, who had received reports of the fugitive murderer driving a blue 1982 Firebird. Wilder reached for a .357 Magnum in the glove compartment and pointed it at Johnson. The 250-pound state trooper grabbed the serial killer in a bear hug. The gun discharged and a bullet passed through Wilder's heart. Two days later Trooper Jellison was proclaimed a hero when the FBI established that he had brought down the most dangerous man in the U.S.

Christopher Bernard Wilder was the son of a U.S. serviceman

who had emigrated to Australia to begin a construction business. In 1970, at the age of twenty-four, Wilder returned to the U.S. to make his fortune. With his partner, L.K. Kimbrell, he started Sawtel Electric and Sawtel Construction, but he paid little attention to the business, preferring to invest in Florida's booming real estate market. Using balloon notes and quit-claim deeds to buy and sell property, he made himself a small fortune by the end of the decade. Articulate and well-mannered, Chris Wilder bought up six parcels of prime Palm Beach County real estate worth an estimated $400,000. Much of his money was used to finance an ostentatious lifestyle. He spent many happy weekends skiing in trendy Vail, Colo., tinkering with his speedboat moored to a private dock in Boynton Beach, Fla., or participating in the amateur race-car circuit. In 1984 he raced his white Porsche 911 in the Miami Grand Prix, finishing seventeenth in the field. It was an impressive showing for a novice. When it came to attracting glamorous women, however, Wilder was in the big leagues. "I want to date and enjoy the company of women. Women with depth. I'm looking for a long-term relationship but not marriage," he said in a 1981 interview with a Florida matchmaking service.

His first known assault was committed in 1976 against the 16-year-old daughter of a Boca Raton family who had hired him to work on their home. Using a tactic that proved successful for him in later years, Wilder lured the girl into his truck, promising to take her to someone who might offer a job. The girl fended him off by saying she was afflicted by venereal disease. Lucky to escape with her life, she related to story to her parents who pressed charges. Court-appointed doctors examined Wilder and concluded that he was psychotic. "Wilder is not safe except in a structured environment and should be in a resident program geared to his needs," said Dr. D.G. Boozer. Despite the warning, Wilder was acquitted on assault charges and never received the treatment he so desperately needed.

Three years later, in 1979, he was arrested and charged with assaulting a 17-year-old Tennessee girl vacationing in Florida. He told her he was a representative of the Barbizon modeling school, and was interested in giving her a tryout. During the "session" Wilder ordered her to pose for cheesecake photos holding a slice of pizza that had been laced with drugs. "He told her to chew it real slowly so that he could see what it would be like," explained Palm Beach detective Arthur Newcombe. Afterward he forced the girl to engage in sex with him in a pickup truck. Wilder was eventually sentenced to five years' probation and was ordered to see a sex therapist twice a month.

Wilder's second encounter with the police and the courts did not deter him from chasing after women. He neglected the construction business to cruise the pickup bars looking for attractive "street type" girls, who were inveigled to return with him to his photography "studio" for fashion-modeling assignments. Many were given hypnotic drugs and then forced to pose for pornographic pictures. In December 1982, Wilder violated the terms of his parole and flew to Sidney, Aus., where he was arrested for abducting and sexually assaulting two 15-year-old girls. Released on $376,000 bail, Wilder negotiated for a postponement of the trial and returned to the U.S. "I didn't really know the man," explained his business partner Kimbrell, "but we did talk about the rape charges. He told me he didn't know the girls were only fifteen, he thought they were twenty. I told him to throw the camera away and be more careful. I could relate to his wanting sex—after all, he was single."

While in Miami for the Grand Prix, Wilder ran into 20-year-old Rosario Gonzalez, an aspiring fashion model who was handing out free samples of aspirin. She had met Wilder two years earlier in 1982, and had posed for the cover of a romance book according to her fiancé. Rosario was never seen after Feb. 26, 1984. She was the first murder victim. A week later, 23-year-old Elizabeth Kenyon vanished from a Coral Gables shopping center. The former Orange Bowl queen was a finalist in the 1982 Miss Florida contest and had been dating Wilder off and on. During the Grand Prix Kenyon spurned his offer of marriage out of respect to the wishes of her parents who objected to the sixteen-year age difference between the two. A gas station attendant told the woman's parents that he had seen Wilder in Elizabeth's company shortly before her disappearance. The distraught father pleaded with the FBI to place Wilder under surveillance, but the agents refused on the grounds of insufficient evidence and hearsay. "We couldn't understand why a man who broke probation four times couldn't be tailed," Dolores Kenyon wondered. "In our justice system the criminal has all the rights and that is why my daughter isn't here tonight."

Teresa Ferguson of Indian Harboor Beach, Fla., left her home on Mar. 18, 1984, to shop at a nearby mall. The body of the dark-haired 21-year-old woman was found three days later in a Florida swamp. The day after the police fished the remains of Ferguson out of the swamp, Wilder claimed his next victim, 24-year-old Terry Diane Walden of Beaumont, Texas. When she failed to pick up her daughter at the local day-care center, school officials phoned her husband, John David, a machine operator at the Goodyear Chemical plant. Her body was found floating face down in the canal. She had been bound, gagged, and knifed to death.

By this time federal authorities were piecing together fragmented information about a dozen rapes, sexual tortures, and murders of young women committed in Florida, Texas, Nevada, and Colorado. A clear pattern had emerged, suggesting that a serial killer similar to Bundy and Seattle's Green River murderer was loose on the land. Several more weeks passed before the FBI assembled enough evidence to finger Wilder as the suspect. Meanwhile, the killer proceeded in a northerly direction. On Mar. 26, a fisherman in Milford Lake, Kan., found the body of Suzanne Logan, a 20-year-old woman Wilder had abducted from an Oklahoma City shopping mall. Logan was another one of Wilder's modeling hopefuls. Three years earlier she had assembled her first portfolio.

Sheryl Bonaventura of Grand Junction, Colo., became Wilder's sixth victim on Mar. 29. Shortly before leaving for Aspen on a pleasure trip, the 18-year-old woman chided her mother for her undue concerns. "Mom, you worry too much," she said. Before meeting with a girlfriend, Sheryl stopped at a local mall where she met Wilder who was looking for a model. "We were always dreaming of someone coming up and saying 'You're found. You're *Vogue* material' I would have done it," said Kristal Cesario, Sheryl's best friend. Two days later Wilder turned up at the Meadows Mall in Las Vegas, Nev., where *Seventeen* magazine was sponsoring a beauty contest. An amateur photographer took a candid shot of Wilder as he was leaving the mall with Michelle Korfman, the 17-year-old daughter of a casino executive. She became the eighth victim.

Wilder continued to California. On Apr. 4 he picked up Tina Marie Riscio, a 16-year-old Torrance girl, at a dress shop. For the next three days he held her hostage, torturing her with a 110-volt prod. Under the penalty of death Wilder made the girl his unwitting accomplice. Together they drove eastward just as the FBI added Wilder's name to its Ten Most Wanted list. "We consider this to be the top fugitive investigation at this time," explained Chris Mazzella, FBI spokesman. "Unlimited resources are being poured into it. This is a truly massive manhunt, stretching from coast to coast." Wilder and Riscio arrived in Merrillville, Ind., a few days later. At an area shopping mall Tina approached 16-year-old Dawnette Sue Wilt and asked if she would like to become a fashion model. The girl followed Riscio back to Wilder's car to sign a consent form. The killer then pulled a gun and ordered her into the car.

Wilder proceeded to Barrington, N.Y., where he repeatedly stabbed Dawnette and left her for dead in a patch of woods on Apr. 12. She broke free of her bonds and flagged down a passing truck. In the hospital the severely wounded girl provided police with enough detail for them to get a fix on Wilder. In Victor, N.Y., he used Riscio to lure 33-year-old Beth Dodge to his car. "He had told Tina he would kill her if she did anything unusual," explained an investigator. "He drove the hostage car with the hostage, and Tina followed in her car. For her to try to escape then would have been foolish. He had told her he was a race-car driver and could easily catch her." Beth Dodge was shot to death near the mall and dumped in a road side gravel pit. Wilder just wanted her car.

In Boston, Wilder bought Tina Riscio an airplane ticket for her return trip to Los Angeles. He handed her some "going-away money" which was later used to purchase lingerie in a tourist shop on Hermosa Beach. After her shopping spree was complete, Tina Riscio notified police about her cross-country trek with the serial killer. During the entire time the girl was away, Tina's mother believed her 16-year-old daughter was out "partying."

Wilder drove Beth Dodge's Firebird north toward the Canadian border. On Friday the thirteenth he made his ill-fated stop at Vic Stanton's Getty Station in Colebrook, N.H., eight miles from the Canadian border. There he was finally apprehended and shot to death by the police.

REF.: *CBA;* Holmes, *Serial Murder.*

Wilford, Thomas, c.1735-52, Brit., mur. Thomas Wilford, born with one arm, served as an errand boy for his parents and the village during his youth. At the age of seventeen, he married Sarah Williams, and the couple moved to St. Giles. On the Sunday following their wedding, Sarah returned home at midnight after being out with an old acquaintance. When asked what she had been doing all evening, she said she went to the park. Wilford, believing that his bride was lying to him, exploded in a jealous rage. He knocked Sarah to the floor, grabbed a knife, and sliced her throat, killing her instantly.

Wilford immediately confessed the murder to a neighbor. He was taken into custody and confined at Newgate. A jury convicted Wilford of the murder and sentenced him to death. He was hanged at Tyburn gallows on June 22, 1752.

REF.: *CBA;* Turner, *The Inhumanists.*

Wilhelm I (Wilhelm Friedrich Ludwig), 1797-1888, Ger., attempt. assass. Wilhelm I acceded to the throne with the support of Chancellor Otto von Bismarck in 1871. In many ways the first Kaiser was a rubber-stamp of the "Iron Chancellor." He brutally suppressed liberal opinion and open dissent within the Reich, while leading the German armies into combat at Gravelotte and Sedan during the Franco-Prussian War of 1871. Within Germany, though, a strong socialist-anarchist movement had already taken shape. Within the ranks of the politically disenfranchised were two socialist agitators who plotted the death of the emperor.

On May 11, 1878, a down-and-out plumber, Max Hödel, fired several errant shots at the Kaiser in Berlin. Then on June 2 anarchist Karl Nobling took aim on Wilhelm I in nearly the exact same spot on the Unter den Linden. His bullets struck the Kaiser in the head and arms, but the ruler miraculously survived. These ill-fated assassination attempts precipitated a wave of similar attacks against the crowned heads of Europe. The anarchist paranoia quickly spread across the continent and into the U.S.

REF.: *CBA;* Thorwald, *The Century of the Detective.*

Wilkerson, James Herbert, 1869-1948, U.S., jur. Served as Illinois state's attorney from 1903-06, and as U.S. Attorney for the northern district court of Illinois from 1911-14. He was nominated judge of the same court by President Warren G. Harding in 1922. REF.: *CBA.*

Wilkes, John, 1725-97, Brit., libel. John Wilkes was a dissident member of the House of Commons, representing the Aylesbury district of England. The outspoken journalist and Parliamentarian who espoused many radical causes, published a paper, *The North Briton,* which stood in opposition to established government policies. His editorial attacks against Lord Bute so offended Lord Earl Talbot, the steward of the household, that the two men exchanged pistol shots in a duel of honor fought at Bagshot Heath on Oct. 5, 1762. The bullets were off the mark, and neither duelist was hurt. Afterward, Wilkes and Talbot repaired to a nearby inn where they resolved their difficulties amicably. In other matters, it was not nearly so easy. In 1763, Wilkes was found to have libeled the king, and all outstanding copies of the paper were ordered burned.

Wilkes was expelled from Parliament on Jan. 20, 1764. A month later he was tried in absentia for publishing an obscene and scurrilous document—the parody of Alexander Pope's *Essay On Man,* which Wilkes called his *Essay On Woman.* The sentence was deferred until he decided which time he decided to return from Paris. He stayed away for the next for years, living a riotous, debauched existence on the continent until finally, his funds were depleted. He returned to London in 1768 hoping to reclaim his seat in Parliament. He failed in his first bid, but was reelected from neighboring Middlesex. The burning of the newspaper had galvanized public support behind Wilkes, and resulted to public disturbances by unruly mobs using the battle cry, "Wilkes and Liberty".

In 1768, copies of the banned publication appeared in public places as a vehicle of dissent. On Apr. 20, Wilkes was ordered tried for this contempt. A week later, after alluding a sheriff with the writ of arrest, Wilkes appeared at King's Bench prison and demanded admittance. Crowds gathered daily outside the prison walls, culminating on May 10, when a riot broke out, resulting in six deaths and multiple injured. This was to be the last instance that Wilkes was seen as the cause for public dissent. After 1779 Wilkes popularity in radical circles began to wane. His support of the government against Catholic insurgents during the 1780 Gordon riots alienated many of his most ardent supporters. By 1790 he realized that the voters from the Middlesex district had turned against him, and therefore announced his intention to withdraw from politics. See: **Gordon Riots.**

REF.: Browne, *The Rise of Scotland Yard; CBA;* Rude, *The Crowd In History: A Study of Popular Disturbances in France and England 1730-1848.*

Wilkey, Malcolm Richard, 1918- , U.S., jur. Served as U.S. Attorney to southern district court of Texas from 1954-58 and as assistant Texas attorney general from 1958-61. He was nominated to the circuit court of Washington, D.C., by President Richard Nixon in 1970. REF.: *CBA.*

Wilkins, Irene, See: **Allaway, Thomas Henry.**

Wilkins, Ross, 1799-1872, U.S., jur. Received three court nominations from President Andrew Jackson. He was appointed to the Michigan Territorial Court in 1832 and 1836, and to the district court of the new state of Michigan in 1836. In 1863 he was nominated to the eastern district court of Michigan by President Abraham Lincoln. REF.: *CBA.*

Wilkins, Walter Keene, 1852-1919, Case of, U.S., suic.-mur. On Feb. 27, 1919, in Long Beach, on New York's Long Island, police found 67-year-old Dr. Walter Keene Wilkins in his driveway, tending to his badly beaten wife. Wilkins said that he and his wife had been attacked by a gang of youths as they returned home and that Mrs. Wilkins had been hit repeatedly on the head. She died the following day. Mrs. Wilkins' initial will left nothing to her husband, but on Mar. 16, 1919, his attorney produced a second will that left the doctor a considerable amount of property. However, the second document was unsigned, and therefore judged invalid. The police became suspicious, and while searching the Wilkin's home, found blood-stained clothing belonging to the doctor, as well as Mrs. Wilkin's hat, gloves, and false teeth. On Mar. 18, the doctor was charged with murder. In June, he was convicted of first-degree murder and sentenced to prison at Mineola. However, he never served his full sentence as he hanged himself in his cell.

REF.: Caesar, *Incredible Detective; CBA;* Hynd, *Murder, Mayhem and Mystery;* Rodell, *New York Murders.*

Wilkinson, Alec, prom. 1955, Brit., mur. At the age of twenty-one, Alec Wilkinson married Maureen Farrell, and the newlyweds moved into a house located down the street from Maureen's mother. Wilkinson's mother-in-law was a foul-mouthed, ill-tempered prostitute who wielded great influence over her daughter. Their marriage quickly deteriorated and Maureen moved in with her mother. On Apr. 30, 1955, Wilkinson called on Maureen, but instead encountered her mother. Mrs. Farrell was abusive and threatened Wilkinson with a carving knife. He eluded her charge and knocked her to the floor, kicked her, and set fire to the house. As he was leaving, his estranged wife walked in; Wilkinson also struck her and left her in the burning house. Wilkinson was arrested for murder, and his defense was unable to convince the court to reduce the charge to manslaughter. He was found Guilty and hanged at Armley prison.

REF.: Butler, *Murderers' England; CBA.*

Wilkinson, Edward C., and **Wilkinson**, Dr. **Benjamin R.**, and **Murdaugh, John**, prom. 1838, Case of, U.S., mur. On Dec. 7, 1838, three Mississippi residents, Judge Edward C. Wilkinson, Dr. Benjamin R. Wilkinson, and John Murdaugh stopped in Louisville on their way to Bardstown, Ky., where Judge Wilkinson was to marry Eliza Crozier on Dec. 18. They registered at the Galt House and went to a tailor named Redding to order clothes for the wedding. On Dec. 15, Dr. Wilkinson returned to pick up the order. He paid for the clothes but was unhappy with the fit of his jacket. He returned an hour later with his two companions, and demanded that the tailor take back the garment and refund the money. Judge Wilkinson and Murdaugh convinced the doctor to cancel the entire order, and Redding admonished the judge for interfering. Incensed, the judge charged at Redding with an iron poker. Redding grabbed the judge, but was knocked to the floor by the three men who had drawn knives. Redding fled the store, but dropped his wallet containing the payment for the clothes. The three men left, and Redding notified police.

In filing his report with the police, Redding had forgotten the names of his assailants and knew only that they were staying at the Galt House. Redding and his brother-in-law, John Rothwell, went to the hotel to search for their names in the register, but while they in the hotel bar, Judge Wilkinson walked in and the argument resumed. The judge disappeared briefly, but reentered with Dr. Wilkinson and Murdaugh, all brandishing knives. During the ensuing knife battle in the crowded bar, Rothwell and a bystander, Alexander H. Meeks, were stabbed to death. Judge Wilkinson was stabbed near the shoulder blade, Murdaugh was bruised and cut on the head, while Dr. Wilkinson received bruises on the head and face.

In court, prosecutor Benjamin Hardin introduced seventeen witnesses who testified against the three attackers. Defense attorney Sergeant S. Prentiss maintained that Redding and his friends had assembled in the bar to cause trouble for the defendants. The jury found Judge Wilkinson, Dr. Wilkinson, and Murdaugh Not Guilty.

REF.: *CBA;* Johnson, *Famous Kentucky Tragedies and Trials.*

Wilkinson, James, 1757-1825, U.S., consp. Brigadier general and secretary on the board of war in 1778. The same year he conspired in the Conway Cabal, a plot to replace General George Washington with General Horatio Gates. He was compelled to step down from his post on the board. He also was involved in a conspiracy with Esteban Miró, the Spanish governor of Louisiana. The conspiracy was formed to establish trade monopolies, but he was also accused of trying to hand over Kentucky to Spain. Additionally, he was thought to be involved in a scheme with Aaron Burr, and he testified at Burr's trial as the primary witness. In 1811 he won an acquittal from a court of inquiry.

REF.: *CBA;* Duke, *Celebrated Criminal Cases of America.*

Wilkinson, Robert, 1950- , U.S., (wrong. convict.) mur. On Oct. 5, 1975, a firebomb exploded in the Philadelphia home of Radames Santiago, killing his wife, three of his children, and a guest. A 14-year-old witness, Nelson Garcia, stated that a neighbor, Robert Wilkinson, had tossed the flaming bottle through the window. The 25-year-old Wilkinson and his wife were arrested and questioned for twenty hours. Wilkinson, who was mildly retarded, eventually confessed to the crime. He was convicted in 1976 on five counts of murder.

Later that year, a neighbor of Wilkinson's, David McGinnis, confessed to the murders, and the original witness admitted that he had lied. A further investigation by the Philadelphia *Inquirer* revealed that Wilkinson's confession had been forced by two detectives who had assaulted him with a blackjack. The Inquirer also found six other incidents of brutality. On June 2, 1977, all charges against Robert Wilkinson were dropped, and he was awarded $325,000 in damages. In March 1978, McGinnis was sentenced to twenty-two years in prison. On Nov. 10, 1979, six detectives found Guilty of maltreating suspects began serving their 15-month prison sentences at the Eglin Federal Prison Camp in Florida. REF.: *CBA.*

Willats, Fleetwood, 1847-1919, Brit., (unsolv.) mur. On the evening of June 13, 1919, in the London district of Tottenham, a 72-year-old widower, Fleetwood Willats, had been drinking beer in a tavern. On the way home he encountered two men who offered him whiskey. The liquor tasted awful and he refused another drink. Willats died the next morning, having been poisoned with hydrochloric acid. His killers were never apprehended.

REF.: Browne and Tullett, *The Scalpel of Scotland Yard; CBA.*

Willebrandt, Mabel Walker, b.1889, U.S., lawyer. Practiced law in Los Angeles, Calif. As assistant attorney general of the U.S. from 1921-29, she handled cases concerning Prohibition, federal taxation, and the bureau of federal prisons. REF.: *CBA.*

Willgoss, Walter William, prom. 1959, Aus., rob.-mur. On May 4, 1959, in the small town of Lara, near Melbourne, Aus., 72-year-old Ivor Lesleigh Gillett was reported missing after he failed to report for work. Gillett was normally quite punctual at his job at a lime merchant's. Concerned fellow employees went to Gillett's home and found his body floating in a well next to the house. A coroner determined he had died of three gunshot wounds, and that the body had been submerged for three to four days. Gillett's truck was missing, as well as the money from a recent paycheck. The truck and two of Gillett's checks were located in Holbrook three days later. On May 8, police received word that a vagrant family had left the main road and were traveling cross-country. The party was easy to apprehend, and the leader, Walter William Willgoss, quickly confessed to Gillett's murder.

In Melbourne, Willgoss had an affair with a married woman. When her husband learned of the affair, he threatened to beat his wife unless she left her lover. Willgoss convinced the woman to divorce her husband and together, with her two children, they left Melbourne. They had run out of money when they encountered Gillett. Gillett refused to help, but Willgoss hid on his property and entered his home when he stepped out. While Willgoss was ransacking the house, Gillett returned and Willgoss shot him. After a five-day trial, he was convicted of murder and sentenced to death. However, upon appeal to the High Court, the sentence was commuted to life imprisonment.

REF.: *CBA;* Clegg, *Return Your Verdict.*

William I (AKA: Longue Épée, Longsword), d.943, Normandy, duke, assass. Duke of Normandy from 927-43. The son of Robert I, he was assassinated by Arnoul II, the Count of Flanders. REF.: *CBA.*

William I (Count of Nassau, AKA: William the Silent), 1533-84, Neth., assass. William I of the Netherlands was among a rare breed of public men who subordinated self-interest to the interest of his people. William championed the rights of religious and political freedom against the kingdom of Spain to become the recognized "father" of Dutch Independence before an assassin cut him down in his fifty-first year.

William, the prince of Orange, was the eldest son of William, count of Nassau-Dillenburg. He was born in a German-Lutheran household, but upon the death of his uncle, René of Orange, the vast family estates fell into the hands of young William, then only eleven years old. The Habsburg emperor Charles V decreed that William's parents should relinquish their guardianship for their son to be raised a Catholic. The Protestant Reformation was sweeping Europe, and while the emperor did not particularly endorse the aims of the movement, he guaranteed the right of religious freedom.

The wealthy young prince, meanwhile, had become a court

favorite, fulfilling all of his political, social, and military obligations both under Charles and his son Philip II, who was cut out of different cloth than the father. Philip demanded unswerving loyalty to the Catholic faith among his subjects. This was especially true after October 1555, when Charles abdicated in favor of his son. King Philip appointed William to the Council of State, and stadholder of Holland, Utrecht, and Zeeland before he himself left for Spain to take his place on the throne. William argued with the new king to respect the rights of the Dutch, but the warnings fell on deaf ears. "I would rather die a thousand deaths and lose every square foot of my empire than permit the least change in our religion!" Philip replied. The Council subjugated the rights of the Dutch Protestants, controlled as it was by the Cardinalistic Party of Spain.

Torn between his conventional Catholic upbringing and the growing feelings of dissatisfaction and alienation felt by his countrymen toward the Council in Brussels, William came to sympathize with the plight of the Protestant majority. In 1561 he was wed to Anne of Saxony, who reenforced his early childhood teachings in the Lutheran Church. The prince argued that it was not morally right to enforce an unpopular rule over his subjects. But in 1565 King Philip ordered that all existing ordinances against heretics be enforced to the letter. Widespread discontent in the Low Countries culminated in bloody rioting in August 1566. The Calvinists entered the Catholic churches where they smashed ecumenical symbols, making peaceful co-existence between the groups impossible. King Philip retaliated in December 1566 by appointing the duke of Alba captain-general in charge of the Netherlands.

William I, assassinated in 1584.

In May 1567, with order seemingly restored, Alba's army entered Brussels. A reign of terror was instituted by the duke. He named a special tribunal composed entirely of Spaniards to hear the cases of those individuals responsible for the "treason." The Council of Troubles, as it was known, condemned to death some 1,000 religious dissenters. William's lands were seized and his son Philip was deported to Spain. Whatever lingering reservations the prince may have had were resolved by the actions of the Spanish king. In April 1568 William of Orange raised an army and led an invasion of the Low Countries but was repelled by the duke of Alba on the banks of the Ems River. The war in the Netherlands had commenced and would drag on until 1576. In April of that year William was recognized as the "Chief and Supreme Authority" after bringing about the union of Holland and Zeeland. A breakdown of Spanish military authority in the Low Countries in 1576 paved the way for negotiations. The Pacification of Ghent and the Union of Brussels signed in 1577 brought to a satisfactory close the first phase of the war.

Inevitably, the Spanish king refused to surrender his claims so quickly and easily. On Mar. 15, 1580, William of Orange was outlawed by Philip II, and a reward of 25,000 ducats was offered for his life. In 1582 a religious fanatic named Juan Jaureguy came forward to answer the king's call. He fired a bullet at the prince which passed under his right ear and exited near his jaw-bone. For days William's life hung in the balance, but he gradually recovered amidst great rejoicing in the provinces. Jaureguy and several accomplices were executed and nailed to the gates of Antwerp as a grim warning to other would-be assassins.

This did not deter a Frenchman named Balthasar Gérard from making one more attempt. On July 10, 1584, the assassin gained admittance to William's residence in Delft, Neth. At the noon hour, Gérard, a fanatical Catholic who had been encouraged by the Jesuits of the College of Trèves, fired three shots at the prince as he made his way to the dining hall. William died instantly and Gérard was quickly seized and forced to undergo a series of heinous tortures. His right hand was burned off and his back broken on the wheel. His head was cut off and impaled on the gate of the Prince's residence. Such was the great animosity felt toward the king of Spain who was responsible for the assassination in the minds of most of the Dutch people. Much of William's task was still incomplete, but he had begun the slow, deliberate path toward independence and for these reasons he was recognized as the rightful founder of the Dutch republic.

REF.: *CBA;* Johnson, *Famous Assassinations of History;* Nash, *Almanac of World Crime.*

William I (Wilhelm Friedrich Ludwig), 1797-1888, Ger., kaiser, attempt. assass. First kaiser of German Empire, ruling from 1871-88. He had ruled Prussia since 1861. Two attempts were made against his life in 1878. REF.: *CBA.*

William II (William Rufus, AKA: **The Red King)**, c.1056-1100, Brit., king, assass. William Rufus was the third son of William the Conqueror, and by all accounts a despotic tyrant whose death was cheered by peasant and nobleman alike. In 1087 William I awarded the Duchy of Normandy to the eldest son Robert II Curthose, with greater England bequeathed to William Rufus. The Norman barons were uneasy with this arrangement, for they envisioned a united England under the rule of Robert. In 1088 there occurred a great uprising in the east, led by William the Conqueror's half brother Odo of Bayeux, the earl of Kent. Realizing that his position was vulnerable, Rufus won over the native English by promising deep tax cuts and an efficiently run government. Once the revolt was suppressed, the King reneged on the agreement, which hastened a second uprising in 1095, led by Robert de Mobray, earl of Northumberland. This too was put down, in a particularly bloodthirsty manner.

In 1089 Rufus began a military action against his brother Robert to secure all of Normandy. The conflict extended over seven years, before the English King was able to pronounce himself the sovereign ruler of all the disputed territories. The tyrant was still not without enemies however. On Aug. 2, 1100 while riding his steed in the New Forest of Hampshire, a knight of the realm named Walter Tirel shot an arrow through William's heart. The assassin explained the shooting was purely accidental, and the King had gotten in the way of a deer he was stalking. Tirel's account was accepted by the people of England and there were no reprisals. Yet it is conceivable that the assassination was ordered by William's younger brother Henry who acceded to the throne of England in his place.

REF.: *CBA;* Nash, *Almanac of World Crime.*

William IX (Count of Poitiers, Duke of Aquitaine), 1071-1127, Brit., morals. Violated church laws against licentiousness and was twice excommunicated. REF.: *CBA.*

William of Norwich, Saint, c.1132-c.1144, Brit., (unsolv.) mur. Tanner's apprentice allegedly martyred on Easter of 1144 or 1145. The boy is popularly believed to be the first victim in a series of ritual killings by Jews. REF.: *CBA.*

William of Saint-Amour, c.1200-72, Fr., her. Scholar at University of Paris whose anti-Dominican publications brought attack. The theologian and philosopher was suspended by Pope Alexander V in 1256, after the publication of one such vitriolic work, and he was exiled from France two years later after contributing text to *De periculis novissimorum temporum.* REF.: *CBA.*

Williams, Ada Chard (AKA: **Mrs. Hewetson**), d.1900, Brit., child abuse-mur. In 1899 in London, the decomposed body of a small girl was found in the Thames River. The girl had been strangled after her head had been beaten against a wall. A servant girl, Florence Jones, admitted to being the mother, but claimed she had given up the girl for adoption to a Mrs. Hewetson. Hewetson, who was really Ada Chard Williams wrote Scotland Yard, stating that she had only acted as a intermediary for another couple who permanently adopted the little girl.

Williams was apprehended, and when unable to produce the name of the other couple, she was charged with the murder. In her trial at Old Bailey, Ada Chard Williams was sentenced to death, and on Mar. 6, 1900, she was hanged at Newgate Prison.

REF.: *CBA;* O'Donnell, *Should Women Hang?*

Williams, Alexander S. (AKA: **Clubber**), 1839-1910, U.S., law enfor. off. One of the most corrupt police officers in the history of New York City, Alexander Williams organized police graft into a business in the late 1800s. Williams moved to New York City from Nova Scotia when he was twenty-seven, joined the Manhattan Police Department, and was assigned to a quiet neighborhood as a patrolman in 1866. Two years later, he was transferred to the high crime area around Broadway and Houston streets. To establish himself in the neighborhood, Williams picked fights with two of the toughest thugs in the area and knocked them unconscious. He then beat their friends unconscious with his nightstick. In the following four years, he averaged one fight a day, earning the name "Clubber Williams." It was Williams who said, "There's more law in the end of a policeman's nightstick than in a decision of the Supreme Court." His tactics were constantly under attack from reformers and clergymen, but Williams continued to assault lawbreakers and occasionally, an innocent victim.

In 1876, Williams was promoted to captain of the twenty-first Precinct, which he cleaned up with his strong-arm techniques. He then did the same in the eighth and fourth precincts, but in 1876, Williams was assigned to the twenty-ninth Precinct, where more than half the buildings were dedicated to some form of vice. Williams coined the term "Tenderloin" for this district when he said, "I've had nothing but chuck for a long time and now I'm going to get the tenderloin." He established set operating prices for brothels, saloons, pool halls, policy shops, and casinos, payable directly to one of Williams' officers. Williams' main source of income in his Tenderloin years was his homemade rot gut whiskey, which he forced saloons to buy by the case.

Alexander "Clubber" Williams, one of the most corrupt police officials in New York for twenty years.

In nine years in the Tenderloin, Williams was tried and acquitted eighteen times for brutality and graft. To get him out of the Tenderloin, the city promoted Williams to inspector in charge of the East Side of Manhattan. He told all captains below him how much money they should expect in graft and how much he expected to receive. Williams appeared before the Lexow Committee in 1894 and his operation was exposed. Officers testified that they received protection money from businesses, then gave it to Williams. One family told the committee that they were evicted after they complained to Williams about the noise coming from the brothel next door. Williams denied everything and was acquitted of the charges. He retired on May 24, 1895, having made an estimated $1 million in police graft.

REF.: Asbury, *The Gangs of New York; CBA;* Logan, *Against the Evidence;* Peterson, *The Mob;* Reppetto, *The Blue Parade;* Servadio, *Mafioso.*

Williams, Ann, d.1753, Brit., mur. Ann Williams, described as a domineering wife, ruled her submissive husband with an iron fist right up until the day she murdered him. Williams and her house servant, who was also her lover, devised a plan to poison her husband by mixing mercury in his dinner. After eating what would be his final meal, Mr. Williams became violently ill. On his deathbed the following day, he explained to his doctor that his wife had poisoned him, because he became sick immediately after eating the food she had prepared. The doctor reported his suspicions, and Williams was immediately taken into custody.

Anne Williams was quickly tried and convicted of the murder. She received the maximum penalty for a wife who murders her husband. She was tied at the stake, strangled to death, and then burned to ashes in Gloucester on Apr. 13, 1753.

Murderess Ann Williams being burned at the stake, 1753.

REF.: *CBA;* Mitchell, *The Newgate Calendar;* Nash, *Look For the Woman;* O'Donnell, *Should Women Hang?;* Poynter, *Forgotten Crimes.*

Williams, Archibald, 1801-63, U.S., jur. Nominated by President Abraham Lincoln to the district court of Kansas in 1861. He had served as U.S. district attorney from 1849-53. REF.: *CBA.*

Williams, Arnold Jason, 1967- , U.S., mur. On Oct. 3, 1987, in Silver Spring, Md., Shannon Anne McMillan, twenty-two, was found stabbed to death in her apartment. A bloody fingerprint was found on a newspaper page. The print belonged to a neighbor, Arnold Jason Williams, a former Marine guard with a notable record. Williams had been stationed at the presidential retreat at Camp David. He originally was charged with murder and rape, but the rape charge was dropped during plea bargaining in exchange for a guilty plea to the charge of first-degree murder. On July 5, 1989, in the Montgomery County Circuit Courtroom of Judge James S. McAuliffe, Williams was sentenced to life imprisonment. REF.: *CBA.*

Williams, Berkeley Cecil, 1900-61, Brit., (unsolv.) mur. In the early morning hours of May 1, 1961, residents of Pennymore, in Devonshire, England, were awakened by an explosion. The body of 61-year-old Exeter grocer Berkeley Cecil Williams was pulled from the passenger's seat. Neither the front nor the rear of the car were in flames, the driver's door was open, and an empty gasoline can with a missing cap was found nearby. Witnesses saw two men in the car earlier in the evening, but the other party was never found, and the mystery of Berkeley Williams' death was never solved.

REF.: *CBA;* Furneaux, *Famous Criminal Cases, vol. 7.*

Williams, Carl, 1954-88, U.S., mur. On Jan. 23, 1988, Dallas police officer John Glenn Chase, twenty-five, was ticketing a motorist for driving without a license when he was accosted by an onlooker who objected to his actions. Carl Williams, a 34-year-old black man, took the white officer's gun during their scuffle. While Chase pleaded for his life, a few members of the a gathering crowd implored Williams to shoot the officer. Williams shot Chase in the face, and returned to fire two more shots, killing the policeman. Williams was later shot to death by two off-duty Dallas policemen. The incident galvanized the racially-polarized city. Police chief Billy Prince blamed black politicians for turning the black community against the force, while civil rights leaders blamed the lack of community influence on the department as the problem. REF.: *CBA*.

Williams, Constance, 1931-45, Brit., (unsolv.) mur. In 1945, near Plymouth, England, the body of 14-year-old Constance Williams was found beside a road near a military base. The initial autopsy stated that the girl, seven months pregnant, had died of asphyxiation. A more seasoned pathologist added that she had been strangled with considerable force. While it was clear that she was killed intentionally, there were no signs of resistance, unusual given the age and health of the girl. Police claimed to have a suspect, but lack of evidence prevented them from making an arrest.

REF.: *CBA;* Simpson, *Forty Years of Murder.*

Williams, David Marshall (AKA: **Carbine Williams**), 1901-75, U.S., firearms-mur. On July 21, 1921, a team of federal agents raided a still in the Five Holly Swamp near Fayetteville, N.C. The still was owned and operated by David M. Williams, a young moonshiner who had been distributing illegal spirits to the county for some time. While trying to escape from the authorities, Williams fired on Deputy Sheriff Al J. Pate of Cumberland County, who was killed instantly. Williams was tracked down in the woods and arrested by local police. Arraigned on a charge of first-degree murder, Williams went on trial before Judge John H. Kerr in Fayetteville on Aug. 31, 1921. Defense attorneys asserted that Williams suffered from paranoia. The jury, upon hearing all the evidence, was unable to reach a verdict and a mistrial was declared on Oct. 17, 1921. The following month the press announced that David Williams would be tried a second time.

Williams withdrew his earlier insanity defense on Nov. 22. He entered a plea of guilty to the lesser charge of second-degree murder. The deal was cut to save Williams from the gallows. Three days later Judge Henry Lane sentenced the defendant to thirty years in jail, the maximum sentence permissible under North Carolina law at the time.

While serving his time in various state prisons, Williams began to tinker with pieces of scrap metal in the blacksmith's shop. With the permission of the prison superintendent, Williams began manufacturing gunmaking tools, which he used to forge a rudimentary design for three innovative weapons that employed the "floating chamber" principle. The Colt Firearms Company heard of his accomplishments and sent a letter of inquiry to George Ross Pou, superintendent of prisons in Raleigh, N.C., in May 1928. The subsequent publicity surrounding Williams' invention of a superior rapid-fire weapon—the carbine rifle—led to his early parole in 1929. Governor Angus W. McLean of North Carolina granted Williams a full and unconditional pardon on Sept. 29 of that year, after the widow of the murdered deputy said Williams might be able to make something of his invention, and his life, if he were released.

David Williams was associated with the carbine, the weapon that helped win WWII, from that day forward. Eight million of these guns were used by U.S. troops in WWII, Korea, and Vietnam. General Douglas MacArthur credited Williams' invention as being "one of the strongest contributing factors to our victory in the Pacific." In his small workshop at the family farm in Camden, S.C., Williams designed the first machine gun capable of firing 2,000 rounds per minute, which brought him one of the seventy weapons patents he held during his lifetime. From his boyhood interest in toy pistols to the time of his death on Jan. 8, 1975, Williams continued to tinker with guns. A Hollywood motion picture titled *Carbine Williams,* starring James Stewart and Jean Hagen, was released in 1952, which profiled the life and times of the inventor.

REF.: *CBA;* Beard, *Carbine: The Story of David Marshal-Williams.*

Williams, Dennis, 1956- , U.S., kid.-rape-mur. Lawrence Lionberg, twenty-nine, and his fiancée, Carol Schmal, twenty-four, were last seen alive on May 10, 1978, at a gas station where Lionberg worked in Homewood, Ill., a southwest suburb of Chicago. Their bodies were discovered two days later, both shot in the back of the head. Schmal had been gang-raped. Five people were arrested for the murders: Dennis Williams, twenty-one, Willie Rainge, twenty-one, Kenneth Adams, twenty, Verneal Jimerson, and Pamela Gray, seventeen. Gray turned state's evidence and testified in court about the murder. She claimed that Williams was the leader of the group who took the couple to an abandoned apartment near Williams' home. While Lionberg was held downstairs, Gray held a cigarette lighter while Williams and the other men repeatedly raped Schmal on the floor of the second-story apartment. Williams then shot Schmal in the back of the head twice with a .38-caliber revolver. He then took Lionberg to a field and shot him twice in the head, then gave the gun to Rainge, who shot the victim once in the back. After her original testimony, Gray recanted and was later convicted of perjury.

Williams, Rainge, and Gray were convicted of aggravated kidnapping, rape, and murder. The charges against Jimerson were dropped, but he was later rearrested, convicted, and in 1985 was sentenced to death. Adams got seventy-five years on two murder counts and sixty years for a rape charge. Williams and Rainge received sixty-year sentences for kidnapping and rape. Also convicted of murder, Rainge was sentenced to life in prison, and on Feb. 6, 1979, Williams was sentenced to die in the electric chair. Williams, Rainge and Gray won new trials from the Illinois Supreme Court on the grounds that their counsel was incompetent, but a jury upheld the verdict on Feb. 13, 1987. On Mar. 4, Williams was sentenced to be executed. As of this writing, Williams and Jimerson are awaiting execution on Illinois' Death Row. REF.: *CBA*.

Williams, Edward, 1872-1924, Aus., mur. Edward Williams, fifty-two, the father of three daughters and the husband of an insane woman, taught music in Sydney, Aus. Depressed about his meager salary and inability to remove his family from hunger and squalor, Williams resorted to drastic means. On Feb. 4, 1924, Williams put his daughters to bed, asked if they wanted to go to heaven, kissed them goodnight, and left the room. As the girls slept, Williams returned to their room and slit their throats. A family friend discovered the bodies of 6-year-old Rosalie, 4-year-old Mary, and 3-year-old Cecilia. The murders were given sensational coverage and Williams became the target of a nationwide manhunt. Six days later, the tired and beleaguered man turned himself in to the police. During his trial, Williams refused to plead insanity, stating calmly that he did not expect to escape punishment. He said, "They went to God with untarnished souls. I was not the callous man they pictured me here today, for when I killed my three children, that was the moment I loved them most intensely." Williams was found Guilty and sentenced to death. He was hanged on Apr. 29, 1924, at the Long Bay jail.

REF.: *CBA;* Clegg, *Return Your Verdict;* Gribble, *Compelled to KIll;* Gurr, *Famous Australasian Crimes.*

Williams, Edward Bennett, 1920-88, U.S., crim. law. Although renowned criminal lawyer Edward Bennett Williams was called "ruthless," a "hypocritical trickster," and "the biggest egotist in the law since William Jennings Bryan," he also had a seventy-percent success rate with the cases he defended and usually earned at least the grudging admiration of his opponents.

Williams was dubbed the nicknames of "the mob's best legal friend" and "the Burglar's Lobby in Washington" for his successful defense of such mob figures as Frank Costello and Jimmy Hoffa. Displaying the philosophy that governed his professional life, Williams answered these intended slights by responding, "The Sixth Amendment of the Constitution guarantees the right of legal counsel to *everyone*. It does not say to everyone *except* people like Frank Costello."

In addition to Hoffa and Costello, Williams also defended Adam Clayton Powell, Bobby Baker, Aldo Icardi, John Connally, Joseph McCarthy, and assorted gamblers and accused Russian spies. Williams so destroyed the government's tax evasion case against Adam Clayton Powell that Powell only ended up paying

$900 in taxes on gross income of $70,000. In the 1950's Williams defended Sen. Joseph McCarthy in the Senate censure hearings and, at virtually the same time, several of the Hollywood writers whom McCarthy had labeled as communists. In one day he was described alternately in two different papers as a "right-wing mouthpiece for the McCarthy fringe," and as a "courtroom apologist for left-wing groups."

Williams' interests also extended into professional sports. He owned the Washington Redskins' football team, and later the Baltimore Orioles baseball team. Williams died at the age of sixty-eight in August 1988. See: **Costello, Frank; Hoffa, James Riddle.** REF.: *CBA.*

Williams, Eleazer, c.1789-1858, U.S., fraud. Indian missionary descended from an American Indian chief and an American woman. He became famous by claiming to be the lost French dauphin, the son of Louis XVI, in 1839. See: **Williams, John.**

REF.: *CBA;* MacDougall, *Hoaxes.*

Williams, Frank C., and Hull, Anna, prom. 1910, U.S., wh. slav. In Summer 1910, Frank Williams met two girls at a picnic in Rock Springs, Ohio. He persuaded them to accompany him to Pittsburgh, Pa., where he turned them over to a woman named Anna Hull who operated a brothel. Williams and Hull were caught and convicted of white slavery. On Oct. 20, 1910, they were sentenced to two-and-a-half years in prison.

REF.: *CBA;* Roe, *The Great War on White Slavery.*

Williams, Gene Howard, 1947- , U.S., (wrong. convict.) rape. In 1972, Gene Howard Williams, twenty-five, was convicted of rape and served more than a year in an Oklahoma prison, including eight-and-a-half months of solitary confinement, because of a clerical error. The actual culprit was 36-year-old Harold Gene Williams, but because both men were known as "Gene," their prison files became mixed up. Although the wrongly accused was released, he was diagnosed as a paranoid schizophrenic. On Oct. 29, 1976, as recompense for his "lost year", Gene Howard Williams was awarded $125,000 in damages by a federal court jury. REF.: *CBA.*

Williams, George Henry, 1823-1910, U.S., atty. gen. George Henry Williams was born in New Lebanon, N.Y., on Mar. 23, 1823, and was educated at schools near Pompey Hills, N.Y. He later studied law and in 1844 practiced law in Fort Madison, Iowa Territory. When Iowa was admitted to the Union, Williams served as a district judge from 1847-52. President Franklin Pierce appointed Williams chief justice of the Oregon Territory in 1853. He held the post for four years. In 1865, Williams was elected to the U.S. Senate from Oregon, where he voted guilty in President Andrew Johnson's impeachment trial. He was appointed attorney general in the cabinet of President Ulysses S. Grant and served from Jan. 10, 1872, until May 15, 1875. Grant nominated him as U.S. Supreme Court chief justice, but Williams asked his name be withdrawn when stiff opposition arose. He served as mayor of Portland, Ore., from 1902-5. Williams lived in Portland until his death on Apr. 4, 1910. REF.: *CBA.*

Williams, Grant, 1872-1937, U.S., law enfor. off. Grant Williams, New York City police officer since 1897, was promoted to sergeant in 1905 and to detective in 1911. He was given the unseemly assignment of identifying the unknown dead, a practice of which he was to become quite adept. He was named lieutenant in 1913, and after the police department's failure to discover the missing Tammany Hall leader Timothy Sullivan, whose body was found awaiting burial in a common grave, Williams was appointed head of the Bureau of Unidentified Dead. In 1914, the bureau became a unit of the Missing Persons Bureau which Williams headed. Williams introduced identification of bodies by using laundry marks from clothing. He also implemented photographing unidentified dead bodies and keeping detailed records. Using plaster and paint, Williams would even reconstruct a corpse's damaged face or head. Poor health forced him to retire in 1918, but until his death in 1937, he would occasionally emerge to help the department on some of the more difficult cases. REF.: *CBA.*

Williams, Hernando, 1955- , rape-kid.-mur. A "monster" with two personalities is how the self-confessed murderer Hernando Williams described himself in the Criminal Court of Chicago. In a thirty-two-page confession given to police on Apr. 2, 1978, following his arrest, the 23-year-old described Linda Goldstone's night of terror that culminated in murder. Williams was sitting on the stairs of a building in Chicago's posh Gold Coast on Mar. 30, 1978, when he decided to rob someone. He found his victim several blocks west of Lake Shore Drive on Superior Street. Linda Goldstone, an instructor in natural childbirth at Prentice Women's Hospital, was abducted by Williams at gunpoint as she parked her car. For the next thirty-six hours the young mother was imprisoned in the trunk of a car, while Williams drove to the South Side, where he drank with friends. Witnesses reported seeing Williams talk to the trunk of his car in the parking lot of the criminal court in suburban Maywood, where he was scheduled to appear on separate rape and kidnapping charges stemming from his abduction of a 24-year-old Evergreen Park woman from a shopping center.

Williams was prepared to release Goldstone on Apr. 1. He drove to the far South Side where he gave her bus fare after she promised not to call police. But a few minutes later he watched her as she solicited the help of a man standing on the back porch of a house. "I stood there looking at her a few minutes and I went to question her why didn't she, you know, get on the bus. That is all she had to do," the killer told police. Instead he dragged her away and shot her to death.

Williams, the son of a South Side minister, pleaded guilty to the charges brought against him. On Dec. 18, 1979, he was sentenced to die in the electric chair after the criminal court jury had spent the previous month deliberating his fate. Judge James Strunck signed the execution order on Jan. 14, 1980, tacking on concurrent prison terms of sixty years for rape and thirty years each for armed robbery and aggravated kidnapping. Strunck decried the "exceptionally cruel and wanton behavior" exhibited by the defendant. REF.: *CBA.*

Williams, John, See: **MacKay, George.**

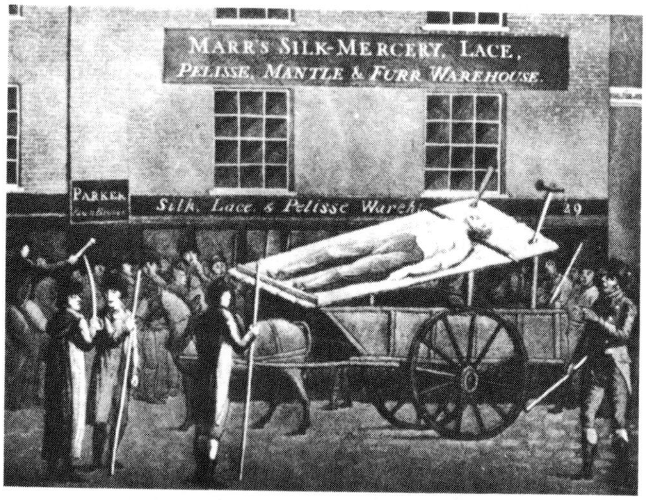

Displaying the body of John Williams, alias Murphy; arrested for the notorious Ratcliff Highway murders of 1811, he committed suicide before trial.

Williams, John (AKA: The Ratcliff Highway Murders), d.1811, Brit., suic.-mur. During the early 1800s, the separate slayings of two families in the East End of London came to be known as "The Ratcliff Highway Murders." The crimes shocked and terrified all of England and were eclipsed only by the Jack the Ripper killings, which began in 1888.

Timothy Marr operated a hosier's shop on Ratcliff Highway and lived there with his wife, Cecilia; their infant daughter; an apprentice, John Goen, about thirteen years old; and a maid, Margaret Jewell, about eighteen years old. On Dec. 7, 1811, as Marr and Goen were closing up the store shortly before midnight,

Jewell was sent out to buy some oysters and was told that the door would be left open for her. When she returned about twenty minutes later, the house was locked and quiet. She rang and knocked at the door, but no one answered. When neighbors arrived and entered the house, they found the entire family slain. Timothy Marr was lying behind the counter, Cecilia Marr was found in the doorway between the back room and the store, and the apprentice, Goen, was at the bottom of the stairs. The killer had battered their heads and slashed their throats. The infant's throat had also been cut. Although the killer may have stolen some pocket change or small items, nothing valuable was taken. He apparently had been looking upstairs when he heard Jewell at the door and fled through the back. A ship's carpenter's maul and a sledgehammer with the initials J.P. on the handle were found.

Londoners were stunned when they learned of the murders, and the entire country, especially the Birmingham region, was gripped with fear. People became cautious, and many equipped their homes with sturdy bolts and chain locks. Door-to-door searches were conducted in the Shadwell area, many tramps were arrested, and rewards were offered for the killer's capture.

On Dec. 19, the killer struck again at the Kings Arms, a pub on Old Gravel Lane, a road that intersected Ratcliff Highway. The pub was operated by an old man, Mr. Williamson, who resided there with his wife; their grandchild, 14-year-old Kitty Stillwell; a maid, 50-year-old Bridget Harrington; and a journeyman carpenter John Turner. Williamson customarily closed the pub and the house door at 11 p.m. He usually left the pub's front door open until 12 a.m. for anyone who wanted a late-night drink. Turner arrived home shortly before 11 p.m., and, exhausted from work, immediately went to his second-floor room and fell asleep. Sometime after 11 p.m. the killer entered the King's Arms and first attacked Harrington, who was setting up the fire for the next morning. When Williamson's wife entered the room, he attacked her as well. He cut both women's throats, nearly severing Harrington's head, and then killed Williamson, who had just returned from the cellar.

At 11:25 p.m., Turner was awakened by the slamming of the outside door. He quietly went downstairs, where he saw "a tall man in a loose, shaggy coat" inside the parlor. The killer, whose back was to Turner, was hovering over a body and going through pockets. When the killer stood up and walked, Turner heard his boots creak. Still undetected, Turner slipped back up to his bedroom, tied sheets together, and climbed out his window. He alerted neighbors, who broke into the house. The killer broke a window at the back of the house and escaped. Kitty Stillwell had escaped injury.

The Williamson slayings caused even greater panic. Notices were circulated, emphasizing the initials, J.P., found on the sledgehammer left at the first murder scene. A man who ran an area pub and inn called the Pear Tree, Mr. Vermiloe, saw the flyers and thought the weapon might belong to a Nordic seaman, John Petersen, who had lodged at his inn and stored a tool chest there. Vermiloe identified the maul as Petersen's, but Petersen had been at sea during the murders.

Another Pear Tree lodger, Irishman John Williams, about twenty or thirty years old, became a suspect and was taken to the Shadwell police station for questioning. Williams had been seen going toward the Kings Arms the night of the slayings and was known to have returned to the inn at about 1 a.m. on the nights of the murders. On the night of the Kings Arms murders, he had asked two other lodgers to snuff out their candles and then gotten into bed in the dark. Williams' shoes and socks were muddy, and he had blood on his shirt, which he said had resulted from a fight. After the first murder, Williams had purchased a new pair of boots, which creaked. Additionally, Williams' coat pocket was stained with blood, as were a pair of his pants found in an outhouse. During questioning, Williams admitted frequenting the Kings Arms. He was arrested and taken to the New Prison at Coldbath Fields.

On Dec. 28, Williams hanged himself in his prison cell. His corpse was placed on a cart and taken to the scenes of the crime. On Dec. 31, his body was taken to the intersection of New Road and Cannon Street, and a stake was driven through his heart before burial. About five or six weeks later, a knife covered with dried blood was discovered in Williams' former room at the Pear Tree. The weapon had been hidden in the floor of the room in a mouse hole. Although Williams was never tried, and the evidence in the case was primarily circumstantial, the slayings stopped after his arrest. In 1849, his remains were disinterred because of street repairs.

Within hours of Williams' death, Sir Thomas Lawrence made a watercolor portrait of him, showing light blue eyes and blond hair, although according to other reports, he had red hair. The case also captured the imagination of Thomas De Quincey (1785-1859), who wrote *On Murder, Considered as one of the Fine Arts,* published in 1827. In an appendix, he composed a descriptive piece recreating murder.

REF.: Atholl, *Shadow of the Gallows;* Brock, *A Casebook of Crime;* Browne, *The Rise of Scotland Yard; CBA;* Critchley, *The Maul and the Pear Tree, The Ratcliffe Highway Murders;* Hibbert, *The Roots of Evil;* Logan, *Masters of Crime;* Pearce, *UNsolved Murder Mysteries;* Potter, *The Art of Hanging;* Roughead, *The Art of Murder;* Snyder and Morris (ed.), *A Treasury of Great Reporting;* Stevens, *From Clue to Dock;* Wilson, *Encyclopedia of Murder;* (FICTION), Shearing, *Orange Blossoms* ("Blood and Thunder")

Williams, John James, 1904- , U.S., polit. corr. In the early 1950s, the offices of Republican Senator John Williams of Delaware became a virtual clearing house for cases involving governmental corruption. He became a reformer a year after his election, in 1947, when his own name wrongly appeared on a delinquent tax list. An investigation led to the discovery of an embezzler in the tax office. Williams suspected further injustices in the Department of Internal Revenue. He quietly built a strong case, using internal sources.

On the Senate floor, he preached of wrongdoing in New York, St. Louis, and San Francisco, which led to further investigation by a House of Representatives subcommittee. Next, he investigated the income tax records of reputed mobsters. In the case of Frank Costello, Williams produced information which had miraculously eluded the Treasury Department for twenty years despite the fact that the information was found in the department's files. He discovered that the Department of Agriculture records had not been scrutinized by Congress for four years, and that the department was missing $81 million. Williams was instrumental in removing a number of corrupt officials. Boston, Mass., tax collector Denis Delaney and James Finnegan of St. Louis were sentenced to two years in prison. Theron Lamar Caudle, Joseph P. Marcelle, James B.E. Olson, and U.S. Attorney General J. Howard McGrath were all fired; and Daniel A. Bolich, Joe Nunan, and Charles Oliphant resigned their posts. REF.: *CBA.*

Williams, Joseph, prom. 1939, Case of, Brit., rob.-mur. On May 21, 1939, in the English town of Bournemouth, Walter Dinivan was found lying in a pool of blood near the fireplace in his home. He had been battered with a blunt object, stabbed ten times, and strangled. Dinivan seemingly knew his attacker, there were no signs of resistance, and there was evidence that Dinivan had drinks with a guest. He died the next morning. A week later, Joseph Williams, who was always broke, began spending a great deal of money. Williams denied the crime, but bloodstains of his type and his thumbprint were found at the murder scene. The bank notes he was spending were traced to Dinivan. Williams was arrested, and the prosecution felt it had an easy case. However, on Oct. 14, 1939, a jury acquitted Williams because they did not understand the fingerprint evidence. Once free, Williams confessed to a journalist that he had indeed murdered Walter Dinivan.

REF.: Burt, *Commander Burt of Scotland Yard; CBA;* Cherrill, *Cherrill of the Yard;* Tullett, *Strictly Murder.*

Williams, Joseph S., prom. 1920, U.S., (wrong. convict.) mansl. In 1920, in Virginia, Joseph S. Williams was convicted of voluntary manslaughter for the murder of his wife and sentenced to five years in prison. She had died of a brain hemorrhage, and Williams was suspected of striking her. However, there was no outward sign of physical violence. When the Virginia Supreme Court ordered a retrial, the state chose not to prosecute and Williams was released. REF.: *CBA.*

Williams, Lionel Ray, c.1957- , U.S., rob.-mur. On Feb. 13, 1976, 37-year-old Sal Mineo, an actor who had acquired fame and Oscar nominations very young and then disappeared from public view, was returning to his small apartment near the Sunset Strip. Lionel Williams, who made a career of robbery along famous Hollywood streets, waited in the carport and attacked Mineo before he reached the door of his apartment, stabbing him in the chest several times with a hunting knife. But before Williams could grab Mineo's money, a neighbor came running and saw Williams briefly. The witness thought the assailant was a white man rather than a light-skinned black. Mineo died within a few minutes of massive hemorrhaging.

Actor Sal Mineo, the murder victim.

A few days later, Lionel Williams was arrested for robbery, but the police paid no attention when he commented that Sal Mineo had been killed over drugs, because they had found no evidence the actor used drugs. More than a year later, Williams' wife reported to police that her husband had killed Mineo. She said he had come home the night of the murder and told her that he had done it. She described exactly the knife he used, and the medical examiner found that such a knife fit the stab wounds in Mineo's chest.

Lionel Williams, the killer, at right, under arrest.

Williams was, at that time, imprisoned in Michigan for passing bad checks. Prison guards there reported that he often bragged about killing Mineo, but no one had believed it. It took until January 1979 for the authorities to get Williams back to California for trial. He was tried for eleven robberies and the murder and found Guilty of all but one robbery. Judge Bonnie Lee Martin sentenced Williams to fifty-one years to life in prison.

REF.: *CBA;* Nash, *Murder Among the Mighty;* Wolf, *Fallen Angels.*

Williams, Margaret, prom. 1949, Aust., mur. Montague Cyril Williams, a British soldier stationed in Austria in 1949, married that spring while he was home on leave. His wife Margaret later admitted that she did not love him, and she only married him because she was tipsy when she said yes, and because he agreed that they would not have sex until she grew to love him. The couple spent the weekend of July 2 drinking at the Grand Hotel in Anneheim. On their return to their base at Klagenfurt, they had a fight, and Margaret went out for a walk. She met some Austrian friends who took her to a nearby inn to drink, but her husband came after her with two friends who physically removed her from the inn and carried her home. Back in their room, her husband beat her up and she told him she was going to leave him. When he slapped her again, she grabbed a knife from the table and stabbed him. She tried to get help for him, but the knife had penetrated his heart and he bled to death.

Margaret Williams was returned to England for trial, which started at the Old Bailey on Sept. 15. Although Justice Streatfeild informed the jury that they could bring in a verdict of manslaughter or self-defense, the jury found Margaret Williams Guilty of murder. She was sentenced to death but was reprieved by the home secretary.

REF.: *CBA;* Harrison, *Criminal Calendar;* Simpson, *Forty Years of Murder.*

Williams, Mary, d.1874, Brit., mur. In 1874, Mary Williams was a housekeeper for a Mr. Higgins and his elderly aunt in Liverpool, England. Williams and her sister, Mrs. Flanagan, poisoned the two, after taking out insurance policies on their lives. They buried the bodies and collected the money. They were not apprehended until they began to argue loudly over the division of the insurance money. A passing policeman overheard them and arrested them. The sisters were found Guilty of the murders, and both were hanged at Kirkdale prison in 1874.

REF.: *CBA;* O'Donnell, *Should Women Hang?*

Williams, Matthew, prom. 1931, U.S., mur. In December 1931, Matthew Williams, a black man, worked in a lumber yard in Salisbury, Md. Angry about his low wages, Williams shot his boss, Daniel Elliott, to death. During an ensuing shootout, Elliott's son wounded Williams in the head, and Williams accidentally shot himself in the chest. Later that day, six men took him from a hospital and delivered him to a throng of 2,000 waiting outside. Williams was blindfolded and hanged from a tree on the courthouse lawn. After twenty minutes, his body was cut down and burned. Nobody was charged with the lynching. REF.: *CBA.*

Williams, Montagu Stephen (AKA: **The Poor Man's Magistrate**), 1835-92, Brit., lawyer. Montagu Williams was a third-generation lawyer, who was admitted to the bar of the Inner Temple on Apr. 30, 1862. He was educated at Eton, and later fought in the Crimean War. Williams' modest academic attainments prevented him from engaging in the more complex civil cases. Nonetheless, he became one of the notable criminal lawyers of his time. Montagu Williams was a revered figure among the poorer classes of London during the fifteen years he practiced law. He championed the cause of the indigent, and recounted their plight in his 1892 book *Round London.*

In 1886, Williams lost part of his larynx to a throat disease. He attempted a comeback, but his oratory skills were so badly impaired that he could no longer practice law. In December of that year, he was appointed metropolitan stipendiary magistrate of Greenwich, and later at Wandsworth, and then Worship Street. In 1888 Williams was made a Queen's counsel. He died on Dec. 23, 1892. REF.: *CBA.*

Williams, Norman, prom. 1904, U.S., big.-mur. In February 1904, George Nesbitt appeared near Hood River, Ore., looking for clues in the disappearances four years before of Alma and Louisa Nesbitt, his mother and sister. He suspected Norman Williams, who had known the Nesbitt family when they had lived in Iowa, followed the women to Oregon, and farmed adjoining land. A search of the Nesbitt homestead revealed a gunnysack which may have contained human blood and hair, but this was hardly enough evidence to convict a suspect. However, it was learned that Williams had married Alma Nesbitt, George's sister, while he was married to a woman in neighboring Dufar, Ore. A Portland chemist determined that the hairs in the gunnysack were human hairs pulled violently from the scalp, and a local liveryman recalled that Williams had leased a buggy at about the time of the disappearances. By killing the women, Williams inherited their land. He was arrested for the murders, convicted, and hanged.

REF.: *CBA;* Hynd, *Murder, Mayhem and Mystery.*

Williams, Patrick, 1949- , Case of, U.S., rape. On May 27, 1976, a man abducted an 8-year-old girl as she was walking home from school on Chicago's South Side. The girl was taken to a nearby apartment, raped, and kept captive for eight hours before being released. Police arrested 27-year-old Patrick Williams five days later, took him to Wentworth District police station, and held him in an interrogation room. While an officer was typing up a report charging Williams with rape, the mother of the victim, Esther Lee Clay, entered the room, aimed a .38-caliber revolver, and shot Williams. Clay said, "You raped my daughter. You raped my baby." Williams was paralyzed from the neck down. Clay was charged with attempted murder and aggravated battery.

In April 1977, State's Attorney Michael Robbins dropped sexual assault charges against Williams on the recommendation of Dr. Douglas Foster, a psychiatrist who determined that Clay and her daughter were emotionally unstable and unable to testify. On Mar. 9, 1978, the state moved to drop the prosecution of Clay, and Circuit Court judge Aubrey F. Kaplan dismissed the charges against her. REF.: *CBA.*

Williams, Renwick (AKA: The Monster), prom. 1790, Brit., asslt. For several months during Winter 1789-90, Renwick Williams attacked unescorted women at knife-point. He committed his attacks seemingly at random, and became known as "The Monster." On the evening of Jan. 18, 1790, Anne Porter, her sister Sarah Porter, and another woman were walking home after a dance. A man jumped from the shadows and stabbed Anne in the right hip with a sharp instrument. The weapon sliced a nine-inch gash in her leg while the man grabbed and ripped at Anne's dress. When Sarah tried to free her sister from the attacker's grasp, he hit her on the head. The attacker fled, but not before the two women saw his face.

Renwick Williams, called "The Monster."

Williams shown stabbing another woman on a London street, 1790.

Five months after the attack, on June 13, Anne, Sarah, their mother, and a man named John Coleman again met the assailant. While walking through St. James Park, Williams violently pushed the woman out of his way. He turned to see what he had done, and Anne Porter recognized him. Williams fled, but Coleman followed him home and authorities later took him into custody.

Williams was tried Dec. 10, 1790. After a parade of witnesses supporting each side testified, the jurors quickly found Williams Guilty. He was charged with two counts of assault, including the "malicious tearing, cutting, spoiling, and defacing of the garments of Anne Porter." He was sentenced to two consecutive two-year terms at Newgate, and upon his release was required to pay £200 in two separate sureties of £100 each to ensure his good behavior on his own recognizance. Many Londoners believed Porter had mistaken Williams for the actual slasher, and that he had been wrongly convicted.

REF.: Atholl, *Shadow of the Gallows; CBA;* Culpin, *The Newgate Noose;* Griffiths, *Mysteries of the Police and Crime;* Mitchell, *The Newgate Calendar;* Potter, *the Art of Hanging.*

Williams, Richard, c.1698-1719, Brit., rob. Richard Williams was born in Hereford where he lived with his father, Roger Williams. When he was fifteen, he moved to London to become a brazier's apprentice. Two years later, he turned from his trade to a career of robbery which ended with his indictment in 1719.

On Apr. 9, 1719, Richard Williams and his father were brought up on charges of stealing forty-two shillings from Ralph Courtney. Courtney alleged that Richard and an accomplice, Thomas Harrich, forced their way into his home and stole money from him. After they fled, Courtney tried to catch them but was stopped by the father, Roger Williams.

In his defense, the younger Williams maintained that Courtney had solicited sex from both himself and Harrich, and that he had willingly admitted them into his house. Once inside, Courtney allegedly paid in advance for sex with Harrich, and when the two men refused to comply with his requests, he agreed to give them additional money to protect his reputation. Once paid, the two thieves left the home unimpeded by Courtney.

The jury found Roger Williams Not Guilty, based on his good-standing reputation in the community, but found his son Richard Guilty. Roger Williams pleaded for leniency for his son, but the judge sentenced Richard Williams to death. REF.: *CBA.*

Williams, Robert, 1938- , U.S., (wrong. convict.) mur. Robert Williams confessed twice to murders he did not commit. In 1956, at age eighteen, Williams confessed to the murder of a Palos Verdes, Calif., man, believing he would never be convicted. He confessed to get the attention of a former girlfriend who was about to marry another man. To prove to authorities that an innocent man could be wrongly convicted, he then confessed to a second murder. He spent the next seventeen years in prison, many of them in solitary confinement. Paroled in 1975, Williams started trying to clear his name. After he produced a letter which placed him in a corrections camp at the time of the first murder, a judge released him from his parole on May 31, 1978.

REF.: *CBA;* Jones, *By Persons Unknown.*

Williams, Roger, c.1603-83, Brit., her. Became a pastor shortly after emigrating from London to Salem in the colony of Massachusetts in 1630. The Massachusetts General Court reacted against his doctrines and criticisms of officials by banishing him from the colony. He later helped found and settle Rhode Island, and was a fervent advocate of religious toleration. REF.: *CBA.*

Williams, Roy Lee, 1915-89, U.S., brib. Roy Williams began his association with the International Brotherhood of Teamsters as a truck driver, and rose to the presidency of the 1.5 million-member union in 1981. The union had fought accusations of corruption for twenty-five years. Williams was indicted in 1982 for bribing U.S. Senator Howard Cannon of Nevada to help defeat legislation that would deregulate the trucking industry. Williams offered Cannon a chance to bid on Teamster property in Las Vegas in return for cooperation. The legislation passed, however, and Cannon did not get the land, nor was he charged in the bribery case. On Dec. 15, 1982, in Chicago, before U.S. District Court Judge Prentice H. Marshall, Williams was sentenced to ten years for bribery, becoming the third Teamster president, after Dave Beck and Jimmy Hoffa, to be imprisoned. He remained free on appeal until 1985, when, because of emphysema and heart ailments, he began serving his sentence at the U.S. Medical Center for Prisoners in Springfield, Mo. Williams served three years of his sentence and was released on Sept. 27, 1988. He had testified for the government at two organized crime trials, and his parole was contingent on future cooperation.

Williams' leadership of the union was also tainted by mob connections. In 1985, in an effort to get his sentence reduced, Williams testified that he helped Kansas City crime boss Nick Civella obtain a $60 million loan from the Teamsters Central States Pension Fund. In return, Williams received $1,500 a month from 1974-81, and Civella's backing in union elections. Allegations of pension fund mismanagement also led to the slaying of Allen Dorfman in Lincolnwood, Ill., on Jan. 20, 1983. On Apr. 28, 1989, Williams died at his farm in Leeton, Mo. REF.: *CBA.*

Williams, Samuel Tito, prom. 1948, U.S., (wrong. convict.) mur. On Mar. 2, 1948, in New York City, Samuel Tito Williams was convicted of the 1947 murder of a 15-year-old Brooklyn girl, and sentenced to death. On Nov. 16, 1949, the day before Williams was to die in the electric chair, Governor Thomas Dewey commuted his sentence to life imprisonment. In 1963, after sixteen years in prison, Williams' conviction was overturned because his confession had been coerced. He was released and later received compensatory damages from the state for his "malicious prosecution." REF.: *CBA.*

Williams, Thomas Joseph, c.1923-42, Brit., mur. On Easter 1942, six members of the Irish Republican Army (IRA) shot to death Constable Patrick Murphy. Murphy was shot five times, three times with one weapon, twice with another. IRA members Thomas Joseph Williams, nineteen, Patrick Simpson, eighteen, William J. Perry, Henry Cordner, John T. Oliver, and Joseph Cahill were arrested. Ballistics tests linked them to the weapons. During the trial, Williams confessed to firing one of the weapons. On July 30, 1942, the six men were sentenced to be hanged. On Aug. 30, five of the men were reprieved. Simpson was resentenced to fifteen years in prison and Williams was condemned to die. REF.: *CBA.*

Williams, Thomas Sutler, 1872-1940, U.S., jur. Nominated to U.S. Court of Claims by President Herbert Hoover in 1929. He served as prosecuting attorney in Clay County, Ill., from 1908-15. REF.: *CBA.*

Williams, Wayne Bertram, 1958- , U.S., mur. Experience has taught the members of the Atlanta Police Department to expect eight, possibly ten child murders in a calendar year. Frequently the victim dies as a result of senseless domestic violence, be it a quarrel between siblings or the act of an abusive parent. These cases are usually cleared within days, freeing the police for other duties. In 1979, however, the city police force was alerted to the presence of a serial killer within the metropolitan area—one who preyed on young black children between the ages of seven and fourteen. Before the nightmare was over, various experts from across the country would be brought in to lend their special talents to a criminal investigation that dragged on for more than two years, one that sorely tested the resources of the city administration and its police force. In March 1981, President Ronald Reagan committed up to $1.5 million in federal funds to help defray costs of the investigation. At that time the death toll stood at twenty-six. It would climb to twenty-eight before a suspect would be formally charged.

The bodies of the first two victims were found lying adjacent to Niskey Lake on July 28, 1979. A man scavenging for tin cans stumbled across the remains of what he first thought to be a dead animal. Upon further investigation he noticed a pair of boy's pants, a belt, and a human torso. Lying in the underbrush some 150 feet away a second body was found. Forensic investigators identified the sets of remains as 13-year-old James Evans and 14-year-old Edward Smith. Both boys had disappeared from their Atlanta homes earlier in the week. Evans by all indications had been asphyxiated, while Smith was shot. The dual murders did not attract much press attention at the time, and neither did the discovery of the skeletal remains of 14-year-old Milton Harvey on Nov. 5. The youth was first reported missing in October after wandering away from his home in northwest Atlanta. The police were unable to determine the precise cause of death. Three days later a fourth black child was found, 9-year-old Yusef Bell, the son of noted civil rights worker Camille Bell from Mechanicsville. The boy disappeared after he had been sent out on an errand and was found in the maintenance shaft of an abandoned schoolhouse.

Nothing more was heard from the unknown assailant until March 1980, when the killing resumed with sickening regularity. Twelve-year-old Angel Lanier, the first female victim, was found tied to a tree with her panties stuffed in her mouth in early March. The fact that she had been raped puzzled the police who had concluded that the killer was a male homosexual. By July 1980, the death toll had climbed to twelve following the discovery of the bodies of Eric Middlebrooks, Christopher Richardson, Aaron Wyche, and LaTonya Wilson. The black community was convinced that the murders were racially motivated and carried out by a white supremacist. The police did not give much credence to this theory, believing that the presence of a white murderer in the all-black neighborhoods where these children lived would have eventually been detected by the local residents. In July, Camille Bell and the parent of Mary Mapp, one of the victims, called a press conference to announce the formation of the Committee to Stop the Children's Murders. Public Safety Commissioner Lee Brown, the first American black to receive a doctorate in criminology, was taken to task for his department's failure to apprehend a suspect by community activists and officials on the federal level. Former Attorney General Griffin Bell remarked, "I think you ought to be able to catch somebody. If you have more than twenty deaths, why isn't at least one person caught? That's what I hear people saying."

Atlanta mass murderer Wayne Williams greeting the press, 1980.

Brown responded by organizing a five-man task force to supplement the police investigation. "I have the utmost confidence in our investigation," Brown said. "I don't believe all knowledge rests in Georgia." By year's end the task force had been expanded in the wake of additional killings. Some of the leading figures in criminal investigation were brought in at Brown's behest, including retired Los Angeles Police Department Captain Pierce Brooks, who cracked the Onion Field murders, Lieutenant George Mayer of Stamford, Conn., who had worked on the "Merritt Parkway Bra" murders, and Lieutenant Gilbert Hill of Detroit who brought the Browning Gang to justice after they had murdered fifteen victims. Their presence failed to mollify anxious members of the black community who believed a policeman was responsible for the slayings. Law enforcement officials replied that the killer was in all likelihood a black teenager who was looked up to and trusted by his victims. A $100,000 reward was posted by the city, and additional cash incentives were put up by three recording companies and celebrities from the world of sports and entertainment. And still it continued. By March 1981, twenty bodies had been found. Autopsies showed that none of the victims to date were drugged or given alcohol. Only 23-year-old Michael McIntosh, found floating in the Chattahoochee River on Apr. 20, 1981, was completely disrobed.

The first major break in the case came on May 22 when police officer Fred Jacobs sat in his patrol car near a bridge spanning the river. He heard a resounding splash and then saw a man get into a station wagon. The information was relayed to a second patrol car driving in the vicinity. Before the station wagon could exit the bridge, the second patrol car stopped the driver for questioning. The police searched the vehicle and found some nylon rope, a pair of gloves, and a blood-stain on the front seat. The driver was identified as 23-year-old Wayne Williams, a black man who lived with his parents in a modest brick home in northwest Atlanta. Williams told the police that he was returning from a musical audition. He denied stopping on the bridge and swore he knew nothing about a bundle being dropped in the river. The police warned him that if a body turned up they would be calling him in for further questioning. Williams drove off.

Two days later the remains of Nathanial Cater, the twenty-eighth and final victim, was removed from the Chattahoochee River. An eyewitness told police that Williams and Cater, a 27-year-old homosexual, were seen leaving a movie theater together. A second witness came forward and told police that Williams had also been keeping company with Jimmy Ray Payne, a 21-year-old man pulled out of the muddy waters of the Chattahoochee on Apr. 27. Payne was reported missing after he failed to show up for a job interview.

Convinced that Williams was their man, police detectives sent the car seat containing the bloodstains to the state crime lab in Atlanta for analysis on June 4. It was found that the blood type matched that of Williams and Cater. Additionally, dog hairs found on the body of Cater were identical to those in Williams' car. The dog in question was Williams' German shepherd.

On June 18 Wayne Williams was indicted for the murders of Nathanial Cater and Jimmy Payne. The accused was the only child of Homer and Fay Williams, two retired schoolteachers from Atlanta. Mrs. Williams described her son as a "miracle child" who was born when she was forty-one. From the time he was a child Wayne's parents encouraged the learning process. They had invested all of their savings into radio equipment Wayne needed to start a radio station. A transmitter was installed in the family home, and it was powerful enough to broadcast a mile in each direction. The project failed and the family suffered financial hardship as a result. Williams was alternately described as a "media junkie" and a frustrated dreamer, obsessed with his own success and failings. He dabbled in photography and promoted himself as a talent scout. Williams printed leaflets offering young black men between the ages of eleven and twenty an opportunity to embark on a musical career through his influence. One of the men answering his ad was Patrick Rogers, an aspiring soul singer who was later murdered. Under heavy security, the murder trial of Wayne B. Williams began at the Fulton County Courthouse on Jan. 5, 1982. Superior Court Judge Clarence Cooper imposed a gag order on district attorney Lewis Slaton and defense attorneys Alvin Binder, and Mary Welcome, preventing them from discussing aspects of this highly controversial case with the media. Legal experts conceded that the prosecution faced an uphill battle trying to secure a conviction based solely on forensic evidence and the testimony of police officers. Though inadmissible in court, the most damaging evidence against Williams was the fact that the killing immediately stopped after he was taken into custody.

Williams took the stand on Feb. 22. He denied he was a homosexual and refuted the testimony of a youth who claimed to have been molested by him. "Ain't no way I'm a homosexual," he said. "I have no grudge against (homosexuals) as long as they keep their hands to themselves. I'm scared," he added. The jury, composed of eight blacks and four whites, retired on Feb. 27, 1982, to consider its verdict. After deliberating for less than twelve hours they returned a verdict of Guilty. Judge Cooper sentenced Williams to two consecutive life sentences. The verdict was upheld by the Georgia Supreme Court, amidst growing doubt that Williams was railroaded through unsupported circumstantial evidence. It was alleged that several of the witnesses were more interested in the reward money than securing justice for the defendant. Commented Homer Williams, "It's impossible to find a young man like this guilty." Since 1981, the city of Atlanta has not experienced a similar outbreak of child murder, suggesting that the police and the courts had been right all along.

REF.: Boar, *The World's Most Infamous Murders;* Cartel, *Serial Mass Murder; CBA;* Fox, *Mass Murder;* Wilson, *Encyclopedia of Modern Murder.*

Williams, William August Helm (AKA: **Lamont Woods, Colonel One**), 1940- , U.S., fraud-extor.-kid. Posing as a benefactor for the needy, William A.H. Williams visited the editor of the Atlanta *Constitution,* John R. "Reg" Murphy, on Feb. 20, 1974. He persuaded the 40-year-old editor to accompany him to his home in an Atlanta suburb to obtain goods for a charity. After the editor got into the car, Williams flashed a gun and informed the newspaperman that he had been kidnapped by a representative of the American Revolutionary Army. Murphy was bound, blindfolded, forced into the trunk of the car, and taken to a house where he was forced to make ransom tapes. The next day, the editor called a lawyer with the $700,000 ransom demand. Murphy and Williams stayed in a hotel the second night, and on Feb. 22, the two drove around for several hours before the abductor then picked up the ransom money. Shortly afterward, Williams released the editor.

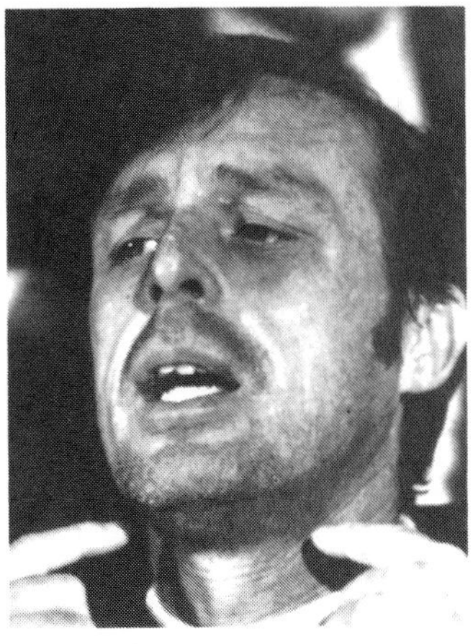

Kidnapped editor Reg Murphy.

Betty and William Williams; he was convicted of extortion.

Acting on a tip, police arrested Williams and his wife at their home in Lilburn, Ga., on Feb. 23, and recovered the ransom money. In custody, Williams, a self-employed contractor, admitted that the A.R.A. was fictitious. On Aug. 4, 1974, he was convicted on charges of extorting $700,000 from the newspaper, using the mails for the ransom demand, and using a firearm. On Dec. 21, 1976, Williams, thirty-six, was sentenced to a total of forty years in prison, twenty years for extortion and ten years each for the firearm and mail charges, all to be served consecutively. His 28-year-old wife, Betty Ruth Williams, was convicted of failing to report Williams' crimes. She was given a three-year suspended sentence with probation.

REF.: *CBA;* Messick, *Kidnapping.*

Williams, William S. (**AKA: Old Bill**), 1787-1849, U.S., rob. William Williams, a horse thief, Army scout, scalp hunter, and accused cannibal, was memorialized in the names of the Bill Williams River, Bill Williams Mountain, and the town of Williams, Ariz. In 1806, Williams stole a horse and left his home in the part of the Louisiana Purchase that is now Missouri. He was a trapper for a time, and from 1813-25 lived with the Osage Indians and scouted for the U.S. Army. Williams began scalping Indians for bounty in the 1830s, and joined scalpers James Hobbs and James Kirker in stealing scalp trophies from Indian camps. With mountain men Jim Beckwourth and "Pegleg" Smith, Williams created the largest horse-stealing band in California in the 1840s. They sold their horses in Utah, but soon disbanded due to stepped-up vigilance activity. Williams returned to scouting, and guided General John C. Fremont's disastrous railroad survey expedition in 1848. When the troops were caught in the La Garita Mountains of Colorado, eleven men froze to death, and Fremont fired Williams for incompetence and cannibalism. Ute Indians killed Williams in March 1849 in revenge for his killing several Utes the previous year. REF.: *CBA.*

Williams, Willie L., 1943- , U.S., law enfor. off. In 1962, Willie L. Williams began a long and meritorious career in public service in Philadelphia when he was employed as a clerk in the Department of Public Policy. Twenty-six years later, he was named police commissioner. He entered the police department in 1964 as a member of the Park Police, and was promoted to detective in 1972, sergeant in 1974, lieutenant in 1976, and captain in 1983 before attaining the rank of commissioner on June 10, 1988. Williams has also served as the executive officer of the Police Training Bureau, and was the commanding officer of the Civil Affairs Division. He is the recipient of ten departmental awards and commendations, and has been recognized by the Crisis Intervention Network, the Guardian Civic League, the Fraternal Order of Police, and the National Organization of Black Law Enforcement Executives. Commissioner Williams holds an associate degree in business administration from the Philadelphia College of Textiles and Science, and has attended the Northwestern University Traffic Institute Police Administration Program and the Harvard University Police Executive Research Forum. REF.: *CBA.*

Williams Farm Murders, 1921, U.S., mur. John Williams, a 58-year-old farmer from Jasper County, Ga., owned a sprawling 2,200-acre plantation thirty-five miles north of Macon. Over the years Williams and his sons ran the farm, and employed a group of poor black field-hands to harvest the crops and tend to chores. Slavery had ended with the collapse of the Confederacy in 1865, but Williams instituted his own system of peonage and involuntary servitude. "Mr. Johnny never did pay us off and we were all too scared of him to ask for money," one aging black man related to federal authorities. "Once he gave me a dollar but that's all the money I ever got. I worked for him in all about six years. Yes, sir, he always gave us plenty to eat and kept us in clean clothes." He neglected to add that Williams, or one of his boys, kept the field-hands shackled in balls and chains and under armed guard in a sweltering stockade by night. The conditions were beyond human endurance. Many of the victims chose death over continued enslavement at the Williams farm.

The bodies of three black men were found weighted down in the murky depths of the Yellow River in early March 1921. From Clyde Manning, a "trustee" on the Williams plantation, the authorities learned that there were other victims, possibly eleven, who had been killed after threatening to escape. Manning's startling confession led to the arrest and indictment of John Williams on Mar. 24. The farmer accused members of the Leverett family of framing these charges against him and his boys. A property dispute dating back nearly seven years was the cause of these present troubles, Williams said. "They also have claimed that I killed some of their live-stock. Last fall the Leverett boys charged my boys with turning up a still to the officers and we almost had a shooting scrape over that," Williams explained.

Manning led a team of federal and state officers to a remote spot in Jasper County where he identified the graves of five farm-hands whose skulls had been split open with an axe. "This is the Negro who would rather be shot than whipped," Manning said. "He ain't been buried long." Three other bodies were found weighted down under the Waters Bridge which spanned the Alcovy River. "Me and Mr. Williams took Charlie (Chisholm) to Waters Bridge. Charlie begged hard but Mr. Williams said: 'Throw him over,' so we weighted him pretty good at both ends and splash! That was the end of Charlie," Manning related in gruesome detail.

The coroner's jury believed that both victims were alive when they were thrown into the river. Manning, the self-confessed murderer of blacks, said that he had stood nearby while his victims were forced to dig their own graves. "Why did I do it? Because the boss Mr. Williams said he wanted to get rid of the Negroes and that if I didn't make them disappear he'd kill me." John Williams was convicted by a jury in Covington, Ga. on Apr. 9, for the murder of Lindsay Peterson, one of eighteen victims found in Newton and Jasper Counties. The conviction carried with it an automatic sentence of life imprisonment. Additional indictments were returned against John Williams' three sons, Hayler, Marvin, and Julius, as well as the field-hand "overseer," Clyde Manning. In his instructions to the jury, Judge Parks of the superior court expressed his sorrow. "Lawlessness in this section has now reached the point where it will cause us to be shunned unless we check it," he said. "We will soon reach the stage where no capital will come here and help us to develop our great natural resources." Williams was convicted of additional murders committed in Newton County on Feb. 1, 1922, and was handed a second life sentence. He passed away on Jan. 26, 1932, while serving his time. Manning was later convicted of murder but under appeal to a higher court the verdict was overturned. REF.: *CBA.*

Williamson, John, d.1767, Brit., mur. Apprenticed as a shoemaker, John Williamson was making an honest living when his wife, and the mother of his three children, died. He remained a widower for some time before meeting a woman whose mental condition bordered upon idiocy, and whose relatives had bequeathed money enough to support her. The cobbler proposed marriage, and though the proposal was opposed by her guardian, Williamson soon obtained a marriage license, and the money on marrying the woman was his.

Approximately three weeks after the wedding, Williamson began to savagely beat and cruelly treat his new bride. He placed the woman in a closet where her hands were shackled with handcuffs behind her back and then raised above her head with a rope looped through a link in the cuffs. Her hands were drawn above her head so tightly that only her toes could touch the floor of the closet. The shoemaker also deprived his wife of nourishment—leaving her a minimal amount of water each day and a tiny piece of bread with butter which he placed just within reach of her mouth. Once, the woman suffered these agonies for an entire month without release.

This cruelty however, did not go unnoticed or without attempts to relieve the woman's pain. A female lodger in the house and Williamson's daughter from his previous marriage gave the woman some assistance. The daughter even freed the woman once and on occasions when her father was absent placed a stool under the woman's feet to ease her pain. These attempts at relief were all met with violence from Williamson, who savagely beat his daughter and threatened to increase the severity of the punishment if she interfered again. Other women in the neighborhood knew of Williamson's barbarous treatment but did nothing to prevent it.

With his second wife in a weakened stage far beyond recovery, Williamson released her, and perhaps with the hope of being spared a murder charge, he gave her meat for Sunday dinner—though she ate very little. Following her meal she was allowed to warm herself in front of the fire, but when Williamson saw her throwing the bugs swarming around her clothing into the fire he sent her back to the closet. The next day she was delirious and at about 2 a.m. on Tuesday she died.

Dr. Barton, a surgeon at Redcross Street, performed the autopsy and declared that the woman had died from a lack of life's necessities. Williamson was arrested. The trial at the Old Bailey was presided over by Lord Chief Baron Parker, who condemned the defendant to death upon hearing the evidence of Williamson's daughter, Barton, and a Mrs. Cole. In his defense, Williamson claimed that his wife provoked him to treat her cruelly by stepping on and killing a kitten, and then upturning the whites of her eyes.

While awaiting execution, Williamson admitted his wrongs to a clergyman, but claimed he never intended to kill his wife. The gallows were erected in Moorfields, opposite Chiswell Street, and after singing a psalm and praying, Williamson was hanged before a large crowd on Jan. 19, 1767. The shoemaker's body was dissected at Surgeon's Hall and his children were sent to Cripplegate workhouse. REF.: *CBA.*

Williamson, Thomas Henry, See: **Benton, Wallace**.

Williamson Family (**AKA: The Terrible Williamsons**), c.1895- , U.S., fraud-rob.-asslt. For almost a century, the con artists descended from Robert Logan Williamson have bilked Americans in every state. Their swindles have changed with the times, but their tight-knit clan continues to expand. Recent estimates put their income at $5 million per year.

Robert Williamson moved from Scotland to Brooklyn in 1895, started his family, and quickly turned them into gypsies, picking up cheap merchandise in one place, and selling the goods elsewhere for fifteen or twenty times the price. The clan centered in Cincinnati, though it cannot be considered their home. The entire family returns there at least once a year. Outside of Cincinnati, they live out of their cars, usually very comfortable and expensive ones, taking over whole motels when they reach a destination.

Every member of the family is expected to return a portion of his or her take to the head of the family. The Williamsons often concentrate on door-to-door sales. Some hunt weathered houses and offer to paint them for a small amount of money. Their paint is adulterated with cheap oil so that by the time the painters have disappeared, money in hand, the paint is already running off the house. Other Williamsons sell bogus Irish lace, Persian rugs, "Harris tweed," or lightning rods sold as metal but made of wood. The most frequent arrests of the Williamsons are for peddling without a license. Usually those arrested put up bail and then disappear. The family regards such expense as a normal cost of doing business. In 1936, George C. Williamson once killed Isaac Cotton Williamson with a knife in an argument over which one had the right to work a certain territory. After attempting suicide, George was sent to jail for two years on a manslaughter conviction. The family is probably better known, however, to the Better Business Bureaus in major cities due to complaints received.

One member of the clan, Charles Williamson, disliked what his family was doing, and in 1938 began to notify Better Business Bureau officials of when the group was about to descend on a city. In 1966, more than 600 clan members swarmed over Los Angeles selling housing repairs.

REF.: *CBA;* Nash, *Hustlers and Con Men.*

Williamsons, Case of the, See: **Williams, John**.

Willis, Frances, and **Artegian, Rodney**, prom. 1975, U.S., mur. On Sept. 25, 1975, Frances Willis told Orlando, Fla., police that her husband James had been beaten and murdered by a group of wild-looking strangers. Police found that the man had been shot while asleep, with no signs of a beating. He had also drunk a can of beer laced with horse tranquilizer. His wife held a $17,000 insurance policy on his life.

Investigators found a handicapped cleaning man, Rodney Artegian, who confessed that Willis gave him $5,000 to kill her husband. Who actually fired the fatal shot was never clear, and Artegian and Willis were both tried for the murder. Artegian, who turned state's evidence, received a plea-bargained verdict of second-degree murder and was sentenced to fifteen years in prison. Willis was convicted of first-degree murder and sentenced to life imprisonment.

REF.: *CBA;* Godwin, *Murder U.S.A.*

Willis, George Henry, 1910- , Case of, Brit., mur. On Feb. 10, 1939, the body of 85-year-old Frederick James Paul was found in a pond near his cottage in Ascot, England. He had been shot in the head and neck with a double-barreled .410-caliber shotgun. George Henry Willis, a 29-year-old laborer, was implicated because he owned a double-barreled .410-caliber shotgun and had been seen near the murder site. However, the weapon was common in the British countryside and the sighting of Willis was not necessarily at the time of the murder, as a coroner stated that Paul had been killed two days before the body was found. In a very popular decision, a jury found Willis Not Guilty of murder.

REF.: *CBA;* Hastings, *The Other Mr. Churchill.*

Willis, James, 1900- , U.S., (wrong. convict.) rob. On Apr. 12, 1927, before Judge J.F. Pullen of the Superior Court of Sacramento County, James Willis was sentenced to San Quentin for from five years to life for first-degree robbery. Willis, twenty-seven, the son of a prominent California physician, was a drug addict, had a police record, and had been convicted twice in Washington state. He was convicted of three separate robbery incidents in Sacramento on Mar. 19, 1927, and was identified by all of the victims. However, at about the same time Vincent Bohac, twenty-three, confessed to Detroit police that he had committed the Sacramento crimes. In turn, Bohac was identified by all three victims, and sentenced in May 1927. Because of Willis' past record, he was not pardoned until Aug. 18, 1927. REF.: *CBA.*

Williston, Samuel, b.1861, U.S., jur. Legal scholar. He was a professor of law at Harvard University from 1895-1938, writing and editing several legal treatises and anthologies. REF.: *CBA.*

Willmott, Donna Jean, 1950- , U.S., pris. esc. Donna Jean Willmott and Claude Daniel Marks were last seen outside a prison wall in Leavenworth, Kan. Willmott is wanted for prison escape, damage and destruction of government property, receipt and transportation of explosives, interstate travel to promote criminal activity, and possession of unregistered firearms. She is proficient in martial arts and the use of firearms. At this writing, Willmott is still at large. REF.: *CBA.*

Willner, Josephine, b.1834, U.S., mur. On Mar. 2, 1876, in Milwaukee, Wis., 42-year-old Josephine Willner shot Dr. Garner at his front door. He died the following day. She left the murder scene and ate dinner at a hotel restaurant before she was apprehended by police. She said she shot the doctor because he had killed her husband, father, uncle, and brother. However, no evidence existed that any family member had been treated by Garner, while many testified to the mental instability of Willner. During her trial, there was no doubt that she had committed the murder, so the jury had to determine her sanity. In May 1876, they found her Guilty of the murder, but Judge James H. Mallory expressed shock that twelve people could find Willner sane. He obtained the certification of two doctors that she was hopelessly insane, and committed her to the Northern Hospital for the Insane at Oshkosh.

REF.: *CBA;* Derleth, *Wisconsin Murders.*

Wilmington Race Riots, 1898, U.S., mob vio. In the 1890s, blacks became more politically active in North Carolina, and Republicans, who promised increased black participation, began winning important seats in the state government. Republican

Daniel Russell, elected governor in 1896, appointed a black collector of customs in Wilmington. The appointments and the election of five blacks to North Carolina's House of Representatives led to the formation of white vigilante groups. One such group, the Red Shirts, used intimidation, assault, and murder to stop blacks from going to the polls. The North Carolina Democrats used "Negro domination" propaganda. One well-known Democrat, Alfred M. Waddell, said, "Go to the polls tomorrow and if you find the negro out voting, tell him to leave the polls and if he refuses, kill him...." The Democrats won the election, and two days later, whites rioted in the streets of Wilmington. They burned out a black newspaper office, began randomly killing blacks, forced all black officials to resign, and initiated the new government at gunpoint. With the old political order restored, blacks were again deprived of voting rights and subject to poll taxes and other abuses. REF.: *CBA*.

Wilmot, Thomas, c.1631-70, Brit. rob.-mur. The eldest son of John Wilmot, Esq. of Suffolk, Thomas Wilmot was easily taken advantage of by women who neither loved nor cared for him, and subsequently he soon squandered the £600 a year left to him upon his father's death. It is rumored that he was born with long hair and fangs with which he drew blood from the breast of the woman who was suckling him; which is believed to be an omen of the blood this adventurous highwayman would one day shed.

Although a brilliant young man capable of reading, writing, and speaking English, Dutch, French, Italian, and Spanish, Wilmot entered upon the life of a highwayman after falling prey to the wiles of women. His boldness was such that he would often assail two or three travelers at a time single-handedly. Once he accosted three women riding on the road between Dorking, Surrey and Petworth, Sussex. These three were soon relieved of about £8, and from one of the ladies he removed a diamond ring–which, unfortunately for the woman, could not be easily removed, whereat Wilmot barbarously removed the victim's finger as well as ring, stating that women especially should suffer his cruelty.

On one outing, Wilmot happened to rob who he presumed to be the wife of Thomas Blood–the man whose attempt to steal the Crown Jewels May 9, 1671, so delighted Charles II that the king pardoned the thief and even granted Blood an estate in Ireland valued at £500 a year. When the lady posing as Mrs. Blood protested to his gentleman qualities not to rob her, Wilmot answered, "As the falsehood of women has been the cause of my misfortune, and the only cross wind that has shipwrecked my felicity, you being one of the perfidious sex, you must not expect any favor at my hands; therefore deliver presently, or else Madam Blood, there will come blood of it indeed."

At being offered a half-crown by the woman, Wilmot added, "as no less than a crown would serve your husband, when he robbed the king, I'll have you to know that I'll not be put off with half a crown." Whereat the highwayman searched her and found 15 guineas and a silver thimble.

Having gambled away his horse, clothing, and most of his money, Wilmot soon found himself at the door of a house in Shropshire, penniless and tired. The owner of the home was entertaining a large party celebrating his wedding anniversary and informed him that no room could be spared; that is, except the room said to be haunted by the ghost of his grandfather's barber who had slit his own throat for the love of a chambermaid. Upon hearing the story and accepting the invitation Wilmot was soon alone in the believed-haunted room. He quickly set about his plan of robbing the revelers who were downstairs playing cards and dice.

By rubbing his face on the white surface of the wall, and arming himself with a razor he had in his pocket–which he spilt blood from his fingers upon–and a chamber pot–to represent the barber's basin–Wilmot was prepared to impersonate the ghost of the barber. Wilmot soon reached the room where the gambling was taking place without being noticed until a servant took fright; which the highwayman took as a cue to utter the phrase the husband of the house had told him the ghost always asks: "Will you be shaved?" It did not take long for the room to be cleared, nor for Wilmot to clear all the winnings from the table and quickly return to his bed laden with loot. In the morning, the erstwhile ghost related how he too had been attacked, having his hands cut while protecting his throat from the razor, and walked away from the house without the least suspicion.

A while later Wilmot fled to Switzerland after committing a robbery, and while there broke into a house at night and murdered three children, their parents, and a maid–for which the authorities executed two innocent people. Returning to England he robbed the Duke of Buckingham in Northamptonshire of more than 200 guineas. Wilmot was shortly arrested, condemned, and hanged for robbery, which was punishable by death at that time, in Northampton on Apr. 30, 1670. REF.: *CBA*.

Wilson, Alexander, prom. 1793, Scot., libel. In 1793, Alexander Wilson, an ornithologist and poet, published some satirical poems about certain manufacturers in Paisley, Scot. The subjects of the poems sued Wilson for libel. He was found Guilty and ordered to pay a small fine, and burn the remaining poems at the public market in Paisley. Unable to pay the fine, Wilson spent a short time in prison, and when released, left Scotland, in disgust, for the U.S.

REF.: Andrews, *Old-Time Punishments; CBA*.

Wilson, Billy, See: **Anderson, David L.**

Wilson, Catherine, 1822-62, Brit., mur. In 1853, Catherine Wilson went to work as a housekeeper for Captain Peter Mawer. He quickly grew fond of her and told her that he was leaving her something in his will. He soon died of an overdose of the colchicum that he was taking for his gout. Wilson took the supply of the virtually undetectable vegetable poison with her when she left. She was next seen at the home of Mrs. Soames with a man named Dixon, to whom she may have been married. Dixon died mysteriously, but an autopsy failed to reveal colchicum. Mrs. Soames died four months later for the £9 Wilson borrowed the previous day plus £10 for which Wilson forged a promissory note.

In 1862 while nursing Sarah Carnell, Wilson switched from colchicum to sulfuric acid. When the patient spat out her "medicine," it burned a hole through the carpet. Wilson was arrested for attempted murder, but the jury found her Not Guilty when the defense attorney convinced them that the pharmacist had made a mistake in filling the bottle of medicine. However, Wilson was immediately rearrested for the murder of Mrs. Soames. This time the jury found her Guilty and she was sentenced to death. Catherine Wilson was hanged on Oct. 20, 1862, before 20,000 people.

REF.: Brock, *A Casebook of Crime; CBA;* Kingston, *A Gallery of Rogues;* ____, *Remarkable Rogues;* Nash, *Look For the Woman;* O'Donnell, *Should Women Hang?;* Thompson, *Poisons and Poisoners;* Twyman, *The Best Laid Schemes.*

Wilson, Charles, See: **Great Train Robbery.**

Wilson, Constance, prom. 1862, Brit., mur. Sarah Carnell had separated from her husband, and in London in 1862, she befriended a widow, Constance Wilson. Carnell became ill after taking medication Wilson had given her for a minor ailment. Poison was found in the glass, and Constance Wilson was arrested for attempted murder. However, the evidence was scant and Wilson was acquitted. Two months later, it was discovered that Wilson was the lover of the Carnell's estranged husband, and she was arrested again. An examination revealed that several people had died under mysterious circumstances in her presence, often leaving a financial reward. She was tried before Justice Byles for the 1856 death of Mary Soames. Wilson was found Guilty and, shortly after, was hanged at Newgate prison.

REF.: *CBA;* Poynter, *Forgotten Crimes.*

Wilson, Dink (AKA: **McCarthy**), and **Wilson, Charles**, prom. 1893, U.S., burg.-rob.-mur. In August 1893, a Syracuse, N.Y., police detective was murdered during an attempted burglary. A suspect who said his name was McCarthy was arrested, but no criminal record for him was found. But Robert Pinkerton saw the suspect's photograph and identified the man as Dink Wilson, wanted for railroad robbery since 1891. Wilson confessed his identity, and further Pinkerton information led to the arrest of the robber's brother, Charles Wilson. They were both convicted of murder. Dink Wilson was electrocuted at Sing Sing, and Charles Wilson was sentenced to life imprisonment.

REF.: *CBA;* Horan, *The Pinkertons.*

Wilson, Earl, 1952- , U.S., mur. On Nov. 18, 1986, on Chicago's South Side, flamboyant drug dealer Willie "Flukey" Stokes, forty-nine, was gunned down, execution-style, while riding in his car. Stokes' driver, 28-year-old Ronald Johnson, was also killed. The three gunmen were not apprehended, but Stokes' bodyguard, 34-year-old Earl Wilson, was arrested for complicity in the murders. He had been in a car following Stokes' on the night of the murder, and was alleged to have communicated with the murderers via car phone. In Wilson's Autumn 1987 trial, the defense claimed that he was working as an informant for the state's attorney and had provided daily information about Stokes. The prosecution countered that Wilson had aspired to Stokes' position as a drug kingpin, noting that he had not released the names of his co-conspirators. On Jan. 7, 1988, in the Cook County criminal courtroom of Judge Ronald Himel, Wilson was convicted of the double murder and sentenced to life imprisonment without the possibility of parole. REF.: *CBA.*

Wilson, Eddie, and **Peters, Warren**, prom. 1975, U.S., burg.-rob.-kid.-rape-mur. On Oct. 22, 1975, Curtis Arrington and Lois Ann Davis were murdered in a Washington, D.C., ghetto apartment. Arrington was found stabbed sixty-one times, and Davis, forty-three times. They were the victims of a gang of drug addicts who were looking for one of Arrington's friends. The killers were apprehended through police contacts, but the trial became somewhat unwieldy. The two suspects, Eddie Wilson and Warren Peters, pleaded guilty to 103 charges each, including kidnapping, rape, armed robbery, burglary, and auto theft, as well as the double murder. Superior Court judge Nunzio, overwhelmed by the number of confessions, accidentally overlooked the murder charges and sentenced the two to only twenty-eight years in prison. When confronted with his oversight, the judge exclaimed, "That was the biggest mistake I ever made. I didn't know then what I know now."

REF.: *CBA;* Godwin, *Murder U.S.A.*

Wilson, Edwin, 1928- , U.S., smug.-mur. A former secret agent for the CIA, Edwin Wilson smuggled explosives into Libya and used U.S. Special Forces personnel to train Libyan terrorists. In 1976, Libyan dictator Muammar Qaddafi agreed to buy Wilson's expertise on the U.S. military, arms, explosives, and covert operations. Wilson organized, financed, and directed a group of ten men with U.S. Army Special Forces experience to work in Libya training terrorists. Wilson also brought to Libya another group of Americans with expertise in explosives. A grand jury indicted Wilson in 1980 for smuggling twenty tons of explosives and other weapons into Libya. Wilson was a fugitive for a few years, but when he was lured back to the U.S., he was arrested. Wilson was convicted in November 1982 and sentenced on Feb. 18, 1983, to seventeen years in prison for smuggling explosives and fifteen years for smuggling weapons.

While in prison awaiting his trial, Wilson had asked fellow inmate Wayne Trimmer to help him find a hit-man to kill the prosecutors, his former business partner, and several witnesses in his case. He offered a total of $1.25 million for seven or eight killings. The inmate went to the federal authorities and became a key witness against Wilson. Wilson then offered two other inmates money to kill Trimmer and to arrange for another hit-man to kill the people involved in his trial. Those two inmates also went to the federal authorities. An undercover FBI agent met Wilson's son, Erik Wilson, in a hotel room and collected a $9,800 down payment from him. Wilson was charged with attempted murder. Following his trial, which began on Oct. 4, 1983, Wilson was convicted and sentenced to twenty years in prison. He was put in solitary confinement at the federal prison in Marion, Ill. REF.: *CBA.*

Wilson, Elizabeth, 1874-1928, Fr., (unsolv.) mur. Elizabeth and Henry Wilson, a British couple, were living in France in the 1920s. Visiting friends at Le Touquet, they played golf on the afternoon of May 19, 1928. Elizabeth, fifty-four, left early, arranging to meet the others at the hotel at 7:30 and she set off at a fast pace along the edge of the golf course. Other friends saw her on the road and offered her a lift, but she turned it down and walked into a wooded area. Her strangled body was found there the next morning. Her underclothes had been removed, but she had not been raped. Stab wounds had been made in her body after death, and her empty purse lay nearby.

The police became convinced that Elizabeth Wilson had had an assignation and that that was why she refused the ride. But the murder remains unsolved.

REF.: *CBA;* Greenwall, *They Were Murdered in France;* Heppenstall, *Bluebeard and After;* Jacobs, *Pageant of Murder;* Morain, *The Underworld of Paris;* Nash, *Look For the Woman;* ____, *Open Files.*

Wilson, Frank J., 1887-1970, U.S., law enfor. off. Before he became chief of the Secret Service in 1936, Frank J. Wilson developed the case that won Al Capone's conviction and imprisonment for tax evasion. Elmer I. Irey, chief of the Internal Revenue Service Enforcement Branch, assigned Wilson to expose Capone's tax evasion. Using a 1927 Supreme Court decision that subjected income acquired from illegal activity to income tax, Irey saw a means of prosecuting the gangster kingpin. As Capone did not file returns, own property, endorse checks, maintain bank accounts, or give receipts, Wilson had to determine Capone's net worth and net expenditure to gather evidence for a case. Wilson had his men infiltrate Capone's organization. Capone became so nervous he ordered five New York gunmen to assassinate Wilson. But federal agents heard of the contract, and eventually Capone's old mentor, Johnny Torrio, convinced him to call off the killers. Wilson's case eventually sent Capone to prison.

As the federal representative in the Lindbergh kidnapping case, Wilson insisted that the serial numbers on the ransom money be recorded. Because this was done, Bruno Richard Hauptmann was arrested, convicted, and executed. Wilson served as chief of the Secret Service from 1936 to 1947, and nearly eliminated the production and distribution of counterfeit money. He also initiated procedures in presidential security that have since become standard practice. He retired in 1947 and died on June 22, 1970. REF.: *CBA.*

Wilson, Frank Wiley, 1917- , U.S., jur. Nominated by President John F. Kennedy to the eastern district court of Tennessee in 1961. He published numerous legal works. REF.: *CBA.*

Wilson, Harriette, 1786-1840s, Brit., pros.-blk. Harriette Wilson, one of the fifteen children of a Swiss watchmaker, found entrance to high society by working as a prostitute. The business was so lucrative that three of her six sisters joined her. At age fifteen, Wilson became the mistress of Lord Craven and began a series of affairs with titled men, culminating in a much-publicized encounter with the Duke of Wellington. Later, Wilson married a bogus colonel, William Henry Rochfort. The two moved to Paris and spent Wilson's fortune on liquor and gambling.

In 1825, Wilson published her *Memoirs,* for which she earned £10,000. She gave each of her famous lovers an opportunity to be excluded from the work—for a price. A large number of noblemen gladly paid the price. However, the Duke of Wellington returned his "extortion" letter without money, stating in red ink: "Publish and be damned." The publisher was sued for libel and other damages, but the book was published in thirty-one editions during the first year alone, and became a popular item in pirated editions all over Europe. Wilson later sank into obscurity, emerging briefly in 1829 to sue her brother for having sexual relations with her maid. She is thought to have returned to England and to have died sometime in the 1840s.

REF.: Bullough, *An Illustrated History of Prostitution; CBA.*

Wilson, Sir Henry Hughes, 1864-1922, Brit., assass. Field-Marshal Henry Wilson was held personally responsible for what came to be known as the "Orange Terror" by members of Sinn Fein. In his capacity as military advisor to the Parliament of Northern Ireland, Wilson raised and organized the Ulster Special Constables to root out and crush the Irish Republican Army (IRA). To the Irish Catholics and Free Staters of Belfast, Wilson was a hated symbol of British oppression. In Spring 1922, he was marked for death by Michael Collins, head of the Irish Provisional Government.

Wilson was born in Currygrane, Edgeworthstown, County Longford, in what later became the Republic of Ireland. He attended Marlborough College, working tirelessly toward a career in the military—a goal seemingly thwarted after he failed to gain admission to Woolwich and Sandhurst. In 1882 Wilson was commissioned in the Longford Militia (then the Sixth Battalion, Rifle Brigade), and later the 18th Royal Irish Regiment. His rise through the ranks was steady if not spectacular. During the Boer War, Wilson was named to the headquarters staff after distinguishing himself under the command of Major-General Neville Lyttelton. In 1913, the year before war broke out on the continent, Wilson was promoted to major-general. Impressed with his gruff, plain-speaking manner, Prime Minister David Lloyd George named Wilson chief of the Imperial General Staff in February 1918. A year later he was made a field marshal.

Throughout his career in public life, Wilson was an uncompromising foe of the Sinn Fein movement, a Protestant who advocated drastic military measures against them. He expressed these views on more than one occasion following his election to Parliament as a conservative member from North Downe in February 1922. In May he toured war-torn Northern Ireland where he delivered several incendiary speeches against the Sinn Fein, and advised the government on the policing of the new frontier. Wilson returned to London the next month, not knowing that Michael Collins had issued secret orders to Sam Maguire, the chief spy in London for the IRA, to execute the Field-Marshal by whatever means necessary.

On June 22, 1922, Wilson appeared in full-dress uniform on Liverpool Street, London, where he dedicated the GER Memorial with great solemnity. When the ceremony ended he returned to his home on Eaton Place by cab. After paying the taxi driver, Wilson turned toward his residence. Before he could enter, two men accosted him with pistols. Sensing the danger, Wilson drew out his sword and prepared to do battle with the assailants but he was cut down in a hail of gunfire. Wilson died a short time later in his residence.

The two IRA assassins were cornered on Ebury Street after they had turned their guns on a police detective and a passerby. The two men were quickly subdued and taken into custody. They were identified as Reginald Dunne and Joseph O'Sullivan, both twenty-four, and recruited from the ranks of the military by the IRA. O'Sullivan lost a leg during the war, while Dunne had attained the rank of lance corporal. Nothing in their past suggested they were members of any criminal group but had acted purely out of political conviction.

The two men were tried before Justice Montague Shearman at the Central Criminal Court on July 2 for murder. Ballistic evidence supplied by Sir Bernard Spilsbury was overwhelming. He told the court in precise detail the position in which the murderers stood when they fired their shots. "Wilson was not shot after he had fallen," Spilsbury wrote. "All nine wounds were inflicted when he was erect or slightly stooping, as he would be when tugging at his sword hilt." The prisoners were found Guilty and hanged at Wandsworth on Aug. 10, 1922. Before he died on the gallows, Dunne wrote a statement to the British courts which read, "The same principle for which we shed out blood on the battleground of Europe led us to commit the act we are charged with. You may by your verdict find us guilty, but we will go to the scaffold justified by the verdict of our conscience." See: **Irish Republican Army**.

REF.: Browne and Tullett, *The Scalpel of Scotland Yard; CBA;* Melville, *Famous Duels and Assassinations;* Nash, *Almanac of World Crime;* Paine, *The Assassins' World;* Sparrow, *The Great Assassins.*

Wilson, James, 1742-98, U.S., jur. James Wilson was one of the original associate justices of the U.S. Supreme Court. Born in Fifeshire, Scot., on Sept. 14, 1742, Wilson was educated at universities in St. Andrews, Glasgow, and Edinburgh before arriving in America in 1766. He was elected to the Second Continental Congress in 1775, but was relieved of the position two years later. For the next ten years, he speculated in questionable business investments which brought great financial reward. But later he was financially ruined and publicly disgraced. In 1789, Wilson was appointed to the Supreme Court by President George Washington, and served until 1798, despite criminal allegations which forced him to flee the capital, and even landed him in jail. While seeking refuge in Edenton, N.C., the hometown of fellow justice James Iredale, Wilson died, at age fifty-five, on Aug. 21, 1798. REF.: *CBA.*

Wilson, James, 1900- , Case of, N. Zea., mur. James Wilson operated a gas station in Auckland, N. Zea., with his 56-year-old wife, Norah. On Aug. 31, 1954, Norah Wilson died from arsenic poisoning found in her stomach medicine. In March, six months after Mrs. Wilson's death, James was placed on trial for her murder. Experts believed she had received small doses of arsenic for an extended time before her death. A month before her death, the doses of medicine had been increased. It was shown that on at least one occasion the accused poisoner had suffered the same symptoms as his wife. The clinical evidence was not conclusive.

The prosecution conceded that the arsenic found in Mrs. Wilson's body could have come from medication she had taken the night before. The source of the arsenic never was clearly established. The woman might have prepared the fatal potion herself from garden weed killer readily available. In October, Wilson was acquitted.

REF.: *CBA;* Dunning, *The Arbor House Treasury of True Crime;* Smith, *Mostly Murder.*

Wilson, James Clifton, 1874-1951, U.S., jur. Nominated to northern district court of Texas by President Woodrow Wilson in 1919. He had served as U.S. Attorney in Ft. Worth, Texas, from 1913-17 and as a U.S. congressman from 1917-19. REF.: *CBA.*

William Wilson, who fired on a group of school children, killing two on Sept. 26, 1988.

Wilson, James William, 1969- , U.S., mur. Described as "difficult to manage" and "volatile" by psychiatrists, James William Wilson more than lived up to his description when, in the fall of 1988, he opened fire on the children and staff of an elementary school in South Carolina, leaving nine people wounded and two children dead.

Wilson was 19-years-old when the shooting took place on Sept. 26, 1988, and had been under psychiatric care from the age of fourteen, being hospitalized six times from May 1983 to April 1988. He lived in Greenwood, S.C., with his paternal grandmother. He had been there ever since his father had asked the boy to move out of the family home—about the time he began psychiatric treatment—because Wilson's father feared for his family's well-being. At seventeen Wilson dropped out of high school and was unable to hold any type of employment.

Between the year he left school, 1986, and the rampage, Wilson's family had twice attempted to have the boy involuntarily committed to a mental institution; each time the court rejected the petition. His grandmother noted that Wilson, who was on medication for his mental state up until two months prior to the killings, would stay awake throughout the night reading, often going to bed at 8 a.m. Wilson would read books and articles on murderers, most notably serial killer John Wayne Gacy (who Wilson read about the night before his shooting spree in Tim Cahill's and Russ Ewing's book, *Buried Dreams: Inside the Mind of a Serial Killer*) and Laurie Dann, whose assault upon a Winnetka, Ill., elementary school was not only similar to Wilson's, but as the killer himself said, in the *People* magazine article on the case, "I read it every day. I had it for a few months. I could understand where she was coming from. I think I may have copied her in a way."

According to forensic psychiatrist Dr. Donald Morgan, Wilson was suffering–and still is–from "borderline personality disorder," which impaired his knowing right from wrong, when he drove to his paternal grandmother's home in nearby Abbeville to arm himself with a nine-shot pistol, his father having removed any guns from the place Wilson currently lived six months previously on account of his son's disposition.

After purchasing two boxes of ammunition at a discount store, Wilson pulled into the front drive of the Oakland Elementary School in Greenwood where he loaded the .22-caliber handgun, placing extra bullets in his shirt pocket, and entered the building through the front door.

It was shortly after 11 a.m. when Wilson appeared in the school's cafeteria and opened fire, wounding three students and a teacher in a crowd of about 100 first-graders and a third-grade class. The gunman left the lunchroom, having discharged all nine shots, making his way down the hallway to a girls' restroom where he reloaded his weapon. Upon leaving the restroom Wilson was confronted by physical education teacher Kat Finkbiener, who was shot in the mouth and hand while attempting to stop him.

Wilson continued down the hall entering a classroom where one of the twenty-two third-graders said that she laughed at his appearance on first seeing the overweight gunman, but added, "I wasn't laughing when he began shooting.

In that room Wilson shot and wounded four children and killed two others: Shequila Bradley, eight, who was shot once in the forehead, and Tequila Thomas, eight, who died three days later from wounds to her neck and chest. When he had run out of ammunition, Wilson dropped the gun and left the room, surrendering himself to principal Eleanor Rice who asked him to stop and held him until the police arrived.

Following a plea of guilty but mentally ill, Eighth Circuit Court Judge James E. Moore sentenced Wilson, who had waived his right to a jury trial, to death by electrocution. The death sentence, which is the first such case for a plea of guilty but mentally ill, has created controversy over the state's law concerning such a plea.

The defense counsel for Wilson, David G. Belser and William H. Nicholson III, argued that a person declared mentally ill should not be sentenced to death because the penalty is too severe for someone who did not know he was breaking a law. Eighth Circuit Solicitor Townes Jones contends for the prosecution that the statute concerning a plea of guilty but mentally ill does allow for a death sentence and added vehemently that "Jamie Wilson decided to act and live in a certain way. He chose to live the way he did. We have a man who chose as his heroes John Wayne Gacy, a serial murderer, and Laurie Dann, a murderer. He didn't choose to save lives. He chose to destroy them."

Along with the death sentence, Wilson was also sentenced to 175 years in prison on various charges stemming from the wounds he inflicted. He is currently awaiting appeal of his sentence on death row at the Central Correctional Institution in Columbia, S.C. See: **Dann, Laurie Wasserman; Gacy, John Wayne, Jr.** REF.: *CBA*.

Wilson, Jerry V., 1928- , U.S., law enfor. off. Jerry Williams spent twenty-five years as a police officer in the District of Columbia, including five years as chief of police. Born Mar. 23, 1928, in South Hills, Va., Wilson served in the U.S. Navy and the U.S. Marine Corps from 1943-47, and joined the Washington, D.C., Police Department in 1949. After attaining various ranks, he was named budget officer in 1960, director of planning in 1965, and assistant chief for field operations in 1968 before becoming the position of chief of police in 1969. He served until 1974, when he retired to his present position, as corporate vice president for security for Peoples Drug Stores, Inc. Wilson authored many books and monographs, including: *Police Report: A View of Law Enforcement* (1975), *Police and the Media* (1975), *The Investigator's Handbook* (1977), and *Terrorism: The Executive's Guide to Survival* (1977). He also wrote a weekly column for the Wasington *Post* in 1974-75. REF.: *CBA*.

Wilson, Jimmie, 1903- , U.S., rob. On July 27, 1957, in Marion, Ala., Jimmie Wilson, a 55-year-old black man, robbed Estelle Barker, an 82-year-old white woman, of $1.95. He was convicted of robbery and sentenced to die in the electric chair. According to Wilson, Barker gave him the money as an advance on what she owed him for yard work. Barker claimed Wilson threatened her and then tried to rape her after she gave him the money. The state supreme court denied Wilson's request for a retrial and scheduled his execution for late October 1958. After overwhelming international protest, Governor James E. Folsom commuted Wilson's sentence to life imprisonment on Sept. 29, 1958. REF.: *CBA*.

Wilson-Lyon Duel, c.1809, Can., Case of, duel-mur. In 1833, John Wilson and Robert Lyon were combatants in Canada's last fatal duel. Wilson was a 24-year-old law student in Perth, Ontario, who had a crush on Elizabeth Hughes, the daughter of the local Unitarian minister. Another student, Henri LeLiévre, was also attracted to Hughes. On Valentine's Day, Wilson sent an unsigned love poem to another romantic interest of his, Caroline Thom, which was intercepted by Simon Robertson, who signed the name Robert Lyon. An irate Lyon learned the identity of the true author, Wilson, and mistakenly challenged him to a duel. Wilson, facing public humiliation, as well as losing the attention of Hughes, was forced to accept the challenge.

On June 13, 1833, amid heavy rain, Lyon and Wilson counted their paces, turned, and fired. Neither was hit, and it was suggested that honor had been restored and the affair was over. But, Leliévre, citing an 1780 Tipperary dueling code, said that since no blood had been drawn or apology offered, the duel must continue. The duelists reluctantly fired a second shot, and Lyon was struck and killed. Wilson and his second, Robertson, surrendered to the police in Perth. During the trial on Aug. 9, 1833, in Brockville, Ontario, it became obvious that the real culprit was LeLiévre, who goaded the two into a second round. The jury found Wilson Not Guilty and he married Hughes.

REF.: *CBA*; Miller, *Twenty Mortal Murders*.

Wilson, John, b.1829, Case of, U.S., mur. On Oct. 28, 1844, in rural downstate Illinois, fifteen-year-old John Wilson, stabbed a man to death with a pitchfork after the man told Wilson he was lazy. During the trial the following spring, the boy did not have an attorney, until Abraham Lincoln rose from the audience and offered to help him. The prosecution built a strong case. Then, Lincoln told of Wilson's life; how he was the victim because he was forced to work like an adult after his father died, and how the man Wilson killed had been repeatedly cruel to the boy. Wilson rightfully belonged in school, not prison, Lincoln told the court. The jury agreed and returned a verdict of Not Guilty, at which Wilson fainted into the arms of Lincoln. REF.: *CBA*.

Wilson, John Gleeson, c.1820-49, Brit., rob.-mur. In March 1849, John Gleeson Wilson was a boarder in the rooming house of a Mrs. Henrickson in Liverpool, England. The woman asked Wilson to leave when he refused to pay a week's rent. Later, as she was out shopping, a delivery man went to the house. Wilson answered the door covered in blood, and soon, Henrickson returned home for the last time. After Wilson was seen leaving, nervous neighbors forced their way into the home and discovered the bodies of Henrickson, and her two sons, ages four and six. Their throats had been slit. Henrickson's maid lived and was able to identify Wilson as the murderer. Four days later, Wilson was apprehended. He was quickly convicted of the murders and sentenced to death. Wilson was hanged in front of a crowd numbering in the tens of thousands at Kirkdale Jail.

REF.: Brock, *A Casebook of Crime;* Butler, *Murderers' England; CBA;* Logan, *Masters of Crime;* ____, *Rope, Knife and Chair.*

Wilson, John Wayne 1949-73, U.S., suic.-mur. On Jan. 1, 1973, Roseann Quinn became New York City's first homicide victim of the year. She was strangled, stabbed eleven times, and mutilated beyond recognition. Six days later, 24-year-old John Wayne Wilson was arrested in Indianapolis, Ind., for the murder. He told homicide detectives that he had picked the girl up in a singles' bar, and after sleeping together, the girl severely scratched his back in an effort to throw him out of the apartment. In addition, Wilson told his attorney that he had been mocked by the girl for being impotent. Prison psychologists diagnosed Wilson as schizophrenic with homicidal and suicidal tendencies. He hanged himself in his cell before he could be brought to trial for Quinn's murder. The case served as a model for the book, and subsequent movie, *Looking for Mr. Goodbar.*

REF.: *CBA;* Godwin, *Murder U.S.A.*

Wilson, Mary Elizabeth (AKA: **The Widow of Windy Nook**), b.1891, Brit., mur. If not for a casual remark said in jest Mary Wilson might have slipped through the hands of British authorities and otherwise been forgotten. Instead, she became the first woman sentenced to death under the terms of the recently enacted Homicide Act and the first person to be convicted and sentenced under it for multiple murder.

Mary Elizabeth Wilson, the merry "widow of Windy Nook," disposed of two of her three husbands in a year's time. In Summer 1956 at age sixty-five, when she was a widow for the first time, (Mary's first husband, John Knowles, was a retired chimney sweep) Wilson was introduced to 76-year-old Oliver James Leonard, a real-estate agent. "Has the old (man) any money?" she asked her friend, Mrs. Alice Mary Connelly, who owned a lodging house where the man lived. "A little as far as I know," came the reply. The widow Knowles and Leonard were married a short time later. The marriage lasted several months. On Oct. 3, 1956, Leonard died unexpectedly. Two days later a death certificate was signed by Dr. John Hubert Laydon listing the cause of death as "degeneration of the heart with some inflammation of the kidneys." Dr. Laydon, who had prescribed some mild cough medicine just two days earlier, said that Leonard was in good health for his age. Asked how he had known the man was dead, Dr. Laydon replied, "Some person came in and told me Mr. Leonard was dead and I filled in the death certificate." Under British law a physician was permitted to issue a death certificate if he had seen the patient within fourteen days of death.

Several weeks after Leonard's death, his son by a former marriage asked the widow about the will. "There wasn't much," she explained. All that was left was £45 to £75. Husband number three was Ernest George Lawrence Wilson, a retired engineer who met Mary while seeking out a housekeeper. He intimated that he was seeking a life companion and had £100 in the Cooperative Society to his name. This, coupled with a small insurance policy, enticed Mary into a marriage with the 76-year-old Wilson. At the reception a wedding guests asked Mary what she planned to do with the cakes and sandwiches that were in abundance. "Just keep them for the funeral, although I might give this one a week's extension," she laughed. Her whimsy was forgotten until Wilson died on Nov. 11, 1957. Earlier that day Dr. William Proudfoot Wallace was summoned to their home by Mrs. Wilson who reported that her husband had become sick during the night. The physician decided that Wilson was suffering from myocardio degeneration of the heart and prescribed a cough medicine and some pills. The next morning he received a second call from Mary Wilson who said that her husband's condition had worsened. By the time he arrived at the home, Ernest Wilson was dead. Dr. Wallace listed the cause of death as cardio-vascular failure on the death certificate. Three days after the body was interred in the ground Mary Wilson drew out £24 on two of her husband's life insurance policies.

These highly suspicious circumstances came to the attention of pathologist Dr. William Stewart, who ordered that the remains of John Knowles, Ernest Wilson, and Oliver Leonard be exhumed. Stewart arrived at the conclusion that Wilson and Leonard had been poisoned. The presence of elemental phosphorus was found in their systems, a substance used in rat and beetle poisons. When confronted about her flippant remarks at the wedding reception, Mary Wilson shot back, "I know I upset some people by that joke at my wedding. But I think that really people are jealous of me because I have always tried to laugh my way through life. I've had plenty of troubles but I believe in keeping cheerful. My conscience is clear. I have looked after all my men as a good wife should." She added that if the right opportunity came along she would consider marrying again.

Mary was indicted for the double murder of Leonard and Wilson. The trial went before Justice Hinchcliffe at the Leeds Assizes in March 1958. In his opening remarks, Geoffrey Veale, representing the Crown, described Mrs. Wilson as a "wicked woman who in succession married two men and then deliberately poisoned them in order to get the paltry benefits she hoped she might obtain from their deaths." In defense of her client, Attorney Rose Heilbron produced scientific evidence to show that phosphorus was commonly used in prescription medicine to cure rickets, nervous disorders, and on occasion could serve as a sexual stimulant. "What more natural than that these old men, finding a wife in the evening of their lives, should purchase these pills for the purpose for which they are apparently known," she concluded. Druggist Angus Fraser McIntosh explained that it would take 150 of these pills to bring on death.

Acting under the advice of her attorney, Mary Wilson did not appear as a witness on her on behalf. This left many unanswered questions. Why wasn't a doctor called in earlier? On the day of Wilson's death she had attempted to sell an expensive gold watch, which was hardly the rational act of a grieving widow. The jury returned a Guilty verdict after debating the matter for an hour and a half. Justice Hinchcliffe sentenced her to death in his first murder trial. Because of her advanced age however, she was eventually reprieved.

REF.: *CBA;* Furneaux, *Famous Criminal Cases, vol. 5.*

Wilson, Nathaniel (AKA: **Buster Wilson**), d.1980, U.S., (unsolv.) mur. Rock and roll singer Buster Wilson, formerly of the 1950s' group The Coasters, was appearing in a Las Vegas lounge in 1980 when he disappeared. No one reported him missing, and six weeks later his mutilated body was found in a canyon near Modesto, Calif. He had apparently been killed elsewhere, his hands and feet were cut off, and he was moved to the canyon.

At the time he died, Wilson shared a house with his manager, Patrick Cavanaugh, who was thoroughly investigated. Cavanaugh was later arrested in San Diego for defrauding businessmen of $500,000, but Wilson's murder remains unsolved.

REF.: *CBA;* Nash, *Open Files.*

Wilson, Norah, See: **Wilson, James.**

Wilson, Ocie, d.1925, U.S., lynch.-mur. In June 1925, in Slater, Mo., Ocie Wilson killed Romeo Logan. Wilson was apprehended, and while on the way to jail, he was kidnapped by twelve men who cornered the squad car. His body was found the next morning, hanging from a tree. In an era of racially motivated lynching, this case is unusual in that both Wilson and Logan were black. REF.: *CBA*.

Wilson, Otto Stephen, c.1910-46, U.S., mur. Although outwardly calm and alluring, Otto Stephen Wilson was capable of murder. He choked to death and mutilated the bodies of two women he met for the first time less than seven hours apart.

Before Wilson began his brutal murder spree he got extremely drunk. Still in a drunken stupor two days later, the former Navy man purchased a butcher knife with a nine-inch blade, and, in this same state he met Mrs. Virginia Lee Griffin, his first victim, in one of Los Angeles' seedier bars.

Although married, the 25-year-old Griffin agreed to accompany Wilson to the Barclay Hotel. She told Wilson as the two entered the hotel that her horoscope said Wednesday was her lucky day. Wednesday Nov. 15, 1944, proved anything but lucky for Griffin. By 8 a.m. the next day she was dead.

Wilson claimed that Griffin, after sharing a few drinks in the hotel room, had demanded more money from him. At that point the shipyard commissary fry cook hit Griffin and choked her until she stopped breathing and then mutilated and dismembered the corpse beyond recognition.

On leaving the room Wilson paid the chambermaid $1 "not to disturb his wife." He ended up in another bar and not long after he and Mrs. Lillian Johnson, thirty-eight, were in a room at the nearby Joyce Hotel. After Johnson removed her clothes, Wilson strangled her. By then he realized the butcher knife had been left behind at the Barclay Hotel, so after giving himself a shave with the razor he carried with him, Wilson slashed Johnson's body, cutting his hand in the process.

When Wilson told the hotel desk clerk not to disturb his sleeping wife it was already 3 p.m. on Thursday, and an hour earlier the police had discovered what was left of Griffin; one-half hour later they would learn of Johnson's murder as well.

The Los Angeles Police Department was quick to track down this homicidal maniac. Patrolman Harry E. Donlan noticed a man with a cut on his hand and blood on his mustache talking to woman in a bar not far from the Joyce Hotel. It was Wilson. Just two hours after the discovery of Johnson's body her murderer was in custody.

At first Wilson denied the bloody crimes but later confessed saying Griffin's demand for more money angered him. As for Johnson he said, "for some reason—just pure cussedness, I guess—I hit her."

Authorities in Tulsa, Okla., suspected Wilson in two other murders when they noted similarities between his brutal acts and the killings of Luzila Stewart and her daughter Georgia Green, on Jan. 14, 1943.

Wilson was convicted of the Griffin and Johnson murders and received the death penalty. He was executed in the gas chamber at San Quentin, Sept. 20, 1946. REF.: *CBA*.

Wilson, Philip Morrel, 1937- , U.S., fraud-org. crime. In 1965, Philip Wilson had the reputation the most prolific writer of substandard insurance policies in Missouri. From these humble beginnings Wilson branched out to international fraud. In 1966 John Christian Konig, a 22-year-old British speculator, founded the offshore bank of Sark in the Channel Islands. Konig gambled with his large inheritance, but proved to be a poor businessman. Offshore banking was considered a lucrative new area of investing despite Konig's inept track record, and Wilson was anxious to cash in. Through an intermediary, John Risely-Pritchard, Wilson acquired the bank in 1969 and advertised it as the perfect "haven" for investors—no matter their reputation. The Bank of Sark backed deals that never would have been sanctioned by any legitimate institution in the U.S. or Europe. In 1969 the London *Sunday Times* identified Wilson and his various enterprises as highly suspect.

Between 1966 and 1970, the Bank of Sark issued $50 million in worthless securities, returning a tidy but illicit profit of $5 million to its directors. In 1972, Wilson and his boss, Louis "the Doctor" Mastriana, a leading figure in New York organized crime, strung out a tangled maze of 150 interdependent companies, including the Transcontinental Casualty Insurance Co., which claimed assets of over $290 million—all of it in worthless paper. Following the publication of the London *Times* exposé, several British investors struck Wilson's companies off their financial register. In 1972, he was arrested in the U.S., and charged with 150 paper frauds. In return for cooperating with the McClellan Rackets Committee, his eight-year sentence was reduced to four months. He was given a new identity in Italy, only to resurface briefly in 1976, to require another new name. Someone, he explained, was trying to kill him.

REF.: *CBA; Rose, The World's Greatest Rip-offs.*

Wilson, Samuel Fell, d.1930, Brit., (unsolv.) mur. On Sept. 24, 1930, a police constable discovered a dead body in a car parked on the side of the road in the small British village of Warsop. In the driver's seat was Samuel Wilson, a young provisions merchant, who had been shot to death with two fully-loaded .12-gauge shotgun cartridges. An order book was found indicating that Wilson had collected at least £20, but only £6 were found on his person. Police speculated that Wilson had been hailed from the side of the road, shot by a gunman at point-blank range as the car slowed down, and then robbed. No suspects were arrested and the case was never solved.

REF.: Butler, *Murderers' England; CBA.*

Wilson, Sarah, b.1755, U.S., fraud. Sarah Wilson thought that being a member of the royal family was better than working for the royal family. Born in 1755, in Staffordshire, England, Wilson moved to London as a 16-year-old, and was employed as a maid to Caroline Vernon, a lady-in-waiting to Queen Charlotte. Wilson was caught stealing a number of jewels, a dress, and a portrait from the queen, and sentenced to death. Vernon interceded, and Wilson was instead exiled to the American colonies, where she was employed by William Devall. Still in possession of the stolen goods, Wilson abandoned Devall and entered Virginia society, posing as the queen's sister. In 1773, after two years as the belle of the south, she was apprehended in Charleston, S.C., and returned to Devall at gunpoint. She remained in his employ until 1775, when she swapped identities with another servant and disappeared to marry British army officer William Talbot. After the Revolutionary War, the two became U.S. citizens and spent the rest of their lives in New York. REF.: *CBA*.

Wilson, Scott, 1870-1942, U.S., jur. Served as attorney general of Maine from 1913-14. He later joined the Maine Superior Court, serving as an associate justice from 1918-25, then served as chief justice from 1925-29. President Herbert Hoover nominated him to the first circuit court of the state of Maine in 1929. REF.: *CBA*.

Wilson, Thomas Stokeley, 1818-94, U.S., jur. Served as prosecuting attorney for territory of Iowa from 1837-38. He was then appointed to territorial court by President Martin Van Buren. He served as judge for the Dubuque District Court in Iowa from 1853-63. REF.: *CBA*.

Wilson, Tug, c.1862-1934, U.S., asslt.-polit. corr. The most famous ruffian in post-Civil War New Orleans, Tug Wilson frequently intimidated voters for corrupt politicians. Wilson appeared in the French Quarter in 1881 and frequented saloons and speakeasies in the red-light district. He carried in the pockets of his long coat shards of beer bottles which he used as weapons. Wilson harassed voters into casting their ballots for the candidate who employed him, sometimes entering the voting booth with them to make sure they voted correctly. He was frequently arrested but rarely spent much time in jail. His experience with voters was too valuable to the politicians. Even through the reforms of the turn of the century and Prohibition, Wilson continued to find work as a strong-arm. Until his death in 1934, Wilson was an infamously feared bouncer at speakeasies. REF.: *CBA*.

Winch, Joel C. C., 1835-80, U.S., jur. Served as U.S. district attorney in the eastern district court of Texas from 1869-70. Earlier, he served as county attorney in Houston and as state district attorney. In 1870, he was nominated by President Ulysses S. Grant to serve as judge in the eastern district court of Texas. REF.: *CBA.*

Winche, Paul (AKA: **John Winter**), b.1862, Brit., extor. In 1920, a well-known British barrister received a threatening letter stating that details of the judge's personal correspondence would be released unless a £50 ransom was paid. A trap was set, and as the ransom was paid, the police arrested 57-year-old Paul Winche, who had access to the judge's quarters through an association with a cleaning lady. Winche, a former professor, had a criminal record for fraud dating to 1896. In 1920, Justice Lawrence sentenced Winche to five years in prison to be followed by deportation for his blackmail.

REF.: *CBA;* Nicholls, *Crime Within the Square Mile.*

Windell, D.S., See: **Isaac, Bernard.**

Windham, Thomas R., 1938- , U.S., law enfor. off. Thomas Windham spent twenty-one years with the Los Angeles Police Department, before being appointed chief of police in Fort Worth, Texas, in 1985. Windham, a native of Hamilton, Texas, joined the LAPD. in 1964, after service in the U.S. Army. He rose through the ranks to become captain in 1978 and Commander in 1980. Windham has both a BA and MA degree from Pepperdine University as well as advanced training from the University of Southern California Managerial Policy Institute and the FBI's National Academy and Executive Institute. In 1988, he was presented with the "Katie Sherrod Award," in recognition of his concern for the victims of family violence. REF.: *CBA.*

Windisch-Graetz, Ludwig, prom. 1920s, Hung., count. Prince Ludwig Windisch-Graetz was a descendant of Hapsburg nobility. He was a grandson of Field Marshal Alfred Candidus Windisch-Graetz, who suppressed an insurrection in Vienna in 1848 that paved the way for the ascendancy of Emperor Franz Joseph I to the throne. Prince Ludwig, owner of the lavish eleventh century castle at Saros-Patak was regarded in all together different terms. In the castles of Europe he was known as a consummate gambler and fascist sympathizer, who had thrown his lot in with Archduke Albrecht.

In the 1920s, Windisch-Graetz and his fascist friends decided the time had come to restore Hapsburg to the Hungarian throne. To finance the overthrow of Admiral Nicholas Horthy, the regent of Hungary who was devoid of any real political power, Windisch-Graetz and his co-conspirators counterfeited 30 billion French francs and then upset the European money markets by passing them in Holland, Italy, and France.

Astute French detectives traced the fraud to three Hungarian partisans operating in Holland: Colonel von Jankovitch, Captain Marsowsky, and George Mankowitz who had 1,000 forged notes in their possession. These three suspects provided enough details of the international forgery to allow detectives to trace their accomplices to Budapest. Details of the crime were laid on the doorstep of the Hungarian government, which promised the French immediate action. The regent was understandably taken aback by the news of the intrigue. He instructed Premier Count Stephen Bethlen to track down the guilty parties regardless of the likely political repercussions.

Windisch-Graetz was identified and jailed at the central Budapest Prison. He named Major Gerö of the Cartographic Institute of Budapest as the principal engraver of the forged notes. The work had been completed on government presses under the nose of the regent's men. The counterfeiters were protected by Chief of Police Emmerich von Nadossy, who tearfully admitted his role in the scheme.

Forty high-ranking officials were jailed, but only twenty-four stood in the dock when the trial opened on May 7, 1926. The verdict was handed down on May 26. Nadossy received the stiffest sentence: four years in prison coupled with a fine of ten thousand crowns. Windisch-Graetz was given the same prison sentence minus the fine. Major Gerö, the engraver, was sent to prison for two years, and his superiors at the Institute, General Hajts and Colonel Kurcz, each received one year. In October 1931, the prince was granted his freedom by the new premier of Hungary. He left Budapest in 1932 for Vienna, where he eventually became a German citizen.

REF.: Bloom, *Money of Their Own; CBA.*

Wing, Francis Joseph, b.1850, U.S., jur. U.S. district attorney in northern district court of Ohio from 1880-81. He served as judge for the common pleas court in Cuyahoga County, Ohio, from 1899-1901, then was nominated federal judge of the northern district of Ohio court by President William McKinley. REF.: *CBA.*

Wing, George Chew, 1904-37, U.S., (wrong convict), mur. On Dec. 18, 1936, in New York, George Chew Wing was convicted of the Nov. 29, 1935, Chinatown murder of Yip Chow. Wing had been identified as one of the four masked men who took part in the first Chinese homicide in more than twenty years. He was executed on Feb. 8, 1937, but later it was discovered that he had been falsely identified and that perjured testimony had been used against him. An alleged co-conspirator had named Wing in exchange for a plea-bargained lower sentence. REF.: *CBA.*

Wingard, Samuel Cyrus, 1825-1910, U.S., jur. Served as U.S. district attorney from 1873-74. He was nominated to the territorial court of Washington by President Ulysses S. Grant in 1875. He was appointed to the same court again in 1878 by President Rutherford B. Hayes, and once more in 1883 by President Chester A. Arthur. REF.: *CBA.*

Wingate, George Wood, 1840-1928, U.S., lawyer. Devised rules for systematic rifle practice and was essential in formation of National Rifle Association in 1871. He served as the NRA's president for twenty-five years and practiced law in New York City. REF.: *CBA.*

Winheld, Oscar, 1868-1933, U.S., suic. In January 1933, in Brooklyn, N.Y., 65-year-old unemployed bricklayer Oscar Winheld spent a day looking for work and had used his last nickel to enter the subway. A policeman however, thought the coin was a slug and arrested Winheld. Later that day, Winheld committed suicide by hanging himself with his belt, looped around a cell crossbar. REF.: *CBA.*

Winkler, Gus, d.1934, U.S., org. crime. In October 1934, the corpse of gunman Gus Winkler was discovered on the street of a Chicago suburb. Winkler was readily identifiable, having been long wanted for murder and bank robbery, yet his fingerprints did not match those in FBI files because Winkler had changed a small line on his fingerprints. He did this instead of attempting to alter the entire print by acid because the prints often return. Whether the prints matched, the body was definitely that of Gus Winkler, a man who had at one time been aligned with Ma Barker, Fred "Killer" Burke, Al Capone, and Rafer Dooley. See: **Capone, Alphonse; Burke, Fred.**

REF.: *CBA;* Thorwald, *The Century of the Detective.*

Winkler, Peter, 1956- , Leb., kid. vict. On Nov. 17, 1988, Peter Winkler, a Swiss official of the International Committee of the Red Cross, was kidnapped in Hisbeh Square in Sidon, Leb. He was kidnapped by the Fatah-Revolutionary Council, headed by Palestinian terrorist Abu Nidal, to insure the fair treatment of a terrorist about to be tried in Switzerland. Winkler was released unharmed on Dec. 16, 1988. REF.: *CBA.*

Winnik, Abraham, and **Meppen, Adele**, prom. 1950, U.S., smug. In May 1950, Adele Meppen, a Brooklyn, N.Y., housewife, was offered a free trip to Europe by diamond courier Abraham Winnik, in return for carrying two suitcases to Winnik's home in Brussels. The trip was completed and five months later, Meppen received another offer; a trip to Montreal. She was to smuggle two packages of diamonds worth $121,000, into the U.S. However, customs officials were waiting at the border, and as she was about to be searched, Meppen flushed the packets down the toilet. The toilet backed up, the police recovered the diamonds, and Meppen was arrested. A few days later, Winnik was arrested while boarding a plane to Europe. He was sentenced to prison for two years. Meppen pleaded guilty, turned state's evidence against Winnik, and was placed on probation for five years.

REF.: *CBA;* Whitehead, *Border Guard.*

Winning Post, See: **Sievier, Robert S.**

Winslow, Angela, prom. 1976, U.S., (unsolv.) asslt.-rape. In September 1976, an intruder broke into the Chicago apartment of Denise Dozier. He raped and beat her friend, Angela Winslow, before throwing her out a fifteenth-floor window. Winslow miraculously survived when she landed on the building's entrance canopy. With a handgun, Dozier was able to wound the assailant, who nevertheless escaped. The man was not found, but Dozier was arrested for failing to have registration for the gun, and for firing the weapon in a confined area.

REF.: *CBA;* Godwin, *Murder U.S.A.*

Winslow, Forbes Benignus, 1810-74, Brit., crim. just. Early advocate of insanity plea in criminal cases. He authored studies on insanity and was also an early advocate for the humane treatment of the insane. REF.: *CBA.*

Winslow, Thomas, prom. 1860, Case of, Brit., mur. Thomas Winslow became friendly with Mrs. Ann James of Liverpool, whose restaurant and inn he managed and lived in. James' relatives were not happy about the relationship. Ann James developed cancer of the bowel and was clearly dying. Wilson got a lawyer to come in and make a will for James, in which she left her businesses to Winslow. During the Spring 1860, she got worse and developed symptoms that her physician thought unusual. His investigation uncovered the presence of the poisonous substance antimony. After James died on June 24, Thomas Winslow was arrested for murder.

At Winslow's trial, expert witnesses disagreed as to whether James had died of her disease or of the slow poisoning by antimony. An attempt was made to prove that Winslow had purchased antimony before, but the prosecution could only show that he had been seen putting some white crystals on bread he was buttering for James. The jury acquitted Winslow and the court did not pursue his contention that James had been murdered by her jealous relatives.

REF.: Browne, *Trials for Murder by Poisoning; CBA;* Pearce, *Unsolved Murder Mysteries.*

Winslow Boy, The, 1946, a play by Terence Rattigan. This drama and film by the same name (1950, directed by Anthony Asquith) is drawn from the celebrated Archer-Shee case. A teen-age cadet was dismissed from the Royal Naval College in 1908 over a minor theft of which he was proved innocent, a case that blossomed into a major court battle involving the British heads of government. See: **Archer-Shee, George**. REF.: *CBA.*

Winsor, Charlotte, b.1822, Brit., mur. On Feb. 15, 1865, the body of 4-month-old Tommy Harris was found wrapped in newspapers beside a road near Torquay, England. The child's unmarried mother, Mary Jane Harris had entrusted his care to Charlotte Winsor, a thrice-married, 43-year-old woman. The mother was arrested the following day, and the police went to question Winsor, who stated that an aunt had taken possession of the child. But when the child's belongings were found in Windsor's cottage, she was arrested.

In July 1865, the prosecution tried Winsor, using Mary Jane Harris as a witness. Harris testified that Winsor had bragged of putting unwanted children to death, and had offered to kill Tommy for a slight fee. Copies of the newspaper and thread used to wrap the body were found in Winsor's home. On July 29, 1865, the jury found Winsor Guilty, and sentenced her to death. On August 2, just before she was to have been executed, she was given a reprieve. However, the verdict was upheld, and a second execution date was set for Feb. 14, 1866. Again, minutes before the scheduled execution, she escaped through a legal technicality. On May 12, 1866, Winsor's sentence was reduced to life imprisonment, through a conditional pardon issued by the Home Office.

REF.: *CBA;* Lambert, *Where Justice Faltered.*

Winstanley, Elijah, and **Kearsley, William**, prom. 1895, Brit., mur. Detective Osborne and Detective Sergeant Robert Kidd, thirty-six, were patrolling the railroad side tracks at Wigan, England, on a September night in 1895, when Osborne noticed a man crouching on the ground. Osborne pinned the suspect against a van, but was attacked by two more thieves. Osborne collapsed and was taken to a hospital; Kidd was found dead, slashed and stabbed nine times.

In less than six hours, information from local bars led to the arrest of William Kearsley, a coal miner. Two days later, William Halliwell and Elijah Winstanley were also in police custody. Halliwell claimed to have met the other men in a tavern earlier on the evening of the killing, and said he had only kept watch while they fought with Osborne and Kidd. Bloodstained clogs found in Winstanley's home linked him with the murder, and all three prisoners were scratched and bruised. The murder weapon, a penknife, was found by workmen about a hundred yards from the spot where Kidd fought for his life. Tried at Liverpool Assizes, Winstanley and Kearsley were found Guilty of first-degree murder by a jury that did not leave the courtroom to argue the case. Halliwell, accused only of unlawful wounding, was discharged. Winstanley was executed, but Kearsley received a reprieve and his sentence was commuted to penal servitude. Interviewed in jail shortly before he died, Winstanley said that it was drink that had caused his downfall, adding, "I would rather meet what I have to meet tomorrow than serve twenty years." REF.: *CBA.*

Winter, Willie, d.1791, Brit., mur. In 1791, Willie Winter was executed for murdering an old woman in Newcastle, England. The name of the victim was forgotten, but the spot of Winter's execution by gibbeting was marked by a rotting wooden head attached to the gruesome apparatus.

REF.: Butler, *Murderers' England; CBA.*

Wintermute, Peter P., prom. 1873, Case of, U.S., mur. Banker Peter Wintermute quarreled bitterly with Edwin S. McCook concerning railroad rights-of-way in the burgeoning Dakota Territory of the 1870s. The protracted legal battle came to an unceremonious end in the district courtroom of Yankton in 1873. Wintermute drew his pistol and shot McCook to death in cold blood. The murder outraged the inhabitants of the territory who remembered McCook fondly from his military days. He was the brother of Major-General Alexander McDowell McCook, hero of Bull Run, Shiloh, and Stones River during the Civil War, and Edward Moody McCook, brigadier general and commander of a cavalry brigade. The "Fighting McCooks" were war heroes, but Wintermute was perceived as a blackguard.

In his first trial Wintermute was convicted of manslaughter, but the decision was reversed under appeal. The jury in the second trial returned a verdict of Not Guilty, amidst public uproar that the well-financed Wintermute had passed bribery money. The defendant snuck out of the Dakota Territory on his pack mule, one step ahead of the lynch mob.

REF.: *CBA;* Nash, *Almanac of World Crime.*

Winters, John, prom. 1901, U.S., rob. On Aug. 5, 1901, $283,005 in gold bullion was stolen from the Selby Smelting Works in Vallejo Junction, Calif., by a thief who had tunneled into the company vault. Police suspected a former employee, John Winters, who lived nearby. While Winters was away from home, mud similar to that found in the tunnel and digging tools was found in his cabin. Winters was traced to San Rafael, Calif., and arrested two days later. He confessed to the crime and the bullion was recovered. On Aug. 21, 1901, in Martinez, Calif., Winters was convicted and sentenced to fifteen years' imprisonment. He was paroled on Nov. 24, 1908.

REF.: *CBA;* Duke, *Celebrated Criminal Cases of America.*

Winterset, 1935, play by Maxwell Anderson. Based on the celebrated Sacco-Vanzetti murder-robbery case (U.S., 1920-27). Anderson also used this case as the basis of an earlier play, *Gods of the Lightning.* See: **Sacco, Nicola**. REF.: *CBA.*

Winthrop, John, 1588-1649, U.S., lawyer-jur. Opposed Anne Hutchinson and presided at court that found her Guilty and sentenced her to banishment. He studied law at Gray's Inn in 1613, and practiced in London before settling in the Massachusetts Bay Colony in 1630. He became its first governor, serving from

1629-49. He also played a vital role in organizing the confederation of New England colonies in 1645. REF.: *CBA.*

Wirt, William, 1772-1834, U.S., atty. gen. William Wirt had one of the longest careers as U.S. attorney general in history, serving two presidents for twelve years. Born in Bladensburg, Md., on Nov. 8, 1772, Wirt was educated at Georgetown University and at an academy operated by Reverend James Hunt in Montgomery County, Md. Admitted to the Bar in 1792, Wirt opened a law office in Culpeper, Va., and moved to Richmond seven years later. In 1802, he became chancellor of the eastern district of Virginia; in 1807 he was named prosecuting attorney by President Thomas Jefferson, in the case of Aaron Burr; and in 1816, was named U.S. District Attorney for Virginia by President James Madison. On Nov. 13, 1817, Wirt assumed the role of attorney general in the cabinet of President James Monroe, and continued through the administration of President John Quincy Adams, until Mar. 3, 1829. He was the first attorney general to preserve his official opinions as precedents for his successors. Wirt lived in retirement in Washington, D.C., until his death on Feb. 18, 1834. REF.: *CBA.*

Wirz, Henry, d.1865, U.S., war crimes. Confederate captain Henry Wirz had been in charge of one of the worst prison camps in the South during the Civil War, a hellish cesspool called Andersonville. Following the end of the war, Wirz was captured and placed on trial, accused of murdering dozens of Union prisoners through beatings, starvation, and summary executions. Many historians claimed that the case against Wirz was trumped up by vengeance-seeking Union officials, including Edwin Stanton, secretary of war. General Lew Wallace, who voted against every one of the Lincoln conspirators, presided in the Wirz case and busied himself during the trial by sketching scenes of death and destruction at Andersonville as they were described by witnesses.

Wirz, a somber, withdrawn man, said little in his own defense, except to deny his guilt. Wirz was born in Zurich, Switz., immigrating to the U.S. in 1849, moving to Louisiana where he became a self-styled doctor on a sprawling plantation; he claimed

The hanging of Henry Wirz, 1865.

to have studied medicine in Europe. Becoming a clerk of the Richmond, Va., prisons at the onset of the war, Wirz was soon commissioned a captain. After being wounded at the battle of Five Oaks–a wound that was still festering when he was hanged for his war crimes–Wirz took a health trip to Europe. Upon his return he was made commandant of the stockade at Andersonville, Ga. For his reported strangling, stabbing, shooting, and starving of prisoners there, Wirz was convicted (historian August Mencken stated "on dubious evidence") and sentenced to hang in Washington, D.C., on Nov. 10, 1865.

The condemned man's wife visited him three times in his cell, the first while his trial was in process. Watched by guards at all times, the couple acted oddly, almost as strangers. At their first reunion, Mrs. Wirz entered the cell with an icy stare and curt tongue. "How are you, Wirz?" she inquired without emotion.

"I am getting along pretty well," he answered, his voice equally dull-toned.

She looked him over and grimaced. "When did you have on a clean shirt last? I never saw you look so dirty in my life."

The second meeting between Wirz and his wife was also a cold event. The last time they met was a few days before Wirz's execution. General Lafayette Baker stood with a number of armed guards at their side. A New York *Tribune* reporter inside the cell noted the couple's strange conduct. So did General Baker who stood very close to them and watched them kiss for the last and only time of Wirz's confinement. Baker lifted an eyebrow of suspicion. "The movement was rather peculiar for kissing." The general was convinced that Mrs. Wirz had passed something from her mouth into her husband's, and he lunged forward, grabbed Wirz by the throat, and shouted: "Spit it out, damn you, or I'll strangle you on the spot." Wirz spat out a little, partly chewed ball which later proved to be smaller than an acorn and coated with oil silk and licorice. Inside the ball was enough strychnine to kill a horse.

Mrs. Wirz was ushered from the cell and ordered to leave the city. When Wirz heard that guards might be placed in his cell at all times, he blurted, "I'm not going to commit suicide. I am not afraid to die and I will not save the government the expense of hanging me. I'm damned if the Yankee eagle has not turned out to what I expected, a damned turkey buzzard!" He watched the gallows constructed in the prison yard.

"You know what this is, Wirz?" a guard asked the prisoner as he stared out of his cell window at the instrument of death.

"Well, you must be putting up a scaffold. I've seen them before." (Wirz had reportedly hanged many a Union soldier from the gallows in Andersonville.)

At 10 a.m. on the appointed day, Wirz was led to the gallows in the Old Capitol prison. He took the stairs quickly, a priest and guards fairly running after him. He sat stoically on the stool as an officer read off the death warrant, tediously detailing his crimes at which Wirz grimaced, shook his head, and seemed on the verge of verbally debating. About 200 spectators stood in the sun-lit yard, most of them reporters, artists, officials, and soldiers. The statue of liberty on the dome of the Capitol looked directly down upon the scene. The rooftops of neighboring houses and sheds and nearby trees were covered with people peering from beyond the prison walls. They had a perfect view of Wirz who finally stood up and had the rope placed about the neck.

He twisted his neck about at the hangman and remarked in irritation: "This is too tight! Loosen it a little." Then he addressed those in the yard. "I am innocent. I will have to die sometime. I will die like a man. My hopes are in the future."

Wirz was sent through the trap at 10:32 a.m. Those in the yard remained gravely silent the moment he fell, but the thousands of spectators outside let out a deafening roar as he dropped downward into death.

REF.: Blay, *The Civil War;* Catton, *Pictorial History of the Civil War; CBA;* Foote, *The Civil War,* vol. 3; Mencken, *By the Neck;* (FICTION), Kantor, *Andersonville.*

Wise, Martha Hasel, b.1885, U.S., rob.-arson-mur. When 40-year-old Martha Wise of Medina, Ohio, fell in love with Walter Johns, her mother spoke scornfully of the romance. On Jan. 1, 1925, she died of poisoning. Lily and Fred Geinke, Wise's aunt and uncle, also died in February after drinking arsenic-laced coffee. Martha Wise admitted murdering her relatives, but blamed it on the devil, whom she saw following her everywhere. She confessed that the devil had also caused her to burgle houses in the area and to set destructive fires.

At Wise's trial, Johns tried to help her defense by testifying that she must be insane, because when they made love she barked. Nevertheless, the jury found Wise Guilty of murder, and she was sentenced to prison for life.

REF.: *CBA;* Nash, *Look For the Woman.*

Wise, Olive Catherine, prom. 1931, Brit., mur. Olive Catherine Wise, an unmarried mother, earned money to feed her four childen by peddling chopped wood. Despondent over a fifth pregnancy, she asphyxiated her fourth-born child in an oven. She was apprehended and sentenced to death. However, a sympathetic judge, John Robert Clynes, decreed the penalty too harsh and reduced the sentence to life in prison. REF.: *CBA.*

Wisecarver, Ellsworth C. Jr. (AKA: **Sonny, The Woo Woo Kid**), c.1929- , U.S., runaway. According to Mrs. Eleanor Deveny, Ellsworth Wisecarver Jr. was "the kind of guy every girl dreams about but seldom finds." This dreamboat caused quite a stir during the waning years of WWII by running off with married women, seven to eight years his senior, on two separate occasions. Truly remarkable about this Southern California heartthrob was his age at the time of his escapades; fourteen and sixteen.

Mrs. Elaine Ludlum Monfredi, twenty-one, and a mother of two, liked the company of younger people, often having teenagers at her home for dancing. One of these teens was Wisecarver. At fourteen, Wisecarver may have acted older than his age, but he was not old enough to marry according to California law.

Neither Wisecarver's age, nor the fact that Monfredi was already married deterred the two as they headed for Yuma, Ariz., on Apr. 28, 1944, for their wedding. On the marriage license the teenager gave his age as twenty-one, but produced a note purportedly signed by his mother and giving him permission to marry. The two left Yuma for Albuquerque, N.M. and then to Denver, Col., where their honeymoon was cut short by police who arrested Monfredi following a telegram to her mother and intercepted by her husband alerted authorities as to the couple's whereabouts. She was held on a charge of child stealing.

A reduction in the child stealing charge was later made to one of contributing to the delinquency of a minor, after Monfredi agreed to have the marriage annulled on Apr. 23, 1945. She was placed on probation for three years, while Wisecarver, charged as a runaway, was allowed to leave juvenile detention if he agreed not to communicate with Monfredi again.

Wisecarver's first marriage was over but his notoriety as a teenage lover was just beginning. He spent some time as a merchant seaman before engaging in his next liaison, at sixteen, with the 25-year-old Deveny, who like Monfredi, had two children and was married. The two met through a mutual friend who each was living with at the time.

Although Wisecarver and Deveny never married, the two ran away together on Nov. 9, 1945. After spending a night in a Long Beach, Cal. hotel they journeyed to Oroville, Cal., about 275 miles to the north. Once again the trip was cut short by the law. This time, however the couple spotted the headlines their romance had produced and decided to return of their own accord. The woman, like her predecessor, was charged with contributing to the delinquency of a minor; Wisecarver was labeled by Juvenile Court Judge A.A. Scott as an "incorrigible and a sexual delinquent."

The boy who stole the hearts of two married women later married a girl his own age; 17-year-old Betty Zoe Reber, who Nevada officials would not allow to wed Wisecarver in their state, resulting in the two being wed at St. George, Utah on Mar. 25, 1947. Wisecarver's youthful romances have since been retold in a movie adaptation entitled *In the Mood,* 1987. REF.: *CBA.*

Wishart, George, c.1513-46, Scot., her. On Mar. 1, 1546, George Wishart was burned at the stake as a religious heretic after being convicted by a convocation of bishops. John Knox, the foremost leader of the Scottish Reformation, had been converted to Protestantism by Wishart, and was one of his disciples.

Wishart and Knox had challenged the doctrines of the Roman Catholic Church in Scotland, when Cardinal David Beaton, the Archbishop of St. Andrews, undertook a massive persecution of Protestant "heretics" in the realm. While Wishart traveled among the diseased and the poor, Beaton sent out emissaries to murder the heretic. These attempts were unsuccessful, but in January 1546, Wishart was arrested by Patrick Hepburn, Third Earl of Bothwell, in the house of Ormiston.

The earl accompanied Wishart to Edinburgh where Wishart was placed on trial for heresy on February 28. Speaking in his defense, the Protestant leader quoted various scriptures, and prophesied the Cardinal's death. "God forgive that yon man that lies so glorious on yon wall head; but within a few days he shall lye as shameful as he lyes glorious now," Wishart said. That same year Beaton was burned at the stake.

REF.: Bierstadt, *Curious Trials and Criminal Cases; CBA.*

Wissinger, Hans, prom. 1932, Ger., (unsolv.) assass. On May 22, 1932, Hans Wissinger, who had recently resigned from the Communist Party was found dead in his Hamburg apartment. He had been responsible for the safe passage of espionage material, and because he knew too much, his resignation was not accepted. Two men, George Mink and Hugo Marx, were suspected of the murder, but no one was ever apprehended and the crime is considered unsolved.

REF.: *CBA;* Dewar, *Assassins at Large.*

Withers, Jack (John Withers), d.1703, and **Edwards, William**, d.1703, Brit., rob.-mur. Apprenticed under his father as a butcher, the skills Jack Withers learned cutting meat did not bring him fortune in a butcher shop, but infamy as a barbarous killer and highwayman.

Following his apprenticeship at home in Staffordshire, Withers headed for London where, unable to find employment, he joined a gang of thieves and soon ended up in Newgate Prison, where he was sent to Flanders to serve as a soldier. Withers' quick wit saved him from punishment in Ghent, when he claimed a statue of the Virgin Mary had commanded him to steal the offertory money with which he was caught red-handed.

Withers returned to England where he started robbing travelers on the highways. He is reputed to have once robbed an old usurer, telling the nearly blind man not to worry, "you don't give me this money, you do but lend it, and I'll be sure to pay you again when the devil's blind."

Withers later teamed up with William Edwards, who was with him when Withers' horse was shot from under him by one of their victims not far from Beaconsfield in Buckinghamshire. Narrowly escaping pursuit, the two were on foot heading for London when they met a penny postman. After stealing eight shillings from the courier, Withers slit the man's throat, disemboweled the body, and filled the body cavity with stones and dirt before tossing it into a pond.

Although the body was discovered the following day, the outlaws evaded capture for about two months, when Withers and Edwards were arrested for robbery. Both highwaymen were condemned at the Lent assizes in Norfolk—robbery being punishable by death at the time. Prior to their execution on Apr. 16, 1703, at Thetford, Withers confessed to the vicious murder. REF.: *CBA.*

Cop killer William Witherspoon; he was paroled in 1979.

Witherspoon, William, 1925- , U.S., mur. Until Apr. 29, 1959, William Witherspoon's criminal record was limited to petty thievery. But on that date, he shot and killed Chicago police officer Mitchell Stone. Although Witherspoon contended that the gun went off accidentally as he handed it to Stone, he was charged with the police officer's murder. Witherspoon was convicted and sentenced to die in the electric chair. However, in 1986, the U.S. Supreme Court replaced the death sentence with a sentence of 100 years in prison. Witherspoon became eligible for parole in 1970, but parole was not granted until 1979. REF.: *CBA.*

Withrington, Jack (John), d.1691, Brit., rob. From early on, Jack Withrington never lasted long at any undertaking. He ran away from an apprenticeship as a tanner, was thrown out of the military–though earned a highly praised reputation as a duelist among officers and whores alike–with less than a year's service upon challenging his captain, and soon had to give up his activities as a card sharp when fellow gamblers became suspicious of his character. Withrington did however, finally find his calling as a highwayman; unfortunately for him this profession led to the same end as his four brothers before him–death by hanging.

As a highwayman, Withrington had a reputation as giving his victims well-reasoned explanations for robbing them. Once, while stealing from Edward Clark, an usher to the Duchess of Mazarin he remarked when asked if were going to rob the man, "indeed I shall, for you get your money more easily than I do; for I'm forced to venture my life for a maintenance." While robbing a tailor who lied to the bandit about possessing more money on his person, Withrington said, "Well, I vow and protest, this is a sad world we live in, when one Christian cannot believe another."

But for all Withrington's clever prating he was finally captured at Malmesbury in Wiltshire when a hue and cry was raised after he robbed a nobleman of £60, 280 guineas, and some valuable clothes and linen. At Newgate he was condemned for his crimes, robbery being punishable by death at the time.

On the way to his hanging at Tyburn, Withrington asked that the cart being driven a different route as he owed money at an inn along the way and he did not want to be arrested for that crime as well. The sheriff's deputy assured him not to worry, and the cart proceeded to the gallows where Withrington was hanged on Apr. 1, 1691.

REF.: *CBA;* Smith, *Highwaymen.*

Withrington, Thomas, prom. 17th Cent., Brit., rob. Thomas Withrington became a highwayman after squandering away the fortune left him by his father on lascivious women, when he discovered that his wealthy wife was being unfaithful to him. He spent from six to seven years earning a living in this fashion before finally being arrested between Acton and Uxbridge, and imprisoned in Newgate until his execution, robbery being punishable by death at that time.

Hanged along with Withrington were Jonathan Woodward and James Philpot. These two were condemned for breaking into houses, having earlier been pardoned by an act of King James I which granted leniency to all but those who committed high treason and murder. These three thieves were the first to receive a special ceremony for condemned prisoners established by the will of Mrs. Elizabeth Elliot, whose son had been pardoned from death by the king.

The ceremony which Elliot instructed the church of St. Sepulchre's in London to oversee called for a man to ring a bell outside Newgate each night before a man was to be executed. This bell ringer would call out to the condemned, and upon a response would exhort to the prisoner to seek repentance and salvation by praying to Jesus for forgiveness. Next day, as the cart passed by the church, the bell would toll and the bell ringer would again pray for the condemned man's soul.

REF.: *CBA;* Smith, *Highwaymen.*

Witmer, Charles B., 1862-1925, U.S., jur. Served as assistant attorney for U.S. government from 1902-04, as marshal for U.S. government from 1906-07, and as district attorney from 1907-11. He was nominated to the middle district court of Pennsylvania by President William Howard Taft in 1911. REF.: *CBA.*

Witt, Johan de, 1625-72, Neth., polit., assass. Held office as grand pensionary of Holland from 1653-72, finalizing the Treaty of Westminster in 1654, and successfully waging the Second Anglo-Dutch War from 1665-67. He created the Triple Alliance with England and Sweden to fight France the following year. He was forced to resign following the French invasion and Orangist riots in 1672. He was slain with his brother, Cornelis Witt, by a mob at The Hague. REF.: *CBA.*

Wittenberg, Solomon, See: **Alexander II.**

Wittman, Manfred (AKA: **The Beast of Oberfranken**), 1945- , Ger., mur. Beginning in 1959, a man known to the local populace as the Beast of Oberfranken had attacked several attractive young women near the small German town of Kaltenbrunn. After forcing his victims to undress and binding them, often with their own undergarments, the attacker stabbed them repeatedly with a 10-inch serrated knife and, finally, slit their throats. His first victim survived, but the subsequent three did not.

Suspicion fell on Manfred Wittman when a resident of Kaltenbrunn told police that she had seen the last victim getting into a car similar to the one driven by Wittman. The description of the attacker, given to police by the surviving victim, suited Wittman, but his popularity in the community initially made him seem less than the perfect suspect. Police ordered a physical examination of Wittman, during which it was discovered that his genitalia were no more developed than that of a 10-year-old. He broke down and confessed to the murders following the examination. In his confession, Wittman claimed that it was frustration over his impotence that led him to murder the women. He was subsequently tried and sentenced to life in prison. REF.: *CBA.*

Wittrock, Frederick, 1858-1921, U.S., rob. In November 1886, Frederick Wittrock, a St. Louis store clerk, armed himself with two revolvers, masked his face with a bandanna, and stole $10,000 from the safe of an express train from San Francisco, after it slowed to enter the St. Louis yards. Returning to his job, he pored over newspaper accounts of his deed. Seeing that detectives had no clues, he sent a letter to a newspaper saying the robbery tools could be found in the baggage room of the local railroad station. The tools were indeed in the baggage room, along with a dime novel with Wittrock's name and address on its cover. As he was arrested, Wittrock implored the officers to address him as "Terrible Fred", his imagined underworld moniker. Wittrock was convicted of robbery and given a long prison sentence.

REF.: *CBA;* Dunning, *The Arbor House Treasury of True Crime;* Heppenstall, *The Sex War and Others;* Nash, *Bloodletters and Badmen.*

Witzke, Lothar, See: **Mare Island Explosion.**

Witzler, Margarete, b.1895, Ger., war crimes. In August 1944, during WWII, citizens of the town of Rüsselsheim, Ger., killed six U.S. airmen shot down during an air strike on Osnabrueck. The crew of a U.S. bomber were captured by the Gestapo and were to be taken to prison. On Aug. 26, the Gestapo paraded the airmen down the main street of Rüsselsheim—a violation of the Geneva Convention, which prohibited the exhibition of prisoners of war. Two housewives, Margarete Witzler and her sister Kathe Reinhardt, ran out of their homes screaming, "There are the terrorizers of last night. Kill the dogs! We can't have any pity!" A mob quickly formed, and the two women forced the servicemen to run a gauntlet in which they were beaten to death with fists, sticks, rocks, and hammers.

After the war, the six bodies were exhumed from a mass grave found in the town cemetery. Only four of the bodies could be identified: William A. Dumont, John N. Sekul, Elmore Austin, and Thomas Williams. Upon their discovery, an investigation was launched that led to the arrest of eleven people for "willfully, deliberately, and wrongfully encouraging, aiding, abetting and participating in the killing of the above named members of the United States Army and two other members of the United States Army whose names are not known, each of whom was then unarmed and a prisoner of war in the custody of the then German Reich." Those charged were 50-year-old Witzler, 38-year-old Reinhardt, Friedrich Wust, Josef Hartgen, Johann Opper, Heinrich

Barthel, Johannes Seipel, George Baum, Philip Gutlich, Karl Fugmann, and August Wolf. A U.S. military commission conducted the trial in Darmstadt, as Rüsselsheim's courthouse and jail were destroyed in a British air strike. Ten of the defendants were convicted. Only Fugmann was found Not Guilty. On July 31, 1945, Witzler, Reinhardt, Hartgen, Wust, Seipel, Opper, and Gutlich were sentenced to hang. Baum was given a twenty-five-year prison sentence, and Wolf and Barthel each received fifteen years. REF.: *CBA.*

Wivallius, Lars, 1605-69, Swed., fraud. Ventured across Europe while masquerading as a nobleman from 1625-29. He was jailed for marrying under an alias and was deported to Finland, where he lived from 1634-41. REF.: *CBA.*

Wojtasik, Gerald, 1950- , U.S., sex. asslt.-rape. Gerald Wojtasik, a former Marine, sexually assaulted six Chicago girls between the ages of nine and seventeen during the summer of 1979. Wojtasik, who lived on South Ashland Avenue in Chicago was convicted by a jury on Feb. 26, 1980, on several counts of deviate sexual assault and taking indecent liberties with a child. At least twice, Wojtasik abducted the girls off the street and took them to an alley or garage where he assaulted them. He was sentenced to thirty years in prison. REF.: *CBA.*

Wolf, Jerome W., c.1939- , U.S., fraud. In April 1983, Jerome W. Wolf, a former Internal Revenue Service agent, was indicted on twenty-two counts of fraud, including tax evasion, failure to file tax returns for the four years ending in 1979, mail fraud, and obstructing an inquiry by the IRS. As a tax preparer, Wolf had his customers give him the money they owed for income tax. He told them he would place the money in a special account from which he would pay their taxes when the time came. One client even mortgaged his home and gave the money to Wolf to invest. Instead, Wolf kept the money, some $560,000, and used it to live extravagantly. He bought furs, jewelry, a yacht, and a mansion in Riverwoods, Ill., an exclusive Chicago suburb. Wolf pleaded guilty to four of the twenty-two counts and received an eight-year prison sentence. The court also ordered him to pay restitution to his clients. REF.: *CBA.*

Wolf, Walter E,, prom. 1931, U.S., embez. An employee of Chicago's Continental Illinois Bank & Trust Company for twenty-six years, Walter E. Wolf had been the manager of the coupon department since 1927. Wolf was also one of the greatest embezzlers in U.S. banking history. From 1919 to 1931, he embezzled nearly $4 million in bonds and securities from the Continental Bank. He confessed after auditors examined his accounts. Wolf pleaded guilty to ten counts of embezzling, and received ten one to ten-year consecutive sentences.

In 1919, Wolf gave a stock broker $5,000, to buy him 100 shares of "good stock," something stable and on which he could collect several years later. Instead, the broker speculated, buying questionable stock on margin. When the stock went down, Wolf had to raise his margin to save the money already invested. He raised all but $500 by legal means. Then, Wolf simply took one of the many bonds that crossed his desk every day. He continued to do so when his investments repeatedly failed. When he stole a bond, he also stole the bank's receipt of the bond. The audit which eventually led to his imprisonment was called for after one of Wolf's stockbrokers became suspicious of the amount of capital Wolf, a bank clerk, was able to generate. REF.: *CBA.*

Wolsey, Thomas, c.1475-1530, Brit., consp.-treas. Ordained in 1498 and served as royal almoner and as dean of Lincoln under Henry VIII. He was placed in charge of public and foreign affairs in 1511 as privy councilor. He behaved arrogantly, giving himself royal privileges while serving as lord chancellor from 1515-29. He ended Britain's alliance with France following Charles V's election as emperor in 1519. He arbitrated Charles V's marriage to Princess Mary, who later became England's Mary I, and tried to manipulate Charles and Francis I so that both, in turn, would support England. According to his critics, he supported Charles to be named pope, but failed to win the emperor's support in 1521 and 1524. He was blamed somewhat for Francis' defeat and capture at Pavia, and completed treaties with him at Amiens in 1527. Two years later, he was divested of most of his authority and titles following his failure to obtain Pope Clement VII's consent for Henry VIII to divorce Catherine of Aragon. He was arrested for high treason, reportedly for appealing to Francis for help, and died en route to London.

REF.: Andrews, *Old-Time Punishments; CBA.*

Wolter, Albert W., 1892-1910, U.S., mur. On Mar. 25, 1910, sixteen-year-old Ruth Wheeler, a recent secretarial course graduate, answered a classified ad for a stenographer. When she failed to return home for dinner that evening, her sister Pearl went to the address on the upper east side of Manhattan and found an apartment that belonged to 18-year-old Albert Wolter.

Pearl became suspicious and called police when Wolter claimed he had never seen or heard of Ruth Wheeler. While police questioned Wolter, the building janitor discovered a package containing the charred remains of a human body in the interior courtyard of the building. A more thorough search of Wolter's apartment uncovered clothing and other items belonging to Wheeler. From evidence within the apartment, it became apparent that Wolter had raped and strangled Wheeler shortly after she arrived at the apartment. He then bound her body and stuffed it into the small fireplace. Although Wolter denied committing the crime, he was convicted of Wheeler's murder, and at the age of eighteen, became the youngest person executed in New York state at that time.

REF.: Carey, *Memoirs of a Murder Man; CBA;* Lebrun, *It's Time to Tell;* Livingston, *The Murdered and the Missing.*

Wolters, Jacob F., prom. 1929, U.S., law enfor. off. In 1926, there was no town of Borger, Texas. Within three short years and with the discovery of oil, not only was there a Borger, but it was a town with a population of 10,000. In true boomtown fashion, Borger also had its fair share of crime. In its first three years, forty murders were committed in Borger, without a single conviction. Finally, the killing of District Attorney John A. Holmes spurred Governor Dan Moody to declare martial law in Borger and send in the National Guard, headed by Brigadier General Jacob F. Wolters.

Wolters, who had twice before been responsible for cleaning up Texas towns, began his clean-up of Borger by replacing corrupt city officials with Texas Rangers. Guardsmen took over all police functions in the city, including traffic control. Bootleggers and prostitutes, unable to work freely, left town. After several weeks, Wolters and his Guardsmen relinquished control to newly installed city officials. REF.: *CBA.*

Woo Bum Kong, 1955-87, Kor., suic.-mur. On Apr. 28, 1982, in an area 170 miles southeast of Seoul, a South Korean police officer went on a rampage killing fifty-eight people before blowing himself up with a hand grenade. The 27-year-old policeman, Woo Bum Kong, reportedly became enraged when his common-law wife, Chun Mal Soon, slapped his chest while trying to kill a fly. Woo became furious, the couple quarrelled, and after several hours of drinking, Woo returned home and beat his wife. When neighbors tried to intercede, Woo began shooting. Chun was shot in the abdomen and was in serious condition after surgery.

After shooting Chun, Woo went on to the police department armory where he equipped himself with two carbine rifles and 180 rounds of ammunition. He also acquired seven hand grenades from a nearby militia station. After leaving the militia station, Woo shot and killed three men in the street. His next stop was the post office where he shot a telephone operator and three other employees. Woo then went to a nearby village where he killed six more people. By this time, police had been alerted and were tracking Woo with orders to shoot to kill. Woo, however, eluded the police and went to yet another village where he killed twelve more people. Woo moved from village to village during the night, randomly killing unsuspecting villagers. After eight hours of attacks, and in his fifth village, Woo exploded a hand grenade, killing himself and three members of a farm family. In addition to the fifty-eight dead, another thirty-seven people were wounded in the rampage. REF.: *CBA*.

Wood, Fernando, 1812-81, U.S., polit. corr. The land-grabbing Fernando Wood, was elected to his post as the "model mayor" of New York City in 1854, the "Bloody Sixth" ward, utterly controlled by political boss Isaiah Rynders, casting 600 more votes that the entire ward contained. One of the staunch leaders of the anti-foreign Know-Nothing party, Wood had imperiously proclaimed on the eve of the election: "The people will elect me mayor though I should commit a murder in my family between this and the election."

Wood was put into office with an edge of 1,456 votes and he promptly joined with the city's board of aldermen in looting New York. The aldermen were then commonly known as "The Forty Thieves." William Marcy "Boss" Tweed, the ringleader of these aldermanic money-grubbers, had, by the advent of Wood's administration, conducted graft and countless other political vices on an unheard-of level. He and his cronies had sold the city's ferry leases and street railway franchises to the highest bidder. They had received $100,000 for the land to be used as a paupers' burial ground, an area not worth more than $30,000. They had charged the city $4,100 for such incidentals as fireworks for the Fourth of July, ten times the amount needed. When the body of Henry Clay lay in state in New York's City Hall, Tweed and his fellow thieves overcharged the city by thousands of dollars for burial arrangements, including $1,400 for cigars and liquor used on the boat that transported Clay's corpse to Albany.

Fernando Wood, one of New York's most corrupt mayors.

The Tammany-supported Wood showed no inclination to depart from such self-enriching procedures. He became adroit in buying up cheap but choice land for himself, using city funds to complete the purchases. Soon the corrupt Tweed was complaining that Wood beat him to all the best properties that could be filched with city funds.

Initially, Wood exemplified the "model mayor" role with superficial vigor and as much publicity as he could muster. He kept a "citizen's complaint" book on his desk and invited any New Yorker to step into his private chamber and register his distemper at various injustices. Many of these cases Wood personally investigated. In the first six months of his term, Wood enforced the law in New York with an iron hand. Brothels and gambling dens were shut down and stayed closed. He enforced the Sunday no-drinking law and only about twenty saloons remained open on the Sabbath out of the 2,300 that usually operated on that day. Rowdyism was suppressed. Hackmen who overcharged their passengers were arrested and fined heavily. Wood publicly stated that he "hated pickpockets," and these criminals were the primary objects of his energetic police in their daily sweeps of the city.

Wood's reputation grew so rapidly and so broadly that he became known across the country as a political leader who knew how to suppress crime. When a passenger on a Michigan train collared a pickpocket and threw the fellow off at one stop, despite the criminal's threat to "cut his throat," other passengers were heard to exclaim: "That must be Mayor Wood." There was much talk of electing him to the governorship of New York and a temperance group from Iowa conducted a pilgrimage to Washington, D.C., to lobby for his nomination for the presidency.

Of course, it was all pretense. Wood's second election to the post of mayor was a bloody farce. Rynders and others supporting the Tammany candidate smashed ballot boxes, beat up voters, and rigged the entire election. One estimate had it that more than 10,000 fraudulent votes were cast for Wood. In 1856, the "model mayor" began selling public offices at staggering amounts for those days. It was a case of the highest bidder getting the job.

John K. Hackett had been promised by Wood the position of corporation counsel but the Mayor changed his mind and sold the office to John E. Devlin for $4,000. Hackett became so incensed at the double-cross that he broke into Wood's office and drew a pistol. When a guard rushed in at Wood's call, Hackett shouted: "If that man comes between us, I shall blow out his brains and cut off your ears." Wood waved the guard away and Hackett lectured the corrupt mayor, ending his indictment by calling him "a scoundrel, a rascal, and a perjured villain." Wood patiently nodded to all these appellations until Hackett exhausted his rancor and left.

Many of the higher city appointments were sold personally by Wood in the Gem Saloon, Rynders and his henchman, John Morrisey, looking on in approval. One of his most profitable deals, settled over drinks in the Gem Saloon, enriched Wood by $70,000. Andrew J. Hackley was awarded the city's street cleaning contract for one year at $279,000. About one-fifth of this sum was kicked back to the mayor. Another reputable firm had offered to do the job for $84,000, but its owners were disinclined to pay off Wood.

Even city hall went on the block during Wood's administration. One of the mayor's cronies, Robert W. Lowber, fraudulently obtained a judgment of $196,000 against the city for a plot of ground that was later properly estimated to be worth less than $60,000. Yet, to satisfy Lowber's phony claim, city hall, with all its furniture and paintings, was auctioned off. Daniel F. Tiemann, later the mayor of New York, put up $50,000 to satisfy the judgment. He was later reimbursed by the city.

Wood is best remembered in history for his prompting the awful Police Riot of 1857, one where he attempted to use his own Municipal Police Department as a private army to control his widespread graft. This truculent, tyrannical politician also earned his historical niche as one of New York's most venal and unscrupulous mayors, accumulating a fortune in payoffs and kickbacks before his death in 1881 when he left to relatives more than $500,000 in cash and property worth twice as much, almost all of this boodle gleaned from his energetic boondoggling. See: **Police Riot; Rynders, Isaiah; Tammany Hall.**

REF.: Asbury, *The Gangs of New York;* Barnes, *The Metropolitan Police;* Booth, *History of the City of New York;* Browne, *The Great Metropolis; CBA;* Costello, *Our Police Protectors, The History of the New York Police;* Greeley, *Recollections of a Busy Life;* Hopkins, *A History of Political Parties in the United States;* Ingraham, *A Biography of Fernando Wood;* Lunch, *"Boss" Tweed;* MacLeod, *Biography of Hon. Fernando Wood;* Myers, *History of Tammany Hall;* Parkhurst, *Our Fight with Tammany;* Stone, *History of New York;* Tilden, *The New York City Ring;* Townsend, *New York in Bondage;* Walling, *Recollections of a New York Chief of Police;* Werner, *Tammany Hall.*

Wood, Harlington, Jr., 1920- , U.S., jur. U.S. Attorney for southern district of Illinois from 1958-61, and associate deputy attorney general from 1969-70 and from 1970-72. He was nominated to the southern district court of Illinois by President Richard Nixon in 1973, and to the seventh circuit court by President Gerald R. Ford in 1976. REF.: *CBA*.

Wood, Isaac, d.1858, U.S., mur. In the largest family poisoning in American history, Isaac Wood poisoned his brother's family as well as his own wife and child. Wood's brother, David, owned an estate in Dansville, N.Y., in the 1850s. In May 1855, David Wood grew ill and died. Within a year, his wife and three children died of the same strange illness. Isaac inherited the estate, then moved with his wife and child to New Jersey, where he killed them as well. Before he left, Wood found a temporary tenant for the estate. In the barn, the tenant found three bags of arsenic wrapped in legal documents which indicated that David's estate would go to Isaac should David and his family die. With this evidence, the state successfully prosecuted Isaac. He was hanged on July 9, 1858.

REF.: *CBA;* Nash, *Bloodletters and Badmen.*

Wood, Ivy Lydia, See: **Beard, Arthur**.

Wood, Robert William Thomas Cavers (AKA: **Scotch Bob**), prom. 1907, Case of, Brit., mur. London prostitute Emily Elizabeth Dimmock moved in with Bertram Shaw, a dining car cook on the Midland Railway, in February 1907. They lived together as man and wife in a shabby, out-of-the-way place in Camden Town, a half-mile from St. Pancras. Dimmock, known to her "customers" as Phyllis, paid the landlady £1 a week in rent from the household money Shaw gave her. On the surface it appeared that the two were happy, though he had refused to marry her.

While Shaw was away Phyllis was sneaking men up to the flat—the typical street trade she encountered during nightly forays into the King's Cross area. On the evening of Sept. 12, 1907, Shaw returned home from his customary trip from Sheffield to St. Pancras only to discover that his doors were bolted shut. He borrowed a duplicate set of keys from Mrs. Sarah Stocks, the landlady, and let himself in. The flat was in a shambles. Furniture was overturned, and the contents of all the drawers were emptied on the floor. In the bedroom he found Phyllis sprawled on the bed naked. Her throat had been slit from ear to ear and blood had coursed through the cracks in the floorboards. Panic-stricken and white with terror, Shaw fled into the street to summon a constable. He was quickly ruled out as a suspect in this tragedy after police verified his whereabouts with railroad officials.

Phyllis Dimmock was an avid collector of picture postcards, then quite the rage in the U.S. and Europe. She had carefully placed them in a scrapbook for safe-keeping. Since the book was stored in a secret place Shaw was doubly alarmed when he found it lying on the floor. The killer had rifled through the contents apparently looking for something. On Sept. 25 Shaw stumbled upon what appeared to be a solution to the riddle. He found a postcard dated Sept. 9, concealed under a drawer lining. This seemed to be the card the killer had looked for so frantically. The London *News of the World* replicated the card in their editions of Sept. 29, asking: "Can You Recognize This Writing?" A young woman named Ruby Young identified it as belonging to her boyfriend, Robert William Thomas George Cavers Wood, a 28-year-old artist employed as a pattern designer by a local glass company.

Emily Dimmock, the murdered prostitute.

Wood was in the habit of picking up prostitutes and on the night of the murder he met Phyllis at the Rising Sun pub in Camden Town. A boy entered the pub hawking picture postcards which caught Phyllis' eye. "Don't buy those. They're common," Wood cautioned. "I have some from Bruges, in Belgium." He produced a card with the illustration of a woman holding a child. Phyllis admired the art work and asked if he would send it to her with a personal message enclosed. He sketched a rising sun on the front of the card, but did not sign his name at the woman's insistence. "Don't do that. The governor might cut up rough. Put my friend's name, Alice," she said. This was essentially the story Wood related to Ruby Young. Fearing that he might be considered a murder suspect, he asked her to keep the facts to herself.

Young could not keep a secret. She told several of her other close male companions, who in turn reported the matter to the police. Wood was arrested on suspicion on Oct. 4. A coroner's jury returned a murder indictment against him on Dec. 4. The trial opened at the Central Criminal Court before Justice William Grantham. The esteemed criminal attorney Edward Marshall Hall represented Wood. There was nothing to suggest that Wood had anything to do with this crime, Hall told the jury. Not a drop of blood was found either on the defendant or any of his razors. It was peculiar given the amount of blood found on the premises. Surely the killer would have emerged from the apartment with at least a modest trace of blood.

Under cross-examination Robert Henry MacCowan, the man who claimed to have observed Wood leaving Dimmick's building that morning, proved to be a lot less sure of himself. Hall asked MacCowan to describe the weather conditions that day. He said that to the best of his recollection it was a gray, drizzly day. Official weather-tracking records were produced which showed that there had been no rain that day, and, in fact it had been quite clear. MacCowan did little for his credibility by describing Wood as "broad-shouldered" when the reverse was true. "Would you describe a bluebottle as an elephant because it is bigger than a fly?" Hall wise-cracked.

Regarding the testimony of Ruby Young, Hall was equally merciless. He portrayed her as a scorned woman bent on revenge. The public, which had followed the case with great interest in the tabloids, became increasingly sympathetic to Wood's plight. Ruby Young was, in their eyes, villainous. When she was excused from the stand she had to be hustled out of the building disguised as a washerwoman. The Camden Town Murder mystery ended when the jury returned a Not Guilty verdict against Wood after just fifteen minutes of deliberation. He became the first person to be acquitted of murder following passage of the Criminal Evidence Act of 1898 which permitted a defendant to testify on his own behalf. The famous London stage actress Mrs. Beerbohm Tree raced back to the West End Theatre to breathlessly convey the happy news. "I was one of those who burst into tears," she said.

REF.: Bishop, *From Information Received;* Bowker, *Behind the Bar;* Brock, *A Casebook of Crime; CBA;* Duke, *Six Trials;* Goodman, *Posts-Mortem: The Correspondence of Murder;* Graham, *Fifty Years of Famous Judges;* Gribble, *They Got Away With Murder;* Hicks, *Not Guilty M'Lord;* Jacobs, *Aspects of Murder;* Lambton, *Echoes of Causes Celebres;* Logan, *Great Murder Mysteries;* Lustgarten, *Defenders' Triumph;* ____, *The Murder and the Trial;* Marjoribanks, *For the Defense, The Life of Sir Edward Marshall Hall;* Nash, *Open Files;* Neil, *Menhunters of Scotland Yard; Notable British Trials;* Pearce, *Unsolved Murder Mysteries;* Rowland, *Murder Mistaken;* Russell, *Best Murder Cases;* Shew, *A Second Companion to Murder;* Warner-Hooke and Thomas, *Marshall Hall;* Wilson, *Encyclopedia of Murder.*

Wood, Sidney, prom. 1923, U.S., (wrong. convict.) rob. On the evening of Nov. 7, 1923, three masked bandits robbed a train running between Los Angeles and Pasadena, Calif. After the robbery, the bandits stopped the train, jumped off, and fled in a car driven by a fourth man. Los Angeles police questioned a young Englishman, Sidney Wood, who had no previous criminal record and produced evidence of an exemplary record in the British military, but had a flimsy alibi for the night of the robbery. On the basis of identifications by the motorman and the conductor, police charged Wood with the crime. The jury was unable to decide the case, but just before the district attorney was about to drop all charges, a passenger on the train positively identified Wood as one of the bandits. A second trial was called, and several passengers identified Wood as one of the robbers based on his physical stature and the resemblance of part of his face to that of one of the masked bandits, whose features had not been fully covered by his disguise.

The jury returned a verdict of Guilty on Mar. 3, 1924, and Wood was sentenced to five years to life at San Quentin Prison. In January 1925, police received a tip regarding the identities of the men who had actually committed the crime. Three of the four, James Hovermale, Mark Godfrey, and Russell Smith were arrested in Idaho and extradited to Los Angeles. Charges were filed against them, and the fourth man, Roy Smith, whose whereabouts were not known. Godfrey, who was only seventeen at the time of the robbery, was acquitted because of his age and his cooperation with the police. Hovermale and Smith were tried, found Guilty, and sent to prison. Sidney Wood's conviction was reversed and he was released from San Quentin on May 5, 1925. REF.: *CBA.*

Woodbury, Levi, 1789-1851, U.S., jur. A graduate of Dartmouth College, Levi Woodbury began his political career in 1816, serving as a clerk of the New Hampshire state senate. In 1817, he was appointed associate justice of the state superior court, and between 1823 and 1824 he served as governor of New Hampshire. Woodbury served a single term in the U.S. Senate and then went on to serve as secretary of the Navy in the Jackson administration and secretary of the Treasury under both President Andrew Jackson and President Martin Van Buren. In 1846, after the death of Associate Justice Joseph Story, President James Polk appointed Woodbury to the Supreme Court.

Woodbury served on the Supreme Court until his death on Sept. 4, 1851. During those six years, he was actively involved in the constitutional debates, often opposing the opinion of the majority of his colleagues. In 1847, however, Woodbury wrote the majority opinion in the case of Jones v. Van Zandt, upholding the Fugitive Slave Act of 1793. While serving on the Supreme Court, Woodbury was seriously considered for the Democratic presidential nomination in 1848. Throughout his life, Woodbury advocated free public schools and cultural activities for the general public. REF.: *CBA.*

Woodfield, Randall Brent (AKA: **I-5 Killer**), prom. 1980, U.S., rape-mur. Throughout 1980 and 1981, newspapers in Oregon and Washington were filled with stories about a phantom murderer, dubbed "the I-5 Killer" because he dumped his victims' bodies along Interstate Highway 5 in those two states. Ex-football player Randall Brent Woodfield was arrested and convicted of the rapes and murders. Woodfield, who had been rejected by the Green Bay Packers after one tryout, was imprisoned in 1982. It was speculated that his violent acts were in part caused by a combination of psychological factors including lack of parental nurturance and an overinflated ego. More than sixty rapes and the murders of twelve to eighteen young women have been attributed to Woodfield.

REF.: *CBA;* Holmes, *Serial Murder.*

Woodhouse, Elinor Drinkwater, See: **Houghton, Charles.**

Woodhouse, Joan, 1921-48, Brit., (unsolv.) mur. The body of 27-year-old Joan Woodhouse was found in a thicket in Arundel Park, Sussex, on July 31, 1948, by Thomas Stillwell, a laborer. She had been strangled, but medical examiners could not determine if she had been raped.

When police failed to find the killer, her elderly aunts hired a private detective. They and Woodhouse's father came to believe that Thomas Stillwell had killed her. In July 1950, the father went before the magistrates to ask for a private warrant for Stillwell's arrest. Although it had been eighty-five years since such a warrant was issued, Woodhouse persuaded the magistrates that he had sufficient evidence. The warrant was issued, and Stillwell was taken before a panel of magistrates. They studied the Woodhouses' circumstantial evidence and dismissed the case. Joan Woodhouse's murder was never solved.

REF.: Butler, *Murderers' England; CBA;* Cuthbert, *Science and the Detection of Crime;* Nash, *Open Files;* O'Donnell, *Cavalcade of Justice;* Shew, *A Companion to Murder;* Simpson, *Forty Years of Murder.*

Woodhull, Victoria, 1838-1927, U.S., pros. Victoria Woodhull's family was run out of Homer, Ohio, in 1849 after her father took out an insurance policy on his wood mill and then burned it down. Her mother was a spiritualist who took money for holding séances to support her husband and their ten children. When Woodhull and her sisters were grown, they supplemented the family income through prostitution. The family moved aimlessly from town to town.

Victoria met and married Dr. Canning Woodhull in 1853. Although he was an alcoholic and spent their wedding night in a brothel, Woodhull took care of him for the rest of his life. They had two children, then moved to Cincinnati, where Woodhull, her mother, and her younger sister, Tennessee Claflin, held séances for wealthy men who, for an extra charge, could buy sexual favors from their hostesses. The setup went bad when Claflin started blackmailing her patrons, and the family was run out of town in lieu of their being lynched.

By this time, Woodhull's political consciousness was awakening. She began advocating free love as a social ideal. She took up with James Harvey Blood, who also embraced the concept, and they lived in common-law marriage although each was already married. They toured the Midwest with a spiritualist show titled "Blood in Tow," then settled in New York City, where Woodhull's career began in earnest.

Woodhull and Claflin cultivated industrialist Cornelius Vanderbilt, who desperately wanted to live as long as he could to debauch as many young women like Claflin as he could. Woodhull used her spiritualist showmanship to convince him he had a long, healthy life ahead of him. Out of gratitude, he told Woodhull about a scheme some other businessmen were hatching to corner the gold market. On his advice, she bought all the stock she could; Woodhull made nearly $1 million on the deal, and Claflin at least $500,000.

Victoria Woodhull, prostitute turned politician.

With the proceeds of this early case of "insider trading," Woodhull entered politics. Beginning small by lecturing on women's rights, she made a giant leap into the public eye on Apr. 2, 1870, when she announced her candidacy for president of the U.S. She lobbied unsuccessfully for support of key congressmen in 1871, but the leaders of the women's movement began to give serious consideration to her candidacy. Her rhetoric as a public speaker was powerful. In an address to women's leaders in May 1871, she proclaimed, "If the very next Congress refuses women all the legitimate results of citizenship, we shall proceed to call another convention expressly to frame a new constitution and to erect a new government...We will overthrow this bogus Republic and plant a government of righteousness in its stead."

Ironically Woodhull's background, which had been the springboard for her dual career in finance and politics, prevented her from getting any farther. Some leaders of the movement knew of her past and opposed her association with the ideals she professed. Her mistake was in taking on reform-minded minister Henry Ward Beecher, whose own affair with a married woman Woodhull exposed in her newspaper, *Woodhull & Claflin's Weekly.* Beecher's friend, Anthony Comstock, pressed charges of obscenity against Woodhull and her co-publisher, Claflin, when they printed details of Beecher's purported liaisons. By the time Claflin and Woodhull were found Not Guilty in court, they had spent six months off and on in jail, and Woodhull's leadership in the women's suffrage movement was permanently discredited. Nevertheless, most of the social changes she advocated were eventually instituted.

REF.: Butterworth, *The American Past; CBA;* Nash, *Zanies;* Sachs, *"The Terrible Siren," Victoria Woodhull.*

Woodmansee, Ernest, 1928- , U.S., (wrong. convict?) mur. On the night of Sept. 9, 1946, San Francisco special police officer Charles Odom interrupted a robbery at Dan's Creamery. His body was found outside the creamery the next morning. Odom had been shot through the heart and had lacerations on his head and face. Various tools were scattered on the ground around the body, and two doors of the building had been forced open. One of the trio arrested in the murder, a man named Foakes, was granted immunity in exchange for his testimony. Foakes implicated two other men, Ernest Woodmansee, and Joseph Trujillo. According to Foakes' testimony, the three had planned to rob the creamery. Foakes was left in the car as look-out but became dizzy after smoking marijuana and put his head down for a few minutes. Odom apparently surprised the two men, they ran back to the car, woke up Foakes, and insisted that he drive off. He said that Woodmansee and Trujillo had killed Odom not knowing he was a police officer. Both Trujillo and Woodmansee were convicted of the murder. Trujillo was executed, and Woodmansee was sentenced to life in prison. Ultimately, Foakes' testimony was impeached by the Court of Last Resort and, in 1956, Woodmansee was released on parole. REF.: *CBA*.

Woods, Dorothy, 1942- , U.S., fraud-forg.-perj. Dorothy Woods bilked Chicago merchants out of $250,000 in a credit card swindle, and then collected $377,000 from the Los Angeles County Department of Public Social Services between 1974 and 1980. Woods used twelve aliases and claimed forty-nine children, collecting as much as $5,200 in one month. She lived in an eighteen-room Spanish-style mansion in Pasadena, Calif., and owned six late-model luxury automobiles, including a Rolls-Royce. Dorothy and her latest husband, John Woods, a real estate broker, owned six other properties in California, one valued at $2 million. In February 1981, police came to the Woods mansion and other properties with warrants to search for evidence of fraud. They confiscated fake drivers licenses, blank birth and baptismal certificates, and many wigs and disguises. The 38-year-old Woods was indicted on forty-one counts of fraud, forgery, and perjury. She pleaded guilty and received an eight-year prison sentence.

In 1971, under the name Dorothy Mae Palmer, Woods moved to Pasadena. Not long afterward, Chicago police arrested her in connection with a credit card swindle Woods perpetrated while living in Chicago. She spent six months in prison, and was released in 1973. Woods returned to Pasadena, married John Woods, and began fraudulently collecting welfare checks. Her husband was convicted of aiding Dorothy in the scheme and ordered to make restitution to the county. Shortly after his arrest, John Woods, fifty-two, filed for bankruptcy. REF.: *CBA*.

Woods, Frank, prom. 1902, U.S., attempt. rob.-mur. On Jan. 20, 1902, six men attempting to rob the safe at a cemetery in San Mateo County, Calif., were foiled by an armed guard. The group next considered breaking into the office of a coal yard. After rejecting this idea, three of the men, William Kennedy, John Courtney, and a man named Goucher, along with William Henderson, William Kaufman, and Frank Woods, attempted to rob a man on the street. As the man fled, Kennedy shot at him. A policeman patrolling the area, Eugene C. Robinson, heard the gunfire, approached the group, and asked about the shots. In response, Woods shot Robinson to death. A second patrolman responded to the shots and opened fire on the men. Only one of the original group of six, William Henderson, was captured, but he identified his accomplices.

Goucher and Kaufman were sentenced to twenty-five years in prison. The case against Kennedy was dismissed due to insufficient evidence. Henderson was released on probation because of his cooperation with police. The case against Courtney was reduced to manslaughter, and he was sentenced to six years in prison. Woods, however, was identified as having fired the fatal shot and was executed on Oct. 6, 1905.

REF.: *CBA;* Duke, *Celebrated Criminal Cases of America.*

Woods, Frederick Newhall, 1951- , and **Schoenfeld, Richard A.**, 1951- , and **Schoenfeld, James L.**, 1954- , U.S., kid. A sixteen-hour kidnapping ordeal ended happily for twenty-six schoolchildren and their bus driver on July 16, 1976, when they tunneled their way out of a truck trailer buried in a stone quarry in Alameda County, Calif.

The bizarre kidnapping occurred on July 15, as school bus driver Franklin Edward Ray was driving the children home from the Dairyland Unified District School, located twelve miles west of Chowchilla. A white van was parked in the middle of the road. When Ray stopped the bus on the highway, three masked men commandeered his vehicle. Ray was ordered into the van, and one of the kidnappers drove the bus to the Berenda Slough, where a second vehicle was waiting. The children were forced at gunpoint into the van, and taken to the California Rock and Gravel Co., near Livermore. The quarry was owned by the father of Frederick Woods, one of the kidnappers.

Ray and the children were told to climb down a ladder into a buried truck trailer. Afterward, the hole was covered with a steel plate and camouflaged with shrubbery before the kidnappers left to negotiate a $5 million ransom demand. The plan went awry when Ray and several of the older children escaped. A night watchman at the quarry was notified, and within minutes the rest of the children were freed. The FBI easily identified the suspects, who had attempted to flee to Canada. Richard Schoenfeld, twenty-six, surrendered to police in Madera County on July 23. Woods reached Vancouver but was arrested and extradited back to the U.S. James Schoenfeld was turned away at the Canadian border by suspicious immigration officials on July 18, and was arrested a few days later. The draft of a ransom note later found on the Woods estate convinced federal authorities they had apprehended the kidnappers.

On Dec. 15, 1977, the three men were found Guilty of kidnapping in a bench trial before Judge Leo Deegan in the Superior Court of Oakland, Calif. The Schoenfeld brothers and Wood each received a mandatory sentence of life imprisonment. Superior Court Judge Deegan removed the possibility of parole for all three because they were also found Guilty of causing bodily harm to three girl captives. REF.: *CBA*.

Woods, William Burnham, 1824-87, U.S., jur. A graduate of Yale University, William Burnham Woods studied law in Newark, Ohio, and was admitted to the bar in 1847. He was elected mayor of Newark in 1856 and to the Ohio legislature the following year, where he became speaker of the house. Although Woods originally opposed Abraham Lincoln, he was a strong supporter of the Union during the Civil War. After the war, Woods settled in Alabama where he served in the Reconstruction government. In 1869, he was appointed U.S. circuit judge for the 5th Judicial Circuit by President Ulysses S. Grant. When Associate Justice William Strong retired from the Supreme Court, Woods was appointed to his seat, filling the need for a Southern justice. As the sole representative of the South on the Supreme Court, Woods actively participated in the civil rights decisions responsible for undermining the effects of the Reconstruction. Woods wrote the majority opinion in the case that ruled the Anti-Klan Act (of 1870) was unconstitutional. He served on the Court until his death in 1887. REF.: *CBA*.

Woodville, Richard (Wydeville, Earl Rivers), d.1469, Brit., consp. Secretly married Jacquetta, the Duke of Bedford's widow, around 1436. He joined the Duke of York in quelling Jack Cade's rebellion in France in 1450, the same year he became privy councilor. At Towton in 1461, he fought for the Lancastrians, but after the battle he ended his ties with Henry VI to side with Edward IV. He became the constable of England in 1467, in which post he became an enemy of the Earl of Warwick, Richard Neville. He and his son, Sir John Woodville, were put to death following Edward's loss at Edgecot. REF.: *CBA*.

Woodward, Raymond L. Jr., c.1925- , U.S., mur. Not one of the hundreds of people searching for a missing 15-year-old girl thought to look in the parsonage across the street from the girl's home. If they had, she would have been spared four days of torture and mutilation at the hands of a 15-year-old boy.

Age and the hometown of Reading, Mass., were about all victim Constance Arlene Shipp and perpetrator Raymond L. Woodward, Jr., had in common. Shipp was a nearly straight-A student at Reading High School, where she was a sophomore.

Woodward had been expelled for misbehavior from Belmont Junior High School before returning to Reading Junior High School, where he had been under the supervision of the superintendent for the past three years.

Before murdering Shipp, whose body was discovered July 19, 1941, Woodward had already been convicted of a charge of accosting a woman on June 27 of that year, for which he received a $10 fine and a year's probation, and he had been indicted two weeks before he was charged with murder for allegedly attacking another woman, a crime for which he had been released on bail.

Faced with a murder charge, Woodward adamantly professed his innocence, telling investigators he did not have a key to the locked parsonage where Shipp's body was found, but was simply working on the lawn for the vacationing reverend. The youth even claimed he had left his chores and went home at the same time Shipp was last seen alive.

Four days passed before the girl's body was found. The corpse was discovered with twenty-two separate wounds resulting form bludgeoning, cutting, and stabbing. An autopsy revealed that some of the wounds were older than others by as much as a day, which meant her attacker had spent a good deal of time mutilating her. Other injuries had been inflicted while she was alive and she had likely been tortured. There were also a number of wounds to the breasts and Shipp's head had been bashed in.

Evidence against Woodward mounted—the clothes he was wearing when Shipp disappeared were stained with blood, fingerprints were found inside the parsonage, and a witness had seen someone leaving the building during the time the girl's body was inside—when the youth confessed to having killed the girl.

Under Massachusetts' law, Woodward's plea of guilty meant that the youth would automatically be sentenced to death under Massachusetts' law, however, at the recommendation of the state's attorney general the governor agreed to commute the boy's sentence to life in prison, thus sparing Woodward from the electric chair in January 1942. He is currently serving his prison sentence at the Southeast Correctional Center in Bridgewater, Mass. REF.: *CBA.*

Woodward, William Carroll (AKA: **Senator Lionel Musgrave, Big Bill Hawley, The Old Boy Himself**), b.c.1860, U.S., fraud. The self-professed "dean of U.S. confidence men," William Carroll Woodward amassed more than $4 million through confidence games on four continents. Arrested thirty-seven times by the age of thirty-seven, Woodward started as a police reporter. He was allegedly involved in a 1916 U.S. gang that blackmailed several prominent people by posing as U.S. marshals with arrest warrants for their participation in white slavery. Woodward opened a gaming parlor in Kensington, England, and came home with $800,000. Woodward swindled jewels valued at $250,000 from an Indian merchant in Ceylon, and collected $50,000 as "The National Old Age Pension Bureau" before it was shut down by Philadelphia police. In 1929, at the age of seventy-one, Woodward sued pulp fiction writer James R. Crowell for $15,000 for detailing his exploits in *Detective Fiction.*

REF.: *CBA;* Thorwald, *Crime and Science.*

Wooldridge, R. Clifton, 1850-1915, U.S., law enfor. off. Known as one of the most colorful and accomplished police officers in the history of American law enforcement, Clifton Wooldridge averaged three arrests a day, for a career total of 19,500. In 1888, while in his thirties, Wooldridge joined the Chicago police force and was made a detective within a year. He had a reputation for fearlessness, and made arrests in places no other police officer dared enter. Wooldridge recovered hundreds of thousands of dollars in merchandise, rescued countless women from prostitution and white slavery, shut down hundreds of phony matrimonial agencies, and never accepted a bribe. He was also an expert marksman who never shot to kill. Though he was wounded twenty-three of the forty-four times he was shot at, and shot and wounded forty-six criminals, he felt a "police officer's job was to protect, not kill."

Wooldridge was Chicago's most successful and diligent campaigner against vice. He humiliated underworld thugs, arrested madams like "Big Susan" Winslow, and imprisoned white slavers such as Mary Hastings. This extraordinary officer was also a comic character given to boasting and outrageous antics. When Wooldridge arrested an underworld hoodlum named Adams who bragged he ate cops for breakfast, Adams carried Wooldridge piggyback to the police lockup. Wooldridge held the butt end of his revolver above Adams' head and threatened to hit him if he even stumbled. Due to deteriorating health, Wooldridge retired in 1910, and later published his memoirs, *Hands Up! In the World of Crime.* REF.: *CBA.*

Woolfe, George, 1880-1902, Brit., mur. George Woolfe, twenty-two, had the dubious distinction of being the last man to be hanged at Newgate before the prison was demolished. Woolfe was convicted of the murder of Charlotte Cheeseman, a young woman with whom Woolfe had been involved. Cheeseman resisted Woolfe's attempts to break off their relationship. On the morning of Jan. 26, 1902, Cheeseman's body was found in a ditch, her head battered with a chisel. Woolfe, who had enlisted in the military, was arrested on Feb. 6. In April, he faced trial at the Old Bailey, was found Guilty of murder, and hanged.

REF.: *CBA;* Felstead, *Sir Richard Muir;* Goodman, *Posts-Mortem: The Correspondence of Murder;* Shew, *A Second Companion to Murder.*

Woolfolk, Thomas, d.1890, U.S., mur. Thomas Woolfolk was convicted of murdering his father, stepmother, two stepbrothers, four stepsisters, and a female visitor to the family's farm. It was surmised that Woolfolk's motive for the murders was to acquire the family property. He was sentenced to death and hanged at Perry, Ga., on Oct. 29, 1890.

REF.: *CBA;* Logan, *Rope, Knife and Chair.*

Woolmington, Reginald, 1914- , Brit., mur. On Dec. 10, 1934, Violet Woolmington was shot to death in her mother's home. Neighbors reported seeing her husband, Reginald Woolmington, leaving the scene of the crime on his bicycle. Woolmington was arrested and brought to trial for the murder. During the course of the trial, it was revealed that Woolmington had become jealous when he heard reports that his wife, who had moved back to her mother's house after only a few weeks of marriage, had been seen out with another man. Woolmington admitted shooting his wife, but insisted that the gun had fired accidentally. The trial ended with a hung jury.

At the end of the second trial, the judge quoted a passage from *Archbold's Criminal Pleading* to the jury which he paraphrased as follows: "If once you find that a person has been guilty of killing another, it is for the person who had been guilty of the killing to satisfy you that the crime is something less than the murder with which he is charged." After these instructions, the jury returned a verdict of Guilty and Woolmington was sentenced to death. Woolmington's counsel appealed the verdict, arguing that the oft-quoted passage offended the very essence of British law—the idea that a person is innocent until the Crown has proved him guilty. After much debate, the Lord Chancellor announced that the jury had been misdirected and the conviction could not stand. Woolmington was released and English legal history was forever amended.

REF.: Butler, *Murderers' England; CBA;* Fay, *The Life of Mr. Justice Swift.*

Woolridge, Charles Thomas, 1866-96, Brit., mur. In 1896, Ellen Wooldridge, the 23-year-old wife of Charles Thomas Woolridge, lived with her husband's niece in a small house in Windsor. Charles, a trooper with the Royal Horse Guards, was stationed in Regent's Park and visited her whenever he could get leave. During his absence, their occasional jealous arguments became more frequent. Woolridge, incensed over reports of her infidelities struck her on one occasion, and she demanded that he sign a document promising never to strike her again. On Mar. 29, 1896, Ellen failed to keep an appointment with her husband, and he left the barracks, saying that he was going to "do some damage." Woolridge traveled to the house in Windsor and, while his niece was upstairs, slit his wife's throat. The defense requested a reduction of the charge to manslaughter because his wife's infidelity had provoked him to kill. Woolridge was found Guilty of murder and hanged in Reading jail on July 7, 1896.

REF.: Butler, *Murderer's England; CBA;* Winterich, *Twenty-Three Books and the Stories Behind Them;* Winwar, *Oscar Wilde and the Yellow Nineties;* (POETRY), Wilde, *The Ballad of Reading Gaol.*

Woomer, Ronald, 1955- , U.S., mur. On Feb. 22, 1979, Ronald Woomer and a companion, Eugene Skaar, went on a crime spree in South Carolina that left four people dead. The two men started off in West Virginia, driving to the South Carolina coast with the intention of robbing some coin dealers. They murdered coin collectors John Turner, Arnie Richardson, Earl Dean Wright, and a convenience store clerk, Mrs. Sellers. In addition to the murders, they also committed armed robbery, attempted murder, and rape.

Skaar shot himself as police surrounded a Myrtle Beach hotel where the two men were hiding. Woomer, who was charged with only one of the murders, remained on Death Row for ten years. The Supreme Court stay of execution that removed him from Death Row came only thirteen hours before Woomer was scheduled to be executed in the electric chair in June 1989. Although the Supreme Court refrained from giving specific reasons for granting the stay, Woomer's attorney indicated that important evidence, withheld during Woomer's trial, had been uncovered.

Shortly after the stay was granted, Senator Strom Thurmond requested that the U.S. Senate introduce legislation to reduce filing of habeas corpus petitions such as the one responsible for Woomer's stay. Using Woomer's case as an example, and citing the statistics that the number of these petitions has increased steadily since 1941, Thurmond requested the legislation as a means of preventing the clogging of the federal courts with petitions used mostly as a delaying tactic. The legislation Thurmond recommended would allow federal courts to deny petitions involving cases that had been fully and fairly adjudicated in state courts, and would permit petitions to be filed only within one year after a defendant exhausted all available state remedies, such as appeals. REF.: *CBA.*

Workman, Charles (AKA: **The Bug**), prom. 1930s, U.S., org. crime. Charles Workman was one of the heaviest hitters in Louis "Lepke" Buchalter's Murder, Inc. Like most of Buchalter's other paid assassins, Workman was Jewish and from the Brownsville section of Brooklyn. He relished his work and the luxurious living it provided. He killed countless victims, the most famous of whom died on Oct. 23, 1935.

Charles "The Bug" Workman, upon his release from prison, 1964.

Along with Emmanuel "Mendy" Weiss and a mobster called "Piggy," Workman was assigned to eliminate mob chieftain Dutch Schultz, who had been ranting dangerously about assassinating U.S. Attorney Thomas Dewey. The three hit men traveled to Newark, N.J., arriving at the Palace Chop House shortly after 10 p.m. Workman and Weiss entered the establishment and opened fire upon three men seated at a rear table, then Workman went into the restroom and fired a shot at the lone occupant, Dutch Schultz. In the confusion Weiss disappeared, fleeing with Piggy back to New York and leaving Workman stranded without transportation. Workman returned by walking across a New Jersey swamp and stealing back into Manhattan across a railway trestle. Soaked and filthy, he called on a friend, who hid him until Buchalter could arrange safe passage to Florida. Schultz's murder remained unsolved until Abe "Kid Twist" Reles became an informant in 1941.

Workman was arraigned for his complicity in the murder. Eyewitnesses at the Palace Chop House failed to identify him, and he had a flimsy alibi about being employed as a funeral home dispatcher on the fatal evening. But under cross-examination, his alleged employer admitted to the lie. Fearing the electric chair, Workman entered a plea of *non vult,* which was close to an admission of guilt, but carried a life sentence rather than death. He served eleven years at the State Prison in Trenton before being transferred to the Rahway State Prison Farm in 1952.

Workman noted with satisfaction that Mendy Weiss, who had abandoned him, was electrocuted in 1944 for the same crime he had committed. Workman was a model prisoner, earning trusty status and working in the library. In 1964, he was returned to Trenton to prepare for parole. On Mar. 10 of that year, Workman's wife picked him up outside the Trenton Prison, making him a free man for the first time in twenty-three years. See: **Buchalter, Louis; Dewey, Thomas Edmund; Murder, Inc.; Reles, Abraham; Schultz, Dutch; Weiss, Emmanuel.** REF.: *CBA.*

Workman, William, 1930-81, U.S., mur. William Workman had a long history of psychiatric disorders before he went on a murder spree in 1973 that left seven people dead. In 1968 Workman, an alcoholic, was readmitted to the Tinley Park, Ill., health center in suburban Chicago for attacking his wife with a butcher knife. On June 27, 1973, after his release from the center, Workman shot and killed seven people: his father, Raymond Workman; his mother, Dena Workman; two neighbors, Henrietta Cliff and her 12-year-old daughter Kimberly; his friend, Paul Clesson, Jr.; and Clesson's parents, Paul Clesson, Sr. and Neta Clesson. After the murders, Workman was committed to the state's maximum security mental institution in Chester without possibility of release or leave. Although Workman requested that he be allowed to stand trial, the state deemed him unfit to stand trial and kept him confined at Chester for most of the next eight years.

Workman was finally brought to trial in 1981. Experts in criminal justice said that he was brought to trial not because of a change in his level of competency, but because society had moved in the intervening years toward demanding greater responsibility of individuals who commit crimes. Workman was convicted of the mass murders and sentenced to three concurrent terms, with a sentence of 100 to 300 years in prison. Workman died in his cell within two weeks of his arrival at the state prison in Joliet, apparently of natural causes. REF.: *CBA.*

World's Fair Bombing, 1940, U.S., (unsolv.) bomb. On July 4, 1940, at the New York World's Fair, electrician William Strachan discovered a small bag in the ventilation room on the second floor of the British Pavilion. He heard it ticking and called the police. Detectives William Federer and Fred Morelock arrived, and Morelock, accompanied by Federer, Strachan, and Sidney Grant Wood, the Pavilion's chief attendant, carried the bag out of the Pavilion, through the crowds of people, to an isolated place. When bomb squad detectives Joseph Lynch and Ferdinand Socha arrived, Socha cut open one end of the bag and saw several sticks of dynamite and a clock. At that moment, the bomb exploded. Lynch and Socha were killed instantly, their bodies severely mangled. Federer and detective Joseph J. Gallagher were severely injured, and Morelock, Strachan, and Wood were also injured in the blast. Police arrested Edward A. Kangesier, a gyroscope mechanic, in connection with the bombing, but no one was charged. REF.: *CBA.*

Worley, Captain, d.1719, U.S. pir. Although Captain Worley began his short-lived career as a pirate with the aid of just eight men and a small open boat, he nevertheless managed to thrive as a pirate along the East Coast of the U.S., plundering ships from as far north as the Delaware River south to the Bahamas, before his capture less than one half year after leaving New York.

Heading south from New York, Worley and his band journeyed about 150 miles before leaving the Atlantic Ocean for quieter waters of the Delaware. On this river the pirates encountered another small boat; this one laden with goods bound for Philadelphia. Not only did the captain and his crew easily acquire the booty, but increased their number by one in the process. Their next encounter proved even more successful; three more men joined the pirates and the captain also took possession of the larger vessel.

It was not long after acquiring a second ship that a third took its place, a sloop of a larger size and more efficient for piracy. With the issuance of a proclamation by the British colonial government calling for the pirates' capture, Worley sailed for the Bahamas, avoiding the twenty gun *Phoenix* which was sent in pursuit. While in the islands they sunk a sloop from New York (to prevent word of their whereabouts) and plundered a brigantine.

Returning to the U.S. coast about six weeks later, with a crew of twenty-five and six cannons on deck, Worley put in at a bay in North Carolina. When word reached the governor of the state, two ships–one with eight guns and the other with six, and a total of seventy men between the two–were sent to capture the pirates. Worley mistakenly viewed the ships as possible plunder, realizing too late his blunder, he was cut off from the open sea and forced to fight.

Remaining loyal to a vow of fighting any adversary to the death rather than surrender, all but Worley and a few wounded were left alive after his ship was boarded. Taken ashore in irons, he and his men were hanged the next day, Feb. 17, 1719, for fear that any delay might allow the wounded men a chance to escape the gallows by dying prior to their execution. REF.: *CBA*.

Worley, Claude M., prom. 1918-30, U.S., law enfor. off. Claude M. Worley, chief of police in Indianapolis, Ind., between September 1927 and January 1930, began his ascent within the department in 1918 with his promotion to detective. In 1922, he was promoted to the rank of captain and assigned to criminal court. In May 1923, he was reduced in rank to sergeant and resigned shortly thereafter. In 1926, he was reinstated and promoted to inspector. Six months later, he was transferred to the detective department as its commanding officer. From the rank of chief of detectives, Worley was again reduced, this time to lieutenant. On Aug. 3, 1927, Worley resigned from the department again. Less than a month later, Worley was appointed police chief, a position he held until Jan. 6, 1930, when he resigned from his post once again. REF.: *CBA*.

Worley, Richard, d.1718, U.S., pir. In September 1718, pirate Richard Worley and eight companions sailed out of New York in a small open boat with scanty provisions and only six muskets. But when they reached the Delaware River, they captured a sloop, which provided them with more of all the proper accouterments for pirates. Two months later, in a brigantine—the *Eagle*—and a sloop—*New York Revenge's Revenge*—Worley and his men waited outside Charleston Harbor for unsuspecting ships. They had a few successes until Governor Robert Johnson of South Carolina personally commanded an expedition of four ships with a combined total of seventy guns and set out after Worley.

Early in the morning of Nov. 5, 1718, the governor's expedition slipped out of Charleston Harbor. Thinking they were merchants, Worley and his pirates attempted to corner them in the mouth of the harbor. When Worley ran up the black flag and demanded the surrender of Johnson's ships, Johnson replied by firing broadside into Worley's ship. The *Eagle* managed to escape temporarily, but Johnson's forces fought *New York Revenge's Revenge* for the next four hours. Worley was killed in the struggle and the remainder of his crew surrendered. Johnson then pursued the *Eagle* and captured it. A total of twenty-seven pirates were killed. Nineteen others were brought ashore and hanged, and five were acquitted.

REF.: *CBA;* Rankin, *The Golden Age of Piracy.*

Worms, Pamela Lee, d.1852, U.S., mur. Pamela Worms, of Pennsylvania, was fed up with her hard-driving husband, Moses, and put arsenic into his dinner. Then, while still angry, she put the poison in her daughter's food, too. Both victims died, and Worms was convicted of murder. She was hanged at Pittsburgh on Jan. 30 before a large crowd.

REF.: *CBA;* Nash, *Look For the Woman.*

Worth, Adam (AKA: **Harry Raymond, Henry Jarvis Raymond**), 1844-1902, Int'l., burg.-rob. Adam Worth was beyond a doubt the greatest criminal mastermind of the nineteenth century. Sir Robert Anderson, chief of the Criminal Investigation Department at Scotland Yard, said of him: "He was the Napoleon of the criminal world. None other could hold a candle to him." Allan Pinkerton, founder of the famed Pinkerton Detective Agency in the U.S., echoed this grudging respect, stating: "He was the Napoleon of crime, the greatest mastermind of them all." These words were not lost on British author Arthur Conan Doyle, creator of Sherlock Holmes. In creating a criminal mind that would match his super-sleuth, Doyle patterned the cunning Professor James Moriarty after Adam Worth. At one point, Holmes tells his loyal associate: "He is the Napoleon of crime, Watson. He is the organizer of half that is evil and nearly all that is undetected in this great city. He is a genius, a philosopher, an abstract thinker. He has a brain of the first order. He sits motionless, like a spider in the center of its web, but that web has a thousand radiations, and he knows well every quiver of each of them."

The Moriarty Doyle created had much in common with his role model. Like the devastatingly clever professor, Worth headed and directed an enormous international network of thieves, planning thefts no other in his day would dare commit and traveling about the globe while living in splendor in the finest hotels or on the high seas aboard his private yacht. He, like Moriarty, enjoyed Oriental decor and the mysticism of the Far East. Also, like the professor, Worth confounded the efforts of police on three continents, evading arrest and escaping prison, except in two instances. Wholly unlike Doyle's fiendish mastermind, Worth abhorred violence and never went armed. He gave strict instructions that none of his men were ever to resort to violence and any man who betrayed this edict was sent from his organization into permanent exile.

Adam Worth at the height of his criminal career.

Worth lived like a rajah, and directed the careers and lives of scores of the world's super thieves, yet he died almost broke, and, as a noble gesture to enrich the lives of his two children, who never knew of his criminal past, returned the greatest treasure of his fifty-year criminal career to its rightful owners. The mastermind could have easily sold this treasure, which one detective tracked him around the world to recapture, adding perhaps a million to the estimated $3-$5 million he gleaned during his long criminal career. But Worth had a deep-rooted sense of honor that compelled him, as it had throughout his life, to perform a final *beau geste*.

The beginnings of this strange and unpredictable man were humble. Worth was born to Jewish parents in New York City and received a good education. He was intelligent and liked reading good books. He began working as a clerk before the outbreak of the Civil War, and in 1861, he accepted the $500 the Union army was paying to recruits. In fact, he took advantage of this mercenary payment *several* times, as a bounty jumper. Worth enlisted, collected his $500, marched off to training camp, then deserted, returned to New York, and enlisted again under a different name. After collecting several thousand dollars, which he banked, Worth stayed in the army and served with distinction until he was mustered out of service in 1864.

Unable to find work, Worth resorted to theft, taking a package from an Adams Express truck. He was caught and sent to Sing Sing for three years, his only arrest, conviction, and prison term in the U.S. At Sing Sing, Worth was put to work with quarry gangs. He was assigned the lethal task of warming up frozen nitroglycerine, used in blasting quarry rock. Worth later told William Pinkerton, one of the detectives who pursued him over the years: "I was a rather stupid young fellow. I never questioned the guard and I always wondered why he left when I put the brittle chunks (of nitro) in the stove. When one of the older inmates told me I could be blown to bits, I decided I had had enough of prison."

With the kind of meticulous care he would take in his later robberies, Worth planned his escape from Sing Sing with split-second timing. He noted that a tug appeared on the Hudson River at a certain hour and then noted the regular times when the guards at the quarry relieved each other. During one of these changings of the guards, Worth, a small man (five feet, seven inches, never weighing more than 130 pounds), slipped into a culvert that led to the river. He crawled past guards and lowered himself into the Hudson, swimming out to the tugboat that had just pulled away from the dock. Climbing aboard, he hid himself among cargo boxes. When the tug approached New York City, Worth slipped over the side and swam to shore.

By 1866, the cautious Worth had decided upon a life of crime. He summoned his brother John from Boston. Worth planned to rob $30,000 from the Atlantic Transportation Company in New York, but his brother proved to be so inept that the two were almost caught entering the building. Worth abandoned this plan and sent his bumbling brother home. He traveled to Cambridge, and after scouting about, learned that an insurance firm in that city kept large amounts of cash on hand. Working alone, Worth disguised himself as a constable and gained admittance to the insurance building, telling a night watchman that he had been tipped that the vault was to be burglarized that night. When the watchman made his rounds, Worth used nitroglycerine, which he had become familiar with in Sing Sing, to blow open a small hole in the door of the vault to open it. He looted the vault of $30,000 and was on his way before the watchman returned.

Using this money to establish his front, Worth took elegant rooms in the Astor House, the finest hotel in New York at the time. He had his clothes custom-made by the most distinguished tailors in the city and then, looking the dandy, began to make the rounds of underworld hangouts, seeking intelligent criminals with his own bent for details and creative crime. He disdained hellholes such as Geohegan's, the Strand, and Allen's, going instead to Shang Draper's elegant saloon. He spent long hours sipping champagne and playing the gentleman scoundrel. He met and bedded many show girls at this time, but his purpose was clear. He wanted to line up a super gang of intellectual criminals who could put inventive schemes to work.

Worth's quest was rewarded when he encountered Charles Bullard, son of a high society New York family who could trace their ancestors back to an officer on the staff of General George Washington. Bullard came into an inheritance when his father died, but he squandered this money on wine and women and was soon looking for ways to make quick cash. He met an apprentice burglar named Ike Marsh and the pair concocted a daring train robbery. On May 4, 1868, Bullard and Marsh, traveling on the Hudson River Railroad Express, slipped into the baggage car and knocked out the guard, John Putnam, then helped themselves to $100,000 in cash and negotiable securities. The Pinkertons were called in on the case, but Bullard and Marsh had left no real clues and the guard was of little help. He stated he had been asleep in the baggage car when he was attacked and knocked out and could not give a description of his assailants. Putnam had been found with froth on his lips, as if in a coma from the attack, yet he bore nothing more than a slight bruise to the right temple. The Pinkertons suspected Putnam of collusion but could prove nothing.

Robert Pinkerton and his chief of the Philadelphia office, Robert Linden, were assigned to the case. They went over every inch of the baggage car, where Linden found a piece of soap. When Putnam was brought in for more questioning, Linden showed him the soap and bluntly told the guard that it had made the froth on his lips and that he, Putnam, was in league with the robbers. Putnam, under relentless interrogation, signed a confession two days later, implicating Marsh and Bullard. The two thieves by then had fled to Canada. Bullard's rooms in New York were searched and some of the stolen securities were found. After a lengthy legal battle, Bullard and Marsh were returned to New York and housed in a White Plains Jail. Bullard and Marsh escaped, however, when their friends dug a hole in the jail and freed them before their trial.

Bullard's adventures caused him to be the toast of New York's underworld. He intrigued the scheming Adam Worth, who admired Bullard's daring. They were introduced to each other in a back room of Draper's saloon and became fast friends. Bullard was by then called "Piano Charley" because he played the instrument well. Worth and Bullard had similar tastes. Both enjoyed high living and preferred the company of elegant people, rather than criminal riffraff. They enjoyed good clothes, food and wine, and the company of beautiful women. They also disdained violence and never went armed. They, like the fictional character Raffles, lived by their wits, not by the gun. In a few days, Worth suggested to Bullard and Marsh that they join him in robbing the Boylston National Bank of Boston. He had recently scouted the bank, Worth told them, and knew that hundreds of thousands of dollars were in its vault. They would rent the house next to the bank and burglarize the bank, Worth explained, by breaking through a common wall and entering the bank at night. Worth had made detailed drawings of the bank, and the shops on either side of it.

Gainsborough's "Duchess of Devenshire."

Bullard and Marsh quickly agreed to take part in the theft. Once in Boston, the thieves encountered a problem. The house next to the bank on Boylston and Washington streets had been rented. The barbershop, which was located on the other side of the bank, however, was another matter. Worth simply bought the shop for $500 and he and his men moved in, changing the store to Judson and Company, Dealers in Wine Bitters. Bullard was the ostensible owner of the shop, using the name William A.

Judson. Worth had carpenters construct a partition that prevented passersby from looking into the shop and in the window he lined up many bottles with dark-looking contents. He was a stickler for fronts and facades and insisted upon having a convincing cover.

Marsh was assigned to keep regular office hours, ready to write an order for bitters if a customer appeared. But none arrived, as Worth expected, since buyers of bitters generally went to available general liquor dealers. Joining the gang were Adam Worth's brother, John, who relieved Marsh in the store clerk role, and Bob Cochran, who was brought in on the caper because of his brawny back and powerful arms. Cochran did most of the tunneling into the bank building. The thieves took their time, coming and going from the shop as would regular businessmen. They lived in the best hotel and frequented the finer Boston restaurants. While the digging went on, Worth and Bullard attended the theater and the opera. They always had lovely ladies on their arms as they strolled from the theater with top hats, silk-lined capes, and gold-knobbed walking sticks.

On the night of Nov. 20, 1869, Cochran sent word to Worth that he was about to break into the bank. Worth, Bullard, Marsh, John Worth, and Cochran gathered in the dark store close to midnight and then punched through the wall of the bank. In minutes, Worth was able to blow off the tumblers and handles of vault doors and the gang entered the spacious vault with large carpetbags, filling them with more than $450,000 in cash and negotiable securities, an enormous haul for those days, equivalent to several million dollars in today's inflated currency.

Returning to New York, the gang stayed in suites at the Astor House, the last place police might think of looking for desperate bank burglars. The newspaper accounts of the great robbery filled the front pages for days. When Bullard read that the Pinkertons—the very agency that had exposed his railway robbery—had been hired to track down the thieves, he grew nervous and urged Worth to leave for Europe. "Those damned detectives will be on to us within a week," Bullard told Worth. "I don't want to be playing a piano in the Ludlow Street Jail."

Worth and Bullard sailed for Liverpool the next day, taking their fabulous spoils with them. Once in Liverpool, the pair rented spacious suites in the American Hotel. In the pub of this hotel, Worth and Bullard were both captivated by a local singer, beautiful 17-year-old Kitty Flynn. Worth was deeply in love with Kitty, but lost her to Bullard, whom she married. The trio then went on to London, where Bullard used the alias Charles Wells. Worth, with his customary wit, used the name Henry J. Raymond, the name of the founder of the New York *Times*. This was the name Worth used in his marriage and the one he handed down to his two children. Both Worth and Bullard posed as wealthy New York merchants and they lived like visiting royalty.

Traveling to Paris, Worth and Bullard opened up an elegant cafe, the American Bar, which offered gambling in its back rooms. The place became the center for U.S. expatriates in Paris and it catered to society clientele. The cream of American criminals also gathered here and came under the direction of Worth. Max Shinburn, who later bought a title and retired as Baron Shindell, enlisted in Worth's company of thieves, as did Walter Sheridan, George McDonald, and Austin and George Bidwell, who were all later to swindle a great fortune from the Bank of England in an elaborate forgery scheme attributed to the ingenious Worth.

The mastermind planned many bank burglaries and security frauds, sending some of his men to Turkey, where they passed fraudulent bank drafts for more than $400,000. Worth received a quarter of all the profits from the crimes he planned and he was soon a millionaire. He returned to London and lived in the best part of the city in a townhouse replete with servants. Next he bought a yacht and christened it the *Shamrock,* a name given to it by Kitty Flynn Bullard. Sailing between European ports, Worth continued planning one spectacular robbery after another, sending his talented lieutenants to Belgium, Holland, Germany, France, and Italy to perform the crimes.

Though fabulously wealthy, Worth occasionally committed crimes alone, purely to "keep my hand in," as he later stated. On one occasion, Worth purchased some items from a London pawnbroker and noticed that the man's safe was brimming with money. He stole the pawnbroker's keys and had copies made, returning the keys, unseen, some hours later. That night Worth entered the shop and removed $20,000 from the safe. He spent the money in a month on lavish parties. Bored with polite London society, Worth decided to sail the *Shamrock* to South Africa. He had read about the fabulous diamonds coming from the Kimberley mines.

Once in Capetown, Worth posed as a retired businessman from the U.S. He took pains to befriend the postmaster of Capetown after learning that all of the Kimberley diamonds were shipped to the post office and from there to London diamond merchants. Some weeks later, Worth mailed three parcels to himself from a distant town and then called for them at the Capetown Post Office just as the place was about the close. The postmaster explained that he would have to return the next day, but the charming Worth prevailed upon the man. As the postmaster went to retrieve the parcels in the absence of departed clerks, Worth quickly made a wax impression of the keys to the building and safe that the postmaster kept on the same ring. A few nights later, Worth entered the building, opened the safe, and removed more than $500,000 to $1 million in diamonds.

A few weeks later Worth returned to London where, using front men, he sold the diamonds for $300,000. Ironically, the diamonds were purchased by the very merchants to whom they had been originally assigned by the Kimberley mine owners. With his coffers brimming, little Adam Worth sailed for New York. Here he married a respectable young woman and moved into a mansion. The couple had two children. Worth's attractive wife knew him only as Henry J. Raymond. He spent six months a year with his family in New York and the other six months roaming around Europe, planning and executing, through his syndicate of crooks, one incredible caper after another. His most celebrated crime had nothing to do with either cash or gems.

Worth shortly before his death in 1902.

On the balmy afternoon of May 27, 1876, Worth, lost in thought, walked along Bond Street in London. At his side was an enormous American thief, Jack "Junka" Phillips. A curiosity even among the underworld, Phillips was a one-time wrestler who stood nearly seven feet tall. He sometimes actually carried away safes too difficult to open with jimmies or crowbars. As he walked with Worth, whom he dwarfed, Phillips chattered about his idiotic plans to commit several robberies, saying that he was going to strike out on his own and that he was "tired of being used like a horse." This unlikely pair paused at Agnew and Company, one of the world's most famous private art galleries.

A big crowd had gathered to buy tickets to see Gainsborough's "The Duchess of Devonshire," which Christie's had just sold to Agnew's for $50,000, the largest amount ever paid for a work of art. The painting was of the wife of the fifth duke, the lovely Georgiana Spencer. Worth seemed to give the crowd little note. The pair moved down the street, but after walking a block, Worth stopped and said: "Junka. I'm going to steal that painting in Agnew's tonight. I'll need your help."

"What? A painting? What for?"

"Because I want it. That's reason enough. Don't ask questions, Junka. Do as you're told."

Following Worth's instructions, Phillips returned to Agnew's and bought two tickets to the exhibit. Worth stood for a long time, admiring the new Gainsborough exhibition on the second floor. Returning to Worth's comfortable town house, Worth summoned Joseph "Little Joe" Elliott, then his right-hand man. He told him that he and Phillips were going to rob Agnew's that night and that he wanted Elliott to stand lookout at the gallery.

"I don't understand, boss," Elliott said. "There's dozens of banks waiting to be taken and you want to steal a painting."

Worth did not explain that he intended to use the painting to bargain for the release of his brother, John, who had again bungled a robbery assignment and was being held without bail, pending trial. That night, while Elliott stood watch, Worth climbed atop Junka Phillips' shoulders and pried open a second-floor window of Agnew's Gallery. He went to the Gainsborough, cut it from its frame, but left one corner of the painting so that the original would match the torn portion and no copy could replace it. Rolling up the Gainsborough, Worth let himself down onto Junka Phillips' shoulders and made off with one of the most priceless art treasures in the world.

Robert Pinkerton, who was in London to help the police obtain evidence against Worth (and was failing to do so), attributed the crime to the American mastermind as soon as he heard of the painting's theft. "There's only one man who would have the nerve to commit such a crime," he told a Scotland Yard official. "That man is Adam Worth. But what puzzles me is that Worth is smart enough to know that no fence in the world will handle such an item as the Gainsborough."

Worth merely hid the painting. Junka Phillips began dunning Worth for his share of the loot, so Worth gave him £50, saying that he had to sell the painting for a small amount. Phillips was dissatisfied and began to extort more money from Worth, who ordered Phillips to keep away from him. Phillips followed Worth to the Criterion Bar one night and loudly began to accuse him of holding out on him and complaining that Worth had made him an accessory in the theft of the painting.

Worth saw the tall figure of Inspector Greenham of Scotland Yard in the bar mirror. He realized that Phillips had turned informer and was trying to force an admission of guilt from Worth in earshot of the detective. Without arguing with Phillips, Worth ordered a bottle of champagne. When it arrived, he suddenly crashed the heavy bottle down on Phillips' head, sending the giant unconscious to the floor. Worth brushed the tiny shards of glass from his expensive frock coat, stepped over the fallen Phillips, and left the Criterion. He was not bothered again by the greedy giant.

Adam Worth held on to the priceless Gainsborough for the next twenty-six years. He carried it with him inside an umbrella, in false-bottom trunks, even down his trouser leg. All the while, assigned by Agnew's to recover the painting whatever the cost, Robert Pinkerton, and later his brother, William Pinkerton, dogged the footsteps of mastermind Worth, waiting for him to slip. For ten years Adam Worth evaded arrest while continuing to manage a network of crooks and thieves in half a dozen countries. Then, in Liege, Belg., Worth, on a whim, decided to rob a mail wagon. As he was about to take a cash shipment, he was caught red-handed and sent to prison for seven years. When he was released, most of Worth's money had vanished, siphoned by confederates. His yacht and London house had been sold by aides to finance robberies and burglaries that failed miserably for lack of Worth's planning and direction.

Adam Worth was a broken man, no longer a mastermind of archcriminals. His associates, Bullard, Shinburn, Sheridan, the Bidwell Brothers, were either dead or in prison. He drifted back to the U.S., and following the death of his wife, wound up in a cheap Chicago rooming house. He nevertheless possessed the Gainsborough. He learned that his son and daughter were in financial distress, and though he vowed he would never give up the painting, he wrote to William Pinkerton. (Robert Pinkerton, the man who had tracked him halfway across the world, was dead by then.) Worth explained that he knew of the painting's whereabouts, although he was not responsible for its theft. He wanted to claim the reward Agnew's had posted for the painting and have this money sent to his son and daughter. Pinkerton wrote to Agnew's and the deal was made. The Gainsborough was sent to Pinkerton, who returned it to Agnew's. The reward was paid to the Worth children and the mastermind then wrote a letter to William Pinkerton thanking him for his kindness. The detective proved as noble as the criminal he and his brother had long sought to jail. After Worth's death, William Pinkerton wrote several letters to Worth's young son, sending him hundreds of dollars, stating that he had obtained this money from "a man who owed your father these sums." The money came from Pinkerton's own wallet.

Earlier, Worth had returned to London, taking an apartment in Regent Park. His return to this city was obviously permitted by the authorities as part of the deal made with Agnew's. He lived in seclusion until he suddenly grew ill and died on Jan. 2, 1902. The greatest criminal of the Victorian era passed on without notice from the press. Five years earlier, his fictional counterpart had met a more spectacular end. Professor Moriarty had died while struggling with the indefatigable Sherlock Holmes, these eternal adversaries crashing to oblivion in the Reichenback Falls. See: **Bullard, Charles; Sheridan, Walter; Shinburn, Max.**

REF.: Barton, *True Exploits of Famous Detectives;* Byrnes, *Professional Criminals in America; CBA;* Dilnot, *Rogue's March;* Horan, *The Pinkertons;* Kingston, *Dramatic Days at the Old Bailey;* ____, *Remarkable Rogues;* Kobler, *Some Like It Gory;* Nash, *Almanac of World Crime;* Rowan, *The Pinkertons.*

Wortham, Quintin (AKA: **Capitol Hill Rapist**), c.1959- , U.S. rape. Labelled a "savage parasite" by the judge who sentenced him to 376 years in prison, Quintin Wortham showed little emotion at hearing the record sentence for raping five women and attempting to rape another in Denver, Col.

By receiving the maximum term of imprisonment for committing fourteen counts of sexual assault, burglary, and theft, the 28-year-old Wortham was sentenced to 152 years more prison time than any other felon in Denver history, making him ineligible for parole until he were to reach the age of 215. District Judge Lynne Hufnagel, considered one of the city's toughest sentencing jurists, made her decision on May 14, 1988, five days after Wortham was found guilty.

From the time he was twelve Wortham had had run-ins with the law, amassing a fifteen year arrest record. During his sentencing trial seven police officers guarded Wortham. His crimes as a rapist in 1985 and 1986 were committed against women he found alone and in the privacy of their own homes, a situation Wortham capitalized on according to Hufnagel, adding that he "immediately blinded his victims by slamming them face forward into a wall or covering their heads."

Wortham's violence was not only physical but the mental anguish he caused his victims was devastating; making threats of death that left one woman "cowering for hours in a shower for fear the rapist would make good his threat to kill her if she moves," said Hufnagel. One of the rapist victims said of her attacker, "He should never be on the streets again." Wortham is currently serving his sentence in Canon City, Col. REF.: *CBA.*

Wortman, Frank (AKA: **Buster**), 1903-70, U.S., org. crime. For many years Frank "Buster" Wortman was the mob boss of the St. Louis and southwestern Illinois territories. His reign was violent, characterized by the ruthless elimination of the men who gave him his first break in the St. Louis rackets—the Shelton brothers.

As an adolescent, Wortman was involved in crime and beginning in 1926, he was arrested many times for robbery. In 1926 he joined the Shelton brothers, an East St. Louis bootlegging gang, who were then associated with a ruthless outfit from across the Mississippi River, the Cuckoos. Jimmy Michaels was the leader of the Cuckoos, and he was entrusted with task of eliminating Charlie Birger's mob, which challenged the Sheltons for control of rum-running operations along the Illinois-Missouri border. Wortman was suspected of carrying out a number of gangland hits against the Birger men. In June 1933 a Prohibition official was murdered after he arrested Wortman and Monroe "Blackie" Armes. The two gangsters were captured and sent to prison for ten years each. Wortman was sentenced to Alcatraz, and Armes went to Leavenworth.

St. Louis gang boss Frank "Buster" Wortman, right, conferring with his attorney.

In 1941 Wortman emerged from prison determined to seize control of Southern Illinois and St. Louis. With an army of hired killers including "Black" Charlie Harris, Monroe and Tony Armes, and Elmer Sylvester "Dutch" Dowling, Wortman began his campaign against the three Sheltons, Bernie, Earl, and Carl, in the early 1940s. The Wortman gang first murdered Carl Shelton in 1947, and then killed Bernie a year later. With his rivals out of the way, Wortman took control of all gambling, narcotics distribution, and vice in Southern Illinois and St. Louis. His political influence on both sides of the Illinois-Missouri line was reportedly considerable. One Illinois politician rumored to be on the Wortman payroll was Auditor Orville Enoch Hodge, who was convicted of skimming more than $1 million in public monies in 1956.

Wortman was convicted of tax evasion on Feb. 26, 1962, but the case was set aside. In 1970 he died of cancer. See: **Birger, Charles; Shelton Brothers**.

REF.: *CBA;* Demaris, *Captive City;* McClellan, *Crime Without Punishment;* Messick, *Secret File;* ____, *Syndicate in the Sun;* Nash, *Bloodletters and Bad Men.*

Wounded Knee Massacre, prom. 1890, U.S., mur. The U.S. government began its most intensive effort to confine the Sioux nation to reservations in the 1870s. Following Sioux victories at Rosebud Creek and Little Bighorn, cold and starvation forced them into reservations in Winter 1876. The whites began systematically "civilizing" the Indians by forcing their educational system and religion on the young. The Teton Sioux were settled on a reservation in 1880, where they were not allowed to hunt, participate in religious rituals such as the Sun Dance, practice any activity relating to war, or educate their children outside the missionary schools. With its people forced to live on handouts from the Indian agents, Sioux society began to deteriorate, and soon turned to messianic religion.

An Indian messiah arose and advocated the Ghost Dance, whose performance was believed to hasten the arrival of a time when all Indians would regain their freedom, the whites would leave the continent and the old Indian ways would be practiced. While in their ornate ghost shirts, ghost dancers believed they were invulnerable to bullets. The Ghost Dance was neither violent nor advocated violence, but whites became nervous about the dance and in a few cases tried to prevent it. The army was called to the Teton reservation on one occasion, and a soldier shot and killed the great Teton Sioux chief, Sitting Bull. Several groups of Indians fled into the badlands following this and other incidents.

One such band, the Miniconjou Sioux, led by Chief Big Foot, were on their way back to the Indian Agency to surrender when they were met by Colonel James W. Forsyth and the Seventh Cavalry, on Dec. 29, 1890, in an area called Wounded Knee in South Dakota. Bigfoot and his people immediately surrendered and held up a white flag. Forsyth thought the Indians were concealing weapons, and ordered a search of their belongings. While the soldiers were looking through the blankets, one Indian pulled out a rifle, held it over his head, and threw it on the ground. A shot was fired, either by the gun striking the earth or by a soldier. At that point, the soldiers opened fire on the Sioux, indiscriminately killing men, women, and children. When the shooting was over, the soldiers had killed 200 to 250 Miniconjou Sioux.

This event marked the final defeat of the Sioux. Forsyth was relieved of his command by General Nelson A. Miles, who considered Wounded Knee a massacre. However, Forsyth was restored by the secretary of war, and eighteen soldiers who participated in the massacre received Congressional Medals of Honor. REF.: *CBA.*

Wren, Margery, d.1930, Brit., (unsolv.) mur. Margery Wren, who ran a sweetshop on Church Road in Ramsgate, Eng., was attacked in the late afternoon of Sept. 20, 1930. Someone beat her with a pair of fire tongs, but she would not say who. "Let him live in his sins," she told the police. Wren had been found by a little girl sent by her mother to buy some sugar. The girl knocked until the injured old lady came to the door and let her in. The child got what she needed and ran home to tell her parents. They called the police, who quickly took Wren to the hospital. She died five days later, having kept her secret.

REF.: Adam, *Murder Most Mysterious;* Brock, *A Casebook of Crime;* Browne and Tullett, *The Scalpel of Scotland Yard; CBA;* Hambrrok, *Hambrook of the Yard;* Nash, *Open Files;* Shew, *A Second Companion to Murder;* Wilson, *Encyclopedia of Murder.*

Wren, William R., prom. 1877, U.S., west. gunman-lawman. William Wren was a cattle rancher in Lampasas County, Texas. He became Pink Higgins' chief lieutenant in a feud with the Horrell brothers. On Mar. 26, 1877, Wren, Higgins, and several others ambushed Mart and Sam Horrell. They shot Sam from his horse, and though they wounded Mart, he charged the ambushers and single-handedly dispersed them. Wren was wounded in a battle with seven Horrell men in Lampasas on June 14. Frank Mitchell, Higgins' brother-in-law, was killed, and Wren was wounded. The following month, Higgins and fifteen men besieged the Horrell ranch. The assault lasted two days, during which two of Horrell's men were wounded. Higgins had to withdraw when his ammunition ran low. Wren was severely wounded in a street fight later that year, and signed a truce at the insistence of Texas Ranger major John B. Jones. Wren later became a county sheriff.

REF.: *CBA;* Gillett, *Six Years with the Texas Rangers;* Sonnichsen, *I'll Die Before I'll Run;* Webb, *Texas Rangers.*

Wright, Bella, See: **Light, Ronald Vivian**.

Wright, Cecil (AKA: **The Brain of Alcatraz**), 1907-87, U.S., burg. In the 1930s, Cecil Wright and three companions burglarized a post office and made off with the not-very-impressive sum of $2.43. The four burglars were arrested and convicted in federal court of the crime. In Leavenworth Prison, Wright began to study law and wrote petitions for other inmates. In 1942, he was transferred to Alcatraz and continued his legal work for inmates and for himself. His efforts on his own behalf eventually resulted in his release. At the time of his release a federal prosecutor called him "the world's greatest authority on habeas corpus." Wright died Aug. 24, 1987. REF.: *CBA*.

Wright, Charles Edward, b.1884, and **Wood, Horace**, b.1878, Case of, Brit., mur. Henry Charles Joyce, a law enforcement official of the Yorkshire, England, sheriff, noticed two men with a gun and a dog during the early hours of May 4, 1911. The officer placed his gun against a tree and, unarmed, went to question the men, 27-year-old Charles Edward Wright and 33-year-old Horace Wood. During a scuffle, a shot was fired and Joyce died from a shotgun wound. The two miners were arrested and police found parts of Wright's gun buried in a garden. Wright and Wood were tried, and their lawyer argued that the gun had accidentally discharged when Joyce tried to take it from Wright. The two men were acquitted.

REF.: *CBA;* Hastings, *The Other Mr. Churchill.*

Wright, Dr. **David**, d.1863, U.S., mur. Until the Civil War, Dr. David Wright conducted a prosperous medical practice in Norfolk, Va. However, his practice dwindled after federal troops occupied the city. The doctor, a Confederate sympathizer, was annoyed by the continual sight of the Union soldiers. One day, spotting a Union regiment of black soldiers, he suddenly pulled his pistol and fatally shot one of the officers, Lieutenant Sanborn. Wright was tried, convicted, and sentenced to death. While awaiting his execution, Wright's friends tried to persuade President Abraham Lincoln to commute the sentence. His daughter switched places with him during a jail visit and he tried to escape in her clothing. His supporters also allegedly tried to bribe the Norfolk telegraph operator to create a phony telegram from the president granting a reprieve. In spite of friends' attempts, he was hanged Oct. 23, 1863.

REF.: *CBA;* Mencken, *By the Neck.*

Wright, David Ray, 1942- , and **Wright, Willye Sue**, prom. 1967-71, and **Wright, Raymond**, prom. 1967-71, U.S., fraud. Mark Hopkins, the California railroad and real estate magnate, died in 1878 but neglected to leave a will for division of his $20 million estate. On Nov. 1, 1883, a California state court adjudicated the estate, distributing one-quarter to Hopkins' brother, Moses Hopkins, and three-quarters to Mary Frances Sherwood Hopkins, the woman assumed by the court to be Hopkins' widow. In 1906, virtually all of the records on Hopkins past were destroyed in the great San Francisco earthquake and fire. Over the years, many people claimed to be the rightful Hopkins' heirs—case after case was dismissed by the courts as being unprovable.

One particularly enterprising family tried another approach. Willye Sue Wright and her 25-year-old son David Ray Wright extracted from 300 victims in at least thirteen states, a sum conservatively estimated at $300,000. Each person who invested with the Wrights was led to believe that they had a legitimate claim on the Hopkins estate and were promised a minimum of $1 million of its "unclaimed assets". While pitching their potential victims, the Wrights carried with them a suitcase full of "documents" intended to convince the victims of the legitimacy of their claim. The Wrights claimed that all of the property Disneyland had been built on, plus seventy acres in downtown San Francisco, were in the estate. They also mentioned the names of other legatees, including Harry S. Truman, Ronald Reagan, and Lady Bird Johnson.

The Wrights often returned to the same people and pitched to their family members for multiple $250 "investments"—parents could be persuaded to register each of their children as well as themselves. One such family, the Forrests, had 112 members who had invested a total of $51,475 with the Wrights without a firm assurance of receiving anything at all in return. Later, several members of the Forrest family contacted the local postal authorities. The ensuing investigation was difficult because of many victims' unwillingness were reluctant to come forward—some out of embarrassment, but still more out of the stubborn belief that they would inherit millions. Eventually, the postal inspectors found a number of victims willing to testify.

On Feb. 8, 1971, the Wrights were indicted by a federal grand jury and on Feb. 22, they were arrested and released on bond. In the months that intervened between their arrests and the scheduling of a trial date, the Wrights continued their con game. In federal court on Dec. 22, David Ray and Willye Sue pleaded guilty on each of twenty counts. David Ray was fined five thousand dollars and sentenced to one year in prison. Willye Sue received the same fine and was put on probation for three years. The IRS had procured indictments against David Ray, Willye Sue, and Willye Sue's husband, Raymond Wright. From this indictment, Raymond Wright drew a $5,000 fine and three years' probation. REF.: *CBA.*

Wright, James Claude, Jr., 1933- , Case of, U.S., polit. corr., Early in 1988, Georgia Republican Representative Newt Gingrich delivered a series of speeches before the House of Representatives that sparked demand for an investigation into the financial affairs of House Speaker Jim Wright. A seven-month inquiry conducted by special counsel Richard Phelan, was completed in February 1989 and delivered to the House Ethics Committee. Phelan's 279-page report was withheld from the public while the twelve-member ethics panel continued the investigation.

One prominent issue under investigation was Wright's complex business dealings with George Mallick, a real estate developer from Wright's home town of Fort Worth, Texas. In 1980, Wright and his wife, Betty Wright, bought a 50 percent interest in Mallightco, a company formed the previous year by Mallick and his wife. The Wrights received stocks valued between $50,000 and $100,000 in return for their investment. Of concern to the committee was that Wright did not detail his holdings in the partnership in his House financial disclosure statements until 1988.

A corollary issue involved a 1979 Cadillac owned by Mallightco, but loaned to Mrs. Wright for her use in Washington, D.C. Mrs. Wright was also paid $18,000 a year from 1979 to 1983 by Mallightco. In addition the Wrights used, free of charge, a Fort Worth condominium owned by Mallick's son, Steven. The committee was concerned with determining whether the car, salary, and use of the condominium were compensation for Mrs. Wright's work for the company or undisclosed gifts.

Also under investigation was the subject of royalties amounting to $55,600, money above and beyond allowed lecture fees for congressmen, from Wright's 117-page book, *Reflections of a Public Man*. The book was printed by Wright's political campaign printer and many were bought in bulk by his political supporters. Another serious charge against him was that he had tried to bully federal investigators into giving favorable treatment to Texas savings and loan associations under government investigation.

Wright has been known as a fierce Democratic partisan with many political enemies on Capitol Hill, even within his party. During the nearly two months between the completion of the special counsel's report and the subsequent completion of the panel's investigation, tension between House Democrats and Republicans ran particularly high. Democrats accused some Republicans of being "zealous partisans" and turning the investigation into a "brazenly political circus." Democratic comments indicated fear that Republicans would hold Wright's conduct to rigorous standards in retaliation for the recent rejection of the nomination of Republican John Tower as secretary of defense.

While the public waited for the panel to announce its findings, a number of individual incidents darkened Speaker Wright's prospects. On Mar. 20, L. William Seidman, chairman of the Federal Deposit Insurance Corp., reported that Wright had placed pressure on federal bank regulator Edwin J. Gray to assist troubled Texas savings and loan associations in the mid-1980s. Further accusations disclosed that at the same time Wright advocated leniency for troubled savings and loan associations, George Mallick was struggling to repay a $2.2 million loan to a troubled S & L. Conceivably, any help given to savings and loans might have reduced the pressure on the Mallicks' lender to foreclose on his loan.

Then, on Mar. 21, conservative activist Paul Weyrich asked Attorney General Dick Thornburgh to name a special prosecutor to investigate an allegation that Wright violated federal criminal law. The Justice Department deferred a decision regarding any criminal charges against Wright until after the House Committee had released its finding.

The House Ethics Committee concluded its exhaustive ten month investigation on Apr. 12, 1989. The 450-page report produced by the panel eliminated a large number of the original allegations against Wright and focused instead on three issues: the royalties on Wright's book, the income his wife received from Mallick, and the possibility that Mallick had a direct interest in legislation authored by Wright. In the case of Wright's book, the panel concluded that it may have been published specifically to circumvent the limit on income that members of the House can receive from interest groups. With regard to Mrs. Wright's earnings from Mallightco, it concluded that the money and benefits may have constituted a gift which, under House rules, should have been reported. The committee further suspected that Mallick had an interest in the legislation authored by Wright in October 1986, that provided a federal grant for development of the old stockyards in Fort Worth.

On Apr. 13, Wright delivered an emotional plea to the American public for fairness. On Apr. 17, the House Ethics Committee announced it had "reason to believe" that Wright violated the rules of Congressional conduct sixty-nine times. The sixty-nine charges fell into two categories: the evasion of House limits on outside income by selling copies of his book in lieu of speaking fees, and the receipt of $145,000 worth of improper gifts from Mallick over the last decade. They voted 12-0 in favor of bringing charges against Wright.

Wright vowed to fight to clear his name and retain his position as speaker of the House. He requested that the panel grant him a hearing at the earliest possible time. But on May 25, his chances of clearing his name seemingly hopeless, Wright offered to resign from his position as Speaker of the House if all the charges were dropped. The panel rejected Wright's offer for a plea bargain, and on May 31, Wright appeared before the full House to announce his resignation as Speaker of the House and as a U.S. Representative. REF.: *CBA*.

Wright, James Skelly, 1911- , U.S., jur. Served as U.S. attorney in New Orleans, La. He was nominated to the eastern district court of Louisiana by President Harry Truman in 1949 and to the District of Columbia Circuit Court by President John F. Kennedy in 1962. REF.: *CBA*.

Wright, Jeanne Anne, 1958- , U.S., mur. A New Jersey mother receiving public assistance drowned her four children because she reportedly thought they would be better off dead. Several times pregnant as a teenager, Jeanne Anne Wright was forced to drop out of high school. Emilio Jaime Andujar fathered three of her four children. Wright lived with her children and her parents in a low-income housing project, but in 1983, she was directed to move because the apartment was occupied by too many people. In October 1983, her food stamps were cut off, and a welfare check arrived two weeks late. Wright, who was later diagnosed as suffering from chronic depression and borderline personality disorders, was also concerned because Andujar, whom she said was abusive, allegedly threatened to take custody of the children.

Late on Nov. 10, 1983, Wright took her four children to the Cooper River, to hide and to think, she later said. She sat on a wooden plank by a railroad trestle for several hours before she dropped the sleeping children into the water. Then she walked to a friend's house, claiming that Andujar had abducted them. On Nov. 27, a gas station attendant spotted the body of 34-month-old Jonathan Wright. On Feb. 21, 1984, Wright pleaded guilty to four counts of murder before a judge. On Apr. 19, 1984, Wright, twenty-six, was sentenced to four concurrent life prison terms. REF.: *CBA*.

Wright, Paul, prom. 1937, Case of, U.S., mur. The marriage of Paul and Evelyn Wright was unbalanced: he worshipped her, and she used him. Wright had gone into debt to supply his dissatisfied wife with expensive clothes, a convertible, and a big house in a fancy Glendale, Calif., neighborhood. After the birth of their daughter, Wright found a surgeon to perform a sterilization—an expensive and risky operation at that time. In the early morning hours of Nov. 9, 1937, Wright woke to hear the repeated sound of a piano key. Walking into the living room he saw his wife and his best friend, John Kimmel, making love on the piano bench. Enraged, Wright returned to his room, picked up a revolver, and went back into the living room to fire nine rounds at his wife and Kimmel. He then called the police and waited on the sidewalk for them to come. After Wright called his father in Milwaukee, Wis., he hired attorney Jerry Giesler. The district attorney contended that Wright had long been aware of the affair between Kimmel and his spouse, and was waiting for the opportunity to murder them.

Giesler maintained that Wright's shooting was a case of temporary insanity. Wright testified, "A white flame exploded in my brain." Bringing the piano and bench into the courtroom to reenact the killings, Giesler demonstrated by falling at the angle Kimmel had dropped, and continuing part of his speech from that position. An important point in Wright's defense was the question of whether he had fired two shots, and then hesitated before continuing, or whether he had fired all nine rounds in a calculated and cold-blooded action at close range. An elderly neighbor testified to the latter but, when the prosecution asked her to demonstrate the firing technique by tapping with a pencil, she considered for a very long time, then tapped out a rhythm that had a lengthy pause after two taps. Wright was found Guilty only of manslaughter. In the second phase of the trial, Giesler managed to switch the burden of proof of sanity at the time of the crime over to the prosecution. After two days of deliberation the jury found Wright Not Guilty by reason of temporary insanity. When psychiatric examination revealed that he was no longer insane, he was released.

Paul Wright, accused killer.

REF.: *CBA; Wolf, Fallen Angels.*

Wright, Peter, See: **Gladstone, Henry Neville.**

Wright, Robert Alderson, 1869-1964, Brit., jur. The son of a Marine Superintendent from South Shields, Robert Alderson Wright went on to become one of Britain's most learned jurists, whose decisions on the bench were guided by his unshakable belief that for each appeal decided a general principle should be established. Wright was called to the bar by the Inner Temple in 1900. In 1925, after a quarter-century in lucrative, private practice he was appointed to the King's Bench and awarded knighthood. Seven years later, at the age of sixty-three, Justice Wright was named Lord of Appeal in Ordinary—a position he would hold until 1947. His tenure in the House of Lords was briefly interrupted in 1935-37, when he succeeded Lord Hanworth as Master of the Rolls in the Court of Appeal.

In 1945, the aging jurist was appointed chairman of the United Nations War Crimes Commission, which gathered evidence to support the charges brought against Nazi leaders at the Nuremberg hearings. In 1946, his article *War Crimes Under International Law* appeared in the *Law Quarterly Review*. REF.: *CBA*.

Wright, Sir **Robert Samuel**, 1839-1904, Brit., jur. Called to the bar by the Inner Temple in 1865, Robert Samuel Wright practiced on the Northern Circuit and was later made junior counsel to the Treasury. Raised to the Bench in 1890, he was a judge of the King's Bench for fourteen years. Wright was a classics scholar who edited the *Golden Treasury of Greek Poetry* and the *Golden*

Treasury of Greek Prose. He was politically liberal and humane in his opinions, for which he drew some criticism. Wright was often lenient in his sentencing at a time when severity was esteemed. A solemn and conscientious jurist, Wright resigned his position in June 1904 because of failing health. His resignation was deferred in the hopes that his condition might improve, but Wright died just two months later, at sixty-five. One of his well-known cases was that of Samuel Herbert Dougal. REF.: *CBA.*

Wright, Samuel, d.1864, Brit., mur. A bricklayer, Samuel Wright was convicted of murder and sentenced to die by hanging on July 12, 1864. Questions about Wright's sanity and reservations about the speed in which the sentence followed the verdict, caused many efforts to commute his sentence. The controversy was further exacerbated by the fact that George Townley, a young man from a wealthy family, had recently had his sentence rescinded on the grounds of insanity. The issue of an unequal system of justice for rich and poor raged, as visiting justices of Horsemonger Lane and tradesmen circulating petitions fought for clemency for Wright. All appeals were rejected by Home Secretary Sir George Grey. Sentiments against the execution were so intense that authorities assigned 1,000 metropolitan police officers in the Horsemonger Lane Jail area where the hanging was to take place. Apparently touched by the sympathetic reaction, Wright bowed repeatedly to the crowd just before he was hanged. REF.: *CBA.*

Wright, Scott Olin, 1923- , U.S., jur. Served as prosecuting attorney in Boone County, Mo., from 1955-59. He was nominated to the western district court of Missouri by President Jimmy Carter in 1979. REF.: *CBA.*

Wright, Tom (AKA: Thomas Curt), d.1882, Brit., burg.-rob.-mur. Tom Wright was the cook on a small ship, the *Lollard,* which sailed a route between Sunderland and London. A heavy drinker with a police record for violence, Wright murdered Maria Fitzsimmons in Sunderland in 1869. Although a sailor was suspected, the captain ordered Wright to stay on board and clean the filthy ship's kitchen and so the cook was able to avoid being seen in Sunderland just after the murder. The ship sailed back to London, and the crew members discussed the case for days, with Wright, enjoying the fact of his secret notoriety, participating in and encouraging the conversations. After arriving in London he wrote a full confession of his crime in the pocket book of another sailor, then threw it into the Serpentine in the West End instead of sending it to the police. A man named Dyson found the confession the next day and turned it in to Scotland Yard.

The London police offered a £100 reward for information that would lead to the arrest and conviction of Fitzsimmons' killer. Wright decided to collect the money, and went to Inspector Hann, saying he would point out the slayer the next day at an East End pub. He fingered a sailor named O'Connor, who had served with him on the *Lollard,* and O'Connor was brought arrested, with Wright scheduled as the principal witness. Visiting Hann just before the case was scheduled in court, Wright was told by Hann that Inspector Elliot from Sunderland was in the next room and would present testimony about the murder. Terrified, since Elliot was the one police officer who knew his entire record and would arrest him immediately, Wright left the police department, and signed on for a steamer bound for Spain, but got into a drunken fight and was jailed briefly. By the time he was released, the steamer had sailed. So Wright remained in the East End, living by stealing scraps of food and renting cheap rooms for several years, becoming a proficient burglar in the process. He was eventually convicted of robbery with violence and, under the assumed name of Thomas Curt was sentenced to fifteen years of penal servitude. In jail he became a model prisoner, educating himself in classic literature and becoming a scholar and a writer. His conscience moved him to write a confession of the murder, and give it to the warden. Tried at the Durham Assizes, Wright was convicted and sentenced to death. He wrote the story of his life and of his time in jail, and was executed on May 16, 1882, thirteen years after he killed Fitzsimmons. REF.: *CBA.*

Wright, Whitaker, 1845-1904, Brit., fraud-forg.-suic. The career of Whitaker Wright was relatively brief but dramatic. Born in Cheshire, England, in 1845, he was trained as a chemist and moved to the U.S. in 1856, becoming an assayer. He became involved in a silver mine, which made him a millionaire. Within a short time, Wright was made president of the Philadelphia Stock Exchange and chairman of the New York exchange. Investing in coal and iron, Wright lost all his money. He relocated to England in 1889, and by 1897, he was a tremendous success, fabulously wealthy and with connections in high society and royalty. He bought racing yachts, and had an extravagant estate with a private theater and stables and a fourteen-mile wall around the property.

Wright had founded forty-two companies with capital of $110 million. When the Boer War caused a major market slump and Wright tried to escape to the U.S., it was discovered that all but $10 million of his capitalization was only on paper. His fictitious London & Globe Finance Corporation collapsed. Wright was charged with making false entries and making false statements with intent to defraud creditors and shareholders. Charged

Swindler Whitaker Wright, center, on trial for fraud, 1904.

initially in a private prosecution by a shareholder on Aug. 5, 1903, Wright was tried on Jan. 11, 1904, before Mr. Justice Bigham and a special jury at the King's Bench Court. Defending attorneys were Lawson Walton, Richard Muir, and F. Cassel, with Guy Stephenson, G.A.H. Branson, and Avory for the prosecution. Wright pleaded not guilty. The jury deliberated for one hour before finding him Guilty on Jan. 26. Protesting his innocence to the end, Wright was sentenced to seven years' penal servitude for his massive financial frauds. Taken to a private room to await an escort to prison, Wright poisoned himself by swallowing cyanide of potassium, also known as prussic acid. Within thirty minutes of his sentencing, Wright was dead.

REF.: Bowker, *Behind the Bar; CBA;* Ellis, *Black Fame;* Lustgarten, *The Story of Crime;* MacDougall, *Hoaxes;* Nicholls, *Crime Within the Square Mile.*

Wright, Willard Huntington (AKA: S.S. Van Dine), 1888-1939, U.S., writer. Created fictional detective Philo Vance under pseudonym S.S. Van Dine. Books authored: *The Canary Murder Case, The Casino Murder case, The Gracie Allen Murder Case,* others. REF.: *CBA.*

Wright, William (AKA: **Fred Evans**), d.1891, U.S., suic.-mur. On Mar. 13, 1891, the corpse of Carl Emanuel Ruttinger, a clerk from Germany, was found floating near the town of Tottenville on Staten Island, N.Y., by a schooner's mate who was clam fishing. Chief of Police Blake took charge of the body, noted two ferry tickets in the pocket, the hands tied behind the back at the wrists and elbows, and a handkerchief with the initials "W.W." stuffed down the throat. In investigating the case, District Attorney Fitzgerald talked with electrician S. Gustave Neu who lived on East 58th Street and had come forward to explain that Ruttinger boarded with him and with William Wright, the dead man's inseparable companion and brother-in-law. Ruttinger left Neu's house on Feb. 2, and never returned. Wright was English, a slight, blond, delicate man; Ruttinger weighed more than 200 pounds, and acted as the spokesman for the pair. Wright, Neu explained, had left on Feb. 1, presumably to return to a job cutting gems in Boston. Ruttinger had taken him to the station and returned to the rooms that night, leaving very early the next morning.

A coroner's jury had gathered to begin to consider the evidence when Fitzgerald remembered a Feb. 2 suicide at New York City's Astor House, of a slight, blond Englishman who registered as "Fred Evans." Checking records, Fitzgerald learned that Evans had destroyed all identifying marks and burned his papers before cutting his throat with a razor. The possessions of "Evans" revealed the initials "W.W." on the dead man's boots, and several other characteristics indicated that he was Wright. The body was exhumed and witnesses identified the corpse as Wright. Ruttinger had been killed after a quarrel. His long-time companion and lover, Wright, enraged at being replaced in his affections by Neu, first gave Ruttinger morphine pills then tied his hands and stuffed a gag down Ruttinger's throat. Having disposed of his former lover, Wright then took his own life.

REF.: *CBA;* Rodell, *New York Murders.*

Wriothesley, Henry (Earl of Southampton), 1573-1624, Brit., consp. Participated in rebellion led by Earl of Essex and was convicted of fueling conspiracy through revival of Shakespeare's *Richard II.* Sentenced to death in 1601, his sentence was commuted to life imprisonment, and he was released after serving only two years. REF.: *CBA.*

Written on the Wind, 1946, a novel by Robert Wilder. Torch singer Libby Holman, accused of murdering her millionaire husband, Zachary Smith Reynolds (U.S., 1932), is the steamy role model for this work of fiction. A 1956 film with the same title, based on the novel and directed by Douglas Sirk, offers a composite portrait of Holman by Lauren Bacall and Dorothy Malone. See: **Holman, Libby.** REF.: *CBA.*

Wrottesley, Sir Frederic John, 1880-1948. Brit., jur. The third son of Reverend Francis John Wrottesley, Sir Frederic John Wrottesley was a barrister and a judge from 1907 until his death in 1948. Called to the Bar in 1907, he practiced parliamentary law exclusively. His career was interrupted by WWI, during which he attained the rank of major, serving in the Royal Field Artillery in France. Appointed to the King's Bench Division of the High Court in 1937, Wrottesley succeeded Justice Talbot. He became adept in criminal and civil law and was raised to the Court of Appeal ten years later. He was made a justice of appeal in October 1948, but was forced to retire due to deteriorating health. He died Nov. 14, 1948. He presided over cases involving such people as George Brain, George Silverosa, Samuel Dashwood, and Harry Dobkin. His works include *The Examination of Witnesses in Court* (1910), and *Letters to a Young Barrister* (1930). REF.: *CBA.*

Wullenwever, Jürgen (Wullenweber), c.1488-1537, Ger., her. Attempted to reinstate Lübeck as chief Baltic power and worked to spread Protestantism. He was imprisoned by the anti-Lutheran Duke Henry of Brunswick-Wolfenbüttel and was tortured, condemned to death, and executed. REF.: *CBA.*

Wupper, Paul (AKA: **Frederick Brinkmann**), b.1874, U.S., embez. The president of Beemer (Neb.) State Bank from 1908, 54-year-old Paul Wupper fled Beemer in 1928 when bank examiners arrived. Wupper, also the mayor of Beemer for more than twelve years, had embezzled around $1 million from the bank. The Beemer State Bank collapsed after his flight, wiping out the savings of hundreds of residents, including his wife. Wupper changed his name to Frederick Brinkmann, married a woman in Trenton, N.J., and took a job as a supervisor in an electrical company. He left his wife after losing his job and moved to New York City. In March 1931, police arrested him for desertion and non-support, but changed the charge to bigamy when they learned he had not divorced his first wife. While awaiting a hearing, Wupper confessed to the Beemer embezzlement and sent a telegram to the Lincoln, Neb., sheriff. He was charged with twenty counts of forgery. He pleaded guilty and was sentenced by Judge Clinton Chase to 110 years in prison, twenty years for the first offense, and ten years for each of the following nine. He was also fined $500 for each offense. REF.: *CBA.*

Würzburg Stones, 18th Cent., Ger., hoax. An over-zealous professor's students perpetrated a hoax which ruined his career. Johann Bartholomaeus Adam Beringer, a professor of natural philosophy, was a deeply religious man, who had a theory that fossils, which were the main subject of attention in the scientific world at that time, were "capricious fabrications of God." Beringer believed fossils were hidden in the earth for some unknown purpose, perhaps to test man's faith. Obsessed with gaining recognition for his theory, Beringer alienated his University of Würzburg students by continually harping on this theme. Imitating a joke played on mathematician Athanasius Kircher in the seventeenth century, the students planted clay tablets inscribed in Arabic, Syriac, Babylonian, and Hebrew on a hillside where Beringer took his classes to search for specimens. After a few easy successes, the students inscribed God's signature on one of the ersatz fossils. Beringer was ecstatic, believing his theories justified by this proof, and began writing a book in Latin about his philosophy and the evidence. At great cost, he had engravings made of the stones and tablets.

The students confessed, but their teacher refused to believe them, accusing them of trying to rob him of the honor of his greatest discovery. *Lithographiae Wirceburgensis* appeared in 1728, with fourteen chapters and twenty-one plates of the figures. Beringer, who became a laughingstock, spent the rest of his fortune buying back the copies and was said to have died of a broken heart. A Hamburg bookseller named Hobard later bought all available copies and reissued them in a second edition under a new title.

REF.: *CBA;* MacDougall, *Hoaxes.*

Würzburg Witch Trials, 1623-29, Ger., witchcraft. In the Würzburg Witch Trials, hundreds of men, women, and children of all ages were implicated, with victims from the clergy and nobility as well as peasants. Three hundred 3- to 4-year-old children were accused of having intercourse with the devil, and children as young as seven were tortured and murdered. Led by two cousins, Prince-Bishop Philipp Adolf von Ehrenberg of Würzburg, responsible for burning 900 witches; and Prince-Bishop Gottfried Johann Georg II Fuchs von Dornheim of Bamberg, who burned 600, the hunt for witches was savage.

The hysteria was started, as it was in Austria and Bavaria, by priests who fanned the flames of irrationality and fear. Although random executions for witchcraft had occurred since 1600, full-blown terror did not take hold until von Ehrenberg succeeded to the throne in 1623. Records reveal the usual techniques of torture and whippings to extract confessions were used, as well as people who insisted on their innocence, capitulating under severe duress, "confessing," and implicating others. A list dated Feb. 16, 1629, detailed twenty-nine separate mass executions at Würzburg, with a total of 157 people killed. The list of victims included highly-placed wealthy people, children—thirteen of them twelve-years-old and younger—and almost as many men as women.

Around this time, a young relative of von Ehrenberg was executed as a witch. Ernest von Ehrenberg had been an excellent student with a bright future, but he left his schoolwork to drink and chase after an older woman. Questioned subtly by the priests, he was denounced, secretly tried, and sentenced, completely unaware of the judgment. One morning Ernest von Ehrenberg was awakened, told he would lead a better life, and led to a castle and into a torture chamber. When he fainted, some of the judges asked the Prince-Bishop for mercy, but the older von Ehrenberg merely renewed the execution order. Resisting the hangman, Ernest von Ehrenberg was hit over the head, then slain. Following this deed, von Enrenberg instituted commemorative services for victims of witch trials. Gradually, the delirium began to diminish, aided by the march of the Swedish Protestant Army which helped stop the executions.

REF.: Burr, *Translations and Reprints, University of Philadelphia; CBA;* Diefenbach, *Der Hexenwahn vor und nach den Katechismen Dr. Martin Luthers und des P. Casinius;* Gropp, *Collectio Scriptorum et Rerum Wirceburgensium;* Hauber, *Bibliotheca, Acta et Scripta Magica;* Lea, *Materials Toward a History of Witchcraft;* Leitschuh, *Beiträge zur Geschichte des Hexenwesens in Franken;* Robbins, *The Encyclopedia of Witchcraft and Demonology;* Snell, *Hexenprozesse und Geistestörung;* Soldan, *Geschichte der Hexenprozesse aus der Quellen dargestellt;* Summers, *The Geography of Witchcraft.*

Wu T'ing-fang, 1842-1922, China, penal reform. Remodeled Chinese penal code while serving as minister of board of punishment from 1905-07. REF.: *CBA.*

Wyatt, John Arthur, c.1904- , and **Bryan, John Henry**, c.1906- , and **Saxton, John William**, c.1913- , and **Allen, George Charles**, c.1907- , and **Howells, James Thomas**, c.1905- , Brit., burg. In 1947, Scotland Yard detectives became aware of a new safe-breaking technique in which burglaries were accomplished by the use of duplicate keys to the safes; the burgled safes were all from one firm. Detectives learned that one of the firm's employees, George Charles Allen, forty, was meeting with John Arthur Wyatt, forty-three, a supposed bookmaker who actually had a long criminal record. Authorities also discovered that Wyatt was meeting with Harry John Bryan, forty-one, another bookmaker with a criminal record. After another safebreaking theft, it was noticed that Wyatt and Bryan had been in the premises not long before the robbery. With lists detailing safe sales and repairs, detectives watched places where the safes were. When it became obvious that the detectives' actions were somehow being leaked from Scotland Yard, Superintendent Lee authorized making incorrect entries in the daily duty books.

In Fall 1950, Wyatt and several other gang members, including John William Saxton, thirty-seven, and James Thomas Howells, forty-five, were seen at the Lloyds Bank at Waterlooville, Hampshire. Scotland Yard detectives and the local police force laid a trap by keeping watch over the bank. Eleven days later, Saxton and Howells were caught with the key as they entered the building. The next morning officers watching Wyatt's house saw Mrs. Wyatt come out with a brown paper parcel, which she dropped at the house of her sister, Mrs. Staggs. Searching the place, police found stolen jewelry, a ring with twenty-five carefully-labeled safe keys, and a book of addresses. Wyatt and his wife were arrested, along with Mr. and Mrs. Staggs, and Allen.

The trial, in April 1951 before Mr. Justice Byrne, with Ewen E. S. Montagu and J.T. Molony for the prosecution, lasted eleven days. All eight defendants were charged with conspiracy to break and enter premises and to steal from safes. All pleaded not guilty, with the exception of Saxton and Howells, who were caught in the act. The Stagg couple were acquitted on all counts. All others were convicted, with Bryan receiving a ten-year sentence and a £2,000 fee to cover prosecution costs; Wyatt was given an eight-year sentence; Saxton got four years of corrective training; and Allen was given a one-year sentence. Wyatt's wife was put on probation.

REF.: *CBA;* Woodland, *Assize Pageant.*

Wyatt, Nathaniel Ellsworth (AKA: **Zip, Wild Charlie, Dick Yaeger**), 1863-95, U.S., west. outl. Nathaniel Wyatt was the son of an Indiana farmer. He turned to outlawry after his brother, Nim "Six Shooter Jack" Wyatt, was killed in Texline, Texas. Nathaniel robbed various U.S. postal stations, retail stores, and trains in the Southwest before retreating to Indiana, where he was arrested and jailed by Chris Madsen. However, he escaped from the jail in Guthrie and returned to Oklahoma, where some his most famous gunfights occurred.

In the little village of Todd, on Mar. 29, 1894, Wyatt and two henchman held up a Blaine County store owned and operated by E.H. Townsend. When the proprietor put up some resistance, the robbers shot him dead in the presence of his wife and children. The next month in Dewey County, Okla., Wyatt murdered County Treasurer Fred Hoffman. After the successful robbery of a Santa Fe train in Whorton, Okla., on May 9, 1894, that left the station master dead, Wyatt and his gang went across the border into Kansas. Wyatt and his gang were cornered in Pryor's Grove by Sheriff Andrew Balfour, who produced an arrest warrant. Wyatt wheeled and fired on the sheriff, instantly killing him.

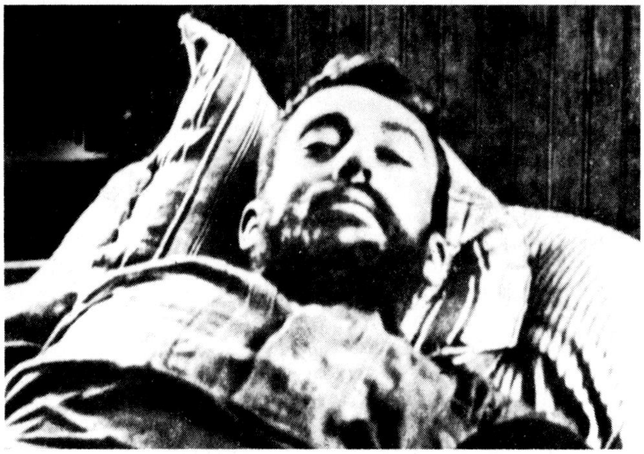

Outlaw Zip Wyatt, photographed only a few hours before he died of wounds.

Wyatt, a trigger-happy gunman, was pursued throughout the Old West for several years before a posse finally caught up with him outside Skeleton Creek, Okla., on Aug. 3, 1895. Wyatt had drifted off to sleep in a cornfield when Ad Poak and Tom Smith crept up on him with their rifles drawn. Without giving him a chance to respond, they opened fire. "Don't shoot any more. I'm bad hit," Wyatt said. He was taken to Enid, Okla., where he died Sept. 7.

REF.: *CBA;* Croy, *Trigger Marshal;* Hanes, *Bill Doolin;* Hunter and Rose, *The Album of Gun-Fighters;* Nix, *Oklahombres;* Shirley, *Six-Gun and Silver Star;* ____, *Toughest of Them All;* Sutton, *Hands Up!.*

Wyatt, Ross, prom. 1938, U.S., attempt. mur. On July 26, 1938, Ray Bonta, a Dallas *News* reporter, drove Mary Jo Miller, twenty-six, a physical education teacher from Chicago, home from a dance and saw her go into her brother's house where she was staying. Miller, getting ready for sleep, heard a thud and a crash from the front bedroom where she slept. Running in, Miller saw a suitcase on the floor under a broken window. As she ran to her brother, J.H. Miller, the house blew up. No one was killed or seriously hurt. Outside, a car drove away. E. Ross Wyatt, thirty-six, a rural school superintendent, was soon charged with "burglary of a private residence at nighttime with intent to commit a felony; to wit, murder."

Wyatt was held in jail for sixteen months. The "love bomb" trial began in mid-December 1939. Miller returned from Chicago, where she had moved two years earlier, to escape Wyatt. On the witness stand, she told of how Wyatt had pursued her for seven years, since she had gone to work for him as his secretary in 1931, and that he had sworn to kill "both of you," meaning her brother as well, if she went out with anyone else. She said there had been no real intimacies outside of kisses and hugs. Several witnesses, including Lela Wyatt, who had divorced the "classroom Casanova" in 1936 after finding him with Miller several times, and waitress Thelma Powell, who had once had an affair with Wyatt, testified.

Wyatt's alibi, that he had been 250 miles from the bombing, was backed by seven witnesses, but detective work placed his car near the scene of the crime. It was proved both that he had purchased dynamite in 1938 in Shreveport, La., and that one of the suitcases in his car had carried that explosive. On the stand, Wyatt told of the intense, very intimate affection between him and Miller. The Texas jury unanimously found him Guilty and he received a fifty-year sentence. REF.: *CBA.*

Wyatt, Sir **Thomas,** c.1503-42, Brit., consp. Accused of being in alliance with Oliver Cromwell and imprisoned in 1541. REF.: *CBA.*

Wyatt, Sir **Thomas the Younger,** c.1521-54, Brit., treas. Involved with forces leading general insurrection attempting to keep Queen Mary from marrying Philip of Spain in 1554. Charged with high treason, he was condemned to death and executed. REF.: *CBA.*

WYCA Murders, See: **Byrne, Patrick Joseph.**

Wyche, Charles Cecil, 1885-1966, U.S., jur. Served as district attorney for U.S. Department of Justice from 1933-37. He was nominated to the western district court of South Carolina by President Franklin D. Roosevelt in 1937. REF.: *CBA.*

Wychford Poisoning Case, 1930, a novel by Anthony Berkeley. This is a mystery based on the Maybrick poison case (Brit., 1889). See: **Maybrick, Florence Elizabeth.** REF.: *CBA.*

Wycliffe, John, c.1320-84, Brit., her. Accused of heresy by Pope Gregory XI in 1377. His trial was suspended due to rioting. He was finally condemned by the Council of Constance in 1415, thirty-one years after his death from a heart attack. As punishment, his remains were exhumed, burned, and thrown into the River Swift. REF.: *CBA.*

Wylie Hoffert Murders, See: **Robles, Richard.**

Wyman, Alfred Lee, 1874-1953, U.S., jur. Served as state attorney in Yankton, S.D., from 1905-08 and from 1915-18. He was nominated to the district court of South Dakota by President Herbert Hoover in 1929. REF.: *CBA.*

Wymer, Eugene William, 1927- , U.S., mur. On Apr. 11, 1943, 15-year-old Eugene Wymer and his brother, George, then nine, were climbing the rocks on Table Mountain near Golden, Colo., when they met two other boys. Wymer first forced 11-year-old Milo Flindt to give up his shoes and stockings, explaining that George needed new ones. Then Wymer made Donald James Mattas, eight, hand over his wrist watch. Deciding to leave no witnesses to the thefts, Wymer wrestled Mattas to the edge of a 175-foot cliff and pushed him over the edge, then turned to Flindt and forced him over, too. On their way back down the Wymer boys came across seven other youths and demanded each pay a 10-cent fee to continue their climb.

The bodies of Flindt and Mattas were found on Apr. 12. Through the testimony of the seven hikers, the Wymers were linked to the crimes, and Eugene Wymer was arrested in a Golden, Colo., hotel. Convicted of first-degree murder, Wymer was sentenced to life imprisonment on July 21, 1943. Except for an escape attempt about a year into his term when he tried to swim through a sewer line but failed, Wymer made, according to Warden Tinsley, "a good adjustment" to prison life. He appealed his conviction in January 1960, and although turned down by then-Governor Steve McNichols, Wymer was commended for his good behavior and urged to try for commutation of his sentence at a later time. Wymer was paroled on July 21, 1968, and was discharged on Mar. 15, 1974. REF.: *CBA.*

Wyndham, Charles, 1710-63, Brit., jur. Served as member of Parliament from 1734-50, and assisted the Earl of Halifax George Montagu Dunk in the prosecution of criminal John Wilkes. REF.: *CBA.*

Wynekoop, Dr. **Alice,** 1870-1952, U.S., mur. Chicago physician Dr. Alice Wynekoop was widely known for her medical career and her charitable activities. She also adored her youngest son, Earle. In the early 1930s, Earle Wynekoop met and married young violinist Rheta Gardner and brought her back to Chicago to live in the family mansion. But Rheta had not turned into the wife Earle wanted, and he began to look elsewhere. Dr. Wynekoop, disturbed that her son was unhappy, began to think about how she could fix things. In the early afternoon of Nov. 21, 1933, she took Rheta into the small surgery attached to her home, shot her dead, and left her lying on the table.

Murderess Dr. Alice Wynekoop, undergoing a lie detector test.

After a leisurely evening, at about 10 p.m., Dr. Wynekoop called Cook County Hospital where her daughter, Dr. Catherine Wynekoop, was on staff and told her that Rheta had been shot dead. The daughter sent the police to investigate. They found Rheta lying naked on the operating table, her clothing heaped on the floor nearby, and Dr. Wynekoop muttering, "It must have been a burglar." Earle Wynekoop was on a train to the Grand Canyon with another woman, but he hurried home when he heard of his wife's death.

Dr. Wynekoop was taken to police headquarters and questioned for many hours. She finally wrote a confession in which she said that Rheta had asked to be examined but wanted some anesthetic to be more comfortable. She had used too much chloroform, Wynekoop said, accidentally killing the girl. Realizing Rheta was dead, Wynekoop then put a bullet in her to "ease the situation."

Earle, too, confessed to killing his wife, but there was plenty of evidence that he had been on the train west. Dr. Alice Wynekoop tried to retract her confession at her trial, but she was convicted and sentenced to life in prison. She was paroled in 1949 at age seventy-nine. She died two years later.

REF.: *CBA;* Halper, *The Chicago Crime Book;* Nash, *Look For the Woman;* Rice, *Forty-five Murderers;* Rodell, *Chicago Murders.*

Wynkeburn, Walter, d.1363, Brit., mur. Hanged for murder in 1363 in Leicester, England, Walter Wynkeburn was cut down and began to revive in the cart as he was being taken to the cemetery. The priest who was to read the burial service over him instead took him into a church and held him there, guarding him against those who wanted to hang him again. He stayed in the church until enough time had passed for King Edward to learn of the case and grant him a pardon.

REF.: Atholl, *Shadow of the Gallows; CBA.*

Wynne, Thomas, prom. 1680s, Brit., burg.-mur. Born at Ipswich in Suffolk, Thomas Wynne went to sea in his mid-teens. After eight years he settled in London where he became an expert burglar, once robbing Queen Elizabeth's lodgings at Whitehall Palace of £400 worth of goods.

Wynne, a notorious ladies' man, became involved with the Countess of Salibury's gentlewoman. When she later spurned his advances, he became so enraged that he attacked her and bit her. Servants using a wooden stick to pry open his jaws finally released her from his bite. Understandably, Wynne was sentenced to severe punishment for his offense. After enduring it for a period, he ran off . Before he left, however, he stole from the coachman, who had been assigned to flog him and several other members of the household.

Wynne's next mode of operations was one that preyed upon the lack of attentiveness of innkeepers. Dressed as a porter, Wynne would go to an inn where he would spot some unattended luggage. Acting as though he had been commissioned to do so, he would throw the luggage on his back and make off with it. Wynne engaged in all manner of burglaries over the next eight years. Most of his work was marked by cleverness in its conception and rarely included any serious violence. However, after breaking into a house in Cheapside, Wynne murdered the elderly couple who lived there. He made off with £2,500 and, taking his wife and children, escaped to Virginia. Another man was arrested and charged with the murder and robbery, and despite his protestations, was convicted and hanged for the crimes.

Wynne, meanwhile, lived a prosperous existence in the colonies for some twenty years. After this period, he decided to return to England for a visit. While in a shop in Cheapside, a prisoner broke loose from his captors in the street outside. Hearing the shouts of "Stop him! Stop him!" Wynne's conscience got the best of him and he ran out of the shop, attempting to escape the pursuing crowd. When they caught up with him, he admitted that he was the one who had murdered the couple twenty years earlier. He was subsequently arrested and taken to Newgate. He was tried and condemned and then hanged in front of the house where he had committed the crimes.

REF.: *CBA;* Smith, *Highwaymen.*

Wyszynski, Stefan, 1901-81, Pol., impris. Roman Catholic cardinal imprisoned by ruling communists in 1953 for refusing to denounce Bishop Kaczmarek. He was released in 1956, and led the Church's long struggle against Polish communist oppression. REF.: *CBA.*

X

X, Malcolm, See: **Malcolm X.**

X, Michael, See: **Malik, Abdul.**

Xerxes I (AKA: **the Great**), c.519-465 B.C., Per., king, assass. Suppressed revolt in Egypt from 485-84 B.C. and continued Darius' legacy of punishing Greeks. He led the great expedition from 483-81 B.C., bridging the Hellespont, marching through Thrace, Macedonia, and Thessaly, winning at Thermopylae in 480 B.C., and also burning Athens. In 480 B.C., however, he was defeated at Salamis and returned to Asia Minor, leaving his army under the command of Mardonius. His army was defeated by the Greeks at Plataea, and on the same day in 479 B.C., his fleet was conquered by the Greeks at Mycale. He spent a degenerate life at Susa until he was murdered by Artabanus, the captain of the guards. REF.: *CBA.*

Xerxes II, d.424 B.C., Per., king, assass. Murdered by half brother Sogdianus. The son of Artaxerxes I, he reigned as king for just a few weeks.

REF.: *CBA;* Nash, *Almanac of World Crime.*

Xiphilinus, John, VIII, c.1010-75, Roman., jur. Head of law faculty at University of Constantinople. He entered the monastery of Holy Spirit on Mt. Olympus in 1054. From 1063 until his death he was the patriarch of Constantinople. Highly regarded, he left an encomium on Eugenius of Trabzon as well as some legal writings. REF.: *CBA.*

Yablonski, Joseph Albert, See: **Boyle, William Anthony.**

Yager, Erastus (AKA: **Red**), d.1864, U.S., west. outl. A nineteenth-century outlaw informant, Erastus Yager revealed the identities of several members of the Innocents outlaw gang, bringing about the gang's destruction. In December 1863, a vigilante committee captured Yager while he was carrying messages to gang agents who held up wagons and stages carrying large sums of money. Yager claimed he worked for Sheriff Henry Plummer, the leader of the Innocents, and told the vigilantes that Sheriff Plummer directed the activity of the Innocents while telling the public he was trying to rid the area of them. Yager also revealed how the organization was structured, how orders were handed down, and the password "innocent." He further revealed the names of twenty-six key members of the gang. The vigilance committee, while appreciating Yager's information, hanged him in Stinkingwater Valley on Jan. 4, 1864. REF.: *CBA.*

Yagoda, Henrikh Gregoryevich, prom. 1938, U.S.S.R., consp.-mur. Henrikh Gregoryevich Yagoda began his ascent within the ranks of the Soviet Secret Service in 1920 when he became a member of the Presidium Cheka, the organization that later became the GPU (Government Political Administration), precursor of the KGB. Yagoda served as vice-chief of the GPU in 1924, but due to the poor health of the chief, he virtually controlled the entire police force. Yagoda, although honored and decorated by Lenin, became best known for the accusations of murder levelled against him in his 1938 trial, which began on Mar. 2, in Moscow.

Before the trial ended on Mar. 13, three prominent Soviet doctors testified that Yagoda, a former pharmacist, had forced them to murder patients deemed dangerous to the state. The physicians, D.D. Pletnev, L.G. Levin, and I.N. Kazakov, admitted murdering writer Maxim Gorky, Gorky's son, Yagoda's predecessor as head of the GPU, Menzhinsky, and Kuibyshev, a former friend and assistant of Stalin who had risen to power after Lenin's death. It was implied, though not directly stated, that the deaths of many others, including many Bolsheviks, and even Lenin himself, were attributable to Yagoda.

Yagoda was found Guilty, condemned to death, and executed. It was generally conceded that, although the witnesses at his trial had fabricated parts of their testimony, Yagoda had, on Stalin's instruction, been responsible for the deaths of a number of "enemies of the state."

REF.: Bornstein, *The Politics of Murder; CBA.*

Yahya (Yahya Mahmud al-Mutawak-kil), 1867-1948, Yemen, imam, assass. Led troops in sporadic warfare against Ottoman Empire from 1904-11 until autonomy was recognized. Following WWI, he was viewed as the independent ruler of Yemen. In 1934, he was defeated by Saudi Arabia and kept his country isolated from the outside world until his assassination. REF.: *CBA.*

Yakshiyants, Pavel, prom. 1988, U.S.S.R., skyjack. On Dec. 1, 1988, four Soviets—later described by Soviet authorities as petty criminals from the southern Transcaucasus region—seized a bus load of Soviet fourth graders and ransomed them for more than $2 million in cash, an unspecified quantity of drugs, and a cargo jet with flight crew. The four men and the wife of one of them fled the Soviet Union aboard an Aeroflot jet after twenty-two hours of negotiations with Soviet officials. The hijackers instructed the crew to fly them to Israel, a destination apparently selected because Israel does not have an extradition agreement with the U.S.S.R.

With cooperation uncharacteristic of the two countries since a break in diplomatic relations following the 1967 Middle East war, Israeli authorities returned the kidnappers to the Soviet Union shortly after their surrender. The gang reportedly offered Israeli Defense Minister Yitzhak Rabin half of the ransom money in exchange for asylum in Israel. Rabin refused, and returned the money, drugs, and the airliner to Soviet officials. The four men were charged with banditry and illegally crossing the Soviet border. The ringleader, Pavel Yakshiyants, was sentenced to fifteen years in prison, while the other three received sentences of fourteen years. The wife of one of the hijackers, who had not taken part in the abduction of the schoolchildren or in the ransom negotiations, was sentenced to three years in prison as an accomplice. REF.: *CBA.*

Yoshio Kodama, left, Yakuza crime boss in Japan during the 1960s, shown with aides.

Yakuza, 1600s- , Japan, secret crim. soc. In 1988, the citizens of Ebitsuka, Japan, launched a campaign to rid their community of some unwanted neighbors. A five-story green building housed what they believed to be the headquarters of a formidable criminal yakuza gang known as *Ichiriki Ikka,* or "One Power Family." The citizens of Ebitsuka erected a two-level shack across the street and videotaped the movements of all visitors entering and leaving the building. After one surly gangster attacked the surveillance team with a sword, the townspeople gathered outside the green building they referred to as the *burakku biru* or "black building." "Get out!" they chanted. "Seek an honorable life!" National media attention was focused on the case, as the town's eight-member police force was bolstered with an additional 300 officers from other communities. The nearby city of Hamamatsu set up a police task force of 120 officers to stand guard against illegal activities.

Yakuza gangsters scuffling during a meeting at the Mitsubishi Shoji Corporation.

Eventually, half of the yakuza in the town were jailed or put in detention. In April 1988, Tetsuya Aono, the chief of the Ichiriki-Ikka, agreed to settle the suit out of court and abandon the headquarters building in Ebitsuka. The anti-yakuza banners were taken down by the happy residents as the gangsters sneaked out of town. It was a small, but important victory in an escalating war against organized crime in Asia—a growing menace—with larger implications for the industrial nations of the west.

The history of the yakuza can be traced back to 1612, during the time of the *machi-yakko*—a popular band of young rebels who defied the murderous Samurai warlords. According to criminologist Kanehiro Hoshino of Japan's Police Science Research Institute, the shogunate rounded up and executed the last of the *machi-yakko* in 1686. The exploits of this gang of "Robin Hoods" are kept alive in the folk tales and kabuki plays of the Japanese. The modern yakuza gangs first appeared in the mid-1700s. Like the Italian Mafia, the gangs were divided into families; however, in the yakuza, the father-child role, or *oyabun-kobun,* which mirrored traditional Japanese society played an important role. Just as the father was the supreme authority figure in the family, he was also the master of the apprentice's destiny in the yakuza. *Oyabun-kobun* provided strength and cohesion, which ultimately translated into blind obedience to the "boss" or criminal ruler. "If the boss says that a passing crow is white, you must agree," states a yakuza adage.

In the late nineteenth century, as Japan threw off the last vestiges of feudalism, a schism developed within the yakuza. Many of its members sided with the Tokugawa shogunate; others joined with the emperor. The ultimate victor was Jirocho no Shimizu, the boss of the *bakuto* or gambling empire. When Jirocho died in 1893 he was revered by the peasant classes as a wise and just bandit leader. In the early years of the twentieth century, Japan modernized, and within a few decades, became the leading industrial power of southeast Asia. The yakuza also adapted to the profound social changes around them. The gangs gained a toehold in the big cities by organizing groups of industrial workers for construction projects. The bosses of the lucrative *bakuto* gangs organized legitimate business fronts to cover their illegal activities, while the *tekiya* factions, which controlled thousands of peddler's stalls in the large cities, cultivated important ties to the politicians and police officials.

Takeshi Takagi, left, Yakuza boss in Honolulu, 1978.

The nationalist fervor that swept Japan in the first two decades of the twentieth century started in the 1880s, when Mitsuru Toyama organized a group of right-wing toughs from Fukuoka into the *Genyosha,* or "Dark Ocean Society"—a reference to the narrow passage of water separating Japan from Korea and China. This group spawned hundreds of secret societies in East Asia including the "Blood Pledge Corps," the "Association for Heavenly Action," and the "Death-Defying Corps"—terrifying names for an organized crime network that oversaw prostitution, gambling, extortion, drugs, and street peddling. The yakuza gangs realized that their success was intrinsically tied to the fortunes of the political right. Neither the yakuza nor the right-wingers wished to see their influence diminished by the socialist coalitions. After WWII, such pre-war nationalists as Kodama Yoshio, Kishi Nobusuke, and Sasakawa Ryoichi forged alliances with the yakuza to vanquish their enemies on the left. In 1960, for example, the rightists assassinated Socialist Party leader Asanuma Inejiro.

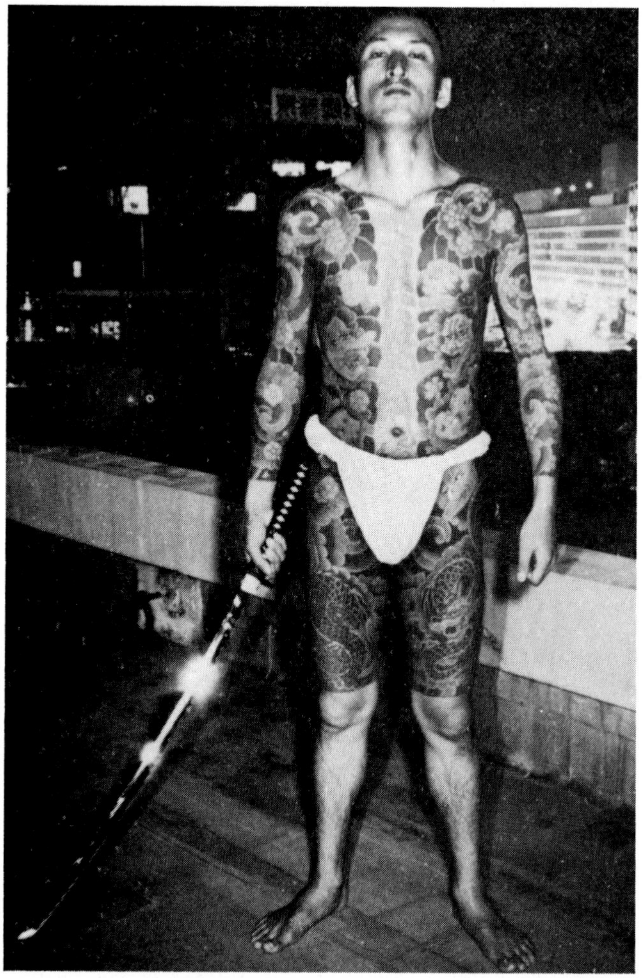

A tattooed Yakuza gangster with samurai sword, Tokyo, Japan, 1988.

The very nature of the yakuza changed after WWII. Swords were replaced by guns and the gangsters assumed a more western appearance. The *kobun* abandoned traditional folk dress in order to copy their counterparts in the Mafia. Dark suits and sunglasses became the preferred attire among a new generation of toughs. By 1958, the Tokyo police estimated that there were 70,000 yakuza in the whole of Japan. Five years later this figure grew to 184,000, by far the largest organized crime network in the world. The most formidable of the gangs to emerge after the war was the *Yamaguchi-gumi*, originally a small waterfront mob in Kobe before it was given direction by Taoka Kazuo, Japan's Al Capone.

Taoka bossed 343 different gangs by 1964. His influence in the Osaka region was particularly strong. Here the syndicate was said to control 80 percent of all cargo loading on the Kobe docks. Across Japan there were other yakuza gangs of lesser stature, which nonetheless employed the same viciousness in their methods. In Yokohama, the ruler of the criminal underworld was Inagawa Kakuji, whose *Kakusei-kai* gang (later called *Kinsei-kai*) claimed 2,700 members by the mid-1960s. The most important source of revenue for Kakusei was gambling. On Oct. 24, 1972, the Inagawa gang and the powerful Yamaguchi were united in a federation by the visionary gangster Kodama Yoshio. As a ranking member of the rightist Liberal-Democratic Party, Kodama desired to bring about permanent harmony between the warring clans. More than anything he feared that the leftists would exploit the factional rivalries and eventually eclipse the LDC in power. The amalgamation of the Yamaguchi and Inagawa empires brought the majority of Japanese gangs under their control.

By the 1970s, yakuza gangs were reported to be active in Thailand, Malaysia, Hong Kong, and Taiwan where they forged important links with the Chinese Triads. The specter of an all-powerful Chinese-Japanese Mafia controlling the international drug trade alarmed western observers who feared that the gangs were on the brink of funding large-scale shipments to the U.S. and Europe. In September 1985 for example, the U.S. and the Hong Kong police took ten people into custody who were charged with smuggling fifty-two pounds of amphetamines and twelve pounds of heroin into the states. Two high-ranking members of *Yamaguchi-gumi* were picked up in Hawaii where they were to serve as "point men" for the deal. As Inagawa Kakuji explained: "Ultimately the yakuza will become like the U.S. Mafia. In the future there'll be one national mob. Like my organization the biggest firms will take over. You can see the move towards a more corporate structure." He warned of a lack of respect for traditional morality, a concern reflected in an ever-increasing murder rate. Today the yakuza accounts for about one-third of all the murders committed in Japan and some 60 percent of blackmail cases. See: **Inagawa Kakuji; Jirocho no Shimizu; Kimura Tokutaru; Kishi Nobusuke; Kodama Yoshio; Machii Hisayuki; Nakasone Yasuhiro; Ogawa Kaoru; Osano Kenji; Sasakawa Ryoichi; Taoka Kazuo; Toyama Mitsuru; Triad Society; Yamaguchi-gumi.**

REF.: Allen, *Japan: The Years of Triumph;* Ames, *Police and Community in Japan;* Anslinger, *The Protectors;* Aoyama, *Yakuza no Seikai: Kenka Jingi Tobaku, Sono Onna;* Arahara, *Dai Uyoku Shi;* Barnett, *The Alliance;* Bayley, *Forces of Order: Police Behavior in Japan and in the United States;* Beasley, *The Modern History of Japan;* Benedict, *The Chrysanthemum and the Sword: Patterns of Japanese Culture;* Berrigan, *Yakuza no Sekai: Nehon no Uchimaku;* Boettcher, *Gifts of Deceit: Sun Myung Moon, Tongsun Park, and the Korean Scandal;* Boulton, *The Grease Machine;* Bresler, *The Chinese Mafia;* Brown, *Nationalism in Japan;* Buruma, *Behind the Mask; CBA;* Craig, *The Fall of Japan;* Crane, *Korea Patterns;* Curtis, *Election Campaigning, Japanese Style;* Deacon, *Kempei Tai: A History of the Japanese Secret Service;* Dore, *Aspects of Social Change in Modern Japan;* Dower, *Empire and Aftermath;* Duus, *The Rise of Modern Japan;* Fujita, *Koan Daiyoran;* ____, *Koan Hyakunenshi;* ____, *Ninkyo Hyakunenshi;* Gayn, *Japan Diary;* Gibney, *Japan: The Fragile Superpower;* Goto, *Koria Uochiya;* Hane, *Peasants, Rebels, and Outcasts: The Underside of Modern Japan;* Haven, *Gentlemen of Japan;* Hobsbawn, *Bandits;* Hougan, *Spooks;* Huddle and Reich, *Island of Dreams: Environmental Crisis in Japan;* Ide, *Jissho: Nihon no Yakuza;* Ino, *Kodama Yoshio no Kzozo to Jitsuzo;* ____, *Nihon no Uyoku;* ____, *Yakuza to Nihonjin;* Kaplan and Dubro, *Yakuza;* Kata, *Nihon no Yakuza;* Johnson, *Conspiracy at Matsukawa;* Kent, *Hawaii: Islands Under the Influence;* Kodama, *I Was Defeated;* Lebra, *Japanese Culture and Behavior;* ______, *Japanese Patterns of Behavior;* Lee, *Koreans in Japan;* Livingston, *Imperial Japan;* ____, *Postwar Japan: 1945 to the Present;* Matsumoto, *Nihon no Kuroikiri;* McCoy, *The Politics of Heroin in Southeast Asia;* Mori, *Kuroikikan;* Morikawa, *Chi no Senkoku: Don Taoka Sogeki Jiken;* Morris, *Nationalism and the Right Wing in Japan;* Nakane, *Japanese Society;* Nishi, *Unconditional Democracy;* O'Callaghan, *The Triads;* Packard, *Protest in Tokyo;* Parker, *The Japanese Police Systems Today;* Roberts, *Mitsui: Three Centuries of Japanese Business;* Rome, *The Tattooed Men;* Sampson, *The Arms Bazaar;* Sansom, *A History of Japan;* Seagrave, *The Soong Dynasty;* Smith, *Minamata;* Statler, *Japanese Inn;* Storry, *A History of Modern Japan;* Takemori, *Miezaru Seiful;* Toland, *The Rising Sun;* Wang, *Hawaii's State and Local Politics;* Wildes, *Typhoon in Tokyo;* Williams, *Japan's Political Revolution under MacArthur.*

Yale, Frankie (AKA: **Frank Uale**), 1885-1927, U.S., org. crime. Frankie Yale came up through the ranks with Johnny Torrio and Al Capone, all of whom belonged to New York's infamous Five Points Gang. In 1908, after having spent several years proving his worth to his superiors, Yale was permitted to join Torrio's Black Hand ring, which extorted thousands of dollars from anyone in the neighborhood with the ability to pay. Yale was more than just a two-bit head-cracking gangster. He attained a guise of respectability in 1918 when he took over the reins of the Unione Siciliane, the fraternal association that had turned criminal under the leadership of Ignazio Saietta (Lupo the Wolf). Yale took over when Saietta was convicted of charges ranging from extortion to murder. If asked about his living, Yale would explain: "I'm an undertaker."

New York gangster Frankie Yale, 1909.

Yale's home base was the Harvard Inn, scene of at least two dozen murders between 1918 and 1928. Torrio was a partner in the operation until he went to Chicago to serve as the "muscle" in his uncle Jim Colosimo's Levee operations. Yale had his hand in a number of illegal ventures. During Prohibition he was a bootlegger, extortionist, and rum-runner. His legitimate business front was a cigar manufacturing concern. Tobacco dealers were forced to purchase the inferior grade cigars or risk reprisals. In the underworld parlance of the day, a "Frankie Yale" came to symbolize anything cheap and inferior.

Yale was also Al Capone's chief liquor supplier. He was sometimes called on by the Chicago crime boss to perform other "services," one of which was the gangland execution of Dion O'Bannion in his flower shop in November 1924. Yale and his bodyguard Sam Pollaccia were arrested at the LaSalle Street train station just hours after O'Bannion was cut down while trimming his roses. The two hoodlums were brought before Chief Morgan Collins and questioned about the gun they found in his coat pocket. "I have a permit from a Supreme Court justice of New York to carry it," Yale beamed. "I collect lots of money in New York." A rift later developed between Capone and Yale when Yale refused to endorse Scarface's choice for the presidency of the Unione Siciliane in Chicago. Then Capone began to suspect treachery involving the shipments of bootleg liquor from the East. Some of Yale's delivery trucks were being hijacked before they left New York. Capone sent James F. DeAmato to New York to spy on Yale, and he discovered what his boss had known all along. The beer trucks were being hijacked by Yale's own men. De Amato, once his mission was revealed to Yale, was murdered. From Chicago, Capone sent an angry message. "Some day you'll get an answer to DeAmato."

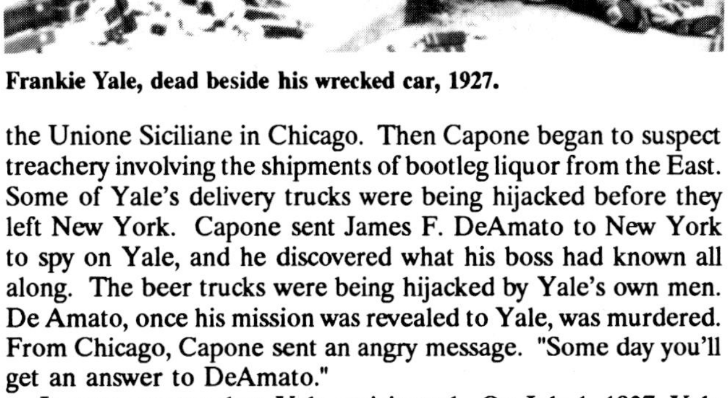

Frankie Yale, dead beside his wrecked car, 1927.

It came sooner than Yale anticipated. On July 1, 1927, Yale was summoned out of a Brooklyn speakeasy by a mysterious caller. Yale climbed into his roadster and drove down Forty-Fourth

Street when a second vehicle pulled up along side. The gunmen riddled Yale's car with rifle, shotgun, and machine bullets. Yale's car crashed into the front of a house.

The machine guns used in this killing—the first ever in New York—were traced to Chicago weapons dealer Peter von Frantzius. Capone, no doubt, wanted his enemies to know who supplied the answer. Frankie Yale's lavish funeral cost thousands of dollars. A wreath placed on the cortege bore the ominous inscription: "We'll See Them, Kid." See: **Capone, Alphonse; O'Bannion, Charles Dion; Torrio, John; Unione Siciliane**.

REF.: Asbury, *Gem of the Prairie;* Bonanno, *A Man of Honor; CBA;* Eisenberg and Landau, *Meyer Lansky;* Fried, *The Rise and Fall of the Jewish Gangster in America;* Gage, *Mafia, U.S.A.;* Gosch and Hammer, *The Last Testament of Lucky Luciano;* Kobler, *Al Capone;* Lait and Mortimer, *Chicago: Confidential;* Landesco, *Organized Crime in Chicago;* Levine, *Anatomy of a Gangster;* Lynch, *Criminals and Politicians;* McPhaul, *Johnny Torrio;* Martin, *Revolt in the Mafia;* Nash, *Bloodletters and Badmen;* Peterson, *The Mob;* Sann, *Kill the Dutchman;* Smith, *Syndicate City;* Spiering, *The Man Who Got Capone;* Thompson, *Gang Rule in New York.*

Yale, Linus, 1821-68, U.S., crime prevention. Invented types of bank, dial, and small cylinder locks. He served as president of Yale Lock Manufacturing Company of Stamford, Conn. The basis for the Yale lock is still used today. REF.: *CBA.*

Yamaga Soko, 1622-85, Japan, banish. Military strategist and philosopher banished to Ako for ten years for offending the shogun. He developed an influential neo-Confucian code of honor for the samurai class which emphasized duty and also proclaimed the superiority of Japanese civilization over that of China. REF.: *CBA.*

Yamagishi, Lieutenant, See: **Inukai Tsuyoshi**.

Japanese war criminal, General Yamashita, hanged in 1946.

Yamashita Tomoyuki (AKA: **Tiger of Malaya**), 1885-1946, Japan, war crimes. General Yamashita Tomoyuki was in charge of the Japanese army in the Philippines at the end of WWII. Prior to assuming this command, he was instrumental in training Japanese soldiers in jungle warfare and helped plan the invasion of the Malay Peninsula of 1941-42. He accepted the surrender of Singapore on Feb. 15, 1942, after a ten-week campaign. Prime Minister Tojo Hideki then removed him from active service, transferring him to a training command in Manchuria. He assumed command in the Philippines in 1944 and surrendered on Sept. 2, 1945.

General Douglas MacArthur ordered that Yamashita be immediately tried as a war criminal. Some of the foulest atrocities in the history of warfare were committed by the Japanese army in the Philippines, including the infamous Bataan Death March of April 1942, when the army was commanded by General Homma Masaharu, in which ten of thousands of U.S. and Filipino soldiers were brutally killed. The Death March was an outgrowth of the Japanese militaristic tradition, which Homma strictly followed by encouraging his men to brutalize enemies who had "disgraced" themselves by surrendering.

Two years later, when Yamashita took command, the Japanese soldiers were still committing atrocities at will. At Yamashita's trial, impassioned testimony from victims revealed that Japanese soldiers had placed candy and whiskey in a dining hall where they had detained 800 civilians, then set off an explosive when the people gathered round, killing hundreds of them. A little girl showed her scars from thirty-eight bayonet wounds to the five U.S. generals presiding over the case. A woman described the bayonetting death of her 9-month-old daughter. The court heard endless horror stories about the estimated 60,000 U.S. and Filipino deaths at Japanese hands that occurred during the eleven months Yamashita was in command. Yamashita's defense was that he had just assumed command at the end. He was unfamiliar with the country in which his troops were fighting, as well as its language and customs, and even his own officers. Though he gave a good account of himself on the stand, it was not enough to counterbalance the stories of brutalities his men had inflicted. The court sentenced him to hang.

The execution was carried out in March 1946. Prior to being hanged, Yamashita thanked his captors for a fair trial. "I know that all you Americans and American military affairs officers always have tolerance and rightful judgment," he wrote. "I can never forget what they have done for me, even if I have died. I don't blame my executioners."

Some jurists disagreed with Yamashita's own assessment of the fairness of his trial, however. His appeal to the U.S. Supreme Court was rejected six-to-two, but the minority opinion written by Justice Frank Murphy stated, "Yamashita was rushed to trial under an improper charge, given insufficient time to prepare an adequate defense...and summarily sentenced to be hanged. In all this needless and unseemly haste there was no serious attempt to charge or to prove that he committed a recognized violation of the laws of war..." Three years after Yamashita's death, U.S. lawyer A. Frank Reed published a book, *The Case of General Yamashita.* Reed cited the opinion of the other dissenting justice, Wiley Rutledge, who described the charges against Yamashita as "vagueness if not vacuity." He was blamed for murder and rape committed by naval forces who were not under his command. He landed in the Philippines only two days before the U.S. landing at Leyte and was never able to make contact with many of the units he was nominally commanding. Most of the testimony was based on hearsay, but none of the judges had legal training, and they allowed the prosecution leeway that experienced jurists would not have. Yamashita was held responsible for troops who were in every practical sense, out of his control. Reel quoted an army lawyer as saying, "Under such a principle, I suppose, even MacArthur should be tried."

When Yamashita went to the gallows, he wore U.S. combat fatigues at MacArthur's orders. Along with having to wear the uniform of the conquering army, the condemned man was also stripped of all symbols of rank and honor, a final humiliation that was not even visited upon General Homma, the architect of the Death March. See: **Bataan Death March**; **Homma Masaharu**; **Tojo Hideki**

REF.: Bergamini, *Japan's Imperial Conspiracy; CBA;* Kenworthy, *The Tiger of Malaya: The Inside Story of the Japanese Atrocities;* Knox, *Death March: The Survivors of Bataan;* Manchester, *American Caesar;* Rutherford, *Fall of the Philippines.*

Yang Chien, 541-604, China, emp., assass. Emperor of China from 581-604 and founder of Sui dynasty. His reign is considered one of the greatest in China. He established a strong centralized government, abolished inheritance of office, introduced a civil service system, and erected a new capital city. He was responsible for conquering southern China and reunifying the country. He was murdered by his son, Yang Kuang. REF.: *CBA*.

Yang Hsiu-ching, d.1856, China, consp. Rose quickly in Taiping military, becoming commander in chief in 1851. He developed an extensive spy system and was instrumental in organizing the army. He won several victories in the Taiping Rebellion and captured Nanking in 1853. He was later made prime minister. When he tried to usurp Hung Hsiu-chuan's position, he was executed. REF.: *CBA*.

Yang Kuang (Yang Ti), 580-618, China, emp., assass. Second and last emperor of the Sui dynasty of China. During his reign, he built a canal system throughout China, erected palaces, founded a second capital at Lo-yang, and extended his rule south to Vietnam and north into Central Asia. His attempts to rule Korea resulted in a people's revolt, and he was assassinated. See: **Yang Chien**. REF.: *CBA*.

Yang Kuei-fei, d.756, China, consp. Killed by imperial guards after An Lu-shan's rebellion. She became the concubine of T'ang emperor Hsüan Tsung. She exercised great influence at court. She made An Lu-shan her protege, adopted son, and according to many, her lover. REF.: *CBA*.

Yang Yen, 727-81, China, brib.-suic. Committed suicide after being accused of bribery and corruption. As chief minister to T'ang emperor Te Tsung, he abolished taxes on peasants and instituted a double tax on land, thus greatly reducing the power of the aristocratic classes. REF.: *CBA*.

Yang Yu-ting, d.1929, China, assass. When Chinese Nationalist armies invaded Peking in June 1928, dictator Chang Tso-lin fled to Manchuria with his son, Chang Hsueh-liang, in an escape engineered by Yang Yu-ting. A long-time advisor to Chang, Yang was influential in Chang's regime. Young Chang assumed the dictatorship of Manchuria when his father died in July 1928. In January 1929, Yang was shot to death by Chang's forces. Various accounts of his death were recorded, but it is widely accepted that Yang was assassinated to prevent him from encroaching on the new dictator's power. See: **Chang Hsueh-Liang.** REF.: *CBA*.

Yankwich, Leon Rene, 1888-1975, U.S., jur. Judge on California Superior Court from 1927-35. He was nominated to the southern district court of California by President Franklin D. Roosevelt in 1935. REF.: *CBA*.

Yarham, Samuel, 1817-1846, Brit., mur. In November 1844, elderly widow Hariette Chandler of Yarmouth, Norfolk, received a package containing a large sum of money. She was not particularly discreet about the cash, and when police found her dead on Nov. 18, in the shop which occupied the lower portion of her house, they determined that burglary was the motive. Police questioned Samuel Yarham, a 27-year-old shoemaker who rented the upper floor of Chandler's house, but he claimed to have heard nothing on the night of the murder.

When Chandler's money was found buried on the beach, Yarham and three other men, Royle, Hall, and Mapes, were arrested. Yarham, however, turned Queen's witness before the trial, claiming that he had seen the other men come out of Chandler's shop on the night of the murder, had heard them discussing the murder, and then saw Chandler's dead body for himself. The three men provided concrete alibis and were acquitted. Yarham, incorrectly thinking himself invulnerable to prosecution for the crime, confessed his part in it to one of the women who had discovered the money. According to her testimony, Yarham told her that Royle, Hall, and Mapes had badgered him to help them rob Chandler. Yarham finally agreed and admitted them to her empty shop. When Chandler returned unexpectedly, the men beat her. Yarham claimed that when he returned and saw her, he cut her throat because he felt she was too badly injured to recover. Yarham was found Guilty of murder and executed at Norwich Castle on Apr. 4, 1846.

REF.: Brock, *A Casebook of Crime*; *CBA*.

Yashvill, Prince, See: **Paul I**.

Yasuhiro, Nakasone, See: **Nakasone Yasuhiro**.

Yates, Lonnie, 1946- , U.S., rob.-mur. Veronica Lee, seventeen, was an honor student who was planning to enlist in the Air Force after her high school graduation. Lee lived with her mother, Ernestine Yancy, on Chicago's West Side and was home alone on July 11, 1977, when she awoke to find Lonnie Yates, thirty-two, burglarizing their home. Yates had a pile of goods by the door when Lee found him. Yates hit the young woman with a steam iron three times, then plunged a pair of scissors into her back. As she staggered into a closet, he plunged the scissors into her heart, then took $17 and fled the house. Lee's cousins, walking up the back stairs of the apartment building, saw a man walking down wiping his hands. They found Lee stuffed upside down in the closet. Yates, an ex-convict, was arrested four days later, and was identified by the two cousins in a police lineup and in court.

The trial lasted for seven days, with state's attorneys Robert Boharic and Frank Patterson for the prosecution, and public defender Richard Kling representing Yates. On Feb. 25, 1979, the jury convicted Yates of burglary and murder, and Circuit Court Judge Sylvestor C. Close sentenced Yates to be electrocuted. Veronica's mother said, "The death penalty—that's the only thing I had. He killed my only daughter. I believe that justice was done." Yates' appeal to the U.S. Supreme Court, contending that his conviction was unconstitutional because blacks were excluded from the jury, was rejected on May 14, 1984. As of this writing Yates is still in prison. REF.: *CBA*.

Yates, Robert, 1738-1801, U.S., jur. Practiced law in Albany, N.Y. He was a justice on the New York Supreme Court from 1777-98, serving as chief justice from 1790. He opposed a federal U.S. constitution, fearing that the constitutional convention was exceeding its powers. REF.: *CBA*.

Yazdegerd I, prom. 399-420, Per., reform. Brought the persecution of Christians to a halt during his reign and kept peaceful relations with the Roman Empire. He tried to free Persia from the domination of Magian priests and nobles. REF.: *CBA*.

Yazdegerd II, prom. 440-57, Per., war crimes. Persecuted Christians and Jews. He was king during the war with Rome from 440-57, and during continuous conflict with eastern tribes. REF.: *CBA*.

Yazdegerd III, d.651, Per., king, assass. Grandson of Khosrau II and last of the Sassanidae dynasty. Although he reigned from 632-641, he was actually too young to rule. He was driven from the throne and murdered at Merv. REF.: *CBA*.

Yazid ibn al-Muhallab, 672-720, Per., polit. corr.-rebel. Known as cruel and corrupt governor of Khorasan. He held various positions, including that of governor of Iraq. He persecuted followers of his enemy al-Hajjaj, former governor of Iraq. He died leading a rebellion against the caliphate. REF.: *CBA*.

Yeager, Dick, See: **Wyatt, Nathaniel Ellsworth.**

Yeh T'ing (Yeh Hsi-ping), 1897-1946, China, rebel. Communist rebel arrested by Nationalists. He was imprisoned from 1941 until his death. REF.: *CBA*.

Yeldham, William James, 1899-1922, Brit., mur. In May 1921, the body of a journeyman printer, George Stanley Grimshaw, was found in Higham's Park, Chingford, a desolate section of Epping Forest. The 54-year-old man had been hit in the head repeatedly with a heavy object and robbed. Police at first surmised that Grimshaw's murder might have been retribution for his spying on couples who frequently came to this secluded part of the woods.

However, when police investigated reports that Grimshaw had been seen recently in the company of a young woman, their appraisal of the motive changed. The young woman, Elsie Yeldham, had married William James Yeldham just three days after Grimshaw's murder. The newlyweds were arrested and quickly confessed to the crime. Elsie lured Grimshaw into the woods, where her fiancé ambushed him. Both husband and wife were convicted of murder and sentenced to death. Yeldham was hanged on Sept. 5, 1922, and Elsie's sentence was commuted.

REF.: *CBA*; Shew, *A Second Companion to Murder*; Wensley, *Forty Years at the Yard*.

Yellow, Marjorie, 1913- , and **Thay, Emily**, prom. 1932, Case of, Brit., mur. Nineteen-year-old Marjorie Yellow, and her sister Emily Thay, ran from Marjorie's house in Birmingham on the evening of Oct. 24, 1932, screaming murder and asking pedestrians to help remove an unwanted man from their house. Before they returned with help, Sidney Marston, twenty-one, staggered out onto the street, bleeding from a stab wound in the chest. He died shortly afterwards.

Yellow and Thay were arrested and tried for Marston's murder in spite of contradictory and confusing evidence. Marston was a very strong man, yet there were no signs of a struggle. A supposedly missing ten-shilling note was found in his pocket along with the blade of a knife. Despite the fact that Yellow claimed Marston stabbed himself and that she took the handle to the knife after it broke off, investigators concluded that the wound was not self-inflicted. Witnesses claimed that Yellow denied knowing Marston, while others stated she had met him at a dance.

On grounds of insufficient evidence, the judge, Sir Travers Humphrey, found the sisters Not Guilty and released them.

REF.: *CBA;* Shew, *A Second Companion to Murder.*

Yellow Henry Gang, prom. 1870s-80s, U.S., org. crime. Named after their leader, Yellow Henry Stewart, the Yellow Henry gang was the most vicious gang of thieves, burglars, cutthroats, and murderers in late nineteenth-century New Orleans. Yellow Henry was nicknamed such because he suffered from malaria, an illness that gave his skin a yellow tint and significantly shortened his life. Understanding this, he became a reckless and violent criminal, given to killing his victims just as frequently as beating them senseless. Henry joined an outlaw gang and inherited the leadership in 1877 from Turpo, who was convicted of murder and sent to prison. Henry planned several successful and lucrative burglaries, hold ups, and protection rackets. It was Stewart's success as a leader that compelled the gang to name themselves after him. He attracted many of the city's most notorious criminals including Joe Martin, the city's most expert garroter, Crooked Neck Delaney, another garroter, Tom McDonald, Prussian Charley Mader, George Sylvester, Garibaldi Bolden, the murderous Red and Blue Haley, Pat Keeley, and Frank Lyons, the famous cop-killer.

Arrested along with three gang members for robbery, Henry was sent to prison in 1884, and died of malaria there in July 1886. The cop-killer Frank Lyons was in prison at the same time, but escaped in 1888. He reorganized the Yellow Henry gang, but was captured and returned to prison. When Louisiana governor Francis T. Nicholls pardoned Lyons in 1890, the cop-killer again began criminal activities with the Yellow Henrys. In 1892, the wrath of the New Orleans Police Department descended on the Yellow Henrys after Lyons shot and killed another police officer. Lyons went to prison for the last time, and the gang was permanently disbanded. REF.: *CBA.*

Yellow Turban Rebellion, 184, China, rebel. Chang Chüeh was a Taoist who developed a following among people who claimed that he had a supernatural gift of healing as well as other powers. Priests and missionaries of the Yellow Turban religion wore yellow robes, while the followers of this movement wore yellow headdresses, thus, the name Yellow Turbans. Chang Chüeh gradually built his following to open rebellion. The Han Dynasty was, during those years, seriously weakened by too many generations of child emperors whose regents cared only for their own aggrandizement. The Yellow Turbans worshipped Huang-lao Chün and gained considerable momentum in eastern and northern China. During a one month period, much of northern China was subdued by the rebellion led by thirty-six field commanders. Though the rebellion was short-lived, it managed to fragment the dynasty's already weak structure and provide a forewarning of nineteenth century secret societies which combined crime, political revolt, and religion. REF.: *CBA.*

Yerevan Bank Robbery, 1977, U.S.S.R., rob. In the city of Yerevan, Armenia, bank robbers took between 1.5 million and 8 million rubles, or about $2 million to $11 million. The stolen money was reportedly part of the payroll for a major Yerevan plant, and was kept in a top floor room of the bank building, which is located near the central square of the city. The thieves bored their way into the room through the building's roof. The Yerevan Bank Robbery was believed to have been the largest bank robbery reported in the Soviet Union, but there were no published accounts of the theft when it happened in October 1977. Sources in Moscow who were in touch with friends in Yerevan, said the robbery was common knowledge. A Ministry of Internal Affairs official admitted in a phone conversation with an interviewer on Oct. 20, 1977, that he was aware of the crime, but refused to comment further.

Although the media in Moscow reported daily on crime in the West, all Soviet crime statistics were censored, making it impossible to estimate the frequency of bank robberies in the U.S.S.R. Published reports of wrongdoing were generally written up to act as a deterrent to would-be criminals; unsolved crimes were not reported. A contemporary report of another burglary around the time of the Yerevan robbery said that the criminals had been captured within ten days and were given ten-to-twelve-year jail sentences. REF.: *CBA.*

Yerkes, Charles Tyson Jr., 1837-1905, embez. The life of financier Charles Yerkes formed the basis of Theodore Dreiser's trilogy of novels, *The Financier, The Titan,* and *The Stoic,* which explored the darker side of the American dream: greed, lust for power, punishment, and ultimate atonement.

Charles Tyson Yerkes, the son of Quaker parents, was born in Philadelphia. His father was the president of the Kensington National Bank and instilled in his son a keen appreciation for American commerce, encouraging him to enter the commission brokerage business after completing his studies. In 1859 after serving his apprenticeship as a clerk for James P. Perot & Brother, Yerkes struck out on his own and opened a brokerage firm. He was soon recognized as a brilliant wheeler-dealer after disposing of a Philadelphia bond issue at par value after the prices had fallen to 65 percent. In 1871 the Chicago Fire sent shock waves through stock exchanges across the U.S. Yerkes, who by now was a major figure in Philadelphia's financial circles, was suddenly placed in a precarious position. Unable to pay monies back to the city administration that he had collected from the sale of municipal bonds, Yerkes was indicted for embezzlement and sentenced to two years and nine months. He served just seven months before being pardoned and released.

The failure of Jay Cooke & Co. precipitated another panic in 1873, which afforded Yerkes the opportunity to buy up stocks at far less than their par value, thus recouping his losses from the prior two years. In 1882, following a scandalous divorce from his wife of many years, Yerkes and the new love interest in his life, Mary Adelaide Moore, moved to Chicago. For the next fifteen years, the wily and devious financier established himself as the "traction" king of Chicago, buying up options on the street-railway lines and using the stock as collateral to purchase the next. Aldermen who were anxious to receive graft that Yerkes threw them like candy to hungry children justified their actions as being consistent with the public good. After all, Yerkes had replaced forty-eight horse-car lines with cable traction and had electrified 240 miles of railway. A byproduct of all the backroom deals was the creation of the "Chicago Loop," the circular elevated train route that traverses the downtown business district to this day.

Yerkes created a maze of holding companies and interlocking directorships that were made possible by a corrupt partnership with the aldermen of Chicago, who were satirized as the "Grey Wolves." Charles Yerkes was an arrogant, defiant financial wizard who traced his business success to a simple, direct philosophy: "Buy old junk, fix it up a little, and unload it on other fellows." Assailed by the press for his unwillingness to provide an adequate number of street cars, Yerkes retorted: "It is the strap-hangers that pay the dividends." Yerkes counted on the greed of the legislators to help him push through the Humphrey Bills in 1895, which would have extended him a 100-year franchise on prime Loop real estate. In the past, the aldermen and many of the downstate politicians had voted his way in return for their usual kickbacks. Governor John Peter Altgeld, a tough-minded reformer who was a breed apart from the Chicago Grey Wolves, refused Yerkes' bribery and vetoed the legislation. The traction magnate retaliated with a smear campaign that effectively ruined Altgeld's chances for re-election. The next governor, William Tanner, was more compliant. In 1897, Yerkes succeeded in getting the City Council to consider the Allen Bills, which were basically a rehash of the failed Humphrey Act. The aldermen were cowed and intimidated by throngs of outraged voters who circled the City Hall. Some were armed with guns and lynching ropes. The bill was defeated, thanks in part to Michael "Hinky Dink" Kenna and "Bathhouse John" Coughlin. These two First Ward political sachems were not role models of civic virtue by any stretch of the imagination, but Yerkes' rapacity was just too much in this instance. "John," Kenna cautioned, "always go after the little stuff."

Identical Allen Bills were introduced in both the General Assembly in Springfield and the City Council in Chicago. The state assembly passed it, but its failure in the council led to its repeal in the State House in 1899. Charles Yerkes was through in Chicago. He was ostracized both socially and politically, which forced him to sell what was left of his shaky traction empire to Peter Widener and William Elkins, two former business partners from Philadelphia, in 1901. Yerkes took some $15,000,000 in cash out of Chicago and retired briefly to New York. He later became the head of a syndicate of London businessmen who converted the steam subway railways to electricity, a dubious venture that severely diminished his remaining fortune. Yerkes died on Dec. 29, 1905, a tarnished figure who symbolized the social ills wrought by the industrial revolution. See: **Altgeld, John Peter; Coughlin, John; Kenna, Michael.**

REF: Asbury, *The Chicago Underworld; CBA;* Dedmon, *Fabulous Chicago;* Demaris, *Captive City;* Harrison, *Stormy Years;* Lait and Mortimer, *Chicago: Confidential!;* Lewis and Smith, *Chicago;* Morgan, *Prince of Crime;* Nash, *People to See;* Reppetto, *The Blue Parade;* Smith, *Syndicate City;* (FICTION), Dreiser, *The Financier;* ____, *The Titan;* ____, *The Stoic.*

Yesh, Robert, prom. 1983, U.S., drugs. In April 1981, former congressional page Douglas Marshall, twenty-seven, and Troy Todd, Jr., twenty-three, of Potomac, Md., were arrested on drug charges. Their arrests led to an investigation of drug use among members of Congress. Charges against Todd and Marshall were dropped, according to Assistant U.S. Attorney Daniel Bernstein, so that the grand jury could investigate without the time pressures of the Speedy Trial Act, which requires prosecutors to bring indictments within thirty days of arrests, with trials commencing within seventy days of the indictments. Before they were indicted in November 1982 on charges of running a Capitol Hill cocaine distributing ring, Todd and Marshall went to Australia, where they were arrested in January 1983.

According to Representative Robert Dornan, investigators discovered that six members of Congress were cocaine users. In early 1983, Robert Yesh, an employee of the House of Representatives doorkeeper's office for thirteen years and former supervisor in the House Democratic cloakroom, admitted that he had personally supplied small amounts of marijuana and cocaine to a U.S. congressman and his aide. In mid-April, Yesh was sentenced to a year in prison followed by three years of probation on one count of possession of cocaine and another of conspiracy to possess the drug. Implicated in Yesh's testimony were Representative Ronald Dellums of California, and his legislative assistant, John Apperson. At a March press conference, Dellums had denied that he or any of his aides had ever bought or used drugs. Polygraph tests given to Yesh indicated that he was telling the truth about supplying drugs.

On July 27, the Justice Department made the statement that it would end the investigation and would not bring charges against Dellums or Barry M. Goldwater, Jr., former Republican representative from California, or Charles Wilson, a Democrat from Texas who also had been under investigation. Wilson, who said all the allegations against him were false, told an interviewer, "I'm not bitter, they haven't got any evidence against me, period, except from a convicted felon trying to cop a plea." The House Ethics Committee cleared Dellums and Wilson on Nov. 17, 1983, concluding that there was no evidence of a Capitol Hill drug ring. Frederick W. Richmond of Brooklyn, a former representative, resigned from Congress on Aug. 25, 1982, the same day he pleaded guilty to marijuana possession, income tax evasion, and improper payments to a federal employee. Richmond was sentenced and served a federal prison term from December 1982 through Sept. 6, 1983. REF.: *CBA.*

Yitzernitsky, Itzhak, See: **Stern, Abraham.**

Yo Fei (AKA: Yüeh Fei), 1103-41, China, gen., assass. General who led Sung forces in effectively prohibiting Juchen advance. Ch'in Kuei stopped his advance northward by ordering his execution. He was long considered a national hero. REF.: *CBA.*

Yoritomo, 1147-99, Japan, mur. First Minamoto shogun and founder of Kamakura shogunate in 1192. Ordered the death of his brother Yoshitsune and the deaths of important members of his family from 1184-93. REF.: *CBA.*

William York, age ten, murdering 5-year-old Susan Mahew.

York, William, b.1738, Brit. mur. As a young child, William York had nowhere to go but the parish poor house in Eye, Suffolk. There he shared a bed with 5-year-old Susan Mahew, another destitute child left at the church doorstep. York cared little for Mahew, however. She wet her bed, and they quarreled frequently. So on May 13, 1748, as the little girl was leaving the house on her way to the manure pile to perform her chores, Will York, then ten, murdered her with a hook and knife and hid her body in the manure. When arrested, all York could say in his defense was that he did not like the girl.

Tried on Aug. 5, 1748, York was convicted and sentenced to die. (During the eighteenth century, it was not uncommon for child murderers to be executed in Britain.) In this case, however, the courts were inclined to show mercy and granted York an official pardon.

REF.: *CBA;* Mitchell, *The Newgate Calendar;* Wilson, *Children Who Kill.*

Yorke, Philip (Earl of Hardwicke), 1690-1764, Brit., atty. gen.-jur. Attorney general from 1720-24, and chief justice and privy councilor in 1733. REF.: *CBA.*

Yorkshire Ripper, The, See: **Sutcliffe, Peter William.**

Yorkshire Witch, The, See: **Bateman, Mary.**

Yoshimitsu, 1358-95, Japan, law enfor. off. Kept piracy in check and diminished power of Kyushu. As the third shogun of the Ashikaga shogunate from 1367-95, he also brought order to his country and ended civil war. REF.: *CBA.*

Yoshio, Kodama, See: **Kodama Yoshio.**

Youmans, Frank A., 1860-1932, U.S., jur. Served as U.S. district attorney from 1887-95 in western district court of Arkansas. He was nominated to the western district court of Arkansas by President William Howard Taft in 1911. REF.: *CBA.*

Young, Alse, d.1647, U.S., witchcraft. Alse Young, a resident of Windsor, Conn., was tried and condemned as a witch, and appears to be the first person on record in New England to be so charged. Young predates Mary Johnson, who was executed in Boston a year later (and, up to now, thought to be the first victim of the U.S. witch mania). Young was hanged at Windsor on May 26, 1647. Existing records give no other details of this precedent-setting case. See: **Johnson, Mary; Salem Witchcraft Trials.** REF.: *CBA.*

Young, Bob, 1941- , U.S., jur. In 1960, nineteen-year-old Bob Young was arrested in Los Angeles for stealing a credit card out of the mail. He was tried, convicted and sent to jail. Young served twenty months in federal prison and four more years on parole. Upon his release, he joined a local motorcycle gang, the Galloping Gooses, and was arrested along with other gang members for attempted murder and assault with a deadly weapon.

According to Young, he had not actually done anything wrong—he had just been in "the wrong place with the wrong people". His parole officer, Walter R. Lumpkin, believed him, and refused to have Young held in custody until trial. Lumpkin's show of faith apparently led Young to rethink his life. When the charges against him were dismissed, he envisioned a more constructive future for himself.

Based on the results of an aptitude test, Young decided to become a lawyer, and applied to eleven different law schools. When they all refused his application, he personally visited each of them. He was eventually accepted by McGeorge School of Law, where he graduated and, in 1970, passed the bar exam. In 1977, after practicing law for seven years, he ran for the Justice Court of Loomis, Calif., and was elected by fifty-two per cent of the vote. REF.: *CBA.*

Young, Danny Jerome, 1960- , U.S., kid.-mur. In March 1980, 10-year-old Ronnie Tolleson disappeared from his West Covina, Calif., home. Eight days later, his body was found in a neighbor's garage, two houses away from his home. Twenty-year-old Danny Jerome Young, who lived at the address where Ronnie's body was found, was arrested in Nevada a month later and charged in the kidnapping and murder. Young maintained his innocence throughout his trial, despite the prosecution's use of his previously taped confession. Young refuted his earlier statements, explaining that police had coerced the confession. Nevertheless, Young was convicted of second-degree kidnapping and murder. He was sentenced to life in prison without possibility of parole.

In April 1989, Young returned to court to testify in a wrongful death suit brought against the police department by Ronald A. Tolleson, Sr., the victim's father. With apparently little to gain, Young testified for the police department and admitted kidnapping and killing Ronnie Tolleson. The senior Tolleson maintained that the West Covina police had acted slowly and ineffectively in investigating his son's disappearance, and in so doing, had contributed to his death. Although Young testified that he had strangled the boy shortly after abducting him and before calling Tolleson to demand a $3,000 ransom, medical examiners testified that Ronnie was not killed until several days after his abduction. Police searched Young's house on the night of Ronnie's disappearance, but failed to check the garage, where the child was hidden. On May 9, 1989, the Superior Court awarded Tolleson a $5.7 million judgment against the city of West Covina, Police Chief Craig Meacham, and former Officer Larry J. Todd. REF.: *CBA.*

Young, Don John, 1910- , U.S., jur. Served as judge on common pleas court of Huron County, Ohio, from 1952-53, and later on probate and juvenile court in the same county from 1953-65. He was nominated to the northern district court of Ohio by President Lyndon B. Johnson in 1965. He published more than fifty publications in the field of law and corrections. REF.: *CBA.*

Young, Earl (AKA: Andrew Riska, Karl Richardson, Lester Byler Young), 1911-38, U.S., rape-mur. Earl Young first went to jail in 1927 for breaking and entering. During the next ten years, Pennsylvania authorities arrested Young on three different occasions for robbery, fencing, illegal possession of firearms, car theft, and criminal assault. On Mar. 18, 1938, he was arrested in Reading, Pa., for carrying concealed weapons. Two months later, on May 18, Young escaped from the Lebanon County jail and drove away.

Known for his tattoos—especially the eagle on his chest and Mickey Mouse and Popeye on his arms—Young arrived in Lyons, Kan., on June 22, 1938, looking for money and women. At gunpoint he held up Marcus Cain and Rosanna Sandberg, a 21-year-old student from Hutchinson. After tying Cain to a telephone pole, Young ordered Sandberg into the trunk of his car. Then, in a wheat field outside Newton, he raped and strangled her, leaving her for dead.

She recovered sufficiently to identify Young from most-wanted posters and newspaper photographs, but the rapist had moved on to Louisville, Ky., where he kidnapped and sexually assaulted Nettie Costin and stole her car.

Young crisscrossed seven states. On July 28, 1938, he arrived in Sioux Falls, S.D., where he broke into the Summit Avenue home of Joseph Floyd. He intended to rape 16-year-old nursemaid Dorothy Monohan, but panicked and fled after she screamed as he was knocking her unconscious with the butt of his gun.

Young proceeded to the nearby residence of Walter Nelson. Pretending to be lost, Young was admitted to the house by 17-year-old Betty Schnaidt, who was babysitting for 5-year-old Jackie Nelson. Gagging Schnaidt with a towel, Young carried her out the back door while Jackie slept soundly in the next room. Four days later, Schnaidt's abused and strangled body was found in St. Charles, S.D., 150 miles from Sioux Falls. Through the license plates on the stolen car, fingerprints found at the scene of the crime, and a sack of old clothing in a motel in Manhattan, Kan., police were able to identify Young as the killer. At the motel, Young had registered as Karl Richardson, one of many aliases. The name Andrew Riska was later found on some items in the smashed and abandoned automobile Young had driven from South Dakota.

Young passed through six midwestern and western states before he was finally apprehended by police in a Hot Springs, Ark., hotel. Spotting Young in a beer hall, Captain Ben Rogers checked wanted posters to make sure he was their man. Satisfied that he was, Rogers and Captain Jerry Watkins followed Young to his hotel. "We knocked on his door and told him to open up," Watkins said. "He asked who we were and we told him police. I peeked through the keyhole and saw him get out of bed. When he opened the door I stuck my foot in the room but he opened fire on us. As we fired back he slammed the door and kept on shooting."

The policemen retreated. A housemaid called the station for reinforcements and back-up. A few minutes passed. Suddenly Young burst out of the room, guns blazing, but his aim was poor. Rogers and Watkins cut him down before he got near the door.

Young was still breathing, but slipping fast. He died on Aug. 5, in a hospital, refusing to the end to confess or offer an alibi. Had he recovered from his gunshot wounds, Young would have faced first-degree murder charges and violations of the Lindbergh Act, a law designed to punish kidnappers, enacted after the abduction of famous aviator Charles Lindbergh's son. REF.: *CBA.*

Young, Edward Louis III, 1943- , U.S., theft. In September 1988, Texas judge Ted Poe sentenced 45-year-old Edward Louis Young III to 600 hours shoveling manure in the Houston Mounted Police stables. Young had stolen two Colt .45-caliber revolvers from Jack Carlson "Clayton" Moore, star of the "Lone Ranger" television series, as Moore signed autographs at Houston Intercontinental Airport on Dec. 24, 1986. In the 1988 trial, Young was also sentenced to ten years' probation and one month in the county jail. REF.: *CBA.*

Young, George, 1819-1907, Scot., atty. gen.-jur. Attorney general of Scotland from 1862-69. He presided as judge of the court of session from 1874-1905. He was the author of the Scottish Education Act in 1872 and the Law Agents Act in 1873. REF.: *CBA.*

Young, Gig, 1913-78, U.S., suic.-mur. At about 2:30 p.m. on Oct. 19, 1978, a resident of the Osborne apartments on Manhattan's upper west side heard what sounded like gunshots. At around 7:30 p.m., visitors to the apartment of actor Gig Young, sixty-four, and Ruth Schmidt, thirty-one, his wife of three weeks, received no answer at the door, and police later discovered the bodies of the newlyweds. According to police sergeant John Murphy, Young had a gun in his hand and had apparently shot his wife and then killed himself. Young had met Schmidt, his fifth wife, in Hong Kong where he was making a movie. The actor's business agent, Ed Traubner, said his client had just recently returned to his New York home from Canada, where he had been performing on stage.

In 1969, Gig Young won an Academy Award for his portrayal of a sadistic dance marathon pitchman in *They Shoot Horses, Don't They?* Critics referred to his performance as "a lifeline for a drowning actor" whose career consisted primarily of "a trail of second leads in second-rate movies." Young described his work in movies prior to winning the coveted award as "thirty years and fifty-five pictures, and there are not more than five that were any good or any good for me." Young had been famous for portraying "the urbane suitor who loses the girl at the end of the picture." Born Byron Barr in St. Cloud, Minn., Young claimed to be a sad and very shy child, saying that he was so grateful to one teacher who liked him, that he used to give her dimes. Moving to Washington, D.C., he performed in school plays and amateur theater, then moved to California after graduation. In Pasadena, Calif., he acted in thirty plays in three years at the Pasadena Playhouse, and was eventually seen by a talent agent who got him his first movie role in *The Gay Sisters* with Barbara Stanwyck. Since there was another actor named Byron Barr, he changed his name to Gig Young.

In WWII, Young enlisted in the Coast Guard and ferried troops across the Pacific. He returned to Hollywood and received his first Academy Award nomination in 1951 for his role as an alcoholic in *Come Fill The Cup.* He hosted "Warner Brothers Presents," and appeared in the TV series "The Rogues," with David Niven and Charles Boyer in the mid-1960s. Young was again nominated for an Oscar for his work in a Clark Gable and Doris Day movie, *Teacher's Pet.* Three of the actor's five marriages ended in divorce. Young was alleged to have had a serious drinking problem. According to his fourth wife, Elaine Young, his role as an alcoholic in *Come Fill The Cup* was "a terrifying symbol of the years ahead." REF.: *CBA.*

Young, Graham, 1948- , Brit., mur. John Hadland, Ltd., a British Photographic Instrument company, employed seventy people in an attractive building at Bovington, near London. In the summer of 1971, 60-year-old head warehouseman Bob Egle, in robust health and looking forward to retirement, developed a serious illness. He died on July 19, after suffering agonizing back and stomach cramps. Another employee, 56-year-old Fred Biggs, became ill with similar symptoms in October 1971, and within a month he too was dead. When four more employees began suffering similar afflictions, the company sought the aid of Dr. Arthur Anderson. While questioning employees, Anderson encountered 23-year-old Graham Young, who had rapt interest in the fate of his fellow workers, as well as a thorough knowledge of the effects of thallium poisoning. Police discovered that Young had been kept at the Broadmoor Institution for the criminally insane between July 1962 and February 1971 for killing his stepmother with poison and attempting to poison his father, sister, and a friend. He had been released as posing no further threat to society and was hired by John Hadland, whose personnel office had no knowledge of his past. Young was arrested on suspicion of murder, brought to trial in June 1972 at St. Albans, Hertfordshire, and convicted of the murders of Egle and Biggs, as well as the attempted murders of Jethro Batt and David Tilson. Far from contrite, Young said that he could have killed the others but had let them live. He soon began serving a sentence of life imprisonment.

REF: Boar, *The World's Most Infamous Murders;* Borrell, *Crime in Britain Today; CBA;* Wilson, *Encyclopedia of Modern Murder.*

Young, Harry, 1904-32, U.S., mur. In a small farmhouse six miles southwest of Springfield, Mo., Mrs. J.D. Young struggled to feed her children. On Mar. 28, 1927, however, 23-year-old Harry Young went to prison for grand larceny. Paroled in 1928, he murdered Republic, Mo., police constable Mark Noe a year later when Noe tried to arrest him for being drunk and disorderly.

For nearly two-and-a-half years Harry Young was the object of a statewide manhunt. Then on Jan. 2, 1932, police stopped two of Young's sisters, Mrs. Loretta Conlon and Vinita Young, when their vehicle was identified as stolen. The women were taken to police headquarters where they confessed that the car belonged to their brother Harry, who, with two other brothers, was hiding out at the family farmhouse. Greene County sheriff Marcell Hendrix organized a seven-man posse to go after the Young boys, believed to be armed and dangerous.

Deputy Wiley Mashburn, Patrolman Virgil Johnson, and Hendrix slowly advanced on the farmhouse, located in a desolate site and surrounded by scrub oak and barbed wire. They kicked in the kitchen door, but were immediately cut down by gunfire. Mashburn and Hendrix were killed instantly. Johnson ran for the car but was shot in the leg just before he closed the door. He did, however, drive to the next house to call for reinforcements. Four other policemen remained pinned down by the hail of gunfire from the house.

Harry Young and his unidentified companions were expert marksmen who picked off the trapped police officers one by one. Chief of detectives Tony Oliver was the third victim. Pinned behind a tree, he got a bullet in the head. "Run before they kill us all!" he cried just before losing consciousness. Officers Charles Houser and Ollie Crosswhite were next, both hit in the forehead and temple. Detective Owen Brown and patrolman Frank Pike were the last two left alive. "We've killed all but you two, and you had better throw down your pistols and come in here," someone in the house cried out. Pike refused, even though their magazines were empty.

By the time reinforcements arrived on the scene, the siege was over. Brown had escaped unhurt, but Pike sustained a bullet wound. The killers had slipped out of the house and into the rugged Ozark hill country, where detection was all but impossible. An angry mob of 350 farmers was immediately pressed into duty by Constable Scott Curtis. "Alright," Curtis said. "You're all deputized. Go as far as you like to catch them, but don't let them get away!" They dispersed across the farms and fields while ambulances carried away the bodies of the five dead men. Detective Dan Bilyeu believed that two of the gunmen holed up in the Young farmhouse were the notorious bandits Fred Barker and Pretty Boy Floyd.

The 68-year-old widowed mother of the Young brothers was taken in for questioning by police. When the tragedy occurred, she had been visiting another son. She expressed the hope that her boys would kill themselves rather than be taken alive.

Two days later, in Houston, Harry and his brother Jennings shot each other in a Magnolia Park rooming house after their landlord, 50-year-old carpenter J.F. Tomlinson, recognized them from photographs in a Houston newspaper. Nine police officers armed with tear gas bombs and shotguns advanced on the one-story dwelling. A dozen shots were fired through the closed doors of the building, but the fugitives did not return fire. "We're dead. C'mon and get us," one of them said. Then there were two quick shots and silence.

Jennings Young lay dead on the bathroom floor. Harry was still breathing, but died soon after at a nearby hospital. Justice of the Peace Campbell Overstreet ruled the shootings a suicide. When the news filtered back to Springfield, Mo., Mrs. Young broke down and cried. "Oh my God, why did they do it?" Reminded of her earlier wish that they not submit to the authorities, she said, "But they're my boys. They're my flesh and blood. Take me away. Take me home God! Father missed all this, why couldn't I?" Paul Young turned himself in to Houston police on Jan. 7, 1932, and was officially charged. It was later revealed that the murder weapons had been supplied by another brother, Oscar Young, a local farmer considered an upstanding member of the community, and thought to be unaware of Harry's murderous tendencies. REF.: *CBA.*

Young, James, prom. 19th Cent., U.S., forg.-embez. After three years as millionaire John Jacob Astor's private secretary, James Young had earned his employer's trust in handling vast financial dealings unsupervised. During this time the young Harvard University graduate also had fallen in love with an actress who required expensive gifts to win her attention; gifts which had already placed Young in considerable debt.

In pursuit of the actress, Young stole from Astor $25,000 in cash, a small amount compared to the large quantity that passed through his hands each day. He assumed that he had seventeen days before Astor would look at his bankbook again. But the very next morning, Astor insisted on pulling in all his available funds for a major purchase of railway stock. That day, Young wrote a check for $150,000, forging Astor's signature, and cashing it at the bank before leaving for South America.

Young traveled to London, England, where within a month a detective discovered Young working in a shoe manufacturing firm. Young escaped though, and remained at large for two years, when he was found again, married to a young Englishwoman and vacationing in Folkestone. Young, however, was released almost immediately as a diplomatic dispute between Britain and the U.S. nullified all extradition treaties. It was two years before a treaty was in place once again. Young was soon arrested in a suburb of Birmingham and returned to New York for trial. He pleaded guilty and was sentenced to fifteen years in prison. REF.: *CBA.*

Young, John, d.1748, Brit., forg. Apprenticed to a linen-draper in Belfast, Ire., John Young remained in his master's employ until he got into trouble with a house servant. Young fled to Dublin, but was waylaid by a regiment of footguards, who recruited him into the service. He stayed, and later was promoted to sergeant. Distinguishing himself in combat at the battle of Fontenoy, Young earned a battlefield promotion to paymaster. As sergeant-major and paymaster for the troops, he handled many large notes drawn on the Bank of Scotland.

One day, while Young was looking over some bank drafts from Edinburgh, a new recruit named Parker told him that with the proper tools he could create forgeries so precise that the untrained eye could never tell the difference. Young at first dismissed the idea, but it played on his mind. So he rented an apartment for Parker and supplied him with the tools to produce likenesses of Scottish bank notes. Six months later, when the regiment received its marching orders, Young decided to cash in the bogus certificates and convinced a Mr. Gordon, a manufacturer from Aberdeen, that the notes were genuine.

Gordon passed the notes in southern Scotland and did not realize he had been swindled until he noticed a small item in the local newspaper about a alleged forgery near Aberdeen. Gordon called the sheriff of Inverness, who arrested Young and found in his possession three £100 notes and some copper plate used in forgery. Parker was also arrested, but he agreed to turn state's evidence against Young in return for his life. Forgery then a capital offense, he was willing to do anything to save his neck.

The trial was held at the High Court of Judiciary in Edinburgh. A Guilty verdict was returned against Young, and he was executed at the Grassmarket on Dec. 19, 1748.

REF.: Atholl, *Shadow of the Gallows; CBA.*

Young, John, d.1750, Scot., forg. In Scotland in the eighteenth century the time as well as the date of a hanging were specified when the sentence was handed down. John Young, a convicted forger, was sentenced to hang between 2 p.m. and 4 p.m. He thought that if he were not hanged by 4 p.m., he would be spared. He locked himself in his jail cell, and when prison guards broke through the wall shortly after 4 p.m., Young triumphantly informed them that they could no longer carry out the sentence. Prison officials informed Young that the specific time meant nothing and that he could, and would, be hanged immediately. Despite Young's attempt to avoid, as he put it, being "an accessory in (his) own murder," he was hanged that afternoon.

REF.: *CBA;* Mitchell, *The Newgate Calendar.*

Young, John Riley, d.1945, Brit., mur. On June 6, 1945, the 17-year-old daughter of Frederick and Cissie Lucas returned to her home in Leigh-on-Sea, England, to find her parents brutally murdered. Lucas, a jeweler, and his wife had been hit repeatedly on the head with at least two different instruments. Lucas had died shortly after the attack, while Cissie, although dead by the time her daughter discovered the bodies, had lived some seven hours. John Riley Young was arrested in connection with the slayings and was convicted at Chelmsford. When arrested, he attempted suicide by slashing his wrists. Young survived the attempt and was executed at Pentonville.

REF.: Brock, *A Casebook of Crime; CBA;* Simpson, *Forty Years of Murder.*

Young, Joseph Louis (AKA: **Yusuf-Ali**), 1946- , U.S., burg.-rob.-asslt.-mansl.-mur. On May 27, 1987, Joseph Louis Young, forty-one, entered the Wyncote, Pa., home of Isma'il al-Faruqui, a 65-year-old proponent of Palestinian rights. Isma'il was a U.S. citizen and had taught, along with his 59-year-old wife, Lois al-Faruqui, at Temple University since 1968. According to police Lieutenant Robert Krauser, Young used a 15-inch knife to murder the couple. He also attacked their pregnant daughter—the mother and baby survived. Washington attorney Jawad George headed a group offering a $50,000 reward for information that would lead to a conviction. George identified Young as a member of the Black Muslims and said the suspect had known the Faruquis and had visited them at their home. Faruqui, who taught religion at the university, was the last governor in the Galilee area prior to the United Nations' creation of Israel in 1948. Young was arrested on Jan. 16, 1987, at a Philadelphia jail, where he was being held on other charges.

Almost 4,000 mourners attended the funeral for the Faruquis at a Philadelphia mosque, with telegrams pouring in from Moslem leaders and dignitaries from South Africa, the Philippines, Jordan, Egypt, Kuwait, Malaysia, and Pakistan. Young was held without bail and was tried in July 1987 at a Montgomery County, Pa., court with Judge William Nicholas presiding. On July 10, Young was found Guilty of both murders and was sentenced to death. He was also sentenced to five to ten years for attempted murder and ten to twenty years for assault, burglary, robbery, reckless endangerment, possession of a deadly weapon, and voluntary and involuntary manslaughter. REF.: *CBA.*

Young, Kenneth, 1956- , U.S., (unsolv.) kid. In the early morning of Apr. 3, 1967, Kenneth Young, the 11-year-old son of Herbert J. Young, president of Gibraltar Savings and Loan Association, was kidnapped from his Beverly Hills, Calif., home. On Kenneth's bed, his mother, Arline Young, found an envelope with a note inside. At the top of the message was typewritten "IMPORTANT IMPORTANT IMPORTANT." The ransom note continued, "Master of the house...I have the merchandise you want. Don't go to the police, your competitor for the merchandise...Otherwise the merchandise will be vindictively destroyed." The note added that $250,000 in $100 bills must be paid for the safe return of the "merchandise"—Kenneth.

Aside from contacting the police and the FBI, the Youngs—who convinced two Los Angeles newspapers not to print stories of the kidnapping—followed the ransom note's instructions. On Apr. 5, Mr. Young drove to a gas station in Westwood Village.

At exactly 6 p.m., the phone in the booth there rang. The caller informed Young to drive to a second gas station some two miles north. Young waited there for forty minutes before a man driving a white Chevrolet Impala motioned for Young to follow in his car. At a secluded stretch along Sepulveda Boulevard, the lead car pulled over. With lights of both cars turned off, Young gave the driver of the Impala a tan overnight bag containing the ransom money. Young then drove home.

At 4 a.m. on Apr. 6, Kenneth called his parents from an apartment in Santa Monica. He had been left tied up and blindfolded inside a garage there. Kenneth had not been physically harmed, but he was drowsy from sleeping pills the kidnapper—Kenneth believed there was just one man who kidnapped him, though the FBI believed more than one person was involved—had given him. He also had had his head shaved to create a snug fit for the blindfold he wore.

Kenneth's safe return marked the highest amount of money ever paid to a kidnapper where the victim was not killed. A ransom of $600,000 had been paid in 1953 to the abductors of 6-year-old Bobby Greenlease in Kansas City, Mo. His body was found later in a shallow grave. In 1963, 19-year-old Frank Sinatra, Jr. had been kidnapped and $240,000 paid before he was returned unharmed. His captors, however, were arrested and most of the ransom money was recovered. Though a list of the serial numbers of the money the Youngs paid was released by the FBI, and more than 300 agents were assigned to the case, the kidnapper was not captured. See: **Hall, Carl Austin**.

REF.: Alix, *Ransom Kidnapping in America; CBA.*

Young, Mary, See: **Diver, Jenny.**

Young, Robert, d.1980, U.S., sod.-necro.-mur. In 1974, Robert Young shot and killed a woman who returned home while he was burglarizing her apartment. He then sodomized the dead body. He was arrested and sentenced to eighteen years in prison for these crimes and for sodomizing an 11-year-old girl in a separate incident. Instead of prison, Young was sent to Matteawan State Hospital for the Criminally Insane. He escaped in a mass breakout in 1977.

After the breakout, Young teamed up with Blanche Wright. On Jan. 21, 1980, the two approached Felipe Rodriguez, a Colombian drug dealer in the Bedford Park district of the Bronx. Wright convinced Rodriguez to allow the two into his apartment to buy drugs. Young pushed his way inside and shot Rodriguez, his common law wife, Maria Navas, and a neighbor, Luis Martin. Wright and Young then looted the apartment, stealing $8,000 in cash and narcotics. Only Rodriguez survived the shootings.

Two weeks later, Wright and Young attacked another drug dealer, Marshall Howell, as he left his apartment with bodyguard Sam Nevins. Young shot at Howell, but when his gun jammed, he was himself shot and killed by Nevins. Wright then shot the already wounded Howell in the head, while Nevins escaped. When police visited the home of the woman who had claimed Young's body, they found Wright. She denied any knowledge of the murder. However, when police suggested she had let her partner down by not firing sooner, she became indignant and replied that her bullets had killed Howell. She then confessed that she and Young were contract killers who had been hired to kill Howell for failing to pay a drug debt. She admitted that they were responsible for the attempted murder of Rodriguez, and the murders of Navas and Martin, as well as the contract killing of another drug dealer, Carlos Medina, in November 1979. Wright was sentenced to eighteen years to life in the Howell slaying and fifteen years to life for her part in the Navas and Martin murders.

REF.: *CBA;* Wilson, *Encyclopedia of Modern Murder.*

Young, S. Glenn, prom. 1924-25, Case of, U.S., secret soc.-attempt. mur. In the small mining town of Herrin, Ill., in January 1924, the Ku Klux Klan faced off with anti-Klan forces in a series of prohibition raids that nearly caused riots. Klan leader S. Glenn Young walked the streets with two guns strapped to his waist, and troops were called in to prevent violence. After troops were withdrawn, gunfire flared up again, with one man killed and several more wounded. In February, Young was arrested. Known as a "man killer" in his activities as a federal prohibition agent against moonshiners in Tennessee and Georgia, he was said to have killed between twenty and thirty men. In May, Young and his wife were shot and wounded as they drove in their car. Within twenty-four hours, a man named Skelcher, who was alleged to have been in the group that fired on the Youngs, was gunned down, his body riddled with thirty bullets. When Young's case came up in late August 1924, he was in Atlanta, Ga. Pleading ill health, he forfeited his $24,000 bond.

During the trial of the men accused of killing Skelcher, a Klan member testified that he did not believe the accused were guilty, and the case was dismissed. That same day the sheriff and two deputies went to the Klan's headquarters at the Smith garage and seized the car allegedly used in the shooting of Skelcher. Klansman Dewey Newbolt and several others opened fire; six were killed, another five wounded. Thirty-two murder warrants were sworn out and troops again were called in to keep the peace. On Oct. 20, Young and KKK members John Crompton and Leonard Barress were arrested by Deputy Sheriff Ora Thomas, Young's fierce enemy. All three were charged with assault with intent to commit murder in an attack on John Garvagalis, former Herrin health officer. In Fall 1924, Thomas left Herrin as part of an armistice agreement signed between the warring factions.

On Jan. 24, 1925, Thomas, who had resigned his post when he left town, returned to fight Young, sending word that the Klan leader could not keep him out. Young, who was living at the Lymar Hotel and writing his autobiography, called his lieutenants together and announced that Thomas would not be permitted in Herrin. Young and his gang paraded the streets all day. At about 8:30 p.m., in front of a restaurant, Young and Thomas faced off and shooting broke out while a crowd watched. Young, Thomas, and Klansmen Ed Forbes and Homer Warren lay dead, with several others wounded. The state militia was again brought in to control the streets. In Marion, Ill., on Feb. 10, 1925, Police Chief Matt Walker and officers Ross Lisenby and Harry Walker were charged with neglect of duty in the January gunfight. By Feb. 12, fifty-seven indictments were returned by a Williamsburg grand jury. As the coroner's jury in Herrin ruled that Thomas killed Young and Young killed Thomas, Sheriff Galligan and Herrin police chief A.M. Walker asked for a declaration of martial law in the strife-torn community. The jury made no recommendations for punishment in their verdict. REF.: *CBA.*

Young, William, 1856-1925, U.S., law enfor. off. William Young joined the St. Louis police force on Dec. 5, 1878. After serving as captain of the force for twenty-one years, Young was promoted to police chief. The *St. Louis Police Journal,* the first weekly newspaper published by a police department in the U.S., began in April 1912, during Young's tenure as chief. Following a board hearing, Young was demoted to the rank of captain in 1919. Shortly after his demotion, he resigned, and in 1921 he was appointed to the board of police commissioners. REF.: *CBA.*

Young, William Hooper, prom. 1902, U.S., mur. In 1902, the body of Mrs. Joseph P. Pulitzer was found in a ditch in New Jersey. The body was held down by a tie-weight, the piece of iron used to keep livery horses standing in one place. By searching area livery stables for a rented rig returned without its tie-weight, police linked Pulitzer's death to William Hooper Young, grandson of Brigham Young. Suspicion of the Mormon religion encouraged speculation that the murder was part of a secret blood ritual conducted by the Mormons. Mormon leaders strenuously denied any connection between William Hooper Young and the Mormon sect, stating that he had long since been disowned for his immoral lifestyle. Young was captured in upstate New York, masquerading as a hobo. He was charged in the murder and found Guilty.

REF.: *CBA;* Rodell, *New York Murders.*

Youngdahl, Luther Wallace, 1896-1978, U.S., jur. Served as Minnesota governor from 1947-51. He also was a judge on the Minnesota State Supreme Court from 1942-46, and was district judge for Hennepin County, Minn., from 1936-42. He was appointed to the district court of Minnesota by President Harry S. Truman in 1951. REF.: *CBA*.

Younger Brothers, prom. 1860s-70s, U.S., west. outl. The four Younger brothers, Thomas "Cole" Coleman, John, Robert, and James, grew up in Kansas in the 1850s when the state was torn between the pro-slavery factions and the abolitionists of the North who sought to keep slavery out of the territories. The Youngers were growing up in Lee's Summit, Mo., when their father was killed, presumably by Northerners. When the Civil War came, Cole Younger joined William Quantrill's band of Confederate marauders who rode through border states creating havoc against the Union. In 1863 Cole met 16-year-old Myra Belle Shirley, while he was stationed in Texas. Their courtship produced an illegitimate child, according to Shirley, who achieved notoriety as the legendary outlaw Belle Starr.

Jim Younger, who was only eleven when the war started, followed his older brother into the ranks of the Quantrill raiders in the vain hope of avenging his father's death. They rode together for the duration of the conflict, until Quantrill was mortally wounded at Smiley, Kan. Jim was captured and jailed at a military prison in Alton, Ill., where he was held until the waning months of 1865. About a year later, Cole Younger was introduced to Frank James, who was also a former member of Quantrill's Raiders.

After gaining his release, Jim returned to the family farm. Cole Younger, his taste for adventure whetted by the Civil War, joined the Frank and Jesse James holdup gang in 1866. They robbed a bank in Liberty, Mo., and then fled to Texas and Louisiana to spend their loot. At an opportune time, Cole returned to Missouri where he inveigled his brothers to join him. Jim left the farm to ride with the newly formed James-Younger Gang.

John and Bob were too young to have fought in the Civil War, but they joined their older brothers in 1868 and 1872 respectively. Jesse James was the acknowledged leader of this Western outlaw gang, but he never got along well with Cole. The Younger Brothers and the James boys committed a string of bank robberies and train holdups throughout Missouri and the surrounding states in the late 1860s, continuing through the next decade. As was their custom when the law was in pursuit, the Younger-James gang retreated to Texas and laid low until things settled down in Missouri.

The highly publicized exploits of this renegade band led to stepped-up pressure for their arrest. By 1874 the Pinkerton National Detective Agency entered the affray, sending several of their best agents to Missouri to capture Jesse James and the Youngers. In March 1874, John and Jim Younger went into hiding at a friend's house in Monegaw Springs, Mo. Having discovered their location, Agents Louis J. Lull and John Boyle disguised themselves as cattle buyers to garner some useful information. The Youngers were in hiding at Theodorick Snuffer's home in Monegaw Springs when the Pinkerton men appeared at the door asking for directions. When they had gone, the Youngers loaded up their weapons and rode off in pursuit. They caught up with them on the Chalk Level Road, and demanded that the "cattle buyers" identify themselves. Jim Younger collected their rifles while John stood guard. A moment later, Agent Lull produced a hidden pistol and shot John Younger through the throat. Before he fell to the ground, he fired several shotgun blasts which killed Lull. Deputy Sheriff Ed Daniels, who accompanied the two Pinkertons, was gunned down in a similar fashion. John Younger, who had killed a man for the first time when he was only fifteen, died of his wounds a short time later.

The three remaining Youngers rode with the James Brothers and three other men into Northfield, Minn., on Sept. 7, 1876, to rob the First National Bank. The ill-timed holdup went awry from the beginning when three bank employees, F.J. Wilcox, A.E. Bunker, and Joseph Lee Heywood, refused to cooperate. Bunker turned and fled out the door, but Wells wounded him with a bullet outside. Jesse James and Bob Younger shot cashier Heywood to death, then ran outside to re-join the gang. Pandemonium broke loose, when the incensed residents of Northfield learned what had transpired. A storekeeper, A.E. Manning, exchanged shots with Bob Younger. Bill Chadwell and Clell Miller, who had re-routed the gang from Mankato to Northfield because they feared the vigilantes there, were shot off their horses. A medical student, Henry Wheeler, took aim on Miller, and leveled him. Chadwell and Charlie Pitts were also killed. Bob Younger, who was severely wounded in the hand, was snatched up by his brother, Cole, who galloped out of town. Jesse and Frank James fled from the area, not really caring about the plight of the Youngers who sought refuge in a thicket near Medalia, Minn.

Cole, Jim, and Samuel Wells did as much as they could for brother Bob, who was weakened by the loss of blood. On Sept. 21, a posse caught up with the Youngers and demanded their immediate surrender. They replied by firing on the lawmen, which commenced one last bloody shoot-out. Wells was killed. Cole was shot eleven times, and James was hit five times. Bob emerged from behind the embankment with his hands raised. "They're all down except me," he said. A final shot clipped Bob in the cheek before the lawmen took the prisoners back to jail.

The three brothers entered a plea of guilty to robbery and murder. All three were sentenced to life in the Stillwater penitentiary. Bob Younger was a model prisoner. He studied medicine and cooperated with the guards in every way. However, his health was frail. He contracted tuberculosis and died on Sept. 16, 1889. Cole and Jim were paroled in 1901, but were required under the terms of the Deming Act to live in Minnesota. The brothers went into business selling tombstone monuments, and later, insurance. Jim fell in love with a newspaper writer, Alice Miller, but was not permitted to marry under the strict parole terms handed down by the state. Despondent, he killed himself on Oct. 19, 1902. Cole Younger received an official pardon in 1903. He eventually reunited with Frank James in a touring Wild West show. Before he died on Feb. 21, 1916, Cole went on the lecture circuit preaching the evils of crime. See: **James, Jesse Woodson**.

REF.: Aikman, *Calamity Jane;* American Guide Series, *Missouri, A Guide to the "Show Me" State;* Appell, *Belle's Castle;* Appleman, *Charlie Siringo;* Appler, *The Guerrillas of the West;* ____, *The Younger Brothers;* Barker, *Missouri Lawyer;* Bartholomew, *The Biographical Album of Western Gunfighters;* ____, *Western Hard-Cases;* Barton, *Three Years With Quantrell;* Beebe, *The American Earth;* Beebe and Clegg, *The American West;* Belden, *Life of David Belden;* Block, *Great Train Robberies of the West;* Booker, *Wildcats in Petticoats;* Botkin, *A Treasury of Southern Folklore;* Bradley, *The Outlaws of the Border;* Breihan, *The Complete and Authentic Life of Jesse James;* ____, *The Day Jesse James Was Killed;* ____, *Outlaws of the Old West;* ____, *Younger Brothers;* Bronaugh, *The Youngers' Fight For Freedom;* Brownlee, *Gray Ghosts of the Confederacy;* Buel, *The Border Outlaws;* ____, *Jesse and Frank James;* Burch, *Charles W. Quantrell;* Burnham, *Taking Chances;* Byers, *With Fire and Sword;* Byrum, *Behind Prison Bars;* Callison, *Bill Jones of Paradise Valley;* Casey, *The Texas Border;* Castel, *A Frontier State at War;* ____, *William Clarke Quantrill; CBA;* Chilton, *The Book of the West;* Clark, *Then Came the Railroads;* Crittenden, *The Crittenden Memoirs;* Croy, *Jesse James Was My Neighbor;* ____, *Last of the Great Outlaws;* Dacus, *Illustrated Lives and Adventures of Frank and Jesse James, and the Younger Brothers;* Dale, *Adventures and Exploits of the Younger Brothers;* Dalton, *Under the Black Flag;* Donald, *Outlaws of the Border;* Doughitt, *Romance and Dim Trails;* Drago, *Outlaws on Horseback;* ____, *Red River Valley;* Duke, *Celebrated Criminal Cases of America;* Edwards, *Noted Guerrillas;* Ellis, *Pioneers;* Elman, *Fired in Anger;* Farber, *Those Texans;* Fellows, *This Way to the Big Show;* Gardner, *The Old Wild West;* Garwood, *Crossroads of America;* George, *Just Memories and Twelve Years With Cole Younger;* Gish, *American Bandits;* Godwin, *Murder U.S.A.;* Graham, *Tales of the Ozark River Country;* Gregory, *True Wild West Stories;* Harrington, *Hanging Judge;* Harrison, *Hell Holes and Hangings;* Hayes, *Iron Road to Empire;* Heilbron, *Convict Life at the Minnesota State Prison;* Henderson, *Keys to Crookdom;* Hendricks, *The Bad Man of the West;* Hicks, *Belle Starr and Her Pearl;* Hill, *The End of the Cattle Trail;* Hill, *Stories of the Railroad;* Holbrook, *The Story of American Railroads;* Holloway, *Texas Gun Lore;*

Cole Younger

Bob Younger

Jim Younger

John Younger

The disastrous raid of the James-Younger gang in Northfield, Minn., 1876, saw the capture of the Younger Brothers.

Cole Younger, 1890.

Bob Younger, 1890.

Jim Younger, 1890.

Cole Younger in old age.

Horan, *Desperate Men;* ____, *Desperate Women;* ____, *The Great American West;* ____, *The Pinkertons;* ____ and Sann, *Pictorial History of the Wild West;* Hough, *The Story of the Outlaw;* Hubbard, *Railroad Avenue;* Hunt, *A Dictionary of Rogues;* Hunter and Rose, *The Album of Gun-Fighters;* Huntington, *Robber and Hero;* Hutto, *The Dallas Story;* James, *James Boys;* Jameson, *Heroes by the Dozen;* Jones, *The Hatfields and the McCoys;* Kane, *100 Years Ago With the Law and the Outlaw;* Kelly, *The Outlaw Trail;* King, *Ghost Towns of Texas;* Lambert, *Stephen Benton Elkins;* Lavender, *The American Hertiage History of the Great West;* Lewis and Smith, *Oscar Wilde Discovers America;* Lieberson, *The Columbia Records Legacy Collection;* Love, *The Rise and Fall of Jesse James;* McCarty, *The Enchanted West;* McCarty, *The Gunfighters;* McCready, *Railroads in the Days of Steam;* McKennon, *Iron Men;* Miller, *Shady Ladies of the West;* Miller, *Pioneering North Texas;* Myers, *Doc Holliday;* Nash, *Bloodletters and Badmen;* Nesbit, *An American Family;* O'Neal, *They Die But Once;* Paxton, *Annals of Platte County;* Phares, *Bible in Pocket, Gun in Hand;* ____, *Reverend Devil;* Potter, *The Autobiography of Theodore Edgar Potter;* Preece, *The Dalton Gang;* Quinn, *Fools of Fortune;* Raine, *Guns of the Frontier;* Rainey, *No Man's Land;* Rascoe, *Belle Starr;* Ray, *The Life of Bob and Cole Younger with Quantrell;* ____, *The Younger Brothers;* Rea, *Boone County and Its People;* Rennert, *Western Outlaws;* Riegel, *America Moves West;* Roe, *The James Boys;* Russell, *The Lives and Legends of Buffalo Bill;* Russell, *Behind These Ozark Hills;* Schrantz, *Jasper County;* Scott, *Some Memories of a Soldier;* Scott, *Belle Starr in Velvet;* Settle, *Jesse James Was His Name;* Shackleford, *Belle Starr;* ____, *Gun-Fighters of the Old West;* Shaner, *The Story of Joplin;* Shirley, *Law West of Fort Smith;* ____, *Outlaw Queen;* Shoemaker, *Missouri Day by Day;* Simpson, *Llano Estacado;* Small, *The Best of True West;* Stambaugh, *A History of Collin County;* Sterling, *Famous Western Outlaw-Sheriff Battles;* Sutley, *The Last Frontier;* Thorndike, *Lives and Exploits of the Daring Frank and Jesse James;* Triplett, *History, Romance and Philosophy of Great American Crimes and Criminals;* Walker, *Jesse James;* Waller, *Last of the Great Western Train Robbers;* Ward, *The James Boys of Old Missouri;* ____, *Jesse James' Dash For Fortune;* ____, *The Younger Brothers;* Waters, *A Gallery of Western Badmen;* Watson, *A Century of Gunmen;* Wellman, *A Dynasty of Western Outlaws;* White, *Lead and Likker;* Williams and Shoemaker, *Missouri, Mother of the West;* Winther, *The Transportation Frontier;* Young, *True Stories of Old Houston and Houstonians;* (FILM), *Bad Men of Missouri,* 1941; *Return of the Badmen,* 1948; *The Return of Jesse James,* 1950; *Best of the Badmen,* 1951; *The Maverick Queen,* 1956; *Cole Younger, Gunfighter,* 1958; *The Outlaws Is Coming,* 1965; *The Great Northfield, Minnesota Raid,* 1972; *The Long Riders,* 1980.

Youngman, William Godfrey, c.1835-60, Brit., mur. William Youngman carried out a plan of murder for insurance. In the process, he killed not only the insured, his fiancée Mary Streeter, but also his mother and two brothers.

Youngman said his mother murdered his two brothers and Streeter and claimed he killed his mother in self-defense. But police discovered in his possession the insurance policy his fiancée had taken out on her life naming Youngman as the beneficiary, as well as numerous letters belonging to Streeter in which Youngman repeatedly urged her to take out a policy. Furthermore, the knife used was his. He was found Guilty of murder and hanged in 1860. REF.: *CBA.*

Youtsey, Henry E., See: **Goebel, William.**

Ypsilanti Ripper, The, See: **Collins, John Norman.**

Yu Chien, 1398-1457, China, treas. Executed as traitor for efforts to save China following kidnapping of Emperor Cheng-t'ung. REF.: *CBA.*

Yu, Ching-man, d.1955, China, (unsolv.) assass. In 1955, emissaries from Communist China and from Chiang-Kai-shek's Formosan stronghold competed for the political loyalty of retired and uncommitted Chinese nationalists. One particularly desirable leader was Ching-man Yu, who had served as commander of the Nationalist 26th Army in Yunnan and as leader of the defense of Changteh against the Japanese in 1943. Yu was visited by General Wei Lihuang, who defected to the Communists in March 1955. Shortly thereafter, General Li Mi, a former commander of Nationalist troops in Burma, visited Yu in his Hong Kong home. Presumably both were seeking a commitment from Yu, who had prospered through investments in Hong Kong real estate, Macao fisheries, and Chinese trading firms.

In September 1955, Yu was ambushed by three men outside his home. They ordered him inside the house and shot him to death. Police killed one of the assailants, but the other two escaped. Police first shied away from the dangerous politics involved, and labeled the crime a murder with a robbery motive. Eventually, however, they acknowledged the probable political nature of the assassination and offered a substantial reward for information leading to the capture of the murderers. REF.: *CBA.*

Yui Shosetsu, d.1651, Japan, consp.-suic. Devised plan to overthrow Tokugawa shogunate, but killed himself when his plot was discovered. REF.: *CBA.*

Yukl, Charles (AKA: **Mr. Williamson**), prom. 1960s-70s, U.S., necro.-mur. In July 1974, a Mr. Williamson of Greenwich Village in New York City, ran ads in which he said he was seeking actresses to audition for a role in a film production. Aspiring actress Karin Schlegel applied and while in Williamson's apartment was strangled and raped. Her mutilated body was left in the building.

Police discovered that Williamson was actually Charles Yukl, who had committed an identical crime in October 1966 and had been paroled after serving only five years of his sentence. This time he received a life sentence. REF.: *CBA.*

Yung-yen (AKA: **Chia-ch'ing** or **Jui Huang-ti**), 1760-1820, China, law enfor. Arrested influential and corrupt minister Ho-shen in 1799. As the fifth emperor of the Ch'ing dynasty, he overwhelmed the White Lotus Rebellion from 1796-1804. He was unsuccessful in both ending corruption and restoring the treasury. He was one of the most disliked Ch'ing emperors. REF.: *CBA.*

Yurovsky, Jacob, See: **Nicholas II.**

Yusupov, Prince **Felix**, See: **Rasputin, Gregory.**

Yusupov, Irina Alexandrovna, prom. 1934, Fr., libel. Fearing that the wily and manipulative faith healer Gregory Rasputin was seriously undermining the Russian monarchy, a group of arch-conservatives led by Prince Felix Yusupov (husband of Czar Nicholas' daughter, Princess Irina Alexandrovna) hatched a conspiracy to eliminate the threat before it could do irreparable damage to the regime. On the night of Dec. 29, 1916, Rasputin visited the prince's home where he was served poisoned wine and tea cakes. When the poison failed to take hold, Yusupov shot him with a pistol. Rasputin, gravely wounded, fled into the courtyard where he was shot again by Vladimir Mitrofanovich Purishkevich. Afterward, he was tossed through the ice in the Neva River, where he drowned.

Prince Felix and his wife were driven into exile by the vengeful Czarina Alexandra, and had settled in Paris by the time the rest of the royal family was executed during the revolution. In 1932, the MGM film company released a motion picture titled *Rasputin and the Empress.* Although Irina's name was changed to "Natasha," the thinly-disguised portrayal failed to still the anger of the real-life princess who objected to a scene where Natasha confesses to having been seduced by Rasputin. Princess Irina claimed never to have met Rasputin. She filed suit against the makers of the film and received £25,000 in libel damages. The offensive scenes were excised from the finished product. REF.: *CBA.*

Yves of Brittany, Saint (AKA: **l'Avocat des Pauvres**), 1253-1303, Fr., lawyer. Known as patron saint of lawyers, and as "the poorman's lawyer," for his many charities. He was also a government official at Rennes, an ordained priest, and the rector of Louannec. REF.: *CBA.*

YWCA Murder, The, See: **Byrne, Patrick Joseph.**

Z

Zaccaro, John A., Jr., 1964- , U.S., drugs. On Feb. 20, 1986, John A. Zaccaro, Jr. was arrested at Middlebury College in Vermont, where he was a senior, and was charged with selling a quarter gram of cocaine. Zaccaro, the son of 1984 Democratic vice-presidential candidate Geraldine A. Ferraro, pleaded not guilty to possession of a regulated drug before Judge Frank Mahady, and was released on his own recognizance. According to Addison County deputy state's attorney John Quinn, police found $2,000 and between six and eight grams of cocaine in Zaccaro's car after he sold cocaine to an undercover officer. After a six-day trial, a Rutland, Vt., jury deliberated for two hours on April 9, 1988, before finding Zaccaro Guilty of selling $25 worth of cocaine to undercover agent Laura Manning.

Following the verdict, Ferraro read a statement outside the courthouse criticizing Quinn for "prolonging the agony for two years" regarding her son's trial. She said the family had tried to set up a plea agreement soon after Zaccaro's arrest, but she and her husband had refused to allow Zaccaro to plead guilty to a felony drug charge because they believed he was innocent.

On June 16, Zaccaro, who had spent the last two years working at a New York City shelter for runaways, was sentenced to four months in prison, a $1,500 fine, and 300 hours of community service. Ferarro found a "house arrest cell" in Burlington, Vt., for her son, installing him in a $1,500-a-month apartment with cable TV and maid service. Ferraro explained that she was only allowed to visit Zaccaro twice a month, and that he was only permitted an hour of shopping time weekly. When not working at the local youth center, he was confined to his apartment. Ferraro said her son's situation was "better than being in jail, but he's by himself; he does his own cooking." After serving 90 days of his 120-day sentence, Zaccaro was released under the supervision of a New York parole officer on Sept. 28, 1988. REF.: *CBA.*

Zaghlul Pasha, Saad, 1857-1927, Egypt, jur. Cairo lawyer appointed judge of Court of Appeals in 1892. He served as minister of justice from 1910-12, but was deported to Malta and later Ceylon. He returned to Egypt in 1921. REF.: *CBA.*

Zaghlul, Saad, prom. 1926, Egypt, fraud. In 1919, an agent acting on behalf of Pasha Saad Zaghlul, leader of the powerful Egyptian Nationalist party known as Wafd, contracted with Joseph Wingate Folk, a U.S. Attorney and governor of the state of Missouri, to further the cause of Egyptian independence by the use of propaganda in the U.S. The agreed upon fee was $5,000 a month and $500,000 upon the successful completion of the work. Folk acted according to plan from July 1919 to January 1921 but had received only $5,000 at the time of his death in 1923. When Wafd later repudiated the debt, Folk's widow accused Zaghlul of fraud and sued for $602,924. In May 1924, the Cairo Mixed Court ordered Zaghlul to pay Mrs. Folk $55,000 in settlement of the debt. REF.: *CBA.*

Zahaby, Mohammed Hussein, 1910-77, Egypt, sheik, assass. On July 3, 1977, Sheik Mohammed Hussein Zahaby, sixty-seven, was sleeping in his home in Helwan, near Cairo, when four men dressed as police officers stormed in and took him away. Zahaby, former Egyptian cabinet minister and an expert in religious affairs and Islam, had been kidnapped by young Muslim extremists from the Jamaat al Takfir wal Hijira sect, also known as the Society for Repentance and Retreat. The extremists threatened to execute Zahaby unless the government paid a $300,000 ransom and released sixty of their comrades from prison. The extremists murdered their hostage three days after his capture. Zahaby's body was found in a house near the Giza pyramids. He had been strangled, tortured, and shot through the eye. The Hijira sect, far more extreme than the fundamentalist, arch-conservative Muslim Brotherhood, bitterly opposed then-President Anwar Sadat's government, saying it had sullied the purity of Islam by increasing the role of women in public life. The leader of the 500-member group of youths was Ahmed Mustapha Shukri, thirty-four. In 1975, townspeople of the village of Minya, in the Nile Valley, claimed that the group was brainwashing young women and taking them away to be concubines. One young woman had been convinced by them to commit suicide as atonement for her alleged sins.

Zahaby's murder provoked major controversy. Islam theologians denounced the extremists, and police arrested nearly 190 sect members. In November 1977, a military tribunal in Cairo, headed by Major General Hassah Sadek, tried forty members of the Takfir wal Hijira group. President Sadat ordered the members tried by military court in order to speed the process, but the defendants were subjected to the civilian penal code. Shukri, Maher Bakri Zanati, Ahmed Tarek Abdel-Alim, Anwar Mamoun Sakr, and Mustafa Ghazi, were found Guilty and sentenced to death by hanging. Thirty-six other convicted members of the group received sentences ranging from three to twenty-five years, and thirteen defendants were acquitted. In addition to the killing of Zahaby, the bombings of at least two Cairo movie theaters were traced to the militant group. On Mar. 19, 1978, the five men were hanged in Cairo. REF.: *CBA.*

Zahle, Carl Theodor, 1866-1946, Den., jur. Served as minister of justice from 1909-1919, and again between 1929-35. REF.: *CBA.*

Zaim, Husni, d.1949, Syria, assass. Syrian strongman Husni Zaim turned over Syrian nationalist leader Antan Saada to Lebanese officials after Saada was charged with engineering a coup in Lebanon. He was executed by the Lebanese, setting in motion a series of retaliatory assassinations that stretched to Brazil. The chain of retribution finally reached back to Zaim in 1949 when another Syrian nationalist, Fadallah Abu Mansur, killed him in revenge for betraying Saada.

REF.: *CBA;* Paine, *The Assassins' World.*

Zaleucus, prom. 7th Cent. B.C., Gr., jur.-suic. Believed to have written Locrian code, the first recorded legal code in Greece. According to legend, he was a slave who committed suicide upon discovering he had broken one of his own laws. REF.: *CBA.*

Zaluski, Andrzej, 1650-1711, Pol., impris. Statesman and prelate ultimately imprisoned over differences with King Augustus II. REF.: CBA.

Zambino, Luigi, prom. 1905, U.S., (wrong. convict.) count.-fraud. In December 1905, a Massachusetts mill hand, Luigi Zambino, was implicated by Frank Manfra in the passing of counterfeit U.S. $5 silver certificates. Manfra was arrested in New York City when he passed the phony bills and identified Zambino as his accomplice. Zambino was jailed in Trenton, N.J., and indicted for counterfeiting and fraud in June 1906 after a grand jury investigation. Zambino's trial began July 11, with Manfra, already convicted, testifying for the prosecution. Also working against Zambino was the testimony of liquor store owner Charles Wyatt, who positively identified Zambino as the man who had accompanied Manfra when the two attempted to pass the counterfeit bills in his store.

Despite Zambino's claims that he had been at work on the day of the incident, he was found Guilty and sentenced to six years at hard labor in the New Jersey State Prison, and fined $500. After Zambino had been convicted and sent to prison, an attorney in Lawrence, Mass., became interested in the case and discovered that Zambino's alibi was sound. Both Zambino's overseer and the timekeeper confirmed with certainty that Zambino had been at the mill on the days in question. The overseer and timekeeper were subpoenaed but failed to appear at the trial. Charles Wyatt's identification was dismissed when it was discovered that Manfra, who by this time had been arrested again for passing the same kind of bad bills, had a brother who closely resembled Zambino. The attorney, J.C. Sanborn, appealed the conviction and Zambino was formally released by a full and unconditional pardon granted by President William Taft on Nov. 24, 1909, after serving more than three years of his sentence. REF.: *CBA.*

Zamora y Torres, Niceto Alcala, b.1877, Spain, consp. Sentenced to prison for involvement in overthrow of Alfonso XIII in 1930. He became president of the Spanish republic a year later and served until 1936. REF.: *CBA.*

Zampano, Robert Carmine, 1928- , U.S., jur. Nominated by President Lyndon B. Johnson to the district court of Connecticut, where he served as U.S. Attorney from 1961-64. Earlier, from 1957-61, he worked as town counsel and judge in New Haven. REF.: *CBA.*

Zane, Charles Shuster, 1831-1915, U.S., jur. City attorney from 1859-61 and later county attorney in Springfield, Ill. He became a judge for the nineteenth judicial district of Illinois in 1873, remaining at that post for eleven years. In 1896, President Chester A. Arthur appointed him chief justice of Utah, a title which he retained until 1899. He authored the Utah State Constitution. REF.: *CBA.*

Zangara, Giuseppe, See: **Cermak, Anton.**

Zangara, Joseph, See: **Roosevelt, Franklin Delano.**

Zantzinger, William Devereux, c.1939- , U.S., asslt.-mansl. On a February evening in 1963, rural aristocrat and owner of a Maryland tobacco operation, William Devereux Zantzinger, and his wife, Jane Zantzinger, went out with friends. The Zantzingers, who frequently got drunk, soon became inebriated, with William becoming quite abusive. In a downtown Baltimore bar, he struck both the hostess and the restaurant sommelier with a wooden cane. Later, at the Emerson Hotel, Zantzinger beat a bellhop, a waitress, and 51-year-old bartender Hattie Carroll, all black, after inciting the hotel employees with racial slurs.

Only until he turned the cane on his wife, was he arrested. Hattie Carroll died later that night of a brain hemorrhage, and Zantzinger was charged with murder. By the time he came to trial in June, the charge against Zantzinger was reduced to manslaughter. Zantzinger was found Guilty, fined $125 for assault and sentenced to six months in jail; he was fined another $500 for the death of Hattie Carroll. The beginning of his sentence was deferred until Sept. 15, to allow Zantzinger time to harvest his tobacco crop. REF.: *CBA.*

Zapata, Emiliano, 1879-1919, Mex., rebel, assass. Emiliano Zapata, Mexico's greatest hero during its revolutionary years, 1910-19, was born a peon with Indian blood. He possessed a native intelligence that reached far beyond his lack of education. (He did not learn to read until his adult years.) Zapata was small and slender with coal black piercing eyes. During his years of prominence, he wore black, with gold and silver trimming on his tight-fitting, ornate finery, and wore huge silver-laden sombreros. He was the dandy of the revolution and the greatest champion of the peon, the landless, and the homeless. Zapata was obsessed with agrarian reform and died fighting for his programs.

Born dirt poor in the village of Anenecuilco in the province of Morelos, Zapata worked in the fields of a great estate from childhood through his teenage years. Industrious and conscientious, the landowner favored Zapata by making him a *mediero,* a tenant farmer of sorts who cultivated a section of land and shared in half the profits from its crops. This position was the highest a man like Zapata could reach in the *hacienda* system of old Mexico. The landowner, Ignacio de la Torre y Mier, who was married to Amada Diaz, daughter of Mexico's dictator, Porfirio Diaz, admired Zapata's expert horsemanship and befriended him.

The *hacendado* invited Zapata to inspect his magnificent stables in Mexico City. Zapata, who had never been outside the state of Morelos until that time, was shocked to see that the landowner's horses lived in stalls that were more spacious and accommodational than the huts in which his fellow peons lived. He became critical of the estate system and openly defied the authorities. The local political chief, after a confrontation with Zapata, branded the outspoken Zapata a troublemaker, and he was conscripted into the army.

Zapata proved an excellent soldier, rising to sergeant. He was fascinated by military tactics and strategy and when he was released from service in 1910, he had expert knowledge of how to organize and deploy troops. The Diaz regime had inadvertently created a brilliant militarist who would, in years to come, out-general and out-maneuver its armies with a motley band of dedicated peons, "Zapatistas" as they were later known. When Francisco I. Madero rose against Diaz in 1910, Zapata was one of the first to embrace Madero's cause, leading his ragged peons against the troops of the dictator in Morelos. When Madero, Zapata, Pancho Villa fighting in the north, and others overthrew Diaz, Madero became president.

The Madero administration was slow to bring about agrarian reform, however, and Zapata rebelled, withdrawing his support but not openly battling Madero's forces. When Madero was assassinated on orders of Victoriano Huerta, Zapata, joined by Villa, Alvaro Obregón, and Venustiano Carranza, continued the revolution, finally overthrowing Huerta, who, like Diaz, fled the country. Zapata then attempted to put his agrarian reforms into effect, following his Plan of Ayala. Carranza, backed by Obregón, seized power and Zapata and Villa continued their revolution on behalf of the peon. From 1914-19, Zapata fought a losing war against overwhelming odds.

In early April 1919, a colonel in the army of Pablo González, a Yaqui Indian named Jesús Guajardo, sent word that he planned to defect from the Carranza forces, taking with him more than 600 battle-trained troops and a huge store of ammunition and guns, all to be placed under Zapata's command. On Apr. 10, 1919, Zapata and ten men rode to the *hacienda* near Chinameca. Zapata alone got off his horse, and while his men stayed outside the walls of the *hacienda,* he walked into the large square where Guajardo awaited him. Colonel Guajardo welcomed Zapata with open arms, embracing him and kissing him on the cheek in an extravagant show of affection that was really a signal to his hundreds of troops who lay in hiding on the walls of the *hacienda.*

A line of troops stood at attention for review by Zapata who marched past them as a bugler blew three long notes. Zapata, who had reached the main house, had one foot on the first step leading to the porchway, when the troops, holding their rifles at present-arms, suddenly shifted their weapons, aiming them at Zapata. They fired a volley that ripped into the revolutionary leader, toppling him dead on the steps. So terrorized were these troops of Zapata's fierce legend, that they continued to pump volley after volley into his quivering corpse until it was rented like a sieve.

Several of Zapata's men were shot dead by other troops with only three who escaped on horseback. For his insidious betrayal of Zapata, Guajardo, whose traitorous actions were backed by Carranza and Obregón, was promoted to brigadier general and given a $50,000 reward. Zapata's tattered body was dumped in the town square of Cuautla, his one-time headquarters. Here his body was taken to the local police station and identified, marked with a tag reading: "Emiliano Zapata, dead." To the poor peons he represented, however, Zapata's legend never died. He remains to this day Mexico's most colorful hero. His prophetic words, written years earlier, came to reality years later: "Though society defames us, history will justify our actions, when the new generations come to enjoy the fruits of our battles, fought with our bodies and the tears of our women. And this same society which attacks us today for our crimes will cover us with blessings." See: **Carranza, Venustiano; Madero, Francisco I.; Obregón, Alvaro; Villa, Pancho.**

REF.: Alba, *The Mexicans;* Alessio, *Historia Politica de la Revolución;* Atkin, *Revolution!;* Baerlein, *Mexico, The Land of Unrest;* Baker, *Woodrow Wilson, Life and Letters;* Barba González, *La Lucha por la tierra: Emiliano Zapata;* Beals, *Porfirio Diaz: Dicatator of Mexico;* Bell, *The Political Shame of Mexico;* Blasco Ibañez, *Mexico in Revolution;* Blum, *Woodrow Wilson and the Politics of Morality;* Braddy, *Cock of the Walk: The Legend of Pancho Villa;* ____, *Pancho Villa at Columbus;* Brand, *Mexico: Land of Sunshine and Shadow;* Breceda, *Méxocp Revolucionario, 1913-1917;* Brenner and Leighton, *The Wind That Swept Mexico;* Bulnes, *The Whole Truth About Mexico;* Bush, *Gringo Doctor;* Calcott, *Liberalism in Mexico, 1857-1919;* Callahan, *American Foreign Policy in Mexican Relations;* Cal-

The noble revolutionary, Emiliano Zapata, 1912.

Porfirio Diáz, Mexico's dictator.

Venustiano Carranza, 1918.

Victoriano Huerta, 1913.

Pancho Villa, in throne chair, and Emiliano Zapata, right, conferring in the National Palace, Mexico City.

Zapata's foe, Alvaro Obregón.

vert, *The Mexican Revolution, 1910-1914;* Camreon, *Mexico in Revolution;* Casasolka, *Historia Gráfica de la Revolución; CBA;* Cline, *The United States and Mexico;* Creel, *The People Next Door;* Creelman, *Diaz: Master of Mexico;* Cumberland, *Mexican Revolution: Genesis Under Madero;* De la Huerta, *Memorias;* Diaz Soto y Gama, *La revolución agraria del Sur y Emiliano Zapata;* Dillon, *Mexico on the Verge;* Dromundo, *Vida de Emiliano Zapata;* Dulles, *Yesterday in Mexico;* Dunn, *The Crimson Jester: Zapata of Mexico;* Estrada, *La Revolución y Francisco Madero;* Evans, *Letters from Mexico;* Flandrau, *Viva Mexico;* Foix, *Pancho Villa;* Fyfe, *The Real Mexico;* Grayson, *Woodrow Wilson;* Grieb, *The United States and Huerta;* Gruening, *Mexico and Its Heritage;* Guzmán, *Memoirs of Pancho Villa;* Haley, *Revolution and Intervention: The Diplomacy of Taft and Wilson with Mexico, 1910-1917;* Hendrick, *Life and Letters of Walter H. Page;* Herrera, *Francisco Villa, Ante La Historia;* Inman, *Intervention in Mexico;* Johnson, *Heroic Mexico;* ____, *Mexico;* King, *Tempest Over Mexico: A Personal Chronicle;* Lara Pardo, *De Porfirio Diaz á Francisco Madero;* Liceaga, *Félix Diaz;* Lord, *The Good Years;* Magaña and Guerrero, *Emiliano Zapata y el Agrarismo en México;* Márquez, *Los Ultimos Dias del Presidente Madero;* Meyer, *Huerta: A Political Portrait;* Moats, *Thunder in Their Veins;* Nash, *Almanac of World Crime;* O'Hea, *Reminiscences of the Mexican Revolution;* O'Shaughnessy, *A Diplomat's Wife in Mexico;* ____, *Intimate Pages of Mexican History;* Palacios, *Emiliano Zapata;* Parkes, *A History of Mexico;* Pinchon, *Viva Villa!;* ____, *Zapata the Unconquerable;* Plenn, *Mexico Marches;* Puente, *Pascual Orozco y la Revuelta de Chihuahua;* Reed, *Insurgent Mexico;* Regler, *A Land Bewitched;* Reyes, *A History of Mexico;* Rippy, *The United States and Mexico;* Robinson, *The Foreign Policty of Woodrow Wilson;* Ross, *Francisco I. Madero: Apostle of Mexican Democracy;* Sherman, *Victoriano Huerta, A Reappraisal;* Simpson, *Many Mexicos;* Smith, *Benighted Mexico;* Sotelo Inclán, *Raiz y razón de Zapata;* Stevens, *Here Comes Pancho Villa;* Strode, *Timeless Mexico;* Tannenbaum, *Peace by Revolution;* ____, *Mexico: The Struggle for Peace and Bread;* Taracena, *Madero, Vida del Hombre y del Politico;* Turner, *Barbarous Mexico;* Turner, *Bullets, Bottles and Gardenias;* Tweedie, *Mexico: From Diaz to the Kaiser;* ____, *Porfirio Diaz;* ____, *Mexico As I Saw It;* Walworth, *Woodrow Wilson;* Wilson, *Diplomatic Episodes in Mexico, Belgium, and Chile;* Womack, *Zapata and the Mexican Revolution;* Zayas, *The Case of Mexico and the Policy of President Wilson;* (FILM), *Viva Zapata,* 1952.

Zasulich, Vera Ivanovna, See: **Trepoff**, General **Dmitri Feodorovich.**

Zavatt, Joseph Carmine, 1900- , U.S., jur. Counsel for New York state legislature from 1948-53. In 1957, President Dwight D. Eisenhower nominated him to the eastern district court of New York. REF.: *CBA.*

Zayas, Fernando, 1962- , U.S., mur. On July 2, 1983, Fernando Zayas, twenty-two, shot and killed Miguel Vargas, twenty in Chicago, Ill. Four years before, Vargas had pleaded guilty to killing Ramon Vasquez, a friend of Zayas'. Zayas, a reputed gang member, ambushed and killed Vargas and two friends, Juis Cuaresma, seventeen, and Ruben Gutierrez, twenty, as they watched TV on Vargas' porch. The killing was motivated by revenge. Zayas was convicted of murder and sentenced to life in prison on May 18, 1984. REF.: *CBA.*

Zebra Killings, 1973-74, U.S., rob.-asslt.-consp.-kid.-mur. In a period of 179 days between late 1973 and early 1974, five men shot twenty-three people in the San Francisco area. The victims, all of whom were white, were chosen at random. The attacks, which resulted in fifteen deaths and several cases of permanent injury, and which included at least one case of torture and dismemberment, were committed by five black men seeking membership in a Black Muslim-backed organization called the Death Angels. The racial crimes motivated a massive, and controversial, manhunt in which some 600 young black men were stopped on the streets of San Francisco, searched and questioned. The manhunt was halted before the killers were found due to concerns about infringement on civil rights.

The crimes, dubbed by police as the "Zebra killings" because of their interracial nature, were solved when 29-year-old Anthony Harris, one of the original participants, confessed and implicated four other men, Manuel Moore, thirty-one, J.C. Simon, twenty-nine, Larry C. Green, twenty-four, and Jessie Lee Cooks, thirty. The doctrine of the Death Angels dictated that all whites were evil and should be destroyed. The killings, an initiation requirement, were viewed as part of a full-scale war against whites. After a trial that lasted a year and six days in which 181 witnesses were called, Moore, Simon, Green, and Cooks were found Guilty and sentenced to life imprisonment.

REF.: *CBA;* Fox, *Mass Murder;* Howard, *Zebra.*

Zechariah, d.744 B.C., Isr., king, assass. Last monarch in Jehu dynasty. He was murdered by Shallum shortly following his ascension to the throne. REF.: *CBA.*

Zedekiah (Mattaniah), d.c.586 B.C., Judah, rebel. Gained throne through nephew, Nebuchadnezzar II, in 597 B.C. In 586 B.C., two years after launching an unsuccessful revolt against Nebuchadnezzar, he was captured and transported in chains to Babylon. REF.: *CBA.*

Zeev, Israel (AKA: **Ira Farkas**), 1950- , Isr., mansl. In December 1988, a U.S.-born Jewish settler, Israel Zeev, became the first Israeli to be convicted of attacking or killing a Palestinian since the Palestinian uprising began in December 1987. Zeev, thirty-eight, who emigrated to Israel from the West Rogers Park area of Chicago in 1968, was convicted in the shooting death of an Arab shepherd, Judeh Abdallah Awad. According to Zeev, he ordered a group of Arab shepherds off of land belonging to the Israeli settlement of Shiloh on the West Bank where he owns a sheep ranch. Zeev claimed that he fired at the group only after firing a series of warning shots into the air when the Arabs began hurling rocks at him. The 28-year-old Awad was killed in the shooting and another Palestinian was injured.

Several days after the conviction, Zeev, who changed his name from Ira Farkas when he moved to Israel, was sentenced to five years in prison and ordered to pay $17,500 compensation to the slain man's family. Two years of the sentence were suspended so that with the seven months Zeev had served prior to trial and additional time off for good behavior, Zeev could become eligible for parole in May 1990. REF.: *CBA.*

Zeigler, J. George, See: **Goetz, Fred.**

Zelea-Codreanu, Cornelius, See: **Codreanu, Cornelius Zelea.**

New York gangster "Big Jack" Zelig, 1911.

Zelig, Jack (William Alberts, AKA: **Big Jack)**, 1882-1912, U.S., org. crime. Born in New York City as William Alberts, Jack Zelig turned to crime in his early teens. After working as a pickpocket and mugger, he assumed the leadership of the Monk Eastman gang after Eastman was sentenced to prison. Along with Jack Sirocco and Chick Tricker, Zelig directed the activities of seventy-five hoodlums, including "Dago" Frank Cirofici, Harry "Gyp the Blood" Horowitz, Jacob Siedenschner (Whitey Lewis), and "Lefty" Louis Rosenberg. Aligned with Charles Becker, a crooked New York policeman, he ordered the killing of gambler Herman "Beany" Rosenthal.

In 1911, Zelig learned that two of his men, Sirocco and Tricker, intended to betray him to gain control of the mob. They refused to bail him out of jail after he was arrested for robbing a brothel. Using his political clout, Zelig was able to free himself, but learned that his two associates intended to kill him, using a gunman named Julie Morrell. On Dec. 2, 1911, Zelig lured Morrell to a Second Avenue nightclub, where the gunman was plied with alcohol, eventually staggering to the dance floor in search of his victim. Morrell drunkenly called for Zelig, whereupon the lights were extinguished and a single shot was fired. Morrell lay dead on the floor from a bullet through the heart. But the following year, Sirocco and Tricker got their revenge. On Oct. 5, 1912, Zelig was shot to death by Red Phil Davidson as he riding a Thirteenth Street trolley car. See: **Becker, Charles.**

REF.: Asbury, *The Gangs of New York; CBA;* Fried, *The Rise and Fall of the Jewish Gangster in America;* Haskins, *Street Gangs;* Logan, *Against the Evidence;* Peterson, *The Mob;* Sann, *Kill the Dutchman;* Thompson, *Gang Rule in New York.*

Zenge, Mandeville, prom. 1935, U.S., mur. On July 31, 1935, Mandeville Zenge, a carpenter from Missouri, kidnapped 38-year-old Dr. Walter J. Bauer from his Ann Arbor, Mich., hotel. Somewhere between Ann Arbor and Chicago, Zenge sexually mutilated Dr. Bauer with a penknife. Zenge had been engaged to Bauer's wife, Louise Schaffer Bauer until a short time before Bauer married her, and became jealous of the recent marriage. Zenge left Bauer's car with the dying Bauer in it at a Chicago garage. Garage attendants who saw a man leave the car, found the mortally wounded Bauer and called police.

Zenge was arrested in Chicago a short time later and charged in the murder. He was found Guilty by a jury and, in November 1935, was sentenced to life imprisonment. REF.: *CBA.*

Zenger, John Peter, prom. 1735, Case of, U.S., libel. John Peter Zenger came to the U.S. from Germany and supported himself with a small printing business located in New York City. In 1735, circumstances conspired to place Zenger at the center of a power struggle between the American colonists and the British rulers—a struggle which presaged the coming revolution.

As was often the case in colonial America, the English governor of New York, William Cosby, was both poorly qualified as an administrator and likely to use his public position for private gain. The citizens of New York saw the need to protect themselves against Cosby's mismanagement and greed. To gain the support of the Assembly, the third arm of government after the King and the governor, the citizens group contracted with John Zenger to publish a weekly journal to voice opposition to the governor's policies. On Nov. 5, 1735, the first edition of the *New York Weekly Journal, containing the Freshest Advices, Foreign and Domestick* appeared. The *Journal's* opposition to the Governor made it extremely popular—so popular, in fact, that the governor targeted the *Journal* and John Zenger as his primary opponents.

After several unsuccessful attempts to bring Zenger to trial on charges of libel, Governor Cosby finally succeeded. Cosby previously had Zenger's two attorneys disbarred to intimidate any attorney who might have considered coming to his aid. He further stacked the deck in his favor by having Zenger represented by an attorney with political ambitions—someone who would therefore be easily manipulated by the governor's representatives. Cosby's attempts to predetermine the outcome of Zenger's trial were thwarted, however, because when Zenger's trial began on Aug. 4, 1735, Andrew Hamilton, a former attorney general of Pennsylvania and an astute litigator, appeared in court to aid in Zenger's defense. Hamilton foiled the prosecution at virtually every turn and Zenger was eventually found Not Guilty and returned to publishing the successful *Journal.*

REF.: *CBA;* Postgate, *Murder, Piracy and Treason.*

Zenner, Albert (AKA: Fat Albert), 1948- , U.S., arson. Twenty-eight-year-old Albert Zenner was arrested at least six times from 1972-76 and charged with arson, but the charges were always reduced for lack of evidence. Zenner set another fire in the early morning hours of Nov. 4, 1976, in the partly demolished Worthington Hotel in Chicago. This time, Zenner was seen by a resident of a nearby high-rise apartment who happened to be looking at the back of the Worthington Hotel through binoculars at the time Zenner left the building. Curious about what someone would be doing in an abandoned hotel at such a late hour, the witness, Richard Whorton, continued to follow Zenner with his binoculars. When smoke began to issue from the building, Whorton called police to report the suspected arson. Whorton tracked Zenner's movements and reported them via telephone to the police, until officers arrested the arsonist.

Zenner was found Guilty of arson in November 1977 and sentenced to two to six years in the penitentiary. In July 1980, he was paroled on the condition that he stay away from fires. When Zenner began showing up at fires that summer, fire buffs took pictures documenting his presence. Zenner's parole officer got word of his activities and Zenner was returned to prison to await a parole-violation hearing. REF.: *CBA.*

Zerajdic, Bogdan, See: **Varesanin, Marijan.**

Zerilli, Joseph, 1897-1977, U.S., org. crime. A respected and honored Mafia don, Joseph Zerilli maintained absolute control over Detroit, Mich. He immigrated to the U.S. from Sicily at the age of seventeen and worked as a laborer before joining the Purple Gang, mostly Jewish gangsters who made nearly all their money from bootleg alcohol. The Purples worked well with the Mafia, and imported St. Louis gunman Yonnie Licavoli when the Detroit gang wars broke out. Over 500 gangland slayings occurred in this time, and Gaspar Milazzo and Zerilli, then a fast-rising mafioso, were hired to help with the killing. Zerilli and the Purples continued to work together in loan-sharking, extortion, narcotics, labor racketeering, and bookmaking, eventually building up a crime empire that netted annual profits of $150 million.

Mafia don Joseph Zerilli.

When Milazzo was killed by New York mafiosi in 1930, and the remaining Purple members moved on to take more lucrative places in the national syndicate's gambling enterprise, Zerilli rose to prominence. He posed as a baker, lived in a $500,000 home, and was one of only two non-New Yorkers to sit on the national commission. Though involved in innumerable murders, he was convicted only twice: once for speeding, the other for carrying a concealed weapon. He was also an advocate for rights of crime bosses to control their own territory. Zerilli was highly respected in the crime world, due, in part to the personal control he held over all organized crime operations in Detroit. He insisted on not only knowledge of all hits in Detroit, but also on participation in and approval of these activities.

Zerilli retired in the early 1970s, having arranged for his son to take control of the crime business—Zerilli was one of the few dons who managed this. Yet he returned to the business in 1975 when his son was sent to prison for four years for conspiring to obtain a hidden interest in a Las Vegas casino. Also, at this time Jimmy Hoffa was released from prison. Hoffa was a former Teamsters boss who began scheming to restore his power in the union. Zerilli told Hoffa, through his top lieutenant Tony Giacalone, to discontinue his efforts, but the old labor boss refused to listen. Hoffa was to meet Giacalone outside a Detroit restaurant on July 30, 1975, but he never arrived. His disappearance and apparent murder have been the source of much speculation. Although popular theory suggested that Pennsylvania-upstate New York boss Russell Bufalino and New Jersey mafioso Tony Provenzano, killed Hoffa, Zerilli's reputation regarding Mafia protocol made him a suspect as well.

Zerilli died on Oct. 30, 1977, taking more crime secrets to his grave than even Frank Costello, according to one official. He never said a word to the authorities about Hoffa's disappearance. See: **Bufalino, Russell; Hoffa, James Riddle**.

REF.: Bonanno, *A Man of Honor; CBA;* Demaris, *The Last Mafioso;* Fried, *The Rise and Fall of the Jewish Gangster in America;* Gage, *Mafia, U.S.A.;* ____, *The Mafia is not an Equal Opportunity Employer;* Gosch and Hammer, *The Last Testament of Lucky Luciano;* McClellan, *Crime Without Punishment;* Maas, *The Valachi Papers;* Reid, *The Grim Reapers;* Servadio, *Mafioso;* Velie, *Desperate Bargain: Why Jimmy Hoffa Had to Die.*

Zevi, Sabbatai, c.1626-76, Turk., her.-rebel. The approach of the year 1666, with its ominous suggestion of the Great Beast prophesied in Revelations, engendered anticipation in Europe of the second coming of Christ, and for the Jews, the coming of the Messiah. Sabbatai Zevi, the educated son of a wealthy Turkish merchant, seized upon the fervor of the time and declared himself the Messiah. Zevi sailed to Palestine where he reformed the synagogue at Jerusalem and was proclaimed Messiah by his disciple, Nathan. He exhorted the Syrian Jews to ready themselves for the struggle against the Turks in the belief that Sultan Mahomet IV would be dethroned at the end of the year and the Jews would assume control of the world.

While sailing to Constantinople, Zevi was arrested by the Turkish ruler. The Jews in Constantinople, convinced of Zevi's prophecies, refused to pay their debts. When Mahomet IV suggested that Zevi be set up as a target for archers and if he survived it would be considered proof that he was the Messiah, Zevi declined the opportunity to prove his divinity.

When offered a choice between impalement or conversion to Islam, Zevi converted. Not one to give up easily, however, Zevi next tried converting all of his Jewish followers, claiming it was all part of the prophecy. Despite the fact that Zevi was deserted by all of his followers, he persisted in calling himself the Messiah. Now known by his Muslim name, Aziz Mehmed Efferidi, he died on the Jewish Day of Atonement, Sept. 17, 1676. REF.: *CBA.*

Zhelyaboff, See: **Alexander II**.

Ziani, Sebastiano, c.1102-c.1180, Venice, jur. Wealthy and influential judge and politician who shaped governmental structure and helped negotiate peace treaty when Emperor Frederick I was defeated in battle by the Lombard League in 1176. REF.: *CBA.*

Zia ul-Haq, Mohammed, c.1924-88, Pak., pres., assass.? On Aug. 17, 1988, Pakistani President Mohammed Zia ul-Haq boarded a C-130 transport plane in Bahawalpur in eastern Pakistan after spending the day watching field tests of the American-made M-1 Abrams tank which he was considering buying for the Pakistani army. Zia ul-Haq's plane climbed to about 5,000 feet before it suddenly lost altitude and exploded in flames. Zia ul-Haq and twenty-nine other passengers on the plane, including U.S. Ambassador Arnold Raphel and Brigadier General Herbert Wassom, the chief military attaché, died in the crash.

A two month-long investigation by Pakistani and American technical experts proved inconclusive. Although popular opinion held that someone had planted a bomb on the plane specifically to assassinate the president, evidence from the crash was insufficient to confirm the theory. Despite the lack of physical evidence, there were many people and groups with motives for wanting Zia al-Haq dead. The Pakistani president had long been a source of serious annoyance to the Soviets for his committed support of the rebels fighting against Soviet troops in Afghanistan. In addition, India's Prime Minister Rajiv Gandhi had recently accused Pakistan of agitating Sikh extremists on the Indian side of the India-Pakistan border. Within Pakistan itself the president also had enemies. The formal opposition was led by the Pakistan People's Party, headed by Benazir Bhutto, whose father, the last freely elected Pakistani prime minister, was hanged by Zia ul-Haq. Additionally, Zia ul-Haq, a devoted Sunni Moslem, was opposed by Pakistani Shiite Moslems. REF.: *CBA.*

Zillman, Bertha, d.1893, Ger., mur. Bertha Zillman, a battered wife, killed her husband by poisoning him with arsenic after he had delivered a particularly severe beating to both Bertha and their children. She was found Guilty of murder and was beheaded on Oct. 21, 1893.

REF.: *CBA;* Nash, *Look for the Woman.*

Zimbabwe Missionary Massacre, 1987, Zimbabwe, (unsolv.) mur. Pentecostal ministers and their families who lived at the Olive Tree and New Adam's farms in southern Zimbabwe chose not to arm themselves against rebellious natives engaged in overthrowing the government. They said they trusted in God for their safekeeping. One night early in December 1987, an armed band of rebels invaded the two farms, roused the missionaries from their beds, bound them with barbed wire, and butchered them with axes. The marauders set fire to the houses, threw the bodies into the flames, and left.

Sixteen men, women, and children were killed in the raid. Only two of the missionaries survived. One of them, a 13-year-old girl, was given a note from the rebels for "all people from Western or capitalist countries" living in Zimbabwe, saying that the rebels were prepared to fight to their last man in reclaiming Zimbabwe from white settlers. Although the rebels had waged a campaign of terror against white settlers since 1982, the immediate cause of the attack appeared to have been an incident in which a group of black squatters were driven off land by white owners. No arrests were made in connection with the murders. REF.: *CBA.*

Zimmerly, Dr. **Harry C.**, prom. 1935, U.S., abor.-mur. In March 1935, Dr. Harry C. Zimmerly performed an illegal abortion on Gladys Lawson, who died as result of the operation. Panicking, two of his employees informed the authorities that the doctor had performed an illegal procedure and then had cut up the body and disposed of it. The police found Lawson's body and the bones of several other women in a grave under the floor of a barn. Zimmerly was convicted of performing an illegal operation and sentenced to seven and one half years in prison. REF.: *CBA.*

Zimmerman, Alfred F.M., 1859-1940, Ger., polit. corr.-treas. Became Secretary of Affairs for Germany in 1916. He used his position to attempt to provoke Mexico into attacking the U.S. during WWI. Upon disclosure of the "Zimmerman note," a document promising huge tracts of land to Mexico, the diplomat was forced into early retirement. REF.: *CBA.*

Zimmerman, Isidore, 1917-83, U.S., (wrong. convict.) mur. In 1937, 20-year-old Isidore Zimmerman was arrested and charged with six other young men in the robbery of a New York restaurant, in which a police detective was killed. Although Zimmerman was not present at the crime, police contended that he supplied the guns that killed the detective. Despite his claim of innocence, Zimmerman was convicted and sentenced to die in the electric chair. He spent nine months on Death Row, receiving a commutation of his sentence to life in prison only two hours before the scheduled execution. For the next twenty-four years, Zimmerman tried to prove his innocence while in jail. Finally, an attorney volunteered to reinvestigate the case and the conviction was overturned when it was shown that the prosecutor knew Zimmerman was innocent, suppressed evidence, and intimidated witnesses into perjuring themselves.

After his release in 1961, Zimmerman spent much of the next seventeen years lobbying for legislation that would permit him to sue the state for damages. In 1981, former New York governor Hugh Carey signed the necessary legislation. Zimmerman received a $1 million settlement, one-tenth of the figure named in his suit, in June 1983. He died four months later on Oct. 12, 1983. REF.: *CBA.*

Zind, Ludwig, b.c.1907, Ger., verbal asslt. After studying at Heidelberg, Ludwig Zind became a Nazi stormtrooper and later, a reserve captain in the Wehrmacht on the Russian front. When he returned from the war, the Allies barred him from resuming his former teaching job. In 1948 he did, however, begin teaching mathematics and biology at a secondary school in the town of Offenburg.

One evening, while having a drink in a local bar, the 51-year-old Zind began talking with another patron. The conversation continued late into the evening. Then Zind began to talk about his hatred of the Jews. His new friend, Kurt Lieser, forty-six, objected, informing Zind that he was a Jew and had spent the war in a concentration camp. Zind replied, "That means they forgot to gas you, too? The Nazis did not gas enough Jews." Lieser later protested to the state government, which tried to arrange a reconciliation between the two men. Instead of apologizing, Zind said, "I would rather clean the streets than crawl to a Jew." Zind was suspended from his job and put on trial in April 1958 under rarely used statutes prohibiting public approval of crimes or slandering the memory of the dead. During his trial, Zind denied nothing. He was found Guilty and sentenced to one year in jail. REF.: *CBA.*

Zinn, Herbert D., 1971- , U.S., computer crime. In the 1980s, technological advances making it possible to link computer systems around the world have made computer hackers potentially dangerous. In Fall 1988, a Cornell University graduate student, Robert T. Morris, Jr., designed a computer "virus" able to destroy the memory of computers it entered. In Los Angeles, 25-year-old Kevin David Mitnick was jailed for tapping into computers run by the National Security Agency. And, in February 1989, 18-year-old Herbert D. Zinn was sentenced in Chicago to nine months at a federal juvenile prison and fined $10,000 for breaking into computers run by the federal government and AT&T and illegally copying more than $1.2 million in software. REF.: *CBA.*

Zinoviev, Grigori Evseevich, 1883-1936, Rus., consp.-mur. Ruled with Lev Borisovich Kamenev and Joseph Stalin as part of triumvirate but was removed from office after conspiring with Kamenev and Leon Trotsky against Stalin. Although he was readmitted to the Communist party, he eventually confessed to complicity in the killing of Sergei Kirov in 1934, and was executed. REF.: *CBA;* MacDougall, *Hoaxes.*

Zinoviev Letter, 1924, Brit., hoax. In 1924, England's first Labor government introduced the issue of entering into a commercial treaty with the U.S.S.R. At the same time, a hoax involving a letter from a high Soviet official was perpetrated. The "very secret" letter, supposedly from a high Soviet official named Zinoviev and addressed to members of the British Communist party, advised open violence, sedition, and subversion in the British army and navy as the first steps toward a British proletarian revolutionary movement.

Prior to a general election in 1924, the forged document was published in the London *Mail* where it was editorialized: "The country now knows that Moscow issues orders to British Communists and they are obeyed by Communists here. British Communists, in turn, give orders to the Socialist government, which it tamely and humbly obeys." The people of England overwhelmingly defeated the treaty favored by the Labor party. REF.: *CBA.*

Zinzendorf, Nikolaus Ludwig von, 1700-60, Saxony, her. Assisted members of the persecuted sect known as *Unitas Fratrum* or *Bohemian Brethren* by harboring them on his Herrnhut estate. He reorganized the church as the Renewed Church of the United Brethren, but was expelled to London in 1737 after being ordained a bishop. Eleven years later he returned to Saxony. REF.: *CBA.*

Zinzigk, Perry, prom. 1963, U.S., mur. On Oct. 24, 1963, a Cincinnati woman notified police that her mother, 46-year-old Lillian Greer, had disappeared. Greer worked as a waitress at the Christoph Cafe and lived in a apartment over the restaurant. Beverly Norman, Greer's daughter, told police that her mother was last seen by another daughter on Oct. 13. When police questioned Greer's employer, Perry Zinzigk, he claimed that the woman told him she had become tired of bearing much of the financial responsibility for her children and had moved to Chicago.

When investigations in Chicago yielded no trace of Greer, Norman insisted to Cincinnati police that her mother would not have left town without notifying her children. The case was taken over by Detective Wilbert Stagenhorst, who repeatedly questioned the restaurant owner for further clues. Zinzigk cooperated thoroughly with the investigation and even passed a lie detector test. Stagenhorst's suspicion of Zinzigk deepened, however, when the detective came across a newly poured concrete slab in the basement of the restaurant. Police workers removed the concrete slab, and found Greer's body. Although Zinzigk claimed he had accidentally shot Greer during an argument, he was charged with second-degree murder and brought to trial on May 15, 1964. Zinzigk was found Guilty and sentenced to fifty years in prison. REF.: *CBA.*

Zirpoli, Alfonso Joseph, b.1905, U.S., jur. Served as counsel for New York state legislature. He was nominated by President John F. Kennedy to the northern district court of California in 1961. REF.: *CBA.*

Zito, Frank, prom. 1950s-70s, U.S., org. crime. Frank Zito was the mob boss of southern Illinois for more than twenty years, beginning in the 1950s. Based in Springfield, he worked closely with the St. Louis mob to oversee the largely rural gambling and drug operations. On Nov. 14, 1957, Zito was a participant in the infamous Apalachin Conference, held at the estate of Canada Dry president Joseph M. Barbara, in upstate Apalachin, N.Y., following the mob assassination of New York Mafia leader Albert Anastasia. State police became suspicious of the large number of hotel reservations made by Barbara, and with federal investigators of the Alcohol-Tobacco Tax Unit, raided the estate. The mobsters scattered, running through the heavily forested area in silk suits, disposing of weapons and cash as they fled. Most were apprehended while looking hopelessly out of place on the country back roads. No charges were filed, but the name of virtually every high-ranking mobster in the U.S. was published. See: **Apalachin Conference.** REF.: *CBA.*

Znidar, Thomas F., 1965- , U.S., mur. On the evening of Mar. 31, 1988, in Anne Arundel County, Md., 23-year-old Thomas F. Znidar strangled his girlfriend of four years, 19-year-old Ilka Dibble. After sodomizing her body, Znidar threw it in the trunk of her car and drove to his parent's home in Clay County, Fla., where he buried the body in a shallow grave. Police at first treated the case as a missing persons case, assuming that she had run away. Ilka's mother, Gisela Dibble, persisted in her attempts to have police treat the case with greater urgency. Three days after the murder, police began questioning Znidar. Although he first denied any knowledge of Ilka Dibble's whereabouts, he eventually broke down and detailed the crime to police in a three-hour taped confession.

The prosecutors entered a charge of first-degree murder against Znidar, but no mention was made in the charges of the sexual assault because Maryland law states that it is not a crime to assault a dead body. When the homicide detective investigating the case testified, but skipped over the sexual assault, Dibble's mother stood up and yelled to the jury, "And then he sexually assaulted her!" Although the defense attorney moved for a mistrial on the basis of the outburst, the presiding judge decided, after polling the jurors, that Dibble's actions would not have any impact on the jury's deliberations. However, the prosecuting attorney felt that Dibble's outburst greatly enhanced the chance of a reversal of a guilty verdict in any subsequent appeal. He further reasoned that a subsequent retrial had a far less substantial chance of resulting in a conviction. On the strength of these beliefs, he accepted a plea bargain that enabled Znidar to escape the otherwise virtually certain sentence of life without parole.

On Apr. 26, 1989, Znidar was sentenced to life in prison. The judge who handed down the sentence, which does allow for the possibility of parole, recommended that Znidar be allowed to serve his time at the Paxutent Institution, a prison which offers therapeutic and educational programs. REF.: *CBA.*

Zodiac Killer, prom. 1960s-70s, U.S., mur. A mass murderer whose *modus operandi* was strangely similar to that of the Monster of Florence—a killer who preyed on couples in parked cars in Italy in the 1960s and 1970s—the Zodiac Killer committed a series of killings in northern California beginning in 1966. Investigators named him the Zodiac Killer due to the signs and cryptograms he mailed to the police. Through descriptions provided by surviving victims, it is fairly certain the Zodiac killer was male. He did not claim responsibility for several murders he most certainly committed, and police could not find bodies of several victims he claimed to have killed. Most of his victims were young women, and the Zodiac killer once claimed he was "collecting slaves for my afterlife." Body counts of Zodiac murders range from nine to over forty.

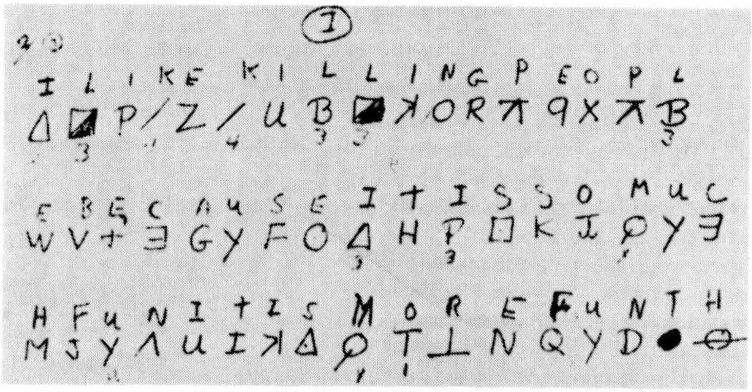

The cryptic message left by California's Zodiac Killer.

The first killing that the Zodiac murderer confessed to occurred on a deserted road outside Vallejo, Calif., on Dec. 20, 1968. The killer approached David Faraday, seventeen, and Bettilou Jensen, sixteen, who were sitting in a parked car. He shot Faraday three times in the head with a .22-caliber pistol, and shot Jensen five times after she jumped out of the car and attempted to run away. The killer struck again on July 4, 1969, killing a 19-year-old girl and critically wounding her companion, who survived but could give only a sketchy description of the attacker, who had blinded him by shining a flashlight in his eyes. He said the attacker was male, fairly heavy, and wore glasses.

A particularly gruesome murder attributed to the Zodiac Killer was that of Cecelia Shephard, who he stabbed twenty-four times in the back. He then carved the outline of a cross into her skin. the killer then shot a taxi driver in the back from the rear seat of the taxi, wiped the car clean of prints, and cut off a bloody piece of the driver's shirt to send to the police. The driver lived and gave the most accurate description to date of the murderer. With the driver's description, a composite of the Zodiac killer was developed and circulated. Police searched for a man approximately five-feet, eight-inches tall with short reddish-brown hair and thick glasses.

Police composite sketches of the Zodiac Killer.

The killer stopped communicating with police in 1975. He claimed to have killed thirty-seven people, though police believed that some of the letters were fakes. While the San Francisco police attributed only six murders to Zodiac, the sheriff of Sonoma County, Don Striepeke, placed the total at more than forty killings in four western states, based on a computer study of similar murders. Striepeke hypothesized that the murderer worked from a large "Z" drawn over a map of several states. Police believe that the murderer either died or was committed to a psychiatric institution. Like the Monster of Florence, he simply ceased killing. See: **Monster of Florence.**

REF.: *CBA;* Nash, *Open Files;* Purvis, *Great Unsolved Mysteries;* Wilson, *Encyclopedia of Modern Murder.*

Zoë, 980-1050, Roman., consp.-mur. Eastern Roman empress from 1028-34. She married Michael IV after conspiring with him to have Romanus killed. REF.: *CBA.*

Zoldoske, Rose, prom. 1891, U.S., mur. On Jan. 8, 1891, 23-year-old Ella Maly, a resident of Richland Center, Wis., attended a birthday party given by another young woman, Rose Zoldoske. Zoldoske, complaining of not feeling well, went to her room to lie down. She asked to see several of the guests at the party who each visited her in turn. One of the women who visited the ailing hostess in her room was Maly. On the walk home, Maly produced some chocolates she said Zoldoske had given her. She offered one to her sister, Lillie Maly, and then finished them herself.

Shortly thereafter, Ella complained of not feeling well. G.R. Mitchell, Zoldoske's landlord and doctor, was called and, after examining Maly, diagnosed poisoning. The young woman died shortly after a second doctor confirmed Dr. Mitchell's diagnosis. The second doctor noticed that her symptoms resembled those manifested by Dr. Mitchell's wife who had died the previous year. When her body was exhumed, an autopsy revealed strychnine in her stomach. When an analysis of the contents of Maly's stomach showed a large quantity of strychnine and investigators learned that Zoldoske allegedly wanted to marry Dr. Mitchell, suspicion of murder focused on Zoldoske.

With this and other circumstantial evidence at hand, Rose Zoldoske was charged in Ella Maly's death. It was hypothesized during the trial that Rose Zoldoske had killed Ella Maly because she suspected that Dr. Mitchell was interested in her, and Zoldoske herself wanted to marry the widowed doctor. A number of witnesses testified that Zoldoske had, on a number of occasions made comments regarding a change in Dr. Mitchell's behavior toward her. On the basis of a large amount of highly circumstantial evidence, Rose Zoldoske was found Guilty of murder in the first degree and was sentenced to life imprisonment. After serving eight years of her sentence, she was pardoned in 1899, and released from prison.

REF.: *CBA;* Derleth, *Wisconsin Murders.*

Zon, Hans von, 1942- , Neth., mur. Hans von Zon, born in Utrecht, Neth., on Apr. 20, 1942, displayed difficulty in distinguishing between fantasy and reality early in life. After he left school, he was dismissed from a succession of jobs for petty dishonesty. At the age of sixteen he went to Amsterdam and claimed to be a student.

In 1964, von Zon committed his first murder. His victim, Elly Hager-Segov, allowed von Zon to stay the night and make love to her. When she refused to allow him to make love to her a second time, he strangled her and slit her throat. Over the next couple of years, von Zon murdered a film director and a long-time lover. While drunk, he boasted about the murders to a convict known as Oude Nol, who blackmailed von Zon into committing murders for him. Von Zon killed two men on Oude Nol's orders and attempted to kill one of Oude Nol's former lovers. The last victim, however, survived the attempt and called police. Both von Zon and Oude Nol were arrested and charged with murder. Oude Nol was sentenced to seven years in prison while von Zon received a life sentence.

REF.: *CBA;* Wilson, *Encyclopedia of Modern Murder.*

Zoot-Suit Riot, 1943, U.S., mob vio. In the early 1940s, racial tension between whites and Mexicans was heightened when underground gangs of Mexican youths formed throughout southern California. Gang members developed their own language—a mixture of Spanish, English, and slang—and dressed in elaborate, broad-shouldered suits with large lapels known as "zoot-suits." In early Summer 1943, zoot-suit gangs clashed with soldiers and sailors stationed in Los Angeles. From June 3, following one particularly vicious assault on a group of sailors, mobs of thousands of civilians, soldiers, and sailors roamed the streets looking for Mexicans. The mob violence was focused on the "zoot-suiters," as the press called them, but it quickly spread to all Mexicans and then to blacks. The press condemned the Mexicans for any action they took to strike back or protect themselves, and police did nothing to stop the angry mobs as they broke into theaters, homes, and streetcars, dragged Mexicans into the street, and beat them. On several occasions, the police arrested the victims. The city of Los Angeles condoned the riots, praised the vigilante character of the military servicemen, and shortly afterwards, made wearing a zoot-suit a misdemeanor. The district attorney claimed "zoot-suits are an open indication of subversive character." REF.: *CBA.*

Zouche, Richard, 1590-1661, Brit., jur. Professor and authority on civil law. He became judge of the high court of admiralty in 1641, but was removed because of his Royalist ties. His position was restored in 1661. He published two important works, *Elementa Jurisprudentiae,* which organized law into categories, and *Jus Feciale,* which was the first publication to present the law of nations as an organized system. REF.: *CBA.*

Zowkowski, John, d.1933, U.S., suic.-mur. In November 1933, the strangled and badly burned body of a young woman was pulled from a fire in a field near Philadelphia. From personal effects found near the scene of the fire, the woman was identified as Tanka Hetman. Hetman's landlady told police that the young woman had left several days earlier with her boyfriend, a racketeer named John Zowkowski. Zowkowski, apparently alerted to the imminent arrival of the police, had fled only moments earlier. The police traced him to a wooded area where Zowkowski and police exchanged gunfire. When Zowkowski stopped firing, the police closed in. Zowkowski was found dead of a bullet wound in the temple. Powder burns on the skin around the wound indicated that the death was a suicide. REF.: *CBA.*

Zrinyi, Peter, 1621-71, Hung., consp. Croatian leader who helped lead a conspiracy of Hungarian magnates. He was captured and beheaded in Vienna. REF.: *CBA.*

Zu Shenatir, prom. 5th cent., El-Yemen, sod.-mur. In the fifth century, Zu Shenatir, the caliph of El-Yemen, lured young men and boys into his palace, where he sodomized them and then tossed them out the window. Zu Shenatir was stabbed in the rectum by a young man named Zerash.

REF.: *CBA;* Masters, *Perverse Crimes in History.*

Zundel, Ernst, 1939- , Can., fraud. In January 1988, German-born publisher Ernst Zundel, forty-nine, was brought to trial in Toronto for deliberately "spreading false news". Zundel published a thirty-two-page pamphlet which claimed that the Nazis did not plan to systematically murder Jews and had not used gas chambers to commit mass murder. Zundel was found Guilty in early May. On May 3, 1988, Judge Ron Thomas sentenced the publisher to a nine-month jail term, saying, "It is not the Holocaust that is a fraud; it is Ron Thomas who is a fraud." Zundel had emigrated to Canada in 1958, but never became a citizen. REF.: *CBA.*

Zuno Hernandez, José Guadalupe, b.1891, Case of, Mex., kid. On Aug. 28, 1974, 83-year-old José Guadalupe Zuno, the father-in-law of Mexican President Luis Echeverriá Alvarez and a former governor of the state of Jalisco, was kidnapped by four leftist guerrillas while being driven through Guadalajara. His captors, identified as the Revolutionary Armed Forces of the People demanded a ransom of $1.6 million and the release of fifteen political prisoners. The government refused to comply and stated that they had the names of seven suspects in the crime. Four men were arrested but not formally charged. On Sept. 7, 1974, eleven days after his abduction, Zuno was released, although no ransom had been paid. Healthy and unharmed, Zuno praised his captors and sharply criticized the reactionary policies of his son-in-law's government. REF.: *CBA.*

Zuta, Jack, d.1930, U.S., org. crime. Jack Zuta was a mob accountant in Chicago during the 1920s, serving as an intermediary between the interests of Al Capone and City Hall. In 1927, Zuta contributed $50,000, known to be Capone's money, to the reelection campaign of Mayor William Hale Thompson. But within a year, Zuta switched allegiances, becoming the business manager for North Side mobsters George "Bugs" Moran and Joey Aiello. In June 1930, he allegedly ordered the murder of Chicago *Tribune* reporter Jake Lingle after Lingle attempted to extort Moran for a share of his gambling profits. On June 30, 1930, Zuta was brought in for questioning, but released the following day. While Zuta was being driven home in a police cruiser, the car was overtaken and fired upon by the occupants of a blue sedan. A streetcar motorman was shot to death, and another man was wounded, before the assailants drove off, escaping in a cloud of smoke. Obviously a marked man, Zuta moved to the shores of Upper Nemahbin Lake, near Milwaukee, Wis., living under the name J.H. Goodman. But on Aug. 1, 1930, as he was about to put a nickle in a mechanical piano at a roadhouse in Delafield, Wis., Zuta was shot to death by eight men, who entered the room armed with sawed-off shotguns, automatic pistols, and a submachine gun.

The dead man's power reached beyond the grave. A meticulous record keeper, he had complete details of mob transactions hidden in various safety-deposit boxes. Police intercepted two shipments of whiskey bound for Bugs Moran, and raided several breweries. Most damaging was a payoff schedule to several politicians and lawmen, including Chicago alderman Dorsey Crowe, Board of Education executive Nate DeLue, former Judge Emanuel Eller, Evanston, Ill., police chief William O. Freeman, Chicago police sergeant Martin C. Mulvihill, Judge Joseph W. Schulman, and state senator Harry W. Starr. All denied any improprieties, some saying they received the money as a campaign contribution. But the name Zuta became synonymous with revenge, and in 1931, when Al Capone learned of a $50,000 bounty placed on his scalp, loudly proclaimed, "Nobody's gonna Zuta me."

Chicago mobster Jack Zuta, murdered in 1930.

REF.: Asbury, *Gem of the Prairie; CBA;* Demaris, *Captive City;* Gage, *The Mafia is not an Equal Opportunity Employer;* Kobler, *Al Capone;* Landesco, *Organized Crime in Chicago;* Morgan, *Prince of Crime;* Peterson, *The Mob;* Sanders, *Murder Behind the Bright Lights;* Smith, *Syndicate City.*

Zvonimir, d.1089, Croatia, king, assass. Killed for supporting anti-nationalist Croatian Latin faction. His death led to civil war and Hungarian domination. REF.: *CBA.*

Zwaiter, Wadal Abdel, d.1972, Italy, assass. Following the massacre of Israeli athletes at the Munich Olympics in September 1972, a new retaliatory Israeli organization, the *Mivtzan Elohim,* or Wrath of God, was formed. The specific purpose of this new group was to meet the threat of Arab terrorism directly. Soon after the Munich massacre, on Oct. 16, 1972, in Rome, Wadal Abdel Zwaiter, the suspected leader of *Al Fatah* was shot twelve times with a .22-caliber Beretta and killed. Zwaiter's assassination opened up a virtual war between *Mivtzan Elohim* and the Palestinians.

REF.: Bell, *Assassin; CBA.*

Zwani, Fikizolo, d.1925, Swaziland, (unsolv.) mur. A superstitious fear of crop failure lead a group of Swazis in 1925 to sacrifice the life of an infant, Fikizolo Zwani, from their community. The child was kidnapped by several men who took him to a cave outside of the village. There they bound and gagged him and, after performing rites intended to prepare him as a sacrifice, left him in the cave for eight days. At the end of the eight days, the child was taken from the cave and one of the men slit his throat. The body was then dismembered and, in ritualistic fashion, cooked. Although several men were arrested and brought to trial in a British court, no witness would incriminate them, and the men were eventually released.

REF.: Bennett, *Up for Murder; CBA.*

Zwanziger, Anna Maria (Anna Maria Schonleben), 1760-1811, Ger., mur. Born in Nuremberg, Ger., Anna Maria Zwanziger married young, but her husband proved to be an alcoholic and she soon left him. She took on a number of odd jobs throughout Germany. Early in the nineteenth century Zwanziger was employed as housekeeper and cook by a Judge Glaser in Pegnitz. In an attempt to become Glaser's wife, Zwanziger poisoned the judge's present wife with arsenic. The woman soon died, but Glaser was not interested in his cook, and Zwanziger moved on. She then became the housekeeper for Judge Grohmann. When again her marital desires proved unrequited, Zwanziger killed Grohmann. She was hired by Judge Gebhard as a nurse for his wife and infant child. Mrs. Gebhard soon met the same fate as Zwanziger's earlier victims.

Courtroom histrionics by murderess Anna Zwanziger.

Zwanziger, however, had no better luck winning the affection of Gebhard than she had in the past. Gebhard's lack of attention toward Zwanziger led her to seek vengeance on all who entered Gebhard's home. Visitors and servants were overcome with pain after eating food Zwanziger prepared. She told her employer that she must have used too much spice or possibly the wrong ingredient. He summarily fired her. Before she left she contaminated the household staples with arsenic, and even fed the baby arsenic-laced candy as a parting gift. The Gebhards became violently ill not long after Zwanziger left. Arsenic was soon discovered in kitchen canisters, and after the exhumation of Zwanziger's previous victims, the police arrested the woman on Oct. 18, 1809.

The trial of Zwanziger took almost two years before completion, as arsenic was not easily detectable at that time. She finally admitted her guilt, however, stating, "Yes I killed them all, and would have killed more if I had had the chance!" Zwanziger was beheaded with a sword in July 1811. REF.: *CBA*.

Zwerbach, Maxwell (Zwerback or **Zweibach,** AKA: **Kid Twist, Kid Slyfox),** 1882-1908, U.S., org. crime. One of the toughest gangsters in New York at the turn of the century, Maxwell "Kid Twist" Zwerbach came up through the ranks of the massive Monk Eastman gang. He became Eastman's right-hand man, and when Eastman was sent to prison in 1904, Zwerbach attempted to take over the Eastman gang. His arch rival for this powerful position was another Eastman lieutenant, Rickie Fitzpatrick. Both men were dedicated killers, but Zwerbach was the more lethal of the two, having murdered at least fifteen men on Monk Eastman's orders and another five or so on his own. His sobriquet was well earned since Zwerbach was the epitome of street craft and cunning. He proved this with deadly accuracy when he sent an emissary to Fitzpatrick, who offered a simple proposal from Kid Twist. The two of them would meet in a Christie Street saloon, have a few beers, and divide up Eastman's territory like gentlemen. Fitzpatrick agreed.

He arrived in the saloon at the appointed time, and just as Kid Twist lifted his glass of beer in a salute to his adversary, the lights went out. Gunfire quickly filled the room, then silence. Police arrived some minutes later to find the place empty, except for Richie Fitzpatrick who lay dead on the floor with a bullet in his heart and his hands crossed neatly over his chest. Zwerbach and his closest ally, Kid Dahl, were picked up for the slaying but provided alibis and were released. For this slaying, Zwerbach gained another nickname, Kid Slyfox. Zwerbach was not without manners. He sent a huge floral wreath to Fitzpatrick's funeral and wore a black mourning arm band for several months to show the world how deeply he had cared for the slain Fitzpatrick.

As Kid Twist rose as gangster star, he sent his considerable forces into the Five Points to establish rackets on the very edge of the criminal domain ruled by super boss Paul Kelly. Some of Kelly's men, who operated lucrative gambling dens, suddenly found themselves taking orders from Kid Twist. Zwerbach and Kid Dahl visited one of Kelly's men, a giant known as The Bottler (he had, at one time, worked in a distillery). They demanded half of The Bottler's profits, threatening him with instant death unless he agreed. The Bottler agreed and Kid Dahl immediately moved in as manager of the operation. Several days later Zwerbach informed The Bottler that another friend, a gambler known as The Nailer, was going to pick up The Bottler's half of the gambling operations and that The Bottler had better leave town.

This was more than the gambler could bear. The Bottler vowed open warfare, and he barricaded his gambling den, challenging Kid Twist and his gangsters to oust him. Zwerbach shrugged and then planned The Bottler's death with his usual murderous guile. Knowing the police were watching him and had been alerted to the fact that he had ordered The Bottler killed, Zwerbach sent for one of his trusted Brooklyn aides, Samuel Teitsch, a carnival strong man known as Cylone Lewis (or Vach Lewis or Cyclone Louie). Lewis was a towering brute who amused customers at Coney Island side shows by bending iron bars around his neck (and sometimes around the necks of those who displeased him). A few nights later Zwerbach made sure that one of his men was locked up for disturbing the peace so that he had an excuse to visit the Delancey Street station where, at precisely 9 p.m., he began a loud argument with the desk sergeant, stating that his man's bail was too high. At the same time, his lieutenant, Kid Dahl, rose from his table in a Houston Street restaurant to tell the owner that his food "ain't fit for pigs to eat!" These disturbances, of course, were planned as memorable alibis. At the same time, Cyclone Louie visited The Bottler and shot him dead in front of twenty men. Because he was a stranger from Brooklyn, no one knew the killer, who promptly returned to his domicile to await the thanks of Kid Twist. In recalling the incident a year or so later, Cyclone Louie stated: "I done the cooking (killing) for the Kid the way any friend would do."

New York gangster and ruthless killer Max "Kid Twist" Zwerbach, 1906.

Cyclone Louie became a permanent member of Kid Twist's gang and the boss' bodyguard. He accompanied Zwerbach to all his meetings with high-ranking Tammany sachems where Kid Twist got his orders regarding upcoming elections. As with Eastman before him, Kid Twist made sure that the votes on election day went in favor of Tammany politicians. Hundreds of goons served as repeat voters and forced any undecided voter at gunpoint to cast his ballot for the Tammany man. In return Kid Twist and his gang received extraordinary treatment from government officials, and most police officers looked the other way when spotting any of Zwerbach's illegal gambling operations, brothels, and drug runners. Zwerbach split his profits with crooked politicians and some police officers, including his considerable take from extortion rackets throughout the Lower East Side.

Zwerbach was not a man to let any lucrative racket slip from his grasp. Being Jewish, he knew since childhood that Jews favored celery tonic, a mixture of syrup and carbonated water, with their meals, and he cornered the market on this item. Within months Zwerbach's dour face adorned the labels of thousands of small bottles containing the soft drink, which proved to be almost as profitable as his many rackets. Kid Twist took great pride in being Jewish, albeit the Jewish merchants he victimized did not esteem him as a member of their culture. Zwerbach told a newsman on one occasion: "De Lower East Side ain't gonna be run by no wop or no mick!"

Such remarks were not lost on Paul Kelly who bore an Irish name but was Italian through and through (real name Antonio Vaccarelli). Following an incident a short time later in Coney Island, Kelly took sly revenge on Kid Twist for his outspoken slurs against his people. Coney Island in the lazy days of 1908 was the resort spot of the Manhattan gangsters. After a busy day at their rackets, the likes of Kid Twist retired to Coney Island for a leisurely dinner and some drinks at the many restaurants and dance halls there. More than good food and liquor caused Kid Twist to visit this haven on the night of May 14, 1908. He had met a beautiful singer-dancer named Carroll Terry at one of halls and seriously thought to make her his wife. She had been going with another New York hoodlum, Louis Pioggi, a 19-year-old gangster who had become infamous as a member of Paul Kelly's Five Points gang, which he had joined in 1906. Pioggi had slain several Monk Eastman thugs and Kelly was grooming him to assassinate none other than the powerful Kid Twist Zwerbach.

Pioggi, who was known as Louie the Lump because of his undersized, slightly bent figure, danced with Carroll Terry early in the evening of May 14, asking her to return to Manhattan with him that night. She told him she would think about it, but about an hour later Pioggi spotted her sitting with none other than Kid Twist and his bodyguard, Cyclone Louie. He realized then that his sweetheart would be going to Manhattan with Kid Twist. He stormed from the Surf Avenue hall to a nearby second-story saloon, where he began to belt down shots of whiskey while gritting out oaths to kill Zwerbach. The bartender overheard him and sent word to Kid Twist who, a short time later, sauntered into the saloon with Cyclone Louie lumbering next to him. The sadist in Kid Twist oozed out of him as he sidled next to Pioggi at the bar, ordering drinks for himself and Cyclone Louie.

Lifting his glass to Pioggi in a mock salute, Kid Twist sneered: "I jus' seen Carroll, Louie. She says youse is the biggest bum she knows."

Pioggi scowled in anger but said nothing. Kid Twist narrowed his eyes and through a thin smile said: "She says you was an active little cuss, always jumpin' aroun'. Let's see how active youse is, kid." Zwerbach paused and then nodded toward an open window which faced the street. "Take a jump out the window!"

With Kid Twist and Cyclone Louie escorting him to the window, Pioggi looked downward to the street, his eyes wide with fear. He stopped for a moment, his hand instinctively reaching for a back pocket and his revolver. Then he noticed Zwerbach and his bodyguard put their hands into their pockets and partially withdraw their own weapons. Pioggi jumped, landing on all fours like a cat but still spraining an ankle. Looking up he could see Kid Twist and Cyclone Louie laughing hysterically. Cyclone Louie snorted to Kid Twist: "He jumps real good, boss—see 'im bounce?" Pioggi limped off, the sound of their laughter in his ears. He went to a phone booth and called Paul Kelly at his headquarters in the Five Points.

Pioggi had been humiliated by Kid Twist and the insult was leveled at the whole Italian nationality, Pioggi explained to his superior, or in words to that effect. Kelly asked him what he wanted to do. Louie the Lump Pioggi did not hesitate. "I got to cook (kill) him, boss," he said.

"Sure you got to cook him," soothed Kelly. "You tail these birds and I'll send a fleet down. When the boys get there, you get these bums into the street and open up with your canisters. The boys'll take care of Twist's mob and any bulls that interfere." With that about ten of Kelly's top gunmen raced to Coney Island. When they located Pioggi on the street, Louie the Lump hailed a stew bum and gave him a dollar to deliver a message to Kid Twist, who was still in the gin mill with Cyclone Louie, celebrating the embarrassment they had caused Louie the Lump.

The drunk staggered up the stairs of the saloon and found Zwerbach, telling him: "Someone named Carroll Terry wants to see you outside for a minute."

"Sure," replied the amorous Kid Twist, "tell her I'll be right out." Finishing his drink and accompanied by Cyclone Louie, Zwerbach went down the stairs and stepped into the gloom of the street.

"Over this way, Kid!" shouted a voice and Zwerbach stepped further into the street where he and Cyclone Louie soon realized that they were ringed by more than a dozen of Paul Kelly's sharpshooters. Kid Twist's hand dove into a pocket for his revolver but he never pulled it forth. Louie the Lump, two guns in his hands, blazed away at the man he hated most on earth, sending a bullet into Kid Twist's brain and another into his heart. The fierce gang leader fell to the ground, dead, while Cyclone Louie began to run. He, too, was shot dead by Kelly's men, toppling over the body of his chief. Just at that minute Carroll Terry arrived, screaming at the sight. Such was Pioggi's wrath that he shot her, too, wounding her in the arm. She fell in a faint on the bodies of Kid Twist and Cyclone Louie.

Pioggi and Kelly's men fled the scene, but an inquisitive officer came running by them, saw the bodies in the street, and turned, ordering the fleeing men to halt. Pioggi, on the run, sent a bullet in his direction, blowing the policeman's helmet off his head. The bullet grazed the man's skull and knocked him senseless.

Once in Manhattan, Pioggi went into hiding. Paul Kelly pulled his usual political strings and then ordered Louie the Lump to give himself up and plead guilty to manslaughter. A deal had already been made and the little killer received an eleven-month sentence. He was sent to Elmira Reformatory instead of Sing Sing Prison because he was still a teenager. Pioggi was now famous as the man who killed one of the most powerful crime bosses in New York, and he acted out the part of the swaggering braggart, telling news reporters before going off to the reformatory: "What's eleven months? I could do that standin' on me head!" Pioggi may have murdered out of passion, but his bullets served Paul Kelly's rackets well. With Zwerbach out of the way, Kelly moved his Five Pointers into the Lower East Side territory to seize the unions, gambling, and prostitution operations that had so carefully been built up by Monk Eastman, Zwerbach, and others. The murder of Max Kid Twist Zwerbach spelled the decline and fall of the overall power of the Jewish gangster in New York, although there would be notable exceptions such as Arnold Rothstein, Dutch Schultz (Arthur Fleggenheimer), and Waxey Gordon (Irving Wexler), who would all come to infamous riches during the Roaring Twenties. See: **Eastman, Edward**; **Kelly, Paul**.

REF.: Asbury, *The Gangs of New York; CBA;* Fried, *The Rise and Fall of the Jewish Gangster in America;* Lewis, *The Apaches of New York;* Nash, *Bloodletters and Badmen;* Peterson, *The Mob.*

Zwillman, Abner (AKA: **Longie**), 1899-1959, U.S., org. crime. During the early decades of the national crime syndicate, Jewish gangsters like Meyer Lansky, Ben "Bugsy" Siegel, and Abner "Longie" Zwillman were on equal footing with their Sicilian counterparts. In the 1950s, the Mafia Ruling Commission—the

"Big Six"—was composed of Frank Costello, Tony Accardo, Joe Adonis, Jake Guzik, Lansky, and Zwillman.

Abner Zwillman, who had risen steadily through the ranks since the days of Prohibition, helped arrange the 1929 sit-down conference in Cleveland, and was admitted to the Big Six a year later. He surrounded himself with loyal henchmen like Willie Moretti. After Dutch Schultz was gunned down in a Newark chop-house in October 1935, Zwillman took over his rackets and became the "Al Capone of New Jersey." Zwillman cloaked his sinister activities in the guise of respectability. When the Lindbergh baby was kidnapped in 1932, the gangster posted a sizeable reward. Years later Zwillman donated $250,000 to finance a Newark slum clearing project. For the next twenty-four years, beginning in 1935, he held virtually every local politician in the palm of his hand. In 1946, Republican Governor Harold G. Hoffman found it useful to solicit Zwillman's support. Three years later Zwillman offered Democratic gubernatorial nominee Elmer Wene $300,000 for the right to nominate the state attorney general. Wene declined Zwillman's offer, and lost the election.

New Jersey crime boss Abner "Longie" Zwillman.

For years Zwillman and Moretti controlled statewide gambling operations. Their Marine Room inside the Riviera nightclub in The Palisades was a syndicate show spot that attracted all the high-rollers from politics, show business, and Manhattan society. According to New York *Times* reporter Meyer Berger, "All players had to be known. Outsiders only saw the dining rooms."

In the late 1950s, Zwillman's star began to fade when the government began to exert pressure. After a government examination of his tax records, the McClellan Senate Committee subpoenaed him to testify. Top gangsters like Meyer Lansky became increasingly nervous that the aging Zwillman would become an informant to avoid a prison term. Within Mafia circles, "Longie" Zwillman had backed a string of losers, including Albert Anastasia, who was gunned down in a Manhattan barber shop on orders from Vito Genovese. When rival mobsters began muscling in on Zwillman's once unassailable New Jersey operations, he found himself in a tenuous position.

On Feb. 27, 1959, shortly before his scheduled appearance before the McClellan Committee, Zwillman was reported to have committed suicide in his twenty-room mansion in West Orange, N.J. He had used a plastic electrical cord. Police investigators found bruises on his wrists, an indication that he had been bound and gagged. Syndicated newspaper columnist Earl Wilson speculated that two hired assassins had visited Zwillman's home that night carrying a bottle of premium brandy, and threatened to kill his wife if he did not kill himself. The assassins offered him brandy as a gesture of respect and to make the ordeal as painless as possible. Zwillman was found the next morning dangling a couple of inches above the floor. Years later Meyer Lansky blamed Genovese for murdering his old comrade. Yet it is doubtful that the Italian Cosa Nostra could have moved against one as powerful as Zwillman without Lansky's blessing. Before he died, exiled gangster Charles "Lucky" Luciano took Meyer Lansky to task for betraying a friend. See: **Anastasia, Albert; Genovese, Vito; Lansky, Meyer; Luciano, Charles.**

REF.: Campbell, *The Luciano Project; CBA;* Demaris, *Captive City;* ____, *The Director;* ____, *The Last Mafioso;* Eisenberg and Landau, *Meyer Lansky;* Fried, *The Rise and Fall of the Jewish Gangster in America;* Gage, *Mafia, U.S.A.;* Gosch and Hammer, *The Last Testament of Lucky Luciano;* Katz, *Uncle Frank;* Kobler, *Al Capone;* Levine, *Anatomy of a Gangster;* McClellan, *Crime Without Punishment;* McPhaul, *Johnny Torrio;* Maas, *The Valachi Papers;* Messick, *Lansky;* ____, *Secret File;* ____ and Goldblatt, *The Mobs and the Mafia;* Peterson, *The Mob;* Reid, *The Grim Reapers;* Sann, *Kill the Dutchman;* Servadio, *Mafioso;* Thompson, *Gang Rule in New York.*

SUPPLEMENTS

ARSON

The willful and malicious burning of property constitutes the crime of arson. In British common law the term is limited to the burning of buildings when it endangers the lives of others. In recent years municipalities have broadly expanded the definition of arson and stiffened penalties for anyone intentionally setting fire to property, whether or not anyone is on the premises. Except in Great Britain, arson that results in a person's death is regarded as murder, whether or not the perpetrator knew that someone was present. Many jurisdictions break the crime down into categories and reserve the stiffest penalties for destruction of public places such as stores, apartment buildings, factories, transport vehicles, bridges or woodlands.

Germany and some jurisdictions in the U.S. have imposed rigid penalties for criminal suspects attempting to destroy evidence of another crime by starting a fire. A fire that is started accidentally or through carelessness is not considered arson, but a person may be accused of arson if his recklessness regarding fire has endangered the lives of others. Typically the arson is committed for financial reasons, usually to defraud an insurance company. However, in cases in which the defendant is proven to be mentally unstable, an insanity plea may be accepted by the courts.

538 B.C.
Babylon, Mesopotamia, was captured by the Persians who torched the city in retaliation for the strong resistance they encountered. Thousands were killed, and most of the buildings, and the hanging gardens were also destroyed.
390 B.C.
Following defeat at the Battle of Allia, Rome was abandoned and the conquering Gauls looted and burnt the city.
146 B.C.
Seventeen days of flames enveloped the African city of Carthage.
58 B.C.
Banished Roman politician, Marcus Tullius Cicero, had his home on the Palatine burned down by tribune of Rome, Publius Clodius.
48 B.C.
Under siege, in Alexandria, Egypt, Julius Caesar commanded his men to burn the Egyptian fleet. The blaze spread to the city and destroyed the Alexandrine library and its contents.
64 A.D.
Emperor Nero ordered the destruction of Rome, Italy, so that he could rebuild it anew. Within eight days 75 percent of the city had been consumed and hundreds of people were dead. Nero blamed the Christians for setting the fire.
1381
John Ball and Wat Tyler led an English peasant revolt which torched the Duke of Lancaster's palace, the Savoy.
1631
May 20: Jan Tzerklas, the Baron of Tilly, commanded the troops of Maximilian, Duke of Bavaria, which burned Magdeburg, Ger., against Tzerklas' orders. He later burned Eisleben, Halle, Merseburg, and other cities.
1653
Several Boston, Mass., homes were set afire and destroyed by arsonists.
1667
June: Sheerness, England, burned by the Dutch fleet.
1676
Jamestown, Va., was burned during the rebellion of Nathaniel Bacon. Fifty buildings, including the church of Increase Mather were burnt to the ground in Boston, Mass. No arrests were made.
1679
In Boston, Mass., eighty homes and several warehouses were ruined by an unidentified arsonist who set fire to a tavern sign. Authorities proclaimed that the death penalty would be implemented for arson.
1681
July 12: Two houses were set on fire in Roxbury, Mass., by a slave named Marja. A child burned to death; Marja was burned at the stake on Sept. 22.
1688
October: French war minister François Michel Le Tellier de Louvois ordered the burning of Heidelberg, Mannheim, Speier, Worms, and the German countryside to the border of Alsace.
1690
Dec. 22: Serving time for stealing, Anne Hereford attempted to escape Newgate by setting the prison on fire.
1724
The New England village of Norridgewock was burned during the war between colonists and natives.
1741
March: A number of fires in New York City were attributed to black slaves plotting mass murder by suspicious whites. Thirty-one slaves were executed and seventy-one were deported.
1749
Apr. 7: John Collington and John Stone were hanged after they were convicted of burning down a church warden's home.
1755
November: Following the earthquake on Nov. 1 in Lisbon, Port., which killed 50,000 people, looters set fires throughout the ruined city.
1776
Sept. 7: After rendering his services as arsonist to the American Revolution, James Hill burned a storage building on Portsmouth dock.
Sept. 21: More than 500 buildings, or one-fourth of New York City, was razed by fire five days after the British arrived. The destruction was apparently ordered by George Washington who was denied permission to do so by the Continental Congress. The British marched suspected arsonists into the flames at bayonet point.
1781
Fall: New London burned during U.S. Revolutionary War.
1791
Buckman, an African slave working as an overseer on the island of Saint-Dominique started an uprising among the other slaves, who set crops on fire and killed the white land owners.
1812
Sept. 15: The day after Napoléon Bonaparte's French troops entered Moscow, retreating Russian generals ordered the city destroyed. More than 31,000 buildings valued at $150 million were burned.
1814
Aug. 24: During the War of 1812, British General Robert Ross ordered the burning of Washington, D.C., as U.S. soldiers retreated from the capitol.
1822
A portion of the Turkish fleet was burned and 3,000 Turks killed by Greek naval commander Canaris.
1830
Peter Comyn, a convicted arsonist, was rescued from the gallows by King George IV, starting a movement to reform sentencing of criminals.
1837
The U.S. steamer *Caroline* is burned by rebellious Canadians.
1842
November: Inventor of the revolver, Samuel Colt, was suspected of setting on fire the Tombs prison in New York City, but there was no proof. Colt was known to be working on a new explosive and his brother, murderer John C. Colt, was scheduled to hang soon.
1849
May 17: A discontent sailor torched the *White Cloud*, moored alongside other vessels in St. Louis, Mo., and the fire soon spread. Twenty-five ships, all piers, and fifteen square city blocks—totalling $4 million in losses—were destroyed.
1853
November: Four miles from Windsor, Burnham Abbey Farm was burned and Moses Hatto was convicted of killing the housekeeper before setting the blaze.
1858
Oct. 5: More than $2 million in antiquities and art were lost during the fire at New york City's Crystal Palace.
1863
Narciso Bojorques, the leader of a group of Mexican desperados, killed a man and his wife and child in Alameda, N.M., then set their ranch house on fire.
July 13-17: In response to the Union army's conscription policy during the U.S. Civil War, many New York City men rebelled and set afire numerous buildings and attacked blacks as part of the Draft Riots. An estimated 2,500 people were killed, more than 7,500 injured, and damages of $5 million incurred.
1864
During Union general William T. Sherman's infamous "March to the Sea," he ordered the destruction of a number of Southern cities including Columbia and Charleston, S.C.
Nov. 15: Union General Sherman broke his promise and razed Atlanta, Ga., destroying more than 5,000 buildings.
Nov. 25: Confederates attempted to burn down New York City in retaliation for General Sherman's burning of the South. Little damage resulted from the eleven hotels, two theaters, and Barnum's Museum that had been set ablaze.
1865
Apr. 2: Rather than allow Union troops to take over Richmond, Va., Confederates burned valuable businesses and industries, but homes were also consumed.
1873
William Udderzook was hanged for murdering his brother-in-law W.S. Goss, whose corpse was used to make insurance claims of the arson he

committed in Baltimore, Md., appear genuine.

1878

Dr. Thomas Neill Cream, who would earn greater infamy as a murderer, set a number of fires in the London, Ontario, area.

July 16: Several bodies were found in and outside a farm house that was set on fire. Joseph Garcia was hanged for the deed even after he pleaded not guilty to the murder charges.

1880's

Albert Bruneau, an ordained priest, was found Guilty of murder, robbery and twice setting his rectory on fire. He was beheaded in 1894.

1883

Jan. 10: A fire at the Newhall House hotel in Milwaukee, Wis., was allegedly started by an arsonist. Seventy-one people were killed.

1884

Count Henri de Tourville, who set fire to his house to collect insurance on the lives of his son and nurse, died in prison while serving a twenty-year sentence for another murder.

September: The entire business section of Silver Plume, Colo., was burned to the ground over a mining claim dispute in the boomtown.

1886

Feb. 4: Edward and Henry Kohout torched a New York City tenement house on 64th Street to collect insurance, but were convicted of murder when Mrs. Fialla and her two children were killed.

1888

To gain control of the milling business in Greensburg, Pa., miller Frank Baer burned down two competing mills which caused their owners to declare bankruptcy. Baer and accomplice William Richardson were found Guilty.

1892

Mass murderer Herman Webster Mudgett torched several heavily-insured buildings he owned on Chicago's South Side and in the following year he attempted to burn down his three-story home known as "Murder Castle."

May 1: Patrick Mullins was caught while setting on fire a New York City stable he owned. After insuring a stable he and four confederates would replace high-priced horses with run-down animals and torch the building. All five men were imprisoned.

1894

After a grand jury trial, Jim French was sentenced, as leader of a group of arsonists working out of St. Louis, Mo., to ten years in prison.

1897

Feb. 4: Civil war began in Canea after a majority of the Christian section was burned.

1899

October: William M. Jacobs, whose fully-insured cigar manufacturing factories were mysteriously destroyed by fire in the early 1890s, was sentenced to prison with five others for counterfeiting.

1900's

A prominent man in Fairburn, Ga., Bill Green was found Guilty of burning the town bank and was sent to prison.

1904

Peter Kurten, future mass murderer, burned several barns and haystacks in Cologne, Ger., to watch the grief of the owners.

1905

July 7: At eleven, Carl Panzram set ablaze a warehouse at the Minnesota Training School in Red Wing, where he was an inmate. Damages totalled $100,000.

1908

Apr. 28: The LaPorte, Ind., home of Belle Gunness burned. The bodies of her three children and a woman were found in the ruins. The woman's body was not positively identified as Gunness', but twenty-eight murdered corpses were discovered about the farm.

1913

Sept. 13: Franz Wagner killed his wife, children, and nine others, then torched a number of homes in Degerloch, Ger., before his arrest. He was sent to an insane asylum.

1914

Apr. 20: Striking miners and their families living in Ludlow, Colo., were attacked by the National Guard under the command of Lieutenant Karl E. Linderfelt, who then set fire to the tent colony. Twenty people were killed, mostly children and women.

1916

Sept. 28: Frederick Small set alight his Mountainview, N.H., home after murdering his wife for the insurance money. He was hanged in 1918.

1917

September 9: During the Russian Revolution, Bolshevik prison escapees set fire to Laishev, Rus., for which twenty were lynched. A few days later, 200 Bolsheviks were killed in a Nicholivak wine cellar when the fire they started got out of control.

1919

July 26: Racial tension was the cause of rioting in Chicago, Ill., that resulted in large areas of the South Side being virtually demolished by arson and looting.

1922

Spring: Katherine Allers burned down a run-down Brooklyn, N.Y., mansion. She had recently insured her home for $5,000 and the furniture inside for $2,500. Allers was sent to prison.

1923

May: A premature explosion in a cabinet making company resulted in Joseph Engelstein and two other men being injured and consequently imprisoned for setting the fire.

1925

Jan. 13: Angry at his mother for having him blacklisted, Petrus Stephanus François Hauptfleisch suffocated her and set her body on fire. Hauptfleisch was hanged in December 1926.

July 30: Chemist Charles Henry Schwartz burned his Walnut Creek, Calif., plant with the murdered corpse of look-alike Gilbert Warren Barbe inside, so his wife could collect the insurance. The ruse was discovered and Schwartz killed himself.

1926

The first confirmed arson committed under the leadership of Leopold Harris of Harris & Company fire assessors netted £3,000 for Harris and his brother. By 1930 the profitable London arson ring was found out and the gang was sent to prison.

May 30: Forest View, Ill., citizens set ablaze Al Capone's Maple Inn, which firefighters allowed to burn down.

1930

Apr. 21: Hugh Gibson, Clinton Grate, and James Raymond, set fire to the Ohio Penitentiary in Columbus, Ohio, in an attempted escape. The buildings were destroyed and 322 inmates killed. The three arsonists were convicted of second-degree murder.

1931

Jan. 6: Otterburn, England, taxi driver Evelyn Foster is attacked and left for dead in her smoldering car. She died some time later and the killer was never found.

Jan. 26: More than $3 million in damages was attributed to the numerous fires set and the subsequent looting throughout Buenaventura, Col.

June 27: The Wonder Apparel Shop in New York City is burned down by garment magnate Sam Sapphine because his partner, Sol Cohen, owed him money.

1932

October: After insuring their photography equipment, George Frederick Fillis and Tom John Lonnen set fire to their studio loft. Though they claimed it was an accident, they were convicted of arson and sent to prison.

1933

Feb. 6: Frederick Ellison Morton is murdered in Yorkshire, England, by Ernest Brown, who then placed his employer in Morton's car and ignited the body. Brown was hanged in 1934.

Nov. 18: Following a series of fires set to collect insurance, New York City businessmen Sam Berliner and Dr. Jerome Garber were arrested. Both were sent to prison.

1936

Dec. 31: On the eve of his wedding, Ralph Hawk set his fiance ablaze along with the rest of her family. He later confessed and was sentenced to death.

1937

Clifford Bramble set thirty-one fires in Sacramento, Calif., and five more in Salt Lake City, Utah, resulting in losses of $2 million. An unhappy home life led him to arson, for which he was committed to an asylum.

1938

Apr. 29: Harvey L. Rousch killed his business partner Homer T. Myers, and his wife, then burned the bodies in his Delaware, Ohio, home. Rousch was executed.

1942

November: Mark Pulliam was imprisoned for life for burning his Chatsworth, Ga., farm house. His wife and five of their eight children were killed.

1944

Mar. 25: During a three-day period, pyromaniac George Holman killed twenty-two people in Oakland and San Francisco, Calif., with the eleven fires he set. He received twenty-two consecutive life sentences.

1948

Mar. 2: The *Barrarolle*, a heavily insured pleasure boat, caught on fire after the owner, Derek Clayton-Wright, made an evening visit. Clayton-Wright was convicted of arson and attempted insurance fraud and was sent to prison.

1949

London police officer Clifford Alexander Weallans torched eight Jewish-owned businesses in England's capital because he "hated the Jews." He was sent to prison.

Sept. 3: The fire lighted by the Communist underground in Chungking, China, blazed for two days and left 1,700 people dead and another 100,000 homeless. One of the arsonists was shot during the blaze.

1950s

William S. Ford exploded the Brooklyn, N.Y., tenement home of George Keim to settle an old debt between former business partners. Ford hanged himself while awaiting trial for the murder of Keim and two others.

1951

July 22: Eight people died in a San Francisco apartment building fire set by 17-year-old Kenneth Skinner, who confessed when a newspaper photo placed him at the scene. He was sent to prison.

1952

Oct. 21: A state of emergency was declared in Kenya when Mau Mau warriors began a murder and arson spree.

1953

May 26: In a suicide attempt Everett D. Green, who was later convicted of murder and had his conviction overturned by the supreme court, set his apartment building on fire which resulted in an 83-year-old woman's death.

Oct. 24: John Maurice Jordan torched three Houston, Texas, lumber yards. In all, he set twenty-two fires with damages exceeding $4 million.

Dec. 4: Vincent Ciucci killed his wife and three children and then burned his Chicago home. Ciucci was electrocuted in 1962.

1955

Mar. 2: George Fisher phoned his home in Chicago from Florida, thereby igniting a special gadget rigged to destroy the twelve-room structure. The wiring was discovered and Fisher did not collect $75,000 in insurance.

1965

Aug. 11: During racial rioting in Watts, Calif., thirty-four people died, 1,033 were wounded, more than 4,000 were arrested, and damages exceeded $34 million. The fire raged four days.

1967

July 13: For two days racial tensions in Newark, N.J., led to riots and arson in which a white fire captain Michael Moran was killed while fighting a fire.

July 16: A riot led to fire at the recently-integrated Road Prison 32 in Jay, Fla., which left thirty-eight of fifty-one inmates dead.

July 23-28: Forty-one people were killed and more than 1,100 fires had been set during racial violence in Detroit, Mich.

1968

Apr. 5: For two days following the assassination of Dr. Martin Luther King, Jr. on Apr. 4, a number of black communities in cities across the U.S. erupted in violence. President Lyndon B. Johnson ordered 6,700 U.S. Army and National Guard troops to defend Washington, D.C. Chicago's West Side suffered over 731 fires in the first two days.

1969

July 7: A Marks and Spencer store was firebombed in London by the PFLP.

Oct. 7: In Buenos Aires, Arg., terrorists firebombed the U.S. Information Service library.

1970

Feb. 13: Seven people died and nine were injured, when arsonists burned a home for the Jewish elderly in Munich, Ger.

Sept. 9: Seven senior citizens were killed and others were injured when a West German old-age home was set on fire.

Oct. 16: In Buenos Aires, the U.S. defense attaché's house was completely destroyed by a firebomb.

Oct. 19: After the blaze was extinguished at Dr. Victor Ohta's home, the bodies of the doctor, his family, and his secretary were found. John Linley Frazier was convicted of the crime and received a life sentence.

1971

Albert Epstein employed Benjamin Warren to burn down his five-story New York City apartment building for insurance money. Warren locked the three boys he hired in a closet where they died during the blaze. Both men went to prison.

Jan. 25: In Ankara, Turk., Molotov cocktails were hurled into the home of a U.S. Foreign Service officer.

Mar. 25: The Movement of Youthward Brothers in War of the Palestinian People firebombed the offices of Bull Computer in France.

July 8: The Londonderry, N. Ire., plant of Essex International Brakelining was firebombed.

July 23: Several Molotov cocktails were hurled at the Jordanian embassy in Paris, Fr. Police wounded and arrested one of the Fatah terrorists.

July 25: In the U.S., members of the JDL destroy a Soviet Embassy official's car with a firebomb.

Nov. 3: The homes of officials of the Swift and Company Chicago Bridge Company in Sao Paulo, Braz., were firebombed.

1972

Feb. 2: In Dublin, Irish terrorists bombed the British Embassy, setting it on fire.

1973

Jan. 7: At the downtown New Orleans, La., Howard Johnson Motel, Mark James Robert Essex set a number of fires during a shooting spree in which he killed five people and wounded sixteen. He was shot to death by police.

Jan. 10: Arsonists torched the Amerika Haus in Frankfurt, Ger., causing $25,000 in damage to its library.

Mar. 21: In Frankfurt, Ger., police discovered Molotov cocktails on a garage roof near the U.S. consulate general's grounds.

Mar. 22: The Greek Anti-Dictatorial Youth firebombed a U.S. government employee's car in Athens, Gr.

Mar. 23: In Brussels, Belg., a Molotov cocktail was hurled into the home of the Greek ambassador. Minor damage was caused.

Apr. 9: Two young men employed incendiary devices to set fire to a USO building in Rome, Italy.

Apr. 23: A crowd hurled firebombs at the U.S. consulate in Frankfurt, Ger.

Apr. 25: An incendiary device was thrown into the main entrance of a U.S. ammunition depot, near Yokosuka Naval Base in Japan. No damage was done.

May 1: In Barcelona, Spain, the British European Airways office was set on fire by incendiary bomb.

May 2: The offices of Pan American Airlines in Barcelona, Spain, were firebombed.

May 18: The Sao Paulo home of a U.S. diplomat was damaged by fire. The fire was believed to have been started by an in incendiary bomb.

June 20: The car of a Soviet mission member was destroyed by fire in New York. The arsonist was believed to be a member of JDL, protesting the treatment of Soviet Jews.

Sept. 26: Barnell Bishop was sentenced to life imprisonment for setting fire to Cantrell Cleaners and killing the owner, his wife and son, and an employee of the cleaners.

1974

Mar. 14: Arsonists set fire to a supermarket in Venezuela. Responsibility was claimed by the Red Flag guerrillas, the National Liberation Armed Forces, and other groups.

Nov. 5: A firebomb burns the Milan Trade Center, operated by the U.S. Department of Commerce, in Milan, Italy.

December: The first of nine arsons—including one business, one home, and seven nightclubs—in the Memphis, Tenn., area were committed. The crimes would last through May 1981 and net more than $1 million for the clients of the two arsonists.

Dec. 30: Olean, N.Y., honor student, Anthony F. Barbaro, torched his school, killed three passersby, and wounded eleven firefighters with a shotgun. He hanged himself in jail.

1975

Sept. 27: A city block in Lowell, Mass., was declared a disaster area by President Gerald R. Ford following a fire which destroyed the block, caused damages in the millions, and injured twenty-three people. A man was sent to prison in 1981.

1976

Oct. 24: José Cordero hired two teenagers to set a Bronx social club on fire. Twenty-five people were killed and another twenty-four were injured. Cordero and one of his accomplices were sent to prison.

1978

Summer: A Honolulu, Hawaii, pornographic bookstore was fire-bombed in an attempt to collect $148,000 in insurance. The organized crime figure and the man he hired were arrested on July 16, 1979.

June 3: Chicago secretary Bobbie Ryan, stripped her drunken date's apartment, then set it on fire. Peter Hoban was killed and Ryan was sent to prison.

1979

The destruction of a Los Angeles garment business by its owners resulted in damages of $250,000. The fraud by the two businessmen was discovered.

January: An investigation by the Bureau of Alcohol, Tobacco, and Firearms was begun in which an a man hired for arson was caught while attempting to torch a Houston, Texas, restaurant. He was sent to prison for life.

Jan. 12: An insurance claim of $1,118,928 was determined fraudulent following an investigation into the Philadelphia, Pa., fire.

Mar. 7: An Arlington, Texas, custom van business was destroyed to collect $400,000 in insurance. The owner, general manager, and hired arsonist were convicted.

May 16: An indictment was handed down for the arson of two Illinois restaurants. Two elderly people were killed in the Maywood fire, but the man responsible was convicted of fire bombing Chicago's Bull and Bear Restaurant.

May 25: Four firefighters and a public official were killed, and thirty-six others injured in a downtown Shelby, N.C., fire. The owner of a clothing store had paid another to burn the property to collect insurance.

June: The owner of the Barn Restaurant in Tuscaloosa, Ala., paid another to burn down the building for insurance reasons. Damages were $265,000, but the arsonists were arrested.

July: Fifteen people were convicted as part of an organized crime arson ring which had fire bombed night clubs in the Seattle and Tacoma, Wash., area.

July 6: The investigation of the twenty-four arsons in the Cleveland, Ohio, area was concluded with the sentencing of a South Euclid resident. Four arsonists were involved in the gang.

July 7: For committing a number of arsons in the Cleveland, Ohio, area to collect insurance money, a Cleveland businessman was sent to prison.

Aug. 24: The Classic Cat II lounge in Nashville, Tenn., was torched and a van loaded with 100 pounds of explosives was found outside. Three people were arrested.

Aug. 27: A profit-motivated arson caused $20,000 in damages to Jordan's Store in Loris, S.C. Two people were arrested in connection with the fire.

Sept. 24: Two suspects were arrested as part of an arson ring and racketeering operation in Philadelphia, Pa.

October: Damages of $1.5 million were incurred from a fire at a shopping center in West Hartford, Conn.

Oct. 10: A fire destroyed the International Market Place in Anchorage, Alaska, causing $3.8 million in damages.

Oct. 14: The arsonist of the Long Beach, Calif., Western Farms, Inc., meat packing plant died from burns suffered during the crime. He accused the owners of trying to obtain the $3 million in insurance.

Oct. 30: A 1-year-old child was killed after falling five floors when his mother attempted to toss him to a fire escape close by during a fire at the Wheeling, W. Va., Kapehart Hotel.
November: Two men pleaded guilty to the attempted torching of the Naples, Fla., Elks Club. The man hired to set the fire was caught in the act.
Nov. 16: The attempted torching of an Ocean City, N.J., residential building by a hired arsonist was thwarted by an Alcohol Tobacco and Firearms undercover agent.
Nov. 21: Muslim students set the U.S. Embassy in Islamabad on fire. One U.S. Marine was killed during the six-hour siege.
Dec. 2: In Tripoli, Libya, the U.S. Embassy is torched by a mob containing Libyan troops.

1980

Feb. 5: French ambassador and staff leave Libya after its Embassy is burned in Tripoli.
Sept. 22: A fire in Braddock, Pa., resulted in $50,000 damages. The Braddock Volunteer Fire Department chief was sent to prison one year later.
Sept. 29: Three children were injured when their Racine, Wis., home was set on fire. The former motorcycle gang member had sought revenge upon the children's father. He was sent to prison.

1981

Jan. 28: One firefighter was killed and eight people were injured during the blaze at Cugee's Restaurant in North Hollywood, Calif. Almost one year later one of the three defendants was convicted.
Feb. 10: Eight people were killed and the Las Vegas Hilton Hotel was destroyed in the fire set by a man who sent to prison for first-degree murder and arson the following spring.
Feb. 12: A man was caught as he entered the garage of the Tulsa, Okla., building he was hired to burn. He was committed to a mental institution for one and a half years.
Feb. 18: A blaze, which preceded three separate explosions, ruined the Highstown, N.J., Jerry Richard's Men's Store, with damage estimated at $215,000. The building was burned for insurance purposes.
Feb. 20: A building in Grand Rapids, Mich., outside the main plant of a company involved in a union strike was set afire by three Molotov cocktails. Two union members pleaded guilty.
Feb. 20: A police outpost in San Juan Comalapa, Guatemala, was attacked and burned by ORPA rebels.
Mar. 1: An incendiary bomb discovered at an Anchorage, Alaska, topless dance bar, exploded as a police bomb technician was placing the device into an explosive disposal container.
May 8: The Popular Revolutionary Struggle claimed responsibility for the firebombing of three police stations in Athens, Gr.
May 8: Slight damage was sustained by a British army building in Glasgow, Scot., hit with three firebombs.
May 15: Killeen Castle in County Meath, Ire., was set on fire and burned for two days causing £2.5 million in damage. On Mar. 12, 1982, Shane Martin Corrigan was sentenced to six years' imprisonment for his involvement.
May 17: In Dungannon, Ire., a movie theater, a toy shop and a brick factory were fire-bombed by masked gunmen. The sum of the damages equalled $2.2 million.
May 17: An incendiary bomb was discovered at a Soviet mission in Riverdale, New York.
May 17: In Dunmurry, Ire., arsonists torched St. Anne's Protestant Church.
May 22: Arsonists ruined twelve buildings during a riot in Londonderry, Ire.
June 12: The Columbus High School in Columbus, Ga., suffered $2.5 million in damages.
June 17: Mark Clements, a mentally disabled 17-year-old, set fire to an apartment building in Chicago, Ill. He was sent to prison after being convicted of murder and aggravated arson.
June 24: Following the detonation of five bombs, Navarra University in Pamplona, Spain was extensively damaged by fire.
July 14: In Northwest Zambia, the Mushala gang set houses on fire, resulting in injuries and deaths of the occupants.
Aug. 8: After joining an IRA hunger strike, Thomas McIlwee died in Maze prison. McIlwee was serving a life sentence for fire- bombing a boutique which resulted in the death of its owner in 1976.
Aug. 17: Seven men were convicted for ten arsons against eight automotive parts companies in Los Angeles from 1973 to 1980. The arson ring had set the fires to force their competitors out of business.
Aug. 19: At the U.S. District Court in Fort Dodge, Iowa, the first of seven suspects was sent to prison for his part in an arson-for-profit gang which operated in several states.
Aug. 31: A Providence, R.I., discount warehouse was burned. The owner was accused of arson.
Sept. 1: In Frankfurt, Ger., the Red Army Faction claimed responsibility for fire-bombing an office of the Social Democratic party.
Sept. 1: Arsonists set several cars on fire on an estate for U.S. servicemen in Weisbaden, Ger.
Sept. 11: A five-alarm fire destroyed a Dallas, Texas, clothing manufacturing business, Altman's of Dallas. The blaze was linked to the owner and caused $1.5 million in damages.
Sept. 13: In Frankfurt, Ger., the home of U.S. consul-general David Betts was fire-bombed.
Sept. 18: The owner of a Wheaton, Wyo., bar was sentenced to prison for conspiracy in the attempted arson of his business and a second bar.
Sept. 21: Two suspects were sentenced for the firebombing of the Sterling, Conn., home of two people who had testified against the defendants during an earlier case.
Sept. 22: Protesters to a game with the South African Springbok rugby team fire-bombed the headquarters of the Eastern Rugby Union in Schenectady, N.Y.
Sept. 24: Iraqis attacked a Turkish convoy on the Turco-Iraqi pike, near Habur. They set nine trucks on fire and took fifteen drivers hostage.
Sept. 25: An explosion, and subsequent fire, at the Evansville "All Whites" Rugby/Football Club, Inc., in Evansville, Ind., caused $250,000 in damages. The owner and a hired arsonist were arrested.
October: Two arsonists were killed while torching a Great Neck, N.Y., diner. Both owners of the diner were sent to prison.
Oct. 26: Welsh nationalists were suspected of planting a fire-bomb at a British army recruiting center in Pontypridd, Wales. The bomb was defused by police.
Nov. 11: During a raid on Ixchiguan, Guat., guerrillas set buildings on fire and coerced residents to attend a political meeting.
Nov. 28: Seventeen buildings were destroyed and six others damaged by fire which caused $80 million damage in downtown Lynn, Mass. President Ronald Reagan designated Lynn a disaster area. The hired arsonist was sent to prison for perjury in 1983.

1982

Two defendants were convicted in the burning of a Spokane, Wash., meat company. Both were sent to prison, while one, the company's original financier, was ordered to pay restitution of $92,000.
Jan. 6: Following the kidnapping of Sister Victoria de la Roca, her abductors set the convent at Equipulas, Guat,, on fire.
Feb. 8: Sentencing took place for the last of three defendants in an arson ring which burned commercial property in Osgood, and Rising Sun, Ind.
Feb. 18: Eight men were charged with setting fifteen fires in the Los Angeles area over a five year period which caused $10 million in damages.
Mar. 18: Seven people were killed, 100 wounded, and twenty vehicles burned by gasoline bombs thrown at a rally for the ruling Golkar Party in Jakarta, Indo.
May 9: Fire destroyed the Jewish Tennis and Social Club in Belfast, N. Ire.
May 15: The arson of an Ogunquit, Maine, retail store caused $1 million in damages when adjacent property was burned.
June 27: Two firefighters were killed and four were wounded when a Sioux City, Iowa, poultry processing plant burned down. The owner of the overly-insured building and an accomplice were sent to prison.
July 15: "Siderurgistes en colere" (Angry Metallurgists) claimed responsibility for torching the Chateau de La Buchere in the Ardennes, Fr.
July 16: An abandoned Miami Beach, Fla., hotel was razed by fire, with damages at $1 million. Three arsonists, who confessed to forty other arsons—fourteen at the same hotel in July 1982—were sent to prison.
July 18: The offices of Honeywell in Padua, Italy, suffered damages of $30,000 from a fire possibly set by the Communist Front for Counter-Power.
Aug. 9: Office equipment and documents in a Beijing, China, embassy were set on fire by four Central African students who sought scholarship money from their country.
Aug. 12: IRA gasoline bombs burn an insurance company's building in Londonderry, Ire., in commemoration of the thirteenth anniversary of renewed sectarian violence in the country.
Aug. 14: A "Jews for Jesus" synagogue in Paris, Fr., was burned.
Aug. 18: Charges were brought against four men in connection with a fire at a Monticello, Ark., restaurant. All were sent to prison.
Sept. 1: Public buildings in Yamabal, El Salvador, were burned by some 200 guerrillas who overran the town.
Sept. 4: A law office next to the High Court in Lahore, Pakistan, was set on fire.
Sept. 18: After a small fire bomb exploded in the lap of Elvin Abellanosa Laurel at the Manilla Hilton, he and his uncle, Santos Abellanosa, were arrested.
Sept. 22: The owner of a fire-destroyed Franklin, Pa., building was indicted. Her husband was indicted on Dec. 3, 1982. The fire occurred thirty-two minutes prior to the expiration of a $1 million insurance policy.
Sept. 27: A West Berlin office of Sperry was damaged by a fire bomb.
Sept. 29: A prison under construction in Pesaro, Italy, was damaged by arson.
Oct. 11: A Wilmington, N.C., elementary school burned down, with damages set at $2 million. The fire was the eighteenth blaze of similar origin since January 1982 in that school district.
Oct. 17: Adverse editorials by the Lakota *Times* newspaper in Pine Ridge, S.D., resulted in three Molotov cocktails being thrown at the paper's building. Little damage resulted.
Nov. 19: A Salt Lake City, Utah, warehouse was destroyed by fire resulting in damages of $500,000 to $1 million.
Nov. 30: The underground garage of an apartment where U.S. military personnel lived was damaged by arson in Eschborn, W. Ger.
Dec. 24: A Minneapolis, Minn., warehouse, insured for $225,000, was destroyed in a five-alarm fire.

1983

June 25: Sisters Zita Blum and Honora Lahmann were found shot and stabbed to death in their Joliet, Ill., home, which was then plundered and set ablaze.

1987

Dec. 31: Ninety-seven people were killed in the blaze which engulfed the Dupont Plaza Hotel in San Juan, P.R. Héctor Escudero Aponte, Jose Francisco Rivera Lopez, and Armando Jimenez Rivera were sent to prison.

1988

Apr. 8: Tegucigalpa and San Pedro Sula, Hond., were declared a state of emergency after rioting students attacked the U.S. embassy annex and set twenty-five cars on fire.

Oct. 5: Three people were killed in a North Side Chicago apartment building fire apparently started after a dispute between the landlord and tenant Frank Creque. Creque was believed to be upset over the termination of his lease.

ASSASSINATION

Assassination is usually carried out for political and ideological reasons. Throughout history, from Brutus' assassination of Julius Caesar to the assassination of Egyptian president Anwar Sadat in October 1981 by men posing as loyal soldiers, assassins have used stealth and treachery to gain access to their targets.

The word "assassin" dates to the eleventh and twelfth centuries to an Islamic sect that considered the murder of one's enemy a religious and sacred rite. Marco Polo told stories about the followers of this Near Eastern cult and their deadly acts carried out after smoking "hashshashin" or hashish. The drug supposedly elevated them to a higher level of paradise that enabled them to fearlessly face "martyrdom." The word "assassin" is derived from the word "hashish." In the eleventh century Hasan-e Sabbah commanded a vast network of professional killers who stalked their enemy all over Persia and Iraq. By the twelfth century their influence extended into Syria. The reign of the assassins lasted until 1256 when the Mongol armies under the leadership of Hülegu seized their castles in Persia and Alamut. After this, the sect became insignificant, but the tales of their infamy were brought back to Europe by the Crusaders.

No culture or people has been immune to political assassination. Four U.S. presidents—Abraham Lincoln, James Garfield, William McKinley, and John F. Kennedy—have been assassinated since 1865. Unsuccessful attempts were made on the lives of Andrew Jackson, Theodore Roosevelt, Gerald Ford, and Ronald Reagan. In 1800 James Hadfield was acquitted of trying to murder King George III on the grounds of insanity. During the sixty-four year reign of Queen Victoria of England, at least six attempts were made on her life. Spencer Percival, the only British Prime Minister to succumb to the assassin's bullet, was shot down by John Bellingham in 1812 in the House of Commons. In 1843 in a case of mistaken identity, Daniel M'Naghten attempted to kill the prime minister, but killed his secretary instead.

Following the 1963 murder of President John F. Kennedy, the U.S. National Commission on the Causes and Prevention of Violence compiled a profile of the individual most likely to become an assassin. The study concluded that this person invariably was a classic loner: alienated from family and friends, unemployed, and desperately in need of a social identity. The commission's profile accurately described John Hinckley, the disturbed young man who shot Ronald Reagan in 1981 to demonstrate his devotion to screen actress Jodie Foster.

1590 B.C.
Mursilis I, Hittite king, was ousted in a coup and murdered in c.1590 B.C.
1200 B.C.
Eglon, king of Moab, was killed in c.1200 B.C. by Ehud, an Israeli chief, biblical.
12th Cent. B.C.
Abimelech, king of Shechem, was slain by an unknown woman, biblical.
Holofernes, Assyrian leader and general of Nebuchadnezzar, was reportedly murdered by Judith, biblical.
Sisera, general of the Canaanites, was murdered by Jael, the wife of Herber, biblical.
11th Cent. B.C.
Abner, an Israeli military commander, was murdered by Joab, David's commander, biblical.
Absalom, an Israeli prince, was killed by Joab while fleeing from battle, biblical.
Amasa, an Israeli prince and captain of Absalom's army, was murdered by Joab, biblical.
Amnon, an Israeli prince, was slain by his brother, Absalom, biblical.
Sheba, Benjamite leader, was killed by Joab, biblical.
911 B.C.
Nadab, king of Israel and son of Jeroboam I, was killed by usurper Baasha, biblical.
900 B.C.
Phales, king of Tyre, was killed by Ethbaal (Ithabalus), who seized the crown c.900 B.C.
10th Cent. B.C.
Adonijah, an Israeli prince, was murdered by Benaiah, at the direction of King Solomon, biblical.
Joab, an Israeli commander, was murdered by Benaiah, at the direction of King Solomon, biblical.
887 B.C.
Elah, king of Israel and son of Baasha, was killed by one of his generals, Zimri, biblical.
844 B.C.
Ahaziah, king of Judah, was assassinated by Jehu in c.844 B.C. and Athaliah succeeded him, biblical.
842 B.C.
Jehoram (Joram), king of Israel, was overthrown and assassinated by Jehu in c.842 B.C., biblical.
Jezebel, queen mother of Jehoram, was brutally murdered by Jehu, biblical.
841 B.C.
Benhadad II (Hadadezer), king of Damascus, was overthrown and killed by Hazael in c.841, biblical.
836 B.C.
Athaliah, queen of Judah and a Baal worshipper, persecuted Jehovahites and was responsible for the deaths of all of the sons of Ahaziah, except Joash, who later became king. Athaliah was killed at the command of Joash, biblical.
830 B.C.
Sicharbus, regent ruler of Tyre for nephew Pygmalion, who was the grandson of Ethbaal, was assassinated by his nephew c.830 B.C.
797 B.C.
Joash (Jehoash, Joas), king of Judah, was slain by officers of his palace guard, biblical.
744 B.C.
Shallum, king of Israel, killed Zechariah and a month later he was murdered by Menahem, biblical.
Zechariah, king of Israel, was assassinated by Shallum, biblical.
738 B.C.
Pekahia, king of Israel, was slain by an army officer, Pekah, biblical.
732 B.C.
Pekah, king of Israel, was murdered by Hoshea, biblical.
730 B.C.
Amaziah, king of Judah, was murdered at Lachish in c.730 B.C. He was succeeded by his son Uzziah, biblical.
8th Cent. B.C.
Amulius, king of Alba Longa, was killed by Romulus, legendary founder of Rome.
681 B.C.
Sennacherib (Sinakhkheeriba), king of Assyria, was assassinated by at least one of his sons. After Sennacherib's death, his son Esarhaddon ruled, biblical.
569 B.C.
Apries (Pharoah Hophra), king of Egypt, was strangled by troops at the command of Amasis, who succeeded him, biblical.
554 B.C.
Phalaris, king of Acragas (Sicily), was slain by Rhodian troops, according to legend.
534 B.C.
Servius Tullius, king of Rome according to legend, was murdered by Tarquin the Proud.
522 B.C.
Bardiya (Smerdis), nobleman of Persia, was reputedly killed by his brother, Cambyses. Bardiya's identity was later believed to be assumed by Gaumata, who usurped his power. Gaumata was eventually murdered by Darius.
Cambyses I, king of Persia and the son of Cyrus the Great, was slain.
514 B.C.
Hipparchus, tyrant and prince of Athens, was murdered by Harmodius, who was slain by a guard, and Arsitogiton, who was tortured and put to death.
500 B.C.
Gautama Buddha (Gotami, Gotama, Prince Siddhartha Gautama), an Indian philosopher and founder of Buddhism, was the target of numerous assassination attempts in c.500 B.C. by Prince Devadetta, his cousin who wanted to succeed him as the head of the order.
473 B.C.
Gnoeus Genucius, Roman tribune, was slain.
465 B.C.
Xerxes I, king of Persia, and his oldest son were slain by Artabanus, his Persian minister.
464 B.C.
Artabanus (Ardaban), Persian minister and ruler of Achaemenian state, was slain by Artaxerxes in c.464 B.C.
460 B.C.
Inaros (Ienharou), an Egyptian leader who led a rebellion against Persia in 465 B.C., was seized and put in prison. Although Artaxerxes I saved him from execution, the monarch's mother, dowager queen Amestris, killed Inaros.
456 B.C.
Ephialtes, a statesman and general of Athens supported a law that established democratic government in Athens. He was slain by unidentified attackers.
450 B.C.
Siccius Dentatus, former Roman tribune, was executed, c.450 B.C.
439 B.C.
Spurius Moelius, a wealthy citizen, was suspected of trying to gain power and was killed by C. Servilius Ahala.
424 B.C.
Sogdianus, king of Persia, was assassinated by Ochus, his half-brother, who became Darius II. Sogdianus was put into a slow-burning furnace.
Xerxes II, king of Persia, reigned only a few weeks before he was murdered by his half-brother, Sogdianus.
413 B.C.
Demosthenes, Athenian commander and general, was taken prisoner as the result of an unsuccessful assault on Syracuse and put to death by the government of Syracuse.

411 B.C.
Hyperbolus, leader of the democratic party in Athens, was killed in Samos by the government.
404 B.C.
Alcibiades, Athenian general, was slain at Phrygia.
Theramenes, Athenian general, was forced to drink hemlock on the orders of Critias, who was later killed.
5th Cent. B.C.
Phrynichus, Athenian general, was reputedly slain.
399 B.C.
Socrates, Greek philosopher, was poisoned with hemlock in Athens.
395 B.C.
Tissaphernes, Persian who reigned in western Asia, lost to Agesilaus and put to death on the orders of Tithraustes.
390 B.C.
The Gauls besieged Rome and murdered numerous senators.
370 B.C.
Jason, king of Pherae, Gr., was murdered by conspirators.
359 B.C.
Cotys I, king of Thrace, conquered Sestos, Turk., jeopardizing the grain shipping of Athens. He was later slain.
356 B.C.
Heraclides, a Greek politician, was slain by Dion.
353 B.C.
Dion, king of Syracuse, was murdered at the direction of his friend, Calippus.
353 B.C.
Clearchus, king of Heraclea, was murdered by Chion and Leonidas.
338 B.C.
Artaxerxes III (Ochus), king of Persia, a despot who killed numerous political rivals and conquered Egypt, was poisoned by one of his Egyptian governors, Bagoas, who was in a conspiracy with Darius III.
336 B.C.
Arses (Xerxes III), king of Persia, was killed by Bagoas, the Egyptian governor who also murdered his father, Artaxerxes III. Bagoas conspired with Darius III, who wanted to ascend to power.
Philip II, king of Macedonia and father of Alexander the Great, was assassinated by Pausanias, apparently acting on orders from his wife, Olympias. Pausanias was executed.
330 B.C.
Darius III (Codommanus), king of Persia, had taken power by conspiring to kill Artaxerxes III and his son, Arses. Darius suffered a military loss to Alexander the Great and he was slain by his own underling, Bessus.
Parmenio, Macedonian general, was put to death at the direction of Alexander the Great because his son, Philotas was charged with conspiracy.
329 B.C.
Bessus, governed Bactria and Sogdiana, assassinated Darius III and took power as Artaxerxes IV. He was later executed for murdering Darius.
323 B.C.
Harpalus, a Macedonian, was placed in charge of the royal treasure by Alexander the Great and absconded with it. He was later killed on Crete.
322 B.C.
Hyperides (Hypereides), Athenian official, encouraged Lamian War, but after Athenians lost at Cranon, he was sentenced to death, caught, and put to death.
321 B.C.
Perdiccas, Macedonian general, ruled as regent for infant Alexander IV, and was slain by his soldiers, who revolted.
317 B.C.
Philip III Arrhidaeus, king of Macedon, was named king by military after the death of Alexander the Great, but was later killed on the orders of Olympias, Alexander's mother.
Phocion, Athenian general, held tyrannical power in Athens, and was put to death by the Democratic party for fraudulent treason charges.
316 B.C.
Olympias, queen mother of Macedonia, wife of Philip II, and mother of Alexander III (Alexander the Great), was stoned to death by those related to her victims.
310 B.C.
Alexander IV, son of Alexander the Great and Roxana, was executed with his mother at the direction of Cassander.
2nd Cent. B.C.
Porus, king of Indian country, was killed at the direction of Eudamus.
294 B.C.
Alexander V, son of Macedonian king, Cassander, was slain on the order of Demetrius.
281 B.C.
Seleucus I (Nicator), king of the Seleucid Empire and of Macedon, was killed by Ptolemy Ceraunus in c.281 B.C.
279 B.C.
Ptolemy Ceraunus, king of Macedonia, was murdered by Gauls.
260 B.C.
Philochorus, politician of Athens, was against procedures of Demetrius Policetes and his son, Antigonus Gonatas, who was responsible for Philochorus' death in c.260 B.C.
259 B.C.
Hannibal, Carthaginian admiral, was crucified by his forces.
250 B.C.
Marcus Atilius Regulus, Roman consul, was captured in Carthage and executed after he unsuccessfully tried to conclude an agreement between Rome and the Carthaginians.
246 B.C.
Antiochus II (Antiochus Theos), king of the Seleucid domain of Syria, was allegedly poisoned by Laodice.
235 B.C.
Diodotus II, king of Bactria, was overthrown and assassinated by Euthydemus in c.235 B.C.
221 B.C.
Berenice II, wife of Egyptian ruler Ptolemy III Euergetes, was poisoned by her son, Ptolemy IV Philopator.
Hasdrubal was a Carthaginian general and leader. After one of Hasdrubal's governors executed the master of a Celto-Iberian slave, the slave killed Hasdrubal in retaliation.
212 B.C.
Two brothers, Gnaeus Cornelius Scipio and Publius Cornelius Scipio, Roman generals, were captured and executed in Spain by the Carthaginian army and Prince Massinissa of Eastern Numidia.
208 B.C.
Li Ssu, minister to Chinese Emperor Cheng, was the target of a successful murder plot by court conspirators.
207 B.C.
Chao Kao, head eunuch to Chinese emperor Shih Huang Ti, arranged for his heir apparent to commit suicide, for co-conspirator Li Ssu to be murdered, and for his infant child Hu Hai to be killed after the ruler's death. Chao Kao was later killed.
206 B.C.
Machanidas, despot of the Spartans, was slain by Greek general Philopoemen.
204 B.C.
Arsinoë III, wife of Egyptian king Ptolemy IV Philopator, her brother, was slain after her husband died by members of the court in c.204 B.C.
192 B.C.
Nabis, a ruler of Sparta and a despot, was assassinated.
182 B.C.
Philopoemen, Greek general, was caught during a battle at Messina and put to death.
181 B.C.
Ptolemy Eupator, king of Egypt, was slain by his uncle, Ptolemy VII.
180 B.C.
Ptolemy V (Ptolemy Epiphanes), king of Egypt, was poisoned by some of his courtiers.
175 B.C.
Seleucus IV (Philopator), king of the Seleucid Empire, was murdered, and his brother, Antiochus IV, became the new ruler.
162 B.C.
Antiochus V (Antiochus Eupator), king of the Seleucid domain of Syria, was deposed and slain by Demetrius I Soter, his cousin.
Gnaeus Octavius, Roman general and consul, was killed in Syria.
Lysias, general and ruler of Syria, was murdered on the orders of Demetrius I.
160 B.C.
Timarchus, self-proclaimed king of Babylonia and Media, was ousted by Syrian Demetrius I, and executed.
144 B.C.
Ptolemy VII (Ptolemy Neos Philopator), king of Egypt, was murdered by his uncle, Ptolemy VIII.
143 B.C.
Jonathan Maccabees, leader of Judea, was apprehended at Bethshean and killed in c.143 by Tryphon, a Syrian who seized power.
139 B.C.
Viriathus (Shepherd of Lusitania) (Portugal), fought in the Punic Wars. During the Numantine Revolt, he was murdered by his own men, who had been bribed by the Romans.
134 B.C.
Simon Maccabees, civil governor of Judea, succeeded Jonathan, his murdered brother, and was assassinated by his son-in-law.
133 B.C.
Tiberius Sempronius Gracchus was a Roman statesman and tribune of the people who supported land reforms. When he illegally tried to run for re-election, he was murdered by a mob.
132 B.C.
Eunus (Antiochus), Syrian leader of the first slave insurrection in Rome-administered Sicily, was caught and killed with other rebels by Roman soldiers.
129 B.C.
C. Carbo, Roman tribune, may have been killed.
Publius Cornelius Scipio Aemilianus Africanus Numantinus, Roman general and consul. It is beleived that Publius may have been assassinated.
125 B.C.
Seleucus V, king of the Seleucid Empire of Syria, was murdered by Cleopatra Thea, his mother, who ruled during the minority of another son, Antiochus VIII.

121 B.C.
Gaius Sempronius Gracchus and M. Fulvius Flaccus, Roman tribunes, and hundreds of others were slain during an election riot.
Cleopatra Thea, queen of Syria, reigned while her son, Antiochus VIII, was a minor. Later, she was later reputedly poisoned by him.
120 B.C.
Mithradates V Euergetes, king of Pontus, was murdered in c.120 B.C.
117 B.C.
Hiempsal I and Adherbal, kings of Numidia, ruled jointly with their cousin, Jugurtha, who assassinated them in c.117 B.C.
111 B.C.
Caius Memmius, Roman tribune, was murdered during a riot instigated by praetor Glaucia in c.111 B.C.
104 B.C.
Antigonus I, king of Judea, was joint ruler with his brother, Aristobulus, until he was slain in a conspiracy by the royal court.
Jugurtha (Iugurtha), king of Numidia, was captured and given to the Romans, who put him in prison and killed him.
100 B.C.
Lucius Appuleius Saturnius, a tribune of Rome, was stoned to death by a group with opposing political views.
2nd Cent. B.C.
Massiva a Roman, was cousin to King Jugurtha of Numidia whose agents killed Massiva.
91 B.C.
Marcus Livius Drusus, a Roman tribune, was killed at the start of the civil war.
89 B.C.
Asellio, praetor of Rome, was slain.
87 B.C.
Marcus Antonius, Roman consul and censor, was put to death at the direction of Gaius Marius and Lucius Cornelius Cinna.
Gnaeus Octavius, consul of Rome, supported Sulla and opposed Lucius Cornelius Cinna. He was killed by agents of Cinna.
84 B.C.
Lucius Cornelius Cinna, Roman general, was about to lead an assault on Lucius Cornelius Sulla when his forces revolted and murdered him.
80 B.C.
Berenice III, Egyptian princess who ascended to power, was killed by Ptolemy Alexander.
Ptolemy XI (Ptolemy Alexander II), king of Egypt, murdered his stepmother, Berenice, and was slain by an angry mob.
72 B.C.
Quintus Sertorius, Roman general, was the victim of a successful murder conspiracy led by Marcus Perperna, who was later put to death by Pompeius.
63 B.C.
Marcus Tullius Cicero, Roman consul, was the target of a failed murder plot during an election by rival Lucius Sergius Catiline. Some of the conspirators were put to death.
57 B.C.
Phraates III, king of Parthia, was assassinated by his sons, Mithradates III and Orodes II in c.57 B.C.
55 B.C.
Berenice IV, Egyptian princess and daughter of Ptolemy XII Auletes, held power while her father was exiled, but he later ousted and killed her.
54 B.C.
Mithradates III, king of Parthia, was slain.
53 B.C.
Marcus Licinius Crassus, Roman praetor, consul, censor, and governor of Syria, attacked the Parthians, but lost and was put to death.
52 B.C.
Publuis Clodius, Roman statesman, was killed by supporters of his rival, Titus Annius Milo, close to Bovillae.
48 B.C.
Gnaeus Pompeius Magnus (Pompey the Great), was murdered by an Egyptian general, Achillas, acting at the direction of Ptolemy.
Marcus Caelius Rufus, Roman tribune, tried to instigate a rebellion, but was later slain by some soldiers whom he had tried to bribe.
47 B.C.
Pharnaces II, king of Bosporus (Pontus) and son of Mithridates the Great, suffered a calamitous defeat to Caesar before he was murdered by one of his own governors.
45 B.C.
Gnaeus Pompeius Magnus, Roman military commander and son of Pompey the Great, lost to Caesar at Munda, was caught and put to death.
Marcus Claudius Marcellus, Roman consul, was traveling to Rome when he was killed by one of his escorts.
44 B.C.
Burebistas (Burebista), king of Dacia, was slain in c.44 B.C.
Ptolemy XIV (Ptolemy Theos Philopater II), king of Egypt, ruled jointly with his sister, Cleopatra VII, who killed him so her son, Ptolemy XV, could reign.
Mar. 15: Gaius Julius Caesar, dictator of Rome, was assassinated in Rome by Marcus Junius Brutus, Gaius Cassius Longinus, Gaius Cassius Parmensis, and other senators as he entered the Senate building. The leaders of the conspiracy were executed.
43 B.C.
Antipater (Antipater the Idumaean), procurator of Rome under Julius Caesar, was killed.
Marcus Tullius Cicero, a Roman statesman, criticized Antony after Caesar was murdered. On Antony's orders, Herennius and Popillius killed Cicero.
42 B.C.
Ariobarzanes III, king of Cappadocia, was executed on the orders of Cassius.
41 B.C.
Arsinoë IV, daughter of Egyptian king Ptolemy XII Auletes, was apprehended by the Romans, paraded through Rome, and murdered at the direction of Cleopatra and Mark Antony.
37 B.C.
Antigonus II (Mattathias), king of Judea, was conquered by the Romans and assassinated at Antioch.
36 B.C.
Orodes II, king of Parthia, was slain by his son, Phraates IV in c.36 B.C.
35 B.C.
Aristobulus III, high priest and member of the Hasmonaean line, was murdered by Herod.
Sextus Pompeius Magnus (Pompey the Younger), Roman military leader, was apprehended and killed by forces under Marcus Antonius.
34 B.C.
Artavasdes III, king of Armenia, was apprehended by Mark Antony during an attack, transported to Alexandria, and murdered by Cleopatra.
30 B.C.
Gaius Cassius Parmensis, Roman politician, participated in the assassination of Gaius Julius Caesar in 44 B.C. He was later executed by Octavian in c.30 B.C.
John Hyrcanus II, leader of Judaea and high priest, was put to death by Herod.
Ptolemy XV (Ptolemy Philopater Philometor Caesar; Caesarion), king of Egypt, was executed on the orders of Octavian.
6 B.C.
Aristobulus, son of Herod the Great and a member of the Hasmonaean line, was charged with treason and assassinated by Herod.
2 B.C.
Phraates IV, king of Parthia, was poisoned by his concubine, Musa, clearing the throne for her son, Phraates V.
7 A.D.
Sadyattes (AKA: Candaules), king of Lydia (Persia), was slain by a palace guard named Gyges.
19 A.D.
Germanicus Caesar, Roman general, died close to Antioch, and may have been poisoned at the direction of Emperor Tiberius.
21 A.D.
Arminius (Armin; Hermann), Cherusci leader, became a Roman citizen and was slain.
23 A.D.
Drusus Caesar (Drusus Junior), the son of Roman Emperor Tiberius and a Roman consul, was reputedly poisoned by Sejanus and Livilla.
Wang Mang, emperor of China, was murdered by Han princes.
31 A.D.
Lucius Aelius Sejanus, Roman consul, was involved in several conspiracies, and was put to death at the direction of Tiberius.
33 A.D.
Agrippina (Vipsania Agrippina), was the mother of Caligula. She was exiled to Pandataria, an island near Naples, where she starved to death, probably at the command of Tiberius.
Drusus, nobleman of Rome and son of Agrippina, was put in prison and starved to death on the orders of Emperor Tiberius, who felt threatened by his popularity.
41 A.D.
Gaius Cassius Chaerea, a Roman soldier who helped murder Caligula, was slain at the direction of Caligula's successor, Emperor Claudius.
Jan. 24: Caligula (Gaius Caesar Germanicus), Roman emperor, was stabbed to death by praetorian guardsmen led by Gaius Cassius Chaerea and Sabinus.
48 A.D.
Valeria Messalina, wife of Roman Emperor Claudius, was slain on his orders.
54 A.D.
Claudius I (Tiberius Claudius Drasus Nero Germanicus), Roman emperor, was poisoned by his fourth wife and niece, Agrippina.
55 A.D.
Britannicus (Claudius Tiberius Germanicus), was poisoned by his stepbrother, Nero.
59 A.D.
Agrippina (Colonia Agrippina, Agrippina the Younger), mother of Nero, had numerous Roman nobles killed, as well as her husband and uncle Claudius I, to install Nero in power. Nero later ordered her execution.
62 A.D.
Octavia, was slain by agents of her husband, Roman Emperor Nero.
65 A.D.
Lucius Annaeus Seneca (Seneca the Younger), Roman praetor, was

suspected of involvement in the plot by Gaius Calpurnius Piso to assassinate Nero and committed suicide at Nero's command.
66 A.D.
Claudia Antonia, daughter of Emperor Claudius, was executed by Nero.
69 A.D.
Aulus Vitellius, Roman consul and emperor, was murdered by supporters of Titus Flavius Vespasianus.
January: Servius Sulpicius Galba, Roman emperor, was murdered by soldiers at the direction of Otho, who once backed him.
93 A.D.
Gnaeus Julius Agricola, Roman consul, may have been poisoned by agents of Domitian.
96 A.D.
Domitian (Titus Flavius Domitianus Augustus), Roman emperor, was murdered by a freedman, Stephanus, an agent of empress Domitia and members of the court.
2nd Cent. A.D.
Apollodorus of Damascus, Greek architect, was exiled and murdered by Emperor Hadrian.
175
Avidius Cassius, soldier of Rome, self-proclaimed emperor, was killed by one of his own soldiers.
192
Tung Cho, a Chinese general, overthrew a Han ruler, became a tyrant, and was slain.
Dec. 31: Commodus (Lucius Aelius Aurelius), Roman emperor and a despot, was strangled by wrestler Narcissus, a member of a conspiracy.
193
Marcus Didius Julianus (Marcus Didius Salvius Julianus), Roman emperor, was attacked and murdered by troops of Lucius Septimius Severus.
Publius Helvius Pertinax, Roman emperor, was assassinated after ruling three months by members of the praetorian guard under Laetus.
194
Pescennius Niger (Gaius Pescennius Niger Justus), Roman general, was named emperor by his troops and after a defeat in battle, he was murdered by Septimius Severus.
212
Papinian (Aemilius Papinianus), Roman praetorian prefect, was put to death by Emperor Caracalla.
Publius Septimus Geta, Roman emperor, ruled jointly with his brother, Septimus Bassianus Caracalla, who had him assassinated.
217
Apr. 8: Caracalla (Marcus Aurelinus Antoninus, Bassianus), Roman emperor, was slain by Macrinus, who became emperor. Macrinus had heard a prediction that he would become the ruler, and he was afraid Caracalla would murder him.
222
Mar. 11: Elagabulus (Varius Avitus Bassianus), was crowned emperor of Rome, Marcus Aurelius Antoninus, by soldiers. A despot responsible for the deaths of numerous Roman senators, he and his mother, Julia Soaemias, were murdered by praetorian guardsmen.
235
Alexander Severus, Roman emperor, was killed by his soldiers who revolted.
238
Gaius Julius Verus Maximinus, Roman emperor, was expelled by the Senate and assassinated by his soldiers.
Marcus Clodius Pupienus Maximus and Decimus Caelius Balbinus, joint Roman emperors, were slain by the praetorian guard, who named Gordianus III the new emperor.
Tiridates II (Khosrow the Great), king of Armenia, was killed by a Persian in c.238.
244
Marcus Antonius Gordianus III (Gordianus Pius), Roman emperor, was murdered by soldiers of Philip the Arabian, praetorian prefect.
253
Gaius Vibius Trebonianus Gallus, Roman emperor, was slain by his soldiers.
267
Odenathus (Odaenathus), king of Palmyra, was slain in c.267.
268
Publius Licinius Valerianus Egnatius Gallienus, Roman emperor, was assassinated by his own soldiers at Mediolanum.
275
Aurelian (Lucius Domitius Aurelianus), Roman emperor, was assassinated by his officers.
Manes (Mani, Manichaeus), a Persian who established the Manichaean religious sect, was put to death.
276
Marcus Claudius Tacitus, Roman emperor, was murdered by his soldiers. His half-brother, Florianus, became emperor after his death.
282
Marcus Aurelius Probus, Roman emperor, was killed during a revolt by his soldiers.
284
Carinus, Roman emperor, was slain by his own soldiers.
Marcus Aurelius Numerianus, Roman emperor, was slain by his father-in-law.
293
Marcus Aurelius Carausius, Roman general and emperor of Britain, was slain by one of his ministers, Allectus.
4th Cent. A.D.
Delmatius and Hannibalianus, nephews of Roman emperor Constantine I who were supposed to become joint rulers with the emperor's sons were put to death by Constantine II in c.337.
The families of Maximus Daia and Galerius Severus were slain by Licinius, who wanted to eliminate rivals for the Roman emperor position.
310
Maximian (Marcus Aurelius Valerius Maximianus), Roman emperor, was apprehended in Massilia and executed on the orders of Constantine.
324
Licinius (Valerius Licinianus Licinius), Roman emperor, lost a war to Constantine, and was put to death.
326
Flavius Julius Crispus, the son of Roman emperor Constantine, was executed on his father's orders through the connivance of his step-mother, Fausta, who was also later killed.
340
Constantine II (Flavius Claudius Constantinus), Roman emperor, ruled jointly with his brothers, Constantius II and Constans, until he was murdered at Aquileia.
350
Constans I (Flavius Julius Constans), Roman emperor, was assassinated by Magnentius' troops.
361
George of Cappadocia, prelate, was slain by a crowd in Alexandria.
383
Flavius Gratianus Gratian, Roman emperor, was overthrown and slain by insurgents led by Maximus, who seized power.
Magnus Clemens Maximus, Roman emperor, was apprehended at Aquileia and slain by Theodosius.
390
In retaliation for a Thessalonica rebellion, Theodosius ordered 7,000 put to death.
392
Valentinian II, Roman emperor, was slain by Arbogastes, the commander of his troops.
395
Flavius Rufinus, Roman praetorian prefect of the East, carried out harsh policies, and was killed by agents of Gainas, an ally of Flavius Stilicho.
399
Bahram IV (Varahran IV), Sassanid king, was slain in an uprising.
408
Flavius Stilicho, Roman general and politician, was thought to possibly be involved in a plot against Emperor Honorius, and was put to death on the order of the emperor.
Heraclian, Roman general, rebelled and was slain at Carthage on the orders of Emperor Honorius.
415
Ataulphus (Atawulf, Ataulf, Athaulf), king of the Visigoths, attacked Spain and was slain at Barcelona.
Hypatia, a Greek philosopher, lectured at Alexandria where he was slain by a crowd led by the archbishop of Alexandria, Cyril.
453
Attila, king of the Huns, murdered by a woman at the direction of Roman General Aetius.
Flavis Maximiana Fausta, Roman empress, was suffocated at the direction of her husband, Constantine, possibly because she falsely accused her stepson, who was put to death.
Thorismond (Thorismund), king of the Visigoths, was killed by usurper Theodoric II, his brother.
454
Flavius Aëtius, a Roman general who planned the successful killing of Attila, was assassinated at the direction of Emperor Valentinian III.
455
Valentinian III, Roman emperor, murdered his general, Flavius Aëtius, and was killed by supporters of Aëtius.
459
Hormizd III, king of the Sasanian Empire of Persia, was ousted and assassinated by his brother, Firuz.
466
Theodoric II, king of the Visigoths, was slain by Euric, his brother.
476
Orestes, regent of the Roman empire, was assassinated by Odoacer.
493
Odoacer (Odovacar, Odovakar), member of the Roman army and king of the Heruli. Odoacer was murdered by Theodoric, king of the Ostrogoths.
524
Albinus, Roman senator and consul, was charged with treason and killed with Boethius and Symmachus in c.524.
Chlodomer, Frankish prince, led assault on and caught Sigismund of Burgundy, but was later slain at Vienne, Fr., by Godomer, Sigismund's brother.

535
Amalsuntha (Amalasuentha, Amalaswintha), the queen of the Ostrogoths, was murdered while she was taking a bath. Her death, on the orders of Theodahad, her cousin, resulted in a calamitous war with Emperor Justinian, an ally of Amalsuntha.
536
Theodahad (Theodat), king of the Ostrogoths, a usurper who ordered the death of Queen Amalasuntha, was killed by an officer in his army.
549
Ly Bon (Ly Ban, Ly Bi, Li Bi, Li Nam-Viet De Bon), emperor of Vietnam, lost struggle to Chinese and escaped to Laos, where he was put to death.
573
Alboin, king of the Lombards, murdered Cunimund, king of the Gepidae. He married Cunimund's daughter, Rosamund, and made her drink wine from the skull of her father. Rosamund's lover, Peredeo, stabbed Alboin to death in his sleep.
575
Sigebert I, Frankish king of Austrasia, was killed by Queen Fredegund of Neustria, the widow of assassinated King Chilperic I. The death of Sigebert resulted in fights between Fredeguad and Queen Brunhilde, the wife of Sigebert.
584
Chilperic I (Chilperich), the Frankish king of Neustria, killed his wife, Galswintha, to mollify his mistress, Fredegund. He was murdered by an unknown assailant, thought to be acting at the direction of Galswintha's sister, Queen Brunhilde.
590
Hormizd IV (Ormazd, Ormizd), king of the Sasanian Empire of Persia, was overthrown and assassinated by rebels under General Bahram Chubin.
592
Sushun, emperor of Japan, was killed on the orders of his uncle, Soga Umako, who placed Sushun's sister, Suiko, in power.
602
Mauricius (Flavius Tiberius Mauricius, Maurice, Markios), emperor of the Eastern Roman Empire, fell from power when the Danube army led by Phocas mutinied. Mauricius fled the capital, but he was chased, and he and his five sons were murdered by the usurpers.
610
Phocas, emperor of the Eastern Roman Empire and a brutal despot, was tortured and decapitated after being ousted by his son, Heraclius and Exarch of Africa, Heraclius.
613
Brunhilde (Brunehilde, Brunechildis, Brunehaut), Queen of Austrasia, was put to death at the order of Chlotar II, king of the Franks.
Sigebert II, Frankish ruler, was reputedly put to death by Chlotar II, king of the Franks.
626
Adaloald, Lombard king of Italy, was overthrown and killed in c.626.
628
Khosrow I (Khosrau II, Khosrau Parucz), king of the Sasanian empire of Persia, was overthrown and murdered by his son, Kavadh II.
630
Ardashir III (Artakhshathra), child king of Persia, was killed by Shahrbaraz, his general.
Shahr-barz, king of the Sasanid empire of Persia, ruled only two months before he was slain by his own soldiers.
634
Caedwalla (Cadwalader, Cadwallon), king of Gwynedd, lost to Oswald, who killed him.
641
Constantine III Heraclius, emperor of the Eastern Roman Empire, shared power with Heracleonas, his half-brother. He was allegedly poisoned.
643
Prince Yamashiro Oe, Japanese heir apparent, was murdered by Soga Iruka, imperial minister who wanted to seize power.
644
Omar I (Umar ibn-al-Khattab), Muslim caliph, was entering a mosque when he was stabbed to death by a Persian Christian slave.
645
Soga Iruka, imperial minister of Japan, was murdered by conspirators Nakatomi Kamatari and Tenchi, who became the emperor several years later.
648
Gyges, king of Lydia, lost to and was killed by Cimmerians.
651
Yazdegerd III (Isdigerd), king of Persia, suffered military defeats, escaped to Media, and was murdered at Merv.
655
Penda, king of Mercia, was attacked, beaten by, and killed by forces under Northumbrian king Oswiu.
656
Othman, third caliph of the Muslims, was murdered in Medina at the direction of Mohammed, son of abu-Bakr, during an insurrection by Othman's Arab army.
661
Ali (Ali ibn-abi-Talib), was the fourth caliph of the Muslims. The son-in-law of Mohammed, Ali became one of his first converts. Ali was slain by three members of the Kharijite sect at Al Kufa.
668
Constans II (Flavius Heraclius), Holy Eastern Roman emperor, was a dictator who killed his brother, Theodosius. Constans was murdered in Syracuse, an ancient city of Sicily, by a discontent attendant of the court.
669
Hasan (Hassan, al-Hasan), caliph, stepped down from his post and was the victim of a successful harem murder conspiracy.
671
Grimoald I, duke of Benevento, usurped Lombard power and was killed.
680
Oct. 10: Husain (Hosein), caliph, was slain by Yazid at Karbala, Iraq.
705
Leontius, emperor of the Eastern Roman Empire, ousted Justinian II, but was himself deposed by Tiberius VII Apsimar, and assassinated by Justinian.
711
Justinian II (Rhinotmetus), emperor of the Eastern Roman Empire, was captured by Philippicus and executed.
721
Anastasius II, emperor of the Eastern Roman Empire, was killed by Leo III.
754
June 5: Saint Boniface (Wynfrid, Wynfrith), archbishop of Mainz, was murdered by a crowd at Dokkum, West Friesland.
757
An Lu-shan (Hsiung Wu, Kang), Chinese general, self-proclaimed emperor of the Great Yen dynasty, was killed by a slave involved in a murder conspiracy.
788
Adelchis, Lombard prince, tried to win power over Italy and was possibly slain during the campaign.
797
Constantine VI, emperor of the Eastern Roman Empire, was a minor during the regency of his mother, Irene. Following disputes, Constantine VI was murdered on his mother's order and she seized power.
813
Amin, al (Muhammad al-Amin), abbasid caliph of Baghdad, surrendered to his brother, al-Mamun, who had attacked Baghdad. Amin was killed because he surrendered.
820
Leo V (AKA: The Armenian), emperor of the Eastern Roman Empire, was murdered by adherents of Michael the Amorian.
861
al-Mutawakkil, caliph of Baghdad, was slain by Turkish mercenaries, agents of his eldest son.
866
Bardas, ruled the Eastern Roman Empire with Theodora during the childhood of Michael III. Michael III later conspired with Basil I to kill Bardas.
867
Michael III (AKA: Michael the Drunkard), a despot, was killed by Basil I, his close companion with whom he jointly ruled.
898
Lambert of Spoleto, Holy Roman Emperor, was possibly murdered.
914
Chu Wen (Chu Ch'üan-chung), emperor of China, was assassinated by his oldest son, who ascended to power.
924
Berengar I, Holy Roman Emperor and king of Italy, was murdered by his associates.
925
Alberic I, nobleman of Lombard, believed murdered by Romans.
928
John X, pope, gained his position with the aid of Theodora, the wife of a senator, Theophylact. Theodora's daughter, Marozia, however, was responsible for having the pope arrested and he was slain.
939
Otto I, king of Germany and Holy Roman emperor, was the target of an unsuccessful assassination plot in c.939, by his brother, Henry, who was pardoned in 941.
942
William I (Longue Épée), duke of Normandy, was murdered by the count of Flanders, Arnoul II.
946
Edmund (Eadmund I; the Deed-doer; the Magnificent), king of England, was stabbed to death by a banished thief at Pucklechurch.
959
Constantine VII (Porphyrogenitus), emperor of the Eastern Roman Empire, was poisoned by his son Romanus II, who usurped the throne.
969
Nasir ad-Dawlah, Muslim prince of the Hamdanid family, was ousted by princes of the same family.
Dec. 10: Nicephorus II Phocas, Holy Roman emperor, was killed in his sleep by his nephew, John Zimisces (John Tzimiskes), and the

Empress Theophano on her orders.
974
Benedict VI, pope, was put in prison and strangled by agents of antipope Boniface VII.
978
Edward (Edward the Martyr), king of England, was murdered at Corfe Castle, maybe on the orders of his stepmother, Aelfthryth, to place her son, Aethelred II, in power.
984
John XIV (Pietro Canepanova), pope, was put in prison and slain by Crescentii, who supported antipope Boniface VII.
985
Boniface VII, antipope, killed Pope Benedict VI to usurp his power. He was later put in prison and slain by Roman masses.
999
Gregory V, the first German pope, quarreled with French King Robert and excommunicated the monarch. The pope died under mysterious circumstances, which some historians attribute to murder, possibly by an agent of Robert.
11th Cent.
Ulf-Jarl unsuccessfully tried to install Hardeknut (later Canute III), as king of Denmark, and was slain on the orders of Canute II king of Denmark.
1002
Ekkard I (Eckard), margrave of Meissen and challenger of Henry II, was murdered in c.1002
1003
Sylvester II (Gerbert of Aurillac), pope, died under mysterious circumstances that some historians believe was murder.
1017
Eadric Streona (Edric Streona), was assassinated by agents of Canute, who doubted Eadric Streona's loyalty.
1034
Romanus III Argyrus, emperor of the Eastern Roman Empire, was purportedly killed by his wife, Zöe, and Michael IV.
1040
Duncan I, king of Scotland, was conquered and killed by clan chief Maelbaethe (or Macbeth, Mormaoe of Moray). The murder was the inspiration for Shakespeare's *Macbeth*.
1051
Drogo de Hauteville, Norman noble and count of Apulia, was the victim of a successful anti-Norman murder conspiracy.
1052
Gaimar V (Guaimar V, Gaimar IV), prince of Salerno and ruler of Capua, overthrew Pandulph III to become the leader of Capua. He was later murdered.
1072
Sancho II, king of Castile, lost in battle and was murdered at Zamora.
1075
Anno (Hanno), archbishop of Cologne and Saint, abducted the child King Henry IV and overthrew his mother, Agnes of Poitou, who was reigning during the king's minority. Anno was later slain.
1076
Sancho IV, king of Navarre, was killed, reputedly by his brothers.
1086
Saint Canute IV, king of Denmark, was slain by insurgents.
1092
October: Nizam-al-Mulk (Abu Ali Hassan ibn-Ali), statesman and vizier of Persia, was in his traveling chair on his way to the tent of his women when he was stabbed to death by members of the Order of the Assassins, whom he was against.
1094
Duncan II, king of Scotland and the son of Malcolm III, was killed by agents of Donald Bane, his uncle.
1100
Aug. 2: William II (Rufus), king of England, was riding home in his private forest close to Winchester when the despot was shot in the chest with an arrow, allegedly by Walter Tirel. Tirel, a Norman knight, was not punished.
1103
Magnus III (Barfot), king of Denmark, was slain on the Irish coast.
1127
Mar. 2: Charles the Good (Count of Flanders), was saying his prayers in the church of Saint Donatien in Bruges, a Flemish city, when he was murdered by swordsmen acting at the direction of Borsiard, a member of the Erembald family involved in a feud with Charles.
1129
Raymond II of Tripoli (Syria), was slain at the gates of Tripoli by the Order of the Assassins because he was an "unbeliever." He was the first "Frankish" person the sect murdered.
1131
Canute Lavard, prince of Denmark, was murdered by Magnus the Strong.
1153
Randulf de Gernons (Fourth Earl of Chester), a military leader, was believed to have been poisoned by a follower of King Stephen.
1155
Sigurd II (Munnr), king of Norway, was a joint ruler with his half-brother Ingi, whose followers killed Sigurd.
1157
Canute V, king of Denmark, was murdered.
Eystein Haraldsson, king of Norway, was slain.
1164
Ingo della Volta, nobleman and ruler of Genoa, faced civil strife and was killed.
1167
Charles VII, king of Sweden, was killed by Knut Eriksson.
1170
Dec. 29: Saint Thomas à Becket, archbishop of Canterbury, was a friend of Henry VIII until the two began to disagree over religious matters. Four of Henry's knights, in an impetuous effort to aid the king, murdered Becket in a cathedral.
1172
Vitale II Michiel, chief magistrate of Venice, was killed by a mob.
1174
Andrew (Andrey Yuryevich Bogolyubsky), Russian prince, was murdered by noblemen.
1183
Alexius II Comnenus, emperor of Eastern Roman Empire, was joint ruler with his uncle, Andronicus I Comnenus, who overthrew and assassinated him.
1185
Andronicus I Comnenus, emperor of Eastern Roman Empire, was deposed by Isaac II Angelus and assassinated by a crowd.
1192
Apr. 28: Conrad (Marquis of Montferrat), lord of Tyre and king of Jerusalem, was killed by two members of the Order of the Assassins. The assailants asserted that King Richard of England paid them to murder Conrad, but actually they acted at the direction of Saladin.
1203
Arthur (Count or Duke of Brittany), made claims to the British thone, but was slain at Rouen, most likely on the orders of his uncle, King John.
1204
Alexius IV Angelus, emperor of the Eastern Roman empire, was executed on the orders of Alexius V.
Alexius V, emperor of the Eastern Roman empire, was put to death.
1206
Mohammed of Ghor (Muizz-ad-din, AKA: Muhammad Ghori), sultan of Ghazni, was murdered.
1207
Han T'o-chou, minister to Chinese emperor Ning Tsung, caused catastrophic war and was put to death by his fellow citizens.
1208
Peter of Castelnau (Pierre de Castelnau), French archdeacon and inquisitor of Raymond VI, who was responsible for Peter's death.
June: Philip of Swabia, Holy Roman emperor and king of Germany, was killed at Bamberg, Ger., by Count Palatine, Otto von Wittelsbach.
1215
Buondelmonte (Buondelmonti), a Florentine and head of the Guelphs, was assassinated. The incident was used to start civil war between the Ghibellines and the Guelphs.
1225
Engelbert I, archbishop of Cologne and saint, was killed by agents of his cousin, Count Frederick of Isenburg.
1231
Jalal-ad-Din (Jelal ad-Din), shah of Khwarazm, was defeated by Mongols led by Ogadai and murdered.
1240
Raziya (Raziyyatuddin), queen of Delhi, was assassinated by Hindus.
1241
Snorri Sturluson, president of the high court of Iceland, conspired against Norwegian King Haakon IV, whose agents killed Sturluson.
1250
Erik IV (Ploughpenny), king of Denmark, was ousted and murdered by his brother, Abel, who became king.
Turan-Shah, sultan of Egypt, was assassinated by officers under Baybars I.
1258
al-Mustasim, caliph of Baghdad, was murdered by Hülegü at Baghdad.
1268
Conradin (Konradin), a German prince, lost a battle to Charles of Anjou, and was apprehended and decapitated.
1277
Constantine Asen (Constantine Tych), czar of Bulgaria, was assassinated by a peasant who took power.
1283
September: Dafydd ap Gruffydd, prince of Gwynedd (Wales), was double-crossed, and hanged, drawn, and quartered.
1290
Ladislas IV, king of Hungary, was slain by a Cuman.
1296
Jalal-un-Din Firuz Khalji, sultan in Delhi, India, was killed by Juna Khan, his son-in-law who seized power.
1305
Roger de Flor, Italian, led mercenaries under Andronicus II and tried

to establish his own kingdom before he was killed at the direction of the emperor.
1306
John Comyn (John the younger), a Scot, argued with Robert the Bruce (Robert I), who fatally stabbed Comyn at Dumfries, Scot.
May 1: Albert I, king of Germany, was killed by his nephew, John the Parracide, who had been denied hereditary rights by Albert. In 1312, John was arrested in Pisa.
1316
Ramon Llull (Raymond Lully), Catalan missionary, tried to win Muslim converts in Asia Minor and North Africa, and he was supposedly stoned to death at Bougie.
1322
March: Thomas, earl of Lancaster, Derby, Lincoln, Leicester, and Salisbury, rebelled against the royal troops and was decapitated.
1326
Hugh Despenser and his son, Hugh, were British court favorites until they were banished in 1321 and later hanged.
1327
Sept. 21: Edward II (of Caernarvon), king of England, was ousted by his wife, Queen Isabella, and her lover, Roger de Mortimer, first Earl of March. Edward was confined in Berkely Castle where he was slain.
1349
Günther of Schwarzburg, king of Germany, may have been poisoned.
1358
Feb. 22: The marshals of Champagne and Normandy were killed by Etienne Marcel in front of French dauphin Charles (King Charles V), after inciting a crowd to storm the palace. Marcel was later killed by Jean Maillart on the orders of Charles.
1369
Pedro el Cruel, king of León and Castile, was murdered by Henry II, count of Trastamara.
1378
Ala-ud-Din Mujahid, sultan of India, was killed by his cousin, Daud.
1382
Joanna I, queen of Naples, Italy, was responsible for the murder of her first husband, Prince Andrew of Hungary. She was assassinated on the order of Charles III, king of Naples.
Kestutis, grand duke of Lithuania, was put to death by Jagiello.
1386
Charles III (Charles of Durazzo), king of Naples, (also Charles II, king of Hungary), came to power by murdering Queen Joanna of Naples. He was assassinated at Buda Castle by agents of dowager Queen Elizabeth.
1397
Thomas of Woodstock, duke of Gloucester, apparently conspired against the king of England, Richard II, who may have ordered his death.
1400
Richard II, king of England, lost in a battle with Henry of Bolingbroke and was incarcerated. He was possibly slain while imprisoned.
1407
Nov. 11: Louis I, duke of Orleans, fought Philip the Bold of Burgundy, whose son, John the Fearless, was responsible for Louis' death. Louis was slashed by swordsmen in Paris.
1415
May 30: Jerome of Prague (Hieronymus of Prague), was burned at the stake as a heretic.
1418
Bernard VII (Comte d'Armagnac), nobleman of France, held great influence in the government of Charles VI until he was killed by a Parisian mob.
1419
Sept. 10: John the Fearless, duke of Burgundy, wielded enormous power in France and opposed the dauphin who later became Charles VII. John met with Charles on the banks of the Seine at Montereau where he was slain on Charles' orders.
1437
James I, king of Scotland, was assassinated at Perth by Sir Robert Graham in a conspiracy with Walter Stewart.
1439
Pietro Loredan, Venetian admiral and general, was killed, possibly by agents of Francesco Foscari, doge of Venice.
1450
John Cade (Jack), a British insurgent, was slain by Alexander Iden.
William Crowmer, sheriff of Kent, James Fiennes, Baron Sele, and Baron Say were slain in London by rebels led by John Cade.
1447
Humphrey, duke of Gloucester, an English Prince, was confined for possibly plotting against the king of England, Henry VI, and died under suspicious circumstances.
1452
William, eighth earl of Douglas, a Scotsman, was slain by agents of James II, king of Scotland.
1460
Richard Plantagenet, third duke of York and heir apparent to the British throne, went to crush the Lancastrian rebellion in northern England and was slain.
1471
Edward, prince of Wales, was slain by Edward IV after a skirmish at Tewksbury.
Henry VI, king of England, was overthrown by Edward IV, put in the Tower of London, reinstated for a short time, and then killed, probably on the orders of Edward.
1476
Dec. 26: Galeazzo Maria Sforza, duke of Milan, Italy, was slain as he walked into the Saint Stephen Church by three aristocratic Milanese youths, including leader Girolamo Olgiati, who was tortured and executed later.
1478
Giuliano Medici, a member of the influential Florentine family, and his brother, Lorenzo Medici, were assaulted when they went to pray at the Duomo on Easter Sunday. Giuliano Medici died, but his brother survived. The attackers were later put to death.
1480
Pino III, member of the Italian Ordelaffi family, ruler of Forli, deposed and killed his brother, Cecco III, and was slain by Lucrezia Pico, his third wife.
1483
Edward V, 12-year-old king of England, and his younger brother, the Duke of York, were taken prisoner by the Richard, Duke of Gloucester and confined in the Tower of London. Probably at the direction of Gloucester, who became Richard III, the children were smothered to death.
1489
Hans Waldmann, mayor of Zürich, Switz., ruled tyrannically and was put to death by a group with opposing political views.
1500
July 15: Alfonso of Aragon, the son of the king of Naples, Alfonso II, was probably slain by agents of Cesare Borgia.
Mohammed X (AKA: The Brave), a Moor who reigned in southern Spain, lost several battles and was killed.
1501
Giovanni Gogliani, prince of Fermo, and his entire family were slain by Oliverotto da Formo, who became prince.
1502
Oliverotto da Fermo was murdered by Cesare Borgia during a dinner at Sinigaglia.
1522
Cuauhtémoc (Guatimozin, Guatemotzin), Aztec emperor, was besieged, tortured, and hanged by Hernán Cortés.
1532
Huáscar (Inti Cusi Huallpa Huáscar), Inca leader, was executed on the orders of his half-brother, Atahualpa, who had revolted against Huáscar and feared Pizarro would reinstall Huáscar to power.
1533
Atahualpa (Atahuallpa, Atahalipa) Inca king of Peru, was strangled on the orders of Spanish conquistador Francisco Pizarro.
1536
Ibrahim (Ibrahim Pasha), grand vizier of Turkey, was strangled by agents of the sultan.
1537
Alessandro Medici, duke of Florence and a despot, was killed by Lorenzino Medici, a relative.
Jürgen Wullenwever, burgomaster of Lübeck, was put in prison and put to death.
1538
Diego de Almagro, a Spaniard who fought in Peru, fought against the Pizarros and was put to death by Hernando Pizarro.
1541
Francisco Pizarro, Spanish conquistador, was murdered in retaliation for Diego de Almagro's execution.
1542
Catherine Howard, queen of England, wife of Henry VIII, was decapitated for adultery.
István Werboczi, chancellor of Hungary, was poisoned by the pasha of Buda.
1546
May: David Beaton (Bethune), a Scottish Roman Catholic Cardinal, denounced George Wishart, a Reformation minister, in 1546 as a heretic and Wishart was later burned at the stake. In retaliation, Norman Leslie and John Leslie murdered Beaton at St. Andrews castle in Scotland.
1547
Pier Luigi Farnese, first duke of Parma and Piacenza, was implicated in the Fiesco conspiracy and was probably killed by Andrea Doria.
Gianettino Doria, the nephew and heir of wealthy Genoese Andrea Doria, was slain in the Fiesco conspiracy.
1550
Jon Arason, bishop of Holar, Ice., was against Lutherans. He was arrested and decapitated.
1551
György Martinuzzi (Juraj Utiesenovic), ruled as regent for young Hungarian King John Sigismund and arranged treaty with Ferdinand I of Austria whose agents later murdered Martinuzzi.
1553
Pedro de Hinojosa, Spanish governor of Charcas and conquistador, was slain by conspirators.

1558
Caupolicán (Quepolicán), Indian chief of Araucanians, hid in mountains after he lost to Don Garcia Hurtado de Mendoza. Caupolicán was caught and slain.
1563
February: François de Lorraine (Francis, duke of Guise, le Balafré), was fatally shot outside of Orleans, Fr., by Jean de Poltrot, Seigneur de Méré, apparently because of his opposition to the Huguenots.
1566
March: David Rizzio (David Riccio), an Italian, became the influential secretary to Mary, Queen of Scots. Armed with daggers, the queen's husband, Lord Darnley, and other noblemen pulled Rizzio from the queen's dinner room at Holyrood Palace and fatally wounded him.
1567
Wilhelm von Grumbach, a German knight, backed John Frederick's bid for elector, but the victor, Augustus I of Saxony, had Grumbach put to death.
Feb. 10: Henry Stewart (Stuart, Lord Darnley), second husband of Mary, Queen of Scots, was involved in a conspiracy to murder David Rizzio, his wife's secretary. Stewart was slain at Kirk o'Field, Edinburgh, Scot.
1568
Don Carlos de Austria, prince of Asturias and heir apparent to the Spanish throne, lost his wife to his father. Afterward, he was put in prison on charges of scheming to kill his father. He later died while in prison and might have been the victim of an assassination.
1569
March: Louis I de Bourbon (Prince de Condé), backed the Huguenots during the war with Catholic Guise supporters. In southwestern France at the battle of Jarnac, Louis I was killed by Montesquiou, a Catholic army officer.
1570
February: James Stewart (Stuart), earl of Moray, advisor to Mary, Queen of Scots, was slain in Linlithgow, Scot., by James Hamilton of Bothwellhaugh and other supporters of Mary.
1571
Matthew Stewart (Stuart), fourth earl of Lennox, was apprehended at Stirling, Scot., and assassinated.
Tupac Amaru, Inca chief, was apprehended by agents of Francisco de Toledo, viceroy, and decapitated at Cuzco.
1572
Gaspard II de Coligny (Coligni), admiral of France and leader of the Huguenots, fought with Catholic supporters of Guise. Coligny was murdered by royal guards at the direction of Henry I of Lorraine, duke of Guise.
1577
Erik XIV, king of Sweden, became insane, was ousted, put in prison, and may have been poisoned.
1578
Juan de Escobedo, representative of John of Austria, was killed on the orders of Philip II.
John Stewart, fourth earl of Atholl, chief counsellor to Mary, Queen of Scots and chancellor, was thought to have been poisoned.
1579
Seigneur Louis de Clermont de Bussy-d'Amboise, French nobleman and governor of Anjou, Fr., murdered a relative to whom he was indebted during the St. Bartholomew's Massacre. Bussy-d'Amboise was later slain by his lover's jealous husband.
Claud Hamilton (Baron Paisley, Lord Claud Hamilton), fourth son of the duke of Châtelherault, left Scotland after charges of conspiracy in a number of intrigues, with his brother John Hamilton, acting as agents of Mary, Queen of Scots. He was implicated in the murders of regents Lennox and Murray.
Mehmed Pasa Sokollu, grand vizier of the Ottoman Empire, was slain.
1582
Nobunaga (Oda Nobunaga), general of Japan, was killed by another general.
1583
Gerald Fitzgerald, fourteenth earl of Desmond, an Irishman, was captured and slain at Glanaginty.
1584
July 10: William I (William the Silent), prince of Orange, founder of the Dutch Republic, was fatally shot in Delft, Neth., by Balthasar Gérards, who was tortured and executed.
1587
Mary, Queen of Scots (Mary Stuart), was found Guilty of involvement in Babington's plot and decapitated at Fotheringhay Castle in Northamptonshire.
1588
Dec. 23: Henri I de Lorraine (le Balafré, duke of Guise), and his brother, Louis II de Lorraine, a cardinal, were stabbed to death a day apart in the Castle of Blois, Fr., by Captain Lorignac, acting on the orders of King Henry III of France.
1589
Aug. 1: Henry III, king of France, fled Paris on the Day of Barricades in 1588. Henry was stabbed to death at St. Cloud by Jacques Clément, a Dominican monk.
1591
Dmitri Ivanovich Demetrius, heir apparent to the Russian throne, was purportedly slain by Boris Godunov and later considered a martyr.
1592
James Stewart (Stuart), a Scot, second earl of Moray, was sought and killed by George Gordon, sixth earl of Huntly.
1594
Dec. 27: Henry IV, king of France, was the target of a failed assassination attempt by French extremist Jean Châtel, who was put to death.
1596
James Stewart of Bothwellmuir, a Scot, earl of Arran, and lord chancellor, was killed by Sir James Douglas.
1601
Michael the Brave (Mihai Viteazul), prince of Walachia, was killed by General Giörgio Basta, a Transylvanian soldier who backed insurrection against the prince.
1603
Mohammad III, sultan of the Ottoman Empire, directed that his nineteen brothers, potential rivals to power, be slain.
1605
Fyodor II Borisovitch, czar of Russia, was assassinated by Russian aristocrats.
1606
István Bocskay, rebel and prince of Transylvania, was reputedly poisoned.
Demetrius I (False Demetrius), (an imposter), possibly Yury Otrepyev, was installed as ruler of Russia by the army, but later slain as a charlatan by Vasily Shuysky, who became czar.
1610
Demetrius II, ruler of Russia, was murdered.
Demetrius III, ruler of Russia and purported son of Demetrius II, was slain.
May 14: Henry IV (Henry of Navarre), king of France, was stabbed to death in Paris by religious zealot François Ravaillac, who was tortured to death.
1613
Gabriel Bathory (Bathori), prince of Transylvania, was assassinated because of his brutality.
Demetrius IV, ruler of Russia and purported son of Demetrius II, was put to death.
1617
April: D'Ancre, Marquis Concino Concini (Maréchal D'Ancre), marshal of Ancre, and prime minister of France, was stabbed to death by Vitry, a royal guardsman, in Paris. Vitry was acting at the direction of King Louis XIII and the Duke of Luynes.
1620
T'ai-ch'ang, Ming emperor of China, was probably assassinated by members of his court with poison.
1628
Aug. 23: George Villiers, English duke of Buckingham, was stabbed to death by John Felton, a former navy officer who had been turned down by Villiers for a captain's post.
1632
Gustavus II Adolph (Adolphus), king of Sweden, may have been slain by Francis Albert, duke of Lauenburg.
1634
February: Albrecht Eusebius Wenzel von Wallenstein, duke of Friedland and Austrian general, was stabbed to death in Eger, Bohemia, by Captain Walter Devereaux and other Scottish and Irish officers.
1635
Fakhr ad-Din II, leader of Lebanon, lost to the Ottomans, and was apprehended and put to death by them.
1643
Miantonomo, U.S. Indian chief, was murdered by Uncas, a chief of the Mahicans.
1646
Chu Yü-chien, Ming emperor, was caught and murdered by Ch'ing troops.
1648
Ibrahim, sultan of the Ottoman Empire, was overthrown in a Janissary revolt and killed.
1649
Isaac Dorislaus, Dutch-English statesman, was slain.
1657
Nov. 10: Giovanni Monaldeschi, marchese of Italy, fell from the graces of Queen Christina of Sweden, who ordered his death.
1660
Thomas Harrison, member of British Parliament, was put in prison, and after the Restoration, he was put to death.
1662
Chu Yu-lang, self-proclaimed Chinese emperor, escaped to Burma, but was apprehended and slain by Ch'ing troops.
1670
Henrietta Anne, duchess d'Orléans, may have been poisoned on the orders of her husband, Philippe, duc d'Orléans.
1672
Aug. 20: Jan and Cornelius De Witt, heads of the Dutch republican party, were killed by a mob at The Hague.
1678
Charles II, king of England, was the target of the purported Popish Plot conspirators.

1679
May 3: Archbishop Sharpe was slain during the religious persecutions perpetrated by Lauderdale.
1685
Charles II, king of England and Ireland, was the target of an unsuccessful attempt on his life by conspirators in the Rye House Plot.
1688
Constantine Phaulkon, Greek chief minister of Siam, helped open the country to outsiders, but he was put to death by General Bedraja, who opposed foreign influences in Siam.
1689
Marie Louise d'Orleans, queen of Spain, may have been poisoned.
1695
William III, king of England, was the target of an unsuccessful attempt on his life by conspirators including Sir John Fenwick.
1696
William III, king of England, was the target of conspirators in Sir George Barclay's unsuccessful plot, including Robert Charnock and Sir John Fenwick, who were later executed.
1707
Melchoir Rakovsky, a Hungarian nobleman, led a rebellion against Prince Rakoczy, whose adherents later slashed the nobleman to death at Onod.
1709
Robert Harley, British nobleman and statesman, was the target of an unsuccessful assassination attempt by a French spy.
1716
Banda Singh Bahadur (AKA: Lachman Das, Lachman Dev, Madho Das), Sikh military chief, was caught and put to death by torture.
Sir James Radcliffe (Radclyffe), British noble, third earl of Derwentwater, helped incite Stuart revolt and was put in prison and decapitated.
1718
Dec. 11: Charles XII, king of Sweden, was shot to death at Friedrichshall.
1726
Shah Sultan Husayn, emperor of Persia, was ousted, put to death, and his son, Tahmasp II became emperor.
1730
Patrona Halil (Khalil), Turkish rebel, headed insurrection and was murdered.
1757
Louis XV, king of France, was the target of an assassination attempt at Versailles, Fr., by Robert Francois Damiens, who was tortured and executed.
1758
Joseph I (Joseph Emanuel, José Manuel), king of Portugal, was the target of gunmen on two occasions, but the assassins were unsuccessful.
1759
Alamgir II (Aziz-ud-Din Alamgir), Mughal emperor of India, was killed at the direction of the vizier, Imad ul-Mulk.
1762
July 17: Peter III, czar of Russia, was ousted July 8, 1762, by nobles conspiring with his wife, Catherine the Great, who succeeded him. Peter was strangled to death at St. Petersburg by Alexis Aleksei Orlov, the brother of Catherine's lover.
1774
Binnya Dala, sovereign of Mon domain of Lower Burma, was conquered by Alaungpaya and slain.
1782
Alexander, Russian prince and son of Peter the Great, was imprisoned and thought to have been poisoned, possibly on his father's orders.
1784
Maung Maung, ruler of Burma, was overthrown by a relative, Bodawpaya, and assassinated.
1786
George III, king of England, was stabbed by Margaret Nicolson, a deranged woman, at the entrance of Saint James Palace in an attempt on the king's life.
1792
Comte Stanislas Marie Adélaide de Clermont-Tonnerre, French noble, was slain by a mob in Paris.
Marie-Thérèse-Louise de Lamballe (nee Savoié-Carignan), princesse de Lamballe, was killed by a crowd after she refused to denounce the royalty.
Mar. 16: Gustavus III, king of Sweden, was shot in the back at a masked ball by Jacob J. Anckarström.
1793
Jeanne du Barry (Comtesse du Barry, nee Bécn), member of the French court and mistress of Louis XV, was condemned by the Revolutionary Tribunal and guillotined.
Nicolas-Jean Hugou de Bassville, diplomat of France, was killed in an anti-French protest in Rome.
Louis-Michel Lepeletier de Saint-Fargeau, a politician of France, was slain.
July 13: Jean-Paul Marat, French politician and revolutionary, was stabbed to death in his bathtub by Marie-Anne-Charlotte Corday d'Armont, who was executed days later.
1794
Apr. 5: Camille Desmoulins (Lucie-Simplice-Camille-Benoit Desmoulins), a rebel, was put to death with fourteen others, and his wife was guillotined on Apr. 13.
1798
Charles Louis d'Erlach, Swiss general in chief of Bernese army, suffered losses and was killed by his own forces.
1799
Apr. 28: Three French ambassadors, Ange Elisabeth Louis Antoine Bonnier, Claude Roberjot, and Jean Debry, were attacked at Rastadt by Hungarian calvary members. Bonnier and Roberjot were killed and Debry was injured.
1800
June 14: Jean-Baptiste Kléber, a Frenchman who served in the French and Austrian military, was killed by an Egyptian extremist.
Dec. 24: Napoleon I (Napoléon Bonaparte), emperor of France, survived a bombing attempt on his life in the Jacobin plot. The ruler survived, but thirteen people were killed and 130 Jacobins were deported.
1801
Mar. 23: Paul I, czar of Russia, and a guard were assassinated at the fortress of Saint Michael by conspirators supported by his son, Alexander, who were not punished.
1802
Napoleon I (Napoléon Bonaparte), emperor of France, was the target of a reputed conspiracy against his life by Italian sculptor Giuseppe Ceracchi, and others, who were put to death.
1803
George III, king of England, was the target of an unsuccessful murder plot headed by Irishman Edward Marcus Despard, who was sentenced to be hanged, drawn, and quartered with six others.
1804
February: Georges Cadoudal, a French rebel, conspired with Charles Pichegru, a French general, to kill the first consul. Cadoudal was guillotined, and Pichegru was sent to prison, where he was later strangled.
1806
Jean-Jacques Dessalines (Jacques I), emperor of Haiti, seized land belonging to whites and urged the slaughtering of whites. He was killed by Henri Christophe and Alexandre Sabès Pétion.
1808
Mustafa IV, sultan of the Ottoman empire, was overthrown and killed by agents of his brother, Mahmud II.
1809
Napoleon I (Napoleon Bonaparte), emperor of France, survived an assassination attempt by Fredrich Staps, who tried to stab the ruler to death in Vienna, Aust.
1810
Andreas Hofer, Tyrolese rebel, lost to Bavarian and French forces, and was caught and put to death.
1811
Miguel Hidalgo y Costilla, Mexican rebel, lost to Spanish troops led by Félix Calleja, and was caught and shot to death.
1812
May 11: Spencer Perceval, prime minister of England, made banknotes legal tender and afterward, he was murdered by John Bellingham, a broker who went bankrupt and blamed Perceval. Bellingham was hanged.
1815
Guillaume-Marie-Anne Brune, general and marshal of France, was slain at Avignon, Fr., during the White Terror by royalist crowds.
1817
Karageorge (Kara George, Karadjordje, Czerny Djordje), Serbian liberator, was assassinated, reputedly at the direction of the leader of the Obrenovich family.
1819
Mar. 23: August Friedrich Ferdinand von Kotzebue, German writer and dramatist, was murdered in Mannheim, Ger., by student Karl Ludwig Sand because the author had criticized the Burschenschaft political movement.
1820
King George IV's ministers were the targets of assassins in the unsuccessful Cato Street Conspiracy led by Arthur Thistlewood, who was executed with four others.
Charles Ferdinand de Bourbon, duc de Berry, was a French prince killed in Paris.
1821
José Miguel Carrera, rebel of Chile, tried to incite a revolt in Chile, but was apprehended and put to death at Mendoza.
May 5: Napoleon I (Napoléon Bonaparte), died in captivity on the island of St. Helena where he was a prisoner of the British, whom some speculate slowly poisoned him to death.
1822
Ali Pasa (The Lion of Janina), Turkish bandit and pasha, killed at the direction of Sultan Mahmud II.
1824
Agustin de Iturbide (Agustin I), emperor of Mexico, forced to step down by rebels, fled the country, but later came back and was caught and shot to death.
1828
Manuel Dorrego, governor of Buenos Aires, was overthrown and assassinated by insurgents backing General Juan Lavalle.

Shaka (Chaka, Tshaka), chief of the Zulus, went mad in 1827 before he was slain by his half-brothers.
1830
José Maria Córdoba, a Columbian general, was killed by members of a conspiracy.
Antonio José de Sucre, Venezuelan general and president of Upper Peru region, was killed.
1831
Vicente Guerrero, president of Mexico, was deposed by insurrectionists under Anastasio Bustamante, and shot to death.
Oct. 9: Ioánnis Antónios Kapodistrias (Johannes Antonius Capodistrias), provisional president of Greece, was slain.
1835
Jan. 30: Andrew Jackson, president of the U.S., was the target of an attempted assassination by Richard Lawrence, who shot at the president in the Capitol because he thought the president was destroying the country. Never tried, Lawrence was deemed insane and institutionalized.
July 28: Louis Philippe, king of France, was the target of an unsuccessful assassination attempt.
1837
Diego José Victor Portales, chief minister of Chile, was despised for his oppressive policies, and murdered.
1838
Pieter Retief (Piet), head of Boers in South Africa and governor and chief of the Great Trek, was put to death by Dingane, Zulu king.
1840
June 10: Victoria (Alexandrina Victoria), queen of England, was the target of a failed shooting attempt on her life by Edward Oxford, who was later declared insane.
1841
Sir William Hay Macnaghten, minister to the court at Kabul, Afg., wanted Shah Shoja as ruler and was slain by suspicious Afghans.
1842
Shah Shoja (Shah Shuja), king of Afghanistan, was murdered by supporters of Dost Mohammed.
May 30: Victoria (Alexandrina Victoria), queen of England, was the target of a failed attempt on her life by John Francis, who was transported for life.
July 3: Victoria (Alexandrina Victoria), queen of England, was the target of a failed assassination attempt by John William Bean, who was sent to prison.
1843
Jan. 20: Edward Drummond, secretary to British prime minister Robert Peel, was murdered by Daniel M'Naghten, who intended to kill Peel. M'Naghten was committed to an asylum.
1844
June 27: Joseph Smith, head of the Mormon Church, was murdered at night in Carthage, Ill., by a mob.
1845
Braulio Carrillo, chief justice of the supreme court and president of Costa Rica, was overthrown in 1841 and later murdered.
James Jesse Strang (Jessie James), founded the Strangite religious group and was murdered by two of his ex-followers.
1848
June: Denis Auguste Affre, archbishop of Paris, and General Bréa were killed by rebels in the Revolution of 1848.
November: Pellegrino Rossi, Italian count and prime minister of Papal States under Pius IX, was murdered.
1849
Lajos Batthyány, premier of ministry of Hungary, was apprehended and put to death by Austrians.
May 19: Victoria (Alexandrina Victoria), queen of England, was the target of a thwarted assassination attempt by William Hamilton, an Irishman who was transported.
1850
May 27: Victoria (Alexandrina Victoria), queen of England, survived an assassination attempt by Robert Pate, an ex-army officer who was transported.
1852
Isabella II, queen of Spain, was the target of an attempted assassination by a fanatical priest.
1854
Abbas I, pasha of Egypt, murdered by slaves.
1856
Charles Sumner, U.S. senator from Massachusetts, was nearly beaten to death with a cane in the Senate chamber in Washington, D.C., by South Carolina Congressman Preston Brooks because of an antislavery speech by Sumner.
1857
Jan. 3: Marie-Dominique-Auguste Sibour, archbishop of Paris, was stabbed to death by Jean-Louis Verger, a fanatical priest who challenged the Immaculate Conception of Mary, a new Catholic idea.
1858
Jan. 14: Napoleon III, Charles Louis Napoleon Bonaparte (Carbonnaro) was riding in a carriage when revolutionaries under Count Felice Orsini tried unsuccessfully to bomb the vehicle. However, eight people were killed and 156 injured. Orsini was executed, and the other revolutionaries were exiled or put in prison.
1860
Danilo I, prince and ruler of Montenegro, was assassinated.
Mar. 23: Ii Naosuke (AKA: Ii Kamon-no-kami), became prime minister of Japan without authorization, signed pacts with several countries, and was slain by conspirators who disagreed with his policies.
1861
William I, king of Prussia and emperor of Germany, survived an attempt on his life when Oscar Becker of Odessa shot at him, grazing his sleeve.
1862
Julio Arboleda, president of Columbia, was assassinated.
Santos Guardiola, president of the Honduras, was murdered.
1864
Tamechika Okada, painter and Japanese courtier, was fraudulently denounced as supporting the shogunate and murdered.
Shozan Sakuma (Sakuma Zozen), Japanese intellectual who welcomed Westernization, was killed by Japanese samurai patriots.
1865
Apr. 14: Abraham Lincoln, president of the U.S., was shot to death by John Wilkes Booth at Ford's Theater in Washington, D.C. Lincoln died on Apr. 15. Booth was reputedly tracked down and killed trying to escape. Four conspirators were hanged and more were sent to prison.
Apr. 14: William H. Seward, U.S. secretary of state, was lying disabled in bed in his Washington, D.C., home when he was attacked by Lewis Paine and David Herold, conspirators in the Lincoln assassination plot. Seward survived and Paine was later hanged.
1866
Alexander II, czar of Russia, was the target of a failed attempt on his life.
Manuel Isidoro Belzú, president and general of Bolivia, was murdered.
1867
G.W. Ashburn, delegate to the Georgia Constitutional Convention, was fatally shot by unknown assailants. Ten leading citizens were implicated.
Almon Case, a state senator, was fatally shot by Frank Farris, a guerilla chief opposed to the Union.
H.W. Fowler, assistant collector of revenues for Texas, was shot dead by D.B. Bonfoey.
L. Harris Hiscox, delegate to the New York Constitutional Convention, was shot dead in New York by M. Cole in a matter concerning Cole's wife.
J.W.C. Horne, a Georgia judge, was shot to death by an unidentified black man.
Ryoma Sakamoto, Japanese rebel, planned to oust the shogun, but was murdered.
John P. Slough, chief justice of the New Mexico Territory, was shot to death by Captain William L. Rynerson, who tried to effect Slough's recall.
June 19: Maximilian (Ferdinand Maximilian Joseph), archduke of Austria and emperor of Mexico, suffered a loss to Juárez at Querétaro where he was executed with Tomás Mejia, a Mexican general.
1868
Samuel W. Beall, ex-lieutenant governor of Wisconsin, assaulted George M. Pinney during a dispute concerning some articles that Pinney had written. Pinney fatally shot Beall in Montana. He was tried and acquitted on the grounds of self-defense.
V. Chase, a Louisiana state judge who supported the Union, was fatally shot by a group of unidentified former Confederates.
Venancio Flores, president of Uruguay, resigned and was slain four days later.
Robert Gray, a Louisiana justice, was shot dead by unknown assailants during the Reformation of the South.
James Hinds, Republican Representative of Arkansas, was shot dead by George M. Clark, secretary of the Democratic Committee, who contended that he was drunk at the time of the murder.
Thomas D'Arcy McGee, a member of the Canadian Parliament, was murdered at Ottawa, most likely because he was opposed to the Fenian attack.
Michael (Mihailo III Obrenovic), prince of Serbia, was murdered.
B. Saulet, sheriff of Caddo Parish, La., was shot to death by unknown assailants.
Mar. 12: Alfred, prince and duke of Edinburgh, was the target of a failed assassination attempt in a Sydney, Aus., suburb by an Irishman, O'Farrell, who was put to death.
1869
Benjamin Ayers, Georgia state legislator, was fatally shot by L. Wilson.
M. McConnel, Illinois state senator, was shot to death by unknown assailants following a dispute concerning reputed property rights.
I. Musajiro, Japanese defense minister, was slain in Japan.
1870
Gaylord Clark, a district judge in Texas, was fatally shot by Frank Williams, a rival who wanted Clark's job.
A.P. Crittenden, a California state judge, was fatally shot by his mistress, Laura D. Fair.
William S. Lincoln, New York state representative, survived an attack in Maryland by Joseph Segar, who beat him with a cane, intending to kill him. Segar had lost his seat as representative.
Ma Hsin-i, prominent Chinese official, was stabbed to death by Chang Wen-hsiang.
John W. Stevens, North Carolina Republican state senator, was stabbed

and hanged by local Democratic Party members.
December: Juan Prim y Prats, prime minister of Spain, was assassinated when he was leaving government buildings in Madrid, Spain. The unidentified assassin avoided capture.

1871
Georges Darboy, archbishop of Paris and senator, was apprehended and shot to death by Communards.
Alden McLaughlin, Texas Customs Inspector, was shot to death by unidentified smugglers.

1872
José Burgos, a Catholic priest in the Philippines, was murdered after soldiers revolted at Cavite, Phil. He became a martyr for the nationalists.
Lord Mayo, viceroy of India, was murdered by Shere Ali.
Agustin Morales, president of Bolivia, was slain.
Feb. 28: Victoria (Alexandrina Victoria), queen of England, survived an attempt on her life by dim-witted Arthur O'Connor.

1873
T.S. Crawford, a Louisiana district county judge, and Arthur H. Harris, a district attorney for Monroe County, La., were shot to death during an ambush. Members of the Tom Wayne gang were suspected to be the attackers.
H.P. Farrow, U.S. district attorney in Georgia, was injured after he was clubbed by unidentified assailants, suspected to be five defendants he had been prosecuting in 1873.
William Pitt Kellog, governor of Louisiana, was voted into office after an election that almost resulted in rebellion. Kellog was wounded by gunshot, but survived the attack by Melvin H. Cohen and others who challenged the election.
Edwin S. McCook, secretary of the Territory of Dakota, was shot to death in the Dakota Territory by P.P. Wintermute over a dispute concerning railroad bonds.
Samuel Clark Pomeroy, former U.S. senator from Kansas, was shot and injured in Washington, D.C., by M.F. Conway, another Kansas politician.

1874
James O'Brien, former state senator for New York, was assaulted after a political dispute by Tammany members, including Richard "Boss" Croker, John Sheridan, Henry Hickey, and George Hickey, who unsuccessfully tried to shoot him in New York.

1875
V. Belden, an ex-parish judge in Louisiana, was shot to death by M. Sherburn, a judge.
Gabriel Garcia Moreno, president of Ecuador, was murdered.
E.G. Johnson, deputy collector of internal revenue and Florida state legislator, was fatally shot by unknown assailants.
Daniel O'Connell, New York City alderman, was threatened by John T. Cox.
G.A. Roderty, tax collector of Grant Parish, La., was shot to death by former sheriff, John B. McCoy.
May: The French and German consuls in Salonica, Gr., were slain.

1876
Abdulaziz (Abdulaziz Oglu Mahumud II), sultan of the Ottoman Empire, was overthrown and possibly murdered.
Hussein Avni Pasha, general and grand vizier of Turkey, was murdered.

1877
Stephen B. Packard, governor of Louisiana, was shot and injured by W.H. Weldon, a member of a group disputing Packard's election to office.

1878
General A. Mezentseff, chief of the Russian secret police, was assassinated by Sergei Kravchinsky in St. Petersburg, Rus.
Toshimichi Okubo, Japanese prime minister, was slain by samurai supporters of insurgent Takamori Saigo.
General Fyodor Fyodorovich Trepov, chief of the St. Petersburg police, was shot and injured in Russia by revolutionary Vera Zasulich, who was acquitted.
May 11: William I, king of Prussia and emperor of Germany, was the target of Hodel, who shot at him four times, but missed.
June 2: William I, king of Prussia and emperor of Germany, was injured in Berlin when Dr. Karl Noberling shot him. The king survived.
Sept. 7: Mehemet Ali Pasha (Karl Detroit), a German native who became a Turkish general, was slain by rebels in Albania.

1879
Prince M. Kropotkin, a Russian general, governor of Kharkov, and relative of rebel Peter Kropotkin, was murdered at Kharkov, Rus.
April: Alexander II, czar of Russia, was the target of a failed attempt on his life.
November: Alexander II, czar of Russia, was the target of an unsuccessful attempt on his life near Livadia.

1881
C. Smith, Tennessee state senator, was shot and injured during a political dispute by John J. Vertress.
Mar. 13: Alexander II (Aleksander Nikolayevich), czar of Russia, was assassinated by Will of the People, an extremist group who planted a bomb in St. Petersburg.
July 2: James Abram Garfield, president of the U.S., was fatally shot by Charles J. Guiteau, a lunatic who had sought a political appointment. Garfield died on Sept. 19, 1881 and Guiteau was hanged on June 30, 1882.

1882
Mar. 2: Victoria (Alexandrina Victoria), queen of England, was the target of a failed assassination attempt by Roderick McLean, who was found insane.
May 6: Lord Frederick Charles Cavendish, chief secretary for Ireland, and Thomas Henry Burke, undersecretary for Ireland, were shot to death in Phoenix Park in Dublin, Ire., by members of the Invincibles, a clandestine Irish political organization.

1885
S. Arinori, minister of education of Japan, was slain because of his liberal opinions.
John B. Bowman, former mayor of East St. Louis, Ill., was fatally shot by unknown assailants.

1887
Mar. 13: Alexander III, Russian czar, was the target of an assassination plot during a trip to St. Petersburg. Some of the St. Petersburg Nihilist conspirators arrested were hanged and others were sent to prison.

1889
Stephen J. Field, California Supreme Court judge, survived an attack by David S. Terry during an argument about a legal matter.
W.L. Pierce, a superior judge of San Diego, Calif., ruled unfavorably in a case affecting W.S. Clendennin, who shot and injured the judge.
Aug. 14: David S. Terry, a California judge, was sitting in a restaurant in Lathrop, Calif., about to assault Supreme Court Judge Stephen Field, when U.S. deputy marshal David Neagle, Field's guard, shot Terry to death. Neagle was not charged.

1890
G. Menendez, former president of El Salvador, was slain.
Sitting Bull (Tatanka Iyotake), chief of the Sioux, was apprehended and shot to death by Indian watchmen.
William P. Taulbee, former U.S. Representative from Kentucky, was shot to death in Washington, D.C., by Charles E. Kincaide.

1892
R.D. McCotter, North Carolina state senator, was shot to death by unknown attackers, suspected to be over a personal matter.

1893
Henry S. Tyler, mayor of Louisville, Ky., survived an assault by P.J. Schwartz, who did not want the city limits to reach his property.
Oct. 28: After answering the door of his mansion, Carter H. Harrison, Sr., mayor of Chicago, Ill., was shot dead on his doorstep by Patrick Eugene Prendergast, a malcontent who sought office.
Nov. 13: Ambassador Georgevitch, Serbian diplomat to Paris was stabbed to death. A man who turned himself in as the culprit signed a note as Lély Lauthier.

1894
Hilarión Daza (Hilarión Grosolé), general and president of Bolivia, was ousted and fled the country, but he went back to Bolivia where he was slain by a crowd.
June 24: Marie François Sadi Carnot, president of France, was riding in a carriage in Lyons, Fr., when Italian anarchist Santo Geronimo Caserio stabbed him to death. Caserio was beheaded on Aug. 16 of the same year.

1895
July 15: Stefan Nikolov Stambolov (Stambouloff), former premier of Bulgaria, was slain.

1896
Colonel Albert Jennings Fountain, ex-state legislator in New Mexico Territory, was shot dead by unknown assailants during a dispute concerning land.
May 1: Nasr-ed-Din (Nasiruddin Shah), king of Persia, was killed.

1898
José Maria Reina Barrios, president of Guatemala, was assassinated.
Sept. 10: Elizabeth (Elisabeth Amalie Eugenie), empress of Austro-Hungary, queen of Hungary, and a member of the Hapsburg dynasty, was murdered in Geneva, Switz., by an Italian anarchist.

1900
Klemens von Ketteler, German minister to Mexico and Peking, was killed in the Boxer Rebellion by a Chinese.
William II (Friedrich Wilheim Viktor Albert), emperor of Germany and king of Prussia, was the target of Frau Schnapka, who threw a hatchet at him.
Jan. 30: William Goebel, governor of Kentucky, was shot dead by Caleb Powers, who challenged Goebel's election.
July 29: Humbert I (Umberto I), king of Italy, was fatally shot at Monza by Gaetano Bresci, an anarchist who had traveled from Patterson, N.J., to carry out the assassination.

1901
Konstantin Petrovich Pobedonostev, chief procurator of the Holy Synod and former tutor to the czar, was attacked for the fifth time in 1901 and injured.
William II (Friedrich Wilheim Viktor Albert), emperor of Germany and king of Prussia, survived an attempt on his life by a Bremen shipyard worker.
Feb. 27: Nicholai Parlovich Bogolepov, minister of education in Russia, was slain by a student who had been expelled.
Sept. 6: William McKinley, president of the U.S., was fatally wounded in Buffalo, N.Y., by Leon F. Czolgosz, an anarchist. McKinley died on Sept. 14, and Czolgosz was executed on Oct. 29.

Sept. 28: Antonio Maggio, notorious anarchist, was apprehended on charges of conspiracy to kill state officials in Santa Fe, N.M.

1902

M. Kanchev, minister of Bulgarian cabinet, was slain.

Prince I.M. Obolensky, governor of Kharkov, Pol. survived two assaults.

Dimitri F. Trepov, police chief of Moscow, Rus., survived three attacks.

V. Wahl, military governor of Vilna, was injured by Lithuanian patriots.

Apr. 15: Dimitri Sergeevich Sipiagin, minister of interior for Russia, was murdered in St. Petersburg, Rus., by a student, S.V. Balmashov.

1903

N.M. Bogdanovich, governor of Ufa, was murdered in Kiev, Rus., by a Social Revolutionary.

June 11: Alexander I (Aleksandar Obrenovic or Alexander Obrenovich), king of Serbia, and his queen, Draga, were assassinated at the palace in Belgrade in their bedroom quarters by army officers of Black Hand, a rebel group under "Colonel Apis," Dragutin Dimitriyevitch.

1904

Nikolai Ivanovich Bobrikov, a Russian general and brutal governor general of Finland, was assassinated by a nationalist Finnish student who committed suicide.

M. Bogoslausky, governor of the Caucasus, was killed by separatists.

July 28: Vyacheslav Konstantinovich Plehve (Wenzel von Plehwe), minister of the interior for Russia during an oppressive administration, was killed in St. Petersburg, Rus., by a bomb.

1905

The chief of police of Warsaw, Pol., was the target of an unsuccessful attempt on his life by two radicals, one of whom was executed.

Five Chinese ministers were the targets of a bombing attempt by Wu Yueh, who died when the bomb exploded. None of the ministers were hurt.

Theódoros Dhiliyiánnis (Diliyiánnis, Deligiánnis), prime minister of Greece, fought and ceded valued land to Turkey before he was slain.

Prof. Mikhail Ia. Gertsenstein, a member of the Russian Duma, was murdered by an anti-Semitic extremist.

Abdul Hamid, sultan of the Ottoman Empire, was the target of a failed attempt on his life by Armenian insurgents.

Pavel Andreevich Shuralov, prefect of police in Moscow, was slain by revolutionaries.

E. Soisalon-Soininen, procurator (attorney general) of Finland, was slain by a radical.

Frank Steunenberg, ex-governor of Idaho, died when his Caldwell, Idaho, home blew up in an explosion from dynamite planted by labor terrorist Harry Orchard, who was sent to prison for life.

Peter Arkadevich Stolypin, premier of Russia, was the target of unsuccessful assassins numerous times, including a bombing of his villa when thirty-two of his guests died.

Feb. 17: Alexandrovich (Grand Duke Sergei), governor general of Moscow, and the uncle of Czar Nicholas II, was murdered by a bomb hurled by Ivan Kalayev.

1906

Polish governor-general Skallon was the target of a failed assassination attempt in Warsaw.

May 31: Alphonso XIII, king of Spain, and his bride, Victoria, were returning from their wedding when a bomb exploded, missing the royal couple, but wounding and killing members of the procession and spectators.

1907

Amin-es-Sultan, premier of Persia, was stabbed to death by a banker who was a religious fanatic.

En-ling, Manchu governor of Chekiang, was killed by Hsu Hsi-lin, an insurgent leader who was executed.

Dimiter Petkov, minister of the Bulgarian cabinet, was murdered.

1908

John F. Fort, governor of New Jersey, was the target of unidentified assailants, reportedly angry with enforcement of liquor laws, who tried to kill him with a bomb.

Kuanghsu (Kwang Su), Chinese emperor, was thought to have committed suicide or to have been slain at the command of Tz'u-hsi, dowager empress.

Andreas Potocki, Polish nobleman and Hapsburg governor of Polish Galicia, was murdered.

Feb. 1: Carlos I (Charles I), king of Portugal, and his son, Crown Prince Luis, were riding in a carriage in Lisbon, Port., when a crowd of insurgents attacked the carriage and the two members of the royal family were fatally shot.

1909

June 26: A major general in the Swedish Marines was shot to death in Stockholm by anarchist Hjalmar Wang, who committed suicide.

July 1: Sir William Hutt Curzon Wylie, former British administrator in India, and a bystander were shot dead by Madar Lal Dhingra because he opposed British presence in India. He was hanged Aug. 17.

Oct. 24: Ito Hirobumi, prince and prime minister of Japan, was assassinated in Harbin, China, by a Korean nationalist.

1910

Butros Ghali Pasha, prime minister of Egypt, was slain by Egyptian nationalists who feared the leader would let foreigners have control of the Suez Canal.

Prince Tsai-feng, Chinese regent, was the target of an unsuccessful assassination attempt by anarchist Wang Ching-wei.

Aug. 6: William Jay Gaynor, mayor of New York City, was wounded by gunfire in New York by John J. Gallagher, a city employee who was angry because he was fired and because of Gaynor's trip to Europe.

Oct. 1: Twenty-one employees of the *Los Angeles Times* were killed by a bomb planted by union supporters in the building housing the *Times*, which was owned by Harrison Gray Otis, a union critic.

1911

Two Manchu provincial authorities, Feng-shan and Fu-ch'i, were slain in China.

Peter Arkadevich Stolypin, premier of Russia, was at the Kiev opera when he was slain by Mordka Bogrov, a police spy who was actually a Bolshevik.

1912

Charles Hardinge, first baron Haardinge of Penshurst, viceroy of India, was the target of an unsuccessful assassination attempt.

Jan. 26: Liang-pi, leader of the Manchu Court, disagreed with other Chinese leaders who wanted a child emperor to abdicate, and was slain by P'eng Chia-chen.

Oct. 14: Theodore Roosevelt, president of the U.S., was shot and injured at a political rally in Milwaukee, Wis., by John Schrank, who claimed the assassinated President McKinley had directed him to avenge his death. Schrank was later pronounced insane.

Nov. 12: Jose Canalejas y Mendez, a Spanish politician, was assassinated by anarchists in Madrid, Spain.

1913

Nazim Pasha, minister of war of Turkey, was slain in a conspiracy led by Enver Pasha.

B.P. Windsor, mayor of Mt. Auburn, Ill., was fatally shot by Fay D. State during a dispute about a political editorial.

Feb. 19: Gustavo Madero, Mexican political leader and brother of the overthrown president of Mexico, was shot at night by agents of Victoriano Huerta.

Feb. 23: Francisco Indalecio Madero, president of Mexico, was ousted on Feb. 13, 1913, by Victoriano Huerta. Madero and Vice President Jose Pino Suárez were slain in Mexico City by Francisco Cardenas and others at the direction of Huerta.

March: Sung Chiao-jen, a cabinet member under Yüan Shih-k'ai, was killed by Yuan Shih-k'ai.

Mar. 7: Abraham Gonzalez, governor of Chihuahua, Mex., and pro-Madero politician, was murdered by Huerta military.

Mar. 18: George I, king of Greece, was murdered at Salonika, Gr.

June 11: Mahmud Sevket Pasa, grand vizier of the Ottoman Empire, was slain.

1914

Mar. 13: Gaston Calmette, editor of *Le Figaro*, was fatally shot by Haughty Henriette Caillaux, wife of the minister of finance of France, because, she said, he libeled her husband. She was acquitted.

June 28: Francis Ferdinand (Franz Ferdinand), archduke of Austria, and his wife, Countess Sophie Chotek, were fatally shot in Sarajevo, Bosnia, Yug., by Gavrilo Princip, in a Black Hand plot. Princip was sent to prison and the assassination touched off WWI.

June 28: Gregori Efimovich Rasputin, Russian monk and favorite of the court, survived an attack.

July 31: Jean-Joseph-Marie-Auguste Jaurès, French socialist leader, was slain in Paris by Raoul Villain.

1915

May 16: Joao Chagas, premier designate of Portugal, was nearly murdered by Senator Joao de Freita, who was slain by bodyguards of Chagas.

July 28: Vilbrun Guillaume Sam, president of Haiti, was ousted and slain by a mob.

1916

Ch'en Ch'i-mei, Chinese rebel against Manchus, was killed by Yuan Shin-k'ai, possibly in retaliation for an alleged assassination plot against Chang Ju-ch'eng.

Oct. 21: Count Karl von Stürgkh, prime minister of Austria-Hungary, was sitting in a Vienna, Aust., restaurant eating dinner when he was fatally shot by Freidrich Adler.

Dec. 29: Gregori Efimovich Rasputin, Russian monk and favorite of the court, was murdered the evening of Dec. 29-30 in St. Petersburg, Rus., by Prince Felix Yussoupov and other Russian noblemen. He was poisoned, stabbed, and shot that night before he finally drowned in the Neva River.

1917

Ivan Logginovich Goremykin, prime minister of Russia, was put in prison after the revolution and assassinated by the Bolsheviks at Caucasus.

Henry Cabot Lodge, U.S. senator from Massachusetts, was attacked in Washington, D.C., by A. Bannwart, Mrs. M.A. Peabody, and Rev. P.H. Drake, pacifists who were angry because Lodge supported war against Germany.

Mar. 10: Alice Wheeldon, Winnie Mason, and Alfred Mason, were convicted and sent to prison for plotting to kill David Lloyd George, prime minister of England, because they blamed him for losing WWI.

1918

Alexandra Feodorovna (Aleksandra Fyodorovna), Russian empress, was put in prison by the Bolsheviks and killed.

Nikolai Lenin (Vladimir Ilich Ulyanov), Russian dictator, was the target of a failed assassination attempt by Dora Kaplan.
Count Stephan (Istvan) Tisza, premier of Hungary, was assassinated by terrorists for backing the Centralists' ambitions of WWI.
Jan. 27: Nikolai Vladimirovich Russki, general of Russia, was slain by the Bolsheviks.
July 6: Count Wilhelm von Mirbach, German ambassador to Russia, was murdered in Moscow by gunmen.
July 12: Grand Duke Michael of Russia, was murdered at Perm, U.S.S.R.
July 16: Nicholas II, czar of Russia, and his entire family, including his son, Alexis Nikolaevich (Czarevitch Alexis), were assassinated at Ekaterinburg, Rus., by Bolsheviks at the direction of Vladimir Lenin.
July 29: F.M. Hermann von Eichhorn, a German field marshal and administrator after the Brest-Litovsk Treaty, was slain in Kiev by a rebel sailor.
Aug. 30: M.S. Uritsky, chief of the Petrograd Cheka (secret police), and high-ranking Bolshevik, was murdered in Petrograd, U.S.S.R., by L. Kenigiessev, a Social Revolutionary student.
Aug. 30: V. Volodarsky, Bolshevik and Petrograd commissar of propaganda, was slain in Moscow by Social Revolutionaries.
Nov. 12: William Frederick was the target of an unsuccessful attempt on his life in the Netherlands.
Dec. 7: Sidonio Bernardino Cardosa da Silva Paes, president of Portugal, was the target of an unsuccessful attempt on his life.
Dec. 14: Sidonio Bernardino Cardosa Paes, president of Portugal, founded a military dictatorship in 1917, and was assassinated by rebels.

1919

Radko Dmitriev (Dimitriev), Bulgarian who served in the army of the U.S.S.R., was most likely slain by the Bolsheviks.
Jan. 15: Rosa Luxemburg (Red Rosa), was a German socialist leader and joint leader of the Spartacus Party with Karl Liebknecht. During the Spartacist revolt in Germany, the two were slain in Berlin by rightist Free Corpsmen.
Jan. 18: Karl Liebknecht was slain in Germany.
Jan. 28: Nikolai Mikhailovich (Nicholas), Russian grand duke, was imprisoned by the Bolsheviks and put to death.
February: Edhard Auer, president of Bavaria, was the target of an unsuccessful assassin.
February: Kurt Eisner, president of the Bavarian Republic and a German politician, was murdered in Munich, Ger., by Lieutenant Count Arco-Valley, an officer of the German army.
Feb. 1: T.H. Wong was assassinated in Washington, D.C.
Feb. 3: Pavel Aleksandrovich (Paul Alexandrovitch), Russian grand duke, was slain in Petrograd, Rus.
Feb. 20: Habibollah Khan (Habibullah Khan), amir of Afghanistan, was murdered. Nasr Ullah Khan was jailed for complicity in the crime.
Feb. 29: Georges Clemenceau, premier of France, was the target of a failed attempt on his life.
Mar. 14: Lugan Baronorsky was murdered in Russia.
Mar. 15: Leon Trotsky (Leon Trotski, Leib or Lev Davydovich Bronstein), Communist leader of Russia, was exiled and was the target of unsuccessful assassins.
April: Otto Neuring, socialist war minister of Saxony, was slain by soldiers because of a pay cut.
Apr. 10: Emiliano Zapata, national hero and Mexican revolutionary leader, was betrayed by Colonel Jesus Guajardo. Zapata was shot to death at the hacienda of San Juan Chiameca outside Cuautla Morelos, Mex., by troops.
Apr. 19: A. Blanquet, a military officer, was killed by assassins in Mexico.
May: Radko Dimitriev, a military officer, was assassinated in Russia.
May 15: Ignacy Jan Paderewski, prime minister of Poland, was the target of unsuccessful assassins.
June 2: A. Mitchell Palmer, U.S. attorney general, was the target of a bombing attempt by an assassin who blows himself up. The incident touches off the arrest of numerous agitators nationwide.
Aug. 15: Joaquin Tinoco was the target of unsuccessful assassins in Costa Rica.
Sept. 2: Mohammed Pasha Said, prime minister of Egypt, was almost assassinated by rebels.
Sept. 4: Baron Saito was the target of an unsuccessful attempt on his life in Korea.
Oct. 8: Hugo Haase, German socialist leader, was murdered in Berlin.
Oct. 27: Ahmed Hati was murdered in Russia.
November: Alexander Hollan was killed in Hungary.
Nov. 5: Sir John Denton Pinkstone French, British viceroy of Ireland, was the target of an unsuccessful attempt on his life in Ireland.
Dec. 19: Sir John Denton Pinkstone French was the target of IRA gunmen in an ambush, but he escaped.

1920

Jesus Guajardo, a military officer, was assassinated in Mexico.
Essad Pasa (Toptani), minister of war and of interior of Albania, devised a plan to attain power after WWI, and was about to become the National Assembly king of Albania before he was slain in Paris by an Albanian.
Jan. 11: A.M. Sullivan was the target of an unsuccessful assassination attempt in Ireland.
Feb. 7: Aleksandr Vasiliyevich Kolchak, Russian admiral, was apprehended and shot by the Bolsheviks.
Mar. 20: T. MacCurtain was slain in Ireland.
May 14: T.G. Wilkinson was murdered in Ireland.
May 20: General Venustiano Carranza, president of Mexico, was shot to death at San Antonio Tlaxcalantongo by troops acting under the direction of traitor Rodolfo Herrero, a conspirator of Alvaro Obregon.
June 13: Tewfik Nessim Pasha was slain in India.
June 16: L. Wilson was assassinated in Ireland.
July 31: F. Brooke was murdered in Ireland.
Aug. 23: Abderhaman was slain in Syria.
Aug. 23: Droubi Pashda was killed in Syria.
Sept. 26: The wife of T. MacCurtain was the target of an unsuccessful attempt on her life in Ireland.
Dec. 24: Dejelal Munif Bey was murdered in Hungary.

1921

A candidate to the State legislature was slain in South Australia by a political rival, who was reportedly insane.
M. Tronkiewitz was killed in Russia.
Jan. 8: Stefan Fatzeas was assassinated in Greece.
Jan. 22: Shir Singh was slain in Germany.
Feb. 2: Captain King was the target of an unsuccessful attempt on his life in Ireland.
Feb. 3: R. Dixon was killed in Ireland.
Feb. 4: F.W. Craven was murdered in Ireland.
Feb. 7: In the battle between two Chicago political rivals, a bomb exploded at a dance, injuring a few campaign supporters.
Mar. 8: Eduardo Dato Iradier, premier of Spain, was fatally shot by an anarchist.
Mar. 10: Angel Gaxiola was murdered in Mexico.
Mar. 15: Mehmet Talaat Pasha (Talaat Bey), grand vizier of Turkey, was killed by an Armenian student in Germany.
Apr. 3: F. Quinones was slain in Cuba.
Apr. 14: Sir A. Vicars was assassinated in Ireland.
May 8: M. Gonzales was the target of an unsuccessful assassination attempt in Mexico.
May 8: J. Moguel was murdered in Mexico.
June: Fernando Viscaino, a military officer, was assassinated in Mexico.
June 10: Karl Gaveis, a political leader of Bavaria, was shot dead outside of his Munich, Ger., home.
July 14: Józef Klemens Pilsudski, Polish general, was the target of an unsuccessful attempt on his life in Poland.
July 22: Milorad Draskovic, minister of interior of Yugoslavia, was murdered by a Bosnian Communist.
Aug. 10: J.A. Robles, a military officer, was killed in Mexico.
Aug. 19: L.H. Ball, U.S. senator, was the target of an unsuccessful assassination attempt in Washington, D.C.
Sept. 26: Count J. Andressy Rakovsky was the target of a failed attempt on his life in Hungary.
Sept. 27: Józef Klemens Pilsudski, general and premier of Poland, was the target of an unsuccessful assassination attempt in Poland.
Oct. 21: Antonio Granjo, former prime minister of Portugal, was slain along with four others by military and civilian vigilantes.
Oct. 21: Machado Dos Santos was assassinated in Portugal.
Oct. 21: Carlos Silva was murdered in Portugal.
Oct. 21: Carlos Mara was killed in Portugal.
Oct. 23: Alexander Dimitroff was slain in Bulgaria.
Oct. 26: Matthias Erzberger, chief of the leftist Center Party and a German statesmen, was shot dead at a Black Forest retreat by two former army officers.
Nov. 4: Takashi Hara (Kei Hara), prime minister of Japan, was at the Tokyo Railroad Station and ready to get on a train when he was stabbed to death by Nakaoka Konichi, a young rightist, who was later sent to prison.
Nov. 20: O. Helst was the target of an unsuccessful attempt on his life in Illinois.
Nov. 21: Dr. Zmable Jones was murdered in Argentina.
Dec. 13: P. Meade was the target of an unsuccessful assassination attempt in Ireland.

1922

Juan Carrasco was killed in Mexico.
Francisco Murguia was slain in Mexico.
Gabrjel Narutowicz, served as Poland's president only a few days before he was assassinated by an insane man.
Ahmed Djemal Pasha, a Turkish general, was murdered.
Francisco Pancho Villa (Doreteo Arango), bandit, revolutionary leader and general of Mexico, was the target of a failed attempt on his life in Mexico.
February: Antonio Pruneda was murdered in Mexico.
February: Antonio Ruiz was slain in Mexico.
Feb. 15: Heikki Ritavouri, minister of the interior for Finland, was slain by a rightist extremist who disagreed with the way Ritavouri handled Red prisoners after the 1918 war.
Mar. 17: Julian Perez Lazono was killed in Spain.
Mar. 22: Tsang Hou was the target of an unsuccessful attempt on his life in France.
Mar. 22: Tcheng Loe was the target of a failed assassination attempt in France.
Mar. 29: Paul N. Milukoff was the target of unsuccessful assassins in Germany.

Apr. 8: Cardinal Pompilj was the target of a failed attempt on his life in Italy.
Apr. 14: P. Conner was murdered in New York.
June: Philipp Scheidemann, former prime minister of the German Republic, survived an attempt on his life in Kassel, Ger., by assailants who used prussic acid.
June 5: W. Flanagan was murdered in Ireland.
June 19: Juan F. Aragone was the target of an unsuccessful attempt on his life in Spain.
June 22: Sir Henry Wilson, who had served as military advisor during the Irish Civil War to Protestant troops in Belfast, Ire., was shot to death by Reginald Dunne and Joseph O'Sullivan, who were executed on Aug. 10, 1922.
June 24: Walter Rathenau, foreign minister of Germany, signed the Rapallo Treaty with Russia and was assassinated by rightist navy officers.
July: Lucio Blanco was slain in Mexico.
July: Candido Martinex was murdered in Mexico.
Aug. 14: Baron Udekem D'Acoz was assassinated in Belgium.
Aug. 22: Michael Collins, prime minister of Free State, Ire., and revolutionary, was shot to death by IRA members at Beal-n-Blath, Cork, Ire.
Dec. 16: Gabriel Narutowicz, president of Poland, was assassinated by anarchist Eligius Niewiadomski several days after he took office.

1923

Salvador Alvarado, a military officer, was slain in Mexico.
Rafael Buelna, a military officer, was killed in Mexico.
Enrique Estrada, a military officer, was assassinated in Mexico.
Nicola Genadiev, Bulgarian cabinet minister, was murdered.
Alois Rasin, minister of finance for Czechoslovakia, was murdered by a Communist insurgent.
Francisco Pancho Villa (Doreteo Arango), bandit, revolutionary leader and general of Mexico, was the target of a failed attempt on his life.
Jan. 11: Mohammed Fenni was the target of an unsuccessful attempt on his life in Switzerland.
Jan. 23: Marius Plateau was murdered in France.
Apr. 1: Ali Chukri Bey was slain in Turkey.
June 5: Soldevilla y Romero Card was assassinated in Spain.
June 14: Alexander Stamboliski (Alexander Stambuliski), the overthrown dictator and premier of Bulgaria, was assassinated.
July 20: Francisco Pancho Villa (Doreteo Arango), bandit, revolutionary leader and general of Mexico, was murdered with his bodyguards when they entered Parral, Mex., by gunmen under Jesus Salas Barraza.
Aug. 27: M. Dashkaloff was killed in Czechoslovakia.
Oct. 4: R. DeLeon was the target of an unsuccessful attempt on his life in Mexico.
Nov. 4: Colonel Krastitch was the target of a failed assassination attempt in Bulgaria.
Nov. 4: A. Rodriguez, a military official, was slain in Mexico.
Nov. 4: Vaslaw Vorovsky was assassinated in Switzerland.
Dec. 23: Giovanni Amendola, minister for colonies, was the target of an unsuccessful assassination attempt in Italy.
Dec. 27: When Hirohito (Showa), emperor of Japan, was Crown prince, he was the target of an unsuccessful assassin, Daisaku Namba, who was executed.

1924

Jose F. Gomez was killed in Mexico.
Robert Imbrie was murdered in Iran.
Heinz Orbis, pro-French Separatist leader, was slain by four nationalist gunmen at Speyer, Ger.
Petko Petkov, leader of the Bulgarian Agranian Party, was murdered.
Robert Young Thomas, Jr., U.S. representative from Kentucky, was attacked by a political rival, G. Baker.
Ramon Trevino was slain in Mexico.
Jan. 6: L. Duparinof was murdered in Bulgaria.
Jan. 18: Philippe Daudet was assassinated in France.
Jan. 23: Francisco Field Jurado was killed in Mexico.
Jan. 31: E. Guminger was slain in Germany.
Feb. 21: N. Buonservici was the target of an unsuccessful attempt on his life in France.
April: Manuel Dieguez, a military officer, was murdered in Mexico.
April: Alredo R. Garcia, a military officer, was killed in Mexico.
April: Cristoforo Ocampo, a military officer, was slain in Mexico.
April: Manuel Vigil Garcia was assassinated in Mexico.
Apr. 7: R.L. Coleman was murdered in Albania.
Apr. 7: G.B. Delong was slain in Albania.
May 14; Fortunato Maycotte, a military officer, was killed in Mexico.
May 30: R.P. Cicaria was killed in Spain.
May 30: Baron Saito was the target of an unsuccessful attempt on his life in Korea.
June 2: Ignatz Seipel, chancellor of Austria, was the target of a failed assassination attempt.
June 10: Giacomo Matteotti, Italian socialist politician, was against Mussolini. He was killed by Mussolini's Blackshirt Fascisti.
July 2: Israel DeHaan was slain in Palestine.
July 13: Said Zaghloul Pasha ibn Ibrahim, premier of Egypt, was the target of an unsuccessful attempt on his life.
September: The Macedonian Revolutionary Organization was responsible for several political slayings in Bulgaria.
Sept. 13: Armando Casalini, Fascist deputy, was shot dead in Rome, allegedly by Giovanni Corvi, who claimed when arrested that he wanted revenge for the death of Giacomo Matteotti, slain in June.
Sept. 16: Todor Aleksandrov, Internal Macedonia Revolutionary Organization leader, was murdered.
Oct. 6: Mario Garcia Menocal, president of Cuba, was the target of a failed attempt on his life.
Nov. 19: Sir Lee Oliver Fitzmaurice Stack, British commander of the Egyptian army, was riding in his car in Cairo, Egypt, when he was shot to death by Egyptian nationalists under Shafik Mansur, who were executed in June 1925.
December: Alejandro Greene, a military officer, was assassinated in Mexico.
December: Carlos Greene, a military officer, was killed in Mexico.
December: Fernando Segouia, a military officer, was slain in Mexico.

1925

Liao Chung-k'ai, influential Chinese member of the Kuomintang, was slain by agents of Hu Han-min.
Jan. 4: M. Selas was murdered in Cuba.
Jan. 11: Takaakira Kato, prime minister of Japan, was the target of a failed assassination attempt.
Jan. 29: Mustapha El Maraghi was the target of an unsuccessful assassination attempt in Egypt.
Feb. 14: N. Mileff was murdered in Bulgaria.
Feb. 19: T. Strachinicoff was slain in Bulgaria.
Apr. 14: Boris III, czar of Bulgaria, was the target of an assassin in Sofia, Bul.,but the attempt was unsuccessful.
Apr. 15: Gen. Kosta Georgiev, a close associate of Boris III, czar of Bulgaria, was slain by Communist terrorists in Sofia, Bul.
Apr. 15: M. Iltcheff was killed in Bulgaria.
Apr. 16: Boris III, czar of Bulgaria, attended the funeral of Gen. Georgiev and was nearly killed by a bomb explosion that demolished Saint Nedelja Cathedral in Sofia, Bul., leaving 125 dead.
Apr. 17: Alex Tsankoff, premier of Bulgaria, was the target of a failed attempt on his life.
Apr. 18: General Davidof was killed in Bulgaria.
Apr. 22: R. Yankoff was assassinated in Bulgaria.
Apr. 29: A. Boumethoka was murdered in Bulgaria.
May 2: Boris III, czar of Bulgaria, was the target of an unsuccessful attempt on his life.
May 10: Todor Panizza was assassinated in Austria.
May 17: F. Amaral was the target of a failed assassination attempt in Portugal.
May 20: Buck Kirk was slain in West Virginia.
May 25: M. Fukuda, a military officer, was the target of an unsuccessful attempt on his life in Japan.
June: Herman Helling was assassinated in Germany.
June 16: P. Mikhailoff was killed in Bulgaria.
July: Giovanni Amendola, minister for colonies, was murdered in Italy.
July 9: Hsu Sung-Chi was the target of a failed attempt on his life in China.
July 9: Wu Hon Min was the target of an unsuccessful assassination attempt in China.
July 19: H.G. Bretherton was the target of an unsuccessful attempt on his life in Mexico.
July 31: A. Kasselo was assassinated in Poland.
Aug. 3: Robert Maurer was slain in Mexico.
Aug. 23: M. Richard was the target of a failed attempt on his life in Martinique.
Sept. 5: M. Perez was murdered in Mexico.
Sept. 11: C. Cruz was killed in Mexico.
Sept. 11: Benito Mussolini, dictator of Italy, was the target of an unsuccessful assassination attempt.
Sept. 13: Carol II, future king of Rumania, was the target of a failed assassination attempt.
Oct. 4: Cavaliere Lupporini was slain in Italy.
Oct. 6: G. Benciolini was murdered in Italy.
Oct. 18: H. Barde was the target of an unsuccessful attempt on his life in Switzerland.
Oct. 30: Danoso Tsankoff was assassinated in Bulgaria.
Nov. 4: Benito Mussolini, dictator of Italy, was the target of a failed assassination attempt.
Dec. 9: Hong Chow-Ling, a military officer, was the target of an unsuccessful attempt on his life in China.
Dec. 12: Heinrich Dammers was killed in Germany.
Dec. 26: Kuo Sing-Ling, a military officer, was assassinated in China.
Dec. 31: Hsu Shu-Cheng, a military officer, was murdered in China.

1926

Todor Panitza was killed in Bulgaria.
Jan. 15: E.C. Sloat, Jr. was the target of an unsuccessful attempt on his life in New Jersey.
Apr. 4: Angel Flores was murdered in Mexico.
Apr. 8: Benito Mussolini, dictator of Italy, was the target of a failed assassination attempt.
Apr. 21: Father Gregorio Esparragoza was assassinated in Mexico.
Apr. 25: William H. McSwiggin, an Illinois state's attorney, was allegedly shot to death in machine gunfire by Al Capone, during an election. Capone was never tried for the slaying, although a dozen witnesses saw

him shoot the gun from a moving car.
May 25: Simon Petlura (Petliura; Petlyura), Ukrainian nationalist leader, was in exile in Paris where he was shot to death by Simon Schwarzbart.
June 5: C. Knight was killed in Mexico.
June 11: Gregoire Beschapely was slain in France.
June 22: Radziwill Oskilko was murdered in Poland.
June 23: A.A. Luter was the target of an unsuccessful attempt on his life in Texas.
July 7: Mordel Vincent was the target of a failed attempt on his life in Mexico.
July 7: Felton Zimmerman was slain in Cuba.
July 11: J. Yerman was murdered in Illinois.
July 17: Don R. Mellett was killed in Ohio.
Aug. 1: Bert Donaldson was assassinated in Georgia.
Aug. 5: Salustio DeLloyd was slain in Mexico.
Aug. 6: S. Dunfee was killed in Ohio.
Aug. 9: Jose Almeida was murdered in Mexico.
Aug. 9: Raymundo Violante was assassinated in Mexico.
Aug. 26: J. Pineda was slain in Mexico.
Sept. 18: Louise, Swedish princess, was the target of an unsuccessful attempt on her life in Japan.
Oct. 13: Benito Mussolini, dictator of Italy, was the target of a failed assassination attempt.
Nov. 4: Coutinho de Azevedo was the target of an unsuccessful attempt on his life in Mozambique.
Nov. 8: Jeff Stone, mayor of Culp, Ill., was shot to death by unknown assailants, suspected to be bootleggers with political ties.
Nov. 18: Marcelos Mejia was the target of a failed assassination attempt in Mexico.
Nov. 26: G.D. Dale was the target of an unsuccessful attempt on his life in Indiana.
Dec. 2: Aldo Cantoni was the target of a failed attempt on his life in Argentina.
Dec. 2: Fernando Marina was slain in Argentina.
Dec. 12: Joe Adams, mayor of West City, Ill., was shot and killed by two youths. The murder was directed by Charles Birger, a gang leader in southern Illinois who was later hanged for this crime.
Dec. 12: Philip A. Atanasoff was the target of a failed assassination attempt in Bulgaria.
Dec. 12: Slawe Ivanoff was the target of an unsuccessful attempt on his life in Bulgaria.
Dec. 24: Adolfo Diaz, president of Nicaragua, was the target of a failed assassination attempt.
Dec. 24: Swami Shradanand was killed in India.

1927

Alberto Salazar was slain in Mexico.
Wlodzimierz Zagorski, ex-chief of the Polish Air Force, was put in prison and he vanished. Some speculate he was slain by supporters of Premier Jósef Pilsudski of Poland.
Li Ta-chao, joint leader of the Chinese Communist party with Mao Tse-tung, was put to death by Chang Tso-lin.
Jan. 24: Antonio Cisneros was assassinated in Mexico.
Feb. 10: T. Hernandez was murdered in Mexico.
Feb. 20: G. Nelson was killed in Mexico.
Mar. 7: M. Ikonomoff was assassinated in Bulgaria.
Apr. 11: Ernst Kantor was the target of an unsuccessful attempt on his life in Germany.
Apr. 16: Father David Uribe was murdered in Mexico.
Apr. 20: Peter Voikoff was slain in Poland.
May 22: Archbishop Chryostomos was the target of a failed assassination attempt in Greece.
July 10: Kevin C. O'Higgins, vice president of Ireland, was slain by IRA gunmen who were never caught.
Aug. 10: L.M. Har, a military officer, was assassinated in Canada.
Aug. 10: W. Park was killed in Canada.
Sept. 5: E. Steger was the target of an unsuccessful attempt on his life in Germany.
Sept. 13: Count Carlo Nardini was slain in France.
October: Artura Lasso de la Vega, a military officer, was murdered in Mexico.
October: Norberto C. Olivera, a military officer, was assassinated in Mexico.
October: Alredo Rodriguez, a military officer, was killed in Mexico.
Oct. 3: Octavio R. Almada was slain in Mexico.
Oct. 3: Carlos B. Ariza, a military officer, was murdered in Mexico.
Oct. 3: Alonso Capetillo was slain in Mexico.
Oct. 3: Otilio Gonzalez was assassinated in Mexico.
Oct. 3: Antonio Jauregui was murdered in Mexico.
Oct. 3: Rafael Martinez de Escobar was killed in Mexico.
Oct. 3: Ernesto V. Mendez was murdered in Mexico.
Oct. 3: Enrique Monteverde was assassinated in Mexico.
Oct. 3: Augusto Pena was slain in Mexico.
Oct. 3: Daniel Peralta, a military officer, was assassinated in Mexico.
Oct. 3: Miguel A. Peralta, a military officer, was killed in Mexico.
Oct. 3: Francisco Serrano, a military officer, was slain in Mexico.
Oct. 3: Carlos A. Vidal, a military officer, was murdered in Mexico.
Oct. 3: Jose Villa Arce was assassinated in Mexico.
Oct. 5: Luis Hermosillo, a military officer, was killed in Mexico.
Oct. 6: Jose C. Moran, a military officer, was slain in Mexico.
Oct. 15: Tsena Bey was murdered in Czechoslovakia.
November: Oscar Aguilar, a military officer of Mexico, was assassinated.
Nov. 2: Mirailo Gavriloff was killed in Yugoslavia.
Nov. 2: Risto Gavriloff was murdered in Yugoslavia.
Nov. 5: Arnulfo Gomez, a military officer, was slain in Mexico.
Nov. 13: Alvaro Obregón, president of Mexico, was the target of an unsuccessful attempt on his life.

1928

Said Mohammed Pasha, prime minister of Egypt, was the target of a near-fatal attempt on his life.
Stefan Radic (Stephen Raditch), leader of the Croatian Peasant party, was assassinated on the floor of the Yugoslavian parliament by a Montenegrin separatist.
May 20: Luis Mena, a military officer, was assassinated in Nicaragua.
June 1: G. Basaritchik was killed in Yugoslavia.
June 4: Chang Tso-lin, a Chinese military leader, was aboard a train in Mukden, Manchuria, when a bomb exploded, killing him.
June 21: P. Raditch was murdered in Yugoslavia.
July 3: Ivan Jacobobovitch was slain in Rumania.
July 9: Alex Protogueroff was killed in Bulgaria.
July 15: Luis Morones was the target of a failed assassination attempt in Mexico.
July 17: Plutarco Elias Calles, president of Mexico, was the target of an unsuccessful attempt on his life.
July 17: Alvaro Obregón, a general and president of Mexico, was sitting in "La Bombita," a San Angel, Mex., cafe when he agreed to let José de Leon Toral draw his picture. Toral, who disagreed politically with Obregon, fatally shot Obregon, and was later executed.
Aug. 6: V. Ristovitch was assassinated in Yugoslavia.
Aug. 30: Luigi Patrezi was killed in Canada.
Nov. 20: G. Nanders was murdered in Yugoslavia.
Dec. 1: A. Bebi was slain in Czechoslovakia.

1929

Julio Antonio Mella was assassinated in Cuba.
Jan. 12: Herbert Hoover, U.S. president, may have been the target of an assassination plot. Jacob B. Sommers, Willis Callahan, and Thomas Mulligan were arrested in Miami on charges of conspiring against Hoover, but they were freed.
Mar. 10: Chu Yun-Fung, a military officer, was murdered in China.
Mar. 23: T. Schlegel was killed in Yugoslavia.
June 8: O.F. Aderholt was slain in North Carolina.
Aug. 22: P. Holt was murdered in Montana.
Sept. 14: J.A. Holmes was assassinated in Texas.
Sept. 15: The wife of E.M. Wiggins was killed in North Carolina.
Oct. 7: T. Krokowski was slain in Pennsylvania.
Oct. 12: Jean Galmot was murdered in French Guinea.
Nov. 2: Antonio R. Zertuche, a military officer, was the target of an unsuccessful attempt on his life in Mexico.
Nov. 25: P.H. Ashby was killed in Kentucky.
December: Sousa Filho was assassinated in Brazil.

1930

Jan. 14: Horst Wessel was slain in Germany.
February: Leon Ibarra was killed in Mexico.
February: F. Melo Viana was the target of an unsuccessful attempt on his life in Brazil.
Feb. 5: Pascual Ortiz-Rubio, president of Mexico, was the target of a failed assassination attempt.
Feb. 9: Christopher Barlow was assassinated in Nigeria.
Feb. 18: Po Ching-King was murdered in China.
Feb. 18: Wang Po-Ling was killed in China.
Feb. 19: A. Florian was slain in Czechoslovakia.
Feb. 19: Emil Kramer was assassinated in Germany.
Mar. 5: V. Poundeff was killed in Bulgaria.
Apr. 22: Ghulum Agha was the target of an unsuccessful attempt on his life in India.
Apr. 26: Augusto Bernardino Leguia y Salcedo, president of Peru, was the target of a failed assassination attempt.
May: Baron Strickland, prime minister of Malta, was the target of a failed attempt on his life. John Miller was a suspect.
May 18: Dr. Rintelen was the target of an unsuccessful attempt on his life in Austria.
May 24: Lord Strickland was the target of a failed assassination attempt in Malta.
June: Liu Huan-yen, governor of Kwangsi province of China, was shot dead outside his home. Evidence pointed to the governor's bodyguard, who confessed.
June 8: Dr. Henry Albert Von Baligand, German minister, was slain in Portugal, apparently by a man who wanted to murder a British, U.S., or German diplomat.
June 29: Giuseppe Chiesti was murdered in Albania.
July: Joao Pessoa was assassinated in Brazil.
July 22: M. Angelescu was the target of an unsuccessful attempt on his life in Rumania.
July 25: E.J. Dennis was the target of a failed assassination attempt in South Carolina.
Aug. 26: Ismail Pasha Sidky was the target of an unsuccessful assassination attempt in Egypt.

Aug. 26: Charles Tegart was the target of an unsuccessful attempt on his life in India.
Aug. 30: Eric Hobson was the target of a failed attempt on his life in India.
Aug. 30: Francis Lowman was murdered in India.
Sept. 1: M. Dabski was the target of an unsuccessful attempt on his life in Poland.
Sept. 8: Hassanand Khaneband was killed in India.
Sept. 9: R.L. Freeman was assassinated in Georgia.
Sept. 9: Max Holtz was the target of a failed attempt on his life in Germany.
Oct. 2: J.B. Jenkins was slain in Georgia.
Oct. 2: Lenox Simpson was the target of an unsuccessful attempt on his life in China.
Oct. 4: Khan Buhadan Aziz was the target of an unsuccessful assassination attempt in India.
Oct. 14: Jósef Pilsudski, general and premier of Poland, was the target of an unsuccessful attempt on his life.
Nov. 14: Yuko Hamaguchi, prime minister of Japan, was shot by Black Dragon gunman, Tomeo Sagoya. Hamaguchi died six months later in 1931 from the injuries and Sagoya was imprisoned for three years before he was pardoned by Emperor Hirohito.
Nov. 21: Said Kirkhan was assassinated in Russia.

1931

T' and Yu-lu, advisors of Chinese minister of finance Tse-ven Soong, were killed.
Jan. 1: Herbert Graf was slain in Germany.
Jan. 1: Willi Schneider was murdered in Germany.
Jan. 8: Hirohito (Showa), emperor of Japan, was the target of an unsuccessful assassin, I Pong-chang, who was later executed.
Jan. 14: S. Ali was the target of an unsuccessful attempt on his life in India.
Jan. 14: Traiiko Moriotcheto was assassinated in Bulgaria.
February: Benito Mussolini, dictator of Italy, was the target of a failed assassination attempt.
Feb. 5: A. Beritch was killed in Yugoslavia.
Feb. 18: Captain Barnes was murdered in India.
Feb. 19: Ercole Guzzi was the target of an unsuccessful attempt on his life in France.
Feb. 21: Major Topola was killed in Austria.
Feb. 21: Zog I, premier and king of Albania, was the target of an unsuccessful assassination attempt.
Feb. 25: Gerardo Machado, president of Cuba, was the target of an unsuccessful attempt on his life in New York.
Mar. 2: Munshi Lal was slain in India.
Mar. 17: E. Henning was murdered in Germany.
Apr. 1: T.H. Stern was assassinated in Iraq.
Apr. 11: Captain G.F. Heaney was killed in Burma.
Apr. 11: James Peddie was murdered in India.
May 9: W.H. Austin was slain in India.
May 14: Chanan Singh was assassinated in India.
June 9: Jawad Husain was killed in India.
July 19: N. Ruseff was slain in Bulgaria.
July 23: Sir J.E.B. Hotson was the target of a failed assassination attempt in India.
July 23: Tse-ven Soong (T.V. Soong), Chinese minister of finance, was the target of an unsuccessful attempt on his life.
July 28: R.R. Garlick was assassinated in India.
July 30: Chiang Kai-Shek, president of China, was the target of a failed attempt on his life.
Aug. 23: Tse-ven Soong (T.V. Soong), Chinese minister of finance, was the target of an unsuccessful attempt on his life.
Aug. 30: Tadeusz Holovko, in favor of friendly Polish Ukranian relations, was murdered in Poland.
Oct. 2: Ismet Inönü, prime minister of Greece, was the target of a failed attempt on his life in Greece.
Nov. 9: Hsüan T'ung, emperor of China, was the target of an unsuccessful attempt on his life.

1932

S. Barakat was the target of a failed attempt on his life in Syria.
Luis M. Sanchez Cerro, president of Peru, was the target of an unsuccessful assassination attempt.
Baron Takuma Dan, Mitsui president in Japan, was slain.
Jan. 3: Tse-ven Soong (T.V. Soong), Chinese minister of finance, was the target of a failed attempt on his life.
Jan. 8: Hirohito, emperor of Japan, was the target of an unsuccessful attempt on his life.
Jan. 9: G. Gentile was the target of a failed assassination attempt in France.
Jan. 16: F. Winkler was the target of an unsuccessful attempt on his life in Austria.
Jan. 17: Antonio Oscar de Fragosa Carmona, president of Portugal, was the target of an failed assassination attempt.
Feb. 7: Ir S. Jackson was the target of an unsuccessful attempt on his life in India.
Feb. 9: Junnosuke Inouye, minister of finance of Japan, was killed by a nationalist group opposed to his policies.
Apr. 9: Hans Luther, ambassador to the U.S., was the target of an unsuccessful attempt on his life in Germany.
Apr. 20: S. Casares Quiroga was the target of a failed attempt on his life in Spain.
May 6: Pasha Sidky was the target of an unsuccessful assassination attempt in Egypt.
May 7: Paul Doumer, president of France, was assassinated by a an anarchist from Russia.
May 15: Ki Tsuyoshi Inukai, prime minister of Japan, was slain by extremist army and navy officers in Tokyo.
May 17: Professor D. Michailoff was the target of an unsuccessful attempt on his life in Bulgaria.
June 6: Benito Mussolini, dictator of Italy, was the target of a failed attempt on his life.
June 10: Chiang Kai-Shek, president of China, was the target of an unsuccessful assassination attempt.
June 11: Gerardo Machado, president of Cuba, was the target of an unsuccessful attempt on his life.
June 23: V. Popovitch was slain in Yugoslavia.
Sept. 22: Wu Kwang-Tsung was murdered in China.
Sept. 29: Sir A. Watson was the target of a failed attempt on his life in India.
Oct. 20: Count Bethlen was assassinated in Hungary.
Nov. 16: G. de Fostoa was murdered in Spanish Guinea.

1933

Feb. 15: Anton Joseph Cermak, mayor of Chicago, and President Franklin Delano Roosevelt were traveling to a political meeting in Miami, Fla., when Joseph Zangara, who intended to shoot Roosevelt, instead hit Cermak. Cermak died on Mar. 6 and Zangara was executed on Mar. 20, 1933.
Mar. 10: Chen Chi-Tang was the target of an unsuccessful attempt on his life in China.
Apr. 30: Luis M. Sanchez Cerro, president of Peru, was killed.
May 6: Yuh Sueh-Chung was the target of a failed assassination attempt in China.
May 8: Chang Ching-Yao was murdered in China.
May 13: P. Napetoff was slain in Bulgaria.
May 17: Pasha Sidky was the target of an unsuccessful attempt on his life in Egypt.
June 7: Mohammad Aziz Khan was assassinated in Germany.
June 7: Eleutherios Venizelos, premier of Greece, was the target of an unsuccessful attempt on his life in Greece.
June 12: R. Steidle was the target of a failed attempt on his life in Austria.
Sept. 3: B.E.J. Burge was murdered in India.
Oct. 4: Engelbert Dollfuss, chancellor and dictator of Austria, was the target of an unsuccessful attempt on his life in Austria.
Oct. 4: Ramon Grau San Martin, provisional president of Cuba, was the target of an unsuccessful attempt on his life.
Oct. 12: Carol II, king of Rumania, was the target of a failed attempt on his life.
Oct. 23: Oscar Raimundo Benavides, president of Peru, was the target of an unsuccessful attempt on his life.
Nov. 8: Nadir Shah was killed in Afghanistan.
Nov. 13: J.A. Primo de Rivera was the target of an unsuccessful assassination attempt in Spain.
Nov. 21: Baron Wakatzuki was the target of an unsuccessful attempt on his life in Japan.
Dec. 25: L.E. Tourian was murdered in New York.
Dec. 30: Ion Duca, prime minister of Rumania, was shot to death by members of the fascist Iron Guard.

1934

Dr. Chaim Arlosoroff, Jewish leader, was shot to death in Tel Aviv. A Zionist was convicted for the murder, but later the decision was reversed.
Ralph Cairns, a British policeman, was working in Palestine under the auspices of the League of Nations when he was murdered by members of Irgun, an Israeli nationalist group.
Arab Kai Khosrow was assassinated in Iran.
Abdul Husayn Taymurtash was slain in Iran.
Jan. 11: Pai-Yuan Chang was killed in China.
Feb. 23: F. Estrada, a military officer, was murdered in Nicaragua.
Feb. 23: Augusto César Sandino, leader of Nicaraguan guerrillas, was assassinated by a member of the national guard.
Feb. 23: J.P. Umanzor, a military officer, was slain in Nicaragua.
Mar. 8: C. de la Torriente was the target of an unsuccessful attempt on his life in Cuba.
Apr. 11: J.A. Primo de Rivera was the target of a failed assassination attempt in Spain.
Apr. 12: Edward Koerbel was murdered in Austria.
Apr. 15: Major Emil Fey, minister of the interior of Austria, was the target of an unsuccessful attempt on his life.
Apr. 18: Huang Shao-Wen was killed in China.
May 9: Sir J. Anderson was the target of a failed attempt on his life in India.
June: Franz von Papen, vice-chancellor of Germany to Adolf Hitler, was the target of an unsuccessful attempt on his life.
June 3: Hwang Fu was the target of an unsuccessful attempt on his life in China.

June 7: Damaso Berenguer was the target of a failed assassination attempt.
June 7: Fernando Berenguer was killed in Spain.
June 10: J.A. Primo de Rivera was the target of an unsuccessful assassination attempt in Spain.
June 16: Carlos Mendieta, provisional president of Cuba, was the target of an unsuccessful attempt on his life in Cuba.
June 16: Colonel Bronislaw Pieracki, Polish minister of the interior, was assassinated in Poland.
June 30: Kurt von Bredow was slain in Germany.
June 30: Lieutenant Edmund Heines was murdered in Germany.
June 30: Gustav von Kahr was killed in Germany.
June 30: Erich Klausener was assassinated in Germany.
June 30: Ernst Röhm (Roehm), German National Socialist leader, and Kurt von Schleicher, former chancellor of Germany, were placed on the Nazis' "enemies lists," and murdered on "The Night of the Long Knives" with about 300 others.
June 30: Bernhard Stempfle was murdered in Germany.
June 30: Gregor Strasser was slain in Germany.
July 25: Engelbert Dollfuss, chancellor and dictator of Austria, was fatally shot by Austrian Nazi SS agents headed by Otto Planetta, in an unsuccessful coup. Planetta and others were executed later.
July 26: J. Wadij was assassinated in Poland.
Oct. 9: Alexander I, king of Yugoslavia, and grandson of Alexander Karageorgevic and Jean Louis Barthou, French foreign minister, were shot to death in Marseilles by Vlada Chernozamsky. Chernozamsky was hired by Ante Pavelic, a Croatian nationalist, and was fatally shot by police the same day.
Oct. 13: Archbishop J. Pommer was killed in Latvia.
Nov. 4: J.C. Moreland was the target of an unsuccessful attempt on his life in Illinois.
Nov. 5: During a political parade in Kelayres, Pa., five participants were fatally shot and others wounded by political rival John J. Bruno and his relatives who were all sent to prison.
Nov. 9: Chiang Kai-Shek, president of China, was the target of a failed attempt on his life in China.
Nov. 28: M. Kolodyer was the target of an unsuccessful attempt on his life in Yugoslavia.
Dec. 1: Sergei Mironovich Kirov, Russian revolutionary leader, was slain at Leningrad, U.S.S.R. His assassin and 116 others were convicted on charges of conspiring to oust the Stalin administration, and thousands of others later allegedly died in the purge. Stalin may have engineered Kirov's death as an excuse to wipe out his rivals.
Dec. 25: George Kondylis, minister of war of Greece, was the target of an unsuccessful assassination attempt in Greece.

1935

Ahmad Kasravi was slain in Iran.
Firuz Mirza was killed in Iran.
Jose A. Miro Quesada was assassinated in Peru.
Wang Ching-wei, Chinese president, was the target of a failed assassination attempt.
Jan. 28: Wilhelm II, king of the Netherlands, was the target of an unsuccessful attempt on his life in the Netherlands.
Feb. 24: M. Shoriki was murdered in Japan.
Feb. 24: Luang Bipul Songram was the target of a failed attempt on his life in Thailand.
Mar. 16: Abdul Aziz was the target of an unsuccessful attempt on his life in Saudi Arabia.
Mar. 25: Thomas J. Courtney, a state's attorney for Illinois, was shot to death by unknown assailants. The members of Al Capone's gang were suspected.
June 3: Gabriel Terra, president of Uruguay, was the target of an unsuccessful assassination attempt in Uruguay.
Aug. 12: Tetsuzan Nagata, a military officer, was killed in Japan.
Aug. 16: L. de Ghilardi, a military officer, was murdered in Albania.
Sept. 5: E.C. Middleton was assassinated in Kentucky.
Sept. 8: Huey Pierce Long, U.S. senator from Louisiana, was shot to death by Dr. Carl Austin Weiss, who was then shot by Long's bodyguards in Baton Rouge, La. Weiss apparently was angry that Long plotted to have his father-in-law's judgeship revoked. Long died on Sept. 9.
Nov. 14: Sun Chuan-Fang was killed in China.
Dec. 26: Tang Yu-Jen was murdered in China.
Dec. 27: John Harrison was the target of an unsuccessful attempt on his life in Ireland.

1936

Sardar Assad was slain in Iran.
J.M. Bolton, Illinois state legislator, was shot dead by unidentified killers, suspected to be gangsters who were associates of politicians.
Eustaquio Gomez was killed in Venezuela.
Abdul Husayn Hazhir was slain in Iran.
Luis De Serval was murdered in Spain.
Jan. 12: J.I. Niemerower was the target of an unsuccessful attempt on his life in Rumania.
Jan. 18: M. Ganeff was killed in Bulgaria.
February: Leon Blum, French political leader, was assaulted and injured in Paris by a nationalist.
Feb. 4: Wilhelm Gustloff, a Nazi official, was killed at Davos, Switz., by David Frankfurter, a Jewish student.
Feb. 7: Chien Wha was assassinated in China.
Feb. 11: R. Donkin was the target of an unsuccessful attempt on his life in Zanzibar.
Feb. 11: C. Eberwein was murdered in New Jersey.
Feb. 11: Ian Humphrey was slain in Zanzibar.
Feb. 11: J.P. Jones was the target of an unsuccessful assassination attempt in Zanzibar.
Feb. 11: Leslie Skinner was the target of a failed assassination attempt in Zanzibar.
Feb. 13: Léon Blum, premier of France, was the target of an unsuccessful attempt on his life in France.
Feb. 21: Rudolfo Graziani, marchese di Neghelli, Italian marshal and administrator and viceroy of Ethiopia, was the target of Ethiopian assassins in a failed attack in Addis Ababa.
Feb. 24: W.H. Aluwihara was the target of a failed attempt on his life in Ceylon.
Feb. 24: E.F. Riggs was killed in Puerto Rico.
Feb. 26: Count Makino was the target of an unsuccessful assassination attempt in Japan.
Feb. 26: Keisuke Okada, prime minister of Japan, was murdered.
Feb. 26: Makoto Saito, former prime minister of Japan, was slain with others during a mutiny by the army. Also killed was Korekiyo Takahashi, former premier of Japan and minister of finance.
Feb. 26: Admiral Suzuki was the target of an unsuccessful assassination attempt in Japan.
Feb. 26: Korekiyo Takahashi, premier and minister of finance of Japan, was the target of an unsuccessful assassination attempt in Japan.
Feb. 26: General Watanake was slain in Japan.
Mar. 13: L.J. Asua was the target of a failed assassination attempt in Spain.
Mar. 23: Dr. Alfredo Martinez was murdered in Spain.
Mar. 25: H.B. Somerville was assassinated in Ireland.
Apr. 5: Count L. Torres de Sanchez was the target of an unsuccessful assassination attempt in Spain.
Apr. 7: Eduardo Ortega Gasset was the target of a failed attempt on his life in Spain.
Apr. 15: M. Pedregal was the target of an unsuccessful assassination attempt in Spain.
Apr. 28: Josep Madia was killed in Spain.
Apr. 28: Miguel Madia was murdered in Spain.
May 11: Major Gonzales was the target of an unsuccessful assassination attempt in Cuba.
May 30: J. Pedraza was the target of a failed assassination attempt in Cuba.
June 1: Li Shengta, a military officer, was slain in China.
June 22: Moritz Schlick was killed in Austria.
June 23: I. Urdaneta was the target of an unsuccessful assassination attempt in Panama.
July 13: Calvo Sotelo was assassinated in Spain.
July 16: Edward VIII, king of England, was at Constitution Hill when Jerome Pannigan hurled a loaded gun at him, causing no harm. Pannigan was sent to prison.
July 16: Michael Stelescu, Rumanian political leader, was recovering in a hospital bed from an appendectomy when eight members of the Iron Guardists shot him to death.
Aug. 18: Garcia Lorca was murdered in Spain.
October: Sayyid Jaefar Al-Askari (Jafar al-Askari), Iraqi minister of defense, was killed during a coup in Iraq.
Oct. 12: M. Falconde was the target of an unsuccessful assassination attempt in France.
Oct. 26: Yang Yung-Tai was slain in China.
Dec. 24: V. Martin was assassinated in Brazil.
Dec. 24: J. Villaboas was killed in Brazil.
Dec. 29: M. Grove was the target of an unsuccessful assassination attempt in Chile.

1937

Lu Po-hung, prominent industrialist in Shanghai, helped hospitals when the Japanese occupied Shanghai, and was slain.
Solat Ed-Dawlah was assassinated in Iran.
Jan. 2: Plutarco Elias Calles, former president of Mexico, was living in exile in the U.S. when he was the target of an unsuccessful assassination attempt in California.
Jan. 23: Suleiman Bey Salah was slain in Palestine.
Jan. 23: Hassan Bey Shukry was the target of a failed assassination attempt in Palestine.
Feb. 4: Wang I-Cheh was killed in China.
Feb. 21: General Rudolfo Graziani (Marchese di Neghelli), was the target of a failed assassination attempt in Addis Ababa, Ethiopia.
Feb. 21: Abuna Kyrillos was the target of an unsuccessful assassination attempt in Ethiopia.
Feb. 21: General Aurelio Leolta was the target of unsuccessful assassins in Ethiopia.
Mar. 14: R. Garcia was slain in Mexico.
Apr. 30: Liu To-Chuan was the target of an unsuccessful attempt on his life in China.
May 7: Francisco Ascasso was assassinated in Spain.
May 7: A. Sesa was killed in Spain.
July 7: Antonio de Oliveira Salazar, premier of Portugal, was the target

of an unsuccessful assassination attempt in Portugal.
July 17: Colonel Adam Koc was the target of a failed assassination attempt in Poland.
Aug. 11: Bakir Sidky Pasha (al-Fariq Bakir Sidqi, Bakr Sidqi), Iraqi dictator, was murdered.
Aug. 12: Muhammad Ali Jawad was slain in Iraq.
Sept. 27: L.Y. Andrews was killed in Palestine.
Sept. 27: P.R. McEwan was murdered in Palestine.
Oct. 13: J.T. Marriner was slain in Lebanon.
Nov. 28: Mustafa an-Nahhas Pasha (Mustafz el-Nahas Pasha), prime minister of Egypt, was the target of an unsuccessful assassination attempt in Egypt.
1938
Nikolay Ivanovich Bukharin, member of the Central Committee of the Communist party in Russia, was ousted, tried, and slain with other Bolsheviks.
Chang Hsiao-lin, Chinese leader in the Green gang, was killed.
Chi Yun-ch'ing, Chinese leader in the Green gang, was slain.
Chou Feng-chi, Chinese politician, may have been assassinated.
Fu Hsiao-an, Shanghai mayor, was murdered.
Ho Tien-fang, radical Chinese government official, was killed.
Liu Chan-en (Herman Liu), influential in Shanghai, was murdered on the orders of the Japanese.
Lu Lien-k'ui, Shanghai investigator, was slain.
T'ang Shao-i, Chinese politician, was murdered.
Feb. 28: Swami Chinna was killed in India.
Apr. 12: J.R. Clark was murdered in Kentucky.
Apr. 12: James Dykes was the target of an unsuccessful assassination attempt in Kentucky.
May 11: Getúlio Dornelles Vargas, dictator of Brazil, was the target of an unsuccessful attempt on his life in Brazil.
July 10: F.O. Epps was slain in Georgia.
Aug. 5: Lee Combs was killed in Kentucky.
Aug. 5: Lewis Combs was the target of an unsuccessful assassination attempt in Kentucky.
Aug. 5: Walter Deaton was the target of a failed assassination attempt in Kentucky.
Oct. 10: Jordan Peeff was assassinated in Bulgaria.
Nov. 7: Ernst von Rath, an official of the German Embassy, was fatally shot by Hershel Grynszpan, a Jewish student. Adolph Hitler used the incident to start the persecution of Jews known as the "Crystal Night."
Nov. 9: Prince Luigi Trivulzio was slain in Italy.
Nov. 29: Cornelius Zelea-Codreanu, a leader of the Rumanian Iron Guard, and seventeen others were shot to death by agents of the Rumanian government.
1939
Ch'en Lu, foreign minister under Wang Ching-wei, was assassinated.
Saturnillo Cedillo was slain in Mexico.
Louis E. Edwards, mayor of Long Beach, N.Y., was shot to death by Alvin Dooley, who was angry because Edwards had blocked Dooley from obtaining a police job.
Jan. 1: G.D. Sanderson was murdered in Palestine.
Jan. 1: Sir C. Tegart was the target of an unsuccessful assassination attempt in Palestine.
Jan. 17: Dr. Shahbandar was the target of a failed assassination attempt in Lebanon.
Jan. 24: Pedro Acosta was murdered in Cuba.
Feb. 3: Hugh Bingham was the target of an unsuccessful assassination attempt in Palestine.
Feb. 7: Chow Chi-Tang was killed in China.
Feb. 7: Koo Pingtsun was murdered in China.
Feb. 10: Hadi Stambouli was the target of an unsuccessful assassination attempt in Palestine.
Feb. 13: M. Calinescu was the target of an unsuccessful assassination attempt in Rumania.
Feb. 13: Dr. Franco Gazzera was killed in Ethiopia.
Feb. 21: Chen Loh was slain in China.
Feb. 22: M. Li was murdered in China.
Feb. 28: N. Kruschev was the target of a failed assassination attempt in Poland.
Mar. 1: Tao Shan-Chen was the target of an unsuccessful attempt on his life in China.
Mar. 6: Adnan Nashashibi was killed in Palestine.
Mar. 7: Dr. Sternberg was the target of an unsuccessful assassination attempt in Palestine.
Apr. 5: G.E.A.C. Monc-Mason was assassinated in Iraq.
Sept. 21: Armand Calinescu, premier of Rumania, was murdered by Rumanian Nazis, the Iron Guardists.
Nov. 8: Adolph Hitler, führer of Germany, was the target of an unsuccessful assassination attempt in Germany.
Dec. 10: Miguel Balmaseda was slain in Cuba.
1940
Juan Andreu Almazan, presidential candidate of Mexico, was the target of an unsuccessful assassination attempt in Mexico.
Marian Bogatko, outspoken Polish critic of U.S.S.R. occupation and husband of writer Wanda Wasilewska, was slain in Lwow.
Jan. 18: Rustum Haydar was killed in Iraq.
Jan. 29: General R. Valazquez Rivera, was murdered in the Dominican Republic.
February: Dr. Taqi Arani was slain in Iran.
Feb. 8: Ivan Bakior was killed in Yugoslavia.
Feb. 9: E. Sumuano was assassinated in Mexico.
Mar. 10: Dr. Oreste Ferrara was murdered in Cuba.
Mar. 10: Lord Lamington was the target of an unsuccessful assassination attempt in England.
Mar. 13: Sir L. Dane was the target of an unsuccessful attempt on his life in England.
Mar. 13: Sir Michael Francis O'Dwyer, former governor of Punjab, was shot to death in London by extremist Udham Singh, a Sikh, who was hanged on June 25, 1940.
Mar. 15: Les Wilson, a candidate for sheriff of Okaloosa County, Fla., was fatally shot at his house by Jessie and Doyle Cayson, so profitable contracts won through political ties would not be jeopardized. The Caysons were given life terms.
Apr. 5: The Duke of Santo Mauro was assassinated in France.
May: Maciej Rataj was killed in Poland.
May 6: E. Leimer was murdered in Czechoslovakia.
June: Italo Balbo, Italian governor of Tripolitania, died in an airplane crash over Tubruq, Libya. The incident was suspected to be sabotage and an assassination plot.
July 7: Felix Rodriguez was killed in Mexico.
Aug. 10: Ma You-Feng was slain in China.
Aug. 16: Dr. R.V. Daussa was murdered in Cuba.
Aug. 20: Chang Han-Yen was assassinated in China.
Aug. 20: Leon Trotsky (Leon Trotski, Leib, Leba, Lev Davidovich Bronstein), Communist leader of Russia, was exiled by Joseph Stalin and assassinated in his villa outside Mexico City by Stalinist Jacques Mornard. Mornard was later sent to prison.
Sept. 18: Count Bombelec was the target of an unsuccessful assassination attempt in Yugoslavia.
Sept. 30: A.M. Garcia Mendez was the target of a failed assassination attempt in Puerto Rico.
Oct. 11: Fu Siau-En was murdered in China.
Oct. 24: Andino Carias, president of the Honduras, was the target of an unsuccessful assassination attempt in the Honduras.
Nov. 13: Alejandro Garcia de Caturla was killed in Cuba.
Nov. 23: R.F. Perry was murdered in Alabama.
Nov. 29: Dr. R. Fernandez Fiallo was assassinated in Cuba.
Nov. 29: Nicola Iorga, former prime minister of Rumania, was slain in Rumania by members of the Iron Guard.
Dec. 31: E. Frugoni was the target of an unsuccessful assassination attempt in Uruquay.
1941
Boris III, czar of Bulgaria, was the target of three unsuccessful assassination attempts in Bulgaria in 1941.
Victor Emmanuel III, king of Italy, was the target of a failed assassination attempt in Albania.
Jan. 14: M. Mandique was slain in Cuba.
Jan. 24: The Earl of Erroll was murdered in Kenya.
Jan. 24: W.J. Keswick was the target of an unsuccessful assassination attempt in China.
Jan. 28: E. Sanchez Errazuriz was killed in Chile.
Feb. 1: J. Baldes Lamas was murdered in Cuba.
Feb. 1: Bernardo Menendez was assassinated in Cuba.
Apr. 1: José Manuel Cortina y Garcia, president of the Cuban delegation to the League of Nations, was the target of an unsuccessful assassination attempt in Cuba.
Apr. 26: J. Ayala was slain in Cuba.
Apr. 30: R. Zaydin Almendares was the target of an unsuccessful attempt on his life in Cuba.
May 17: F. Pinto was murdered in Chile.
May 18: Sepulveda Fernando Pinto was killed in Chile.
June 3: M. Faget was the target of an unsuccessful assassination attempt in Cuba.
June 18: J. Kusocinski was assassinated in Poland.
Aug. 14: Baron Kiichiro Hiranuma, former premier of Japan, was killed.
Aug. 28: Marcel Deat was the target of a failed assassination attempt in France.
Aug. 28: P. Durvez was the target of an unsuccessful assassination attempt in France.
Aug. 28: Pierre Laval, future premier of France, was the target of an unsuccessful assassination attempt in France.
Sept. 6: M. Gitton was killed in France.
Oct. 7: K.H. Frank was the target of a failed assassination attempt in Czechoslovakia.
Oct. 21: K.F. Holtz was murdered in France.
Nov. 17: Ernst Udet, German Luftwaffe (air force) general, offended Adolf Hitler and apparently was directed to commit suicide or be killed because of his drunkenness.
Dec. 6: Arturo Alessandri Palma, former president of Chile, was the target of an unsuccessful assassination attempt in Chile.
Dec. 21: S. Okanda was murdered in California.
1942
Hendrik Josephus Franciscus Marie Sneevliet, member of the Dutch Parliament, was put to death by the Germans.
Jan. 6: Y. Paringaux was killed in France.

Feb. 25: Franz von Papen, former German vice chancellor under Adolf Hitler, was the target of an unsuccessful assassination attempt in Turkey.
Mar. 7: Governor A. Zarate-Albarran was murdered in Mexico.
Mar. 28: Marcel Deat was the target of an unsuccessful assassination attempt in France.
Apr. 14: Ebeid Pasha was the target of a failed assassination attempt in Egypt.
May 27: Reinhard Heydrich (der Henker, the hangman), deputy chief of the Gestapo and Reich "protector" of Czechoslovakia, was wounded in a Prague suburb by Jan Kubis, Josef Gabcik, and others. He died on June 4, 1942. In retaliation, the Nazis killed hundreds of people and razed Lidice, Czech.
May 31: General Enriquez was slain in Ecuador.
June 3: A. Clement was murdered in France.
June 11: J. Louer was assassinated in France.
July 9: Jean Demaret was killed in Belgium.
Aug. 3: Frank Waldo was the target of an unsuccessful assassination attempt in Argentina.
Aug. 8: H. Gachelin was slain in France.
Aug. 10: Dr. Griffiths was murdered in Iran.
Aug. 13: Hideki Tojo, prime minister of Japan, was the target of an unsuccessful assassination attempt in Japan.
Aug. 28: Dr. Drosch was killed in Yugoslavia.
Aug. 31: General Mulletti was the target of an unsuccessful assassination attempt in Albania.
Sept. 9: Hideki Tojo, prime minister of Japan, was the target of an unsuccessful attempt on his life in Japan.
Sept. 10: D. O'Brien was murdered in Ireland.
Sept. 26: Marcel Rondoz was slain in Belgium.
Oct. 1: Ion Antonescu, dictator of Rumania, was the target of an unsuccessful assassination attempt in Rumania.
Oct. 19: John M. Box was murdered in Mississippi.
Nov. 21: J. Teughels was slain in Belgium.
Dec. 6: Ion Antonescu, dictator of Rumania, was the target of a failed attempt on his life in Rumania.
Dec. 24: Jean Louis Xavier François Darlan, a French admiral and high commissioner for the French Vichy administration in North and West Africa, was murdered in Algiers by Fernand Bonnier de la Chapelle, who was later executed.

1943

Jean Verdier was the target of an unsuccessful assassination attempt in France.
Yang Chien, secretary of Academia, may have been assassinated.
Jan. 11: Carlo Tresca, anti-Communist editor, was fatally shot in New York City.
Jan. 12: Henri Beraud was the target of a failed assassination attempt in France.
Jan. 22: Wilhelm Haas was killed in Belgium.
Feb. 4: Manuel Avila Camacho, president of Mexico, was the target of an unsuccessful assassination attempt in Mexico.
Feb. 5: General Hendrik Alexander Seyffardt was assassinated in the Netherlands.
Feb. 6: J. Fernandez Pelaez was murdered in Cuba.
Feb. 11: Enrique Ruiz Guiñazu, foreign minister of Argentina, was the target of an unsuccessful assassination attempt in Argentina.
Feb. 12: C. Van Ravenzwaai was killed in the Netherlands.
Feb. 12: Dr. H. Reydon was murdered in the Netherlands.
Feb. 18: M. Desslain was slain in Belgium.
Feb. 21: Albrecht Van Stenlandt was assassinated in Belgium.
Feb. 26: Dr. Wolfgang Glad was murdered in Belgium.
Mar. 9: Jan Akkers was slain in Belgium.
Mar. 21: G. Savo was killed in Albania.
Apr. 9: J.E. Brynder was assassinated in Belgium.
Apr. 9: Julien Curvers was murdered in Belgium.
Apr. 15: Sotir Janeff was slain in Bulgaria.
Apr. 16: Paul Colin was killed in Belgium.
Apr. 17: Isoroku Yamamoto, a military officer, was assassinated in Japan.
Apr. 20: K. Hoffman was murdered in Poland.
Apr. 21: Maurice Chevalier was the target of an unsuccessful assassination attempt in Belgium.
Apr. 21: Cyrille Corteville was killed in Belgium.
Apr. 25: Paul Gassowski was slain in France.
Apr. 29: L. Fischer was the target of an unsuccessful assassination attempt in Poland.
May 1: Pierre Cathala was the target of a failed attempt on his life in France.
May 1: P. Laval was the target of a failed assassination attempt in France.
May 2: Hugo Dietz was murdered in Poland.
May 2: B. Kurtz was killed in Poland.
May 6: Georg Nitsche was slain in Norway.
May 6: Kurt Olitsch was assassinated in Norway.
May 10: General W. Krueger was killed in Poland.
May 15: K.B.A. Baksh was slain in India.
May 15: O. Rebus was murdered in Poland.
May 18: Raymond Dirr was killed in France.
May 18: Michel Guerin was assassinated in France.
May 30: Leng Yun was slain in China.
May 31: Jean Bouisson was murdered in France.
May 31: Pierre Haudevin was the target of an unsuccessful assassination attempt in France.
June 1: Sapria Klevkoff was killed in Bulgaria.
June 5: Abdul Ilah was the target of an unsuccessful assassination attempt in Iraq.
June 8: Dr. F.E. Posthuma was assassinated in the Netherlands.
June 9: Vassal Joltekenoff was murdered in Bulgaria.
June 26: L. Ehrenlichter was slain in Russia.
June 28: F. Schmidt was killed in France.
June 30: Paul Tissot was murdered in France.
July 4: Maurice Labreau was slain in Belgium.
July 4: Wladyslaw Sirkorski, a general and statesman of Poland, and during WWII, head of the Polish government in exile, was killed in an airplane crash, possibly an assassination plot.
July 17: Carolino Arrarista was killed in Mexico.
July 22: L. Aletrino was murdered in Rumania.
Aug. 16: Andrew and Elizabeth Toth, fanatic anti-Nazi immigrants from Hungary, disappeared from New York City, possibly killed by members of the German-American Bund, a Nazi dominated group.
Aug. 24: Boris III, czar of Bulgaria, was assassinated.
Aug. 26: Francois Cinquin was slain in France.
Aug. 26: Jose DelaPlace was murdered in France.
Sept. 21: Marcel Varoteaux was killed in France.
Sept. 22: Wilhelm Kube, a German commissioner general for the White Russian Republic at the time of WWII, died in an explosion set by Russian operatives in Minsk, U.S.S.R.
Sept. 29: Julius Ritter was assassinated in France.
Oct. 1: Dr. Jolicoeur was slain in France.
Oct. 10: Lucie Darbelle was killed in France.
Oct. 12: Paul Lespinasse was the target of an unsuccessful assassination attempt in France.
Oct. 20: Adrianus M. De Jong was slain in the Netherlands.
Oct. 27: Jean Barthelet was killed in France.
Nov. 8: Eugene Escofier was murdered in France.
Nov. 14: Emile Edde was the target of a failed assassination attempt in Lebanon.
Nov. 16: J. Philippon, a military officer, was slain in France.
Nov. 18: Andre Bonamy was killed in France.
Dec. 7: Jean Verdier was murdered in France.

1944

Jan. 3: J. Marion was slain in France.
Jan. 5: Hans Hobel was killed in Italy.
Jan. 6: K. Munk was murdered in Denmark.
Jan. 14: Leo Kaerra was the target of an unsuccessful assassination attempt in Denmark.
Jan. 15: J. Serlin was assassinated in France.
Feb. 13: J. Harvey was murdered in France.
Feb. 14: Tan Shu-Kuei was killed in China.
Feb. 18: H. Ludberg was slain in Poland.
Feb. 22: Colonel Rodolfo Loaiza was murdered in Mexico.
Feb. 29: D. Tommasini was assassinated in France.
Mar. 26: S. Thompson was killed in Denmark.
Apr. 4: I. Herrerias was murdered in Mexico.
Apr. 4: P. Marion was slain in France.
Apr. 7: Chen Yao-Tsu was killed in China.
Apr. 9: Jense Albert Ibsen was slain in Denmark.
Apr. 10: Manuel Avila Camacho, president of Mexico, was the target of an unsuccessful assassination attempt in Mexico.
Apr. 25: Benito Mussolini, dictator of Italy, was the target of a failed attempt on his life in Italy.
Apr. 30: Colonel Ingarano was the target of an unsuccessful assassination attempt in Italy.
May 1: O. Grunwald was murdered in Poland.
May 1: Metropolitan of Vilna Sergius was killed in Poland.
June 10: Humbert, prince of Italy, was the target of an unsuccessful assassination attempt in Italy.
June 14: E. Herland was killed in Norway.
June 20: Adolf Hitler, German chancellor and dictator, was the target of a failed assassination attempt by military and civilian conspirators who blew up his headquarters in Rastenburg, East Prussia. Afterward, hundreds of people were executed for treason.
June 22: Lieutenant Koch was murdered in Italy.
June 27: T. Norse was killed in Norway.
June 28: Philippe Henriot, minister of propaganda for the French Vichy government, was slain.
July 6: S. Rolls was murdered in Norway.
July 7: Georges Mandel, ex-French minister of the interior, was killed in France.
July 8: Edward DeGrelle was assassinated in Belgium.
July 10: Jose A. Arze was the target of an unsuccessful assassination attempt in Bolivia.
July 10: Georges Bartelemy was killed in France.
July 20: Adolph Hitler, German chancellor and dictator, was the target of a failed bombing attempt against his life.
Aug. 7: Benito Mussolini, dictator of Italy, was the target of an unsuccessful assassination attempt in Italy.

Aug. 13: Sir Harold McMichael was the target of a failed assassination attempt in Palestine.
Aug. 13: P. Sandhoe was killed in Denmark.
Aug. 28: Charles-André-Marie-Joseph de Gaulle, president of France, was the target of an unsuccessful assassination attempt in France.
Sept. 19: D. Carretta was slain in Italy.
Sept. 21: Etienne Lahs was murdered in France.
Sept. 21: Andre Picout was slain in France.
Oct. 3: Alejandro Cordova was killed in Guatemala.
Oct. 12: Sir Harold MacMichael was the target of an unsuccessful assassination attempt in Palestine.
Oct. 12: T.J. Wikin was murdered in Palestine.
Oct. 15: H. Gilbert was the target of a failed assassination attempt in Denmark.
November: L. Calvo was slain in Bolivia.
November: F. Capriles was assassinated in Boliva.
Nov. 1: Jean Paul Boncour was the target of an unsuccessful assassination attempt in France.
Nov. 6: Walter Edward Guinness (Lord Moyne), former chief of the Irish House of Lords and British minister of state for the Middle East, was killed in Cairo, Egypt.
Nov. 11: Wilhelm Keitel, German field marshal, was the target of an unsuccessful assassination attempt in Germany.
Nov. 19: J.E. Stahr was murdered in Denmark.
Dec. 10: R. Voigt was killed in Norway.

1945

W.J. Fitzpatrick was assassinated in New York.
Jan. 12: Warren G. Hooper, Michigan state senator, was shot to death by conspirators Harry Fleisher, Sam Fleisher, Pete Mahoney, and Mike Selik, because Hooper was an important witness in an investigation.
Jan. 15: Joachim von Ribbentrop, minister of foreign affairs of Germany, was the target of an unsuccessful assassination attempt in Germany.
Jan. 29: E.J. Pospichal was assassinated in New York.
Jan. 30: Rosendo G. Castro was killed in Mexico.
February: Adolf Hitler, führer of Germany, was the target of an unsuccessful assassination attempt in Germany.
February: Giulio Loret was murdered in Italy.
Feb. 4: Y. Fujui was slain in Macao.
Feb. 8: General Carl Martinsen was assassinated in Norway.
Feb. 17: Josef Fitzhum was killed in Austria.
Feb. 24: Ahmed Maher Pasha, Egyptian premier, was murdered in Egypt by a nationalist.
Feb. 25: Nicolae Radescu, premier of Rumania, was the target of an unsuccessful assassination attempt in Rumania.
March: Maurice Sarraut was assassinated in France.
Mar. 12: Count Carlos Sforza was the target of an unsuccessful assassination attempt in Italy.
Mar. 14: M. Berlinguer was the target of a failed assassination attempt in Italy.
Mar. 16: Dr. Eugenio Llanillo was murdered in Cuba.
Mar. 25: Franz Oppenhof was killed in Germany.
Mar. 25: Baldur von Schirach was the target of an unsuccessful attempt on his life in Germany.
Apr. 19: Sepp Dietrich was the target of an unsuccessful assassination attempt in Austria.
Apr. 25: E. Enriquez was assassinated in Cuba.
Apr. 28: Benito Mussolini, dictator of Italy, Clara Petacci, his mistress, and others were assassinated by Italian Communists as they tried to flee to Switzerland.
May: Edvard Benes, president of Czechoslovakia, was the target of an unsuccessful assassination attempt in Czechoslovakia.
June: E. Moravec was killed in Czechoslovakia.
June 18: S. Sokol was slain in Poland.
July 31: General M. Hill was the target of a failed assassination attempt in Chile.
August: M. Jean Passalides was the target of an unsuccessful attempt on his life in Greece.
Aug. 30: Klement Gottwald, deputy premier of Czechoslovakia, was the target of a failed assassination attempt in Czechoslovakia.
Aug. 30: Z. Nejedly was the target of an unsuccessful assassination attempt in Czechoslovakia.
Sept. 27: Victor Basch was killed in France.
Oct. 2: Theophilus Anba was slain in Egypt.
Oct. 3: Alcide De Gasperi, prime minister of Italy was the target of an unsuccessful assassination attempt in Italy.
Oct. 18: R. Lassen was murdered in Denmark.
Nov. 29: Colonel A. Brito was killed in Cuba.
December: E.N. Ostrom was murdered in Indonesia.
Dec. 7: Mustafa an-Nahhas Pasha, prime minister of Egypt several times, was the target of an unsuccessful assassination attempt in Egypt.
Dec. 22: Nan Ung was the target of a failed attempt on his life in Korea.

1946

Li Chao-liu, Chinese head of Communist guerrillas, was slain in Harbin.
Li Kung-p'o, Democratic League leader, was assassinated.
Wen I-to, head of the Chinese Democratic League, was murdered, most likely by members of the Kuomintang (Chinese Nationalist Party).
Jan. 6: Osman Pasha was slain in Egypt.
Jan. 13: E. Cofran was murdered in Germany.
Jan. 13: Tarrad Moulheim was killed in Syria.
Jan. 20: R.D. Joglar was assassinated in Cuba.
Jan. 28: Chang Hsi-Fu was murdered in Manchuria.
Mar. 9: Sung Chu-Hsiang was killed in Manchuria.
Apr. 10: M.M. Baig was slain in India.
Apr. 11: Song Chin-Woo was assassinated in Korea.
Apr. 24: R. Imperial was killed in the Philippines.
June 9: Rama VIII (Ananda Mahidol), king of Siam (Thailand), was shot dead by unknown assailants at the palace in Bankok.
June 12: T. Atherton was slain in Yugoslavia.
July 10: Nevzat Tandogan was murdered in Turkey.
July 16: Dr. P.M. Roxas was killed in the Philippines.
July 21: Gualberto Villaroel was assassinated in Boliva.
Aug. 26: Sir S.A. Khan was slain in India.
September: T. Monje Gutierrez was the target of an unsuccessful assassination attempt in Bolivia.
Sept. 1: E.Y. Hartshorne was killed in Germany.
Sept. 8: L.J. Martinez Fernandez was the target of a failed assassination attempt in Cuba.
Sept. 18: Chakravarti Rajagopalachari was the target of an unsuccessful assassination attempt in India.
Sept. 24: B. Scioborek was assassinated in Poland.
Sept. 28: T.S. Donald was murdered in India.
Oct. 4: A. Rodrigues Araya was the target of an unsuccessful assassination attempt in Argentina.
Oct. 22: Chang Taik Sang was the target of a failed assassination attempt in Korea.
Oct. 31: Sir Noel Charles was the target of an unsuccessful attempt on his life in Italy.
Nov. 12: J. Scottoriggio was assassinated in New York.
Nov. 24: Fawzi Husseini was killed in Palestine.
Nov. 27: D. Gonzalez Piloto was murdered in Cuba.
Dec. 27: I. Levin was killed in Palestine.
Dec. 27: Emir Mohammed Zeinati was slain in Palestine.

1947

John William Bricker, a U.S. Senator from Ohio, was shot and injured by William L. Kaiser in Washington., D.C., as the result of a feud stemming from when Bricker served as attorney general.
Hubert H. Humphrey, mayor of Minneapolis, Minn., was the target of unsuccessful assassins several times during 1947. One shooting attempt was suspected to have been engineered by members of a crime-labor syndicate that Humphrey had uncovered.
Feb. 1: Camille Sachs was the target of an unsuccessful assassination attempt in Germany.
Feb. 11: R.W.M. DeWinton, a military officer, was slain in Italy.
March: General Karl Swerozewski was murdered in Poland.
Mar. 10: George P. McNear was slain in Illinois.
Mar. 21: John Zeugous was killed in Greece.
April: Christos Contopoulos was murdered in Greece.
Apr. 15: Peter Davey was assassinated in Aden.
Apr. 26: Dermott Fawsitt was the target of a failed assassination attempt in Ireland.
Apr. 28: A.E. Lonquest was killed in Palestine.
May: Thomas Anglin, Oklahoma state senator, was shot and injured by Jim Scott, after Anglin's law firm advised Scott's wife during a divorce.
May 5: Ernest Bevin, British secretary of state for foreign affairs, was the target of a failed assassination attempt in England.
May 5: Sir Robert Anthony Eden, former secretary of state for foreign affairs, was the target of an unsuccessful assassination attempt in England.
June: Antonio Santin was the target of an unsuccessful assassination attempt in Italy.
July 19: Abdul Bazak was killed in Burma.
July 19: Mahn Ba Khaing was murdered in Burma.
July 19: Aung San, head of the Anti-Fascist People's Freedom League, virtual prime minister of the interim Burmese government, was slain by conspirators under U Saw, former prime minister. U Saw was executed.
July 19: Sao Sam Heun was murdered in Burma.
July 19: Thakin Mya was assassinated in Burma.
July 19: U Ba Choe was killed in Burma.
July 19: U Ba Win was murdered in Burma.
August: U Tin Tut was the target of an unsuccessful assassination attempt in Burma.
Aug. 11: Stanislaw Tonski was killed in Poland.
Aug. 11: Tadeusz Zeglicky was slain in Poland.
Aug. 27: Abbe Buselitch was assassinated in Trieste, Italy.
Aug. 27: Abbe Khristian was murdered in Trieste, Italy.
September: Sami Taha was slain in Palestine.
Sept. 12: Jan Masaryk was the target of a failed assassination attempt in Czechoslovakia.
Sept. 23: Paul I, king of Greece, was the target of an unsuccessful attempt on his life in Greece.
Oct. 7: Paul Ramadier, former French premier, was the target of an unsuccessful assassination attempt in France.
Oct. 10: Truong Dinh Tri was murdered in Indochina.
November: Nu Thakin was the target of a failed assassination attempt in Burma.

December: Chang Duk Soo was killed in Korea.
Dec. 5: Nizam of Hyderabad was the target of an unsuccessful assassination attempt in India.
1948
Muhammad Masud was assassinated in Iran.
Thomas C. Wasson was murdered in Palestine.
Jan. 20: Mohandas Karamchand Gandhi, a religious and political leader of India, was the target of an unsuccessful assassination attempt in India.
Jan. 30: Mohandas Karamchand Gandhi, a religious and political leader of India, was fatally shot in New Delhi, India, by Nathuram Vinayak Godse and others. Godse was executed on Nov. 15, 1949.
Feb. 17: Yahya Mahmud al-Mutawak-kil (Mohammed ton Yahya), imam (ruler) of Yemen, was killed in Yemen.
Apr. 9: Jorge Eliécer Gaitán, Columbian presidential candidate, was murdered in Colombia.
Apr. 20: Walter Reuther was the target of an unsuccessful assassination attempt in Michigan.
Apr. 25: Mustafa Nahas Pasha was the target of a failed assassination attempt in Egypt.
May 1: Christos Ladas was killed in Greece.
September: U Tin Tut was assassinated in Burma.
Sept. 1: Juan Arevalo Y Veitia was slain in Cuba.
Sept. 17: Count Folke Bernadotte af Wisborg, a mediator for the United Nations, arranged for a truce between Israelis and Arabs. He was slain in Jerusalem by Israeli fanatics.
Sept. 17: Colonel Andre Serot was murdered in Israel.
Dec. 28: Mahmoud Nukrashy Pasha, premier of Egypt, was killed in Egypt by members of the Muslim Brotherhood.
1949
Mohammad Reza Pahlavi, shah of Iran, was the target of an unsuccessful assassination attempt in Iran.
Jan. 9: Dr. Ivov O.G. Kostelnik was slain in Russia.
Jan. 9: Sir John Lucie-Smith was the target of a failed assassination attempt in Sierra Leone, Africa.
Jan. 21: Ede Raulin-Laboureur was assassinated in France.
February: Hasan al-Banna, Egyptian politician who established the Muslim Brotherhood, was killed in a plot involving the Egyptian administration.
Feb. 17: A.C. Maule was murdered in Poland.
Apr. 26: Elihu H. Bailey, mayor of Evarts, Ky., was the target of unknown assailants, suspected bootleggers, who unsuccessfully tried to kill him with dynamite.
Apr. 29: The wife of Manuel Quezon was killed in the Philippines.
June 7: Victor Reuther was the target of an unsuccessful assassination attempt in Michigan.
June 20: Alessandro Torlonia was murdered in Italy.
July: Antun Saada (Antan Saada), Syrian nationalist leader, was assassinated in Lebanon.
July 19: Francisco Javier Arana was killed in Guatemala.
Aug. 14: Muhsin Al-Barazi was murdered in Syria.
Aug. 14: Colonel Husni Zaim was slain in Syria by Fadlallah Abu Mansur, apparently for handing Antun Saada to Lebanese officials.
December: Duncan George Stewart was killed in Malaysia.
Dec. 12: F.J. Christenson was murdered in Illinois.
1950
Abdul-Husayn Hazhir was murdered in Iran.
March: Jose Gallostra was assassinated in Mexico.
Mar. 4: Do Van Nang was slain in Vietnam.
Mar. 7: Sheikh Adil Alwani was killed in Syria.
Mar. 10: Riad El Solh was the target of an unsuccessful assassination attempt in Lebanon.
Mar. 12: V.S. Armstrong was slain in Pennsylvania.
July 26: J. Weston, a military officer, was killed in South Africa.
July 31: Muhammad Nasir was murdered in Syria.
Sept. 4: C. Graile was slain in Cuba.
Oct. 31: Colonel Sami Al-Hinnawi was assassinated in Lebanon by Ahmad al-Barazi, who was avenging his cousin's death.
Nov. 1: Harry S. Truman, president of the U.S., was the target of a failed assassination attempt by Puerto Rican nationalists Griselio Torresola and Oscar Collazo. Torresola and a guard, Private Leslie Coffelt, died. Collazo's death sentence for Coffelt's murder was commuted to life imprisonment.
Nov. 13: Carlos Delgado Chalbaud, colonel and president of Venezuela, was murdered in Caracas.
1951
Mar. 8: General Ali Razmara, prime minister of Iran, was assassinated in Iran.
Mar. 20: Abdul Hamid Zangareh was the target of an unsuccessful assassination attempt in Iran.
June 15: J. Rincon was murdered in Colombia.
July 16: Riad Al-Sulh (Riad Solh Bey), prime minister of Lebanon, was murdered in Amman, Jor., by a supporter of Antun Saada.
July 20: Abdullah (Abdul ibn Hvssein, Abd Allah ibn al-Husayn), king of Jordan, was murdered by a Palestinian nationalist.
July 31: Thai Lap-Thanh was assassinated in Vietnam.
Sept. 23: H.J. Mazuera was killed in Colombia.
Oct. 16: Liaquat Ali Khan, prime minister of Pakistan, was murdered in Pakistan.
Oct. 19: C. Ousman was slain in Saudi Arabia.
1952
Si Sliman Ben Hamouda was assassinated in Tunisia.
Feb. 16: Hussein Fatemi, minister of foreign affairs, was killed in Iran.
March: Farouk I, king of Egypt, was the target of an unsuccessful assassination attempt in Egypt.
March: Bernard Rosselin was killed in France.
Mar. 10: Colonel Palmer was assassinated in Jordan.
May 21: Colonel Harjono was the target of an unsuccessful assassination attempt in the Netherlands.
June 21: Zvi Pinkas was the target of a failed assassination attempt in Israel.
July 16: Paul Didier was the target of an unsuccessful attempt on his life in France.
July 28: Chedly Hayder was the target of a failed assassination attempt in Tunisia.
Aug. 5: Sir Jack Drummond was murdered in Switzerland.
October: Alejandro Carrion was the target of an unsuccessful assassination attempt in Ecuador.
Dec. 5: Ferhat Hached was murdered in Tunisia.
1953
Lavrenty Pavlovich Beria, deputy prime minister of U.S.S.R., was slain in U.S.S.R.
Anastasio Somoza, president of Nicaragua, was the target of an unsuccessful assassination attempt in Nicaragua.
Apr. 15: Juan Domingo Perón, president of Argentina, was the target of a failed assassination attempt in Argentina.
May 1: Dr. Ben Rais was the target of an unsuccessful assassination attempt in Tunisa.
May 2: Chedly Kastalli was murdered in Tunisia.
July 2: Azzedine Bey was slain in Tunisia.
August: The wife of Bernard Peck was killed in Spain.
Sept. 11: Sidi Muhammad ben Moulay Arafa, sultan of Morocco, was the target of a failed assassination attempt in Morocco by Allal ben Abdallah, a Moroccan nationalist who was shot during the attack.
Sept. 13: Hedi Chakir was assassinated in Tunisia.
Oct. 25: G.R.G. Sierra was murdered in Cuba.
November: Jose Velasco Ibarra (Belasco), president of Ecuador, was the target of an unsuccessful assassination attempt in Ecuador.
1954
Konrad Adenauer, chancellor of West Germany, was the target of an unsuccessful assassination attempt in West Germany.
Feb. 19: Si Hadi Thami Galoui was the target of a failed assassination attempt in Morocco.
Mar. 1: Puerto Rican nationalists sprayed gunfire into the House of Representatives, injuring Representatives Alvin Morell Bentley, Clifford Davis, George Hyde Fallon, Benton Franklin Jensen, and Kenneth Allison Roberts. The attackers, including Lolita Lebron, were sent to prison.
Mar. 5: Muhammad V (Sidi Muhammad ben Yusuf), Sultan of Morocco, was the target of an unsuccessful assassination attempt in Morocco.
Mar. 16: J. Montalvo was the target of a failed assassination attempt in Guatemala.
Mar. 22: Sir Winston Churchill, prime minister of England, may have been the target of a failed assassination attempt when a bomb arrived by mail.
Mar. 24: Faisal II, king of Iraq, was the target of an unsuccessful assassination attempt in Pakistan.
June 19: A.L. Patterson was slain in Alabama.
June 20: General Hauteville was the target of an unsuccessful assassination attempt in Morocco.
June 30: Dr. Eyraud was killed in Morocco.
Aug. 5: Carlos Lacerda, journalist who was an outspoken critic of the Brazilian government, was injured in an unsuccessful attempt on his life in Brazil. An air force major accompanying him died.
Aug. 5: Ruben Florentino Vaz was murdered in Brazil.
Sept. 20: Kow Worawong was slain in Laos.
Oct. 27: Ismail Azhari, prime minister of Sudan, was the target of an unsuccessful assassination attempt in Sudan.
Oct. 27: Gamal Abdel Nasser, president of Egypt, was the target of a failed assassination attempt in Egypt.
1955
Jan. 2: Jose Antonio Remon, president of Panama, was visiting a Panama race track when he was shot dead in machine-gun fire.
Jan. 4: Abdallah Ben Shain was killed in Morocco.
Jan. 8: Arthur Cutino was the target of an unsuccessful assassination attempt in Morocco.
Feb. 5: J. Hoffman was the target of a failed assassination attempt in Germany.
Feb. 8: Ibrahim Al-Shalky was murdered in Libya.
March: Tran Van Lam was the target of an unsuccessful assassination attempt in Vietnam.
Mar. 2: Moulay Idriss was assassinated in Morocco.
Mar. 12: Motilal Nehru, prime minister of India, was the target of a failed assassination attempt in India.
Mar. 13: F.L. Quiroz was slain in Bolivia.
Apr. 2: Sir Robert Armitage was the target of an unsuccessful attempt on his life in Cyprus.

Apr. 19: Victor Paz Estenssoro, president of Bolivia, was the target of an unsuccessful assassination attempt in Bolivia.
Apr. 22: Lieutenant Colonel Adnan Al-Malki, Syrian ruler, was killed in Syria by a nationalist sergeant in the Syrian army.
May 14: Konrad Adenauer, chancellor of West Germany, was the target of an unsuccessful assassination attempt in West Germany.
May 24: Sir Robert Armitage was the target of a failed assassination attempt in Cyprus.
May 24: Eric Ellis was the target of an unsuccessful attempt on his life in Bermuda.
June: Ridoub Amar Ben Naceur was slain in Algeria.
June 3: Mekki Ben Azouz was the target of an unsuccessful assassination attempt in Tunisia.
June 14: Jacques Lemaigre-Dubreuil was killed in Morocco.
June 16: Juan Peron, president of Argentina, was the target of a failed assassination attempt in Argentina.
June 16: Tomas Russo, a military officer, was assassinated in Argentina.
June 17: Mark Desanti was the target of an unsuccessful assassination attempt in Morocco.
June 20: Said Allal was the target of an unsuccessful attempt on his life in Morocco.
June 25: William Vacanarat Shadrach Tubman, president of Liberia, was the target of an unsuccessful assassination attempt in Liberia.
June 27: Mohamed Naciri was the target of an unsuccessful assassination attempt in Morocco.
July 5: Matus Cernak was slain in West Germany.
Sept. 16: Michael Talow was killed in Morocco.
Oct. 24: Raymond Courvoisier was the target of an unsuccessful assassination attempt in Lebanon.
Nov. 3: Joseph Gallo was the target of a failed assassination attempt in Algeria.
Nov. 11: Kwame Nkrumah, future president of Ghana, was the target of an unsuccessful assassination attempt on the Gold Coast.
Nov. 17: Hussein Ala, premier of Iran, was the target of an unsuccessful assassination attempt in Iran.
Nov. 21: K. Djurhuus was the target of a failed assassination attempt in Denmark.
Nov. 26: Sir John Harding was the target of an unsuccessful attempt on his life in Cyprus.
Nov. 30: Mustapha Diouri was the target of a failed assassination attempt in Morocco.
Nov. 30: Mohammed Mouakit was the target of an unsuccessful assassination attempt in Morocco.

1956

Jesus de Galindez was assassinated in the Dominican Republic.
Feb. 28: Mao Tse-tung, chairman of China and the Communist party, was the target of an unsuccessful assassination attempt in China.
Apr. 6: V. Riesel was the target of an unsuccessful assassination attempt in New York.
June 4: Sir John Harding was the target of a failed assassination attempt in England.
June 26: Fulgencio Batista, dictator and president of Cuba, was the target of an unsuccessful assassination attempt in Cuba.
June 26: Bernard V. Shaw was the target of an unsuccessful attempt on his life in Cyprus.
Sept. 6: J.T. Hernandez was killed in Mexico.
Sept. 21: Anastasio Somoza, president and dictator of Nicaragua, was shot in León, Nicaragua, and died on Sept. 29.
Sept. 28: John M. Chang was the target of an unsuccessful assassination attempt in South Korea.
October: R. Salas Canizares was slain in Cuba.
October: Antonio Blanco Rio was assassinated in Cuba.

1957

Octavio de la Maza was killed in the Dominican Republic.
Jan. 13: Orlando Piedra was the target of an unsuccessful assassination attempt in Cuba.
Feb. 19: Ghassan Jahid was murdered in Lebanon.
Feb. 23: Ngo Dinh Diem, president of Vietnam, was the target of an unsuccessful assassination attempt in Vietnam.
Mar. 13: Fulgencio Batista, president of Cuba, was the target of a failed assassination attempt in Cuba.
Apr. 17: Nnamdi Azikiwe, premier of the Eastern Region of Nigeria, was the target of an unsuccessful assassination attempt in Nigeria.
Apr. 17: Kamal Eddine Salah was killed in Somalia.
May 25: Kliment Yefremovich Voroshilov, chairman of the Russian presidium, was the target of an unsuccessful assassination attempt in Indonesia.
May 27: Ali Chekhol was slain in France.
June 5: Addi Koussa was assassinated in Algeria.
June 24: J. Massu was the target of a failed assassination attempt in Algeria.
June 24: Isaac Rojas was the target of an unsuccessful attempt on his life in Argentina.
July 12: Mohammed Zahir Shah, king of Afghanistan, was the target of an unsuccessful assassination attempt in Afghanistan.
July 12: Sardar Mohammed Daud Khan, prime minister of Afghanistan, was the target of a failed assassination attempt on his life in Afghanistan.
July 26: Carlos Castillo Armas, president of Guatemala, was slain by one of his own guards in Guatemala City.
Aug. 8: Si Henni Jah Ahmed was slain in Algeria.
Nov. 1: Henri Borgeaud was the target of an unsuccessful assassination attempt in France.
Nov. 28: Abdelkader Barakrok was the target of an unsuccessful attempt on his life in France.
Dec. 1: A. Sukarno (Kusnasosro), president of Indonesia, was the target of a failed attempt on his life in Djakarta, Indo., but ten people died and others were injured in gunfire and grenade blasts.

1958

Paul A. Wallace, South Carolina state senator, was shot to death by Henry Rogers, who was later found insane and committed to an institution for the mentally ill, where he hanged himself.
February: Paramo Arias was the target of a failed assassination attempt in Colombia.
February: Sardi Garces was the target of an unsuccessful attempt on his life in Colombia.
February: Arboleda de Uribe was the target of an unsuccessful assassination attempt in Colombia.
Feb. 8: Jacques Soustelle, minister of information of France, was the target of a failed assassination attempt in France.
Mar. 12: Fabio Arbelaez-Cifuentes was slain in Colombia.
Mar. 14: Jose Figuerola was the target of an unsuccessful assassination attempt in Argentina.
Mar. 14: Emilio Sevillano was the target of an unsuccessful attempt on his life in Argentina.
Mar. 26: Jean Chapel was the target of an unsuccessful assassination attempt in Algeria.
Mar. 27: Henri Pharaon was the target of a failed assassination attempt in Lebanon.
Apr. 7: Burhanuddin Harahap was killed in Indonesia.
Apr. 10: Dr. Ernst Guenther Mohr was the target of an unsuccessful assassination attempt in Germany.
Apr. 14: Samuel Devieux was murdered in Washington, D.C.
Apr. 20: Sami El-Solh, premier of Lebanon, was the target of an unsuccessful attempt on his life in Lebanon.
May 4: Louis Dejoie was slain in Haiti.
May 4: Victor Duncan was killed in Haiti.
May 4: Ernst Sabalat was murdered in Haiti.
May 7: Gerald A. Drew was the target of an unsuccessful assassination attempt in Haiti.
May 8: Nasib El-Mitry was assassinated in Lebanon.
May 9: Dr. Khan Sahib was murdered in Pakistan.
May 11: Arthur D. Haas was the target of an unsuccessful assassination attempt in Haiti.
June 13: Santiago Rey was assassinated in Cuba.
June 18: Angelico Balboalopez was the target of a failed assassination attempt in Cuba.
June 22: Jose de Jesus Marquez Monreal was slain in Mexico.
June 29: F.L. Shuttlesworth was the target of an unsuccessful attempt on his life in Alabama.
July 1: Nicolas Rivero Aguero was the target of a failed assassination attempt in Cuba.
July 11: Abboud Abdul Arzzak was the target of an unsuccessful assassination attempt in Lebanon.
July 14: Ibrahim Hashim, past regent and uncle of King Faisal, was assassinated in Iraq.
July 14: Abdul Ilah, past regent and uncle of King Faisal, was killed in Iraq.
July 14: Khulousy El-Khalry was slain in Iraq.
July 14: Suleiman Toukan was murdered in Iraq.
July 14: Faisal II, king of Iraq, was assassinated at the Baghdad palace during a military coup led by General Kassem (Qassim), who was later ousted and executed on Feb. 9, 1963.
July 15: General Nuri as-Said, premier of Iraq, was killed by insurgents under General Kassem in Baghdad.
July 29: Sami El-Solh, premier of Lebanon, was the target of an unsuccessful assassination attempt in Lebanon.
Aug. 30: Salah Samarai was killed in Lebanon.
Sept. 15: Jacques Soustelle, minister of information of France, was the target of a failed assassination attempt in France.
Sept. 18: John Page Wentworth was the target of an unsuccessful attempt on his life in Cyprus.
Sept. 20: Reverend Martin Luther King, Jr., civil rights leader, was the target of an unsuccessful assassination attempt in New York.
Sept. 21: Mohammed Chmine was murdered in France.
Sept. 29: Anibal Vega was slain in Cuba.
Oct. 13: El-Sohl Wadih was the target of an unsuccessful assassination attempt in Lebanon.
Nov. 5: Ait Ahcene Ameziane was killed in Germany.
Nov. 6: Ah Ann was slain in Malaya.
Nov. 6: Chai Swee Sang was murdered in Malaya.
Nov. 23: Auguste Thuveney was slain in Morocco.

1959

P'eng Teh-huai, Chinese official, vanished and may have been assassinated.
February: Teofilo Guerrero Rosario was murdered in the Dominican Republic.

Mar. 7: Rafael Altamirano Herrera was killed in Mexico.
Mar. 16: El Aris was the target of an unsuccessful assassination attempt in Lebanon.
Apr. 12: James Lindsay Almond, Jr., governor of Virginia, was the target of unsuccessful assassins, possibly segregationists, who attempted to shoot him during an era of school integration.
May 3: Rodriguez Echazabal was the target of an unsuccessful attempt on his life in Haiti.
May 3: Ismet Inönü, former president and future premier of Turkey, was the target of an unsuccessful assassination attempt in Turkey.
May 19: Rashid Karami, prime minister of Lebanon, was the target of a failed assassination attempt in Lebanon.
June 7: Rodriguez Echazabal was the target of an unsuccessful attempt on his life in Haiti.
June 8: Luis A. Somoza Debayle, president of Nicaragua, was the target of an unsuccessful assassination attempt in Nicaragua.
June 22: G.D. Shakerch was killed in Iraq.
July 10: Dale R. Buis was murdered in Vietnam.
July 29: N. Moghabghab was slain in Lebanon.
Sept. 1: Norodom Suramarit was the target of an unsuccessful assassination attempt in Cambodia.
Sept. 25: Solomon West Ridgeway Dias Bandaranaike, prime minister of Ceylon, was killed by a Buddhist monk in Colombo.
Oct. 8: Abdul Karim Kassem, prime minister of Iraq, was the target of an unsuccessful assassination attempt in Iraq.
Nov. 24: Sardar Mohammed Naim was the target of an unsuccessful attempt in Afghanistan.
Dec. 4: M. Reyes Rodriguez was the target of a failed assassination attempt in Mexico.
Dec. 13: Bin Ibrahim was the target of an unsuccessful attempt on his life in Oman.
Dec. 19: A. Hakim was the target of a failed assassination attempt in Lebanon.

1960

Jan. 9: Jose Pardo Llada was the target of an unsuccessful attempt on his life in Cuba.
Jan. 13: Daniel Kemajou was the target of a failed assassination attempt in Cameroon.
Feb. 6: Laercio Lemos was murdered in Brazil.
Feb. 18: Norodom Sihanouk, king of Cambodia, was the target of a failed assassination attempt in Cambodia.
Mar. 2: Dr. Roger Rousseau was slain in Haiti.
Mar. 9: A. Sukarno (Kusnasosro), president of Indonesia, was the target of an unsuccessful assassination attempt in Indonesia.
Mar. 12: Rene Cabrera was the target of a failed assassination attempt in Argentina.
Mar. 27: Juan Lagalaye, a military officer, was the target of a failed attempt on his life in Argentina.
Mar. 28: Arturo Frondizi, president of Argentina, was the target of an unsuccessful assassination attempt in Argentina.
Apr. 1: Dr. Oscar Sevilla Sacasa was the target of an failed assassination attempt in Nicaragua.
Apr. 9: Hendrik Frensch Verwoerd, prime minister of South Africa, was critically wounded by gunshot by a white farmer opposed to apartheid in Johannesburg. Verwoerd survived.
Apr. 14: Jairo Alberto Calderon Forero was assassinated in the Dominican Republic.
Apr. 21: Paul-Emile Chabert was killed in Laos.
May 4: Robert Abdesselam was the target of an unsuccessful assassination attempt in France.
May 19: Ben Mahmoud was murdered in Algeria.
June 17: Jotaro Kawakami, Japanese socialist, was stabbed to death in Japan.
June 24: Ramon Armas Perez was assassinated in Venezuela.
June 24: Romulo Betancourt, president of Venezuela, was wounded in Caracas in a bomb blast that killed an aide.
June 24: Josue Lopez Henriques was the target of an unsuccessful assassination attempt in Venezuela.
June 24: Francisco R. Sequero was the target of an unsuccessful attempt on his life in the Dominican Republic.
July 8: Patrice Lumumba, prime minister of the Congo, was the target of an unsuccessful assassination attempt in the Congo.
July 14: Nobusake Kishi, premier of Japan, was stabbed in a failed assassination attempt in Japan.
July 23: Sir Edward D. Asafu-Adjaye was the target of an unsuccessful attempt on his life in England.
July 25: Mark H. Higgins was slain in the Congo.
July 28: Alberto J. Altamirano was murdered in Mexico.
Aug. 9: Sounthone Pathammavong, a military officer, was killed in Laos.
Aug. 29: Zuha Iddin Hammoud was slain in Jordan.
Aug. 29: Mamdoh Ishasat was assassinated in Jordan.
Aug. 29: Hazza Majali, premier of Jordan, was in his Amman office when he and ten others died in a bomb explosion.
Aug. 29: Assem Taijo was murdered in Jordan.
Sept. 15: Patrice Lumumba, prime minister of the Congo, was the target of an unsuccessful assassination attempt in the Congo.
Sept. 29: Raoul Zevaco was murdered in Algeria.
Oct. 12: Inejiro Asanuma, secretary-general of the Socialist Party in Japan, was stabbed to death by a radical in Japan.
Oct. 16: Dr. Felix Moumie was slain in Switzerland.
Oct. 26: Boniface Kalowa was assassinated in the Congo.
Nov. 12: Roby H. Heard was murdered in California.
Nov. 23: Edward Hodgson was slain in the Congo.
Nov. 23: Elton G. Knauf was assassinated in the Congo.
Nov. 29: Patricia Mirabel de Gonzales was slain in the Dominican Republic.
Nov. 29: Maria Teresa Mirabel de Gozman was murdered in the Dominican Republic.
Nov. 29: Dr. Minerva Mirabel de Tavarez was killed in the Dominican Republic.
Dec. 24: Germane Newaye was slain in Ethiopia.
Dec. 25: Carl W. Strom was the target of an unsuccessful assassination attempt in Bolivia.

1961

Salah Ben Youssef was killed in Germany.
Jan. 17: Patrice Hemery Lumumba, prime minister of the Congo (now Zaire), was arrested by agents of President Joseph Kasavubu, and slain in Katanga Province.
Jan. 17: Maurice Mpolo was assassinated in the Congo.
Jan. 17: Joseph Okito was murdered in the Congo.
Jan. 26: Habib ibn Ali Bourguiba was the target of an unsuccessful assassination attempt in Tunisia.
February: Joseph Finant was slain in the Congo.
February: Alphonse Songolo was murdered in the Congo.
Mar. 27: Imam Ahmed Ibn Yahya, of Yemen, was shot and critically injured at Hodeida, but he survived. Five assailants received the death penalty.
May 30: Rafael Leónidas Trujillo Molina, dictator of the Dominican Republic, was in his car when he was murdered by assassins under Pedro Cedeno and Lieutenant Amado Garcia in an unsuccessful coup.
May 31: Ernesto de la Maza was killed in the Dominican Republic.
June: Miguel A. Baez Diaz was slain in the Dominican Republic.
June: Juan Tomas Diaz, a military officer, was murdered in the Dominican Republic.
June: Amado Garcia Guerrero was slain in the Dominican Republic.
June: Juan Haviera was killed in the Dominican Republic.
June: Segundo Imbert Berrera, a military officer, was assassinated in the Dominican Republic.
June: Antonio de la Maza was killed in the Dominican Republic.
June: Jose R. Roman Fernandez was slain in the Dominican Republic.
Sept. 9: Charles-André-Marie-Joseph de Gaulle, president of France, was the target of an unsuccessful assassination attempt in France.
October: Louis Rivagasore was slain in Burundi, Africa.
Nov. 18: Luis M. Caceres was killed in the Dominican Republic.
Nov. 18: Modesto Diaz was murdered in the Dominican Republic.
Nov. 18: Salvador Estrella Sadhala was assassinated in the Dominican Republic.
Nov. 18: Pedro Livio Cedeno was slain in the Dominican Republic.
Nov. 18: Roberto Pastoriza was murdered in the Dominican Republic.
Nov. 18: Huascon Tejeda Pimentel was killed in the Dominican Republic.
December: Members of the Ikeda Cabinet in Japan were the targets in an assassination plot, authorities discovered.

1962

Jan. 22: Sylvanus Olympio, president of Togo, was the target of an unsuccessful assassination attempt in Togo.
Jan. 24: Mahendra, king of Nepal, was the target of an unsuccessful assassination attempt in Nepal.
Jan. 28: Antoine Gizenga was the target of a failed assassination attempt in the Congo.
Feb. 15: H.D. Stogner was slain in the Congo.
Feb. 27: Ngo Dinh Diem, president of Vietnam, was the target of an unsuccessful attempt on his life in South Vietnam.
May: R. Salan was the target of an unsuccessful assassination attempt in France.
May 14: A. Sukarno (Kusnasosro), president of Indonesia, was the target of an unsuccessful assassination attempt in Indonesia.
May 22: Charles-André-Marie-Joseph de Gaulle, president of France, was the target of a failed assassination attempt in France.
May 31: Charles-André-Marie-Joseph de Gaulle, president of France, was the target of a failed attempt on his life in France.
June 15: Charles-André-Marie-Joseph de Gaulle, president of France, was the target of an unsuccessful attempt on his life in France.
June 16: N. Tovey was slain in the Bahamas.
Aug. 23: Charles-André-Marie-Joseph de Gaulle, president of France, was the target of an unsuccessful assassination attempt in France.
Sept. 13: Charles-André-Marie-Joseph de Gaulle, president of France, was the target of a failed assassination attempt in France.
Sept. 28: Muhammad Al-Badr, imam (ruler) of Yemen, was the target of an unsuccessful assassination attempt in Yemen.
Sept. 29: Kwame Nkrumah, president of Ghana, was the target of an unsuccessful attempt on his life in Ghana.
Oct. 22: Charles-André-Marie-Joseph de Gaulle, president of France, was the target of a failed attempt on his life in France.
Oct. 23: Paul Joachim was assassinated in Illinois.
Dec. 6: James Hoffa, labor leader, was the target of an unsuccessful

assassination attempt in Tennessee.
Dec. 27: Habib ibn Ali Bourguiba was the target of an unsuccessful assassination attempt in Tunisia.

1963

Jan. 13: Sylvanus Olympio, president of Togo, was slain at Lomé, Togo, by former soldiers.
Jan. 29: Charles-André-Marie-Joseph de Gaulle, president of France, was the target of an unsuccessful attempt on his life in France.
Feb. 8: General Abdul Karim Kassem (Quassim), prime minister of Iraq, was ousted and murdered in a military takeover in Baghdad, Iraq.
Feb. 15: Charles-André-Marie-Joseph de Gualle, president of France, was the target of a plot to assassinate him while he visited the Ecole Militaire in Paris.
Mar. 1: Charles-André-Marie-Joseph de Gaulle, president of France, was the target of an unsuccessful attempt on his life in France.
Mar. 6: Henri Lafond was slain in France.
Apr. 1: Quinim Pholsena, foreign minister of Laos, was murdered in Vientiane by Chy Kong, a neutralist soldier and his personal guard who confessed to the crime.
Apr. 11: Felix Houphouet-Boigny was the target of an unsuccessful assassination attempt on the Ivory Coast.
Apr. 11: Mohammad Khemisti, foreign minister of Algeria, was shot to death in Algiers, Alg., by a Muslim.
Apr. 17: Abdul Aziz Ben Saud Djalawi was killed in France.
Apr. 17: Shavarsh Kouyoumjian was the target of a failed assassination attempt in Syria.
May 28: Frederick Nolting was the target of an unsuccessful attempt on his life in South Vietnam.
June 12: Medgar W. Evers, Mississippi field secretary for the National Association for the Advancement of Colored People, was shot to death in Jackson, Miss., by unknown assailants.
June 13: Romulo Betancourt, president of Venezuela, was the target of an unsuccessful assassination attempt in Venezuela.
Oct. 31: Savang Vathana was the target of an unsuccessful assassination attempt in Laos.
Nov. 2: Ngo Dinh Diem, president and dictator of South Vietnam, and his brother, Ngo Dinh Nhu, were murdered in the back of an armored personnel carrier by an unnamed South Vietnamese army officer.
Nov. 22: John Fitzgerald Kennedy, president of the U.S., was fatally shot, and John B. Connally, governor of Texas, was injured in Dallas, Texas, by political subversive Lee Harvey Oswald, who was killed two days later by Jack Ruby. Ruby was given the death penalty.
Dec. 10: George Henderson was slain in Aden, Yemen.

1964

Lieutenant General Rene Barrientos Ortuno was the target of two unsuccessful assassination attempts in Bolivia.
Jan. 18: Charles-André-Marie-Joseph de Gaulle, president of France, was the target of a failed attempt on his life in France.
Jan. 24: Marc Blitzstein, U.S. composer, was slain in Martinique.
Feb. 4: Hassan II, king of Morocco, was the target of an unsuccessful assassination attempt in Morocco.
Feb. 12: Ketsana Vongsonavanh was killed in Laos.
Feb. 13: Charles-André-Marie-Joseph de Gaulle, president of France, was the target of an unsuccessful assassination attempt in France.
Feb. 22: Ismet Inonu, premier of Turkey, was the target of a failed assassination attempt in Turkey.
Mar. 19: Charles-André-Marie-Joseph de Gaulle, president of France, was the target of a failed attempt on his life in France.
Mar. 24: Edwin Reischauer was the target of an unsuccessful assassination attempt in Japan.
Mar. 25: Charles-André-Marie-Joseph de Gaulle, president of France, was the target of an unsuccessful assassination attempt in France.
Apr. 1: Charles-André-Marie-Joseph de Gaulle, president of France, was the target of a failed assassination attempt in France.
Apr. 5: Jigme P. Dorji was killed in Bhutan, Asia.
Apr. 11: Verda Welcome was the target of an unsuccessful assassination attempt in Maryland.
May 21: Roberto Arias was the target of an unsuccessful attempt on his life in Panama.
May 21: Escolastico Calvo was the target of a failed assassination attempt in Panama.
June 1: A. Ben Bella, president and premier of Algeria, was the target of an unsuccessful assassination attempt in Algeria.
June 5: Abate Agede was murdered in Sweden.
September: H.N. Sanyal was killed in India.
Sept. 27: General Adib Al-Shishakli, overthrown Syrian leader, traveled to Brazil where he was slain by a Druse who thought that the Druse in Syria had been persecuted by the general.
Dec. 20: Simon Wiesenthal, Nazi hunter, was the target of an unsuccessful assassination attempt in Austria.

1965

Mohammed Reza Pahlavi, shah of Iran, was the target of an unsuccessful assassination attempt in Iran.
Jan. 15: Pierre Ngendandumwe was slain in Burundi, Africa.
Jan. 21: Hassan Ali Mansour (Ali Mansur), premier of Iran, was murdered in Teheran. Four assassins were executed.
Feb. 6: Pratap Singh Kairon was murdered in India.
Feb. 9: Colonel Harold Hauser, head of the U.S. military mission to Guatemala, was the target of an unsuccessful assassination attempt by Movimiento Revolucionario-13 terrorists.
Feb. 15: Anselme Massouemi was slain in the Congo.
Feb. 15: Lazare Matsokota was killed in the Congo.
Feb. 15: Joseph Pouabou was murdered in the Congo.
Feb. 21: Malcolm X, black nationalist, was shot to death in New York City, allegedly by Black Muslims. Three assailants were sent to prison.
Mar. 9: Reverend James J. Reeb was assassinated in Alabama.
Mar. 21: Lieutenant General Rene Barriento Ortuno was the target of an unsuccessful assassination attempt in Bolivia.
Mar. 25: Viola Liuzzo was killed in Alabama.
Mar. 28: Charles-André-Marie-Joseph de Gaulle, president of France, was the target of a failed assassination attempt in France.
Apr. 1: Mohammed Al-Zubairy was slain in Yemen.
Apr. 14: Hamani Diori was the target of an unsuccessful assassination attempt in Niger.
May 21: Colonel Ernesto M. Arreaga was slain in Guatemala.
May 24: Charles-André-Marie-Joseph de Gaulle, president of France, was the target of an unsuccessful assassination attempt in France.
July 17: Charles-André-Marie-Joseph de Gaulle, president of France, was the target of a failed assassination attempt in France.
July 20: General Maxwell D. Taylor was the target of an unsuccessful attempt on his life in Vietnam.
July 27: Emilio Aragones was the target of an unsuccessful assassination attempt in Cuba.
July 27: Fidel Castro, premier of Cuba, was the target of a failed assassination attempt in Cuba.
August: Jonathan M. Daniels was murdered in Alabama.
Aug. 7: Abdullah Al-Sallal was the target of a failed assassination attempt in Yemen.
Sept. 13: Sir Arthur Charles was slain in Aden.
Oct. 20: John Kilpatrick, president of the United Industrial Workers' Union, was fatally shot in Chicago by Dana H. Nash, who was sent to prison.
Oct. 29: Diosdado Macapagal, president of the Philippines, was the target of an unsuccessful assassination attempt in the Philippines.
Oct. 31: Mario Mendez Montenegro was slain in Guatemala.
Nov. 4: Ali Benahmed was killed in Aden.

1966

Manuel Isidoro Belzú, ex-president of Bolivia, was assassinated.
Jan. 15: Sumuel L. Akintola was killed in Nigeria.
Jan. 15: Sir Abubakar Tafawa Balewa, prime minister of Nigeria, was assassinated in Nigeria.
Jan. 15: Sir Ahmadu Bello was slain in Nigeria.
Jan. 15: Festus Okotie-Eboh was murdered in Nigeria.
Apr. 13: Abdullah El-Airiny was killed in Yemen.
Apr. 14: Abdul Iriani was assassinated in Yemen.
Apr. 14: Ahmed Rahoumi was the target of an unsuccessful attempt on his life in Yemen.
May 18: General Maximliano Hernandez Martinez was assassinated in the Honduras.
June 6: James Meredith, civil rights activist, was the target of a failed assassination attempt in Mississippi.
June 19: Arthur Calwell, head of the Labor party, was the target of an unsuccessful assassination attempt in Australia by Peter R. Kocan, who was sent to prison for life.
July: Thanom Kittakachorn, premier of Thailand, was the target of an unsuccessful attempt on his life in Thailand.
July: Gamal Abdel Nasser, president of Egypt, was the target of a failed assassination attempt in Egypt.
July 30: J.T.V. Ironsi Aguiyi was slain in Nigeria.
August: Ahmed Bassendawah was killed in Aden.
August: Arthur Costa E Silva, minister of war of Brazil, was the target of an unsuccessful assassination attempt in Brazil.
Sept. 6: Hendrik Frensch Verwoerd, prime minister of South Africa, was stabbed to death in parliament at Capetown by an itinerant, Dimitri Stifanos, who was later judged insane.
Sept. 13: J. Van der Poel, was murdered in England.
Dec. 7: Tran Van Van was slain in South Vietnam.

1967

Dr. Herbert Aptheker was the target of an unsuccessful assassination attempt in New York.
Jan. 3: Mohammed Khider was murdered in Spain.
Feb. 2: Abdul Q. Mackawee was the target of a failed assassination attempt in Aden.
Feb. 3: Demba Diop was killed in Senegal.
Feb. 26: Sayed Mohammed Hassan was slain in Aden.
Mar. 5: Mohammed Nagi was killed in Aden.
Mar. 20: Abdurrahman Girgerah was murdered in Aden.
Mar 22: Léopold Sédar Senghor, president of Senegal, was the target of an unsuccessful assassination attempt in Senegal.
Mar 23: Léopold Sédar Senghor, president of Senegal, was the target of a failed attempt on his life in Senegal.
Apr. 4: Haider Shamshair was slain in Aden.
Apr. 5: Hubert Humphrey, vice president of the U.S., was the victim of an apparent murder plot during his visit to West Berlin by eleven conspirators, who were arrested.
Apr. 19: Sheik Salem Al-Amoodi was assassinated in Aden.

Apr. 19: Abdurrahim Qassem was killed in Aden.
Apr. 24: Etienne Eyadema was the target of an unsuccessful assassination attempt in Togo.
May 8: Haidera Saleh Mohammed Yafai was slain in Aden.
May 28: Rodolfo Gonzalez was murdered in Venezuela.
June 9: Charles Eustis Bohlen, U.S. ambassador to Paris, was the target of an unsuccessful assassination attempt in France.
June 22: Roy Wilkins, civil rights leader, was the target of an unsuccessful attempt on his life in New York.
June 25: Francois Duvalier, president of Haiti, was the target of an unsuccessful attempt on his life in Haiti.
July 3: Sheik Ali Salih Fedama was murdered in Aden.
August: Lam Bun was killed in Hong Kong.
Aug. 26: George Lincoln Rockwell was slain in Virginia.
Sept. 28: Levi Eshkol, prime minister of Israel, was the target of an unsuccessful assassination attempt in Israel.
November: Che Guevara, revolutionary hero, was assassinated in Bolivia.
Dec. 14: Bui Quang San was murdered in South Vietnam.

1968

Than Tun (Thakin Than Tun), head of White Flag Communist party of Burma, led a failed rebellion, and was slain.
Jan. 16: Colonel John D. Webber, Jr., commander of a U.S. squad in Guatemala, and Lieutenant Commander Ernest A. Munro were shot to death in Guatemala.
Apr. 4: Reverend Dr. Martin Luther King, Jr., civil rights leader, was shot to death in Memphis, Tenn., by James Earl Ray, who was sent to prison.
Apr. 25: Houari Boumedienne, president of Algeria, was the target of an unsuccessful assassination attempt in Algeria.
May 25: Modesto Chiari was assassinated in Panama.
May 31: Camille Chamoun, president of Lebanon, was the target of a failed assassination attempt in Lebanon.
June 5: Robert Francis Kennedy, U.S. senator from New York, was shot to death in Los Angeles by Sirhan Bishara Sirhan, a Palestinian, because of comments on foreign policy in regard to the Middle East. Sirhan was later sent to prison.
July 7: Abdul Rahman Al-Iryani was the target of an unsuccessful attempt on his life in Yemen.
July 26: Yevgeny N. Kachailov was murdered in Russia.
Aug. 2: Militon Manzanas was killed in Spain.
Aug. 13: George Papadopoulis, premier of Greece, was the target of a failed assassination attempt in Greece.
Sept. 16: Shawki El-Farrah was assassinated in Gaza.
Oct. 12: Charles R. Chandler, U.S. Army captain, was slain outside his home in Sao Paulo, Braz., apparently by Vanguarda Popular Revolucionaria (VPR) terrorists.
Oct. 21: Jose Roman was killed in the Philippines.
Oct. 23: El Poder Cubano terrorists allegedly responsible for trying to kill the Cuban ambassador to the United Nations were apprehended.
Oct. 26: Three Croatian leaders who opposed Communism were discovered slain in Munich, Ger.
Dec. 14: Charles Senecal, director of Chanbly Transport, was the target of bombings in Canada.

1969

Feb. 3: Dr. Eduardo Mondlane, president of the Mozambique Liberation Front, was killed when he received a bomb by mail at Dar es Salaam, Tanzania, sent by unknown killers.
Mar. 1: Clay Shaw was acquitted on charges of conspiring to assassinate President John F. Kennedy.
June 30: The chief of the Yugoslavian mission in West Berlin, was critically wounded in an attempt on his life and another was injured by a Croation nationalist.
July 5: Tom Mboya, minister of economic planning and development of Kenya, was murdered in Nairobi by members of the Kikuyu Tribe.
July 30: A.H. Meyer, U.S. ambassador to Japan, was the target of a failed attempt on his life when he was accosted in Japan by a Japanese citizen armed with a knife.
Oct. 17: Abdi Rashid Ali Shermarke, president of Somalia, was killed at Las Anos, Somalia.

1970

Jan. 30: A state of siege was declared in Guatemala following the attempted assassination of a presidential candidate and the murder of a newspaper editor who opposed Communism.
Mar. 8: Makarios III, president of Cyprus, was the target of an unsuccessful assassination attempt in Nicosia. Polycarpos Georghadjis, ex-minister of interior, was thought to be involved.
Mar. 27: General al-Numeiri, Sudan leader, was the target of a failed attempt on his life by adherents of Imam al-Hadi al-Mahdi.
May 4: The wife of the first secretary of the Israeli embassy in Asunción, Para., was shot to death and another person was injured in the embassy, allegedly by Al Fatah terrorists.
May 29: Pedro Eugenio Arambaru, former president of Argentina, was abducted and murdered by terrorists whose demands for freeing political inmates were denied.
June 10: Major Robert Perry, military attaché in Amman, Jor., was at home when he was fatally shot by terrorists.
Aug. 15: Alfredo Stroessner, president of Paraguay, was the target of a failed assassination attempt.
November: Amilcar Cabral, prominent African nationalist, was the target of a failed attempt on his life by Portuguese commandos.
November: Sákou Touré, president of Guinea, was the target of an unsuccessful assassination attempt by Portuguese raiders.
Nov. 1: The deputy foreign minister of Poland was slain by a Pakistani in Karachi, Pak.
Nov. 27: Paul VI, pope, was threatened, but not hurt in the Manila, Phil., airport by Benjamin Mendoza, a Bolivian who was armed with a knife.

1971

Mar. 6: Colonel Delgado Villegas, former prominent Guatemalan police official, was fatally shot following three previous attempts on his life.
Apr. 7: The Yugoslavian ambassador to Sweden was killed and two other Yugoslavian statesmen were injured in Stockholm, Swed., by Croatian terrorists.
Aug. 21: Assassins tried to slay numerous members of the Liberal Party (in opposition) in Manila, Phil.
Sept. 29: Mullah Barzani, head of the Kurdistan Democratic Party was the target of an unsuccessful assassination attempt in Iraq.
Oct. 6 Yasser Arafat (Yasir), chairman of the Palestinian Liberation Organization, was the target of a failed attempt on his life.
Oct. 18: Alexei Kosygin, premier of the U.S.S.R., was unhurt by an attack near the Canadian Parliament in Ottawa by a protester.
Nov. 28: Wasfi Tal, prime minister of Jordan, was assassinated in Cairo by Black September Palestinian guerrillas.
Dec. 15: Zaid Rifai, Jordan ambassador in London was injured by gunshot in a failed attempt on his life by Black September Palestinian terrorists.
Dec. 16: The Jordan ambassador in Geneva, Switz., was the target of an unsuccessful attempt on his life.

1972

Mar. 3: Black September Palestinian terrorists tried to assault the London quarters of Hussein I, king of Jordan.
Apr. 8: Sheik Abeid Amani Karume, leader of Zanzibar, was slain.
May 15: George Wallace, governor of Alabama, was shot and severely crippled in Laurel, Md., by Arthur Bremer, who was sent to prison.
Sept. 9: Dr. Ami Shachori, agricultural advisor of the Israel Embassy, was slain by a mail bomb in London sent by Black September terrorists.
Sept. 11: Salvador Allende Gossens, president of Chile, was ousted in a military coup under General Ugarte Augusto Pinochet and he either committed suicide or was put to death.
Oct. 16: Wael Zuaiter, Fatah official in Rome, was fatally shot near his apartment in Rome by Mossad terrorists.
Dec. 7: Imelda Marcos, wife of Philippine president Ferdinand Edralin Marcos, was stabbed and critically injured, but survived, an attack in Pasay City, Phil.
Dec. 8: Mahmoud Hamshari, the primary official of Al Fatah and the Palestinian Liberation Organization in Paris died when a bomb exploded at his Paris apartment. Mossad members were allegedly responsible.

1973

Jan. 20: Amilcar Cabral, politician and prominent African nationalist, was murdered outside his home in Conakry, Guinea, by Innocencio Canida.
Feb. 9: Hussein I, king of Jordan, was a likely target of Black September assassin suspects who were arrested.
Mar. 2: Cleo A. Noel, Jr., U.S. Ambassador, George C. Moore, U.S. Charge d'Affaires, and Guy Eid, Belgian Charge d'Affaires, were murdered in Khartoum, Sudan, by Palestinian guerrillas.
Apr. 1: Ziyad Al Hilu, a member of the Black September Organization who allegedly helped kill Prime Minister Wasfi Tal of Jordan, was the target of Jordan intelligence assassins in a bombing, according to the BSO.
Apr. 9: Kamal Adwan, head of Al Fatah, was slain in Beirut by Israeli terrorists.
June 2: Lieutenant Colonel Lewis Hawkins, U.S. military adviser in Iran, was shot to death by those thought to be left-wing terrorists.
June 28: Mohammed Boudia, most prominent Arab terrorist in Europe, was murdered by a car bomb in Paris.
July 1: Colonel Yosef Alon, Israeli military attache in Washington, D.C., was fatally shot at his house in Chevy Chase, Md., and Arab terrorists were suspected.
Sept. 17: The British ambassadors in Lisbon, Port., and Kinshasa, Zaire, and a high-ranking government administrator in Gibralter were sent letter bombs. Only one exploded, injuring a security official in Kinshasa.
Nov. 22: John A. Swint, general manager of a Ford subsidiary, Transax, was shot to death with three bodyguards in Cordoba, Arg. The Fuerzas Armadas Peronistas (FAP) took credit.
Dec. 20: Luis Carrero Blanco, prime minister, was slain in a bomb blast and ETA terrorists claim credit.
Dec. 30: Teddy Seiff, prominent British Zionist, was slain in London by a PFLP terrorist.

1974

Feb. 12: Federal officials in Buenos Aires detected a terrorist plot to murder Juan Perón, president of Argentina, and his wife, Isabel, and Uruguayan President Juan M. Bordaberry.
Aug. 15: Park Chung Hee, president of South Korea, was the target of a failed attempt on his life by assassins who fatally shot his wife instead.

Aug. 19: Rodger P. Davies, U.S. ambassador to Cyprus, was shot to death in Nicosia.
Sept. 12: Ahmed al-Ghafour, head of NAYLP and terrorist, was fatally shot by Fatah terrorists.
October: Yasser Arafat, chairman of the Palestinian Liberation Organization, and Executive Committee member, Abu Mazin, were the targets of a failed assassination attempt, attributed to Abu Nidal terrorists.
Oct. 1: Hussein I, king of Jordan, was the target of a murder plot by Black September Palestinian assassins in Rabat, Mor.
Nov. 11: Gunter von Drenkmann, president of the German Supreme Court, was slain by members of the Second of June Movement.

1975

A U.S. Senate report outlined attempts by the CIA to assassinate Fidel Castro, prime minister of Cuba.
Feb. 11: Richard Ratsimandrava, president of Madagascar, was shot dead in Tananarive.
March: Herbert Chitepo, ex-chairman of the Zimbabwe African National Union, was murdered in Lusaka, Zambia.
Mar. 25: Faisal, king of Saudi Arabia, was killed in the royal palace at Riyadh by Prince Faisal Bin Musaed Bin Abdulaziz in retaliation for the murder of his brother nine years before.
Aug. 15: Sheik Mujibur Rahman (Sheikh Mujib), president of Bangladesh, was assassinated during a coup.
Sept. 5: Gerald Rudolph Ford, president of the U.S., survived an attack in Sacramento, Calif., by Charles Manson devotee Lynette Alice (Squeaky) Fromme. She was sent to prison.
Sept. 22: Gerald Rudolph Ford, president of the U.S., was assaulted by armed political activist Sarah Jane Moore, but the attack was thwarted and she was sent to prison.
Dec. 23: Richard S. Welsh, chief of the CIA in Athens, Gr., was fatally shot as he arrived home by unknown attackers.

1976

Fidel Castro, prime minister of Cuba, asserted that the CIA was still trying to assassinate him. Henry A. Kissinger, U.S. secretary of state, denied the allegations.
Francis Meloy, Jr., ambassador, was slain.
Feb. 13: General Murtala Ramat Mohammad, president of Nigeria, was killed by rebels during a coup attempt.
Apr. 7: Hugo Carlos Sardan, a Pfizer executive, was the target of an unsuccessful assassination attempt in Argentina. One guard was murdered and another injured.
Apr. 21: The president of Chevron Oil Italiana was injured in Rome, Italy, apparently by members of the Armed Communist Formations.
July 31: Christopher Ewart-Biggs, British ambassador to Ireland, was slain by a bomb in Dublin, Ire., planted by PIRA terrorists.
Sept. 21: Orlando Letelier, former foreign minister of Chile, died when his car blew up in Washington, D.C., the victim of unknown assailants.
Nov. 3: Carlos Souto, Argentine executive of Chrysler, was shot close to his house in Buenos Aires, Arg.
Dec. 27: Abd al-Halim Khaddam, Syrian foreign minister, was the target of an unsuccessful murder plot in Damascus, allegedly by the Abu Nidal terrorists.

1977

Feb. 3: Brigadier General Teferi Bante, Ethiopian head of state, and six others on the military council in power, were murdered during a coup led by Lieutenant Colonel Mengistu Haile-Mariam.
Mar. 16: Kamal Jumbat, Lebanese Druse leader, was shot to death close to Beirut.
Mar. 18: Marien Ngouabi, Congo president, was shot to death in Brazzaville.
April: Siegfried Buback, German public prosecutor, was slain by terrorists.
Apr. 10: Abdullah al-Henjiri, ex-prime minister of Yemen, his wife, and the Yemen embassy minister were fatally shot in London by Zohair Akache, a Palestinian terrorist.
July 30: Jürgen Ponto, prominent German banker, was slain in Frankfurt by Red Army Faction terrorists.
October: Sayf bin Sa'id al-Ghubash, the foreign minister of the United Arab Emirates, died in an assault at the Abu Dhabi airport, apparently by the Abu Nidal terrorists in an unsuccessful attempt to kill Abd al-Halim Khaddam, the Syrian foreign minister.
Nov. 15: Muhammad Salah, director of the Arab Library in Paris, was slain, reportedly by the Abu Nidal terrorists.

1978

Sardar Mohammad Daud Khan, prime minister and president of Afghanistan, overthrew King Mohammad Zahir Shah, but was ousted and murdered in a left-wing military coup.
Jan. 1: Said Hammami (Hamami), Palestinian Liberation Organization agent in London, was killed in London by Abu Nidal terrorists.
Jan. 10: Pedro Chamorro, opposition newspaper editor and publisher, was murdered in Nicaragua.
Feb. 18: Yusuf Siba'i (Yousseff el-Sebai), leader of the Committee for Afro-Asian Solidarity and editor of *Al Ahram*, an Egyptian newspaper, was murdered in Nicosia, by Abu Nidal Palestinian terrorists.
Mar. 6: Aldo Moro, former prime minister of Italy, was kidnapped for political ransom. The abductors the Red Brigade, murdered him about two months later and his body was found in Rome on May 9, 1978. Thirty-three members of the Red Brigade were sent to prison.
Mar. 27: Chief Kapuuo, who was appointed president of Namibia by South African officials, was killed.
May 11: Marzio Astarita, Italian manager of the Chemical Bank of New York, was shot in the legs in Milan, Italy, apparently by members of the Front Line and Fighting Communist Formations.
June 15: Ali Yasin, an agent of the Palestinian Liberation Organization, was slain in Kuwait by Abu Nidal terrorists.
June 24: President Ghashmi of North Yemen was assassinated at a conference in Beirut.
June 26: Ali, president of South Yemen, was killed following a Soviet National Liberation Front coup.
July 9: Abdul Razak Al-Naif, ex-premier of Iraq, was shot dead in London by members of the Iraqi secret service.
July 21: Juan Sanchez, brigadier general, and Lieutenant Colonel Juan Perez Rodriguez were murdered in Spain and a man was sent to prison.
July 31: Two Arabs took hostages in the Iraqi Embassy in Paris. One fled and the other demanded the freedom of an Arab woman held for trying to kill the Iraqi ambassador in London.
Aug. 3: Adnan Hamid, journalist for the Palestine news organization and Ezzedine Kalak, director of the Palestinian Liberation Organization in Paris, were killed by the Abu Nidal terrorists.
November: Albert Miles, deputy governor of Maze Prison, was slain close to his house in Belfast, Ire. An alleged member of the IRA was charged with murder.
Nov. 27: Harvey Milk, supervisor of San Francisco, a professed homosexual, and George Moscone, San Francisco mayor, were shot to death in City Hall by Daniel James White, former supervisor of the city. White was sent to prison for manslaughter, a verdict which sparked riots by the homosexual community on July 15, 1979.
December: A retired Army colonel was slain in San Sebastian, Spain, and three men were sent to prison.
Dec. 7: Abdul Wahhab Kayali, former leader of the Pro-Iraqi Liberation Front, was shot in his office in Beirut.
Dec. 11: Ayatollah Abdol Hossein Dastgheib, an aide to Ayatollah Ruhollah Khomeini, was killed in a bomb blast near his home in Shiraz, Iran.
Dec. 17: Ronald Reagan, U.S. president, was the target of an attempt on his life when he received a letter bomb, which was disarmed.
Dec. 23: Paul Grimm, manager of the Oil Service Company of Iran, was shot dead in Ahwaz, Iran, as he drove to work.

1979

Jan. 12: Ali Hassan Salemeh, organizer of the Munich massacre, was slain in Beirut by a car bomb planted by members of Mossad.
February: Abdi Ipekci, chief editor of *Milliyet*, a newspaper of Istanbul, was killed by Mehmet Ali Agca.
Feb. 14: Adolph Dubs, U.S. ambassador, was shot dead in Kabul, Afg., by Afghan Muslim fanatics.
Mar. 22: Sir Richard Sykes, British ambassador to the Netherlands, was fatally shot at his home at the Hague by terrorists.
Mar. 25: Manuel Colom Argueta, head of the Opposition United Front of the Revolution party of Guatemala, was shot to death by unknown assassins.
Mar. 30: Airey Neave, Tory member of parliament of England, was slain when a bomb exploded in his car, reputedly planted by the IRA.
April 4: Zulfikar Ali Bhutto, president and prime minister of Pakistan, was overthrown in 1977, and put to death in Rawalpindi, Pak.
May 29: John H. Wood, Jr., a U.S. judge, was shot to death by Charles V. Harrelson, a professional killer. Harrelson was sent to prison for life.
May 30: The Swiss chargé d'affaires was shot to death in El Salvador by unknown assailants.
June 29: General Alexander Haig, NATO commander, was the target of a failed attempt on his life with a car bomb in Belgium.
July 25: Zuhair Moshin, head of the Syrian dominated Sa'ika, was fatally shot near his Cannes, Fr., apartment by Abu Nidal terrorist acting for the Iraqi secret service.
Aug. 27: Louis Mountbatten, first Earl of Mountbatten of Burma (formerly Prince Louis Francis Albert Victor Nicholas of Battenberg), was killed on his yacht off the coast of County Sligo, Ire., in a bomb explosion. The IRA claimed responsibility.
Oct. 26: Park Chung Hee, president of South Korea, and several aides and bodyguards were shot to death in Seoul by Kim Jae Kyu, Korean intelligence chief, and others during a military coup. Kyu was sentenced to death Dec. 20.
Nov. 13: Efraim Eldar, Israeli ambassador was the target of an unsuccessful attempt on his life in Lisbon, Port. by Abu Nidal terrorists.

1980

A Cuban diplomat at the United Nations was slain by Omega 7 terrorists, whose chief, Eduardo Arocena, was sent to prison for life for the killing.
The director of the San Sebastian, Spain telephone company was slain by ETA terrorists.
Feb. 6: Dogan Turkmen, Turkish ambassador to Bern, was the target of an attempt on his life by conspirators including Max Kilnndjian.
Mar. 3: Max Mazin, a leader a local Jewish community, was apparently the target of the Abu Nidal terrorists, who unintentionally murdered Adolfo Cottelo instead.
Mar. 24: Oscar Arnulfo Romero, archbishop of San Salvador who had publicly denounced the oppressive military, was killed.

Apr. 12: William Richard Tolbert, Jr., president of the Republic of Liberia, was killed after he was overthrown in a military coup by Sergeant Samuel Doe.
Apr. 14: Indira Gandhi, prime minister of India, was the target of an unsuccessful attempt on her life in New Delhi, when a man hurled a knife at her.
Apr. 22: Salah Khalaf (Abu Iyad), chief of the Palestinian Liberation Organization's military department and deemed to be Yassar Arafat's deputy, was the target of an attempted bombing, apparently by Abu Nidal terrorists in Belgrade, Yug. One person was tried by Fatah.
May 10: Omran el-Mehdawi, ex-finance attache and second secretary of the Libyan Embassy in Bonn, Ger., was killed in Bonn.
May 29: Vernon E. Jordan, Jr., civil rights leader and president of the National Urban League, was shot and injured, but survived an attack in Ft. Wayne, Ind.
June: John Turnly, a leader in the Irish Independence Party, was slain.
June 2: Bassam Shaka, mayor of Nablus, lost both of his legs when a car bomb exploded.
July 18: Shahpur Bakhtiar, premier of Iran, was the target of a failed assassination attempt in Paris and five men were sent to prison.
July 19: Nihat Erim, ex-premier of Turkey, was slain and a Marxist group took credit.
Sept 15: According to reports, Serbian terrorists planned to assassinate or kidnap Edward R. Vrdolyak, Chicago alderman, on or near this date.
Sept. 17: Anastasio Somoza, ex-president of Nicaragua, was ousted in 1979 by the Sandinistas. He fled, but was shot to death in Paraguay.
October: Mario Amato, judge in Rome, was slain.
October: Ronnie Bunting, influential in Republican party and alleged high-ranking IRA member.
November: More than twenty leaders of the Democratic Revolutionary Front were kidnapped in El Salvador and six were later slain.
December: Ayatollah Moussavi Ardebeli, prosecutor general of Iran, was the target of Forgan terrorists who placed a bomb at Teheran University.
December: Sultan Ibraimov, chairman of the council of ministers of the Kirgiz Republic, U.S.S.R., was slain.
December: Christopher Tugendhat, British official of the European Community Commission, was the target of an unsuccessful assassination attempt in Brussels, Belg.
Dec. 25: Karim Khalaf, mayor of Ramallah, was injured by a car bomb.
Dec. 31: General Enrico Galvaligi, chief of security for prisons confining terrorists in Italy, was shot to death in Italy.

1981

Jan. 3: Jose Rodolfo Viera, president of the Salvadoran Institute for Agrarian Transformation, Michael Peter Hammer, U.S. agrarian reform authority, and Mark David Pearlman, U.S. attorney, were shot to death in San Salvador, El Sal.
Jan. 12: Sheik Hammad Abu Rabia, chief of one of the biggest Negev tribes, was shot to death in Jerusalem.
Jan 16: Muhammad Hamud Khamis, minister of local government in the Yemen Arab Republic, was murdered during a trip from Sana'a to Hodeida.
Jan. 16: Bernadette Devlin McAliskey, Irish political activist, and her husband, Michael, survived an attack after they were shot and injured in County Tyrone, Ire., by three members of a protestant paramilitary organization.
Jan. 21: Sir Norman Stronge, Protestant speaker of the Northern Ireland Parliament, and his son, James, former member of the Stormont Parliament, were shot to death in their home in Armagh.
February: Two Palestinian bodyguards of Ruholla Khomeini, Ayatollah, were put to death for plotting to murder the Iranian leader.
Feb. 6: Mahmut Dikler, deputy director of police for Istanbul, and a bodyguard were shot to death in Instanbul. Left-wing terrorists were thought to be responsible.
Feb. 6: Jose Maria Ryan, head engineer of a nuclear plant being built in Lemoniz, was killed by members of the Basque Fatherland and Liberty Group (ETA) terrorists.
Feb. 7: A retired colonel was killed in Istanbul and left-wing terrorists were thought responsible.
Feb. 16: John Paul II, pope, was the probable target of a bomb that exploded in Pakistan just before an appearance by the pope.
Feb. 17: A newspaper announced that several Syrians were apprehended in Jordan for trying to kill Mudar Badran, the prime minister of Jordan.
Feb. 17: Luigi Marangoni, head of the Polyclinic Hospital in Milan, Italy, that was operated by the state, was fatally shot by four attackers after attempts had been made to restructure the government health service.
Feb. 28: The director of posts and telecommunications of Uganda was murdered.
Mar. 5: The Turkish labor attache in Paris was killed and his assistant injured by gunshots near the Turkish Embassy.
Mar. 5: Jose-Maria Moya, commissioner of police in a section of Bilboa, Spain, was shot dead.
Mar. 10: John Gunther Dean, U.S. ambassador, was the target of an unsuccessful assassination attempt in Beirut.
Mar. 15: Wilfred Hawker, U.S. Army sergeant major, was injured in a failed attempt on his life in Surinam.
Mar. 18: The head of the national militia training in Nicaragua was shot to death in Chinandega province, Nic.
Mar. 19: Lieutenant Colonel Ramon Romero Rotaeche, was murdered in Bilbao, Spain.
Mar. 21: Lieutenant Colonel Jose Luis Prieto Garcia, retired chief of the Navarre, Spain, regional police, was slain.
Mar. 29: Rabbani Shirazi, ayatollah and emissary of Ayatollah Ruhollah Khomeini was injured in Shiraz, Iran.
Mar. 30: Ronald Reagan, president of the U.S., Press Secretary James Brady, police officer Thomas Delahanty, and Secret Service agent Timothy J. McCarthy were shot and injured, but survived an attack in Washington, D.C., by John W. Hinckley, Jr., who was sent to an institution for the mentally ill.
April: Jill Knight, Tory member of the British Parliament, was sent a letter bomb by the English Republican Army (ERA).
Apr. 7: Edward Michael Richardson, armed with a gun, was arrested in New York and indicted two days later for threatening the life of President Ronald Reagan.
Apr. 14: Giuseppe Salvia, deputy director of Poggioreale Prison was shot to death in his car in Naples, Italy.
Apr. 16: Joseph Munhangi, member of the Ugandan Parliament, was assassinated in Kampala, Uganda.
Apr. 25: Barry Porter, member of Parliament and British conservative, was sent a letter bomb, possibly by members of the IRA. The bomb did not explode.
Apr. 30: Jose Barrera Aguilar, production manager of a coffee company, was fatally shot near his home in Guatemala City, Guat.
May: Juan Carlos, king of Spain, was the probable target of a murder plot, police theorized after finding a tunnel built beneath the road the king would be traveling in a May 31 parade.
May 1: Heinz Nittel, Vienna Councilman and president of the Austrian-Israeli Friendship League, was shot to death near his apartment in Vienna, Aust. A member of Al-Asifa later admitted to the murder.
May 4: Andreas Gonzalez de Suso, brigadier general, was shot to death near his apartment in Madrid, Spain, by leftist terrorists.
May 4: Three of the king of Spain's personal aides were slain in a bomb blast in Spain.
May 5: Indira Gandhi, prime minister of India, planned to travel from May 5-13 on an airplane. Officials found that someone had tried to sabotage the plane before the flight.
May 6: Roy Hattersley, British shadow home secretary and Jim Kelfedder, Unionist member of Parliament, were sent letter bombs.
May 6: David Thebehali, mayor of Soweto, S. Afri., was the target of an unsuccessful assassination attempt when a grenade exploded under his car.
May 11: Heinz Herbert Karry, minister of economics of Hesse, West Ger., was shot to death in his bedroom in Frankfurt.
May 12: Otto Walter Garcia, one of the leaders in the Leftist United Revolutionary Front, was killed in Guatemala.
May 13: John Paul II, pope, and two others were shot and injured in St. Peter's Square, Rome, by Mehmet Ali Agca, a Turkish terrorist acting on orders from Communist leaders. Agca was sent to prison.
May 14: Carlos Humberto Mendez Lopez, deputy commander of the private army of the National Liberation Movement, was fatally shot in Guatemala City, Guat., by two attackers.
May 22: Military conspirators failed in a bid to take power of Libya and assassinate Muammar Gaddafi, president of Libya.
May 30: Ziaur Rahman, president of Bangladesh, was murdered in Chittagong, Bangladesh, with six bodyguards and two aides in a short-lived coup under Major General Abul Manzur, who was killed by guards on June 1.
June: Ayatollah Ruhollah Khomeini, Iranian leader, was the target of conspirators who planned to have him slain by members of Savama, a secret service, during the first week in June.
June 1: Na'im Khadir, agent of the Palestinian Liberation Organization in Brussels, Belg., was killed, reputedly by the Abu Nidal terrorists.
June 3: The first secretary of the Iraqi Embassy in Beirut was injured by gunmen in Beirut.
June 6: Uberto Siola, a Communist councilman of Naples, Italy, was shot in his legs by Red Brigades terrorists.
June 13: Lord Gardiner, British ex-lord chancellor, was the target of a failed assassination attempt when a bomb fell off his car and was disarmed. The IRA claimed credit.
June 22: Luis de la Parra Urbaneja, retired army colonel, was murdered in Irun, Spain. Members of the Basques terrorist group were suspected.
June 24: The governor of Mahabad, Iran, six guards, and others, were injured in a funeral procession when they were attacked by members of the Kurdistan Democratic Party.
June 24: Juan Carlos, king of Spain, was apparently the target of a murder plot by three Spanish officers who were taken into custody.
June 25: Ferdinand Marcos, president of the Philippines, was allegedly the target of a murder plot by conspirators, several of whom were arrested.
June 28: Muhammad Kacu'i, governor of Evin Prison, was murdered in Teheran on June 28 or June 29.
Aug. 1: Abu Da'ud (Abu Daoud), a leader of Black September and the Palestinian Liberation Organization (PLO), was slain in Warsaw by Abu Nidal terrorists.
Aug. 9: Samuel K. Doe, president master sergeant, was the target of

a failed attempt on his life by People's Redemption Council members, five of whom were put to death in Liberia.
Aug. 12: Sirimavo Bandaranaike, ex-prime minister of Sri Lanka, was serving as chairman of a Freedom party meeting close to Colombo, Sri Lanka, when a bomb was detonated. She was not injured, but seventy people were hurt in the chaos that followed.
Aug. 15: An Iranian mullah in Sanandaj, Iran, was killed.
Aug. 15: Hojatoleslam Towhidi, Iranian mullah, was in his car when he was shot to death in Babol, Iran.
Aug. 16: Saleh Khosravi, Iranian mullah, and his son, were murdered as they left a mosque.
Aug. 18: Rosa Judith Cisneros, civil rights leader and legal advisor to the Salvadoran Communal Union, was assassinated in San Salvador, El Sal., as she left her home.
Aug. 30: Mohammed Ali Rajai, president of Iran, and Mohammed Javar Bahonar, prime minister, were murdered and other officials were injured in a bomb blast in Teheran. Colonel Vahid-Dastgerdi, chief of the Teheran police, died Sept. 6.
Aug. 31: Hojatoleslam Mortraza Ayatollahi Tabataba Yazdi, prominent religious leader, and Hojatoleslam Nasser Jamali, court official in Teheran, were slain in Teheran.
September: General Enrique Briz Armengol was slain in Barcelona, Spain by terrorists.
Sept. 2: Hojateslam Morteza Khodad, a close aide to the Ayatollah Ruhollah Khomeini, was assassinated by a grenade at Bandar Enzeli.
Sept. 3: A bomb attached to a Soviet diplomat's car parked close to the U.S.S.R. mission in New York exploded, and an alleged JDL terrorist took credit.
Sept. 4: Louis Delamare, French ambassador to Lebanon, was shot to death while driving in his car in Beirut.
Sept. 5: Hojatoleslam Ali Ghodussi, ayatollah and general revolutionary prosecutor of Iran, was slain by a bomb at his office.
Sept. 9: A Hindu newspaper editor who disagreed with the Sikh policy of separatism was shot to death shortly after an article appeared expressing his view on the subject.
Sept. 11: Assodollah Mandani, ayatollah and aide to Ayatollah Ruhollah Khomeini, was killed by a hand grenade blast.
Sept. 15: General Frederick J. Kroesen, commander of U.S. troops in Europe, was the target of a failed assassination attempt in Heidelberg, Ger.
Sept. 16: Hojatoleslam Nematollah Adib, high-ranking Muslim, was injured by gunshot as he was leaving a mosque in Shiraz, Iran.
Sept. 18: Samuel Rodolfo Gutierrez Obregon, secretary-general of the Bank Employees Federation, was shot to death near his home in Guatemala.
Sept. 29: Hojatoleslam Abdulkarim Hashemi-Nejad, secretary-general of the Islamic Republic Party, was killed and others were wounded in Mashad, Iran, by a hand grenade held by Hadi Alavai Fitilechi, a Mujahedeen terrorist.
October: The Iranian charge d'affaires was riding in a car in West Beirut when gunshots were fired at his car.
Oct. 6: Anwar Mohammad as-Sadat, president of Egypt, was reviewing a military parade in a Cairo suburb when he was shot to death by Khaled Ahmed Shawki Islambouly and other guerrillas.
Oct. 7: Teng Hsiao-ping (Deng Xiaoping), Chinese leader, was wounded in gunshot, apparently by a Maoist organization.
Oct. 8: Abu Tariq, Palestinian Liberation Organization agent in Libya, was allegedly the target of a murder plot by Abu Nidal terrorists in Valletta, Malta.
Oct. 9: Majed Abu Sharar, a member of the Al Fatah Central Committee, may have been shot to death before a bomb exploded in his Rome hotel room.
Oct. 10: Officials attending the funeral of Anwar Mohammad as-Sadat were reportedly the target of a bomb plot by conspirators.
Oct. 10: Nabawy Ismail, minister of interior of Egypt, was the target of an assassination attempt when gunmen shot at his home with machine-guns.
Oct 16: George Bush, U.S. vice-president, was apparently the target of a failed assassination attempt. A bomb was discovered underneath the runway of an airport in Bogota, Col. A caller said the Workers Self-Defense was responsible.
Oct. 17: Sir Stuart Pringle, lieutenant general and ex-commandant of the British Marines and Northern Ireland commando leader, lost part of a leg when a bomb planted by IRA terrorists exploded in his car.
Oct. 21: Maxwell M. Rabb, U.S. ambassador to Italy, was reportedly the target of an assassination plot by Libyans after the U.S. shot down two Libyan jets on Aug. 19.
Nov. 4: Roland Smith received a three-year sentence for threatening U.S. President Ronald Reagan's life.
Nov. 6: Israel Borquez, president of the Supreme Court of Chile, was slightly wounded in Santiago by gunmen.
Nov. 12: Christian Chapman, U.S. charge d'affaires in Paris, was the target of an unsuccessful attempt on his life by gunmen in Paris.
Nov. 14: Reverend Robert Bradford, member of the British Parliament and Ulster Unionist, was fatally shot in Belfast, Ire.
Nov. 21: NBC News announced that the security of high-level U.S. government officials had been expanded because of reported murder plots by Libyan president Muammar Qaddafi.
Dec. 19: Muammar Gaddafi, president of Libya, was injured and his driver slain by Khalifa Khadir, Libyan army colonel.
Dec. 27: Eight high-ranking members of the Baha'i National Spiritual Assembly in Iran were reportedly put to death.
Dec. 28: Muhammad Taki Behsharat, Majlis deputy, was assassinated and others wounded by gunmen in Teheran.

1982

January: Ronald Reagan, president of the U.S., was apparently the target of several assassination plots and several people were deported in late 1981 and in January 1982.
January: Lech Walesa, Polish labor leader, visited Rome and was the target of a murder plot, apparently by Red Brigade members and Bulgarians.
Jan. 4: Cesare Romiti, well-known in the Italian Association of Industrialists was probably the target of Red Brigade members who were arrested outside his Rome house.
Jan. 6: Dr. James Donovan, chief of the Garda Siochana Forensic Science Laboratory, was hurt in Clondalkin, Ire., when his car exploded.
Jan. 6: Nicola Simone, deputy head of the Rome anti-terrorist police, was injured at his home. The First Line Armed Cell claimed responsibility.
Jan. 10: Hojjatoleslam Muhadi Kermani, deputy of the Majlis, was the target of an unsuccessful assassination attempt in Iran.
Jan. 10: Mohammad Khamenei, brother of Iranian President, Ali Khameini, and deputy to Parliament, was shot and injured in Tehran near his home.
Jan. 11: Hojjatoleslam Hassan Monfared, deputy industrial minister of Iran, was wounded in his shoulder in Tehran.
Jan. 13: Rabeh Jerwa, minister plenipotentiary of the Algerian Embassy in Beirut, was kidnapped from his apartment and shot three times in the head.
Jan. 18: Lieutenant Colonel Charles Robert Ray, U.S. military attache, was shot to death near his Paris apartment by FARL terrorists.
Jan. 28: Kemal Arikan, consul general of Turkey, was shot to death in Los Angeles in his car. Armenian terrorists took credit for the incident.
Jan. 29: John McKeague, Loyalist leader and possibly chief of clandestine Red Hand Commandos, was shot to death in Belfast.
Jan. 29: Peter Robinson, deputy chief of the Irish DUP, was the target of an unsuccessful British assassin in New York.
Feb. 4: George Bamuturaki, member of Parliament, Zeb Okao, general manager of the National Housing Corporation, were shot to death in Kampala, Uganda, and others were wounded.
Feb. 5: Roberto Giron Lemus, editor of *La Nacion*, was going to work when he was assassinated in Guatemala City.
Feb. 8: Mussa Kheyyabani, operational commander of the Mujahedeen Khalq, was slain by rebel guards in Tehran.
Feb. 8: Jens Petersen, West German ambassador to Iran, was wounded with two others in his car in Tehran.
Feb. 8: The wife and child of Massoud Rajavi, leader of the Mujahadeen in exile, were slain in Tehran.
Feb. 16: Max Martin, director of the Societe d'exploitation de fruits and legumes, was killed in Capesterre, Guadeloupe.
Feb. 24: Hussein ali Montazeri, ayatollah and likely successor to Ruholla Khomeini, was assassinated by the Mujahedeen in Tehran, apparently in retaliation for the slaying of Mussa Kheyyabani).
Feb. 25: Colonel Seyyed Ibrahim Hejazi, chief of the Tehran police administration was wounded with two others by gunshot in a failed assassination attempt in Tehran.
Feb. 26: Tucapel Jimenez, trade union leader, was found dead near Santiago, Chile.
Mar. 2: Lord Lowry, chief justice of Ireland, was not wounded in an unsuccessful assassination attempt in Belfast, but another was hurt.
Mar. 7: Hojatoleslam Muhammad Chavushi, Iranian navy official in the political-ideological section, was shot and another was wounded in Tehran. Chavushi died on Mar. 8.
Mar. 7: Karim Shahrkandi, mullah, was fatally shot in Iran.
Mar. 22: Ali Hajem Sultan, third secretary of the Iraqi Embassy in Beirut, was slain near the embassy.
Mar. 26: The head of the San Sabastian, Spain, telephone company was shot dead, apparently by ETA terrorists. His predecessor was also killed by the ETA in 1980.
Mar. 28: Muammar Gaddafi, president of Libya, was nearly killed at the navy base at Tobruk.
Apr. 3: Yacov Barsimantov (Ya'acov Bar Simantov), second secretary of the Israel embassy in Paris, was shot to death in his Paris apartment.
Apr. 3: Wandee Thongprapa, managing editor of *Tawan Siam*, a Bangkok newspaper, was shot to death in his office.
Apr. 9: Kani Gungor, a commercial officer of the Turkish Embassy in Ottawa, was injured by gunshot and the Secret Army for the Liberation of Armenia took credit.
Apr. 14: Taha Talib, ex-speaker of the Negri Sembilan State Assembly, was shot to death in Malaysia. Implicated for killing their political rival, Mokhtar Hashim, Malaysia cultural minister, and others were tried.
Apr. 22: Elias al-Atesh, a Fatah official, and his wife, were killed by a bomb in a hotel in West Beirut.
Apr. 26: Sheikh Ahmad Assaf, Sunni leader in Lebanon, was shot to death in West Beirut as he left a mosque.
Apr. 27: Raffaele de Cogliano, Christian Democrat and commissioner

of the Campania administration, and his driver were fatally shot in Naples, Italy by terrorists.
Apr. 27: Saudi Arabia was implicated in a plot to assassinate Ayatollah Ruhollah Khomeini by a relative of Ayatollah Kazem Shariat Madari.
Apr. 28: Pio La Torre, member of parliament and leader of the Communist Party in Sicily, and his driver, were shot to death in Palermo.
May 4: Orhan R. Gunduz, honorary Turkish consul to New England, was shot to death in Somerville, Mass., a Boston suburb. The Justice Commandos of the Armenian Genocide claim credit.
May 5: Angel Pascual Mugica, general manager of the Lemoniz nuclear plant, was driving outside of Bilbao, Spain, when he was shot to death.
May 8: Sayyed Serajulddin, executive of a textile plant, and his son, were murdered by a bomb at his home.
May 12: John Paul II, pope, was threatened, but unhurt, by Juan Fernandez Krohn, a Spanish priest who was armed with a knife and subdued by guards in Portugal.
May 20: Reverend William Beattie, head of the Democratic Unionist Party in Belfast, Ire., was the target of a failed attempt on his life. A bomb on his doorstep was disarmed and the INLA took credit.
May 26: The deputy commander of the U.S. military organization in El Salvador was slain in San Salvador, El Sal.
June: General Yekotiel Adam former deputy chief of staff and leader of the Israel intelligence agency, Mossad, was murdered by members of the Palestinian Liberation Organization.
June 3: Shlomo Argov, Israeli ambassador to England, was shot and critically injured, but survived an attack in London by Abu Nidal terrorists who were sent to prison.
June 4: Mustafa Marzook, first secretary of the Kuwaiti Embassy in New Delhi, India, was shot to death at his home. The Arab Brigades Movement took credit.
June 4: Petrus Nyaose, secretary general of the African National Congress, and his wife, Jabu, were murdered by a car bomb in Swaziland.
June 10: Rocco Polimeni, alleged head of Prima Linea, was found shot to death in Milan, Italy.
June 15: Ahmad Khomeini, the son of Ayatollah Ruhollah Khomeini, was the target of a failed murder attempt when assassins attacked his car in Tehran.
June 17: Kamal Hussein, deputy director of the Palestinian Liberation Organization Office in Rome, was slain by a car bomb in Rome.
June 23: Dom Mintoff, prime minister of Malta, might have been the target of assassins when a bomb exploded at the Karachi Airport close to a car he was supposed to use.
July 2: Mohammed Sadduqi, ayatollah and member of Parliament, and three women were slain by a grenade during a prayer meeting in Yezd, Iran. Members of the Mujahedden Khalq were suspected.
July 6: Ali Akhavein-Ansari, governor general of Gilan Province, Iran, was shot to death in Rasht, Iran.
July 6: Giuseppe Taliercio, manager of a Montedison petrochemical complex, was found dead after he had been kidnapped and "sentenced to death" by Red Brigades terrorists.
July 12: General Fateh Mohammed Ferqameshr, established the National Fatherland Front, and was killed at his house in Kabul, Afg., by terrorists.
July 16: An executive of a tobacco company was slain by the ETA terrorists.
July 17: Zenon Palomino Flores, a district governor, was fatally shot in Callera, Peru.
July 19: The head of the Divandarren Department of Education in Kurdistan was slain.
July 20: Habibollah Asghar Owladi Musulman, Iranian presidential candidate and deputy speaker of the Iranian Majlis, was injured in Teheran.
July 21: Kenalettin Demirer, Turkish consul general, was the target of a failed assassination attempt in Rotterdam, Neth., by four assailants.
July 23: Hojatoleslam Seyyed Hasan Behesti, candidate for the Iranian Parliament, and his nephew were shot to death at Behesti's Isfahan home.
July 23: Fadel el-Dani, deputy director of the Palestinian Liberation Organization Office in Paris was slain when assassins threw a bomb in his car in Paris.
July 28: Hashemi-Rafsanjani, Iranian Majlis speaker, said the U.S. tried to plot to murder Ayatollah Ruhollah Khomeini.
July 29: Reza Saadati, a leader of the Mujahedeen, was put to death by Iran, according to *L'Humanite*.
July 29: Fernando Belaunde Terry, president of Peru, might have been the target of assassins when a bomb exploded not far from where he had been watching a parade a few minutes beforehand.
July 31: Joe Goabi, an African National Congress official, was the target of a shooting attempt on his life in Salisbury, Zimbabwe. The Zimbabwe government thought South Africa might have been involved in the incident.
Aug. 4: *Pravda* notes people recently slain in Kabul, including, People's Army Major Sher Aqa, well-known singer Khan Karabaghi, and Director of the city council's administrative department Adel Zumati. Deputy Minister of Higher and Vocational Education Wali Yusufi, was the target of a failed attempt on his life.
Aug. 5: Dr. Hasan Ayat, member of the Central Council of the ruling Islamic Republican Party and a member of the Islamic Majlis, was shot to death in Teheran near his home.
Aug. 8: A bomb exploded in a conference room where the Syrian cabinet was planning to meet and three ministry workers died.
Aug. 9: Hojatoleslam Haj Ahmad Faqihi, chief judge of the Islamic Revolutionary Court for six cities in Fars province, was fatally shot by two attackers.
Aug. 20: Darbara Singh, head minister of Punjab, was wounded with thirty others when a grenade exploded at a building dedication ceremony.
Aug. 26: The Abu Nidal terrorists apparently tried to assassinate the consul of the United Arab Emirates in Bombay, India.
Aug. 27: Colonel Atilla Atikat, the Turkish military attache in Ottawa, Can., was fatally shot in his car. The Justice Commandos of the Armenian Genocide took credit.
Aug. 30: Nhem Heng, Kampuchean deputy minister of Agriculture and three others were murdered in Kompong Cham, Kampuchea.
Sept. 3: General Carlo Alberto Dalla Chiesa, chief of an anti-Mafia effort, his wife, and a bodyguard, were slain in Sicily by the mafia.
Sept. 13: Zahur Hassan Bhopali, member of the Advisory Council, was killed in Karachi, Pak.
Sept. 14: Bashir (Bishin) Gemayel, president-elect of Lebanon, was murdered in east Beirut by a bomb, reportedly planted on the orders of the Syrian secret service.
Sept. 14: Hamad Jutaili, acting consul general of the Kuwaiti Embassy in Karachi, Pak., was shot at a service station.
Sept. 15: Sedegh Ghotbzadeh, former Iranian foreign minister, was executed after admitting to a plot to assassinate Ayatollah Ruhollah Khomeini.
Sept. 16: Najeeb Sayeb Refai, first secretary of the Kuwaiti Embassy in Madrid, was fatally shot by gunmen, including Abu Nidal terrorist Ibrahim Nasser Hamdan.
Sept. 27: Abu Walid (Kafr Kalil), brigadier general and Palestinian Liberation Organization chief of operations, was slain in Lebanon.
Oct. 4: A.S. Malik, deputy commander of Indian troops, was found shot to death in Meerut, India.
Oct. 15: Ashrafi Isfahani, ayatollah, was hugged by an assassin carrying a grenade and blown up in Bahtaran, Iran. The assassin may have been a member of the Mujahedeen Khalq.
Oct. 20: James Molyneaux, Official Unionist Party leader, was the target of assassins who planted a bomb, which was disarmed, near his home in Northern Ireland. The INLA claimed credit for the attempt.
Oct. 22: The FBI disclosed on Oct. 5, that five Armenians had been arrested in connection with assaults in southern California on Turkish statesmen.
Nov. 4: General Victor Lago Roman, commander of the Brunete First Armored Division of Spain, was assassinated in Madrid, Spain by terrorists.
Nov. 6: Two reputed leaders of the ETA terrorists were arrested in St. Jean de Luz, Fr., for possibly plotting to kill Pope John Paul II.
Nov. 7: Noor Ahmed Dalily, former deputy minister of transportation of Afghanistan, and his son, were murdered.
Nov. 9: The U.S. State Department notified Iraq that the U.S. did not agree with the Iraqi decision to allow Abu Nidal, who reportedly had plotted to kill Yasser Arafat, to move his headquarters.
Nov. 26: Adamson Mushala, leader of the rebel Mushala group, was slain in the Lunga National park in Zambia.
Nov. 29: Gloria Lara de Echeverry, director of the Community Action in the Ministry of Interior and wife of a Columbian senator, was found slain in Bogota, Col.
Dec. 1: Walid Jumblatt, Druse Muslim leader, was injured with thirty-eight others and four were killed when a bomb exploded near his car in Lebanon.
Dec. 9: Zola Ngini, Adolph Mpongosohe, and Jackson Tayo, leaders of the African National Congress, were slain with thirty-nine others when South African raiders attacked an ANC camp in Lesotho.
Dec. 15: Howard Bromberg, U.S. army captain, is injured in Darmstadt, West Ger., when a bomb in his car explodes.
Dec. 31: Erich Honecker, East German statesman, might have been the target of Paul Essling, who purportedly shot guards protecting Honecker and then killed himself.

1983

Mar. 9: Galip Balkar, Turkish ambassador to Yugoslavia, was fatally shot and his driver critically wounded in Belgrade, Yug. Balkar died Mar. 11 and two terrorists groups took credit.
Apr. 10: Dr. Issam Sartawi, prominent Palestinian Liberation Organization moderate, was shot to death in Albufeira, Port., by Abu Nidal terrorists.
May 26: U.S. deputy commander of armed forces was murdered in San Salvador.
June 7: Abu Nidal terrorists were apparently responsible for injuring a Fatah employee and an associate in Barcelona, Spain.
Aug. 21: Benigno S. Aquino, Jr., a Filipino politician, returned to the Philippines and was fatally shot at the Manila International Airport. A leftist rebel was responsible, according to the Marcos administration, but a military assassination was suspected.
Oct. 9: Four cabinet ministers of South Korea and fifteen others died in a bomb explosion in Rangoon, Burma. President Chun accused North Korea.
Oct. 19: Maurice Bishop, premier of Grenada, was placed under house arrest on Oct. 13, and slain by insurgent military members.

Oct. 21: Henry A. Gentile, a Chicago, Ill., judge, was murdered in his Chicago courtroom and divorce attorney James A. Piszcor was wounded by ex-Chicago police officer Hutchie T. Moore.
Oct. 25: Abu Nidal terrorists allegedly attempted to assassinate the Jordanian ambassador in New Delhi, India.
Oct. 26: Abu Nidal terrorists reportedly injured the Jordanian ambassador and his driver in an attempt on the diplomat's life in Rome.
Nov. 15: George Tsantes, U.S. Navy captain, was shot to death in Athens by left-wing terrorists.

1984

Jan. 29: Guillermo Lacaci, Spanish lieutenant general, was fatally shot in Madrid by terrorists.
Feb. 2: Abu Nidal terrorists reputedly killed the United Arab Emirates ambassador in Paris.
Mar. 8: Kiichi Miyazawa, prominent political figure in Japan, was attacked and wounded with a knife by Hirosato Higashiyama.
Mar. 14: Gerry Adams, head of the Provisional Sinn Fein, was injured, but survived, an attack in Belfast, Ire., by Ulster freedom fighters.
Mar. 14: Hector Flores Larin, head of the Salvadorean National Conciliation Party, was slain by unknown assassins.
Mar. 24: Elizabeth II, queen of England, received threats on her life during her trip to Jordan, allegedly by Abu Nidal terrorists.
Mar. 28: Kenneth Whitty, first secretary of the British embassy in Athens, was fatally shot in Athens and the Revolutionary Organization of Socialist Muslims took credit for the murder.
Apr. 2: A prominent Hindu politician was slain by Sikh terrorists, causing Hindus to riot in Punjab.
May 5: Abu Nidal terrorists were apparently responsible for killing the chairman of the Arab Writers Union in Nicosia, Cyprus.
May 10: The ex-high priest of the Amritsar Golden Temple in India was slain by Sihk terrorists, causing strikes and rioting.
June 16: Hardayal Singh, chief of the Jullundur district committee of the Congress Party, was shot to death in Goraya, India, by Sikh terrorists.
Sept. 5: The Palestinian Liberation Organization agent in Bucharest, Rum., was allegedly killed by three members of the Abu Nidal terrorists.
Oct. 12: Margaret Thatcher, prime minister of England, and members of the British cabinet were the target of PIRA terrorists who planted a bomb at Brighton. Five people died and others were injured.
Oct. 25: The second secretary of the United Arab Emirate embassy in Rome was the target of an assassination attempt, reputedly by the Abu Nidal terrorists.
Oct. 31: Indira Gandhi, prime minister of India, was shot to death in New Delhi, India, by two of her Sikh bodyguards.
Nov. 27: Percy Morris, British deputy high commissioner, was fatally shot in Bombay, India, by Abu Nidal terrorists.
Dec. 29: Fahd Qawasma (Fahd Kawasmeh), ex-mayor of Hebron, was nominated as a member of the Palestinian Executive Committee and shortly afterward, he was slain in Amman, Jor., reportedly by Abu Nidal terrorists.

1985

Jan. 25: General René Audran, chief of the French international arms sales group, was fatally shot in Paris by Action Directe.
Feb. 1: Ernst Zimmermann, president of the West German Aerospace and Armaments Association, was fatally shot in Munich by Red Army Faction terrorists.
Mar. 13: Abu Nidal terrorists were apparently responsible for shooting into the home of the Jordanian ambassador in Rome in an unsuccessful attempt on his life.
Mar. 24: Arthur Nicholson, U.S. Army major whom the U.S.S.R. said was a spy, was slain in Ludwigslust, Ger., by a Russian guard.
Apr. 1: Liberian president Samuel Doe was the target of an unsuccessful attempt on his life by chief bodyguard, Colonel Flanzamaton, who was put to death on Apr. 7.
Apr. 23: Ahmad Jarallah, editor of *al-Siyasa*, a Kuwaiti newspaper, was the target of an attempted assassination, reputedly by Abu Nidal terrorists.
June 5: Mustafa Ali Mustafa, Palestinian Liberation Organization agent in Greece, was the target of a failed attempt on his life in Athens, reportedly by Abu Nidal terrorists.
July 24: Abu Nidal terrorists were allegedly responsible for murdering a Jordanian diplomat in Ankara, Turk.
Aug. 20: Albert Atrakchi, first secretary of the Israeli embassy in Cairo, was shot to death, and his wife and another woman were injured. The Egyptian Revolution took credit.
Aug. 20: Sant Harchard Singh Longowal, prominent Sikh moderate, was murdered.
Sept. 4: Arjun Dass, high statesman, was assassinated by Sikh radicals during elections in Delhi.
Sept. 15: Abu Nidal terrorists allegedly tried to kill the editor of an Arabic newspaper in Athens.
Sept. 18: Michel Namari, publisher of the anti-Syrian Arab News Letter in Athens, was slain, reportedly by Abu Nidal terrorists.
Nov. 24: Hussein Ali Ibrahim al-Bitar, was involved in a quarrel with Sabri al-Banna, who asserted he owned al-Bitar's home. Al-Bitar was murdered by three assailants, apparently Abu Nidal terrorists, in Amman, Jordan.

1986

Jan. 13: Nasser Mohammad, president of South Yemen, was the target of an unsuccessful assassination attempt.
Feb. 6: Cristobal Colon, vice admiral, was murdered by ETA terrorists who threw grenades at his car in Madrid.
Feb. 22: Antonio Da Empoli, economic aide to Italian Prime Minister Bettino Craxi, was the target of a failed attempt on his life by Red Brigade terrorists in Rome.
Feb. 28: Olaf Palme, prime minister of Sweden, was shot dead in Stockholm.
Mar. 2: Zafr al-Masri, mayor of Nablus, was fatally shot by Palestinian terrorists.
Mar. 19: Etti Tal-Or, Israeli diplomat's wife, was shot to death in Cairo, and three other Israelis were injured. The Egyptian Revolution took credit.
Sept. 7: General Augusto Pinochet Ugarte, president of Chile, was riding in a car when he was assaulted by insurgents armed with grenades, guns, and rockets. He survived but six bodyguards died.
Oct. 2: Rajiv Gandhi, prime minister of India, was the target of an unsuccessful assassination attempt by Sikhs.
Oct. 3: The police chief of Punjab, India, was the target of a failed attempt on his life.

1987

Mar 20: Licio Giorgieri, chief air force general in charge of space research for Italy, was slain by Italian terrorists.
June 1: Rashid Karami, premiere of Lebanon, was traveling in a helicopter when a bomb detonated, killing him.
Oct. 15: President Sankara of Burkina Faso was overthrown and slain by Captain Blaise Compaoré, his deputy.

1988

Trying to impede elections, Farabundo Marti National Liberation Front guerrillas murdered a mayor in El Salvador in early 1988, and carried out other terrorists acts.
Jan. 25: Carlos Hoyos, attorney general of Columbia, was abducted and murdered close to Medellin, Col., by drug traffickers. Two of the official's bodyguards were also killed.
Mar. 29: Dulcie September, European agent of the outlawed African National Congress, was fatally shot near her Paris office.
Apr. 7: Albie Sachs, well-known South African lawyer who opposed apartheid, was apparently the target of an assassination attempt when critically wounded in Maputo, Mozambique by a car bomb.
Apr. 16: Khalil al-Wazir (Abu Jihad), military leader of the Palestinian Liberation Organization, a gardener, and two bodyguards were shot to death at his home near Tunis. Tun.
June 18: Turgut Ozal, prime minister of Turkey, was not seriously injured by gunshot fired by Kartal Demirag, reportedly a member of the Grey Wolves.

BALLISTICS

Ballistics is the study of flight and propulsion of projectiles. Forensic ballistics is the scientific study of guns and ammunition, often applied to murder and other criminal cases. Terminal ballistics, a sub-category within the discipline deals with the impact of the projectile when it strikes its target. Forensic ballistics and forensic pathologists' reports taken together enable investigators to reconstruct the crime.

Ballistics became a viable field of study when spent bullets were found to have unique marks, or "fingerprints," a discovery made in the U.S. Because of the marks, bullets can be linked to specific guns. Guns are categorized as smooth-bore or rifled. The shotgun is an example of the smooth-bore class. The inside of the barrel is smooth all the way through. Shotguns are the preferred weapons of game hunters and sportsmen. They fire a spray of pellets accurate to a range of about fifty yards. The shotgun contains one or two barrels which fire hand-loaded cartridges. The empty cases remain inside the gun after the shot is fired. The shell travels at a speed of 1,100 feet per second, but after three feet, the pellets spread out, creating a multiple shot effect. By contrast, a rifled weapon "spins" a bullet, stabilizing the flight and providing a greater degree of accuracy. The rifled class includes long-barreled rifles (two to three feet) or a short-barreled pistol (typically one to twelve inches). Pistols are classified as either revolvers or automatics. The revolver was the preferred weapon of the western gunslingers and cowboys. The circular chamber revolves around an axis and brings the cartridge into position after the last shot has been fired. The user must then manually remove the cartridge cases. The spent cartridges in an automatic pistol are ejected automatically. The ammunition for this type of weapon is usually housed in the butt of the pistol.

Weapons manufacturers have known since the sixteenth century that the range and accuracy of a gun can be improved by cutting spiraled grooves into the barrel. The machines that create the spiraling have flaws that are transferred to the gun, which in turn make marks called striations on the bullets. The gun itself is a kind of heat engine that partially converts the chemical energy of a propellant into the kinetic energy of a projectile. Combustion results from a build-up of pressure from hot gasses generated by the propellant. This intense pressure causes the burning rate to increase. The shot moves when the pressure finally overcomes the resistance to motion. Before the bullet exits the chamber, a precursor blast occurs, followed by a discharge of compressed gasses behind the shot. The blast shockwave travels at a speed greater than sound, hence the sharp report of gunfire. The heat generated by the exiting bullet causes a momentary flash near the muzzle. Silencer devices can be affixed to muffle the sound of the blast by scattering the shock waves. The path the bullet travels before striking its target is known as the trajectory. Such atmospheric forces as drag, lift, and gravity influence the trajectory.

Bullets are manufactured in various sizes and shapes depending on usage and ballistic requirements. Before 1900, the traditional bullet was made of lead and fitted to the black powder cartridge, adopted for use in small handguns and rifles. With the introduction of smokeless powder at the turn of the century, manufacturers were forced to change the composition of the bullet because lead proved too pliable to be used with any degree of accuracy. This led to the invention of the "jacketed" bullet, in which the lead center was encased with a hard veneer of cupronickel. The resilient jacketed bullet will not strip as it exits the barrel. Once it strikes the intended target it will not fragment or deform. Bullets are manufactured slightly larger than the weapon, even though the caliber will always match that of the gun.

When a bullet is retrieved from a victim or a crime scene, it can be matched against a bullet test-fired from the type of gun believed used in the crime. The suspect weapon is first taken to the laboratory where technicians examine it for possible design flaws, or mechanical imperfections. Next, the "rifling" characteristics will be measured with highly sophisticated instruments before the firing test is finally performed. Years ago the test bullet was discharged into a barrel of water or a pile of oiled sawdust. Currently, a box filled with cotton wool is commonly used as the target, in order to prevent possible distortion. The firing test is the only way to accurately determine whether the bullet removed from the crime scene is compatible.

The area of wound ballistics basically concerns itself with the medical aspects of a bullet wound sustained by the human body. After the projectile penetrates the skin, the force and momentum of the blast on surrounding tissues creates a cavity. The severity of the injury has everything to do with the measurable size of this cavity. Ballistic researchers have shown that the seriousness of the wound is increased when the bullet "mushrooms" or tumbles following impact. Very often shattered bone fragments will maximize the severity of the injury. Medical experts who study bullet wounds are interested in two critical factors: the point of entry and where the shot exited. The differences between these two wounds will help investigators determine whether or not a victim perished by his own hand or was murdered. Ballistics experts will closely examine the entry wound for scorching or powder residue. A dermal nitrate test is often administered to the victim and assailant to detect the presence of these residues on the hand. The test results often show whether the victim struggled with the killer or the distance the shot was fired.

Gunshot wounds are categorized by the distances from which the weapon was fired. There are three basic types: (1) contact, in which the muzzle of the gun is pressed against the skin surface or an inch or two away; (2) close discharge, in which the gun is fired from close range, typically six inches to two feet away; (3) distant discharge, in which the shot emanates from more than two or three feet. A skilled detective may be able to identify the type of weapon used in a homicide by determining the distance from which the shot was fired.

The reality of a ballistics investigation is quite a bit different from the fictional portrayal in popular films and novels. Once the doctor has pronounced the victim dead, the murder scene is photographed by detectives, and a chalk outline is drawn on the floor around the body prior to removal. The crime scene investigators are careful not to disrupt the room or immediate surrounding areas. The positioning of every item found near the corpse is carefully recorded and catalogued for future reference. A search is made for spent shell casings or bullets lodged in the walls and furniture. The distance between the shots is measured to help determinine bullet trajectories. Contrary to popular belief, a detective will not attempt to remove a gun from the murder scene by slipping a pencil through the barrel. Instead, the detective will don kid gloves to avoid smudging, and carefully place the murder weapon in a cotton-wool lined box. The same delicate care is shown during the post-mortem examination. Items of clothing are thoroughly examined for bullet-holes and powder burns. The "wet blot" is employed to trace the powder pattern in close-discharge gunshot wounds. Such a test will reveal the direction the fatal shot came from. Removing the bullet from a victim is another delicate procedure involving the greatest care and attention to detail. Frequently an X-Ray will be taken of the body in order to reveal the precise location of the bullet. This way the chances of the bullet being damaged during surgical removal will be minimized.

In 1889, Professor Alexandre Lacassagne employed a crude version of ballistic theory. While working on a murder case, Lacassagne observed that a bullet taken from the victim had seven marks, and a gun found in the suspect's apartment had the same number of grooves in the barrel. Using this evidence, the suspect was tried and found guilty. As the field developed, the most pivotal breakthroughs were made in the U.S. Charles E. Waite, an attorney with the New York prosecutor's office, made an important contribution by cataloguing guns. In 1923, in New York, Waite and Dr. Philip Gravelle founded the Bureau of Forensic Ballistics, the first facility for ballistic study.

Another major advance occurred when Gravelle invented the comparison microscope. Previously, only one bullet at a time could be observed under a microscope, making it difficult for precise comparison between two bullets. The comparison microscope allows the crime bullet and the test bullet to be examined at the same time, greatly increasing the accuracy of the comparison.

After the landmark conviction of Nicola Sacco and Bartolomeo Vanzetti, two Italians charged with the April 1920 murders of a paymaster and guard at a Braintree, Mass., shoe company, Calvin Goddard, an army doctor, was called on to examine the forensic evidence in the case. The prosecution tried to establish that Sacco's .32-caliber pistol was used to kill the guard. Goddard demonstrated with his comparison microscope that the bullet that killed F.A. Parmenter and Alessandro Berardelli could have come only from Sacco's pistol. The two men died in the electric chair on Aug. 23, 1927. Goddard was next summoned to Chicago in 1929 to lend his special talents to solving the infamous St. Valentine's Day Massacre, in which seven hoodlums were gunned down in a Clark Street Garage. Though the killers were never brought to justice, Goddard identified the caliber of the bullets and the type of guns from which they were fired. His work on this case made him nationally famous and resulted in his appointment to head up the Chicago Scientific Crime Detection Laboratory.

Pathologist Sir Sydney Smith helped identify the assassins of Sir Lee Stack, British Sirdar of Egypt in 1924. Smith went on to establish a forensics laboratory that was certainly the equal of Goddard's in terms of prestige and innovative breakthroughs. Britain's Robert Churchill ranks as one of the most famous ballistics experts of the twentieth century. Churchill's painstaking work helped convict Frederick Guy Browne and William Henry Kennedy of murdering Police Constable George Gutteridge in Essex on Sept. 27, 1927. Churchill pinpointed a unique mark on a cartridge case found in their abandoned car. He test-fired fifty Webley revolvers similar to Guy Browne's to see if a breech mark could be recreated to match the bullet fired from the murder weapon. No comparable marks could be found, proving that Browne had fired his Webley at Officer Gutteridge on the night in question. Consequently, both men were tried for murder, found Guilty, and hanged. In 1934, FBI director J. Edgar Hoover recognized the intrinsic value of the ballistics research conducted by these early pioneers in the field and created a separate ballistics branch within the bureau.

BOMBINGS

Bombing, as a method of political and criminal terror came into prominence in the late nineteenth century, notably in Russia when anarchists attempted to assassinate Czar Alexander II. The dynamite terror soon swept to the U.S. where labor leaders and radical socialists found it an effective weapon against management seeking to curb the power of the fledgling trade unions. In the 1920s, the criminal underworld of Chicago used bombs or "pineapples" to intimidate honest politicians or those persons inimical to their interests.

By the 1960s, hand grenades and bombs had become a standard weapon of terror in the hands of political groups and extremists on the outermost fringe of society. The campaign of bombings accelerated, particularly after the 1967 Arab-Israeli War. The methods of the Palestinian Liberation Organization (PLO) and other pro-Palestinian factions were soon copied by the worldwide terrorist network whose influence extended into virtually every country in the world at one time or another. What follows is a chronological listing of bombings, attempted bombings, and terrorist incidents involving the use of explosives.

1854
June 26: Medical student William Arrison sent a homemade bomb to Superintendent Isaac Allison of the Cincinnati College of Medicine and Surgery in Ohio. Allison was killed, and Arrison was convicted of murder.
1879
November: Czar Alexander II of Russia narrowly escaped death when a dynamite charge exploded along the route he was taking to Livadia.
1880s
Two Americans named Callan and Harkins, agents of a mad doctor in the U.S., attempted to blow up the Houses of Parliament, Buckingham Palace, and Westminster Abbey, but were arrested and sent to prison.
1880
Following the November attack near Livadia, a bomb was set off in the czar's winter palace. Ten of the czar's guards were killed, and fifty-three people were injured.
1881
March: Czar Alexander II of Russia was assassinated in St. Petersburg, by a bomb thrown at his carriage. His death sentence had been passed two years earlier by the "People's Will."
1886
May 4: Seven Chicago police officers were killed in the West Side Haymarket Square when an anarchist's dynamite bomb exploded after a labor rally had been ordered to disperse. Four were hanged on Nov. 11, 1887.
1887
June: Scotland Yard was alerted to an underground bomb plot which was to take place in Westminster Abbey during Queen Victoria's fifty-year Jubilee celebration on June 20. Consequently, a number of Irishmen were arrested, and the Jubilee took place without incident.
Nov. 10: The day before he was to hang for his role in the Haymarket Riot, Louis Lingg blew himself up with a bomb in his jail cell in Chicago.
1892
Mar. 11: Ravachol, an anarchist, bombed the home of a judge and the home of a prosecutor in France for their roles in the sentencing of two anarchists, who had used explosives against the prime minister and the president of the chamber.
Nov. 8: Emile Henry, bomb designer and anarchist, was responsible for the deaths of six police officers at the Rue des Bons Enfants police station in Paris.
1894
Feb. 12: Emile Henry, an anarchist, bombed the Cafe Terminus in Paris, killing two people and injuring seventeen. Henry was convicted and put to death May 21, 1894.
1903
Apr. 29: Bulgarian revolutionaries randomly exploded bombs in various public places during the Salonica Coup aimed at undermining Turkish rule.
Nov. 21: Acting under orders from Bill Haywood, founder of the Industrial Workers of the World (IWW), Harry Orchard blew up the shaft of the Vindicator Mine in Cripple Creek, Colo.
Harry Orchard, IWW terrorist, blew up the train that conveyed strike-breakers in Independence to their dwellings. Twenty-six men were killed and fifty other men were maimed.
Harry Orchard attempted to assassinate Fred Bradley, member of the Mine Owner's Association in San Francisco. A bomb blew Bradley across the street and destroyed his home, but he survived.
1904
Judge Luther M. Goddard of the Colorado Supreme Court was the target of an attempted bombing by the Wobblies (IWW) after he had handed down several unfavorable rulings against them. Goddard survived, but Merritt W. Walley was accidentally killed in the blast.
1905
Feb. 4: Grand Duke Sergei Alexandrovich, the uncle of Czar Nicholas II and the governor of Moscow, was assassinated by a bomb thrown by Ivan Kalayev, a revolutionary.
Dec. 30: IWW terrorist Harry Orchard killed former Idaho governor Frank Steunenberg with a dynamite blast at Steunenberg's house in Caldwell.
1906
Jan. 6: Ten people died in Chicago from bomb explosions in a single twenty-four hour period.
1907
May: Between May and October, rival gambling syndicates in Chicago hurled thirty-two dynamite bombs at each other's pool rooms and off-track betting parlors, causing substantial property damage but no injuries.
Sept. 30: A bomb linked to the Industrial Workers of the World (IWW) killed Sheriff Harvey K. Brown of Baker City, Idaho. His murder was never solved.
1908
John F. Fort, governor of New Jersey, was the target of an unknown dynamite bomber believed to have been a crackpot or an opponent of the rigid state liquor laws.
M. Silverstein threw a homemade bomb into a squad of New York City police in Union Square to protest the harassment of local prostitutes by corrupt law enforcement officers. One pedestrian was killed.
Dec. 13: The Chicago First Ward political ball was not postponed, even though a bomb was detonated in the Coliseum two days before the traditional fund raising event was to take place.
1910
Oct. 1: The Los Angeles *Times* building was bombed, killing twenty-one employees. Perpetrators James and John McNamara, labor union agitators, were eventually arrested.
1916
Beverly Wyly Dunn, inventor of the high explosive, was an instigator of the Black Tom explosion at Jersey City, N.J.
July 22: A bomb exploded in downtown San Francisco during a Preparedness Day Parade. Nine people were killed and forty-one people were injured. Labor leader Tom Mooney and his associate Warren Billings were wrongly convicted for the bombing and were eventually released.
1917
Nov. 16: Reinhold Faust planted a bomb in Chicago's Auditorium Theatre, but it was defused by fireman Michael Corrigan.
1918
Sept. 23: The first of six bombs was thrown at the home of a black citizen in Chicago who had moved into a previously all-white neighborhood.
1919
Jan. 21: Racial tensions in Chicago resulted in more than thirty bombs being thrown at the homes of black residents.
May: Chicago whites bombed a building rented to blacks by William Austin.
June: The home of Chicago attorney William Austin was bombed after he had rented a building on the West Side to a black family.
June 2: The Washington, D.C., home of U.S. attorney general Mitchell Palmer was bombed by an anarchist who was the only casualty of the affray.
Aug. 12: Jim O'Leary's saloon at 4183 Halsted, Chicago, was bombed.
Aug. 19: A bomb exploded in the front yard at Mont Tennes' Chicago home.
1920
Sept. 16: Thirty-eight people were killed when a horse-drawn wagon loaded with dynamite and scrap iron exploded outside the Assay Building at the corner of Broad and Wall streets in New York City.
Sept. 28: In a series of bombs that were exchanged on Chicago's Near South Side between the rival gangs of Alderman Johnny Powers and the D'Andrea family, fighting for control of the Nineteenth Ward, no one was killed, but a restaurant was destroyed.
1921
Feb. 7: The Powers-D'Andrea political feud in Chicago escalated after a bomb exploded at a Blue Island dance hall when a number of D'Andrea supporters were present.
1922
Dec. 27: John Magnuson of Marshfield, Wis., sent a letter bomb to James A. Chapman because of a dispute over water rights. Chapman survived but his wife was killed. Magnuson went to prison for life.
1926
Aug. 24: The Farmer's National Bank of Pittsburgh was destroyed when robbers set off a bomb, injuring twenty-three people.
1927
April: Gangster James "Mad Bomber" Balcastro planted bombs in various Chicago polling places and on the front porches of political opponents of the Al Capone-backed candidate for mayor, William Hale Thompson. Five people were killed and hundreds of people were injured.
1928
May 18: The home of Sing Sing executioner Robert G. Elliott was bombed. No injuries were reported, and the culprit was never found.

June 4: Chinese military leader Chang Tso-lin was killed when a bomb planted by an assassin blew up his train as it made its way through Mukden.
1930
June 27: A.D. Payne of Amarillo, Texas, planted a bomb in his own car, which killed his wife and young son. Payne wanted to live with his mistress. He committed suicide while awaiting trial.
1937
May 2: An incendiary bomb exploded on board the *Hindenberg*, a German airship, killing twenty-two crewmen including two officers, Captain Ernest Lehmann and Colonel Erdmann, and thirteen passengers. The alleged saboteur was Eric Spehl, a crew member, who had become disheartened with Nazi policies.
1939
Mar. 20: To cash in on a life insurance policy, Alice Austin and her lover, Ted Simmons, of Hardin County, Ill., had farmer Ira Scott plant a bomb in the car of her husband, Earl Austin. He and Lacene McDowell were both killed. The conspirators were sentenced to fourteen-year prison terms.
Aug. 25: A bomb planted by the Irish Republican Army (IRA) members Peter Barnes and James Richards exploded in Coventry, England, killing five and wounding fifty others.
1943
July 23: A London soldier named Eric Brown placed a land mine underneath his father's wheelchair, killing the invalid instantly. Brown was convicted and sent to an asylum.
1944
July 20: An attempt to blow up German Chancellor Adolf Hitler at Rastenburg failed. Hitler sustained minor injuries. The assassin, Count Claus Schenk von Stauffenberg, was executed that night.
1948
May 3: Captain James Farran was killed by a letter bomb at his residence in Wolverhampton, Scot. The unknown bomber was avenging the death of a Jewish freedom fighter murdered in Palestine by Farran.
1949
Elihu H. Bailey, mayor of Evarts, Ky., survived an assassination attempt by a dynamiter, who was thought to be a local bootlegger.
May 7: The first bomb placed on board a commercial airliner exploded over the Philippines, killing thirteen people. Crispin Vergo was sent to jail for planting the bomb aboard the Philippine Airlines jet en route from Daet to Manila.
Sept. 9: Albert Guay of Québec City, Can., planted a bomb on board a Canadian Pacific airliner to do away with his wife. The explosion killed Rita Morel Guay and twenty-two other people. Guay and two other conspirators were subsequently hanged.
1950
Feb. 6: A rival gangster exploded a bomb in front of Mickey Cohen's Los Angeles home, but no one was injured.
Apr. 13: One person was injured when a bomb placed inside a towel holder in the lavatory of a British European airliner bound from London to Paris exploded.
1952
Sept. 24: A Mexicana DC-3 jet landed safely after a bomb exploded in the luggage compartment. Two people were injured. Both of the men responsible for the bombing were sentenced to thirty years in prison.
1953
Jan. 11: New York's "Mad Bomber" George Peter Metesky exploded a bomb at New York's Pennsylvania Station, injuring several people.
1955
Apr. 11: A time bomb placed inside the wheel well of an Air India Constellation jet exploded over Great Natuna Island in the South China Sea. Sixteen people were killed, but three passengers survived.
Nov. 1: Forty-four people on board a United Airlines jet were killed instantly when a bomb planted by Jack Gilbert Graham in his mother's luggage exploded over a Colorado beet farm. Graham planned to collect insurance money on his mother. He was executed.
1956
Mar. 4: A Skyways Ltd. jet from Great Britain exploded while on the ground in Cyprus. There were no injuries or casualties.
1957
Forty-five bombings in the South beginning in January 1957 were believed to be the work of the Ku Klux Klan.
July 25: A Western Airlines plane bound from Las Vegas, Nev., to Los Angeles, Calif., was forced to land when a minor explosion blew a hole in the lavatory. The perpetrator was blown out of the aircraft and died. There were no other injuries.
Aug. 4: Three men fire bombed a neighborhood bar in Los Angeles, Calif., killing six people. Clyde Bates, Manuel Chavez, and Manuel Hernandez were convicted of first-degree murder on Aug. 16.
Dec. 19: An Air France plane landed safely at the Lyons airport after a passenger set off a bomb in the lavatory. None of the eighty-nine passengers was hurt.
1958
May: Bomb blasts damaged the Jacksonville, Fla., Jewish Community Center, and the all-black James Weldon Johnson High School. Demanding segregation be restored, the Confederate Underground claimed responsibility.
August.: The son of a Palestinian refugee was accused, with his girlfriend, of bombing an Amman, Jor., office building. Stepho Stephan was sentenced to death and Nadia Salti was sent to prison.
1959
Feb. 1: George Puchert, a West German arms dealer, was blown up by unknown assassins, thought to be Algerian nationals.
Sept. 8: A bomb tore a hole in the fuselage of a Mexicana jet flying over central Mexico, killing the person who detonated the bomb and wounding eight other people. A small fire was extinguished and the plane landed safely.
1960s
The headquarters of the Royal Mounted Canadian Police was dynamited in Westmount, Can., by the Front de Libération du Québec (FLQ). Bombs placed in the Central Station of Montreal were defused before they had a chance to go off.
Following the attack against the Central Service Station of Montreal, there were more bombings carried out against various national symbols by the FLQ.
Members of the FLQ bombed a factory at LaGrenade, Quebec, Can., killing two people.
Jean Corbo, FLQ terrorist, was accidentally killed by his own bomb, while on his way to the Dominion Textile factory in Quebec.
A bomb exploded at the monument of Dollard des Ormeaux at Park Lafontaine in Quebec.
During an election rally at which former Quebec Premier Jean Lesage was speaking, a bomb was set off in the washroom of Paul Sauve Arena.
1960
Fall: On Sundays and holidays several bombs were planted in and around New York City. One nearly wrecked the Staten Island Ferry. The worst bombing killed or injured eighteen people at a subway station. The "Subway Bomber" was never caught.
Jan. 6: A National Airlines jet flying en route from New York to Miami exploded over Bolivia, N.C., and crashed after a passenger set off a dynamite bomb in the forward fuselage. Thirty-four people were killed.
Apr. 28: A bomb which went off in the cockpit destroyed a Linea Aeropostal jet bound from Caracas to Puerto Ayacucho, Venez. Thirteen people were killed.
June 24: President of Venezuela Romulo Betancourt received minor injuries when a bomb that killed his aide exploded in Caracas, Venez.
Aug. 29: Jordanian Premier Hazza Majali and ten others were killed when a time bomb exploded in his Amman office.
1961
A voiceprint convicted Joseph Worley of Orlando, Fla., who had phoned in a bomb threat to local police.
1962
February: A bomb exploded outside the San Fernando Valley, Calif., home of the Reverend Brooks R. Walker, opponent of the political right.
February: A second bomb went off at the home of the Reverend John Simmons, who was participating in the same panel discussion with the Reverend Walker.
May 22: A bomb placed inside in the towel holder in the rear lavatory of a Continental Airlines jet bound from Chicago, Ill., to Kansas City, Mo., killed all forty-five passengers on board.
1963
Mar. 8: The Front de Libération du Québec (FLQ), threw molotov cocktails at military establishments in Canada. This marked the start of a wave of FLQ bombings throughout Canada.
Apr. 20: An FLQ bomb exploded at the Army Recruitment Centre in Montreal, Can. A guard named O'Neil was killed.
April-May: The FLQ tried to blow up the Dominion Monument in Montreal. During the next few weeks, the FLQ attacked the Selbec Copper mines and bombed mailboxes in predominantly English Westmount, Can. Police sergeant M. Leja, of the bomb-detonation squad, was killed.
Sept. 15: The 16th Street Baptist Church in Birmingham, Ala., was bombed by white supremacists who were never caught. Four schoolgirls, Addie Mae Collins, Denise McNair, Carole Robertson and Cynthia Wesley, were killed.
1964
Dec. 8: A dynamite charge apparently planted by a passenger who had insured himself for a large amount of money killed fifteen passengers aboard an Alas Airlines jet bound from Tipuani to LaPaz, Bol.
1965
July 8: A Canadian Pacific Airliner flying over British Columbia crashed on its way to Whitehorse in the Yukon. A bomb planted in the fuselage was blamed for the tragedy that killed all fifty-two passengers.
1966
Jan. 10: Black activist Vernon Dahmer was killed by a Ku Klux Klan bomb in Hattiesburg, Miss.
Jan. 29: Five Yugoslavian consulates in the U.S. were bombed by political dissidents. It was the first massive political bombing in the U.S.
May 6: A Front de Libération du Québec (FLQ) bomb at the La Grenade Factory killed Therese Marin. The bomb was the FLQ's first attack in three years.
June: An FLQ attack against Canadian symbols began with the explosion of a bomb near the monument at Dollard des Ormeaux at Park Lafontain, Can.
June 3: An FLQ bomb exploded in the lavatory of the Paul Sauve Arena in Canada during an election rally. Former Quebec premier Jean Lesage

was present at the rally, but was not hurt.
July 14: FLQ activist Jean Corbo was killed by a bomb he was taking to the Dominion Textile factory in Canada.
Nov. 13: A bomb blew up on *The Grand Integrity* five days after the ship sailed from Portland, Ore. Captain Ho Lien-Siu and a motorman were killed as they inspected the device. The ship was not seriously damaged.
Nov. 22: An Aden Airways jetliner crashed in Southern Yemen after an explosive device hidden in a piece of carry-on luggage was detonated. Twenty-eight people were killed.

1967

Jan. 7: Army deserter Richard James Paris detonated a dynamite bomb with a .38-caliber pistol in the honeymoon suite of the Orbit Inn, in Las Vegas, Nev., killing himself, his wife, and five other newlyweds.
Feb. 24: A love triangle allegedly prompted Lorain, Ohio banker Albert Ricci to send a package bomb to his rival Samuel Hammons of Avon, Ohio. Hammons died opening the box.
May 29: A time bomb exploded, but did not cause serious damage to an Aercondor jet flying between Barranquilla and Bogota, Col. The plane landed safely with no casualties.
June 30: A plastic explosive placed inside the forward compartment of an Aden Airways jet on the ground in Southern Yemen resulted in damage to the craft, but no casualties.
Oct. 12: A British European Airways jet flying over the Mediterranean Sea exploded in midair when a bomb planted in the passenger cabin went off. Sixty-six lives were lost, with no survivors.
Nov. 12: An American Airlines jet flying over Alamosa, Colo., on its way to San Diego, Calif., was damaged when a small bomb exploded in the luggage compartment. No casualties were reported, and the plane landed on schedule.

1968

The Angry Brigade, student terrorists, began a three-year bombing campaign against British public and government buildings. The leaders were arrested, and the movement died.
Jan. 9: The anti-Castro group El Poder Cubano sent a letter bomb from the U.S. that exploded in a Havana post office.
Jan. 25: Two parcel bombs en route to Cuba detonated in Miami injuring one person. The bombs were hidden in shipments of packages sent by El Poder Cubano.
Feb. 8: El Poder Cubano was believed to be responsible for the bombing of the British Consulate in Miami.
Feb. 18: One person was killed and fourteen others injured when a bomb exploded in the basement of the Yugoslav ambassador's home in Paris.
March: El Poder Cubano launched a bombing attack that continued until fall against U.S. businesses engaged in trade with Communist Cuba.
Apr. 22: El Poder Cubano bombed the Mexican mission to the U.S.
Apr. 22: El Poder Cubano bombed the Spanish National Tourist Office in New York City.
May 6: A drunken patron, ejected from a Fort Worth, Texas, nightclub, returned with a fire bomb that killed seven customers and horribly burned six others.
May 11: A bomb was placed in a bottle by the Front de liberation du Quebec (FLQ) at the headquarters of the Quebec branch of the Seven Up Co. as a protest against a labor dispute going on at the time.
May 26: A bomb placed by El Poder Cubano exploded at the Mexican consul general's home in Miami.
June 21: For the second time in 1968, the Spanish National Tourist Office in New York City was bombed by El Poder Cubano.
June 30: Two Ku Klux Klan (KKK) sympathizers, Thomas Albert Tarrant and Kathy Ainsworth, were arrested outside the home of a Jewish businessman in Meridian, Miss., as they were attempting to plant dynamite. Ainsworth was killed trying to escape.
July 4: El Poder Cubano bombed both the Canadian consulate and tourist office, and the Australian National Tourist Office in New York City.
July 7: The Japanese National Tourist Office in New York City was bombed by El Poder Cubano.
July 9: El Poder Cubano bombed the Cuban and Yugoslav missions to the United Nations in New York.
July 14: The Mexican National Tourist Office in Chicago was bombed by members of El Poder Cubano.
July 15: The New York Police removed a bomb placed by El Poder Cubano at the French National Tourist office before it could do any damage.
July 16: Police in Newark, N.J., dismantled a bomb placed at the Mexican consulate by El Poder Cubano.
July 19: The Mexican National Tourist office and the Japan Air Lines office in Los Angeles were bombed by El Poder Cubano terrorists.
July 30: The British consulate in Los Angeles was bombed by an anti-Castro faction.
Aug. 3: El Poder Cubano bombed the New York branch of the Bank of Tokyo Trust Company.
Aug. 8: A British vessel off the coast of Miami was damaged by an underwater bomb placed by El Poder Cubano.
Aug. 17: El Poder Cubano set off a bomb at a Mexican airline office in Miami.
Aug. 27: Gambling magnate Richard Chartrand was killed by a car bomb in Lake Tahoe, Nev.
Sept. 8: The FLQ planted a bomb at a Liquor Commission store in Quebec, Can., in support of striking workers.
Sept. 20: The barracks of the Black Watch Regiment in Quebec was bombed by the FLQ.
Sept. 26: A second FLQ bomb went off at a Liquor Commission store in Quebec.
Oct. 14: Two political clubs, the Club Renaissance and the Reform Club, were bombed by the FLQ in Quebec.
Oct. 27: A Sears, Roebuck store in Brazil was bombed.
Nov. 19: A fire and explosion caused only minor damage to a Continental Airlines jet flying over Gunnison, Colo. The plane landed safely with no injuries reported.
Nov. 20: A third Liquor Commission Store in Quebec, Can., was bombed by the FLQ.
Nov. 22: Twelve people were killed and fifty-two more were injured when a bomb exploded in Jerusalem's busiest open-air market.
Dec. 12: The Montreal residence of the president of Structural Steel was bombed by FLQ terrorists.
Dec. 14: The FLQ continued its bombing campaign with an attack against Chanbly Transport and its director, Charles Senecal.
Dec. 26: Two Habash Front terrorists, armed with hand grenades and small arms, attacked an El Al jetliner in Athens, Gr. An Israeli passenger was killed.

1969

January: The Front de Libération du Québec (FLQ) attacked numerous Anglo-Saxon companies in Montreal with bombs in January and February.
Feb. 3: President of the Mozambique Liberation Front Dr. Edwardo Mondran was killed by a bomb in Tanzania detonated by an unknown assailant.
Feb. 14: A number of people were wounded, and substantial damage was reported after an FLQ bomb demolished part of the Montreal Stock Exchange building.
Feb. 18: Four terrorists belonging to the Habash Front attacked an El Al jet in Zurich, Switz. They were armed with guns and hand grenades. The co-pilot was killed and five passengers were injured.
Feb. 21: Two persons were killed and eight were wounded when a bomb went off in a Jerusalem food store.
Feb. 25: The Popular Front for the Liberation of Palestine (PFLP) claimed responsibility for the bombing of the British consulate in Jerusalem.
Mar. 11: An Ethiopian Airlines jet exploded on the ground at Frankfurt, Ger. There were no injuries.
Apr. 15: Cameron David Bishop, member of Students for a Democratic Society (SDS), was placed on the FBI's Ten Most Wanted List for bombing a defense plant in Colorado in January.
May 20: Two Cubans were arrested in New Jersey after attempting to bomb the Cuban consulate in Montreal.
May 30: A section of the Trans-Arabian pipeline was bombed by the Popular Front for the Liberation of Palestine (PFLP) in the Golan Heights, Israel.
June 8: A bomb exploded at Loew's Orpheum Theater in New York City causing only minor damage. The bomb was allegedly planted by anti-Castro dissidents angry about the showing of the movie *Ché*.
June 9: The Yugoslav consulate in Sydney, Aus., was bombed, possibly by Croatian militants.
June 26: During a visit to Argentina by New York Governor Nelson Rockefeller, several U.S.-owned Minimax supermarkets were bombed.
June 26: The Fuerzas Armadas Rebeldes (FAR) bombed fourteen minimax supermarkets in Argentina, causing $3 million in damages.
July 18: PFLP terrorists fire-bombed two London department stores which had connections with Israel.
Aug. 5: A Philippine Airlines jet exploded over Zamboanga, Phil. The bomb detonated in one of the restrooms, killed the person who set it off, and injured four other people.
Aug. 9: A bomb exploded at the Olympic Airways facility in Athens, Gr., injuring two American tourists.
Aug. 18: A bomb placed by the Habash Front inside the Israel tourist office in Copenhagen, Den., was dismantled.
Aug. 18: The Habash Front set off explosions in a Marks and Spencer store in London.
Aug. 23: A Jewish school in Teheran, Iran, was bombed, with only light damage resulting.
Aug. 23: An explosive charge went off in the hands of a Hawatmah Front terrorist trying to sabotage the Israeli pavilion in Izmir, Turk.
Aug. 25: The PFLP claimed responsibility for the bombing of the Israeli Zim Lines London office, which injured one person.
Aug. 29: A TWA jet bound from Rome to Athens was hijacked by Arab terrorists and diverted to Damascus, Syria. One hijacker threw hand grenades into the cockpit which destroyed the front of the plane.
Sept. 8: The PFLP claimed responsibility for hand-grenade attacks against Israeli offices in Brussels, Bonn, and The Hague.
Oct. 6: The Haymarket Statue, a memorial to slain Chicago police officers who died from an anarchist bomb in 1886, was dynamited by radical student groups, believed to be the Students for a Democratic Society (SDS), and its Weathermen faction.
Oct. 6: The corporate offices of General Motors, Pepsi, Dunlop Tires, Squibb, and the First National City Bank of Córdoba, Arg., were bombed. The offices of IBM and General Electric in San Miguel de

Tucumán, Arg., were also bombed.
Oct. 7: The Buenos Aires, Arg., library of the U.S. Information Service was bombed.
Oct. 8: The Buenos Aires, Arg., branch of the Bank of Boston was bombed. In Santa Fe, Arg., the office of Remington Rand was also bombed.
Nov. 9: A time bomb was discovered in a Jewish Community Center in West Berlin.
Nov. 20: The Peronist Armed Forces (FAP) bombed the offices of fifteen foreign companies doing business in Argentina, nine of them U.S.-owned.
Nov. 27: Two Jordanian terrorists launched a hand grenade attack on the El Al Israel Airlines office in Athens, Gr., killing a Greek child and wounding thirteen other people.
Nov. 29: The Yugoslav embassy in Canberra, Aus., was bombed by Croatian militants.
Dec. 12: The Baader-Meinhof Gang planted three bombs in West Berlin at the El Al Office, the America House, and the U.S. Officer's Club. The first two were defused, but the Officer's Club was damaged by an explosion.
Dec. 12: The Red Brigades exploded a bomb in the Piazza Fontana, in Milan, Italy, that killed sixteen people. Their trial did not begin until 1978. Five defendants were eventually acquitted, and on Mar. 20, 1981, two others sentenced to prison on lesser charges.
Dec. 22: A lavatory explosion on an Air Vietnam jet killed thirty -two people near Nha Trang, S. Viet. The landing brakes were damaged by the bomb, and the plane careened into a school while landing.
Dec. 24: Three Arabs were arrested in Athens, Gr., after attempting to smuggle explosives and guns on board a TWA jet bound for Rome and New York.

1970

A bomb was planted by Silas Trim Bissell (AKA: Terry Jackson) and his wife Judith Emily Bissell, former members of the Weathermen, in the ROTC facility at the University of Washington campus in Seattle. The bomb failed to detonate.
Three members of the Black Panther Party, David Rice, Edwin Poindexter, and Duane Peak planted a bomb in an empty house in Omaha, Neb. The blast seriously wounded two policemen, and a third was killed. All three men were sent to prison.
In a five-day period, student agitators exploded bombs in a New York courthouse, near the Haymarket statue in Chicago, Ill., in an armory in Santa Barbara, Calif., a courtroom in San Rafael, Calif., and a ROTC building on the University of Washington campus.
A San Francisco police station was bombed by political activists, killing one officer.
Jan. 20: A branch of the Bank of America in Turin, Italy, was bombed.
February: Just before robbing a bank, two robbers set off bombs in a police station, the local bank, and a parking lot in Danbury, Conn. Twenty-six people were injured in the police station blast and the building was levelled.
Feb. 10: A bus at the Munich, Ger., airport was attacked by three Arab terrorists with grenades. An Israeli citizen was killed, and eleven other passengers were wounded.
Feb. 21: A Swissair jet flying from Zurich, Switz., to Tel Aviv, Isr., was blown up in midair, claiming forty-seven lives. It was believed that the bomb had been placed by Abu Ibrahim of the Popular Front for Liberation of Palestine (PFLP), who might also be a member of Fedayeen.
Feb. 21: A bomb exploded in the freight hold of an Austrian Airlines jet twenty minutes after takeoff from the Frankfurt Airport. The plane returned to the airfield and landed safely without casualties.
Feb. 24: Two bombs in parcels destined for Israel were defused in Frankfurt, Ger.
Mar. 1: A bomb was removed from an Ethiopian jetliner in Rome, Italy. The device was placed there by the Eritrean Liberation Front (ELF).
Mar. 7: A hand grenade was tossed into the courtyard of Israel's honorary consul in Guatemala.
Mar. 14: As a United Arab Airlines jet prepared to land in Cairo, Egypt, an explosion damaged the rear landing well. The plane managed to land safely.
Apr. 6: A bomb factory in New York's Greenwich Village exploded. It was previously used by student radicals.
Apr. 21: Seventy-five miles north of Manila, a bomb hidden in the lavatory of a Philippine Airlines jet exploded in midair, killing all thirty-six passengers.
Apr. 24: The Popular Front for the Liberation of Palestine (PFLP) bombed the El Al Airline office in Istanbul, Turk., and the Pan American offices in Izmir. No injuries were reported.
May 8: The offices of Bank of America, American Express, the Armed Forces Network and Pan Am, and the Bank of America were firebombed, in Munich. Ger.
May 22: Members of the Fedayeen crossed into Israel from Lebanon and fired three bazooka rockets at a school bus. Eight children were killed in the attack, and twenty-two were injured.
May 24: A series of bomb attacks perpetrated by various Quebec separatist groups began in Montreal, Can.
June 2: One person was killed and twelve others were injured when a hand grenade exploded underneath a seat on a Philippine Airlines jet en route to Bacolad Negros Island. The plane landed safely at Roxas, Phil.
June 18: The Parke-Davis plant in Buenos Aires, Arg., was bombed, killing three employees.
June 27: Nine buildings, including several belonging to U.S. companies, were bombed in Buenos Aires, Rosario, and Cordoba, Arg.
Aug. 24: Karleton Armstrong, David S. Fine, and fellow members of the Students For a Democratic Society (SDS) detonated a bomb at the University of Wisconsin, killing Robert Fassnacht and injuring several other people. Armstrong was sent to prison.
Sept. 7: A Pan Am Boeing 747 was destroyed on the ground in Cairo, Egypt, after two Popular Front for the Liberation of Palestine (PFLP) terrorists hijacked the plane when it took off from the Amsterdam Airport. The plane was diverted to Beirut, then to Cairo, where it was blown up after the passengers and crew had been evacuated.
Sept. 12: A TWA jet bound from Tel Aviv, Isr., to New York, was hijacked by the PFLP on Sept. 6, and forced to land at Dawson Field in Zerka, Jor., where it was blown up. There were no casualties.
Sept. 12: PFLP terrorists blew up a Swissair jet hijacked on Sept. 6. Between Zurich and New York, they forced the craft to land at Dawson Field in Jordan where it was destroyed. No one was killed or injured.
Sept. 12: The PFLP blew up a third jetliner, this one belonging to British Overseas Airways. The plane was hijacked Sept. 9, and the pilot was forced to fly to Dawson Field, Jor., where the plane was blown up on the ground. No casualties were reported.
Oct. 2: A bomb exploded outside a U.S. Air Force commissary in Izmir, Turk. A second, unexploded dynamite bomb was found outside the commissary.
Oct. 3: The CENTO headquarters in Ankara, Turk., was bombed, causing substantial damage to the building, but no casualties.
Oct. 6: An unexploded bomb was found underneath a vehicle belonging to a U.S. airman in Ankara, Turk.
Oct. 6: Letter bombs sent to the Israeli embassy and the offices of El Al Airlines in London were intercepted.
Oct. 8: The Ford Motor Company offices in Santiago, Chile, were bombed.
Oct. 15: More letter bombs were uncovered, this time destined for the Israel Masada exhibition in West Berlin, Ger.
Oct. 16: The Buenos Aires, Arg., home of the U.S. defense department attaché was firebombed.
Oct. 20: The homes of two U.S. officials in Buenos Aires, Arg., were bombed.
Nov. 6: The Tel Aviv, Isr., central bus station was rocked by two explosions that killed two people and wounded twenty-four others.
Nov. 21: A dynamite charge exploded outside the fence of the U.S. embassy in Ankara, Turk.
Nov. 27: U.S. military bases in Ankara, Turk., were damaged minimally by a series of bombs.
Dec. 1: The Tupamaros were blamed for the bombing of an ITT office in Montevideo, Uruguay.
Dec. 24: Two students from Ankara University in Turkey were arrested while trying to explode a charge of dynamite at the U.S. Air Force Tuslog Detachment 30.

1971

During racial disturbances n Wilmington, N.C., a grocery store was firebombed. Nine black men and one woman were jailed in a case that had strong political overtones.
Jan. 8: The Jewish Defense League (JDL) bombed the Soviet cultural offices in Washington, D.C.
Jan. 22: The headquarters of Caltex and Esso were bombed by the People's Revolutionary Front in Manila, Phil., resulting in the death of one employee.
Jan. 23: Unexploded bombs were found at the U.S. embassy and the U.S. Information Service in Ankara, Turk.
Jan. 25: The residence of a U.S. Foreign Service officer in Ankara, Turk., was firebombed with two Molotov cocktails.
Feb. 1: The Popular Front for the Liberation of Palestine (PFLP) tried to bomb an El Al airliner en route from London to Tel Aviv. A Peruvian girl was asked to take a suitcase aboard the plane. Alert security guards found the suitcase and the explosives hidden inside.
Feb. 2: An Indian Airlines jet on the ground in Pakistan was blown up by two Kashmiri nationalists after the Indian government refused to release thirty-six political prisoners.
Feb. 8: A gift-wrapped bomb exploded in the apartment of a U.S. soldier stationed in Turkey. There were no fatalities.
Feb. 17: Turkish terrorists exploded a bomb outside the fence of U.S. Air Force Tuslog Detachment 29 in Istanbul. There were no casualties.
Feb. 19: A passenger boat belonging to the U.S. Army was damaged by a terrorist bomb in Istanbul, Turk.
Feb. 20: Plastic explosives placed outside the U.S. Information Service in Ankara, Turk., failed to detonate after the fuse had been lit.
Mar. 13: The offices of Esso-Pappas in Athens, Gr., were bombed by the Greek Militant Resistance.
Mar. 14: The Palestinian terrorist group El Fatah, assisted by French sympathizers, blew up fuel tanks in Rotterdam, Neth.
Mar 15: The left-wing Turkish People's Liberation Army (TPLA) movement of Turkey bombed the U.S. consulate in Ankara.
Mar. 25: The U.S. consulate in Izmir, Turk., was rocked by a pipe bomb

that caused little or no damage.
Mar. 25: An Arab group known as the Movement of Youthward Brothers in War of the Palestinian People claimed responsibility for the office bombing of Bull Computer in France.
Apr. 2: One bomb exploded outside the CENTO headquarters in Ankara, Turk., and five others were found and defused. Four Turkish students attacked a U.S. officer's mess in Ankara with two black powder bombs.
Apr. 2: The Arab Fedayeen bombed a section of the Trans-Arabian pipeline to the Zarka refinery in Jordan.
Apr. 27: Various American offices were bombed by Luis Blanco and Bello units of Ejercito Revelucionario del Pueblo (ERP) in Rosario, Arg.
May 4: A bomb set off by Turkish terrorists at an empty U.S. Air Force barracks in Ankara shattered all of the windows in the building but injured no one.
May 26: An explosion occurred at the JNF offices in Rio de Janeiro, Braz.
July 8: Railway tracks and a tank truck belonging to Esso-Pappas of Athens, Gr., were bombed.
July 8: The Essex International Brakelining plant of Londonderry, Ire., was bombed.
July 23: Molotov cocktails were thrown at the Jordanian embassy in Paris by the El Fatah organization.
July 25: A JDL firebomb demolished the automobile of a Soviet embassy official in the U.S.
July 28: In a "surrogate" bombing attempt, the PFLP handed a suitcase filled with dynamite to a Dutch woman just before she was to board an El Al jetliner, Tel Aviv, Isr. The woman was stopped and the plot thwarted.
Aug. 24: An explosive device placed inside the lavatory of a Royal Jordanian jet by El Fatah exploded on the ground at Madrid Airport in Spain. There were no casualties.
September.: Cambodian terrorists hurled a bomb onto a softball field at a U.S. military installation, killing two people and wounding ten others.
September.: The vehicle of U.S. Ambassador Emory Swank was attacked by Cambodian insurgents. The bomb they hurled did not go off.
Sept. 1: A "surrogate" attempt to place a bomb on board an El Al jet, this time in London, failed. A Peruvian woman was solicited by a member of the PFLP.
Oct. 12: A car belonging to an employee of the U.S. consulate in Istanbul, Turk., was bombed.
Oct. 14: A Sinclair pipeline in Colombia was bombed by the United Front for Guerrilla Action.
Nov. 3: Molotov cocktails damaged the car of the U.S. consul general and houses belonging to officials from Swift & Company and Chicago Bridge Company in Sao Paulo, Braz.
Nov. 10: Four bombs exploded at the Intercontinental Hotel in Amman, Jor.
Nov. 20: An explosion of mysterious origin ripped apart a China Airlines Caravelle over the South China Sea. There were twenty-five fatalities and no survivors.
Nov. 24: Claiming to have a bomb, D.B. Cooper threatened the pilot of a Northwest Orient jet. Cooper later parachuted out of the plane and was never found.
Dec. 16: A bomb exploded at the Jordanian embassy in Geneva, Switz., wounding four people.
Dec. 28: The Jibral Front sent was held responsible for several letter bombs intercepted in Austria.
Dec. 29: An Arrow II Turbo Commander jet belonging to General Aviation was blown up in the hangar at Elkhart, Ill.

1972

January: The residence of a U.S. businessman in Guatemala was bombed.
Jan. 22: The New York offices of the Portuguese Airlines was bombed in protest of Portuguese colonial rule in Guinea.
Jan. 26: A homemade bomb placed in the luggage compartment of a Yugoslavian jet en route from Copenhagen, Den., to Zagreb, Yug., killed twenty-seven people. One person survived.
Jan. 26: A Stockholm-to-Belgrade jetliner was blown up by Croatian emigrés, killing twenty-six passengers.
Jan. 26: The Jewish Defense League (JDL) fire-bombed the New York offices of Sol Hurok, who had managed the performances of Soviet entertainers in the U.S.
Jan. 27: Six people were injured by a bomb on a train en route from Vienna, Aust., to Zagreb, Yug. Croatian terrorists were suspected.
Feb. 2: The British embassy in Dublin, Ire., was fire-bombed.
Feb. 5: Black September, Palestinian terrorists, blew up two natural gas installations in Holland.
Feb. 18: Black September bombed a Hamburg, Ger., factory which made electric generators for Israeli aircraft. There was extensive damage.
Feb. 22: The Irish Republican Army (IRA) set off a bomb at the Parachute Regiment headquarters in Aldershot, England, killing nine soldiers and civilians, and injuring three other people.
Mar. 8: A bomb exploded in cockpit of a TWA jet parked on the ground at the airport in Las Vegas, Nev. There were no casualties.
Mar. 22: IRA bombs exploded in one of the largest hotels in Belfast, N.Ire., and in the central train station.
Apr. 4: The Cuban Trade Office in Montreal was bombed. One person was killed and seven others injured.
Apr. 29: The Jibral Front sent several parcels of bombs to the Israeli Pavilion at the Hanover, Ger., fair.
May 3: Four Turkish gunmen planted bombs in the parking lot of the U.S. base civil engineering facility in Ankara. The bombs did not detonate.
May 11: The Fifth U.S. Army Headquarters in Frankfurt, Ger., was bombed by a terrorist group believed to be the Baader-Meinhof gang. Colonel Paul Bloomquist was killed, and thirteen others were wounded.
May 12: The Comite Argentino de Lucha Anti-Imperialista was blamed for the bombing of four U.S. firms and a Dutch company in Argentina.
May 23: The offices of ITT in Caracas, Venez., were bombed.
May 24: The JDL bombed the Long Island, N.Y., residence of the Soviet Mission to the U.N.
May 24: Two car bombs exploded outside the U.S. Army's European headquarters in Heidelberg, Ger., killing one soldier and wounding two others. The attack was attributed to the Baader-Meinhof gang.
May 25: Four bombs exploded in Paris: one each at the offices of the American Legion, the U.S. consulate, Pan American World Airways, and TWA.
May 25: A homemade pipe bomb placed in the water fountain of a Lan-Chile jet flying over the Caribbean Sea exploded. The plane landed safely in Montego Bay, Jam., with no casualties.
May 31: One person was killed and two more injured when Iranian terrorists bombed the U.S. Information Service in Teheran, Iran.
June 3: The offices of Honeywell, IBM, and the Bank of America and Italy were bombed in Milan, Italy.
June 9: On the sixtieth anniversary of the abortive Peronist coup, four American firms were bombed in Buenos Aires, Cordoba, Rosario, and Santa Fe, Arg.
June 10: The West German embassy in Dublin, Ire., was the site of a bomb explosion set off by the Baader-Meinhof gang.
June 15: A CV-880 jet belonging to Cathay Pacific Airways of Hong Kong exploded over the central highlands of South Vietnam, killing eighty-one people. The bomb was placed under the passenger seat by a police officer whose fiancee and daughter were aboard.
July 8: The Israeli Mossad detonated a car bomb that killed Ghassan Kanafani of the Popular Front for the Liberation of Palestine (PFLP) in Beirut.
Aug. 16: A bomb on an El Al Israeli Airlines jetliner on its way to Tel Aviv, Isr., from Rome exploded minutes after takeoff. It blew a hole in the aft baggage compartment. The aircraft landed safely with no casualties.
Aug. 29: The Popular Revolutionary Resistance Group of Greece exploded a bomb at the U.S. embassy in Athens, causing minor damage.
September: A bomb damaged the car of Thomas Enders, U.S. Chargé of Affairs in Cambodia. Several bystanders were killed.
Sept. 9: Dr. Ami Shachori, agricultural counselor at the Israeli embassy in London, was killed by a letter bomb sent by Black September. Forty-nine other letter bombs were intercepted.
Sept. 16: An Air Manila Fokker F-27 landed safely in Roxas, Phil., after a hand grenade exploded in the cargo compartment. There were no casualties.
Sept. 16: Twelve businesses, including seven U.S. branch offices, were bombed in four different cities on Mexican Independence Day.
Sept. 18: Letter bombs were sent from Amsterdam to Israeli legations in Geneva, Paris, Brussels, Ottawa, Buenos Aires, Phnom Penh, Montreal, Vienna, and Washington, D.C., by Black September.
Sept. 19: The economic advisor to the Israeli embassy in London was killed by a letter bomb.
Oct. 4: An Arab bookstore was destroyed in Paris by a group known as Masada, Action and Defense Movement.
Oct. 4: Letter bombs sent by Black September from Malaysia were sent to various Jewish addresses throughout the world. One of the bombs exploded in the New York Post Office, wounding one employee.
Oct. 13: A bomb was defused in the El Al offices in Paris.
Oct. 16: Two Americans staying at the Sheraton Hotel in Buenos Aires, Arg., were injured in a bomb blast carried out by the Maximo Mena Command. One Canadian citizen was killed.
Oct. 17: A bomb was discovered in the entrance of a building that housed the Rotterdam offices of the Bank of America and Zim Airlines.
Oct. 24: The Israeli Mossad retaliated against the PFLP by dispatching letter bombs from Belgrade, addressed to Arab leaders in Egypt, Algeria, Libya, and Lebanon.
Oct. 25: Letter bombs earmarked for President Richard Nixon, Secretary of State William Rogers, and Secretary of Defense Melvin Laird were intercepted in the U.S. by police.
Oct. 29: A Lufthansa jet bound from Beirut to Ankara, Turk., was hijacked by Black Septembrists who demanded the release of three terrorists imprisoned for the massacre at the Olympic Village in Munich. The three were freed after negotiations.
Oct. 30: Black September sent letter bombs from Malaysia and Singapore to Israel.
Oct. 31: The Israeli embassy in Nigeria received a Black September letter bomb.
Nov. 2: The French consulate in Zaragoza, Spain, was bombed by three youths. The French honorary consul was killed.

Nov. 3: A French woman attempting to plant a bomb at the U.S. embassy in Amman, Jor., was killed while trying to set it off.
Nov. 4: A Jewish Zionist Youth Group in Frankfurt, Ger., received a letter bomb.
Nov. 5: The Pan Am ticket office in San Salvador, El Sal., was demolished by a terrorist bomb. There were no casualties.
Nov. 6: A letter bomb exploded in a Bombay, India, post office, injuring one worker.
Nov. 9: The IBM offices in San Miguel de Tucumán, Arg., were damaged by a terrorist bomb.
Nov. 11: Five letter bombs were received by the Israeli delegation to Jewish organizations in Geneva, Switz.
Nov. 11: Fourteen letter bombs were received by Jewish organizations and people in London. One rigged envelope mailed from India seriously injured a Jewish diamond seller when it exploded in his hands. Fifty-two other similar bombs were intercepted in Bombay and New Delhi by British officials.
Nov. 15: The Argentine-Brazilian pavilion at the Fifth International Trade Fair in San Salvador, El Sal., was damaged when a bomb exploded in an adjacent restroom.
Nov. 21: Letter bombs sent to prominent Jewish citizens in Toronto, Can., were found.
Nov. 23: Agents of El Fatah threw a bomb into the residence of the Arab National Union in Amman, Jor.
Dec. 7: An underground Greek terrorist movement called Independence, Liberation, Resistance set off time bombs under the cars of two U.S. servicemen in Athens, Gr.
Dec. 7: The Jibral Front sent several letter bombs from Singapore to public institutions in Israel.
Dec. 8: A U.S. businessman vacationing in Brisbane, Aus., was killed by a car bomb outside a Serbian Orthodox church.
Dec. 8: Mossad detonated an electronic telephone bomb in Paris that killed Mahmoud Hamshari of the Palestinian Liberation Organization (PLO).
Dec. 8: Seven terrorists tried to hijack an Ethiopian Airlines craft over Addis Ababa, Eth. The plane landed safely despite a hand-grenade blast. Eleven people were injured.
Dec. 12: The Cuban Secret Government was blamed for the bombing of a travel agency and other offices in New York, Miami, and Montreal.
Dec. 20: The U.S. embassy in Beirut was struck by two rockets fired by Black September.
Dec. 26: Two members of Black September were arrested in Turkey while attempting to convey a plastic bomb into Paris.

1973

Jan. 1: Several letter bombs were mailed to various Jordanian citizens by Black September, Palestinian terrorists.
Jan 8: The Paris offices of an agency that arranged the emigration of Jews to Israel was destroyed by a bomb set off by Black September.
Jan. 24: Black September mailed letter bombs to Israeli consulates in Australia, Canada, and Chile.
Jan. 24: The Pan Am offices in Teheran, Iran, were bombed.
Jan. 29: Letter bombs arrived in Israel from Turkey. Black September was responsible.
Jan. 31: Envelope bombs were sent from Rome to the Israeli embassy in Ruanda by Black September.
Feb. 5: Black September mailed letter bombs from Rome to the Israeli embassy in Guatemala.
Feb. 8: Letter bombs were sent from Germany to the Israeli embassy in Banqui, the capital of the Central African Republic.
Feb. 21: A Libyan Boeing 727 jet was shot down by the Israelis over the Sinai, killing 106 passengers and crew. The Israelis believed that the plane was a "flying bomb."
Mar. 6: A time bomb planted in a rental car outside the El Al terminal at New York's Kennedy Airport was safely removed. Black September was suspected.
Mar. 7: Two more time bombs were defused in New York. They were placed in rental cars parked outside of Israeli-owned banks.
Mar. 8: Two Irish Republican Army (IRA) bombs exploded in London, killing one person and injuring 200.
Mar. 10: An IRA bomb exploded in a Glasgow, Scot., dance hall where Protestant supporters were to stage a dance.
Mar. 15: Two Arabs were arrested by the French police after failing in their attempt to smuggle explosives into the country so they could blow up the Israeli embassy in Paris.
Mar. 19: An Air Vietnam passenger jet was blown apart over Ban Me Thuot when a bomb exploded in the cargo area. Fifty-nine people were killed.
Mar. 21: Two local terrorists fired a gun and threw several Molotov cocktails at the offices of the U.S. consulate general in Frankfurt, Ger.
Mar. 22: An incendiary bomb damaged the vehicle of a U.S. government official in Athens, Gr. The bombs was placed by the Greek Anti-Dictatorial Youth(EAN).
Mar. 23: Terrorists threw a Molotov cocktail through the window of the Greek ambassador's home in Brussels, Belg., on Greek Independence Day.
Mar. 28: A Jewish nursery school in Rosario, Arg., was bombed.
Apr. 1: An explosion that destroyed several automobiles in central Beirut was attributed to Jordanian government agents who planned to assassinate Ziyad Al Hilu, a Black Septembrist.
Apr. 4: Armenian terrorists threw tear-gas grenades into the Turkish consulate general and Turkish airline offices in Paris.
Apr. 5: The living quarters of the U.S. embassy Marine Guard in Rome was bombed, causing only minor damage.
Apr. 9: Arab terrorists blew up the entrance to the apartment of the Israeli ambassador in Nicosia, Cyprus. Three Arabs were arrested on the scene. A subsequent airport attack was blamed on the National Organization of Arab Youth.
Apr. 9: A USO facility in Rome was firebombed by two young terrorists.
Apr. 12: A bomb destroyed the car of a British NATO official in La Spezia, Italy.
Apr. 12: An Arab terrorist who was carrying a Jordanian passport was killed in an Athens, Gr., hotel room when a bomb accidentally went off in his luggage.
Apr. 14: A bomb attached to the Trans-Arabian pipeline near Rafha, Saudi Arabia, was disarmed by the Saudi Arabian National Guard.
Apr. 16: Two Popular Front for the Liberation of Palestine (PFLP) terrorists tried to blow up the Trans-Arabian Pipeline, but only caused minor damage. The terrorists were sentenced to seven years in prison.
Apr. 21: The National Youth Resistance Organization of Greece set off a bomb underneath the car of the Italian vice consul in Athens, Gr. There were no injuries or casualties reported.
Apr. 23: Rocks and firebombs were thrown at the U.S. consulate in Frankfurt, Ger.
Apr. 23: A Russian Aeroflat TU-104 was threatened over Leningrad by a hijacker carrying a bomb in the passenger compartment. The bomb exploded, killing two people, but the aircraft landed safely.
Apr. 24: The Dominican Republic consulate in San Juan, P.R., was bombed by exiles.
Apr. 25: The U.S. ammunition storage area fifteen miles from Yokosuka Naval Base in Japan was damaged by a firebomb.
Apr. 27: Three Arabs who were about to board an Air France jet in Lebanon were arrested after their luggage was found to contain explosives and timing devices.
Apr. 29: IBM offices in San Salvador, El Sal., were damaged in an explosion.
Apr. 29: The residence of the Jordanian ambassador in Beirut escaped serious damage when a stick of dynamite exploded harmlessly in a vacant lot.
Apr. 30: The Goodyear Rubber plant in Cordoba, Arg., was bombed by the Ejercito Revolucionario del Pueblo (ERP).
May 1: For the second time in two days, Goodyear Rubber in Cordoba, Arg., was bombed by the ERP.
May 1: The Barcelona, Spain, offices of British European Airways were firebombed.
May 2: Two firebombs damaged offices of Pan Am Airlines in Barcelona, Spain.
May 2: The U.S. ambassador's home in Beirut was bombed by two rockets. There was no damage.
May 7: A car belonging to a U.S. European Exchange System vendor in Athens, Gr., was damaged by a pipe bomb.
May 7: While parked at the airport in Athens, Gr., a car belonging to a U.S. citizen employed there was bombed.
May 13: Two U.S. soldiers and a Greek-American movie producer were the targets of terrorists who bombed their automobiles.
May 18: A firebomb thrown at the home of a U.S. diplomat in Sao Paulo, Braz., caused moderate property damage.
May 23: A bomb was found in the Ford Motor Plant in Buenos Aires, Arg. Ford officials agreed to pay for medical help demanded by Ejercito Revolucionario del Pueblo (ERP) terrorists in Argentina.
May 24: The Senegalese embassy in Paris was rocked by an explosion, possibly a bomb.
June 8: A weapons production plant in Berlin was blown up by Black September.
June 13: A car bomb exploded next to the El Al offices in Rome, wounding two Black Septembrists.
June 17: Two Arabs were injured when they accidentally detonated a car filled with explosives in Rome.
June 20: The Jewish Defense League (JDL) firebombed the car of a Soviet diplomat in New York as a protest against the impending visit of Leonid Brezhnev to the U.S.
June 28: The Israeli Mossad placed a car bomb in Paris under the vehicle driven by Mohammed Boudia, the top-ranking Arab terrorist in Europe. Boudia was killed instantly.
July 1: The front gate of the French embassy in Lima, Peru was destroyed by a bomb believed to have been placed by anti-nuclear protestors.
July 6: The Ejercito Revolucionario del Pueblo (ERP) threw incendiary bombs at the home of the Uruguayan ambassador in Buenos Aires, Arg.
July 20: A Japan Air Lines 747 on its way to Anchorage, Alaska, from the Netherlands was hijacked. An in-flight explosion killed one of the hijackers. The plane was later diverted to Benghazi, Libya, where it was blown up after being evacuated.
July 22: The Colombian embassy and the Peruvian-North American Cultural Institute in Peru were bombed by someone in a passing automobile.
July 24: An anti-Castro group set off a bomb on the top floor of a Times

Square office building in New York where a Cuban exposition was going to be held.
July 25: The Czechoslovakian embassy in Santiago, Chile, was damaged in a bomb explosion.
July 26: A terrorist fired a tear-gas bomb into the offices of the Organization of American States in Tegucigalpa, Hond.
July 27: The residence in Chile of the second secretary of the Democratic People's Republic of Korea was bombed. There were no injuries.
Aug. 2: Juan Felipe de la Cruz Serafin, a member of the anti-Castro Cuban Revolutionary Directorate, was killed in a bomb explosion in his Avrainville, Fr., hotel room.
Aug. 4: The Belgrade, Yug., railroad station was bombed by terrorists. One person was killed, and seven were injured.
Aug. 5: The Libyan-based National Arab Youth for the Liberation of Palestine (NAYLP) carried out a machine-gun and hand grenade attack against a TWA jet at the Athens Airport. Five passengers were killed, and fifty-five wounded.
Aug. 12: The U.S. consulate in Guayaquil, Ecu., was bombed, causing minor property damage.
Aug. 15: A bomb thrown from a speeding automobile damaged the U.S. Consular Agency in Christchurch, N. Zea. No fatalities or injuries were reported.
Aug. 15: Pipe bombs found at the residence of three U.S. embassy officials in Santiago, Chile, were disarmed.
Aug. 18: The IRA launched a fire- and letter-bomb attack in the British cities of London, Manchester, and Birmingham. Letter bombs were later discovered at the British embassies in Paris and Lisbon, Port. In the following six weeks, at least twenty-nine people were injured.
Aug. 27: Nora Murray, secretary to the British military attaché in the U.S., was injured by a letter bomb. The IRA was blamed for the incident.
Aug. 27: The homes of two Cuban diplomats were bombed in Chile. No one was killed or injured.
Sept. 7: Black September was blamed for a bomb blast that destroyed the Israeli exhibit at the West Berlin International Radio and Television Fair.
Sept. 8: Irish Republican Army (IRA) terrorists exploded bombs at the King's Cross and Euston railway stations in London. Two men and one woman were seriously injured in the blasts.
Sept. 11: A parcel bomb in Zambia killed a British employee of the Zambian Ministry of Information, and injured his wife and son, shortly after the package had been retrieved from the post office.
Sept. 17: Three letter bombs were sent to British officials. The British security officer at the British embassy in Kinshasa, Zaire, was killed. The bombs sent to Lisbon, Port., and Gibraltar were intercepted by police.
Sept. 17: Two bombs exploded in Mönchen-Gladbach, Ger., adjacent to the British army compound on the Rhine. The IRA was believed to be responsible.
Sept. 21: A bomb exploded on the engine manifold of a private aircraft parked on the ground in Crestwood, Ill.
Sept. 28: The radical Weathermen faction of the Students for a Democratic Society (SDS) was believed to be responsible for the bombing of the Latin American section of ITT corporate headquarters in Manhattan. The attack was said to be a protest against ITT activity in Chile.
Sept. 28: A gasoline bomb exploded outside the office of ITT Standard S.A. in Rome. Damage was minor.
Oct. 5: The Proletarian Action Group, linked to Chile, placed two gasoline bombs near the front door of the U.S. consulate general in Genoa, Italy.
Oct. 8: Two of twelve rockets fired by terrorists struck the Sheraton Hotel in Buenos Aires, Arg.
Oct. 8: The Bank of America in Buenos Aires, Arg., was damaged by firebombs on the anniversary of the death of Che Guevara.
Oct. 9: The Cordoba, Arg., offices of U.S.-owned Coca-Cola and Firestone and German-owned Mercedes-Benz were bombed.
Oct. 18: Four terrorists about to blow up El Al locations in West Berlin were arrested with a briefcase full of explosives.
Oct. 26: The Yanikian Commandos sent a smoke bomb to the Turkish Information Office in New York. The bomb never exploded.
November: A letter bomb detonated in the Rio de Janeiro, Braz., offices of the Chilean LAN-Chile Air Company.
Nov. 17: ITT offices in Nuremberg, and West Berlin, Ger., were bombed.
Nov. 27: Five Black September letter bombs addressed to Israeli government installations and the Eilat hotel in Geneva, Switz., were defused.
Nov. 29: Six Black September letter bombs sent from Holland to Israel were defused.
Dec. 3: Two bombs exploded in Greece, one at the Bank of America branch in Piraeus, the other at the Commercial Bank of Greece in Athens. An anti-government group, the Greek People, claimed responsibility for the blasts.
Dec. 14: Nine Black September letter bombs sent from England to Israel were discovered.
Dec. 17: Five NAYLP terrorists carried out an unauthorized operation in the Rome airport. They hurled thermite bombs into a Pan Am jetliner, burning thirty-two passengers to death, and injuring eighteen others.
Dec. 18: Two car bombs and a parcel bomb exploded in London, injuring sixty people.
Dec. 20: A land mine exploded underneath the car of Spanish Prime Minister Luis Carrero Blanco in Madrid. Basque separatists claimed responsibility for the assassination.
Dec. 21: The IRA exploded two bombs in the bar of the London Hilton Hotel.
Dec. 31: Three buildings of ITT were bombed in Rome, Italy.
Dec. 31: Six booby-trapped packages were discovered in the Geneva, Switz., train station and defused.

1974

Jan. 24: The international terrorist Carlos (Illich Ramirez Sánchez) threw a bomb into the Israeli Bank Hapoalim in London, wounding one woman.
Feb. 1: The Pepsi-Cola and Union Carbide plants in Guadalajara, Mex., were bombed. The Coca-Cola plant in Oaxaca, Mex., was also bombed.
Feb. 4: A letter bomb exploded in the offices of the London *Daily Express* newspaper, injuring a security guard.
Feb. 11: The Jewish Defense League (JDL) was suspected of setting off bombs at the Baptist House, Zion House Bible Shop, and the Swedish Theological Institute Chapel in Jerusalem, Isr.
Feb. 12: The Irish Republican Army (IRA) bombed the Latimer National Defense College in Britain, injuring ten people.
Feb. 20: A hijacker demanding to be flown to Dong Hoi, N. Viet., was fooled by the pilot, and the craft landed instead at Hue, S. Viet. Realizing this, the hijacker detonated his explosives, killing himself and two other passengers, and wounding six others.
Feb. 23: While attempting to defuse a bomb placed at the Dow Chemical plant in Lavrion, Gr., two demolitions experts were killed when the device exploded.
Mar. 3: A British Airways VC-10 was hijacked by Arab terrorists on its way to London from Bombay. The plane landed at Amsterdam's Schiphol Airport where it was emptied and blown up on the ground by members of the National Arab Youth for the Liberation of Palestine (NAYLP).
Mar. 3: A suitcase bomb, hidden by the IRA in the luggage compartment of a bus carrying British military personnel and their families, killed twelve people, including two small children.
Mar. 8: The IRA exploded a bomb in front of the British army headquarters in Belfast, Ire. There were no injuries.
Mar. 14: Incendiary bombs were disarmed at Sears department stores in El Marques and Bello Monte, Venez. A Sears store was bombed in Caracas, allegedly by the Fuerzas Armadas de Liberacion Nacional (FALN) and Red Flag.
Mar. 22: A bomb placed in the forward landing gear of an Air Inter jetliner on the ground at Bastia, Corsica, exploded, causing substantial damage to the craft but no injuries.
Mar. 23: A disgruntled patron, turned away from an Allentown, Pa., bar, returned with a Molotov cocktail. He killed eight people and wounded a dozen more. The man was never found.
Mar. 26: The headquarters of an army bomb-disposal unit in northern England was bombed by terrorists. One person was injured.
Apr. 14: The Jewish Defense League (JDL) exploded a bomb at the Lebanese consulate in Los Angeles, Calif., in retaliation for the Apr. 11 Arab guerrilla raid on Qiryat Shemona. No one was injured in the JDL blast.
Apr. 22: Two Palestinian terrorists were convicted in West Germany of conspiring to bomb several Berlin buildings. They were released after terrorists threatened to disrupt the World Cup Soccer Tournament.
May 29: The Habash Front exploded a bomb near the Japanese Airline offices in West Berlin.
June 19: Eight bombs exploded at various firms, including the Bank of America and Coca-Cola, in Buenos Aires, Arg.
July 17: An IRA bomb exploded in the Tower of London, killing one person, and wounding forty-one others.
Aug. 3: Three Habash Front car bombs exploded in Paris, the first near the Jewish Welfare Office, the second adjacent to the newspaper offices of *L'Aurore*, and the third near right-wing journal *Minuit*.
Aug. 4: The neo-Fascist Ordine (Black Order) of Italy exploded a bomb on a Rome to Munich train, killing twelve people and injuring forty-eight others. The incident occurred outside Bologna, Italy.
Aug. 26: Shortly after a TWA jet landed at the Rome airport, a fire was detected in one of the baggage compartments. The fire was caused by an explosive device that malfunctioned. No casualties were reported.
Aug. 26: The Habash Front exploded a bomb near the Israel Tourist Office in Frankfurt, Ger.
Aug. 31: A bomb was detonated at the Lincoln Center in New York by FALN radicals.
Sept. 8: The NAYLP planted a bomb on board a TWA jet bound from Athens to Rome. The bomb damaged an engine, and the plane crashed into the Ionian Sea, claiming the lives of all eighty-eight people aboard.
Sept. 11: The offices of several foreign firms based in Argentina were bombed to coincide with the anniversary of the overthrow of Allende in Chile.
Sept. 15: An Air Vietnam jet was hijacked over Phan Rang, and while the plane circled above the Phan Rang landing strip, the hijacker exploded two hand grenades. The plane crashed, killing all seventy people on board.
Sept. 16: Forty bombs exploded inside the offices of various foreign firms

in Argentina, protesting celebrations marking the revolt which ended Juan Peron's first regime. Among the U.S. offices hit were those of Goodyear, Firestone, Ford, Riker, Eli Lilly, Bank of Boston, Chase Manhattan, Xerox, Coca-Cola, Pepsi-Cola, and Union Carbide.
Oct. 5: Three British soldiers and two women were killed when IRA bombs ripped through several pubs in Guildford, Ire., that catered to military personnel. Fifty-four patrons were injured.
Oct. 6: The offices of Avis in Milan, Italy, were bombed.
Oct. 10: A boy died when the office of the National Cash Register Company in Damascus, Syria, was bombed by the Arab Communist Organization.
Oct. 11: The First National Bank of Chicago branch office in Beirut, Leb., was bombed by the Arab Communist Organization.
Nov. 5: The Milan Trade Center operated by the U.S. Department of Commerce in Milan, Italy, was firebombed.
Nov. 18: Sears department stores in Mexico City, Mex., were bombed.
Nov. 21: The IRA exploded a series of bombs in Birmingham, England, which killed twenty-one people and wounded 168.
Nov. 25: Bombs exploded at the offices of the First National City Bank of New York and at two General Motors showrooms in Buenos Aires, Arg.
Dec. 15: The Youth Action Group bombed the offices of TWA and Coca-Cola in Paris, Fr.
Dec. 16: The offices of 3M in Paris, Fr., were bombed by the Youth Action Group.

1975

Jan. 24: A bomb thrown by the radical Puerto Rican group, Fuerzas Armadas de Liberacion Nacional (FALN), killed four people and injured fifty-one others at the Fraunces Tavern in New York City.
Feb. 3: Two explosions occurred inside the restrooms of a Pan Am jet en route from Bangkok, Thai., to Delhi, India. The passenger ignited the explosions by pouring gasoline into the toilet bowls and lighting it with a butane refill cartridge. One person was injured.
Feb. 11: The Arab Communist Organization bombed the American Life Insurance Company office in Tyre, Leb.
Feb. 29: The Weather Underground claimed responsibility for a bomb explosion at the U.S. State Department. There were no casualties.
Apr. 11: The offices of the American Life Insurance Company in Kuwait were bombed by the Arab Communist Organization.
May 31: The Beirut, Leb., offices of ITT were bombed.
June 3: A Philippine Airlines passenger jet made a safe emergency landing after a bomb planted in the lavatory exploded, killing one person and injuring forty-five others, 200 miles southwest of Manila.
June 19: A McDonald's restaurant in Stockholm, Swed., was bombed.
June 23: In Tel Aviv, Isr., a bomb destroyed the car of a TWA employee near the U.S. embassy.
July 5: A bomb placed under the passenger seat of a Pakistan Airlines jetliner parked on the ground at Rawalpindi, India, damaged the fuselage but injured no one.
Aug. 19: A McDonald's restaurant in Stockholm, Swed., was bombed a second time.
Aug. 23: Two American employees of Collins International Service Company in Asmara, Eth., died when their car struck a land mine.
Sept. 15: Four Arab terrorists took over the Egyptian embassy in Madrid, Spain, threatening to detonate a bomb unless the ambassador signed a statement renouncing the Sinai agreement with Israel. The signed statement was later described as "worthless" by an embassy official.
Sept. 24: The offices of Xerox in Cordoba, Arg., were bombed.
Sept. 27: A bombing in a Lowell, Mass., cafe injured twenty-three people and caused millions of dollars in damage. A Massachusetts man who had hired two people to open up a gas main in the cafe was sent to prison.
Sept. 30: A Hungarian passenger jet making its way from Budapest, Hung., to Beirut, Leb., exploded over the Mediterranean Sea and crashed, killing all sixty-four people on board.
Dec. 19: A military helicopter on the ground at Angels Camp, Calif., was blown up, causing $10,000 damage to the craft. No injuries were reported.
Dec. 29: Eleven people were killed at New York's LaGuardia Airport, and seventy more were injured when a bomb went off in one of the terminals. The killer was never found.

1976

Jan. 1: A Lebanese jetliner flying between Saudi Arabia and Kuwait exploded in midair, killing all eighty-two people on board. The bomb was in the baggage compartment of the plane.
Jan. 7: Anti-communist groups bombed left-wing installations at Oporto in northern Portugal.
Jan 29: A new wave of anti-communist bombings occurred in Braga, Port.
Feb. 27: The offices of American Express and Chase Manhattan in Athens, Gr., were bombed.
Mar. 13: A Sears department store in San Salvador, El Sal., was firebombed by the Farabundo Marti Liberation Labor Forces.
Mar. 31: The offices of Pan Am and Philips Electronic were bombed in Ankara, Turk.
Apr. 2: A branch office of the First National City Bank in Bogota, Col., was bombed.
Apr. 3: The offices of American Express in Athens, Gr., were bombed.
Apr. 14: The Armed Communist Formations group firebombed the offices of Texaco in Florence, Italy.
Apr. 22: The First National City Bank in Athens, Gr., was bombed.
May 4: Gudrun Ensslin of the Baader-Meinhof gang confessed to three bombings for which his group had been charged.
May 21: Moslem rebels hijacked a Philippine Airlines jetliner at Zamboanga, Phil., and exploded hand grenades on board, killing thirteen people and wounding fourteen others.
June 2: Don Bolles, a reporter investigating organized crime in Phoenix, Ariz., was blown up in his automobile. John Harvey Adamson was sentenced to a twenty-year term for planting the bomb.
July 2: Twenty-five policemen were killed by a bomb blast at the Federal Security Building in Buenos Aires, Arg.
July 2: An Eastern Airlines craft parked at Boston's Logan Airport was completely destroyed by a bomb inserted between the strut and the landing gear. One person was injured.
July 31: British Ambassador Christopher Ewart-Biggs was assassinated by a culvert bomb in Dublin, Ire.
Aug. 20: Ten bombs exploded in Buenos Aires, Arg., killing forty-seven people, reflecting the continued strife between Argentine left-wing and right-wing terrorist groups.
Sept. 7: Seven masked men set off dynamite charges on board an Air France jetliner parked at Ajaccio, Corsica. There were no injuries.
Sept. 22: The regional office of Westinghouse in Rome, Italy, was bombed.
Sept. 25: The Ghassan Kanafani Commandos bombed various U.S., Jewish, and Lebanese Christian facilities in Rome, Italy, including the offices of Avis.
Sept. 28: An Army bomb expert was killed and a state arson expert injured in the last of five dynamite explosions rocking the Quincy Compressor Company in Quincy, Ill., shortly after a visit by Republican vice-presidential candidate Robert Dole. The explosions were not politically motivated. Jeffery Lewis, Stanley Stock, and Robert Motley were sentenced for murder and arson.
Oct. 6: Nine minutes after taking off from Barbados, West Indies, a Cuban jet bound for Kingston, Jam., exploded. All seventy-three passengers were killed.
Oct. 13: The Sheraton and Ritz hotels in Lisbon, Port., were bombed.
Oct. 17: A movie theater was destroyed and fifty people were injured when a bomb exploded in Buenos Aires, Arg., during a Peronist "Loyalty Day" celebration.
Dec. 15: Fifteen people were killed and thirty more were wounded when a dynamite bomb exploded in the Defense Ministry building in Buenos Aires, Arg. Leftist Montoneros guerrillas were responsible for the attack.
Dec. 16: A bomb exploded in the pocket of a boy walking in an American-owned store in Chapinero, Col. Seventeen other unexploded bombs were found planted in the store.

1977

Jan. 25: The vacated home of a Goodyear executive in Buenos Aires, Arg., was bombed and machine-gunned by the Juan Jose Valle Montoneros.
Mar. 27: Six bombs exploded at the Sheraton Hilton in Buenos Aires, Arg., injuring nine people.
Apr. 11: The offices of Pan Am Airlines and Henderson and Company in San Jose, Cos., were bombed by the Revolutionary Commandos of Solidarity in reprisal for the death of FSLN leader Carlos Aguerero Echeverria.
May 1: Five Bell helicopters belonging to General Aviation exploded on the ground in Salinas, Calif., causing only minor damage.
Summer: The Puerto Rican independence group Fuerzas Armadas de Liberacion Nacional (FALN) planted bombs in two Manhattan skyscrapers, which killed one person and injured seven others.
July 14: The offices of American Express were bombed in Athens, Gr.
Aug. 6: A bomb exploded in a Woolworth store in Salisbury, Rhod., killing eleven people and wounding seventy-six.
Sept. 6: A Sears store in Cali, Col., was bombed, injuring three people.
Sept. 14: Bombs exploded in a Sears Store and in the Mexican-American Cultural Institute. Other bombs were found at the offices of General Motors and Colgate-Palmolive in Mexico.
Oct. 13: A car bomb which exploded near the residence of an Argentine executive of the Chrysler Corporation killed two people and wounded two others.
Oct. 13: Palestinian terrorists hijacked a Lufthansa jet bound from Majorca to Frankfurt by threatening to blow up the jet unless an $18 million ransom was paid, and jailed leaders of the Baader-Meinhof gang were released. The terrorists were overpowered after the airliner landed in Somalia.
Dec 18: France was accused of sending military fighters to bomb Polisario guerrilla installations.

1978

Jan. 19: Offices of the Discount Bank and a suburban affiliate in Paris, Fr., were bombed.
Feb. 16: The Puerto Rican branch offices of Chase Manhattan, Citibank, Barker, and Woolworth were bombed in Santurce, Rio Piedras, and San Juan.
Mar. 12: An El Fatah (Palestinian Liberation Organization) PLO unit dispatched from South Lebanon blew up a public bus in Tel Aviv, Isr.,

killing thirty-seven people.
May 24: Four people flying in a small Piper Aztec airplane were killed in an explosion over Nairobi, Kenya.
Aug. 18: An explosion in the rear lavatory of a Philippine Airlines jetliner en route from Cebu to Manila killed the bomber and wounded three other people.
Aug. 27: An extortion gang in Stateline, Nev., threatened to bomb several large casinos unless a $3 million ransom demand was met. After delays, they detonated a bomb, severely damaging Harvey's hotel-casino.
Sept. 7: Shortly after all the passengers had disembarked at the Colombo, Sri Lanka Airport, a bomb blast destroyed an Air Ceylon HS-748 jetliner. There were no casualties.
November: A firebomb was thrown at a car driven by George Link, the manager of Oil Service Company offices in Ahwaz, Iran. Link was not injured.
Nov. 22: A Sears, Roebuck store in Lima, Peru was bombed. Several people were injured.
Dec. 8: The company headquarters of Grumman Inc., in Isfahan, Iran, were destroyed by firebombs.
1979
Authorities in Rochester, N.Y., concluded an investigation of six organized crime bombings with convictions of seven underworld figures. The bombs killed two rival gang members in Rochester.
Jan. 22: After a seven-year chase, the Israeli Mossad assassinated Ali Hassan Salameh in Beirut. Salameh and six passersby were killed by a car bomb.
Feb. 11: A coal company in Hazard, Ky., was destroyed by a bomb concealed in a briefcase. The company accountant was killed in the blast. Four Kentucky men were convicted of murder.
Feb. 13: A bomb exploded in the Sheraton Hotel in Cairo, Egypt, injuring five people.
Feb. 19: The offices of Pan Am in Alsancak and Izmir, Turk., were bombed.
Mar. 15: A pipe bomb exploded in an automobile belonging to a Mt. Clemens, Mich., resident suspected of being a drug dealer.
Mar. 30: A mercury-fused car bomb brought instant death to British Parliament member Airey Neave in the parking lot underneath the House of Commons in London.
Apr. 19: A Ford showroom in Valencia, Spain, was damaged by a bomb.
Apr. 23: A subsidiary of Babcock and Wilson in Dusseldorf, Ger., was bombed.
Apr. 26: An Indian Airlines jetliner flying over Madras, India, sustained minor damage when a bomb exploded in the forward washroom. Eight people were injured, but the plane landed safely.
May: Maria del Carmen Lopez Anguita was sentenced to 280 years in prison for the May 1979 bombing of a cafe in Madrid, Spain.
May 10: A Baltimore, Md., resident was killed instantly when a bomb blew up his truck in Sparrow's Point, as he prepared to leave work. A suspect was arrested, and sentenced to thirty years in prison.
May 16: A Chicago man was indicted by a federal grand jury for the firebombing of two restaurants in Chicago and in west suburban Maywood that killed two elderly people.
May 31: Forty-two bombs were exploded by Corsican separatists in Paris. No one was killed, and injuries were minor.
June: Five bombs were sent to the headquarters of neo-Nazi political groups in the U.S. Two of them were directed to Frank Collin, leader of the Chicago chapter of the Nazi party.
June 29: U.S. General Alexander Haig, then serving as NATO commander, survived a bomb explosion under his car. The German Red Army was thought to be responsible.
July: A joint Federal Bureau of Investigation and Bureau of Alcohol, Tobacco, and Firearms (FBI-ATF) investigation into various night club bombings in the Seattle, Wash., area concluded with the arrest of fifteen suspects who belonged to a criminal arson ring.
July 16: The Honolulu Police and Fire Departments arrested two men and charged them with the incendiary bombing of a pornographic bookstore. The suspects hired a "torch" to destroy the building in order to collect insurance money.
July 24: A bomb exploded inside a Wells Fargo Bank in Istanbul, Turk.
Aug. 8: Lord Louis Mountbatten and three friends were killed when an IRA radio-detonated bomb exploded on board their fishing boat off the Irish coast.
Aug. 22: Convicted airplane hijacker James Albee was sentenced in Oregon to sixty years in prison for threatening the pilot of a Los Angeles-bound jet with a bomb.
Aug. 22: A Lexington, Ky., woman who had just purchased ten sticks of dynamite at a local outlet was killed when the explosives blew up in her car on the way home. The woman's 9-year-old son also died.
Aug. 24: A 100-pound bomb that had been placed in a van outside the Classic Cat II Lounge in Nashville, Tenn., was defused by police fifteen minutes before it was to detonate. On Aug. 14, 1980, three suspects were arrested and charged with arson and attempted bombing in connection with the incident.
Aug. 25: A bomb blew up a car in Pascagoula, Miss., killing a local woman.
Aug. 27: Eighteen British soldiers were killed by two Irish Republican Army (IRA) bombs in Warrenpoint, Ire.
Oct. 10: An Oklahoma man was arrested after he attempted to deliver ninety-four pounds of military explosives to an undercover agent of the Bureau of Alcohol, Tobacco, and Firearms, in San Diego, Calif.
Oct. 28: The offices of Bank of America in San Salvador, El Sal., were bombed.
November: An explosion destroyed Jake's Cafe in Lowell, Mass., and sixty-eight adjoining businesses. Twenty-three people were injured and the owner of the cafe was arrested.
November: Two men stationed at Ft. Bragg, N.C., were arrested and charged with the theft and unlawful sale of military explosives, including seventy-five claymore mines and hand grenades.
Nov. 8: A bomb exploded underneath a vehicle in Richmond Heights, Mo., killing the driver.
Nov. 15: Thirty minutes after leaving Chicago, a bomb placed inside a mail bag of an American Airlines 727 exploded. The aircraft sustained only minor damage, and it landed safely at Dulles International Airport, near Washington, D.C.
Nov. 21: A bomb thrown from a passing car into Junior's Lunch Cafe in Lynchburg, Va., injured three people and caused $28,000 worth of damage. Two suspects were eventually taken into custody.
Nov. 23: A bomb exploded at the residence of Lopez Akimenco, a manager of the Swift meat packing plant in La Plata, Arg.
Nov. 26: The Madrid, Spain, offices of TWA and Western Airlines were bombed.
Nov. 29: A 17-year-old boy was killed while attempting to place a bomb inside a soda-pop machine in St. Stephens, S.C.
Dec. 3: A branch office of Morgan Guaranty Trust in Frankfurt, Ger., was bombed.
Dec. 5: The W.R. Grace fertilizer plant in Trinidad was bombed.
Dec. 11: The Russian mission in New York City was seriously damaged by a bomb.
Dec. 16: Two Bloomington, Minn., police cars were destroyed by a homemade bomb. Two suspects were arrested.
Dec. 23: The offices of Air France and TWA in Rome, Italy, were bombed by the Armenian Secret Army for the Liberation of Armenia (ASALA).
Dec. 24: A bomb wrapped as a Christmas present exploded in the home of a Dublin, Ga., paraplegic. The recipient and one other person were injured.
Dec. 25: The El Salvador offices of Citibank and ITT were bombed.
Dec. 28: The People's Liberation Forces of San Salvador, El Sal., tried to bomb a branch office of the First National City Bank, killing a watchman, one of the terrorists, and a passerby.
1980
Mar 6: The whaling ship *Sierra* was sunk in Lisbon, Port., by a conservationist group.
March 10: A Paris synagogue was bombed by the PFLP. The device was placed on the back of a motorcycle. Four people were killed.
April: The Computer Liquidation and Hijack Committee (CLODO), bombed the Phillips Data System in Toulouse, Fr. The group believed that computers were the vehicle of government repression.
Apr. 22: A bomb placed in the car of PLO military chief Salah Khalaf in Belgrade, Yug., exploded harmlessly. One of the conspirators was caught by the Yugoslav police and handed over to El Fatah for justice.
Apr. 25: The suburban offices of an American agricultural firm in Toulouse, Fr., was damaged by a bomb planted by an Iranian terrorist group calling itself the Self-Defense against All Authority.
May: Bassam Shaka, mayor of Nablus, lost both his legs in a bomb blast.
June 1: The African National Congress (ANC) claimed responsibility for a bomb blast that destroyed three oil refineries in South Africa.
June. 3: A Nevada man and his wife bombed the offices of a U.S. magistrate in Elko, Nev. They were later convicted for the bombing.
June 10: A pipe bomb thought to have been packaged and posted by a disgruntled employee, exploded in the home of Percy A. Wood, president of United Airlines, in Lake Forest, Ill. Wood suffered minor injuries.
June 24: Non-union garbage trucks in College Park, Ga., were bombed by two Teamster Union officials after non-union members were hired. The two men were sent to prison.
June 27: A bomb or a missile explosion caused a DC-9 jetliner to crash ninety miles southwest of Naples, Italy. The crash claimed eighty-one lives.
July: Police in Brussels, Belg., thwarted an attempt to attack an El Al jetliner. Explosives found in the room of a suspect were seized.
Aug. 2: The Armed Revolutionary Nuclei (NAR) a neo-fascist Italian terrorist group, was held responsible for the bombing of the Bologna railway station, which killed seventy-six people and wounded 186.
Aug. 22: The wife of a U.S. businessman was killed during bombings by the April 6 Liberation Movement of businesses tied to the interests of the Marcos family in Manila, Phil.
Aug. 27: A well-made homemade bomb exploded in Harvey's Casino in Stateline, Nev., causing $18 million in damage. No one was hurt in the blast.
Sept. 9: An explosion rocked the cargo hold of a United Airlines jet at the boarding gate of the Sacramento, Calif., airport. Two people were slightly injured.
Sept. 20: An Olathe, Kan., man sent a bomb to his ex-wife, killing her and five other people. He was convicted.

Sept. 26: A member of the neo-Nazi Wehrsportsgruppe (Military Sports Group) exploded a bomb at Bierfest in Munich, Ger., killing himself and twelve other bystanders. Over 300 people were injured.
Sept. 29: The residence of a Racine, Wis., man was fire-bombed. Three children were injured. A member of a motorcycle gang was sent to prison for the attack.
Oct. 19: A bomb planted by the April 6 Liberation Movement at the opening session of the American Society of Travel Agents in Manila, Phil., injured eighteen people.
Oct. 22: The Galilee Baptist Church in Birmingham, Ala., was bombed. The suspect taken into custody had been active in the Black Panther Party.
Dec. 31: The PFLP avenged itself for the Entebbe raid by blowing up the Zionist-owned Norfolk Hotel in Nairobi. Sixteen to twenty people were killed and eighty-five people were injured in the resulting fire.

1981

The Wehrsportgruppe, a Neo-Nazi group, planted bombs in the automobiles of U.S. servicemen stationed in West Germany.
Jan. 1: The Liberation Army of Martinique exploded a bomb at the Palace of Justice at Fort-de-France.
Jan. 4: The Groupe de Liberation armee de la Guadeloupe was suspected of blowing up the Boutique Chanel on the Rue Cambon in Paris.
Jan. 5: To disrupt power in Rollo, Mo., during a jewelry store robbery, a bank and the Show Me Power Corporation were bombed. One man was later sentenced to ten years in prison.
Jan 8: A microwave transmitting tower was blown up by the Enlightened Path terrorist group in Ayacucho, Peru.
Jan. 8: The IRA bombed the Uxbridge Air Force Base near London. Two people were injured during evacuation of the facility.
Jan. 10: Arab commandos threw a hand grenade into the car of an Israeli couple driving through the Gaza Strip. The couple was seriously wounded.
Jan. 12: Leftist guerrillas calling themselves the Macheteros exploded twenty-six bombs at the U.S. Air Force base in San Juan, P.R. Nine aircraft were destroyed and two were damaged in the attack.
Jan. 26: In a two-hour period, industrial and commercial sites in five of six counties in Northern Ireland were bombed resulting in extensive property damage and injuries to at least twelve people.
Jan. 29: A furniture store in Belfast, Ire., was bombed. No injuries were reported.
Jan. 30: The Corsican National Liberation Front and the Guadeloupe Liberation Army both claimed responsibility for the bombing of the Paris courthouse.
Feb. 6: The Taiwanese embassy in the Vatican was bombed by a Marxist-Leninist revolutionary who demanded the release of Jiang Qing, held in the People's Republic of China.
Feb. 8: A New Orleans, La., man was killed instantly when a bomb in his car exploded outside his residence. The victim had recently been convicted of federal narcotics violations.
Feb. 9: Eighteen peasants riding in a truck in Suchitoto, El Sal., were killed when a bomb struck the vehicle. Thirty other people were injured.
Feb. 12: Forty-five bombs exploded in scattered locations in Ajaccio, Porticco, and Propriano, Corsica. No injuries or serious damage were reported.
Feb. 16: A rocket attack against the Paris Embassy of the People's Democratic Republic of Yemen was thought to be the work of Jewish terrorist groups.
Feb. 16: A terrorist bomb exploded prematurely at the Karachi stadium in Pakistan where Pope John Paul II was to celebrate mass. The perpetrator was killed.
Feb. 17: Muslim rebels were suspected of exploding a bomb in Davao, Mindanao, Phil., two days before Pope John Paul II was to arrive. One person was killed and eleven were wounded.
Feb. 19: The Soviet government denied an earlier published report of a bomb explosion at the KGB headquarters in Moscow which was said to have killed an army officer and his driver.
Feb. 20: Three Molotov cocktails were thrown into the main plant of a Grand Rapids, Mich., corporation involved in a labor dispute. One defendant was subsequently found Not Guilty and two others received prison terms.
Feb. 20: A bomb exploded on a crowded bus in Teheran, Iran, injuring fifteen people.
Feb. 21: Two people were killed and sixteen were injured in two separate bomb explosions in Teheran, Iran.
Feb. 23: The Munich offices of Radio Free Europe and Radio Liberty were bombed by agents of an East Bloc country. Eight people were injured.
Feb. 26: Bombings and shootings at Karachi University in Pakistan claimed the life of one student leader. Twelve of his followers were injured. A bomb also exploded in Quetta, killing one person and wounding another.
Mar. 1: A police technician was seriously injured while attempting to defuse an incendiary bomb that had been placed inside a topless dancing bar in Anchorage, Alaska.
Mar. 1: Two remote-controlled land mines were detonated on the road between Sestao and Portugalete in Spain, fatally injuring one policeman. Basque separatists were blamed.
Mar. 9: A hand grenade thrown at an Israeli military patrol in the Gaza strip wounded five Arabs.
Mar. 11: The M-19 movement of Colombia exploded a bomb at Bogota's El Dorado International Airport.
Mar. 16: A train carrying jet fuel to the international airport in Tokyo at Narita was fire-bombed. There was minimal damage.
Mar. 17: A bazooka shot fired at a U.S. embassy van in San Jose, Cos., injured three Marines and their Costa Rican driver.
Mar. 24: The party headquarters of the Revolutionary Committees was bombed in Teheran, Iran.
Mar. 25: The April 6 Liberation Group of Manila, Phil., threatened the government with a rash of new bombings.
Mar. 25: A rocket grenade attack against the U.S. embassy in San Salvador, El Sal., caused extensive damage. The attack, the second in three years, was the work of the leftist Popular Liberation Forces.
Mar. 26: Three people believed to be terrorists were killed in San Salvador, El Sal., when a bomb blew up in their car.
Mar. 26: A bomb planted in the Legislative Palace in Tegucigalpa, Hond., exploded while the seventy-one members were in session. Three civilians were injured.
Mar. 27: A car bomb exploded in San Salvador, El Sal., killing a woman and a boy. A second bomb went off at a runway on a military airfield east of San Salvador, causing no damage.
Mar. 29: The U.S. Army security office in Giessen, Ger., sustained heavy damage when a bomb was set off by the Heart of the Beast terrorist group. No injuries were reported.
Apr. 1: Scattered bombings occurred in El Salvador to mark the anniversary of the founding of the Popular Liberation Forces, an opposition group. Two rocket grenades were fired at the U.S. embassy with no injuries reported.
Apr. 2: A bomb demolished a garage in Newport, Ken., killing two people and injuring twenty-one others. The blast caused over $1 million in property damage.
Apr. 2: The IRA claimed responsibility for the car bombing that took the life of Kenneth John Acheson, a member of the Royal Ulster Constabulary.
Apr. 3: A coffee warehouse and various shops in Kampala were bombed by the Uganda Freedom Movement.
Apr. 3: Scattered bombings and rioting in West Bengal, India, killed eight people and left 200 others injured.
Apr. 3: Four of six bombs planted under automobiles at the Ellinikon U.S. Air Base in Greece exploded, causing minor damage.
Apr. 3: Two bombs exploded in Qom, Iran, wounding twenty people.
Apr. 7: A department store in Frankfurt, Ger., was fire-bombed, causing extensive damage.
Apr. 8: A bomb placed inside a locker in an underground railroad station in Cologne, Ger., exploded and injured seven people. The bombing was connected to the RAF hunger strike going on at the time.
Apr. 8: The Uganda Freedom Movement bombed the Indian embassy in Kampala after receiving reports that President Milton Obote was about to receive a shipment of arms from India.
Apr. 8: A terrorist flung a hand grenade into a crowded courtyard during a wedding ceremony in Jerusalem's Old City. An Arab waiter was killed and a child was injured.
Apr. 10: A dynamite bomb ripped apart the headquarters of the Christian Democratic Party in Padua, Italy.
Apr. 10: A store owned by an Indian in Kampala was bombed by the Uganda Freedom Movement.
Apr. 13: A car bomb exploded in the Syrian-controlled city of Aley, east of Beirut, Leb. Two people were killed and sixteen more were wounded.
Apr. 14: Miami, Fla., police arrested two men in the city's Little Havana section. Both men were in possession of guns and explosives.
Apr. 15: A building on the campus of Hamburg University in Germany was bombed.
Apr. 16: A bomb placed at U.S. Army headquarters in Wiesbaden, Ger., was defused. It had been placed by friends of leftist Sigurd Debus, who had died the previous day after a ten-week hunger strike.
Apr. 16: A nine-pound dynamite bomb exploded in a luggage locker at the Campo Dell'Oro airport in Ajaccio, Corsica, killing one person and wounding seven. The bomb exploded minutes before French President Valery Giscard d'Estaing was scheduled to arrive in Corsica.
Apr. 16: The office of the administrative head of Upper Assam, India, was bombed by an opposition political party after the government refused to discharge officials in Assam.
Apr. 17: A fifteen-pound bomb exploded at the Max Planck Institute in West Berlin, causing $5,000 in damage. No injuries were reported.
Apr. 19: Thirteen people were killed and 177 injured when terrorists threw hand grenades into a Roman Catholic church in Davao, Phil., during Easter Mass. The New People's Army of the outlawed Communist Party was responsible.
Apr. 20: Two employees were killed when a bomb exploded at the Hyatt Regency Hotel in Dubai, Oman.
Apr. 22: A bomb went off near the private residence of the Ayatollah Khomeini, killing two people and wounding ten others.
Apr. 23: Naser Almaneih, a former Iranian police chief, was sentenced to fifty years in prison in California for the Aug. 20, 1980, bombing of a high school in Berkeley, Calif., and for conspiring to bomb an Iranian meeting at San Jose State University.

Apr. 25: A car bomb killed seven people and wounded thirty-five others in the Iranian city of Kermanshah.
Apr. 25: Barry Porter, a Conservative Member of Parliament, received a letter bomb from the IRA that failed to detonate.
Apr. 28: Sixty bombs scattered anti-government leaflets in Guatemala City.
May 5: A letter bomb sent to Prince Charles of England was intercepted by Scotland Yard.
May 5: The British Chamber of Commerce in Milan, Italy, sustained minor damage when a bomb planted by the Red Brigades exploded.
May 5-6: One British soldier was injured when a bomb filled with nails exploded in the Catholic area of Belfast, Ire.
May 6: The Royal British Club in Lisbon, Port., was damaged by a bomb planted by the Popular Forces of April 25.
May 6: Letter bombs sent by the IRA to Home Secretary Roy Hattersley, and to Jim Kelfedder, a Member of Parliament, were intercepted before they could go off.
May 6: A hand grenade destroyed the car of Mayor David Thebehali of Soweto, S. Afri. Militant blacks were said to be behind the attack.
May 7: Three Spanish military officers were killed in Madrid by a bomb lobbed by Basque separatists at a staff car waiting at a red light. Eleven other people were injured.
May 7: An explosion in the Belfast, Ire., market district killed one Catholic youth who was thought to have been carrying the bomb.
May 8: A British Army building in Glasgow, Scot., sustained minor damage from three bombs.
May 8: Irish terrorists fired mortar shells at a police-army post in Newtownhamilton, near the border. Two British soldiers were injured.
May 8: The Popular Revolutionary Struggle fire-bombed three police stations in Athens, Gr.
May 9: While touring an oil terminal in the North Sea, Queen Elizabeth escaped injury when an IRA bomb exploded at another terminal at Voe. There were no injuries and little damage.
May 14: A rocket grenade launched by the Provisional wing of the IRA struck a moving Land Rover in Ulster, Ire., seriously wounding two members of the Royal Constabulary.
May 15: Following the death of hunger striker Francis Hughes, the IRA fired a rocket through the roof of a police car in West Belfast, Ire., killing one officer and wounding three others.
May 15: The El Al Airlines offices in Rome were bombed by the May Arab Movement for the Liberation of Palestine.
May 16: An explosive device detonated next to the El Al offices in Istanbul, Turk. Arab terrorists were held responsible.
May 16: The Puerto Rican Armed Resistance Group claimed responsibility for a pipe-bomb explosion that killed Alex McMillan, an employee at Kennedy Airport in New York. Two other bombs were found in the airport during the next twenty-four hours.
May 17: A toy store and a movie house were bombed in Dungannon, twenty-five miles southwest of Belfast, Ire. Additional bomb blasts destroyed a brick factory and ten trucks. Total damage was estimated to be $2.2 million.
May 17: Time bombs were used to shatter six oil and natural gas pipelines in the Khuzistan province in Iran.
May 17: A bomb destined for the Soviet mission's living quarters in Riverdale, N.Y., was intercepted before it could do any damage.
May 20: Four-hundred-eighty-seven bomb threats were received by New York police in the wake of the May 16 attack at Kennedy Airport.
May 21: A pipe bomb placed underneath a garbage truck making the rounds at UN headquarters in New York was defused.
May 24: Kurd rebels blew up the main Baghdad to Basra Railway, ninety miles south of Baghdad.
May 25: A commuter rail line used by mainly black residents of South Africa was blown up. No injuries were reported.
May 27: The British Council offices in Thessaloniki, Gr. were bombed by local supporters of the Irish Republican Army (IRA).
May 28: Two people were killed by a car bomb in Beirut.
May 31: Warrant Officer Michael O'Neill, a member of the British bomb disposal unit, was killed near Newry, Ire., while he was examining a suspicious car.
June: An auditorium in Anaheim, Calif., was bombed. A performance by the Turkish Folkloric Ballet was subsequently cancelled.
June 2: A bomb partially destroyed an armored police vehicle in Londonderry, Ire. One policeman was injured.
June 3: Time bombs destroyed two department stores and six adjacent buildings in Athens, Gr., resulting in millions of dollars in property damage. The Revolutionary Anti-Capitalist Action and the New Organization claimed responsibility.
June 6: An Israeli was killed and another wounded when a grenade exploded inside a vehicle driven in the Gaza Strip.
June 7: Israel bombed an Iraqi nuclear reactor, an action which the United Nations promptly condemned.
June 8: A land mine set off by Guatemalan leftists killed an army lieutenant in northern Guatemala.
June 11: A bomb explosion at the Arab Socialist Union in Tyre, Leb., killed twenty-five people.
June 12: A car bomb exploded in a parking garage at Sandston, Va., injuring the driver. The victim's business partner was convicted and sentenced.
June 13: The Irish Republican Army (IRA) attached a bomb to the car of former Lord Chancellor Gardiner. The bomb fell free and was quickly defused.
June 16: An explosion occurred at the Salt Lake City County Jail in an aborted attempt to free two robbery suspects imprisoned inside. Six people were convicted.
June 16: A Romanian jetliner with 140 passengers aboard was diverted to Turkey when a bomb scare was reported. No bombs were found on the craft after it landed.
June 23: An explosion at the Qom Railroad Station in Iran killed four people and wounded fifty-eight.
June 24: Five bombs exploded in the basement of Navarra University in Pamplona, Spain, injuring four people.
June 26: Five bombs exploded near public buildings in Kuwait.
June 27: A bomb exploded inside a Teheran mosque injuring Hojatoleslam Seyyed Ali Khamenei, a high-level aide to Ayatollah Ruhollah Khomeini. Another bomb went off near Teheran University, and a third bomb was found and defused. Counter-revolutionary groups were blamed.
June 27: An Illinois mob figure and another man were fatally injured when a car bomb exploded in the parking lot of the Tamarac County Club in Oakland Park, Fla.
June 28: The Teheran, Iran, headquarters of the Islamic Republican Party, was bombed. Seventy-two lives were lost, including that of Ayatollah Beheshti, Chief Justice of the Supreme Court, and those of four cabinet ministers.
June 29: Giuseppe Santangelo of Salerno, Italy, was arrested in St. Peter's Square after attempting to set off a homemade bomb in front of 20,000 worshippers.
July 1: A baggage handler was killed in the Guatemala City Airport when a suitcase bomb destined for a Miami-bound Eastern Airlines jetliner exploded prematurely. The Guerrilla Army of the Poor was responsible.
July 2: Fifty people were arrested in Iran in connection with a plot to blow up the Parliament building following the ouster of President Bani-Sadr.
July 9: A pipe bomb exploded at a private residence in Oregon City, Ore. The bomb was coupled with an extortion demand for $450,000. A local school board member and the person he hired to throw the bomb were sent to prison.
July 10: An Eastern Airlines jetliner bound from Chicago to Miami was hijacked and forced to fly to Cuba by two men armed with Molotov cocktails with burning wicks.
July 11: An IRA bomb factory with 250-pound explosives was discovered on Clifton Road in Belfast, Ire.
July 11: A hand grenade was thrown at an Israeli jeep in the Gaza Strip. No damages or injuries were reported.
July 13: A vehicle belonging to the prosecuting attorney of Bonner County, Idaho, was destroyed by a dynamite bomb. No one was in the car at the time of the explosion.
July 14: Dynamite and blasting caps were stolen from a construction site in Warwick, R.I. Two suspects were sentenced two weeks later.
July 14: A movie theater in Banqui, in the Central African Republic, was bombed. Three people were killed.
July 15: Two terrorists disguised as deliverymen left a bomb at the Wellington Park Hotel in Belfast, Ire. Two people were injured in the blast.
July 17: The Dublin-Belfast Railroad line in Ireland re-opened following two bomb blasts in two days.
July 20: The Italian Village Restaurant in Boone, N.C., was blown up, causing $500,000 in damages. The next day the restaurant manager was arrested by Boone police.
July 20: Several people were injured when a bomb exploded in front of the Ministry of Economic Aid and Financial Affairs in Teheran, Iran.
July 20: The June 9 Organization, an Armenian terrorist group, bombed the airport in Zurich, Switz., injuring five people.
July 22: Two bombs exploded at the Geneva, Switz., train station and injured five people. It was the work of the June 9 Organization, protesting of the arrest of Mardiros Sankodigian by the Swiss police.
July 24: Basque Separatists in northern Spain bombed two electrical substations in Iberduero. The explosions caused damage, but there were no injuries.
July 24: Iranian embassies in Ankara, Bonn, Munich, and Vienna, were bombed on the day of the national elections in Iran.
July 28: A 400-pound bomb was defused near the border of the Irish Republic. The bomb was intended for a passing army patrol.
July 30: A pipe bomb on a butane tank in a Great Falls, Mont., railroad yard exploded. A second device was found attached to another butane tank, which did not go off.
July 30: A land mine injured two policemen at Newry, Ire.
July 30: Three bombs containing Communist propaganda leaflets exploded in downtown Capetown, S. Afri.
July 31: The International Seaman Corp. in Great Falls, Mont., suffered minor damage when a bomb connected to the natural gas line exploded.
July 31: The Denver Police Bomb Squad successfully defused a bomb found underneath a police vehicle in the parking area of the Longmont, Colo., Department of Public Safety.
July 31: Four explosions damaged public buildings in Bolzano, Italy. The bombings were believed to have been the work of a group opposed to

the area residents' desire for autonomy.
Aug. 1: A second explosive device was diffused in the public safety garage at Longmont, Colo.
Aug. 2: Two policemen were killed, and two more injured when 100 pounds of explosives went off under their car sixty miles west of Belfast, Ire.
Aug. 2: The Arab Steadfastness Front was blamed for a bomb explosion at a wedding ceremony at the Christian Coptic Church in Cairo, Egypt. Three people died, and fifty-six others were wounded.
Aug. 3: A bomb exploded near the presidential offices in Teheran, Iran, killing the newly-installed President Rajai, prime minister Javad Bahonari, and twelve other people.
Aug. 4: An explosion at the home of an Olney, Ill., woman caused extensive property damage, with minor injuries suffered by the victim. Three suspects were arrested and indicted by a grand jury in late August.
Aug. 5: Several people were injured in Northern Ireland and extensive property damage was reported when ten terrorist bombs exploded. Prior warnings of where the bombs were to explode resulted in relatively few injuries.
Aug. 5: The offices of Pan Am in Guatemala City, Guat., were bombed, causing $200,000 in damages.
Aug. 8: Three employees of the Syrian Ministry were killed when a bomb destroyed a conference hall in the prime minister's building.
Aug. 9: The El Al Airlines office in the Rome Airport was bombed by the 15th of May Arab Movement for the Liberation of Palestine.
Aug. 10: The garden of a building adjacent to the Israeli Embassy in Vienna, Aust., was bombed by the 15th of May Arab Movement for the Liberation of Palestine.
Aug. 10: The Israeli diplomatic mission in Athens, Gr., the El Al Airlines office in Rome, Italy, and the Israeli embassy in Vienna, Aust., were all bombed by the 15th of May Arab Organization.
Aug. 11: A reputed organized crime figure was injured when a bomb exploded in his parked car in St. Louis, Mo.
Aug. 11: The Swissair offices in Copenhagen were bombed by Armenian terrorists demanding the release of Madiros Jamkodjian, who was awaiting trial for shooting a Turkish consular employee in Geneva.
Aug. 12: A meeting of the Sri Lankan Freedom Party in Colombo was disrupted by three bomb blasts. Seventy people were injured as they made their way to the exits. The blast was blamed on the leftist JVP People's Liberation Front.
Aug. 13: Members of the Free People's Party, a pro-drug coalition, detonated three bombs in Wenatchee, Wash. on Aug. 13, and Sept. 13, 1981, and ten suspects were later charged.
Aug. 14: An IRA bomb factory was uncovered in the Shantallow district of Londonderry, Ire.
Aug. 16: Two beer kegs laden with explosives detonated outside a dance hall in Londonderry, Ire.
Aug. 17: The first of twelve bombs exploded in El Salvador. The last explosion was on Aug. 26.
Aug. 19: The African National Congress exploded a bomb on a section of rail line in East London, S. Afri.
Aug. 20: A meat packing plant in Seaman, Ohio, was the scene of a bomb explosion that caused $500,000 in property damage.
Aug. 22: Two IRA bombs exploded and rioting ensued in Belfast, Ire., following the death of hunger striker Michael Devine. Forty-eight people were wounded.
Aug. 28: Several children playing near Sword's Castle, Dublin, uncovered two IRA bombs attached to a black flag.
Aug. 29: The Iranian Radio and Television Offices in West Beirut were destroyed by a bomb. One man was killed.
Aug. 30: President of Iran Mohammed Ali Raji and Premier Mohammed Jad Bahonar were killed in a bomb blast in Teheran.
Aug. 30: Eighteen people were injured when a bomb exploded in the lobby of the Intercontinental Hotel in Paris.
Aug. 31: A car bomb, planted by the German Red Army at the U.S. Air Force Base in Ramstein, wounded twenty people.
Aug. 31: Dynamite exploded in the compound of the U.S. Ambassador to Lima, Peru. A second bomb exploded in the back yard of Ambassador Edwin Corr. The Lima offices of Ford, Coca-Cola, the Bank of America, and Carnation also were bombed.
Aug. 31: A bomb damaged an empty jetliner parked at Beirut Airport. Lebanese Shiite Moslems were blamed.
September: A fifteen-year prison sentence was handed down to a Maryland man for his involvement in a plot to bomb the National Association for the Advancement of Colored People (NAACP) headquarters in Catonsville. The suspect had given an incendiary device to an undercover agent on May 20, 1981.
Sept. 1: The regional offices of the Social Democratic Party in Frankfurt, Ger., were fire-bombed by the Red Army Faction.
Sept. 2: A grenade-throwing assailant killed Hojatesiam Morteza Khodad, a top Khomeini aide, at the Caspian Sea resort of Bandar Enzeli, Iran.
Sept. 3: A car bomb exploded in front of the Syrian Air Force Headquarters in Damascus, killing twenty people and wounding fifty others.
Sept. 3: Bombs exploded outside the U.S. International Communications Agency and a public bar in Maseru, Lesotho.
Sept. 3: A bomb exploded underneath a car belonging to a diplomat at the Soviet mission in New York. An unidentified man took credit for the attack, promising that Russian blood would flow in New York streets.
Sept. 5: Prosecutor General of Iran Ayatollah Ali Ghoddusi was killed in a bomb blast in Teheran.
Sept. 6: The head of the Teheran police, Colonel Vahid-Dastgerdi, died of wounds sustained in a bomb blast Aug. 30.
Sept. 6: The Jewish Defense League (JDL) was suspected of bombing the Four Continents Book Store in New York. The store sold Soviet books.
Sept. 9: Twenty buildings were demolished and $1 million in property damage was reported when terrorists dynamited the fashionable Escalon district in San Salvador. No injuries were reported.
Sept. 11: A top Khomeini aide, Ayatollah Assodollah Mandani, was killed in a hand grenade blast in Tabriz. The assailant had strapped the grenades to his waist.
Sept. 12: An Arab terrorist hurled a grenade into a street near the New Gate in Jerusalem, killing an Italian pilgrim. A bomb was found the same day by a policeman near the Lion's Gate of the Old City.
Sept. 13: Terrorists threw three fire-bombs at the home of David Betts, U.S. Consul General in Frankfurt, Ger. No injuries resulted.
Sept. 13: A hand grenade thrown into a restaurant in Zamboanga City, Phil., wounded eight people.
Sept. 16: Two bombs found next to a railroad line near the Rhine-Main air base in Frankfurt, Ger., were defused before they could cause any damage.
Sept. 17: A car bomb blew up in Sidon, Leb., killing twenty-three civilians. A right-wing political group, the Front for the Liberation of Lebanon, took credit.
Sept. 18: A car rigged with bombs exploded in West Beirut on a street infested with drug dealers. Three people were killed. A group calling itself the Front For the Liberation of Lebanon From Foreigners took credit. The Palestinian Liberation Organization (PLO) claimed the group was an Israeli front.
Sept. 18: Six neo-Nazis were convicted of conspiring to blow up various locations of Greensboro, N.C., in November 1980.
Sept. 19: A Tel Aviv bus driver uncovered a bomb in the rear of his vehicle after reaching his last stop in Bat Yam.
Sept. 20: A bomb exploded in the Muslim section of Beirut killing four people and wounding thirty-five others. The Front for the Liberation of Lebanon from Foreigners claimed credit.
Sept. 21: Two bombs exploded inside the Turquoise Bar in Waterflow, N.M., resulting in $5,000 damage. A third bomb was defused by the Albuquerque Police bomb squad.
Sept. 21: Two suspects were sentenced to four years in prison following their conviction on charges of fire bombing a home in Sterling, Conn. No one was killed or injured in the blast.
Sept. 21: Three bombs exploded in Lebanon causing minimal damage. The Front for the Liberation of Lebanon from Foreigners claimed responsibility.
Sept. 22: Four people were arrested in Nitro, W. Va., and charged with attempting to sell stolen dynamite. Two defendants pleaded guilty to lesser charges and testified against the other two, who were later sent to prison.
Sept. 23: Five employees at the Shoham-Zim offices in Limasol, Cyprus, were injured by a bomb planted by Abu Nidal terrorists.
Sept. 23: A car bomb exploded outside the headquarters of the Progressive Socialist Party in Beirut, Leb. No injuries were reported.
Sept. 25: The clubhouse of an all-white Rugby-football team in Evansville, Ind., was fire-bombed, causing $250,000 damage to the structure and adjacent buildings. A professional arsonist and one of the owners of the facility were arrested and charged.
Sept. 27: The life of Queen Elizabeth was threatened by an anonymous caller who reported that a bomb had been placed in a church in Melbourne, Aus., across the street from where the Queen was visiting. No bomb was found.
Sept. 28: Constable Alexander Beck of the Royal Ulster Constabulary was killed by a rocket fired at his Land Rover by Irish Republican Army (IRA) members along the Suffolk Road.
Sept. 28: A car bomb exploded at the Palestinian checkpoint in Zrariyeh, Leb., killing fifteen patrons at an adjacent restaurant. The pro-Amal Shi'ites were believed to be responsible.
October: Soviet KGB agents arrived in Teheran, Iran, to help establish a security and intelligence force for the Khomeini government. They defused a bomb found in their hotel room.
Oct. 1: A car bomb exploded next to the PLO offices in Beirut, Leb. Fifty people were killed and 250 wounded. The attackers were believed to be from the Front for the Liberation of Lebanon from Foreigners.
Oct. 2: A 165-pound bomb destroyed an empty school in the Shi'ite Muslim village of Jargou. No one was killed.
Oct. 3: A courthouse and a post office in Geneva, Switz., were bombed by the June 9 Organization. No casualties were reported.
Oct. 5: A crowded apartment house in Damascus, Syria, was damaged by a bomb that killed two people and wounded several more. The Muslim Brotherhood was blamed.
Oct. 7: The tourist information office of El Al Airlines in Rome was bombed, injuring eight people. Later that day a post office in Rome was bombed. It was the favored meeting place for Jewish immigrants from the USSR. Two were wounded.
Oct. 8: A government office in Lerida, Spain, was bombed by Catalan separatists.

Oct. 9: Justice Leonei Carias Delgado of the Supreme Court of El Salvador was wounded in a bomb attack on his courtroom. The device had been left behind in a briefcase.
Oct. 9: Three IRA bombs exploded in Strabane, Londonderry, and Armagh, Ire. No one was hurt.
Oct. 10: A nail-bomb attack was launched by the Provisional wing of the IRA on a London bus returning from ceremonies at the Tower of London. The device killed two people and wounded thirty-five others.
Oct. 10: Two suspects were arrested in Little Rock, Ark., after selling a total of five pipe bombs in June and July to undercover officers of the Arkansas State Police and the Bureau of Alcohol, Tobacco, and Firearms.
Oct. 12: A Catholic church at Limavady, Ire., was bombed by the Ulster Freedom Fighters.
Oct. 12: A Teheran, Iran, poorhouse was bombed by leftist guerrillas. Two people were hurt.
Oct. 12: The death of PLO leader Majead Abu Sharar in a Rome hotel on Oct. 9 was ruled a murder. Sharar was a bomb victim.
Oct. 13: Ten people were charged by a Spokane, Wash., grand jury for bombings in Washington between August and September 1981. The defendants were known to be active in an anti-gun, anti-drug law group.
Oct. 13: A bomb placed in a baggage cart below an Air Malta plane at the Cairo Airport killed an employee and wounded another person. A second bomb exploded at the airport fourteen minutes later, but no one was killed or injured.
Oct. 15: The Golden Bridge over the Lempa River in El Salvador was blown up by the Farabundo Marti National Liberation Front. The bridge's destruction cut off one-third of the country.
Oct. 16: The defendant accused of bombing the Galilee Baptist church in Birmingham, Ala., in October 1980 was sentenced under the Multiple Offender Act to twenty years in prison. He had been previously convicted for gun control violations.
Oct. 16: A New York State Trooper was seriously injured when an explosive device detonated inside his car in Wolcott, N.Y.
Oct. 16: Shortly before Vice-President George Bush was scheduled to arrive Bogota, Col., a twenty-two pound dynamite bomb was found buried along the runway of El Dorado Airport. It was placed there by the Worker's Self Defense group.
Oct. 17: Commanding General Sir Stuart Pringle of the Royal Marines lost a leg when an IRA car bomb exploded in London.
Oct. 17: A golf course in Northern Ireland was bombed with no reported damages and only one injury.
Oct. 17: A generator at Santa Cruz del Quinche, Guat., was bombed by rebels, knocking out power in six towns.
Oct. 20: A van loaded with explosives blew up outside a synagogue in Antwerp, Belg., killing two people and wounding 100. The Direct Action Group, Section Belgium, claimed responsibility.
Oct. 23: Three U.S. companies in Rome and the Chilean embassy to the Vatican were bombed by the Communist Groups for Proletarian Internationalism.
Oct. 24: An Argentine business, the Guatemalan mission to the Vatican, and an American Express office were bombed by the Communist Groups for Proletarian Internationalism.
Oct. 24: Four bombs exploded harmlessly outside buildings in Barcelona and Alicante, Spain.
Oct. 24: The suburban Rome, Italy, office of American Express was bombed by the Communist Groups For Proletarian Internationalism.
Oct. 26: Kenneth Howorth, an expert in bomb-disposal was killed by a booby-trapped IRA bomb at the Wimpy Hamburger Bar on Oxford Street in London. A second bomb found down the street was defused.
Oct. 26: Welsh nationalists were blamed for planting fire bombs at a British recruiting center in Pontypridd, Wales, on the eve of a visit by Prince Charles and his wife, Lady Diana.
Oct. 26: A car bomb filled with nails exploded on a street in East Beirut, killing one person and wounding twenty others.
Oct. 27: Two suspicious looking packages were exploded by police on Oxford Street, London. Scotland Yard were looking for six IRA terrorists who they thought were at large in the area.
Oct. 28: The London *Financial Times* received a bomb threat.
Oct. 29: An Iranian terrorist was arrested in Edison, N.J., and charged with the pipe bombing on Sept. 29 of an anti-Khomeini newspaper in Washington, D.C. The blast caused $3,000 damage. A second suspect was arrested on Oct. 13 in New York City.
Nov. 1: The Army For the Liberation of Lesotho exploded several land mines, killing several people.
Nov. 3: Four defendants were sentenced for the theft of 13,150 pounds of explosives and 6,300 blasting caps in Floyd County, Ken., on Mar. 27, and Apr. 27, 1980.
Nov. 7: Three British soldiers were wounded by an IRA bomb that exploded in the border village of Crossmagien, Ire.
Nov. 8: A 17-year-old boy, Trevor Foster, was killed when he entered his father's booby-trapped car outside Armagh, Ire.
Nov. 10: Charles Neville, a member of the Ulster Defense Regiment (UDR), was killed in his car by a hand grenade in Armagh, Ire.
Nov. 13: Thomas Quigly and Paul Kavanagh of the IRA were jailed for thirty-five years after blowing up the home of British Attorney General Sir Michael Havers in London. Havers and his wife escaped injury.
Nov. 13: The Wimbledon, England, home of Attorney General Michael Havers was bombed. No one was injured.
Nov. 16: London police searched more than 300,000 buildings and closed all roads as far away as Manchester in a futile search for 500 pounds of IRA bombs believed to be hidden in the city.
Nov. 20: The Turkish Consulate in Los Angeles was bombed by a group calling itself the Justice Commandos of the Armenian Genocide. The building sustained property damage.
Nov. 24: Three people were killed when a bomb exploded in front of a Teheran, Iran, railway station.
Nov. 25: Several explosions occurred in Khartoum, Sudan.
Nov. 27: Four of seven bombs planted in the commercial district of Teheran exploded, causing significant damage to a department store and a passing bus. At least two people were killed and fifteen were injured.
Nov. 28: A car bomb set off in Damascus by the Moslem Brotherhood as a part of its campaign against the Syrian government killed sixty-four people.
Nov. 28: The Macheteros claimed responsibility for the destruction of two electric substations in San Juan, P.R., which knocked out power for eighteen hours.
Nov. 28: A land mine in Kalasa, Uganda, was destroyed by a bomb. One soldier was killed and several others wounded.
Nov. 29: Sixty-four people were killed when a Peugeot sedan exploded in a Damascus, Syria, neighborhood. Four apartment buildings were destroyed and 135 people were injured.
Dec. 5: Three Irish terrorists, Gerard Bradley, Gerard McKee, and John Connolly, were arrested and charged with the November 28 explosion that killed a Belfast policeman.
Dec. 7: A bomb placed inside a fire extinguisher was hurled into the commander's office at the U.S. Army base in Kassel, Ger. Two officers were injured when the detonator exploded.
Dec. 10: Three bombs exploded in Tripoli, Leb., killing fifteen people and injuring twenty-four.
Dec. 11: Ayatollah Abdol Hossein Dastgheib, an aide to Ayatollah Khomeini, was killed by a bomb that exploded outside the main mosque in Shiraz, Iran. Seven others were killed in the blast.
Dec. 13: A car bomb exploded in Connaught Square in London, killing two passengers from the Middle East, and wounding the driver.
Dec. 15: A suicide car loaded with explosives was driven into the Iraqi Embassy in Beirut, Leb. killing thirty-seven people and injuring fifty. The Kurdistan Liberation Army took credit.
Dec. 17: A letter bomb sent to President Ronald Reagan from San Juan, P.R., was defused by the Secret Service.
Dec. 18: The headquarters of the Zimbabwean African National Union in Salisbur was destroyed by a bomb. At least six people were killed, and 150 were wounded
Dec. 19: A time bomb placed inside a pick-up truck in Beirut exploded killing five policemen and injuring six pedestrians. In the Bekaa Valley in East Lebanon, a Syrian helicopter gunship was destroyed by a bomb.
Dec. 20: A British soldier working on the damaged Old City walls in Londonderry, Ire. was killed by a terrorist nail bomb.
Dec. 21: The Pan-American building in Guatemala City was damaged by a bomb. A parking attendant was killed.
Dec. 26: A bomb exploded in the National Congress building in Guatemala. A museum in the adjacent law school of the University of San Carlos sustained heavy damage.
Dec. 27: An explosion rocked a racetrack in Beirut, causing a stampede of horses. There were no injuries reported.
Dec. 27: Salvadorian rebels blew up the San Francisco Bridge between Santa Ana and Metapan.

1982

A grenade attack against a Jewish synagogue in the heart of Rome killed a 2-year-old boy and wounded thirty-four other persons. The attack was believed to have been carried out by Abdel Osama el-Zomar of the Abu Nidal group.
The Croation Freedom Fighters (CFF) claimed responsibility for two bomb attacks.
January: Five persons were injured when a bomb went off in a railroad station in Nawabshah, north of Karachi, Pak.
Jan. 1: A car bomb in County Down, Ire. killed, Samuel Pollack David Brady, a UDR member thought to be the target, was badly hurt.
Jan. 3: The Kirkuk-Banias oil pipeline near Tall Abbas al-Gharbo, Leb., was bombed by the Iraqi Mujahedeen movement.
Jan. 5: Twelve explosions rocked the city of in San Salvador, El Sal. One of the explosions occurred at a Volkswagen dealer near the U.S. embassy compound.
Jan. 6: The 609-mile oil pipeline between Kirkuk and Ceyhan, Turk., was bombed.
Jan. 6: A car bomb wounded Dr. James Donovan head of the Garda Forensic Science Laboratory in Clondalkin, Ire.
Jan. 13: Socialist Party offices in Libourne, Fr., were bombed and several area buildings were damaged.
Jan. 13: A telephone kiosk near the Polish Central Committee building in Warsaw was wrecked by a bomb.
Jan. 15: Twenty-five persons were injured by an explosion at the Mifgash-Israel Restaurant in Berlin. The 15th of May Arab Organization for the Liberation of Palestine exploded the bomb.
Jan. 16: Communist insurgents favoring martial law in Poland threw five nail bombs into the U.S. Consulate in Calcutta, India.

Jan. 17: The Lufthansa office building in Tel Aviv was damaged by a small bomb.
Jan. 17: Two explosions were set off by Armenian terrorists in Geneva, Switz. No injuries were reported.
Jan. 18: A local ecology group fired five rockets at the Creys-Malville nuclear breeder-reactor, under construction in Lyon, Fr. Minor damage was sustained.
Jan. 19: The Armenian Orly Group exploded a bomb inside a coin-operated baggage locker in the Air France bus terminal on the western edge of Paris. No one was hurt.
Jan. 20: A car bombing in San Cristobal, Guat., killed seven and injured four.
Jan. 21: Rebels blew up an aqueduct in Guatemala servicing the village of Huehuetenango, north of Guatemala City.
Jan. 26: A Romanian physician named Ioan Servan was injured in Geneva, Switz., when a car bomb blew up in the parking lot of his hotel.
Jan. 31: The Moroccan Embassy in Beirut was bombed, but there were only minor damages.
Feb. 4: A crudely made bomb exploded outside the residence of Rabbi Bela Akiba Eisenberg in Vienna, Aust. Only minimal damage was reported.
Feb. 9: Leftist guerrillas in set off explosions that rendered much of Guatamala City and surrounding area without electrical power.
Feb. 10: Kai Mierenforff, known for smuggling refugees out of East Germany, was injured when he opened a letter bomb in his hotel room in Bavaria.
Feb. 11: A dozen explosions in France and Corsica were the work of the Corsican National Liberation Front. Two other bombs went off at the office of a meat importer in Paris.
Feb. 12: A bomb blasted the former home of the Ayatollah Khomeini in the Paris suburb of Neauphle-le-Chateau.
Feb. 13: A car bomb exploded in a Palestinian refugee camp in Sidon, while it was being dismantled by a PLO team. The blast killed four people and wounded five.
Feb. 16: The Corsican National Liberation Front planted nineteen terrorist bombs in Paris and its suburbs. There was some property damage.
Feb. 18: After a shotgun was taken from a Patterson, N.J. man, he placed a bomb inside a car belonging to an alleged thief. The blast killed the suspected thief's girlfriend. Convicted of the manufacture and possession of a bomb, the suspect was found innocent of homicide.
Feb. 18: A caller identifying herself as a member of the militant Jewish Defense League claimed responsibility for a bomb blast that damaged the offices of the Soviet Aeroflat Airlines in Washington, D.C.
Feb. 18: A suitcase bomb exploded in a building housing the Syrian Ministry of Information and the publication *Baath* in Damascus, Syria. Several people were killed.
Feb. 22: Fifteen people were killed and sixty-one injured when a bomb exploded in a garbage truck in Teheran's Seapah Square during rush hour. Twenty vehicles were destroyed.
Feb. 23: Two car bombs exploded in Beirut killing thirteen and wounding sixty others. An emerging terrorist group, the Al Jihad Al Mudaddas Front (Holy War Front) claimed responsibility.
Feb. 24: The militia offices in Beirut, Leb., were damaged by a bomb that killed at least one person and wounded others.
Feb. 27: The Front for the Liberation of Lebanon from Foreigners claimed responsibility for a car bomb explosion at the Syrian army checkpoint in West Beirut that killed eight and wounded thirty-five.
Feb. 28: A bomb inside a loaf of bread exploded harmlessly aboard a parked bus in a Tel Aviv garage.
Feb. 28: The Puerto Rican terrorist group Fuerzas Armadas de Liberacion Nacional (FALN) set off four explosions in New York's Wall Street financial district, causing property damage to the American Stock Exchange, Chase Manhattan Bank, and Merrill Lynch.
Mar. 3: Disguised as electrical appliances, several incendiary devices were sent through the mail to four people on Maui and Oahu. Three bombs exploded injuring three people. No common motive was apparent.
Mar. 3: Two Sequoyah County, Okla., deputy sheriffs attempted to serve an arrest warrant on a suspected bomber. As they approached the dwelling, an explosive device in the ground was detonated by remote control. The defendant was charged with attempted murder.
Mar. 4: A Lorraine, Wyo., tax violator was taken into custody after nineteen explosive devices rigged up at the windows of his residence were successfully defused by local law enforcement officers.
Mar. 4: A powerful TNT bomb exploded in a parked car in a beach resort outside Beirut, Leb., killing three and injuring nine.
Mar. 5: Rebels in Kabul, Afg., exploded a bomb on the ground floor of the Ministry of Education shattering windows in several shops.
Mar. 6: Col. Julio Eduardo Lopez, a retired military officer and presidential candidate, was killed in a car bomb blast in Guatemala City.
Mar. 8: The Zurich, Switz., Stock Exchange was bombed.
Mar. 9: An Irish Republican Army (IRA) bomb was defused on the Belfast railway line near Meigh, in South Armagh, Ire. Earlier, three bombs had exploded on the line at Knockmore junction near Lisburn.
Mar. 10: A car rigged with bombs was driven into the front yard of the Presidential palace in Bogota, Col. The 19 of April Movement claimed responsibility for the blast which injured five persons.
Mar. 10: Dynamite sticks exploded at the government palace in Lima, Peru, causing slight damage.
Mar. 11: Four bombs exploded at the entrance of several public buildings in Pamplona, Spain, injuring one man. The Euzkadi ta Azkatazuna (ETA) was believed responsible.
Mar. 13: The French cultural center in Beirut was bombed.
Mar. 14: A bomb blast killed three persons in the Egyptian section of the French embassy in Beirut.
Mar. 14: The offices of the African National Congress in London was destroyed by a ten-pound bomb.
Mar. 14: Mohammed Salem Hosni and two guards were killed in central Teheran, Iran, by a bomb explosion.
Mar. 15: An IRA car bomb exploded in Banbridge, Ire., killing an 11-year-old boy and wounding two women.
Mar. 16: A car bomb exploded outside the former Egyptian embassy in West Beirut, killing one person and injuring fifteen others.
Mar. 17: London police blew up a suspicious looking automobile on the road about to be traveled by Queen Elizabeth and the Sultan of Oman.
Mar. 17: Defense Secretary John Nott received a letter bomb at the House of Commons from the Scottish Liberation Army.
Mar. 18: Several persons hurled gasoline bombs at a political rally for the Functional Groups Party in Jakarta, Indo. Seven people died and 100 were injured.
Mar. 19: The Scottish Liberation Army sent two letter bombs to SDP offices in Edinburgh and Glasgow.
Mar. 22: A golf club on the outskirts of Newry, County Down, in Ire., was robbed and then bombed by two men.
Mar. 22: Leftist guerrillas bombed eighteen buses in San Salvador, El Sal. Many of the bus lines closed down out of fear.
Mar. 24: An oil pipeline operating from Iraq to Tripoli was bombed at the village of Tall Abbas, Leb.
Mar. 25: Fifty members of the Shiv Sena organization in Bombay, India attacked the U.S. consulate with stones and firebombs.
Mar. 29: The international terrorist Carlos (Illich Raminez Sánchez) claimed responsibility for bombing a Paris-Toulouse express train near Limoges. Six people were killed and another fifteen were wounded.
Apr. 1: A bomb planted outside the residence of U.S. ambassador to Greece, Monteagle Stearns, was defused in Athens.
Apr. 7: A hand grenade attack on the Greek Orthodox Jacob's Well Monastery near Nablus injured two people.
Apr. 7: The American Library in West Berlin was blown up with high explosives, causing $21,000 in damage. The American cultural center in West Berlin was also bombed.
Apr. 15: Two mosques in Iran were bombed. The explosion at the Kaseh-Frushan Mosque in Rasht injured ten people including Hojatoleslam Ehsanbakhsh. The Mujahedeen Khalq was believed to be responsible.
Apr. 15: An explosion at an apartment house in West Beirut killed five people.
Apr. 18: A bomb was defused that had been placed inside the Dog's Head Inn pub in Newcastle, County Down, Ire.
Apr. 18: One white and two blacks died from land mines planted by SWAPO guerrillas in Windhoek, Nambia.
Apr. 18: A series of dynamite charges set off by four members of the ETA in Madrid, Spain, wiped out telephone service to 700,000 people and caused $10 million in property damage.
Apr. 19: The Islamic Revolutionary Guard claimed responsibility for two bomb explosions that damaged the Air France offices in Vienna, Aust.
Apr. 20: Two men died in a car bomb in County Derry, Ire. The IRA claimed credit for its attack against "commercial targets." Causing substantial property damage six other bombs exploded in Northern Ireland in Strabane, Ballymena, Derry, Armagh, Bessbrook, and Belfast.
Apr. 21: An unidentified person lobbed a hand grenade into the square in Nablus along the West Bank. Five persons were injured.
Apr. 22: A rented car parked on the rue Marbeuf in Paris exploded, killing one woman. The blast that occurred across the street from the Lebanese newspaper *Al Watan Al Arabi* was attributed to Carlos, a terrorist.
Apr. 22: An elderly man was injured when a nail bomb exploded outside a store in Derry, Ire. The Irish National Liberation Army (INLA) apologized for the casualty but reminded people that warnings had been issued.
Apr. 22: Elias al-Atesh, an official of El Fatah, was killed with his wife in a bomb blast at a hotel in West Beirut.
Apr. 24: Aa embittered former employee detonated a car bomb in Odessa, Texas, killing his employer instantly. The accused murderer was arrested soon afterward.
Apr. 24: A bomb was discovered in a Turkish-owned bank in Cologne, Ger. A store, also owned by Turks, was bombed in Dortmund.
Apr. 27: A man exploded a grenade in Hanoi, Viet., killing himself and injuring three others.
Apr. 28: A pipe bomb blew out the front door of the Lufthansa offices in New York City. The Jewish Defense League claimed responsibility. Two other bombs were exploded in front of the Iraqi mission to the U.N.
Apr. 28: Masked gunmen blew up twenty-four buses at the Loughgall Road deport in Armagh, Ire. causing £750,000 damage.
May 1: A bomb explosion destroyed a railway link between Zimbabwe and South Africa, and a power plant at the Beit Bridge.

May 2: Two youths were arrested and held for the bombing of the Soviet Cultural Center in Vientiane, Laos.
May 4: The police confiscated 3,000 pounds of gasoline bombs in Belfast on the anniversary of the death of IRA hunger striker Bobby Sands.
May 5: A guerrilla bomb damaged Guatemala's only oil pipeline.
May 5: A letter bomb sent to Professor Patrick Fischer at the Computer Science Department, Vanderbilt University in Nashville, Tenn., injured the secretary who opened it.
May 6: Two Louisiana defendants were placed on probation after pleading guilty to theft of electric blasting caps from Fairfield Industries in Verrette, La.
May 8: A textile plant executive in Sayyed, Serajulddin, and his son were killed in a bomb attack at Kabul, Afg.
May 9: The Syrian embassy in Teheran, Iran, was destroyed by a car bomb. Sixteen pedestrians were injured.
May 12: A rocket grenade fired at the Iraqi Airways office in Beirut injured one person.
May 15: A maintenance depot in Kabul, Afg., that served as the residence of Soviet soldiers was blown up. Five to ten Afghan guards were killed.
May 16: A bomb planted near the front door of the home of a retired Ulster Assistant Chief Constable slightly injured the man's wife, May Bradley. A second bomb was found under a car nearby, but was defused.
May 16: The police headquarters in Ioannina, Gr., was damaged by a time bomb that exploded in the basement. All the windows were blown out of the buildings.
May 18: Two students were arrested in conjunction with the fire bombing of the Ionian and Popular Bank in downtown Athens, Gr. The police academy and the Public Works Ministry had been bombed a day earlier, suffering minor damage.
May 20: A gelignite bomb laid at the doorstep of the Rev. William Beattie of the Democratic Unionist Party of Belfast was defused. The bomb had been placed there by the INLA.
May 21: A dairy building at the U.S. airbase in Athens, Gr., was bombed, causing the air-conditioning system to malfunction. No one was hurt.
May 21: A bomb placed inside a telephone booth next to the Beit Yoel office building in Jerusalem was defused by a capper after it was broken apart by a remote-controlled robot.
May 24: A bomb hidden in a car belonging to the secretary of the French embassy in Beirut was detonated as the vehicle entered the embassy gates. Fourteen people were killed, and twenty-one were injured.
May 26: The offices of two English-language newspapers in Rome, Italy, the *Daily News*, and the *Daily American*, were damaged by bomb blasts. No injuries were reported.
May 29: The offices of Pan Am Airlines and a U.S. insurance company were damaged by bombs in Rome, Italy.
May 30: Los Angeles police defused a bomb placed near the Air Canada terminal at the L.A. International Airport. Three members of the Armenian Secret Army for the Liberation of Armenia (ASALA) were arrested by the FBI.
June 1: Four bombs exploded at U.S. military bases in Hanau, Frankfurt, Bamberg, and Geinhausen, Ger., causing substantial property damage. An IBM office in Dusseldorf was also bombed, resulting in $50,000 damage. The Revolutionary Cells, a radical left-wing group, claimed responsibility.
June 1: Several men broke into the Breenbank industrial estate in Newry, Ire., to set off a bomb. A bonding warehouse and several other buildings were damaged.
June 2: An oil depot outside Paulpietersburg, S. Afri., was bombed by the outlawed African National Congress (ANC). Seven tankers were destroyed.
June 2: Two automobiles belonging to the U.S. embassy in Athens, Gr., were destroyed by bombs. A third bomb exploded at the Athens offices of Honeywell.
June 3: A 16-year-old boy was killed when a bomb exploded on the Rugby Road, in Belfast, Ire. The INLA was responsible.
June 4: The ANC was blamed for a bomb explosion that damaged the offices of the President's Council of Cape Town, S. Afri.
June 4: ANC Secretary General Petrus Nyaose and his wife were killed in a car bombing in Swaziland.
June 5: The ETA exploded a bomb in Santurce, Spain, that killed a wine merchant. The next day two bombs were exploded at Spanish power facilities.
June 8: A hand grenade thrown at an army patrol in Gaza missed the target and killed an Arab shopper.
June 9: Six members of the First of October Anti-Fascist Resistance Group (GRAPO) movement of Spain received lengthy prison sentences for terrorist bombing attacks and political assassinations dating back to July 1978.
June 10: A bomb planted in a chocolate box exploded on board a bus traveling the Malone-Silverstream route in Belfast, Ire. The driver and seven passengers were injured.
June 11: The Derry Brigade of the IRA Provos accepted responsibility for a bomb explosion that killed Detective Constable David Reeves in Shantallow, Ire. The bomb was hidden inside a television set.
June 12: A powerful bomb containing 350 pounds of explosives was found and defused near the border at Crossmaglen, County Armagh, Ire.
June 17: A "sophisticated" car bomb killed Kamal Hussein, Deputy Director of the Palestinian Liberation Organization (PLO) in Rome, Italy.
June 18: A band of neo-Nazis exploded a bomb on the doorstep of Simon Wiesenthal's home in a Vienna suburb. Damage was estimated to be at least $40,000.
June 18: Three people were killed and several more wounded when a fragmentation grenade exploded at the election board of Santo Domingo, Dom. The Armed Nationalist Revolutionary Group took responsibility.
June 22: A storage tank belonging to Shell Oil on the Bay Road in Derry, Ire., was fire bombed.
June 23: A car bomb demolished a parked car at the Karachi Airport. The intended target, Prime Minister Dom Mintoff of Malta, was late in arriving.
June 25: A blue Renault, hijacked earlier from Andersontown, Ire., exploded in front of the Brunswick House hostel in Belfast, injuring twenty-four nurses and one man. The IRA Provos claimed responsibility.
June 25: Three Shi'ite Muslims set off car bombs in a seafront area of Beirut, burying a number of people under tons of debris. The three later said they were intimidated by Israeli officers into driving the car bombs into Beirut.
June 25: The Italian-Israeli Chamber of Commerce and the Hebrew Immigrant Aid Society in Rome were slightly damaged by two bombs.
June 26: Three large bombs exploded in Kampala, Uganda, killing ten people and injuring several others. It was later discovered that a bomb squad led by former minister of internal affairs Andrew Kayira was responsible for the blasts.
June 28: A bomb placed at a construction site in Ulster, Ire., exploded after experts failed to defuse the device. No one was killed or injured, but 300 homes were damaged, their roofs blown off and their windows shattered.
June 28: A Protestant group took credit for a bomb explosion at a Catholic Church in Belfast.
June 30: An underground political movement led by the former Minister of Internal Affairs, Andrew Kayira, planted a time bomb that damaged three cars and a hotel in Kampala, Uganda.
July 2: The Revolutionary Popular Struggle bombed the offices of American Express and Chase Manhattan Bank in Athens, Gr. Also hit in the attack was the Amcor-Israel Solar Energy Company and a travel agency.
July 2: Alexander Giese, an Austrian television figure narrowly escaped death when a bomb exploded in Vienna in the doorway of his apartment building. Giese was a member of the Austria-Israeli Society.
July 3: Three bombs were detonated outside the stadium in Seville, Spain, where the semi-finals of the World Cup soccer tournament were to be played. Several other bombs exploded in the Basque region of northern Spain.
July 3: The offices of Honduran Airlines in San Jose, Cos., were bombed. Three Nicaraguan diplomats were expelled in retaliation.
July 4: Power was lost in Tegucigalpa, Hond., when ten bomb explosions damaged two power plants outside the city.
July 4: The Frlan Travel Agency in Queens, N.Y., was bombed by Croatian terrorists. A gasoline bomb was discovered later in the doorway of Yugoslav Airlines on 51st Street in Manhattan. It was defused before it could go off.
July 7: In connection with hostility toward a nonunion marine contractor, three Milwaukee, Wis., residents were indicted for attempting to plant an explosive device on the Dan Horn Bridge.
July 9: IRA Provos planned to bomb the Annandale Embankment, where the Royal Ulster Constables Brass Band was scheduled to perform July 9. The bomb exploded prematurely and three men were arrested.
July 9: The Angry Merchants of France bombed the collection offices at La Tour du Pin.
July 13: A bomb factory in the Andersontown area of Belfast, Ire., was discovered by the Royal Ulster Constables.
July 15: The Red Placard faction of France set off two explosions at the Lesieur et la Compagnie generale sucriere, a sugar company in Lyon.
July 15: Seventeen bombs placed in various public buildings in northern Spain exploded, but no one was injured. The bombings were the work of the (ETA).
July 17: Basque separatists exploded a series of bombs in Pamplona, San Sebastian, Bilbao, and Vitoria. One man was injured, and public buildings were damaged.
July 18: The Israeli pavilion at the Biennale art exhibit in Venice, Italy, was bombed, resulting in damage to two paintings. The Communist Front for Counter Power was blamed.
July 19: An Armenian terrorist group claimed responsibility for bombing a Parisian bank and a business with ties to Israel.
July 20: Fifteen people were injured when a bomb exploded at the Sainte-Severin cafe in the Place Saint-Michel in the Latin Quarter of Paris.
July 21: An apartment complex where Regis Debray had recently lived was bombed by the right-wing French Revolutionary Brigades.
July 20: IRA bombs meant for the Queen's Household Cavalry in Hyde Park and the Royal Greenjackets Band in Regent's Park killed eight people and injured forty-seven others.
July 20: A bomb explosion damaged a facility of Shell France in the

Edouard-Herriot port of Lyon, Fr.
July 20: The Maghrebian bar of Bastia, Corsica, was bombed.
July 21: The British Armed Forces Radio in Cologne, Ger., was warned of a bomb on the premises, but none was found.
July 23: Three bombs exploded at Bastia and Ajaccio, Corsica.
July 24: Three plastic bombs exploded in Bastia and Ajaccio, aimed at the Societe Phenix.
July 24: The Orly Group, an Armenian terrorist organization, exploded a bomb in the washroom of the Pub Saint-Germain in Paris.
July 25: The Coca-Cola bottling plant in Lima, Peru was bombed by the Front for Counter Power, and dynamite was thrown at the U.S. embassy.
July 26: A property owner in Boise, Idaho, became the target of extortionists seeking to take over his property in order to operate a massage parlor. A dynamite bomb and threatening note had been left in his car.
July 26: A villa at Sanary, Fr., which belonged to a textile industrialist was bombed.
July 26: Seven bombs exploded in Bastia, and Ajaccio, Corsica at commercial establishments over a two-day period.
July 27: Four bombs exploded, including one at the residence of the British ambassador in Lima, Peru. A fifth bomb found at the office of *La Prensa* was defused.
July 27: A bomb destroyed the studio of Radio-Soleil in Menilmontant, Fr.
July 27: Four to five tons of explosives, taken at a robbery in Newcomb, Ky., were recovered by agents of the Bureau of Alcohol, Tobacco, and Firearms in Glasgow, Ky.
July 28: Six bombs in two days exploded in Ajaccio, Corsica, and three more in Bastia.
July 29: Ten minutes after Peruvian President Fernando Belaunde Terry left a reviewing stand where he watched a parade, a bomb planted by his opponents exploded, causing damage to nearby buildings.
July 29: Radio Tiers-Monde, a pro-Palestinian station in Paris was bombed, causing slight damage.
July 30: Two bombs exploded in Bastia, Corsica, causing damage to a Maghrebian bar and a police car.
July 31: Three more bombs exploded in Ajaccio, Corsica. Four other bombs planted near commercial buildings in Bastia exploded in the next five days.
July 31: A bomb concealed in luggage in the Munich Airport exploded. Several passengers waiting to board an El Al jetliner to Israel were injured by flying glass.
Aug. 1: A car bomb exploded in front of the Iraqi Planning Ministry in Baghdad, killing several employees and wounding passersby.
Aug. 1: A firebomb was thrown at a Jewish-owned bank in Vienna, Aust., causing some damage.
Aug. 2: A pipe bomb exploded in a parked automobile in Minot, N.D. causing $3,000 damages. Two juveniles charged in the incident were placed on probation and ordered to make restitution.
Aug. 2: A lounge at the Lahore, Pak. airport was damaged by a car bomb. Eight people were injured. The targets of the blast were three cabinet ministers whose plane had departed fifteen minutes earlier.
Aug. 3: The U.S. military base in Schwabisch-Gmund, Ger., was bombed. One truck was damaged.
Aug. 4: Three locations in Tegucigalpa, Hond. were bombed by the leftist Lorenzo Zelaya Front, including the Pan American Life Insurance Building which housed the offices of IBM, the British embassy, and UN organizations.
Aug. 5: The officer's club at a U.S. military base in Karlsruhe, Ger., was bombed.
Aug. 5: A bomb exploded outside the Alexandre Hotel in East Beirut, injuring several journalists. An Arab group called the hotel a military target given the presence of Israeli military officers.
Aug. 5: The Belfast, Ire., residence of William Meharg, a former assistant chief constable of the RUC was nail bombed by the INLA, causing damage to twelve other structures.
Aug. 5: Four bombs exploded in Corsica.
Aug. 6: Bombs exploded at a hotel in Ajaccio, and at town halls in Porto-Vecchio, Lecci, Figari, and San Gavino-di-Carbini, Corsica.
Aug. 6: A car bomb was defused in the shopping district of downtown Vienna, Aust.
Aug. 7: A bomb thrown by two members of the Armenian Secret Army for the Liberation of Armenia into a crowded waiting room at the Esemboga Airport in Ankara killed three Turkish policemen and an American. Seventy-two others were wounded.
Aug. 7: The Direct Action group of France exploded a bomb at the Discount Bank of Paris, on the rue de Turenne.
Aug. 8: A second bomb attack carried out by Direct Action damaged the Societe Nemor, a Jewish-owned business on the rue Saint-Maur.
Aug. 8: Two bombs exploded in front of U.S.-owned business in Spain: one at a Sears, Roebuck outlet in Barcelona, and another at a branch of the Bank of America in Madrid. No one was hurt.
Aug. 8: A pier in San Sebastian, Spain, was destroyed by a terrorist bomb. The target was a naval patrol boat.
Aug. 8: The Orly Group of France unsuccessfully tried to bombed the central telephone exchange in Paris.
Aug. 8: Three vehicles were bombed in Corsica.
Aug. 9: An apartment belonging to a Moroccan family in Bastia, Corsica, was damaged by a dynamite bomb.
Aug. 9: The fifth bombing in less than a week injured ten people in a crowded shopping plaza in Cotabato, Phil.
Aug. 9: A terrorist flung a bomb into the Jo Goldenberg kosher restaurant in Paris. As patrons fled, the gunman opened fire, killing six people and injuring twenty-two.
Aug. 10: A young black man in Johannesburg, S. Afri., was killed when he opened the pin on his hand grenade when police tried to arrest him.
Aug. 10: The Mozambique Resistance Movement fired a bazooka shell at a passing train near Beira, in Mozambique. Fourteen people were killed and fifty were wounded.
Aug. 11: A truck bomb exploded outside the Iraqi Embassy in Paris, injuring six people. The eight-story building was engulfed in flames. A fundamentalist Muslim sect was believed to be responsible.
Aug. 11: A Jewish-owned bank on the rue de la Baume was bombed by the Direct Action group.
Aug. 11: A 16-year-old boy on board a Pan Am jetliner bound from Tokyo to Honolulu was killed by a bomb that exploded under his seat. Fifteen other passengers were slightly injured.
Aug. 11: A citrus import company in Paris was bombed by the left-wing Direct Action group. The company was engaged in trade with Israel.
Aug. 11: The Banque de Gestion Privee in Paris was bombed by the anti-Semitic Direct Action group. A female pedestrian was injured.
Aug. 12: The IRA exploded a remote-controlled bomb on a train bound for Belfast, Ire., as it crossed into south Armagh. A Londonderry insurance office was torched with IRA gasoline bombs.
Aug. 17: A letter bomb sent to the African Studies Center of the University of Maputo, in Mozambique detonated and killed Ruth First, a Communist member of the outlawed African National Congress (ANC).
Aug. 18: A car bomb exploded outside the Palestine Research center in the Hamra business district of Beirut.
Aug. 19: A powerful car bomb containing 220 pounds of gelignite was defused outside the Lebanese Ministry of Information in Beirut.
Aug. 19: The offices of *Minuit* magazine near the Arch of Triumph in Paris was bombed by Direct Action, recently outlawed in France.
Aug. 20: The Corsican National Liberation Front exploded 100 bombs at various commercial sites on the island.
Aug. 21: A bomb placed under the vehicle of Roderick Grant, an American commercial attache in Paris, exploded near the Eiffel Tower. Two policemen died in the blast, which was attributed to Direct Action.
Aug. 24: A bomb was found on board a Pan Am jetliner as it arrived in Rio de Janeiro from Miami. Thirteen days earlier a passenger had been killed by a bomb on board a Pan Am jet.
Aug. 26: Two officers were killed in Munguia, Spain, while attempting to defuse a bomb.
Aug. 27: Electrical devices used to set off firebombs were found in the Maze Prison in Ireland where IRA prisoners were incarcerated.
Aug. 28: A gelignite dump and a warehouse of ammunition was found in the Dublin Mountains near Glencree. An additional ton and a half of explosives was confiscated by the Gardai when they stopped a truck at Lenaderg, Ire.
Aug. 30: Two men were arrested and later convicted in Denver, Colo., in connection with a bombing-for-hire scheme to defraud an insurance company and to move high grade heroin between Los Angeles and Denver.
Sept. 6: A truck bomb exploded on the Avenue Khayyam, opposite the Ministries of Justice and Interior in Teheran, Iran,killing twenty people and wounding 100 more.
Sept. 11: A bomb blast outside an employment agency in Manila, Phil. killed two employees and wounded twenty-five other people.
Sept. 14: The Syrian Secret Service assassinated President-elect Bashir Gemayel at his office in east Beirut. The 440 pound bomb planted by Habib Shartouni, killed eight other people and wounded more than fifty.
Sept. 16: Two boys were killed by an INLA bomb that exploded prematurely on the balcony of a building near a Belfast, Ire., retail store. The bomb was intended for local security forces.
Sept. 17: An embassy official attached to the Israeli mission in Paris was wounded when a car bomb exploded. Forty other people were hurt by flying glass.
Sept. 18: A crudely made bomb exploded in a Japanese department store in Causeway Bay, Hong Kong. Several other bomb threats were phoned in to two other Japanese stores which closed for the day.
Sept. 18: A bomb exploded in the lap of a patron in the lounge of the Hilton Hotel in Manila, Phil.
Sept. 20: Basque separatists exploded bombs in front of six banks in San Sebastian, Spain, and two other towns. No injuries were reported.
Sept, 20: Four men believed to be members of the INLA seized a Mount Gabriel radar station in Schull, County Cork, Ire. Explosives were placed inside the installation, which attackers thought was a NATO facility. No one was hurt in the ensuing blast.
Sept. 26: After a meat cutter crossed picket lines, his car was destroyed by an explosive device in Lincoln, Neb. Two coworkers who were members of the meat cutter's union were implicated.
Sept. 27: The German branch of Sperry in West Berlin was firebombed eleven days after being bombed by a pro-Palestinian group.
Sept. 27: A bomb hidden in a barrier separating the Catholic and

Protestant areas of Belfast exploded, killing a soldier.
Sept. 27: Two bombs exploded in Frankfurt, Ger. killing a man and seriously wounding a woman. The bombing target was the Pan Am office, but a passerby carried the bomb to a trash can near the Iran Air offices, where it exploded. A second bomb went off near the Mayco Touristik Travel Agency.
Sept. 28: The main sports stadium in Brisbane, Aus., was evacuated when a bomb threat was phoned in during the Commonwealth Games. No bomb was found.
Sept. 28: A bomb was found at the offices of the Philippine Airlines in Frankfurt, Ger. The device was defused.
Sept. 29: The Costa Rican Ministry of Defense accused Dagoberto Zambriano and Eduardo Alfonso Avila of the car bombing on Aug. 4 that inured Luis Medina Perez, a Cuban-American arms who was suspected by Avila of smuggling weapons into El Salvador.
Sept. 29: Sixteen bomb explosions in Madrid, Tarragona, Barcelona, Vigo, Leon, Seville, Cordoba, and Oviedo in Spain caused property damage to a number of government and industrial sites.
Sept. 29: A bomb damaged an empty synagogue in Milan, Italy.
Sept. 29: A prison under construction in Pesaro, Italy, was damaged by firebombs.
Oct. 1: A TNT-bomb blast at the Imam Square in Teheran, Iran, killed, or injured most of the passengers riding on three double-decked buses. Sixty people were killed, and two more were injured. A five-story hotel was completely destroyed.
Oct. 3: A female passenger was arrested on board a Lufthansa jetliner parked on the ground in Munich she threatened to blow the craft up. No explosives were found.
Oct. 4: A Boeing 747 jet bound from Rio de Janeiro, Braz., to New York was threatened with a bomb, but no explosives were found.
Oct. 7: A bomb threat was made on the jetliner carrying Portugal's Prime Minister Francisco Balsemao from New York to Lisbon. The plane returned to Kennedy Airport safely, and no bomb was discovered.
Oct. 8: A bomb inside a lady's handbag exploded in the President Department Store in Kaohsiung, Taiwan, killing one employee and wounding another.
Oct. 9: Four members of the S. Korean cabinet and fifteen civilians were killed in a bomb blast in Rangoon, Burma.
Oct. 12: Pierluigi Pagliai, suspected of masterminding the 1980 bombing of the Bologna, Italy railway terminal was returned to Rome from La Paz, Bol., to stand trial.
Oct. 14: A remote controlled bomb exploded in a garden hedge in the Whiterock district of Belfast, Ire. A British Army patrol was the intended target.
Oct. 15: The Leftist Direct Action group of Canada claimed credit for a car bomb explosion that damaged the Litton Systems factory in Toronto. The plant was a leading manufacturer of radar-evading guidance systems for cruise missiles like those stationed in Western Europe.
Oct. 16: The ETA was suspected of attempting to bomb the residence of the provincial governor of Vitoria, Spain, with a rocket grenade. The grenade bounced harmlessly off a lamppost without exploding.
Oct. 16: A former Washington, D.C. police officer pleaded guilty to federal firearms and explosives charges after blowing up a Milford, Del., gas station in March 1982. Six other defendants from four different states were also identified and sentenced.
Oct. 17: The remains of three Molotov cocktails recovered from the extinguished fires at a newspaper office in Pine Ridge, S.D. The ATF assisted Pine Ridge Police in locating the suspects, who were believed to have carried out the attack in retaliation for earlier uncomplimentary editorials.
Oct. 17: The offices of the Socialist Party in nine Spanish towns were the targets of random bombings.
Oct. 18: An individual was sentenced to three years in prison after pleading guilty in U.S. District Court to possession of an explosive device used in the April 1980 attempted bombing of a bingo parlor in Belvedere, S.C.
Oct. 20: Two women seen leaving the Lebanese embassy in Rome were thought to be responsible for a bomb blast which occurred shortly before the arrival of Lebanese President Amin Gemayel.
Oct. 20: A bomb placed near Official Unionist Party leader James Molyneaux in Northern Ireland was defused. Three other bombs were planted the same day, in an attempt to discourage voter turnout for the elections to the National Assembly.
Oct. 21: Two explosive devices were set off in a high school in Wasilla, Alaska. No one was injured in the blast. Evidence gathered at the scene indicated that students were responsible.
Oct. 21: Several Basque towns in northern Spain were rocked by eighteen terrorist bombs.
Oct. 22: A pipe bomb activated by a mouse trap contained in an ammunition canister exploded and critically injured a worker at an apartment complex in Albuquerque, N.M. Investigation resulted in an indictment of the man who rigged the device.
Oct. 24: A movie theatre in a fourteen-story office building was damaged by a bomb that exploded in Kabul, Afg.
Oct. 27: An ex-convict pleaded guilty to possession of three homemade bombs which he planned to use in an extortion attempt against a Mundelein, Ill., motel owner. The ex-con was sent to prison.
Oct. 27: A band of fifteen secessionist rebels carrying guns and explosives attacked a police station in the Jaffna Peninsula in Sri Lanka. Three policeman and one rebel were killed.
Oct. 31: A car bomb exploded in front of a U.S. housing complex in Giessen, Ger., causing damage estimated to be $157,000.
Nov. 1: Leftist guerrillas set off two bombs which destroyed the El Burro railway bridge in the Tecoluca province, east of San Salvador, El Sal.
Nov. 4: Two successive explosions in a commercial building in Parkersburg, W. Va. caused extensive damage but no one was killed or injured. The suspect, a former city councilman, was trying to assassinate a local attorney and his secretary.
Nov. 7: A Soviet-made hand grenade was thrown into an Israeli jeep in the Gaza Strip. The soldier threw the grenade back into the street, killing one Arab and wounding four others.
Nov. 12: Rebel forces dynamited four pylons supplying electrical power from the Fifth of November Dam to San Salvador, El Sal. The blasts caused the most serious blackout in the region in the previous six months.
Nov. 14: Four restaurants in Kabul, Afg., that were frequented by Communist Party officials were hit by terrorist bombs. At least twenty-four people perished in the blasts.
Nov. 16: A government office building in Swansea, Wales, was bombed by the Worker's Army of the Welsh Republic. No one was injured.
Nov. 17: A former CIA agent was found guilty of illegally exporting explosives to Libya. In a separate trial the same individual was sentenced to fifteen years in prison for sending weapons to a Libyan intelligence officer in Bonn, Ger.
Nov. 19: Leftist rebels fired a rocket-grenade at the Defense Ministry in Bogota, Col.
Nov. 20: Two bombs exploded in Paris, one at the offices of the Outspan Organization, a South African fruit trading concern, and another at the Promo-Chimie, a French chemical company. No injuries were reported.
Nov. 21: A bomb exploded at the main railway station servicing the Haifa-Tel Aviv road in Israel. The bus shelter collapsed, injuring one woman.
Nov. 22: Abu Nidal terrorists Muhammad al-Fayiz al Zomaria and Osama Abd al-Hayy were arrested near the Turkish-Greek border when explosives they intended to use against the Israeli embassies in Athens and Rome were found in their car. They each received five-year prison sentences.
Nov. 23: Three gunmen robbed a geophysical explosives magazine in Amita County, Miss., of 500 pounds of high explosives and sixty electric blasting caps. The merchandise was eventually recovered at Golden Beach, Fla.
Nov. 24: A New Yorker was convicted in Baltimore for attempting to detonate a device involving nine pipe bombs at the home of an attorney who had handled a divorce case for the family. The detonation was incomplete.
Nov. 25: A bomb wrecked a building in the suburb of Shiyah, outside Beirut. Six people were killed and twenty more injured.
Nov. 25: Two terrorist bombs exploded in a shopping center in Kabul, Afg., killing five people and injuring thirty-two others.
Nov. 30: One security officer was injured when a letter bomb exploded at 10 Downing Street, London. Similar devices were sent to other political leaders. The Animal Rights Militia, opposed to seal hunting in northern Scotland, was responsible.
Dec. 1: A Michigan probation violator taped high explosives to his body and when four Grand Blanc Township police officers tried to arrest him, he held them hostage for several hours before surrendering. No one was hurt.
Dec. 1: Walid Jumblatt, a Druse Muslim leader, was injured by a car bomb in Lebanon. His bodyguard and a policeman were among four people killed in the blast.
Dec. 3: The first high level mobster of Syrian factions in the St. Louis, Mo., area convicted on bombing and conspiracy charges was sent to prison.
Dec. 3: Two power stations in Lima, Peru, were bombed, causing power outages in the city.
Dec. 5: A travel agency in Nicosia, Cyprus, was damaged by a bomb.
Dec. 6: Sixteen people at the Razzmatazz Disco in Ballykelly, Ire., were killed when a small bomb, possibly smuggled in by an INLA member, exploded. The disco was popular with British soldiers and their dates.
Dec. 7: A car bomb exploded in Tripoli, Leb., killing eight people. A second explosion in the Bekaa Valley, twenty miles to the east, killed one person and injured another.
Dec. 8: Norman Mayer, an anti-nuclear protestor, drove his truck to the base of the Washington Monument and threatened to blow it up unless a ban on nuclear weapons would began to be discussed. Mayer tried to drive away in the afternoon, but police opened fire and fatally wounded him. There was no dynamite in the truck.
Dec. 12: Two Israelis were injured by hand grenades thrown into their jeep near Nabatiye, Leb.
Dec. 14: A bomb exploded on board a bus in Herzliya, a suburb of Tel Aviv. Passengers evacuated the bus before the detonation of the bomb.
Dec. 14: A vehicle owned by an American serviceman in Butzbasch, Ger., was bombed just as the man entered the car.
Dec. 15: A car bomb exploded near the Iraqi News Agency in Baghdad, killing at least seven people and injuring a number of employees.

Dec. 15: A pressure sensitive bomb placed under the driver's seat of a car seriously injured U.S. Army Captain Howard Bromberg in Darmstadt, Ger. It was the sixtieth attack against an American on German soil in 1982.
Dec. 16: A bomb exploded outside the IBM offices in Harrison, N.Y., and a second in front of the South African Airways in Elmont, Long Island. The Freedom Front-Revolutionary Fighting Group was suspected.
Dec. 17: IBM offices in White Plains, N.Y., and on Madison Avenue in Manhattan were cleared after a bomb threat was reported. No bombs were found at either location.
Dec. 18: Two bombs were planted at the Koeberg nuclear power station under construction outside Capetown, S. Afri. The African National Congress was responsible for the planting of the bombs. Major plant damage was reported.
Dec. 19: The Göttingen, Ger., police station was bombed, causing $40,000 in damages. A police school in Wolfenbüttel, Lower Saxony, was bombed the next day.
Dec. 21: On the third anniversary of the Soviet invasion of Afghanistan, several bombs exploded in Kabul.
Dec. 23: The Israeli consulate in Sydney, Aus., was rocked by a bomb placed in a seventh floor office. Three people were injured. Five hours later two smaller bombs exploded in a car parked at the Hakoah Club in a predominately Jewish section of Sydney.
Dec. 23: Two Israeli soldiers were killed by explosives placed inside their observation post at the Hilwe refugee camp in Sidon, Leb.
Dec. 26: Leftist guerrillas dynamited a power line near San Esteban Catarina, east of San Salvador. The eastern portion of El Salvador was without power for much of the year as a result of rebel attacks.
Dec. 27: A Springfield, Ore. man was killed instantly in a car explosion. The bomb had been placed under the seat by his wife and two accomplices who were indicted for aggravated murder.
Dec. 31: Five government buildings in New York City were bombed in a campaign of terror attributed to the Puerto Rican FALN group. A security officer and two policemen were injured by the bombs.

1983

Jan. 5: Anti-government guerrillas in Mozambique bombed portions of the Beira-Mutare oil pipeline.
Feb. 13: A bomb of mysterious origin blew up at a fuel dump in Lesotho. The South Africans were held responsible.
Feb. 28: Malfunctioning bombs were found outside three Las Vegas, Nev., hotels. Federal prison escapee Dennis Waugh, was the prime suspect in what appeared to be extortion attempts.
Apr. 3: Three died and sixteen were injured when a car bomb exploded in Durban. The work was allegedly done by the ANC.
Apr. 9: Tamil Separatists in Vaffna, Sri Lanka, wounded nine soldiers in a bomb attack.
Apr. 13: A car rigged with bombs by Abu Nidal terrorists exploded near the Saudi Arabian embassy in Athens, Gr.
Apr. 18: Forty-seven people were killed at the U.S. Embassy in Beirut when a bomb planted by the Islamic Jihad exploded.
Apr. 30: Eden Pastora, leader of Nicaraguan rebels, sustained injuries from a bomb explosion at a press conference.
May 22: A bomb exploded in downtown Pretoria, South Africa. The outlawed African National Congress (ANC) took credit for the blast, which killed nineteen persons and wounded 200.
July: Corsican National Liberation Army (ALNC), seeking political independence from France, claimed responsibility for a series of random bombings.
July 15: Orly Airport in Paris was bombed by a nationalist group known as Armenian Secret Army (ASALA). Seven died, and sixty more were injured.
Sept. 29: A Gulf Air jetliner of the United Arab Emirates was blown up in midair by Abu Nidal terrorists, killing all 122 passengers.
Oct. 9: North Korean army officers tried to assassinate President Chun Doo Hwan. Their bomb killed four South Korean Cabinet ministers and fifteen other people at Rangoon, Burma, instead. Burmese forces killed one assassin.
Oct. 23: Two-hundred-forty-one U.S. Marines and fifty-eight French soldiers were killed at their Beirut headquarters by a truck laden with bombs. The attack was the first phase of the Islamic Jihad's campaign to rid Lebanon of the multi-national peacekeeping force.
Oct. 31: A car loaded with explosives was detonated by the Abu Nidal Group near a Jordanian military base in Zarqa.
Nov. 4: Sixty Israelis were killed when a suicide truck bomb exploded in Tyre.
Nov. 9: An Abu Nidal bomb was located in time, and defused near a Saudi Arabian travel agency in Amman, Jor.
Nov. 10: A second Abu Nidal bomb was found and defused in Amman, this time near the Chinese embassy.
Nov. 12: A car booby-trapped by the Abu Nidal Group was defused in a residential area of Amman.
Dec. 9: A Burmese court sentenced two North Korean military officers to death for the Oct. 9 bombing in Rangoon.
Dec. 12: A suicide truck driven by members of the Al-Dawa movement attacked the U.S. embassy in Kuwait. The French embassy was also attacked, leaving four people dead and at least fifty injured.
Dec. 17: A car bomb exploded outside of the London department store Harrods killed six people and wounded ninety-four. The IRA disclaimed responsibility after universal condemnation for the outrage was expressed by world leaders.
Dec. 29: An Abu Nidal bomb was defused near the American officer's club and the French cultural center in Izmir, Turk.

1984

Jan. 29: Bombs exploded at the offices of Panhard-Levassor, manufacturers of military arms in Paris. The Action Directe, opposed to French operations in the African nation of Chad, was held responsible.
Mar. 10: Several bombings, attributed to the Libyan Secret Service, were set off at Arab businesses in London. The most serious incident occurred in Berkeley Square, where twenty-seven were injured. Gaddafi opponents were singled out for assassination.
Mar. 24: Two days before the state visit of Queen Elizabeth II of Great Britain to Jordan, a bomb exploded outside the Intercontinental Hotel. Twenty British journalists were inside at the time.
Apr. 3: A car bomb thought to be planted by the outlawed African National Congress (ANC) exploded in Durban, S. Afri., killing three people and wounding sixteen others.
Apr. 9: Tamil separatists bombed a military installation in Jaffna, Sri Lanka. Nine soldiers were killed.
May 30: Eden Pastora, Nicaraguan rebel commando, was injured by a bomb blast during a press conference.
June 24: The theft of 1,800 pounds of explosives was reported in the small village of Ecaussines, near Brussels, Belg. Earmarked for the European terrorist network, the explosives and were later used in a series of bombings.
Aug. 30: A bomb blast rocked the Varna Airport, Bul. A Turkish group was responsible.
Sept. 20: The Islamic Jihad attempted a suicide bombing of the U.S. embassy annex in Beirut. The driver of the truck, which was filled with explosives, was killed before he reached his target. The truck swerved off course and exploded, killing at least fourteen people.
October: An anti-NATO group based in Belgium, and calling itself the Cellules Communistes (Communist Fighting Cells) carried out a bombing campaign. The perpetrator was believed to have been Pierre Carette.
Oct. 12: A time bomb exploded at the Grand Hotel in Brighton, England, where Prime Minister Margaret Thatcher and her cabinet were holding high level conferences. The IRA claimed responsibility for the blast which killed five people including John Wakeham, chief whip of the Tory Party.
Dec. 11: Six bombs caused serious damage to a secret NATO pipeline outside Brussels, Belg., signaling the start of a "Christmas campaign" by a coalition of Euro-terrorists.
Dec. 25: Three abortion clinics were bombed by pro-life activists in Pensacola, Fla.

1985

Fall: A splinter group of the Irish Republican Army (IRA) known as the Irish National Liberation Army (INLA) began a series of bomb attacks against British installations.
Jan 10: The government of Sri Lanka announced that its internal security forces had bombed the base of the Liberation Tigers of Tamil Eelam. Fourteen Tamil rebels were killed.
Jan 20: The Tamil guerrillas of Sri Lanka retaliated for the Jan. 10 aerial attack of their commando base by blowing up a train. Thirty-three soldiers were killed.
Jan. 21: A bomb blast in Sidon, Leb., seriously injured Mustapha Saad, leader of the Sunni Muslims in Southern Lebanon.
Feb.: The Red Army Faction (RAF), the successors to the Baader-Meinhof Gang of West Germany killed Ernest Zimmerman, and claimed responsibility for a series of bombings.
Feb. 3: A terrorist bomb exploded near the Athens, Gr. air base where U.S. military personnel were stationed. Seventy-nine people were injured.
Feb. 22: A bomb planted by the Abu Nidal Group was discovered near the American cultural center in Amman, Jor., before it could go off.
Mar. 9: An Alia Jordanian jetliner exploded on the ground at Abu Dhabi airport. A suitcase booby-trapped by Abu Nidal terrorists had been smuggled on board. There were no casualties.
Mar. 10: A suicide truck driven by a member of the Syrian National Socialist Party crashed into an Israeli military convoy in Metullah, killing twelve.
Mar. 21: Three pedestrians were wounded when an Abu Nidal bomb exploded near the Alia offices in Athens, Gr. Two workers at the Alia Jordanian offices in Rome were injured in an Abu Nidal grenade attack.
Mar. 26: A Turkish terrorist group set off a bomb on a train bound from Burgos, Bul. to Sofia, killing seven.
Apr. 4: Abu Nidal fired at an Alia plane with rocket launchers as it was about to take off in Athens, Gr. The 100 passengers on board somehow survived the rocket blasts.
Apr. 12: The Islamic Jihad bombed a Spanish restaurant that was popular with U.S. Air Force servicemen. Eighteen people were killed, and eighty-two people were injured,
Apr. 20: The Revolutionary Front for Proletarian Action (FRAP) bombed the headquarters of the North Atlantic Assembly in Brussels.
Apr. 21: FRAP claimed responsibility for a bomb attack against the AEG-Telefunken offices in Brussels.
May 10: Two days of terrorist bombings in New Delhi and other cities in northern India left eighty-five people dead and hundreds more injured.
May 22; A car rigged with explosives by the Abu Nidal Group was

detoured before it reached the U.S. Embassy in Cairo, Egypt.
June 23: Sikh extremists were held responsible for the in-flight explosion of an Air India 747, bound from Toronto to London. All 329 passengers were killed. The same day, a bomb in the luggage of another Air India flight from Canada exploded in Tokyo, killing two baggage handlers.
July 1: One person was killed and twenty-four people were injured in an Abu Nidal bomb and grenade attack at the Alia and British Airway offices in Madrid, Spain.
July 1: Twelve baggage handlers were injured in a bomb explosion at the Rome Airport.
July 11: Fifteen people were killed and ninety more were wounded at Abu Nidal bomb explosions in two Kuwait cafes.
July 21: Abu Nidal set off a bomb outside the Kuwaiti Airlines office in Beirut, Leb.
Aug. 8: Rote Armee Fraktion (RAF) terrorists gained entrance to a U.S. Air Force Base in Rhine-Main, Ger. They planted a car bomb which killed a U.S. soldier and a female companion.
Aug. 8: The British-owned London Hotel in Athens, Gr., was the scene of an Abu Nidal bomb blast that wounded thirteen guests.
Aug. 14: A car bomb in the Christian section of East Beirut, killed fifteen people and wounded at least 120 others.
Aug. 17: A second bomb, in Christian East Beirut, killed fifty-five Christians and wounded at least seventeen more.
Aug. 19: The Christians exploded a bomb in the Muslim suburbs. The blast left twenty-nine people dead and nineteen injured.
Aug. 20: Forty-four people were killed when a car bomb detonated in Tripoli.
Sept. 28: Ten persons were wounded after Abu Nidal terrorists exploded three bombs at the British Airways office in Rome.
Sept. 30: A bomb was set off at night by Abu Nidal terrorists outside the El Al offices in Amsterdam.
Nov. 23: Libyan terrorists under Abu Nidal hijacked an Egyptair 737 bound from Athens to Cairo. The plane was forced to land at Luqa, Malta, where it was stormed by an Egyptian anti-terrorist group. The hijackers blew open the cargo doors killing nine people.
Dec. 15: African National Congress (ANC) guerrillas planted a land mine in Transvaal, S. Afr., which killed six whites, prompting an angry warning from President P.W. Botha to officials of Zimbabwe.
Dec. 23: The outlawed African National Congress (ANC) was blamed for a bomb explosion at a shopping center in Durban, S. Afri., that killed six whites, and wounded forty-eight others.

1986

Feb. 3: A bus transporting English soldiers and their families was targeted by a suitcase bomb. The explosion en route killed nine soldiers, a mother and her two children.
Feb. 6: A hand grenade attack in Madrid, Spain killed Vice Admiral Cristobal Colon, a descendent of Christopher Columbus. The Euzkadi ta Azkatazona (ETA) was responsible for the attack.
Feb. 6: France announced its intention to beef up security procedures after a terrorist bomb injured twenty-one persons in Paris.
Feb. 17: In response to the French attack on the Chad air base, rebel factions attacked the Ndjamena airport.
Mar. 22: Suspected Irish Republican Army (IRA) bomber Evelyn Glenholmes was freed by a Dublin, Ire., court on the grounds that an arrest warrant issued by Scotland Yard was incorrectly sworn.
Mar. 26: A Dutch court in Amsterdam refused to extradite IRA terrorist Gerard Kelly on the grounds that his crimes were political.
Apr. 2: Killing four people, a bomb blew a hole in a TWA 727 jet approaching the Athens airport. The plane landed safely. May Mansur, the widow of a Syrian Socialist National Party member, was held responsible. Mansur was on the flight at the time of the explosion, but denied planting the bomb.
Apr. 5: A U.S. soldier and a Turkish woman were killed and 204 people were injured by a bomb blast at the La Belle disco in West Berlin. Intercepted messages from the Libyan embassy in East Berlin indicated that Libya was responsible for the bomb.
Apr. 17: A bomb was found in the luggage of a pregnant Irish woman by El Al security guards at London's Heathrow Airport. The woman, Anne-Marie Murphy, was unaware that her Jordanian lover Nezar Narwas Mansur Hindawi had planted the explosive. Hindawi's brother was arrested in West Berlin as an accessory to the La Belle disco bombing.
Apr. 18: Two Libyan extremists were arrested in Ankara after attempting to throw a suitcase bomb and hand grenades into a wedding party at a U.S. military base in Ankara.
May 3: The Liberation Tigers of Tamil Eelam (LTTE) exploded a bomb on board an Air Lanka Tristar in Colombo, killing seventeen. The attack was aimed at influencing Prime Minister Margaret Thatcher to aid the Sri Lankan government.
May 3: Two IRA terrorists, Seamus McElwaine and Kevin Lynch, were shot in an ambush in Dublin, Ire., as they were about to set off an 800-pound boobytrap bomb.
May 7: The Central Telegraph office in Colombo, Sri., was bombed by the LTTE. Fourteen were killed, and 100 more injured.
June 14: A car bomb explosion in Durban, S. Afri. killed three persons and injured sixty-nine more.
June 23: IRA terrorist Patrick Magee was sentenced to thirty-five years in a London prison for his role in the Brighton bombing.
June 26: Seven people were killed on a tourist train en route to the Inca ruins of Machu Pichu in Cuzco, Peru. The Sendero Luminoso was blamed for the attack.
Sept. 4: Three French soldiers assigned to the UNIFL peace-keeping force in Lebanon were killed in a bomb attack.
Sept. 8: Ten days of terrorist bombings by the Solidarity Committee of Arab Political Prisoners commenced in Paris. The French government announced tough new measures to combat terrorism including visa requirements for all foreigners except EEC and Swiss nationals.
Sept. 17: A bomb blast in a crowded department store in Paris killed five and wounded sixty-one. The Lebanese Armed Revolutionary Faction (FARL) carried out the attack in order to force the French to release their imprisoned leader Georges Abdallah.
Oct. 15: Palestinian guerrillas threw hand grenades during an Israeli military ceremony in front of the Wailing Wall in Jerusalem. One person was killed and sixty-nine people were injured. Israel responded by bombing Palestinian camps near the Lebanese port of Sidon.

1987

Mar. 18: A bomb exploded underneath the bandstand of a military academy where Philippine President Corazon Aquino was scheduled to speak to a graduating class in a few days
June 1: Rashid Karami, premier of Lebanon was killed by a bomb planted in a helicopter in which he was traveling.
July 30: Sixty-eight people were injured in the bombing of a military barracks in Johannesburg, S. Afri.
Aug. 18: A bomb exploded in the Sri Lankan Parliament building killing one person and injuring fifteen others.
Nov. 8: Remembrance Day ceremonies in Northern Ireland were disrupted by a bomb blast that killed eleven people and wounded sixty-one others.
December: Korean Air Flight 858 was destroyed in midair by a bomb.

1988

Mar. 6: The British Special Air Service (SAS) shot and killed three suspected Irish Republican Army (IRA) terrorists in Gibraltar whom they believed were about to detonate a car bomb with a remote controlled device.
Mar. 20: Marxist guerrillas attempted to disrupt El Salvador's national election by detonating six terrorist bombs in San Salvador. Electricity was interrupted in eighty percent of the country,and almost all highway traffic was halted.
Apr. 7: Albie Sachs, a South African lawyer involved in the anti-apartheid movement was badly injured in a car bomb attack in Maputo, Mozambique.
Apr. 12: A Japanese native, Yu Kikumura, thought to be a member of the Red Army Faction, was arrested in New Jersey with three pipe bombs in his possession.
Apr. 14: Five were killed in a nightclub catering to U.S. servicemen in Naples, Italy, by a car bomb driven by Junzo Okudaira of the Japanese Red Army to observe the second anniversary of the Libyan bombing attack by U.S. planes.
Apr. 23: A truck carrying 300 pounds of TNT exploded in a crowded marketplace in Tripoli, Leb., killing scores of people.
Nov. 11: Animal rights activist, Fran Stephanie Trutt, was arrested outside the headquarters of the U.S. Surgical Corporation in Norwalk, Conn., after placing a crude bomb near the company. Her legal defender raised the issue of entrapment.
Dec. 21: A Pan Am Boeing 747 was blown up by unknown terrorists over Scotland, killing 259 passengers, and nine persons on the ground. The plane was on its way from London to New York City.

1989

Nov. 30: The presidential palace in Manila was bombed during an attempted coup by military commandos, and several radio stations were seized before the disturbance was quelled.

BURGLARY

1850s
Atwell was a petty thief for forger James "Jim the Penman" Saward. He stole from an ironworker's shop in the 1850s and delivered checks and bank drafts to assist his boss in illegal bank transactions.
1869
June 27: George Leonidas Leslie and accomplices broke into the Ocean National Bank, New York, and stole $786,879.
Dec. 14: Mosher and Douglass were killed trying to burglarize a Long Island, N.Y., home. Mosher died instantly; Douglass lived long enough to tell police he and Mosher had kidnapped little Charles Ross, but died before he could tell where the boy was hidden. The boy was never found.
1878
May 25: In London, Adam Worth broke into a building owned by art dealers Agnew and Agnew, stole Gainsborough's priceless *The Duchess of Devonshire*, and sent it to the U.S.
Oct. 27: George Leonidas Leslie and accomplices stole $2,747,000 from the Manhattan Savings Institution.
1892
Frank C. Almy, (AKA: George Abbott), was convicted of several thefts in New England in the 1880s. He escaped from prison, murdered a young woman, and was executed in 1892.
1893
Henry Cochrane spent several decades beginning in 1893 taking gold bars home after work each day at the Philadelphia Mint. He amassed, melted down, and exchanged for gold coins between $50,000 and $60,000 worth of gold before he was caught and sent to prison.
1900
Apr. 17: George "Flat Nose" Currie, train robber and member of the Wild Bunch, was caught stealing cattle near Castle Gate, Utah, and killed by a posseman.
1901
Apr. 26: "Chicago May" Churchill, Eddie Guerin, and accomplices burglarized Paris' American Express office, stealing more than $100,000 in francs and checks. Churchill and Guerin were imprisoned.
1902
Sept. 2: Jackson's burglary conviction in London was the first fingerprint conviction in history.
1906
Apr. 16: A British burglar was arrested in New York City and identified as Henry Johnson after his fingerprints were sent to Scotland Yard. The case was an early victory for fingerprint identification, not yet adopted in the U.S.
1908
May 25: Expensive church belongings were stolen from Paris' Limoges Cathedral and never retrieved.
Aug. 5: Priceless church objects were taken from Paris' Cathedral of St. Viance between Aug. 5 and Aug. 16. They were never recovered.
Oct. 26: Unidentified burglars stole jewel-encrusted statues, goblets, and other items from the Church of St. Vaury, Creuse.
1909
Mar. 25: Burglars entered the Church of the Soulerraine Creuse, Paris, and walked off with precious chalices.
Apr. 27: Burglars in Paris stole valuable artifacts from a private museum.
Nov. 11: William Butler killed an elderly man and his wife while burglarizing their home in Monmouthshire of £3. Butler was arrested, convicted, and hanged.
Dec. 16: Several Russian anarchist jewel thieves robbed the H.S. Harris Jewelry Co. store, killing three London policemen. Two of the men were killed on Jan. 3, in a gun battle with police.
1911
Aug. 21: Charles Arthur was sentenced to penal servitude for life in England for shooting at a policeman during a burglary.
Aug. 21: Vincenzo Peruggia stole Da Vinci's *Mona Lisa* from the Louvre in Paris and hid it in his room for the next two years, when he took it to Florence, Italy and was arrested.
1912
Oct. 9: George Mackay, shot Inspector Arthur Walls to death after being caught burglarizing a mansion. Mackay was convicted and hanged in 1913.
1914
Feb. 4: Young Jack "Legs" Diamond, who later become an influential underworld figure, was arrested in New York City for burglary and sentenced to an indefinite prison term.
May 7: Charley Jones, a black man arrested for shoplifting a pair of inexpensive shoes in Groveton, Miss., was lynched by an angry mob.
July 14: James Bailey, a black man accused of stealing three mules in the Lake Cormorant, Miss., area, was hanged before he could stand trial.
1917
Feb. 13: Charles Dion O'Bannion united Earl "Hymie" Weiss, George "Bugs" Moran, and others in a burglary gang that became the center of underworld activities in Northside Chicago in the 1920s.
1918
Jan. 29: Charles "The Ox" Reiser, notorious safecracker, joined Dion O'Bannion, Bugs Moran, and Hymie Weiss and blew up a safe at the Chicago's Western Dairy Company and stole $2,000.
May 24: George "Bugs" Moran was imprisoned for attempting to burglarize a safe.
Nov. 5: The Reiser safecracking gang broke into the Chicago Prudential Life Insurance Company through a fire escape, exploded the safe, and left with $3,865.
Dec. 2: The Reiser gang burglarized the Borden Farm Products Company in Chicago, taking $594.61.
1919
Jan. 18: The La Villette robbery gang of Paris blew open the Bank of Blache & Gravereau safe and stole 510 francs.
Feb. 10: Wilbur Underhill, or the "Tri-State Terror" robber, was given a short sentence for burglarizing a Joplin, Mo., store.
Dec. 2: Ambrose Small, millionaire, disappeared forever and his employee, John Doughty, was later imprisoned for stealing more than $100,000 in negotiable bonds from Small's account.
1920
Mar. 23: Harvey Bailey, who had been burglarizing small banks throughout the Southwest, was arrested and sentenced for hijacking and burglary in Omaha.
Apr. 25: Percy Toplis, who burglarized homes throughout Wales, England, and Scotland, was fatally shot by police after murdering a taxi driver he was attempting to rob.
Aug. 4: Frank "Jelly" Nash was caught attempting to burgle and blow up a vault in a small bank. He was imprisoned.
1921
Jan 15: Arthur "Dock" Barker burglarized a Muskogee, Okla., bank. Arrested under the alias Claude Dale, he was imprisoned as Bob Barker, released under court order six months later, and vanished before being tried.
Mar. 7: John Mahoney was discovered attempting to blow the same Chicago Masonic Temple safe for the ninth time in two years. He posted bond and was found murdered on Apr. 30.
June 1: Charles Dion O'Bannion, Charles "The Ox" Reiser, and Earl "Hymie" Weiss were caught attempting to crack the safe in Chicago's Postal Telegraph offices. They were acquitted of all charges.
Oct. 10: Charles "The Ox" Reiser killed watchmen Steve Pochnal and is himself wounded while burglarizing the Cooke Cold Storage Company in Chicago. Several days later Reiser, recovering in the hospital, is shot ten times, allegedly by his wife, although it is ruled suicide.
Oct. 27: Jack "Legs" Diamond was arrested for burglarizing a store in New York City. The charge was dismissed.
Nov. 18: Jack "Legs" Diamond was arrested after burglarizing a jewelry store in New York City. Diamond was released the next day by Judge Mancuso.
1923
July 21: John Dillinger, twenty-three, committed his first crime when he stole a car in Mooresville, Ind. He abandoned it and was not arrested.
1924
Nov. 26: Joseph "Doc" Stacher was arrested for burglarizing a store in New York City. The charge against Stacher, who will become a powerful syndicate boss in Las Vegas, was dropped.
1925
Apr. 9: Joe Valachi was sent to Sing Sing for a New York City burglary.
1926
Feb. 25: Alvin Karpis, a budding bank and train robber, was sentenced to the reformatory at Hutchinson, Kan., for five years for burglarizing a store.
1927
Aug. 15: Joseph "Doc" Stacher received a light prison sentence for burglarizing a Newark, N.J., store.
1928
June 15: Joseph Valachi, serving a prison term for burglary, was paroled.
July 28: Pochetti Attilie and Suput Branco burglarized Mrs. Vanderbilt's Paris home, taking jewels valued at a total of 1,000,000 francs.
Aug. 16: Carl Panzram, mass murderer, was given a light jail term for breaking and entering a Washington, D.C. home.
Sept. 14: Pochetti Attilie and Suput Branco stole jewels valued at 300,000 francs from the Heidelbach home in Paris.
1929
Oct. 13: Clyde Barrow was arrested for a burglary in Dallas, but was released just days later due to lack of evidence.
1930
James Biscoff Whitehead and Hugh Middleton broke into a Newcastle, England public house and stole £55 and three bottles of beer from a safe.
Mar. 2: Clyde Barrow, alias Elvin Williams, burgled a store in Waco, Texas. He escaped soon after being jailed, was recaptured, and paroled two years later.
Mar. 23: Alvin Karpis was caught burglarizing a store in Kansas City and stealing a getaway car. He was confined but later escaped.
Sept. 17: O'Connor, Lee, and Britt stole $2,702.796 in cash and securities from the Lincoln National Bank & Trust in Lincoln, Neb. O'Connor and Lee were imprisoned but were later found innocent.

Oct. 19: Frank "Jelly" Nash stole a three-volume set of Shakespeare from the prison library while serving a long sentence in Leavenworth for bank robbery. He escaped and was recaptured after robbing several Southwest banks.
Oct. 28: Willie "The Actor" Sutton and Marcus Bassett burglarized M. Rosenthal & Sons Jewelers in New York City and left with more than $30,000 worth of gems. Bassett was later caught.
1932
Feb. 2: Clyde Barrow was paroled from the Texas State Penitentiary at Huntsville, where he was serving a term for burglary.
Sept. 16: René Anchisi, Adolphe Guillemenot, and Serge Sauvageot stole a loaf of bread from Donald Ross. They ransacked his Paris home while he lay in a drunken stupor. The men were also convicted of his Sept. 16 or 17 murder.
Nov. 14: It was reported that Whitney Endt, wife of an insurance broker, had stolen her best friend's jewels.
1935
Sir Harry Lloyd Verney's home in South Kensington, England was burglarized of jewelry worth £329 by Joseph Sinclair, who had broken into the house with a crowbar.
1938
Oct. 17: It was reported that in Calder, Wisc., burglars thwarted by a safe's tear gas device stole gas masks from the nearby firehouse and then returned to finish the job. They got $400 in cash, $2,800 in non-transferable stock.
1939
Feb. 13: Burglars stole 149 sewing machines, valued at $17,000, from two Brooklyn trade high schools.
1940
Aug. 5: Greenfield Tap & Die Corp. in New York City was burglarized of $75,000 worth of drills used in the manufacture of airplanes.
1942
Jan. 26: It was reported that porter Charles Beverly Grayson allegedly burglarized the FBI headquarters in New York City, taking expensive camera equipment.
1944
Oct.19: Joseph Stepka and Stanley Patrek were indicted for stealing a safe and the $9,000 in it from the Whitestone Savings and Loan Association, Queens County, Flushing, N.Y.
1947
Feb. 10: It was reported that burglars took $435,000 worth of jewels and cash from the Paris hotel in which Lucienne Benitez Rexach was staying.
1951
Oct. 20: More than $230,000 in jewels and furs were stolen from Chicago's Congress Hotel Jewel & Fur Shop owned by Mrs. Pearl Lowenberg Robinson. The valuables were never retrieved.
October: Albert Covner, a Nahant, Mass., physician, and his wife reported $18,000 in cash and several dresses stolen from their home.
1952
May 26: Leland Ferre was reported to have repeatedly left his jail cell in Monticello, Ill., to burglarize local establishments.
1953
May 18: It was reported that Clyde B. Hamblin and Frederick Hamelin, prisoners in Burlington, Vt., burglarized local stores by slipping out of jail at night, then returning before morning.
1958
Aug. 10: Burglars shattered display windows at New York City's Fifth Avenue Tiffany's and took $163,000 in insured jewels. The jewels were never recovered.
1961
July 1: Georges Lemay led a group in burglarizing a branch of the Bank of Nova Scotia that took a total of $633,605 in cash, negotiable securities, and jewels-the largest theft in Canada history to that date.
Sept. 8: Jewels worth $120,000 were stolen from Mary Lasker's Cap Ferret home. Gérald van der Kemp's apartment key was also missing, as was $14,000 worth of gems from Princess Marcia Stranahan's Villa Mayou home.
1963
Sept. 21: French police broke into Nikola Franusic's home and recovered more than $2 million in rare books and other art objects the Yugoslavian house painter had stolen more than thirty years earlier.
1965
Winter: Allen Leroy Anderson spent eleven years in prison for forgery, auto theft, and burglary.
1966
Ninety million S & H Green Stamps worth $250,000 were stolen from a Sperry & Hutchinson warehouse in Chicago. The burglars were never apprehended.
1970
June 12: Tupamaros sneaked into the Swiss embassy in Montevideo, Urug., and stole typewriters, a photocopying machine, and official papers.
Dec. 11: The offices at the Inter-American Development Bank in Montevideo, Urug., were vandalized. The unidentified intruders destroyed furniture and stole documents.
1971
Dec. 31: The Hotel Pierre, New York City, was robbed of gems held in a safe and reportedly worth $5 million. The burglars were not caught.
1973
Dec. 2: Carl Dixon, Louis Mathis, and Anthony B. Vaglica burglarized Harvard University's Fogg Museum, making off with $5 million worth of antique coins. The men were caught while attempting to fence the goods.
1974
Apr. 26: Bridget Rose Dugdale and four armed men stole nineteen paintings worth a total of $19.2 million from the home of English millionaire, Sir Alfred Beit. Dugdale was imprisoned for nine years and the paintings were recovered undamaged.
Oct. 20: Six burglars blew through a wall of Chicago's Purolator Company and stole $4.3 million. They were caught while trying to escape to Latin America, and most of the money was retrieved.
1975
Feb. 27: Joseph Brown was sentenced to three to fifteen years in prison for burglary and vandalism one week after winning $300,000 in the Ohio lottery.
Aug. 14: The negatives of Federico Fellini's *Casanova* and other films in production were stolen from the refrigerated vaults of the Technicolor Company, Rome. Italy's Kidnap, Inc., was accused of stealing the seventy-four reels of film.
September: John Thomas committed eleven burglaries in his South Side Chicago neighborhood.
1976
Jan. 28: Guerrilla terrorists blew open vaults in the British Bank of the Middle East, Bab Idriss, Leb., and stole between $20 million and $50 million. The money was never recovered.
Apr. 14: Burglars involved in the largest hotel robbery to date, in which approximately $6 million worth of gems were taken from safe-deposit boxes in the Palm Towers Hotel, Palm Beach, Fla., have never been caught.
June 1: Allen Leroy Anderson stole credit cards and a car from a halfway house director and started a five-month killing and robbing spree over at least twenty states that included the burglary of a California man's van and trailer.
July 16: Albert Spaggiari and nine accomplices were charged with stealing about $10 million worth of jewels, cash, bonds, and securities from safe-deposit boxes in a branch of the Société Générale in Nice, Fr. Spaggiari escaped before he could be tried.
August: A thief dubbed the "Termite burglar" burglarized Florida apartments and houses tented for fumigation, taking off with a total of $4,500 worth of goods.
1977
May 27: Approximately 7,000 watches worth a total of $1 million were stolen from a Queens, N.Y., warehouse.
1978
May 17: An unidentified person, or persons, removed the body of Charlie Chaplin, silent-film comedian, from his grave and dumped it in a Swiss cornfield.
Oct. 25: Stanley Mark Rifkin silently transferred $10.2 million to his New York bank account from the Security Pacific National Bank. Most of the money was returned after what was the largest bank theft in U.S. history to date.
1980
Sept. 6: Gerald Shallow, former Chicago police sergeant, received a fifteen-year prison term for stealing $2 million worth of gold and jewelry from Donald Bruce Co., Chicago.
1982
July 9: Michael Fagan tried to burglarize Buckingham Palace. He broke into Queen Elizabeth's bedroom and encountered the Queen, who talked with him until guards arrived. He was sent to an asylum for life.
1983
Randy Marsh, nineteen, was imprisoned for burglarizing northwest Chicago suburban homes of crystal, jewelry, and expensive figurines. He was suspected of committing more than 200 burglaries and claimed to have been involved in almost 1,000.
1984
Apr. 29: Burglars escaped with $3 million in jewelry from a vault in the Diamond Tower Exchange, Manhattan.
1986
Paul Centanni and his brother Ray were convicted of burglarizing homes throughout Chicago suburbs. Paul was suspected of committing 200 break-ins. He and his brother were imprisoned.
September: Michael Sherrill, twenty-five, claimed to have burglarized between 5,000 and 8,000 homes in several Chicago counties since he was twelve. He was convicted of four and imprisoned.
1987
Judy Amar burgled a string of Florida homes, taking between $3 million and $6 million in property over five years. She escaped in 1984 and continued her burglaries until being rearrested in 1987 and convicted of burglary and grand theft.

CAPITAL PUNISHMENT

The United States is one of only a handful of nations which continue to regard the death penalty as a natural deterrent to crime. Forty-one countries, including England, West Germany, Italy, the Netherlands, Israel, Switzerland, Ecuador, Costa Rica, and Honduras have now outlawed capital punishment on humanitarian grounds. Within the U.S., advocates of the death penalty argue that the checks and balances within the judicial system are exact and that the chances of the "wrong man" being put to death are remote. However, the history of the capital punishment in the U.S. is full of incidents which contradict this assertion. There was reasonable doubt about the guilt of the four Haymarket men, executed in Chicago in 1887, and the two Italians, Nicola Sacco and Bartolomeo Vanzetti, both accused of murdering a payroll guard in South Braintree, Mass., in 1920. Pennsylvania banned public executions in 1834. Michigan was the first to abolish the death penalty in 1847. Other states soon followed suit, but after periods of great political and social upheaval such as the Civil War and WWI, capital punishment regained popular support. As late as 1971, thirty-nine of fifty-four jurisdictions in the U.S. mandated the death penalty for such crimes as murder, rape, treason, arson, kidnapping, espionage, and train wrecking.

Although after 1947 the number of executions in the U.S. declined dramatically, the fierce debate on capital punishment reached the Supreme Court in 1972. That year, the justices found the death penalty was unconstitutional, ruling that it violated the Eighth Amendment's proviso against cruel and unusual punishment. The sentences of 648 convicted murderers were immediately commuted to life imprisonment. However, public opinion shifted in the next four years, so that by 1976 there was a strong outcry that the legislatures re-institute the death penalty. The Supreme Court reversed its earlier view and decided that capital punishment was not inherently cruel, supporting this viewpoint with statistics that showed a majority of Americans favoring execution by a 2-1 margin. On Jan. 17, 1977, Utah murderer Gary Gilmore's execution by a firing squad marked the return of the death penalty after nearly ten years.

MODERN METHODS

ELECTRIC CHAIR

Electrocution or death in the electric chair became a feasible form of capital punishment in the final quarter of the 19th century. The concept of using a charge of alternating current (AC) as a clean and humane means of executing a condemned criminal is said to have its origin in the marketplace. When attempting to demonstrate the dangers of alternating current, a supplier of direct current (DC) executed stray animals during a traveling exhibition. Once it had been shown that an orangutan the size of a small human could be killed instantly with an electrical charge, preparations were undertaken for the official use of an electric chair in carrying out a death sentence. The first electrocution took place at Auburn Prison, N.Y., on Aug. 6, 1890.

The chair usually is two-legged in back with a single, heavier leg in front. Extra-wide arms are fitted with straps to hold the arms of the criminal rigid, and other straps encase his chest and stomach. A tight mask is fitted over the face. Electrodes are fastened to one leg, and a "death cap" is attached to the shaved head. Once sure that everything is ready, the executioner throws a switch releasing 2,000 volts into the prisoner's body for fifty-seven seconds. The jolt pitches him against his bindings, makes his hair stand up, and turns his flesh the color of beets. Jolts of 1,000 volts, reduced to prevent unnecessary burning of the body, are used thereafter until the prisoner is dead. A post-mortem follows in a morgue attached to the execution chamber.

An efficient electrocution ideally is a three-minute affair. The lights never dim, as Hollywood would have you believe, since the juice to the chair is powered by a source separate from the room. Most experts insist electrocution is immediate and painless. Dr. Harold W. Kipp of Sing Sing, who attended more than 200 executions, said: "The effect of electricity is instantaneous brain death, What observers see are muscle contractions, not agony."

The electric chair has never been adopted outside the U.S.

GAS CHAMBER

In an attempt to provide a more humane method of executing prisoners, the state of Nevada introduced the gas chamber in 1924, and the method eventually was adopted by eleven other U.S. states. The most famous gas chamber in the world, outside of Germany's Holocaust sites during WWII, is the one at San Quentin. Since it was built in 1938, some dramatic executions have occurred there, among them Barbara Graham and Caryl Chessman.

The gassing takes place in a specially constructed "chair room." Under a chair in the chamber are shallow pans connected by tubing to a container outside the room. Above distilled water and sulfuric acid hangs a gauze bag filled with sixteen one-ounce pellets of cyanide. The prisoner is placed on the chair, his arms and legs are strapped, and a stethoscope is attached to his chest. A physician monitors the prisoner's condition by the connecting wire fed through a seal outside the chair room. The room itself is then sealed and the air drawn out by a powerful fan to let the gas fumes take effect more quickly.

At this juncture, the executioner pulls a lever which lowers the deadly gauze bag into the acid bowl. The gas fumes rise from beneath the prisoner's chair. Death comes quickly and painlessly in ten seconds if the prisoner breathes deeply, as he is advised to do. Frequently the will to live is so strong that he ignores the advice, thus suffering a pitiful death.

The doctor listens through his remote-control stethoscope for the cessation of heartbeats. When the prisoner is pronounced dead, the gas is sucked out of the room by a fan and the body sprayed with liquid ammonia to neutralize any lingering trace of hydrocyanic gas.

GUILLOTINE

The modern guillotine was introduced in France on April 25, 1792. A highwayman, Nicholas-Jacques Pelletier, became its first victim. Dr. Joseph-Ignace Guillotine, often but inaccurately called the device's inventor, merely advocated its adoption by France. He watched the initial proceedings, and felt pleased with the effectiveness and humaneness of the method. Later he said: "The victim does not suffer at all. He is conscious of nothing more than a slight chill on his neck." Previous to this time, beheading machines had been used in Persia, where they supposedly originated, and then in Scotland, England, Ireland, and various European countries.

The guillotine consists of two fifteen-foot upright posts surmounted by a crossbeam and grooved so as to guide a triangular steel blade. The honed metal is mounted on a weight which travels in the grooved uprights, which are greased with tallow. The prisoner, who has no knowledge that he is to die that day until he was awakened at dawn, is strapped to a tilting table positioned so that when it is turned horizontally his shaved neck fits into a notch, where it is ready to receive the death blow.

England had a beheading machine similar to the guillotine in the 16th century. Called the "Halifax Gibbet," it was a simple construction of two uprights and a crossbeam holding an ax. Attached to the ax and held to it by a pin was a long rope, which, at the appointed time, was pulled by the executioner, allowing the ax to fall, severing the prisoner's head. "The Iron Maiden" in Scotland at the same time, with minor adaptations, came into vogue after a Scottish nobleman, Earl of Morton, witnessed the "Halifax Gibbet" during a visit to England and was so impressed with its efficiency that he had a model of it made. The guillotine was consigned to history in 1981 when France abolished the death penalty.

HANGING

The ancient method of lawfully killing criminals by hanging (lynching is a hanging without legal sanction) is thought to have originated in Persia, from where it was carried to Europe by the Huns and to England by the Anglo-Saxons in the twelfth century. The early settlers introduced it to North America where it continued in vogue until the advent of the new execution methods of the gas chamber and the electric chair.

The earliest hangings were carried out simply by stringing up a felon to the branch of a tree, a process lynching mobs still used well into the 20th century. The first innovation, probably designed in England, consisted of a gallows fashioned from two poles supporting a crossbeam from which dangled a rope with a noose tied at its end. The prisoner would mount a ladder placed against a pole, the noose would be placed around his neck, and then the hangman would push the ladder away, leaving the felon suspended in the air to slowly strangle to death.

Experiments designed to make hanging more humane were carried out in the 18th century. They resulted, first, in the trap door method, a procedure that utilized a violent drop through space which would dislocate the prisoner's cervical vertebrae and ideally cause instant death. Further refining the goal of a "clean death," James Berry, the Yorkshire executioner from 1884 to 1892, devised a gallows with a series of drops based on a prisoner's weight, eight feet for a man weighing 196 pounds, for example. Finally it was found that if the knot of the noose were placed high up under the left jaw the drop would result in a violent snapback of the chin and a rupturing of the spinal cord, cutting off oxygen to the brain and paralyzing the rest of the body. Brain death would follow rapidly.

Modern-day hangings follow a set procedure. The execution hour is usually set for 8 a.m. First the noose, made of Italian hemp and consisting of five strands each capable of holding a one-ton dead weight, is dropped around the doomed man's neck and a black hood placed over his head. The hangman fixes the knot and binds the prisoner's legs together to prevent his kicking. The felon's body is centered over the trap door. On a signal, three men in a booth on the gallows platform each cut a string, one of which springs the trap door. The victim's thrashing at the end of the rope lasts for a few minutes. Finally, his violent shudders subside. There is one final twitch, then stillness.

INJECTION

Putting a criminal to death by injection—a procedure some death row prisoners refer to sardonically as "the ultimate high"—is the most recent "mercy" method of capital punishment being utilized in the U.S. Receiving a continuous intravenous injection of a barbiturate with a chemical paralyzing agent, the condemned man merely falls asleep and dies, officially of "coronary arrest."

The routine already is quite formalized. The doomed man is strapped to a wheelchair and carried to the execution site. There, three medical technicians stand behind a panel through which a tube connected to the prisoner's arm or leg has been passed. The technicians insert a dark liquid into the tube, and the injection into the doomed man is released. As in the outdated military firing squad technique, in which one of ten marksmen was supplied with a blank bullet, only one of the three technicians actually handles the lethal substance. Who administered the lethal injection is never known.

Though the argument is made that execution by injection is the most humane method of lawful killing, the American Medical Association stands staunchly against it. The Association passed a resolution in 1980 categorizing injection executions as unethical.

SHOOTING

Considering the widely held opinion that death by firing squad is as humane as "mercy killing" by injection, if not more so, it is surprising that death by bullet wounds never gained popularity in English-speaking countries. Favored among Russians from 1927 to 1947, and by Axis powers in WWI and WWII, the firing squad was re-introduced in 1951 by Josef Stalin for crimes involving national security. Reasons advanced for this include the fact that shooting executions are bloody affairs and too much like slaughter for society to generally accept. Another is that sometimes a marksmen will aim off target to make sure he does not fire the fatal bullet.

The firing squad follows an official procedure. The prisoner is strapped in a chair placed against a canvas-covered wall. Twenty feet away five marksmen holding .30-caliber rifles stand behind a canvas shroud, each rifle loaded with a single cartridge with one a blank so that all five men can later rationalize that they did not kill the prisoner. A doctor locates the heart of the felon and pins a cloth target over it. The marksmen then insert their weapons into slits in the canvas, and when the order is given they fire in unison. Four bullets then strike the prisoner in the area of the heart, bringing instantaneous and painless death.

ANCIENT METHODS

BEATING

The leaders of Imperial Rome selected their methods of capital punishment to impress upon the people the perils of breaking the law and to encourage them to become accessories after the fact of murder. An effective method was beating the felon to death.

A sentence of death by beating was, in most cases, an invitation for the populace to join in the act. Armed with staves they would gather at the site of the execution and greet the prisoner with verbal abuse as he was led before them. The shouting would increase as the prisoner was bound and the binding passed through a metal ring set in the wall. Two guards then would break the prisoner's legs with heavy sticks and motion the spectators forward, who would obey with alacrity, hitting him on every part of his body until he was a broken, bloody mess of bones and flesh when he would be left to die.

BEHEADING

Beheading was the first form of public execution. As a method of capital punishment beheading took place in the Egyptian empire in 1580 B.C. It is mentioned in the Ancient Laws of China as the prescribed mode of legal executions. The ancient Greeks and Romans regarded beheading as the most honorable form of death.

Originally the executioner used an ax. Later the Romans adopted the sword, considering it a more refined instrument of death. Dexterity in using it, especially at a chopping block, was regarded a special skill in the army, as is marksmanship today. When the practice was adopted in England by William the Conqueror in 1076 it was reserved for prisoners of high rank. One consequence of the French Revolution, was to spread the punishment to offenders of ordinary birth by means of the beheading machine, the guillotine,

The practice is now rare in European countries but still is used occasionally in some Muslim nations. It was the prescribed method of execution in the German Penal Code until Germany abolished the death penalty after WWII. It was used extensively by Japanese officers against allied prisoners during WWII.

BLACK MASS

A blasphemous and usually obscene burlesque of a Roman Catholic requiem mass by depraved religious apostates is called a Black Mass. The celebrant wears black vestments.

In the satanic Black Mass of the Dark Ages, the execution of a virgin for the purpose of violating her body was an integral part of the performance, with the murder and the following copulation called "worship." In the proceedings, a group of naked women fall to the floor of the "church" and roll, writhing, on the carpet, inhaling an anesthetizing substance. One woman is then selected for the sacrifice, and, probably numbed by the incense and in the grip of religious frenzy, is stretched across the top of an altar. A priest then kills her by plunging a cross sharpened to a dagger-like point into her heart.

The priest, naked under his robe, then performs cunnilingus on the corpse, followed by coitus, both witnessed by the "congregation," which then plunges into a sexual orgy among themselves.

Charges of holding blasphemous black masses have been made against the clergy and against heretics and persons accused of witchcraft since early Christian times. During the 19th century, Freemasons were suspected of engaging in sexual satanism, a form of necrophilia inspired by the close relationship between threatened death and abnormal sexual cravings that is a long-established psychological fact.

BLEEDING

Though many capital punishment deaths caused by bleeding have occurred, most of them were accidental when the executioner or the weapon used were at fault. Few recorded bleedings have been as deliberate as one that occurred in Gascony in the 16th century. For simplicity and directness, it cannot be excelled. The condemned man, convicted of sodomy, was led through the streets on horseback clothed in black and the horse covered in a black saddle cloth. At the execution site the prisoner was made to kneel against a railing, his throat was carefully cut, and then he was laid out on black, cloth-covered boards to bleed to death.

Another hideous method was one reported in China, where, the condemned was placed against a crosspiece and his hands cut off at the wrists. These were stanched with a flaming torch to prevent him from bleeding to death too quickly. Then, the executioner carefully made razor-like incisions the full length of the body and the thief slowly bled to death.

BOILING

The direct burning of a lawbreaker was thought barbaric in 15th century England, so a method was devised to parboil the offender first before gibbeting and hanging him in chains. The method adopted was fiendish. A public place was selected and the felon hung over it while a cauldron of water heated to a boil under him. Then a signal was given, and the man was dropped into a pot. If he tried to grab the hot sides of the cauldron to try to escape, the executioner poked him back into the water with a long pole. Fished out finally, he was hauled off to his doom.

In 1531 Henry VIII made boiling legal. The first culprit killed under the new law, a cook accused of attempting to poison the Bishop of Rochester's household, was publicly boiled to death in a cauldron suspended from an iron tripod over a pile of burning logs. Another boiling death, of a servant who had poisoned her mistress, took place the same year, and a third, another servant, was boiled to death in 1542. Edward VI repealed the law in 1547 and substituted hanging or burning.

Boiling condemned persons to death has long been an accepted practice in Africa and some parts of Asia, notably among the Japanese who used the method on the Christian clergy and sailors during the Kamakura shogunate of 1603-1867 during its policy of isolation.

BURIAL ALIVE

A particularly grotesque method of putting prisoners to death originated in the 15th century among the Chinese to punish captured marauders operating along the rich trade routes leading to the Chinese capital of Peking. The soil of the Mongolian lowlands when mixed with straw and water hardened to a cement-like substance. Into this soil and along the trade route, the bandits would be encased up to their necks, straw and water added, and the pressure of the slowly hardening soil slowly choked them to death, making them useful into eternity as signposts guiding the way north and south.

Far to the west at the same time, Persian courts were sentencing criminals to a Wailing Wall, a double wall that lined a road on the outskirts of the city, the felons' hands and feet tightly pinned by the walls. Unable to eat food lying inches from their mouths, and frequently taunted by passing townspeople, the wailing, crying, starving men met a slow, excruciating death or went insane.

Burial alive never was adopted in the Western world until Germany resorted to the practice for many of its genocide victims in WWII.

BURNING

No use of burning as punishment has ever rivaled those that took place during the 500 years of the dread Inquisition, when the Spanish went so far as to erect *braseros,* or "burning places," in every one of its major cities. Here as many as hundredd of people, Jews, Mohammedans, convicts, and heretics, would be burned at one time before witnesses from every class of society, since attendance at these mass burnings was made obligatory by the authorities. When a particularly large burning was scheduled, a front section of the spectator gallery was cordoned off for members of the clergy, who thus had a front-row seat of the flaming pyres. In the eleven years of the reign of Grand Inquisitor Tomás de Torquemada (1483-1494) more than 10,000 persons were burned, and this was only at the beginning of the Inquisition.

Fire as a method of killing people has been used through the ages. Two thousand years before Christ, King Hammurabi of Babylonia decreed burning as punishment for anybody who destroyed a neighbor's possessions by arson. Assyrians used it as an instrument of terror in their conquest of Israel. French and Spanish inquisitors broadened and refined the ordeal. And in North America, the Puritans stoically burned "witches" while across the woods Indians war-danced around a pyre containing whites.

CRUCIFIXION

Jesus Christ, the most famous victim of crucifixion, followed a line of similar victims from the 6th century B.C. in one of the most significant methods of capital punishment among the Persians, Seleucids, Jews, Carthaginians, and Romans. Regarded as degrading and most painful, it was reserved for slaves and the worst of felons, and finally was abolished in the Roman Empire in 337 A.D. by Constantine the Great.

There were many methods of performing the punishment, but usually the condemned man was forced to drag the crossbeam of his cross to the place of punishment, where a shaft already was fixed to the ground. He was then nailed by the wrists to the crossbeam, the beam raised nine to twelve feet high against the shaft, and the man's feet bound or nailed to the shaft. Over his head was placed a notice stating his name and his crime. Death was caused by exhaustion or heart failure.

A particularly hideous form of crucifixion was carried out in Japan until the 19th century featuring a combination of crucifixion and impalement. The condemned man was tied to a cross by ropes and the executioner given four light spears with which, depending on whether he had been bribed or not, he quickly ended the man's life with the first spear, which struck his heart. If the prisoner was poor or had committed a particularly heinous crime, the four spears were inserted slowly into his body, carefully aimed to miss the vital spots, and death came with painful slowness.

DISEMBOWELMENT

A distinctly English punishment for treason, drawing and quartering was first inflicted in 1283 on the Welsh prince David and in 1305 on a Scotch patriot, Sir William Wallace. In 1351 the Statute of Treason was passed, which ordained that the method of punishment should be, first, that the traitor was drawn to the execution site, hung until nearly dead, then cut down and his entrails cut out of his body and burned. Following this his head would be cut off, the body divided into four parts, and afterward set out in an open space to be viewed by the public. The sentence was last passed on two Irish Fenians in 1867 but never carried out.

DRAWING AND QUARTERING, See: **DISEMBOWELMENT.**

DUCKING AND DROWNING

Though the Roman punishment for parricides was to throw them into the water in a sack containing also a dog, a cock, a viper, and an ape who all would struggle in the sack to survive, ducking and drowning was a peculiarly English and Scottish sentence inflicted on convicted witches along with burning. Four and a half centuries before Christ, the Britons inflicted death on felons by drowning them in a quagmire. Then it was in vogue from 1556 until 1697 when a woman convicted of theft was sentenced in Scotland and was drowned in the Loch of Spyne. Most barons had a drowning pit on their land, and one, the owner of a castle in London, was given the right by King John to drown traitors in the Thames.

Drowning also was the fate of sorcerers and witches in France, and Phillippe Auguste used this punishment on persons who swore. Under Charles VI, drowning was the penalty for sedition, a form of capital punishment that did not disappear until the end of Louis XI's reign in the late 15th century.

In England and Scotland the drowning procedure seldom varied. The man or woman was led to the water's edge, placed on a ducking stool, which was a seat attached to a plank, and there tied by the hands to the seat. The executioner then lifted the farther end of the plank, submerging the prisoner and the seat until the felon was dead.

EXPOSURE

Capital punishment by exposure was often the fate of criminals or slaves when undergoing crucifixion by the Romans. It was a highly specialized performance with a whipping as a preliminary to crucifixion. This was done with the scourge, a many-tailed whip with small pieces of bone embedded in the tips to tear the flesh. Once hoisted to the cross, the condemned man's bones were broken throughout his body and he would live for two or three days exposed to the elements before he died.

FLOGGING

Whipping a criminal or a slave to death commonly took place in the ancient world, especially when slaves were sufficiently numerous to be of little value. However, in general, flogging has been used in the home, school, the armed forces, and in prisons as a form of punishment and to preserve discipline. Flogging to death flourished in France in the 14th century and was not legally abolished until 1791. In Scotland alone among the British Isles it still is used as capital punishment for mutiny, incitement to mutiny, or gross personal violence to an officer of a prison when committed by a male.

The instruments used for flogging to death include the lash, most notably its wicked elaboration, the cat-o'-nine-tails, nine knotted cords or thongs of rawhide attached to a handle. Even more painful and deadly is the Russian knout, which consists of dried and hardened thongs of rawhide interwoven with wire, the wires often hooked and sharpened. Flogging to death is a method of killing that lends itself to great brutality, such as pouring salt into the prisoner's lacerations during the beating to increase the pain.

GARROTTING

To Austria and Spain goes the onerous distinction of developing probably the cruelest death-dealing method ever devised, and to the Spanish descendants of the Inquisition its most sadistic application.

A comparatively modern mode of legal killing and still the official method of execution in Spain, garroting (called hanging in Austria) is an offshoot of the wheel, a torturous form of execution once popular in Germany and France. The simplest form of garotte is a double cord passed through a hole in an upright post. The loop of the cord goes around the victim's neck, the free ends are pulled, and the man dies of strangulation. Modifications led to an iron collar passed around the felon's neck and the upright post. A screw is passed through the collar and slowly tightened against the post until death ensues.

Presently, two more "humane" garrotes have been adopted. In one, the collar contains two rings, an upper and a lower, both operated in opposing directions by screws. Tightening the screws simultaneously draws the upper part of the vertebra forward and the lower one back, snapping the spinal column and causing instant death. In the other, the screw presses against a knife which projects through the post. As the screw is turned, the knife advances, finally to pierce the victim's neck, splitting the spinal column.

The garotte was introduced to North America following the Spanish-American War, and four prisoners were executed by this method in Puerto Rico in 1902. Official photographs were taken of the event, a gala occasion for the populace, and the embarrassment this caused resulted in ending this form of punishment forever in the U.S.

GIBBETING

A form of execution with a macabre twist, gibbeting, a post-hanging ritual, was well advanced in England before the "lynch law" in the wild American West began leaving rustlers, murderers, and card sharks swinging from the trees to amuse or terrorize the settlers. Usually in Britain a hanged prisoner was exhibited in an iron cage placed on a roadside. Another form of exhibiting the dead culprit was to throw the body into a cauldron of boiling tar to preserve it for a length of time. Then the body was taken out of the vat, placed in symbolic chains, riveted into a "suit" of crisscrossing metal strips, and exhibited along a well-traveled road. See: **GUILLOTINE.**

IMPALEMENT

Casting a criminal on pointed stakes is an execution method going as far back as Nero, the extravagant debaucher who ruled Rome from 54-68 A.D. As punishment for a slave caught in the act of theft, he ordered him to dig his own grave. A sharp stick then was embedded in the bottom of the grave, with its point facing upward. At Nero's pleasure, the executioner would then hurl the victim into the grave groin first, to lie there in agony for more than a day before dying, or, on simpler occasions, the victim would be thrown into the grave so that the stick pierced his heart and killed him instantly.

Impalement also was practiced as late as 1876 in the Balkan Peninsula of Albania, Bulgaria, Rumania, and Yugoslavia, and under Charles V of England in the 16th century. Impalement as a form of death-dealing also was widely practiced by the Japanese in WWII and by the Viet Cong during the Vietnam War.

MAZZATELLO

A decidedly brutal method of execution was developed by the Italians in the papal states, the "States of the Church" in central Italy ruled by the popes until 1870.

The mazza or mazzatello, named after the mallet or poleax used in the killing, began with the prisoner, accompanied by a priest, being led to a scaffold erected in a public square. On the platform lay a coffin. Above it the executioner, masked and dressed in black, raised the mallet or poleax, swung it round in the air to gain momentum, and brought it down on the head of the prisoner, much like the mallet swingers in a stockyards on the heads of cattle. Finally the executioner would cut the throat of the fallen man to make sure the job was done. Not until the coming of the Italian patriot and master of guerrilla warfare Giuseppe Garibaldi and the formation of a United Italy in 1861 was the practice abolished.

MUTILATION

Dismembering a prisoner's body after death by hanging or torture or any of the other modes of capital punishment was meant to inspire fear or provide a catharsis over a particularly ignoble crime. William the Conqueror ordered that no person should be hanged or otherwise put to death for any offense whatsoever, but that did not prevent prisoners from being mutilated and dying as a result.

In England parricide often was punished by mutilation. In one case, a man found guilty of cursing his father and suspected of murdering him, was punished by having his tongue cut out, his right hand cut off and his body carried to the scaffold in chains. In France in 1757, Robert-François Damiens, a French fanatic who attempted to kill Louis XV by stabbing and was condemned as a regicide, was pulled to pieces by horses in the Place de Grève. Before Damiens was executed, the hand that had tried to kill the king was burned off. He was tortured for four hours with red-hot pincers, and molten wax, lead, and boiling oil were poured into his wounds.

POISONING

Banishment was the punishment for heinous crimes and burning and crucifixion were the accepted modes of capital punishment in the Greece of Socrates' time. However, Socrates the philosopher was held in such high regard that he was given a relatively painless way to die by swallowing hemlock. The result of the drink was a gradual deadening of his feet and hands, followed by the limbs, and finally the heart. For society, Socrates' death was a unique event, since poisoning had never been a formalized way of legal execution.

PRESSING

Less a legal form of execution in English law than any other method, pressing a felon to death became a regular mode of punishing persons who, arraigned for felony, refused to plead or wilfully stood in contempt of court.

This horrible death finds the naked offender placed on his back on the floor and then his body loaded with iron weights and stones which press him down until he cannot move. Thereafter he is fed morsels of bread and water until he dies.

Illegal pressing was a feature adopted by jailers during the Inquisition in Spain. A young woman suspected of trying to report the jailers' licentious conduct toward her would be stripped and placed on her back in a dungeon fitted with four metal rings on the floor. Her arms and legs were stretched out and she was tied to the metal hoops by her wrists and ankles so that she lay spread-eagled. A series of stones then was piled on her breasts and abdomen, with the pressure being added gradually until one weight too many was placed on her, and she met an "accidental death."

STARVATION

Starvation as a mode of capital punishment among the Romans was a minor method of disposing of the guilty in an empire noted for its brutal attitude toward capital punishment and methods of execution. Chiefly starvation deaths were committed on a hymen-less Vestal Virgin, who would be denounced for her corrupting influence and sentenced to death. Her execution, conducted on a hillside far from the city and witnessed by as many people as possible, would take place in a cave or a hole dug in the hill. After incantations were said, she would be consigned to the cave without food or water and wearing only a light garment. The hole then was closed with stones and earth, a guard posted, and death would follow from starvation, exposure, or suffocation.

STONING

The ancient laws of Moses, which have exerted a lasting influence on the religious life, moral concerns, and social ethics of Western civilization, contained a long list of civil offenses the Jewish prophet said should be punished by stoning. The method prescribed was for the guilty person to be taken to a location marked for such executions by a pile of stones waiting on the ground and a crowd of executioners standing around it, each one holding a heavy stone in his hand. Into this throng would come the accuser, dressed in white, whose role by law was that he should cast the first stone. That done, the surrounding throng would hurl their stones at the victim, again and again even after the condemned was dead, as the continuing hail of stones formed an execution mound. To complete the harshness of the sentence, his property was confiscated and sometimes his relatives were stoned to death as well.

STRANGLING, See: GAROTTING, THE WHEEL.

TORTURE

No crueller time in the history of capital punishment existed than in the period just prior to and during the Middle Ages, when, as the number of capital crimes increased, so did the sadistic ingenuity of the authorities in dealing with them. Torture was in evidence and soon became, if not the chief mode of execution, a necessary part of it. Not standing alone as a class itself of executions, so many persons died undergoing torture before they were to be killed that it deserves mention in any classification of ancient methods of legal killing. See: **BOILING, DISEMBOWELING, IMPALEMENT, MUTILATION, PRESSING, STONING, THE WHEEL.**

THE WHEEL

This fiendish method of punishing criminals, an offshoot of crucifixion and a forerunner of the garotte, underwent several transformations. First used in Germany and France, it featured a large oak wheel placed in the center of town where the prisoner was led. Stripped to a loin cloth, the prisoner was tied to the wheel with his wrists and ankles extending over the rim. An executioner first smashed the arms and legs with an iron bar so that the pulverized bones fitted around the outside of the wheel, and then he wheeled the culprit around town. Finally, the executioner would strike the man solidly on the rib cage with the iron bar and death came soon after.

A modification to this method later was adopted when it became too obvious to ignore that it was extremely brutal. A rope was attached to the rim of the wheel close to the victim's neck so that when it was determined that he had suffered enough, the executioner could pull on the rope and strangle the man.

The Spanish Inquisitors also used the Wheel in their rape and blood-letting exploitation of the Netherlands in the middle of the 16th century, a mass murder orgy that rivals anything of its kind in human history, including the WWII atrocities by the Germans and Japanese. See: **CRUCIFIXION, GAROTTING.**

PUNISHMENTS

BRANK

Sometimes called "the gossip's bridle," the brank was first described in England in 1623, though there are hints of one form of it being used earlier in Scotland. It was last used in Altrincham, England, in 1824.

Used chiefly on outspoken women who had offended a town official, spoken out to a wrongdoer, or scolded their husbands, the brank was a face cage made of iron in front of which was a spiked piece of iron. The spike was so placed that if the woman attempted to move her tongue in any way it would be severely injured. The woman then would be led through the streets by a chain, subjected to the taunts of the townspeople and sometimes their physical abuse. In some towns, she would be chained to a pillory, whipping post, or market cross. The shapes, sizes, and tongue-restraining devices in the mask were as varied as men's imaginations could devise. Sometimes, but rarely, the brank was used on male paupers and blasphemers.

BOOK BURNING

Authors whose words incensed the authorities frequently were brought into public contempt by the Greeks and Romans of antiquity who burned their books or scrolls. In the days of Augustus, for example, 20,000 volumes were thrown into the flames on one occasion. Throughout the centuries the Bible itself has often been publicly burned.

In England, Milton's books were burned by a hangman in 1659, and subsequently publishers joined their authors in being nailed to the pillory by the ears. Frequently the ears would be cut off and left hanging on the post when the culprits finally were freed. Book burning was a frequent tactic resorted to by the Puritans in North America to silence heretical writers. A large number of monastery books, up to 4.1 million, were burned in France in 1790. Germany, singular in the civilized world, burned books they found politically or morally inciting as recently as 1945.

DRUNKARD'S CLOAK

The practice of clothing a drunkard or some other social nuisance in a barrel and parading him through the streets seems to have originated in Holland and Germany in the middle of the 17th century. From there it passed on to a section of England called Newcastle-on-Tyne and thence, briefly, to the U.S. During the Civil War a soldier in punishment drill was seen by an observer of the federal army with his head poking through one end of a barrel from which the bottom end had been sawed off.

Generally the barrel had a hole cut out at one end through which the culprit's head would protrude, and two holes cut in the sides for his hands. The bottom of the barrel was cut out so that the barrel would cover the body down to the small of the legs. Thus arrayed, the victim would be forced to march before the townspeople.

FINGER PILLORY

An extremely painful punishment administered in England during the latter half of the 17th century as domestic punishment for relatively minor offenses such as roistering about on feast days or servants breaking the rules of Christmas was the finger pillory.

Made of oak and clamped to a wall, the stock has two sections, a hinged top and a rigid bottom in which holes have been dug to hold the fingers down to the second joint. When the stock is closed the finger of the culprit is confined in the holes and if held long in this posture it could result in excruciating pain.

JOUGS

Employed in Holland and probably other European countries, jougs as a form of punishment was most often used in England and Scotland for a hundred or so years beyond the 16th century. It was a popular means of enforcing ecclesiastical discipline and for punishing persons guilty of small infractions of the law or of household rules.

The jougs consist of an iron ring or collar with a hinge to enable it to be opened or closed, like a key chain ring. Affixed to it are loops for a padlock to secure it around the neck of the culprit. The jougs themselves are attached to an iron chain leaded into a wall, and here the offender stands whatever hours the sentence reads.

PILLORY

Many of England's noblest personages have suffered the pain and indignity of the pillory as a mode of punishment. Although in use in other European countries, the pillory became the chief form of punishment in England, even by lords of manors who enjoyed the right of a pillory on their lands. In use from the 14th century to 1837, the pillory was abolished by an act of Parliament.

In the earlier times, a pillory, a whipping post, and stocks generally were combined in one torture post. As the pillory became more popular, it soon was accorded its own structure and usually one could be seen in every market place in the kingdom. Though many variations of it existed, including one in Touraine in west-central France which was designed to hold a number of persons, the pillory is a wooden frame with holes in which the prisoner's head and hands can be locked. It was not uncommon for offenders to be killed on the pillory by the rock-throwing they were subjected to by furious crowds of onlookers.

PUBLIC PENANCE

Religious discipline is behind this humbling form of punishment, and even kings and queens have suffered it. Most notably was England's Henry II, who caused the murder of St. Thomas Becket. Afterward, King Henry visited Becket's grave in Canterbury Cathedral, spent the day in fasting, and then, in the presence of the monks, disrobed and presented his shoulders for them to lash.

Early penance was done in many ways. The lash was used, as in King Henry's case. Carrying extremely heavy weights to an altar was another, as was carrying faggots round and round a church and the wearing of white sheets to symbolize unchastity. During most of these penances, the body was symbolically humbled by the penitent walking barefoot and wearing a cloth over the head.

REPENTANCE STOOL

Persons guilty of adultery frequently were sentenced to the repentance stool in the middle of 16th century Scotland. This was a wooden stool with four legs and a crude footrest jutting out from the stool. Here the penitents were forced to sit in open view of the congregation during a church ceremony and suffer in silence the opprobrium of having done something wrong.

RIDING THE STANG

The Stang was an English punishment for husbands who beat their wives or cheated on them or allowed themselves to be henpecked. The method of carrying out the punishment was for young men in the village to gather as public censors against the man accused and ride the stang for three successive nights. The stang was a pole or ladder on which the wittiest man in the village sat as it was carried through town atop the shoulders of the others. As he went, with stick and pan, he led the music of the crowd who beat kettles, pans, pots, or anything else that would make a din. About every fifty yards the processions stopped and the mounted man read a proclamation or proclaimed a rhyme suitable for the occasion. Thereafter, the gathering retired to an open space and burned an effigy of the accused man.

STOCKS

Stocks were used at an early period in England and Scotland as a means of punishing lawbreakers and also as a means of securing offenders. Villages were by law compelled to erect stocks at their own expense and at that time the chief constable could hold offenders in them but could not use them for punishment. This had changed by 1605, when it was decreed that persons convicted of drunkenness should be fined and placed in the stocks. By the 18th century the list of offenses deserving of the stock had widened to include drunkenness in church and public swearing, card sharking and gambling in general, disorderly conduct, and even spreading scandal.

Stocks usually were placed in the center of town and consisted of two slabs of oak indented similarly so that when joined they allowed holes through which a man's legs could protrude. Sentences to be spent in them ranged from hours to days, depending on the severity of the offense.

WHIPPING

Whipping was another peculiarly English custom for punishing the errant in its communities, and for a long time payments for private citizens using the lash against children and servants formed important contributions to parish accounts. The Whipping Act was passed in 1530, during the reign of Henry VIII, making it law that vagrants be beaten with whips until their bodies were bloodied. Various modifications to the law followed until the reign of Queen Elizabeth, when some alterations were made easing the cruelties of some whippings. Thereafter persons were not to be publicly whipped while naked, except from the middle upward, and the whipping post was substituted by the whipping cart, to whose rear end the offender was tied while receiving the lashing with a whip composed of three cords.

COMPUTER CRIME

Computer fraud is the newest, and therefore most difficult, crime to detect. The scope of technology in the last forty years has brought the computer to the forefront of business and industry, and with it, new opportunities for enterprising thieves. Because there is no fool-proof way to ensure the absolute security of a system, computer hackers with a criminal bent have found it easy to tap into a system, sometimes as easily as dialing up a phone number and touch-toning coded instructions. In one instance a bank employee simply transferred $120,000 from various accounts to those belonging to several friends.

One of the earliest computer frauds involved the Equity Funding Corporation. Between 1964 and 1973 a skilled computer con man created 64,000 fake insurance policies in an operation that involved $2 billion in funds. To combat the growing menace of computer fraud, the FBI has worked closely with business and industry to develop the necessary hardware to circumvent would-be thieves. Of course the discovery of each new criminal method brings with it corresponding breakthroughs in technology to ensure that such a thing cannot occur twice. However, we are still a long way from solving all the inherent security problems that plague the computer industry.

1964
$5 million of stolen computer software was sold to Texaco by Robert F. Hancock.

1968
A man walked into the State Unemployment Office in Olympia, Wash., shooting an IBM 1401 computer twice with a pistol. The computer was dented but continued functioning.

1970s
The United States Army in South Korea lost $18 million worth of supplies which were diverted by computer technicians, who later resold the material.

1970
Damages were estimated at $400,000 when computers at Fresno State College were bombed.
Students at New York University placed gasoline bombs on a computer belonging to the Atomic Energy Commission. They demanded $100,000 to pay bail for a jailed member of the Black Panthers. The bombs were defused without incident.
Aug. 24: Computers at the Army Mathematics Research Center at the University of Wisconsin were damaged by an exploded bomb. One person was killed and three injured. Physical damage was $2.5 million. Estimated damage due to loss of data was $16 million.

1971
Honeywell employees, angered with the company, sabotaged its Metropolitan Life computer network, shutting it down for over a month.
Feb. 19: An unidentified man was arrested in Palo Alto, Calif. for the theft of the "Plot/Trans" computer program from Information Systems Design, Inc. valued at $1 million. He was fined $5,000 and was put on three years' probation.

1972
An unidentified computer operator was arrested for short-circuiting a National Farmers Union Service Corporation computer with a car key.
A computer operator for the New York City Board of Elections was arrested for vote-fraud after padding a computerized list of registered voters with the names of unregistered ones.
Feb. 17: Jerry Neal Schneider was indicted for theft in Los Angeles and later sentenced to sixty days on a prison farm. He had placed false orders through a computer at Pacific Telephone & Telegraph and later resold the electronic equipment.

1973
A clerk for the A. Cowen & Co. brokerage house in New York was arrested for embezzling $170,000.
A Burke Sales Co. employee awaits sentencing in Washington after pleading guilty to embezzling $21,000 over a two-year period.
Two Consolidated Edison employees pleaded guilty in New York to embezzling $25,000 by using a computer to change accounting records.
A list of drivers' names and addresses was stolen from a computer at the Illinois Driver Registration Bureau by an unidentified man. The list, valued at $70,000, was used for direct-mailing.
Twenty-nine people were involved in a conspiracy to embezzle $2.8 million from the Steel City National Bank in Chicago.
August: An employee of Westinghouse was indicted in New York for embezzling $1 million. He and six accomplices, also indicted, manipulated the company's computer to issue them forged drafts.
Nov. 1: Stanley Goldblum, the chairman of the board of Equity Funding Corporation of America, and several other corporate officers were indicted on computer-fraud charges. For several years, Equity Funding had listed $185 million-worth of fake insurance policies to drive up stock prices.

1974
Two Department of Motor Vehicles employees were arrested in New York and charged with bribery and forgery for selling drivers licenses.
A Digital Equipment Corp. employee was arrested in Maynard, Mass., for stealing $750,000 worth of computer components.
A Massachusetts State Police officer and the president of a detective agency were found not guilty. They had been charged with selling computerized police records for credit and employee-screening purposes.
Computers at Wright-Patterson Air Force Base were sabotaged in four separate incidents over a six-month period, one using a magnet to destroy stored data. No suspects were apprehended.
July: The head of Dataspecs Computer Services, Inc., his wife and an employee were indicted on arson charges in Santa Ana, Calif., after Computeristics, Inc. was destroyed by fire.
Aug. 15: Masatoshi Tashiro kidnapped a baby in Tokyo and attempted to collect a $16,500 ransom through an automated teller machine. He was arrested as he collected the money.

1975
Bertram Seidlitz was convicted of fraud in Maryland. He had stolen the WYLBUR computer program from Optimum Services, Inc.
$190,500 was stolen from Electrolux Corp. in Georgia by computer file tampering. A former payroll supervisor pleaded guilty to the theft.
Three unidentified men were arrested and charged with the theft of $20 million worth of fuel from the Exxon Corporation in Linden, N.J. The men had manipulated computer records of fuel transfers for seven years and siphoned off the fuel for later resale.
Nine men were arrested in Germany for selling IBM technical secrets to Eastern European spies.
A Michigan Welfare Department worker was convicted of mail fraud after having entered false information into a computer, causing fifteen of her friends to receive checks worth more than $25,000.
March: An employee of TRW Credit Data was indicted for credit-fraud. He had, since August, 1974, altered computerized credit histories.
December: An unidentified Los Angeles man was arrested for theft of computer time. The man illegally gained access to a Manufacturing Data Systems, Inc. computer for 143 hours, valued at $15,000.

1976
Two Blue Cross employees were indicted for creating false insurance claims on a computer.
A former employee of Sears Roebuck and a police officer were arrested and charged with larceny. The employee had entered false merchandise information into a computer, stealing $10,000.
A University of Maryland Hospital employee caused $100,000 worth of damage after ripping out wires and a master switch from the hospital's computer. He was charged with malicious vandalism.
May: Fifteen armed terrorists belonging to Unita Combattenti Communiste firebombed computers at a government tax office in Rome.

1977
An AT&T clerk pleaded guilty to grand theft and served thirty days in jail after she processed false overtime reports for herself.
Two employees at the California Department of Justice pleaded no contest to malicious mischief after they erased information from a file of criminal histories.
A Drug Enforcement Agency agent stole computer printouts for the purpose of helping drug smugglers identify informants. The agent pleaded not guilty to the charges in New Haven, Conn.
The president of Executive Securities Corp. was indicted in Newark, N.J., for securities fraud and other charges. He had attempted to cover up the company's failure to make a stock acquisition.
The First National Bank of Boston Assistant Controller pleaded guilty to embezzling $350,000 by transferring funds into his personal account.
A Fort Meyers, Fla., School Board payroll supervisor embezzled $109,000 by overcharging schools and altering computer records.
Two computer programmers stole computer time from Sperry Univac. The used the company's computers to run a sheet music business.
The Union Planters National Bank was the victim of fraud in Tennessee. Two men were indicted for making false deposits at an automated teller machine and later withdrawing $3,885 of the money.
January: An unidentified programmer for Imperial Chemical Industries, Ltd. was arrested in London. The man had stolen computer-tape records, demanding a ransom of £200,000.
June: Three women and one man, suspected of belonging to the terrorist group Unita Combattenti Communiste, firebombed an academic computer facility in Rome. Damage was reported above $2 million.

1978
Oct. 25: Stanley Mark Rifkin stole $10.2 million from the Security Pacific National Bank in Los Angeles by transferring money via computer into a personal account in New York. He was later caught with diamonds he had bought with the stolen money.

1980
September: DePaul University computers were accessed through a modem by two Illinois high school students who threatened to disable the system unless they were given access to a special program.

1981
January: Boxing promoter Harold J. Smith and accomplice Benjamin Lewis were wanted by the FBI for the fraudulent transfer of $21 million from the Wells Fargo Bank of San Francisco into personal accounts.
December: Two employees of the Central Fidelity Bank in Lynchburg, Va., were convicted for stealing a computer list of securities customers.

1982
January: An employee of the People's Savings Bank in Bridgeport,

Conn., was arrested. She used a computer to divert $37,487 into her personal account.
May: It was reported that a Magnetic Peripherals, Inc. employee stole $155,000 by creating false invoices on her computer.
May: Several employees of the University of Maryland Hospital were charged with embezzlement. They had used the hospital's computers to process false invoices.
June: A Texaco, Inc. employee and his wife were charged with theft. The man had put his wife's name on a computer list of accounts payable. He then ordered the computer to pay his wife $18,000.
August: A former supervisor at the Bank of New England was indicted in Boston for embezzling $30,000. He substituted his name for the names on customer accounts.
August: False invoices were used by the head of the development laboratory at Gould, Inc. to steal $300,000 in cash and computer equipment.
November: Theodore C. Langevin was arrested for illegally gaining access to a Federal Reserve Board computer to obtain money-supply figures for investment use.
December: Two insiders attempted to defraud the Bank of America and Merrill Lynch of $200,000. The two altered computerized account records and attempted to draw on those accounts. Only $17,000 was taken before the scheme was uncovered.
1983
Southern Illinois University was the victim of fraud. Two employees pleaded guilty to buying and leasing computer equipment at inflated prices from false companies. Damages were estimated at $1.3 million.
March: The head of the foreign transfer department of the Slavenburg Bank in Rotterdam, Neth. was arrested for embezzling $65 million. He had broken a computer code which allowed him to transfer bank funds to personal accounts.
August: The FBI investigated Gerald R. Wondra in connection with computer-hacking incidents at the Sloan-Kettering Cancer Center in New York. Wondra allegedly tampered with patients' files for fun.
1984
Two members of the 414 computer hackers' group pleaded guilty in Wisconsin to two counts of using their computer modems to make prank telephone calls.
April: Ronald Austin was arraigned in Los Angeles on twelve counts of illegally accessing an airline computer to order tickets.
1985
The computer files of the Los Angeles Department of Water and Power were frozen when a "logic bomb," an illegal software coding, was activated.
August: Jefferson County, Colo., District Attorney Nolan Brown was convicted of computer crime, forgery and abuse of public records. He attempted to delete two speeding tickets to reduce his insurance rate. He was sentenced to five days in jail, four years probation, a $2,000 fine and 200 hours of community service.
1987
June: It was reported that Robert Post jumped bail in New York. He was arrested for gaining access to automated teller machines and stealing $86,000 from other peoples' accounts.
1988
May 13: Gabriel Taylor, aided by six other men, illegally made an electronic transferral of $68.7 million from First National Bank of Chicago to personal accounts in Vienna.
December: A computer hacker violated federal laws by gaining unauthorized access to the computer at the Lawrence Livermore National Laboratory. No files were altered. The hacker was not caught.

DRUGS

According to an ancient Egyptian papyrus, drug prescriptions were big business as early as 3700 B.C. Initially used in religious rites and as poison, narcotics quickly developed into an extremely profitable business venture. Today, trafficking in drugs is a multi-billion dollar international operation, and over the past two decades, strong evidence exists suggesting that the drug trade is promoted as a political and economic weapon by one country against another.

10,000 B.C.
Evidence suggests that the use of cannabis occurred for the first time on an island in what is now Taiwan.
c.3000 B.C.
Sumerians and Assyrians used opium in religious rituals.
2800 B.C.
Marijuana was used as a curative drug by Chinese emperor Shen-Nung.
1000 B.C.
Earliest known drug-taking Indians in America, the Oaxacas of Mexico, used mushrooms as hallucinogens.
800 B.C.
Cannabis was referred to in the "Soma," included in the Rig-Veda, which contains hymns and prayers used in worship in ancient India.
The mention of *nepenthe* in Homer's *Odyssey* was thought by many scholars to refer to hashish.
700 B.C.
The Persian prophet Zoroaster was thought to be a user of bhanga, a cannabis derivative.
Marijuana was used in Scythian funeral rites as homage to the dead.
600 B.C.
Greek merchants thrived on the transportation of cannabis between Asia Minor and Greece.
500 B.C.
Through the examination of burial sites, archaeologists have determined that cannabis was used in Northern Europe in an area which is now Brandenburg, Germany.
430 B.C.
Cannabis first appears in ancient records; Herodotus' *Histories* describes the use of hemp in purification rites.
400 B.C.
Greeks used opium for hypnosis, as an analgesic, and as poison for political enemies.
100 B.C.
The Egyptian use of cannabis to forget sorrows is documented by the Greek historian Diodorus.
According to the Greek hisorian Herodotus, the Thracians burned the tops of the cannabis plant after their meals, inhaling its fumes until they became tired and went to sleep.
38 B.C.
Marc Antony's Roman troops accidentally ate *datura stramonium* while retreating from Parthis. They fell into a stupor and were slaughtered by their enemies. Thousands died.
70 A.D.
Cannabis was listed in a Roman medical book by Dioscorides, who described its juices as beneficial in curing earaches and diminishing sexual desire.
79 A.D.
In the writings of Roman Pliny the Elder, cannabis is said to relieve gout and cause impotence.
c.100
Taoists burned cannabis in the belief that they would achieve immortality.
c.160
The Roman physician Galen warned that dehydration and impotence were the result of overindulgence in cannabis seeds.
c.200
Cannabis was used as a sedative during surgery by the Chinese surgeon Hua T'o.
c.300
As a means of collecting revenue, the Romans imposed a tax on Egyptian cannabis.
c.400
Roman court physician Oribasius warned that cannabis seeds hurt the head, produced a warm feeling, and promoted weight loss.
570
Evidence indicates that the tomb of Queen Arnegunde, who died in 570 A.D., contained traces of cannabis.
c.600
Marijuana use was discouraged by the Taoists, who worried about its effect on thought processes.
Chinese physician Meng Shen claimed that eating cannabis seeds for 100 days would allow one to see spirits.
Cannabis was used by followers of the Tantric religion in Tibet in rites designed to overcome fear of demons.
c.700
Opium was brought into Europe by Moslem doctors.
c.850
Archaeologists have found traces of cannabis on the remnants of Viking ships circa 850 A.D.
c.1000
Coca, a drug stimulant, was cultivated in Peru.
Chinese physicians claimed that cannabis cleared the blood, lowered body temperature, and cured rheumatism. It was also acknowledged as a general cure for injuries and disease.
In India, cannabis was extolled as the food of the Gods.
Arab physician Ibn Wahshiyah warned that the odor of hashish was lethal.
The collection of Arab stories, *The Thousand and One Nights*, which was collected over 700 years, included references to drugs in stories such as "The Tale of the Hashish Eater."
1155
According to Persian legend, hashish was first used by Haydar, the founder of the Sufi religion.
c.1200
Ganja, a drink derived from cannabis, was used as an elixir for warriors in India.
The Moslem botanist Ibn al-Baytar noted that hashish was eaten in Egypt.
1253
Worried about the excessive use of hashish in his city, the governor of Cairo, Egypt, ordered the area's entire supply thrown onto a massive pyre.
1256
According to Marco Polo, a terrorist ruler in Northern Persia, Hasan-ibn-Sabah, the founder of a band of cutthroats called the Assassins, used cannabis to prove to his men that he could guarantee their entry to Paradise if they stayed loyal and died in his service.
1300s
Cannabis began to be used in Ethiopia.
In the *Decameron*, Boccacio referred to a mysterious potion that seemed to be hashish, although he never named the drug.
Stories of the opium use of Nasreddin Hodja became part of the folklore of several Middle Eastern countries.
1324
The governor of Cairo, Egypt, ordered troops to destroy all hashish plants growing on neighboring farms.
1378
Troops were again ordered to destroy the cannabis fields near Cairo, Egypt.
1400s
Francois Rabelais, the French writer and physician, wrote about cannabis.
1484
Pope Innocent VIII condemned the use of cannabis and witchcraft in the Satanic mass.
c.1500
The use of cannabis was central to the plot of *Dhurtasamagama*, a light farce popular in India.
Jean Weir, a demonologist, stated that cannabis use caused the loss of speech, uncontrollable laughter, and marvelous visions.
1510
Leo Africanus wrote that people in Tunis, Morocco, used cannabis, which caused them to burst into laughter and act as if they were half-drunk.
1511
Explorer Ferdinand Magellan noted opium use during his travels through India and Persia.
1532
Francisco Pizarro conquered Peru, giving Spain a coca monopoly.
1545
Cannabis smoking was introduced to South America by the Spaniards.
1548
An Italian herbologist, Mattioli, described characteristics of male and female hemp plants.
1563
Portuguese doctor, Garcia Da Orta, published *Colloquies on the Simples and Drugs of India*, a report on hallucinogenics and cannabis.
1578
Portuguese doctor, Cristobal Acosta, published *On the Drugs and Medicines from the East Indies*, a detailed analysis of cannabis.
1585
Thomas Heriot reported to Sir Walter Raleigh that cannabis grew in abundance in what was to become the Virginia colony.
1591
Prosper Alpini, in the book *Medicines of the Egyptians*, stated that hashish caused men to revel in ecstasy.
1596
John Huyghen van Linschoten, a Dutchman, published *Itinerario*, a book which perpetuated the myth that opium and cannabis were identical in their effects.
1600s

West African tribesmen traded slaves among themselves, as well as with the Arabs. Later, they were themselves traded to the colonists of the New World. Slaves consumed massive quantities of cannabis in an attempt to endure terrible hardships.
The curative and ecstatic powers of cannabis were extolled in the *Rajvallabha*, a medical text in India.
Englebert Kaempfer, a German physician, wrote of rituals in India which included the use of cannabis.
1609
Joao dos Santos, a Dominican priest, wrote of the intoxicating practice of eating cannabis by the Kafir tribe in Africa.
1615
Giovanni De Ninault, an Italian physician and demonologist, listed cannabis as an ingredient for witches' potions used in the Black Mass.
1619
Colonists in Jamestown, Va., were asked by the directors of the Virginia Company to grow hemp.
1620
Cannabis was one of the first crops planted by the Pilgrims at Plymouth Colony who used the hemp for clothes.
1621
Robert Burton wrote that cannabis might be of value in the treatment of depression.
1626
The use of cannabis by American Indians was detailed by a French physician named Leander.
1628
Peter Mundy, a British East India Company employee, wrote a tract describing the effects of cannabis and opium.
1640
Colonists in Connecticut were urged to grow hemp.
1649
Fray Sebastien Manrique, a Portuguese missionary, wrote of his belief that opium and cannabis were the same, something he came to believe during his travels to India.
1658
Jan van Riebeeck, the governor of a Dutch colony at Africa's Cape of Good Hope, wrote of the use of cannabis by the Hottentot tribe.
1666
Laurent D'Arvieux, a Frenchman, wrote of his experiences with hashish in *Voyage to Palestine, To the Grand Emir, Chief of the Arabian Princes of the Desert, Known as the Bedouins*.
1680
Thomas Bowrey, a British sea captain, described the use of cannabis as an elixir in *Geographical Account of Countries Round the Bay of Bengal*.
1681
Pere Ange, a Frenchman, noted that the effects of the Persian mixture of opium and cannabis were similar to the published accounts by Herodotus of similar use by the Scythians in ancient Greece.
1682
Cannabis was designated as a cure for coughs and jaundice in the *New London Dispensatory*.
Incentives to grow hemp were offered to farmers in Virginia and Maryland.
1686
Jean Chardin, a Frenchman, wrote his observations of cannabis use in *Voyages to Persia and Other Parts of the Orient*.
1695
A physician named Rumphius, while living in India, prescribed the use of cannabis as a treatment for everything from diarrhea to gonorrhea.
1698
John Freyer, a physician with the British East India Company, wrote of the effects of cannabis and opium.
1700s
At "drugging houses" in New Orleans, opium and cannabis were smoked openly.
India provided the greatest supply of opium to America.
1700
Englishman John Jones wrote an early book depicting the agony of opium withdrawal.
1720
Cannabis was condemned as a treatment for jaundice in the *Complete English Dispensatory*.
1729
The Portuguese sold more than 1,000 chests of opium to China.
1753
The variety of hemp plants later to be known as marijuana were formally christened *cannabis sativa* by Carl Linnaeus.
1764
The use of boiled hemp root as a cure for skin inflammation was described in the *New English Dispensatory*.
1765
George Washington recorded in his diary his methods of growing cannabis, or hemp.
1772
Carsten Niebuhr, a Danish mathematician, wrote of hashish intoxication by Sufis in his *Travels in Arabia*.
1783
Jean Lamarck, a French biologist, contended that European and Indian hemp plants were different. He reserved the name of *cannabis sativa* for the European hemp and named the Indian hemp *cannabis indica*.
1794
The medicinal uses of cannabis were described in the *Edinburgh New Dispensary*.
1798
The British Parliament attempted to tax India's manufacture and distribution of cannabis.
1800
October: Napoleon outlawed the use of hashish by his troops, who had begun using the drug, after the French invaded Egypt.
1803
Poet Samuel Taylor Coleridge admitted in a letter that he used opium and cannabis derivatives.
A French doctor named Virey attempted to analyze the active principal of cannabis. He concluded that the drug was the mysterious *nepenthe* administered by Helen of Troy.
Morphine, the active ingredient of opium, was isolated as a separate drug.
1809
Silvestre de Sacy, a French scholar, stated that the name of the Assassins, the Arab cutthroats who had terrorized the Middle East centuries earlier, was derived from the word "hashish."
1811
Dutch explorer C.P. Thunberg wrote about the cannabis-smoking habits of the Hottentot tribe in Africa.
1817
On her deathbed, the Queen of Portugal was given a concoction of marijuana and arsenic to ease her pain.
1818
Joseph von Hammer-Purgstall, an Austrian writer, established the link between hashish and the Assassins terrorist gang, in his *History of the Assassins*.
1820s
As opium became widely used, fake opium, such as wooden nutmegs, were sold to the unsuspecting.
1821
Thomas De Quincey, British essayist, wrote *Confessions of an English Opium Eater*, becoming the first author to write openly in favor of drugs.
1823
In an early account on opium use, the *Boston Medical Intelligencer* wrote of the agony of drug withdrawal.
1830s
Morphine became a staple drug for family use as a pain-killer.
1830
The Municipal Council of Rio de Janeiro prohibited the importation of marijuana.
1838
The smoking of cannabis before a battle became a Zulu ritual, most evidently at Blood River, where they attacked the Dutch.
A British colonial officer in India urged a ban on cannabis because illicit sales were discovered in avoidance of tax laws.
1839
The first Opium War between Britain and China began in 1839 and continued until 1842. Britain forced China to open its port to trade.
The *American Provers' Union*, a homeopathic journal, published a report on the effects of cannabis.
1840s
Pierre Jules Theophile Gautier, a French novelist, poet, and painter, founded the Hashish Club, which met in monthly sessions in the Latin Quarter of Paris.
A chapter detailing the use of hashish was included in Alexander Dumas' *The Count of Monte Christo*.
1842
In the *New Homeopathic Pharmacopoeia and Posology*, recipes for the homeopathic uses of cannabis were included.
1843
Francois Lallemand, a French writer, incorporated the use of hashish into the plot of *Le Hachych*.
French artist Pierre Jules Theophile Gautier published an article titled *Le Hashish*.
Irish physician Dr. William O'Shaughnessy wrote of the therapeutic potential of cannabis.
The use of cannabis became prevalent in South Africa, following the importation of Indian "coolies" to work in the fields.
Cannabis is mentioned as a medicinal agent for the first time in an American medical text.
1845
Dec. 23: In a letter to a friend, French author Honore de Balzac confessed that he had used hashish.
Thomas de Quincey announced that he would follow his opium opus with a volume detailing his use of hashish, but the book never materialized.
The hypodermic syringe was invented.
1846
A French doctor, Jacques-Joseph Moreau published his *Hashish and Mental Illness*, an analysis of the drug's interaction with sensory processes.
French painter and poet Pierre Jules Theophile Gautier wrote an article detailing the activities of the Hashish Club.

Dr. Amariah Brigham noted in the *American Journal of Insanity* that cannabis was a likely cure for insanity.

1847

French novelist Gerard de Nerval detailed his involvement with hashish and double consciousness in his *Voyages to the Orient*.

The Pharmaceutical Society of Paris announced that they would give an award to the person who discovered the active principal of cannabis.

1848

A Frenchman named DeCourtive wrote the first doctoral thesis about hashish.

An anonymous article published in Edinburgh, Scotland, warned of the evils of hashish, then popular in France.

1849

The word hashish was prominently emblazoned on an illustrated banner in a French occult publication, *The Prophet's Almanac*.

1850s

Millions of Chinese men were addicted to smoking and eating opium, which was referred to as a "stomach habit." The drug was considered an aphrodisiac.

Dozens of opium dens were opened to Chinese and white patrons in New York City, many of them around Pell and Doyer streets. Opium traffic was controlled by two powerful tongs which fought a long, violent war for control of the lucrative business.

The use of cannabis was said to have turned Africa's Bashilange tribe from an aggressive group to a peaceful one.

The major alkaloid of the coca bush's leaves was extracted and dubbed "cocaine" by European chemists.

1850

David Urquhart, a member of the British Parliament, included his experiences with hashish in his two volume book, *Pillars of Hercules*.

The use of hashish as a sexual stimulant was advised in Frederick Hollick's *Marriage Guide*.

1852

Dr. John Grigor, an English physician, pioneered the obstetrical use of cannabis as a means of reducing pain during childbirth.

An Ohio doctor reported on the effectiveness of opium in preventing him from contracting dysentery from his many sick patients.

1853

Chinese coolies first came to America to work on railroads, bringing opium with them.

1854

American poet John Greenleaf Whittier wrote about hallucinations caused by hashish in his collection of *Anti-Slavery Poems*.

Cannabis was listed as a medicinal drug in *The Dispensatory of the United States*.

1855

Bayard Taylor, an extremely popular writer in his day, became the first author in America to extol drugs when he wrote about his experiences eating hashish in Egypt and Damascus.

1856

The second Opium War between Britain and China began in 1856 and continued until 1858.

Scribner's Magazine published the first addict experience article by Poughkeepsie, N.Y., cannabis smoker Fitzhugh Ludlow.

1857

David Livingston wrote about the use of cannabis by Africa's Sotho tribe in his *Missionary Travels and Research in South Africa*.

American writer Fitz Hugh Ludlow published *The Hashish Eater: Being Passages from the Life of a Pythagorean*.

1858

French author Charles Baudelaire published *Artificial Paradises*, which contained the "Poem of Hashish," as well as a translation of de Quincey's *Confessions of an Opium Eater*.

Cocaine was isolated from coca for the first time by Dr. K. Niemann, and was soon touted as a cure for morphine addiction.

The anonymous author of a British magazine article stated that opium was used by 400 million people, and cannabis by 200 to 300 million, but that the threat of either drug to the British Isles was nonexistent.

1859

Dr. John P. Gray, future president of the American Psychiatric Association, wrote of his clinical experience with cannabis, and noted its widespread use.

1860s

Morphine was used as a pain killer for almost 500,000 men wounded during the Civil War. The resulting addiction became known as "soldiers disease."

The acceptable medicinal uses for cannabis were published by the Ohio Medical Society.

The extensive use of hashish by Americans was noted by British writer Mordecai Cubitt Cooke.

1860

Oliver Wendell Holmes warned his colleagues of the dangers of drugs, but called opium "God's own medicine."

1867

June: The article "Opium Eating and Eaters" was included in *Harper's* magazine.

1868

A researcher estimated that 80,000-100,000 Americans were opium addicts.

Possession of hashish became a capital offense in Egypt.

1869

Scientific American noted in an article that hashish was in abundance in America.

Chloral hydrate, more commonly known as "knockout drops," was developed.

The U.S. Marines were sent to Brooklyn to destroy illegal distilleries.

1870s

San Francisco's Chinatown flourished as the hub of opium eating and smoking, with a minimum of 200 dens operating twenty-four hours a day. Many high society matrons and daughters became addicted there.

After railroad construction work disappeared, industrious Chinese immigrants opened opium dens in the western U.S. to profit from their impoverished fellow immigrants.

Pioneer photographers like Bellocq and Brassai used opium smokers as early subjects.

Hashish was introduced to Greece through the Aegean seaport of Piraeus.

1870

The financial secretary of India urged a ban on cannabis, attributing crime and insanity to its use.

A Japanese anti-drug law decreed decapitation by samurai sword as the punishment for drug trafficking.

South Africa outlawed the sale, possession, or use of cannabis by any Indian "coolie."

1874

Thomas Bailey Aldrich included a poem about hashish in his collection, *Cloth of Gold and Other Poems*.

To increase tax revenue, importation of hashish was tolerated by Egypt, although possession of the drug remained illegal.

1875

San Francisco enacted a ban on the smoking and possession of opium.

The narcotic and medicinal properties of hashish were acknowledged for the first time in Greek medical texts.

1876

American Indian Chief Sitting Bull was suspected of smoking cannabis, after he went into a trance during pipe smoking rituals.

A 106-year-old British sea captain attributed his long life and good health to the pacifying effects of opium.

Virginia City, Nev., banned the possession and use of opium.

Pharmacists sold hashish in Philadelphia during the American Centennial Exposition.

Dec. 2: The *Illustrated Police News* contained an article about hashish use by New York City women.

1877

A special task force was commissioned in India to examine the effects of excessive use of cannabis.

The Sultan of Turkey ordered all hashish confiscated and destroyed.

British writer W. Laird-Clowes stated emphatically that no professional Englishman had fallen prey to the ravages of hashish.

Dec. 30: The New York *Times* published a lengthy article about drug addiction.

1878

Edward Levinstein, a German physician, suggested going "cold turkey" in order to cure drug addiction in a work translated as *The Morbid Craving for Morphine*.

1879

The Sultan of Turkey, also ruler of Egypt, outlawed the importation of hashish.

1880s

Cannabis was introduced to the southwestern U.S. by Mexicans.

The founder of psychoanalysis, Sigmund Freud, applauded cocaine's medicinal virtues in his treatise *Uber Coca*. Other European writers were known to have used drugs, including Robert Louis Stevenson, occultist Aleister Crowley, James Joyce, who smoked cannabis, Stéphane Mallarmé, philosopher Friedrich Nietzsche, and poet Guillaume Apollinaire.

1882

Dr. Leslie Keeley, originator of addiction cures, estimated that 500,000 Americans were opium addicts.

Paraldehyde was introduced to the international drug market.

1883

Dr. John Brown and Dr. Robert Batho, both English obstetricians, used cannabis to quell excessive menstrual bleeding.

Harper's New Monthly Magazine ran an article about a hashish house in New York.

1884

Confessions of an English Hashish-Eater was published anonymously.

Cocaine appeared in the U.S. with the reputation of being another wonder drug.

Growing cannabis became a capital offense in Turkey and Egypt, but customs officers were allowed to sell the drug abroad.

1885

A cigar containing cocaine was introduced by the Parke-Davis drug company.

A special committee in San Francisco found that twenty-six opium dens were segregated for use by whites only.

1886
Coca-Cola, containing cocaine and sold as a brain tonic, was introduced by Dr. J.C. Pemberton.
Vin Mariani, a tonic and digestive aid made from coca and wine, was manufactured in France for worldwide sale.
Hashish use at Cambridge and Oxford universities was acknowledged when students became ill with overdoses of the drug.
1887
The Wragg Commission of South Africa outlawed the sale, possession, or use of cannabis by any Indian "coolie."
1888
Explorer Hermann von Wissmann wrote of the hashish smoking rituals of the Baloubas, a Bantu tribe in the Belgian Congo.
1889
German philosopher Friedrich Nietszche was known to have used a Javanese sedative which contained hashish.
Sulphonal was introduced to the international drug market.
1890s
Three Cambridge University chemists obtain a pure extract of cannabis named "cannabinol." Two of them were killed during a laboratory explosion, and the third almost died after imbibing the concoction and losing consciousness in his burning laboratory.
Writers Havelock Ellis and William Butler Yeats were known to enjoy using mescaline.
French authors Arthur Rimbaud and Paul Verlaine used hashish. The experience inspired some of the poetry in Rimbaud's *Illuminations*.
Michael Abrams terrorized New York City's Chinatown for ten years, operating opium dens and killing his rivals. Abrams was eventually murdered by Chinese gang members.
1890
Court physician Dr. J.R. Reynolds was suspected of prescribing cannabis to Queen Victoria.
In Greece, the cultivation, importation, and use of hashish was officially outlawed.
1891
Dr. Leslie Keeley became a national sensation for his controversial "Bichloride of Gold" cures for alcoholics and drug addicts.
1893
The Temperance League, concerned about cannabis abuse, urged the British Parliament to form the Indian Hemp Drugs Commission. The commission concluded that moderate cannabis use had no appreciable physical, mental, or moral effects.
Edmund Burke Delabarre, a psychologist at Brown University, began noting the effects of cannabis on himself in a study which continued until 1931.
Aug. 3: The Indian Hemp Drugs Commission met for the first time. In the next year, the testimonies of 1,193 witnesses would be heard.
1896
During the two-year Spanish-American War, morphine was used extensively to treat the wounded. Army physicians have continued to use opiates as painkillers ever since.
Cannabis derivatives, including cannabin, cannabindon, cannabine, and cannabinon were developed by American drug companies.
1897
The Sears Roebuck catalogue offered three types of hypodermic needle kits for sale.
Jan. 2: The *New York Herald* detailed rampant cocaine use by residents of Manchester, Conn.
Oct. 10: A front page story in the *New York Herald* detailed English crusader Lily Dewhurst's visit to a local opium den.
1898
In Egypt, 500 businesses were closed when more than 10,000 kilos of hashish were found on their premises.
Heroin was synthesized from morphine. Although heralded as a cure for morphine, its addictiveness turned out to be far more deadly.
A cough syrup named "Heroin" was marketed by the Bayer Company.
Veronal was introduced to the international drug market.
Pope Leo XIII awarded a gold medal as a "benefactor to humanity" to Angelo Mariani, who produced a popular cocaine-laced tonic wine.
20th Cent.
Once out of the drug trade on New York's lower east side, Alphonse Attardi, (alias "The Peacemaker") informed on major drug traffickers and capos for ten months before collecting a reward and leaving the country.
During the building of the Panama Canal, cannabis was smoked as openly and casually as cigarettes are today.
U.S. jazz musicians, particularly in New Orleans, began widespread use of drugs, especially cocaine, cannabis ,and to a lesser extent, heroin.
1900
One million Americans were said to be addicted to opium or morphine.
In New York City's Chinatown between 1900-06, a bloody tong war raged. Hundreds of people were murdered until a peace treaty between warring factions was signed in 1906 by Tom Lee of the On Leongs and Mock Duck of the Hip Sings faction at the home of Judge Warren W. Foster of the Court of General Sessions.
An Arab medical text prescribed cannabis seeds mixed with bread as a treatment for tuberculosis.
1902
The Ja-Luo tribe in Eastern Uganda prohibited its warriors from using cannabis.
1904
Jan. 10: The *Boston Globe* reported that the U.S. government was growing cannabis and opium in gardens along the Potomac, to be used later for tests of the drugs' therapeutic potential.
1905
Sears Roebuck sold a bottled antidote for sixty-nine cents for those addicted to opium or morphine.
May 12: Herbert Croker, the son of former Tammany Hall leader Richard Croker, was found dead of a drug overdose.
1906
The American Medical Association endorsed small doses of heroin in cough syrups, sedatives, and relaxants.
Congress enacted the District of Columbia Pharmacy Act, which regulated the use of chloral, cocaine, and opiates.
The Pure Food and Drug Laws of 1906 caused the highly addictive coca stimulant to be taken out of home remedies and soft drinks.
The cultivation of the federal narcotics fields along the Potomac was terminated by the U.S. government.
1907
China and India reached a "Ten Year Agreement" to reduce the cultivation and importation of opium by ten percent a year until it ceased.
Feb. 22: Natale Evola, an important N.Y. syndicate sub-boss in narcotics and labor racketeering, was born in New York City.
1908
Canada outlawed the import, sale, possession for sale, or manufacture of opiates for nonmedical use.
Chinese troops began to behead opium growers under orders from the emperor to stop opium trade.
In Egypt 2,000 businesses were closed because hashish had been sold on their premises.
Apr. 3: Five San Francisco pharmacists who had supplied addicts with drugs were arrested on a warrant from the California State Board of Pharmacies.
1909
Led by President Theodore Roosevelt, the U.S. convened an international conference in Shanghai which attempted to eradicate China's opium problem.
When Comanche chief Quanah Parker fell ill, he took peyote given to him by a Mexican woman in Texas. After his cure, use of the drug spread throughout his tribe.
Apr. 10: Roy Carlisi, a syndicate narcotics trafficker, was born in Chicago.
1910
Jan. 31: "Vasta Herne," a play chronicling a woman's involvement with drugs, premiered.
1911
A second international conference concerning the world's opium problem was held at the Hague.
Canada passed the Opium and Drug Act, adding morphine and cocaine to a list of previously banned opiates.
Aug. 20: Joseph Sica was born in Newark, N.J. He became a syndicate subchieftain, and was later charged with narcotics crimes, murder, robbery, and extortion.
1912
"An Essay on Hashish," by Dr. Victor Robinson, was included in the *Medical Review of Reviews*.
Cannabis was used as a sedative for human sacrificial victims during the rituals of witch doctors in the French Congo.
Aug. 1: John Ormento, a syndicate narcotics overlord and labor racketeer, was born in New York City.
1913
Feb. 8: Carmine Lombardozzi, a narcotics smuggler and syndicate gambling boss and labor racketeer, was born in New York City.
1914
Lucky Luciano was arrested in New York for possession of heroin.
El Paso, Texas, banned the sale or possession of marijuana.
The New York City Board of Health banned cannabis.
December 17: The Harrison Act made it a federal offense for physicians to administer morphine except under special circumstances.
Dec. 18: Police in San Francisco made massive raids on opium-den brothels, arresting scores of Oriental prostitutes.
1915
A naive marijuana horror story called "The Poison Ship" was published in *Harper's*.
California, Utah, and Wyoming outlawed the possession of cannabis, unless prescribed by a physician.
Mar. 1: The U.S. Anti-Narcotic Act, which called for more scrupulous record keeping for prescribed narcotics, became effective.
Apr. 5: Six members of a Paris drug ring were apprehended in the city's Latin Quarter.
Apr. 15: Hundreds of drug addicts flooded New York's public hospitals, due to their inability to obtain narcotics under the recent U.S. Anti-Narcotic Act.
Sept. 8: Henry Goddard Thomas, known as the "King of Cocaine," was

arrested in New York.
1916
Pershing led his punitive expedition against Mexican revolutionary Pancho Villa. Pershing's soldiers, including Lieutenant George Smith Patton, were generously supplied with marijuana by the natives.
The federal case, *U.S. vs. Jim Fuey Moy*, ruled that a physician could not be arrested for providing narcotics to addicts.
June 10: Peter Joseph LoCascio, a syndicate figure in narcotics, conspiracy, and liquor violations, was born in New York City.
June 26: After pleading guilty to unlawful possession of narcotics in New York City, Salvatore Charles "Lucky" Luciano was sentenced to a one-year prison term. He was paroled after six months.
1917
It was estimated that 300,000 people in New York City were opium addicts.
Spicy-Adventure Stories published a thriller about Scotland Yard detectives who plied a suspect with hashish in order to solve a murder.
1918
Apr. 28: Joseph Paul LoPicolo, who became a syndicate sub-boss in narcotics smuggling, was born in Chicago.
1919
Dope, a story which detailed the effects of opium, was published by Sax Rohmer, author of the *Fu Manchu* mysteries.
The federal case, *U.S. vs. Doremus*, ruled that physicians must pay taxes on narcotics, and record the dispensation of the drugs.
The federal case, *U.S. vs. Webb*, ruled that narcotics could only be administered to addicts in cases of senility or intractable pain.
Texas outlawed the possession of cannabis not prescribed by a doctor.
January: Seventy-five tins of opium were found by a customs inspector in the Nogales, Ariz., hotel room of Gilda Monheim and Lazaro Vargas.
Jan. 16: Congress passed the Volstead Act, which initiated Prohibition. The law became effective Jan. 16, 1920.
1920s
Cannabis became the drug most routinely used by those involved in the U.S. black national movement, particularly by the followers of Marcus Garvey's Back-to-Africa movement.
Greece became one of the primary producers of hashish, as the drug's cultivation became an accepted part of everyday life.
Receipts from the U.S. drug smuggling business were estimated at $20 million annually.
1920
Opium poppy production was brought into Mexico by Chinese immigrants.
Dr. Oscar Dowling of the Louisiana State Board of Health warned Gov. John M. Parker of the effects of marijuana, with regard to its use by New Orleans musicians.
Actress Olive Thomas accidentally killed herself while injecting heroin in Paris.
May 8: The House of Delegates of the AMA vowed to eliminate heroin from all medical preparations.
June 14: Two inspectors for the California State Board of Pharmacy, Emile Coret and John De Vries, were implicated as leaders of a drug ring.
July 20: While inspecting cracked paint on the side of the Chinese mail liner *Nilo*, federal agents discovered $40,000 in smuggled opium.
Sept. 19: California's San Clemente Island was proposed as a sight for a drug addiction withdrawal center.
Dec. 14: Denver hoodlum "Big Time" Charlie Allen was sentenced to five years for drug trafficking.
1921
Marijuana was officially forbidden on the grounds of Fort Sam Houston.
Aug. 30: Several thousand dollars worth of opium bound for prisoners in San Quentin was intercepted by agents from the California State Board of Pharmacy.
Sept. 8: Federal agents confiscated opium, heroin, and cocaine worth hundreds of thousands of dollars after a wild shoot-out with the crew of the S.S. *King Alexander*, docked in New York Harbor.
Nov. 1: Dr. Royal Copeland stated that drug use in the U.S. was ten times greater than that of any other nation.
Dec. 8: An exposé detailed how U.S. drug manufacturers circumvented federal anti-narcotics laws by exporting narcotics and then smuggling them back across the border.
1922
The anti-drug writings of a Canadian judge, Emily F. Murphy under the name "Janey Canuck," were published in a book, *The Black Candle*.
A leading marijuana expert, Dr. M.V. Ball, representing the AMA, visited Mexican border towns to study the effects of marijuana use.
Feb. 26: U.S. opium importation was estimated at seventeen times that of any other nation.
May 21: A fortune in hard drugs smuggled from the steamship *China* was seized by federal agents in New York Harbor.
May 26: Congress passed the Jones-Miller Narcotic Drug Import and Export Act, which controlled the importation of opium and its derivatives for medical uses, and banned the import or export of opium for smoking.

May 30: Opium valued at $100,000 was seized from a ship in San Francisco, the first such seizure under the new Jones-Miller Anti-Narcotic law.
Dec.: A detailed account of movie star Wallace Reid's drug addiction was published.
Dec. 12: The name of Evelyn Nesbit was found on a narcotic ledger seized during a drug raid in New York's Greenwich Village.
1923
South Africa tried to get help from the League of Nations in their attempt to affect a world-wide ban on cannabis.
The U.S. had an estimated population of one to four million drug users.
The Army prohibited possession of marijuana by U.S. military personnel in the Panama Canal Zone.
The International Narcotic Education Association was organized.
Arkansas, Iowa, Nevada, Oregon, and Washington outlawed the possession of cannabis not prescribed by a doctor.
Two French physicians, Bonnamour and Pic, wrote extensively of the cerebral effects of hashish use.
Jan. 2: John Barker, who ran dope traffic from a fraudulent Oakland, Cal., clinic, was arrested on federal drug charges.
Jan. 11: The *New York Times* proclaimed marijuana the city's "latest habit-forming drug."
Jan. 18: Wallace Reid, a drug-addicted movie star, died in an asylum in California. Although no charges were ever brought in his death, it was later claimed that movie moguls had ordered that Reid be injected with a fatal dose of morphine to prevent him from embarrassing the industry.
Jan. 28: Boston narcotics agent Ralph A. Fry was convicted for taking bribes from a Portland, Maine, drug ring.
Mar. 29: The drug addiction of film actress Juanita Hansen was exposed.
June 5: Under the name "Luciana," heroin-carrying Charles "Lucky Luciano was arrested by police. Charges were dropped when he led lawmen to a stash of heroin belonging to enemy gangsters.
July 1: The prosperous king of Paris' biggest cocaine ring, "Big Raoul," received a short jail sentence.
1924
Britain established the Departmental Committee on Morphine and Heroin Addiction.
July 25: Raw opium valued at $100,000 was seized on a New York City pier by federal agents.
1925
The Second Geneva Opium Conference, concerned with quelling worldwide drug use, convened in Geneva, Switz.
Characters in Carl Van Vechten's *Peter Whiffle* experimented with hashish and other mind-expanding drugs.
Mexico outlawed the cultivation of marijuana.
Apr. 1: A committee was formed to investigate marijuana traffic in the Panama Canal Zone.
1926
Dr. W.W. Stockberger, representing the U.S. Bureau of Plant Industry, stated that marijuana use was detrimental to the social conditions of Mexican border towns.
Hashish production was banned in Lebanon.
The prohibition against marijuana was rescinded in the Panama Canal Zone.
Depictions of hashish use were included in *Tai Fu* and *Pansy Greers*, by Thomas Burke.
Jan. 11: American sculptor William Ordway Partridge was discovered to be a drug addict through the medical records of a New York hospital.
Sept. 9: Jack "Legs" Diamond was discharged hours after being arrested for smuggling narcotics in Mount Vernon, N.Y.
1927
Robert Kingman published "The Green Goddess: A Study in Dreams, Drugs, and Dementia," in the *Medical Journal and Record*.
Notch Number One, a film about a rancher attempting to prevent marijuana use by his ranch hands, was released.
The World Narcotic Defense Association was organized.
The state of Nebraska outlawed possession of cannabis unless prescribed by a physician.
June 3: The Chicago *Tribune* accused the city's Mexican community of bringing marijuana into the city's classrooms.
1928
The *Kansas City Star* published an exposé about school children using marijuana.
South Africa passed another in a series of ineffectual laws banning cannabis.
Experts stated that sixty-nine percent of all violent crimes in New York City could be traced to cocaine use.
A detailed analysis of hashish was included in Boericke's *Materia Medica*.
May 15: A grand jury was empaneled in New York to investigate drug trafficking among prisoners at Welfare Island.
June 30: Four New York narcotic detectives were demoted to street patrol after drugs were found in their police lockers.
Oct. 3: More than $1,500,000 worth of opium was found behind false partitions on the ocean liner *President Harrison*, after it docked in Jersey City, N.J. It was the largest opium seizure of its time.
Dec. 8: More than $5 million worth of heroin was confiscated in raids on hotel rooms in New York and Chicago, and a passenger train in Buffalo, N.Y. It was called the first big narcotics bust of the century.
1929
Canada added marijuana to its list of banned drugs in the Opium and

Narcotics Drug Act of 1929.
A new Army investigation into the effects of marijuana was opened in the Panama Canal Zone.
Jan. 18: The Narcotics Farm Act passed, establishing facilities for the treatment of addicts.
July 10: The wife of former Chinese consul Yin Kao admitted smuggling more than $600,000 worth of opium into the U.S. "for friends." She was deported later in the year.
July 20: Heiress Dolores Elizabeth Ford claimed her marriage to a black man had taken place while she was under the influence of narcotics.
Sept. 10: The *Tulsa Tribune* published details of a drug salesman in the city's schools.
Sept. 20: The League of Nations adopted a plan to curtail the world's drug trade.
Dec. 16: Arnold Rothstein, who was alleged to be the largest drug supplier in New York, was murdered.
1930s
"Reefer songs" became the rage in the jazz world.
Two Frenchmen, Pierre Aunay and Jean Leni, smuggled drugs from Turkish poppy fields to the port of Marseilles.
1930
Antone "Black Tony" Parmagini, a West Coast mob boss, was convicted of drug smuggling.
Feb. 23: Film actress Mabel Normand died a drug-related death.
July 5: Following the mysterious disappearance of Reginald Arthur Lee, British acting consul-general in Marseilles, Fr., there was speculation that he was the victim of the drug smugglers he was investigating. Lee's body was never found.
Aug. 12: The Federal Bureau of Narcotics, headed by Harry J. Anslinger, was formed as a branch of the Treasury Department.
December: The U.S. Army prohibited the use of marijuana in the Panama Canal Zone after an investigation determined that its use impaired the efficiency of soldiers.
Dec. 5: U.S. Customs agents discovered a huge morphine shipment on board the S.S. *Alesia*, a Turkish freighter docked at a Brooklyn, N.Y., pier.
1931
The California State Narcotic Committee warned of widespread marijuana use by the Mexican population in Southern California.
Jan. 5: Alma Ruben, a film star, was arrested for drug smuggling. She never went to trial, dying of an overdose on Jan. 21.
Mar. 26: Eight men were arrested for peddling as much as $500,000 worth of heroin at a Brooklyn high school.
June: The Army convened a third investigation into marijuana use in the Panama Canal Zone.
June 16: Starr Faithful, reportedly the mistress of a Boston politician, drowned after being rendered unconscious with drugs.
Sept. 23: In Shanghai, customs officers seized a huge heroin shipment. No arrests were made.
Nov. 30: August "Little Augie" Del Gracio was arrested as the Simplon Express arrived in Berlin and police discovered 250 kilos of morphine in his luggage.
Dec. 28: Customs officers in Hamburg, Ger., seized 1,513 kilos of raw opium discovered in a shipment of gum on the S.S. *Ceres* of Istanbul.
1932
The Federal Bureau of Narcotics expressed alarm about the increased use of marijuana.
"Smokin' Reefers," a musical number, was included in a Broadway revue.
1933
Writer George Bernard Shaw called himself the world's "cosmic dentist" for his use of laughing gas to alleviate toothaches.
Members of a dope ring that specialized in marijuana, were arrested in Longmont, Colo.
Oct. 16: Marijuana use was determined to be a contributing factor when Victor Licata murdered five family members with an ax in Tampa, Fla.
1934
Mario Balestreri, a West Coast mobster, was convicted for drug trafficking and sentenced to twenty-seven years in prison.
Gertrude Michael sang "Sweet Marijuana" in the film *Murder at the Vanities.*
The *Canadian Medical Association Journal* published an editorial against marijuana.
Jan. 24: A dope ring that included hundreds of prisoners and guards and the deputy warden, was uncovered at Welfare Island Prison in New York.
July 9: Former Russian Princess Concordia di Melikoff received a suspended sentence, following her arrest for drug possession.
September: The New York *Times* noted widespread use of marijuana in Colorado.
Oct. 17: A 125-by-100-foot cannabis field was discovered near the Brooklyn Bridge.
1935
The *American Mercury* included an article entitled "The Menace of Marijuana."
The *New York Times* reported on the sale of marijuana to school children in Sacramento, Cal.
June 27: John Wallace, an inmate at the workhouse on New York's Welfare Island, was convicted for drug possession. A Welfare Island employee was sought as the ringleader of a gang which brought $500,000 worth of narcotics into the prison.
Sept. 20: The handlers of boxer Joe Louis implored the New York State Athletic Commission to be aware of suspected drug use by Louis' upcoming opponent, Max Baer.
1936
The Conference for the Suppression of Illicit Traffic in Dangerous Drugs convened in Geneva, Switz.
William Wolf published "Uncle Sam Fights a New Drug Menace: Marijuana" in *Popular Science Monthly.*
C.M. Weber wrote of marijuana use by school children in New Orleans for *Health Digest.*
Feb. 22: Melody Maker, a British music magazine, published an exposé on marijuana use by British musicians.
Mar. 21: The top racketeer in Manhattan's Chinatown, Harry Gee, arrested with a massive amount of opium, received a long jail term.
May 14: The New York *Times* reported that an American woman was selling marijuana in the Detroit school system for local Mexicans.
Dec. 18: Seven members of a dope ring headed by Morris Schatz were convicted of trafficking in opium and sentenced to federal prison.
1937
Harry Anslinger, commissioner of the Federal Bureau of Narcotics, wrote an article entitled "Marijuana, Assassin of Youth" for *American Magazine.*
Courtney R. Cooper warned of insanity and sexual promiscuity induced by marijuana in his *Here's to Crime.*
Earle Rowell published an anti-drug parable, *The Dope Adventures of David Dare.*
A man arrested with sixty ounces of narcotics was executed under orders of the Chinese government, the first such execution under new laws.
A report in the *International Medical Digest* detailed drug abuse by teenage youngsters in St. Louis, Mo.
Big Bill Hildebrandt, a Minneapolis drug trafficker, was convicted and sentenced to twenty years in prison.
The Marijuana Tax Act made it illegal to use cannabis not prescribed by a doctor and levied a heavy tax on marijuana transactions. The Federal Bureau of Narcotics promised strict enforcement of the law.
In 1937, the Chinese government rescinded a centuries-old law which made death the penalty for uncured addicts.
Mar. 24: Exotic dancer Angelina Rivoti and four men were arrested, and $25,000 worth of narcotics were seized during a New York drug raid.
1938
Drug Kingpin Lucky Luciano was convicted of distributing drugs. He was deported to Italy when paroled seven years later.
Louis "Lepke" Buchalter, Lucky Luciano's drug supplier, became a fugitive after he was sentenced to twelve years for conspiracy to violate federal narcotic laws.
Thomas Nelson, a St. Paul mobster, was convicted of drug trafficking and sentenced to fifteen years in prison.
Dr. Henry Smith Williams cited marijuana's abundance and widespread popularity as reasons why its federal prohibition would only foster profitable illegal trade.
January: The use of marijuana was alleged to be the cause of murder in the Newark, N.J., trial of Ethel "Bunny" Sohl.
April: The use of marijuana was alleged to be the cause of murder in the New York City trial of Arthur Friedman.
1939
On the Trail of Marijuana, the Weed of Madness, by Earle and Robert Rowell, warned of the insidious tricks of marijuana peddlers.
The use of hashish during black magic rituals was the subject of Algernon Blackwood's *A Psychic Invasion.*
A Malayan medical text included cannabis seeds in a recipe for a leprosy treatment.
1940
Dr. Arthur La Roe, president of the American Narcotic Defense Association, wrote an article entitled "Growth of the Marijuana Habit Among Our Youth" for *American Weekly.*
1941
Oct. 28: M. Elias, Harlem's biggest drug dealer was arrested and charged with drug smuggling. He was not convicted.
1942
The Opium Poppy Control Act strictly regulated the nation's opium supply, which included a three year supply kept with the nation's gold at Fort Knox.
New York hoodlum Joseph "Pip the Blind" Gagliano was convicted for drug trafficking.
Feb. 19: During a lecture on cannabis, Dr. Roger Adams decried the medical profession's inability to find the plant's active ingredient, the lack of an animal test that paralleled the drug's effect on humans, and the absence of controlled clinical experiments.
1943
1943: Jazz musician Gene Krupa was arrested for narcotics violations in San Francisco.
Raymond Chandler's *Lady in the Lake* included description of the squalor of drug parlors.
The effects of LSD began to be analyzed by Dr. Albert Hofmann of Sandoz Laboratories in Basel, Switz.
1944
Methadone was created by German scientists during WWII, as a

substitute for the depleted supply of opium.
While at war, the U.S. condemned Japan for its drug trafficking.
The La Guardia Commission published a report on marijuana use called "The Marijuana Problem in the City of New York."
Nov. 1: Joseph Valachi was arrested in Brooklyn for selling narcotics. Charges against him were dismissed later.
1945
Dr. Leopold Brandenburg, a physician for the underworld, was convicted and sentenced for a drug violation.
The American occupation government in Japan banned cannabis, cocaine, and opium.
In China, the Triad KMT reemerged as a major distributor of heroin in Europe years after its 1912 formation.
Oct. 19: Frank Caruso, a Brooklyn racketeer devoted to the smuggling and distribution of narcotics, was sentenced to eight years in prison.
Nov. 21: In Palermo, Sicily, the top Mafia dons met to organize their plan for international drug trafficking following World War II.
1946
"Personalty Studies of Marijuana Addicts," an analysis of drug use, was published in the *American Journal of Psychiatry*.
"The Marijuana Addict in the Army" was published in *War Medicine*.
A Commission on Narcotic Drugs was created by the economic and social council of the United Nations.
1947
Apr. 8: Boss of one of the biggest drug smuggling rings in the U.S., Joseph "Pip the Blind" Gagliano hanged himself in Manhattan before being sent to Sing Sing on a narcotics conviction.
May 28: Blues singer Billie Holiday was convicted for being a drug addict and sentenced to a year and a day in federal prison.
1948
The United Nations included synthetic drugs, which had been manufactured since WWII, under the same controls and restraints as other narcotics.
June 15: Jazz musician Charlie "Bird" Parker was arrested in Manhattan's Dewey Square Hotel for drug violations.
Aug. 31: Along with several others, actor Robert Mitchum was arrested at a Laurel Canyon, Calif., party for smoking marijuana. Sentenced to two years in prison, which was reduced immediately to sixty days, Mitchum served fifty days with time off for good behavior.
1949
Jan. 8: Several importers of a $300,000 cache of opium were arrested by New York City Customs agent Charles E. Wyatt. Wyatt's claim that "Lucky" Luciano was behind the smuggling went unproved.
Aug. 20: A United Nations drug investigation that uncovered a $500,000-a-month smuggling operation between Peru and the U.S., resulted in the arrest of the ringleader.
1950s
The Gambino, Genovese, and Lucchese crime families in New York were hampered in their drug distribution efforts by the vigorous pursuit of the Federal Bureau of Narcotics, which successfully prosecuted between nineteen and forty percent of the members of each "family."
Writer Aldous Huxley wrote of his drug experiences with peyote and mescal.
Jazz musicians Charlie "Bird" Parker and Fats Navarro both succumbed to heroin addiction. Jazzman Stan Getz almost destroyed his career when addiction motivated him to attempt armed robbery.
In the 1950s, Marius Alsaldi, a major supplier of drugs in France, was captured in Montgeron, while manufacturing drugs. Alsaldi, Antonie Bergeret, and the rest of Alsaldi's gang were convicted and sent to the penitentiary at Melun.
1950
Sept. 24: Federal agent Anker M. Bangs was shot to death by John Wong, a suspected drug dealer, during a raid in St. Paul, Minn.
Sept. 28: Drug dealers William Carter, George Mallock, and John Mallock were arrested in Vancouver, B.C., and charged with conspiracy to sell drugs.
1951
Charles Siragusa was assigned by the Federal Bureau of Narcotics to establish foreign offices from a headquarters in Rome.
The Boggs Act, which called for stiff sentences in drug convictions, was enacted by Congress.
Apr. 24: Over 3,000 heroin tablets were stolen from a London hospital by Kevin Patrick Saunders.
August: Mariano Rubino was arrested after being discovered selling heroin from a waiting room at New York's Bellevue Hospital.
1952
The Federal Bureau of Narcotics published *Living Death: The Truth About Drug Addiction*, which linked drug addiction to the "first puff of a marijuana cigarette."
Pancho Trevino, a purported Mexican drug kingpin from Nuevo Laredo, was arrested and imprisoned.
1954
Federal agents investigated the administration of Houston mayor, Judge Roy Hofheinz, following disclosures that many police officers were involved in narcotics trafficking, and that the chief of police was himself a drug user.
1955
The government of Iran banned the cultivation of opium.
The effects of cannabis on aggressive human behavior such as homicide, suicide, and sexual assault, were analyzed by Drs. Alfred Gilman and Louis Goldman.
Dec. 25: Massive drug raids in Houston by customs officers snared dozens of dealers and pushers, and collected drug caches and millions of dollars.
1956
Jazzman Dick Twardzik died in Paris of a heroin overdose.
The Narcotic Control Act of 1956 was passed by Congress, raising the mandatory minimum sentence for drug possession.
1957
Mobsters Frankie "The Bug" Caruso, Salvatore Maneri, Vincent Mauro, and John Papalia were convicted for conspiracy to smuggle $150 million worth of heroin into the U.S.
Drugs and the Mind was published by Robert De Ropp.
Feb. 28: Anthony Carminati the Bronx Mafia representative of the 187the Street mob and one of New York's largest heroin wholesalers, was sentenced to 10 years in prison. Carminati's criminal career dated to 1931.
November: The FBI raided and arrested thirty-eight participants of a Mafia conference in Apalachin, N.Y., called by Vito Genovese to organize a nation-wide drug network. The men were indicted for conspiring to smuggle 200 pounds of heroin from Europe via Cuba.
1958
Britain established the Interdepartmental Committee on Drug Addiction, chaired by Sir Russell Brain.
Captain of the Tramunti crime family, Andimo "Tommy Noto" Pappadio was arrested in connection with a heroin conspiracy that led to the imprisonment of mob boss Vito "Don Vitone" Genovese. Pappadio was convicted of selling heroin but was later pardoned.
Mobsters Peter Casella, Joseph Lo Piccolo, Anthony Napolitano, Ignazio Orlando, James Santore, and Anthony Tarlentino were arrested while in possession of opium and heroin.
June 2: Leroy Jefferson, reportedly a leading U.S. drug seller, was arrested in New York City but released due to lack of evidence.
Dec. 13: The Italian Court of Appeals freed "Lucky" Luciano, declaring that he had "nothing to do with murder, narcotics, or illegal rackets."
1959
Mobster Vito Genovese and fourteen associates were convicted of conspiracy to smuggle heroin into the U.S.
The U.S. cheered Castro's takeover of Cuba because it was thought that the Mafia's drug distribution would be effected.
Members of the Union Corse, a French underground organization, aligned with members of a newly formed Cuban Mafia to establish a cocaine distribution network.
Synanon, a support organization for recovering drug addicts, was founded in Santa Monica, Calif.
Thailand agreed to a ban on opium smoking, thus making the policy uniform for all United Nations countries.
1959: Marcantonio Orlandino, associate of the Tramunti crime family, was described in 1959 as the mastermind of a multimillion dollar heroin operation. Orlandino was sentenced to ten years in federal prison for possessing $200,000 worth of heroin.
Mar. 10: West Coast mobster Anthony Marcello was arrested in Los Angeles for drug trafficking.
1960s
The San Francisco suburb of Haight-Ashbury became the American Mecca for marijuana and LSD.
By the late 1960s, LSD was widely available in the drug marketplace, and "dropping acid" became a familiar term.
1960
Joseph Valachi was convicted of dealing heroin and was sentenced to fifteen years in prison.
Mobsters Guiseppe Cotroni, Carmine Galente, Angelo Loicano, John Ormento, Rocco Sancinella, and Angelo Tuminaro were arrested for heroin trafficking.
Sept. 3: Mobsters Frank Borelli and Anthony DeGeorge were arrested for drug trafficking when found in a laboratory where morphine was being processed into heroin.
Oct. 3: U.S. Narcotic Bureau agents arrested drug trafficker Adolphe Tarditi, Guatemalan Ambassador Muricio Rosal, and an airline steward, confiscating 100 pounds of heroin valued at $20 million, and $26,000 in cash, at a New York City intersection.
1961
Strict penalties for the possession of marijuana were included in Canada's Narcotic Control Act.
Mar. 30: The United Nations adopted the Single Convention, which allowed each country to adopt its own laws against the cannabis plant.
Apr. 18: During a hearing regarding the medical ethics of Britain's doctors who prescribed narcotics, one pharmacist stated that he had filled a prescription calling for thirty grains of cocaine and fifty grains of heroin.
1962
An Ad Hoc Panel on Drug Abuse formed by President Kennedy determined that the link between marijuana, criminality, and sexual abuse was minimal.
Ninety-seven pounds of heroin were confiscated in New York from a drug ring later popularly known as "The French Connection."

The Supreme Court overturned a California ruling which made addiction a criminal offense.
Jan. 24: Mafia members Mario Caruso and Salvatore Mamesi were arrested in Madrid, Spain, for narcotics violations and bail-jumping. Each received a 15-year jail sentence.
1963
The President's Advisory Commission on Narcotics and Drug Abuse decried the fact that similar penalties were given for the sale of marijuana or heroin.
Researchers in New York first told of their successes with methadone in the treatment of heroin addiction.
Mafia informant Joseph Valachi testified before a Congressional Subcommittee on Organized Crime and Narcotics.
A "special employee" of the Federal Bureau of Narcotics was killed during a raid on a Mafia drug warehouse. The man's widow sued for compensation, and the court ruled she was entitled to it because her husband was an FNB "informant."
Mar. 22: Drug trafficker Alvin Beigel was arrested in Queens, N.Y., in possession of more than $3 million worth of heroin.
Mar. 29: Rock and roll singer Jimmy "Baby Face" Lewis was arrested in New York City on drug possession charges. Police later said that his arrest led to the uncovering of a nationwide narcotics ring.
May 10: Professional football player, Eugene "Big Daddy" Lipscomb, died of a suspected heroin overdose.
1964
An official of the Federal Bureau of Narcotics stated that 206 Mafia members, or 25 percent of the known total, had been successfully prosecuted for their involvement in the drug trade.
Drs. R.D. Laing and A. Esterson wrote impassioned pleas to others in the medical profession asking them to allay the fears of police about the dangers of marijuana.
Jan. 21: On the orders of Michael Gargano, a syndicate terrorist, Chicago policemen and mob drug-pusher Thomas N. Durso killed heroin addict and informant Anthony "Lover" Moschiano.
Apr. 21: Colorado District Judge William E. Buck declared a state narcotics law unconstitutional, and dismissed twelve defendants arrested on marijuana charges.
1965
Salvatore Aparo, a soldier in the Caetana crime family, was charged with participation in a heroin importing ring that brought more than $90 million in narcotics into the country in the late 1960s. A State Supreme Court Judge from Brooklyn dropped the charges. Aparo was been convicted of selling narcotics.
Despite being a proponent of drug use, beat poet Allen Ginsberg decried the use of amphetamines.
At a diplomatic dinner in Cairo, Egypt, Chinese Premier Chou En-lai allegedly stated that American soldiers in Viet Nam were being given China's best opium, in an effort to undermine the U.S. war effort.
1966
Hallucinogenic drugs, depressants, and stimulants were added to the list of substances controlled by Federal narcotics legislation.
In an essay, psychiatrist Phillip Epstein correlated the folk story "Jack and the Beanstalk" to a psychedelic drug experience.
Thomas Mattio, a known underworld figure in Central Islip, N.Y., was tried with mob underboss John (Sonny) Franzese for murder. Mattio was suspected of involvement in heroin trafficking with Charles Indiviglio, who was linked to convicted heroin smuggler Louis Cirillo.
Jan. 7: In a lecture in London, Dr. S.H. Groff analyzed the similarities between the use of hallucinogens and high-altitude flying.
May: A British tourist and an American were sentenced to fifteen years in prison in Nigeria for growing and smoking cannabis.
1967
With the aid of a Cuban-French underworld consortium, Frank "Pee Wee" Matthews successfully established an Eastern drug distribution network in direct competition with that of the New York crime families.
The Commission on Law Enforcement and Administration of Justice formed by President Johnson criticized the classification of marijuana as an opiate.
In Bangkok, William Herman Jackson opened Jack's American Star Bar, which served as a drug transaction center between heroin dealers from Asia's Golden Triangle and American servicemen.
May: Lady Frankau, a British physician known to prescribe narcotics liberally for addicts, died.
1968
The Federal Bureau of Narcotics was abolished by President Lyndon Johnson and was replaced by the Bureau of Narcotics and Dangerous Drugs, headed by John M. Ingersoll.
Jan. 11: Dr. John Petro, a British physician known to prescribe narcotics generously to drug addicts, was arrested for failing to keep a drug registry.
1969
It was estimated by the *New York Times* that at least seventy percent of college students had tried marijuana.
As an acknowledgement of his country's drug addiction problem, the Shah of Iran allowed limited cultivation of opium.
Captain of Catena family, Matthew "Matty The Horse" Ianniello was suspected of financial involvement in heroin deals. He had one arrest but no convictions on drug-related charges.
Ralph "Ronnie" Esposito, an ally of the Colombo family, was arrested for conspiracy in the nationwide narcotics investigation *Operation Flanker*. Charges were later dismissed.
Pasquale Ruffino was arrested in Queens, N.Y., and charged with plotting to murder a narcotics peddler. He served seven and a half years on a heroin selling conviction.
Feb. 11: An all-out war on organized crime was declared by President Richard M. Nixon, who asks Congress for $61 million to combat drug trafficking. Governments of several other nations were asked to cooperate with the U.S.
July 15: Attorney General John Mitchell suggested that the drug laws of the fifty states be updated and consolidated into a federal effort.
1970s
The tranquilizing drug Valium became one of the most widely used drugs in history.
1970
Congress passed the Comprehensive Drug Abuse Prevention and Control Act, which gave the attorney general the power to reclassify certain drugs as "dangerous."
A lobbying group, The National Organization for the Reform of Marijuana Laws, was organized.
Diconal, an analgesic preferred to heroin by some addicts, was introduced to the drug market.
Canada softened the penalties for marijuana possession.
Dec. 1: In Denver, Colo., Blanca A. Uriarte De Lopez, Ismael Jaquez-Diaz, Marciano Barraza-Sanchez, and others were arrested after delivering 784 grams of heroin to Bureau of Narcotics and Dangerous Drugs undercover agents. All of the defendants posted bond and fled to Mexico.
Dec. 8: Alan Murray Morris was arrested in Detroit, Mich., for possession of heroin. He was released and arrested eleven months later in Toledo, Ohio, on similar charges. He was arrested again in June 1972 in possession of both heroin and dynamite. Morris was freed on bond two days later.
1971
As much as 25 percent of the American military population in Viet Nam was suspected of using heroin.
The government of Turkey outlawed poppy cultivation, in return for a $35 million subsidy from the U.S.
Marijuana possession was decriminalized from a felony to a misdemeanor in Ann Arbor, Mich.
Marijuana was determined to have a positive effect in the treatment of glaucoma.
Michael Casale, a captain in the Joseph "Joe Bananas" Bonanno crime family, was arrested in 1971 during a nationwide crackdown on narcotics known as *Operation Flanker*. Casale was charged with conspiracy to sell heroin, but the charges were later dropped.
As associate of the Tramunti crime family, Peter Kourakas was identified as a major trafficker in heroin for the last ten years. At a 1971 hearing of the State Joint Legislative Committee on Crime, he invoked the Fifth Amendment repeatedly when asked about his convictions for dealing narcotics.
Paul Sciacca became the first crime boss since Vito Genovese to be charged with heroin conspiracy. Although the charges were dismissed, Sciacca is suspected of having continued to finance occasional heroin deals.
Feb. 6: Joaquim Gonzales, chief of air traffic control at Panama's international airport, was arrested in the Canal Zone. He was convicted and sentenced in Texas for his role in the passage of narcotics.
Feb. 10: Maurice Gregory was arrested in Boston after an investigation named him as head of group that had been selling heroin. After Gregory was freed, he moved to the New York area and continued to sell heroin to a Boston associate. On Nov. 13 he was arrested delivering 75 bundles of heroin to a New Jersey drug courier.
Feb. 21: The Convention on Psychotropic Substances, concerned with the increased usage of hallucinogens, depressants, and stimulants, was held in Vienna.
Apr. 21: Curry Williams was arrested in New Orleans after selling heroin to an undercover agent. Freed on bond, he was subsequently arrested for the sale of heroin on Dec. 9.
June 17: President Nixon established the Special Action Office for Drug Abuse Prevention.
June 28: Albert Bennett was arrested in Gary, Ind., for the possession of several ounces of pure heroin. Released on bond, he was arrested again on Aug. 15 in New York City by U.S. Marshals. In an altercation, Bennett disarmed a marshal and fled. Bennett continued to sell heroin until he was convicted.
June 30: The Board of Narcotics and Dangerous Drugs stated that almost 400 kilos of heroin had been confiscated during the previous twelve months. An estimated 180 kilos of the haul were returned to the streets by crooked policemen.
1972
The National Commission on Marijuana and Drug Abuse determined that about eight million Americans were using marijuana, and twenty-four million over the age of eleven had sampled the drug.
Canada amended its Criminal Code to reduce the penalty for possession of marijuana to a small fine.
Both Anthony Caccavale, enforcer, and Ralph Eboli, brother of deceased

crime boss Thomas "Tommy Ryan" Eboli, were convicted of trying to muscle into the heroin trafficking business at a Port Jefferson, N.Y., bar.
Ernest "Pop" Nelson was arrested in Miami several times throughout the year on charges of possession and sale of cocaine and heroin.
January: Eight Cuban members of Frank "Pee Wee" Matthews' drug ring were arrested, and 385 pounds of heroin valued at $76 million were seized in Miami.
Jan. 9: A "dope war" began in Detroit. It claimed 200 victims in nine months.
Jan. 18: Charles Steven Baken was arrested in Seattle, Wash., after selling heroin and cocaine to undercover agents through one of his dealers.
Jan. 28: Tiring of conflicts between the Bureau of Narcotics and Dangerous Drugs and customs officials, President Nixon established the Office for Drug Abuse Law Enforcement.
Jan. 30: Jose Garcia Leyva was arrested in San Antonio, Texas, after selling heroin to an undercover agent. He failed to appear for sentencing but was arrested on Sept. 19, 1972, in Mexico, for possession of heroin.
Feb. 3: New York City drug dealer Barry Glen Lipsky began confessing his crimes to police. His information led to one of the largest roundups of drug dealers in U.S. history.
Mar. 11: William Jacobs was arrested in Pittsburgh, Pa., in connection with the sale of heroin to Bureau of Narcotics and Dangerous Drugs Division undercover agents. Jacobs was released the same day on $5,000 bond. He was arrested again on Apr. 21 for illegal possession of heroin and was again released. Jacobs was arrested a third time on Aug. 14 by FBI agents as he tried to negotiate for purchase of narcotics being shipped to Pittsburgh.
May 2: FBI Director J. Edgar Hoover died.
May 9: Robert A. Murry was arrested at Los Angeles Airport with 30,000 amphetamine and 1,300 secobarbital tablets. He was released on bond and arrested again in Florida on May 22, as he delivered 450,000 amphetamine tablets to an undercover agent.
May 16: Enrique Barrera was arrested in Manhattan as he attempted to receive a 100 kilogram shipment of heroin. Four months later, U.S. customs agents intercepted several South American couriers in Miami as they tried to bring in cocaine. Barrera was identified as the intended recipient, and was arrested again on Sept. 12.
August: The Office of National Narcotics Intelligence was founded.
September: Charles Indiviglio of East Northport, N.Y., was arrested when $350,000, heroin processing equipment, and a seriously wounded man were found in his basement. Indiviglio's brother was the late Benedetto "Benny the Cringe" Indiviglio, who was named in 1964 by a Senate subcommittee as a narcotics smuggler involved in interstate distribution of drugs.
Sept. 1: "International drug czar" Auguste Ricord was successfully extradited from Paraguay to New York, where he was arrested.
Sept. 15: One of Frank "Pee Wee" Matthews' drug processing mills was raided in New York, netting small amounts of cocaine and heroin, as well as $148,000 found in a pillow case.

1973

Marijuana possession was decriminalized to a misdemeanor in Oregon.
The lenient marijuana laws in Ann Arbor, Mich., were rescinded.
Nepal banned the production of hashish, but later rescinded the edict when the censure threatened the nation's economy.
Jan. 1: East coast drug czar Frank "Pee Wee" Matthews was arrested in Las Vegas, Nev.
April: Drug busts in Collinsville and Edwardsville, Ill., received national attention when the occupants of the raided houses claimed that narcotics agents had used excessive force.
June: Michael Rebozo, the 25-year-old nephew of Nixon confidante Bebe Rebozzo, was sentenced to one year in jail for the possession of eight ounces of cocaine.
July 1: The Drug Enforcement Administration (DEA) was formed by President Nixon.

1974

In Ann Arbor, Mich., possession of marijuana was again reduced to a misdemeanor, subject to a five dollar fine.
Jan. 23: Carmine "The Cigar" Galante was paroled in New York after spending several years in prison for dope smuggling.
Nov. 20: Indictments were issued in a Brooklyn Federal Court, naming fifty-eight suspected heroin and opium smugglers, and twenty-five co-conspirators. Stemming from the investigation of a global network led by Wong Shing Kong, the cartel used Scandinavian seamen and Chinese distributors to import drugs into New York, San Francisco, and Canada.

1975

The Ethiopian Zion Coptic Church, which used marijuana for its worship rituals, bought extensive real estate on Miami's Star Island.
Leslie "Ike" Atkinson was convicted and sentenced to federal prison for operating a drug pipeline between Bangkok and army bases in North Carolina.
January: Thirty-seven people were arrested in a massive drug raid in Miami, signalling the start of Operation Hawk.
February: Miami drug dealer Kenneth Burnstine and drug-running pilot William Klein were convicted of conspiracy involving a drug operation and sentenced to seven years in prison.

1976

Jan. 9: A Malaysian stevedore, Teo Hock-Song, was sentenced to death in Singapore for morphine smuggling.
Apr. 2: James "Big Jim" Capotorto, a cocaine dealer, was shot to death while attempting to collect $20,000 from a client in Fort Lauderdale, Fla.
Apr. 2: John Thomas Jova, the son of the U.S. ambassador to Mexico, was sent to prison in Maidstone, Eng., for two-and-a-half years for drug smuggling.
May 1: Actress Louise Lasser was arrested on charges of cocaine possession in Beverly Hills, Calif.
June 17: Free on appeal, convicted drug king-pin Kenneth Burnstine was killed in a plane crash in the Mojave Desert.
July: The Company, the largest illegal drug smuggling operation ever broken by the DEA, was started in Alton, Ill.
July 18: Agents of the DEA arrested six members of a drug ring led by Oscar Mancillas, in Joliet, Ill. The ring was reputed to have imported $12 million worth of heroin a month to the Chicago area.
Oct. 16: The U.S. Coast Guard intercepted a Panamanian freighter, the *Don Emelio*, off the coast of the Bahamas. Early reports estimated that the ship carried as much as eighty tons of marijuana and 400 pounds of cocaine. At the time, it was the largest seizure of contraband ever recorded.
Oct. 28: Japanese police arrested 2,489 people in Tokyo in drug raids. They confiscated large amounts of illegal drugs.
Nov. 19: Chow Sae Choorachait and Supol Laohavichairat, two Thai citizens, were arrested in Atlanta, Ga., in possession of $3 million worth of heroin carried in hollowed-out books.
Dec. 9: Francois Chiappe and Miguel Russo were convicted in Federal Court in Brooklyn, N.Y., of conspiring to import and distribute heroin. The two, along with Michel Nicoli, formed the "Latin-American Triangle" which brought more than six tons of drugs into the U.S.

1977

Columbia consolidated the efforts of five anti-drug agencies into a single agency, the Federal Judicial Police.
Elvis Presley died, in large part due to an addiction to amphetamines, barbiturates, and sedatives.
Jan. 27: Bales of marijuana were found floating in the Gulf of Mexico after the sinking of the shrimp-boat *Gunsmoke*.
Feb. 1: The Coast Guard apprehended a drug boat, the *Night Train*, and arrested thirteen men, while seizing fifty-four tons of marijuana valued at $21.6 million.
Feb. 2: Police found $200,000 worth of drugs and a large cache of counterfeit $20 bills in the home of Virgil Hewell in Burke, Va. Hewell was sent to prison.
Feb. 13: The DEA arrested six Cubans who had just unloaded a boat filled with marijuana, and two more in a camper that contained seven tons of the drug. Most of the contraband, loaded into two large trucks, eluded the federal agents.
Feb. 20: Marijuana smuggler Robert Yuckman was murdered by one of his employees at his home in Coconut Grove, Fla.
Late Feb.: 120 tons of marijuana, valued at $48 million, were seized by the Coast Guard during a raid on the cargo ship *Calabres*.
Mar. 11: Actress Angelica Huston was arrested for cocaine possession in the home of actor Jack Nicholson while police were searching the house for evidence related to charges that film director Roman Polanski had drugged and raped a 13-year-old girl there the previous night. Nicholson was in Europe at the time.
Mar. 16: Nicky Barnes, purported to be one of New York's biggest heroin dealers, was arrested after a Federal Grand Jury indictment.
Mar. 23: Twenty-one people in a heroin-smuggling ring centered in Ypsilanti, Mich., and headed by Richard Phillips, were arrested at several sites in Cleveland, Los Angeles, Pittsburgh, and Washington.
Apr. 10: Four members of the Rastafarian cult, a sect which included marijuana smoking in its ritualistic worship, were found murdered in Brooklyn, N.Y. At least two of the members were known marijuana dealers.
May 15: The Airport Narcotics Unit was established at Miami International Airport, where over one hundred pounds of uncut heroin was suspected of entering the U.S. annually.
July: Livingston Stocker was one of six men killed during a drug transaction at his Carol City, Fla., home.
July 3: Three men were killed during the sale of $60,000 worth of marijuana near Turkey Point, in the Florida Keys.
August: Manuel Villarreal-Valdez and Emma Quintana-Molina were arrested by Mexican officials at their heroin laboratory in Guadalajara.
August: Robert Reid Topping, who within a year would have inherited $1 million, was stabbed to death in Miami. The son of the former owner of the New York Yankees, he had regularly travelled to Florida to buy large amounts of cocaine.
August: President Jimmy Carter suggested to Congress that possession of an ounce of marijuana should be punished by a fine, rather than a prison sentence.
Aug.7: The bodies of four people, including two missing girls, were found by divers exploring a sinkhole in Taylor County, Fla. The murders were tied to the Jan. 27 sinking of the *Gunsmoke*, a shrimp boat known to be involved in smuggling.
Aug. 14: More than $365,000 and assorted narcotics were confiscated by police in Warwick, R.I., after a chain of events unraveled a large drug distribution network which included Meyer Lansky and Robert Vesco.

November: Michael Rossin, a drug dealer and the son of a Miami restaurateur, was killed as he attempted to rob a potential customer.
Nov. 28: Sixteen tons of marijuana valued at $8 million was seized, and seven people were arrested, including five who were members of the Ethiopian Zion Coptic Church, in a drug raid on Miami's Star Island.
Nov. 30: A Bay County, Fla., grand jury indicted four men for the murder of the four people found in a Taylor County sinkhole. The murders were tied to the sunken shrimp boat *Gunsmoke*. Forty tons of marijuana had been on board the boat, and rumors included hints of state and FBI corruption and a cover-up.
December: John and Lynn Scarborough, the son and daughter of Florida State Senator Dan Scarborough, were arrested and charged with conspiracy in a cocaine ring.
Dec. 2: The Coast Guard intercepted the freighter *Diana Cecelia* and found fifteen tons of marijuana aboard.
Dec. 20: As part of Operation Snowbird, a drug "sting" operation, planes used for marijuana smuggling were seized at Pompano and Sebring, Fla.
Dec. 30: As part of Operation Snowbird, a plane containing seventeen tons of marijuana was captured in Florence, S.C., while a yacht with two tons of marijuana aboard was captured in Ft. Lauderdale, Fla.

1978

More than $3 billion in cash from the sale of drugs was waiting to be deposited in Florida banks. An economist stated that if the drug money was removed from the economy, the state would suffer a severe recession.
After announcing that close to seventy tons of cocaine were being exported annually, the DEA placed agents in ten South American countries.
The DEA estimated that four tons of heroin were imported annually from Mexico. More than 70,000 poppy fields had been eradicated by a government spraying effort during the previous three years.
Chinese drug lord Khun Sa brashly offered the Carter administration a five year opium supply in return for $30 million.
Hawaiian police announced that marijuana had replaced sugar as the state's largest cash crop, netting close to $400 million annually.
Jan. 3: Nearly fifty pounds of cocaine and $36,000 in cash were discovered on a boat near Ft. Lauderdale, Fla.
Jan. 10: Eight people were arrested and 19,000 pounds of marijuana were confiscated in a drug raid in Charleston, S.C., as part of the government's Operation Snowbird.
Jan. 18: Fifty pounds of cocaine were found in life preservers on a boat which had just arrived in Miami.
Jan. 18: More than 2,000 pounds of marijuana were found floating in the Gulf of Mexico, dropped from a plane which was seized in St. Petersburg, Fla.
Jan. 19: New York drug kingpin Nicky Barnes was sentenced to life imprisonment and fined $125,000 for operating a "continuing criminal enterprise."
Jan. 25: Twenty-five boxes of marijuana were seized and two men were arrested, when a plane with two blown tires was traced to an airstrip near Tampa, Fla.
February: Seventeen people, including Ethiopian Zion Coptic Church leader Keith Gordon, were arrested in Miami during the seizure of twenty tons of marijuana.
February: At a trial in Bristol, England, testimony indicated that two laboratories on the outskirts of London made England the largest producer of LSD in the world.
March: Nicholas Christoff, a high school senior, was shot in Pompano Beach, Fla., while discussing a drug deal.
Mar. 26: Drug dealers Carlos Fernando Quesada and Rodolfo Rodriguez were arrested in Miami. Officials seized fifty-six pounds of cocaine valued at $14 million, as well as over $900,000 in cash.
Apr. 6: Drug kingpin and government informant Ricardo "Monkey" Morales and three others were arrested in a Miami raid which also netted 5000 pounds of marijuana.
Apr. 15: Fifty-seven tons of marijuana were seized by the DEA on a tip from the Florida Marine Patrol during a raid on the freighter *Moctezuma*, near the Bahamas.
Mid-April: The Coast Guard seized thirty-seven tons of marijuana, valued at $74 million, in a raid of the freighter *Helena Star*, off the coast of Washington.
June 12: Police arrested two men and seized $1.5 billion worth of cocaine, after blocking the take-off of a private plane on Great Exuma island in the Bahamas.
June 28: Former TV newsman Jack Kelly was one of five men murdered in Boston after a dispute involving cocaine.
August: One hundred twelve tons of marijuana were seized during a raid by the DEA of the freighter *Heidi*, off the coast of Cape Canaveral, Fla.
Aug. 15: Officers of the Alabama Bureau of Investigation found an abandoned DC-3 with the residue of marijuana in its interior, resting in a farm field near Hurtsboro, Ala.

1979

Dutchmen Albertus Merks, Dick Ruiter, and Jan Stuurman were arrested at their amphetamine factory in Scotland. Police confiscated 60 million tablets worth $92 million, as well as material used to manufacture synthetic heroin.
President Zia of Pakistan banned opium production.
Jan. 16: Fifteen members of a huge drug ring known as the Company were arrested in Darlington, S.C., following the seizure of almost 1,400 pounds of marijuana.
Apr. 29: Six and a half tons of marijuana valued at $5.3 million were discovered on a yacht in Chesapeake Bay, near Smith Point, Md.
May 30: Six members of the Company, a large drug ring, were arrested, and 15,000 pounds of marijuana were confiscated at a warehouse in Conley, Ga.
July 19: Giorgio Guiliano, deputy chief of police in Sicily who successfully undermined numerous Mafia drug operations, was murdered in a Palermo cafe.
Sept. 7: Twenty members of a heroin distribution ring led by Armando Quintero-Medina were indicted in a Federal Court in Chicago. He and three other smugglers fled to Mexico to avoid arrest.
Sept. 26: Casare Terranova, a 58-year-old judge appointed to investigate the murder of policeman Giorgio Guiliano, was murdered by armed Mafia motorcyclists in Palermo, Sicily.
December: Sheriff A.J. O'Tuel of Darlington County, S.C., was indicted on five counts of bribery in connection with the DEA dismantling of a huge drug smuggling operation known as the Company. O'Tuel was later found not guilty.
Dec. 14: Three Iranians, Alimaghi Bahman Mazarei, Hashem Mohamad Tavakolian, and Kazem Mohaman Tavakolian, were arrested in California, attempting to smuggle 35 pounds of opium concealed in hollowed-out packets of pictures of Ayatollah Khomeini.

1980s

Drug sales in the U.S. were estimated at $100 billion a year.

1980

Florida attorney general James Smith stated that the drug business was the largest retail enterprise in his state.
In Los Angeles alone, 448 pounds of cocaine valued at $112 million were confiscated.
The DEA offered a $25,000 reward for the capture of Asian drug lord Khun Sa. Shortly thereafter, the wife of a DEA agent was shot to death on a street in Chiang Mai.
One-thousand seven-hundred twenty-six servicemen guilty of drug use were transferred away from nuclear weapons work.
January 17: Former Beatle Paul McCartney was arrested for marijuana possession and jailed for ten days in Tokyo.
Jan. 6: Gaetano Costa, a Sicilian prosecutor of numerous Mafia drug dealers, was murdered in Palermo, Sicily.
May 4: Sicilian police captain Emanuele Basile, who uncovered a Mafia drug operation between Rome and New York, was murdered in Monreale, Sicily.
May 22: In Kendall, Fla., the DEA confiscated 580 pounds of cocaine during a sting operation aimed at stopping drug traffic between Bolivia and the U.S.
June: Comedian Richard Pryor almost died after accidentally setting himself on fire while freebasing cocaine.
June: Over 5000 pounds of marijuana were seized from a boat abandoned near Ocean City, Md.
June 3: Bolivian drug czar Roberto Suarez, Sr. was indicted by a federal grand jury, although he was not in U.S. custody.
July: Dr. Peter Bourne, a presidential advisor who was the former head of the Office of Drug Abuse Policy resigned after admitting that he had obtained methaqualone for a White House assistant by using a fictitious name to fill a prescription.
July: Robert Evans, who produced *Chinatown*, *The Godfather*, and *Love Story*, pleaded guilty to agreeing to buy $19,000 worth of cocaine. Evans later produced an anti-drug TV special called *Get High on Yourself*.
Aug. 12: Robert Steinberg was arrested by agents of the DEA after surrendering in Chicago. He had sold 111 grams of cocaine to an undercover agent, and was further alleged to have imported marijuana by the ton, using semi-trailer trucks.
October: Irish police arrested Larry Dunne, considered to be Ireland's biggest drug dealer, and charged him with possession and intent to supply nearly $80,000 of cannabis, cocaine, and heroin.
Oct. 7: Film producer Robert Evans was given a year's probation in New York City for cocaine possession.
Oct. 20: Seventeen pounds of 100 percent pure heroin were discovered in a car involved in an auto accident in Vientiane, Laos.
Nov. 8: William and Tracy Melton, facing minimum sentences for cocaine and marijuana possession, swallowed cyanide and died in a Rockville, Md., courtroom.
Dec. 4: James Anderson Mitchell and Bryan O'Neal Sullivan, leaders of the drug ring known as the Company, were arrested in Montgomery, Ala.

1981

Phencyclidine (PCP), also known as "angel dust", a drug which affects the central nervous system, began being widely used.
Fumiko Taoka, the leader of the Yakuza which controlled drug traffic, died in Japan.
Methyl analog of fentanyl, an analgesic known as "China White," became a popular drug in Hollywood despite thirty deaths attributed to its use.
Feb. 26: Isaac Kattan, a Columbian drug financier, known as South Florida's "Al Capone," was arrested in possession of twenty kilos of cocaine at an intersection in Miami.
May: Autopsies revealed that six victims of a plane crash on the U.S. aircraft carrier *Nimitz* had marijuana in their systems.
May 29: In federal court in Alton, Ill., Marvin Zylstra, a member of the

drug ring the Company, was sentenced to 210 years in prison on racketeering, conspiracy, and violation of interstate commerce charges.
Aug. 4: Bolivian President Luis Garcia Meza resigned after his government was charged with human rights violations and cocaine trafficking.
November: Tired of waiting for action from federal or state anti-drug programs, the Miami Chamber of Commerce established its own Citizens Against Crime.
Nov. 29: Mario Estebes Gonzalez, a Cuban drug runner, was arrested by the U.S. Coast Guard in possession of 2,500 pounds of marijuana.

1982

Blaming marijuana use, officials noted that the SAT scores on verbal ability had dropped forty percent, and on mathematics twenty-five percent, during the previous fifteen years.
The drug MPTP was accidently invented by chemists trying to synthetically reproduce Demerol. Twenty users contracted Parkinson's Disease.
A Thai informant was buried alive by drug lord Khun Sa.
Edwin Shore, the head of the police authority in the West Midlands, England, admitted to smoking marijuana, stating that he didn't believe it would cause physical harm.
January: Texas millionaire Rex Cauble was convicted for his complicity in a marijuana enterprise.
January: Cocaine dealer Orlando Galvez was murdered in New York City.
Jan. 21: The FBI replaced the DEA as the head of the U.S. anti-drug campaign.
Jan. 28: President Reagan announced a plan for a federal task force headed by Vice-President George Bush, to examine the problem of drugs in south Florida.
February: An American and Columbian undercover operation named Operation Tiburon arrested 500 people and confiscated 6.4 million pounds of marijuana.
Feb. 20: Former basketball star James Bradley was killed by members of the syndicate on a Portland, Ore., street. According to police, the syndicate feared Bradley would reveal their drug trafficking methods to avoid a jail term for drug possession.
March: Comedian John Belushi died after injecting a mixture of cocaine and heroin.
Mar. 9: Almost two tons of cocaine, valued at $1.3 billion, were seized by Customs officers at Miami Airport, mixed in with a clothing shipment from Columbia.
Mar. 12: Cuba was charged with marijuana smuggling and arms running operations when Assistant Secretary of State of Inter-American Affairs, Thomas Enders, told a Senate committee that Columbian drug smuggler, Jaime Guillo Lara, had confessed to helping smuggle weapons to Colombian guerrillas. Lara was aided by Cuba in smuggling marijuana into the U.S.
April: U.S. Customs officials seized more than 500 pounds of cocaine valued at $166 million from an airplane in Bimini.
Apr. 1: U.S. Customs officials seized 70,000 pounds of marijuana, valued at over $54 million, from the trawler *Misfit* off the coast of Florida.
June: President Reagan appointed Dr. Carlton Turner, a scientist who had conducted experiments with marijuana, as his presidential adviser on narcotics.
June 30: Sepala Ekanayaka, who seized a 747 Alitalia jet just after takeoff from New Delhi, was later identified by narcotics officials in Columbo as having been involved in hashish smuggling in Yugoslavia in 1974 and morphine smuggling in 1981.
August: Michael Dunne, a member of Ireland's largest drug-selling family, was arrested for possession of and the intent to supply heroin.
Sept. 2: Police officer Carlo Alberto Della Chiesa was murdered in Palermo while investigating Sicilian Mafia drug money laundering operations.
Sept. 30: Federal agencies announced that they had seized 1.7 million pounds of marijuana and 6,565 pounds of cocaine during the previous seven months, a marked increase over previous years.
Sept. 30: Baseball star Ron LeFlore was arrested in Chicago and accused of possessing illegal drugs and weapons.
October: President Reagan stated that the successful south Florida drug raids were convincing him to try crippling the mob in America.
October: Twenty thousand people marched through the streets of Verona, Italy, protesting against drug dealers, the "merchants of death."
October: Thai police, prodded by the DEA, raided a drug operation run by Asian drug lord Khun Sa, forcing him to relocate in Burma.
Oct. 19: Car manufacterer John DeLorean was arrested in the Sheraton Plaza Hotel in Los Angeles for trying to buy and sell millions of dollars' worth of cocaine. Authorities claim his "buy" was meant to shore up his collapsing financial empire.
November: President Reagan stated that the south Florida task force against drugs was a clear and unqualified success.
November: Over thirty tons of marijuana were seized by U.S. Customs officials when they raided the *Shooting Star*, a vessel sailing north of Puerto Rico.
November: Robert Dunne, a member of Ireland's biggest drug ring, was arrested for possession of and intent to supply heroin.
Nov. 17: William R. Johnson, arrested in connection with the 1981 robbery of a Brink's truck in Nyack, N.Y., was extradited to the U.S. after he was arrested on drug charges in Belize.
December: U.S. Customs officials confiscated twenty-eight tons of marijuana during raids on three vessels sailing near Fort Myers, Fla.
Dec. 3: Customs officials seized 700 pounds of cocaine, valued at $214 million, from a freighter, the *Mal Azul*, in Miami harbor.
Dec. 8: Norman Mayer threatened to blow up the Washington Monument unless a ban on nuclear weapons became "the first order of business on every agenda of every organization." He was fatally wounded by police. Mayer had been arrested in 1976 in Hong Kong for possessing forty-four pounds of marijuana.
Dec. 20: Business man John DeLorean was charged by the U.S. government with promoting a $24 million cocaine deal. DeLorean was also charged with receiving money from the Irish Republican Army to finance the drug deal.

1983

U.S. Customs officials in Miami estimated that more than $100 billion worth of drugs were smuggled into the country annually.
U.S. Customs claimed to have seized more than 2.7 million pounds of marijuana and 20,136 pounds of cocaine during the year.
More than $81 million worth of narcotics were confiscated by British customs officials.
Four hundred fifty-five American servicemen were accused of drug offenses while working near cruise missiles and nuclear-equipped bombers in England.
January: In Alexandria, Va., Barry Toombs was sentenced to fifteen years without parole, Julian Pernell to ten years without parole, for racketeering and possession of 33,000 pounds of marijuana.
March: William Wendell Ylvisaker, a millionaire friend of Britain's Prince Charles, died of a cocaine overdose in Palm Beach, Fla.
April: U.S. Attorney General William French Smith and DEA administrator Francis Mullen traveled to Bolivia and offered the government $40 million in crop restitution for halting some of the growth of coca.
Apr. 29: Sae Henk Wakin and Vichai Phongchaivararith, two Thai nationals, were arrested after being caught shipping pure heroin worth $58 million to various apartments in the Los Angeles area.
May 5: Sheik Juamir, 35-year-old Pakistani "heroin king," was turned over to authorities by tribal elders at the Khyber Pass in Pakistan.
June: As a result of a five-year probe by Italian police and the DEA, sixty-five members of three Sicilian Mafia families were imprisoned for drug trafficking.
July: Shamie Dunne, a member of Ireland's largest drug distribution family, was arrested with more than $500,000 worth of heroin in his possession.
July 9: In London, Michael Fagin, a drug addict, was found with his hand dripping blood, talking to the Queen in her bedroom at Buckingham Palace.
Sept. 12: Federal officials claimed that Robert Vesco, who had fled the U.S. for South America in 1972 with an estimated $60 million in stolen money, had set up a drug ring involving the Cuban coast guard and Nicaraguan leftists to bring heroin and cocaine to the U.S.
October: Five Bahamian government officials suspected of taking bribes from drug traffickers were unseated following an official investigation.

1984

U.S. Customs said they had seized more than 2.9 million pounds of marijuana and 33,080 pounds of cocaine.
The government of Singapore executed twelve people for trafficking drugs in the nine years following a 1975 mandate.
January: A spokesman for the British Police Federation stated that police could neither contain the distribution of marijuana nor enforce anti-usage laws.
March: Two British judges ruled that a person intoxicated by sniffing glue could not be charged with being drunk and disorderly.
Mar. 10: Columbian police seized 13.8 tons of cocaine worth $1.2 billion from a jungle complex near the Yari river in Caqueta.
April: David Anthony Kennedy, son of assassinated Sen. Robert Kennedy, died of an overdose of cocaine and Demerol in Palm Beach, Fla.
April: Columbian Justice Minister Rodrigo Lara Bonilla, who had attempted to quell drug trafficking, was murdered in Bogota.
May: The government of Pakistan considered mandating the death penalty for drug trafficking.
July: Tommasso Buscetta, a Mafia member about to be imprisoned for drug trafficking, confessed to illegal dealings which implicated more than 350 mobsters in New York and Italy.
August: It was determined that Bahamian Premier Lyndon Pindling had spent eight times his official salary during the previous seven years. He was suspected of accepting bribes from drug traffickers.
Dec. 24: The second secretary of the Columbian Embassy in Madrid, Gustavo Jacome Lemus, was arrested on drug smuggling charges.

1985

Designer drugs, produced in laboratories with up to a thousand times the potency of heroin, were created.
A report issued by the House Select Committee on Narcotics Abuse and Control stated that 20 million Americans regularly used marijuana, between 8 and 20 million regularly used cocaine, 1 million used hallucinogens, and a half-million used heroin.
In Los Angeles, 556 pounds of cocaine valued at more than $168 million were confiscated during a single drug raid.
Jan. 26: Masahisa Takenaka, the leader of the Yakuza, which controlled

Japanese drug traffic, was shot to death along with two body guards in Osaka, Japan.
February: Ten top-ranking members of New York crime families were indicted for conspiracy to operate a criminal enterprise, after a five-year undercover investigation by the FBI.
February: Billionaire drug dealer Mustaq Malik was arrested in Karachi by Pakistani police.
March: Zambian Government Commissioner Godfrey Lubinga resorted to diplomatic immunity to avoid questioning in London concerning a $640,000 shipment of heroin. Kenneth Kaunda, President of Zambia, lifted that immunity.
March 6: The bodies of two DEA agents were found in Guadalajara, Mexico, following their kidnapping by Mexican drug traffickers the previous month.
April: The synthetic drug, 3-methyl-fentanyl was created. Although a thousand times stronger than heroin, the drug was legal because it was not banned under the Controlled Substances Act.
May: In a massive eleven-state raid which included a thousand agents, the FBI arrested more than 100 members of the Hell's Angels motorcycle gang and confiscated $2 million worth of drugs.
July: Jamaican Government Minister Norman Saunders was convicted in Miami for complicity in a drug operation.
August: In an interview published in *Playboy* magazine, Cuban Premier Fidel Castro stated that his government had halted drug production and severely punished traffickers, despite accusations by the U.S. government that Cuba was an active conspirator in the international drug trade.

1986

Jan. 7: The Foreign Minister of Mauritius and three other ministers resigned after Mauritian members of parliament were arrested in the Netherlands for smuggling drugs.
Dec. 14: A police and army drug raid in Karachi, Pak., triggered five days of rioting during which at least 180 people were killed.
Dec. 20: The cabinet of Karachi, Pak., resigned after five days of drug riots, but was reconstituted two days later with the same members.

1987

Mar. 19: Kirtanananda Swami Bhaktipada, the leader of the West Virginia faction of the Hare Krishna cult, was expelled following an investigation into many illicit practices, including drug dealing.
November: U.S. Supreme Court nominee Douglas H. Ginsburg withdrew his nomination, following a public furor created by the admission that he had smoked marijuana as a college student.
Dec. 15: Benjamin Herrera, a Columbian drug smuggler suspected of being the founder of a cartel supplying 80 percent of the cocaine brought into the U.S., was arrested in Davie, Fla.
Dec. 31: The U.S. protested the release of a jailed Columbian drug baron who was freed instead of being extradited to the U.S.

1988

Jan. 25: Attorney General Carlos Hoyos of Columbia and two bodyguards were killed by drug traffickers near Medellin. Hoyos sought to allow the U.S. to extradite members of the Medellin cartel.
Feb. 5: Suspected of taking bribes from international drug traffickers, Panamanian General Manuel Noriega was indicted by federal grand juries in Tampa and Miami, Fla.
April: The FBI arrested thirty-nine people in the U.S., while Italian authorities arrested another sixty-two, breaking a Sicilian Mafia drug ring. After two years and more than 200 agents and dozens of wiretaps, the search culminated in a Manhattan motel room, with arrest warrants extending from Cleveland to Puerto Rico.
July 26: U.S. Marshals confiscated the pizza parlor and the bar of Dante Autullo, Jr. in Orland Park, Ill., on rumors that both were meeting places for million-dollar cocaine deals. Although Autullo confessed to selling sixty kilograms of cocaine a month, with a monthly return of $175,000, charges against him were dismissed on Jan. 23, 1989.
Sept. 28: Roman Alvarez-Quiroga, Juiliana Alvarez-Quiroga, and Roman Alvarez Quiroga, Jr. were arrested for speeding near Pontiac, Ill. Search of their station wagon revealed 160 pounds of cocaine worth between $7 and $12 million under the roof liner of their car. Charges against them were dismissed by Judge Harold Frobish on Dec. 1, 1988.
Oct. 11: Nine executives and seventy-six employees of the Luxembourg-based Bank of Credit and Commerce International S.A., were charged by the U.S. government with conspiracy to launder millions of dollars deposited by cocaine dealers.
Oct. 22: The U.S. Congress, in an attempt to limit the supply and consumption of drugs, passed a comprehensive drug bill, which among other things, sanctioned the death penalty in the case of slayings by those involved in two or more ongoing unlawful drug operations.

1989

Mar. 26: Richard Wallstrum was convicted as the ringleader of a $33 million cocaine ring which operated between South America and California from 1974 to 1984. He and eleven others were charged with trafficking in December 1987.

DUELING

Duels of honor have been fought at least since the time of Caesar and Tacitus. Though the practice has been outlawed by most nations, the traditions are kept alive in the German universities where the "Verbindungen" (fighting corps) engage in fencing, adhere to strict rules of sportsmanship, and participate in regimens of the secret society.

Duels were originally fought to settle legal disputes or tribal quarrels between two antagonists. According to Caesar's reports, the early Germanic tribes resolved differences with a decisive battle of swordsmen. The judicial duel sprang from the solemn swearing of oaths, when it was often difficult to determine which of the two participants had perjured themselves. If one party to the dispute swore to a judge that the other had committed a certain crime, and the accused denied it, the judge often ordered them to settle the matter on the field of honor.

The challenger would "throw down the gauntlet." Acceptance of the terms of the duel were signified by the second party picking it up. The victor of the duel was deemed to have been worthy of God's judgment, and therefore absolved of wrongdoing, or vindicated depending on the circumstances of the dispute. Dueling, "the manly art," was the inherent right of all free men, and in some cases was open to the serfs. Women, members of the clergy, minors under the age of twenty, and those past the age of sixty were exempted from the ritual. The judicial duel was introduced to England by William I in the 11th century. It lasted until 1819. In France, the last duel to be sanctioned by the King took place on July 10, 1547.

The famous "duel of honor" dates back to 15th-century Italy. Duels of this nature were fought over the slightest pretext or insult. As the custom evolved, the duelist would designate a second, who often would engage their counterpart to prove their worthiness. King Charles IX's decree that anyone caught fighting a duel would be executed did not entirely discourage men from settling accounts in this fashion. Duels were fought in Europe and in the U.S. throughout the nineteenth century. Alexander Hamilton and Aaron Burr fought a celebrated duel in Weehawken, N.J., in 1804 which resulted in Hamilton's death. Political duels of this nature were common in the 19th century, but were no longer in vogue by the 1900s.

432
Aëtius, Roman general, killed Bonifacius, ruler of Africa.
1356
French soldier Bertrand du Guesclin dueled Thomas Canterbury.
16th Cent.
Azevedo fought Sainte-Croix with dagger and sword in Italy. Sainte-Croix surrendered and Azevedo declined to cut off his opponent's head.
Bayard killed Alonso de Sotomayor, a Spanish captain, in a duel on horseback.
Chateauneuf ran his sword through his elderly guardian, Lachesnaye in a duel fought over rude remarks.
Perault and Aldano dueled in the public square, with permission of De Chaumont, representative to the King of France at Milan. Both men survived.
Four were killed in a duel in which the seconds began fighting before the main participants, D'Entragues and Caylus. Only D'Entragues and Maugerin, one of Caylus' seconds, survived.
1513
In Padua, Domenico Colliva killed Jerónimo de Valencia, a Spanish captain, in a duel fought during a battle between Spaniards and Venetians.
1529
Mar. 12: Giovanni Bandini killed Lodovico Martelli but his second, Albertino Aldobrandi was killed by Martelli's second, Dante di Castiglione.
1547
Comte Guy Chabot de Jarnac killed Comte de la Châteigneraie, who refused to apologize for spreading rumors about Jarnac even after his hamstrings had been sliced and he could not stand.
1572
Bussy d'Amboise was known as a frequent sword duelist.
17th Cent.
Savinien de Cyrano de Bergerac, a French soldier, became known as a prominent duelist in the house of Duc d'Arpajon.
1667
The Duke of Buckingham shot and killed the Earl of Shrewsberry and rode off with the Earl's adulterous wife, for whom the duel was fought.
1712
James Douglas,the 4th Duke of Hamilton and Duke of Brandon and Charles Mohun, dueling over land owned by Douglas, killed each other.
c. 1718
Disguised as a man, Mary Read dueled "Calico Jack" Rackham. Read, after shooting Rackham in the neck, cut his throat. He survived and was later hanged as a pirate.
1728
July: In Boston, Henry Phillips killed Benjamin Woodbridge.
1752
Nov. 26: In the West Indies, young lawyer John Barbot killed Matthew Mills in a duel to settle a debt. Barbot was tried and executed.
1762
September: Magazine editor John Wilkes fought Lord Talbot with pistols. Both walked away from the duel unharmed.
1763
April: John Wilkes was shot and injured by Samuel Martin, secretary of the treasury, in a duel brought on by remarks printed in Wilkes' newspaper, the *North Briton.*
1765
May: Lord Kilmaurs, whose deafness caused him to speak loudly, was stabbed in a duel by a French officer who took offense at his loud voice during a play.
1769
In Ireland, Henry Flood shot and killed James Agar, after the two men decided to settle a long standing conflict with a duel.
1770s
Brigadier general John Cadwalader challenged General Thomas Conway to a duel after discovering Conway's plot to oust George Washington. Conway received serious injuries and dishonor.
1770
Nov. 17: A duel between actors George Garrick and Mr. Baddeley over Baddeley's wife resulted in no injuries for its participants.
1771
Jan. 29: Lord Milton, after asking that his opponent, Lord Poulett, fire the first shot of their duel, was wounded in the stomach.
1772
In Scotland, Mr. M'Lean was killed by Mr. Cameron.
1777
Jan 13: Captain Stoney and newspaper editor Mr. Bate, dueled with guns and swords. An interruption saved Stoney from death, and he married the woman for whom he fought.
May 16: In Georgia, General Lachlan McIntosh and Hon. Button Gwinnett, who signed the Declaration of Independence, wounded each other in a duel. Gwinnett died from his injuries on May 19.
1778
A fake duel was arranged between Comte d'Artois, Charles Phillipe and the Duc de Bourbon, Louis Phillipe d'Orleans in order to appease the public, after a face slapping at the Paris Opera.
Nov. 23: Viscount du Barry and Count Rice finished an argument with pistols and swords at dawn. The Viscount begged for his life but it was too late. The Count was found guilty of Manslaughter.
Dec 31: No injuries resulted from a duel between General Horatio Gates, of the Patriot Army, and John Carter.
1779
British official Sir Philip Francis was wounded by challenger Warren Hastings, who Francis accused of being corrupt.
Aug. 25: Two British military men fought a duel after one accused the other of provoking a mutiny. The accuser was shot and killed.
November: A lawyer who shot a man was found Guilty of premeditated murder, not manslaughter, which was the usual charge for dueling. The judges asked the jury not to impose a sentence of death, and they complied.
Nov. 30: Mr. Adam shot and wounded Charles James Fox.
1780
March: General James Jackson, governor of Georgia, killed George Wells. Jackson was wounded.
March 22: The Earl of Shelborne and Colonel Fullarton ended a conflict after the Earl was shot in the stomach.
April: Mr. Donovan was found Guilty of manslaughter and fined £10 for killing Captain James Hanson.
Sept. 7: Reverend Mr. Bate shot and wounded a St. John's College student.
1782
June 26: Reverend Mr. Allen shot and killed Lloyd Dulany. Allen was convicted of manslaughter, fined three shillings, and sentenced to six months in prison.
1783
Mar. 9: A clergyman stopped a duel in a field and the disagreement was settled peacefully.
Apr. 21: Mr. Cunningham shot and killed George Riddell, and was found Guilty of manslaughter.
June 31: Colonel P-- shot and wounded Captain I-- in the thigh. Captain I-- returned fire, but missed.
Sept. 4: Colonel Cosmo Gordon killed Lt. Col. Thomas.
October: Marine Lt. Harrison wounded M. Harman Van Berkensham in the cheek in a duel with guns. Harrison fired his second shot in the air and ended the conflict.
1784
April: A duel between Sir James Lowther and Sergeant Bolton ended with no injuries on either side.
June 18: Richard England shot and killed Mr. Rowlls after insulting him at the race track. England was convicted of manslaughter and sentenced to twelve months in prison.
August: The second meeting of British naval officer and a German officer was fought with pistols and swords. Both were injured.
Sept. 24: Mr. Sadleir shot and wounded Lord Macartney.

1785
February: A duel between Captain Brises and Captain Bulkley left both parties unharmed.
March: Lt. F-- and Mr. Gordon fought a duel to resolve a dispute over a game of cards. Gordon was shot and had to have his leg amputated.
1786
June 8: Lord Macartney was wounded by General Stewart. The seconds declared that honor had been served.
1787
Robert Keon was sentenced to death for the dueling death of George Nugent Reynolds. Keon was executed on Oct. 16.
May: Counsellor Hutchinson shot and wounded Lord Mountmorris.
June: A button on the coat of Chevalier La B-- deflected a bullet from the gun of British Captain S--. Chevalier La B-- then shot into the air, and the two left the field as friends.
Sept. 10: Sir John Macpherson was shot and injured by Major Browne.
1788
Dec. 21: Thomas Purefoy shot and killed Colonel Roper. He was indicted for the murder and found Not Guilty.
1789
May: The Duke of York and Colonel Lennox dueled.
June: Captain Edward Pellew and Lt. I.M. Northey dueled with pistols. They were unharmed.
June 19: Captain Tongue was shot in the side by Captain Paterson.
July 1: Lt. Col. Lennox shot and wounded Theophilus Swift, who had written negative comments about Lennox in a pamphlet.
1790
Apr. 1: J.P. Curran dueled Major Hobart with no injuries on either side.
Apr. 14: In Scotland, James Macrae fatally shot Sir George Ramsay. Macrae, charged with murder, failed to show for his court appearance and was declared a fugitive.
June 25: Captain H. Ashton was wounded in the neck during a duel with Lt. Fitzgerald.
Aug. 1: Captain James Strong was fatally wounded by Henry Craig, who received a minor leg injury, in Kentucky's first recorded duel.
Sept. 20: Mr. Stephens shot and killed Mr. Anderson. A murder charge against Stephens was dropped by a jury in favor of manslaughter.
1791
July 19: Mr. Graham was shot and killed by Mr. Julius after an argument about religion.
1792
General James Jackson dueled Thomas Gibbons, a distinguished lawyer.
Summer: John Thruston and John Harrison, both of Louisville, Ky., dueled over twelve cents and a jug of whiskey. Harrison won.
March: Mr. Kemble and Mr. Aikin, both actors, fought a duel with no injuries.
June: Two law students, Mr. Frizell and Mr. Clark fought a duel. Frizell received a fatal gunshot wound, Clark was found Guilty of murder.
June 9: The Earl of Lonsdale and Captain Cuthbert fought a duel without injuries.
July 2: Lord Lauderdale and General Arnold settle an argument with a duel.
Nov. 8: A dispute between M. de Chauvigny and M. C. Lameth was reconciled after C. Lameth was shot and wounded in the stomach.
1794
Oct. 21: General Thomas Kennedy killed William Gillespie on the first shot of their duel.
1796
Jan. 26: Captain Watson shot and killed Major Sweetman in a duel brought on by an incident at the opera. Watson was tried for murder and acquitted.
June 28: A duel was fought between Lord Valentia and Henry Gawler, who was having an affair with Valentia's wife. The Lord was wounded.
Aug. 20: Americans John Pride and William Carpenter dueled. Carpenter died from a gunshot wound and Pride was found Guilty of murder.
1797
May 4: On the second round of shots, Lt. Fitzgerald wounded Lt. Warrington.
Aug. 5: Foul language and a slap to the face incited a duel between Captain Smith and Lt. Francis Buckley. Buckley was shot and killed.
Oct. 1: Colonel King shot Colonel Fitzgerald to death. Fitzgerald had dishonored King's sister.
1798
May 21: W. Pitt and G. Tierney dueled without causing injury to anyone involved.
Dec. 23: Major Allen shot and killed Colonel Harvey Aston.
19th Cent.
While dueling with another woman for the hand of gentleman Cort Thomson, Denver madame Katie Fulton shot Thomson. He was only slightly injured.
French journalist and politician Nicolas Armand Carrel was severely injured in a duel.
1800
March 13: In Ireland, Mr. Coolan shot fellow student Mr. Morcan in the temple, killing him instantly.
May 10: Mr. J. Corry shot Mr. Newburgh to death in the second round of a duel.
1801
Feb. 3: Lawyer John Rowan killed Dr. James Chambers. Rowan was charged with murder, but released.
Nov. 24: Lawyer George I. Eaker killed Philip Schuyler Hamilton in Weehawken, New Jersey.
1802
August: Lawyer David Mitchell killed William Hunter, a jury foreman, in a duel.
1803
William H. Crawford, once a member of the U.S. Senate, killed Peter Lawrence Van Alen, a lawyer.
March: A bloody duel left both participants, Lt. W. and Capt. I., dead, one on the eve of his wedding.
Apr. 6: Captain Macnamara shot and killed Lt. Col. Montgomery in a duel over fighting dogs. Macnamara was tried for murder, and the jury found him Not Guilty.
July 31: DeWitt Clinton, who served as the governor of New York, shot and wounded Colonel John Swartwout.
1804
March: Captain Best shot and killed Lord Camelford in a duel incited by a young lady. No charges were brought against Best due to lack of evidence.
Mar. 14: Thomas Reed and John Carr, both of Lexington, Ky., dueled. Both men received minor injuries.
July 11: U.S. vice president Aaron Burr shot and killed secretary of the treasury Alexander Hamilton in a duel brought on by comments made by Hamilton. Murder charges were brought against Burr in both New York and New Jersey and he left Washington to avoid imprisonment.
July 17: William Lowrey dueled Thomas Hurd after an argument about politics, and died the following day from a gunshot wound.
Sept. 18: Fredrick C. DeKraft, later to become a rear admiral in the U.S. Navy, killed William R. Nicholson.
1806
Jan. 1: Lt. Butler shot Ensign Browne to death in a duel. A jury decided that the death was "wilful murder".
Jan. 4: After an agreement to let a year of peace pass before resolving a conflict, Major Brookes and Colonel Bolton dueled, resulting in the death of Brookes.
Mar. 22: Lt. Turrens died from a gunshot wound to the groin in a duel with Mr. Fisher. Fisher, and the two seconds, were charged with murder.
May 3: In Dublin, Mr. Rogers and Mr. Long received fatal gunshot wounds while dueling.
May 29: Andrew Jackson shot and killed Tennessee lawyer Charles Dickinson, who insulted Jackson's wife. A bullet hit Jackson so close to his heart that it was never removed.
August: Francis Jeffreys and Thomas Moore were arrested and fined for attempting to duel. On examining the weapons, police found Jeffreys'gun was empty, and Moore's gun loaded only with paper.
Sept. 22: Mr. Richardson was shot and killed by Baron Hompesch, in a duel challenged after the near-sighted Baron bumped into Richardson in the street.
Dec. 16: William H. Crawford was wounded by General John Clark.
1807
Summer: William C.C. Claiborne dueled Daniel Clark, in New Orleans. Both men left the field of honor uninjured.
May 5: Sir Francis Burdett and Mr. Paull received minor leg injuries while dueling.
June: In Ireland, Major Campbell shot and killed Captain Boyd in an argument over the proper form of a command. Campbell was convicted, sentenced, and executed.
1808
Sept. 25: Lt. William E. Finch, of the U.S. Navy, killed Lt. Francis B. White, of the U.S. Marines in East Boston.
1809
Jan. 19: Henry Clay, the prominent politician, dueled Federalist Humphrey Marshall in Indiana. Both men received minor injuries.
May: Lord Paget and Captain Cadogan left the field unharmed after a duel caused by Paget's seduction of the Captain's sister.
Aug. 30: Lawyer David Trimble shot and wounded lawyer Henry Daniel in Ohio.
Sept. 21: In a duel over politics, Lord Castlereagh wounded Mr. Canning in the leg.
1810
Sept. 6: Mr. Clark shot George Payne, who had an affair with Clark's sister. Clark escaped after the duel.
1811
In a duel over political differences, John Alcock shot and killed Mr. Colclough in a well attended match. Alcock was tried for murder but found not guilty.
Jan. 15: Captain Bordman shot and killed Ensign De Betton in the West Indies. Following the duel, Bordman left the island.
Nov. 1: Englishman Thomas Fuller survived a bullet to the chest in his duel with James Allen, of Kentucky, by stuffing his shirt with padding.
1812
Jan. 7: Captain Nathaniel G.S. Hart dueled Samuel E. Watson resulting in no injuries.
Feb. 19: Major Thomas Marshall was shot in the leg in his duel with Colonel Charles S. Mitchell, of Kentucky.

Oct. 7: Lt. Stewart killed Lt. Bagnall, dueling over a woman.
1813
M.Dupont and M.Fournier, having agreed to duel each time they met, ended the 19-year-old conflict when Dupont won, but declined to shoot his adversary.
July 12: Mr. Maguire shot and killed Lt. Blundell on the Isle of Wight.
1815
Feb. 14: The duel between William Henry and Lieutenant James Haydon was called off after all rounds had been fired without causing injury.
1817
Aug. 17: Thomas Hart Benton shot and wounded fellow lawyer Charles Lucas in St. Louis.
Sept. 26: Thomas Hart Benton and Charles Lucas duel a second round. Lucas is killed.
1818
Apr. 18: John Boswell was fatally wounded by Charles Durand while dueling in Kentucky.
August: In Kentucky, Dr. Benjamin W. Dudley shot Dr. William H. Richardson in the groin, and saved his life by stopping the bleeding.
October: Commo. Oliver Hazard Perry, whose seconds were Stephen Decatur and James Hamilton, dueled Captain John Heath at ten paces. Heath missed his target, and Perry had Decatur read a prepared statement that settled the conflict.
1819
Feb. 6: Colonel John McCarty dueled his cousin, Senator Armistead T. Mason with guns at a close four paces. Mason was killed immediately and McCarty was critically wounded.
July 16: Jacob H. Holeman shot and killed Francis G. Waring in a duel that was challenged after Waring killed Holman's dog. Holman and his second, Wilson P. Greenup became the first men in Kentucky to be tried for murder after winning a duel. They were found Not Guilty.
July 23: In a duel to reconcile an ongoing conflict, lawyer Samuel Q. Richardson suffered a broken arm, while opponent Bushrod Boswell eluded injury.
1820
Mar. 22: Commissioner of the U.S. Navy Stephen Decatur was shot and killed by James Baron, who made the challenge after years of conflict between Decatur and himself.
1821
Feb. 16: Christie shot and killed John Scott, editor of *London Magazine*, who demanded the duel after a conflict over articles published in a magazine managed by Christie's friend. Christie was tried with two other participants and found Not Guilty.
1826
Apr. 8: Politician Henry Clay and Sen. John Randolph dueled without injuries to either man.
Sept. 22: General Sam Houston seriously injured General William A. White in a duel over Tennessee politics.
1827
Mar. 27: Lawyers Calvin M. Smith and Robert M. Brank fought a duel over a court case. Brank was killed instantly.
1828
George William Finch-Hatton, the Tenth Earl of Winchelsea, and Arthur Wellesley, the First Duke of Wellington, dueled with no injuries.
1829
George J. Trotter, editor of the Kentucky *Gazette*, shot and killed Charles Wickliffe, who had challenged the duel.
1833
May 10: Sir John Jeffcot challenged Dr. Peter Hennis to a duel, in which Hennis was killed. Jeffcot, charged with murder fled the country.
1835
John Rowan, Jr. shot Thomas F. Marshall in the hip, in a duel which started as an argument about politics. Marshall was crippled for life.
1837
Feb. 5: General Felix Huston and General Albert Sidney Johnston dueled to settle a dispute over a change in command of Texas forces. Johnston was injured and the two agreed to work together.
1838
Feb. 24: Two members of the House of Representatives, William J. Graves from Kentucky, and Jonathan Cilley from Maine, dueled with rifles. Cilley was killed.
1839
Dec. 29: Alexander Keith McClung, known as the Black Knight of the South, shot and killed John Menifee with a bullet wound to the forehead.
1840
Sept. 12: James Thomas Brudenell, the Seventh Earl of Cardigan, shot Lieutenant Harvey Tuckett for publishing letters that maligned his character. Brudenell was tried and found Not Guilty of intent to murder.
1841
May 15: A duel between Cassius M. Clay and Robert Wickliffe, Jr. was stopped by friends of the participants, in Indiana.
Sept. 27: Edward Heyward shot August Belmont in the thigh.
1842
In Vicksburg, Mississippi, newspaper writer James Fall was wounded in a duel with a bank president.
June 25: Kentucky congressman Thomas F. Marshall shot newspaper editor James W. Webb in the leg.
1843
Dr. James Hagan, editor of the Vicksburg Sentinal, is shot down while unarmed after a series of duels over his editorial policies, including one with the editor of a rival paper.
1845
Jan. 13: Police stopped a duel between two Congressmen, Thomas L. Clingman, from North Carolina, and William L. Yancey, from Alabama, after one shot by each had been discharged. There were no injuries.
Mar. 11: French journalist Rosamond de Beauvallon, of *Le Globe*, shot and killed Alexandre Henri Dujarier, manager of *La Presse*, when a game of baccarat turned unfriendly. De Beauvallon was tried for murder and found Not Guilty, but later was sentenced to eight years for perjury after it was proven that he tested the guns before the duel, violating the rules.
Sept. 6: With pistols at thirty yards, Dr. J.D. Taylor shot and killed his brother-in-law, John M. Harrison.
1846
J. M. Downes killed Vicksburg Sentinel editor T. E. Robins at ten paces.
May 20: James S. Jackson and Robert Patterson resolved their conflict without bloodshed, after each fired once.
Oct. 6: Captain Thomas F. Marshall dueled Second Lieutenant James S. Jackson. Both men escaped injury.
1848
Jan. 15: Lieutenant Roger Hansom fought a duel at ten paces with William M. Duke.
Sept. 6: William O. Smith and Thomas H. Holt exchanged shots without injury.
1849
June 14: Captain Henry C. Pope and John T. Gray dueled after a fight while drinking. Pope, the challenger, was shot and killed.
1852
British revolutionary Emmanuel Barthélemy killed a French naval officer named Cournet in a duel over leadership of a group of exiles. A jury acquitted him of murder, even though his opponent's guns had been sabotaged.
Oct. 5: Benjamin Johnson and Thomas White, both students at Transylvania University in Lexington, Ky., dueled with double barreled shotguns. White received a head wound and died.
1855
In San Francisco, Judge William M. Gwin, later to become the first senator of California, dueled Joseph McCorkle to settle an ongoing dispute.
Feb. 16: Medical student Theophilus Steele shot law student James Blackburn in the thigh. The men went home as friends.
1858
Drama critic Emile Hirairt was challenged to several duels after criticizing a singer's performance. In his second duel, Hirairt killed his opponent. Captain Harry Maury fought Baron Henry Arnous deRiviere in Mississippi, over a young woman. A coin in the Baron's pocket shielded him from the first shot, which hit him in the chest. In the second exchange, he was shot in the mouth, but survived to marry the woman several years later.
Aug. 21: Judge George Pendleton Johnston, author of an anti-dueling law, shot and killed William Ferguson in California, the state where his law had just been passed.
1859
Sept. 13: In California, state supreme court justice David S. Terry killed U.S. senator David C. Broderick in a duel fought with pistols.
1860
Felice Carlo Emmanuele Cavalloti, a member of parliament and Italian left wing leader, dueled Giuseppe Garibaldi. They fought again in 1866.
1862
May 8: Former mayor of Maysville, Ky., William T. Casto was killed by Colonel Leonidas Metcalfe.
1866
Mar. 26: In Kentucky, Confederate Joseph Desha and Unionist Alexander Kimbrough fought a duel over political differences, leaving Kimbrough with a wounded hip. Desha escaped to Canada.
Nov. 12: Two soldiers in the Confederate army, John H. Grasscup and John Blair fought a duel over a woman. Both men were injured.
1867
Apr. 27: In Kentucky, Isaac Hanson shot Noah S. Alexander in a duel. They left the field as friends.
May 7: W.L. Grinnan and D.B. Ridgly dueled without injury.
July 22: Littleton Wells and Saford P. Roberts shot each other to death while dueling over a woman.
1873
June: In Newton, Kansas, Arthur McCluskie, seeking revenge for the death of his brother, and Hugh Anderson killed each other in a duel.
1877
Jan. 7: James Gordon Bennett, Jr. and Frederick May each fired one shot and missed in a duel caused by inappropriate behavior by May while at Bennett's home. Both men left with honor, neither with injuries.
1888
French politician Charles Thomas Floquet wounded George Boulanger.
1889
August: Patrick Calhoun and John D. Williamson resolved their differences over the sale of a railroad, after missing each other with pistols on the Georgia state line. Williamson suffered a minor facial injury from a piece of tree bark.

FORENSICS

Forensic science, or criminalistics, deals with the scientific examination of evidence as it relates to the law. The word is a derivative of the Latin *forensis*, which means "of the forum"—the place in Rome where important civic matters were debated by the leading citizens of the day. Forensics, as a modern scientific procedure, dates back to the seventeenth century when German scholars made it a viable field of study in their universities. The first chair in forensic medicine was established at Edinburgh University in 1807 by George III. It was then known as "medical jurisprudence," but more recently as legal medicine, covering a wide variety of scientific disciplines, including physics, biology, and chemistry.

Forensic scientists work from the smallest clues left at a crime scene: fingerprints, hairs, bloodstains, and fibers. The union of science and law caused much debate and many pioneers are responsible for its advancement. In 1598, Fortunatus Fidelis presented the first survey of the field in Italy. The first English book on the subject, written by Samuel Farr, was published in 1788. The science moved forward with American brothers T.R. and J.B. Beck's *Elements of Medical Jurisprudence* (1823) and what is considered the bible of forensic medicine, Alfred Swaine Taylor's *Principles and Practice of Medical Jurisprudence* (1865).

As forensic science became integral to the investigation of crimes, it became more specialized, creating some of the staples of the criminologist's arsenal. Through dozens of important criminal investigations in Great Britain, the famous pathologist Sir Bernard Spilsbury towers above his peers. According to the crime writer Edgar Lustgarten, Spilsbury stood for pathology "as Hobbs stood for cricket or Dempsey for boxing or Capablanca for chess." In 1924, he conducted the first post mortem on a convicted murderer, Patrick Herbert Mahon, who decapitated his girlfriend, Emily Kaye.

The autopsy remains the most useful method a criminologist has to determine the cause of a death. The ancient Greeks conducted the first dissections of the human body, but it wasn't until the fifteenth century that the practice became standard procedure. Florentine physician Antonio Benivieni conducted fifteen such autopsies to learn the cause of death, and in 1761, his countryman Giovanni Morgagni, known as the father of modern pathology, first described to the scientific community what could be observed in the human body by the naked eye. Since that time the autopsy, or post mortem examination has become standard procedure in any murder investigation.

Dr. Milton Helpern, Chief Medical Examiner in New York City, played a major role in the growth of the forensic pathology and worked on many famous cases in his fifty years of service. The acceptance of fingerprint identification was a milestone for forensic science, replacing the antiquated system of anthropometry, which required the measurement of fourteen body parts and was developed in 1879 by one of fingerprinting's harshest critics, Alphonse Bertillon. The esteemed French criminalist determined that the odds against any two men having the exact same body measurements was 286,435,456 to one. Bertillon was dismissed as a crank by a succession of French police chiefs, who told him to stop wasting time and go back to his regular duties. Not until 1892, when he identified the French terrorist Ravachol using his anthropometric devices, did *bertillonage* gain widespread acceptance. Anthropometry enjoyed only a brief period of notoriety. It was a clumsy, imprecise science that was eclipsed by fingerprinting by the turn of the century. William Herschel of the Indian Civil Service, Sir Edward Henry, and Juan Vucetich pioneered the technique of thumb printing which was universally adopted by police departments around the world by 1910.

Ballistics, another area of forensic science, came into prominence when Dr. Calvin H. Goddard—appointed to head up the Chicago Crime Detection Laboratory at Northwestern University—studied the connection between a bullet and the gun from which it was fired. In a celebrated case, Charles E. Waite's discovery that a gun leaves distinctive marks on a bullet saved the life of Charles E. Stielow. Stielow was actually strapped in the electric chair when Waite's evidence won his reprieve.

Forensic science also encompasses the fields of biology, dentistry, chemistry, and genetic DNA identification. Two highly specialized fields include forensic toxicology, which uncovers drug use, malicious poisonings, and environmental poisonings; and forensic psychiatry, which attempts to determine the mental state of a suspect at the time of a crime. The role of psychiatry in criminal cases cannot be discounted. Since 1780 when the English first concerned themselves with the concept of *mens rea*, or guilty intent, the finest legal .ninds have debated the extent to which a criminal is responsible for his or her actions. In 1843, the M'Naghten Rules were passed by Parliament in an effort to create a test for right and wrong which would stand up under the law. Under the terms of this landmark statute, it had to be proved that the defendant, through a defect in reasoning, did not understand the extent to which he was doing wrong when he committed the crime. Over the years this law was modified. In the U.S. for example, the Durham Rule of 1954 was adopted by the District of Columbia, according to which a person was not responsible for his actions if the unlawful act was the product of mental disease or a mental defect. Britain's Homicide Act of 1957 permitted a defendant to enter a plea of diminished responsibility which allowed for a middle ground—substantial capacity—between mental illness and crime. These interpretations continue to stir up much controversy between adherents of law and order who see this as a means for a criminal offender to escape punishment, and those members of the academic community concerned with the principles of modern psychiatry.

Since the late nineteenth-century, forensic science has played an important role in fighting crime. However, it is estimated that between only three and ten per cent of useful evidence at a crime scene in the U.S. is actually collected and analyzed by laboratory technicians. The problem rests with the policeman on the scene, and his ability or lack there of, to recognize and preserve evidence. According to Dr. Ray Williams, Director of the Metropolitan Police Forensic Laboratory: "the technical limitation in forensic science is the ability to pick out the vital piece of evidence in the initial search." This problem can only be addressed through improved training methods, and the recruitment of qualified personnel. In many large cities in the U.S., administrators have attempted to deal with this problem by funding the mobile laboratory, which provides on-the-spot chemical and forensic analysis of evidence during the initial investigation.

FRAUD

Criminal fraud falls into two broad categories. The most common form involves the issuance of a check for which there are not sufficient funds. The other is the confidence game, dependent upon the victim's gullibility and greed. Over the years the exploits of many famous confidence men have become legendary. Victor "the Count" Lustig taught himself to speak German, Italian, and French and then embarked on a life of crime in Europe and the U.S. He once tried to sell the Eiffel Tower for scrap metal. Joseph "Yellow Kid" Weil and Fred "the Deacon" Buckminster were legendary Chicago con men who practiced their humbuggery for years.

In Europe, the criminal statutes also define fraud to include any misunderstandings arising out of normal business transactions. An omission or concealment that allows one party to take advantage of another may also constitute fraud. Similarly, the embezzlement of money is regarded in the same manner.

Most people arrested and convicted of embezzlement committed their crime while employed by a financial institution. Before computerization significantly altered the rules of the game, there were at least 200 estimated ways to embezzle funds without being immediately detected. Industry executives blame the high incidence of embezzlement on the courts, claiming that the light sentences given for fraud convictions encourage the commission of these crimes.

Sometimes it takes months, even years for an embezzlement to be detected. But with the advent of sophisticated computer systems, the methods have changed. It is now possible for programmers to divert vast sums of money with a few simple keystrokes. John Rankine of IBM said, "The data security job will never be done—after all, there will never be a bank that absolutely can't be robbed."

Biblical
Isaac's youngest son, Jacob, and his wife Rebekah, defrauded the eldest son Esau out of his father's blessing and inheritance, by having Jacob dress up as Esau and fool Issac, the blind father.
3rd Cent. B.C.
In Athens, Demosthenes was defrauded of his father's fortune by the three executors of the estate. Demosthenes sued for repayment at the age of twenty. Later in life, he was exiled for fraud.
1271
Roger Bacon wrote that fraud was rampant among merchants and craftsmen, as well as the rest of society.
1716
March: The Regent of France, Philippe, Duke of Orleans, established the Chambre de Justice to probe people suspected of defrauding the government. A year later the Chambre was dissolved.
1720
Sept. 29: Stock prices for the South Seas Company, which was largely controlled by the British government, dropped from £1,000 to £135 per share. A number of officials were sent to prison in the fraudulent investment scandal.
Dec. 20: Scotland's John Law was dismissed as the president of France's Royal Bank. Law became a scapegoat for the Duke of Orleans' defrauding the bank of some 3 million francs.
1738
Joanna Stephens stated in a *Gentleman's Magazine* ad that she would reveal her kidney stone cure for £5,000. A year later, the British parliament approved of paying for the cure, which turned out to be bogus.
1743
June 8: John Breeds was hanged for the murder of a man who put him in jail by testifying that Breeds, a butcher, weighted his scale to defraud customers.
1747
Charles Julius Bertram claimed to find a fourteenth-century manuscript. It was found in 1866 to be a fraud.
1749
John Berry assembled a group of thief-takers who would entice honest men to commit crimes and then turn them in for the reward money.
1750
Nov. 16: John Carr was hanged for forging the wills of sailors.
1768
Thomas Chatterton "discovered" the alleged work of Thomas Rowley, a priest during the time of Henry II of England. This is one of several forged books he invented.
1772
Mar. 18: James Balland was hanged for robbery and fraud. He was included in many scams ranging from card games and horse theft to setting up his own private jail.
1780
William Beckford wrote a book about famous painters that turned out to be a fraud.
1791
June 28: From June through October Samuel Chitney, one of England's greatest jockeys, fixed a series of races.
1800
Rattlesnake Root, used to allegedly cure pleurisy, was promoted by Virginia charlatan Dr. John Tennant, one of many wonder drugs he sold. Mail-order swindles were first employed, such as Perkins' Metallic Tractors, which reportedly cured diseases with electric currents.
1811
Edward Tinker scuttled his commercial ship off Roanoke Island to collect insurance on the cargo and vessel. He killed a crew member who would not verify his claim. Tinker was hanged.
1815
Daniel Drew convinced wealthy cattlemen in New York, including Henry Astor, to purchase run-down cattle.
1818
An article by *Republican Chronicle* editor Charles N. Baldwin exposed the New York Lottery as being rigged. Baldwin was acquitted of the subsequent libel charge when, on Apr. 6, 1819, John H. Sickles was convicted of providing friends with winning numbers in advance.
1820
A dishonest Washington, D.C., gambling den was opened by Samuel Shirley, who profited from fraudulent faro games.
The Balm of Gilead health tonic was introduced by swindler Samuel Solomon. Solomon created an empire in Great Britain, the U.S., Bengal, Nassau, and Quebec, selling his alleged ancient elixir which was 90 percent brandy.
1823
The contractor of the Congress-sponsored Grand National Lottery absconded with about $300,000.
1830s
Mathew Brady (AKA: Gentleman Matt) was charged with more than 350 crimes including forgery. He was hanged.
George de Luna Byron made claims against the publisher of Lord Byron, saying he was an illegitimate son. He also forged letters by Byron, Shelley, and Keats, and sold them.
1830
"Reformed Gambler" Jonathan H. Green informed Louisville, Ky., police of "The Secret Band of Brothers," which was a New Orleans-based group of some 1,000 cardsharps and con men who shared combined earnings. This group was believed to have begun in 1798.
Shell game operator "Umbrella Jim" Miner opened up business along the Mississippi River.
Cardsharp Elijah Skaggs operated his rigged faro games in Nashville, Tenn. Over the next twenty years, working especially on Mississippi riverboats, he raked in millions.
1832
A gambling saloon, with fixed banco, faro, and roulette tables was opened by Colonel J.J. Bryant in Vicksburg, Miss.
1834
Phony remedies, including Moore's Essence of Life, promising cures for all illnesses are reintroduced creating enormous health-scare sales.
1835
Cardsharp James Ashby worked the Mississippi riverboats preying upon other hustlers with the help of a younger confederate. Ashby played his fiddle to signal the youth, who had been asked to play cards.
Every rigged faro game in Natchez, Miss., was fleeced by 18-year-old Charles Cora, netting him $50,000 in one week.
The Drake inheritance con game, which was played for centuries in Europe, was introduced in the U.S.
July 6: Dutch Bill, D. Hullum, Sam Smith, and gambling den operator John North are hanged by Vicksburg, Miss., vigilantes, known as the Volunteers.
1839
In Huntsville, Ala., Colonel J.J. Bryant beat wealthy saddler Allen Jones at cards so impressively that Jones asked Bryant to teach him how to cheat.
1840
Swindler Charles Legate began working along, and on, the Mississippi River.
1841
Ben Burnish, Johnny Chamberlin, Jimmy Fitzgerald, Gabe Foster, Allen Jones, John Lawler, Price McGrath, Henry Perritt, and Tom Wicks, under John Powell's leadership, operated a cardsharping headquarters established at the Planters Hotel in St. Louis.
1842
"The Sands" gambling section of Chicago, which was located on wooden piers on Lake Michigan, served as headquarters for cardsharps until Mayor Long John Wentworth ordered the area burned in 1857.
1843
Martin Curtis opened a faro gambling hall in Milwaukee. He dominated the city's crooked gambling for the next ten years, and built the 136-room Kirby House hotel in 1845.
1849
A Spaniard named Louis Alvarez and three others defrauded priests in Peru out of an Inca treasure. The treasure was then secretly buried, but never recovered, as two of the men were imprisoned and two died.
The gold-brick con began during the California Gold Rush.
July: Albert Blandig, claiming to be a doctor, though he had no medical background, killed his second wife May when his first wife Jane dis-

covered the bigamy. He committed suicide.

1850

Cardsharpers William "Canada Bill" Jones, Tom Brown, Holly Chappell, George Devol, and others began working the Mississippi riverboats employing three-card monte.

1854

New York and New Haven Railroad president Robert Schuyler issued a large number of phony stocks and escaped to Europe with tens of thousands of dollars.

1856

May 20: Con man Charles Cora was lynched by the San Francisco Vigilance Committee for shooting U.S. marshal General W.H. Richardson. Cora had swindled miners since the California Gold Rush had begun.

1859

Julian Cinquez arrived in New York from Cuba and, posing as Colonel Novena, bilked the wealthy through large real-estate swindles.

1862

George Trussell, along with Old Bill Leonard and Otis Randall operated most of Chicago's fixed gambling dens, and employed people to bring clients from legitimate gambling halls.

Con artist Sophie Lyons began her career in New York.

1863

The first big store with rigged foot and horse races was opened in Denver by Ben Marks.

The U.S. enacted the False Claims Act to curb military contractors from defrauding the government's purchases of military supplies. The law enabled the person informing the government to share in any damages collected from a lawsuit.

1864

Banco and other con games operated by "Hungry Joe" Lewis and others, appeared in New York City.

1866

John Flanagan opened two gambling dens in Minneapolis and employed cardsharps to run his rigged games of banco, faro, three-card monte, and the shell game. He amassed $1 million by his retirement in the late 1880s.

The green-goods game was introduced by James "King" McNally.

1867

Jim Fisk and Jay Gould are appointed by big-time con man Daniel Drew as directors of the Erie Railroad. The two quickly undermined the business with fraudulent stock deals.

1868

Georgia farm hand James Addison Reavis began forging documents which claimed hundreds of miles of Arizona land belonged to a fictitious Spaniard named Miguel de Peralta, who of course, was Reavis.

Giovanni Bastianini, a sculptor who forged the work of Renaissance masters, died. Some of his works were displayed in London's Victoria and Albert Museum before the forgeries were discovered.

1869

Jim Fisk and Jay Gould cornered the U.S. gold market and swindled millions.

1870

Hustler and political manipulator Mike McDonald began his career in Chicago. For the next three decades his army of con men reigned supreme.

"The Crying Kid," a recruiter of swindle victims, began working in New York.

1871

Summer: The San Francisco diamond mine scam was begun by Philip Arnold and John Slack.

1872

Jay Gould was swindled out of $500,000 by "Lord Gordon-Gordon," whose scheme began the previous year.

John E.W. Keely introduced the first phony energy-producing machine.

Charles Becker (AKA: The Prince of Forgers) committed his first major crime, the robbery of a Baltimore, Md. bank. He went on to defraud banks of more than $200,000.

1873

William Udderzook was hanged for murdering his brother-in-law W.S. Goss, whose corpse was used to make insurance claims of the arson he committed in Baltimore appear genuine.

Jack Canter was involved in the Central Fire Insurance Company Frauds. He helped transform one-and two-share stock certificates into 300 and 500 share certificates.

1874

Con artist Ross Saulsbury murdered a Chicago saloon owner, but received a light prison term due to Mike McDonald's influence.

1875

Mar. 12: Edgerton & Co. was prohibited from picking up money orders or registered mail by U.S. postal authorities because of past fraudulent activities in Camden, N.J.

Apr. 17: James W. George & Co. was prohibited from picking up money orders or registered mail by U.S. postal authorities because of past fraudulent activities in New York City.

July 2: L.D.S. Bishop (AKA: L.D. Sine) was prohibited from picking up money orders or registered mail by U.S. postal authorities because of past fraudulent activities in Cincinnati.

Sept. 23: The Texas Gift Concert Association was prohibited from picking up money orders or registered mail by U.S. postal authorities because of past fraudulent activities in Dennison, Texas.

October: John C. Bond was caught by Canadian authorities for his escape one year earlier with the proceeds of a $1500 mortgage.

Oct. 22: Giovanni Patroni (as Cosmopolitan Stamp, Philadelphia Stamp Company) was prohibited from picking up money orders or registered mail by U.S. postal authorities because of past fraudulent activities in Camden, N.J., and Philadelphia.

Nov. 6: Frank Stewart was prohibited from picking up money orders or registered mail by U.S. postal authorities because of past fraudulent activities in Philadelphia, N.Y.

Dec. 9: F.E.G. Lindsey (as E. Gustavus & Company) was prohibited from picking up money orders or registered mail by U.S. postal authorities because of past fraudulent activities in Holston, W. Va.

Dec. 21: Wilcox & Co. was prohibited from picking up money orders or registered mail by U.S. postal authorities because of past fraudulent activities in Windsor, Ohio.

1876

In Spain, Dona Baldomera Larra introduced the first Peter-to-Paul swindle.

Tourists were swindled at New York's Centennial Exposition by "Paper Collar Joe" Kratalsky.

Crooked get-rich-quick advertisements appeared across the U.S. in record numbers.

Jan. 31: H.J. Hall & Co. was prohibited from picking up money orders or registered mail by U.S. postal authorities because of past fraudulent activities in Baltimore.

Apr. 13: Clarence W. Miller (AKA: J.C. Henry & Co.) was prohibited from picking up money orders or registered mail by U.S. postal authorities because of past fraudulent activities in Chester, Pa., and Glens Falls, N.Y.

Apr. 13: C.W. Whitney & Co. was prohibited from picking up money orders or registered mail by U.S. postal authorities because of past fraudulent activities in Chester, Pa., and Glens Falls, N.Y.

June 1: F.E.G. Lindsey was prohibited from picking up money orders or registered mail by U.S. postal authorities because of past fraudulent activities in Abingdon, Va.

June 10: J.B. Hamilton & Co. was prohibited from picking up money orders or registered mail by U.S. postal authorities because of past fraudulent activities in New York City.

June 10: James A. Tomlinson was prohibited from picking up money orders or registered mail by U.S. postal authorities because of past fraudulent activities in New York City.

June 12: J.M. Royce was prohibited from picking up money orders or registered mail by U.S. postal authorities because of past fraudulent activities in Grafton, W. Va.

June 29: V.D. Benton was prohibited from picking up money orders or registered mail by U.S. postal authorities because of past fraudulent activities in Laramie City, Wyo.

June 29: John W. Magee was prohibited from picking up money orders or registered mail by U.S. postal authorities because of past fraudulent activities in Laramie City, Wyo.

Aug. 11: John Burrow was prohibited from picking up money orders or registered mail by U.S. postal authorities because of past fraudulent activities in Bristol, Tenn.

Sept. 15: Marshall S. Pike was prohibited from picking up money orders or registered mail by U.S. postal authorities because of past fraudulent activities in Cheyenne, Wyo., and Topeka, Kan.

Oct. 3: J.M. Pattee was prohibited from picking up money orders or registered mail by U.S. postal authorities because of past fraudulent activities in Cheyenne, Wyo.

1877

The Humbert swindle was begun in Paris by Therese Dauignac, who netted $14 million by 1902 when the fraud was exposed.

June 1: Russell, Hopping & Co. was prohibited from picking up money orders or registered mail by U.S. postal authorities because of past fraudulent activities in Riverside, N.J.

July 6: J.C. Tyner & Co. (AKA: Freshman & Co., American Coral, Florence Jewelry, Premium Art Cos.) was prohibited from picking up money orders or registered mail by U.S. postal authorities because of past fraudulent activities in Pittsburgh.

July 19: Jace Marks (AKA: A.B. Bennington & Co.) was prohibited from picking up money orders or registered mail by U.S. postal authorities because of past fraudulent activities in Lansing, Iowa.

Sept. 8: William H. Hurlburt (as Western Gun Co.) was prohibited from picking up money orders or registered mail by U.S. postal authorities because of past fraudulent activities in Chicago.

Oct. 16: B.C. Bartelle & Co. was prohibited from picking up money orders or registered mail by U.S. postal authorities because of past fraudulent activities in Gloucester, N.J.

Dec. 1: Ellis H. Elias (as Russell & Co.) was prohibited from picking up money orders or registered mail by U.S. postal authorities because of past fraudulent activities in New York City.

Dec. 3: Edgar W. Jones (as Harry J. Littleton & Co., Magnetic Watch Co., Union Publishing Co., Union Purchasing Agency) was prohibited from picking up money orders or registered mail by U.S. postal authorities because of past fraudulent activities in Ashland and South Farmington, Mass.

1878

Apr. 28: George W. Franklin was prohibited from picking up money orders or registered mail by U.S. postal authorities because of past fraudulent activities in Louisville and Glasgow, Ky.

June 5: Clark & Co. (AKA: Silver Mining Co.) was prohibited from picking up money orders or registered mail by U.S. postal authorities because of past fraudulent activities in New York City.

June 22: Reade & Co. was prohibited from picking up money orders or registered mail by U.S. postal authorities because of past fraudulent activities in New Haven, Conn.

July 19: Jace Marks was prohibited from picking up money orders or registered mail by U.S. postal authorities because of past fraudulent activities in La Crosse, Wis.

July 30: A. Jones & Son was prohibited from picking up money orders or registered mail by U.S. postal authorities because of past fraudulent activities in Hopkinton, Mass.

July 30: Webber & Co. (AKA: National Art and Union Silver Plating Cos.) was prohibited from picking up money orders or registered mail by U.S. postal authorities because of past fraudulent activities in Cincinnati.

Aug. 21: The Eastern Manufacturing Co. was prohibited from picking up money orders or registered mail by U.S. postal authorities because of past fraudulent activities in Boston, Chicago, and Rockland, Maine.

Oct. 12: W.J. Hill (as C.W. Whitney & Co.) was prohibited from picking up money orders or registered mail by U.S. postal authorities because of past fraudulent activities in Elkhart, Ind., and Augusta and Battle Creek, Mich.

Oct. 12: C. Wade (AKA: C.H. Walker) was prohibited from picking up money orders or registered mail by U.S. postal authorities because of fraudulent activities in Elkhart, Ind., and Augustana and Battle Creek, Mich.

Oct. 13: John Crest (AKA: W.J. Hill, C.H. Walker, C. Wade) was prohibited from picking up money orders or registered mail by U.S. postal authorities because of past fraudulent activities in Elkhart, Ind., and Augusta and Battle Creek, Mich.

Nov. 28: John C. Brain (as Excelsior Manufacturing Co., Sheffield Firearms Agency) was prohibited from picking up money orders or registered mail by U.S. postal authorities because of past fraudulent activities in Chicago.

Dec. 11: H.D.P. Allen was prohibited from picking up money orders or registered mail by U.S. postal authorities because of past fraudulent activities in New York City.

Dec. 11: John C. Brain (as Excelsior Manufacturing Co., Sheffield Firearms Agency) was prohibited from picking up money orders or registered mail by U.S. postal authorities because of past fraudulent activities in New York City.

Dec. 11: W.P. McCall was prohibited from picking up money orders or registered mail by U.S. postal authorities because of past fraudulent activities in New York City.

Dec. 11: The National Banking Co. was prohibited from picking up money orders or registered mail by U.S. postal authorities because of past fraudulent activities in New York City.

1879

Jan. 24: H.J. Hall & Co. was prohibited from picking up money orders or registered mail by U.S. postal authorities because of past fraudulent activities in New York City.

Apr. 18: Leavitt & Co. (AKA: Russell & Co., Sunbeam Publishing Co.) was prohibited from picking up money orders or registered mail by U.S. postal authorities because of past fraudulent activities in New Bedford, Mass.

Apr. 22: H.A. Burnett was prohibited from picking up money orders or registered mail by U.S. postal authorities because of past fraudulent activities in New York City.

May 19: The Royal Manufacturing Co. was prohibited from picking up money orders or registered mail by U.S. postal authorities because of past fraudulent activities in Brooklyn, N.Y.

May 27: The Arizona Lottery conducted in Prescott, Ariz., was prohibited from picking up money orders or registered mail by U.S. postal authorities because of past fraudulent activities.

May 28: Edward A. Eggleston was prohibited from picking up money orders or registered mail by U.S. postal authorities because of past fraudulent activities in Rosita, Colo.

June 5: The Kentucky Land Co. was prohibited from picking up money orders or registered mail by U.S. postal authorities because of past fraudulent activities in Louisville, Ky.

June 11: The Bristol Piano Co. was prohibited from picking up money orders or registered mail by U.S. postal authorities because of past fraudulent activities in New Bedford, Mass.

June 21: Michael Goldwater was prohibited from picking up money orders or registered mail by U.S. postal authorities because of past fraudulent activities in Prescott, Ariz.

Aug. 7: The Long Island Shirt Co. was prohibited from picking up money orders or registered mail by U.S. postal authorities because of past fraudulent activities in Brooklyn, N.Y.

Aug. 8: J.E. Edmunds & Co. was prohibited from picking up money orders or registered mail by U.S. postal authorities because of past fraudulent activities in Webster, Mass.

Aug. 12: Charles E. Heister (as U.S. Syndicate) was not allowed to pick up money orders or registered mail by U.S. postal authorities because of past fraudulent activities in New York City.

Aug. 21: The Paris Novelty Co. was prohibited from picking up money orders or registered mail by U.S. postal authorities because of past fraudulent activities in Boston and Rockland, Mass., and Chicago.

Aug. 21: E. Ellsworth Slocumb, who used thirteen aliases, was prohibited from picking up money orders or registered mail by U.S. postal authorities because of past fraudulent activities in Chicago, and Boston, Brockton, Rockland, and Weymouth, Mass.

Sept. 3-4: E. Ellsworth Slocumb was again prohibited from picking up money orders or registered mail by U.S. postal authorities because of past fraudulent activities.

Sept. 20: The Great Western Distribution Co. (AKA: Mathews & Co., Kunnecke & Co.) was prohibited from picking up money orders or registered mail by U.S. postal authorities because of past fraudulent activities in Cheyenne, Wyo.

Oct. 10: A. Chase & Co. was prohibited from picking up money orders or registered mail by U.S. postal authorities because of past fraudulent activities in New Haven, Conn.

Oct. 17: L.A. Kendall (AKA: L.A. Ashman) was prohibited from picking up money orders or registered mail by U.S. postal authorities because of past fraudulent activities in Boston.

Oct. 29: I.G. Remis & Co. was prohibited from picking up money orders or registered mail by U.S. postal authorities because of past fraudulent activities in Chicago.

Nov. 3: N.M. Cole & Son was prohibited from picking up money orders or registered mail by U.S. postal authorities because of past fraudulent activities in Detroit.

Nov. 3: S.A. Grant (as Denver Land Co.) was prohibited from picking up money orders or registered mail by U.S. postal authorities because of past fraudulent activities in Denver.

Nov. 10: J.J. Hetsch & Co. (AKA: *People's Literary Journal, Kentucky State Journal,* Newport Paper and Printing Co.) was prohibited from picking up money orders or registered mail by U.S. postal authorities because of past fraudulent activities in Newport, Ky.

Nov. 13: W.C. Creighton (as B.H. Porter & Co.) was prohibited from picking up money orders or registered mail by U.S. postal authorities because of past fraudulent activities in New York City.

Nov. 13: B. Nathan was prohibited from picking up money orders or registered mail by U.S. postal authorities because of past fraudulent activities in New York City.

Nov. 13: J. Tator (AKA: W. Porter, W.R. Porter, B.H. Porter & Co.) was prohibited from picking up money orders or registered mail by U.S. postal authorities because of past fraudulent activities in New York City.

Nov. 13: Williamson & Co. was prohibited from picking up money orders or registered mail by U.S. postal authorities because of past fraudulent activities in New York City.

Nov. 13: Theodore Zchoch was prohibited from picking up money orders or registered mail by U.S. postal authorities because of past fraudulent activities in New York City.

Nov. 14: Under the alias of Waschmann & Co., Moses Bogart, Max Borger, and Theodore Eixmer were prohibited from picking up money orders or registered mail by U.S. postal authorities because of past fraudulent activities in New York City.

Nov. 14: J. Duff and J. Duff & Co. were prohibited from picking up money orders or registered mail by U.S. postal authorities because of past fraudulent activities in New York City.

Nov. 14: Manning Duffree (as C. Bell & Co.) was prohibited from picking up money orders or registered mail by U.S. postal authorities because of past fraudulent activities in New York City.

Nov. 14: Joseph Emerson and Emerson & Goss were prohibited from picking up money orders or registered mail by U.S. postal authorities because of past fraudulent activities in New York City.

Nov. 14: Orlando A. Jackson and Jackson & Co. were prohibited from picking up money orders or registered mail by U.S. postal authorities because of past fraudulent activities in New York City.

Nov. 14: Charles D.J. Noelke was prohibited from picking up money orders or registered mail by U.S. postal authorities because of past fraudulent activities in New York City.

Nov. 14: Samuel Webb (AKA: William S., Samuel Wilson, Luthy & Co.) was prohibited from picking up money orders or registered mail by U.S. postal authorities because of past fraudulent activities in New York City.

Nov. 18: The Great Western Distribution Co. (AKA: Mathews & Co., Kunnecke & Co.) was prohibited from picking up money orders or registered mail by U.S. postal authorities because of past fraudulent activities in Cheyenne, Wyo.

Nov. 18: Taylor & Co. was prohibited from picking up money orders or registered mail by U.S. postal authorities because of past fraudulent activities in New York City.

Nov. 18: J.F. Tully (as C. Bell & Co.) was prohibited from picking up money orders or registered mail by U.S. postal authorities because of past fraudulent activities in New York City.

Nov. 21: Murray, France & Co. was prohibited from picking up money orders or registered mail by U.S. postal authorities because of past fraudulent activities in Louisville, Ky.

Nov. 25: Hugh McKay and Hugh McKay and Co. of St. Stephen, New Brunswick were prohibited from picking up money orders or registered

mail by U.S. postal authorities because of past fraudulent activities in Calais, Maine.
Nov. 25: Henry G. and F.G. Waterson were prohibited from picking up money orders or registered mail by U.S. postal authorities because of past fraudulent activities in Calais, Maine.
Nov. 28: John P. Joyce was prohibited from picking up money orders or registered mail by U.S. postal authorities because of past fraudulent activities in Covington, Ky.
Nov. 28: F. Kennucke, Kennucke & Co., and The Messieurs Kennucke, were prohibited from picking up money orders or registered mail by U.S. postal authorities because of past fraudulent activities in Cheyenne, Wyo.
Dec. 1: Jacob and John Clute, and J.J. Clute & Co., were prohibited from picking up money orders or registered mail by U.S. postal authorities because of past fraudulent activities in New York City.
Dec. 1: Charles F. Lindauer was prohibited from picking up money orders or registered mail by U.S. postal authorities because of past fraudulent activities in New York City.
Dec. 11: Charles E. and Nettie W. Hunt were prohibited from picking up money orders or registered mail by U.S. postal authorities because of past fraudulent activities in Philadelphia.
Dec. 11: John A. Roarty was prohibited from picking up money orders or registered mail by U.S. postal authorities because of past fraudulent activities in Philadelphia.
Dec. 15: The Kansas Land Co. was prohibited from picking up money orders or registered mail by U.S. postal authorities because of past fraudulent activities in Topeka, Kan.
Dec. 20: John Dayton (as R. Field & Co., Field & Co.) was prohibited from picking up money orders or registered mail by U.S. postal authorities because of past fraudulent activities in New York City.
Dec. 20: Ciricaco Veadero (AKA: Emilio M. Castillo, Martinez & Co.) was prohibited from picking up money orders or registered mail by U.S. postal authorities because of past fraudulent activities in New York City.
Dec. 30: Lawrence & Co., which used four aliases, was prohibited from picking up money orders or registered mail by U.S. postal authorities because of past fraudulent activities in New York City.
Dec. 30: T. Potter Wight & Co. was prohibited from picking up money orders or registered mail by U.S. postal authorities because of past fraudulent activities in New York City.

1880

Flim flam operations were established in Denver by French-Canadian swindler Lou Blonger, whose ring ruled the city for forty years.
At McTague's Saloon in Kansas City, Al Burgess began his swindling career as a steerer for the renowned sharper's hall. He became an eminent hustler at eight-dice cloth.
Middle-aged Ellen Peck bilked a New York millionaire, beginning her con career.
Reed Waddell sold his first brick in New York. He became one of the leading gold brick sellers, before he was shot to death in Paris by Tom O'Brien in 1895.
Jan. 7: Wall Street's Baxter & Co. was prohibited from picking up money orders or registered mail by U.S. postal authorities because of past fraudulent activities.
Jan. 9: Benedict & Co. was prohibited from picking up money orders or registered mail by U.S. postal authorities because of past fraudulent activities in New York City.
Jan. 9: Evarts, Barnes & Co. was prohibited from picking up money orders or registered mail by U.S. postal authorities because of past fraudulent activities in New York City.
Jan. 9: Charles Foxwell & Co. was prohibited from picking up money orders or registered mail by U.S. postal authorities because of past fraudulent activities in New York City.
Jan. 9: Thatcher, Belmont & Co. was prohibited from picking up money orders or registered mail by U.S. postal authorities because of past fraudulent activities in New York City.
Jan. 10: B.H. Burton & Co. was prohibited from picking up money orders or registered mail by U.S. postal authorities because of past fraudulent activities in Chicago.
Jan. 13: J.P. Conlon was prohibited from picking up money orders or registered mail by U.S. postal authorities because of past fraudulent activities in New York City.
Jan. 13: H.H. Hull (as U.S. Agency) was prohibited from picking up money orders or registered mail by U.S. postal officials because of past fraudulent activities in Mount Winans, Md.
Feb. 2: A. Henley (as Michael & Co.) was prohibited from picking up money orders or registered mail by U.S. postal authorities because of past fraudulent activities in Atlanta, Ga.
Feb. 16: S.A. McCaulay was prohibited from picking up money orders or registered mail by U.S. postal authorities because of past fraudulent activities in New York City.
Feb. 16: George R. Smith was prohibited from picking up money orders or registered mail by U.S. postal authorities because of past fraudulent activities in Covington, Ky.
Feb. 17: W. Scott Glore was prohibited from picking up money orders or registered mail by U.S. postal authorities because of past fraudulent activities in Louisville, Ky.
Feb. 18: Bornio & Brother was prohibited from picking up money orders or registered mail by U.S. postal authorities because of past fraudulent activities in New Orleans.
Feb. 18: D.P. Herrick & Co. was prohibited from picking up money orders or registered mail by U.S. postal authorities because of past fraudulent activities in New York City.
Feb. 18: M.V. Wagner (as Sherman & Co.) was prohibited from picking up money orders or registered mail by U.S. postal officials because of past fraudulent activities in Marshall, Mich.
Feb. 19: Smalley & Gale was prohibited from picking up money orders or registered mail by U.S. postal authorities because of past fraudulent activities in New York City.
Feb. 25: B.H. Martin & Co. was prohibited from picking up money orders or registered mail by U.S. postal authorities because of past fraudulent activities in Chicago.
Mar. 11: Marcotte & Co. was prohibited from picking up money orders or registered mail by U.S. postal authorities because of past fraudulent activities in New York City.
Mar. 24: F.H. Parsons was prohibited from picking up money orders or registered mail by U.S. postal authorities because of past fraudulent activities in Westborough, Mass.
Mar. 31: Jorda & Puig was prohibited from picking up money orders or registered mail by U.S. postal authorities because of past fraudulent activities in New Orleans.
Apr. 12: E.N. Carr & Co. (AKA: E.J Price & Co., Emery & Co.) was prohibited from picking up money orders or registered mail by U.S. postal authorities because of past fraudulent activities in New York City.
Apr. 12: I. Garcia was prohibited from picking up money orders or registered mail by U.S. postal authorities because of past fraudulent activities in New Orleans.
Apr. 12: Massich & Cossulth was prohibited from picking up money orders or registered mail by U.S. postal authorities because of past fraudulent activities in New Orleans.
Apr. 12: S. Plassans was prohibited from picking up money orders or registered mail by U.S. postal authorities because of past fraudulent activities in New Orleans.
May 24: The Chichester Rifle Co. was prohibited from picking up money orders or registered mail by U.S. postal authorities because of past fraudulent activities in Jersey City, N.J.
May 24: W.N. Fichett was prohibited from picking up money orders or registered mail by U.S. postal authorities because of past fraudulent activities in Jersey City, N.J.
May 27: Charles O. Brookes was prohibited from picking up money orders or registered mail by U.S. postal authorities because of past fraudulent activities in New York City.
May 27: James Harris was prohibited from picking up money orders or registered mail by U.S. postal authorities because of past fraudulent activities in New York City.
May 27: William Lee (AKA: Huff, Stephens) was prohibited from picking up money orders or registered mail by U.S. postal authorities because of past fraudulent activities in New York City.
May 27: Howitt Perkins was prohibited from picking up money orders or registered mail by U.S. postal authorities because of past fraudulent activities in New York City.
May 27: B. and S. Rand were prohibited from picking up money orders or registered mail by U.S. postal authorities because of past fraudulent activities in New York City.
June 14: Professor John Buchanan, who used four academic aliases, was prohibited from picking up money orders or registered mail by U.S. postal authorities because of past fraudulent activities in Philadelphia.
June 14: The Reverend James Murray (as Livingston University of America) was prohibited from picking up money orders or registered mail by U.S. postal authorities because of past fraudulent activities in Haddenfield, N.Y.
June 15: J.C. Wilson was prohibited from picking up money orders or registered mail by U.S. postal authorities because of past fraudulent activities in Austin and Ladonia, Texas.
July 22: P. Ballard was prohibited from picking up money orders or registered mail by U.S. postal authorities because of past fraudulent activities in New York City.
July 22: D.A. Kratzer was prohibited from picking up money orders or registered mail by U.S. postal authorities because of past fraudulent activities in Iowa.
July 22: George Martin was prohibited from picking up money orders or registered mail by U.S. postal authorities because of past fraudulent activities in New York City.

1882

Oscar Wilde was swindled by "Hungry Joe" Lewis and others during the poet's tour of the U.S.
Mail-order bucket shops in New York produced a list of dupes.

1883

Boston Globe Hoax. Soames, an assistant telegraph editor at the *Boston Globe* invented an interview with a ship's captain about a volcano eruption.

1884

The Edwards Inheritance fraud was begun by Cleveland's Herbert H. Edwards.
May 4: Former U.S. President Ulysses S. Grant loaned $150,000 to Ferdinand Ward, who, with Grant's son, ran the Grant and Ward investment firm. Ward was caught fleeing to Canada to avoid repaying investors the $2 million he had defrauded.

May 13: The Second National Bank's president escaped to Canada after defrauding the bank of $4 million.
May 14: The Metropolitan Bank closed after its funds had been used fraudulently by the bank president in purchasing railroad stock.
1886
After placing an ad in the *Pall Mall Gazette*, Mary Ann Bruce Sutherland (AKA: Mrs. Gordon-Baillie) and Percival Frost defrauded several Scottish merchants while posing as wealthy benefactors. Both were later imprisoned.
The Chicago court house was painted with mystical "preserving fluid" by con man Harry Holland.
1889
John Reginald Birchall ran ads in London newspapers looking for investors in a Canadian farm. It was a fraud, and one of the investors, Frederick Benwell, was killed when he went to see the farms.
1890s
In the late 1890s, Fred Buckminister, a former police officer teamed up with con man Joseph Weil. They ran "big store" cons together for forty years.
1890
One of the first spiritual swindles was begun in Harlem, N.Y., by Elizabeth Fitzgerald (AKA: Madam Zingara).
Eminent European figures are defrauded by American Ross Potter, who used a number of aliases.
A group of swindlers in Chicago, under the guise of Flemming and Merriam's Mutual Cooperative Fund, bilked thousands of dollars from the $2 million invested in a few months' time.
1893
Dr. Albert Abrams entered into quackery traveling the U.S. with such devices as the Dynamizer, which allegedly determined ailments from a blood sample or a signature. He left an estate of $2 million upon his death in 1924.
Victims lost $500,000 at the World's Fair in Chicago to Tom O'Brien.
William and Soloman Barmash and Hyman and Phillip Bernstein were sentenced by the British Crown to penal servitude for currency forgery.
Edward Beall (AKA: The Black Prince) and three accomplices opened the London and Scottish Banking and Discount Corp. Ltd. which they used to bilk investors of £30,000.
1894
Inventor of numerous phony machines, engineer W.C. Crosby, started his swindling career in Philadelphia.
1895
James Addison Reavis was found Guilty and sent to prison in Santa Fe, N.M., for the Peralta land grant scheme in Arizona. He had defrauded the Southern Pacific Railroad, the Silver King Mine, and others who paid him for use of "his" land.
The Scottish fraud gang, the Williamsons, immigrated to Brooklyn, N.Y.
1896
"E.S. Dean Safe System of Speculation," the $5 million stock fraud which offered returns of 300 to 400 percent, was introduced by Leopold Balbach. More than 10,000 people were swindled at a rate of $25,000 per day. A year later, Balbach fled the law never to be arrested.
July: Shares were sold at £5 each by the Camden Town, England piano-manufacturer, Thomas Edward Brinsmead. By the year's end the fraudulent operation was uncovered and Brinsmead and his associates were sent to prison.
1897
Inventor Prescott Ford Jernegan of Connecticut bilked more than $350,000 out of people who invested in his "gold accumulator."
May 14: The *New York World* ran a story about the rescue of two balloonists off the coast of Sandy Hook. The story was a fraud invented by a press agent.
1898
The first wire to acquire race results in advance was tapped by "Paper Collar Joe" Kratalsky.
1899
The Franklin Syndicate business investment scam was begun by William Franklin Miller and Robert A. Ammon, who promised 10 percent returns per week.
New York bucket shop con men Henry Allen and Julius Price were convicted for selling phony Rapid transit stock.
A St. Louis pawnbroker was hustled out of $200,000 by the Gondorf brothers in a big store operation.
George Smith operated an insurance claim scam whereby he obtained up to $50,000 per phony claim he filed against Manhattan, N.Y., transportation companies for the "injuries" he sustained.
Former Minnesota senator Alonzo J. Whitman was arrested, and later imprisoned, for falsely securing loans and defrauding hotels with bad checks. His victims included Atlantic City's Isleworth Hotel, Boston's Parker House, Chicago's Grand Pacific, and New York's Bartholdi.
Oct. 24: J.W. Blackridge, David D. Duff, and C.F. Taylor allegedly incorporated a fraudulent investment firm, the Cooperative Trust Co. in Chicago.
1900
The smack was invented by con man Buck Boatright.
Bogus race-track park concessions were sold for a $5,000 apiece by Joseph "Yellow Kid" Weil and Bob Collins.
Sigmund Engel began his career of marrying women and bilking them of their fortunes in Vienna, Aust.
Quack J.H. Kelly obtained $1 million from his mental healing swindle.
Joseph Weil launched a number of short scams.
1901
New York City green-goods operator George Lehman, whose scam was exposed by reformer Anthony Comstock, was convicted of fraud.
Society and literary personalities in Ireland were defrauded con man Count Zuboff, whose real name was Lipman.
Feb. 14: Counterfeiter George Lehman (AKA: Nigger Baker) was convicted of fraud in New York City.
1902
"The Professional Fit-Thrower," George Gray, who swindled victims by feigning epileptic seizures, was arrested in Manhattan, N.Y.
Frederick Emerson Peters began his lengthy con career by cashing his first bad check.
Medicinal and spiritual swindles sprang up across the U.S.
Feb. 15: The first wire store was opened by Jim Roofer in Chicago.
Apr. 10: The Colonel Jacob Baker inheritance con was begun. Victims, who shared the last name of Baker, were led to believe that they would inherit all of Philadelphia—worth $3 billion.
1903
The marriage swindling careers of New York sisters, Charlotte and Katherine Poillon, was begun when Katherine sued William G. Brokaw for $250,000 for breach of promise. An out-of-court settlement of $170,000 was reached.
The first fight store was opened in Colorado Springs, Colo.
Jan. 14: Edgar Zug was found Guilty in Newark, N.J., of perpetrating a witchcraft fraud, in which victims paid to drive away evil spirits.
June 1: From June 1 to July 8, Sophie Beck defrauded $2 million from Philadelphia's Story Cotton Co.
Oct. 3: "King of the Ringers" Benjamin A. Chilson won a fortune in the last race at New Orleans' Morris Park by disguising racehorse McNamara as a long-shot named Fiddler.
1904
Feb. 10: "Kid Duffy" joined Lou Blonger's as a full-time partner of the Denver con empire.
Dec. 8: Cassie Chadwick, born Elizabeth Bigley, was arrested for swindling millions from Cleveland banks which were convinced that she was Andrew Carnegie's illegitimate daughter. She died in prison in 1907.
1905
Feb. 2: William Crane, Christopher Tarcy, and Wyatt swindled John Felix out of $50,000 in an elaborate phony off-track betting scam.
Feb. 18: Charles Ponzi, who later would swindle thousands of people in a "Peter to Paul" scheme, was arrested for check forgery.
Mar. 27: Martin Vzral was poisoned to death in Chicago by Herman Billik, who collected the $2,000 insurance that an infatuated Mrs. Vzral gave to him.
Dec. 11: Mrs. E. Stevens was killed in her Wadhurst, England, home. Her son, James Stevens, was convicted of her murder in an apparent attempt to collect life insurance.
1906
George H. Munroe sold millions of dollars in worthless Montreal and Boston Consolidated Copper Co. stock. He threw lavish $20,000 banquets and took investors to British Columbia aboard the private railroad car of James J. Hill, enticing them with views of others' mining property.
A permanent big store was opened in Manhattan, N.Y., by Charley Gondorf.
Baltimore magic dealer Dr. Theodore White was found Guilty of swindling his "students" of large sums of money.
The first big stores were opened in Oakland, Calif., Salt Lake City, Seattle, and Spokane, Wash.
1907
Edward Pape, who filed phony claims against public transportation companies for his broken neck, was arrested in New York.
1908
Joseph Weil defrauded saloon owners of thousands of dollars by borrowing against a real diamond ring and then selling an imitation ring.
Joseph Weil teamed up with Fred "The Deacon" Buckminster, who, as a policeman, had arrested Weil, but changed his mind when offered a bribe.
Jan. 27: Money box master Victor "The Count" Lustig was arrested for the first time in Prague, Czech., for counterfeiting.
1909
Novice composers were enticed by Tin Pan Alley hustlers who offered to publish music. Scores of these swindlers were arrested.
March: Henry Peter Bernard was tried at the Old Bailey for swindling investors out of £60,000 with his phony company, the City of London Investment Corp.
Mar. 15.: Eddie Jackson, a big-store operator, was sent to prison in Illinois for a green-goods fraud.
June 3: Philip Musica was sent to prison in New York for a swindle in which he had bribed a customs official to allow smuggled sausages into the U.S. for little or no fee.
1910
The Benan Letter, a letter purporting to be a chronicle of the life of Jesus was published. It was exposed as a fake by Dr. Carl Schmidt and

Dr. Herman Grapon.
Eugene and Shelton Burr sold millions of phony stocks in New York.
Halley's Comet produced fears of the world's end in many, and con man William Elmer Mead played upon these fears with his magic-wallet scam.
A majority of the selling stiffs confidence games were introduced by A.L. "Dead" Hicks.
June 1; Cam Spears earned a fortune selling lists of victims to New York bucket shops.
Nov. 1: W.T. Wintemute was arrested in New York, as was his London accomplice, Herman Warszawiak, who supplied Wintemute with some 12,000 victims. Wintemute netted $1.3 million selling bogus shares for $100 and then reselling them for a quarter.
1911
The phony stock investment scam of Eugene and Shelton Burr was exposed and the two were arrested, after they obtained $50 million.
Postal frauds reaped $77 million.
A Baltimore fight store opened and reaped $100,000 per week.
Feb. 13: Seymour Ernest J. Cox was arrested in Michigan for selling phony oil leases.
June 1: Railroad mogul E.H. Harriman was coaxed into purchasing an estimated $250,000 in worthless paintings.
Oct. 20: Cardenio F. King was arrested and sent to prison in Boston for publishing a weekly stock advice newspaper which promoted phony stock.
1912
Jules W. Arnstein defrauded William E. Shinks of $15,000 and then fled from New York to London. He was sent to prison in 1916.
George Munroe was convicted for defrauding hundreds of thousands from investors who purchased phony Marconi Wireless stock.
Philip Musica was sent to prison for cheating several banks of $500,000 with fraudulent shipping information.
Feb. 1: Gustav Aufrecht, Sam Biddison, and others sold fraudulent stock in long-deserted mining operations under the guise of the Avalon Oil Lands. They were later arrested.
Apr. 14: The ocean liner *Titanic* sank. Survivor Alvin Clarence Thomas soon earned his nickname "Titanic Thompson" by filing false insurance claims on victims of the wreck.
June 1: Between June 1 and Nov. 1 Los Angeles real estate swindler Clarence Hillman defrauded thousands from victims with crooked land promotions.
July 13: George Joseph Smith murdered his first wife, Beatrice Constance Annie "Bessie" Mundy, in a bathtub at Herne Bay, England. He collected insurance on her life and his next two wives before he was hanged in 1915.
Dec. 1: Henri Girard killed his friend Louis Pernotte in Paris to collect insurance. He attempted to poison the entire Pernotte family and did murder another person before committing suicide in 1921.
1913
Imposter Luodovic Radzevil swindled fellow immigrants with farcical, but profitable, cons.
Mar. 1: Sweden's Ivar Krueger began his match-making business using phony Italian bonds. This scam would inevitably become history's largest business swindle.
1914
Marcus Garvey arrived in Harlem, N.Y., and inaugurated black-confederation swindles.
After breaking into the offices of con artist James W. Ryan (AKA: The Postal Kid), postal detectives discovered a card catalog of easy con targets.
Earl Barnes was arrested for passing bad checks in Boston.
Mar. 9: Charley Gondorf was convicted following a raid upon his Manhattan, N.Y., big store.
April: Edward Hayes, a millionaire sex medicine promoter, was fined $5,000 for fraud.
July 20: Henri Desire Landru, who later became France's "Bluebeard," was convicted of fraud in Paris and sent to prison.
Oct. 25: Con artist Thomas "Mournful" Meeker was arrested for collecting money from mourners at the wake of an affluent New Yorker.
1915
In New York, Charlotte and Katherine Poillon were arrested for defrauding an elderly man who had paid for their favors.
Feb. 15: Joseph Weil and Fred Buckminster opened a big store in Chicago, swindling about $200,000 in phony stocks.
May 1: Henri Desire Landru placed an advertisement in Paris' *Le Journal* to attract wealthy women he could defraud and murder. He committed eleven known murders for money between 1915 and 1919.
June 23: Police closed down Fred Gondorf's big store and he was sent to Sing Sing where his brother Charley Gondorf was already incarcerated.
Nov. 26: Baltimore playboy Dwight Mallory disappeared while hunting, giving con artists a chance to defraud large sums for his safe return.
1916
Feb. 3: William Rickson was convicted in Maryland of defrauding the family of Dwight Mallory by posing as a private detective who would find the missing man for $500. He was sent to prison.
Apr. 11: In Farmingdale, N.Y., Louis Enricht announced his ability to change water into gasoline. The fraudulent inventor swindled a number of manufacturing magnates.
Sept. 28: Frederick Small murdered his wife to collect insurance. The fire he set at their Mountainview, N.H. home, did not conceal his crime and Small was hanged in 1918.
1917
Fort Worth, Texas, barber J.W. Carruth (AKA: Hog Creek Carruts) bilked tens of thousands of dollars from investors in bogus oil fields. His fraud was disclosed the following year.
A Cheyenne, Wyo., rancher was defrauded of $35,000 by William Elmer Mead's magic-wallet swindle.
Alfred Banker Post (AKA: Colonel Alfred Lindsay) impersonated an intelligence officer probing German spy activity in Washington, D.C. Though charges against him were dropped, he was again arrested for fraud in 1922 and sentenced to prison.
Feb. 17: Lawrence Merle Carroll (AKA: Harold Heck, John O. King) was born. He would later become involved in credit card fraud in Illinois and Indiana.
July 15: Heiress Maude King was defrauded of $150,000 by self-proclaimed detective Gaston Bullock Means. Means was later acquitted of any wrongdoing in King's "accidental" death.
Oct. 7: Dr. John R. Brinkley arrived in Milford, Kan., where he began a number of medical frauds.
Oct. 22: Harry Benson died just moments before Scotland Yard detectives moved in on him for setting up a phony organization, the Prisoners' Aid Society.
1918
Alfred Banker Post was arrested for impersonating a federal agent.
Eric Brotherton tried to charge personal and business expenses to His Royal Majesty in England as a part of a ship building and repair contract he had with the crown. He was caught and jailed.
Feb. 10: A campaign was waged against oil-leasing con artists by the Oklahoma City *News*, which also convinced police to arrest swindlers.
July 18: A bogus cure for tuberculosis, "Tuberclecide," was introduced by quack Charles Aycock.
Aug. 1.: From Aug. 1 to Nov. 1, Gaston Means sold his spy services to British and German agents, who paid him for useless information about each other.
Aug. 19: Joseph J. Kopernik (AKA: Joe Kopinek, Joseph Kipirnik) was born. He would later become involved in credit card fraud in Illinois.
1919
The Hartzell family in Iowa fell victim to the Drake inheritance scam perpetrated by Milo F. Lewis and Sudie Whiteker. Oscar Hartzell inevitably developed the scam on a greater scale.
In three months' time, Max Klante defrauded more than one million marks from bettors at the Karlshorst racetrack in Germany by posing as a tipster. By 1920, he had swindled twelve million marks.
A warning to banks across the U.S. about a multitude of bad-check swindlers was issued by William Allan Pinkerton.
Feb. 27: Dr. Walter K. Wilkins murdered his wife in Long Beach, N.Y., for insurance reasons. He was arrested again, and committed suicide in his jail cell.
May 30: Colonel Bermondt-Avalon defrauded Berlin and London banks of investments in his takeover of Latvia to prevent Bolsheviks from overrunning the country. He looted the treasury and left before Allied forces arrived.
July 18: Cleveland publisher Daniel Kaber was murdered by Salvatore Cala and Vittoria Pisselli at the bidding of Mrs. Eva Catherine Kaber, who had her husband killed to collect his fortune. All were sent to prison.
Dec. 20: Charles Ponzi opened a bank in Boston and reintroduced the Peter-to-Paul swindle. His promise to double investors' money in ninety days, and later in forty-five days, brought him $200,000 a day.
1920
S.C. Pandolfo, under the auspices of the Commercial Club of St. Cloud, defrauded St. Cloud, Minn., residents of $4.8 million in Pan Motor Co. stock. He was sent to prison later by Judge Kenesaw Mountain Landis.
The Automobile League, a bogus car club, was begun by A.C. Bidwell, who obtained millions.
Working under the protective cloak of Denver's Lou Blonger, Joe Furey, and four others defrauded J. Frank Norfleet of $45,000 in Fort Worth, Texas, touching off a great manhunt.
Jean Pierre Lafitte, who claimed the pirate brothers were his ancestors, began his career of fraud.
Antoinette Bonner (AKA: The Diamond Queen) was caught by police when she tried to sell some uncut diamonds she had taken from prominent jewelers.
A Chicago lawyer was swindled of $57,000 by Gaston Means.
Celedonia Sevilla entered into the Spanish prisoner swindle.
Posing as a physician, Stanley Clifford Weyman was sent by a development company to aid Peruvian natives.
Joseph Weil and Sam Banks operated a medium scam, where the mystic wore a microphone in his turban, through which information concerning the victim was relayed. At least $1,000 per session was swindled.
The American State Bank in Chicago was purchased by Joseph Weil and John Worthington, who defrauded creditors of $300,000 with ingeniously fabricated letters of credit.
The Cook family tree fraud was introduced.
August: A run on Charles Ponzi's company—which was really a front for his Peter-to-Paul scheme begun the previous June—was created by a Boston *Globe* exposé on Aug. 2. He repaid $15 million of $20 million he took in, and was sent to prison.

1921
An additional $1 was levied—bringing in millions—upon members of the Negro Improvement Association and African Communities League by Marcus Garvey.
William Elmer Mead swindled $11,600 from a Jacksonville, Fla., resident with his magic-wallet con.
May 3: The wealthy Albright sisters of Chicago were duped of $180,000 by Joseph Weil and others in a phony oil stock scam.
Dec. 12: Future con artist and imposter Ferdinando Waldo Demara was born in Lawrence, Mass.
1922
Horatio William Bottomley was found guilty of bilking the poor out of £150,000 for phony Liberty bonds. This was just one part of a long career as one of England's most successful con-men.
The number of swindlers working for Lou Blonger's Denver operation increased to 500.
Alberto Santos Guimaires employed Dorothy "Dot" King to defraud a Boston banker. He figured prominently in King's murder in 1923 and in the death of Washington socialite Aurelia Drefus, whom he had swindled.
Police brought an end to a profitable Manhattan, N.Y., magic-wallet gang led by William Kent.
Victor Lustig defrauded the American Savings Bank of Springfield, Mo., of $10,000. While using the alias Robert Duval, Lustig switched envelopes during a real estate transaction.
William Elmer Mead was sent to prison after swindling a Colorado victim.
W.H.H. Miller was fired as head of the Illinois Department of Registration and Education for issuing dubious medical licenses.
Giovanni Mogavec Minneci defrauded tens of thousands of dollars from people who paid $1 a month for life insurance. The policies contained minute print which nullified most claims. He was later sent to prison.
Tens of thousands of dollars were defrauded from blacks who contributed to the Mutual Burial Society in New York.
A phony "Federal Secret Service" was established in Trenton, N.J., by Peter Pollack to defraud businessmen.
Feb. 15: Three Miami were swindled of $345,000 by Jackie French's big store horse-racing wire operation.
Mar. 22: Katherine Allers purchased a run-down building in Brooklyn, N.Y., and after insuring the building and furniture for $7,500, she burned it down. She was sent to prison.
June 1: Between June 1 and Oct. 1, Chicago swindler Leo Koretz defrauded more than $1 million with phony oil leases.
Oct. 22: John Earl Alexander (AKA: Johnnie Dollar) was born. He would later become involved in credit card fraud.
1923
Dr. John Romulus Brinkley began advertising his phony goat gland implant procedure on the radio. The operation was claimed to rejuvenate elderly men and cure the sexually impotent.
Durrell Gregory & Co., run by R.H. and John M. Gregory, defrauded millions from stock investors. Only about 10 percent of the stock purchased was legitimate.
Dr. Frederick A. Cook, Seymour Ernest J. Cox, and others were sent to prison for selling fraudulent Texas oil leases.
Jan. 31: Girard and Company, Inc., a bogus Mount Vernon, N.Y. firm, was established by Philip Musica (AKA: F. Donald Coster), who used the profits from selling alcohol to bootleggers to purchase McKesson and Robbins in 1927.
Feb. 28: Louis Enricht was sent to prison for attempting to sell his bogus formula which he claimed changed water into gas.
May 19: Philip Musica buys raw alcohol to make a bogus hair tonic, but sells it to bootleggers instead.
July 21: Lendsay Merrill (AKA: Leroy Merrill, Roy Patillo) was born. He would later become involved in credit card fraud in Chicago.
Aug. 24: Magic-wallet con victim J. Frank Norfleet completed his three-year crusade to track down the five con men in Lou Blonger's gang who had swindled him.
Oct. 15: Publication by the St. Louis *Star* of Harry Thompson Brundige's exposé on fraudulent sales of medical degrees ended Dr. Robert Adcox's diploma swindle. He and his confederates were sent to prison.
1924
More than $150 million in worthless stock was sold in Iowa, Kentucky, Michigan, and Ohio by con artists who convinced country bankers to finance the initial stock purchase.
Marcus Garvey was sent to prison in Atlanta for fraud.
Oscar Hartzell journeyed to London from Iowa on the pretense of finding the heir to his widespread Drake inheritance scam. He was himself swindled by an English medium.
Gramercy Park socialites, Mrs. Van Hilt and Miss Holden, were left homeless after purchasing $60,000 of bogus stock.
Joseph Weil swindled $500,000 from twenty victims in Chicago big-store cons.
A Chicago confidence gang forced prostitutes to provide them with lists of possible victims.
Feb. 14: Davis Rowland MacDonald faked his drowning death in the Allegheny River near Pittsburgh, so that his wife, Clara MacDonald, could collect insurance and remarry. Fourteen years later the fraud was discovered, but MacDonald was not prosecuted.
June 23: Richard Barry pleaded guilty to passing forged money orders in Philadelphia and New York. He was imprisoned.
July 2: Lee T. Brooks was arrested in New York City for listing phony stocks he received from stock swindlers on the exchange. He was sent to prison.
Aug. 6: Lawrence Simmerman (AKA: Charles Hagerty, Tracy Randall) was born. He would later become involved in credit card fraud in Illinois.
1925
Robert Boulton and two partners were charged with bank fraud in London because of their dealings with the Bank of Silma in India. They were acquitted.
Lulu Cummings dined with Clarence Darrow in Chicago and then swindled scores of socialites.
During a raid upon one of New York's largest bucket shops, police arrested super con men Charles Greehaus, Sigmund Levy, Louis Manes, and Edward Rosenberg, who were all directors of the fraudulent stock firm of J.F. Townsend and Co..
A simple investment con was used by Victor Lustig on Al Capone.
Charles Ponzi was arrested in Florida for attempting to defraud real estate investors.
February: Portuguese swindler Alves Reis used the counterfeit currency he printed the previous November to convince Waterlow and Sons, Ltd., of London to print new currency for him.
Feb. 9: Will Barrett was brought to trial in Nashville, Tenn., for check forgery.
Mar. 26: "Colonel" Robert W. Hayes (AKA: Robert Wilbur Hay) was born. He would later be arrested several times for fraudulent activities in Arizona, California, Mississippi, Ohio, and Tennessee.
July 30: Charles Schwartz tried to collect life insurance on himself and on his Walnut Creek, Calif., plant by burning the building down with the corpse of a look-alike inside. He killed himself before being taken captive.
Nov. 26: Real estate broker Charles A. Lee faked his death in Rochester, N.Y., to collect $22,000 in life insurance. He was sent to prison after his arrest three months later in Louisiana.
December: Portuguese officials discovered the counterfeit fraud perpetrated by Alvis Reis, who had amassed 580,000 bank notes totalling $200 million, with which he purchased numerous valuables.
1926
Phony promoters, brokers, and securities salesmen defrauded some $500 million from investors in New York.
Apr. 27: Patrick Henry "Packy" Lennon began his three-year swindle of U.S. tycoon A.J. Cunningham. He obtained millions from Cunningham.
Summer: William N. Coffey married and ran off with Hattie Hales. He killed her and forged a document signing several hundred thousand dollars of stock over to him. He was jailed.
Aug. 18: Charles Ponzi was arrested in Florida for real estate fraud. He was sent to Massachusetts to serve time for his Peter-to-Paul scam of 1919 and 1920.
1927
Hugh Garland began fraudulent pyramid of companies by greatly exaggerating the worth of his Automatic Signal Co. to $32.5 million.
Oscar Hartzell demanded that investors in the U.S. send him money in London to finance his search for the Drake heir in his inheritance scam.
Hugh B. Monjar established his fraudulent Mantle Clubs and became a millionaire.
After a year in the Paris prison, Serge Stavisky continued his con career by placing top French leaders on his immense payroll.
Columbus, Ohio, was invaded by scores of the "Terrible Williamsons" confidence clan, who proceeded to swindle residents.
Feb. 13: Walter Hohenau arrived in Houston, where he introduced a machine to turn water into gasoline. He fled to Mexico when his fraud was revealed.
May 15: Between May 15 and July 25, the "Terrible Williamsons" invaded Cleveland and defraud residents with home-repair scams.
May 17: Walter D. Pritchard, who was later arrested for mail fraud and credit card fraud in Illinois, was born.
Oct. 1: Robert Boltz introduced the Peter-to-Paul scheme in Philadelphia. He made millions for thirteen years.
1928
Charles Aycock's bogus cure for tuberculosis, "Tuberclecide," was determined useless. He was fined and the fraud ended.
Liberian President Charles King, who won re-election by 600,000 votes from an electorate of 15,000, was charged with election fraud by his opponent Thomas Faulkner. King resigned in 1930.
Serge Stavisky monopolized the pawnshop securities with the help of French premier Camille Chautemps. He used phony collateral and stolen jewelry to reap millions.
Spring: Sam Abrams attempted to defraud his insurance company by disappearing after a swim in Rockaway, N.Y. The claim was not paid, and Abrams was later sent to prison.
Summer: The National Surety Co. opened an investigation into a nationally-run check cashing fraud scheme, where forty girls were used to write fraudulent checks over the purchase price at stores.
January: The French Secret Service discovered a $12 million reparations fraud being conducted between French and German merchants during the sale of coal, hops, and seed.

Mar. 17: Samuel Reese (AKA: Candies Wheeler, Jr.) was born. He would later become involved in credit card fraud in Chicago.
Aug. 23: A skeleton, reputedly the body of kidnap victim Heinrich Alberding, was discovered in Saalfeld, Ger. Alberding and his insurance fraud were discovered in 1934 and he was sentenced to death.
1929
Gilbert Carstairs dressed as a military man and stole subscription dues checks from West End clubs.
Leonard Alfred Cline (as One-Man Crime Inc.) was convicted of the first of many forgeries, the forgery of a widow's will.
W.H.H. Miller and his accomplices were indicted in Chicago for operating a counterfeiting ring which made and sold fraudulent medical diplomas for $2,000 each.
To offset losses of $640,000 in Wall Street speculation, Philip Musica issued thousands of inventory invoices against a McKesson & Robbins subsidiary.
An exorbitant amount of worthless stock sold prior to the stock market crash.
Apr. 26: Robert Arthur Tourbillon was arrested in New York for defrauding an apple farmer of his property. He was sent to prison.
June 1: Russian exile Serge Rubinstein, as manager of the Banque Franco-Asiatique in Paris, began confiscating $60,000 in deposits and used money to purchase a restaurant chain worth $450,000 and loot that as well.
Dec. 1: From London, Oscar Hartzell asked Drake inheritance victims in the U.S. to send money to thwart President Herbert Hoover, who he claimed caused the stock market crash to prevent them from obtaining their fortunes.
1930
Abraham Abraham began his forty-year criminal career which included credit card and mail fraud in Illinois, Michigan, Ohio, Pennsylvania, and Texas.
Readers of the New York *Evening Journal* were warned not to buy stock from Patrick Henry Lennon.
Victor Lustig gave up money-box fraud to pursue counterfeiting.
Odie Moore began his Choctaw Indian settlement swindle in Mississippi.
Serge Rubinstein was deported from France for manipulation of the franc.
March: Maude and Robert Eugene Ault were charged with mail fraud for their hoax of being heirs to $50 million if investors would defray litigation costs. Both were sent to prison and fined.
May: Alves Reis was sent to prison for his Portuguese bank note scam.
October: Benito Mussolini decreed penalties and prison terms which would be meted out for corporate and stock frauds in Italy.
November: G. Lisle Ferman and Morrison B. Orr of Prince & Whitely Trading Corporation were expelled from the New York Stock Exchange for fraudulent stock dealings.
Dec. 15: Danzig, Pol., casino owners were swindled by Abram Sykowski, who claimed he controlled Al Capone's millions, but needed more money to bribe officials to obtain the fortune. He used this scam for twenty-five years.
1931
Gilbert H. Beesemyer was sent to prison for defrauding $8 million from Los Angeles' Guaranty Building and Loan Association, of which he had been general manager. The company collapsed.
Hundreds of con artists attempted to obtain the reported $150,000 that Manhattan youth Edward F. Dougherty had recently received.
The Philadelphia Co. for Guaranteeing Mortgages fraudulently reported losses of $40,790 to the U.S. government, while reporting earnings of $725,000 to investors.
A Yonkers, N.Y., construction site was passed off as a newly developed gold mine by con artists who sold $135,000 in phony stock.
January: Wisconsin senator John J. Blaine charged the Chicago-based investment bank of Halsey, Stuart & Co. with defrauding its investors.
Oct. 3: Peter C. "Paddy" Barrie garnered more than $1 million betting on a ringer horse he raced at Havre de Grace in France.
1932
Following a successful stint using the magic-wallet con, William P. Hunt was arrested.
Evelyn Walsh McLean was defrauded by Gaston Means in a spurious search for the missing Lindbergh baby. Means was sent to prison.
Jan. 5: Harry Green, Tony Marino, Dan Kreisberg, Joe Murphy, and Frank Pasqua murdered Michael Malloy to collect insurance money. All but Green were executed.
Mar. 4: A St. Louis financier lost more than $200,000 to William Elmer Mead's magic-wallet scam.
Mar. 5: Rhodes Cecil Cowle was poisoned by his mother, Mrs. Daisy Louisa Cowle de Melker, who also had murdered husbands William Cowle in 1923 and Robert Sproat in 1927 for insurance. She was hanged on Dec. 30.
May 24: George Baker (AKA: Father Devine) was put on trial for defrauding followers at revival meetings.
June: John Bain was convicted of defrauding 150,000 bank depositors out of more than $12 million.
October: President of Chicago investment bank of Halsey, Stuart & Co. Harold Leonard Stuart and two executives were indicted for mail fraud in the sale of $13.5 million in Wardman Real Estate bonds.
Oct. 19: Forger Charles J. Drossner was sent to a Wisconsin prison. Scotland Yard obtained his fingerprints and determined that he was really swindler José de Braganca, wanted in Paris and Rome. He was sent to prison in Europe following his release.
1933
The Harriman National Bank was defrauded by owner Joseph Harriman to manipulate the stock market. He was sent to prison.
Angered at organized crime's invasion of their business, con artists held a convention in Chicago.
A con man drove his car to every gas station in Poughkeepsie, N.Y., filled his tank with water, and then placed a pill into the tank, claiming the water would become gas. He sold hundreds of pills for $13.50. The tank was a false one next to the real gas tank.
In San Francisco, four doctors and five hospital employees were suspended for informing shyster lawyers of accidents from which the lawyers could defraud victims.
Mar. 12: "Swedish Match King" Ivar Krueger killed himself after his fraud was exposed.
April: U.S. collector of customs in Haiti David P. Johnson confessed to defrauding the Haitian government by under weighing merchandise for Syrian-American merchants, the Brothers Zrike.
November: Oscar Hartzell entered Leavenworth prison following his conviction of fraud for his Drake inheritance scam, and his earlier extradition from England.
Nov. 18: Sam Berliner and Dr. Jerome Garber were arrested for burning down buildings they owned in New York City to collect insurance. Both were sent to prison.
Dec. 24: Con man Serge Stavisky was exposed, but escaped arrest. A number of his confederates were arrested when his scams were exposed in France.
1934
Abram Sykowski sold phony passports to refugees from Russia and elsewhere.
Jan. 8: Police officials watched as Serge Stavisky committed suicide. His nine-year swindle of the French government caused the demise of Camille Chautemps' cabinet.
February: U.S. president Franklin D. Roosevelt ordered all airmail contracts cancelled as a means of fining the industry for fraudulent methods.
Feb. 3: Jospeh Weil swindled $50,000 from an investor who believed the con man to be a bank president since Weil was in the office of the real president.
May: Eight members of Japanese Prime Minister Mykato Saito's cabinet were indicted for stock fraud in the Bank of Taiwan Scandal.
June 15: Eva Coo of Cooperstown, N.Y., murdered Harry Wright to collect insurance. She was executed on June 28, 1935.
July 4: William J. Cressy, who made millions on his mail-order swindles, began to sell phony Indian head pennies.
Oct. 15: Lonnie Johnson was born. He would later become involved in credit card fraud in Chicago.
1935
John J. Burke & Co. engineered a massive stock swindle involving Stutz Motor stock, selling more than 160,000 nonexistent shares.
Joseph Hauber, Lester Kirkendall, and Delmar Short—confederates in Oscar Hartzell's Drake inheritance fraud—were arrested in Chicago. All were sent to prison.
William Elmer Mead was sent to prison for fraud.
Wealthy Warren Edmunds from Manhattan, N.Y., was duped into investing in nonexistent property by Joseph Weil, Richard Hampton, and Harris Norris, who posed as geologists.
Joseph Weil convinced numerous victims that he was traveling to Europe to have Adolf Hitler invest in mythical copper mines.
A feud broke out amongst the "Terrible Williamsons" which spread from Georgia to Pennsylvania.
Aug. 15: Robert James murdered his wife Mary, with the help of Charles Hope, to collect insurance. He had previously murdered his nephew for the same reason. He was hanged on May 1, 1942.
1936
Memberships in phony nationwide patriotic clubs in the U.S. were sold by "The Frisco Kid." Branch managerships were offered for $300.
Italy's Benito Mussolini was defrauded by Abram Sykowski, who used his swindle about obtaining Al Capone's millions. He later swindled Barcelona's police chief.
After buying 173,000 shares of the Chosen Corporation mining company, Serge Rubinstein set up six bogus corporations and sold millions of shares through French associates.
William Cameron Morrow Smith reintroduced the Baker inheritance swindle in Pennsylvania, but was arrested and sent to prison.
Feb. 5: Con man Sülün Osman from Turkey sold the *Orient Express* for $75,000, for which he was sent to prison.
Apr. 5: David John Cantrell (AKA: David John Carlino) was born. He later became involved in credit card fraud and forgery in Illinois.
July 18: William Elmer Mead was arrested for fraud in New York City and sent to prison.
Sept. 14: Lucille Francis Jannece (AKA: Lillian Bruno, Lucille Tito) was born. She would later become involved in credit card fraud and be arrested for possession of stolen cards in Illinois.
Sept. 18: Indictments for mail fraud and conspiracy against the Philadelphia Co. for Guaranteeing Mortgages were handed down. More indict-

ments were made on Sept. 28, and in November the charges were made public.
December: A number of ambulance-chasers were reported attempting to defraud victims of an elevated train accident in Chicago.
1937
Wallace G. Garland was sent to prison for a $4.5 million pyramid swindle.
Joseph Weil sold $300,000 in phony hair mattress stock.
Police finally caught up with Morris Bolber and several accomplices who killed at least thirty people over a five-year-long insurance scam.
Mar. 24: In Japan, Serge Rubinstein sold his Korean-based Chosen Corporation. Forbidden from taking money out of the country, he smuggled out 3.5 million yen, leading to the yen's collapse on the market.
June 1: Anna Marie Hahn poisoned Jacob Wagner in Cincinnati, and later poisoned George Opensdorfer; both for insurance. She was executed.
June 3: Archie J. Weathington (AKA: Archie Rowland) was born. He later became involved in credit card fraud and bad check writing in Chicago.
July 8: Marie Petitjean Becker was convicted of poisoning at least twelve people to collect insurance. She was sent to prison.
1938
During questioning by FBI agents Gaston Means died without revealing the whereabouts of money he swindled from Evalyn Walsh McLean.
In England, Rupert Gordon Russell was charged with fraudulently converting £20,140 worth of Commonwealth Treasury Bonds and Miller Anderson Ltd., certificates.
A member of the Williamson confidence ring informed authorities in Pittsburgh of the clan's operations.
The Womack family—including John and Bertha Mae Womack, their three daughters, and their husbands—which operated in Illinois, Indiana, Michigan, Missouri, and Tennessee, was tried for insurance fraud in committing at least 65 phony accidents for $2,085.
November: John Woolcott Forbes, who was charged with defrauding £130,000 from people in Australia, England, France, and India, jumped bail in Bombay.
Dec. 16: Philip Musica (AKA: Frank Donald Coster) killed himself in New York when a federal marshall arrived to arrest him for his McKesson and Robbins fraud.
1939
As part of a general crackdown on con artists, Manhattan's "High-Ass Kid" was sent to prison for working a short con.
Apr. 23: Payoff store swindlers William Graham and James McKay were arrested in Reno, Nev., and sent to prison.
Sept. 1: Ralph Wilby (AKA: James W. Ralston) was arrested for fraud in Colton, Calif. He was sent to prison.
1940
In San Francisco, Juan Barrena and Camilo Lopez Vasques were convicted for operating one of the century's most infamous Spanish prisoner frauds.
W.H. Bruce and H. Vaughan were arrested in London for forging checks totalling more than £7,000. They were sentenced to jail.
John Weiss sold vast sections of track owned by the Long Island Railroad to junk dealers. One dealer, Michael Palermo, was arrested when he began tearing up the track he purchased.
Feb. 10: George Ashley started his fraudulent lonely hearts club.
1941
The U.S. Food and Drug Administration condemned and destroyed the Happy Day Headache Powders produced by quack medicine salesman Dudley J. LeBlanc.
Jan. 8: Ronald J. Circelli was born. He later became involved in credit card fraud and used deceptive practices to obtain narcotics in Illinois.
Mar. 1: Serge Rubinstein was investigated by immigration officials after he boasted of carrying a phony passport. He was released.
May: Dr. Leopold W. August Brandenburg helped Robert J. Phillips alter his fingerprints.
May 10: Marie Fuller convinced victims that Henry Ford was divesting himself of the stock he owned in his car business. She made more than $200,000 before she was indicted nine years later.
Dec. 20: Dennis Eugene "Purple" Kraska was born. He later became involved in credit card fraud in Illinois.
1942
Spring: Alfred Banker Post defrauded $30,000 from a Chicago mother and daughter with the promise of reaping fortunes from Oklahoma oil wells.
Feb. 11: Merle Allen "Buddy" Wagner was born. He later became involved in credit card fraud in Illinois.
Feb. 15: Mildred Hill began her nationwide matrimonial swindle based out of Washington, D.C., by passing herself off as her own daughter.
Sept. 24: Vincent Frank Provenzano, who used several aliases, was born. He would later become involved in fraud throughout the U.S.
Nov. 21: Shirley Ann Notree, who used a number of aliases, was born. She later became involved in credit card fraud in Chicago.
1943
Dudley J. LeBlanc claimed to have been cured from a fatal illness in New Orleans by a quack drug which he would market as "Hadacol," and sell as a miracle elixir.
Apr. 16: Lowell Birrell obtained the directorships of a number of millionaire Cecil B. Stewart's firms before Stewart's death. Birrell swindled the firms for a decade.
Oct. 1: Edward Allen "Fast Eddie" Donaldson, Jr. was born. He later became involved in credit card fraud in Illinois and check forgery in Iowa.
1944
Bebe and Carl Thomas Patten arrived in Oakland, Calif., where he established his evangelism swindle.
Alfred Banker Post defrauded $30,000 from ten Baltimore businessmen who were interested in establishing a shoe factory with his help.
Mar. 15: Cheryl Negorski, who used a number of aliases, was born. She later became involved in credit card fraud in Illinois.
Apr. 29: Robert Jerald Myers was born. He later became involved in credit card fraud in Indiana.
May 31: Samuel Gene Priest (AKA: Samuel G. Johnson, Robert Johnson) was born. He later became involved in credit card fraud in Chicago.
Aug. 19: Alexander J. Lewus, Jr. was born. He later became involved in credit card fraud in Illinois.
Oct. 22: Sharelle Josephine Mazzone (AKA: Sharelle Josephine Bragile) was born. She later became involved in credit card fraud in Illinois.
1945
By selling bogus mining stock through the mail, 272 Canadian swindlers acquired $1 million per week.
Joseph Esposito used a money-box scheme to defraud $15,000 from Providence, R.I., grocer Joseph Tutalo.
Matrimonial con artist Mildred Hill was arrested in Chicago.
June 13: Francis Gross was convicted in Utica, N.Y., and sent to prison for defrauding relatives of U.S. sailors lost at sea.
Aug. 10: From Aug. 10 to Sept. 30 Norman D. Harris of Cleveland defrauded deposits of $100 to $1,500 from people who thought he would build them a home in ninety days. Through stalling he obtained up to $30,000 from individuals. He was sent to prison.
1946
Hundreds of blacks in Philadelphia were defrauded of $150,000 in a construction swindle by Howard Clements and Charles Richman.
Will H. Johnson impersonated Adolf Hitler and defrauded U.S. and Canadian victims of more than $15,000 for the next ten years from his home in Middlesboro, Ky.
Based in Edwardsville, Ill., Robert L. Knetzer used a Peter-to-Paul scheme with automobiles.
Samuel Mussman connived $37,000 from Philadelphia's Bohdan Katamay by selling him buildings in the capital that the government would soon vacate.
Samuel Mussman defrauded Boston businessman Joseph Bennett of $22,765 by telling Bennett he would direct government contracts his way.
Abram Sykowski was arrested by the FBI for fraud after flying from South America under the alias Antonio Novarro Fernandez.
A number of cons were perpetrated against WWII veterans returning to the U.S. A Brooklyn con man offered nonexistent jobs, while a Chicago con man sold an unpopular restaurant as a popular one.
A five-year psychiatric study of con artists was released by doctors Walter Bromberg and Sylvan Keiser.
Feb. 1: Between Feb. 1 and June 15 Serge Rubinstein defrauded U.S. investors of $5 million by using the millions he had swindled in Europe and the Orient. He evaded government investigators' claims of fraud.
April: Samuel Missmen swindles foreign businessmen by leasing unusable government buildings.
Oct. 1: From Oct. 1 to Dec. 30, Robert Lyman Seibert (AKA: Paul J. Black) averaged $11,000 a week in collections from a mail-order nylon stocking fraud based in New Orleans.
1947
Oakland, Calif., evangelistic swindler C. Thomas Patten defrauded followers of almost $1 million and sold church property for $450,000 to the Loyal Order of the Moose.
Howard Clements defrauded leaders in the Dominican Republic of $100,000 with promises of constructing housing projects. He was sent to prison.
Charles Richman conned black pastors out of $28,000 with promises of building cathedrals. He was sent to prison.
Jan. 12: Sam S. De Cesare was born. He would later become involved in credit card fraud in Chicago.
June 26: Boston mayor James Curley was sent to prison for mail fraud.
1948
Ruth Bourjaily called upon Chicago advertisers who had placed help wanted ads to verify the information, and then send a bill for her verification services—as much as $5,000—a few days later which the victims usually paid.
A phony diabetes cure made millions for the Kaadt brothers of Indiana who defrauded hundreds.
Midwest selling-stiff con man Jake Max Landau sold alleged secret insurance policies to relatives of the deceased.
An investigation into evangelist con artists Bebe and C. Thomas Patten was begun by the Oakland, Calif., district attorney.
Tens of thousands of dollars were defrauded from Michigan residents by the "Terrible Williamsons" con ring.
A Boston confidence gang sold tropical plants which disintegrated in water.
Houston merchants defrauded customers by injecting water into poultry

to increase their weight and price.
A medical rebate scheme which defrauded elderly and invalid patients was discovered by the Los Angeles Better Business Bureau.
Norfolk, Va., undertakers sold flowers at funerals for a 20 percent increase after promises of wholesale prices.
Fraudulent repairmen began making needless repairs on furnaces, and roofs, which they had torn apart to fix the furnaces.
Used car swindles were inaugurated with additional costs added arbitrarily.
Nov. 16: Fiore F. Gabriele was born. He later became involved in credit card fraud in Illinois.
1949
Carnival swindles became prevalent. Games were made impossible to win, such as weighted milk bottles which no one could knock over with a baseball.
Nimrod T. Solomon, whose criminal career included counterfeiting and check forgery in Illinois, was first arrested.
1950
Marie Fuller was tried for her fraudulent sale of phony Ford Motor Co. stock. She had taken in more than $200,000.
The pigeon-drop hustle was used most successfully by "Boss" Harvey Caldwell, Emmet Cobb, and Oakey Jackson.
Dudley J. LeBlanc grossed more than $20 million from sales of his alleged miracle drug "Hadacol" throughout twenty-two U.S. states. He toured eighteen southern U.S. cities with a star-studded show promoting his elixir.
February: C. Thomas Patten was tried for his evangelistic fraud. He was later sent to prison.
Mar. 10: From Mar. 1 to May 1 Joseph Levy impersonated prison officials ordering supplies. He wrote bad checks over the amount of the merchandise and pocketed the difference.
April: Stanley Klinger and three fellow Office of Price Administration employees, and three sugar dealers were indicted on charges of defrauding the U.S. government of $300,000 by selling sugar on the black market.
July: The entire town of Wetumka, Okla., was swindled by J. Bam Morrison into believing that a circus was coming.
1951
Patrick Henry Lennon and his gang began swindling millionaire A.J. Cunningham with a stock market fraud which netted $439,121 in four years.
Samuel Mussman convinced the Order of St. Basil the Great to purchase 99-year leases on government buildings in New York.
Spring: The Illinois General Assembly ordered Dudley J. LeBlanc to end testimonials by children promoting the quack elixir "Hadacol," because of the drug's alcohol content.
Summer: Dudley J. LeBlanc toured the U.S. West Coast promoting his miracle drug "Hadacol" in a special seventeen-car train.
Jan. 19: John Patrick and Dorothy Ethel Connolly, and John Joseph Duggan were charged with falsely racing the experienced horse Newton Rock under the name of novice Liffey Valley at tracks in England.
Feb. 15: Rita A. Holmes (AKA: Rita A. Moore) was born. She later became involved in credit card fraud in Illinois and Indiana.
Mar. 8: Martha Julie Beck and Raymond Martinez Fernandez were electrocuted for killing the women Fernandez had married to bilk out of money.
August: Dudley J. LeBlanc sold his "Hadacol" drug company to the Tobey-Maltz Foundation of New York for $8 million. LeBlanc failed to inform the buyers the company was $4 million in debt.
1952
David Beck, head of the Teamsters Union from 1952-1958, embezzled more than $370,000 of union funds. He was convicted of tax evasion.
King Farouk of Egypt was defrauded of $200,000 on the French Riviera by Abram Sykowski.
Three con artists were sent to prison for defrauding London bookmakers by forging racing tickets to appear as winning tickets.
In Miami Beach the "Terrible Williamsons" confidence ring was exposed when a fight broke out amongst members.
Dec. 31: The uranium fraud perpetrated against Baron Scipion du Roure de Beruyère was exposed when his name did not appear on a list of French Legion of Honor recipients.
1953
To pay for $132,000 in jewels he had purchased, Robert Schlesinger convinced his employers that his mother, Countess Mona Bismarck, was investing $500,000 in a Louisiana oil field. The fraud was discovered and Schlesinger fled the country.
Virgil David Dardi and Alexander Guterma, accomplices of Lowell Birrell, were sent to prison for fraud.
Nathaniel Herbert Wheeler swindled his 150th female victim as part of his matrimonial fraud.
June 5: French con men Raymond Alberto and Jean Berthier were sent to prison for convincing Baron Scipion du Roure de Beruyère into purchasing uranium for the good of France.
Oct. 1: Abram Sykowski, who was under house arrest pending investigation of his confidence career, fled custody never to emerge again.
1954
The "Paddy hustle," in which soldiers or sailors were led to believe a woman awaited them in a hotel room and were convinced to leave their valuables with a bogus hotel manager, was used extensively. In one week, $40,000 was taken by San Francisco con men.
Samuel Reese, whose criminal record includes credit card fraud, was first arrested in Chicago.
May 30: From May 30 to Aug. 1 farmers in Iowa and Minnesota were defrauded by the "Terrible Williamsons."
1955
After defrauding A.J. Cunningham for four years, Patrick Henry Lennon and his confederates were arrested.
January: George Lester Belew was arrested after several years of passing false checks.
1956
The Great Sweet Grass stock scam defrauded the public of $12 million. Before its removal from the New York Stock Exchange, the stock was valued at $84,583.
Apr. 18: From Apr. 18 to Sept. 1, N. James Elliot encouraged sale of his phony American Silver Mine stock by having twenty movie stars drive ten tons of silver across the U.S. and dump the load on Wall Street. The New York *Journal American* exposed the fraud.
August: The Bristol, Va., victim, who sent Will H. Johnson more than $4,000 of $15,000 the con man made impersonating Adolf Hitler, died and police discovered the mail fraud.
1957
In an attempt to corner the cottonseed and soybean markets, Anthony "Tino" DeAngelis began his "Great Salad Oil Swindle," which involved fraudulent information concerning his salad oil business, to defraud $219 million.
Robert Sherwood Miller (AKA: Bobby Lee, Jack Henry Olson, Charles Rogers, Robert Webster) was sent to prison in Kentucky for writing fraudulent checks.
Doranne Virginia Riggio (AKA: Margaret Chenowith) was sent to jail in Chicago for her participation in a swindle.
Oct. 4: Edward Calloway (AKA: John C. Gallaway) was arrested in Chicago. For the next fourteen years he was arrested for fraud, and theft of credit cards from the mail.
1958
Earle Belle fled to Rio de Janeiro with the $2 million he and an accomplice defrauded from their company, the Cornucopia Gold Mines of Pittsburgh, with fraudulent bank loans.
Edmund Joseph "Mickey" Bryson (AKA: Nicholas Castoldi), whose extensive criminal record for the next twenty years included fraudulent use of credit cards, was arrested in Missouri.
Hundreds of nonexistent anhydrous ammonia tanks were sold in Pecos, Texas, by Billie Sol Estes, who then leased the equipment to cotton farmers. Estes mortgaged the leases and made about $15 million.
1959
Kenneth Thomas Starr was sent to prison in Illinois for an attempted confidence game and burglary.
1960
Illinois police arrested Charles Frank Pinkas, whose arrest record later included credit card fraud.
Equity Funding Corporation of America was formed by Stanley Goldblum and Mike Riordan, after two other partners left. The company would later defraud millions by clever manipulation of accounting books.
June 23: Angelo Inciso was convicted in Chicago of collecting false insurance claims of $420,267. He was sent to prison and fined $22,000.
1961
Doranne Virginia Riggio was sent to jail in Chicago for involvement in a confidence game.
Oct. 27: Patrick Shearer (AKA: Donald Gervais, Patrick Shurer) was arrested in Illinois. He was later sent to jail for fraud.
Nov. 22: Joseph Michael Riggio, Jr. was sentenced to prison in Illinois for a confidence game and statutory rape.
1962
A U.S. federal court determined that the Micro-Dynameter, a quack medical device invented by F.C. Ellis, was completely useless and unsafe, thus ending a thirty-year fraud.
Robert Sherwood Miller was sent to prison in Georgia for writing fraudulent checks.
Mar. 29: Billie Sol Estes was indicted for transporting fraudulent mortgages of anhydrous ammonia tanks across state lines in his cotton fertilizing and leasing scam in Alabama, Georgia, Oklahoma, and Texas, in which he obtained more than $22 million.
1963
Anthony DeAngelis' "Great Salad Oil Swindle," had obtained $87 million in receipts from American Express Field Warehousing, representing nine times what DeAngelis' oil inventory actually was.
Mar. 28: Billie Sol Estes was convicted of mail fraud and conspiracy.
May 3: Michael Scott (AKA: Michael Andrew Seay, Michael Arrington), who would later be arrested for defrauding an innkeeper and converting bank funds for personal use, was arrested for the first time.
Nov. 18: Anthony DeAngelis filed bankruptcy for his salad oil company when his check-kiting scheme backfired.
1964
Anthony D. "Chucky" Circelli was placed on probation in Illinois for fraud. His arrests for fraud included fraudulent credit card use, obtaining drugs by fraud, and defrauding an inn keeper.
Stanley Goldblum of Equity Funding Corporation of America ordered treasurer Jerome Evans to increase the company's reported earnings, and

thus began a multi-million defraudation of investors.
Soviet con men Grigoryev and Sobolev fraudulently resold a combined total of twenty-five television sets until 1967, marking up the prices for profits of fifty to sixty rubles per set.
Mar. 27: George F. Knoop fakes his drowning at Lake Mead, Nev., to collect life insurance for his wife. The scam was exposed in 1967.
Apr. 16: Texas Gulf Sulphur Co. publicly announced the discovery of large mineral deposits in Ontario, Can. Several company employees were later found Guilty of purchasing Texas Gulf stock based on this discovery, prior to the public announcement.
July 26: Teamsters Union president James Hoffa was convicted of conspiracy and fraud for misuse of union money.
September: Stanley William Grear, whose criminal history incudes arrests for fraudulent activities, was arrested in Illinois.
1965
Anthony DeAngelis was sent to prison for his salad oil swindle. Of the money defrauded, $1 million was never recovered.
Williamson clan leader Donald Williamson bought a Flint, Mich., department store and pulled off a gigantic credit fraud.
April: A false car accident claim gang was begun by St. Charles, N.Y., brothers Kenneth and Larry DeMary. The scam netted $235,000 in bogus insurance claims in eighteen months.
June 14: The Atlantic Acceptance Corporation's fraud was exposed when a bad check of $5 million was written. The Canadian finance company, formed in 1961, caused losses of more than $70 million.
1966
Chicago Credit Card Case. Chicago banks lost $2 to $3 million when they sent out credit cards unsolicited which were used fraudulently.
Dr. Andrew Ivy was acquitted on federal fraud charges for trying to market the drug "Krebiozen," which he developed and used on cancer patients in Chicago.
The ghost town of Death Valley Junction, Calif., was sold by two con men to a retired school teacher for $200,000.
Feb. 3: Chicago police arrested Henry L. "Tony" Hoosier, who later became involved in credit card fraud.
June 1: From June 1 to Oct. 1, Los Angeles was overrun by hundreds of "Terrible Williamsons," who perpetrated dozens of high-priced swindles.
July: Illinois police first arrested James Douglass Ingbretson. His record includes several arrests for fraud, forgery, and fraud in obtaining narcotics.
July 15: From July 15 to Oct. 15, Willard Talbot defrauded more than 4,000 parents of more than $1.5 million by selling them music packages for $489, including cheap accordions and lessons. He promised that their children would play in a Rose Bowl concert.
1967
Francis E. and Guy A. Onesti were sent to prison for stealing mail to obtain credit cards for fraudulent use in Illinois.
Phillip Peter Speciale (AKA: Phillip Peter Spectale) was arrested for fraud in Illinois. He was placed under supervision.
The Blackstone Rangers, a Chicago gang, began the Woodlawn Poverty Organization, which they used to divert $50,000 from the federal War on Poverty program.
January: Police learned that John L. Deviland of El Segundo, Calif., was really George F. Knoop, who had allegedly drowned in Lake Mead, Nev., in 1964. His wife, Janice Knoop, collected $23,000 in insurance. Both were given suspended sentences.
May: Allen Barry Lowenthal was placed under supervision for fraudulent use of credit cards.
May: Cheryl A. Owens (AKA: Linda Larsen, Cheryl Owen) was placed on probation for fraudulent use of credit cards in Chicago.
July: Steven Randolph Zatz was arrested in Chicago for attempted credit card fraud. He was placed on probation.
Sept. 11: Four Seasons Nursing Centers of America, Inc., which built nursing homes and defrauded investors of millions by 1970, was founded.
October: Equity Funding Corporation of America expanded its fraud of investors by purchasing an Illinois insurance company, which would inevitably lead to fraudulent life insurance claims.
October: Dennis Platt was placed under supervision in Chicago for credit card fraud.
October: Monte William "William M." Zatz, was convicted of credit card fraud in Illinois.
November: Anthony Constantine Kallas was placed under supervision for fraudulent use of credit cards.
November: George J. Santopietro, who used several aliases, was placed under supervision for credit card fraud.
1968
New Mexico and Texas were used extensively for real estate fraud. A group of victims from Renton, Wash., were led to believe apartments would be built on the desolate land.
Vincent Lombardo, Jr., who used several aliases, was placed on probation for fraudulent activities.
James Allan Mack (AKA: Joseph Edward Boogaard, John Caine, George Learson) was arrested in Illinois for credit card fraud.
Chicago police arrested Godfrey Jerome "Pooky" Poston, whose arrest record would later include fraud.
Joseph D. Volpe was placed on probation in Illinois for fraud.
Joan Webster, who used several aliases, was placed on probation in Illinois for mail fraud.
May: Bennie "Big Ben" Bradley (AKA: Bennie Currey) was convicted of stealing credit cards for fraudulent use.
June: Carmen Arthur Migliore was arrested in Chicago for credit card fraud.
Sept. 23: As part of a massive exporting fraud, bizarre ingredients such as tar acid, seaweed, and banana paste were found in millions of quarts of Vino Ferrari by Italian wine inspectors.
Oct. 21: Milton Curtis Avant, whose criminal record included fraudulent practices, was first arrested in Illinois.
November: John Payne was placed under supervision in Illinois for using credit cards for fraudulent purposes.
1969
Anthony D. Circelli was sent to jail in Dade County, Fla., for defrauding an innkeeper.
International Gift Shows, operated by Robert Craven and Edward Nelson, defrauded $250,000 from victims who purchased the vacation package for a phony Las Vegas exposition the two offered.
Gust Koroveses was placed on probation for deceptive practices in Illinois.
William "Fat Man" Lamnatos (AKA: William Reno) was placed on probation for fraudulent activities.
James Allan Mack was arrested fraudulent use of credit cards.
John W. Valsamoulis, (AKA: John W. Vale), was placed on probation in Illinois for fraud.
February: Melvin Pumphrey, who used several aliases, was placed under supervision in Chicago for credit card fraud.
Mar. 31: Joseph Burke McClure was sent to federal prison in Sandstone, Minn., for conspiracy to purchase, sell, and transfer phony obligations.
Apr. 28: Milton H. Foster was arrested in Evergreen Park, Ill., for fraudulent credit card use.
June 18: Phillip Merlin Jones (AKA: Tom Jordan, Phillip John Ossley) was placed on probation for fraudulent use of credit cards.
July 23: Gerald Andrew Nannemann was arrested for credit card fraud in Illinois. He pleaded guilty Oct. 17 and was fined.
August: Mary L. Pumphrey, who used several aliases, was placed on probation in Chicago for fraudulent use of credit cards.
October: Thomas E. "Tommy" Gallagher was convicted of interstate wire fraud and sent to prison in Florida. Eight months later he was convicted of credit card fraud.
October: Donald William Starr (AKA: Donald William Cole) was arrested in California for fraudulent use of credit cards.
November: Carmen Arthur Migliore was arrested in Chicago for mail fraud. On Feb. 10, 1970, he was placed on probation.
1970
Equity Funding Corporation of America's insurance companies began selling insurance policies to nonexistent people.
Glenn Turner distributorship frauds, "Kosmetics for the Kommunities of Tomorrow" (Koskot) and "Dare-to-be-Great," ran rampant.
Patrick Lee McWhorter (AKA: Richard Vincent Bernoski, James Carrille) was sent to jail in Chicago for credit card fraud.
The lost-wallet scam went unchecked in Chicago and New York.
Jan. 26: Riotous demonstrations against President Ferdinand Marcos occurred in the Philippines following accusations of voter fraud in November 1969 election.
February: Howard Meisel (AKA: Howard Meiser) was sent to jail in Detroit for check fraud. By 1973, he had been arrested in Illinois for credit card fraud.
March: Charles E. Greller was placed on probation for the fraudulent use of credit cards in Chicago.
April: Brett Francis Benning, whose lengthy arrest record includes fraud, was arrested in Chicago.
April: Gus Robert Kanakes was sent to jail in Chicago for writing fraudulent checks.
May: William Lamnatos was sent to federal prison in Sandstone, Minn., for mail fraud.
May 14: Gust Koroveses was sent to federal prison in Sandstone, Minn., for mail fraud.
June: Fred A. Harvey (AKA: Frank Henderson) was sent to prison for credit card fraud and forgery.
June 21: The Penn Central Railroad filed bankruptcy. Prior to the filing, more than 40,000 shares of Penn Central stock had been sold by fifteen company officers. Based on inside information of the impending bankruptcu, another 2 million were sold before the announcement by large-block shareholders.
June 24: John W. Valsamoulis was sentenced to federal prison in Sandstone, Minn., for mail fraud.
June 26: Four Seasons Nursing Centers of America, Inc., filed bankruptcy, after almost three years of fraudulent practice in the construction of nursing homes. Its subsidiaries soon filed too.
July: Bennie Bradley was convicted and sent to prison for mail fraud involving credit cards.
August: Frank Joseph Wing, Jr., who used a number of aliases, was fined for a credit card fraud operation that he ran in Chicago.
September: Eugene Edward "Geno" Gretchokoff was placed under supervision for credit card fraud that he committed in Illinois.
November: Melvin Pumphrey was sent to jail in Chicago for credit card fraud.

1971
James Michael "Toes" Blenner (AKA: Thomas Vernon Olson) was convicted and fined for fraudulent use of credit cards.
Donald William Starr was arrested for credit card fraud.
Feb. 12: James Allan Mack was sent to jail in Chicago for credit card fraud, forgery, and theft.
Feb. 15: Between Feb. 15 and Aug. 10, a group of con artists used the McCulloch Corporation's successful development at Lake Havasu City, Ariz., to sell desert plots of land under the guise of Lake Havasu Estates.
March: Patrick Lee McWhorter was arrested in Chicago for credit card fraud. He was arrested again in May for theft by deception, and in November for credit card fraud.
March: Mary L. Pumphrey was arrested in Chicago for credit card fraud. She was also arrested one month later for the same offense.
April: Leslie Ann Balonick was charged with using a credit card for fraudulent purposes.
April: Kevin Bruce MacGregor was arrested in Illinois for fraudulent use of a credit card.
Apr. 2: Edmund Joseph Bryson was convicted and sent to prison in Missouri for fraudulent credit card use, narcotics violations, and burglary.
Apr. 28: Michael Karl Stehl was arrested in Niles, Ill., for credit card fraud.
May: Doranne Virginia Riggio was arrested six times in the Chicago suburban area for fraud.
June: Bennie P. Childs (AKA: Leslie Reynolds) was briefly sent to jail and placed on probation in Chicago for the fraudulent use of credit cards.
June: Leonard B. Eaglin (AKA: Richard Ray) was convicted for unlawful possession of credit cards, which were to be used fraudulently.
June: Randolph Merrill was placed on probation in Chicago for fraudulent use of credit cards.
June: John C. Price was placed on probation in Chicago for credit card fraud.
June 16: Bonnie Susan Hicks, who used a number of aliases, was convicted in Chicago of deceptive practice.
July: Benny "Little Ben" Curry (AKA: Benny Perry, Leonard Myrick) was convicted for fraudulent use of credit cards in Chicago.
July 22: Glenn David Horton was arrested in Elmhurst, Ill., for fraudulent use of a credit card.
Aug. 18: Myrna Delores Flanagan, who used several aliases, was arrested for using credit cards to defraud.
Sept. 5: Between Sept. 5 and Oct. 22, Jack Hamblen sold twenty-eight stolen credit cards for fraudulent use in Chicago. He was sent to prison.
Sept. 21: LeRoy Earl Rea, Jr. was arrested in Chicago for credit card fraud. He was placed on probation and ordered to pay $2,600 restitution.
Sept. 26: Lyons, Ill., police arrested Carl J. Kruger (AKA: Carl Cooper, Carl J. Shannon, Anthony De Pento, Jr.) for possession of stolen credit cards for fraudulent use.
Oct. 5: Joseph Burke McClure of Chicago sold one stolen credit card for fraudulent use.
Oct. 5: Richard James Killeen of Bollingbrook, Ill., sold two stolen credit cards for fraudulent use. He sold two additional cards on Feb. 26, 1972.
Oct. 14: Stanley Grear of Hoffman Estates, Ill., sold two stolen credit cards for fraudulent use.
Oct. 19: Thomas Neal French was arrested for deceptive use of credit cards.
Oct. 21: Donald G. Edwards of Chicago sold ten stolen credit cards for fraudulent use. He sold another seven five days later.
Oct. 29: Joseph Michael Riggio, Jr. was convicted of fraud and forgery in Illinois. He was placed on probation.
November: Vito J. Lombardi was sent to federal prison in Indiana for mail fraud involving credit cards.
Nov. 8: Chicago police arrested Patrick Lee McWhorter for credit card fraud.
Nov. 12: Archie Weathington of Chicago sold one stolen credit cards for fraudulent use. He also sold a stolen card on Dec. 8 and Dec. 27.
Nov. 15: Henry Hoosier of Chicago sold eight stolen credit cards for fraudulent use. On Nov. 18 he sold three stolen cards.
Nov. 18: Robert Jerold Myers of East Chicago, Ind., sold seven stolen credit cards for fraudulent use.
Nov. 30: Italian police arrested Elizabeth Ravasio, who, while impersonating a nun, defrauded $3.2 million from charitable people in Rome, by forcing real nuns to beg for the needy.
Dec. 8: Robert Clemens (AKA: Bruce Beecher, Hutson) was arrested in Chicago for fraudulent credit card use.
Dec. 23: Joel Dean Ritter pleaded guilty to fraud following his six arrests by five suburban Chicago police departments. He was sent to the Cook County Jail.
1972
The "Great Salad Oil Swindler" Anthony DeAngelis was released from prison and began a campaign attacking con men like himself.
Chicagoans Sandra and Walter D. Pritchard, who both used several aliases, were indicted for mail fraud involving the use of credit cards.
Using the alias Mr. Zyglit, a bank computer operator rigged the computer to automatically credit the last account on record alphabetically. He was exposed when a man named Zyzow queried of the additions to his account.
Summer: Equity Funding Corporation of America's insurance companies began filing fraudulent death claims for nonexistent people.
January: Leslie Ann Balonick (AKA: Helen Skubikowski) was charged with using a fictitious name and possession of a credit card.
January: Mary L. Pumphrey was arrested in Chicago for credit card fraud. She was also arrested two months later for the same crime.
January: Ernest P. and Becky D. Rushing were arrested in Chicago for fraud involving checks in Indiana. The charges were dropped.
Jan. 11: Brian Kevin McLoughlin was arrested in Illinois. A search of his home revealed several credit cards and proof of his fraudulent use of them.
Jan. 11: Lowell McAfee Birrell was finally jailed after fifteen years of efforts by the government. He set up numerous phony businesses and swindled more than $25 million.
Jan. 30: Virginia L. Sollis (AKA: Virginia Giovenco) was arrested in Chicago for fraud.
February: Gus Robert Kanakes was sent to prison in Indiana on charges including credit card and mail fraud.
Feb.14: A phony investment firm, REFA, was begun by Jerome Hoffman, who obtains $150 million from the scam. He was later sent to prison.
Feb. 18: John Alexander of Chicago sold eight stolen credit cards for fraudulent use.
Feb.28: Edward Allan Donaldson of Summit, Ill., used four credit cards fraudulently. He sold one card on Feb. 28, used four cards fraudulently on Mar. 3, and used one card fraudulently on Mar. 13 and Mar. 14.
Mar. 6: Patrick Lee McWhorter was placed on probation in Chicago for possession of credit cards for fraudulent use.
Mar. 7: Richard Killeen was arrested for stealing a credit card.
Mar. 13: Alexander Lewus of Downers Grove, Ill., used a credit card for fraudulent purposes.
Mar. 15: Rosemary Flores of Chicago used a credit card for fraudulent purposes.
May: Maurice Townsend was arrested in Chicago for fraudulent use of checks.
May 24: Betty Levenhagen was sent to prison for theft of credit cards from the mail for fraudulent purposes.
September: Charles Geotis entered prison for credit card and mail fraud after selling vast areas of land in Maine.
1973
Mar. 7: Ronald Secrist informed the New York State Insurance Department of the fraudulent practices of his former employers at Equity Funding Corporation of America. By Apr. 5, the company had filed bankruptcy.
Apr. 15: A group of wine merchants and brokers in Bordeaux, Fr., were charged with exporting cheaply made wines under the Bordeaux label, obtaining $800,000 in the scandal known as Winegate.
Apr. 19: Dairylea Cooperative, Inc., of Pearl River, N.Y., was fined $150,000 for the adulteration of milk in its dairy processing plants over a six-year period.
November: Nineteen executives, including president Stanley Goldblum, of Equity Funding Corporation of America were indicted on charges which included bank fraud, mail fraud, securities fraud, and falsification of documents. All pleaded guilty.
1974
The bogus oil company Home-Stake Production Co., founded by Robert S. Trippet, was charged with fraud by the Securities and Exchange Commission. Home-Stake investors, lured by hefty tax breaks, were defrauded of $130 million.
Former McClean, Va., telephone employee Robert Dale Johnson defrauded investors of $26 million with his Peter-to-Paul swindle purporting to corner the European industrial wine market.
Sept. 2: In Switzerland, Mark Colombo was convicted of defrauding £33 million from Lloyd's Bank International, Ltd.
Oct. 10: The shipping fraud of Bangkok's Chern Chernratanarak was exposed when the *Lord Byron* of Greece docked in Berbera, Somalia. He absconded with the $5.9 million the Somalian government gave him for 10,000 tons of sugar which did not exist.
Nov. 15: A New York grand jury indicted Dairylea Cooperative, Inc. for filing false reports as a result of the company's adulteration of milk.
December: Cortes W. Randell, Anthony Natelli, and Joseph Scansaroli were sent to prison for Randell's fraudulent National Student Marketing Corporation. Randell had falsified documents since the company's inception in 1968.
1975
Hoyt Torrey of Chicago allegedly took money to secure loans for investors between 1975 and 1978. He was indicted with four others in 1981.
The cargo ship, *Brilliant*, whose owners also owned the *Alexandros K* which sank in 1979, mysteriously sank off the coast of Sicily. Lloyd's of London had insured the ship for $600,000.
Dale Otto Remling, who wrote bad checks totalling $35,000 in Sidney, Mich., escaped in a helicopter from the prison at Jackson, Mich. He was caught thirty hours later.
Mar. 17: Stanley Goldblum and other officials of Equity Funding Corporation of America were sentenced to prison for their part in the company's defrauding investors of more than $100 million.
1976
Rabbi Bernard Bergman pleaded guilty in a $3 million nursing home scandal. He promised to make restitution of $250,000.

Manuel Jose Pires of Spain and Doraldo Perriera Lima of Germany defrauded the Angolan government of more than $6 million when they failed to produce thirteen tons of promised groundnuts. Owners of the ships used and a Swiss bank repaid the loss.
July 14: Black Hebrew Israelites' Chicago leader Bernard "Bennie" Bradley was arrested for bank fraud in connection with the theft of credit cards, and bank and welfare checks from the mail.
Nov. 8: Investment broker Don Everett Luna was arrested in Birmingham, Ala., for embezzlement and misleading investors.
1977
Reputed organized crime member Ned Warren, Sr. was accused of masterminding a multi-million dollar Arizona land fraud operation.
The American Society for Industry Security caught 223 stores who attempted to redeem coupons for the non-existent detergent "Breen" in an elaborate sting operation.
Feb. 4: Businessman Alvin N. Roth and lawyer Richard Prescott, both from Minneapolis, were indicted in Manhattan, N.Y., for filing fraudulent loans of up to $300,000.
Feb. 18: Former Chemical Bank loan officer William H. Hockridge and two others were convicted of defrauding $1.2 million through faulty loans from the Manhattan branch where Hockridge worked.
Mar. 2: Former Chemical Bank loan officer Julian R. Fillipone, Jr. was indicted with two others on charges of defrauding the Brooklyn, N.Y., branch of $1.5 million.
Mar. 3: Claude Arpels, president of the exclusive jewelry firm Van Cleeft Arpels was indicted for offering "gratuities" to IRS agents. He pleaded guilty and was fined.
Mar. 30: The deputy director of the Illinois Bureau of Employment Security, Charles Edward Bennett, was arrested for defrauding the state of more than $1 million by issuing and cashing unemployment checks for ineligible people.
April: Accusations were leveled against illegal aliens who entered the U.S. solely to collect federal aid.
October: James Forman, who possessed two fraudulent death certificates for himself—dated February and December 1975—was arrested in New York for defrauding banks of up to $300,000.
Nov. 1: The *M.V. Mariner* of Athens, Gr., was chartered by Asteris S.A. to deliver $1.3 million worth of tomato paste to Tripoli, Libya. The shipment was diverted to other ports by changing the ship's name several times.
1978
Aug. 7: George E. Allen, impersonating Dr. Jesse Fairchild Adams, was hired as chief physician by the Tennessee Department of Corrections. He was sent to prison for the fraud in July 1980.
1979
January: Ray Blanton, governor of Tennessee, was forced out of office in a parole selling scandal.
Feb. 14: Five men were charged in defrauding the late Frederick Lundy of $11 million. Lundy's former servant, Josep Ramaglia, impersonated the deceased Brooklyn, N.Y., restauranteur during transactions.
Mar. 1: The Internal Revenue Service revealed that the Chicago brokerage of Price & Co. was charged with having reported more than $2.4 million in phony losses in 1977 to avoid taxation.
May: While traveling from Bulgaria to Egypt, the freighter *Alexandros K* was reputedly sunk (by the man who captained the *Salem* in 1980) for more than $1 million in insurance.
Nov. 23: Marvin Barnes, who wrote the book which explained methods of fraud, *100 Ways to Disappear and Live Free*, was arrested in Columbus, Ohio, for filing forty-seven fraudulent tax returns.
Nov. 27: The corpse of Carmela Santimauro, who died in January 1976, was discovered in the Bronx, N.Y., home of son and grandson Michael and William Santi Massino, who had been collecting her social security checks since her death.
1980
Jan. 1: The Beverly Hills, Calif., home of Sheik Mohammed al-Fassi burned to the ground, exposing the fraud of the sheik's former driver, Michal Ivan Luterlof, who posed as an agent of the sheik in selling items from the deserted home.
Jan. 17: Supertanker *Salem* was sunk off the coast of Senegal in an attempt to defraud Lloyd's of London of more than $84 million in insurance.
July 24: Former Michigan U.S. representative Charles C. Diggs was sentenced to prison for mail fraud and receiving kickbacks from employee payrolls.
Aug. 17: Owner of Royal Chrysler in Shinnston, W.Va., Jerry Miller attempted to fake his own death to avoid financial and marital problems by burning a corpse wearing his watch and ring.
Sept. 29: Former FBI informer Joseph Meltzer pleaded guilty to using the mail to defraud Californians of more than $150,000 by using the FBI's Abscam operation as a front.
November: Hector Nunez was arrested in El Paso, N.M., after swindling more than $1,000 from members of the city's high school class of 1955 who, after he convinced them were old classmates of his, gave him money he allegedly needed to pay his rent.
1981
March: The Des Plaines Bank of Illinois collapsed and it was discovered former bank president Anthony G. Angelos had defrauded the bank of more than $5 million. He was sent to prison.
Mar. 18: John Henry Owens and his wife were arrested for murder and insurance fraud in faking Owens' death on Nov. 13, 1972, in Martinez, Ga.
July: Hoyt Torrey and Erik DeLafayette were indicted in Chicago for collecting more than $400,000 in loan fees without producing loans.
1982
The FBI reported that embezzlement and fraud of banking institutions was down from 1981 to 1982, but during the same period, losses rose from $200 million to $450 million. Of these frauds, 83 percent were committed by employees.
The *Wall Street Journal* reported three incidents of "High Performance Fakery," which entails the understating of costs or overstating of sales for a corporation.
Apr. 12: Margaret Barbera, who was to have testified in the fraud trial of Irwin M. Margolies, her employer and owner of New York City's Candor Diamond Co., was murdered.
May: In New York City four former employees of Bankers Trust Co., and two others were indicted for embezzling $1.2 million.
May: Two former Chase Manhattan Bank commercial loan officers were indicted for fraudulently channeling $18 million in unsecured loans to a Florida land developer, who split the loans with the two.
May: Chromalloy American Corporation and its auditors were charged in a class action suit with overstating the company's assets and earnings.
May: The former president and vice president of sales for Pentron Industries, Inc., were sued by the company for defrauding $500,000 through suspect sales commissions.
June: A shareholder sued Data Terminal Systems, Inc., of Boston for allegedly misleading investors by failing to disclose the company's slowing growth in 1980.
June: A former vice president of Midlothian State Bank of Illinois pleaded guilty to embezzling $1.3 million over a nine-year period.
June 30: Charles W. Baker and four others were charged with committing mail fraud at the Indiana State Prison in Michigan City, while all five were prisoners there.
July 6: Sheik Mohammed al-Fassi was arrested for defrauding the Diplomat Hotel in Hollywood, Fla., of more than $1 million.
August: A former Bank of New England supervisor was indicted in Boston on federal charges of embezzling $30,000.
August: A stockholder sued Datapoint Corporation of San Antonio, Texas, for fraudulently misrepresenting its financial outlook.
August: A development laboratory director for Gould Inc. was indicted in St. Louis for defrauding $300,000 from the company with phony invoices.
August: For failing to properly report a $235,000 embezzlement from Hermitite Corporation, the Securities Exchange Commission penalized a small Waltham, Mass., CPA firm.
September: The Bank of Nova Scotia and seven tax shelter promoters were indicted in Washington, D.C., on federal charges of providing a questionable tax shelter which led to $122.5 million in deductions.
September: A congressional committee cited that the collapse of Penn Square Bank in Oklahoma City was due to fraudulent practices including bank fraud, wire fraud, and falsified books.
September: The former chief executive officer of Rusco Industries was accused of defrauding the company of $2.7 million.
September: The Securities and Exchange Commission cited Saxon Industries, Inc., and three former executives for falsification of company records.
September: A former Texaco, Inc. employee and his wife were indicted for defrauding Texaco of $18,000 by the employee instructing a company computer to pay his wife money.
September: A Valley Industries, Inc. vice president was fired when the steel firm discovered he had diverted $2.6 million using bogus invoices for services never rendered.
Sept. 30: Fourteen illegal aliens were arrested in Chicago for defrauding the U.S. government out of grants for college students.
October: Jack R. Bernhardt was found guilty of security and mail fraud in relation to the unauthorized trading of $8 million in his clients' stocks between June 1976 and February 1977.
October: In Philadelphia, an employee of ARA Services, Inc. was indicted for defrauding the company of more than $250,000.
November: A Nabisco Brands, Inc. accounting manager was charged with defrauding $2.1 million from the company by creating a fictitious firm to bill Nabisco for imaginary services.
November: A National Association of Securities Dealers former vice president was charged with mail fraud for allegedly billing the company for $45,000 in nonexistent equipment.
November: The Securities and Exchange Commission charged Ronson Hydraulic Units Corporation in California with stating false sales figures and understating expenses from 1975 to 1980.
Nov. 29: John H. Brandl was indicted on eleven counts of bank fraud relating to a phony loan scam that cost a Glenview, Ill. bank $7 million.
December: A former Federal Reserve economist was discovered attempting to fraudulently access the Reserve's computers to obtain inside information for his Wall Street firm.
December: A scheme to defraud $200,000 from Merrill Lynch and Bank of America was exposed when a bank computer operator was arrested. He had transferred money into his partner's account at Merrill Lynch.
December: A class action suit was filed against Pepsico, Inc. by share-

holders who alleged that the company had overstated earnings by $92.1 million and assets by $79.4 million over a five-year period in its overseas operations.

1983

A former director at the New York City office of Ernest & Whinney was convicted of insider trading, which had garnered him about $46,000, which he repaid.

January: Banker Deil O. Gustafson was convicted in St. Paul, Minn., of check kiting. He attempted to save his failing Tropicana Hotel in Las Vegas by allowing overdrafts to be made.

January: Chicago lawyer Robert L. Tucker was convicted on ten counts of fraud in connection with a $5.1 million fraudulent black bean deal between Deborah Bell and the Guatemalan government.

January: Two Dean Witter stockbrokers began to illegally access and manipulate the company's new twenty-four hour brokerage service. They amassed $14 million before their termination.

March: A former American Bank & Trust Co. loan officer of Reading, Pa., was accused of attempting to embezzle $9.5 million through unauthorized transactions and false loans.

March: An Ohio State Treasurer's office cashier pleaded guilty to embezzling $1.5 million.

March: Seagrave Corporation sued Touche Ross for misleading the company as to its predecessor's finances.

March: The Securities and Exchange Commission accused the former president and vice president of Security America Corporation of falsifying records to show inflated net worth and earnings.

March: An audit uncovered an embezzlement operation by the head of the foreign transfer department of the Slavenburg Bank in Rotterdam, Neth., which could have netted $65 million.

March: An accounting supervisor for the United Way in Cleveland was indicted for embezzling $63,000 through phony building contracts.

Mar. 14: American Cotton Yarns vice president Ronald J. Hurley pleaded guilty to defrauding the U.S. government in rope contracts.

April: Milton Dorison and Richard Firestone were found Guilty of publicizing deceptive coal mine tax shelters, defrauding hundreds with the lure of $100,000 deductions.

April: The Federal Savings & Loan Insurance Corporation charged two executives of the Downers Grove, Ill., First Financial Savings & Loan with embezzling $2.5 million through fake bank entries.

Apr. 13: Joseph Calandra and three codefendants were tried on charges of fraud for attempting to pass false test results at their medical and research testing lab International Bio-Test Inc. in Northbrook, Ill.

Apr. 20: Chicago attorney Vincent Lopez was convicted of embezzling more than $115,000 between April 1968 and August 1979 from the Heineman Family Foundation, which he oversaw.

Apr. 30: Cargo Fashions, Inc., president John Esposito surrendered to federal officials in New York City to face charges of defrauding banks of $10 million.

May: The former director of Southern Illinois University's data processing department and eight others were accused of defrauding the school by purchasing phony equipment at inflated prices.

May: The Securities and Exchange Commission alleged that AM International had fraudulently inflated its 1980 and 1981 profits by $23 million.

May 11: Television weatherman Jim Tilmon was acquitted of defrauding the Chicago Federal Savings & Loan and Banco di Roma's Chicago office by allegedly falsifying loan applications.

June: A former Mr. Coffee executive was indicted for embezzling $884,000.

June: The former manager of the Phoenix office of Walter E. Heller International was indicted for embezzling $1.9 million.

August: Licio Gelli escaped from a Swiss jail where he was in custody for bank fraud.

Sept. 28: Founder of the Bullion Reserve of North America precious metals firm Alan D. Saxon committed suicide in Marina del Ray, Calif., prior to a New York investigation into the company which reported actual assets of $1 million as $1 billion.

Oct. 9: Bernard Whitney was arrested in Los Angeles for an estimated $2 billion land fraud. He sold land to investors in Belgium, the Netherlands, and the U.S. with unfulfilled promises of development.

1984

Feb. 8: Former American Cotton Yarns president Barry W. Splinter was sentenced to prison and fined for defrauding the U.S. government in selling 2.4 million yards of low-quality rope.

May 5: Illinois prison inmate Harry J. Martin and an accomplice were charged with collecting thousands of dollars from fraudulent tax returns in eleven states. He also defrauded Social Security benefits.

June 4: Six of fourteen people charged with defrauding the U.S. in a massive nationwide money-laundering operation were arrested in Miami.

September: Stephen L. Wallis and Shron Willey, who used inside information from a proofreader to trade, were sentenced.

Nov. 2: Velma Margie Barfield was executed for poisoning Stuart Taylor and her mother after forging a $300 check on Taylor's account.

1985

July: Aaron M. Binder and Frederick G. Celari set up a phony high-tech company where a number of television stars were given fake tax shelters.

1986

Congress adopted a series of amendments to protect the jobs of people who expose fraudulent practices by their employers.

Oct. 15: Following the Bangladesh election of President Ershad, the opposition party declared election fraud and ballot-rigging had taken place.

Nov. 14: Ivan Boesky pleaded guilty to one felony count and agreed to pay a $100 million fine for his part in a stock and junk bond scandal. He was jailed.

1987

Los Angeles financial planner Stephen H. Henry was sent to prison for defrauding clients of more than $4 million.

The Federal Trade Commission accused Schoolhouse Coins, Inc., of defrauding $6 million from 2,000 customers through telemarketing sales.

Aug. 30: Mohammad Charafeddine was arrested for $10,000 worth of purchases he made on stolen credit cards.

Dec. 7: From Dec. 7 to Dec. 19, $5,430 in telephone charges were made to the calling card of Donna Plybon, apparently by people who overheard the card's secret code.

Dec. 10: Charles A. Atkins, William S. Hack, and Ernest Grunebaum were convicted of running a fraudulent tax shelter scheme.

1988

Chrysler Motors Corp. agreed to refund customers a total of $16.3 million for their fraudulent selling of cars as brand new, cars which may have been driven 300 miles during testing.

After winning his second car in a sweepstakes, James Lee and the marketing executives who ran both promotions, John Curtin III and Kevin Kissane, were indicted on charges of mail fraud.

Mar. 16: Oliver North, John Poindexter, Richard Secord, and Albert Hakim were indicted for defrauding the U.S. government in the sale of weapons to Iran and the secret transfer of money to Contra rebels in Nicaragua.

Mar. 31: Former South Korean president Chun Doo Hwan's brother, Chun Kyung Hwan, was arrested for embezzlement of funds from the rural development program Saemaul while he headed that program.

June: The FBI's and Naval Investigation Service's two-year long Operation Ill Wind revealed fraudulent passing of information from within the Pentagon to defense firms seeking government contracts.

June: Japanese prime minister Noboru Takeshita was implicated in a stock market scandal involving the apparent sale of unlisted shares of a real estate company, Recruit Cosmos Co.

September: The Securities Exchange Commission filed suit against six people accused of insider trading in connection with the securities firm of Drexel Burnham Lambert, Inc.

Sept. 5: South Korean Chun Kyung Hwan was convicted of embezzlement and other charges. He was sent to prison and fined almost $5.8 million.

Sept. 29: Zenith Electronics Corporation filed suit in Chicago against Brookhurst Partners L.P., which owned 6.1 percent of the company's stock, for allegedly manipulating Zenith stock.

Oct. 12: Sundstrand Corporation of Rockford, Ill., agreed to plead guilty to defrauding the U.S. government and repay more than $127 million obtained in overcharging for military aircraft. It was charged an additional $39.2 million plus interest, a month later.

Oct. 21: Former Philippine president and spouse Ferdinand and Imelda Marcos and eight others were indicted in New York City for racketeering from Ferdinand's embezzlement of more than $100 million from the Philippines.

November: Under a False Claims Act lawsuit, Genisco Technology Corp. was ordered to pay $725,000. Former employee Roland Gibeault was awarded $131,250 for informing the U.S. government of Genisco falsification of military equipment test data.

Nov. 18: Mario Biaggi, a Democratic congressman from New York, was sentenced to prison in the Wedtech Scandal.

Nov. 19: Prime Minister Ranasinghe Premadasa of Sri Lanka was elected president amidst allegations of election fraud by opponent and former prime minister Sirimavo Bandaranaike.

December: Former U.S. Drug Enforcement Administration official Jerry Ramusack was indicted for the defrauding $185,000 from the agency by selling property confiscated in drug raids between 1983 and 1988.

Dec. 21: The securities firm of Drexel Burnham Lambert, Inc. pleaded guilty to insider trading and agreed to pay $650 million as a result of a Securities and Exchange Commission investigation.

1989

A gang of con artists preyed on elderly Chicago residents, netting $100,000.

Angelo Commito, Carl Mattison, and William Wire were acquitted of charges of trying to defraud a janitors' union pension fund in a kick-back scheme.

Mar. 16: Joseph J. McCarthy, Ray John Chapel, Jr., and Ralph G. Hamann, all former executives with Sundstrand Corporation in Rockford, Ill., were indicted as part of the company's military defrauding of the U.S. government.

HIJACKING

1961
Feb. 2: Henrique Galvao, Jorge de Souto, and Jose Velo of the *Santa Maria* crew hijacked the 600-passenger ocean liner to sell its cargo. They were imprisoned after the ship docked at Recife, Braz.
1970
Feb. 23: Jordanian guerrillas attacked a tourist bus near Hebron, Jor., and killed an American woman.
1971
June 11: The Israeli tanker *Coral 10* was damaged in the Bab el-Mandab straits of South Yemen by four Habash "Front" terrorists who then escaped to the South Yemen coast.
1973
Sept. 28: Three Soviet Jews and an Austrian customs official were kidnapped from a train by two armed members of the Eagles of the Palestinian Revolution who then commandeered a car to the Vienna airport. Austria closed Schoenau Castle, a Jewish-run transit camp, to secure the hostages' release.
1974
Feb. 2: Three Arab National Youth for the Liberation of Palestine seized a Greek ship, demanding the release of two imprisoned terrorists. The prisoners were released.
1975
Dec. 2: Six armed South Moluccan extremists hijacked a Dutch train, demanding the release of imprisoned Moluccans, recognition of their government, and a plane. They killed two passengers and the driver before surrendering on Dec. 14.
1977
May 23: South Moluccans hijacked a Dutch passenger train, demanding the release of twenty-one imprisoned South Moluccans and transportation to the Amsterdam airport. They were overpowered. Two hostages and six terrorists were killed.
1981
Feb. 3: Israelis ambushed a PLO vehicle in southern Lebanon, north of Sidon, and killed all its occupants.
Feb. 7: Seven armed IRA terrorists overtook a British ship docked off Donegal, Ire. The crew boarded a raft before the terrorists bombed the ship.
May 5: Rioters attempting to hijack a milk truck in Belfast fatally wounded the driver, 45-year-old Eric Guiney, and his 14-year-old son, Desmond.
May 8: In Londonderry, Ire., eight vehicles were hijacked and burned. Trucks were also seized and burned in Belfast's Lower Falls Road and Andersonstown districts.
Oct. 8: Six armed terrorists forced the engineer of a two-car electric commuter train near Valparaiso, Chile, to stop. The thirty-six passengers and two crewmen were released before the terrorists ignited the vehicle.
1982
Feb. 23: IRA terrorists hijacked a 1,200-ton cargo vessel loaded with coal, in Lough Foyle, Ire. The crew was released before the vessel, worth $1.85 million, was blown up.
Apr. 27: A hijacked truck parked in Belfast, N. Ire., was rigged with a bomb which exploded when police attempted to move the vehicle. The Irish National Liberation Army took responsibility for the act that killed one and injured two.
May 4: Three gunmen hijacked a van in Desertmartin, Ire. Two of the gunmen jumped out of the vehicle to shoot and kill Policeman Samuel Alan Victor Caskey, twenty-one, and wound a 19-year-old policewoman.
July 3: Keith and Kate Haigler hijacked a Continental Trailways bus bound for Wichita, Kan., with fourteen aboard. They demanded an interview with a Springfield, Mo., reporter to discuss their "prophet," Emory Lamb. Kate shot her husband and then killed herself.
1984
Two Arabs were killed after being kidnapped from a hijacked bus in the Gaza strip.
1985
Oct. 7: The *Achille Lauro*, an Italian cruise ship, while carrying 454 passengers, was hijacked by Palestinians. Leon Klinghoffer, an American, was killed before the hijackers gave themselves up at Port Said. The leader, Abu Abbas, was released.
1988
Mar. 7: Three Palestinians seized a bus in southern Israel. The hijackers and three Israeli passengers died when Israeli forces regained control of the bus.
September: A bus taking seventy persons to Maseru, S. Afri., to see Pope John Paul II was hijacked by four alleged members of the Lesotho Liberation Army. A shootout ensued in which three hijackers and two hostages were killed.

IDENTIFICATION SYSTEMS

BERTILLONAGE

Alphonse Bertillon, who is credited with being the founder of modern forensic science, developed a system of body measurements to aid in criminal investigations in the late 1870s. Known as bertillonage, the system employed precise measurement of fourteen body parts, including circumference of the head and chest, and length of arms, legs, feet, fingers, nose, and ears. The system was an early success when Bertillon proved that a man arrested under the alias of Dupont was already on file with the Paris police under his real name of Martin. Bertillon's reputation was further solidified by his identification of the terrorist Koenigstein, who had been arrested under the name of Ravachol, in 1892. Bertillonage was adopted in several countries as the official criminal identification system, but it was soon superseded by the more precise technology of fingerprinting. The credibility of bertillonage suffered a blow in 1903, when two convicts in Leavenworth Penitentiary, Kansas—both, coincidentally, named West—were found to have precisely the same bertillon measurements but, of course, entirely different fingerprints. By the time of Bertillon's death in 1914, his system had already been abandoned by its former advocates.

BLOOD

The ABO blood-typing system, developed by Dr. Karl Landsteiner in 1900, divides human blood into four types based on the presence or absence of a substance called agglutinogen in red blood cells. The system is simple: agglutinogen takes two forms, labeled A and B. Blood with just one of these two forms is typed either A or B; blood with both forms is typed AB; and if neither form is present, the blood is type O. The forensic application of this system is limited but important. While it cannot positively identity a suspect, it can eliminate suspects from investigation, since a blood sample might come from any number of people with the same blood type, but cannot possibly come from a person of a different type. Further divisions of blood typing include the M, N, or MN factor, discovered by Dr. Landsteiner in 1927, the P factor, and the Rhesus factor (Rh positive or negative), discovered in 1940.

Several other forensic tests involving blood are regularly used in criminal investigations. The Kastle-Meyer test uses a control substance which changes color in the presence of blood, but not in the presence of dyes or fruit stains, for example, that might look like blood to the naked eye. The precipitin test, which utilizes a serum taken from rabbits injected with human blood to develop antibodies, determines whether a blood sample is of human or animal origin. The presence of certain antigens, such as the Kell antigen, which appears almost exclusively in whites, or the Duffy antigen, which never appears in whites, makes it possible to some extent to discover the racial origin of an unknown blood sample. A structure called the Barr body in white blood cells indicates a female donor.

DNA PRINTS

Deoxyribonucleic acid, the basic genetic code of life, is unique to each human body (excluding identical twins). Dr. Alec Jeffreys, a British geneticist, published findings in 1985 on a process that broke down organic samples into constituent DNA patterns. These genetic "fingerprints," which resemble a supermarket bar code, are identical regardless of where in the body a tissue sample is taken. Dr. Jeffreys estimated the chances of any two individuals having identical codes are conservatively one in one nonillion (a nonillion being a million million million million million).

Another genetic identification system, the polymerase chain reaction, was developed in California in 1985. At first, considered a rival to Dr. Jefferey's system, it is now regarded as complementary to it. The polymerase chain reaction cannot identify an individual with the same certainty DNA printing can, but it works with far less genetic material, and the material itself can be in far less pristine condition than is required for DNA printing. Thus, unlike DNA testing, the polymerase chain reaction test works where tissue samples are old or degraded.

In two landmark cases, one in Britain and one in the U.S., DNA testing led to the release of innocent men. In 1987, a Leicestershire bakery employee, Colin Pitchfork, was proven to be the serial killer of two young women after DNA printing proved conclusively that prime suspect Richard Buckland was innocent of the crimes. Later, in Virginia, DNA printing exonerated unjustly convicted David Vasquez of a murder committed by serial killer Timothy Spencer, whose guilt in four other murders was also proven by DNA testing.

FIBERS

Forensic scientists can find clues to violent crimes through contact traces of cloth or other material transferred between victim and assailant during an attack. Analysis of both the victims' and suspects' clothing may reveal traces of fiber that place a suspect at the scene of a crime.

A case in which this occurred was the murder of Mabel Tattershaw in Nottingham, England, in 1951. Despite his denial of guilt, Herbert Leonard Mills was convicted when an analysis showed that a thread found under Mrs. Tattershaw's fingernail matched that of Mills' suit.

FINGERPRINTS (DACTYLOGRAPHY)

The forensic use of fingerprinting, or dactyloscopy, had its roots in an 1880 article in *Nature* by Dr. Henry Faulds, a Scotsman working in Japan, that suggested that fingerprints might be used for identification purposes. Faulds' findings were supported by Sir William Herschel, a British colonial administrator, who demonstrated how he had used thumb impressions as identification of illiterates in India. Then Sir Francis Galton, in his landmark 1892 work *Fingerprints*, demonstrated that not only were prints unique to each individual—including identical twins--but that they were permanent as well. The first system of fingerprint classification was developed by Sir Edward Henry of Scotland Yard, when he established arches, tented arches, whorls, and two types of loops as the essential ridge patterns to examine.

A suspect's prints are taken by first cleaning the fingers, then rolling them in printer's ink and rolling them again on a card to produce a clear image of the pattern. Prints can be lifted from the site of a crime by dusting the surface where the print has been left with a fine black or gray powder.

The first crime solved primarily with fingerprint evidence was based on the work of Juan Vucetich of La Plata, Argentina, in 1892. Inspector Carlos Alvarez, a colleague of Vucetich, was called in to investigate a murder in a village in a rural Buenos Aires province. A woman's two small children had been bludgeoned to death, and she accused a male acquaintance, whom she claimed she had seen running away from the scene of the crime. Alvarez used a bloody thumbprint left on a door to prove that the killer was the woman herself. Largely on the strength of this case, Vucetich was able to convince the Argentine government to become the first in the world to abandon bertillonage and adopt fingerprinting as its primary method of criminal identification.

Criminals were quick to catch on to fingerprinting and some thwarted it by wearing gloves while committing crimes. Others took more drastic measures. The American gangster John Dillinger hired a doctor to burn away his fingerprints with acid, but when his fingers healed months later, his prints grew back as before. Another criminal of the same era, Robert James "Roscoe" Pitts, succeeded in eradicating his prints to the first knuckle, but then automatically became the prime suspect in any robbery in New York City in which there were no prints left. Ultimately, Pitts was convicted because he left prints of his fingers between the first and second knuckles.

Fingerprinting has long since become an international activity, with organizations such as Interpol, based in Paris, serving as clearing houses of information for law enforcement agencies around the world.

Electron autography, scanning for prints with X-rays, is a new technology. X-rays reveal prints on materials that had been unyielding of them before, most notably—skin. An FBI computer system uses lasers to scan through thousands of prints per minute, making it possible to match prints from crime scenes with those on file without having to look to a specific suspect.

FOOT PRINTS

The footprints of a perpetrator wearing shoes will not yield a specific identity, as DNA or fingerprints will, but they do offer surprisingly subtle clues to identity. The size of shoe and depth of imprint reflect the size of the person who made the print, and the type and condition of footwear (running shoes, high heels, new or worn-out leather soles, etc.) may provide suggestions as to age, sex, or socio-economic status. Among the details footprint specialists examine are: direction line, which reveals, among other things, whether a person was walking singlemindedly in a straight line or deviated either due to impulse or distraction; foot angle, which can point to the age of a suspect—for example, older people tend to walk more with their toes pointed outward than young—width apart, a possible indication of weight or speed (a person running is likely to keep his feet closer together, and a heavy-set person or one carrying a load is likely to have his feet farther apart); and length of stride, which indicates height.

Bare footprints, of course, are subject to the same set of observations, but instead of the condition and type of shoe soles, the prints of bare feet are subject to the same type of forensic measurement as traces of palms, fingers, teeth, lips, or any other body part.

HAIR ANALYSIS

Contact traces of hair are often evident in violent crimes. A single sample of a victim's hair on a suspect's person, or vice-versa, presents circumstantial evidence of violent contact. However, at the present time, hair cannot be used for conclusive identifications, as fingerprinting or DNA printing can. Progress in this area has been made in recent years, though. Analysis of hair can determine whether a sample is human or animal, and, if human, the race of the person and part of the body it came from; whether it fell out, was cut, or pulled; and whether (and how) it was styled. Chemical analysis of hair relies on trace elements, such as gold, molybdenum, zinc, mercury, and selenium, that are found in minute but varying quantities. It has been estimated that if nine such trace elements are found in comparable proportions in different hair samples, the chance that they came from different heads are about three in 100 million. Of commoner elements found in hair, there tends to be a greater concentration of manganese and cobalt in dark hair, iron in red hair, and nickel in gray hair.

GRAPHOLOGY (HANDWRITING) AND TYPEWRITING

Handwriting has been described as "the conditioned reflex of a person using a writing instrument," and the degree to which the mechanical motions of writing are unconscious is the degree of difficulty in forging another person's writing. It is further complicated by the fact that although any individual's handwriting is an expression of style rooted in muscular coordination and early training, it is also heavily influenced by factors such as age, emotional state, or speed at which a person is writing. Thus, while graphological analysis reflects a person's general style of handwriting, no one's signature—or any other sample of writing—is likely to be identical on separate occasions. This point is illustrated by the 1902 New York case in which a lawyer named Albert Patrick forged the will of William Rice, a Texas millionaire. Patrick was caught when it was found that the four signatures he contended were Rice's were identical, leading authorities to believe that he had traced them from an authentic signature.

Typewriting is also subject to graphic analysis. Aside from different manufacturers choosing different type faces, size, lettering, and such, all typewriters wear differently—letters become damaged in different ways and to different degrees; alignment is thrown slightly off; or footing (the tendency of a letter to strike harder on the left, right, or bottom) varies from key to key. Typewriting analysts have estimated the chances of two typewriters that have both been in use a few years to type identically at about one in three trillion. It was typewriter analysis that provided the breakthrough in the Leopold and Loeb murder case, as authorities examined typing samples of friends of Nathan Leopold who had borrowed his typewriter and found that they matched the ransom note sent to the kidnapped boy's father.

TEETH

Professor Francis Camps, referring to the problems murderers have in disposing of bodies, pointed out that "teeth are the most difficult things to destroy." In forensic terms, teeth are invaluable artifacts for identification purposes. Even if the rest of a body is badly decomposed, its teeth will remain in the same condition they were in at time of death, thereby allowing a forensic odontologist to identify them with dental charts. Teeth also yield useful evidence to a suspect's identity in the rare cases where teeth marks are left on the victim, as in the 1967 British murder case in which Gordon Hay was found to have bitten the breast of a girl he had killed. The chances of two people with complete sets of thirty-two teeth having identical dental marks are estimated at approximately one in 2.5 billion.

VOICE PRINTS

Dr. Lawrence Kersta first published findings on his new process of spectrographic voice analysis in 1962, but it was several years before his system of audio graphics was admitted as court testimony. Although Kersta's researchers were able to analyze 25,000 spectrograms with 97 percent accuracy, Kersta's own first court appearance to give expert testimony was ultimately disregarded. A young man who had taken part in the 1965 Watts riot and subsequently allowed himself to be interviewed anonymously on network television was arrested on the basis of voice analysis, but his conviction was overturned in 1968 because of the lack of acceptance of the voiceprinting method in the scientific community. In the early seventies, however, voiceprinting was a crucial adjunct in exposing the famous Clifford Irving/Howard Hughes hoax. Hughes, a devout recluse, would submit to being interviewed only by telephone, leaving Irving the opportunity to claim that the man on the other end of the line was an impostor. After Dr. Kersta and a colleague were called to give expert testimony on the telephone speaker's voiceprint, they determined it was Hughes' voice. Clifford Irving confessed to the hoax.

While the advances in voiceprinting have benefitted the potential for legitimate law enforcement, it is also the most controversial method of identification in terms of civil liberties. Any recorded voice can be identified by voiceprinting, opening the door for law enforcement abuses. An early case cited by opponents of a national computer bank of voiceprints occurred in the early 1970s when the FBI approached a New York City radio station, WMCA, for a tape of a talk show during which a caller had made threats against President Richard Nixon.

X-RAYS

X-rays, accidentally discovered by Dr. Wilhelm Röntgen in 1895, are a physical phenomenon caused by streams of fast-moving electrons that pass through loose solids but are stopped or bent by denser solids. The medical uses for them are well known—examination of broken bones, damaged organs, or carious teeth, for example—but their forensic uses are just as significant. Pathologists use X-rays in identifying corpses by noting items such as healed bone tissue (signifying injuries recorded on medical charts), size of bones (indicating height and build of a person whose remains are partial), and abnormalities in organs and bones (revealing unusual medical conditions). They are also used in a number of other investigatory areas, such as checking the authenticity of materials used in suspect paintings, and identifying watermarks, paper, and ink in documents and currency.

KIDNAPPING

To seize or unlawfully detain a person against his will is a serious offense in the civilized nations of the world punishable by long imprisonment or death. In past eras, kidnapping most often was equated with the forcible impressment of adult males into military service. When the British Navy routinely began stopping U.S. merchant ships on the high seas and forcing sailors into duty against their will, impressment became one of the major issues leading to the War of 1812.

By the 1850s, the practice of "shanghaiing" had become well established in San Francisco. Waterfront thugs and Barbary Coast saloon owners tricked or forced able-bodied men into shipping off to the Orient as merchantmen. Around the turn of the century, the forcible abduction of young women for immoral purposes became an issue of national concern in the U.S. Typically, young immigrant girls or recent arrivals from rural areas were lured into prostitution by smooth-talking criminal panderers. The passage of the Mann Act in 1910, and the gradual demise of "red light districts" effectively ended the "white slavery" scourge.

Kidnapping for ransom came into real prominence in the late nineteenth century, beginning with the abduction of 4-year-old Charles Ross in Germantown, Pa., in 1874. The Ross boy was never found, but the crime attracted widespread publicity and led to a spate of copycat abductions in subsequent years. The most famous of these involved aviator Charles Lindbergh's infant son, who was snatched from his home in 1932 by Bruno Richard Hauptmann. The Lindbergh case and others like it spurred legislators to enact tough anti-kidnapping statutes. It became a federal crime punishable by death to transport a kidnap victim across state lines; and for the first time, the FBI was involved in the investigation of these crimes.

The 1970s and 1980s saw a fresh outbreak of kidnapping incidents around the world. In France and Italy individual financial gain motivated the kidnapping of the children of wealthy businessmen. In the Middle East, however, political and ideological motives were behind the may ransom kidnappings of Muslim Shiite groups demanding concessions from the U.S., Israel, and its European allies were frequently behind these abductions.

12 Cent. B.C.
Helen, the legendary Greek beauty, was kidnapped as a child in Sparta by Theseus.
923
Charles III, (Charles the Simple), French king, was abducted by Herbert of Vermandois and put in prison, where he died in 929.
1186
The son of Khusru, the Turk ruler of what is now India, was seized by Afghan Muhammad Ghori.
1192
Dec. 20: Richard I, king of England, was abducted in Vienna, Aus., by Leopold, an Austrian duke, on the orders of Emperor Henry VI of Austria, who demanded 150,000 marks. The British people raised the ransom and paid Henry in 1194. Richard was freed.
1223
May: Waldemar II, king of Denmark, his son, and others were kidnapped by Count Henry of Schwerin. He was kept at the castle of Dannenberg-on-Elbe for two-and-a-half years. He paid a high ransom and gave up most of the lands he had conquered before he was freed.
1356
September: John II, (John the Good), king of France, lost a bottle to Edward the Black Prince of England and was held for 3 million crowns. He was freed and paid 400,000 crowns, but when he couldn't pay the rest and his son, still hostage, escaped, John returned to England.
1360
Mar. 1: The British king gave £16 toward the ransom of Geoffrey Chaucer, the future poet, who had been captured near Reims by the French.
1471
May: Margaret of Anjou, queen of England, was seized at Tewkesbury and held for five years. She was ransomed by Louis XI under the terms in the Treaty of Pecquigny and released.
1519
Montezuma II, Aztec emperor, attempted unsuccessfully to keep Hernando Cortes from traveling to Mexico City and was taken hostage by Cortes. The Aztecs attacked the Spaniards and Montezuma was fatally injured while he was still held captive.
1532
Atahualpa, Inca king of Peru, was kidnapped by the soldiers under Spanish Conquistador Francisco Pizarro, who demanded an enormous sum in gold and silver. The Incas raised the ransom, but their king was put to death.
1779
Apr. 14: Ann Kennedy and Catherine Kennedy, teenagers in a wealthy Irish family, were kidnapped and forced into marriage by Garret Byrne and James Strange, poor men who wanted to marry into money. The women were rescued and the men were hanged for theft of property charges.
19th Cent.
In San Francisco, "Calico Jim" Reuben allegedly coerced men into sea duty aboard merchant ships bound for Southeast Asia and China. He fled to Chile and was reportedly shot there by a San Francisco policeman.
1822
Mar. 4: Honora Gould, teen from a wealthy Glangurt, Ire. family, was kidnapped by the White Boys, raped, and freed three weeks later. Walter Fitzmaurice and William Costello stood trial and were sentenced to death. Costello was hanged, but Fitzmaurice was reprieved.
1860s
The Charlton Street Gang acquired a boat and sailed around New York City, robbing homes and holding people for ransom.
1861
Cochise, leader of the Chiricahua Apaches in their battles against white settlers, was taken into custody for abducting a settler's child. He was held in a territorial prison, but he escaped, taking with him several hostages who were killed. Ten years later the U.S. Army captured him.
1870
Apr. 11: Lord and Lady Muncaster of England and other tourists were abducted in Greece by Takos Arvanitákis and his Greek outlaws who demanded one million drachmas in ransom. Four victims were killed and the others were released. Takos escaped.
1874
July 1: Charles B. Ross, was kidnapped from Germantown, Pa., and $20,000 ransom was demanded, but not paid. The child was never located and William Mosher and Joseph Douglass, the alleged culprits were shot during a burglary. William Westervelt was sent to prison for the crime.
1886
Aug. 21: Alexander I, (Alexander Joseph of Battenberg), prince of Bulgaria, was abducted by revolutionaries. The kidnappers were captured and the prince returned to his throne, but one month later he stepped down.
1891
Mar. 20: A well-to-do bachelor from Detroit was abducted and $15,000 was demanded. The ransom was not paid and the Detroit man was freed.
1892
March: Ward Waterbury, the child of a wealthy farmer, was kidnapped from Longridge, N.Y., by his cousin and two others, who demanded $6,000. No money was paid, the child was freed, and the culprits were sent to prison.
1897
August: John Conway, the child of a train dispatcher, was kidnapped from his home in Albany, N.Y., by his uncle and two others who demanded $3,000 ransom. The child was rescued, no ransom was paid, and the three culprits were sent to prison.
1899
May 21: Marion Clarke, the infant of a New York City family, was kidnapped by her nurse, Bella Anderson, and George and Addie Barrow, who planned to demand $300. The baby was found, and the three culprits were sent to prison.
20th Cent.
During the early 1900s, members of the Black Hand were responsible for numerous kidnappings.
Sara Domini, four, was kidnapped in Italy during the mid-1900s.
Giovanna Amati, teenaged daughter of the proprietor of a theater in Italy, was abducted and ransomed for $2.1 million ransom in about the 1970s. She was freed and at least one kidnapper was arrested.
The son of Francesco de Martino a socialist politician in Italy, was kidnapped during the mid-1900s.
Vincenzo Guida, baby of a wealthy family in Italy, was kidnapped and about $300,000 ransom was demanded during the mid-1900s.
Nicolletta de Nardi, child of a diamond authority from Milan, Italy, was kidnapped and 2 billion lire ransom was demanded during the mid-1900s.
The Berenguer Gang, active in Italy around 1975, abducted five people in Rome and collected 4.5 billion lira, about $5.54 million, in ransom.
1900
Dec. 18: Edward A. Cudahy, Jr., the teenaged son of an Omaha, Neb., millionaire, was abducted and ransomed for $25,000 in gold. Patrick Crowe and James Callahan, were tried and both were acquitted.
1901
As a result of the Cudahy kidnapping, the states of Alabama, Indiana, Oklahoma, and South Dakota instituted ransom kidnapping laws with life imprisonment as the maximum penalty.
The Cudahy case caused the states of Delaware, Illinois, Missouri, Nebraska, and Tennessee to enact ransom kidnapping laws with the death penalty as the maximum punishment.
Washington, D.C., passed a law against abducting citizens from the capitol. The penalty was set between one and seven years with a fine. Ten years later, the law was amended to include ransom kidnapping in Washington, D.C., and the territories.
1902
As a consequence of the Cudahy abduction, the states of Connecticut and Iowa enacted ransom kidnapping laws with a life term as the maximum sentence.

1904
Reports of Black Hand kidnappings in the U.S. began appearing in the New York *Times*.
June: Ion Perdicaris, a rich U.S. citizen, was kidnapped from his villa near Tangier, Mor., by Rassouli, a local chief who wanted to disgrace the Moroccan sultan. Perdicaris was freed after several days.
1906
June 13: Freddie Muth, child of a jeweler in Philadelphia, was abducted by John Keene, who demanded $500. Keene and the child were found and Keene was sent to prison.
1907
Jan. 31: Martha Erbelding was abducted by Albert Soleilland. The girl was never found and Soleilland was imprisoned for life.
Mar. 7: Horace Marvin, Jr., the child of a Kittshammock, Del. doctor, was apparently kidnapped. No ransom was demanded and the child was never found. The case caused several states to increase ransom kidnapping punishments.
1909
Feb. 8: Tony Reddes was kidnapped in New York City from his father's meat store. No ransom was demanded and the child was never located.
Mar. 18: Willie Whitla, child of a wealthy lawyer in Sharon, Ohio, was abducted from school by Helen and James Boyle, who received $10,000 in ransom. Willie was freed and the Boyles were later sent to prison.
Mar. 23: A bill was presented to the U.S. House of Representatives which would make ransom kidnapping of children a capital offense in Washington, D.C., and the territories. The bill did not become a law.
1910
Between 1910 and 1934 Albert Fish abducted and murdered children—four hundred by his account. He went to the electric chair in 1936.
1911
July: In an effort to try to stop Black Hand kidnappings, New York state increased the punishment for kidnapping from ten to fifty years in prison.
1913
May 25: Peter Kurten of Dusseldorf, Ger., abducted and murdered an 8-year-old girl. He continued to kidnap and slay at least fifteen children until his capture in May 1930.
1914
Aug. 7: Katherine C. Larkin, a Bronx teenager, was abducted and raped by George Webb, a custodian at her school. She was later found and Webb was sent to prison.
1915
Dec. 17: Cordella Stevenson, a black woman, was kidnapped from her house, raped, and lynched by a group of white men in Columbus, Miss.
1917
After IWW members working for Phelps-Doge Copper in Bisbee, Ariz., went on strike, the company had more than 2,000 strikers abducted and put into cattle cars, which were sent to New Mexico.
May 30: Lloyd Keet, baby of a rich banker in Springfield, Mo., was kidnapped. A $6,000 ransom was demanded, which the parents unsuccessfully tried to deliver. The child was found dead. A mob nearly lynched one suspect but apparently no one was convicted.
June 10: A man named Piersol, a suspect in the Lloyd Keet kidnapping was almost lynched by a mob. He admitted involvement in plotting three other kidnappings and he was sent to prison.
1920
June 2: Blakely Coughlin, the baby of a rich Norristown, Pa., family, was kidnapped from his home and killed by August Pascal. The father paid $12,000 in ransom and Pascal was imprisoned for life.
1921
Gladys Julia Witherall was kidnapped in California and $50,000 ransom was demanded. She was rescued and the culprits were sent to prison.
May: Giuseppi Verotta, child of an Italian pushcart operator, was kidnapped from his New York City home by Black Hand members who demanded $2,500 ransom. The child was strangled and several of the culprits were sent to prison.
Aug. 21: Father Patrick E. Heslin, was abducted close to San Francisco by William Hightower. No ransom was paid, Heslin was killed, and Hightower was sent to prison for life.
1922
Oct. 14: Gordon Duffield, heir to wealth in Chicago, was kidnapped from a New Jersey private school. Neither he nor his abductor were ever located.
1924
May 21: Robert Franks, a teenager, was kidnapped in Chicago by University of Chicago students Richard Loeb and Nathan Leopold, Jr. They demanded $10,000 from Frank's rich father after murdering the youth. The boy's body was found before the parents paid the ransom, and the perpetrators were sent to prison for life.
Aug. 8: Aaron A. Graff, Manhattan, N.Y., entrepreneur, was apparently kidnapped from his home and killed. The criminals were not caught.
1925
Mary Pickford was the target of a failed kidnapping plot in the U.S. The culprits, who planned to demand $200,000 ransom, were sent to prison.
Mar. 15: Madge Oberholtzer was kidnapped by Ku Klux Klan Grand Dragon David C. Stephenson and two others. The KKK leader repeatedly raped and drugged her. She died soon after her release and Stephenson was sent to prison.
Mar. 29: Raimonde von Maluski was abducted by Mary Jones because the Maluskis had accused her of stealing from their house. The child was never found and Jones was sent to prison.
September: Mary Daly, child of a well-to-do businessman of Montclair, N.J., was abducted and killed by Harrison Noel, who was convicted for another murder in connection with the kidnapping and sent to an asylum.
1927
Mar. 9: Virginia Jo Frazier, child of the city commissioner of Chattanooga, Tenn., was abducted by a teenager who received $3,333 ransom. The child was freed and the youth was sent to prison.
Dec. 5: Marian Parker, the child of a well-to-do Los Angeles lawyer, was abducted by William E. Hickman. The $7,500 ransom was paid, but Marian had been murdered. Hickman was hanged, the first criminal to be executed for ransom kidnapping in the U.S.
1928
May 23: A bank in Lamar, Colo., was robbed and when one of the criminals was injured, Dr. W.W. Weininger was kidnapped to treat him. The doctor was slain and his killer was executed.
Nov. 19: Dr. Charles Brancati, thought to be involved with bootleggers, was last seen at a subway in New York City. Police suspect he was abducted.
1929
Gill Jamieson, the child of a bank vice president, was kidnapped in Hawaii. The child was killed and the culprit, a teenager, was executed.
April: The Indian ruler of Jammu and Kashmir decreed that the punishment for kidnapping Kashmiri women be increased from three to seven years in prison in addition to a lashing.
April: The government in British India approved extradition of criminals who kidnapped women or children from Kashmir and Jammu.
June: W.B. Kinne, lieutenant governor, was abducted as he drove between Lewiston to Orofino in Idaho. He was released and the kidnapping suspects were arrested.
1930
Feb. 17: Charles Pershall, well-to-do banker of Granite City, Ill., was abducted by kidnappers who ransomed him for $40,000. They were never caught.
Mar. 18: Michael Katz was kidnapped in Kansas City, Mo., and he was freed after $100,000 ransom was paid.
July 5: Reginald Arthur Lee, British acting consul-general in Marseilles, Fr., may have been kidnapped. He vanished and was never located.
Dec. 16: Nell Quinlan Donnelly, rich Kansas City clothing entrepreneur, and her driver were kidnapped, and $75,000 ransom was demanded. After the case received wide publicity and the victim's husband publicly threatened the criminals, no ransom was paid and Donnelly and the driver were released.
1931
In late April or early May, Dr. Isaac Dee Kelley, Jr. of St. Louis was ransomed and freed in East St. Louis, Ill.
In about May, James Hackett, a gambler, was kidnapped close to Chicago. After $150,000 ransom was paid, Hackett was released.
Patrick McGee, race track enthusiast, was abducted in Flushing, N.Y., and a $50,000 ransom was demanded but reduced to $18,000, which was paid. McGee was freed.
R.W. Oxford was kidnapped in St. Petersburg, Fla., and beaten by six men and a woman.
January: Adolphus Busch Orthwein, teenaged grandson of the president of Anheuser-Busch, Inc., was kidnapped.
Apr. 20: Fred J. Blumer, a Monroe, Wis., brewery owner, was abducted from his offices by kidnappers who demanded $150,000. A smaller sum was reportedly paid. Blumer was freed and the criminals were never caught.
June 15: George J. DeMange, an organized crime figure, was kidnapped by New York City mobster Vincent Coll and his henchmen, who received $35,000 ransom. DeMange was freed. Coll was later shot to death by Dutch Shultz's executioner.
August: John J. "Jack" Lynch, of Lake Geneva, Wis., a partial owner of a news service, was kidnapped by seven men. After his release, he denied reports that $50,000 ransom had been paid.
August: Charles Marvin Rosenthal, a stockbroker, was kidnapped and held captive in New York City until the kidnappers received $50,000 ransom. Police traced several suspects.
October: A St. Paul, Minn., businessman was abducted.
November: A wealthy fur tradesman from St. Louis was kidnapped by armed men, and a $100,000 ransom was demanded, but not collected. St. Louis and Chicago gang members were suspected.
December: A Chicago doctor and his wife were kidnapped and the abductors demanded $25,000, but received $2,000. Two culprits were sent to prison for life.
Dec. 15: Vera Page, ten, was abducted, sexually abused, and strangled to death. Percy Orlando Rush was arrested but not indicted for the crime.
Dec. 17: Marian McLean was kidnapped near her Cincinnati, Ohio, home, attacked, and killed by Charles Bischoff, who was sent to an institution for the mentally ill.
Dec. 21: Robert G. Fitchie, president of the Milk Wagon Drivers Union, was abducted in Chicago by Murray Humphreys and others, who

demanded and received $50,000. Fitchie was freed.

1932

Jan. 19: Benjamin Bower, a well-to-do banking executive, was abducted by kidnappers who ransomed him in Colorado for $50,000 and were never caught.

Jan. 23: A Chicago reporter alerted a senator that General Charles G. Dawes, chief of the Federal Reconstruction Finance Corporation, was the target of a kidnapping plot.

Jan. 26: A well-known South Bend, Ind., businessman was kidnapped. A ransom was demanded.

Feb. 2: A well-known banker from Tucson, Ariz., was kidnapped. A $60,000 ransom was demanded.

March: Two men were tried in Warren, Ohio, and sent to prison on charges of kidnapping James Dejute, Jr., the son of a contractor in Niles, Ohio.

March: A criminal who kidnapped a butcher for ransom was sent to prison by a Manhattan, N.Y., court.

March: Diane Johnson, infant of the vice president of Johnson & Johnson, was the target of a failed kidnapping attempt near Highland Park, N.J. Police arrested a suspect.

Mar. 1: Charles A. Lindbergh, Jr., infant son of Charles A. Lindbergh, was kidnapped from his home in Hopewell, N.J. Bruno Richard Hauptmann demanded $70,000, but only $50,000 was delivered by an intermediary. The child was killed and Hauptmann was executed on April 3, 1935.

June 17: Three women employees were taken hostage during a bank robbery in Fort Scott, Kan., by members of the Barker Gang and Harvey John Bailey, who was convicted.

June 22: U.S. President Herbert Hoover signed a noncapital federal kidnapping bill, which became known as the "Lindbergh Federal Kidnapping Law."

June 30: Haskell Bohn, the son of a wealthy industrialist of St. Paul, Minn., was abducted by kidnappers who demanded $35,000 but received $12,000. The youth was freed and Verne Sankey later confessed to involvement in the crime.

July 6: Joseph Myda was kidnapped from his home by gunmen who apparently planned to murder him. When they made a wrong turn onto a golf course in Elyria, Ohio, golfers attacked the car and Myda was saved. He said the attackers were from Cleveland.

1933

Spring: A committee under Senator Copeland of New York was designated by the U.S. Senate to inquire into kidnapping and racketeering.

Feb. 12: Charles Boettcher II, a rich Denver businessman, was abducted from his house by Verne Sankey and Gordon Alcorn who received $60,000 ransom. The broker was freed and four of the kidnappers were sent to prison.

May 2: Margaret McMath was kidnapped in Harwichport, Mass., by Kenneth Buck, who received $60,000 ransom for the child. She was freed and Buck was convicted.

May 27: Mary McElroy, daughter of the Kansas City city manager, was kidnapped from her house by Clarence Stevens and Walter McGee who received half of a $60,000 ransom demand. The young woman was freed and four kidnappers were sent to prison.

June 15: William A. Hamm, Jr., a rich brewer, was kidnapped in St. Paul, Minn., by the Alvin Karpis-Ma Barker Gang, who demanded and received $100,000 ransom. Hamm was freed and two gang members were sent to prison.

June 16: Jack Killingsworth, Bolivar, Mo., sheriff, was abducted by Charles "Pretty Boy" Floyd and Adam Richetti, who later released the law officer.

July: Frank A. McClatchy, a wealthy real estate broker, was showing a house near Haverford, Pa., to two men when they tried to kidnap him. When he resisted, they shot him and fled. McClatchy died four days afterward.

July: John King Ottley, a well-to-do banker from Atlanta, was kidnapped and the abductors demanded $40,000 ransom. The culprits were arrested.

July 7: John J. "Butch" O'Connell, Jr., nephew of the Democratic leaders in Albany, N.Y., was abducted in Albany by kidnappers who received $42,500 ransom. The young man was freed and the abductors were convicted.

July 10: August Luer, a banker, was kidnapped in Alton, Ill., and later freed. No ransom was paid and four kidnappers were sent to prison.

July 11: John "Jake The Barber" Factor, associate of Alphonse Capone, was allegedly kidnapped close to Chicago by Roger Touhy and others. Factor was freed after $70,000 ransom was paid and Touhy was sent to prison.

July 22: Charles F. Urschel, a rich oilman, was abducted by George "Machine Gun" Kelly and Albert Bates from his Oklahoma City home. They demanded and received $200,000 ransom. Urschel was freed and the abductors and several accomplices were sent to prison.

July 29: J. Edgar Hoover was appointed director of the Division of Investigation, which was created to fight kidnapping, racketeering, and other crimes.

Nov. 9: Brooke Hart, son of a rich San Jose, Calif., department store proprietor, was kidnapped and killed by Thomas M. Thurmond and John Maurice Holmes, who demanded but did not receive a $40,000 ransom. They were arrested and lynched.

1934

Bills strengthening penalties for kidnapping and racketeering, and extending federal jurisdiction in kidnapping cases were introduced in the U.S. Senate.

Jan. 17: Edward G. Bremer, president of Commercial Bank in St. Paul, Minn., was kidnapped by the Alvin Karpis—Ma Barker Gang, who demanded and received $200,000 ransom. Bremer was freed and Alvin Karpis and Harry Campbell were sent to prison.

March: Kid Boots Ace, AKA:(Timmie), a prize-winning Boston Terrier from Massachusetts, was taken from his owner, Louis Rudginsky, in Chicago. The kidnapper demanded $500.

Apr. 25: June Robles, child of rich Tucson, Ariz., ranchers, was abducted by kidnappers who demanded but did not receive $15,000. The child was found alive.

May 9: William F. Gettle, rich oilman, was abducted from his house in Arcadia, Calif., by kidnappers who demanded $80,000. Gettle was found, no ransom was paid, and three were sent to prison.

May 18: President Franklin D. Roosevelt signed into law kidnapping bills, which included provisions for the death penalty.

Oct. 10: Alice Speed Stoll, a well-to-do woman, was kidnapped in Louisville, Ky., by Thomas H. Robinson, Jr., who demanded $50,000. Stoll was freed, no ransom was paid, and Robinson was sent to prison.

1935

May 24: George Weyerhaeuser, the child of a rich Tacoma, Wash., family, was kidnapped from his home by William and Margaret Mahan. The family paid $200,000 ransom, the child was freed, and William Mahan was sent to prison.

Nov. 26: Arthur Gooch and an accomplice abducted two police officers in Paradise, Texas, and forced their hostages to drive them to Oklahoma. The accomplice was killed and Gooch was captured in an ensuing gunfight. On June 19, 1936, Gooch became the first man executed under federal kidnapping laws.

December: Nicolas Castano Padilla, Havana businessman and banker, was kidnapped in Cuba and $300,000 ransom was demanded. He was freed and denied that ransom had been paid.

1936

In early 1936, Cecil Rich and Edward McCune, Kansas college students, were arrested near New Orleans on charges of auto theft, robbery and the kidnapping of a service station attendant.

Dec. 12: Chiang Kai-shek, Chinese generalissimo, was kidnapped in Sian, China, by Chang Hsueh-liang, a warlord who disagreed with his policies. Chiang was freed and his captor was arrested and put under house arrest.

Dec. 27: Charles Mattson, child of a well-known Tacoma, Wash., surgeon, was kidnapped from his home, and the abductors demanded but did not receive $28,000. The child was slain and the culprits were never caught.

1937

June: The wife of William H. Parsons of Long Island, N.Y., disappeared, apparently kidnapped. A note demanded $25,000 ransom which was never paid. She never reappeared and the case remained unsolved.

Aug. 7: Jean de Koven, a dancer from the U.S., was kidnapped from a Paris hotel by Eugene Weidmann who demanded $500 ransom. The young woman was killed and Weidmann confessed to other kidnappings and was guillotined.

Sept. 25: Charles S. Ross, rich, retired manufacturer, was kidnapped close to Franklin Park, Ill., by John H. Seadlund and James A. Gray, who had planned to rob him. They demanded and received $50,000. Seadlund killed Ross and Gray. He was later executed.

Nov. 4: Dr.James Seder, a well-to-do Huntington, W. Va., doctor, was abducted from his house by Orville Adkins, John Travis, and Arnett Booth, who demanded $50,000. Seder was rescued, but later died from pneumonia and the kidnappers were all hanged.

1938

Feb. 24: Peter Levine, a New Rochelle, N.Y., boy, was abducted from his home. A $30,000 ransom was demanded. The child was murdered and the culprit was never apprehended.

May 28: James Bailey Cash, the child of a Princeton, Fla., businessman, was kidnapped and killed by Franklin Pierce McCall, who received $10,000 ransom. McCall was later executed.

1939

Aug. 7: Jean Bolton and Francis Dunn were abducted in Florida by Thomas Ashwell. Ashwell killed Dunn and authorities later rescued Bolton. The killer was executed.

1940

Nicola Iorga, ex-prime minister of Rumania, was kidnapped and slain by the Iron Guardists.

Sept. 20: Marc de Tristan, a child of a well-to-do Hillsborough, Calif., family, was kidnapped by Wilhelm J. Muhlenbroich, who demanded but did not receive $100,000 in ransom. The child was rescued and the kidnapper was sent to prison for life.

1942

Oct. 12: Daniel Joseph Scanlon, an infant, was kidnapped from a hospital nursery in Columbus, Ohio, by Ruby Evelyn Cremeans, who was sent to prison.

1943

Apr. 1: Lee A. Burton admitted to police that he had committed numerous rapes in Pasadena, Alhambra, and Los Angeles. He was sent

to prison on rape and kidnapping charges.
1946
Jan. 7: Suzanne Degnan, six, was kidnapped from her Chicago apartment by William Heirens. He demanded $20,000 ransom, killed the girl, and was sent to prison.
1949
Aug. 17: A housewife was kidnapped from her Fort Wayne-area house and raped by Franklin Click. She later identified Click, who confessed to three 1944 sex murders and was executed.
1950
July 4: Salvatore Giuliano, leader of a Sicilian gang, was slain. He allegedly abducted both mafia leader Don Carlo and the archbishop of Monreale.
Nov. 9: Linda Stram was kidnapped in Santa Fe, N.M., by Dr. Nancy Campbell, who was arrested when she tried to collect $20,000 ransom for the girl. Campbell was sent to prison.
Dec. 30: Nine people, including the Carl Mosser family were kidnapped and six murdered within twenty-two days by William Edward Cook, who was convicted and executed.
1952
Dr. Walter Linse, a lawyer, a leader of the Committee of Free Jurists, and an anti-Communist, was kidnapped from his home in West Berlin. Kurt Knobloch and Siegfried Benter were arrested for the crime.
1953
Sept. 28: Robert C. Greenlease, Jr., was abducted from a private school in Kansas City, Mo., by Bonnie Brown Heady and Carl A. Hall. They killed the child, then demanded and received $600,000 ransom. They were later executed.
1954
Jan. 16: Leonard Moskovitz was kidnapped in San Francisco by Harold Jackson and Joseph Lear. He was rescued before the demanded ransom, first $500,000 then $300,000, was paid. The two kidnappers were sent to prison.
June 9: Evelyn Ann Smith, wife of Herbert Smith, an executive of a Phoenix, Ariz., pipe and steel company, was kidnapped in Phoenix and a $75,000 ransom was demanded and paid. She was freed and Daniel Joseph Marsin was arrested.
1955
Apr. 28: Stephanie Bryan was abducted from Berkeley, Calif., and murdered by Burton W. Abbott.
June 20: Patricia Ann Waters was kidnapped from her home near Rome, Ga., and raped and murdered by Willie Grady Cochran. He was convicted and executed.
Aug. 4: Wilma Frances Allen was kidnapped from a shopping center in Kansas City, Mo., robbed, and killed by Arthur Ross Brown. He was executed.
1956
February: Robert Bialek, inspector general of the East German "People's Police," disagreed with party policy and defected to West Berlin in 1953. He later disappeared, and East Germans were thought to be responsible.
July 4: Peter Weinberger, a Long Island, N.Y., infant, was abducted from the porch of his home by Angelo John LeMarca, who left a note demanding $2,000. The baby was left in a thicket where he died of exposure. LeMarca was executed.
Aug. 6: President Dwight D. Eisenhower signed into law a bill which permitted the FBI to begin investigating a kidnapping case twenty-four hours after the kidnapping.
1957
Sept. 22: Lee Crary, an Everett, Wash., child, was kidnapped from his home by George Edward Collins, Jr., who demanded $10,000 ransom. The child escaped and led police to Collins, who was sent to prison for life.
October: Ng Sen Choy, a well-to-do tailor living in the Singapore region, was kidnapped by members of the 18 Group led by Ah Chai, who was later executed.
1959
Jan. 2: Lisa Rose Chionchio, a newborn, was kidnapped from a hospital in Brooklyn, N.Y., by Jean Iavarone. The child was located and Iavarone was sent to prison.
June 4: Becky Holt was slain in Philadelphia, Pa., after she was abducted by 15-year-old Edward Cooney. He was sent to a juvenile facility and freed when he reached the age of twenty-one.
1960
Feb. 10: Adolph Coors III, a rich brewer, was kidnapped near Golden, Colo., and killed by convicted murderer Joseph Corbett, Jr., who had planned to demand $500,000. Corbett was sent to prison for life.
Apr. 12: Eric Peugeot, the child of the French car industrialist, was abducted from a playground at a Paris golf course. His kidnappers demanded and received $300,000 ransom. Eric was freed and two of the culprits were sent to prison.
July 4: Pietro Crasta, a cheese seller, was driving toward Nuoro, Italy, when he was kidnapped. A $6,000 ransom was demanded. His body was found Aug. 16 and three suspects were arrested.
Aug. 16: The son of Graeme Thorne, a Sydney, Aus., lottery winner, was found dead after having been kidnapped by Stephen Leslie and Magda Bradley, who had demanded £25,000 ransom. They were sent to prison for life.
1961
July: Andrew Ashley, a North Buffalo, N.Y., toddler, was found dead. He was one of several children that were abducted in that region in Summer 1961.
September: John William Clouser (AKA: Jack Clauser; Chuck A. Williams), was arrested for robbing, kidnapping, and beating two theater managers from Orlando, Fla. He was convicted in 1962.
1963
New York state abolished a law requiring the death penalty in cases of premeditated murder or kidnapping in which the victim was hurt.
Dec. 8: Frank Sinatra, Jr., the teenaged son of singer Frank Sinatra, was abducted from a hotel in State Line, Calif., by Joseph C. Amsler, John W. Irwin, and Barry W. Keenan. They received $240,000 ransom, the youth was freed, and the abductors were sent to prison.
1964
Mar. 31: The body of a Mount Pleasant, S.C., child, David Robinson was found. He had been kidnapped by Joseph Francis, Jr., who was imprisoned.
Apr. 2: John William Clouser and three others escaped from the mental ward of the Florida State Hospital and allegedly hijacked a car with two hospital employees and held them hostage. The employees were freed and the car was later found.
May 23: Madeleine Dassault, wife of a plane manufacturer, was kidnapped in Paris and located unharmed the following day. Three suspects were apprehended.
Oct. 9: Michael Smolen, U.S. Air Force lieutenant colonel, was abducted in Caracas, Venez., by Castroite terrorists. They demanded freedom for a terrorist held in Saigon, S. Vietnam, whose execution was then delayed. Smolen was freed.
Dec. 26: Lesley Ann Downey was kidnapped by Manchester, England, residents Ian Brady and Myra Hindley. Downey was murdered and the abductors were sent to prison for life.
1966
From 1966-76, at least four executives of Fiat, the biggest and most influential company in Italy, were kidnapped. Fiat employees were attacked and murdered, and Fiat-owned buildings were bombed.
Mar. 18: Daniel Jesse Goldman, eighteen, was kidnapped from his house near Bal Harbour, Fla.
May 17: Joseph Bonanno, head of a New York City Mafia family, turned himself in to police authorities after allegedly having been kidnapped by Mafia members and held for nineteen months.
Dec. 17: Stephen Shea, a service station attendant, was abducted, raped, and murdered by Myron Lance and Walter Kelbach, who were given life prison terms.
1967
Jan. 6: Betty Hill was held captive in her home in Boulder, Colo. Her husband paid $50,000 ransom and she was freed.
Apr. 3: Kenneth King, a Beverly Hills, Calif., boy, was abducted from his home and $250,000 ransom was demanded and received. King was freed. A suspect was later arrested.
Aug. 19: Christine Anne Darby, seven, was kidnapped, sexually assaulted, and suffocated by Raymond Leslie Morris, in Walsall, England. He was sentenced to life in prison.
1968
Fernando Tondi, businessman, was the target of a failed kidnapping attempt at his home near Nuoro, Italy, in the spring. Six months later, his kidnappers returned, and this time they were successful. The ransom was paid and he was freed.
Mar. 26: Graziano Mesina, a Sardinian outlaw, was arrested. He confessed to the kidnappings of Nino Petretto, son of an auto dealer, and Giocanni Campus, land holder, both from Ozieri, Italy. The kidnappings had occurred not long before his arrest.
Apr. 8: The death penalty clause in the federal Lindbergh kidnapping law was ruled unconstitutional by the U.S. Supreme Court.
Aug. 28: John Gordon Mein, U.S. ambassador to Guatemala, tried to evade a kidnapping attempt in Guatemala City by FAR (Revolutionary Armed Forces) guerrillas and was fatally shot.
Dec. 17: Barbara Jane Mackle, daughter of a rich Miami building contractor, was kidnapped in Atlanta by Ruth Eisemann-Schier and Gary Steven Krist. The $500,000 ransom was paid, the young woman was found alive, and the abductors were sent to prison.
1969
Apr. 10: Camellia Jo Hand was kidnapped in Ocoee, Fla., by Kenneth Ray Wright. The child was murdered and Wright was given a life term.
May 10: Anne Katherine Jenkins was kidnapped from her Baltimore, Md., apartment, allegedly by Marie Calvert and Edward Lee Hull. Her father paid $10,000 ransom and the young woman was freed.
May 14: The wife of Roy Fuchs, a bank manager, and their three children were held captive by abductors who received $129,000. The family was freed and the culprits were later arrested.
September: Enzo Boschetti was kidnapped in Cagliari, Italy, by abductors who collected $115,500.
Sept. 4: Charles Burke Elbrick, U.S. ambassador to Brazil, was abducted in Rio de Janeiro by MR-8 (Revolutionary Movement of the Eighth) and ALN terrorists. As demanded, several political prisoners were freed and the group's manifesto was printed. Elbrick was freed.
Sept. 7: Mary Nelles was abducted near Toronto, Ontario, by kidnappers who demanded and received $200,000 ransom. Nelles was freed and the criminals were sent to prison.

Oct. 6: José Straessle, son of the Swiss consul in Cali, Col., and Hermann Buff, consul secretary, were kidnapped by The Invisible Ones in Columbia and later freed. Officials denied media reports that a ransom of several thousand dollars had been paid.
Oct. 24: Sophie Duguet, daughter of a wealthy farmer, was abducted in Soissons, Fr. by Michel Fauqueux. The equivalent of £75,000 ransom was paid and the girl was released.
Nov. 5: The body of Patrick Dolan, teenage son of a U.S. businessman, was located near Sao Paulo, Braz. He had been abducted and $12,500 ransom paid.
Dec. 29: Muriel MacKay, was mistakenly abducted and slain in London by Arthur and Nizamodeen Hosein, who had wanted to kidnap the wife of media tycoon Rupert Murdoch. Their final demand was £1 million. They were given a life prison term.
Dec. 29: Two children, Peggy Rahn and Wendy Brown Stevenson, were last seen at Pompano Beach, Fla., and were apparently abducted.
1970
Feb. 27: Fuentes Mohr, Guatemalan foreign minister, was abducted by leftist FAR terrorists. He was released when a terrorist leader was freed from prison.
Mar. 6: Sean M. Holly, U.S. labor attaché in Guatemala, was kidnapped in Guatemala by FAR terrorists. Three terrorists were released from prison according to the abductors' demands and Holly was then freed.
Mar. 11: Nobuo Okuchi, Japanese consul general in Sao Paulo, Braz., was kidnapped in Brazil by VPR terrorists who demanded the release of prisoners. The demand was met and the diplomat was released.
Mar. 24: Lieutenant Colonel Donald J. Crowley, U.S. air attaché to the Dominican Republic, was kidnapped. He was freed after twenty political prisoners were permitted to exit the country.
Mar. 24: Joaquin Waldemar Sanchez, Paraguayan consul in Ituzaingo, Arg., was kidnapped by FAL terrorists. Their demands for the release of two terrorists in prison were refused and the diplomat was freed.
Mar. 29: Yuri Pivovarov, U.S.S.R. assistant commercial attaché in Argentina, was the target of a kidnap attempt in Argentina by MANO terrorists. Police rescued Pivovarov after a car chase.
Mar. 31: Count Karl von Spreti, West German ambassador to Guatemala, was abducted and the kidnappers demanded $700,000 and the release of twenty-two political prisoners. The Guatemalan government refused and Spreti was slain.
April: Jack Fry, official of the Peace Corps, was abducted in Ethiopia by terrorists and later freed.
Apr. 5: Curtis S. Cutter, U.S. consul general in Brazil, was nearly kidnapped in Pôrto Alegre, but escaped. Three UPR terrorists were arrested.
Apr. 23: Rudy W. Martinez, Guatemalan exporter of coffee, was kidnapped by terrorists who demanded and received a large ransom. Martinez was freed.
May 29: Pedro Eugenio Arambaru, ex-president of Argentina, was kidnapped in Argentina by terrorists, who murdered Arambaru in retaliation for the execution of General Juan José Valle. Three men were sent to prison.
June 7: Morris Draper, U.S. political secretary, was abducted in Amman, Jor., by PFLP terrorists and later freed.
June 11: Ehrenfried von Holleben, West German ambassador to Brazil, was kidnapped by abductors who demanded that forty prisoners be released. The demand was met and Holleben freed.
July 9: Fernando Londone y Londone, ex-foreign minister of Colombia, was kidnapped by Colombian terrorists who demanded and received $200,000 ransom.
July 21: Two West Germans were kidnapped in Teoponte, Bol., by ELN terrorists whose demands for the release of prisoners was met and the Germans were freed.
July 24: Police saved Donner Lyon, U.S. consul in Recife, Braz., from being kidnapped by terrorists, who were arrested.
July 31: Aloisio Mares Dias Gomide, Brazilian vice-consul in Uruguay, was kidnapped by Tupamaros terrorists who received an alleged $250,000 ransom. Gomide was freed.
July 31: Michael Gordon Jones, second secretary to the U.S. embassy in Montevideo, Urug., was kidnapped by Tupamaros terrorists, but escaped.
July 31: Daniel A. Mitrione, U.S. diplomat, was abducted by Uraguayan terrorists, Tupamaros, who demanded the release of all Tupamaros held in prison. The demand was refused and Mitrione was slain.
July 31: Nathan Rosenfeld, U.S. cultural attaché in Uruguay, was almost kidnapped with Michael Jones, U.S. diplomat, but escaped.
Aug. 7: Claude L. Fly, U.S. agronomist, was abducted in Montevideo, Urug., by terrorists who demanded that 150 prisoners be freed. Fly suffered a heart attack and was freed.
Sept. 12: Three hostages were taken at the Egyptian embassy in London by members of the Jewish Defense League who demanded the release of airplane passengers that were held hostage in Jordan.
Oct. 5: James R. Cross, trade commissioner of England, was abducted from his Montreal, Que., home by five Front de Libération Québec members who demanded about $4 million and the release of FLQ prisoners. Cross was freed and the kidnappers were all sent to prison.
Oct. 10: Pierre Laporte, minister of labor and immigration of Quebec, was abducted by FLQ members to emphasize their demands after having kidnapped James Cross. After Canada suggested freeing only five FLQ prisoners, Laporte was slain. The kidnappers were sentenced to life in prison.
November: Douglas MacArthur II, U.S. ambassador, was the target of a failed kidnap attempt in Iran.
Dec. 1: Eugene Beihl, a West German consul, was abducted in San Sebastián, Spain, by members of a Basque splinter group, ETA, who wanted political concessions. Beihl was freed on Dec. 25.
Dec. 7: Giovanni Enrico Bucher, Swiss ambassador to Brazil, was abducted in Rio de Janeiro by members of National Liberation Alliance (ALN). Seventy political prisoners were freed and Bucher was released.
1971
Jan. 8: Geoffrey M.S. Jackson, British ambassador to Uruguay, was abducted in Montevideo, Urug., by Tupamaro terrorists who demanded the release of political prisoners. Jackson was freed after 106 prisoners escaped from jail.
Feb. 10: The Yugoslavian consulate in Gothenburg, Swed., was taken over by two Croatians who demanded that prisoners in Yugoslavia be freed. Their demands were not met and they gave themselves up.
Feb. 15: James Finlay, U.S. air force security officer in Ankara, Turk., was abducted by TPLA terrorists who demanded nothing and Finlay was freed.
Mar. 4: Four U.S. air force members were kidnapped in Ankara, Turk., by TPLA terrorists who demanded but did not receive $400,000 ransom. The airmen were freed and the culprits convicted.
Mar. 10: Berro Oribe, attorney-general of Uruguay, was abducted by Tupamaro terrorists. After he was grilled about legal cases against terrorists, Oribe was freed.
April 5: Renate Putz, sixteen, was kidnapped in Munich, Ger., and about DM 300,000 was demanded. Her parents did not return from a vacation until ten days later to find the note, and by that time she had been slain.
May 12: The manager for a U.S.-owned gold mine was abducted in Bolivia by poor people who demanded a tractor to build roads. They received a tractor and freed the manager.
May 17: Ephraim Elrom, Israeli consul general in Istanbul, Turkey, was abducted in Istanbul by terrorists whose demands for the release of imprisoned terrorists were refused. Elrom was fatally shot.
May 23: Stanley Sylvester, honorary British consul and administrator of Swift & Co. in Rosario, Arg., was abducted by ERP terrorists whose demands for the distribution of $62,500 in goods to the poor were met and Sylvester was freed.
May 29: Henri Wolimer, French consul in San Sebastian, Spain, evaded a kidnapping attempt by Basque terrorists.
June 2: Raul Guerra, honorary Uruguayan consul in Cordoba, Arg., was the target of a kidnap attempt by ERP members.
June 7: Alfred Kuser, Swiss chief of Volcan, a metallurgy company, was abducted in Boliva and freed after the firm paid about $40,000 in ransom.
June 23: Alfredo Cambon, legal adviser to some U.S.– financed companies in Uruguay, was abducted in Uruguay by OPR-33 terrorists and freed.
July 14: Jorge Berembau, Argentine businessman, was kidnapped by Tupamaro terrorists in Montevideo, Urug., whose ransom demand was not paid. Berembau was freed.
Nov. 19: Jaime Castrejon Diez, rector of the State University of Guerrero, Mex., was abducted by terrorists. After nine political prisoners were freed and $500,000 ransom was paid, Diez was released.
Nov. 30: Michele Ray, French reporter, claimed she was kidnapped by OPR-33 terrorists in Uruguay, but officials thought Ray may have planned the kidnapping to interview the terrorists.
1972
A teacher and six students were abducted by Edwin John Eastwood, of Melbourne, Aus.
March: A written plan by ERP terrorists that outlined possible ways to kidnap a certain U.S. businessman was seized in Argentina.
Mar. 21: Oberdan Sallustro, president of Fiat of Argentina, was kidnapped by ERP terrorists in Argentina whose demands included $1 million in goods ransom and the release of terrorist prisoners. Although Fiat agreed to the demands, the government refused and the executive was killed.
Mar. 27: One Canadian and two British NATO radar technicians were abducted in Turkey by TPLA terrorists whose demands for the release of prisoners were refused. The victims were murdered, and the terrorists were slain in a police raid.
June: The nephew of an alleged New York City mob syndicate leader was kidnapped by other mafia members.
June 30: Ernanno Barca, president of the Buenos Aires branch of the Italian bank Banco di Napoli, was abducted. The bank gave the kidnappers $200,000 ransom and Barca was freed.
July 27: Virginia Piper was kidnapped from her suburban Minneapolis house. After the kidnappers received $1 million ransom, Piper was freed.
July 28: Hector Menoni, director of a United Press International in Uruguay, was abducted in Uruguay by OPR-33 terrorists and later freed.
August: A businessman from the U.S. was abducted in Guatemala and freed after the kidnappers received ransom money.
Aug. 30: The son of the Jordanian ambassador to France was kidnapped. The diplomat paid the kidnappers about $40,000 and his son was freed.

Sept. 5: Two people were killed and nine hostages were taken at the Israeli athletic dormitory at the Munich, W. Ger., Olympics by Black September terrorists whose demands for 200 Palestinians to be freed were refused. At an airport, five terrorists, all hostages, and a police officer were slain.
Sept. 5: Jan J. Van de Panne, Dutch chief of Philips Argentina electronics company, was kidnapped by Montoneros terrorists in Argentina. The firm paid $500,000 ransom and Panne was freed.
Oct. 6: The West German consulate in Algiers was taken over for about an hour by Palestinian students who wanted freedom for three Arabs held in connection with the Munich Olympic situation. The students then left.
Nov. 7: Enrico Barrella, industrialist from Italy, was abducted in Buenos Aires, Arg., by kidnappers who received $500,000. He was freed.
Dec. 6: Felix Azpiazu, industrialist from Spain, was abducted in Argentina by kidnappers who demanded $180,000, but accepted $100,000 ransom. Azpiazu was freed.
Dec. 10: Donald Grove, executive of Vestey Industrial Group, a British company, was abducted by ERP terrorists. The firm allegedly paid $1 million ransom and Grove was freed.
Dec. 27: Vicente Russo, director general of a subsidiary of ITT Corp. in Argentina was abducted in Argentina and freed after the kidnappers were reportedly paid between $500,000 and $1 million ransom.
Dec. 28: Six hostages at the Israeli embassy in Bangkok, Thai., were taken by members of Black September whose demands for the freedom of Arab prisoners in Israel were not met. They withdrew the demands and were allowed to leave the country.

1973

Members of Syrian-based Saiga abducted two Russian Jews travelling to Israel and an Austrian official. They demanded that the Austrian government close the Schonau transit camp. The Austrians complied.
Larry Gene Bell, armed with a gun and knife, tried to abduct two women in South Carolina. He was sent to prison and an institution for the mentally ill.
John Edward Copeland, Jr., suspected of kidnappings and other crimes in California during mid-1973, was arrested in July 1975.
Raul Hernandez, a Mexican businessman vanished. Kenneth B. Krohn and Thurston Drew Schrader were suspects in the case.
Jan. 23: Clinton Knox, the U.S. ambassador to Haiti and Ward Christensen, the U.S. consul general, were abducted by three armed people who demanded the release of prisoners and ransom. The prisoners were released and the ransom partially paid. The kidnappers were allowed to leave the country.
Jan. 23: Two Italian businessmen in Eritrea, Eth., were kidnapped by ELF terrorists. The hostages were released, apparently after ransom was paid.
Feb. 3: Norman Lee, administrator of a Coca-Cola plant, was kidnapped in Buenos Aires, Arg., by terrorists and freed after ransom was paid.
Feb. 20: The child of the president of a Dallas bank was kidnapped. The kidnapper demanded $200,000, but was arrested several hours later by the FBI.
Feb. 20: The teenaged son of a businessman in Bethesda, Md., was abducted and $200,000 ransom was demanded.
Feb. 20: Hostages were taken at the Indian High Commission in London by three Pakistanis who demanded the release of Pakistanis imprisoned in India. Their demands were not met and two of the culprits were shot and another placed under arrest.
Feb. 24: The wife of a bank president in Bath, Pa., was kidnapped and $40,000 ransom was demanded. She was freed before the ransom was paid.
March: The wife of a businessman from Roanoke, Va., was abducted and the kidnappers demanded $25,000, one of whom was captured almost one year later.
Mar. 1: About ten hostages in the Saudi Arabian embassy in Khartoum, Sudan, were taken by members of Black September who demanded the release of prisoners in several countries. Their demands were not met and they killed three diplomats before giving themselves up.
Mar. 28: Gerardo Scalmazzi, manager of the First National Bank of Boston's Rosario branch, was kidnapped in Rosario, Arg., and released after the terrorists received ransom allegedly between $500,000 and $1 million.
April: Two abductors unsuccessfully tried to collect $20,000 ransom for a college student from Macomb, Ill.
April: A gambler from New Rochelle, N.Y., was rescued after having been kidnapped. The abductors had demanded $250,000.
Apr. 2: Anthony R. DaCruz, Eastman Kodak technical operations manager, was abducted in Argentina by terrorists and freed after the firm paid $1.5 million.
Apr. 8: Francis Victor Brimicombe, president of Nobleza Tabacos, a subsidiary of the British-American Tobacco Co., was kidnapped in Buenos Aires, Arg., and freed after the kidnappers were paid ransom between $1.5 and $1.8 million.
May 1: The son of the Swiss chairman of an Italian bank and electric company in Buenos Aires, Arg. was abducted. He was freed after $1.5 ransom was paid.
May 4: Terrance G. Leonhardy, U.S. consul general in Guadalajara, was abducted in Mexico by the People's Revolutionary Armed Forces, whose demands included the release of political prisoners and $80,000 ransom. The demands were met and Leonhardy freed.
May 4: Two Soviet doctors working in Burma were abducted by members of the Shan tribe who demanded the release of Chang Chipo, Shan leader.
May 21: Oscar Castel, president of a Coca-Cola bottling plant in Córdoba, Arg., was abducted in Córdoba and freed after the kidnappers received $100,000 ransom.
May 21: Luis Giovanelli, administrator at a Ford Motor plant, was fatally shot during a kidnapping by ERP terrorists in Buenos Aires, Arg. ERP stated that they would continue kidnapping Ford employees unless $1 million ransom was paid and the company complied.
June: Kidnappers failed to collect $1.5 million ransom they had demanded for the return of Melvin Zahn, president of a pharmaceutical company in Chicago. The kidnappers were sent to prison.
June 6: Charles Lockwood, British executive of an Acrow Steel division in Argentina, was abducted. A ransom of $2 million was paid, and Lockwood was freed.
June 10: J. Paul Getty III, teenaged grandson of rich J. Paul Getty, was abducted close to his quarters in Rome. His grandfather paid 3 billion lire ($2.9 million) and the youth was freed. Authorities later determined that the Calabrian Mafia had been involved.
June 18: Roberto Galvez, manager of a U.S. company, was abducted in Guatemala by FAR terrorists, who were paid $50,000 ransom. Galvez was freed.
June 18: Hans Kurt Gebhardt, West German businessman, was abducted in Argentina by guerrillas who were paid $100,000 ransom. Gebhardt was freed.
June 18: John R. Thompson, president of a Firestone subsidiary in Argentina, was kidnapped in Buenos Aires, Arg., by ERP terrorists and freed after they received $3 million ransom.
June 25: Mario Baratella, vice-president of the Italian-owned Bank of Rio de la Plata in Buenos Aires, Arg. was abducted and released after the kidnappers, who demanded $2 million, were paid an unspecified ransom.
July 2: Raul Bornancini, assistant manager of the Córdoba, Arg. branch of the First National City Bank of New York, was kidnapped in Argentina and freed after the kidnappers were paid a reported $1 million ransom.
July 4: An accountant for a subsidiary of the British-American Tobacco Co., Nobleza Tobacos, was abducted in Buenos Aires, Arg., and freed after the kidnappers received ransom.
July 14: Mark Matson and his girlfriend, both teens, were held prisoner by Albert Brust at Brust's house in a Miami, Fla. suburb. Matson was shot dead, the girl released, and Brust committed suicide.
Aug. 27: Ian Martin, British manager of a meat firm, was abducted in Asunción, Para. Two kidnappers died and others were arrested when police rescued Martin.
Sept. 5: Thirteen hostages at the Saudi Arabian embassy in Paris were taken by Palestinians who demanded that Jordan free Abu Daoud, a Palestinian leader. Daoud was not released, but the terrorists surrendered and all the hostages were freed.
Sept. 23: David George Heywood, employee of a British-American Tobacco Co. subsidiary, Nobleza Tobacos, was abducted in Buenos Aires, Arg., by kidnappers who receive $300,000. Heywood was freed.
Oct. 4: Two U.S. citizens, employees of International Mining, were abducted in Columbia by ELN terrorists, who demanded $168,990 ransom. The army rescued the two.
Oct. 10: Anthony Williams, British consul in Mexico, was kidnapped in Mexico by terrorists whose demands for the release of political prisoners were not met. Whether the $200,000 ransom demand was paid was undisclosed. Williams was freed.
Oct. 15: The Belgian and French ambassadors to Cuba were held captive at the French embassy in Havana by a Cuban who was against Fidel Castro and wanted to leave Cuba. The demand was not met, the Cuban was slain by rescuers, and the diplomats were freed.
Oct. 22: Kurt Schmid, executive of Swissair, was abducted in Argentina by ERP terrorists who demanded $10 million. An unspecified ransom was paid and Schmid was freed.
Oct. 23: David Wilkie, Jr., president of an Amoco International Oil Co. subsidiary, was abducted in Buenos Aires, Arg., and freed after ransom was paid, which was allegedly $3.5 million.
November: Nyborg Anderson, regional manager of the Bank of London, was abducted in Argentina and $1.2 million ransom was demanded.
Nov. 7: Florencio Crespo, Argentine army colonel, was abducted by ERP terrorists.
Nov. 20: Kurt Nagel, honorary West German consul in Maracaibo, was abducted in Venezuela by terrorists and freed.
Dec. 1: Two boys from the Detroit area, Keith Arnold, child actor, and a friend, Gerald Kraft, were kidnapped and killed. Byron Smith, Geary Gilmore, and Jerome Holloway, who demanded $53,000, but reduced ransom to $15,000, were convicted.
Dec. 6: Victor E. Samuelson, U.S. administrator of Exxon Co., was abducted in Buenos Aires, Arg., by ERP terrorists who demanded $14.2 million, which was paid by his firm. Samuelson was freed.
Dec. 12: Terrorist operations of Algerians and Turks and the Habash Front were discovered close to Paris and police learned they planned to kidnap the son of an Israeli diplomat.
Dec. 21: Charles Robert Hayes, construction superintendent for McKee-

Tesca, was kidnapped in La Plata, Arg., and freed after the kidnappers received ransom.
Dec. 27: Thomas Nedermayer, West German businessman and honorary consul in Ireland, was kidnapped, apparently by the IRA.
Dec. 29: Yves Boisset, director of Peugeot of France's Argentine subsidiary, was kidnapped in Buenos Aires. His captors demanded $4 million, and Boisset was released after an unnamed sum was paid. FAR terrorists were thought to be responsible.

1974

Judge Sossi was kidnapped by members of the Italian Red Brigades, who demanded the release of imprisoned Red Brigades. Their demands were not met and Sossi was released.
From 1974 to 1979, Theodore "Ted" Bundy abducted, attacked, and murdered a series of women. He was sentenced to death in Miami, and after confessing to additional murders, was executed.
The wife of the president of a St. Paul, Minn., bank was ransomed for $200,000 of the bank's money.
An assistant vice-president of a bank in Fort Lauderdale, Fla., was abducted by kidnappers who demanded $60,000 from the bank.
The wife and children of the manager of a Grass Lake, Mich., bank were kidnapped. The manager paid $35,000 ransom, using the bank's money.
The program director of a Deland, Fla., radio station was kidnapped and killed by kidnappers who received $10,000 ransom.
Sometime in late 1974, Angela Armellini, a teenager, was almost kidnapped in Rome. The abductors fled when she fought.
January: Thomas Niedermayer, West German consul, was abducted from his house in Belfast, Ire. No demands were made and he was never found.
Jan. 3: Douglas Roberts, executive of Pepsi-Cola, was abducted in Buenos Aires, Arg., and freed after ransom was paid.
Feb. 4: Patricia Campbell Hearst, daughter of newspaper tycoon Randolph Hearst, was kidnapped in Berkeley, Calif., by Symbionese Liberation Army (SLA) terrorists who demanded that $400 million in food be given to the poor. More than $200 in food was distributed. Later the girl was allegedly brainwashed into joining the SLA.
Feb. 6: About twelve hostages were taken at the Japanese embassy in Kuwait by PFLP terrorists whose demands that four other PFLP be flown from Singapore to Kuwait were met. The hostages were freed and all the terrorists left Kuwait.
Feb. 20: John Reginald "Reg" Murphy, editor of the Atlanta *Constitution*, was abducted from his home by William H. and Betty Ruth Williams who demanded and received $700,000 ransom. Murphy was freed and the two culprits were sent to prison.
Mar. 20: During an attempt to kidnap Princess Anne of England in London, three were shot by Ian Ball. Ball, who had planned to demand £3 million, was sent to an institution for the criminally insane.
Mar. 25: John Patterson, U.S. vice consul in Hermosillo, Mex. was abducted by the Mexican People's Revolutionary Army and a ransom note demanding $500,000 was found.
Mar. 26: Three employees of a U.S. oil company and two other people were kidnapped in Ethiopia by ELF terrorists.
April: Françoise Claustre, French archeologist, was kidnapped and her husband, Pierre, was later taken hostage in Chad by Hissen Habre to get money and military supplies from France for his rebels fighting Chad. The rebels got $800,000 and medical supplies and the Claustres were freed.
Apr. 12: Alfred Albert Laun III, chief of the U.S. Information Service section in Córdoba, Arg., was severely hurt when he was abducted by ERP terrorists. He was freed the next day, seemingly because of his injuries.
Apr. 29: Members of the Pattani Liberation Front claimed they had kidnapped two female missionaries in Thailand.
July 24: Fifteen hostages were taken by convicted murderer Fred G. Carrasco and two other inmates at the Huntsville, Texas, prison. Two hostages and captors Carrasco and Rodolfo Dominguez died in a shootout with guards.
Aug. 28: J. Guadalupe Zuno Hernandez, father-in-law of Luis Echeverria Alvarez, president of Mexico, was kidnapped by terrorists, but freed after the government declined to negotiate.
Sept. 7: Barbara Hutchison, head of the U.S. Information Service in the Dominican Republic, was abducted and at the Venezuelan consulate, and the terrorists took six more hostages. Their demands that prisoners be freed and $1 million demand were not met. The hostages were freed and the terrorists left the country.
Sept. 13: Eleven hostages were taken at the French embassy at The Hague, Neth., by the Japanese Red Army, the German RAF, and the PFLP, who demanded that a terrorist held in Paris be freed. The hostages were freed, and the terrorists were allowed to leave the country.
Sept. 16: Jorge and Juan Born, sons of the chairman of Argentina's biggest company in Argentina, Bunge Born, were abducted by Monteneros terrorists who received $60 million. The brothers were freed.
Sept. 30: E.B. Reville, a banker of Hepzibah, Ga., and his wife, Jean, were abducted by kidnappers who received $30,000 ransom. The banker was alive when he was located, but Jean Reville did not survive.
Oct. 17: Fabrizio Mosna, the child of a wealthy furniture manufacturer, was abducted as he was going to school in Trento, Italy. He escaped before his parents received a $130,000 ransom demand.
Oct. 19: Emmanuele "Lele" Riboli, teenaged son of a well-to-do family, was kidnapped near Varese, Italy. The family paid 200 million lire and raised another 97 million lire. The youth was apparently slain. Niccolo Floris, Ugo Schirra, and Guiseppe Vitzizai were accused of the kidnapping.
Oct. 26: Fifteen hostages were taken by four inmates demanding release from Scheveningen Prison, in the Netherlands. Authorities recaptured the convicts and no hostages were injured.
Nov. 12: Jack J. Teich, steel industry executive, was kidnapped from his home in Kings Point, Long Island, N.Y., but freed after the kidnappers received $750,000 ransom. Richard W. Williams was imprisoned.
Nov. 14: United Popular Liberation Army members abduct the wife of an American real estate agent in Cuernavaca, Mex.
Nov. 18: The Philippine ambassador to the U.S. was taken hostage and another person injured by an armed man whose demand that his son be allowed to leave the Philippines was met. The diplomat was freed and the man gave himself up.
Dec. 5: Two hostages were taken at the French embassy in Mexico City by one September 23 terrorist whose demand for political asylum was agreed to and he was arrested.

1975

After having kidnapped Vittoria Vallarina Goncia in Italy, terrorist Margherita Curcio died in a shootout with police who freed Goncia.
Jan. 13: Lesley Whittle, a Kidderminster, England, teenager from a well-to-do family, was kidnapped from her home and killed by Donald Neilson, who demanded £50,000. He did not receive the money and was given a life term in prison.
Feb. 27: Peter Lorenz, German politician, was kidnapped in Berlin by terrorists. The West German government released five members of the Baader-Meinhof gang and paid DM 20,000.
Mar. 25: Two Kensington, Ill., girls, Sheila and Katherine Lyon, twelve and ten, were last seen at a shopping mall and were apparently kidnapped.
Apr. 24: Twelve hostages were taken at the German embassy in Stockholm, Swed., by RAF terrorists whose demands for $500,000 ransom and that terrorists in a West Germany prison be freed were not met. Four terrorists were arrested and two killed. One hostage was slain and others were wounded.
June 30: Cristina Mazzotti, a teenager, was kidnapped and murdered in Italy by a drug overdose. The kidnappers received more than $1.8 million ransom and twenty-four culprits were tried.
July: Ralph Murphy was given the death penalty after kidnapping and killing a mother and her son in Indiana.
July 14: Two employees of Collins International Service Co. and four Ethiopians were abducted in Asmara, Eth., by terrorists and later freed. The company may have paid ransom.
July 30: James Hoffa, leader of the Teamsters Union, was apparently abducted from a Detroit suburb. He was never found.
Aug. 3: Fifty-three hostages were taken at the U.S. embassy in Kuala Lampur, Malaysia, by Japanese Red Army members whose demands that Japan release some terrorists were met. The hostages were freed and the terrorists left Malaysia and gave themselves up in Libya.
Aug. 5: Donald Cooper, executive of Sears Roebuck, was abducted in Bogota, Col., and later released.
Aug. 9: Samuel Bronfman, heir to wealth from Seagram liquor company, disappeared in Purchase, N.Y., and his father paid $2.3 million ransom. Dominic Byrne and Mel Patrick Lynch said the crime was Bronfman's idea. They were sent to prison for extortion.
Aug. 30: Two U.S. employees of Boise-Cascade were abducted in Zamboanga, Phil., by Muslims and later freed.
Sept. 15: The Egyptian ambassador and two others were taken hostage at the Egyptian embassy in Madrid by Arabs who demanded that Egypt repudiate the Sinai agreement with Israel. Several diplomats signed such a statement, which Egypt later refused to recognize as valid. The hostages were freed after being flown to Algeria.
Oct. 3: Dr. Tiede Herrema, manager of a steel plant in Limerick, Ire., was kidnapped on his way to work by Eddie Gallagher, Marion Coyle, Kevin Mallon, and Jim Hyland, who demanded the release of prisoners. Herrema was freed and the kidnappers were arrested.
Nov. 6: Alio Kaloghirou, a teenager originally from Cyprus, was abducted from her London home and £60,000 ransom was demanded. She was freed, and the five kidnappers were arrested.
Dec. 2: About fifty travelers aboard a train were taken hostage near Beilen, Neth., by six South Moluccans who wanted independence for their homeland. Three hostages were slain before the hijackers gave themselves up on Dec. 14.
Dec. 4: Forty-seven hostages were taken at the Indonesian consulate in Amsterdam, Neth., by Moluccan terrorists whose demands for South Moluccan autonomy were refused. The hostages were freed and the terrorists gave themselves up on Dec. 19.
Dec. 21: Sixty hostages, including eleven OPEC delegates, were taken at an OPEC meeting in Vienna, Aus., by Arab, Latin, American, and German terrorists, whose demands that a statement be broadcast and that they be flown from Austria were met. The hostages were freed.
Dec. 22: Ronald Michalke, an executive at Collins Int. Service Co. was kidnapped in Asmara, Ethiopia. He was later released.
Dec. 24: Filiberto Fraccari, dealer in gold, was abducted on his way to his Verona, Italy, house. The initial $3 million ransom demand was reduced to $600,000, which was paid.

Dec. 24: Louis Hazan, administrator of a French record company, was abducted by kidnappers who received $3.5 million ransom. Hazan was found alive and several culprits were caught.

1976

Feb. 27: William Niehous, executive of Owens-Illinois Glass Co., was kidnapped from his home in Caracas, Venez. The kidnappers demanded $3.5 million ransom and bonuses for company employees. Niehous was later freed.
Mar. 10: Abby Drover was abducted, by Donald Alexander Hay and confined for six months underneath his garage in Port Moody, British Columbia, where he sexually assaulted her repeatedly. Policeman found the teenager alive and Hay was given a life prison term.
Apr. 20: Joe Morris, reporter for the Los Angeles *Times*, was kidnapped close to his home in Beirut, Leb.
May 23: Gayle Moony, daughter of a U.S. businessman, was abducted in Acapulco, Mex., by Armed Vanguard of the proletariat terrorists and later freed.
July 15: Twenty-six children were aboard a school bus abducted close to Chowchilla, Calif., by kidnappers Richard and James Schoenfeld and Fred Woods who demanded $5 million. The kidnappers were caught before the ransom was paid and the children were released.
Sept. 26: Francois Feriel, well-to-do businessman, was kidnapped from a villa on the French Riviera where he was a guest. The gunmen also robbed the villa's owners.
Sept. 28: Gustave George Curtis, manager of Grancolombia Industries, a subsidiary of Beatrice Foods, was abducted in Bogota, Col.
Oct. 11: Palestinian terrorists unsuccessfully tried to seize the Syrian embassy in Islamabad, Pak. Two terrorists were injured and the other one died in a shootout with police.
Oct. 11: Five hostages were taken at the Syrian embassy in Rome by Palestinian Black June terrorists who wanted to emphasize that the Palestinians had not been treated fairly by Syria. One hostage was critically injured before the terrorists gave themselves up.
Oct. 20: Tulio Oneto, Argentine financier held in Buenos Aires, Arg., by the People's Revolutionary Front, is slain. His family had refused to pay $2 million ransom.
Oct. 20: Carlos Macri, nephew of Tulio Oneto, also held by the PRA, is released when a $750,000 ransom is paid.
Dec. 13: The teenaged daughter of a Helene Curtis employee was abducted in Milan, Italy and later freed.

1977

Patrizia Spallone, abducted on the way to school, was rescued by Italian police.
Jan. 29: Mary L. Treadway, of Galesburg, Ill., was kidnapped from a shopping mall in Galesburg and later found dead. Donald Eugene Kennedy and Linda Mae Brunner of North Dakota were indicted.
Feb. 8: Richard O. Hall was abducted in Indianapolis by Anthony Kiritsis, who later gave himself up. Hall was freed.
Feb. 11: Eight hostages were taken at a Cincinnati home for unwed mothers by Jesse Coulter and his former wife, Rita Gibbeon of Detroit, who demanded information about a son he had given up for adoption in 1957. They surrendered when a police officer pretended to be their son.
Feb. 12: Daniel R. Evans, of Hyattsville, Md., held his son, age six, hostage at the home of his estranged wife for five hours before releasing the child. Evans was arrested.
Feb. 14: A Melbourne, Aus., resident, Edwin John Eastwood, began a kidnapping spree in which he seized sixteen people. He was sent to prison.
Mar. 8: At three locations in Washington, D.C., a total of 134 hostages were taken by Hanafi Muslims whose demands for the release of five Black Muslims were refused. The hostages were freed, but one who had been injured died from a heart attack.
Mar. 17: Michael Guile, a convicted robber, fatally shot himself after he attempted a robbery and held Pauline Gomez, her husband, and a neighbor's baby hostage in San Francisco for fourteen hours.
Mar. 17: Teenager Hector Lopez, Reverend James Lodwick, and television reporter John Johnson were held hostage in an East Harlem, N.Y., church by Charles "Reggi" Butts, who demanded custody of his daughter, who had been taken away by welfare officials when he was in jail. A policeman seized him and the hostages were rescued.
Mar. 19: Joseph Poore, manager of a Lyons, Ill., bar, was held hostage for several hours by Harold Merryfield who said he wanted police to kill him. Poore was freed and Merryfield arrested.
Mar. 19: Carlo Colombo, a businessman, was freed in Bornago, Italy, after kidnappers collected $1.2 million.
Mar. 21: Thirty-five city employees of Baltimore and family members of Anthony Patrick Griffin were held hostage by Griffin, who, unable to pay rent and gas bills, wanted to publicize his plight. The hostages were freed and he surrendered after a few hours.
Mar. 22: Paolo Lazzaroni, wealthy co-director of a biscuit business in Milan, Italy, was abducted and $5 million was demanded, but $730,000 was agreed to and paid. Lazzaroni was freed.
Apr. 3: Piero Scosta, son of a rich Italian ship-owner, was kidnapped and freed following the payment in Genoa of $1.6 million ransom.
Apr. 13: Luchino Revelli-Beaumont, head of a French Fiat subsidiary, was kidnapped near his apartment in paris by nine South Americans calling themselves the Committee for Socialist Revolutionary Unity and reportedly $2 million ransom was paid. The executive was later freed.
Apr. 18: Lou Adler, president of Ode Records, was abducted by Zoltan Kakash and Veronica Franovic who demanded and received $25,000. Adler was freed and the criminals were sent to prison.
May 23: About fifty-five hostages on board a train close to Glimmen, Neth., were taken by South Moluccan terrorists who wanted a bus and freedom for South Moluccans in Dutch prisons. In a police raid, two hostages died and six terrorists were killed.
May 23: South Moluccans took over a Bovensmilde, Neth., elementary school, holding 125 Dutch children and five teachers hostage. The children were freed and later police rescued the other hostages and captured the assailants.
May 24: Gertrude Resnick Farber, daughter of a wealthy television antenna entrepreneur, was kidnapped from her Monticello, N.Y, home and buried alive in a wooden box. The $1 million ransom was not paid. Ronald Harrison Krom, charged in the case, led police to her body.
May 29: Eduardo Casanova, Salvadoran ambassador to Guatemala, was abducted by guerrillas whose propaganda was read at a banking conference and Casanova was freed.
June 14: In a failed attempt to take control of the Yugoslavian mission to the United Nations, reportedly to call attention to the Croation Separatist Movement, three armed Croatians wounded one person and later gave themselves up.
June 19: Roberto Rischer Sandhoff, son of a Ford company executive, was the target of a kidnapping attempt in Guatemala City and he died several days later.
July: Patrizia Vallisi was abducted in Italy and her kidnappers demanded $10 million. The young woman was rescued before the ransom was paid.
July 31: Jürgen Ponto, powerful German banker, was slain during an apparent kidnapping attempt by RAF terrorists.
Aug. 9: William Weinkamper, manager of a subsidiary of Gould, Inc., Clevite de Mexico, was kidnapped in Mexico City and released after the kidnappers received ransom.
Sept. 5: Dr. Hanns-Martin Schleyer, chief of the West German Industrial Assoc., was kidnapped in Cologne by terrorists who demanded the release of RAF terrorists. Schleyer was slain.
Sept. 6: The wife of a U.S. businessman was abducted outside the company's offices in El Salvador.
Sept. 17: Kirk Anderson, a Mormon missionary from the U.S., was allegedly kidnapped in Epson, England, by Joyce McKinney and Keith Joseph May, and raped by McKinney, his former girlfriend. Free on bond, McKinney fled the country.
October: Graziella Ortiz Patino, a child, was kidnapped close to Geneva, Switz., by Italians and $2 million was demanded and paid. The girl was freed.
Oct. 25: Stephanie Lyng, daughter of Chicago newspaper columnist Dorsey Connors, was apparently kidnapped from her Palatine, Ill., home. She had received death threats prior to her disappearance.
December: Lotte Bohm was kidnapped in Vienna, Aus., by RAF terrorists.
December: Richard Oetker was kidnapped in Munich by members of the RAF.
December: Walter Michael Palmers was kidnapped in Vienna, Aus., by RAF terrorists.
Dec. 14: Achilleas Kyprianou, son of the Cyprus president, was abducted by terrorists who demanded political concessions, which were met. Kyprianou was freed.

1978

Jan. 23: A rich Belgian, Baron Empain, was abducted near his Paris apartment by a gang led by Alain Caillol who reduced their demand from $20 to $8 million. Empain was freed and the culprits were caught.
Feb. 2: Seven hostages were taken at the United Nations office in San Salvador by Popular Revolutionary Bloc members whose demands for the release of political prisoners were not met. A U.N. inquiry into human rights violations in the country was promised.
March: Michela Marconi, teenaged daughter of Italian businessman Sergio Marconi, was kidnapped in Italy. Three kidnappers were arrested and the girl was rescued.
Mar. 13: Seventy-two hostages were taken at Assen, Neth., government offices by South Moluccans who wanted a bus, $12 million ransom, and the release of their associates. One hostage was slain and the three terrorists were apprehended.
Mar. 16: Aldo Moro, ex-prime minister of Italy, was kidnapped in Rome by members of the Red Brigades, whose demands for the release of other terrorists from prison were refused. Moro was found dead May 9.
Apr. 10: Linda Goldstone, wife of a well-known Chicago doctor, was kidnapped, raped, and murdered by Hernando Williams, who was sent to prison for life.
May 24: The honorary Mexican consul and four others were taken hostage at the consul's Recife, Braz., office by an armed man who demanded permission to leave Brazil. The hostages were freed and the culprit was placed under arrest.
May 29: Juan Nicolas Escobar Sota, manager for Texas Petroleum, was abducted by M-19 terrorists and he was later found dead.
July 3: Four hostages were taken at the Chilean consulate in San Juan, P.R., by two armed people whose demands for the release of Puerto Rican terrorists imprisoned in the U.S. were not met. The hostages were

freed and the culprits gave themselves up.
July 31: Several hostages were taken at the Iraqi embassy in Paris by two armed Arabs. One kidnapper fled, and the other's demands for the release of an Arab in the United Kingdom were refused. The hostages were freed and the Arab surrendered. However, a shootout ensued after the surrender and one hostage was killed and three others were wounded.
Aug. 17: Eight hostages were taken at the West German consulate in Chicago by two Croatians who demanded that a Croatian in Cologne be freed and that he not be extradited to Yugoslavia. Later, the hostages were freed and the two gave themselves up.
Oct. 4: Tammy Wynette, country singer, was kidnapped in Nashville, Tenn., for two hours and then freed. The kidnapper has not been caught.
Dec. 11: Robert Piest, fifteen, was abducted, sodomized, and murdered by John Wayne Gacy. The search for Piest led to Gacy's arrest and conviction for twenty-seven murders.
1979
Jan. 16: More than 100 hostages were taken from the Mexican embassy, Red Cross, and the Organization of American States in El Salvador by United Popular Action Front terrorists who demanded the release of prisoners and other political concessions. The hostages were released and the terrorists left the country.
Feb. 14: About 100 hostages were seized at the U.S. embassy in Teheran by radicals for approximately two hours. Before they left, an Iranian worker at the embassy was slain.
Mar. 8: Frankie and Tammy Galleshaw, children of a wealthy Burrillville, R.I., restaurant owner, were kidnapped by three of their father's golfing companions. While Michael Ballard and Allen Gomet were demanding $500,000 ransom, the teenagers persuaded Salvatore Savastano to free them.
Mar. 27: The Egyptian embassy in Teheran was taken over by Arab students who did not support the Egyptian-Israeli peace treaty.
Mar. 27: The Egyptian embassy in Kuwait was taken over by Palestinians who objected to the Egyptian-Israeli peace treaty.
Mar. 27: The ambassador at the Egyptian embassy in Dacca, Bangladesh, was seized for a few hours by Arab terrorists who were against the conclusion of the Egyptian-Israeli peace treaty.
Apr. 28: The body of Terry Lee Chasteen, of Indianapolis, Ind., and her three children were found. Steven Judy had kidnapped the four and raped the woman. He was executed.
May 4: The Metropolitan Cathedral in San Salvador was seized by Popular Revolutionary Bloc terrorists who demanded the release of five people in El Salvador and an investigation of reported human rights violations in El Salvador. Seventeen people died and thirty-five were injured when police raided the building.
May 4: Five hostages were taken at the Costa Rican embassy in El Salvador by Popular Revolutionary Bloc terrorists who wanted freedom for five El Salvador prisoners and an investigation of reported El Salvador human rights violations. The hostages escaped and the terrorists were allowed to leave the country.
May 4: Six hostages were taken at the French embassy in San Salvador by Popular Revolutionary Bloc terrorists who wanted five people in El Salvador released and an investigation of reported human rights violations in El Salvador. An embassy guard was wounded.
May 7: Mrs. Harry Chaddick, wife of a Chicago real estate developer, is kidnapped in Palm Springs, Calif. FBI agents rescued her and killed the kidnappers.
May 11: Eight hostages were taken at the Venezuelan embassy in San Salvador by Popular Revolutionary Bloc terrorists who wanted five El Salvador prisoners freed and an investigation of reported El Salvador human rights violations. Five hostages fled and the terrorists were permitted to leave El Salvador.
May 15: Farabundo Marti Popular Liberation Forces terrorists failed to take over the South African embassy in San Salvador. Two police officers died in a shootout and the terrorists escaped.
June 15: William Rocha, Nicaraguan manager of National Cash Register, was abducted in San Salvador, El Sal., and later released.
June 26: About fifteen hostages were taken at the Mexican embassy in Guatemala by native workers who wanted Guatemala to account for a labor leader that had vanished.
July 13: Twenty hostages were seized at the Egyptian embassy in Ankara, Turk., by Palestinian terrorists who wanted Turkey to cease diplomatic avenues with Egypt and other political concessions. One hostage was freed, four others escaped, and the terrorists gave themselves up.
Oct. 16: Alonzo Daniels was kidnapped from his house in Salt Lake City by Arthur Gary Bishop, who was executed after conviction on multiple murder and kidnapping charges.
Oct. 30: About 300 leftwing gunmen unsuccessfully tried to take over the U.S. embassy in San Salvador. Two U.S. Marines were injured.
Oct. 30: Alfredo Battaglia, son of a well-to-do jeweler, was abducted in Bovalino, Italy. The kidnappers received $300,000 and the teen was freed.
Oct. 31: The Guatemalan embassy in San Salvador was the target of an unsuccessful takeover by unknown assailants.
Sept. 21: Dennis McDonald, executive of Aplar, and Fausto Buchelli were abducted in San Salvador, El Sal., by terrorists whose demands for placing ads in newspapers were me and the men were freed.
Nov. 4: Sixty-three hostages were taken at the U.S. embassy in Teheran by Iranian radicals who demanded the return to Iran of the Shah of Iran. Though their demands were not met and a rescue attempt failed, the hostages were later released.
Nov. 5: Twenty-seven hostages were seized at the British embassy in Teheran by activists who made no demands and left the embassy.
1980
Jan. 11: Seven hostages were taken at the Panamanian embassy in San Salvador by about fifty February 28 Popular League terrorists whose demands for the release of other terrorists were met. The hostages were freed.
Jan. 31: Eight hostages were taken at the Spanish embassy in Guatemala City by protesters and left-wing terrorists. During a fight with police, the building was set on fire and only one protester and the Spanish ambassador survived.
Feb. 4: Eleven hostages were taken at the Spanish embassy in San Salvador by February 28 Popular League terrorists who demanded that El Salvador free several prisoners and that Spain cease diplomatic relations with El Salvador. The prisoners and hostages were released.
Feb. 13: Three hostages were seized at the Panamanian embassy in San Salvador by left-wing radicals. The Panamanian ambassador agreed to try to win the release of several prisoners in El Salvador and the radicals left.
Feb. 27: Fifty-seven hostages were taken at the Dominican Republic embassy in Bogotá, Col., by M-19 terrorists who wanted a $50 million ransom and political concessions. They agreed to $2 million ransom and permission to leave the country. One diplomat escaped and others were freed.
Feb. 28: The Salvadoran embassy in Panama City was taken over for three and a half hours by Panamanian students who wanted some of their associates freed.
Apr. 27: Jack Miller, Jr. was kidnapped from his father's home in Schaumburg, Ill. When he was rescued, he was in the company of his mother, Lillian Miller, and Charles Lurie, who were charged with child abduction.
Apr. 30: Twenty-six hostages were taken at the Iranian embassy in London by Arabs from Iran who demanded freedom for prisoners held in Iran. Two hostages were slain, five freed, and the others rescued in a raid by British authorities. Two Arabs died and the other three were arrested, one of whom died.
May 29: Edward Kvavli, a wealthy Illinois real estate investor, was abducted and released by kidnappers who demanded that he raise $600,000. Police arrested Leo Bonuini and Trenton Nelson, who tried to collect the money.
June 8: Oron Yarden, a boy from a well-to-do Tel Aviv suburb, was abducted and slain by kidnappers who received $40,000 ransom. They were never caught.
June 12: The president of a subsidiary of Nestle in Guatemala was abducted in Guatemala City by FAR terrorists who allegedly received $4.7 million. The executive was later freed.
June 27: Guards rescued Sergeant Stan Fitts, who had been taken hostage by inmates at the Oregon State Penitentiary. Six convicts were injured.
Sept. 15: According to reports, Serbian terrorists planned to kidnap or assassinate Edward R. Vrdolyak, Chicago alderman, on or near this date.
Sept. 15: According to reports, Serbian terrorists planned to assault the Yugoslavian consulate in Chicago and take hostages on or near this date.
October: A British diplomat and Quebec cabinet minister were abducted by members of the Quebec Liberation Front. The diplomat was freed but the minister was killed.
November: Countess Giovanna di Porta Puglia was rescued from the castle of Castell'Arguato, south of Milan, Italy, after she was held captive for more than forty years. Her brothers, Luigi and Alfredo Puglia, and Luigi's wife, were arrested.
Nov. 14: Sixteen children, a school bus driver, and a teacher were taken hostage in Vielsalm, Belg., by Mark Frank, Michael Stree, and another hijacker, who demanded social reforms. They drove the bus to Brussels where police captured them.
Nov. 27: Carmen Ortiz, a first-grader, was abducted, murdered, and sexually assaulted in Chicago by Jose Davis, a man who lived in her building. Davis later admitted to the crime.
Nov. 27: Kim Peterson was kidnapped by Arthur Gary Bishop, who was executed after conviction on multiple murder and kidnapping charges.
Dec. 2: Gianluca Grimaldi, son of a shipping magnate, was abducted in Naples and later released.
Dec. 7: Clifford Bevens, U.S. manager of a Goodyear subsidiary, Ginsa Tire, was kidnapped from his Guatemala City apartment and $10 million ransom was demanded. Bevens and five kidnappers died when soldiers attacked the hideout.
Dec. 12: Giovanni D'Urso, magistrate, was abducted in Rome by Red Brigade terrorists who demanded that the prison at Asinara be shut down. He was later released.
1981
Dr. Julio Iglesias, father of singer Julio Iglesias, was kidnapped by December 29-ETA terrorists who demanded $2 million ransom. He was later freed in Trasmoz, Spain.
Tanya Nix, fourteen, and Valerie M. Sellers, seventeen, were kidnapped

and slain in Richland, Ga., in what authorities believe were related cases. The killers were not found.
Jan. 18: Facundo Guardado, Salvadoran terrorist, was apprehended by the Hondurus' National Intelligence Division. After he was freed, he asserted that he had been kidnapped and tortured.
Jan. 19: Chester A. Bitterman III, U.S. linguist, was abducted from the Summer Institute of Linguistics in Bogota, Col., by terrorists who claimed he was a CIA agent. Bitterman was slain.
Feb. 3: Lori Hocum was kidnapped from her home in Metairie, La., and found in a shopping mall the same day. Her father, Ronald Hocum, was convicted for masterminding the plot. No ransom was demanded.
Feb. 6: Hisham al-Moheisen, the Jordanian charge d'affaires in Beirut, and his maid were kidnapped from his apartment, apparently by the Organization of the National Confrontation Front. He was later freed.
Feb. 13: Perez Concha, Ecuadorean ambassador, and others were taken hostage at the Ecuadorean embassy in Havana, Cuba, by about thirty Cubans who wanted political asylum and to leave Cuba. Their demands were refused and they were apprehended.
Feb. 19: The honorary consuls of Uruguay, Gabriel Biurrum, of Austria, Hermann Diez de la Sel Korsatko, and of El Salvador, Antonio Amparo Fernandez, were abducted in Spain by ETA terrorists and later freed.
Feb. 22: A 27-year-old woman from Steger, Ill., a suburb of Chicago, was kidnapped and raped. She was later rescued and two men were charged in the case.
Apr. 1: Monique Huguette Gauthier, Canadian biologist in San Salvador, El Sal., disappeared and may have been kidnapped.
Apr. 14: Francis Tiernan was abducted from his Foukhill, South Armagh house and the IRA took credit.
Apr. 27: Ciro Cirillo, commissioner of the regional government of Campania, Italy, was going to his house in Naples when he was abducted by Red Brigades terrorists. Ransom of about $1 million was reportedly paid and Cirillo was freed.
May 1: Fluvio Alirio Mejia Milian, a journalist, was kidnapped. He was found dead two weeks later.
May 8: Teofilo Siman, vice-president of the El Salvador Red Cross, was kidnapped at his home in San Salvador by armed men.
May 15: Three terrorists were sentenced in West Berlin for kidnapping Walter Palmers, Austrian businessman, and Peter Lorenz, a Christian Democratic politician.
May 19: Three teenagers were kidnapped and murdered in the Vancouver, British Columbia, area by unknown assailants between May 19 and July 30.
May 20: Cesare Menasci, heir to a clothing business, was kidnapped in Rome.
May 20: Giuseppe Tagliercio, an administrator of a Montedison petrochemical firm, was kidnapped from his apartment in Mestre, Italy, by members of the Red Brigades and was later found dead.
June 3: Renzo Sandrucci, administrator of Alfa Romeo Motor Co., was abducted by Red Brigades terrorists whose demands for his resignation were met. He was released in Milan.
June 4: Edwin Paz Belteton, brother-in-law of Nery Grauc, reportedly tried to escape from kidnappers and was killed in Guatemala.
June 4: Nery Lucas Grauc, nephew of Fernando Romeo Lucas Garcia, president of Guatemala, was kidnapped in Guatemala by armed men.
June 17: Julio Cesar Difuentes Anleu, head of planning for the National Electrification Institute in Guatemala City, was abducted and he was later found dead.
June 26: Four Fijans with a military force in Lebanon were abducted from their headquarters in Kana by Palestinian Liberation Organization members. Four were murdered, two of them trying to escape.
July 17: Mirta Corsetti, was kidnapped in Torvaianica, Italy, from her millionaire father's restaurant by four men. Police freed the girl, found $250,000 of the ransom, and arrested six.
July 27: Adam Walsh, six, was kidnapped from a department store and found dead close to Fort Pierce, Fla.
Aug. 2: Reverend Carlos Perez Alonzo (Alonso), Spanish Jesuit, was abducted in Guatemala and later freed.
Aug. 24: Hostages were taken at the Iranian embassy in a Stockholm, Swed., suburb, by Iranian students who demanded political concessions. The students were arrested by riot police and the Iranian ambassador and his wife were freed.
Aug. 25: Claude Jacqueman, French diplomat, was kidnapped by armed men in Beirut who diverted his journey to work, took his car, and then freed him.
Aug. 31: Roquelino Recinos Mendez, minister of public health of Guatemala, was kidnapped in Guatemala City by armed men and later freed.
Sept. 14: E.R. Okrimiuk, a Soviet geologist working in Afghanistan, was kidnapped by Hezbe Islami guerrillas who wanted the release of fifty insurgents.
Sept. 24: Fifteen drivers operating Turkish trucks were abducted along the Turco-Iraqi highway by Iraqis.
Oct. 12: Three Iranians who were to buy arms were abducted in London.
Oct. 16: Ben Dunne, owner of supermarkets and department stores, was abducted in Northern Ireland.
Oct. 20: Danny Davis was kidnapped by Arthur Gary Bishop, who was executed after conviction on multiple murder and kidnapping charges.
Nov. 19: Helen Lavalley and Jean Reimer, Catholic nuns from the U.S., were on their way from Panjachel to Acatenango, when they disappeared in Guatemala.
Dec. 14: Alfonso Lopez, ex-president of Columbia, and Belisario Betancur, Conservative Party member, were the targets of kidnapping plots by guerrillas, according to the Columbian government report.
Dec. 17: James L. Dozier, U.S. general and chief U.S. Army officer at the Verona headquarters of NATO, was abducted in Verona, Italy, by Red Brigades terrorists. He was rescued by police and numerous Red Brigades members were sent to prison.
Dec. 17: Moises Carril Maquehue, math teacher from Chile, and John Burlison, ecologist from England, were kidnapped from the Wildlife School at the Gorongosa National Park in Mozambique.

1982

Jan. 1: Fifty residents of San Francisco El Tablon, Guat., were kidnapped, and most were tortured and shot to death.
Jan. 5: Jose Lipperheide, a Basque businessman, was abducted near Bilbao, Spain by ETA terrorists who received about $1.2 million. The industrialist was later freed after the ransom was paid.
Jan. 5: Reverends Roberto Paredes, of Guatemala, and Paul Gerard Schildermans, of Belgium, were abducted in Nuevo Concepcion, Guat.
Jan. 6: Sister Victoria de la Roca was kidnapped in Esquipalas, Guat.
Jan. 13: Rabeh Jerwa, minister plenipotentiary of the Algerian Embassy in Beirut, Leb., was abducted from his apartment in west Beirut and fatally shot.
Jan. 26: Jacobo Ramon Larach, general manager of the Pepsi Cola bottling company in San Pedro Sula, Hond., was fatally shot when kidnappers tried to seize him.
Jan. 29: Roberto Palomo Salazar, industrialist, was the target of a failed kidnapping attempt in Costa Rica in which three leftists were slain and three others were arrested.
Feb. 4: Ana Maria Martinez, a member of the leftist Socialist Workers Party, was abducted in a suburb of Buenos Aires, Arg., and slain.
Feb. 6: Peter Lengene, citizen of South Africa residing in Botswana, was purportedly abducted in Botswana by security officials of South Africa.
Feb. 8: Tommy Manotoc, son-in-law of Ferdinand Marcos, president of the Philippines, was found in an area about fifty-five miles east of Manila after having been kidnapped.
Feb. 24: One hundred and five passengers are held hostage by twelve Shiite Muslim gunmen aboard a hijacked Kuwaiti B-707. The hijackers surrender Syrian troops in Beruit and the hostages are freed unharmed.
Feb. 26: Eighty-two people are held hostage when a Tanzanian plane is hijacked to Kenya, Saudi Arabia, Greece, and England. The hostages are released but four passengers suffer shock and the co-pilot is wounded.
Mar. 1: One hundred and one people aboard a United B-727 flying from Chicago to Miami are briefly held hostage by a hijacker demanding to go to Cuba. The man is subdued and the flight went on to Miami.
April: Jean-Edern Hallier, a left-wing author, was abducted by members of the French Revolutionary Brigades who demanded the french minister of the interior and four Communist ministers be discharged.
Apr. 3: Wanda Faye Reddick was found dead. The teenager had been kidnapped a few days before from her home in Richland, Ga.
Apr. 26: Four people were kidnapped by James B. Moran in Akron, Ohio, and forced to go with him to Pittsburgh. There he kidnapped another woman and drove her and her car to Aurora, Colo. He was later sent to prison.
Apr. 27: Frances Julia Slater, an heiress, was kidnapped in Stuart, Fla., during a robbery by J.B. Parker, Alphonso Cave, and two others. The teen was slain and the men were convicted.
May 12: Eight people including ambassador Antonio Carlos de Abreu e Silva are taken hostage at the Brazilian embassy in Guatemala City, to protest the new military government. The hostages were freed and the terrorist flown to Mexico.
June 15: A businessman's wife was apparently abducted in Spain by ETA terrorists.
June 22: Victor Kaire Bassin, the member of a well-known banking family, was kidnapped in Guatemala City.
June 22: Julio Flores Toledo, an exporter of coffee, was kidnapped at gunpoint in Guatemala City.
June 23: Ricardo Mendez, son of the Guatemalan minister of the interior, was abducted near the University of San Carlos in Guatemala.
June 24: Horacio Ruiz, an editor of *La Prensa* in Managua, Nic., was abducted by four armed men and beaten.
July: Marta Corsetti was kidnapped in Rome. No ransom was paid and she was released.
July 12: Fiona Brown, whose husband was involved in failed bomb plot in Ireland, was last seen at her Twinbrook house and was suspected to have been kidnapped by IRA Provos.
July 14: Dutch Prime minister Andries van Agt and Queen Beatrix were apparently the target of a kidnapping plot, which was detected by police.
July 19: David Dodge, president of the American University of Beirut, was on his way to work when he was abducted by armed men.
July 23: Six western tourists were abducted in Zimbabwe by gunmen demanding the release of Joshua Nkumo.
July 28: Mauricio Cuellar, administrator of the Salvadoran Industry Association, and his daughter, Patricia, were abducted in El Salvador.

Aug. 1: Alison Jones and Richard and Nicola Prankard, British tourists, were found dead in Zimbabwe after having been kidnapped about two weeks previously.
Aug. 13: Dr. Hector Zevalloses, abortion clinic operator, and his wife were abducted in Edwardsville, Ill., but later freed by anti-abortionist Army of God members under Don Benny Anderson, several of whom were sent to prison.
Aug. 31: Six Bulgarian civil engineers were purportedly abducted by guerrillas in Mozambique who wanted members of their group released from prison.
Oct. 3: Gaby Kiss Maerth, teenaged daughter of a British businessman, was released by her kidnappers in Como, Italy, after they allegedly received $119,000 of the demanded $3.5 million ransom.
Oct. 22: Five leaders of the leftist Democratic Revolutionary Front in El Salvador are reported kidnapped.
Nov. 3: Maria Josefina Morales de Palozzi, publisher of *Quorum*, was the target of an attempted kidnapping in Buenos Aires, Arg.
Dec. 5: One hundred and thirty-seven people on a bus bound for a soccer game are kidnapped by Salvadoran rebels trying to recruit forces for their ranks. One person is killed trying to escape, the rest are freed within a few days.
Dec. 14: Dr. Judith Xiomara Suazo Estrada, daughter of the president of Honduras, was going to a hospital in Guatemala City when she was kidnapped by terrorists. She was released after their leftist manifesto was printed by the government.

1983

Jan. 13: Robert S. Hester, Memphis police officer, was taken hostage by six religious cult members under Lindberg Sanders. Hester was slain and about twelve hours later a Memphis SWAT team killed all of the kidnappers.
Jan. 19: Eleanor M. Mitchell was arrested in Baltimore, Md., on charges of kidnapping elderly men, drugging them, and robbing them.
Feb. 28: Kenneth Bishop, U.S. executive of an oil company, was kidnapped and two bodyguards were slain in Bogota, Col.
June 22: Troy Ward was kidnapped by Arthur Gary Bishop, who was executed after conviction on multiple murder and kidnapping charges.
July: Emanuela Orlandi, teenaged son of a low-ranking Vatican official, was abducted by terrorists who demanded the release of Mehmet Ali Agca, who injured Pope John Paul II.
July 14: Graeme Cunningham was kidnapped by Arthur Gary Bishop, who was executed after conviction on multiple murder and kidnapping charges.

1984

Robert Biddings was charged with assaults of nineteen women that occurred between 1984 and 1988. He was convicted for forty counts of kidnapping, rape, and aggravated robbery.
February: An Indian diplomat was abducted and killed in Birmingham, Eng., by the Kashmiri Liberation Army (KLA).
May 29: Vernita Wheat of Kenosha, Wis., was abducted and strangled by Alton Coleman in a series of murders, robberies, and rapes. Coleman and Debra Brown were given multiple sentences, including death sentences.
June 30: Hernán Siles Zuazo, president of Bolivia, was kidnapped during a coup attempt. The kidnappers apparently were members of a narcotics police squad. The leader was freed.
July 5: Umaru Dikko, ex-cabinet member of Nigeria, was abducted from his house in London, but he was rescued by police at an airport.
July 6: Between July 6 and Aug. 5, 1987, six men were held prisoner, tortured, and murdered by Robert Berdella in the Kansas City, Mo. area. After another victim escaped, Berdella was sent to prison for life.
Oct. 19: Jerzy Popieluzsko, backer of the Polish trade union Solidarity, was kidnapped by Polish secret police and later found dead.

1985

Feb. 7: Enrique Camarena Salazar, U.S. drug enforcement agent, and Alfredo Zavala Avelar, his pilot, were kidnapped in Mexico, tortured, and slain by Raul López Alvarez and two others acting on the orders of drug king Rafael Cáro Quintero.
Mar. 16: Terry Anderson, journalist, was kidnapped in Lebanon by Islamic Jihad members. As of this writing, he is still captive.
Mar. 28: A reporter from Beirut was abducted in Lebanon. The kidnapping was attributed to the Abu Nidal group.
June 7: Twenty Finns in UNIFIL were abducted by members of the South Lebanon Army who demanded the release of eleven SLA members, who actually had defected. When the truth was learned, the Finns were freed.
Sept. 10: The daughter of José Napoleón Duarte, president of El Salvador, was kidnapped by guerrillas.
Sept. 30: Four diplomats of the U.S.S.R. were kidnapped in Beirut, Leb., by Sunnis who demanded that the U.S.S.R. force Syria to halt attacks on Tripoli. One diplomat, Arkady Kathov, was slain and the other three were freed.

1986

Apr. 17: Two British citizens and a U.S. citizen who had been kidnapped were slain in Beirut after the U.S. and England bombed two Libyan cities, a response to Libya's bombing of a disco in West Berlin.
June 20: After France altered its Middle East policy, two people in a hostage French television crew were freed. Another was released on Dec. 24.
Oct. 27: Two children, Samuel Johnson, Jr. and Emmanuel Dalieh, were abducted at a parade in Harper City, Liberia, Africa, for sacrificial use by several people, including Joshua Bedell and Samuel Cummings. They were all sentenced to death.
Nov. 11: After France promised to repay some of a $1 billion loan to Iran, two Frenchmen kidnapped in Lebanon were freed in Syria.

1987

Jan. 12: Bakr Damanhuri, a Saudi diplomat, was abducted in Beruit, Leb.
Jan. 13: Roger Augue, a French journalist, was abducted in Beruit, Leb.
Jan. 16: Ecuador President Cordero was abducted by kidnappers whose demands for the release of General Vargas were met. Cordero was freed. The kidnappers were later jailed.
Jan. 17: Rudolf Cordes, West German businessman, was abducted in Beirut, Leb.
Jan. 20: Alfred Schmidt, West German engineer, was kidnapped in Beirut, Leb., and later freed.
Jan. 20: Terry Waite, a special envoy to the Archbishop of Canterbury, met with terrorist intermediaries in Beruit, Leb., and was abducted.
Jan. 24: Four professors at the Beirut University College in west Beirut, Leb., Alann Steen, Mithileshwar Singh, Jesse Turner, and Robert Polhill, were abducted and Islamic Jihad for the Liberation of Palestine demanded that the U.S. acknowledge Palestinian rights.
Apr. 27: Larry Gene Bell was sentenced to die for the kidnap-murder of Debra May Helmick, who had been abducted from her house in Richland Co., S.C.
Apr. 28: An Iranian consul officer was arrested after a British diplomat was kidnapped in Tehran.
May: A British diplomat in Beruit, Leb., was held hostage for twenty-four hours by Iranians.
May 17: Maybelle Martin, a modeling agent, Dorothy Walsh, and two teenaged modeling students left Reno, Nev., to go to Lake Tahoe with Herbert James Coddington. There, he murdered Martin and Walsh and sexually attacked the students. He was convicted and sentenced to death.
June 8: Julie Magliulo, a toddler, was abducted and she was later found dead near Broward County, Fla.
June 18: Charles Glass, a reporter, and Ali Osseiran, son of the defense minister of Lebanon, were abducted in Beirut. Osseiran was freed on June 24.

1988

Farabundo Marti National Liberation Front guerrillas carried out terrorists acts in El Salvador, including kidnapping four mayors in early 1988 to try interfere with elections.
January: A divorced Jordanian man illegally took his daughter, Lauren Mahone, to Jordan. Her mother, Cathy Phelps Mahone, with the help of antiterrorist experts, successfully seized her from a school bus in Jordan.
Jan. 25: Carlos Hoyos, attorney general of Colombia, was abducted and killed outside Medellin, Col., by drug traffickers. Two of his bodyguards were also slain.
February: Seventeen employees of a Lumberton, N.C., newspaper were seized by Tuscarora Indian Eddie Hatcher and Timothy Jacobs, whose demands for a gubernatorial inquiry of alleged maltreatment of Native Americans and blacks by the local sheriff were agreed to.
February: Eighty students and four teachers were held hostage at a school in Tuscaloosa, Ala., by James Harvey and John Rhodes, who wanted to gain attention for the homeless and unemployed. They gave up and were arrested..
February: Lucas Mangope, president of Bophuthatswana, a homeland established by South Africa, was seized by insurgents during a coup attempt. He was rescued by South African forces and reinstated to power.
Mar. 6: The body of prostitute Kimberly Ann Hanlon was found in a freezer in the home of James W. Bailey. She had been seized, raped, and shot several years earlier. Bailey, Irvin Riley, and James Whyte were sent to prison.
May 21: Jan Marcel Maria Robert Cools, a Belgian physician, was abducted near Tyre, Leb., and the Soldiers of Justice Organization claimed responsibility.
July 13: William Hope (AKA: Ernest Holt), Chicago gang leader, was arrested on charges of giving orders to abduct and beat three of his own gang members after they sold guns to members of another gang.
November: After mercenaries failed in a coup attempt in the Maldives, a group of islands near India, they held approximately thirty hostages on a cargo ship.
Nov. 30: Lotti Margaret "Maggie" Rhodes, a child from Arlington, Texas, was kidnapped from her home, raped, and murdered. Jackie Barron Wilson was tried.

LOOTING

390 B.C.
July 18: Rome, after being defeated, was abandoned by its citizens. It was seized by the Gauls, looted, then burned, and the senators were killed.
79 A.D.
Aug. 24: Hundreds of years after Naples' Mount Vesuvius volcano erupted, archaeologists discovered many well-preserved victims in Pompeii, many of whom, clutching handfuls of valuables, were apparently in the process of looting.
1069
Devastation following the Norman Conquest and the great famine of 1069 resulted in massive looting by bands who stole valuables and food from the homes and bodies of victims.
1203
Following the revolt of the Greek population, and the capture by the Latin empire of the city of Constantinople, there was plundering, and fires destroyed many pieces of ancient literature.
1348
The Black Death, or bubonic plague, swept through Asia, Africa, and Europe, leaving 22 million people dead. Survivors looted the affected areas.
1568
Pervasive destruction of churches accompanied the War of Liberation in the Netherlands.
1644
Sept. 13: Widespread looting followed the entrance of James Graham Montrose, First Marquess, into Aberdeen, Scot., during the Great Rebellion.
1688
During the Third War's invasion and devastation of the Palatinate, the entire country, extending to the Alsace borders, was pillaged and burned.
1755
Nov. 1: An earthquake and consequential seismic sea wave and fire destroyed the prison in Lisbon, Port., from which hundreds of criminals escaped. Many set fires and looted homes. They were captured and hanged.
1761
The five India invasions by Ahmad Shah Durani, the Afghan ruler of Kandahar, resulted in the destruction and looting of the city of Delhi.
1765
March: With the passage of the Stamp Act in the U.S., and the arrival of stamp officers, the people started to riot and ransack houses.
1806
Nov. 10: After Napoleon seized Berlin, picture galleries and museums were robbed of their treasures.
1871
Oct. 8: The massive fire that virtually wiped out Chicago set off widespread looting, especially in the red-light district known as Conley's Patch. Jacob Klein, dry goods store owner, suffered a crushed skull at the hands of looters seeking two bolts of cloth.
1875
Dec. 6: After the *Deutschland,* a huge passenger liner on its way to the U.S., crashed into England's Kentish Knock shoals during a storm, looters searched victims, mainly poor immigrants, for wedding rings, watches, and small amounts of money. Many looters were imprisoned.
1889
May 31: Looters waded through the water that had finally settled after the 100-foot-high earthen dam above Johnstown, Pa., broke. As many as a dozen looters were sent to prison.
1895
Sept. 30: As a result of Armenian demonstrations at Constantinople, thousands were massacred by the Kurds, Circassians, and Turkish soldiers, leaving hundreds of thousands destitute from extensive pillaging that lasted throughout the year.
1900
Sept. 8: Looters rumaged through Galveston, Texas, following a hurricane until the mayor assembled troops against the plunderers, and in a ruthless effort against them, instructed the troops to shoot at will. Approximately 500 people were executed.
1902
April: As the result of labor strikes throughout Russia, famine was the motivation behind the looting of large estates.
May 8: The eruption of the volcano Pelée on Martinique island destroyed St. Pierre and the surrounding villages and spurred rampant looting. Twenty-seven people caught prying open safes were arrested. Two looters were killed.
1903
Dec. 23: Looters searched for valuables among the sixty-four bodies following a Pennsylvania passenger train derailment. The looters were arrested.
1906
Apr. 18: Plundering followed a massive San Francisco earthquake. Mayor Eugene E. Schmitz ordered execution squads to take action against the pillagers. More than 100 were killed for alleged looting.
1908
Dec. 28: An underwater earthquake in the Strait of Messina left 160,000 dead in Messina, Reggio di Calabria, and the surrounding area. Looters combed through the rubble. Russian sailors were ordered to execute approximately 500 of the looters.
1911
September: Following a flood in which the Yangtze River engulfed Shanghai and four surrounding Chinese provinces, killing at least 100,000 in the 700 square miles affected, hundreds pillaged for food.
1913
Mar. 23: Looters discovered searching through homes destroyed by one of the worst tornadoes in Omaha, Neb., were arrested by National Guard troops.
1919
Sept. 9: Looters took advantage of a Boston police strike, freely stealing from shops in daylight. Governor Calvin Coolidge ordered troops in to combat the crime.
1923
Much looting was reported following the Great Kwanto Earthquake which destroyed Japan's entire Eastern Plain, wiping out the Tokyo-Yokohama region. The Black Dragon Society blamed Koreans for the looting, arrested more than 4,000 of them, and had them beheaded.
1924
June 28: Lorain, Ohio's chief of police gave policemen orders to shoot to kill anyone seen looting dead bodies following a brutal tornado which left 700 office buildings and homes ruined. Many were arrested but no one was shot.
1925
Sept. 3: When the dirigible *Shenandoah* was ripped apart in an Ava, Ohio, storm, leaving fourteen crew members dead, looters swarmed over the ruins allegedly for souvenirs. Gunfire used to keep looters away served only as a warning; no one was shot.
1946
June 5: Pillagers crowded the wreckage following the La Salle Hotel fire in Chicago. Looters stole wallets and jewelry. Several were arrested, including two men found with suitcases full of stolen goods valued at $200,000.
1953
Apr. 14: An unidentified looter yelled, "Fire!" in a crowded Caracas, Venez., church, starting a stampede. Fifty-three people died, twenty-two of them children. The looter stole valuables from the bodies.
1959
Sept. 26: Hurricane *Vera* ravished Nagoya, Japan, killing more than 5,000 persons. Looters searched bodies and homes for goods. At least 100 looters were executed.
1960
May 21: Earthquakes in central Chile spurred volcanic eruptions which killed almost 6,000 persons. Homeless victims looted for food and were killed by troops.
1964
July 16: Looters descended on Harlem, N.Y., stores after a 15-year-old boy was shot to death and a looter was killed by police officers. A full-fledged race riot ensued and 140 more people were injured.
1977
Jan. 31: Following a heavy snowfall in Buffalo, N.Y., dozens of homes, businesses, and stalled vehicles were looted by thieves. Police borrowed snowmobiles and four wheel drive trucks, but were unable to keep up with the looters.
1978
Sept. 25: A Pacific Southwest Airlines jet collided with a small private plane over a residential section of San Diego, killing 144 persons. The bodies and aircraft were looted. Fifteen were arrested and released.
1982
July 17: Fifteen gunmen killed Peruvian governor Zenon Palomino Flores, fifty-five, in Callera and then looted stores in the mountain village.
Aug. 20: An estimated $4 million worth of valuables was looted throughout Lima, Peru, during an Aug. 20-22 blackout caused by Sendero Luminoso blasts.
Nov. 27: Thousands of anti-Ku Klux Klan demonstrators vandalized downtown Washington, D.C., and looted stores during a Klan rally in Lafayette Park.

LYNCHING AND VIGILANTISM

As a method of vigilante "justice" commonly practiced in the United States, lynching dates back to the settlement of the original thirteen colonies. In Pennsylvania during the French and Indian War, for example, Dutch-German settlers seized twenty Conestoga Indians, including women and children, near Lancaster in 1763, and hanged them without benefit of trial. This incident was not the first reported lynching in North America. The name was borrowed from two Virginians, Colonel Charles Lynch and Captain William Lynch who seem to have initiated the practice years earlier.

In the 1830s the Vicksburg Volunteers employed the technique against the riverboat card sharps and "blacklegs" corrupting the citizens of that city. Twenty years later, the San Francisco Vigilance Committees, which enjoyed a measure of popular support among California legislators, took the law into their own hands, and snatched a number of criminals from their jail cells, hanging them in a public place. In Montana during the Civil War there was a fresh outbreak of lynching when a vigilante group seized twenty-six members of the Innocents outlaw gang and hanged them.

Since the Civil War the practice has been confined mostly to the southern part of the U.S. The Ku Klux Klan, in particular, has used it as an instrument of terror against black Americans, Jews, Catholics, various left-wing groups, and during National Prohibition, bootleggers. A study conducted by the Tuskegee Institute estimates that of 4,672 persons lynched between 1882 and 1936, nearly three-quarters of them 3,383—were black. Between 1886 and 1916, the height of Ku Klux Klan activity in the South, 2,605 blacks were lynched. From 1930 until 1937 the rural South accounted for 97 percent of all reported lynchings in the U.S. With the advent of the Civil Rights movement after WWII the figures begin to decline; between 1952 and 1954 no lynchings were reported in the South. The 1968 Civil Rights Act, which has since made it a federal offense for two or more persons to conspire to violate a person's constitutional rights, regardless of whether death occurs, has become an effective deterrent against this kind of lawlessness.

13th Century
German Vehmic courts combat anarchy, plundering, and heretical behavior through vigilante style secret courts.
1752
Dec. 18: A vigilante group, the Denomination of "Regulars", dressed in women's clothing and wearing face paint, tortured other men accused of such crimes as wife beating.
1763
December: Fourteen Conestoga Indians accused of scalping white settlers were massacred after a gang of fifty men broke into the Paxtang, Pa., jail, where the Indians were being detained by Quaker lawmen.
1767
October: South Carolina farmers, tired of being beseiged by bandits, retaliate by forming a vigilante group, named the "Regulators". When their efforts became excessive, a counter-vigilante group named the "Moderators" was formed.
1768
Sept. 7: A custom house waiter accused of being an informant to the English crown was tarred and feathered in Salem, Mass.
1768: South Carolina regulators lynched sixteen members of an outlaw band near Mount Airy, N.C.
1769
Nov. 6: A soldier accused of rape was tarred and feathered near Boston.
1780
Sept. 22: William Lynch of Pittsylvania, Va., offers in a manifesto a ritual of vigilante justice to combat lawlessness in the area. The rules became known as Lynch laws, from which the term "lynching" is derived.
1798
Groups of regulators were organized in Tennessee.
1814
A Committee for Vigilance and Safety was formed in Baltimore.
1815
Groups of regulators were organized in St. Louis.
1816
Groups of regulators were organized in Illinois and Kentucky.
1818
Groups of regulators were organized in Indiana and Tennessee.
1820
Groups of regulators were organized in Kentucky.
1825
Groups of regulators were organized in Ohio.
1831
Groups of regulators were organized in Illinois.
1835
Twenty-one alleged outlaws were hanged by regulators in Hinds and Madison counties, Miss.
1837
Groups of regulators were organized in Ohio.
1838
Vigilance committees to aid runaway slaves were formed in New York and Philadelphia.
1840
Regulators pronouncing instant vigilante justice infested Shelby and Harrison counties in Texas, as well as the Oklahoma Indian Territories.
1841
July 14: Charles W. Jackson, accused of murdering a man in cold blood, escapes justice when he enters the Harrison County, Texas, courtroom of Judge John M. Hansford with 150 armed "regulators."
Oct. 9: Two white "Moderator" leaders, "Buckskin Bill" McFaddin and Squire Humphreys, were hanged in Shelbyville, Texas, by 300 "Regulator" sympathizers.
1843
1843: In Shelby County, Texas, a white man named Stanfield was hanged by friends of Samuel Hall, who had been shot to death by Stanfield following allegations of livestock theft.
1843: Henry Runnells, a regulator, was murdered in Texas for his complicity in the murder of Samuel Hall.
1843: James Hall, the brother of Samuel Hall, was murdered in Texas, following the murder of regulator Henry Runnells.
1844
1844: John M. Bradley was murdered by Regulator Watt Moorman in San Augustine Texas.
July 28: Regulators meet in Shelby County, Texas, to order the evacuation of twenty-five Moderators.
Aug. 9: "Colonel" Davidson and as many as fifteen other Regulators were killed when they were ambushed by Moderators in Hilliard Springs, Texas.
1847
May: Twenty-three people died at a wedding reception of a former Regulator in Shelby County, Texas, the result of poisoned food inflicted by a former Moderator.
1851
June 9: The First Committee of Vigilance was formed in San Francisco following the slow process of legal justice, after a series of merchant robberies.
June 10: John Simpton, accused of stealing a safe, was hanged after being pronounced guilty by the Committee of Thirteen in San Francisco.
July 5: A woman named Juanita was lynched in Downieville, Calif., after stabbing a man who was attempting to rape her.
July 11: James Stuart, accused of being an outlaw, was lynched by the Committee of Vigilance in San Francisco.
Aug. 24: Robert McKenzie and Sam Whittaker, accused of murder, were lynched by the Committee of Vigilance in San Francisco.
1856
A group of wealthy cattlemen form the Committee of Vigilance in Leavenworth, Kan.
May 14: The Second Committee of Vigilance was formed in San Francisco following the shooting of a newspaper editor and the police protection of the alleged culprit.
May 22: James P. Casey and Charles Cora, both convicted of murder by the Second Committee of Vigilance, were hanged in San Francisco.
July: Philander Brace and Joseph Hetherington, both accused of murder, were hanged by the Second Committee of Vigilance in San Francisco. Francis Murray "Yankee" Sullivan died of stab wounds while awaiting deportation by the same committee.
1858
In Northern Indiana, a vigilante group of "Regulators" was organized to dispense justice at no cost to the county.
1859
The Denver Vigilantes were formed as a miner's court.
1863
Thirty-five people in Montana accused of being horse thieves were killed with vigilante justice during a two year period, after the local sheriff was suspected of complicity with the thieves.
Dec. 19: George Ives was lynched in Nevada, Mont., after a vigilante trial conducted by a hastily organized Masonic posse following the murder of Nicholas Tiebalt.
Dec. 20: The Montana Vigilantes were formed by five men who took an oath in Virginia City, Mont.
1864
Jan. 4: George Brown and Erastus "Red" Yager, accused of murder by the Montana Vigilantes, were hanged near Virginia City, Mont.
Jan. 10: Ned Ray and Buck Stinson, accused of murder by the Montana Vigilantes, were hanged near Virginia City, Mont.
Jan. 10: Henry Plummer, a lawman accused of complicity with outlaws, was lynched by a vigilante mob in Bannack, Mont.
Jan. 11: "Dutch John" Wagner, accused of attacking a wagon train and horse stealing, was lynched by the Montana Vigilantes near Virginia City, Mont.
Jan. 11: Joe "Greaser" Pizanthia, accused of being an outlaw, was shot to death in his cabin following a shoot-out with the Montana Vigilantes

near Virginia City, Mont.
Jan. 14: Five outlaws: Jack Gallagher, Boone Helm, "Clubfoot" George Lane, Hayes Lyons, and Frank Parish; were hanged by the Montana Vigilantes in Virginia City, Mont.
Jan. 16: Steve Marshland, accused of robbing a wagon train, was hanged by the Montana Vigilantes near Big Hole River, Mont.
Jan. 19: Billy Bunton, accused of being an outlaw, was hanged by the Montana Vigilantes near Cottonwood, Mont.
Jan. 24: George Shears, accused of being an outlaw, was hanged by the Montana Vigilantes near Virginia City, Mont.
Jan. 25: Four men accused of being outlaws: Alex Carter, John Cooper, Cyrus Skinner, and Bob Zachary; were hanged by the Montana Vigilantes near Virginia City, Mont.
January: "Whisky Bill" Graves, accused of being an outlaw, was lynched by the Montana Vigilantes near Fort Owen, Mont.
Feb. 3: Bill Hunter, accused of being an outlaw, was lynched by the Montana Vigilantes near Virginia City, Mont.
Feb. 10: James A. Slade, a rancher who held a gun to the head of a local judge, was lynched by members of the Montana Vigilantes in Virginia City, Mont.
Sept. 19: Tommy Cooke was lynched as a pickpocket in Helena, Mont.

1866
James Daniels, accused of killing a man during a card game, was lynched by vigilantes in Montana.

1868
Four men were victims of vigilante hangings in Cheyenne, Wyo.

1870
Two men were lynched at the "hanging tree" in Helena, Mont.

1877
The Committee of Vigilance resurfaced briefly in San Francisco.

1880
Apr. 15: James Webster Smith, a black West Point cadet, was gagged, bound, beaten, and his ears slit after being taken from his barracks. When he couldn't identify his assailants, he was accused of attacking himself.

1881
William Coons, a white man, was lynched in Lincoln County, N.M., by friends of a man he had recently shot in self-defense.
In Rawlins, Wyo., "Big Nose" George Parrott was lynched by vigilantes, including the future governor of the state, Dr. John E. Osborne.

1882
October: George Johnson was lynched in Tombstone, Ariz., after he was mistakenly thought to have murdered a stage coach passenger during an armed robbery. The victim had died of a heart attack. A tombstone epitaph acknowledged that Johnson had been hanged by mistake.

1883
July: Residents of Miles City, Mont., announced they would retaliate against men threatening to form a vigilante organization.

1884
Thirty-five outlaws were hanged by armed posses in Montana. Theodore Roosevelt, while admitting that some innocent men had been hanged, stated the the mob action was "in the main wholesome."
Feb. 22: John Heath, a white man convicted of murder, was lynched by a mob of miners in Tombstone, Ariz.

1885
January: The Bald Knobbers, a vigilante group comprised of Baptist fundamentalists, was formed in Taney County, Mo.
January: Frank and Tubal Taylor, accused of shooting a local shopkeeper and his wife, were lynched by the Bald Knobbers in Forsyth, Mo.
September: The Christian County Knobbers, a group aligned with the Bald Knobbers, was formed in Missouri.
Sept. 18: Lee Kee Nam, accused of murdering a rival merchant, was lynched with two other men by vigilantes near Pierce City, Idaho.
Nov. 22: The wrong black man was lynched in Madisonville, Texas, after a little girl was trampled by a horse allegedly ridden by the victim. The actual rider escaped.

1886
March: Andrew Cogburn, accused of being a "rowdy", was killed in a duel with Captain Kinney, the Bald Knobbers' leader, in Forsyth, Mo.

1887
Mar. 11: William Edens and Charles Green, accused of making disparaging remarks about the Bald Knobber Vigilantes, were murdered by the group in their cabin at Smelter Hollow, Mo.

1889
Jan. 7: Alfred Shafford, a white man accused of murder, was lynched at Gilman, in the Washington Territory.
Jan. 15: George Meadows, a black man accused of rape, was lynched in Pratt Mines, Ala.
Jan. 15: Dean Reynolds, a black man accused of jilting a girl, was lynched in Arkansas.
Jan. 19: Two men and a woman, all white, accused of robbery and murder, were lynched in Tiptonville, Tenn.
Jan. 21: Henry Thomas, a black man accused of murder, was lynched in Bolar, Mo.
Jan. 25: Samuel Wakefield, a black man accused of murder, was lynched in New Iberia, La.
Jan. 26: William Brewington, a black man accused of murder, was lynched in Wadis Station, S.C.
Feb. 1: A black man named Rosemond, accused of stealing cattle, was lynched in New Iberia, La.
Feb. 5: George Haggerman, a white horse thief, was lynched in Schuyler, Neb.
Feb. 7: An unknown black man accused of rape was lynched in Amite County, Miss.
Feb. 10: Hayward Handy, a black man who defended himself, was lynched in Houghton, La.
Feb. 13: Charles Stein, a white man accused of murder, was lynched in the Oklahoma Territory.
Feb. 19: Two black men accused of murder were lynched in Liberty, Texas.
Feb. 20: Two white men, Asa Bown and W.L. Smith were lynched in San Saba County, Texas.
Feb. 20: John Puckett and his wife were lynched at Lyon Creek, in the Oklahoma Territory.
Feb. 22: D.H. Smith, a black man, was lynched in Artesia, Miss., for attempting to form a black colony.
Feb. 23: Thomas Wesley, a black man accused of attempted rape, was lynched in Port Gibson, Miss.
Feb. 28: A black man named Perkins was lynched in Port Gibson, Miss.
Mar. 5: Three white men accused of stealing horses were lynched at a site unknown.
Mar. 8: J.E. Robinson, a black man accused of rape, was lynched in Texarkana, Ark.
Mar. 14: Magruder Fletcher, a black man accused of rape, was lynched in Tasley, Va.
Mar. 18: B.S. Sprague, a white man accused of murder, was lynched in Garvanza, Calif.
Mar. 28: Three white men named Babcock, Gannon, and Remus, were lynched in Ainsworth, Neb., after being accused of stealing horses.
Apr. 3: Martin Roland, a black man accused of murder, was lynched in Abington, Va.
Apr. 5: John Wolfenberger, a white man accused of murder, was lynched in Rutledge, Tenn.
Apr. 7: Daniel Beeler, a white man accused of murder, was lynched in Rutledge, Tenn.
Apr. 15: George Driggs, a black man accused of rape, was lynched in Hempstead, Texas.
Apr. 18: A black man named Hector accused of murder, was lynched in New Iberia, La.
Apr. 19: An unidentified black man accused of rape was lynched in Bayou Desard, La.
Apr. 23: Scott Bailey, a black man, was lynched in Halifax, Va.
Apr. 23: An unknown black man accused of murder was lynched in Oklahoma.
May 7: Three white brothers named Corber, accused of murder, were lynched in Tiptonville, Mo.
May 17: Tut Danford, a black man, was lynched in Mt. Carmel, S.C., for turning state's evidence.
May 17: An unknown black man suspected of rape was lynched in Millican, Texas.
May 18: An unidentified black man accused of burglary was lynched in Columbia, La.
May 19: A.M. Neely, a black man accused of causing political trouble, was lynched in Forest City, Ark.
May 20: Joseph Thornton, a black man accused of rape, was lynched in Wickliffe, Ky.
May 21: James Mitchell, a black man accused of rape, was lynched in Kosciusko, Miss.
May 22: Noah Dickson, a black man accused of rape, was lynched in Walnut Grove, Ala.
May 22: Frank Pekwek, a white man accused of beating his wife, was lynched in Weston, Neb.
May 27: Albert Martin, a black man accused of rape, was lynched in Port Huron, Mich.
May 31: John T. Newell, a white man, was lynched by vigilantes in Deyapaha County, Neb.
May 31: An unknown black man accused of rape was lynched in Thomastown, Miss.
June 1: Robert Herron, a black man, was lynched in Eureka, Miss.
June 4: Nathaniel Oliphant, a white man accused of murder, was lynched in Topeka, Kan.
June 4: Patrick Cleary, a white man accused of murder, was lynched in Lincoln, Kan.
June 5: Dick Conley and a man named Huey, both black, were lynched in Tangipahoa, La.
June 5: Two white highway robbers were lynched in Marysville, Mont.
June 7: Thomas J. Loyd and E.R. Reynolds, both white men accused of murder, were lynched in Scott County, Tenn.
June 11: John Forbes, a black man suspected of rape, was lynched in Petersburg, Va.
June 12: James Devine and Charles Tennyson, two white men accused of murder, were lynched in Corydon, Ind.
June 13: Armstead Johnson, a black man accused of theft, was lynched in Pine Bluff, Ark.
June 21: Alfred Grizzard, a black man accused of gambling, was lynched in Tiptonville, Mo.

June 22: Andy Caldwell, a black man accused of rape, was lynched in Ridgewater, S.C.
June 22: Nicholas Foley, a white man accused of murder, was lynched in Elgin, Neb.
June 24: Tony Cravasso, a white man, and his brother, were lynched for murder in Shepherdsville, Ky.
June 28: John Hock, a white man accused of murder, was lynched in Piegan, Mont.
June 28: A black man named A. McNight was lynched for quarreling in Union County, S.C.
July 1: An unknown black man accused of rape was lynched in Irwinville, Ga.
July 1: An unknown Indian man accused of rape was lynched in Gravity, Iowa.
July 11: Martin Love, a black man accused of rape, was lynched in Tunnell Hill, Ga.
July 12: Felix Keyes, a black man accused of murder, was lynched in Lafayette, La.
July 12: Prince Luster, a black man accused of rape, was lynched in Iuka, Miss.
July 14: Henry Davis, a black man, was lynched in Waco, Texas.
July 15: H.A. Mandin, a white man accused of horse stealing, was lynched in Bassett, Neb.
July 16: Swan Burres, a black man accused of murder, was lynched in Iuka, Miss.
July 20: James Averill, a cattle rancher and Ella Watson, a prostitute, were hanged in Sweetwater, Wyo. by a group of fellow ranchers who suspected the couple of harboring stolen cattle as well as luxury items, during otherwise poor economic times.
July 20: Peter Willis, a black man accused of rape, was lynched in Warsaw, Ind.
July 20: Three black men accused of murder were lynched in Clinton, Miss.
July 22: Two white men accused of stealing horses were lynched in Kelly, N.M.
July 23: Daniel Malone, a black man accused of rape, was lynched in Covington, Ky.
July 23: James Kelly, a black man accused of rape, was lynched in Paris, Ky.
July 24: John Carter, a white man accused of murder, was lynched in Hinton, W.Va.
July 26: Joseph Chacha, a white man accused of murder, was lynched in Wallace, N.M.
July 26: George Lewis, a black man accused of poisoning well water, was lynched in Belen, Texas.
July 28: George Lindley, a black man, was lynched in Greenville, Texas.
July 31: Thomas Talbot, a black man accused of rape, was lynched in Kemper County, Miss.
Aug. 3: Benjamin Smith, a black man accused of rape, was lynched in La Plata, Mo.
Aug. 14: Keith Bowen, a black man accused of rape, was lynched in Aberdeen, Miss.
Aug. 14: James Brooks, a black man accused of rape, was lynched in Orange, Texas.
Aug. 23: Sherman Lewis, a black man accused of rape, was lynched in Luccalena, Miss.
Aug. 30: Thomas Harris, a white man suspected of burglary, was lynched in Amory, Miss.
Aug. 30: John Turner, a black man, was lynched in Fayetteville, W.Va.
Sept. 2: Two black men accused of murder were lynched in Montevallo, Ala.
Sept. 4: Warren Powers, a black man accused of rape, was lynched in East Point, Ga.
Sept. 9: George Allen, a black man accused of incendiarism, was lynched in Le Flore County, Miss.
Sept. 9: Richard Fisher, a black man accused of stealing horses, was lynched in Hiawatha, Kan.
Sept. 9: John Sigmond, a black man accused of rape, was lynched in Stanley Creek, N.C.
Sept. 10: Two white brothers named Hall, accused of rape and murder, were lynched in West Virginia.
Sept. 11: David Boone, a black man, and Frank Stack, a white, were lynched in Morganton, N.C., after being accused of murder.
Sept. 12: John Davis, a white man accused of murder, was lynched in Stafford, Mo.
Sept. 12: Lewis Mortimer, a black man accused of murder, was lynched in Shell Mound, Miss.
Sept. 16: Samuel Garner, a black man, was lynched in Bluefield, Va.
Sept. 17: George Burke, a black man accused of rape, was lynched in Columbia, Mo.
Sept. 27: John Steele, a black man accused of murder, was lynched in Birmingham, Ala.
Oct. 1: John Duncan, a black man, was lynched in Spring Place, Ga., for living with a white woman.
Oct. 4: Stark, a black man accused of murder, was lynched in Alabama.
Oct. 12: William Moore, a black man accused of throwing stones, was lynched in Jesup, Ga.
Oct. 12: Biggs Robert, a black man accused of rape, was lynched in Hernando, Miss.
Oct. 21: An unknown black man accused of rape was lynched in Lake Comorant, Miss.
Oct. 25: Robert Berrier, a white man accused of murder, was lynched in Lexington, N.C.
Oct. 25: Green McCoy, a white man accused of murder, was lynched in Hamlin, W.Va.
Oct. 26: Joseph Harrold, a black man accused of rape, was lynched near Columbus, Miss.
Oct. 27: Milton Haley, a white man accused of murder, was lynched in Hamlin, W.Va.
Nov. 8: Owen Anderson, a black man accused of attempted rape, was lynched in Leesburg, Va.
Nov. 10: John Thomas, a black man accused of rape, was lynched in Midville, Ga.
Nov. 15: Two black brothers named Stanford, accused of murder, were lynched in Hazelhurst, Miss.
Nov. 16: John Anthony, a black man accused of attempted rape, was lynched in Lincolnton, Ga.
Nov. 16: George Washington, a black man accused of attempted murder, was lynched in Magnolia, Miss.
Nov. 16: An unknown black man accused of murder was lynched in Hazelhurst, Miss.
Nov. 17: Joseph Gebhart, a white man accused of breaking into a safe, was lynched in Kennett, Mo.
Nov. 18: An unknown black man accused of incendiarism was lynched in Vidalia, La.
Nov. 23: Robert Bland, a black man, was lynched in Petersburg, Va.
Nov. 24: Joseph A. Smith, a white man accused of murder, was lynched in Trenton, Ky.
Nov. 25: Hans Jacob Olsen, a white man, was lynched in Preston, Wisc.
Dec. 3: Joseph Vermillion, a white man accused of arson, was lynched in Marlboro, Md.
Dec. 9: John Turner, a white man accused of murder, was lynched in Greensburg, Ky.
Dec. 11: Eleven white men accused of murder were lynched in Big Horn Basin, Wyo.
Dec. 12: William Carden, a white man accused of rape, was lynched in Cleveland, Tenn.
Dec. 14: Two white outlaws were lynched in White Rock, Texas.
Dec. 16: Four unidentified white outlaws were lynched in Maumelle, Ark.
Dec. 19: Doc Jones, a black man accused of murder, was lynched in Owensboro, Ky.
Dec. 26: Two black men, William Hopps and Peter Jackson, were lynched for racial hatred in Jesup, Ga.
Dec. 27: Bud Wilson, a black man accused of attempted rape, was lynched in Tuscaloosa, Ala.
Dec. 28: Eight black men: Michael Adams, Peter Bell, Hugh Furz, Hudson Johnson, Ripley Johnson, Judge Jones, Rafe Monoll, and Robert J. Phoenix; were lynched for murder in Barnwell, S.C.
Dec. 28: Two white outlaws named O'Dell were lynched in Uvalde, Texas.

1890

An Indian man was lynched at a site unknown.
Jan. 1: An unidentified black man accused of being an accessory to a murder was lynched at Turner, Ark.
Jan. 3: Henry Holmes, a black man, was lynched in Bossier Parish, La.
Jan. 7: Alfred Shafford, a white man accused of murder, was lynched in Klichitat County, Wash.
Jan. 8: Henry Ward, a black man accused of murder, was lynched in Bayou Sara, La.
Jan. 11: William Black, a black man accused of burglary, was lynched in Barnwell, S.C.
Jan. 15: George Smith, a black man, was lynched in Iowa.
Feb. 8: Eli Ladd, a black man, was lynched in Blountsville, Ind.
Feb. 14: William Larkin, a black man accused of murder, was lynched in Camden, Ark.
Feb. 19: Jacob Staples, a black man accused of rape, was lynched in Heiskell's Station, Tenn.
Feb. 28: Washington Brown, a black man accused of rape, was lynched in Athens, Ga.
Mar. 2: Burke Martin, a black man accused of murder, was lynched in Greenville, Miss.
Mar. 15: Philip William, a black man accused of rape, was lynched in Napoleanville, La.
Mar. 16: Henry Williams, a black man accused of rape, was lynched in Gadsen, Tenn.
Mar. 22: Robert Moseley, a black man accused of rape, was lynched in Huntsville, Ala.
Mar. 24: Samuel Martin, a black man accused of murder, was lynched in Wrightsville, Ga.
Mar. 27: An unknown black man accused of murder was lynched in Hedsville, Texas.
Mar. 29: Simmons Simpson, a black man accused of murder, was lynched in Marianna, Fla.
Mar. 31: Frank Griffin, a black man accused of rape, was lynched in Stanton, Ala.
Apr. 2: An unknown black man accused of murder was lynched in

Brantley, Ala.
Apr. 5: A black man named Williams, accused of rape, was lynched in Kosse, Texas.
Apr. 5: An unknown black man accused of rape was lynched in Thornton, Texas.
Apr. 5: An unknown white man accused of murder was lynched in Rutledge, Tenn.
Apr. 18: Samuel Moody, a black man accused of murder, was lynched in Auburn, Ky.
Apr. 20: Simeon Garrette, a black man accused of attempted murder, was lynched in San Augustine, Texas.
Apr. 20: Stephen Jacobs, a black man accused of incendiarism, was lynched in Fay, Texas.
Apr. 24: Jerry Teel, a black man accused of attempted murder, was lynched in San Augustine, Texas.
Apr. 24: An unknown black man was lynched for rape in Cameron Station, Texas.
May 5: Willie Leaphart, a black man wrongly accused of rape, was lynched in Lexington, S.C.
May 12: Edward Bennett, a black man accused of rape, was lynched in Hearne, Texas.
May 22: Grant Anderson, a black man suspected of rape, was lynched in Columbus, Miss.
May 30: Robert Weaver, a black man accused of racial prejudice, was lynched in Arkansas.
June 1: Thomas Brown, a black man accused of murder, was lynched in Hooks Ferry, Texas.
June 3: George Stevenson, a black man suspected of rape, was lynched in Hattiesburg, Miss.
June 10: George Prince, a black man accused of rape, was lynched in Elbert County, Ga.
June 10: Jesse Poke, a black man accused of murder, was lynched in Eastman, Ga.
June 10: Rich Perry, a black man, was lynched in Marion County, Ga.
June 13: George Penner, a black man accused of rape, was lynched in Elberton, Ga.
June 16: George Swayey, a black man, was lynched in East Feliciana, La., for political causes.
June 20: A black man accused of murder was lynched in Livingston, Texas.
June 28: Andrew Roberts, a black man accused of rape, was lynched in Waycross, Ga.
June 28: An unknown black man was lynched in Antlers, Texas.
June 29: John Coleman, a black man accused of murder, was lynched in Shreveport, La.
July 3: Patrick Henry, a black man accused of gambling, was lynched in Nechesville, Texas.
July 10: A black man accused of making threats was lynched in Lebanon, Va.
July 11: James Harmon, a black man accused of rape, was lynched in Social Circle, Ga.
July 13: John Jones, a black man accused of robbery, was lynched in Anniston, Ala.
July 18: Green Jackson, a black man accused of murder, was lynched in Ft. White, Fla.
July 22: Andy Young, a black man accused of racial prejudice, was lynched in Red River County, Texas.
July 25: An unknown black man was lynched in Riverton, Ala.
July 30: William Hawkins, a black man accused of theft, was lynched in Cypress, Texas.
Aug. 4: John Brown, a black man accused of rape, was lynched in Navasota, Texas.
Aug. 8: An unknown black man accused of rape was lynched in Anderson, Texas.
Aug. 12: Isaac Cook, a black man, was lynched in Montgomery, Ala.
Aug. 14: Two unknown black men accused of rape were lynched in Mexia, Texas.
Aug. 15: A white man named Lashman, accused of murder, was lynched in Roslyn, Wyo.
Aug. 17: John Henderson, a black man accused of murder, was lynched in Midway, Ky.
Aug. 18: Thomas Woodward, a black man accused of robbery, was lynched in Humboldt, Tenn.
Aug. 21: Fox Henderson, a black man accused of robbery, was lynched in Trenton, Tenn.
Aug. 22: William Alexander, a black man accused of attempted rape, was lynched in Baton Rouge, La.
Sept. 3: Thomas Smith, a black man accused of murder, was lynched in Poplar Bluff, Mo.
Sept. 4: John Rogers, a black man accused of attempted rape, was lynched in Water Valley, Miss.
Sept. 11: Two black men accused of rape, George Bolter and Stephen Crump, were lynched in Amory, Miss.
Oct. 2: Ernest Humphreys, a black man accused of murder, was lynched in Princeton, Ky.
Oct. 12: Frank Wosten, a black man accused of incendiarism, was lynched in Homer, Ga.
Oct. 24: John Williams, a black man accused of murder, was lynched in Waynesboro, Ga.
Oct. 31: A black man named Polasco, accused of rape, was lynched in Valdosta, Ga.
Oct. 31: Two black men accused of rape were lynched in Barton, Ga.
Nov. 1: Owen Jones, a black man accused of rape, was lynched in Pulaski, Ga.
Nov. 14: A black man named Mc Gregory, accused of rape, was lynched in Water Valley, Miss.
Nov. 17: Edward Stevens, a black man accused of murder, was lynched in Savannah, Tenn.
Nov. 18: Henry Smith, a black man accused of rape, was lynched in Indiana.
Nov. 18: Sandy Wallace, a black man accused of rape, was lynched in Longstown, Miss.
Nov. 19: John Simmons, a black man accused of rape, was lynched in Cairo, Ga.
Dec. 3: Henry Johnson, a black man accused of rape, was lynched in Central, S.C.
Dec. 3: An unknown black man was lynched in Rome, Ga.
Dec. 7: Dennis Martin, a black man accused of murder, was lynched in Roebuck Landing, Miss.
Dec. 9: Moses Lemon, a black man accused of making threats, was lynched in Roebuck Landing, Miss.
Dec. 10: Richard Lumdy, a black man accused of murder, was lynched in Edgefield County, S.C.
Dec. 11: Daniel Williams, a black man accused of incendiarism, was lynched in Florida.
Dec. 24: Kinch Freeman, a black man accused of murder, was lynched in Winton, N.C.
Dec. 24: Five black men accused of murder were lynched in Mecklenburg County, Va.

1891

Jan. 1: Charles Bealle, a black man accused of rape, was lynched in Lang, Texas.
Jan. 2: A black man named Sharp, accused of robbery, was lynched in Neshoba County, Miss.
Jan. 3: An unknown white man was lynched in Neshoba County, Miss.
Jan. 10: An unknown Indian accused of murder was lynched in Neshoba County, Miss.
Jan. 20: Olli Truxton, a black man accused of rape, was lynched in Glasgow, Mo.
Feb. 6: Green Jackson, a black man suspected of murder, was lynched in Greenville, Miss.
Feb. 7: Jesus Salceda, a white man, was lynched in Knickerbocker, Texas.
Feb. 16: William Brown, a black man accused of rape, was lynched in Roxie, Miss.
Feb. 16: Frinch Haynie, a black man accused of rape and incendiarism, was lynched in Hendersonville, Tenn.
Feb. 17: Thomas Rebin, a black desperado, was lynched in Douglas, Texas.
Feb. 18: Two outlaws, a black man named Champion and Michael Kelly, a white man, were lynched in Gainsville, Fla.
Feb. 19: John Bull, an Indian man accused of murder, was lynched in Battlefield, Miss.
Feb. 21: Wesley King, a black man accused of murder, was lynched in Georgia.
Feb. 22: Oliver Reilly, a white man accused of murder, was lynched in Salado Independence County, Calif.
Feb. 23: Scott Bishop, a black man accused of robbery, was lynched in Blackstone, Va.
Feb. 24: Thomas Rowland, a black man accused of robbery, was lynched in Douglas, Texas.
Feb. 26: Allen West, a black man accused of rape, was lynched in Abbeville, Ga.
Feb. 27: White men named Jasper, Williams, and two others, were lynched by vigilantes at Sea Junction, Texas.
Mar. 3: An unknown black man accused of rape was lynched at Woodward, in the Oklahoma Territory.
Mar. 7: Louis Hodge, a black man accused of attempted rape, was lynched in Louisville, Miss.
Mar. 10: Bradford Scott, a black man, was lynched in Pinson, Tenn.
Mar. 13: The New Orleans Vigilance committee was formed.
Mar. 13: Henry Sanders, a black man accused of rape, was lynched in Lavernia, Tenn.
Mar. 14: White men accused of conspiring to murder, Antonio Bajnetti, Loretto Conritez, James Comso, Tocco Guacci, Joseph Maclecha, Antonio Marchesi, Pietro Monastero, Manuel Palitz, Frank Romero, Antonio Scaffedi, and Charles Trahina, were lynched in New Orleans, La.
Mar. 18: Nograde Bela, a white man accused of stealing, was lynched in Branchville, Va.
Mar. 26: Thomas Huntley, a black man accused of murder, was lynched at Cumberland Gap, Tenn.
Mar. 28: Elrod Hudson, a black man accused of murder, was lynched in Russellville, Okla.
Apr. 1: William Field, a white man accused of attempted rape, was lynched in Mineola, Texas.
Apr. 2: Zachioli Grohan, a black man accused of rape, was lynched in Whistler, Ala.

Apr. 2: Martin Mayberry, a black man accused of rape, was lynched in Bryant Station, Tenn.
Apr. 6: Thomas Pumill, a white man accused of robbery, was lynched in Gladys, Va.
Apr. 10: William Boles, a white man accused of murder, was lynched in Kenton, Ohio.
Apr. 12: John Rose, a white man accused of murder, was lynched in Seabury, Wash.
Apr. 13: Alexander Foote, a black man accused of murder, was lynched in Princeton, W.Va.
Apr. 15: Roxie Elliott, a black woman suspected of robbery and murder, was lynched in Centerville, Ala.
Apr. 16: William Skapp, a black man accused of murder, was lynched in Old Union, Ky.
Apr. 21: Charles Curtis, a black man accused of rape, was lynched in Liberty, Miss.
Apr. 24: A.J. Hunt, a white man accused of murder, was lynched in Oregon.
Apr. 25: A black man named Randall, suspected of robbery and murder, was lynched in Winfield, Ala.
Apr. 30: William Taylor, a black man accused of robbery and murder, was lynched in Franklin, Tenn.
May 2: Monroe Walters, a black man suspected of murder, was lynched in Hudson, Miss.
May 11: John Barrentine, Wesley Lee, and Monroe Walker, all black and accused of murder, were lynched in Loundes County, Miss.
May 12: Asbury Green, a black man accused of rape, was lynched in Centerville, Md.
May 15: A white man named Juiden, accused of murder, was lynched in Dewey, Mont.
May 22: James Jennings, a black man accused of rape, was lynched in Indiana.
May 22: A white man named Lupersky was lynched at a site unknown.
May 22: Hy Wilcox and John Wilcox, two white men accused of rape, were lynched in Sandy Hook, Ky.
May 23: Two white men accused of rape, John Anderson and William Anderson, were lynched in Louisiana.
May 23: Dennis Hampton, a white man accused of murder, was lynched in Barnsley, Penn.
May 26: Green Wells, a black man accused of murder, was lynched in Tennessee.
May 28: Monroe Sheppard, a white man, was lynched in Belton, Texas.
May 30: Turnip Hampton, a black man accused of larceny, was lynched in Claiborne, La.
June 2: Three black men, Samuel Hummel, accused of murder, and Alex Campbell and another unknown, accused as accessories, were lynched in Point Cenpee Parish, La.
June 8: Evan E. Shelby, a black man accused of murder, was lynched in Wickliffe, Texas.
June 13: Robert Clark, a black man accused of rape, was lynched in Bristol, Tenn.
June 15: Ah Anong Ti, an oriental man accused of murder, was lynched in Bridgeport, Calif.
June 15: An unknown black man accused of rape was lynched in Brookhaven, Miss.
June 17: An unknown black man was lynched in Fort White, Fla.
June 18: James Waggoner, a white man accused of stealing horses, was lynched in Cook County, Wyo.
June 22: Charles Griffen, a black man accused of murder, was lynched in Florida.
June 25: Henry Jones, a black man accused of murder, was lynched in Hamburg, Ark.
June 28: William Hartfield and Munn Sheppard, both black men accused of being troublesome, were lynched in Cass County, Texas.
June 29: Royal Frisby, a white man, was lynched in Sparland, Ill.
July 1: Daniel Buck, a black man accused of rape, was lynched in Bluffton, Ga.
July 1: William Gates, a black man accused of rape, was lynched in West Point, Miss.
July 5: A black man named Thompson, accused of murder, was lynched in Dyer, Tenn.
July 6: Calvin Brown, a black man accused of rape, was lynched in Alabama.
July 6: Robert Brown, a black man accused of rape, was lynched in Alabama.
July 6: Henry Centry, a black man accused of murder, was lynched near Vicksburg, Miss.
July 7: James Bailey, a black man accused of rape, was lynched in Beebe, Ark.
July 7: Wallace Douglas, a black man accused of robbery, was lynched in Whitaker Station, Miss.
July 14: Sam Gillespie, a black man accused of racial prejudice, was lynched in De Soto, Miss.
July 17: Frank Rossimus, a white man accused of attempted murder, was lynched in Arkansas City, Ark.
July 18: Frank Rice, a white man accused of attempted murder, was lynched in Arkansas City, Ark.
July 19: John Darmer, a white man accused of murder, was lynched in Arkansas City, Ark.
July 19: Ben Walling, a black man accused of rape, was lynched in Decaturville, Tenn.
July 20: Mark Brown, a black man accused of rape, was lynched in Shelbyville, Ky.
July 22: William Johnson, a black man accused of rape, was lynched in Henderson, Texas.
July 25: John Grange, a black man accused of making threats, was lynched in Franklin, Ky.
July 26: John Brown, a black man accused of murder, was lynched in Jackson, Tenn.
July 26: Joseph Clancy, a white man accused of murder, was lynched in Billings, Mont.
July 26: Jesse Underwood, a black man accused of rape, was lynched in Tuscumbia, Ala.
Aug. 1: Eliza Lowe, Willis Lowe, Ella Williams and William Williams, black persons accused of incendiarism, were lynched in Henry County, Ala.
Aug. 21: Ray Porter, a black man, was lynched in Clanton, Ala.
Aug. 22: Charles Hawkins, a white man accused of murder, was lynched in Shelbyville, Ind.
Aug. 24: Lucius Andrews, a black man, was lynched in Magnolia, Miss.
Aug. 25: Andy Ford, a black man, was lynched in Gainsville, Fla., for having a bad reputation.
Aug. 25: William Lewis, a black man, was lynched in Tullahoma, Tenn., for drunkenness.
Aug. 25: Lee Oman, an oriental man accused of rape, was lynched in California.
Aug. 28: James Dudley, a black man accused of murder, was lynched in Georgetown, Ky.
Aug. 29: William Owens, a black man accused of rape, was lynched in Jesup, Ga.
Aug. 30: Charles Mulligan, a black man accused of murder, was lynched in Conway, Ark.
Sept. 1: Andrew Murrell, a white man accused of bank robbery, was lynched in Conden, Miss.
Sept. 2: Two unknown black men accused of murder were lynched in Maybee Station, Mich.
Sept. 2: Three white men accused of stealing cattle were lynched in Custer County, Mont.
Sept. 3: James Sims, a white man accused of murder, was lynched in Choctaw County, Ala.
Sept. 5: A black man accused of rape was lynched in Oxford, Miss.
Sept. 8: Mack Bess, a black man accused of attempted rape, was lynched in Nearland, N.C.
Sept. 15: James H. Gilliland and Josiah Gilliland, two white men accused of murder, were lynched in Somerset, Ky.
Sept. 21: Anton Siebolt, a white man accused of murder, was lynched in Darlington, Wisc.
Sept. 25: Hezekiah Rankin, a black man accused of murder, was lynched in Asheville, N.C.
Sept. 26: Charles Mack, a black man accused of rape, was lynched in Swainsboro, Ga.
Sept. 28: Louise Stevenson, a black person accused of being an accessory to a murder, was lynched in Hollandale, Miss.
Sept. 29: Lee Barley, a black man accused of rape, was lynched in De Land, Fla.
Sept. 29: Two unknown black men accused of murder were lynched in Georigiana, Ala.
Oct. 1: John Brown, a black man who testified against whites, was lynched in Childersburg, Ala.
Oct. 1: Ben Patterson, a black man accused of strike rioting, was lynched in Hackette, Ark.
Oct. 1: Edward Peyton, a black man accused of strike rioting, was lynched near Marianna, Ark.
Oct. 9: Joseph Coe, a black man accused of rape, was lynched in Omaha, Neb.
Oct. 15: Sam Wright, a black man accused of rape, was lynched in Helena, Ala.
Oct. 17: James Scott, a black man, was lynched in Clifton Forge, Va.
Oct. 20: John Russ, a white man accused of murder, was lynched in Columbia, La.
Oct. 26: Leo Green, a black man accused of murder, was lynched in Linden, Texas.
Oct. 30: A black man named Snowden was lynched for incendiarism in Monroe, La.
Oct. 30: Jack Parke, a black man accused of murder, was lynched in Abitz Springs, La.
Oct. 31: An unknown black man was lynched in Poole's Landing, La.
Nov. 2: Larkin Nix, a white man accused of murder, was lynched in Decatur County, Ga.
Nov. 4: W.S. Felton and J.T. Smith, two white men accused of murder, were lynched in Morehouse Parish, La.
Nov. 8: William Rice, a black man, was lynched in Arkansas.
Nov. 10: John Hagle, a black man, was lynched in Homer, La.
Nov. 13: Joseph Mitchell, a black man accused of rape, was lynched in McConnell, Tenn.
Nov. 13: Two black men were lynched in Burnet, Texas.

Nov. 20: Nat Hadley, a black man accused of murder, was lynched in Gurdon, Ark.
Nov. 21: An unknown black man accused of racial prejudice was lynched near Baton Rouge, La.
Nov. 22: William Black, a black man accused of making insulting remarks, was lynched in Moscow, Texas.
Nov. 22: Daniel Gladney, a black man accused of racial prejudice, was lynched in Atlanta County, Miss.
Nov. 27: A black man named Mixy, accused of rape, was lynched in Many, La.
Nov. 28: A white man named Jones, accused of stealing cattle, was lynched at Cherry Creek, S.D.
Nov. 30: Arthur Rainsey, a black man accused of racial prejudice, was lynched in Meridian, Miss.
Dec. 10: Richard Lundy, a black man accused of murder, was lynched in Edgefield, S.C.
Dec. 12: Three white men named Hand, Lovett, and a third unknown, accused of stealing horses, were lynched in Deadwood, S.D.
Dec. 14: Robert Kingut, a black man accused of rioting, was lynched in Waycross, Ga.
Dec. 14: An unknown black man was lynched in Newton County, Ark.
Dec. 15: An unknown black man accused of robbery was lynched in Florida.
Dec. 15: Two unknown black men accused of murder were lynched in Live Oak, Fla.
Dec. 15: An unknown black man accused of burglary was lynched in Camak, Ga.
Dec. 16: Welcome Golden, a black man accused of rioting, was lynched in Waycross, Ga.
Dec. 17: John R. Ely, a black man accused of murder, was lynched in Holloway, La.
Dec. 18: An unidentified white vagrant accused of rape was lynched in Emmett, Neb.
Dec. 20: An unknown black man accused of rape was lynched in Meridian, Miss.
Dec. 21: Two white men, J.A. Smith and Floyd Gregory, accused of murder, were lynched in Dewitt, Ark.
Dec. 21: Moses Henderson, a black man accused of rape, was lynched in Dewitt, Ark.
Dec. 22: Jesse Miller, a white outlaw, was lynched in Bibb County, Ala.
Dec. 26: Five white outlaws, Robert Sims and four brothers named Savage, were lynched in Choctaw County, Ala.
Dec. 27: John Sims and Mosely Sims, white outlaws, were lynched in Choctaw County, Ala.
Dec. 30: An unidentified black man accused of murder was lynched in Blackwater, La.

1892

Jan. 7: L.N. Descharner and Calvin Foster, two black men accused of murder, were lynched in Rayville, La.
Jan. 9: Nathan Andrews, a black man accused of murder, was lynched in Caddo Parish, La.
Jan. 9: A white man named Nux, accused of murder, was lynched in Mitchell County, Ga.
Jan. 12: Henry Henson, a black man accused of murder, was lynched in Micanopy, Fla.
Jan. 14: Henry Corbin, a black man accused of murder, was lynched in Oxford, Ohio.
Jan. 16: Augustus Hehman, a white man accused of murder, was lynched in Rosalia, Kan.
Jan. 18: Henry Hinton, a white outlaw, was lynched in Choctaw County, Ala.
Jan 18: A white man named Johnson and a woman named Baker, suspected of murder, were lynched in Northern Arkansas.
Jan. 22: Robert Hepler, a white man accused of murder, was lynched in Nevada, Mo.
Jan. 28: Lee Gibson, a black man accused of murder, was lynched in Owenton, Ky.
Jan. 29: Joseph Shields, a white man, was lynched in Thompsons, Texas.
Jan. 30: Four white men accused of stealing horses were lynched in Montana.
Feb. 3: A black woman named Martin, accused of racial prejudice, was lynched in Sumner County, Tenn.
Feb. 3: Amos Miller, a white man accused of murder, was lynched in Cairo, Ill.
Feb. 9: Henry Beavers, a black man accused of assaulting a woman, was lynched in Wilmar, Ark.
Feb. 10: Hamp Briscoe, his wife, and their son, were lynched in Arkansas because of racial prejudice.
Feb. 12: Lewis Gordon, a white man accused of rape, was lynched in Carrollton, Mo.
Feb. 12: William Lavender, a black man accused of attempted rape, was lynched in Roanoke, Va.
Feb. 13: Two unknown black men accused of incendiarism were lynched in Sylvan, Ala.
Feb. 14: John F. Bright, a white man accused of murdering his wife, was lynched in Taney County, Mo.
Feb. 14: Two black men, John Kelly, accused of murder, and Gulbert Harris, accused as an accessory, were lynched in Pine Bluff, Ark.
Feb. 14: Wiley Webb, a black man accused of rape, was lynched in Selma, Ala.
Feb. 18: Walter Austin, a black man accused of murder, was lynched in Arcadia, Fla.
Feb. 20: Ed Coy, a black man accused of rape, was lynched in Texarkana, Ark.
Feb. 23: George Harris, a black man accused of murder, was lynched in Varner, Ark.
Feb. 28: John Robinson, a black man accused of robbery, was lynched in Shaw Station, Miss.
Feb. 30: James Lytle, a white man accused of murdering his wife, was lynched in Findlay, Ohio.
Mar. 1: A white man named Jones accused of murder was lynched in Ware County, Ga.
Mar. 4: An unknown black man accused of robbery was lynched in Waynesboro, Tenn.
Mar. 8: Richard Center and John Rice, two black men accused of incendiarism, were lynched in Boyle Station, Miss.
Mar. 8: Calvin McDonnell, Thomas Moss, and William Stuart, all black men accused of murder, were lynched in Memphis, Tenn.
Mar. 10: An unknown black man accused of assault was lynched in Macon County, Ala.
Mar. 13: A black person named Ella, accused of attempted murder, was lynched in Rayville, La.
Mar. 18: Joseph Dye and Lee Heplin, black men accused of murder, were lynched in Farquhar County, Va.
Mar. 28: Jack Tillman, a black man accused of racial prejudice, was lynched in Gretna Parish, La.
Mar. 30: Denniss Cobb, a black man, was lynched in Arcadia, Fla.
Apr. 1: John Mullens, a white man accused of murder, was lynched in Alabama
Apr. 1: Charles Stuart, a white man accused of attempted rape, was lynched in Arkansas.
Apr. 1: An unknown black man was lynched in Millersburg, Ohio.
Apr. 5: Five black men accused of rape were lynched near Lithonia, Ga.
Apr. 6: Four unidentified black men accused of murder were lynched in Fishville, La.
Apr. 9: Isaac Brandon, a black man accused of attempted rape, was lynched in Charles City, Va.
Apr. 14: William West, a black man accused of murder, was lynched in Georgia.
Apr. 19: Four black men accused of murder, George Davis, Albert Roberts, Jerry Williams, and William Williams, were lynched in Inverness, Ala.
Apr. 23: A white man named Freeman accused of murder was lynched in Smithland, La.
Apr. 26: A black man accused of murder was lynched in Riesil, Texas.
Apr. 27: David Sims, a black man, was lynched in Clarkton, Mo.
Apr. 27: A white tramp accused of robbery and murder was lynched at Point Conpee, La.
Apr. 28: Henry Griggard, a black man accused of rape, was lynched in Goodlettsville, Tenn.
Apr. 30: A black man named Ephraim Groggard, accused of rape, was lynched in Nashville, Tenn.
May 2: An unknown black man accused of rape was lynched in Greenville, Miss.
May 3: Lyman Purdee, a black man accused of murder, was lynched in Elizabethtown, N.C.
May 5: Charles Miller, a white man accused of murder, was lynched in Blunt County, Tenn.
May 8: George Hoes, a black man accused of rape, was lynched in Butler, Ala.
May 9: A black man accused of murder was lynched in Berkley County, S.C.
May 13: James Henry, a black man accused of rape, was lynched in Little Rock, Ark.
May 13: Mills Luther, a black man, was lynched in Mercer County, W.Va.
May 15: "Red" Smith, a black man accused of murder, was lynched in Naugatuck, W.Va.
May 16: William Cantor, Berry Rowder, and James Rowder, all black men accused of robbery, were lynched in Childersburg, Ala.
May 16: A black man accused of murder was lynched in Berkley County, S.C.
May 17: Three black men suspected of robbery were lynched in Clarksville, Ga.
May 18: James Taylor, a black man accused of rape, was lynched in Chestertown, Md.
May 19: Charles Everett, a black man accused of attempted robbery, was lynched in Manchester, Tenn.
May 21: Serborn Smith, a black man accused of rape, was lynched in Covington, Ga.
May 21: Charles Stewart, a black man accused of murder, was lynched in Morrillton, Ark.
May 22: A black man accused of murder was lynched near Monroe, La.
May 23: A black man accused of murder was lynched near Bastrop, La.
May 25: Two black men, James Williams and another unidentified, were lynched in Florida.

May 27: James Smith, a black man accused of murder, was lynched in Logan County, W.Va.
May 31: Three white men named McArthur, accused of advising murder, were lynched in Perryville, Ark.
May 31: David Shaw, a black man accused of larceny, was lynched in Gray Court, S.C.
May 31: Heck Willis, a black man accused of rape, was lynched in Lebanon, Tenn.
June 1: A black man named Walker, suspected of rape, was lynched in Sparta, La.
June 1: Nick Willis, a black man accused of rape, was lynched in Lebanon, Ky.
June 2: Robert Lewis, a black man accused of rape, was lynched in Port Jervis, N.Y.
June 7: William Kaneker, a black man accused of rape, was lynched in Apalachicola, Fla.
June 8: Austin Porter, a black man accused of murdering his wife, was lynched in Grayson, Ky.
June 10: Tobe Cook, a black man accused of rape, was lynched in Bastrop, Texas.
June 10: Charles Hill, a black man accused of rape, was lynched in Paducah, Ky.
June 10: Alex Wentely, a white man accused of murder, was lynched in Charlotte, N.C.
June 11: Anderson Moreland, a black man accused of rape, was lynched in Forsythe, Ga.
June 12: J.A. Burris, a black man accused of murder, was lynched in Albermarle, N.C.
June 16: Four white men accused of murder were lynched near Seattle, Wash.
June 19: John Johnson, a black man accused of murder, was lynched in McComb City, Miss.
June 22: Henry Carson, a white man accused of murder, was lynched in Moark, Ark.
June 22: Two white men accused of stealing horses were lynched in Calabasas, Ariz.
June 23: Christopher Chamblers, a white man accused of attempted murder, was lynched in Red Creek Bay, Ala.
June 27: Thomas Bates, a white man accused of murdering his wife, was lynched in Shelbyville, Tenn.
June 28: Henry Gaines, Thomas Smith, and Prince Wood, all black men accused of rape, were lynched in Spurger, Texas.
July 1: Thomas Lillard, a black man accused of rape, was lynched in Woodbury, Tenn.
July 2: An unidentified black man accused of rape was lynched in Wynne, Ark.
July 2: Robert Donnelly, a black man accused of rape, was lynched in Union Township, Ark.
July 5: Smith Tooley, a black man accused of murder, was lynched in Vicksburg, Miss.
July 5: An unknown black man accused of attempted rape was lynched in Jasper, Ala.
July 6: Edgar Jones, a black man accused of murder was lynched in Weston, W.Va.
July 8: Henry McDuffie, a black man accused of stealing, was lynched in Orlando, Fla.
July 8: Edward Prater, a black man accused of rape, was lynched in Clay County, Ala.
July 9: William Anderson, a black man accused of rape, was lynched in Louisa County, Va.
July 12: J.R. Redfern, a white man accused of murder, was lynched in Franklin, Ky.
July 14: Julian Moseley, a black man accused of rape, was lynched in Arkansas City, Ark.
July 19: Doc Davis, a black man accused of rape, was lynched near Jackson, Miss.
July 21: An unidentified black man was lynched in Jesup, Ga.
July 24: Charles Ruggles and John Ruggles, both white, were lynched for murder and robbery in Redding, Calif.
July 25: J.H. Wynne, a white man accused of murder, was lynched in Burns, Tenn.
July 29: Andy Beshears and John Willis, both white men accused of rape, were lynched in Jacksonboro, Tenn.
July 29: Lee McDaniels, a black man accused of attempted rape, was lynched in Oaks Crossing, Ky.
July 30: Eugene Baker, a black man accused of defending himself, was lynched in Monticello, Ark.
Aug. 1: Loeb Landers, a black man accused of attempted rape, was lynched in Dresden, Tenn.
Aug. 4: Allen Carter, a black man accused of rape, was lynched in Wynne, Ark.
Aug. 10: Robert Jordon, a black man accused of insulting a woman, was lynched in Camden, Ark.
Aug. 14: Port Magee, a black man suspected of rape, was lynched in Westville, Miss.
Aug. 16: Logan Murphy, a black man accused of murder, was lynched in Mt. Sterling, Ky.
Aug. 16: Three white highwaymen were lynched at Nassau Creek, Wyo.
Aug. 23: A black man named Bowles, accused of rape, was lynched in Gurdon, Ark.
Aug. 25: Benjamin Howard, a black man accused of murder, was lynched in Josselin, Ga.
Aug. 29: Dennis Blackwell, a black man accused of attempted rape, was lynched in Alamo, Tenn.
Aug. 30: John Jessy, a black man accused of rape, was lynched near Forsythe, Ga.
Sept. 2: John Wilcoxson, a black man accused of murder, was lynched in Edmonton, Ky.
Sept. 6: William Armor, John Ransom, and John Walker, all black men accused of rioting, were lynched in Paris, Texas.
Sept. 6: Ed Laurent and Gabriel Magloire, both black, were lynched in Bunkie, La., for making threats.
Sept. 7: An unidentified black man accused of incendiarism was lynched in Waldo, Fla.
Sept. 8: Sam Dixon, a black man accused of attempted murder, was lynched in Kenner, La.
Sept. 8: Jesse Williams, a black man accused of attempted rape, was lynched in Eastman, Ga.
Sept. 13: Thomas N. Allison, a white man accused of murder, was lynched in Mt. Airy, N.C.
Sept. 14: James Thompson, a black man accused of rape, was lynched in Larned, Kan.
Sept. 15: James Patton, a black man accused of murder, was lynched in Bonita, La.
Sept. 19: A black man accused of rape was lynched in Paris, Texas.
Sept. 20: A black man named Harrison, accused of racial prejudice, was lynched in Champagnolle, Ark.
Sept. 23: William Sullivan, a black man accused of rape, was lynched in Plantersville, Texas.
Sept. 30: J.W. Smith, a white man, was lynched for murder in California.
Oct. 5: Alexander Bell, a black man accused of insulting a woman, was lynched in Mt. Pelia, Tenn.
Oct. 5: Four black desperadoes were lynched near Beandon, Miss.
Oct. 6: Benjamin Walker, a black man accused of attempted rape, was lynched in Concordia, La.
Oct. 6: Two black desperadoes were lynched in Copiah County, Miss.
Oct. 12: Two white men accused of stealing horses were lynched in Casper, Wyo.
Oct. 13: Four black men, Burrell Jones, Moses Jones, and two unidentified men, all accused of murder, were lynched in Monroeville, Ala.
Oct. 16: J.S. Bedford, a black man accused of stealing horses, was lynched in Big Horn, Wyo.
Oct. 17: Eight horse thieves were lynched in Deer Flat, Idaho.
Oct. 18: An Indian man accused of rape was lynched in Ash Fork, Ariz.
Oct. 25: James Courtney, a white man accused of attempted rape, was lynched in Plaquemine, La.
Oct. 26: James Wilson, a black man accused of racial prejudice, was lynched in Dalton, Ga.
Oct. 30: Allen Parker, a black man accused of incendiarism, was lynched in New Monroesville, Ala.
Nov. 1: Two white brothers named Burgess, accused of murder, were lynched in Lebanon, Va.
Nov. 2: The son and daughter of John Hastings were lynched in Calahoula, La.
Nov. 5: John Hastings, a black man accused of murder, was lynched in Calahoula, La.
Nov. 8: James Talbert, a white man accused of murder, was lynched in Fort Stephens, Miss.
Nov. 11: Henry Planz, a black man, was lynched in San Jose, Calif.
Nov. 15: William Burnett, a black man accused of rape, was lynched in Oxford, N.C.
Nov. 16: Two white men accused of stealing horses were lynched in Fremont County, Wyo.
Nov. 18: Duncan McFatton, a black man accused of murder, was lynched in Cheraw, S.C.
Nov. 26: Gester Scott, a white man accused of murder, was lynched in Calhoun, Ga.
Nov. 28: Nathan White, a black man accused of incendiarism, was lynched in Quaker Creek, S.C.
Nov. 29: Commodore True, a black man accused of murder, was lynched in Hiawatha, Kan.
Nov. 30: Richard Magee and a man named Carmichael, both white, were lynched for murder in Benton, La.
Dec. 5: Cornelius Coffee, a black man accused of murder, was lynched in Keystone, W.Va.
Dec. 7: A black man named Lightfoot, accused of fraud, was lynched near Newport, Ark.
Dec. 7: A black man and a white man, both accused of rape, were lynched in Jellico, Tenn.
Dec. 14: Jesse E. Reed, a black man accused of murder, was lynched in Tennessee.
Dec. 15: A black convict accused of murder was lynched in Greenwood, Miss.
Dec. 15: A black man accused of rape was lynched in Nashville, Tenn.
Dec. 17: Irwin Roberts, a black man accused of murder, was lynched in Shady Valley, Tenn.

Dec. 19: James Bond, a black man accused of attempted rape, was lynched in Guthrie, Ky.
Dec. 21: A white man named Cora was lynched by Indians near Guthie, Okla.
Dec. 28: An unidentified black man accused of rape was lynched in Bowling Green, Ky.
Dec. 29: Lewis Fox and Adam Gripson, two black men accused of murder, were lynched in Luling, La.
Dec. 30: Two white men, James Hopp and Charles Kelly, accused of murder, were lynched in Greenville, Ala.

1893

Jan. 3: Henry Duncan, a white man accused of murder, was lynched in Loudon, Tenn.
Jan. 5: Albert Roberts, a white man accused of murder, was lynched in Idaho.
Jan. 6: Two black men, Henry Allen and Paul Scroggs, both accused of murder, were lynched in Brinkley, Ark.
Jan. 6: Ben Lafargues, a white man accused of murder, was lynched in Avengeles Parish, La.
Jan. 6: An unknown black man accused of murder was lynched in Pocket Township, N.C.
Jan. 12: Edward Moorman and Richard Moorman, two white men accused of murder, were lynched in Guston, Ky.
Jan. 19: James Williams, a black man accused of rape, was lynched in Pickens County, Ala.
Jan. 21: Richard Davis, "Chicken" George, and Robert Landry, three black men accused of murder, were lynched in St. James Parish, La.
Jan. 25: William Fisher, a black man accused of murder, was lynched in Algiers, La.
Jan. 26: Patrick Wills, a black man accused of incendiarism, was lynched in Quincy, Fla.
Jan. 30: Thomas Carr, a black man accused of racial prejudice, was lynched in Kosciuscko, Miss.
Jan. 31: Henry Smith, a black man accused of murder, was lynched in Paris, Texas.
Feb. 1: Four black men accused of murder: Spencer Branch, Jerry Brown, Sam Ellerson, and John Johnson; were lynched in Richmond, Va.
Feb. 7: Ireno L. Gonzalez, a white desperado, was lynched at a site unknown.
Feb. 9: Frank Harrel and a man named Felder, both black and accused of incendiarism, were lynched in Dickey, Miss.
Feb. 11: A black man accused of rape was lynched in Forest Hill, Tenn.
Feb. 14: Andy Blount, a black man suspected of rape, was lynched in Chattanooga, Tenn.
Feb. 16: Richard Forman, a black man accused of burglary, was lynched near Granada, Miss.
Feb. 17: William Butler, a black man accused of racial prejudice, was lynched in Hickory Creek, Texas.
Feb. 18: John Hughes, a black man accused of insulting whites, was lynched in Moberly, Mo.
Feb. 21: Richard Mayes, a black man accused of attempted rape, was lynched in Springfield, Mo.
Feb. 24: Thomas Whitson and Wilson Whitson, both black men accused of murder, were lynched in Asheville, N.C.
Feb. 26: Joseph Hayne, a black man accused of rape, was lynched in Jellico, Tenn.
March: William Frazier, a white man accused of murder, was lynched in Albia, Iowa.
Mar. 1: Abner Anthony, a black man accused of rape, was lynched in Hot Springs, Va.
Mar. 1: Thomas Hill, a black man accused of rape, was lynched in Spring Place, Ga.
Mar. 19: Jessie Jones, a black man accused of murder, was lynched in Jellico, Tenn.
Apr. 7: Jesus Fulzen, a white man accused of murder, was lynched in San Bernadino, Calif.
Apr. 14: William Hardin, a white man accused of murder, was lynched in Monticello, N.M.
Apr. 14: Ed Onlu, a black man accused of murder, was lynched in Eufala, Ala.
Apr. 19: Flannegan Thornton, a black man accused of murder, was lynched in Morrillton, Ark.
Apr. 20: Dan Adams, a black man accused of murderous assault, was lynched in Salina, Kan.
Apr. 24: John Peterson, a white man accused of rape, was lynched in Denmark, S.C.
Apr. 24: A white man named Tarpley was lynched in Verona, Tenn.
May 3: James Collins, a white man accused of stealing horses, was lynched in Sherman, Ky.
May 6: John Demean, a white man accused of rape, was lynched near Duluth, Minn.
May 6: Sam Gaillard, a black man accused of rape, was lynched in South Carolina.
May 7: Victoriano Anjou, Antonio J. Barceloz, and Antonio Martinez, all white men accused of murder, were lynched in Los Lunas, N.M.
May 9: Two black men, "Doc" Henderson and John Stewart; and a white man, A.B. Cram, all accused of murder, were lynched in Bearden, Ark.
May 10: Hayward Banks, a black man accused of rape, was lynched in Columbia, S.C.
May 12: Israel Haloway, a black man accused of rape, was lynched in Napoleanville, La.
May 12: A black man accused of rape was lynched in Wytheville, Va.
May 23: Two black men, Ephrim Muchlea and another unknown, were lynched for murder in Hazelhurst, Ga.
May 28: An Indian man accused of murder was lynched in Cass Lake, Minn.
May 30: Celio Lucero, a white man accused of murder, was lynched in Las Vegas, N.M.
May 31: John Wallace, a black man accused of rape, was lynched in Jefferson Springs, Ark.
June 2: Isaac Lincoln, a black man accused of insulting women, was lynched in Ft. Madison, N.C.
June 3: Sam Bush, a black man accused of rape, was lynched in Decatur, Ill.
June 8: L.C. Dumas, a black man accused of rape, was lynched in Gleason, Tenn.
June 13: William Shorter, a black man accused of rape, was lynched in Winchester, Va.
June 14: George Williams, a black man accused of rape, was lynched near Waco, Texas.
June 17: Camp Reese, a black man, was lynched in Wetumpka, Ala.
June 19: An unknown white cowboy accused of murder was lynched in Dunseath, N.M.
June 21: James Harr, a white man in a case of mistaken identity, was lynched in Gleason, Tenn.
June 24: Dan Edwards, a black man accused of rape, was lynched in Selma, Ala.
June 27: Ernest Murphy, a black man accused of rape, was lynched in Daleville, Ala.
July 6: Unidentified black men accused of rape were lynched in Poplar Head, La.
July 7: Charles Miller, a black man suspected of rape, was lynched in Bardwell, Ky.
July 12: Henry Flemming, a black man accused of murder, was lynched in Columbus, Miss.
July 12: Robert Larkins, a black man accused of rape, was lynched in Ocala, Fla.
July 14: Allen Butler, a black man accused of criminal abortion, was lynched in Lawrenceville, Ill.
July 16: A white man named Jazo, accused of murder, was lynched near El Paso, Texas.
July 17: Warren Dean, a black man accused of rape, was lynched in Georgia.
July 17: An unknown black man accused of murder, was lynched in Brierville, Ala.
July 18: Dub Meetze, a black man accused of stealing horses, was lynched in Lexington County, S.C.
July 26: Nocolai Arata, a white man accused of murder, was lynched in Denver, Colo.
Aug. 3: Felix Poole, a white man accused of rape, was lynched in Owensboro, Ky.
Aug. 13: Kurt Chambers and Lee James, two white desperadoes, were lynched in Coffeyville, Ala.
Aug. 14: Monroe Smith, a black man accused of rape, was lynched in Springfield, La.
Aug. 18: Charles Walton, a black man accused of murder, was lynched in Morganfield, Ky.
Aug. 19: A black vagrant accused of rape was lynched in Paducah, Ky.
Aug. 21: Charles Tait, a black man accused of murder, was lynched near Memphis, Tenn.
Aug. 21: John Wilson, a black man accused of rape, was lynched in Leavenworth, Kan.
Aug. 22: Charles Hart, a black man accused of racial prejudice, was lynched in Lyons Station, Miss.
Aug. 23: Jacob Davis, a black man accused of rape, was lynched in Greenwood, S.C.
Aug. 28: Leonard Taylor, a black man accused of murder, was lynched in Newcastle, Ky.
Aug. 31: An unknown black man was lynched in Yarborough, Texas.
Sept. 1: Judge McNeal, a black man accused of attempted rape, was lynched in Cadiz, Ky.
Sept. 2: William Arkinson, a black man accused of rape, was lynched in McKinney, Ky.
Sept. 6: An unknown black man accused of rape was lynched in Centerville, Ala.
Sept. 8: Benjamin Jackson, a black man accused of murder, was lynched in Quincy, Miss.
Sept. 11: Frank Smith, a black man accused of attempted rape, was lynched in Newton, Miss.
Sept. 14: John Williams, a black man accused of murder, was lynched in Jackson, Tenn.
Sept. 15: Paul Archer, Emma Fair, and Paul Hull, all black persons accused of arson, were lynched in Carrolton, Ala.
Sept. 15: Rufus Beagley, Louisa Carter, W.A. Healey, Benjamin Jackson, and Mahala Jackson, all black and accused of poisoning well water, were lynched in Jackson, Miss.

Sept. 16: Redmond Burke, a white man accused of beating his wife, was lynched in Breckenridge, Mo.
Sept. 18: A white man named A. Youmans was lynched in Oklahoma.
Sept. 22: Five Indians were lynched in Oklahoma.
Sept. 24: An unknown white man was lynched in Hennessey, Okla.
Sept. 29: A white man accused of murder was lynched in Alva, Okla.
Oct. 2: George McFadden, a black man accused of rape, was lynched in Moore's Cross Roads, Va.
Oct. 17: A white man accused of robbery was lynched in Pullman, Wash.
Oct. 22: John Gamble, a black man accused of rape, was lynched in Pikeville, Tenn.
Oct. 22: Edward Jenkins, a black man accused of murder, was lynched in Clayton County, Ga.
Oct. 24: Two black men accused of stealing were lynched in Knoxpoint, La.
Nov. 1: Abraham Redmond, a black desperado, was lynched in Charlotte County, Va.
Nov. 4: Three black men suspected of barn burning: Sam Motlow, Edward Wagner, and William Wagner; were lynched in Lynchburg, Va.
Nov. 8: Robert Kennedy, a black man accused of attempted rape, was lynched in Spartanburg, S.C.
Nov. 9: Henry Boggs, a black man accused of murder, was lynched in Fort White, Fla.
Nov. 14: A black man named Nelson, accused of murder, was lynched in Varner, Ark.
Nov. 14: Three black men accused of murder were lynched in Lake City Junction, Fla.
Nov. 18: A white man accused of stealing horses was lynched near Ponca, Okla.
Nov. 21: F.O. Johnson, a white man accused of rape, was lynched at a site unknown.
Nov. 29: Newton Jones, a black man accused of murder, was lynched in Boxley, Ark.
Dec. 2: Lucius Holt, a black man accused of murder, was lynched in Concord, Ga.
Dec. 7: Robert Greenwood, a black man accused of racial prejudice, was lynched in Cross County, Ark.
Dec. 8: Joseph Giohen, Benjamin Minty, and Robert Wilkins, all black men accused of murder, were lynched in Berlin, Ala.
Dec. 10: Two unknown black men accused of murder were lynched in Alabama.
Dec. 12: Four unknown black men accused of attempted robbery were lynched near Selma, Ala.
Dec. 16: Henry Givens, a black man accused of poisoning livestock, was lynched in Nebo, Ky.
Dec. 19: William Ferguson, a black man, was lynched in Adel, Ga., for turning state's evidence.
Dec. 23: Sloan Allen, a black man suspected of murder, was lynched in West, Miss.
Dec. 23: An unknown black man suspected of robbery was lynched in Fannin, Miss.
Dec. 25: Calvin Thomas, a black man, was lynched in Georgia.
Dec. 28: Tillman Green, a black man accused of attempted assault, was lynched in Columbia, La.
Dec. 28: Mack Segars, a black man, was lynched in Brantley, Ala.

1894

Jan. 5: Alfred Davis, a black man accused of stealing, was lynched in Lonoke County, Ark.
Jan. 7: Judas Miller, a white man, was lynched in Ft. Reynold, Texas.
Jan. 7: Joshua Mitchell, a white man, was lynched in Leesburg, Ky.
Jan. 9: Samuel Smith, a black man accused of murder, was lynched in Greenville, Fla.
Jan. 11: Sherman Wagoner, a white man accused of murder, was lynched in Mitchell, Ind.
Jan. 12: Roscoe Parker, a black man accused of murder, was lynched in West Union, Ohio.
Jan. 14: Charles Willis, a black desperado, was lynched in Ocala, Fla.
Jan. 17: John Buckner, a black man accused of rape, was lynched in Valley Park, Mo.
Jan. 18: An unknown black man suspected of incendiarism was lynched in Bayou Sara, La.
Jan. 21: M.G. Gumble, a black man accused of rape, was lynched in Jellico Mines, Ky.
Jan. 22: An unknown black man accused of rape was lynched in Verona, Mo.
Feb. 2: George Hurst, a black man accused of murder, was lynched in Neely, Neb.
Feb. 6: A white man named A. Pikkarien, accused of rape, was lynched in Ewen, Wisc.
Feb. 9: Henry Bruce, a black man, and Charles and Robert Plunkett, both white, were lynched in Gulch County, Ark, after being accused of murder.
Feb. 10: A black man named Collins, accused of enticing a servant away, was lynched in Athens, Ga.
Feb. 10: Jesse Dillingham, a black man accused of wrecking a train, was lynched in Smokeyville, Texas.
Feb. 11: Henry McGreeg, a black man accused of rape, was lynched in Pioneer, Tenn.
Feb. 14: A white vagrant accused of murder was lynched in Quito, Tenn.
Feb. 15: Robert Collins, a black man accused of racial prejudice, was lynched in Oglethorpe, Ga.
Feb. 17: Three white men accused of murder, Hendricks, W. George and A. Seddon, were lynched in Stanton, Ala.
Feb. 25: A white man named P. Slaughter, accused of murder, was lynched in Sparta, N.C.
Feb. 26: A white man named T.Douglas, accused of murder, was lynched in Alabama.
Feb. 27: Two white men named A. Carter and B. Montgomery, accused of murder, were lynched in West Plaines, Mo.
Mar. 2: Len Tye, a black man accused of kidnapping, was lynched in Hariem, Ky.
Mar. 5: Sylvester Rhodes, a black man accused of murder, was lynched in Collins, Ga.
Mar. 6: Lampson Gregory, a black man, was lynched in Bells Depot, Tenn.
Mar. 6: John Rodgers, a white man accused of larceny, was lynched at a site unknown.
Mar. 6: An unidentified black woman was lynched near Marche, Ark.
Mar. 15: Richard Puryea, a black man accused of murder, was lynched in Pennsylvania.
Mar. 29: Oliver Jackson, a black man accused of murder, was lynched in Montgomery, Ala.
Mar. 30: A black man named Saybrick, accused of murder, was lynched at Fishers Ferry, Miss.
Apr. 2: Holland English, a black man accused of murder, was lynched in Bakerhill, Ala.
Apr. 5: Two unidentified black men accused of murder were lynched near Selma, Ala.
Apr. 6: Daniel Ahren, a black man accused of rape, was lynched in Greensboro, Ga.
Apr. 10: Edward Cash, a white man accused of rape, was lynched in Greensboro, Ga.
Apr. 14: Alfred Bren, a black man, was lynched in Gatesville, Texas.
Apr. 14: Jack Crews, a white man accused of murder, was lynched in Gainsville, Texas.
Apr. 14: William Lewis, a black man accused of murder, was lynched in Lamison, Ala.
Apr. 15: Seymour Neville, a black man accused of rape, was lynched in Rushsylvania, Ohio.
Apr. 18: Henry Montgomery, a black man accused of larceny, was lynched in Lewisburg, Tenn.
Apr. 19: Two white men, Dock Bishop and another named F. Latham, accused of stealing horses, were lynched in Wakongo, Okla.
Apr. 20: Henry Worley, a white man, was lynched in Murry County, Ga.
Apr. 20: A white man known as "Dutch John", accused of stealing cattle, was lynched at Tukon, in the Oklahoma Territory.
Apr. 22: Thomas Black, Tony Johnson, and John Williams, all black men accused of barn burning, were lynched in Tuscumbia, Ala.
Apr. 23: Thomas Claxton, David Hawkins, and Samuel Stangate, three black men accused of murder, were lynched in Tallulah, La.
Apr. 24: Jeff Luggle, a black man accused of murder, was lynched in Cherokee, Kan.
Apr. 26: Robert Evarts, a black man accused of rape, was lynched in Georgia.
Apr. 26: Seven white men accused of stealing horses, were lynched in Hennessey, Okla.
Apr. 27: Camp Claxton, Thell Claxton, Scott Harvey, and Jerry McCly, four black men accused of murder, were lynched in Tallulah, La.
Apr. 27: James Robinson and Benjamin White, both black men accused of rape, were lynched in Manassas, Va.
Apr. 30: Reddy Nilson, a white man accused of murder, was lynched in Missouri Valley, Iowa.
May 7: A white man named A. Hicks, suspected of arson, was lynched at Rocky Springs, Miss.
May 9: Lewis and W. McKindley, accused of murder, were lynched in Sharon Springs, Kan.
May 9: An unknown black man was lynched in West Texas for writing a letter to a white woman.
May 13: George Rose, a white man accused of rape, was lynched in Florida.
May 15: Coat Williams a black man accused of murder, was lynched in Pine Grove, La.
May 15: Nim Young, a black man accused of rape, was lynched in Ocala, Fla.
May 17: Henry Scott, a black man accused of murder, was lynched in Jefferson, Texas.
May 17: Samuel Wood, a black man, was lynched in Gate City, Va.
May 22: A black man accused of rape was lynched in Miller County, Ga.
May 23: William Brooks, a black man accused of asking a white woman to marry him, was lynched in Palestine, Ark.
May 26: Two Indian men accused of rape were lynched in Hennessey, Okla.
May 29: J.T. Burgis, a black man accused of conspiracy, was lynched in Palatka, Fla.
May 29: Henry Smith, a black man accused of burglary, was lynched in Clinton, Miss.

June 1: Frank Ballard, a black man accused of attempted murder, was lynched in Jackson, Tenn.
June 2: Jeff Crawford, a black man accused of murder, was lynched in Bethune, S.C.
June 2: Two white men named Hill and Parker, accused of murder, were lynched in Colfax, Wash.
June 2: Alex McCurdy, a white man accused of murder, was lynched in Golden, Colo.
June 3: Harry Gill, a black man, was lynched in Lancaster, S.C.
June 3: An unknown black man accused of highway robbery was lynched in Lancaster, S.C.
June 4: Ready Murdock, a black man suspected of rape, was lynched in Yazoo City, Miss.
June 4: Thomas Underwood, a black man accused of murder, was lynched in Monroe, La.
June 8: Isaac Kemp, a black man accused of murder, was lynched in Cape Charles, Va.
June 9: Lewis Williams, a black man suspected of rape, was lynched in Hewitt Springs, Miss.
June 10: Mark Jacobs, a black man accused of racial prejudice, was lynched in Bienville, La.
June 10: James Perry, a black man accused of spreading smallpox, was lynched in Knoxville, Tenn.
June 13: Bascom Cook and Lon Hall, both black men accused of murder, were lynched in Sweet Home, Texas.
June 13: A black man accused of rape was lynched in Blackshear, Ga.
June 14: J.H. Day, a black man suspected of arson, was lynched in Monroe, La.
June 15: Luke Thomas, a black man accused of murder, was lynched in Biloxi, Miss.
June 18: Owen Opietress, a black man accused of rape, was lynched in Forsythe, Ga.
June 20: Archie Haines and William Haines, two white men accused of horse stealing, were lynched in Mason County, Ky.
June 21: Burt Haines, a white man accused of horse stealing, was lynched in Mason County, Ky.
June 22: Henry Capus, a black man accused of rape, was lynched in Magnolia, Ark.
June 24: Caleb Godly, a black man accused of rape, was lynched in Bowling Green, Ky.
June 25: William Stacey, a white man accused of swindling, was lynched in Iowa Falls, Iowa.
June 26: William Pinkerton, a white man accused of rape, was lynched in Spring Valley, Ill.
June 28: Fayette Franklin, a black man accused of rape, was lynched in Mitchell County, Ga.
June 28: George Linton, a black man accused of attempted rape, was lynched in Brookhaven, Miss.
June 28: Edward White, a black man accused of attempted rape, was lynched in Hudson, La.
June 29: Ulyssess Haydon, a black man accused of murder, was lynched in Monett, Mo.
June 29: John Williams, a black man accused of murder, was lynched in Sulphur Springs, Texas.
July 2: Three white men accused of arson, Rapple Hills, his son, and a third unknown, were lynched at Bush Creek, Neb.
July 2: Joseph Johnson, a black man accused of rape, was lynched at Hillers Creek, Mo.
July 6: George Pond, a black man accused of attempted rape, was lynched in Fulton, Miss.
July 6: Lewis Barkhead, a black man accused of rape, was lynched in Amite County, Miss.
July 6: A black man named Hood, accused of murder, was lynched in Amite County, Miss.
July 7: James Ball, a black man accused of murder, was lynched in Charlotte, Tenn.
July 7: Augustus Pond, a black man accused of attempted rape, was lynched in Tupelo, Miss.
July 14: William Bell, a black man accused of burning a barn, was lynched in Dixon County, Tenn.
July 14: James Mason, a black man accused of being an informant, was lynched in Abbeville County, S.C.
July 14: An unknown black man accused of attempted rape was lynched in Biloxi, Miss.
July 16: Marion Howard, a black man accused of rape, was lynched in Scottsville, Ky.
July 19: John Brownlee, a black man, was lynched for political reasons in Oxford, Ala.
July 20: William Griffith, a black man accused of rape, was lynched in Woodville, Texas.
July 20: Allen Myers, a black man accused of witchcraft, was lynched in Rankin County, Miss.
July 24: An unknown black woman accused of racial prejudice was lynched in Simpson County, Miss.
July 26: Vance McClure, a black man accused of attempted rape, was lynched in New Iberia, La.
July 26: William Tyler, a black man accused of attempted rape, was lynched in Carlisle, Ky.
Aug. 2: Anderson Holliday, a black man, was lynched in Elkhorn, W.Va.
Aug. 2: W.S. Thompson, a white man accused of murder, was lynched in Lake View, Ore.
Aug. 12: William Nershbred, a black man accused of rape, was lynched in Rossville, Tenn.
Aug. 14: Marshall Boston a black man accused of rape, was lynched in Frankfort, Ky.
Sept. 1: Edward Hall, Daniel Hawkins, John Hayes, Robert Haynes, Graham White, and Warner Williams, all black men accused of barn burning, were lynched in Millington, Tenn.
Sept. 4: A white man named Bourke, accused of rape, was lynched in Watertown, S.D.
Sept. 9: Link Waggoner, a black man accused of murder, was lynched in Minden, La.
Sept. 14: James Smith, a black man accused of attempted rape, was lynched in Starke, Fla.
Sept. 14: Robert Williams, a black man accused of murder, was lynched in Concordia Parish, La.
Sept. 16: In Ki Wish, an Indian policeman, was lynched by desperadoes in the Oklahoma Territory.
Sept. 19: David Goosenby, a black man accused of rape, was lynched in Atlanta, Ga.
Sept. 21: James Darcey, a white man accused of being an informant, was lynched near Bristol, Tenn.
Sept. 22: Three black men, Henry Crobyson, Luke Washington, and another man named Washington, all accused of murder, were lynched in McGehee, Ark.
Sept. 26: A white man accused of stealing horses was lynched in Lincoln, Okla.
Oct. 1: Berry Rich, a white man suspected of robbery, was lynched in Marion County, Ky.
Oct. 8: Henry Gibson, a black man accused of attempted rape, was lynched in Fairfield, Texas.
Oct. 8: Al Richardson, a white man accused of rape and murder, was lynched in Irvine, Ky.
Oct. 14: Oscar Morton, a black man accused of murder, was lynched in Stanton, Ky.
Oct. 15: Willis Griffey, a black man accused of attempted rape, was lynched in Princeton, Ky.
Oct. 20: A black man named Williams, accused of attempted rape, was lynched in Upper Marlboro, Md.
Nov. 5: An unknown white man was lynched in Roscoe, Mo.
Nov. 8: Lee Lawrence, a black man accused of murder, was lynched in Jasper County, Ga.
Nov. 8: Gabe Nalls and Ulyssess Nalls, two black men accused of incendiarism, were lynched in Blackford, Ky.
Nov. 10: Needham Smith, a black man accused of rape, was lynched in Tipton County, Tenn.
Nov. 10: Charles Williams, a white man, and Lawrence Younger, a black man, both accused of murder, were lynched in Lloyds, Va.
Nov. 14: Robert Moseley, a black man accused of rape, was lynched in Dolimite, Ala.
Nov. 29: An unknown black man was lynched in Landrum, S.C.
Dec. 4: William Jackson, a black man accused of rape, was lynched in Ocala, Fla.
Dec. 5: A white woman named Mrs. T. Arthur was lynched in Lincoln County, W.Va.
Dec. 11: George Bronson, Lee Brown, and Charles Smith, all white men accused of murder, were lynched in Clarke County, Ala.
Dec. 17: An unidentified black man accused of rape, was lynched in Marion County, Fla.
Dec. 20: James Allen, a black man accused of arson, was lynched in Brownsville, Texas.
Dec. 23: George King, a black man accused of assault, was lynched in New Orleans, La.
Dec. 23: Seven black men accused of murder; Charles Frazier, Samuel Pike, Harry Sherard, Samuel Taylor, and three unknown; were lynched in Brooks County, Ga.
Dec. 26: William Carter, a black man accused of murder, was lynched in Winston, County, Miss.
Dec. 28: Scott Sherman, a black man, was lynched in Morehouse Parish, La.

1895

Jan. 1: Thomas Blau, a white man accused of murder, was lynched in Mt. Sterling, Ky.
Jan. 1: Barret Scott, a white man accused of fraud, was lynched in O'Neill, Neb.
Jan. 1: Three white men accused of stealing horses were lynched in Kingfisher, Okla.
Jan. 4: John F. Begeron, a white man accused of murder, was lynched in Idalit, N.C.
Jan. 7: Spencer Costello, a black man accused of murder and robbery, was lynched in Flora, Miss.
Jan. 9: Thomas Boyd, a white man suspected of murder, was lynched in Bowie, Texas.
Jan. 9: George Coldhand, a black man accused of murder, was lynched in Colquitt County, Ga.
Jan. 9: George Witherell was lynched in Canon City, Colo.

Feb. 17: George Tracy, a white man accused of murder, was lynched in Kingston, Mo.
Mar. 2: Charles Robertson, a black man accused of murder, was lynched in Allendaletown, Ga.
Mar. 11: Isaac Manion, a black man accused of murder, was lynched in Athens, Texas.
Mar. 12: Six white men accused of murder: Antonio Apoletti, Pietro Giaconino, Antinio Lorenzo, Francisco Rochetti, Stanislaus Vettari, and Joseph Welsby, were lynched in Walsenburg, Colo.
Mar. 12: Two white men accused of stealing horses were lynched at Enterprise, in the Oklahoma Territory.
Mar. 14: Armor Gibson, a black man accused of rape, was lynched in Forsythe, Ga.
Mar. 18: A white woman, Mrs. W.E. Holton, was lynched by vigilantes in Keyapaha County, Neb.
Mar. 19: Daniel Dawson, Joseph Holman, and Robert Holman, all black men accused of arson, were lynched in Tyler, Ala.
Mar. 20: Harriet Talley, a black woman suspected of arson, was lynched in Petersburg, Tenn.
Mar. 29: Robert Betat, a black man accused of arson, was lynched in Bluff Creek, Miss.
Apr. 2: William Rawles, a black man accused of murder, was lynched in Florida.
Apr. 3: Newton Walters, a white man accused of murder, was lynched in Kansas.
Apr. 12: Nelson Calhoun, a black man accused of rape, was lynched in Corsicana, Texas.
Apr. 14: Frederick Chamberlain and Dean Powell, both white men accused of rustling cattle, were lynched in Keyapaha County, Neb.
Apr. 15: Manuel Dunegan, a black man, was lynched to prevent evidence in Chilton County, Ala.
Apr. 21: Zeb Colley, Mary Deane, Alice Green, Martha Green, and John Rattler, all black persons accused of murder, were lynched in Greenville, Ala.
Apr. 25: An unknown black man was lynched in Parsons, Tenn.
Apr. 26: George Ray, a black man accused of being disreputable, was lynched in Gensonton, Ky.
Apr. 28: Thomas Gibson, a white man, was lynched in Sevierville, Tenn.
Apr. 30: George Jones, an Indian man accused of assault, was lynched in Devers, Texas.
May 2: Thomas Brownlee, a black man accused of being an informant, was lynched in Butts County, Ga.
May 5: Andy Hames, a white man accused of murder, was lynched in Stevenson, Ala.
May 15: John Calvin and William Dunn, both white men accused of being informants, were lynched near Ingalls, Okla.
May 16: John Howeston, a white man accused of rape, was lynched in Marion, Ky.
May 19: John Brooks, Simeon Crowley and Samuel Echols, all black, were lynched for rape near Ellaville, Fla.
May 19: Jerido Shivers, a black man accused of rape, was lynched in Coffee County, Ala.
May 22: William Connell, a white man accused of murder, was lynched in Montgomery County, Ga.
May 23: Claude Thompson, a black man accused of attempted rape, was lynched in De Koven, Ky.
May 23: An unknown black man accused of rape, was lynched in Rodney, Miss.
May 25: John Crocker, a white man accused of murder, his wife and his son, were lynched in Wharton, Texas.
May 25: John Halls and William Royce, two white men accused of rape, were lynched in Danville, Ill.
May 27: Jacob Henson, a black man accused of murder, was lynched in Elliot City, Md.
May 30: Three unidentified black men suspected of rape were lynched in Bartow, Fla.
May 31: James Freeman, a black man accused of rape, was lynched in Columbus City, Ala.
May 31: Nelson Weatheroff, a white man accused of attempted rape, was lynched in Logan, Ohio.
June 5: James Powell, a black man accused of attempted rape, was lynched in Alabama.
June 9: William Collins, a black man accused of attempted rape, was lynched in Mayo, Fla.
June 11: John Cherry and Alexander White, both black men accused of murder, were lynched in Keno, Texas.
June 11: William Johnson, a black man accused of rape, was lynched in Lufkin, Texas.
June 11: Two unidentified black men accused of harboring a criminal were lynched in Mayo, Fla.
June 13: J.M. Alexander, a black man accused of protecting another black man, was lynched in Tuskegee, Ala.
June 17: R.W. Dawson, a white man accused of murder, was lynched in Natchez, Miss.
June 18: George Harris, a black man accused of attempted rape, was lynched near Dublin, Ga.
June 19: William Chandler, a black man accused of attempted rape, was lynched in Abbeyville, Miss.
June 20: Frank King, a black man accused of murder, was lynched in Little Rock, Ark.
June 24: John Fry, a white man accused of arson, was lynched in Gretna, La.
June 26: Thomas Browne, a black man accused of burglary, was lynched in Point Clear, Ala.
June 26: William Stokes, a black man accused of attempted rape, was lynched in Colleton County, S.C.
June 29: Thomas Bowen, a black man accused of rape, was lynched in Brook Haven, Miss.
July 1: Abithal Colston, a white man, and Mollie Smith, a black man, both accused of murder, were lynched in Trigg County, Ky.
July 1: Two white men accused of stealing horses were lynched near Guthrie, Okla.
July 2: Samuel Chandler, a black man, was lynched in Monroe, Ga.
July 2: Marshal C. Price, a white man accused of murder, was lynched in Denton, Md.
July 4: Robert Bennet, a black man accused of attempted rape, was lynched near Lake City, Fla.
July 6: Theodore Picket, a black man accused of larceny, was lynched in Jackson, Miss.
July 9: A white man, Howton Howlett, and his son, were lynched in Lewiston, Ky.
July 14: Two unidentified black men suspected of rape were lynched in Hampton, Ark.
July 15: Robert Huggard, a black man suspected of rape, was lynched in Winchester, Ky.
July 15: Ira Jackson, a black man suspected of rape, was lynched in Piedmont, S.C.
July 18: Andrew Thomas, a black man accused of rape, was lynched in Scranton, Miss.
July 20: Six black people accused of racial prejudice: Benjamin Johnson, Abe Phillips, Jr., Mrs. Abe Phillips, Edward Phillips, Hannah E. Phillips, and K.D. Taylor; were lynched in Mant. Texas.
July 23: An unknown black woman accused of racial prejudice was lynched in Brenham, Texas.
July 24: Ovide Belzaire, a black man accused of racial prejudice, was lynched in Youngsville, La.
July 25: Thomas Johnson, a black man accused of murder, was lynched in Hattiesburg, Miss.
July 27: Victor Adams, a white man accused of murder, was lynched in O'Neals Madera County, Calif.
July 28: Charles Burwell, a black man accused of assault, was lynched in Meridian, Miss.
July 29: Squire Loftin, a black man accused of rape, was lynched in Lexington, Texas.
Aug. 2: A black couple, Mr. and Mrs. James Mason, were lynched in Daingerfield, Texas.
Aug. 12: William Harris, a black man accused of attempted rape, was lynched in Colquitt County, Ga.
Aug. 12: An unknown black man accused of racial prejudice was lynched in Delta County, Texas.
Aug. 14: Charles Vinson and Samuel Vinson, both white men accused of murder, were lynched in Ellensburg, Wash.
Aug. 15: Emmett Divens, a black man accused of murder, was lynched in Fulton, Mo.
Aug. 16: Two white brothers named Bidderly, accused of stealing cattle, were lynched in Buffalo County, S.D.
Aug. 18: Samuel Lewis, a black man accused of murder, was lynched in Florida.
Aug. 21: Noah Anderson, a black man accused of murder, was lynched in New Richmond, Ohio.
Aug. 22: James Jones, a black man accused of murder, was lynched in Arkansas.
Aug. 22: An unknown black man accused of murder was lynched in Wharton, Texas.
Aug. 26: Jefferson Cole, a black man accused of racial prejudice, was lynched in Paris, Texas.
Aug. 26: Four white men; Lawrence Johnson, Louis Moreno, William Null, and Harland Seemler, accused of murder, were lynched in Yreka, Calif.
Aug. 26: Harrison Lewis, a black man accused of murder, was lynched in Springfield, Ky.
Sept. 2: William Butcher, a black man accused of murder, was lynched in Hickman, Ky.
Sept. 2: An unknown black man accused of miscegenation was lynched in Simpson County, Miss.
Sept. 3: Jerry Johnson, a black man accused of making insulting remarks, was lynched in Farmington, Tenn.
Sept. 5: Aaron Freeman, a white man accused of rape, was lynched near Hot Springs, Ark.
Sept. 6: "Doc" King, a black man accused of attempted rape, was lynched in Fayetteville, Tenn.
Sept. 10: Wesley Wingfield, a black man accused of attempted rape, was lynched in Lunenburg, Va.
Sept. 10: Lum Wood, a white man accused of giving evidence, was lynched in Union City, Tenn.
Sept. 11: Two black men, William Caldwell and John Thomas, accused

of murder, were lynched near Osceola, Ark.
Sept. 19: An unknown black man accused of rape was lynched in Arkansas.
Sept. 22: William Smith, a black man accused of murder, was lynched in Hammond, La.
Sept. 26: Felician Francis, a black person was lynched near New Orleans, La.
Sept. 27: William Archor, an indian man accused of murder, was lynched in Bakersfield, Calif.
Oct. 1: John Littlefield, a white man accused of murder, was lynched in Round Valley, Calif.
Oct. 4: Neal Smith, a black man accused of rape, was lynched in Georgia.
Oct. 5: Tobe McGrady, a black man accused of rape, was lynched in Perote, Ala.
Oct. 11: William Henderson, a black man accused of rape, was lynched in Jackson, Mo.
Oct. 14: Floantina Suitta, a white woman accused of murder, was lynched in Catula, Texas.
Oct. 15: Jeff Ellis, a black man accused of murder, was lynched in Braden, Tenn.
Oct. 15: Eugene Vancy, a black man accused of rape, was lynched in Manchester, Tenn.
Oct. 17: William Blake, a white man accused of murder, was lynched in Hampton, S.C.
Oct. 17: Daniel E. Young, a white man, was lynched in Oak Canon, N.M.
Oct. 22: John Henderson, a white man accused of attempted rape, was lynched in Vinegar Bend, Ala.
Oct. 22: Two white men accused of stealing cattle, James Umbra and another known as Mexican John, were lynched in Hennessey, Okla.
Oct. 29: Henry Hilliard, a black man accused of murder, was lynched in Tyler, Texas.
Nov. 4: Albert England, a black man accused of burglary, was lynched in Wynne, Ark.
Nov. 4: Lewis Jefferson, a black man accused of rape, was lynched in Homersville, Ga.
Nov. 17: James Bowens, a black man accused of rape, was lynched in Frederick, Md.
Nov. 21: Charles Hurd, a black man accused of murder, was lynched in Wartburg, Tenn.
Nov. 21: Two black men accused of rape were lynched in Henderson, Ky.
Nov. 21: A black man was lynched in Madison County, Texas.
Nov. 23: L.W. Perdue, a white man accused of rape, was lynched in Georgia.
Nov. 24: John Richards and Thomas Watts, both black men accused of murder, were lynched in Abbeville, S.C.
Nov. 25: Balam Hancock, a black man accused of attempted rape, was lynched in Gibson, Ga.
Nov. 25: An unidentified black man accused of train-wrecking was lynched in Calvert, Ky.
Nov. 29: Ozias McGahey and Joseph Robinson, both black men accused of murder, were lynched in Fayetteville, Tenn.
Nov. 29: Cad Smith, a white man accused of attempted rape, was lynched near Ootlewah, Tenn.
Nov.29: A white man named Yarborough, accused of murder, was lynched in Crystal Springs, Miss.
Dec. 1: Two white desperadoes, Henry Sutton and Long Sutton, were lynched in Unadilla, Ga.
Dec. 2: Two black men named Henrip and Poss, accused of murder, were lynched in Fairfax County, Va.
Dec. 5: A black couple, Isom Kearse, accused of larceny; and Hannah Kearse, accused of having knowledge of the larceny, were lynched in Colleton County, S.C.
Dec. 7: William Blake, a black man suspected of murder, was lynched in Hampton, S.C.
Dec. 8: James Smith, a white man accused of being an informer, was lynched in Monticello, Ga.
Dec. 29: William Dever, a white man accused of murder, and Mrs. T.J. West, a white woman accused of mob indignation, were lynched in Lebanon, Ky.

1896

Jan. 8: Harrison Fuller and Frank Simpson, both black men accused of rape, were lynched in Lexington, Tenn.
Jan. 10: A.L. Smart, a black man accused of murder, was lynched near Monroe, La.
Jan. 10: George H. Smith, a white man accused of murder, was lynched in Ransonville, N.Y.
Jan. 12: Three members of the Patrick Morris family, accused of miscegenation, were lynched near New Orleans, La.
Jan. 13: Harry Jordon, a black man accused of murder, was lynched in Alachua, Fla.
Jan. 15: Four highwaymen, Thomas Foley, a man named "Wild Horse," an Indian, and another unknown, were lynched at Ft. Holmes, Okla.
Jan. 18: An unknown black man accused of assault was lynched in Mitchelville, Iowa.
Jan. 28: Alexander Jones, a black man accused of murder, was lynched in Bluefield, W.Va.
Feb. 1: An unknown black man accused of murder was lynched in Bramwell, W.Va.
Feb. 9: Hy Blake, a white man accused of illicit distilling, was lynched in Georgia.
Feb. 10: James Leeds, a white man accused of attempted assault, was lynched in Seddon, Ala.
Feb. 12: A white man named Grant, accused of murder, was lynched in Sullivan, Ill.
Feb. 17: Fomit Martin, a black man accused of burning a barn, was lynched in Monticello, Ky.
Feb. 17: Robert Wilson, a white man accused of murder, was lynched in Montgomery, Ala.
Feb. 20: A white man named T. Lewis, accused of robbery and murder, was lynched in Wichita Falls, Texas.
Feb. 29: Foster Crawford, a white man accused of robbery and murder, was lynched in Wichita Falls, Texas.
Feb. 29: Two white men, Gilbert Francis and Paul Francis, accused of robbery and assault, were lynched in St. James, La.
Feb. 29: Melville Kennedy, a black man suspected of rape, was lynched in Windsor, S.C.
Mar. 16: Bird Love, a black man accused of robbery, was lynched in Rayville, La.
Mar. 22: William Murphy, a white man accused of murder, was lynched in Huntsville, Tenn.
Mar. 23: Isaac Pizer, a black man accused of attempted rape, was lynched near Shreveport, La.
Mar. 24: Louis Senegal, a black man accused of rape, was lynched in Carencro, La.
Apr. 3: Harvey Mayberry, a black man accused of rape, was lynched in Teysels, Miss.
Apr. 12: Reddrick Adams, a black man accused of murder, was lynched in Seale, Ala.
Apr. 15: Sam Covington, a white man accused of murder, was lynched in Central City, Colo.
Apr. 17: York Douglas, a black man accused of incendiarism, was lynched in McMinnville, Tenn.
Apr. 18: Sterling Savage, a white man accused of distilling moonshine, was lynched in Irving College, Tenn.
Apr. 20: John Van Brunt, a black man accused of disorderly conduct, was lynched in De Land, Fla.
Apr. 22: Robert Charmers, a black man accused of incendiarism, was lynched in Cranberry, N.C.
Apr. 23: Thomas Price, a black man accused of assault, was lynched in Westville, S.C.
Apr. 26: Victor Hillis and William Hillis, both white men accused of murder, were lynched in Shellsford, Tenn.
Apr. 27: O.H. Givens, a white man accused of murder, was lynched in Dandridge, Tenn.
May 3: William Benby, a black man accused of murder, was lynched in Beaumont, Texas.
May 7: Charles Jones, a black man, was lynched in MacClenny, Fla.
May 9: Eden Williams, a white man accused of incest, was lynched in Manitua, Ala.
May 11: Harry Wilson, a black man, and a white man named Murray, were lynched in Madison County, Fla.
May 11: An unknown black man accused of murder was lynched in Fulton, Ky.
May 12: William Hardee, a black man accused of assault, was lynched in Nichols, Ga.
May 19: Joseph Dazzele, a black man accused of attempted rape, was lynched in St. Bernard Parish, La.
May 21: An unknown black man was lynched in Bossier Parish, La.
June 1: Two black men, William Miles and Jesse Slayton, accused of rape, were lynched in Columbus, Ga.
June 10: George J. Johnson and Louis Whitehead, both black men accused of rape, were lynched in Bryan, Texas.
June 12: Samuel Clay, a black man accused of attempted rape, was lynched in Martin, Tenn.
June 12: Walter Starkes, a black man accused of rape, was lynched in Baldwin, La.
June 20: Leon Orr, a black man accused of rape, was lynched in Alabama.
June 24: William Westmoreland, a black man accused of murder, was lynched in Montgomery, Ala.
June 27: James Cockling, a white man accused of murder, was lynched in La Plata, Mo.
June 27: Perry Young, a black man accused of rape, was lynched in Winona, Miss.
June 30: Cecil Wayland, a white man accused of rape, was lynched near Hannibal, Mo.
June 30: An unknown black man accused of rape was lynched near Trenton, Tenn.
July 6: Nimrod Cross, a black man accused of rape, was lynched in Sardis, Tenn.
July 6: Jacob Williams, a black man accused of rape, was lynched in Madison County, Fla.
July 6: An unknown black man accused of rape was lynched in Lincoln County, S.C.
July 13: Mond Dunley and James Porter, two black men accused of

murder, were lynched in Minden, La.
July 13: Courtney Rendrick, a black man accused of murderous assault, was lynched in Monroe, La.
July 14: Three white men accused of stealing horses were lynched at Reagan, in the Oklahoma Territory.
July 15: Frank James, a black man accused of murder, was lynched in Bayou Sara, La.
July 18: Daniel Dicks, a black man accused of rape, was lynched in Ellenton, S.C.
July 27: A white man named M. Crawford, accused of attempted rape, was lynched near Tipton, Mo.
July 27: Isaac McGee, a black man accused of rape, was lynched in Homer, La.
July 31: Gidfrey Gould, a black man accused of rape, was lynched in Clarendon, Ark.
Aug. 1: William Hunter and Isadore Moreley, black men accused of attempted murder, were lynched near Selma, Ala.
Aug. 3: Louis Mullen, a white man accused of attempted rape, was lynched in Bunkie, La.
Aug. 5: Hiram Weightman, a black man accused of attempted murder, was lynched in Franklin, La.
Aug. 9: Decimo Loceno, Angelo Marcuso, and L. Saladino, three white men accused of murder, were lynched in Halumlee, La.
Aug. 13: Benjamin Gay, a black man accused of arson, was lynched in Hopkins County, Texas.
Sept. 4: Thomas Larkin, a white man accused of rape, was lynched in Vineland, Mo.
Sept. 10: Two white vagrants accused of murder were lynched in Glencoe, Minn.
Sept. 14: Thomas White, a black man, was lynched in Aurora, Ky.
Sept. 16: James McCauley, a black man accused of rape, was lynched in Monroe, La.
Sept. 16: B.S. Morris, a black man accused of murder, was lynched in Watonga, Okla.
Sept. 16: Lem Warren, a black man accused of rape, was lynched in Terrell County, Ga.
Sept. 19: Elmer Coax, a white man accused of murder, was lynched in Pawnee, Okla.
Sept 23: Two black men, Charles Harris and Anthony Johnson, accused of rape, were lynched near De Land, Fla.
Sept. 24: Alexander Hawkins, a black man accused of slapping a child, was lynched in Gretna, La.
Sept. 27: Harrison Boone, a black man accused of shooting at an officer, was lynched in Sparta, Ga.
Sept. 27: John Fitch, a black man accused of attempted rape, was lynched in Alabama.
Oct. 7: Charles Williams, a black man accused of murder, was lynched in Georgia.
Oct. 9: Louis Hamilton, a black man accused of arson, was lynched in Bossier Point, La.
Oct. 10: James Anderson, a black man suspected of murder, was lynched in Taylor Ferry, Ala.
Oct. 10: A black man named Henry Cyat, accused of murder, was lynched in Henry, Ala.
Oct. 12: An unknown black man accused of murder was lynched in Ala.
Oct. 14: George Harris, Charles Jones, and William Smith, three white men accused of bank robbery, were lynched in Meeker, Colo.
Oct. 14: An unknown black man accused of murder was lynched in Toadvine, Ala.
Oct. 15: Henry Milner, a black man accused of rape, was lynched in Griffin, Ga.
Oct. 21: A white man named Hollinshead was lynched for turning state's evidence in Washington county, Ala.
Oct. 21: A unknown black man accused of murder was lynched in Sunnyside, Miss.
Nov. 15: Charles Allen, a black man accused of rape, was lynched in McKenzie, Tenn.
Nov. 18: Mimms Collier, a black man accused of attempted rape, was lynched in Steenston, Miss.
Nov. 19: Samuel M. Donald, a black man accused of making threats, was lynched in Huntingdon, Tenn.
Nov. 28: Alfred Daniels, a white man accused of arson, was lynched in Gainsville, Fla.
Dec. 6: James Nelson and Jessie Winner, two white men accused of murder, were lynched in Lexington, Mo.
Dec. 7: William Wardley, a black man accused of passing counterfeit money, was lynched in Irondale, Ala.
Dec. 9: A black man known as Crazy Jim, accused of murder, was lynched in Milton, Ark.
Dec. 17: An unknown black man accused of murder was lynched near Pine Bluff, Ark.
Dec. 18: Arch Proctor and Pink Proctor, two white men accused of murder, were lynched near Russellville, Ky.
Dec. 21: James Stone, a black man accused of rape, was lynched in Mayfield, Ky.
Dec. 22: Jerry Burke, a black man accused of attempted murder, was lynched in Clio, La.
Dec. 22: George Finley, a black man accused of theft, was lynched in Mayfield, Ky.
Dec. 22: Joseph James, a black man accused of rape, was lynched in Woodstock, Ala.
Dec. 26: Alfred Holt, a black man accused of murder, was lynched in Owensboro, Ky.

1897

Jan. 5: Sidney Gust, a black man accused of racial prejudice, was lynched in Georgia.
Jan. 6: Lawrence Brown, a black man suspected of arson, was lynched in Stilton, S.C.
Jan. 8: An unknown black man suspected of arson was lynched in Orangeburg, S.C.
Jan. 8: Simon Cooper, a black man accused of murder, was lynched in Sumter, S.C.
Jan. 9: Anthony Henderson, a black man accused of murder, was lynched in Unadilla, Ga.
Jan. 10: Two black men accused of murder and robbery were lynched in Vardaman, Miss.
Jan. 17: An unknown black highwayman was lynched in White Castle, La.
Jan. 19: Gus Johnson, Archie Joiner, and Gus Williams, black men accused of murder, were lynched in Amite City, La.
Jan. 20: Peter Henderson, a black man accused of murder and assault, was lynched in Itta Bena, Miss.
Jan. 22: Two black men, Charles Forsythe and William White, accused of murder, were lynched in Jeffersonville, Ga.
Jan. 24: Pierce Taylor, a black man accused of attempted rape, was lynched in Tallahassee, Fla.
Jan. 25: Eugene Washington, a black man accused of rape, was lynched in Bryan, Texas.
Jan. 27: George Brannan, a black man accused of assault, was lynched in Georgia.
Jan. 31: James Jackson, a black man accused of murder, was lynched in Bibb County, Ala.
Feb. 4: Henry Linton and Joseph Robinson, both white outlaws, were lynched in Oklahoma.
Feb. 4: Robert Morton, a black man accused of writing insulting letters, was lynched in Rockford, Ky.
Feb. 13: An unknown black man accused of rape was lynched in Saluda, S.C.
Feb. 17: Two black men accused of arson were lynched in Webb City, Tenn.
Feb. 26: Charles Brown, a black man accused of attempted rape, was lynched in Soddy, Tenn.
Mar. 2: An Indian doctor and a white girl were lynched in Morganton, N.C.
Mar. 3: A white man, William Whaley, and his wife, were lynched in Sevierville, Tenn.
Mar. 5: Five black men accused of murder; Henry Edwards, Jack Green, Sam Jones, Wash Melton, and Otea Smith, were lynched in Juliette, Fla.
Mar. 5: An unknown black man accused of burglary was lynched in Elgin, Texas.
Mar. 8: An unknown black man accused of stealing was lynched in Rock Springs, Ky.
Mar. 14: William Clement, a black man accused of a felony, was lynched in Lynchburg, Va.
Mar. 15: Three black men accused of murder; James Gilmore, James Miley, and Otis Miller, were lynched in Juliette, Fla.
Mar. 18: Andy Beard, a black man who eloped with a white girl, was lynched in Kennedy, Ala.
Mar. 20: John Smith, a black man accused of rape, was lynched in Scottsboro, Ala.
Mar. 26: John Marritt, a black man accused of assault, was lynched in Pickens County, Ala.
Mar. 28: T.W. Hollinshead, a black man accused of being an informer, was lynched in Waynesboro, Miss.
Apr. 2: Joseph McCoy, a black man accused of rape, was lynched in Alexandria, Va.
Apr. 3: A black man named Haines, accused of murder, was lynched in Belen, Miss.
Apr. 10: An unknown black man was lynched near Vicksburg, Miss.
Apr. 14: William Braydee, a white man accused of murder, was lynched near Middleboro, Ky.
Apr. 16: Jesse Evans, a black man accused of rape, was lynched in Edwards, Miss.
Apr. 27: Rob Brown, Hal Wright, and Russell Wright, three black men accused of robbery and arson, were lynched in Harrison County, Texas.
Apr. 30: Seven black men accused of murder: William Gates, Fayette Rhone, Aaron Thomas, Benjamin Thomas, James Thomas, Lewis Thomas, and William Williams; were lynched in Sunnyside, Texas.
May 12: Amanda Franks and Molly White, both black women accused of murder, were lynched in Jefferson, Ala.
May 13: James Nance, a black man accused of murder, was lynched in Jefferson, Ala.
May 14: Three black men accused of attempted rape: David Cotton, Sabe Stewart, and Henry Williams; were lynched in Rosebud, Texas.
May 15: An Indian man named Alivate, accused of murder, was lynched at a site unknown.

May 15: Charles Jackson, a black man accused of train wrecking, was lynched in Redwood, La.
May 18: A black man known as Captain Lewis was lynched in Lumpkin, Ga., because of alleged arson.
May 18: Three men named White, accused of murder, were lynched in San Augustine, Texas.
May 20: Presley Oates, a black man accused of theft, was lynched in Arkansas.
May 21: A white man named Peter was lynched in Brown County, Texas.
May 22: Jack Coffman and John Mitchell, two white men accused of larceny, were lynched in Mountain Grove, Mo.
May 23: William Jones, a black man accused of murder, was lynched in Tyler, Texas.
May 27: James Cooper, a black man accused of attempted murder, was lynched in Hemlock, Miss.
May 29: Thomas Johnson and Joseph Kiser, both black men suspected of murder, were lynched in Concord, N.C.
June 1: John Hayden, a black man, was lynched in a case of mistaken identity, in Lamar County, Ala.
June 4: Charles Mitchell, a black man accused of rape, was lynched in Urbana, Ohio.
June 5: Isaac Barrett, a black man accused of murder, was lynched in Orange Dale, Fla.
June 9: William Anderson, a black man accused of rape, was lynched in Princess Anne, Md.
June 10: An Indian man known as Mouse, accused of murder, was lynched at Muddy Creek, Nev.
June 23: An unknown black man accused of murder was lynched in Newcastle, Tenn.
June 25: John M. Moses, a black man accused of murder, was lynched in Crystal Springs, Miss.
June 28: Pary Giliam, a black man accused of assault and robbery, was lynched in Aberdeen, Miss.
July 9: James Thomas, a black man, was lynched in Blossburg, Ala., for refusing to give evidence.
July 10: Erastus Brown, a black man accused of rape, was lynched in Villa Ridge, Mo.
July 13: Atticus Thompson, a black man accused of insulting a white woman, was lynched in Forest, La.
July 15: Tony Williamson, a black man accused of murder, was lynched in West Point, Tenn.
July 16: A black man named Terrill, accused of murder, was lynched in Elba, Ala.
July 19: W.L. Ryder, a white man accused of murder, was lynched in Waverly, Ga.
July 20: James Daniel, a black man accused of attempted rape, was lynched in Goose County, Ala.
July 21: James Speaks, a black man accused of rape, was lynched in Riverton, Ala.
July 22: Ephraim Brinkley, a black man, was lynched in Madison, Ky.
July 23: James Gray, a black man accused of rape, was lynched in Golboro, S.C.
July 23: Oscar Williams, a black man accused of attempted rape, was lynched in Griffin, Ga.
July 24: Jack Davis, a black man accused of rape, was lynched in Baldwin, La.
July 28: James Sellers, a black man accused of murder, was lynched in Pittsboro, Miss.
Aug. 6: Esseck White, a black man accused of rape, was lynched in Nacogdoches, Texas.
Aug. 10: John Gordon, a black man accused of murder, was lynched in Louisiana.
Aug. 10: Rev. Captain Jones, a white man, was lynched for eloping, in Paris, Texas.
Aug. 15: George Wilson, a black man, was lynched in Meyers, Ky.
Aug. 19: An unknown white vagrant accused of murderous assault was lynched in Mannheim, Ill.
Aug. 20: John E. Nowhir, a white man accused of being a revenue informer, was lynched in Runneybag, Va.
Aug. 20: An unknown black man accused of attempted rape was lynched in Apalachicola, Fla.
Aug. 21: A unknown white man accused of larceny was lynched in Skaguay, Alaska.
Aug. 22: Eleany Sullivan, a white man accused of rape, was lynched in Williamsburg, Ky.
Aug. 23: Andrew Green, a black man accused of murder, was lynched in Lovett, Ga.
Aug. 24: William Wyatt, a black man, accused of murder, was lynched in Rison, Ark.
Aug. 26: A black man named Bonner, accused of rape, was lynched in Bellville, Texas.
Aug. 26: Wesly Johnson, a white man accused of attempted rape, was lynched in Mooreville, Texas.
Aug. 26: Edward Williams, a black man accused of rape, was lynched in Baxter, Ark.
Aug. 30: Jack Pharr, a black man accused of robbery, was lynched in Claiborne, Ala.
Sept. 2: Ben Scott, a black man accused of stealing cattle, was lynched in Echols County, Ga.
Sept. 2: An unknown black man accused of assault was lynched in Excel, Ala.
Sept. 5: An unknown black man was lynched in Robroy, Ark.
Sept. 6: Henry Wall, a black man accused of rape, was lynched in Friends Mission, Va.
Sept. 11: William G. Martin, a white man accused of larceny, was lynched in Lake Bennett, Alaska.
Sept. 12: Charles Gibson, a black man accused of murder, was lynched in Mason, Ga.
Sept. 15: Five white men accused of burglary: Robert Andrews, Clifford Gordon, William Jenkins, Lyle Levi, and Heine Shuble; were lynched in Valparaiso, Ind.
Sept. 16: D.L. Watson, a black man accused of racial prejudice, was lynched in Hamilton, Ark.
Sept. 18: An unknown white man accused of larceny was lynched in Skaguay, Alaska.
Sept. 18: Two white cattle rustlers were lynched at Morea River, S.D.
Sept. 26: Raymond Brushrod, a black man accused of rape, was lynched in Hainsville, Ky.
Oct. 1: William Oliver, a black man, was lynched in Jefferson, La., for disobeying ferry regulations.
Oct. 2: Peb Falls, a white woman, was lynched in Cowans Depot, Va.
Oct. 2: Washington Furran, a black man accused of rape, was lynched in Monroe, La.
Oct. 2: Frank Johnson, a black man accused of rape, was lynched in Georgia.
Oct. 6: Henry Crower, a black man accused of rape, was lynched in Hernando, Miss.
Oct. 11: Robert Carter, a black man accused of murder, was lynched in Brenham, Texas.
Oct. 15: Douglas Bolte, a black man, was lynched for running in Quarantine, La.
Oct. 15: Thomas Parker, a black man accused of killing a white cap, was lynched in Kendall, Ark.
Oct. 16: William Williams, a black man accused of rape, was lynched in Hamburg, Miss.
Oct. 17: A white man named Cole, accused of murder, was lynched in Wilmot, Ark.
Oct. 28: Juan Madera, accused of murder, was lynched in Morenci, Ariz.
Nov. 14: Two Indians, Alex Condout and Paul Holy Track, and a white man, Philip Ireland; all accused of murder, were lynched in Williamsport, S.D.
Nov. 15: Henry Philkips, a black man accused of murder, was lynched in Osceola, Ark.
Nov. 18: Silas P. Fargo, a white man suspected of arson, was lynched in Liberty, Mo.
Nov. 18: Joshua Ruff, a black man accused of rape, was lynched in Gibson, Ga.
Nov. 18: Thomas Sweat, a black man accused of murder, was lynched in Bryan, Texas.
Nov. 19: William Connell, a white man accused of murder, was lynched in Dublin, Ga.
Nov. 25: Hicks Price, a black man accused of rape, was lynched in Starke, Fla.
Nov. 27: Nathan Willis, a black man accused of murder, was lynched in Town Creek, N.C.
Nov. 29: Henry Abrams, a black man accused of murder, was lynched in Montgomery, Ala.
Dec. 7: Adam Uber, a white man accused of murder, was lynched in Genoa, Nev.
Dec. 8: A white man named Murray was lynched in Jenny Lind, Ark., for arresting a miner.
Dec. 10: Charles Jones, a black man accused of murder, was lynched in Weanon, Miss.
Dec. 13: Three black men accused of murder: Charles Alexander, James Alexander, and Joseph Thomas, were lynched near Plaquemine, La.
Dec. 16: John Bonner and Louis Bonner, both black men accused of giving evidence, were lynched in Kennedy, Ala.
Dec. 16: Thomas Waller, a black man accused of murder, was lynched near Brookhaven, Miss.
Dec. 17: Bud Beard, a black man accused of rape, was lynched in Carrolton, Ala.
Dec. 23: Chadwick Marshall and Joseph McDonald, both white men accused of murder, were lynched in Colfax, Wash.
Dec. 27: James Hopkins, a black man accused of murder, was lynched in Glendora, Miss.
Dec. 29: Sam Turner, a black man accused of murder, was lynched in Kingstree, S.C.

1898

Jan. 1: James Jones, a black man accused of arson, was lynched in Macon, Miss.
Jan. 1: An unidentified black man accused of theft was lynched in Sherrill, Ark.
Jan. 4: David Hunter, a black man accused of violating a contract, was lynched in Clinton, S.C.
Jan. 7: Sam Cole and James Watts, two black men who made insulting remarks, were lynched in Pea Ridge, Miss.

Jan. 8: Marshall Chadwick, a white man accused of murder, was lynched in Colfax, Wash.
Jan. 8: Black men named Daval and Huntley and two unidentified, were lynched near Reader, Ark., after being accused of murder.
Jan. 8: John McGeesey and Palmer Simpson, both Indian men accused of murder, were lynched at Maud, in the Oklahoma Territory.
Jan. 26: Mary Pearson, a white woman accused of murder was lynched near Natchez, Miss.
Feb. 1: John Belin, a black man accused of murder, was lynched in Georgia.
Feb. 2: M.F. Tanner, a white man accused of murder, was lynched in Alaska.
Feb. 2: A black man named Ward, accused of murder, was lynched in Galena, Mo.
Feb. 13: Whit Dillard, a white man accused of murder, was lynched in Blue Ridge, Ga.
Feb. 20: John Kellog, a black man accused of attempted rape, was lynched in Blanche, Ala.
Feb. 22: F.B. and Dora Baker, a black couple accused of racial prejudice, were lynched in Lake City, S.C.
Feb. 23: Two black men, Richard Allen, accused of robbery; and Thomas Holmes, accused of murder; were lynched in Mayfield, Ky.
Mar. 2: Frederick Moore, a white man accused of murder was lynched in Senatobia, Miss.
Mar. 6: William Jones, a black man accused of rape, was lynched in Lake Cormorant, Miss.
Mar. 7: Louis P. Johnson and a man named Banvret, both white and accused of murder, were lynched near Cheyenne, Wyo.
Mar. 9: William Harris and Andrew Pigge, two black men accused of robbery, were lynched near New Orleans, La.
Mar. 15: An unknown black man accused of robbery was lynched in Marcella, Ark.
Mar. 20: Alex Anderson, a black man accused of attempted rape, was lynched in Grenada, Miss.
Mar. 21: John Calloway, a black man accused of paying attention to a white girl, was lynched in Calhoun County, Ala.
Mar. 21: John Collar, a black man accused of attempted rape, was lynched in Godson, Tenn.
Mar. 24: Joseph Allen, a black man accused of attempted murder, was lynched in Moultrie, Ga.
Apr. 2: William Bell, a black man accused of murder, was lynched in Amite, La.
Apr. 3: William Mercer, a white man accused of murder, was lynched in Ark.
Apr. 5: Carlos Guilen, a black man accused of murder, was lynched in Brownsville, Texas.
Apr. 26: Columbus Lewis, a black man, was lynched in Lincoln Parish, La., for resisting arrest.
Apr. 29: Paris Smith, a white man accused of murder, was lynched in Coeburn, Va.
May 6: Dennis Burrel, a black man accused of murder, was lynched in New Orleans, La.
May 26: Garfield King, a black man accused of murder, was lynched in Salisbury, Md.
May 27: Joseph Mitchell, a black man accused of murder, was lynched in Rives, Tenn.
May 27: Richard Olliver, a black man accused of murder, was lynched in Donaldsonville, Ga.
June 3: Levi Hayden, a black man accused of assault, was lynched in Texarkana, Ark.
June 3: William Street, a black man accused of attempted murder, was lynched in Doyline, La.
June 6: George Washington, a black man accused of murder, was lynched in Wemar, Texas.
June 6: Curtin Young and Sam Young, both black men accused of murder, were lynched in Clarkville, Mo.
June 13: John Becker, a white man accused of murder, was lynched in Great Bend, Kan.
June 15: An unidentified black man accused of assaulting a police officer was lynched in Oak Ridge, La.
June 16: Gams Calls, a black man accused of rape, was lynched in Glasgow, Ky.
June 17: Five black men accused of murder: Soloman Jackson, William Jackson, Camp Reese, Louis Spier and Jesse Thompson; were lynched in Wetumpka, Ala.
June 23: Charles Washington, a black man accused of rape, was lynched in Mine Lick, Tenn.
June 26: George Scott, a black man accused of rape, was lynched in Russellville, Ky.
June 30: Henry Williams, a black man accused of rape, was lynched in Macon, Mo.
July 1: Goode Gray, a black man accused of murder, was lynched in Rison, Ark.
July 12: Wesley Gould, a black man in a case of mistaken identity, was lynched in Leland, Miss.
July 12: John H. James, a black man accused of rape, was lynched in Charlottesville, Va.
July 12: Sidney Johnson, a black man accused of rape, was lynched in Coaling, Ala.
July 14: Two black men, Alexander Johnson and James Reid, accused of murder, were lynched in Monticello, Ark.
July 19: William Patterson, a black man, was lynched in Westville, Miss.
July 27: Lee Elmer, a white man accused of murder, was lynched in Wahpeton, S.D.
Aug. 8: John Meadows, a black man accused of attempted rape, was lynched in Carmel, Ga.
Aug. 8: Dan Ogg, a black man accused of rape, was lynched in Palestine, Texas.
Aug. 8: Richard Thurmond, a black man, was lynched in Ripley, Tenn.
Aug. 9: Four black men: Castle Manse, Dennis Ricord, William Saunders, and Rilla Weaver; accused of murder, were lynched in Clarendon, Ark.
Aug. 9: William Nail, a white man accused of murder, was lynched at Braggs, in the Oklahoma Territory.
Aug. 11: Benjamin Jones, a white man accused of murder, was lynched in Liberty, Mo.
Aug. 11: Mulloch Walker, a black man accused of robbery, was lynched in Corinth, Miss.
Aug. 20: A black man accused of murder was lynched in Americus, Ga.
Sept. 7: John Williams, a black man accused of rape, was lynched in Fowlstown, Ga.
Sept. 11: George Burton, a black man accused of rape, was lynched in Digbey, Ga.
Sept. 13: Albert Anderson, a black man accused of murder, was lynched in Alabama.
Sept. 15: A white man named Wise, accused of stealing horses, was lynched at Turtle Mountains, S.D.
Sept. 26: John Williams, a black man accused of rape, was lynched in Mountain City, Tenn.
Oct. 1: Peter Johnson, a black man accused of larceny, was lynched in Edmond, Okla.
Oct. 2: John Anderson, a black man accused of murder, was lynched in Lafayette, Ala.
Oct. 2: Arch Bauer, a black man accused of murderous assault, was lynched in Tompkinsville, Ky.
Oct. 2: Wright Smith, a black man accused of attempted rape, was lynched in Annapolis, Md.
Oct. 23: Joseph Mackie and Luther Sullivan, both black men suspected of murder, were lynched in Edgefield, S.C.
Oct. 23: An unknown black man accused of murder was lynched in Lafayette, Ala.
Nov. 6: Arthur Williams, a black man accused of murder, was lynched in Wellborne, Fla.
Nov. 7: F.W. Stewart, a black man accused of rape, was lynched in Lacon, Ill.
Nov. 9: Six black people suspected of murder: Jeff Darling, Rose Etheridge, Columbus Jackson, Hampton McKenny, Drayton Williams, and Jesse Williams; were lynched in Phoenix, S.C.
Nov. 10: Benjamin Collins and Essex Harrison, both black men suspected of murder, were lynched in Phoenix, S.C.
Nov. 17: Charles Morrell, a black man accused of burglary, was lynched in Edgard, La.
Nov. 18: Eliza Goode, a black man accused of racial prejudice, was lynched in Greenwood, S.C.
Nov. 19: John Smart, a black man accused of racial prejudice, was lynched in Chapelton, Tenn.
Nov. 23: Edward Merriweather, a black man accused of rape, was lynched in Monticello, Ga.
Nov. 27: Three black men accused of assaulting a white man were lynched near Meridian, Miss.
Nov. 29: A unidentified black man accused of murder was lynched near New Madrid, Mo.
Dec. 6: Newton Gaines, a black man accused of rape, was lynched in Arkansas.
Dec. 6: Jacob Glover, a black man accused of murder, was lynched in Monticello, Ga.
Dec. 6: James Anderson, a black man accused of murder, was lynched in Georgia.
Dec. 6: Two black men named Hearn and Richardson, accused of murder, were lynched in Benton, La.
Dec. 6: A black man named White, accused of murder, was lynched in Tallahatchie County, Miss.
Dec. 10: Eli Fisher, a white man, was lynched in Montana, in a case of mistaken identity.
Dec. 16: Pleas Goin, a white man accused of murder, was lynched near Middletown, Ky.
Dec. 21: William Simms, a white man accused of murder, was lynched near Decatur, Ill.
Dec. 24: Marion Tyler, a white man accused of murderous assault, was lynched in Scottsburg, Ind.
Dec. 26: Jeff Bolton, a white man accused of arson, was lynched in Harmony Grove, Ga.

1899

Jan. 5: Marsal McGregor, a black man suspected of arson, was lynched in Banks, Ala.
Jan. 11: Henry Jones, a black man accused of murder, was lynched in

Harps Cross, N.C.
Jan. 17: Two black men, George Call and John Shaw, were lynched in Lynchburg, Tenn.
Feb. 1: Charles Martin, a black man, was lynched in Madison, Fla.
Feb. 11: Three black men accused of rape; George L. Bivins, George Foot, and William Holt; were lynched in Leesburg, Ga.
Mar. 11: Thomas Allen, a black man, was lynched in McGee, Miss.
Mar. 16: Five black men accused of arson: John Bigley, Henry Bingham, Edward Brown, Bud Catlen, and Tip Hutson; were lynched in Palmetto, Ga.
Mar. 23: Three black men accused of racial prejudice: Willis Boyd, C.C. Reed, and Minor Wilson; were lynched in Silver City, Miss.
Mar. 23: Seven black men: General Duckett, Edward Goodwin, Benjamin Jones, Joseph Jones, Moses Jones, Joseph King, and another unidentified; all accused of murder, were lynched in Little River County, Ark.
Mar. 28: Henry Sanderson, a white man accused of murder, was lynched in Kansas.
Apr. 6: Two black men accused of murder, Moses Anderson and Forest Jameson, were lynched in Brookfield, Miss.
Apr. 18: W.H. Harkin, a white man accused of murder, was lynched in Clinton, Ark.
Apr. 18: A.M. Larne, a white man accused of murder, was lynched in Henderson, Tenn.
Apr. 23: Sam Holt was doused with kerosene and burned at the stake after being mutilated by knives near Newnan, Ga. He was accused of murdering Alfred Cranford and raping his wife.
Apr. 25: Elijah Strickland was hanged in Palmetto, Ga., after being implicated in the murder of Alfred Cranford, by Sam Holt, who was lynched April 23.
Apr. 25: Samuel Hose, a black man accused of murder and rape, was lynched in Newman, Ga.
Apr. 25: Charles Williams, a black man accused of murder, was lynched in Galena, Kan.
Apr. 27: Mitchell Daniel, a black man, was lynched in Leesburg, Ga., for using inflammatory language.
May 1: Willie Dees, a black man accused of arson, was lynched in Osceola, Ark.
May 11: Walter Holland, a white man accused of rape, was lynched in Meyers, Ky.
May 11: Two black men accused of murder were lynched in Pitt County, N.C.
May 22: Thomas Linton, a black man accused of racial prejudice, was lynched in Georgia.
May 23: A white man named Humphry and his two sons, were lynched in Ally, Texas, for abetting the escape of a murderer.
June 7: William Hill, a white man accused of being a murder accomplice, was lynched in Bibb County, Ala.
June 11: Simon Brooks, a black man accused of robbery, was lynched in Sardis, Miss.
June 13: A black man accused of murder and two others accused of racial prejudice were lynched in Dunellon, Fla.
June 14: Edward Gray, a black man accused of racial prejudice, was lynched in St. Peter, La.
June 16: Two black men, David Clark, accused of resisting arrest, and a man named Williams, accused of rape, were lynched near Odum, Ga.
June 18: Louis Patrick, a black man accused of murder, was lynched in Bayne, S.C.
June 20: Daniel Patrick, a black man accused of rape, was lynched in Scranton, Miss.
June 27: Henry Stevens, a white highway robber, was lynched in Fulton, Ky.
July 1: Allie Thompson, a black man accused of rape, was lynched in Waskom, Texas.
July 9: Bud Brake, a white man accused of being an accomplice in a murder, was lynched in Corning, Texas.
July 14: Abe Brown, a black man accused of rape and murder, was lynched in Gilead, Texas.
July 14: An unknown black man accused of murder, was lynched in Iola, Texas.
July 16: Six white men accused of being accomplices in a murder: Joseph Cereno, Charles Defalta, Frank Defalta, Joseph Defalta, Sy Deferroch, and Si Smith; were lynched in Tallulah, La.
July 16: George Jones, a black man, was lynched in St. Charles Parish, La.
July 16: Harry McGee, a black man accused of murder, was lynched in Navasota, Texas.
July 23: Frank Embree, a black man accused of rape, was lynched in Steinmetz, Mo.
July 23: Six black men accused of robbery and murder: Gus Fish-Head, Washington Johnson, Charles Mack, Louis Sammin, and two unknown men, were lynched in Safford, Ga.
July 24: Chich Davis, a black man accused of rape, was lynched in Wilmot, Ark.
July 24: An unknown black man accused of rape was lynched in Pushington, Miss.
July 25: An unknown black man accused of complicity in a murder was lynched near Leesburg, Ga.
July 25: Henry Hamilton, a black man accused of incendiarism, was lynched near Navasota, Texas.
July 25: Henry Noark, a black man accused of attempted rape, was lynched in Hattiesburg, Miss.
July 26: Stanley Hayes, a black man accused of attempted rape, was lynched near Brandon, Miss.
July 27: In a case of mistaken identity, a black man was lynched in Lindsay, La.
Aug. 1: Solomon Jones, a black man accused of attempted rape, was lynched in Forrest, Ga.
Aug. 2: Taylor Kirk, a white man accused of murder, was lynched in Cloud Chief, Okla.
Aug. 3: Louis Henderson, a black man accused of rape, was lynched in Blakely, Ga.
Aug. 8: Benjamin Thompson, a black man accused of rape, was lynched in Alexandria, Va.
Aug. 9: Echo Brown, a black man accused of various crimes, was lynched in Amite City, La.
Aug. 9: An unknown black man accused of rape was lynched in Jasper, Fla.
Aug. 11: William Chambers, a black man accused of rape, was lynched in Bellbuckle, Tenn.
Aug. 11: William McCue, a black man accused of attempted rape, was lynched in Clem, Ga.
Aug. 11: Man Singleton, a black man accused of attempted rape, was lynched in Grant Point, La.
Aug. 11: William Wilson, a black man accused of attempted rape, was lynched in Port Gibson, Miss.
Aug. 17: Charles Hunt, a black man accused of attempted rape, was lynched in Brantley, Ala.
Aug. 21: A white man, Peter Lonin, and his son, both suspected of murder, were lynched in Electric, Ala.
Sept. 6: William Stern, a black man accused of murder, was lynched in Rosemeath, Miss.
Sept. 14: An unidentified black man accused of rape was lynched in Ty Ty, Ga.
Sept. 20: William Otis, a black man, was lynched in Rawles Springs, Miss.
Oct. 10: Basil Laplace, a white man, was lynched in St. James Parish, La.
Oct. 15: James L. Smith, a white desperado, was lynched in Wilson, La.
Oct. 21: Joseph Luflore, a black man accused of arson and murder, was lynched in St. Anne, Miss.
Oct. 24: John Goosby, a black man accused of attempted murder, was lynched in Georgia.
Oct. 30: George Mills, a black man accused of murder, was lynched in Weir, Kan.
Nov. 1: Thomas Hayden, a black man accused of murder, was lynched near Fayette, Mo.
Nov. 2: Albert Sloss, a black man accused of attempted rape, was lynched near Courtland, Ala.
Nov. 16: William Huuf, a white man accused of murder, was lynched in Bloomfield, Mo.
Nov. 22: Lawrence West, a black man accused of rape, was lynched near Pensacola, Fla.
Nov. 23: An unknown black man accused of attempted rape was lynched in Jackson, Ga.
Dec. 6: Richard Coleman, a 20-year-old black man, was intercepted by an angry mob as he was being delivered from a prison cell to be tried for the murder of a white woman, in Maysville, Ky.
Dec. 13: David Pierce, a black man accused of murder, was lynched in Dunbar, Penn.
Dec. 13: An unknown black man accused of rape was lynched in Jones, La.
Dec. 23: James Martin and Frank West, both black and accused of murder, were lynched in Bolton, Miss.

1900

John Gambola, a white man accused of murder, was lynched in Hackensack, N.J.
Jan. 5: W.W. Wates, a white man accused of rape, was lynched in Newport News, Va.
Jan. 9: Henry Giveney and Roger Giveney, both black men accused of murder, were lynched in Ripley, Tenn.
Jan. 11: Rufus Salter, a black man suspected of arson, was lynched in West Springs, S.C.
Jan. 16: Anderson Ganse, a black man accused of abetting the escape of a murderer, was lynched in Henning, Tenn.
Jan. 20: Two white men accused of murder, Edward Smith and George Smith, were lynched at Fort Scott, Kan.
Jan. 26: Thomas Reynolds, a white man accused of murder, was lynched in Canon City, Colo.
Feb. 11: James Sweeney, a white man accused of murder, was lynched in Port Arthur, Texas.
Feb. 17: In Columbia, S.C., William Burts, a 19-year-old black man accused of attacking Mrs. C.L. Weeks, was lynched.
Mar. 4: James Crosby, a black man accused of making murderous threats, was lynched in Tutwiler, Miss.
Mar. 4: George Ratcliffe, a black man accused of rape, was lynched in Clyde, N.C.
Mar. 10: Thomas Clayton, a black man accused of rape, was lynched in

Hernando, Miss.
Mar. 11: An unidentified black man accused of murder was lynched in Jennings, Fla.
Mar. 18: John Barley, a black man accused of attempted rape, was lynched in Marietta, Ga.
Mar. 18: Charles Humphries, a black man accused of attempted rape, was lynched in Lee County, Ala.
Mar 22: George Ritter, a black man accused of being an informer, was lynched in Carthage, N.C.
Mar. 23: Lewis Rice, a black man, was hanged in Ripley, Tenn., for testifying in favor of another black man, alleged to have murdered a white man named Goodrich.
Mar. 24: Walter Colton and Brandt O'Grady, both black men accused of murder, were lynched in Emporia, Va.
Mar. 26: Lewis Harris, a black man accused of rape, was lynched in Belair, Md.
Mar. 27: William Edward, a black man accused of murder, was lynched at Deep Creek Bridge, Miss.
Apr. 3: Allen Brooks, a black man accused of rape, was lynched in Berryville, Ga.
Apr. 5: A unknown black man accused of arson was lynched in Southampton County, Va.
Apr. 16: Moses York, a black man accused of murder, was lynched near Tunica, Miss.
Apr. 19: Henry McAfee, a black man accused of attempted rape, was lynched in Brownsville, Miss.
Apr. 22: Edward Ames and John Hugerly, two black men accused of plotting to kill whites were lynched in Allentown, La.
Apr. 22: John Peters, a black man accused of rape, was lynched in Tazewell, Va.
Apr. 28: Mundee Chowagee, a black man accused of murder, was lynched in Marshall, Mo.
May 1: George Gordon, a black man accused of attacking a white man, was lynched in Albin, Miss.
May 1: Henry Ratcliff, a black man accused of attacking a white man, was lynched in Gloster, Miss.
May 4: Henry Darley, a black man accused of rape, was lynched in Liberty, Mo.
May 4: Marshall Jones, a black man accused of murder, was lynched in Douglas, Ga.
May 7: An unknown black man accused of rape was lynched in Geneva, Ala.
May 7: An unknown black man was lynched in Amity County, Miss.
May 11: William Lee, a black man accused of attempted rape, was lynched in Hinton, W.Va.
May 13: Alex Whitney, a black man accused of murder, was lynched in Harlem, Ga.
May 14: William Willis, a black man accused of murder, was lynched in Grovetown, Ga.
May 14: Two unknown black men accused of murder were lynched in Brooksville, Fla.
May 15: Henry Harris, a black man accused of attempted rape, was lynched in Lena, La.
May 16: Samuel Hinson, a black man accused of assault, was lynched in Cushtusha, Miss.
May 22: Calvin Kunblern, a black man, was lynched in Pueblo, Colo.
May 26: An unknown black man accused of robbery was lynched in West Point, Ark.
June 3: Dago Pete, a black man accused of rape, was lynched in Tutwiler, Miss.
June 9: Simon Adams, a black man accused of attempted rape, was lynched near Columbus, Ga.
June 10: A black man named Askew was lynched in Mississippi City, Miss., after being suspected of murdering a schoolgirl.
June 10: John Sanders and another black man were shot to pieces in Sneads, Fla. They were believed to be accessories to the murder of Ernest Hardwick, a white farmer who was beaten to death by a gang of black men.
June 11: Lenny Jefferson, a black man accused of attempted rape, was lynched in Metcalf, Ga.
June 12: John Brodie, a black man accused of attempted murder, was lynched in Lee County, Ark.
June 12: Seth Cobb, a black man accused of making threats, was lynched in Devail Bluff, La.
June 17: Nat Mullens, a black man accused of murder, was lynched in Earle, Ark.
June 19: William Woodward, a white man accused of murder, was lynched in Searcy County, Ark.
June 23: Frank Gilmore, a white man accused of rape, was lynched in Livingston Parish, La.
June 27: Robert Davis, a black man accused of murder, was lynched in Mulberry, Fla.
June 27: Jordan Hines, a black man, was lynched in Molena, Ga.
June 27: Jack Thomas, a black man accused of attempted rape, was lynched in Live Oak, Fla.
June 29: James Barco, a black man, was lynched in Panasoffkee, Fla.
July 23: Elijah Clark, a 20-year-old black man, was abducted from a Huntsville, Ala., jail by 150 cotton mill workers and shot to death, following his arrest for the assault of 13-year-old Susan Priest.
Aug. 13: Jack Betts, a black man accused of rape, was lynched in Corinth, Miss.
Sept. 1: Thomas J. Amos, a black man accused of murder, was lynched in Cheneyville, La.
Sept. 1: An unknown black man accused of murder was lynched in Forest City, N.C.
Sept. 8: Grant Welly, a black man accused of assaulting a white man, was lynched in Thomasville, Ga.
Sept. 10: Logan Reams, a black man accused of attempted rape, was lynched in Duplex, Tenn.
Sept. 12: Zed Floyd, a black man accused of murder, was lynched in Tunica, Miss.
Sept. 14: Frank Brown, William Brown, and David Moore, all black and accused of murder, were lynched in Tunica, Miss.
Sept. 19: An unknown black man accused of rape was lynched in Arrington, Va.
Sept. 21: Four black men accused of burglary: George Bickham, Nathaniel Bowman, Charles Elliott, and Isaiah Rollins were lynched in Ponchatonia, La.
Sept. 26: An unknown black man accused of rape was lynched near South Pittsburg, Tenn.
Oct. 2: Winfield Townsend, a black man accused of attempted rape, was lynched in Eclectic, Ala.
Oct. 3: A black man named Williams, accused of robbery, was lynched in Tiptonville, Tenn.
Oct. 18: Fraten Warfield, a black man accused of attempted rape, was lynched in Elliston, Ky.
Oct. 19: Frank Hardeman, a black man accused of rape, was lynched in Willaston, Ga.
Oct. 19: Nubry Johnson, a black man accused of murder, was lynched near Baton Rouge, La.
Oct. 23: Gloster Barnes, a black man accused of murder, was lynched near Vicksburg, Miss.
Oct. 24: Two black men, James Caleaway and James Guer, accused of racial prejudice, were lynched in Liberty Hill. Ga.
Oct. 30: A black man named Abernathy, accused of assault, was lynched in Duke, Ala.
Nov. 8: Kit Nabors, a white man accused of murder, was lynched in Coahoma, Miss.
Nov. 15: Three black men accused of attempted murder were lynched in Jefferson, Texas.
Nov. 16: Preston Porter, a white man accused of murder, was lynched in Colorado.
Nov. 27: Spencer Williams, a white man accused of murderous assault was lynched in Lake City, Fla.
Dec. 8: Daniel Long, a black man, was lynched in Wythe County, Va.
Dec. 8: Bud Rufus, a white man accused of murder, was lynched near Rome, Ga.
Dec. 16: Thomas Henderson and Bud Rowland, two black men accused of murder, were lynched in Rockport, Ind.
Dec. 17: John Rollo, a black man accused of complicity in a murder, was lynched in Booneville, Ind.
Dec. 19: Two black men accused of murder were lynched in Arcadia, Miss.
Dec. 20: A black man named Lewis, accused of murder, was lynched in Gulfport, Miss.
Dec. 21: An unknown black man accused of rape was lynched in Arkadelphia, Ark.
Dec. 28: George Fuller, a black man accused of arson, was lynched in Marion County, Ga.

1901

Jan. 3: In Rome Ga., a black man, George Reed, was shot and hanged after being released by Superior Court Judge Hudson. Reed, accused of assaulting Mrs. J.M. Locklear, was released to the mob of 150 men, in spite of the fact that the woman was unable to identify her assailant.
Jan. 3: Louis McAdams, a black man accused of murderous assault, was lynched in Wilsonville, Ala.
Jan. 3: Nelson Simpson, a black man accused of racial prejudice, was lynched in Neelyville, Mo.
Jan. 3: Sterling Thompson, a black man accused of racial prejudice, was lynched in Campbell County, Ga.
Jan. 5: An unidentified black man accused of rape was lynched near Quitman, Ga.
Jan. 7: James Denson, a black man, and his stepson, accused of murder, were lynched in Madison, Fla.
Jan. 15: Fred Alexander, a black man accused of murder and rape, was lynched in Leavenworth, Kan.
Jan. 16: Norman McKinney, a black man accused of train wrecking, was lynched in Dunnellon, Fla.
Jan. 16: Charles Robinson, a black man accused of rape, was lynched in Elko, S.C.
Jan. 24: An unknown black man accused of rape was lynched in Doylands, La.
Feb. 1: Warner Matthews, a black man accused of rape, was lynched in Ocean Springs, Miss.
Feb. 8: Sam Williams and William Wright, black men accused of complicity in a murder, were lynched in Dade City, Fla.

Feb. 11: George Carter, a black man accused of rape, was lynched in Paris, Texas.
Feb. 17: Thomas Jackson, a black man accused of murder, was lynched in St. Peter, La.
Feb. 18: Fred Isham and Henry Isham, two black men accused of arson, were lynched in Macon, Miss.
Feb. 18: Fred King, a black man accused of attempted rape, was lynched in Dyersburg, Tenn.
Feb. 20: Peter Berryman, a black man accused of assaulting a white person, was lynched in Mena, Ark.
Feb. 21: Thomas Vital, a black man accused of rape, was lynched in Fenton, La.
Feb. 26: John Knox, a white man accused of murder was lynched in Scranton, Miss.
Feb. 26: George Ward, a black man, was dragged from his Terre Haute, Ind., prison cell and hanged from a tree at the banks of the Wabash river. He was accused of murdering Ida Finkelstein, a school teacher.
Feb. 28: Johnson Miller, an Indian man accused of murder, was lynched at Holdenville, in the Oklahoma Territory.
Mar. 2: Arthur McNeal, a black man accused of murder, was lynched in Richmond, Mo.
Mar. 2: John Moody, a black man, was lynched in Bryan County, Ga.
Mar. 5: William Davis, a black man accused of rape, was lynched in Blanchard, La.
Mar. 6: Bud Davis, a black man, was lynched in Moulton, Ala.
Mar. 13: Sherman Harris, a black man accused of murder, was lynched in Shellman, Ga.
Mar. 13: In Corsicana, Texas, John Henderson, a black man, was burned at the stake before 5000 persons for rape.
Mar. 16: Ballie Crutchfield, a black woman in Rome, Tenn., was abducted from her cabin at midnight, shot in the head, and thrown in a nearby creek. She was attacked after her brother escaped from a mob that was attempting to execute him for theft.
Mar. 17: Isaac Fitzgerald, a white man accused of rape, was lynched in Tiptonville, Tenn.
Mar. 18: An unknown black man accused of murder was lynched in Randolph County, Ga.
Mar. 20: Terry Bell, a black man accused of racial prejudice, was lynched in Terry, Miss.
Mar. 22: An unknown black man was lynched for arson in Halifax County, Va.
Mar. 23: George Stunly, a white man accused of murder, was lynched in Pocohantos, Ark.
Apr. 2: Charles Davis, a white man accused of rape, was lynched in Smithville, Tenn.
Apr. 6: May Hearn, a white woman accused of murder, was lynched in Osceola, Ark.
Apr. 15: Kennedy Gordon, a black man accused of attempted rape, was lynched in Portal, Ga.
Apr. 25: Henry Noles, a black man accused of murder, was lynched near Winchester, Tenn.
Apr. 29: William Grouslsby, a black man accused of murderous assault, was lynched in Elberton, Ga.
Apr. 29: Wyatt Mallory, a black man accused of murder, was lynched in Springfield, Tenn.
May 4: Felton Brigman, a black man accused of rape, was lynched in Rodessa, La.
May 4: Grant Johnson, a black man accused of running a gambling house, was lynched in Alden Bridge, La.
May 6: Three black men, Robert Dawson, "Dic" Mayes, and Ed Mayes, accused of sheltering a murderer, were lynched in Selma, Ala.
May 10: J.L. Chandler, a white man suspected of killing cattle, was lynched in Oklahoma.
May 10: Henry Johnson, a black man accused of murderous assault, was lynched in Valdosta, Ga.
May 11: A black man, thought to be James Brown, was shot to death by a number of white men near Leeds, Ala. The victim was accused of assaulting Della Garrett, but the local coroner thought the mob had killed the wrong man.
May 11: William Williams, a black man accused of theft, was lynched in South Side, Ala.
May 13: A black man named Dr. Herman, accused of racial prejudice, was lynched in Topeka, Kan.
May 13: Lee Key, a black man accused of racial prejudice, was lynched in Knoxville, Ark.
May 22: Milt Calvert, a white man accused of attempted rape, was lynched in Griffith, Miss.
May 22: An unknown black man accused of arson was lynched in Halifax County, Va.
May 25: William Campbell, a black man accused of murder, was lynched in Pond Creek, Okla.
May 30: Frank Reeves, a black man accused of attempted rape, was lynched in Butler County, Ala.
May 30: Fred Rochelle, a black man accused of murder, was lynched in Bartow, Fla.
May 31: Five white men: Calvin Hale, Frank Hale, James Hale, Martin Hale, and B.D. Tantis, accused of theft, were lynched in Lookout, Calif.
June 5: "Dic" Dickson, a black man accused of murder, was lynched in Minden, La.
June 16: George Harris, a black man accused of arson, was lynched in Limestone, Ala.
June 19: A mob of approximately 200 armed men in Benton, La., lynched two black men, Frank "Prophet" Smith and F.D. McLand, arrested for murdering a white man, John Gray Foster.
June 29: An unknown black man accused of attempted rape, was lynched in Georgetown, Ga.
July 1: A black man named Walker, accused of rape, was lynched in Lawrenceville, Va.
July 10: Tung Fook, a Chinese man, was lynched in California.
July 11: Five white men, including John Ameo and a man named Victor, accused of stealing cattle, were lynched in Erwin, Miss.
July 14: A black man named Haines, accused of murder, was lynched in Thickety, S.C.
July 15: Louis Thomas, a black man accused of theft, was lynched in Girard, La.
July 16: Alexander Herman, a black man accused of murder, was lynched in Courtland, Ala.
July 16: Salvator Librero, a white man, was lynched in Judith, Mont.
July 19: An unknown black man accused of resisting rape was lynched in Crowley, La.
July 20: Jesse P. Philips, a white man accused of murder, was lynched in Cleveland, Miss.
July 21: William Cornish, a black man accused of murder, was lynched in Port Royal, S.C.
July 22: William Brooks, a black man accused of murder, was lynched in Elkins, W.Va.
July 25: Frank Erle, a black man accused of robbery, was lynched in Vidalia, Ga.
July 26: John Mack, a white man, was lynched in Missouri.
July 27: Ignacio Rivera, accused of being a horse thief, was lynched at Hent's Ranch, Ariz.
Aug. 1: Three black women, Belfield, Betsy, and Ida McCray, all implicated in a murder, were lynched in Carrolton, Miss.
Aug. 1: A white man named Seigler, accused of murder, was lynched in Rosston, Ark.
Aug. 1: An unknown black man accused of insulting a white woman was lynched in Mobile, Texas.
Aug. 2: Charles Bentley, a black man accused of murder, was lynched in Leeds, Ala.
Aug. 4: William Price, a black man accused of complicity in a murder, was lynched in Carrolton, Miss.
Aug. 5: William Heffen, a black man accused of murder, was lynched in Moscow, Iowa.
Aug. 7: John Pennington, a black man, was chained to a tree and burned to death near Enterprise, Ala. He was caught in a swamp by a mob using bloodhounds after an attack on a white woman, Mrs. J.C. Davis.
Aug. 10: An unknown black man accused of rape, was lynched in Ways Station, Ga.
Aug. 19: Three black men, French Godley, William Godley, and Peter Hampton, were lynched for suspicion of murder in Lexington, Mo.
Aug. 20: In Pierce City, Mo., a mob of white men terrorized the black community for fifteen hours, burning the homes of five black families and causing the death of 71-year-old Peter Hampton. The violence occurred in the aftermath of the murder of Casselle Wilds, for which two men were lynched the previous day.
Aug. 20: Abe Wilder, a black man accused of murder, was lynched in Dexter, Texas.
Aug. 21: Luke Hough, a black man accused of murder, was lynched in Wadesborough, N.C.
Aug. 25: Felix Martinez, a white man, was lynched in Kenedy, Texas.
Sept 1: Richard Hill, a black man accused of murder, was lynched in Philadelphia, Miss.
Sept. 1: Sam West, a black man accused of attempted rape, was lynched in Louisiana.
Sept. 3: William Fournay, a black man accused of rape, was lynched in Chestnut, Ala.
Sept. 7: An unknown black man accused of rape was lynched in Chipley, Fla.
Sept. 12: Three black men accused of murder: Ernest Harris, Frank Howard, and Sam Reed, were lynched in Wickliff, Ky.
Oct. 2: James E. Brady, a white man accused of rape, was lynched in Helena, Mont.
Oct. 2: Jumbo Fields and Clarence Garnett, two black men accused of murder, were lynched in Shelbyville, Ky.
Oct. 3: Five black men were lynched in Harrison, Texas, after quarreling over a profit sharing arrangement
Oct. 4: Walter McClennon, a black man accused of assaulting a white man, was lynched in Huntingdon, Tenn.
Oct. 7: Matthew Wilson, a white man accused of attempted rape, was lynched in Helena, Mont.
Oct. 7: Four black men accused of theft, were lynched in Caney Springs, Tenn.
Oct. 8: The wife of the jailer of Shelbyville, Ky., died in the aftermath of a jail attack in which two black men were taken and lynched. Mrs. Ben C. Perkins apparently died of shock and fright after the abduction.
Oct. 12: William Morris, a black man accused of rape, was lynched in

Balltown, La.
Oct. 21: An unknown black man accused of burglary, was lynched in Hampton, S.C.
Oct. 25: Galner Gordon, a black man accused of murder, was lynched in Quitman, Texas.
Oct. 31: Silas Esters, a white man who forced a boy to commit a crime, was lynched in Hodgenville, Ky.
Nov. 1: An unknown black man accused of attempted rape, was lynched in Allentown, Ga.
Nov. 4: A unknown black man accused of rape was lynched in Perry County, Miss.
Nov. 24: John Ladison, a black man accused of murder, was lynched in Anderson County, S.C.
Nov. 24: Frank Thompson, a black man accused of murder, was lynched in Shreveport, La.
Dec. 6: Three unknown black men accused of racial prejudice, were lynched in Covington County, Ala.
Dec. 7: Sam Poydrass, a black man accused of murderous assault, was lynched in Lake Charles, La.
Dec. 25: J.H. McClinton, a black man, was lynched in Paris, Texas.

1902

Jan. 11: Mays, a black man accused of criminal assault, was lynched in Spyfield, Ky.
Jan. 18: John Yellowwolf, a white man accused of stealing horses, was lynched in Rosebud, S.D.
Jan. 26: Two black men accused of murder were lynched in West Carrol Parish, La.
Feb. 6: Thomas Brown, a black man accused of criminal assault, was lynched in Nicholasville, Ky.
Feb. 6: Enless Whitaker, a black man accused of murder, was lynched in Lynchburg, Tenn.
Feb. 7: A black man named T. Williams was lynched in Glen Jean, W.Va.
Feb. 15: Bell Duly, a black man suspected of murder, was lynched in Fulton, Ky.
Feb. 17: Louis Wright, a black man accused of assaulting a white man, was lynched in New Madrid, Mo.
Feb. 20: Oliver Bibb, a black man accused of being an accessory to a murder, was lynched in Winona, La.
Feb. 26: Woodford Hughes, a black man, was lynched in Illinois.
Mar. 10: Horace McCoy, a black man accused of criminal assault, was lynched in Foreman, Ark.
Mar. 11: Nathan Bird, a black man, was lynched along with his son, in Luling, Texas.
Mar. 19: John Woodward, a black man accused of murder, was lynched in Vidalia, La.
Mar. 20: Elijah Drake and James Stewart, two black men suspected of larceny, were lynched in Madrid Bend, Ky.
Mar. 24: William Ziegler, a black man accused of criminal assault, was lynched in Alabama.
Mar. 25: James Walker, a black man accused of murder, was lynched in Washington, N.C.
Mar. 25: Washington H. Wallace, a black man accused of assault, was lynched in La Junta, Colo.
Mar. 26: Oliver Wright, a black man, was lynched in Higbee, Mo.
Mar. 28: Charles Woodward, a white man accused of murder, was lynched in Casper, Wyo.
Mar. 29: Richard Young, a black man accused of murder, was lynched near Savannah, Ga.
Mar. 30: A black man, mistaken for one Richard Young, was burned to death by a posse near Savannah, Ga. Young was sought for the murder of Dower Fountain.
Apr. 1: A crowd of 4,000 battered down the jail doors in Rome, Ga., and seized prisoner Walter Allen. Allen, a black man, had been charged with assaulting 15-year-old Blossom Adamson. After hanging the man from an electric light pole, the mob fired over a thousand shots into the dead body.
Apr. 1: George Franklin, a black man accused of attempted murder, was lynched in Homer, La.
Apr. 6: James Carter, a black man accused of murderous assault, was lynched in Amherst, Va.
Apr. 6: William Reynolds, a black man accused of murder, was lynched in Tuscumbia, Ala.
Apr. 10: Thomas Blambard, a black man accused of murder, was lynched in Fulton, Ky.
Apr. 10: An unknown black man accused of murder was lynched in Victoria, La.
Apr. 22: Harry Young, a black man, was lynched in Georgia.
Apr. 30: Ernest Dewley, a black man accused of murderous assault, was lynched in Brandenburg, Ky.
May 4: John Sims, a white man accused of sheltering a murderer, was lynched in Oak Ridge, La.
May 12: James Underwood, a black man accused of making threats, was lynched in Decatur, Tenn.
May 13: Nicholas Dublano, a black man accused of attempted criminal assault, was lynched in Loreauville, La.
May 13: Horace Muller, a black man accused of attempted murder, was lynched in Cookamie County, Miss.
May 22: Dudley Morgan, a black man accused of assaulting Mrs. McKay, was snatched from the sheriff in Lansing, Texas, by a mob of 4000. Morgan was tortured and finally burned to death at the stake.
May 25: Abraham Witherups, a white man accused of murder, was lynched in Paris, Mo.
June 5: James Black, a black man accused of murder, was lynched in Ravenals, S.C.
June 6: Wiley Gam, a black man accused of attempted rape, was lynched in Toms Brook, Va.
June 11: Harrison Gillespie, a black man accused of murder, was lynched in Salisbury, N.C.
June 11: An unknown black man was lynched near Newport News, Va.
June 25: Willy Campbell, a black man accused of attempted murder, was lynched in Alabama.
July 15: William Ody, a black man accused of attempted rape, was lynched in Clayton, Miss.
July 17: Joshua Anderson, a white man accused of murder, was lynched in Lexington, Mo.
July 20: Two black men accused of racial prejudice were lynched at Cross Roads, Miss.
July 25: Five black men accused of murder: William Carroll, Rudolph Clements, Peter Jackson, and two others unidentified; were lynched in Wanelsdorf, W.Va.
July 28: Arthur McCauley, a black man accused of murder, was lynched in Georgia.
July 28: John Wise, a black man accused of rape, was lynched in Pembroke, Ga.
July 28: An unknown black man was lynched in Bluff Springs, Fla.
July 31: Charles Craven, a black man accused of murder, was lynched in Leesburg, Va.
Aug. 1: Lee Newton, a black man accused of attempted rape, was lynched in Arkansas.
Aug. 1: Alonzo Williams, a black man accused of rape, was lynched in San Antonio, Fla,
Aug. 4: John McDaniel, a black man accused of lawlessness, was lynched in Smithdale, Miss.
Aug. 12: Harry Gates, a black man, was lynched in Lexington, Mo.
Aug. 12: Charles Salyers, a white man accused of murder, was lynched at a site unknown.
Aug. 17: Charles Johnson, a black man accused of rape, was lynched in Walnut Grove, Miss.
Aug. 25: Thomas Jones, a black man accused of rape, was lynched in Seven Springs, N.C.
Aug. 29: John Labarge, a white man was lynched in Michigan.
Aug. 31: John Brosin, a black man accused of attempted rape, was lynched in Monticello, Ga.
Sept. 1: Manny Price and Robert Scruggs, both black, were lynched for murder in Newberry, Fla.
Sept. 3: Hog Wilson, a black man accused of rape, was lynched in Stephens, Ark.
Sept. 4: Edward Brown, a black man accused of attempted rape, was lynched in Illinois.
Sept. 4: Jesse Walker, a black man accused of rape, was lynched in Hempstead, Texas.
Sept. 8: William Mobley, a black man accused of attempted rape, was lynched in Winona, La.
Sept. 15: Alonzo Fisher, a black man accused of rape, was lynched in Mansfield, Ore.
Sept. 28: The execution of a black man, Tom Clark, was carried out in Corinth, Miss., after a vigorous argument as to whether he should be hanged or burned. He had confessed to the August 10 murder of Mrs. Carey Whitfield.
Oct. 4: Utt Duncan, a black man accused of attempted rape, was lynched in Columbus, Texas.
Oct. 8: Curtis Brown and Garfield Burley, both black men accused of murder, were lynched in Newburn, Tenn.
Oct. 17: An unknown black man accused of murder was lynched in Calcasieur, La.
Oct. 20: Charles Young, a black man accused of rape and murder, was lynched in Forrest City, Ark.
Oct. 20: An unknown black man accused of attempted rape was lynched in Estabutchie, Miss.
Oct. 21: Reddish Barton and Joseph Wesley, both black men accused of rape, were lynched in Hempstead, Texas.
Oct. 23: Benjamin Brown, a black man accused of rape, was lynched in Tallapoosa, Ga.
November: In Stujely, Hung., a burgermeister was lynched by townspeople after he set fire to his own house, killing his wife, parents, and three children.
Nov. 1: An unknown black man accused of murder was lynched in Darling, Miss.
Nov. 3: Samuel Harris, a black man accused of murder, was lynched in Salem, Ala.
Nov. 13: John Davis, a black man accused of murder, was lynched in Lewisburg, Tenn.
Nov. 16: Harlan Buckles, a white man accused of murder, was lynched in Elizabethtown, Ky.
Nov. 20: James Dillard, a black man accused of rape, was lynched in Sullivan, Ind.

Nov. 20: Elijah Wells, a black man accused of murderous assault, was lynched in Wynne, Ark.
Nov. 20: Two black men, John Youngblood and another unknown, were lynched in Summit, Miss. for complicity in a murder.
Nov. 26: Joseph Lamb, a black man accused of attempted rape, was lynched in Francisville, La.
Dec. 20: Scott Bishop, a black man accused of murder, was lynched in Marbury, Ala.
Dec. 25: Montgomery Godley, a black man accused of murder, was lynched in Pittsburg, Kan.
Dec. 27: Oliver Wideman, a black man, and his wife, were lynched for murder in Troy, S.C.

1903

Jan. 10: John Hollins, a black man accused of attempted assault, was lynched in Drew, Miss.
Jan. 14: Ransom O'Neal and Charles Tunstall, both black men accused of murder, were lynched in Angleton, Texas.
Jan. 19: An unknown white man was lynched in Louisiana.
Jan. 21: Andy Clark, a black man accused of murder, was lynched in Leeper, Mo.
Jan. 26: Joseph Momas, a black man accused of murder, was lynched in Luling, La.
Feb. 4: Frank Brown, a black man accused of murder, was lynched in Madison, W.Va.
Feb. 7: Lee Hill, a black man accused of murder, was lynched in Wrightsville, Ga.
Feb. 7: Cornelius Lee, a black man accused of murderous assault, was lynched in Plaquemine, La.
Feb. 24: William Fambro, a black man accused of insulting a white woman, was lynched in Griffin, Ga.
Mar. 9: Henry Thomas, a black man accused of rape, was lynched in Parish, Fla.
Mar. 20: Frank Robertson, a black man accused of arson, was lynched in Bradley, Ark.
Apr. 6: John Turner, a black man accused of attempted rape, was lynched in Warren, Ark.
Apr. 15: Thomas Gilyard, a black man accused of murder, was lynched in Joplin, Mo.
Apr. 22: Alexander Thompson, a black man accused of murderous assault, was lynched in Gurdon, Ark.
Apr. 23: Andrew Rainey, a black man accused of arson, was lynched in Bainbridge, Ga.
Apr. 26: Hensley Johnson, a black man accused of attempted rape, was lynched in Carthage, Texas.
Apr. 26: Joe Shively, a 50-year-old black man, was whipped with barbed wire and hit in the eye with brass knuckles when a mob of thirty-eight men broke into the house where Shively was lodged. Two white sisters, Rebecca and Ida Stephens were also whipped by the assailants, who objected to a black boarder living with a white family.
Apr. 26: An unknown black man accused of attempted rape, was lynched in Thebes, Ill.
May 3: Robert Bryant, a black man accused of murder, was lynched in Vicksburg, Miss.
May 3: Dan Kennedy, a black man accused of murder, was lynched in Mulberry, Fla.
May 3: Two black men, D. Malone and W.J. Mooneyhon, were lynched in Caruthersville, Mo., after being accused of racial prejudice.
May 19: Washington Jarvis, a white man accused of murder was lynched in Madison, Fla.
May 20: Two black men, Henry Gordon and Amos Randall, accused of murder, were lynched in Mulberry, Fla.
May 20: Mose Hart, a black man accused of murderous assault, was lynched in Corinth, Miss.
May 22: William Hopkins, a black man accused of rape, was lynched in New Bainbridge, Ga.
May 27: W.C. Clifton, a white man accused of murder, was lynched in Newcastle, Wyo.
May 27: An unknown black man accused of rape, was lynched in Kemp, Texas.
May 28: An unknown black man accused of arson was lynched in Woodville, Miss.
June 1: Benjamin Gorman, a black man accused of murder, was lynched in Georgia.
June 4: Robert Dennis, a black man suspected of rape, was lynched in Greenville, Miss.
June 6: David Wyatt, a black man accused of murder, was lynched in Bellville, Ill.
June 8: Banjo Peavy, a black man accused of murder, was lynched in Fort Valley, Ga.
June 8: Four black men and a black woman, accused of complicity in a murder, were lynched in Smith County, Miss.
June 12: Frank Dupree, a black man accused of murder, was lynched in Forest Hill, La.
June 12: George Kincaid, a black man accused of murderous assault, was lynched near Cleveland, Miss.
June 12: George White, a black man accused of rape and murder, was lynched near Wilmington, Del.
June 19: John Brown, a white man accused of murder, was lynched in Bad Lands, Mont.
June 24: Three black men accused of murder: Wiley Annett, Garfield McCoy, and George McKinney, were lynched in Newton, Ga.
June 24: Andrew Diggs, a black man accused of attempted rape, was lynched in Scottsboro, Ala.
June 24: Jack Harris and Lamb Whittle, twp black men accused of assaulting a white man, were lynched in Concordia Parish, La.
June 24: Charles Jones, a black man accused of rape, was lynched in Elk Valley, Tenn.
July 1: Charles Evans and two other black men were lynched on suspicion of murder in Norway, S.C.
July 1: A mob of fifty men shot and killed a black man, Ruben Elrod, at his home in Piedmont, S.C. Three women who lived in the house were stripped, flogged, and warned to leave the county.
July 7: Cato Jarrett, a black man accused of murder, was lynched in Stouts Crossing, Miss.
July 14: A man falsely believed to be Ed Claus was tied to a tree and shot to death after being apprehended by an angry mob in Eastman, Ga. The black man was apprehended after the attack on Susie Johnson, a schoolteacher. It was later determined that the mob had killed the wrong man, when Claus was located in Darien, Ga., on July 26.
July 14: William Thackson, a white man accused of murder, was lynched in Maysville, Ky.
July 18: A black man named Adams, accused of rape, was lynched in Lake Butler, Fla.
July 19: James Gorman and J.P. Walters, both white men accused of murder, were lynched in Basin, Wyo.
July 20: Jesse Butler and Dennis Head, both black men, were lynched in Aiken County, S.C., in a case of mistaken identity.
July 21: Crane Green, a black man accused of rape, was lynched in Pine Barren, Fla.
July 22: Two black men, John Gilbert and another unidentified, accused of murder, were lynched in Arkansas.
July 23: Moony Allen, a black man accused of murder, was lynched in Beaumont, Texas.
July 23: I.D. Mayfield, a black man accused of murder, was lynched in Danville, Ill.
July 26: Jennis Sturs, a black woman, was hanged from a tree on a plantation near Shreveport, La., where she was accused of poisoning 16-year-old Elizabeth Dolan with a tainted glass of lemonade.
July 31: An unknown black man accused of assault, was lynched near Alto, Texas.
Aug. 5: William Hamilton, a white accused of murder, was lynched in Asolo, Wash.
Aug. 5: Two unknown black men were lynched in Lewisburg, Tenn.
Aug. 12: Eight black men were arrested for the attack on Mrs. Hart in Whitesboro, Texas. Seven men were released but the eighth man was hanged from a tree, after which the black community was terrorized by the white mob.
Aug. 14: An unidentified white man was lynched in Dupyer, Mont.
September: A black man named Hellem was lynched in Luxora, Ark., for sexual assault of black girls.
September: An unknown black man accused of rape, was lynched in Whigham, Ga.
September: George Jones, a black man accused of arson, was lynched in Mayersville, Miss.
September: Allen Small, a black man accused of attempted rape, was lynched in Lynchburg, Tenn.
September: Will Williams, a black man accused of murder, was lynched in Centerville, Miss.
Sept. 17: A Chinese man accused of racial prejudice was lynched in Tonopah, Nev.
Oct. 1: Walker Davis, a black man accused of murder, was lynched in Marshall, Texas.
Oct. 6: Edward McCollum, a black man accused of murderous assault, was lynched in Sheridan, Ark.
Oct. 9: Thomas Hall, a black man accused of murder, was lynched in Kevil. Ky.
Oct. 9: Samuel Williams, a white man who refused to supply information, was lynched in Lawby, Fla.
Oct. 14: Walter Jackson, a white man accused of murder, was lynched in Hamilton, Mont.
Oct. 16: George Kenny, a black man accused of murderous threats, was lynched in Taylor Town, La.
Oct. 16: An unknown black man was lynched in Cordele, Ga.
Oct. 27: William McAlpin, a white man accused of murder, was lynched in Smith County, Miss.
Oct. 29: An unknown black man accused of attempted rape, was lynched in Hattiesburg, Miss.
Nov. 2: Joseph Craddvels, a black man accused of murder, was lynched in Taylor Town, La.
Nov. 3: Henry Johnson, a black man accused of murder, was lynched in Lake Village, Ark.
Nov. 5: Samuel Adams, a black man accused of rape, was lynched in Pass Christian, Miss.
Nov. 8: Z.C. Cadle, a white man accused of murder, was lynched in Brinkley, Ark.
Nov. 15: Charles Young, a black man accused of attempted rape, was

lynched in Ala.
Nov. 24: Charles Nelson, a black man accused of rape, was lynched in Jefferson, S.C.
Nov. 28: John Fagler, a black man accused of attempted rape, was lynched in Ross Station, S.C.
Nov. 30: Three black men, Walter Carter, Phillip Davis, and Clinton Thomas, accused of murder, were lynched in Alabama.
Dec. 5: Jackson Lewis, a black man accused of attempted rape, was lynched near Tampa, Fla.
Dec. 10: Joseph Brake, a black man accused of murder, was lynched in Ripley, Tenn.
Dec. 24: Eli Hilson, a black man accused of racial prejudice, was lynched in Brookhaven, Miss.
Dec. 27: James Carr, a black man accused of murder, was lynched in Millview, La.

1904

Jan. 3: Robert Alexander, a black man accused of racial prejudice, was lynched in Ripley, Tenn.
Jan. 14: Elmer Moseley, a black man accused of murder, was lynched in Sussex County, Va.
Jan. 14: Bush Riley, a black man accused of murder, was lynched in Tallula, Miss.
Jan 15: Jumbo Clark, a black man accused of rape, was lynched in High Springs, Fla.
Jan. 15: "General" Lee, a black man accused of attempted rape, was lynched in Dorchester, S.C.
Jan. 24: Lewis Radford, a black man accused of murder, was lynched in Guthrie, Ky.
Feb. 7: A mob of 200 men and two packs of bloodhounds caught Luther Holbert and his wife near Doddsville, Miss., following the murders of plantation owner James Eastland and a black employee, John Carr. The black couple was and burned at the stake.
Feb. 7: Posses pursuing Luther Holbert lynched three unknown black men near Doddsville, Miss.
Feb. 19: Glenco Days, a black man accused of murder, was lynched in Crossett, Ark.
Mar. 7: Richard Dixon, a black man accused of murder, was lynched in Springfield, Ohio.
Mar. 8: Richard Dickerson, a black man, was lynched in retaliation for the murder of a white policeman, causing a race war in Springfield, Ohio.
Mar. 12: An unidentified black man was lynched in Majane, Calif.
Mar. 17: An unknown black man accused of murder was lynched in Saucier, Miss.
Mar. 19: Two black men accused of murder, Burke Harris and Fayette Sawyer, were lynched in Cleveland, Miss.
Mar. 26: Thirteen black men: Mack Baldwin, William Baldwin, Abe Bailey, Perry Carter, Garrett Flood, Randall Flood, Henry Griffin, Walter Griffin, Aaron Hinton, Killis Johnston, William Madison, Charles Smith, and James Smith; accused of racial prejudice, were lynched in St. Charles, Ark.
Apr. 16: Ruben Sims, a black man accused of murder, was lynched in Little River, Ala.
Apr. 16: A white man named Petrie accused of rape, was lynched in Dunsmuir, Calif.
Apr. 29: Thomas Seacey, a black man accused of rape, was lynched in Haywood, Tenn.
May 1: Caines Hall, a black man accused of rape, was lynched in Kingston, Ala.
May 8: Frank Piper, a black man accused of making threats, was lynched in Alexandria, La.
May 15: John Cummings, a black man accused of rape, was lynched in Appling, Ga.
May 19: A black man named Whitehead, accused of rape, was lynched in Virginia.
May 19: An unknown black man accused of rape was lynched in Seaboard, N.C.
May 20: An unidentified black man was lynched in Mulberry, Fla.
May 24: An unknown black man was lynched for murder in O'Neil, Miss.
June 1: Arthur Thompson, a black man accused of murder, was lynched in Arlington, Ga.
June 3: T.M. Myers, a white man accused of murder, was lynched in Grangeville, Idaho.
June 3: Three black men accused of murder, named Clark, Mayfield, and Van Horne, were lynched at Trail Lake, Miss.
June 14: Marie Thompson, a black woman accused of murder, was lynched in Lebanon Junction, Ky.
June 22: Ephreim Pope, a black man accused of rape, was lynched in Lamison, Ala.
June 26: Sterling Dunham, a black man, was lynched in Europa, Miss., after being accused of rape.
June 30: Cairo Williams, a black man accused of murder, was lynched in Scranton, S.C.
July 1: Jon Jones, a black man accused of rape, was lynched in Altoona, Ala.
July 5: John Taylor, a black man accused of attempted rape, was lynched in Chesterfield County, S.C.
July 9: An unknown black man accused of attempted rape was lynched in Mississippi.
July 10: Jesse Tucker, a black man accused of attempted rape, was lynched in Houston, Miss.
July 17: An unidentified black man accused of murder was lynched in Kentucky.
July 30: John Larremore, a black man accused of racial prejudice, was lynched in Lockhart, Texas.
Aug. 4: Andrew Dudley, a black man accused of attempted rape, was lynched in Greenfield, Va.
Aug. 7: Ed Bell, a black man accused of murder, was lynched in Selma, Ala.
Aug. 16: Two black men accused of murder, William Cato and Paul Reed, were lynched in Statesboro, Ga.
Aug. 17: Two black men, Albert Rogers and his son, were lynched in Statesboro, Ga., for exhibiting racial prejudice.
Aug. 17: Rufus Lesuere, a black man accused of assault, was lynched in Thomaston, Ga.
Aug. 22: James Glover, a black man accused of rape, was lynched in Georgia.
Aug. 28: A black man named Scott, accused of murder, was lynched in Rebecca, Ga.
Aug. 30: Joe Bumpass, a black man accused of rape, was lynched near Hickman, Ky.
Aug. 30: John Martin, a black man accused of assault, was lynched in Laramie, Wyo.
Aug. 30: Sebastian McBride, a black man accused of racial prejudice, was lynched in Portal, Ga.
Aug. 31: Oscar Turner, a black man accused of attempted rape, was lynched in Weimer, Texas.
Aug. 31: Two unidentified black men, accused of insulting a white woman, were lynched in Stephens, Ark.
Sept. 1: Oscar Tucker, a black man accused of rape, was lynched in Weimer, Texas.
Sept. 5: An unknown black man accused of assault, was lynched in Crossett, Ark.
Sept. 6: Washington Bradley, a black man accused of murder, was lynched in Bronson, Fla.
Sept. 7: Horace Maples, a black man accused of murder, was lynched in Huntsville, Ala.
Sept. 18: John Allison, a white man accused of murder, was lynched in McGhees Station, La.
Sept. 18: John Ware, a black man accused of murder, was lynched in Royston, Ga.
Sept. 21: Jack Troy, a black man, and Edward Weaver, a white man, were lynched for murder in Talbotton, Ga.
Sept. 24: An unknown black man accused of rape, was lynched in Waterloo, S.C.
Oct. 1: John Morrison, a white man accused of murder, was lynched in Kershaw, S.C.
Oct. 2: Frank Wigfall, a black man accused of murder, was lynched in Rawlins, Wyo.
Oct. 4: A white man named Rivers, accused of attempted rape, was lynched in Perry, Fla.
Oct. 12: Moses Weaver, a black man accused of murder, was lynched in Tifton, Ga.
Oct. 24: George W. Blunt, a white man accused of assaulting a policeman, was lynched in Berkely, Va.
Nov. 29: Hurbert Simmons, a black man accused of murder, was lynched in Neal, Ga.

1905

Jan. 1: Louis Allwhite, a white man accused of murder, was lynched in Newport, Ark.
Jan. 4: White Jetton, a black man accused of murder, was lynched in Spring Hill, Ark.
Jan. 4: An unknown black man was lynched in Benoit, Miss.
Feb. 16: Carlos Munoz, a white man accused of rape, was lynched near Dale, Texas.
Feb. 17: William Johnson, a black man accused of rape, was lynched in Smithville, Texas.
Feb. 20: Henry Henderson, a black man accused of racial prejudice, was lynched in Ingram, Va.
Feb. 22: An unknown white man accused of robbery was lynched in Hazen, Nev.
Mar. 5: An unknown black man accused of murder was lynched at Helm Station, Miss.
Mar.8: Ronce Gwyn, a black man accused of theft, was lynched in Tullahoma, Tenn.
Mar. 14: Two black men accused of murder, Edward Plowly and William Plowly, were lynched in Pine Apple, Ala.
Mar. 14: Julius Stevens, a black man accused of murderous assault, was lynched in Long View, Texas.
Apr. 20: John Barrett, a black man accused of murder, was lynched in Askew, Ark.
Apr. 26: A white man named R. Craighead, accused of murder, was lynched in Homer, La.
May 12: Robert Pettigrew, a black man accused of kidnapping, was lynched in Belmont, Mo.
May 22: Robert Shaw, a black man accused of murder, was lynched in Waitman, Ky.

June 1: Thomas Wilson, a black man accused of murder, was lynched in Batchelor, La.
June 20: Ford Simon, a black man accused of rape, was lynched in Riverside, Texas.
June 25: Pierce Moberly, a black man accused of murder, was lynched near Meridian, Miss.
June 29: Eight black men accused of murder: Rich Allen, Lon J. Aycock, Claude Elder, Robert Harris, Lewis Robinson, Rich Robinson, and Gene Yerly; and Sandy Price, accused of attempted murder; were lynched in Watkinsville, Ga.
July 1: Doc Peters, a black man accused of murder, was lynched in Cottondale, Fla.
July 6: James Woodman, a black man, was lynched in Arkansas for eloping with a white girl.
July 7: Leon Beard, a black man accused of rape, was lynched in Normandy, Ky.
July 14: Frank Mason, a black man accused of rape, was lynched in Golmada, Texas.
July 19: Henry Harris, a black man accused of murder, was lynched near Glendora, Miss.
July 20: Sam Green, a black man accused of rape, was lynched in New Braunfels, Texas.
July 25: William Harris, a black man accused of murder, was lynched near Glendora, Miss.
July 29: An unknown black man accused of rape, was lynched in Avery, Texas.
Aug. 4: Kid George and Edward Lewis, both black and accused of murder, were lynched in Hattiesburg, Miss.
Aug. 8: Sank Majors, a black man accused of rape, was lynched in Waco, Texas.
Aug. 11: Thomas Williams, a white man accused of attempted rape, was lynched in Sulpher Springs, Texas.
Aug. 12: An unknown black man accused of murder was lynched in Eros, La.
Aug. 14: Thomas Williams, a black man accused of attempted rape, was lynched in Sulpher Springs, Texas.
Aug. 16: Henry Young, a black man accused of murder, was lynched in Lake Cormorant, Miss.
Aug. 23: Oliver Latt, a black man accused of murder, was lynched in Tunnel Springs, Ala.
Aug. 27: John Moore, a black man accused of murderous assault, was lynched in Clark, N.C.
Sept. 1: Alt Rees, a black man accused of rape, was lynched in Rosetta, Miss.
Sept. 2: Arthur Woodward and Talcum Woodward, both black men accused of murderous assault, were lynched in Silver City, N.M.
Sept. 7: Stephen Davis, a black man accused of rape, was lynched in Italy, Texas.
Sept. 14: William James, a black man accused of being an informant, was lynched in Tallahatchie County, Miss.
Sept. 19: John McDowell, a black man, was lynched in Rankin County, Miss.
Sept. 20: Allen Pendleton, a black man accused of murder, was lynched in Abbeville, S.C.
Sept. 22: Frank Brown, a black man, was lynched in Conway, Ark., in a case of mistaken identity.
Oct. 8: Thomas Seabright, a black man accused of rape, was lynched in Bainbridge, Ga.
Oct. 10: Luther Billings, a black man accused of attempted rape, was lynched in Brunswick, Tenn.
Oct. 10: John James, a black man accused of attempted rape, was lynched in Woodville, Miss.
Oct. 12: Frank Leavell, a black man accused of attempted rape, was lynched in Elkton, Ky.
Oct. 29: Augustus Goodman, a black man accused of murder, was lynched in Bainbridge, Ga.
Nov. 11: Three black men accused of murder: Robert Askew, John Reese, and a third unknown; were lynched in Henderson, Texas.
Nov. 22: David Simms, a black man accused of murder, was lynched in Coahoma, Miss.
Nov. 26: Monsie Williams, a black man accused of attempted rape, was lynched in Tangipahoa, La.
Dec. 11: James Green, a black man accused of rape, was lynched in Boyle, Miss.
Dec. 20: Frank Da Loach and John Da Loach, both black men accused of murder, were lynched in Barnwell, S.C.

1906

Jan. 10: Benjamin Harris, a black man accused of murder, was lynched in Moscow. Texas.
Jan. 17: An unknown black man accused of attempted rape, was lynched in Penola, Miss.
Jan. 22: Ernest Baker, a black man accused of murder, was lynched in Cadiz, Ky.
Feb. 7: James Calton, a black man accused of murderous assault, was lynched in Elmarth, Ark.
Feb. 11: Bunkie Richardson, a black man accused of murder and rape, was lynched in Gadsden, Ala.
Feb. 20: A black man named Pedigrie, accused of rape, was lynched in Andalusia, Ala.
Feb. 24: Wiltzie Page, a black man suspected of rape, was lynched in Bienville, La.
Mar. 17: William Carr, a black man accused of stealing a white man's cow, was hanged from a railway trestle by a mob of thirty masked men in Planquemines, La.
Mar. 19: Ed Johnson was taken from jail and lynched in Knoxville, Tenn., shortly after the black man was granted an appeal by the U.S. Supreme Court.
Mar. 28: A black man named "Cotton", accused of attempted rape, was lynched in Carrolle, La.
Apr. 4: Harry Duncan, a black man suspected of rape, was lynched in Springfield, Mo.
Apr. 14: James Copeland, a black man accused of rape, was lynched in Springfield, Mo.
Apr. 15: William Allen, a black man accused of murder, was lynched in Springfield, Mo.
Apr. 24: A black man accused of rape was lynched in Groesbech, Texas.
Apr. 25: A black man accused of rape was lynched in Oakwood, Texas.
Apr. 29: William Brown, a black man accused of murder, was lynched in Rienzi, Ala.
May 8: Sam Simms, a black man accused of killing a horse, was lynched in Jackson, Miss.
May 8: George Whitney, a black man accused of insulting a woman, was lynched in Ethel, La.
May 14: William Womack, a black man accused of rape, was lynched in Eastman, Ga.
May 17: Frank Jordan, a black man accused of murder, was lynched in Inverness, Fla.
May 23: John Irwin, a white man accused of murder, was lynched in Chipley, Ga.
May 23: Thomas Jackson, a black man accused of robbery, was lynched in Blanchard, La.
May 23: George Younger, a black man accused of murder, was lynched in Columbus, Miss.
May 23: An unknown black man accused of murder was lynched at Choctsaw Nation, Okla.
May 28: J.V. Johnson, a white man accused of murder, was lynched in Wadesboro, N.C.
May 29: R.T. Rogers, a black man accused of murder, was lynched in Tallulah, La.
June 8: James Davis, a black man accused of murder, was lynched in Inverness, Fla.
June 11: Wood Ambrose, a black man accused of murder, was lynched in Prentiss, Miss.
June 14: Moses Hughes, a black man suspected of arson, was lynched in Union, S.C.
June 14: Ed Watson, a black man accused of murderous assault, was lynched in Pokomoke City, Md.
June 30: An unknown black man suspected of rape was lynched in De Kalb, Miss.
July 2: An unknown black man accused of rape was lynched in Chickasha, Okla.
July 8: William Anderson, a black man accused of rape, was lynched in Pillar, Ark.
July 11: Ed Pearson, a black man accused of murderous assault, was lynched in Swainsboro, Ga.
July 12: An unknown black man accused of attempted rape was lynched near Junction City, Ark.
July 27: Two black men, John Black and William Reagin, accused of murder, were lynched in Florida.
July 31: Floyd Carmichael, a black man accused of rape, was lynched in Lakewood, Ga.
Aug. 6: Three black men accused of murder: Jack Dillingham, John Gillespie, and Nease Gillespie; were lynched in Salisbury, N.C.
Aug. 20: Robert Davis, a black man accused of rape, was lynched in Greenwood, S.C.
Aug. 20: Robert Ethridge, a black man accused of attempted rape, was lynched in Mont Willing, S.C.
Aug. 21: John Bapes, a black man accused of murderous assault, was lynched in Mulberry, Fla.
Aug. 22: William Spain, a black man accused of attempted rape, was lynched at St. George, S.C.
Aug. 26: Alfred Shaufilet, a black man accused of attempted rape, was lynched in Calhoun, La.
Sept. 7: Two unknown black men accused of attempted rape were lynched in Laurel, Miss.
Sept. 10: Charles Miller, a black man accused of attempted rape, was lynched in Culloden, Ga.
Sept. 15: Mitchell Frazier, a black man accused of murderous assault, was lynched in Rosebud, Texas.
Oct. 6: Henry Peters and Richard Robinson, black men accused of rape, were lynched in Prichard Station, Ala.
Oct. 6: An unknown black man accused of rape was lynched in Basin, Miss.
Oct. 7: H. Blackburn, a black man accused of murderous assault, was lynched in Argenta, Ark.
Oct. 8: Anthony Davis, a black man accused of attempted rape, was

lynched in Texarkana, Ark.
Oct. 20: Daniel Dove, a black man accused of attempted rape, was lynched in Alabama.
Oct. 25: Thomas Crompton, a black man accused of murder, was lynched in Centerville, Miss.
Oct. 26: "Slab" Pitts, a black man, was lynched in Toyah, Texas, after marrying a white woman.
Oct. 29: George Estes, a black man accused of murder, was lynched in Hales Point, Tenn.
Nov. 8: "Jet" Hinks, a black man accused of murder, was lynched in Lee County, Miss.
Nov. 9: An unknown black man accused of rape was lynched in Madison, Fla.
Nov. 15: Mark Davis, a black man accused of murderous assault, was lynched near Newberry, S.C.
Nov. 15: William Harris, a black man accused of murder, was lynched near Asheville, N.C.
Nov. 29: Anton Domingo, a black man accused of disorderly conduct, was lynched in Lafayette, La.
Nov. 29: An unidentified black man accused of attempted rape was lynched in Hot Springs, Ark.
Dec. 5: Wes Young, a black man, was lynched near Valley Park, Miss.
Dec. 21: Henry Davis, a black man accused of rape, was lynched in Annapolis, Md.
Dec. 27: Laurence Leborg, a white man accused of murder, was lynched in Las Animas, Colo.

1907

Jan. 4: An unknown black man accused of attempted rape was lynched in Midway, Ala.
Jan. 9: James Cullen, a white man accused of murder, was lynched in Charles City, Iowa.
Jan. 23: Henry Bell, a black man accused of rape, was lynched in Greenwood, Miss.
Mar. 15: Two black men accused of murder, Henry Gardner and Flint Williams, were lynched in Monroe, La.
Mar. 20: Two unidentified black women, accused of murderous assault, were lynched in Stamps, Ark.
Mar. 24: Cleveland Harding, a black man accused of attempted rape, was lynched in Florence, Ala.
Mar. 26: An unknown black man accused of rape was lynched in Hartford, Ala.
Mar. 31: James Williams, a black man accused of attempted rape, was lynched in Colbert, Okla.
Apr. 16: Charles Strauss, a black man accused of attempted rape, was lynched in Bunkie, La.
Apr. 17: Fred Kilbourne, a black man accused of attempted rape, was lynched in Clinton, La.
Apr. 29: Eben Calhoun, a black man accused of murderous assault, was lynched in Pittsview, Ala.
May 3: Silas Ealy, a black man accused of rape, was lynched in Bossiers City, La.
May 7: Charles Harris, a black man accused of murder, was lynched in Dearing, Ga.
May 7: An unknown black man accused of rape was lynched in Marion County, S.C.
May 21: Five black men accused of inciting a race riot were lynched in Reidsville, Ga.
June 1: Henry Johnson, a black man accused of attempted rape, was lynched in Echo, La.
June 2: George Hudson, a black man accused of attempted rape and murder, was lynched in Trenton, S.C.
June 8: Two black men, Abe Johnson and Henry Johnson, were lynched near Yazoo City, Miss., for participating in a race riot.
June 9: Lee Fox, a black man, was lynched near Yazoo City, Miss., for participating in a race riot.
June 10: James Wilson, a black man accused of attempted rape, was lynched in Gibsland, La.
June 28: Ralph Dorans, a black man accused of rape, was lynched in Ruby, La.
June 28: Mathias Jackson, a black man accused of rape, was lynched near Alexandria, La.
July 1: "Dock" Posey, a white man accused of rape, was lynched in Dalton, Ga.
July 2: George Herbert, a black man accused of murderous assault, was lynched in Cowen, Ga.
July 14: Fred Wilson, a black man accused of murder, was lynched in Del Rio, Texas.
July 16: Frank Bailey, a black man accused of murder, was lynched near Oklahoma City, Okla.
July 20: Andrew Trice, a black man accused of murder, was lynched in Olive Branch, Miss.
July 22: Two black men were lynched in Lake County, Tenn., after fighting with a white man.
July 28: James Reed, a black man accused of murder, was lynched in Crisfield, Md.
July 29: Sam Washington, a black man accused of murder, was lynched near Vicksburg, Miss.
August: Louis Higgins, a white man accused of rape, was lynched in Bancroft, Maine.
Aug. 6: Thomas Hall, a black man accused of attempted assault, was lynched in Goliad, Texas.
Aug. 16: William Clifford, a black man accused of rape and murder, was lynched in Maple Grove, Ky.
Aug. 27: John Lipsey, a black man accused of rape, was lynched in Pickensville, Ala.
Sept. 3: Jerry Johnson, a black man accused of rape, was lynched in North Birmingham, Ala.
Sept. 22: Moses Dossett, a black man accused of attempted murder, was lynched in Prichard Station, Ala.
Oct. 5: William Burns, a black man accused of murder, was lynched in Cumberland, Md.
Oct. 11: Three black men accused of burglary, William Jackson, George Robinson, and James Shoots, were lynched in Tunica, Miss.
Oct. 23: Henry Sykes, a black man accused of insulting a woman, was lynched in Van Vleet, Miss.
Oct. 27: A black man named Meyer, accused of complicity in a murder, was lynched in Carrollton, Miss.
Oct. 27: John Wilks, a black man accused of robbery, was lynched in Byron, Ga.
Oct. 29: Charles German, a black man accused of rape, was lynched near Belen, Miss.
Nov. 2: Henry Lucas, a black man accused of complicity in a murder, was lynched in Vinegar Bend, Ala.
Nov. 2: Abram Sumroll, a black man accused of murder, was lynched in Vinegar Bend, Ala.
Nov. 3: Fred Quigleton, a black man accused of murder, was lynched in Talledaga, Ala.
Nov. 4: Alex Johnson, a black man accused of attempted rape, was lynched in Caneron, Texas.
Nov. 30: Newt Saunders, a black man accused of rape, was lynched in Covington County, Ala.
Dec. 5: Washington Mussay, a black man accused of murder, was lynched in Augusta, Ark.
Dec. 13: An unknown black man accused of murderous assault was lynched in Mer Rouge, La.
Dec. 16: Pat Husband, a black man accused of rape, was lynched in McHenry, Miss.
Dec. 24: James Garden, a black man accused of murder, was lynched in Muskogee, Okla.
Dec. 26: Anderson Callaway, a black man accused of attempted rape, was lynched in Marques, Texas.

1908

Jan. 2: An unnamed black man accused of murder was lynched in Brookhaven, Miss.
Jan. 9: Thomas Coley and Isaac Webb, black men accused of murderous assault, were lynched in Goldsboro, Ga.
Jan. 12: An unnamed black man was lynched by blacks in Pine Level, N.C., for being a poor performer.
Jan. 21: Walter Cole, a black man accused of murder, was lynched in Morgan County, Tenn.
Jan. 28: Two unnamed black men accused of murder were lynched near Commerce, Miss.
Feb. 2: Charles Pitman, a black man suspected of murder, was lynched in Greenville, Fla.
Feb. 5: Robert Mitchell, a black man accused of murder, was lynched in Oak Grove, La.
Feb. 10: Eli Pigatt, a black man accused of rape, was lynched in Brookhaven, Miss.
Feb. 17: An unidentified black man accused of rape was lynched in Stateboro, Ga.
Feb. 24: Gilbert Thompson, a black man wrongly accused of rape, was lynched in Stateboro, Ga.
Feb. 26: An unknown black man accused of conspiracy to do violence was lynched in Valdosta, Ga.
Feb. 28: Clem Scott, a black man accused of attempted rape, was lynched in Conroe, Texas.
Mar. 5: John Long, a white man accused of murder, was lynched in Newberry, Fla.
Mar. 6: Robertson Curry and John Henry, two black men accused of murder, were lynched in Hawkinsville, Ga.
Mar. 10: John Campbell, a black man accused of murderous assault, was lynched in Navosota, Texas.
Mar. 10: Presler Jackson, a white man accused of murder, was lynched in Bristol, Va.
Mar. 10: David Poe, Thomas Ranston, and two brothers named Jenkins, all black and accused of incendiarism, were lynched in Van Cleave, Miss.
Mar. 24: An unnamed black man accused of attempted rape was lynched in Conroe, Texas.
Mar. 24: Two unnamed black men accused of attempted rape were lynched in Magnolia, Texas.
Apr. 5: John Burr, a black man accused of murder, was lynched in Wesson, Miss.
Apr. 6: Walter Clayton, a black man accused of rape, was lynched in Bay Minett, Ala.
Apr. 9: Albert Fields, a black man accused of rape, was lynched in Long View, Texas.

Apr. 19: Jasper Douglas, a black man accused of rape, was lynched in Atlanta, Texas.
Apr. 23: Joseph Simpson, a white man accused of murder, was lynched in Sikdoo, Calif.
May 7: John Williams, a black man accused of murder, was lynched in Naples, Texas.
May 8: Elmo Garvard, a black man accused of attempted rape, was lynched in Pulaski, Tenn.
May 31: Jacob McDowell, a black man accused of murder, was lynched in Providence, Ky.
June 4: Bird Cooper, a white man accused of murder, was lynched in Homer, La.
June 20: Ernest Williams, a black man accused of using offensive language, was lynched in Parkdale, Ark.
June 22: Nine black men accused of murder: Jerry Evans, William Johnson, William Manuel, "Rabbit Bill" McCoy, Moses Spellman, Cleveland Williams, Frank Williams, and two others unknown; were lynched in Hemphill, Texas.
June 27: Albert Baker and Walter Wilkins, two black men accused of rape, were lynched in Waycross, Ga.
June 27: An unidentified black man accused of complicity in a rape was lynched in Hickox, Ga.
July 14: Hugh Jones, a black man accused of attempted rape, was lynched in Middleton, Tenn.
July 15: An unnamed black man was lynched in Beaumont, Texas, in a case of mistaken identity.
July 18: Three unknown black men suspected of arson were lynched in Jonesville, La.
July 28: Tad Smith, a black man accused of rape, was lynched in Greenboro, Texas.
July 29: Leander Shaw, a black man accused of attempted rape, was lynched in Pensacola, Fla.
July 29: Alonzo Williams, a black man accused of attempted rape, was lynched in Ohoopee, Ga.
Aug. 1: Four black men: Robert Jones, Thomas Jones, Virgil Jones, and Joseph Riley; were lynched in Russellville, Ky., for expressing sympathy with the murder of a white man.
Aug. 3: Andrew Harris, a black man accused of attempted rape, was lynched in Bethany, La.
Aug. 6: William Miller, a black man accused of dynamiting, was lynched in Brighton, Ala.
Aug. 7: Charles Lokie, a black man accused of insulting a white woman, was lynched in Tifton, Ga.
Aug. 15: Scott Burton, a black man who participated in a race riot, was lynched in Springfield, Ill.
Aug. 15: Moses Jackson, a black man, was lynched in Bellville, Texas.
Aug. 16: George Donigan, a black man who participated in a race riot, was lynched in Springfield, Ill.
Aug. 25: Vance Williams, a black man accused of murder, was lynched in Louisville, Ga.
Aug. 28: George Johnson, a black man accused of attempted rape, was lynched in Murfreesboro, Tenn.
Aug. 28: John Williams, a black man accused of arson, was lynched in Ittababa, Miss.
Sept. 5: John Towne, a black man accused of rape, was lynched in Damascus, Ga.
Sept. 8: Lawson Patton, a black man accused of murder, was lynched in Oxford, Miss.
Sept. 13: Daniel Newton, a black man accused of murder, was lynched in Brodeshire, Texas.
Sept. 19: John Miles, a black man accused of assault and robbery, was lynched in Louisiana.
Sept. 20: Charles Jones, a black man accused of murder, was lynched in Yazoo City, Miss.
Sept. 22: George Thomas, a black man accused of murderous assault, was lynched in Fort Gaines, Ga.
Oct. 4: David Wallace, his wife and two children, were lynched for making threats in Hickory Grove, Ky.
Oct. 5: Benjamin Price, a black man accused of rape, was lynched in Florida.
Oct. 10: Dee Dawson, William Fuller, and Frank Johnson, all black and suspected of complicity in a murder, were lynched in Hickory, Miss.
Oct. 11: Two black men accused of murder, Frank Davis and Joseph Davis, were lynched in Lula, Miss.
Oct. 11: Henry White, a black man accused of murderous assault, was lynched in Younker, Ga.
Oct. 12: Nicholas Hector, a black desperado, was lynched in New Iberia, La.
Oct. 15: W.J. Jackson, a black man accused of theft, was lynched in Hernando, Miss.
Oct. 19: Two black men, Quinten Rankin and R.E. Taylor, were lynched by night riders in Walnut Log, Tenn.
Oct. 21: A black man named Stover, accused of attempted rape, was lynched in Halselle, Ala.
Oct. 30: George Cook, a white man accused of murder, was lynched in Kingston, Tenn.
Nov. 2: William Hodges, a black man accused of rape, was lynched in Union, Miss.
Nov. 10: Henry Leidy, a black man accused of rape, was lynched in Biloxi, Miss.
Nov. 24: Edward Stineback, Marshall Stineback and Tennes Stineback, all black men accused of murder, were lynched in Tiptonville, Tenn.
Dec. 17: Elmer Hill, a white man, was lynched in Monticello, Ky.
Dec. 19: Cleveland Franklin, a white man accused of murderous assault, was lynched at a site unknown.

1909

Jan. 6: Arthur Davis, a black man, was lynched in Florence, S.C., following a dispute with a white man.
Jan. 6: An unnamed black man accused of rape was lynched in Lexington, S.C.
Jan. 16: "Pink" Willis, a black man accused of attempted rape, was lynched in Poplarville, Miss.
Jan. 18: A black man named Hilliard, accused of insulting a white girl, was lynched in Hope, Ark.
Jan. 22: Douglass Robertson, a black man accused of murder, was lynched in Mobile, Ala.
Jan. 24: A black man named Davenport, accused of barn burning, was lynched in Leighton, Ala.
Feb. 1: An unknown black man accused of attempted rape was lynched in Bolivar, Ala.
Feb. 9: Robby Buskin, a black man accused of murder, was lynched in Houston, Miss.
Feb. 13: Jacob Nader, a black man accused of rape, was lynched in Lakeland, Fla.
Feb. 19: Rolley Wyatt, a black man accused of murder, was lynched in Georgia.
Feb. 22: Three white men accused of rape were lynched in Mineral Bluff, Ga.
Mar. 2: Joseph Fowler, a black man accused of murder, was lynched in Blakely, Ga.
Mar. 7: Anderson Ellis, a black man accused of rape, was lynched in Rockwall, Texas.
Mar. 8: William Ramsay, a black man, was lynched in Rosedale, Md.
Mar. 12: Joseph Gordon, a black man accused of murder, was lynched in Greenwood, Miss.
Mar. 19: Joseph Brown, a white man accused of murder, was lynched in Whitmore, W.Va.
Apr. 5: David Alexander, a black man accused of murder, was lynched in Pensacola, Fla.
Apr. 9: Benjamin Brame, a black man accused of attempted rape, was lynched in Hopkinsville, Ky.
Apr. 10: John Smith, a black man accused of rape, was lynched in Arcadia, Fla.
Apr. 11: Horace Montgomery, a black man, was lynched in Mississippi.
Apr. 19: Four white men: J.B. Miller, accused of murder; and three others, Joseph Allen, D.B. Burrell, and Jesse West; accused of complicity in a murder, were lynched in Ada, Okla.
Apr. 25: A black man named Thomas, accused of murder, was lynched near Birmingham, Ala.
Apr. 27: James Hodges, a black man accused of rape, was lynched in Marshall, Texas.
Apr. 30: Three black men accused of murder: Matthew Chase, "Pie" Hill, and a third known as "Creole Mose"; were lynched in Marshall, Texas.
May 9: An unidentified black man accused of rape was lynched in Duval County, Fla.
May 24: Albert Aikens, a black man accused of rape, was lynched in Pine Bluff, Ark.
May 28: Thomas Burnett, a white man accused of murder, was lynched in Abilene, Texas.
May 30: Joseph Blakely, a black man accused of murder, was lynched in Portland, Ark.
June 3: John Maxey, a black man accused of murder, was lynched in Frankfort, Ky.
June 6: Maik Morris, a black man accused of murder, was lynched in Tallahassee, Fla.
June 11: Frank Samuels and Tuillie Simmons, both black men accused of murder, were lynched in Branchville, S.C.
June 15: An unidentified black man accused of attempted rape was lynched in Arcadia, Fla.
June 22: Two black men, William Cornaker and Joseph Hardy, were lynched in Talbotton, Ga.
June 25: Albert Reese, a black man accused of murderous assault, was lynched in Cuthbert, Ga.
June 26: Sylvester Shennien, a black man accused of murder, was lynched in Wilburton, Okla.
July 1: An unidentified black man accused of burglary was lynched in Barnett, Ga.
July 20: King Green, a black man accused of insulting women, was lynched in Gum Branch, Ga.
July 20: Albert Lawson, a black man accused of murder, was lynched in Paris, Tenn.
July 30: Two black men accused of murder, Emile Antoine and Onexzime Thomas, were lynched in Grand Prairie, La.
July 31: Simon Anderson, a black man accused of window peeping, was lynched in Wellston, Ga.
Aug. 1: George Johnson, a white man accused of murder, was lynched

in Platte City, Mo.
Aug. 10: Wallace Miller, a black man accused of attempted rape, was lynched in Cadiz, Ky.
Aug. 15: An unidentified black man was lynched in Morehouse Parish, La., after suing a white man.
Aug. 17: William Robinson, a black man, was lynched in Greenville, Miss.
Aug. 24: William Way, a black man accused of murderous assault, was lynched in Monroe, La.
Aug. 27: Two black men, Benjamin Clark, accused of murder; and John Sweeney, accused of complicity; were lynched in Tarrytown, Ga.
Aug. 27: A black man named Clark, suspected of murder, was lynched in Sopertown, Ga.
Sept. 4: Two black men, Lewis Balaam and Joshua Balaam, accused of murder, were lynched in Jackson, Ala.
Sept. 8: Henry Hill, a black man accused of rape, was lynched in Mangham, La.
Sept. 11: John Spencer, a white man accused of murder, was lynched in Jonesboro, Tenn.
Sept. 13: An unnamed black man accused of murder was lynched in Bellamy, Texas.
Sept. 13: Two unnamed black men accused of murder were lynched at Sandy Point, Texas.
Sept. 26: Charles Anderson, a black man accused of murder, was lynched in Perry, Fla.
Oct. 1: Aps Ard, a black man accused of murder, was lynched near Greensburg, La.
Oct. 12: Michael Rodriguez, a white man accused of robbery, was lynched in Slabtown, La.
Oct. 27: Joseph Gifford and Alex Hill, both black and accused of murder, were lynched in Floyd, La.
Oct. 28: Four unnamed black men accused of murder were lynched in Kemper County, Miss.
Nov. 3: William Jones, a black man accused of murder, was lynched in Cairo, Ill.
Nov. 3: Charles Lewis, a black man accused of rape, was lynched near Sutton, W.Va.
Nov. 20: James Estes, a black man accused of murder, was lynched in Delhi, La.
Nov. 24: Ray Rolston, a black man accused of murderous assault, was lynched in Anniston, Ala.
Nov. 25: Morgan Chambers, a white man accused of robbery, was lynched in Meehan, Miss.
Nov. 27: Henry Rachel, a black man accused of rape, was lynched in Shreveport, La.
Dec. 1: John Harvard, a black man accused of murder, was lynched in Cochran, Ga.
Dec. 20: George Baily, a black man accused of murder, was lynched in Devil's Bluff, Ark.
Dec. 20: Cope Mills, a black man accused of murder, was lynched in Rosebud, Texas.
Dec. 20: Clinton Montgomery, a black man accused of murder, was lynched in Magnolia, Ala.
Dec. 26: Henry Remington, a white man accused of murder, was lynched in Menley, Va.
1910
Feb. 2: An unknown black man accused of rape was lynched in Beaumont, Texas.
Feb. 20: Dan Lumpkin, a black man accused of complicity in a murder, was lynched in Columbus County, Ga.
Mar. 2: An unidentified black man accused of attempted rape and murder was lynched in Vidalia, Ga.
Mar. 3: Holland Brooks, a black man accused of rape, was lynched in Dallas, Texas.
Mar. 7: Sam Ellis and Wade Ellis, both black, were lynched for murder in Tampa, Fla.
Mar. 8: An unknown black man accused of murder was lynched in Tampa, Fla.
Mar. 14: Ely Denton, a black man accused of murder, was lynched in Rayville, La.
Mar. 19: Two black men, Robert Austin and Charles Richards, accused of murder, were lynched in Marion, Ark.
Mar. 25: In Pine Bluff, Ark., "Judge" Jones, a black man was accused of improper conduct with a white woman, was removed from jail by a mob of forty men and hanged.
Apr. 1: A white man named Carroll was lynched in Goff, Ky.
Apr. 5: Frank Bates, a black man accused of murder, was lynched in Centerville, Texas.
Apr. 5: Laura Mitchell and Frank Pride, both black and accused of murder, were lynched in Arkansas.
Apr. 11: James Tabor, a black man accused of rape, was lynched in Alamo, Ga.
Apr. 15: Charles Jackson and Albert Royal, two black men accused of rape, were lynched in Amboy, Ga.
Apr. 19: Thomas O'Neil, a black man accused of murder, was lynched in Meridian, Miss.
May 14: "Dock" McLane, a black man accused of murderous assault, was lynched in Ashdown, Ark.
May 26: Jesse Matson, a black man accused of murder, was lynched in Calera, Ala.
May 26: A black man accused of rape was lynched in Charlotte, N.C.
May 27: Charles Wilson, a black man accused of rape, was lynched in Albany, Ga.
May 30: An unidentified black man accused of murderous assault was lynched in New Madrid, Mo.
June 11: Robert Matthews, a black man accused of rape, was lynched in Florida.
June 12: Elmer Curl, a black man accused of murder, was lynched in Mastadon, Miss.
June 14: William Hunter, a black man accused of insulting a white woman, was lynched in Star City, Ark.
June 15: Otto Mitchell, a black man accused of attempted murder, was lynched in Durant, Miss.
June 26: Leonard Johnson, a black man accused of murder, was lynched in Rusk, Texas.
June 28: A black man named Jones, accused of murder, was lynched in Braxton, Miss.
July 3: Robert Coleman and Sam Field, both black men accused of murder, were lynched in Charleston, Mo.
July 3: Henry McKenney, a black man accused of attempted rape, was lynched in Dothan, Ala.
July 5: An unnamed black man accused of attempted rape was lynched in Rodney, Texas.
July 6: Sam Powell, a black man accused of robbery and arson, was lynched in Huttig, Ark.
July 8: Carl Etherington, a white man accused of murder, was lynched in Newark, Ohio.
July 9: Sam McIntosh, a black man accused of attempted murder, was lynched in Kathleen, Fla.
July 10: J.D. Freeman, a white man, was lynched in Rayville, La.
July 12: Henry Gentry, a white man suspected of murder and rape, was lynched in Belton, Texas.
July 27: Evan Ralent, a black man accused of attempted rape, was lynched in Georgia.
July 30: Two unknown black men accused of murder were lynched in Bonifay, Fla.
July 31: Between 15 and 20 unarmed black men were killed during race rioting by a mob of white men in Palestine, Texas.
July 31: An unidentified black man accused of rape was lynched near Cairo, Ga.
Aug. 1: An unidentified black man was hanged by a posse in Dady, Fla., following the murder of a school girl, Bessie Morrison.
Aug. 1: William Wallace, a black man accused of rape, was lynched in Axis, Ala.
Aug. 2: Four unidentified black men, accused of complicity in a murder, were lynched in Bonifay, Fla.
Aug. 15: Joseph Buckley, a white man accused of murder, was lynched in Weleetka, Okla.
Aug. 25: Laura Porter, a black woman accused of keeping a house of prostitution, was lynched in Monroe, La.
Sept. 1: Nicholas Thompson, a black man accused of rape, was lynched in Armory, Miss.
Sept. 2: Two black people, Edward Christian, suspected of murder, and Hattie Bowman, suspected of complicity, were lynched in Graceville, Fla.
Sept. 6: Two black men accused of attempted burglary and murder were lynched in Clark County, Ga.
Sept. 13: Robert Bruce and William Sharp, black men accused of attempted rape, were lynched in Tiptonville, Tenn.
Sept. 14: Isaac Glover, a black man accused of murder, was lynched in Springfield, La.
Sept. 20: Two white men, Angelo Albano and Castenego Ticoretea, were lynched for attempted murder in Tampa, Fla.
Oct. 4: Bush Withers a black man accused of rape, was lynched in Sanford, Ala.
Oct. 8: An unknown black man accused of rape was lynched in McFall, Ala.
Oct. 8: A black man accused of robbery was lynched in Pelham, N.C.
Oct. 9: John Dell, a black man accused of murder, was lynched in Montgomery, Ala.
Oct. 12: A black man, Grant Richardson, was accused by a white woman, Mrs. Crow of assaulting her and fathering her child in Centreville, Ala. While being taken to jail he was seized by an angry mob and shot to pieces.
Oct. 14: A black man accused of murder was lynched in Huntington, W.Va.
Nov. 8: William Barnes and John Walker, two black men accused of murder, were lynched in Montezuma, Ga.
Nov. 8: Antonio Rodiguez, a white man accused of murder, was lynched in Rock Springs, Texas.
Nov. 15: A black man accused of murder was lynched in Mannford, Okla.
Nov. 26: Oscar Chitwood, a white man accused of murder, was lynched in Hot Springs, Ark.
Nov. 26: Flute Clark, a black man accused of murder, was lynched in Little Mountain, S.C.
Nov. 26: Richard Lowe, a black man accused of attempted rape, was

lynched in Mayo, Fla.
Nov. 26: Robert Matthews, a black man accused of rape, was lynched in Gull Point, Fla.
Nov. 30: Mach Neal, a black man accused of murder, was lynched in Warren, Va.

1911

Jan. 15: Three black men, Wade Patterson and James West, accused of insulting women, and Gene Marshall, accused of murder, were lynched in Shelbyville, Ky.
Jan. 20: Oval Poulson, a black man accused of murder, was lynched in Opelousas, La.
Jan. 22: William Johnson, a black man accused of murder, was lynched in Georgia.
Feb. 12: Iver Peterson, a black man accused of attempted rape, was lynched in Eufala, Ala.
Feb. 25: Robert Jones and John Vease, two black men accused of murder, were lynched in Augusta, Ga.
Mar. 5: Galvin Baker, a black man accused of making threats, was lynched in Marianna, Fla.
Apr. 2: An unknown black man accused of rape was lynched in Union Springs, Ala.
Apr. 7: Charles Hale, a black man accused of rape, was lynched in Lawrenceville, Ga.
Apr. 8: Murray Burton, Dawson Jordan, and Charles Pickett, three black men accused of murder, were lynched in Ellaville, Ga.
Apr. 21: William Potter, a black man accused of murder, was lynched in Livermore, Ky.
Apr. 25: Four unidentified white people were lynched in Campton, Ky.
May 18: John McLeod, a black man accused of murder, was lynched in Swainsboro, Ga.
May 21: Benjamin Smith, a black man accused of murder, was lynched in Swainsboro, Ga.
May 21: Six unidentified black men accused of murder were lynched in Lake City, Fla.
May 22: Joseph Moore, a black man accused of murder, was lynched in Crawfordsville, Ga.
May 25: Laura Nelson, a black woman accused of murder, and her son, were lynched in Okemah, Okla.
May 25: James Sweet, a black man accused of murder, was lynched in Gallatin, Tenn.
June 1: Patrick Crump, a black man accused of attempted rape, was lynched in White Haven, Tenn.
June 8: John Winston, a black man accused of murder, was lynched in Lafayette, Tenn.
June 16: William Bradford, a black desperado, was lynched in Chunky, Miss.
June 19: Charles Sellers, a white man accused of murder, was lynched near Cody, Neb.
June 20: A Mexican boy accused of murder was lynched in Thorndale, Texas.
June 27: An unnamed black man accused of murder was lynched in Cleveland, Ohio.
June 30: Thomas Allen and Foser Watts, two black men suspected of rape, were lynched in Monroe, Ga.
July 11: William McGroff, a black man accused of murder, was lynched in Baconton, Ga.
July 24: Miles Taylor, a black man accused of murder, was lynched in Claiborne Parish, La.
Aug. 4: Sam Verge was lynched by a mob in Demopolis, Ala., after they were unable to locate his brother, Richard Verge, wanted for the murder of planter Vernon Tutt.
Aug. 12: "Commodore" Jones, a black man accused of insulting women, was lynched in Farmersville, Texas.
Aug. 14: Zachariah Walker, suspected of murdering policeman Edgar Rice and in a Coatesville, Pa., hospital from a self-inflicted wound, was snatched by a masked mob and burned to a crisp while still on his mattress.
Aug. 18: An unnamed black man accused of murder was lynched in Durant, Okla.
Aug. 24: Peter Carter, a black man accused of rape, was lynched in Purcell, Okla.
Aug. 29: Peter Davis, a black man accused of murder, was lynched in Ft. Gaines, Ga.
Aug. 30: An unknown black man accused of murder was lynched in Clayton, Ala.
Sept. 9: Arthur Dean, a black man accused of rape, was lynched in Augusta, Ark.
Sept. 9: Peter Hallick, a white man accused of wife beating, was lynched in Grangeville, Idaho.
Sept. 15: Walter Byrd, a black man accused of murderous assault, was lynched in Winnsboro, La.
Sept. 20: Charles Molpass, a white man accused of murder, was lynched in Ala.
Oct. 5: An unidentified black men accused of attempted rape was lynched in Dublin, Ga.
Oct. 10: Willis Jackson, a black man accused of rape, was lynched near Greenville, S.C.
Oct. 11: Andrew Chapwan, a black man accused of attempted rape, was lynched in Georgia.
Oct. 11: Two black men, A.B. Richardson, accused of armed robbery, and Benjamin Woods, accused of rape, were lynched in Caruthersville, Mo.
Oct. 16: Nathan Lucey, a black man accused of rape, was lynched in Forrest City, Ark.
Oct. 19: Terry Lovelace, a black man accused of murderous assault, was lynched in Manchester, Ga.
Oct. 20: Charles Lewis, a black man accused of insulting women, was lynched in Hope, Ark.
Oct. 22: Edward Suddeth, a black man accused of murder, was lynched in Corneta, Okla.
Oct. 28: Daniel Walker, a black man accused of murder, was lynched in Washington, Ga.
Oct. 29: An unnamed black man accused of attempted rape was lynched in Marshall, Texas.
Nov. 7: "Judge" Moseley, a black man accused of murderous assault, was lynched in Lockhart, Miss.
Nov. 8: Riley Johnson, a black man accused of attempted rape, was lynched in Clarksville, Texas.
Nov. 8: William Nixon, a black man accused of murder, was lynched in Delhi, La.
Nov. 10: A black man was lynched in Honea Path, Ga., after Governor Cole L. Blease refused to order state police to stop the lynch mob. Blease stated he would have "resigned the office and come to Honea Path and led the mob myself."
Dec. 6: Bud Walker, a black man accused of murder, was lynched in Mannford Creek, Okla.
Dec. 6: Three unnamed black men accused of racial prejudice were lynched near Clifton, Tenn.
Dec. 21: John Warren, a black man accused of murder, was lynched in Donald, Ga.
Dec. 25: King Davis, a black man accused of murder, was lynched in Brooklyn, Md.

1912

Jan. 1: Sam Turner, a black man accused of murder, was lynched in Muldrow, Okla.
Jan. 15: Neeley Giles, a black man accused of murder, was lynched in Sucarnoochee, Miss.
Jan. 23: Belle Hathaway, John Moore, Eugene Hamming and "Dusty" Cruthfield all black and arrested for the murder of a young farmer, Norman Hadley, were lynched in Hamilton, Ga.
Jan. 28: John Chandler, a white man accused of murder, was lynched in Bessemer, Ala.
Feb. 4: Charles Powell, a black man accused of assault and robbery, was lynched in Macon, Ga.
Feb. 13: George Saunders, a black man accused of complicity in a murder, was lynched in Marshall, Texas.
Feb. 14: Mann Hamilton, a black man accused of rape, was lynched in Starkesville, Miss.
Feb. 14: Mary Jackson, a black woman accused of complicity in a murder, was lynched in Marshall, Texas.
Feb. 15: An unnamed black man accused of rape was lynched in Memphis, Tenn.
Feb. 19: Green Boman, Walter Grer, and David Neal, all black men accused of murder, were lynched in Shelbyville, Tenn.
Feb. 19: An unnamed black man accused of murder was lynched in Dothan, Ala.
Mar. 13: Aldred Dublin, Richard Dublin, and Peter Rivers, three black men accused of arson, were lynched in Olar, S.C.
Mar. 21: Homer Burk, a black man accused of murder, was lynched in Cochran, Ga.
Mar. 23: Sanford Lewis, a black man accused of murder, was lynched in Arkansas.
Mar. 29: Joseph Bronson and Fred Whisonant, both black men accused of murder and assault, were lynched in Blacksburg, S.C.
Apr. 3: Alex Coleman, a black man accused of attempted rape, was lynched in Starkesville, Miss.
Apr. 9: In Shreveport, La., a 29-year-old black man, Tom Miles, was hanged and his body filled with bullets after being acquitted of writing "insulting letters" to a white girl.
Apr. 15: Sam Arline, a black man accused of murder, was lynched near Tampa, Fla.
Apr. 18: Harry Hofner, a white man accused of murder, was lynched in Forsyth, Mont.
Apr. 25: An unnamed black man was lynched in Delhi, La.
Apr. 26: Henry Etheridge, a black man attempting to secure recruits for a proposed African colony, was lynched near Jackson, Ga.
May 3: Ernest Allums, a black man accused of insulting a white woman, was lynched in Louisiana.
May 7: G.W. Edd, a black man accused of murder, was lynched near Macon, Miss.
May 7: An unnamed black man accused of attempted rape was lynched in Greenville, Miss.
May 25: Dan Davis, a black man accused of rape, was lynched in Tyler, Texas.
May 27: Jacob Samuels, a black man accused of rape, was lynched in Robertson County, Tenn.

June 25: Ann Bostwick, a black woman accused of murder, was lynched in Georgia.
July 4: William English, a black man accused of insulting a white woman, was lynched in Bradentown, Fla.
July 5: A black man named Williams, accused of murder, was lynched in Plummerville, Ark.
Aug. 8: An unnamed black man accused of rape was lynched in Richmond, Va.
Aug. 13: T.Z. Cotton, a black man accused of murder, was lynched in Columbus, Ga.
Aug. 20: Monroe Franklin, a black man accused of rape, was lynched in Russellville, Ark.
Aug. 28: An unnamed black man accused of murder was lynched near Gadsen, Ala.
Sept. 4: Willis Perkins, a black man, was murdered for no apparent reason while walking on a railroad track near Hackleburg, Ala.
Sept. 7: A mob mistakenly lynched a black man, Walter Johnston, for the murder of 14-year-old Nite White, in Bluefield, W. Va. A statement issued by public officials said there was plenty of evidence that Johnston didn't commit the crime.
Sept. 10: Robert Edwards, a black man accused of complicity in a murder, was lynched in Cummings, Ga.
Sept. 14: A black man named Murphy, accused of rape, was lynched in Atlon, Fla.
Sept. 25: Sam Johnson, a black man accused of murder, was lynched in Grand Cane, La.
Oct. 5: A black man named Yarborough accused of rape, was lynched in Americus, Ga.
Nov. 2: William Smith, a black man accused of murder, was lynched in Wetumpka, Ala.
Nov. 7: George Baker, a white man accused of murder, was lynched in Steele, N.D.
Nov. 14: Preech Nellis, a black man accused of murder, was lynched in Ocala, Fla.
Nov. 18: A black man named Berney, accused of murder, was lynched in Wetumpka, Ala.
Nov. 19: John Archer, a black man accused of murder, was lynched in Ocala, Fla.
Nov. 23: William Thomas, a black man accused of murder, was lynched in Newberry, S.C.
Nov. 28: Wood Burke, James Heard, and Silas Jimmerson, all black and accused of murderous assault, were lynched in Benton, La.
Nov. 30: Chesbley Williams, a black man accused of murder, was lynched in Cordele, Ga.
Dec. 7: Azariah Curtis, a black man accused of murder, was lynched in Butler, Ala.
Dec. 17: An unnamed black man accused of murderous assault was lynched in Jackson, Miss.
Dec. 20: An unknown black man accused of murder was lynched in Cuba, Ala.
Dec. 21: Henry Fitts, a black man, was lynched in Norway, S.C., for refusing to repay a loan.
Dec. 28: Norm Cadore, a black man accused of murder, was lynched in Baton Rouge, La.

1913

Jan. 2: An unnamed black man accused of rape was lynched in Wagoner County, Okla.
Jan. 3: A black man named Carson was lynched in Selma, Alabama.
Jan. 17: Henry Monson, a black man accused of murder, was lynched in Paris, Texas.
Jan. 23: Richard Stanley, a black man accused of rape, was lynched in Fullbright, Texas.
Jan. 30: An unnamed black man accused of murder was lynched in Drew, Miss.
Feb. 7: Andrew Williams, a black man falsely accused of murder, was lynched in Houston, Miss.
Feb. 9: David Rucker, a 30-year-old black man, was found guilty of murdering Mrs. J.C. Williams in a mock trial conducted by a mob of 1000, in Houston. Rucker was chained to a steel pump, soaked in oil, and burned alive.
Feb. 14: The body of a black preacher, Charles Tyson, was found hanging from a tree near Myrtis, La., after his wife had reported him missing.
Feb. 23: Willie Webb, a black man accused of murder, was lynched in Drew, Miss.
Feb. 25: Two black men were lynched in Marshall, Texas. Robert Perry was shot to death for horse stealing, and a man named Anderson was hanged for unknown reasons.
Mar. 4: Two unidentified black men accused of murder were lynched in Cornelia, Ga.
Mar. 5: Samuel Owensby, a black man accused of murder, was lynched in Hogansville, Ga.
Mar. 12: The wife and child of Joe Perry were killed, and Perry and his brother John critically burned when when their home was set afire in Henderson, N.C.
Mar. 21: John Gregson, a black man accused of murder, was lynched in Union City, Tenn.
June 4: An unnamed black man accused of murderous assault was lynched in Beaumont, Texas.
June 5: Richard Galloway, a black man accused of racial prejudice, was lynched in Newton County, Texas.
June 6: Richard Galloway, a black man, was shot to death after posting bail at a Beaumont, Texas. jail. He and two others were accused of attacking a party of white men.
June 13: Dennis Simmons, a black man accused of murder, was lynched in Anadarko, Okla.
June 19: William Norman, a black man, was lynched near Hot Springs, Ark.
June 21: William Redding, a black man, was seized by a mob of 500, strung up to an overhead cable, and fired upon from every direction in Americus, Ga. The victim incurred the wrath of the crowd by shooting at police chief William Barrow.
June 21: An unidentified black man accused of murder was lynched in Americus, Ga.
June 27: William Robinson, a black man accused of murder, was lynched in Lambert, Miss.
July 6: Roscoe Smith, a black man accused of murder, was lynched in Yellow River, Fla.
July 7: An unidentified black man accused of rape was lynched in Bonifay, Fla.
July 10: Kid Tempers, a black man accused of murder, was lynched in Blountstown, Fla.
July 15: Samuel Towner, a black man accused of murder, was lynched in Alligator, Miss.
July 28: John Shake, a black man accused of murderous assault, was lynched in Georgia.
Early August: Two black farm hands were lynched near Germantown, Tenn., for no apparent reason.
Aug. 5: J.C. Collins, a black man accused of murder, was lynched in Mondak, Mont.
Aug. 12: Richard Puckett, a black man, was abducted from a Laurens, S.C., jail by a mob of 2000 men, hanged from a railway trestle, and shot with several hundred bullets. Puckett was accused of attacking a woman on a rural road.
Aug. 14: Sanders Franklin and Henry Ralston, both black men accused of murder, were lynched in Paul's Valley, Okla.
Aug. 15: Robert Lovett, a black man accused of murder, was lynched in Morgan, Ga.
Aug. 24: A young, retarded black man, Wilson Gardner, was beaten to death and hanged with his belt from a railway trestle near Kilgore, Ala., after threatening to hang his attackers with a rope which he carried.
Aug. 25: An innocent black man, Virgil Swanson, was lynched in Greenville, Ga., for the murder of planter L.C. Marchman. Later, Walter Brewster, also black, confessed to the crime.
Aug. 26: Joseph McNeely, a black man accused of murder, was lynched in Charlotte, N.C.
Aug. 27: James Comeaux a black man jailed for striking a merchant, A.W. Joseph, was taken from his cell by a mob and shot to death, in Jennings, La.
Aug. 28: An unknown black man was lynched in Kilgore, Ala.
Sept. 5: Lee Simms, a black man accused of rape, was lynched in Little Rock, Ark.
Sept. 12: Two black men accused of murderous assault were lynched in Tamms, Ill.
Sept. 21: Henry Crosby, a black man, was found hanged from a tree in Parkinsville, Ky., after he had appeared in the home of Mrs. J.C. Carroll.
Sept. 21: William Davis, a black man accused of murder, was lynched in Franklin, Texas.
Sept. 26: Joseph Richardson, a black man accused of rape, was lynched in Leitchfield, Ky.
Sept. 28: Walter Jones and William Jones, both black men accused of murder, were lynched in Harriston, Miss.
Oct. 15: Walter Brownlee, a black man wrongly accused of rape, was lynched in Hinchcliff, Miss.
Oct. 22: Warren Eton, a black man, was taken from his Monroe, La., jail cell by two armed masked men and hanged from a telephone pole. Eton had been jailed for making an insulting remark to a white woman.
Nov. 4: John Cudjo, a black man accused of murder, was lynched in Wewoka, Okla.
Nov. 7: John Talley, a black man accused of attempted rape, was lynched in Dyersburg, Tenn.
Dec. 16: Clive Kulbertson, a white man accused of murder, was lynched in Williston, N.D.
Dec. 16: Ernest Williams and Frank Williams, both black and accused of murder, were lynched in Blanchard, La.

1914

Jan. 8: David Lee, a black man accused of murderous assault, was lynched in Jefferson, Texas.
Jan. 27: Benjamin Dickerson, a black man accused of murder, was lynched in Noble, Okla.
Jan. 27: James Wilson, a black man accused of murder, was lynched in Wendell, N.C.
Feb. 16: Johnson McQuirk, a black man accused of murder, was lynched in Love Station, Miss.
Feb. 24: Sam Petty, a black man accused of murder, was lynched in Leland, Miss.

Mar. 13: William Williams, a black man accused of murder, was lynched in Hearne, Texas.
Mar. 19: Dallas Shields, a black man accused of murder, was lynched in Fayette, Mo.
Mar. 29: Charles Young, a black man accused of murder, was lynched in Clayton, Ala.
Mar. 31: Adolfe Padilla, a white man accused of murder, was lynched in Santa Fe, N.M.
Mar. 31: A dozen armed men overpowered a one-armed jailer, and abducted a black woman, Marie Scott, from a Muskogee, Okla., jail. Scott, accused of stabbing a young white man, was hanged from a telephone pole.
Mid-April: A 17-year-old black girl was lynched near Wagner, Okla. Two drunken white men who attempted to rape her were fired upon by her brother. She was arrested after her brother shot one of the men, but was taken from her cell by a mob later that night.
Apr. 29: In Marshalltown, Texas, a mob mutilated Charles Fisher, a black youth, after he kissed the white daughter of a local farmer.
May 7: Charley Jones, a black man suspected of stealing a pair of shoes, was taken from two police officers in Groveton, Ga., and lynched by a number of white men.
May 7: An unknown black man accused of murder was lynched in St. James, La.
May 12: Edward Hamilton, a black man accused of rape, was lynched in Shreveport, La.
June 7: William Robertson, a black man accused of murder, was lynched in Navasota, Texas.
June 17: A black couple, Isaac and Paralee Collins, were lynched in West Plains, Mo.
June 30: Fred Young accidentally shot James Jolly to death near Shaw, Miss. Both men were members of a posse seeking a black man, Jack Farmer, who was being sought for the murder of a prominent citizen, Earl Chase. Jennie Collins, a black woman, was killed for aiding Farmer.
July 13: Rose Carson, a black man accused of murder, was lynched in Elloree, S.C.
July 14: Accused of stealing three mules, a black man, Joseph B. Bailey, was hanged in Lake Cormorant, Miss., by a mob of twenty masked men.
July 17: An unknown white man accused of rape was lynched in Whitney, Ore.
Aug. 7: Three black men, Charles Griffin, Presto Griffin, and Henry Holmes, accused of murder, were lynched in Munroe, La.
Aug. 7: Crockett Williams, a black man accused of murder, was lynched in Eufala, Okla.
Aug. 9: An unknown black man suspected of murder was lynched in Munroe, La.
Aug. 12: A black man named Romeo, accused of murder, was lynched in Slidell, La.
Sept. 20: Nathan Brown, a black man accused of murder, was lynched in Rochells, Ga.
Oct. 14: Albert Claza, a white man accused of murder, was lynched in Willisville, Ill.
Oct. 14: Joseph Durfee, a black man, was hanged in Angleton Texas, after having his death sentence commuted to life imprisonment by Governor Colquitt of Texas.
Oct. 17: Joseph Durfee, a black man accused of murder, was lynched in Angleton, Texas.
Oct. 25: Mayshe Miller, a black man accused of murderous assault, was lynched in Aberdeen, Miss.
Oct. 28: Howard Davis, a black man accused of murder, was lynched in Newport, Ark.
Nov. 3: Thomas Burns, a black man accused of murder, was lynched in Hernando, Miss.
Nov. 13: Henry Alley, a black man, was lynched in Hillside, Ky.
Nov. 13: Ten unidentified black men were lynched in Rochester, Ky.
Nov. 14: John Evans, a black man accused of murder, was lynched in St. Petersburg, Fla.
Nov. 24: Dillard Wilson, a black man accused of murder, was lynched in Shiloh, S.C.
Nov. 25: A black man, Fred Sullivan, and his wife, accused of burning a plantation barn, were hanged in Byhalia, Miss., by a mob that forced the deputy sheriff and his posse to watch the lynching.
Early December: Three black men were lynched in Sylvester Station, La., for the murder of postmaster Charles Hicks. On December 12, the charred remains of Watkins Lewis were found bound to a tree. Tobe Lewis and Monroe Lewis were lynched a week earlier.
Dec. 2: Two black men accused of murder, Munroe Durden and Tobe Lewis, were lynched at Sylvester Station, La.
Dec. 3: Kane McKnight, a black man accused of murder, was lynched in Sylvester Station, La.
Dec. 4: William Grier, a black man accused of frightening a woman, was lynched in Coward, S.C.
Dec. 5: Willie Green, a black man accused of attempting to steal chickens, was lynched at Cowards, S.C.
Dec. 11: Bread Henderson and Charles Washington, both black and accused of murder, were lynched in Mooringsport, La.
Dec. 16: Allen Seymour, a black man accused of rape, was lynched in Hampton, S.C.
Dec. 19: William Jones, a black man accused of murder, was lynched in Fort Deposit, Ala.

1915

Jan. 4: Two black men, Edwin Smith and William Smith, accused of murder, were lynched in Wetumpka, Ala.
Jan. 15: Two black men, Jesse Barker and Samuel Barker, and a black woman, Eula Charles, were lynched in Monticello, Ga., when they resisted arrest for murderous assault.
Jan. 15: A white man named Molinndro was lynched in Lovelaceville, Ky.
Jan. 18: Herman Deeley, a black man accused of murder, was lynched in Taylorsville, Ala.
Jan. 20: Edward Johnson, a black man accused of murder and stealing cattle, was lynched in Vicksburg, Miss.
Jan. 23: Peter Morris, a black man accused of murder, was lynched in Arlington, Ga.
Feb. 4: A.B. Culberson, a black man accused of rape, was lynched in Evens, Ga.
Feb. 10: Alexander Hill, a black man accused of murder, was lynched in Brookville, Miss.
Feb. 13: Houston Underwood, a white man, was lynched in Irvine, Ky.
Feb. 14: Thomas Tinker, a white man accused of murder, was lynched in Mayfield, Ky.
Feb. 17: John Richards, a black man accused of insulting a white woman, was lynched by a mob near Sparr, Fla.
Feb. 21: W.F. Williams, a black man accused of murder, was lynched in Mt. Pleasant, Mo.
Feb. 28: William Reed, a black man accused of rape, was lynched in Kissimmee, Fla.
Apr. 17: Caesar Sheffield, a black man accused of stealing meat from a smokehouse, was taken from a jail and found shot to death in a field in Valdosta, Ga.
Apr. 20: Juan Leon and Jose M. Leon, both alleged bandits, were lynched at Lonely Gulch, Ariz.
Apr. 28: Thomas Brooks, a black man accused of murder, was lynched in Somerville, Tenn.
May 9: Dr. E.B. Ward, a black man accused of murder, was lynched in Norman, Okla.
May 9: An unidentified black man accused of murder was lynched in Big Sandy, Texas.
May 15: An unnamed black man accused of insulting a white woman was lynched in Louisville, Miss.
June 4: Arthur Bell, a black man accused of rape, was lynched in Princeton, Ky.
June 10: Joseph Strands, a black man accused of murder, was lynched in Johnston City, Ill.
June 14: Samuel Hevens, a black man accused of rape, was lynched in Toccoa, Ga.
June 14: Jules Smith, a black man accused of rape, was lynched in Winnsboro, S.C.
June 15: Loy Haley, a black man accused of murder, was lynched in Hope, Ark.
June 28: An unnamed black man accused of attempted rape was lynched in Cedar Bluffs, Miss.
July 5: Two white men, William Green and his son, suspected of murder, were lynched in Macon, Ga.
July 11: An unnamed black man accused of theft was lynched in De Kalb, Miss.
July 16: Thomas Collins, a black man accused of murderous assault, was lynched in Bunkie, La.
July 16: William Mitchell, a black man accused of murderous assault, was lynched in Sardis, Miss.
July 21: Peter Flambe and a man named Jackson, both black, were lynched in Cochran, Ga., accused of being accessories to a murder.
July 23: H.M. Owens, a black man, was lynched in Trenton, Fla.
July 29: Adolfo Munz, a white man accused of murder, was lynched in Brownsville, Texas.
Aug. 6: Edward Berry, a black man accused of rape, was lynched in Shawnee, Okla.
Aug. 6: William Leach, a black man accused of rape, was lynched in Dade City, Fla.
Aug. 10: James Fox, a black man accused of murder, was lynched in Alabama.
Aug. 12: Audry Crum, a white man accused of murder, was lynched in Osceola, Fla.
Aug. 16: A Jewish man, Max Leo Frank, convicted of the Apr. 27, 1913, murder of 14-year-old Mary Phagan, was dragged from the Milledgeville, Ga., jail and lynched after his death sentence was commuted to life imprisonment.
Aug. 17: "Kid" Jackson, Henry Russell, and a third man, all black and accused of poisoning mules, were lynched in Hope Hull, Ala.
Aug. 17: John Riggins, a black man accused of rape, was lynched in Bainbridge, Ga.
Aug. 20: Six Mexican men accused of pillage and murder were lynched in San Benito, Texas.
Aug. 21: An unnamed black man accused of attempted rape was lynched in Grand Bayou, La.
Aug. 24: John Slovak, a white man accused of beating his wife, was lynched in Shiner, Texas.

Aug. 26: An unnamed black man accused of attempted rape was lynched in Conshama, La.
Aug. 29: King Richmond, a black man, was lynched in Sulphur Springs, Texas.
Aug. 29: Three white night riders were lynched in Graham County, N.C.
Sept. 1: Rudd Lane, a black man accused of theft, was lynched in Louisiana, Mo.
Sept. 3: Three Mexican men accused of murder were lynched in Texas.
Sept. 4: George Washington, a black man accused of attempted rape, was lynched in Wagoner, Okla.
Sept. 4: A black man named Wilson, accused of rape, was lynched in Dresden, Tenn.
Sept. 8: In Dresden, Tenn., Mallie Wilson, a black man accused of entering a room occupied by a white woman, was taken from a jail cell and hanged.
Sept. 10: Claude Johnson, a white man accused of murder, was lynched in Hickman, Ky.
Sept. 12: Jacob Bowers, a black man accused of murder, was lynched in Carlisle, Ark.
Sept. 14: Six Mexican bandits were lynched in San Benito, Texas.
Oct. 10: Ten Mexican men accused of train wrecking and murder were lynched near Brownsville, Texas.
Oct. 11: Two unnamed black men accused of murder were lynched in Clarksdale, Miss.
Oct. 21: Two black men, Alonzo Green and his son, accused of murder, were lynched in Wayside, Ga.
Oct. 30: Joseph Huyler, a white man accused of murder, was lynched in Columbus, Miss.
Nov. 12: John Taylor, a black man accused of murderous assault, was lynched in Aberdeen, Miss.
Nov. 26: Ellis Buckner, a black man accused of rape, was lynched in Henderson, Ky.
Dec. 3: William Patrick, a black man accused of murder, was lynched in Forrest, Ark.
Dec. 9: An unnamed black man accused of theft was lynched in Hopeful, Va.
Dec. 17: Near Columbus, Miss., a black woman, Cordella Stevenson was hanged for suspected complicity in the barn fire of a white man, Gabe Frank.
Dec. 20: Two black men, Samuel Bland and William Stewart, were lynched in Eastman, Ga.
Late December: Six black men were killed following the murder of Henry J. Villipique in Early County, Ga.

1916

Jan. 2: Two black men were lynched and a black woman beaten in Anderson County, S.C., after one of the men allegedly made an offensive remark to a white woman.
Jan. 3: Samuel Sykes, a black man accused of attempted murder, was lynched in Hayti, Mo.
Jan. 12: John Richards, a black man accused of murder, was lynched in Goldsboro, N.C.
Jan. 21: Five innocent black men: Felix Lake, his three sons Frank, Dewey, and Major, and Rodium Seamore, accused of having knowledge of the murder of Lee County Sheriff Moreland were hanged near Starkville, Ga.
Jan. 22: An unidentified white highwayman was lynched in Vandervoort, Ark.
Jan. 24: W.J. Maxfield, a white man accused of murder, was lynched in Boston, Texas.
Jan. 28: Richardson Anderson, a black man accused of murder, was lynched in Ocala, Fla.
Jan. 28: Richard Burton, a black man accused of burglary, was lynched in Boyds, Ala.
Feb. 12: Harvin Harris, a black man accused of murder, was lynched near Macon, Ga.
Feb. 25: Jess McCortele, a black man accused of attempted rape, was lynched in Cartersville, Ga.
Mar. 1: William Whitley, a black man accused of murder, was lynched in Lebanon, Tenn.
Mar. 19: William Thomas, a black man accused of shooting a police officer, was lynched in Dyersburg, Tenn.
Mar. 20: Jeff Brown, a black man accused of attempted rape, was lynched in West Point, Miss.
Mar. 31: In Cedar Bluff, Miss., Jeff Brown, a black man who accidentally brushed against a white women while attempting to board a freight train, was beaten and hanged by a gang who witnessed the incident.
Apr. 3: Fayette Chandler, a black man accused of murder, was lynched near St. Charles, Mo.
Apr. 3: Oscar Martin, a black man on trial in Idabel, Okla., for the attack on a 13-year-old girl, was hanged from a second story balcony by a mob of 500 men who overpowered court officers.
Apr. 5: Joseph Black, a black man accused of attempted murder, was lynched in Kinston, N.C.
Apr. 9: Carl Dudley, a black man accused of murder, was lynched in Lawton, Okla.
Apr. 16: John Duke, a white man accused of murder, was lynched in Bonifay, Fla.
Apr. 17: John Dykes, a white man accused of murder, was lynched in Vernon, Fla.
May 5: Thomas Dixon, a black man accused of rape, was lynched in Hempstead, Texas.
May 15: Jesse Washington, an 18-year-old black man, was burned to death in front of a crowd of 15,000 in Waco, Texas. He was dragged from the courtroom after being convicted of the murder of Lucy Fryer.
May 25: U.G. Tally, a black man accused of attempted rape, was lynched in McNary, La.
May 27: Felix Gilman, a black man accused of murder, was lynched in Prescott, Ark.
June 20: Jeronimo Lerma, a black man accused of murderous assault, was lynched in Brownsville, Texas.
July 1: Lemuel Weeks, a black man accused of murder, was lynched in Pickensville, Ala.
Aug. 7: Stephen Brown, a black man accused of murder, was lynched in Seymour, Texas.
Aug. 9: A black man accused of attacking the daughter of a white planter was lynched in Stuttgart, Ark.
Aug. 19: Edward Lang, a black man accused of murder, was lynched in Rice, Texas.
Aug. 19: Three men and two women, all black, were lynched in Newberry, Fla., after being accused of aiding a black man suspected of murder to escape.
Aug. 21: A black man named Lewis, accused of burglary, was lynched in Valdosta, Ga.
Aug. 26: Jess Hammet, a black man accused of assaulting a white woman, was hanged from a telephone pole after being taken from a jail in Vivian, La.
Aug. 31: Sheriff Sherman Ely of Lima, Ohio was nearly lynched by a mob of 3000, when he refused to divulge the location of Charles Daniels, a black Man, who was accused of assaulting Mrs. John Barber, a white woman.
Sept. 21: Bert Dudley, a white man accused of murder, was lynched in Olathe, Kan.
Sept. 21: Henry White, a black man accused of rape, was lynched in Durand, Ga.
Sept. 26: Peter Hudson and Elijah Sturgis, twp black men accused of murder, were lynched in Cuthbert, Ga.
Sept. 29: Two black men, John Foreman and another unnamed, suspected in the shooting of Nowata, Okla., deputy sheriff James Gibson, were saved from one mob by the plea of a minister, but hanged by a second.
Sept. 29: Moxie Shuler, a black man accused of rape, was lynched in Bainbridge, Ga.
Sept. 29: Two black men accused of being accessories to a murder were lynched in Gordon, Ga.
Oct. 4: In Leary Ga., Sam Conley, a black man, was charged with the beating death of white planter E.M. Melvin. Conley escaped, but his mother, Mary Conley was arrested and subsequently shot to death after being abducted by an angry mob.
Oct. 5: William Spencer, a black man suspected of murder, was lynched in Graceton, Texas.
Oct. 6: Allen Nance, a black man accused of murderous assault, was lynched in Greenwood, Miss.
Oct. 7: Charles Smith, a black man accused of murder, was lynched near Sandersville, Ga.
Oct. 9: Frank Dodd, a black man accused of insulting two women, was hanged and shot after being abducted from his cell in DeWitt, Ark.
Oct. 16: In Paducah, Ky., two black men were lynched and their bodies burned. Brock Henley was accused of attacking a white woman, Mrs. George Rose, and James Thornhill for voicing approval.
Oct. 21: Anthony Crawford, a black man attempting to defend himself, was lynched in Abbeville, S.C.
Nov. 5: Joseph Johnson, a black man accused of murder, was lynched in Bay City, Texas.
Nov. 29: Buck Thomas, a black man accused of murderous assault, was lynched in Clarksville, Texas.
Dec. 14: Paulo Boleta, a white man accused of murderous assault, was lynched in Greenwich, N.Y.

1917

Jan. 10: An unidentified black man accused of rape was lynched in Greeley, Ala.
Feb. 8: James Smith, a black man accused of murder, was lynched in Proctor, Ark.
Mar. 1: Linton Clinton, a black man accused of rape, was lynched in Meigs, Ga.
Mar. 1: Emma Hooper, a black woman accused of murder, was lynched in Hammond, La.
Mar. 12: William Sanders, a black man accused of robbery, was lynched in Mayville, Ky.
Mar. 28: Joe Nowling, a black man, was lynched in Pelham, Ga.
Mar. 29: S.G. Garner, a black man who refused to give up his farm, was lynched in Kissimmee, Fla.
May 6: Star Daley, accused of murder, was lynched in Florence, Ariz.
May 11: Henry Brooks, a black man accused with intimacy with a white woman, was lynched in Shreveport, La.
May 18: Ell Persons, a black man, was burned to death and his head severed, in Memphis, Tenn. A photograph of the mutilated head was

widely circulated in the black press in the north, as a grim reminder of Southern racial attitudes.
May 20: Laurence Dempsey, a white man accused of murderous assault, was lynched in Fulton, Ky.
May 22: Ell Person, a black man suspected of rape and murder, was lynched in Memphis, Tenn.
June 2: Van Hayes and Pratt Hempton, two black men accused of murder, were lynched in Columbia, Miss.
June 10: A man named Piersol, the primary suspect in the May 30, 1917 kidnapping and murder of the 14-month-old son of a Springfield, Mo. banker, was dragged from a sheriff's car by a mob and strung from a tree, while protesting his innocence. His life was spared and he was eventually sentenced to thirty-five years for the kidnapping.
June 16: Henry Conly, a black man accused of rape, was lynched in Holdenville, Okla.
June 22: Benjamin Harper, a black man accused of murder, was lynched in Courtney, Texas.
June 23: Elijah Hays, a black man accused of striking a white woman, was lynched in Reisel, Texas.
June 25: Charles Sawyer, a black man accused of rape, was lynched in Galveston, Texas.
June 25: Shepherd Trent, a black man accused of attempted rape, was lynched in Punta Gorda, Fla.
June 29: Robert Jefferson, a black man, was lynched in Temple, Texas.
July 3: Gilbert Guidry, a black man accused of attempted rape, was lynched in Orange, Texas.
July 10: Marvell Ruffin, a black man accused of vagrancy, was lynched in Edgard, La.
July 16: An unidentified black man accused of burglary was lynched in Reform, Ala.
July 23: Three black men, Poe Hibbler, accused of attempted rape, Jesse Powell, and William Powell, both accused of threatening to kill, were lynched in Pickens County, Ala.
July 23: An unnamed black man was lynched in Elysian Fields, Texas, for entering the room of a white woman.
July 29: Two black men accused of murder, Daniel Rout and Jerry Rout, were lynched in Amite, La.
July 31: Andrew Avery, a black man accused of robbery, was lynched in Garland City, Ark.
Aug. 1: Frank Little, a white union organizer, was lynched in Butte, Mont.
Aug. 9: Aaron Jimerson, a black man accused of murderous assault, was lynched in Ashdown, Ark.
Aug. 17: William Page, a black man accused of attempted rape, was lynched in Lilian, Va.
Aug. 22: Charles Jones, a black man accused of attempted rape, was lynched near Marshall, Texas.
Aug. 24: Lawrence Sheppard, a black man accused of larceny, was lynched near Memphis, Tenn.
Aug. 24: W.D. Sims, a black man, was lynched in York, S.C., for advocating sedition.
Sept. 3: Charles Jennings, a black man, was lynched in Beaumont, Texas.
Sept. 9: Twenty Bolsheviks are lynched after breaking jail and torching Laistiev, Kazan, Russia.
Sept. 13: Samuel Gates, a black man accused of insulting girls, was lynched in England, Ark.
Sept. 18: Rufus Moncrief, a black man accused of rape, was lynched in Whitehall, Ga.
Sept. 21: Bert Smith, a black cook at an oil reservation in Goose Creek, Texas, accused of assaulting a white woman, was seized by 800 fellow workers and hanged. His body was then riddled with bullets, and mutilated with sledgehammers and knives.
Oct. 8: An unidentified black man accused of robbery was lynched in Arkansas.
Oct. 12: Fred Johnson, a black man accused of robbery, was lynched in New Orleans, La.
Oct. 13: Walter Clark, a black man accused of murder, was lynched in Danville, Va.
Nov. 16: Jesse Staten, a black man accused of insulting a white woman, was lynched in Quitman, Ga.
Nov. 17: Two black men, Collins Johnson and D.C. Johnson, were lynched in Sale City, Ga., for disputing a white man's word.
Nov. 22: An unidentified black man accused of attempted rape was lynched in Welch, W.Va.
Dec. 2: Ligon Scott, a black man accused of rape, was lynched in Dyersburg, Tenn.
Dec. 14: Wade Hampton, a black man, was lynched in Rock Springs, Wyo.
Dec. 15: Claxton Dekle, a black man, was lynched in Metter, Ga.

1918

Jan. 17: Sam Edwards, a black man accused of murder, was lynched in Hazlehurst, Miss.
Jan. 26: Jim Hudson, a black man accused of living with a white woman, was lynched in Benton, La.
Feb. 7: "Bud" Crosby, a black man accused of intending to rob and kidnap, was lynched in Fayetteville, Ga.
Feb. 7: Ed Dansy, a black man accused of killing two police officers and wounding two others, was lynched in Willacoochee, Ga.
Feb. 10: G.W. Lych, a black man accused of aiding a black man to escape, was lynched in Estill Springs, Tenn.
Feb. 12: Jim McIlherron, a black man accused of killing two white men and wounding another in Estill Springs, Tenn., was abducted from a train by twelve masked men, tortured with a red-hot crowbar, and burned to death.
Feb. 23: Walter Bess, a black man accused of murder, was lynched in Fairfax, S.C.
Feb. 26: Jim Jones, Jim Lewis, and Will Powell, three black men accused of stealing hogs, were lynched in Rayville, La.
Mar. 16: George McNeel and John Richards, two black men accused of attacking a white woman, were lynched in Monroe, La.
Mar. 22: Spencer Evans, a black man accused of assaulting a black woman, was lynched in Crawfordsville, Ga.
Mar. 26: Peter Bazemore, a black man accused of attacking a white woman, was lynched in Lewiston, N.C.
Apr. 4: Robert P. Praeger, a white man accused of making disloyal remarks was lynched in Collinsville, Ill.
Apr. 20: Claud Singleton, a black man accused of murdering a white man, was lynched in Poplarville, Miss.
Apr. 22: Berry Noyes, a black man accused of murdering a sheriff, was lynched in Lexington, Tenn.
Apr. 22: Clyde Williams, a black man accused of shooting a white man, was lynched in Monroe, La.
May 17: Eleven black persons accused of murdering a white man: Will Head, Sydney Johnson, Eugene Rice, Chime Riley, Simon Schuman, Will Thompson, Hayes Turner, Mary Turner, and three unidentified others, were lynched in Brooks and Lowndes counties, Ga.
May 20: Thomas Devert, a black man accused of murdering a white girl, was lynched in Erwin, Tenn.
May 22: Henry Jackson, a black man accused of throwing a white man under a train, was lynched in Miami, Fla.
May 22: John Womack, a black man accused of assaulting a white woman, was lynched in Redlevel, Ala.
May 23: James Cobb, a black man accused of murdering a white woman, was lynched in Cordele, Ga.
May 25: John Calhoun, a black man accused of murdering a white man, was lynched in Barnesville, Ga.
May 27: Kirby Goolsie, a black man accused of attacking a white girl, was lynched in Beaumont, Texas.
June 4: Six members of the Cabaniss family, Bessie, Cute, Pete, Sarah, Tenola, and Thomas, were lynched in Huntsville, Texas, for threatening a white man.
June 4: Edward Valentine, a white man accused of murder, was lynched in Sanderson, Texas.
June 13: Allen Mitchell, a black man accused of wounding a white woman, was lynched in Earle, Ark.
June 18: George Clayton, a black man accused of murdering a white man, was lynched in Mangham, La.
June 29: A black man named Magill, accused of assaulting a white woman, was lynched in Madill, Okla.
July 27: Gene Brown, a black man accused of assaulting a white woman, was lynched in Benhur, Texas.
Aug. 7: Bubber Hall, a black man accused of attacking a white woman, was lynched in Bastrop, La.
Aug. 11: Ike Radney, a black man accused of killing one policeman and wounding another, was lynched in Colquitt, Ga.
Aug. 28: Frederick Wagner, a white man accused of making disloyal remarks, was lynched near Hot Springs, Ark.
Sept. 3: Marion Czerich, a white man accused of murder, was lynched in San Pedro, Calif.
Sept. 3: John Gilham, a black man accused of attacking a white woman, was lynched in Macon, Ga.
Sept. 18: Abe O'Neal, a black man accused of shooting a white man, was lynched in Buff Lake, Texas.
Sept. 24: Sandy Reeves, a black man accused of assaulting a white girl, was lynched in Waycross, Ga.
Nov. 5: George Taylor, a black man accused of rape, was lynched in Rolesville, N.C.
Nov. 11: William Bird, a black man accused of creating a disturbance, was lynched in Sheffield, Ala.
Nov. 12: George Whiteside, a black man accused of murdering a policeman, was lynched in Sheffield, Ala.
Nov. 14: Charles Shipman, a black man, was lynched in Ft. Bend, Texas, after a disagreement with a white man.
Nov. 24: Allie Thompson, a black man accused of assaulting a white woman, was lynched in Culpepper County, Va.
Dec. 10: Edward Woodson, a black man accused of murder, was lynched in Green River, Wyo.
Dec. 16: Charles Lewis, a black man accused of beating a sheriff, was lynched in Hickman, Ky.
Dec. 18: Willis Robinson, a black man accused of murdering a policeman, was lynched in Newport, Ark.
Dec. 21: Andrew Clark, Major Clark, Alma House, and Maggie House; four black people accused of murdering a white man, were lynched in Shubuta, Miss.

1919

Apr. 4: William Little, a black soldier home shortly from WWI, was

found beaten to death outside Blakely, Ga., while still wearing his army uniform. Local whites had objected to it.
Apr. 29: George Holden, already wounded from two previous lynching attempts, was taken from a train in Monroe, La., by an armed mob and shot to death. Holden was accused of writing an insulting note to Onlie Elliot, a white woman.
May 14: Lloyd Clay, a 24-year-old innocent black man accused of the attempted rape of 19-year-old Lulu Belle Bishop was hunted down with bloodhounds in Vicksburg, Miss., abducted from a jail, covered with oil, set aflame, hanged from a tree, and his body riddled with bullets.
July 1: Cleveland Butler, an innocent black man who resembled another wanted for a crime, was shot to death by four white men in Dublin, Ga.
Aug. 29: Eli Cooper, a black community leader in Ocmulgee, Ga., was attacked in a church and shot to death. Other black churches and lodges were also burned.
Sept. 29: Joe Coe, a black man wrongly accused of assaulting a 5-year-old girl was taken from a Omaha jail by a crowd of 1000, dragged down the crowded street and hanged from a corner telephone pole.
Sept. 29: Omaha Mayor Edward P. Smith died from injuries suffered as he attempted to prevent the lynching of Joe Coe. The crowd then began to lynch him.
Oct. 3: The body of a black man, Ernest Glenwood, missing since Sept. 22, was found in a river, a rope around his neck, and another binding his wrist near Americus, Ga.

1920

May 8: Henry Scott, a black railway porter accused of insulting a white woman, was taken from a train near Tampa, Fla. He was taken from the sheriff by a mob of white men in three cars, and lynched.
June 16: Three black circus workers, Isaac McGhie, Elmer Jackson and Nate Green, accused of attacking a 17-year-old white girl in Duluth, Minn., were taken from jail and hanged at eight minute intervals from a telephone pole.
June 20: Philip Gathers, a black man accused of murdering Anza Jaudon near Stilson, Ga., was captured, mutilated, saturated with gasoline and burned, before being riddled with bullets.
July 6: In Paris, Texas, 28-year-old Herman Arthur and his brother, 19-year-old Irving Arthur, accused of the murder of their landlord and his son, were burned at the stake by an angry mob of 3000.
July 7: Edward Roach, a 24-year-old black man wrongly imprisoned for the attack on a 14-year-old white girl, Annie Lou Chambers, was taken from the county jail in Roxboro, N.C. by masked men, and hanged from a tree in a rural black churchyard.
Oct. 28: Cooksie Dallas, accused of either making improper advances towards a white woman or refusing to sell moonshine to white soldiers, was lynched by a mob in Johnson City, Tenn.
Early November: Ben Jacobs, a black man, was lynched in Tylertown, Miss., for the assault of a white man.
Nov. 23: Harry Jacobs a black man and the brother of Ben Jacobs was taken from the Tylertown, Miss. courtroom and hanged by a lynch mob. He was on trial for the assault of a white woman.
Nov. 24: In Dewitt, Ga., the body of a black man, Curley McKelvey, whose brother killed a white man, was found riddled with bullets, hanging from a tree.
Nov. 30: Charles E. Davis, a white N.C. farmer, hanged himself in a Raleigh jail cell after failing to convince authorities that his wife had been murdered by a "lecherous looking black man."

1921

Jan. 27: Henry Lowry, a black man accused of the murder of a white man and his daughter in Wilson, Ark., was burned at the stake in Nodena, Ark., after being seized from a train and returned near the scene of the alleged crime.
Feb. 1: In Camillia, Ga, Jim Roland, a well-to-do black farmer who shot Jason I. Harvel, a wealthy white farmer, was lynched after being apprehended by a posse.
Mar. 13: A mob of fifty men overpowered a jailer in Versailles, Ky., seized black prisoner Richard James, and hanged him from a tree. James was accused of the murders of Ben T. Rogers and Homer Nave.
Mar. 15: William Bowles, a black man accused of making improper remarks to a white woman, was lynched near Eagle Park, Fla.
Mar. 17: Howard Hurd, a black railroad brakeman, was lynched after he and other black railroad employees were warned to quit their jobs. His bullet riddled body was found with a note saying his death was a warning to other black men.
Mar. 21: In Monticello, Ark., Phil Slater, a 50-year-old black man who confessed to the attack of a white woman, was lynched after being taken from his jail cell.
May 21: At McGhee Ark., Leroy Smith, a 14-year-old black youth, was lynched after being suspected of an attack on a white couple.
June 20: John Henry Williams a black man convicted of the murder of an 11-year-old white girl, was seized while leaving the courtroom in Moultrie, Ga., and burned at the stake.
Aug. 15: Alexander Winn, a black man accused of assaulting a seven-year-old girl was hanged by a mob in Datura, Texas. Another mob burned his body after it had been taken to a funeral parlor.
Aug. 18: In Winston, N.C., Jerome Withfield, a black man suspected of assaulting the wife of a white farmer, was hanged even though the woman doubted that he was her assailant.
Oct. 1: Ray Newsome, a black man accused of insulting a white girl, was shot to death on a Pinetta, Fla., farm.
Oct. 11: In Leesburg, Texas, Wylie McNeely, a 19-year-old black man, was burned at the stake before a mob of 500 after being suspected of assaulting a 18-year-old girl.
Nov. 18: In Marianna, Ark., Will Turner, a black man accused of assaulting a white woman, was seized by a mob and shot to death. Afterwards, his body was burned in a city park.
Nov. 25: In Lake Village, Ark., Robert Hicks, a 25-year-old black man was lynched after he appeared at the home of a white woman, asking her about a note he had previously written.
Dec. 11: In Fort Worth, Texas, Fred Rouse, a black packing house worker, in the hospital with a fractured skull from a melee in which he had wounded two colleagues, was taken from his bed and hanged on a nearby tree.

1922

Jan. 13: In Florence S.C., a black man known as Ed accused of having a sexual relationship with a white women was lynched, and another man wounded by a white mob.
Jan. 17: Jake Brooks, a black employee of a packing house involved in a strike, was kidnapped from his Oklahoma City home and lynched by a mob.
Mar. 22: Alex Smith, an elderly black man who ran a house of prostitution in Gulfport, Miss., was hanged from a bridge after two white girls were found in his establishment.
May 6: Three black men: "Shap" Curry, twenty-six; Mose Jones, forty-four; and John Cornish, nineteen, were tied together and burned in the city square of Kirvin, Texas, after being accused of murdering 17-year-old Eula Ausley. Two white men were later arrested for the crime.
May 18: 15-year-old Charles Atkins, one of four black men arrested for the murder of 20-year-old mail carrier Elizabeth Kitchens, was brought to the murder scene and burned at the stake.
May 27: Jesse Thomas, a wrongly accused black man was burned in the public square in Waco, Texas, after being identified by a woman he allegedly attacked.
June 24: Warren Lewis, an 18-year-old black man who confessed to the attack of a white woman, was hanged before a mob of 300 persons in New Dacus, Texas.
July 28: John West a black laborer, was shot to death after a quarrel over the use of a drinking cup, at a road paving site near Guernsey, Ark.
Aug. 22: Parks Banks, a black man in Yazoo City, Miss., was hanged after he disregarded a warning to leave town.
Dec. 11: The uncle of a black man wanted for the attack on a local sheriff in Streetman, Texas, was lynched after a posse was unable to locate his nephew.
Dec. 14: George Gay, a 25-year-old black man accused attacking a white woman, was abducted by a mob of 1500 from the penitentiary in Huntsville, Texas, and shot to death.
Dec. 14: Charles Wright, a 21-year-old black man who confessed to the murder of white school teacher Ruby Hendry, was burned at the stake in Perry, Fla.
Dec. 15: Arthur Young, a black man accused of the murder of Ruby Hendry, was lynched by a mob in Perry, Fla., even though Charles Wright, had confessed to the crime.
Dec. 29: In Pilot Point, Texas, two black men accused of stealing two horses, were missing from their jail cells and were believed to have been lynched.

1923

Jan. 9: Leslie Legget, mistaken for a black man, was accused of consorting with white women and shot to death in Shreveport, La.
Feb. 16: In Milledgeville, Ga., two black men who may have been wrongly accused of killing a white grocer, were lynched and dismembered.
Apr. 29: James T. Scott, a black janitor at the University of Missouri in Columbia, was abducted by a mob of 500 and hanged from a bridge, after being accused of attempting to assault the 14-year-old daughter of a faculty member.
June 13: The body of Henry Simmons, an outspoken black man, was found strung from a tree, riddled with bullets, in Palm Beach Island, Fla.
July 4: Samuel Carter, a 46-year-old black man, was shot to death in Bronson, Fla., after attempting to aid his son, suspected of assaulting a white woman.
Aug. 6: The burning of Willie Minnifield caused a mass exodus of black people from Yazoo City, Miss. Minnifield was accused of attacking a woman with an axe.
Aug. 25: Len Hart, a 34-year-old black man was lynched after being accused of peeping in the window of a girl in Jacksonville, Fla.
Nov. 7: Dallas Sewell, a black man accused of "passing for white and associating with white women," was lynched in Eufala, Okla., by a mob wearing the garb of the Ku Klux Klan.

1924

Oct. 8: William Bell, a black man, was beaten over the head with a baseball bat and died at the hands of a mob of 100 people in Chicago. He was accused of assaulting two girls, but his guilt was later questioned.

1925

Dec. 19: Lindsay Coleman, a black man, was lynched in Clarksdale, Miss., shortly after being acquitted of the murder of a local plantation store manager, Grover C. Nicholas.

1926

June 2: Albert Blazes, a 22-year-old black man was hanged and his body

burned in Osceola, Ark., after being accused of assaulting a white girl. It was thought the girl was merely frightened.
Oct. 8: In Aiken, S.C., three blacks were lynched following the murder of sheriff H.H. Howard. Demon and Bertha Lowman, a brother and sister and their cousin Clarence, were shot to death by a mob. Demon had been cleared of the murder charge.
1927
Mar. 11: Clarence Darrow, in Mobile, Ala., to condemn the practice of lynching and other atrocities, and stressing the importance of mutual respect and cooperation through tolerance and less mob activity, was forced to leave the podium with the protection of a squad of special police, who shepherded him through an unruly mob.
June 13: In Louisville, Miss., two black brothers, Jim and Mark Fox accused of killing a sawmill foreman, were seized by an angry mob, soaked in gasoline, and burned to death.
Nov. 11: Henry Choate, an 18-year-old black accused of attacking a white girl, was hanged from a courthouse balcony in Colombia, Tenn.
1928
June: Two black brothers, Lee and David Blackman, were lynched by a mob in Rapides Parishes, La., after a shooting incident involving another brother. William Blackman was shot to death by police officers shortly after he killed a white deputy sheriff.
1929
June: Joe Boxely, nineteen and black, accused of attacking Mrs. John James, was taken from jail and killed near Alamo, Tenn.
Dec. 28: Chester Rugate, a farmer accused of murdering Clay Watkins, was taken from his jail cell, beaten, and shot to death.
1930
Jan. 11: Will W. Alexander, director of the Commission on Inter-Racial Cooperation, stated that lynching would disappear by 1940, wiped out by radio, good roads and the newspapers.
Feb. 1: James Irwin, a black man accused of rape and murder, was lynched in Ocilla, Ga.
Apr. 23: David Harris, a black man accused of murder, was lynched in Rosedale, Miss.
Apr. 24: Allen Green, a black man accused of rape, was lynched in Walhalla, S.C.
Apr. 28: John Houdaz, a white man accused of bombing, was lynched in Plant City, Fla.
Late April: Dane Harris, a black man suspected of murder and stealing groceries, was shot to death near Rosedale, Miss.
Late April: Allen Green, a black man accused of raping a white woman was shot to death by a midnight mob.
May 9: George Hughes, a black man who pleaded guilty to assaulting a white woman, was incinerated in Sherman, Texas, when a mob burned down the courthouse he was being held in.
May 18: George Johnson, a black man accused of murdering his landlord, was lynched in Honey Grove, Texas.
May 31: Henry Argo, a 19-year-old black man accused of attacking a white woman, was seized by a mob in his Chickasha, Okla., jail cell, shot in the head and stabbed twice in the heart.
June 17: William Roane, a black man accused of attempted rape, was lynched in Bryan, Texas.
June 21: Daniel Jenkins, a black man accused of attacking two white sisters, was lynched in Union, S.C.
July 4: Esau Robinson, a black man accused of murder, was lynched in Emelle, Ala. Five other persons, two white men, two black men, and one black woman were also killed.
July 29: S.S. Mincey, a black man, was lynched in Ailey, Ga.
Aug. 7: Thomas Shipp and Abraham Smith, both black men accused of rape and murderous assault, were lynched in Marion, Ind.
Aug. 15: George Robinson, a black man accused of resisting arrest, was lynched in Raymond, Miss.
Aug. 19: Oliver Moore, a black man accused of rape, was lynched in Tarboro, N.C.
Sept. 9: An articulate Atlanta police captain Grover C. Fain was able to quell a disturbance and disperse a mob intent on apprehending Robert Glaze, a black man being held in connection with the murder of a street car operator.
Sept. 10: In Darien Ga., two black men, George Grant and Willie Bryan, were apprehended for the murder of police officer Bob Freeman. Both were lynched, after which it was proven that at least one and possibly both were innocent.
Sept. 10: Pig Lockett and Holly White, both black and accused of robbing tourists, were lynched on the way to Scooba, Miss.
Sept. 25: Willie Kirkland, a young black man suspected of attacking a young white girl was wrested from jail by a mob of seventy-five and hanged from a tree in Magnolia Gardens, Ga.
Sept. 28: Lacy Mitchell, a black man, was lynched in Thomas County, Ga.
Oct. 1: John William Clark, a black man accused of killing a police officer, was lynched in Cartersville, Ga.
1931
Jan. 12: Raymond Gunn, a black man accused of murder, was lynched in Maryville, Mo.
Jan. 29: Charles Bannon, a white man accused of murder, was lynched in Schafer, N.D.
Mar. 22: Steve Wiley, a black man accused of attempted rape, was lynched in Inverness, Miss.
Mar. 29: Elijah Johnson, a black man accused of attempted rape, was lynched in Vicksburg, Miss.
April: Steve Wiley, a black man accused of attacking a white woman, was hanged from a railroad trestle in Inverness, Miss.
Apr. 17: George Smith, a black man accused of attempted rape, was lynched in Union City, Tenn.
Aug. 2: Oscar Livingston, a black man accused of attempted rape, was lynched in Point a la Hache, La.
Aug. 5: Neal Guinn, a black man accused of attempted rape, was lynched in Haynesville, Ala.
Aug. 28: Richard Smoke and Charles Smoke, a black father and son, accused of assault, were lynched in Blountstown, Fla.
Early December: Tom Jackson and George Links, suspected of shooting two officers, were hanged and shot in Lewisburg, W. Va.
1932
June 14: Sheriff Hood of Winnsboro, S.C. was killed and six deputies wounded while attempting to stave off a lynch mob attempting to wrest a black prisoner from their possession. The mob extracted the prisoner and shot him to death.
1933
Feb. 19: Nelson Nash, a 24-year-old black man, allegedly killed a bank president and assaulted his wife during a robbery attempt. Nash was lynched in Ringgold, La., after confessing to the crime. He was later proved innocent.
Mar. 26: In Lowell, N.C., a 20-year-old black man accused of assaulting a 16-year-old white girl, was saved from a lynch mob by Dr. James W. Reid, who harbored the youth in his basement.
July 5: Norris Bendy, a black truck driver, was arrested after a fight with Marvin Tollis, a white truck driver, in Clinton, S.C. Later he was seized from his cell, shot, beat and strangled, before being hanged from a tree.
July 21: An unidentified black man was hanged in Caledonia, Miss., after being accused of insulting a white woman.
August: A.T. Harden, Elmore Clark, and Dan Pippen, blacks accused of murder, were taken from Sheriff R.L. Shamblin. Two were found shot to death, the third wounded, in Tuscaloosa, Ala.
Oct. 9: Bennie Thompson, a young black man was taken from jail in Ninety Six, N.C., and beaten to death. Four white men were subsequently arrested, one of whom implicated the police force.
Oct. 11: Two innocent black men were attacked in Labadieville, La. after being accused of murdering a white girl. Freddy Moore was lynched by the mob, while Norman Thibodeaux managed to escape. Later, the slain girls' stepfather admitted to the murder.
Oct. 18: George Armwood, a 24-year-old black man accused of murdering 82-year-old Mary Denston, was lynched in Princess Anne, Md. A mob of 3000 overpowered fifty state troopers to extract Armwood from his cell.
Nov. 26: Thomas Harold Thurmond and John Maurice Holmes, accused of the murder of 22-year-old Brooke Hart in San Jose, Calif., were lynched after 15,000 irate citizens stormed their prison cell.
Nov. 28: Seven reporters and a photographer were forced to flee a Salisbury, Md. hotel. A mob of 500 sought to attack the press, after successfully forcing armed soldiers to leave the town.
Nov. 29: Lloyd Warner, a black man, was burned alive in St. Joseph, Mo.
Dec. 8: David Gregory, a black man who resisted arrest by a posse, was burned and mutilated by a mob in Kountze, Texas. Gregory was accused of killing a white woman.
Dec. 15: Cord Cheek, a 20-year-old black man was lynched in Columbia, Tenn., after a Grand Jury refused to indict him for molesting an 11-year-old white girl.
1934
June 9: Two black men, Joe Love and Isaac Thomas, who allegedly confessed to the assault of a white woman, were taken from a sheriff in Clarksdale, Miss. by a mob of 150, and hanged from a railway trestle.
June 21: John Criggs, a black man accused of associating with a white women, was hanged and shot in Newton, Texas, after being seized from two deputies by a mob of 200 armed men.
July 9: Andrew McCloud, a 26-year-old black man suspected of attempting to assault a white girl, was hanged in the public square of Bastrop, La., after a mob of 3000 dragged him from the Morehouse parish jail.
July 16: James Sanders, a 25-year-old black man accused of writing an indecent and insulting letter to a white girl, was shot to death by a mob in Bolton, Miss.
Oct. 27: Claude Neal, a 23-year-old black man who confessed to the murder of a white girl, was hanged from a tree on the courthouse lawn in Marianna, Fla. Newspapers printed the planned itinerary of the lynching ritual.
1935
Jan. 11: In Franklinton, La., a black man whose conviction for murder was reversed by the Louisiana Supreme Court on the grounds that his trial was unfair, was shot to death in his jail cell by an angry mob.
Mar. 12: Ab Young a black man suspected in the murder of a state highway worker, was hanged by a mob of 50 white men near Slayden, Miss.
Mar. 25: R.J. Tyrone, a black farmer in Hattiesburg, Miss., who had been having financial difficulty with a neighboring white farmer, was found dead from multiple gunshot wounds near his home after a visit from a white mob. A coroner ruled that he had committed suicide.

Sept. 19: As a jury was deliberating his fate in a murder trial in Osford, Miss., Ellwood Higginbotham, the black defendant, was taken from his cell and lynched.

1936

Apr. 28: Lint Shaw, a black farmer from Colbert, Ga., was shot to death by a mob of forty men eight hours before he was be tried on the charge of attempted criminal assault.

May: Willie Kees, a nineteen-year-old black man accused of assaulting a white woman, was taken from the sheriff and shot in Lepanto, Ark.

June: Frank Weems, a black sharecropper, was flogged to death by unknown vigilantes in Earle, Ark.

June 18: A mob of 300 persons attempted to lynch five men and four women, all black, for a murder in a El Campo, Texas, cafe. After the Texas Rangers prevented the lynching, the mob vented its anger by burning the cafe.

1937

Feb. 2: Wesley Johnson, a black man accused of attacking a white woman, was lynched in Henry County, Ala. Four months later Sheriff J.L. Corbitt was charged with failing to protect Johnson from the mob, and that the mob had lynched the wrong man.

Apr. 13: Two black men named "Bootjack" McDaniels and Roosevelt Townes were lynched and another severely whipped by a mob of 100 white men in Winona, Miss., after being suspected of murdering a white man.

May 25: Willie Reid, a 24-year-old black man arrested for the murder of a white woman, was shot as he attempted to escape from the custody of a sheriff's deputy in Bainbridge, Ga. Later, a mob burned the corpse in a public display.

July 20: Richard Hawkins and Ernest Ponder, black men, were lynched in Tallahassee, Fla., for attacking a white policeman.

Aug. 17: Albert Gooden, a black man, was lynched in Covington, Tenn.

Oct. 4: J.C. Evans, a black man, was lynched in Milton, Fla.

1938

June 10: Washington Adams, a black man, was lynched in Columbus, Miss.

July 6: Tom Green, a black man, was lynched in Rolling Fork, Miss.

July 9: John Dukes, a black man, was lynched in Arabi, Ga.

Oct. 13: R.C. Williams, a black man, was lynched in Ruston, La.

Nov. 21: Wilder McGowan, a 24-year-old black man accused of assaulting a 74-year-old white woman, was hanged after being hunted with bloodhounds by a mob of 200 white men near Wiggins, Miss.

1939

Mar. 2: Members of the Ku Klux Klan whipped a couple parked on a "lovers lane" to death, for violating the Klans "Moral Kode."

Apr. 20: Lee Snell, a black man, was lynched in Daytona Beach, Fla.

May 8: Joe Rodgers, a black man, was lynched in Canton, Miss.

1940

May 9: O'Dee Henderson, a black man, was lynched in Fairfield, Ala.

June 22: Jesse Thornton, a black man, was lynched in Crenshaw County, Ala.

June 22: Elbert Williams, a black man, was lynched in Brownsville, Tenn.

Sept. 8: Austin Callaway, a black man, was lynched in La Grange, Ga.

1941

Feb. 15: Bruce Tisdale, a black man, was lynched in Andrews, S.C.

Apr. 13: Robert Melker, a black man, was lynched in Cherryville, N.C.

May 6: Robert Sapp, a black man, was lynched in Blakely, Ga.

May 13: A.C. Williams, a 22-year-old black man charged with assaulting a 12-year-old white girl in Quincy, Fla., was abducted from his jail cell, shot in the head and left for dead. While being taken to the hospital he was again seized and shot to death.

1942

Jan. 16: A letter to a congressman alleged that vigilante groups were forming to take action against Japanese held in detention camps following the attack on Pearl Harbor the previous month.

Jan. 25: Cleo Wright, a black man, was lynched in Sikeston, Mo.

July 13: Willie Vinson, a black man, was lynched in Texarkana, Texas.

Oct. 12: Ernest Green, a black man, was lynched in Quitman, Miss.

Oct. 12: Charles Lang, a black man, was lynched in Quitman, Miss.

Oct. 12: Edward Person, a black man, was lynched in Paris, Ill.

Oct. 17: Howard Wash, a black man, was lynched in Laurel, Miss.

Mid-October: Two unidentified 14-year-old black boys accused of attempting to rape a white girl were hanged in Shubuta, Miss.

1943

Jan. 30: Robert Hall, a black man, was lynched in Newton, Ga.

June 16: Cellos Harrison, a black man, was lynched in Marianna, Fla.

Nov. 7: Hallery Willis, a black man, was lynched in Camp Ellis, Ill.

1944

Mar. 26: Rev. Isaac Simmons, a 66-year-old black minister and farmer who suspected there was oil on his property, was lynched in Amite county, Miss., after he hired a lawyer to safeguard the title to his property.

Nov. 23: James Scales, a black man, was lynched in Pikeville, Tenn.

1945

Oct. 12: Jesse James Payne, a black man, was lynched in Madison, Fla.

1946

July 22: Leon McTatie, a black man, was lynched in Lexington, Miss.

July 26: Two 27-year-old black men, Roger Malcolm and George Dorsey, and their wives, were shot to death by twenty unmasked white men near Monroe, Ga. One of the victims was suspected of stabbing his former employer.

Aug. 8: John C. Johnson, a black man, was lynched in Minden, La.

1947

Feb. 17: Willie Earle, a black man, was lynched in Pickens County, S.C.

1948

Nov. 20: Robert Mallard, a black man, was lynched in Lyons, Ga.

1949

May 30: Caleb Hill, Jr., a black man, was lynched in Irwinton, Ga.

July 9: Malachi Wright, a black man, was lynched in Houston, Miss.

Sept. 3: Hollis Riles, a black man, was lynched in Bainbridge, Ga.

1951

Mar. 31: Melvin Womack, a black man, was lynched in Winter Garden, Fla.

1955

May 7: Rev. George W. Lee, a 51-year-old black man who refused to withdraw his name from a voting list, was shot to death in Bezoni, Miss.

Aug. 6: Lamar D. Smith, a 63-year-old black man who was encouraging other blacks to register to vote, was shot to death on the courthouse lawn at Brookhaven, Miss.

Aug. 31: Emmett Louis Till, a 15-year-old black man accused of whistling at a white woman, was found shot through the head, floating in the Tallahatchie river near Greenwood, Miss.

1959

Apr. 24: Mack Charles Parker, a black man, was lynched in Poplarville, Miss.

1960

Mar. 8: In Houston, Felton Turner, a 27-year-old black man was hung from his heels from a tree and had a series of KKK's carved into his chest and stomach by four masked white men.

1964

May: The Maccabees, a vigilante force of Hassidic Jews, was formed in the Crown Heights section of New York City.

June: Three civil rights workers, James Chaney, Andrew Goodman, and Michael Schwerner were lynched by the Ku Klux Klan in Neshoba County, Miss.

December: Following increased robberies by heroin addicts, residents of many New York neighborhoods organized foot patrols.

1965

May: A black vigilante organization, Deacons for Defense and Justice, was formed in Louisiana to protect black residents as well as white civil rights activists.

1967

Mar. 3: Thirty-five residents of New York City's Peter Cooper housing project, organized a temporary vigilante committee to prevent increased rapes and muggings.

June: Private armed guards began patroling the streets of Houston.

July: Italians in Newark, N.J. threaten to oppose blacks with vigilante gangs in response riots during the summers.

October: Oberia D. Dempsey, a Harlem minister, organized Operation Interruption, an armed vigilante group which attemped to counteract drug addicts.

1968

Summer: White vigilante groups were formed in Cleveland.

October: Blacks in Pittsburgh formed unarmed vigilante patrols.

1969

January: Twenty men uniformed in paramilitary clothing formed the vigilante Community Patrol Corps in Detroit.

Dec. 4: Fred Hampton, a leader of the Illinois chapter of the Black Panther Party, was one of two men killed by police armed with pistols, shotguns, and submachine guns, when they stormed his apartment on Chicago's West Side.

1974

April: Police in Fort Worth, Texas, were forced to add private citizens to its patrol force because of increased crime.

Apr. 24: An attempt to reformulate the Montana Vigilantes was announced by Captain Loren J.B. Nedley of Stevensville, Mont.

July 31: Edward Foster, a policeman in Portland, Maine, was detained in a psychiatric ward after the suggestion that department should institute a vigilante "death squad."

Oct, 10: Julio Torres, suspected of being a drug addict, was beaten to death by self-styled vigilantes in New York City.

1975

Private "Towne Watch" patrols began in Camdem, N.J., following increased crime and allegations of police corruption.

February: Private patrols were instituted in Duluth, Minn., following a rash of gas-station hold-ups.

June 21: After claims of a national vigilant force numbering two million, nine people attend the first convention of the Posse Comitatus of Montana and the USA, held in Virginia City, Mont.

September: For three days, a group of forty armed vigilantes in response to a strike by the United Farm Workers held union organizers at bay with threats of violence.

1979

Tony Cimo, a South Carolina man whose parents were murdered in their grocery store, killed their accused murderer, 19-year-old Rudolph Tyner, with a bomb concealed in a radio, after the state refused to pronounce the death penalty. Cimo pleaded guilty to the retaliatory murder and

sentenced to eight years.
November: Five Communist Workers Party members were killed in Greensboro, N.C. Six members of the Ku Klux Klan were implicated in the slayings, but were acquitted a year later.

1983

Roberta Leonard, a 67-year-old grandmother who was partially blind, held twelve muggers at bay with an unlicensed pistol after she was accosted on a New York street. She obtained the weapon after having been a mugging victim two months earlier.

Willie E. Williams, a Buffalo, N.Y., man whose daughter was kidnapped and sexually molested, beat her attacker and stabbed him in the stomach.

1984

Dec. 22: Bernhard Goetz armed with an unlicensed .38-caliber pistol, shot four black youths who accosted him on a New York subway train.
December: Harold Brown, a Chicago man, shot two black youths, killing one, after they attempted to rob him at knifepoint.

MOB VIOLENCE

A breach of the public order by three or more persons employing violence constitutes a riot according to prevailing criminal statutes in the U.S. The riot differs from an unlawful assembly in the sense that it incorporates violent acts. Rioting encompasses a wide range of illegal acts, ranging from an angry clash between labor union picketers and strike breakers to angry crowds robbing and looting store fronts, as happened during the civil disturbances in the large metropolitan areas of the U.S. in the late 1960s.

England, the U.S., and India treat rioting as a misdemeanor punishable by light prison sentences. In Great Britain, however, there is an important distinction. Rioters who refuse to disperse after being ordered to do so by the magistrate face stiffer penalties. In West Germany in order for a demonstration to be termed a riot, the participants must resist arrest or otherwise assault an officer of the law. The ringleader of the riot faces a harsher penalty in Germany than he or she would elsewhere. These distinctions concerning liability are also a part of Japanese law. From the worker uprisings of the mid-nineteenth up to the early twentieth centuries have evolved the urban race riots and civil demonstrations that characterized the 1960s. Beginning in the early 1910s, U.S. blacks in Omaha, and Chicago expressed their discontent toward white society through simultaneous acts of violence in the urban core. By the 1960s, the cities of Newark, Detroit, Los Angeles, and Chicago were in flames during the "long hot summers" of that era. The Vietnam War and protest against the draft laws occasioned fresh outbreaks of mob violence on the nation's campuses during this same time.

133 B.C.
Roman Election Riot. A Roman statesman, Tiberius Sempronius Gracchus, was killed by a mob while seeking reelection.
121 B.C.
Roman Election Riot. Gaius Sempronius Gracchus, a Roman tribune who instituted land reforms, was murdered in an election riot by troops belonging to Opimus.
1526
November: The first recorded slave revolt in North America occurred in a tiny Spanish colony at the mouth of the Pedee River in what is now present-day South Carolina. The 150 Spanish settlers sailed to Haiti the next month.
1663
A conspiracy hatched by indentured white servants and black slaves to gain their freedom in Gloucester County, Va., was crushed by local authorities. A white servant named Berkenhead revealed the plot to the legislature resulting in the execution of several of the ringleaders.
1672
Aug. 27: Dutch Riot. Jan DeWitt and his brother Cornelius, heads of the Dutch republican party, were killed by a mob at the Hague.
1676
Bacon's Rebellion. Nathaniel Bacon and 400 Virginia frontiersmen angered by the colonial government's refusal to provide protection against Indian attacks held the governor and the entire assembly at gunpoint while reiterating their demands. When refused, they burned Jamestown to the ground. In retaliation, the governor hanged many of the frontiersmen.
1687
A conspiracy to kill all the white slave owners in the Northern Neck region of Virginia was uncovered. The council then decreed that there would be no more public slave funerals.
1708
A small group of slaves rebelled against their masters in Newton, L.I. Seven whites were killed. Three slaves and an Indian were executed for their part in the uprising.
1710
April: A slave uprising in Surry and James City Counties, Va., was betrayed by a black man named Will before it could start.
1711
Spring: A slave named Sebastian led a small insurrection in South Carolina before he was tracked down and killed by an Indian hunter.
1712
Pilgrim-Puritan Controversy. Rivalry over the Indian fur trade sparked a dispute between the Pilgrims of Plymouth and the Puritans of the Massachusetts Bay Colony in which two men were killed.
Apr. 6: New York Slave Revolt. A group of blacks and Indians ambushed nine whites. Eighteen of the twenty-four blacks sentenced to death were not reprieved, and were hanged, tortured, or burned to death.
1713
May 19: Boston Bread Riot. In the midst of a severe food shortage in Boston, a crowd rioted when some merchants exported corn.
1715
English Political Riots. With Tory influence, London crowds took to the streets of London, Holborn, and Whitechapel, shouting "High Church and Ormonde" and attacking a Presbyterian meeting house.
Riot Act. Enacted in Great Britain during the reign of George I, it stipulated that when twelve or more persons were unlawfully gathered they must disperse "on proclamation" or be guilty of a felony. The ceremony of reading the Riot Act at such gatherings became routine law enforcement in the American colonies.
1720
July: French Financial Riots. In massive riots sparked by John Law's financial operations, 15,000 people gathered in the Rue Vivienne, sixteen were trampled to death, Law's coachman was lynched and the Palais Royal was threatened with destruction.
1721
During a succession of disturbances caused by the severity of punishments inflicted on domestic servants, 5,000 gathered on one occasion to protest the public punishment of a coachman. Five people were killed and several wounded.
1727
English Anti-Turnpike Riots. Mobs destroyed most of the turnpikes and toll gates on all roads leading into Bristol, England.
1725
August: French Food Riots. When the price of bread exceeded those of the famine year of 1709, riots occurred at Caen in Normandy and throughout the Paris region, resulting in the resignation of the responsible minister.
1729
June: A large number of Virginia slaves fled into the Blue Ridge Mountains in a vain attempt to gain their freedom. After a short but violent skirmish with white men, the slaves were captured and returned to bondage.
1733
London Anti-Tax Riot. Crowds in London beseiged Parliament and mobbed Robert Walpole in protest of his Excise Tax bill, crying "No slavery—no excised—no wooden shoes!" He was forced to withdraw the bill.
1734
April 23: Mast Tree Riot. Residents of Exeter, N.H., drove off British troops enforcing the law reserving the best New England trees for masts for the Royal Navy.
1735
Anti-Turnpike Riots. Riots against turnpikes occurred sporadically over a two period around Hereford and Worcester in England.
1736
Anti-Irish Riots. Two days of rioting in Shoreditch, Spitalfields, and Whitechapel, England, were sparked when Irish workmen were hired at substantially lower pay to replace English workmen. A crowd of 4,000 destroyed several Irish homes and taverns. Nine prisoners were taken, of whom five later stood trial at the Old Bailey.
1737
Boston Brothel Riot. Crowds in Boston destroyed several brothels.
1738
Spring: Prince George's County Slave Revolt. Several slaves broke free from their jail cell in Prince George's County, Md. They fomented a revolt against the white slave owners of the county before the sheriff and his men were able to quell the disturbance.
December: Wiltshire Weavers Riot. In Wiltshire, England, the weavers and shearmen engaged in widespread riots, attacking the homes of clothiers and destroying their property. Subsequently the clothiers acceded to the rioters demands.
1739
French Food Riots. Successive outbreaks of food riots occurred in Bordeaux, Caen, Bayeux, Angouleme, and Lille.
March: One white man was killed and three others wounded in a slave insurrection near Purysburgh, S.C. It foreshadowed a larger revolt that occurred six months later.
Sept. 9: Led by a black man named Jemmy, a group of slaves from Stono, S.C., seized a quantity of arms and powder from a warehouse and rampaged through the countryside. They were joined by seventy to eighty other slaves before the rebellion was put down by militiamen ten miles outside of Stono. About forty Negroes were shot dead, and many more were hanged and gibbeted.
1740
June: A slave conspiracy was uncovered in Charlestown, S.C. Fifty blacks were rounded up and hanged as an example to other slaves contemplating escape.
September: When the price of a four-pound loaf of bread rose to equal the daily wage of an unskilled laborer, King Louis XV and his ministers were mobbed by crowds and a prison riot over bread resulted in the deaths of fifty prisoners.
1741
Apr. 13: Negro Riots of New York. A number of fires of mysterious origin were set in New York City in late March and early April. Soon there were unfounded rumors that the entire city was to be burned to the ground. Believing that this was the work of the Negro population, the white residents of New York fled the city. At least 200 blacks were publicly hanged (200 more were burned at the stake) for inciting a panic. Many other prisoners were transported for life.
1742
Philadelphia Election Riot. The Quaker and Proprietary parties, divided over using force against Indians in the West, clashed in Philadelphia in an election riot. A number of Quakers were injured by sailors hired by the Proprietary party.

1743
Parisian Draft Riots. Riots occurred over the practice of balloting for the militia.
1745
Jan.15, 1746: New Jersey Tenant Riots. Tenants and law enforcement officers clashed over tenants imprisoned for disputes with proprietors. There were several injuries, but no deaths.
1746
Anti-Catholic Riots. In the English towns of Sunderland and Liverpool, Roman Catholic chapels were destroyed in anti-Catholic riots.
1747
French Food Riots. Food riots occurred at Toulouse and Guyenne.
Nov. 16: Boston Anti-Impressment Riot. In opposition to impressment, several hundred armed sailors in Boston wounded a sheriff, put a deputy in the stocks, stormed the General Court, and demanded seizure of the impressment officers.
1750
The arrest in Paris of a large number of children on vagrancy charges caused a week of rioting in which four to eight police were killed. Later, three men were publicly executed amid scenes of rioting and rumors of a planned march to Versailles to burn it down.
1752
French Food Riots. Food riots occur in numerous towns including Rouen where cotton workers held the city for three days and raided granaries and warehouses, Fifteen people were killed. In Paris, bread riots were coupled with protest against the Archbishop of Paris.
French Draft Riots. Riots at Vincennes ocurred over the practice of balloting for the militia.
1753
June: English Anti-Turnpike Riots. Rioting crowds pulled down every turnpike near Leeds, Wakefield, and Beeston. Ten people were arrested, ten were killed and twenty-four were wounded.
1757
Anti-Militia Act Riots. The Militia Acts sparked riots in the English towns of East Anglia, Lincoln, Northampton, and Yorkshire East Riding.
1761
March: 5,000 Northumberland, England, miners, marching to Hexham to stop the ballot for recruits, were fired on by the Yorkshire militia, who killed forty-two of them and wounded forty-eight.
1763
Anti-Irish Riots. Disguised as an industrial dispute, Irish citizens were attacked in Covent Garden in England.
October: Weavers Riots. During a wages dispute, 2,000 journeymen weavers disguised themselves as sailors and broke into the house of journeymen who refused to join them, smashed their looms, wounded several, and burned a master weaver in effigy.
1764
The Paxton Riots. Residents of the frontier town of Paxton, Pa., murdered a small group of Indians and later tried to kill another group being sheltered in Philadelphia, but were stopped by a group headed by Benjamin Franklin.
1765
Doctors' Riot. A mob outraged by the practice of robbing graves to supply corpses for anatomy courses attacked the property of Dr.William Shippen.
English Anti-Workhouse Riots. Attacks on workhouses occurred in several Suffolk villages .
August: Stamp Act Riots. Boston gangs protesting the Stamp Act on Aug. 14 and 26 damaged or destroyed the houses of several English officials and the future office of the stamp master. For the first time "respectable" citizens not only fomented the disturbances, but participated in them.
Nov. 1: New York Stamp Act Riot. On Nov. 1, the effective date of the Stamp Act, about 3,000 New York men—workers and sailors inspired by the Sons of Liberty—assaulted the army headquarters, burned effigies of the devil and the lieutenant governor, and sacked the home of the ranking British colonel.
1766
Summer: English Food Riots. Rapidly ascending prices of bread and other staples inspired a riot which spread over large parts of England's west country. Sporadic outbreaks over three months included the burning of flour mills, the seizure of farmers' wheat, and the attack and looting of food merchants
June 26: New York Agrarian Rebellion. Tenant rebellion against landowners in New York climaxed when a sheriff trying to evict settlers was met by sixty armed men. Seven of the militia were wounded and one killed. Three farmers were killed and many wounded.
Nov. 15: In Ludlow, England, coal miners protesting the use of wheat in distilling when people were hungry, marched into town and destroyed the local distillery.
1767
Fall: Virginia Slave Revolt. Black slaves from Alexandria, Va., (some of them belonging to George Mason) poisoned several overseers as a part of a planned larger rebellion. At least four slaves were executed and their heads were cut off and put on public display.
1768
Wilkite Riots. When John Wilkes, a vocal opponent of the British monarchy was elected to Parliament, tumultuous riots occurred in London and Westminster. The Austrian Ambassador was dragged from his coach and homes were vandalized. Two further weeks of riots occurred when Wilkes was imprisoned, culminating in the massacre at St. George's Fields when guards shot into a crowd surrounding the prison, killing eleven and wounding twelve.
French Food Riots. When the price of bread exceeded the high of 1725, riots occurred at Le havre and at Mantes where crowds sacked a warehouse and sold its contents at half market price.
Sawmill Riot. Charles Dingley's new mechanical sawmill in Limehouse was attacked and partially destroyed by a mob of five hundred sawmill workers.
April: Coal Heavers' Riot A coal heavers' dispute in Shadwell and Wapping in England turned into a riot when strike break organizer John Green, was attacked in his public house. Subsequently, seven coal heavers were sentenced to death and hanged before a crowd of 50,000.
May: Coal Heavers' Riot. Coal heavers boarded a ship and threatened the lives of any sailor continuing to unload. In a two week period, one sailor was killed and two others were beaten. The military was finally called in, one man was hanged and the riots came to an end.
July 26: English Weavers Riot. An armed and disguised mob broke into the homes and shops of several journeymen weavers in and near the town of Spitalfields and destroyed the silk on nine different looms.
Aug. 20: English Weavers Riots. A mob of weavers in Spitalfields, England, broke into the house of Nathaniel Farr, cut the silk in two looms into pieces and shot and killed 17-year-old Edward Fitch.
1769
English Weaver Riots. Weaver John Valline headed a crowd of 1,500 weavers who attacked the house of silk handkerchief weaver, Lewis Chauvet, and cut the silk in seventy-six looms when Chauvet failed to contribute to a weavers' strike fund.
1770
French Food Riots. Spinners and weavers at Rheims sacked a warehouse and sold its contents.
Mar. 5: Boston Massacre. After months of violent protest of the Townsend Acts, a Boston crowd attacked some English sentries. When someone shouted "Fire," the soldiers shot into the crowd, killing five men and wounding six.
Anti-Loyalist Riot When a Boston customs officer confiscated an illegal cargo of sugar, 2,000 people dragged him through the street, and stripped, tarred, feathered, and set him on fire.
1772
English Food Riots. Nine food riots occurred between 1772-73.
1773
Dec. 16: Boston Tea Party Boston patriots dressed as Indians boarded a British ship in Boston Harbor and dumped 342 chests of tea overboard in protest of English taxation of the colonies.
English Weavers Riots. Riots revived when the number of unemployed journeymen weavers in key English towns reached 12,000. Parliament subsequently passed protective legislation. The weavers also developed the "Union," a negotiating entity anticipatory of modern arbitration procedures.
1774
Anti-Loyalist Riots. Anti-Loyalist crowds attacked the Cambridge, Mass., home of Attorney General Sewall, and caused him to flee to British protection in Boston.
French Food Riots. Food Riots occurred at Tours and Bordeaux.
November: Anti-Loyalist Riot. When an ensign in the militia refused to surrender his military insignia, an anti-Loyalist mob in Hallifax rode him on a rail and beat him for two hours.
November: Georgia Slave Revolt. A group of slaves from St. Andrew's Parish, Ga., rebelled against their masters. Before the revolt was quelled four whites were killed and three others wounded.
1775
Anti-Loyalist Riot. In East Haddum, Conn., an anti-Loyalist mob dragged a 70-year-old Episcopal Church clerk from his bed, beat him and paraded him naked. When the clerk's nephew, Dr. Abner Beebe, complained, he was beaten, tarred, and smeared with hog manure.
Philadelphia Anti-Loyalist Riot. In Philadelphia, anti-Loyalists dragged John Kearsley from his home and carted him through the streets.
Apr. 27: French Corn Riots. Popular alarm over an abrupt rise in prices of grain, flour, and bread led to a riot in Beaumont-Sur-Oise, twenty miles north of Paris which soon spread to other towns. In a two week period hundreds of rioters were arrested.
1778
French Bread Riots. Bread Riots occurred at Grenoble and Toulouse.
1779
English Spinners' Riot. Irate spinners destroyed innovative equipment in spinning concerns in Chorley.
1780
June 2: Gordon Riots. When Lord George Gordon, head of the London Protestant Association, led a crowd to Parliament to protest the passage of the Catholic Relief Act, and Parliament refused to consider their petition, riots, possibly the worst in London's history, erupted. In the course of a week of rioting that spread to neighboring towns, Catholic schools, dwellings, and pubs and the houses of both government and opposition supporters were damaged or destroyed. Six prisons were destroyed and their inmates released, and assaults were made on Blackfriars Bridge and the Bank of England. Property damage exceeded

£100,000, 285 rioters were killed, and another 173 were wounded. Gordon was imprisoned although later acquitted. Of 450 prisoners taken, 160 were tried; of those, twenty-five were hanged and another twelve were imprisoned.

1782

Aug.: A group of rampaging whites, and about fifty fugitive slaves attacked several plantations in City County, Va.

1784

French Bread Riot. Bread riot occurred at Bayeux.

1785

French Bread Riot. Bread riot occurred at Rennes.

1786

Fall: Shay's Rebellion. Farmers forced courts to close in protest of suits for debts incurred as a result of rising taxes. Shay's army of 1,000 was routed in December.

1787

Fall: Pre-French Revolution Food Riot. Riots broke out in Paris when the price of bread rose steeply. Guard posts on both sides of the Pont Neuf were ransacked and burned to the ground. 600 demonstrators were fired on by troops, killing seven or eight. The riots continued for two weeks with more casualties.

1788

April 13-14: New York City Doctors' Riot (Anti-Dissection Riot). Part of a New York hospital was destroyed by crowds angered over the practice of graverobbing to supply corpses for anatomy courses. At least five people were killed and more were wounded before the state militia quelled the riots.

November: French Spinners Riot. Cotton machinery was wrecked by the spinners of Falaise in France.

1789

April 28: Réveillon Riot. Five or six hundred workers incensed by anti-labor remarks attributed to major French manufacturer, Réveillon, rioted, destroyed Réveillon's house and that of another manufacturer. The Garde Francaises fired on the mob on the second day killing and wounding many.

July 14: Storming of the Bastille. In Paris, a mob of insurgents searching for arms stormed the Hotel des Invalides where they seized 30,000 muskets. Once armed, they pressed on across the river where they seized control of the Bastille.

July 14: While the Bastille was being stormed in Paris, mobs in Rouen destroyed machinery.

Oct.5: Parisian Women's March. A food riot of angry market women developed into the great women's march which, supported by the battalions of the National Guard, brought the King back in triumph to the capital.

1790

January: French Labor Riot. Operators of cotton machinery in Louviers in France rioted and destroyed machinery.

March: Brussels Church and King Riot. Houses of wealthy "Vonckists," members of the pro-French democratic or "patriot" party were looted and destroyed in Brussels.

1791

Louisiana Slave Uprising. Slave revolts occurred in Lower Louisiana.

July 14: English Church and King Riot. In Birmingham, a crowd angered over the observation by a group of Unitarians of the second anniversary of the fall of the Bastille rioted for five days. Four dissenters' meeting houses were damaged or destroyed; houses of twenty-seven persons were looted, demolished, or burned. Property damage reached £100,000. Seventeen rioters were tried, of whom four were found guilty and two were hanged.

Dec. 10: English Church and King Riot. A crowd shouting "God save the King" attacked the offices of the local radical newspaper and the homes of two men thought to be anti-monarchy. Two of the rioters were wounded.

1792

Louisiana Slave Revolt. Slave uprisings were reported in Lower Louisiana.

January: Paris Sugar Riots. When the price of sugar nearly tripled in three days in Paris, riots broke out throughout Paris. The rioters, many of them women, forced merchants to sell sugar at reduced prices or seized the sugar and sold it themselves. A large military force dispersed the rioters. Fourteen were arrested .

February: Beauce Food Riots. Hoarding of grain by large producers and the depletion of stocks by sales to other areas caused food riots in the Beauce, an area northwest of Paris.

November: Beauce Food Riots. An enlarged version of the February riots, mobs of 5,000-10,000 rural craftsmen and glassworkers raided local markets.

1793

Viennese Church and King Riot. The Viennese poorer classes, staunchly "Church and King" and anti-Jacobin in their loyalties, rioted against the execution of Louis XVI.

New York City Brothel Riot. In New York City, several people were wounded in fights between angry mobs and defenders of brothels.

February: Paris Food Riots. Rapidly increasing prices of sugar, coffee, and candles brought on riots more extensive than the previous year. Virtually all of Paris was involved, and again, mobs forced merchants to sell goods at reduced prices.

1794

August: English Anti-Recruitment Riots. A crowd of men, women and children defied the milita for three days and attacked and destroyed army recruitment centers.

July 17: Whiskey Rebellion. Protesting a tax on whiskey, 500 Pennsylvanians led by James McFarland attacked the home of an excise inspector. George Washington faced the rebels with 12,990 men and dispersed them. Of twenty prisoners taken, two were convicted of treason, but later pardoned by Washington.

1795

English Food Riots. Fifteen food riots occurred throughout the year.

Spring: A slave uprising in Pointe Coupée Parish, La., was crushed before it could start. Three whites implicated in the conspiracy were banished. Twenty-five Negroes who resisted capture were killed.

Apr. 1: 12th Germinal Riot. The National Convention at Paris was invaded by an angry mob shouting for bread and wearing the slogan, "Bread and the Constitution of 1793."

1799

Naples Church and King Riots. The lower classes of Naples rioted against the French and their own French-collaborating officials.

Fall: Virginia Slave Revolt. Two whites were killed in Southampton County, Va., when several slaves resisted an attempt to transport them to Georgia. Four to ten slaves were executed.

1800

Aug. 30: Gabriel's Insurrection. A Henrico County, Va., slave by the name of Gabriel incited about 1,000 blacks to rebel against their masters. Armed with homemade weapons, the mob was discouraged from carrying out the plan by the presence of 650 militia men. Gabriel and thirty-five other rebels were hanged in October 1800.

November: Continued slave unrest in Norfolk, Richmond, and Nottoway County, Va., led to the arrest of dozens of blacks. In January 1801, two slaves were convicted of conspiring to rebel, and were hanged nine days later.

1803

February: Pennsylvania Negro Riots. A black woman named Margaret Bradley was convicted of attempted murder in York, Penn. This precipitated a minor riot among Negores who burned down eleven buildings over a three-week period. Twenty blacks were eventually convicted of arson.

Apr. 25: Black residents of Warrenton, N.C., spent the night rioting.

1807

Baltimore Doctors' Riots. A mob destroyed a new medical college in protest of the practice of robbing graves to supply corpses for use in anatomy courses.

1811

English Luddite Riots. In 1811-12, a major wave of labor violence (named for Ned Ludlam, an apprentice credited with smashing his master's stocking frames) took the form of machine breaking and food riots. In the summer of 1812 more than 12,000 troops were stationed in the Luddite districts between Leicester and York. Property damage amounted to £100,000.

January: Louisiana Uprising. Five hundred sugar plantation slaves wounded the owner and killed his son, then marched on New Orleans, recruiting more slaves and burning four or five plantations on the way. Sixteen leaders were executed, their heads mounted on poles along the Mississippi River.

1812

Winter: English Luddite Riots. One of three minor waves of labor violence following the major wave of 1811-12, all of which were characterized by machine breaking predominantly by weavers as a means of gaining concessions from employers.

1813

Mar.-Apr.: Virginia Slave Revolt. The Lancaster, Va., militia was ordered to put down a slave uprising in the county. Three Negroes were held on conspiracy charges.

1814

Summer: English Luddite Riots. The second of three minor waves of labor violence following the major wave of 1811-12, characterized by machine breaking predominantly by weavers as a means of gaining concessions from employers.

1816

Summer: English Luddite Riots. The third of three minor waves of labor violence following the major wave of 1811-12, characterized by machine breaking predominantly by weavers as a means of gaining concessions from employers.

1820

March: One Negro was killed and other casualties reported when a contingency of newly arrived Jamaican slaves revolted in Florida.

1821

Aug.-Sept: Three hundred militia men from Onslow, Bladen, and Carteret Counties in North Carolina were called on to suppress a rebellion of freed slaves, runaways, and abolitionists, responsible for the murder of a slaveholder. Twelve militia men were wounded when they accidentally began firing on each other.

1822

May 30: Denmark Vesey, a freed African slave from South Carolina, conspired with Peter Poyas and Mingo Harth to lead a slave insurrection in Charleston. The plan was betrayed by a slave named William, which led to the arrest of 131 blacks. Thirty-seven were hanged between June 18 and August 9.

1825

Boston Brothel Riots. In Boston, over 2,000 rioters destroyed several brothels and assaulted police trying to intervene.

Portland, Maine, Brothel Riots. After each of three successive riots in Portland, Maine, in which mobs attacked brothels, the prostitutes relocated and went back into business.

1826

Decatur Incident. Twenty-nine slaves shipped from Maryland to Georgia on board the ship *Decatur* rebelled. Two crew members were killed, and a third was ordered to sail toward Haiti. The slavetrader was captured and towed into New York. All but one of the slaves escaped. William Bowser was caught and executed in New York on Dec. 15, 1826.

1829

Charlestown Anti-Catholic Riots. The purchase of three acres of land on Bunker Hill by the Bishop sparked three nights of rioting in Boston, as the homes of many Irish Catholics were stoned. A stable on the convent grounds was burned to the ground to protest a decision to convert a portion of Bunker Hill into a Catholic cemetery.

Pennsylvania Brothel Riot. In Lenox, Pa., crowds attacked a brothel.

1830

August: English "Swing" Riots. The introduction of the threshing machine and of cheaper Irish labor on farms in southern England sparked riots among farm laborers already contending with high rents, low wages and an agricultural depression which moved throughout sixteen counties for five months. Threshing machines were destroyed, barns were burned and ministers were forced to reduce tithes. In all, 1,406 rioters were brought to trial, of whom nine were hanged, 657 sent to prison and 464 transported to Australia.

1831

St. Louis Brothel Riots. Crowds attacked and damaged a brothel in St. Louis, Mo.

Aug. 21-23: Nat Turner Rebellion. In Virginia, black slave Nat Turner murdered his master, Joseph Travis, and Travis' family. In two days, Turner and his band of seventy-five slaves murdered fifty-seven whites including women and children over a twenty-mile area. The group's capture began a retaliatory massacre of at least 100 blacks.

November: French Silk Weavers Riot Silk weavers in Lyon, France rioted under the slogan, "*Vivre en travaillant ou mourir en combattant*," in response to difficult economic conditions. The insurrection however had social aims and therefore is considered the birth of the modern labor movement.

1832

June 5: Paris Political Riots. The most violent in a series of riots and armed insurrections took place in the cloisters of St. Méry in Paris between government troops and a crowd of workers seeking political as well as economic change. In two days of fighting, seventy troops and eighty rioters were killed.

1833

Oct. 2: A crowd of Southern sympathizers in New York City attempted to disrupt a planned abolitionist meeting organized by David Lloyd Garrison. However the situation was quickly difused when Garrison cancelled the assemly.

1834

April: French Silk Weavers Riot. The second riot by silk weavers in Lyon, France seeking social as well as economic change.

Apr. 8: Political antagonisms between Whigs and Democrats led to three days of street fighting in New York City. Fifteen thousand enraged Whigs blocked the streets, forcing the Mayor to call on the militias for help.

July 8: Anti-Abolitionist Riot. A violent anti-abolitionist crowd, allegedly provoked by New York political boss Isaiah Rynders, vandalized the inside of the Bowery Theater and the home of Lewis Tappan, brother of abolitionist Arthur Tappan. $20,000 worth of damage property was damaged.

Aug. 11: Massachusetts Convent Burning. A mob of Charlestown, Mass., Protestants, operating in a paranoid frenzy about Roman Catholics, sacked and burned the Ursuline convent. Sixty children and ten adults escaped without injury but three buildings were destroyed. Bishop Fenwick was shot in effigy.

September: A fight between resident blacks and white sailors in Snow Town, the black district of Providence, R.I., erupted into a riot in which considerable property was destroyed, four people were killed, and fourteen were wounded.

October: In Philadelphia, disputes between Whigs and Democrats turned into a bloody riot with one man killed, up to twenty wounded, and considerable property destroyed.

1835

When the building contractors working on the New York University buildings announced that they were purchasing cheaper, dressed stone produced by inmates of the Sing Sing Penitentiary, a group of tradesmen camped out in Washington Square for four days causing a near riot.

June: Dr. W.M. Caffrey was killed in the Five Points riot of New York City, pitting native born Americans against foreign immigrants.

Aug. 6, 8 & 9: Baltimore Anti-Bank Riots. An angry Baltimore crowd attacked the homes of bankers accused of fraud in the collapse of the Bank of Maryland. When confronted by the militia, ten to twenty were killed and about a hundred wounded.

December: A slave rebellion was crushed before it got started in East and West Feliciana, La. A number of whites were held responsible for fomenting the trouble.

1837

Illinois Anti-Abolition Violence. When abolitionist publisher Elijah P. Lovejoy moved to Alton, Ill., pro-slavery mobs destroyed his press at least three times. On Nov. 7, Lovejoy was killed while defending it.

Feb. 13: New York Flour Riot. A New York protest of food prices turned into an assault on local flour merchants and the sack of a warehouse. National Guardsmen finally restored order to the city.

1838

Oct. 30: Anti-Mormon Riot. A mob led by three state militia captains attacked a colony of Mormons at Haun's Mill, Mo., after an incendiary statement by the governor. All the Mormons were killed or wounded.

1839

January: Welch "Rebecca" Riots. Beginning in January 1839, with the erection of four new toll gates, mobs of men dressed in women's clothing and with blackened faces, ranging in size from forty to 250, staged nocturnal raids in which they destroyed toll gates on all but the "Queen's Highway." The raids, which continued until September 1844, were organized with military precision and claimed only one life.

Ohio Doctors' Riot. A mob in Worthington, Ohio, forced the closing of a college over the practice of graverobbing to supply corpses for anatomy courses.

1841

Sept.: Cincinnati Race Riot. Irish workers fearing job competition clashed with blacks. A number of men were killed and wounded on both sides .

1842

July: The Plug-Plot Riots. A sharp rise in wheat prices and threats of lower factory wages sparked riots in which crowds of men marched from town to town stopping work by pulling the plugs on factory boilers. Hundreds of mill and factories were shut down and some pillaging occurredinManchester,Yorkshire,Cheshire,Staffordshire,Warwickshire, the Potteries and Wales.

1844

May 6-8: Philadelphia Anti-Catholic Riots. A mob of anti-Irish Catholic Nativists (American Republicans) prevented from meeting in a Catholic neighborhood burned over thirty homes and tenements, and two churches.

June 27: Carthage, Ill., Mormon Riot. After fleeing persecution in Missouri, Mormon leader Joseph Smith and his followers moved to Carthage, Ill., where he ordered his men to destroy a newspaper that had criticized him. Smith and his brother were jailed for inciting a riot and were killed by a mob.

July 5-8: Philadelphia Anti-Catholic Riots Philadelphia Protestants attacked a Catholic church containing weapons and armed Irish volunteers. Both sides had cannon. In these and the May riots as many as twenty-four were killed and more than a hundred were wounded.

1847

Scottish Food Riot. Food riots occurred in the Scottish Highland towns of Castletown, Avoch, Beuly, Thurso, Invergordon, and Black Isle. In some cases, prisoners were taken, and at Thurso, stoning occurred.

1848

French Revolution of 1848. A demonstration in Paris in favor of an extension of suffrage developed in stages into a popular revolution which claimed a number of lives and caused the King to abdicate.

August: A white college student named Patrick Doyle led a slave insurrection in Fayette County, Ky. Two gun battles were fought in which a black man and two whites were killed. Doyle was captured and sent to prison for twenty years. Three slaves were hanged.

1849

Doctors' Riot. A crowd in St. Charles, Ill., killed the anatomy professor of Franklin Medical College and one of his students in protest of the practice of graverobbing to supply corpses for anatomy courses.

May 7 and *May 10:* Astor Place Riots. On May 7, anti-British New Yorkers jeered British actor William C. Macready at the Astor Place Opera House and slightly damaged the interior of the theater. On May 10, Macready returned and the theater was set on fire. A crowd of 10,000 to 15,000 rioted until the National Guard opened fire, killing twenty-two and injuring thirty.

1850

Troy, N.Y., Brothel Riot. A crowd attacked a brothel in Troy, N.Y.

January: Missouri Slave Revolt. Thirty Negro slaves in Lewis County, Mo., attempted an insurrection against their masters. One of the slaves were killed in a pitched gun battle with whites. The leaders were captured and shipped to St. Louis to be sold.

Aug. 14: Squatters' Riots. Several men were killed or injured when squatters in California, tried to retake property from which John F. Madden had been evicted.

1851

May 26: Hoboken Anti-German Riot. German workers and their families in Hoboken, N.J., celebrating Pentecost Sunday, were attacked by a mob of nativists and Irish Catholic immigrants. One person was killed and dozens were injured.

September: Christiana Affair. Blacks and whites in the black town of Christiana, Pa., refused to assist Maryland slave owner Edward Gorsuch in capturing some of his slaves hiding there. Gorsuch was killed and his sons were wounded. Thirty-eight townspeople were indicted for treason but all were acquitted.

1855

Aug. 6: Louisville Anti-German Riots. Anti-German nativists of the Know-Nothing party attacked immigrants in voting lines in Louisville, Ky. Twenty people were killed and many were injured.

1856

May 21: Kansas Slavery Riots. A pro-slavery crowd burned several houses in Lawrence, the stronghold of the "free-soil" contingent in Kansas. Violence continued there through the Civil War, although Kansas became a free state in January 1861.

September: Baltimore Election Riots. The Know-Nothing party used Baltimore street gangs to intimidate immigrant voters. In the resulting riots, more than a dozen people were killed and hundreds were injured.

1857

Detroit Brothel Riots. In Detroit rampaging mobs destroyed six brothel houses.

Baltimore Election Riot. In Baltimore, the Know-Nothing party hired street gangs to intimidate immigrant voters. Numerous casualties resulted from the riots.

April: In Chicago, volunteers led by Mayor John Wentworth burned down the "Sands" vice district.

June: The passage of the Metropolitan Police Bill in New York led to several days of protest-rioting by supporters of Democratic Mayor Fernando Wood, who stood in opposition to the Republican sponsored measure. By the July 1, the Seventh Regiment had quelled the distrubance.

July 4: A gang fight between the Dead Rabbits and the Roach Guards erupted into a deadly melee in Manhattan. Two bodies of police, assisted by the Seventy-first and Eighth Regiments, restored order to the areas most affected by the gang violence; White and Worth Streets.

Fall: New York Bread Riot. A financial panic and worsening economic conditions threw 10,000 people out of work. Hungry, desperate mobs gathered in Central Park demanding bread. Soup kitchens were established for the homeless.

September: Mountain Meadows Massacre. In Utah, Mormons colluded with Indians to massacre 120 California-bound pioneers. Mormon John Lee was executed twenty years later at the site of the massacre.

1858

Baltimore Election Riot. Continued intimidation of immigrant voters in Baltimore by the Know-Nothing Party resulted in riots and ensured victory for the party.

1859

Baltimore Election Riot. In Baltimore, the Know-Nothing Party again caused election riots,but the state legislature invalidated their victories.

Oct. 16: Harpers Ferry Raid. John Brown and his supporters seized control of the federal arsenal at Harper's Ferry, Va. His plans for a massive slave uprising failed to materialize. Government troops led by Robert E. Lee surrounded the arsenal and forced Brown and his men to surrender. Brown was hanged on December 2.

December: Missouri Slave Revolt. One man was killed and several white men were injured when a gang of black slaves in Bolivar, Mo., revolted.

1861

April: Charleston Slave Revolt. Seven slaves were hanged in Charleston, S.C., when their attempted rebellion was crushed.

1863

Apr. 2: Richmond, Va., Bread Riot. A crowd of hungry men, women and children in Richmond, Va., looted stores of food and supplies until threatened by Confederate troops led by Confederate president Jefferson Davis. Several rioters were later tried and given the maximum sentence of three years in prison.

July 13-16: New York Draft Riots. In a race riot in New York City exacerbated by labor unrest and Civil War draft laws, a mob of Irish laborers destroyed draft headquarters, burned down an entire block between Broadway and Twenty-eighth, closed factories and shops, cut telegraph lines, and destroyed railroad tracks, and then massacred from 300 to 1200 of the city's blacks.

1864

December: The last known slave revolt in the U.S. was thwarted in Troy, Ala.

1866

July 30: New Orleans. When radical Democrats reconvened the 1864 Convention in New Orleans to enfranchise blacks, whites assaulted the hall. Thirty-eight men were killed and 146 were wounded.

1870

January: Paris Riots. When Pierre Bonaparte, a cousin of Napoleon Bonaparte, killed a radical journalist, riots broke out in Paris. Bonaparte was acquitted by a court in Tours.

July 12: New York City Orange Riot. Commemoration in New York of the Battle of the Boyne provoked bloody clashes between Irish Catholics and Protestants along Fourth Street, in which five people died.

1871

July 12: Second New York City Orange Riot. On the anniversary of the 1870 Orange Riot, Catholics harassed a parade of Irish Protestants (Orangemen) in New York City who were defended by 5,000 militia. When a bullet was fired, the soldiers returned the volley. Thirty-one rioters were killed and sixty-seven were wounded.

Oct.24: Los Angeles Anti-Chinese Riot. After several policemen were wounded trying to stop a Tong war in Los Angeles' Chinatown, the Chinese barricaded themselves in their district as white mobs attacked and killed between twenty and twenty-five Chinese, including an elderly doctor named Gene Tong, who pleaded with the angry rioters to spare his life.

1874

January: Tompkins Square Riot. Seven thousand immigrant demonstrators during the depression of 1873 were repeatedly attacked by police in Tompkins Square Park in New York City.

Dec. 7: Vicksburg Race Riot. Reconstruction whites forced black sheriff Peter Crosby of Vicksburg, Miss., to resign. When armed blacks rallied to his defense, whites jailed Crosby and attacked the blacks, shooting or lynching more than thirty.

1877

Railroad Strike. A strike on the Baltimore and Ohio railroad spread and in Pittsburgh the militia killed ten to twenty strikers and injured sixty or seventy. The crowd then attacked the militia and destroyed 104 locomotives, 2,152 cars, and the entire depot.

1884

Mar. 28-30: Cincinnati Riot. Following a mass protest in Cincinnati of a lenient sentence for a confessed murderer, William Berner, a crowd of several thousand broke into the jail where he was kept and set it on fire. In three days of rioting, at least fifty people were killed.

1885

Sept. 2: Rock Springs Massacre. When Chinese miners in Rocks Springs, Wyo., resisted unionization, other miners attacked them, killing twenty-eight, wounding fifteen, and driving away hundreds. Federal troops stopped the violence, and forty-five whites were fired by Union Pacific. In 1887, the Chinese government was granted an indemnity by Congress.

Sept. 10: A vigilante mob in Pierce City, Idaho, avenged the murder of a white merchant named D.M. Fazier by lynching five Chinese men. The wholesale expulsions of many other Chinese from the Idaho towns followed.

1886

May 4: Haymarket Square Riots. In Chicago, seven policemen were killed and sixty were wounded in an anarchist riot. Violence by some Knights of Labor discredited the organization and led to the formation the American Federation of Labor (AFL).

1887

Oct. 4: Louisianna Sugar Strike. When sugar field workers, mostly blacks, went on strike, the militia attacked the strikers, killing four. Thirty-five unarmed blacks were killed and two black strike leaders lynched.

1891

May: Anti-Missionary Riots in China. Anti-missionary rioting in May and June broke out in China. On June 13 the government issued an ineffectual decree against the rioters. Gunboats patrolled offshore.

Oct. 16: Anti-American Mob Violence in Valparaiso, Chile. A mob and police attacked U.S. sailors in Valparaiso, Chile, killing or wounding several. The Chilean government apologized on Jan. 25, 1892, and paid an indemnity.

Mar. 14: New Orleans Anti-Italian Riot. When nineteen Italians, suspected Mafia members, were acquitted of murdering the mayor of New Orleans, 6,000 citizens protested and attorney William Parkerson led fifty to the jail where they killed eleven of the Italians. The Italian government received an indemnity of 125,000 lire.

1892

July: Homestead Steel Riot. The Carnegie Phipps Steel Company in Homestead, Pa., brought in Pinkerton agents on barges to break the union. Striking employees attacked them but were later defeated by the National Guard and indicted for conspiracy, murder and rioting. The union was broken in November.

July 7-11: Coeur d'Alene Mine Strike The Homestead Riot spurred strikes in Idaho. Five miners and one guard were killed and more than thirty others wounded before the National Guard and federal troops defeated the miners.

1894

May 1: Coxey's Army's March on Washington. A group of unemployed and homeless men led by Populist businessman Jacob Coxey, in Washington demanding a $1.50 an hour minimum wage for public works, scuffled with police. Some of the demonstrators received light fines or jail terms.

June 28-July 7: Chicago Pullman Strike. A strike against the Pullman Palace Car Company stopped rail traffic out of Chicago, and when President Grover Cleveland sent in federal troops, crowds burned freight cars and stoned trains. Four were killed and twenty were wounded.

1898

Nov. 10: Wilmington, N.C., Race Riot. White Democrats, faced with increasing black political activity, rioted two days after a decisive Democratic victory, burned down a black newspaper and killed between twenty and 100 blacks.

1899

Apr. 29: Coeur d'Alene, Idaho, Miners' Strike. Approximately 1,000 members of the Western Federation of Miners armed with guns and dynamite came into Wardner, Idaho, on a hijacked train and blew up the Bunker Hill and Sullivan Company mine, the only remaining non-union mine in the Coeur d'Alene district. Two men were killed. One union organizer was sentenced to seventeen years prison. Ten miners were also found Guilty and given short prison terms.

1901

Mar. 4: Denver Riots. When immigrant Frank Latito was shot to death in Denver in broad daylight, crowds almost rioted. Police arrested Frank Sposato and rushed him out of the Italian colony. Sposato was acquitted on Nov. 19.

Aug. 15: New York Race Riots. Theater mobs tried to kill several black entertainers, including Ernest Hogan, Williams & Walker, and Coke & Johnson.

Aug. 20: Pierce City, Mo., Riots. White citizens rioted and injured several blacks.

1902

July: French School Riots. Riots in Brittany and Savoy over the closing of unauthorized religious schools closed about 3,000 schools.

Sept. 25: Liverpool Riots. Catholics attacked John Kensit, founder of the Protestant Truth Society. Kensit was struck in the eye and later died of the injury. John McKeever was tried for the murder but acquitted.

1903

Apr. 19-20: Russian Anti-Jewish Riots. A planned riot against the Jews in the Russian town of Kishinef attracted worldwide attention when authorities sympathized with the rioters.

Apr. 26: Bloomington, Ind., Racial Violence. Thirty-eight white men broke into a Bloomington, Ind., home and whipped owners Rebecca and Ida Stephens and their black boarder, Joe Shively.

June 7: Motormen's Riot. A motormen's riot in Richmond, Va., left dozens injured.

1904

Nov. 11-12: Brazil Riots. In Brazil, President Rodriquez Alves' policy of compulsory innoculation during a smallpox epidemic caused riots which were quickly suppressed.

1905

French Anti-clerical Riots. In the midst of strong anti-clerical feeling in France, riots broke outgovernment inventory takers were opposed by parishioners protecting their churches.

Jan. 22: Bloody Sunday Massacre. Following Red Sunday, when strikers in St. Petersburg, Russia, were fired upon by czarist forces, sympathetic outbreaks occurred throughout Russia, all of which were quickly suppressed.

1906

Sept. 22: Atlanta Race Riots. Twelve purported assaults by black men on white women reported in "extras" in the Atlanta press resulted in a wave of violence against blacks in which twelve were killed and over seventy wounded.

1913

Aug. 3: Wheatland Riot. Protesting migrant workers in California clashed with the authorities. A district attorney, a deputy, and two workers were shot to death.

September: Ludlow, Colo., Mine Strike. Industrial workers worldwide supported the striking Ludlow miners. Seventy-four people were killed in violence that ended in December 1914 when the strike was broken.

1916

Washington Anti-Wobblies Violence. Wobblies (IWW) supporting a strike in Everett, Wash., were attacked by residents and police. When 280 Wobblies were repulsed, seven were left dead and many injured.

1917

May: When black and white strikebreakers and the militia broke a strike in St. Louis, the union blamed blacks. A riot broke out during which buildings were demolished and solitary blacks were attacked.

May 28: East St. Louis, Ill., Race Riot. Racial tension fueled by rumors that blacks were perpetrating crimes against whites, particularly white women, brought 3,000 whites into the downtown area. Scores of blacks were beaten but there were no fatalities.

May 30: Springfield, Mo., Riot . After suspects in the kidnapping and murder of 14-month-old Lloyd Keets were captured, thousands of people almost rioted in downtown Springfield, Mo. Angry crowds pulled suspect Piersoll the sheriff's car and twice threatened to lynch him before returning him to the sheriff.

July 2: East St. Louis, Ill. Race Riot. Amidst continuing racial tensions, a black man shot his white attacker. When whites then drove through the black district, shooting into homes, blacks returned fire and killed two policemen. The white rioters were particularly brutal, killing women and children and tossing bodies onto large bonfires. Over 300 buildings were burned, eight whites and thirty-nine blacks were killed, and hundreds of blacks were wounded.

1918

Apr.: Quebec City Riots. Several citizens were killed in Quebec City during riots over of conscription.

1919

May 1: May Day Riots. Crowds attacked Socialists' May Day celebrations throughout the U.S. In Cleveland, socialist offices were wrecked, one person was killed, and forty were injured when army veterans attacked a parade.

July 30: Chicago Race Riots. A black youth on Chicago's South Side in which a black youth swam in waters reserved for whites and was stoned and drowned. The ensuing race war left twenty-two blacks and fourteen whites dead, and more than 500 wounded.

September: Washington Anti-Wobblies Riot. When American Legion members in Centralia, Wash., attacked the IWW hall, the Wobblies fired on the Legionnaires, killing three. The hall was destroyed and Wobblies throughout the state were jailed.

Sept. 9-12: Boston Police Strike. When more that three-fourths of the Boston police force walked off the job striking for higher wages, the city was overrun by criminals. Governor Calvin Coolidge called out the national guard who shot thieves and looters on sight. Nine rioters were killed and fifty-eight were wounded.

Sept. 22-Oct. 5: Pennsylvania Steel Strike. A strike by 250,000 U.S. Steel workers, opposed by thr state militia and special police, resulted in several deaths and many injuries. The steel company invoked racial and anti-communist bias.

1922

June 22: Herrin Mine Massacre. Union miners in Herrin, Ill., attacked strikebreakers. Men were told to run and then shot. Some were tied together and shot, others' throats were slit, and some were hanged. Nineteen men were murdered.

1926

Aug. 24: Eighty-thousand movie fans caused a near-riot on Broadway near 66th Street in New York City, as they pushed and shoved their way forward to view the corpse of actor Rudolph Valentino. A task force of 200 policemen eventually brought the unruly crowd (mostly women) under control. However, crowds continued to mill in the street all night long.

1929

June 7: Police chief Orville Aderholt was killed and three policemen were wounded in a fight with striking workers at a North Carolina textile mill. Fred Erwin Beale and six other textile workers were convicted of second degree murder and sentenced to seventeen to twenty years in prison.

July 28: Auburn Prison Riot. Overcrowding caused 1,700 convicts to seize the New York prison arsenal and try to escape. During the five-hour riot, two prisoners were killed and eleven escaped. Damage to the prison was estimated at between $450,000 and $470,000. Six convicts were sentenced for leading the riot.

Dec. 11: Auburn Prison Riot. Fifty men in solitary confinement for their part in the July 28 riot broke out and took the prison warden hostage. Police fired on the prisoners and a six-hour seige left nine guards and prisoners dead and many wounded. Three were executed on Aug. 28, 1930.

1930

May 10: Sherman, Texas, Race Riot. Mobs of whites rioted and burned down several blocks of blacks' homes.

1931

Mar. 14: Joliet, Ill., Prison Riot A meal that inmates at the Joliet, Ill., prison called "goat stew" caused a riot in the mess hall.

Aug. 3: Chicago Eviction Riot. When a mostly black crowd of 5,000 in Chicago tried to prevent an eviction, police fired into the crowd, killing three and wounding many more. Twenty thousand whites and 40,000 blacks marched to the funeral.

Sept. 14: Hawaii Riot. Lieutenant Thomas Massie of the U.S. Navy in Hawaii killed Joseph Kahawawai, accused of raping Massie's wife. Massie and three others were convicted, but after they were sentenced to only one hour in the dock, the locals almost rioted.

1932

Mar. 7: Dearborn Massacre. Thousands of unemployed workers marched on the Ford plant in Dearborn, Mich., where firehoses, pistols, and a machine gun were used to repulse them. Four marchers were killed and twenty or more were injured.

July 28: Bonus Army Riot. Cavalry, infantry, and six tanks lead by General Douglas MacArthur, Dwight Eisenhower, and George Patton attacked the temporary camp in Washington, D.C., of the Bonus Expeditionary Force, jobless veterans demanding payment of a promised bonus. Soldiers burned the camps to the ground, killed an infant, and wounded several people.

1933

Oct. 27: Arab Riot. Refusing an order to disperse, 9,000 Arabs were attacked by club-wielding police in Palestine. The Arabs were protesting Jewish settlement in the country. A score of rioters were killed by police bullets.

1934

Apr. 8: U.S. Nazi Riot. A pro-Nazi rally in New York City ended in eighteen separate clashes between Nazis and 200 or so Communists. The Nazis were seeking to end the boycott on German goods. Twelve persons were arrested.

1935

Southern Tenant Farmers' Union Violence. In Arkansas and neighboring states, local whites and absentee corporations, terrorized the 10,000-members of the interracial Southern Tenant Farmers' Union, for two and a half months. Its members were murdered, harassed, attacked and jailed.

Mar. 19: Harlem Race Riot. The arrest of a sixteen-year-old black, Lino Rivera, for shoplifting set off riots in Harlem in which 200 stores were gutted, $2 million in property was destroyed, one black was shot, and more than 100 people were injured.

1937

May: Memorial Day Massacre. Police fired on a crowd of 3,000 striking employees of the Republic Steel Company in South Chicago, killing ten strikers, six of them shot in the back. Fifty-eight strikers and sixteen policemen were injured in the struggle.

1938

Oct. 30: A radio airing of the "War of the Worlds" on CBS radio's *Mercury Theatre* touched off wide-spread panic across the nation as thousands of Americans erroneously believed they were being invaded by Martians. In Jersey City, N.J., the police had to clear the streets of hysterical citizens who thought the world was ending.

Nov. 9: Kristallnacht (Night of the Broken Glass). In a massive planned display, mobs of Nazis throughout Germany destroyed synagogues, ransacked Jewish homes and vandalized Jewish businesses.

1943

June 3-8: Zoot Suit Riots. Rioting broke out in Los Angeles when soldiers began fighting Mexicans wearing zoot suits. Many were injured and the City Council banned the zoot suit.

June 20: Detroit Race Riots. Following a racial fight in an amusement park, riot began in which blacks sacked white stores and whites randomly attacked blacks. Nine whites and twenty-five blacks were killed.

1946

Mar.: Mink Slide Riots. When blacks in the Mink Slide area of Columbia Tenn., shot four policemen, whom they mistook for part of a rampaging white mob, 104 black men were rounded up for interrogation. Two were killed allegedly while trying to escape, and police caused substantial property damage. Twenty-three blacks were acquitted and two were convicted of attempted murder.

1949

Sept. 4: Peekskill Riot. At a Communist Party-sponsored concert in Peekskill, N.Y., were assaulted by American Legionnaires, Westchester police, and local anti-Communists damage cars and assaulted a number of people.

1952

Apr. 20-24: Jackson, Mich., Prison Riot. Two inmates at the Southern Michigan Prison, Earl Ward and "Crazy" Jack Hyatt, led detention block prisoners in a five-day seige which eventually spread throughout the prison and involved over 2,500 inmates. Armed troopers finally subdued the rioters but Ward and Hyatt used thirteen guards taken hostage to bargain for an eleven-point agreement which included a promise that no reprisals be taken against the rioters. One convict was killed, nine were wounded, and $2,500,000 in damage was done to the prison. The riot, until then the largest in U.S. history, inspired significant changes in the U.S. prison system, both in terms of facilities and techniques of inmate control.

1953

June 19-21: East Berlin Riot. Anti-Communist riots broke out in East Berlin, and spread across the Soviet sector. Twenty people were killed and 200 more were injured. Soviet authorities declared martial law and announced a strict curfew.

Oct. 25: Anti-Italian protests broke out in Belgrade, Yug., following a speech by Marshal Tito. The conflict stemmed from Italy's proposal that both countries withdraw their troops from a common frontier.

1954

Dec. 18: Nicosia Riots. Greek Cypriots took to the streets of Nicosia to protest the U.N.'s refusal to allow Cyprus' right of self-determination. British troops fired into the crowd of student demonstrators.

1955

July 14-17: Moroccan Riots. Casablanca was placed under marshal law following three days of rioting between Europeans and native Moroccans. Six Europeans were killed in a café bomb blast on Bastille Day, which sparked the violence.

1956

June 28-29: Anti-Soviet Riots in Poland. Political riots began in Poznan, Pol., when workers walked off their jobs at the Stalin engineering works. Demanding bread and other commodities, the rioters roamed the streets of the city chanting anti-Communist slogans while tearing down red banners.

Oct. 30: Anti-Soviet Riots in Hungary. The streets of Budapest erupted in violence as thousands of protestors clashed with Soviet troops. The rioters demanded a free and independent Hungary.

1957

Sept. 2: Governor Orval Faubus defied federal law by sending in state militia troops to Little Rock's Central High School on September 2, in a vain attempt to block nine Negro students from enrolling in classes. A protest demonstration ensued on september 25, in which seven whites were arrested, and one man was struck down in the streets.

1958

Jan. 23: A hundred persons were killed during two days of street rioting in Caracas, Venez. The dictatorship of General Marcos Perez Jimenez was overthrown.

May: Anti-U.S. Demonstrations. Vice-President Richard Nixon was denounced as an imperialist in a series of angry demonstrations that threatened to become violent in Latin America. Nixon was completing a diplomatic tour designed at shoring up strained relations with the South American governments.

May 13: French-Algerian Riots. French protestors seized control of key government buildings in Algeria to indicate their displeasure toward their government's shift in policy. The French Cabinet indicated its willingness to acquiese to Algerian nationalists seeking political autonomy.

1959

Aug. 12: Twenty-one segregationists were arrested outside Central High School in Little Rock for refusing an order to disperse. The 250 demonstrators were protesting school integration.

1961

May 4: Civil Rights Violence. Two buses carrying thirteen freedom riders to New Orleans were firebombed in Alabama and the demonstrators were beaten several times.

1962

Sept. 30: Mississippi Integration Violence. A mob attacked federal marshals escorting black student James Meredith to the University of Mississippi. The fifteen-hour attack was finally halted by 3,000 U.S. troops and the National Guard. Two people were killed and over seventy were wounded.

1963

Sept. 15: Alabama Race Riot. Fourteen-year-old Virgil Lamar Ware was killed during a wave of racist violence in Birmingham, Ala.

1964

Jan. 10: Panama Riots. In Panama dozens were killed in anti-American riots provoked by inflammatory radio broadcasts.

July 1: Philadelphia Race Riots. One hundred fifty were injured and 165 arrested for attacking police during race riots in Philadelphia.

July 16: Harlem Race Riots. When a 15-year-old black was shot to death while attacking a policeman, looters gutted Harlem stores. One looter was killed and 140 other people were injured.

July 27: Rochester Race Riot. Governor Nelson Rockefeller called up the National Guard to quell a race riot in Rochester, N.Y. One-hundred-twenty rioters were arrested.

Aug. 2: Chicago Race Riots. Race riots broke out in Chicago when three black families moved into white neighborhoods. Several people were injured.

1965

Aug. 8: Watts Race Riots. Rioting blacks in the Watts area of Los Angeles set fires, then cut the fire hoses, gutting half of the entire area. Thirty-four died, 1,032 were injured, 4,000 were arrested, and damages exceeded $34 million.

Aug. 11: Cape Town Race Riots. Race riots on the outskirts of Cape Town, S. Afr., left seventeen blacks dead and fifty more injured.

1966

July: Race Riots. Cleveland, New York, and Chicago were the battlegrounds in the latest outbreak of racial warfare in the U.S. In Chicago 4,000 National Guardsmen were called into the affray before order was restored.

July 31: A black protest march through white neighborhoods in Chicago sparked an angry rock throwing melee. Fifty-four people were injured.

August: Chinese Cultural Revolution. Thousands of zealous young Chinese and Red Guards took to the streets to denounce U.S. "imperialism" and Soviet "revisionism" in demonstrations that received the whole-hearted endorsement of the Central Committee of the Communist Party.

Sept. 29: San Francisco Race Riot. Dozens were injured in a race riot in San Francisco before National Guardsmen restored order.

1967

July 12: U.S. Race Riots. One hundred twenty-seven separate race riots broke out across the U.S. within six days, leaving scores injured and causing millions of dollars of property damage.

July 23: Detroit Race Riot. Crowds angered by police raids on area clubs began looting Detroit stores. Overreaction and abuse by police and National Guardsmen followed. Thirty-three blacks and ten whites were killed, over 600 were injured, and 3,800 people were arrested. Property loss was estimated at $46 million.

Oct. 21: Pentagon Anti-War Protest. Some 250 anti-war demonstrators were arrested outside the Pentagon in Washington D.C. after a peaceful demonstration turned violent. No shots were fired, but federal marshals and U.S. soldiers used their guns to club the activtists over the head.

1968

There were more than 300 major anti-war protests staged on college campuses in the U.S. during the 1968-69 school year. Sit-down protests, classroom takeovers, and random violence on the part of the students forced many institutions of higher learning to temporarily suspend classes. Among the prestigious universities plagued by civil disobedience included: the City College of New York, Brandeis, Cornell, Harvard, Duke, San Francisco State College, Wisconsin, and the Berkeley campus in California.

Apr. 5: Chicago King Riots. Following the assassination of the Reverend Dr. Martin Luther King, the West Side of Chicago exploded in a riot. Hundreds of stores were looted and burned by angry blacks, forcing Mayor Richard Daley to call up the National Guard to restore order.

Apr. 5-9: King Riots. Racial violence erupted in Baltimore, Washington, and Cincinnati in the wake of King assassination. Thirty-one persons died in the combined riots.

Apr. 23-28: Columbia University Riots. On Apr. 23, 200 members of the Students for a Democratic Society in disagreement with the school's "racial policies" took over five campus buildings, holding three officals hostage. After six days, New York City police dispersed the crowds. More than 130 people were injured and 700 people, mostly students, were arrested during six days of rioting.

May 21-22: Columbia University Riot. After four student leaders were suspended for their role in the April riot, the SDS seized the main class-

room building on May 21. Sixty-eight persons were injured and 177 more were arrested. Property damage was estimated to be $300,000.
May 11-30: Paris Worker's Strike. Millions of workers and student radicals staged a nationwide protest that closed down most of France's major industries. Low wages, and other grievances led to the declaration of a general strike on May 11.
Aug. 28: Chicago Police Riot. Anti-Viet Nam war demonstrators trying to march on the Democratic Convention clashed with Chicago police. As demonstrators threw sticks and bottles, police attacked demonstrators and journalists, injuring many.
Oct. 5: Northern Ireland Riots. Police clubbed protestors during riots in Derry.
1969
Jan. 12: Rhodesia and South Africa Race Riots. Hundreds were injured in the smashing of police lines in Rhodesia and South Africa.
Mar. 30: New Africa Organization. A gun battle which broke out after a meeting of the New Africa organization in Detroit resulted in the death of one policeman, the wounding of four black militants, and the arrests of 135 people.
Apr. 19: Northern Ireland Riots. Riots broke out between Paisleyites and Civil Rights supporters in Derry.
Apr. 19: Cornell Takeover. One-hundred blacks seized the Student Union at Cornell University to protest the arrest and detention of several student activists the previous December.
May 13: Malaysian Race Riots. Race riots in Kuala Lumpur, Malaysia, resulted in more than 100 deaths.
Aug. 2: Northern Ireland Riots. Police arrested more than 100 in a violent outbreak between factions in Belfast.
Aug. 12: Northern Ireland Riots. A riot broke out at the Apprentice Boys march in Derry.
Sept. 21: Moslem-Hindu Riots in India. Moslems and Hindus in western India rioted over alleged mistreatment of sacred Hindu cows and Hindu spiritual leaders. More than 1,000 people were killed.
Oct. 5: British troops used teargas to disperse a mob of Protestants who who marched through the streets of Belfast in the wake of five hours of street fighting with Catholics.
Oct. 15: Vietnam Moratorium Day. A massive nationwide protest against the Vietnam War was staged in the U.S.
Nov. 15: At least ninety-three persons were arrested in the nation's capitol, following a day long peace march down Pennsylvania Avenue to the Washington Monument. At dusk, the radicals began throwing rocks and bottles at the Justice Department.
1970
Mar. 17: West Bengal Riots. After two days of fighting, the Indian Central government ended violence provoked by a Marxist Communist strike.
May 4: Kent State Student Demonstration. During a demonstration against U.S. action in Cambodia, the Ohio National Guard opened fire on students, killing four.
May 11: Georgia Race Riots. Six black demonstrators were killed and twenty-five were injured in race riots in Augusta, Ga.
May 20: Okinawa Anti-U.S. Riots. U.S. troops confronted extensive anti-U.S. rioting in Koza, Okinawa.
June 11: Italian Riots. Rioting broke out in Pescara, Italy, when the rival city of L'Aquila was chosen as regional capital.
July 3: Northern Ireland Riots. Five people were killed in a clash between troops and the Provisional IRA in Belfast.
July 14: Italian Riots. Rioting broke out in Reggio Calabria, Italy, when its rival city of Catanzaro was selected as regional capital.
Oct 7: Italian Riots. Rioting in Reggio Calabria broke out again, lasting until Oct. 18.
Dec. 14-19: Polish Food Riots. Rioting by Polish workers over increased food prices was quelled by armed security forces.
1971
Jan. 23: Northern Ireland Riots. Riots lasting two days occurred in Belfast.
June 17: Okinawa Treaty Riots. Riots broke out in Japan on the signing of the Okinawa Reversion Treaty, which returned Okinawa to Japan in 1972 but left U.S. bases there.
Aug. 9: Northern Ireland Riots. Twelve people were killed, 300 arrested, and 150 houses burned during riots in Belfast.
Sept. 9: Attica Prison Riot. Inmates angered over overcrowding and harsh treatment seized the state prison near Buffalo, N.Y., and took fifty hostages. Twenty-nine inmates and ten hostages were killed and eighty-five inmates, three hostages, and a state trooper were wounded when law police opened fire. None of the prisoners were punished.
Dec. 1: Chilean Political Riots. Pro- and anti-government groups rioted in Santiago, Chile, for first time since President Salvador Allende took office.
1972
Jan. 29: Northern Ireland Riots. Civil Rights marchers in Dungannon, N. Ire., were dispersed with rubber bullets and gas.
Jan. 30: Northern Ireland Riots. British troops killed thirteen at a rally in Derry. The day later became known as "Bloody Sunday."
Feb. 2: Northern Ireland Riots. Marchers burned the British Embassy in Dublin.
1973
Feb. 7: Northern Ireland Riots. Belfast Loyalists rioted after Loyalist Association of Workers called a one-day strike.
1975
Jan. 20: Walpole, Mass., Prison Riots. Dozens were injured in a five-day riot at the Walpole, Mass., Prison.
1976
Mar. 8: West Bank Riots. Brutality by Israeli troops in the West Bank town of Nablus resulted in riots and the resignation of the town council.
Mar. 17: West Bank Riots. Rioting in the Israeli-occupied West Bank spread when an Israeli soldier killed an Arab boy.
Mar. 21: West Bank Riots. Israeli troops were ordered out of Hebron after severe rioting.
Apr 5: Chinese Riots. Riots broke out in Beijing as demonstators protested against Teng Hsiao-ping.
June 16: Anti-apartheid Riots. One hundred seventy-six people were killed in rioting in Soweto, S. Afri., which later spread to Transvaal, Natal, and Pretoria.
July 2: Peruvian Food Riots. A state of emergency was declared in Peru after rioting over food prices broke out.
Aug. 4: Anti-apartheid Riots. New riots broke out in Soweto, S. Afri., and spread to black townships near Cape Town.
Dec. 29: Chinese Political Riots. Political riots broke out in Paoting, 110 miles south of Beijing.
1977
Jan. 18: Egyptian Food Riots. President Anwar Sadat revoked food price increases that caused riots in Cairo and Alexandria.
Dec.2: Bermuda Riots. The governor of Bermuda declared a state of emergency after an all-night riot. On Dec. 5, 250 troops arrived and were removed two days later.
1978
Feb.3: Nicaraguan Riots. Ten people were killed when demonstrators opposing the Somoza regime in Nicaragua clashed with the National Guard.
Mar. 8: Anti-Somoza Demonstrations. An aide to Nicaraguan dictator Anastasio Somoza was killed during widespread demonstrations.
May 20: Peruvian Riots. President Bermudez declared martial law to control trade strikes and pre-election rioting.
Aug. 12: Iranian Riots. The Shah of Iran declared martial law in four cities as violent demonstrations continued.
Dec. 26: Turkish Political Riots. Turkey imposed martial law in thirteen southeastern districts following political rioting.
1979
July 12: Chicago Disco Demolition Riot. A between games "anti-disco" rally staged by a local radio station in Chicago's Comiskey Park resulted in forfeiture of the second baseball game between the White Sox and Detroit, and considerable property damage to the grounds.
July 15: San Francisco Riots. San Francisco homosexuals, enraged by the lenient sentence given Supervisor Daniel James White for the Nov. 27, 1978, murders of Mayor George Moscone and gay City Supervisor Harvey Milk, staged mass riots in protest.
Sept. 23: Statesville Prison Riot. A three-hour riot by the inmates of the Statesville Correctional Center outside Joliet, Ill., caused substantial damage to the prison.
Nov. 21: Islamabad Riots. Muslim students attacked and burned the U.S. embassy in Islamabad. Pakistani troops rescued 100 U.S. citizens. One U.S. marine was killed.
Dec. 3: Who Concert Stampede. Eleven people were trampled to death when fans tried to enter a Cincinnati rock concert given by the rock-and-roll group, The Who.
1980
Feb. 3: New Mexico State Prison Riot. Thirty-two people were killed and scores were injured in a riot at the New Mexico State Prison.
May 13: South Africa Riots. The most violent rioting since the 1976 Soweto riots broke out.
May 14: South Korean Anti-Government Riots. Following anti-government demonstrations in Seoul, S. Kor., rebellion broke out against the military government in Kwangju as 100,000 citizens battled riot police and troops.
May 18: South Africa Riots. Forty-two people were killed and 200 were wounded during two days of rioting on Cape Peninsula on the anniversary of the 1976 Soweto riots.
May 19: Miami Race Riots. Race riots in Miami in which eighteen people were killed and more than 1,300 were arrested were quelled by 3,500 National Guard troops. Economic damage reached $100 million.
June 1: Cuban Refugee Riots. Hundreds of Cuban refugees, including criminals deported by Castro rioted at a relocation center in Ft. Chaffee, Ark. Fifteen lawmen were wounded.
July 18: Northern Ireland Riots. Thousand of IRA hunger strike supporters clashed with police in Dublin while trying to demonstrate outside the British Embassy.
July 22: Chattanooga, Tenn., Riots. Racial violence continued in Chattanooga, Tenn., for four days after two Ku Klux Klan members accused of shooting four black women were acquitted by an all-white jury. At least eight police officers were injured.
Aug. 20: Northern India Riots. Civil riots between Moslems and Hindus lasted several days in more than a dozen north India towns and left 150 people dead in the rioting.
Aug. 27: Philadelphia Race-Related Violence. In Philadelphia, two days of violence erupted when a police officer shot and killed a black youth.

1981

Jan. 12: Nigerian Riots. Muslim rioting in Kano, Nig., left 7,000-10,000 dead.

Jan. 27: Irish Prison Riot. Some 400 Irish Republican Army (IRA) members imprisoned in Maze Prison smashed furniture and windows and two days later resumed smearing the walls with their own excrement.

Feb. 6: Pakistani Riots. The Movement for Restoration of Democracy staged riots against President Mohammed Zia-ul-Haq.

Feb. 13: Spanish Basque Riots. Following the death, apparently from political torture, of Basque separatist Jose Ignacio Arregui Izaguirre, rioting occurred in Basque towns.

Mar. 11: Yugoslavian Riots. The Communist Party Presidium held an emergency session when riots protesting the high cost of living broke out at the University of Pristina.

Apr. 1: Yugoslavian Riots. Nine people were killed in fighting between police and some 10,000 protestors seeking independence for the largely Albanian province of Kosovo.

Apr. 3: Indian Riots. Bombing and rioting in West Bengal killed at least eight people and left 200 injured.

Apr. 19: Northern Ireland Riots. Two 18-year-olds were killed in Londonderry when a British army vehicle rammed into a crowd of rioters throwing gas bombs.

May 5: Belfast Riots. A boy and his father were fatally injured when a rioting crowd hijacked their milk truck.

May 8: Northern Ireland Riots. Vehicles were burned in rioting in Londonderry and Belfast.

May 20: Honduran Peasant Riot. Several hundred machete-wielding Honduran peasants stormed the National Agrarian Institute demanding the release of 105 peasants.

May 22: Northern Ireland Rioting. One man was killed and five British soldiers were injured in rioting following the death of IRA hunger striker Patrick O'Hara.

July 5: British Anti-Thatcher Riots. More than 200 people were injured in Liverpool, England, in riots protesting the policies of Margaret Thatcher's government.

July 10: Northern Ireland Riots. The funeral of IRA hunger striker Joe McDonnell became a riot when British troops tried to ambush three IRA gunmen.

July 18: Dublin Riots. Supporters of Maze Prison's IRA hunger strikers clashed with police and 170 were injured at the British Embassy in Dublin.

Aug. 9: Belfast Riots. Two people were killed in Belfast during riots following the death of hunger striker Thomas McIlwee.

Aug. 22: Belfast Riots. Forty-eight people were wounded in riots and bombings following the death of hunger-striker Michael Devine.

1982

June 14: Polish Riots. Rioting broke out in the Polish cities of Wroclaw, Gdansk, Nowa Huta, and Cracow.

Aug. 13: Polish Solidarity Riots. Three people died and more than 4,000 were detained while tens of thousands demonstrated in Poland on Solidarity's second anniversary.

Oct. 8: Polish Solidarity Riots. Riots at the Lenin Shipyard in Gdansk in response to the Polish parliament's dissolution of Solidarity were met with army rule.

Oct. 26: Nigerian Riots. Hundreds were killed, including at least 100 riot police in riots in Nigeria instigated by Islamic fundamentalists.

1983

Jan. 10: Sing Sing Prison Riot. Five hundred-fifty prisoners at Sing Sing Prison in New York held seventeen guards hostage for twenty-four hours until prison officials promised reforms.

Feb. 14: Indian Hindu-Muslim Riots. Hindus and Muslims battled in India over elections. By the end of the month as many as 1,500 had been killed.

April 4-5: Brazilian Unemployment Riots. High unemployment caused rioting and looting in Sao Paulo, Braz.

May 1: Polish Pro-Solidarity Riots. Pro-solidarity demonstrations broke out in twenty Polish cities. One person died and at least 11,000 people were held.

July 24: Sri Lanka Riots. Rioting against the Tamil minority in Sri Lanka broke out after Tamil separatists killed thirteen government soldiers. By the end of the month, 100 people had been killed.

1984

Jan. 3: Tunisian Food Riots. Food riots in Tunisia caused President Bourguiba to declare a state of emergency, and ended when planned food price increases were cancelled.

Feb. 18: Libyan Riots. The burning of the Jordanian embassy in Tripoli caused Jordan to break diplomatic relations with Libya.

Apr. 2: The killing of a prominent Hindu politician by Sikh extremists led to rioting by Hindus in Punjab. Sikhs retaliated with fires in 40 railway stations. Two hundred Sikhs were arrested.

May 10: Hindu-Muslim Rioting Rioting in Bombay, India, killed 230 people in eleven days.

Aug. 12: Northern Ireland Riots. One man was killed and more than twenty were injured in an attempt to arrest a Noraid leader during an anti-internment commemoration in West Belfast.

Nov. 4: Indian Hindu-Muslim Riots. Order was finally restored after 2,000 Sikhs were killed following the assassination of Prime Minister Indira Gandhi by two Sikh bodyguards.

1985

Mar. 26: Sudanese Food Riots. Two days of food riots paralyzed the Sudanese capital of Khartoum.

June 3: Sri Lanka Riots. Eighty people were killed and hundreds wounded when Sinhalese mobs attacked Tamil villagesin Sri Lanka.

June 25: Guadeloupe Riots. Rioting in the capital of Guadeloupe over the detainment of separatist leader Georges Faisans brought French troops to the Caribbean island.

Aug. 8: South African Riots. At least sixty people were killed in five days of rioting around Durban, S. Afri.

Aug. 30: South African Riots. Twenty-eight more people died in rioting in the Cape Town area.

Oct. 9: South African Riots. The execution of black dissident poet Benjamin Moloise set off rioting in Johannesburg.

1986

Feb. 15: South African Riots. At least fourteen people were killed in riots in black townships in South Africa.

Feb. 25: Egyptian Conscription Riot. The Egyptian Army ended a riot begun by conscripts of the Central Security Force.

May 3: South Korean Student Riots. Students in Inchon, S. Kor. rioted.

June 9: South African Riots. Rioting between rival black groups in the Crossroads squatters' camp left twenty dead, hundreds wounded and 20,000 homeless. South Africa declared a nationwide state of emergency.

June 21: Spanish Riots. Spanish riot police quelled a two-day riot between right-wing Spaniards and Muslims.

Aug. 13: Pakistani Political Riots. The arrest of opposition leader Benazir Bhutto on the eve of Independence Day sparked six days of riots in Pakistan in which sixteen people were killed.

Aug. 18: South African Riots. In Soweto, S. Afri., blacks protesting evictions of rent boycotters clashed with police, resulting in twenty-one dead and 100 injured.

Oct. 28: South Korean Student Riots. South Korean student protests calling for President Chun's resignation led to 1,200 arrests during five days of rioting in Seoul and Pusan.

Oct.31: Pakistani Riots. Fifty-three people were killed in riots in Karachi and Hyderabad, Pak.

Nov. 27: French Student Riots. Demonstrations by French university students protesting an education reform bill resulted in the death of one student.

Dec. 16: Soviet Riots. Two days of rioting in the Soviet republic of Kazakhstan were sparked by a change in party leadership.

1987

June 10: South Korean Riots. Riots in Seoul, S. Kor., erupted in the streets when President Chun named Roh Tae Woo as the presidential candidate.

June 12: Anti-American Berlin Riots. Anti-American riots occurred in West Berlin before, during and after a visit by U.S. President Ronald Reagan.

July 5: South Korean Student Riots. South Korean student riots continued.

July 31: Saudi Arabian Riots. Iranian pilgrims to Mecca clashed with Saudi security forces resulting in 400 deaths.

Dec. 9: Palestinian anti-Israeli demonstrations on the East Bank and the Gaza Strip begin. Two dozen Palestinians will be killed by Jan. 3 and nine Palestinian "instigators" will be deported.

1988

January: Brazilian Prison Riot. The siege of a prison near Porto Alegre, Braz., led to its occupation by 350 police and the death of two prisoners.

Feb. 10: Bangladesh Election Riots. Two hundred persons were killed and thousands injured when rival factions in Bangladesh fought one another during nationwide elections for positions in 4,376 village governments.

Feb. 28: Soviet Ethnic Riots. An anti-Armenian mob in Sumgait, U.S.S.R., stormed seventeen apartment buildings, killing seven people. The ethnic riots, caused a reported thirty-two fatalities when the Soviets rejected an Armenian demand for the mostly-Armenian district of Nagorno-Karabakh. Akhmedov received the death penalty.

Feb. 29: Senegalese Election Riots. Police occupied Dakar University in Senegal when riots broke out after President Abdou Diouf, also head of the Socialist party, was reelected. Many rioters were arrested.

June: Soviet commandos stormed the jail at Komsomolsk-na-Amure after six prisoners seized a guard and five women.

Aug. 19: Burmese Riots. Hundreds of people protesting a change in the Burmese government were shot by the military under orders of then president U Sein Lwin, successor to Ne Win.

Aug. 22: Burundi Ethnic Riots. At least 5,000 people were killed during a week of ethnic violence between the majority Hutu tribe and the smaller Tutsi tribe of Burundi.

Dec. 7: Guayama, P. R. Prison Riot. A gang war in a penitentiary in southern Puerto Rico turned into a riot in which the warden was taken hostage. A wing of the prison was burned and thirteen inmates were wounded. Prisoners released the warden unharmed.

1989

Mar. 5: Tibetan Anti-China Riot. Chinese police fired on an illegal Buddhist parade in Lhasa, Tibet. Eleven people died and more than 100 were injured as rioters looted shops and vandalized police cars.

ORGANIZED CRIME

What follows is a compilation of important organized crime figures comprising the twenty-six Mafia families in the U.S. and major criminal gangs active in the U.S. and abroad since the mid-nineteenth century. Also included are significant events, and figures from law enforcement and criminal justice who had a particular bearing on organized crime.

STRUCTURE OF A MAFIA CRIME FAMILY

The Honored Society, as the Mafia is known among its members, is structured much like a modern corporation in the sense that duties and responsibilities are disseminated through a "chain of command," organized in pyramid fashion.

1. Capo Crimini (Super Boss)
2. Consigliere (Trusted advisor, or family "counselor")
3. Capo Bastone (Underboss, the second in command)
4. Contabile (financial advisor)
5. Caporegime or Capodecina (Lieutenant, typically heads a faction of ten or more foot "soldiers")
6. Sgarrista (a foot soldier, carries out the day to day business of the family. A "made" member of the Mafia. Has taken the secret oath-bound initiation)
7. Picciotto (lower ranking soldiers; enforcers. Also known in the streets as a "button")
8. Giovane D'Honore (Mafia associate, typically a non-Sicilian, or non-Italian member)

BOSTON-NEW ENGLAND ORGANIZED CRIME

Abrams, Hyman, prom. 1930s-40s. Lieutenant of Charles Solomon. He later joined Meyer Lansky in the operation of various Las Vegas and Havana gambling casinos.

Angiulo, Gennaro J. (AKA: **Jerry**), 1919- . Caporegime of the Patriarca syndicate when Philip Bruccola fled to Italy to avoid prosecution for income tax violations. He was demoted in 1984 and is now in jail.

Baharoian, John, 1923- . Roxbury gambler and bookmaker who ran gaming establishments in Dorchester and the South End of Boston from 1982-88.

Barboza, Joseph (AKA: **The Animal**), d.1976. New England mob enforcer who was imprisoned in the 1970s for murder. He was beaten to death in San Francisco, in 1976, after joining the Federal Witness Protection Program and testifying against Raymond Patriarca.

Bennett, Edward (AKA: **Wimpy**), prom. 1960s. Foot soldier in the Patriarca crime family who was assassinated.

Bianco, Nicholas, prom. 1950s-80s. One-time member of the Colombo family in New York. Bianco is now the reigning underboss of the New England family, based in Providence, R.I.

Bruccola, Philip, prom. 1930s-50s. Successor to Joseph Lombardo. Policy boss and gang chief in Boston. He presided over a de-centralized confederation of Italian gangs for much of the time he served as boss. Forced to flee to Sicily after being indicted for income tax evasion, Bruccola turned the operation over to Raymond Patriarca in 1950.

Bulger, Stephen J. (AKA: **Whitey**), prom. 1980s. South Boston mobster allied with Stephen Flemmi. These two men reportedly control the non-Mafia rackets in Boston.

Burke, Elmer (AKA: **Trigger**), 1917-58. New England hitman executed on Jan. 9, 1958, for the murder of bartender Edward Walsh.

Cardillo, Robert, prom. 1950s-60s. Associate of the Patriarca family who was imprisoned for a securities swindle.

Castagna, John F. (AKA: **Sonny**), 1941- . Associate of the New England Mafia based in Hartford, Conn. He was convicted of manslaughter in 1972.

Castucci, Richard, prom. 1950s-60s. Operated a nightclub for Vincent Teresa.

Cataldo, Anthony (AKA: **Maxie Baer**), prom. 1950s-60s. New England mobster and enforcer.

Cesario, Salvatore, prom. 1950s-60s. Loan shark and enforcer who served as a bodyguard for Gennaro Angiulo.

Combat Zone, prom. 1970s. Segregated vice district in downtown Boston that was the scene of numerous assaults, robberies, and murders.

Cortese, Joseph (AKA: **Little Bozo**), prom. 1950s-60s. Triggerman for mobster Michael Rocco.

Cucchiara, Frank (AKA: **Frank Caruso, Frank Russo, Frank the Spoon**), b.1895. Gambling boss and narcotics trafficker in the North End of Boston who functioned as Raymond Patriarca's right-hand man.

Cufari, Salvatore (AKA: **Big Nose Sam**), prom. 1940s-60s. Springfield, Mass., crime boss.

Daddieco, Robert, prom. 1950s-70s. Associate of the Patriarca family who turned informant against the mob.

D'Aquila, Salvatore (AKA: **Butch**), 1941- . Associate of the New England mob based in Middletown, Conn., who was charged with running an illegal gambling operation at the Saybrook Yacht Club in 1975. He has also sponsored gambling junkets for his Mafia associates.

David, Waddy, prom. 1950s-60s. Numbers racketeer in Boston under Ilaro Zannino.

DeChristoforo, Benjamin, prom. 1960s-70s. Mafia enforcer for Gennaro Angiulo.

Dellarusso, Anthony (AKA: **Chickie Spar**), prom. 1950s-60s. Owned the Frolics Nightclub in Revere, Mass.

Deprisco, Thomas (AKA: **Richard Dipiescia**), prom. 1950s-60s. One time partner of the late Joseph Barboza.

DiGiacomo, Biagio, 1945- . Caporegime in the Patriarca crime family.

DiPietro, Robert A. (AKA: **Tony**), prom. 1950s-60s. Boston gambling boss for Carlo Mastrototaro.

Failla, Louis R., 1928- . Resident of East Hartford, Conn. Failla was a soldier in the Patriarca crime family. In 1980, he was charged with attempting to bribe the East Hartford Police chief.

Farrell, John E. (AKA: **Fast Jack**), 1938- . Associate of the Patriarca family, headquartered in Manchester, Conn., and reputedly one of the best card and dice "mechanics" in the country.

Fiumara, Peter (AKA: **Skinny Pete**), prom. 1960s-70s. Associate of the Patriarca family. He owned a nightclub outside Boston.

Flemmi, Stephen J. (AKA: **The Rifleman**), prom. 1950s-80s. New England hitman, the brother of Vincent Flemmi, and an associate of Stephen Bulger.

Flemmi, Vincent (AKA: **The Butcher**), prom. 1950s-60s. Brother of Steve Flemmi and a New England hitman.

Fox, Louis, prom. 1930s-50s. Accountant and financial wizard for the New England mob. He took over the Revere, Mass., territory following Charles Soloman's death.

French, Roy, prom. 1950s-60s. Enforcer for Gennaro Angiulo who was sent to prison.

Fucillo, Theodore (AKA: **Teddy**), prom. 1930s-40s. Elder statesman of the Boston mob.

Gagliardi, Carmine, prom. 1950s-60s. Enforcer under Gennaro Angiulo.

Garrett, Oliver B., prom. 1920s. Boston policeman who supplied dairy products to the city bordellos and gambling dens as a sideline.

Gioachinni, Vincent C., 1952- . Soldier in the Patriarca family, serving under Biagio DiGiacomo.

Giso, Nicola, prom. 1950s-60s. Boston bookmaker and loan shark who worked for Joseph Lombardo.

Grasso, William P. (AKA: **The Wild Guy**), d.1989. Underboss in the New England crime family following the elder Patriarca's death. He was murdered and his body was dumped in the Connecticut River, on June 17, 1989.

Grieco, Louis (AKA: **Lou, The Gimp**), prom. 1960s-70s. New Hampshire Mafia figure who was imprisoned.

Gugliemetti, Matthew, Jr., prom. 1970s-80s. Rhode Island resident who currently serves as caporegime in the Patriarca family.

Imbruglia, Frank, 1932- . East Boston Mafia figure, Imbruglia emerged as a suspect in several gang-related shootings in 1989, including that of Francis Salemmi.

Johns, John (AKA: **Jackie**), 1960- . Son of John Castagna. He is also an associate of the Patriarca crime family who ran an illegal gambling club in Manhattan.

Kattar, George, prom. 1960s-70s. Financier who was indicted for income tax evasion. He is also an associate of the Patriarca family.

Krikorian, Joseph (AKA: **Joe Kirk**), prom. 1950s-70s. Gambling boss. He resides in Rhode Island.

Lamattina, Joseph (AKA: **Joe Black**), prom. 1950s-60s. New England mob figure who fled to Sicily following a securities theft.

Lerner, Maurice (AKA: **Pro**), prom. 1950s-60s. Hit man for the Patriarca family.

Limone, Peter, prom. 1960s-70s. Associate of Gennaro Angiulo.

Linsey, Joseph, prom. 1920s-40s. Russian-born lieutenant of Charles Solomon. He became a mob boss in his own right, controlling several New England dog tracks and country clubs.

Lombardo, Joseph, prom. 1930s-60s. Policy boss in Boston. Lombardo died of natural causes, in 1969.

McCarthy, William, prom. 1980s. Reigning boss of the Teamsters Union, accused of consorting with New England organized crime figures by Jackie Presser.

McLaughlin, Bernard, d.1961. Boston mobster who ran the Charlestown Mob, New England's "Irish faction" of organized crime. He was killed on Oct. 31, 1961, in a gang war against the Italians.

McLean, James (AKA: **Buddy**), prom. 1960s. Irish gang leader who went to war against the Patriarca clan in the 1960s. He led the Winter Hill Gang of Somerville, Mass.

Marfeo, Rudolph, prom. 1960s. New England mob figure who was murdered in Providence, R.I., in 1968.

Martinelli, Peter, prom. 1950s-60s. Pimp and loan shark under Vincent Teresa.

Mastrotaro, Carlo, prom. 1950s-60s. Replaced Henry Tameleo as underboss of the Patriarca crime family.

Milano, Gaetano J., prom. 1980s. Soldier in the Patriarca crime family. Milano resides in East Longmeadow, Mass.

Modica, Joseph (AKA: **Don Peppino**), prom. 1940s-50s. Old-line Mafia boss in New England.
Morelli, Frank (AKA: **Butsey**), prom. 1940s-50s. First crime boss of Rhode Island.
Mustone, Christopher, prom. 1950s-60s. Thief and armed bandit. Mustone was a partner of Vincent Teresa.
Nazarian, John (AKA: **Jackie, Mad Dog**), prom. 1950s. Mafia assassin who was allegedly hired by Raymond Patriarca to kill Albert Anastasia in 1957.
Palladino, Joseph (AKA: **Joe Beans**), prom. 1940s-60s. Prominent Boston bookmaker and syndicate gambler.
Palladino, Joseph, Jr. (AKA: **Little Beans**), prom. 1960s-70s. Son of Joseph Palladino, Sr. and partner of Vincent Teresa.
Palombo, Joseph, prom. 1950s-60s. Former rackets boss of Gloucester, Mass.
Patriarca, Raymond Loredo Salvatore, 1908-84. Ruler of the New England crime family beginning in the 1950s, when he succeeded Philip Bruccola. He owned a share of the Dunes Hotel in Las Vegas and was involved in gambling in Haiti. His influence in New England stretched from Portland, Me., to New Haven, Conn. Patriarca was jailed in 1968.
Patriarca, Raymond, Jr. (AKA: **Junior**), 1945- . Son and successor of Raymond Patriarca, Sr. Raymond, Jr., functions as head of the New England crime family. He replaced his father on the National Commission.
Petrillo, Americo (AKA: **Rico, The Cigar**), 1934- . Resident of Old Saybrook, Conn. He is a soldier in the Patriarca crime family, and former associate of William P. Grasso.
Pugliano, Frank A. (AKA: **Frankie Pugs**), 1929- . Associate of the New England mob. He ran a gambling club in West Springfield, Mass.
Puleo, Stephen, 1923- . Belmont, Mass., bookmaker. He is associated with reputed Mafia figure Stephen Flemmi.
Rocco, Michael (AKA: **Mike the Wiseguy**), prom. 1950s-60s. Leading associate of Joseph Lombardo. He died of natural causes.
Rossi, Alfredo (AKA: **The Blind Pig**), prom. 1950s-60s. Fence man for the Patriarca mob. He died of natural causes.
Russo, Joseph (AKA: **J.R.**), prom. 1970s-80s. Currently serves as family consigliere in the Patriarca crime family. He was implicated in the 1976 murder of Joseph Barboza.
Salemmi, Francis P. (AKA: **Cadillac Frank**), 1934- . Mafia soldier who was severely wounded in a shootout in Saugus, Mass., in June 1989.
Samenza, Al (AKA: **Fat Al**), prom. 1950s-60s. Racetrack fixer at Suffolk Downs.
Sciarra, Rudolph, prom. 1960s-70s. Credit card counterfeiter and assassin for the New England mob.
Simonelli, Joe (AKA: **Blondy**), prom. 1950s-60s. Race fixer who worked for the New England mob.
Solomon, Charles (AKA: **King**), prom. 1920s-30s. Prohibition gang leader in Boston who was gunned down at the Cotton Club in South Boston, on Jan. 24, 1933.
Spagnolo, Antonio L., 1941- . Soldier in the Patriarca family who serves under Biagio DiGiacomo.
Taglianetti, Louis (AKA: **Louie the Fox**), prom. 1950s-60s. New England mafia enforcer who was a gambling boss in Rhode Island who was murdered by the mob.
Tameleo, Enrico Henry (AKA: **The Referee**), prom. 1950s-60s. Underboss in the Patriarca crime family. He was sentenced to death for murder.
Teperow, Leonard, 1931- . West Roxbury bookmaker and Mafia associate.
Teresa, Vincent (AKA: **The Fat Man**), prom. 1960s-70s. Former number three man in the Mafia family headed by Raymond Patriarca. He published a memoir titled, *My Life in the Mafia.*
Turrussa, Nazzarene (AKA: **Nene**), prom. 1950s-60s. Member of the New England mob advisory council and a cousin of Joseph Modica.
Zannino, Ilario (AKA: **Larry Baiona**), prom. 1950s-80s. Number two man in the New England Mafia until 1984. Following the death of Raymond Patriarca, Sr., he was awarded control of the Boston region.

BUFFALO-WESTERN NEW YORK ORGANIZED CRIME

Agueci, Albert, d.1961. Brother of Vito Agueci. He was a heroin smuggler for the Genovese family. He was murdered in 1961.
Agueci, Vito, prom. 1950s-60s. Operated the drug trafficking business in the Toronto-Buffalo, and Western New York markets, under Stefano Magaddino. Sent to prison, he avenged his brother's death by "helping" Joe Valachi turn informant against Magaddino and others.
Bonito, Salvatore, prom. 1960s-70s. Section leader in the Magaddino family.
Briandi, Paul, prom. 1960s-70s. Served as a section leader in the Magaddino crime family.
Brocato, Salvatore, prom. 1960s. Section leader for the Magaddino crime family.
Cammillieri, John, prom. 1960s. Lieutenant in the Magaddino crime family.
Canal Street, prom. 1860-1915. Vice-district in Buffalo that catered to the river traffic on the Erie Canal.
Cannarozzo, Steven, prom. 1960s. Lieutenant in the Magaddino crime family.
Carlisi, Roy, prom. 1960s. Lieutenant in the Magaddino crime family.
DiCarlo, Joseph J. (AKA: **Jerry the Wolf, Joe the Gyp**), b.1899. Top gunman for Stefano Magaddino. He was driven out of Buffalo by police. He took up residence in Miami, where he was a gambling boss.
Fino, Joseph, prom. 1960s-70s. Underboss of the Magaddino crime family during the 1970s.
Lagattuta, Samuel, prom. 1960s-70s. Section leader in the Magaddino family.
Magaddino, Antonio, prom. 1960s-70s. Son of Stefano Magaddino.
Magaddino, Gaspare, d.1968. Younger brother of Peter Magaddino who was imported from Sicily to work as a syndicate assassin. He was shot to death in Brooklyn in 1968.
Magaddino, Peter, 1902- . Nephew of Stefano Magaddino who later served as Joe Bonanno's bodyguard.
Magaddino, Stefano (AKA: **Steve**), b.1891. Long-time boss of the Buffalo-Eastern Ohio rackets, allied with Salvatore Maranzano during the 1930-31 Castellammare War.
Miano, Salvatore, prom. 1960s-70s. Section leader in the Magaddino crime family.
Natarelli, Pascal, prom. 1960s. Lieutenant of Stefano Magaddino's in the 1960s.
Perna, Anthony, prom. 1960s-70s. Section leader in the Magaddino crime family.
Politano, Pascal, prom. 1960s-70s. Section leader in the Magaddino crime family.
Randaccio, Federico, prom. 1960s. Underboss for Stefano Magaddino during the 1960s.
Rizzo, Salvatore, prom. 1960s-70s. Section leader in the Magaddino crime family.
Russotti, Samuel, prom. 1970s-80s. Boss of the Rochester, N.Y., crime family.
Sansanese, Daniel, prom. 1960s-70s. Section leader in the Magaddino family.
Scro, Vincent, prom. 1960s-70s. Family consigliere to Stefano Magaddino during the 1970s.
Tascarella, Michael, prom. 1960s-70s. Section leader in the Magaddino crime family.
Todaro, Joseph E. (AKA: **Lead Pipe Joe**), 1923- . Buffalo mob boss who is active in the labor unions.
Tranalone, John (AKA: **Peanuts**), prom. 1960s-70s. Soldier in the Buffalo crime family. Later, he was active in Miami, where he operated a travel agency.
Valenti, Frank, prom. 1960s-70s. Boss of the Rochester, N.Y., crime family.

CANADA ORGANIZED CRIME

Bouchard, Conrad, prom. 1960s. Right-hand man to Canadian mob boss Pepi Catroni.
Boyd, Murray Allen, 1940-70. Gunman and drug trafficker killed in a police shootout on Apr. 21, 1970.
Catalanotte, Joseph, prom. 1960s-70s. Lieutenant in the Windsor, Ont., branch of the Detroit mob.
Cicchini, Nicolas, prom. 1960s-70s. Lieutenant in the Windsor, Ont., branch of the Detroit mob.
Cotroni, Pepi, prom. 1960s. Montreal Mafia boss and international drug trafficker.
Cotroni, Vincent, prom. 1960s-70s. Ruling Mafia don in Montreal, with business interests in Florida.
Greco, Louis, prom. 1960s-70s. Montreal Mafia boss and narcotics trafficker.
Mayer, Lucien Joseph, prom. 1960s. Montreal heroin trafficker and gangster.
Minaudo, Onofrio, prom. 1960s-70s. Lieutenant in the Windsor, Ont. branch of the Detroit mob.

CHICAGO ORGANIZED CRIME

Abatte, Frank, d.1944. Crime boss of Calumet City, Ill. He was murdered on Apr. 22, 1944.
Accardo, Anthony Joseph (AKA: **Joe Batters, Big Tuna**), 1906- . Number-two man behind Paul Ricca in the mob hierarchy in 1941. By 1950, he was in virtual command of all gambling operations in Chicago. He stepped aside in favor of Sam Giancana, in 1956, but remained a power behind the throne until 1975. Accardo resumed joint command of the syndicate in 1975 with Joseph "Doves" Aiuppa. Currently, Accardo is in prison, but retains his status as "chairman of the board."
Ackerman, Frederick P., prom. 1950s-60s. Lawyer and one-time associate of Sam De Stefano. After turning informant in 1966, he was relocated under the witness protection program.
Adams, Kitty, prom. 1880s-90s. White slaver, and brothel keeper on State Street after 1886. She died in prison.
Adams, Phyllis, prom. 1910s. Levee brothel madame.
Adams, Red, prom. 1880s. Con man and bunko artist.
Adler, John (AKA: **Jakie**), prom. 1910s-20s. Pimp, police fixer, and

liaison between the Al Capone mob and police officials. He was kidnapped and held for ransom by the South Side O'Donnell Gang, in 1927, although he was later released.

Aiello, Andrew, prom. 1920s. Brother of Joe Aiello. In 1928, he was chased out of Chicago by Al Capone.

Aiello, Anthony, prom. 1920s. Fled Chicago with brothers Joe and Dominick, in 1928.

Aiello, Dominick, prom. 1920s. Brother of gang boss Joe Aiello. He was murdered in Chicago.

Aiello, Joseph, 1891-1930. Bootlegger and rival of Al Capone, who rose to prominence on the West Side in the early 1920s. Joe Aiello's ruthless ambition to control the Unione Siciliano led to his death. He was cut down on a city street on Oct. 23, 1930.

Aiuppa, Joseph (AKA: **Doves, The Pope, Joe O'Brien**, 1907- . Joined the Al Capone mob in 1935, as a triggerman protecting the Cicero strongholds. By the 1950s, he was the number-three man in the Outfit behind Gus Alex and Murray Humphreys. Through the 1970s, Aiuppa was boss of Cicero vice operations. He is currently in prison.

Alderisio, Felix Anthony (AKA: **Milwaukee Phil, Phil Aldonese, Phil Alderisio, Phillip Aldi, Phil Gato, Felix Alerise, Alderist, Aldresse, Aldrise, Phil Elderise**), 1922-71. Messenger boy for the Al Capone syndicate. He later worked as the syndicate bagman, carrying payoff money to the local police. In the 1950s and 1960s, he worked as an enforcer and triggerman. Alderiso died in prison in 1971.

Aleman, Harry (AKA: **The Hook**), 1940- . Top triggerman for the Chicago mob in the 1970s. Aleman is considered to be the prime suspect in the 1975 murder of Mafia boss Sam Giancana.

Alex, Gus (AKA: **Sam Taylor, Paul Benson, Gus Johnson, John Alex, Gussie, Shotgun, Slim, The Muscle, Mr. Ryan**), 1916- . Allegedly responsible for murdering five people. At present he shares the number two spot with Joseph Aiuppa. He is not in jail.

Alfano, Pietro (AKA: **Pete**), 1939- . Husband of Gaetano Badalamenti's niece. His Oregon, Ill., pizzeria was the center of midwest operations for the Sicilian-U.S. Pizza Connection. He was sentenced to fifteen years in prison for narcotics conspiracy on Oct. 21, 1987.

Algano, Lorenzo, prom. 1920s. Former member of the Genna gang. Lorenzo was assassinated by Al Capone gunmen.

Allegretti, James (AKA: **Jimmy the Monk**), 1905- . North Side vice boss, union racketeer, bagman, and syndicate bookmaker.

Allen, Lizzie (**Ellen Williams**), 1858-96. Congress Street brothel owner who operated in tandem with Christopher Columbus Crabb, from 1872 until the early 1890s.

Almeida, Louis, prom. 1970s. Syndicate hitman and mob associate of Harry Aleman. He became an important government informant in the mid-1970s.

Aloisio, William (AKA: **Smokes**), 1906- . Owner of the bowling alley where Jack McGurn was slain. He was a hitman and one-time member of the Al Capone gang, who ruled the 34th Ward in later years.

Alterie, Louis (**Leland Varain**, AKA: **Two-Gun**), 1886-1935. Top gunman for Dion O'Bannion's North Side mob. Just before the gang was vanquished by Al Capone, Alterie retired from Chicago. Unfortunately, he kept returning to attend to union business and was gunned down on July 18, 1935.

Amato, Joseph (AKA: **Black Jack**), prom. 1960s-70s. Chicago mob figure allegedly involved with the Laborer's International Union.

Amatuna, Samuzzo (AKA: **Samoots**), 1899-1925. Member of the alky-cooking empire forged by the Genna Brothers in the early 1920s. He became a powerful leader of the Unione Siciliano but was gunned down in a West Side barber shop on Nov. 13, 1925, by the Weiss-Moran mob.

Ambrosia, John, prom. 1940s. Syndicate gambling boss in Chicago during the 1940s.

Anderson, Katherine, prom. 1870s. Owner of the Senate, a Chicago brothel, which operated after the Chicago fire.

Andrews, Shang, prom. 1870s. Publisher of the *Chicago Sporting Gazette* that provided listings of brothels, gambling dens, and houses of vice in the Levee district.

Angelini, Donald (AKA: **Don Angel, The Wizard of Odds**), 1929- . Syndicate gambling boss based in West Suburban Elmhurst. He ruled a sports betting empire with Dominic Cortina before he was sentenced to prison on Mar. 21, 1990.

Annenberg, Moses L., 1878-1942. Street thug and hired newspaper slugger. He became boss of the racing wire in 1922 after purchasing the *Daily Racing Form* with money borrowed from Johnny Torrio. With the help of the national crime syndicate, his Nationwide News Service established a monopoly over the distribution of racetrack information.

Annixter, Julius (AKA: **Lovin Putty**), prom. 1900s-10s. Syndicate gambler and Levee vice boss in the pre-Prohibition era.

Anselmi, Albert, d.1929. Partner of John Scalise. Anselmi helped form the nucleus of one of the most feared hit teams in Chicago. He is thought to be one of the gunmen who shot Dion O'Bannion in his flower shop in 1925. He was murdered by Al Capone on May 7, 1929, after failing in an attempt to depose him.

Ansoni, Robert J. (AKA: **Robert Taylor**), prom. 1950s-60s. Co-owner, with Joseph Aiuppa, of Taylor and Company, manufacturers of gambling casino equipment. He was the gambling boss of Cicero in the 1960s.

Anton, Theodore (AKA: **The Greek**), d.1927. Managed a restaurant above the Hawthorne Inn, which was a popular rendezvous for Al Capone. He was abducted and murdered by the Moran gang on Jan. 6, 1927.

Appetite Bill, prom. 1880s. Con man and bunko artist.

Arlington, Jim, d.1875. Con man and swindler who was murdered by White Pine Martin.

Armato, Dominic, prom. 1920s. Chicago hoodlum killed in retaliation for the 1923 murder of Thomas Keane.

Arnold, Joseph (AKA: **Jerry Voltaire**), 1917- . Bodyguard and chauffeur for Jimmy "The Monk" Allegretti. He became the gambling overlord of the 38th Ward when Allegretti was sent to prison.

Attlominonte, Diego, prom. 1920s. Member of the Genna gang who was murdered by Capone gunmen.

Austin Avenue Gang, prom. 1900s. Chicago street gang around the turn of the century.

Bacino, Philip (AKA: **Tony Cello**), b.1902. Bootlegger and mob figure who operated behind the scenes for many years. He was arrested at a Mafia meeting in Cleveland, in 1928.

Bad Lands, the, prom. 1870s-80s. Vice-ridden district bounded by Clark, Van Buren, and Taylor streets, on Chicago's West Side.

Baldelli, Edward (AKA: **The Eagle**), d.1926. Member of the Genna gang who was killed in Chicago and dumped in a rural ditch on Feb. 23, 1926.

Barker, George (AKA: **Red**), prom. 1920s. Teamsters Union boss and racketeer, affiliated with the West Side O'Donnell mob.

Barko, Louis, prom. 1920s. Gangster and triggerman who belonged to the Capone gang.

Baron, Charles, prom. 1929. Murdered bootlegger James Walsh following a prize fight in December 1929.

Barry, John, prom. 1920s. Member of the Sheldon bootlegging gang. He was sent to prison for two years, in 1925, for violations of the Volstead Act.

Barry, James, prom. 1890s. Pickpocket who operated in Chicago's Loop.

Bartlett, "Soup", prom. 1920s. Dynamite specialist who worked for Jim Sweeney.

Bas, Marvin, 1905-50. Chicago lawyer. He was murdered before he could appear before the Kefauver Committee, in 1950.

Bascone, Vito, d.1926. West Side "alky cooker" allied with the Genna Brothers. He was murdered in Stickney, Ill., on Feb. 24, 1926.

Basile, James (AKA: **Duke**), 1936- . Chicago bookmaker who became a government informant in 1989. He identified a mob "graveyard" in suburban Hillside.

Bates, Karl (AKA: **Big Karl**), prom. 1920s. Professional killer employed by the Ralph Sheldon gang in the 1920s. He was killed by the Saltis-McErlane gang in 1925.

Battaglia, Anthony J., 1914-75. Brother of Sam Battaglia. He was murdered outside his West Suburban home on Apr. 29, 1975.

Battaglia, Samuel (AKA: **Teetz**), 1908- . Muscleman and juice collector for the Chicago mob on the West and North Sides. He was also a confederate of Sam Giancana.

Bed Bug Row, prom. 1900s-10s. Section of the South Side Levee featuring twenty-five cent brothels, occupied by young black girls.

Beidler, Jacob, prom. 1877. Chicago alderman who owned Noah's Ark, a three-story assignation house located in the Black Hole, west of the Chicago Loop.

Beige, Frank, prom. 1920s. Triggerman for the Al Capone mob.

Belcastro, James (AKA: **Rocco, Mad Bomber**), prom. 1920s. Black Hand extortionist. Belcastro later became the leader of Al Capone's demolition squad.

Belknap, James, prom. 1880s. Gambler and sporting house proprietor.

Bennett, Benjamin, d.1930. New York mobster brought to Chicago to provide "muscle" for Moran's interests. He disappeared sometime in 1930.

Benvenuti, Caesar, prom. 1920s. Numbers runner and brother of Julius and Leo Benvenuti.

Benvenuti, Julius, d.1950. Numbers racketeer who ran the Erie-Buffalo policy wheel. He was one of three brothers who operated under the protection of Al Capone.

Benvenuti, Leo, prom. 1920s-40s. Syndicate numbers runner and brother of Julius and Caesar Benvenuti.

Bernstein, Eugene, prom. 1940s. Former IRS accountant who went to work for Paul "the Waiter" Ricca and Louis "Little New York" Campagna.

Bernstein, Leo, prom. 1900s. Brothel owner in the Levee district.

Bertsche, Christian (AKA: **Barney**), prom. 1910s-20s. West Side gambler, swindler, and triggerman allied with William Skidmore.

Bertsche, Joseph, d.c.1930. Brother of Christian Bertsche. He was killed during the "Fox Lake Massacre," June 1, 1930.

Big Maud, prom. 1870s. Black woman who ruled the Bad Lands during the 1870s.

Biler Avenue, prom. 1870s-90s. Section of Pacific Avenue lined with bordellos and cheap tenements. It was nicknamed Biler Avenue because of the presence of steam locomotive boilers rumbling past.

Bills, Charles (AKA: **Guy**), prom. 1980s. South suburban "chop shop" operator and bagman for Albert Tocco.

Bim Boom Gang, prom. 1920s. Committed robberies on the South

Side of Chicago.

Black Eyed Johnny, prom. 1880s. Con man and bunko artist.

Black Ghost Shadows, prom. 1970s. Tong, active in Chicago's Chinatown.

Black Hole, prom. 1870s. West Side vice district composed of black saloons and brothels.

Black Horton, prom. 1890s-1900s. Lawyer, politician, and bondsman who worked for pickpocket Eddie Jackson.

Blackstone Rangers (AKA: **Black P-Stone Nation, El Rukns**), prom. 1960s-80s. Powerful South Side street gang involved in drug trafficking, extortion, terrorism, and murder. At various times this black inner-city gang has disguised its activities as community work.

Blanchey, Marie, prom. 1910s. Levee brothel madame.

Blasi, Dominic (AKA: **Joe Bantone**), 1911- . Private chauffeur and bodyguard for Sam Giancana.

Blaudins, Giovanni, prom. 1920s. Member of the Genna gang, who was murdered by Capone triggermen.

Block, William, prom. 1946. One of three hoodlums arrested for the murder of James Ragen in 1946. The case was nol-prossed.

Bloody Maxwell, prom. 1900s-20s. Name given to the Maxwell Street Police District, located on Chicago's West Side. It was a haven for criminals, pickpockets, and murderers.

Bloom, Ike (AKA: **Isaac Gittelson**), d.1930. Owner and operator of several brothels and a nightclub in Chicago's Levee district in the early 1900s. He was a top lieutenant for Big Jim Colosimo.

Boettiger, John, prom. 1930. Chicago newspaper reporter. He tracked down the killer of Jake Lingle and then wrote a book about it.

Bolton, "Red", prom. 1900s. Commander of the Valley Gang after Heinie Miller and Jimmy Farley went to jail.

Bovo, Joseph, prom. 1900s. Member of the Van Bever white slave gang.

Bracy, William, prom. 1970s. Professional hitman. He was a member of the Royal Family gang of assassins and hold-up men.

Brady Gang, prom. 1900s. Milwaukee Avenue street gang.

Brancata, Dominick (AKA: **Nags**), 1906- . Hitman and former juice collector for the Capone mob. He was active on the city's Near North Side.

Bratz, Albert, prom. 1930. North Side gangster who was affiliated with Jack Zuta.

Bravos, George, 1911-88. North Side gambling boss and loan shark, who was sent to prison in 1965.

Briggs, Hattie, prom. 1870s-90s. Black woman, ran a twenty-five-cent brothel in Little Cheyenne, near Clark and Polk Streets.

Briscoe Gang, prom. 1900s. Street gang headquartered on Fortieth Street on Chicago's South Side.

Brodkin, Michael, prom. 1950s-60s. Syndicate lawyer. He got his start through William Skidmore, a long-time political fixer and gambling boss. He formed a criminal law practice with George Bieber. They have represented Tony Accardo, Paul Ricca, Claude Maddox, and Murray Humphreys.

Brooks, Joseph (AKA: **Dynamite Joe**), d.1925. Member of the Saltis-McErlane gang. He was allegedly assassinated by Pete Kunski out of professional jealousy. He died in December, 1925.

Brooks, Virginia, prom. 1912. Chicago reformer. She fought to close the vice district in Hammond, Ind., in 1912.

Brothers, Leo Vincent (AKA: **Louis, Buster Bader**), 1909-51. Labor union racketeer who was convicted and sent to prison for the murder of Alfred "Jake" Lingle.

Brown, Jim (AKA: **General**), prom. 1840s. Boss of a gang of Chicago counterfeiters and footpads.

Brush, William, prom. 1880s. Member of John Turner's gang of bunko men and swindlers.

Buccieri, Fiore (AKA: **Fifi**), 1904-73. Proclaimed the "lord high executioner" of the Chicago mob in 1966. Buccieri began working for the Capone syndicate in the mid-1920s.

Buchalsky, "Izzy the Rat", prom. 1910s. Labor union thug.

Bucher, George (AKA: **Spot**), d.1923. Member of the Spike O'Donnell gang. He was killed with George Meeghan on Sept, 17, 1923.

Buonaguidi, Lawrence (AKA: **Larry the Hood**), 1915- . Terrorist and hitman working under Jimmy "the Monk" Allegretti.

Burnish, Benjamin, prom. 1860s. Professional gambler and partner of Gabe Foster.

Burrough, David, prom. 1850s. Owner of a Randolph Street gambling house, closed down by Mayor Wentworth in 1857.

Butler, Benjamin, prom. 1920s. Member of the Ralph Sheldon bootlegging gang.

Buxbaum, Ferdinand, prom. 1900s-10s. Owner of a dive in the Marlborough Hotel.

Cada, Joseph, d.1930. Associate of Jimmy Walsh. He was murdered on Feb. 3, 1930.

Caifano, Marshall Joseph (AKA: **Johnny Marshall**, 1911- . Syndicate executioner and gambling boss in Chicago. He is currently in prison.

Caifano, Leonard (AKA: **Fat Lenny**), d.1951. Brother of Marshall Caifano killed on June 18, 1951 while attacking policy boss Theodore Roe.

Cain, Richard, 1924-73. Chicago policeman and investigator for the State's Attorney's office. He turned mobster and was murdered in a West Side snackshop in 1973.

Calabrese, Frank James, prom. 1980s. Syndicate loan shark and mob hitman.

Calabriese, Joseph (AKA: **Little Joe**), d,1925. Collector and enforcer for the Genna Brothers gang. He was shot to death in 1925.

Callahan, Gerald Michael (AKA: **Cheesebox**), 1909- . Wire tapper and electronics expert employed by the Capone mob in the 1930s.

Cameron, Theodore, prom. 1860s. Owner of two gambling resorts.

Campagna, Louis (AKA: **Little New York**), prom. 1920s-40s. Former member of the Five Points Gang of New York. Campagna was brought to Chicago to kill Joe Aiello in 1928. He became a boss in his own right during the 1930s and 1940s.

Campagna, Anthony, d.1925. Independent alcohol manufacturer from Chicago's "Little Italy." He was killed by the Capone mob July 10, 1926.

Campione, Frank, d.1921. Member of the Sam Cardinelli gang and was executed in 1921.

Canale, Salvatore, d.1928. Member of the Joe Aiello gang. He was murdered in front of his home on July 25, 1928.

Capezio, Anthony (AKA: **Tough Tony**), prom. 1920s. Triggerman and member of the Al Capone gang.

Capise, Jasper, d.1983. Hitman named by Ken Eto as one of the men who tried to have him killed, Capise was himself the victim of mob vengeance in 1983 for failing to carry out the "hit."

Capone, Alphonse (AKA: **Scarface, Al Brown**), 1899-1947. Mob boss. Brooklyn born Al Capone arrived in Chicago c.1919 and in six short years established himself as the undisputed boss of the Chicago underworld. Sent to prison for income tax evasion in 1931, Capone died of venereal disease at his Florida estate in 1947.

Capone, Ermino John (AKA: **John, Mimi, Miami**), b.1904. Younger brother of Al Capone. He supervised various syndicate gambling dens in Chicago and Miami.

Capone, Frank, d.1924. Younger brother of Al Capone. He was killed during a gun battle with Chicago police in 1924.

Capone, Ralph (AKA: **Bottles**), d.1974. Brother of Al Capone. He ran the syndicate bottling operations in the 1920s. He died of natural causes.

Car Barn Bandits, prom. 1903. Street gang headquartered at Monticello Ave. and the Chicago River.

Cardinelli, Sam, prom. 1910s. Black Hand extortionist and ruler of his own criminal gang. He was executed on the gallows.

Carlisi, Samuel (AKA: **Wings**), 1921- . Former mob courier. Carlisi took over the daily operations of the Chicago mob following the death of Joseph Ferriola in March 1989. A convicted tax cheat and one-time protege of Joseph Aiuppa, Carlisi was allegedly pushed aside by John "No Nose" DiFronzo.

Carr, Charles, prom. 1920s. Agent of Johnny Torrio.

Caruso, Frank (AKA: **Frank Spino**), 1911- . South Side gambling boss and former member of the Forty-Two Gang along with Sam Giancana.

Casselli, Michael, prom. 1920s. Manufacturer and distributor of bombs to the Chicago gangland.

Catuara, James (AKA: **The Bomber**), d.1977. South Side mob boss involved in the "chop shop" rackets. He was murdered in 1977.

Cavallaro, Louis (AKA: **Blind Louie**), prom. 1970s. Syndicate extortionist who was sent to prison for eighteen months in 1978.

Cawley, Frank (AKA: **Si**), d.1929. Henchman of the West Side O'Donnells. He was murdered on Sept. 4, 1929.

Cerone, Frank (**Francesco Cironato**, AKA: **Skippy**), 1913- . Mafia hitman and gambling boss, and a cousin of John Cerone.

Cerone, John (AKA: **Jackie the Lackey**), 1917- . Gambling boss of Chicago with interests in Las Vegas. He is number three in the modern day Chicago mob. He is currently in prison.

Cesario, Samuel. 1918-71. Chicago gangster murdered on Oct. 19, 1971, after marrying a former girlfriend of "Milwaukee" Phil Alderiso.

Chamberlain, Henry Barret, prom. 1919. Operating director of the Chicago Crime Commission.

Channel, William, prom. 1920s. Underworld figure allied with Frankie McErlane.

Chicago Crime Commission, 1919- . Independent civilian agency monitoring vice and crime conditions in the city, organized on Jan. 1, 1919.

Chicago Vice Commission, prom. 1910. Commission organized as a civic crusade on Mar. 15, 1910 in order to close the brothels and panel houses in Chicago's red-light district known as the Levee.

Cicero, Ill., prom. 1920s. Chicago suburb where the Al Capone gang set up headquarters in 1923.

Cinderella, Dominic, prom. 1920s. Genna gunman, killed by the rival Capone mob.

Circella, Nicholas (AKA: **Nick Dean**), prom. 1941. Partner of Willie Bioff and George Browne in the multi-million dollar Hollywood extortion plot, run through the syndicate controlled Projectionist Union.

Circus Gang, prom. 1920s. North Side criminal gang who often supplied the firepower to Al Capone's mob.

Clafin, Dora, prom. 1890s. A white slaver and operator of a bordello in Hell's Half Acre.

Clark, James (**Albert Katchelak**), d.1929. One of Bugs Moran's top triggermen and lieutenants. He was killed in the St. Valentine's Day Massacre of 1929.

Clark, Jennifer, prom. 1880s-90s. Worked in tandem with Kitty Adams in her streetwalker's crib on Satan's Mile.

Clements, Hilary, d.1923. Beer-runner for the Ralph Sheldon gang. He was executed on Dec. 30, 1923, on orders from Joe Saltis.

Clifford, George, d.1929. Triggerman for the West Side O'Donnell mob. Clifford killed William J. Vercoe on Mar. 15, 1929 before being murdered himself on April 14.

Clifford, Elizabeth, prom. 1865-71. Owner of one of Chicago's first panel houses in 1865.

Cobras, prom. 1980s. Black street gang active in the North Side Cabrini Green housing project.

Coli, Eco James, 1922- . Labor racketeer from the West Side of Chicago with more than twelve arrests. Coli was convicted of armed robbery in 1952, and sent to prison for eight to ten years. He was released after three years by order of the Illinois Supreme Court.

Collins, Morgan A., prom. 1920s. Chicago Police Chief from 1923-27. Collins drove the Capone gang into Cicero in 1923.

Collins, Roger Lee (AKA: **Cochise**), prom. 1970s-80s. Leader of the Royal Family criminal gang. Collins cultivated ties to the Chicago Mafia in the early 1970s.

Colosimo, James (AKA: **Big Jim**), 1877-1920. Notorious figure in Chicago's Levee district before WWI. Colosimo ruled the prostitution and gambling rackets before his assassination in his own restaurant on May 11, 1920.

Colvin, Harvey Doolittle, prom. 1873-75. Corrupt mayor of Chicago 1873-75, who permitted the Mike McDonald syndicate to operate with minimal interference.

Condon, John (AKA: **Blind John**), d.1915. Racing boss, bookmaker, and syndicate gambler.

Conley's Patch, prom. 1860s. Vice district located at Adams and Franklin Streets, presided over by a black woman nicknamed the Bengal Tigress.

Conlish, Peter, prom. 1880s. Conman and bunko artist.

Conlon, Frank, d.1926. Chauffeur for Joe Saltis, until he was gunned down by Mitters Foley on July 20, 1926.

Connelly, Frank, prom. 1860s. Owner of the Senate, a deluxe gambling emporium in downtown Chicago during the Civil War.

Connolly, Al, prom. 1890s. First Ward Democratic Committeeman. Connolly was a political "fixer" for Whisky Row vice operatives.

Conroy, William, prom. 1900s. Proprietor of two Levee brothels near Armour Ave. and Dearborn Street.

Cooney, Dennis (AKA: **The Duke**), prom. 1900s-20s. Owner of the Rex Hotel, a bawdy house in the Chicago Levee in the early 1900s. He joined the Capone mob in the 1920s.

Coon Hollow, prom. 1870s. Post-fire Chicago vice-district.

Cooper, Abraham, prom. 1920s. Racketeer who attempted to go straight. He murdered Leo Mangovin in 1928.

Corrozzo, Michael (AKA: **Dago Mike**), prom. 1910s-20s. Corrupt labor union boss. Corrozzo was an associate of James Colosimo.

Cortina, Dominic (AKA: **Dom**), prom. 1980s. Syndicate gambling boss from South Suburban Oak Brook who operates in tandem with Don Angelini and Joseph Spadavecchio. He was formerly allied with Joseph Ferriola in a sports betting enterprise that netted him $20 million a year, but has since been sentenced to prison.

Cosgriff, Mollie (AKA: **Irish Mollie, Mollie Trussel**), prom. 1860s. Prostitute and bordello keeper. Cosgriff shot and killed her lover George Trussell in 1866 because of his undue attentions to his racehorse, Dexter.

Cosmano, Vincent (AKA: **Sunny Jim**), prom. 1920. Labor union racketeer and syndicate gunman. Cosmano was arrested for the murder of Maurice "Mossie" Enright in 1920. He was later acquitted.

Costello, Charles, prom. 1920s. Capone mob bootlegger, and owner of the Chicago Heights Distributing Company, a liquor wholesaler.

Costello, Jennifer, prom. 1890s. Brothel keeper in the Custom House Levee.

Costenaro, John, d.1927. Barkeeper Costenaro bought his supply of beer from the Ralph Sheldon gang. As a result, he was murdered by a rival gang in January 1927.

Cota, Joseph, prom. 1920s. Member of the Al Capone gang. He shot and killed gambler Jimmy Walsh in 1929.

Coughlin, John (AKA: **Bathhouse**), prom. 1890s-1930s. Ruler of the First Ward with Mike "Hinky Dink" Kenna for nearly forty years. He was a colorful but corrupt alderman who licensed vice and gambling in his ward.

Courtney, Thomas J., prom. 1932-44. Illinois State's Attorney for twelve years. Courtney escaped assassination at the hands of the syndicate in 1935.

Covelli, Gerald, prom. 1930s-50s. Associate of Jimmy Allegretti and Jackie Cerone. Covelli managed three syndicate nightclubs until he was jailed in 1959 for possession of stolen whiskey.

Crabb, Christopher Columbus, prom. 1880s-90s. Department store clerk who managed the affairs of Lizzie Allen and Mollie Fitch, who made him a wealthy man.

Craig, Andrew, prom. 1890s-1910s. Bondsman, pickpocket, criminal panderer and burglar along Whisky Row in the early 1900s. Craig owned the Tivoli cabaret.

Cremaldi, J., d.1926. Genna "alky cooker". Cremaldi was murdered after he attempted to peddle his product on the North Side.

Crockett, Clarence, 1939- . Collector and bagman for Albert "Caesar" Tocco. Crockett fled to Kentucky after being indicted on income tax evasion charges in 1986.

Crowe, Robert Emmet, prom. 1920s. Illinois State's Attorney during the Prohibition gang wars. Crowe prosecuted the Leopold-Loeb case in 1924.

Cullet, Harry (AKA: **Chicken Harry**), prom. 1914-20. Former Chicago policeman turned hoodlum. Cullet was active in the Levee under James Colosimo.

Cullotta, Frank, prom. 1970s-80s. West Suburban Chicago mobster who turned government informant against Joseph Lombardo and other local kingpins.

Custom House Levee (Fourth Avenue), prom. 1860s-90s. Vice-district adjacent to the Polk Street train station in Chicago's South Loop.

Cutter, Oscar, prom. 1930s-40s. Top commission boss for the Chicago syndicate in the 1930s and 1940s.

Daddano, William, Sr. (AKA: **Willie Potatoes, Dado**), 1912-75. Enforcer, professional thief, and Western Suburban gambling boss until his death in 1975.

Daly, John , prom. 1890s. Co-leader of the Maxwell Street gang with his brother Tom. He was sent to prison in 1905 for burglary.

Daly, Thomas, prom. 1890s. Brother of Jack Daly. He was sent to prison in 1905.

D'Andrea, Anthony, d.1921. Three-time aldermanic candidate from the 19th Ward who was shot to death in the Powers-D'Andrea feud of 1921.

D'Andrea, Joseph, prom. 1910s. Labor racketeer and president of the Sewer Digger's and Tunnel Miner's Union.

D'Andrea, Nicholas, 1932-81. Mafia assassin employed by Albert Tocco. He was murdered on Sept. 13, 1981.

D'Andrea, Philip, prom. 1920s-40s. Bodyguard of Al Capone. He rose through the syndicate ranks to become president of the Unione Siciliane.

Dannenberg, William C., prom. 1914. Chicago Police Department Morals Inspector. He helped close down the Levee following the shooting of Patrolman Stanley Birns, in July 1914.

D'Arco, John, prom. 1950s-60s. Long time alderman of Chicago's syndicate-controlled First Ward, allegedly a member of the Chicago mob.

Darrow, George, prom. 1928. Member of the Dingbat Oberta gang who tried to kill Spike O'Donnell on Oct. 11, 1928 in Wisconsin.

Dauber, William, d.1980. Chicago racketeer active in suburban "chop shop" operations and drug trafficking. He was murdered while driving away from the Will County Courthouse on July 2, 1980.

Davenport, Julia, prom. 1850s. Owner of the Green House brothel on State Street.

Davenport, Elizabeth, prom. 1890s. Owner of several panel houses in the Custom House Levee.

Davies, "Parson", prom. 1880s. Gambling boss who took over Mike McDonald's Store.

Dead Man's Alley, prom. 1870s-90s. Post-fire Chicago vice-area located within the boundaries of Hell's Half Acre.

Deadshots, prom. 1920s. Chicago street gang that waged constant warfare with the Bim Booms.

DeAmato, James, d.1927. Chicago gunman sent to New York by Al Capone to check up on the bootleg operations of Frankie Yale. DeAmato was shot to death in Manhattan, on June 10, 1927.

Death Corner, prom. 1900s-10s. Intersection of Milton and Oak, in the heart of "Little Italy" on the near West Side. The site of numerous murders and Black Hand extortions.

DeBiase, John (AKA: **Johnny Banana**), b.1901. West Side juice collector, gambler and drug peddler. He bankrolled a number of hijacking and robbery operations.

Deckman, Alfred, d.1924. Allegedly murdered in 1924 by Walter O'Donnell, who was subsequently acquitted.

DeGeorge, James (Vincenzo DeGiorgi), b.c.1898. Grape peddler to Italian wine makers and bootleggers. He became a dominant force in Lake County, Ind., and Wisconsin rackets. He was a one-time member of the Mafia ruling commission.

de George, Marie, prom. 1900s. Owner of Twentieth Street brothel in the South Side Levee district.

DeGrazia, Rocco, b.1897. Member of the Capone gang active in gambling, loan sharking, and drugs. He owned the Casa Madrid restaurant, a syndicate haunt.

DeLaurentis, Frank, prom. 1920s. Gunman for the Ralph Sheldon bootlegging gang.

Del Bono, Frank, prom. 1930. Gunman believed to have murdered three Capone gunmen on the Easter holiday, 1930.

de Muncey, Anne, prom. 1900s-10s. Levee brothel madame.

DePietto, Americo, 1913- . Syndicate extortionist, narcotics boss, and West Side terrorist.

DeStefano, Rocco Nicholas, 1913- . Cousin of Al Capone and Joe Fusco. He engaged in real estate development and nightclub acquisition for the syndicate.

DeStefano, Samuel (AKA: **Mad Sam**), 1909-73. Chicago's most efficient hit man for nearly three decades. He executed his own brother on orders from Sam Giancana.

Diamond, Frank (Frank Maritote), prom. 1920s-40s. Captain of the Capone bodyguards in the 1920s. He was convicted in 1943, and sentenced to ten years in prison, for involvement in the Hollywood extortion plot.

DiBella, Dominick, b.1902. Important North Side vice and gambling operative active in bookmaking and wire rooms. He was suspected of ten gangland murders.

Dickman, William, d.1925. One-time member of the Saltis gang, murdered because he joined the Ralph Sheldon mob.

DiFronzo, John (AKA: **No Nose**), 1928- . Loan shark, hitman, and heir apparent to Joseph Ferriola as head of the Chicago mob.

DiVarco, Joseph Vincent (AKA: **Little Caesar**), 1911- . Syndicate underling in charge of lucrative Near North Side vice operations. He is also a major figure in Las Vegas gambling on behalf of the Chicago mob.

Doherty, James (AKA: **Red**), d.1926. Member of the West Side O'Donnell gang. He was killed with Assistant State's Attorney William McSwiggin in Cicero, 1926.

Donovan, "Stink Bomb", prom. 1920s. Beer-runner and gunman for the Sheldon mob.

Dorfman, Allen, d.1983. Son of Paul "Red" Dorfman, a union organizer and early backer of James Hoffa. Manager of the Teamster's Pension fund and a convicted extortionist. Murdered gangland style in the parking lot of a suburban Chicago hotel, Jan. 20, 1983.

Dowling, John, prom. 1870s-80s. Gambling house proprietor. Ally of Mike McDonald.

Drucci, Vincent (AKA: **The Schemer**), 1885-1927. Criminal associate of North Side crime boss Dion O'Bannion. Shot and killed by Chicago policeman Dan Healy on Apr. 4, 1927.

Drucker, Charles, prom. 1880s. Conman and bunko artist.

Druggan, Terry, d.1950. Bootlegger who teamed up with Frankie Lake and former members of the Valley Gang to dispense liquor on the West Side. After making a fortune, Druggan retired to New York State, where he died.

Druggan, George, prom. 1920s. Brother of Terry Druggan. Mortally wounded in the "Fox Lake Massacre," June 1, 1930.

Drury, William, d.1950. Former Chicago Police captain. Murdered by Mafia hitmen in his garage, Sept. 25, 1950.

Duffy, Thomas (AKA: **Red**), d.1926. Irish mobster hooked up with the West Side O'Donnells. Killed with William McSwiggin on Apr. 17, 1926. Son of a Chicago policeman.

Dulfer, William, prom. 1900s. One of three leaders of the Formby Gang. Killed two men while holding up a saloon.

Duncan, Robert (AKA: **King of the Pickpockets**), prom. 1890s. Owner of two saloons on Whisky Row, favored by the hobo trade. Political fixer and bail bondsman.

Dunn, Jere, prom. 1860s. Gambler who worked Chicago's Hairtrigger Block during the 1860s. Killed Jim Elliot.

Dunn, Sonny, prom. 1920. Lieutenant in the Johnny Torrio gang.

"Old Man" Dunne, prom. 1870s. Chicago gambling house proprietor.

Durso, Natale, prom. 1920s. Small-time gangster murdered while parked at a red light.

Durso, Thomas N., prom. 1960s. Chicago policeman and syndicate drug dealer. Murdered Anthony "Lover" Moschiano on Jan. 21, 1965.

Dutch Bill, prom. 1880s. Conman and bunko artist.

Dutch Frank, prom. 1850s. Owner of a stable of racing dogs, a gambling house, and a saloon.

Duval, Emma (AKA: **French Em**), prom. 1900s. Owner of a Levee bordello.

Eboli, Louis (AKA: **the Mooch**), prom. 1970s-80s. Syndicate boss of the Western Suburbs of Chicago. An "aide-de-camp" to Joseph Lombardo. In retirement.

Edwards, Maggie, prom. 1890s. Brothel keeper in the Custom House Place district.

Egan, William (AKA: **Shorty**), d.1923. Beer-runner for the South Side O'Donnell mob. Murdered on Dec. 1, 1923 with Morrie Keane.

Eisen, Maxie, prom. 1920s. Labor racketeer and president of the Kosher Meat Peddler's Association. Affiliated with the Saltis-McErlane gang on the West Side.

Elizabeth Street Gang, prom. 1900s. Chicago street gang.

Eller, Morris, prom. 1920s. Corrupt Prohibition-era politician who bossed the 20th Ward. Allied with Al Capone.

Emery, James (Vincenzo Ammeratto), prom. 1930s. Mafia boss of south suburban Chicago Heights, which was under the aegis of the Al Capone gang.

English, Charles Carmen (Charles Inglise), (AKA: **Chuckie**), 1914-85. North Side racketeer who specialized in jukeboxes and vending machines. English was also active in Phoenix, Ariz. before being shot to death in a Chicago restaurant in 1985.

Enright, Maurice (AKA: **Moss, Mossie**), d.1920. Labor racketeer and strong arm gunman responsible for the murders of at least a half-dozen union rivals, was gunned down on Feb. 2, 1920.

Enright, Thomas, prom. 1920. Member of the John Torrio gang.

Epstein, Joseph, 1901-76. Chicago bookie and wire service boss for Jake Guzik. Virginia Hill's first gangster boyfriend.

Esposito, Joseph (AKA: **Diamond Joe**), 1872-1928. Chicago political leader and labor racketeer from the West Side. Esposito ran for committeeman in 1928, against Al Capone's wishes, and was gunned down in front of his house on March 21.

Eto, Ken, prom. 1980s. Japanese gambler and member of the Chicago syndicate. Survived three gunshot wounds in the head, on Feb. 10, 1983.

Everleigh, Ada, 1867-1960. Famous South Side brothel madame. Opened up the Everleigh Club with her sister Minna on Feb. 1, 1900.

Everleigh, Minna, 1878-1948. Owner of the Everleigh Club brothel on Dearborn Street with her sister Ada, until it was closed by police order in 1911.

Fagan, William, prom. 1850s. Gambler and card sharp. Owner of the House of David.

Fanelli, Rocco, prom. 1920s. Gunman for Al Capone. Emerged as a prime suspect in the St. Valentine's Day Massacre.

Farley, James, prom. 1900s. Pickpocket, burglar, and an early ruler of the West Side Valley Gang.

Farmer, Margaret (AKA: **Margaret Walsh**), prom. 1930. Girlfriend of killer Leo Brothers. Arrested for complicity in the Lingle murder.

Fay, James, prom. 1880s. Member of the John Turner gang.

Feinberg Gang, prom. 1900s. Street gang located on Twenty-third Street on Chicago's South Side.

Ferrari, Joseph, d.1930. Hitman and soldier in the Joe Aiello mob. Killed on May 31, 1930.

Ferraro, Joseph, prom. 1928. Bodyguard of Tony Lombardo. Ferraro was with him the day he was killed in 1928.

Ferriola, Joseph (AKA: **Joe Nagall**), 1927-89. Top ranking Mafia kingpin in Chicago, who relinquished power to Rocco Infelice a year before his death, in March 1989. Considered to be the top "enforcer" in the 1970s. Took on a more active role in the mob hierarchy in 1981, when Tony Accardo went into semi-retirement. Controlled a sports gambling empire that handled $40 million in bets each year.

Fewer, Michael, prom. 1900s. Saloon owner, and owner of two concert halls in the West Side Levee.

Ficke, Steven, prom. 1920s. Manufacturer and distributor of bombs to Chicago gangland.

Fields, Vina, prom. 1890s. Black woman who owned a brothel adjacent to that of Mary Hastings.

Finalli, Anthony, d.1926. Member of the Genna gang, murdered on Mar. 7, 1926.

Finkelstein, Henry, prom. 1927. Henchman of Northside mobster Vincent "Schemer" Drucci.

Finn, Mickey, prom. 1890s. Barkeep and owner of the Lone Star Saloon. Invented a potent knockout drink bearing his name.

First Ward Ball, 1897-1908. Annual fund raising event held in the Chicago Coliseum to line the political coffers of Aldermen John "Bathhouse" Coughlan and Michael "Hinky Dink" Kenna.

Fischetti, Charles, prom. 1920s-1950s. Cousin of Al Capone. Supervised liquor distribution in Chicago. Later purchased the first machine guns for the mob.

Fischetti, Rocco (AKA: **Rocks**), prom. 1920s-60s. First cousin of Al Capone. Top mob figure through the 1950s in Chicago.

Fitzgerald, James (AKA: **Red**), prom. 1880s. Conman and swindler.

Fitzsimmons, James, prom. 1870s. Bought out the Oyster Parlor founded by Jerry Monroe.

Foley, John (AKA: **Mitters**), d.1924. Member of the Sheldon booze gang. Shot and killed by Frank "Lefty" Koncil on Aug. 6, 1926.

Ford, Emma, prom. 1890s. Pickpocket and panel worker active in the Custom House Levee.

Formby Gang, prom. 1910s. Fullerton Avenue street gang.

Formby, James, prom. 1900s. Teen-age gang leader. Murdered a street car conductor in 1904.

Forsythe, James (AKA: **Red**), prom. 1920s. Chicago mobster many consider to be the real killer of newspaper reporter [Alfred "Jake" Lingle], who was gunned down in June 1930. Forsythe disappeared soon afterward.

Forty-Two Gang, prom. 1900s-20s. West Side Street gang that expanded during prohibition in the 1920s. Sam Giancana was an early member.

Four Deuces, prom. 1920s. 2222 S. Wabash Street. Al Capone's Chicago headquarters.

Foster, Frank (Frank Citro), prom. 1920s. Sicilian-born mobster who worked for Dion O'Bannion. One of the first to import Canadian-made whisky during Prohibition.

Foster, Gabe, prom. 1860s. St. Louis gambler who arrived in Chicago in the 1860s.

Foster, Henry (the Black Bear), d.1895 Black gang boss who commanded footpads in the vicinity of Dead Man's Alley. Executed on July 1, 1895 for murder.

Frabotta, Albert (Albert Fravatto), 1911- . Graduate of the "42 Gang," which was involved in burglary, auto theft, and strongarm tactics. Revenue collector for Marshall Caifano in the 1960s.

Franche, James (AKA: **Duffy the Goat**), prom. 1914. Murderer of Isaac Henagow in Roy Jones' Levee saloon in 1914.

Frantzius, Peter von, d.1968. Supplied machine guns and armaments to the Chicago mobs.

Fratto, Frank (AKA: **One Ear Frankie**), 1915- . North Side mobster active in the aluminum siding and storm window business.

Friedberg, Lesser, prom. 1870s. Fence, pawnbroker and murderer of Patrolman Albert Race in 1878.

Friedman, Solly, prom. 1900s. Brother-in-law of Ike Bloom. Co-proprietor of Freiberg's Dance Hall, one of the best-known resorts in the Levee.

Funkhouser, Metellius C., prom. 1911-15. Civilian Morals Inspector of the Chicago Police Department, assigned to investigate conditions in the South Side Levee.

Fusco, Joseph Charles, 1902-76. Named "Public Enemy Number One" in 1931. Supervised a string of Capone breweries.

Fyffe, Isabelle (AKA: **Dummy**), prom. 1900s. House girl at Mickey Finn's saloon who later testified against him at aldermanic hearings.

Gagliano, Joseph (AKA: **Joey G., Joe Gags**), 1914-71. Triggerman for Joey Glimco and Chuckie English. West Side loan shark and drug trafficker.

Galiano, Dominic, d.1966. Syndicate hoodlum murdered in Chicago on Mar. 11, 1966.

Gamblers Row, prom. 1860s-70s. Section of Clark Street from Randolph to Monroe that featured gambling resorts, low-life entertainment, and bordellos.

Garrity, Leona (AKA: **Mrs. Lemuel Schlotter**), prom. 1907. Owner of a vicious Peoria Street bordello who posed as a society matron in posh Glencoe until her identity was revealed in 1907.

Gary, "Red", prom. 1880s-90s. Member of the Johnson Street Gang.

Gaston, Lucy Page, prom. 1910s. Chicago reformer who believed that all social problems were tied to cigarette smoking. Founder of the Anti-Cigarette League.

Gattuso, John, d.1983. Former Cook County policeman turned mobster. Executed for botching the "hit" on Ken Eto.

Gavin, Larry, prom. 1870s. Owner of a gin-mill in Little Cheyenne that was frequented by street walkers and footpads.

Gaynor, Thomas, prom. 1890s. Partner and successor of Mary Hastings in the brothel business.

Gazzola, John, prom. 1900s. West Side gambling boss and bookie.

Genaro, John, d.1931. Robber and Capone gunman. Executed gangland style in 1931.

Genero, Joseph (AKA: **Peppy**), prom. 1920s. Lieutenant of the Capone Gang responsible for mob operations in Calumet City, Ill.

Genite, Joseph, prom. 1900s. Reputed bomb supplier to Chicago's Black Hand.

Genker, Charles (AKA: **Monkey Face**), prom. 1900s-20s. Levee pander and brothel keeper allied with Mike Heitler. Remained an independent through the 1920s.

Genna Brothers, prom. 1920s. Angelo, Pete, Michael, Tony (the Gentleman), Vincenzo, and Sam migrated from Sicily to Chicago where they became the leading dispensers of homemade liquor on the West Side. Angelo, Mike, and Tony were eventually killed, forcing the other three into hiding.

Gentlemen, Peter, prom. 1910s. Son of a policeman who became a labor slugger. Killed by Walter Stevens during Prohibition.

Giancana, Sam (AKA: **Momo, Mooney**), 1908-75. West Side gangster who ruled the Chicago mob from 1957-66. Assassinated at his west suburban home in 1975.

Gianola, Leonard (AKA: **Needles**), 1910- . West Side labor racketeer and narcotics trafficker.

Gioe, Charles (AKA: **Cherry Nose**), d.1954. Chicago mob boss convicted of extorting millions of dollars from Hollywood movie moguls on Oct. 5, 1943. Shot to death in 1954.

Gistenson, Leo, d.1924. Member of Spike O'Donnell's gang. Murdered by the Saltis mob on Dec. 19, 1924.

Giunta, Joseph (AKA: **Hop Toad**), 1907-29. President of the Unione Siciliane, prior to his execution at the hands of Al Capone on May, 8, 1929. Conspired with Scalise and Anselmi to murder the Chicago gang boss.

Glimco, Joseph Paul (AKA: **Giuseppe Glielmi**), 1909- . Top labor racketeer in the 1950s. Boss of fifteen Teamster's Locals. Vicious and depraved Mafia don disguising his illegal activities with many legitimate business fronts.

Gnolfo, Phillip, d.1930. Associate of Angelo Genna, and syndicate gunman, murdered on May 31, 1930.

Gold, William, prom. 1940s-50s. Intermediary and bagman between the 42nd Ward politicians and the syndicate gambling bosses.

Goldstein, "Bummy", d.1925. Mobster allied with Sam Amatuna. Murdered in 1925.

Gonsky, Paul M., d.1976. Owner of a Chicago porno theatre. He was gunned down by mob rivals on Sept. 21, 1976.

Gorman, John Paddy, prom. 1890s. Loop pickpocket.

Grabiner, Joseph (AKA: **Jew Kid**), prom. 1910s-20s. Levee vice-lord and gambling boss before WWI.

Graver, Clem, d.1953. Chicago politician abducted on June 11, 1953. The body was never found.

Gray, Robert (AKA: **Blubber**), prom. 1900s. Operated the California, a tough Levee brothel.

Gray Shadows, prom. 1970s. Tong active in Chicago's South Side Chinatown district.

Greenberg, Alec Louis, d.1955. Accountant for the Capone gang murdered in a Chicago café in 1955.

Green Street Gang, prom. 1900s. Chicago street gang.

Grisafe, Joseph, d.1974. Mafia enforcer whose mangled body was found on July 6, 1974.

Grogan, Barney, prom. 1900s. West Side politician and vice boss.

Guilfoyle, Martin, prom. 1910s-20s. West Side gambler and bootlegger, loosely affiliated with the Capone syndicate, but more properly tied in with Al Winge and Matt Kolb.

Gunn, Curt, prom. 1870s-80s. Owner of a gambling resort.

Gusenberg, Frank, and **Gusenberg, Peter**, d.1929. Two triggermen for Bugs Moran's North Side bootlegging gang. The Brothers Gusenberg were lined up against the wall and shot during the St. Valentine's Day Massacre, Feb. 14, 1929.

Gussler, Eva (AKA: **Eva the Cow**), prom. 1890s. Pickpocket, shoplifter, and member of the White Gang.

Guzik, Harry (Harry Cusick), prom. 1910s. Brothel keeper in the Chicago Levee. Brother of Jake Guzik.

Guzik, Jake (Jake Cusick), (AKA: **Greasy Thumb**), d.1956. Business manager and long time accountant for the Al Capone mob. Prior to this time he ran a string of Levee brothels with his brother Harry.

Guzzino, Sam, d.1981. Long time associate of Alfred Pilotto. Murdered on Oct. 3, 1981, allegedly by Albert Tocco hitmen.

Hairtrigger Block, prom. 1860-70s. Section of Randolph Street between Clark and State, dotted by gambling dens, bagnios, and faro banks.

Hankins, Al, prom. 1860s-80s. One of three brothers who owned a string of "dinner pail" gambling resorts in downtown Chicago that catered to the working men.

Hankins, Effie, prom. 1890s. Leased the House of Mirrors from Lizzie Allen following her retirement in 1896.

Hankins, George, prom. 1860s-80s. Brother of Al and Jeff Hankins, Clark Street gambling bosses. Died a pauper in 1912.

Hankins, Jeff, prom. 1860s-80s. Brother of George and Al Hankins in the gambling syndicate.

Hanley, Edward T., prom. 1980s. President of the Hotel and Restaurant Employees and Bartenders International Union. Alleged to have ties to organized crime leaders, including Anthony Accardo.

Hare, Sam, prom. 1900s-20s. Brothel manager for James Colosimo in the old Levee. Active in Capone vice operations in the 1920s.

Harmening, Edward, d.1925. Independent bootlegger killed in his car with Joe Brooks in 1925.

Harper, Louis, prom. 1860-70s. Owner of the Mansion, an elegant post-fire brothel located on Monroe Street.

Harmon, John, prom. 1870s. Owner of Chicago's first "concert saloon" in the Black Hole district featuring six to eight prostitutes.

Harrison, Carter Jr., prom. 1897-1915. Son of former mayor Carter Harrison Sr. Served as mayor himself from 1897-1905; 1911-15. Closed the Levee by decree in 1912.

Harrison, Carter Sr., d.1893. Powerful five-term mayor of Chicago who permitted the McDonald syndicates to flourish in the 1880s. Assassinated in 1893.

Hartrauft, Julia, prom. 1900s. Levee brothel keeper. Later sold her resort to Ed Weiss.

Hart, Michael, prom. 1900s. Member of the Van Bever white slave gang.

Hart, Mollie, prom. 1900s. Wife of Mike Hart. Procured girls from St. Louis, and forced them into white slavery in the Chicago Levee.

Hasmiller, Henry, d.1924. New York gunman hired by the South Side O'Donnell gang in Chicago. Murdered in 1924.

Hastings, Mary, prom. 1890s. Brussels-born brothel madame who opened a dive in the Custom House Levee in 1892. Forced to leave Chicago in 1897.

Hawkins, Katherine, prom. 1860-70s. Owner of Ramrod Hall, the largest Chicago bordello before the Great Fire of 1871.

Hayes, John, prom. 1920s. Leader of a bombing-extortion gang.

Hedlin, David, prom. 1920s. Member of the Al Capone gang.

Heeney, William, prom. 1920s-50s. Syndicate gambling boss believed responsible for carrying out the assassination of Assistant State's Attorney William McSwiggin.

Heffrous, Patrick, prom. 1880s. Gambling house proprietor.

Heitler, Michael (AKA: **Mike the Pike**), d.1931. Longtime Levee panderer and white slave trafficker who became a bootlegger during prohibition. Murdered by the Capone syndicate in April 1931, after volunteering evidence to the State's Attorney.

Hell's Half Acre, prom. 1870s-90s. One of a dozen Chicago vice-districts to organize after the Chicago Fire. Located on Plymouth Place in the South Loop.

Henry Street Gang, prom. 1880s-90s. Street gang active in the Maxwell Street district.

Herbert, Earl (AKA: **Big Earl**), prom. 1926. Syndicate gunman allied with the Saltis gang. Indicted for the murder of Mitters Foley in 1926.

Herrick, Eleanor (AKA: **Mother Herrick**), prom. 1850s. Owner of the Prairie Queen, a State Street brothel.

Heyer, Adam (AKA: **John Snyder**), d.1929. Chicago racketeer and owner of the North Side garage where he was killed during the St. Valentine's Day Massacre of 1929.

Higgins, Buff, prom. 1880s-90s. Thief, juvenile delinquent and the leader of the Johnson Street Gang. Executed on Mar. 23, 1894 for murder.

Higgins, Harry, d.1929. St. Paul bootlegger murdered on the North Side of Chicago.

Hill, John, prom. 1850s. With his wife Mary, the first to run the "badger game" in Chicago.

Hitchcock, Frank, prom. 1920s. Bootlegger from Burnham, Ill. who defied the Capone mob and was murdered.

Hoban, John, (AKA: **Red**), prom. 1920s. North Side bootlegger.

Hoffman, Peter B., prom. 1920-24. Corrupt Sheriff of Cook County in league with the Torrio-Capone mob. Allowed Frankie Lake and Terry Druggan "furloughs" from the County Jail.

Holbrook, Buck, prom. 1860s. Gambler, safe-robber, and owner of a Randolph Street gambling emporium. His wife Mollie turned prostitute in 1871 after he went to jail.

Holbrook, Mollie, prom. 1870s-90s. Wife of Buck Holbrook. Organized fellow prostitutes into a gang of pickpockets. Sent to prison, but eventually pardoned by President Grover Cleveland.

Holt, George, prom. 1870s. Chicago gambling house proprietor.

Hooper, Murray, prom. 1970s. Ranking member of the Royal Family street gang. Professional assassin.

Hopkins, Harry, prom. 1900s. Partner of Jakie Adler in the Levee. Co-owner of the Silver Dollar.

Howard, Joseph (AKA: **Ragtime Joe**), d.1924. Small-time underworld figure murdered by Al Capone on May 8, 1924, in a Chicago saloon, after he roughed up syndicate bookkeeper Jake Guzik.

Hrubec, Charles (AKA: **Big Hayes**), d.1927. Member of the Saltis gang. Shot and killed with Lefty Koncil on Mar. 11, 1927, while driving through the domain of the South Side O'Donnell gang.

Hubacek, Hayes, prom. 1920s. Member of the Joe Saltis gang. Murdered by Ralph Sheldon's gang.

Hughes, William (AKA: **Tootsie**, prom. 1900s. Maxwell Street thief, and member of the Valley Gang.

Humphreys, Murray Llewellyn (AKA: **The Camel**), 1899-1965. Emerged as a top syndicate boss in Chicago following the death of Frank Nitti, in 1943. Active through the 1960s.

Hunt, Samuel McPherson (AKA: **Golf Bag**), d.1955. Capone gangster and rackets boss who concealed his shotgun in a golf bag.

Hustion, Eugene, prom. 1900s. Operator of a vicious dive on Bed Bug Row with his wife. Morphine and cocaine supplier in the Levee.

Hyman, Cap, d.1876. Owner of a string of gambling resorts on Randolph Street during the Civil War. Husband of brothel keeper Gentle Annie Stafford.

Inendino, James (AKA: **The Boy**), 1932- . Mafia hitman and associate of Harry Aleman.

Infelice, Ernest Rocco (AKA: **Henry Marks**), 1922- . River Forest mobster allied with Americo DePietto. Narcotics and gambling boss rumored to have taken control of the Chicago rackets, from Joseph Ferriola, in 1988.

Inserro, Vincent Joseph (AKA: **The Saint**), 1911- . Labor racketeer and West Side hitman, who free-lanced in burglary.

Jackson, Edward, prom. 1890s-1930s. Loop pickpocket who led a gang of four men. Arrested at least 2,000 times. Died a pauper in 1932.

Jackson, William (AKA: **Action**), d.1961. Loan shark and assassin. Murdered by the mob in August 1961.

Jacobson, Benjamin (AKA: **Buddy**), prom. 1920s-50s. Bodyguard of Earl "Hymie" Weiss. Graduated from gangland to become secretary of the First Ward Democratic Organization. Convicted on a vote fraud indictment in 1931.

Jahoda, William (AKA: **B.J.**), 1942- . Former syndicate bookmaker and associate of Joseph Ferriola who turned government informant in the Summer of 1989.

Jamericco, Numio, prom. 1920s. Genna gang member shot down by Al Capone gunmen.

Johnson, John V. (AKA: **Mushmouth**), prom. 1890s-1910s. Black gambler and policy boss of South State Street.

Johnson Street Gang, prom. 1880s-90s. Gang of young toughs who frequented the Maxwell Street Police district on the West Side.

Jones, Roy, prom. 1900s-10s. Owner of a Wabash Avenue saloon and brothel. A power in the Levee District for many years. Married to Victoria Shaw.

Jordan, John (AKA: **Pops**), prom. 1900s. Husband of Georgie Spencer. Proprietor of a Twentieth Street resort.

Judd, James, prom. 1860s. Partner of George Trussell, Civil War gambling boss.

Juliano, Lorenzo, prom. 1920s. Chicago gangster, murdered and dumped in a junk heap.

Jungle, the, prom. 1900s. Brothel district bordered by Monroe and Peoria Streets on the near West Side.

Kauffman, Julian (AKA: **Potatoes**), prom. 1920s-30s. Gambler and fence allied with the O'Bannion mob. Operated the Sheridan Wave Tournament Club, a Chicago gambling emporium, with Bugs Moran and Joey Brooks.

Kaufman, Louis, prom. 1943. Chicago gangster convicted in 1943 of shaking down Hollywood movie moguls of millions of dollars.

Keane, Thomas (AKA: **Morrie**), d.1923. Beer-runner for Spike O'Donnell. Killed by Frank McErlane during a hijack attempt on Dec. 1, 1923.

Kearney, Aloysius, d.1930. Labor racketeer and associate of Red McLaughlin. Murdered on June 9, 1930.

Kelly, Daniel, prom. 1890s. Loop pickpocket.

Kelly, David, prom. 1900s. Co-leader of the Formby gang with Bill Dulfer and Jimmy Formby.

Kenna, Michael (AKA: **Hinky Dink**), prom. 1890s-1930s. Democratic alderman and political boss of the vice-ridden First Ward for nearly forty years. Systemized the payoffs and graft collection.

Kennedy, Patrick, prom. 1890s. Downtown pickpocket.

Kilmas, Leo, d.1924. Waiter at the Hawthorne Inn, Al Capone's suburban headquarters. Killed by the West Side O'Donnells in 1924.

King, Patrick, d.1930. Small time hood found murdered in Terry O'Connor's gambling den in December 1930.

King, Patsy, prom. 1900s. West Side gambler and bookmaking boss.

Kinzie Street Gang, prom. 1900s. Chicago street gang.

Kolb, Matthew, d.1931. Left the Al Capone mob to join Roger Touhy's suburban bootlegging gang. Kidnapped by Capone men, released, and then later killed.

Koncil, Frank (AKA: **Lefty**), d.1927. Private chauffeur for Joe Saltis. Executed by Capone gunmen on Mar. 11, 1927 after being acquitted of murdering Mitters Foley.

Konvalinka, Edward, prom. 1923. Cicero politician who promised Al Capone a free hand if he could help get him elected to office in 1923.

Korocek, Alex, prom. 1920s. Supplier of tommy guns and ammunition to the Capone gang.

Kruse, Leslie Earl (AKA: **Killer Kane**), 1906- . One-time bodyguard of Jake Guzik. Became syndicate chieftain in the Lake County-Waukegan area.

Kunski, Peter (AKA: **Three Finger**), prom. 1920s. Bomber and terrorist affiliated with the Joe Saltis mob. Killed when one of his devices accidentally went off.

Laborer's International Union, prom. 1970s-80s. Tenth largest labor union in the U.S., allegedly controlled by Chicago gangsters Al Pilotto, and Vincent Solano.

Labriola, Paul (AKA: **Needlenose**), d.1921. Political lieutenant of Alderman Johnny Powers. Murdered by the Genna brothers on Mar. 28, 1921.

LaBarbera, Joseph Anthony (AKA: **Joe the Barber**), 1910- . New York hoodlum, who moved to Chicago, in the mid-1940s, to become active in North Side Chicago vice operations.

LaCava, Joseph, prom. 1920s. Brother of Louis LaCava, and a syndicate presence in Cicero.

LaCava, Louis, prom. 1920s. Capone gangster banished to obscurity in 1927 after attempting to appropriate the Cicero territory.

Lake, Frank, prom. 1920s. Partner of Terry Druggan, and ruler of the West Side Valley Gang. Went to jail with his partner in 1924 for violation of the Volstead Law. Convicted of income tax evasion and sent to a federal prison in 1932.

LaPietra, Angelo, 1920- . South Side mob boss. Currently in prison.

LaPietra, James, 1927- . Brother of Angelo LaPietra. Boss of South Side mob operations.

LaPorte, Frank (**Francesco Liparota**), b.1901. Former syndicate boss of South Cook and Will Counties. Ruled vice and gambling from Calumet City to Kankakee, Ill.

Lardino, John (AKA: **John Nardi**), 1908- . Syndicate gunman and labor racketeer. Boss of several retail and service unions.

Lattyak, Edward, prom. 1920s. Professional gunman who worked for the Ralph Sheldon gang.

Lavenuto, Sam, d.1926. West Side "alky cooker" killed by the Capone mob on July 15, 1926.

Lawrence, Harry, prom. 1880s. Business partner of Mike McDonald. Co-owner of the "Store," McDonald's deluxe downtown casino.

Leathers, William, prom. 1910s-20s. Levee hoodlum who joined forces with Dion O'Bannion in the 1920s.

Lehman, "Dutchy", prom. 1880s. Conman and bunko artist.

Leonard, William (AKA: **Old Bill**), prom. 1860s. Partner of George Trussell, Civil War gambling boss.

Le Presti, Felix, prom. 1920s. Mob figure who was tortured and killed.

Levee, the, prom. 1890-1920. Famous South Side vice district for nearly three decades. Located in the politically sensitive First Ward, controlled by Aldermen Hinky Dink Kenna and Bathhouse John Coughlan.

Levine, Hymie (AKA: **Loud Mouth**), prom. 1920s-40s. Capone gunman who became a gambling boss in the 1930s.

Lewis, Frank (AKA: **Dago Frank**), prom. 1900s. One of the rulers of the South Side Levee. Owner of a saloon and bordello.

Lewis, Joseph (AKA: **Hungry Joe**), prom. 1880s. Conman who swindled Oscar Wilde out of several thousand dollars in 1882.

Lewis, Joseph E., prom. 1920s. Popular nightclub entertainer of the 1920s, who was viciously knifed in a Chicago hotel by "Machine Gun" Jack McGurn for allegedly breaking his contractual obligations with the Capone mob.

Lewis, Samuel, prom. 1930s-50s. Syndicate juice operator and political associate of Donald Parrillo, syndicate-controlled alderman who succeeded John D'Arco in the First Ward.

Lingle, Alfred (AKA: **Jake**), d.1930. Sixty-five dollar a week reporter for the Chicago *Tribune*, who earned a fortune through his secret dealings with the mob. Murdered by Leo Brothers on June 9, 1930, in a crowded subway tunnel.

Little Cheyenne, prom. 1870s-80s. One of a dozen vice-districts to organize after the Chicago Fire. Located north of the Badlands.

Little, George, prom. 1890s-1900s. Owner of the Imperial, a Levee bordello located on Armour Ave.

Little Hell, prom. 1870s. West Side district, located near Crosby and Larrabee Streets populated by underworld figures and fugitives in the years following the Chicago Fire.

Little Hell, prom. 1900s-1920s. North Side district south of Division Street to the Chicago River. Notorious haven for strong-arm burglars, sexual degenerates, and tough criminal gangs.

Ljubas, Ante, prom. 1970s. Hit man allegedly retained by Harry Aleman to assassinate John Badovinac, Croatian nationalist, in 1975.

Loesch, Frank, prom. 1920s. President of the Chicago Crime Commission who solicited Al Capone for a "fair and honest" election in 1928.

Lolordo, Joseph, prom. 1928. Body guard of Tony Lombardo. Elder brother of Pasquale Lolardo.

Lolordo, Pasquale (AKA: **Patsy**), d.1929. Successor to Tony Lombardo as the head of the Unione Siciliano. Murdered in his apartment on Jan. 8, 1929, allegedly by Joe Aiello working in tandem with the Bugs Moran gang.

Lo Mantio, Angelo, prom. 1927. Milwaukee hoodlum hired by the Aiello gang to try to kill Al Capone.

Lombardi, Frank, d.1916. Nineteenth Ward politician who became the first casualty of the Powers-D'Andrea feud in February 1916.

Lombardo, Antonio, d.1928. Briefly ruled the powerful Unione Siciliano until he was shot in the back of the head in downtown Chicago, Sept. 7, 1928, by Joseph Aiello and his brothers, who desired to take over the organization themselves.

Lombardo, Joseph (AKA: **Joey the Clown**), prom. 1960s-80s. Extortionist, labor union racketeer, and long-time Mafia assassin. Convicted in December 1982 of attempting to bribe Sen. Howard Cannon of Nevada.

Lovejoy, Rose, prom. 1870s. Owner of a Fourth Avenue brothel.

Lowry, Eva, prom. 1900s. Manager of a Levee bordello on behalf of Maurice Van Bever.

Ludlum, Lou, prom. 1880s. Conman and bunko artist.

Luzi, Frank, prom. 1960s. Nephew and chauffeur of Frank LaPorte. Ran a bail bonding company.

McCafey, Therese, prom. 1900s. Wife of Bob Gray. Proprietress of the Levee brothel California.

McCann, Edward C., prom. 1909. Chicago Police Inspector sent to prison in 1909 for accepting bribes from West Side Levee bosses.

McCarthy, Daniel, prom. 1920s. Member of Dion O'Bannion's North Side gang.

McCue, "Rags", d.1924. Rum-runner for the West Side O'Donnell gang. Murdered by James "Red" Doherty in 1924.

McCullough, Robert (AKA: **Big Bob**), prom. 1924. Cicero bootlegger named as one of the killers of Assistant State's Attorney William McSwiggin.

McDonald, Michael Cassius, d.1907. Powerful gambling boss during the 1870s and 1880s. Owner of a lavish "resort" called the "Store."

McElligot, Thomas, d.1929. Member of the West Side O'Donnell mob, murdered in a Loop saloon on May 29, 1929.

McErlane, Frank, prom. 1920s. Chicago bootlegger and professional killer. Was the first to use a Thompson sub-machine gun on Sept. 7, 1923, when he murdered Jerry O'Connor, from a moving car.

McErlane, Vincent, prom. 1920s. Younger brother of Frankie McErlane. Co-ruler of the Saltis-McErlane mob, who narrowly escaped assassination, in July 1926.

McFall, Daniel, prom. 1920s. South Side Chicago gangster affiliated with the Saltis-McErlane bootlegging gang.

McGann, James, prom. 1890s. Local gangster in the Maxwell Street district. Worked in tandem with his five sons.

McGarigle, William, prom. 1880s. Police chief of Chicago in 1882. Allied with Mike McDonald. Indicted for graft in 1882. Fled to Canada.

McGeoahegan, Daniel, prom. 1920s-30s. Beer runner, murderer, and bank robber from the South Side "Back of the Yards" district.

McGinnis, Thomas, prom. 1900s. Gambling boss and bookmaker in the downtown Loop district.

McGovern, Hugh (AKA: **Stubby**), prom. 1920s. Gambler, swindler, and hired gunman. Left Ragen's Colts to join Ralph Sheldon's gang.

McGraw, Bill, prom. 1840s. Gambler, and bookmaker. One of the first operators of a roulette wheel in Chicago.

McGraw, John, prom. 1890s. Co-ruler of the Mortell-McGraw gang.

McGurn, Jack (**James DeMora**) (AKA: **Machine Gun Jack**), 1904-36. Former prize fighter who went to work as a gunman for Al Capone. Believed to have planned the 1929 St. Valentine's Day Massacre. Killed in a Milwaukee bowling alley on Feb. 14, 1936.

McLaughlin, Eugene (AKA: **Red**), d.1930. Petty gangster murdered in June 1930, and dumped into the river.

McLaughlin, John J. (AKA: **Boss**), prom. 1930. State legislator and backer of the Bugs Moran Gang. Opened a deluxe gambling emporium in 1930.

McNally, James, prom. 1880s. Conman and bunko artist.

McNichols, Thomas, d.1930. Small-time bootlegger killed during a shootout on Madison Street with Jimmy Schupe on July 31, 1930.

McPadden, William (AKA: **Gunner**), d.1929. One-time member of Ragen's Colts and professional killer; worked for the Sheldon booze gang in the 1920s. Killed by George Maloney on Jan. 1, 1930.

McSwiggin, William H., d.1926. Chicago Assistant State's Attorney thought to be mixed up with the Klondike O'Donnell booze gang in some way. Machine gunned to death in Cicero, Ill. on Apr. 27, 1926.

Maddox, Claude (**John Edward Moore**, AKA: **Screwy Moore, John Manning**), prom. 1920s-30s. Leader of the Northwest Side Circus Gang, which was allied with Al Capone.

Madigan, Harry, prom. 1920s. Owner of the Pony Inn, a syndicate hangout during the 1920s. Arrested on kidnapping and extortion charges in 1923.

Magnabosco, Marco, prom. 1920s. Chicago hoodlum murdered by the Aiello gang.

Malaga, Samuel, prom. 1920s. Bodyguard of John "Dingbat" Oberta.

Malloy, John (AKA: **Snapper**), prom. 1880s. Conman and bunko artist.

Maloney, George, 1892-1930. Chicago gunman who was the first to saw off both barrels of a .38 revolver. Formed his own bootlegging gang with Michael "Bubs" Quinlan.

Maloy, Thomas, d.1935. Labor union boss murdered on Feb. 4, 1935 by Frank Nitti gunmen.

Mangano, Lawrence (AKA: **Dago**), d.1944. Manager of beer and liquor distribution for the Al Capone syndicate. In later years a West Side gambling boss before his assassination in August 1944.

Manno, Nicholas (AKA: **Jeff**), prom. 1950. One of three Manno brothers named in the Kefauver Report as policy bosses.

Manno, Patrick, prom. 1940s. Chicago policy boss and numbers racketeer who ran the Roman Silver Wheel.

Manno, Thomas (AKA: **Mousey**), prom. 1950. Brother of Pat Manno. Syndicate policy boss.

Manson, Rose, prom. 1890s. Owner of the Looking Glass House, a mirrored brothel.

Manzie, Frederick (AKA: **Rick**), d.1976. Husband of entertainer Barbara McNair, suspected of having strong ties to the Chicago Crime Syndicate. Murdered in Las Vegas Dec. 15, 1976.

Marcello, Sam, d.1974. Chicago Mafia loanshark murdered with Joseph Grisafe on July 6, 1974.

Marchone, Pasqualino (AKA: **Pat Marcy**), prom. 1930s-60s. Political henchman of First Ward Alderman John D'Arco in the 1950s. Imprisoned for robbery in the 1930s.

Marcus, Leonard, d.1957. Chicago banker shot to death in 1957, allegedly by Sam Giancana.

Marcus, Sam, prom. 1920s. Chicago gunman. Bodyguard to Al Capone.

Market Streeters, prom. 1910s-20s. Street gang, active near Market Street and Chicago Avenues.

Marks, William, prom. 1920s. High level associate of Bugs Moran. Active in the mob-run Central Cleaning Company.

Martin, John, prom. 1880s. Conman and bunko artist.

Martin, Morris, prom. 1880s. Business partner of Mike McDonald, and co-owner of the "Store."

Marx, Gustave, d.1904. One of the four Car Barn Bandits that committed a series of robberies and murders in 1903. Executed Apr. 22, 1904.

Masterson, "Paddy", prom. 1890s. Loop pickpocket.

Matrisciano, George (AKA: **Martini**), prom. 1920. Little Italy bombmaker who worked for Joseph Sangerman.

May, John, d.1929. Car mechanic for the Bugs Moran gang who happened to be in the garage on the day of the St. Valentine's Day Massacre, in 1929. Shot and killed with the others.

Maybaum, Charles, prom. 1910s. Levee brothel keeper. Leader of one of three vice rings in the South Side district.

Maybaum, Julius, prom. 1910s. Brother of Charles Maybaum. Co-owner of a Levee resort.

Meeghan, George, d.1923. South Side bootlegger allied with Edward "Spike" O'Donnell. Murdered on Sept. 17, 1923.

Merlo, Michael, d.1924. Boss of the Unione Sicilane until he died of natural causes in November 1924. A peacemaker who abhorred violence, Merlo was thought to be Dion O'Bannion's only ally in the Italian underworld.

Merry, Christopher, prom. 1890s. Leader of the Henry Street Gang. Executed for murdering his wife.

Mesi, Sam, b.1900. Third generation gangster, prominent on Chicago's West Side. Owner of three off-track betting operations that grossed $800,000 annually.

Messino, William (AKA: **Wee Willie**), 1917- . "Juice" collector for the Chicago mob. Later convicted of armed robbery.

Micello, Giuseppe, prom. 1920s. Murdered in the presence of 200 spectators. The killers got away.

Millard, Zoe, prom. 1910. Owner and proprietor of a Levee bordello.

Miller, Bob, prom. 1900s. Saloon keeper in the West Side Levee.

Miller, Davy, prom. 1920s. Gambler and bootlegger hooked up with Dion O'Bannion.

Miller, George, prom. 1890s. Titular head of the White Gang in the 1890s.

Miller, "Big Heinie", prom. 1900s. Early leader of the Valley Gang.

Miller, "Kid", prom. 1880s. Conman and bunko artist.

Miller, Mary, prom. 1890s. Co-ruler with her husband George, of the White Gang in the 1890s.

Mirro, James (AKA: **Cowboy**), 1913- . West Suburban loan shark, and gambler. Convicted of transporting and concealing stolen goods.

Monahan, Michael, prom. 1890s-1900s. Footpad and Levee brothel keeper.

Mondi, James, prom. 1920s. Gambling boss in the Al Capone syndicate.

Mongoven, Leo, prom. 1920s. George "Bugs" Moran's personal bodyguard.

Monistero, Samuel, d.1930. Mobster in the Joe Aiello gang. Murdered on May 31, 1930.

Monroe, Jerry, prom. 1870s. Dive-keeper and owner of the Oyster Palace on Van Burne Street, in the Little Cheyenne district.

Moore, Edward, prom. 1920s. Capone mobster implicated in the shooting death of William McSwiggin.

Moore, Flossie, prom. 1889-93. Pickpocket, hold-up woman, and panel worker in the Custom House Levee. Sent to prison for five years in 1893.

Moore, Mollie, prom. 1870s. Chicago brothel madame.

Moore, "Pony", prom. 1910. Black gambler and owner of a Levee saloon and bagnio, the Turf Exchange.

Moran, George (AKA: **Bugs**), 1893-1957. Former bank robber turned bootlegger. Moran took over the reins of Chicago's North Side mob following the assassinations of Earl "Hymie" Weiss, and Dion O'Bannion. Capone ordered the St. Valentine's Day Massacre in an attempt to kill Moran. Moran survived and died of natural causes in 1957.

Moreci, Agostino, and **Moreci, Antonio**, d.1926. Yeast and sugar suppliers to the Genna gang. The Morecis were murdered on Jan. 27, 1926.

Moresci, Joseph, prom. 1920. Brother-in-law of James Colosimo. A prime suspect in his murder on May 11, 1920.

Moresco, Victoria, prom. 1895-1920. Wife of James Colosimo. Managed several Levee brothels with her husband.

Morgan Street Gang, prom. 1900s. Chicago street gang.

Morris, Evander, prom. 1860s. Gambler and card sharp active on the Hairtrigger Block in the 1860s.

Mortell, William, prom. 1890s. Gang boss of the Mortell-McGraw outfit, active in the Maxwell Street District.

Mortell, John, prom. 1880s-90s. Member of the Johnson Street Gang.

Morton, Samuel (AKA: **Nails**), prom. 1920s. War hero turned prohibition bootlegger. Kicked to death by his horse, which in turn was shot by vengeful O'Bannion gunmen.

Mosel, Emma, prom. 1900s. White Slaver in the Levee district.

Mott, Robert, prom. 1907. Saloon owner and gambler who took over Mushmouth Johnson's rackets in 1907.

Murphy, William, prom. 1900s. Saloon owner in the West Side Levee.

Murphy, Timothy (AKA: **Big Tim**), d.1928. Strong arm killer and labor union organizer. He was believed responsible for the 1920 murder of rival Moss Enright. Assassinated in his South Side home on June 26, 1928.

Murray, Patrick (AKA: **Paddy**), d.1926. Bodyguard of Earl "Hymie" Weiss. Killed with his boss outside Holy Name Cathedral on Oct. 11, 1926.

Myrick, W.F., prom. 1844. Chicago bookmaker and gambler who laid out the city's first racetrack in 1844.

Neglia, Thomas, d.1943. Prohibition-era gangster murdered in a Chicago barbershop in December 1943.

Neidermeyer, Peter, 1881-1904. One of the four Car Barn Bandits that committed robbery and murder in 1903. Executed on Mar. 1, 1904.

Nerone, Joseph (AKA: **Spano, the Cavalier**), d.1926. Betrayed the Genna gang. Killed Tony Genna in 1925, and in turn was murdered a year later.

Neubeck, Richard, prom. 1980s. Jewel thief indicted in April 1981 for a $1 million theft shipped through the United Airlines terminal at O'Hare Airport.

Neumann, Lawrence, prom. 1983. First Chicago hitman to face the death penalty after being convicted of murdering Robert Brown, a Chicago jeweler in 1979.

Newberry, Ted, prom. 1920s. Right-hand man of George "Bugs" Moran who defected to the Capone mob following the St. Valentine's Day Massacre. Ranked number two on the public enemies list in 1931.

Newmark, Benjamin (AKA: **Jew Ben**), prom. 1920s. Former investigator for the State's Attorney's office who became a syndicate gunman, extortionist and counterfeiter.

Nicoletti, Charles, d.1977. Associate of Sam Giancana. Ranked number four in the Chicago mob at the time of his murder on Mar. 29, 1977—one thought to be carried out by Tony Spilotro.

Niemoth, Willie, prom. 1920s. Member of the Joe Saltis gang. Suspected of having murdered John "Dingbat" Oberta.

Nitti, Frank (Frank Nitto), (AKA: **The Enforcer**), d.1943. Triggerman and later mob treasurer for Al Capone. In 1932 Nitti was appointed head of the Chicago family at an "organizational meeting". Facing a lengthy prison sentence, he committed suicide in April 1943.

Noonan, Mary, prom. 1880s. Wife of Mike McDonald. Shot and wounded a Chicago police officer on Nov. 23, 1878.

Nootbar, Max, prom. 1914. Incorruptible Chicago police captain sent in to clean up the Levee, in July 1914.

Norton, John, prom. 1880s. Conman and swindler who bilked Charles Francis Adams out of $7,000 in 1882.

Nuccio, Dominick, b.1895. Chicago hitman, who joined Al Capone in the 1920s after leaving the Gloriana Gang. A prime suspect in at least ten murder investigations.

O'Bannion, Charles Dion, 1892-1924. One-time altar boy who rose steadily through the ranks, until he controlled his own Chicago mob. O'Bannion was killed in his flowershop by Capone gunmen, in 1924.

Oberta, John (AKA: **Dingbat**), prom. 1920s. West Side Polish gangster allied with Joe Saltis. Accused of murdering Mitters Foley.

O'Brien, Michael, prom. 1850s. Burglar, and vice-boss of the Sands District in the 1850s.

O'Brien, Thomas (AKA: **King of the Bunko Men**), prom. 1880s. Expert swindler who fled to Paris in 1895.

O'Brien, William W., prom. 1926. Chicago criminal attorney wounded by gunshots while in the company of Earl "Hymie" Weiss, on Oct. 11, 1926.

O'Connor, Jerry, d.1923. Henchman of Edward "Spike" O'Donnell, murdered Sept. 7, 1923.

O'Donnell, Edward (AKA: **Spike**), prom. 1920s. Former bankrobber turned bootlegger. Together with his three brothers, Spike O'Donnell challenged Al Capone for supremacy on the South Side, but was driven out of Chicago in 1925 after being shot at by Frankie McErlane.

O'Donnell, Steven, prom. 1920s. Brother of Edward "Spike" O'Donnell.

O'Donnell, Thomas, prom. 1920s. Brother of Edward "Spike" O'Donnell.

O'Donnell, Walter, d.1925. Brother of Edward "Spike" O'Donnell. Murdered in 1925.

O'Donnell, William (AKA: **Klondike**), and **O'Donnell, Miles**, and **O'Donnell, Barnard**, prom. 1920s. A West Side Irish gang who controlled the bootleg rackets between Chicago Avenue and Madison Street. The brothers rebelled against Al Capone's rule in 1926, and were deposed following the assassination of William McSwiggin.

O'Hara, Daniel, prom. 1920s. Chicago street gang leader.

O'Hare, Edward J. (AKA: **Artful Eddie**), d.1939. Lawyer, and business partner of Al Capone in several dog tracks. Murdered by the syndicate on Nov. 8, 1939 after his cover as an informant was blown.

O'Leary, James, d.1926. South Side gambling boss, poolroom, and racing wire promoter. Rival of Mont Tennes, and a partner of John Condon.

Oliver, Michael, d.1979. Associate of Gerald Scarpelli involved in shaking down suburban porno book store operators. Assassinated in 1979.

O'Malley, John, prom. 1900s. Loop gambler and bookmaker.

O'Malley, Patrick, prom. 1900s. Saloon owner and gambling boss.

Oaks, Daniel, prom. 1860s-70s. Early partner of Mike McDonald. Opened a gambling resort in Chicago in 1867.

Original Andrews, prom. 1870s. Partner of Lesser Friedberg.

Orlando, Andrew, d.1921. Associate of Nineteenth Ward boss Anthony D'Andrea. Assassinated by the Powers forces in July, 1921.

Owens, Thomas, prom. 1910s. Owner of a Levee café on Armour Ave.

Paine, "Ginger Heel", prom. 1870s. Partner of Hattie Briggs. Ran her Customs House Place brothel.

Palermo, Dominick (AKA: **Tootsie**), 1918- . South Suburban crime boss who succeeded Albert Tocco after he was indicted on extortion charges in October 1988.

Panice, Herbert, 1922- . Chicago Heights brothel-keeper who became a government witness against Albert Tocco in 1989.

Patrick, Leonard, 1913- . One of three hoodlums indicted for the murder of James Ragen, in 1946. The case was nolle prossed. Current boss of the far North Side to the Wisconsin border.

Patton, John (AKA: **The Boy Mayor**), prom. 1918-30. Mayor of Burnham, Ill. in 1918. A youthful thug who permitted the Capone syndicate to operate in his town without interference. Active in Miami gambling in later years.

Pellar, Sam, prom. 1926. Private chauffeur for Earl "Hymie" Weiss. Badly wounded by gunshots outside Holy Name Cathedral on Oct. 11, 1926.

Pentenza, Rocco, prom. 1950s-60s. Member of the Forty-Two Gang and associate of Sam Giancana.

Percy, Valerie, d.1966. Daughter of Senator Charles Percy. Murdered in 1966, allegedly by Chicago organized crime figures.

Perry, Frank, prom. 1920s. Bodyguard of Al Capone.

Perry, Harry, prom. 1900s-10s. Policy gambler and partner of Social Smith in the operation of the *City of Traverse*, a Chicago gambling ship.

Petrocelli, William (AKA: **Butch**), prom. 1980s. South Suburban mobster accused of masterminding the 1980 assassination of fellow gangster William Dauber and his wife by FBI informant Gerald Scarpelli.

Pettit, Larry, 1925- . Mob boss in the far northern sections of Cook and Lake County, extending to the Wisconsin border.

Phillips, Richard, prom. 1920s. One-time business partner of James Colosimo and prohibition bootlegger.

Pierce, Ralph (AKA: **Robert Symons**), b.1903. South Side gambling boss formerly associated with Al Capone. In later years, a lieutenant of Sam Battaglia and Sam Giancana.

Pilotto, Alfred, prom. 1970s-80s. Boss of Chicago's South Suburban rackets. Survived an assassination attempt on July 25, 1981. Received a twenty year prison sentence in 1982.

Pinelli, Anthony R., Sr., b.1899. Rackets boss of Lake County, Ind., in the 1940s. Moved to California in 1953, but maintained an influence in the Midwest. Former member of the "board of directors" of the Chicago crime syndicate.

Pitt, John, prom. 1900s. Owner of the Why Not?, a Levee brothel. Arrested for white slavery in 1907.

Plant, Daisy, prom. 1870s-90s. Daughter of Roger Plant. Owned a bordello with her sister Kitty in the South Clark Street Levee.

Plant, Roger, prom. 1850s-60s. Englishman who owned the "Under the Willow" gambling resort and brothel on Wells Street.

Plant, Roger, Jr., prom. 1868-94. Took over his father's business in 1868, and ran the bordello and saloon into the 1890s.

Plescia, Peter, d.1930. Collector for the Joe Aiello gang, murdered on May 31, 1930.

Polito, Joseph, d.1967. Murdered on Mar. 7, 1967 after testifying about the $50,000 Vogue Jewelry fraud.

Pontelli, Michael, d.1944. Bodyguard of Lawrence Mangano. Assassinated with his boss in Cicero, in August 1944.

Pope, Frank (AKA: **The Millionaire Newsboy**), prom. 1920s. Chicago gangster who belonged to the Torrio gang. Manager of the Hawthorne Smoke Shop in Cicero.

Porto, Pietro, prom. 1920s. Murdered outside a Chicago cigar store.

Post, George, prom. 1880s. Conman and bunko artist.

Potenza, Rocco (AKA: **The Parrot**), 1912- . Rackets boss of Northwest Cook County. Specializes in dice and card games.

Powell, Maurice (AKA: **Pimp**), prom. 1970s. Original leader of the Royal Family criminal gang.

Powers, John (AKA: **Johnny de Pow**), prom. 1888-1921. Chicago alderman and political boss of the West Side 19th Ward for nearly forty years. Engaged in a protracted "war" with the Italian underworld faction led by Philip D'Andrea in 1921.

Pranno, Rocco Salvatore, 1916- . Prominent in the western suburbs of Chicago. A vicious syndicate hoodlum arrested at various times for bombing, armed robbery, and murder.

Prignano, Albert, prom. 1920s-30s. Twentieth-Ward alderman who was an agent of the Al Capone gang. Assassinated by syndicate gunmen in 1935.

Prio, Ross (Rosario Fabricini, Rosario Priolo), 1900-72. North Side boss of vice and gambling. Identified as one of seven "power" mobsters by Joe Valachi in 1962.

Pulizzi, Peter, prom. 1920s. Gangster murdered in his own car on the Chicago's West Side.

Quan, "Dinky", prom. 1920s. Labor union thug who attempted to muscle in on the Tire Workers and Vulcanizer's Union. Killed by Chicago Police.

Quinlan, Michael (AKA: **Bubs**), prom. 1920s. Former bodyguard of gambler Tommy Tuit. Organized his own booze gang with George Maloney, specializing in Canadian whisky.

Quinlan, Walter (AKA: **The Runt**), prom. 1910s-20s. Saloon owner and gunman. Killed by Paddy Ryan's son as an act of vengeance.

Quinn, James (AKA: **Hot Stove**), prom. 1900s. Political boss, and gambler affiliated with Mont Tennes on the North Side.

Quirk, Michael, Member of the West Side O'Donnell gang. Died in the Fox Lake Massacre, June 1930.

Rafferty, John, prom. 1893-1910. Assumed leadership of Chicago's bunko men following Mike McDonald's retirement in 1893. A fixture on Whisky Row after 1893.

Ragen, Frank, prom. 1900-20. President and co-founder of Ragen's Colts Street gang, active on Chicago's South Side. Later a force in local politics.

Ragen, James, Sr., d.1946. Boss of the syndicate racing wire in Chicago. Brother of Frank Ragen. Executed by the mob on June 24, 1946.

Ragen, Michael, prom. 1900s. Brother of Frank and James Ragen. Co-founder of the Colts.

Ragen's Colts, prom. 1902-1925. Organized as Ragen's Athletic and Benevolent Association. Devolved from a sports club to a vicious South Side German-Irish street gang active in bootlegging.

Ragucci, Anthony, d.1953. Syndicate subboss found murdered on Oct. 1, 1953.

Randall, Otis, prom. 1860s. Partner of George Trussell, Civil War era gambling boss.

Rappaport, John, d.1924. Member of the South Side O'Donnell gang. Killed by Saltis men on Dec. 19, 1924 in retaliation for shooting Mitters Foley.

Rayola, Albert John (Alberto Capone), d.1980. Brother of Al Capone. Involved in south suburban gambling operations. Described as an "overlord" of vice and gambling in the Hickory Hills area according to published reports in 1969. Last of the active Capones.

Raymond, Anthony, d.1923. Chicago bootlegger. Murdered in 1923.

Reagan, Timothy, prom. 1860s. Owner of a Clark Street grog shop and vice den.

Reilly, Michael, d.1929. Former member of the West Side O'Donnell mob, who was murdered with his partner George Clifford on Apr. 14, 1929.

Ricca, Paul (Paul DeLucia) (AKA: **The Waiter**), 1897-1972. Selected by Meyer Lansky to head up the Chicago crime syndicate, Ricca played the "waiting game" to eventually become top boss of the outfit in the late 1940s. He was succeeded by Sam Giancana for a few years in the 1950s, but regained the top position and held on until his death in 1972.

Riley, William (AKA: **Silver**), prom. 1890s. One of the first professional gamblers to specialize in racetrack bookmaking.

Rio, Frank (AKA: **Frank Kline, Slippery**), prom. 1920s. Bodyguard of Al Capone and top triggerman for the mob. Named as one of the killers of Assistant State's Attorney William McSwiggin.

Ritchie, Emma (AKA: **French Em**, prom. 1870s-90s. Owner of the largest brothel in Chicago following the 1871 fire.

Rito, John (AKA: **Billiken**), d.1929. A former Genna Bootlegger who hooked up with Ted Newberry. Found murdered on Nov. 17, 1929.

Robbins, Watt, prom. 1860s. Gambler and card-sharp prominent on the Hairtrigger Block of the 1860s.

Roderick, Ike, prom. 1910s-20s. Professional bondsman who supplied cash bonds on demand to any gangster with the ability to pay.

Rodgers, Alva, prom. 1970s-80s. Car thief, mafia henchman, and government informant.

Roeski, Emil, prom. 1903. Associate of the Car Barn Bandits. Sent to prison for life in 1904.

Rogers, John, prom. 1900s. Chicago alderman and gambling boss on the West Side.

Rolfe, Louise, prom. 1929. Girlfriend of Jack McGurn who became known as the "Blonde Alibi" after covering for him during the St. Valentine's Day Massacre investigation.

Romaine, Harry, prom. 1880s. Gambling house proprietor.

Romano, Frank, prom. 1920s. Lieutenant in the Al Capone gang.

Romano, Louis, prom. 1930s. Agent of Frank Nitti, who assumed control of Local 278 of the Chicago Bartenders and Beverage Dispenser's Union. Indicted for murder in 1922, but cleared.

Rosanova, Lou, prom. 1970s. Labor racketeer identified by the Chicago Crime Commission as Chicago Mafia figure.

Rosenberg, Alan, d.1967. Chicago businessman who was in debt to Felix Alderiso. Beaten to death on Mar. 16, 1967.

Rosenberg, Moe, prom. 1920s-30s. Ex-convict and junkyard owner who became the syndicate political boss of the Twenty-Fourth Ward. A powerful backer of Mayor Anton Cermak.

Rosenheim, Julius, d.1930. Gangster turned informant. Murdered in Chicago Feb. 4, 1930.

Roti, Fred, prom. 1960s-80s. Alderman of the syndicate-infested First Ward of Chicago. Alleged to have ties to the mob.

Routzong, Andrew, prom. 1860s. Owner of a Clark Street saloon and hang out for Civil War bounty jumpers.

Royal Family, prom. 1970s-80s. Black criminal gang patterned after the U.S. Mafia. Involved in armed robbery, drug trafficking and contract murder.

Rugendorf, Leo, prom. 1960s-70s. Bail bondsman and an associate of Phil Alderisio.

Ruse, "Boss", prom. 1880s. Conman and bunko artist.

Russo, Anthony K., d.1927. St. Louis gunman hired by the Aiello gang in 1927. Murdered by the Capone gang on Aug. 10, 1927.

Russo, James, d.1926. Independent manufacturer of bootleg liquor in the "Little Italy" section of Chicago. Murdered by Capone gunmen on July 15, 1926.

Ryan, William, prom. 1890s. Loop pickpocket.

Ryan, John, prom. 1860s. Owner of the Concert Saloon, a vice den and hangout for Chicago hoodlums.

Ryan, Frank (AKA: **Chew Tobacco**), prom. 1920s-30s. Chicago hoodlum and First Ward political figure.

Ryan, Michael, prom. 1914. Corrupt police captain who commanded the Levee district before being ousted in 1914.

Ryan, "Paddy" (AKA: **Paddy the Bear**), d.1920. Took over the Valley Gang from Red Bolton. Assassinated by Walter Quinlan in 1920.

Ryan, Robert Emmet, prom. 1920s. Member of the Al Capone gang. Murdered gambler Jimmy Walsh in 1929.

Ryan, William, prom. 1920s. Labor racketeer killed by Chicago Police during a protracted shootout.

Saffo the Greek, prom. 1914. Levee vice-lord. Forced to flee the district in 1914.

St. Valentine's Day Massacre, 1929. Seven members of the Bugs Moran gang were machine gunned to death in a North Clark Street garage by rival mobsters posing as policemen. The gunmen are commonly believed to have been members of the Al Capone Gang.

Saltis, Joseph (AKA: **Polack Joe**), prom. 1920s. Southwest Side gang boss, bootlegger, and partner of Frankie MacEarlane.

Salvatore, Rocco, 1911- . Former chauffeur for Sam Battaglia. North Side gambling figure.

Sammons, James (AKA: **Fur**), Labor racketeer allied with the West Side O'Donnells. One of twenty-eight hoods named to the first "Public Enemies" list by the Chicago Crime Commission in 1923.

Sands, the, prom. 1850s. Early Chicago vice-district torn down by order of Mayor John Wentworth in 1857. Located on the near-North Side.

Sangerman, Joseph, prom. 1920. Official of the Chicago Barber's Union. Organized a bombing-terrorist squad that supplanted Jim Sweeney's.

Satan's Mile, prom. 1870s-80s. South Side vice-district; State Street from Van Buren to Twenty-Second.

Saulsbury, Ross, prom. 1880s. Member of the John Turner gang. His wife was often recruited to carry out the various swindles.

Scalise, John, d.1929. Teamed with Albert Anselmi to form a deadly assassination team. Murdered by Al Capone in May 1929 after attempting to usurp the gang lord's power.

Scalise, Joseph (AKA: **Jerry**), prom. 1970s-80s. Mafia associate of Gerald Scarpelli. Currently in a British prison for the theft of the Marlborough Diamond.

Scarpelli, Gerald, 1938-89. Mafia assassin who turned FBI informant. Committed suicide in the Chicago Metropolitan Correctional center on May 2, 1989.

Schoemaker, William (AKA: **Shoes**), prom. 1920s. Longtime Chief of Detectives in Chicago. A resolute foe of the syndicate.

Schupe, James (AKA: **Bozo**), d.1930. West Side bootlegger killed in a shootout with Tommy McNichols on July 31, 1930.

Schwimmer, Reinhart, d.1929. Retired optometrist who befriended the Bugs Moran gang. Happened to be in the North Side garage on Feb. 14, 1929, and was killed by Capone triggermen.

Sears, John, prom. 1840s-50s. Gambler and card sharp.

Serritella, Daniel, prom. 1920s-40s. Politically connected gangster. City Sealer of Chicago in the 1920s. Gambling boss in the Capone syndicate in the 1930s and 1940s.

Shaw, Victoria, prom. 1900-30. Owner and proprietor of a South Dearborn Street brothel. Bitter rival of the Everleigh sisters.

Shea, Cornelius (AKA: **Con**), prom. 1900s-20s. Labor thug, and professional bomber, he was first president of the Teamster's Union until he was jailed for assaulting his mistress with a knife.

Sheedy, Patrick, prom. 1880s. Gambling house proprietor.

Sheeney George, prom. 1870s. Partner of Lesser Friedberg.

Shefferman, Nathan. b.1888. Teamster's Union organizer and longtime associate of Dave Beck. Called before the 1957 McClellan Committee to testify about alleged misappropriation of union funds and Beck's ties to organized crime.

Sheldon, Ralph, prom. 1920s. Former member of Ragen's Colts who organized his own bootleg gang when Prohibition went into law in 1920.

Shotgun Man, prom. 1910-11. Unknown Black Hand assassin who killed at least thirty-eight persons at Milton and Oak—Death Corner—between Jan. 1, 1910, and Mar. 26, 1911.

Shouse, Minnie, prom. 1890s. Black woman who worked in partnership with Henry Foster.

Sinacola, Joseph, d.1921. Gunned down during the Powers-D'Andrea feud, in August 1921.

Skar, Manny, d.1965. Syndicate gambler and nightclub operator murdered on Sept. 11, 1965 before he could give evidence to the government.

Skidmore, William, prom. 1910s-30s. Syndicate gambler, bail bondsman, and political fixer for nearly forty years.

Small, Lennington (AKA: **Len**), prom. 1920s. Republican governor of Illinois, 1921-28. Ally of Mayor William H. Thompson. Indicted for many frauds. Issued over 1,000 pardons to syndicate killers and bombers, including Spike O'Donnell.

Smith, Charles (AKA: **Social**), prom. 1900s-10s. South Side gambling boss, and co-proprietor of the *City of Traverse*, a floating poolroom.

Smith, "Gipsy", prom. 1909. English reformer who led a march against the South Side Levee in October 1909.

Solano, Vincent, 1919- . Chicago labor racketeer, and gambling boss on the North Side. Longtime head of Local One of the Laborer's Union.

Somnerio, Thomas, d.1930. Capone lieutenant strangled to death on the West Side, in June 1930.

Soteras, Charles, prom. 1980s. Bagman for Albert Tocco. South suburban "chop shop" operator.

Spadavecchio, Joseph (AKA: **Spa**), prom. 1980s. Syndicate gambling boss aligned with Donald Angelini.

Spencer, George, prom. 1910. Dearborn street brothel keeper and rival to the Everleigh sisters.

Spicuzza, Vincent, d.1927. St. Louis gunman, hired by the Aiello brothers to wage war on Al Capone. Murdered with Anthony Russo on Aug. 10, 1927.

Spilotro, Victor, prom. 1980s. Brother of Anthony Spilotro. Involved in credit card laundering in Chicago's South Suburbs.

Spingola, Henry, d.1926. Brother-in-law of the Terrible Genna Brothers on Chicago's West Side. Was shot and killed by Capone gunmen on Jan. 19, 1926.

Stafford, Annie, prom. 1860s-70s. Brothel keeper wedded to Cap Hyman.

Standish, Jennifer, prom. 1870s. Owner of a Wells Street bordello.

Stanton, Danny, prom. 1920s-40s. West Side triggerman who joined the Ralph Sheldon gang in the 1920s. Served as interim boss of the Saltis gang in 1929.

Stead, William T., prom. 1890s-1900s. English reformer. Author of *If Christ Came To Chicago*, a look at vice conditions in Chicago in 1893.

Stege, John, prom. 1920s. Chief of Detectives, and a resolute foe of the Capone syndicate.

Stein, Benjamin, prom. 1960s. Labor racketeer sent to prison for eighteen months on May 23, 1966.

Stenson, Joseph, prom. 1920s. Wealthy independent businessman who was a private backer of Johnny Torrio's bootleg gang.

Stevens, Walter, 1877-1939. Labor slugger and hired gunman for the Torrio-Capone mob. Credited with personally killing sixty men in his long career. Retired in 1924.

Stewart, Anne, prom. 1862-74. Famous Chicago madame who owned a resort on South Clark Street. Shot and killed Constable Marcus Donahoe on July 11, 1868.

Sullivan, Manley, prom. 1927. Bootlegger indicted for tax evasion in 1927. The Sullivan case established the precedent that illegal income was taxable. Became a powerful weapon in the battle against organized crime.

Sullivan "Paddy", prom. 1920s. Member of the Dingbat Oberta gang.

Sutherland, Ida, prom. 1870s. Proprietor of a "goosing slum" on North Clark Street.

Sweeney, James, prom. 1920s. Gang boss and professional bomber headquartered near Harrison and Halsted Streets. Jailed in 1921.

Tancl, Edward, d.1924. A one-time Cicero prizefighter and saloon owner who was murdered by Miles O'Donnell in 1924.

Tennes, Jacob (AKA: **Monte**), prom. 1900-25. Powerful gambling boss of the Racing Wire, in Chicago, for nearly twenty-five years. Sold his interests to Moses Annenberg in 1927.

Testa, Albert, d.1961. Four-foot midget who was an associate of William "Action" Jackson, syndicate hitman. Burglar, and counterfeiter; Testa was murdered by the mob in November 1961.

Thistles, prom. 1920s. Chicago street gang.

Thompson, William Hale (AKA: **Big Bill**), prom. 1915-31. Flamboyant, but corrupt mayor of Chicago, 1915-23; 1927-31. Permitted the criminal bootlegging gangs latitude in his "wide open town".

Thornton, Mary (AKA: **Gold Tooth**), prom. 1900s. House girl at Mickey Finn's saloon, who later testified against him at aldermanic hearings.

Tocco, Albert (AKA: **Caesar**), Top-ruling mob boss in the South Suburbs. Involved in extortion and racketeering, fled to Greece until he was abducted by Athens Police and returned to the U.S. to stand trial in January 1989.

Tolizotte, Pasquale, d.1926. Chicago bootlegger affiliated with the South Side O'Donnell gang. Killed in 1926.

Torello, James Vincent (AKA: **Turk**), 1930- . Cicero mob boss, loan shark, and syndicate assassin.

Torrio, John (AKA: **Johnny, the Fox, Terrible John, Frank Langley**), d.1957. Nephew of Big Jim Colosimo. Succeeded his uncle as boss of the South Side Chicago rackets, until he was nearly killed by Weiss-Moran bullets in 1925. Moved to New York, where he helped Lucky Luciano and Meyer Lansky organize the national crime syndicate.

Touhy, Roger (AKA: **the Terrible**), 1898-1959. Bootlegger active in the Northwest suburbs of Chicago. Went to jail for the 1933 abduction of Jake "the Barber" Factor. Assassinated in 1959 after winning parole.

Touhy, Thomas, prom. 1920s-30s. Brother of Roger Touhy. Active in bootlegging and labor racketeering.

Tremont, Fred, prom. 1940s-50s. Policy gambler. Brother of Nick, Peter, and Tom Tremont.

Tremont, Nicholas, prom. 1940s-50s. Policy gambler. One of four Tremont brothers.

Tremont, Peter, prom. 1950s. Numbers racketeer employed by the Manno Brothers. Boss of the Roman Silver Wheel, on Chicago's South Side.

Tremont, Thomas (AKA: **Mousey**), prom. 1940s-50s. Brother of Peter Tremont. Policy boss.

Trilby Gang, prom. 1900s. Street gang, active near Carroll and Elizabeth Streets.

Tropea, Urazio (AKA: **The Scourge**), d.1926. Affiliated with the Genna Brothers, Urazio Tropea was gunned down by men in a speeding car on Feb. 15, 1926.

Trussell, George, prom. 1850s-60s. Powerful gambling boss along the "Hair trigger" Block, Randolph Street. Shot and killed by his estranged lover, Mollie Cosgriff, on Sept. 4, 1866.

Tuccello, John, prom. 1920s. Professional gunman who worked for the Ralph Sheldon bootleg gang. Killed by the McErlane gang in 1926.

Tuckhorn, Sime, prom. 1900s. Owner of a Whisky Row dive. Opened the Olympis Café in 1901 catering to the white slave traders.

Turner, John (AKA: **Hank Davis**), prom. 1870s-80s. Conman, thief, forger, and associate of Mike McDonald. Sent to prison for murder in 1875.

Tyler, Richard, prom. 1900s. Member of the Van Bever white slave gang.

Unione Siciliane, prom. 1880s-1930s. Began as a fraternal society in New York, but was converted to a criminal cartel by Ignazio Saietta in 1914. Chicago became a battleground in the 1920s, as rival Sicilians killed each other in order to accede to the presidency which carried with it control of the rackets.

Valley Gang, prom. 1890s-1920. West Side street gang that evolved into a bootlegging operation by 1920.

Van Bever, Julia, prom. 1900-10. Convicted with her husband Maurice of Mann Act violations.

Van Bever, Maurice, prom. 1900-10. White Slaver, convicted of the Mann Act and sent to prison in 1909.

Van Dine, Harvey, 1881-1904. One of the four Car Barn Bandits who committed a string of robberies and murders in 1904. Executed on Mar. 1, 1904.

Vanilli, Roxie, prom. 1914. Cousin of John Torrio. New York gunman brought to Chicago by John Torrio, in 1914. Arrested for the murder of a Chicago policeman in the Levee, July 1914.

Varnell, Harry (AKA: **Prince Hal**), prom. 1880s-90s. Gambling house owner active in local politics.

Vercoe, William J. (AKA: **Clown for the Hoodlums**), d.1929. Poetry-reciting thug, gunned down in the Pony Inn in Cicero by George Clifford on Mar. 15, 1929.

Viana, Nicholas (AKA: **The Choir Boy**), d.1921. Triggerman in the Sam Cardinelli gang. Hanged in 1921.

Vice Lords, prom. 1980s. Inner-city black street gang.

Vine, Irving, 1904-63. Low-ranked henchman of Eddie Vogel and Ralph Pierce. Volunteered to appear as an unfavorable witness against Murray Humphreys for the IRS. Murdered in a South Side hotel on May 6, 1963.

Vinci, James, prom. 1920, in Chicago labor union racketeering. The only man to go to jail for the murder of Maurice "Moss" Enright in 1920.

Vision, Solly, prom. 1930. Criminal associate of Jack Zuta.

Vitaco, John, prom. 1920s. Extortionist and syndicate bomber killed by police in the apartment of Jack Hayes.

Vogel, Edward (AKA: **Dutch, Five-by-Five**), b.1895. Slot machine and gambling boss of Cook County for nearly forty years. Affiliated with the Capone mob in the 1920s. Engineered the takeover of Cicero in 1923.

Volpe, Anthony (AKA: **Mops**), prom. 1920s. Syndicate gunman and bootlegger who belonged to the Capone gang.

Von Frantzius, Peter, prom. 1920s. Owner of a Chicago sporting goods store who sold machine guns to the Capone mob.

Wagner, Ed, prom. 1880s. Gambling house proprietor.

Wallace, John, prom. 1880s. Conman and bunko artist. Brother of Tom Wallace.

Wallace, Thomas, prom. 1880s. Conman and bunko artist.

Walpole, John, prom. 1880s. Gambling house proprietor.

Walsh, James, d.1929. Small-time bootlegger murdered by Charles Baron in December 1929.

Waterford Jack, prom. 1870s. Streetwalker and procuress. Organized a band of prostitutes in the mid 1870s.

Watson, Carrie (Caroline Victoria Watson) b.1850. Arrived in Chicago in 1866. Owner of a lavish bordello on South Clark Street, in Little Cheyenne.

Wayman, John E.W., prom. 1908-12. Republican State's Attorney who closed the Levee District in September 1912, shortly before his term was to expire.

Webster, Daniel, prom. 1870s-90s. Keeper of a large brothel and gambling den on Biler Avenue in the 1870s.

Webster, Fred, prom. 1850s. One of the rulers of the Sands vice-district in the 1850s. Owner of a twenty-five-cent resort.

Weiner, Irwin S., prom. 1950s-60s. Bail bondsman and associate of Sam Giancana. Involved in medicare fraud, gambling, bribery, and murder.

Weinshank, Albert, d.1929. Member of the North Side mob. Killed in the St. Valentine's Day Massacre of 1929.

Weiss, Earl (Earl Wajeichowski, AKA: **Hymie, Little Hymie)**, d.1926. Successor to Dion O'Bannion as the head of Chicago's North Side mob. Murdered by Al Capone's gunmen while entering Holy Name Cathedral on Oct. 11, 1926.

Weiss, Ed, prom. 1910. Owner of the Capitol, a Levee saloon and assignation house.

Weiss, Louis, prom. 1900s. Brother of Ed Weiss. Owner of a string of saloons and bordellos in Chicago.

Welch, Nellie, prom. 1870s. Chicago brothel madame.

Wentworth, John (AKA: **Long John**), prom. 1857-61. Two-term mayor of Chicago. Closed the Sands District in April 1857. Fired the Police Department en masse in 1861.

West, Charles, prom. 1910s. South State Street saloon owner.

Whisky Row, prom. 1900-10. Section of State Street, from Van Buren to Harrison, populated by saloons, cheap vaudeville, and assignation houses.

White, Bud, prom. 1900s. Proprietor of the *City of Traverse* gambling vessel until it was put out of business, in 1907.

White Gang (Weiss Gang), prom. 1866-1899. Maxwell Street gang founded in 1866 by the six sons of Widow Margaret Weiss.

White Hand Society, prom. 1907. Opposition group to the Black Hand, organized in Chicago in 1907 by the fraternal societies to combat the organized terror and extortion.

White, "Limpy", prom. 1920s. Member of a Chicago extortion gang that used bombs as a method of terror. Killed by police in the apartment of Jack Hayes.

White, William (AKA: **Three Finger Jack**), prom. 1920s. Bodyguard of Al Capone who always wore gloves in public after losing two fingers.

Willard, May, prom. 1870s. West Side streetwalker and pocket book snatcher.

Williams, Jennifer, prom. 1870s-90s. Brothel keeper. Owner of a parlor house, the Golden Gate, on Biler Avenue.

Williams, Judith, prom. 1910s. Independent brothel keeper in the South Side Levee.

Wilson, Anna, prom. 1850s. Brothel keeper and one of the co-rulers of the Sands vice-district.

Wilson, Mamie, prom. 1910s. Levee brothel keeper.

Wilson, William, prom. 1920s. Killed with Dinky Quan and William Ryan in a shootout with Chicago Police.

Winkler, Gus, prom. 1920s-30s. West Side gambler, and bootlegger allegedly involved in the planning of the St. Valentine's Day Massacre. Machine-gunned in 1933.

Winslow, Susan (AKA: **Black Susan**), prom. 1870s-90s. Brothel keeper whose two-story shack at Clark and Twelfth Street was among the worst dives in Chicago's Bad Lands.

Wright, Frank, prom. 1890s. Owner of the Library, a Randolph Street brothel.

Wright, Seneca, prom. 1860s. Owner of the Randolph Street Saloon where George Trussell was shot in 1866.

Yaras, David (AKA: **David Miller**), 1912- . West Side gambling boss indicted for the 1946 murder of James Ragen. The case was nol-prossed.

Yattaw, John (AKA: **Black Jack**), prom. 1860s. Bounty jumper and bumboat pirate.

Zammuto, Joseph, prom. 1970s. Mob boss of Rockford, Ill.

Zapas, Gus (AKA: **Windshields**), prom. 1950s-60s. Business agent and personal associate of Teamster's boss James Hoffa. Arrested over forty times in Chicago. Linked to the kidnap murder of Robert Greenlease by the Senate McClellan Committee.

Zion, Edward, d.1925. An associate of Sam Amatuna. Murdered in 1925.

Zuckerman, Benjamin (AKA: **Zookie the Bookie**), prom. 1930s-40s. Gambling and syndicate boss. Assassinated in 1944.

Zuta, John (AKA: **Jack**), d.1930. Brothel keeper and one-time business manager for the Bugs Moran gang. Murdered in a Delafeld, Wis., roadhouse on Oct. 23, 1930.

CHINESE TRIADS (Hong Kong, Imperial China, Korea, Singapore, Shanghai, Malaya)

Big Swords, prom. 19th Cent. Chinese Triad Society.

Chiu Chao (Chao Zhou), prom. 1970s-80s. Triad society headquartered in Hong Kong, but active in the heroin traffic of Thailand. Current membership estimated to be 16,000 broken down into six different sub-gangs.

Dragon Flower Sacred Religious, prom. 19th Cent. Chinese Triad Society.

Four Seas (Shih Hai), prom. 1970s-80s. Taiwanese triad group.

14-K Association, prom. 1950s. Comprised of members of the peasant class in Hong Kong committed to the anti-Communist cause. Became a powerful criminal gang after 1953, with a total membership of 80,000. Largest and most important Triad today.

Fuk Yee Hing Triad Society, prom. 1950s-60s. A secret triad officially listed as the Fuk Yee Industrial and Commercial Association, which assisted members of the Hoklo dialect group to attain employment and housing in Hong Kong. Three-thousand of its members also belonged to the Triad.

Great Circle Triad, prom. 1980s. The Great Circle Triad is based in Hong Kong and regulates the flow of heroin between East and Southeast Asia and entry ports in Belgium and the Netherlands.

Green Pang, prom. 1940s-60s. Organized in Shanghai and Hong Kong. Attained their greatest power after the 1949 Revolution. Popularized the use of heroin, armed robbery, and pickpocketing. Organized prostitution and drug trafficking on a larger scale than any other single Triad society.

Heaven and Earth Society, prom. 1786-89. Instigated a popular revolt against the Manchu dynasty in 1786.

Hung League, prom. 19th Cent. Chinese Triad Society.

Khun Sa (AKA: **Prince of Death**), prom. 1950s-80s. Powerful opium warlord based in the mountainous regions of Thailand, near the Mekong and Hok Rivers. Said to control 60 percent of the world's opium production for the past twenty-five years. Recruited by the CIA in the 1960s to fight the Communist leader Pathet Lao in return for guarantees to peddle drugs in South Vietnam without U.S. interference.

Limpy Ho, prom. 1960s-70s. Godfather of the Chiu Chao Triad until his downfall.

Luen Group, prom. 1970s-80s. Hong Kong triad with 5,000 active members who belong to four different sub-gangs.

Nine Mansions Sects, prom. 1786-88. Chinese Triad at the forefront of the 1786 uprising against the Manchu dynasty.

Niu-Pu Gang, prom. 1970s-80s. Taiwanese triad with 1,000 members.

Red Pang, prom. 1940s-60s. A Shanghai-based Triad.

Red Spears, prom. 19th Cent. Chinese Triad Society.

Shan United Army, prom. 1950s-80s. Organized network of guerilla fighters belonging to opium trafficker Khun Sa. Membership in this private army numbers 4,000.

Single Hearted Celestial Principles, prom. 19th Cent. Chinese Triad Society.

Small Daggers, prom. 19th Cent. Chinese Triad society.

Tung Group, prom. 1970s-80s. Hong Kong trial with 3,000 members active in Southeast Asia and overseas.

United Bamboo of Taiwan (Chu Lien Pang), prom. 1980s. Taiwanese Triad that is beginning to establish bases of drug operation and money laundering operations in the U.S. and Europe. Current membership estimated to be between 10,000 and 15,000.

Yellow Beards, prom. 19th Cent. Chinese Triad society.

Yuet Tung Society, prom. 1940s-50s. Triad society that battled the 14K for autonomy in the Kowloon in the early 1950s.

White Lotus, prom. 1700s-1800s. Religious and mystical triad that engineered a revolt in 1794 against the Ch'ing Emperor Ch'ien Lung.

White Yang Sect, prom. 18th-19th Cent. Chinese Triad Society.

Wo Group, prom. 1970s-80s. Hong-Kong based Triad, with 29,000 members divided into ten different gangs.

CLEVELAND-NORTHEAST OHIO ORGANIZED CRIME

Angersika, John, prom. 1940s. Cleveland gambling racketeer.

Angersola, Fred, prom. 1917-40s. One-time bodyguard of Al Polizzi. Brother of John Angersola and top ranking member of the Cleveland mob.

Angersola, George (AKA: **King**), prom. 1930s-40s. Brother of John Angersola. Indicted for numbers running in 1939.

Angersola, John, prom. 1930s-40s. Cleveland gambler and a partner in the Miami Wofford Hotel operation in 1941.

Anthony, Mark (AKA: **Mark Petercupo**), prom. 1950s-60s. Cleveland Mafia associate who managed Bob Hope Enterprises. Close friend of Los Angeles mobster Jimmy Fratianno.

Biondo, Lorenzo, prom. 1919. Acting on orders from Rosario Borgio, Lorenzo Bionde was one of four gunmen who murdered several Akron police officers in return for a $250 bounty.

Biondo, Pasquale, prom. 1910s. Brother of Lorenzo Biondo. Imprisoned for the 1918 murder of an Akron policeman.

Birns, Shonder, prom. 1930s-40s. Gambler and racketeer, indicted for numbers running in 1939.

Borgio, Rosario, prom. 1910s. Black Hand leader of Akron, Ohio. Went to the electric chair after ordering the murders of several policemen interfering in his enterprises.

Boyle, Anthony, prom. 1960s-70s. Boss of the United Mine Workers who was voted out of office in 1972 after being accused of murdering Jock Yablonski and his family.

Brink, James H., 1904- . Gambler, bootlegger, and horse promoter who became the Cleveland Syndicate's junior partner in the Kentucky-Southern Ohio region.

Calandra, John, prom. 1950s-60s. Soldier in the Cleveland crime family.

Cammerata, Frank, prom. 1930s-40s. Bank robber and mob figure. Brother-in-law of Pete Licavoli. Deported in 1937, but returned to Cleveland in 1939 where he was protected by James Hoffa.

Carabbia, Ronald, prom. 1950s-60s. Associate of the Cleveland Mafia.

Cavallaro, Charles (AKA: **Cadillac Charley**), prom. 1940s. Mafia boss of the Youngstown, Ohio area until his assassination.

Chiavaro, Paul, prom. 1919. Chiavaro was sent to the electric chair along with Rosario Borgio, for the contract killing of Akron policemen.

Cisternino, Pasquale (AKA: **Butchie**), prom. 1950s-60s. Associate of the Cleveland Mafia.

Colletti, Charles, prom. 1920s. Member of the Mayfield Road Mob.

Cutty, Thomas, prom. 1940s. Supervised operations in Nevada and Florida for the Cleveland mob.

Dalitz, Louis, b.1897. Brother and business partner of Moe Dalitz in a chain of syndicate laundries in Cleveland.

Dalitz, Morris (AKA: **Moe, Moey Davis**), 1899-1989. Began his criminal career as a member of the Purple Gang. Later organized the Cleveland Mayfield Road mob, after vanquishing the Lonardo and Porello families. Forged a criminal alliance with Al and Chuck Polizzi before expanding the business to encompass Las Vegas gambling in the 1940s. Majority owner of the Desert Inn and Stardust Hotels.

Delsanter, Anthony (AKA: **Tony Dope**), prom. 1960s-70s. Appointed consigliere of the Cleveland family in 1975. Deceased.

Farah, John, Brother of Mike Farah. Syndicate gambler.

Farah, Michael, Gambling boss.

Ferritto, Raymond, prom. 1950s-60s. Burglar from Erie, Penn., hooked up with the Cleveland mob.

Friedman, Harold, 1923- . President of the Ohio Council of the Teamsters. Indicted for racketeering and embezzlement in Cleveland in 1989.

Giesey, Alvin E., prom. 1933. IRS agent who quit the service to become a tax advisor for Al Polizzi, Morris Kleinman and others.

Greene, Daniel (AKA: **Danny**), prom. 1960s-70s. Powerful Irish gang leader who survived several assassination attempts only to be blown up in his car.

Haas, Sam, prom. 1919-30. Son of Adolph Haas, Ohio political boss. Considered to be a "quiet brain" behind the Cleveland mob.

Hayes, James, d.1931. Boss of Toledo gambling operations. Murdered by Joe Massei in 1931.

Hughes, Anthony, 1937- . Recording Secretary for the Teamster's 507 local. Indicted with Harold Friedman for racketeering and for accepting pay without working. Alleged government informant against organized crime figures.

Kleinman, Edward, prom. 1940s. Nephew of Morris Kleinman. Took over a part of Nate Weisenberg's gambling empire after his death.

Kleinman, Morris, prom. 1920-40s. Powerful bootlegger and crime boss in partnership with the Dalitz Brothers. Indicted for income tax evasion in 1936.

Kommissarow, Morris, d.1930. Cleveland rum-runner aligned with Moe Dalitz. Murdered in August 1930, and dumped in Lake Erie.

Liberatore, Anthony, prom. 1960s-70s. Soldier in the Cleveland Mafia family.

Licavoli, James, prom. 1930s-40s. Cousin of Peter Licavoli. Rackets boss of Youngstown, Ohio.

Lonardo, Joseph (AKA: **Big Joe, Peppino**), prom. 1920s. Bootlegger and syndicate gangster who was gunned down by the Porello mob on Oct. 13, 1927.

McBride, Arthur B. (AKA: **Mickey**), prom. 1900-39. Cleveland sportsman who bought the Continental Press, a racing wire, from Moe Annenberg, in 1939. Organized the Mayfield Road Mob to "slug" for the Cleveland *News* circulation, department in the early 1900s.

McGinty, Thomas Jefferson, prom. 1913-50. Cleveland gangster who recruited a gang of sluggers to compete with Arthur McBride in 1913. Mentioned in the 1950 Kefauver Report.

Mayfield Road Mob, prom. 1910-20. Newspaper sluggers and street thugs that evolved into the Cleveland Mafia during Prohibition.

Mezzano, Vito, prom. 1919. One of four men executed in the electric chair for murdering several Akron policemen.

Milano, Antonio, prom. 1920s-70s. Brother of Frank Milano. Remained in Cleveland to supervise the Brotherhood Loan Company, a syndicate fronted operation. Underboss of the Cleveland Mafia until his retirement in 1975. His son Peter currently heads up the Los Angeles crime family.

Milano, Frank, prom. 1920s-60s. Member of the Mayfield Road Mob, and one-time boss of the Cleveland Mafia. Escaped to Mexico in 1934 to avoid income taxes. Later involved in the management of the Desert Inn in Las Vegas.

Milano, Jerry, prom. 1950. Cleveland gangster mentioned in the 1950 Kefauver Report.

Miller, Samuel (AKA: **Gameboy**), prom. 1950. Named as a member of the Cleveland syndicate, in 1950. Developed the Empire News division of Continental Press.

Moceri, Leo (AKA: **The Lips**), d.1976. Hitman associated with James Licavoli. Named underboss of the Cleveland family in 1975. Secret informer for the DEA. Murdered on Aug. 22, 1976.

Nardi, John, prom. 1970s. Labor boss of the Cleveland Teamster's Union. Began a war against the bosses in 1976. Was murdered.

Polizzi, Al (AKA: **The Owl, Big Al**), b.1900. One of the founding fathers of the national Crime Syndicate. A henchman of Moe Dalitz, Polizzi arrived in the U.S. from Siculiana, Sicily, in 1900. Later moved to Coral Gables, Fla.

Polizzi, Joseph, prom. 1940s. Brother of Al Polizzi. Took over a portion of Nate Weisenberg's gambling territory after his death.

Porello, Angelo, prom. 1920s. One of seven brothers whose bootlegging gang was vanquished by the Mayfield Road Mob in the early 1930s.

Porello, James, d.1930. Brother of Joseph Porello. Murdered by the Mayfield Road Mob three weeks after his brother

Porello, Joseph, d.1930. One of seven brothers from Sicily who waged war with the Mayfield Road Mob in the 1920s. Murdered on July 5, 1930, allegedly by Al Polizzi.

Porello, Raymond, d.1932. Murdered during a blackjack game with his brother Rosario on Feb. 25, 1932.

Porello, Rosario, d.1932. One of seven brothers from Licati, Si. Assassinated on Feb. 25, 1932 by the Mayfield Road Mob.

Presser, John (AKA: **Jackie**), 1926-88. Teamster's boss who succeeded Roy L. Williams in 1983. Became an FBI informant in the mid-1970s against rival Teamsters with ties to the Mafia.

Rockman, Milton (AKA: **Maishe**), prom. 1970s-80s. Labor racketeer identified to the government as a Mafia figure by Jackie Presser. Convicted of racketeering.

Rothkopf, Louis (AKA: **Lou Rhody, Zarumba, Uncle Louie**), prom. 1930-50. One of the co-rulers of the Cleveland syndicate. Served as a link to Frank Costello and the New York mobs. Associated with Moe Dalitz in the Las Vegas Desert Inn. Died mysteriously in 1956.

Scalish, John, 1912- . Syndicate labor racketeer. Boss of the Cleveland family from 1953-75. Arrested at the 1957 Apalachin meeting. Deceased.

Swarts, William, prom. 1930s. Wire service operator and lieutenant of Thomas McGinty. Supervised the Mounds Club, a Lake County casino for the syndicate.

Tronolone, John (AKA: **Peanuts**), prom. 1980s. Mob associate of Milton Rockman.

Tucker, Garson, prom. 1940s-50s. Brother of Sam Tucker. Managed syndicate businesses in Miami.

Tucker, Samuel, prom. 1930s-50s. Identified in the 1950 Kefauver Report as one of the original four founders of the Cleveland syndicate; along with Morris Kleinman, Moe Dalitz, and Louis Rothkopf.

Valente, Sam, d.1927. Gunman and hired assassin. Moved to Chicago in 1927, to work for the Joe Aiello gang. Machine gunned to death on the day he arrived.

Weisenberg, Nathan (AKA: **Slots King of Ohio**), d.1945. Gambling and vending and slot machine boss whose influence extended into Colorado and Arizona. Murdered by the Cleveland syndicate on Feb. 24, 1945.

Wexler, Morris (AKA: **Mushy**), prom. 1910s-50s. Cleveland crime boss. Took over the local wire services with his brother-in-law Sam "Gameboy" Miller.

Zucker, Joseph (AKA: **Joe Baker**), b.1890. Polish-born racketeer sent to Cleveland by Frank Costello in the 1930s to serve as liaison between the New York mob and Moe Dalitz's gang.

CORSICA-FRANCE ORGANIZED CRIME

Blémant, Robert, d.1965. Police Superintendent of Marseilles, who joined forces with crime boss Antoine Guérini. Assassinated in 1965.

Bocognani, Roger, prom. 1960s. French drug smuggler named by British television as one of President John F. Kennedy's assassins.

Caetti, Andrien, prom. 1940s. Corsican gangster shot to death by Napoléon Jean Corticchiato.

Carbone, Paul, prom. 1930s. Ruler of the Marseilles underworld during the 1930s.

Corsican Vendetta, prom. 1944-54. Blood vendetta between two rival gangs fighting for control of the French narcotics traffic.

De Lussatz, Gaetan, prom. 1930s. Marseilles gangster affiliated with Paul Carbone.

Guérini, Antoine, prom. 1950s-60s. French crime boss.

Paterni, Laurant, prom. 1930s. Corsican gangster murdered by Napoléon-Jean Corticchiato.

Pironti, Sauveur, prom. 1960s. Marseilles drug smuggler. Accused of complicity in the 1963 Kennedy Assassination by British Central Television in 1988.

Ricord, Auguste, prom. 1960s-70s. Kingpin of the French Connection. Sentenced to life in prison by the U.S. courts.

Sarti, Lucien, prom. 1960s. French contract killer.

Spirito, François, prom. 1930s. Criminal associate of Paul Carbone and a major figure in the Marseilles underworld.

CUBA AND THE BAHAMAS ORGANIZED CRIME

Batista, Fulgencio, 1901-73. Batista was the political dictator of Cuba who ruled the gambling rackets with Meyer Lansky beginning in 1932.

Casino Internacional, prom. 1950s. The Casino Internacional was a famous Havana casino and nightclub founded by Meyer Lansky. It was taken over by Moe Dalitz and Sam Tucker on Aug. 25, 1955, and later sold to Mike McLaney just six months before the Cuban revolution began.

Cellini, Dino, prom. 1940s-50s. Cellini was a syndicate gambler who helped George Raft open up the Colony Club, in England, following his deportation from the Bahamas.

Cellini, Edward, prom. 1940s-50s. Ohio-born gambler who managed the Paradise Island casino in Nassau. Brother of Dino Cellini.

Chesler, Louis Arthur (AKA: Uncle Lou), 1913- . Toronto financial speculator who moved to Miami Beach in 1946, where he became an intimate of "Trigger" Mike Coppola and Meyer Lansky. Involved in show lounges, hotels, and films. Helped Wallace Groves establish the Bahamas as a "swinger's paradise" and gambler's haven fronted by the Grand Bahama Development Company.

Falcon, Sicilia, prom. 1970s-80s. Cuban drug trafficker.

Groves, Wallace, prom. 1940s-60s. Former bond salesman from Baltimore. Purchased the Little Whale Cay in the Bahamas in 1937. Imprisoned in 1941 for mail fraud. Later went into business with Stafford Sands to organize Nassau Securities, Ltd., and North American, Ltd.

McLaney, Michael Julius, 1915- . One-time New Orleans deputy sheriff who went on to become a Havana casino operator. Had close ties to Santo Trafficante and Meyer Lansky.

Peters, Daniel (Samuel Lepides), (AKA: **Dusty**), b.1903. Supervised syndicate gambling operations in Havana for Meyer Lansky during the pre-Castro days of the 1950s.

Sands, Stafford, 1913- . As director of development in the Bahamas, Sands created the legal machinery that made gambling legal on the islands. By the mid-1950s, he was one of the most powerful political figures on the islands. Sands ran gambling casinos on Paradise Island in Nassau until he fled to Spain in 1967. For many years he provided a legitimate business front for Meyer Lansky's many criminal operations.

DALLAS-HOUSTON ORGANIZED CRIME

Binion, Lester (AKA: **Benny, Cowboy**), prom. 1930s-50s. Numbers runner and bookie, driven out of Dallas in 1936. Continued to run his hotel and operations from Las Vegas.

Campisi, Joseph, prom. 1960s. Ranked number two in the Dallas Mafia in the 1960s, behind Joseph Civello.

Campisi, Samuel, prom. 1960s. Brother of Joseph Campisi. Co-owner of the Egyptian Lounge, a Dallas Mafia hangout.

Civello, Joseph, prom. 1957. Crime boss of Dallas in the 1950s. A lieutenant of Carlos Marcello. Arrested at the Apalachin Meeting of 1957.

Halfen, John (AKA: **Jack**), prom. 1940s-50s. Political fixer and top associate of Carlos Marcello in Dallas.

Jones, Paul Roland, prom. 1950s. Dallas gangland figure. Private conversations were taped by the Kefauver Committee in 1950.

LaMonte, Frank, prom. 1960s. Business partner of Joseph Civello. Suspected of narcotics trafficking.

West, John (AKA: **Zip**), prom. 1950. Bookmaker involved in the 1950 NCAA point-shaving scandal. Associate of Jack Ruby.

DETROIT ORGANIZED CRIME

Allevato, Dominic J., prom. 1960s-70s. Mafia figure and gambler. Associated with Sol Shindel.

Axler, Abraham, d.1933. Member of the Purple Gang. Assassinated in 1933.

Baker, Barney, prom. 1950s. Ally of James Hoffa. Described in Robert Kennedy's book *The Enemy Within* as an "ambassador of violence."

Bannerman, John, prom. 1930s. Member of the Michigan Black Legion.

Barbara, Joseph Jr., prom. 1960s-70s. Underboss in the Detroit mob. Son of Joseph Barbara of New York, who convened the 1957 Apalachin meeting.

Bernstein, Abraham, prom. 1920s-30s. Leader of the Purple Gang. A 1934 partner of Meyer Lansky and Joe Adonis after 1934.

Bommarito, Benedict, prom. 1960s-70s. Lieutenant in the Detroit crime family.

Bommarito, Joseph, prom. 1960s-70s. Underboss of the Detroit mob.

Caruso, Sam, prom. 1960s-70s. Lieutenant in the Detroit mob.

Cavataio, Dominic, prom. 1960s-70s. Lieutenant in the Detroit mob.

Cavataio, Julian, prom. 1960s-70s. Lieutenant in the Detroit mob.

Cavataio, Peter, prom. 1960s-70s. Lieutenant in the Detroit mob.

Cellura, Leo (AKA: **Black Leo**), prom. 1920s. Directed field operations in Detroit following the conviction of Peter Licavoli on bribery charges.

Cimini, Anthony, prom. 1960s-70s. Underboss in the Detroit mob.

Corrado, Dominic P., prom. 1960s-70s. Capo in the Detroit mob.

Davis, Harvey, (AKA: **Colonel**), prom. 1930s. Founded the white supremacist Michigan Black Legion in 1933.

Dean, Dayton, prom. 1930s. Revealed the existence of the Michigan Black Legion to police, in 1933.

Evangelista, Benjamin, d.1929. Religious cultist and real-estate mogul who was murdered along with his wife and four children on July 2, 1929. The killings were believed to be connected to organized crime.

Finazzo, Sam, prom. 1960s-70s. Lieutenant in the Detroit crime family.

Fletcher, Ed, d.1933. Leader of the Purple Gang. Assassinated in 1933.

Galbo, Joseph, prom. 1920s. Bootlegger and business agent for the Cleveland mob who handled Detroit operations. Went to jail on bribery charges in 1928.

Giacalone, Anthony (AKA: **Tony**), prom. 1960s-70s. Capo in the Detroit crime family.

Giacalone, Vito (AKA: **Billy**), prom. 1960s-70s. Brother of Anthony Giacalone. Enforcer for the Detroit mob.

Guarella, Eddie, prom. 1960s-70s. Lieutenant in the Detroit mob.

Hoffa, James Riddle, 1913-75. Powerful boss of the Teamster's Union from 1955 until his imprisonment in 1967. Abducted in Bloomfield Township, Mich., on July 30, 1975. He was never seen again.

Keywell, Harry, prom. 1920s-30s. Member of the Purple Gang. Brother of Phil Keywell.

Keywell, Philip, prom. 1920s-30s. Member of the Purple Gang. Suspected of complicity in the Chicago St. Valentine's Day Massacre of 1929.

Lee, Erwin, prom. 1930s. Member of the Michigan Black Legion.

Lewis, George F., prom. 1920s-30s. Member of the Purple Gang. Questioned by police about the 1929 Chicago St. Valentine's Day Massacre.

Licavoli, Dominic, prom. 1940s. Brother of Peter Licavoli. Son-in-law of Joseph Zerilli.

Licavoli, Peter Joseph, d.1984. Ruled the Detroit mob jointly with Joseph Zerilli and John Prizola. Leader of the Purple Gang, until he was driven out of the city in 1930. Established autonomy in Tucson, Ariz., in the 1940s. Also maintained business dealings in Cleveland with Moe Dalitz and Al Polizzi.

Licavoli, Thomas (AKA: **Yonnie**), prom. 1920s-30s. Founder of the Detroit Purple Gang. Relinquished control to brother Peter after he was sent to prison for the murder of Toledo bootlegger Jackie Kennedy.

Little Jewish Navy, prom. 1920s. Rival bootlegging gang, vanquished by the Purple Gang in the 1931 Collingwood Manor Apartments Massacre.

Lucido, Salvatore, prom. 1960s-70s. Capo in the Detroit mob.

Massei, Joseph, prom. 1930s-70s. Partner in the Licavoli Brothers gambling empire that extended to Las Vegas. Arrested for murder in 1933, but the charges were dropped. Served as consiglieri to Joseph Zerilli in the 1970s.

Meli, Angelo, prom. 1950s-70s. Consiglieri to mob boss Joseph Zerilli in the 1970s.

Meli, Frank, prom. 1960s-70s. Lieutenant in the Detroit crime family.

Meli, Salvatore Angelo, prom. 1950s-60s. Son of Angelo Meli. Married to one of the daughters of Frank Livorsi.

Meli, Vincent (AKA: **Little Vince**), 1927- . Current mob boss of Detroit. Involved in the lucrative steel hauling industry. Married to Pauline Perrone, daughter of Bonanno associate Santo Perrone.

Moceri, Joseph, prom. 1960s-70s. Underboss in the Detroit mob.

Moss, Abraham, prom. 1920s-40s. Bootlegger and gambling boss who was an original member of the Purple Gang. Supervised Detroit operations for the Cleveland syndicate.

Perrone, Santo, prom. 1960s-70s. Underboss in the Detroit crime family.

Polizzi, Michael, prom. 1960s-70s. Underboss of the Detroit Mafia family.

Priziola, John, prom. 1950s-70s. Underboss of Joseph Zerilli's in the 1970s.

Purple Gang, the, prom. 1920s-30s. Tough bootlegging and extortion mob led by Abe Bernstein. Supplied the Chicago criminal gangs with Canadian liquor during Prohibition. Absorbed into the modern crime syndicate after 1934.

Quasarano, Raffaele (AKA: **Jimmy Q, Gino**), 1910- . Former drug trafficker and top crime boss of Detroit, with important ties to New York mobsters Frank Costello and Frank Coppola. His father-in-law is Sicilian Mafia boss Vito Vitale.

Rubino, Michael (AKA: **Mike**), prom. 1960s-70s. Detroit Mafia chieftain associated with Sol Shindel.

Serra, Salvatore, prom. 1960s-70s. Lieutenant in the Detroit mob.

Shindel, Sol, prom. 1960s-70s. Gambler and Mafia figure indicted in the 1970s along with sixteen Detroit police officers for running an illegal operation at the downtown Anchor Bar. Assassinated in Southfield, Mich.

Stein, Sammy, b.1896. Russian-born gangster involved in smuggling gold into the U.S. from Canada. Close friend of Moe Dalitz in Cleveland.

Teramine, Anthony, prom. 1960s-70s. Underboss in the Detroit mob.

Tocco, Giacomo (AKA: **Jack Tocco**), 1926- . Member of the Detroit mob. Lives in Grosse Point, Mich.

Tocco, William (AKA: **Black Bill**), prom. 1930s-40s. Shared joint rule of the Detroit syndicates with Joseph Zerilli. Rose to power in the 1930s, when the Italian mobs took over the territories of the Purple Gang. Deceased.

Triglia, Joseph, prom. 1960s-70s. Underboss in the Detroit mob.

Vitale, Paul, prom. 1950s-60s. Underboss in the Detroit mob.

Vitale, Peter, prom. 1960s-70s. Underboss in the Detroit mob.

Wertheimer, Mert, A Detroit gambler.

Williams, Roy L., 1916- . President of the Teamster's Union from 1981-83. Linked to major organized crime figures by FBI informant Jackie Presser. Jailed in 1985 for attempting to bribe a U.S. Senator. Released in October 1988.

Zerilli, Anthony (AKA: **Tony**), prom. 1950s-60s. Son of Joseph Zerilli. Boss of the Detroit family.

Zerilli, Joseph (AKA: **The Old Man**), b.1897. An original member of the Purple Gang. Identified as a ruling "don" of the Detroit syndicate by the McClellan sub-committee. Deceased.

FLORIDA ORGANIZED CRIME

Alo, Vincent (AKA: **Jimmy Blue Eyes**), prom. 1940s-60s. Henchman of Charles "Lucky" Luciano, and the liaison to the syndicate "banker" Meyer Lansky. Boss of Miami for the Genovese family, and successor to Frank Costello on the National Commission. Resident of Broward County.

Arnstein, Peter (AKA: **Petey Arnold**), prom. 1940s-50s. Operated a call-girl ring in Chicago before moving to Miami in the 1940s where he opened Mother Kelly's Nightclub, a syndicate operation controlled by Joe Sonken.

Beckley, Gil (AKA: **The Brain**), prom. 1950s-60s. Ran a national sports-betting operation from his apartment north of Miami Beach. Arrested in 1965 and sentenced to prison for ten years.

Bedami, Angelo, prom. 1960s-70s. Underboss in the Trafficante crime family.

Blackburn, Harlan, prom. 1960s-70s.

Carter, George R.K., prom. 1930s. Proprietor of a South Miami Beach gambling casino that was taken over by the Cleveland and New York mobs.

Carfano, Anthony (AKA: **L'il Augie Pisano**), 1899-1959. Florida gambling boss murdered at New York's LaGuardia Airport for attempting to oust Meyer Lansky from power.

Catena, Gerardo Vito, 1905- . Ranked number four in the national crime syndicate hierarchy. Longtime member of the Vito Genovese crime family, now operating out of Boca Raton, Fla.

Cohen, Sam, prom. 1940s. Co-founder of the S & G bookmaking operation in Miami in 1944, which grossed between $30 and $40 million a year.

Coticchia, Louis (AKA: **Lou Brady**), 1920- . Associate of Santo Trafficante. Given the job of courier by Trafficante. Worked in the Cuban casinos at one time.

Diecidue, Frank, prom. 1960s-70s. Underboss in the Trafficante crime family.

Ehrenberg, Nathan, prom. 1950s-60s. Assumed control of the numbers racket after Hymie Martin went to jail for five months for contempt of court. After his release, Ehrenberg was murdered, and his remains thrown into Biscayne Bay.

Erickson, Frank, prom. 1920s-50s. Bookmaker and gambling boss in association with Frank Costello. Arrested and sent to prison in New York in 1950.

Friedman, Charles, prom. 1944. Co-founder of the Miami S & G bookmaking syndicate in 1944.

Gagliano, Charles Joseph, prom. 1970s. Member of the New York based Galente mob. Active in Miami.

Garrett, George Nathaniel, prom. 1970s. Associate of Charles Gagliano, and supplier of "assassination kits" to Florida gangsters. Sent to prison for fifty years in 1977.

Hart, Leon, prom. 1950s-60s. Real-estate promoter, and backer of various lotteries, bolita games, and illegal gambling in Broward County. Disappeared from Ft. Lauderdale in 1965 on the eve of his scheduled grand jury appearance.

Kovolick, Phil (AKA: **The Stick**), prom. 1920s-60s. Prohibition-era mobster from New York who re-located to Hollywood, Fla. where he was employed by Meyer Lansky.

Lansky, Jacob, prom. 1930s-50s. Brother of Meyer Lansky. Established casino operations in south Broward County in the late 1930s. A long-time resident of Hollywood, Fla.

Lazzara, Augustine Primo, prom. 1960s-70s. Underboss in the Trafficante crime family.

Levitt, Jules, prom. 1940s. One of the partners in the S & G bookmaking syndicate, founded in Miami.

Lombardo, Philip (AKA: **Benny Squirt**), 1911- . Genovese crime boss in Miami. Loan shark, gambler, construction mogul.

Longo, James Costa, prom. 1960s-70s. Underboss in the Trafficante crime family.

LoPiccolo, Joseph, 1918- . Narcotics peddler in South Florida. Sent to prison in 1958 on federal drug charges.

Loscalzo, Vincent Salvatore, 1935- . Mafia boss of Tampa, Fla., believed to be the successor of Santo Trafficante.

Lumia, James, d.1950. Top-level mobster murdered in Tampa, June 5, 1950.

Martin, Hymie (AKA: **Fat Hymie**), prom. 1930s-50s. One-time Pittsburgh mobster who muscled in on the South Florida numbers racket in the 1940s.

Mistretta, Gaetano, prom. 1960s-70s. Consigliere (or "elder") to Santo Trafficante Jr..

Plate, Anthony (AKA: **Tony**), prom. 1960s-70s. Member of the Gambino crime family of New York. Sent to Miami by Aniello Dellacroce.

Prokos, John (AKA: **The Greek**), prom. 1950s-60s. With his brother Chris, Prokos ran the largest bookie operation in Miami, bankrolled by the same syndicate that backed Gil Beckley. Ran a café as a legitimate business front.

Rainwater, Houston (AKA: **Red**), prom. 1940s-50s. Gambling boss, and syndicate bagman in Miami.

Randazzo, Anthony (AKA: **Tony**), prom. 1960s-70s. Former member of the Cleveland Mafia. Became an underboss in the Tampa crime family.

Rosenbaum, Edward (AKA: **Lucky Eddie**), prom. 1940s. Helped found S & G bookmaking, in Miami, in 1944.

Salvey, Harold, prom. 1940s. Miami gambler and racketeer. A partner in S & G bookmaking.

Scaglione, Salvatore, prom. 1960s-70s. Consigliere to Santo Trafficante Jr..

Silesi, Joseph Albert (AKA: **Joe Rivers**), prom. 1970s. Mafia chieftain in Miami Beach allied to the Gambino-Lucchese families of New York.

Silvers, Louis (AKA: **Babe**), d.1960. Dade County bookie and Mafia henchman who disappeared mysteriously in 1960. Believed murdered by Mafia thugs and dumped into the Intercoastal Waterway.

Sonken, Joseph, prom. 1950s. Owner of the Gold Coast Lounge, unofficial syndicate headquarters in Miami during the 1950s. Former partner of Peter Arnstein, who ran a call-girl racket in Chicago before coming to Florida.

Trafficante, Sam Cacciatore, prom. 1960s-70s. Underboss in the Trafficante family. Responsible for Central and East Florida.

Trafficante, Santo Jr., 1914- . Boss of the Mafia-run Cuban gambling casinos, until Fidel Castro came to power, in 1959. Florida rackets boss, based in Tampa, during the 1950s and 1960s. Born in Tampa.

Trafficante, Santo Sr., d.1954. Father of future Florida mob boss, Santo Jr. Passed the mantle to his son in 1954.

Vaught, Red (AKA: **Little Red**), prom. 1940s-60s. Miami Beach vice-boss who owned a string of brothels in Dade and Broward Counties.

Velsco, James, d.1948. Syndicate hoodlum murdered in Tampa, Dec. 12, 1948.

Wolinsky, Moe (AKA: **Dimples**), prom. 1930s-40s. Co-owner of a South Miami Beach gambling resort along with Meyer Lansky and members of the Cleveland mob.

GREAT BRITAIN-UNITED KINGDOM ORGANIZED CRIME

Barrie, John, prom. 1960s. Member of the Kray criminal gang. Sent to prison in 1969 in connection with the murder of Jack "the Hat" McVitie.

Birmingham Boys, prom. 1920s. British street gang involved in bookmaking and horse racing.

Castucci, Richard, prom. 1950s-60s. U.S. gangster deported from

England for rigging games at the London Villa Casino.

Colony Sports Club, prom. 1960s. London gambling casino opened up by Meyer Lansky and Angelo Bruno. Fronted by U.S. actor George Raft.

Cornell, George, d.1965. Member of the Richardson Gang. Murdered by Ronald Kray in 1965.

Comer, John (AKA: **Jack Spot**), 1912- . British gambling boss and black marketeer.

Dimes, Albert (AKA: **Italian Albert**), prom. 1950s. Chief enforcer for Billy Hill.

Hill, William, prom. 1940s-50s. Rival gang leader of Jack Comer. Fled to Australia, where he hired thugs to try to have Comer assassinated.

Hoxton Gang, prom. 1940s. Soho street gang.

King's Cross Gang, prom. 1940s. Soho street gang.

Kray, Reginald, 1933 . East End gang leader. Brother of Ronald Kray. Imprisoned in 1969 for the murder of Jack McVitie.

Kray, Ronald, 1933- . Twin brother of Reggie Kray. Provided the strong-arm for their East End extortion gang. Murdered George Cornell in 1965.

Messina Brothers, prom. 1940s-50s. Five brothers of Italian-Arabic extraction who ran a powerful white slave ring in the West End of London in the 1950s. Alfredo, Carmelo, Attilio, Eugene and Salvatore Messina were all eventually jailed or deported.

Napolitano, Joey, prom. 1950s-60s. U.S. gangster deported from England for rigging card games at the Villa Casino.

Richardson, Charles, prom. 1950s-60s. Rival gang leader of the Kray brothers. By 1965 his gang was put out of business by the London police.

Richardson, Eddie, prom. 1950s-60s. Co-leader of an East End criminal gang, along with his brother Charles.

Russo, Victor (AKA: **Scarface Jack**), prom. 1950s. London gangster affiliated with Billy Hill.

Sabini, Darby, prom. 1920s. Italian gang leader, whose mob waged war with the Birmingham Boys.

JAPAN ORGANIZED CRIME (Last Name Shown First)

Banzuiin Chobei, prom. 17th cent. Legendary outlaw-bandit considered to be the earliest known predecessor to the modern day yakuza.

Dai Nippon Heiwa-kai, 1965- . Kobe, Osaka, criminal gang founded in 1965. Active in thirteen prefects with a total membership of 914.

Genyosha (AKA: **Dark Ocean Society**), prom. 1880s-1900s. An ultranationalist political society, founded in 1881. It fused the extremes of the political right with members of the yakuza criminal gangs.

Hasegawa Shunji, prom. 1960s. A ranking lieutenant in the Inagawa criminal organization.

Hayashi Shotaro, prom. 1970s-80s. Hayashi is the eighth boss of the Doshida family, a 200-man Tokyo gang under the umbrella of Sumiyoshi-rengo.

Hori Masao, prom. 1950s-80s. Boss of the Sumiyoshi-rengo criminal confederation.

Ichiwa-kai, prom. 1984- . An Osaka-based criminal gang that splintered from the Yamaguchi-gumi, the Ichiwa-kai went to war with the Yamaguchi-gumi in 1985-87, a conflict that cost twenty-six lives.

Inagawa Kakuji, prom. 1940s-80s. Yokohama-based gang lord who founded his own yakuza gang in 1945. Today he is one of the respected elder statesmen of the Japanese underworld.

Inagawa-kai (Kakusei-kai), prom. 1945- . Toyko criminal gang founded after WWII by Kakuji Inagawa with a current membership of 4,347. The Ingawa-kai were involved in a turf war with the Yamaguchi-gumi in the late 1980s.

Ishii Susumu, prom. 1970s-. Number-two ranking gangster in the Inagawa-kai.

Jirocho Shimizu no, 1820-93. A legendary gambler who is celebrated as a hero by many modern day Japanese. In the 1860s, Jirocho helped to bring an end to the feudal rule of the Tokugowa Shoguns by joining forces with the emperor.

Katsuyoshi Hirata, prom. 1980s. Ruling boss of the Dai Nippon Heiwa-kai gang of Kobe, Japan.

Kimura Tokutaro, prom. 1950s. Minister of justice under Prime Minister Shigeru Yoshida.

Kodama Yoshio, d.1984. Former Japanese war criminal and right-wing politician who consolidated the Yamaguchi-gumi and the Inagawa gang into a temporary alliance in October 1972. Kodama is considered a "godfather" of the yakuza.

Kyo Koo-soo (AKA: **Seikichi Kimura**), prom. 1980s. Boss of the Nippon Kokusui-kai gang of Tokyo.

Machii Hisayuki (Yong Chong Gwon), (AKA: **the Ginza Tiger**), prom. 1950s-70s. Korean born gangster who organized the Tokyo-based Tosei-kai (Voice of the East Gang) in 1948. Machii is a blood brother to Kazuo Taoka and has been the godfather of the Towa Yuai Jigyo Kumiai (East Asia Friendship Enterprise Association) since 1965, when Tosei-kai was disbanded due to police crack downs.

Matsuba-kai, prom. 1953- . Criminal gang founded in Tokyo in 1953. Current membership stands at 2,147.

Matsuda-gumi, prom. 1970s. Rival gang faction that waged a war of attrition against the Yamaguchi-Gumi in the 1970s. Membership at that time barely exceeded thirty.

Meiraki-gumi, prom. 1940s. Yakuza gang used by Kodama Yoshio against the labor unions at the Hokutan Coal mine in 1949.

Motokyokuto Aioh (Rengo Kai), prom. 1930- . Third largest yakuza gang in Japan with 4,416 members in twenty-two prefectures.

Nakanishi Kazuo, 1923- . Elected to succeed Masahisa Takenaka as head of the Yamaguchi-gumi in 1985, following the gang lord's assassination.

Nibiki-kai, prom. 1970s- . Criminal gang headquartered in the city of Shizuoka. Engaged in a gang war with the Yamaguchi-gumi, for control of the Tokyo markets.

Nippon Kokusui-kai, prom. 1958- . Criminal gang organized in Tokyo in 1958, with a membership of 943 spread across ten prefectures.

Ogawa Kaoru, prom. 1970s-80s. Powerful Japanese racketeer who relocated his operations to Hawaii in 1978. Involved in various extortion schemes known in Japan as "sokaiya."

Ono Toshifumi, 1927-86. Leader of the Ichiwa-kai gang, assassinated in 1986 in apparent retaliation for the murder of Masahisa Takenaka.

Ozu Kinosuke, prom. 1950s. The Tekiya boss of the Shinjuku section of Tokyo often called the "Al Capone" of his city. Ozu controlled thousands of street peddlers and bakuto gangs. In 1947, he ran unsuccessfully for a seat in the diet.

Sumiyoshi-rengo, prom. 1958- . Based in Tokyo, Sumiyoshi-rengo is the second largest underworld organization in Japan, with 6,723 members in twenty prefectures.

Takenaka Masahisa, 1915-85. Succeeded Kazuo Taoka as godfather of the Yamaguchi-gumi. Takenaka was murdered by rival members of the Ichiwa-kai gang on Jan. 26, 1985.

Tanaka Haruo, prom. 1980s. Current syndicate boss of the Motokyouto Aioh gang.

Tanaka Keizo, prom. 1970s-80s. Top ranking lieutenant in the Inagawa gang.

Taoka Kazuo (AKA: **the Bear**), 1913-81. Ruler of the Yamaguchi-Gumi for thirty-two years until he was shot and wounded in a Kyoto, Japan, nightclub in July 1975.

Toa Yuai (Jigyo Kumiai), prom. 1966- . Tokyo criminal gang organized in 1966. Current membership numbers 796.

yakuza, prom. 1600s- . The Japanese Mafia. Its origins date to the 1600s.

Yamaguchi-gumi, prom. 1915- . Powerful underworld organization with a total membership of 10,400 members active in twenty-nine of Japan's forty-seven prefectures. Their drug traffic, illegal gambling operations, and prostitution rackets are fronted by legitimate real estate offices and consulting firms.

Yamamoto Hiroshi, prom. 1980s. Current boss of the Ichiwa-kai gang in Kobe.

Yamamoto Kenichi, prom. 1950s-70s. Ranking member of the Yamaguchi-Gumis.

KANSAS CITY, MO., ORGNAIZED CRIME

Anthon, Ferris, d.1933. A lieutenant of Joe Lusco; assassinated by Lazia gunmen on Aug. 12, 1933.

Balestrere, James, prom. 1950. Named by the Senate Kefauver Committee in 1950 as one of the "Five Iron Men" of K.C.

Benintende, Joseph (AKA: **Joe Granza**), prom. 1950. Kansas City mobster sentenced to prison in 1953 for the NCAA point shaving scandal.

Binaggio, Charles, 1909-50. Syndicate boss of Kansas City. Successor of Johnny Lazia, found murdered outside Democratic Headquarters, Apr. 6, 1950.

Cammisano, William (AKA: **Willie**), 1918- . Powerful gambling boss, loan shark, and fence.

Carrollo, Charles, prom. 1930s. Right hand man and successor to Johnny Lazia. Convicted of income tax evasion in 1939.

Civella, Nicholas (AKA: **Mr. Nichols**), 1912-83. Reputed boss of the Kansas City crime syndicate until he died in prison in 1983. Died of natural causes on Mar. 12, 1983.

Coleman, Frank (AKA: **Weinie**), prom. 1920s. Petty hoodlum and bank robber. Shot to death near White Bear Lake, Minn.

DeLuna, Carl (AKA: **Toughy**), 1930- . Rackets boss of Kansas City. Currently in jail.

DiGiovanno, Joseph (AKA: **Scarface**), b.1888. Black Hand extortionist who ruled the Italian-Sicilian community for nearly five decades.

Di Giovanino, Peter (AKA: **Sugarhouse**), 1910s-40s. Brother of Joseph DiGiovanni. Black Hand enforcer for nearly five decades. Named by the Kefauver Committee as a member of the Kansas City Mafia in 1950.

Fascone, Gus, d.1933. Top triggerman in the Johnny Lazia mob. Murdered Ferris Anthon on Aug. 12, 1933, and was shot and killed by police while trying to escape.

Gargotta, Charles, d.1948. One of the "Five Iron Men" of Kansas City. One-time henchman of Charlie Binaggio and Johnny Lazia. Murdered in 1948.

Gizzo, Anthony, prom. 1950. Identified as one of the "Five Iron Men" of Kansas City by the Kefauver Committee in 1950.

Higgins, Otto, prom. 1930s. Corrupt police chief of Kansas City who owed allegiance to Tom Pendergast and Johnny Lazia. Jailed for income tax evasion in 1939.

Kansas City Massacre, 1933. On June 17, 1933, three gun-men led by Verne Miller, shot and killed four law enforcement officers outside of Kansas City's Union Station in an all-fated attempt to free bank-robber Frank "Jelly" Nash.

Klein, Morris (AKA: **Snag**), prom. 1950. Kansas City gangster and gambler.

La Capra, Michael James (AKA: **Jimmy Needles**) d.1935. Former associate of Johnny Lazia, suspected of masterminding his death. Hunted down and killed on Aug. 21, 1935.

Lazia, John (AKA: **Johnny**), 1897-1934. A petty hoodlum who became the principal enforcer and gang boss of the rackets controlled by Democratic political boss, Tom Pendergast. Lazia was assassinated on July 10, 1934.

Lococo, Tano, prom. 1950. Named as one of the "Five Iron Men" of Kansas City.

Lusco, Joseph, prom. 1930s. Rival bootlegger who challenged Johnny Lazia for supremacy in the 1930s.

Miller, Vernon, prom. 1930s. Former sheriff turned bootlegger. Purported to have been one of the trigger men who carried out the Union Station Massacre.

Moretina, Charles, prom. 1980s. Lieutenant of Nicholas Civella. Imprisoned for conspiracy in 1983.

Nash, Frank (AKA: **Jelly**), d.1933. Escaped bankrobber with syndicate ties. Nash was shot to death in the Kansas City Massacre, June 17, 1933.

Osadchey, Edward P. (AKA: **Eddie Spitz**), prom. 1950. Testified before the Kefauver Committee in 1950.

Pendergast, Thomas Joseph, 1870-1945. Boss of the Kansas City Democratic Machine until his imprisonment on income tax evasion charges in 1939.

Richetti, Adam, prom. 1930s. Professional assassin, allegedly hired by Johnny Lazia to carry out the Union Station Massacre.

Rusick, Michael, prom. 1920s. Member of the Sammy Stein gang. Murdered in Minnesota.

Scola, Sam, d.1933. A Lazia gunman who was killed by police on Aug. 12, 1933, after murdering Ferris Anthon.

Stein, Samuel (AKA: **Ten Dollar Kid**), prom. 1928. Hoodlum accused of murdering Kansas City police officer "Happy" Smith in 1928. Mob double-crosser, found murdered at White Bear Lake, Minn.

Thomas, Carl, prom. 1980s. Casino boss and associate of Nicholas Civella. Imprisoned in 1983 for conspiracy.

Weissman, William (AKA: **Solly**), prom. 1930s. Mob enforcer who served under Johnny Lazia.

LAS VEGAS ORGANIZED CRIME

Baron, Charles (AKA: **Babe**), prom. 1920s-60s. Chicago gunman and member of the Al Capone mob. Worked for Meyer Lansky in the Cuba casinos before becoming the official "greeter" at the Sands Hotel in Las Vegas.

Beasley, Milton (AKA: **Art Norris, Duke, Mel Norris**), 1933- . Hitman convicted of murdering Bill Green in Las Vegas in August 1961. Beasley was sentenced to life imprisonment.

Berman, David (AKA: **Davie the Jew**), 1903-57. One-time member of Murder, Inc., who went to Las Vegas in 1944 to help the New York mobs stake their claim in the gambling casinos.

Clark, Wilbur Ivern, prom. 1940s-50s. Member of the Cleveland syndicate, and associate of Moe Dalitz who invested in the Desert Inn and other Las Vegas gambling casinos in the 1940s.

Cohen, Yale, prom. 1940s-50s. Former inmate with Jimmy Fratianno at the Ohio Penitentiary. Later an executive with the Stardust Hotel.

Conforte, Joseph, prom. 1950s-60s. Owner of the Mustang Ranch, a Reno brothel.

Culotto, Frank, 1937- . Lieutenant of Tony Spilotro. Became a mob informant in 1982.

Danolfo, Nicholas (AKA: **Peanuts**), prom. 1940s-60s. A former doorman at a Cleveland bookie joint. Later managed the Desert Inn and Stardust Hotels.

Glick, Allen, prom. 1970s. San Diego businessman who secured $95 million in loans from the Central States Teamster's Pension fund in 1974 to finance his purchase of the Stardust, Fremont, Hacienda, and Marina hotels of Las Vegas.

Goldbaum, Hy, prom. 1950s-60s. Los Angeles bookmaker who moved to Las Vegas. Goldbaum started up a sports bookie operation at the Flamingo.

Graham, William (AKA: **Bill**), prom. 1950s-60s. Political fixer of Nevada. Operated out of Reno. Supplied many mob-fronted business with gambling licenses. Deceased.

Greenbaum, Gus, prom. 1940s-50s. Arizona mob figure brought to Las Vegas in 1947, to succeed Bugsy Siegel as the manager of the Flamingo Hotel.

Kolud, Ruby, prom. 1950s. affiliated with Moe Dalitz and the group that bought the Desert Inn.

Levinson, Ed, prom. prom. 1940s-50s. Principal investor in the Fremont hotel and casino. Associate of Meyer Lansky, Bobby Gene Baker, and "Trigger" Mike Coppola.

Ponti, Phil, prom. 1970s. Foot soldier in the Chicago crime family who worked as an executive at the Stardust Hotel.

Rosenthal, Frank (AKA: **Lefty**), prom. 1970s. Envoy of the Chicago mob who was Allen Glick's "silent partner" in the hotel casino operations.

Rothkopf, Bernard (AKA: **Bernie**), prom. 1960s-70s. Nephew of Cleveland mob boss Louis Rothkopf. Allied with Moe Dalitz in Las Vegas. President of the MGM Grand.

Royal Casino, prom. 1980s. Allegedly the headquarters for drug traffickers and mob figures who used it for money laundering schemes in 1983.

Shapiro, Irving (AKA: **Slick**), prom. 1970s. Toledo bookmaker who moved to Las Vegas in 1975.

Siegel, Benjamin (AKA: **Bugsy**), 1906-47. Born in Brooklyn, Siegel became the first boss of the West Coast crime operations. His operations were centered primarily in Las Vegas, where he built and ran the Flamingo Resort Hotel until the mob ordered his assassination in 1947.

Spilotro, Anthony (AKA: **The Ant, Little Guy**), prom. 1970s. Chicago mobster sent into Las Vegas to oversee gambling operations. Succeeded John Roselli as Chicago's "point man." Murdered.

Stacher, Joseph (AKA: **Doc**), b.1902. Syndicate gambling boss for Meyer Lansky, who began his criminal career as a New Jersey thief. Helped build the Sands Hotel. Deceased.

Vallardo, Michael, prom. 1950s-60s. Youngstown, Ohio native who ran Caesar's Palace. An intimate of Jimmy Fratianno.

LOS ANGELES-SOUTHERN CALIFORNIA ORGANIZED CRIME

Adamo, Joseph, prom. 1940s-50s. Brother of Momo Adamo. Former capo in the Los Angeles crime family. Supervised operations in San Diego.

Adamo, Momo, prom. 1940s-50s. Underboss in Jack Dragna's family. Committed suicide.

Aguayo, Robert, 1959- . Robert Aguayo has served as a member of the El Centro del Pueblo, a counseling organization aimed at providing jobs and opportunity for former L.A. gang members.

Albanese, Vinnie, prom. 1950s-70s. San Diego Mafia associate. A friend of Frank Sinatra.

Alessio, John, prom. 1940s-60s. San Diego gambling boss who was a close friend of Mickey Cohen. Sentenced to prison in 1966 for skimming millions of dollars in racetrack profits. Alessio reportedly donated significant amounts of money to Richard Nixon's 1968 presidential bid.

Araujo, Jaime, prom. 1980s. Araujo invested $1.5 million from his $33 million narcotics trafficking empire into prime U.S. real estate. Much of this land was later confiscated by the government.

Battaglia, Charles (AKA: **Charley Bats**), prom. 1950s-60s. Buffalo mobster who became a soldier in the Los Angeles crime family. Later joined up with Joseph Bonanno in Arizona.

Bloods, prom. 1980s. Los Angeles street gang. Bitter rivals of the Crips. Identified by the red colored clothing they wear.

Bompensiero, Frank (AKA: **The Bump**), 1905-77. Triggerman for the California mob. Bompensiero was capo in San Diego, until his imprisonment, in 1955. Demoted to status of lowly soldier after his release. Later, a top FBI informant until his murder.

Bonventre, Biaggio, prom. 1940s-50s. A soldier in Jack Dragna's crime family.

Brancato, Anthony, prom. 1950. Mafia triggerman believed responsible for the shotgun murder of lawyer Samuel Rummel on Dec. 11, 1950. Assassinated by Mickey Cohen.

Brooklier, Dominick (AKA: **Jimmy Regace**), prom. 1940s-70s. Began as a bookmaker with Jimmy Fratianno in the 1940s. Boss of the Los Angeles Mafia since 1974. Indicted in 1979 for racketeering, conspiracy, obstruction of justice and murder.

Bruno, Sam, prom. 1940s-50s. Soldier in Jack Dragna's family.

Buccieri, Frank (AKA: **The Horse**), 1919- . Brother of Chicago mobster Fifi Buccieri, he was nicknamed the "Horse" because he gave a racing horse to Pattie Reynolds, former *Playboy* playmate of the month. Sent by the ruling Mafia commission to the West Coast to head up syndicate operations. Thought to be active in Milwaukee, Wis., organized crime at the present time.

Cesar, Thane, prom. 1960s. Long-time associate of John Alessio. Strongly suspected of complicity in the 1968 assassination of Senator Robert Kennedy.

Cohen, Mickey, 1913-76. Trigger happy boss of the Los Angeles and Las Vegas underworld, following the 1947 assassination of Benjamin "Bugsy" Siegel. One of Cohen's rackets was to sexually blackmail Hollywood stars. Eclipsed in power by Jack Dragna and John Roselli.

Coronado White Boys, prom. 1980s. San Diego youth gang headquartered on Coronado Island.

Crips, prom. 1980s. Los Angeles street gang engaged in drug trafficking and extortion. Identified by the blue colored clothing they wear.

DeMayo, Thomas, prom. 1950s. Los Angeles racketeer.

DeSimone, Frank, d.1968. Took over the reins of the Los Angeles crime family in 1957, following the death of Jack Dragna. Subordinated to the role of "junior partner" by the New York mob.

Dippolito, Charles, prom. 1940s-50s. Soldier in the Los Angeles crime family. Deceased.

Dippolito, Joseph, prom. 1950s-60s. Son of Charles Dippolito. Also deceased

Dragna, John (Antonio Rizzoti), 1891-1957. Known as the "Al Capone of Los Angeles," Dragna ruled the Southern California rackets for about twelve years in the 1940s and 1950s. He was never a forceful, or resolute leader.

Dragna, Louis Tom (AKA: **The Reluctant Prince**), 1920- . Nephew of Jack Dragna. Assumed control of the crime family from Frank DeSimone and Nick Licata by default. A hesitant and unsure ruler of the West Coast Mafia.

Fiato, Anthony Craig, 1944- . Los Angeles loan shark who turned government informant in 1984. With his brother Lawrence, he went undercover to gather evidence on Peter Milano and his associates.

Fiato, Lawrence, 1955- . Brother of Craig Fiato. Ran a loan sharking operation until 1984 when they agreed to supply information to the FBI about the Milano crime family.

Fine, Mickey (Mickey Feinberg), prom. 1960s-70s. Los Angeles mob figure involved in the pornography industry.

Fratianno, Aldena (AKA: **Jimmy the Weasel**), 1913- . Became a capo in the Dragna crime family in the late 1950s, and boss a decade later before turning government informant in 1970.

Iannone, James (AKA: **Danny Wilson**), prom. 1950s-60s. Los Angeles racketeer. Soldier in the L.A. crime family

Jefferson, Leroy, 1919- . Leading narcotics trafficker in the black community of Los Angeles and greater Southern California. Convicted in three separate conspiracy cases in 1958.

Korshak, Sidney, prom. 1950s-60s. Powerful attorney who specialized in labor law. The Chicago mob's "advance" man on the West Coast. Brother of Marshall Korshak, Democratic Committeeman from Chicago's South Side, and a political wheelhorse in City Hall.

LaVerne Gang, prom. 1980s Latino street gang based in Los Angeles.

Licata, Carlo, prom. 1950s-60s. Son of Nicholas Licata. Married the daughter of Detroit mobster William Tocco.

Licata, Nicholas (AKA: **Nick**), 1897-1974. Assumed control of the Southern California rackets from Frank DiSimone, in January 1968. His criminal record was relatively clean, with one conviction in 1945.

LoCicero, Giocchino (AKA: **Jack**), prom. 1970s. Foot soldier in the Brooklier crime family.

Lo Cigno, Sam, prom. 1950s-60s. Low-ranked Mafia figure employed by Mickey Cohen. Alleged to have been sexually involved with Marilyn Monroe for purposes of blackmail.

Marcello, Anthony, prom. 1960s. Mafia boss of Southern California and drug trafficker.

Meltzer, Harold (AKA: **Happy**), prom. 1950s. Gambling boss, and drug trafficker in Southern California. A close associate of Meyer Lansky, and Mickey Cohen.

Milano, Peter (AKA: **Pete**), 1929- . Son of Cleveland racketeer Anthony Milano. Current Mafia kingpin in Los Angeles. Convicted of racketeering, loan sharking, and fraud after a lengthy investigation, in 1984.

Mohesky, Joseph Lee, d.1976. Owner of a Fresno adult theatre before being gunned down by his mob associates on Sept. 1, 1976.

Monica, John (AKA: **Sparky**) prom. 1950s-70s. One of the most influential sports bookmakers in Los Angeles.

Nealis, Edward (AKA: **Eddie**), prom. 1950s-60s. Los Angeles gambler who attempted a buyout of the Las Vegas Tallyho Hotel.

Palermo, Thomas, prom. 1960s-70s. Consigliere in the Los Angeles crime family.

Petti, Chris (Chris Poulos), 1942- . Affiliated with the Chicago mob, but headquartered in San Diego, where he oversees gambling operations.

Pinelli, Salvatore (AKA: **Sal**), prom. 1960s-70s. A soldier in the Los Angeles crime family.

Piscitelle, George, prom. 1950s-60s. Gangster employed by Mickey Cohen. Allegedly involved at one time with Marilyn Monroe.

Piscopo, Salvatore (AKA: **Dago Louie**), prom. 1940s-60s. Soldier in the Los Angeles crime family. A close friend of Jimmy Fratianno.

Pisello, Salvatore, prom. 1980s. Reputed member of the Gambino crime family of New York. Convicted in Los Angeles in 1988 of evading taxes on hundreds of thousands of dollars of income earned through deals with MCA Records.

Polizzi, Angelo, prom. 1960s-70s. Buffalo mobster who joined the Los Angeles family as a soldier.

Rand, Tamara, d.1975. San Diego businesswoman and girlfriend of Allen Glick. Also a Justice Department informant. Murdered by the mob on Nov. 9, 1975.

Ricciardi, Thomas, prom. 1970s. Soldier in the Brooklier crime family. Indicted with Brooklier, Sam Sciortino, Jack Lo Cicero, and Louis Tom Dragna, for racketeering, conspiracy, and murder in 1979.

Rizzitello, Michael (AKA: **Mike Rizzi**), prom. 1960s-70s. A capo in the Brooklier crime family. Indicted with his boss in 1979, for racketeering, conspiracy, and obstruction of justice.

Roselli, John (Fillippo Sacco), 1905-76. Syndicate underling of Jack Dragna. Sentenced to ten years in prison in 1944, for his role in the movie extortion case. Served only three years. One of the Mafia suspects in alleged plots to kill Fidel Castro and John F. Kennedy. Murdered in 1976.

Rummel, Samuel, prom. 1940s. Attorney for Mickey Cohen and police fixer. Murdered.

Sciortino, Samuel, prom. 1960s-70s. Underboss of the Los Angeles Mafia under Dominick Brooklier. A cousin of New Orleans mobster Philip Rizzuto.

Shenker, Morris, prom. 1970s. Influential attorney for the Mafia.

Sica, Joseph, 1911- . Narcotics trafficker, hired killer, and extortionist employed by Mickey Cohen. Sent to the Leavenworth Penitentiary in the 1950s for criminal extortion.

Stellino, Frank, prom. 1960s-70s. Son-in-law of Nick Licata. Member of the Los Angeles family.

Stompanato, John, d.1958. Bodyguard of Mickey Cohen. Murdered by 14-year-old Cheryl Crane, daughter of actress Lana Turner.

Todd, Thelma, d.1935. Film actress murdered in Santa Monica, Calif., supposedly by the mob after she refused to permit a gambling den to operate above her restaurant.

Tripoli, Mimi, prom. 1960s-70s. Pizzeria owner and member of the Los Angeles mob.

Trombino, Anthony, prom. 1950. Reputed to be one of the two gunmen who killed Samuel Rummel, lawyer for Mickey Cohen. Assassinated on orders from Cohen.

Werber, Victor, prom. 1960s-70s. Los Angeles bookie and loan shark. Also involved in the garment industry.

MEXICAN-SOUTH AMERICAN DRUG CARTELS-ORGANIZED CRIME

Abello Silva, José, 1954- . Considered to be the number four ranking member of the Medellin drug cartel. Responsible for smuggling thousands of pounds of cocaine and marijuana into the U.S. during 1983-84. Captured and extradited to Tulsa, Okla. where he was indicted in 1989.

Aldana Ibarra, Miguel, prom. 1980s. Former primer commandante of the Mexican Federales, and chief of INTERPOL in Mexico who was linked to the Rafael Cáro Quintero drug cartel.

Antonio Ruiz, Camilo, prom. 1980s. Former top aide to murdered Colombian drug trafficker José Gonzalo Rodriguez Gacha. Financial officer for the Medellin Cartel. Arrested on Dec. 30, 1989 by Colombian military authorities.

Barba-Hernández, Javier, d.1986. Mexican lawyer on the payroll of the Guadalajara Drug Cartel. Killed by the police in 1986.

Barragan, Ismael, 1914- . Associated with Juan and Roberto Hernandez, narcotics traffickers out of Guadalajara. Imported tons of marijuana across the U.S. border.

Camarena, Enrique (AKA: **Kiki**), 1948-85. DEA agent abducted and murdered by the Guadalajara drug cartel in February 1985.

Cáro-Quintero, Rafael (AKA: **Rafa**), 1952- . Ruler of the Guadalajara drug cartel. Imprisoned for complicity in the murder of DEA agent Enrique Camarena.

Cebellos, Martin, 1956- . Son of a former Colombian legislator who was also imprisoned for drug smuggling. Cebellos Jr. is a drug trafficker and associate of José Abello Silva. Arrested in Miami, Fla., in October 1988.

Emilio Zapata, Jesus, prom. 1980s. Drug overlord of the Bogotá Cartel of Columbia. Wanted in the U.S. for drug trafficking.

Escobar Gaviria, Pablo, 1949- . Drug trafficker and member of the Medillin Col. Cartel.

Esparragoza Moreno, Juan José (AKA: **El Azul**), prom. 1985. Drug trafficker and member of the Guadalajara, Mex. cartel.

Felix Gallardo, Miguel Angel (AKA: **El Padrino**), 1946- . Former Mexican police official turned drug trafficker. Has cultivated ties to the Medellin Cartel.

Felix Guitterrez, Jesus, 1960- . Los Angeles businessman convicted of aiding and abetting Rafael Cáro Quintero in the kidnap-murder of Enrique Cammarena Salazar.

Fonseca Carrillo, Ernesto (AKA: **Don Neto**), 1931- . Drug trafficker and senior adviser to Rafael Cáro-Quintero.

Gallardo Parra, José Luis (AKA: **El Guero**), prom. 1985. Drug trafficker aligned with Ernesto Fonseca Carrillo.

Gomez, Luis Arce (AKA: **the Minister of Cocaine**), prom. 1980s. Bolivian army colonel who conspired with local drug traffickers in 1980-81 to ship cocaine into the U.S. Captured and extradited to the U.S. in December 1989.

Herrera Family, prom. 1950s-80s. Family of heroin and marijuana traffickers from Los Herreras Durango, Mex. and Chicago, Ill.

Ibarra Herrera, Manuel, prom. 1982-85. Appointed Director of the Mexican Federales Judicial Police in 1982. Suspected of having ties to the Guadalajara Cartel.

Lehder Rivas, Carlos, 1947- . Major Colombian drug trafficker. One of the co-rulers of the Medellin Cartel.

López Alvarez, Raul, 1959- . Former Mexican state police officer convicted of murdering Enrique Cammarena Salazar. Received a 240 year prison sentence.

Matta Ballesteros, Juan Ramón, prom. 1985-86. Drug chemist formerly aligned with Sicilia Falcon, Cuban trafficker. Later a member of the Guadalajara Cartel.

Noriega, Manuel, prom. 1980s. Political dictator of Panama who gave aid and comfort to members of the Medellin Drug Cartel. Overthrown by U.S. troops in December 1989.

Ocampo Obando, José, prom. 1980s. Fifth ranking member of the Medellin drug cartel. Captured by Colombian police on Dec. 29, 1989.

Ocaña Garcia, Gilberto, prom. 1986. Brother of the former Governor of Sonora, Mex., Samuel Ocaña Garcia. Arrested in October 1986, and accused of running several large marijuana growing farms in Sonora.

Ochoa Restrepo, Fabio, 1924- . One-time Colombian cattle breeder who became a major figure in the Medellin drug cartel.

Ochoa Vásquez, Jorge Luis, 1949- . Son of Fabio Restrepo Ochoa. Member of the Medellin cartel who established the eastern U.S. drug routes for the cartel. Wanted in the U.S. on drug trafficking charges.

Ontiveros, Gilberto, prom. 1980s. Head of a large drug ring in Ciudad Juárez.

Quintero Payán, Emilio, prom. 1960s-80s. An uncle of Rafael Cáro Quintero. Active in the Guadalajara Cartel.

Quintero Payán, Juan José, prom. 1960s-80s. Uncle of Rafael Cáro Quintero. Member of the Guadalajara Cartel.

Rodriguez Gacha, José Gonzalo, d.1989. Medellin drug trafficker killed in a shootout with police on Dec. 15, 1989.

Rodriguez Orejuela, Gilberto, prom. 1980s. Brother of Jorge Rodriguez Orejuela. Reputed to be the number two man in the Medellin cartel, based in Cali, Col.

Rodriguez Orejuela, Jorge, prom. 1980s. One of three brothers involved in the manufacture and distribution of cocaine in Cali, Col. Arrested in August 1989 for carrying illegal weapons and false papers. Illegally freed by a Colombian judge.

Rodriguez Orejuela, Miguel Angel, prom. 1980s. Brother of Gilberto Rodriguez Orejuela. Cali drug trafficker.

Salcido Uzeta, Manuel (AKA: **Cochi Loco**), 1947- . Drug boss in Sinaloa, Mex.

Suárez Gomez, Roberto (AKA: **Papito**), 1932- . Drug overlord of Santa Ana de Yacuma, Bol.

Tejeda Jaramillo, Francisco (AKA: **Paco**), prom. 1970s-80s. Top enforcer and money courier for Rafael Cáro Quintero.

Valenzuela, José, prom. 1970s-80s. Headed up a heroin smuggling operation, extending from Mexico to New York, from his home in San Marino, Calif. Convicted of drug trafficking.

Verdugo Urquiquez, Rene Martin, 1952- . Lieutenant of Rafael Cáro Quintero, convicted in 1988, by a Los Angeles jury, for complicity in the Enrique Camarena Salazar murder.

MILWAUKEE-MADISON, WIS., ORGANIZED CRIME

Alioto, John, prom. 1950s-60s. Former boss of the Milwaukee crime family.

Balistrieri, Frank (AKA: **Frankie Bal**), 1921- . Boss of the Milwaukee rackets, sent to prison for his role in the Central States Teamster Pension Fund shakedown.

Balistrieri, John, 1949- . Son of mob boss Frank Balistrieri. Convicted of extortion on May 30, 1984.

Balistrieri, Joseph, 1941- . Son of Frank Balistrieri. Convicted of extortion on May 30, 1984.

Caputo, Carlo, prom. 1970s. Syndicate boss of Madison, Wis. operations.

Miniaci, August (AKA: **Augie**), d.1975. Mobster turned FBI informant. Murdered on Sept. 11, 1975.

MISCELLANEOUS ORGANIZED CRIME

Cosa Nostra, prom. 1920s- . Euphemism for the Mafia, meaning "this thing of ours."

Kefauver, Carey Estes, prom. 1950. U.S. Senator from Tennessee. Conducted Senate hearings into national organized crime in various cities in 1950.

Kefauver Committee, prom. 1950. Senate hearings chaired by Estes Kefauver, Democratic Congressman from Tennessee. The Committe delved into the inner workings of the national racing wire and related organized crime activities. The hearings were conducted in various U.S. cities in the Summer and Fall of 1950.

McClellan Committee, prom. 1957-63. U.S. Senate Select Committee empowered to investigate labor racketeering and organized crime in the U.S. Chaired by Senator John L. McClellan of Arkansas, and spearheaded by Robert F. Kennedy, the committee revealed for the first time the existence of the "Cosa Nostra" from informant Joseph Valachi, who provided members with a detailed organizational "chart" of ranking mobsters in the U.S.

Mafia Induction Oath, The initiate's trigger finger is cut. Blood is then drawn and a holy card with an image of the family's patron saint is burned. According to secret FBI recordings made in Connecticut, in 1989, the oath is as follows: "I (NAME GIVEN) want to enter into this organization to protect my family and to protect my friends. I swear not to divulge this secret and to obey with love and omerta. As burns this saint so will burn my soul. I enter alive into this organization and leave it dead."

Nixon, Richard M., 1913- . U.S. President who received the political support of Frank Fitzsimmons, president of the Teamster's Union, and assorted organized crime figures involved in the Central States Pension fund.

RICO (Racketeer Influenced and Corrupt Organizations), prom. 1970- . Enacted in 1970, RICO legislation is designed to circumvent the infiltration of legitimate business by organized crime figures. The law carries with it stiff penalties, including asset forfeiture, and the right of injured parties to file civil suits in the courts for attorneys fees and treble damage.

Thornburgh, Richard (AKA: **Dick**), prom. 1980s. U.S. Attorney General appointed by President Ronald Reagan. Merged the fourteen regional organized crime strike forces with the U.S. Attorney's offices in February 1989.

NEW ORLEANS, LA., ORGANIZED CRIME

Anderson, William (AKA: **Crazy Bill**), prom. 1860s-80. Member of the Live Oaks gang.

Anderson, Thomas C., prom. 1890s-1910s. Fourth-Ward political boss and owner of a string of saloons and bordellos in Storyville.

Ardotta, Giutano, prom. 1880s. Mafia assassin. Killed Tony Labruzzo on Bienville Street, in July 1881.

Arlington, Josie (Mary Deubler), 1864-1914. Famous brothel keeper on Basin Street. Her gaudy establishment was gutted by fire in 1905.

Bagnetto, Antonio, prom. 1890. One of nineteen Mafiosi indicted for the murder of Police Chief David Hennessy. Lynched on Mar. 14, 1891.

Bailey, William, d.1930. Rival gangster of Sylvestro Carolla, murdered in 1930.

Barton, Leila, prom. 1870s. Basin Street brothel madame.

Basin Street, prom. 1860-1900. Gaudy boulevard of saloons, bordellos, and dance halls extending from St. Peter St., southward to Canal.

Belmont, Frankie, prom. 1880s-90s. Proprietress of a Customhouse Street brothel.

Béluche, René, prom. 1810s. New Orleans pirate headquartered on Grand Terre Island.

Bertin, Pierre, prom. 1860s. Burglar and underworld figure. Sent to prison in 1871.

Bison Williams, prom. 1860s. Proprietor of the Buffalo Bill House, a concert saloon and dance house at Franklin and Dryades Sts.

Black Hand, prom. 1890s-1920s. Secret Italian terrorist society. Composed of many splinter groups, the Black Hand was active in sections of Chicago, Philadelphia, St. Louis, Kansas City, San Francisco, Detroit and New York.

Blue Book, prom. 1890s-1900s. Guidebook to Storyville and other New Orleans red light attractions. Later supplanted by the Green Book, and the Red Book.

Bolden, Garibaldi, prom. 1880s. Member of the Yellow Henry Gang.

Bridget Fury (Delia Swift), prom. 1859. Opened a bordello on Dryades Street in 1859.

Brown, Thomas, prom. 1850s-60s. Riverboat gambler and card sharp.

Bruneau, Emile, prom. 1960s. Associate of Carlos Marcello who furnished bail bond for Lee Harvey Oswald following his 1963 arrest in New Orleans for fighting.

Capdeville, Jean, prom. 1860s. Conman and burglar who worked in tandem with Pierre Bertin. Sent to prison in 1871.

Capro, Joseph, prom. 1930s-40s. Underboss in the Sam Carolla crime family. Attended the secret Black Diamond meeting of 1947.

Caracci, Frank, prom. 1960s-80s. Mafia boss of the French Quarter since 1986. An intimate of Carlos Marcello. Was questioned about the Kennedy Assassination by the Warren Commission in 1964.

Carolla, Anthony, prom. 1940s-60s. Son of Sam Carolla. Underboss in his crime organization.

Carolla, Sylvestro (AKA: **Sam, Silver Dollar**), 1896-1972. Boss of the New Orleans Mafia from 1925 until 1947, at which time he was deported. Formerly served under Charles Matranga as the French Market supervisor.

Cassidy, Charles (AKA: **Larkin**), prom. 1850s. Newspaper reporter turned gambling boss. Partner of Augustus Lauraine.

Chappell, Holly, prom. 1850s-60s. Riverboat gambler and card sharp.

Chighizola (AKA: **Cut Nose**), prom. 1810s. Lieutenant and criminal associate of the pirate Jean Lafitte.

Christmas, Anne, prom. 1800s. A black woman who maintained a floating brothel near the New Orleans Levee.

Cohern, Gib, prom. 1840s. Riverboat gambler and conman.

Committee of One Hundred, prom. 1886. Reform group aimed at stopping police corruption and reducing crime.

Contreras, Juan, d.1822. Leased the Sure Enuf Hotel from Mother Colby in 1822. Killed by Bill Sedley in 1822.

Corduroy Alley, prom. 1860s. Narrow alleyway extending from St. Thomas to Rousseau Sts., lined with gin mills and vice dens.

Curtius, prom. 1850s. Owner of an exclusive gambling house at Toulouse and Chartres Streets, where the only games allowed were chess, boston, and poker.

Davis, John, prom. 1820s-30s. Politically connected owner of a gambling house at Orleans and Bourbon Streets, opened in 1827.

Dean, Julia, prom. 1890s. Storyville brothel madame.

Decker, Fanny, prom. 1880s-90s. Customhouse Street brothel keeper.

Deckert, Anne, prom. 1880s-90s. Proprietress of a Customhouse Street brothel.

Deering, Eunice, prom. 1890s. Storyville brothel madame.

Delaney, "Crooked Neck", prom. 1880s. Member of the Yellow Henry Gang.

Denham, James Cole (AKA: **King Cole**), prom. 1870s-80s. Last of the Gulf of Mexico pirates. Imprisoned in 1881.

Desfargues, Jean, prom. 1810s. A follower of Jean Lafitte. Hanged as a pirate in 1819.

Devol, George prom. 1840s-80s. Notorious "head-butting" steamboat gambler and card sharp. Formed a partnership with two other gamblers, Tom Brown and Holly Chappell.

DiPiazza, Salvatore (AKA: **Sam**), prom. 1970s. Gambler and bookmaker who worked for Carlos Marcello.

Dix, Gertrude (Gertrude Hoffmire), prom. 1910s. Basin Street brothel madame and wife of Tom Anderson.

Doran, S.A. (AKA: **Major**), prom. 1870-83. Tennessee gunman who opened a gambling den on Royal Street.

Emerson, William, prom. 1860s-80s Member of the Live Oaks gang.

Esposito, Giuseppi (AKA: **Radzo**), prom. 1880s. New Orleans Mafia chieftain, who arrived from Sicily, in 1881. Arrested by Police Chief David Hennessy in 1881. Deported to Italy.

Ferrie, David, prom. 1960s. Legal researcher on the staff of Carlos Marcello. Implicated in the assassination of President John F. Kennedy.

Fitzgerald, James, prom. 1840s. New Orleans steamboat gambler and card sharp.

Fluger (AKA: **Colonel Plug**), prom. 1800s-10s. Riverboat pirate who robbed and sank flatboats. The passengers were killed or left to drown.

Franklin, William, prom. 1870s. New Orleans gambling boss, whose establishment was located at Common St. and Charles Ave.

Freeman, Caroline, prom. 1890s. Customhouse Street brothel madame.

French Quarter, 1700s- , Original settlement of New Orleans. Became notorious for its many gambling dens and saloons following the passage of a bill legalizing gambling in 1869.

Gagliano, Frank, prom. 1920s-50s. Original member of the Sam Carolla gang in the "pre-Marcello" era.

Gallatin Street, prom. 1840s-70s. Vice district located within the Vieux Carré, between Ursuline Ave. and Nicholls St. Gallatin Street was notorious for its gin mills, bordellos, and barrel houses.

Gambi, Vincent, prom. 1810s. Italian pirate and lieutenant of Jean Lafitte.

Gambino, Anthony Peter, d.1976. Cousin of New York mobster Carlo Gambino. Murdered after informing on the mob, in November 1976.

Garbright, Nettie, prom. 1890s. Customhouse Street brothel madame.

Graffagnini, Nicholas, prom. 1960s. Associate of Carlos and Peter Marcello. Managed the Sho-Bar on Bourbon Street.

Grey, Anne, prom. 1870s. Brothel madame and mistress of Tom O'Brien.

Grifazzi, Nicholas, prom. 1930s-40s. Underboss in the Sam Carolla crime family. Attended the 1947 Black Diamond meeting.

Haley, Nellie (AKA: **Queen of the Procuresses**), prom. 1880s-90s. White slaver and procuress. Arrested in Chicago in 1893, but acquitted.

Hamilton, Hattie (Hattie Peacock), d.1882. Owner of the Twenty-One, a Basin Street bordello. Allegedly shot and killed Senator James D. Beares on May 26, 1870.

Hargraves, Richard, prom. 1840s-70s. Successful riverboat gambler whose worth was estimated to be $2 million.

Hennessy, David C., 1857-90. Chief of Police who was murdered by the Mafia on Oct. 15, 1890.

Hennessy, Michael, d.1886. Cousin of David Hennessy. Murdered in Houston, by a New Orleans assassin.

Hewlett, James, prom. 1830s-40s. Proprietor of Hewlett's Exchange, a sporting house and saloon where slave auctions were held.

Incardona, Bastion, prom. 1890. One of nineteen Mafiosi indicted for the murder of Police Chief David Hennessy. Prosecution was later abandoned.

Italian Vigilance Committee, prom. 1900. Organized by local Italian businessman to track down Black Hand extortionists.

Jackson, Mary Jane (AKA: **Bricktop**), prom. 1850s. Famous red-haired prostitute who worked in Archie Murphy's establishment. Murdered three men, but served a four year prison sentence, earning her release, in 1862.

Jackson, Nina, prom. 1890s. Customhouse brothel madame.

John, Joseph, prom. 1880s. Member of the Yellow Henry Gang.

Johnson, Emma, prom. 1880s-90s. Procuress and brothel keeper of the Studio on Basin Street.

Johnson, Kitty, prom. 1870s. Proprietress of a bordello on Customhouse Street.

Johnson, Robert, prom. 1810s. A lieutenant of pirate Jean Lafitte.

Jones, William (AKA: **Canada Bill**), prom. 1850s-60s. Riverboat gambler and monte player.

Karno, Nicholas, prom. 1980s. Lieutenant and right hand man of Frank Caracci in the French Quarter.

Kastel, Philip (AKA: **Dandy**), prom. 1950s. Slot machine boss and point man for Frank Costello in New Orleans.

Keeley, Patrick, prom. 1880s. Member of the Yellow Henry Gang.

Knuckley, William, prom. 1860s-80s. Member of the Live Oaks gang.

Knuckley, Michael, prom. 1860s-80s. Member of the Live Oaks gang. Brother of Bill Knuckley.

Krause, Frederick (AKA: **Crazy Bill**), d.1855. Girod Street figure who bought the Sure Enuf Hotel from Mother Colby.

Labruzzo, Anthony, prom. 1880s. Early leader of the New Orleans Mafia. Deposed by Giuseppi Esposito, and gunned down by Giutano Ardotta in July 1881.

Lauraine, Augustus, prom. 1850s. Partner of Charles Cassidy, and co-owner of a New Orleans keno parlor.

Lehde, George, prom. 1880s. Member of the Yellow Henry Gang.

Leigh, Madge, prom. 1880s-90s. Owner of a Customhouse Street brothel.

Leoni, prom. 1880s. First boss of the New Orleans Mafia. Emigrated from Sicily. Succeeded by Giuseppe Esposito.

Levy, Sally, prom. 1890s. Customhouse Street brothel madame.

Lewis, Thomas, prom. 1860s-80s. Member of the Live Oaks gang.

Liberto, Frank, prom. 1950s-60s. Member of a New Orleans-based Mafia family which was heavily involved in the city's produce markets.

Liberto, Salvatore, prom. 1950s-60s. Brother of Frank Liberto. Identified as a member of the Carlos Marcello organization by the House Select Committee on Assassinations in 1979.

Live Oak Boys, prom. 1860s-80s. Street gang headquartered on Gallatin Street. Nicknamed for their habit of using oak truncheons as their favored assault weapon.

Livingston, Gertrude (AKA: **Queen Gertie**), prom. 1890s. Took over management of Abbie Reed's brothel in 1893.

Lockerby, Charles (AKA: **Lagerbeer**), prom. 1860s-80s. Member of the Live Oaks Gang. Killed in a saloon brawl.

Lombardino, Frank, prom. 1930s-40s. Underboss in the Sam Carolla crime family. In attendance at the 1947 Black Diamond conclave.

Long, Huey Pierce (AKA: **Kingfish**), 1893-1935. Governor of Louisiana, 1928-31. Helped Carlos Marcello establish his gambling rackets in Louisiana.

Louisiana State Lottery Co., prom. 1868-1907. Organized in 1868 following passage of a state bill legalizing gambling. A power in nationwide gambling until 1907 when it dissolved.

Lowe, John, prom. 1860s-80s. Member of the Live Oaks gang.

Lynch, Barry, prom. 1860s-80s. Member of the Live Oaks gang.

Lyons, Frank, prom. 1880s. Member of the Yellow Henry Gang. Son of Jack Lyons. Assumed leadership of the gang from Henry Stewart in 1890.

Lyons, John, prom. 1860s-80s. Member of the Live Oaks gang.

McDonald, Thomas (AKA: **Tom the Dog**), prom. 1880s. Member of the Yellow Henry Gang.

McGrath, Price, prom. 1850s. Opened a deluxe keno hall in partnership with James Sherwood and Henry Perritt.

McLane, James, prom. 1840s. Riverboat gambler and card sharp.

Macheca, Joseph, prom. 1890. One of nineteen Mafiosi indicted for the murder of Police Chief David Hennessy.

Mackey, Thomas, prom. 1840s. Riverboat gambler and card sharp.

Mader, Charles, prom. 1880s. Member of the Yellow Henry Gang.

Marchese, Paulo (Paul di Cristina), prom. 1910-20s, Ordered the murder of New York City police lieutenant Joseph Petrosino while still residing in Sicily in 1909. Later became the ruler of the New Orleans Black Hand.

Marcello, Anthony prom. 1950s-80s. Brother of Carlos Marcello. Underboss of the New Orleans Mafia.

Marcello, Carlos (Caloreo Minicari) (AKA: **The Little Man**) 1910- . Supreme boss of the New Orleans Mafia since 1947; his name has often been linked to the assassination of President John F. Kennedy.

Marcello, Joseph Jr., prom. 1950s-60s. Younger brother of Carlos Marcello. Functioned as the immediate underboss in the family, and helped Joseph Poretto run the Nola wire service.

Marcello, Nicholas, prom. 1930s-40s. Cousin of Carlos Marcello. Underboss in the Sam Carolla organization.

Marcello, Pasquale (AKA: **Pascal**), 1925- . Younger brother of Carlos Marcello. Operator of a syndicate gambling den in Gretna, Jefferson Parish.

Marcello, Peter Jr., 1961- . Nephew of Carlos Marcello. Arrested for distributing 500,000 tablets of the drug ecstasy in January 1990.

Marcello, Peter Sr., 1921- . Younger brother of Carlos Marcello. Proprietor of the Sho-Bar, a New Orleans strip joint in the French Quarter.

Marcello, Salvadore (AKA: **Sammy**), prom. 1940s-60s. Youngest of the seven Marcello brothers. Restaurateur, and slot machine boss of Jefferson Parish.

Marcello, Vincent, prom. 1940s-60s. Brother of Carlos Marcello. Ran a jukebox and pinball business known as Jefferson Music. One of the prime targets of Attorney General Robert Kennedy's war on organized crime.

Marchesi, Asperi, prom. 1890. Fourteen-year-old boy indicted for the murder of David Hennessy in 1890.

Maroney, James, prom. 1880s. Member of the Yellow Henry Gang.

Marshall, Mattie, prom. 1890s. Customhouse Street brothel madame.

Martin, Joseph, prom. 1880s. Expert garroter, and a member of the

Yellow Henry Gang.

Mason, Samuel, prom. 1820s. Former Justice of the Peace turned bandit along the Natchez Trace.

Matranga, Charles, prom. 1880s-90s. Brother of Tony Matranga. Co-leader of the emerging New Orleans Mafia. Acquitted of murdering Police Chief Hennessy in 1891.

Matranga, Anthony, prom. 1880s-90s. Took over leadership of the New Orleans Mafia after Giuseppi Esposito was deported.

Merritt, Anne, prom. 1880s-1910s. Owner of a brothel on Customhouse Street.

Miller, Charles P. (AKA: **King of the Banco Men**), prom. 1870s. Associate of S.A. Doran. Later went to New York to start his own bunko racket.

Miner, James (AKA: **Umbrella Jim**), prom. 1850s. Shell-player and big time conman on board the Mississippi River steamboats.

Miss Carol, prom. 1890s. Baronne Street procuress who also supplied young boys to homosexual patrons of an assignation house on Lafayette St.

Monasterio, Pietro, prom. 1890. One of nineteen Mafiosi indicted for the murder of Police Chief David Hennessy.

Moran, James (James Brocatto), (AKA: **Diamond Jim**), prom. 1930s. Former bodyguard of Huey Long. Lieutenant of Sam Carolla.

Morris, Frances, prom. 1890s. Storyville brothel keeper.

Mother Colby, prom. 1820s-30s. Proprietress of the Sure Enuf Hotel, a bordello located in the Swamp district of New Orleans.

Murphy, Archie, prom. 1850s-60s. Owner of a Gallatin Street bordello.

Murrel, John A., prom. 1820s-30s. Murderer, highwayman, and trafficker in Negro slaves. Imprisoned in 1834 for stealing slaves.

Nolan, Eugene, prom. 1970s. Gambler and bookmaker allied with Carlos Marcello.

O'Brien, Hugh, prom. 1860s-80s. Brother of Jimmy O'Brien. One of the leaders of the Live Oaks.

O'Brien, James, prom. 1860s-80s. Member of the Live Oaks. Killed Henry Thompson in 1867. Died in prison.

O'Brien, Mary, prom. 1890s. Customhouse Street brothel madame.

O'Brien, Matthew, prom. 1880s. Son of Hugh O'Brien. Member of the Live Oaks.

O'Brien, Monk, prom. 1880s. Gang leader and thief.

O'Brien, Thomas, prom. 1870s-80s. Bunko artist and swindler who later traveled to Paris to set up operations.

Oster, Philip, prom. 1870s-80s. Burglar, and gang leader.

Owens, Ray, prom. 1890s. Owner of the Star Mansion, a Storyville brothel.

Pecora, Nofio J., prom. 1940s-60s. Regarded as one of Carlos Marcello's most trusted lieutenants, ranked number three in the outfit.

Perritt, Henry, prom. 1850s. St. Louis gambler who opened a keno hall on Carondelet Street with Price McGrath and James Sherwood.

Petrie, Henry, prom. 1860s. Member of the Live Oaks gang.

Petrie, "Redhead", prom. 1860s. Member of the Live Oaks gang.

Petrie, "Whitehead", prom. 1860s. Member of the Live Oaks gang.

Piazza, William (AKA: **Countess**), prom. 1890s-1900s. Storyville brothel madame.

Pickett, Thomas, prom. 1872-76. Last owner of the Green Tree dive. Sent to prison for the murder of Mike Knuckley.

Pinchback, Pinckney Benton Stewart (AKA: **Pinch**), prom. 1840s-70s. Protegé of George Devol. Cardsharp and river boat gambler who preyed on freed blacks. Later became acting governor of Louisiana.

Politz, Manuel, prom. 1890. One of nineteen Mafiosi indicted for the murder of Police Chief David Hennessy. Lynched on Mar. 14, 1891.

Poretto, Joseph Albert, prom. 1940s-60s. Top lieutenant and business associate of Carlos Marcello. Ran the family's horse-racing interests in New Orleans.

Powell, John, prom. 1840s-50s. Riverboat gambler who won $100,000 from Jules Devereaux in a poker marathon, 1858.

Provenzano, Joseph, prom. 1880s-90s. One of three brothers who owned an import fruit business in New Orleans. Indicted for the ambush shooting of Tony Matranga in 1880. His 1890 trial led to the murder of Police Chief David Hennessy.

Provenzano, Peter, prom. 1880s-90s. Brother of Joe Provenzano, and an ally of David Hennessy.

Quadroon Balls, prom. 1800-50. Annual social function designed to provide white men with Quadroon mistresses. It was little more than a licensed slave-market, usually held at the top hotels in New Orleans.

Reed, Abbie (Mary Hines), prom. 1890s. Owner of two bordellos on Burgundy Street and Delord. Forced to retire in 1893.

Rice, Harry, prom. 1860s. Owner of the Green Tree brothel. Driven out of town in 1864 by a mob of riotous sailors.

Rich, Mary (AKA: **One Legged Duffy**), prom. 1865. Purchased the Green Tree from Harry Rice in 1865, but was murdered by her lover Charley Duffy.

Rigaut, Pierre (Marquis de Vaudreuil), prom. 1751-53. Corrupt French governor of New Orleans. With his wife, Rigaut sold drugs to the townspeople and permitted the prostitution rackets to flourish.

Rizzuto, Philip, prom. 1960s-70s. Cousin of Los Angeles mob boss Sam Sciortino. A trusted member of Carlos Marcello's inner circle. Indicted in 1981 for conspiring to bribe a federal judge.

Rizzuto, Thomas, prom. 1930s-40s. Underboss in the Sam Carolla Mafia family. Attended the 1947 Black Diamond conclave.

Rousell, Louis, prom. 1950s-60s. New Orleans financier and money launderer closely allied with Carlos Marcello.

Santa Hermandad (Holy Brotherhood), prom. 1769. Early law enforcement agency, committed to vigilantism as a means of combatting crime.

Scaffedi, Antonio, prom. 1890. One of nineteen Mafiosi indicted for the murder of Police Chief David Hennessy.

Schoenhausen, Otto Henry, prom. 1867-69. Owner of the Royal Palace Beer Saloon. Imprisoned for murder in 1869. Later organized the Actor's Benevolent Association in an effort to evade the Sunday closing laws.

Sedley, William, prom. 1820s. Kentucky riverboat man who murdered Juan Contreras in 1822.

Shakespeare, Joseph, prom. 1881-87. New Orleans mayor whose "Shakespeare Plan" licensed large gambling dens. Under Mayor Shakespeare, proceeds were funneled into the Shakespeare Almshouse, subsequent administrations abused the fund. After a grand jury investigation in 1897, the system ceased to work.

Sherwood, James, prom. 1850s. One of three partners of McGrath & Co., a deluxe keno hall opened in the 1850s.

Smoky Row, prom. 1870-85. Burgundy Street, between Bienville and Conti, lined by Negro bordellos and vice dens.

Spanish Agnes. prom. 1880s-90s. Ran an "employment agency" for prostitutes on Burgundy Street. Bought and sold girls for the brothel keepers of Galveston and New Orleans.

Spiders, the, prom. 1880s. Criminal gang whose headquarters on Franklin St. was called the "Web."

Starr, Charles (AKA: **Colonel**), prom. 1850s. Flamboyant riverboat gambler.

Stewart, Henry (AKA: **Yellow Henry**), prom. 1880s. Took over as leader of the Yellow Henry gang of thieves and pickpockets in 1877. Died of malaria in 1886.

Stoppagherra Society, prom. 1869. Early Mafia faction prominent in the Second District.

Story, Sidney, prom. 1890s. New Orleans alderman whose 1897 City Council resolution permitted vice and prostitution to flourish in a controlled district.

Storyville, prom. 1897-1917. Notorious red light district of New Orleans located in a section of the French Quarter. Named for Alderman Sidney Story.

Struve, William, prom. 1890s-1910s. Right hand man of political boss Tom Anderson in the Storyville district.

Swamp, the, prom. 1820s. Six-block vice district located near Cypress and South Liberty Streets in New Orleans; favored rendezvous of the flatboat men.

Swan, William, prom. 1860s-80s. Saloon keeper whose establishment served as the meeting place for the Live Oaks.

Sweet, Fannie (Mary Robinson), b.1827. Owner of a Basin Street brothel. Indicted for murder in 1861, but acquitted. Retired to Florida in 1889.

Sylvester, George, prom. 1880s. Member of the Yellow Henry Gang.

Tannenbaum, Harold, prom. 1950-60s. New Orleans nightclub owner, and associate of Carlos Marcello.

Termine, Samuel, prom. 1950s-60s. Served as Carlos Marcello's chauffeur and bodyguard. Involved in syndicate gambling and prostitution in New Orleans and Waco, Tex.

Thompson, Henry, d.1867. Member of the Live Oaks. Killed by Jimmy O'Brien in 1867.

Timphony, Frank, prom. 1970s. Gambler and bookmaker who belonged to the Carlos Marcello syndicate.

Todaro, Frank, 1920-30s. Underboss to Sam Carolla during the 1920s. Attended the 1947 Black Diamond meeting.

Townsend, Katherine, prom. 1860s-80s. Owner of one of the original bordellos on Basin Street. Murdered by her lover, Treville Sykes on Nov. 1, 1883. Sykes was acquitted.

Tregle, Bernard, prom. 1940s-60s. Owner of a string of New Orleans restaurants and bars backed by the Marcello organization. Tregle ran a horse book operation, and his restaurants were stocked with syndicate jukeboxes and slot machines.

Tuckers, John, prom. 1810s. Pirate who served under Jean Lafitte.

Vieux Carré, prom. 1820s-40s. Vice-district located in the American section of New Orleans above Canal Street.

Vigilance Committee, prom. 1881. Organized to fight crime and corruption in New Orleans.

Walker, Joseph, prom. 1860s. Saloon keeper and founder of the Citizen's Protective Association, opposed to the Sunday closing laws.

Walla, William, prom. 1880s. Gang leader and burglar.

White, George M., 1805-1900. Faro dealer and riverboat gambler. Ran a large faro bank in New Orleans.

White, Lulu, prom. 1890s-1900s. Brothel keeper of an octoroon house in Storyville.

White, Napoléon Bonaparte (AKA: **Poley**), d.1889. Operated a gambling house on St. Charles Avenue. Committed suicide after the resort was forced to close.

Williams, Nellie, prom. 1890s. Customhouse Street brothel madame.

Williams, Samuel, prom. 1860s-80s. Business partner of Poley White.

Wilson, "Bully", prom. 1800s-10s. Riverboat pirate whose Cave-in-the Rock served as a safe haven for other buccaneers.

Wilson Rangers, prom. 1861-65. Confederate cavalry composed entirely of Gulf Coast blacklegs and card sharps.

You, Dominique (AKA: **Captain Dominique**), 1775-1830. Former soldier in Napoléon's army, turned pirate. Lieutenant of Jean Lafitte.

NEW YORK CITY-NEW JERSEY ORGANIZED CRIME

Abbandando, Frank (AKA: **the Dasher**), 1910-42. Frankie Abbandando was the top triggerman for Murder, Inc. In 1940, Abe "Kid Twist" Reles turned informant, revealing to federal prosecutors dozens of executions Abbandando and "Happy" Maione had carried out. Was put to death at Sing Sing, on Feb. 19, 1942.

Abbatemarco, Anthony, b.1922. Son of Frank Abbatemarco. Top ranking lieutenant in the Colombo crime family.

Abbatemarco, Frank (AKA: **Frankie Shots**), d.1959. A member of the Joseph Profaci crime family, Frank Abbatemarco was a policy bank operator until he was assassinated in the Spring of 1959, by the Gallo Brothers, for failing to pay $50,000 in protection money to his superiors.

Abrams, Michael (AKA: **Big Mike**), prom. 1900s. Owner of a string of opium dens in Chinatown.

Accardi, Settimo (AKA: **Big Sam**), 1902- . A mob boss in New Jersey, where he was both a heroin trafficker and a Mafia enforcer.

Accetturo, Anthony, 1938- . A member of the Thomas Lucchese crime family. Accetturo still directs the activities of his New Jersey faction from his home in Hollywood, Fla.

Adams, Albert J., d.1906. Adams was boss of the New York numbers racket with over 800 policy shops under his control. He was sent to prison for eighteen months in the spring of 1903. On Oct. 1, 1906, he shot himself to death in the Hotel Ansonia.

Addonizio, Hugh J., prom. 1960s. A one-time mayor of Newark, N.J., Addonizio was sent to prison in 1972 after being convicted of accepting kickbacks from Mafia boss Angelo De Carlo.

Adler, Polly, prom. 1930s. Notorious Manhattan brothel madame whose 1935 arrest contributed to Lucky Luciano's downfall.

Adonis, Joseph (Giuseppe Antonio Doto) (AKA: **Joey A. Adone, Joe Arosa, James Arosa, Joe DeMio**), 1902-72. A top Mafia boss in New York for nearly thirty years; rose to prominence in the bootlegging racket with Waxey Gordon and Charles "Lucky" Luciano, in the 1920s. Adonis led a gang called the "Broadway Mob," but his influence in New York was much wider than the name of his gang suggested. Deported to Italy in 1956, along with his secret fortune, Adonis died during a police interrogation.

Agnello, Carmine, prom. 1970s-80s. Brother-in-law of John Gotti. Co-owner of the Jamaica Auto Salvage in Queens, reputed "clearing house" for a stolen auto parts ring.

Agone, Joseph (AKA: **Curly**), d.1971. New York City mobster shot and killed on July 26, 1971.

Agron, Evsei, d.1985. Leningrad-born extortionist, contract killer, and professional thief who was murdered in Brooklyn in 1985. Helped found the "Soviet Mafia."

Alaimo, Dominic, 1910- . Syndicate labor racketeer, born in Pittston, Pa.

Albanese, Salvatore (AKA: **Phil Katz**), prom. 1970s. New York City mobster allied with Anthony Abbatemarco. Disappeared in 1977.

Allen, John, prom. 1850s-60s. Proprietor of a notorious Fourth Ward dance house. Scene of revivalist meetings in later years.

Aloi, Sebastiano, prom. 1970s. Capo in the Giuseppe Magliocco family.

Alongi, Dominick (AKA: **Fat Dom**), prom. 1960s. Foot soldier, and later a capo in the Genovese Crime family.

Alpert, Alex (AKA: **Red**), d.1933. Killed by Murder, Inc., on Nov. 25, 1933.

Amato, Baldassare (AKA: **Baldo**), 1951- . Carmine Galante's bodyguard. Was present when Galante was killed on July 12, 1979. Escaped unhurt. Sentenced to five years in prison in 1988, for his part in the Pizza Connection conspiracy.

Amberg, Joseph C. 1892-1935, and **Amberg, Louis** (AKA: **Pretty**), 1899-1935. The Ambergs ran a protection racket in Brooklyn, but the more powerful syndicates pushed them aside. The brothers came to a violent, gruesome end in 1935, at the hands of Murder, Inc.

American Guards, prom. 1830s-50s. Bowery street gang connected with the Native American Party of New York.

Amuso, Victor, 1934- . In the 1970s, Victor Amuso left the crime family headed up by Joe Gallo to accept work as a foot soldier in Carlo Gambino's organization. Arrested for heroin trafficking in 1977.

Anastasia, Albert (Umberto Anastasio), (AKA: **Lord High Executioner, The Mad Hatter, Big Al**), 1903-57. A protegé of Brooklyn crime boss Joe Adonis, Albert Anastasia assembled a group of killers in the late 1920s that came to be known as Murder, Inc. He emerged as a top Mafia Don in the 1940s and 1950s, but was murdered in the barbership of a New York hotel on Oct. 25, 1957.

Anastasia, Anthony (AKA: **Tough Tony**), 1906-63. Brother of Albert Anastasia; boss of the International Longshoreman's Association for many years. Allegedly arranged for the French luxury liner *Normandie* to be blown up in protest against Charles "Lucky" Luciano's imprisonment in Dannemora. Died of natural causes in 1963.

Andolino, Simone, prom. 1960s-70s. Capodecina in the Magliocco-Profaci crime family.

Angelina, James (AKA: **Jimmy**), prom. 1970s. Caporegime in the Vito Genovese crime family.

Apacalo, Anthony, 1867-c.1904. Apacalo financed the criminal activities of Paul Kelley, leader of the Five Points Gang. Became a leading Mafia figure in New York by 1897; and was reputed to be the major bankroll behind the city bordellos, gambling dens, and fencing operations.

Argone, Joseph, d.1971. Mobster killed in Greenwich Village on July 26, 1971.

Armone, Joseph, prom. 1970s-80s. Underboss in the Gambino family. Currently in prison on racketeering charges.

Arnstein, Nicholas, prom. 1920s. New York City gambler, jailed in 1928, for bond forgery. Husband of Fanny Brice.

Arra, Frank (Frank Nunzio), prom. 1970s. A soldier in the Lucchese crime family.

Atlantic Guards, prom. 1830s-40s. Irish street gang headquartered in the Five Points.

Attardi, Alphonse (AKA: **the Peacemaker**), b.c.1892, in New York. Mob informant. Facing bankruptcy he reluctantly agreed to tell what he knew about drug trafficking on the Lower East Side in the 1950s.

Aurelio, Thomas A., prom. 1945-53. Aurelio was a judge of the New York State Supreme Court who secured his appointment through the efforts of mob boss Frank Costello.

Baby Faced Willie, prom. 1870s. Leader of the Baxter Street Dudes.

Bagdonowitz, John, d.1933. New Jersey racketeer shot by Murder, Inc., in 1933.

Baker, Joseph, prom. 1910s. Captain of an East Side gang. Battled Joe Morello for supremacy in 1912.

Baker, Lewis, prom. 1855. Tammany Hall politician and gangster. Murdered Bill Poole in 1855.

Balagula, Marat, 1943- . Soviet émigré who became a power in Brooklyn organized crime after arriving in the U.S. in 1977. Helped form a "Soviet Mafia" in New York.

Baldinucci, Giuseppe, prom. 1970s-80s. Mafia ssociate of the Bonanno family. Drug trafficker involved in the Pizza Connection.

Banana War, 1964-69. Gang war instigated by Joseph Bonanno against the principal leaders of the other four New York families in order to gain absolute control of the rackets. Bonanno fled to Arizona in 1968, bringing the war to a premature end.

Baratta, Peter (AKA: **Bull, Peter Barato**), prom. 1970s. Soldier in the Gambino crime family.

Barbara, Joseph Sr., 1905-59. Born in Sicily, Barbara became a prominent labor racketeer and gambling boss, but was better known as the host of the November 1957 Apalachin crime conference at his lavish upstate New York resort.

Barcellona, Charles (AKA: **Charlie the Wop, Sleepy**), prom. 1970s. Foot soldier in the Gambino crime family.

Barnes, LeRoy (AKA: **Nicky**), 1933- . Harlem drug boss groomed for duty by Joseph Gallo.

Barrese, Michael, prom. 1950s. Gunman for the Genovese mob. Allegedly murdered the husband of the woman Vito Genovese later married.

Barreto, Gregario, d.1971. New York mobster shot down in Manhattan on July 6, 1971.

Bartolf, James, prom. 1851. Owner of a gambling resort on Park Place.

Basto, Frank (AKA: **The Bear**), prom. 1970s. Member of Carlo Gambino's assassination team. Resides in New Jersey.

Batavia Street Gang, prom. 1900s. Small sized gang that owed allegiance to the Five Points organization.

Battle Annie (AKA: **Queen of Hell's Kitchen**), prom. 1900s. Leader of the Lady Gophers gang.

Baxter Street Dudes, prom. 1870s. Juvenile street gang who opened their own theater on Baxter Street.

Becker, Charles, 1869-1915. A New York police lieutenant who ran a "protection" racket for city gambling operations. Ordered the 1912 assassination of informant Herman "Beansie" Rosenthal. Executed at Sing Sing July 7, 1915.

Bergens Gang, prom. 1910s. New York City street gang.

Berger, Paul, prom. 1940. Brooklyn mobster who turned state's evidence in 1940.

Berman, Otto (AKA: **Abbadabba**), 1881-1935. Accountant for the Dutch Schultz mob who was killed with his boss in Newark, N.J. on Oct. 23, 1935.

Bernow, Harry (AKA: **The Hawk**), prom. 1960s. New York City gambler and mob figure.

Bernstein, Sholem, prom. 1920s-30s. Brooklyn gangster, car thief, and loan shark. Became a police informant.

Berry, James, prom. 1850s. Gambling house proprietor.

Biedler, Art, prom. 1910s. Triggerman in Owney Madden's mob.

Biello, John (AKA: **Futto**), prom. 1960s. Capo in the Genovese mob. Murdered in Miami, Fla.

Bioff, William Morris, d.1955. Labor union racketeer who extorted millions of dollars from the Hollywood movie industry through his control of the Projectionists Union. Assassinated by the Chicago mob after turning informant.

Biondo, Joseph (AKA: **Joe Bandy**), prom. 1940s-50s. Henchman of Albert Anastasia, suspected of murdering his boss. Later affiliated with the Gambino crime family.

Blind Mahoney, prom. 1870s. Pickpocket and co-captain of the Molasses Gang.

Bloody Angle, prom. 1900s. Section of New York's Chinatown on Doyers Street. A preferred escape route of the hatchet men in the criminal Tong gangs.

Blumenfield, Harry (AKA: **Yiddy Blum**), prom. 1970s. Mid-town gambling boss and racketeer.

Boccia, Ferdinand (AKA: **The Shadow**), d.1934. Old fashioned Mafia boss murdered by Vito Genovese hitmen on Oct. 9, 1934.

Boiardo, Ruggiero (AKA: **Richie the Boot**), 1891-1984. New Jersey crime boss associated with Abner "Longy" Zwillman.

Bongiovi, Robert (AKA: **Bobby Darrow**), prom. 1970s. Hitman for the Joey Gallo mob. Convicted and sent to prison after murdering a Times Square tavern owner.

Bonina, Nicholas (AKA: **The Baron**, prom. 1970s. A foot soldier in the Lucchese crime family.

Bonventre, Cesare (AKA: **the Tall Guy**), 1951-84. Youngest capo in the Mafia at the time of his murder in April 1984. Member of the Bonanno-Galante crime family. He was seated with Galante when Galante was shot to death in a Brooklyn restaurant on July 12, 1979.

Bonventre, John, prom. 1930-50. Cousin of Joseph Bonanno, and underboss in the crime family. Returned to Sicily, in 1950, where he became a leader in the local Mafia.

Boodle Gang, prom. 1870s. Gang of thieves headquartered near Greenwich, Washington, Spring, and Canal Streets.

Border Gang, prom. 1850s. Fourth Ward street gang.

Borelli, Patsy, prom. 1950s. Gambler and Manhattan policy boss.

Bowdach, Gary, prom. 1980s. Drug dealer, loan shark, and mob hit man. Released from the Atlanta Penitentiary in 1978 through the intervention of Sen. Sam Nunn, (D. Ga.).

Bowe, William, prom. 1850s. Brother of Martin Bowe. Engaged in fencing stolen merchandise from the cargo holds of East River vessels.

Bowe, John, prom. 1850s. Brother of Martin Bowe.

Bowe, James, prom. 1850s. Brother of Jack and Martin Bowe.

Bowe, Martin, prom. 1850s. Owner of Glass House, a tough Fourth Ward saloon. With his three brothers, Bowe stole merchandise from ships moored in the East River, and then sold the goods.

Bowery Boys, prom. 1820-70s. Famous Bowery street gang that waged constant warfare with the Dead Rabbits for over forty years. Politically allied with Tammany Hall.

Bowery Indians, prom. 1900s. Social-political club organized by Tammany Hall politicians.

Bow Kum, d.1909. Chinese slave girl, whose murder in August 1909 commenced a Tong War in New York.

Brady, Denny, prom. 1870s. River pirate and co-leader of the Patsy Conroy gang.

Brady, James, prom. 1870s. Member of the George Leslie hold-up gang.

Brady, "Yakey Yake", prom. 1900s. Leader of the Yakey Yakes street gang until he died from tuberculosis.

Brancato, Joseph, prom. 1960s-70s. Assumed command of the Colombo family in 1971 following the assassination of Joseph Colombo on Italian Unity Day.

Bray, Thomas, prom. 1870s. Proprietor of a resort on Thompson Street near the Mulberry Police Station.

Brennan, Martin, prom. 1900s. Member of the Gophers street gang.

Bridge Twisters, prom. 1910s. New York street gang active near the Queensboro Bridge.

Browne, George, prom. 1930s-40s. Associate of Willie Bioff involved in the movie extortion racket. Later killed on orders of the Chicago mob.

Brunder, Wilfred, prom. 1920s-30s. A Harlem numbers kingpin who was later dominated by the Dutch Shultz mob.

Buchalter, Louis (AKA: **Lepke**), 1897-1944. Garment industry racketeer; an early partner of Jacob "Gurrah" Shapiro. Chief assassin for Murder, Inc. Executed in Sing Sing.

Buckoos, prom. 1840s. Fourth Ward street gang, involved in the scuttling of vessels sailing in and out of the East River.

Burns, Kit, prom. 1850s. Owner of Sportsman's Hall, a Water Street dive frequented by the gangs of the Fourth Ward.

Busteed, William, prom. 1900s. Owner of a gambling resort on Broadway in Manhattan.

Calderazzo, Vincent (AKA: **Gazut**), d.1977. New York mobster turned informant. Found in a desert grave in San Bernadino, Calif., on Apr. 4, 1977.

Calterone, Anthony, d.1920s. Mobster killed during a Brooklyn gang war.

Camarda, Emile, prom. 1940s. Longshoreman's union racketeer.

Campanello, Frank (AKA: **F Bell**), prom. 1970s. Soldier in the Lucchese crime family.

Canfield, Richard, prom. 1902. Owner of a deluxe gambling resort in New York City; raided by District Attorney William Traver Jerome on Dec. 1, 1902.

Cangiano, Cosmo (AKA: **Gus**), prom. 1960s-70s. Colombo family soldier, swindler, and criminal fence.

Canone, Steven (AKA: **Stevie Beefs**), prom. 1970s. Elected consigliere in the Bonanno crime family, 1978.

Cantalupo, Joseph, prom. 1970s-80s. Owner of a mob-fronted real-estate firm in Brooklyn. One-time associate of Joseph Columbo who turned government informant. Author of *Body Mike: An Unsparing Exposé by the Mafia Insider Who Turned On the Mob.*

Cantellops, Nelson, prom. 1959. Small time drug pusher who turned informant against the Bonanno and Lucchese families, in 1959.

Capone, Louis, d.1944. New York mobster (no relation to Al) executed in 1944, for the murder of Joseph Rosen.

Capuzzi, Nicholas (AKA: **The Thief**), prom. 1920s. Allied with Joe "the Boss" Masseria during the Castellammarese War.

Car Barn Gang, prom. 1911-14. Street gang that congregated near the East River Docks.

Carbo, Frankie (John Paul Carbo), 1904-76. Gunman for Lepke Buchalter. A crooked fight promoter in later years.

Cardinali, James, prom. 1970s-80s. Mafia assassin and drug trafficker. Appeared as a prosecution witness in the government trial of John Gotti. In prison for murder.

Carfaro, Vincent (AKA: **The Fish**), 1934- . Protege of Anthony "Fat Tony" Salerno. Inducted into the mob in the early 1970s. Turned informant against John Gotti in 1989.

Carillo, Anthony, prom. 1960s. Foot soldier in the Genovese crime family.

Carlino, Leo, prom. 1960s-70s. Capo in the Magliocco-Profaci crime family.

Carlisi, Roy, 1909- . Carlisi was a Mafia drug trafficker and labor union racketeer in New York for many years.

Carna, Joseph (AKA: **Little Lollypop**), prom. 1950s-60s. Member of the Gallo gang in Brooklyn.

Carna, Larry, (AKA: **Big Lollypop**), prom. 1950s-60s. Brother of Joseph Carna and a triggerman for the Gallo gang.

Carnera Boxing Scandal, 1930s. Named for boxer Primo Carnera whose prize fights were rigged by the New York mob.

Carpenters, prom. 1910s. Small New York street gang active south of Fourth Avenue.

Carrao, Joseph (AKA: **Joe Butch**), prom. 1970s-80s. Caporegime in the Gambino family. Close friend of John Gotti. Currently in prison.

Carrigio, James (AKA: **Gold Mine Jimmy**), prom. 1910s. Captain of the Jimmy Curley Gang.

Carrillo, Anthony (AKA: **Tony the Shiek**), prom. 1970s. New York City mobster.

Caruso, Angelo, prom. 1950s-60s. Trusted sidekick of Joe Bonanno. Supported the son Bill, as the family's heir and successor in 1962.

Caruso, Frankie (AKA: **The Bug**), prom. 1970s. New York City mobster.

Cascioferro, Vito, 1862-1945. Sicilian Mafiosi who emigrated to the U.S. in 1900. Established a protection racket in New York, and was later implicated in the murder of New York policeman Joseph Petrosino. Arrested in Italy in 1926 by Benito Mussolini's government. Died in prison.

Cassese, Vincent, prom. 1967. Foot soldier in the Bonanno crime family of New York. Wounded in October 1967 during the Banana War.

Castellammarese War, 1928-31. Mafia war of succession which pitted the forces of Joe "the Boss" Masseria against those who were loyal to Salvatore Maranzano. In time both leaders were assassinated by the "Young Turk" element within the New York mobs.

Castellano, Paul (AKA: **Big Paul**), 1912-85. Became the heir and successor to the crime family headed by his brother-in-law Carlo Gambino. Head of the Mafia Commission until he was assassinated outside a New York steak house, in 1985.

Castronovo, Frank (AKA: **Ciccio l'Americano**, 1934- . Co-owner of a New Jersey restaurant. Sentenced to prison for twenty-five years for his role in the Pizza Connection conspiracy.

Catalano, Salvatore (AKA: **Sal, Toto**), 1941- . A Queens, N.Y., baker who negotiated the overseas distribution of heroin for the Pizza Connection. Arrived in New York in 1961. Admitted to the Bonanno crime family. Took over Pietro Licata's operations in Brooklyn. Sentenced to forty-five years in Leavenworth, on June 22, 1987.

Catalino, Julie, prom. 1930s. Syndicate assassin for Murder, Inc. Testified before the Turkus Commission in 1940.

Catania, Joseph (AKA: **Joe the Baker**), d.1931. Fought on the side of Joe Masseria in the Castellammarese War. Shot to death as he bid his wife farewell, one morning, in 1931.

Cavalieri, Sam (AKA: **Big Sam**), prom. 1970s. Soldier in the Lucchese crime family.

Cecere, Daniel (AKA: **Red**), prom. 1960s-70s. Newark, N.J. mobster sentenced to twelve years in prison for extortion in 1970.

Charley the Cripple (Charles Vitoffsky), prom. 1910s. Gangster and slugger who worked the seltzer and soda water dealers in tandem with Yoske Nigger and Johnny Levinsky.

Charlton Street Gang, prom. 1860s. Fourth Ward pirate gang that preyed upon commercial shipping along the Hudson River.

Cherry Hill Gang, prom. 1890s. A gang of hold-up men and jewel thieves.

Chichester Gang, prom. 1820s-60s. Five Points street gang allied with the Dead Rabbits.

Chieppa, Angelo (AKA: **Chippo**), prom. 1950s-60s. Former bodyguard of Ruggiero Boiardo.

Chin, Frank, 1929-77. Foot soldier and electronics expert in the DiGilio-Galante family. Murdered after turning informer.

Chisel Gang, prom. 1910s. Lower East Side street gang.

Circular Jack, prom. 1890s. One of the founders of the Hudson Dusters street gang.

Cirofici, Frank (AKA: **Dago Frank**), prom. 1910s. One of four mobsters to be found guilty of murdering Herman Rosenthal on July 15, 1912. He was executed for the crime.

Clegg, Ellen, prom. 1870s. Thief and con artist.

Coakley, Abraham, prom. 1870s. Member of the George Leslie hold-up gang.

Cocchiaro, Carmelo, 1935- . Member of the DeCavalcante crime family of New Jersey.

Coco, Ettore, prom. 1960s-70s. Capodeceine in the Lucchese crime family.

Coffee, James, prom. 1870s. One of the co-leaders of the Hooker Gang.

Cohen, Louis, and **Friedman, Isadore**, d.1939. Two witnesses against Louis "Lepke" Buchalter murdered in New York City, on Jan. 28, 1939.

Colazzo, Joseph, prom. 1960s-70s. Capodeceine in the Gambino crime family.

Coleman, Edward, d.1839. Gangster from the Paradise Square section of the Five Points. One of the first to be executed in the Tombs on Jan. 12, 1839.

Coll, Vincent (AKA: **Mad Dog**), 1909-32. Hired gunman who worked for Dutch Schultz. Decided to break off and form his own mob in 1931. Killed in a phone booth by four of Schultz's men.

Colontuono, Emile d.1963. Member of the Joe Gallo gang, murdered in Manhattan on June 6, 1963.

Colombo, Anthony, prom. 1970s. Son of Joe Colombo. Accused of melting down silver coins by the FBI in 1970.

Colombo, Joseph A., d.1978 Took over control of the Profaci Crime Family. Re-named it the Colombo family. Shot by Jerome A. Johnson at the Italian Unity Day Parade in New York, June 28, 1971. Remained in a coma for seven years.

Colton, Harry, prom. 1850s. Owner of a gambling resort on Barclay Street.

Connolly, "Baboon", prom. 1870s. Member of the Whyos Gang.

Connolly, "Slops", prom. 1870s. Member of the Whyos gang. Professional killer.

Connors, Chuck (George Washington Connors), 1852-1913. Political organizer in Chinatown in the 1880s. Connected to the Bowery Boys and leaders of Tammany Hall.

Consalvo, Carmine, d.1975. Member of the Gambino crime family. Opened up Mexico for drug trafficking operations before being thrown out of a window on Sept. 7, 1975.

Consalvo, Frank, d.1975. Brother of Carmine Consalvo. Murdered by Gambino gangsters for trying to avenge his brother's death.

Consolo, Michael, 1902-68. One-time member of the Bonanno crime family, who defected to Gasper DiGregorio. Murdered in 1968.

Cooney, James, prom. 1960s-80s. Co-founder of the Westies, a powerful Irish West Side street gang.

Coppolla, Leonardo (AKA: **Nino**), prom. 1970s. Bodyguard of Carmine Galante. Shot with his boss on July 12, 1979.

Coppola, Michael (AKA: **Trigger Mike**), 1904-66. Brutal and sadistic henchman of Vito Genovese. Helped Genovese take over Dutch Schultz's rackets in 1935. Drove second wife Ann to suicide.

Corallo, Anthony (AKA: **Tony Ducks**), 1914- . Head of the Thomas Lucchese crime family, and a ranking member in the Mafia Commission. Extortionist who is also active in Long Island.

Corcoran, "Googy", prom. 1870s. Member of the Whyos Gang.

Corcoran's Roosters, prom. 1910s. Street gang, whose turf was Third Avenue.

Corcoran, Thomas, prom. 1910. Leader of Corcoran's Roosters.

Corlear's Hook, prom. 1860s-70s. Where the Fourth Ward river gangs sought refuge after being chased out of the district by the New York Police.

Costello, Frank (Francesco Saveria), (AKA: **the Prime Minister**), 1893-1973. Powerful mob boss who rose to power under William "Big Bill" Dwyer and Charles "Lucky" Luciano. His span of control in the gambling rackets extended from New York, to Florida, to Las Vegas. Deposed by Vito Genovese in the late 1950s.

Costello, Michael, prom. 1900s. Member of the Hudson Dusters street gang.

Costello, Richard, 1936-89. President of Local 1964 of the International Longshoreman's Union Association, a syndicate controlled union in New Jersey. Associate of Thomas Gambino, reputed Mafia capo, and Paul Castellano. Assassinated on Aug. 9, 1989.

Country McCleester, prom. 1850s. Gang leader affiliated with Isaiah Rynders and the Nativist movement.

Crazy Butch Gang, prom. 1890s. Pickpocket gang active on the Lower East Side. Crazy Butch was an early associate of Monk Eastman.

Croker, Richard, 1841-1922. Boss of Tammany Hall, 1886-1902. One-time leader of the Fourth Avenue Tunnel Gang.

Curry, John F., prom. 1930s. Tammany Hall political leader until he was deposed in 1934.

Dahl, Kid, prom. 1900s. Gangster associate of Max "Kid Twist" Zweibach. Partner in a Five Points gambling racket.

Daly, John, prom. 1900s. Owner of a Broadway gambling resort.

D'Ambrosio, Alphonse (AKA: **Funzied**), prom. 1970s. Soldier in the Colombo crime family.

Dangarro, Charles, prom. 1960s-70s. Capodeceine in the Carlo Gambino family.

Daniello, Ralph (AKA: **Ralph the Barber**), prom. 1910s. Independent gang leader on the Lower East Side.

D'Argenio, Edward, prom. 1970s. Foot soldier in the Lucchese crime family.

Davidson, Jo Jo, prom. 1960s. New York City gangster.

Davidson, Philip (AKA: **Red Phil**), prom. 1900s. Murdered Jack Zelig on board a Second Avenue Trolley car, Oct. 5, 1912.

Davis, "Dinky", prom. 1900s. Owner of a Broadway gambling resort.

Davis, Julius Richard (AKA: **Dixie**), 1905-70. Served as legal counsel for Dutch Schultz. Sent to prison in 1938. Died in 1970.

Daybreak Boys, prom. 1840s-50s. Fourth Ward street gang that scuttled ships in the East River for criminal plunder. Dissolved in 1859.

Dead Rabbits Gang (AKA: **Black Birds**), prom. 1850s. Welsh-Irish street gang that terrorized the Lower East Side. They marched into battle with a dead rabbit mounted high on a spear.

DeCarlo, Angelo (AKA: **The Gyp**), 1902-73. New Jersey Mafia boss jailed in 1970 for extortion.

DeCavalcante, Simone Rizzo (AKA: **Sam the Plumber**), prom. 1960s. Mafia chieftain of New Jersey who served on the national commission. Intermediary between the warring factions in the Banana War. Sent to prison for fifteen years, in 1969.

DeCicco, Frank, d.1986. Associate of Paul Castellano, who he betrayed to John Gotti. Was murdered in 1986.

Defeo, George, d.1930. Gunman for Murder, Inc. Killed, in 1930, by the Shapiro Brothers.

Defeo, Peter, prom. 1970s. New York City mobster.

Dellacroce, Aniello (AKA: **Mr. Neil, Father O'Neill**), 1914-85. Underboss in the Carlo Gambino family until his death in 1985. A powerful, respected capodecine.

Dellacroce, Armond (AKA: **Buddy**), d.1988. Son of Aniello Dellacroce. Drug trafficker and user who died of an overdose in 1988.

DeLutro, Charles (AKA: **Charlie West**), prom. 1970s. Soldier in the Gambino crime family.

DeMange, George Jean (AKA: **Big Frenchy**), prom. 1920s-30s. Bootlegger and racketeer involved in the Carnera Boxing Scandal.

DeMeo, Roy, d.1983. Long Island milkman who headed up an elite execution squad for the Gambino crime family in the 1970s and 1980s. Murdered on Jan. 10, 1983.

DePalma, Gregory, prom. 1970s. Became a soldier in the Gambino crime family in June 1977.

DeQuatro, Dominick (AKA: **Dom the Sailor**), prom. 1930s-70s. Shared the command of the Luciano crime family when Lucky Luciano went to jail, in 1936. Later a top boss in the Genovese family.

Devery, William S., prom. 1890s. Corrupt New York City police captain in charge of the Eleventh Ward vice areas. Evidence of his graft was supplied by the Lexow Investigating Committee. Dismissed from the force in 1894.

Devinish, Fritz, prom. 1970s. Numbers and policy gangster in Central Harlem.

Diamond, John (John T. Nolan), (AKA: **Legs**), 1896-1931. Legs Diamond graduated from small-time burglary and armed robbery to become one of the top crime kingpins of New York in the 1920s and 1930s. Murdered in Albany in 1931, allegedly by Dutch Schultz.

Diamond, Morris, d.1939. Teamster's boss murdered by Louis "Lepke" Buchalter's men on May 25, 1939.

Di Angelo, James, d.1967. Together with his brother Thomas, James Di Angelo left the Bonnano crime family to join Gaspar DiGregorio. Murdered for his betrayal.

Di Angelo, Thomas, d.1967. Defected from the Bonanno crime family, in 1967. Murdered with Frank Telleri and his brother James, at the Cypress Garden Restaurant, in Queens, in October 1967.

Diapoulas, Peter (AKA: **Pete the Greek**), prom. 1972. Bodyguard of Crazy Joe Gallo. Wounded in a shootout at Umberto's Clam House on Apr. 7, 1972.

DiBello Thomas, b.1903. Underboss in the Joseph Colombo crime family. Negotiated a peace with the Gallo Brothers in 1971 following the death of Joseph Colombo.

DiBernardo, Robert (AKA: **Dee-Bee**), d.c.1986. Caporegime in the Gambino family responsible for pornography operations. Disappeared in 1986.

DiBiasio, John, d.1948. A lieutenant of Jersey City, N.J. crime boss Charles Yarnowsky. Murdered twenty-five days after his boss.

DiCarlo, John, prom. 1970s. Soldier in the Lucchese crime family.

DiGilio, John, prom. 1970s. New Jersey mobster convicted in 1977, on a 1975 charge of plotting to steal federal records dealing with his loan sharking activities. Murdered.

DiGregorio, Gasperino (AKA: **Gaspar**), 1905- . Top henchman of Joseph Bonanno, who ruthlessly formed his own mob, in 1964, when the boss was kidnapped. Brother-in-law of Stefano Magaddino.

DiGilio, John (AKA: **Johnnie Dee**), 1936- . Member of the Genovese crime family, active in New Jersey waterfront unions and loan sharking.

DiNapoli, Vincent (AKA: **Vinnie**), 1937- . A ranking lieutenant of the Genovese crime family of New York. Labor union and construction racketeer considered to be the tenth most influential Mafiosi in the U.S. Convicted on racketeering charges in 1988 and sentenced to twenty-four years in prison.

Ding Dong, prom. 1900s. Skilled thief who belonged to the Hudson Dusters gang.

Dio, Johnny (John Dioguardi), 1915-79. Labor racketeer and sidekick of Jimmy Hoffa. Assisted Hoffa in his attempt to take over the New York local of the Teamster's Union.

Dio, Tommy (Thomas Dioguardia, prom. 1970s. Foot soldier in the Lucchese crime family. Married to one of the daughters of Frank Livorsi.

DiPalermo, Charles, prom. 1970s. Soldier in the Lucchese crime family.

DiPalermo, Joseph (AKA: **Joey Beck**), 1907- . New York City mobster and narcotics dealer targeted by Vito Genovese and Joseph Valachi for assassination. Member of the Lucchese family. Valachi murdered the wrong man.

Dirty Face Jack, prom. 1850s. Gang chieftain and lieutenant of Isaiah Rynders, leader of the Nativist movement in New York.

Dobbs, John (AKA: **Mike Kerrigan**), prom. 1870s. One-time river pirate and member of the Patsy Conroy Gang who opened a vicious saloon on Mott Street.

Dock Rats, prom. 1910s. Lower East Side street gang.

Dolan, John (AKA: **Dandy Johnny**), b.c.1850-76. Burglar and member of the Whyos Gang. Hanged on Apr. 21, 1876.

Dongarro, Charles (Rosario), prom. 1970s. A capodecine in the Gambino crime family.

Donovan, "Wreck", prom. 1870s. Member of the Patsy Conroy Gang.

Douglas, Joseph, d.1874. Abducted little Charley Ross in July 1874. Killed before he could reveal the whereabouts of the boy.

Doyle, Patsy (AKA: **Little Patsy**), prom. 1910s. One-time member of the Gophers, who was murdered in November, 1914, after staging an insurrection against Owney Madden.

Draper, Shang, prom. 1870s-80s. Saloon owner and gang leader. His Twenty-Ninth Street resort was a notorious location for badger game swindles. Later joined George Leslie's robbery gang.

Driscoll, Daniel, d.1888. Ruled the Whyos Gang jointly with Danny Lyons. Executed in 1888.

Duck, Mock, prom. 1900s. Leader of the Chinese Hip Sings in New York City; wounded in a gunfight on Pell street Nov. 4, 1904.

Duffy Hills, prom. 1900s. Street gang that battled the Red Peppers for control of East 102nd Street.

Duffy, Thomas, prom. 1920s. Gangster who was shot to death on Long Island.

Dunn, John (AKA: **Cockeye**), prom. 1940s. Longshoreman's union racketeer.

Dunnigan, James, prom. 1870s. Co-captain of the Molasses Gang.

Dutch Mob, prom. 1860s. New York City pickpocket gang that operated east of the Bowery.

East Side Crashers, prom. 1900s. Social-political club organized by Tammany Hall politicians.

Eastman, Edward (Edward Osterman), (AKA: **Monk**), 1873-1920. Monk Eastman's gang dominated the area between the Bowery and the East River. He was a powerful turn-of-the-century gangster who enjoyed the protection of Tammany Hall political boss Tim Sullivan until he went off to jail for ten years. Murdered on Dec. 26, 1920.

East Side Dramatic and Pleasure Club, prom. 1900s. Social-political club organized by Tammany Hall politicians.

Eboli, Thomas (AKA: **Tommy Ryan**), d.1972. Ruled the Genovese family when Vito went to prison, in 1959. Shot to death dead in 1972 by Gambino assassins.

Egan, Edward, prom. 1910s. Lieutenant of Owney Madden for a brief period.

Egan, Patsy, prom. 1870s. Owner of saloon at Broadway and Houston Street.

Ellison, James (AKA: **Biff**), prom. 1900s. Member of the Five Points Gang in the early 1900s. Sent to Sing Sing, in 1911, for shooting Paul Kelly.

Emerson, Peter (AKA: **Banjo Pete**), prom. 1870s. Member of the George Leslie robbery gang.

Emery, Samuel, prom. 1900s. Owner of a Broadway gambling den.

Entratta, Charles (AKA: **Charlie Green**), d.1931. Chief enforcer and partner of Jack "Legs" Diamond. Assassinated in Brooklyn in 1931.

Eppolito, James, 1946-80. New York mobster with a dual identity. A member of the Carlo Gambino crime family, Eppolito was photographed with First Lady Rosalynn Carter, in 1979, in recognition for his charitable work in Manhattan. Murdered with his father in March, 1980.

Erickson, Frank, prom. 1930s-50s. Powerful New York City mobster.

Espy, Benjamin A., prom. 1940s. Mafia underling.

Evola, Natale (AKA: **Joe Diamond**), 1907-73. Labor racketeer and drug trafficker in New York. Head of one of the five families in the early 1970s.

Failla, James (AKA: **Jimmy Brown**), 1922- . Former chauffeur of Carlo Gambino. Labor union racketeer and capo in the Gambino crime family. Betrayed Paul Castellano, in 1985, in order to hook up with John Gotti.

Farace, Costabile (AKA: **Gus**), prom. 1980s. Brooklyn mob boss implicated in the murder of DEA agent Everett Hatcher. Killed in his parked car in Brooklyn.

Farrell, "Red", prom. 1900s. Member of the Hudson Dusters street gang.

Farrell, "Red Rocks", prom. 1870s. Assassin and bank robber. A member of the Whyos.

Farrell, "Spick", prom. 1970s. New York City mobster.

Fashion Plates, prom. 1900s. Small West Side gang that challenged the Hudson Dusters for supremacy.

Fatico, Carmine (AKA: **Charley Wagons**), prom. 1950s-80s. Long-time capo in the Gambino organization. Close associate of John Gotti.

Fatico, Donato (AKA: **Danny Wags**), prom. 1970s-80s. Brother of Carmine Fatico. Arrested in 1971, on hijacking charges. One of John Gotti's early sponsors.

Featherstone, Thomas Francis (AKA: **Mickey**), prom. 1970s-80s. Bodyguard of James Coonan. Became his partner in 1976, and then jointly ruled the Westies, a powerful Irish street gang active in the Hell's Kitchen section of New York City. Arrested for murder in 1979, became a government informant.

Fein, Benjamin (AKA: **Dopey Benny**), prom. 1910s. Gang leader and labor union thug who directed activity on the lower half of Manhattan. Sent to prison in 1914 on an assault charge.

Feinstein, Irving (AKA: **Puggy**), d.1939. Racketeer who was tied to a chair and burned to death by Abe "Kid Twist" Reles, Happy Maione and others, on Sept. 6, 1939.

Feinstein, "Tootsie", d.1939. One-time associate of Louis "Lepke" Buchalter, murdered on his orders May 10, 1939.

Feraco, James (AKA: **Dizzy**), d.1940. Brooklyn racketeer murdered by rival gang members.

Ferrara, Peter (AKA: **Petey Pumps**), prom. 1970s. A capodecine in the Gambino crime family.

Ferriano, Frank, d.1972. New York mobster murdered near the Holland Tunnel, Apr. 10, 1972.

Ferigno, Steven (Steven Fennuci), d.1930. Member of the Mafia "old guard", led by Joe Masseria. Shot to death by Maranzano gunmen on Nov. 5, 1930.

Fialla, James, 1921- . Staten Island gangster affiliated with the Gambino crime family. Involved in in the private carting industry in New York.

Filipone, George, prom. 1960s. New York City mobster.

Fitzpatrick, Richard, 1880-1905. Top lieutenant of Monk Eastman. Murdered in 1904 by rival gangsters.

Fiumara, Tino (AKA: **George Grecco**), 1943- . Boss of the New Jersey waterfront unions. Currently in jail.

Five Points Gang (AKA: **Five Pointers**), prom. 1900-19. A criminal street gang active in the Sixth Ward of the Lower East Side. Successors to the Dead Rabbits. The Five Points spawned such Prohibition racketeers as Al Capone, Lucky Luciano, and Johnny Torrio. The gang dissolved on the eve of Prohibition.

Flaherty, "Porkie", prom. 1910s. Lower East Side gang leader.

Flying Dragons, prom. 1970s. Tong gang active in New York's Chinatown.

Folly Gang, prom. 1910s. Lower East Side street gang.

Fontana, Harry, prom. 1960s-70s. Capo in the Profaci-Magliocco family.

Forlano, Nicholas (AKA: **Jiggs**), prom. 1960s. Capo in the Magliocco-Profaci crime family.

Forty Little Thieves, prom. 1850s-60s. Gang of children who copied the exploits of the Forty Thieves.

Forty Thieves, prom. 1820s-50s. One of the original Five Points gangs headquartered in Rosanna Peers saloon on Center street.

Four Brothers, prom. 1900s. Chinese Tong Gang allied with the Hip Sings during the 1909 gang war.

Fourteenth Street Gang, prom. 1900s. Small East Side gang that was active in the territory of the Five Points.

Fourth Avenue Tunnel Gang, prom. 1850s. Juvenile street gang active along Fourth Avenue from Thirty-Fourth to Forty-Second.

Franse, Stephen, 1895-1953. Police informant murdered by Joseph Valachi on June 19, 1953.

Franzese, John (AKA: **Sonny**), prom. 1950s-60s. Father of Michael Franzese. Former mob captain in the Colombo family involved in receiving kickbacks from the recording industry. Imprisoned from 1970 until 1979.

Franzese, Michael, 1953- . Capo in the Colombo family active in Long Island auto dealerships, movies, and bootleg gasoline. Currently in prison.

French José, prom. 1850s. Gambling house proprietor in business with Jimmy Berry.

Friedman, Abraham (AKA: **Whitey**), d.1929. Murdered by Louis "Lepke" Buchalter's men on Apr. 28, 1939.

Frog Hollows, prom. 1910-13. Lower East Side street gang.

Fuca, Patsy, prom. 1970s. Brooklyn mobster and drug trafficker. Convicted in the French Connection smuggling case.

Fucceri, Louis (AKA: **Louie Beans**), prom. 1970s. Soldier in the Lucchese crime family.

Fuchs, David, prom. 1920s. Killed by police while trying to hold up a store in New York.

Furnari, Christopher (AKA: **Christie Tick**), 1927- . Top ranking member of the Lucchese crime family of New York. Loan shark, gambling boss, construction tycoon.

Gaggi, Anthony F., 1924-86. Captain of the DeMeo "hit squad" which carried out planned assassinations for the Gambino crime family in the 1980s. A close advisor of Mafia boss Paul Castellano. Died of natural causes.

Gagliano, Gaetano, prom. 1920s-30s. One of the founding fathers of the modern New York crime syndicate. His family was taken over by Thomas Lucchese in 1931.

Galante, Carmine (AKA: **Lillo, the Cigar**), 1910-79. Former associate of Joseph Bonanno who took control of the family, in 1974. Became the top Mafia boss of New York City, shortly before he was murdered, in 1979.

Galgano, Michael (AKA: **Blackie, Black Mike**), prom. 1970s. Foot soldier in the Gambino crime family.

Galione, Ralph (AKA: **Ralphie Wags**), d.1973. Mafia triggerman who was murdered in 1973. Believed responsible for the execution of James McBratney, who kidnapped and murdered Carlo Gambino's son.

Gallagher, Newburg, prom. 1900s. Member of the Gophers street gang.

Gallo, Albert (AKA: **Kid Blast**), prom. 1960s. Brooklyn based mobster who was a brother of Crazy Joe Gallo. Inherited the rule of the gang when Joe was killed, in 1972.

Gallo, Joseph N., prom. 1960s-80s. Consigliere in the Gambino crime family, until he was deposed by John Gotti in 1986. Sentenced to ten years in prison. Not related to Joseph Gallo.

Gallo, Joseph (AKA: **Crazy Joe**), 1929-72. Member of the Carlo Gambino crime family. With his brothers Larry and Albert, Gallo waged constant war against the Profaci family for the better part of three decades.

Gallo, Lawrence (AKA: **Larry**), prom. 1960s. Brother of Joey Gallo. Former member of the Gambino family.

Gallus Mag, prom. 1850s. Englishwoman who ran the Hole-In-the Wall saloon on Dover Street, with Charley Monell.

Gambino, Carlo, 1902-76. Boss of one of the five families of Manhattan during much of the 1960s and 1970s; died of natural causes in 1976. Former director of the National Crime Commission.

Gambino, Emmanuel, d.1973. Nephew of Carlo Gambino. Murdered in New Jersey, in 1973.

Gambino, Giuseppe, prom. 1980s. Nephew of Carlo Gambino. Arrested in December, 1988, for importing cocaine and heroin into the U.S.

Gambino, Paolo, prom. 1960s-70s-. Capodeceine in the Gambino crime family.

Gambino, Thomas, prom. 1960s-80s. Son of Mafia don Carlo Gambino. Married to Frances Lucchese, daughter of Mafia boss Thomas Lucchese.

Ganci, Giuseppe (AKA: **Il Bufalo**), d.1986. Soldier in the Santa Maria di Gesu Mafia family of Sicily before he emigrated to the U.S. in 1965. Owner of a Queens pizzeria. Major drug trafficker indicted for buying and selling heroin during the days of the Pizza Connection. Died of lung cancer in 1986.

Garofalo, Frank, prom. 1950s. Top lieutenant in the Bonanno crime family until moving back to Sicily, in 1957.

Garofalo, Vincent, prom. 1960s. Soldier in the Bonanno crime family. Wounded with Vincent Cassese in October 1967, during the Banana War.

Gas House Gang, prom. 1890s-1900s. Gang of 200, organized in the Gas House district of East Thirty-Fifth Street. Specialized in nocturnal burglary.

Gassell, Mandel, d.1933. Racketeer tied in with Waxey Gordon. Shot and killed by Dutch Schultz gunmen at the Carteret Hotel, in Elizabeth, N.J., on Apr. 12, 1933.

Gee, Harry, prom. 1930s. Chinatown drug trafficker.

Genovese, Michael, prom. 1950s-60s. Messenger, in the Vito Genovese crime family.

Genovese, Vito (Don Vitone), 1897-1969. Born In Sicily, Genovese arrived in the U.S., in 1913. By the 1940s, he was one of the top crime bosses in New York. Died in prison in 1969.

Gentile, Nicole (AKA: **Culicchia**), prom. 1930s. Agent for the International Mafia, elected to the National Commission, in the 1930s. Jumped bail in New York, in 1937, and returned to Sicily.

Geoheghan, Owney, prom. 1870s. Owner of a vicious dive in Satan's Circus.

Ghost Shadows, prom. 1970s. Tong Gang active in New York's Chinatown district.

Giaccone, Philip (AKA: **Lucky**), d.1981. Giaccone failed in his attempt to oust Philip Rastelli as head of the Bonanno crime family in 1980. He disappeared on May 5, 1981.

Giannini, Eugenio, d.1952. Shot to death, in East Harlem, on Sept, 20, 1952, by Tony Strollo's gunmen.

Gigante, Vincent (AKA: **the Chin**), b.c.1926- . A soldier in the Vito Genovese crime family who advanced himself to a position of power. Failed in his attempt to murder Frank Costello May 2, 1957.

Giordano, John (AKA: **Handsome Jack**), 1941- . Captain in the Genovese crime family, headed by John Gotti. Reputed boss of a Manhattan sports-gambling ring.

Gioerelli, Joseph (AKA: **Joe Jelly**), d.1962. New York City hitman allied with the Gallo gang. Turned informant. Murdered on Aug. 17, 1962.

Giovanelli, Frederico, 1932- . Reputed member of the Genovese crime family convicted in November, 1989, of murdering police detective Anthony Venditti.

Glover, James Jr., prom. 1970s. Harlem gambling and policy boss.

Go-Aheads, prom. 1900s. Social-political club organized by Tammany Hall.

Goldstein, Martin (AKA: **Bugsy**), d.1936. Assassin for Murder, Inc. Executed in Sing Sing on June 12, 1936.

Goodie, Edward, prom. 1870s. Sneak thief and bank robber who belonged to George Leslie's gang.

Gophers, prom. 1890s-1910s. Street gang headquartered in Hell's Kitchen, from Seventh to Eleventh and Fourteenth to Forty-Second Streets.

Gordon, Waxey (Irving Wexler), 1889-1952. Top Prohibition bootlegger. Sided with Joe "the Boss" Masseria during the Castellammarese War. Jailed for narcotics violations in 1951.

Gorillas, prom. 1900s. Hell's Kitchen street gang.

Gotti, Gene, prom, 1960s-80s. Brother of John Gotti. Heroin trafficker who is currently serving a fifty-year prison sentence.

Gotti, John J., 1940- . Top ranked Gambino family crime boss. Loan shark, professional thief and phonograph industry mogul. Assumed control of the crime family in 1985 following the murder of Paul Castellano which he was reputed to have engineered. Has emerged as one of the most important drug traffickers in the U.S. today.

Gotti, John A. Jr. (AKA: **Junior**), 1964- . Son of Gambino crime family boss John Gotti. Reputed boss of a contingency of Mafia soldiers who make money for the family through construction extortion, auto crime, and loan sharking.

Gotti, Peter, prom. 1960s-80s. Brother of John Gotti. Bookmaker and hijacker. Managed the Hunt and Fish Club, where the family conducted its business.

Gotti, Richard, prom. 1960s-80s. Brother of John Gotti. Member of the Gambino crime family.

Grady, John D. (AKA: **Travelling Mike**), prom. 1860s-70s. Professional fence.

Gravano, Salvatore (AKA: **Sammy the Bull**), prom. 1970s-80s. Burglar, extortionist and associate of John Gotti. Replaced Joseph N. Gallo as Gambino family consigliere in 1986.

Greenberg, Harry (AKA: **Big Greenie**), d.1939. Murdered in Los Angeles, on orders from Meyer Lansky, after stealing syndicate money.

Greenberg, Max, (AKA: **Big Maxie**), d.1933. Member of Waxey Gordon's gang; murdered in an Elizabeth, N.J., hotel room by Dutch Schultz gunmen on Apr. 12, 1933.

Greene, Thomas, prom. 1970s. Policy and numbers racketeer in Central Harlem.

Griffin, Larry, prom. 1870s. River pirate, footpad, and one of the leaders of the Patsy Conroy Gang.

Gualtiere, Carmine, 1931- . Reputed member of the Genovese crime family. Convicted of racketeering charges and murder in November, 1989, and sentenced to twenty years in prison.

Guerrieri, Anthony (AKA: **Tony Lee**), prom. 1980s. Associate of John Gotti involved in airport trucking. Labor union extortionist acquitted of assault charges with Gotti in 1990.

Gurino, Vito, prom. 1930s. Assassin for Murder, Inc., and baker's union racketeer. Killed John Bagdonowitz, in 1933.

Hales, Clarence (AKA: **Crappy**), prom. 1970s. Numbers runner in Central Harlem.

Hamley, Joseph, prom. 1920s. Associate of Legs Diamond. Shot to death in Milburn, N.J.

Harrington, William, prom. 1900s. Five Points gangster murdered by Biff Ellison and Razor Riley at the New Brighton saloon in 1904.

Harrison, Richard, prom. 1900s. Member of the Hudson Dusters street gang.

Hartley Mob, prom. 1870s. Street gang active near Broadway and Houston Street. Used a funeral hearse to transport them into battle.

Haskins, Hester Jane (AKA: **Jane the Grabber**), prom. 1870s. Procuress and white slaver. Arrested and sent to prison.

Haymarket, prom. 1870-1913. Famous dance hall and saloon located on Sixth Avenue, in Satan's Circus.

Hedmano, Geraldo, prom. 1920s. Syndicate hoodlum murdered in a New York taxi-cab.

Heinrichs, "Dutch", prom. 1860s-70s. Leader of the Hell's Kitchen Gang. Imprisoned for assaulting a policeman.

Hell Cat Maggie, prom. 1840s. Gang woman who fought with the Dead Rabbits during many of their wars with the Bowery Boys.

Hell's Kitchen, prom. 1860s-1930s. Original name of a saloon in Corlear's Hook, but since the 1860s it has come to mean the section of Manhattan north and south of West Thirty-Fourth Street and west of Eighth Avenue. A high crime area, populated by numerous street gangs and criminals.

Hell's Kitchen Gang, prom. 1860s-70s. Extortion gang that terrorized the neighborhood of the same name.

Herne, Patrick, prom. 1850s. Owner of a gambling resort on Lower Broadway.

Hewitt, Abram Stevens 1822-1903. Reform mayor of New York, 1887-88. Closed down the saloons of Harry Hill, and Billy McGlory.

Hicks, Albert E. (AKA: **Hicksie**), prom. 1850s. Fourth Ward river pirate and gangster. Executed on Bedloe's Island in 1860.

Hill, Harry, prom. 1860s-80s. Proprietor of a dance house and saloon on West Houston Street.

Hines, "Big Josh", prom. 1870s. Member of the Whyos Gang. Professional killer.

Hines, James J., 1877-1957. Mob controlled leader of Tammany Hall. Sent to prison in 1940 for protecting Dutch Schultz's Harlem numbers racket.

Hip Sings, prom. 1900s. New York City Tong gang.

Hogan, Pat (AKA: **Rough House**), prom. 1900s. Five Points gangster in attendance at the New Brighton when Paul Kelly was shot.

Holtz, "Curly", prom. 1920. New York city hoodlum who served as a lieutenant in Augie Orgen's gang.

Honeymoon Gang, prom. 1850s. Eighteenth Ward street gang driven for cover by Police Chief George Walling.

Hookers, prom. 1850s-60s. Fourth Ward street gang headquartered on Stanton Street near the East River.

Hope, James, prom. 1870s. Member of the George Leslie hold-up gang.

Horowitz, Harry (AKA: **Gyp the Blood**), prom. 1910s. Manhattan mobster convicted of murdering Herman Rosenthal on July 15, 1912. Was later executed.

Howlett, William, d.1853. Co-leader of the Daybreak Boys. Executed in the Tombs when he was nineteen.

Hudson Dusters, prom. 1890s-1910s. Street gang organized in the 1890s near the corner of Hudson and Thirteenth Streets. Many of the members were cocaine addicts.

Hurley, "Bull", prom. 1870s. Member of the Whyos Gang.

Hurley, "Pugsy", prom. 1870s. Member of the Patsy Conroy Gang.

Hyland, "Chick", prom. 1900s. Lieutenant of Owney Madden.

Iacovetti, David, prom. 1960s. Gambino family soldier. Jailed for securities fraud.

Ianniello, Matthew (AKA: **Matty the Horse**), 1923- . Loan shark. Overseer of New York topless bars and labor union boss for the Genovese crime family. Under indictment.

Illiano, Frank (AKA: **Punchy**), prom. 1950s-60s. Member of the Gallo crime family.

Impastato, Nicolo, 1900- . International drug trafficker deported to Italy, by the Mexican government, in 1955.

Indelicato, Alphonse (AKA: **Sonny Red**), d.1981. Father of Anthony Indelicato. Headed up the faction within the Bonanno crime family that opposed the takeover of Philip Rastelli. Murdered with Dominick Trinchera and Philip Giaccone on May 5, 1981.

Indelicato, Anthony (AKA: **Bruno**), 1950- . Bonanno crime boss in New York specializing in narcotics. Escaped an attempted hit in 1981, and went into hiding. Currently on trial.

Irving, John, prom. 1880s. Gang leader shot down by Johnny Walsh in Shang Draper's saloon.

Ison, Joseph, prom. 1930s. A Harlem numbers racketeer who was taken over by the Dutch Shultz mob in the early 1930s.

Italian Dave Gang, prom. 1850s. A Paradise Square criminal whose gang of youthful pickpockets roamed the Five Points in search of victims.

Jackson, Humpty, d.1914. Turn of the century gang boss and murderer whose mob controlled the area bound by First and Second Avenues and Twelfth and Thirteenth. Imprisoned in 1909 for attempted murder. Died in jail.

James, Richard (AKA: **Goldfinger**), prom. 1970. Harlem gunman.

Jefferson, Leroy, prom. 1950s. New York City drug trafficker.

Jimmy Curley Gang, prom. 1910s. New York street gang.

Johnson, William, prom. 1850s. Member of the Daybreak Boys.

Johnson, David, prom. 1900s. Owner of a Broadway gambling resort.

Johnson, Jerome, d.1971. Black gunman who shot and fatally wounded Joseph Colombo. Shot and killed June 28, 1971.

Johnson, Nathan, prom. 1970s. Numbers runner and racketeer in Central Harlem.

Johnson, Wilfred (AKA: **Willie Boy**), prom. 1950s-80s. Lifelong friend of John Gotti who became a valuable FBI informant in 1969 after the Mafia went back on its promise to provide for his wife while he was in prison. Murdered on Aug. 29, 1988.

Jolly Forty-Eight, prom. 1900s. Social-political club organized by Tammany Hall politicians.

Jones, William, prom. 1900s. New York gangster imprisoned in 1910. Member of the Gas Housers.

Judson, Edward Z.C. (AKA: **Ned Buntline**), prom. 1850s. Gang leader allied with Isaiah Rynders and the Native American movement.

Kane, Beeny, prom. 1870s. Member of the Patsy Conroy gang.

Kaplan, Louis Nathan (AKA: **Kid Dropper**), d.1923. New York City gangster and ruler of the mid-town bootlegging rackets until he was murdered outside the courthouse by Louis Kushner on Aug. 28, 1928.

Katharane, Nicholas, prom. 1970s. East Village racketeer.

Kavolick, Philip (AKA: **Little Farfel**), d.1949. Member of the Meyer Lansky gang assassinated in Valley Stream, N.Y., on Sept. 16, 1949.

Kelly, William, prom. 1878. Member of the George Leslie holdup gang. Sent to prison in 1878.

Kelly, James, prom. 1900s. Owner of a bowery saloon, and leader of a small independent gang.

Kelly, John (AKA: **Honest John**), 1856-1926. Owner of a string of gambling houses in New York. One of the most influential gambling bosses of the early twentieth century.

Kelly, Paul (Paolo Antonini Vaccarelli), prom. 1900s. Kelly was a New York organized crime figure who ruled the notorious Five Points Gang.

Kerrigan, Daniel, prom. 1870s. Tammany Hall politician who operated the Strand dance hall in Satan's Circus.

Kerryonians, prom. 1820s-30s. Street gang composed of immigrants from County Kerry, Ire.

Kid Yorke, prom. 1890s. Organized the Hudson Dusters street gang.

Kim Lan Wui Saw, prom. 1910s. Chinese Tong gang.

Kleinschmidt, Lena (AKA: **Black Lena**), prom. 1870s. Thief and blackmailer. Later attained social prominence in Hackensack, N.J.

Knox, Goo Goo, prom. 1900s. Member of the Gophers street gang. Later helped found the Hudson Dusters.

Konigsberg, Harold (AKA: **Kayo**), prom. 1960s. New Jersey loan shark jailed in 1966.

Krakower, Whitey, d.1940. Murdered by Ben "Bugsy" Siegel on July 31, 1940, in revenge for acting as an informant.

Krompier, Martin (AKA: **Little Marty**), prom. 1930s. Chief enforcer and top lieutenant for Dutch Schultz in the Harlem policy rackets. Badly wounded by gunmen in 1935, but he survived the attack. By 1960 he was reduced to working as a delivery man for a New York camera store.

Kurtz, Michael (AKA: **Sheeny Mike**), prom. 1870s. Bank robber. Leader of the Dutch Mob.

Kushner, Louis (Louis Cohen), prom. 1920s. A crime syndicate underling of Legs Diamond, Louis Kushner murdered Nathan "Kid Dropper" Kaplan, on Aug. 28, 1923. He was sentenced to life imprisonment in Sing Sing.

LaBruzzo, Frank, d.1968. Brother-in-law of Joseph Bonanno, and a partner in the family undertaking business. Appointed leader of the gang, in 1964, when Bonanno disappeared, but he was voted down by the ruling commission.

Lady Barker's Association, prom. 1900s. Adjunct of the Tammany Hall social clubs for women.

Lady Flashers, prom. 1900s. One of several women's clubs organized to promote Tammany Hall's political agenda.

Lady Gophers (AKA: **Battle Row Ladies Social and Athletic Club**), prom. 1900s. Female chapter of the Gophers street gang.

Lady Liberties of the Fourth Ward, prom. 1900s. Female social-political club organized by Tammany Hall.

Lady Locusts, prom. 1900s. Adjunct of the Tammany Hall social clubs organized for women.

Lady Truck Driver's Association, prom. 1900s. Political club organized to promote the aims of Tammany Hall.

Laietta, Donato (AKA: **Dempsey**), prom. 1970s. Soldier in the Lucchese crime family.

Lamberti, Giuseppe (AKA: **Joe**), 1932- . Cousin of Salvatore Lamberti. Convicted of narcotics conspiracy, RICO violations, and a continuing criminal enterprise in drug trafficking in 1987. Sentenced to thirty years in the federal penitentiary in Terre Haute, Ind.

Lamberti, Salvatore, 1932- . Emigrated to the U.S. from Sicily in 1982. Convicted of narcotics conspiracy and violation of the RICO laws for his role in the Pizza Connection. Sentenced to twenty years at a minimum security detention center in 1987.

Langella, Gennaro (AKA: **Jerry Long**), 1942- . Syndicate boss of the Colombo family in Brooklyn. Ranked number five in the national crime syndicate despite the fact that he is currently in prison.

Lansky, Meyer (Maier Suchowljansky, AKA: Little Man, Maier Suchow, the Genius), prom. 1902-83. The most powerful Jewish gangster in the U.S. Charter member of Murder, Inc.; later organized the syndicate gambling operations in Miami, and Cuba.

Landau, Abraham (AKA: **Misfit**), d.1935. Shot down with Dutch Schultz, Lulu Rosencrantz, and Otto Berman at the Palace Chophouse in Newark, N.J., on Oct. 23, 1935.

Lanza, Joseph (AKA: **Socks**), prom. 1942. Labor racketeer and fishing industry organizer. Worked with the government in 1942, to prevent wartime sabotage on the New York piers.

LaRasso, Louis, prom. 1965. Petty mob figure whose conversations were taped by the FBI, in 1965.

Laratro, Joseph (AKA: **Joey Narrow**), prom. 1970s. Capodecine in the Lucchese crime family.

La Salle, Stefano, prom. 1970s. Retired underboss of the Gaetano Lucchese crime family.

Lascari, Michael, prom. 1940s. Mafia associate.

LaTempa, Peter, prom. 1940s. Witness to the murder of Ferdinand "the Shadow" Boccia. Poisoned in his jail cell.

Latini, Bruno, d.1971. New York City mobster shot in his car on Dec. 25, 1971.

Laydon, "Pickles", prom. 1910s. New York gang leader.

Leary, Red, prom. 1870s. Member of the George Leslie hold-up gang.

LeCicero, Charles, d.1966. Member of the Colombo crime family. Murdered in 1966.

Lee, Thomas, prom. 1890s-1900s. Boss of the On Leong Tong gang, and a political power in Chinatown.

Leese, George (AKA: **Snatchem**), prom. 1850s. Fourth ward brawler who belonged to the Slaughter House Gang.

Lenox Avenue Gang, prom. 1900s. Gang of pickpockets and burglars active on 125th Street. Captained by Harry Horowitz.

Leo, Arthur, prom. 1960s-70s. Capodeceine in the Gambino crime family.

LeSalva, Joseph, prom. 1970s. Underboss in the New Jersey crime family headed by Simone DeCavalcante.

Leslie, George Leonidas (AKA: **George Howard, Western George**), prom. 1870s-80s. Leader of a large and powerful bank robbing gang responsible for the 1878 holdup of the Manhattan Savings Institution. Murdered in 1884.

Le Strange, Terry, prom. 1870s. Waterfront thief who served as one of the leaders of the Hooker Gang.

Levine, Samuel (AKA: **Red, Joseph Brown**), b.1903. Brooklyn gambler, narcotics trafficker, and a member of Murder, Inc. Alleged to have been one of the four who assassinated Salvatore Maranzano.

Levinsky, Benjamin, d.1922. New York City gangster murdered by William Lipshitz on Dec. 5, 1922.

Levinsky, John, prom. 1910s. Gangster who specialized in stealing and poisoning horses. Entered into a partnership with Charley the Cripple and Yoske Nigger.

Lewis, Joseph, (AKA: **Hungry Joe**), prom. 1880s-90s. Bunko artist and conman. Once almost swindled Oscar Wilde out of $5,000.

Lewis, Vach (AKA: **Cyclone Louie**), prom. 1900s. Gangster and professional assassin allied with Max "Kid Twist" Zweibach.

Lexow Committee, prom. 1894. Special investigative committee created by the Republican-dominated state legislature to ferret out police and municipal graft in New York City. Chaired by Senator Clarence Lexow, the committee demonstrated that the NYPD was in the "iron grip" of Tammany Hall, and that the city suffered under a staggering weight of political graft. Before it was over in December 1894, Lexow issued 3,000 subpoenas, heard 678 witnesses, and recorded 10,576 pages of testimony.

Liberito, Joseph (AKA: **The Baker**), prom. 1930s. Member of Murder, Inc. Turned state's evidence against Kid Twist Reles.

Liberty Athletic Club, prom. 1900s. Social-political club organized by Tammany Hall.

Licata, Pietro, prom. 1930s-70s. Underboss in the Bonanno family. Maintained control of the Knickerbocker Avenue neighborhood of Brooklyn, even after Bonanno was forced into exile. Murdered on Nov. 4, 1976, a hit allegedly ordered by Sal Catalano.

Ligammari, Giovanni, 1939- . Partner in the syndicate-run Pronto Demolition. Convicted of narcotics conspiracy for his part in the Pizza Connection case. Sentenced to fifteen years in a federal prison in Alabama.

Limburger Roarers, prom. 1900s. Social-political club organized by Tammany Hall.

Lingley, William, prom. 1911. Reputed to have organized the Car Barn Gang. Executed for murder along with Freddie Muehfeldt.

Lisi, Anthony (AKA: **Tony**), prom. 1970s. Member of the Gaetano Lucchese crime family.

Little Dead Rabbits, prom. 1850. Gang of children who emulated the Dead Rabbits Gang.

Little Doggies, prom. 1910s. Lower East Side street gang.

Little Freddie, prom. 1870s. Co-leader of the Dutch Mob.

Little Mike, prom. 1870s. Leader of the Nineteenth Street Gang.

Little Plug Uglies, prom. 1850s. Gang of Children who emulated the Plug Uglies.

Little Rhody, prom. 1910s. Gang chieftain, and labor union thug.

Livin, Charles (AKA: **Ike the Blood**), prom. 1900s. Ally of Monk Eastman. Killed in a Seventh Avenue saloon by the Gophers.

Livorsi, Frank, prom. 1930s. Fought with Joe Masseria during the Castellammarese War, but changed sides and joined up with Salvatore Maranzano.

Lobster Kid, prom. 1900s. Member of Humpty Jackson's gang.

LoCascio, Peter Joseph (AKA: **Mr. Bread**), 1916- . New York City narcotics peddler and syndicate goon active on the Lower East Side.

Lollie Meyers, prom. 1900s. Lower east side street gang.

Lombardozzi, Carmine (AKA: **The Doctor**), 1913- . Drug trafficker, labor racketeer and gambling boss who formerly worked with Meyer Lansky. A capodecine in the Gambino crime family.

Lonergan, Richard (AKA: **Peg Leg**), prom. 1900s. Took over control of the White Hand Gang from Wild Bill Lovett. Killed during a Brooklyn gang war.

Lonzo, Antonio, d.1932. Veteran Mafiosi, assassinated on Mar. 16, 1932, by order of Vito Genovese.

LoPiccolo, Joseph Paul, 1918- . Narcotics boss who lives in New York, but maintains business interests in Hardin County, Ill. An associate of Santo Trafficante.

Lo Pinto, Anthony (AKA: **Tea Bags, Tony Pinto**), prom. 1970s. Ranking member of the Gaetano Lucchese crime family.

Lo Proto, Salvatore (AKA: **Sally**), prom. 1970s. Member of the Gaetano Lucchese crime family.

Lo Verde, Toto, prom. 1910s-20s. Member of the Mafia National Commission during the Castellemmarese War of 1928-31.

Lovett, William (AKA: **Wild Bill**), prom. 1900s. Extortionist and co-leader of the White Hand Gang. Murdered in 1923.

Low Hee Tong, prom. 1900s. High ranking member of the Four Brothers Tong gang. His "purchase" of the slave girl Bow Kum led to a vicious Tong war in 1909.

Lowrie, William, prom. 1850s. Assumed leadership of the Daybreak boys following the executions of Nicholas Saul and William Howlett.

Lucchese, Joseph, prom. 1960s-70s. Capodeceine in the Lucchese crime family.

Lucchese, Thomas (**Gaetano Lucchese**, AKA: **Three Finger Brown**), 1903-67. One of Charles "Lucky" Luciano's top gunmen, in the 1930s. Later crowned the head of the New York crime family founded by Gaetano Gagliano, in 1931.

Luciano, Charles (**Salvatore Luciana**, AKA: **Lucky**), 1897-1962. All powerful rackets boss of New York City, until Prosecutor Thomas Dewey sent him to prison in 1936. Later paroled and deported to Italy. Died Jan. 26,1962.

Luciano, Frank (AKA: **Frank Miller**), prom. 1970s. Foot soldier in the Gambino crime family.

Lustig, William, prom. 1910. Captain of a gang of labor union thugs.

Lynch, Thomas, d.1914. The last chieftain of the Gas House Gang, killed in a gun battle with the Jimmy Curley Gang.

Lyons, Daniel, prom. d.1888. Leader of the Whyos Gang. Executed on Aug. 21, 1888 after murdering a Five Points girl.

Lyons, Sophie, prom. 1870s. Con artist. Married to Ned Lyons, a bank robber.

McArdle, John, prom. 1910s. Triggerman in Owney Madden's mob.

McCabe, William (AKA: **Tough Willie**), prom. 1940s. Underworld figure active in Harlem.

McCarthys, prom. 1900s. Street gang of lesser influence, but owing allegiance to the Five Points led by Monk Eastman.

McCarthy, Samuel (AKA: **Cow Legged**), prom. 1850s. Member of the Daybreak Boys.

McCoy, Frank (AKA: **Big Frank**), prom. 1870s. Bank robber.

McCray, Edward, prom. 1970s. Harlem gambler and racketeer.

McGerald, "Fig", prom. 1870s. Member of the Whyos Gang.

McGloin, Michael, d.1883. Member of the Whyos. Hanged in the Tombs Prison on Mar. 8, 1883.

McGlory, William, prom. 1870s. Former member of the Forty Thieves. Opened a notorious concert saloon called Armory Hall on Hester Street.

McGrath, E.J. (AKA: **Eddie**), prom. 1940s. Longshoreman's union racketeer.

McIntosh, Hugh (AKA: **Apples**), d.1963. Mobster killed during the Gallo-Profaci War; July 1963.

McManus, George (AKA: **Hump**), prom. 1928. New York City gambler indicted for the 1928 murder of Arnold Rothstein. McManus never went to trial for lack of evidence.

McManus, John (AKA: **Eat 'Em Up**), prom. 1900s. Prize-fighter turned gangster. Member of the Five Points Gang.

Macchiarole, Pasquale (AKA: **Paddy Mac**), d.1977. Lieutenant of Funzi Tieri, head of the Genovese crime family. Assassinated by order of Carmine Galante, in 1977.

Madden, Owen (AKA: **Owney, The Killer**), 1892-1964. Prohibition bootlegger and one of the major crime bosses of New York, in the 1920s. He boasted of having personally killed each of the thugs who shot him at a 52nd Street dance, on Nov. 6, 1912.

Madden, "Punk", prom. 1910s. Independent gang leader. No relation to Owney Madden.

Madden, Sow, prom. 1850s. Member of the Daybreak Boys.

Maffetore, Anthony (AKA: **Dukey**), prom. 1930s. Brooklyn associate of Kid Twist Reles. Turned informant in 1940.

Magliocco, Ambrose, prom. 1960s-70s. Capo in the Magliocco-Profaci family.

Magliocco, Joseph, d.1963. New York City crime boss who took over the Profaci Family, in 1962. Member of the National Commission. Died of a heart attack on Dec. 28, 1963.

Magnasco, Joseph, d.1961. Henchman of Joey Gallo murdered during the Profaci-Gallo war, on Oct. 4, 1961.

Magoon, Seymour (AKA: **Blue Jaw**), prom. 1930s. Heavy-handed Brooklyn mobster who informed on Murder, Inc., in 1940.

Mahaney, John (AKA: **American Jack Sheppard**), b.1844. Youthful street thief who worked for Italian Dave. Later organized his own Five Points Gang.

Mahoney, Bum, prom. 1870s. Fourth Ward gangster who joined the Hooker gang. Later assumed leadership of the gang.

Maione, Harry (AKA: Happy), d.1942. Deadly Brooklyn assassin for Murder, Inc. Executed in 1942, for killing Puggy Feinstein.

Majuri, Frank, prom. 1950s-70s. One-time member of the Bonanno crime family. Underboss of Simone DeCavalcante in the 1970s.

Malarkey, "Stumpy", prom. 1900s. Member of the Gophers street gang.

Maltese, Stephen, 1933- . Reputed member of the Genovese crime family. Sentenced to twenty years in prison in November, 1989, on racketeering charges and murder.

Mancuso, Rosario, 1907- . New York City labor racketeer.

Mancuso, Thomas (AKA: **Teaballs**), prom. 1960s. New York City mobster.

Mandelbaum, Fredericka (AKA: **Marm**), prom. 1860s-80s. Ran a large fencing operation on Rivington Street for the burglary gangs of New York.

Mangano, Benjamin, (AKA: **Benny Eggs**), prom. 1970s. Soldier in the Genovese crime family.

Mangano, John, prom. 1950s. Syndicate policy boss in Manhattan.

Mangano, Philip, d.1951. With his brother Vincent, Philip Mangano headed up his own family in the 1930s and 1940s. Murdered in 1951 by Albert Anastasia hitmen.

Mangano, Vincent, d.c.1951. Brother of Philip Mangano. Allegedly murdered and buried in the concrete foundation of a housing project by Albert Anastasia.

Mangiaracnina, Salvatore, prom. 1910s-20s. Member of the Mafia National Commission during the Castellemmarese War of 1928-31.

Manna, Louis (AKA: **Bobby**), 1929- . Genovese crime boss active in New Jersey; specializes in construction, gambling, and loan sharking.

Marangello, Nicholas (AKA: **Nicky Cigars, Nicky Glasses**), prom. 1970s-80s. Capo in the Bonanno crime family. Operated the Toyland Social club in Manhattan. Demoted in 1979 from capo to soldier.

Maranzano, Salvatore, 1868-1931. A founding father of the modern crime syndicate. Organized the Sicilian Mafia in the U.S., along traditional old world values of discipline, respect, and the code of silence. Involved in gambling, bootlegging, and burglary until his assassination on Sept. 10, 1931, at the hands of Luciano gunmen.

Marginals, prom. 1900s. Street gang active near the Hudson River waterfront.

Mari, Frank, d.c.1967. Defected from the Bonanno gang to join up with the DiGregorio forces during the Banana War. Disappeared in 1967.

Marino, James (AKA: **James LaPore**), d.1931. Maranzano lieutenant shot and killed outside a Bronx barber shop on Sept. 10, 1931.

Marquez, Raymond (AKA: **Spanish Raymond**), prom. 1965. Son of one of Vito Genovese's top aides. Ran a Puerto Rican numbers game in 1965.

Mas, Radames, prom. 1970s. Underboss of Raymond Marquez near Eighth Avenue and 113th Street in Manhattan.

Masseria, Giuseppe (AKA: **Joe the Boss**), d.1931. A top crime boss of New York in the 1920s, he lost the Castellammarese War fought against Salvatore Maranzano and his minions. Shot to death at Coney Island by Bugsy Siegel, Vito Genovese, Joe Adonis, and Albert Anastasia on Apr. 15, 1931.

Massina, Joseph, prom. 1970s-80s. Capo in the Bonanno crime family and a friend of John Gotti.

Massotta, Thomas, prom. 1970s. New York city mobster.

Mazzara, Gaetano (AKA: **Tommy**), 1936-86. Business partner and cousin of Frank Castronovo. Arrested for drug-trafficking in the Pizza Connection case. Murdered in Brooklyn on Dec. 1, 1986.

Mazzie, Rocco, prom. 1960s-70s. Capodeceine in the Gambino crime family.

Mazzurco, Salvatore, 1936- . Brother-in-law of Giuseppe Lamberti, who he organized a construction company with. Sentenced to twenty years on a narcotics conspiracy charge and fifteen years for RICO violations for his part in the Pizza Connection case.

Meehan, Dinny, prom. 1900s. Co-leader of the White Hand Gang, active in the Red Hook section of Brooklyn.

Meehan, Red Shay, prom. 1870s. Leader of the Potash Gang.

Mercaldo, Joseph, prom. 1930s. Brooklyn-based assassin for Murder, Inc.

Merrick, Suds, prom. 1870s. Co-captain of the Hooker Gang.

Migliore, Neil, prom. 1970s. Member of the Gaetano Lucchese crime family.

Milgram, Arthur, d.1977. New York businessman who owned a lottery ticket distribution service. Murdered by the mob on Feb. 2, 1977.

Miller, Charles P. (AKA: **King of the Banko Men**), prom. 1870s. New Orleans conman and swindler, whose gang worked the Astor House and Fifth Avenue Hotel in Manhattan.

Miller, Joseph, d.1939. Labor union racketeer killed by Murder, Inc.

Mineo, Alfred (**Al Manfredi**), d.1930. Long-time Mafia boss allied to Joe Masseria. Influence extended from Manhattan to the Bronx. Albert Anastasia and Frank Scalise were members of Mineo's organization. Gunned down with Steve Ferigo on Nov. 5, 1930.

Miranda, Michele (AKA: **Mr. Big**), b.1896. Top ranking Mafiosi connected with New York's garment racket. Succeeded Vito Genovese, in 1969.

Mirra, Anthony, prom. 1970s-80s. Soldier in the Bonanno crime family. Owner of a luncheonette in Lower Manhattan.

Molasses Gang, prom. 1870s. Gang of sneak thieves and pickpockets who utilized sorghum molasses and a soft hat as their decoy.

Molinas, Jacob (AKA: **Jake**), d.1975. Convicted briber of New York basketball players. Murdered by New York mobsters in his Los Angeles home on Aug. 2, 1975.

Monaco, Samuel, d.1931. Maranzano lieutenant tortured to death and found floating in Newark Bay.

Mondello, Alfred, d.1963. Gunman for Joey Gallo. Murdered during the Gallo-Profaci War on June 6, 1963.

Monell, Charles, prom. 1850s. Proprietor of the Water Street resort, Hole-In-the Wall, frequented by various Five Points gangs.

Monroe Street Gang, prom. 1890s. Lower East Side street gang that waged war with the Cherry Hill mob.

Montana, John, prom. 1950s. Buffalo mobster arrested at the 1957 Apalachin meeting.

Montemorano, Donald (AKA: **The Shack**), prom. 1960s. New York mobster.

Moore, Orlando, prom. 1850s. Owner of a gambling resort on Lower Broadway.

Morale, John, prom. 1960s. Ranked second in the Bonanno crime family, in 1966.

Morello, Giuseppi, prom. 1900s. Mafia killer who worked for Ignazio Saitta.

Morello, Peter (AKA: **Piddu, The Clutching Hand**), d.1930. Old time Black Hand-Mafia boss murdered on Aug. 15, 1930, by Albert Anastasia and Frank Scalise.

Moretti, William (AKA: **Willie Moore**), d.1951. Syndicate boss of New Jersey. Murdered in a Cliffside Park restaurant, on Oct. 4, 1951.

Morgan, William, prom. 1870s. Co-captain of the Molasses gang.

Morrell, Julie, d.1911. Hired by Chick Tricker to kill Jack Zelig, but was himself the victim on Dec. 2, 1911.

Morris, Joseph, (AKA: **Fat Joe**), prom. 1970s. Harlem gambler and racketeer.

Morrissey, John, prom. 1850s-70s. Prize fighter, fierce opponent of Isaiah Rynders and his backers, and New York gambling boss. Opened a deluxe resort in Saratoga Springs that was later sold to Richard Canfield.

Mose (AKA: **Mose the Fireboy**), prom. 1840s-50s. Legendary leader of the Bowery Boys, whose true identity is a matter of conjecture. A fearsome gang leader celebrated in many published novels and stories.

Mosher, William, prom. 1870s. With Bill Douglas, Mosher kidnapped 4-year-old Charley Ross on July 1, 1874. Killed during a robbery attempt on Dec. 14, 1874.

Mott, William (AKA: **Willie the Sailor**), prom. 1910s. Mob associate of Owney Madden.

Muehfeldt, Frederick (AKA: **The Kid**), prom. 1911. Co-founder of the Car Barn Gang. Executed along with Bill Lingley for the murder of a Bronx liquor dealer.

Mulraney, John (AKA: **Happy Jack**), prom. 1900s. Member of the Gophers sent to prison for the murder of saloon owner Paddy the Priest.

Murderer's Alley, prom. 1830s. Gathering place for thieves, killers, and prostitutes in the Five Points section.

Murder, Inc., prom. 1930s. Crack Mafia assassination squad organized in New York by Charles "Lucky" Luciano, Vito Genovese, Louis Buchalter, Abner "Longy" Zwillman, Meyer Lansky, and Frank Costello to eliminate "independents." Top gunmen included: Harry "Pittsburgh Phil" Strauss; Benjamin "Bugsy" Siegel; Frank Abbandando; Abe "Kid Twist" Reles; Phil and "Happy" Maione.

Mussachio, Salvatore (AKA: **Sally the Shiek**), d.1963. Nominal head of the Magliocco family, after Giuseppe died, in 1963. Associate of Frank Livorsi.

Musumeci, Joseph, prom. 1950s-60s. Member of the Brooklyn-based Gallo gang.

Nani, Sebastiano, prom. 1950s. Brooklyn mobster who ran a large-scale narcotics operation.

Napoli, James (AKA: **Jimmy Napp**), 1914- . Member of the Genovese crime family. Gambler and loan shark.

Napoli, Vincent, 1931- . Brooklyn-based drug smuggler and member of the Gambino crime family.

Napolitano, Dominick (AKA: **Sonny Black**), d.1982. Capo in the Bonanno crime family. When schisms developed in the Bonanno organization in 1980, Black tried to win the support of Carmine Persico, head of the Colombo family of Brooklyn. In 1982, was murdered and buried in a shallow grave in Staten Island.

Nayfeld, Benjamin, prom. 1986. Soviet émigré convicted in 1986 for his role in a credit card scheme to bilk Merrill Lynch customers. Member of the emerging "Soviet Mafia" of Brooklyn.

Nayfeld, Boris, prom. 1980s. One-time bodyguard of Soviet-born gangster Evsei Agron. Went to work for Marat Balagula after Agron was murdered.

Neighbor's Sons, prom. 1910s. New York street gang.

Nineteenth Street Gang, prom. 1870s. Particularly vicious gang from Poverty Lane and Misery Row.

Nizich, Emil, 1915-41. Small-time mobster murdered in February 1941.

Noles, "Piggy", prom. 1970s. Member of the Hookrs Gang.

Notaro, Joseph, d.1966. One of Joseph Bonanno's top ranking lieutenants.

O'Brien, "Buck", prom. 1910s. Assumed control of one of three factions of the Gophers gang. Controlled the district from Forty-Second to Fifty-Ninth and from Ninth Avenue to the Hudson River.

O'Brien, Tom, prom. 1880s-90s. Bunko artist and conman who preyed upon bankers.

O'Connell Guards, prom. 1830s-40s. Irish street gang from the Bowery.

Oddo, John, prom. 1960s. Capo in the Magliocco-Profaci crime family.

O'Dwyer, William (AKA: **Big Bill**), prom. 1930s-40s. Brooklyn District Attorney who attempted to secure a release for Louis "Lepke" Buchalter in 1943. Later, mayor of New York.

Old Flaherty, prom. 1860s. Seventh Ward thug, whose family comprised the criminal gang.

One Lung Curran, prom. 1900s. Member of the Gophers, who first popularized the gang's habit of assaulting a policeman for his tunic.

On Leongs, prom. 1900. Chinese Tong gang.

Orgen, Jacob (Jacob Orgenstein, AKA: Little Augie), d.1927. Augie Orgen was a New York City bootlegger and garment industry strongman, who groomed Jack "Legs" Diamond to become his right hand man. Orgen was killed on Oct. 15, 1927, in Manhattan, and Diamond took over.

Ormento, John (AKA: **Big John**), 1912- . New York City labor racketeer and drug trafficker. Caporegime in the Lucchese crime family.

Ormento, Thomas, prom. 1950s-60s. Son of John Ormento. Married to the daughter of Frank Livorsi.

Pacella, Louis (AKA: **Louie Dome**), prom. 1960s-70s. Soldier in the Genovese crime family. An intimate of Frank Sinatra.

Pacelli, John (AKA: **the Ape**), prom. 1920s. New Jersey racketeer who cornered the grape market. Killed in his hospital bed.

Palermo, Thomas J., d.1977. Mob informant found murdered on Apr. 1, 1977.

Panica, Vic, prom. 1970s. Member of the Gaetano Lucchese crime family.

Pansies, prom. 1900s. Independent street gang active near Avenue A and Eighty-First street.

Papadia, Andinno (Andimo Papadio, AKA: **Pop Wilson)**, prom. 1970s. Member of the Gaetano Lucchese crime family.

Paradiso, Michael (AKA: **Mickey Boy**), prom. 1970s-80s. Heroin trafficker and associate of John Gotti.

Pariano, Giuseppe, d.1930. Bodyguard for Peter Morello. Killed with his boss in 1930.

Parisi, John (AKA: **Dandy Jack**), prom. 1930s. Affiliated with Louis Capone and Murder, Inc.

Parlor Mob, prom. 1900s. Hell's Kitchen Street gang.

Parsons, Reuben, prom. 1850s-60s. Gambling kingpin who backed a number of policy and raffling houses in New York.

Pasqua, Frank (AKA: **Big Frank**), prom. 1970s. Foot soldier in the Gambino crime family.

Patsy Conroys, prom. 1840s. Fourth Ward street gang named for their founder Patsy Conroy.

Patsy the Barber, prom. 1850s. Member of the Daybreak Boys. Slashed to death by Slobbery Jim at the Hole-In-the-Wall saloon.

Patterson, James Dura, prom. 1970s. Gambling and policy boss in Harlem.

Pearl Buttons, prom. 1900s. Waterfront street gang conquered by the Marginals.

Pecoraro, Michael (AKA: **Skinny Mike**), prom. 1970s. Foot soldier in the Gambino crime family.

Peers, Rosanna, prom. 1820s-30s. Owner of a Five Points grocery store and grog shop frequented by the Forty Thieves gang, and the Kerryonians.

Pelligrino, Rocco, (AKA: **The Old Man**), prom. 1970s. Acting boss of the Genovese family in the 1970s.

Pendola, Teddy, prom. 1920s. New York city gangster shot down in the streets.

Peroff, Frank P., prom. 1970s. Drug smuggler, con man, and government informant who provided transportation in and out of the U.S. for major Mafia figures.

Perris, Samuel (AKA: **Worcester Sam**), prom. 1870s. Bank robber suspected of murdering George Leslie.

Perrone, Santo (AKA: **Sam**), d.1968. Member of the Bonanno crime family. Owned a Brooklyn trucking company. Murdered by the DiGregorio interests, in March, 1968.

Persico, Carmine (AKA: **the Snake, Junior**), 1936- . Underboss of the Colombo crime family of Brooklyn. Assumed control in the 1970s. Currently ranked number six in the outfit.

Petrilli, Dominick (AKA: **The Gap**), d.1953. Brought Joe Valachi into the mob. Was later deported to Italy, but snuck back into the U.S., in 1953, only to be shot to death by rival gangsters.

Pinchey Paul, prom. 1910s. Lower East Side gang leader and union racketeer who was murdered by Joseph Rosensweig in 1915.

Pinzolo, Joseph, d.1930. One of the original "Mustache Petes" of New York; murdered on Sept. 9, 1930 by Thomas Lucchese.

Pioggi, Louis (AKA: **Louie the Lump**), prom. 1908. A tough New York city gangster who murdered Max "Kid Twist" Zwerbach and Vach "Cyclone Louie" Lewis after they had forced him to jump out of a second story window in Coney Island, 1908.

Plug Uglies, prom. 1820s-60s. Irish street gang in the Five Points. Named for the plug hats they wore, stuffed with wool and leather.

Plumeri, James, prom. 1960s-70s. Capodeceine in the Lucchese crime family.

Polizzi, Francesco, (AKA: **Frank**), 1934- . New Jersey millionaire who solved the "pipeline" problems for the Pizza Connection. He was sentenced to twenty years in prison for violation of the RICO laws, and drug trafficking.

Pompez, Alexander, prom. 1930s. A Harlem numbers boss who joined Dutch Shultz' gang.

Poole, William (AKA: **Butcher**), d.1855. Bowery Boy gangster and ward healer. Shot by Lew Baker in 1855.

Potashes, prom. 1900s. Lower West Side street gang who prowled the vicinity of the Babbitt Soap Factory on Washington Street.

Potenza, Vincent (AKA: **Jimmy Jones**), prom. 1970s. Ranking member of the Gaetano Lucchese crime family.

Presenzano, Angelo, prom. 1950s-60s. Soldier in the Bonanno crime family. Defected to the DiGregorio camp during the Banana War.

Profaci, Joseph (AKA: **The Olive Oil King**), 1897-1962. Boss of one of New York City's five families. Controlled Staten Island and a part of Brooklyn. Waged war against the Gallo brothers in Brooklyn. Died of natural causes on June 7, 1962.

Provenzano, Anthony (AKA: **Tony Pro**), 1920-88. Professional killer. Labor union racketeer. Genovese family crime boss in New Jersey.

Provenzano, Nunzio, prom. 1970s. Brother of Anthony Provenzano. Served as president of New Jersey Teamster's Local 560.

Provenzano, Salvatore, prom. 1970s. Brother of Anthony Provenzano. Long-time secretary-treasurer of Teamster's Local 560.

Rag Gang, prom. 1870s. Bowery street gang.

Rampino, Anthony (AKA: **Tony Roach**), prom. 1970s-80s. Foot soldier and private assassin in the employ of John Gotti. Currently in prison for narcotics trafficking.

Rand, Jake (AKA: **Greedy Jake**), prom. 1870s. Thief, who robbed financier Rufus Lord of $1,900,000 in 1866.

Rao, Joseph (AKA: **Joseph Cangro**), b.1901. Drug trafficker and one-time associate of Dutch Schultz. Arrest record dates back to 1920; including arrests for burglary, robbery, and homicide.

Rao, Vincent John (AKA: **Frank Arra, Nunzio Arra**), b.1898. Former consiglieri in the family of Thomas Lucchese. Owned vast acreage in East Harlem, and was an associate of Willie Moretti.

Rastelli, Philip (AKA: **Rusty**), 1918- . Became boss of the Bonanno family of New York, after Joe was deposed. Loan shark, drug trafficker, and labor union racketeer. A rival faction, headed by five capos initially opposed Rastelli's ascendency. Ranked number nine in the mob hierarchy.

Rava, Armand, b.1911. Boss of syndicate gambling in New York. Top lieutenant of Aniello Dellacroce until his disappearance.

Raymond, Nathan (AKA: **Nigger Nate**), prom. 1928. California gangster who sat in on the fatal poker game of Nov. 4, 1928, in New York City, that claimed the life of Arnold Rothstein. Raymond never went to trial.

Reardon, "Duck", prom. 1900s. Member of the Batavia Street gang.

Reddy the Blacksmith, prom. 1870s. Member of the Bowery Boys. Killed Philadelphia gangster Jimmy Hagerty at Patsy Egan's resort.

Red Light Lizzie, prom. 1860s-70s. Procuress and owner of six bordellos in New York. Supplied girls to other establishments as well.

Red Onions, prom. 1900s. Lower East Side street gang.

Red Peppers, prom. 1900s. Street gang whose turf was 102nd Street on the East Side.

Reina, Gaetano (AKA: **Tom**), d.1930. Old-time Black Hand-Mafia "don" who controlled the Bronx. Murdered on Feb. 26, 1930, by Vito Genovese, during the Castellammarese War.

Reinfeld, Joseph H., prom. 1920s-30s. Liquor distributor who supplied Prohibition alcohol to Waxey Gordon and other New York mobsters. Organized a "combine" with Abner "Longy" Zwillman headquartered in New Jersey and Manhattan.

Reles, Abraham (AKA: **Kid Twist**), d.1941. Small-time killer who revealed the existence of Murder, Inc., to the government in 1941. Allegedly committed suicide by jumping out of a Coney Island hotel on Nov. 12, 1941.

Rhodes Gang, prom. 1900s. Hell's Kitchen street gang.

Riccobono, Joseph, prom. 1950s-60s. Consigliere in the Gambino crime family until his retirement in the late 1960s.

Riggi, John Sr., 1928- . New Jersey crime boss allied with Simone DeCavalcante. Active in north and central N.J. waterfront racketeer.

Riley, "Rags", prom. 1900s. Leader of the Pansies street gang.

Riley, "Razor", prom. 1900s. Member of the Gophers. Murdered Paul Kelly.

Ritter, Frank (AKA: **Red Reed**), prom. 1970s. Mid-town Manhattan gambling boss.

Rivera, Pedro, prom. 1970s. Latin gangster associated with Raymond Marquez.

Roach Guards, prom. 1820s-30s. Five Points street gang that spawned the Dead Rabbits.

Robilotto, John (AKA: **Johnny Roberts**), d.1958. Believed responsible for Willie Moretti's murder. He was murdered shortly after Albert Anastasia was hit, in 1957.

Rodriquez, Benjamin (AKA: **Benny**, prom. 1970s. A lieutenant in the Raymond Marquez crime organization controlling gambling in the vicinity of Eighth Avenue and 113th Street.

Romanello, Anthony, prom. 1900s. Member of Owney Madden's gang.

Romano, Pasquale, prom. 1950s. Policy racketeer in New York.

Romero, Anthony, prom. 1930s. Criminal associate of Lepke Buchalter.

Ronsisvalle, Luigi, prom. 1970s-80s. Contract killer and Mafia drug runner who became a key government informant during the Pizza Connection hearings in 1985-86. Served as the "mule" for the Connection, delivering 300 kilos of heroin to Chicago in 1977 and 1978.

Rooney, Al, prom. 1900s. Leader of the Fourteenth Street gang.

Rosato, Joseph, b.1904. Born in Naples, Italy. Rosato was a long time narcotics peddler and labor racketeer in New York. Capodecine in the Lucchese crime family.

Rosen, Joseph, d.1936. A courtroom eyewitness against Lepke

Buchalter. Murdered by Mendy Weiss before he could give testimony on Sept. 12, 1936

Rosenberg, Louis (AKA: **Lefty Louie**), prom. 1910s. New York City mobster convicted and executed for the 1912 murder of Herman Rosenthal.

Rosenkrantz, Bernard (AKA: **Lulu**), d.1935. Member of the Dutch Schultz mob. Murdered with Schultz, Abe Landau, and Otto Berman on Oct. 23, 1935.

Rosensweig, Joseph (AKA: **Joe the Greasor**), prom. 1910s. New York street gang chieftain.

Rosenthal, Herman (AKA: **Beansie**), d.1912. A New York City gambler and police informant shot to death by Harry Horowitz, Frank Cirofici, Louis Rosenberg, and Jacob Siedenshner on July 15, 1912.

Rothstein, Arnold (AKA: **The Brain**), 1882-1928. An influential New York gambler known simply as "A.R." to his associates. Rothstein was the man who engineered the 1919 World Series fix. He was shot in a poker game in New York, in 1928.

Rough Riders, prom. 1917. Jewish street gang organized by Nathan "Kid Dropper" Kaplan after the death of Johnny Spanish.

Round Back Rangers, prom. 1900s. Social-political club organized by Tammany Hall.

Rubber Shaw, prom. 1900s. Member of the Hudson Dusters street gang.

Rubin, Max, prom. 1940. A New Jersey racketeer who turned state's evidence in 1940, after being wounded by the mob.

Rubinov, Boris, d.1987. Russian-born Brooklyn gangster murdered in 1987 following his arrest on gun-running charges.

Rudnick, George (AKA: **Whitey**), d.1940. Brooklyn loan shark, murdered by Dasher Abbandando and Happy Maione, for which they went to the electric chair.

Rudolph, Harry, prom. 1940. Sent to prison in 1940, for theft. While there, he revealed important information about Abe "Kid Twist" Reles, and other members of Murder, Inc.

Ruggiero, Angelo, prom. 1970-80s. Capo in the Gambino crime family, and noted labor racketeer. Died of cancer in 1989.

Ruggiero, Benjamin (AKA: **Lefty**), prom. 1970s-80s. Soldier in the capodecine of Dominick Napolitano. Ran a bookie operation in a Lower Manhattan "social club."

Ruggiero, Salvatore, prom. 1970s-80s. Brother of Angelo Ruggiero. A major heroin trafficker who died in a plane crash in 1982.

Rullo, Jerry, prom. 1930s. New Jersey mob figure affiliated with Willie Moretti.

Runnelli, Steven, prom. 1930s. Gunman employed by Salvatore Maranzano.

Rupolo, Ernest (AKA: **The Hawk**), d.1964. Top triggerman for Vito Genovese, found murdered, in 1964.

Russo, Louis, d.1931. Maranzano lieutenant, who was tortured and murdered by the Luciano-Lansky factions in 1931.

Ryan, "Piker", prom. 1870s. Professional killer and bank robber. Member of the Whyos Gang.

Rynders, Isaiah, prom. 1850s. Political boss of the Sixth Ward and "protector" of the Five Points Gangs. Used the street gangs to further the aims of the Nativist movement.

Sabatino, Thomas (AKA: **Big Tom**), prom. 1920s. New York City mobster murdered in his car.

Sabella, Michael, prom. 1970s. Underboss in the Bonanno crime family.

Sadie the Goat, prom. 1869. Fourth Ward gang woman, who took over leadership of the Charlton Street Gang.

Sage, Walter, d.1933. Member of the Reles-Maione gang, in Brooklyn. Stabbed by Phil Strauss, in 1933, after his duplicity was discovered by his bosses.

Saietta, Ignazio (AKA: **Lupo the Wolf**), prom. 1890s-1910s. Vicious boss of the Black Hand, in Harlem, for nearly three decades. Sent to the Sing Sing Penitentiary, in 1918.

Salerno, Anthony (AKA: **Fat Tony**), 1914- . Head of the Vito Genovese crime family. Member of the ruling commission, and one of the most important mobsters in the U.S. today. Gambling, loan-sharking, and labor union racketeering is his specialty.

Salter, Michael (AKA: **Nigger Mike**), prom. 1900s. Owner of a resort in Pell Street.

Santoro, Salvatore (AKA: **Tom Mix**), 1919- . Ranked number eight in the national crime syndicate hierarchy. Capodeceine of the Thomas Lucchese crime family.

Santucci, Girolamo (AKA: **Bobby Doyle**), prom. 1930s. New York gangster, who fought on the side of Salvatore Maranzano, in the Castellammarese War. Was in Maranzano's presence the day he was killed, on Sept. 10, 1931.

Satan's Circus, prom. 1860s-70s. Collection of bordellos, and vice dens located between Twenty-Fourth and Fortieth Streets and Fifth and Seventh Avenues. Dubbed the "Tenderloin" by Police Inspector Alexander "Clubber" Williams" because of its graft potential.

Saul, Nicholas, 1833-53. Shared leadership of the Daybreak Boys with William Howlett. Hanged in the Tombs Prison with Howlett.

Saupp, John, d. 1962. Killed by mistake, in 1962, by Joe Valachi, while the two men were serving time in the Atlanta Penitentiary.

Scalise, Frank (AKA: **Don Cheech**), d.1957. Lieutenant in the Anastasia crime family. Murdered in 1957, after it was learned that he had been selling Mafia memberships for $50,000, a piece.

Scalise, Joseph, prom. 1950s. Brother of Frank Scalise. Assassinated when he threatened to avenge his brother's death.

Scalise, George, prom. 1940. Labor racketeer who headed up the Building Service Employee's International Union of New York before his indictment on extortion charges in April, 1940.

Schapiro, Solomon, prom. 1917. Headed up an Italian street gang that challeged the Rough Riders of Kid Dropper.

Schlitten, Moishe, prom. 1940s. One of two brothers running a numbers racket on behalf of Vito Genovese.

Schlitten, Samuel, prom. 1940s. Brother of Moishe Schlitten.

Schmertzler, Morris (AKA: **Max Courtney**), prom. 1970s. New York City gambler active in mid-town Manhattan.

Schultz, Dutch (Fleggenheimer, Arthur), 1902-35. Prohibition bootlegger, and violent killer; gunned down by members of the Albert Anastasia gang in a New Jersey snack shop, in 1935.

Schwartz, Martin (AKA: **Red**), prom. 1970s. Mid-town Manhattan gambler.

Sciacca, Paul, prom. 1960s. One time member of the Bonanno family. Defected to the DiGregorio forces, in 1964. Failed in an attempt to take over the DiGregorio family.

Sciarra, Daniel, prom. 1980s. Brother of Michael Sciarra. Assumed control of New Jersey Teamster's Local 560 in 1988, allegedly controlled by Anthony Provenzano.

Sciarra, Michael, prom. 1980s. New Jersey Teamster's boss allegedly hand picked to head up Local 560 by Anthony "Tony Pro" Provenzano.

Scimone, John, prom. 1950s. Member of the Gallo family, who joined the Profacis during the war.

Sclafani, Joseph, prom. 1980. Mob associate of Costabile Farace. Wounded during a Mafia shootout in 1989 that took Farace's life.

Scoperto, Charles (AKA: **Scoops**), prom. 1970s. Member of the Gaetano Lucchese drime family.

Scopo, Ralph, 1932- . Member of the Colombo family of Brooklyn. Labor union racketeer currently on trial.

Scotchy Lavelle, prom. 1910s. One-time river pirate who opened a saloon dive in Chatham Square in Chinatown.

Seabury, Samuel, 1873-1958. Justice of the New York Supreme Court, whose penetrating 1930 investigation into the criminal-politico tie-up in New York, led to the resignation of Mayor Jimmy Walker.

Sedotto, Anthony, prom. 1960s-70s. Capodeceine in the Gambino crime family.

Segal, Harry (AKA: **Champ**), prom. 1970. Frank Costello's favorite bookmaker.

Shapiro, Irving, prom. 1920s. Brother of Meyer Shaprio. Killed during the 1931 takeover attempt, by Kid Twist Reles.

Shapiro, Jacob (AKA: **Gurrah, Jake**), prom. 1920s-30s. Prominent Jewish gangster who was a lieutenant in Murder, Inc., and a sidekick of Louis "Lepke" Buchalter. Died in prison in 1947.

Shapiro, Meyer, d.1931. East side gambling, bootlegging, and vice boss. Eldest of three brothers who owned a string of bordellos. Murdered by two former associates: Kid Twist Reles and Bugsy Goldstein.

Shapiro, Willie, prom. 1920s. Brother of Meyer Shapiro. Buried alive by Kid Twist Reles and his associates.

Sharpton, Al, prom. 1980s. Activist black preacher who supplied the government with information about New York drug dealers and organized crime figures.

Shay, Thomas, prom. 1870s. Leader of the Hooker gang, which moved from the Fourth Ward to Corlear's Hook.

Shea, William, prom. 1900s. One-time gambling partner of Arnold Rothstein. The partnership dissolved in the early 1900s.

Sheeney Mike, prom. 1870s. One of the leaders of the Dutch Mob.

Sherman, Albert (AKA: **Plug**), d.1939. Assassinated by Allie Tannenbaum and "Knuckles" Mitzberg on Jan. 29, 1939.

Shillitani, Salvatore (AKA: **Sally Shields**), prom. 1970s. Member of the Gaetano Lucchese crime family.

Shinburn, Mark, prom. 1870s. Bank burglar who sailed to Europe and became a Baron in Monaco.

Shirt Tails, prom. 1820s-60s. Five Points street gang, so named because they wore their shirts outside their trousers.

Short Tails, prom. 1840s. Fourth Ward street gang.

Sica, Joseph, 1911- . Sica was active in New Jersey organized crime from 1928 on, as a thief, drug pusher, extortionist, and syndicate killer.

Siedenshner, Jacob (AKA: **Whitey Lewis**), prom. 1910s. Participated in the murder of rival gambler Herman Rosenthal on July 15, 1912. Was tried, found guilty, and later executed for the crime.

Silesi, Joseph Albert (AKA: **Joe Rivers**), prom. 1970s. Member of the Gaetano Lucchese crime family.

Silver Gang, prom. 1870s. Lower West Side burglary gang.

Simmons, Zachariah, prom. 1900. A turn-of-the-century policy boss in Manhattan, exposed by the New York *Times* as an influence peddler and bribe giver.

Simpson, William, prom. 1920s. Waterfront rackets boss. Assassinated.

Siracusa, Pepino, prom. 1910s-20s. Old-line Mafiosi who served on the National Commission prior to and during the Castellemmarese War.

Sirocco, John, prom. 1910s. One of the last leaders of Monk Eastman's Five Points gang.

Sister's Row, prom. 1860s. A row of bordellos run by seven sisters from New England; located on West Twenty-Fifth Street near Seventh Avenue in Manhattan.

Slater, Sidney, prom. 1970s. New York City racketeer.

Slaughter Housers, prom. 1850s. New York street gang.

Slobbery Jim, prom. 1850s. Member of the Daybreak Boys. Killed Patsy the Barber at the Hole-in-Wall Saloon.

Smith, Norman E., prom. 1970s. Gambling and policy boss in Harlem.

Snyder, Benjamin (AKA: **Nigger**), prom. 1910s. Henchman of Joseph Rosensweig. Sent to prison for twenty years in 1915 for murder.

Socco the Bracer (Joseph Gayles), 1844-73. River pirate. Top lieutenant of Patsy Conroy. Killed by police on May 29, 1873.

Soresi, Giuseppe, prom. 1970-80s. Borghetto, Si., drug trafficker who moved his operations to Queens, N.Y. Accused of being the alternative heroin supplier to Gaetano Badalamenti during the height of the Pizza Connection.

Soup Greens, prom. 1900s. Social-political club organized by Tammany Hall politicians.

Spanish, John (Joseph Weyler, AKA: **Johnny)**, d.1917. Boss of most of the New York City rackets until he was gunned down by Nathan "Kid Dropper" Kaplan on July 29, 1917.

Spanish Louie, prom. 1900s. Member of Humpty Jackson's gang.

Squab Wheelmen, prom. 1900s. Gang organized by Crazy Butch.

Stable Gang, prom. 1870s. Lower West Side gang that preyed on newly arrived immigrants.

Stein, Ruby, prom. 1970s. New York City mobster.

Stewart, Honey, prom. 1900s. Member of the Hudson Dusters street gang.

Straci, Joseph (AKA: **Joe Stretch**), prom. 1920s. A member of Joe Masseria's outfit at the start of the Castellammarese War, but changed sides midway through, to hook-up with the Manganos.

Strauss, Hershel (AKA: **Pittsburgh Phil, Harry**), d.1936. Professional assassin for Murder Inc., executed in Sing Sing, on June 12, 1936.

Strollo, Anthony C. (AKA: **Tony Bender**), 1899-1962. Syndicate gunman, bootlegger, and lieutenant in the Luciano Crime Family. Boss of the Greenwich Village rackets following the assassination of Salvatore Maranzano in 1931. Vito Genovese's underboss in Manhattan. Disappeared in 1962.

Stuart, Frank, prom. 1850s. Owner of a gambling resort on Park Place.

Sullivan, Jeremiah J., prom. 1940s. Longshoreman's union racketeer.

Sullivan, Timothy D. (AKA: **Big Tim**), d.1946. Corrupt political boss of Tammany Hall in the early 1900s.

Sutton, Robert, prom. 1970s. Numbers boss of Central Harlem in the early 1970s.

Swamp Angels, prom. 1850s. Fourth Ward street gang.

Tambone, Peter (AKA: **Little Pete**), prom. 1970s-80s. Drug trafficker who was banished by Paul Castellano after his role in the Ruggiero-Gotti heroin operation was revealed. Reinstated by Gotti in 1986.

Tammany, William, prom. 1900s. Lieutenant of Owney Madden. Arrested and sent to Sing Sing.

Tammany Hall, prom. 1789-1970. Executive committee of the New York Democratic Party, named after a Delaware Indian chief. Taken over by Irish immigrants in the 1830s, and converted into a potent, and often corrupt political machine that guided the city politics, vice, and gambling for decades.

Tannenbaum, Albert (AKA: **Tick Tock**), prom. 1930s. New York hitman who killed on orders from Louis "Lepke" Buchalter.

Tannenbaum, Benjamin (AKA: **Benny the Boss**), d.1941. Mafia aide to Lepke Buchalter and Jake "Gurrah" Shapiro. Murdered at a New York State resort in February 1941.

Tarolino, Salvatore, d.1920s. Shot down in a Brooklyn gang war.

Tarricone Alphonse (AKA: **Funzi**), prom. 1970s-80s. Loan shark, extortionist, and strong-arm soldier who rejected an FBI offer to inform against John Gotti.

Tartamella, John, prom. 1930s-50s. Ranked number three in the Bonanno crime family until ill health forced him to step down in 1964.

Telleri, Frank (AKA: **The 500**), d.1967. Defector from the Bonanno camp. Joined DiGregorio, but was murdered at the Cypress Garden Restaurant, in Queens, in 1967.

Tenth Avenue Gang, prom. 1870s. Street toughs who were later absorbed into the Hell's Kitchen gang.

Terranova, Ciro (AKA: **the Artichoke King**), 1891-1938. Powerful Prohibition-era hoodlum who cornered the market on artichokes in New York City. Deposed by Lucky Luciano and Vito Genovese, in the 1930s.

Terry Reilleys, prom. 1910s. Third Avenue street gang.

Testa, Joseph Jr., prom. 1980s. Member of the Gambino crime family. Carried out Mafia assassinations for the DeMeo hit squad in the 1970s.

Teti, Felice, prom. 1970s. Foot soldier in the Gambino crime family.

Thieves' Exchange, prom. 1870s. Rendezvous for the burglary gangs, located near Broadway and Houston Street.

Tieri, Frank (AKA: **Funzi**), prom. 1960s-70s. Served as acting boss of the Vito Genovese crime family.

Tinerello, James, prom. 1920s. Gangster and convict murdered in New York.

Tolentino, Nicholas (AKA: **Big Nose Nick**), prom. 1970s. Member of the Gaetano Lucchese crime family.

Toplitz, Alfred, prom. 1952. Democratic leader of the First Assembly District in Manhattan. Reputed associate of "Trigger" Mike Coppola and Frank Erickson. Appeared before the New York Crime Commission in 1952.

Torchio, Antonio, prom. 1927. New York based gunman hired out to the Chicago Joe Aiello gang, in 1927. Murdered as he stepped off the train in Chicago, by Capone gunmen.

Torti, Charles, prom. 1910s. Member of the Jack Sirocco gang. Shot Jack Zelig outside the Criminal Courts Building.

Tourine, Charles (AKA: **The Blade**), prom. 1960s. New York City mobster.

Traina, Giuseppe (AKA: **the Peasant**), prom. 1910s-20s. Member of the National Commission during the Castellemmarese War of 1928-31.

Tramunti, Carmine (AKA: **Mr. Gribs**), prom. 1972. New York gang boss who assumed control of the Lucchese family in 1972

Tresca, Carlo, d.1943. Socialist newspaper editor murdered in Manhattan on Jan. 1, 1943, allegedly by Carmine Galante.

Tricker, Chick, prom. 1910s. One of the last rulers of the Monk Eastman gang. Owner of a dive on Park Row that was closed down by the Committee of Fourteen in 1910.

Trinchera, Dominick, d.1981. One of the malcontents within the Bonanno crime family who engineered a coup against Philip Rastelli in 1980. Disappeared on May 5, 1981.

Troia, Vincenzo, prom. 1910s-20s. Member of the ruling National Commission during the Castellemmarese War of 1928-31.

True Blue Americans, prom. 1830s-40s. Irish street gang from the Bowery that expressed anti-English sentiment.

Tuminaro, Angelo (AKA: **Little Angie**), 1908- . Lucchese family drug trafficker. Currently a fugitive from justice.

Tunnel Gang, prom. 1910s. Third Avenue street gang that waged constant warfare with Corcoran's Roosters.

Turkis, Burton B., prom. 1940. New York prosecutor who received the confession of Abe "Kid Twist" Reles of Murder, Inc.

Turner, James, prom. 1850s. Tammany Hall politician and street thug.

Turnio, Joseph, d.1925. New York longshoreman murdered in 1925. Albert Anastasia and Jimmy Florio were tried and convicted for his murder. They were released after a retrial.

Tweed, William Marcy (AKA: **Boss Tweed**), 1823-78. Corrupt political boss of Tammany Hall through the 1860s. Imprisoned in 1875 for graft and embezzlement.

Twin Oaks, prom. 1900s. Social-political club organized by Tammany Hall.

Ullo, Joseph Spencer, prom. 1950s-70s. Soldier in the Genovese family. Fled to Los Angeles, after failing to repay his juice loans.

Vadala, Anthony (AKA: **Grio**), prom, 1970s. Member of the Gaetano Lucchese crime family.

Valachi, Joseph, 1904-71. Syndicate foot soldier who revealed the existence of the Cosa Nostra to a Senate Subcommittee, in 1962. Died in prison.

Valente, Samuel, prom. 1970s. Member of the Gaetano Lucchese crime family.

Valente, Thomas, prom. 1970s. Member of the Gaetano Lucchese crime family.

Valenti, Frank Joseph, 1911- . Syndicate gambling chieftain, born in Rochester, N.Y. Imprisoned in 1972.

Valenti, Umberto, prom. 1920s. Attempted to murder Joe Masseria, in 1922. After failing in this attempt, he was shot dead during peace talks with Masseria.

Vario, Paul Sr., 1917- . Lucchese crime boss currently residing in prison.

Varriale, Carmine, d.1987. Brother of Pasquale Varriale, and a made member of the Lucchese family. Gunned down in September 1987.

Varriale, Pasquale (AKA: **Paddy Bulldog**), d.1987. Small-time gambler and hustler who received $10,000 from the Bonanno family to bribe a Pizza Connection juror. When he backed out of the deal in February, 1987, he was assassinated.

Vento, Joseph (AKA: **Babe**), prom. 1970s. Member of the Gaetano Lucchese crime family.

Vernotico, Gerard, d.1932. Murdered with Antonio Lonzo by Vito Genovese gunmen.

Vintaloro, James (AKA: **Jimmy the Sniff**), prom. 1970s. Member of the Gaetano Lucchese crime family.

Vollero, Alessandro, prom. 1919. New York hoodlum sent to prison in 1919. Educated Joe Valachi in the ways of the Cosa Nostra.

Waddell, Reed, d.1895. Conman and swindler. Killed in Paris in 1895.

Waffa, Ali, d.1963. Killed during the Gallo-Profaci War in July 1963.

Wagner, Abe, prom. 1930s. Bootlegger and mob associate of Dutch Schultz.

Wah Kee, prom. 1860s-70s. China town gambling boss and opium dealer.

Wallace, Chris, prom. 1900s. Member of the Monk Eastman gang.

Wallis, John, prom. 1850s. Chinese gambler who took over the gambling dens of Jimmy Berry and French José after winning a coin toss.

Walsh, "Hoggy", prom. 1870s. Member of the Whyos Gang.

Walsh, John (AKA: **Johnny the Mick**), prom. 1880s. Pickpocket and gang leader. Killed Johnny Irving.

Walsh, Michael, prom. 1900s. Member of the Batavia Street Gang.

Walters, Norby, prom. 1988. Professional sports agent convicted of fraud and racketeering in April 1988 for signing college players to pro contracts before their eligibility expired. Alleged to have connections with mobster Michael Franzese.

Ward, Slipsley, prom. 1860s. Lieutenant of Bum Mahoney in the Hooker Gang.

Weiss, Emmanuel (AKA: **Seymour, Mendy**), d.1944. A henchman of Lucky Luciano, who murdered Dutch Schultz at the Palace Chophouse, in Newark, N.J., on Oct. 23, 1935. Executed in 1944.

Weinberg, Abraham (AKA: **Bo**), d.1935. Ran the Dutch Schultz rackets when the boss went into hiding, in 1933. Secretly negotiated with Lepke Buchalter and Lucky Luciano, not expecting Schultz to return. When he did, Weinberg was murdered.

Weinberg, George, d.1938. Numbers racketeer who committed suicide before his scheduled court appearance in which he was to testify against Dutch Schultz.

Weingarten, Benjamin, prom. 1970s. Gangster active in the East Village of Manhattan.

Westies, prom. 1960s-80s. Powerful Irish street gang active in the Hell's Kitchen section of Manhattan. Forged an alliance with Paul Castellano of the Gambino crime family in 1978. The gang was broken up in 1987-88 following a long series of criminal trials that resulted in long prison terms for the top ranking leaders.

White Hand Gang, The, prom. 1900-25. An extortion gang active in the East River docks for a quarter century. The White Hand was ruled at various times by Wild Bill Lovett, Dinny Meehan, and Richard "Peg Leg" Lonergan.

Whyos Gang, the, prom. 1860s-1900. Tough street gang organized after the Civil War. Active in the vicinity of the Fourth Ward on the Lower East Side. Eclipsed at the turn of the century by the gangs of Monk Eastman and Paul Kelly.

Williams, Alexander (AKA: **Clubber**), prom. 1887-1894. Corrupt Police Inspector who collected graft from the vice areas. Implicated by the Lexow Committee of 1894.

Wolinsky, Moey (AKA: **Dimples**), d.1942. Served as manager for the empire of Louis "Lepke" Buchalter. Lied to his boss in 1939, saying that a deal had been cut to reduce Buchalter's sentence. Wolinsky was shot dead, in 1942.

Wolosky, David, d.1972. Murdered outside the Beth Israel Hospital in Manhattan on Apr. 19, 1972.

Wong Get, prom. 1900s. Rival of Tom Lee for leadership of the On Leong Tong gang. Allied himself with Mock Duck.

Woods, Arthur, prom. 1914. New York Police commissioner who imprisoned more than 200 gang leaders in his first year in office.

Woods, William, prom. 1870s. Member of the Patsy Conroy Gang.

Woods, Morris (AKA: **Big Mo**), prom. 1970s. Harlem gunman.

Workman, Charles (AKA: **The Bug**), prom. 1930s. Syndicate killer, who took part in the assassination of Dutch Schultz, at the Palace Chophouse, in Newark, N.J. Sent to prison in 1941.

Yacovelli, Joseph (AKA: **Joey Yac**), prom. 1970s. Consiglieri in the Colombo crime family. A bitter foe of Thomas DiBella.

Yakey Yakes, prom. 1900s. Street gang whose territory was near the Brooklyn Bridge.

Yale, Frankie (Frank Uale), 1885-1927. Contract killer, born in Brooklyn. President of the Union Siciliano from 1918 until his death at the hands of Al Capone gangsters in 1927. Believed to be one of the triggermen sent into Chicago to murder Dion O'Bannion in November 1924.

Yankee Doodle Boys, prom. 1900s. Social-political club organized by Tammany Hall politicians,

Yarnowsky, Charles, d.1948. Syndicate hood active in Jersey City, N.J., found murdered on July 16, 1948.

Yoske Nigger (Joseph Toplinsky), prom. 1910s. Gangster who extorted money from produce dealers, truckmen, and livery stables. Worked in tandem with Charley the Cripple and Johnny Levinsky.

Yuran, Hyman, d.1938. Former associate of Louis "Lepke" Buchalter; shot by Murder, Inc., and dumped into a limepit near Lake Sheldrake, N.Y., on Aug. 21, 1938.

Zaffarano, Michael (AKA: **Mickey**), prom. 1970s. Capo in the Bonanno family, (later ruled by Carmine Galente.) Involved in the pornography industry. Suspected of murdering Jake Molinas in 1975.

Zangarra, Anthony, prom. 1960s-70s. Capo in the Gambino crime family.

Zappi, Ettore (AKA: **Tony Russo**), 1904- . Brooklyn racketeer and blood relative of Carlo Gambino. Served as bodyguard to Anthony Anastasia, boss of the Brooklyn waterfront. Capo in the Gambino family.

Zelig, John (William Alberts), (AKA: **Big Jack**), 1882-1912. Powerful New York City mob boss who took over Monk Eastman's gang. Murdered on a street car trolley, Oct. 5, 1912 by Red Phil Davidson.

Zelmanowitz, Gerald (AKA: **Paul Maris**), prom. 1970s. One-time mobster whose testimony helped convict his associates Angelo "Gyp" DeCarlo and Daniel "Red" Cecere in 1970. Was given a new identity and moved to San Francisco under the witness re-location program. Became a successful businessman.

Zicarelli, Joseph, prom. 1940s-60s. Foot-soldier in the Joseph Bonanno crime family. During the "Banana War" he defected to the Mafia gang headed by Gaspar DiGregorio.

Zingara, Joseph, 1911- . Member of the Carlo Gambino family. Oversaw mob activity in Westchester County.

Zummo, Thomas, d.1969. Lieutenant in the DiGregorio-Bonanno family. Last gangster to die in the "Banana War:" Feb. 6, 1969.

Zwerbach, Max (AKA: **Kid Twist**), 1882-1908. One of Monk Eastman's top assassins in the early 1900s. Responsible for the murders of at least ten New York City gangsters.

Zwillman, Abner (AKA: **Longy**), 1899-1959. Established autonomy in New Jersey, in the 1930s, after being pushed out of New York by Lucky Luciano. Became supreme boss of the Newark rackets after the death of Dutch Schultz, in 1935. Killed on orders from Meyer Lansky, though his death was made to look like a suicide.

OMAHA-ROCKY MOUNTAIN ORGANIZED CRIME

Biase, Anthony Joseph, 1908- . Boss of the Omaha faction of the National Crime syndicate. Took control of the rackets after his associate Anthony Marcella went to prison.

Coletti, James, prom. 1950s. Crime boss of Colorado. In attendance at the 1957 Apalachin meeting.

Smaldone, Eugene, prom. 1970s-80s. Reigning Mafia kingpin of Denver.

Spinuzzi, Joseph, prom. 1970s. Head of Cosa Nostra operations in Denver in the 1970s.

PHILADELPHIA-NORTHERN & EASTERN PA. ORGANIZED CRIME

Allen, Charles, prom. 1980. Mob hitman hired by Frank Sheeran in 1980 to commit murder and assault.

American Blackies, prom. 1920s. Prohibition-era bootleg gang that competed with Max Hoff's mob.

Blavat, Jerry, prom. 1970s-80s. Member of the Bruno-Testa crime family.

Bouras, Chelsais (AKA: **Steve**), d.1981. Drug trafficker and loan shark who was boss of Philadelphia's "Greek mob." Assassinated in a South Philadelphia restaurant on May 27, 1981, allegedly by hitmen employed by Nicodemo "Little Nicky" Scarfo.

Bruno, Angelo (Angelo Bruno Analoro), 1911-80. Former boss of one of three Pennsylvania crime families. Operated out of Philadelphia. Assassinated Mar. 21, 1980.

Bufalino, Lawrence, prom. 1980s. Relative of Russell Bufalino, owned and operated a food importing company in Williamsport, which was destroyed by fire in December 1980.

Bufalino, Russell, 1903- . One of three powerful syndicate bosses of Pennsylvania. Operates out of Pittstown. Arrested and imprisoned at Danbury in 1977.

Caponigro, Antonio, d.1980. Served as consiglieri to the Bruno-Testa family before being murdered on Apr. 17, 1980.

Caramandi, Nicholas, prom. 1980s. Moster who turned informant against Nicodemo Scarfo Jr. in 1988. Sentenced to eight years in prison in 1989.

Casella, Peter, prom. 1981. Became underboss of the Bruno-Testa family following the death of Angelo Bruno in 1980.

Ciancaglini, Joseph, prom. 1980. Enforcer and hit man who took over Frank Sindone's loan sharking operations. Convicted on conspiracy charges in November 1988.

D'Alfonso, Frank (AKA: **Frankie Flowers**), d.1985. Member of the Bruno-Testa crime family. Assassinated in 1985 by Eugene Milano and seven other Scarfo mobsters.

DelGiorno, Thomas, prom. 1980s. Reputed mob figure who became a government informant against Nicodemo Scarfo Jr. Currently serving a five year sentence.

Denano, Ignazio, prom. 1970s. Underboss of the Bruno crime family in the early 1970s.

Duffy, Mickey, prom. 1930s. Irish mob boss, assassinated by Italian gangsters in Atlantic City.

Elfman, Louis R., prom. 1920s. Lieutenant of Max Hoff who turned state's evidence against his boss in 1928.

Farrell, Martin, prom. 1930s. Member of the Tri-State Gang of Bucks County. Convicted in April 1935 of the kidnap-murder of William Weiss, a Philadelphia racketeer.

Grande, Wayne, prom. 1988. Philadelphia mobster convicted of racketeering and conspiracy charges in November 1988.

Guarnieri, Anthony F., prom. 1970s-80s. A capo in the Bufalino crime family, now operating out of Florida.

Hoff, Maxie (AKA: **Boo-Boo**), prom. 1920s. Bootleg boss of the criminal underworld during the Prohibition era.

Iannece, Charles, prom. 1988. Philadelphia mobster convicted of racketeering and conspiracy charges in November 1988.

Iannarella, Francis Jr., prom. 1988. Philadelphia mobster convicted of conspiracy and racketeering charges in November 1988.

Ida, Joseph, prom. 1950s. Philadelphia gang boss arrested at the 1957 Apalachin meeting.

Idone, Sando, prom. 1980s. Member of the Bruno-Testa mob.

Inadi, Joseph, prom. 1980s. Former Philadelphia police officer who turned drug dealer. Later became a federal witness.

Ippolito, Carl (AKA: **Pappy**), prom. 1980. Headed the Bruno-Testa gambling operations in Bucks County. Eclipsed in power.

LaFontaine, James, prom. 1932. Ran a gambling club in Washington, D.C., before being kidnapped by Philadelphia gangsters, in 1932.

Lazar, Samuel, prom. 1920s. Philadelphia crime boss. Attended the Atlantic City Conference of 1929.

Legenza, Walter, d.1935. Co-leader of the Tri-State Gang with Robert Mais. Executed in Richmond, Va.

Leonetti, Philip, prom. 1988. Nephew of Nicodemo Scarfo, and one-time underboss in the crime family. Convicted of racketeering and conspiracy charges in November 1988.

McCullough, John, d.1980. Boss of the Roofer's Union, Local 30 and an associate of Angelo Bruno. Murdered in December 1980 by a man posing as a florist.

Mais, Robert, d.1935. Co-leader of the Tri-State Gang of Bucks County, with Walter Legenza. Executed in Richmond, Va., in 1935 after being convicted of murder.

Martorano, George (AKA: **Cowboy**), prom. 1980s. Son of Raymond Martorano. Currently serving a life term in prison for violation of federal drug racketeering laws.

Martorano, Raymond (AKA: **Long John**), 1930- . Boss of local narcotics, several labor unions, and the vending machine racket for the Bruno-Testa family. Allegedly set up Steve Bouras, for assassination by the Scarfo mob, in 1981. Currently in jail.

Merlino, Lawrence, prom. 1988. Philadelphia mobster convicted of racketeering and conspiracy in November 1988.

Milano, Eugene, prom. 1970s-80s. Soldier in the Scarfo crime family. One of seventeen local mobsters convicted in the federal racketeering case of 1988. Appeared as a government witness against eight other associates for the 1985 murder of Frank D'Alfonso. Testified against his brother Nicholas. Currently in prison.

Milano, Nicholas, prom. 1970s-80s. One of seven men convicted of murdering Frank D'Alfonso. Brother of Eugene Milano.

Miller, Frank, prom. 1970s-80s. Delaware County gambling boss.

Moran, Willard (AKA: **Junior**), prom. 1980s. Mob hit man convicted of the 1980 contract killing of Union boss John McCullough. Allegedly hired to carry out the 1981 assassination of Steve Bouras.

Nacrelli, John, prom. 1980. Former mayor of Chester, Penn., convicted of accepting bribes from Frank Miller. Convicted and sent to jail for six years on Mar. 21, 1980.

Narducci, Frank, Jr. (AKA: **Chuckie**), prom. 1980s. Member of the Bruno-Testa family. Convicted of racketeering and conspiracy charges in November 1988.

Narducci, Frank, Sr., d.1982. Father of Frank Jr. Assassinated by members of the Scarfo mob in 1982.

O'Leary, Daniel, prom. 1920s. Prohibition gang boss and rival of Max "Boo-Boo" Hoff.

Outlaws, the, prom. 1970s-80s. A motorcycle gang.

Pagans, the, prom. 1970s-80s. A motorcycle gang.

Pontani, Albert (AKA: **Red**), prom. 1970s-80s. Member of the Bruno-Testa family. Considered to be a syndicate up-and-comer under the aegis of Nicky Scarfo.

Pungitore, Anthony, Jr., prom. 1988. Philadelphia mobster convicted of racketeering and conspiracy charges in November 1988.

Raiton, Ronald (AKA: **Silver Fox**), prom. 1980s. Drug dealer who supplied Steve Bouras with phenyl-2 propanone, a key ingredient of methamphetamine. Later turned government informant.

Riccobene, Harry, prom. 1970s-80s. Member of the Bruno-Testa family. Convicted for narcotics and gambling law violations.

Riccobene, Mario (AKA: **Sonny**), prom. 1970s-80s. Brother of Harry Riccobene. Has appeared as a government witness in several Mafia trials.

Rosen, Nig (Harry Stromberg), prom. 1920s-40s. Philadelphia crime boss allied with Meyer Lansky. One of the "Big Seven" appointed to head up the Mafia ruling commission at the Atlantic City Conference of 1929.

Rugnetta, Joseph, prom. 1970s. Family consigliere to Angelo Bruno in the 1970s.

Salerno, Alfred, d.1980. Chauffeur to Antonio Caponigro. Murdered with his boss on the same day.

Scafidi, Salvatore, prom. 1988. Philadelphia mobster convicted of racketeering and conspiracy charges in November 1988.

Scalleat, Joseph, prom. 1980s. Political fixer for the Bufalino family. Operates out of Hazelton.

Scarfo, Nicodemo (AKA: **Nicky**), 1932- . Boss of the Philadelphia-South New Jersey crime family, with responsiblity for the Atlantic City rackets. Convicted in November, of 1988, on charges of murder and conspiracy.

Scarfo, Nicodemo, Jr. (AKA: **Little Nicky**), prom. 1980s. Son of Nicky Scarfo. Acquitted of conspiring to murder Salvatore Testa on Sept. 14, 1984. Part of a younger generation of mobsters taking control of the Philadelphia and Atlantic City rackets.

Schwartz, Charles, prom. 1929. Gang leader present at the 1929, Atlantic City, conference.

Sciandra, Edward, prom. 1980s. A capo in the Russell Bufalino family who took over operations in 1981.

Shapiro, Kenneth, prom. 1970s-80s. Land speculator in Atlantic City, reputed to be the chief financial officer for the Scarfo mob.

Sheeran, Frank, prom. 1980. Teamster's boss in Wilmington, Del. Acquitted of conspiring to commit murder, assault, and bombing in 1980.

Simone, John, d.1980. Capo in the Bruno-Testa family. Murdered in New York on Sept. 19, 1980.

Sindone, Frank, d.1980. In charge of loan sharking operations for the Bruno-Testa family. Murdered in south Philadelphia on Oct. 30, 1980.

Staino, Ralph, prom. 1988. Philadelphia mobster convicted of racketeering and conspiracy charges in November 1988.

Stanfa, John, prom. 1970s-80s. Bodyguard of Angelo Bruno.

Testa, Philip C. (AKA: **Chicken Man**), 1925-81. Underboss and successor to Angelo Bruno. Owned Virgillio's Restaurant in Philadelphia. Killed by a bomb on Mar. 15, 1981.

Testa, Salvatore, prom. 1980s. Son of Philip Testa. Involved in the South Philadelphia rackets.

Vadino, Frank, prom. 1970s-80s. Convicted drug dealer and longtime bodygyard of George "Cowboy" Martorano.

Virgilio, Nicholas, prom. 1988. Philadelphia mobster convicted of racketeering and conspiracy charges in November 1988.

Weiss, William, d.1934. Philadelphia racketeer kidnapped and murdered in October 1934 by members of the Tri-State Gang.

Wiley, Francis, prom. 1935. Member of the Mais-Legenza Tri-State Gang. Convicted in April 1935 of the kidnap-murder of Philadelphia mobster William Weiss.

Zeid, Charles, prom. 1930s. Member of the Tri-State Gang.

Zito, Benito, prom. 1980s. Sicilian Mafia figure who emigrated to Philadelphia. Sold 2.5 kilos of heroin to DEA Agent Stephen Hopson between June and August 1983.

PHOENIX, TUCSON, AND THE SOUTHWEST ORGANIZED CRIME

Battaglia, Charles, prom. 1960s. Top lieutenant of Joseph Bonanno in Tucson. Sentenced to ten years in Leavenworth in the 1960s.

Bonanno, Joseph (AKA: **Joe Bananas**), 1905- . Boss of a powerful New York crime family for nearly thirty years, until he was vanquished in the "Banana War" of the 1960s, and forced into semi-retirement in Tucson, Ariz. Quickly established autonomy over the organized crime rackets of the Southwest, with his son Bill.

Bonanno, Salvatore Vincent (Bill), 1931- . Son of Joseph Bonanno. Took over as family consigliere in 1964, when John Tartamella was forced to step down. Married the niece of Mafia boss Joseph Profaci.

Fischer, Harold, prom. 1940s. Partner of Edwin Loewenstein in the Tucson bookmaking operation known as E.R. Lowe & Co.

Gordon, George (**George C. Burslem**), 1911- . Member of the Cleveland mob who served as the Tucson "front" for Moe Dalitz and Morris Kleinman in a string of mob-run hotels.

Kreisler, Fred, prom. 1940s. Partner of Edwin Loewenstein, until he was forced out of the gambling and bookmaking operations.

Lazar, Edward, d.1975. Government witness against Ned Warren. Murdered before he could testify on Feb. 19, 1975.

Loewenstein, Edwin Rogers (AKA: **Butts Lowe**), prom. 1940s. Established a book-making operation in Tucson and Albuquerque in 1947, on behalf of Peter Licavoli and Moe Dalitz.

Schiro, Paul (AKA: **Paulie**), 1944- . Chicago gambling boss headquartered and overseeing operations in Phoenix.

Warren, Ned, prom. 1970s. Racketeer. Called the "land-fraud godfather" of the Southwest.

PITTSBURGH-SOUTHWEST PA. ORGANIZED CRIME

Amato, Frank D., Jr., prom. 1980s. Brother-in-law of the late Gabriel Mannarino. Operated Catoris Candies as his legitimate business front.

Bazzano, John, Jr., prom. 1980s. Son-in-law of Antonio Ripepi, a capo in the LaRocca crime family. Reportedly was to succeed Gabriel Mannarino as capo.

Ciancutti, Thomas A., prom. 1980s. Syndicate boss of the New Kensington region, previously controlled by Gabriel Mannarino.

DeLucia, Nicholas A., Jr., prom. 1980s. Owner and manager of a string of Pittsburgh massage parlors. Sent to prison in 1980 for tax fraud.

Genovese, Michael James, 1924- . A cousin of Vito Genovese, Labor racketeer, current underboss of Pittsburgh operations.

Gentile, Nicola, prom. 1950s. Mafia member active in Pittsburgh, Cleveland, and Kansas City, until he fled to Sicily in the early 1960s to avoid prosecution on a narcotics charge.

LaRocca, Sebastian, prom. 1950s-80s. Aging crime boss of the Pittsburgh region. Still runs one of the three Pennsylvania crime families.

Mannarino, Gabriel (AKA: **Kelly**), d.1980. Capo in the LaRocca crime family. Died of natural causes on July 11, 1980.

Marchese, Richard, prom. 1980s. Manager of several of the DeLucia massage parlors.

Ripepi, Antonio, prom. 1980s. Ranking capo in the LaRocca organization.

Rosa, Frank J., prom. 1980s. Capo in the LaRocca crime family.

Verilla, John A., prom. 1980s. Boss of Altoona, Penn. operations. Co-owner of Jaye's Bar, cited for violations of Pennsylvania gambling laws on several occasions.

ST. LOUIS-SOUTHERN ILL., ORGANIZED CRIME

Ajilonny, Kustandy, d.1926. Affiliated with the Green Ones Gang, Ajilonny was murdered by the Cuckoos on Oct. 15, 1926.

Amato, Benedetto, d.1927. Leader of the Green Ones gang of St. Louis. Amato was shot in the back on Nov. 15, 1927.

Birger, Charles, 1884-1928. A bootlegging kingpin in Southern Illinois during the 1920s. Ordered the execution of Mayor Joe Adams of West City, Ill., for which he was tried and found guilty. Executed on Apr. 21, 1928.

Buffa, Thomas, d.1946. Narcotics trafficker allied with Tony Lapiparo. Assassinated in Lodi, Calif., in 1946.

Burke, Fred (AKA: **Killer, Frederick Dane**), 1893-1940. A member of Egan's Rats, hired out as a professional killer to various other gangs. Believed to have been one of the triggermen in the Chicago St. Valentine's Day Massacre of 1929.

Christian, Frank, d.1926. St. Louis gangster hooked up with the Green Ones. Murdered in the Submarine Bar, in 1926, by the Cuckoos.

Corsiglio, Joseph, d.1926. Affiliated with the St. Louis Cuckoo Gang. Murdered by the Green Ones on Sept. 22, 1926.

Dattalo, Anthony, d.1926. Member of the Green Ones, killed in a gang war with the Cuckoos, in 1926.

Deluca, Mariano, d.1926. After refusing to pay extortion money to the criminal gang known as the "Green Ones," Deluca was shot to death on May 21, 1926.

Dunn, Harvey J., d.1926. Murdered by the Green Ones after refusing to surrender his distillery, June 27, 1926.

Egan's Rats, prom. 1910s-20s. A street gang organized by Jellyroll Egan in the early 1900s. Dormant by WWI, but given new life in Prohibition. The top bootlegging gang of the 1920s in St. Louis.

Giamonco, Benjamin (AKA: **Melonhead**), d.1927. After promising to avenge the deaths of Shorty Russo, and Vincent Spicuzza, Giamonco was shot to death on Aug. 24, 1927.

Giordano, Anthony, 1914- . Counterfeiter and syndicate gangster. Reputed mob boss of St. Louis. Enjoys close ties to the New Orleans Crime family.

Hyland, Ray, prom. 1920s. Henchman of Charles Birger. Tried for murder and found Guilty in July, 1927. Sent to prison for life.

Krueger, Smitty, prom. 1930s. Safe-cracker and jewel thief who did work for the Detroit Purple Gang.

Lapiparo, Anthony, prom. 1930s-40s. Mafia chieftain and narcotics trafficker in St. Louis.

Newman, Arthur, prom. 1920s. Criminal associate of Charles Birger. Tried for murder in July, 1927, and found guilty. Sent to prison for life.

Palmisano, Charles, d.1927. St. Louis businessman, gunned down on Oct. 27, 1927, for refusing to pay extortion to the Green Ones Gang.

Ray, Earl, d.c.1929. Rumored to have been one of the triggermen brought to Chicago to carry out the 1929 St. Valentine's Day Massacre. Vanished shortly afterward.

Rudensky, Morris (AKA: **Red**), prom. 1920s-30s. Safe cracker and jewel thief who accepted occasional work from the Detroit Purple Gang.

Russo, Anthony F. (AKA: **Shorty**), and **Spicuzza, Vincent**, d.1927. Russo and Spicuzza were tied in with the Green Ones of St. Louis. They were lured to Chicago to murder Al Capone by the Cuckoos but were murdered on Aug. 24, 1927.

Schamora, Joseph, d.1926. St. Louis gangster murdered by the Green Ones on Aug. 21, 1926.

Shelton, Bernard, prom. 1920s. Williamson County, Ill. bootlegger, whose gang waged war with Charles Birger for control of liquor distribution.

Shelton, Carl, prom. 1920s. Brother of Bernie and Earl Shelton. The Shelton bootleg gang was composed of fifty seasoned gunmen and bootleggers dedicated to the elimination of the rival Birger gang.

Shelton, Earl, prom. 1920s. The third of three brothers who vied for control of the Southern Illinois bootleg rackets during a seven year period in the 1920s.

Spica, John Paul, 1937-79. Co-owner of a cigarette and amusement machine company controlled by Anthony Giordano. Was strongly suspected of complicity in the 1968 assassination of Dr. Martin Luther King. He was himself the victim of an assassin on Nov. 9, 1979 when a car bomb went off in his Cadillac.

Trupiano, Matthew, Jr., prom. 1970s-80s. Top ranking Mafia figure in St. Louis.

Vitale, John, prom. 1930s-40s. Directed the St. Louis Mafia family in the 1930s.

Webbe, Peter, d.1926. Member of the Cuckoos gang of St. Louis. Murdered by the Green Ones on Sept. 5, 1926.

Wortman, Frank (AKA: **Buster**), 1903-70. Member of the Shelton bootlegging gang. Later attempted to take over their rackets. Murdered Carl Shelton in 1947, and his brother Bernie a year later. Wortman dominated syndicate gambling and vice in St. Louis until his death.

Zito, Frank, prom. 1970s. Crime boss of Springfield, Ill., in the 1970s.

SAN FRANCISCO-NORTHERN CALIF., ORGANIZED CRIME

Ah Toy, prom. 1850-70. One of the first Chinese prostitutes to arrive in San Francisco. Later became a brothel madame and procuress.

Alhambra, the, prom. 1850s. Deluxe Barbary Coast gambling house.

Allen, Ned, prom. 1860s. Owner of the Bull Run, a Barbary Coast dive at Pacific and Sullivan alley. Killed by Bartlett Freel, a Barbary Coast Ranger.

Barbary Coast, prom. 1860-1917. The San Francisco waterfront, extending from Broadway and Pacific to the slopes of Telegraph Hill. In later years, the single block of Pacific Street from Kearney to Montgomery. Prominent vice area for nearly eighty years. The original settlers were Australian immigrants, who dominated the criminal underworld in the 1840s and 1850s.

Barrish, Benjamin, prom. 1960s-70s. Bookmaker and juice collector for Jimmy Fratianno.

Bassity, Jerome (Jere McGlane), prom. 1901-07. Powerful political ruler of the Barbary Coast in the early 1900s. Member of the Abe Reuf political machine. Died in 1929.

Beck, David, b.1894. Elected president of the Teamster's Union in 1952. Commanded a "goon squad" of West Coast organizers in the 1930s. Brought before the McClellan Rackets Committee in March 1957, where his misappropriation of union funds and long-time ties to organized crime were exposed by Senator Robert Kennedy. Imprisoned in 1957.

Bella Union, prom. 1849-1906. Famous Barbary Coast gambling resort and concert hall. Re-built several times at Washington and Kearney Streets. Destroyed in the 1906 earthquake.

Bloom, Lloyd, prom. 1988. Sports agent convicted in April 1988 of signing college athletes to pro contracts before their eligibility expired. Associated with Norby Walters of New York, and mobster Michael Franzese. Heads up Bloom Entertainment, Inc.

Briggs, William, prom. 1850s-70s. Gambling boss and faro dealer. Owner of a sporting house on Montgomery Street.

Broderick, David C., d.1859. Transplanted New York Tammany politician who took over the political machinery of San Francisco, and ruled the city from 1851 until his death in a duel, in 1859.

Bryant, J.J. (AKA: **Colonel**), prom. 1850s. Politician and gambling promoter. Owner of a large gambling house and hotel.

Calamia, Leonard, 1911- . Drug trafficker and syndicate gunman. Acquitted of murdering Nick DeJohn in San Francisco, in 1947.

Calico Jim, prom. 1880s. Saloon keeper reputed to have "shanghaied" six San Francisco policeman sent out to arrest him.

Carr, William, prom. 1850s. Member of the David Broderick machine. Expelled by the second Vigilance Committee in 1856.

Cerrito, Joseph, prom. 1970s. Boss of organized crime in San Jose, Calif. in the 1970s. Deceased.

Chapman, Abraham (AKA: **Trigger Abe**), prom. 1930s-50s. Former member of Brooklyn's Murder, Inc. Re-located to San Francisco.

Dah Pa Tsin, prom. 1890s. Chinese slave trader and trafficker in under-age prostitutes.

DeJohn, Nicholas, d.1947. Mafia boss in Chicago and San Francisco, murdered on May 9, 1947 by killers unknown.

Devil's Acre, prom. 1886. Dangerous vice area of the Barbary Coast running along Kearny Street, from Broadway to Montgomery.

Devine, Johnny (AKA: **Shanghai Chicken**), prom. 1870s. Pimp, thief, and blackjack artist whose special talent was forcing men into sea duty against their will.

Duane, Charles P. (AKA: **Dutch**), prom. 1850s. Right-hand man of political boss David Broderick. Expelled by the second Vigilance Committee in 1856.

El Dorado, prom. 1850. First gambling house opened after the discovery of gold in 1848.

Fung Jing Toy (AKA: **Little Pete**), prom. 1880s-90s. Leader of the Sum Yops. Murdered at least a dozen men during the Tong Wars. Killed by Le-Lum Jung and Chew Tin Gop on Jan. 23, 1897.

Garcia, Manuel (AKA: **Three Fingered Jack**), prom. 1850s. Chief lieutenant of Joaquin Murieta.

Harrington, John (AKA: **Happy Jack**), prom. 1860s-70s. Owner of the Opera Comique, a famous Barbary Coast concert hall. Later sent to San Quentin for manslaughter.

Hop Sings, prom. 1860s-1900s. Chinese Tong gang organized in the gold fields of Marysville, Calif.

Hounds (AKA: **San Francisco Society of Regulators**), prom. 1848-49. Para-militaristic gang of thieves and bullies who preyed on Spanish-speaking foreigners.

Hung, Charles, prom. 1890s. Chinese slave dealer who bought and sold under-age prostitutes.

Kearney, "Woolley", prom. 1850s. Member of the David Broderick machine. Expelled by the second Vigilance Committee in 1856.

Kelly, Margaret (AKA: **Cowboy Maggie**), prom. 1890s. Proprietor of the Cowboy's Rest, on the Barbary coast, until it was destroyed by the 1906 earthquake.

Kwong Ducks, prom. 1875. Chinese Tong gang.

Lanza, James J. (AKA: **The Hat**), prom. 1950s-70s. Top Mafia boss of Northern California. Resides in San Mateo.

Lasala, James V., b.1904. One-time boss of the narcotics racket of Northern California; born in Brooklyn, N.Y.
Lima, Anthony, prom. 1970s. Ruled San Francisco's crime family in the 1970s.
Little Dick, prom. 1878. Thirteen-year-old girl who commanded a youthful street gang.
Low Sing, d.1875. Member of the Suey Sings tong gang. Murdered by Ming Long during the first U.S. Tong War.
McAlear, Thomas (AKA: **Dirty Tom**), prom. 1850s. Member of the Sydney Ducks.
McKenzie, Robert, d.1851. Member of the Sydney Ducks. Hanged by the Vigilance Committee in 1851.
Magee, Thomas, prom. 1906-08. Opened the Seattle Saloon with Ed Pincus, one of the first vice dens to be built after the 1906 earthquake, and one of the early "B-Girl" establishments.
Maguire, Thomas, prom. 1851. Gambler and sportsman. Opened the first brick theatre in the city.
Maita, Filippo, prom. 1930s-40s. Mafia soldier in the San Francisco crime family.
Maita, Philip, prom. 1960s-70s. Grandson of Filippo Maita. Proprietor of a porno theatre in Redwood, Calif.
Maloney, Reuben, prom. 1850s. Member of the David Broderick machine. Expelled by the second Vigilance Committee in 1856.
Marino, Angelo, prom. 1960s-70s. Capo in the San Jose crime family. Son of Pittsburgh mobster Salvatore Marino.
Ming Long, prom. 1875. Member of the Kwong Ducks. Murdered Low Sing over the favors of a slave girl named Kim Kum.
Miss Piggott, prom. 1880s. Operated a saloon on Davis Street where men were forcibly impressed into sea duty aboard ocean vessels.
Mulligan, William, prom. 1850s. Gambler, and associate of political boss David Broderick until his expulsion by the second Vigilance Committee in 1856. Keeper of the city jail.
Murieta, Joaquin (Joaquin Carillo), prom. 1850s. Mexican outlaw who terrorized the gold fields and mining camps during the early 1850s. Killed in July 1853.
Nikko, prom. 1880s. Streetwalker who enticed potential "shanghai" victims into Miss. Piggot's saloon.
One Year Tim, prom. 1860s. Proprietor of the Bull Run, a saloon and bordello on the Barbary Coast.
Pincus, Ed, prom. 1906-08. Co-owner of the Seattle Saloon, a post-earthquake dance hall, with Tom Magee. Murdered in 1909.
Portsmouth Square, prom. 1850s. Early San Francisco vice district.
Reuf, Abraham, prom. 1900s. Political boss of the Workingman's Party, who regulated the Barbary Coast vice district with Jerome Bassity.
Riley, James (AKA: **Butt Riley, King of the Hoodlums**), prom. 1870s. Street brawler and habitue of the Barbary Coast brothels.
Roberts, Samuel, prom. 1848-49. Leader of the Hounds.
San Francisco Vigilance Committee, prom. 1851-56. Organized with connivance of the local politicians to eradicate crime and vice in the community. There were two such groups in the 1850s.
Schmitz, Eugene, prom. 1901-07. Corrupt mayor of San Francisco put in office by Abe Reuf. Indicted for malfeasance in 1906.
Sciortino, Gaspare (AKA: **Bill**), prom. 1960s-70s. Underboss of the San Francisco crime family.
Selina, prom. 1880s. Chinese prostitute and brothel keeper.
Shanghai Kelly, prom. 1880s. Barbary Coast Irishman who drugged unwilling sailors in his saloon and shipped them off to sea against their will.
Sing Dock (AKA: **Scientific Killer**), prom. 1880s. Chinese Tong assassin.
Smith, William, prom. 1870s. Leader of the Valley Boys gang. Sent to prison on assault charges in 1871.
Spanish Kitty (AKA: **Kate Lombard, Kate Edington**), prom. 1886-1906. Owner of the Strassburg Music Hall, a brothel and concert hall destroyed in the 1906 earthquake.
Stevenson, Jonathan D., prom. 1848-49. Organized the Hounds along military principles. Succeeded by Sam Roberts.
Stuart, James (AKA: **English Jim**), prom. 1850s. Australian convict deported from England for forgery. Joined the Sydney Ducks in San Francisco. Executed on the gallows in 1851.
Suey Hin, prom. 1890s. Slave trader and trafficker in Chinese prostitutes.
Sue Yops, prom. 1870s. Chinese Tong gang.
Suey Sings, prom. 1875. Chinese Tong gang.
Sum Yops, prom. 1870s. Chinese Tong gang.
Sydney Ducks (AKA: **Sydney Coves**), prom. 1850s. Australian immigrants who formed a criminal association on the original Barbary Coast, known in the 1850s as Sydney Town.
Telegraph Hill, prom. 1850s. Waterfront vice-district.
Tetlow, Samuel, prom. 1860s. Proprietor of the Bella Union concert hall.
Uptown Tenderloin, prom. 1900s. Vice district bounded by Mason, Larkin, Eddy, Ellis, Powell, and other thoroughfares north of Market Street. Came into prominence after the 1906 earthquake.
Valley Boys (AKA: **Rising Star Club**), prom. 1870s. San Francisco street gang numbering 200 members. Commanded by Billy Smith.
Vanderah, the, prom. 1850s. Barbary Coast gambling resort.
Wall, Tessie, prom. 1900s-20s. Brothel keeper in the Uptown Tenderloin for many years. Died in 1932.
Whipple, Steven, prom. 1850. Owner of a gambling emporium on Commercial Street.
Whittaker, Samuel, d.1851. Member of the Sydney Ducks. Hanged by the Vigilance Committee in August 1851.
Yee Toy, prom. 1880s. Chinese Tong assassin.
Zoccoli, Steven, prom. 1970s. Consigliere in the San Jose crime family, headed by Joseph Cerrito in the 1970s.

SICILIAN MAFIA

Albano, Domenico, prom. 1940s. Mafia leader of Borgetto. Formerly allied with the Giuliano bandit gang. Served as the treasurer.
Amendolito, Salvatore, 1934- . Money launderer and crooked financier who appeared as a witness in the Pizza Connection trial in New York in 1986.
Badalamenti, Antonino, prom. 1960s-70s. Cousin and arch-enemy of Gaetano Badalamenti. In 1978, he took over the Cinisi family after Gaetano was ousted and forced to flee Sicily.
Badalamenti, Gaetano (AKA: **Don Tanino, The Old Man**), 1923- . Sicilian Mafia boss from Cinici, who emigrated to the U.S. in 1946, but was deported back to Sicily a short time later. Narcotics trafficker who headed the Mafia Commissione from 1969-78. Extradited to the U.S. from Spain in 1984 to stand trial for his role in the "Pizza Connection" case. Currently in a U.S. prison.
Badalamenti, Vito, 1957- . Eldest son of Gaetano Badalamenti. Extradited to the U.S. in 1984, and charged with negotiating the South American end of the "Pizza Connection" drug smuggling ring. Only defendant to be found Not Guilty.
Barbaccia, Francesco, prom. 1910s-30s. Head of a Mafia family headquartered in Godrano, near Palermo. Kidnapped and murdered by unknown assassins.
Barbino, Domenico, prom. 1970s. Calabrian Mafia member who "fingered" J. Paul Getty III for abduction in 1973.
Bonanno, Salvatore, 1878-1915. Father of Joseph Bonanno. A much respected Mafia leader in Castellammare, Si., before his death in 1915.
Bontade, Giovanni, 1946-88. Mafia leader killed with his wife on Sept. 27, 1988 at the family villa outside Palermo.
Bontade, Stefano, prom. 1970s. Palermo Mafia boss assassinated in 1979 after bilking his U.S. contacts out of a $20 million cocaine shipment. Member of the ruling Mafia triumverate.
Bottaro, Angelo, 1939-88. Mafia gangster from Siracusa, Si., who was killed in his hospital room on Dec. 3, 1988.
Buscetta, Tommasso, prom. 1988. Mafia drug runner from Sicily, who fled to Brazil in 1982. He was extradited to the U.S. where he became the highest ranking member of the outfit to turn government informant. Buscetta testified in 1985, against twenty-two defendants charged with smuggling $1.65 billion worth of heroin into the U.S.
Cascioferro, Vito (or **Cascio Ferro**), 1862-1945. Mafia don who served as a link between Sicily and the U.S. Black Hand. Deported to Sicily where he became a top Mafia boss.
Castronovo, Carlo, prom. 1980s. Sicilian drug runner and a cousin of Francesco Castronovo, defendant in the 1985 Pizza Connection case in New York.
Cavatajo, Michele, d.1969. Mafia boss shot down while driving his car in Palermo, Dec. 10, 1969.
Ciaculli Massacre, 1963. On June 30, 1963, a car bomb exploded in Ciaculli, Si., killing seven police officers. It was the climax of the Greco-Corleonese War. Hundreds of Mafia members were arrested and imprisoned in a general crackdown that decimated the ranks of the families.
Ciccu, V. d.1961. Top Mafia don in Sicily. Died of natural causes on Sept. 13, 1961.
Contorno, Salvatore, prom. 1970s-80s. Member of the Santa Maria di Gesu Family, headed by Stefano Bontade. Survived an assassination attempt by the rival Corleonese in 1981, to become a government informant for U.S. and Italian officials investigating the "Pizza Connection."
Coppola, Frank (AKA: **Three Fingers**), prom. 1970s. Deported to Italy by U.S. authorities. Active in the Sicilian Mafia.
Corleone, Si., prom. 1870s. Village in Sicily, located forty-two miles south of Palermo. Birthplace of many U.S. mobsters.
Cuccia, Ciccio, prom. 1920s-30s. Mafia boss who served as Mayor of Piana dei Greci during the rule of Benito Mussolini.
Cuini, Candido, d.1975. Sicilian Mafia chieftain murdered while recovering from an earlier wound in a Palermo hospital, Oct. 8, 1975.
Cutolo, Don Raffaele (AKA: **Don Raf**), 1941- . Mafia boss of Naples imprisoned for murder.
Esposito, Carmine, 1956- . Naples crime boss who fled to the U.S. in 1984 after committing thirteen murders, and embezzling $2 million from Mafia coffers. Arrested by the FBI in 1987.
Falconieri, Michelangelo, prom. 1960s-70s. Calabrian Mafia boss imprisoned for murder. Eventually relinquished control to his wife Concetta Rottura.
Ferro, Vito Cascio, prom. 1910s. Highly respected Mafia Don, on the island of Sicily, who ruled the organization for twenty-five years. Died in 1920, after being sentenced to prison.

Giampaolo, Antonio, 1953- . Mafia boss in southern Calabria. Accused of murdering Dr. Gino Marino, the surgeon who operated on his 4-year-old daughter in October 1988.

Giuliano, Salvatore, prom. 1940s. Powerful Sicilian bandit king who led rebel bands against the Communist strongholds on the island in the 1940s. Murdered on July 4, 1950 near Portella della Ginestra by Gaspare Pisciotta.

Grasso, Mommo, prom. 1940s-60s. Mafia leader in Misilmeri until he disappeared with his son in the early 1960s.

Greco, Giuseppina, d.1945. Daughter of a powerful Sicilian Mafia family. Became the first woman to be murdered in a Mafia vendetta.

Greco, Leonardo, prom. 1940s-70s. Head of a powerful Mafia family in Ciaculli, Si., and second only to Luciano Liggio in the hierarchy of the Corleonese faction.

Greco, Michele (AKA: **the Pope**), prom. 1960s-80s. Following the reorganization of the Mafia ruling Commissione in 1978, Greco was named "boss of bosses." He was a leading figure in the powerful Corleonese alliance.

Inzerillo, Pietro, prom. 1970s. Brother of Salvatore Inzerillo. Boss of a small Mafia clan that attempted to garner control of the French Connection. Assassinated in New York by the rival Corleonese in 1979.

Inzerillo, Salvatore, d.1981. Ally of Stefano Bontade. Head of the Rigano Mafia family, before being assassinated by the Corleonese on May 10, 1981.

LaBarbera, Angelo, prom. 1950s-60s. Mafia chief of Palermo-Central, considered to be the richest of all Sicilian families. Fronted his operations with a successful building firm. Driven into exile in Milan.

LaBarbera, Salvatore, prom. 1950s-60s. Brother of Angelo LaBarbera and co-leader of the Palermo-Central family. Died under mysterious circumstances.

LaMattina, Nuncio, prom. 1980s. Mafia tobacco smuggler who switched to heroin trafficking. He was a major figure in the Pizza Connection before being murdered.

LiCausi, Girolamo, prom. 1940s. Outspoken Sicilian political leader opposed to the Mafia. Attacked and beaten by Mafia men on Sept. 16, 1944.

Liggio, Luciano (AKA: **The Faceless One**), prom. 1940-60s. Powerful leader of the Corleonese faction in Palermo. Captured on May 15, 1965.

Mammoliti, Saverio, prom. 1970s. Member of the Calabrian Mafia. Indicted for the 1973 kidnapping of J. Paul Getty, III.

Mammoliti, Vincenzo, prom. 1970s. Brother of Saverio Mammoliti. Indicted for the kidnapping of J. Paul Getty III.

Mangano, Angelo, prom. 1970s. Mafia chief in Palermo, Si.

Mannoia, Francesco Marino (AKA: **Mozzarella**), prom. 1980s. Sicilian chemist who earned $4,000 a day processing heroin earmarked for distribution in U.S. pizzerias in 1979.

Manseuto, Simone, prom. 1963. The first Sicilian to testify in a Mafia trial. Gave evidence in 1963 against the murderers of Paolo Riccobono.

Manzella, Cesare, d.1963. One-time gambling boss in Chicago. Attempted to take over the narcotics trade following Lucky Luciano's death in 1962. Assassinated by a car bomb at his home in Sicily in April 1963.

Minasola, Don Nitto, prom. 1940s-50s. Mafia chieftain in Monreale, Si., outside Palermo. Masterminded the 1950 assassination of the bandit Salvatore Giuliano. Later assassinated in the streets of Giuseppe Jato.

Muratore, Giorgio, prom. 1980s. Drug trafficker and member of the Sicilian Mafia.

Navarra, Michele, prom. 1940s. Mafia member who was also a physician. Served as a Medical Officer of Health and chairman of a local branch of the Christian Democratic Party.

Palazzolo, Vito Roberto, prom. 1980s. Sicilian money launderer involved in Swiss banking operations.

Petrosino, Joseph, d.1909. New York City Police Lieutenant who headed the "Italian Squad" organized to investigate Black Hand terror. He traveled to Palermo, Si., to identify the ranking Mafia criminals, but was murdered there on Mar. 12, 1909.

Pirmalli, Gerolamo (AKA: **Momo**), prom. 1970s. Calabrian Mafia boss. Masterminded the 1973 abduction of J. Paul Getty III.

Pisciotta, Gaspare, d.1954. Cousin of Salvatore Giuliano and a Sicilian Mafiosi. Murdered Giuliano in his bed, July 4, 1950, and was then poisoned in his jail cell four years later.

Randazzo, Vincenzo (AKA: **Enzo**), 1941- . Nephew of Gaetano Badalamenti. Arrested in Zurich on Apr. 5, 1984, and extradited to the U.S. to stand trial for drug smuggling and conspiracy. Sentenced to time served. Deported in 1988. Currently resides in Milan.

Riccobono, Francesco, prom. 1940s-50s. Headed an influential Mafia family outside Tommaso Natale, Si. Murdered during a vendetta.

Riccobono, Paolo, d.1963. Fourteen-year-old son of Francesco Riccobono. Last male member of the Riccobono family. Murdered in September 1963.

Riina, Salvatore, prom. 1970s. Leader of the Corleonese faction of the Sicilian Mafia. One of three members of the ruling triumverate. Allegedly ordered the assassinatiopn of Stefano Bontade in an effort to return control of the commission to the Corleonese.

Rottura, Concetta, prom. 1970s. Wife of Calabrian Mafia boss Michelangelo Falconieri. Became a Mafia boss in her own right, and was sentenced to three years in exile in 1976 for extortion.

Russo, Giuseppe Genco, prom. 1930s-50s. Top ranked "rural" Mafiosi. Considered to be the second in command behind Don Calogero Vizzini. Shot to death by Pino Greco, an ally of the Corleonese.

Sacco, Vanni, prom. 1940s. Post WWII Mafia boss of Camporeale who joined the Christian Democratic Party.

Scaglione, Pietro, d.1970. Sicilian judge who presided over several Mafia trials. Assassinated in Palermo on May 5, 1970.

Sicilian Commissione, 1957-63; 1969- . Organized by Charles "Lucky" Luciano and Joseph Bonnano, in 1957, to arbitrate disputes and prevent fresh outbreaks of war between the ruling families. Membership is composed of the ruling capos from each family. The commission was temporarily forced out of existence in 1963, following the Ciaculli Massacre. In 1969, the commissione was re-structured. A ruling triumverate was appointed to establish policy and by 1975 the triumverate was controlled by the Corleonese.

Tognoli, Oliviero, prom. 1980s. Milanese businessman who rules the Ciaculli crime family in tandem with Leonardo Greco.

Vitale, Vito, prom. 1940s. Father-in-law of Detroit mobster Raffaele Quasarano. Mafia don in Sicily.

Vizzini, Don Calogero (AKA: **Don Calo**), 1877-1947. Mafia mayor of Villalaba, Si. Undisputed leader of the entire Sicilian Mafia during the 1940s.

A ROGUES' GALLERY OF ORGANIZED CRIME

Frank Abbandando

Anthony J. Accardo

Joseph Adonis

Joseph Aiello

Joseph Aiuppa

Felix A. Alderisio

Gus Alex

Louis Alterie

Samuel S. Amatuna

Albert Anastasia

Anthony Anastasio

Albert Anselmi

Gaetano Badalamenti

Barney Baker

Joseph Barbara, Sr.

George Barker

Charles Battaglia

Gil Beckley

James Belcastro

Joseph Bertsche

William Bioff

Dominic Blasi

Frank Bompensiero

Joseph Bonanno

Cesare Bonventre

Dominick Brooklier

Leo Vincent Brothers

Angelo Bruno

Fiore Buccieri

Louis Buchalter

Russell Bufalino

Elmer Burke

Fred Burke

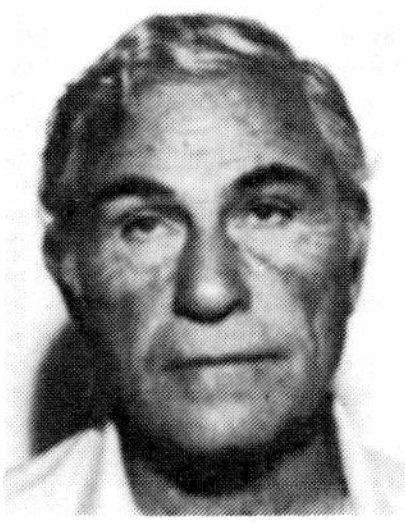
Marshall J. Caifano

Richard Cain

Louis Campagna

Anthony Capezio

Alphonse Capone

Ermino John Capone

Louis Capone

Ralph Capone

Frankie Carbo

Anthony Carfano

Vito Cascioferro

Paul Castellano

John Cerone

Joseph Civello

Mickey Cohen

Vincent Coll

Anthony Colombo

Joseph A. Colombo

James Colosimo

Jack Comer

Frank Coppola

Michael Coppola

Anthony Corallo

Frank Costello

Philip D'Andrea

Morris Dalitz

Angelo DeCarlo

S.R. DeCavalcante

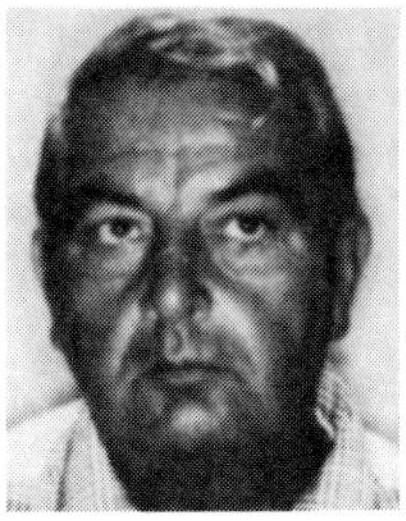
Anthony Delsanter

George J. DeMange

Gregory DePalma

Frank DeSimone

Sam DeStefano

Frank Diamond

Jack Diamond

Joseph DiGiovanni

Johnny Dio

Joseph DiPalermo

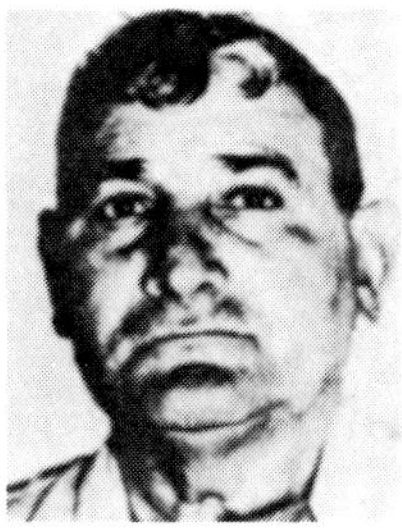
Charles Dippolito

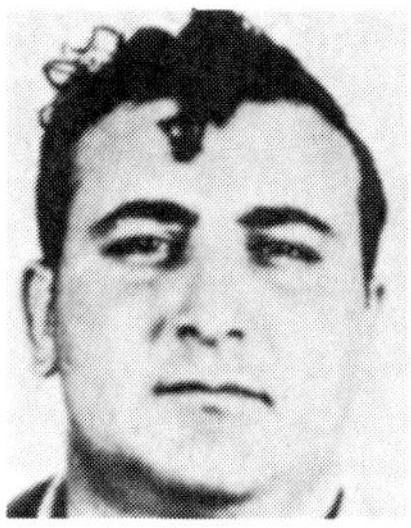
Joseph Dippolito

Jack Dragna

Louis Tom Dragna

Vincent Drucci

Terry Druggan

Charles C. English

Charles Entratta

Frank Erickson

Joseph Esposito

Natale Evola

Rocco Fanelli

Benjamin Fein

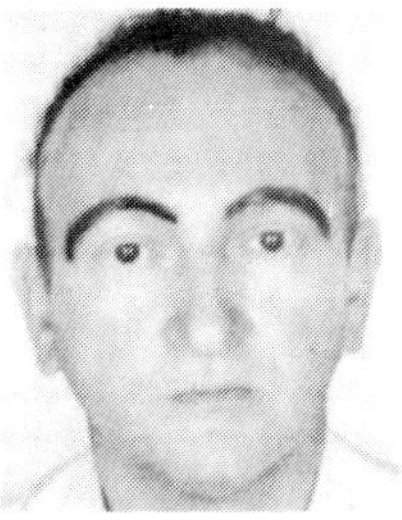
David Ferrie

Raymond Ferritto

Charles Fischetti

Rocco Fischetti

John Foley

James Forsythe

Peter von Frantzius

Joseph Gagliano

Carmine Galante

Joseph Gallo

Lawrence Gallo

Carlo Gambino

Angelo Genna

James Genna

Pete Genna

Sam Genna

Tony Genna

Vito Genovese

Sam Giancana

Vincent Gigante

Charles Gioe

Salvatore Giuliano

Joseph Giunta

Tony Gizzo

Joseph Paul Glimco

Martin Goldstein

Waxey Gordon

John Gorman

Leonardo Greco

Max Greenberg

Jake Guzik

Michael Heitler

James J. Hines

James Riddle Hoffa

Pat Hogan

Harry Horowitz

Murray L. Humphreys

Samuel M. Hunt

Philip Kastel

Julian Kauffman

Morris Kleinman

Sidney Korshak

Martin Krompier

Angelo LaBarbera

Frank Lake

Abe Landau

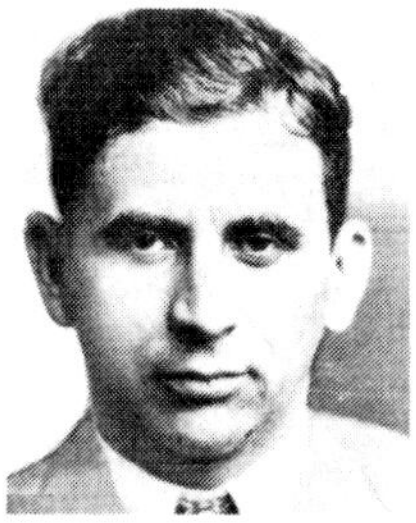
Meyer Lansky

Joseph Lanza

Ed Levinson

Nicholas Licata

James Licavoli

Peter Joseph Licavoli

Luciano Liggio

Alfred Lingle

Giocchino Lo Cicero

Antonio Lombardo

Joe Lonardo

Thomas E. Lucchese

Charles Luciano

Arthur B. McBride

Frank McErlane

Thomas J. McGinty

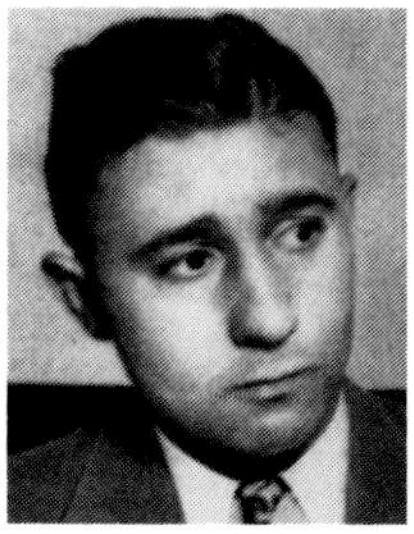
Jack McGurn

Owen Madden

Stefano Magaddino

Joseph Magliocco

Frank Majuri

Lawrence Mangano

Carlos Marcello

Sam Marcello

Vincent Marcello

Angelo Marino

Giuseppe Masseria

George Meeghan

Harold Meltzer

Onofrio Minaudo

Michele Miranda

Leo Mocari

John Montana

George Moran

William Moretti

Samuel Morton

Art Newman

Charles Nicoletti

Frank Nitti

Charles D. O'Bannion

John O'Berta

Jerry O'Connor

Edward O'Donnell

Wiliam O'Donnell

Jacob Orgen

John Ormento

Edward P. Osadchey

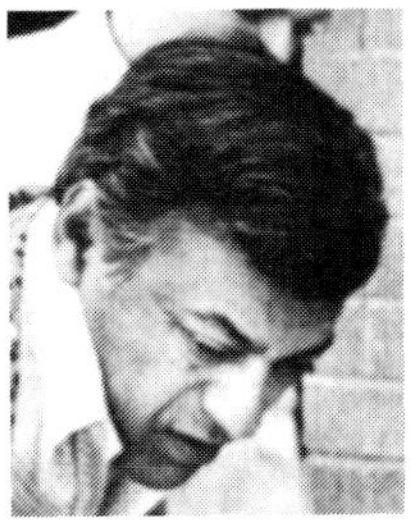
Louis Pacella

Johnny Patton

Sam Pellar

Carmine Persico

Gaspare Pisciotta

Al Polizzi

Rocco Potenza

Rocco S. Pranno

Ross Prio

Joseph Profaci

Abraham Reles

Paul Ricca

Thomas Ricciardi

Frank Rio

Michael Rizzitello

John Roselli

Nig Rosen

Louis Rosenberg

Bernard Rosenkrantz

Louis Rothkopf

Arnold Rothstein

Ernest Rupolo

Mike Rusick

Giuseppe G. Russo

Robert Emmet Ryan

Ignazio Saietta

Joseph Saltis

James Sammons

John Saupp

Pietro Scaglione

Frank Scalise

John Scalise

Dutch Schultz

Sam Sciortino

Irving Shapiro

Jacob Shapiro

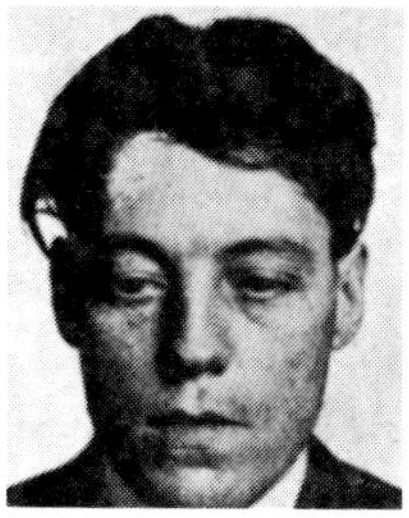
Ralph Sheldon

Carl Shelton

Earl Shelton

Joseph Sica

Benjamin Siegel

Charles Solomon

Anthony Spilotro

Danny Stanton

Sammy Stein

Timothy D. Sullivan

Albert Tannenbaum

John Tartamella

Ciro Terranova

Frank Tieri

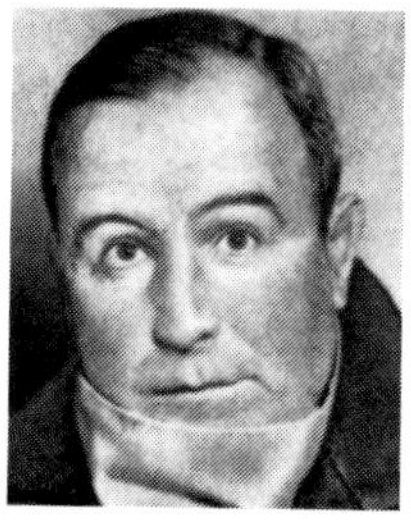
John Torrio

Santo Trafficante, Sr.

Samuel Tucker

Joseph Valachi

Don Calogero Vizzini

Eddie Vogel

Anthony Volpi

Abe Weinberg

George Weinberg

Earl Weiss

Emmanuel Weiss

Morris Wexler

William White

Charles Workman

Frankie Yale

Jack Zelig

Joseph Zerilli

Jack Zuta

Abner Zwillman

POLICE

U.S. POLICE CHIEFS

BALTIMORE, MD.

Commissioners	Tenures
Charles Howard	1850-61
Nicholas L. Wood	1862-64
Samuel Hindes	1864-66
James Young	1866-67
Jarrett Le Fevre	1867-70
John W. Davis	1870-71
William H.B. Fusselbaugh	1871-81
George Colton	1881-87
Edson M. Schryver	1887-97
Daniel C. Heddinger	1897-1900
George M. Upsher	1900-04
George R. Willis	1904-08
Sherlock Swann	1908-10
John B.A. Wheltle	1910-12
Morris A. Soper	1912-13
James McEvoy	1913-14
Daniel C. Ammidon	1914-16
Lawrason Riggs	1916-20
Charles D. Gaither	1920-37
William Lawson	1937-38
Robert F. Stanton	1938-43
Hamilton R. Atkinson	1943-49
Beverly Ober	1949-55
James M. Hepbron	1955-61
Bernard Schmidt	1961-66
George M. Gelston	1966
Donald D. Pomerleau	1966-81
Frank J. Battaglia	1981-84
Bishop L. Robinson	1984-87
Edward J. Tilghman	1987-present

BOSTON, MASS.

Commissioners	Tenures
Henry S. Russell	1878-80
Samuel R. Spinney	1878-80
James M. Bugbee	1878-79
Henry Walker	1879-82
Edward J. Jones	1880-82
Thomas J. Gargan	1880-82
Thomas L. Jenks	1882-85
Nathaniel Wales	1882-85
Benjamin D. Burley	1882-83
Michael P. Curran	1883-85
Albert T. Whiting	1885-95
William H. Lee	1885-94
William M. Osborne	1885-93
Robert F. Clark	1893-1903
Augustus P. Martin	1894-99
Charles P. Curtis, Jr.	1895-1905
Harry F. Adams	1899-1906
William H.H. Emmons	1903-06
Charles H. Cole, Jr.	1905-06
Stephen O'Meara	1906-18
Edwin U. Curtis	1918-22
Herbert A. Wilson	1922-30
Eugene C. Hultman	1830-34
Joseph J. Leonard	1934-35
Eugene M. McSweeney	1935-36
Joseph F. Timilty	1936-43
Thomas F. Sullivan	1943-57
Leo Sullivan	1957-62
Francis J. Hennessey	1962
Edmund J. McNamara	1962-72
William J. Taylor (acting)	1972
Robert J. diGrazia	1972-76
Joseph M. Jordan	1976-85
Francis M. Roache (acting)	1985
Francis M. Roache	1985-present

CHICAGO, ILL.

Chiefs	Tenures
Cyrus Bradley	1861-63
William Turtle	1863-66
Jacob Rehm	1866-71
W.W. Kennedy	1871-72
Elmer Wasburn	1872-73
Jacob Rehm	1873-75
Michael C. Hickey	1875-78
Valorious A. Seavey	1878-79
Simon O'Donnell	1879-80
William J. McGarigle	1880-82
Austin J. Doyle	1882-85
Frederick Ebersold	1885-88
George W. Hubbard	1888-90
Frederick H. Marsh	1890-91
Robert W. McClaughry	1891-93
Michael Brennan	1893-95
John J. Badenoch	1895-97
Joseph Kipley	1897-1901
Francis O'Neill	1901-05
John M. Collins	1905-07
George M. Shippy	1907-09
Leroy T. Steward	1909-11
John McWeeny	1911-13
James Gleason	1913-15
Charles C. Healy	1915-17
Herman F. Schuettler	1917-18
John J. Garrity	1918-20
Charles C. Fitzmorris	1920-23
Morgan A. Collins	1923-27

Commissioners	Tenures
Michael Hughes	1927-28
William R. Russell	1928-30
John H. Alcock (acting)	1930-31
James P. Allman	1931-46
John C. Prendergast	1946-50
Timothy J. O'Connor	1950-60

Superintendents	Tenures
Orlando W. Wilson	1960-67
James B. Conlisk, Jr.	1967-74
James M. Rochford	1974-77
Michael A. Spiotto	1977-78
James E. O'Grady	1978-79
Samuel W. Nolan	1979
Joseph G. DiLeonardi	1979-80
Richard J. Brzeczek	1980-83
Fred Rice, Jr.	1983-87
LeRoy Martin	1987-present

CINCINNATI, OHIO

Marshals	Tenures
Samuel R. Miller	1819-21
John C. Avery	1821-24
William C. Anderson	1824-25
Joseph Martin	1825
William C. Anderson	1825-26
Zebulon Byington	1826-29
William Doty	1829-33
Jesse Justin	1833-35
James Saffin	1835-47
Ebenezer Hulse	1847-49
James L. Ruffia	1849-55

Chiefs	Tenures
Jacob Kiefer	1853
Thomas Locken	1853-54
David Hoke	1854-55
Edward Hopkins	1855-57
James L. Ruffin	1857-59
Lewis Wilson	1859-61
J.W. Dudley	1861-62
Lawrence M. Hazen	1862-63
James L. Ruffin	1863-67
Robert McGrew	1867-68
James L. Ruffin	1868-71
David M. Blocks	1871-73

Superintendents	Tenures
Jeremiah Kiersted	1873-75
Thomas E. Snelbaker	1875-76
Ira Wood	1876-78
George W. Ziegler	1878-80
Charles Wappenstein	1880
Enoch T. Carson	1880-81
Jacob Gossert	1881
M.F. Reilley	1881-85
Edwin Hudson	1885-86
Arthur C. Moore	1886
Philip P. Deitsch	1886-1903

Chiefs	Tenures
Paul M. Milliken	1903-10
William H. Jackson	1910-12
William Copelan	1912-35
Eugene T. Weatherly	1935-51
Stanley R. Schrotel	1951-67
Jacob W. Schott	1967-71
Carl V. Goodin	1971-76
Myron J. Leistler	1976-85
Lawrence E. Whalen	1985-present

DALLAS, TEXAS

Town Marshals	Tenures
Andrew W. Moore	1856
M.M. Thompson	1857
Andrew M. Moore	1858

City Marshals	Tenures
William Moon	1858
M.M. Thompson	1859
Stephenson	1860
Andrew M. Moore	1861
Barbier	1862
Thomas Flynn	1872-74
June Peak	1874-76
W.F. Morton	1876-81

Chiefs	Tenures
J.C. Arnold	1881-98
M.W. Kirby	1898
E.G. Cornwell	1898-99
Sterling Price	1900-02
R.L. Winfrey	1902-04
E.G. Knight	1904-05
R.B. Keith	1905-06
B.F. Brandenburg	1906-08
R.L. Cornwell	1908-09
J.W. Ryan	1909-21
Elmo Strait	1921-22
J.H. Tanner	1922-23
L.W. Brown	1923-24
C.W. Trammel	1924-35
R.L. Jones	1935-39
J.M. Welch	1939-45
C.F. Hansson	1945-60
J.E. Curry	1960-66
Charles T. Batchelor	1966-69
Frank Dyson	1969-73
Don A. Byrd	1973-79
Glen D. King	1979-82
Billy D. Prince	1982-88
Mack M. Vines	1988-present

INDIANAPOLIS, IND.

Chiefs	Tenures
James F. Quigley	1897-1902
G.A. Taffe	1902-03
Christian L. Kruger	1903-05
Robert Metzger	1906-10
Martin Hyland	1910-13
Samuel V. Perrott	1913-17
James F. Quigley	1917-18
George V. Coffin	1918-19
Jeremiah Kinney	1919-22
H.F. Riekhaff	1922-26
Claude F. Johnson	1926-27
Cland M. Worley	1927-30
Michael F. Morrisey	1931-42
Clifford Beeker	1943-44
Jesse McMurtrey	1945-47

Howard L. Sanders	1947
Edward Rauls	1948-51
John J. O'Neal	1951
John E. Ambuhl	1952-56
Frank Mueller	1956-58
Robert Reilly	1959-64
Noel Jones	1964-67
Daniel T. Veza	1967-68
Winston Churchill	1968-74
Kenneth B. Hale	1974-75
Eugene Gallagher	1976-80
Joseph G. McAtee	1981-84
Paul A. Annee	1986-present

LOS ANGELES, CALIF.

Chiefs	Tenures
Alexander W. Hope	1851
Jacob T. Jerkins	1876-77
Emil Harris	1877-78
Henry King	1878-80
George E. Gard	1880-81
Henry King	1881-83
Thomas J. Cuddy	1883-85
Edward McCarthy	1885
John Horner	1885
J.W. Davis	1885-86
John K. Skinner	1886-87
P.M. Darcy	1887-88
Thomas J. Cuddy	1888
H.H. Benedict	1888-89
Terrence Cooney	1889
J.E. Burns	1889
John M. Glass	1889-1900
Charles Elton	1900-04
William A. Hammell	1904-05
Walter H. Auble	1905-06
Edward Kern	1906-09
Thomas Broadhead	1909
E.F. Dishman	1909-10
Alexander Galloway	1910
Charles E. Sebastian	1911-15
C.E. Snively	1915-16
John L. Butler	1916-19
George K. Home	1919-20
A.W. Murray	1920
Lyle Pendegast	1920-21
Charles A. Jones	1921-22
James W. Everington	1922
Louis D. Oaks	1922-23
August Vollmer	1923-24
R. Lee Heath	1924-26
James E. Davis	1926-29
Roy E. Steckel	1929-33
James E. Davis	1933-38
D.A. Davidson	1938-39
Arthur C. Hohmann	1939-41
Clarence B. Horrall	1941-49
William A. Worton	1949-50
William H. Parker	1950-66
Thad F. Brown	1966-67
Thomas Reddin	1967-69
Roger E. Murdock	1969
Edward M. Davis	1969-78
Daryl F. Gates	1978-present

MIAMI, FLA.

Chiefs	Tenures
F.B. Hardee	1905-11
Robert Ferguson	1911-13
W.J. Whitman	1913-15
William Curry	1915-19
Raymond F. Dillon	1919-21
Howard L. Quigg	1921-28
Guy Reese	1928-37
Howard L. Quigg	1937-46
Charles L. Nelson	1946-47
Frank Mitchell	1947-48
Walter Headly	1948-68
Paul Denham	1968-69
Bernard Garmire	1969-75
Garland Watkins	1975-78
Kenneth Harms	1978-84
Herbert Breslow	1984-85
Clarence Dickson	1985-88
Perry L. Anderson	1988-present

MINNEAPOLIS, MINN.

Chiefs	Tenures
H.H. Brackett	1867
Daniel A. Day	1868
H.H. Brackett	1869
Daniel A. Day	1870
Cortez L. Peck	1871
George C. Kent	1872
Randall W. Hasden	1873
Michael Hoy	1873
John H. Noble	1874-75
A.S. Munger	1877-82
A.C. Berry	1883
John West	1884-85
Charles R. Hill	1886-88
Winslow Brackett	1889-90
R.R. Henderson	1891-92
Vernon M. Smith	1893-98
James Doyle	1899-1900
Fred Ames	1901-02
Ed J. Conroy	1903-04
James Doyle	1905-06
F. Corriston	1907-10
Michael Mealey	1911-12
Oscar Martinson	1913-16
Louis Harthill	1917-18
J. Frank Walker	1919-21
Anton Henson	1921-23
Frank Brunskill	1923-28
Harry Lindholm	1929-31
W.J. Meehan	1931-33
Joe Lehmeyer	1933
John Hart	1934
Mike Johannes	1935
Frank Forrestal	1935-40
Edward Hansen	1941-42
Joe Jonas	1942
Elmer Hillner	1943-45
Edward Ryan	1945-46
G.W. McLean	1946-49
Thomas R. Jones	1949-56
E.I. Walling	1956
Milton Winslow	1957-60
Kenneth Moore	1960
E.I. Walling	1961-64
Calvin Hawkinson	1964-68
Donald Dwyer	1968
B.J. Lutz	1969-71
Gordon Johnson	1971-74
Jack L. McCarthy	1974
John P. Jensen	1974-76
Carl E. Johnson	1976-78
Elmer C. Nordlund	1978-79
Donald Dwyer	1979-80
Anthony V. Bouza	1980-88
John T. Laux	1989-present

NEW YORK, N.Y.

Commissioners	Tenures
Michael C. Murphy	1901-02
John N. Partridge	1902-03
Francis V. Greene	1903-04
William McAdoo	1904-06
Theodore A. Bingham	1906-09
William F. Baker	1909-10
James C. Cropsey	1910-11
Rhinelander Waldo	1911-13
Douglas I. McKay	1913-14
Arthur Woods	1914-18
Frederick H. Bugher	1918
Richard E. Enright	1918-25
George V. McLaughlin	1926-27
Joseph A. Warren	1927-28
Grover A. Whalen	1928-30
Edward P. Mulrooney	1930-33
James S. Bolan	1933
John F. O'Ryan	1934
Lewis J. Valentine	1934-45
Arthur W. Wallander	1945-49
William P. O'Brien	1949-50
Thomas F. Murphy	1950-51
George P. Monaghan	1951-53
Francis W.H. Adams	1954-55
Stephen P. Kennedy	1955-61
Michael J. Murphy	1961-65
Vincent L. Broderick	1965-66
Howard R. Leary	1966-70
Patrick V. Murphy	1970-73
Donald F. Cawley	1973
Michael J. Codd	1974-77
Robert J. McGuire	1978-83
William J. Devine	1983
Benjamin Ward	1984-present

PHILADELPHIA, PA.

Superintendents	Tenures
Kernard Jones	1872-1879
Samuel I. Givin	1879-1884
James Stewart	1884-87
James Lamond	1887-92
Robert Linwood	1892-99
Harry M. Quirk	1899-1904
John B. Taylor	1904-12
James Robinson	1912-20
William B. Mills	1920-31
Joseph E. LeStrange	1931-36
James H. Malone	1936-37
Edward Hubbs	1937-40
Howard P. Sutton	1940-52

Commissioners	Tenures
Thomas J. Gibbons	1952-60
Albert N. Brown	1961-63
Howard R. Leary	1963-65
Edward J. Bell	1965-67
Frank L. Rizzo	1967-71
Joseph F. O'Neill	1971-80
Morton B. Solomon	1980-83
Gregory Sambor	1983-85
Kevin Tucker	1986-88
Willie L. Williams	1988-present

PORTLAND, ORE.

City Marshals	Tenures
Hiram Wilbur	1851
William Higgins	1851-53
William Grooms	1853-54
William Higgins	1854
R.S. Perkins	1854
Thomas Holmes	1854-56
William Higgins	1856-58
S.B. Holcomb	1858-59
James H. Lappeus	1859-61
William Grooms	1861-63
William Clark	1863-65
Henry L. Hoyt	1865-67
A. Rosenheim	1867
David Jacobi	1867-68
James H. Lappeus	1868-69
Phillip Saunders	1869-70

Chiefs	Tenures
Phillip Saunders	1870
James H. Lappeus	1870-77
Lucerne Besser	1877-79
James H. Lappeus	1879-83
William Watkins	1883-84
Samuel B. Parrish	1884-92
Ernest W. Spencer	1892
Charles H. Hunt	1892-94
John W. Minto	1984-96
D.W. Robertson	1896-97
John Myers	1897
Patrick J. Barry	1897-98
Michael J. Clohessy	1897-98
Michael J. Clohessy	1898
Daniel M. McLauchlan	1898-1903
Charles H. Hunt	1903-05
Charles Gritzmacher	1905-09
A.M. Cox	1909-11
Enoch A. Slover	1911-13
John Clark	1913-17
Nelson F. Johnson	1917-19
Leon V. Jenkins	1919-33

Burton K. Lawson	1933-34
Harry M. Niles	1934-46
Leon V. Jenkins	1946-48
James Fleming	1948
Charles P. Pray	1949-51
Donald I. McNamara	1951-53
Jim Purcell	1953-56
William J. Hilbruner	1957-60
David H. Johnson	1960-64
Donald I. McNamara	1964-74
Bruce R. Baker	1974-81
Ronald R. Still	1981-85
Gary M. Haynes	1985
Penny Harrington	1985-86
Robert M. Tobin	1986
James T. Davis	1986-87
Richard D. Walker	1987-present

ST. LOUIS, MO.

Chiefs	Tenures
James McDonough	1861
John E.D. Couzens	1861-65
Bernard Laibold	1865-66
William P. Fenn	1866-68
William Lee	1868-70
James McDonough	1870-74
Laurence Harrigan	1874-75
James McDonough	1875-81
Ferdinand B. Kennett	1981-82
John W. Campbell	1882-83
Bernard (Barney) P. Taafee	1883-84
Laurence Harrigan	1884-86
Anton Huebler	1886-90
Laurence Harrigan	1890-98
John W. Campbell	1898-1901
Mathew Kiely	1901-06
Edmund P. Creecy	1906-10
William Young	1910-19
Martin O'Brien	1919-25
Joseph A. Gerk	1925-34
John J. McCarthy	1934-37
John H. Glassco	1937-43
James J. Mitchell	1943-46
Jeremiah O'Connell	1946-59
Joseph E. Casey	1959-60
Curtis Brostron	1960-70
Eugene J. Camp	1970-82
John F. Berner	1982-85
Robert E. Scheetz	1985-present

SAN DIEGO, CALIF.

Chiefs	Tenures
Joseph Coyne	1889-91
William H. Crawford	1891
W.H. Pringle	1891
Jacob Brenning	1891-97
James Russell	1897-99
E.W. Bushyhead	1899-1903
Albert A. Thomas	1903-07
George W. Moulton	1907
William T. Neely	1907-09
J. Keno Wilson	1909-17
Joseph Steer	1917
James Patrick	1917
S.P. McMullen	1917-19
James Patrick	1919
James Patirck	1919-27
Joseph W. Doran	1927-29
Arthur R. Hill	1929-31
Percy J. Benbough	1931
James Patrick	1931
Harry H. Scott	1931-32
John T. Peterson	1932
Robert P. Newsom	1932-33
Harry J. Raymond	1933
John T. Peterson	1933
John T. Peterson	1933-34
George M. Sears	1934-39
Harry J. Kelly	1939
John T. Peterson	1939-40
Clifford E. Peterson	1940-47
A. Elmer Jansen	1947-62
Wesley S. Sharp	1962-68
O. Jimmy Roed	1968-71
Ray L. Hoobler	1971-75
W.B. Kolender	1975-76
W.B. Kolender	1976-88
Robert W. Burgreen	1988
Robert W. Burgreen	1988-present

SAN FRANCISCO, CALIF.

Chiefs	Tenures
J. Curtis	1855-57
M. Burke	1858-65

City Marshals

M. Fallon
B. Sequine
J. McKenzie

Chiefs	Tenures
P. Crowley	1865-74
T. Cockrill	1874-75
H. Ellis	1876-77
F. Kirkpatrick	1878-79
P. Crowley	1880-97
I. Lees	1897-1900
W. Sullivan	1900-01
G. Wittman	1901-05
J. Dinan	1905-07
William Biggy	1907-08
J. Cook	1908-10
J. Martin	1910
J. Seymour	1910-11
D. White	1911-20
D. O'Brien	1920-28
William Quinn	1928-40
C. Dullea	1940-47
M. Riordan	1947
M. Mitchell	1948-51
M. Gaffey	1951-55
G. Healy	1955-56
F. Ahern	1956-58
T. Cahill	1958-70
A. Nelder	1970-71
D. Scott	1971-76
C. Grain	1976-80
C. Murphy	1980-86
Frank M. Jordan	1986-Present

WASHINGTON, D.C.

Chiefs	Tenures
William B. Webb	1861-64
A.C. Richards	1864-78
Thomas P. Morgan	1878-79
William G. Brock	1879-83
William M. Dye	1883-86
Samuel H. Walker	1886
William C. Moore	1886-98
Richard Sylvester	1898-1915
Raymond W. Pullman	1915-20
Harry L. Gessford	1920-21
Daniel Sullivan	1922-25
Edwin B. Hesse	1925-29
Henry G. Pratt	1929-31
Pelham D. Glassford	1931-32
Ernest W. Brown	1932-41
Edward J. Kelly	1941-46
Harvey G. Callahan	1941-47
Robert J. Barrett	1947-51
Robert V. Murray	1951-64
John B. Layton	1964-69
Jerry V. Wilson	1969-74
Maurice J. Cullinane	1974-78
Burtell M. Jefferson	1978-81
Maurice T. Turner, Jr.	1981-present

FBI

Directors	Tenures
Stanley W. Finch	1908-11
Alexander Bruce Bielashi	1912-18
William E. Allen	1919
William J. Flynn	1919-21
William J. Burns	1921-24
J. Edgar Hoover	1924-72
Louis Patrick Gray	1972
William D. Ruckelshaus	1973
Clarence Marion Kelley	1973-78
William H. Webster	1978-87
John Otto (acting)	1987
William Steele Sessions	1987-present

DEA

Commissioner of Narcotics	Tenures
Harry Jacob Anslinger	1930-62
Henry H. Fowler	1962-

Director of the Bureau of Narcotics and Dangerous Drugs	Tenures
John E. Ingersoll	1968-73

DEA administrator	Tenures
John R. Bartels, Jr.	1973-75
Henry S. Dogin	1975
Peter B. Bensinger	1976-81
Francis M. Mullen Jr.	1981-85
John C. Lawn	1985-90

U.S. SECRET SERVICE

Directors	Tenures
William V. Wood	1865-69
Herman C. Whitley	1869-74
Elmer Washburn	1874-76
James J. Brooks	1876-88
John S. Bell	1888-90
A.E. Drummond	1891-94
William P. Hazen	1894-98
John E. Wilkie	1898-1911
William J. Flynn	1912-17
William H. Moran	1917-36
Frank J. Wilson	1937-46
James J. Maloney	1947-48
H.E. Baughman	1948-61
James J. Rowley	1961-73
H. Stuart Knight	1973-82
John R. Simpson	1982-present

SCOTLAND YARD

Commissioners of Police	Tenures
Sir Charles Rowan	1829-50
Sir Richard Mayne	1829-50
Sir Richard Mayne	1850-55
William Hay	1850-55
Sir Richard Mayne	1855-68
Sir Edmund Henderson	1869-86
Sir Charles Warren	1886-88
James Monro	1888-90
Sir Edward Bradford	1890-1903
Sir Edward Henry	1903-18
Sir Nevill Macready	1918-20
Sir William Horwood	1920-28
Viscount Byng of Vimy	1928-31
Lord Trenchard	1931-35
Sir Philip Game	1935-45
Sir Harold Scott	1945-53
Sir John Nott-Bower	1953-58
Sir John Simpson	1958-68
Sir John Waldron	1968-72
Sir Robert Mark	1972-77
Sir David McNee	1977-82
Sir Kenneth Newman	1982-87
Sir Peter Imbert	1987-present

PRISONS

PRISON ESCAPES

1788
Thirty-three members of the Doane gang escaped from Philadelphia's Walnut Street Prison. Infantry soldiers tracked down most of the escapees.
1789
March: Six inmates at the Walnut Street Prison in Philadelphia escaped by stealing keys from a drunk warden. They were recaptured.
September: Five inmates of the Walnut Street Prison, Philadelphia, escaped and were recaptured.
1808
Mar. 14: Sixteen inmates escaped from a Baltimore, Md., jail after killing a guard. Four were recaptured and hanged for the guard's murder.
1835
Dec. 6: Ten prisoners in a Baltimore, Md., jail escaped.
1838
December: Six convicts escaped from a new prison in Alton, Ill.
1864
April: All San Quentin, Calif., prisoners escaped. At least fifty were fatally shot by local citizens. Some were recaptured; others escaped.
1874
Alfred Packer escaped from the Los Pinos Indian Agency, Colo., where he awaited being tried for murder. He was recaptured in 1883.
1881
Apr. 28: William H. Bonney, or Billy the Kid, escaped from the Mesilla, N.M., jail, killing deputies J.W. Bell and Bob Olligner in the process. Sheriff Pat Garrett fatally shot Billy the Kid three months later.
1895
Apr. 10: Train robber Oliver Curtis Perry escaped from the State Hospital for the Criminally Insane at Matteawan, N.Y. He was quickly captured and put in a maximum security prison in Dannemora, where he remained in solitary confinement for twenty-five years.
1902
June 9: Dave Merrill and Harry Tracy, convicted murderer and members of Butch Cassidy's Wild Bunch, escaped from the Colorado State Prison. Tracy murdered Merrill and later committed suicide.
1904
Jan. 10: Jack Stewart and Billy Roberts escaped from the prison in Dannemora, N.Y.
1907
May 14: Five convicts probably drowned after their escape from the French Guiana penal colony at Cayenne.
1910
Dozens of Leavenworth prisoners escaped. They were all recaptured.
1912
Sept. 2: Reynold Forsbrey was captured following his escape from a solitary confinement cell at Sing Sing.
1913
January: Herbert Repsold escaped San Quentin by jumping over the prison wall into San Francisco Bay into an awaiting boat. Something went wrong and Repsold's drowned body was found the next morning.
Aug. 17: Harry K. Thaw, convicted of murdering Stanford White, fled to Canada following his escape from the Matteawan State Prison Hospital in New York. He was soon captured and returned to the hospital.
1915
Jan. 1: German immigrant Frederick Mors, a male nurse who had killed seventeen patients, escaped from the state prison in Matteawan, N.Y. He was never apprehended.
1917
Sept. 9: Twenty Bolsheviks were executed after being captured following an escape from the jail in Laishev, Rus.
1918
May 21: "The Gorilla Murderer," Earle Leonard Nelson, who was charged with assault in San Francisco escaped from an asylum.
July 4: Arthur "Dock" Barker was arrested for auto theft in Tulsa, Okla. He escaped from custody as he was being brought to court.
1921
December: Thomas "Terrible Tommy" O'Connor, escaped from the Criminal Courts Building in Chicago just days before O'Connor was given the death penalty for murder. He was never found.
1922
Sept. 20: Emile Courgibet, imprisoned for theft, escaped from Dutch Guiana's Camp Colbert.
1926
Bernard Roa, inmate at Illinois' Stateville Prison, escaped, killing Deputy Warden Peter Klein on his way out. Roa was recaptured. He later escaped from a jail in Will County, Ill., and returned to Mexico, his native country.
James D. Price, who escaped from the Stateville Prison in Illinois, was later found at the Clinton State Prison using the alias Frank Meadows. He was returned to Stateville.
1928
Mar. 9: John Leonard Whitfield, imprisoned for the murder of a Cleveland police officer, was shot to death as attempted to escape from the Ohio Penitentiary.
1930
Oct. 19: Oklahoma bank robber Frank "Jelly" Nash escaped from Leavenworth after being entrusted to cook for the warden's family outside the prison walls. He returned to a life of crime, dying in a gun battle on June 17, 1933, in Kansas City.
1931
July 14: Murderer and bank robber Wilbur Underhill escaped from the state prison in McAlester, Okla.
Dec. 11: Seven Leavenworth inmates tried to escape. Whitey Lewis was killed by a deputy during the break. Grover Durrel and Bill Green killed themselves. Tom Underwood, Charles Berta, and Stanley Brown were quickly recaptured. Earl Thayer, was caught four days later.
1932
July 7: Bank robbers Harvey Bailey, Tommy Holden, and Francis Keating; all recently escaped from prison, were recaptured by FBI agents on a golf course near Kansas City.
Dec. 12: Willie "the Actor" Sutton and John Eagan escaped from Sing.
1933
May 31: Harvey Bailey led ten inmates in an escape from the Kansas State Penitentiary. Wilbur Underhill, "Big Bob" Brady, Frank Sawyer, Ed Davis, and Jim Clark were among the eleven escapees. All were recaptured within a year.
Sept. 26: Ten men received smuggled guns from paroled John Dillinger and escaped from the Michigan City Prison through the front door. Escapee James Jenkins was killed the same day. Five were recaptured; four were not caught.
Oct. 12: Charles Makley, Jim "Oklahoma Jack" Clark, Harry Pierpont, and Russell Clark broke John Dillinger out of a Lima, Ohio, jail, after killing Sheriff Jess Sarber.
1934
Mar. 3: John Dillinger became Public Enemy No. 1 when he escaped with Herbert Youngblood from the jail in Crown Point, Ind. Youngblood was shot and killed by deputy sheriffs on Mar. 16 in Port Huron, Mich.
1935
January: Four San Quentin inmates took the warden and three prison official hostage, and escaped from the prison, leading authorities on a wild chase through northern California. Two hours later the convicts were apprehended after a shootout which left one dead and the warden wounded.
1936
Mar. 2: The author of *Dry Guillotine*, Rene Belbenoit, escaped from a penal colony in French Guiana.
1937
September: Convicts Charles Bird, Frank Bird, Theodore Slapik, and James Widmer, escaped from the Municipal Jail in Cleveland.
September: Three inmates escaped from newly constructed "escape proof" state prison in Tattnall, Ga.
September: Seven convicts in California's Folsom Prison, armed with knives, overpowered guards and attempted to escape. During an ensuing shootout in the prison yard, two were killed and the others recaptured, while Warden Clarence A. Larkin died from a stab wound.
September: Alcatraz warden James A. Johnston was beaten during an unsuccessful escape attempt by convicted kidnapper Burton Phillips.
December: Six Columbia, S.C., State Prison inmates failed in their escape attempt when they were forced with tear gas to abandon the room in which they had taken a guard hostage. However, the guard was stabbed to death during the siege.
Dec. 16: Ralph Roe and Theodore "Sunny Boy" Cole escaped from Alcatraz by breaking a window and jumping into the San Francisco Bay. Authorities never saw them again.
1938
July: Due to severe overcrowding, 200 trusted inmates of the Arizona State Prison in Phoenix were allowed to sleep outside the prison walls. The solution failed when twenty inmates proved they were falsely trusted and disappeared during a two month period.
1939
Jan. 13: Arthur "Dock" Barker, William Martin, William Rufe McCain, Dale Stamphill, and Henry Young, escaped from Alcatraz. Martin, McCain, and Young quickly surrendered, while Stemphill was shot in the legs, and Barker, resisting further, was shot to death.
1941
April: Charles McGale, Joseph Riordan, and James Waters shot their way out of Sing, killing a guard and a police officer. Waters was killed during the exchange of gunfire, while McGale and Riordan were apprehended by a posse later in the day.
April: Sixty youthful inmates at a reform school in Whittier, Calif., escaped, shortly after hearing a motivational speech about reform, given by Boys Town's Father Flanagan.
1942
Oct. 9: Inmates Basil "The Owl" Banghart, Eddie Darlok, St. Clair McInerney, Martlick Nelson, Gene O'Connor, and Roger "The Terrible" Touhy escaped from Stateville Prison, near Joliet, Ill. McInerney and O'Connor were killed in an ensuing gun battle, while the others were

eventually captured and returned to custody.
1943
January: Musician Michael Neely Bryan, imprisoned on drug charges, escaped from the Miami Beach Army Stockade, aided by author Ursula Parrott.
1945
January: Bandits Edgar Cook and John Giles escaped the jail in Council Bluffs, Iowa. They were apprehended in Concord, N.H., two months later.
May 7: Bank robber Willie "The Actor" Sutton was apprehended by police after he tunneled his way out of Philadelphia's Eastern State Penitentiary.
1946
May 2: Clarence Carnes, Bernard Paul Coy, Joseph Cretzer, Miran Thompson, Marvin Hubbard, and Sam Shockley attempted to escape from Alcatraz. Two guards, as well as Coy and Cretzer were killed while the others were recaptured.
1947
Feb. 9: Bank robber Willie "The Actor" Sutton scaled the walls of Philadelphia's Holmesburg Prison. He remained free until his apprehension in New York City on Mar. 8, 1952.
Sept. 3: Emile Buisson, imprisoned for bank robbery, escaped from an asylum in Paris.
1948
January: Twelve inmates, including Richard Heilman, Werner Schwartzmiller, Jimmy Sherbondy, A.B. Tolley, and Orville Turley, escaped from the state prison in Canon City, Colo. All were recaptured within two days following a massive manhunt.
1951
July 17: Inmate Romeo Martin lost his designation as a trusty, when he escaped from the prison in Walla Walla, Wash. during a baseball game. He was apprehended four months later.
1952
Sept. 8: George Lemay and three other bank robbers escaped from prison in Toronto, only to be recaptured a few weeks later.
1953
Oct. 1: Abram Sykowski, imprisoned for swindling, escaped from the police in Paris, and was never apprehended.
1954
Oct. 9: Charles Rape, serving a sentence for grand larceny, escaped from the Elmore State Prison in Atmore, Ala. He eluded authorities for 27 years, marrying and raising a family, until his apprehension in Dothan, Ala. on Aug. 25, 1981. Three days later, after being termed a "model citizen", Rape was released on probation.
1955
January: Walter Harold Balben, Teddy Green, Joseph "Red" Flaherty, and Fritz Swenson, four inmates attempting to escape from state prison in Boston, took eleven hostages and staved off police and the National Guard, until they were recaptured three-and-a-half days later.
June 15: Roger Dekkar escaped from Fontevrault Prison, near Paris, by wearing a guard's uniform. He was shot to death by police officers two days later.
November: Ten prisoners escaped from the state prison in Walla Walla, Wash.
1957
May: Teddy Green and two others were apprehended as they attempted to escape from Alcatraz. Green had been sent to the island after a 1955 escape attempt from the Massachusetts State Prison.
1960
Feb. 5: Five inmates, including burglar Jean-Louis Andre, escaped from the Fresne Prison in France, only to be apprehended a few weeks later.
1962
June 12: Clarence Anglin, Joseph Anglin, and Frank Lee Morris crawled through ventilating ducts to escape from Alcatraz. The escape was presumed successful, as their bodies were never found in San Francisco Bay.
1963
July: As many as 400 inmates, led by drug dealer Jose Rafael Cariola escaped from the La Planta jail in Caracas, Venez.
1964
Apr. 2: John William Clouser, self-named the "Florida Fox", escaped with three others at knife point from the Florida State Hospital in Chattahoochie, where he was detained on a breaking and entering charge. The accomplices were apprehended shortly thereafter, but Clouser outwitted authorities for more than a decade, until he surrendered voluntarily on Aug. 22, 1974.
1965
Sept. 21: George Lemay, imprisoned for bank robbery, escaped from Miami's Dade County Jail.
1966
Oct. 17: Convicted spy George Blake escaped from England's Wormwood Shrubs Prison.
1967
Apr. 23: James Earl Ray escaped from the Missouri State Prison by managing to secrete himself in a delivery truck. Days later, Ray was recaptured.
Dec. 26: Five inmates escaped from England's Dartmoor Prison.
1971
Aug. 18: Carlos Castro and Joel D. Kaplan escaped by helicopter from the prison in Mexico City. The CIA was suspected in the $1 million caper.
1972
Aug. 15: Six ERP terrorists escaped from the Rawson prison in Argentina. They hijacked an airliner, fleeing to Santiago, Chile.
Nov. 11: Mass-murderer Charles Schmid escaped from the Arizona State Prison with killer Raymond Hudgens, causing mass panic until he was apprehended shortly thereafter.
1973
May 14: Prison escapees Wayne Coleman, George Dungee, Billy Isaacs, and Carl Isaacs, murdered seven members of a family in Seminole County, Ga. They were recaptured and sentenced to death.
1974
Oct. 26: Four inmates took fifteen hostages and barricaded themselves in a chapel, as they attempted to escape from the Scheveningen Prison in the Netherlands. The siege ended five days later when the four surrendered and the hostages were released unharmed.
1975
June 6: Dale Otto Remling escaped by helicopter from the state prison in Jackson, Mich. He was apprehended the following day while sitting in a bar in nearby Leslie, Mich.
Nov. 15: Five psychopathic inmates escaped from the State Hospital for the Criminally Insane, in Lima, Ohio.
1976
Aug. 25: Charles Wayne Adams was apprehended as he was attempting to hitchhike back to the state prison in Michigan City, Ind., from which he had earlier escaped.
1977
Mar. 6: Robert Perry and Glenn Wise escaped from the Rahway Prison in New Jersey. They were apprehended the same day after raping a woman and assaulting a visitor at the adjoining Marlboro State Hospital.
May 26: David Kimes, a 27-year-old man charged with armed robbery, theft and forgery, escaped from authorities after being transferred from his cell to the Kane County courthouse in Geneva, Ill. He was apprehended later that day after being injured in an automobile accident and taking two hostages in neighboring Aurora.
June 15: James Earl Ray, convicted of killing Dr. Martin Luther King, Jr., escaped from Tennessee's Brushy Mountain State Prison. He was recaptured a short time later.
1979
Nov. 2: Terrorist and police killer Joanne Chesimard escaped from prison in New Jersey.
1980
Mar. 3: Three inmates escaped from the Rikers Island prison in New York City by secreting themselves in a guard's automobile.
May 31: Donald Reynolds, a former police officer, escaped from the County Courthouse in Peoria, Ill.
1981
June 10: Eight IRA terrorists escaped from the Crumlin Road Prison in Belfast.
Sept. 6: Everett L. Cameron, John E. Kitchell, Robert Bentley and four other inmates escaped from the Kansas State Penitentiary. Cameron and Kitchell eluded police for eight days until they were captured Sept. 13, 1981 near Goodman, Mo., while Bentley was captured a day earlier at Noel, Mo.
1982
Jan. 4: Terrorist Susanna Ronconi was one of four women who escaped from the prison in Rovigo, Italy, abetted by outsiders who dynamited the prison walls and tossed the women sub-machine guns. One person died and six others were wounded in the crossfire.
Jan. 11: Twenty guerrillas escaped from the Imphal Central Jail in India, killing a guard in the exchange of gun fire.
Mar. 2: As many as 250 inmates escaped from prison in Ayacucho, Peru, after rebels assaulted the facility and engaged the guards in a five hour gun battle. Twenty-two died and another twelve were wounded in the battle.
1984
Jan. 23: Robert Vance Latimer and Kenneth Lundien escaped from the state prison in Florence, Ariz. On Mar. 8, 1984, in Springfield, Va., they wounded FBI agent Carl Swanson in a shootout. Lundien was apprehended in New York City two days later, while Latimer was shot to death in Nashville, Tenn. on Apr. 15, 1984 during a second shootout with FBI agents.
May 31: Six murderers escaped from death row at the prison in Mecklenburg, Va. Willie Leroy Jones and Lem Tuggle, Jr. were apprehended on June 8, 1984, near the Canadian border at Woodford, Vt. The other four were also eventually recaptured.
July 1: Three inmates escaped from the state prison in Only, Tenn.
1988
Aug. 26: Victor Thomas escaped from Chicago's Cook County Jail, using a bar of soap shaped like a gun and coated with black ink, as a weapon.
Sept. 26: Murderer Jesse Sumner, imprisoned at the Pontiac, Ill., Correctional Center, escaped from guards, taking four people hostage, as he was being driven to Joliet. He was apprehended four hours later.
Dec. 13: More than 200 prisoners escaped from the prison in Colombo, Sri Lanka, during an attack by leftist guerrillas. Thirty others were shot to death by guards during the escape attempt.

UNITED STATES PRISONS

ALABAMA:

Boot Camp (Kilby CC)
Minimum security
Lt. Beutler, Unit Commander
Capacity: 64
Established in 1988

Bullock Correctional Facility
Union Springs
Leoneal Davis, Warden
Medium-minimum security
Capacity: 689
Established in 1987

Draper Correctional Center
Elmore
Dale Howard, Warden
Medium-minimum security
Capacity: 1,029
Established in 1939

Elmore Correctional Facility
Elmore
Ron Jones, Warden
Minimum security
Capacity: 524
Established in 1982

Escambia Correctional Center
Atmore
I. Brown, Warden
Minimum security
Capacity: 208
Established in 1984

Frank Lee Youth Center
Deatsville
Kathleen Holt, Warden
Minimum security-ages 16-25
Capacity: 200
Established in 1964

G.K. Fountain Correctional Center
Atmore
J.O. Davis, Warden
Medium-minimum security
Capacity: 772
Established in 1936

Hamilton A&I
Hamilton
W.C. Berry, Warden
Medium-minimum security
Capacity: 168
Established in 1981

Holman Prison
Atmore
Charlie Jones, Warden
Maximum-medium-minimum security
Capacity: 648
Established in 1969

Julia Tutwiler Prison for Women
Wetumpka
Jean Hare, Warden
Maximum-medium-minimum security
Capacity: 504
Established in 1942

Kilby Corrections Facility
Mt. Meigs
Lynn Harrelson, Warden
Maximum-medium-minimum security
Capacity: 884
Established in 1970

Limestone Correctional Center
Capshaw
J.D. White, Warden
Maximum-medium-minimum security
Capacity: 1,030
Established in 1985

Red Eagle Honor Farm
Montgomery
James Cooke, Warden
Minimum security
Capacity: 225
Established in 1972

St. Clair Correctional Facility
Springville
Larry Burton, Warden
Maximum-medium-minimum security
Capacity: 1,032
Established in 1983

State Cattle Ranch
Greensboro
Charles A. Farquhar, Warden
Minimum security
Capacity: 85
Established in 1982

Thomas F. Staton Correctional Center
Elmore
Jim Morrison, Warden
Medium-minimum security
Capacity: 561
Established in 1978

West Jefferson Correctional Facility
Bessemer
Eddie Nagle, Warden
Maximum-medium-minimum security
Capacity: 1,352
Established in 1982

ALASKA:

Anchorage, Sixth Avenue Annex
Anchorage
Chester Chiara, Superintendent
Medium security
Capacity: 116
Established in 1973

Anvil Mountain Correctional Center
Nome
Myron Michaels, Superintendent
Medium-minimum security
Capacity: 102
Established in 1985

Eagle River, Hiland Mountain Correctional Center
Eagle River
Frank Sauser, Superintendent
Maximum-medium security
Capacity: 229
Established in 1974

Eagle River, Meadow Creek Correctional Center
Eagle River
Mike Wehrer, Assistant Superintendent
Medium security
Capacity: 56
Established in 1981

Fairbanks Correctional Center
Fairbanks
Gail Frank, Superintendent
Maximum-medium-minimum security
Capacity: 200
Established: 1967

Kenai, Wildwood Correctional Center
Kenai
Russ Moody, Superintendent
Medium-minimum security
Capacity: 204
Established in 1983

Ketchikan Correctional Center
Ketchikan
Nan Bailey, Superintendent
Medium-minimum security
Capacity: 63
Established in 1983

Lemon Creek Correctional Center
Juneau
Dan Carothers, Superintendent
Maximum-medium-minimum security
Capacity: 174
Established in 1969

Palmer Correctional Centers
Palmer
Art Schmidt, Superintendent
Medium-minimum security
Capacity: 295
Established in 1962 (min.), 1983 (max.)

Spring Creek Correctional Center
Seward
Richard Schoffel, Superintendent
Maximum security
Capacity: 96
Established in 1988

Yukon-Kuskokwim Correctional Center
Bethel
James Symbol, Superintendent
Medium security
Capacity: 88
Established in 1984

ARIZONA:

Alhambra Reception and Treatment Center
Phoenix
Richard Ward, Acting Deputy Warden
Maximum-medium-minimum security
Capacity: 254
Established in 1979

Arizona Center for Women
Phoenix
Mary Vermeer, Deputy Warden
Minimum security
Capacity: 350
Established in 1982

Arizona State Prison Complex-Douglas
Douglas
George Herman, Warden
Medium-minimum security
Capacity: 1,768
Established in 1983

Arizona State Prison Complex-Florence
Florence
Robert Goldsmith, Warden
Maximum-medium-minimum security
Capacity: 3,006
Established in 1912

Arizona State Prison Complex-Perryville
Goodyear
William Rhode, Warden
Medium-minimum security
Capacity: 1,400
Established in 1981

Arizona State Prison Complex-Phoenix
Phoenix
Hal Cardin, Warden
Capacity: 1,004
Established in 1978

Arizona State Prison Complex-Tucson
Tucson
Roger Crist, Warden
Medium-minimum security
Capacity: 2,095
Established in 1978

Arizona State Prison Complex-Winslow
Winslow
Charles Ryan, Warden
Medium-minimum security
Capacity: 50
Established in 1986

Arizona State Prison-Fort Grant
Ft. Grant
Duane Vild, Warden
Minimum security
Capacity: 503
Established in 1912

Arizona State Prison-Safford
Safford
Earl Dowdle, Warden
Minimum security
Capacity: 384
Established in 1970

Arizona State Prison-Yuma
Yuma
William Huston, Warden
Minimum security
Capacity: 250
Established in 1988

Aspen-DWI
Phoenix
Tim Murphy, Administrator
Minimum security
Capacity: 200
Established in 1982

Coronado Unit
Winslow
Charles Ryan, Warden
Medium-minimum security
Capacity: 650
Established in 1988

ARKANSAS:

Benton Work Release and Pre-Release Center
Benton
Bruce Collins, Warden
Minimum security
Capacity: 225
Established in 1974

Cummins Unit
Grady
Willis Sargent, Warden
Maximum-medium-minimum security
Capacity: 1,650
Established in 1902

Diagnostic Unit
Pine Bluff
Ed Lagrone, Warden
Maximum-medium-minimum security
Capacity: 488
Established in 1981

Maximum Security Unit
Tucker
Larry B. Norris, Warden
Maximum security
Capacity: 432
Established in 1982

Mississippi County Work Release Center
Luxora
Jim Lowe, Supervisor
Minimum security
Capacity: 66
Established in 1975

Modular Minimum Security Unit
Grady
Minimum security
Capacity: 200
Established in 1983

Northwest Arkansas Work Release Center
Springdale
Jerry Price, Supervisor
Minimum security
Capacity: 16
Established in 1980

Texarkana Regional Correction Center
Texarkana
Rick Hart, Supervisor
Minimum security
Capacity: 119
Established in 1983

Tucker Modular Barracks
Tucker
Maximum-medium-minimum security
Capacity: 120
Established in 1982

Tucker Unit
Tucker
G.D. Guntharp, Warden
Maximum-medium-minimum security
Capacity: 676
Established in 1916

Varner Unit
Grady
M.D. Reed, Warden
Minimum security
Capacity: 700
Established in 1987

Women's Unit
Pine Bluff
Virginia Wallace, Warden
Maximum-medium-minimum security
Capacity: 288
Established in 1976

Wrightsville Unit
Wrightsville
Tim B. Baltz, Warden
Medium-minimum security
Capacity: 420
Established in 1981

CALIFORNIA:

Avenal State Prison
Avenal
Al Gomez, Superintendent
Medium security
Capacity: 3,034
Established in 1987

California Correctional Center
Susanville
William Merkle, Superintendent
Medium-minimum security
Capacity: 3,102
Established in 1963

California Correctional Institution
Tehachapi
B.J. Bunnell, Superintendent
Maximum-medium-minimum security
Capacity: 2,757
Established in 1955

California Institution for Men
Chino
Otis Thurman, Superintendent
Medium-minimum security
Capacity: 2,778
Established in 1941

California Institution for Women
Corona
Sue Poole, Asst. Superintendent
Maximum-medium-minimum security
Capacity: 1,026
Established in 1936

California Medical Facility
Vacaville
Eddie Yost, Superintendent
Medium-minimum security
Capacity: 4,730
Established in 1950

California Men's Colony
San Luis Obispo
Wayne Estelle, Warden
Medium-minimum security
Capacity: 3,859
Established in 1954

California Rehabilitation Center
Norco
Leonard Chastain, Superintendent
Medium security
Capacity: 2,385
Established in 1963

California State Prison
Corcoran
Bernie J. Aispuro, Superintendent
Maximum-medium-minimum security
Capacity: 2,916
Established in 1988

California State Prison at Folsom
Represa
Robert Borg, Warden
Maximum-minimum security
Capacity: 3,796
Established in 1880

California State Prison at San Quentin
San Quentin
Dan Vasquez, Warden
Maximum-medium-minimum security
Capacity: 2,267
Established in 1852

Chuckawalla Valley State Prison
Blythe
Vern Smith, Superintendent
Medium-minimum security
Capacity: 2,002
Established in 1988

Correctional Training Facility
Soledad
Eddie Myers, Superintendent
Medium-minimum security
Capacity: 3,285
Established in 1947

Deuel Vocational Institution
Tracy
Midge Carroll, Superintendent
Medium security
Capacity: 1,506
Established in 1953

Mule Creek State Prison
Ione
Roger Schaufel, Superintendent
Medium-minimum security
Capacity: 1,600
Established in 1987

Northern California Women's Facility
Stockton
Teena Farmon, Superintendent
Maximum-medium-minimum security
Capacity: 400
Established in 1987

Richard J. Donovan Correctional Facility at Rock Mountain
San Diego
John Ratelle, Superintendent
Medium-minimum security
Capacity: 2,200
Established in 1987

COLORADO:

Arkansas Valley Correctional Facility
Crowley
Jim Brittain, Superintendent
Medium security
Capacity: 942
Established in 1987

Buena Vista Correctional Facility
Buena Vista
Warren T. Diesslin, Superintendent
Medium security
Capacity: 842
Established in 1892

Centennial Correctional Facility
Canon City
Ben Johnson, Superintendent
Maximum security
Capacity: 336
Established in 1980

Colorado Correctional Center
Golden
William Bokros, Superintendent
Medium security
Capacity: 108
Established in 1969

Colorado Territorial Correctional Facility
Canon City
R. Mark McGoff, Superintendent
Medium security
Capacity: 571
Established in 1871

Colorado Women's Correctional Facility
Canon City
Richard G. Mills, Superintendent
Maximum-minimum security
Capacity: 184
Established in 1968

Columbine Correctional Center
Denver
Ruben Avila, Supervisor
Minimum security
Capacity: 28
Established in 1984

Delta Correctional Center
Delta
Pat Marah, Superintendent
Minimum security
Capacity: 120
Established in 1967

Four Mile Modular Unit
Canon City
Thomas I. Cooper, Superintendent
Minimum security
Capacity: 100
Established in 1983

Fremont Correctional Facility
Canon City
Lou Hesse, Superintendent
Medium security
Capacity: 657
Established in 1962

Pre-Release Unit
Canon City
Lou Hesse, Superintendent
Minimum security
Capacity: 82
Established: 1983

Rifle Correctional Facility
Rifle
Wallis Gunnells, Superintendent
Minimum security
Capacity: 120
Established in 1979

Shadow Mountain Correctional Facility
Canon City
Thomas I. Cooper, Superintendent
Medium-minimum security
Capacity: 384
Established in 1981

Skyline Correctional Center
Canon City
Ben Johnson, Superintendent
Minimum security
Capacity: 165
Established in 1964

CONNECTICUT:

Carl Robinson Correctional Institution
Enfield
Edward Gaudet, Warden
Minimum security
Capacity: 650
Established in 1985

Connecticut Correctional Center
Cheshire,
Victor Liburdi, Warden
Maximum-medium security
Capacity: 615
Established in 1982

Connecticut Correctional Institution
Enfield
Richard Wezowicz, Warden
Medium security
Capacity: 474
Established in 1930

Connecticut Correctional Institution
Niantic
Marie Cerino, Warden
Minimum security
Capacity: 400
Established in 1930

Connecticut Correctional Institution
Somers
George Bronson, Warden
Maximum security
Capacity: 1,397
Established in 1963

J. Bernard Gates Correctional Unit
Niantic
Dennis Guay, Warden
Minimum security
Capacity: 206
Established in 1982

John R. Manson Youth Institution
Cheshire
Michael Bonzagni, Warden
Medium security
Capacity: 472
Established in 1982

DELAWARE:

Delaware Correctional Center
Smyrna
Walter W. Redman, Warden
Maximum-medium-minimum security
Capacity: 1,604
Established in 1971

Morris Correctional Institution
Dover
Robert Snyder, Warden
Maximum-medium security
Capacity: 88
Established in 1977

Multi-Purpose Criminal Justice Facility
Wilmington
Howard Young, Warden
Maximum security
Capacity: 678
Established in 1982

Pre-Trial Annex
Wilmington
John Webb, Warden
Maximum-medium security
Capacity: 81
Established in 1975

Sussex Correctional Institution
Georgetown
John C. Ellingsworth, Warden
Maximum-medium-minimum security
Capacity: 372
Established in 1932

Women's Correctional Institution
Claymont
Elizabeth Neal-Reed, Warden
Maximum-medium-minimum security
Capacity: 150
Established in 1975

DISTRICT OF COLUMBIA:

Central Facility
Lorton, Va.,
David D. Roach, Administrator
Medium security
Capacity: 1,166
Established in 1916

Maximum Security Facility
Lorton, Va
Bernard L. Braxton, Administrator
Capacity: 536
Established in 1923

Minimum Security Facility
Lorton, Va
James W. Bragg, Acting Administrator
Capacity: 600
Established in 1910

Modular Facility
Lorton, Va
John W. Lattimore, Administrator
Medium security
Capacity: 500
Established in 1986

Occoquan Facility
Lorton, Va
Douglas W. Stemson, Administrator
Medium security
Capacity: 1,568
Established in 1982

Youth Center I
Lorton, Va
John S. Henderson, Administrator
Medium security
Capacity: 440
Established in 1960

Youth Center II
Lorton, Va
John S. Henderson, Administrator
Medium security
Capacity: 286
Established in 1972

FLORIDA:

Apalachee Correctional Institution
Sneads
C.W. Sprouse, Superintendent
Medium-minimum security
Capacity: 1,257
Established in 1949

Avon Park Correctional Institution
Avon Park
David E. Watson, Superintendent
Maximum-medium-minimum security
Capacity: 1,245
Established in 1957

Baker Correctional Institution
Olustee
O.J. Phillips, Superintendent
Maximum-medium-minimun security
Capacity: 626
Established in 1978

Brevard Correctional Institution
Sharpes
Jerry, W. Hicks, Superintendent
Maximum-medium-minimum security
Capacity: 483
Established in 1976

Broward Correctional Institution
Pembroke Pines
Marta Villacorta, Superintendent
Maximum-medium-minimum security
Capacity: 336
Established in 1977

Calhoun Correctional Institution
Blountstown
Joseph Thompson, Superintendent
Medium-minimum security
Capacity: 840
Established in 1987

Corrections Mental Health Institution
Chattahoochee
Jim Ivey, Superintendent
Between maximum and medium security
Capacity: 135
Established in 1985

Cross City Correctional Institution
Cross City
Randall Music, Superintendent
Maximum-medium-minimum security
Capacity: 609
Established in 1973

Dade Correctional Institution
Florida City
Paul Sheffield, Superintendent
Maximum-medium-minimum security
Capacity: 400
Established in 1976

DeSoto Correctional Institution
Arcadia
John Shaw, Superintendent
Maximum-medium security
Capacity: 580
Established in 1969

Florida Correctional Institution
Lowell
James E. Curington Jr., Superintendent,
Maximum-medium-minimum security
Capacity: 510
Established in 1956

Florida State Prison
Starke
Tom L. Barton, Superintendent
Maximum-medium-minimum security
Capacity: 1,468
Established in 1960

Glades Correctional Institution
Belle Glade
Chester Lambdin, Superintendent
Maximum-medium security
Capacity: 886
Established in 1932

Hamilton Correctional Institution
Jasper
C.R. Cason, Superintendent
Medium-minimum security
Capacity: 574
Established in 1987

Hendry Correctional Institution
Immakolee
Jerry Wade, Superintendent
Maximum-medium-minimum secuity
Capacity: 1,223
Established in 1979

Hillsborough Correctional Institution
Riverview
Don M. Dean, Superintendent
Medium-minimum security
Capacity: 210
Established in 1976

Holmes Correctional Institution
Bonifay
Ronnie K. Griffis, Superintendent
Maximum-medium-minimum security
Capacity: 768
Established in 1988

Indian River Correctional Institution
Vero Beach
David Hemme, Superintendent
Medium-minimum security
Capacity: 155
Established in 1976

Lake Correctional Institution
Clermont
G.W. Bedingfield, Superintendent
Maximum-medium-minimum security
Capacity: 411
Established in 1973

Lancaster Correctional Institution
Trenton
Bradley Carter, Superintendent
Medium-minimum security
Capacity: 417
Established in 1979

Lantana Correctional Institution
Lantana
Ray Henderson, Superintendent
Medium-minimum security
Capacity: 187
Established in 1975

Lawtey Correctional Institution
Lawtey
G.S. "Sid" Fortner, Superintendent
Medium-minimum security
Capacity: 554
Established in 1977

Marion Correctional Institution
Lowell
Gerald Collins, Superintendent

Maximum-medium-minimum security
Capacity: 642
Established in 1976

Martin Correctional Institution and Vocational Center
Indiantown
Bill Rouse, Superintendent
Maximum security
Capacity: 1,033
Established in 1985

Mayo Correctional Institution
Mayo
Hamilton D. Mathis, Superintendent
Medium-minimum security
Capacity: 552
Established in 1984

New River Correctional Institution
Raiford
James T. Wainwright, Superintendent
Maximum-medium-minimum security
Capacity: 768
Established in 1987

Okaloosa Correctional Institution
Crestview
Carl W. Kirkland, Superintendent
Maximum-medium-minimum security
Capacity: 150
Established in 1982

Orange Correctional Institution
Orlando
Dennis T. O'Neill, Superintendent
Maximum-medium-minimum security
Capacity: 1,257
Established in 1988

Polk Correctional Institution
Polk City
Everett I. Perrin Jr., Superintendent
Maximum-medium-minimum security
Capacity: 814
Established in 1978

Putnam Correctional Institution
East Palatka
James R. Reddish, Superintendent
Maximum-medium-minimum security
Capacity: 204
Established in 1961

Reception and Medical Center
Lake Butler
George Denman, Superintendent
Capacity: 897
Established in 1968

River Junction Correctional Institution
Chattahoochee
Jimmy D. Folsom, Superintendent
Medium-minimum security
Capacity: 460
Established in 1974

South Florida Reception Center
Miami
Dr. Ana I. Gispert, Superintendent
Maximum security
Capacity: 609
Established in 1985

Sumter Correctional Institution
Bushnell
Paul Worthington, Superintendent
Maximum-medium-minimum security
Capacity: 1,140
Established in 1965

Tomoka Correctional Institution
Daytona Beach
Leonard Dugger, Superintendent
Maximum-medium-minimum security
Capacity: 727
Established in 1981

Union Correctional Institution
Raiford
W. Marion Ellis, Superintendent
Maximum-medium-minimum security
Capacity: 1,279
Established in 1913

Zephyrhills Correctional Institution
Zephyrhills
Sterling Staggers, Superintendent
Maximum-medium-minimum security
Capacity: 360
Established in 1977

GEORGIA:

Al Burruss Correctional Training Center
Forsyth
Tommy Payne, Superintendent
Medium security
Capacity: 300
Established in 1986

Augusta Correctional/Medical Institution
Grovetown
Charles Burden, Superintendent
Maximum-medium-minimum security
Capacity: 390
Established in 1983

Bostic Correctional Center
Hardwick
Tom Jones, Superintendent
Medium security
Capacity: 504
Established in 1987

Central Correctional Institution
Macon
Truett Goodwin, Superintendent
Maximum-medium security
Capacity: 546
Established in 1978

Coastal Correctional Institution
Garden City
Barry Gaither, Superintendent
Medium security
Capacity: 758
Established in 1981

Dodge Correctional Institution
Chester
Curtis Scott, Superintendent
Maximum-medium-minimum security
Capacity: 386
Established in 1983

Georgia Diagnostic and Classification Center
Jackson
Walter Zant, Superintendent
Maximum security
Capacity: 1,381
Established in 1969

Georgia Industrial Institute
Alto
Garrison Parker, Superintendent
Maximum security
Capacity: 1,443
Established in 1946

Georgia State Prison
Reidsville
Jerry Thomas, Superintendent
Maximum security
Capacity: 812
Established in 1936

Georgia Training and Development Center
Buford
Rick Abbott, Superintendent
Maximum-medium security
Capacity: 240
Established in 1951

Jack T. Rutledge Correctional Institution
Columbus
Paul Ford, Superintendent
Maximum-medium security
Capacity: 580
Established in 1976

Lee Correctional Institution
Leesburg
Ira Kelso, Superintendent
Maximum-medium security
Capacity: 640
Established in 1956

Lowndes Correctional Instituion
Valdosta
David Thompson, Superintendent
Maximum-medium security
Capacity: 121
Established in 1959

Men's Correctional Institution
Hardwick
Jim Wharton, Superintendent
Maximum-medium-minimum security
Capacity: 585
Established in 1983

Metro Correctional Institution
Atlanta
Mary Esposito, Superintendent
Maximum-medium security
Capacity: 690
Established in 1980

Montgomery Correctional Institution
Mt. Vernon
Jack Todd, Superintendent
Maximum-medium security
Capacity: 425
Established in 1972

Putnam Correctional Institution
Eatonton
Larry Hurt, Superintendent
Maximum-medium security
Capacity: 100
Established in 1976

Rivers Correctional Institution
Hardwick
Calvin Green, Superintendent
Maximum-medium-minimum security
Capacity: 880
Established in 1983

Rogers Correctional Institution
Reidsville
Jackie Trimm, Superintendent
Medium-minimum security
Capacity: 430
Established in 1983

Stone Mountain Correctional Institution
Stone Mountain
Elie Jones, Superintendent
Maximum-medium security
Capacity: 228
Established in 1970

Walker Correctional Institution
Rock Springs
James Wilson, Superintendent
Maximum-medium security
Capacity: 324
Established in 1972

Ware Correctional Institution
Waycross
Doug Williams, Superintendent
Maximum-medium security
Capacity: 97
Established in 1951

Wayne Correctional Institution
Odum
Thomas Wallace, Superintendent
Maximum-medium security
Capacity: 192
Established in 1949

Women's Correctional Institution
Hardwick
Gary Black, Superintendent
Maximum security
Capacity: 660,
Established in 1957

Youthful Offender Correctional Institution
Hardwick
Grady Lewis, Superintendent
Maximum-medium security
Capacity: 874
Established in 1975

HAWAII:

Halawa High Security Facility
Oahu,
William Oku, Administrator
Maximum security
Capacity: 90
Established in 1962

Halawa Medium Security
Aiea
William Oku, Administrator
Medium security
Capacity: 496
Established in 1987

Hawaii Community Correctional Center
Hilo
Donald Kobatake, Administrator
Medium-minimum security
Capacity: 32
Established in 1975

Kauai Community Correctional Center
Lihue
John Smythe, Administrator

Medium-minimum security
Capacity: 45
Established in 1977

Kulani Correctional Facility
Hilo
Peter McDonald, Administrator
Medium-minimum security
Capacity: 160
Established in 1946

Maui Community Correctional Center
Wailuku
Marye Deming, Administrator
Medium-minimum security
Capacity: 78
Established in 1973

Oahu Community Correctional Center
Honolulu
Edwin Shimoda, Administrator
Medium-minimum security
Capacity: 709
Established in 1918

Waiawa Correctional Facility
Pearl City
Eric Penarosa, Acting Administrator
Minimum security
Capacity: 120
Established in 1985

Women's Community Correctional Center
Kailua
Renee Colster, Acting Administrator
Maximum-medium-minimum security
Capacity: 143
Established in 1983

IDAHO:

Idaho Correctional Institution
Orofino
Jim Hope, Warden
Maximum-medium security
Capacity: 196
Established in 1984

Idaho State Correctional Institution
Boise
Dave Paskett, Warden
Maximum-medium-minimum security
Capacity: 495
Established in 1870

South Idaho Correctional Institution
Boise
Larry Wright, Warden
Medium-minimum security
Capacity: 194
Established in 1986

ILLINOIS:

Centralia Correctional Center
Centralia
Ronald Haws, Warden
Medium security
Capacity: 993
Established in 1980

Danville Correctional Center
Danville
Michael V. Neal, Warden,
Medium security
Capacity: 900
Established in 1985

Dixon Correctional Center
Dixon
Richard Gramley, Warden
Medium security
Capacity: 845
Established in 1983

Dwight Correctional Center
Dwight
Jane E. Huch, Warden
Maximum-medium-minimum security
Capacity: 596
Established in 1930

East Moline Correctional Center
East Moline
Odie Washingtom, Warden
Minimum security
Capacity: 736
Established in 1980

Graham Correctional Center
Hillsboro
Alethea T. Camp, Warden
Medium security
Capacity: 1,008
Established in 1980

Hill Correctional Center
Galesburg
Jerry D. Gilmore, Warden
Medium security
Capacity: 320
Established in 1986

Jacksonville Correctional Center
Jacksonville
Kenneth McGinnis, Warden
Minimum security
Capacity: 499
Established in 1984

Joliet Correctional Center
Joliet
J.W. Fairman, Warden
Maximum security
Capacity: 1,201
Established in 1860

Lincoln Correctional Center
Lincoln
Kenneth P. Dobucki, Warden
Minimum security
Capacity: 549
Established in 1984

Logan Correctional Center
Lincoln
Stephen McEvers, Warden
Medium security
Capacity: 1,037
Established in 1977

Menard Correctional Center
Menard
James A. Buch, Warden
Maximum security
Capacity: 2,411
Established in 1878

Menard Psychiatric Center
Menard
Dr. Mary Flannigan, Administrator
Capacity: 365
Established in 1970

Pontiac Correctional Center
Pontiac
Howard Peters III, Warden
Maximum security
Capacity: 1,722
Established in 1871

Shawnee Correctional Center
Vienna
James Thieret, Warden
Medium security
Capacity: 1,046
Established in 1984

Sheridan Correctional Center
Sheridan
James A. Chrans, Warden
Medium security
Capacity: 904
Established in 1973

Stateville Correctional Center
Joliet
Michael O'Leary, Warden
Maximum security
Capacity: 1,920
Established in 1925

Vandalia Correctional Center
Vandalia
Alfred E. Buscher, Warden
Minimum security
Capacity: 858
Established in 1921

Vienna Correctional Center
Vienna
Larry Mizell, Warden
Minimum security
Capacity: 871
Established in 1965

INDIANA:

Branchville Training Center
Tell City
Paul W. Kranning, Superintendent
Medium security
Capacity: 476
Established in 1982

Indiana State Farm
Greencastle
H. Gene Combs, Superintendent
Medium security
Capacity: 1,650
Established in 1914

Indiana State Prison
Michigan City
Jack Duckworth, Superintendent
Maximum-medium security
Capacity: 1,615
Established in 1859

Indiana State Reformatory
Pendleton
Edward L. Cohn, Superintendent
Maximum-medium security
Capacity: 1,615
Established in 1923

Indiana Women's Prison
Indianapolis
Clarence E. Trigg, Superintendent
Maximum security
Capacity: 144
Established in 1973

Indiana Youth Center
Plainfield
Thomas Richards, Superintendent
Medium security
Capacity: 864
Established in 1965

Reception Diagnostic Center
Plainfield
Donald L. Hudkins, Director
Maximum security
Capacity: 204
Established in 1971

Westville Correctional Center
Westville
G. Michael Broglin, Superintendent
Maximum-medium security
Capacity: 1,932
Established in 1977

IOWA:

Correctional Treatment Unit
Clarinda
Mark Lund, Superintendent
Medium security
Capacity: 120
Established in 1980

Iowa Correctional Institution for Women
Mitchellville
Barbara Olk, Superintendent
Medium-minimum security
Capacity: 100
Established in 1982

Iowa Medical and Classification Center
Oakdale
Russell E. Rogerson, Superintendent
Medium security
Capacity: 300
Establisehd in 1968

Iowa State Penitentiary
Fort Madison
Crispus Nix, Warden
Maximum-medium-minimum security
Capacity: 780
Established in 1839

Medium Security Unit
Mt. Pleasant
David Scurr, Superintendent
Medium security
Capacity: 528
Established in 1977

North Central Correctional Facility
Rockwell City
John F. Ault II, Superintendent
Medium-minimum security
Capacity: 100
Established in 1982

Riverview Release Center
Newton
John Mathas, Superintendent
Minimum security

Capacity: 96
Established in 1965
The Men's Reformatory
Anamosa
John Thalacker, Warden
Minimum security
Capacity: 840
Established in 1872

KANSAS:

El Dorado Honor Camp
El Dorado
Harold Samuels, Director
Minimum security
Capacity: 97
Established inn 1982
Ellsworth Correctional Facility
Ellsworth
Michael Nelson, Director
Medium-minimum security
Capacity: 461
Established in 1988
Forbes Correctional Facility
Topeka
Norman Bacon, Director
Minimum security
Capacity: 76
Established in 1972
Hutchinson Correctional Work Facility
Hutchinson
Gary Rayl, Director
Medium-minimum security
Capacity: 380
Established in 1988
Hutchinson Work Release Center
Hutchinson
Gail Voss, Supervisor
Minimum security
Capacity: 19
Established in 1977
Kansas Correctional Institution at Lansing
Lansing
Barbara Carter, Director
Maximum-medium-minimum security
Capacity: 159
Established in 1917
Kansas Correctional-Vocational Training Center
Topeka
George W. Thompson, Director
Minimum security
Capacity: 173
Established in 1974
Kansas Industrial Reformatory
Hutchinson
Robert D. Hannigan, Director
Maximum-medium-minimum security
Capacity: 897
Established in 1895
Kansas State Penitentiary
Lansing
Steven J. Davies, Director
Maximum-medium-minimum security
Capacity: 1,428
Established in 1864
Norton State Correctional Facility
Norton
Louis E. Bruce, Director
Minimum security
Capacity: 228
Established in 1987
Osawatomie State Correctional Facility
Osawatomie
Thomas Vohs, Director
Minimum security
Capacity: 76
Established in 1987
State Reception and Diagnostic Center
Topeka
Leo Taylor, Director
Maximum security
Capacity: 206
Established in 1962
Topeka Correctional Facility
Topeka
Robert Harrison, Director
Minimum security
Capacity: 105
Established in 1984
Toronto Honor Camp
Toronto
Harold Samuels, Director
Minimum security
Capacity: 67
Established in 1963
Wichita Work Release Center
Wichita
Elizabeth Gillespie, Director
Minimum security
Capacity: 95
Established in 1976
Winfield Correctional Facility
Winfield
Gordon Hetzel, Director
Minimum security
Capacity: 276
Established in 1984

KENTUCKY:

Bell County Forestry Camp
Pineville,
Lloyd Fletcher, Warden
Minimum security
Capacity: 200
Established in 1988
Blackburn Correctional Complex
Lexington
Ralph Evitts, Warden
Minimum security
Capacity: 390
Established in 1972
Frankfort Career Development Center
Frankfort
Paul Kavanaugh, Acting Warden
Minimum security
Capactiy: 180
Established in 1976
Kentucky Correctional Institution for Women
Pewee Valley
Betty Kassulke, Warden
Medium security
Capacity: 202
Established in 1938
Kentucky State Penitentiary
Eddyville
Bill Seabold, Warden
Maximum security
Capacity: 803
Established in 1888
Kentucky State Reformatory
LaGrange
Al Parke, Warden
Medium security
Capacity: 1,429
Established in 1939
Luther Luckett Correctional Complex
LaGrange
Stephen T. Smith, Warden
Capacity: 623
Established in 1980
Northpoint Training Center
Burgin
Dewey Sowders, Warden
Medium security
Capacity: 822
Established in 1983
Roederer Farm Center
LaGrange
Mike O'Dea, Warden
Medium-minimum security
Capacity: 247
Established in 1976
Western Kentucky Farm Center
Eddyville
John W. Duncan, Warden
Minimum security
Capacity: 330
Established in 1976

LOUISIANA:

Avoyelles Correctional Center
Cottenport
Medium security
Capacity: 600
Established in 1989
Dixon Correctional Institute
Jackson
Burl Cain, Warden
Medium security
Capacity: 873
Established in 1976
Hunt Correctional Center
St. Gabriel
John P. Whitley, Warden
Maximum-medium-minimum security
Capacity: 1,843
Established in 1979
Louisiana Correctional and Industrial School
DeQuincy
Steve Radar, Warden
Medium security
Capacity: 928
Established in 1958
Louisiana Correctional Institute for Women
St. Gabriel
Johnnie Jones, Warden
Maximum-medium-minimum security
Capacity: 414
Established in 1961
Louisiana State Penitentiary
Angola
Hilton Butler, Warden
Maximum security
Capacity: 4,747
Established in 1866
State Police Barracks
Baton Rouge
Minimum security
Capacity: 170
Established in 1988
Wade Correctional Center
Homer
Richard Stalder, Warden
Medium security
Capacity: 1,181
Established in 1980
Washington Correctional Institute
Angie
J.F. "Jack" Donnelly, Warden
Medium security
Capacity: 1,120
Established in 1983
Winn Correctional Center
Winnfield
Medium security
Capacity: 600
Established in 1989
Work Training Facility - North
Pineville
Larry Jeane, Warden
Minimum security
Capacity: 450
Established in 1970
Work Training Facility - South
New Orleans
Frank Jobert, Warden
Minimum security
Capacity: 300
Established in 1976

MAINE:

Charleston Correctional Facility
Charleston
Jeffrey Merrill, Director
Minimum security
Capacity: 93
Established in 1980
Downeast Correctional Facility
Bucks Harbor
C. Mark Caton, Director
Medium-minimum security
Capacity: 96
Established in 1985
Maine Correctional Center
Windham
James Clemons, Superintendent
Medium-minimum security
Capacity: 208
Established in 1919
Maine State Prison

Thomaston
Martin A. Magnusson, Warden
Maximum-medium security
Capacity: 400
Established in 1842

Maine Youth Center
South Portland
Richard J. Wyse, Superintendent
Minimum security
Capacity: 250
Established in 1853

MARYLAND:

Baltimore City Correctional Center
Baltimore
Pat Conroy, Unit Manager
Minimum security
Capacity: 250
Established in 1984

Baltimore Pre-Release Unit
Baltimore
George W. Redd, Unit Manager
Capacity: 166

Brockbridge Correctional Facility
Jessup
William Filbert, Asst. Warden
Medium-minimum security
Capacity: 512

Central Laundry Correctional Facility
Sykesville
Marsha Maloff, Unit Manager
Minimum security
Capacity: 192

Eastern Correctional Institution
Westover
Medium security
Capacity: 1,440
Established in 1987

Eastern Pre-Release Unit
Church Hill
Earl Runde, Unit Manager
Capacity: 135

Jessup Pre-Release Unit
Jessup
Sandra Thacker, Unit Manager
Minimum security
Capacity: 166

Maryland Correctional Adjustment Center
Baltimore
Sewall Smith, Asst. Warden
Maximum security
Capacity: 300
Established in 1988

Maryland Correctional Institution
Hagerstown
John N. Brown, Warden
Medium security
Capacity: 748
Established in 1931

Maryland Correctional Institution
Jessup
Medium security
Capacity: 512
Established in 1981

Maryland Correctional Institution for Women
Jessup
Sharon Johnson, Warden
Maximum-medium-minimum security
Capacity: 258
Established in 1939

Maryland Correctional Pre-Release System
Jessup
John P. Wilt, Warden
Medium-minimum security
Capacity: 1,884

Maryland Correctional Training Center
Hagerstown
Lloyd L. Waters, Warden
Medium security
Capacity: 1,617
Established in 1966

Maryland House of Correction
Jessup
Terrie Chavis, Warden
Medium-minimum security
Capacity: 1,409
Established in 1878

Maryland Penitentiary
Baltimore
James N. Rollins, Warden
Maximum security
Capacity: 1,053
Established in 1811

Poplar Hill Pre-Release Unit
Quantico
George Kaloroumakis, Unit Manager
Capacity: 135

Pre-Release Unit for Women
Baltimore
Barbara Shaw, Unit Manager
Capacity: 31

Reception Diagnostic and Classification Center
Baltimore
Merry L. Coplin, Warden
Maximum security
Capacity: 400
Established in 1981

Roxbury Correctional Institution
Hagerstown
Jon P. Galley, Warden
Medium security
Capacity: 720
Established in 1983

Southern Maryland Pre-Releases Unit
Charlotte Hall
Major Raymond Grimes, Unit Manager
Capacity: 135

MASSACHUSETTS:

Bay State Correctional Center
Norfolk
George Grigas, Superintendent
Minimum security
Capacity: 72
Established in 1977

Boston Pre-Release Center
Dorchester
Abu Hanif Abdul Khallaq, Superintendent
Minimum security
Capacity: 55
Established in 1972

Bridgewater State Hospital
Bridgewater
Gerald Boyle, Superintendent
Capacity: 337
Established in 1855

Lancaster Pre-Release
Lancaster
Paul Dickaut, Superintendent
Minimum security
Capacity: 95
Established in 1976

Massachusetts Correctional Institution
Bridgewater
John Noonan, Superintendent
Capacity: 955
Established in 1855

Massachusetts Correctional Institution
Framingham
Barbara Young, Superintendent
Minimum security
Capacity: 139
Established in 1877

Massachusetts Correctional Institution
Norfolk
Norman Butler, Superintendent
Medium security
Capacity: 799
Established in 1931

Massachusetts Correctional Institution
Orange
Jon Cooke, Superintendent
Minimum security
Capacity: 50
Established in 1964

Massachusetts Correctional Institution
South Carver
John Tucker, Superintendent
Minimum security
Capacity: 51
Established in 1952

Massachusetts Correctional Institution
South Walpole
Michael Maloney, Superintendent
Maximum security
Capacity: 562
Established in 1956

Massachusetts Correctional Institution
West Concord
Norman Carver, Superintendent
Medium security
Capacity: 255
Established in 1878

Medfield Prison Project
Medfield
Alicia Ryan, Superintendent,
Minimum security
Capacity: 36
Established in 1976

Norfolk Pre-Release Center
South Walpole
Judi Cyr, Superintendent
Minimum security
Capacity: 26
Established in 1975

North Central Correctional Institution
Gardner
James Bender, Superintendent
Medium security
Capacity: 166
Established in 1981

Northeastern Correctional Center
West Concord
Paul Raikey, Superintendent
Minimum security
Capacity: 152
Established in 1977

Old Colony Correctional Center
Bridgewater
Joseph Ponte, Superintendent
Medium security
Capacity: 400
Established in 1987

OUI-Longwood
Boston
David MacDonald, Superintendent
Capacity: 125
Established in 1985

Park Drive Pre-Release Center
Boston
Timothy App, Superintendent
Minimum security
Capacity: 50
Established in 1977

Shirley Pre-Release Center
Shirley
Richard Grelotti, Superintendent
Minimum security
Capacity: 250
Established in 1972

South Middlesex Pre-Release Center
Framingham
Ernest Vandergriff, Superintendent
Minimum security
Capacity: 75
Established in 1976

Southeastern Correctional Center
Bridgewater
Ron Amaral, Superintendent
Medium security
Capacity: 179
Established in 1977

MICHIGAN:

Cassidy Lake Technical School
Chelsea
Minimum security
Capacity: 266
Established in 1944

Corrections Camp Program
Grass Lake
William F. Grant, Warden
Minimum security
Capacity: 1,104
Established in 1948

Florence Crane Women's Facility
Coldwater
Carol Howes, Warden
Medium security
Capacity: 300

Established in 1985
G. Robert Cotton Correctional Facility
Jackson
Elton Scott, Warden
Medium security
Capacity: 612
Established in 1985
Huran Valley Men's Facility
Ypsilanti
Gene Borgert, Warden
Maximum security
Capacity: 411
Established in 1981
Huran Valley Women's Facility
Ypsilanti
Tekla Miller, Warden
Maximum-medium security
Capacity: 262
Established in 1977
Ionia Temporary Facility
Ionia
Medium security
Capacity: 480
Established in 1985
Kinross Correctional Facility
Kincheloe
Robert LeCureaux, Warden
Medium security
Capacity: 1,108
Established in 1978
Lakeland Correctional Facility
Coldwater
Robert Redman, Warden
Medium security
Capacity: 500
Established in 1985
Michigan Dunes Correctional Facility
Holland
Martin Makel, Warden
Medium security
Capacity: 480
Established in 1978
Michigan Reformatory
Ionia
Pam Withrow, Warden
Maximum-medium security
Capacity: 1,232
Established in 1877
Michigan Training Unit
Ionia
James Yarborough, Warden
Capacity: 1,110
Established in 1985
Muskegon Correctional Faciltiy
Muskegon
H. Gary Wells, Warden
Medium security
Capacity: 669
Established in 1974
Phoenix Correctional Facility
Plymouth
Emmett R. Baylor Jr., Warden
Medium security
Capacity: 311
Established in 1980
Reception and Guidance Center
Jackson
John Prelesnik, Warden
Capacity: 540
Established in 1956
Reception and Guidance Center - Riverside
Ionia
Robert J. Mayer, Administrator
Capacity: 94
Established in 1979
Riverside Correctional Facility
Ionia
Maximum-medium security
Capacity: 512
Established in 1977
Scott Correctional Facility
Plymouth
James Stegall, Acting Warden
Maximum-medium-minimum security
Capacity: 528
Established in 1986
State House of Correction and Branch Prison
Marquette
Theodore Koehler, Warden
Maximum security
Capacity: 749
Established in 1889
State Prison of Southern Michigan
Jackson
John Jabe, Warden
Maximum-medium-minimum security
Capacity: 4,729
Established in 1839
Western Wayne Correctional Facility
Plymouth
Emmett Baylor, Warden
Medium security
Capacity: 650
Established in 1985

MINNESOTA:

Minnesota Correctional Facility - Lino Lakes
Lino Lakes
Fred A. Holbeck, Superintendent
Medium-minimum security
Capacity: 202
Established in 1963
Minnesota Correctional Facility - Oak Park Heights
Stillwater
Frank W. Wood, Warden
Maximum security
Capacity: 400
Established in 1982
Minnesota Correctional Facility - Red Wing
Red Wing
Gerald O'Rourke, Superintendent
Minimum security
Capacity: 170
Established in 1889
Minnesota Correctional Facility - Sauk Centre
Sauk Centre
Dale Ulrich, Superintendent
Minimum security
Capacity: 70
Established in 1912
Minnesota Correctional Facility - Shakopee
Shakopee
D. Jacqueline Fleming, Superintendent
Maximum-medium-minimum security
Capacity: 132
Established in 1986
Minnesota Correctional Facility - St. Cloud
St. Cloud
W.F. McRae, Superintendent
Maximum security
Capacity: 700
Established in 1889
Minnesota Correctional Facility - Stillwater
Stillwater
Robert A. Erickson, Warden
Maximum-minimum security
Capacity: 1,250
Established in 1913
Thistledew Camp
Togo
Derwood J. Lund, Superintendent
Minimum security
Capacity: 60
Established in 1956
Willow River Camp
Willow River
Gothriel "Fred" LaFleur, Superintendent
Minimum security
Capacity: 100
Established in 1951

MISSISSIPPI:

Mississippi State Penitentiary
Parchman
Steve Puckett, Superintendent
Maximum-medium-minimum security
Capacity: 4,716
Established in 1900
Rankin County Correctional Facility
Pearl
Joseph Cooke, Superintendent
Maximum-medium-minimum security
Capacity: 562
Established in 1986

MISSOURI:

Algoa Correctional Center
Jefferson City
Carl White, Superintendent
Medium security
Capacity: 1,150
Established in 1932
Boonville Correctional Center
Boonville
David C. Miller, Superintendent
Minimum security
Capacity: 620
Established in 1983
Camp Hawthorne
Kaiser
Ron Schmitz, Unit Manager
Minimum security
Capacity: 40
Established in 1982
Central Missouri Correctional Center
Jefferson City
Gerald Higgins, Superintendent
Medium-minimum security
Capacity: 1,200
Established in 1938
Chillicothe Correctional Center
Chillicothe
Donald M. Camper, Superintendent
Maximum-medium-minimum security
Capacity: 430
Established in 1981
Farmington Correctional Center
Farmington
Denis D. Dowd, Superintendent
Medium security
Capacity: 1,750
Established in 1986
Missouri Eastern Correctional Center
Pacific
Myrna Trickey, Superintendent
Medium security
Capacity: 1,000
Established in 1981
Missouri State Penitentiary for Men
Jefferson City
William Armontrout, Warden
Maximum security
Capacity: 2,100
Established in 1835
Missouri Training Center for Men
Moberly
Jimmie M. Jones, Superintendent
Medium security
Capacity: 1,800
Established in 1963
Ozark Correctional Center
Fordland
James Purkett, Superintendent
Minimum security
Capacity: 408
Established in 1961
Potosi Correctional Center
Mineral Point
Paul Delo, Superintendent
Maximum security
Capacity: 500
Established in 1989
Renz Correctional Center
Cedar City
William R. Turner, Superintendent
Minimum security
Capacity: 400
Established in 1961
State Correctional Pre-Release Center
Tipton
Paul Caspari, Superintendent
Minimum security
Capacity: 275
Established in 1960
Western Missouri Correctional Center
Cameron
Mike Kemna, Superintendent
Medium security
Capacity: 1,900
Established in 1989

MONTANA:

Montana State Prison
Deer Lodge
Jack McCormick, Warden
Maximum-medium-minimum security
Capacity: 744
Established in 1869

Swan River Forest Camp
Swan Lake
Gerald E. Underwood, Superintendent
Minimum security
Capacity: 54
Established in 1968

Women's Correctional Center
Warm Springs
Steven MacAskill, Director
Maximum-medium-minimum security
Capacity: 40
Established in 1982

NEBRASKA:

Hastings Correctional Center
Hastings
Mike Kenney, Superintendent
Minimum security
Capacity: 160
Established in 1987

Lincoln Correctional Center and Evaluation Unit
Lincoln
John J. Dahm, Warden
Maximum-medium-minimum security
Capacity: 468
Established in 1979

Nebraska Center for Women
York
Linda Leonard, Asst. Superintendent
Maximum-medium-minimum security
Capacity: 84
Established in 1920

Nebraska State Penitentiary
Lincoln
Harold W. Clarke, Warden
Maximum-medium security
Capacity: 500
Established in 1869

Omaha Correctional Center
Omaha
Karen Shortridge, Superintendent
Minimum security
Capacity: 240
Established in 1984

Omaha Correctional Center Work Release Unit
Omaha
Karen Shortridge, Superintendent
Maximum-medium security
Capacity: 219
Established in 1985

NEVADA:

Nevada State Prison
Carson City
Harold Whitley, Warden
Maximum-medium security
Capacity: 658
Established in 1861

Nevada Women's Correctional Center
Carson City
Margaret Knapp, Warden
Maximum-medium-minimum security
Capacity: 227
Established in 1964

Northern Nevada Correctional Center
Carson City
Brenda Burns, Warden
Medium security
Capacity: 793
Established in 1964

Northern Nevada Restitution Center
Reno
Gerald Stephan, Manager
Capacity: 60
Established in 1979

Reno Correctional Facility
Reno
Pat Anderson, Captain
Maximum-medium security
Capacity: 96
Established in 1988

Southern Desert Correctional Center
Indian Springs
George Deeds, Warden
Medium security
Capacity: 1,306
Established in 1982

Southern Nevada Correctional Center
Jean
Walt Luster, Warden
Medium security
Capacity: 519
Established in 1978

Southern Nevada Restitution Center
Las Vegas
Florozeen Gray, Manager
Capacity: 60
Established in 1980

NEW HAMPSHIRE:

Concord Community Corrections Center
Concord
Bryant Frost, Unit Manager
Minimum security
Capacity: 24
Established in 1973

Manchester Community Corrections Center
Manchester
Lee Martin, Unit Manager
Minimum security
Capacity: 45
Established in 1979

New Hampshire State Prison Complex
Concord
Michael Cunningham, Warden
Maximum-medium-minimum security
Capacity: 774
Established in 1880

New Hampshire State Prison-Women's Facility
Goffstown
Edda Cantor, Unit Manager
Maximum-medium security
Capacity: 60
Established in 1988

Secure Psychiatric Unit
Concord
Dr. David E. Rosengard, Director
Maximum security
Capacity: 60
Established in 1986

NEW JERSEY:

Albert C. Wagner Youth Correctional Facility
Bordentown
Donald E. Lewis, Superintendent
Medium security
Established in 1937

Adult Diagnostic and Treatment Center
Avenel
Sally Scheidementel, Superintendent
Medium-minimum security
Capacity: 180
Established in 1976

Bayside State Prison
Leesburg
E. Calvin Neubert, Superintendent
Minimum security
Established in 1970

East Jersey State Prison
Rahway
John J. Rafferty, Superintendent
Medium security
Established in 1901

Garden State Reception and Youth Correctional Facility
Yardville
Donald D. Zelinski, Administrator
Medium security
Established in 1968

Edna Mahan Correctional Facility for Women
Clinton
Robert R. Walton, Superintendent
Medium-minimum security
Established in 1913

Mid-State Correctional Facility
Wrightstown
Robert Barker, Superintendent
Medium security
Capacity: 500
Established in 1982

Mountainview Youth Correctional Facility
Annandale
Stephen M. Domovich, Superintendent
Minimum security
Established in 1929

New Jersey State Prison
Trenton
Howard L. Beyer, Administrator
Maximum security
Established in 1798

Northern State Prison
Newark
Robert E. Stephens, Administrator
Medium security
Capacity: 1,000
Established in 1987

Riverfront Correctional Facility
Camden
Thomas Hundley, Superintendent
Medium security
Capacity: 400
Established in 1985

Southern State 1 & 2
Delmont
Robert D. Edmiston, Superintendent
Medium security
Capacity: 1,008
Established in 1983

NEW MEXICO:

Camp Sierra Blanca
Ft. Stanton
Bob Marrs, Warden
Minimum security
Capacity: 65
Established in 1976

Central NM Correctional Facility
Los Lunas
Dareld L. Kerby, Warden
Medium-minimum security
Capacity: 480
Established in 1980

Los Lunas Correctional Center
Los Lunas
Ken Rommel, Warden
Minimum security
Capacity: 230
Established in 1940

Penitentiary of New Mexico
Santa Fe
Robert Tansy, Warden
Maximum-medium-minimum security
Capacity: 419
Established in 1884

Penitentiary of New Mexico - North
Santa Fe
Robert Tansy, Warden
Maximum security
Capacity: 288
Established in 1985

Penitentiary of New Mexico - South
Santa Fe
Robert Tansy, Warden
Minimum security
Capacity: 288
Established in 1987

Roswell Correctional Center
Hagerman
Jan Thomas, Warden
Minimum security
Capacity: 120
Established in 1978

Southern New Mexico Correction Facility
Las Cruces
Donald Dorsey, Warden
Medium security
Capacity: 480
Established in 1983

Western New Mexico Correctional Facility

Grants
John Shanks, Warden
Maximum-medium-minimum security
Capacity: 278
Established in 1984

NEW YORK:

Adirondack Correctional Facility
Raybrook
James Racette, Superintendent
Medium security
Capacity: 609
Established in 1972

Albion Correctional Facility
Albion
Sunny Schriver, Superintendent
Minimum security
Capacity: 523
Established in 1893

Altona Correctional Facility
Altona
William Donahue, Superintendent
Medium security
Capacity: 452
Established in 1983

Arthur Kill Correctional Facility
Staten Island
Raymond Bara, Superintendent
Medium security
Capacity: 776
Established in 1976

Attica Correctional Facility
Attica
Walter Kelley, Superintendent
Maximum security
Capacity: 2,135
Established in 1931

Auburn Correctional Facility
Auburn
Robert J. Henderson, Superintendent
Maximum security
Capacity: 1,727
Established in 1817

Bedford Hills Correctional Facility
Bedford Hills
Elaine Lord, Superintendent
Maximum security
Capacity: 787
Established in 1933

Cape Vincent Correctional Facility
Cape Vincent.
John O'Keefe
Superintendent,

Clinton Correctional Facility
Dannemora
Eugene LeFevre, Superintendent
Maximum security
Capacity: 2,815
Established in 1945

Collins Correctional Facility
Helmuth
Charles James, Superintendent
Medium security
Capacity: 1,103
Established in 1981

Coxsackie Correctional Facility
West Coxsackie
John Twomey, Superintendent
Maximum security
Capacity: 968
Established in 1935

Downstate Correctional Facility
Fishkill
Stephen Dalsheim, Superintendent
Maximum-medium security
Capacity: 1,162
Established in 1979

Eastern Correctional Facility
Napanoch
Robert Hoke, Superintendent
Maximum-medium security
Capacity: 987
Established in 1900

Elmira Correctional Facility
Elmira
Ronald Miles, Superintendent
Maximum security
Capacity: 1,765
Established in 1876

Fishkill Correctional Facility
Beacon
Dean Riley, Superintendent
Medium security
Capacity: 1,767
Established in 1982

Franklin Correctional Facility
Malone
Peter J. Lacy, Superintendent
Capacity: 798
Established in 1986

Great Meadow Correctional Faciltity
Comstock
Arthur Leonardo, Superintendent
Maximum-medium security
Capacity: 1,560
Established in 1911

Green Correctional Facility
Coxsackie
David Harris, Superintendent
Medium security
Capacity: 781
Established in 1984

Green Haven Correctional Facility
Stormville
Charles Scully, Superintendent
Maximum-medium security
Capacity: 2,052
Established in 1949

Groveland Correctional Facility
Sonyea
Bert Ross, Superintendent
Medium security
Capacity: 843
Established in 1982

Hudson Correctional Facility
Hudson
Richard VanZandt, Superintendent
Medium security
Capacity: 515
Established in 1976

Lyon Mountain Correctional Facility
Lyon Mountain
Ismael Colon, Superintendent
Minimum security
Capacity: 151
Established in 1984

Mid-Orange Correctional Facility
Warwick
Joseph Snow, Superintendent
Medium security
Capacity: 778
Established in 1977

Mid-State Correctional Facility
Marcy
Wayne Barkley, Superintendent
Medium security
Capacity: 1,405
Established in 1983

Mt. McGregor Correctional Facility
Wilton
Joseph Kennedy, Superintendent
Medium-minimum security
Capacity: 502
Established in 1976

Ogdensburg Correctional Facility
Ogdensburg
Francis Latourelle, Superintendent
Medium security
Capacity: 580
Estasblished in 1982

Oneida Correctional Facility
Romel
Edward Reynolds, Superintendent
Capacity: 836
Established in 1988

Orleans Correctional Facility
Albion
Sally Johnson, Superintendent
Medium security
Capacity: 814
Established in 1984

Otisville Correctional Facility
Otisville
David Hood, Superintendent
Medium security
Capacity: 624
Established in 1977

Queensboro Correctional Facility
Long Island City
Kenneth Dunham, Superintendent
Capacity: 466
Established in 1977

Shawangunk Correctional Facility
Wallkill
Louis F. Mann, Superintendent
Maximum security
Capacity: 544
Established in 1985

Sing Sing Correctional Facility
Ossining
James Sullivan, Superintendent
Maximum-medium security
Capacity: 1,760
Established in 1825

Sullivan Correctional Facility
Fallsburg
Robert Kuhlmann, Superintendent
Maximum security
Capacity: 557
Established in 1985

Taconic Correctional Facility
Bedford Hills
Charles Hernandez, Superintendent
Medium security
Capacity: 429
Established in 1901

Wallkill Correctional Facility
Wallkill
William Kirk, Superintendent
Medium security
Capacity: 561
Established in 1932

Washington Correctional Facility
Comstock
Everett Jones, Superintendent
Medium security
Capacity: 998
Established in 1985

Watertown Correctional Facility
Watertown
Andrew Peters, Superintendent
Medium security
Capacity: 651
Established in 1982

Wende Correctional Facility
Alden
Dominic J. Mantello, Superintendent
Maximum security
Capacity: 784
Established in 1983

Woodbourne Correctional Facility
Woodbourne
Carl Berry, Superintendent
Medium security
Capacity: 893
Established in 1932

Wyoming Correctional Facility
Attica
Frederick Richardson, Superintendent
Medium security
Capacity: 882
Established in 1984

NORTH CAROLINA:

Alamance Correctional Center
Graham
Larry L. Tingen, Superintendent
Minimum security
Capacity: 142
Established in 1930s

Alexander Correctional Center
Taylorsville
W.F. Watkins, Superintendent
Medium security
Capacity: 100
Established in 1936

Anson Correctional Center
Polkton
Benjamin Brooks, Superintendent
Minimum security
Capacity: 122
Established in 1937

Avery Correctional Center
Newland
Thomas Laws, Superintendent
Medium security
Capacity: 124
Established in 1936

Black Mountain Advancement Center for Women
Black Mountain
Michele Reichert, Superintendent
Minimum security
Capacity: 50
Established in 1986

Bladen Correctional Center
Elizabethtown
C.L. Sparkman, Superintendent
Minimum security
Capacity: 108
Established in 1939

Buncombe Correctional Center
Asheville
Sam W. Reed, Superintendent
Minimum security
Capacity: 104
Established in 1988

Cabarrus Correctional Center
Mt. Pleasant
A.J. Threatt, Superintendent
Minimum security
Capacity: 198
Established in 1929

Caswell Correctional Center
Yanceyville
P.M. Rogers, Superintendent
Medium security
Capacity: 124
Established in 1930s

Caldwell Correctional Center
Hudson
Grant Spicer, Superintendent
Minimum security
Capacity: 142
Established in 1936

Caledonia Correctional Institution
Tillery
Randy Lee, Superintendent
Maximum-medium security
Capacity: 592
Established in 1892

Carteret Correctional Center
Newport
C.L. Meeks, Superintendent
Minimum security
Capacity: 208
Established in 1940

Catawba Correctional Center
Newton
Boyce C. Lambert, Superintendent
Minimum security
Capacity: 220
Established in 1929

Central Prison
Raleigh
Gary T. Dixon, Warden
Maximum-medium security
Capacity: 925
Established in 1884

Charlotte Correctional Center
Charlotte
J. Baxter Bridges, Superintendent
Minimum security
Capacity: 174
Established in 1930

Cleveland Correctional Center
Shelby
R.S. Whitaker, Superintendent
Medium security
Capacity: 128
Established in 1937

Columbus Correctional Center
Brunswick
William R. Barker, Superintendent
Medium security
Capacity: 156
Established in 1939

Craggy Correctional Center
Asheville
Sherrill G. Allen, Superintendent
Medium security
Capacity: 119
Established in 1936

Currituck Correctional Center
Maple
L.E. Cherry, Superintendent
Medium security
Capacity: 158
Established in 1949

Davidson Correctional Center
Lexington
David Murphy, Superintendent
Minimum security
Capacity: 184
Established in 1939

Davie Correctional Center
Mocksville
Wayne Moore, Superintendent
Medium security
Capacity: 128
Established in 1939

Duplin Correctional Center
Kenansville
Dallas C. Weaver, Superintendent
Minimum security
Capacity: 146
Established in 1939

Durham Correctional Center
Durham
G.H. Newkirk, Superintendent
Minimum security
Capacity: 204
Established in 1939

Eastern Correctional Institution
Maury
Talmadge Barnett, Superintendent
Maximum-medium security
Capacity: 480
Established in 1983

Forsyth Correctional Center
Winston-Salem
Zeb S. Crews, Superintendent
Minimum security
Capacity: 159
Established in 1939

Fountain Correctional Center for Women
Rocky Mount
W. Keith Hester, Superintendent
Minimum security
Capacity: 200
Established in 1984

Franklin Correctional Center
Bunn
Raymond Hayes, Superintendent
Medium security
Capacity: 160
Established in 1939

Gaston Correctional Center
Dallas
C.A. Meares, Superintendent
Minimum security
Capacity: 200
Established in 1930

Gates Correctional Center
Gatesville
Van Barnes, Superintendent
Minimum security
Capacity: 108
Established in 1939

Goldsboro Correctional Center
Goldsboro
E.S. Banks, Superintendent
Minimum security
Capacity: 100
Established in 1955

Granville Correctional Center
Oxford
T.C. Smiley, Superintendent
Minimum security
Capacity: 60
Established in 1931

Greene Correctional Center
Maury
Joseph Szilagyi, Superintendent
Minimum security
Capacity: 104
Established in 1939

Guilford Correctional Center
McLeansville
Tommy Lee, Superintendent
Minimum security
Capacity: 220
Established in 1950

Halifax Correctional Center
Halifax
Lonnie Edwards, Superintendent
Minimum security
Capacity: 160
Established in 1925

Harnett Correctional Institution
Lillington
L.V. Stephenson, Superintendent
Medium security
Capacity: 600
Established in 1936

Haywood Correctional Center
Hazelwood
W.H. Caldwell, Superintendent
Minimum security
Capacity: 117
Established in 1936

Henderson Correctional Center
Hendersonville
J.E. Baine, Superintendent
Minimum security
Capacity: 142
Established in 1937

Iredell Correctional Center
Statesville
Jerry L. Moore, Superintendent
Medium security
Capacity: 120
Established in 1939

Johnston Correctional Center
Smithfield
James Thornton, Superintendent
Medium security
Capacity: 208
Established in 1930

Lincoln Correctional Center
Lincolnton
J.G. Pickelsimer, Superintendent
Medium security
Capacity: 145
Established in 1930

McCain Correctional Hospital
McCain
Herbert A. Rosefield, Superintendent
Minimum security
Capacity: 300
Established in 1983

McCain Correctional Institution
McCain
J.H. Griffin, Superintendent
Medium security
Capacity: 526
Established in 1923

McDowell Correctional Center
Marion
Ken Setzer, Superintendent
Medium security
Capacity: 124
Established in 1931

Martin Correctional Center
Williamston
A. Hathaway III, Superintendent
Minimum security
Capacity: 84
Established in 1932

Mecklenburg Correctional Center
Huntersville
L.H. Cashion, Superintendent
Minimum security
Capacity: 138
Established in 1930

Montgomery Correctional Center
Troy
D.G. Luther, Superintendent
Minimum security
Capacity: 176
Established in 1939

Moore Correctional Center
Carthage
Waylon B. Collins, Superintendent
Medium security
Capacity: 92

Established in 1939
Nash Correctional Center
Nashville
J.K. Edwards, Superintendent
Minimum security
Capacity: 92
Established in 1939
New Hanover Correctional Center
Wilmington
Sam Stallings, Superintendent
Minimum security
Capacity: 262
Established in 1926
North Carolina Correctional Center for Women
Raleigh
Fay D. Lassiter, Superintendent
Maximum-medium-minimum security
Capacity: 544
Established in 1934
Odom Correctional Institution
Jackson
Harry Allsbrook, Superintendent
Maximum-medium security
Capacity: 550
Established in 1956
Orange Correctional Center
Hillsborough
Mike Thumm, Superintendent
Minimum security
Capacity: 164
Established in 1930
Pender Correctional Center
Burgaw
J.V. Turlington, Superintendent
Medium security
Capacity: 126
Established in 1937
Person Correctional Center
Roxboro
A.K. Pruitt, Superintendent
Minimum security
Capacity: 76
Established in 1938
Piedmont Correctional Institution
Salisbury
R.M. Jarvis, Superintendent
Maximum-medium security
Capacity: 480
Established in 1980
Raleigh Correctional Center for Women
Raleigh
Joy Barefoot, Superintendent
Minimum security
Capacity: 100
Established in 1988
Randolph Correctional Center
Asheboro
J.W. Iddings, Superintendent
Medium security
Capacity: 150
Established in 1930s
Richmond Correctional Center
Rockingham
R.D. Trask, Superintendent
Minimum security
Capacity: 52
Established in 1939
Robeson Correctional Center
Lumberton
Joseph Brooks, Superintendent
Minimum security
Capacity: 256
Established in 1939
Rockingham Correctional Center
Reidsville
David Osborne, Superintendent
Medium security
Capacity: 100
Established in 1930s
Rowan Correctional Center
Salisbury
James F. Bame, Superintendent
Minimum security
Capacity: 180
Established in 1935
Rutherford Correctional Center
Spindale
Joe Huntley, Superintendent
Minimum security
Capacity: 142
Established in 1933
Sampson Correctional Center
Clinton
James Bullock, Superintendent
Medium security
Capacity: 84
Established in 1939
Sandy Ridge Correctional Center
High Point
Herman Bridges, Superintendent
Minimum security
Capacity: 142
Established in 1939
Sanford Correctional Center
Sanford
Joe Beach, Superintendent
Minimum security
Capacity: 184
Established in 1950
Scotland Correctional Center
Wagram
J.E. Osborne, Superintendent
Medium security
Capacity: 108
Established in 1939
Southern Correctional Institution
Troy
Michael E. Bumgarner, Superintendent
Maximum-medium security
Capacity: 480
Established in 1983
Stanly Correctional Center
Albermarle
Larry L. Shoe, Superintendent
Medium security
Capacity: 116
Established in 1935
Stokes Correctional Center
Walnut Cove
H.B. Shepherd, Superintendent
Minimum security
Capacity: 142
Established in 1939
Tillery Correctional Center
Tillery
Robert W. Smith, Superintendent
Minimum security
Capacity: 200
Established in 1988
Triangle Correctional Institution
Raleigh
George Currie, Superintendent
Minimum security
Capacity: 470
Established in 1963
Umstead Correctional Center
Butner
Don Wilson, Superintendent
Minimum security
Capacity: 134
Established in 1949
Union Correctional Center
Monroe
Jack C. Ward, Superintendent
Medium security
Capacity: 94
Established in 1930
Vance Correctional Center
Henderson
James Hayes, Superintendent
Medium security
Capacity: 132
Established in 1939
Wake Correctional Center
Raleigh
W.K. Jones, Superintendent
Minimum security
Capacity: 304
Established in 1966
Warren Correctional Center
Warrenton
H.J. Carter, Superintendent
Minimum security
Capacity: 88
Established in 1931
Washington Correctional Center
Creswell
E.R. Sutton, Superintendent
Medium security
Capacity: 126
Established in 1931
Watauga Correctional Center
Boone
Daniel Johnson, Superintendent
Minimum security
Capacity: 128
Established in 1940
Wayne Correctional Center
Goldsboro
David Chester, Superintendent
Medium security
Capacity: 175
Established in 1979
Wilkes Correctional Center
North Wilkesboro
James Holloway, Superintendent
Minimum security
Capacity: 192
Established in 1938
Wilmington Residential Facility for Women
Wilmington
Laura B. Overstreet, Superintendent
Minimum security
Capacity: 14
Established in 1986
Yadkin Correctional Center
Yadkinville
Gilbert Brown, Superintendent
Medium security
Capacity: 124
Established in 1939
Yancey Correctional Center
Burnsville
Ernest Hughes Jr., Superintendent
Medium security
Capacity: 100
Established in 1940

NORTH DAKOTA:

Men's Medium Security Unit
Bismarck
Maximum-medium-minimum security
Capacity: 63
Established in 1987
North Dakota State Farm
Bismarck
Tom Powers, Warden
Capacity: 97
Established in 1943

OHIO:

Allen Correctional Institution
Lima
C.E. Humphreys, Superintendent
Maximum-medium security
Capacity: 720
Established in 1987
Chillicothe Correctional Institute
Chillicothe
Art Tate Jr., Superintendent
Maximum-medium security
Capacity: 1,508
Established in 1966
Correctional Reception Center
Orient
David Baker, Superintendent
Maximum-medium security
Capacity: 806
Established in 1987
Dayton Correctional Institution
Dayton
Reggie Wilkinson, Superintendent
Medium security
Capacity: 500
Established in 1987
Franklin Pre-Release Center
Columbus
Christine Money, Superintendent
Minimum security
Capacity: 250
Established in 1988

Grafton Correctional Institution
Grafton
Norm Hills, Superintendent
Medium security
Capacity: 700
Established in 1988

Hocking Correctional Facility
Nelsonville
Carole J. Shiplevy, Superintendent
Medium-minimum security
Capacity: 205
Established in 1983

Lebanon Correctional Institution
Lebanon
W.H. Dallman, Superintendent
Medium-minimum security
Capacity: 1,434
Established in 1959

Lima Correctional Institution
Lima
H.K. Russell, Superintendent
Medium-minimum security
Capacity: 1,200
Established in 1982

London Correctional Institution
London
A.R. Jago, Superintendent
Medium-minimum security
Capacity: 1,800
Established in 1925

Madison Correctional Institution
London
George D. Alexander, Superintendent
Medium-minimum security
Capacity: 1,000
Established in 1986

Marion Correctional Institution
Marion
Norris McMackin, Superintendent
Maximum-medium-minimum security
Capacity: 1,584
Established in 1955

Northeast Pre-Release Center
Cleveland
Ronald Edwards, Superintendent
Minimum security
Capacity: 350
Established in 1988

Ohio Reformatory for Women
Marysville
Harrison L. Morris, Superintendent
Maximum-medium-minimum security
Capacity: 925
Established in 1916

Ohio State Reformatory
Mansfield
Eric Dahlberg, Superintendent
Maximum-medium-minimum security
Capacity: 1,800
Established in 1896

Orient Correctional Institution
Columbus
Thomas Stickrath, Superintendent
Medium security
Capacity: 1,500
Established in 1984

Pickaway Correctional Institution
Orient
James Jackson, Superintendent
Minimum security
Capacity: 1,100
Established in 1984

Ross Correctional Institution
Chillicothe
Gary C. Mohr, Superintendent
Medium security
Capacity: 1,008
Established in 1987

Southeastern Correctional Institution
Lancaster
B.G. Bower, Superintendent
Medium-minimum security
Capacity: 1,609
Established in 1980

Southern Ohio Correctional Facility
Lucasville
Terry L. Morris, Superintendent
Maximum security
Capacity: 1,645
Established in 1972

Warren Correctional Institution
Lebanon
Anthony Brigano, Superintendent
Maximum-medium-minimum security
Capacity: 766
Established in 1988

OKLAHOMA:

Dick Conner Correctional Center
Hominy
Ronald Champion, Warden
Medium security
Capacity: 720
Established in 1979

Howard C. McLeod Correctional Center
Farris
Earl Allen, Warden
Minimum security
Capacity: 410
Established in 1961

Jackie Brannon Correctional Center
McAlester
Sonny Scott, Warden
Minimum security
Capacity: 230
Established in 1974

James Crabtree Correctional Center
Helena
Michael D. Parsons, Warden
Medium-minimum security
Capacity: 375
Established in 1982

Jess Dunn Correctional Center
Taft
Michael Cody, Warden
Minimum security
Capacity: 799
Established in 1980

John H. Lilley Correctional Center
Boley
Howard Ray, Warden
Minimum security
Capacity: 500
Established in 1983

Joseph Harp Correctional Center
Lexington
Jack Cowley, Warden
Medium security
Capacity: 720
Established in 1978

Lexington Assessment asnd Reception Center
Lexington
Steve Kaiser, Warden
Maximum-medium-minimum security
Capacity: 1,034
Established in 1978

Mabel Bassett Correctional Center
Oklahoma City
Mary Livers, Warden
Maximum-medium-minimum security
Capacity: 269
Established in 1973

Mack H. Alford Correctional Center
Stringtown
Richard Barnhard, Deputy Warden
Medium security
Capacity: 227
Established in 1955

Oklahoma State Penitentiary
McAlester
James Saffle, Warden
Maximum security
Capacity: 555
Established in 1908

Oklahoma State Reformatory
Granite
Steve Hargett, Warden
Medium-minimum security
Capacity: 534
Established in 1909

Ouachita Correctional Center
Hodgen
William Yeager, Warden
Minimum security
Capacity: 410
Established in 1970

OREGON:

Eastern Oregon Correctional Institution
Pendleton,
Robert L. Wright, Superintendent
Medium security
Capacity: 400
Established in 1985

Oregon State Correctional Institution
Salem
Carl Zenon, Superintendent
Maximum-medium-minimum security
Capacity: 476
Established in 1959

Oregon State Penitentiary
Salem
Manfred Maass, Superintendent
Maximum-medium-minimum security
Capacity: 1,650
Established in 1853

Oregon Women's Correctional Center
Salem
Robert Scheidler, Superintendent
Maximum-medium-minimum security
Capacity: 80
Established in 1965

PENNSYLVANIA:

Regional Correctional Facility at Mercer
Mercer
Gilbert A. Walters, Superintendent
Medium-minimum security
Capacity: 464
Established in 1978

State Correction Institution (and Diagnostic and Classification Center) at Camp Hill
Camp Hill
Robert M. Freeman, Superintendent
Medium-minimum security
Capacity: 1,826
Established in 1941

State Correctional Institution at Cresson
Cresson
Dr. Jeffrey A. Beard, Superintendent
Medium-minimum security
Capacity: 499
Established in 1987

State Correctional Institution at Dallas
Dallas
Joseph M. Ryan, Superintendent
Maximum-medium-minimum security
Capacity: 1,457
Established in 1960

State Correctional Institution at Frackville
Frackville
Raymond E. Clymer, Superintendent
Medium security
Capacity: 540
Established in 1987

State Correctional Institution (and Diagnostic and Classification Center) at Graterford
Graterford
Charles H. Zimmerman, Superintendent
Maximum-medium-minimum security
Capacity: 2,144
Established in 1929

State Correctional Institution at Greensburg
Greensburg
Laurence J. Reid, Superintendent
Medium-minimum security
Capacity: 461
Established in 1966

State Correctional Institution at Huntingdon
Huntingdon
Thomas A. Fulcomer, Superintendent
Maximum-medium-minimum security
Capacity: 1,347
Established in 1889

State Correctional at Muncy
Muncy
Ann M. Goolsby, Superintendent
Medium-minimum security
Capacity: 344
Established in 1920

State Correctional Institution (and Diagnostic and Classification Center) at Pittsburgh
Pittsburgh
George Petsock, Superintendent
Maximum-medium security
Capacity: 1,140
Established in 1826

State Correctional Institution at Retreat
Humlock Creek
Dennis R. Erhard, Superintendent
Medium-minimum security
Capacity: 480
Established in 1988

State Correctional Institution at Rockview
Bellefonte
Dr. Joseph F. Mazurkiewicz, Superintendent
Medium-minimum security
Capacity: 1,250
Established in 1912

State Correctional Institution at Smithfield
Huntingdon
Margaret A. Moore, Superintendent
Medium security
Capacity: 556
Established in 1988

State Correctional Institution at Waynesburg
Waynesburg
Fredric A. Rosemeyer, Superintendent
Medium-minimum security
Capacity: 144
Established in 1984

RHODE ISLAND:

High Security Center
Cranston
William A. Quattrocchi, Associate Director
Maximum security
Capacity: 96
Established in 1980

Intake Service Center
Cranston
Ronald Detonnancourt, Associate Director
Maximum security
Capacity: 168
Established in 1982

Intake Service Center Annex
Cranston
Maximum security
Capacity: 90
Established in 1987

Maximum Security Facility
Cranston
James Berard, Associate Director
Capacity: 450
Established in 1956

Medium Security Facility
Cranston
Ronald Brule, Associate Director
Capacity: 220
Estalished in 1956

Minimum Security Facility
Cranston
Dennis Papa, Associate Director
Capacity: 150
Established in 1973

Women's Division
Cranston
Gloria McDonald, Associate Director
Maximum-medium-minimum security
Capacity: 125
Established in 1978

Work Release Unit
Cranston
Charles Brown, Associate Director
Minimum security
Capacity: 150
Established in 1982

SOUTH CAROLINA:

Aiken Youth Correction Center
Aiken
George T. Hagan, Warden
Minimum security
Capacity: 310
Established in 1975

Blue Ridge Pre-Release/Work Center
Greenville
James H. Whitworth, Superintendent
Minimum security
Capacity: 208
Established in 1968

Broad River Correctional Institution
Columbia
George N. Martin III, Warden
Maximum-medium security
Capacity: 370
Established in 1988

Byrnes Clinical Center
Columbia
Robert E. Elgin, Warden
Established in 1987

Campbell Work Center
Columbia
George Roof, Superintendent
Minimum security
Capacity: 150
Established in 1975

Catawba Work Release Center
Rock Hill
Gene J. Bradshaw, Superintendent
Minimum security
Capacity: 144
Established in 1971

Central Correctional Institution
Columbia
Kenneth D. McKellar, Warden
Maximum-medium security
Capacity: 1,364
Established in 1868

Coastal Work Center
Charleston
Frank A. Smith, Superintendent
Minimum security
Capacity: 158
Established in 1970

Cross Anchor Correctional Institution
Enoree
Phoebe B. Johnson, Warden
Minimum security
Capacity: 528
Established in 1983

Dutchman Correctional Institution
Enoree
Glenn T. Davis, Warden
Minimum security
Capacity: 528
Established in 1980

Givens Youth Correction Center
Simpsonville
Robert H. Mauney, Warden
Minimum security
Capacity: 131
Established in 1969

Goodman Correctional Institution
Columbia
Louisa D. Brown, Warden
Minimum security
Capacity: 466
Established in 1970

Greenwood Correctional Center
Greenwood
Frankie L. Rickenbaker, Warden
Minimum security
Capacity: 94
Established in 1974

Kirkland Correctional Institution
Columbia
Laurie Bessinger, Warden
Maximum-medium security
Capacity: 612
Established in 1975

Lieber Correctional Institution
Ridgeville
P. Douglas Taylor, Warden
Maximum-medium security
Capacity: 696
Established in 1986

Livesay Work Release Center
Spartanburg
Robert L. Rice, Superintendent
Minimum security
Capacity: 96
Established in 1982

Lower Savannah Work Release Center
Aiken
John H. McCall, Superintendent
Minimum security
Capacity: 81
Established in 1974

McCormick Correctional Institution
McCormick
Richard S. Lindler, Warden
Maximum-medium security
Capacity: 600
Established in 1987

MacDougall Youth Correction Center
Ridgeville
Edsel T. Taylor, Warden
Minimum security
Capacity: 565
Established in 1966

Manning Correctional Institution
Columbia
William C. Wallace, Warden
Medium security
Capacity: 486
Established in 1963

Northside Correctional Center
Spartanburg
Frank H. Horton Jr., Warden
Minimum security
Capacity: 290
Established in 1974

Palmer Work Center
Florence
Thomas Lesesne, Superintendent
Minimum security
Capacity: 100
Established in 1975

Perry Correctional Institution
Pelzer
S.R. Witkowski, Warden
Maximum-medium security
Capacity: 768
Established in 1981

State Park Correctional Center
State Park
Judy C. Anderson, Warden
Capacity: 250
Established in 1984

Stevenson Correctional Institution
Columbia
George Hampton Jr., Warden
Minimum security
Capacity: 170
Established in 1964

Walden Correctional Institution
Columbia
Rickie Harrison, Warden
Minimum security
Capacity: 306
Established in 1951

Wateree River Correctional Institution
Rembert
John H. Carmichael, Warden
Minimum security
Capacity: 630
Established in 1892

Watkins Pre-Release Center
Columbia
Jerry D. Spigner, Warden
Minimum security
Capacity: 144
Established in 1983

Women's Correctional Center
Columbia
Vannie M. Toy, Warden
Medium-minimum security
Capacity: 437
Established in 1973

SOUTH DAKOTA:

South Dakota Penitentiary
Sioux Falls
Herman S. Solem, Warden
Maximum security
Capacity: 468
Established in 1882

South Dakota Training School
Plankinton
Herman Venekamp, Superintendent

Minimum security
Capacity: 85
Established in 1887

Springfield Correctional Facility
Springfield
Lynne DeLano, Superintendent
Medium security
Capacity: 418
Established in 1984

TENNESSEE:

Brushy Mountain State Penitentiary
Petros,
Otie Jones, Warden
Maximum-medium-minimum security
Capacity: 408
Established in 1896

Carter County Work Camp
Roan Mountain
Edward Arbogast, Warden
Medium-minimum security
Capacity: 180
Established in 1986

Chattanooga Community Service Center
Chattanooga
John Patterson, Warden
Minimum security
Capacity: 120

Deberry Correctional Institute
Nashville
Aileene Love, Warden
Maximum-medium-minimum security
Capacity: 265
Established in 1978

Fort Pillow Prison and Farm
Henning
Billy Compton, Warden
Maximum-medium-minimum security
Capacity: 610
Established in 1938

Knoxville Community Service Center
Knoxville
Ray Hatfield, Warden
Minimum security
Capacity: 150

Lake County Regional Correctional Facility
Tiptonville
Billy McWherter, Warden
Medium-minimum security
Capacity: 725
Established in 1981

Mark H. Luttrell Reception Center
Memphis
Bruce MacDonald, Warden
Medium-minimum security
Capacity: 411
Established in 1976

Middle Tennessee Reception Center
Nashville
Larry Lack, Warden
Capacity: 600
Established in 1979

Morgan County Regional Correctional Facility
Wartburg
Herman Davis, Warden
Medium-minimum security
Capacity: 815
Established in 1980

Nashville Community Service Center
Nashville
Charles Bass, Warden
Minimum security
Capacity: 300

Southeastern Tennessee State Regional Correctional Facility
Pikeville
Gary Livesay, Warden
Medium-minimum security
Capacity: 806
Established in 1980

Tennessee Prison for Women
Nashville
Eileen Hosking, Warden
Maximum-medium-minimum security
Capacity: 374
Established in 1898

Tennessee State Penitentiary
Nashville
Jack Morgan, Warden,
Maximum-medium-minimum security
Capacity: 1,068
Established in 1898

Turney Center Industrial Prison
Only
Donal Campbell, Warden
Medium-minimum security
Capacity: 782
Established in 1970

Wayne County Work Camp
Clifton
James Bowlen, Warden
Medium-minimum security
Capacity: 120
Established in 1985

TEXAS:

Beto I Unit
Tennessee Colony
Terry L. Terrell, Warden
Maximum security
Capacity: 3,616
Established in 1980

Beto II Unit
Palestine
Michael Countz, Warden
Maximum security
Capacity: 1,075
Established in 1982

Central Unit
Sugar Land
Lepher Jenkins, Warden
Maximum security
Capacity: 932
Established in 1902

Clemens Unit
Brazoria
David Moya, Warden
Maximum security
Capacity: 1,051
Established in 1902

Coffield Unit
Tennessee Colony
Jimmy Alford, Warden
Maximum security
Capacity: 3,000
Established in 1965

Darrington Unit
Rosharon
Keith Price, Warden
Maximum security
Capacity: 1,810
Established in 1919

Diagnostic Unit
Huntsville
Billy R. Ware, Warden
Maximum security
Capacity: 1,364
Established in 1964

Eastham Unit
Lovelady
George Waldron, Warden
Maximum security
Capacity: 2,250
Established in 1917

Ellis I Unit
Huntsville
Jerry Peterson, Warden
Maximum security
Capacity: 2,081
Established in 1963

Ellis II Unit
Huntsville
Randy McCloud, Warden
Maximum security
Capacity: 2,081
Established in 1983

Ferguson Unit
Midway
Wesley Warner, Warden
Maximum security
Capacity: 2,300
Established in 1962

Gatesville Unit
Gatesville
Susan C. Cranford, Warden
Maximum security
Capacity: 1,182
Established in 1980

Goree Unit
Huntsville
Richard Fortenberry, Warden
Maximum security
Capacity: 992
Established in 1901

Hilltop Unit
Gatesville
Jerry Gunnells, Warden
Maximum security
Capacity: 1,248
Established in 1981

Huntsville Unit
Huntsville
Jack B. Pursley, Warden
Maximum security
Capacity: 1,900
Established in 1849

Jester I Unit
Richmond
Morris M. Jones, Warden
Maximum security
Capacity: 448
Established in 1885

Jester II Unit
Richmond
Morris M. Jones, Warden
Maximum security
Capacity: 431
Established in 1885

Jester III Unit
Richmond
Morris M. Jones, Warden
Maximum security
Capacity: 1,028
Established in 1982

Michael Unit
Tennessee Colony
Jack M. Garner, Warden
Maximum security
Capacity: 2,250
Established in 1987

Mountain View Unit
Gatesville
Catherine M. Craig, Warden
Maximum security
Capacity: 653
Established in 1975

Pack I Unit
Navastoa
Bobby D. Morgan, Warden
Maximum security
Capacity: 1,063
Established in 1981

Pack II Unit
Navasota
Ron Drewry, Warden
Maximum security
Capacity: 1,334
Established in 1982

Ramsey I Unit
Rosharon
James A. Shaw, Warden
Maximum security
Capacity: 1,400
Established in 1908

Ramsey II Unit
Rosharon
Michael Wilson, Warden
Maximum security
Capacity: 850
Established in 1908

Ramsey III
Rosharon
Arthur Velasquez, Warden
Maximum security
Capacity: 1,495
Established in 1983

Retrieve Unit
Angleton
Bobby Crawford, Warden
Maximum security
Capacity: 770
Established in 1919

TDC Hospital/Galveston
Galveston
Fred Becker, Warden
Maximum security
Capacity: 96
Established in 1982

Wynne Unit
Huntsville
Lester Beaird, Warden
Maximum security
Capacity: 2,500
Established in 1899

UTAH:

Iron County/Utah State Correctional Facility
Cedar City
James Stewart, Director
Maximum-medium-minimum security
Capacity: 154,
Established in 1987

South Point Prison
Draper
Jerry Cook, Warden
Capacity: 876
Established in 1868

Women's Facility
Draper
Betty Gaines-Jones, Warden
Capacity: 132
Established in 1988

Young Adult Correctional Facility
Draper
Jeff Galli, Warden
Medium security
Capacity: 288
Established in 1984

VERMONT:

Chittenden Correctional Center
South Burlington
Philip Scripture, Superintendent
Maximum-medium-minimum security
Capacity: 128
Established in 1975

Northwest State Correctional Facility
St. Albans
Heinz Arenz, Superintendent
Maximum-medium-minimum security
Capacity: 15
Established in 1969

Rutland Correctional Center
Rutland
Michael O'Malley, Superintendent
Maximum-medium-minimum security
Capacity: 99
Established in 1969

St. Johnsbury Correctional Center
St. Johnsbury
Raymond J. Pilette, Superintendent
Maximum-medium-minimum security
Capacity: 99
Established in 1969

Windsor Correctional Facility
Windsor
T. Michael Coxon, Superintendent
Minimum security
Capacity: 68
Established in 1973

Woodstock Correctional Center
Woodstock
Lawrence McLiverty, Acting Superintendent
Maximum-medium-minimum security
Capacity: 44
Established in 1969

VIRGINIA:

Appalachian Correctional Unit (Unit 29)
Honaker
Robert J. Beck, Superintendent
Medium-minimum security
Capacity: 43
Established in 1986

Augusta Correctional Center
Craigsville
Larry Huffman, Warden
Maximum-medium-minimum security
Capacity: 500
Established in 1986

Baskerville Correctional Unit (Unit 4)
Baskerville
J.D. Netherland, Superintendent
Medium-minimum security
Capacity: 104

Bland Correctional Center
Bland,
W.D. Blankinship, Warden
Medium-minimum security
Capacity: 440
Established in 1946

Botetourt Correctional Unit (Unit 25)
Troutville
J.D. Terry, Superintendent
Medium-minimum security
Capacity: 58

Brunswick Correctional Center
Lawrenceville
Ellis B. Wright Jr., Warden
Maximum-medium-minimum security
Capacity: 500
Established in 1982

Buckingham Correctional Center
Dillwyn
James E. Johnson, Warden
Maximum-medium-minimum security
Capacity: 500
Established in 1982

Capron Correctional Unit (Unit 20)
Capron
Herbert Bryant, Superintendent
Medium-minimum security
Capacity: 85

Caroline Correctional Unit (Unit 2)
Hanover
Eddie Pearson, Superintendent
Medium-minimum security
Capacity: 130

Chatham Correctional Unit (Unit 15)
Chatham
Christopher Webb, Superintendent
Medium-minimum security
Capacity: 95

Chesterfield Work Release
Chesterfield
Wendy Hobbs, Superintendent
Minimum security
Capacity: 100

Culpeper Correctional Unit (Unit 11)
Culpeper
G.P. Dodson, Superintendent
Medium-minimum security
Capacity: 65

Deerfield Correctional Center
Capron
Robert Kelly, Warden
Medium-minimum security
Capacity: 290
Established in 1977

Dinwiddle Correctional Unit (Unit 27)
Church Road
Samuel Batts, Superintendent
Medium-minimum security
Capacity: 90

Fairfax Correctional Unit
Fairfax
Robert Kline, Superintendent,
Medium-minimum security
Capacity: 120

Fluvanna Correctional Unit (Unit 12)
Troy
C.W. Mitchell, Superintendent
Medium-minimum security
Capacity: 90

Greenville Correctional Unit (Unit 10)
Greenville
Cornel Nulty, Superintendent
Medium-minimum security
Capacity: 85

Halifax Correctional Unit (Unit 23)
Halifax
W.J. Towknley, Superintendent
Medium-minimum security
Capacity: 184

Harrisonburg Correctional Unit (Unit 8)
Harrisonburg
W.J. White, Superintendent
Medium-minimum security
Capacity: 100

Haymarket Correctional Unit (Unit 26)
Haymarket
Morrell Woods, Superintendent
Medium-minimum security
Capacity: 90

Haynesville Correctional Unit (Unit 17)
Haynesville
Medium-minimum security
Capacity: 85

James River Correctional Center
State Farm
John B. Taylor, Warden
Medium-minimum security
Capacity: 321
Established in 1895

Marion Correctional Treatment Center
Marion
Gerald Deans, Warden
Maximum-medium-minimum security
Capacity: 160
Established in 1980

Mecklenburg Correctional Center
Boydton
Charles E. Thompson, Warden
Maximum security
Capacity: 335
Established in 1977

Nansemond Correctional Unit (Unit 3)
Walters
Medium-minimum security
Capacity: 90

New Kent Correctional Unit (Unit 16)
Barhamsville
J.E. Lightfoot, Superintendent
Medium-minimum security
Capacity: 95

Nottoway Correctional Center
Burkeville
David A Garraghty, Warden
Maximum-medium-minimum security
Capacity: 500
Established in 1984

Patrick Henry Correctional Unit (Unit 28)
Ridgeway
B.C. Plageman, Superintendent
Medium-minimum security
Capacity: 102

Pocahontas Correctional Unit (Unit 13)
Chesterfield
Joseph F. Lewis, Superintendent
Medium-minimum security
Capacity: 210

Powhatan Correctional Center
State Farm
David A. Williams, Warden
Maximum-medium-minimum security
Capacity: 933
Established in 1895

Pulaski Correctional Unit (Unit 1)
Dublin
H.L. Underwood, Superintendent
Medium-minimum security
Capacity: 50

Rustburg Correctional Unit (Unit 9)
Rustburg
C.A. Hollar, Superintendent
Medium-minimum security
Capacity: 100

St. Brides Correctional Center
Chesapeake
Alton Baskerville, Warden
Medium-minimum security
Capacity: 423
Established in 1973

Smith Mountain Lake Correctional Unit (Unit 24)
Moneta
G.G. Wagner, Superintendent
Medium-minimum security
Capacity: 83

Southampton Correctional Center
Capron
Eugene M. Grizzard, Warden

Medium-minimum security
Capacity: 690
Established in 1937

Stafford Correctional Unit (Unit 21)
Stafford
C.A. Neff, Superintendent
Medium-minimum security
Capacity: 90

Staunton Correctional Center
Staunton
Thomas Israel, Warden
Medium-minimum security
Capacity: 522
Established in 1976

Tazewell Correctional Unit (Unit 31)
Tazewell
L.R. Ross, Superintendent
Medium-minimum security
Capacity: 100

Tidewater Correctional Unit (Unit 22)
Chesapeake
J.H. Snodgrass, Superintendent
Medium-minimum security
Capacity: 95

Virginia Correctional Center for Women
Goochland
Shirley P. Burton, Warden
Maximum-medium-minimum security
Capacity: 325
Established in 1932

Virginia State Penitentiary
Richmond
R.M. Muncy, Warden
Maximum-medium-minimum security
Capacity: 868
Established in 1800

White Post Correctional Unit (Unit 7)
White Post
Gary Keyser, Superintendent
Medium-minimum security
Capacity: 75

Wise Correctional Unit (Unit 18)
Coeburn
Sherman L. Townley, Acting Superintendent
Medium-minimum security
Capacity: 90

WASHINGTON:

Cedar Creek Corrections Center
Littlerock
James Blodgett, Superintendent
Minimum security
Capacity: 103
Established in 1980

Clallam Bay Corrections Center
Clallam Bay
Robert Moore, Superintendent
Medium security
Capacity: 500
Established in 1986

Clearwater Corrections Center
Forks
Neal Brown, Superintendent
Minimum security
Capacity: 113
Established in 1987

Indian Ridge Corrections Center
Arlington
Richard Bosse, Superintendent
Minimum security
Capacity: 81
Established in 1969

Larch Corrections Center
Yacolt
Jerry Minaker, Superintendent
Minimum security
Capacity: 114
Established in 1956

McNeil Island Corrections Center
Steilacoom
William L. Callahan, Superintendent
Maximum-medium-minimum security
Capacity: 779
Established in 1981

Olympic Corrections Center
Forks
Neal Brown, Superintendent
Minimum security
Capacity: 111
Established in 1981

Pine Lodge Corrections Center
Medical Lake
James Heffernan, Superintendent
Minimum security
Capacity: 104
Established in 1978

Purdy Corrections Center for Women
Gig Harbor
Sue Ellen Clark, Superintendent
Maximum-medium-minimum security
Capacity: 142
Established in 1970

Special Offender Center
Monroe
Donald Bonamy, Superintendent
Maximum-medium security
Capacity: 144
Established in 1980

Twin Rivers Corrections Center
Monroe
Janet Barbour, Superintendent
Medium security
Capacity: 500
Established in 1984

Washington Corrections Center
Shelton
Kurt Peterson, Superintendent
Maximum-medium security
Capacity: 902
Established in 1964

Washington State Penitentiary
Walla Walla
Lawrence Kincheloe, Superintendent
Maximum-medium-minimum security
Capacity: 1,284
Established in 1887

Washington State Reformatory
Monroe
Kenneth DuCharme, Superintendent
Maximum-medium security
Capacity: 751
Established in 1908

WEST VIRGINIA:

Anthony Center
Neola
Michael Richmond, Superintendent
Minimum security
Capacity: 120
Established in 1970

Beckley Work/Study Release Center
Beckley
Wyetta Fredericks, Administrator
Minimum security
Capacity: 60
Established in 1974

Charleston Work/Study Release Center
Charleston
Robert McElrath, Administrator
Minimum security
Capacity: 70
Established in 1972

Davis Center
Davis
William Duncil, Superintendent
Minimum security
Capacity: 60
Established in 1956

Huntington Work/Study Release Center
Huntington
Karen Spoor, Administrator
Capacity: 63
Established in 1983

Huttonsville Correctional Center
Huttonsville
C.M. "Bud" White, Warden
Medium security
Capacity: 490
Established in 1939

Industrial Home for Youth
Salem
Ronald Gregory, Superintendent
Minimum security
Capacity: 92
Established in 1899

West Virginia Penitentiary
Moundsville
Jerry Hedrick, Warden
Maximum security
Capacity: 575
Established in 1866

WISCONSIN:

Columbia Correctional Institution
Portage
James Murphy, Superintendent
Maximum security
Capacity: 450
Established in 1986

Dodge Correctional Institution
Waupun
Gordon A. Abrahamson, Superintendent
Maximum-medium-minimum security
Capacity: 309
Established in 1978

Fox Lake Correctional Institution
Fox Lake
Darrell Kolb, Superintendent
Medium security
Capacity: 576
Established in 1962

Green Bay Correctional Institution
Green Bay
Donald Clusen, Superintendent
Maximum-medium security
Capacity: 584
Established in 1898

Kettle Moraine Correctional Institution
Plymouth
Richard Franklin, Superintendent
Medium-minimum security
Capacity: 375
Established in 1962

Oakhill Correctional Institution
Oregon
Catherine Farrey, Superintendent
Minimum security
Capacity: 321
Established in 1977

Oshkosh Correctional Institution
Oshkosh
Donald Gudmanson, Superintendent
Medium security
Capacity: 300
Established in 1986

Taycheedah Correctional Institution
Taycheedah
Nona Switala, Superintendent
Maximum-medium-minimum security
Capacity: 126
Established in 1921

Waupun Correctional Institution
Waupun
Maximum-medium-minimum security
Capacity: 840
Established in 1851

Wisconsin Correctional Center System
Oregon
Minimum security
Capacity: 802
Established in 1962

WYOMING:

Wyoming Boys' School
Worland
David Renaud, Superintendent
Minimum security
Capacity: 140
Established in 1915

Wyoming Girls' School
Sheridan
Jack Geisler, Superintendent
Minimum security
Capacity: 90
Established in 1925

Wyoming Honor Farm
Riverton
James Gamble, Superintendent
Minimum security

Capacity: 90
Wyoming State Hospital
Evanston
Dr. John Doidge, Superintendent
Capacity: 30
Established in 1979
Wyoming State Penitentiary
Rawlins
Duane Shillinger, Warden
Maximum-medium-minimum security
Capacity: 675
Established in 1892
Wyoming Women's Center
Lusk
Judith Uphoff, Warden
Maximum-medium-minimum security
Capacity: 90
Established in 1977

UNITED STATES PENITENTIARIES:

Alcatraz
Capacity: 300
Established in 1933
Closed in 1963
Atlanta, Georgia
Joe Petrovsky,Warden
Capacity: 1,614
Established in 1902
Leavenworth, Kansas
Robert L. Matthews,Warden
Capacity: 1,190
Establihed in 1895
Lewisburg, Pennsyvania
Patrick W. Keohane, Warden
Capacity: 1,187
Established in 1932
Lompoc, California
Richard H. Rison, Warden
Capacity: 1,519
Established in 1959
Marion, Illinois
Gary Henman, Warden
Capacity: 574
Established in 1963
Terre Haute, Indiana
Calvin R. Edwards, Warden
Capacity: 973
Established in 1940

FEDERAL CORRECTIONAL INSTITUTIONS:

Alderson, West Virginia
Ron Burkhart, Warden
Capacity: 572
Established in 1927
Ashland, Kentucky
William Story, Warden
Capacity: 401
Established in 1940
Bastrop, Texas
Roderick D. Brewer, Warden
Capacity: 456
Established in 1979
Butner, North Carolina
Kathleen M. Hawk, Warden
Capacity: 303
Established in 1976
Danbury, Connecticut
Dennis Luther, Warden
Capacity 643
Established in 1940
El Reno, Oklahoma
Tommy C. Martin, Warden
Capacity: 958
Established in 1933
(Englewood) Littleton, Colorado
Tony Belaski, Warden
Capacity: 393
Established in 1940
Ft. Worth, Texas
D.C. Kastner, Warden
Capacity: 587
Established in 1971
La Tuna, Anthony, New Mexico-Texas
Thomas R. Kindt, Warden
Capacity: 478
Established in 1932
Lexington, Kentucky
Patrick R. Kane, Warden
Capacity: 911
Established in 1974
Loretto, Pennsylvania
Robert J. Barncastle, Warden
Capacity: 500
Established in 1984
Marianna, Florida
F.P. "Sam" Samples, Warden
Capacity: 750
Established in 1988
Memphis, Tennessee
O.I. White, Warden
Capacity: 429
Established in 1977
Milan, Michigan
John C. Gluch, Warden
Capacity: 587
Established in 1933
Morgantown, West Virginia
Michael B. Cooksey, Warden
Capacity: 344
Established in 1968
Otisville, New York
Jesse James
Capacity: 431
Established in 1980
Oxford, Wisconsin
E.J. Brennan, Warden
Capacity: 494
Established in 1973
Petersburg, Virginia
Jeff Clark, Warden
Capacity: 529
Established in 1930
Phoenix, Arizona
Peter M. Carlson, Warden
Capacity: 509
Established in 1985
Pleasanton, Dublin, California
Rob Roberts, Warden
Capacity: 335
Established in 1974
Ray Brook, New York
John T. Hadden, Warden
Capacity: 480
Established in 1980
Safford, Arizona
Roger F. Scott, Warden
Capacity: 188
Established in 1958
Sandstone, Minnesota
John J. Sullivan, Warden
Capacity: 347
Established in 1959
Seagoville, Texas
W.L. Garrison, Warden
Capacity: 250
Established in 1940
Talladega, Alabama
Donald J. Southerland, Warden
Capacity: 507
Established in 1979
Tallahassee, Florida
R.E. Honsted, Warden
Capacity: 527
Established in 1938
Terminal Island, California
Dutch Brewer, Warden
Capacity: 578
Established in 1955
Texarkana, Texas
Jim Swinson, Warden
Capacity: 558
Established in 1940
Tucson, Arizona
William A. Perrill, Warden
Capaciity: 181
Established in 1982

METROPOLITAN CORRECTIONAL CENTERS:

Chicago, Illinios
A.F. Beeler, Warden
Capacity: 363
Established in 1975
Los Angeles, California
Margaret Hambrick, Warden
Capacity: 588
Established in 1988
Miami, Florida
John L. Clark, Warden
Capacity: 326
Established in 1976
New York, New York
George C. Wigan, Warden
Capacity: 407
Established in 1975
San Diego, California
Al Kanahele, Warden
Capacity: 559
Established in 1975

MEDICAL CENTERS:

Rochester, Minnesota
Dr. Joseph B. Bogan, Warden
Capacity: 500
Established in 1985
Springfield, Missouri
Alan Turner, Warden
Capacity: 838
Established in 1933

PRISON CAMPS:

Big Spring, Texas
Philip M. Spears, Superintendent
Capacity: 486
Established in 1979
Boron, California
Larry F. Taylor, Superintendent
Capacity: 243
Established in 1979
Duluth, Minnesota
G.R. Gasele, Superintendent
Capacity: 500
Established in 1983
Eglin AFB, Florida
George E. Killinger, Superintendent
Capacity: 486
Established in 1962
George AFB, Victorville, California
Jon Dobre, Superintendent
Capacity: 300
Established in 1988
Lowry AFB, Denver, Colorado
Paul Thomas, Superintendent
Capacity: 300
Established in 1988
Lompoc, California
Harvey R. Cox, Superintendent
Maxwell AFB, Montgomery, Alabama
Wayne H. Seifert, Superintendent
Capacity: 240
Established in 1930
Montgomery, Pennsylvania (Allenwood)
Joe Class, Superintendent
Capacity: 374
Established in 1952
Saufley Field, Pensacola, Florida
Mark Henry, Superintendent
Capacity: 228
Established in 1988
Tyndal, Panama City, Florida
Greg Bogdan, Superintendent
Capacity: 120
Established in 1988

DETENTION CENTERS:

Oakdale, Louisiana
O.C. Jenkins, Warden
Capacity: 900
Established in 1986

UNITED STATES EXECUTIONS

DATE NAME (STATE)

01/17/77Gary Gilmore (UT)
05/25/79John Spenkelink (FL)

10/22/79Jesse Bishop (NV)
03/09/81Steven Judy (IN)
08/10/82Frank Coppola (VA)
12/07/82Charlie Brooks (TX)
04/22/83John Evans (AL)
09/02/83Jimmy Lee Gray (MS)
11/30/83Robert Sullivan (FL)
12/14/83Robert Wayne Williams (LA)
12/15/83John Eldon Smith (GA)
01/26/84Anthony Antone (FL)
02/29/84John Taylor (LA)
03/14/84James Autry (TX)
03/16/84James Hutchins (NC)
03/31/84Ronald O'Bryan (TX)
04/05/84Arthur Goode (FL)
04/05/84Elmo Sonnier (LA)
05/10/84James Adams (FL)
06/20/84Carl Shriner (FL)
07/12/84Ivon Stanley (GA)
07/13/84David Washington (FL)
09/07/84Ernest Dobbert (FL)
09/10/84Timothy Baldwin (LA)
09/20/84James Dupree Henry (FL)
10/12/84Linwood Briley (VA)
10/30/84Thomas Barefoot (TX)
10/30/84Ernest Knighton (LA)
11/02/84Velma Barfield (NC)
11/08/84Timothy Palmes (FL)
12/12/84Alpha Otis Stephens (GA)
12/28/84Robert Lee Willie (LA)
01/04/85David Martin (LA)
01/09/85Roosevelt Green (GA)
01/11/85Joseph Carl Shaw (SC)
01/16/85Doyle Skillern (TX)
01/30/85James Raulerson (FL)
02/20/85Van Roosevelt Solomon (GA)
03/06/85Johnny Paul Witt (FL)
03/13/85Stephen Peter Morin (TX)
03/20/85John Young (GA)
04/18/85James Briley (VA)
05/15/85Jesse de la Rosa (TX)
05/29/85Marvin Francois (FL)
06/25/85Morris Mason (VA)
06/25/85Charles Milton (TX)
07/09/85Henry Martinez Porter (TX)
09/11/85Charles Rumbaugh (TX)
10/16/85William Vandiver (IN)
12/06 85Carroll Cole (NV)
01/10/86James Terry Roach (SC)
03/12/86Charles William Bass (TX)
03/21/86Arthur Lee Jones (AL)
04/15/86Daniel Thomas (FL)
04/16/86Jeffrey Allen Barney (TX)
04/22/86David Funchess (FL)
05/15/86Jay Pinkerton (TX)
05/20/86Ronald Straight (FL)
06/09/86Rudy Esquivel (TX)
06/18/86Kenneth Brock (TX)
06/24/86Jerome Bowden (GA)
07/31/86Michael Smith (VA)
08/20/86Randy Woolls (TX)
08/22/86Larry Smith (TX)
08/26/86Chester Wicker (TX)
09/19/86John Rook (NC)
12/04/86Michael Wayne Evans (TX)
12/18/86Richard Andrade (TX)
01/30/87Ramon Hernandez (TX)
03/04/87Elisio Moreno (TX)
05/15/87Joseph Mulligan (GA)
05/20/87Edward Earl Johnson (MS)
05/22/87Richard Tucker (GA)
05/28/87Anthony Williams (TX)
05/29/87William Boyd Tucker (GA)
06/07/87Benjamin Berry (LA)
06/09/87Alvin Moore (LA)
06/12/87Jimmy Glass (LA)
06/16/87Jimmy Wingo (LA)
06/24/87Elliott Johnson (TX)
07/06/87Richard Whitley (VA)
07/08/87Connie Ray Evans (MS)
07/08/87John R. Thompson (TX)
07/20/87Willie Celestine (LA)
07/24/87Willie Watson (LA)
07/30/87John Brogdon (LA)
08/24/87Sterling Rault (LA)
08/28/87Wayne Ritter (AL)
08/28/87Dale Pierre Selby (UT)
08/28/87Beauford White (FL)
09/01/87Billy Mitchell (GA)
09/10/87Joseph Starvaggi (TX)
09/21/87Timothy McCorquodale (GA)
01/07/88Robert Streetman (TX)
03/15/88Willie Darden (FL)
03/15/88Wayne Felde (LA)
04/13/88Leslie Lowenfield (LA)
04/14/88Earl Clanton (VA)
06/10/88Arthur Bishop (UT)
06/14/88Edward Byrne (LA)
07/28/88James Messer (GA)
11/03/88Donald Gene Franklin (TX)
11/07/88Jeffrey Daugherty (FL)
12/13/88Raymond Landry (TX)
01/06/89George "Tiny" Mercer (MO)
01/24/89Theodore Bundy (FL)
03/22/89Leon Rutherford King (TX)
05/04/89Aubrey Adams (FL)
05/18/89Henry Willis (GA)
05/24/89Stephen McCoy (TX)
05/26/89Michael Lindsey (AL)
06/19/89William Paul Thompson (NV)
06/21/89Leo Edwards (MS)
06/23/89Sean Patrick Flannagan (NV)
07/14/89Horace F. Dunkins (AL)
08/18/89Herbert Lee Richardson (AL)
08/30/89Alton Waye (VA)
09/20/89James E. Paster (TX)
11/17/89Arthur Julius (AL)
12/07/89Carlos de Luna (TX)
01/18/90Gerald Smith (MO)
04/21/90Jerome Butler (TX)
04/27/90Ronald Raymond Woomer (SC)

U.S. DEATH ROW INMATES

ALABAMA (Electrocution)

Adkins, Ricky
Arthur, Thomas
Baldwin, Brian
Bankhead, Grady
Bell, Randy
Boyd, William
Bradley, Danny Joe
Brown, Gary Leon
Brown, Raymond
Brownlee, Virgil Lee
Bui, Quaing
Cade, Clyde
Callahan, James
Clisby, Willie
Cochran, James
Coral, Robert
Coulter, David
Daniel, George
Daniels, John R.
Davis, Jimmy Wayne
Davis, Kenneth
Davis, Timothy
Dill, Jimmy
Duncan, Joseph Cecil
Duren, David
Flowers, Clayton
Floyd, Tommy
Ford, Pernell
Fortenberry, Tommy Jerry
Freeman, Darryl
Freeman, David
Gentry, Ward
Giles, Arthur
Grayson, Darrell
Gurley, Wilson
Guthrie, Colon
Hadley, J.C.
Hallford, Phillip
Hamilton, Tommy
Hamm, Doyle Lee
Haney, Judie
Harrell, Ed
Harris, Louise
Hays, Henry
Heath, Larry
Henderson, Curtis Lee
Henderson, Jerry
Henderson, Joe
Hill, Walter
Hinton, Anthony Ray
Holladay, Glenn
Hooks, Joseph
Horsley, Edward
Hubbard, J.B.
Jackson, Willie
Jefferson, Albert
Johnson, Anthony Keith
Johnson, Rickie Lee
Jones, Aaron
Kennedy, Victor
Kuenzel, William
Lawhorn, James
Luke, Johnny
Lynn, Frederick
McGahee, Earl
McMillan, Walter
McWilliams, James
Magwood, Billy Joe
Magwood, Kenneth
Martin, James
Morrison, Jesse
Murry, Paul
Musgrove, Donnis
Neelley, Judith
Nelson, David
Nicks, Harry
Parker, John
Peoples, John
Rogers, David
Russaw, Henry
Rutledge, Mitchell
Siebert, Daniel Lee
Singleton, Cornelius
Smith, James Wyman
Smith, Kenneth E.
Stephens, Victor
Tarver, Bobby
Tarver, Robert Lee
Thomas, Kenneth Glenn
Thomas, Patricia
Thomas, Wallace
Thompson, Michael Eugene
Thompson, Steven Allen
Tomlin, Philip
Waldrop, Billy
Walker, Altione
Watkins, Darryl
Weeks, Varnell
Wesley, Ronald
Whisenhant, Thomas
White, Leroy
Wilson, Shepp
Windsor, Harvey
Wright, Freddie

ARIZONA (Gas Chamber)

Adamson, John
Amaya-Ruiz, Jose
Arnett, James
Atwood, Frank
Beaty, Donald
Bishop, Ronald
Blazak, Mitchell
Bracey, William
Brewer, John
Brown, John G.
Carriger, Paris
Ceja, Jose
Chaney, Anthony
Clabourne, Scott
Clark, James Dean
Comer, Robert
Connor, Ronnie
Cook, Daniel Wayne
Correll, Michael
Davis, Michael
Epperson, George
Fierro, Jose
Fischer, James
Fisher, James C.
Gerlaugh, Darrick
Gillies, Jesse
Greenawalt, Randy
Greenway, Richard H.
Gretzler, Douglas
Harding, Donald

Henry, Graham
Herrera Jr., William
Herrera, Michael
Herrera Sr., William
Hinchey, John
Hooper, Murray
James, Steven
Jeffers, Jimmy
Jimenez, Jesus
Lagrand, Karl
Lagrand, Walter
Lambright, Joe
Lavers, Alfred E.
Libberton, Lawrence
Lopez, Samuel
McCall, Edward
McMurtrey, Jasper
Martinez-Villareal, Ramon
Mata, Luis
Mathers, Jimmy Lee
Medrano, Angel
Moormann, Robert Henry
Nash, Viva Leroy
Ortiz, Ignacio
Poland, Michael
Poland, Patrick
Richmond, Willie Lee
Robinson, Fred
Roscoe, Kevin
Rossi, Richard
Running Eagle, Sean
Salazar, Alphonso
Schaaf, Steven R.
Schad, Edward
Serna, John
Shackart, Ronald
Smith, Bernard
Smith, Joe
Smith, Robert
Smith, Roger Lynn
Stanley, Milo
Summerlin, Warren
Tison, Ricky
Vickers, Robert
Villafuerte, Jose
Wallace, James
Walton, Jeffrey
Washington, Theodore
West, Thomas
White, Michael
Williams, Ronald Turney
Woratzeck, William
Zaragosa, Ruben

ARKANSAS (Lethal Injection or Choice of Electrocution for Sentences Before Mar. 4, 1983)

Clark, Antonio
Clements, Kenneth W.
Clines, Hoyt
Coulter, Rodger
Fairchild, Barry
Ford, Clay Anthony
Fretwell, Bobby Ray
Gardner, Mark
Hayes, T.J.
Henderson, Wilbur
Hill, Darrell
Hill, Steven Douglas
Holmes, James W.
Hulsey, Dewayne
Miller, Eddie Lee
O'Rourke, Michael
Orndorff, Michael
Parker, William Frank
Perry, Eugene
Pickens, Charles
Pruett, Marion
Rector, Ricky
Remeta, Daniel
Richley, Daryl
Ruiz, Paul
Simmons, Ronald
Simmons, Thomas
Singleton, Charles
Snell, Richard Wayne
Starr, David Lee
Swindler, John
Van Denton, Earl
Wainright, Kirt
Whitmore, Jonas Hotan

CALIFORNIA (Gas Chamber)

Adcox, Keith
Ainsworth, Steven
Alcala, Rodney
Allen, Clarence R.
Allison, Watson
Alvarez, Manuel M.
Anderson, James
Anderson, Stephen
Andrews, Jesse J.
Ashmus, Troy
Avena, Carlos
Ayala, Ronaldo M.
Babbitt, Manuel
Bacigalupo, Miguel
Barnett, Lee Max
Bean, Anthony
Beardslee, Donald
Beeler, Rodney
Bell, Ronnie
Belmontes, Fernando
Benson, Richard Allan
Berryman, Rodney
Bittaker, Lawrence
Blair, James N.
Bloom, Robert S.
Bloyd, Dale
Bonillas, Louis
Bonin, William
Boyd, Juan
Boyde, Richard
Bradford, Bill
Breaux, David
Brown, Albert
Brown, John
Bunyard, Jerry
Burgener, Michael
Burton, Andre
Cain, Tracy
Caro, Fernando
Carpenter, David
Carrera, Constantino
Champion, Steve
Clair, Kenneth
Clark, Douglas
Clark, John William
Clark, Richard
Coddington, Herbert
Coffman, Cynthia
Coleman, Calvin
Coleman, Russell
Cooper, Kevin
Cox, Michael
Cox, Tiequon A.
Crandell, Kenneth
Crittenden, Steven E.
Cudjo, Armenia
Cummings, Raynard
Cunningham, Albert
Daniels, Jackson
Danielson, Robert
Davenport, John
Davenport, John
Day, Christopher
Deere, Ronald
Dennis, William
Desantis, Stephen
Diaz, Robert R.
Douglas, Fred Berre
Duncan, Henry Earl
Dunkle, Jon S.
Dyer, Alfred
Easley, Elbert
Edelbacher, Peter
Edwards, Thomas F.
Espinoza, Antonio
Fairbank, Robert
Farmer, Lee
Farnam, Jack Gus
Fauber, Curtis
Fields, Stevie
Fierro, David
Frank, Theodore
Freeman, Fred
Frierson, Lavell
Frye, Jerry G.
Fudge, Keith
Fuentes, Jose
Gallego, Gerald
Garceau, Robert
Garrison, Richard
Gates, Oscar
Gay, Kenneth
Ghent, David
Gonzalez, Jesse
Gonzalez, Martin
Gordon, Patrick
Grant, Richard
Griffin, Donald
Guzman, Gary
Haley, Kevin
Halvorsen, Arthur
Hamilton, Bernard Lee
Hamilton, Billy Ray
Hamilton, Michael
Hardy, James
Harris, Robert
Harris, Von M.
Hart, Joseph
Haskett, Randy
Hawthorne, Anderson
Hayes, Blufford
Hayes, Royal
Heishman, Harvey
Hendricks, Edgar
Hernandez, Francis
Hill, Michael
Hill, Shawn
Hines, Gary
Hithchings, Keith
Holloway, Duayne
Horton, James
Hovey, Richard
Howard, Albert C.
Howard, Gary
Hunter, Michael
Jackson, Earl
Jackson, Michael
Jackson, Noel
Jenkins, Daniel
Jennings, Michael
Jennings, Wilbur
Johnson, James
Johnson, Joe
Johnson, Laverne
Johnson, Willie D.
Jones, Earl
Jones, Jeffrey
Jones, Troy
Karis, James
Kaurish, Jay
Keenan, Maurice
Kelly, Horace
Kimble, Eric
Kipp, Martin
Kirkpatrick, Willaim
Kolmetz, Jeffrey
Kraft, Randy
Lang, Kenneth
Ledesma, Fermin
Lewis, Robert
Livaditis, Steven
Lucas, David A.
Lucas, Larry
Lucero, Philip
Lucky, Darnell
McDowell, Charles
McLain, Robert
McPeters, Ronald
Malone, Kelvin
Marlow, James
Marquez, Gonzalo
Marshall, George
Marshall, Ryan
Marshall, Sam
Mason, David
Massie, Robert
Mattson, Michael
Mayfield, Demetrie
Mayfield, Dennis

Medina, Teofilo
Melton, James
Memro, Harold
Mendoza, Manuel
Mickey, Douglas
Mickle, Denny
Miller, Donald
Milner, Lynn
Mincey, Bryan
Miranda, Adam
Mitcham, Stephan
Montiel, Richard
Moore, Charles
Morales, Michael
Morris, Bruce
Murtishaw, David
Myers, Venson
Neely, Charles
Nicolaus, Robert Henry
Noguera, Willaim
Ochoa, Lester
Odle, James
Osband, Lance
Payton, William
Pensinger, Brett
Phillips, Richard
Pinholster, Scott
Poggi, Joseph
Price, Curtis
Pride, Timothy
Proctor, William
Quartermain, Drax
Raley, David
Ramirez, Anthony Richard
Ramirez, Richard
Ramos, Marcelino
Ray, Clarence
Reilly, Mark
Rich, Darrell
Riel, Charles D.
Robbins, Malcolm
Roberts, Larry
Robertson, Andrew
Rodriguez, Jose
Rodriguez, Luis
Rogers, David
Ross, Craig
Rowland, Guy Kevin
Ruiz, Alejandro
Rundle, David
Samayoa, Richard
Sanchez, Teddy
Sanders, Ricardo
Sanders, Ronald
Sandoval, Alfred
Schmeck, Mark
Scott, James
Seaton, Ronald H
Sheldon, Jeffrey
Silva, Benjamin
Silva, Mauricio
Sims, Mitchell
Siripongs, Jaturun
Smithey, George H
Stankewitz, Douglas
Stanley, Gerald
Stansbury, Robert
Sully, Anthony Jack
Taylor, Freddie Lee
Thomas, Donrell
Thomas, Ralph
Thompson, Robert
Thompson, Thomas Martin
Tuilaepa, Paul
Turner, Melvin
Turner, Richard
Turner, Thaddeus Louis
Viscotti, John
Wade, Melvin
Wader, Michael
Walker, Marvin
Wash, Jeffrey David
Weaver, Ward Francis
Webb, Dennis
Webster, Larry
Welch, David E.
Wharton, George
Whitt, Charles
Williams, Barry
Williams, Darren C.
Williams, Keith
Williams, Kenneth
Williams, Michael
Williams, Stanley
Wilson, Robert
Wrest, Theodore
Wright, Bronte
Zapien, Conrad J

COLORADO (Lethal Injection)

Daivs, Gary
O'Neil, John
Rodriguez, Frank

CONNECTICUT (Electrocution)

Breton, Robert
Ross, Michael

DELAWARE (Lethal Injection or Choice of Hanging for Those Sentenced Before June 13, 1986)

Bailey, Billy
Dawson, David
Deputy, Andre
Deshields, Kenneth
Flamer, William
Riley, James
Sanders, Reginald

FLORIDA-ELECTROCUTION

Agan, James
Aldrich, Leon
Alvord, Gary
Amos, Vernon
Anderson, Richard
Asay, Marc
Atkins, Phillip
Bedford, Michael
Bello, Carlos
Beltran-Lopez, Mauricio
Bertolotti, Anthony
Blakley, Robert
Blanco, Omar
Boggs, John
Bolender, Bernard
Booker, Stephen
Bottoson, Linroy
Bowden, Roosevelt
Breedlove, McArthur
Brown, Larry
Brown, Paul A.
Bruno, Michael
Bryan, Anthony
Bryant, Robert
Buenoano, Judi
Buford, Robert
Burns, Daniel
Burr, Charlie
Bush, John Earl
Byrd, Milford
Campbell, James
Capehart, Gregory
Card, James
Carter, Antonio
Carter, Charles
Caruso, Michael
Castro, Edward
Cave, Alfonso
Chandler, James
Cherry, Roger L.
Cheshire, Steven E.
Christopher, William
Clark, Larry
Clark, Raymond
Coleman, Michael
Colina, Manuel
Cook, David
Cooper, Richard
Cooper, Vernon
Copeland, Johnny
Correll, Jerry
Craig, Donny Gene
Craig, Robert
Crossman, Martin Edward
Crump, Michael
Cruse, William B.
Czubak, Walter
Dailey, James
Davis, Allen
Davis, Henry
Davis, Mark
Deaton, Jason P.
Delap, David
Demps, Bennie
Derrick, Samuel
Diaz, Angel
Dolinsky, Raymond
Dougan, Jacob J.
Douglas, Howard
Douglass, Howard V.
Downs, Bobbie Lee
Downs, Ernest
Doyle, Danny
Duckett, James
Duest, Lloyd
Dufour, Donald
Dupocher, Michael A.
Durocher, Michael
Elledge, William
Ellis, Ralph
Engle, Gregory
Espinosa, Henry
Eutzy, William
Farinas, Alberto
Ferguson, John
Floyd, James
Ford, Alvin
Foster, Charles Kenneth
Francis, Bobby
Frazier, Darrell
Freeman, John D.
Garcia, Enrique
Garcia, Henry
Garcia, Rolando
Gilliam, Burley
Glock, Robert D.
Gore, David
Gorham, David
Green, Alphonso
Griffin, Frank
Griffin, Kenneth
Groover, Tommy
Grossman, Martin Edward
Gunsby, Donald
Hakim, Yaqub
Haliburton, Jerry
Hall, Anthony
Hall, Freddie Lee
Hallman, Darrell
Hamblen, James W.
Happ, William
Hardwick, John Gary
Hardwick, Kenneth
Hargrave, Lenson
Harich, Roy
Harris, Theodore
Harvey, Harold
Hayes, Tony
Hegwood, Bernell
Heiney, Robert
Henderson, Robert D.
Henderson, Thomas
Henry, Robert Lavern
Herring, Ted
Hildwin, Paul
Hill, Clarence
Hill, George A.
Hitchcock, James Ernest
Hodges, George M.
Hoffman, Barry
Holton, Rudolph
Hooper, Harold
Hudson, Timothy
Huff, James
Jackson, Andrea H.
Jackson, Carl
Jackson, Clarence
Jackson, Clinton L.
Jackson, Douglas
Jackson, Etheria

Jackson, Nathaniel
Jackson, Ronald
Jacobs, Eligaah
James, Davidson
Jennings, Bryan
Johnson, Larry Joe
Johnson, Marvin
Johnson, Paul Beasley
Johnson, Terrell
Johnston, David E.
Jones, Clarence J.
Jones, Leo
Jones, Leslie
Jones, Randall Scott
Jones, Ronnie Lee
Justus, Buddy
Keen, Michael Scott
Kelley, William
Kennedy, Edward Dean
Kight, Charles
King, Amos Lee
Kloklec, Victor
Knight, Thomas
Koenig, Kenneth
Kokal, Gregory
Koon, Raymond
Lambrix, Cary
Lambrix, Michael R.
Lara, Mario
Lecroy, Cleo
Lewis, Lawrence
Lightbourne, Ian
Livingston, Jessie, J.
Lockhart, Michael
Long, Robert
Long, Robert
Lopez, Eduardo
Lucas, Harold
Lusk, Bobby
McCrae, James
Maharaj, Krishna
Mann, Larry
Maquiera, Jose
Marek, John R.
Marshall, Matthew
Martin, Nollie
Mason, Oscar
Maulden, Charles
Maxwell, Chester
Medina, Pedro
Meeks, Douglas
Melendez, Juan Roberto
Mendyk, Todd
Merritt, John
Michael, John
Middleton, William
Mikenas, Mark
Mills, Gregory
Mills, John
Mitchell, Willie
Morgan, Floyd
Morgan, James
Morris Jr., George
Muehleman, Jeffrey A.
Muhammad, Askari
Nibert, Billy Ray
Nixon, Joe Elton
Nowitzke, Frederick
O'Callaghan, John
Oats, Sonny Boy
Occhicone, Dominick
Omelus, Ulrick
Owen, Duane
Pace, Bruce
Pardo, Manuel
Parker, J.B.
Parker, Norman
Parker, Robert Lacey
Patten, Robert
Peede, Robert
Penn, James
Pentecost, David
Pettit, Manuel
Phillips, Harry
Ponticelli, Anthony
Pope, Thomas Dewey
Porter, George
Porter, Raleigh
Preston, Robert A.
Provenzano, Thomas
Puiatti, Carl
Quince, Kenneth
Ragsdale, Edward
Randolph, Richard
Reaves, William
Reed, Grover
Remeta, Daniel
Rhodes, Richard
Riechmann, Dieter
Riley, Wardell
Rivera, Michael
Rivera, Samuel
Roberts, Rickey
Robertson, Lavarity
Robinson, Johnny J.
Robinson, Timothy
Rogers, Jerry Layne
Rose, James
Rose, Milo A.
Routly, Daniel
Ruffin, Mack
Rutherford, Arthur
Sanchez, Rigoberto
Santos, Carlos
Savage, James
Schafer, Arthur
Scott, Abron
Scott, Bradley
Scott, Jeremy L.
Scott, Paul
Scull, Jesus
Shere, Richard E.
Sims, Terry
Sireci, Henry
Smith, Frank
Smith, Frank L.
Smith, Jimmy Lee
Sochor, Dennis
Songer, Carl
South, George
Spaziano, Joseph
Spencer, Leonard
Squires, William
Steinhorst, Walter
Stephen
Stevens, Rufus
Stewart, Kenneth
Stewart, Roy
Stone, Raymond
Suarez, Ernesto
Swafford, Roy
Tafero, Jesse
Taylor, Perry A.
Teffeteller, Robert
Thomas, Edward
Thompson, Charlie
Thompson, Joey
Thompson, Raymond
Thompson, William
Tillman, Gary
Tompkins, Wayne
Torres-Arboledo, Oscar
Trawick, Gary
Trotter, Melvin
Turner, William
Valle, Manuel
Van Poyck, William
Ventura, Peter
Walls, Frank
Walton, Jason Dirk
Warfielod, Mike
Waterhouse, Robert
Watts, Tony R.
Way, Fred
White, Jerry
White, Reginald
White, William
Wickham, Jerry
Wickham, Jerry
Wilke, Warfield R.
Williams, Andrew
Williams, Freddie Lee
Williamson, Johnny
Woods, Ronald
Wright, Joel
Wright, Mack Ray
Young, David
Zeigler, William

GEORGIA (ELECTROCUTION)

Alderman, Jack
Allen, Stanley
Baxter, Norman
Beck, Eli
Birt, Billy Sunday
Black, Robert
Blankenship, Roy
Blanks, Kenneth
Brantley, Jeffery David
Brown, Nathan
Burden, Jimmy
Burger, Christopher
Buttrum, Janice
Cargill, David
Chenault, Marcus
Childs, Johnny
Cohen, Michael Anthony
Collier, Robert
Collins, Roger
Conklin, Robert
Connor, John Wayne
Cook, James
Crawford, Eddie
Cunningham, James
Davis, Curfew
Davis, George
Davis, John Michael
Devier, Darrell
Dobbs, Wiley
Felker, Ellis
Ferrell, Eric
Finney, Eddie
Fleming, Son
Ford, James Arthur
Ford, Melbert Ray
Foster, Timothy
Frazier, Leonard
Gaddis, Bobby Gene
Gary, Carlton
Gates, Johnny Lee
Gilreath, Fred
Hall, Willie James
Hance, William Henry
Hardy, Kenneth
Harrison, Aden
Hatcher, Ricky
Hicks, Robert Karl
High, Jose
Hightower, John
Hill, Floyd
Holiday, Dallas
Horton, Jimmy
Housel, Tracey Lee
Ingram, Nicholas
Isaacs, Carl
Jarrell, David
Jarrells, Jonathen
Jefferson, Lawrence
Jones, Brandon
Justus, Buddy
Kinsman, Ronald
Lee, Jessie
Lee, Larry
Legare, Andrew
Lipham, William
Lonchar, Larry Grant
Mathis, James
Meders, Jimmy F.
Miller, Michael
Mincey, Terry
Mitchell, Nelson E.
Moon, Larry Eugene
Moore, Carzell
Morgan, Alfonso
Nelson, Gary
Newland, Robert
Parker, Byron
Patillo, Keith
Peek, David
Pitts, James L.
Potts, Jack
Presnell, Virgil
Putman, William

Roberts, Victor
Rogers, James
Romine, Larry
Ross, Eddie Lee
Smith, William
Spencer, James
Spivey, Ronald
Stephens, W. Kenny
Stevens, Thomas
Stripling, Alfonso
Todd, William L.
Walker, Richard
Waters, Eurus
Williams, Alexander
Williams, Harold
Wilson, Willie

IDAHO (Lethal Injection or Firing Squad)

Beam, Albert Raymond
Card, David L.
Charbeneau, Jaimi Dean
Creech, Thomas
Fetterly, Donald
Gibson, Thomas Henry
Hoffman, Maxwell
Lankford, Brian
Lankford, Mark
Leavitt, Richard
McKinney, Randy
Paradis, Donald
Paz, Federico
Pizzuto, Gerald
Pratt, James
Rhoades, Paul
Sivak, Lacey
Stuart, Eugene

ILLINOIS (Lethal Injection)

Albanese, Charles
Allen, Kenneth
Ashford, James
Barrow, Ronald
Bean, Harold
Boclair, Stanley
Bracey, William
Brisbon, Henry
Britz, DeWayne
Burrows, Joseph
Byron, Robert
Caballero, Juan
Chandler, Mark
Coleman, Alton
Collins, Roger
Crews, William
Cruz, Rolando
Davis, Girvies
Delvecchio, George
Easley, Ike
Eddmonds, Durlyn
Edwards, Daniel
Emerson, Dennis
Ennis, Tony
Enoch, Willie
Erickson, Paul
Evans, Johnnie Lee
Eyler, Larry
Fields, Nathson
Flores, Mario
Foster, James
Franklin, William
Free, James
Gacho, Robert
Gacy, John Wayne
Gibson, Sherman
Gosier, Harry
Griffin, Henry
Guest, Anthony
Hall, Anthony
Harris, James
Harris, Terry
Hawkins, Earl
Hayes, Clarence
Henderson, Demetrius
Holman, Tafford
Hooper, Murray
Hope, Edgar
House, Derrick
Howard, Stanley
Jackson, Lawrence
Jimerson, Verneal
Johnson, Andrew
Johnson, Mark
Johnson, Milton
Jones, Andre
Jones, Ronald
Jones, William
King, Derrick
Kokoraleis, Andrew
Kubat, Robert
Leger, William
Lego, Donald
Lucas, John
Lucas, Roosevelt
Mack, Larry
Madej, Gregory
Mahaffey, Jerry
Maxwell, Andrew
Melock, Robert
Montgomery, Ulece
Morgan, Derrick
Morgan, Samuel
Neal, John
Nitz, Richard
Odle, Thomas
Olinger, Perry
Orange, Leroy
Owens, Robin
Pasch, John
Patterson, Aaron
Pecoraro, John
Perez, Domingo
Phillips, John Paul
Pitsonbarger, Jimmy
Porter, Anthony
Pugh, Willie
Ramey, Irving
Richardson, Floyd
Ruiz, Luis
Salazar, Manuel
Sanchez, Hector
Scott, Larry
Seuffer, James
Shurn, Keith
Silagy, Charles
Simms, Darryl
Smith, David
Smith, Steven
Spreitzer, Edward
St. Pierre, Robert
Steidl, Gordon
Stewart, Raymond
Stewart, Walter
Strickland, Tyrone
Sutherland, Cecil
Szabo, John
Tenner, James
Terrell, Drew
Thomas, Walter
Thomas, Willie
Thompkins, Willie
Titone, Dino
Turner, Robert
Tye, Jimmy
Walker, Charles
Ward, Jerry
West, Paul
Whitehead, John
Wiley, Howard
Williams, Bennie
Williams, Dennis
Williams, Eddie
Williams, Hernando
Wright, Patrick
Young, William

INDIANA (Electrocution)

Allen, Howard
Averhart, Rufus
Baird, Arthur
Bellmore, Larry
Benefiel, William
Bernischke, William
Bieghler, Marvin
Boyd, Russell
Brewer, James
Brown, Debra
Burris, Gary
Canaan, Keith
Castor, Marvin
Coleman, Alton
Conner, Kevin
Daniels, Michael
Davis, Frank
Davis, Greg
Evans, Charles
Fleenor, D.H.
Games, James
Harris, James
Hough, Kevin
Huffman, Richard
Jackson, Donald
Johnson, Gregory Scott
Kennedy, Stuart
Landress, Cindy
Lockhart, Michael
Lowery, James
Lowery, Terry
McCullom, Phillip
Minnick, William
Moore, Richard
Potts, Larry
Resnover, Gregory
Roark, Dennis
Rondon, Reynaldo
Rouster, Gregory
Schiro, Thomas
Smith, Charles
Smith, Tommie
Spranger, William
Thacker, Lois
Townsend, Johnny
Trueblood, Michael
Underwood, Herbert
Van Cleave, Greg
Wallace, Donald
Williams, Darnell
Williams, Larry
Wisehart, Mark
Woods, David

KENTUCKY (Electrocution)

Clark, Michael
Epperson, Roger Dale
Foster, Lafonda Fay
Gall, Eugene
Halvorsen, Leif
Harper, Eddie Lee
Hodge, Benny Lee
Jacobs, Clawvern
Kordenbrock, Paul
Marlowe, Hugh
Matthews, David
McQueen, Harold
Moore, Brian Keith
Sanders, David Lee
Simmons Beoria
Skaggs, David
Slawter, James
Smith, David
Smith, Robert
Stanford, Kevin
Taylor, Victor
Thomas, Alfred
Thompson, William
White, Gene 'Karu'
Willoughby, Mitchell
Wilson, Gregory

LOUISIANA (Electrocution)

Bates, Wayne
Brooks, George
Brown, John
Burrell, Albert Ronnie
Cage, Tommy
Comeaux, Adam
Copeland, James
Deboue, Thomas
Dugar, Troy
Eaton, Winthrop

El-Mumit, Abdullah Hakim
Ford, Glenn
Graham, Michael
James, Antonio
Jones, Andrew Lee
Kirkpatrick, Frederick
Kyles, Curtis
Lee, Tracy
Lindsey, Tyronne
Loyd, Alvin
Messiah, Keith
Perry, Michael Owen
Prejean, Dalton
Sawyer, Robert
Scire, Anthony
Smith, Clarence
Sullivan, John
Tassin, Robert
Thompson, John
Ward, Thomas Lee
Welcome, Herbert
Williams, Dobie
Willie, John Francis

MARYLAND (Gas Chamber)

Booth, John
Bruce, Kirk
Calhoun, James
Collins, Kenneth
Colvin, Eugene
Evans, Vernon
Gilliam, Tyrone
Grandison, Anthony
Huffington, John
Hunt, Flint
Mills, Ralph
Thomas, Donald
Tichnell, Richard
Trimble, James
White, Derrick
Wiggins, Kevin

MISSISSIPPI (Gas Chamber)

Abram, Donald
Berry, Earl
Bevill, Randy
Billiot, James
Booker, John
Clemons, Chandler
Cole, West
Culberson, Alvin
Davis, Gregory
Dufour, Donald
Feraga, Lazaro
Foster, James Henry
Gilliard, Robert
Hansem, Tracy
Hill, Alvin
Holland, Gerald
Irving, John Buford
Johnson, Samuel
Jones, Gregory M.
Jordan, Richard
King, Mack Arthur
Ladner, Jeffrey
Lanier, Arthur Ray
Lockett, Carl
Mackabee, Frank
Minnick, Robert
Neal, Howard
Nixon, John
Pinkney, Bobby Joe
Shell, Robert Lee
Smith, Willie Albert
Stringer, James R.
Thorson, Roger
Tokman, George
Turner, Kevin
Wheat, Kenneth
Wilcher, Bobby
Wiley, William
Williams, Jesse
Woodward, Paul

MISSOURI (Lethal Injection)

Amrine, Joseph
Antwine, Calvert
Bannister, Alan
Battle, Thomas
Blair, Walter
Bolder, Martsay
Boliek, William
Brown, Vernon
Byrd, Maurice
Chambers, James
Clemmons, Eric
Davis, Ralph
Debeler, Shelby
Driscoll, Robert
Feltrop, Ralph
Fix, Andrew
Foster, Emmitt
Gilmore, George
Griffin, Larry
Griffin, Milton
Griffin, Reginald
Grubbs, Ricky Lee
Guinan, Frank
Hunter, Burt
Irvin, Thomas
Johns, Stephen
Jones, Marvin
Jones, William
Kenley, Kenneth
Kilgore, Bruce
Larette, Anthony
Lashley, Frederick
Laws, Leonard
Leisure, David R.
Lingar, Stanley
McDonald, Sam
McMillan, Richard
Mallett, Jerome
Malone, Kelvin
Mathenia, Charles Lee
Murray, Robert "Tony"
Nave, Emmett
Newlon, Rayfield
O'Neal, Robert
Oxford, Richard
Parkus, Steven J.
Petary, Donald
Pollard, Roosevelt
Preston, Elroy
Reese, Donald
Roberts, Roy
Rodden, James
Sanders, Clindell
Schlup, Lloyd
Schneider, Eric
Schnick, James
Shaw, Robert
Shurn, Daryl
Sidebottom, Robert T.
Sloan, Jeffrey
Smith, Gerald
Smith, Samuel D.
Stokes, Winford
Sweet, Glennon
Twenter, Virginia
Walls, Robert
Weaver, William
Wells, Luther
Whitfield, Joseph
Wilkins, Heath
Williams, Doyle
Young, Moses
Zeitvogel, Richard

MONTANA (Hanging or Lethal Injection)

Dawson, David T.
Kills On Top, Vern
Kills On Top, Lester
Langford, Terry
McKenzie, Duncan
Smith, Ronald

NEBRASKA (Electrocution)

Anderson, C. Michael
Harper, Steven
Hochstein, Peter
Joubert, John
Moore, Carey
Otey, Harold
Palmer, Charles
Reeves, Randolph
Rust, John
Ryan, Michael
Victor, Clarence
Williams, Robert

NEVADA (Lethal Injection)

Adams, Larry
Baal, Thomas
Beets, Edward
Bejarano, John
Bennett, Edward
Browning, Paul Lewis
Canape, Richard
Cavanaugh, Patrick
Collier, Gregory
Crump, Thomas
Dawson, Henry
Depasquale, Vince
Emil, Rodney
Emmons, Mark
Farmer, Robert
Flanagan, Dale
Ford, Priscilla
Gallego, Gerald
Haberstroh, Richard
Hardison, Richard
Hill, James E.
Hogan, Michael Ray
Homick, Steven
Howard, Samuel
Jimenez, Victor
Kirksey, Jimmy
Lopez, Manuel
Lord, Thomas
McKague, Kenneth
McKenna, Patrick
Mazzen, John
Milligan, Ronnie Gayle
Miranda, Roberto
Moore, Randolph
Moran, Richard
Neuschafer, Jimmy
Nevius, Thomas
Padilla, Daniel
Pelligrini, David
Perdgen, Wes
Petrocelli, Tracy
Riggins, David
Robins, Charles Lamont
Rogers, Mark
Sechrest, Ricky
Snow, John
Stevens, Dwayne
Valerio, John
William, Leonard
Williams, Cary
Wilson, Edward
Ybarra, Robert

NEW JERSEY (Lethal Injection)

Bey, Marko
Clausell, James
Coyle, Bryan
Dixon, Philip
Erazo, Samuel
Harvey, Nathaniel
Hightower, Jacinto
Hunt, James
Jackson, Kevin
Johnson, Walter
Long, Ronald
McDougald, Anthony
Marshall, Robert
Moore, Samuel Leon
Ogelsby, Walter
Pennington, Frank
Perry, Arthur
Pitts, Darryl Lee
Purnell, Braynard
Savage, Roy
Zola, James E.

NEW MEXICO (Lethal Injection)

Clark, Terry
Henderson, Thomas

NORTH CAROLINA (Gas Chamber or Lethal Injection)

Adams, Thomas
Ali, El-Amin Ahmad
Allen, Timothy
Anthony, Francis
Artis, Roscoe
Bacon, Robert Jr.
Barnes, Elwell
Bonney, Thomas
Boyd, Arthur Martin
Boyd, Kenneth
Bridges, Wilfred
Brogden, Donald R.
Brown, Bobby Ray
Brown, David Junior
Brown, Thomas Jack
Brown, Willie
Buchanan, Lenwood E.
Case, Jerry Douglas
Coffey, Fred
Cole, Wade L.
Cox, Sue
Craig, Andrew
Cummings, Edward Lee
Cummings, Jerry Ray
Davis, Eugene
Fullwood, Michael Lee
Gardner, John
Green, Alton Garner
Green, Harvey Lee
Greene, Gary
Handy, William
Heatwole, George
Hedgepeth, Roland
Hightower, Bobby Ray
Holden, Russell
Huff, Everett R.
Huffstetler, David
Hunt, Henry Lee
Johnson, Ceasar L.
Johnston, Joe C.
Jones, William Q.
Joyner, Richard
Laws, Wayne Alan
Lawson, David
Lloyd, Oscar
Lynch, Gregory
McCarver, Ernest
McDougall, Mike
McKoy, Dock
McLaughlin, Elton
McNeil, Leroy
McPhail, Frederick W.
Maynard, Anson
Meyer, Jeffrey
Monroe, Casey Jack
Moore, George
Moss, Bobby R.
Noland, John
Oliver, John Wesley
Payne, Randy Joe
Pinch, Michael
Pope, Jimmie
Porter, William Howard
Price, Ricky Lee
Quesinberry, Michael
Quick, Harold
Robbins, Phillip
Robinson, Dwight
Robinson, Eddie
Roper, James E.
Sanders, Stanley
Sanderson, Ricky Lee
Simpson, Perrie Dyon
Smith, Kermit
Smith, Roger
Smith, Rowland
Smith, Terry William
Spruill, Jonnie Lee
Stager, Barbara
Taylor, Norris
Thomas, James Edward
Turner, Claude
Upchurch, James
Williams, Douglas
Williams, Larry Darnel
Willis, James Earl
Wilson, Michael
Wynne, Carl
Zuniga, Bernardino

OKLAHOMA (Lethal Injection)

Allen, Gary
Allen, John C.
Allen, Wanda Jean
Banks, Anthony
Barnett, Larry
Battenfield, Billy
Berget, Roger
Boltz, John
Booker, Winfred
Bowie, Benito
Boyd, Ronald Lee
Brecheen, Robert
Brewer, Benjamin
Brown, David
Cannon, Randy
Cartwright, Timothy
Castro, John
Clayton, Robert W.
Coleman, Charles
Cooks, Cornell
Cravatt, Darias Jr.
Crawford, Joseph
Cyril, Wayne
Davis, Charles
Duckett, Robert D.
Duvalle, John
Fisher, James
Fontenot, Karl
Foster, Charles
Fowler, Mark
Fox, Billy
Green, Michael
Hain, Scott Allan
Hale, Alvie
Harjo, Jerald
Hatch, Steven
Hawkins, Don Wilson
Hayes, Roger Dale
Hays, Thomas "Sonny"
Hogan, Kenneth
Hooker, John
Howell, Michael
Humphrey, Jackie
Hunter, Thomas
Jackson, Simon
James, Terrence
Johnson, Malcolm
Johnson, Robert Grady
Jones, D.L.
Jones, Patricia B.
Lafever, Lloyd
Lambert, Robert
Liles, Mark
Long, Michael Edward
Mann, Anthony
Marquez, Howard
Martinez, Gilberto
Miller, Robert Lee
Moore, Dewey
Moore, Scott Lee
Munson, Adolf
Neill, Jay Wesley
Newstead, Norman Lee
Nguyen, Tuan
Nolte, Michael
Nuckols, Kenneth
Parker, Henry
Parks, Robin Leroy
Paxton, Kenneth W.
Plantz, Marilyn K.
Porter, Roger
Revilla, Daniel
Roberts, Michael
Robison, Olan Randle
Rojem, Richard
Romano, John
Ross, Bobby Lynn
Roubeaux, James
Salazar, Maximo
Sellers, Sean
Smith, Bobby D.
Smith, Henry
Smith, Lois Nadine
Smith, Mikell P.
Smith, Phillip
Smith, Richard
Snow, Rocky D.
Stafford, Roger
Stiles, Russell
Stouffer, Bigler
Stout, Billy Gene
Tate, Kenneth
Thomas, Darrell
Tibbs, Derek
Trice, Eddie
Valdez, Geraldo
Van Woudenbert, Sammy
Wade, Forrest K.
Walker, Gary Alan
Walker, Jack D.
Washington, John Paul
White, Stephen
Wilhoit, Gregory
Williams, Melvin
Williamson, Robert
Woodruff, David
Workman, Wendell

OREGON (Lethal Injection)

Brown, Cornelius
Douglas, Rickey
Farrar, Stephen L.
Guzek, Randy
Isom, Michael
Johnson, Stressla
Langley, Robert
Langley, Robert
McDonnell, Michael
Miranda, Reyes
Moen, Ronald H.
Montez, Marco
Nestead, Stephen
Pinnel, Mark
Rogers, Dayton
Rose, Jason
Simonsen, David
Smith, Charles F.
Stevens, Dallas Ray
Tucker, Michael
Wagner, Jeffrey Scott
Walton, Tyrone
Williams, Jeffrey

PENNSYLVANIA (Electrocution)

Abu-Jamal, Mumia
Albrecht, Alfred
Appel, Martin
Atkins, Robert
Baker, Herbert
Baker, Lee
Banks, George
Bannerman, Samuel
Basemore, William
Beasley, Leslie
Birdsong, Ralph
Blystone, Scott
Breakiron, Mark
Bricker, Robert
Bryant, James
Bryant, Robert Pernell
Buehl, Roger
Carpenter, James
Carter, Darryl
Chambers, Karl
Chester, Frank
Chmiel, David
Christy, Lawrence
Clayton, Willie
Cook, Robert
Copenhefer, David C.
Cox, Russell
Crawley, Dewitt

Cross, Charles
D'Amato, Carmen
Daniels, Henry
Dehart, Robert
Draighton, Erik
Duffey, Steven
Edwards, George
Fahy, Henry
Faulkner, Arthur
Fisher, Robert
Frey, Roderick
Gorby, Thomas
Graham, Harrison
Green, Samuel Lee
Green, William
Grier, Eric J.
Griffin, Rodney
Haag, Randy
Hachett, Richard
Hall, Donald
Hardcastle, Donald
Henry, Joseph
Hiednik, Gary
Holland, William
Holoway, Arnold
Howard, Melvin K.
Hughes, Kevin
Jasper, Alfred
Jermyn, Frederic
Jones, Damon
Jones, James
Jones, Thomas
Judge, Roger
Kindler, Joseph
Laird, Richard
Lambert, James
Lark, Robert
Lee, Percy
Lesko, John
Lewis, Reginald
Logan, Ronald
Ly, Cam
McNair, Nathaniel
Marshall, Jerome
Marshall, Jerry J.
Matthews, Kevin
Maxwell, Fred
Mayhue, Fred
Mikell, William
Moore, Tyrone
Morales, Salvador
Morris, Kelvin
Moser, Leon
Murphy, Craig
O'Shea, Ronald
Pelzer, Kevin
Peterkin, Otis
Porter, Ernest
Powers, Alphonso
Proctor, Roger
Pursell, Alan
Rivers, Delores
Rolan, Florencio
Rollins, Saharris
Rompilla, Ronald
Santiago, Salvadore
Smith, James
Sneed, Willie
Spence, Morris
Starr, Gary
Steele, Roland
Stokes, Ralph
Strong, Jafes
Szuchon, Joseph
Tedford, Donald
Terry, Benjamin
Thomas, Brian
Thomas, Leroy
Tilley, William
Travaglia, Michael
Wallace, William
Watson, Herbert
Wharton, Robert
Whitney, Ray
Williams, Craig
Williams, Kenneth
Williams, Terrance
Wilson, Harold C.
Wilson, Zachary
Yarris, Nicholas
Young, Joseph
Zettlemoyer, Keith

SOUTH CAROLINA (Electrocution)

Adams, Sylvester
Arnold, John
Atkins, Joseph
Bell, Larry Gene
Bell, William H.
Butler, Horace
Cain, Russell
Caldwell, Rickie Tim
Chaffee, Jonathan
Damon, Shellie
Drayton, Leroy
Elmore, Edward Lee
Farrell, Dallas
Gaskins, Donald
Gathers, Demetrious
Gilbert, Larry
Gleaton, J.D.
Green, Anthony
Howard, Ronnie
Johnson, Richard
Jones, Donald Allen
Koon, Paul
Kornahrens, Fred
Lucas, Cecil
Manning, Warren
Matthews, Earl
Orr, Ronald
Owens, Alvin
Patterson, Raymond
Plath, John
Riddle, Ernest
Roberts, Sammy
Sims, Mitchell
Singleton, Fred
Smith, Andy Laverne
South, Robert
Spann, Sterling
Torrence, Michael
Truesdale, Louis
Victor, William
Weldon, Dana
Wilson, James William
Yates, Dale Robert
Yound, Kevin D.
Young, Kevin D.

TENNESSEE (Electrocution)

Adkins, Carl Wayne
Alley, Sedley
Austin, Richard
Barber, Terry
Bates, Wayne Lee
Bell, Roger Morris
Black, Byron
Bobo, Tony L.
Boyd, Michael Joe
Brown, Mack Edward
Caldwell, Richard
Campbell, Kenneth
Carter, James David
Caruthers, Walter
Coe, Glen
Coker, Rocky
Coleman, Michael Angelo
Cone, Gary
Cooper, Vernon Franklin
Dicks, Jeffrey
Duncan, David
Evans, Jonathan
Goad, William W. Jr.
Groseclose, William
Hale, Thomas
Harbason, Edward
Harries, Ronald
Harris, Edward
Hartman, Eddie
Henley, Steve
Hines, Anthony
House, Paul Gregory
Houston, Richard
Howell, Michael W.
Irick, Billy Ray
Johnson, Donnie Edward
Johnson, Erskine Leroy
Johnson, Walter
Jones, James Lee
King, Terry
King, Thomas
Laney, Thomas Gerald
McCord, J.B.
McCormick, Michael
McKay, William
McNish, David
Matson, Michael
Melson, Hugh
Middlebrooks, Donald
Miller, David
Morris, Timothy
O'Guinn, Kenneth W.
Owens, Gaile
Payne, Pervis
Poe, David
Porterfield, Sidney
Rickman, Ronald
Sample, Michael
Simon, Richard
Smith Leonard
Smith, Ricky
Sparks, Willy
Strouth, Donald
Sutton, Nicholas
Taylor, Darryl
Taylor, Richard C.
Teel, Bouldin
Thompson, Gregory
Tran, Heck Van
West, Steven
Wilcoxson, Bobby
Workman, Phillip
Wright, Charles
Zagorski, Edmund

TEXAS (Lethal Injection)

Adanandus, Dwight
Alexander, Guy
Allridge, James
Allridge, Ronald Keith
Amos, Bernard
Anderson, Johnny Ray
Anderson, Larry Norman
Andrews, Maurice
Aranda, Arturo
Baldree, Ernie
Banks, Dema
Barber, Danny Lee
Barefield, John Kennedy
Barnard, Harold
Barnes, Willis J.
Barrientes, Antonio
Beathard, James Lee
Beavers, Richard Lee
Beets, Betty Lou
Behringer, Earl
Bell, Walter
Beltran, Noe
Belyeu, Clifton
Bennett, Baby Ray
Bird, Jerry Joe
Black, Robert
Blackmon, Ricky
Blue, Michael
Boggess, Holt
Bonham, Antonio
Bower, Lester L.
Boyd, Charles
Boyle, Benjamin
Bradford, Gayland
Briddle, James
Bridge, Warren
Brimage, Richard
Burdine, Calvin
Burks, John
Burns, William
Butler, Jerome
Butler, Steven
Buxton, Lawrence
Cannon, Joseph J.

Cantu, Domingo
Cantu, Ruben
Cardenas, Francisco
Carter, Johnny Ray
Carter, Robert Anthony
Cass, Mark R.
Castillo, David Allen
Chambers, Ronald
Chappell, William
Clark, David M.
Clark, Herman Robert
Clayton, James
Cockrum, John
Cole, Ted Calvin
Cook, Anthony
Cook, Kerry Max
Cooks, Vincent
Cordova, Joseph Angel
Corley, Edward
County, Charles
Crane, Alvin W.
Crank, Denton Alan
Cruz, Oliver D.
Cuevas, Ignacio
Cumbo, Sam Edward
Davis, James Carl Lee
Davis, William Prince
De La Cruz, Jose
Deblanc, David Wayne
Deeb, Muneer M.
Degarmo, Roger
Delk, Monty Allen
Demouchette, James
Derrick, Mikel
Draughon, Martin
Drew, Robert
Drinkard, Richard
Duff-Smith, Markham
Duhamel, Emile Pierre
Dunn, Kenneth D.
Earhart, James
Earvin, Harvey
East, Wayne
Ellason, Thomas
Elliott, John
Ellis, Edward
Emery, Jeff
Farris, Troy Dale
Faulder, Joseph
Fearance, John
Felder, Sammy
Fierro, Cesar
First, Kenneth
Foster, Richard Donald
Fronckiewicz, Mark
Fuller, Aaron
Fuller, Tyrone
Garcia, Fernando
Gardner, Billy Conn
Gardner, David
Garrett, Daniel
Garrett, Johnny F.
Gentry, Kenneth
Gibbs, David Earl
Goodman, Michael
Goodwin, Alvin
Gosch, Lesley Lee
Goss, Cornelius
Graham, Gary
Granviel, Kenneth
Green, G.W.
Gribble, Timothy
Griffin, Jeffery
Guerra, Ricardo
Gunther, James Lee
Hafdahl, Randall Wayne
Hammond, Karl
Harris, Curtis Paul
Harris, Danny Ray
Harris, David R.
Harris, Kenneth
Havard, Patrick Curtis
Hawkins, Samuel
Hawthorn, Gene Willford
Hernandez, Juan
Hernandez, Rogelio
Hernandez, Rudolfo Baiza
Herrera, Leonel
Hicks, David
Hill, Mack O.
Hogue, Jerry
Holland, David Lee
Holloway, Emmett
Hughes, Billy George
Hughes, Preston
Jackson, Tommy Ray
Jacobs, Bruce
Jacobs, Jesse Dewayne
James, Johnny
Jenecka, Allen
Jennings, Robert M.
Jernigan, Joseph
Johnson, Carl
Johnson, Curtis
Johnson, Dorsie
Johnson, Eddie
Johnson, Gary
Joiner, Orien
Jones, Michael Steven
Jones, Raymond
Jones, Richard
Kelly, Carl E.
Kemp, Emanuel
Kinnamon, Raymond
Kitchens, William
Knox, James Roy
Kunkle, Troy
Lackey, Clarence
Lamb, John Michael
Lane, Harold
Lauti, Asua
Lewis, Andre
Lewis, David Lee
Lincecum, Kevin
Little, William Hamilton
Livingston, Charles
Lockhart, Michael
Long, David Martin
Losada, Davis
Lucas, Henry Lee
McBride, Michael
McFadden, Jerry
McFarland, Frank
McGee, Jewel R.
McGowen, Roger Wayne
McKay, David Wayne
Macias, Frederico
Madden, Robert
Madison, Daryl
Mann, Fletcher
Marquez, Mario
Martinez, Raymond
Mata, Ramon
Matson, John, Jr.
May, Justin Lee
Mayo, Randy
Mays, Nobel
Meanes, James R.
Medina, Javier
Miller, Donald A.
Miller, Garry
Miller-El, Thomas Joe
Mines, Charles
Miniel, Peter
Mitchell, Andrew L.
Mitchell, Gerald Lee
Modden, Willie Max
Montoya, Irineo
Montoya, Ramon
Moody, John
Mooney, Nelson W.
Moore, Bobby James
Moreland, James
Moreno, Jose
Motley, Jeffrey
Muniz, Pedro Cruz
Napier, Carl
Narvaiz, Leopoldo
Nelson, Marlin
Nelson, Peter D.
Nethery, Stephen
Newton, Frances
Nichols, Joseph B.
Nobles, Jonathan
Norris, Michael
Payne, Edward
Penry, Johnny Paul
Perez, Manuel J.
Perillo, Pamela
Phillips, Clifford X.
Pierce, Anthony Leroy
Powell, David Lee
Purtell, Robert Michael
Pyles, Johnny
Rabbani, Syed
Ramirez, Carlos
Ransom, Kenneth Ray
Rector, Charles
Reed, Jonathan
Rice, Tony
Richards, Michael
Richardson, Damon
Richardson, James
Richardson, Miguel A.
Riddle, Franville
Riles, Raymond
Riley, Michael Lynn
Rios, Joe
Rivera, Angel
Rivers, Warren
Roberson, Brian
Robinson, William
Robison, Larry
Rogers, Patrick
Romero, Jesus
Rosales, Mariano Juarez
Rougeau, Paul
Rousseau, Anibal
Rudd, Emerson
Russell, Clifton Charles
Russell, James C.
Santana, Carlos
Satterwhite, John
Sattiewhite, Vernon
Sawyers, John
Selvage, John Henry
Session, James
Sharp, Michael
Skelton, John
Smith, Charles
Smith, Jack Harvey
Smith, James E.
Soffar, Max
Soria, Juan
Sosa, Pedro S.
Spence, David Wayne
Sterling, Gary
Sterling, Terry Nash
Stewart, Darryl E.
Stocker, David
Teague, Delbert Boyd
Tennard, Robert
Thomas, Danny Dean
Thomas, Kenneth Wayne
Tompkins, Phillip D.
Trevino, Jose Mario
Tucker, Jeffery
Tucker, Karla Fay
Turner, Jessel
Upton, Jackie Wayne
Urbano, Gilbert
Valdez, Alberto
Vanderbilt, Jimmy
Vega, Martin
Vigneault, Donald L.
Vuong, Hai Hai
Washington, Terry
Washington, Willie
Webb, Freddie
West, Robert W.
Westley, Anthony Ray
White, Billy Wayne
White, Excell
White, Larry Wayne
Wilkens, James Jay
Wilkerson, Richard
Williams, Arthur Lee
Williams, Calvin Joseph
Williams, Toby Lynn
Williams, Walter Key
Williams, Willie Ray
Willis, Ernest Ray
Wills, Bobby Joe
Wilson, Jackie B.

Woods, Billy Joe
Wyle, James

UTAH (Firing Squad or Lethal Injection)

Andrews, William
Archiletta, Michael
Gardner, Ronnie Lee
Holland, James
Lafferty, Ron
Menzies, Ralph W.
Parsons, Mitchell
Tillman, Elroy
Young, David

VIRGINIA (Electrocution)

Barnes, Herman
Bassett, Herbert
Beaver, Gregory
Bennett, Ronald
Boggs, Richard
Buchanan, Douglas
Bunch, Timothy
Cheng, Dung Quang
Clozza, Albert
Coleman, Roger
Correll, Walter
Delong, Wayne
Eaton, Dennis W.
Edmonds, Dana
Evans, Wilburt
Fisher, David Lee
Fitzgerald, Edward
Fruett, David Mark
Giarratano, Joseph
Gray, Coleman Wayne
Hoke, Ronald Lee
Jones, Willie Leroy
Justus, Buddy
Mackall, Tony
O'Dell, Joseph
Payne, Joseph
Peterson, Derrick
Pope, Carlton
Poyner, Syvasky
Pruett, David Mark
Savino, Jospeh J.
Smith, Roy B.
Spencer, Timothy
Stamper, Charles
Stockton, Dennis
Stout, Larry Alan
Townes, Richard
Tuggle, Lem
Turner, Willie Lloyd
Washington, Earl Jr.
Watkins, Johnny
Watkins, Ronald
Williams, Terry
Wise, Joe

WASHINGTON (Lethal Injection)

Campbell, Charles
Furman, Michael
Harris, Benjamin
Jeffries, Patrick
Lord, Brian Keith
Mak, Kwan
Rice, David Lewis
Rupe, Mitchell

WYOMING (Lethal Injection)

Engberg, Roy
Hopkinson, Mark

FEDERAL JURISDICTIONS (Lethal Injection)

Curtis, Ronnie Allen
Gray, Ronald
Loving, Dwight J.
Murphy, James
Thomas, Joseph L.

ROBBERY

1671
May 9: Colonel Thomas Blood and two others stole the British Crown Jewels from the Tower of London. King Charles II pardoned Blood after his capture.
1719
Mar 23: Christopher Banister, British thief, was hanged for attempting to rob Dorothy Thompson of her muslin hood, valued at only four shillings.
1721
January: Convicted highwayman Thomas Spigot was sentenced in London to torturous treatment in which his limbs were extended and heavy weights were placed upon his chest.
1759
May 31: Margaret Barrack, Mary Duncan, and Janet Shinney stood in the Market Cross at Aberdeen, Scot. wearing nameplates showing their guilt for pilfering tea and sugar from a resident businessman.
1823
Oct. 23: William Weare died after his throat was slit by John Thurtell, during a robbery attempt in London.
1855
William Pierce and Edward Agar committed the first recorded train robbery, known as the Great Train Robbery. The two threw gold bars from the South Eastern Railway train as it left London. Agar turned in Pierce and others later.
1858
Dionysius Wielobychi, Scottish physician, was brought to justice for robbing his patients in Portobello by fraudulent investments.
1863
Dec. 15: Edward W. Green robbed the Malden, Mass., bank of $5,000 after he killed Frank Converse, son of the bank's president. He was executed on Feb. 27, 1866.
1864
Oct. 18: Twenty-two Confederate soldiers robbed three banks in St. Albans, Vt., of $114,522, then fled to Canada, where fourteen were later arrested. Neither the gold nor the cash was recovered.
1866
Feb. 13: Jesse and Frank James, Cole Younger, and others stole $60,000 from the Clay County Savings Bank in Liberty, Mo. Liberty resident George Wymore was shot dead as the bandits rode off.
Oct. 6: Frank, John, Simon, and William Reno, and six others stopped a train bound from Ohio to Mississippi and stole $10,000 in cash and gold from the Adams Express car on a train outside of Seymour, Ind.
1868
May 22: The Reno brothers and their gang boarded a train of the Jefferson, Mo., and Indianapolis Railway, uncoupled the passenger cars, and robbed the express car of $96,000 twenty miles down the tracks. All were hanged by vigilantes Dec. 11.
1869
June 27: George Leonidas Leslie and his gang robbed the Ocean National Bank in New York City of $786,879.
1871
June 3: Jesse and Frank James, the Younger brothers, and three others robbed the Ocobock Brother's Bank in Corydon, Iowa, of $45,000.
1875
July 7: The James gang robbed the United Express car on the Missouri Pacific train of $75,000 outside Otterville, Mo.
1876
May 27: Adam Worth, accompanied by two men, stole the Gainsborough painting "The Duchess of Devonshire" from a London gallery.
Sept. 7: The James-Younger gang robbed the First National Bank of Northfield, Minn. After a seven-minute fusillade outside the bank, the gang fled. Some were wounded but none killed.
1877
Sept. 18: Sam Bass and five others stole $60,000 in gold and $1,000 from passengers from the Union Pacific train, outside of Big Springs, Neb.
1878
Oct. 27: George Leonidas Leslie and four others stole $2,747,000 from the Manhattan Savings and Loan in New York City.
1884
December: After being robbed, a Newark laundry owner was stabbed and left for dead.
1885
Oct. 28: £400 of jewelry were illegally taken by James Baker and Anthony Benjamin Rudge, who injured two officers and killed a constable while making their escape.
1886
October: Thieves stole $88,000 in cash and securities from an Adams Express Company car, near St. Louis. Four months later, Fred Wittrock was arrested and charged with masterminding the operation.
1895
July 1: A female robber named Frankie Smith was apprehended in Chicago by Detective Clifton Wooldridge.
1896
Oct. 27: Delia Foley, a prostitute, and George Mead, were arrested on robbery charges, by Chicago detectives. The two were turned in by another prostitute, with whom Foley had had a disagreement.
1900
Robert Owen Bain stole several thousand dollars from a bank and a steel company in Chicago.
Jan. 11: After serving time in the Utah State Penitentiary for robbery and murder, William Wall and Wild Bunch member Matt Warner were released.
Feb. 28: Wild Bunch member Lonnie Logan was shot to death outside Dodson, Mont., by a posse after him for bank robbery.
Apr. 17: Wild Bunch member and train robber George "Flat Nose" Currie was shot to death near Castle Gate, Utah, by a posse after him for cattle rustling.
May 16: Sheriff John Tyler and Deputy Sam Kenkins were murdered by Harvey "Kid Curry" Logan in Moab County, Utah, when they tried to arrest Logan for robbery.
May 23: Thomas Jones, Fred L. Rice, Frank Rutledge, and another man, robbed a bank in Aurora, Ontario.
May 24: Herman Boppart, "Pony" Moore, and Bessie Mitchell were indicted for a series of jewel robberies in Chicago.
Aug. 29: The Wild Bunch, including Butch Cassidy, O.C. "Deaf Charley" Hanks, Harvey Logan, and Harry "the Sundance Kid" Longbaugh, robbed $5,014 from the Union Pacific No. 3 Train between Tipton and Table Rock, Wyo.
Sept. 19: Butch Cassidy and Harry Longbaugh robbed several thousand dollars from the First National Bank of Winnemuca, Nev.
1901
Jan. 17: Wealthy farmer William Pearson was shot to death on a London-bound train by George Henry Parker, who stole the man's purse. Parker was hanged on Mar. 19.
Apr. 9: "Pony" Moore was indicted for the robbery of jewelry in Chicago.
Apr. 25: In Clayton, N.M., Black Jack Ketchum was hanged for train robbery.
Apr. 26: The Paris American Express office was robbed of $100,000 by "Chicago May" Churchill, Eddie Guerin, and others. On June 14, 1902, Churchill and Guerin were sent to prison.
June 17: "Old Bill" Miner was released from San Quentin after serving twenty years for robbing the Sonora, Calif., stagecoach.
July 3: Butch Cassidy, O.C. Hanks, Harvey Logan, Harry Longbaugh, Ben "the Tall Texan" Kilpatrick, and others stole $40,000 from the Great Northern train outside Wagner, Mont. Kilpatrick and his wife were arrested Nov. 8 and sent to prison.
1902
Apr. 15: Police caught up with Wild Bunch member O.C. Hanks two years after he robbed a train. Hanks was killed resisting arrest.
May 8: After an earthquake leveled St. Pierre, Martinique, dozens of looters descended upon the city and robbed the banks.
Sept. 21: Eugenie Fourgè\re was strangled to death by her companion Madame Giriat, who then stole her jewelry. Giriat was sent to prison for life.
Nov. 30: Harvey Logan was sent to prison for twenty years and fined $5,000 for train robbery.
Dec. 28: George Collins and Bill "the Missouri Kid" Rudolph blew open the vault of a Union, Mo., bank and stole $28,000.
1903
Jan. 16: President Theodore Roosevelt pardoned Henry Starr and the robber and murderer was released from the Ohio State Penitentiary.
July 8: In Chicago, Gustave Marx, Peter Neidermeyer, and Harvey Van Dine, called the "Automatic Trio" or "Car Barn Bandits," began their spree of eight robberies, in which eight men were killed. They were arrested Nov. 27.
Sept. 23: A train was stopped and robbed of a few hundred dollars outside Corbett, Ore., by lone robber Old Bill Miner.
Dec. 7: Notorious bank robber and burglar Jimmy Dunlap was released from prison in Joliet, Ill., after serving only three years.
1904
Jan. 19: Pitchfork-wielding farmers prevented Bill Rudolph from robbing the National Bank of Louisburg, Kan. He was captured and sent to prison.
June 7: Harvey "Kid Curry" Logan and two others robbed the Denver & Rio Grande Railroad at Parachute, Colo. The next day, a posse wounded Logan, who committed suicide.
Aug. 3: A postman was robbed of 400 francs and killed in Paris by Jean-Baptiste Detollenaere, who was guillotined in 1905.
Sept. 3: A Canadian Pacific train was robbed of $10,000 at Missouri Junction, B.C., by Old Bill Miner.
1905
Feb. 11: Butch Cassidy, Harry Longbaugh, and others robbed several sacks of gold from the bank in Lourdes, Arg.
Mar. 23: Robert Butler robbed and killed William Munday near Tooringa, Aus. He was later executed.
1906
Jan. 10: After serving five years for an 1897 train robbery, Wild Bunch member Elza Lay was released from New Mexico State Prison.
Mar. 2: Butch Cassidy, Harry Longbaugh, and others robbed gold and bank notes from the bank in Via Mercedes, Arg.

May 8: Outside Furrer, B.C., the Canadian Pacific's Transcontinental Express was robbed of several hundred dollars by Old Bill Miner, who was sent to prison on June 1.
Oct. 16: Posing as an army captain, Wilhelm Voight took over Kopeneck, Ger., and ordered deluded soldiers to bring him the city's funds of 4,000 marks which he ran off with.
1907
Feb. 13: After serving time for robbery in Wyoming State Penitentiary, Wild Bunch member Bob Lee was released.
Apr. 20: The U.S. Army court-martialed Carl Panzram for stealing government property. He was sent to prison.
June 25: Semyon A. Ter-Petrossian, a friend of Joseph Stalin, stole $341,000 from two bank guards in Tiflis, Russia.
1908
Mar. 3: Bolivian troops interrupted Butch Cassidy, Harry Longbaugh, and others while they were robbed a pack train near La Paz. Longbaugh was killed at San Vincente, while Cassidy either escaped or killed himself.
Mar. 13: Henry Starr and Kid Wilson robbed $2,500 from the State Bank of Tyro, Kan.
1909
Jan. 24: Paul Hefeld and Jacob Meyer stole eighty gold sovereigns from Schurmann's Rubber Co. in London. Two in pursuit were shot to death as the gunmen escaped. Later, Hefeld killed himself, and Meyer was shot to death by police.
Feb. 16: Leslie Coombs was sentenced to death for robbing and killing a man in St. Lawrence County, N.Y.
June 28: The bank of Amity, Colo., was robbed of $1,100 by Henry Starr and Kid Wilson. Both were later imprisoned.
July 30: A Portland, Ore., bank was robbed of $12,000 by Old Bill Miner.
Dec. 29: The Mercantile Co. of Rio Pescado, Arg., was robbed by U.S. outlaws, who killed Lloyd Apjuan before fleeing with little money.
1910
Mar. 18: Cashier John Nisbet was robbed of his company's wages by John Alexander Dickman while riding the train to Widdrington Station, England. Dickman was hanged.
Sept. 17: Future Chicago gangster George "Bugs" Moran was sent to prison in Joliet, Ill., for robbing a store.
1911
Jan. 18: The Southern Railroad Express was robbed at White Sulphur Springs, Ga., of $3,500 by Old Bill Miner and others. Miner was caught and sent to prison.
June 11: Ben Kilpatrick was released from Atlanta Federal Penitentiary after serving a sentence for robbery.
June 15: New York's Roy Hotel was robbed of $160 by Robert Arthur Tourbillon.
Aug. 21: Vincenzo Peruggia, a janitor at the Louvre in Paris, stole the Mona Lisa. He was arrested in 1913 and given a light sentence.
Sept. 5: A jewelry store was robbed at Wood Green, England.
Dec. 21: A gang led by Jules Joseph Bonnot, the first European to use a car in a robbery, stole $333,500 in paper and gold from the Saint-Ouen Branch of the Société Général Bank in Paris.
1912
A Chantilly, Fr., bank was robbed of 80,000 francs by Jules Joseph Bonnot, who shot and killed three people before fleeing by car.
Jan. 3: Jules Bonnot and his gang robbed and killed a wealthy senior citizen and his servant in Paris.
Jan. 8: The Jules Bonnot gang robbed the Smith & Wesson gun shop in Paris.
Mar. 12: David A. Trousdale, the guard on the Southern Pacific's Sunset Flyer, killed Ben Kilpatrick and Howard Benson as they tried to rob the train's express car.
Mar. 14: Floyd Allen and his gang were found guilty of bank robbery in Richmond, Va. In an attempt to escape, Allen and his men shot up the courtroom, killing Judge Thornton L. Massie, before they were subdued.
Mar. 25: The Jules Bonnot gang stole a car for an upcoming robbery, and killed the occupants. Bonnot killed himself on Apr. 29 when surrounded by police, who also killed an accomplice.
June 14: The scheduled execution of Mexican general Pancho Villa was halted when the charge of stealing horses was dropped.
1913
Feb. 26: Surviving members of the Jules Bonnot gang—Callemin, Dieudonne, Monier, and Soudy—were sentenced to death in France for robbery and murder. Dieudonne was later reprieved.
October: Paul Markowitz was apprehended for the robbery of a Berlin apartment after it was found that minute particles of lignite ash found on his shoes matched samples taken at the crime scene.
1914
Sept. 30: The Kiefer Central Bank in Kiefer, Okla., was robbed of $6,400 by Henry Starr and others, who escape by car—the first time in the U.S. a getaway car was used in a bank robbery.
Oct. 6: Henry Starr and his gang stole $800 from the Farmers' National Bank in Tupelo, Okla.
Oct. 14: Henry Starr and his gang robbed the Pontotoc Bank in Pontotoc, Okla., of $1,100.
Oct. 20: The Byars State Bank in Byars, Okla., was robbed of $700 by Henry Starr and his gang.
Nov. 13: Henry Starr and his gang stole $2,400 from the Farmers' State Bank in Glencoe, Okla.
Nov. 29: Henry Starr and his gang robbed the Citizens' State Bank in Wardville, Okla., of $800.
Dec. 16: The Prue State Bank in Prue, Okla., was robbed of $1,400 by Henry Starr and his gang.
Dec. 29: Henry Starr and his gang stole $2,853 from the Carney State Bank in Carney, Okla.
1915
Jan. 4: Henry Starr and his gang blew open the vault at the Oklahoma State Bank in Preston, Okla. The blast burned most of the currency and caused $1,200 damage. They fled as police arrived.
Jan. 5: The First National Bank in Owasso, Okla., was robbed of $1,500 by Henry Starr and his gang.
Jan. 12: Henry Starr and his gang stole $1,800 from the First National Bank in Terlton, Okla., and $2,500 from the Garber State Bank in Garber, Okla.
Jan. 13: Henry Starr and his gang robbed the Vera State Bank in Vera, Okla., of $1,300.
1916
May 12: In New York City, Jack "Legs" Diamond was arrested for robbery and assault.
Sept. 3: Dwight Dilworth was robbed and killed by three gunmen while he was sitting in his stalled car in New York City's Cortland Park.
1917
Aug. 28: "Blackie" Wheed and others robbed $9,100 from a Brink's truck in Chicago, killing the driver and a guard as well. Wheed was later executed, two others were sent to prison, and the fourth escaped. Only half of the money was recovered.
Dec. 12: Johnny Lazia was sent to the Missouri State Penitentiary for robbing a Kansas City, Mo., store.
1918
Jan. 20: Joseph and Helen Holbach were robbed of several hundred dollars and killed in their roadhouse outside South Ozone Park, N.Y., by Mike Casalino, Giuseppe Zambelli, and two others. Casalino and Zambelli were executed; the others were sent to prison.
Mar. 13: For attempting to rob a New York City jewelry store, Jack Diamond was arrested, but the charge was dropped.
Apr. 16: Jack Diamond was arrested for attempted robbery in New York City. The charge was dropped.
Apr. 24: The La Villette gang stole 94,000 francs from Mme. Dreyfus after killing her in her Paris apartment.
Sept. 24: Kansas City police cornered bank robbers Dale Jones and Roscoe Lancaster, and their driver Margie Dean. Lancaster was killed as Dean and Jones escaped.
Nov. 24: Police cornered and killed bank robbers Margie Dean and Dale Jones in a shootout in Arcadia, Calif.
1919
Oct. 18: In Cordell, Okla., Frank "Jelly" Nash was arrested for robbing several hundred dollars from the local bank a week earlier. The charges were dropped.
Dec. 30: After knocking out the driver, Chicago crook Charles Dion O'Bannion stole a truck filled with liquor.
1920
Apr. 15: The $15,776.51 payroll for the Slater and Morrill shoe factory in South Braintree, Mass., was robbed by four gunmen who killed paymaster Frederick Parmenter. Nicola Sacco and Bartolomeo Vanzetti were executed for the crime.
Apr. 25: Percy Toplis killed a taxi driver when he resisted the robbery. Toplis was killed at Penrith, Scot., in a shootout with police.
Aug. 10: The Lesieur banking firm in Paris was robbed of more than 30,000 francs by the La Villette gang.
Oct. 11: In a robbery attempt, René Jean and La Villette gang members threw pepper in the eyes of a bank messenger carrying 225,000 francs on a Paris street.
Oct. 21: Thousands of francs were stolen from Mme. Dessene in Paris after René Jean and other La Villette gang members killed her.
Nov. 5: Wilbur Underhill was sent to the Jefferson City, Mo., state prison for robbery.
1921
Feb. 18: Henry Starr was shot by Peoples Bank president W.J. Meyers as the lone gunman fled the Harrison, Ark., bank. Starr died four days later.
July 25: After leaving Paris, wealthy passengers on the Express No. 5 train were robbed by five bandits who killed an officer trying to stop them. All robbers were later tracked down.
Oct. 14: In New York City, Gerald Chapman and Charles Loeber robbed a mail truck of more than $2.4 million in negotiable securities.
Oct. 15: "Terrible Tommy" O'Connor was convicted of a murder committed during the robbery of the Illinois Central a year earlier. He escaped before his scheduled execution.
Oct. 24: Gerald Chapman and others robbed securities from a New York City mail truck.
Oct. 27: A mail truck in New York City was robbed of $1,424,129 by Gerald Chapman and two others. Chapman was hanged on Apr. 5, 1926, for killing a guard.
Nov. 9: Ex-politician "Big Tim" Murphy was convicted and sent to prison for participating in a $360,000 mail robbery the year before.

1922
The Denver U.S. Mint was robbed of $500,000 in gold by Harvey Bailey and James Ripley.
Feb. 10: Arthur "Dock" Barker was sent to Oklahoma State Penitentiary in McAlester for bank robbery and murder.
Apr. 16: Following a New York City robbery, Jack Diamond was held as material witness, but released the next day.
Apr. 19: The La Villette gang robbed the Paris post office of an unknown sum of money.
Nov. 28: The last of the La Villette robbery gang, led by René Jean, was arrested. All were sentenced to death.
1923
Feb. 14: Wilbur Underhill was sent to prison in Jefferson City, Mo., for bank robbery.
June 12: Jewels worth 800,000 francs were stolen from a French diamond broker by a thief named Kleinberg, who swapped bags with the broker. Kleinberg and his accomplice were arrested July 29.
July 20: Pancho Villa, bandit and revolutionary leader of Mexico, was killed as he drove into Parralll.
Aug. 20: The *Katy Limited* train was robbed of $20,000 in Liberty bonds and cash near Okesa, Okla., by George Curtis, Grover Durill, Curtis Kelly, Frank Nash, Al Spencer, Earl "Dad" Thayer, and Wilbur Underhill. Police killed Spencer Sept. 20.
Oct. 11: Hugh, Ray, and Roy D'Autremont killed four crew members of the Southern Pacific Railroad No. 13 train outside Siskiyou, Ore., in a failed robbery attempt. They were later sent to prison.
Nov. 28: Jack Diamond was arrested for robbing a New york City store. He was released four months later.
1924
Jan. 5: Cecilia and Ed Cooney stole $688 from a Brooklyn, N.Y., store. They were caught in Florida and sent to prison.
Sept. 6: John Herbert Dillinger's attempt to rob a Martinsville, Ind., grocery was foiled by the owner. Dillinger was sent to prison.
Oct. 24: Three robbers tried to steal thousands of dollars from Brink's guards Franklin Good and John Callanan in New York City. Good was killed, and though shot, Callanan retrieved the money.
1925
Mar. 20: Marcel Pierson and two others robbed a Paris post office and killed a postman. The trio were sent to prison.
Sept. 16: For robbing a St. Louis payroll, Charles Arthur "Pretty Boy" Floyd was sent to prison in Jefferson City, Mo.
1926
Apr. 5: Gerald Chapman was hanged for killing a police officer who chased him following an attempted robbery of a New Britain, Conn., department store.
Apr. 21: In Newark, N.J., Joseph "Doc" Stacher was arrested for robbery, but he was released on Apr. 22.
July 11: Lester Gillis, later known as "Baby Face" Nelson, was paroled from his third robbery conviction in Illinois.
Aug. 24: Making good his threat if he were not given $2,000, a robber in the Farmers' National Bank in Pittsburgh, Pa., dropped the bag containing a bomb. Twenty-three people were injured, and the robber and a guard were killed.
1927
Matt and George Kimes and Ray Terrill drove their truck through the window of the Pampa, Texas, bank, tied the safe to a winch and drove off with $35,000 trailing behind.
Jan. 7: Following an aborted bank robbery in Tulsa, Okla., Wilbur Underhill stole a car and killed the driver. He was caught and sent to prison.
Mar. 11: Explosives planted by Paul Jawarski and nine other Flathead Gang members turned a Brink's car over near Pittsburgh, Pa. The robbers stole more than $104,000 after breaking through the truck's wooden bottom. Brink's armored cars were soon revamped.
Sept. 19: Herman Barker committed suicide when police closed in on his car used in a robbery in Newton, Kan.
1928
May 23: William Harrison and Ralph Emerson Fleagle, and Howard Royston, and George Johnson Abshier robbed the First National Bank in Lamar, Colo., of $218,000 and killed A.N. and N.J. Parrish and Dr. W.W. Weininger. Three robbers were hanged, while William Fleagle was killed by police.
1929
Mar. 9: Charles Arthur Floyd was arrested for robbery in Kansas City, but the charge was dropped, as were similar charges on three more arrests during the year.
Mar. 15: Joseph Valachi was released from custody in New York City following his arrest Mar. 14 for armed robbery.
June: Toyoshi Nakamura was arrested in Tokyo, and charged with the series of robberies which occurred at geisha houses.
October: Six armed men robbed patrons of Chicago's Palm Gardens night club. They tempered the loss by buying a round of drinks and returned jewelry to the women who consented to dance with them.
December: After derailing a Union Pacific train near Cheyenne, Wyo., Tom Vernon robbed its passengers of $800.
1930
March: After convincing a teller they could tell his fortune after placing a handkerchief over the money, two women stole $1,000 from the East Orange, N.J., Trust Company.
Mar. 11: Thousands of dollars were stolen from the Sylvania, Ohio, bank by Charles Arthur Floyd, Jack Atkins, and Tom Bradley. Bradley was executed for killing officer Harlan F. Manes as they escaped; Atkins was sent to prison, and Floyd escaped.
Sept. 10: Oliver Curtis Perry, 1890s train robber, died after blinding himself in his cell at Clinton Prison in Dannemora, N.Y.
Sept. 17: Edward Wilhelm Bentz, Harvey Bailey, and Ed Fitzgerald were arrested for the robbery of the Lincoln National Bank and Trust Co. of more than $2.6 million.
Oct. 28: New York City's M. Rosenthal & Sons Jewelers was robbed of more than $30,000 by Willie "The Actor" Sutton, who posed as a telegraph messenger to gain entrance, and Marcus Bassett.
Nov. 28: Marcus Bassett was arrested for robbery in New York City, and confessed to eight holdups garnering $214,000 committed with Willie Sutton.
Dec. 16: Herman K. Lamm, James "Oklahoma Jack" Clark, Walter Dietrich, and G.W. "Dad" Landy stole $15,567 from the Citizens State Bank in Clinton, Ind. Lamm and the gang's driver were killed by police, Landy killed himself, and Clark and Dietrich were sent to prison.
1931
Harvey Bailey, Eddie Bertz, and others stole more than $1 million from the Lincoln National Bank in Lincoln, Neb.
Jan. 15: "Baby Face" Nelson robbed a few gems from a Chicago jewelry store.
Feb. 23: "Iron Irene" Schroeder was executed at Pennsylvania's Rockview Penitentiary for killing a guard during an escape. She and her condemned husband, Walter Glenn Dague, had committed numerous bank robberies across the U.S.
May 2: After serving time for robbery in the Kansas State Penitentiary, Alvin Karpis was released.
July 17: "Baby Face" Nelson was sent to the state prison in Joliet, Ill., for robbery.
Dec. 12: Charles Arthur Floyd and George Birdwell stole a few hundred dollars from two banks, one in Castle, Okla., and the other in and Paden, Okla.
1932
Mar. 9: Police arrested bank robber Adam Richetti in Sulphur, Okla. He jumped bond and joined up with Charles Arthur Floyd.
Mar. 25: Clyde Barrow stole $300 from the Sims Oil Co. in Dallas, Texas.
May: The home of Portuguese couple with a royal lineage, "King" Manoel and "Queen" Augusta Victoria, was robbed in London.
June 17: Fred Barker, Harvey Bailey, Phil Courtney, Larry Devol, Tommy Holden, and Alvin Karpis stole $47,000 from the Fort Scott, Kan., Bank.
July 7: The FBI arrested bank robbers Harvey Bailey, Tommy Holden, and Francis Keating while they golfed at the Old Mission Country Club near Kansas City.
July 25: Fred Barker, Earl Christman, Larry Devol, Jess Doyle, Alvin Karpis, and Frank Nash stole more than $250,000 from the Cloud County Bank in Concordia, Kan.
Aug. 8: Fred Barker, Volney Davis, and Larry Devol stole $1,000 from the Citizens Security Bank in Bixby, Okla.
September: Eight men stole $250,000 from a safe at Koch & Company, a Chicago real estate office, after breaking through the floor of an apartment located above the office.
October: Four men robbed the county jail at Crookston, Minn., of money, arms, ammunition, liquor and confiscated slot machines.
Oct. 8: Bonnie Parker, Clyde and Buck Barrow, Ray Hamilton, W.D. Jones stole $1,400 from the Abilene State Bank in Abilene, Texas.
Nov. 1: Charles Arthur Floyd, George Birdwell, and Aussie Elliot stole $2,530 from the Sallisaw, Okla., Bank.
Nov. 7: Charles Arthur Floyd, George Birdwell, and Aussie Elliot stole $11,352.20 from the Henryetta, Okla., bank.
Nov. 9: Bonnie Parker, Clyde Barrow, and others stole $200 from the Orenogo, Mo., bank.
Nov. 30: Charles Arthur Floyd, George Birdwell, and Aussie Elliot stole $50,000 from the Citizens State Bank in Tupelo, Miss.
December: A robber using a piece of gum on the end of a stick extracted $500,000 in government bonds from a tellers window at the Continental Bank & Trust Company in New York City.
Dec. 16: Arthur and Fred Barker, Larry Devol, Jesse Doyle, Alvin Karpis, Verne Miller, and Bill Weaver stole $20,000 from the Third Northwestern Bank in Minneapolis, Minn.
Dec. 23: Clyde Barrow killed Doyle Johnson in Temple, Texas, and then stole his car.
1933
May 8: Clyde Barrow, Bonnie Parker, and others stole $300 from the Lucerne, Ind., State Bank.
May 16: Bonnie Parker, Clyde Barrow, and others stole $1,500 from the First State Bank in Okabena, Minn.
June 10: John Dillinger, Paul "Lefty" Parker, and William Shaw stole $10,600 from the National Bank in New Carlisle, Ind.
June 22: Clyde Barrow, Bonnie Parker, and others robbed the Alma, Texas, State Bank of a few hundred dollars.
June 23: Clyde Barrow and Bonnie Parker stole about $50 from a Fayetteville, Texas, grocery store, and killed Marshal H.D. Humphrey.

July 6: In Kansas City, FBI agents arrested James "Fur" Sammons, who was wanted for a 1926 robbery of $85,000 from International Harvester Co. in Chicago, and a Baltimore, Md., robbery of $47,000.
July 17: John Dillinger and Harry Copeland robbed the Danville, Ind., Commercial Bank of $3,500.
July 18: The Clyde Barrow gang stole less than $100 from three Fort Dodge, Iowa, gas stations.
Aug. 4: John Dillinger and Harry Copeland stole $10,110 from the First National Bank in Montpelier, Ind.
Aug. 14: John Dillinger, Harry Copeland, and Sam Goldstein robbed the Citizens National Bank in Bluffton, Ohio, of $2,100.
Aug. 15: Arthur and Fred Barker, Larry Devol, Charles J. Fitzgerald and Alvin Karpis stole $30,000 from the Swift Co. payroll in St. Paul, Minn.
Aug. 22: Arthur and Fred Barker, Monty Bolton, Fred "Shotgun Ziegler" Goetz, and Bill "Lapland Willie" Weaver robbed a Federal Reserve bank mail truck in Chicago, but obtained only canceled checks in killing policemen Miles A. Cunningham.
Sept. 6: John Dillinger, Harry Copeland, and Hilton Crouch stole $24,000 from the Massachusetts Avenue State Bank in Indianapolis, Ind.
Nov. 2: Wilbur Underhill, Ford Bradshaw, and others robbed the Citizens National Bank of Okmulgee, Okla., of $13,000.
Nov. 15: Basil "the Owl" Banghart, "Hill Billy" Costner, Charles "Ice Wagon" Connors, and "Dutch Louie" Schmidt stole $100,000 from a mail truck in Charlotte, N.C. Connors was later found murdered, while the others were sent to prison.
Nov. 20: John Dillinger, Harry Pierpont, Charles "Fat Charley" Makley, Russell Clark, and "Three-Finger Jack" Hamilton, stole $20,736 from the American Bank & Trust Co. in Racine, Wis.
1934
January: Four armed men stole $8,000 from a bank in Nauvoo, Illinois.
January: John Dillinger and John Hamilton stole $20,376 from the First National Bank of East Chicago, Ind., using the bank vice-president as a shield to escape waiting police officers.
Jan. 1: FBI agents and local police surrounded bank robber Wilbur Underhill's honeymoon cottage in Shawnee, Okla., and blasted it apart, wounding Underhill, who died five days later.
Jan. 19: A posse near Paola, Kan., killed "Big Bob" Brady, prison escapee who had robbed banks with James Henry "Blackie" Audett.
Jan. 20: Clyde Barrow and Bonnie Parker robbed the State Bank of Lancaster, Texas, of only a few hundred dollars.
Feb. 14: Willie "The Actor" Sutton was convicted in Philadelphia of bank robbery and sentenced to twenty-five to fifty years in prison.
Feb. 17: A massive raid on Cookson Hills, Okla., failed to net Bonnie Parker and Clyde Barrow or Charles Arthur "Pretty Boy" Floyd, but Aussie Elliott, Raymond Moore, and Ed Newt Clanton died and Sheriff Will Harper killed Ford Bradshaw.
Mar. 5: Harry Wells stole $2,482 from the Citizens' Bank of Luling, Texas. Ten days later he was captured in his Gladwater, Texas, hideout and sentenced to ninety-nine years in prison.
Mar. 6: John Dillinger and his gang robbed the Security National Bank of SIoux Falls, S.D., of $49,000.
Mar. 13: The Dillinger Gang robbed the First National Bank of Mason City, Iowa, of $52,000. Dillinger and John Hamilton were wounded and Hamilton later died and was buried in secret by the gang.
June 30: John Dillinger and his gang robbed the Merchants National Bank of South Bend, Ind., of $18,000.
Aug. 21: Machine gun-toting thieves robbed $427,950 from a U.S. Trucking Corporation armored car in Brooklyn, N.Y. The money was not recovered, but the robbers were sent to prison.
1935
Reese Bailey and others held up the Rosalia State Bank in Rosalia, Wash. He was caught and sent to prison one year later.
Mar. 22: Five unidentified bandits were driven away by Brinks guards when they tried to rob Wilson & Co. meatpackers in Chicago.
April: Roy Peters assaulted a woman on an Atlanta street by attempting to steal her purse. He was stopped by an elegantly dressed man who leaped from a passing car and slit Peter's throat.
Apr. 25: Alvin Karpis, Harry Campbell, and Joseph Rich stole a payroll of $70,000 from the Youngstown Sheet & Tube Plant in Youngstown, Ohio.
June 7: In New York City, William Schweitzer robbed lawyer Howard Carter Dickinson of $135 and killed him. Schweitzer was later arrested in Chicago and sentenced to life in prison.
July 7: Alvin Karpis, Harry Campbell, Fred Hunter, Ben Grayson and another man took $34,000 from Erie Mail Train No. 622 in Warren, Ohio.
November: George Albert Boyog, a Navy enlisted man, was arrested after he attempted to rob the paymaster of the *U.S.S. California*, while the ship was at sea.
Dec. 5: Several thieves robbed a bank car of the Hull Branch of the Banque Provinciale de Canada in Québec of $16,000 and killed guard Armand Nadeua. The robbers were never identified.
1936
Jan. 25: International jewel thief André Cartier killed and robbed French-Canadian jeweler Emil Haye outside London. By the time police found Cartier in Paris he was already serving twenty years for another robbery.
February: Robber Clayton Clawson, while at trial in Cleveland, produced a vial of liquid, claiming it was nitroglycerin. It proved to be merely ammonia when he dropped the container after being wounded by courtroom deputies.
May 1: The FBI arrested bank robbers Alvin Karpis and Fred Hunter in New Orleans and both were sentenced to Alcatraz. Karpis was later released and died in Europe in 1979.
November: William T. Moyers and his 18-year-old son, Marshall, robbed a Georgia bank president of $30,000 at gunpoint. They were arrested by FBI agents five days later.
December: French auto executive Emile E.C. Mathis and his wife, foiled a robbery attempt, when they beat off gunmen who attacked them as they rode in a New York City taxicab.
1937
Jan. 7: Prominent real estate man Harry Linton Butler robbed the Colorado-Mentor branch of the Bank of America of $4,000 and was shot dead by policemen as he fled.
Jan. 31: Bill Dainard and an accomplice robbed the Oakville State Bank of Oakville, Wash., of $5,000. Dainard was later captured and imprisoned.
1938
Jan. 12: Joseph Bates and Robert Clement robbed loan society manager Anthony Bocchini of $125,000 in jewelry in Alton, Fla., in a scheme masterminded by William H. Connelly. Bates and Clement were caught and given life sentences, and Connelly later got ten years.
Aug. 25: Teenagers Estelle Mae Irwin and Bennie Dickson began a crime spree by robbing the Corn Exchange Bank of Lake Benton, Minn., of over $2,000. The FBI killed Dickson in St. Louis on Apr. 6, and Irwin later went to jail for ten years.
October: Inmates Jim Godwin and Bill "Bad Eye" Wilson coerced the daughter of the county jailer in Lexington, N.C. to aid in their escape. They were both apprehended after they shot a man to death as they were stealing his automobile.
1939
Feb. 6: Wanted robber Joseph Ricardo held up the Mistele Coal Company in Detroit and got away with $10,000. He then impersonated an FBI agent in Milwaukee and committed more robberies in a hotel. He was captured after a gun battle with police in Milwaukee and sentenced to ten years in prison.
Feb. 21: Allen Reed killed auto mechanic Sam Salone during an attempted robbery in Geneva, N.Y.
1940
April: Anthony Buccolo, Doyle Gazaway and John Serido were arrested and charged with a series of gas station robberies in New Jersey.
May 30: James Henry "Blackie" Audett was released from Alcatraz after serving five years for bank robbery.
1941
Jan. 14: Horace Blacock was arrested for a series of robberies in Atlanta.
Feb. 24: Two guards pushing nearly 4 million francs in a cart—to conserve on gas—from the Crédit Industriel & Commercial to the Bank of France in Paris were robbed by Emile Buisson and two accomplices. One of the guards was killed by Buisson.
Nov. 21: Mrs. Ethel Leta Juanita "Duchess" Spinelli, leader of a 1930s San Francisco robbery gang, became the first woman executed in San Quentin's gas chamber for her part in the murder of gang member Robert Sherrard.
Dec. 19: Inga Arvidsson was murdered during a robbery attempt in Trollsborg, Sweden.
1942
Sept. 6: John Elbert and Phil Ferdinand killed Giovanni Leonidas while trying to rob him of the gold he was rumored to have hoarded. Their companion Josephine Humphrey informed on them and both were given life sentences.
Oct. 30: Police in Tacoma, Wash., arrested Jake Bird, who then confessed to killing ten robbery victims with an ax in Illinois, Washington and elsewhere. He was hanged in Washington in 1948.
1944
Oct. 7: Stripper Elizabeth Marina Jones met GI Gustave Hulten in London and together they robbed and murdered cab driver George Edward Heath on King Street. The killers were apprehended two days later. Hulten got the death penalty and Jones was sentenced to life in prison.
1945
June 3: William Heirens, seventeen, committed a series of burglaries in Chicago and murdered Josephine Alice Ross, Evelyn Petersen, Frances Brown, and finally 6-year-old Suzanne Degnan. Heirens was caught during a burglary on June 26 and sentenced to three consecutive life terms.
Dec. 15: William "Treetop" Turner was convicted of five counts of burglary and murder, but the convictions would later be overturned.
1946
Mar. 13: War veteran Erwin Walker initiated a series of holdups of dozens of stores in Los Angeles. With a submachine gun he killed police officer Loren C. Roosevelt. Convicted and sentenced to death, Walker would later be found insane and transferred to an asylum.
June 26: Former bootlegger George "Bugs" Moran, with Virgil Summers and Albert Fouts, robbed a bank messenger in Dayton, Ohio, of $10,000.

Moran was captured and sent to Leavenworth, where he died in February 1957.
Aug. 18: Justin William McCarthy, better known as the Park Avenue Bandit, robbed the passengers of a limousine parked on Park Avenue in New York City. He stole more than $200,000 in furs and jewelry before his arrest.
1947
Apr. 29: Charles Henry Jenkins, Terence Peter Rolt, and Christopher James Geraghty killed Alec de Antiquis when he tried to stop them from robbing a West End London jewelry store. Jenkins and Geraghty were hanged Sept. 17, but Rolt was only seventeen and went to prison.
November: Abe Greenburg and Joe Miller stole $125,000 in jewelry from the California home of Sayde Genis. Brothers Moe and Gail Reingold were charged with masterminding the plot.
1948
Jan. 23: Caryl Chessman was arrested in Los Angeles while he was driving a stolen car. He was identified as the Red Light Bandit who had been committing robberies and rapes for months. Convicted on May 18, Chessman received the death sentence in 1960.
Jan. 26: Sadimacha Hirasawa impersonated a doctor and told fourteen employees of the Teikoku Imperial Bank in Tokyo that they must drink a "medicine" he provided to prevent dysentery. the potion contained cyanide and thirteen people died as Hirasawa robbed the bank of 180,000 yen ($600). The lone survivor later identified him, and Hirasawa was imprisoned for life.
Feb. 13: London burglar Donald George Thomas shot to death a policeman who had stopped him for questioning. Thomas was soon arrested and sentenced to life in prison.
1949
June 25: Five men robbed the South Chicago Savings Bank and killed two Brink's guards. The net was only $920 in cash and many worthless checks. Jakalski was later extradited from Wyoming. Although acquitted of the murders, he was convicted of robbery and given 199 years.
Nov. 7: Prostitute Jean Lee, pimp Robert David Clayton, and Norman Andrews tortured wealthy bookmaker William George Kent with a broken bottle in a Carlton, Aus., hotel room until he told them where his money was. He later died and the three thieves were captured in Sydney and hanged on Feb. 19, 1951.
1950
Jan. 17: Joseph F. "Big Joe" McGinnis, Anthony Pino, and their gang robbed Brink's armored car service center in Boston. They made off with more than $2.7 million, but were turned in later by gang member Joseph "Specs" O'Keefe.
Mar. 13: Three armed men attempted to rob the Maybrook, N.Y. National Bank, only to be foiled by a teller who released tear gas into their faces. The three and their driver were apprehended a short time later.
Aug. 13: Rudi Brettinger committed the first of a series of robberies in Baltimore, for which he was apprehended three days later.
1951
July 8: Three bandits attacked a Brink's armored car parked in front of the Bowman Dairy Company in Chicago. They struck driver Julius Blanchart on the head with a rifle butt, but he remained conscious and killed one robber and wounded another before help arrived and the robbery was thwarted.
Oct. 20: Burglars stole more than $230,000 in goods from the Congress Hotel Jewel & Fur Shop in Chicago. The merchandise was never recovered.
1952
February: Robert Henry Bondurant was accosted and apprehended by an armed citizenry, after he robbed the bank in Middleton, Tenn.
February: Three unemployed "sharpies"—Joseph Guidice, Joseph Paladino, and Carmine Zoccollo—were arrested two days after stealing $115,000 in cash and jewelry from the Park Avenue apartment of Mollie Parnis, a New York fashion designer.
March: Thieves in Reno, Nev., stole $2 million in negotiable securities, as well as $350,000 in cash and jewelry, from the home of financier Verne Redfield.
April: More than $680,000 was taken from a Brink's armored truck in Danvers, Mass., while all three guards sipped coffee at a nearby restaurant.
June: Three armed men methodically robbed tenants of the Emerson Hotel in New York City of more than $3,000. They accosted the residents as they entered the lobby.
July 16: Alice Wiltshaw of Staffordshire, England was murdered and robbed of £3,000 in jewelry. The criminal's apparent knowledge of the household routine led police to Leslie Green, the Wiltshaw's former chauffeur, who was hanged on Dec. 23.
August: John Green and Barry Jacobs shot a man to death, during a thwarted robbery attempt in the Bronx.
Sept. 12: Jeweler Fred Wasserman's sample case containing $30,000 in jewels was stolen on Milwaukee Avenue in Chicago. The robber was never found.
October: Ethel Arata, a 52-year-old woman nicknamed "Grandma" by authorities, stole $2,600 at gunpoint from the Union Bank & Trust Co. in Los Angeles.
Nov. 2: While robbing a London warehouse, teenagers Derek Bentley and Christopher Craig were surprised by police. Craig killed Constable Sydney Miles and then jumped from a roof and broke his spine. Bentley was charged with murder because he supposedly encouraged Craig to shoot. Bentley's hanging on Jan. 23, 1953, aroused protest which resulted in the suspension of capital punishment in England.
Nov. 13: Brink's guards Bud Murray and Al Pukay interrupted a bank robbery in Walkerville, Ontario, and chased off the two robbers, who fled with no money and were never captured.
Nov. 26: Ethel Arata committed her second bank robbery, stealing $257 from the Citizens National Trust & Savings Bank in Los Angeles.
December: Ethel Arata was arrested as she attempted to rob a bank in Arcadia, Calif. The 52-year-old "Grandma" confessed to two earlier robberies.
1953
Apr. 14: A pickpocket attending Holy Week church services in Caracas, Ven., shouted "Fire!" and fifty-three people were killed in the ensuing stampede.
July 31: William Kampf was arrested after he commandeered a Brooklyn diner. He robbed the register, while staying to serve free food to twenty apprehensive customers.
Dec. 4: Chicago robber Richard Carpenter killed Officer Murphy and hid in the home of Leonard Powell. Carpenter was captured after a shootout and went to the electric chair on Mar. 16, 1956.
1954
Feb. 22: David Daniel Keegan and two accomplices killed a farmer in Mondamin, Iowa, while robbing his house of $17,000 in cash and government bonds.
1955
April: After kidnapping employees as they arrived at their jobs, three men armed with machine-guns, robbed New York City's Bank of Manhattan of more than $300,000.
Aug. 3: Three robbers hid in a Brink's garage in Buffalo and when a truck returned, they held up the guards and stole $489,500. The guards chased the robbers and captured two of them. Eugene Francis Newman fled and was subsequently named to the FBI's list of ten most wanted fugitives.
November: Maggie O'Connor was arrested by Chicago police for her participation in more than 100 armed robberies.
1956
July 18: Car salesman William Liebscher, Jr., robbed the Bank of America in Daly City, Calif., of $1,750.
December: John Robert Wagner, a student at M.I.T., was arrested in Oklahoma City, and charged with the robbery of the Richmond, Ill., State Bank.
1957
May 10: William Liebscher, Jr., robbed the Napa City, Calif. bank of $2,555. He was sentenced to fifteen years.
June 14: William Liebscher, Jr. robbed the Western bank in Fairfield, Calif., of $2,500.
July 10: William Leibscher, Jr. robbed a teller of $700 at the American Trust Company. He was apprehended by two FBI agents and was eventually sentenced to prison.
1958
In Mexico, robber and murderer Robert J. Thompson was convicted of assaulting American tourists in six separate incidents over three months.
Feb. 27: A delivery van from the Popular Bank of Milan, Italy, was stopped by robbers who took $182,400 in cash and about $750,000 in securities. All six gunmen were later arrested.
May 3: Five men, including Rene Martin, stole $3.5 million in negotiable bonds, as well as $55,000 in cash and jewelry, from the vault of the Brockville, Ontario Trust & Savings Bank.
Aug. 10: Unidentified burglars smashed the display windows of Tiffany's main store on Fifth Avenue in New York and got away with $163,000 in jewels.
1959
Jan. 30: British mobster Brian Donald Hume robbed a bank in Zurich, Switz., of $50,000 and then killed a cab driver who refused to drive him to safety. Hume was imprisoned for life for the murder.
July 16: Guenther Fritz Erwin Padola robbed Mrs. Verne Schiffman of £2,000 then fatally shot Detective Raymond Purdy and escaped. Padola was later captured and hanged on Nov. 5.
1960's
Serge Barany and Noël Marcucci, two Frenchmen, robbed a post office at Noailles.
1961
July 1: A team of burglars organized by Georges Lemay stole $633,605 from the Bank of Nova Scotia in Montréal.
September: John William Clouser, who later spent seven years on the FBI's Most Wanted List, was arrested for his complicity in the robbery and assault of two theater managers in Orlando, Fla.
1962
Aug. 14: The White Glove Gang, named for their practice of wearing white gloves, robbed $1,551,277 from a mail truck traveling to Boston. The robbers were not caught.
Nov. 27: Five robbers overcame guards at Heathrow Airport in London and stole £62,000. Of the five, Charles Wilson, Gordon Goody, and Mickey Ball were caught. Only Ball was convicted.
1963
Aug. 8: Bruce Reynolds and eleven masked men stopped the Glasgow-

to-London train near Cheddington, and drove off with $7,368,715. All were arrested, but less than $1 million was recovered.
Sept. 21: French police found $2 million worth of stolen books and art objects in the apartment of house painter Nikola Franusic.
1964
December: Six gunmen robbed a Brink's truck of $285,000 as it was parked at a church rectory in Norridge, Ill.
1965
Jan. 31: Moments after they had successfully held up a Chicago convenience store, three teenagers—George Del Vecchio, Joseph A. Varchetto, and Eugene Waswil—killed the man they were attempting to rob.
November: The FBI arrested two prominent Georgians, William T. Moyers and his son Marshal in downtown Atlanta, and charged them under the National Robbery Act.
1966
Aug. 19: The FBI captured bank robber Georges Lemay in Las Vegas and sent him back to Montréal where he was convicted and imprisoned. He was released in 1976.
1967
Sept. 22: Burglar V.I. Samarsky of Leningrad, U.S.S.R., was sentenced to three years in prison.
1970
June 23: Tupamaros guerrillas robbed the Palestine Bank in Uruguay of $72,000.
Sept. 11: Tuparmaro guerrillas robbed Esso, and Standard Oil of $1,800.
1971
July 9: Gordon Coggswell and an accomplice robbed a bank in Norwalk, Conn. Coggswell and police officer Nicholas Fera were fatally shot to death during an ensuing gun battle.
Aug. 2: Frederick Joseph Sewell and others robbed a jewelry store in Blackpool, Eng, of £106,000 and shot several policemen while escaping. Sewell was caught and sentenced to thirty years.
Oct. 10: Gunmen David Bozeman and Carlos Hawes were shot to death as they attempted to rob a pharmacist at his home in Keystone Heights, Fla.
Nov. 24: Aboard a flight from Portland, Ore., to Seattle, D.B. Cooper demanded $200,000 and four parachutes, which he was given when the plane landed. It took off again with only Cooper aboard, but when it landed in Reno, Cooper and the money were gone. Children later found some of the marked bills along the river in Vancouver, Wash., but Cooper was never found.
December: Thomas Givens, turned in by his female companion, was arrested and charged with the robbery and murder of salesman Charles Farmer in rural north Georgia.
1972
Jan 2: Robert Comfort and four associates robbed the Pierre Hotel in New York of about $5 million in jewels, cash, and securities. Comfort and two others were sent to prison.
Mar. 24: Money and valuables worth over $1.4 million were stolen out of the Laguna Niguel branch of the United California Bank by Ronald L. Barber and six accomplices.
November: Texas family members Sherman McCrary, Carolyn McCrary, Danny McCrary, Ginger McCrary Taylor, and Carl Taylor were indicted in Denver, for a series of murders, kidnappings, and robberies that occurred in Colorado, Oregon, Texas, and Utah.
Nov. 5: The Barn restaurant in Braintree, England was robbed of £900 and owner Bob Patience and his wife and child were killed. George Ince was tried and acquitted twice, then look-alike John Brook and partner Nicholas de Clare Johnson were caught. Brook got life in prison, and Johnson ten years.
1973
Winter: A young police constable was honored for his bravery in responding to a robbery in progress at the National Westminster Bank in London. He killed one of the bandits and wounded another.
Spring: Two young Pakistanis were killed and a third wounded in an attempt to rob the indian High Commission. Members of the Special Patrol Group in London were praised.
July 20: Martan A. Williams was arrested in Chicago and charged with the robberies of ten New York banks during the prior three months.
Dec. 2: Carl Dixon, Louis Mathis, and Anthony B. Vaglica stole $5 million in antique coins from Harvard University's Fogg Museum. They were later caught trying to fence the coins and sent to prison.
1974
Oct. 20: Six men used a bomb to blast through the wall of the Purolator Company office in Chicago and stole $4.3 million, but they were later captured and most of the money was recovered.
1975
Feb. 3: Four armed members of the Irish Republican Army took $80,000 from a bank outside London.
July 30: Arthur Byrd and Reginald Lewis, both prisoners at a halfway house, executed four persons following a robbery of an apartment in Washington, D.C.
Aug. 18: Wayne Donald Horton was arrested for robbing a taxi driver in Las Vegas. He confessed the murders of three people and the wounding of another.
September: Three gunmen took six hostages during a failed attempt to rob a restaurant in London.
Sept. 18: Patricia Hearst was arrested and charged with the robbery of a San Francisco bank.
1976
Eight men stole $13.6 million from Bank of America's Mayfair branch in London. All robbers were sent to prison.
Jan. 28: Robbers blew open vaults of the British Bank of the Middle East in Bab Idriss, Leb., and stole between $20 million and $50 million, which was never recovered.
Feb. 7: Melvin Douglas Downing and two accomplices, killed three men and wounded another, during the robbery of a food store in Washington, D.C.
Mar. 30: More than $2.8 million was stolen from a Brink's armored car in Montreal, Quebec, when five men ambushed the truck and pointed an anti-aircraft gun at the vehicle.
Apr. 7: James Melvin Keyes killed a man during the course of five armed robberies, committed with an accomplice in Washington, D.C.
Apr. 14: Burglars stole $6 million in gems from the Palm Towers Hotel in Palm Beach, Fla., and were never caught.
July 16: Albert Spaggiari and his gang tunneled into the branch bank of the Societé Général in Nice, Fr., and stole over $8 million. Spaggiari was later captured but escaped before trial.
Sept. 26: Four gunmen stole $200,000 in cash and jewels, and forced wealthy patrons to sign blank checks. They kidnapped a guest during a robbery of a villa on the French Riviera.
Oct. 1: Steven Brown stole $7,000 from a bank in Evanston, Ill. It was later discovered that the teller, Lorene P. Gooden, was an accomplice to the crime.
Dec. 20: Raymond Jordan was charged in the robbery and murder of a Transit Authority patrolman in Queens as he drove a taxi during off hours.
Dec. 25: Walter Guyton was apprehended shortly after he robbed a sandwich shop in Danbury, Conn.
1977
Feb. 1: Robber and rapist Robert J. Tannehill was sentenced to fifteen concurrent prison terms in Chicago, for crimes committed during the previous year.
Mar. 17: Michael Guile shot himself to death after a fourteen hour siege. He had taken two hostages during a failed robbery attempt in San Francisco.
Apr. 9: George William Brady and Leroy Marshal'l killed three people and wounded another as they robbed a bank in Kodak, Tenn. They were apprehended the following day.
Apr. 12: A lone gunman stole $2,050 from the Sterling Savings & Loan Assn. in Chicago. Frederick J. Pickler was arrested six hours later and charged with the robbery.
Apr. 15: Curtis Davis and Eddie Jackson killed two people during a robbery of a plumbing and heating supply company on the South Side of Chicago.
Apr. 15: New York optometrist Dr. Herbert Lauring was murdered after a $75 robbery. Rafael Santiago was charged with the crimes two days later.
Apr. 22: An armored truck was robbed of $80,000, including $60,000 in coins, at a tollway plaza near Chicago.
May 1: Convicted robber Richard Gantz, out on a work-release program, robbed three gas stations, stole three cars, and kidnapped and raped a 19-year-old student before his capture and return to prison.
May 7: The body of Marjorie Jackson was discovered, following a $1 million robbery in Indianapolis. Howard Russell Willard and Marjorie Louise Pollitt were arrested shortly thereafter.
May 24: An armored truck carrying $288,000 and two guards, disappeared in Phoenix. It was found empty the following day.
May 25: Using a blowtorch to break into a dynamite warehouse in Hunnerberg, Swed., two burglars blew themselves and the building to pieces.
June 6: Thieves kill West Virginia jeweler Aubrey Hawkins and his wife Alberta in Jacksboro, Tenn., and steal $176,000 in jewelry.
Oct. 7: An employee of the First National Bank of Chicago stole exactly $1 million from a vault. The bank dismissed him several months later, but under FBI surveillance the suspect did not touch the money or attempt to flee.
1978
Oct. 25: Computer consultant Stanley Mark Rifkin learned a secret code and illegally transferred $10.2 million from the Security Pacific National Bank to New York where he collected it and used it to buy diamonds in Switzerland. The money was recovered, and Rifkin was caught and sentenced to ten years.
Dec. 11: Six masked men stole $5 million in cash and $1 million in gold and jewels from the Lufthansa Airlines cargo hold at Kennedy International Airport in New York.
Dec. 19: Three men stole $3 million from a Wells Fargo armored car in Staten Island, N.Y., while the guards were at lunch. Joseph "Pepe" Marino was later convicted of the robbery.
1979
Nine Buffalo, N.Y., banks were robbed of $150,000 by one bank robbery gang.
Jan. 30: Gerald and Tommy Ortiz, two brothers charged with armed robbery, escaped from the Cook County Sheriff's van in Chicago.
February: Thieves stole $140,000 from the Morton Grove, Ill., Bank

and $550,000 in jewelry from nearby Angelic Enterprises.
May 3: Prostitute Cathy Nathaniel murdered and robbed Steven Ticho in his Chicago apartment, allegedly helped by her friend Berniece Albright. Nathaniel got thirty-five years and Albright was not charged.
July 24: Michael Brown held five people hostage in two homes in Chicago and demanded unsuccessfully that they withdraw money from local banks. He was captured and sentenced to twenty-five years.
Aug. 21: Eleven banks were robbed within seven hours in New York City.
Sept. 5: Benjamin and Lonny Steele robbed a bank in Rockingham, N.C., only to be apprehended when their dog was discovered carrying a wig that one of the brothers had used as a disguise.
Sept. 12: Two gunmen robbed the Barclay's Bank in New York City. James Taylor was arrested at the scene, while an accomplice escaped with $200,000 in cash.
Nov. 25: Five men stole $200,000 in cash and jewels from safety-deposit boxes at the Mayfair Regent Hotel in New York City.
Dec. 3: Robert Hanahan, Paul "Peanuts" Panczko, Robert Pullia, Robert Siegal, and Gerald Tomasek were arrested as they prepared to rob a bank in Des Plaines, Ill.
1980
Jan. 16: Two thieves, disguised as airport mechanics, stole $2.2 million from the cargo hold of a Swissair jet as the plane sat on a runway in Rome.
February: Two gunmen stole $324,000 from an armored truck, parked outside an Elmwood Park, Ill., bank.
Mar. 2: Ten armed men stole $90,000 from guests and safety-deposit boxes at the Miramar Palace Hotel in Rio De Janeiro, Braz.
May 9: Four men—Manny Delgado, Christopher Harven, Russell Harven, and Gregory Smith—robbed the Security Pacific Bank of Norco, Calif. Delgado was shot to death by authorities the following day, while the others were taken into custody.
Aug. 16: George Bosque, a Brink's guard, absconded with $1.85 million from his armored vehicle. He was arrested in November 1981, but only $34,000 was recovered.
Aug. 19: Three gunmen stole $450,000 in gold salts and $36,400 in cash, from an armored truck in East Killingly, Conn.
Sept. 13: Four armed men stole $400,000 in money and jewels from guests at a private dinner party in Sherman Oaks, Calif.
1981
Feb. 22: Two men robbed a food store in Fish Lake, Ind., leading to the death of a county sheriff who was struck at a roadblock. Steven Cary and Russell Wright were arrested shortly thereafter.
Aug. 21: Thieves stole $2,800 from the Sooner Federal Savings & Loan Assn. in Oklahoma City. David B. Jones, Frank Marino, and Timothy Waldron, suspects in a Bank of America robbery in Sacramento, Calif., were arrested in connection with the crime.
Sept. 4: Thomas E. Hustead was wounded by authorities after he robbed the North Bank's branch office, on the Near North Side of Chicago.
Sept. 16: An estimated three carloads of thieves stole $1.8 million from an armored truck in a forested area near London.
Oct. 10: A nun was robbed and raped, in the rectory of a church in New York City. Max Linderman and Harold Wells were apprehended and charged with the crimes.
Oct. 20: Kuwasi Balagoon, a member of the Black Liberation Army, and Weather Underground members David Gilbert and Judith Clark killed two police and a Brink's guard in Nanuet, N.Y., and stole $1.6 million in cash. Each was sentenced to twenty-five years to life.
Dec. 16: Forty gunmen stole $125,000 from four banks in Digos Town, in the Philippines.
Dec. 17: John Sherman was arrested for his complicity in a series of West Coast armed robberies during the 1970s.
Dec. 26: Police arrested two men who raped and robbed a Chicago woman. Derrick Montgomery and Gaelord Overton were charged with the assault and robbery.
1982
Jan. 8: Anthony LaBorde was arrested and charged with stealing $1.6 million from Brink's in Nyack, N.Y.
Feb. 14: Two robbers surprised a single guard at the Sentry Armored Car Courier Company in the Bronx, N.Y., and got away with $5.3 million in cash. The robbers have never been caught.
Oct. 5: Four bank robbers were allowed to escape with an undetermined amount of money from a bank in Koblenz, W. Ger., after they threatened to kill their nine hostages.
Oct. 8: Five gunmen stole $28,000 from the Banca di Santo Spirito in Rome.
Oct. 29: The Reverend Jasper J. Taylor was shot to death by two thieves who robbed him of $8,000 on the West Side of Chicago. Joseph Gardner and Sidney Portis were arrested and charged with the crimes.
Nov. 20: Ray C. Greer killed an off-duty police officer during an attempted robbery on the South Side of Chicago.
Dec. 23: Pointing to an arrest and conviction, a stolen automobile was discovered in the garage of Frank Wilson on the West Side of Chicago, He was suspected of more than 1,000 similar thefts.
1983
Jan. 16: Nicky Cozart and Darnell Davis shot police officer Larry J. Vincent to death, as they were committing a robbery at an apartment building on the South Side of Chicago.
Jan. 19: Eleanor M. Mitchell, 63, was arrested in Baltimore and charged with the robberies of four elderly men. She would lure a man into her car, give him a drugged beer, and steal his money.
Feb. 26: Police surrounded several robbers trying to hold up a bank in Tegucigalpa, Hon., and after a gunfight, forced them to surrender. Police Captain Louis Moran Morel was killed in the fight.
May 24: Four gunmen stole $10.7 million in cash from an armored vehicle in the suburbs of Paris.
Aug. 5: Two men tried to rob the safe deposit boxes at the Sofitel Hotel in Avignon, Fr., but when they failed, killed four guests and three hotel employees before escaping. The robbers' identities are still unknown.
Aug. 30: Joseph "Pops" Panczko and George Schnell were arrested for stealing $200,000 in gold and diamonds from a jewelry salesman's car near Springfield, Ill.
Nov. 28: Career thief Paul "Peanuts" Panczko was the primary suspect in a $500,000 jewelry robbery at a warehouse on Chicago's North Side.
1984
July: John and Julia Gavis robbed their father's remains to recover teeth they thought bore the number of a secret bank account.
1986
June 17: Michael Thomas Karalis was arrested in Chicago for complicity in a $250,000 jewel robbery in Indiana in 1981.
1987
July: A New York street thief attacked and stole a watch from Attorney Barry Slotnick, who was defending subway vigilante, Bernhard Goetz.
July: Hermes 1A1 and the thirteen claimed responsibility for robbing the grave of Juan Perón in Argentina. Taken were the late president's saber and severed hands.
1988
A ring of "Rolex bandits" operating throughout the U.S. was discovered. The female thieves stole men's valuables after they had slipped knockout drops into their drinks.
July 8: Attempting to garner money needed to repair an automobile, five teenagers, Barry Bootan, James Cooney, Danny Florio, Jason Katanic, and Brendan Moynahan robbed a convenience store in New York City. During a second robbery attempt, Cooney was shot to death by an off-duty police officer. The others were apprehended shortly thereafter.
July 20: Robert Roy Woodard stole $30,000 from the Midwest Bank of Zion branch in Waukegan, Ill., only to be apprehended as he went on a clothing and car buying spree.
Dec. 12: Three paintings by Vincent van Gogh were stolen from the National Museum at Otterlo, in the Netherlands.

SKYJACKING

While scattered reports indicated commercial aircraft were being hijacked as early as the 1930s, air piracy did not become a serious problem until the early 1960s. The decade spawned a rash of these crimes, many of them involving young leftists, who for political and ideological reasons commandeered U.S. commercial aircraft and directed them to land in Cuba. American fugitives also found Cuba to be a safe haven. In response to this, "sky marshals" were assigned to a number of sensitive flights as a way of discouraging air piracy in the late 1960s.

At first Cuban premier Fidel Castro showed his willingness to accept skyjackers into his country, but in 1973, after years of delicate negotiation, an agreement was struck between the island nation and the U.S. to discourage acts of air piracy. The agreement crumbled three years later, when Castro accused the CIA of bombing a Cuban passenger jet. In 1980 the skyjackings to Cuba resumed, with most of them carried out by disenchanted Cuban exiles who wanted to return home.

The 1970s and 1980s witnessed a fresh spate of terrorist hijackings. In the Middle East, Arab groups such as the Palestine Liberation Organization and its affiliated Black Septembrist faction attempted to dramatize their plight by seizing Western aircraft and using the planes and passengers as bargaining chips against the U.S. and Israel. The U.S. and its allies responded by instituting tough security measures. Guns were outlawed on all commercial craft. The U.S. Federal Aviation Administration ordered that the cockpits on jetliners be locked during flight. Before boarding an aircraft, passengers were required to pass through security checkpoints.

1931

February: Skyjackers on a Peruvian domestic flight attempted to force pilot, Captain B.D. Richards, to drop propaganda over Peruvian cities and to transport troops. Richards refused.

1947

July 25: Three men skyjacked a Rumania plane to Canakkale Province, Turk. One crew member was killed.

1948

Apr. 6: A Czechoslovakian plane was skyjacked by seventeen people, including the pilot and two members of the crew. The plane landed in the U.S. zone of Germany.

May 4: Two men skyjacked a Czechoslovakian aircraft and forced it to land in the U.S. zone of Germany.

June 4: Two men took over a Yugoslavian plane traveling from Belgrade to Sarajevo, Yug. They forced it to land in Bari, Italy.

June 17: A Soviet-Rumanian Airways C-47 was skyjacked to Salzburg, Aust.

June 30: Mihalakev, Strahil, and others skyjacked a Bulgarian Junkers 52 scheduled to fly from Varna to Sofia, Bulg., and forced it to land in Istanbul, Turk. The pilot was killed and two crew members were wounded.

July 16: Wong Io, Chio Tok, Chio Choi, and Chio Cheong skyjacked a Cathay Pacific Catalina flying from Macao, Japan, to Hong Kong. The pilot and copilot were killed. The plane crashed, killing twenty-five people. Only one skyjacker survived.

Sept. 12: Eight people took control of a Greek Dakota plane flying from Athens to Salonika, Gr. They forced it to land in Tetovo, Yug.

1949

Jan. 4: Janos Majoros, pilot Milos Kuhn, and twenty others skyjacked a Hungarian plane going from Peos to Budapest, Hung. They landed in the U.S. zone of Germany.

Jan. 30: Six people skyjacked a China National Aviation Corp. plane flying from Shanghai to Taingtao, China. The plane landed in Tainan, China. The passengers were held for one month, released, and sent to Taingtao. The plane was retained.

Apr. 29: Korm and Stoyan took control of a Soviet-Rumanian Dakota jet flying from Timisoara to Bucharest, Rom. It landed in Salonika, Gr. One skyjacker, a female passenger, and a security guard were granted political asylum.

Sept. 16: Five men skyjacked a LOT Polish plane flying from Gdansk to Lodz. It landed at Nykoeping Military airfield, sixty-five miles south of Stockholm, Swed.

Dec. 9: Four people took control of a Soviet-Rumanian DC-3 scheduled to fly from Sibiv to Bucharest, Rum. They killed a security guard before landing in Belgrade.

Dec. 16: Sixteen people skyjacked a Polish plane flying from Lodz to Gdansk. It landed in Roenna, Bornholm Island, Den.

1950

Mar. 24: Vit Angetter and Mraz Kamil skyjacked a Czechoslovakian DC-3 flying from Brno to Prague. It landed in the U.S. zone of Germany.

Mar. 24: Vladimir Svetlik and Viktor Popelka skyjacked a Czechoslovakian DC-3 flying from Ostrava to Prague. It landed in the U.S. zone of Germany.

Mar. 24: Oldrich Dolezel, Morijov Smid, Stanislav Sacha, and Jan Kralovansky skyjacked a Czechoslovakian DC-3 flying from Bratislava to Prague. It landed in the U.S. zone of Germany.

Aug. 11: Two people skyjacked a Czechoslovakian Transport plane. It landed in Pottmes, in the U.S. zone of Germany.

1951

Oct. 17: The pilot and copilot skyjacked a Yugoslav National Airlines DC-3 domestic flight. The plane landed in Zurich, Switz. and the skyjackers, their wives, and two boys, requested political asylum. The rest of the crew, passengers, and the plane were returned to Yugoslavia.

1952

June 26: Vilim Inkret, Josip Tevek, and Bogdan Zigic took control of a Yugoslav National Airlines plane flying from Belgrade to Poland. Inkret took over the controls and flew to Folingo, Italy, where the skyjackers requested political asylum. The passengers, crew, and plane were returned to Yugoslavia.

Dec. 30: Ang Tie Cho skyjacked a Philippines DC-3 traveling from Laoag to Aparri, demanding to go to Red China. The pilot and purser were killed. The copilot landed at Quemoy and Tie-Cho was arrested.

1953

Mar. 23: Miroslav Slovak, Helmut Cermiak, Hana Cermiakova, and one other man took over a Czechoslovakian C-47 going from Prague to Brno, Czech. The plane, piloted by Slovak, landed in Frankfurt, Ger.

1956

July 13: Georg Polyak, Joseph Jakaby, Gabor Kiss, Karl Tinter, Joseph Balla, and Mr. and Mrs. Franz Isar skyjacked a Hungarian Twin Engine plane. One of the skyjackers took control of the plane, landed it in West Germany, and requested political asylum. The other passengers and crew were returned to Hungary.

1958

Feb. 16: Five men and two women skyjacked a South Korean DC-3 bound for Seoul and forced it to land in Pyongyang, N. Kor. The passengers and crew returned to South Korea.

Apr. 9: A Cubana plane leaving Havana was forced to land in Merida, Mex. The plane and passengers were returned to Cuba.

Apr. 10: One man skyjacked a South Korean C-46 traveling from Taegu to Seoul, S. Kor., demanding the plane fly to North Korea. The craft landed it Pyongtaek, S. Kor. The radioman was killed and the pilot and copilot were wounded. The skyjacker was arrested.

Apr. 13: Carlos Villamar and two other men, part of the plane's crew, skyjacked a Cubana DC-3 and forced it to land in Miami. The twelve passengers, crew, and plane were returned to Cuba.

June 2: Jaroslav Vydra and Mr. and Mrs. Josef Hornik took control of a chartered Czechoslovakian domestic flight. Armed with a broken pistol, they forced the plane to land in Vienna, Aust. They were arrested, but the charges were dropped.

Oct. 22: Three Cuban rebels skyjacked a Cubana DC-3 domestic flight. The aircraft disappeared.

Nov. 1: Five men skyjacked a Cubana Viscount flying from Miami to Havana. The plane crashed and seventeen of the twenty aboard were killed.

Nov. 6: A Cubana DC-3, while flying from Manzanillo to Holguin, Cuba, was skyjacked and held on a rebel airstrip. The twenty-five passengers were returned.

1959

Apr. 10: Six men skyjacked a Haitian DC-3 flying from Auxcayes to Port Au Prince, Haiti. The pilot was killed and the copilot flew to Cuba.

Apr. 16: Leonard Serrate, Jesus Mason y Serrate, and Alfredo Sanchez skyjacked a Cuban Aerovias DC-3 flying from Havana to the Isle of Pines, Cuba. It landed in Miami where the men were taken into custody.

Apr. 25: Antonio Rodrigues Diaz, a general under the deposed Cuban president, Fulgenico Batista, and several others skyjacked a Cuban Vicker Viscount flying from Varadero Beach to Havana. At gunpoint, the pilot was ordered to fly to Miami, but landed the plane in Key West, Fla. due to lack of fuel.

July 8: Cuckovic Obrad skyjacked a Yugoslavian plane headed to Belgrade from Cattaro. The plane landed in Bari, Italy.

Oct. 2: Estaban and Gloria L. Betancourt and Osvaldo Hernandez took control of a Cubana Viscount heading to Santiago from Havana. The plane landed in Miami.

Dec. 2: Eight men skyjacked a Brazilian Constellation flying to Belem from Rio De Janeiro. They landed in Aragarcas, Braz, where the skyjackers unsuccessfully attempted to revolt against the Brazilian government.

1960

Apr. 21: Gonzalo Herrera, Francisco Monnar, Angel E. Lopez, and Pedro Enrique commandeered a domestic Cuban flight to Miami. The pilot and two crewmen were among the skyjackers.

July 5: Miguel Acosta and Leslie Norbregas skyjacked a Cubana plane on its way to Havana from Madrid. The plane landed in Miami. The copilots were the skyjackers.

July 17: Jose P. Menendez, pilot of a Cubana Viscount, veered from his scheduled flight from Havana to Miami, and landed in Jamaica.

July 18: Jose F. Cardenas Adeas skyjacked a private Cuban single-engine plane flying from Havana. He forced it to land in Fort Lauderdale, Fla.

July 19: Alex Hildebrant skyjacked a Trans-Australia Electra L-188 headed for Brisbane, Aus. He was overpowered by the copilot and taken into custody in Singapore, and imprisoned.

July 28: Three men, including the pilot and two passengers, veered a

Cubana jet scheduled to fly to Havana off course and landed it in Miami.
Aug. 21: A man and a woman attempted to skyjack a U.S.S.R. domestic flight, but were overpowered by the crew.
Oct. 29: Nine men, including a copilot, skyjacked a Cubana DC-3 on its way to Isle of Pines, Cuba. It landed in Key West, Fla. A security guard was shot and killed. The pilot, copilot, and one passenger were injured.
Dec. 8: Five people skyjacked a domestic Cuban flight. The pilot crash-landed, killing one and injuring four.

1961

Jan. 1: Two men skyjacked a Cubana domestic flight. The plane landed in New York. The skyjackers, pointing a pistol at the pilot in the Havana terminal, forced him to fly a group of Fulgencio Batista supporters out of Cuba.
May 1: Antulio Ramirez Ortiz took control of a National CV-440 with thirteen aboard destined for Key West, Fla., from Miami as later arrested in Miami and imprisoned.
July 3: Eleven men and three women skyjacked a Cubana DC-3 headed for Veradero, Cuba. The plane landed in Miami. A security guard was shot and wounded.
July 24: Wilfredo Oquendo skyjacked an Eastern PAC L-188, carrying thirty-three passengers and five crew en route from Miami to Tampa, Fla. He forced the pilot to land in Cuba and escaped.
July 31: Bruce Britt skyjacked a DC-3 Chico, Calif., to San Francisco flight. He shot and injured a ticket agent and the pilot. Britt was arrested and imprisoned.
Aug. 3: Leon F. Bearden and his son, Cody, took over a Continental B-707 carrying ninety-three people to El Paso, Texas, from Phoenix, Ariz. They told the pilot to fly to Cuba. The Beardens were overpowered in El Paso. Leon was sent to prison and Cody was placed in a juvenile detention center.
Aug. 9: Albert Cadon skyjacked a Pan American DC-8 with seventy-nine aboard flying from Mexico City to Guatemala. He ordered the pilot to land in Cuba. Cadon was deported to Mexico and imprisoned.
Aug. 9: Five men skyjacked a Cuban C-46 on its way to the Isle of Pines. The pilot and two others were killed, and six were wounded. The copilot made a crash landing.
Sept. 10: Serge Tumanyan, Henrik Sekoyan, and Haregin Movseyan skyjacked a chartered U.S.S.R. YAK-12 flying from Erwan to Yekhegnadzor, U.S.S.R. They wounded the pilot. One of the skyjackers was killed when the plane crashed in Armenia. The other two were sentenced to death.
Nov. 10: Six men took control of a Transportes Aereos Portuguese L-1049 on its way to Lisbon. The plane circled its destination dropping leaflets before landing in Tangier, Mor. The skyjackers were granted asylum in Brazil.
Nov. 27: Five men skyjacked a Venezuelan DC-6B on its way to Maracaibo. It landed in Curacao. The men were extradited and imprisoned.

1962

Mar. 17: One man skyjacked a French plane carrying thirty-two prisoners from Paris to St. Martin De L'Ardoise. One prisoner was shot and wounded by a guard.
Apr. 13: David Healy and Leonard Oeth skyjacked a chartered plane over Miami to Cuba. They deported to the U.S. and imprisoned.
Apr. 16: Edgar Da Silva skyjacked a Royal Dutch Airlines plane heading for Lisbon. He wanted to go to East Berlin. The craft landed in Holland where he was taken into custody.

1963

Aug. 5: A Venezuelan air carrier was skyjacked to Trinidad.
Nov. 28: "Commander" Dilma, Olga Dilma, Jose Marin, Alberto Kojas, Patrick Toledo, and Armando Rojas skyjacked a Venezuelan Convair Twin Engine plane. It landed in Trinidad and the skyjackers were extradited.

1964

Feb. 18: Enrique Castillo Hernandez and Reinaldo Lopez Rodriguez, armed with pistols, skyjacked a chartered Piper with two passengers and a one-man crew, flying from Miami to Key West, Fla. They ordered it flown to Cuba. Hernandez was returned to the for trial.
Oct. 19: Two men skyjacked a U.S.S.R. AN-2 and wounded the pilot and copilot before the plane landed in Kishinev.

1965

Spring: A man and woman attempted to take control of a domestic U.S.S.R. flight but were overpowered by crew members. The flight engineer was killed.
Aug. 31: Harry F. Fegerstrom, armed with a knife and glass from a broken bottle, skyjacked a Hawaiian DC-3 scheduled to fly from Honolulu to Kauai, Hawaii. He ordered the pilot to return to Honolulu. Fegerstrom was caught and sent to correctional school.
Oct. 11: Lawrence D. Heisler and Richard K. Boyd, both Navy seamen, skyjacked an Aloha F-27 en route from Molokai, Hawaii, to Honolulu. They were imprisoned and dishonorably discharged from the Navy.
Oct. 26: Luis Medina Perez attempted to skyjack a National L-188 with thirty-three aboard, heading for Key West, Fla., from Miami. He used a "BB" pistol to order the pilot to land in Cuba. He was found mentally incompetent and acquitted.
Nov. 17: Thomas H. Robinson, brandishing two revolvers, took over a National DC-8 flight carrying ninety-one people from Houston to New Orleans. He ordered the pilot to land in Cuba. He was sent to correctional school.

1966

Spring: A Soviet plane en route from the U.S.S.R. to Turkey was unsuccessfully skyjacked.
Mar. 27: Angel Betancourt Gueto, flight engineer, skyjacked a Cubana IL-18 heading for Havana. The pilot and a guard were killed after the plane landed in Cuba. The copilot was wounded. The skyjacker, who thought they had landed in Miami, was captured.
July 7: Nine people, including the pilot, skyjacked a Cubana IL-18. It landed in Jamaica. The copilot was wounded.
Aug. 9: Three men skyjacked a U.S.S.R. domestic flight. The plane landed in Batumi. One passenger was wounded. The skyjackers were captured.
Sept. 28: Maria Varrier and nineteen others skyjacked an Argentine DC-4. It landed in the Falkland Islands. The three leaders of the skyjackers were sentenced to death, the others to prison.

1967

Feb. 7: Riyad Kamal Hajjaj skyjacked an Egyptian AN-24 domestic flight and forced the plane to land in Jordan. He escaped to Sweden and was arrested for other crimes.
Apr. 23: Five men took over a Nigerian F-27 traveling to Lagos. The plane landed in Enugu, Nig.
June 30: Francois Bodenan skyjacked a private United Kingdom jet carrying Moise Tshombe, former prime minister of the Congo. The plane landed in Algeria where Tshombe was held captive until his death on June 29, 1969.
Aug. 6: Pedro Buendia, Fermina Rojas, Roberto Lopez, Julian Alvarez, and one other man skyjacked a Columbian DC-4 scheduled to fly from Barranquilla to the San Andres Islands, Col.
Sept. 9: Ramino Garcia, Fernando Garcia, and Joaquin Garcia skyjacked a Colombian DC-3 flying from Barranquilla to Magangue, Col.
Nov. 20: Louis G. Babler took control of a chartered Piper Apache, taking three people from Hollywood, Fla., to Bimini, Bahama Islands. He demanded the plane be flown to Cuba where he escaped.

1968

Feb. 9: William Clark, a Marine, skyjacked a Pan American military chartered DC-6, flying from South Vietnam to Hong Kong. Clark was court-martialed and sentenced, but charges were dropped when Clark was diagnosed as schizophrenic.
Feb. 18: James Boynton skyjacked a one-passenger, one-crewmember Miami-bound Piper Apache to Cuba. He was returned to the U.S. sentenced for kidnapping.
Feb. 21: Lawrence M. Rhodes skyjacked a Delta DC-8 flying to West Palm Beach, Fla., from Tampa. He ordered the pilot to fly to Cuba. He was committed to a mental institution.
Mar. 5: Sami Awadalla, Aristides Villalobos-Rico, and Jairo Ortiz-Acosta, members of the ELN, took control of a Colombian DC-4 flying to Baranquilla and ordered it flown to Cuba.
Mar. 12: Jesus Armenteros, Gilberto Carrazana Y Gonzales, and Ramon Donato-Martin, armed with two pistols, skyjacked a Miami-bound National DC-8, carrying fifty-eight people to Cuba. The skyjackers escaped.
Mar. 16: Two American men and one American woman skyjacked a private Mexican twin engine plane flying to Merida Cozumel, Mex.
Mar. 21: Three men skyjacked a Venezuelan CV-440 flying to Maracaibo, Venez. They demanded it land in Cuba.
June 19: Radhames Mendez-Vargas skyjacked a Venezuelan DC-9 flying from the Dominican Republic to Curacao, Netherland Antilles. He was imprisoned in the Dominican Republic.
June 29: E.H. Carter, armed with a revolver, skyjacked a Southeast DC-3 carrying seventeen people from Miami to Key West, Fla., to Cuba. He escaped.
July 1: Mario Velasquez Fonseca skyjacked an eighty-five passenger Northwest B-727 en route from Chicago to Miami. He forced the pilot to land in Cuba and then escaped.
July 4: John H. Morris attempted to skyjack a TWA B-727 flying from Kansas City, Kan., to Las Vegas, Nev. Claiming he had a gun and dynamite, Morris ordered the pilot to fly to Mexico. He had no weapons, was overpowered, and imprisoned.
July 12: Leonard S. Bendicks skyjacked a private Cessna-210 with two people aboard, flying to Miami from Key West. He ordered the pilot to fly to Cuba. He was deported back to the U.S. and imprisoned.
July 12: Oran D. Richards skyjacked a forty-eight passenger Delta CV-880 en route from Baltimore to Houston. He ordered the pilot to land in Cuba. He was hospitalized in a mental institution.
July 17: Rogelio Hernandez Leyva, armed with a pistol, skyjacked a fifty-seven passenger National DC-8 en route from Los Angeles to New Orleans. He ordered the pilot to land in Cuba and escaped.
July 22: Three terrorists took control of an El Al plane traveling from Rome to Tel Aviv, Isr. They forced the pilot to land in Algeria. The Habash "Front" skyjackers were imprisoned.
Aug. 4: Willis Jessie took his three-year-old daughter along when he skyjacked a chartered Cessna 182 flying from Naples, Fla. He ordered the pilot to fly to Cuba. He was imprisoned for kidnapping.
Aug. 22: Bill McBride, wielding a revolver, skyjacked a chartered Cessna 336 flying en route from Nassau, Bahama Islands, to Georgetown. He diverted the plane to Cuba and escaped.
Sept. 11: Charles Beasley took control of an Air Canada plane flying

to Toronto and demanded to be flown to Cuba. He was imprisoned.
Sept. 20: Jose A. Suarez Garcia skyjacked a forty-six passenger Eastern B-720 San Juan, P.R., to Miami flight, diverting it to Cuba. He escaped.
Sept. 22: Ramon Garcia took over a Colombian B-727 on its way to Cartagena and demanded to be flown to Cuba. He escaped.
Sept. 22: Carlos London skyjacked a Colombian DC-4 flying to Santa Marta, Cuba, and demanded to be flown to Cuba. He escaped.
Oct. 6: Judy Vazquez skyjacked a Mexican HS-748 flying to Merida, Mex., and forced it to be flown to Cuba. She escaped.
Oct. 23: Alben W. Truitt took over a chartered Cessna 177 flying from Key West, Fla., and skyjacked it to Cuba. He was imprisoned.
Oct. 30: Juan Francisco Garcia Zurita skyjacked a Seasa C-46 flying to Reynosa, Mex. It landed in Brownsville, Texas. Zurita was extradited to Mexico.
Nov. 2: Roger A. Pastorcich took control of an Eastern DC-9 with fifty-four aboard flying to Chicago from Birmingham, Ala. He demanded it be flown to South Vietnam. His demand was rejected. He was placed in a juvenile detention center.
Nov. 4: Raymond Johnson, Jr. skyjacked a National B-727 carrying sixty-five people from New Orleans to Miami. He ordered to be flown to Cuba and escaped.
Nov. 6: Four men took control of a Philippines Fokker twin engine. The plane landed in Manila after one passenger was killed, another wounded, and all were robbed. The skyjackers escaped.
Nov. 8: Umberto Giovine and Maurizio Panichi skyjacked an Olympic B-707 en route from Paris to Athens. They distributed handbills publicizing opposition to the military junta in Greece, and forced the plane to return to Paris. They were imprisoned.
Nov. 18: Two men skyjacked a Mexican DC-6 scheduled to land in Mexico City and commandeered it to Cuba.
Nov. 23: Aramis Suarez Garcia, Miguel Mayor Velasques, Alberto Arroyo Quintero, Irardo Mendoza Viera, Teresa Nunez de Mendoza, and Moises Rodriguez Rodriguez, armed with four pistols, took over an Eastern B-727 Chicago to Miami flight with ninety aboard. They ordered the pilot to fly to Cuba and escaped.
Nov. 24: Jose Rios Cruz, Luis A. Pena Soltren, and Miguel I. Castro Cruz, armed with three pistols, took control of a ninety-six-passenger Pan American B-707 New York to San Juan, P.R., flight. They ordered the pilot to fly to Cuba. All were imprisoned except Soltren.
Nov. 30: Miguel Montesino Sanchez skyjacked an Eastern B-720 flying thirty-eight passengers from Miami to Dallas. Wielding a pistol, he ordered the pilot to fly to Cuba. He escaped.
Dec. 3: Nicasio M. Cadahia Delgado took over a twenty-eight-passenger National B-727 en route from Tampa to Miami. Carrying a pistol and a hand grenade, he skyjacked the plane to Cuba.
Dec. 11: Armed with a revolver, James and Gwendolin Patterson skyjacked a St. Louis to Miami TWA B-727 flight carrying thirty-nine people to Cuba. They remain fugitives.
Dec. 19: Thomas G. Washington, carrying a fake pistol and phony nitroglycerin, took 142 passengers and nine crew hostage when he skyjacked a Miami-bound Eastern DC-8 to Cuba. He was returned to the U.S. and imprisoned.
Dec. 26: Two skyjackers commandeered an El Al plane wielding small arms and hand grenades. One Israeli passenger was killed and two flight attendants were injured in this Habash "Front" attack. The skyjackers were held by Athens police.

1969

Jan. 2: Tyrone and Linda Austin, armed with a pistol, took control of a 138-passenger, Eastern DC-8 heading for Miami from New York. They ordered the pilot to land in Cuba and escaped. Tyrone was later killed in a bank robbery.
Jan. 2: George Flamourides (AKA: G. Paravolidakis) skyjacked a Greek DC-6B flying to Athens. The plane landed in Cairo. He was imprisoned.
Jan. 7: One man skyjacked a Colombian DC-4 flying for Maicao and diverted it to Cuba.
Jan. 9: Ronald T. Bohle, wielding a knife, skyjacked a seventy-three-passenger Nassau-bound Eastern B-727 to Cuba. He was imprisoned.
Jan. 11: Robert M. Helmey, brandishing a revolver, skyjacked a B-727 Jacksonville to Miami flight taking twenty people to Cuba. He was found insane and acquitted.
Jan. 11: Jesus Anaya Roseque took over a Peruvian CV-990 en route from Buenos Aires to Miami. He ordered the plane to land in Havana. He was returned to Mexico and imprisoned.
Jan. 13: Kenneth E. McPeek took over a Delta CV-880 en route from Detroit to Miami carrying seventy-seven people. Wielding a shotgun, he unsuccessfully attempted to skyjack the plane to Cuba. He was imprisoned.
Jan. 19: Aristoarez A. Navarro Payano, brandishing a hand grenade, held 171 passengers and crew hostage when he skyjacked an Eastern DC-8 New York to Miami flight to Cuba. He was sentenced in the Dominican Republic.
Jan. 19: Four armed skyjackers overtook an Ecuadorian Electra L-88 flying from Quito, Ecu. to Miami and diverted it to Havana. All were convicted.
Jan. 24: A man knmown as "Ayre," wielded a knife to skyjack a National B-727 Key West, Fla., to Miami flight with forty-seven people aboard to Cuba. He escaped.
Jan. 28: Clinton R. Smith and Byron V. Booth, armed with a revolver and dynamite, skyjacked a National DC-8 Miami-bound flight with thirty-two people aboard to Cuba. The skyjackers escaped.
Jan. 28: Larry F. Brooks, Noble B. Mason, and Everett L. White took control of an Eastern DC-8 Atlanta to Miami flight and its 105 passengers, wielding three revolvers. They forced the pilot to fly to Cuba. They were imprisoned.
Jan. 31: Allan C. Sheffield skyjacked a fifty-five passenger, National DC-8 en route from San Francisco to Tampa, Fla., and forced it to land in Cuba. He was arrested and sentenced.
Feb. 3: Joaquin Babin Estrada and Garcia W. and Marina L. Hernandez took control of an Eastern B-727 flying from Newark, N.J., to Miami. Threatening the pilot with a knife and alleged bomb, they forced him to fly to Cuba. They escaped.
Feb. 3: Michael Anthony Peparo and Tasmin Rebecca Fitzgerald, armed with a knife and an aerosol insecticide cylinder, attempted to skyjack a National B-727 New York to Miami flight carrying seventy passengers and crew to Cuba. They were arrested and sentenced.
Feb. 5: A Colombian DC-4 was skyjacked while flying to Medellin, Col., and diverted to Havana, Cuba.
Feb. 6: Seven men skyjacked a Venezuelan plane to Havana.
Feb. 8: Victor Romo attempted to skyjack a Mexican DC-6 while on its way to Villa Hermosa. He was overwhelmed by passengers.
Feb. 10: Pedro Alvarez de Quesada skyjacked an Eastern DC-8 carrying 111 passengers from San Juan, P.R., to Miami. He forced the pilot at gunpoint to land in Cuba and escaped.
Feb. 11: Three men skyjacked a Venezuelan DC-9 en route to Caracas, Venez., demanding it be flown to Cuba. They escaped.
Feb. 18: Four armed Palestinian Freedom Front terrorists took over an El Al plane and killed the Israeli co-pilot and injured five passengers. One of the skyjackers was killed before the remaining three were arrested by Swiss authorities.
Feb. 25: Lorenzo Ervin, Jr. used a revolver to take over an Eastern DC-8 Atlanta to Miami flight carrying sixty-seven people and forced the pilot to land in Cuba. He was imprisoned.
Mar. 5: Anthony G. Bryant took over a National B-727 New York to Miami flight carrying twenty-six people. Threatening the pilot with a revolver, he forced him to land in Cuba. Bryant was arrested and sentenced.
Mar. 11: Juan Caro Montoya took over a Colombian DC-4 en route to Cartagena, Col. The plane landed as scheduled after an airline mechanic was killed and Montoya was wounded and overpowered.
Mar. 15: One man skyjacked a Colombian DC-6 en route to the San Andres Islands and diverted it to Cuba.
Mar. 17: Four men skyjacked a Peruvian B-727 flying to Arequipa, Peru, and diverted it to Cuba.
Mar. 17: Robert L. Sandlin, claiming to have a bomb, skyjacked a Delta DC-9 carrying sixty-three people from Atlanta to Augusta, Ga., and diverted it to Cuba. The alleged bomb was a fake. Sandlin was institutionalized.
Mar. 19: Douglas A. Dickey used a revolver to skyjack a Delta CV-880, with ninety-seven people aboard, scheduled to fly to New Orleans from Dallas. He ordered the pilot to fly to Cuba. He was later found insane and institutionalized.
Mar. 25: Luis A. Frese skyjacked a Delta DC-8 scheduled to fly 114 people to San Diego from Dallas. At gunpoint, Frese ordered the pilot to land in Cuba. He was imprisoned in Cuba where he died.
Apr. 11: Three men skyjacked an Ecuadorian DC-6 flying to Quito and diverted it to Cuba.
Apr. 13: Hiran Courouneaux Sanchez, Manuel Vargas Agueros, Jose Diaz Claro, Esmeraldo Ramirez Castaneda, brandishing pistols and a knife, skyjacked a Pan American B-727 scheduled to fly eighty-four passengers from San Juan, P.R., to Miami. They diverted the flight to Cuba and escaped.
Apr. 14: Three men took control of a Colombian DC-4 flying to Barranquilla, Col., and diverted it to Cuba.
May 5: Jean P. Charrette and Alain Allard used two revolvers and a knife to take hostage seventy-five people aboard a National B-727 flying to Miami from New York. They demanded to land in Cuba. They were sentenced in Canada.
May 20: Luis Eduardo Martinez Rusinke and two other men skyjacked a Colombian jet in Bogotá and commandeered it to Cuba.
May 26: Crecencio Parra Zamora, Roberto Romero Gracial, and Marino Bolivar Samon skyjacked a Northeast B-727 scheduled to fly twenty people to New York from Miami. The skyjackers used pistols and a knife to force the pilot to land in Cuba. They escaped.
May 30: Terrance Niemeyer attempted to skyjack a Texas International CV-600 New Orleans to Alexandria, La., flight carrying forty-four people, to Cuba. He falsely claimed to have a hand grenade. He was institutionalized.
June 4: Three men overtook an Angolan DC-3 flying to Cabinda, Angola. It landed in the Congo.
June 8: Two armed Africans disguised in Portuguese Army uniforms skyjacked a Portuguese plane in Angola and diverted it to Pointe-Noire, Congo Republic.
June 17: William L. Brent used a revolver to skyjack a TWA B-707 Oakland, Calif. to New York flight, carrying ninety people, to Cuba. He escaped.
June 20: Three men and one woman skyjacked a Colombian DC-3 flying

to Monterrey, Col., and diverted it to Santiago, Chile.
June 22: Agustin Esquivel Medrano skyjacked an Eastern DC-8 traveling from Newark, N.J., to Miami. He wielded a knife and jar labeled "poison" to coerce the pilot to land in Cuba. He escaped.
June 25: John Marques skyjacked a United DC-8 carrying fifty-eight people from Los Angeles to New York. He forced the pilot at gunpoint to land in Cuba and escaped.
June 26: Raymond Anthony, wielding a pocketknife, skyjacked a Miami-bound Eastern Airlines B-727 to Cuba. The plane's crew and ninety-six passengers returned to the U.S. He was later returned to the U.S. and jailed.
July 3: Thirteen people commandeered an Ecuadorian DC-3 flying to Quito, Ecu., and demanded to be flown to Cuba. They escaped.
July 10: Luis Herrera attempted to skyjack a Colombian DC-4 flying to Santa Marta, Col., and demanded to be flown to Cuba. He was overpowered by the pilot and returned to Barranquilla, Col.
July 10: David Olarte attempted to skyjack a Colombian DC-4 destined for Bogota, Col. He was overpowered by flight attendants and passengers and the plane landed as scheduled.
July 26: David Carrera-Vasquez skyjacked a Mexican DC-6 flying to Hermosa, Mex. and diverted it to Cuba. He escaped.
July 26: Joseph C. Crawford skyjacked a Continental DC-9 destined for Midland from El Paso, Texas. Brandishing a knife, he forced the pilot to land in Cuba. He was returned to the U.S. and imprisoned.
July 29: A man, dressed as a woman, attempted to skyjack a Nicaraguan jet. He demanded to be flown to Cuba. He was overpowered.
July 31: Lester E. Perry skyjacked a TWA B-727, flying 123 passengers from Pittsburgh to Los Angeles. Threatening the pilot with a razor blade, Perry forced him to land in Cuba. Perry escaped.
Aug. 4: Three men skyjacked a Colombian DC-4 flying to Riohacha, Col., and demanded to be flown to Cuba. They escaped.
Aug. 5: John S. McCreery attempted to skyjack an Eastern DC-9 flying from Philadelphia to Tampa, to Cuba, wielding a knife and razor blade. He was institutionalized.
Aug. 12: Seven student members of the ELF took over an Ethiopian DC-3 flying to Addis Ababa, Eth. The plane landed in Khartoum, Sudan.
Aug. 14: Domingo Torres Diaz and Julio L. Mena Prez skyjacked a Northeastern B-727 flying forty-five passengers from Boston to Miami. They used a revolver and knife to coerce the pilot to fly to Cuba where they escaped.
Aug. 16: Vassilies Tsironis, his wife, and two of their sons skyjacked a Greek DC-3 flying from Athens to Agrinion, Gr. They demanded to fly to Albania where they escaped. They were imprisoned two years later in Sweden.
Aug. 18: Mohamed Hashem El Moneiry and Soliman El Moneiry and his wife, along with their three children, skyjacked an Egyptian Anatov flying from Cairo to Luxor, Egypt. The plane landed in El Wagah, Saud. The skyjackers were arrested.
Aug. 23: Two men skyjacked a Colombian AV-748 flying to Bogota, Col., and took it to Santiago, Chile.
Aug. 29: Jorge Carballe Delgado used a revolver to skyjack a forty-nine passenger National B-727 to Cuba while en route from Miami to New Orleans. He escaped.
Aug. 29: Leila A. Khaled and Salim K. Essawai of the PFLP skyjacked a TWA B-707 flying from Rome to Athens with 127 people aboard. Armed with pistols and hand grenades, they ordered the plane flown to Syria. In Damascus, two passengers were exchanged for two Syrian pilots. Everyone aboard deplaned and the skyjackers demolished the cockpit, and escaped.
Sept. 6: Six men skyjacked an Ecuadorian Tame Commercial Airline DC-3 operated by the air force and ordered it flown to Cuba. The copilot was killed and the radio man wounded when the plane refueled in Tumaco. The aircraft was abandoned.
Sept. 6: An Ecuadorian air carrier was unsuccessfully skyjacked to Cuba.
Sept. 7: Felix Peterson-Coplin used a revolver to skyjack an Eastern DC-8, scheduled to fly ninety-six people from New York to San Juan, to Cuba. He escaped.
Sept. 10: Jose Gonzalez Medina unsuccessfully attempted to skyjack an Eastern DC-8 flying 194 passengers to San Juan, P.R., from New York. He used no weapon when ordering the pilot to land in Cuba. He was institutionalized.
Sept. 13: Three members of the ELF skyjacked an Ethiopian DC-6 flying from Addis Ababa to Dijibouti, Fr. One skyjacker was shot and the other two taken into custody when the plane landed in Aden, S. Yemen.
Sept. 13: Carlos Huete skyjacked a Honduran DC-3 flying to Teguciagalpa, Hond. He was arrested after the plane landed in San Salvador, El. Sal.
Sept. 16: Sadi Toker skyjacked a Turkish Viscount flying from Istanbul to Ankara, Turk. The plane landed in Sofia, Bul., and Toker was institutionalized.
Sept. 24: Alfredo A. Hernandez, brandishing a pistol and alleged bomb, diverted a National B-727 scheduled to fly eighty-four people to Miami from Charleston, S.C., to Cuba. He was returned to the U.S. and arrested in 1980.
Sept. 29: A TWA plane flying from Rome to Lod, Italy, was skyjacked by two Habash "Front" terrorists who forced it to land in Damascus. Two Israeli passengers were freed in exchange for the release of two Syrian pilots being held in Israel.
Oct. 8: Four men skyjacked a Brazilian Caravelle flying to Manaus, Braz., to Cuba. They escaped.
Oct. 8: E. Ugartteche skyjacked an Argentinian B-707 en route to Miami and forced it to Cuba.
Oct. 9: Francisco Rivera Perez skyjacked a National DC-8 scheduled to fly from Los Angeles to Miami. He used a revolver to divert the flight to Cuba, where he escaped.
Oct. 19: P. Klemt and H.U. Von Hof skyjacked a Polish IL-18 flying from Warsaw to East Berlin. It landed in West Berlin and the skyjackers were imprisoned.
Oct. 21: Henry Shorr skyjacked a Pan American B-720 scheduled to carry its twenty-eight passengers from Mexico City to Merida, Mex. Shorr wielded a revolver to divert the plane to Cuba. He committed suicide a year later.
Oct. 28: Two men skyjacked a Colombian Beachcraft flying from Buenaventura to Bogota, Col., and demanded to be flown to Cuba. They escaped.
Oct. 31: Raphael Minichiello skyjacked a TWA B-707 set to fly its forty passengers from Los Angeles to San Francisco. He pulled out a rifle and forced the pilot to fly to Italy. The skyjacker was imprisoned in Italy.
Nov. 4: Jose Juan Quezada Maldonado and Rena Lugo Alencia skyjacked a Nicaraguan BAC-11 flying to San Salvador, El Sal. Everyone except the crew was let off the plane at Grand Cayman Island.
Nov. 4: Five men and one woman skyjacked a Brazilian B-707 flying from Buenos Aires, Arg., to Santiago, Chile, and ordered the plane landed in Cuba.
Nov. 4: Two armed men skyjacked a Nicaraguan plane flying from Miami to Mexico and diverted it to Cuba.
Nov. 8: Luis Melgarejo tried to skyjacked an Argentinian BAC-111 en route to Buenos Aires. He was convinced to surrender while the plane refueled in Montevideo.
Nov. 10: David Booth, fourteen, attempted to skyjack a Delta DC-9 en route from Cincinnati, Ohio, to Chicago with seventy-five people aboard. He wielded a knife, but failed to force the pilot to land in Sweden or Mexico. He was put in a juvenile detention center.
Nov. 12: Pedro Varas Flores and Patricio F. Degach Vergue attempted to skyjack a Chilean Caravelle to Cuba. They were overpowered by the crew.
Nov. 12: One man skyjacked a Brazilian YS-11 flying from Manaus to Belem, Braz. He demanded to fly to Cuba and escaped.
Nov. 13: Six men skyjacked a Colombian DC-4 flying to Bogota, Col., and demanded to be flown to Cuba. A pregnant woman and another person were allowed to leave when the plane refueled in Barranquilla. The skyjackers escaped in Cuba.
Nov. 18: A Mexican general aviation plane was skyjacked to Cuba.
Nov. 20: W. Szymankiewicz and R. Zolotucho skyjacked a Polish AN-24 flying from Wroclaw, Pol., to Bratislava, Czech. The plane landed in Austria and the skyjackers were imprisoned.
Nov. 29: One man skyjacked a Brazilian B-707 en route from London to Rio de Janeiro and demanded to be flown to Cuba. He escaped.
Dec. 2: Benny R. Hamilton skyjacked a TWA B-707 flying from San Francisco to Philadelphia. Armed with a knife, he forced the pilot to fly to Cuba. He was imprisoned in the U.S.
Dec. 11: One man skyjacked a South Korean YS-11 flying from Kangnung to Seoul. The plane landed in North Korea and the skyjacker escaped.
Dec. 12: Two men skyjacked an Ethiopian B-707 flying from Madrid to Addis Ababa, Eth.
Dec. 19: Patricio Alarcon skyjacked a Chilean B-727 en route from Santiago to Arica, Chile, and demanded to be flown to Cuba. He escaped.
Dec. 21: Three Habash "Front" terrorists, planning to skyjack a TWA plane arriving from Tel-Aviv, Isr., were apprehended by Athens, Gr., police and released in July 1970.
Dec. 23: One man skyjacked a Costa Rican C-46 en route from Puerto Limon to San Jose, Cos. He demanded to be flown to Cuba and escaped.
Dec. 24: Athens police arrested three armed members of the PFLP as they prepared to board a TWA plane scheduled to fly to Rome and New York. They had planned to take the plane to Tunis. They were arrested and later freed.
Dec. 26: M. Martinez, used a revolver to skyjack a United B-727 Chicago-bound flight carrying thirty-two people. He forced the pilot to land in Cuba, where he escaped.

1970

Jan. 1: Eight members of VAR-Palmares skyjacked a plane en route from Montevideo to Rio de Janeiro. They ordered the plane be flown to Cuba "to pay homage" to dead guerrilla leader Ché Guevara.
Jan. 6: Anton Funjek skyjacked a Delta DC-9 taking sixty passengers from Orlando to Jacksonville, Fla. Brandishing a knife, Funjek attempted to force the pilot to land in Switzerland. He was imprisoned.
Jan. 7: A Spanish air carrier was unsuccessfully skyjacked to Albania.
Jan. 8: Christian Belon skyjacked a TWA 707 carrying twenty people from Paris to Rome to "spite Americans and Israelis for their aggression in the Middle East." Belon ordered the pilot at gunpoint to fly to Beirut.

He was arrested in Lebanon and sentenced.
Jan. 9: A Panamanian air carrier was unsuccessfully skyjacked to Cuba.
Jan. 25: A Dutch Antilles Airways plane was skyjacked over Haiti and taken to Cuba.
Feb. 6: A Chilean air carrier was unsuccessfully skyjacked to Cuba.
Feb. 10: Three agents of the Executive Committee for the Liberation of Palestine shot and threw grenades at El Al passengers. One Israeli passenger was killed and eight were injured. A skyjacker was injured. The three were arrested and later released.
Feb. 16: Daniel Lopez del Abad diverted an Eastern Airlines B-727, carrying 100 people from its Newark, N.J., to Miami route. Carrying a pistol, knife, and incendiary bomb, he ordered the pilot to fly to Cuba and escaped.
Mar. 3: Kozo Okamoto's older brother, Takeshi, a member of the Japanese Red Army, brandishing a samurai sword, forced a Japanese jet to fly to North Korea.
Mar. 10: An East German air carrier was unsuccessfully skyjacked.
Mar. 11: A Colombian Avianca plane was skyjacked to Cuba.
Mar. 11: Clemmie Stubbs skyjacked a United B-727, scheduled to fly from Cleveland to Atlanta to Cuba. He threatened the 106 passengers and crew with a revolver. He was imprisoned in Cuba where he died in an escape attempt.
Mar. 12: A Varig Brazilian Airlines plane en route from Santiago, Chile, to Buenos Aires, Arg., was skyjacked to Cuba.
Mar. 17: John Divivo unsuccessfully tried to skyjack an Eastern DC-9 flight taking seventy-three passengers and crew from Newark, N.J., to Boston. Divivo shot and killed the copilot and wounded the pilot. He was overpowered and later imprisoned where he killed himself.
Mar. 24: An Argentine plane was skyjacked to Cuba.
Mar. 31: Nine URA members skyjacked a Japan Air Lines plane and ordered it flown to Pyongyang, N. Kor. Seoul's airport was disguised to look like Pyongyang's and although the skyjackers were not mislead, they let the plane land, and freed the passengers. The skyjackers flew to Pyongyang.
Apr. 22: Ira D. Meeks and Dianne V. McKinney, wielding a revolver, skyjacked a chartered Cessna 172 from Gastonia, N.C., to Cuba. Meeks was found mentally incompetent and charges against both were dropped.
Apr. 23: Joseph A. Wagstaff unsuccessfully attempted to divert a DC-9 en route from Pellston to Sault St. Marie, Mich., to Detroit using a toy pistol and an alleged bomb. He was later institutionalized.
Apr. 26: Joaquim Terreira skyjacked a Brazilian VASP plane and ordered it flown to Cuba. The passengers were released in Guyana.
May 1: Two Americans skyjacked a British West Indian Airways plane flying from Jamaica to Miami. The plane refueled in Havana where the skyjackers surrendered.
May 5: A Czech uranium plant official skyjacked a company airplane to Austria.
May 13: A Dutch Antilles Airways plane was taken over by eight armed Dominican nationals who ordered the plane flown to Cuba.
May 14: A Brazilian plane was skyjacked to Cuba.
May 21: A Colombian plane was skyjacked to Cuba.
May 24: A Mexican plane was skyjacked to Cuba.
May 25: Nelson Molina skyjacked an American Airlines B-727 en route from Chicago to New York. With a pistol, he commandeered the plane and its seventy-four passengers and crew and forced the pilot to land in Cuba. He escaped.
May 25: Graciella C. Quesada Zamora skyjacked a ninety-six-passenger Delta CV-880 en route from Chicago to Miami. Flashing a revolver, she forced the pilot to land in Cuba. She was returned to the U.S. in 1980 and imprisoned.
May 30: An Italian plane was skyjacked to Egypt.
May 31: A Colombian plane was skyjacked to Cuba.
June 4: Arthur Barkley attempted to hold hostage the fifty-seven people aboard a TWA B-727 en route from Phoenix, Ariz., to St. Louis, Mo. Wielding a revolver, razor blade, and bottle of gasoline, he demanded a $100 million ransom. He was found temporarily insane and acquitted.
June 5: A Polish plane was skyjacked to Denmark by people seeking asylum.
June 8: A Czech plane was skyjacked to West Germany by people seeking asylum.
June 9: A Swissair plane was skyjacked flying to Amman, Jor.
June 21: An Iranian 727 was skyjacked to Baghdad by three armed Iranians who asked for asylum in Iraq.
June 22: Haxhi H. Xhaferi skyjacked a Pan American plane carrying 133 passengers from Beirut to Rome. Flashing a pistol, he ordered the plane flown to Cairo. He was sentenced three years later.
June 26: A Venezuelan plane was skyjacked to Colombia.
July 1: George E. Lopez skyjacked a National Airlines DC-8 flying from Las Vegas, Nev., to Tampa, Fla., was skyjacked to Cuba. He used a pistol to take control of the thirty-two passengers and seven crew members. He escaped.
July 1: A Brazilian plane was unsuccessfully skyjacked to Cuba.
July 4: A Brazilian plane was unsuccessfully skyjacked to Cuba.
July 8: Eight men and women forced a two-engine aircraft en route from Prague, Czech., to Carlsbad, Yug., to divert its course to West Germany. They were imprisoned.
July 12: A Saudi Arabian plane was skyjacked to Syria by someone seeking political asylum.
July 22: Six Palestinian Popular Struggle Front terrorists skyjacked an Olympic Airways plane flying from Beirut to Athens and ordered it flown to Cairo. The terrorists were released by the Greek government.
July 22: A South Vietnamese plane was unsuccessfully skyjacked to Hong Kong.
July 25: A Mexican plane was skyjacked to Cuba.
July 25: Three Dominican Republic nationals and one Mexican skyjacked a Mexican plane to Cuba.
Aug. 2: Rudolfo Rivera Rios skyjacked a Pan American B-747 scheduled to fly from New York to San Juan, P.R., to Cuba. He threatened 360 passengers and seventeen crew members with a pistol and alleged nitroglycerin. He was later imprisoned.
Aug. 8: Three men seeking political asylum skyjacked a Czech plane to Austria.
Aug. 19: Five people seeking political asylum skyjacked a Polish plane to Denmark.
Aug. 19: Jose Arrue Martinez, Jesus Ramos Cobas, and Brilan Torres Llurdan skyjacked a Trans Carribean Airways plane. They armed themselves with a pistol and two hand grenades to overpower the 154 passengers and crew. They escaped.
Aug. 20: Gregory A. Graves skyjacked a Delta DC-9 scheduled to fly from Atlanta to Savannah, Ga., to Cuba. He commandeered the eighty-two passengers and crew with an alleged bomb. He was returned to the U.S. five years later and imprisoned.
Aug. 24: Robert J. Labadie skyjacked a TWA B-727, scheduled to fly from Chicago to Philadelphia, to Cuba. He took control of the eighty-six passengers and crew with an alleged bomb. He was institutionalized.
Aug. 30: Johan Huber unsuccessfully attempted to skyjack a Pan American B-727 en route from Munich to West Berlin with 125 people aboard. Wielding a starter pistol, he tried to force the pilot to fly to Budapest, Hung. He was institutionalized.
Aug. 31: Three armed Algerians seeking political asylum skyjacked an Algerian plane to Albania. The plane went to Yugoslavia when officials refused to allow the plane to land in Albania.
Sept. 6: Sa'id Ali Ali, Samir Abdel Ibrahim, and Mazin Abu Khalil, of the Habash "Front" used pistols and hand grenades to overpower 171 passengers and crew to skyjack a Pan American 747 to Beirut and then Cairo. The plane was then vacated and blown up.
Sept. 6: A Swissair DC-8 flying from Zurich, skyjacked by members of the Habash "Front", was landed in Dawson Field in the Jordanian desert near Zarka.
Sept. 6: A TWA 707 en route from Frankfurt, Ger., to New York was diverted by members of the Habash "Front" to Dawson Field where passengers and crew were released and the plane was blown up.
Sept. 6: Habash "Front" terrorists made an abortive attempt to skyjack an El Al plane en route to London from Amsterdam. Terrorist Patrick Arguello was killed. Terrorist Leila Khaled, an Israeli flight attendant, and four passengers were injured. Khaled was released in exchange for hostages from a another skyjacking.
Sept. 8: Two ELF members attempted to skyjack an Ethiopian plane in Athens but were thwarted by security guards.
Sept. 9: A British Overseas Airways VC10 jet was skyjacked and forced to land at Dawson field in Jordan.
Sept. 14: A group of Hungarians seeking political asylum skyjacked a Romanian plane to Munich.
Sept. 15: Donald B. Irwin attempted to skyjack a TWA B-707, scheduled to fly from Los Angeles to San Francisco, to North Korea. He used an unloaded pistol to commandeer fifty-nine passengers and crew. He was imprisoned.
Sept. 19: Richard D. Witt skyjacked a B-727 flying from Pittsburgh to Philadelphia. Using a pistol and alleged bomb, he commandeered the aircraft and its ninety-eight passengers and crew to Egypt and then to Cuba. He was later imprisoned in the U.S.
Sept. 22: David W. Donovan failed to skyjack an Eastern DC-8 en route from Boston to San Juan, P.R. He threatened to set the plane on fire if his demands, which he failed to state, were not met. Skyjacking charges were dropped, but he was imprisoned for an unrelated robbery and murder.
Oct. 9: An Iranian plane was skyjacked to Baghdad by Iranian terrorists seeking the release of twenty-one prisoners held in Iran.
Oct. 15: Two Lithuanians skyjacked a Soviet Aeroflot plane to Turkey. A flight attendant was killed and the pilot and navigator were wounded. The skyjackers were tried and released.
Oct. 22: Skyjackers, demanding the release of four Nicaraguan guerrillas held in Costa Rica, took over a Costa Rican plane. The guerrillas, members of the FSLN, were released and flown to Cuba with the skyjackers.
Oct. 27: Two Soviet students seeking asylum skyjacked an Aeroflot plane to Turkey.
Oct. 30: "L. Rosas", skyjacked a National DC-8, flying from Miami to Tampa, to Cuba. He wielded a pistol to commander the fifty-one passengers and seven crew members.
Nov. 1: Felipe F. Larrazolo skyjacked a United B-727, scheduled to fly from San Diego to Los Angeles, to Cuba. He wielded a pistol and razor to overpower the seventy-one passengers and crew and force the pilot to land in Cuba. He escaped.
Nov. 13: "G. Jones", skyjacked an Eastern DC-9, scheduled to fly from Raleigh, N.C., to Atlanta, to Cuba. He overpowered the seventy-eight

passengers and crew with a pistol. He escaped in Cuba.
Dec. 19: Carlos Denis claimed to have a pistol when he attempted to overpower thirty passengers and crew members to skyjack a DC-9, scheduled to fly from Albuquerque, N.M., to Tulsa, Okla., to Cuba. He had no weapon and was overpowered and later imprisoned.
Dec. 21: Victor Lopez Morales attempted to divert to Mexico a Prinair 157 en route from San Juan to Ponce, P.R., by threatening the nineteen passengers and two crew with an alleged bomb. He was overpowered, found to have no weapon, and institutionalized.
1971
Jan. 3: Arthur J. Wilson, Lolita K. Graves, Carl White, and Norma Jean White skyjacked a National DC-8, scheduled to fly eighty-nine passengers from Los Angeles to Tampa, Fla., to Cuba. Three were imprisoned and charges against Norma White were dropped.
Jan. 21: An Ethiopian plane was skyjacked to Libya by four ELF members.
Jan. 22: Garland J. Grant skyjacked a Northwest B-727, scheduled to fly sixty people from Milwaukee, Wis., to Detroit, to Cuba. He came aboard armed with a hatchet and an alleged bomb. He was returned to the U.S. and imprisoned.
Jan. 23: A South Korean attempted to skyjack a South Korean plane to North Korea but the craft was forced to make an emergency landing after the skyjacker blasted through the cockpit with hand grenades.
Feb. 1: Jibril "Front" terrorists attempted to blow up an El Al plane en route form London to Lod via a rigged suitcase. The girl unwittingly targeted to carry the suitcase aboard was released and the terrorists were not caught.
Feb. 2: Two armed Kashmiri nationalists skyjacked an Indian Airlines plane to Pakistan, demanding the release of thirty-six prisoners in Kashmir. After passengers and crew deplaned and the skyjackers demands were rejected, they blew up the plane.
Feb. 4: Walter C. Hines, allegedly armed with nitroglycerin, skyjacked a Delta DC-9, set to fly twenty-seven people from Chicago to Nashville, Tenn., to Cuba. He was imprisoned.
Feb. 25: Chappin S. Paterson, allegedly carrying a bomb, commandeered a B-737, scheduled to fly ninety-eight people from San Francisco to Seattle. He skyjacked it to Cuba and then Canada. He was deported to the U.S. and imprisoned.
Mar. 8: Thomas K. Marston, seventeen, attempted to skyjack a B-727, flying forty-six people from Mobile, Ala., to New Orleans. Armed with a pistol, he ordered the pilot to fly to Canada. Overpowered, the minor was given an indeterminate sentence.
Mar. 30: Six members of the Philippine leftist student group Kabataang Makabayan, skyjacked a Philippine Air Lines domestic flight to Peking.
Mar. 31: Diego Ramirez, claiming to have a pistol and bomb, skyjacked an Eastern Airlines DC-8 to Cuba. The plane was scheduled to fly seventy-four passengers to San Juan, P.R., from New York. He was later returned to the U.S. three years later and put on probation.
Mar. 31: John M. Mathews, Jr., fourteen, armed with a pistol, attempted to divert a Delta DC-9 Birmingham, Ala., to Chicago flight to Cuba. He was put on three-years' probation for carrying a weapon aboard an airplane.
Apr. 5: Carlos L. Hernandez Trahns skyjacked an American Air Taxi-208 Cessna 402 en route from Key West, Fla., to Miami. He overpowered the pilot with a pistol and commandeered the aircraft to Cuba, where he escaped.
Apr. 21: Francisco Anile failed to skyjack to Italy an Eastern Airlines DC-8 en route from Newark, N.J., to Miami. Claiming to have a pistol and hand grenade, he was overpowered and found to possess no weapons. He was imprisoned.
May 27: Six armed skyjackers forced a Romanian national airlines plane to be flown to Vienna where they requested political asylum.
May 28: James E. Bennett, allegedly armed with acid and explosives, attempted to skyjack an Eastern B-727 with 138 people aboard to divert the Miami to New York flight, to the Bahamas and Ireland. He was institutionalized.
May 29: Ivan G. Garcia Landaeta diverted a Pan American B-707 Caracas, Venez., to Miami flight to Cuba. He overpowered the sixty-nine passengers and crew with a pen knife and a hunting knife. He was returned to Venezuela from Cuba five years later.
June 4: Glenn E. Riggs attempted to skyjack a United Airlines B-737 flying sixty-seven people from Charleston, W.V., to Newark, N.J. Wielding a revolver, Riggs tried to divert the flight to Israel. He was imprisoned.
June 11: Gregory L. White skyjacked a TWA B-727 en route from Chicago to New York. Holding twenty-six people hostage with a pistol, White demanded a $75,000 ransom and to be flown to North Vietnam. He was put in an institution where he killed himself.
June 18: Bobby R. White attempted to skyjack a B-737 Winston-Salem, N.C., chartered flight to Cuba, claiming to have acid and a bomb. He was imprisoned.
July 2: Robert L. Jackson and Ligia Sanchez Archila skyjacked a B-707 en route from Mexico city to San Antonio, Texas. Wielding pistols and alleged nitroglycerin, they overpowered the 110 passengers and crew and demanded a $100,000 ransom and to be flown to Brazil, Argentina, and Algeria. They were imprisoned.
July 23: Richard A. Obergfell was killed attempting to divert a TWA B-727 New York to Chicago flight to Italy with sixty-one people aboard. Although he claimed he had a pistol and a bomb, no weapons were found.
July 24: Santiago M. Guerra Valdez skyjacked a National DC-8, carrying eighty-three people to Cuba. He diverted the Miami to Jacksonville, Fla., flight by flashing a pistol and stick of dynamite.
July 28: A Jibril "Front" terrorist tried to demolish an El Al plane traveling from Rome to Lod via a rigged suitcase. The would-be skyjacker got away.
August: Two El Fatah skyjackers commandeered a plane to Algeria.
Sept. 3: Juan M. Borges Guerra attempted to skyjack an Eastern DC-9 Chicago to Miami flight to Cuba. He overpowered the eighty-six passengers and crew with an ice pick. He was imprisoned.
Sept. 8: An El Fatah member skyjacked a Jordanian Alia plane to Libya.
Sept. 16: El Fatah terrorists made a foiled attempt to take over a Jordanian Alia plane en route to Beirut.
Sept. 24: Barbara H. Pliskow attempted to skyjack an American Airlines B-727 Detroit to New York flight to Algeria. Pliskow wielded a pistol and dynamite and demanded that specified prisoners be released. She was put on probation for two years.
Oct. 4: George Giffe, Jr. and Bobby Wayne Wallace, armed with pistols, tried to skyjack a chartered Big Brother Inc. Aero Commander Hawk 681 to the Bahamas. Giffe killed his wife and the pilot of the Nashville, Tenn., to Atlanta flight before committing suicide.
Oct. 9: Richard F. Dixon skyjacked an Eastern B-727 Detroit to Miami flight to Cuba by overpowering the forty-six passengers and crew members with a revolver. He was imprisoned five years later.
Oct. 18: Del L. Thomas skyjacked a B-737 Anchorage, Alaska, to Bethel, Ark., flight to Cuba. He overpowered the thirty-five passengers and crew with a pistol. He was imprisoned.
Oct. 25: Angel Lugo Casado skyjacked an American Airlines B-747 New York to San Juan, P.R., flight to Cuba. He overpowered the 236 passengers and crew with a pistol that turned out to be a fake. He was returned to the U.S. seven years later and imprisoned.
Nov. 24: "D.B. Cooper", skyjacked a Northwest B-727 Portland, Ore., to Seattle, Wash., flight carrying forty-two passengers and crew. Claiming to carry a bomb, he demanded $200,000 and four parachutes. He parachuted and escaped.
Nov. 27: Michael R. Finney, Charlie R. Hill, and Ralph L. Goodwin commandeered a TWA B-727 en route from Albuquerque, N.M., to Chicago. Brandishing two pistols and a knife, they diverted the flight to Cuba. Goodwin drowned trying to swim to shore and Finney and Hill became fugitives.
Dec. 24: Everett L. Holt skyjacked a B-707 taking thirty-five people from Minneapolis, Minn., to Chicago. He wielded a revolver and an alleged bomb and demanded a $300,000 ransom and two parachutes. He was institutionalized.
Dec. 26: Donald L. Coleman attempted to skyjack an American Airlines B-707 en route from Chicago to San Francisco. He tried to overpower the eighty-five people aboard with a knife, toy pistol, and fake bomb. He demanded a $200,000 ransom. He was imprisoned.
1972
Jan. 7: Allen G. Sims and Ida P. Robinson skyjacked a B-727 San Francisco to Los Angeles flight to Africa and then Cuba. They brandished a pistol and shotgun to overpower 151 people. Sim was sentenced. Robinson escaped.
Jan. 12: Billy E. Hurst, Jr. skyjacked a B-727 en route from Houston to Dallas. He brandished a pistol and an alleged bomb to overpower the 100 people aboard. He demanded a $1 million ransom and ten parachutes. He was imprisoned.
Jan. 20: Richard C. LaPoint skyjacked a DC-10 Las Vegas to Reno, Nev., flight. Claiming to have a bomb, he held the seventy-three people aboard hostage and demanded $500,000 and two parachutes. He parachuted, was captured, and imprisoned.
Jan. 26: Merlyn L. St. George, armed with a starter pistol and alleged bomb, was killed attempting to skyjack an FH-227 plane flying forty-six people from Albany to New York. He had demanded $200,000 and four parachutes.
Jan. 26: Patrick H. McAlroy attempted to skyjack an SFO helicopter about to leave Berkeley, Calif., for San Francisco. He carried a pistol and attempted to take off for Cuba. He was committed to a mental institution.
Jan. 29: Garrett B. Trapnell, armed with a pistol and phony bomb, failed to skyjack a B-707 en route from Los Angeles to New York with 101 people aboard. He demanded $306,800 ransom, the release of a Dallas prisoner, and flight to Europe. He was shot, captured, and later imprisoned.
Feb. 19: A thwarted attempt was made to skyjack a Jordanian plane flying from Cairo to Amman, Jor.
Feb. 22: A German Lufthansa Airlines plane en route from New Deli to Athens was skyjacked and ordered to Aden, South Yemen by Habash "Front" terrorists. The plane, passengers, and crew were released. The West German government paid a $5 million ransom and let the terrorists go.
Mar. 7: James W. Brewton and Joseph T. Bennett, armed with guns, skyjacked to Cuba a Chalk's Flying Service Grumman 73 scheduled to fly to the Bahamas from Miami. Bennett escaped in Cuba. Brewton was fatally shot in Jamaica three years later.

Mar. 7: Edmond M. McKee, Jr., armed with a pistol, attempted to skyjack to Sweden a B-727 en route from Tampa to Melbourne, Fla., carrying seventeen passengers and seven crew. Charges against him were dismissed and he was institutionalized.

Mar. 19: John H. Jennings and Janyce Reed skyjacked a Tortuga Airways Cessna 206 to Cuba while en route from Key West, Fla., to Tortugas Island. They used a pistol and knife to overwhelm the pilot and four passengers. Both were sentenced.

Apr. 7: Richard F. McCoy skyjacked a United B-727 taking ninety-one people from Denver to Los Angeles. He used a pistol, hand grenade, and a phony bomb and demanded a $500,000 ransom and six parachutes. He escaped and was later killed resisting arrest.

Apr. 9: Stanley H. Speck, claiming to have a hand grenade, attempted to skyjack a B-727 with ninety-two people aboard en route from Oakland to San Diego, Calif. He demanded a $500,000 ransom and four parachutes. He was captured in San Diego and institutionalized.

Apr. 13: Ricardo Chavez-Ortiz skyjacked a B-737 en route from Albuquerque, N.M., to Tuscon, Ariz., to Mexico. He overpowered the thirty-two people aboard by wielding a pistol. He was imprisoned.

Apr. 16: Uriel Ojeda Perez, carried explosives that were later found to be fake, to skyjack a chartered Prinair 179 scheduled to fly from Ponce to San Juan, P.R. He was overpowered by a passenger and mechanic and imprisoned.

Apr. 17: Kenneth L. Smith forced his way aboard a B-727 scheduled to fly from Seattle to Annette Island, Ark. Claiming to carry a pistol, he was unsuccessful in forcing the pilot to fly to Cairo, Egypt. He was institutionalized.

Apr. 17: William H. Greene III attempted to skyjack a Delta CV-880 en route from West Palm Beach, Fla., to Chicago. Threatening the seventy-six people aboard with a phony pistol, he demanded $500,000 ransom and a flight to Nassau, Bahamas. He surrendered and was imprisoned.

Apr. 18: Two Czech miners skyjacked a Czech plane to Nuremberg, W. Ger., requesting political asylum. The co-pilot was wounded.

May 3: Four TPLA members, demanding the release of three prisoners in Turkey, skyjacked a Turkish plane to Sofia, Bulg., where they surrendered. The crew and passengers were released the next day.

May 5: Frederick W. Hahneman, armed with a pistol and fake bomb, skyjacked an Eastern B-727 carrying forty-nine passengers from Allentown, Pa., to Washington, D.C. He demanded $303,000, a flight to Central America, and six parachutes. He later surrendered and was imprisoned.

May 5: Michael L. Hansen, armed with a pistol, skyjacked a B-737 en route from Salt Lake City, Utah, to Los Angeles. He diverted the seventy-five passenger craft to Hanoi, N. Viet., and Cuba. He was later imprisoned.

May 8: Four members of Black September were responsible for skyjacking a Sabena Belgian World plane on its way from Vienna to Tel Aviv. Two of the skyjackers were caught and imprisoned. The others were killed by Israeli forces.

May 30: Three young Japanese student members of the Red Army brandished three submachine guns at the Lod Airport and fired into the crowd, killing twenty-four people and injuring seventy-six. The one surviving terrorist, Kozo Okamoto, was tried.

June 2: William Holder and Katherine Kerkow, armed with a fake bomb, skyjacked a B-727 en route from Los Angeles to Seattle carrying ninety-seven people. They demanded to be flown to Algeria, a $500,000 ransom, and five parachutes. The ransom was returned, Holder was given a suspended sentenced, and Kerkow escaped.

June 2: Robb D. Heady skyjacked a United Airlines B-727 en route from Reno, Nev., to San Francisco. He held six people hostage with a pistol and demanded a $200,000 ransom. He was captured after his parachute jump and imprisoned.

June 23: Martin J. McNally and Walter J. Petlikowsky skyjacked an American B-727 en route with 101 people from St. Louis to Tulsa, Okla. Wielding a submachine gun, a hand grenade, and a phony bomb, they demanded $502,000 ransom and five parachutes. They were imprisoned.

June 30: Daniel B. Carre skyjacked a DC-9 en route to Portland, Ore., from Seattle. Claiming to have a knife, he demanded a $50,000 ransom and a parachute. He was institutionalized.

July 2: Thai Binh Nguyen skyjacked a Pan American B-747 en route from Honolulu, Hawaii, to Saigon, S. Viet., with 135 passengers. Wielding a knife and alleged hand grenades, he demanded to be flown to Hanoi, N. Viet. He was killed in Saigon by another passenger.

July 5: Charles E. Smith attempted to skyjack an American Airlines B-707 on the ground in Buffalo, N.Y. He brandished a knife and demanded to be flown out of the U.S. He eventually surrendered and was sentenced to probation.

July 5: Dimitz K. Alexiev and Michael D. Azmanoff, armed with pistols, skyjacked a B-737 en route with eighty-six people aboard from Sacramento, Calif., to San Francisco. They demanded $800,000 ransom and two parachutes. The skyjackers and one passenger were killed. Lubomir Peichev, a conspirator, was imprisoned.

July 6: Francis M Goodell skyjacked a B-727 en route from Oakland to Sacramento, Calif., with fifty-eight people aboard. Goodell wielded a pistol and demanded $455,000 in ransom and one parachute. He eventually surrendered and was imprisoned.

July 12: M. Fisher skyjacked an American B-727 en route from Oklahoma City to Dallas with fifty-seven people aboard. He brandished a pistol and an alleged bomb and demanded a $550,000 ransom and a parachute. He eventually surrendered and was imprisoned.

July 12: Michael S. Green and Lulseged Tesfa skyjacked a B-727 en route from Philadelphia to New York. They brandished a pistol, shotgun, and fake bomb. They held 120 people aboard hostage and demanded $600,000 ransom and three parachutes. Both surrendered and were imprisoned.

July 31: Melvin and Jean McNair, George Wright, George Brown, and Joyce Burgess, members of the Black Panther Party, skyjacked a Delta DC-8 en route from Detroit to Miami with 101 people aboard. They carried handguns and demanded a $1 million ransom and a flight to Algeria. All but Wright were imprisoned.

Aug. 18: Frank M. Sibley, Jr. skyjacked a United Airlines B-727 en route from Reno, Nev., to San Francisco. He carried a shotgun and demanded a $2 million ransom for the thirty-three people he held hostage. He was imprisoned.

Oct. 29: Charles, Brice, and Jonathan Tuller and Willaim W. Graham skyjacked an Eastern B-727 with forty-seven people aboard going from Houston to Atlanta. Armed with guns and a knife, they demanded to be flown to Cuba. The Tullers were imprisoned. Graham escaped.

Oct. 29: A Lufthansa Boeing en route to Munich was skyjacked after leaving Beirut by two members of Black September flashing revolvers and hand grenades and demanding to be taken to Nicosia, Cyprus. The plane landed in Libya and the skyjackers were arrested.

Nov. 10: Henry D. Jackson and Melvin C. and Louis D. Cale skyjacked a DC-9 en route from Birmingham to Montgomery, Ala., with thirty-three people aboard. Wielding pistols and phony hand grenades, they demanded $10 million ransom and parachutes. The copilot was wounded and the skyjackers were imprisoned.

1973

Jan. 2: Charles A. Weinge skyjacked a YS11A en route from Washington, D.C., to Baltimore, Md. He wielded a pistol and demanded to be flown to Toronto, Can. He was imprisoned.

June: A Colombian plane was skyjacked for two and a half days by two men who claimed to be members of the National Army, a Colombian guerilla group.

July 11: Daniel Clark skyjacked a privately chartered JDJ Flying Service Helicopter Bell 47G5 over Gainesville, Texas. Wielding a pistol, he demanded to be flown to Wichita Falls. Texas. He was imprisoned.

July 21: A Japan Airlines plane traveling from Paris via Amsterdam to Tokyo with 137 passengers was skyjacked by four terrorists who forced the pilot to land in Dubai. The plane was flown to Libya, passengers and crew deplaned, and the craft was blown up.

1974

Feb. 22: Samuel J. Byck, armed with a gun and bomb killed a policeman in the Baltimore, Md., terminal before forcing his way aboard a Delta DC-9 scheduled to fly to Atlanta with fourteen people aboard. He killed the copilot, wounded the pilot, and then killed himself.

Mar. 30: Ernest J. Smith, wielding a shotgun, attempted to skyjack a National Airlines B-727 on the ground in Sarasota, Fla. He was imprisoned.

May 23: David F. Kamaiko skyjacked a Wall Street Bell 206A helicopter in New York. He used a rifle, zip gun, and alleged dynamite to hold the three people aboard hostage. He demanded a $2 million ransom before being overpowered. Prosecution was declined.

June 26: Edwin C. Rowell skyjacked an Air Charter Inc., Piper en route from Alexandria to Angola, La. He wielded a pistol and demanded to be flown to Hammond, La. He was caught and later imprisoned.

June 27: Douglas A. Kirkaldie, William H. Beck, and Stanley D. Naylor skyjacked a chartered Big Horn Airways Cessna 172 en route from Ashland, Mont., to Sheridan, Wyo. Using three pistols, they demanded to be flown to Yellowtail Dam, Mont. They were imprisoned.

Sept. 4: Marshall Collins, III skyjacked an Eastern DC-9 en route with 100 people from New York to Boston. Wielding a razor blade and nail, he demanded a $10,000 ransom and flight to New York. He was institutionalized.

Dec. 14: Donald L. Rider skyjacked a chartered Tampa Flying Service Piper Seneca en route from Tampa to Naples, Fla. He wielded a pistol and ordered the pilot to fly to Cuba, where he escaped.

1975

Jan. 3: Paul T. Landers, armed with a rifle, skyjacked an out-of-service National B-727 in Pensacola, Fla., to draw attention to himself. He was imprisoned where he killed himself.

Jan. 13: Laughlin Wright attempted to skyjack an Eastern B-727 en route from Atlanta to Philadelphia with sixty people aboard. He demanded to be flown to San Juan, P.R. He was institutionalized.

Mar. 2: Alexander P. Grosser attempted to skyjack a Twin Otter plane on the ground in Hyannis, Mass., and scheduled to fly to Nantucket. He wielded a knife and demanded to be flown to New Haven, Conn. He was put on probation.

Mar. 6: Ralph Gonzales and Edward Rodriguez skyjacked a chartered Sawyer Aviation Cessna 310 en route from Phoenix to Tuscon, Ariz. They wielded a pistol and demanded the pilot fly to Nogales, Mex. They were imprisoned.

Apr. 25: Francis P. Covey skyjacked a United B-727 en route with sixty-seven people from Raleigh, N.C., to Newark, N.J. He demanded to go to Cuba. He was imprisoned.

May 15: Deborah L. Crawford attempted to skyjack a United B-737 en route from Eugene, Ore., to San Francisco with eighty people aboard. Claiming she had a knife, she forbade the pilot landing in San Francisco. She was hospitalized.
June 6: Morris E. Colosky, wielding a knife, skyjacked a chartered helicopter en route from Plymouth to Lansing, Mich. He demanded that the pilot pick up an escaped prisoner. Colosky, the convict, and six accomplices were captured. Colosky was imprisoned.
Aug. 16: Roper McNair skyjacked a Woodbridge Airport, Inc., Piper Cherokee flying over Woodbridge, Va. He wielded a pistol and demanded to be flown to Jamaica, Puerto Rico, and Madrid, Spain. He was institutionalized.
Sept. 15: Frederick Saloman attempted to skyjack an out-of-service B-727 in San Jose, Calif. He took four hostages. Two hostages escaped, one was released, and the other was wounded by Saloman, who was then fatally shot.
Oct. 7: Ronald E. Ralph, David P. Burke, and Jeffrey W. Murphy skyjacked a chartered Atlantic Aero Cessna 177 en route from Greensboro, N.C., to Atlanta. They ordered the pilot at gunpoint to fly to Florida. Only Ralph and Burke were imprisoned.
Nov. 8: Jack R. Johnson skyjacked a chartered Tri State Aero Cessna flying over Evansville, Idaho. Wielding a pistol, he ordered the pilot to dive in to the ground. The pilot struggled with Johnson, finally pushing him out of the plane. Johnson died.
Nov. 24: Gary W. Schmidt skyjacked a chartered California Air Charter Piper Navajo en route from Palomar, Calif., to Dallas, Texas. He wielded a rifle and two shotguns and demanded to be flown to Mazatlan, Mex. He escaped.

1976

Apr. 18: Roger L. Lentz skyjacked a Heinzmann Engineering Co., Piper Navajo PA 31 over Grand Island, Neb. He threatened the pilot with a revolver and shotgun and demanded to be flown to Mexico. Lentz was fatally shot by a police officer.
May 13: Franklin M. Solesby, armed with a pistol, tried to skyjack a chartered Royal American Fliers Cessna 210 en route from Denver to Houston. Solesby already faced murder charges so skyjacking charges against him were dropped.
June 24: Two West Germans and five PFLP members skyjacked an Air France Airbus en route from Tel Aviv to Paris with 245, passengers. They ordered the pilot to fly to Entebbe, Uganda, where they held the mainly Israeli passengers until Israeli commandoes rescued them. Two captives died while being held. The skyjackers died in the raid.
Sept. 10: Julienne and Zvonko Busic, Peter Matanic, Frane Pesut, and Mark Vlasic skyjacked a TWA B-727 en route from New York to Chicago. Armed with phony explosives, they wanted to distribute Croatian independence propaganda. They were imprisoned.
Dec. 21: Palm J. Hinnant attempted to skyjack an out-of-service United DC-8 in San Francisco. Armed with two revolvers and a knife, he demanded to be flown to the East Coast. He was institutionalized.

1977

Jan. 8: Guy Elmore and Oscar Kuykendall, wielding a revolver, tried to skyjack a privately chartered Iredell Aviation Piper Arrow 200 en route from Statesville, N.C., to Raleigh. They were ordered to pay for damages to the plane and placed on probation.
Jan. 11: William Saupe attempted to skyjack a TWA B-747 en route from New York to London. Claiming he had hand grenades, he held the 333 passengers hostage and demanded to be taken to Uganda. He was put on probation.
Mar. 15: Luciano Porcari skyjacked an Iberia Airlines B-727 scheduled to take thirty-seven people from Barcelona to Palma, Majorca, forcing the pilot to fly to the Ivory Coast. He said he wanted $120,000 to recover his daughter from her mother. He was arrested.
May 8: Bruce J. Trayer, armed with a razor blade, tried to skyjack a Northwest B-747 en route from Tokyo to Honolulu with 262 aboard. He demanded to be taken to Moscow. Trayer was overpowered and the plane returned to Tokyo. He was institutionalized.
Jun. 6: Nasser Mohammed Ali Abu Khaled skyjacked a Lebanon Middle East Airways B-707 bound for Baghdad, Iraq. He held 115 hostages and demanded a $5 million ransom. He was subdued by commandoes but released for health reasons. The hostages were released unharmed.
Aug. 20: Jerry R. Mills skyjacked a B-707 en route from San Diego to Denver with thirty-one people aboard. He claimed to be carrying a bomb and ordered the pilot to fly to Mexico. He was put on probation and ordered to obtain psychiatric care.
Sept. 28: JRA members skyjacked a Japanese plane, demanding $6 million and the release and flight to Aden of five JRA prisoners. The demands were met.
Oct. 13: PFLP and Baader-Meinhof terrorists skyjacked a Lufthansa plane with eighty-four on board after it took off from Palma, Majorca. The skyjackers demanded $15 million and the release of RAF prisoners. They fatally shot the captain. The plane was stormed and four skyjackers were killed.
Oct. 20: Thomas M. Hannan skyjacked a B-737 en route from Grand Island to Lincoln, Neb., with thirty-four on board. He wielded a shotgun and demanded to be flown to Atlanta to pick up a convict. He also demanded two parachutes, two pistols, two submachine guns and $3 million ransom. The hostages were released and the skyjacker fatally shot himself.
Dec. 25: Nikolai Wischnewski skyjacked an Eastern DC-9 en route from Jacksonsville, Fla., to Atlanta with thirty-six aboard. He wielded a toy pistol and a phony bomb, and demanded to be flown to Cuba. He was imprisoned.

1978

Jan. 24: Harold L. Starry attempted to skyjack a Nampa Aero Club Cessna 205 in Homedale, Idaho. He wielded a pistol and demanded to be flown to Mexico. He was imprisoned.
Jan. 28: Sam Dawkins skyjacked a YS-11 en route from Greensboro to Wilmington, N.C., with fourteen people aboard. Claiming to carry a gun, Dawkins demanded to be flown to Cuba. He was imprisoned.
Mar. 13: Clayton Thomas skyjacked a United B-727 en route from San Francisco to Seattle with seventy-five people aboard. Claiming to have a bomb, he demanded to be flown to Cuba. He was institutionalized.
Apr. 1: Richard Bland, sixteen, tried to skyjack a B-737 en route with sixty-six people aboard from Richmond to Norfolk, Va. Wielding a rifle, he demanded $1 million ransom and to be flown to New York, and then France. He was put under psychiatric care.
May 24: Barbara A. Oswald, armed with three pistols, skyjacked a chartered helicopter out of St. Louis. She demanded the release of G. Trapnell, a federal prisoner. The pilot struggled with her, grabbed her gun, and fatally shot her.
June 30: Francis J. Bond, Adelado S. Trujillo, and Richard J. Mascarenas, armed with a pistol and knife they wrestled from the pilot, skyjacked a chartered Colorado Air Transport Piper Seneca II en route from Pueblo to Greeley, Colo. Bond was found mentally incompetent. Only Trujillo and Mascarenas were imprisoned.
Aug. 25: Rudi S. Kreitlow attempted to skyjack a TWA B-707 with eighty-eight people aboard, en route to Geneva, Switz., from New York. He claimed to carry explosives and firearms and demanded the release of several individuals. He was imprisoned.
Aug. 27: Diana L. Benson skyjacked a United DC-8 en route from Denver to Seattle with 159 people aboard. Claiming to possess a bomb, Benson demanded to be flown to Vancouver, Can. She was found mentally incompetent and released.
Sept. 13: George T. Bonds, Larry P. Chism, Ronald L. Lyons, and Floyd R. Brewer, convicts armed with guns, skyjacked a Dickson Flying Service Cessna 182 out of Dickson, Tenn., to escape prison. Chism escaped. The others were captured and imprisoned.
Nov. 23: John R. Prindle attempted to skyjack a DC-9 en route with twenty-three people to Milwaukee from Madison, Wis. He had a knife and claimed to have a bomb, but unintelligibly declared where he wanted to go. He was found mentally incompetent.
Dec. 14: Gerald E. Casey attempted to skyjack a National B-727 taking fifty-four people from New York to Miami. Claiming to have a gun, he ordered the pilot to go to Cuba. His demand was unmet and he was put on probation.
Dec. 16: Walter H. Scott, engaged in an instructional flight over Rural Retreat, Va., brandished a pistol and attempted to skyjack the Mt. Empire Flying Service Cessna 172 to Camden, S.C. He was imprisoned.
Dec. 21: Robyn S. Oswald, claiming she carried a bomb, skyjacked a TWA DC-9 en route from St. Louis to Kansas City, Mo., to help G. Trapnell escape from prison. She was put in a juvenile home and placed on probation.

1979

Jan. 27: Irene McKinney, claiming to have nitroglycerin, skyjacked a United B-747 carrying 131 people from Los Angeles to New York. She demanded specified celebrities read a message on television. She was placed on probation.
Feb. 23: A man and woman skyjacked a chartered helicopter scheduled to fly from Montreal to Quebec City and forced its pilot, at gunpoint, to land at a shopping center in St. Laurent. There, the couple robbed a bank and disappeared in a subway station.
Mar. 16: John C. Kivlen, saying he had a knife, skyjacked a B-727 en route from Los Angeles to Tuscon, Ariz., carrying ninety-four people. He demanded $200,000 ransom and a flight to Cuba. He was sent to a hospital for mental care.
Apr. 4: Domenico Speranza attempted to skyjack a Pan American B-747 in Sydney, Aus., set to fly to Auckland, N. Zea. He wielded a knife and two cans of gunpowder and demanded flight to Moscow via Rome. He was killed before the plane left Sydney.
Apr. 15: Belgian Police and Israeli guards prevented the skyjacking of an El Al plane at Brussels.
June 11: Eduardo Guerra Jimenez skyjacked a Delta L-1011 en route from New York to Fort Lauderdale with 204 aboard. He carried a pocketknife and claimed to have a bomb and gun. He demanded to go to Cuba, where he escaped.
June 20: Nikola Kavaja skyjacked an American Airlines B-727 en route from New York to Chicago. Using two ground burst simulator projectiles and claiming to have dynamite, he held 136 people hostage. He demanded the release of a prisoner and flight to Ireland. He was imprisoned.
June 30: Rigoberto Gonzalez Sanchez attempted to skyjack an Eastern Airlines L-1011 en route from San Juan, P.R., to Miami carrying 306 people. Threatening to ignite a bottle of rum, he ordered the pilot to fly to Cuba. Gonzalez was overpowered. He was institutionalized.
July 20: Ronald A. Rimerman skyjacked a United B-727 en route from Denver to Omaha, Neb. He threatened the 126 passengers and crew with

alleged plastic explosives and ordered the pilot to fly to Cuba. He was found insane.
Aug. 16: Alfred R. Kagan skyjacked an Eastern B-727 en route from Guatemala City, Guat., to Miami. Threatening the ninety-one people aboard with a penknife and an alleged bomb, he demanded to go to Cuba. He was institutionalized.
Aug. 22: James R. Allbee skyjacked a United B-727 en route with 120 people from Portland, Ore., to Los Angeles. Claiming he had a bomb, Allbee ordered the pilot to return to Portland. He was imprisoned.
Aug. 25: Rudi S. Kreitlow skyjacked a plane. He was imprisoned.
Sept. 12: Rafael Keppel skyjacked a Lufthansa B-727 flying from Frankfurt, Ger. Wielding a toy pistol, he held the 119 passengers and eight crew seven hours at Bonn-Cologne Airport, and read demands for a more "humane world." He surrendered.
Oct. 16: Joann Thedorf skyjacked a privately owned Piper Cherokee in Lower Lake, Calif., and ordered the pilot at gunpoint to fly to Napa, Calif. She was declared insane.
Oct. 30: John E. Gray skyjacked a B-727 en route from Los Angeles to San Diego. Claiming he had a bomb, he held the 108 people on board hostage and ordered the pilot to fly to Mexico. He was imprisoned.
Nov. 24: Gerald J. Hill, claiming to carry a knife and dynamite, skyjacked an American Airlines B-727 en route from San Antonio, Texas, to El Paso with seventy-four aboard. He demanded to go to Iran. He was imprisoned.
Dec. 12: Michael L. Magruder skyjacked a privately chartered Island City Flying Service Cessna 172 scheduled to fly over Key West, Fla. At knifepoint, he ordered the pilot to fly to Cuba. Magruder was institutionalized.

1980

Jan. 14: A man who said he was a member of the unknown group called Les Vivants, threatened the pilot of an Alitalia plane, saying an accomplice had explosives. He demanded the release of twenty-five prisoners in Tunisia and flight to Tripoli. After negotiations in Sicily, the skyjacker surrendered and asked for political asylum. No accomplice or explosives were found.
Jan. 18: A Middle East Airlines plane was taken over by a man claiming he wanted to determine the fate of a missing Muslim spiritual leader. He ordered the plane to be flown to Iran but allowed it to return to Beirut for refueling. There he surrendered after being allowed a press conference.
Jan. 25: Samuel A. Ingram, claiming to have a pistol and bomb, forced a Delta L-1011 pilot to fly sixty-three people to Cuba where the crew and most of the passengers escaped. He demanded flight to Iran and then surrendered. He was imprisoned.
Jan. 30: Two men who attempted to skyjack an East German Illyushin-18 plane were overpowered by the crew and passengers.
Feb. 29: A man at an Ecuadorian terminal attempted to climb aboard a plane with hostages, including two women and two children. He pounded on the plane's locked doors and shot at the pilot before surrendering.
Mar. 10: A man took over a plane en route to Beirut with a toy gun. The skyjacker held a press conference after the plane had landed in Beirut and attempted to create interest in the fate of a missing Muslim spiritual leader. He was then arrested.
Apr. 9: A skyjacker sneaked aboard an American B-727 in Miami, attacked seven crew members and demanded to be flown to Cuba. They landed in Havana after refueling in Dallas-Fort Worth and he surrendered.
Apr. 14: Thomas C. Wiltgen, claiming to be an IRA member, boarded a Continental B-727 in Denver. Carrying a knife, he demanded the plane fly to Libya. The seventy-five passengers deplaned, Wiltgen surrendered and was imprisoned.
May 1: Stephen W. Bilson sneaked on to a Pacific Southwest B-727 in Stockton, Calif., and took the flight engineer hostage, who disarmed him. Bilson read a statement concerning Iran and hostages in Iran, and was arrested and imprisoned.
May 6: An Air Portugal TAP B-727 headed for Faro, Port., was taken over by a skyjacker who threatened the pilot with a pistol and demanded $10 million and flight to Madrid and then to Switzerland. In Madrid, the skyjacker dropped his demands. He was taken into custody in Lisbon.
May 15: James T. Wright, armed with guns, forced a maintenance employee aboard an out-of-service Grumman 73 in Miami and demanded a pilot. Claiming he had been cheated out of $3,000 in welfare payments, Wright demanded to fly to Capetown, S. Afri., "to dig for diamonds." Before the plane departed, he surrendered.
June 30: An Aerolineas Argentinas B-737 en route to Buenos Aires with forty-five passengers was skyjacked by one man. Using a pistol, he demanded $100,000 and a flight to Mexico. The man took the pilot and one flight attendant hostage until he surrendered.
July 11: Glen K. Tripp, threatening to blow up a Northwest B-727 about to depart for Portland with sixty-four people, demanded $100,000 and two parachutes. He later demanded a car and was arrested on his way to the automobile. He was imprisoned.
July 12: A Philippine airplane traveling to Manila was taken over by a man claiming to have two confederates aboard armed with a bomb. He demanded $6 million, flight to Libya, and ten American hostages. The crew locked him out of the cabin and returned to Manila where he was arrested.
July 22: Silvio Mesa Cabrera took control of a 144-passenger Delta L-1011 en route from Miami to San Juan, P.R. He demanded the craft be taken to Havana. Weather conditions prohibited that, so the plane landed in Camaguey, Cuba, where he escaped.
July 24: Skyjackers aboard a Kuwaiti jet ordered the aircraft to Kuwait and demanded a Kuwaiti businessman pay a debt. Some passengers were released, and finally, in Kuwait, the pilot and copilot escaped. The skyjackers surrendered.
Aug. 10: Manuel Soto, threatening to blow up a Key West-bound Air Florida plane, demanded the pilot land in Cuba. The plane, carrying thirty passengers and five crew, landed in Havana where Soto surrendered. His "bomb" was a box of soap.
Aug. 13: Seven males on an Air Florida plane en route with sixty-eight passengers from Key West, Fla., to Miami, poured gasoline in the plane, walking the aisle with lighters shouting, "Cuba." The plane landed in Havana where the skyjackers were arrested.
Aug. 14: Two males on a National DC-10 headed for San Juan, P.R., with 224 aboard, demanded to be taken to Cuba. Threatened with gasoline and lighters, the pilot landed the plane in Havana and the men were arrested.
Aug. 16: Geraldo Guerra and three others skyjacked a Delta L-1011 en route from San Juan, P.R., to Miami with 179 passengers aboard. They threatened to blow up the plane with gasoline and a lighter. They were arrested in Havana.
Aug. 16: An Eastern B-727 flying forty-six passengers and seven crew to Orlando, Fla., was taken over by six males armed with a fake bomb and demanding to be flown to Cuba. The plane landed in Havana and the men were taken into custody.
Aug. 16: Eduardo Lopez, Ramon E. Lopez, Roberto Lopez, and Orlando Perez took over a Republic DC-9 scheduled to fly 116 people from Miami to Orlando, Fla. They threatened to set the craft on fire unless it was flown to Cuba. The plane landed in Havana and the men were taken into custody.
Aug. 18: Herald H. Blum, claiming to have a bomb on an Eastern DC-9, demanded $3.4 million, the release of two prisoners, and flight to Cuba. The plane landed in Atlanta, the crew and passengers deplaned, and Blum was arrested.
Aug. 26: Mariano Avila Cables, Gilberto Cables Calero, and Miguel Yurubi Toledo skyjacked an Eastern L-1011. They threatened to blow up the Miami-bound aircraft unless it was flown to Cuba. In Havana, the men escaped.
Aug. 29: Approximately 168 Cubans stormed onto a Braniff DC-8 in Lima, Peru, flashing knives. They took eighteen hostages. Threatening to burn the plane, they demanded to be flown to Miami, but later surrendered. Two were allegedly shot and one injured.
Sept. 8: Jose Espinosa Garcia skyjacked an Eastern B-727 scheduled to fly to Tampa, Fla. He threatened to start the eighty-three passenger aircraft on fire unless it was taken to Cuba. The plane landed in Havana and the man was arrested by Cuban authorities.
Sept. 12: Guillermo Lima Hernandez skyjacked an Eastern B-727 en route from Newark, N.J., to Miami. Armed with phony dynamite, he threatened to blow up the aircraft and its eighty-five passengers and crew unless he was flown to Cuba. He was overpowered and arrested.
Sept. 13: Miguel and Roberto Aguiar Rodriguez skyjacked a Delta B-727 en route from New Orleans to Atlanta with eighty-eight people aboard. They demanded to be flown to Cuba. They escaped.
Sept. 14: Carlos J. Figueroa skyjacked an Eastern B-727 en route with 106 people to Miami from Tampa. He threatened to detonate an alleged bomb in Tampa unless he was taken to Cuba. The pilot landed in Miami, the man was taken into custody, and no bomb exploded.
Sept. 17: Juan Adega Fresneda and Crecencio Perez Perez skyjacked a Delta B-727, en route with 104 passengers to Columbia, S.C., from Atlanta. They demanded to be flown to Cuba. In Havana the skyjackers were taken into custody and extradited to South Carolina.
Oct. 13: Four men armed with guns took control of a Turkish jet after it left Istanbul. They demanded to be flown to Jidda, Saud. Fifty-five passengers were freed before military personnel overpowered the skyjackers. A passenger allegedly died.
Oct. 25: Rafael A. Castanedo Reyes took over a 125-passenger Continental B-727 en route to Houston, Texas, from Miami. He threatened to ignite the plane if he were not taken to Cuba. Reyes was overpowered and given to the FBI.
Nov. 6: A Venezuelan Airlines plane was taken over shortly after it left Caracas by skyjackers claiming to have explosives and demanding to be taken to Cuba. The plane landed in Havana where the skyjackers were taken into custody.
Nov. 12: Orlando Castro skyjacked a Uruguayan plane en route from Colonia, Urug., to Buenos Aires, Arg. He threatened to demolish the plane. His demands to be taken to several countries were refused so he requested asylum. He released thirty-two passengers, wounded one hostage, and surrendered. He was arrested.
Nov. 25: A Dominican Republic Air Taxi Service plane was taken over by a man with a bottle of gasoline who demanded to be taken to Cuba. The plane landed at Port-Au-Prince, Haiti. The man was taken into custody.
Dec. 4: A Polish aircraft was skyjacked by a man who demanded to be flown to West Berlin. The plane landed at Tempelhof where the

skyjacker requested asylum and was taken into custody.
Dec. 5: A Venezuelan Aeropostal plane traveling to Caracas was taken over by four men who demanded to be flown to Higuerote, Venez. They took about $1.75 million in Bolivars from the plane's cargo. They money was located and thirty-five people were arrested.
Dec. 15: Seven armed men, claiming membership to the 19th of April Movement, took control of an AVIANCA Colombian jet. Passengers were freed during four stopovers. When the plane landed in Havana, the skyjackers surrendered.
Dec. 29: Four skyjackers forced a helicopter pilot to fly to a farm south of San Jose, Cos. Three skyjackers disembarked with a Philippines corporation payroll of about $404,000. The fourth released the pilot and helicopter nearby. The New People's Army reportedly got the money.

1981

February: Four young gunmen attempted to skyjack a Moscow plane to the West on an unspecified date. An assault group stormed the plane with tear gas grenades and automatic rifles. The skyjackers were shot.
Mar. 2: Salaamullah Tippu and others skyjacked a Pakistani International Airlines plane after takeoff from Karachi. One hostage of 148 died, and fifty-four were freed in Damascus when fifty-four political prisoners were released and $50,000 ransom was received.
Mar. 27: A Tansahsa Airlines B-737 en route from Honduras to New Orleans was skyjacked by five demanding the release of sixteen Salvadoran Leftists in Honduras. The plane was flown to Managua, Nic., where they surrendered.
Mar. 28: An Indonesian Airways jet flying within Sumatra was overpowered by Jihad Command skyjackers who demanded the release of eighty political prisoners in exchange for the fifty-seven hostages. Four terrorists died in a gun battle.
Apr. 10: Rafael Fredesvindo Pellerano Albantosa, a Cuban refugee, was killed in a fight when he attempted to skyjack an Eastern flight from New York to Miami.
May 2: Laurence James Downey, an Australian, skyjacked an Aer Lingus B-737 flying from Dublin. He demanded publication of *The Third Secret of Fatima*, a prophecy of global war. Antiterrorist police captured Downey.
May 24: A Turkish Airlines DC-9 with 112 people aboard flying to Ankara from Istanbul, was skyjacked by two Dev Sol members demanding the release of prisoners in Turkey and $500,000. The plane landed in Burgas, Bul. The siege ended. No demands were met.
July 10: Two men armed with Molotov cocktails forced an Eastern L-1011 en route from Chicago to Miami to fly to Cuba.
July 22: Bernhard Pientka commandeered a Polish airplane to West Berlin because he was disgusted with conditions in Poland. He was imprisoned.
Sept. 18: Twelve students skyjacked a LOT Polish Airlines plane en route from Katowice to Warsaw. Armed with broken glass and razor blades, they demanded to go to West Berlin where they sought political asylum.
Sept. 22: Four Polish skyjackers attempted to take control of a Polish plane by wielding "sharp instruments." They demanded the plane fly to West Berlin. Instead, the pilot returned to Warsaw, where the police took the plane by force, injuring one skyjacker.
Sept. 26: A Yugoslav B-727 en route from Dubrovnik to Belgrade was skyjacked by three Croatians. Denied landing rights in Israel, the plane landed in Larnaca, Cyprus. All passengers and crew escaped after feigning fire. The skyjackers surrendered.
Sept. 29: An India B-737 was skyjacked by five Sikhs after takeoff from New Delhi and forced to land in Lahore, Pak. The skyjackers demanded $500,000 and the release of Sant Jarnail Singh Bhindranwale and others. The terrorists were overpowered and arrested.
Sept. 29: Marek K., alias, tried to skyjack a LOT AN-24 about to depart Warsaw for Szczecin. He demanded to go to West Berlin, but was overpowered by the passengers and police.
Oct. 29: Five people took control of a flight from Puerto Quepos, Nic., en route to San Jose, Cos. They demanded the release of seven prisoners in Costa Rica. Hostages were exchanged for the prisoners. The group was arrested.
Dec. 8: Three Venezuelan planes were skyjacked by eleven members of Venezuela's Red Flag who forced the planes to first land in Barranquilla, Col., and finally to be flown to Cuba where the skyjackers surrendered.

1982

Jan. 1: Amado Jose Flores and Daniel de Jesus Rivera Gonzalez, Nicaraguan Air Force members, attempted to skyjack the Nicaraguan junta's jet to Miami and were killed trying to escape from custody.
Jan. 7: Jairo Hernandez Martinez took over an Aerotal airliner after it left Barranquilla, Col. He demanded it fly to Aruba and that authorities release his brother, who skyjacked a plane in May 1978. Passengers subdued the skyjacker.
Jan. 27: Nine Leftist Colombian skyjackers held seventy-four hostages aboard an Aerotal Boeing 727 on route from Bogota to Pereira. They released the prisoners the next day and were flown to San Andres Island.
Feb. 2: A male "homesick Cuban" took control of an Air Florida Boeing 737 from Miami to Havana in the first successful U.S. skyjacking in six months.
Feb. 12: Czeslaw K., alias, a Polish pilot, flew to Tempelhof Airport in West Berlin, purposely diverting a Warsaw to Wroclaw flight to defect with seven others. Fourteen passengers returned to Poland.
Feb. 24: Hamza led several Shiite Muslims who took over a Kuwaiti Boeing 707 in Beirut to publicize the claim Libya seized Shiite Muslim leader, Imam Moussa Sadr. The skyjackers were flown to Iran, surrendering when they learned the plane was not Libyan.
Feb. 26: Four men commandeered a Tanzanian passenger plane and forced it to Kenya, Saudi Arabia, Greece, and England and demanded the resignation of President Julius Nyerere. The skyjackers turned themselves in. Their demands were not met.
Mar. 1: A man attempted to hijack a plane to Cuba, but was overwhelmed by a passenger and crew members on the Chicago to Miami flight.
Apr. 5: Rogelio Vincente Otano, Vincente Rego Otano, and Fidel Rego Otano skyjacked a Delta plane leaving Chicago for Cuba. They were arrested.
Apr. 28: A Honduran Air Service plane was skyjacked by four Leftists in Tegucigalpa who demanded the release of political prisoners and ransom. Eventually, all hostages were released and the skyjackers were flown to Cuba.
May 10: Francisco Arce Lopez and Camilo Martin Walter Hurtado took over an Aeronica plane going from Bluefields, Cos., to Corn Island. The plane was diverted to Puerto Limon, where the skyjackers sought protection.
May 21: Juan Cleano skyjacked a Philippine Airlines BAC-111 before it landed at Cebu and demanded 60,000 pesos ($7,270) and political reforms. He was overpowered.
May 27: Hamid Alaoui skyjacked a Royal Air Morocco B-727 after it left Athens and demanded a flight to Tunis and improvements in the morality of observance of Islam in Morocco. He surrendered to Tunisian officials.
July 22: Two men skyjacked an Air Florida plane flying from Miami to Key West and ordered it to Havana. They were arrested.
July 25: Five workers from Xian took control of a Chinese passenger plane heading from Xian to Shanghai and demanded to go to Hong Kong. Passengers and crew fought the skyjackers, an explosion ensued and caused the plane to make an emergency landing. The terrorists were arrested.
July 30: Chinese skyjackers seized control of a Viscount heading from Shanghai to Beijing. The terrorists were overcome in a fight and the plane landed in Nanking.
Aug. 4: Gurbax Singh demanded an Indian Airlines B-737 in flight be taken to Lahore, Pak. The plane wasn't allowed to land there and instead went to Amritsar, India, where Singh demanded to talk to a Sikh leader. Police overpowered him.
Aug. 20: M. Sigh skyjacked an Indian Airlines B-737 headed from Bombay to New Delhi. He diverted it to Amritsar and demanded that India transfer political power in Punjab to the Sikh-controlled Akali Dal party and that jailed Sikhs be released. He was killed by security guards after the plane landed.
Aug. 25: S. Franciszek and P. Ryszard took control of a Polish plane and ordered it to be flown to Munich, where the men were taken into custody.
Sept. 25: Igor Shkuro took control of an Alitalia B-727 shortly after it took off from Algiers demanding to go to Tripoli, Libya, and Valette, Malta. The plane was denied landing permission at both airports and landed in Catania, Sicily, where the passengers and some of the crew were released. The remaining crew attacked Shkuro and had him arrested.
Oct. 3: A woman threatened to blow up a Lufthansa plane heading from Hamburg to Munich and demanded it return to Hamburg. She was ignored by the pilot. The plane landed in Munich as scheduled and no explosives were found.
Oct.3: Two Iranian officers and the wife and son of one skyjacked an Iranian military plane, freed all passengers but one, and flew around the Gulf in search of a country that would let them land. Iranian jets forced the plane back to Iran.
Oct. 14: Zbigniew Purgall skyjacked a Bulgarian TU-134 on a Warsaw to Burgas flight. He injured a flight attendant and forced the plane to Vienna where he sought political asylum.
Nov. 7: Three Soviets skyjacked a plane flying from Novorossiisk to Odessa. They stabbed the pilot, wounded two passengers, and forced to plane to land in Sinop, Turk. They were arrested.
Nov. 22: Piotr Windgrodzki ordered a Warsaw-bound Polish plane to fly to West Berlin. At Tempelhof, he was wounded by security guards, and turned over to West Germany.
Nov. 27: An armed skyjacker was apprehended in the Warsaw Airport after he attempted to overtake a Hungarian plane en route from Moscow to Budapest.
Dec. 7: Muslims skyjacked a Libyan plane, demanding an inquiry of Imam Moussa Sadr's disappearance. They forced the plane to land in Beirut three times, and in Damascus and Teheran before surrendering.

1983

Feb. 20: A Libyan Arab Airways B-727 en route from Sebha, Libya to Tripoli was skyjacked by two Libyan army officers who held the 158 passengers hostage at the airport in Valletta, Malta for three days. They surrendered on the promise of political asylum.
Apr. 26: Gene B. Katz attempted to skyjack a commuter plane in Albany, N.Y. He planned to commandeer the Mall Airways craft to Portland, Maine.

May 1: A Capitol Air DC-8 carrying 214 people to Chicago from San Juan, P.R., was skyjacked to Cuba by a man claiming to carry a gasoline bomb. He was arrested.
May 5: Tjou Chang-Jen skyjacked a jet en route from Manchuria to Shanghai, China. He demanded to be flown to Taiwan. Instead, the jet flew to S. Korea where he was imprisoned.
1984
July 31: An Air France B-737 was skyjacked to Tehran en route from Frankfurt to Paris by Islamic Jihad terrorists demanding the release of terrorists jailed in France. Two people were killed. The skyjackers' demands were not met.
Dec. 3: Five Arabs skyjacked a Kuwaiti jet flying from Dubai to Karachi and ordered it flown to Teheran, demanding freedom for Shi'ites held in Kuwait for bombing the U.S. embassy. They killed two U.S. officials. Iranian troops captured them.
1985
June 14: Mohamed Ali Hamadi led several Lebanese Shi'ites who diverted to Beirut a TWA plane carrying 153 passengers from Athens to Rome. They demanded the release of 700 Lebanese Shi'ites held in Israel. One hostage was killed. All but forty-two hostages were freed in Beirut. The others were freed after Israel released thirty-one Shi'ites. Hamadi was later imprisoned.
Nov. 23: Abu Nidal terrorists forced an EgyptAir B-737 en route from Athens to Cairo to land in Valletta, Malta. Egyptian forces stormed the plane, which caught fire, and fifty-nine, including all but one skyjacker, died.
1986
Sept. 5: Four men from Abu Nidal skyjacked a Karachi Pan Am B-747 carrying 389 passengers. The crew escaped, the plane was immobilized, and the terrorists killed twenty passengers before being arrested.
Dec. 25: An Iraqi plane was skyjacked while en route from Baghdad to Amman. It crashed and sixty-two were killed.
1987
July 24: Hussein Ali Hariri, Lebanese Shi'ite, skyjacked a plane to Geneva, where he demanded the release of a Lebanese terrorist held in West Germany. One French passenger was killed, the rest escaped when Swiss police stormed the plane.
Dec. 23: Zino Scioni, falsely claiming to carry a bomb, skyjacked to Rome a KLM B-737 en route to Milan from Amsterdam. Holding the ninety-seven people aboard hostage, he demanded $1 million. He was arrested four hours later.
1988
Apr. 5: Eight Arabs skyjacked a Kuwaiti B-747 going from Thailand to Kuwait, demanding the release of some Arab terrorists held in Kuwait. Two passengers were killed, others were freed in Iran, Cyprus, and Algeria. The skyjackers were allowed to exit Algeria.
Sept. 24: Raimundo Alves da Conceicao, took control of a Brazilian B-737 en route from Porto Velho to Rio de Janeiro. He shot the copilot and was shot and wounded trying to board a smaller plane he agreed to take.
1989
Jan. 31: Alvin Antonio Siu, a Nicaraguan Indian exiled in Colombia, skyjacked a Costa Rican Ace Airline B-727 carrying 122 people to Medellin, Col., by threatening to set a passenger on fire. An antiterrorist squad arrested the skyjacker in Costa Rica.
July 5: An Indian Airlines A-300 Airbus carrying 255 from Srinager, Kashmir to New Delhi, was skyjacked to Pakistan by suspected Sikh extremists threatening to blow up the plane. They demanded $25 million from India and the release of some political prisoners.

TERRORISM

Terrorism defies exact definition. It has been variously described as wanton acts of violence; irrational, senseless barbarism, and insidious vandalism. Terrorism differs from other crimes in that its main objective is to evoke panic, disorder, and intimidation within society. Terrorist tactics are calculated to destroy order, paralyze activity within a community, and inflict suffering and pain. Mexico's penal code describes terrorism as any act of violence "against persons, things or public services, that may produce alarm, fear, or terror in the population...to disturb the public peace or to try to undermine the authority of the state, or exert pressure on the authorities in order for them to take a decision." Most governments agree that terrorism includes any act of violence committed by their political opponents.

International terrorism is an issue necessarily and inextricably intertwined with international politics. Outside of obvious and universally accepted acts like airline hijacking and the kidnapping of diplomats, what qualifies as terrorism stirs debate and invites dissent. The violence in terrorist acts is usually aimed at civilian targets. Attacks are frequently committed in a manner that will garner extensive publicity, especially as they concern specific demands and threats on the lives of the hostages. Often, the victims are random targets. The incidents of violence can be isolated and single, or serial in a campaign that functions outside all laws and procedures for diplomacy and war. The violence is designed to attract international attention and is often carried out for effect.

From an historical perspective, terrorism was used by Medieval rulers hiring assassins to slay their opponents, and by the Inquisitors' mass burnings of citizens to inspire more "confessions" during the infamous four centuries of the Spanish Inquisition. During the Russian Revolution, as during any struggle for independence, assassinations and random murders were a major part of the great political upheaval. With modern technology, terrorists' capabilities have escalated. Air travel gives them increased mobility and dramatic possibilities for targets anywhere in the world. The media provides immediate exposure; modern society's dependence on technology makes it increasingly vulnerable to such attacks. New weaponry further increases the danger and odds for disaster.

1905
1905: A plot by two members of the militant Polish Socialist Party to kill the Police Chief of Warsaw failed. Both men lost their own lives.
1906
Aug. 15: On a day that became known as Bloody Wednesday, several terrorist attacks were directed at individual police officers in Warsaw, Pol.
1931
February: A Peruvian Airlines domestic flight was hijacked.
1934
Ulrike Marie Meinhof, of the Baader-Meinhof gang, was born.
1935
January: Wolfgang Huber, a German terrorist, was born.
July: Ursula Huber, a German terrorist, was born. She made bombs in Heidelberg.
1936
Eric Grusdat, altered stolen cars and took part in Berlin bank raids, was born.
Peter Homann, affiliate of the Baader-Meinhof gang, was born.
January: Horst Mahler, who established the Red Army Faction, was born.
1938
Karl-Heinz Ruhland, a German terrorist, was born.
1939
April: Hans-Jürgen Bäcker, tried and acquitted of taking part in the 1970 freeing of Andreas Bernd Baader, was born.
October: Marianne Herzog, who worked with Baader-Meinhof gang in Frankfurt and Berlin, was born.
1940
Gudrun Ensslin, RAF leader found guilty of arson and tried for murder, forming criminal association, and bank robbery, was born.
March: Jörg Lang, who headed the Red Army Faction, was born.
April: Angela Luther, an affiliate of the Red Army Faction and Movement Second June, was born.
1941
August: Holger Klaus Meins, Red Army Faction terrorist, was born.
1942
Monika Klara Berberich, member of Horst Mahler's "Socialist Lawyers' Collective," who was convicted of bank robbery, was born.
January: Rolf Pohle, who purchased guns for terrorists, was born.
August: Alfred Mahrländer, German terrorist, was born.
1943
February: Katharina Hammerschmidt, supporter of the Baader-Meinhof, was born.
March: Eberhard Becker, Heidelberg partnership member, was born.
May: Andreas Bernd Baader, arsonist who was tried for murder, organizing a criminal association, and bank robbery with Ulrike Meinhof, Ensslin, and Raspe, was born.
June: Fritz Teufel, a German terrorist who was later accused of kidnapping, was born.
1944
Karl Heinz Roth, Red Army Faction affiliate, was born.
January: Inge Viett, German terrorist affiliate, was born.
March: Lutz Manfred Taufer, a German terrorist, was born.
June: Ingrid Siepmann, a Movement Second June terrorist, was born.
July: Jan-Carl Raspe, Red Army Faction terrorist, was born.
November: Ingrid Schubert, a German terrorist, was born.
1945
March: Siegfried Haag, lawyer who went underground and was arrested in 1976 for smuggling arms, was born.
October: Hanna-Elise Krabbe, a German terrorist, was born.
1946
Ulrich Wessel, a German terrorist, was born.
February: Bernhard Braun, mixed up in SPK and Movement Second June, was born.
October: Manfred Grashof, German army deserter and member of Berlin Kommune I, was born.
October: Bernd Maria Rössner, a German terrorist, was born.
1947
April: Werner Sauber, allegedly sold guns to terrorist, was born.
May: Irmgard Möller, reputedly a German terrorist, was born.
May: Astrid Proll, allegedly a German terrorist, was born.
July 25: A Rumanian airliner was hijacked by three men who diverted the plane to the Canakkale Province of Turkey. One crewman was killed during the incident.
August: Michael Baumann, early Movement Second June member, was born.
September: Klaus Jünschke, a German terrorist, was born.
September: Carmen Roll, a German terrorist, was born.
October: Brigitte Asdonk, who played a role in the Berlin bank raids with Horst Mahler, was born.
December: Hans-Joachim Klein, who later helped attack the Vienna offices of OPEC, was born.
December: Ulrich Scholtze, Red Army Faction terrorist, was born.
1948
February: Heinrich Jansen, a Red Army Faction member, was born.
March: Margrit Schiller, a German terrorist, was born.
Apr. 6: In a plot that included the pilot and two other crew members, a Czechoslovakian Airlines flight was hijacked to The U.S. zone of Germany.
May 4: A Czechoslovakian Airlines flight was hijacked by two men and diverted to the U.S. zone of Germany.
June: Gerhard Müller, a German terrorist, was born.
June: Wolfgang Grundmann, arrested for connection with Berlin subversive paper *Agit 883*, was born.
June 4: A Yugoslavian Airlines flight was hijacked by two men after taking off from Belgrade and diverted to Bari, Italy.
June 17: A Soviet-Rumanian Airways flight was hijacked to Salzburg, Austria.
June 30: A Bulgarian Airlines pilot was killed and two crew members wounded during a hijacking by several men who diverted the flight to Istanbul, Turk.
July: Ingeborg Barz, Wolfgang Grundmann's girlfriend and suspected murder victim, was born.
July 16: A Cathay Pacific airliner crashed at sea after the pilot and co-pilot were shot to death by four
hijackers after taking off from Macao.
August: Ralf Reinders, who headed the Movement Second June, was born.
Sept. 12: After taking off from Athens, a Salonika-bound Greek Airline flight was diverted by eight hijackers to Tetovo, Yug.
1949
Jan. 4: A Hungarian Airlines domestic flight was diverted to the U.S. zone of Germany, by a group of twenty-three people, including the pilot.
Jan. 30: A China National Aviation Corporation flight was hijacked shortly after takeoff from Shanghai by six people who diverted the plane to Tainan, China. The passengers were held hostage for a month.
February: Wilfried Böse, RAF victim killed during raid on Entebbe 1976, was born.
February: Werner Hoppe, a German terrorist, was born. He was arrested July 15, 1971.
February: Thomas Weissbecker, a German terrorist, was born.
Apr. 29: Two people hijacked a Soviet-Rumanian Airliner to Salonika, Gr., shortly after taking off from Timisoara. One hijacker was granted political asylum.
Sept. 16: A LOT Polish Airlines flight was hijacked by five men after taking off from Gdansk and diverted to a military base near Stockholm.
Dec. 9: A Soviet-Rumanian Airlines flight en route to Bucharest was hijacked by four people who diverted the plane to Belgrade, Yug. A security guard was killed.
Dec. 16: Shortly after takeoff from lodz, a group of sixteen people hijacked a Polish Airlines flight to Roenna, Den.
1950
Kay-Werner Allnach, associate of Margrit Schiller, was born.
Christa Eckes, accused of partaking in the Hamburg bank raid in 1973, was born.
Mar. 24: Three Czechoslovakian Airlines domestic flights were hijacked to the U.S. zone of Germany.

August: Petra Schelm, who was shot to death by police when she broke through a roadblock with Werner Hoppe in 1971, was born.
Aug. 11: Two hijackers diverted a Czechoslovakian Airlines flight to the U.S. zone of Germany.

1951
Roland Otto, a German terrorist, was born.
Beate Sturm, a Red Army Faction terrorist, was born.
April: Irene Goergens, Meinhof protégée arrested in 1970, was born.
May: Gabriele Kröcher-Tiedemann, Movement Second June terrorist, was born.
August: Ulrich Schmücher, a Movement Second June terrorist, was born.
Oct. 17: The pilot and the copilot of a Yugoslav National Airlines plane hijacked their own flight to Zurich, Switz., where they sought political asylum.

1952
January: Siegfried Hausner, a Meinhof backer, was born.
June 26: Shortly after takeoff from Belgrade, three men seeking political asylum hijacked a Yugoslavian National Airlines flight to Foligno, Italy.
July: Verena Becker, Movement Second June member who was sentenced to six years in jail, was born.
April: Karl-Heinz Dellwo, implicated with SPK and invasion of German embassy in Stockholm in 1975, was born.
Dec. 30: The pilot and a crew member of a Philippine Airline plane were killed when a hijacker attempted to divert the domestic flight to China. The hijacker was arrested after the copilot landed the aircraft in Quemoy.

1953
Juliane Plambeck, Movement Second June terrorist, was born.
Gabriele Rollnick, who was later accused of kidnapping, was born.
Mar. 23: Shortly after taking off from Prague, a pilot hijacked his own Czechoslovakian Airlines flight to Frankfurt, Ger. He was seeking political asylum.

1954
May: Ilse Stachowiak, Red Army Faction terrorist, was born.

1956
July 13: Seven people seeking political asylum hijacked a Hungarian Airlines flight to Ingolstadt, Ger.

1958
Feb. 16: A South Korean Airlines domestic flight was hijacked by a group and diverted to Pyongyang, N. Kor. Among the hijackers was a woman with a baby.
Apr. 9: A Cubana Airlines flight between Havana and Santa Clara, Cuba, was hijacked to Merida, Mex.
Apr. 10: The pilot and copilot were wounded, and a radioman was killed, when a hijacker attempted to divert a South Korean Airlines flight to North Korea. The hijacker was arrested when the plane landed at Pyongtaek, S. Kor.
Apr. 13: The three man crew of a Cubana Airlines domestic flight hijacked their own aircraft to Miami.
June 2: Three people hijacked a Czechoslovakian Airlines charter flight and diverted the plane to Vienna, Aust.
Oct. 22: A Cubana Airlines plane disappeared after being hijacked by three Cuban rebels during a flight from Cayo Mambi to Moa Bay.
Nov. 1: Seventeen of twenty people aboard were killed when a Cubana Airlines flight which was being hijacked by five men, crashed shortly after taking off from Miami.
Nov. 6: A Cubana Airlines flight was detained by rebels on an airstrip in Manzanillo, Cuba.

1959
Apr. 10: The pilot of a Haitian Airliner flight was killed by six hijackers who then ordered the copilot to fly to Cuba.
Apr. 16: Three Cuban defectors hijacked an Aerovias Airline flight to Miami shortly after it took off from Havana.
Apr. 25: Two men and two women, including a deposed Cuban general, hijacked a Cuban Airliner to Key West, Fla., from Varadero Beach.
July 8: A Yugoslavian Airlines flight en route to Belgrade was hijacked by one man, who diverted the plane to Bari, Italy.
Oct. 2: Three people hijacked a Cubana Airlines flight to Miami shortly after take-off from Havana.
Dec. 2: Eight Brazilian rebels hijacked a Panair Do Brazil Airlines flight to Buenos Aires, Arg.

1960
Apr. 21: The pilot and two crew members of a Cubana Airlines domestic flight hijacked their own plane to Miami.
July 5: The copilots of a Cubana Airlines flight from Madrid, Spain, to Havana, Cuba, hijacked their own plane to Miami.
July 17: The pilot of a Cubana Airlines flight from Havana to Miami hijacked his own flight to Jamaica.
July 18: A noncommercial Cuban aircraft was hijacked to Fort Lauderdale, Fla.
July 19: The hijacking of a Trans-Australia Airlines flight was averted when the copilot overpowered a man attempting to divert the flight to Singapore.
July 28: Shortly after taking off in the Oriente province, three men, including the pilot, hijacked a Cubana Airlines flight to Miami.
off in the Oriente Province.
Aug. 21: The crew members of a domestic Soviet flight were wounded, but they were able to overpowere a man and a woman who were attempting to hijack the plane.
Oct. 29: Shortly after taking off from Miami, nine men, including the copilot, hijacked a Cubana Airlines flight to Key West, Fla. A security guard was killed, and the pilot, copilot and a passenger were wounded.
Dec. 8: One person was killed and four others wounded in a crash landing, after four men attempted to hijack a Cubana Airlines domestic flight.

1961
Jan. 1: Two men commandeered a Cubana Airlines plane at the terminal in Havana, and ordered the pilot to fly a group of Batista supporters to New York.
May 1: A National Airlines flight from Marathon to Key West, Fla., was hijacked to Miami.
July 3: A security guard was wounded when fourteen people hijacked a Cubana Airlines domestic flight to Miami.
July 24: After taking off from Tampa, Fla., an Eastern Airlines flight en route to Miami was hijacked by one man.
July 31: A pilot and ticket agent were wounded in the failed hijacking attempt of a San Francisco-bound flight from Chico, Calif.
Aug. 3: Two men were arrested in their failed attempt to hijack a Continental Airlines flight from Los Angeles to Houston.
Aug. 9: A man was arrested after a failed attempt to hijack a Pan American Airlines flight from Mexico City to Guatemala.
Aug. 9: The pilot and two others were killed, as five men hijacked an Aerovias Cuban Airline domestic flight. The copilot was forced to make a crash landing.
Nov. 10: A Transportes Aereos Portuguese airline flight from Casablanca to Lisbon, Port., was hijacked by six men and diverted to Tangier, Mor.
Nov. 27: Five men hijacked a domestic Avensa Venezuelan Airlines flight to Curacao. They were later extradited and imprisoned.

1962
Mar. 17: While being transported on a domestic flight in France, a prisoner was wounded when he attempted to hijack the plane.
Apr. 13: Two men failed in their attempt to hijack a charter flight in Miami.
Apr. 16: A Portuguese man attempted to hijack an Amsterdan to Lisbon Royal Dutch Airlines flight to East Berlin. He was arrested, however, when the plane returned to Holland.

1963
Nov. 28: Six men hijacked an Avensa Venezuelan Airlines domestic flight to Trinidad.

1964
Members of the Armee de Liberation Quebecois (ALQ) staged raids at an industrial complex in Shawinigan Falls and at various military bases around Montreal.
Autumn: The pilot and copilot of a Soviet domestic flight were wounded by two unsuccessful hijackers. The plane landed in Kishinev, U.S.S.R.
Feb. 18: Two men hijacked a private charter flight between Miami and Key West, Fla.
Aug. 28: Two workers were killed when ALQ members invaded an armament factory in Montreal. Five terrorists were arrested.

1965
In Trois Riviere, Quebec, members of the Front de Liberation National (FLN) burned the car of Progressive Conservative Party leader Leon Balcer.
Spring: A flight engineer was shot to death during the attempted hijacking of a Soviet aircraft in the Balkin region. After the shooting, the hijacker was disarmed.
Jan. 18: The Reverend Martin Luther King was assaulted as he attempted to be served along with eleven other blacks at a white restaurant in Selma, Ala.
Feb. 16: Four people were arrested for plotting to blow up the Statue of Liberty, the Liberty Bell, and the Washington Monument.
Feb. 21: Black activist Malcolm X was shot and killed as he addressed a rally in New York City.
Mar. 5: A school for black children in Indianola, Miss., was destroyed by fire.
Mar. 21: A Ku Klux Klan (KKK) firebomb destroyed a desegregated restaurant in Vicksburg, Miss.
Mar. 21: Four KKK timebombs were discovered planted throughout black neighborhoods in Birmingham, Ala.
Mar. 22: The KKK attempted to detonate two bombs in the black neighborhoods of Birmingham, Ala.
Mar. 25: A white civil rights marcher was shot to death following a rally in Selma, Ala.
Mar. 29: Two black churches were destroyed by firebombs in Meridian, Miss.
Apr. 1: The KKK was suspected to have bombed the home of a black accountant in Birmingham, Ala. Similar attempts on the homes of the mayor and a city council member were made.
June 2: A black deputy sheriff was shot to death while on patrol in Bogalusa, La.
July 8: Following a civil rights rally in Bogalusa, La., a white man was shot and seriously wounded by two black marchers.
July 15: A black man named Willis Brewster was shot by white gunmen driving through Anniston, Ala.
July 16: Civil rights demonstrators were attacked seven times by white gangs in Bogalusa, La.

July 21: The headquarters of the Council of Federated Organizations in Columbia, Miss., was firebombed and riddled with bullets.
July 27: Two homes in Ferriday, La., inhabited by blacks were damaged by firebombs.
July 28: In retaliation for an earlier stone-throwing incident, a white man was killed by black gunmen in a passing car in Americus, Ga.
Aug. 3: Two black churches were burned in Slidell, La.
Aug. 11: Thirty-four people were killed and more than 4,000 arrested during a three-day riot in the Watts section of Los Angeles.
Aug. 11: A hotel and a motel used by civil rights workers were bombed in Baton Rouge, La.
Aug. 11: Seven people were injured and eighteen blacks arrested during a riot on Chicago's West Side.
Aug. 13: Sixty people, including eighteen police officers, were injured and 104 people arrested during a three-day racial riot on Chicago's West Side.
Aug. 13: Two stores owned by whites were destroyed by fire during racial demonstrations in Springfield, Mass.
Aug. 16: Property was destroyed during racial unrest in Philadelphia.
Aug. 18: Four people were injured and fifty-nine arrested during a clash between Black Muslims and police in Los Angeles.
Aug. 22: An 87-year-old civil rights opponent was found with his body beaten and his tongue severed in Greensboro, Ala.
Aug. 22: A white minister was wounded by shotgun blasts in Jackson, Miss.
Aug. 26: Twenty-eight civil rights workers were attacked by members of the KKK in Plymouth, N.C.
Aug. 27: Local NAACP leader George Metcalf was injured in a car-bomb explosion in Natchez, Miss.
Aug. 31: A white man was shot and another stabbed as a crowd of whites intimidated black civil rights marchers in Plymouth, N.C.
Aug. 31: A juvenile hijacked a Hawaiian Airlines flight in Honolulu. He was arrested and sent to reform school.
Oct. 4: A black teenager was assaulted by KKK Grand Dragon Calvin Craig in Crawfordsville, Ga.
Oct. 10: The homes of two black families were burned in a predominantly white section of Lakewood, N.J.
Oct. 11: Two U.S. sailors were thwarted in their attempt to hijack an Aloha Airlines flight from Molokai to Honolulu. They were imprisoned and given dishonorable discharges from the Navy.
Oct. 12: A Southern Christian Leadership Conference photographer was attacked by a member of the KKK in Crawfordsville, Ga.
Oct. 17: Three KKK members were arrested and a cache of arms confiscated following the intimidation of a black man in Crawfordsville, Ga.
Oct. 22: Black civil rights marchers were attacked by white segregationists in Lincolnton, Ga.
Oct. 23: A car was overturned in Lincolnton, Ga., injuring seven civil rights workers.
Oct. 26: A mentally disturbed man attempted to hijack a National Airlines flight from Miami to Key West, Fla.
Nov. 7: A black man in Detroit was shot and killed by a group of white youths.
Nov. 8: A black church in Twiggs County, Ga., and two buildings in neighboring Jones County were destroyed by fires set by a white physician named Dr. Beverly Holland White.
Nov. 11: The home of a black family in a predominately white neighborhood was attacked on Chicago's South Side.
Nov. 17: A juvenile was unsuccessful in his attempt to hijack a National Airlines flight from New Orleans to Florida.
Nov. 21: The home of the president of the Freedom Movement in Ferriday, La., was damaged by a gasoline bomb.
Nov. 22: Four black activists' homes were bombed in Charlotte, N.C.
Nov. 24: Three guards were killed during a four-hour prison riot at the state penitentiary in Menard, Ill.
Nov. 29: Three people were injured when a bomb exploded near a black grocery store in Vicksburg, Miss.

1966

Jan. 2: Fire damaged a black church in Newton, Ga.
Feb. 2: Two civil rights workers were injured by shotgun blasts in Kosciusco, Miss.
Feb. 6: The home of a black man was bombed in Zachary, La.
Feb. 21: Five black people were wounded when a white gunman fired eight shots at 150 civil rights picketers in Birmingham, Ala.
Feb. 24: A school which had recently admitted black students was bombed in Elba, Ala.
Mar. 14: Two black youths were wounded by shotgun blasts in the Watts section of Los Angeles.
Mar. 15: Two people were killed, twenty injured, and forty-nine arrested during riots that caused extensive property damage in the Watts section of Los Angeles.
Mar. 17: Two *Newsweek* reporters were attacked and injured at a protest rally in the Watts section of Los Angeles.
Mar. 27: The flight engineer of a Cubana Airlines domestic flight attempted to hijack the plane to Miami. He killed the pilot and a guard when they refused and landed the plane in Cuba himself.
May 22: Policemen in Bakerfield, Calif., were pelted with rocks and bottles by 200 black protesters.
June 6: Black civil rights marcher James Meredith was wounded in Hernando, Miss.
June 12: Forty-nine people were arrested during a Puerto Rican riot in Chicago.
June 12: Police discovered the body of a black person hit by sixteen shotgun blasts in Natchez, Miss. Three Ku Klux Klan (KKK) members were arrested.
June 13: Seven protesters were shot and several police officers and reporters injured by bricks during a riot in a Puerto Rican neighborhood of Chicago.
June 20: Cars were pelted with rocks in Jersey City, N.J., during a riot between black and Puerto Rican groups.
June 21: Six hundred blacks rioted in Pompano Beach, Fla., after a white grocer slapped a 10-year-old black youth.
June 26: A grocery store was firebombed in Cleveland following racial disturbances.
June 28: Following a racial disturbance at a desegregated swimming pool, a ninety-minute exchange of gunfire occurred in Cordele, Ga.
July 3: A police car was attacked by black youths in Omaha, Neb.
July 7: Nine people, including the pilot, hijacked a domestic Cubana Airlines flight to Jamaica. The copilot was wounded during the incident.
July 12: More than 500 were arrested during four days of rioting in a predominately black area of Chicago.
July 15: In Brooklyn, warfare between black and Italian, and black and Puerto Rican, gangs, occurred for a week.
July 18: During racial violence in CLeveland, one person was killed and eleven injured, including six police officers.
July 18: During racial violence in Jacksonville, Fla., a Klansman was arrested as he attempted to serve a KKK warrant on a NAACP official.
July 19: One person was killed and two others wounded during a sniper attack in Cleveland.
July 19: Firebombing and vandalism occurred in the black neighborhood of Jacksonville, Fla.
July 22: In Cleveland, a black man was shot at a bus stop by whites in a passing car.
July 23: A black man was shot to death by a shotgun blast from a passing car in Cleveland.
July 28: Racial violence occurred in a black neighborhood in Baltimore.
July 30: Eight people were arrested during a bottle and rock throwing incident in racially divided area on Chicago's Southwest Side.
July 30: Thirty-seven people were injured and forty-one were arrested in a clash between Puerto Rican youths and police in Perth Amboy, N.J.
July 31: Extensive property damage occurred during a confrontation in Chicago between a black protest caravan and white hecklers.
Aug. 3: Looting and window smashing occurred in a black neighborhood of Minneapolis.
Aug. 6: Members of the Front du Libération du Québec (FLQ) terrorist organization committed several holdups and armed robberies in a three-week spree to obtain money and weapons for the attack of industrial enterprises.
Aug. 7: Black youths hurled stones and firebombs at white hecklers and police during two days of racial violence in Lansing, Mich.
Aug. 9: A police officer was stabbed as he attempted to arrest three blacks in Detroit; subsequent violence led to the arrests of seven black youths.
Aug. 9: A NAACP office in Milwaukee was bombed.
Aug. 10: A black person was shot and two firebombs exploded during racial violence in Detroit.
Aug. 12: Five blacks were injured during racial violence in Muskegon, Mich.
Aug. 14: Whites assaulted blacks marching through white neighborhoods in Chicago.
Aug. 26: NAACP officials were pelted with rocks as they picketed in Milwaukee, Wis.
Aug. 26: Fourten people were injured and eighty arrested when black gangs rioted during three days in Waukegan, Ill.
Aug. 28: Black youths threw stones and bottles during four nights of racial violence in Benton Harbor, Mich.
Sept. 1: Two days of racial violence followed the fatal shooting of a black man in Dayton, Ohio.
Sept. 4: Fifteen people were injured and thirty-four arrested during a civil rights march in Cicero, Ill.
Sept. 6: Racial violence exploded in Atlanta after a black man was shot and wounded by a police officer.
Sept. 7: A firebomb damaged a building in the black area of Atlanta, and police forced a crowd of 400 to disperse.
Sept. 10: The fatal shooting of a black man and the wounding of another by a white man precipitated an outburst of racial violence in Atlanta.
Sept. 11: Twenty people were injured and fifty-eight were arrested during racial violence in Atlanta.
Sept. 12: Black school children were attacked by mobs of whites in Grenada, Miss. Police were called in on Sept. 13 to keep order.
Sept. 17: The Reverend Melvin Dewitt Bullock, ex-president of the NAACP chapter in New Rochelle, N.Y., was beaten to death.
Sept. 27: A black youth was shot to death by a San Francisco police officer, an act which precipitated two days of rioting and looting. The National Guard was called in on Sept. 28.
Sept. 28: Twenty dissidents hijacked a domestic Argentinian Airlines

flight to the Falkland Islands. The hijackers were subsequently extradicted and sent to prison.
Sept. 28: Rioting occurred in St, Louis following the shooting of a black robbery suspect.
Oct. 2: Twenty people were arrested during three days of racial violence in Philadelphia after a black family attempted to move into a white neighborhood.
Oct. 5: A bomb exploded at a black church in Richmond, Va.
Oct. 18: Two days of racial violence occurred in Oakland, Calif.
Oct. 31: Nineteen members of the right-wing paramilitary Minuteman organization were arrested as they attempted to firebomb four offices in New York City.
Oct. 31: Four hundred black youths rioted in Ossining, N.Y.
Nov. 5: Student Nonviolent Coordinating Committee (SNCC) chairman Stokely Carmichael and two other blacks were arrested in Selma, Ala., and charged with inciting a riot.
Nov. 21: Eighteen inmates and three guards were injured during a prison riot at the Essex Coty Penitentiary in Caldwell, N.J.
Dec. 9: Following the acquittal of a white youth on a murder charge, blacks rioted and looted in Tuskegee, Ala.
1967
Jan. 2: Seventy-two people, including three CBS cameramen, were arrested as they prepared to invade Haiti.
Jan. 21: A black church was destroyed by fire in Collins, Miss.
Jan. 29: Yugoslavian embassies were bombed in Chicago, New York, Ottawa, San Francisco, Toronto, and Washington, D.C.
Feb. 6: Yugoslvian missions were bombed in Chicago, New York, San Francisco, and Washington, D.C.
Feb. 7: One man hijacked an Egyptian Airlines domestic flight to Jordan. The hijacker escaped to Sweden where he was imprisoned for other crimes.
Feb. 27: NAACP treasurer Wharlest Jackson was killed by a truck-bomb in Natchez, Miss.
Mar. 4: A black church, headquarters for the Southern Christian Leadership Conference, was damaged by fire in Grenada, Miss.
Mar. 12: A church used by civil rights organizers was destroyed by fire in Hayneville, Miss.
Mar. 13: A bomb exploded at a Head Start office in Liberty, Miss.
Mar. 13: A black church was destroyed by fire in Fort Deposit, Ala.
Apr. 3: Terrorists bombed the Cuban Mission to the United Nations in New York City.
Apr. 8: Three days of racial violence exploded in Nashville, Tenn.
Apr. 11: Demonstrations led by the Reverend A.D. Williams King sparked ten days of racial violence in Louisville, Ky. Hundreds were arrested.
Apr. 16: Four people were arrested during racial violence in Cleveland.
Apr. 23: Five men hijacked a Nigerian Airlines domestic flight to Enugu, E. Nig.
Apr. 25: The home of Court Judge Frank M. Johnson was bombed in Montgomery, Ala.
May 9: Three days of racial violence occurred in Jackson, Miss., leaving two dead.
May 16: A police officer was killed during a protest at Texas Southern University in Houston.
June 2: A Mothers for Adequate Welfare sit-in led to three days of racial violence in Boston.
June 5: Forty members of the Political Confederation of Free City States invaded a courthouse in Rio Arriba County, N.M., and freed eleven rebels.
June 11: Snipers fired on police in Prattville, Ala.
June 12: Following a speech by H. Rap Brown, blacks attacked whites in Dayton, Ohio.
June 15: A riot broke out at a prison workhouse in Cincinnati, Ohio.
June 17: A man was killed during four days of racial violence in Atlanta.
June 20: Four homes and a barbershop were bombed by alleged KKK members in McComb, Miss.
June 21: Sixteen members of the Revolutionary Action Movement (RAM) were arrested in New York for plotting to murder two black civil rights leaders.
June 21: Four RAM members were arrested in Philadelphia for plottong to cotaminate the city's water supply.
June 27: Black youths hurled stones and set fires in Buffalo, N.Y.
June 30: A French terrorist hijacked a private flight carrying former Congo Prime Minister Moise Tshombe to Spain. After landing in Algeria, Tshombe was held in captivity until his death on June 29, 1969.
July 3: Looting and vandalism lasted two days in a black neighborhood of Cincinnati.
July 12: Twenty-three people were killed during three days of rioting and looting in Newark, N.J.
July 15: A police officer was shot and beaten as a mob of black youths rioted for two days in Plainfield, N.J.
July 17: Racial violence erupted at a housing project in Cairo, Ill. During the two-day riot, vandals set fire to a warehouse and damaged stores.
July 19: Racial violence occurred in Durham, N.C.
July 19: Rioters threw firebombs and fought in the street during seven days of racial violence in Minneapolis, Minn.
July 21: Eight police officers were injured during mob violence in Englewood, N.J.
July 23: Thirty-eight people were killed during six days of racial riots in Detroit.
July 23: Three people were killed during three days of racial violence in Harlem.
July 23: Incidents of firebombing and looting occurred for three days in Rochester, N.Y.
July 24: Two people were killed during racial violence in Pontiac, Mich.
July 24: Three men were wounded during racial violence in Grand Rapids, Mich.
July 24: More than twenty fires were set during racial violence in Toledo, Ohio.
July 24: Police remained in Mount Vernon, N.Y., during five days of rioting.
July 25: Two days of racial violence occurred in Cambridge, Md.
July 26: Racial violence occurred in Philadelphia, Pa.
July 26: Incidents of looting and arson occurred in Cincinnati.
July 27: Thirty-five people were arrested during riots in Chicago.
July 28: Incidents of arson, looting and sniper attacks continued for two days in Wilmington, Del.
July 29: A store was bombed with five molotov cocktails on the West Side of Chicago.
July 30: Two people were killed and eighty-three injured during rioting in Milwaukee. Twenty-eight fires were set.
July 31: Nineteen people were arrested surrounding firebombing and rock-throwing incidents in Wichita, Kan.
July 31: Violence erupted between white gangs, black gangs, and police in South Providence, R.I.
Aug. 1: Incidents of arson, looting, and vandalism occurred in Washington, D.C.
Aug. 1: Sporadic sniper attacks broke out in Milwaukee.
Aug. 2: Several fires were set amid racial tension in South Providence, R.I.
Aug 4: Twenty people were wounded during four days of racial violence in Wichita, Kan.
Aug. 6: Five men hijacked an Aerocondor Columbian Airlines domestic flight to Cuba.
Aug. 15: Twenty black marchers were attacked by fifteen whites in Holden, La.
Aug. 16: Twenty-five black marchers were attacked by seventy-five whites in Satsuma, La.
Aug. 18: Black marchers were pelted with bottles and eggs in Denham Springs, La.
Aug. 19: Four days of racial violence in New Haven, Conn., followed the fatal shooting of a Puerto Rican by a white restaurant owner.
Aug. 25: American Nazi Party leader George Lincoln Rockwell was shot to death in Arlington, Va., by a former party captain.
Aug. 28: Racial violence occurred in Milwaukee in response to a protest march, led by Father Groppi, seeking equal housing opportunities.
Sept. 7: The office of the mayor of Milwaukee was vandalized by seventy-five members of the Youth Council, a black commando organization.
Sept. 9: Three men hijacked an Avianca Columbian Airlines domestic flight to Cuba.
Sept. 10: One person was killed in racial violence following a speech by H. Rap Brown in East St. Louis, Ill.
Sept. 13: A white mob, waiting to attack black marchers, clashed with police in Milwaukee.
Sept. 14: Following a Student Nonviolence Coordinating Committee (SNCC) rally, rioting and sniping occurred in Chicago.
Sept. 18: Demonstrations led to mass vandalism in Hartford, Conn. Twenty-five were arrested.
Sept. 19: Looting and vandalism followed a demonstration protesting the death of a civil rights worker in Dayton, Ohio.
Oct. 16: Bombs exploded near the Cuban, Finnish and Yugoslav missions to the U.N. in New York City.
Oct. 17: Four hundred police and highway patrol officers broke up an anti-war demonstration with clubs and chemical sprays in Oakland, Calif.
Oct. 18: Seventy people were injured during riots at an anti-war protest in Madison, Wis.
Oct. 19: One hundred anti-war protesters attempted to break into a Chicago induction center.
Oct. 19: Fights broke out between student demonstrators and police at a Naval recruiting station in Brooklyn.
Oct. 20: Seven KKK members were convicted in Meridian, Miss., for the 1964 murders of three civil rights workers.
Oct. 21: A massive three-day anti-war demonstration was held in Washington, D.C.
Oct. 28: One police officer was killed, another wounded, and black activist Huey Newton also wounded, in a gun battle in Oakland, Calif.
Nov. 2: Black gangs roamed the streets, rioting and looting, in Winston-Salem, N.C.
Nov. 13: Students pelted police with rocks during a sit-in at Wilburforce University in Ohio.
Nov. 20: A charter flight out of Hollywood, Fla., was hijacked to Cuba.
1968
Jan. 9: In Havana, a parcel bomb sent by the anti-Castro El Poder Cubano group exploded in a post office.

Jan 16: In Guatemala, Colonel John D. Webber, commander of a U.S. military group there, and Lieutenant Commander Ernest A. Munro, head of the Navy section in Guatemala, were shot to death. The Fuerzas Armadas Rebeldes (FAR) claimed responsibility.
Jan. 25: Parcel bombs sent from Cuba were placed by El Poder Cubano and two exploded in Miami. One person was injured.
Feb. 8: A bomb thought to have been planted by anti-Castro terrorists exploded at the British Consulate in Miami.
Feb. 8: Thirty-seven South Carolina State College students were wounded by state troopers during an anti-segregation protest march.
Feb. 9: A U.S. Marine unsuccessfully attempted to hijack a Saigon to Hong Kong Pan American military charter. He was subsequently courtmartialed and sentenced.
Feb. 17: A charter flight between Marathon, Fla., and Miami was hijacked to Cuba.
Feb. 18: In the Yugoslavian ambassador's residence in Paris, a bomb blast in the basement killed one person and injured fourteen.
Feb. 21: A mentally disturbed man hijacked a place from Tampa, Fla., to Cuba.
Feb. 23: Police and striking sanitation workers clashed in Memphis, Tenn.
Mar. 5: A Colombian airlines plane was hijacked by three Ejercito de Liberacion National (ELN) terrorists who demanded it be flown to Cuba.
Mar. 12: Three men hijacked a plane from Tampa, Fla., to Cuba.
Mar. 19: Students seized the adminisration building at Howard University in Washington, D.C.
Mar. 21: In Venezuela an airplane was hijacked and taken to Cuba.
Mar. 22: Three hundred students staged a three-day protest in Cheyney, Pa.
Mar. 28: A boy was shot and sixty people injured during a protest march by Dr. Martin Luther King in Memphis, Tenn.
Mar. 29: Students seized the administration building at Bowie State College in Maryland.
Apr. 4: Dr. Martin Luther King was shot to death in Memphis, Tenn.
Apr. 4: Preceding three days of rioting and looting, a march led by Stokely Carmichael was held in Washington, D.C.
Apr. 4: A Cornell University professor was held hostage for six hours, protesting another professor's allegedly making racist remarks.
Apr. 4: One person was killed and more than thirty were injured in three days of rioting in Memphis, Tenn.
Apr. 5: Eleven blacks were killed in three days of race riots in Chicago.
Apr. 6: Five people were killed in four days of racial violence in Baltimore.
Apr. 6: Three police officers and three Black Panther members, including Eldridge Cleaver, were wounded in a gun battle in West Oakland, Cal.
Apr. 6: Ninety people were injured during race riots in Pittsburgh, Pa.
Apr. 7: Students at the Tuskegee Institute held college trustees hostage for twelve hours.
Apr. 8: A couple was attacked by black youths in Mount Auburn, Ohio.
Apr. 8: Following a memorial service for Dr. Martin Luther King, two people were killed in riots in Cincinnati.
Apr. 9: Incidents of arson and looting occurred in Newark, N.J.
Apr. 9: A student was killed by a police officer during demonstrations in Trenton, N.J.
Apr. 10: Five blacks were shot to death in two days of race riots in St. Louis.
Apr. 18: El Poder Cubano, an anti-Castro group, bombed the Mexican mission to the U.S..
Apr. 22: El Poder Cubano bombed the Spanish National Tourist Office in New York City.
Apr. 23: Students at Columbia University occupied several campus buildings for a week. Police were called in on Apr. 29.
Apr. 26: Students at Ohio State University seized the administration building and held two administrators and four employees hostage for several hours.
May 3: The finance building at Northwestern University was seized by black students in Evanston, Ill., and held until May 4.
May 5: Students occupied the administration building at Cheyney State College in Pennsylvania for two days.
May 9: Sixteen students barricaded themselves in the president's office at Roosevelt University in Chicago.
May 17: For destroying draft board files, nine people, including the Reverend Philip Berrigan, were arrested in Catonsville, Md.
May 18: Three hundred blacks demonstrated in Salisbury, Md. Police countered with tear gas and dogs.
May 26: El Poder Cubano planted a bomb to damage the Mexican consul general's residence in Miami, Fla.
June 5: Senator Robert F. Kennedy was shot to death by Sirhan Bishara Sirhan in Los Angeles.
June 19: A Viasa Airlines flight out of Santo Domingo, Dom., was hijacked to Cuba.
June 21: El Poder Cubano bombed the Spanish National Tourist Office in New York City.
June 22: In Spokane, Wash., seven members of the Minutemen paramilitary organization were convicted for conspiracy to commit bank robberies.
June 28: Demonstrations sponsored by the Young Socialist Alliance lasted three days at the University of California in Berkeley.
June 29: A Miami to Key West Southeast Airlines flight was hijacked to Cuba.
July 1: A man named Velasquez Fonseca hijacked a plane from Chicago to Cuba.
July 4: In New York City, El Poder Cubano bombed the Canadian tourist office and consulate, as well as the Australian National Tourist office.
July 4: A prisoner being transported tried to hijack a flight between Kansas City and Las Vegas.
July 7: In New York City, the Japanese National Tourist Office was bombed by El Poder Cubano.
July 9: In New York the Yugoslavian mission to the United Nations was bombed by El Poder Cubano.
July 9: The Yugoslavian and Cuban missions to the United Nations were bombed by El Poder Cubano.
July 12: A man named Leonard Bendicks hijacked a plane from Key West, Fla., to Cuba.
July 12: A man named Oran Richards was unsuccessful in his attempt to hijack a plane from Baltimore to Cuba.
July 14: The Mexican National Tourist Office in Chicago was bombed by El Poder Cubano.
July 15: In New York a bomb placed by El Poder Cubano was removed from the French National Tourist Office by police.
July 16: Police found and disarmed a bomb placed by El Poder Cubano in the Newark, N.J., Mexican Consulate.
July 17: A flight out of Los Angeles was successfully hijacked to Cuba.
July 17: More than 100 people were arrested in two days of rioting in Akron, Ohio.
July 19: In Los Angeles an Air France ticket office was damaged by an El Poder Cubano bomb.
July 19: El Poder Cubano members bombed the Los Angeles Mexican National Tourist Office.
July 19: The Japan Air Lines office in Los Angeles was bombed by El Poder Cubano.
July 22: An El Al Israel Airlines flight on its way from Rome to Tel Aviv was hijacked and taken to Algeria with forty-eight people on board.
July 23: Seven people were killed during a gunfight between police and Black Nationalists in Cleveland. Three more died in subsequent rioting and looting.
July 27: A black motorcycle gang, Sin City Disciples, clashed with police and incited three days of rioting and looting in Gary, Ind.
July 30: The British Consulate in Los Angeles was bombed by anti-Castro Cuban terrorists.
July 30: Sporadic rock throwing and gunfire violence occurred in Peoria, Ill.
Aug. 2: Two police officers were wounded by shotgun blasts allegedly fired by Black Panther members in Brooklyn.
Aug. 3: El Poder Cubano bombed the Bank of Tokyo Trust Company in New York.
Aug. 4: A charter flight in Naples, Fla., was hijacked to Cuba by a man who was carrying his 3-year-old daughter.
Aug. 5: Three Black Panther members were killed and two police officers wounded during a gun fight in the Watts area of Los Angeles.
Aug. 6: Six police officers were injured during racial disturbances in two Chicago suburbs.
Aug. 6: Three people were killed and two police officers injured during a in the second gunfight in two days, between police and Black Panther members in the Watts section of Los Angeles.
Aug. 8: An underwater bomb planted by El Poder Cubano exploded in Miami, damaging a British vessel.
Aug. 8: Three blacks were killed by police amid public violence in Miami.
Aug. 8: Anti-Castro Cubans bombed the British consulate in Los Angeles.
Aug. 11: Three people were killed and another forty-four injured during a riot which occurred at a summer festival in the Watts section of Los Angeles.
Aug. 11: Police in New York were shot at by alleged Black Panther snipers.
Aug. 17: In Miami, a Mexican airline office was damaged by an El Poder Cubano bomb.
Aug. 22: A Bahamian charter flight was hijacked to Cuba.
Aug. 24: The administration building at Boston University was occupied by 300 black students.
Aug. 24: Six alleged Minutemen fought a gun battle with state troopers in Voluntown, Conn.
Aug. 26: A week of violence began in Chicago, as thousands of people seeking to stage a protest at the Democratic National Convention clashed with police at several sites around the city.
Aug. 28: As he tried to avoid being kinapped, John Gordon Mein, the U.S. Ambassador to Guatemala, was killed by submachine gun fire in downtown Guatemala by FAR members.
Aug. 30: Fifty-two people were injured when a riot erupted at a dance in St. Paul, Minn.
Aug. 30: A four-day demonstration against U.S. involvement in Vietnam and Chicago Police brutality was held in Berkeley, Calif.
Sept. 1: Racial violence followed the fatal shooting of a black man by a white policeman in Newport News, Va.
Sept. 4: Nine Black Panther members were attacked by a white mob

as they attended a criminal court hearing in Brooklyn, N.Y.
Sept. 9: The student union at the University of Illinois in Urbana was occupied by black students for two days.
Sept. 11: A U.S. citizen named Charles Beasley failed in his attempt to hijack a domestic Air Canada flight.
Sept. 12: Alleged Black Panther snipers wounded two police officers in Brooklyn, N.Y.
Sept. 16: Members of El Poder Cubano fired on a Polish ship in Miami.
Sept. 20: A flight out of San Juan, P.R., was hijacked by a man named Suarez Garcia and diverted to Cuba.
Sept. 22: An Avianca Columbian Airlines domestic flight was hijacked to Cuba by a man named Ramon Garcia.
Sept. 22: An Avianca Columbian Airlines domestic flight was hijacked to Cuba by a man named Carlos London.
Sept. 24: A Milwaukee draft board was seized and records destroyed by Catholic protesters.
Sept. 25: Snipers shot at police and stores were looted during a race riot in the Roxbury section of Boston.
Oct. 5: Incarcerated Black Panther members led a prison revolt at the Queens House of Detention in Kew Gardens, N.Y.
Oct. 6: An Argentine woman with two children successfully hijacked a domestic Aeromaya Mexican Airlines flight to Cuba.
Oct. 8: A race riot occurred in Washington, D.C., after a black man was fatally wounded by a white police officer.
Oct. 12: Vanguarda Popular Revolucionaria (VPR) terrorists fatally shot U.S. Army Captain Charles R. Chandler in front of his São Paulo home. Leaflets left near the body accused Chandler of being a "Vietnamese war criminal" sent to Brazil to train right-wing terrorists.
Oct. 14: A classroom building was seized by members of the Black Students Union, in Santa Barbara, Calif.
Oct. 23: El Poder Cubano terrorists were captured by police in New York after an unsuccessful attempt to assassinate the Cuban ambassador to the United Nations.
Oct. 23: A man named Alben Truitt hijacked a Key West charter flight to Cuba.
Oct. 27: A Sears Roebuck store was bombed in Brazil.
Oct. 30: A Seasa Mexican Airlines flight was diverted to Brownville, Texas. The hijacker was extradited to Mexico.
Nov. 2: A juvenile was unsuccessful in his attempt to divert to Cuba an Eastern Airlines flight en route to Chicago.
Nov. 2: Racial violence occurred in Washington, D.C., following an altercation between two black women and a white policeman.
Nov. 4: A flight out of New Orleans was successfully hijacked to Cuba.
Nov. 4: Three hundred students seized thirty-six hostages and held the administration building at the San Fernando Valley State College in California.
Nov. 6: One passenger was killed and another wounded when four men hijacked a Philippine Airlines domestic flight.
Nov. 6: Three student factions organized a strike at San Francisco State University in California.
Nov. 8: A Paris to Athens Olympic Greek Airlines flight was forced to return to Paris by two Italian men who distributed handbills.
Nov. 11: Eleven people were arrested for conspiring to bomb various government buildings in and around Detroit.
Nov. 12: Four police officers were among the ten people wounded in a gun battle with Black Panther members in Carbondale, Ill.
Nov. 13: A police officer and a Black Panther member were both wounded during a shootout in Berkeley, Calif.
Nov. 13: Three blacks were killed and two wounded during a gun battle at a ghetto self-help organization in Boston.
Nov. 16: Black students staged a violent demonstration at the Bluefield State College in West Virginia.
Nov. 18: Two men hijacked a CMA Eastern Airlines flight from Mexico to Cuba.
Nov. 19: Two police officers were wounded by Black Panther gunfire in San Francisco.
Nov. 22: In Jerusalem's most populated outdoor market a bomb exploded. Twelve were killed and fifty-two were wounded.
Nov. 22: A bomb exploded at the physical education building on the campus of the Bluefield State College in West Virginia.
Nov. 23: Nine people, including a woman and three children, hijacked a Chicago to Miami Eastern Airlines flight to Cuba.
Nov. 24: A flight out of New York was hijacked by three man and diverted to Cuba.
Nov. 29: A police station in Jersey City, N.J., was attacked by alleged Black Panther machine-gun fire.
Nov. 30: A flight out of Miami was successfully hijacked to Cuba.
Dec. 1: Four Black Panther members were injured when a firebomb exploded at their headquarters in Newark, N.J.
Dec. 3: A plane was hijacked from Tampa, Fla., to Cuba.
Dec. 5: Twenty-five students were arrested during demonstrations at San Francisco State College.
Dec. 5: Black students attacked a black teacher amid rioting at a middle school in the Roxbury section of Boston.
Dec. 11: A Nashville to Miami TWA flight was hijacked to Cuba by James and Gwendolyn Patterson.
Dec. 13: Twelve white students were beaten as more than 150 minority students rioted in San Mateo, Calif.
Dec. 19: An Eastern Airlines Philadelphia to Miami flight was hijacked to Cuba by a man carrying his infant daughter.
Dec. 19: Black Panther member Frank Diggs was discovered shot to death in the Watts area of Los Angeles.
Dec. 26: In a shooting attack on an El Al Israel Airlines plane at Athens airport a flight attendant and an Israeli passenger were wounded. Israeli commandos retaliated by attacking Beirut Airport two days later, damaging thirteen airplanes.

1969

Jan. 2: A couple carrying an infant daughter hijacked an Eastern Airlines New York to Miami flight and diverted the plane to Cuba.
Jan. 2: An Olympic Greek Airlines domestic flight was hijacked to Cairo, Egypt.
Jan. 3: Members of the SEEK student organization invaded various buildings at Queens College, N.Y.
Jan. 6: Members of SEEK committed various acts of vandalism on the Queens College campus in New York.
Jan. 7: A Columbian domestic flight was hijacked to Santiago, Chile.
Jan. 8: The campus communications center at Brandeis University in Waltham, Mass., was seized and held for eleven days by members of that school's Afro-American Society.
Jan. 9: An Eastern Airlines Miami to Nassau, N.Y., flight was hijacked to Cuba.
Jan. 9: The administration building at Swarthmore college was seized by students and held for seven days.
Jan. 9: Two hundred and thirty-five people were arrested during a protest rally at the San Fernando Valley State College in California.
Jan. 11: A Mexican man hijacked a Panama City-Miami APSA Peruvian Airlines flight to Cuba.
Jan. 12: A hijacker seized a Peruvian airliner and diverted it to Cuba.
Jan. 13: A man was unsuccessful in his attempt to hijack a flight out of Detroit.
Jan. 13: The office of the president of Queens College in New York was ransacked by black students.
Jan. 13: Two fugitive leaders of the paramilitary Minutemen organization were arrested near Truth or Consequences, N.M.
Jan. 14: The administration building at the University of Minnesota was seized by black students and members of Students for a Democratic Society (SDS).
Jan. 17: Students vandalized buildings on the campus of the San Jose State College in California.
Jan. 17: Two Black Panther members were shot and killed on the campus of UCLA by alleged members of US, a rival black militant group.
Jan. 19: An Ecuadorian airliner en route to Miami was seized by four armed terrorists and taken to Cuba.
Jan. 20: Anti-war protestors threw rocks and bottles at President-elect Richard Nixon as he rode to his Inauguration in Washington, D.C.
Jan. 23: Almost 500 people were arrested at a Third World Liberation Front rally at the San Francisco State College.
Jan. 23: Violence broke out in Jacksonville, Fla., after a white man was acquitted of murdering a black man.
Jan. 24: A flight out of Key West, Fla., was successfully hijacked to Cuba.
Jan. 26: Seattle Urban League director Edwin T. Pratt was shot to death at his home in Richmond Heights, Wash.
Jan. 28: A flight out of New Orleans was hijacked to Cuba.
Jan. 28: An flight out of Atlanta was hijacked to Cuba.
Jan. 30: The administration building of the University of Chicago was seized by more than 400 student protesters who occupied it until Feb. 14.
Jan. 31: A flight out of San Francisco was successfully hijacked to Cuba.
Feb. 3: A couple with a small child hijacked a Newark-Miami Eastern Airlines flight to Cuba.
Feb. 3: Two Cubans hijacked a flight in Newark, N.J., and diverted the plane to Cuba.
Feb. 4: Twenty people were arrested during campus protests in Berkeley, Calif.
Feb. 5: A hijacker diverted to Havana a Colombian airliner on a domestic flight.
Feb. 5: Student protesters ransacked the office of the Queens College president in New York.
Feb. 6: A Venezuelan airliner was hijacked to Havana, Cuba, by seven men.
Feb. 7: The administration building at North Carolina A & T College was occupied by 125 student demonstrators.
Feb. 8: The hijacking attempt of a Mexican Airlines domestic flight was foiled when passengers overpowered the hijacker.
Feb. 9: State police broke up a student demonstration at the Mississippi Valley State College in Itta Bena, Miss.
Feb. 10: A flight out of Atlanta was hijacked to Cuba.
Feb. 11: Three men hijacked to Cuba an Aeropostal Venezuelan Airlines domestic flight.
Feb. 12: Student continued to take over classes at Roosevelt University in Chicago.
Feb. 12: National Guard troops were activated to quell an uprising of more than 2,000 students in Madison, Wis.
Feb. 13: Twenty people were injured when students clashed with police

in Durham, N.C.
Feb. 13: The administration building at the City College of New York was occupied by 200 black and Puerto Rican students.
Feb. 17: Student demonstrators threw rocks and stench bombs in Berkeley, Calif.
Feb. 18: Black students seized campus buildings at Wiley College in Marshall, Tex.
Feb. 18: Students seized the law school building at Howard University in Washington, D.C.
Feb. 18: Preparing to take off from Zurich for Tel Aviv an El Al Israel Airlines jet was machine gunned by four Popular Front for the Liberation of Palestine (PFLP) Arab terrorists. One Arab commando was killed and four crew members and three passengers were wounded.
Feb. 20: Demanding retention of an assistant dean, students seized the library at the State University of New York at Stony Brook.
Feb. 20: Students were thwarted in their attempt to seize the administration building at Eastern Michigan University at Ypsilanti.
Feb. 20: Students demonstrated violently at Roosevelt University in Chicago.
Feb. 21: In a Jerusalem supermarket, a bomb killed two and wounded eight.
Feb. 24: Student demonstrators barred Army recruiters from the State University of New York at Stony Brook.
Feb. 24: Black students seized a campus building at Rutgers University in Newark, N.J.
Feb. 24: Students seized the administration building at Pennsylvania State University in University Park, Pa.
Feb. 25: At the British consulate in Jerusalem a bomb exploded, with the PFLP taking the credit.
Feb. 25: A flight out of Atlanta was hijacked to Cuba.
Mar. 5: A National Airlines New York to Miami flight was hijacked to Cuba.
Mar. 11: A man attempted to hijack a SAM Columbian Airlines domestic flight. He was overpowered and wounded after he killed an airline mechanic when the plane landed in Cartagena.
Mar. 11: Students seized numerous buildings on the campus of Howard University in Washington, D.C.
Mar. 15: An Aerocondor Columbian Airlines domestic flight was hijacked to Cuba.
Mar. 16: In Colombia, a hijacker seized a Columbian airliner to divert it to Cuba.
Mar. 17: A Peruvian airliner was hijacked to Cuba by six armed men.
Mar. 17: A flight out of Dallas was hijacked to Cuba.
Mar. 17: A flight out of Atlanta was hijacked to Cuba.
Mar. 19: A Delta Airlines Dallas to New Orleans flight was hijacked to Cuba.
Mar. 25: A Delta Airlines Dallas to San Diego flight was hijacked to Cuba.
Mar. 25: SDS members peacefully picketed eight buildings at Columbia University in New York.
Mar. 29: A police officer was killed and another wounded during a shootout with members of the Republic of New Africa in Detroit.
Mar. 29: Thirty-nine students were arrested at a sit-in at Queens College in New York.
Apr. 3: The National Guard was summoned to quell rock and bottle throwing incidents at Chicago high schools.
Apr. 9: Following a SDS rally at Harvard University, 300 students seized the administration building and hold it until the next day.
Apr. 11: An Ecuadorian airliner bound for Cuba was hijacked by three men with machine guns.
Apr. 13: Four hijackers successfully diverted a plane in San Juan, P.R., to Cuba.
Apr. 14: A Colombian airliner was commandeered to Cuba by three men armed with knives.
Apr. 14: Members of the student Afro-American Society seized the admissions office at Columbia University in New York.
Apr. 16: Students occupied the administration building at Queens College in New York.
Apr. 17: Members of the Student-Faculty Coalition to End Political Suppression staged a sit-in at the Queensborough Community College in New York in response to the hiring of an English professor.
Apr. 17: Members of SDS seized Philosophy Hall at Columbia University in New York.
Apr. 17: Students set fires, vandalized buildings, and disrupted classes at Brooklyn College in New York.
Apr. 19: Members of the Expansion Committee, a radical faction of SDS, seized a campus building at Columbia University in New York.
Apr. 19: Black students occupied the student union for thirty-six hours at Cornell University in Ithaca, N.Y.
Apr. 21: Students began a four-day strike at Queens College in New York.
Apr. 21: Students staged a sit-in at the Queensborough Community College in New York.
Apr. 21: Students of the School of Social Work boycotted classes at Howard University in Washington, D.C.
Apr. 22: The City College of New York was closed after black and Puerto Rican students barricaded themselves inside campus gates.
Apr. 22: Students staged a six-hour sit-in at Brooklyn College in New York.
Apr. 23: Three thousand students staged a sit-in at Cornell University in Ithaca, N.Y.
Apr. 26: Incidents of sniping and firebombing lasted three days in Cairo, Ill.
Apr. 27: Inciting three days of rioting, a black fugitive wounded a black policeman in Winston-Salem, N.C.
Apr. 28: The administration building at Queens College in New York was occupied by members of the Ad Hoc Committee to End Political Suppression.
Apr. 28: Armed students seized the administration building at Voorhees College in Denmark, S.C., and were arrested by state police.
Apr. 30: Students vandalized the office of the president of Brooklyn College in New York.
Apr. 30: Members of SDS seized two buldings on the campus of Columbia University in New York and held it overnight.
May 1: Black students vandalized campus buildings at Queens College in New York.
May 5: An airplane in New York was successfully hijacked to Cuba.
May 7: Black and white students battled each other at the reopening of the City College of New York.
May 7: Students forced the closure of Howard University in Washington, D.C., occupying eight campus buildings for three days.
May 7: Students occupied eight campus buildings for three days, forcing the closure of Howard University in Washington, D.C.
May 15: One person was killed and seventy injured during student riots in Berkeley, Calif.
May 16: One person was killed and forty-eight arrested during riots and looting in Burlington, N.C.
May 19: A riot occurred in Newark, N.J., after a black youth was killed by a black police officer.
May 20: In New Jersey, two Cuban refugees were arrested after they tried to bomb the Cuban consulate in Montreal.
May 20: Students demonstrated at the home of the University Chancellor in Berkeley, Calif.
May 20: An Avianca Columbian Airlines domestic flight was hijacked to Cuba.
May 21: High school and college students rioted in Greensboro, N.C. One student was killed in a gun battle with police.
May 21: The body of a Black Panther murder victim was discovered floating in a river in New Haven, Conn. Two Black Panthers were convicted of the crime.
May 22: Five hundred demonstrators were arrested during a march in Berkeley, Calif.
May 22: Three Habash Front terrorists were arrested in Copenhagen and accused of conspiring to assassinate David Ben Gurion.
May 23: Black Panther member John Savage was shot to death in San Diego. The murder provoked gun fights between Panthers and US, the rival black militant organization, throughout the summer.
May 30: A portion of the Trans-Arabian pipeline was bombed by PFLP terrorists in the Golan Heights, Isr.
June 3: A Texas International Airlines flight from New Orleans to Alexandria, La., was hijacked and diverted to Cuba.
June 4: Three men hijacked a DTA Angolan Airlines flight to the Congo.
June 5: Numerous stores were looted in the black and Puerto Rican neighborhoods of Hartford, Conn.
June 5: The offices of the Black Panthers were raided by police in Denver.
June 8: A Portuguese airliner in Angola was hijacked by two Africans armed with grenades and machine guns, who diverted it to the Congo Republic.
June 8: A bomb was detonated at New York City's Loew's Orpheum Theater to protest the screening of the movie *Che*. Minor damage resulted.
June 9: An Ethiopian airliner at the Karachi airport was attacked by three armed Eritrean Liberation Front (ELF) members.
June 9: A bomb exploded at the Yugoslavian Consulate in Sidney, Aus.
June 16: Thirteen police officers were wounded in a shootout with Black Panthers in Sacramento, Calif.
June 17: A TWA Oakland to New York flight was hijacked to Cuba.
June 18: An Ethiopian Airliner in Karachi, Pak., was attacked by members of the ELF.
June 19: Four fires erupted during a race riot in Cairo, Ill.
June 20: A facility of General Motors in Montevideo, Urug., was attacked by three terrorists of Tupamaros Movimento de Nacional (MLN). Damage was estimated at $1 million.
June 20: A Colombian airliner bound for Santiago, Chile, was hijacked by three armed men and one woman.
June 20: Twelve hostages were taken during a prison riot at St. Cloud, Minn.
June 22: A flight out of Newark, N.J., was hijacked to Cuba.
June 23: Three police officers were wounded by gunfire in Cleveland.
June 24: Looting and firebombing in Omaha, Neb., continued for two days.
June 25: A flight out of Los Angeles was successfully hijacked to Cuba.
June 26: In U.S.-owned Minimax supermarkets in Argentina, a series of bombings occurred during the official visit by New York State

Governor Nelson Rockefeller.
June 27: A General Motors plant in Penarol, Urug., was robbed.
June 28: A flight out of Baltimore was successfully hijacked to Cuba.
June 30: The head of the Yugoslavian mission in West Berlin was seriously wounded by a Croatian nationalist.
July 3: Thirteen people hijacked a Saeta Ecuadorian Airlines flight to Cuba.
July 10: The pilot overpowered a man attempting to hijack an Avianca Columbian Airlines flight to Cuba.
July 10: A flight attendant and passengers overpowered a man attempting to hijack a SAM Columbian Airlines flight to Cuba.
July 15: A terrorist named Sam Melville bombed a military arsenal in New Jersey.
July 15: Looting and firebombing continued three days in Youngstown, Ohio.
July 17: A National Guardsman and a black woman were killed during racial violence in York, Pa.
July 18: Two London department stores were firebombed by terrorists known to be linked with Israel. The attack was later claimed by the PFLP.
July 20: One U.S. Marine was killed during racial violence at Camp Lejeune, N.C.
July 22: A man was killed by sniper fire and thirty-six others were injured during racial violence in Columbus, Ohio.
July 26: A Mexican airliner on a domestic flight was taken by a hijacker to Cuba.
July 26: A Continental Airlines El Paso to Midland, Texas, flight was hijacked to Cuba.
July 26: A terrorist named Sam Melville bombed the United Fruit Company pier in New York.
July 29: A man dressed as a woman was subdued as he attempted to hijack a Nicaraguan Airlines flight to Cuba.
July 30: In Japan an unsuccessful assassination attempt was made by a knife-wielding Japanese youth on U.S. Ambassador to Japan A.H. Meyer, on his way to the Tokyo airport with Secretary of State William Rogers.
July 31: A flight out of Pittsburgh was successfully hijacked to Cuba.
July 31: Five police officers were wounded during a shootout with Black Panther members in Chicago.
Aug. 3: Rioting occurred in the Puerto Rican neighborhood of Passaic, N.J.
Aug. 4: Three men hijacked an Avianca Columbian Airlines flight to Cuba.
Aug. 5: A man named John McCreery was remanded to a mental institution after he failed in his attempt to hijack a Philadelphia to Tampa, Fla., Eastern Airlines flight to Cuba.
Aug. 8: A state trooper in Michigan was wounded by sniper fire.
Aug. 9: At an Olympic Airways facility in Athens a bomb exploded, injuring two U.S. tourists.
Aug. 10: Sixteen people were injured in a clash between black and white marines at a base near Honolulu.
Aug. 12: Prompting several days of picketing, a white man and his son bludgeoned two black women in Somerville, Tenn.
Aug. 12: An Ethiopian airliner going to Khartoum, Sudan, was hijacked by seven Ethiopian students.
Aug. 14: A flight out of Boston was hijacked to Cuba.
Aug. 15: A man distributing a Black Panther newspaper was shot to death in San Diego.
Aug. 16: A couple with two children hijacked an Olympic Greek Airlines domestic flight and diverted the plane to Albania.
Aug. 17: Black and white gangs clashed in Niagara, N.Y. Vandalism and looting followed.
Aug. 18: Sniper fire followed a clash between black and white gangs in Tacoma, Wash.
Aug. 18: Six people, including a woman and three children, hijacked a Misrair Egyptian Airlines flight and diverted the plane to El Wagah, Saud.
Aug. 18: A bomb placed by the Habash Front was defused before it detonated at an Israeli tourist office in Copenhagen.
Aug. 18: A bomb placed by the Habash Front exploded in a London department store.
Aug. 19: A black mob battled with police in Lakewood, N.J.
Aug. 20: A terrorist named Sam Melville was suspected of bombing the Marine Midland Grace Trust Company in New York City.
Aug. 23: A Colombian airliner was hijacked by two men and taken to Santiago, Chile.
Aug. 23: One Hawatmah Front terrorist was killed and another wounded, when their bomb exploded prematurely in Izmir, Turk.
Aug. 23: A bomb exploded at a Jewish school in Teheran, Iran.
Aug. 25: The Israeli Zim Lines office in London was bombed, with one person injured; the PFLP claimed the act.
Aug. 25: Fifty people were injured during three days of racial violence in downtown Pittsburgh.
Aug. 27: A mob of 1,000 whites called for the lynching of three black men accused of rape in Forrest City, Ark.
Aug. 29: A flight out of Miami was successfully hijacked to Cuba.
Aug. 29: A TWA 707 en route between Paris and Athens was hijacked by two PFLP members who demanded that it be flown to Syria, where the passengers were removed and the plane destroyed.
Aug. 29: Six people, including four police officers, were injured during rock-throwing incidents in Grand Rapids, Mich.
Aug. 29: The Jewish Defense League was suspected of stealing Palestine Liberation Organization (PLO) files in New York City.
Aug. 30: Blacks confronted police amid sniper fire and rock-throwing in Fort Lauderdale, Fla.
Aug. 30: The offices of the black militant US organization were bombed in San Diego.
Sept. 1: Puerto Rican demonstrators besieged a fire station and rioted for four days in Hartford, Conn.
Sept. 2: The National Guard was called to quell violence in Fort Lauderdale, Fla.
Sept. 2: A white police officer and a black young girl were killed during four days of sniper fire in Camden, N.J.
Sept. 4: Charles Burke Elbrick, U.S. Ambassador to Brazil, was kidnapped by members of the Acao Libertadora Nacional (ALN) and the Moviment de Accion Revolucionaria (MR-8). Elbrick was released on Sept. 7. His abduction was the first diplomatic kidnapping, a practice that spread rapidly throughout Latin America.
Sept. 6: An Ecudorian Air Force transport was hijacked by thirteen terrorists with machine guns; the copilot was murdered and one crew members was wounded.
Sept. 6: Racial violence occurred during a protest march in Somerville, Tenn.
Sept. 7: A lone hijacker diverted a flight out of New York to Cuba.
Sept. 8: Israeli embassies in The Hague and Bonn and the El Al Israel Airlines office in Brussels were bombed by three Arab terrorists.
Sept. 10: A man failed in his attempt to hijack a San Juan, P.R., flight to Cuba.
Sept. 10: Guns and bombs belonging to Loyalist factions were confiscated by British troops in Belfast, Ire.
Sept. 13: An Ethiopian airliner was hijacked by three armed members of the ELF and diverted to Aden, Southern Yemen.
Sept. 14: A Honduran airlines on a domestic flight was taken by a hijacker to San Salvador, El Sal.
Sept. 16: A Turkish airliner was hijacked by a Turkish student and taken to Sofia, Bul.
Sept. 16: A woman was wounded during a gunfight between blacks and whites in Cairo, Ill.
Sept. 19: The terrorist Sam Melville, was suspected of bombing a federal office building in New York City.
Sept. 24: A flight out of Charleston, S.C., was successfully hijacked to Cuba.
Sept. 24: An ROTC office was bombed on the campus of the University of Wisconsin in Madison.
Sept. 24: A federal building was bombed in Milwaukee, Wis.
Sept. 24: A time bomb was discovered at the Civic Center in Chicago.
Sept. 26: Students seized a campus building at the University of Michigan in Ann Arbor.
Sept. 29: A TWA flight between Rome and Lod, Isr., was hijacked by two Habash Front terrorists and diverted to Damascus, Syria. Two Israeli passengers were exchanged for two Syrian pilots.
Oct. 4: A police officer was wounded during a gun battle with Black Panther members in Chicago.
Oct. 5: Two people were killed during racial violence in Las Vegas, Nev.
Oct. 6: In Cali, a gang called The Invisible Ones attacked a car carrying Swiss consul Enrique Strassle, his son José, and Herman Buff, Consul Secretary in Colombia. The captives were released after a large ransom was allegedly paid.
Oct. 6: In Córdoba, Arg., the offices of Pepsi-Cola, Squibb, First National City Bank, and Dunlop Tires were damaged by bombs.
Oct. 6: In San Miguel de Tucumán, Arg., the offices of IBM and General Electric were damaged by bombs.
Oct. 7: In Buenos Aires, the U.S. Information Service library was bombed.
Oct. 7: The terrorist Sam Melville allegedly bombed a military recruiting station in New York City.
Oct. 7: A police statue in Chicago was bombed by members of the Weather Underground.
Oct. 8: In Buenos Aires, a branch of the Bank of Boston was bombed.
Oct. 8: In Santa Fe, Arg., a Remington Rand office was bombed.
Oct. 8: A Brazilian airliner on a domestic flight was seized by a hijacker and taken to Cuba.
Oct. 8: An Aerolineas Argentinas airliner was hijacked by a lone terrorist and taken to Cuba.
Oct. 8: Members of the Weather Underground clashed with police in downtown Chicago during the so-called "Days of Rage."
Oct. 9: A flight out of Los Angeles was successfully hijacked to Cuba.
Oct. 12: Demanding the release of the Fort Dix 38, four thousand people demonstrated at Fort Dix, N.J.
Oct. 14: The Swiss embassy in Bogotá was fired on, but no one was wounded.
Oct. 18: Police and two Black Panther members were involved in a shootout in Los Angeles.
Oct. 19: A Polish airliner going from Warsaw to East Berlin was hijacked by two East Germans who diverted it to West Berlin.
Oct. 21: A flight from Mexico City to Miami was successfully hijacked to Cuba.

Oct. 28: Two men hijacked a Columbian Air Taxi to Cuba.
Oct. 30: Students occupied the administration building at Vassar College in Poughkeepsie, N.Y.
Oct. 31: A TWA Los Angeles to San Francisco flight was hijacked to Rome.
Nov. 3: Sixty members of SDS seized a personnel office at Yale University in New Haven, Conn. Four hostages were taken.
Nov. 4: A Nicaraguan airliner in flight from Miami to Meixco was seized by two armed men and diverted to Cuba.
Nov. 4: A lone gunman hijacked a Brazilian airliner en route from Buenos Aires to Santiago, Chile, and took it to Cuba.
Nov. 5: The son of a U.S. businessman was kidnapped and killed in Brazil when ransom demands were not met.
Nov. 8: A hijacker was dissuaded during a refueling stop as he attempted to divert an Austral Argentinian Airlines flight to Cuba.
Nov. 8: Twenty-three members of the Weathermen organization were arrested following a sniper attack on the police headquarters in Cambridge, Mass.
Nov. 9: A timebomb planted by the Habash Front was found in a West Berlin Jewish Community Center.
Nov. 10: A juvenile who had taken a girl hostage in an airport terminal failed in his attempt to hijack a Delta Airlines Cincinnati to Chicago flight.
Nov. 11: An undetonated Habash Front time bomb was discovered at a Jewish community center in West Berlin.
Nov. 11: The terrorist Sam Melville was suspected of bombing the offices of RCA and General Motors in New York City.
Nov. 11: The Chase Manhattan Bank was bombed in New York City.
Nov. 12: Two juveniles were overpowered by the crew when they attempted to hijack a LAM Chilean Airlines flight to Cuba.
Nov. 12: A Cruzerio du Sol Brazilian Airlines flight was hijacked to Cuba.
Nov. 12: The terrorist Sam Melville was suspected of bombing a courthouse and an army vehicle in New York City.
Nov. 13: Six men hijacked an Avianca Columbian Airlines flight to Cuba.
Nov. 13: Two police officers were killed and another was wounded during a gun battle with Black Panthers in Chicago.
Nov. 13: The two-day March Against Death, an anti-war rally in Washington, D.C., culminated in rock throwing and teargassing.
Nov. 18: A Mexican Airlines domestic flight was hijacked to Cuba.
Nov. 19: SDS members held a campus dean hostage at Harvard University in Cambridge, Mass.
Nov. 20: Alacatraz Island was seized by eighty-nine Indian protesters who sought to claim it by right of discovery.
Nov. 20: The Fuerzas Armadas Peronists (FAP) claimed responsibility for bombing fifteen firms in Argentina. Nine of them were U.S.-owned.
Nov. 20: A LOT Polish Airlines flight was hijacked to Austria.
Nov. 27: Two Jordanian terrorists were involved in the hand grenade attack on an El Al Israel Airline office in Athens, Gr.
Nov. 29: The Yugoslavian embassy in Canberra, Aus., was bombed by Croatian extremists.
Nov. 29: A Varig Brazilian Airlines London to Rio de Janeiro, Braz., flight was hijacked to Cuba.
Dec. 2: A TWA flight from San Francisco to Philadelphia was hijacked to Cuba.
Dec. 4: Black Panther members Fred Hampton and Mark Clark were killed during a police raid in Chicago.
Dec. 5: Members of the Organization for Black Unity seized a building at Harvard University in Cambridge, Mass.
Dec. 8: Six people were wounded, including three police officers, in a gun battle with Black Panther members in Los Angeles.
Dec. 11: A South Korean Airlines domestic flight was hijacked to North Korea.
Dec. 11: Members of the Revolutionary Armed Independence Movement allegedly bombed five hotels in San Juan, P.R.
Dec. 12: Two men were killed by security guards when they attempted to hijack an Ethiopean Airlines flight between Madrid, Spain and Addis Ababa.
Dec. 12: In West Berlin, a bomb placed by Baader-Meinhof terrorists exploded at a U.S. Army officers' club, while others were defused at another military building and at an El Al Israel Airlines office.
Dec. 19: A LAN Chilean Airlines flight was hijacked to Cuba.
Dec. 21: Three Habash Front terrorists were arrested in Athens for conspiring to hijack a TWA flight arriving from Israel.
Dec. 23: A LACSA Costa Rican Airlines flight was hijacked to Cuba.
Dec. 24: Three Arabs were arrested by Athens police as they tried to board a TWA plane bound for Rome and New York. Armed with guns and explosives, the three men said they were PFLP members and had orders to divert the plane to Tunis where they planned to unload the passengers and destroy the plane.
Dec. 26: A United Airlines New York to Chicago flight was hijacked to Cuba.
Dec. 28: Members of the Young Lords, a militant Puerto Rican organization, began an eleven-day occupation of a church in New York City.
Dec. 29: The Jewish Defense League was suspected of sabotaging a Soviet Airline office in New York City.

1970

Jan. 1: An airplane en route from Montevideo to Rio de Janeiro was hijacked by eight members of the Vanguarda Armada Revolucionaria-Palmares (VAR-Palmares) and was flown to Cuba.
Jan. 2: Country prosecutor Joseph Laurita was injured by a car-bomb explosion in Morgantown, W.Va.
Jan. 5: Members of the Students for a Democratic Society Weathermen attempted to bomb an ammunition factory in Baraboo, Wis.
Jan. 9: Christian Belon, a Frenchman, hijacked a TWA 707 airliner en route from Paris to Rome to protest U.S. and Israeli aggression in the Middle East. Belon was sentenced to a nine-month jail term, which he had served while awaiting trial. He was returned to France where he received another eight-month term for illegal possession of weapons.
Jan. 11: In Ethiopia, gunmen shot and killed a U.S. soldier. The Eritrean Liberation Front (ELF) was suspected.
Jan. 20: In Guatemala City unidentified gunmen entered the British consulate and murdered the consul's bodyguard.
Jan. 20: A branch office of the Bank of America was bombed in Turin, Italy.
Jan. 20: A fire was set at the Black Panther Party headquarters in Jersey City, N.J.
Jan. 25: Over Haiti, a Dutch Antilles Airways plane was diverted and flown to Cuba.
Jan. 30: An anti-Communist newspaper editor was killed and a Christian Democratic presidential candidate was wounded by gunmen in Guatemala.
Feb. 6: Twelve dynamite bombs exploded in Denver, destroying one third of the city's school buses.
Feb. 10: In a grenade attack on an El Al Israel plane in the Munich airport, three Arab terrorists killed an Israeli citizen and wounded others. The Executive Committee for the Liberation of Palestine (ECLP) was responsible.
Feb. 13: At a Jewish home for the elderly in Munich, arsonists set a fire; seven people were killed and nine were wounded.
Feb. 13: Seven officers were injured when two bombs exploded in a police station parking lot in Berkeley, Calif.
Feb. 13: Twenty-six people were injured after terrorists exploded bombs and robbed a bank in Danbury, Conn.
Feb. 16: A police sergeant was killed by a bomb explosion outside a police station in San Francisco.
Feb. 16: Two department stores in Berkeley, Calif., were bombed.
Feb. 16: In the U.S., an Eastern Airlines plane was hijacked and taken to Cuba.
Feb. 17: A live bomb was discovered at a paint factory in Oakland, Calif.
Feb. 21: Near Frankfurt, Ger., a bomb exploded in the cargo hold of an Austrian Airlines plane. The Jibril Front was responsible.
Feb. 21: In Austria a bomb, planted by the Popular Front for the Liberation of Palestine (PFLP), exploded in an plane carrying mail to Tel Aviv.
Feb. 21: Thirty-eight passengers and nine crew members were killed when a Swissair flight from Zurich to Lod exploded in midair. The Jibril Front terrorist organization was the primary suspect for the explosion.
Feb. 23: Near the town of Hebron in Jordan, guerrillas ambushed a tourist bus and murdered a U.S. woman.
Feb. 24: Two Jibril Front parcel bombs were defused before they detonated in Frankfurt, Ger.
Feb. 25: Student protesters burned a branch of the Bank of America in Isla Vista, Calif. After three days of violence, Governor Ronald Reagan called out the National Guard.
Feb. 25: Students threw rocks and exploded firebombs on the campus of the State University of New York at Buffalo.
Feb. 27: In Guatemala, members of the left-wing Revolutionary Armed Forces kidnapped Foreign Minister Fuentes Mohr. He was released in exchange for an imprisoned guerrilla leader the following day.
Feb. 27: Students seized the administration building at the State University of New York in Buffalo.
March: Five members of a National Geographic film crew were held hostage for seventeen days in Ethiopia by ELF terrorists.
Mar. 1: A bomb planted by the ELF was discovered in luggage on board an Ethiopian airliner in Rome.
Mar. 3: A white mob attacked a school bus transporting black children in Lamar, S.C.
Mar. 3: An FBI informer named Jeffrey Paul Desmond bombed a construction company and a mailbox of the University of Seattle.
Mar. 6: Sean Holly, a U.S. labor attaché, was kidnapped by members of the Fuerzas Armadas Rebeldes (FAR) in Guatemala. The kidnappers' demands for the release of four prisoners held by Guatemalan authorities was agreed to, and Holly was released on Mar. 8.
Mar. 6: Three Weathermen terrorists were killed manufacturing bombs at a townhouse in New York's Greenwich Village.
Mar. 7: Terrorists tossed a hand grenade at the home of the Israeli consul in Guatemala.
Mar. 9: Arson caused extensive damage to the library at University of California-Berkeley.
Mar. 10: More than 1,200 students rampaged near the campus of the San Francisco State University.

Mar. 10: Two associates of H. Rap Brown were killed by a car-bomb explosion in Bel Air, Md.
Mar. 11: In Brazil, Vanguarda Popular Revolucionaria (VPR) members seized Nobuo Okuchi, Japan's consul general in São Paulo. Ransom demands for the release of five prisoners, immunity from retaliation, and suspension of a massive government search for the kidnappers were met. The prisoners were released on Mar. 14. Okuchi was released unharmed ten hours after the prisoners reached Mexico by plane.
Mar. 11: In Colombia, an Avianca jet was hijacked to Cuba.
Mar. 11: A United Air Lines jet was hijacked to Cuba.
Mar. 11: A bomb explosion destroyed a courthouse in Cambridge, Md.
Mar. 12: En route from Santiago, Chile, to Buenos Aires, Arg., a Varig Brazilian Airlines jet was hijacked to Cuba.
Mar. 12: Bombs set by the Revolutionary Force 9 terrorist organization exploded at the corporate headquarters of GTE, IBM and Socony Mobil in New York City.
Mar. 17: Intending to commit suicide, a passenger killed the co-pilot and wounded the pilot during a flight from Newark to Boston.
Mar. 20: Michigan Civil Rights Commission director Burton Bordin was shot to death in Detroit.
Mar. 21: Two department stores were bombed in New York City.
Mar. 22: Fifteen people were injured when a bomb exploded in a New York City nightclub.
Mar. 24: In Argentina an airliner was hijacked and flown to Cuba.
Mar. 24: Six members of a group called the United Anti-Reelection Command, a leftist group opposed to President Balaguer's reelection, kidnapped Lieutenant Colonel Donald J. Crowley, the U.S. air attaché in the Dominican Republic. Demanding that twenty-one prisoners be set free in a ceremony in Santo Domingo's main square, the kidnappers swore that Crowley would be released ten hours after the ceremony. The government agreed to release twenty prisoners, flying them to Mexico. After their release was confirmed, Crowley was also released on March 26.
Mar. 24: Fuenta Argentino de Liberation (FAL) members in Argentina kidnapped Paraguayan consul Joaquin Waldemar Sanchez in Ituzaingo. They threatening to murder him if two of their members were not released from Argentine prison. When their demand was rejected by the government the kidnappers extended their deadline several times. They released Sanchez unharmed on Mar. 28 but vowed to slay police and government officials.
Mar. 24: Eighty students were arrested following the occupation of a campus building at the University of Maryland in College Park.
Mar. 27: Right wing terrorist group Movimento Argentino Nacional Organisacion (ANO) threatened to kill Argentina's Soviet ambassador and his family in reprisal for the Mar. 24 kidnapping of the Paraguayan consul.
Mar. 27: Followers of Imam al-Hadi al-Mahdi were unsuccessful in their attempt to assassinate Sudanese leader General al-Numeiri. Four days later, Imam was shot to death as he attempted to escape to Ethiopia.
Mar. 28: One person was killed and another injured when a bomb exploded in an apartment building on New York's Lower East Side.
Mar. 29: In Argentina four MANO members kidnapped Soviet assistant commercial attaché Yuri Pivovarov at gunpoint. Police chased the kidnappers and fired into their car. When the abductor's car crashed, three of the assailants were captured and a fourth escaped. Pivovarov was not badly injured. A deputy police officer was found to be involved in the kidnapping attempt.
Mar. 31: A Japan Air Lines plane was hijacked by members of the United Red Army (URA) and ordered to be flown to Pyongyang in North Korea. Officials disguised the Seoul airport to make it look like Pyongyang. The kidnappers, who were not fooled, allowed the passengers to disembark and then flew on to Pyongyang on Apr. 3.
Mar. 31: FAR members in Guatemala kidnapped West German ambassador Count Karl von Spreti by taking him at gunpoint from his car. Their threat to kill von Spreti unless seventeen prisoners were released by the government was soon increased to a demand for the release of twenty-five prisoners and a $700,000 ransom. Facing pressure from the West German government, the Guatemalan government rejected the demands. On Apr. 5, the Guatmalen government received an annonymous call telling them where to find the ambassador's body.
April: A Peace Corps official, Jack Fry, was kidnapped from an Ethiopian train by terrorists and was released five days later.
April 5: In Brazil, U.S. Consul General Curtis S. Cutter avoided a kidnapping attempt in Pôrto Alegre. As Cutter drove home from a dinner, his car was blocked by another from which four or five men carrying machine guns emerged. Cutter knocked one of them down with his auto, was wounded, but drove away while the kidnappers escaped. Three members of the VPR were later arrested.
Apr. 13: Berkeley, Calif., was without power for one hour after a high voltage power line was bombed.
Apr. 15: High school students demonstrated violently against an ROTC office in Berkeley, Calif. Rock throwing and teargassing continued until Apr. 17.
Apr. 16: Four women were wounded during demonstrations in Isla Vista, Calif.
Apr. 20: A campus fire caused more than $2 million in damages at the University of Kansas at Lawrence.
Apr. 20: A dynamite explosion damaged the Louisiana State capitol in Baton Rouge.
Apr. 24: Terrorists staged several attacks in Santo Domingo coinciding with the fifth anniversery of the 1965 Dominican civil war.
Apr. 24: The Pan Am office in Izmir, Turk., was bombed by members of the Popular Struggle Front.
Apr. 24: A fire caused extensive damage to a campus building of Stanford University in Palo Alto, Calif.
Apr. 24: A police officer was shot while he was responding to a civil disturbance call in Baltimore.
Apr. 25: In the Istanbul, Turk., offices of El Al Israel Airlines were the target of a bomb explosion.
Apr. 26: Armed hijacker Joaquim Terreira, hijacked a Brazilian VASP airliner and ordered it to be flown to Cuba. Passengers were permitted to disembark in Guyana.
Apr. 26: The Louisiana State Capitol was damaged by the explosion of thirty sticks of dynamite. The incident followed the killings of three blacks by police officers.
Apr. 27: Black and white students clashed at a high school in River Rouge, Mich. Firebombing and looting followed. Seventeen people were injured.
Apr. 29: Twenty students were wounded as they protested the presence of an ROTC installation on campus at Ohio State University in Columbus.
May 1: A British West Indian Airways flight was hijacked by two U.S. citizens. When the craft landed in Havana to refuel, Cuban and British authorities convinced the hijackers to abandon their plan to fly to Senegal and surrender.
May 1: An ROTC office was ransacked by students at the University of Maryland.
May 3: Member of the British High Commission in Kampala Brian Lea staged his own abduction to call attention to the plight of Asians in Uganda.
May 4: Four students were killed and another wounded by National Guardsmen during demonstrations at Kent State University in Ohio.
May 4: In the Israeli embassy in Asunción, Para., two Arabs from Palestine shot and killed the first secretary's wife and wounded an employee. Arrested later, the assailants were alleged to be members of Al Fatah.
May 5: The company plane of a uranium plant in Czechoslovakia was hijacked by a company official and taken to Austria.
May 5: Students attempted to raid a Selective Service office in Madison, Wis., and were teargassed by local police.
May 5: A computer center was firebombed on the campus of the University of Miami at Coral Gables, Fla.
May 5: The National Guard was summoned to halt a demonstration by students at the University of Kentucky.
May 5: Two National Guardsmen were injured after their unit was activated to halt student demonstrations at Ohio State University in Columbus.
May 6: Three students were stabbed in a flag-raising dispute on campus at the University of New Mexico.
May 8: The offices of four U.S. firms were bombed in Munich, Ger.
May 8: The National Guard was activated to disperse student demonstrators at Southern Illinois University in Carbondale.
May 8: Seven students at the University of New Mexico were reportedly stabbed by bayonet-wielding National Guardsmen.
May 8: Seventy people, including three police officers, were injured during a clash between student demonstrators and construction workers in the Wall Street district of New York City.
May 8: A peaceful mass protest at George Washington University in Washington, D.C., turned violent as demonstrators stoned police and firemen.
May 9: A police officer was killed by sniper fire in Sacramento, Calif.
May 10: Members of the Weather Underground bombed a National Guard building in Washington, D.C., in response to the killings at Kent State on May 4.
May 11: Thousands of construction workers staged a counter-demonstration in the Wall Street district of New York City.
May 12: More than a dozen people were killed during rioting and looting in Augusta, Ga.
May 13: Police teargassed student demonstrators at Eastern Michigan University in Ypsilanti.
May 13: The National Guard was activated to quell racial disorders in Athens, Ga.
May 13: A Dutch Antilles Airways plane was hijacked by eight Dominican nationals who ordered it to be flown to Cuba.
May 14: Student demonstrations to block a nearby highway led to the summoning of the National Guard to the University of Maryland at College Park.
May 14: One person was wounded and six others injured during racial violence in Syracuse, N.Y.
May 14: The assistant dean of Illinois State University was injured during a clash between police and student protesters.
May 14: Two black students were shot to death by police on the campus of Jackson State College in Mississippi.
May 15: Three students were injured during a campus explosion at Southern Illinois University in Carbondale.
May 15: Student demonstrators forced the closing of Ohio University

in Athens, Ohio.
May 17: Racial violence broke out following a local election in Lake Providence, La.
May 17: Extensive looting occurred in the black neighborhoods of Hot Springs, Ark.
May 20: A firebomb destroyed the computer center at the Fresno State College in California.
May 20: Fifty-one people were arrested during racial violence at a high school in Rahway, N.J.
May 21: In Colombia, an airliner was hijacked and flown to Cuba.
May 22: Crossing the border from Lebanon into Israel, Fedayeen members fired three bazooka rockets at a school bus. Eight children were killed and another twenty-two wounded.
May 22: A police officer was hit by sniper fire in St, Paul, Minn.
May 24: In Mexico an airliner was hijacked and flown to Cuba.
May 24: The first of many bombs placed by members of Quebec Separatist groups exploded in Montreal.
May 26: After several weeks of racial violence, two tobacco warehouses were destroyed by firebombs in Oxford, N.C.
May 27: Rioting and vandalism broke out in Melbourne, Fla.
May 28: Six Black Panther members were suspected in the fatal shooting of a police officer in Sacramento, Calif.
May 29: Former Argentine President General Aramburu was kidnapped by members of the National Command for National Liberation. His body was found on July 16, 1970.
May 29: A black youth was shot to death by a white clerk. The incident precipitated a week of racial violence in Alexandria, Va.
May 31: In Colombia, a plane was hijacked and ordered flown to Cuba.
June 4: A lone gunman hijacked a flight between Phoenix and St. Louis. He diverted the plane to Washington, D.C., and demanded $100 million.
June 5: In Poland, an airliner was hijacked and taken to Denmark by people who were seeking asylum.
June 7: In Amman, Jor., members of the PFLP kidnapped Morris Draper, U.S. political secretary. They released him unharmed the next day.
June 7: U.S. military attaché in Jordan, Captain Robert Potts, and his wife were wounded by gunfire when their car was stopped by a roadblock in Amman.
June 8: People seeking asylum hijacked seized a Czech airliner and took it to West Germany.
June 8: PFLP terrorists held sixty hostages in two Amman hotels and threatened to blow them up if Jordanian PFLP camps were smashed. The hostages were released unharmed four days later.
June 8: SDS members were primary suspects in the bombing of the National Socialist White People's Party headquarters in Chicago.
June 9: Members of the Weathermen bombed police headquarters in New York City.
June 10: In Amman, Jor., U.S. military attaché Major Roebert Perry was fatally shot by guerrillas.
June 11: West German ambassador to Brazil Ehrenfried von Holleben was kidnapped by Acao Libertadora Nacional (ALN) and Vanguarda Popular Revolucionaria (VPR) terrorists. Forty prisoners were released from jails and flown to Algeria on June 15. Hollenben was released unharmed the next day.
June 12: The Swiss embassy in Uruguay was raided by Tupamaros who seized office supplies and documents.
June 12: Extensive looting and rioting occurred in the Brownsville section of Brooklyn, N.Y.
June 14: Three police officers and four firemen were injured during rioting in the Puerto Rican section of Harlem.
June 15: Twelve Jewish dissidents hijacked a Soviet aircraft during a flight from Leningrad to Serdobol. The attempt failed and all of the participants were arrested in Leningrad and Priozersk.
June 16: Four days of looting, firebombing, and rock throwing occurred in Miami, Fla.
June 18: Three people were killed when a Parke-Davis plant was bombed in Buenos Aires, Arg.
June 19: Bombs exploded at two branches of the Bank of America in Berkeley, Calif.
June 19: A police officer was shot to death in his patrol car in Chicago.
June 21: An Iranian 727 plane flying to Baghdad was hijacked by three armed Iranians who sought political sanctuary in Iraq.
June 22: A Pan American jet was hijacked by a U.S. citizen with an Albanian passport who ordered it flown to Cairo.
June 23: The New York offices of Amtorg Trading Corporation were damaged by Jewish Defense League (JDL) terrorists.
June 23: Robbing the Palestinian bank in Uruguay, Tupamaros escaped with $72,000.
June 24: A woman was killed in Ottawa, Can., when a bomb placed by Front du Libération du Québec (FLQ) terrorists exploded at a government office building.
June 27: Nine buildings, including the branch offices of many U.S. corporations, were bombed in three Argentinian cities.
June 28: Three Detroit police officers were wounded by members of the National Committee to Combat Fascism.
July 1: In the U.S., a National Airlines jet was hijacked to Cuba.
July 1: A bomb explosion destroyed reference material in a campus building at the University of California at Berkeley.
July 1: A police officer was shot to death as he aided firefighters who were being fired upon by snipers in Plainfield, N.J.
July 1: A bank was firebombed in Walnut Creek, Colo.
July 1: Members of the Revolutionary Force 7 bombed the headquarters of the Inter-American Defense Board in Washington, D.C.
July 2: A man was killed when a bomb he was carrying exploded as he neared police headquarters in Compton, Calif.
July 2: Members of the Revolutionary Force 7 bombed the Argentinian, Dominican, Haitian, and Uruguayan embassies in Washington, D.C.
July 2: A black-owned business was bombed in Omaha, Neb.
July 3: Five people were killed during a conflict between the Provisional IRA and the British Army in Belfast, Ire.
July 3: A warehouse and drug store were bombed in Leavenworth, Kan.
July 3: Bombs exploded near the University Federal Savings and Loan in Seattle, Wash.
July 4: The headquarters of the Democratic Committee in Long Beach, N.Y., was bombed.
July 4: A British Airlines office was bombed in New York City.
July 5: Police in New York City discovered undetonated time bombs beneath five squad cars.
July 6: A bomb exploded in a drug store in Kansas City, Mo.
July 6: The National Shawmut Bank was firebombed in Boston.
July 7: A pipe bomb exploded at the Haitian consulate in New York City, injuring three people.
July 7: The Portuguese Travel and Information Agency was bombed in New York City.
July 7: A bombing attempt failed at the South African consulate in New York City.
July 7: An Atlas missile replica was bombed at the World's Fair Grounds in New York City.
July 7: The offices of the Southeastern Community Organizations were firebombed in Chicago.
July 9: In Columbia, members of the National Liberation Army kidnapped former Foreign Minister Londono y Londono. He was released on July 19, 1970.
July 11: Twelve businesses were firebombed in Charleston, W.Va.
July 12: A person seeking political shelter hijacked a Saudi Arabian airliner from Lebanon to Syria.
July 12: A branch office of the Bank of America was bombed in Palo Alto, Calif.
July 14: A Marine Corps recruiting office was firebombed in New York City.
July 14: The offices of the Tri-City Human Relations Council were firebombed in Chicago.
July 15: An explosion occurred near the Chase Manhattan Bank in New York City.
July 16: Two teenagers were killed and a policeman was wounded during five days of racial disorders in Lawrence, Kan.
July 16: A Selective Service office was firebombed in South St. Paul, Minn.
July 16: A Marine Corps recruiting office was firebombed in Brooklyn.
July 17: Two police officers were killed by sniper fire in Chiacgo.
July 18: A draft board office was firebombed in Des Plaines, Ill.
July 21: Five days of looting and vandalism occurred in New Brunswick, N.J.
July 21: In Teoponte, Bol., Ejercito de Liberacion National (ELN) terrorists kidnapped two West German technicians, burning the U.S.-owned South American Placers, Inc., a gold mining firm, and demanding that the government release ten prisoners within forty-eight hours. On July 22 the demands were met, and the technicians were released unharmed.
July 21: A branch office of the Bank of America was bombed in San Diego.
July 22: An Olympic Airlines plane en route to Greece was hijacked by six Arab guerrillas who demanded and obtained the release of eight other Arab guerrillas by the Greek government. The hijackers and liberated terrorists flew to Cairo, Egypt. The Palestinian Popular Struggle Front claimed responsibility.
July 22: Two police vehicles were bombed in New York City.
July 23: A firebomb exploded at police headquarters in Wellesley, Mass.
July 23: The headquarters of the highway patrol was bombed in Oakland, Calif.
July 24: The attempted kidnapping of Doner Lyon, U.S. consul in Recife, Braz., was foiled by police; three terrorists were arrested.
July 25: In Mexico an airliner was hijacked to Cuba.
July 25: A Mexican airplane was hijacked and taken to Cuba by three Dominican Republic nationals and one Mexican.
July 26: Continental Telephone Company president Phillip Lucier was killed when his car exploded in St. Louis, Mo.
July 26: A power transformer was sabotaged at the Camp McCoy Army Base in Sparta, Wisc.
July 27: Members of the Weather Underground bombed a branch office of the Bank of America, in the Wall Street district of New York City.
July 27: Members of the Weather Underground bombed a display missile at the Presidio military installation near San Francisco.
July 27: Twenty-five people were injured, including ten police officers, during a riot following the cancellation of a rock concert in Chicago.

July 27: A bank and a market were firebombed in Houston after the fatal shooting of People's Party member Carl Hampton.
July 27: A power station and a telephone exchange were bombed by three soldiers in Sparta, Wis.
July 28: The offices of the Associated Testing Labs was firebombed in Houston, Tex.
July 29: Looting and mass vandalism occurred in a Puerto Rican neighborhood in Hartford, Conn.
July 29: Nineteen blacks were arrested by state police as sniper fire lasted three days in New Bedford, Mass.
July 30: Members of a Weather Underground faction firebombed the Alameda County Courthouse in Oakland, Calif.
July 30: Members of the Black Panthers attempted to destroy the power lines of an electric railroad in Chicago.
July 31: Daniel A. Mitrione, U.S. public safety adminstrator, Aloisio Mares Dias Gomide, Brazilian consul, and Claude Fly, U.S. agricultural ambassador, were kidnapped in a series of Tupamaros raids in Uruguay. The kidnappers' demands were not met, the President of Uruguay refused to negotiate, and Mitrione's body was found on Aug. 10. Dias Gomide was released six months later.
July 31: A Tupamaros attempt to kidnap Michael Gordon Jones, secretary to the U.S. embassy in Montevideo, failed when Jones escaped by throwing himself from the back of a pickup truck into which he had been tossed in Montevideo. Cultural attaché Nathan Rosenfeld eluded capture.
August: In Uruguay a public safety officer for the U.S. Agency for International Development was held by Tupamaros while his car was commandeered for a bank robbery. He was later released.
Aug. 1: A Puerto Rican man was killed in Hartford, Conn., precipitating three days of rioting.
Aug. 1: Members of the Revolutionary Affinity Group 6 claimed responsibility for bombing the office of the Bank of Brazil in New York City.
Aug. 2: In the U.S., a 747 Pan American World Airways jet was hijacked to Cuba.
Aug. 6: Three days of racial disorders followed the fatal shooting of a black woman in Lima, Ohio.
Aug. 6: A branch office of the Bank of America was firebombed in Placentia, Calif.
Aug. 7: Claude Fly, U.S. agricultural adviser, was kidnapped by Tupamaros and released to a physician on Mar. 2, 1971, after he had a heart attack.
Aug. 7: Four people, including Superior Court Judge Harold Haley were killed in a courtroom shootout in Marin County, Calif., during the Soledad Brother trial.
Aug. 8: A Czech airplane flying to Austria was hijacked by three men who sought political asylum.
Aug. 8: A Selective Service office was firebombed in Dundalk, Md.
Aug. 11: A Selective Service office was firebombed in Portland, Ore.
Aug. 13: A police detective was shot to death by sniper fire on the South Side of Chicago.
Aug. 15: Following an assassination attempt on Paraguay's President Stroesser, more than 100 students were arrested.
Aug. 17: A Selective Service center was damaged by a dynamite explosion in Minneapolis, Minn.
Aug. 17: A police officer in Omaha, Neb., was killed by a Black Panther bomb.
Aug. 18: A man named Leon Zelwanski, seeking to avenge the death of 250 relatives during WWII, fired four shots at two German consulate attaches in New York City.
Aug. 19: In Poland five people seeking political asylum hijacked a Polish airliner to Denmark.
Aug. 19: A Trans-Carribean Airways jet in the U.S. was hijacked to Cuba.
Aug. 20: In the U.S. a flight out of Atlanta was successfully hijacked to Cuba.
Aug. 20: A police officer was shot to death in Berkeley, Calif., by a man who casually approached him on a street.
Aug. 21: A campus building was firebombed at the University of Oregon in Eugene.
Aug. 22: A National Guard vehicle was firebombed in Baltimore.
Aug. 24: A TWA jet in the U.S. was hijacked to Cuba.
Aug. 24: A physics researcher was killed when a bomb exploded at a University of Wisconsin Research Center in Madison.
Aug. 25: District Court Judge Fred Nelson was injured by a car-bomb explosion in Tulsa, Okla.
Aug. 25: A firebomb exploded at the police headquarters in Burlington, Mass.
Aug. 28: A bomb exploded at the JFK School of Government in Cambridge, Mass.
Aug. 28: A National Guard installation was firebombed in Walnut Creek, Calif.
Aug. 29: A police sergeant was shot to death after being lured to an isolated area at a public park in Philadelphia.
Aug. 29: A branch office of the Bank of America was firebombed in Berkeley, Calif.
Aug. 29: The Portuguese embassy and the Rhodesian Information office in Washington, D.C., were bombed by members of the Revolutionary Action Party.
Aug. 29: A firebomb exploded at a courthouse in Walnut Creek, Calif.
Aug. 30: Two police officers were wounded by unprovoked gunfire while on patrol in Philadelphia.
Aug. 30: Terrorists attempted to bomb the Portuguese embassy in Washington, D.C.
Aug. 31: In Turkey, a U.S. Air Force facility in Ankara, the Tuslog Detachment 30, was bombed.
Aug. 31: In Algeria, a plane hijacked by three armed Algerians seeking political asylum was flown to Albania. After authorities refused to let it land, the airliner was taken to Yugoslavia.
Aug. 31: Three Philadelphia police officers were wounded during a raid on the home of three Black Panther Party members.
Sept. 1: A terrorist named Susan Saxe robbed the Bell Federal Savings and Loan at gunpoint in Philadelphia.
Sept. 4: An oil storage depot was bombed in St. Paul, Minn.
Sept. 5: A bomb exploded at the police department in Dewitt, Iowa.
Sept. 5: A bomb exploded at the Hall of Justice in Los Angeles.
Sept. 5: Terrorists attempted to bomb the Orange County Courthouse in Santa Ana, Calif.
Sept. 6: Terrorists attempted to bomb the police station in Fitchburg, Mass.
Sept. 6: PFLP terrorists hijacked three airliners. One plane was blown up in Cairo after the passengers were evacuated, and two landed at Dawson Field in the Jordanian desert. An attempt to hijack an El Al Israel aircraft flying from London to Amsterdam was foiled when terrorist Patrick Arguello was killed by a security guard.
Sept. 8: Security guards stopped an attempt by ELF terrorists to hijack an Ethiopian airliner in Athens.
Sept. 8: Terrorists failed in their attempt to sabotage an El Al Israel Airline office in Athens.
Sept. 9: A BOAC VC-10 was commandeered by PFLP terrorists and taken to Jordan, where a total of 300 hostages, from other hijacked planes as well, were being held in the desert. On Sept. 12, the three captured planes were blown up. By Sept. 30 all of the hostages were released.
Sept. 9: In Argentina, the U.S. Information Service office in Córdoba was raided and bombed by three armed men.
Sept. 9: Seven people died and others were injured when an arson fire destroyed an old-age home in West Germany.
Sept. 9: A firebomb exploded near the office of an underground newspaper in Madison, Wis.
Sept. 10: A firebomb exploded at the ROTC building on the campus of the University of Florida at Gainsville.
Sept. 11: The Esso Standard Oil offices in Uruguay were robbed of $1,800 by terrorists.
Sept. 12: In the United Kingdom, JDL terrorists announced that they had captured three Egyptian embassy employees and would not release them until the Jordanian airlines passengers (see Sept. 6 and 9) were released.
Sept. 13: Members of the Weather Underground aided the escape of Timothy Leary from the San Luis Obispo Mens' Colony in California.
Sept. 14: Seeking political asylum, a Hungarian group forced a Romanian airliner to fly to Munich.
Sept. 15: A lone gunman failed in his attempt to hijack a Los Angeles-bound flight to North Korea.
Sept. 18: A police officer was shot to death by an unprovoked assailant while he was on patrol in Toledo, Ohio.
Sept. 19: A flight out of Pittsburgh was successfully hijacked to Cuba.
Sept. 19: A firebomb exploded at a National Guard armory in Newburyport, Mass.
Sept. 20: Terrorists Susan Saxe and Katherine Ann Power were charged with robbing a National Guard armory in Newburyport, Mass.
Sept. 22: A man wanted for robbery and murder was arrested as he attempted to hijack a plane in Boston.
Sept. 23: A Brighton, Mass., police officer was shot to death during a bank robbery committed by five terrorists. The group included Susan Saxe.
Sept. 24: Offices of the Japanese and Kuwaiti governments were bombed in New York City.
Sept. 25: Members of the Weather Underground bombed an Army recruiting station in the Bronx.
Sept. 26: A bomb exploded near the Ivory Coast mission to the U.N., in New York City.
Sept. 30: A police officer was shot while on patrol in Atlantic City, N.J.
Oct. 1: A bomb exploded at the police headquarters in Kearney, N.J.
Oct. 2: Outside the U.S. Air Force commissary in Izmir, Turk., an explosive device was discharged.
Oct. 2: A bomb exploded in a campus building at the University of Oregon in Eugene.
Oct. 3: In Ankhara, Turkey CENTO headquarters were bombed; there were no injuries.
Oct. 3: A firebomb exploded at the U.S. Mint in Denver.
Oct. 5: In Canada, FLQ terrorists kidnapped Quebec Province British trade minister James R. Cross. The Canadian government refused their demands. On Oct. 10 FLQ members captured Pierre LaPorte, Quebec's minister of labor. Their demands were again rejected. On Oct. 18 LaPorte's corpse was found in the trunk of a car. More than 500

suspects were arrested. Cross was released unharmed on Dec. 3. LaPorte's abductors were later arrested, tried, and sentenced to life imprisonment.
Oct. 5: Members of the Weather Underground bombed the Haymarket statue in Chicago.
Oct. 5: A bomb exploded in a campus building at the Bluefield State College in West Virginia.
Oct. 6: An undetonated bomb was discovered under the car of a U.S. Air Force member who lived nearby in Ankara, Turk.
Oct. 6: Letter bombs addressed to the Israeli Embassy and an El Al Israel Airline office were intercepted in London.
Oct. 6: A PLO office was bombed in New York City.
Oct. 6: A bomb exploded at a state office building in Annapolis, Md.
Oct. 7: Racial violence followed the shooting of a black youth in Pontiac, Mich.
Oct. 8: The offices of the Ford Motor Company were bombed in Santiago, Chile.
Oct. 8: Members of the Weather Underground bombed the Marin County Courthouse in California.
Oct. 8: A bomb placed by members of the Perfect Park Home Garden Society exploded at a National Guard facility in Santa Barbara, Calif.
Oct. 8: A bomb placed by members of the Quarter Moon Society exploded at an ROTC office in Seattle.
Oct. 8: A bomb placed by members of members of Purple Sunshine failed to detonate at a University of California building in Berkeley.
Oct. 9: Iranian terrorists seeking the release of twenty-one prisoners held in that country hijacked an Iranian airliner and ordered it flown to Baghdad.
Oct. 10: A bomb exploded at the Long Island City Courthouse in New York.
Oct. 12: Five public buildings were bombed in Rochester, N.Y.
Oct. 14: A bomb placed by the Proud Eagle Tribe faction of the Weather Underground exploded at a Harvard University Library in Cambridge, Mass.
Oct. 15: A bomb placed by the Proud Eagle Tribe faction of the Weather Underground exploded at an MIT campus building in Cambridge, Mass.
Oct. 15: During the hijacking by two Lithuanians of a Soviet Aeroflot plane heading for Turkey, a flight attendant was slain and two crew members wounded. Tried on hijacking charges in May 1974, the two were released under a Turkish amnesty law.
Oct. 15: A letter bomb addressed to an Israeli trade exhibition was intercepted by authorities in West Berlin.
Oct. 16: In Buenos Aires the U.S. defense attaché's residence was firebombed and destroyed.
Oct. 17: A bomb exploded at the county courthouse in Worcester, Mass.
Oct. 18: A bomb exploded at the Stanford Research Institute in Irvine, Calif.
Oct. 19: For the second consecutive day, a bomb exploded at the Stanford Research Institute in Irvine, Caif.
Oct. 20: In Argentina bombs exploded at the Buenos Aires homes of two U.S. officials.
Oct. 22: Terrorists in Costa Rica hijacked an airliner and diverted it to Cuba. They demanded the release of four guerrillas in Nicaragua, Frente Sandinistande Liberacion Nacional (FSLN) members who were being held in Costa Rica. The guerrillas were freed and flew to Cuba along with the hijackers.
Oct. 22: A bomb exploded outside a church in San Francisco.
Oct. 22: A firebomb exploded at the city hall in Racine, Wis.
Oct. 24: A firebomb exploded at a post office in Norfolk, Va.
Oct. 24: A police officer was shot to death and another wounded in Detroit, near the office of the National Committee to Combat Fascism.
Oct. 24: Gangs of blacks dressed in military fatigues attacked the police headquarters three times over a two-day period in Cairo, Ill.
Oct. 25: A bomb exploded at the main post office in Washington, D.C.
Oct. 25: Terrorists attempted to bomb a university gymnasium in Berkeley, Calif.
Oct. 26: A branch office of the Bank of America was destroyed by fire at the University of California Irvine campus.
Oct. 27: Two Soviet students seeking political asylum hijacked an Aeroflot plane and ordered it flown to Turkey.
Oct. 27: A 14-year-old student threatened to exploded a hydrogen bomb in Orlando, Fla., if a $1 million ransom was not paid.
Oct. 28: A bomb exploded at the county courthouse in Stuart, Fla.
Oct. 29: Twenty-five people were injured in street fighting between blacks and whites in Trenton, N.J.
Oct. 29: A firebomb exploded at a Marine Air Station in El Toro, Calif.
Oct. 30 : In the U.S., a National Airlines jet was hijacked and flown to Cuba.
Oct. 30: Bombs exploded at two National Guard facilities in Queens, N.Y.
November: A kidnap attempt on U.S. Ambassador Douglas MacArthur II failed after at least one shot was fired at him and an axe was thrown through the rear window of his limousine.
Nov. 1: In Karachi, Pak., the Polish deputy foreign minister was assassinated by a Pakistani who drove a truck into an airport reception line.
Nov. 1: In the U.S., a United Air Lines flight was hijacked to Cuba.
Nov. 1: Bombs exploded at a newspaper office and a Selective Service center in Fresno, Calif.
Nov. 1: A firebomb exploded in an ROTC vehicle in Ann Arbor, Mich.
Nov. 5: Disputes over school desegregation policies led to violence in Henderson, N.C.
Nov. 6: At Tel Aviv's crowded central bus station, explosives killed two people and wounded twenty-four.
Nov. 7: Twelve stores were firebombed during racial disorders in Daytona Beach, Fla.
Nov. 8: A lumberyard owned by the leader of a vigilante group was burned in Cairo, Ill.
Nov. 12: Firebombs exploded at several Selective Service offices in Chicago.
Nov. 13: In the U.S., an Eastern Airlines plane was hijacked and taken to Cuba.
Nov. 14: Five bombs placed by members of the Armed Commandos of Liberation exploded in San Juan, P.R.
Nov. 18: White revolutionaries firebombed a police patrol car in St. Petersburg, Fla.
Nov. 21: Outside the fence of the U.S. embassy in Ankara, Turk., a dynamite charge was exploded.
Nov. 21: A bomb was found in the city hall of Portland, Ore.
Nov. 22: A bomb exploded at a National Guard armory in Whitefish Bay, Wis.
Nov. 23: Members of the Armed Commandos of Liberation bombed the Dominican consulate in San Juan, P.R.
Nov. 25: The JDL was the suspected in the bombings of the Aeroflot and Intourist offices in New York City.
Nov. 27: At the U.S. military installations in Ankara, Turk., a series of bombs were exploded.
Dec. 1: Capturing Eugene Beihl, honorary West German consul in San Sebastian, Spain, (ETA) terrorists said that Beihl's survival was dependent on the sentences meted out to fifteen Basques accused of murdering a chief of police. Beihl was released on Dec. 24. On Dec. 28 the Basques were sentenced, six of them to death. Generalissimo Franco commuted the death sentences two days later.
Dec. 1: The Montevideo, Braz., offices of the ITT Corporation were bombed by the Tupamaros.
Dec. 1: A bomb exploded in a campus building at the University of Oregon in Eugene.
Dec. 7: Giovanni Enrico Bucher, Swiss ambassador to Brazil in Rio de Janeiro, was captured by VPR and ALN terrorists who murdered his bodyguard. The Brazilian goverment met the kidnapper's demands to release seventy prisoners on Jan. 14, 1971. Bucher was released unharmed two days later.
Dec. 11: The offices of the Inter-American Development Bank in Montevideo, Urug., were attacked by vandals who stole documents and destroyed furniture.
Dec. 11: Three people were injured when an explosion occurred on the campus of the University of Kansas in Lawrence.
Dec. 14: An anti-poverty organization office was firebombed in Bridgeport, Conn.
Dec. 14: A bomb placed by the Movimento Independista Revolucionario Armada (MIRA) Puerto Rican militant organization exploded at the headquarters of General Electric in New York City.
Dec. 15: A bomb exploded in the ROTC offices at the University of Connecticut in Storrs.
Dec. 15: A firebomb exploded at a politician's office in Havana, Ill.
Dec. 15: A branch office of the Bank of America was bombed in Isla Vista, Calif.
Dec. 16: A bomb exploded at a Selective Service office in Hollywood, Fla.
Dec. 18: A bomb exploded at a Selective Service office in San Mateo, Calif.
Dec. 19: Bombs exploded at a San Francisco police station and housing authority office.
Dec. 19: A man was arrested in Tulsa, Okla., after failing in his attempt to hijack a plane to Cuba.
Dec. 22: A bomb exploded at a National Guard armory in Whitefish Bay, Wis.
Dec. 24: While attempting to dynamite the U.S. Air Force Tuslog Detachment 30 in Ankara, Turk., two Ankara University students were arrested.
Dec. 31: A bomb exploded near the Municipal Courthouse in El Monte, Calif.
Dec. 31: Three gunmen who were planning to hijack two planes in New York were apprehended following a bank robbery in Locust Valley, N.Y.

1971

Jan. 3: In the U.S., a National Airline aircraft was hijacked to Cuba.
Jan. 4: A bomb exploded at a military induction center in Oakland, Calif.
Jan. 5: A ROTC office was bombed on the campus of the Clairmont Men's College in California.
Jan. 5: A military induction facility was bombed in Oxnard, Calif.
Jan. 7: An explosion occurred at the headquarters of the Campfire Girls in Pomona, Calif.

Jan. 8: British ambassador to Uruguay, Geoffrey M. S. Jackson was kidnapped by Tupamaros. When the government rejected demands for the release of 150 prisoners, Jackson was held for eight months and was released on Sept. 9, three days after 106 of the prisoners escaped from jail.
Jan. 8: Jewish Defense League (JDL) terrorists were responsible for a bomb explosion in the Soviet cultural offices in Washington, D.C.
Jan. 12: Police in Winston-Salem, N.C., fought a gun battle with local Black Panther Party members.
Jan. 12: Firemen were pelted with rocks and bottles as they attempted to put out fires at two Black Panther buildings in New Orleans.
Jan. 12: A bomb exploded at the Chamber of Commerce office in Rolling Hills Estates, Calif.
Jan. 13: A police officer was wounded by members of the BLA in Hunters Point, Calif.
Jan. 15: Bombs exploded at two military recruiting stations in New York City.
Jan. 17: A firebomb exploded at the United Arab Republic mission in New York City.
Jan. 19: Two San Francisco police officers were wounded by BLA members.
Jan. 20: A hijacker named Richard LaPoint was apprehended in Sterling, Colo., after he parachuted with $50,000 ransom money from a flight from Las Vegas to Reno, Nev., that he had commandeered.
Jan. 21: Eritrean Liberation Front (ELF) members hijacked an Ethiopian airliner and ordered it flown to Libya.
Jan. 21: After three days of campus unrest at the University of Arizona, the mayor of Tuscon declared martial law.
Jan. 22: A Northwest Airlines jet in the U.S. was hijacked to Cuba.
Jan. 22: One person was killed when members of the Philippines People's Revolutionary Front bombed two U.S. branch offices in Manila.
Jan 23: A South Korean attempted to hijack a South Korean plane. His plans to get to North Korea ended as the plane made an emergency landing.
Jan. 23: Bombs were found on the grounds of both the U.S. embassy and the U.S. Information Service in Turkey.
Jan. 23: Rioting lasted two days in Belfast, Ire.
Jan. 25: Two molotov cocktails were thrown onto the balcony of the residence of a U.S. Foreign officer in Ankara, Turk.
Jan. 29: One person was killed when a bomb placed by members of the Chicano Liberation Front exploded at a Federal Building in Los Angeles.
Jan. 31: Fifty people were injured and ninety arrested during a clash between police and chicano demonstrators in East Los Angeles, Calif.
February: Three members of the Black Panther Party were convicted of killing a police lieutenant in High Point, N.C.
Feb. 1: A bomb placed by Jibril Front terrorists was discovered and defused on an El Al flight between London and Lod.
Feb. 2: An Indian Airlines plane was hijacked by two Kashmiri gunmen and taken to Pakistan. When their demands that the Indian government release thirty-six prisoners held in Kashmir were rejected, they freed the passengers and crew and blew up the aircraft.
Feb. 4: In the U.S. a Delta Airlines plane was hijacked to Cuba.
Feb. 4: A bomb placed by members of the Bay Bombers exploded at a military induction center in Oakland, Calif.
Feb. 4: The office of a civil rights lawyer was destroyed by an arsonist in Charlotte, N.C.
Feb. 5: A ROTC building was burned on the California campus of the University of Santa Barbara.
Feb. 5: Four days of racial violence began in Wilmington, N.C.
Feb. 6: A British soldier was killed in Belfast, Ire. His death was the first since troops were moved into the area in 1969.
Feb. 7: Windows were broken during a protest march on the campus of Stanford University in Palo Alto, Calif.
Feb. 8: Four sticks of dynamite were ignited in the apartment of a U.S. soldier in Turkey with no casualties.
Feb. 10: In Sweden, two Croatian emigrés took control of the Yugoslavian consulate in Gothenburg in an unsuccessful effort to trade the occupants for convicted terrorists in Yugoslav jails.
Feb. 10: Two people were shot during a campus protest at Stanford University in Palo Alto, Calif.
Feb. 12: Three police officers and a student were injured when protesters attacked a campus building at Columbia University in New York City.
Feb. 12: A firebomb exploded at a military recruiting office in Santa Cruz, Calif.
Feb. 13: Bombs exploded at two military offices in Atlanta.
Feb. 14: The files at a draft board were burned in Bristol, Pa.
Feb. 14: Twenty-one people were arrested following a violent clash between members of the Black Muslims and the Black Panthers in Atlanta.
Feb. 15: James Finlay, a U.S. Air Force security officer, was kidnapped by the Turkish People's Liberation Army (TPLA) while on his Ankara Air Station beat. No ransom demands were made, and Finlay was freed seventeen hours later.
Feb. 17: In Turkey, a bomb was detonated outside the U.S. Air Force Tuslog Detachment 29 in Istanbul; no damage resulted.
Feb. 17: A bomb exploded on the Milwaukee campus of the University of Wisconsin.
Feb. 19: In Istanbul, Turk., a U.S. Army passenger boat was damaged by an explosion.
Feb. 20: In Ankara, Turk., a plastic explosives device was found on the property of the U.S. Information Service. Although the fuse had been lit, the bomb had not exploded.
Feb. 22: Members of the Chicano Liberation Front bombed a realty office in Los Angeles.
Feb. 25: A man successfully hijacked a flight from San Francisco to Cuba.
Feb. 27: A bomb exploded at a municipal building in Berkeley, Calif.
Mar. 1: A bomb placed by members of the Weather Underground caused extensive damage after exploding in the Senate wing of the U.S. Capitol.
Mar. 1: Members of the Puerto Rican Resistance Movement bombed the New School for Social Research in New York City.
Mar. 1: Members of the Chicano Liberation Front failed in their attempt to bomb a bank in Vernon, Calif.
Mar. 2: A firebomb exploded at the Iraqi mission to the U.N. in New York City.
Mar. 3: An explosion destroyed an electrical transformer on the Santa Barbara campus of the University of California.
Mar. 3: A branch office of the Bank of America was bombed in Berkeley, Calif.
Mar. 4: Four U.S. servicemen stationed near Ankara, Turk., were kidnapped by five TPLA members. On Mar. 8, the kidnappers freed the four servicemen.
Mar. 5: A campus building was burned at the University of Hawaii in Honolulu.
Mar. 6: Guatemalan police official Colonel Delgado Villegas was shot to death after he had survived three other assassination attempts.
Mar. 8: In protest of the government's African policy, the Revolutionary Armed Action sabotaged a Portugese aircraft near Lisbon.
Mar. 8: Ten people were injured during the bombings of a ROTC office and government record center in St. Louis.
Mar. 8: Members of the Citizens' Commission to Investigate the FBI stole almost 800 documents from an FBI office in Media, Pa.
Mar. 8: A juvenile failed in his attempt to hijack a flight from Mobile, Ala., via New Orleans to Canada. He was arrested in Miami.
Mar. 9: A man was killed during a dispute between warring factions of the Black Panther Party in New York.
Mar. 9: A bomb exploded at the police headquarters at Fort Lupton, Calif.
Mar. 9: A bomb exploded in a campus building at Woodbury College in Los Angeles.
Mar. 10: Uraguayan Attorney General Berro Oribe was kidnapped by Tupamaro guerrillas. After being interrogated about governmental legal tactics, he was released thirteen days later.
Mar. 11: Two police officers and a student were killed during campus riots at the University of Puerto Rico in Rio Pedras.
Mar. 12: A bomb exploded at a police community-relations office in Portland, Ore.
Mar. 12: A bombing attempt failed on the California campus of the East Los Angeles Junior College.
Mar. 13: The branch office of Esso-Pappas was bombed by the Greek Militant Resistance in Athens, Gr.
Mar. 14: Fatah terrorists blew up fuel tanks in Rotterdam, Neth.
Mar. 15: The U.S. consulate in Ankara, Turk., was bombed by TPLA members.
Mar. 15: A bomb exploded at a Selective Service office in San Mateo, Calif.
Mar. 16: Members of the Weather Underground failed in their bombing attempt of the Hall of Justice in San Francisco.
Mar. 17: An ROTC classroom was damaged by fire on the campus of Cornell University, in Ithaca, N.Y.
Mar. 18: A bomb exploded at an Army recruiting office in Jacksonville, Fla.
Mar. 19: A laboratory was bombed at the Oakland Community College in Detroit.
Mar. 21: A campus building was burned at Tufts University in Medford, Mass.
Mar. 23: A bank on campus at the California Lutheran College in Los Angeles was bombed.
Mar. 23: A bomb exploded in a campus building at Wayne State Universty in Detroit.
Mar. 23: Members of the Weather Underground bombed the Mill Valley, Calif., branch office of the Bank of America.
Mar. 25: In the U.S. consulate in Izmir, Turk., a pipe bomb went off.
Mar. 25: At the Bull Computer Company, a General Electric Subsidiary in France, forty protestors threw molotov cocktails. The Movement of Youthward Brothers in War of the Palestinian People claimed credit for the assault.
Mar. 26: A bomb exploded at the Brooklyn Community College in New York.
Mar. 27: An electric power station was burned in Baltimore.
Mar. 27: A bomb exploded at a Firestone plant in Riverview, Mich.
Mar. 28: A bombing attempt failed at a gas and electric utility center in Dundalk, Md.
Mar. 30: A Philippine Air Lines domestic flight was hijacked by six

members of Kabataang Makabayan, a leftist student group, and was ordered flown to Peking, China.
Mar. 30: Members of the Secret Cuban Government bombed the offices of the Cuban Health Exchange in New York City.
Mar. 30: The firebombing of the courthouse failed, during the trial of Lieutenant William Calley at Fort Benning, Ga.
Mar. 30: Bombs exploded at the city hall and the police station in Bradford, Pa.
Mar. 30: Members of the Black Liberation Army (BLA) attempted to bomb a police station in San Francisco.
Mar. 31: In the U.S., an Eastern Airlines jet was hijacked to Cuba.
Mar. 31: A lone gunman failed in his attempt to hijack a flight from Birmingham to Cuba.
Mar. 31: Terrorists attempted to bomb a police station in San Francisco.
Mar. 31: A firebomb exploded at a minority recruiting office in Denver.
Mar. 31: A letter bomb exploded at a government office building in Boston.
Apr. 1: Former Bolivian Secret Service agent Roberto Quintanilla was shot to death by members of the Ejercito Liberacion Nacional (ELN).
Apr. 1: A bomb exploded at city hall in Los Angeles.
Apr. 2: Terrorist Fedayeen members in Jordan damaged a pipeline transporting crude oil to the Zarka refinery. The Arabian-American Oil Corporation owned the pipeline.
Apr. 2: Near the CENTO secretariat building in Ankara, Turk., five smoking bombs were found. Four Turks hurled two black powder bombs into the U.S. Officers Open Mess in Ankara.
Apr. 3: A branch office of the Bank of America was firebombed in Los Angeles.
Apr. 3: A firebomb exploded at the campus police headquarters of the University of Oklahoma in Norman.
Apr. 5: A man successfully hijacked a plane from Key West, Fla., to Cuba.
Apr. 6: A branch office of the Bank of America was bombed again in Los Angeles.
Apr. 6: A bomb exploded at a branch office of the Bank of America in San Jose, Calif.
Apr. 7: In Sweden, the Yugoslavian ambassador was murdered by Croatian terrorists. Two Yugoslav diplomats in Stockholm were injured.
Apr. 8: The administration building at the University of California in Santa Cruz was destroyed by arsonists.
Apr. 8: A bomb exploded at a county courthouse in Fresno, Calif.
Apr. 10: A firebomb exploded at a power station in Stanford, Calif.
Apr. 12: A bomb allegedly placed by Black Revolutionary members exploded at the South African consulate in New York City.
Apr. 13: A New York City bank manager and thirteen others were held hostage, as three gunmen stole $400,000 from the Community National Bank at Fort Hamilton.
Apr. 14: The home of the Uruguayan naval attachè in Buenos Aires, Arg., was attacked by ERP terrorists.
Apr. 14: The campus police station was firebombed at Stanford University in Palo Alto, Calif.
Apr. 15: Sixty-seven members of the Black Student Union were arrested during a sit-in on the Gainsville campus of the University of Florida.
Apr. 15: A bomb exploded at a draft board in Los Angeles.
Apr. 17: A Black Panther Party member was shot and an office burned in New York, during a feud between warring East and West Coast factions.
Apr. 19: A bomb exploded at the South African Tourist Corporation in New York City.
Apr. 19: Two police officers were shot as they attempted to question three BLA members in New York City.
Apr. 20: A firebomb exploded at a draft board in Richfield, Minn.
Apr. 21: A lone gunman was umsuccessful in his attempt to hijack a flight from Newark to Italy.
Apr. 21: A Selective Service office was bombed in Fresno, Calif.
Apr. 22: Equipment was stolen from a Parke-Davis laboratory by ERP terrorists in La Plata, Argentina.
Apr. 22: Seven members of the JDL bombed a Soviet trade agency in New York City.
Apr. 23: Members of the Chicano Liberation Front bombed a parole office in Fresno, Calif.
Apr. 23: A bomb exploded in the president's office on the campus of Stanford University.
Apr. 24: A bomb exploded at a National Guard armory in Youngstown, Ohio.
Apr. 25: Firebombs exploded at the ROTC building at Claremont College and the administration building at adjacent Pomona College, in Claremont, Calif.
Apr. 26: A firebomb exploded in the president's office at Harvey Mudd College in Clairmont, Calif.
Apr. 27: U.S. business offices were bombed by ERP terrorists in Rosario, Arg.
Apr. 30: A draft board was bombed in Braintree, Mass.
May 1: Members of the People's Revolutionary Party bombed a branch office of the Bank of America in Santa Cruz, Calif.
May 2: Authorities evicted 30,000 protesters from a public park in Washington, D.C., shortly before a massive demonstration.
May 3: More than 2,000 anti-war demonstrators were arrested during a massive rally in Washington, D.C.
May 4: Another 2,000 anti-war demonstrators were arrested by authorities in Washington, D.C.
May 4: At the Tuslog Department 30 airman's quarters in Ankara, Turk., a bomb was detonated. There were no casualties.
May 4: A firebomb exploded at a post office in Los Angeles.
May 4: A branch office of the Bank of America survived a firebombing attempt in San Bruno, Calif.
May 5: More than 1,000 anti-war protesters were arrested by authorities in Washington, D.C.
May 5: Student riots occurred on the College Park campus of the University of Maryland.
May 5: Students rioted on the Madison campus of the University of Wisconsin.
May 5: Seventy-six anti-war demonstrators were arrested in San Francisco.
May 5: A building was firebombed on the Tempe campus of Arizona State University.
May 5: A bombing attempt failed at a bank in Boulder, Colo.
May 5: A firebomb exploded at a Federal building in Kansas City, Kan.
May 6: More than 125 protesters were arrested during an anti-war demonstration in Boston.
May 6: A firebomb exploded at a military recruiting center in Burlingame, Calif.
May 6: One person was killed and another injured when a bomb exploded at an ammunition depot in Hawthorne, Nev.
May 6: A campus bombing attempt failed at the Cuyahoga Community College in Cleveland.
May 6: A bomb exploded at a power station in Monte Vista, Calif.
May 7: The National Guard was reactivated to quell student anti-war demonstrations on the College Park campus of the University of Maryland.
May 7: Members of SDS allegedly bombed the City Civic Center in Iowa City, Iowa.
May 7: Stinkbombs exploded at the South Vietnameses government offices in San Francisco.
May 8: A bomb exploded at a social services agency in Los Angeles.
May 9: A bomb was discovered near the Greensboro home of the president of the A & T State University of North Carolina.
May 11: Three banks were bombed in Los Angeles.
May 11: Military vehicles were firebombed in Baltimore.
May 12: Bolivian peasants abducted the manager of a U.S.-owned gold mine and swapped him for a tractor with which to make roads.
May 12: A bomb exploded in the car of the county school superintendant in West Palm Beach, Fla.
May 13: Three police officers were wounded by sniper fire on the South Side of Chicago.
May 15: Police and demonstrators clashed at an anti-war rally near the Berkeley campus of the University of California.
May 17: Ephraim Elrom, the Israeli consul general in Istanbul, Turk., was kidnapped by the Turkish People's Liberation Front (TPLF). Their demand for the release of all guerrillas being held by the government was turned down. Elrom's body was found in an apartment on May 23. Two of the kidnappers were killed in gunfights with the police.
May 19: Two police officers were lured into a Black Liberation Army ambush in New York City.
May 19: A firebomb and a smokebomb exploded at an office building in Syracuse, N.Y.
May 20: A firebomb exploded at an IBM division office in San Jose, Calif.
May 20: Terrorists attempted to bomb a police station in Washington, D.C.
May 21: Two police officers were killed by members of the Black Liberation Army during an ambush in New York City.
May 22: A police officer was killed by a guerrilla land mine in South-West Africa.
May 22: After four days of disturbances, a firebomb exploded at a National Guard armory in Kent, Ohio.
May 23: Stanley Sylvester, a Swift & Co. exeuctive in Rosario, Arg., was kidnapped by ERP terrorists. Their demands for the company to donate $62,500 worth of clothing, food, and school supplies were met and Sylvester was freed on May 30.
May 23: A branch office of the Bank of America was firebombed in Oakland, Calif.
May 25: A bomb exploded at the Pacific Gas and Electric Company in Walnut Creek, Calif.
May 26: A bomb exploded in a J.N.F. office in Rio De Janeiro, Braz.
May 27: A Romanian national airlines plane was hijacked by six armed people and taken to Vienna, Aust., where the hijackers demanded political sanctuary.
May 28: In Turkey, the Israeli Counsul General was killed by members of the Turkish Liberation Army.
May 28: A dynamite time bomb was discovered shortly before detonation near a sheriff's office in Bedford Park, Ill.
May 28: A lone hijacker was arrested and deported after he diverted a flight from Miami to Nassau.
May 29: The French consul in Spain, Henri Wolimer, fled and resisted a kidnapping attempt by Basque nationalists.

May 29: Bombs exploded at two Tucson branches of the Southern Arizona Bank and Trust Company.
June 2: In Cordoba, Arg., members of the ERP failed in a kidnapping attempt of Uraguayan Consul Raul Guerra.
June 3: A bomb exploded at the United California Bank in El Sereno, Calif.
June 4: A lone hijacker failed in his attempt to divert a Charleston-Newark flight to Israel.
June 5: One person was killed when members of the Black Liberation Army attempted to hold up a night club in New York City.
June 6: A bomb exploded at a branch office of the Wells Fargo Bank in Menlo Park, Calif.
June 7: In Bolivia, the head of the Volcan metallurgy company, Swiss industrialist Alfred Kuser, was kidnapped and ransomed by his firm, which paid approximately $40,000 for his release on June 9.
June 10: A bomb explosion damaged a branch office of the Bank of America in Petaluma, Calif.
June 11: An Israeli tanker was bombed by four PFLP terrorists off the coast of South Yemen in the straits of Bab el Mandeb.
June 11: A passenger was killed as a man failed in his attempt to hijack a plane from Chicago to North Vietnam.
June 13: A bomb exploded at the Mexican government tourist office in Los Angeles. The explosion was in retaliation for the deaths of six students in Mexico City riots.
June 16: A bombing attempt was discovered at a government building in Santa Cruz, Calif.
June 17: In what emerged as the Watergate scandal, five men were arrested as they attempted to burglarize the offices of the Democratic National Committee in Washington, D.C.
June 18: A man was arrested and charged with air piracy in Winston-Salem, N.C., after he failed to hijack a plane to Cuba.
June 18: A New York City bank was robbed by members of the BLA.
June 21: Terrorists attempted to bomb the city council chambers in San Jose, Calif.
June 22: President Torres of Bolivia survived a coup attempt.
June 22: Members of the JDL bombed Soviet property in Glen Cove, N.Y.
June 23: In Uruguay, Organization of the Popular Revolution-33 (OPR-33) terrorists captured Alfredo Cambon, legal counselor to several U.S.-backed companies. He was freed on June 25.
June 24: A branch office of the Bank of America was bombed in Oakland, Calif.
June 24: A bomb exploded at the Essex County Corrections Center in North Caldwell, N.J.
June 25: A Selective Service office was firebombed in Freeport, N.Y.
June 26: Four prisoners in Buenos Aires were rescued by guerrilla members of the Eva Peron Commando.
June 26: A bomb exploded at the Security Pacific National Bank in Los Angeles.
June 27: A bomb exploded at the National Bank of Detroit.
July: A bomb placed by members of the Secret Cuban Government, exploded at a theater in New York City.
July 3: A bomb exploded at a military training center in Beverly Hills, Calif.
July 4: A bomb exploded at a federal office building in San Jose, Calif.
July 8: Esso-Pappas property was bombed in Athens, Gr.
July 8: An Essex Corporation plant was firebombed in Londonderry, Ire.
July 8: A bomb placed by members of the Chicano Liberation Front exploded at the Pan American National Bank in East Los Angeles, Calif.
July 9: A bomb exploded at the city hall of Providence, R.I.
July 9: A bomb exploded at a draft board in San Diego, Calif.
July 14: Argentine industrialist Jorge Berembau was kidnapped by Tupamaro terrorists in Montevideo. Although the kidnappers demanded a huge ransom, Berembau was released without a payment on Nov. 26, 1971.
July 20: Fatah terrorists attacked the Rome office of Alia, the Jordanian airline.
July 23: Fatah terrorists threw Molotov cocktails into the Jordanian embassy in Paris.
July 23: A man was killed as he attempted to hijack a New York bound flight to Italy.
July 24: In the U.S., a National Airlines plane was hijacked and flown to Cuba.
July 24: A Jordanian Alia airliner was bombed by Fatah terrorists while on the ground at the airport in Cairo, Egypt.
July 24: A bomb exploded at a National Guard armory in Santa Cruz, Calif.
July 25: JDL terrorists planted a bomb which demolished a Soviet embassy official's car.
July 26: Nine imprisoned Black Panther Party members took two guards hostage, as they staged a prison uprising in New Orleans.
July 27: The Jordanian Embassy in Paris was bombed by members of the Fatah terrorist organization.
July 28: Israeli officials in Tel Aviv, Isr., intercepted a bomb given to an unsuspecting girl by Popular Front for the Liberation of Palestine-General Command (PFLP-GC) terrorists; it was supposed to explode on an El Al aircraft.
July 28: A bomb exploded at a courthouse in Torrance, Calif.
July 28: A branch office of the Bank of America was bombed in Ben Lomond, Calif.
July 30: Thirty-eight female prisoners were freed by Tupamaro guerrillas from the Montevideo jail in Argentina.
July 30: A bomb placed by members of the JDL exploded at a travel agency in Beverly Hills, Calif.
August: Two Al Fatah terrorists hijacked a flight to Algeria.
August: A unknown gunman wounded a security guard at a nuclear power plant in Vernon, Vt.
August: An Atlanta police officer was shot to death and a bank was robbed by twenty members of the Black Liberation Army operating out of a farmhouse in Fayetteville, Ga.
Aug. 9: Twelve people were killed and 300 were arrested during a dawn raid by British troops in Northern Ireland. More than 150 homes were burned in the subsequent rioting.
Aug. 10: A firebomb exploded in a campus building at the University of Californai in Berkeley.
Aug. 11: Members of the JDL bombed a trucking company in New York City.
Aug. 12: A branch office of the Bank of America was bombed in Pittsburg, Calif.
Aug. 16: Rumors of police brutality sparked eight days of violence in the Puerto Rican neighborhood of Camden, N.J.
Aug. 18: Two police officers were killed, and an officer and FBI agent wounded during a raid on the residence of the Republic of New Africa leader, in Jackson, Miss.
Aug. 18: A bomb exploded at the headquarters of the Black Panther Party in Cleveland.
Aug. 19: A police officer was hit by sniper fire in Corpus Christi, Texas.
Aug. 20: Twenty people were arrested as they attempted to raid a Selective Service office in Camden, N.J.
Aug. 21: Soledad Brother George Jackson, as well as two other inmates and two prison guards, died in a shootout as a prison escape failed at San Quentin.
Aug. 22: Nine firebombs placed by members of the Movimiento Independisto Revolucionario Armado (MIRA) Puerto Rican Independence Group exploded at grocery stores in New York City.
Aug. 23: Members of the Black Liberation Army robbed the Bankers Trust Company in Queens, N.Y.
Aug. 24: A firebomb exploded at a federal building in Hammond, Ind.
Aug. 24: In Madrid, Spain, an Al Fatah bomb damaged a Jordanian airliner.
Aug. 27: A firebomb allegedly placed by members of the Chicano Liberation Front exploded at a real estate office in Los Angeles.
Aug. 28: Members of the Weather Underground bombed the Department of Corrections office in San Francisco, and the office of California Prisons in Sacramento.
Aug. 28: Two Black Liberation Army members were arrested in San Francisco after they attempted to ambush a patrol car with machine guns.
Aug. 29: A San Francisco Police Department desk sergeant was shot to death. Members of the Black Liberation Army were suspected of the killing.
Aug. 29: A bomb reportedly placed by members of the Weather Underground exploded at a bank in San Francisco.
Aug. 29: A bomb placed by members of the Chicano Liberation Front exploded at a branch office of the Bank of America in Vernon, Calif.
Aug. 30: Firebombs placed by six members of the Ku Klux Klan (KKK) exploded beneath ten school buses in Pontiac, Mich.
September: In Cambodia, terrorists threw explosives onto a softball diamond. Two U.S. embassy employees were killed and ten were injured.
September: Near the U.S. embassy in Cambodia, a bicycle bomb was thrown at Ambassador Emory Swank's car; it did not explode.
Sept. 1: Israeli security intercepted a bomb that was intended to explode on an El Al aircraft flying from London to Tel Aviv.
Sept. 1: Two classrooms of a desegregated school were damaged by dynamite bombs in Columbus, Ga.
Sept. 2: A bombing attempt failed in a barracks building at Fort Bragg, N.C.
Sept. 3: A lone hijacker failed in his attempt to divert a flight from Chicago to Cuba.
Sept. 4: Eight firebombs exploded at a desegregated school in Kannapolis, N.C.
Sept. 5: Eight police officers were injured during two days of violence in the Puerto Rican neighborhood of Hoboken, N.J.
Sept. 6: ERP guerrilla rescued seventeen prisoners from a Tucuman, Arg., jail.
Sept. 6: Tupamaro guerrillas freed 106 inmates from a Montevideo, Arg., maximum security prison.
Sept. 7: A time bomb placed by a man named Ronald Kaufman exploded prematurally at a branch office of the Bank of America in San Francisco.
Sept. 8: A Jordanian Alia airliner was hijacked and diverted to Libya by Al Fatah.
Sept. 9: The Trans-Arabian Pipeline in Jordan was damaged three times in two months by the Fedayeen.
Sept. 9: A black student was killed and three police officers were

wounded during two days of racial violence in Lubbock, Texas.
Sept. 13: Thirty-two inmates and eleven guards were killed during a prison riot in Attica, N.Y.
Sept. 16: Al Fatah terrorists unsuccessfully attempted to hijack a Jordanian Alia flight en route to Beirut.
Sept. 17: A bomb placed by members of the Weather Underground exploded at the New York Deptartment of Corrections office in Albany.
Sept. 18: A police officer was shot to death as he directed traffic in Plainfield, N.J.
Sept. 19: Terrorists failed in their attempt to bomb a savings and loan office in Washington, D.C.
Sept. 20: Members of the Black Revolutionary Assault Team (BRAT) bombed the Zaire Mission to the United Nations in New York City.
Sept. 20: Members of BRAT attempted to firebomb the Malawi Mission to the United Nations in New York City.
Sept. 24: A molotov cocktail exploded at the Chase Manhattan Bank in New York City.
Sept. 24: A bomb placed by members of the Weather Underground exploded at the Chase Manhattan International Banking Corporation office in Los Angeles.
Sept. 24: Members of the Quarter Moon Tribe bombed a military recruiting center in Portland, Ore.
Sept. 24: Two members of the White Panthers attempted to hijack a flight from Detroit to Algeria.
Sept. 27: Mexican Civil Aviation Services Director Julio Hirschfeld was kidnapped by members of the Movimiento de Accion Revolucionario (MAR) guerrilla organization and ransomed for $250,000.
Sept. 29: Kurdish Democratic Party leader Mullah Barzani survived an assassination attempt in Iraq.
Oct. 3: A firebomb exploded at the ROTC building on the campus of Tampa University in Florida.
Oct. 4: A General Aviation pilot was shot to death as two men unsuccessfully attempted to hijack the flight from Nashville to the Bahamas. One hijacker committed suicide during the incident after killing his own wife.
Oct. 6: PLO leader Yasir Arafat survived an assassination attempt.
Oct. 7: Members of the Black Liberation Army reportedly robbed a branch office of the Fultan National Bank in Atlanta.
Oct. 9: A man successfully hijacked a flight from Detroit to Cuba.
Oct. 11: A bomb exploded at a branch office of the Wells Fargo bank in Santa Cruz, Calif.
Oct. 12: A car belonging to a U.S. consulate employee in Istanbul was bombed by Turkish terrorists.
Oct. 14: A Sinclair Oil pipeline was bombed in Columbia by members of the United Front for Guerrilla Action.
Oct. 14: A bomb exploded at the home of the Iranian consul in San Francisco.
Oct. 15: Members of the Proud Eagle faction of the Weather Underground bombed a MIT campus building in Boston.
Oct. 16: H. Rap Brown was shot twice as he attempted to hold up a bar in New York City.
Oct. 18: A member of the Canadian Hungarian Freedom Fighters Federation assaulted Soviet premier Aleksei N. Kosygin in Ottawa, Ontario.
Oct. 18: A man was arrested in Vancouver after he failed to hijack a flight from Anchorage to Cuba.
Oct. 18: Members of the JDL bombed a travel agency in Los Angeles.
Oct. 20: In the U.S. JDL terrorists rifled shots into an apartment containing Soviet delegation members to the United Nations.
Oct. 24: The Trans-Arabian pipeline was damaged by Fedayeen terrorists in Jordan.
Oct. 25: In the U.S., an American Airlines 747 plane was hijacked and flown to Cuba.
Oct. 29: A man and three youths successfully hijacked a plane to Cuba, after they had killed a ticket agent at an airport in Houston.
Oct. 31: A firebomb allegedly placed by members of SDS exploded in a college building in Nassau County, N.Y.
Oct. 31: Seven grocery stores were firebombed in Hoboken, N.J.
October: The offices of Coca-Cola were robbed by PGT/FAR terrorists in Guatemala.
Nov. 2: A bomb allegedly placed by members of the Weather Underground exploded at a branch office of the Bank of America in Los Angeles.
Nov. 3: In Brazil, molotov cocktails damaged the residences of officials of Swift & Co. and Chicago Bridge Company and a car of the U.S. consul general in São Paulo.
Nov. 3: A police officer was shot to death by alleged members of the Black Liberation Army in Atlanta.
Nov. 4: An arsonist attacked a nuclear power plant in Buchanan, N.Y.
Nov. 10: In Amman, Jor., four bombs exploded at the U.S.- managed Intercontinental Hotel, which had once been backed by U.S. funds.
Nov. 10: A bomb was planted at a National Guard armory in New York City.
Nov. 15: Members of the Sons of Liberty claimed credit for bombing a bank in Cambridge, Mass.
Nov. 17: A branch office of the Bank of America was firebombed in San Francisco.
Nov. 17: A bomb exploded at an induction center in Boise, Idaho.
Nov. 18: A bomb exploded at a bank in Deer Park, N.Y.
Nov. 18: A bomb exploded at the office of Honeywell Corporation in Wellesley, Mass.
Nov. 18: A firebomb exploded in a campus building at the University of Oklahoma in Norman.
Nov. 19: Coca-Cola plant owner and Guerrero Mexico University Rector Dr. Jaime Castrejon Diez was kidnapped. He was released on Dec. 1, 1971, for a $200,000 ransom and nine prisoners who were later transported to Cuba.
Nov. 22: Reputed members of the Puerto Rican Liberation Front firebombed a bank and an office building in Camden, N.J.
Nov. 22: A bomb exploded at the district attorney's office in San Bernadino, Calif.
Nov. 24: A train was blown up by a guerrilla bomb in Malawi, Mozambique.
Nov. 24: After hijacking a flight over Portland, Ore., a man using the alias D.B. Cooper parachuted from a plane with $200,000 ransom money.
Nov. 27: A TWA jet in the U.S. was hijacked to Cuba by three armed members of the Republic of New Africa.
Nov. 28: Wasfi Tal, the Prime Minister of Jordan, was assassinated by four terrorists from the Black September Organization (BSO).
Nov. 30: In Uruguay, French journalist Michele Ray said she had been abducted and held captive for thirty-eight hours by members of the OPR-33. Officials raised speculation that Ray had engineered her kidnapping to obtain interviews from the guerrillas.
Nov. 30: A bomb exploded in a classroom at the Nassau Community College in New York.
Nov. 30: A firebomb exploded at an Army Reserve building in Akron, Ohio.
Dec. 4: Fifteen people were killed when a UVF bomb exploded in a pub in Belfast, Ire.
Dec. 5: Members of the Jewish Armed Resistance bombed a Russian gift shop in New York City.
Dec. 6: Members of the Jewish Armed Resistance bombed a Russian gift shop in Shakopee, Minn.
Dec. 7: A bomb exploded at Stanford Linear Accelerator in California.
Dec. 12: Five prisoners, including three members of the Black Liberation Army, escaped from the DeKalb County jail in Atlanta.
Dec. 15: Members of the BSO in England tried to kill the Jordanian Ambassador, Zaid Rifai, in London.
Dec. 18: Five members of the East Coast Conspiracy to Save Lives were arrested as they attempted to pour concrete on railroad tracks in York, Pa.
Dec. 20: A bomb exploded at the police headquarters in Cambridge, Mass.
Dec. 21: Two police officers were injured when a hand grenade exploded during the pursuit of two Black Liberation Army members in New York City.
Dec. 22: Tupamaro guerrillas blew up a golf course in Punta Carretas, Arg.
Dec. 22: Alleged members of the Puerto Rican Liberation Front bombed two buildings in Camden, N.J.
Dec. 24: A man unsuccessfully attempted to hijack a plane in Minneapolis.
Dec. 26: In Canada, a solitary gunman hijacked an Air Canada jet and had it flown to Cuba after releasing the passengers in Toronto. The hijacker remained in Cuba and allowed the plane and crew to return.
Dec. 26: A man unsuccessfully attempted to hijack a plane in Chicago.
Dec. 28: Jibril terrorist letter bombs were intercepted by authorities in Austria. A policeman was wounded while attempting to defuse one of the bombs.
Dec. 31: Members of the Black Liberation Army and a rival Youth in Action militant group staged a shootout in Brooklyn, N.Y.
Dec. 31: Black Liberation Army member Frankie Fields was shot to death by FBI agents in Odessa, Fla.

1972

January: The home of a U.S. businessman was bombed in Guatemala.
January: The Kuwait Oil Company facilities were bombed.
Jan. 5: A State Correctional Services office was bombed in Buffalo, N.Y.
Jan. 6: Political activist Paula Tharp was wounded by Secret Army Organization snipers in San Diego.
Jan. 7: Bombs with nine-month timing devices were discovered in Chicago, New York, and San Francisco. Ronald Kaufman was arrested as the perpetrator on Jan. 13, 1972.
Jan. 7: A man and a woman successfully hijacked a flight from San Francisco to Cuba.
Jan. 10: Four people, including two police officers were killed during a shootout between Black Muslims and police in Baton Rouge, La.
Jan. 12: A man was arrested in Dallas after hijacking a plane in Houston and demanding $1 million and ten parachutes.
Jan. 16: During a terrorist attack in the Israeli-occupied Gaza strip, a U.S. nurse was killed and several people were injured.
Jan. 17: A bomb exploded at a Stanford University office in Palo Alto, Calif.
Jan. 19: Two members of the Black Liberation Army, carrying a large cache of weapons, were arrested in Philadelphia.
Jan. 20: A man was arrested near Denver after he had parachuted with $50,000 ransom money from a plane he hijacked in Las Vegas.

Jan. 22: In protest of Portuguese rule in Portuguese Guinea, a pipe bomb was detonated at the New York offices of the Portuguese airlines.
Jan. 26: The New York offices of the late Sol Hurok, a theatrical impresario who managed U.S. tours by Soviet performers, were bombed by JDL members.
Jan. 26: Merlyn St. George was shot to death by FBI agents, as he attempted to hijack a plane in Albany, N.Y.
Jan. 26: Twenty-six people died when Croatian emigres engineered the bombing and subsequent crash of an airliner en route from Sweden to Yugoslavia.
Jan. 26: A man failed in his attempt to hijack a helicopter in Berkeley, Calif.
Jan. 27: A bomb exploded in an Austrian train en route from Vienna to Zagreb, Yug., wounding six people. Croatian terrorists were suspected of the assault.
Jan. 27: Two New York City police officers were shot to death. Four members of the Black Liberation Army were named as suspects.
Jan. 27: A police officer was seriously wounded after stopping a vehicle for a minor traffic violation in New York City.
Jan. 29: British troops used rubber bullets and tear gas to disperse civil rights marchers in Dungannon, Ire.
Jan. 29: A man demanding the release of Angela Davis as ransom was wounded after hijacking a plane in Los Angeles.
Jan. 30: British troops killed thirteen protesters at a rally in Derry, Ire., in what came to be known as "Bloody Sunday."
February: Numerous objects, including a molotov cocktail were thrown at a police car in Modesto, Calif.
Feb. 2: The British embassy in Dublin was bombed by Irish militants.
Feb. 5: Machine gun fire from a car killed a British sailor on shore leave in Rio de Janeiro. A handbill signed by four Brazilian radicals was left behind to claim responsibility for the murder.
Feb. 5: Six Fatah-Black September terrorists sabotaged two gasoline storage installations in Holland.
Feb. 6: Near Cologne, West Germany five Jordanian workers who were thought to be spying for Israel were slain. The BSO was regarded as responsible.
Feb. 6: Two gas-processing plants in Rotterdam were blown up by Black September terrorists.
Feb. 8: A plant near Hamburg, Ger., which produced electrical generators for Israeli aircraft, was damaged; the BSO terrorists were suspected.
Feb. 16: A member of the Black Liberation Army was shot to death while he was resisting arrest in St. Louis.
Feb. 16: Bombs placed by members of the People's Liberation Army exploded at the police and fire departments in Manchester, N.H.
Feb. 19: A hijacking attempt aboard a Jordanian airliner destined for Amman was unsuccessful.
Feb. 22: At the Aldershot army base in England, an Irish Republican Army (IRA) bomb exploded, killing seven and wounding five. Two more later died.
Feb. 22: Five guerrillas, who identified themselves as members of the Organization for Victims of Zionist Occupation hijacked a Lufthansa German Airlines plane en route from New Delhi to Athens and ordered the jet flown to Aden, South Yemen. The next day, the passengers, crew, and jet were released. The West German government later said it had paid a $5 million ransom. The hijackers were not captured.
Feb. 22: Black September terrorists bombed an Esso Oil pipeline in Hamburg, Ger.
Feb. 27: Sniping and arson occurred in a neighborhood of Wilmington, N.C.
Feb. 28: A prison guard was stabbed to death in Trenton, N.J.
March: Members of the Secret Cuban Government bombed a theater in New York City.
March: Members of the Secret Cuban Government bombed two drug stores in San Juan, P.R.
Mar. 4: Two people were killed and 130 injured by a bomb which exploded at a crowded restaurant in Belfast, Ire.
Mar. 7: A bomb was discovered in a plane at Kennedy Airport in New York.
Mar. 7: Two men successfully hijacked a private plane from Miami to Cuba.
Mar. 7: A man failed in his attempt to hijack a flight from Tampa to Sweden.
Mar. 8: A bomb exploded in a TWA plane at the airport in Las Vegas.
Mar. 8: Two people were wounded and ten arrested during a day of racial violence in Key West, Fla.
Mar. 11: An attempt by Black September terrorists to attack King Hussein's London home failed.
Mar. 19: A man and a woman hijacked a private plane from Key West to Cuba.
Mar. 20: Six people were killed by a Provisional IRA bomb that exploded on a street in Belfast, Ire.
Mar. 21: In Argentina, Ejercito Revolucionario del Pueblo (ERP) terrorists kidnapped Oberdan Sallustro, the president of the Italian-owned Fiat of Argentina Company. Although Fiat met the ransom demand of $1 million, they were unable to meet the kidnappers' demands to free 50 guerrillas. In April, just before their capture by police, the terrorists executed Sallustro.
Mar. 27: In Turkey, three NATO radar technicians were kidnapped by TPLA members who demanded the release of three terrorists sentenced to death. When the government refused to negotiate with the abductors or to allow them safe conduct out of the country, and police surrounded their hideout, the terrorists murdered their hostages. Ten terrorists died in the battle that ensued.
Mar. 27: Members of the Commission to Demilitarize Industry and the Citizen's Commission to Investigate the FBI sabotaged an ammunition factory in York, Pa.
Mar. 29: Alleged members of the anti-Castro Cuban group JCN bombed a Russian ship off the coast of Biscayne, Fla.
Apr. 4: In Montreal, a bomb detonated in the Cuban Trade Office, with one person slain and seven others injured.
Apr. 7: A man was arrested in Provo, Utah, after he parachuted from a plane he had hijacked in Denver.
Apr. 9: A man who hijacked a plane in Oakland, Calif., was arrested upon landing in San Diego.
Apr. 13: A man surrendered to authorities after hijacking a plane to Los Angeles.
Apr. 14: A police officer was killed and five others wounded during a shootout with Black Muslims in New York City.
Apr. 17: Sixteen people were arrested following the occupation of a military recruiting office in San Francisco.
Apr. 17: A hijacker failed in his attempt to divert a flight from Seattle to Cairo.
Apr. 17: A man was arrested in Chicago after he had attempting to extort $500,000 during the hijacking of a Delta Airlines flight.
Apr. 17: Anti-war demonstrators clashed with police during a four-day protest at College Park, Md. The National Guard was called in on Apr. 20.
Apr. 18: A Czech airliner was hijacked by two Czechoslovakian miners and flown to Nuremberg, Ger., where they asked for political sanctuary.
Apr. 18: Offices at Harvard University were ransacked in Cambridge, Mass.
Apr. 18: A bomb exploded at an office building in Bellflower, Calif.
Apr. 20: A University Senate meeting at Columbia University in New York City was disrupted by 250 demonstrators.
Apr. 20: Offices were ransacked on the campus of Boston University.
Apr. 20: More than 150 Antioch College students were arrested for attempting to block the gates of an Air Force base in Dayton, Ohio.
Apr. 20: Black students began a week-long occupation of a campus building at Harvard University in Cambridge, Mass.
Apr. 21: Almost 100 demonstrators were arrested as they attempted to block the gates of an Air Force base in Chicopee, Mass.
Apr. 21: A large anti-war demonstration following the ransacking of the ROTC offices at the University of Michigan in Ann Arbor was dispersed by club-wielding police officers.
Apr. 21: Army Chief of Staff General William Westmoreland was struck by a tomato during an anti-war demonstration in El Paso, Texas.
Apr. 22: Students staged a twelve-hour occupation of the Woodrow Wilson School of International Affairs at Princeton University in Princeton, N.J.
Apr. 25: Students occupied the administration building at Reed College in Portland, Ore.
Apr. 26: Forty-two people were arrested as they attempted to blockade the Groton, Conn., submarine base.
Apr. 26: Students seized the library at Cornell University in Ithaca, N.Y.
Apr. 27: A campus building at the University of Pennsylvania was seized by 400 student demonstrators.
Apr. 29: Jibril Front letter bombs were sent to the Israeli pavilion at a fair in West Germany.
May 3: Bombs planted on the U.S. Base Civil Engineering facility in Ankara, Turk., by four armed gunmen failed to detonate.
May 3: A Turkish airliner was hijacked by four TPLA members, all students, and forced to fly to Sofia, where they surrendered to Bulgarian officials. The following day, the passengers and crew were released.
May 4: A hijacker named Michael Hansen successfully diverted a Salt Lake City-Los Angeles flight to Cuba.
May 5: A man surrendered in Honduras after he had attempted to extort $300,000 ransom following the hijacking of a flight in Allentown, Pa.
May 8: A Sabena Belgian World Airlines plane en route from Vienna to Tel Aviv was hijacked by four BSO members. At the Lod Airport in Tel Aviv, paratroopers dressed as mechanics gained entry to the plane. They killed two hijackers and wounded a third. Five passengers were wounded; one later died. Two female hijackers were later sentenced to life in prison.
May 9: An arson fire damaged two military facilities in San Jose, Calif.
May 9: Authorities arrested 395 University of Florida students during a demonstration in Gainsville.
May 9: Protestors burned cars and blocked traffioc in Boulder, Colo.
May 9: Two thousand students rioted at the Champaign-Urbana campus of the University of Illinois.
May 9: Federal buildings in Binghamton, N.Y., were blockaded by anti-war protestors.
May 10: Twenty-five students and three police officers were injured during campus protests at the University of Minnesota.
May 10: Federal buildings were blocked by demonstrators in Burlington, Vt.

May 10: Protestors forced the closing of the public gallery at the U.S. House of Representatives in Washington, D.C.
May 10: Four members of the Black Liberation Army were arrested in Columbia, S.C.
May 10: Nine people were injured during a two-day riot at the University of New Mexico in Albuquerque.
May 11: At the Fifth U.S. Army Corps headquarters in West Germany, a series of bombs planted by the Baader-Meinhof Gang in retaliation for U.S. action against North Vietnam exploded. Colonel Paul Bloomquist was killed and thirteen others were wounded.
May 11: Three police officers were shot during demonstrations at the University of Wisconsin in Madison.
May 11: Fifty-two people were injured during rioting in Berkeley, Calif.
May 11: Seventy-two people were arrested for refusing to vacate the U.S. Capitol in Washington, D.C.
May 12: Terrorists from the Comité Argentino de Lucha Anti-Imperialisto bombed one Dutch and four U.S. companies in Argentina.
May 12: Anti-war demonstrators battled construction workers near the U.N building in New York City.
May 14: A bomb explosion destroyed a military vehicle at the McDonald Army Reserve Center in Jamaica, N.Y.
May 15: Democratic Presidential aspirant George Wallace was shot and seriously wounded by Arthur Bremer while the candidate was delivering a campaign speech in Laurel, Md.
May 16: Authorities arrested 120 demonstrators during a sit-in at the U.S. Capitol in Washington, D.C.
May 18: A molotov cocktail was thrown at a police car during a demonstration in Blythe, Calif.
May 19: A bomb placed by members of the Weather Underground exploded at the Pentagon building in Arlington, Va.
May 20: A motel in Dorado, P.R., was bombed during the Miss U.S.A. beauty pageant.
May 22: Washington, D.C., Police Chief Jerry Wilson was among those injured during aa anti-war demonstration near the U.S. capitol.
May 23: The branch office of ITT Corp. was bombed in Caracus, Venez.
May 24: The residence of the Soviet mission to the United Nations on Long Island, N.Y., was bombed by JDL terrorists.
May 24 : At the U.S. Army's European headquarters in Heidelberg, Ger., two car-bombs exploded; one soldier was killed and two others were wounded. The Baader-Meinhoff gang was suspected.
May 25: In France, the offices of the American Legion, Pan American World Airways, the U.S. consulate, and TWA in Paris were bombed.
May 26: A South African Airways jet was hijacked by two Lebanese who were captured. No injuries were inflicted.
May 26: Two Lebanese terrorists attempted to extort money from the Anglo-American Mining Company in Rhodesia-Malawi.
May 27: Black Panther Party member Isaiah Rowley was shot to death in Jersey City, N.J.
May 27: The shooting of a black by a white store owner sparked three days of looting and vandalism in Concord, N.C.
May 27: Explosions damaged two buildings at Columbia University.
May 31: In Israel, at Tel Aviv's Lod Airport, three Japanese terrorists attacked passengers with machine guns and hand grenades; twenty-five were killed and seventy-six wounded. Members of the Japanese URA, the assailants, had been recruited for the assault by the Popular Front for the Liberation of Palestine, which claimed responsibility for the attack.
May 31: The U.S. Information Services office in Teheran, Iran, was bombed by Iranian terrorists. One person was killed and two were wounded.
May 31: The police community relations office was bombed with a molotov cocktail in Denver, Colo.
June: A letter bomb was delivered to a County police station in Los Angeles.
June 1: In Frankfurt, Ger., police captured Andreas Baader, the leader of the Baader-Meinhof Gang. Two weeks later Ulrike Meinhof, coleader, was arrested.
June 2: Robb Heady was arrested after he parachuted from a plane he had hijacked in Reno, Nev.
June 3: In the U.S., a solitary hijacker who claimed to be a member of the Black Panther Party took over a Western Airlines plane and ordered it flown to Algeria after he had received $500,000 in ransom. In Algeria, he was arrested and the money was returned.
June 3: The branch offices of IBM, Honeywell, and Bank of America were bombed in Milan, Italy.
June 8: A Czecholsovakian airline was hijacked by ten people who ordered it flown to West Germany where they sought political sanctuary. The pilot of the craft was killed.
June 9: Four U.S.-owned companies in Argentina were damaged by bombings, coinciding with the 60th anniversary of a thwarted Peron coup.
June 10: In Dublin, the West German embassy was damaged by a bomb allegedly planted by Baader-Meinhof Gang terrorists.
June 14: Members of the Anti-Communist Commandos bombed a liquor store in San Juan, P.R.
June 15: West German terrorist Ulricke Meinhof was arrested in Hanover after he had been betrayed by a commrade.
June 19: A pornographic theater in San Diego was bombed by Yakopec, a member of the Secret Army Organization.
June 20: Before their defeat, nineteen Croatian guerrillas who had infiltrated into Herzegovina and western Bosnia, assaulted and murdered thirteen security guards near the town of Bugojno.
June 23: A man named Martin J. McNally was arrested after he hijacked a plane from St. Louis to Peru, Ind.
June 30: Ernanno Barca, president of the Buenos Aires branch of the Italian bank, Banco di Napoli, was abducted by four armed men and was later released unhurt when the bank paid a $200,000 ransom.
June 30: A man named David B. Carre was arrested as he attempted to hijack a plane in Seattle.
July 2: A Pan American World Airways jet was hijacked by a South Vietnamese student after it took off from Saigon. The student, who wanted the plane flown to Hanoi, was killed by another passenger.
July 4: Nine police officers were injured during a riot in New York City incited by a routine arrest.
July 5: A man was arrested as he attempted to hijack a plane in Buffalo, N.Y.
July 5: Three hijackers and a passenger were killed during an attempt to divert a flight from Sacramento to Russia.
July 6: A man was arrested in Oakland, Calif., after collecting ransom money in a hijacking attempt.
July 6: A firebomb exploded at the police department in Connellsville, Pa.
July 10: An Algerian hijacked a Lufthansa German Airlines plane en route from Cologne to Munich and demanded a $100,000 ransom; he was captured by German police.
July 10: Groups of whites and Puerto Ricans clashed in Long Branch, N.J.
July 12: A man was arrested in Norman, Okla., after he parachuted from a plane that he hijacked in Oklahoma City.
July 12: Two hijackers surrendered in Lake Jackson, Texas, after diverting a New York bound flight.
July 17: The first secretary of the Swedish embassy in Bogotá, Col., Kjell R. Haeggloef, was murdered by a gunman.
July 21: In what became known as Bloody Friday, eleven people were killed and 130 injured by twenty-two Provisional IRA bombs that exploded throughout Belfast, Ire.
July 21: A molotov cocktail and other objects were thrown at a police patrol car in Washington, D.C.
July 28: Terrorists from the OPR-33 group kidnapped the manager of the United Press International in Uruguay, Hector Menoni, releasing him unharmed the next day.
July 30: A time bomb was discovered near a police station in East St. Louis, Ill.
July 31: Five blacks were wounded on the streets of Dayton, Ohio, by an armed motorist in a manner that would be repeated twenty-five times over the next years.
July 31: A Delta Airlines jet flying over Florida was seized by hijackers claiming to be Black Panther Party sympathizers. They ordered the plane to Algeria upon receiving a ransom of $1 million. In Algeria, authorities took the ransom money, arrested the hijackers, and returned the money to Delta. The hijackers were released later.
Aug. 5: In Trieste, Italy BSO members set fire to an oil storage facility because it provided oil for Austria and Germany; both countries were Israeli allies. An estimated $7 million in damage was caused.
Aug. 8: Black Liberation Party fugitive Robert Vickers was apprehended in Newark, N.J.
Aug. 15: Escaping from Rawson prison in Argentina, six ERP members hijacked an aircraft to Santiago, Chile.
Aug. 16: Shortly after departure from Rome, an El Al Israel Airlines plane was damaged by a bomb concealed in the luggage compartment. The Nationalist Group for the Liberation of Palestine accounted for the attack.
Aug. 18: A man was arrested in Seattle after hijacking a flight in Reno, Nev.
Aug. 22: Three armed men, saying they were members of the Eagles of National Unity, hijacked a Southern Yemen DC-6 plane en route from Beirut to Cairo and ordered it flown to Benghazi, Libya, where the hijackers asked for asylum. Later. they were freed by the Libyan government.
Aug. 22: In an incident that would become the basis for the film "Dog Day Afternoon", two gunmen held several employees hostage during a foiled bank robbery in Brooklyn, N.Y.
Aug. 28: A police officer was wounded during an ambush in Columbus, Ohio.
Aug. 29: A bomb detonated at the U.S. embassy in Athens, causing minor damage; the Popular Resistance Group accounted for the act.
Aug. 30: In France, the Jordanian ambassador's son was kidnapped and promptly released following his father's payment the next day of a ransom believed to be $40,000.
September: In Cambodia, the car in which U.S. Chargé Thomas Enders was riding, en route to the U.S. embassy, met with extensive damage from a bomb explosion which killed several bystanders.
Sept. 5: At the Olympic Games in Munich, Ger., eight BSO guerrillas killed two Israeli athletes and took nine others hostage. The German government granted them safe passage to Egypt and escorted them to the airport where a gun fight resulted in the deaths of five terrorists and

all nine hostages.
Sept. 5: In Argentina, Jan J. Van de Panne, a Dutch citizen who was in charge of the Philips Argentina electronics firm, was captured by the Monteneros who demanded and received a $500,000 ransom; they released Van de Panne, unharmed, two days later.
Sept. 8: A fight at a high school football game escalated to rock-throwing and sniper fire over the course of two days in Gainesville, Ga. Sixty-six people were arrested.
Sept. 9: Dr. Ami Shachori, agricultural counselor at Israel's London Embassy, was killed by a letter bomb mailed by Black September terrorists.
Sept. 9: Three members of the Black Liberation Army, including one escaped convict, were apprehended in Brooklyn, N.Y.
Sept. 11: At a Brussels cafe in Belgium, an Israeli official was shot and critically wounded after he had been lured there by an anonymous call. Initial reports indentified the gunman as an Arab guerrilla, but later information implied that he was a Moroccan who formerly worked for Israeli intelligence.
Sept. 14: A bomb exploded at the apartment of a Palestinian Arab in Hollywood, Calif.
Sept. 15: A Scandinavian Airlines System (SAS) plane was hijacked by three Croatian emigrés who ransomed the passengers for six Croatian terrorists jailed in Sweden. The plane was routed to Madrid where the terrorists surrendered.
Sept. 16: The offices of twelve businesses, including branches of seven U.S. firms, were bombed in four Mexican cities, coinciding with the celebration of Mexican Independance Day.
Sept. 17: The Yugoslav tourist agency in Sydney, Australia was bombed by Croatian militants.
Sept. 19: In the Israeli embassy in London a letter bomb mailed by BSO guerrillas exploded, killing a diplomat. Almost fifty such bombs, all posted from Amsterdam on Sept. 16, were intercepted in the next few days, sent to Israeli officials worldwide, and another eight, all mailed from Malaysia, were discovered in the first part of October.
Oct. 1: Members of the Afro-American Liberation Army bombed a police garage in Los Angeles.
Oct. 4: When a bomb detonated in an Arab bookstore in Paris, the Masada, Action and Defense Movement claimed responsibility. Israel denied awareness of the group.
Oct. 4: A postal employee was wounded by a letter bomb addressed to a Jewish organization in New York. The parcel was one of several postmarked in Malaysia that were sent to Jewish organizations worldwide. The BSO took credit.
Oct. 4: Rioting and vandalism erupted from a routine arrest of one youth in Newburgh, N.Y.
Oct. 6: In Algeria's West German consulate, Palestinian students detained several hostages for an hour, demanding that three imprisoned terrorists be released from jail in Munich.
Oct. 7: Members of the Black Liberation Army bombed a police car in Los Angeles.
Oct. 11: Forty-six persons were injured in a racial fight involving 100 persons aboard the U.S.S. *Kitty Hawk* aircraft carrier off the coast of North Vietnam.
Oct. 13: A bomb was discovered at the offices of El Al Airlines in Paris.
Oct. 16: A bomb planted in the Buenos Aires Sheraton Hotel exploded, killing a Canadian tourist. Supporters of Juan Perón were responsible.
Oct. 16: Racial fighting broke out on a U.S. Navy tanker as it sailed near the Philippines.
Oct. 17: A bomb was found at the Bank of America office in Rotterdam, Neth.
Oct. 22: A Turkish airliner bound for Bulgaria was hijacked by four men who threatened to detonate the plane containing sixty-nine passengers unless Turkey released twelve terrorist prisoners, reorganized the universities, and restored workers' rights to strike. The hijackers surrendered when their demands were refused.
Oct. 23: A PLO representative was arrested for the possession of letter bombs in Brussels.
Oct. 24: The Israelis retaliated for a series of letter bomb attacks, by sending similar missives to Palestinian leaders in Algeria, Egypt, Lebanon, and Libya.
Oct. 25: In the U.S., police officers seized letter bombs mailed from Israel which were addressed to Secretary of Defense Melvin Laird, President Richard Nixon, and Secretary of State William Rogers.
Oct. 26: A Houston police officer was shot to death by two men who followed him from a restaurant.
Oct. 29: A Lufthansa German Airlines 727 en route from Beirut to Ankara was hijacked by two BSO members and ordered flown to Munich. Threats to blow up the plane caused the West German government to release three BSO terrorists who were delivered to the hijackers in Zagreb, Yug. The hijacked plane, carrying all the terrorists, was flown to Libya and released.
Oct. 29: Four men hijacked a plane from Houston to Cuba, after killing a ticket agent and wounding another employee.
Oct. 30: Fatah-Black September letter bombs mailed from Malaysia and Singapore were discovered in Israel.
Oct. 31: A letter bomb was received at the Israeil embassy in Nigeria.
Nov. 2: In Zaragoza, Spain, three youths bombed the French consulate, killing the honorary consul and injuring two others.
Nov. 2: The Bureau of Indian Affairs building in Washington, D.C. was seized by 500 members of AIM and held for seven days.
Nov. 3: In Amman, Jor., a French girl, identified as a PFLP member, was killed while handling a bomb, which police reported she had intended to plant at the U.S. embassy.
Nov. 4: A letter bomb was received by a Jewish Zionist Youth Group in Frankfurt, West Germany.
Nov. 5: The Pan American World Airway ticket office in San Salvador, El Sal., was bombed, causing appreciable damage but no injuries.
Nov. 6: A Bombay, India, post office was the site of a letter-bomb explosion; a post office worker was wounded.
Nov. 7: A $500,000 ransom was paid for the release of Italian industrialist Enrico Barrella, who was captured in Buenos Aires and released three days later.
Nov. 8: A Mexican airliner was hijacked by four Armed Communist League members whose demands for $330,000, the release of five jailed guerrillas, and the promise to drop accusations against two fugitives who joined them were met by the government. The plane flew to Cuba where the eleven guerrillas were given asylum.
Nov. 9: An IBM branch office was bombed in San Miguel de Tucuman, Arg.
Nov. 10: A letter-bomb from India being opened by the managing director of a London diamond firm detonated. Fifty-two more letter-bombs mailed to Jewish companies throughout Europe were seized in New Delhi and Bombay, with twenty more intercepted in Britain and five intercepted in Switzerland.
Nov. 10: Three men hijacked a flight from Birmingham, Ala., to Cuba.
Nov. 11: Five letter bombs addressed to the Israeli delegation of Jewish organizations were intercepted in Geneva, Switz.
Nov. 13: A Syrian journalist was murdered by three Fatah-Black September terrorists in Paris.
Nov. 14: The American Information Center was sabotaged in Ankara, Turkey.
Nov. 15: At the Argentine/Brazilian pavilion of the Fifth International Trade Fair in San Salvador, El Sal., a small bomb detonated in the women's bathroom.
Nov. 15: Two white police officers were shot by a sniper in Kennett Square, Pa.
Nov. 16: Two Southern University students were shot to death during a clash with police in Baton Rouge, La.
Nov. 21: Four letter bombs sent to Jewish targets were intercepted in Toronto.
Nov. 23: An Al Fatah operation bombed an Arab National Union official's house in Amman, Jor. Three people were arrested and confessed to the assault.
Nov. 25: Four abandoned suitcases filled with weapons were confiscated at the airport in Rome.
Nov. 27: Five people were wounded during a riot in Pontiac, Mich.
December: Members of the anti-Castro group FIN bombed a travel agency in Queens, N.Y.
Dec. 1: As an Egyptian plane took off, fifteen machine-gun shots were fired at it. Not until the aircraft's landing in Cairo did the crew become aware of the incident.
Dec. 5: In Venezuela, the Honduran ambassador's residence was peppered with machine-gun fire; no one was hurt.
Dec. 6: Two days after his company paid $100,000 of a $180,000 ransom demand ($800,000 was the original demand), Spanish industrialist Felix Azpiazu was released unharmed.
Dec. 7: The Singapore Jibril Front directed letter bombs to public organizations in Israel.
Dec. 7: In Athens, Gr., timed bombs exploded under two U.S. servicemen's cars, with the Independence, Liberation, Resistance organization claiming a protest against U.S. support of the Greek government.
Dec. 8: In Paris, the principal representative of the Al Fatah and the PLO was mortally wounded when an explosion tore apart his apartment.
Dec. 8: A U.S. businessman died when a car bomb detonated in Brisbane, Aus.
Dec. 10: A British Vestey Industrial Group executive, Donald Grove, was kidnapped by the ERP who released him unhurt after the company paid an estimated $1 million ransom.
Dec. 11: A bomb placed by members of the anti-Castro group, FIN, exploded at the VA-Cuba Forwarding Company in New York City.
Dec. 12: Bombs that exploded in package offices in New York, Miami, and Montreal were believed to be sent by the Cuban Secret Government.
Dec. 20: In an attack alleged to be the action of the BSO, the U.S. Embassy in Beirut, Leb., was fired on by two rockets.
Dec. 20: Secret Army Organization member Gregory Thorpe killed his wife and another couple before turning his gun on himself in Phoenix, Ariz.
Dec. 24: A terrorist intending to bomb Israeli embassies in Scandinavia was arrested in London.
Dec. 27: An executive of the Argentine subsidiary of ITT Corp., Vicente Russo, was kidnapped in Argentina and was released uninjured two days later. The company would not reveal whether or not the $500,000 to $1 million ransom had been paid.
Dec. 27: A police officer was killed and his partner was wounded, as they attempted to apprehend three fugitives in Detroit.
Dec. 27: In Argentina an administrator of Standard Electric of Argentina

was abducted by Descamisados Peronistas Montoneros terrorists and freed three days later after a ransom was paid.
Dec. 28: At the Israeli embassy in Bangkok, Thai., four BSO members held six people captive for nineteen hours, requesting freedom for several Arab guerrillas in Israeli jails, threatening to blow up the embassy. They agreed to release the hostages upon their safe arrival in Cairo, Egypt. On Jan. 5 Thailand disclosed that Israel had consented to release the bodies of two Palestinian hijackers to their families.
Dec. 28: Members of the Black Liberation Army kidnapped a tavern owner in Brooklyn, N.Y.
December: A terrorist squad attempting to reach Israel by boat was arrested by authorities in Greece.
December: An car filled with explosives intended for various Israeli embassies was seized by authorities in Europe after its arrival from Lebanon.
1973
Jan. 1: A Syrian and a Palestinian who had been ordered from Syria into Jordan by Al Fatah to serve the Trans-Arabian Pipeline were caught by an army patrol in Jordan.
Jan. 1: Fatah-Black September letter bombs were intercepted by police in Kuwait, Jordan.
Jan. 2: A man unsuccessfully attempted to hijack a plane in Baltimore.
Jan. 2: A person was shot to death as members of the Black Liberation Army robbed a social club in Brooklyn, N.Y.
Jan. 5: Terrorists tossed molotov cocktails into the police station in Port Clinton, Ohio.
Jan. 7: In Athens, Gr., two cars belonging to U.S. government employees were set on fire by incendiary devices; no one was hurt.
Jan. 7: Six people, including two police officers, were killed by snipers in New Orleans. One gunman was subsequently shot to death by a police marksman.
Jan. 8: The Paris offices of an agency that coordinated plans for emigration of Jews to Israel was demolished by a bomb explosion for which the BSO claimed responsibility.
Jan. 9: The Black September terrorist organization sabotaged a building occupied by a Jewish group.
Jan. 9: Four Habash Front terrorists were thwarted in their attempt to carry out a suicide mission in Haifa when they were detained by authorities in Cyprus.
Jan. 10: The West Germany Amerika Haus library in Frankfurt was set on fire by arsonsists, with $25,000 in damages.
Jan. 10: A member of the Black Liberation Army fired a shot at a police officer in pursuit and escaped in a Brooklyn subway tunnel.
Jan. 11: At a Kaiserslautern restaurant in West Germany a group of alleged Arab terrorists assaulted a group of foreigners. One tourist was killed and several others were hurt.
Jan. 12: Two members of the Black Liberation Army shot two Housing Detectives on a Brooklyn street.
Jan. 17: In Lebanon, a dynamite explosion destroyed a restroom of the American University in Beirut.
Jan. 17: Four U.S. military cars were set on fire in Terrania, Italy.
Jan. 18: Seven members of the Washington D.C. Hanafi Muslims were murdered by five Philadelphia Muslims.
Jan. 18: Molotov cocktails were thrown into a police community relations center in Pueblo, Colo.
Jan. 19: Three Black September terrorists were arrested in Vienna as they attempted to attack an immigrant transit facility.
Jan. 19: A man was disarmed by a policewoman as he attempted to hijack a plane in Louisville, Ky.
Jan. 19: Following the fatal shooting of a New York City police officer and the wounding of two others, four gunmen held twelve people hostage but surrendered two days later.
Jan. 20: A priest was assaulted by a member of the right-wing group, Breakthrough, at an anti-war rally in Detroit.
Jan. 21: An American Indian was stabbed to death in Buffalo Gap, S.D. The subsequent charge of manslaughter against the assailant provoked much protest from AIM.
Jan. 22: A molotov cocktail was thrown towards a police station in Alton, Ill.
Jan. 23: In Ethiopia, two businessmen from Italy acting as negotiators in talks with a guerrilla group were kidnapped by ELF
members.
Jan. 23: The U.S. ambassador and the U.S. counsul general to Haiti were held hostage as three gunmen negotiated the release of twelve prisoners and ransom money.
Jan. 23: Two members of the Black Liberation Army were killed and two police detectives wounded during a shoot-out in Brooklyn, N.Y.
Jan. 24: The offices of Pan Am Airlines were bombed in Teheran, Iran.
Jan. 24: Black September letter bombs sent to Israeli consulates were seized in Australia, Canada, Chile, and Greece.
Jan. 25: In Nicosia, Cyprus, one person linked to Al Fatah died after a time bomb went off in his hotel room. Palestinians believed Israeli agents were the culprits.
Jan. 25: Members of the Black Liberation Army machine-gunned a patrol car in Brooklyn, N.Y.
Jan. 26: Black September terrorists killed Baruch Cohen, an Israeli intelligence officer, as he was sitting in a cafe in Madrid, Spain.
Jan. 26: Three Fatah-Black September terrorists, intending to attack Soviet Jewish emigrants in Vienna, were arrested by authorities at the Italian border.
Jan. 27: The Turkish consul general and the vice consul were murdered by an Armenian gunman in Los Angeles.
Jan. 28: Members of the Black Liberation Army machine-gunned two police officers on patrol in Queens, N.Y.
Jan. 29: Fatah-Black September letter bombs with Israeli addresses were intercepted in Turkey.
Feb. 1: Fights and bomb threats disrupted classes at several schools in Oklahoma City.
Feb. 3: Coca-Cola executive Norman Lee was kidnapped by FAL terrorists in Buenos Aires, Arg., and released after a $1 million ransom was paid.
Feb. 5: Fatah-Black September letter bombs intended for the Israeli embassy in Guatemala were intercepted en route from Rome.
Feb. 5: An incendiary bomb was discovered in the Paraguayan ambassador's car in Argentina.
Feb. 6: Thirty-seven Indians were arrested after a violent clash with police at the Chamber of Commerce building in Custer, S.D., stemming from the Jan. 21 killing of an Indian by a white man.
Feb. 8: Fatah-Black September letter bombs intended for the Israeli Embassy in Bangui, Central Africa, were intercepted en route from Germany.
Feb. 9: Seventeen members of the BSO were arrested by Jordanian officials before they could attack the U.S. Embassy and government building in Amman.
Feb. 9: Indians clashed with whites at a tavern in Rapid City, S.D.
Feb. 9: A bank in the Bronx, N.Y., was robbed by members of the Black Liberation Army
Feb. 20: Police in London shot two Pakistani terrorists and arrested a third, during an occupation attempt at the Indian embassy.
Feb. 21: In retaliation for the murder of eleven Israeli athletes by the BSO at the 1972 Olympic Games in Germany, Israel raided Lebanese refugee camps and slaughtered thirty-one people. One hundred and six passengers died when a Libyan Aircraft was shot down after it had strayed into Israel and was suspected to be a flying bomb.
Feb. 21: In Athens, two U.S. servicemen's cars were bombed by a group who opposed the Greek regime.
Feb. 23: Two members of the Black Liberation Army were arrested with a large cache of explosives in Brooklyn, N.Y.
Feb. 27: Seeking a Senate investigation into Indian affairs, 200 members of AIM took eleven hostages, raided a trading post, and occupied a church in Wounded Knee, S.D. Hostages were released on Mar. 1, but the occupation did not end until Mar. 9.
Mar. 1: The Saudi Arabian Embassy in Khartoum, Sudan, was invaded by eight Black September terrorists, who after demanding the release of Palestinian and European terrorists, shot U.S. ambassador Cleo A. Noel, U.S. deputy chief of mission, George Curtis Moore, and Belgian chargé d'affaires Guy Eid.
Mar. 1: The house of an AIM member was firebombed in Wounded Knee, S.D.
Mar. 2: Members of the Black Liberation Army engaged in a shootout with police in Brooklyn, N.Y.
Mar. 3: The Habash Front sank a Cypriot passenger ship named *Sunyon.*
Mar. 3: A bomb hidden in a shoe box was found under the car of the U.S. consul in Casablanca, Mor.
Mar. 3: A time bomb allegedly placed by members of the Black September Organization was discovered outside the El Al terminal at Kennedy airport in New York City.
Mar. 4: Members of the Black September Organization bombed an Israeli bank in New York City. An undetonated bomb was discovered at another bank.
Mar. 4: BSO took responsibility for an explosion aboard a Greek charter ship conveying 250 U.S. passengers to Israel from Beirut, Leb. No one was injured.
Mar. 4: A bomb exploded at a police community relations center in San Diego.
Mar. 5: In Casablanca, Mor., a bomb inside a package was found in a washroom at the U.S. Information Service Cultural Center.
Mar. 6: At the El Al Israel Airlines air terminal at Kennedy Airport in New York a time bomb was discovered in a deserted rental car. The BSO was suspected.
Mar. 6: Three members of the Black Liberation Army and two police detectives staged a shootout in the Bronx, N.Y.
Mar. 7: Outside Israeli banks in New York two undetonated bombs were found in deserted rental cars. Letterhead stationery from the BSO was found in the autos.
Mar. 8: In London, two bombs, suspected to have been planted by the IRA, exploded, killing one person and injuring two hundred.
Mar. 8: Two Indians were shot during an extended protest and occupation in Wounded Knee, S.D.
Mar. 10: At a Glasgow, Scot., hall a bomb allegedly hidden by the IRA exploded. The hall had been rented by Protestant supporters of British rule in Northern Ireland for a scheduled dance.
Mar. 11: An FBI agent and an Indian were shot during a clash in Wounded Knee, S.D.
Mar. 12: In Cyprus the BSO took credit for the assassination of an

Israeli businessman; he was later named by Cairo's fedayeen radio as a "Zionist intelligence officer."
Mar. 14: Two BSO terrorists were arrested by French authorities for a plot to sabotage the Israeli embassy in Paris.
Mar. 15: Two Arabs who purportedly were trying to smuggle explosives into France in order to blow up the Israeli Embassy in Paris were arrested by French police.
Mar. 17: Two firebombs exploded at a police community relations bureau in North Denver, Colo.
Mar. 17: Eight police officers were injured during a clash with militant Mexican-Americans in Denver.
Mar. 21: In West Germany, the premises of the U.S. consulate general in Frankfurt, were invaded by two people firing a pistol. Several molotov cocktails were found on the roof of a nearby garage. Many windows were broken at businesses throughout the city.
Mar. 22: The private car of a U.S. government employee in Athens was damaged when an incendiary device was exploded. EAN, (Greek Anti-Dictatorial Youth), was believed to be responsible.
Mar. 23: Minor damage was caused when a molotov cocktail was tossed through the basement window of the Brussels, Belgium Greek ambassador's residence. The incident occurred while the embassy was celebrating Greek Independence Day.
Mar. 26: A U.S. marshal was wounded during disturbances at Wounded Knee, S.D.
Mar. 27: A Brooklyn, N.Y., food store was robbed by members of the Black Liberation Army.
Mar. 28: A Jewish nursery school in Rosario, Arg., was damaged by terrorist bombs. No one was injured.
Mar. 28: Gerardo Scalmazzi, the branch manager of the First National Bank of Boston office in Rosario, Arg., was kidnapped, and released after a ransom between $500,000 and $1 million was paid.
Mar. 28: PIRA weapons from Libya were discovered in a Cypriot vessel moored near County Waterford, Ire.
Mar. 28: Members of the Secret Cuban Government bombed the Center for Cuban Studies in New York City.
Mar. 29: Members of the Cuban National Front attempted to bomb a bookstore in Union, N.J.
Apr. 1: In Beirut, Leb. several cars were destroyed in an explosion. The bombing allegedly was an attempt by Jordanian intelligence officers to murder BSO official Ziyad Al Hilu.
Apr. 2: In Argentina, Anthony R. DaCruz, a U.S. citizen, was kidnapped on his way to work as a technical operations manager at Eastman Kodak Company. A $1.5 million ransom was paid by Kodak, and DaCruz was released on Apr. 7.
Apr. 4: Tear gas grenades were tossed, allegedly by Armenians, into the Turkish airlines office and the Turkish consulate general in Paris.
Apr. 5: Minor damage was caused by an exploded bomb at the U.S. embassy Marine Guard quarters in Rome.
Apr. 5: After an Iraqui law professor, Basil Raoud Al Kubaisi, was shot and killed in Paris by two gunmen, the PFLP in Beirut issued a statement to say Kubaisi had been slain while on a PFLP mission.
Apr. 6: In Rome, an incendiary device cause a fire at the U.S. Information Service library.
Apr. 8: The president of Argentina's largest tobacco company, Francis Victor Brimicombe, was kidnapped near his home in Buenos Aires. An estimated $1.5 to $1.8 million ransom was paid, and he was released.
Apr. 9: Nine Arabs attacked the Israeli ambassador's residence and later an Israeli plane in Nicosia, Cyprus. Seven were arrested. One was killed, and one escaped. The BSO was suspected but the National Organization of Arab Youth claimed responsibility.
Apr. 9: A USO facility in Rome was firebombed by two young men who disarmed a policeman outside the building.
Apr. 10: Seventeen people were killed in an Israeli commando raid in Beirut. Three high-ranking Palestinian guerrilla leaders were slain and several others were wounded.
Apr. 10: Members of the Black Liberation Army robbed a bank in Queens, N.Y.
Apr. 12: In La Spezia, Italy, a British NATO official's car was destroyed in a bomb explosion. There were no injuries.
Apr. 12: A bomb exploded in an Athens hotel room killing an Arab. The man, carrying a Jordanian passport, had hidden the bomb in his luggage.
Apr. 12: Two men, suspected of being police officers, were held at gunpoint by members of the Black Liberation Army in Brooklyn, N.Y.
Apr. 14: In Lebanon, a U.S.-owned oil storage tank was destroyed by masked raiders who damaged three others, one in Sidon.
Apr. 14: An explosive device wired to an oil pipeline in Saudi Arabia, near Rafha, was discovered by the Saudi Arabian National Guard and was disconnected.
Apr. 16: When two Palestinian guerrillas tried to destroy the Trans-Arabian Pipeline to Zahrani, Leb., they succeded only in denting it. The terrorists, who were alleged to have been working for the PFLP and the PFLP-GC, were sentenced to seven years in jail.
Apr. 16: In Washington, D.C., a shot was fired through the bedroom window of the New Zealand chargé d'affaires' house. The words "Black September" were painted on the house.
Apr. 17: An Indian was killed during a shoot-out at Wounded Knee, S.D.
Apr. 21: In Athens, a bomb exploded under the Italian vice consul's car causing severe injuries to a passerby, and a car owned by a U.S. employee of the European Exchange Service was damaged by another explosion. The National Youth Resistance Organization claimed responsibility.
Apr. 23: In Frankfurt, Ger., protestors threw firebombs and rocks at the U.S. consulate.
Apr. 23: In an attempt to hijack an Aeroflot plane flying from Leningrad to Moscow, a terrorist exploded a device which killed him and the co-pilot. The flight returned safely to Leningrad.
Apr. 24: In San Juan, P.R., a bomb blast at the Dominican Republic consulate caused minor damage. An unidentified man called, claiming the action as that of Dominican Republic exiles.
Apr. 25: A U.S. ammunition storage area near the Yokosuka Naval Base in Japan was firebombed, but there were no injuries and no damage.
Apr. 25: Sixty-eight people were arrested during a demonstration at Wounded Knee, S.D.
Apr. 27: In Rome, an Italian El Al Israel Airlines employee was shot to death outside a department store. A BSO member from Lebanon was arrested and said he had orders to murder the Italian because he was an Israeli spy who had killed an Al Fatah official.
Apr. 27: When three Arabs about to board an Air France flight to Paris were arrested in Lebanon, their luggage was found to contain timing devices and explosives.
Apr. 27: An Indian protester was killed and another wounded during a shoot-out with U.S. marshals at Wounded Knee, S.D.
Apr. 29: The IBM Corporation offices in San Salvador, El Sal., were damaged by a bomb.
Apr. 29: The trading post at Wounded Knee, S.D., was destroyed by fire.
Apr. 29: The Jordanian ambassador's residence in Beirut, Leb., was the target of a bombing.
Apr. 30: The ERP bombed a Goodyear Rubber Company-owned building in Córdoba, Arg., causing serious damage but no casualties.
Apr. 30: Four suspected BSO members riding in a car with explosives, weapons, and a radio transmitter were arrested by Lebanese troops near the U.S. embassy in Beirut. Five other armed Palestinians were arrested in connection with the planned assault.
May 1: An assistent manager at the Indian Airlines in Kabul, Afg., overpowered a Pakistani Black December member who had shot at him.
May 1: The chairman of the Italo-Argentine Electric Co. and an Italian bank in Buenos Aires, Arg., was kidnapped. He was released on May 4 after payment of $1.5 million.
May 1: In Barcelona, Spain, the British European Airways office was firebombed.
May 1: The offices of Goodyear Rubber were bombed by ERP terrorists in Córdoba, Arg.
May 1: Malcolm X Foundation leader H.A. Jamal was shot to death by members of a rival Muslim group in New York City.
May 2: Two firebombs shattered windows and caused extensive damage to the Pan American World Airways office in Barcelona, Spain.
May 2: No one was injured and no damage occurred at the U.S. ambassador's residence in Beirut, Leb., after it was fired upon with rockets.
May 2: A police officer and a Black Liberation Army member were killed during a shoot-out on the New Jersey Turnpike.
May 4: Two Soviet doctors working in Burma were abducted by rebel Shan tribesman who demanded that imprisoned Shan leader Chang Chipu be released. Government troops attacked on May 30, but the kidnappers had fled with the hostages.
May 4: U.S. consul general in Guadalajara, Mex, Terrance G. Leonhardy, was kidnapped by members of the People's Revolutionary Armed Forces, who released Leonhardy on May 6 after a number of demands were met, including the release of thirty political prisoners.
May 7: A car carrying official nondiplomatic tags owned by a U.S. European Exchange System vendor was hit by a pipe bomb in Athens, Gr.
May 7: Police in Paris arrested two terrorists who were about to fire upon the Israeli embassy from a nearby building.
May 7: A U.S. citizen's car was damaged by a pipe bomb at the Athens, Gr., airport.
May 8: Members of the Weather Underground bombed police cars and a corporate office in New York City.
May 13: Cars belonging to a Greek-American movie producer and to two U.S. military men were damaged by pipe bombs in Athens, Gr.
May 15: A molotov cocktail was thrown at a police department office in Denver, Colo.
May 18: A U.S. diplomat's home in São Paulo, Braz., was set on fire, purportedly from an incendiary device thrown at the residence.
May 18: Four members of the leftist guerrilla organization, People's Revolutionary Army (Zero Point), hijacked a Venezuelan aircraft and asked for the release of seventy-nine Venezuelan prisoners. The demand was rejected by the government, and the hijackers flew to Havana, Cuba, where they were given poltical asylum.
May 18: Members of Weather Underground Organization were suspected of bombing two patrol cars in New York City.

May 19: Two police officers, interrupting a robbery, were shot by members of the Black Liberation Army in Mount Vernon, N.Y.
May 21: Oscar Castel, manager of the Coca-Cola bottling plant in Córdoba, Arg., was kidnapped by armed men and released on June 2 after a $100,000 ransom had been paid.
May 21: In Argentina, an executive and an employee of Ford Motor Argentina were wounded during a kidnap attempt by ERP terrorists, who warned on May 23 that abductions would continue unless a $1 million ransom were paid. Luis Giovanelli later died.
May 23: A bomb was defused at the Buenos Aires Ford offices and the $1 million ransom demanded by ERP to halt kidnappings was paid in the form of medical supplies for provincial hospitals, and goods for the poor.
May 30: Two armed men hijacked a Colombian airliner ordering it flown to several South American countries before landing in Paraguay where they escaped with $50,000 after their demands for the release of forty-seven guerrillas and a $200,000 ransom were refused.
May 31: Argentina's Otis Elevator Co. executives and their families were threatened with kidnapping by the ERP unless $500,000 in charitable contributions was made and employees salaries were doubled. Thirteen executives and their families were flown to Sao Paulo, Braz., when Otis refused.
May 31: Imprisoned Black Muslim members stabbed a warden and deputy warden to death at Holmesburg Prison in Philadelphia.
May 31: Two youths surrendered after holding twenty-four people hostage during a failed bank robbery attempt in Rancho Cordova, Calif.
June 2: Gunmen, alleged to be part of a leftist guerrilla group in Iran, shot and killed U.S. military adviser Lieutenant Colonel Lewis Hawkins.
June 5: Two members of the Black Liberation Army shot a transit detective to death in New York City.
June 6: British businessman Charles Lockwood was kidnapped by terrorists in Buenos Aires, Arg. He was released on July 30 after a $2 million ransom was paid.
June 9: The Fritz Werner GMBH West Berlin arms plant was seriously damaged by the BSO, which claimed responsibility for the incident and said it was because Werner dealt with Israel.
June 10: Three armed men hijacked a Royal Nepal Airlines domestic flight, seized the $400,000 bank shipment on board, and flew to India where they escaped.
June 13: Two BSO terrorists were wounded when an explosion occurred in their auto close to the El Al Rome office.
June 13: The brother of Sirhan Sirhan was convicted of threatening the life of Golda Meir in a letter sent to U.S. secretary of state William Rogers.
June 17: The apparent detonation of a bomb inside an explosive filled car in Rome seriously injured two Arabs.
June 18: A West German clothing manufacturer, Hans Kurt Gebhardt, was kidnapped in Argentina by guerrillas who were paid a $100,000 ransom for his June 25 release.
June 18: John R. Thompson, president of Firestone Tire and Rubber Company's Argentinian subsidiary, was abducted by the ERP and released on July 6 after a $3 million ransom had been paid.
June 18: The general manager of a U.S. firm in Guatemala, Roberto Galvez, was released after his FAR abductors received a $50,000 ransom.
June 19: Police officer Larry Barkwell was shot to death in Atlanta.
June 20: The car of a member of the Soviet mission to the United Nations was firebombed in New York. The car was allegedly destroyed by the JDL as a protest against the treatment of Jews in the U.S.S.R. and Leonid Brezhnev's visit to the U.S.
June 21: Two reputed Teamster members stabbed a citrus ranch foreman during a kidnap attempt in Coachella Valley, Calif.
June 25: Alleged ERP members in Buenos Aires, Arg., kidnapped Mario Baratella, vice president of the Italian-owned Bank of Rio de la Plata. After an undiclosed amount was paid, Baratella was released on July 5.
June 28: A car bomb explosion in Paris killed Mohammed Boudia, Algerian supporter of fedayeen terrorist operations and an alleged BSO member.
June 29: A group of Teamsters were arrested after attacking a UFW picket during a labor dispute in the San Joaquin Valley of California.
June 30: Two molotov cocktails were thrown at a police car in Rochester, N.Y.
July: The son of a U.S. businessman was killed in Guatemala.
July 1: In Lima, Peru, a small bomb destroyed the French embassy gate. Planned nuclear tests in the Pacific were believed to have provoked the attack.
July 1: Israeli military attaché in Washington, D.C., Lieutenant Colonel Yosef Ayalon was shot and killed. According to a Voice of Palestine radio broadcast, the execution was in revenge for the June 28 killing of Mohammed Boudia.
July 2: Kidnappers demanded a $1 million ransom after abducting Raul Bornancini, assistant manager of the First National City Bank of New York in Córdoba. A ransom was paid and Bornancini was released on July 13.
July 4: An Argentine aircraft was hijacked by a man claiming to be an ERP member and was flown to Santiago, Chile, and then to Cuba. His demand for $200,000 to be paid to charitable organizations was refused. The ERP denied the hijacker was a member.
July 4: A British-American Tobacco Co. accountant was abducted in Buenos Aires, and released after a $300,000 ransom was paid.
July 6: Incendiary bombs were thrown and bullets fired at the residence of the Uruguayan ambassador in Buenos Aires by ERP members, but no injuries were sustained.
July 8: In La Plata, Arg., the Uruguayan consulate was seized for fifteen minutes by two men and one woman, alleged ERP members, who painted slogans on the walls.
July 11: A man was captured in Dallas after hijacking a helicopter in Gainsville, Tex.
July 18: Members of the Black Liberation Army robbed a bank in the Bronx, N.Y.
July 19: The El Al Israel Airlines office in Athens, Gr., was attacked by a single Palestinian guerrilla, who when unable to enter the office took seventeen hostages from a nearby hotel and was flown to Kuwait, where he disappeared.
July 20: A Japan Air Lines 747 was hijacked after taking off from Amsterdam by three Arabs and one Japanese. A fifth terrorist was killed soon after the takeover when a grenade she was carrying exploded. The plane was eventually flown to Benghazi, Libya, where it was destroyed after release of the passengers. The incident was allegedly in retaliation for Japan's payment to victims of the Lod Airport attack on May 21, 1972.
July 21: A Moroccan waiter in Oslo, Norway, believed to be involved in the BSO, was killed, reportedly by the JDL's Wrath of God or Israeli counter-terrorists agents. On July 26 two Israelis and four other people were arrested.
July 22: An annex of Columbian embassy and the Peruvian-North American Cultual Institute were attacked with bombs tossed from a passing car.
July 24: A maintenance worker was injured when the top floor of a Times Square New York office building where a pro-Casro Cuban exposition was scheduled to take place was bombed. Cuban refugees were believed responsible.
July 25: In Santiago, Chile, the offices of the Czechoslovakian embassy were damaged by a bomb.
July 26: A tear-gas bomb exploded in the offices of the Organization of American States in Tegucigalpa, Hond.
July 27: A car in front of the home of the second secretary of the Democratic People's Republic of Korea was destroyed by a thrown bomb.
July 28: Mexican-Americans enraged by the killing of a 12-year-old boy by police rioted in Dallas.
Aug. 2: A member of the militant anti-Castro Cuban Revolutionary Directorate, Juan Felipe de la Cruz Serafin, was killed when a bomb exploded in his Avrainville, Fr., hotel room.
Aug. 4: One person was killed and seven people wounded by an explosion at the Belgrade, Yug., railroad station.
Aug. 5: At the Athens, Gr., Airport, at least three people were killed and fifty-four wounded when two Arabs with hand grenades and machine guns opened fire on passengers. They seized thirty-five hostages before surrendering to police. On Aug. 8 the Seventh Suicide Squad claimed responsibility and on Aug. 24, two men were sentenced to death for the attack.
Aug. 7: A sheriff's office and a deputy's home were the targets of bombing attempts in Kern County, Calif.
Aug. 12: An explosion near the U.S. consulate in Guayaquil, Ecu., shattered windows but injured no one.
Aug. 15: A bomb thrown from a car caused damage to the U.S. Consular Agency's office in Christchurch, N. Zea.
Aug. 15: Pipe bombs were disarmed at the Santiago, Chile, homes of three U.S. embassy officials.
Aug. 18: A fire and letter bomb campaign was launched by IRA sympathizers in Birmingham, London, and Manchester, with more than forty bombs exploded by Sept. 28 and at least twenty-nine people injured. Letter bombs were found at British embassies in Paris, Lisbon, Zaire, Gibraltar, and Brussels.
Aug. 20: Six members of ERP took over the airfield at La Plata, Arg., forcing a pilot to fly over La Plata and shower the city with propaganda leaflets.
Aug. 27: A letter bomb detonated in the hands of Nora Murray, British military attaché's secretary, as she flew to the U.S. on a Royal Air Force plane from Britain.
Aug. 27: Liegib's Meat Company manager, Ian Martin, was abducted. An ERP ransom note was found, but authorities believed the abduction was the work of MoPoCo. Two kidnappers were killed and several others arrested when Martin was rescued on Sept. 6.
Aug. 27: Bombs caused extensive property damage to the homes of two Cuban diplomats and the car of another in Santiago, Chile.
Aug. 30: Two Saiqa terrorists were arrested in Beirut, Leb. before they could board a flight to Czechoslovakia.
September: Racial violence plagued the openings of schools in Oklahoma City.
Sept. 3: A deputy sheriff, responding to a robbery call, was shot to death on a reservation in Apache County, Ariz.
Sept. 4: The Nation of Islam leader, Reverend James Shabazz, was shot to death by suspected members of a rival Muslim sect in Newark, N.J.
Sept. 5: Thirteen people were taken hostage at the Saudi Arabian

embassy in Paris by five Palestinians, who demanded the release of Al Fatah leader Abu Daoud. The request was denied, but the terrorists and four hostages left France. On Sept. 8, the terrorists surrendered.
Sept. 5: Five Arab terrorists who had planned to shoot down an El Al Israel airliner in Rome were arrested by military police. All five, two in absentia, were sentenced to prison terms, but released on bond.
Sept. 7: The Israeli exhibit at the West Berlin International Radio and Television Fair was destroyed by a bomb. The BSO later claimed responsibility.
Sept. 8: At least thirteen people were injured when two bombs exploded in London's King's Cross and Euston railway stations. The IRA was believed responsible for the bombings.
Sept. 11: A British employee of the Zambian Ministry of Information and his wife were killed, and their son injured, when the parcel the victim placed in his car exploded.
Sept. 17: British ambassadors in Kinshasa, Zaire, and Lisbon, Port., as well as a senior government official in Gibraltar, Spain, received letter bombs. The Kinshasa bomb exploded, injuring a British security officer.
Sept. 23: David George Heywood, an employee of Nobleza Tabacos Co., a subsidiary of British-American Tobacco Co. in Buenos Aires, Arg., was abducted. On Oct. 20 he was released after his family paid a $300,000 ransom. Two of the seven abductors were later captured.
Sept. 24: Terrorists attempted to destroy a Tapline Co. oil pipeline in An-Nabityah, Leb.
Sept. 26: Hundreds of students were involved in an interracial fight at a Boston high school.
Sept. 28: A time bomb destroyed four rooms at the New York headquarters of ITT Corporation's Latin American section. Reported to be a protest against ITT's activities in Chile, the assault was believed to be linked to the SDS's Weatherman faction.
Sept. 28: Four people en route from the U.S.S.R. to Israel were seized aboard a train in Austria by two people claiming to be members of Eagles of the Palestinian Revolution, an alleged offshoot of Al Fatah. The terrorists' demand that Austria close Schoenau Castle, a Jewish emigrés transit camp, was agreed to, the hostages were released, and the terrorists flown to Libya.
Sept. 28: In the Dominican Republic the twelve-year-old son of Francisco Garcia, the Mexican ambassador, was held hostage by a left-wing revolutionary who threatened to murder the boy unless he was given safe passage to Spain. He released the boy unharmed at the Santo Domingo Airport after the demand was granted.
Sept. 28: At the ITT Standard S.A. in Rome there was a blast outside the office after, according to police, unidentified suspects poured gas on the main doors and lit it. The fire was extinguished and there was little damage.
October: Members of the Death Angel cult committed the first of fourteen murders which would become known as the Zebra killings.
October: Black parents clashed with school board officials in Dearborn Heights, Mich.
October: Racial fighting erupted at John Marshall High School in Oklahoma City.
Oct. 1: A group identifying itself as a faction of the ERP sent notes to the Argentinean offices of both Pan American World Airlines and Braniff International demanding $1 million payments from each. Neither company revealed what the terrorists threatened to do if the demand was not met.
Oct. 2: Snipers shot down a police helicopter in Oakland, Cal.
Oct. 4: In Colombia two U.S. citizens employed by Frontino Goldmines were abducted. The kidnappers, believed to be ELN members, sent a letter the next day to International Mining Company in New York demanding a $168,990 ransom which the board of directors agreed to pay.
Oct. 5: In an attack that was believed to be related to Chilean politics two gas bombs were planted at the front door of the Genoa, Italy, U.S. consulate general, with leaflets bearing the name of the Proletarian Action Group left at the scene. There were no injuries.
Oct. 6: A white man was shot to death in a black area of Boston, following the assault of a white woman by black youths, who set her on fire.
Oct. 8: Coinciding with the anniversary of the death of Che Guevara, the Buenos Aires office of the Bank of America and a Sheraton Hotel were hit by rockets and fire bombs.
Oct. 9: In Córdoba, Arg. bombs were detonated in front of three companies: U.S. owned Coca-Cola and Firestone Tire & Rubber, and the German-owned Mercedes-Benz. There were no casualties.
Oct. 10: British consul in Mexico Anthony Williams was kidnapped, with terrorists demanding a $200,000 ransom plus the release of fifty-one political prisoners. On Oct. 14 Williams was freed; it was not known if a ransom had been paid. The 23rd of September Communist League claimed responsibility.
Oct. 15: An anti-Castro gunman was killed in a shoot-out with Cuban security forces, after he kidnapped the Belgian and French ambassadors in Havana.
Oct. 18: A Bank of America office in Beirut was seized by five guerrillas who claimed to be members of the Lebanese Socialist Revolutionary Organization and demanded $10 million to finance the Arab war effort against Israel, the release of Palestinian guerrillas in Lebanon, and safe passage to Southern Yemen or Algeria. Twenty-five hours later army commandos and police went in. U.S. citizen John Crawford Maxwell had been murdered by the terrorists; killed in the battle were one police officer and two guerrillas. Surviving terrorists were tried and sentenced, with Adel Najin Abu-Asi condemned to die for murdering Maxwell.
Oct. 18: Four Fatah-Black September terrorists were arrested with a suitcase filled with explosives in West Berlin.
Oct. 18: Two Black Muslim members were murdered reportedly by members of a rival sect.
Oct. 20: Four armed terrorists, self-proclaimed Tupamaros, hijacked an Argentine Airlines 737 flying from Buenos Aires to Salta. The plane landed in the border town of Yacuiba, and forty-eight hours later the terrorists accepted the promise of safe passage to Cuba in exchange for release of the hostages.
Oct. 20: A bomb made of firecracker powder exploded at a business establishment in New York City.
Oct. 21: In the first reported case of Arab guerrilla activity in the Soviet Union two Palestinians, calling themselves BSO members, warned dissident Soviet physicist Andrei Sakharov and his wife to stop making statements in support of Israel.
Oct. 22: Kurt Schmid, a Swissair executive, was kidnapped by the ERP, who demanded a $10 million ransom. An undisclosed sum was paid and Schmid was released on Nov. 29.
Oct. 23: Amoco executive David Wilkie, Jr. was kidnapped in Buenos Aires, Arg., and released after a ransom between $1 million and $3.5 million was paid.
Oct. 25: In Buenos Aires David Wilkie, Jr., the president of Amoco Argentina, an Amoco International Oil Company subsidiary, was kidnapped. Three and a half million dollars was reportedly given for his release, and he was freed on Nov. 11.
Oct. 25: A bomb was discovered at the police headquarters in Denver.
Oct. 26: The Yanikhan Commandos mailed a smoke bomb, which did not explode, and letter, to the Turkish Information Office in New York City.
November: Fifteen people were injured when a letter bomb exploded at the LAN-Chile Air Company office in Rio de Janeiro, Braz.
November: Black and Spanish-speaking students seized the student union at Ramapo College in Mahwah, N.J., and held it twenty-eight hours.
Nov. 1: The Pan American offices were bombed with a molotov cocktail in Hato Ray, P.R.
Nov. 4: A firebomb exploded in a police car near the police headquarters in Madison, Wis.
Nov. 6: Oakland Calif., school superintendent Marcus Forter was shot to death by members of the Symbionese Liberation Army.
Nov. 6: A Wadena, Minn., family was held hostage for three days by two escaped convicts.
Nov. 7: Argentinean infantryman Colonel Florencio Crespo was abducted by left wing guerrillas, with the ERP accusing him of collaborating with the U.S. by accepting instruction in U.S. military schools.
Nov. 14: Twymon Myers, a member of the Black Liberation Army, was killed by police during a shootout in the Bronx, N.Y.
Nov. 17: The branch offices of ITT Corp. were bombed in Nuremburg and West Berlin.
Nov. 20: In Maracaibo, Venez., the honorary West German consul, Kurt Nagel, was abducted by armed men and released two days later. The Bandera Roja, a leftist group, was believed to be responsible.
Nov. 22: John A. Swint, a U.S. executive of Ford Motor Argentina, and three bodyguards were murdered in Córdoba, with the FAP claiming responsibility.
Nov. 25: A KLM jumbo jet was hijacked by three Palestinian guerrillas of the Arab Nationalist Youth for the Liberation of Palestine not long after take-off from Beirut, with the hijackers demanding poltical concessions. On Nov. 27 all 247 passengers and seventeen crew members were released and the terrorists surrendered, receiving safe passage from Dubai.
Nov. 27: Five letter bombs addressed to Israeli government branches were intercepted in Geneva. Three similar parcels were found in Israel.
Nov. 27: A bomb placed by the group, Americans for Justice, exploded in San Francisco.
Nov. 29: Six letter bombs mailed from Holland were intercepted in Israel.
December: Members of the Secret Cuban Government bombed a business office in New York City.
December: Members of the FLNC bombed a Bahamian vessel off the coast of Miami.
Dec. 3: Outside the building where the Bank of America was housed in Piraeus, Gr., a bomb exploded causing damage but no injuries. The same day a bomb exploded in a Comercial Bank of Greece branch building in Athens. The anti-government group Greek People claimed the actions.
Dec. 4: Independent truckers protesting the speed limit blockaded several highways in Delaware, Ohio, and Pennsylvania.
Dec. 6: In Argentina a U.S. executive from the EXXON Corporation, Victor Samuelson, was abducted by ERP members who demanded $10 million in medicine and food to be given to the poor with another $4.2 million in services, medicine and supplies for flood-torn northwest Argentina. The company paid $14.2 million in cash, the highest amount ever paid for a single victim, and Samuelson was released on April 29, 1974.

Dec. 14: Nine letter bombs mailed from England to Jewish targets in Israel were discovered.
Dec. 17: Five Arab guerrillas attacked a Pan American airliner killing at least thirty-two and wounding forty at the Rome airport. A Lufthansa plane was then commandeered by the guerrillas and flown to Kuwait, where they surrendered.
Dec. 18: Sixty people were wounded when two PIRA car bombs and a parcel bomb exploded outside the Old Bailey courthouse.
Dec. 19: A plot by a joint squad of Habash Front, Algerian, and Turkish terrorists to kidnap an Israeli diplomat's son and attack the Israeli embassy failed when the group was arrested in Paris.
Dec. 20: French officials uncovered near Paris a sabotage headquarters that was used by several international terrorist organizations.
Dec. 20: Spanish Premier Luis Carrero was assassinated when his car was bombed by ETA Basque terrorists.
Dec. 21: Two IRA bombs exploded in the bar of the Hilton Hotel in London.
Dec. 21: McKee-Tesca Corp. employee Charles Hayes was abducted in La Plata, Arg. He was released on Jan. 31, 1974, after a $1 million ransom had been paid.
Dec. 25: Four Fatah-Black September terrorists were arrested in England, for conspiring to commit assaults.
Dec. 27: Three Black Liberation Army sympathizers were arrested as they attempted to aid the escape of BLA members from a prison in New York City.
Dec. 30: A Jewish man, Harold Seiv, was wounded by Habash Front terrorists in London.
Dec. 30: Members of the National Integration Front bombed a Britsh vessel off the coast of Miami.
Dec. 31: British Zionist Joseph E. Sieff was shot and wounded in his London mansion. The PFLP credited itself for the attack.
Dec. 31: Three offices of the ITT Corp. were bombed in Rome.
Dec. 31: Six parcel bombs were defused at a railway station in Geneva, Switz.

1974

Jan. 1: A bomb exploded near a classroom in San Jose, Calif.
Jan. 2: Another bomb exploded at a school in San Jose, Calif.
Jan. 3: Pepsi-Cola executive Douglas Roberts was kidnapped in Buenos Aires, Arg. He was released on Feb. 2, 1974, following payment of a ransom.
Jan. 12: A bomb explosion damaged a school in San Jose, Calif.
Jan. 12: A bomb exploded at a post office in Matheny, W.Va.
Jan. 20: A Libyan terrorist was arrested in London as he was about to attack an El Al Airline office.
Jan. 23: A pipe-bomb exploded at a high school in Lancaster, Calif.
Jan. 24: A woman was wounded by a hand grenade explosion at an Israeli bank in London. The international terrorist Carlos took credit for the incident.
Jan. 29: A building was bombed on the campus of the University of Kansas in Lawrence.
Jan. 31: Palestinian and Japanese terrorists seized fuel installations in Singapore.
February: Racial violence broke out during Black Heritage Week at a high school in Oklahoma City.
Feb. 1: Pepsi-Cola and Union Carbide plants were bombed in Guadalajara, Mex.
Feb. 1: A Coca-Cola plant was bombed in Oaxaca, Mex.
Feb. 2: Three members of the Arab National Youth for the Liberation of Palestine commandeered a Greek ship in Karachi, Pakistan, demanding the release of imprisoned terrorists.
Feb. 3: A bank at Stansted Airport, near London, was robbed of $80,000 by four men who claimed to be IRA members.
Feb. 3: Eleven people were killed in England when an bomb exploded on a bus filled with soldiers and their families. The IRA was blamed for the attack.
Feb. 3: A bomb that was discovered beneath a police vehicle was successfully dismantled in Laurel, Md.
Feb. 4: At the *Daily Express*, a London newspaper, a letter bomb exploded, injuring a guard.
Feb. 4: In Berkeley, Calif., heiress Patricia Hearst was kidnapped by members of the Symbionese Liberation Army.
Feb. 4: Four members of a Sunni Muslim sect were murdered by rival Black Muslims in Brooklyn, N.Y.
Feb. 6: Five Japanese Red Army and PFLP terrorists occupied the Japanese Embassy in Kuwait and successfully negotiated the release of four imprisoned colleagues.
Feb. 11: Three buildings affiliated with religious organizations were bombed in Jerusalem. The JDL was suspected.
Feb. 11: An independent truckers' strike ended after violence in twenty states and two killings during the labor dispute.
Feb. 12: Buenos Aires federal police uncovered a plot by left-wing Peronist guerrillas and guerrillas from Uruguay to assassinate President Juan Perón, his wife Isabel Perón and Uruguay's president Juan M. Bordaberry. Thirty Uruguayans were arrested, as well as Peronist guerrilla Carlos ALberto Caride, an FAR member.
Feb. 12: A firebomb exploded at the school administration building in Middletown, Ohio.
Feb. 16: The University of Cali in Colombia was occupied by members of the M-19, who painted slogans on the walls and issued a proclamation demanding the release of twenty leftists from jail.
Feb. 17: An Army private was shot down and apprehended after he commandeered a helicopter and hovered near the White House in Washington, D.C.
Feb. 20: Four members of the American Revolutionary Army kidnapped *Atlanta Constitution* editor J. Reginald Murphy. He was released two days later, after a $700,000 ransom was paid by the newspaper.
Feb. 22: A police officer and a copilot were shot to death and a pilot wounded by a man who in turn killed himself during a hijacking attempt in Baltimore.
Feb. 23: While attempting to defuse a bomb found at the U.S.-owned Dow Chemical plant in Lavrion, Gr., two demolition experts were killed. The bombs allegedly were planted by people protesting U.S. support of the government in Athens.
Feb. 24: A bomb exploded at a school in Boulder, Colo.
Mar. 1: A terrorist fire destroyed a Sonolar Corp. plant in Paris. We Must Do Something was linked to the attack.
Mar. 1: An attempted bombing occurred at the police headquarters in Kingsport, Tenn.
Mar. 3: A British airplane en route from Bombay to London was hijacked by two Arabs at the Beirut airport and forced to land at the Schiphol Airport in Amsterdam, where ninety-two passengers and twenty crew members were freed before the aircraft was bombed.
Mar. 3: A bomb placed by members of Americans for Justice exploded in San Francisco.
Mar. 6: A high school student was caught with twenty-four pipe bombs in Johanna, Ohio.
Mar. 7: Members of the Weather Underground bombed the Department of Health, Education, and Welfare building in San Francisco.
Mar. 7: A bomb exploded at a state office building in Portland, Ore.
Mar. 8: A bomb exploded in front of the British Army headquarters in central Belfast, Ire., with no injuries reported. The IRA was believed responsible.
Mar. 8: A pipe bomb exploded at a reformatory in Lorton, Va.
Mar. 9: Terrorists attempted to cause a gas explosion in Beverly Hills, Calif.
Mar. 14: In Venezuela a new supermarket owned partly by the U.S. Rockefeller family was set on fire with the Red Flag guerrilla group claiming the action, as did the National Liberation Armed Forces.
Mar. 14: Six Arab terrorists were caught smuggling weapons onto a KLM plane which they allegedly planned to hijack from Beirut.
Mar. 15: A bomb exploded at a police station in Pasadena, Calif. A man who called himself the Phantom claimed responsibility.
Mar. 15: Six Arabs were arrested by police after they tried to smuggle explosives and arms above a KLM Royal Dutch Airlines plane in the Beirut airport. The would-be hijackers included a Lebanese employee of KLM, a Jordanian, an Egyptian, and a man from Yemen.
Mar. 16: Another bomb exploded at a police station in Pasadena, Calif.
Mar. 16: A bomb exploded at the University of Colorado police Department in Boulder, followed by an explosion at the Boulder Courthouse minutes later.
Mar. 17: In Northern Ireland a hijacked truck driven by four masked guerrillas infiltrated the U.S. Navy communications center outside Londonderry and opened fire on a guard in an attempt to steal weapons. The terrorists took one U.S. hostage, but he escaped, and the men fled on foot. There were no injuries.
Mar. 18: A bomb was discovered and defused in an office at Fort Rucker, Ala.
Mar. 21: Firebombs exploded at two grocery stores in Stockton, Calif.
Mar. 21: A bomb exploded at the police station in Folcroft, Pa.
Mar. 25: U.S. Vice Consul John Patterson was kidnapped in Hermosillo, Mex. Abductors left a note, signed by the Mexican People's Revolutionary Army, demanding a $500,000 ransom.
Mar. 25: A fake bomb was used to extort money from a bank in Houston.
Mar. 26: The headquarters of an army bomb-disposal regiment in northern England was hit by terrorist bombs; one person was wounded.
Mar. 26: In Ethiopia three employees of U.S. oil company Tenneco, Inc., and two other people were captured by ELF members. Negotiation talks came to a halt when a person sent to get the company employees was also kidnapped and a Dutch nurse was killed. A U.S. nurse was kidnapped by the ELF on May 27, and medical aid and equipment were demanded for her release.
Mar. 26: A bomb exploded and twelve more discovered in a bomb factory in Arlington Heights, Ill.
Mar. 30: A man was arrested after being disarmed as he attempted to hijack a plane in Sarasota, Fla.
Mar. 31: Two members of the terrorist organization US escaped from San Quentin prison in California.
April: Racial tensions in the classrooms in Osawatomie, Kan., fomented violence in the streets, resulting in ten arrests.
Apr. 4-10: Members of an anti-Castro organization, Abdala, bombed eight buildings in San Juan, P.R.
Apr. 8: A bombing attempt failed at a diplomatic residence in Washington, D.C.
Apr. 8: A molotov cocktail exploded near a police station in Bradenton, Fla.

Apr. 11: A resident building in Qiryat Shemona, Isr., was stormed by three Arab guerrillas, leaving eighteen people killed and sixteen wounded. The terrorists, believed to be part of the PFLP-GC died in a gun and grenade battle with Israeli troops.
Apr. 12: In Argentina Alfred Laun, head of the U.S. Information Service branch in Córdoba, was captured and wounded by the ERP. Although the guerrillas announced that Laun would be questioned for "counter-revolutionary activities" in several countries, he was released on Apr. 13, presumably because of his serious wounds.
Apr. 13: Former Cuban government minister Jose de la Torriente was shot to death in Miami, by members of Zero, a pro-Castro group.
Apr. 14: At the Lebanese consulate in Los Angeles a bomb exploded, apparently in retaliation for the raid by Arab guerrillas on Qiryat Shemona in Israel on Apr. 11. There were no injuries and $1,500 in damages. The JDL was suspected in the action.
Apr. 15: Members of the SLA, including kidnapped heiress Patricia Hearst, robbed a branch office of the Hibernia Bank in San Francisco.
Apr. 18: The Technical Military Academy in Cairo was attacked by an extremist organization connected with Libya and led by an Iraqui national. Eleven people were killed in the attack, and twenty-seven were injured.
Apr. 18: Two buildings in Burlingame, Calif., were damaged by a bomb.
Apr. 18: A bomb destroyed a police car in Prosser, Wash.
Apr. 19: A tear-gas grenade exploded at a high school in Ocala, Fla.
Apr. 19: A riot developed in Union City Calif., after police officers shot a suspected shoplifter.
Apr. 22: A plot to blow up an El Al Israel Airlines office, a police registration for foreigners office, a Jewish owned nightclub, and a hotel was uncovered. Two Palestinian terrorists were convicted but then released on June 9, following threats that other terrorists would strike at West Berlin's World Cup soccer matches if the imprisoned Arabs were not released.
Apr. 23: In southern Thailand the Pattani Liberation Front, a Muslim separtist movement, claimed credit for kidnapping two women missionaries and demanded that Britain and the U.S. stop all economic and military aid to Thailand.
Apr. 24: A police car was damaged by an explosion in Cecil County, Md.
Apr. 25: Racial tensions developed into fistfights at a high school in Salinas, Calif.
Apr. 25: A fake bomb was discovered on a campus in University Park, Texas.
Apr. 26: In a raid on the home of English millionaire Sir Alfred Beit five people, including Bridget Rose Dugdale, were arrested for stealing nineteen paintings valued at $19.2 million. A week later a letter demanded the transfer of IRA guerrillas Doulours and Marion Price, Hugh Tenny and Gerald Kelly from England to prisons in Ulster, demanding also $1.2 million in cash by May 14 and threatening to destroy the paintings unless the demands were met. On May 3 all of the stolen art was recovered. Dugdale was later given a nine year jail sentence.
Apr. 28: A fake bomb was discovered at a newspaper office in Dallas.
Apr. 29: A fake bomb was discovered at a court house in Washington, D.C.
Apr. 30: A manufacturing plant was damaged by a dynamite blast in Cleveland.
Apr. 30: Rioting occured surrounding the trial of AIM leader Russell Means in Sioux Falls, S.D.
May 1: A bomb explosion injured two people at an airport in New York City.
May 3: A bomb exploded at a police station in Lexington, Ky.
May 3: Members of the Black Liberation Army shot a police officer and robbed a bank in New Haven, Conn.
May 4: A bomb exploded in a public park in New York City.
May 13: Two people were wounded as fifty Mohawk Indians seized state-owned land in Eagle Bay, N.Y.
May 16: SLA terrorists Bill and Emily Harris, as well as kidnapped heiress Patricia Hearst, kidnapped a student in Los Angeles and held him hostage for twelve hours.
May 17: Six Symbionese Liberation Army members were killed during a shootout with police in Los Angeles.
May 17: Four Loyalist bombs killed thirty people in Dublin and Monaghan, Ire.
May 20: A bomb exploded beneath a police car in Yuba City, Calif.
May 21: A state office in Yuba City, Calif., was damaged by a molotov cocktail explosion.
May 23: A man was arrested in New York City after he wounded a helicoptor pilot during a hijacking attempt.
May 29: A bomb placed by the Habash Front exploded near a Japanese Airline office in West Berlin.
May 31: Members of the Weather Underground bombed the offices of the California Attorney General in Los Angeles.
May 31: A pipe bomb exploded at a police station in Chicago.
June: Sixteen bombs were planted at nine department stores in New York City.
June 2: Two members of the Black Liberation Army were arrested following an attack on police officers in New York City.
June 6: Terrorists attempted to bomb an oil storage tank in Detroit.
June 11: A court house was bombed in San Pedro, Calif.
June 11: A pipe bomb was discovered at a foreign embassy in New York City.
June 11: The private vehicle of a police officer was bombed in St. Louis.
June 11: Police Chief William Cann was shot to death by snipers in a church in Union City, Calif.
June 13: A bomb placed by WU terrorists exploded at the offices of Gulf Oil in Pittsburgh.
June 14: Members of the FALN Puerto Rican Nationalists set off two bombs in Chicago.
June 19: The offices of Bank of America and Coca-Cola were bombed in Buenos Aires, Arg.
June 26: A man being escorted to prison was able to produce a gun and hijack a flight after taking off from Alexandria, La. He was recaptured upon landing in Hammond, La.
June 26: A bomb exploded beneath a city vehicle in Las Vegas, Nev.
June 27: Three men were arrested after they robbed a bank and hijacked an aircraft in Ashland, Mont.
June 28: A bomb was discovered on the campus of a community college in Hazard, Ky.
July 6: A huge cache of weapons, including machine guns, grenades, and rocket launchers, was stolen from a National Guard Armory in Compton, Calif.
July 11: Two prisoners took seven hostages as they seized a courthouse for four days in Washington, D.C.
July 12: Members of the White Panthers fought a gun battle with police in San Francisco.
July 14: Three bombs exploded at a housing development in Strongville, Ohio.
July 14: A bomb exploded beneath a city employee's vehicle in South Greensburg, Pa.
July 23: A pipe bomb exploded at a foreign mission in Washington, D.C.
July 25: A bombing attempt failed at a foreign embassy in Washington, D.C.
July 26: Japanese Red Army terrorist Yoshiaka Yamada was arrested at Orly Airport in Paris.
August: Racial violence broke out in response to the fatal shooting of a black youth by police in Savannah, Ga.
Aug. 3: Car bombs placed by members of the PFLP and the terrorist Carlos exploded outside the offices of three Paris newspapers.
Aug. 5: Members of the New World Liberation Front attempted to bomb an insurance agency in Burlingame, Calif.
Aug. 6: A bomb placed by a member of the Aliens of America, exploded at Los Angeles International Airport.
Aug. 7: Terrorists failed in the bombing attempt of the United Nations building in New York City.
Aug. 8: Members of the New World Liberation Front attempted to bomb an auto agency in San Francisco.
Aug. 23: Racial violence occurred after a black man was shot by a police officer in Herndon, Va.
Aug. 23: Spectators disrupted the trial of AIM leaders in St. Paul, Minn.
Aug. 26: The Israel Tourist Office was bombed by members of the Habash Front in Frankfurt.
Aug. 26: The factory of an Israeli industrial concern was bombed by Habash Front terrorists in Mannheim, Ger.
September: Racial fighting between students broke out at two high schools in Oklahoma City.
September: Racial fighting lasted five days at a high school in West Pittsburg, Calif.
Sept. 1: Three people were shot during a Puerto Rican festival in Newark, N.J.
Sept. 2: Two people were killed during rioting in a Puerto Rican neighborhood in Newark, N.J. Eighteen firebombings occurred in the ensuing violence that lasted five days.
Sept. 3: Members of the New World Liberation Front bombed a stock brokerage office in San Francisco.
Sept. 4: A man was arrested after attempting to hijack a flight in Boston.
Sept. 7: U.S. Information Services director Barbara Hutchison and six others were kidnapped in the Dominican Republic and held at the Venezuelan consulate. They were released thirteen days later, despite the refusal of a $1 million ransom and the release of prisoners.
Sept 8: The Arab Nationalist Youth Organization for the Liberation of Palestine caused the death of eighty-eight passengers when a TWA aircraft exploded off the coast of Greece, en route from Lod to New York.
Sept. 10: Members of the Weather Underground bombed a corporate office in San Leandro, Calif.
Sept. 11: The offices of several foreign companies were bombed in Argentina, coinciding with the anniversary of the ouster of Allende in Chile.
Sept. 12: Rocks were thrown at buses carrying black school children in Boston. The incident was repeated the next day.
Sept. 12: Four men were arrested after taking two hostages during a robbery attempt in the Bronx, N.Y.
Sept. 13: Terrorist Yoshiaka Yamada was freed in exchange for hostages after three Japanese Red Army terrorists invaded the French Embassy in The Hague, Neth.
Sept. 15: Two people were killed and another thirty-four wounded when

the terrorist Carlos tossed a bomb into a Paris drug store.
Sept. 16: Several U.S. companies were the targets for more than forty bombs which exploded in Argentina, commemorating the revolt which ended the regime of Juan Peron.
Sept. 16: Eight police officers were among the ten people injured in a riot outside a police station in Brooklyn, N.Y.
Sept. 19: Racial violence occurred in the Brownsville neighborhood of Brooklyn, N.Y.
Sept. 28: A bomb exploded between the city hall and police department in Newark, N.J.
Oct. 1: Fifteen Fatah-Black September terrorists were arrested in Rabat, Mor., and charged with conspiring to assassinate Jordan's King Hussein.
Oct. 2: Members of the New World Liberation Front bombed a hotel in San Francisco.
Oct. 5: Members of the New World Liberation Front bombed a hotel in Los Angeles.
Oct. 6: An Avis office and an ITT plant were firebombed in Milan, Italy.
Oct. 8: Racial violence broke out at a high school in the Roxbury section of Boston.
Oct. 9: Members of FLNC bombed a theater in San Juan, Puerto Rico.
Oct. 10: A boy was killed when an Arab Communist Organization bomb exploded at a National Cash Register office in Damascus, Syria.
Oct. 11: In Beirut, the office of the First National Bank of Chicago was bombed by the Arab Communist Organization.
Oct. 26: Members of FALN bombed the entances of five banks in New York City.
Oct. 28: A firebomb exploded at a police community relations office in El Paso, Tex.
Oct. 30: Members of the New World Liberation Front bombed the home of a former ITT executive in Los Altos Hills, Cal.
Nov. 2: Terrorists tossed a molotov cocktail towards a police community relations office in El Paso.
Nov. 5: A U.S. Dept. of Commerce Trade Center was firebombed in Milan, Italy.
Nov. 9: Members of the FLNC anti-Castro group bombed the Organization of American States building in Washington, D.C.
Nov. 10: The Jewish Defense League was the primary suspect for a bomb that exploded at the U.N. Information Center in Los Angeles.
Nov. 14: The wife of a U.S. real-estate agent was kidnapped in Cuernavaca, Mex., by members of the United Popular Liberation Army.
Nov. 18: A Sears store in Mexico City was bombed by the 23rd of September terrorist organization.
Nov. 18: A Philippine embassy official was wounded and the ambassador kidnapped by a gunman in Washington, D.C. The hostage was released when the gunman's son was allowed to emigrate to the U.S.
Nov. 21: Twenty-one people were killed and 182 injured when two Provisional IRA bombs exploded at pubs in Birmingham, Eng.
Nov. 22: Two Abu Nidal terrorists were freed from Dutch prisons and fifteen from Rabat, in exchange for passengers who became hostages during the hijacking of a British Airways airliner in Dubai.
Nov. 25: The office of First National City Bank of N.Y. and two General Motors showrooms were bombed in Buenos Aires, Arg.
December: Two gas utility cooling towers and twenty gas transmission lines were damaged by bomb explosions in Kentucky.
Dec. 2: Two gunmen were arrested after taking seven people hostage during a failed robbery attempt at a grocery store in San Francisco.
Dec. 5: Two hostages were taken by a September 23 guerrilla terrorist requesting political asylum, who occupied the French embassy in Mexico City. He was arrested after authorities gave in to his demands.
Dec. 11: A police officer was injured by an FALN bomb explosion, after being lured to a building in New York City.
Dec. 11: A white mob held a group of black captive for four hours at a high school in South Boston.
Dec. 14: A man successfully hijacked a private plane from Tampa, Fla., to Cuba.
Dec. 15: The Youth Action Group bombed Coca-Cola and TWA offices in Paris.
Dec. 16: The Youth Action Group bombed a 3M Corp. office in Paris.
Dec. 19: Members of the New World Liberation Front bombed an office building in San Francisco.
Dec. 20: Four Indian gunmen were arrested after taking forty people hostage during a thwarted robbery at a grocery store in Richfield, Minn.
Dec. 28: A man was arrested as he attempted to escape from authorities after hijacking a plane to Grand Forks, N.D.
Dec. 29: Two days of racial violence occured in Port Arthur, Tex., after a black youth was shot as he fled from police headquarters.

1975

Ten members of the FALN,Armed Forces of National Liberation of Puerto Rico, committed terrorist acts over a four-year period related to planting bombs in twenty-eight Chicago buildings. All served state prison terms for weapons violations, armed robbery, and conspiracy; all were sentenced by a Federal judge to terms ranging from fifty-five to ninety years.
Jan. 1: A Roman Catholic abbey in Gresham, Wis., was seized by forty-five members of the Menominee Warrior Society.
Jan. 3: A man was overpowered and arrested as he attempted to hijack a flight in Pensacola, Fla.
Jan. 4: A bomb exploded at a police station in Columbus, Ohio.
Jan. 13: A Yugoslav plane was damaged in Paris by the terrorist Carlos, who was attempting to destroy a neighboring El Al aircraft with hand-held missiles.
Jan. 13: Three persons were injured in racial violence at a high school in Boston.
Jan. 13: A man was arrested on a plane in Washington, D.C., as he was attempting to hijack a flight to San Juan, P.R.
Jan. 19: Carlos-PFLP terrorists escaped to Iraq after taking hostages at Paris' Orly Airport during an thwarted bombing attempt.
Jan. 22: Two gunmen escaped after taking six people hostage during a thwarted robbery attempt of a clothing store in South Bend, Ind.
Jan. 24: Four people were killed and fifty-three were injured when a FALN bomb exploded at Fraunces Tavern in New York.
Jan. 29: A bomb placed by the Weather Underground exploded at the U.S. State Department, causing extensive damage.
Jan. 29: A bomb placed by members of the Weather Underground failed to detonate at a Federal building in Oakland, Calif.
Feb. 1: Members of the anti-Castro group Abdala bombed the Venezuelan Consulate in New York City.
Feb. 2: Members of the National Socialist Liberation Army tear-gassed a leftist rally in Santa Monica, Calif.
Feb. 3: Members of the New World Liberation Front bombed a corporate office building in San Jose, Calif.
Feb. 3: Four people were injured when a bomb placed by members of the Continental Revolutionary Army, exploded at a Securities and Exchange Commission office in Denver.
Feb. 4: Members of the New World Liberation Front bombed an Air Force facility and an asphalt company in El Granada, Calif.
Feb. 4: The National Socialist Liberation Front was the primary suspect in the bombing of the Socialist Workers Party office in Los Angeles.
Feb. 5: Members of the New World Liberation Front bombed a foundry in Oakland, Calif.
Feb. 6: A bomb placed by members of the New World Liberation Front exploded at a television station in San Francisco.
Feb. 6: The Cuban Action Commandos were the primary suspects for the bombing of a socialist book store in Los Angeles.
Feb. 11: The Arab Communist Organization bombed an American Life Insurance Company office in Tyre, Leb.
Feb. 11: Members of two anti-Castro groups were suspected of a bombing incident in Elizabeth, N.J.
Feb. 14: Violence broke out in the courtroom of a Menominee Indian trial in Shawano, Wis.
Feb. 26: Members of the Cuban Action Commandos bombed a radio station in Los Angeles.
Feb. 27: Five West German terrorists were freed in exchange for politician Peter Lorenz, who was kidnapped by Baader-Meinhof terrorists.
March: Herbert Chitepo, former chairman of the Zimbabwe African National Union, was murdered in Lusaka, Zambia.
Mar. 1: A guard was stabbed with a pencil as two SLA members on trial for murder attempted to escape from a courtroom in Oakland, Calif.
Mar. 1: A bomb destroyed a sheet metal company in Shelton, Conn.
Mar. 2: A man was overpowered as he attempted to hijack a small plane in Hyannis, Mass.
Mar. 3: Members of the AIM occupied a manufacturing plant in Shiprock, N.M.
Mar. 6: Two men hijacked a private plane to Nogales, Mex., shortly after takeoff from Phoenix, Ariz.
Mar. 8: Police confiscated seventy-five pounds of explosives on the Lower East Side of New York.
Mar. 10: A young girl was injured when two hand grenades exploded at the home of a private investigator in Staten Island, N.Y.
Mar. 10: Pipe bombs placed by members of the Chicano Liberation Front exploded at a bank, grocery store, and corporate headquarters in San Francisco.
Mar. 12: A transmission line was bombed in San Bruno Hills, Calif.
Mar. 14: A terrorist with four molotov cocktails in his possession was arrested in Miami.
Mar. 17: Members of the Eagle Warrior Society occupied a food processing plant and held it for three days in Wagner, S.D.
Mar. 20: Members of the New World Liberation Front bombed six electric utility towers in San Bruno, Calif.
Mar. 26: Police discovered a pipe bomb near a station house in New York City.
Mar. 27: Members of the New World Liberation Front bombed a utility power facility in San Jose, Calif.
Mar. 27: A bomb placed by members of the Red Guerrilla Family exploded at an FBI office in Berkeley, Calif.
Mar. 27: Members of the Cuban Action Commandos bombed two foreign government offices in Los Angeles.
Mar. 29: Terrorists bombed an electrical utility transformer in Sacramento, Calif.
Apr. 2: FALN terrorists bombed four buildings in New York City.
Apr. 3: The Cuban Action Commandos were suspected of a bombing attempt at the Communist Party headquarters in Los Angeles.
Apr. 4: A Standard Oil Company office was bombed in San Francisco as President Gerald Ford was delivering a speech less than a mile away.
Apr. 5: A member of the Jewish Defense League attempted to bomb

a travel agency in Los Angeles.
Apr. 5: A bomb exploded at the Iraqi Airways office in Los Angeles.
Apr. 8: Members of the New World Liberation Front bombed a utility substation in San Jose, Calif.
Apr. 9: Members of two tribes seized and occupied the Bureau of Indian Affairs office in Horton, Kan.
Apr. 11: The Arab Communist Organization bombed an American Life Insurance office in Kuwait.
Apr. 13: Members of the Cuban Action Commandos bombed a left-wing book store in Los Angeles.
Apr. 21: One person was killed as a SLA terrorist robbed a bank near Sacramento, Calif.
Apr. 24: Two diplomats in the West German embassy in Stockholm, Swed., were killed by six Baader-Meinhof terrorists after the demand to free twenty-six imprisoned terrorists was not met. As police approached, the Embassy was blown up, killing two of the invaders. The remaining four were taken into custody.
Apr. 25: A man was arrested after failing in his attempt to hijack a United Airlines flight bound for Newark, N.J.
Apr. 28: Bombs exploded at the home of a CIA employee and at a bank in Denver.
May 1: Members of the Nat Turner-John Brown faction of the New World Liberation Front bombed a California Department of Corrections office in Sacramento, Calif.
May 2: Members of the Cuban Action Commandos bombed a left-wing book store in Santa Monica, Calif.
May 2: Armed Indian protesters occupied a food processing plant in Wagner, S.D.
May 7: A bomb exploded at a left-wing book store in Los Angeles.
May 9: Members of the New World Liberation Front bombed a utility office in Berkeley, Calif.
May 15: A female passenger was arrested after making a hijacking threat on a United Airlines flight to San Francisco.
May 25: A member of the Black Liberation Army fell to his death during an attempted escape from the Brooklyn House of Detention in New York.
May 31: An ITT Corp. office was bombed in Beirut, Leb.
May 31: Members of the George Jackson Brigade bombed a correctional institution office in Olympia, Wash.
June 6: Racial violence broke out in Hamlet, N.C., following the allegation by a black woman that a white police officer had beaten her.
June 6: A convict was captured after he escaped from prison in a helicopter hijacked by an accomplice in Plymouth, Mich.
June 7: American Indian Movement leader Russell Means was wounded during a clash with agents of the Bureau of Indian Affairs at the Standing Rock Reservation in North Dakota.
June 8: The leader of the United Prisoner's Union and a school teacher were shot to death in San Francisco by alleged members of the New World Liberation Front.
June 14: Bombs placed by FALN members exploded at a bank and an outdoor plaza in Chicago, coinciding with the celebration of Puerto Rican Day.
June 16: Members of the Weather Underground bombed a Puerto Rican branch bank in New York City.
June 17: Cuban-American demonstrators clashed with police in Elizabeth, N.J.
June 19: A McDonald's restaurant was bombed in Stockholm, Swed.
June 23: A bomb destroyed a TWA employee's car in Tel Aviv, Isr.
June 24: FBI agents were besieged by gun fire and a pipe bomb as they attempted to apprehend members of a terrorist group in Chicago.
June 26: Two FBI agents and an AIM member were killed during a gun battle at the Pine Ridge Indian Reservation in South Dakota.
June 27: Two police officers and a PFLP liaison officer were killed as French authorities sought to apprehend the terrorist Carlos in Paris. Following the shoot-out, Carlos escaped to Algeria.
June 27: Members of the New World Liberation Front bombed the Bureau of Indian Affairs in Alameda, Calif.
June 27: A bomb exploded near the Mount Rushmore memorial in South Dakota.
July 2: Four members of the Black Muslims were shot by passers-by in Chattanooga, Tenn.
July 14: Six people were kidnapped by ELF-Revolutionary Council guerrillas in Asmara, Eth. They were released on May 3, 1976.
July 14: A bomb exploded at the headquarters of the Revolutionary Black Guard in Cleveland.
July 15: A bomb placed by a consortium of three terrorist groups exploded at the Mexican consulate in Los Angeles, injuring four persons.
July 18: A bomb partially detonated near the Costa Rican embassy in Washington, D.C.
July 21: A bomb placed by members of the Red Guerrilla Family exploded near U.S. Treasury Department offices in San Francisco.
July 28: Two days of rioting occurred in Detroit, following the fatal shooting of a black youth by a white tavern owner.
July 31: Three people were killed by UVF terrorists in Armagh, Ire.
Aug. 2: Looting and vandalism followed the conclusion of the All Nations' Festival in Cleveland, Ohio.
Aug. 3: The Japanese Red Army seized the U.S. Consulate in Kuala Lumpur, Malaysia, taking fifty-three hostages.
Aug. 5: Sears, Roebuck executive Donald Cooper was kidnapped by five terrorists in Bogota, Col. He was released on Nov. 2, 1975.
Aug. 5: Bombs placed by a member of the George Jackson Brigade exploded at a courthouse and a Bureau of Indian Affairs office in Tacoma, Wash.
Aug. 8: A bomb exploded at the U.S. Courthouse in Denver.
Aug. 8: The estate of a director of a supermarket chain was bombed by members of the New World Liberation Front in California.
Aug. 10: Blacks trying to use a beach in a white neighborhood led to three days of violence in Boston.
Aug. 12: The shooting of a black youth by a white police officer provoked three days of racial violence in Elyria, Ohio.
Aug. 15: Five people were killed when a Provisional IRA bomb exploded at a pub in Belfast, Ire.
Aug. 16: National Student Liberation Front leader Joseph Tommassi was shot to death by members of the American Nazi Party, which he had headed at one time.
Aug. 16: A pilot landed his plane on a highway when it ran out of fuel after being hijacked from Woodbridge, Va.
Aug. 17: Police in Wilmington, Del., use tear gas to quell a disturbance after a black woman was shot by a white man.
Aug. 19: A McDonald's restaurant was bombed for the second time in Stockholm, Swed.
Aug. 20: Members of the NWLF and SLA bombed two police cars in San Rafael, Calif. Kidnapped heiress Patricia Hearst admitted to being present during the incident.
Aug. 23: A land-mine explosion killed nine employees of the Collins International Services Co. in Asmara, Eth.
Aug. 30: Muslim dissidents kidnapped two Boise-Cascade employees in Zamboanga, Phil. They were released two days later.
September: Two students were shot during rioting at an Oklahoma City high school.
Sept. 2: Six Protestants were shot to death by Provisional IRA members in South Armagh, Ire.
Sept. 2: A hostage was killed and a police officer wounded during an lengthy shootout with a man who attempted to rob a motel in Lake Tahoe, Calif.
Sept. 2: Four members of the right-wing Posse Comitatus were arrested for blockading union organizers in the San Joaquin Valley of California.
Sept. 4: A man surrendered after taking ten people hostage during a thwarted bank robbery in Albany, N.Y.
Sept. 4: Thirty-five people were injured during two days of rioting at a high school in Louisville, Ky.
Sept. 5: Lynette "Squeaky" Fromme was arrested after she attempted to assassinate President Gerald Ford.
Sept. 5: Members of the Weather Underground bombed an office building in Salt Lake City.
Sept. 5: Racial fighting erupted during a high school football game in Raleigh, N.C.
Sept. 6: Seventy-five anti-busing demonstrators were arrested as National Guardsmen converged in Louisville, Ky.
Sept. 9: An oil company office was bombed in Carteret, N.J.
Sept. 11: Bombs exploded at a gas station and an oil company office in Chamblee, Ga.
Sept. 12: A Federal building in Seattle was bombed by the People's Forces Unit IX division of the New World Liberation Front.
Sept. 12: Rocks, bottles, and firebombs were thrown at police officers in two Boston neighborhoods.
Sept. 12: Members of the People's Forces Unit IX of the NWLF failed in their attempt to bomb a Federal building in Phoenix, Ariz.
Sept. 12: Racial violence occurred at a high school in Winchester, Va.
Sept. 15: The Egyptian embassy in Madrid was invaded by four Arab terrorists who took three hostages. The siege ended after four Middle-Eastern ambassadors signed an accord denouncing the Sinai agreement, and the gunmen were given passage to Algeria.
Sept. 15: A man was shot to death by police in San Jose, Calif., after wounding one of the four hostages he took during a hijacking attempt.
Sept. 15: A terrorist named Ralph Patrick Ford was killed when his own bomb exploded at a grocery store in Seattle.
Sept. 16: Police disarmed a bomb that was about to explode near a meeting of the International Association of Police Chiefs in Denver.
Sept. 16: A second incident of racial violence forced the closure of a high school in Winchester, Va.
Sept. 16: A student was injured during racial violence at a high school in South Boston.
Sept. 16: Members of the Socialist White People's Party and the Progressive Labor Party attempted to lynch a black minister in Pasadena, Calif.
Sept. 18: A former Philadelphia police officer was arrested after he threatened to kidnap a U.S. Representative in Washington, D.C.
Sept. 18: Hostage-turned-revolutionary Patricia Hearst and three members of the Symbionese Liberation Army were arrested for bank robbery in San Francisco.
Sept. 18: Nine people were injured when a bomb placed by members of the George Jackson Brigade exploded at a grocery store in Seattle.
Sept. 18: A student was killed and another wounded during a riot at an Oklahoma City high school.
Sept. 20: Racial violence broke out at a high school in Suitland, Md.,

with students throwing rocks and bottles and swinging chains.
Sept. 21: A gunman held tavern employees hostage during a robbery in Boston.
Sept. 22: Sara Jane Moore was arrested after she attempted to assassinate President Gerald Ford in San Francisco.
Sept. 24: The offices of Xerox Corp. were bombed in Córdoba, Arg.
Sept. 24: Weather Underground founder Larry Handelsman was arrested by police in Seattle.
Sept. 26: Student demonstrators were dispersed with tear gas, at a high school in Louisville, Ky.
Oct. 1: Twelve people were injured during racial violence at a high school in Danbury, Conn.
Oct. 2: Twelve people were killed and forty-six injured by UVF members in a series of attacks in Northern Ireland. The UVF was declared an illegal organization the next day.
Oct. 5: A firebomb damaged a truck in Kalamazoo, Mich. Five strikers were arrested.
Oct. 6: A bomb placed by members of the FINC-Youth of the Stars, exploded at the Dominican consulate in Miami.
Oct. 6: A gunman was arrested after taking ten people hostage at a bank in New York City.
Oct. 7: Three people were arrested after attempting to hijack a plane in Greensboro, N.C.
Oct. 8: Twenty-three people were arrested during racial conflict at a high school in the Bronx, N.Y.
Oct. 10: Members of the anti-Castro group FLNC bombed a courthouse in Fort Lauderdale, Fla.
Oct. 10: Students rioted at a high school in Boston.
Oct. 13: Two people were injured during racial violence at a high school in Baltimore.
Oct. 13: A bomb exploded at the Bureau of Indian Affairs at the Pine Ridge Reservation in South Dakota.
Oct. 13: A bomb was discovered near an electric utility tower in Redwood City, Calif.
Oct. 13: Members of the Emiliano Zapata Unit attempted to bomb a utility tower in Belmont, Calif.
Oct. 17: A bomb exploded at Miami International Airport.
Oct. 20: Rioting broke out in a Wilmington, Del., Puerto Rican neighborhood following the arrest of two youths for loitering.
Oct. 21: A bomb exploded at a Safeway store in Oakland, Calif.
Oct. 22: Two right-wing terrorists were arrested in Phoenix, Ariz., for plotting to assassinate government agents.
Oct. 24: Another bomb exploded at a Safeway store in Oakland, Calif.
Oct. 27: Members of the FALN bombed a bank and two office buildings in Chicago, two government buildings in Washington, D.C., and four banks and a U.N. Mission in New York City.
Oct. 29: A paroled man surrendered after taking nine hostages during a thwarted bank robbery in Cleveland, Ohio.
Oct. 31: A car bomb exploded in Miami, killing Cuban vigilante Rolando Masferrer.
Oct. 31: Members of the New World Liberation Front bombed a storage building at Fort Ord, Calif.
Oct. 31: Members of the Emiliano Zapata Unit bombed a grocery store in Oakland, Calif.
Nov. 5: Police used tear gas on a rioting crowd of demonstrators in Louisville, Ky.
Nov. 8: A young man fell to his death after being pushed out of a plane he was attempting to hijack over Evansville, Ind.
Nov. 11: Five people were shot during disturbances at the White Earth Indian Reservation near Mahnomen, Minn.
Nov. 11: Fighting broke out between white and black students at a high school in Annapolis, Md.
Nov. 19: Twenty Indian demonstrators were arrested while attempting to enter a John Birch Society meeting in Milwaukee.
Nov. 21: Two CBS employees suspected of being CIA agents were detained by MPLA guerrillas in Angola. They were released on Dec. 11, 1975.
Nov. 24: A man hijacked a chartered plane from Palomar, Calif., to Mazatlan, Mex.
Nov. 27: A time bomb placed by members of Cuban Power '76 exploded in a Bahamas Airline plane while it was on the ground in Miami.
Nov. 27: Members of the Emiliano Zapata Unit bombed a Safeway store in San Francisco.
Nov. 30: The car of a hospital equipment firm owner was bombed in San Francisco by members of the New World Liberation Front.
Dec. 2: South Moluccan terrorists seized the Indonesian Embassy in the Hague as well as a train in Beilen, Holland, demanding Moluccan independence from Indonesia.
Dec. 2: A car at the former home of the San Francisco Police Officers' Association was bombed by members of the New World Liberation Front.
Dec. 3: Five government office building were bombed in Miami.
Dec. 4: Members of the anti-Castro group JIN bombed the police department and the Metropolitan Justice building in Miami.
Dec. 9: A bomb exploded at the home of a Boston clergyman.
Dec. 10: A bomb exploded at the NAACP office in Boston.
Dec. 21: Three people were killed and eleven kidnapped when the OPEC headquarters in Vienna was seized in a collective raid by the PFLP, German terrorists, and Carlos. The hostages were released for ransom in Algeria.
Dec. 22: A Collins International Service Co. executive was kidnapped by five terrorists in Asmara, Eth. He was released on June 3, 1976.
Dec. 23: A bomb placed by members of the Continental Revolutionary Army exploded at a Federal building in Denver.
Dec. 28: Members of the Emiliano Zapata Unit bombed a Safeway store in Belmont, Calif.
Dec. 29: A bomb exploded at the Chicago home of a Yugoslav consular official.
Dec. 29: Eleven people were killed when a bomb exploded at New York's LaGuardia Airport.
Dec. 29: Members of the JDL were arrested after spray-painting pro-Israeli slogans inside the Mexican consulate in Philadelphia.
Dec. 30: Members of the Emiliano Zapata Unit bombed a branch office of the Bank of America in Berkeley, Calif.
Dec. 31: Members of the George Jackson Brigade bombed a Safeway store in Bellevue, Wash., and a utility substation in nearby Laurelhurst.

1976

January: One person was killed during clashes between union and non-union personnel at a chemical company in Shreveport, La.
Jan. 1: Members of the Native Underground Red Cloud Group attempted to bomb the Bureau of Indian Affairs building in Parker, Ariz.
Jan 4: Five Catholics were shot to death by the Protestant Action Force in Northern Ireland.
Jan 5: Ten Protestants were machine-gunned to death by Provisional IRA terrorists in County Armagh, Ire.
Jan. 5: Three students were injured during a racial clash at a Chicago high school.
Jan. 7: Numerous left-wing headquarters were bombed in northern Portugal.
Jan. 7: Two sticks of dynamite placed by Byron G. Birch exploded near the Standard Oil storage tanks in Richmond, Calif.
Jan. 8: A member of the Society for International Involvement bombed a service station in Livermore, Calif. Police suspected Byron G. Birch as the culprit.
Jan. 9: A man kidnapped a Belle Vernon, Pa., store manager and his wife, releasing them after obtaining ransom money.
Jan. 10: Members of the New World Liberation Front sent bombs disguised as boxes of candy to two members of San Francisco's Board of Supervisors.
Jan. 11: A firebomb exploded at a community development center in Anaheim, Calif.
Jan. 12: Members of the Young Croatian Republican Army and the Jewish Armed Resistance Strike Movement placed three pipe bombs at the United Nations headquarters in New York City.
Jan. 12: Members of the Jewish Underground Army attempted to bomb the Iraqi Mission to the U.N. in New York City.
Jan. 13: A bomb placed by members of the Emiliano Zapata Unit exploded at a Safeway store in Novato, Calif.
Jan. 14: Two people were injured when a bomb placed by members of the Red Guerrilla Family explode at the Iranian consulate in San Francisco.
Jan. 14: A molotov cocktail was discovered at the home of a labor dispute participant in Deer Park, Texas.
Jan. 14: Terrorists attempted to bomb a diner in Hartford, Conn.
Jan. 16: A bomb planted beneath a police car in Union City, Calif., failed to explode.
Jan. 16: Members of the Jewish Armed Resistance bombed the Polish consulate in New York City.
Jan. 20: A bomb exploded at a non-union barbershop in Hendersonville, Tenn.
Jan. 21: Terrorists attempted to bomb the B'Nai Israel Temple in Sacramento, Calif.
Jan. 22: Police in San Jose, Calif., confiscated a large cache of weapons belonging to the Nuestra Familia, a prison-based gang.
Jan. 23: A member of the George Jackson Brigade was killed by police during a foiled bank robbery in Tukwila, Wash.
Jan. 28: A terrorist attempted to bomb the U.S. Public Health Center in Phoenix, Ariz.
Jan. 29: Two Bendix Corp. executives were killed by terrorists who invaded their offices in Buenos Aires, Arg.
Jan. 30: A pipe bomb placed by members of the Emiliano Zapata Unit, exploded at a Safeway store in Santa Clara, Calif.
Jan. 30: Six dynamite bombs were dismantled during a labor dispute at a construction site in Media, Pa.
Feb. 1: A bomb failed to detonate at the home of the owner of Gaitland Apartments in San Francisco.
Feb. 1: A bomb placed by members of the New World Liberation Front damaged a car in San Francisco.
Feb. 1: A bomb was discovered at a utility company in San Geronimo, Calif.
Feb. 1: The home of the Board Chairman of the Bank of California was set afire at Pebble Beach, Calif.
Feb. 3: A police officer was injured during a protest by Indians at a school in Anadarko, Okla.
Feb. 4: An arson fire destroyed the home of a black contractor in

Keyes, Calif.
Feb. 4: Two members of the Menominee Warrior Society were killed during a shootout with authorities in Keshena, Wis.
Feb. 12: Imprisoned IRA terrorist Frank Stagg died after a sixty-day hunger strike in Northern Ireland's Wakefield Prison. His death set off widespread shootings and bombings.
Feb. 12: A bomb placed by members of the New World Liberation Front exploded at the Hearst mansion in San Simeon, Calif.
Feb. 13: Terrorists attempting to bomb a power company fired at a deputy sheriff in San Mateo, Calif.
Feb. 16: Seventy police officers were among the 110 people injured during anti-busing demonstrations at a high school in South Boston, Mass.
Feb. 17: Members of the New Dawn Collective, posing as FBI agents, were involved in a shootout at the home of a reported drug dealer in Marin County, Calif.
Feb. 19: Four members of the Revolutionary Student Brigade were arrested during a demonstration of 5,000 students at the State House in Trenton, N.J.
Feb. 21: Members of the New World Liberation Front sabotaged eleven utility poles in San Francisco.
Feb. 21: Six members of the Emiliano Zapata Unit were arrested and a large cache of explosives seized by FBI agents and a SWAT team in Richmond, Calif.
Feb. 27: The branch offices of American Express and the Chase Manhattan Bank were bombed in Athens, Gr.
Feb. 27: Owens-Illinois Glass Company executive William Niehous was kidnapped by members of the Revolutionary Commandos in Caracas, Venez.
Mar. 3: Two workers were killed during a labor strike in the Basque region of Spain.
Mar. 5: Members of the Red Guerrilla Family bombed a Hewlitt-Packard laboratory in Palo Alto, Caif.
Mar. 5: A bomb placed by a consortium of three terrorist organizations exploded at a facility of the San Francisco Housing Authority.
Mar. 5: A mob of white people attacked the home of a black family in Philadelphia.
Mar. 8: The home of the only black family in a white neighborhood in Louisville, Ky., was dynamited.
Mar. 8: A teenager took two hostages while attempting to engage police in a shoot-out at Vista, Calif.
Mar. 9: Members of the New World Liberation Front bombed William Randolph Hearst's mountain retreat in Redding, Calif.
Mar. 10: Former UDA Chairman Sammy Smyth was shot to death in Northern Ireland.
Mar. 10: A member of the George Jackson Brigade shot a police officer and escaped custody as he was being delivered to a county jail in Seattle.
Mar. 11: IRA terrorists Eddie Gallagher and Marian Coyle received lengthy prison sentences in Dublin for the kidnapping of Dutch industrialist Tiede Herrema.
Mar. 13: A Sears store was firebombed by members of the Farabundo Marti Liberation Labor Forces in San Salvador, El Sal.
Mar. 14: Members of Save Our Israel smashed the windows of ten branch banks in New York City.
Mar. 17: A member of the group Vanguard surrendered after holding a hostage for two hours at the State Labor Department in New York City.
Mar. 20: Patricia Hearst was found guilty of armed robbery by a jury in San Francisco.
Mar. 23: Eight people were released after being held hostage at a hospital in Jefferson City, Mo.
Mar. 25: A time bomb placed by members of the Jewish Armed Resistance was discovered at a Soviet trade agency in New York City.
Mar. 26: Two Ford Motor Co. security guards were killed by machine-gun fire in Argentina.
Mar. 31: The branch offices of Pan Am and Philips Electronic were bombed in Ankara, Turk.
Apr. 2: The branch office of the First National City Bank was bombed in Bogota, Colombia.
Apr. 3: American Express offices were bombed in Athens, Gr.
Apr. 5: A black person was attacked and beaten by several white high school students during an anti-busing demonstration in Boston, Mass.
Apr. 7: A guard was killed and another injured when leftist terrorists attacked the Argentine home of Pfizer executive Hugo Carlos Sardan.
Apr. 7: A Philippines Airliner was hijacked by Muslim separatists. They released the hostages and surrendered to authorities in Libya on May 3, 1976.
Apr. 13: Two guards were killed by machine-gun fire when terrorists attacked the home of a Goodyear executive in Buenos Aires, Arg.
Apr. 14: The Armed Communist Formations firebombed the Texaco offices in Florence, Italy.
Apr. 14: A Chrysler executive, a Navy captain, and three police officers were shot to death in Buenos Aires, Arg.
Apr. 20: News correspondent Joe Morris was abducted from his car in Beirut, Leb.
Apr. 21: The president of Chevron Oil Italiana was wounded in Rome, by members of the Armed Communist Formations.
Apr. 22: A branch office of the First National City Bank was bombed in Athens, Gr.
May 8: Imprisoned West German terrorist Ulricke Meinhof committed suicide by hanging herself from a cell window in Stammheim, Ger.
May 23: South Moluccan terrorists seized a train in Assen, Neth., and held the passengers hostage for twenty days. Six terrorists and two hostages were killed during a successful rescue by the Dutch Marines.
May 23: An American businessman's eight-year-old daughter was abducted in Acapulco, Mex., by members of the Armed Vanguard of the Proletariat. She was released on June 15, 1976, after a $400,000 ransom had been paid.
June 18: Brazil's Federal Police Chief General Cesareo Cardoza was killed when a bomb planted by an ERP terrorist friend of his daughter exploded beneath his bed in Buenos Aires.
June 27: An Air France flight was hijacked by West German and Palestinian terrorists and diverted to Entebbe, Uganda. The hostages were later released in an Israeli commando raid on the airport.
July 2: Twenty-five police officers were killed when a bomb exploded in Buenos Aires.
July 10: The newly appointed British ambassador to Ireland was killed by IRA terrorists.
July 19: ERP terrorist leader Robert Santucho was killed in a gun battle with authorities in Argentina.
July 21: Christopher Ewart-Biggs, British ambassador to Ireland, was killed by a PIRA culvert bomb in Dublin, Ire.
Aug. 10: Three children died when a Provisional IRA terrorist was shot to death by British troops in Belfast, Ire.
Aug. 13: Terrorists destroyed equipment at an American firm in Jenin, Israel.
Aug. 28: Three Rockwell International missile experts were shot to death by Mujahedeen Khalq terrorists in Teheran, Iran.
Sept. 15: The home of a Ford Motor executive was attacked with submachine guns and hand grenades in Buenos Aires, Arg.
Sept. 22: A branch office of Westinghouse Corp. was bombed in Rome.
Sept. 25: An Avis Corp. branch office was bombed by Ghassan Kanafani Commandos in Rome.
Sept. 28: Beatrice Foods executive Gustave George Curtis was kidnapped in Bogota, Col. He was released after an estimated $140,000 ransom was paid.
Oct. 6: A bomb destroyed a Cuban aircraft shortly after takeoff from Barbados. President Fidel Castro accused the CIA of complicity in the incident.
Oct. 11: Three Black June Palestinian terrorists infiltrated the Syrian embassy in Rome and took five hostages. They surrendered to authorities two hours later.
Oct. 11: A Palestinian terrorist was killed and two others were wounded in an unsuccessful attempt to occupy the Syrian embassy in Islamabad, Pakistan.
Oct. 13: The Sheraton and the Ritz hotels were bombed in Lisbon, Port.
Oct. 28: Provisional IRA leader Maire Drumm was shot to death in a Belfast, Ire., hospital by a member of UDA.
Nov. 3: Chrysler executive Carlos Souto was shot by two leftist terrorists at his home in Buenos Aires, Arg.
Dec. 13: A Helene Curtis representative's seventeen-year-old daughter was kidnapped in Milan, Italy. She was released unharmed on Jan. 27, 1977.
Dec. 16: A bomb exploded in a boy's pocket as he walked through a store in Chapinero, Col. Seventeen more bombs were discovered in the store.

1977

A bomb explosion in a department store in Zimbabwe killed eleven and wounded seventy-six.
Jan. 20: Duraflex Corp. president Mitchell Andreski and a colleague were killed as they attempted to stop members of the 23rd of September Armed Communist League from distributing leaflets at a construction site.
Jan. 24: Two Warriors of Christ the King, armed with submachine guns, killed five communist lawyers at an office in Madrid.
Jan. 25: The empty home of a Goodyear executive was attacked in Buenos Aires by members of the Montoneros terrorist organization.
Mar. 9: Hanafi Muslim gunmen seized three Washington, D.C., buildings and held 134 people hostage for thirty-nine hours.
Mar. 16: A leftist leader named Jumblatt was shot to death in Beirut, Leb.
Mar. 27: Nine persons were hurt when six bombs exploded at the Sheraton Hilton Hotel in Buenos Aires, Arg.
Apr. 7: Siegfried Buback, chief police prosecutor of West Germany, was shot to death by Baader-Meinhof terrorists in Karlsruhe.
Apr. 10: In London, PFLP terrorists killed former Yemeni Prime Minister Abdullah al-Hejiri, his wife, and a minister at the Yemeni Embassy.
Apr. 11: The Pan Am and Henderson Co. branch offices in San Jose, Cost., were bombed by the Revolutionary Commandos of Solidarity, purportedly in retaliation for the death of FSLN leader Carlos Aguerero Echeverria.
Apr. 11: A General Motors executive was murdered by leftist Montoneros terrorists in Buenos Aires, Arg.
Apr. 28: West German terrorist Andreas Baader was sentenced to life

imprisonment.
May 11: An Aramco production center was ravaged by fire in Saudi Arabia.
June 14: A Yugoslav embassy employee was wounded as three Croatian terrorists attempted to occupy the building. No hostages were taken, and the terrorists surrendered two hours later.
June 19: The son of a Ford dealer and hotel director, was kidnapped by four men in Guatemala City, Guat. The victim and one of the kidnappers were killed during a rescue effort two days later.
July 14: An American Express branch office was bombed in Athens, Gr.
July 31: West German banker Juergen Ponto was murdered in Frankfurt by a Baader-Meinhof terrorist who entered his home with the aid of his goddaughter.
Aug. 3: One person was killed and seven others injured when two New York City office buildings were bombed by FALN terrorists.
Aug. 6: Windows in the Intercontinental Hotel in Istanbul, Turk., were shattered by machine-gun fire from the Turkish People's Liberation Party.
Aug. 6: Eleven people were killed and another seventy-six hurt when a bomb exploded at a Woolworth store in Salisbury, Rhodesia, S. Afri.
Aug. 9: Gould Inc. executive William Weinkamper was kidnapped while in his car in Mexico City, Mex. He was released after a $2 million ransom had been paid. On Aug. 19, the police arrested two suspects and $100,000 was retrieved.
Sept. 5: In an effort to free imprisoned members of West Germany's Baader-Meinhof terrorist gang, urban guerrillas kidnapped West German businessman Dr.Hans-Martin Schleyer. His body was discovered in France on Oct. 19, 1977.
Sept. 6: Guerrillas kidnapped an American industrialist's wife in El Salvador.
Sept. 6: Three people were hurt when a bomb exploded at a Sears store in Cali, Col.
Sept. 14: The Mexican-American Cultural Institute and a Sears store were bombed in Mexico. More bombs were discovered at the branch offices of General Motors and Colgate Palmolive.
Sept. 28: A Japanese Airlines plane was hijacked by Japanese Red Army terrorists in Bombay, Ind. They successfully negotiated the release of six imprisoned comrades and a ransom of $6 million, escaping to Baghdad.
Oct. 13: In West Germany, PFLP terrorists hijacked a Lufthansa Airliner. Anti-terrorist police rescued the eighty-six passengers on Oct. 18, 1977.
Oct. 13: Two people were killed and two others injured when a car bomb exploded at the home of a Chrysler administrator in Argentina.
Oct. 17: Two leftists who shot at police while distributing leaflets at a Chrysler plant in San Justo, Arg., were in turn shot to death.
Oct. 20: Three West German Baader-Meinhof terrorists committed suicide in their prison cells in Stammheim, Ger. Andreas Baader, Gudrun Ensslen, and Jan-Carl Raspe had expected to be freed through negotiations in other terrorist hostage situations.
Dec. 2: Two bodyguards were killed and another one injured, when terrorists attacked a Chrysler administrator with machine-gun fire in Buenos Aires, Arg.
Dec. 7: London *Sunday Times* Middle East expert David Holden was killed in Cairo by an unknown assailant.
Dec. 15: The son of Cypriot President Kyprianou was kidnapped by members of the EOKA-B Movement. He was released unharmed three days later.
Dec. 31: Two Syrian diplomats were killed in the Mayfair district of London when a bomb exploded in their car.

1978

Jan. 4: PLO representative Said Hammami was killed by either PFLP or Black June terrorists in London.
Jan. 10: Opposition newspaper publisher Pedro Chamorro was shot to death in Nicaragua at the orders of General Somoza.
Jan. 14: Four security guards were killed by rebels at a B.F. Goodrich rubber plantation at Basilan in the Philippines.
Jan. 19: A branch office of the Discount Bank was bombed in Paris.
Feb. 2: The United Nations office in San Salvador was occupied by twenty-four members of the leftist Popular Revolutionary Bloc, who took seven persons hostage. They were released when the U.N. agreed to investigate human violations in El Salvador.
Feb. 16: The branch offices of Chase Manhattan and Citibank, as well as a Woolworth and a Barker store, were bombed at various sites in Puerto Rico.
Feb. 17: Twelve people were killed and another twenty-three injured when a Provisional IRA fire-bomb exploded at a restaurant in County Down, Ire. IRA member Robert Murphy was sentenced to twelve life sentences for causing the explosion, and for other terrorist activities.
Feb. 18: Egyptian newspaper editor Yusuf Seba was murdered by two PFLP terrorists in Nicosia, who escaped by hijacking a Cypriot airliner. Fifteen people died when an Egyptian commando unit attempted to capture the terrorists.
Mar. 9: The trial of forty-eight Red Brigades members, including leader Renato Curcio, began in Turin, Italy.
Mar. 10: In Rome, Judge Rosario Berardi and a prison official were killed by members of the Red Brigades.
Mar. 12: Thirty-seven people were killed when an Al Fatah bomb exploded on an Israeli bus, near Tel Aviv.
Mar. 16: As he was being driven through Rome, former Italian Premier Aldo Moro was kidnapped and five of his bodyguards were killed by members of the Red Brigades.
Mar. 25: The Red Brigades announced the kidnapped former Italian Premier Aldo Moro would be tried by a "People's Court."
Mar. 27: Chief Kapuuo, the intended President of Nambia, was assassinated by terrorists.
Apr. 1: PFLP operational commander and co-founder Wadi Haddad died of cancer in East Berlin.
Apr. 7: Pope Paul VI issued an urgent plea to Red Brigades terrorists to spare the life of former Italian Premier Aldo Moro.
Apr. 7: Four people were shot to death while riding in a B.F. Goodrich truck at Zamboanga Del Sur province in the Philippines.
Apr. 13: Argentine terrorist banker David Graiver was indicted in absentia in New York.
Apr.15: Former Italian Premier Aldo Moro was reportedly condemned to death by a Red Brigades "People's Court."
Apr. 24: Twenty-four members of a terrorist ring organized by Abu Nidal of the Al Fatah, were arrested by Egyptian authorities in Cairo.
May 10: The body of former Italian Premier Aldo Moro was found in the trunk of a car in Rome.
May 11: The manager of the Milan, Italy, branch of the Chemical Bank of New York was shot by two members of the Front Line and Fighting Communist Formations.
May 12: A Honeywell Corp. warehouse was set on fire in Italy.
May 24: A terrorist took five hostages as he occupied the Mexican Consulate in Recife, Brazil. He was arrested after accepting the promise of safe passage out of the country.
May 29: A Texas Petroleum Corp. manager was kidnapped in Bogota, Col., by eight members of the M-19 guerrilla organization. On Jan. 3, 1979, his corpse was found in a guerrilla hideout.
June 15: PLO representative Aly Yasin was killed by Black June terrorists in Kuwait.
June 23: In Turin, Italy, Red Brigades leaders Renato Curcio and Pietro Bassi received fifteen year prison sentences.
June 24: The Iraqi Embassy in Brussels was bombed by PLO terrorists.
June 24: North Yemeni President Ghashmi was assassinated by terrorists in Beirut, Leb.
July 3: The Chilean consulate in San Juan, Puerto Rico, was occupied and four hostages taken by a man and woman demanding the release of four political prisoners in the U.S. They were persuaded to give up seventeen hours later.
July 9: Former Iraqi Prime Minister General al-Naif was assassinated by Iraqi Secret Service agents outside a London hotel.
July 26: The British government expelled eleven Iraqi diplomats because of suspected involvement in terrorist activities.
July 28: In London, a hand grenade was thrown by a PLO terrorist at the car of the Iraqi ambassador.
July 31: PLO terrorists launched an unsuccessful machine-gun attack on the Iraqi ambassador in Beirut, Leb.
July 31: An Arab gunman seized the Iraqi embassy in Paris, taking eight hostages. Gunfire between the French police and Iraqi guards following the gunman's surrender left two dead and four wounded.
July 31: A French police official and an Iraqi diplomat died in a gun battle after PLO terrorists invaded the Iraqi Embassy in Paris.
August: Lebanese spiritual leader Imam Moussa Sadr disappeared. Although Libya denied it, Sadr's followers believed Libya was responsible.
Aug. 2: The Iraqi Consulate in Karachi was attacked by two PLO gunmen. During an ensuing gun and bayonet fight, one terrorist was killed, while a diplomat and consulate guard were wounded.
Aug. 3: PLO representative Izz al-Din Qalaq was killed by Black June terrorists in Paris.
Aug. 5: Four men died when four Black June terrorists attacked a PLO office in Islamabad.
Aug. 7: An inter-Arab battle between PLO and Iraqi factions broke out at Lebanese refugee camps.
Aug. 17: Eight hostages were taken at the West German consulate in Chicago by two Croatian terrorists demanding the release of an imprisoned colleague. The two surrendered peacefully ten hours later.
Aug. 20: An El Al stewardess was killed and another wounded in London when an airline bus was attacked by Black June terrorists.
Sept. 6: West German Baader-Meinhof terrorist Peter Stoll was killed at a Dusseldorf restaurant by police who were attempting to arrest him.
Sept. 13: Red Brigades terrorist Corrado Alunni, a primary suspect for the murder of Aldo Moro, was arrested in Milan.
Sept. 15: West German Baader-Meinhof terrorist Astrid Proll was arrested in London.
Sept. 24: West German Baader-Meinhof terrorists Michael Knoll and Angelika Speitel were arrested by police after being wounded in a gun battle in Dortmund, Ger.
November: Albert Miles, the deputy governor of Maze Prison, was murdered outside his Belfast, Ire., home. IRA member Kevin Artl was charged with the slaying three years later.
November: Terrorists threw a fire-bomb at the car of a manager of the Oil Service Company in Ahwaz, Iran.
Nov. 9: In Bogota, Col., M-19 guerrillas burglarized a Chrysler Colmotores Company warehouse and took radio equipment.

Nov. 22: Several people were injured when a bomb exploded at a Sears, Roebuck store in Lima, Peru.
December: Ten people were injured by IRA bombs aimed at five cities.
Dec. 8: The headquarters of the Grumman Corporation was firebombed in Isfahan, Iran.
Dec. 23: An Oil Service Company manager and his production superintendent were killed in separate incidents by terrorists in Ahwaz, Iran.

1979

Jan. 6: Five men armed with knives, guns, and fake grenades were arrested at the airport in Leningrad, U.S.S.R., for planning to hijack a Soviet aircraft to Oslo, Nor., and requesting the freedom of political prisoners.
Jan. 14: Parsons-Jurdon employee Martin Berkowitz was fatally stabbed in his home in Kerman, Iran.
Jan. 16: As many as 156 hostages were taken by forty United Popular Action Front terrorists when they invaded the Mexican embassy, and the offices of the Red Cross and the Organization of American States in El Salvador. Although authorities refused to release seventy-two prisoners, the siege ended two days later, when the terrorists were given safe passage to Mexico.
Jan. 22: Al Fatah terrorist Ali Hassan Salameh, who allegedly plotted the 1972 Munich Olympic massacre, was killed by a car-bomb in Beirut, Leb.
Feb. 13: Five people were injured when a bomb exploded in a Sheraton Hotel in Cairo, Egypt.
Feb. 14: An Iranian employee was killed, two Marine guards were wounded, and about 100 employees were taken hostage when armed militants occupied the U.S. embassy in Teheran.
Feb. 14: In Afghanistan, U.S. ambassador Adolph Dubs was killed during a rescue effort, after he had been kidnapped by Muslim dissidents.
Feb. 19: An office of Pan Am Airlines was bombed in Alsancak, Izmir, Turk.
Feb. 27: Three non-Soviet representatives of the Way of Eternal Bliss hijacked an Oslo-to-Stockholm flight and ordered the pilot to fly to Moscow, where they planned to burn the plane. However, they were forcibly detained by passengers and crew members, and arrested in Stockholm, Swed.
Mar. 25: United Front of the Revolution Party leader Manuel Colom Argueta was shot to death in Guatemala.
Mar. 27: The Egyptian ambassador to Bangladesh was held hostage for several hours by Arab militants in Dacca.
Mar. 27: The Egyptian embassy was seized by students in Teheran, Iran.
Mar. 27: The Egyptian embassy was attacked by Palestinians in Kuwait.
Mar. 30: Conservative spokesman Airey Neave was killed by an Irish National Liberation Army car-bomb, which exploded outside the House of Commons in London.
Apr. 1: Former Pakistani prime minister Zulfikar Ali Bhutto was executed.
Apr. 15: An El Al Airline hijacking was thwarted by authorities in Brussels.
Apr. 19: A Ford Motor Co. showroom was bombed in Valencia, Spain.
Apr. 23: A Babcock & Wilson West German subsidiary was bombed in Dusseldorf.
May: In Tiberias, Isr., a marketplace bomb explosion killed two people and wounded thirty-six. Ziad Abu Eian, a terrorist, was suspected.
May 4: A guard was wounded as six hostages were taken by sixteen members of the Popular Revolutionary Bloc (BPR), who occupied the French embassy in San Salvador.
May 4: The Metropolitan Cathedral in San Salvador was occupied by members of the BPR. Seventeen people died and another thirty-five were wounded on May 9 as police attempted to end the siege.
May 4: Five people were taken hostage as four members of the BPR occupied the Costa Rican embassy in El Salvador. The hostage escaped on May 9 while the kidnappers were eating dinner.
May 11: Eight hostages were taken when nine BPR terrorists occupied the Venezuelan embassy in San Salvador. Five hostages escaped on May 20 and the others were released on June 1 when the kidnappers were given political asylum in Mexico.
May 15: Two police officers were shot to death in a gun battle with eight members of the Farabundo Marti Popular Liberation Forces who attempted to occupy the South African embassy in San Salvador.
May 20: An IBM branch office was hit by gunfire in San Salvador, El. Sal.
May 26: As a result of a business disagreement, the sports car of Robert Manina was set on fire and exploded in Canada.
June 15: National Cash Register branch manager William Rocha was kidnapped in San Salvador, El. Sal. He was released on June 27, 1979.
June 26: As many as twenty hostages were taken by a group of workers who occupied the Mexican embassy in Guatemala.
July 13: Two Turkish guards were killed and a policeman wounded when four Palestinian terrorists seized the Egyptian embassy in Ankara. The hostages were released and the siege ended forty-five hours later.
July 24: A bomb exploded at the Wells Fargo Bank in Istanbul, Turk.
August: Two members of the Weather Underground were indicted. They were charged with possession of bombs linked to a Hoboken, N.J., bombing.
Aug. 14: The general manager of Apex Textile Co. was held hostage for nine days, after his factory was taken over by terrorists in El Salvador.
Aug. 27: Lord Mountbatten was killed by a Provisional IRA bomb, while aboard his yacht in Mullaghmore Harbor, County Sligo, Ire.
Aug. 27: Eighteen British soldiers were killed by Provisional IRA terrorists near Warrenpoint, Ire.
Sept. 16: Afghan President Taraki was killed when his regime was toppled by one led by Hafizullah Amin.
Sept. 21: Two Beckman Instruments executives were kidnapped and their driver was killed by members of the Revolutionary Party of Central American Workers. The hostages were freed on Nov. 7, 1979.
Oct. 22: South Korean President Park was killed by a member of the Korean CIA.
Oct. 26: The deputy manager of a Citicorp branch office was fatally wounded in San Salvador, El. Sal.
Oct. 28: A branch office of Bank of America was bombed in San Salvador, El. Sal.
Oct. 30: Two U.S. Marines were injured as 300 leftists attempted to attack the U.S. embassy in San Salvador.
Oct. 31: A group of terrorists failed in an attempt to occupy the Guatemalan embassy in San Salvador.
Nov. 4: Sixty-three people were taken hostage as Iranian militants seized the U.S. embassy in Teheran.
Nov. 5: Twenty-seven hostages were taken when militant Iranians occupied the British embassy in Teheran.
Nov. 20: The Grand Mosque in Mecca was seized by members of a fanatical Moslem sect.
Nov. 23: The home of Swift Co. plant manager Lopez Akimenco was bombed in La Plata, Argentina.
Nov. 26: The offices of TWA and Western Airlines were bombed in Madrid, Spain.
Dec. 2: The U.S. embassy in Tripoli, Libya, was burned during a protest by more than 2,000 people.
Dec. 3: The branch office of the West German Morgan Guaranty Trust Co. was bombed in Frankfurt.
Dec. 5: A W.R. Grace fertilizer plant was bombed in Trinidad.
Dec. 14: In Istanbul, Turk., three Boeing employees and a member of the U.S. armed forces were shot to death by members of the Marxist-Leninist Armed Propaganda Unit of the Turkish People's Liberation Front Party.
Dec. 18: U.S. businessman Jeremy Cross was shot by rebels on motorcycles in Pasay City in the Philippines.
Dec. 23: The Air France and TWA offices in Rome were bombed by the Armenian Secret Army for the Liberation of Armenia.
Dec. 25: The offices of the ITT Corp. and Citibank were bombed in El Salvador.
Dec. 28: Three people were killed, including a terrorist, when a People's Liberation Forces bomb exploded at the First National City Bank in San Salvador, El. Sal.

1980

January: Former Iranian police chief Naser Almaneih was accused of bombing Berkeley High School and of attempting to bomb an Iranian meeting at San Jose State University in California. He was later sentenced to fifty years in a Federal prison.
Jan. 11: Seven hostages were taken as fifty members of the 28 February Popular League occupied the Panamanian embassy in San Salvador, demanding the release of political prisoners. The government acceded to the demands, and the hostages were released on Jan. 14, 1980.
Jan. 14: A man requiring the release of 25 Tunisian prisoners attempted to hijack a Alitalia flight to Tripoli, Libya. When bad weather forced the pilot to land in Palermo, Si., the hijacker surrendered after ten hours and asked for political asylum.
Jan. 25: A Delta flight was hijacked to Cuba by a man armed with a small pistol. After landing there, the hijacker decided to go to Iran, but surrendered when an airport vehicle was not removed from the runway.
Jan. 28: After a Middle East Airlines flight landed in Beirut, Leb., a man armed with a knife demanded a press conference to plea for information about a missing Muslim spiritual leader. He was arrested after being allowed to read a speech.
Jan. 31: Thirty-nine people died in a fire at the Spanish embassy in Guatemala City, set by members of the Guerrilla Army of the Poor, who were attempting to occupy the building.
Feb. 4: Eleven people were held hostage and the release of political prisoners demanded as thirty members of the leftist Popular League occupied the Spanish embassy in San Salvador. The siege ended Feb. 18 when the El Salvadoran government acceded to the terrorists' demands.
Feb. 5: The French embassy was attacked and burned in Tripoli, Libya.
Feb. 13: Three hostages were taken by leftist militants as they briefly occupied the Panamanian embassy in San Salvador.
Feb. 27: Fifty-seven people were taken hostage by sixteen members of the M-19 guerrilla terrorist organization, which seized the Dominican embassy in Bogota, Columbia. They demanded the release of 311 prisoners and a $50 million ransom. The siege ended sixty-one days later when the guerrillas accepted a lesser demand of $2 million and safe passage to Cuba.
Feb. 28: The Salvadoran embassy in Panama City was briefly occupied by seventeen student militants.
March: Le Phenix, a Paris bookstore carrying literature from the

People's Republic of China was destroyed.
Mar. 10: Shortly before landing in Beirut, Leb., a Middle East Airlines flight was seized by a man brandishing a toy pistol. He demanded a press conference to plead for information about a vanished Muslim spiritual leader, but was arrested when the plane landed.
Mar. 24: Archbishop Romero was shot to death in San Salvador. He had been a severe critic of the government.
Apr. 7: Five Arab terrorists and two Israeli commandos were killed during an effort to free hostages taken from a kibbutz dormitory near the Lebanese border.
Apr. 12: Liberian President Tolbert was assassinated by members of the People's Redemption Council during a military coup.
Apr. 14: A man armed with a knife and claiming to be associated with the IRA, planned to hijack a Continental Airlines flight to Libya, but was dissuaded by the pilot when strange sounds were heard in the back of the airplane.
Apr. 25: A bomb placed by the Self-Defense Against All Authority exploded at an American Agricultural Equipment Corporation office in Toulouse, Fr.
Apr. 30: Twenty-six hostages were taken as Iranian Arabs occupied the Iranian embassy in London. On May 5, following the execution of two of the hostages, British commandos raided the building, killing five terrorists and capturing the others.
May: Six Jewish settlers, including two U.S. citizens, were killed and sixteen others wounded in a PLO ambush near Hebron on the West Bank. Four Palestinian guerrillas were brought to trial for the slayings.
May 1: A Pacific Southwest Airlines flight engineer disarmed a man who was attempting to hijack the vacant plane to Iran.
May 5: In London, the seizure of the Iranian Embassy was ended by Britain's Special Air Service (SAS).
May 6: A man armed with a pistol, hijacked a TAP Air Portugal flight bound for Faro, Port., and requested $10 million and passage to Madrid, Spain, and eventually, Switzerland. In Madrid, he dropped his demands, and was arrested in Lisbon by Portuguese authorities.
May 17: An undetonated bomb was discovered in the Bronx, at the compound of the Soviet Mission to the United Nations.
June: John Turnly, a leader of the Irish Independence Party, was killed by an assassin.
June: Miriam Daly, past member of the Irish Republican Socialist Party, was assassinated.
June 1: African National Congress terrorists bombed three oil storage tanks in South Africa.
June 2: Bassam Shaka, the mayor of Nablus, lost both of his legs in a car-bomb explosion.
June 12: A Nestlé subsidiary president was kidnapped by FAR terrorists in Guatemala City, Guat. He was freed following the payment of an estimated $4.7 million ransom.
June 18: Forty-two people were killed and more than 200 wounded during fighting between police and rioters at Cape Peninsula, South Africa.
June 30: A man fired a shot on a Aerolineas Argentinas flight bound for Buenos Aires, demanding $100,000 and passage to Mexico. In Buenos Aires, Brazilian troops used tear gas to free the passengers, and after several hours, the pilot convinced the hijacker to surrender.
July 12: A man claiming to possess a bomb entered the cockpit of a Philippine Airlines plane en route to Manila, requesting $6 million and passage to Libya. However, he left the cockpit, whereupon the pilot landed in Manila, and the hijacker was arrested.
July 19: Marxist terrorists assassinated former Turkish Premier Nihat Erim.
Aug. 2: Eighty-four people were killed and almost 200 injured when a bomb placed by the Armed Revolutionary Nuclei exploded at a train station in Bologna, Italy.
Aug. 18: A note delivered aboard an Eastern Airlines flight in Atlanta stated that a remote-control bomb was stashed in the cargo hold. A man requested $3.4 million and freedom for two prisoners. Before the pilot could take off for Cuba as directed, the crew discovered the threat was a hoax. The man was arrested by authorities in Atlanta.
Aug. 22: The wife of a U.S. businessman was killed by an April 6 Liberation Movement bomb in Manila, in the Philippines.
September: The Defense Sport Group Hoffmann, a neo-Nazi group, was connected to the bombing at Oktoberfest. Twelve people were killed.
October: Ronnie Bunting, allegedly a leader of the IRA who caused the murder of a House of Commons member, was assassinated.
Oct. 3: A bomb explosion in a hotel room led to the arrest of two Armenians.
Oct. 13: Four armed men hijacked a Turkish Airlines flight shortly after takeoff from Istanbul, and demanded the pilot fly first to Teheran, Iran, and later to Jidda, Saudi. The siege ended in a furious gun battle after Turkish troops stormed the plane. One passenger was allegedly killed and ten people, including a hijacker, were wounded.
Oct. 19: Eighteen people were hurt when a bomb placed by the April 6 Liberation Movement, exploded at a travel agents' convention in Manila, in the Philippines.
Nov. 12: A man hijacked a Arco Uruguayan flight and asked for asylum. A woman was wounded when three passengers attempted to seize his gun. After passage to Cuba and other destinations was denied, the hijacker's uncle was brought aboard, and the man surrendered.
December: In Brussels, Belg., an effort to assassinate Christopher Tugendhat, delegate of the European Community Commission was thwarted. The IRA claimed responsibility for the attack.
December: Sultan Ibraimov, the chairman of the Council of Ministers of the Kirgiz Republic, was murdered. Six months later, the killing was alleged to be a conspiracy.
Dec. 2: In Naples, Italy, a university student Gianluca Grimaldi was kidnapped.
Dec. 4: A LOT Polish Airlines flight was hijacked to West Berlin by a man seeking political asylum.
Dec. 5: Four men hijacked an Aeropostal Venezuelan Airline flight en route to Caracas and ordered the pilot to fly to Higuerote, Venez. Upon landing, the hijackers removed $1.75 million and disappeared. The money was recovered the next day and thirty-five people were arrested.
Dec. 7: Fifteen terrorists disguised as policemen kidnapped Goodyear employee Clifford Bevens from his apartment in Guatemala City. Bevens and five of his captors were killed during a rescue attempt on Aug. 13, 1981.
Dec. 12: Judge Giovanni D'Urso was kidnapped by Red Brigades members.
Dec. 15: Seven terrorists purportedly belonging to the 19th of April movement hijacked a AVIANCA Colombian Airlines plane. After stops in Santa Marta and Barranquilla, Col., Panama City, Panama, and Mexico City, Mex., the plane landed in Havana, where the terrorists surrendered to Cuban authorities.
Dec. 29: In Italy, a revolt by Red Brigades members held in Trani Prison, was successfully suppressed.
Dec. 29: A helicopter about to deliver a corporate payroll was hijacked by four armed men at the Philippines airport in Magat. After forcing the pilot to fly to a nearby farm, the men escaped with more than $400,000, purportedly destined for the New People's Army.
Dec. 31: In Nairobi, Kenya, the famous Norfolk Hotel, owned by a Jewish family with ties to Israel, was bombed on New Year's Eve; twenty people were killed and eighty-five were injured in a fire. The Habash Front was suspected in the assault.
Dec. 31: Head of security for Italian prisons holding terrorists, General Enrico Galvaligi was assassinated by Red Brigade members who shot him, apparently in retaliation for the Dec. 29 suppression of a Trani Prison revolt.

1981

January: Nicaraguan rebels allegedly bombed a leftist radio station in Costa Rica.
January: A Pakistan Airlines DC-10 airplane was destroyed in its hangar with Al Zulfikar, a movement led by the son of the slain Prime Minister of Pakistan, claiming responsibility.
January: From late January to early February Chinese newspapers reported bombings and protests in Shanghai, the Yunnan and Shanxi provinces, Xinjiang, and the Tibetan autonomous region.
Jan. 1: At the Palace of Justice at Fort-de-France in Martinique, a bomb exploded. Suspected was the Groupe de Liberation armee de la Martinique.
Jan. 2: A threat to "attack all Swiss diplomats worldwide" was made by the Secret Army for the Liberation of Armenia because the Swiss reportedly mistreated prisoners.
Jan. 2: Jordan alleged that Syrian troops slaughtered 200 civilians in Aleppo the previous week. Syria denied the charges, but admitted that nine Muslim Brotherhood terrorists were killed there.
Jan. 2: After serving three years of a thirty-six to 108 year sentence for a March 1977 assault on the Washington, D.C., headquarters of B'nai B'rith, Abdul Hamid, Hanafi Muslim, was freed.
Jan. 3: *L'Espresso* Magazine published a seventy-page report on terrorism following exclusive reporting on the kidnapping of Judge Giovanni D'Urso.
Jan. 3: In San Salvador, two U.S. agrarian reform experts, Michael Hammer and Mark Pearlman, were shot to death in the Sheraton Hotel coffee shop. Jose Rodolfo Viera, president of the Agrarian Reform Institute, was also murdered.
Jan. 4: At the Boutique Chanel in Paris a bomb exploded. The Groupe de Liberation armee de la Guadeloupe, (GLAG), was suspected, with the actual target thought to be the nearby Archives of the Ministry of Justice.
Jan. 4: In Switzerland, the Secret Army for the Liberation of Armenia declared a truce and ordered that all raids in Switzerland be halted until Jan. 15.
Jan. 4: Bassam Shaka, the Mayor of Nablus, returned to the West Bank. The Mayor of Ramallah, Karim Khalaf, had returned ten days earlier; he had lost a foot in another explosion the same day.
Jan. 5: The Libyan mission in Lagos, Nig., was expelled after it became a People's Bureau. Three Libyan diplomats were reported to have been expelled from Mauritania in late 1980.
Jan. 5: The Italian Ministry of Justice decided to bulletproof their offices, buying 900 bulletproof cars for key executives. A sum of $6.5 million was spent in the process.
Jan. 5: Milan, Italy, newspaper *Corriere della Sera* and *Radiotelevisione Italiana* decided to end coverage of the Red Brigades abduction of Judge Giovanni D'Urso. The terrorists had demanded that television stations and seven Italian newspapers publicize prisoner's declarations from the

Trani and Palmi jails.
Jan. 6: In Chicago, Cathlyn Platt Wilkerson was given a nine month-sentence after pleading guilty to resisting arrest, jumping bail and aggravated battery in connection with the 1969 "Days of Rage" at the Democratic Convention in Chicago.
Jan. 6: In Italy, alleged informer Luca Perucci, was killed by the Armed Revolution Squads, a right-wing organization.
Jan. 7: In Guatemala, an army convoy traveling the Santiago Atitlan and San Pedro La Laguna roads was ambushed by the Revolutionary Organization of the People in Arms. There were fifty-five army casualties.
Jan. 8: In Ayacucho, Peru, Enlightened Path terrorists, allegedly responsible for 300 bombings in six months, destroyed a microwave tower after a Jan. 5 increase in food and fuel prices. More than 100 were arrested.
Jan. 8: In the outlying area northwest of London the Uxbridge Air Force Base was bombed. Explosives were found, a building was evacuated, and gasoline barrels were removed. There was extensive building damage and two civilians were injured. The IRA claimed responsibility for the assault.
Jan. 9: The U.S. Justice Department ended its second investigation into the 1978 police slayings of Dario Rosado and Carlos Soto Arrivi, suspected terrorists.
Jan. 10: In Belfast, Ire., two policemen were injured in different attacks.
Jan. 10: In the Gaza Strip, an Israeli couple was seriously harmed when a grenade was thrown into their car.
Jan. 10: In El Salvador, a twelve-day leftist offensive began. The government estimated that 1,000 rebels were slain in the battles.
Jan. 11: The PLO was suspected in the shooting death of an Israeli cab driver in the Gaza Strip.
Jan. 11: In Nambia, South African forces invaded southern Angola over a ten-day period.
Jan. 12: In El Salvador, Ian Mates, a South African working for a London television company, was fatally wounded when his car hit a land mine. *Newsweek* photographer John Hoagland and *Time* photographer Susan Meiselas were injured in the accident.
Jan. 12: Street fighting in Kano, Nig., between police and army and members of Islamic cults resulted in a reported 1,000 or more people being killed. The riots began on Dec. 18 with a Muslim rampage through the Kano marketplace. Journalists estimated that as many as 7-10,000 were killed. The government of Nigeria claimed Libya was involved in the violence.
Jan. 12: An Army transport along the road from Quezaltenango to San Marcos, Guat., was ambushed by ORPA rebels; there were twelve casualties.
Jan. 12: Authorities ruled that kidnapping charges would be filed against eighty alleged terrorists imprisoned in connection with Judge Giovanni D'Urso's abduction.
Jan. 12: In his car outside Jerusalem's Holy Land Hotel, Sheik Hammad Abu Rabia, a Bedouin member of Parliament, was murdered when shots were fired from a military jeep. Arrested were Daish, Seif and Hail Muadi, sons of Jaber Muadi, the Druse sheik who would inherit the slain parliamentarian's seat.
Jan. 12: At the U.S. Air Base in San Juan, P.R., leftists exploded twenty-six bombs, destroying nine planes and damaging two, with estimated damages of $45 million. The Macheteros claimed responsibility, with one of their trademark machetes tied with a ribbon left behind at the bombing scene.
Jan. 13: In a published interview in the Egyptian weekly, *The People*, Chairman of the Executive Committee of the PLO, Yasir Arafat rejected Palestinian autonomy.
Jan. 13: Two Italian newspapers, *Il Messaggero* and *Secolo XIX*, agreed to print statements of the Red Brigades after an appeal from kidnapped Judge Giovanni D'Urso, who was abducted on Dec. 12, 1980.
Jan. 13: Arrested in October, 1980 in Geneva, Switzerland, after a bomb exploded in her hotel room, Suzy Mahseredjian was convicted of helping to extort $6,000 from a Geneva businessman and was given an eighteen-month suspended sentence. Mahseredjian's cause was championed by the Secret Army for the Liberation of Armenia.
Jan. 13: About one hundred guerrillas, believed to have come from Nicaragua, landed on an eastern beach in El Salvador.
Jan. 13: On charges of aggravated battery and jumping bail from the 1969 "Days of Rage" in Chicago, Bernadine Dohrn was given a $1,500 fine and three years probation.
Jan. 15: *Newsweek* reporter Olivier Rebbot was shot in San Francisco, the provincial capital of El Salvador; he died on Feb. 9 in Miami.
Jan. 15: In the first case of soldiers convicted of murder during the conflict in Northern Ireland, a Belfast court sentenced Sgt. John Byrne, Staff-Sgt. Stanley Hathaway, Iain Chestnut, and Captain Andrew Snowball to jail terms for the murders of IRA suspects Michael Naan and Andrew Murray.
Jan. 15: Judge Giovanni D'Urso, who was kidnapped by the Red Brigades in a highly publicized Italian abduction, was freed in Rome. Police arrested one suspect and issued warrants for six others the same day that D'Urso was freed.
Jan. 15: On a boat in a Florida cove, seven members of the anti-Castro group Alpha 66 were arrested, armed with machine guns and bombs and apparently on their way to invade Cuba.
Jan. 15: A nine-week hunger strike by six Corsicans held in prison for kidnapping and for being members of an armed group ended with the terrorists explaining, "Our suffering has become useless."
Jan. 15: The murders of nine leaders of the Bolivian Revolutionary Left Movement, the MIR, found outside a house in La Paz, Bol., were blamed on paramilitary and security forces.
Jan. 16: Muhammad Hamud Khamis, Yemen Arab Republic Minister of Local Government, was killed as he traveled from Sana'a to Hodeida. One assailant was killed and another was arrested.
Jan. 16: Following his policy of not negotiating with terrorists, Arnaldo Foriani, the Christian Democrat Premier of Italy, received a vote of confidence in the Chamber of Deputies.
Jan. 16: In County Tyrone, Ire., three gunmen invaded the isolated farmhouse of former Parliament member Bernadette Devlin McAliskey, seriously wounding McAliskey and her husband. Three men were arrested for the assault.
Jan. 16: In Warrenpoint, County Down, Ire., two young men held up the customs office and shot Ivan Toombs, 42, part-time major in the Ulster Defense Regiment, who became the first IRA victim of the year.
Jan. 17: Martial law in the Philippines, in effect since September 1972, was ended by President Ferdinand Marcos. Of 341 prisoners released, 159 had been charged with violating public security.
Jan. 18: Facundo Guardado, a Salvadoran, was captured by members of the Honduras National Intelligence Division. Guardado, who was released seventy-two days later as part of a demand by hijackers of a Sahsa Airlines Boeing 737 on March 27, said he was tortured and held incommunicado.
Jan. 18: According to a London *Sunday Times* report, Saudi Arabia offered Pakistan $800 million for assistance in helping to build an H-bomb.
Jan. 18: On the La Vina estate in Colomba, Quezaltenango in Guatemala ORPA guerrillas assaulted an outpost, with twenty-eight casualties, one of them a guerrilla.
Jan. 19: Near Tarish, Leb., three Sengalese soldiers in the United Nations Interim Force in Lebanon were slain. Fifty-four soldiers died there since March 1978.
Jan. 19: The Summer Institute of Linguistics in Bogota, Col., which translates the Bible into Indian dialects, was broken into by guerrillas who kidnapped U.S. linguist and lay missionary Chester A. Bitterman, III.
Jan. 19: In El Salvador, Defense Minster Colonel Jose Guillermo Garcia said that ninety-seven government troops had been slain and around 1,000 Leftists had died since the offensive began on January 10.
Jan. 20: At a security gate between Londonderry and the Bogside, an IRA sniper killed one soldier and wounded another.
Jan. 20: According to The Voice of Palestine, Japan granted full diplomatic status to the PLO representative in Tokyo.
Jan. 20: The IRA said that a corpse found in South Armagh near the border was that of a police informer.
Jan. 20: In Iran, fifty-two U.S. hostages were released after 444 days of captivity.
Jan. 21: Patrick Pimbert, an alleged activist of the neo-Fascist Federation Action National European, FANE, was arrested in Italy. Pimbert's associates, Ciro Lai and Giuseppe Fioravanti were arrested in March and February, with all the arrests allegedly occurring after PLO faction Fatah provided Italian authorities with information on terrorists.
Jan. 21: In an attack on their Armagh home, Sir Norman Stronge, the Protestant speaker of the Parliament in Northern Ireland for twenty-six years, and his son, James, a Stormont Parliament member, were slain by gunmen, with the IRA taking responsibility for the assault. The gunmen escaped.
Jan. 22: In Germany, Peter Boock, a member of the Baader-Meinhof Gang, was arrested in connection with the 1977 murders of Jurgen Ponto and Hanns-Martin Schleyer.
Jan. 22: In Turin, two Red Brigades leaders were given seven-year sentences for illegal possession of firearms. They were allegedly leaders of the Veneto column of the Red Brigades.
Jan. 23: San Mateo, Quezaltenango in Guatemala was occupied by the Revolutionary Organization of the People in Arms.
Jan. 24: The Guadeloupe Liberation Army claimed responsibility for a concrete block dropped on a passing suburban train; the conductor was killed.
Jan. 24: In an interview in *Die Welt*, President Sandro Pertini said he believed that the headquarters of the Red Brigades were not in Italy but abroad, implicating the U.S.S.R after further questioning.
Jan. 24: Martial law in Korea was lifted by President Chun Doo Hwan; it had been extended after riots in May 1980.
Jan. 24: In the San Rafael Panam rural estate in Chicacao, ORPA rebels set the offices on fire after seizing ammunition and four guns.
Jan. 26: The head of the Foreign Affairs Department of the PLO, Karouk Kadoumi, was elected Vice-President both of the Islamic Conference in Taif, Saud., and of the Non-Aligned Summit meeting in New Delhi.
Jan. 26: Throughout Northern Ireland bombs exploded between 6 a.m. and 8 p.m. in five of six counties, with more than twelve people hurt in the attacks.
Jan. 26: After receiving a death threat, a candidate of the Official Unionist Party, which supported the union of Northern Ireland and

England, withdrew from the Belfast City Council election.
Jan. 26: Kamal Hasan Ali, the Egyptian foreign minister and Deputy Prime Minister, urged the PLO to reject conflict with Israel and to begin a dialogue with the U.S. to work on solving the problem in Palestine.
Jan. 27: Yitzhak Shamir, Israel's foreign minister, rejected a U.S. Department of State spokesman's assertion that Israeli settlement policies were interfering with peace in the Middle East and that some PLO factions were moderate. Shamir said that the PLO is a terrorist group.
Jan. 27: In Guatemala, San Pablo Jocopilas and Samayac were seized by ORPA guerrillas. Six army troopers and one guerrilla were killed.
Jan. 28; In an interview in *L'Umanita* Ruggero Puletti, Vice-Secretary of the Italian Social Democratic Party, said there were connections between Czechoslovakia and Italian terrorists.
Jan. 29: PLO bases in southern Lebanon were shelled by Israelis, with ten killed and fifteen injured when planes attacked Tyre, Saida, and Nabatiyeh.
Jan. 29: A furniture store in Belfast, Ire., was bombed. A fire was started, but there were no casualties.
Jan. 29: In Maze Prison, ninety-six prisoners spread excrement throughout their cells after a two-week halt in a "dirty protest" with more than 400 suspected IRA members involved in the present campaign.
Jan. 29: The municipality of San Martin Zacatepequez in Quezaltenango, Guat. was taken by ORPA rebels.
Jan. 30: In San Salvador, El Sal., nine civilians were killed in cross fire when a van transporting security forces was ambushed.
Jan. 30: Three guerrilla bases in Maputo, Mozambique, were destroyed by South African commandos. Several African National Congress members were reported killed, along with one South African and a civilian; there were a total of thirteen deaths.
Jan. 30: Early in the day the main courthouse in Paris was bombed with two groups–the Corsican National Liberation Front and the Guadeloupe Liberation Army–claiming responsibility. No one was injured
Jan. 31: Two military police platoons in Nuevo Progreso, department of San Marcos in Guatemala, were attacked by ORPA units, with police suffering twenty-three casualties.
February: Two Palestinian bodyguards of Ayatollah Khomeini were arrested and executed in an Iraqi scheme to kill the head of Iran.
February: Oualid Abu Dahr, director of an Arab magazine, was threatened with death for his pro-Iraqi stance in relation to Syria and Iran.
February: Between 100-200 armed M-19 guerrillas secretly entering Colombia to set up a people's army were captured. Among those arrested was the M-19 leader Rosenberg Pabon.
Feb. 2: A hunger strike was begun by Red Army member Sigurd Debus, who had been sentenced to twelve years in jail for robberies and bombings. Debus died on April 16, 1981.
Feb. 3: At the Seventh-Day Adventist Church mission school 125 miles southeast of Salisbury, Zimbabwe Donald Lale and his wife, Anne Lale were killed, reportedly in revenge for the South African raid on Mozambique.
Feb. 3: In southern Lebanon north of Sidon, a PLO vehicle was ambushed by Israelis. All the passengers were killed.
Feb. 4: In Guatemala, an army transport in the village of Palin, San Marcos was ambushed by ORPA guerrillas. Fourteen soldiers were killed and nine wounded. Other army transports were hit that same day along the road to San Marcos.
Feb. 4: Palestinians claimed, for the second night, to have shot at Israeli boats in an area south of Beirut.
Feb. 4: A report on missing persons issued by the United Nations Human Rights Commission says that between 11-13,000 persons reported missing are believed to be victims of political violence, with Argentina topping the list of countries with missing persons.
Feb. 5: In a gunfight on the outskirts of Padua, in Italy, two carabinieri were killed, with the terrorists suspected of being Third Position members.
Feb. 5: After a gunfight in Turin, Italy, the suspected leader of the Prima Linea, Maurice Bignami, was wounded and arrested.
Feb. 5: At the Breda Steel Factory in Milan, Italy, a foreman was chained to a steel gate by two youths.
Feb. 6: In the Etiler district of Istanbul, Turk., Deputy Director of Police Mahmut Dikler was ambushed and killed by three gunmen, with his bodyguard also slain. Leftists were allegedly responsible for the attack.
Feb. 6: The Jordanian embassy in Beirut, Leb., was attacked by four cars of gunmen. One guard was killed and a policeman was wounded. Diplomat Hisham al-Moheisen was abducted from his apartment and an anonymous call four days later reported that he was executed after a 48-hour deadline established by his abductors expired.
Feb. 6: The chief engineer at a nuclear plant under construction at Lemoniz, Jose Maria Ryan, was killed by the Basque Fatherland and Liberty Group, ETA, after he refused to dismantle the project.
Feb. 6: The Taiwan embassy at the Vatican was bombed. No casualties occurred, but massive damage was done to property. A caller claiming to be a Marxist-Leninist called for Jiang Qing's release in the People's Republic of China.
Feb. 7: In Turkey, terrorists killed a retired colonel in an Istanbul coffee shop. Leftists were allegedly responsible for the murder.
Feb. 7: Seven masked members of the IRA, armed with guns, commandeered a pilot launch. They boarded a British coal ship off the coast of Donegal, the *Nelly M.*, forced the crew into a raft while they planted bombs, and left the ship partially submerged. There were no injuries.
Feb. 7: Near Bulawayo, Zimbabwe, guerrilla groups fought, with the newly banded National Army of Robert Mugabe clashing with Joshua Nkomo's former guerrillas. After a cease-fire arranged on Feb. 13, around 150 people were reported killed.
Feb. 8: In Chicacao, Suchitepequez, Guat., Revolutionary Organization of the People in Arms guerrillas ambushed a troop transport, with twenty-six resulting army casualties.
Feb. 8: Former Moro National Liberation Front commander Unad attempted to move weapons from the Philippine island of Pata to Bubuan.
Feb. 9: Terrorists from the Arab Revolution Vanguards Organization reported storming a Syrian intelligence headquarters in Aleppo, and capturing ten officers.
Feb. 9: More than 300,000 people were involved in a general anti-terrorist strike in Vasco, Spain, protesting the Feb. 6 murder of nuclear engineer Jose Maria Ryan.
Feb. 9: In Suchitoto, El Sal., eighteen peasants were killed and thirty others wounded when a terrorist threw a bomb at a truck.
Feb. 9: In Uganda enemies of the Obote regime attacked army barracks and police stations.
Feb. 10: The head of Istanbul's Electricity and Transport Authority, Colonel Cezmi Olcay was wounded by two gunmen as he drove through morning rush hour traffic.
Feb. 10: In Guatemala, between the municipalities of Comalapa and San Jose Poaquil in Chimaltenango ORPA rebels attacked a troop transport, resulting in twenty-eight army casualties.
Feb. 10: Shot and killed in Londonderry, Ire., was Samuel Montgomery, a part-time member of the Ulster Defense Regiment.
Feb. 10: In a shoot-out with a night guard in Rome, a member of the Rightists, a Third Position organization, was wounded, as was the guard.
Feb. 11: A story in *Foreign Report* which reported that Israel had 200 nuclear weapons and was developing a cruise missile was denied by the Israeli foreign ministry.
Feb. 11: When a detachment of Treasury police in Tacana, San Marcos, Guat., was attacked by ORPA, there were ten police casualties.
Feb. 12: The Federal Republic of Germany repealed two laws prohibiting oral or written descriptions of how to commit serious crimes, or verbally favoring violence.
Feb. 12: In the Philippines, on the southern island of Pata, Muslim guerrillas led by former Moro National Liberation Front commander Unad killed 118 army troopers. Government troops had desecrated mosques, raped village women, and ransacked homes. The Navy sank six boats and killed Unad's son. Unad's guerrillas opened fire when the 124-man assault party landed, and Unad and forty-six followers were slain. The number of civilian dead ranged from 400 to 2,000.
Feb. 12: In Corsica, forty-five bombs exploded; no injuries or serious damages occurred. The bombs were probably set to protest the Feb. 11 Paris court decision to imprison thirteen Corsicans for terrorism for a January, 1980 hotel siege during which three people were killed.
Feb. 13: Jose Ignacio Arregui Izaguirre, an ETA member who allegedly killed two guards, died in a Madrid prison hospital, apparently from political torture. Two days of rioting and strikes in Basque towns followed his death. On Feb. 17, five police inspectors were arraigned in the case.
Feb. 13: Arrested as propagandists for the Red Brigades were attorneys Eduardo di Giovanni and Giovanna Lombardi. Both had defended the founder of the Brigades, Renato Curcio. Editor of the Left-Wing newspaper *Controcorrenti*, Carmine Fiorillo was also arrested.
Feb. 13: In the village of Pojopon, Esquipulas Palo Gordo, San Marcos, an anti-guerrilla unit suffered twenty-three casualties. When additional guerrillas joined the fray, the army sustained thirty-five casualties; one transport and an armored vehicle were destroyed.
Feb. 13: In Havana, around thirty armed Cubans broke into the Ecuadorian embassy, seized Ambassador Perez Concha and several others, and offered to exchange the hostages for safe conduct out of Cuba and political asylum. The Cuban government rejected negotiations, stormed the embassy, and arrested twenty-nine people.
Feb. 15: According to The Voice of Lebanon, eight Syrian soldiers were slain in a Muslim Brotherhood of Aleppo ambush. Eight members of the Brotherhood and twenty civilians were later killed by the Syrian army.
Feb. 16: In Paris, the Embassy of the People's Democratic Republic of Yemen was damaged by a rocket. A note left nearby said, "Remember Copernic." A Jewish synagogue had been bombed on the Rue Copernic in Paris in 1980.
Feb. 16: Just before Pope John Paul II celebrated a mass in Karachi stadium in Pakistan, a bomb exploded prematurely, killing its bearer. The Al Zulfikar later claimed the action.
Feb. 16: The Prosecutor's Office in Cairo, Egypt, charged three Palestinians and two Egyptians of conspiracy to blow up both the Israeli Embassy and a Cairo synagogue.
Feb. 17: In twenty-four hours of political violence in Guatemala, thirty-seven people died, with Rightists allegedly responsible for the deaths, most of them by torture.
Feb. 17: In El Salvador, fifteen guerrillas were reported killed in a fight

with government troops at a Santo Domingo hideout. Seven dissidents died elsewhere.
Feb. 17: In Davao, one person was killed and eleven wounded in a bombing that occurred two days prior to Pope John Paul II's visit to the Philippines. Muslim groups were allegedly responsible.
Feb. 17: Several Syrians were arrested in Jordan in an assassination attempt on the life of Prime Minister Mudar Badran, according to *Al-Ittihad* newspaper of Abu Dhabi. The *Al-Ray* newspaper of Amman claimed that Syria was responsible for the February 6 kidnapping in Beirut of the *chargé d'affaires*.
Feb. 17: After four gunmen assassinated Luigi Marangoni, the Director of the Polyclinic Hospital in Milan, Italy, a leaflet found the next day said his murder was a protest against efforts to reorganize the state medical service. The Walter Alasia column of the Red Brigades was suspected.
Feb. 18: Kurdish rebels in Iraq took nine persons hostage, including a British subject, according to the British Foreign Ministry.
Feb. 19: In Spain, the honorary consuls of Austria, El Salvador, and Uruguay were kidnapped, allegedly for the purpose of publicizing the treatment of Basque prisoners. All were released unharmed in San Sebastian by the ETA.
Feb. 20: A police outpost in San Juan Comalapa, Chimaltenango in Guatemala was burned by ORPA rebels.
Feb. 20: In the Alto Adige region of northern Italy, two pylons were felled by explosions. A leaflet signed "Tyrol" left at the scene demanded that the area be returned to Austria.
Feb. 20: In Suratthani province in Thailand, guerrillas shot down an army helicopter and killed twelve people, while Communist and Muslim guerrillas killed fifteen others in a raid south of Bangkok.
Feb. 20: In Beirut, Leb., Maximov Hakim, Bishop of the Greek Orthodox Eastern Church, escaped an assassination attempt.
Feb. 20: An explosion on a Teheran bus injured fifteen people, five seriously.
Feb. 21: Thirty Cubans who had entered the Ecuadorian embassy in Cuba to seize the ambassador and others on Feb. 13 were arrested by security forces. Twenty-nine people were arrested.
Feb. 21: In Teheran, Iran, two bombs exploded killing two and injuring sixteen.
Feb. 21: Factions in the Lebanese civil war staged a shoot-out in front of the French embassy in Beirut.
Feb. 22: At a Palestinian base inside Lebanon, Israelis killed ten suspected guerrillas. The base was controlled by the Iraqi Arab Liberation Front.
Feb. 23: Eight persons were injured by a bomb planted outside the offices of Radio Free Europe and Radio Liberty in Munich, Germany.
Feb. 23: During an ultimately unsuccessful coup attempt led by Lieutenant Colonel Antonio Tejero Molina and others in Madrid, Spain, the cabinet and 350 legislators were taken hostage.
Feb. 23: A police station surrendered its weapons when ORPA guerrillas took over the town of Pueblo Nuevo, Suchitepequez in Guatemala.
Feb. 26: Bombings and shooting at Karachi University in Pakistan claimed one student's life and left twelve others wounded. In anti-government demonstrations in Quetta, one person was killed and another wounded by a bomb explosion.
Feb. 27: In West Beirut, two Iraqi Embassy officials were killed when unidentified gunmen shot into the Ambassador's car from a passing automobile.
Feb. 27: Argentinian national police arrested human rights movement leaders and seized files on over 6,000 persons.
Feb. 28: Soviet news sources reported an unsuccessful hijacking attempt on an unspecified date in Moscow. Four armed men insisting on flight to the West held a plane with thirty passengers. The hijackers were shot by militiamen who assaulted the plane.
Feb. 28: A Ugandan government official was killed and four others wounded when their car was fired upon.
March: Six people were killed in an attack on a hydroelectric plant near Havana, Cuba.
Mar. 1: Four inmates of the Maze Prison near Belfast, Ire., began a new hunger strike seeking political status for IRA prisoners.
Mar. 1: After a week's hiatus from violence, Spanish terrorists exploded two land mines, injuring three policemen and one passerby. The act was attributed to either the ETA military wing, or the Autonomous Commando Group.
Mar. 2: After three days of artillery exchanges, Israeli planes bombed Palestinian-dominated areas north of Tyre, Leb., killing fifteen.
Mar. 2: Three members of Al Zulfikar, a Pakistani group headed by Murtaza Bhutto, the son of the slain former Pakistani prime minister, whose aim was the overthrow of President Zia ul-Haq, hijacked a Pakistani jet, taking 148 hostages. The hijackers, armed with pistols and hand grenades, insisted upon the release of ninety-two political prisoners. They flew first to Kabul, Afg., and then to Damascus, Syria. After killing one hostage, a Pakistani diplomat, and threatening to blow the plane up with all hostages on board, they reduced the number of prisoners they wished released to fifty-five. Finally after thirteen days, fifty-four prisoners were exchanged, a $50,000 ransom paid, and the hijackers left for asylum in Libya.
Mar. 3: In answer to Israeli air raids, the Palestinians fired rockets into northern Israeli settlements. The Israelis responded with artillery fire.
Mar. 4: Police arrested three supposed members of the Basque Spanish Battalion.
Mar. 4: No injuries resulted when gunmen fired on the U.S. Embassy in San Salvador. Right-wing leader Robert D'Aubuisson was suspected of instigating the attack.
Mar. 5: Victor Malasauskas hijacked a Continental Airlines jet, demanding $3 million and threatening to detonate a remote-control bomb. Malasauskas held several passengers hostage for eleven hours at Los Angeles International airport before the hostages escaped and he surrendered. He later received a life sentence.
Mar. 5: Two gunmen shot two Turkish diplomats in Paris, killing one and wounding the other. The Secret Army for Liberation of Armenia was allegedly responsible for the attack.
Mar. 5: The Spanish police commissioner, Jose-Marie Moya, was shot and killed in Bilboa, Spain. The Basque ETA was suspected of the attack.
Mar. 6: Salaamullah Tippu, a member of Al Zulfikar, hijacked a plane, killing Pakistani diplomat Tariq Rahim.
Mar. 6: Five government soldiers were killed when rebels in El Salvador attacked a small town north of the capital.
Mar. 6: Two Iraqi Embassy employees in Beirut, Leb., were not injured when machine gun fire hit their car.
Mar. 7: Ammar Ouzegane, a theoretician and leader of the *Front de liberation nationale* (FLN) of Algeria, who also acted as Secretary General of the Algerian Communist Party and Minister of Agriculture in the Ben Bella government was buried.
Mar. 8: A man stating that he was a Turk named Hassan apparently made his way into Israel via hang-glider, kidnapped an Israeli man, and held him for several hours before he was captured.
Mar. 9: The Ugandan Patriotic Movement claimed responsibility for an ambush outside of Kampala in which seventy-three Ugandan government soldiers were killed.
Mar. 9: A horse was killed and five Arabs were wounded in Gaza when a grenade was thrown at an Israeli military patrol.
Mar. 10: Gonzalvo Yurrita, a Guatemalan minister and his driver were killed in a terrorist attack. Also in Guatemala City, four bombs exploded injuring one passerby.
Mar. 10: The U.S. ambassador to Lebanon, John Gunther Dean, was uninjured when a bullet hit his limousine during his twice daily drive between his home and the U.S. embassy.
Mar. 11: The Colombian government reported that M-19 guerrillas raided two towns and set off an explosion at Bogota's international airport.
Mar. 11: Over 100 M-19 guerrillas seized the town of Mocoa near the Ecuadorian border where they held up two banks and killed three civilians. Forty-eight guerrillas were captured while crossing the border.
Mar. 11: The Jihad Command stormed a police station in Bandung, Indo.
Mar. 12: Timur Selcuk, a member of the neo-Fascist Democratic Idealist Turkish Association was arrested by Turkish authorities for assisting Mehmet Ali Agca, the man who would try to assassinate the pope on May 13, 1981, to flee Turkey for Iran in 1980.
Mar. 12: Police and rebels exchanged gunfire in San Salvador, El Sal., when rebels shot at army men displaying captured guerrilla weapons.
Mar. 12: A force of seventy ORPA guerrillas stormed a police station in Puerto Limon, Guat. No one was injured in the attack.
Mar. 14: Three assailants, reportedly Palestinians, machine-gunned a bus passing through a Jewish neighborhood in northern Jerusalem, injuring one person. The guerrillas escaped.
Mar. 14: Seventy-five alleged members of the Italian terrorist group Prima Linea were indicted on charges ranging from attacks on buildings to murder.
Mar. 16: Slight damage resulted from the fire-bombing of a jet-fuel train headed for Tokyo's international airport at Narita.
Mar. 16: The *New York Times* reported that 600 Nicaragua-bound terrorists were training in Florida, New Jersey, and Los Angeles.
Mar. 17: The IRA took credit for the wounding of a reserve policeman in Londonderry, Ire.
Mar. 17: South African jets attacked a SWAPO guerrilla base north of the Angola-Namibia border. Two South Africans were killed in fights with Mozambique's border guards.
Mar. 17: Two gunmen in a speeding truck fired approximately ten shots at the U.S. embassy in San Salvador, El Sal., after U.S. Representative Clarence Long held a news conference there.
Mar. 17: The Carlos Aguero Echeverria commando group took credit for bomb attacks in San Jose, Cos., on a van driven by U.S. embassy security guards and on the Honduran embassy. The attacks, in which six people were wounded, were thought to be in retaliation for the government's sanction of a visit of U.S. warships to Puerto Limon.
Mar. 18: The Nicaraguan national militia head of training was murdered by six gunmen whom the government believed entered from Honduras.
Mar. 18: South African and Mozambican forces clashed near Porto do Ouro, Mozambique.
Mar. 18: The Ecuadorian army effectively wiped out the guerrilla group M-19 when they killed nineteen and captured seventy-four of their number.
Mar. 19: A woman terrorist shot and fatally wounded Spanish army officer, Lieutenant Colonel Ramon Romero Rotaeche in Bilbao, Spain. She and a male companion then escaped. Police blamed the ETA.

Mar. 20: An Italian appeals court acquitted five defendants of charges in the Dec. 12, 1969 bombing in Milan's Piazza Fontana in which sixteen people were killed and ninety injured. The acquittals, on grounds of insufficient evidence, sparked demonstrations.
Mar. 20: The IRA apologized for mistakenly killing Gerry Roland in an ambush. They wanted to kill, but only wounded Roland's friend, Maurice Lutton, an ex-soldier in the Ulster Defense Regiment.
Mar. 20: Gunmen shot six soldiers patrolling an area near Guatemala City and then murdered ten peasants who saw the soldiers' murders.
Mar. 20: Soldiers of the Ulster Defense Regiment fatally wounded a 17-year-old in a car chase.
Mar. 21: The retired chief of police of the Navarre area in Spain Lieutenant Colonel Jose Luis Prietogaria was killed in Pamplona while heading to church with his family.
Mar. 21: Rightists and Basque separatists fought a gun battle in the town of San Jean de Luz on the French border. Several were injured.
Mar. 22: Following Leftist criticism of the U.S. for its failure to approve censure of Israel involvement in the bombing of southern Lebanese villages by Christian militia, gunmen in a passing car fired at the U.S. Embassy in West Beirut. No one was injured.
Mar. 23: Growing terrorism and an attempted coup in Spain motivated the organization of a special anti-terrorist unit.
Mar. 24: The Farabundo Marti National Liberation Front in El Salvador called a 24-hour truce to commemorate the first anniversary of the assassination of Archbishop Oscar Arnulfo Romero. An attack on a police station south of San Salvador violated the truce.
Mar. 24: Philipine government forces reportedly killed seven Muslim rebels, all members of the Moro National Liberation Front on the southern island of Siasi.
Mar. 24: Power stations were blown up, Uganda Radio was knocked off the air, and the Kampala headquarters of the Obote Party sustained machine gun shots. Ninety were later detained in regard to the guerrilla activities.
Mar. 24: A British businessman, Ross McMahon, was shot in both legs in Dublin by gunmen shouting "H-block," the section in which IRA prisoners are held near Belfast, Ire.
Mar. 24: Syrian President Hafez al-Assad announced that he would permit the PLO to launch raids against Israel from Syria.
Mar. 24: In Iran, a bomb damaged the headquarters of the Revolutionary Committees in Teheran.
Mar. 25: Eighteen alleged members of the April 6 Liberation Group threatened more bombings in Manila if "tangible concessions" by the Philippine government were not made.
Mar. 25: For the third time during March, the U.S. Embassy in San Salvador, El Sal., was attacked, this time by three separate groups. The terrorists attacked with rifles, submachine guns, and grenade launchers. The Leftist group, Popular Liberation Forces, claimed responsibility.
Mar. 26: A car in San Salvador, El Sal., exploded killing its three occupants and a nearby motorcyclist. The police suspected the three were terrorists whose bomb went off prematurely.
Mar. 26: Three people were injured when a bomb exploded in the Honduran Legislative Palace of Tegucigalpa at its opening session.
Mar. 26: U.S. National Security Adviser Richard Allen charged the USSR with sponsoring the PLO.
Mar. 26: The Spanish army arrested fifty Basque suspects believed to be Herri Batasuna.
Mar. 26: IRA sympathizers tore down the statue of Queen Victoria in Dun Laoghaive near Dublin, Ire.
Mar. 27: A Basque soldier, Jesus Urbien Orbegozo, suspected of links to a radical branch of the ETA, was killed in a shootout with civil guards in Madrid, Spain.
Mar. 27: New Orleans bound Honduran jet was hijacked by four men and a woman demanding the release of sixteen Salvadoran Leftists jailed in Honduras. The plane landed in Nicaragua, and then went on to Panama where the hijackers surrendered to Col. Manuel Noriega. None of the forty-nine hostages were injured.
Mar. 27: In San Salvador, El Sal., a bomb in a parked car exploded, killing two bystanders and injuring four others.
Mar. 27: A bomb exploded under an overpass near a runway at a military airfield east of San Salvador. No damage was reported.
Mar. 28: The Jihad Command claimed responsibility for hijacking an Indonesian airliner leaving Sumatra with fifty-seven persons on board. After raising their original demands, four of the hijackers were killed by a U.S.-trained Indonesian commando unit in Bangkok, Thai.
Mar. 29: Manuel Aristimuno Mendizabal, a suspected Basque terrorist, was killed by police, and a second unidentified suspect was wounded.
Mar. 29: In Shiraz, Iran, Ayatollah Rabbani Shirazi, who represented Ayatollah Khomeini, was wounded while sitting in his car. The assailant was on a motorcycle.
Mar. 29: A bomb exploded outside a security office at the U.S. Army base in Giessen, Ger. Heart of the Beast group claimed responsibility on behalf of hunger strikers.
Mar. 30: Israelis trapped at a roadblock on the West Bank wounded an Arab woman near Ramallah, during an anti-Israeli demonstration.
Mar. 30: U.S. President Ronald Reagan was shot in the chest by John Warnock Hinckley as he emerged from the Hilton Hotel in Washington D.C. Press Secretary James Brady was shot in the head, and a Secret Service agent and a policeman were also wounded.
Apr. 1: Eleven protesters and two policemen were killed during a protest demanding autonomy for Pristina, a province in Kosovo, Yug., with a large Albanian population.
Apr. 1: Bombings and random violence took place in El Salvador on the eleventh anniversary of the formation of the Popular Liberation Forces. Monique Huguette Gauthier, a Canadian biologist, disappeared during the violence.
Apr. 1: Thai Prime Minister Prem Tinsulanonda was the victim of a military coup, when Army generals, led by Sant Chitpatima established a Revolutionary Committee. The following day Prem's forces recaptured Bangkok and arrested four of the military leaders.
Apr. 1: No one was injured during a grenade attack on the U.S. Embassy in San Salvador, El Sal.
Apr. 2: Kenneth John Acheson of the Royal Ulster Constabulary was killed by an IRA car bomb.
Apr. 3: A bomb intended to destroy Uganda's coffee supply was detonated by the Ugandan Freedom Movement at a Kampala warehouse.
Apr. 3: Eight people died and two hundred were injured as bombs exploded during a general strike in West Bengal, India.
Apr. 3: Cars were damaged when four bombs exploded at the U.S. Air Base in Ellinikon, Greece.
Apr. 3: Two bombs exploded in Qom, Iran, injuring twenty people.
Apr. 6: A car containing four U.S. military specialists was shot at in Istanbul, Turkey.
Apr. 7: Joanna Mathers, an Irish census worker, was shot to death in Londonderry, Ire. Although the IRA denied responsibility, they had stated an intent to disrupt the census.
Apr. 7: In retaliation for the arrest of Mario Moretti, the Italian Red Brigades killed prison guard Raffaele Cinotti near his home in Rome.
Apr. 7: Extensive damage was caused by two fire bombs which exploded in a department store in Frankfurt, Ger.
Apr. 8: A bomb exploded, injuring seven people and causing extensive damage to a railroad station in Cologne, Ger.
Apr. 8: Two people were injured when a bomb exploded at the Indian Embassy in Kampala, Uganda.
Apr. 8: One man was killed and a child injured when a hand grenade exploded during a Jewish wedding near Jerusalem's Old City.
Apr. 9: Police officer Vincente Sanchez Vicente was killed by four masked gunmen in Baracaldo, Spain.
Apr. 10: Extensive damage was caused by a dynamite explosion at the Christian Democratic Party Headquarters in Padua, Italy.
Apr. 10: Two people were injured when a Uganda Freedom Movement bomb exploded in the Indian community of Kampala, Uganda.
Apr. 10: IRA member Bobby Sands, who was in the fifth week of a hunger strike after being arrested for the illegal possession of firearms, was elected to parliament.
Apr. 10: Cuban refugee Rafael Fredesvindo Pellerano Albantosa died during a scuffle as he attempted to hijack an Eastern Airlines flight to Miami, after its takeoff from New York.
Apr. 11: In Chuabajito, Guat., soldiers massacred Indians who had recently joined leftist organizations.
Apr. 12: Shots were fired at the door of the Soviet Consulate in San Francisco.
Apr. 12: A U.S. military train was detained when a cable was placed over an electrified railway line in Bonn, Ger. Supporters of jailed hunger strikers were responsible.
Apr. 13: A car-bomb exploded in Aley, Leb., killing two people and wounding sixteen others. The attack occurred during a five day cease-fire between warring Lebanese and Syrian forces and the Christian militia.
Apr. 13: Ernano Puzzi, who was imprisoned at Novara for a 1974 terrorist bombing which killed eight, was strangled in the exercise yard.
Apr. 14: The Farabundo Marti Liberation Front, which claimed to control eleven areas in El Salvador, carried out ten terrorist operations over seven days, including the bombing of a movie theater in San Salvador, and clashing with government troops in Guarnecia, Santa Ana, and Puente Bordon.
Apr. 14: Three people were killed in Spain in separate incidents coinciding with the fiftieth anniversary of the second Spanish Republic.
Apr. 14: In Miami's Little Havana, Franklin Joseph Camper and Robert Lee Lisenby were arrested in possession of an explosive device. The two had been arrested the previous month, with eleven others, for practicing jungle warfare.
Apr. 14: Jordanian government minister Hisham Mohaisen, who had been kidnapped in Beirut by armed members of the Organization of the National Confrontation Front, was released in Lebanon after sixty-six days in captivity.
Apr. 14: Deputy Director of the Poggioreale Prison Giuseppe Salvia was shot and killed while he was driving in Naples, Italy. His car was forced off the road by the assailant's car.
Apr. 14: Assailants armed with a rocket launcher and Soviet rifles attacked a police station in Johannesburg, South Africa.
Apr. 14: The IRA kidnapped Francis Tiernan from his home in Foukhill, Ire.
Apr. 14: During a clash between the Lebanese Army and leftist terrorists, the U.S. Embassy in Beirut was struck by machine gun fire.
Apr. 15: Several buildings in Londonderry, Ire., were set on fire, after demonstrations supporting imprisoned IRA member Bobby Sands.

Apr. 15: In the southern Philippines, Godfredo Alingal, a Jesuit priest who witnessed an alleged rape related to the army, was killed by five gunmen at his monastery.
Apr. 15: A bomb exploded on the campus of Hamburg University, West Germany.
Apr. 16: A bomb was found at the U.S. Army Base in Wiesbaden, Ger., in retaliation for the hunger strike death the same day of terrorist Sigurd Debus.
Apr. 16: Ugandan Parliament member Joseph Muhangi was killed by an unidentified assailant in Kampala.
Apr. 16: A guerrilla organization attacked a government military patrol in northern Guatemala, leaving eighteen leftist guerrillas and six soldiers dead.
Apr. 16: A bomb exploded, killing one and wounding seven others at the airport in Ajaccio, Corsica, coinciding with the arrival of French President Valery Giscard d'Estaing.
Apr. 16: A bomb killed Indian administrative official E.S. Parthasarthi at his office in the Upper Assam province.
Apr. 16: Ulster Defense Regiment member Jack Donnelly, who campaigned against IRA member Bobby Sands, was shot to death in Moy, Ire.
Apr. 16: Two terrorists who were attempting to enter Israel in a balloon were killed by gunfire near Houle, Leb.
Apr. 16: A Cypriot freighter, thought to be loaded with weapons, was blown up by Israeli frogmen in the port of Sidon, Leb.
Apr. 17: A bomb exploded at West Berlin's Max Planck Institute, a research facility, in apparent retaliation for the hunger strike death of RAF member Sigurd Debus.
Apr. 19: Two Catholic youths were killed when rammed by British vehicles during a march in Londonderry, Ire., commemorating the 1916 Easter Rebellion in Dublin.
Apr. 19: Thirteen people were killed and 177 wounded when members of the outlawed Philippines New Peoples's Army tossed hand grenades and fired guns into a crowded church during an Easter mass in Mindanao.
Apr. 20: Two people died and another was hurt following a hotel bombing in Dubai, Oman.
Apr. 21: Two suspected neo-fascist terrorists were wounded and another captured following a gunfight with police at the Italian-Swiss border.
Apr. 21: Israeli cities in Galilee were attacked for two days by Lebanese rockets.
Apr. 22: In response to opposition of Syrian President Hafez Assad, government troops massacred several hundred people in the Hama area during a six-day period.
Apr. 22: Beirut Airport was closed and two aircraft were damaged by artillery fire.
Apr. 22: Two people were killed and ten others wounded when a bomb exploded near the home of Ayatollah Khomeini in Teheran, Iran.
Apr. 23: In Northern Ireland, a former Ulster Defense Regiment member was killed during a riot supporting imprisoned IRA member Bobby Sands.
Apr. 23: In conflicting reports, Lebanese officials stated that the Israelis had shelled the city of Tyre, while the Israelis claimed that they sank terrorist vessels off Lebanon.
Apr. 23: Eighteen Columbian soldiers were killed and ten were wounded after being ambushed by M-19 guerrillas at numerous sites over a six-day period in the Columbian jungle.
Apr. 24: Sixteen members of Turkey's leftist Revolutionary Sympathizers Union were charged with the murders of four people in Istanbul.
Apr. 25: A car bomb exploded in Kermanshah, Iran, killing seven and wounding thirty-five.
Apr. 25: A letter-bomb which did not explode was received by British Parliament member Barry Porter.
Apr. 26: Forty IRA sympathizers were arrested in London for violating a ban on marches.
Apr. 26: An IRA arsenal which contained numerous explosives, weapons, and ammunition, was discovered in Charlemont, County Armagh, Ire.
Apr. 27: Irish soldier Kevin Joyce was shot to death during gunfire between terrorist factions near Deir Antar, Leb.
Apr. 27: One person died when members of the pro-Iranian government Islamic Hezbollahis attacked members of the leftist People's Fedayeen Movement, who were gathered for a commemorative rally.
Apr. 27: Red Brigades terrorists kidnapped Italian government official Ciro Cirillo near Naples. Two others were killed during the abduction. He was released several months later for a ransom of $800,000 to $1.2 million.
Apr. 27: Belfast, Ire., police officer Gary Martin died and two other officers were wounded when a truck bomb exploded.
Apr. 28: Ulster Defense Regiment member Richard McKee died when his car crashed during a sniper attack.
Apr. 28: Sabotage was attempted on an aircraft about to fly Indian Prime Minister Indira Gandhi to Switzerland.
Apr. 28: One soldier was killed and another wounded near Belfast, Ire.
Apr. 29: Buses were burned in Guatemala City by members of the January 31 Popular Front. They also exploded twenty propaganda bombs in other provinces of Guatemala.
Apr. 30: Five people were killed, including two armed with home-made bombs, in Guatemala City, Guat.
Apr. 30: The Guatamalan Work Party claimed responsibility for the shooting death of Jose Barrera Aguilar, a coffee company production manager.
May: The Yugoslav Embassy in Tirana, Alb., was bombed.
May 1: In his automobile outside his apartment, the president of the Austrian-Israeli Friendship League, Heinz Nittel, was shot to death by Husham Mohammed Rajih, a member of the Al-Asifa terrorist organization.
May 1: Four members of the Costa Rican Carlos Aguero Echeverria terrorist organization were arrested and accused of attacking a U.S. Marine barracks in April.
May 1: Journalist Fluvio Alirio Mejia Milian was kidnapped. Several weeks later his body was found in Guatemala, along with fifteen others. All had been tortured.
May 1: During the first twenty-four hours following the death of hunger striker Bobby Sands, injuries numbered two dozen, and forty-eight people were arrested.
May 2: Seven members of the Falangists, a right-wing terrorist organization, seized an Occidental Petroleum camp near Santa Cruz, Bol. They were arrested two days later.
May 4: Spanish Brigadier General Andreas Gonzalez de Suso was shot to death by three assailants outside his Madrid apartment. Policeman Ignacio Garcia was also killed during an ensuing chase. Five days later, three members of the leftist First of October Autonomous Revolutionary Group (GRAPO), were apprehended.
May 4: Sergeant Justiniano Fernandez and Guardsman Francisco Montenegro were shot in the back of their heads by two terrorists in Barcelona, Spain.
May 5: Scotland Yard intercepted a letter bomb intended for Britain's Prince Charles.
May 5: A bomb accompanied by a note from the Red Brigades exploded at the British Chamber of Commerce in Milan, Italy. Two bomb threats were also received at the British Consulate in New York.
May 5: During the night, a bomb filled with nails injured a British soldier at a roadblock in Belfast, Ire.
May 5: A milk truck driver and his son died after being assaulted by rioters in the Catholic area of Belfast, Ire.
May 6: In Lisbon, Portugal, the Royal British Club was bombed by members of the Popular Forces of April 25th.
May 6: A terrorist group called the English Republican Army sent letter bombs to two British politicians. No damage occurred.
May 6: A hand grenade exploded beneath the car driven by David Thebehali, the mayor of Soweto, S. Afri.
May 6: Royal Ulster Constabulary member Philip Ellis was killed and five others were wounded by IRA snipers in Northern Ireland.
May 7: In Dublin, Ire., the wife of Fine Gael leader Dr. Fitzgerald thwarted an assassination attempt by slamming the door on two armed men who appeared at her residence.
May 7: In Madrid, Spain, two terrorists on a motorcycle threw a bomb into an Army vehicle, killing Lieutenant Colonel Guillermo Tevar Saco and two other soldiers, while wounding eleven bystanders and the personal bodyguard to King Carlos.
May 7: A young man was killed when the bomb that he was carrying exploded in Belfast, Ire. Twelve others were injured.
May 8: At gunpoint, the Vice-President of the Red Cross of El Salvador, Teofilo Siman, was kidnapped from his home in San Salvador.
May 8: A British Army building in Glasgow, Scot., was damaged by three fire-bombs.
May 8: Two British soldiers were wounded by guerrilla mortar fire in Newtownhamilton, Ire.
May 8: The Popular Revolutionary Struggle claimed responsibility for the fire-bombing of three police stations in Athens, Gr.
May 8: More than eight vehicles were seized and burned during riots in Belfast and Londonderry, Ire.
May 9: A bomb exploded at a Scottish oil terminal a quarter mile from where Queen Elizabeth was having lunch. The IRA had issued numerous bomb threats, one of which led to the evacuation of 600 persons from a nursing home and an orphanage near Belfast, Ire.
May 9: A hand-grenade injured five policemen and a soldier was shot in two incidents in Belfast, Ire.
May 10: West Germany's Minister of Economics Heinz Herbert Karry died in his bed after being shot four times by a sniper.
May 11: Two British soldiers were wounded by snipers in West Belfast, Ire.
May 12: Six people were arrested in Houston, Texas, in possession of over 1000 M-16 rifles allegedly bound for South Africa.
May 12: A priest, Carlos Galvez Galindo was shot to death in his parish home in Tecpan, Guatemala.
May 12: The leftist leader of the United Revolutionary Front, Otto Walter Garcia, was murdered in Guatemala.
May 13: Nine members of the radical group MOVE, including the group's leader Vincent Leaphart, were arrested in Philadelphia and charged with conspiracy, possession and manufacture of bombs and other explosive devices.
May 13: Pope John Paul II was shot six times as he rode through St. Peter's Square in the Vatican. Mehmet Ali Agca, a Turkish terrorist who had recently escaped from prison, was charged with the shooting. He was sentenced to life imprisonment.

May 14: Five members of the Royal Ulster Constabulary were injured when their vehicle was hit by a rocket launched by the IRA Provos.
May 14: Two members of a police convoy were killed and another wounded when Basque terrorists detonated remote-controlled explosives near Bilbao, Spain.
May 14: The Deputy Commander of the National Liberation Movement, Carlos Humberto Mendez Lopez, was shot to death by two gunmen in a car in Guatemala City, Guat.
May 14: Carlos Galvez, a priest in Tecpan, Guatemala, was fatally shot in the head as he was going to a baptism at his church.
May 15: A police officer was killed and three others were injured by an IRA rocket that was fired through the roof of their vehicle in West Belfast, Ire.
May 15: The 15th of May Arab Movement for the Liberation of Palestine was suspected of the bombing of an El Al Airlines office in Rome.
May 16: A bomb exploded near the El Al Airlines office in Istanbul, Turkey. As in the previous day, the 15th of May Arab Movement for the Liberation of Palestine was the primary suspect.
May 16: An airport worker at New York's Kennedy Airport was killed when a pipe bomb exploded shortly after a phone call from the Puerto Rican Armed Resistance Group warned of such an attack.
May 16: Patrick Martin, a Belfast butcher who refused to close his store in honor of an IRA funeral, was found shot to death in his home in Ardoyne, Ire.
May 17: As a security precaution in the Gaza Strip, Israeli security forces destroyed the houses of five recently arrested terrorists who were suspected of causing fourteen deaths.
May 17: More than $2 million in damage was caused by fire bombs that exploded in a movie theater, a toy shop, and a brick factory in Dungannon, Ire.
May 17: Four people were injured when time bombs exploded near six oil and gas pipelines in the Khuzistan province of Iran.
May 17: Thirty-two police officers, investigating the murder of a Sunni clergyman, were killed in ambushes in the Sistan and Baluchistan provinces of Iran.
May 17: A protestant church in Dunmurry, Ire., was set on fire by arsonists.
May 17: Members of a British patrol killed a man in apparent self-defense, in Belfast, Ire.
May 19: An 11-year-old girl was wounded as British troops fired into a mob in Belfast, Ire. The troops also avoided injury when they were fired upon by two snipers.
May 19: Five British soldiers were killed when a land mine destroyed their armored vehicle near Camlough, Ire.
May 19: The director of Germany's Haus Waelischmiller Company received a death threat for shipments of nuclear-related materials to Pakistan; the firm had been bombed as well.
May 20: Several hundred members of the National Peasant Union, armed with machetes, stormed the office of the Honduran National Agrarian Institute in Comayagua province, demanding the release of a hundred comrades held in custody.
May 20: Clothing store heir Cesare Menasci was abducted from his car in Rome.
May 20: Petrochemical executive Giuseppe Tagliercio was abducted from his home near Venice by four gunmen dressed as customs police.
May 21: In New York City, a pipe bomb was discovered in a garbage truck as it was making a pickup at the United Nations building.
May 21: Imprisoned IRA members Raymond McCreesh and Patrick O'Hara both died in Maze Prison on the sixty-first days of their hunger strikes. Nine days earlier, Francis Hughes died on the fifty-ninth day of his hunger strike.
May 22: The Director of Rome's employment office, Enzo Retrosi, was shot twice in each leg by three Red Brigades gunmen.
May 22: A Catholic rioter was killed and five British soldiers were injured during demonstrations in Londonderry, Ire., following the death of hunger striker Patrick O'Hara.
May 22: In contradictory reports, the PLO claimed to have shot down three Israeli planes over Bekaa Valley, Syria, while the Israeli's countered that one pilotless plane had been lost.
May 23: A small group of armed right-wing terrorists took two hundred people hostage in a crowded Barcelona, Spain, bank, demanding the release of four imprisoned military officers. The thirty-seven hour siege ended when police stormed the bank and apprehended nine of the terrorists.
May 23: A British soldier was wounded amidst rioting in Belfast, Ire.
May 24: Joseph Lynch of West Belfast, Ire., was killed during a riot when he was run over by a British troop vehicle.
May 24: A Turkish Airlines plane bound for Ankara with 112 passengers and six crew members aboard, was hijacked by two members of Dev Sol, shortly after takeoff from Istanbul. The hijackers demanded the release of forty-seven prisoners and $500,000 in ransom. Although the demands were rejected, the siege ended the following day.
May 24: In Iraq, Kurdish terrorists blew up the railway tracks on the main route between Baghdad and Basra.
May 24: A member of the Royal Ulster Constabulary was wounded by two gunmen in a milk truck during his patrol through Belfast, Ire.
May 24: Terrorists were caught during an attempted takeover of Banco Central in Barcelona, Spain.
May 25: Automatic weapons were fired at the police, during the funeral of IRA hunger striker Patrick O'Hara.
May 25: One member of the Ulster Defense Regiment was killed and three others wounded, after they were ambushed by members of the Provisional wing of the IRA, in Ballaghy, Ire.
May 25: A commuter rail line, predominantly used by blacks, was bombed in South Africa. No one was hurt.
May 27: Royal Ulster Constabulary member Mervyn Basil Robinson was shot to death while sitting in his car in South Armagh, Ire. The Provisional IRA took credit.
May 27: The British Council offices in Thessaloniki, Gr., were bombed by members of the Greek Armed Group for the Support of the Northern Irish Struggle.
May 27: A military recruiting office was bombed and forty-eight people in Cape Town were arrested, following demonstrations commemorating South Africa's twentieth anniversary of independence from the commonwealth.
May 28: A British soldier killed two IRA gunmen and wounded another as he was being ambushed in Londonderry, Ire.
May 28: In Beirut, Leb., two people were killed by a car bomb.
May 29: In Lebanon near Damur, Israelis bombed missile sites allegedly run by Libya in retaliation for attacks on their planes. An estimated twenty to eighty people were killed and 100 wounded.
May 29: Honduran professor Antonio Teruel was killed by shots fired from a passing car, as he drove through Guatemala City, Guat.
May 29: Giuseppe Magagna, an Italian teacher, was shot in the legs by four members of the Red Brigades.
May 30: Almost one hundred people were killed during a clash between rebel and government forces near the Indian-Burmese border.
May 31: A member of the Royal Ulster Constabulary was shot to death by two men and a woman as he was guarding a hospital intensive care ward in Belfast, Ire.
May 31: British Bomb Disposal Unit member Michael O'Neill was killed as he examined an abandoned car near Newry, Ire.
June: A bomb was set off in an Anaheim, Calif., auditorium where the Turkish Folkloric Ballet was to have performed. No injuries occurred, but that performance and others in the area were called off.
June: An Armenian church in close proximity to Paris was bombed by the Turkish-Islamic Underground Organization.
June 1: Police in Jamaica killed eight suspected terrorists during a raid of a building in Kingston. Also found were M-16 rifles, small arms, gas masks, and military uniforms. Terrorist Anthony "General Starkey" Tirgle was among those killed.
June 1: The PLO lobbyist to the Common Market Naim Khader was shot to death by a single gunman as he walked near his home in Brussels, Belg. The PLO suspected the murderer to be an Israeli agent, while Israel suspected Arab extremists.
June 2: Six people were killed and forty-five wounded when six Israeli aircraft bombed a regional Al Fatah headquarters near Tyre, Leb.
June 2: A remote-controlled bomb misfired, injuring a police officer in Londonderry, Ire.
June 3: The Revolutionary Anti-Capitalist Action and the New Organization both took credit for the fire bombing of two department stores in Athens, Gr. Six buildings were ultimately leveled and damage was estimated in the millions of dollars.
June 3: Joseph Lynn of Derry, Ire., was shot to death in the crossfire between snipers and a British foot patrol.
June 3: The First Secretary of the Iraqi Embassy was shot twice in the arm by a gunman in a passing car, as he drove through the streets of Beirut, Leb.
June 4: Nery Lucas Grauc and Edwin Paz Belteton, both relatives of Guatemalan president General Fernando Romeo Lucas Garcia, were kidnapped by terrorists armed with machine guns in Guatemala City. Belteton was killed as he tried to escape.
June 4: Guatemalan national police detective Marco Tulio and medical student Raul Falla were murdered by gunmen in separate incidents on the campus of the San Carlos National University.
June 4: Seven civilians died, including the mayor of a small town, in a shoot-out with guerrillas in Guatemala. Three guerrillas also died in the crossfire.
June 4: Two people were killed and twelve more wounded at the American University Hospital in West Beirut, Leb., during a vicious gunfight between Kurdish and Mourabetoun forces.
June 5: One policeman was killed and several others were injured when a land mine blew up underneath a police bus in San Sebastian, Spain. The ETA took credit for the attack the next day.
June 5: Ulster Defense Regiment member Ronald Graham was killed in his home in Fermanagh County in Ireland, by two gunmen who had taken his wife hostage.
June 5: As a result of a two-day guerrilla attack near Chichontepee volcano in El Salvador, army sources reported that 100 people died.
June 6: An Israeli driver was killed and a passenger injured when a hand grenade was tossed into their vehicle as they were driving in the Gaza Strip.
June 6: In Naples, Italy, Uberto Siola, a Councilman, was wounded by gunshots fired at his legs by Red Brigades members.
June 7: Israeli aircraft bombed the Iraqi nuclear reactor being built near

Baghdad, Iraq.
June 8: An army lieutenant was killed when a land mine exploded as he was driving in northern Guatemala.
June 9: Turkish consular employee Mehmet Yerguz was killed in Geneva, Switz.
June 10: Eight IRA prisoners escaped from the Crumlin Road jail in Belfast. Three lawyers suspected of smuggling arms to the prisoners were arrested the following day.
June 11: In Paris, a Turkish Airlines office was invaded by sixteen Armenian terrorists. They were removed later without incident.
June 11: Imprisoned IRA terrorist Kieran Doherty, in the midst of a hunger strike, was elected to the Irish Parliament.
June 11: Twenty-five people were killed in an explosion at the Arab Socialist Union, in Tyre, Leb.
June 13: A IRA plan to kill Lord Gardiner, the former lord chancellor of London, with a car bomb, failed when the bomb fell from the car and was defused.
June 13: Three Costa Rican guards were killed by four gunmen in San Jose. A taxi driver was also killed during the escape.
June 13: Marcus Simon Sarjeant was arrested after he fired six blank shots at Queen Elizabeth as she rode on horseback through St. James Park.
June 15: Six people were killed, and many others wounded when Philippine troops shot at a crowd protesting against upcoming presidential elections.
June 15: The ETA was suspected in the wounding of three civil guards in Spain.
June 15: At an alleged ETA hideout in San Sebastian, Spain, police inspector Maria Jose Garcia was killed during a midnight raid.
June 16: A bomb threat forced a Romanian airplane on a flight from Bucharest to Tel Aviv with 140 passengers and fifteen crew members aboard, to land at the Konya Military Airport in Turkey. No bomb was found, but four passengers were injured as they jumped to the tarmac.
June 17: A bomb exploded at a NATO arms depot near Hanover, Ger.
June 17: The planning chief of the National Electrification Institute, Julio Cesar Difuentes Anleu, was kidnapped in Guatemala City. His body was discovered five days later.
June 18: In two separate incidents near Barcelona, Spain, civil guards killed four members of the leftist GRAPO terrorist organization.
June 18: According to the National Association of Educators, five teachers were killed and another thirteen kidnapped by Salvadorian security forces during the previous week.
June 19: Deputy Police Superintendent Sebastiano Vinci was killed and his driver seriously injured by members of the Red Brigades as they were driving through Rome.
June 19: Publishing executive Giuseppe Franconieri was wounded by members of the Communist Armed Nuclei in Rome.
June 19: Antonio De Vita, the attorney of a former Red Brigades member who turned informer, was wounded in Rome.
June 20: In New York, the FBI arrested three men for supplying arms to the IRA. More than forty automatic weapons were confiscated.
June 20: The MacRoy Park Army Base in Belfast, Ire., was besieged by IRA guerrillas who wounded five soldiers and a young boy with mortar fire.
June 20: Off-duty police officer Neal Quinn was shot to death in a pub in Newry, Ire.
June 22: The Polisario Front reported victories in their two-day battles with Moroccan troops.
June 22: Basque terrorists were suspected in the shooting death of retired Army Colonel Luis de la Parra Urbaneja in Irun, Spain.
June 22: A travel agency in Pireus, Gr., was attacked by terrorists armed with handguns. The Habash Front was suspected of the assault in which two died and seventy were wounded.
June 23: Four people were killed and fifty-eight wounded in an explosion at a railroad station in Qom, Iran.
June 24: Ugandan troops killed fifty-five people and wounded 100 more, at a Catholic mission near Arua, that was suspected of harboring terrorists.
June 24: Kurdish guerrillas attacked a funeral procession in Mahabad, Iran, wounding the city's governor as well as six Revolutionary Guards.
June 24: Basque terrorists were suspected of the shooting deaths of two men and the wounding of another, in Tolosa, Spain.
June 24: Four people were injured when a bomb exploded in a campus basement of Navarra University in Pamplona, Spain.
June 25: Nine Croatian nationalists, suspected of murder, arson, and extortion, were arrested by authorities in the U.S. and Canada.
June 25: Two people died and two were injured when a hand grenade exploded at the Chad Embassy in Khartoum, Sudan. A terrorist, who was also wounded, was suspected of the attack. He claimed Libya was responsible for the attack.
June 26: Two Fijian members of the UN Interim Force were killed after they were kidnapped by PLO members near Bayyada, Leb.
June 26: The governor of Mahabad, Iran, was one of six people killed when Kurdish terrorists attacked members of the Revolutionary Guards.
June 26: Five bombs were set off in public areas of Kuwait.
June 27: A bomb exploded at a mosque in Teheran, Iran, injuring Hojatoleslam Seyyed Ali Khamenei, an aide to Ayatollah Khomeini.
June 28: The governor of Evin prison, Muhammad Kacu'i, was killed in Teheran, Iran, according to Radio Teheran. Another source reported that his death occurred the following day.
June 28: In Teheran, seventy-four people, including the Chief Justice of the Iran's Supreme Court and leader of the Islamic Republican Party, and thirty-three other political leaders, were killed when a bomb exploded at the Islamic Party headquarters.
June 29: Giuseppe Santangelo was arrested in Rome after he unsuccessfully attempted to detonate a home-made bomb at St. Peter's Square in the Vatican.
July 1: A suitcase bomb exploded at the Guatemala City Airport, killing a luggage handler. Had the Miami-bound flight not been delayed forty-five minutes, the bomb would have exploded in mid-air.
July 2: Following the ouster of Iranian President Bani-Sadr, seventeen leftists were executed and fifty more were arrested for an alleged attempt to blow up Parliament.
July 3: In Belfast, Ire., shots were fired at Ian Paisley by members of the INLA as he was returning home after a BBC interview.
July 5: An Iranian Revolutionary Guard was wounded when members of that group attacked the headquarters of the leftist Mujahedeen Khalqs. Three guerrillas were killed, including two who blew themselves up with hand grenades.
July 5: Five commandos, who were allegedly attempting to assassinate Fidel Castro, were arrested near Havana.
July 6: The body of a Red Brigades kidnapping victim, Giuseppe Taliercio, was found in the trunk of a car.
July 6: The Governor of Iran's Gilan Province, Ali Akhavein-Ansari, was shot to death by two motorcyclists armed with Uzi machine guns as he drove to his office.
July 6: Chilean secret police employee Carlos Tapia Barraza was killed by gunmen armed with automatic weapons as he left his home in Santiago.
July 8: Imprisoned IRA terrorist Joe McDonnell died in Maze prison on the 61st day of his hunger strike. Five days later, IRA terrorist Martin Hurson died on the 45th day of his hunger strike in Maze.
July 9: Two people were killed and a member of the Royal Ulster Constabulary was wounded in gun battles around Belfast, Ire.
July 10: Mourners began pelting police with bricks and stones in Northern Ireland during the funeral of IRA hunger striker Joe McDonnell. The police also wounded two men and captured a third during an attempted ambush.
July 10: A stray bullet killed Hugh O'Neill in Belfast, Ire.
July 10: Two hijackers, wielding molotov cocktails, commandeered an Eastern Airlines Chicago-to-Miami jet, carrying 180 passengers and a crew of twelve, and ordered the pilot to fly to Cuba.
July 11: Almost 100 leftist guerrillas were killed by the Salvadoran Army in the Cabanas and Cuscatlan districts.
July 11: Occupants of an Israeli Army jeep were not harmed in a hand grenade attack in the Gaza Strip.
July 12: In Angola, 114 black nationalist Namibian guerrillas were killed during raids by South African soldiers.
July 12: The founder of the National Fatherland Front, General Fateh Mohammed Ferqameshr, was killed by terrorists in Kabul, Afg.
July 12: A man named George Joseph Hall was stabbed to death near his home in Belfast, Ire.
July 13: Mauritanian dissidents occupied their own embassy in Moscow, holding the staff members hostage, in protest of delays in processing their study grants.
July 14: Residents of Northwest Zambia were terrorized by members of the Mushala gang.
July 14: Police in Portadown, Ire., were attacked by gunfire and gasoline bombs during demonstrations surrounding the funeral of IRA hunger striker Martin Hurson.
July 14: Three people died in a movie theater bombing in Bangui, Central African Republic.
July 15: Two people were injured and extensive damage was caused by a bomb that exploded in a hotel kitchen in Belfast, Ire.
July 16: In Ruacana, Namibia, more than 100 South African soldiers were killed or wounded by members of the SWAPO terrorist organization.
July 16: Army Corporal Gavin Dean was killed and two other soldiers were wounded by IRA snipers using automatic weapons at an observation post in Glassdrummond, Ire.
July 16: Two explosions in two days destroyed railroad tracks, temporarily closing the Dublin-Belfast Railroad.
July 17: Israeli forces staged air and ground raids on Lebanon over a five-day period, and the PLO countered with shelling in several different locations, injuring fifty-eight people and killing three.
July 17: Six government vehicles were stolen and subsequently burned in Northern Ireland.
July 17: In Beirut, Leb., 200 people were killed and 600 were injured when the PLO headquarters was attacked by Israeli jets.
July 18: In Dublin, Ire., 120 police officers and fifty protesters were injured during a demonstration by 15,000 people supporting the IRA hunger strikers in Belfast's Maze prison.
July 19: The Kurdish head of the Divandarren Department of Education was assassinated in Iran.
July 20: Iranian Presidential candidate Habibollah Asghar Owladi was

wounded by three gunmen in Teheran, Iran. One attacker was fatally shot, another wounded, while the third man escaped.
July 20: Three bombs placed by members of the M-19 guerrilla movement exploded on the Presidential Palace grounds in Bogota, Columbia.
July 20: In Teheran, Iran, several people were wounded by a bomb that exploded at the Ministry of Economic and Financial Affairs.
July 20: Five people were injured when a bomb set by the June 9 terrorist organization exploded at the airport in Zurich, Switzerland.
July 21: Land mines set by the African National Congress damaged two power stations in South Africa.
July 22: The PLO methodically launched rockets into two Israeli coastal settlements, killing three people and wounding twenty-five.
July 22: The June 9 Organization, an Armenian terrorist group, exploded two bombs which injured five people at a railway station in Geneva, Switz.
July 23: Iranian Parliamentary candidate Hojatoleslam Seyyed Hasan Behesti and his four-year-old nephew were shot to death at his home in Isfahan, Iran.
July 23: Auto executive Renzo Sandrucci, who had been kidnapped by the Red Brigades fifty days earlier, was found unharmed in a car near Milan, Italy.
July 23: Twenty-four members of the Marxist Peykar and Mujahedeen terrorist groups were executed at the Evin prison in Teheran, Iran.
July 24: Two power stations in northern Spain were bombed by Basque terrorists.
July 24: A stray bullet killed Peter Doherty in his apartment building near Belfast, Ire.
July 24: Thirteen people were killed, including twelve members of the Revolutionary Guards, in violence occurring on Iran's election day.
July 24: Coinciding with Iran's national elections, bombs exploded at the Iranian embassies in Ankara, Turk., Munich, Ger., Bonn, and Vienna.
July 25: In Teheran, Iran, members of the Revolutionary Guards arrested several Peykar organization terrorists and confiscated handguns, rifles, submachine guns, and hand grenades.
July 25: In Namibia, the SWAPO people's liberation army claimed to have killed 146 government troops the previous May.
July 25: In violence surrounding Iran's national elections, a man was shot to death by a submachine gun.
July 28: Police patrols in Belfast survived heavy IRA sniper attacks without casualties.
July 28: A 400-pound bomb was defused after being discovered in Northern Ireland.
July 28: U.S. missionary, Stanley Rother was killed at his mission in Santiago Atitlan, Guat.
July 28: Protesting their transfer between two Spanish prisons, fourteen Basque terrorist prisoners began a hunger strike.
July 29: Three gunmen killed Antonio Caputo, the driver for the chief attorney of Salerno, Italy.
July 29: Four people were wounded and an unborn baby was killed on a bus that was attacked by Palestinian guerrillas near Jerusalem.
July 29: Mujahedeen leader Reza Saadati was executed on orders of the Iranian government.
July 30: Armed civilians and paramilitary police attempted a coup on the Gambian government when President Dawda Kairaba Jawara was in London attending the royal wedding. They took control of the radio station and the airport, and released prisoners. More than 2,000 civilians died before the coup attempt ended a week later.
July 30: Twenty-nine people, including women and children, were massacred by the police in El Salvador.
July 30: Two police officers in Newry, Ire., were injured when a land mine exploded underneath their vehicle.
July 31: Ulster Defense Regiment member Thomas Harpur was shot to death by two IRA gunmen in Strabane, Ire.
July 31: Five people were killed and eight injured during an attack on a dormitory in Lahijan, Iran.
July 31: In Bolzano, Italy, four public buildings were damaged extensively by explosions.
July 31: African National Congress official Joe Goabi was wounded as he was driving in Salisbury, Zimbabwe. The Zimbabwe government believes South Africa was responsible for the attempt on Goabi's life.
August: A large cache of Soviet arms was seized by South African troops during invasions of SWAPO bases.
August: A petroleum depot in Lesotho was damaged by South African mortar fire.
Aug. 1: Imprisoned IRA terrorist Kevin Lynch died in Northern Ireland's Maze prison, on the 71st day of his hunger strike. Four other hunger strikers died within the next two weeks.
Aug. 1: Muhammad Daoud Odeh, the Black September terrorist suspected of plotting the West German 1972 Olympics massacre in Munich, was shot five times at close range in a cafe in Warsaw, Pol.
Aug. 1: Mujahedeen terrorists killed two revolutionary guards and wounded three more, in an ambush in Amol, Iran.
Aug. 2: Imprisoned IRA terrorist Kieran Doherty died in Belfast's Maze prison, on the 73rd day of his hunger strike.
Aug. 2: Police officers John Smyth and Andrew Woods were killed when a land mine exploded beneath their patrol car near Belfast, Ire. Two other police officers in a separate car were wounded.
Aug. 2: The Arab Steadfastness Front was blamed for the bombing of the Christian Coptic Church in Cairo, Egypt. Three people died and fifty-six more were wounded by the explosion during a wedding ceremony.
Aug. 3: A car bomb exploded near the prime minister's office in Teheran, Iran, killing as many as four persons.
Aug. 3: Thirteen people were killed when a bomb exploded in the public square of Kermanshah, Iran.
Aug. 3: Clergyman Hojatoleslam Abdul-Karim Dehkadian was shot to death in Teheran, Iran.
Aug. 3: In the West German capital of Bonn, the Iranian Embassy was besieged by 100 dissidents opposing the regime of Ayatollah Khomeini.
Aug 3: Former Red Brigades member Roberto Peci, whose brother, Patrick Peci, was suspected of being an informant, was shot to death in Rome. He was found handcuffed and holding a sign which said "Death to Traitors."
Aug. 4: Following the arrest of a Thai Communist Party leader Surachai Sae Dan, rebels took control of a railroad station and demolished a locomotive.
Aug. 5: An unborn child died when terrorists fired shots into a bus near Jerusalem.
Aug. 5: Islamic parliament member Doctor Hasan Ayat was shot to death outside his home in Teheran, Iran.
Aug. 5: Following the deaths of two IRA hunger strikers, ten explosions which injured numerous persons, occurred throughout Northern Ireland.
Aug. 5: A young rioter was injured at the Belfast, Ire., funeral of hunger striker Kieran Doherty by security officers firing plastic bullets into the crowd.
Aug. 5: Ninety-six citizens were killed by the Salvadorian Army in the Chaparral province.
Aug. 5: An explosion caused extensive damage at the Pan American World Airlines office in Guatemala City, Guat.
Aug. 7: Two police officers and two guerrillas were killed in a shoot-out in Transkei, S. Afri.
Aug. 7: Kidnapped Jesuit priest Carlos Perez Alonso was freed by his captors in Guatemala.
Aug. 8: Imprisoned IRA terrorist Thomas McIlwee died in Belfast's Maze prison, on the 62nd day of his hunger strike.
Aug. 8: Three persons were killed when a bomb destroyed the conference hall of the Syrian Ministry.
Aug. 9: In Liberia, an alleged attempt to assassinate President Samuel K. Doe was foiled.
Aug. 9: Two people died and two police officers were injured by sniper fire, in demonstrations in Belfast, Ire., following the death of an IRA hunger striker.
Aug. 9: The 15th of May Arab Movement for the Liberation of Palestine was the primary suspect in the bombing of the Israeli Consulate in Athens, Gr.
Aug. 9: The Chief Judge of the Islamic Revolutionary Court, Hojatoleslam Haj Ahmed Faqihi was fatally wounded by two motorcyclists in Iran.
Aug. 9: The 15th of May Arab Movement for the Liberation of Palestine was the primary suspect in the bombing of an El Al Airplane office in Rome. One person was injured.
Aug. 10: The 15th of May Arab Movement for the Liberation of Palestine was probably responsible for two bombs set off near the Israeli Embassy in Vienna, Aust.
Aug. 10: A British soldier was shot to death by IRA Provos in Belfast, Ire.
Aug. 11: A Belfast, Ire., travel agent, who was probably mistaken for his Royal Ulster Constabulary member brother, was shot to death by a gunman on a motor bike.
Aug. 11: The June 9 Armenian group bombed the Swissair offices in Copenhagen, Switz.
Aug. 12: Four people were executed after terrorists took over the Salvadorian village of Perquin. Army troops recaptured the village a week later.
Aug. 12: Seventy people were injured in a stampede following the bombing of a Freedom Party meeting near Colombo, Sri Lanka. Thirteen members of the JVP-People's Liberation Front were arrested for the incident.
Aug. 13: Near East London, S. Afri., two guerrillas were killed and one police officer was wounded. The guerrillas were allegedly responsible for shopping center bombings in Durban and East London.
Aug. 13: African National Congress members fired rockets into a military base near Pretoria, S. Afri. One person was hurt in the explosion and one was shot by the riflemen.
Aug. 13: U.S. tire company manager Clifford Bevens, who was kidnapped by the Guerrilla Army of the Poor, was killed in a shoot-out as Guatemalan soldiers attempted to rescue him. Twelve guerrillas also died in the raid.
Aug. 13: Twenty-three people in an area almost fifty miles west of San Salvador, El Sal., were murdered after being abducted from their homes.
Aug. 13: An Iranian gunboat was hijacked by members of the monarchist group Azadegan. A week later the hijackers were given political asylum by the French government.
Aug. 13: Thirty guerrillas and nine government troopers were killed in a gun battle in northwestern Guatemala. The guerrillas also injured nineteen.
Aug. 14: Five People's Redemption Council members were executed in Liberia for the attempted assassination of President Samuel K. Doe.

Aug. 14: An IRA bomb factory was discovered in a Londonderry, Ire., apartment.
Aug. 15: Iranian Mullah Hojatoleslam Towhidi was shot to death by three assailants as he was driving in Babol.
Aug. 15: A clergyman was murdered in Sanandaj, Iran.
Aug. 15: Terrorists attacked the Maryknoll Rural Education Institute near Juli, Peru. A bomb explosion injured many bystanders.
Aug. 16: Two bombs exploded outside a dance hall in Londonderry, Ire. No one was injured.
Aug. 16: Saleh Khosravi, an Iranian clergyman, and his son were shot to death as they were leaving a mosque. Three other Iranians were injured.
Aug. 16: Seven people were shot in the kneecaps by IRA terrorists.
Aug. 17: Twelve bombs exploded in El Salvador over an eleven-day period during the civil war.
Aug. 18: Salvadoran Communal Union legal adviser and civil rights leader Rosa Judith Cisneros was murdered at her home in San Salvador, El Sal.
Aug. 19: In the Gulf of Sidra, near Libya, two U.S. planes drop two Libyan planes after Libyan leader Moammar Khadafy widened Libya's offshore territory.
Aug. 19: A railway track in East London, S. Afri., was blown up, on the very day that three African National Congress members received death sentences.
Aug. 19: Leftist guerrillas murdered two national guards and ten were killed in preliminary fighting after army troops recaptured Perguin, El Sal., allegedly over a two-day period.
Aug. 20: Thirty-four headless corpses, the work of right-wing death squads, were discovered near Santa Ana, El Sal.
Aug. 20: Seven Revolutionary Guards and five Mujahedeen members were killed during a prolonged two-day shoot-out in Teheran, Iran.
Aug. 21: Imprisoned IRA terrorist Michael Devine died in Maze prison on the 60th day of his hunger strike.
Aug. 22: Forty-eight people were injured by bombs throughout Northern Ireland, during demonstrations following the death of an IRA hunger striker.
Aug. 22: Thirteen members of the anti-Castro Cubans United died when their shrimp boat exploded en route to Guantanamo Bay off the coast of Cuba, from Miami.
Aug. 22: Two police officers were injured by IRA machine-gun fire in Londonderry, Ire.
Aug. 23: Two men blasted the residence of Teheran's governor.
Aug. 23: Five people were killed and fifteen wounded when three Romanian terrorists commandeered a bus in Timisoara, Rom.
Aug. 24: Thirty-four unarmed student members of the leftist Peykar and Fedayeen groups, seized the Iranian Embassy in Stockholm, Swed.
Aug. 24: Anti-Khomeini protesters took over the Amnesty International office in Paris.
Aug. 24: In Brussels, Belg., twenty Iranian students briefly took over the Iranian mission.
Aug. 24: Seventy-two executions took place in Iran.
Aug. 24: Three terrorists were arrested following the machine-gun assault on the residence of Iran's general prosecutor, Ayatollah Rabbani Amlashi. The home of Teheran's deputy, Goharo Sharia Dastgheib was also blasted.
Aug. 25: After an unsuccessful attempt to take over their Embassy in the Hague, Neth., eighteen Iranians, unarmed, were arrested.
Aug. 25: In Beirut, Leb., French diplomat Claude Jacquemain was kidnapped briefly and had his car stolen by four gunmen.
Aug. 25: In El Salvador, the bodies of twenty-six people were found along a highway between San Salvador and Santa Ana over a two-day period.
Aug. 25: A teacher and a shop owner were killed by terrorists in Bonjuro, Iran.
Aug. 25: A hand grenade was thrown into a news agency in Teheran.
Aug. 26: Four people were murdered after being tortured in an area close to San Martin, El Sal.
Aug. 27: A tunnel dug by members of the ETA terrorist organization was discovered beneath Carabanchel Prison in Spain.
Aug. 27: The pro-Iranian Mujahedeen Saff launched a rocket attack on the Saudi Arabian Embassy in Beirut, Leb.
Aug. 29: One person was killed and three injured when a bomb exploded at the Iranian Radio and Television office in West Beirut, Leb.
Aug. 29: Fourteen people were wounded when two Arab terrorists attacked a synagogue in Vienna shot and threw grenades at a synagogue in Vienna, Aust.
Aug. 30: A young girl was killed and fourteen people were wounded when a bomb exploded in a pushcart in Nablus, Jor.
Aug. 30: President Muhammed Ali Rajai and Prime Minister Muhammed Javar Bahonar of Iran were among eight people killed by a bomb placed in the prime minister's office. Twenty-three others were injured in the blast. Security Council Secretary Masoud Keshmiri, who was suspected of placing the bomb in the chambers, also died.
Aug. 30: Eighteen people were injured when a bomb exploded at the Intercontinental Hotel in Paris.
Aug. 31: In Lima, Peru, bombs exploded at the home of the U.S. Ambassador and at the offices of four companies affiliated with the U.S. Nobody was hurt in the explosions.
Aug. 31: In Beirut, Leb., a bomb exploded on an unoccupied Middle East Airlines jet. Lebanese Shiite groups were the primary suspects.
Aug. 31: A family of four from London was shot at in Ballybrittas, Ire., after their British accents were detected.
Aug. 31: The Guatemalan minister of public health Roquelino Recinos Mendez was abducted from his car in Guatemala City, Guat. His captors released him several months later.
Aug. 31: Twenty people were injured when a bomb exploded at the U.S.-NATO headquarters on the Ramstein Air Force Base in West Germany. The Baader-Meinhof Gang was apparently responsible for the attack.
Aug. 31: Teheran court official Hojatoleslam Nasser Jamali and Irani religious leader Hojatoleslam Mortraza Ayatollahi Tabataba Yazdi were murdered in Iran.
September: A television series devoted primarily to the exploits of terrorist organizations, appeared in Spain.
Sept. 1: The Red Army Faction fire-bombed a West German Social Democratic Party office in Frankfurt, Ger.
Sept. 1: The cars of many U.S. military personnel were set on fire at the army base in Wiesbaden, Ger.
Sept. 2: A hand grenade explosion killed Hojateslam Morteza Khodad, an assistant to Ayatollah Khomeini.
Sept. 2: Members of the exiled Lesotho Liberation Army were believed to be responsible for an explosion at the airport in Maseru, Lesotho.
Sept. 3: Twenty people were killed and another fifty wounded when a car bomb exploded at the Damascus headquarters of the Syrian Air Force.
Sept. 3: A bomb probably set by members of the Lesotho Liberation Army, exploded at the U.S. International Communications Agency in Maseru, Lesotho.
Sept. 3: Four persons, including two black police officers, were killed when black guerrillas attacked a police station in Bophuthatswana, S. Afri.
Sept. 3: A bomb allegedly set by the Jewish Defense League, exploded beneath a Soviet diplomat's car in New York.
Sept. 4: French ambassador to Lebanon, Louis Delamare, was shot to death by four gunmen in Beirut, Leb.
Sept. 5: Iranian general revolutionary prosecutor, Ayatollah Hojatoleslam Ali Ghodussi, was killed by a bomb in his office in Teheran.
Sept. 5: Enrique Cerden Calixto, a Spanish terrorist who had escaped from prison, was killed by police in Barcelona, Spain.
Sept. 5: A British soldier was killed and another wounded by IRA Provos gunmen after two women led them into a Belfast, Ire., apartment.
Sept. 6: The Jewish Defense League was suspected in the bombing of a New York bookstore which specialized in Soviet books.
Sept. 7: Two police officers were killed by an IRA Provo land-mine explosion near Belfast, Ire.
Sept. 9: In El Salvador, at least sixty people died in politically related violence.
Sept. 9: Approximately $1 million in damages was caused by a dynamite blast in the Escalon district of San Salvador, El Sal.
Sept. 11: In Tabriz, Iran, a man detonated a hand grenade attached to his waist, killing himself and six others, including Ayatullah Assodollah Mandani, an aid to Ayatollah Khomeini.
Sept. 12: A man was killed and twenty-eight people were injured when an alleged Arab terrorist tossed a grenade into a heavily populated street in Jerusalem.
Sept. 12: A British soldier was fatally wounded by a gunman in a passing car in Ulster, Ire.
Sept. 13: A bomb was tossed into a restaurant in the Philippine city of Zamboanga, injuring eight people.
Sept. 13: Two U.S. missionaries were shot, one fatally, after gunmen abducted them from their home in Palama, Guat.
Sept. 13: The charred and mutilated bodies of forty-one men were found on roadsides throughout Guatemala.
Sept. 13: In Frankfurt, three fire-bombs were hurled into the West German home of David Betts, the U.S. consul-general.
Sept. 14: Soviet geologist E.R. Okrimiuk was kidnapped by Hezbe Islami guerrillas in Afghanistan. His captors demanded the release of fifty rebels in return for his release.
Sept. 15: In West Germany, the European commander of U.S. forces, General Frederick J. Kroesen, escaped injury when his bulletproof limousine was attacked by terrorist rocket-fire in Heidelberg.
Sept. 16: Eight people were killed by gunfire when Iran's revolutionary guards attempted to halt a Mujahedeen demonstration in Teheran.
Sept. 16: In West Germany, two time-bombs that were set to detonate on a rail line that served the U.S. Air Base in Frankfurt, were defused.
Sept. 16: In Shiraz, Iran, Muslim leader Hojatoleslam Nematollah Adib was wounded by gunmen as he left his mosque.
Sept. 17: A bomb set by the right-wing Front for the Liberation of Lebanon from Foreigners exploded in Sidon, Leb., killing twenty-three people and wounding another ninety. The group set off another bomb in Chekka, Leb., killing ten and injuring ten more.
Sept. 18: A car-bomb exploded in West Beirut, killing three people. The Front for the Liberation of Lebanon from Foreigners admitted responsibility for the blast.
Sept. 18: A part-time member of the Royal Ulster Constabulary was wounded by a Tyrone Brigade gunman in a passing car in Ballygawley,

Ire. He died two months later
Sept. 18: A Guatemalan Union Secretary General, Samuel Rodolfo Gutierrez Obregon, was shot to death as he walked near his home.
Sept. 19: The Ulster Freedom Fighters killed Eugene Mulholland as he was walking down a road in Belfast.
Sept. 19: Israeli commandos broke up a Fatah cell that was responsible for seven fatal terrorist attacks that left twenty-seven wounded.
Sept. 19: Thirteen Arab suspects were arrested after an undetonated bomb was discovered on a bus in Tel Aviv, Israel.
Sept. 20: A Sikh terrorist named Jarnail Singh was arrested for masterminding the murder of a Hindu newspaper editor. Nine people were killed and fourteen were injured when supporters rioted the following day. Masked men on a motor bike killed three in a Hindu area.
Sept. 20: Nearly 200 children of Mujahedeen members were executed by authorities in Iran, and thirty of their Militia Girls were executed several days later.
Sept. 20: Four people were killed and another thirty-five wounded when a bomb placed by the Front for the Liberation of Lebanon from Foreigners exploded in the Muslim district of Beirut, Leb.
Sept. 20: In Kabul, Afg., terrorists launched rockets at the Soviet Embassy, destroying the trade section building.
Sept. 20: Four people were killed and another thirty wounded when a bomb placed by the Front for the Liberation of Lebanon from Foreigners exploded in a Beirut, Leb., movie theater.
Sept. 21: The Front for the Liberation of Lebanon from Foreigners admitted committing a series of bombings around the country.
Sept. 22: In Schenectady, N.Y., a fire-bomb exploded in the office of the Eastern Rugby Union in protest of an appearance of a South African rugby team.
Sept. 22: Two British soldiers were wounded by gunmen as they drove through Belfast, Ire., in their jeep.
Sept. 22: Anarchists caused extensive damage when they detonated a smoke bomb in a fashionable Parisienne restaurant and demanded freedom for Direct Action political prisoners.
Sept. 23: Two U.S. soldiers were wounded when their van was ambushed by members of the Lorenzo Zelaya Popular Revolutionary Command, near Tegucigalpa, Hond.
Sept. 24: Nine trucks were set on fire, and fifteen drivers were kidnapped when terrorists attacked a Turkish convoy along the Iraqi border.
Sept. 24: In Paris, a guard was killed and the vice-consul wounded as four Armenian terrorists seized the Turkish Consulate and demanded the release of Armenian, Turkish and Kurd prisoners from Turkey. The siege ended peacefully fifteen hours later.
Sept. 25: A firebomb destroyed the office of the Evansville Rugby Club in Illinois in protest of an exhibition game scheduled against a touring South African team.
Sept. 26: Police officer John Stewart was shot to death at point-blank range in Killough, Ire.
Sept. 26: A JAT Yugoslavian Airliner on a flight from Dubrovnik to Belgrade, Yug., was hijacked by three Croatians and detoured to Cyprus, Gr. The three surrendered after the passengers and crew escaped via emergency chutes.
Sept. 26: Six people died in sporadic gun battles between Iran's Revolutionary Guards and the Mujahedeen Khalq guerrillas shortly before the country's general elections.
Sept. 27: Royal Ulster Constabulary informer Anthony Braniff was shot to death in Belfast, Ire.
Sept. 27: A bomb threat was received near the site where Queen Elizabeth was attending a church service during a visit to Melbourne, Aus.
Sept. 28: Royal Ulster Constabulary member Alexander Beck was killed and three others were injured when their police vehicle was hit by an IRA rocket. Seven men were arrested for the attack, and the rocket launcher and additional rockets were seized.
Sept. 28: Fifteen people were killed when a car-bomb exploded at a checkpoint in Zrariyeh, Leb. Shiite terrorists were the primary suspects.
Sept. 29: An India Airlines jet was hijacked, after taking off from New Delhi, India, by five Sikhs who were armed with daggers and a hand grenade. They forced a landing at Lahore, Pak., where they made demands. During negotiations, commandos stormed the plane and ended the nineteen hour siege.
Sept. 29: In Mashad, Iran, the secretary-general of the Islamic Republic Party, Hojatoleslam Abdulkarim Hashemi-Nejad, was killed and two others injured by a hand grenade. It was thrown by Mujahedeen guerrilla Hadi Alavai Fitilechi, whose hand was blown away in the explosion, and he later died.
Sept. 30: Two Northern Irish Protestant prisoners, seeking segregation from Catholic prisoners, fired shots and seized six prison guards, holding them hostage for two hours.
October: M-19 rebels hijacked a cargo plane.
October: A mother and her two daughters were injured when a hand grenade exploded near the Western Wall of the Old City of Jerusalem.
October: Two hand grenades were hurled at a truck near the Nablus-Jenin road in Israel.
October: Shots were fired at the Iranian *Charge d'Affaires* as he was being driven through Beirut.
October: El Salvadorian bridge was destroyed by members of the Farbundo Marti National Liberation forces.
October: Soviet KGB agents discovered a bomb in their Teheran hotel room.
October: Two feminists and a university professor were arrested in Madrid on suspicion of aiding the ETA terrorist organization.
Oct. 1: Fifty people were killed and more than 250 were wounded when a car-bomb exploded outside the PLO headquarters in Beirut, Leb.
Oct. 2: An empty school was bombed in the Shiite Muslim village of Jargou, Leb.
Oct. 2: A bomb planted by the ETA exploded on a Spanish naval destroyer in the port of Santander, Spain.
Oct. 3: The IRA announced that it was ending its hunger strike which had claimed ten victims at Belfast's Maze prison.
Oct. 3: Bombs planted by the June 9th Organization exploded at a court house and a post office in Geneva, Switzerland.
Oct. 4: IRA terrorist Gerald Tuite gave a radio interview shortly after he and two accomplices escaped from Northern Ireland's Brixton prison.
Oct. 5: Sixty-one Iranian guerrillas were executed by firing squad at the Evin Prison in Teheran. Another sixty-eight leftists were executed in similar fashion throughout Iran.
Oct. 5: Two people were killed and several others injured when a bomb exploded in Damascus, Syria. The Muslim Brotherhood was strongly suspected.
Oct. 6: Egyptian President Anwar Sadat was assassinated by three men who emerged from a military vehicle which stopped in front of his reviewing stand during a parade in Cairo, Egypt. Three others died and thirty-eight were wounded in the attack which was believed to be precipitated by Muslim fundamentalists.
Oct. 7: Eight people were injured in Rome when a bomb exploded at the El Al Airline office.
Oct. 7: Two people were wounded when a bomb exploded at a Rome post office which was known to be a gathering place for U.S.S.R. Jewish emigrants.
Oct. 7: Muslim fundamentalists attacked police in Assyut, Egypt. The two-day battle left 118 people dead; close to half were police officers. Six days later, two of five extremists captured in a shoot-out with police near the Giza Pyramids appeared to be the perpetrators in the earlier attack.
Oct. 8: A two-car commuter train was burned near Valparaiso, Chile, after being commandeered by six terrorists wielding pistols and a submachine gun.
Oct. 8: A bomb thought to be placed by Catalan separatists exploded at a government office in Lerida, Spain.
Oct. 8: Two terrorists killed four people with machine gun fire at a pub in Belfast's Catholic area.
Oct. 9: Salvadoran Supreme Court Justice Leonel Carias Delgado was injured when a briefcase bomb exploded in his office.
Oct. 9: Three bombs exploded in Northern Ireland after warnings had been issued, precluding injuries.
Oct. 9: PLO official Majed Abu Sharar was killed in Rome when a bomb, placed by the Asifa Revolutionary Council, exploded in his hotel room. Police later concluded that he was killed prior to the bombing.
Oct. 10: The home of Egyptian Minister of the Interior Nabawy Ismail was sprayed with machine-gun fire.
Oct. 10: A police officer was killed in Cairo, Egypt, during a clash with Muslim fundamentalists who refused to leave a mosque.
Oct. 10: Police officer Eduardo Rocael Giron Lopez was killed outside the U.S. Embassy in Guatemala City by gunmen firing automatic weapons as they sped past in several vehicles.
Oct. 10: A woman was killed and thirty-nine others, including twenty-two Irish Guards, were wounded in London when the IRA bombed a bus carrying the Guards and their families.
Oct. 11: Eighty-two leftists, including seventy-three members of the Mujahedeen Khalq, were executed by firing squad in Iran, and another nine were slain in four other cities.
Oct. 12: A Catholic church in Limavady, Ire., was bombed by the Ulster Freedom Fighters.
Oct. 12: Three Iranians in London to buy weapons were kidnapped by one Iranian and three Britons.
Oct. 12: Robert Ewing, a Catholic, was shot to death at his home in Belfast.
Oct. 12: Two people were injured when a leftist bomb exploded in Teheran, Iran.
Oct. 13: A baggage handler was killed and four persons were wounded when a bomb exploded at Cairo International Airport near a plane which had just landed from Libya. Nobody was hurt when a second bomb subsequently exploded.
Oct. 13: Two police officers and a soldier were injured in a gunfight as they arrested five Muslim extremists near Cairo.
Oct. 13: Three Moroccan aircraft were shot down over Mauritania by Polisario missiles.
Oct, 15: A soldier was killed in El Salvador when four guerrilla units of the Farabundo Marti National Liberation Front blew up a bridge spanning the Lempa River.
Oct. 16: A bomb placed by the Workers Self-Defense was discovered at the airport in Bogota, Col., shortly after U.S. vice president George Bush was diverted to an alternate landing site.
Oct. 16: Ben Dunne, the son of a well-to-do department store owner, was kidnapped in Ulster, Ire.

Oct. 17: British Marine commandant Lieutenant General Steuart Pringle lost part of his right leg when his house in West Dulwich, Eng., was bombed by the IRA.
Oct. 17: One person was hurt when a bomb exploded at a golf course parking lot in Northern Ireland.
Oct. 17: Six towns were blacked out when a rebel bomb destroyed a generator in the Santa Cruz del Quiche province of Guatemala.
Oct. 17: Spanish civil guardsman Santiago Gonzalez de la Paz was shot to death by three ETA terrorists in Santurce, P.R.
Oct. 19: Digos agents Carlo Buonantuono and Vincenzo Tumminello were killed and Franco Epifanio was wounded when they were shot by a gunman in a speeding car, in Milan, Italy.
Oct. 19: Shrines of the Polisarian Front were bombed by Moroccan fliers in Mauritania after the two groups fought over an outpost across of Bir Moghrein.
Oct. 20: Two terrorists were killed and two police officers wounded during a shoot-out near Munich, Ger., which occurred after five members of the neo-Nazi Socialist People's Movement of Germany were stopped by police.
Oct. 20: Members of the radical Weather Underground were blamed for a $1.5 million Brink's heist in Rockland County, N.Y. In the chase, two police officers were killed and a third was wounded before four of the robbers were apprehended.
Oct. 20: Two people died and nearly 100 were injured when a bomb placed by members of the Direct Action Group, exploded in the diamond district of Antwerp, Belg.
Oct. 21: Maxwell M. Rabb, U.S. ambassador to Italy, was forced to return home, after he was named the primary assassination target of Libya's President Khadafy.
Oct. 21: In Belfast, Ire., an Ulster Defense Regiment member was shot to death by a gunman disguised as a mailman.
Oct. 23: April 19 Movement members kidnapped a Colombian official in the Amazon jungle.
Oct. 23: Basque ETA Madrid terrorist leader Jose Andres Eizaguirre Gogorza and an associate, were killed in a shoot-out at a police roadblock in Spain.
Oct. 23: Weather Underground terrorist Samuel Smith, a suspect in the Oct. 20 Brink's robbery, was killed in a shoot-out with police in Queens, N.Y. Nat Burns, another suspect, was arrested.
Oct. 23: Bombs placed by the Communist Groups for Proletarian Internationalism exploded at three U.S. corporate offices in Rome and at the Chilean Embassy in the Vatican.
Oct. 23: Three crew members were killed when Polisario guerrillas hit a Moroccan helicopter in the Sahara.
Oct. 24: Bombs placed by the Communist Groups for Proletarian Internationalism exploded at Argentine and Guatemalan offices in the Vatican, and at an American Express office in the suburbs of Rome.
Oct. 24: Four bombs exploded in public areas of Barcelona and Alicante, Spain.
Oct. 26: Police arrested two IRA members as they were waiting to detonate a land mine on a road in Northern Ireland.
Oct. 26: In Northern Ireland, a bomb hidden in the bushes was defused. Police captured two alleged IRA members who were asleep near the detonator.
Oct. 26: Royal Army Ordnance Corps member Kenneth Robert Howorth was killed in a London restaurant by the explosion of an IRA bomb he was attempting to defuse.
Oct. 26: Police in East Orange, N.J. uncovered a bomb factory operated by the Weather Underground and the Black Liberation Army.
Oct. 26: A fire bomb allegedly planted by Welsh nationalists was defused in Pontypridd, Eng., near a road Prince Charles and Princess Diana were to travel on three days later.
Oct. 26: One person was killed and twenty more wounded when a car bomb exploded in the Christian sector of East Beirut, Leb.
Oct. 27: Two suspicious looking packages, possibly delivered by the IRA, were deliberately exploded by police in the Oxford Street section of London.
Oct. 28: Twenty-four people were killed during two attacks by Leftist terrorists in Solola, Guat.
Oct. 28: The INLA took responsibility for the shooting death of a man whose body was discovered in a garbage dump near Londonderry, Ire.
Oct. 29: Five hijackers demanding the release of seven Nicaraguan prisoners in Costa Rican prisons, commandeered a flight between Nicaragua and Costa Rica. Six of the prisoners were released, but the hijackers were arrested in San Miguel, El Sal.
Oct. 30: Two government buildings were bombed in Thailand.
Oct. 30: Six members of the Argentinian Revolutionary Workers Party, ARWP, were arrested in Mexico City for the kidnapping of the daughter of a wealthy businessman. One of those arrested was Roberto Guevara de la Serna, the brother of Ernesto "Che" Guevara.
November: In Guatemala, five police officers dozing in a park were killed when hand grenades were tossed and machine guns were fired at them.
Nov. 1: The Army for the Liberation of Lesotho killed several people with land mine explosions.
Nov. 4: An Ulster Defense Association member, suspected of being an informant, was killed in Northern Ireland by Ulster Freedom Fighters.
Nov. 6: Chilean Supreme Court President Israel Borquez was wounded in the shoulder near his home in Santiago.
Nov. 7: Dozens of people were killed or wounded when Kurdish and Mujahedeen rebels invaded the city of Bukan, Iran.
Nov. 7: An IRA bomb wounded three British soldiers in Crossmaglen, Ire.
Nov. 8: The son of an Ulster Defense Regiment member was killed by a bomb placed in the family's car in Lisnadell, Ire.
Nov. 8: Seventy-four people were killed in Bukan, Iran, in fighting between the government and rebels.
Nov. 9: Ulster Defense Regiment member Cecil Graham was shot to death at Lisnaskea, Ire.
Nov. 10: Ulster Defense Regiment member Charles Neville was killed when a hand grenade was hurled at his car and guns were fired in Armagh, Ire.
Nov. 10: An Ulster Defense Regiment member was wounded in an ambush near Fivemiletown, Ire.
Nov. 11: Guerrillas burned several building during a raid in the San Marcos province of Guatemala.
Nov. 12: In Paris, shots were fired at Christian Chapman, the U.S. charge d'affaires, as he was walking near his home. He was unharmed. Libya's President Khadafy was suspected of ordering the attack.
Nov. 13: A bomb exploded at the home of British Attorney General Michael Havers in the Wimbledon section of London. No one was injured by the blast.
Nov. 14: British Parliament Unionist member Rev. Robert Bradford, was killed in Belfast, Ire., by three IRA gunmen as he spoke with constituents at a community center.
Nov. 14: A man was wounded by gunfire when he answered his door in the Protestant section of North Belfast, Ire.
Nov. 14: Three Lebanese soldiers were killed when their vehicle hit a land mine.
Nov. 14: Two police officers were wounded by sniper fire in the Catholic section of West Belfast.
Nov. 14: Two people were shot in the legs by IRA gunmen near Londonderry, Ire.
Nov. 14: In Glen Cove, N.Y., members of the Jewish Defense League fired shots into the home of the Soviet Ambassador to the United Nations.
Nov. 17: An Ulster Defense Regiment member was shot to death by the IRA in Maguiresbridge, Ire.
Nov. 17: A Northern Ireland Housing Executive who was Catholic was killed by the IRA in Lurgan, Ire.
Nov. 17: A police reservist was killed by an IRA motorcycle gunman in Newry, Ire.
Nov. 17: Palestinian leader Yusuf Khatib was wounded and his son was killed by gunfire as they drove toward the Ramallah region near Jerusalem.
Nov. 17: Six towns were blacked out when a bomb exploded and disabled a generator in Santa Cruz del Quiche, Guat.
Nov. 18: According to the Sidamo Liberation Movement, 615 people were massacred by Ethiopian government troops in the Sidamo province.
Nov. 19: Ulster Defense Regiment member John McKeegan was killed by the IRA after he was lured to a home where a family had been taken hostage.
Nov. 19: An attempt to murder an Ulster Defense Regiment member was foiled.
Nov. 20: More than thirty suspected IRA terrorists were arrested in Ire.
Nov. 20: Twenty-three diplomatic vehicles were stolen by armed terrorists in Kampala, Uganda, during the previous two weeks.
Nov. 20: A bomb placed by the Justice Commandos of the Armenian Genocide exploded at the Turkish Consulate in Los Angeles.
Nov. 21: The Secret Service increased security around President Reagan and his Cabinet members when U.S. intelligence learned of death threats by Libya's President Khadafy.
Nov. 22: Three Protestant members of the newly formed Third Force were arrested with a van full of explosives in Newry, Ire.
Nov. 23: Nineteen members of the Leftist Patriotic Honduran Front were arrested when police raided their office in San Pedro Sula, Hond.
Nov. 23: One hundred fourteen SWAPO guerrillas were killed by South African troops during the previous two weeks.
Nov. 24: Three people were killed when a bomb exploded at the railroad station in Teheran, Iran.
Nov. 25: Several bombs exploded and many were defused near Khartoum, Sudan.
Nov. 25: Forty-four mercenary members of the Rhodesian and South African Armies attempted a military coup in Seychelles. About thirty-six escaped by plane after they were discovered with explosives contained in false-bottom luggage, but they were arrested in Durban, S. Afri.
Nov. 27: Two people were killed and another fifteen injured in Teheran, Iran, when four bombs exploded near Quds, the city's department store.
Nov. 27: A police officer and a leftist terrorist were killed and five people were injured during a gun battle which occurred when Honduran police raided a house in Tegucigalpa, Hond.
Nov. 28: Royal Ulster Constabulary member William Coulter was killed after he was lured with five other officers into an IRA stronghold.
Nov. 28: A police officer died after a bomb exploded under his car in Belfast, Ire.
Nov. 28: Two bombs placed by the Macheteros exploded at power sta-

tions in San Juan, P.R., cutting off power to a tourist area for eighteen hours.
Nov. 28: Israeli military bases near Haifa were damaged by bombs placed by the PLO.
Nov. 28: A soldier was killed and several others were wounded in Kalasa, Uganda, when an army truck was destroyed by a land mine. The army retaliated by killing seventeen civilians during the following week.
Nov. 29: Sixty-four people were killed and another 135 wounded when a car-bomb exploded in Damascus, Syria.
Nov. 30: Thirty-one suspected terrorists were arrested in Iran when government forces conducted raids in the Khorasan and Nowshahr provinces.
Nov. 30: An oil refinery in Luanda, Angola, was burned by UNITA guerrillas.
Dec. 5: During a shoot-out in Rome, two police officers and a right-wing guerrilla were wounded.
Dec. 7: Former leader of the Pro-Iraqi Arab Liberation Front Abdul Wahhab Kayali was killed by two gunmen in Beirut, Leb.
Dec. 7: Two U.S. Army officers were injured when a detonator exploded on a West German base in Kassel.
Dec. 7: A Libyan airliner was hijacked by Muslim terrorists protesting the 1978 disappearance of Shiite spiritual leader Imam Moussa Sadr. After landing at three different airports, the hijackers surrendered three days later in Beirut, Leb.
Dec. 8: Eleven members of the Leftist Red Flag organization hijacked three Venezuelan airliners and forced them to land in Barranquilia, Col. After several other stops, the planes were flown to Cuba, and the hijackers surrendered.
Dec. 9: Twenty-two alleged M-19 terrorist rebels were killed by Columbian troops in the Caqueta and Putumayo provinces.
Dec. 10: Fifteen people were killed and another twenty-four wounded in Tripoli, Leb., when a car-bomb exploded near a packed cafe.
Dec. 10: Five members of the Mujahedeen Khalq were killed and 293 leftists were arrested by Iranian troops in Teheran and the Gilan province.
Dec. 11: Eight people, including Ayatollah Abdol Hossein Dastgheib, were killed in Shiraz, Iran, when a bomb exploded at the main mosque.
Dec. 12: A helicopter crewman was killed by rebel snipers as ten reporters were being flown through a flooded area of southern Thailand.
Dec. 13: Two people were killed when a car-bomb exploded in London's West End.
Dec. 14: A Salvadorian rebel radio station was captured by government troops in the Morazan province.
Dec. 15: Thirty-seven people were killed and another fifty wounded when bombs placed by the Kurdistan Liberation Army exploded at the Iraqi Embassy in Beirut, Leb.
Dec. 16: Four banks were robbed in Digos Town in the Philippines by forty men in military dress who took three hostages and $125,000.
Dec. 16: The corpses of six people were found in the San Agustin and Nejapa provinces of El Salvador.
Dec. 16: Power was lost for several hours in San Salvador, El Sal., after guerrillas severed two main electrical cables.
Dec. 17: The Secret Service defused a letter bomb intended for President Reagan. The envelope was sent from San Juan, P.R.
Dec. 17: U.S. Brigadier General James Dozier was kidnapped by Red Brigades terrorists from his apartment in Verona, Italy. He was rescued by Italian police on Jan. 28, 1982.
Dec. 18: Six people were killed and 150 were wounded when a bomb exploded at the headquarters of the African National Union in Salisbury, Zimbabwe.
Dec. 19: Eleven people, including five police officers, were killed and thirty were injured when a truck bomb exploded in midday traffic in Beirut, Leb.
Dec. 19: A Syrian helicopter was demolished when a bomb exploded at the Rayak Air Force Base in eastern Lebanon. An additional two helicopters were damaged.
Dec. 19: Three people were killed and ten wounded during a coup attempt in Roseau, Dominica.
Dec. 20: One person was hurt when a nail bomb exploded among British soldiers in Londonderry, Ire.
Dec. 21: One person was killed when a bomb exploded at the Pan-American building in Guatemala City, Guat.
Dec. 26: A bomb exploded at the headquarters of the Guatemalan National Congress.
Dec. 27: A bomb exploded at a Beirut race track, causing horses to stampede and spectators to panic. No one was injured.
Dec. 27: Eight Baha'i National Spiritual Assembly members were executed in Iran.
Dec. 27: The vital San Francisco bridge was destroyed by Salvadorian rebels in Santa Ana, El Sal.
Dec. 28: In Teheran, Iran, gunmen killed Khomeini loyalist Muhammed Taki Behsharat and wounded a member of the Revolutionary Guards.
Dec. 31: Ghana President Hilla Limann was ousted in a military coup and replaced by Jerry J. Rawlings, a former flight lieutenant who became President for the second time.

1982

January: A Nawabshah, Pak., railroad station was bombed, wounding five.
January: Fifteen Mozambican National Resistance guerrillas were injured and ten were slain by Mozambican troops searching for two abducted teachers.
Jan. 1: A car bomb exploded in Newcastle, Ire., killing Samuel Pollock, and critically injuring UDR member David Brady. Brady and the driver were probably the intended victims.
Jan. 1: Daniel de Jesus Rivera Gonzalez and Amado Jose Flores, of the Nicaraguan Air Force, attempted to skyjack a jet to Miami. Taken into custody, they died trying to escape.
Jan. 1: Armed men forced sixty San Francisco El Tablon, Guat., residents from the town, torturing and murdering fifty. The others were not located.
Jan. 2: In Tripoli, Leb., rockets were fired at a Panamanian tanker scheduled to deliver a shipment to a Lebanese refinery.
Jan. 3: In Lebanon, the Kirkuk-Banias oil pipeline was bombed and the Mujahedeen Movement of Iraq took credit.
Jan. 3: Accused as an informer by the IRA, John Joseph Torbitt was fatally shot at his West Belfast, Ire., house.
Jan. 4: The government of Italy announced that more than 1,100 terrorists were imprisoned as of November 1981.
Jan. 4: Two armed members of the Red Brigades were waiting outside the house of Cesare Romiti, well-known member of the Italian Association of Industrialists, when they were arrested. An accomplice was caught later.
Jan. 5: In Northern Ireland, the RUC warned that the IRA Provos might increase mortar attacks.
Jan. 5: The Reverends Roberto Paredes, of Guatemala, and Paul Gerard Schildermans, of Belgium, were kidnapped in Guatemala.
Jan. 5: San Salvador, El Sal., suffered twelve bombings, including the houses of two judges.
Jan. 5: ETA terrorists kidnapped industrialist Jose Lipperheide near Bilbao, Spain. He was released after about $1.2 million ransom was paid.
Jan. 6: In Turkey, a pipeline between Ceyhan and Kirkuk was bombed.
Jan. 6: Dr. James Donovan, chief of the Garda Siochana Forensic Science Laboratory was injured in Ireland when a bomb attached to his car exploded.
Jan. 6: Deputy head of the Rome anti-terrorist police, Nicola Simone, was shot and wounded. The First Line Armed Cell took credit.
Jan. 6: Victoria de la Roca, a nun, was abducted from Esquipalas, Guat., and the convent there was set on fire.
Jan. 7: Armed with gasoline and dynamite, Jairo Hernandez Martinez skyjacked a plane that departed from Barranquilla, Col., demanded the release of his skyjacker brother and to be flown to Aruba. Martinez was subdued by passengers.
Jan. 7: The West Berlin homes of twelve teenage members of the German People's Socialist Movement were searched by police, who made no arrests.
Jan. 7: Terrorists blew up the primary oil pipeline between Turkey and Iraq.
Jan. 9: Giovanni Senzani, Red Brigades leader linked to the kidnapping of Brigadier General James Dozier, was arrested in Italy.
Jan. 10: Mohammad Khamenei, brother of President Ali Khamenei of Iran, was injured and two of his bodyguards were killed in Teheran.
Jan. 10: Police arrested two who planned to murder Hojjatoleslam Muhadi Kermani, deputy of the Majlis in Iran.
Jan. 10: Six soldiers were slain by about 100 members of the People's Liberation Army at Kingtuang, Burma.
Jan. 12: In La Gomera, Guat., twelve Alvarez Barillas family members were murdered.
Jan. 11: A soldier was injured when twenty Manipur terrorists escaped from the Imphal Central Jail in India.
Jan. 11: Hajjatoleslam Hassan Monfared, deputy industrial minister of Iran, was injured in the shoulder by gunmen in Teheran.
Jan. 13: In Libourne, Fr., a bomb damage the office of the Socialist Party, whose agenda on agriculture had been opposed by farmers. Pamphlets in the area said, "The farmers are not Poles."
Jan. 13: After martial law was established in Poland in December 1981, the first bombing afterward in Warsaw near the Polish Central Committee building caused minor damage.
Jan. 13: Algerian diplomat Rabeh Jerwa was kidnapped from his apartment in West Beirut and fatally shot.
Jan. 13: Five Lopez Yon family members were slain in Coban, Guat., by unknown killers.
Jan. 15: In Berlin, a Jewish restaurant was bombed, wounding 25 people. The 15th of May Arab Organization for the Liberation of Palestine reportedly took credit.
Jan. 15: In a report, Judge Ferdinando Imposimato charged that Libya and the U.S.S.R. were supplying arms to Leftist Italian terrorists.
Jan. 16: All-India Communist Party backers bombed the U.S. Consulate General's facilities in Calcutta.
Jan. 16: The ex-leader of the IRA Provos, Seamus Twomey, was freed from prison in Ireland.
Jan. 17: Patrick Trainor, thought to have informed on the IRA Provos, was found dead in Belfast.
Jan. 17: The Tel Aviv offices of Lufthansa were damaged by a bomb.
Jan. 17: Two bombs exploded in Geneva. They were planted by Armenian terrorists who wanted an imprisoned murderer freed.
Jan. 17: Mario Lopez Lara was shot to death in Cuilapa, Guat.

Jan. 18: Near Lyon, Fr., four of five rockets struck the Creys-Malville nuclear plant, which sustained minimal damage. Ecology activists claimed credit.
Jan. 18: Lieutenant Colonel Charles Robert Ray, U.S. citizen, was shot to death outside his apartment in Paris. The Lebanese Armed Revolutionary Faction took credit.
Jan. 19: In Paris, a bomb exploded in the Air France bus terminal, causing some damage. No one was hurt. The Armenian Orly Group claimed credit.
Jan. 19: In a raid on Turkish terrorists' homes, Ankara officials apprehended fifty-one members of Dev-Yol (Revolutionary Path).
Jan. 20: Officials confiscated five tons of ETA terrorist arms near Bilbao, Spain.
Jan. 20: In San Cristobal, Guat., a car bomb, apparently planted by guerrillas, wounded four and killed seven.
Jan. 21: An aqueduct supplying Huehuetenango, Guat., was bombed with dynamite by guerrillas.
Jan. 22: Two IRA members were arrested attempting to travel from Canada to N.Y., according to the FBI. Bomb threats were made to seven area British-owned restaurants.
Jan. 24: Romanian Dr. Joan Servan, living in exile, was injured in Geneva by a car bomb, according to a Turkish newspaper report.
Jan. 26: During an attempted abduction in Honduras, Jacobo Ramon Larach, general manager of the Pepsi-Cola bottling firm in San Pedro Sula, was fatally shot.
Jan. 27: At the edge of San Salvador, El Sal., the Ilopango Air Force base was assaulted by leftist insurgents, who demolished several aircraft.
Jan. 27: A police officer, Benigno Garcia, was fatally shot in a Bilbao, Spain, suburb.
Jan. 27: A bomb threat caused a Syrian Air Lines Boeing 747 to stop in Istanbul, but no bombs were discovered.
Jan. 27: An Aerotal Boeing 727 en route from Bogota, Col., to Pereira was skyjacked by nine leftists. All hostages were released and the skyjackers eventually flew to San Andres Island.
Jan. 28: Kemal Arikan, Turkish consul general, was shot dead in Los Angeles as he drove to work. Armenians took credit.
Jan. 29: Loyalist leader John McKeague, suspected chief of the Red Hand Commandos, was fatally shot in Belfast.
Jan. 29: Deputy leader of the DUP in Ireland, Peter Robinson, announced that the FBI told him he apparently had been the target of an assassination attempt in the United States.
Jan. 29: Roberto Palomo Salazar, industrialist, was the target of a failed abduction attempt in Costa Rica. Three leftists were slain and three more were apprehended.
Jan. 30: On the West Bank, three armed Al Fatah terrorists were apprehended after having set mines.
Jan. 31: On the anniversary that the Spanish Embassy in Guatemala City was attacked by police, a Guatemala City supermarket was set on fire by Guerrilla Army of the Poor members and buses were spray-painted by January 1st Popular Front members.
Jan. 31: The Moroccan Embassy in Beirut was bombed. Windows were broken but no one was hurt.
February: PLO guerrillas Marwan Muhammed Sartawi and Abdelhakim Suleiman sought asylum in Israel.
February: On the Panamerican and Riverside highways, terrorists demolished thirty Salvadoran buses.
Feb. 1: As Saiqa and Al Fatah guerrillas clash in suburban Beirut refugee camps Shatila and Sabra.
Feb. 1: In Emyvale, Ire., officials find enormous stores of ammunition and arms.
Feb. 2: In Hama, Syria, fighting broke out when a weapons stockpile of the Muslim Brothers was stormed by troops, continuing for three weeks. Three hundred were ordered to be put to death on Feb. 19.
Feb. 2: An Air Florida Boeing 737 carrying seventy-seven people was en route to Key West from Miami when a Cuban man skyjacked the plane to Havana. No one was hurt.
Feb. 4: In Donegal, Ire., 100 pounds of gelignite stored by the IRA were found by officials.
Feb. 4: In Kampala, Uganda, George Bamuturaki, Parliament member and opposition leader, and Zeb Okao, general manager of the National Housing Corporation, were shot to death. More were injured.
Feb. 4: In Vienna, a bomb exploded near the apartment of Bela Akiba Eisenberg, chief rabbi in Vienna. Little damage resulted.
Feb. 4: A one-year truce with the Spanish government was called off by Basque ETA terrorists and a grenade launcher was fired at a civil guard station.
Feb. 4: A Red Brigades arms storehouse was found close to Treviso, Italy.
Feb. 4: Ana Maria Martinez, member of the Left-wing Socialist Workers Party, was abducted from a Buenos Aires, Arg., suburb. She was later found dead.
Feb. 5: In north Guatemala City, Roberto Giron Lemus, editor of *La Nacion*, was slain.
Feb. 6: Peter Lengene, a South African residing in Botswana, was abducted by South African officials, according to reports.
Feb. 6: Desmond Ellis, James Kelly, William O'Neill, William Gilroy, and Edward Howell were arrested at Niagara Falls in the U.S. They apparently planned to buy arms for the IRA.
Feb. 8: In Guatemala, FAR, OPRA, EGP, and the Guatemalan Labor Party's National Directorate Nucleus join, forming the Guatemalan National Revolutionary Unity.
Feb. 8: In Teheran, Mussa Kheyyabani, chief of the Mujahedeen Khalq, was slain by revolutionary guards.
Feb. 8: In northern Teheran, revolutionary guards killed Mujahedeen leader in exile Massoud Rajavi's wife and child, as well as ten Central Committee members.
Feb. 8: In Iran, Jens Petersen, West German ambassador to Iran, and two others were traveling to the embassy when they were attacked and wounded.
Feb. 9: In Guatemala, industrialist Abud Zaid was shot to death.
Feb. 9: Antigua, Chimaltenango, and Guatemala City, Guat., were bombed, causing power outages. The union of four Guatemalan terrorist groups was announced by radio.
Feb. 9: In Caserta, north of Naples, Italy, Red Brigades terrorists steal arms from an army barracks.
Feb. 10: In Bavaria, Ger., Kai Mierendorff, who had led a West German effort to secretly help more than 1,000 people flee East Germany, was wounded by a letter bomb.
Feb. 10: In Santa Clara, San Salvador, and San Vicente, El Sal., about twenty-two buses were demolished by terrorist firebombs.
Feb. 11: Following more than twelve bombings in Corsica and France, the Corsican National Liberation Front (FLNC) took credit. In addition, a non-commissioned Air Force officer was shot and injured and after a Foreign Legion station outside Bastia was attacked, one Leqionaire died and another was injured.
Feb. 12: In Neauphle-le-Chateau, a Parisian suburb, a previous quarters of the Ayatollah Ruhollah Khomeini was demolished by a bomb.
Feb. 12: In Beirut, Leb., the Palestinian Communist Party formed.
Feb. 13: James Alfred Miller, a U.S. missionary, was fatally shot in Huehuetenango, Guat.
Feb. 13: Terrorists plotted to destroy the primary power station in Aden, South Yemen, and a storage tank for oil. However, police arrested them before the plan was carried out and ten terrorists pleaded guilty to sabotage charges.
Feb. 13: Near a Palestinian refugee camp in Sidon, a car bomb killed four and injured five.
Feb. 15: In El Salvador, rebels assaulted five military outposts and in Apopa, five city offices were set on fire. Thirty rebels were reported dead by the government.
Feb. 15: In Calante, Guat., forty-three were murdered. Other accounts claimed fifty-three Quiche Indians were slain.
Feb. 16: Magdalena Kopp, member of the Baader-Meinhoff gang, and Bruno Breguet were arrested in Paris with numerous arms in their possession.
Feb. 16: In Capesterre, Guadeloupe, Max Martin, director of the Societe d'exploitation de fruits et legumes, was found murdered. The Union de travailleurs agricoles was suspected.
Feb. 16: Nineteen bombs were placed in and around Paris by FNLC terrorists, resulting in damage.
Feb. 17: In Mexico City, the People's Front 31st January, the Democratic Front Against Repression, and two other groups combine to create the Guatemalan Committee of Patriotic Unity.
Feb. 18: Giovanni Marceddu and Tiziana Marceddu, suspected Red Brigades members were arrested, according to the *Turkish Daily News*.
Feb. 18: At Rathmore Crescent, Derry, Ire., a family was held captive overnight and their car was taken by four men. The intruders appeared to have planned to attack British military or security members.
Feb. 18: In Washington, D.C., a bomb was detonated near the Soviet Aeroflot Airlines office, causing slight damage. A woman claimed the Militant Jewish Defense League wanted a teenager in the U.S.S.R. freed.
Feb. 18: In a building containing the offices of *Baath*, a Party publication, and the Syrian Ministry of Information, a bomb exploded, killing a few.
Feb. 20: Patrick Reynolds, Gardai officer, was slain in Tallaght, County Dublin, Ire. The INLA disavowed involvement, claiming that former members may have been responsible.
Feb. 22: In the Revolutionary Guards' barracks in Teheran, a bomb detonated inside a garbage truck, killing fifteen, wounding sixty-one, and causing extensive damage.
Feb 22: Major Sergio Vecchioni was arrested and charged with helping a right wing terrorist group, according to reports.
Feb. 22: In Kampala, Uganda, rebels assaulted several military targets. Some of the rebels and two soldiers died over the course of two days.
Feb. 23: Sergeant Zdzislaw Karos, a police officer, was fatally shot. On Mar. 5, five men were arrested in Poland.
Feb. 23: In Lough Foyle, Ire., the British cargo ship, *St. Bedan*, was taken over by IRA members. After the crew was put in a lifeboat, the ship was blown up.
Feb. 23: In Beirut, Leb., two car bombs exploded, killing thirteen and injuring sixty. The Al Jihad Al Mudaddas Front takes credit, claiming the bombings were a protest against Syrian forces killing "innocent families in Tripoli."
Feb. 24: Apparent replacement to Ayatollah Ruhollah Khomeini, Ayatollah Hussein ali Montazeri, was killed by the Mujahedeen in Teheran, seemingly in retaliation for the death of Mussa Kheyyabani, who was slain by Revolutionary Guards.
Feb. 24: Several were injured and one may have been killed by a bomb

that exploded in Beirut, Leb., near militia offices.
Feb. 25: In Beirut, a Kuwaiti Boeing 707 was mistakenly skyjacked by twelve Shiites. They had wanted to skyjack a Libyan plane, saying that Libya had taken Immam Moussa Sadr, a Shiite Muslim leader. After freeing all 105 hostages, the skyjackers evidently were freed by Syrian forces in Beirut.
Feb. 25: Gunmen shot at Colonel Seyyed Ibrahim Hejazi, an Iranian police chief in Teheran, in an unsuccessful assassination attempt. A police officer was slain and two others were injured.
Feb. 25: In Zimbabwe, a large weapons storehouse was found on land belonging to Joshua Nkomo, ex-cabinet minister.
Feb. 26: Iraq was taken off a list of countries favoring terrorism by the U.S., facilitating U.S. deliveries of military equipment to Iraq.
Feb. 26: Tucapel Jimenez, head of a Chilean trade union, was found dead near Santiago.
Feb. 26: A Tanzanian plane with eighty-two on board was diverted to Kenya and finally to England by four skyjackers who demanded that President Julius Nyerere step down. Passengers were gradually released, four suffering from shock.
Feb. 27: Eight were killed and thirty-five injured by a car bomb that was detonated in West Beirut at a checkpoint of the Syrian Army.
Feb. 28: Inside a garage close to Tel Aviv, Isr., a bomb was discovered aboard a bus. The device was exploded, causing no harm.
Feb. 28: FALN, Puerto Rican terrorists apparently set off four bombs in New York, causing damage to several financial institutions.
Mar 1: A man tried to skyjack to Cuba a United Airlines Boeing 727 en route from Chicago to Miami but was overpowered by the crew and a passenger.
Mar. 1: In the French embassy at The Hague, a letter was found demanding two suspected terrorists be freed. The letter contained thumb prints of Ilich Ramirez Sanchez, or "Carlos."
Mar. 2: In Belfast, a professor was hurt by a gunshot intended for Lord Lowry, chief justice of Northern Ireland.
Mar. 2: In Peru, during assaults on police stations and an Ayacucho, Peru, prison by Sendero Luminoso guerrillas, about 250 prisoners were released. Twelve were wounded and twenty-two died in the clash.
Mar. 4: In Beirut, three died, nine were wounded, and extensive damage resulted from a bomb placed in a car.
Mar. 5: In Kabul, Afg., a bomb damaged the Ministry of Education and broke windows of other area buildings.
Mar. 6: A meeting to consider backing arms to the PLO from Bulgaria, East Germany, and Hungary took place between Saudi Arabian and PLO officials.
Mar. 6: In Guatemala City, Julio Eduardo Lopez, retired colonel and head of security for a presidential candidate, died in a car bomb blast. Four bodyguards were wounded.
Mar. 7: In Teheran, Hojatoleslam Muhammad Chavushi, a member of the Navy, was fatally shot on a highway.
Mar. 8: The U.S. was not covertly backing paramilitary Iranian exiles in Turkey, according to Illhan Oztrak, acting Turkish foreign minister.
Mar. 8: In Zurich, Switz., the stock exchange was bombed, causing damage to other buildings.
Mar. 9: At the port city of Tyre, Leb., *Rashed*, a Lebanese freighter was destroyed by a bomb. Israelis were thought to have been responsible.
Mar. 9: Saudi Arabia presented $28.5 million to the PLO, according to PLO official Rafiq Al-Natsha.
Mar. 9: In South Armagh, Ire., a bomb was discovered on a railroad line and earlier, three other bombs exploded close to Lisburn, Ire.
Mar. 10: In Bogota, Col., five were injured by a car bomb that exploded at the presidential palace. The 19 of April Movement took credit.
Mar 10: In Lima, Peru, minimal damage was caused when two dynamite sticks were tossed at the governmental palace.
Mar. 11: Lieutenant General Lookout Masuku, deputy commander of the army, and two others who headed the ZAPU Patriotic Front were arrested, according to a Zimbabwe official.
Mar. 11: In Pamplona, Spain, one was injured when four bombs exploded. ETA terrorists were thought responsible.
Mar. 13: Austria was considering selling weapons to Libya, according to Bruno Kreisky, Austrian chancellor.
Mar. 13: In Beirut, a bomb exploded at the French cultural center.
Mar. 14: In Beirut, three died in a bomb blast at the French embassy in an Egyptian affairs department.
Mar. 14: In London, the African National Congress office was demolished by a bomb.
Mar. 14: In Teheran, a mullah, Mohammed Salem Hosni, and two guards died when a bomb was tossed into his car.
Mar. 15: In Banbridge, Ire., a child died and two women were wounded by an IRA car bomb.
Mar. 16: In Beirut, one died and fifteen were wounded by a car bomb blast near the previous site of the Egyptian embassy.
Mar. 16: According to reports, four of nine suspects arrested in San Jose, Costa Rica, were accused of planning to abduct a U.S. diplomat and charged with smuggling weapons to El Salvador.
Mar. 17: Close to San Nicolas Piedras Gordas, El Sal., four Dutch newsmen accompanying leftist guerrillas were slain, including Jacobs Jan Willensen, Hans Lodewijk Ter Laag, Andries Koster, and Jan Kornelius Kuyper. Government forces were responsible.
Mar. 17: A letter bomb arrived for John Nott, defense secretary in the United Kingdom, it was sent by the Scottish National Liberation Army, apparently to protest the Trident missiles.
Mar. 17: The commander-in-chief of Salvadoran group Farabundo Marti National Liberation Front, Lieutenant Colonel Martell, reportedly met with Abu Iyad and Yasser Arafat.
Mar. 18: In Belfast, a reserve member of the RUC was injured by armed assailants.
Mar. 18: In Jakarta, Indo., seven were killed, 100 were wounded, and twenty autos were damaged by bombs during a gathering for the party in power, Golkar Party.
Mar. 19: SDP offices in Glasgow and Edinburgh received letter bombs comparable to one previously sent to an SDP office in Edinburgh protesting British influence.
Mar. 19: In Saint Etienne de Baigorry, Fr., a French riot police officer was slain and one other died from injuries. Iparretarrak and the Spanish Basque Battalion were suspected.
Mar. 20: Harold McCusker, Peter Robinson, and the Reverends Martyn Smith and Ian Paisley were reportedly at the top of those the IRA planned to kill.
Mar. 20: In four El Salvador provinces, power pylons were damaged for several days beginning on Mar. 20, causing power outages.
Mar. 20: In Dublin, Brendan Sowney and Jimmy Mullen were wounded by gunmen. Officials thought common criminals using IRA techniques or IRA members may have been responsible.
Mar. 21: A U.S. citizen who had resided in Guatemala for eight years, J. Pittes Harvies, Jr., was slain and some buildings on his property were set on fire.
Mar. 22: In eastern Beirut, third secretary of the Iraqi embassy Ali Hajem Sultan was murdered close to the embassy.
Mar. 22: Near San Salvador, eighteen buses were bombed by guerrillas.
Mar. 22: In a suburb of Bilbao, Spain, two police officers and a woman were slain and two were injured by gunmen. ETA terrorists were thought to be responsible.
Mar. 22: In Iran, mullah Karim Shahrkandi was fatally shot.
Mar. 24: IRA and INLA informants' tips led to the charges and convictions of about 200 terrorists, according to the RUC chief constable.
Mar. 24: At Tall Abbas, Leb., the Kirkuk-Banias oil pipeline carrying oil to Tripoli, Leb., from Iraq was damaged by a bomb.
Mar. 25: At al-Abdah, Leb., the oil pipeline from Iraq to Tripoli, Leb., sustained minor damage.
Mar. 25: In Bombay, Ind., one was killed during an assault with fire bombs and rocks on the U.S. consulate.
Mar. 25: IRA gunmen ambushed two Land Rovers in Belfast, killing three soldiers and wounding two civilians.
Mar. 26: The head of the telephone firm in San Sebastian, Spain, was shot to death. In 1980, his predecessor was slain by ETA terrorists.
Mar. 26: In Peru, five mining workers were wounded at Ayacucho, Peru, when rebels made assaults there and at Huancavelica to steal large amounts of dynamite.
Mar. 27: In East Belfast, Ire., Stephen Boyd was discovered dead. He was thought to have been linked to the Ulster Volunteer Force.
Mar. 27: In Kuala Lumpur, Malaysia, nine Crypto members were arrested. They were charged with plotting to oust the government.
Mar. 28: In France, assassins tried unsuccessfully to kill Moammar Khadafy, president of Libya.
Mar. 28: In Derry, Ire., RUC member Norman Duddy was fatally shot and the IRA Provos took credit.
Mar. 29: Outside Limoges, Fr., five died and twenty-seven were injured in a bomb blast aboard the Capitole Express going between Paris and Toulouse. No one claimed responsibility and some thought the explosives had been placed on board by terrorists to be carried to another destination, but inadvertently blew up.
Mar. 30: In San Sebastian, Spain, Ramiro Carasa, a physician, was slain, apparently by the ETA, for informing on a terrorist he attended, or for declining to treat a terrorist.
Mar. 31: The IRA Provos announced that, contrary to past policy, they would not abort missions in regions covered by RUC members and British forces if children happened to be present.
Mar. 31: At a meeting in Bantry, Ire., the Association of Garda Sergeants and Inspectors recommended that definition of "political offence" be altered so that extradition to Northern Ireland and England would be possible.
Mar. 31: In Paris, the Israeli trade office was sprayed by machine gun fire, but no one was hurt.
April: James Neilson, editor of the Buenos Aires *Herald*, (printed in English), and his family left the country.
April: In Barcelona, Spain, armed ETA terrorists injured one police officer and killed police officer Antonio Queralt Colom.
April: In Hanoi, Viet., one died and three were wounded by a hand grenade blast.
April: Four top members of the Ulster Defence Association, a Loyalist paramilitary organization, were arrested, including John McClatchey, Andy Tyrie, Sammy McCormick, and John McMichael.
Apr. 1: Near the quarters of Monteagle Stearns, U.S. ambassador in Athens, Gr., a bomb was disarmed.
Apr. 3: Yacov Barsimantov, diplomat in the Israeli embassy in Paris, was fatally shot by a woman. The Lebanese Armed Revolutionary Brigades claims credit.

Apr. 3: The managing editor of *Tawan Siam*, a Bangkok newspaper, Wandee Thongprapa, was shot dead in his office.
Apr. 4: A Palestinian and two Libyans, armed with guns and explosives, were arrested near the Dhahran Airfield in Saudi Arabia.
Apr. 5: In Tegucigalpa, Hond., the U.S. embassy was attacked by gunmen who drove past. Slight damage resulted.
Apr. 5.: Vicente Rego Otano, Fidel Rego Otano, and Rogelio Vincente Otano skyjacked to Cuba Delta Flight 591 from Chicago. They were arrested in Cuba.
Apr. 7: Close to Nablus, Sister Philathea Kapische and an Arab were wounded by a hand grenade tossed at the Greek Orthodox Jacob's Well Monastery.
Apr. 7: The American Library and the American cultural center in West Berlin were bombed. No one was hurt, but the library was extensively damaged.
Apr. 7: Former Iranian Foreign Minister Ghotbzadeh was arrested and accused of plotting to assassinate Ayatollah Khomeini. He was executed on Sept. 15, 1982.
Apr. 8: A weapons cache was discovered in an underground garage in Paris and police arrested Mohand Hamami.
Apr. 9: In Ottawa, Can., Turkish Embassy official Kani Gungor was shot and seriously injured as he left his garage to go to work. The Secret Army for the Liberation of Armenia took credit.
Apr. 12: In Kotompoki, India, eleven rebels and two soldiers died when Indian forces raided houses of the Manipur Liberation Army.
Apr. 15: In Iran, the Jameh Mosque of Mababad was damaged by a bomb, but no one was injured.
Apr. 15: In Rasht, Iran, Hojatoleslam Ehsanbakhsh and ten more were wounded at the Kaseh-Frushan Mosque. A boy who had a hidden bomb hugged Ehsanbakhsh prior to the blast. Mujahedeen Khalq were thought responsible.
Apr. 15: In West Beirut, five were killed and others wounded when an apartment building was bombed.
Apr. 15: In west Beirut, French consulate code clerk Guy Cavallot and his wife were fatally shot at home. Illich Ramirez Sanchez ("Carlos") was a suspect.
Apr. 17: A death threat was issued against Eden Pastora Gomez, a leader of the Sandinista revolution.
Apr. 17: Sonia Benedetti, Loredana Biancamano, and Raffaele de Blasi, suspected members of Prima Linea, were arrested in Turin, Italy.
Apr. 17: In South Armagh, Ire., five mortar rounds hit inside an old RUC station and caused slight damage to the new one.
Apr. 18: In Newcastle, County Down, Ire., a bomb that had been planted in a pub was disabled.
Apr. 18: In Windhoek, Namibia, land mines set by SWAPO members killed a farmer and two children.
Apr. 18: Six SWAPO members who had entered northeast Namibia from Angola died in two fights.
Apr. 18: In Madrid, disrupted telephone service, four injuries, and $10 million worth of damage was caused when the primary telephone substation in Madrid was bombed several times. Basque ETA members were suspected.
Apr. 19: A Polisario Front official in Algiers threatens that if the U.S. persisted in giving military aid to Morocco, his organization would request arms from the U.S.S.R.
Apr. 19: Beginning in 1981, forty clandestine organizations working against the Yugoslavian government have been established, according to *Business Week.*
Apr. 19: In Eibar, close to San Sebastian, Spain, ETA members assaulted a civil guard command post, injuring one.
Apr. 19: In Vienna, the French embassy and the Air France office were bombed. No one was hurt. The Islamic Revolutionary Guard took credit.
Apr. 19: Ayatollah Ruhollah Khomeini was the target of assassins, according to Sedegh Ghotbzadeh, ex-foreign minister of Iran. He said he initially supported the plan, but later did not.
Apr. 19: In Magherafelt, County Derry, Ire., a car bomb blast killed Wilbert Kennedy and Noel McCulloch. The IRA took credit.
Apr. 20: In Strabane, Ire., a bomb exploded near a bank, injuring a few people. The IRA was probably responsible.
Apr. 20: In Belfast, Ire., a bomb exploded. The IRA was probably responsible.
Apr. 20: In Ballymena, Ire., a car bomb exploded, causing some damage to nearby buildings. The IRA was probably responsible.
Apr. 20: In Bessbrook, Ire., a bomb exploded in the garage of an Official Unionist councilor. The IRA was probably responsible.
Apr. 20: In Derry, Ire., a car bomb damaged property, but injured no one. The IRA was probably responsible.
Apr. 20: In Armagh, Ire., a fire bomb demolished a store. The IRA was probably responsible.
Apr. 20: In Belfast, Ire., a car bomb close to the offices of the newspaper *News Letter* was disarmed. The IRA was probably responsible.
Apr. 21: In Vienna at the French trade mission, security guard Peter Siegl was discovered dead.
Apr. 21: At Nablus, on the West Bank, five were injured when a grenade was apparently thrown at Arab police and exploded.
Apr. 22: In Paris, a passerby was killed and sixty-three wounded by a car bomb that detonated near *Al Watan Al Arabi*, a Lebanese newspaper. Illich Ramirez Sanchez ("Carlos") might have been behind the attack.
Apr. 22: In Derry, Ire., an INLA nail bomb detonated, critically wounding one.
Apr. 22: Ali Zarkesh was made the new chief of staff for the Mujahedeen Khalq in exile.
Apr. 22: In a West Beirut hotel, a bomb killed Elias al-Atesh, Al Fatah representative, and his wife and injured more people.
Apr. 24: SWAPO chiefs went to the U.S.S.R. for the twenty-second anniversary of SWAPO.
Apr. 24: On Apr. 24 and 25, in Cologne, Ger., a bomb was found in a Turkish bank and in Dortmund, a bomb hit a Turkish business. Armenians claim credit.
Apr. 25: Jose Miguel Munoz Echaniz and other suspected ETA members were arrested in Hendaye and Dax, Fr.
Apr. 26: With 104 aboard, a Chinese airplane crashed at Gongcheng, close to Guilin, China. The plane may have been sabotaged. Some speculated that skyjackers tried to take control of the plane; others thought the co-pilot, son of an adversary of Deng Xiaoping, had been the target of assassins.
Apr. 26: In a west Beirut mosque, Sheikh Ahmad Assaf, chief of Muslim organizations in Lebanon, was fatally shot.
Apr. 26: At the suggestion of the Committee for Solidarity with Asian and African Countries, George Habash, general secretary of the PFLP, traveled to Moscow, staying until Apr. 30.
Apr. 27: According to reports, in West Beirut, a French U.N. official was shot and injured by assailants who appeared to be attempting to take his car.
Apr. 27: In Derry, Ire., a Waterside family was held hostage by four armed men. The next morning, the assailants took the family's car, traveled to a supermarket, and, at close range, fatally shot Leslie Hamilton, a bread delivery man.
Apr. 27: Saudi Arabia planned to back an assassination attempt against Ayatollah Ruhollah Khomeini, according to Ayatollah Kazem Shariat Madari's son-in-law. Saudis refuted the allegation.
Apr. 27: Raffaele de Cogliano, commissioner of the Campania regional government and Christian Democrat, and his car driver were fatally shot in Naples, Italy. The Red Brigades claim responsibility.
Apr. 28: In New York City, a pipe bomb damages the Lufthansa offices and the Jewish Defense League reportedly claimed responsibility.
Apr. 28: The Iraqi mission to the United Nations was slightly damaged by two pipe bomb blasts.
Apr. 28: In Armagh, Ire., twenty-four buses at the Loughgall Road station were demolished by fire bombs.
Apr. 28: In Palermo, Italy, gunmen fatally shot Pio La Torre, member of Parliament and leader of the Communist Party in Sicily, and his car driver. Mafia members were thought responsible.
Apr. 28: In Tegucigalpa, a Honduran Air Service airplane was skyjacked by four leftists who held twenty-one hostage and demanded ransom and the release of political prisoners. Finally, all hostages were freed and the skyjackers, alleged members of the Revolutionary Popular Forces-Lorenzo Zelaya, were flown to Cuba.
Apr. 29: The general secretary of the Polisario Front and leader of the Democratic Saharawi Arab Republic (DSAR), Mohamed Abdelaziz, traveled to Cuba for a visit.
Apr. 30: The Honduran Congress passed the country's first anti-terrorist law, Decree-33, which called for a minimum of three-to-fifteen year prison sentences for defendants convicted on terrorism charges. A Honduran plane skyjacking on Apr. 28, 1982, led to the measure.
May: In Rome, a U.S. insurance firm and the Pan Am office were allegedly bombed.
May 1: The South African government said four African National Congress members had been arrested, thus diverting a "May Day terror campaign."
May 1: In Zimbabwe, a Beit Bridge power installation and a railroad between South Africa and Zimbabwe, were bombed, causing damage.
May 1: In the Pakhoi Phu region in Sayaboury province of Laos, Laotian rebels assaulted a military camp.
May 2: In the Pakhoi Phu region in Sayaboury province of Laos, Laotian rebels raided a military camp a second time. Four soldiers died.
May 2: In Oslo, Norway, the building housing the Storting (Norwegian parliament) was damaged by a bomb and night watchman Hans Rovold was injured.
May 2: In Peshawar, Pak., the Islamic Unity of the Mujahedeen was created when seven Afghan rebel groups joined. Abdur Rasul Sayaf became the president.
May 2: In Vientiane, Laos, the Soviet Cultural Center was damaged in a hand grenade blast. Two were arrested.
May 2: Near Oncarroa, Spain, a civil guard was slain by an armed assailant.
May 4: In Somerville, Mass., a Boston suburb, honorary Turkish consul to New England Orhan R. Gunduz was shot dead. The Justice Commandos of the Armenian Genocide claim credit.
May 4: Constable Samuel Alan Victor Caskey was shot and killed and a policewoman was injured by gunmen in Desertmartin, County Derry, Ire.
May 4: In Belfast, more than 3,000 gasoline bombs were seized by police officials on May 4 and 5.
May 5: In Guatemala, leftist guerrillas set a bomb that damaged the

country's sole oil pipeline.
May 5: A bomb sent to Professor Patrick C. Fischer was opened at Vanderbilt University in Nashville, Tenn., by secretary Janet Smith. Smith was wounded.
May 5: Ten miles outside Bilbao, Spain, Angel Pascual Mugica, general manager of the Lemoniz nuclear plant, was slain by gunmen and his son was injured. ETA terrorist may have been responsible.
May 6: The top positions of the Ulster Defence Association, a Loyalist paramilitary organization, were filled with more radical leaders.
May 8: In Kabul, Afg., Sayyed Serajulddin, executive of a textile facility, and his son died when a bomb exploded at their home. Several other people were injured.
May 9: Sixteen were injured and the Syrian embassy in Teheran was demolished by a bomb.
May 9: In Belfast, Ire., a fire demolished the Jewish Tennis and Social Club.
May 10: An Aeronica plane en route from Bluefields to Corn Island, near Nicaragua, was forced to fly to Puerto Limon, Costa Rica. Francisco Arce Lopez and Camilo Martin Walter Hurtado requested asylum in Costa Rica.
May 12: In Portugal, Juan Fernandez Krohn, armed with a knife, tried to attack Pope John Paul II. Krohn was an ex-member of a group that was against policy changes instituted by the Vatican II council.
May 12: One day after resuming flights to Egypt, Iraqi Airways in Beirut was the target of a grenade that was rocket propelled.
May 12: In Northern Ireland, Thomas Cunningham, former UDR member, was shot and killed by IRA Provos members.
May 12: In north Belfast, Ire., Francis Toner, store helper, was shot to death.
May 12: The Brazilian embassy in Guatemala City was taken over and eight were held hostage by members of three alleged terrorist groups who denounced the new military government. All hostages were freed and a flight to Mexico was arranged for the terrorists.
May 14: Representatives of the African National Congress met with a Russian official in the U.S.S.R.
May 15: Close to Luwero, Uganda, a land mine likely planted by the National Resistance Army killed forty-five Ugandan soldiers and wounded seventeen.
May 15: A residential facility in Kabul, Afg., housing numerous Soviet citizens was bombed. As many as ten Afghan guards died.
May 16: A bomb exploded outside the home of a retired RUC assistant chief constable, injuring his wife and damaging the home. A second bomb was found on the same street beneath the car of a UDR member and disarmed in Northern Ireland.
May 16: Close to Londonderry, Ire., a bomb exploded near the home of a female reserve member planning to marry a police officer. She was wounded.
May 16: In San Juan, Puerto Rico, three U.S. sailors were injured and another was slain. Two groups, the Macheteros and the Vieques Group, claimed responsibility.
May 16: In Ioannina, Gr., a bomb blast damaged police headquarters.
May 18: Athens, Gr., suffered several bombings on May 18 and 19. A bank branch, the Police Academy, and a suburban office of the Public Works Ministry were bombed. Two students, Sophia Dimou and Fotios Daniatis, were arrested.
May 20: A bomb was planted but disarmed near the home of the Reverend William Beattie, head of the Democratic Unionist Party in Belfast.
May 21: No one was injured, but some damage was caused when the U.S. air base in Athens was bombed.
May 21: Near Cebu, Phil., a Philippine Airlines BAC-111 was skyjacked by Juan Cleano who was captured.
May 21: In Jerusalem, outside the Beit Yoel offices, a bomb was disarmed.
May 24: Fourteen died and twenty-one were wounded by a bomb blast at the French embassy in Beirut.
May 26: In Rome, offices of the *Daily News* and the *Daily American*, both printed in English, were bombed.
May 27: After flying from Athens, a Royal Air Moroc B-727, a Moroccan plane, was diverted by skyjacker Hamid Alaoui to Tunis. He wanted greater adherence to Islam in Morocco. Alaoui turned himself over to Tunisian officials.
May 29: The offices of Pan Am and a U.S. insurance company were bombed in Rome.
May 30: At the Los Angeles International Airport, a bomb planted at the Air Canada terminal was disarmed. The Armenian Secret Army for the Liberation of Armenia took credit. Varant Berkev Chirinian and Hratch Kozibioukian and his wife were arrested.
June: Mossad Israeli intelligence organization chief, General Yekotiel Adam, was assassinated by PLO members.
June: In Madrid, Spain, near the Ministry of Defense, bombs went off in mid-June. They may have been set by ETA or others.
June: In Binihesar, two officers in the Afghan army were slain in mid-June.
June: In Afshar, four members of the Communist Party were fatally shot in mid-June.
June: A professor at Kabul University who had become a member of the People's Democratic Party of Afghanistan was murdered in mid-June.
June 1: In West Germany, U.S. military bases at Gelnhausen, Frankfurt, Bamberg, and Hanau, a Control Data facility, and IBM in Dusseldorf were bombed. Another bomb was discovered in Berlin near a U.S. Army radio tower. The Revolutionary Cells took credit.
June 1: Close to Newry, Ire., the Breenbank industrial complex was bombed, causing extensive damage.
June 2: Just outside Paulpietersburg, S. Afri., a Total gas station was bombed. The African National Congress was suspected.
June 2: In Athens, Gr., two cars used by the U.S. embassy and a car belonging to a Bulgarian were firebombed.
June 2: Near the Honeywell offices in Athens, Gr., bombs exploded.
June 3: In Belfast, a bomb rigged on a parked motorcycle exploded, killing a passerby, 16-year-old Patrick Smith, and injuring two other youths. The INLA was thought responsible.
June 3: Two power line supports located between Soweto and Johannesburg were bombed. The Umkonto Wesizwe, an arm of the African National Congress, was suspected.
June 3: In London, a Jordanian shot Shlomo Argov, Israeli ambassador to England. Three of four arrested were charged. Abu Nidal and the Lebanese Revolutionary Armed Faction claimed credit, but Israel said the PLO was responsible.
June 4: One was killed in Cape Town, South Afri., when the President's Council of Cape Town offices were bombed. The ANC was suspected.
June 4: First secretary of the Kuwaiti embassy in New Delhi, India, Mustafa Marzook was shot to death at his house. The Arab Brigades Movement claimed credit.
June 4: In Dublin, Ire., James Patrick Flynn, thought linked to the INLA, was fatally shot. He may have been a fatality in a feud between Irish Republican Socialist Party (of which the INLA is an arm) and the Official Sinn Fein.
June 5: In Santurce, Spain, a wine dealer died in a bomb blast. The ETA took credit.
June 7: Attache Erkut Akbay to the Turkish mission to Portugal was fatally shot near his Lisbon house and his wife, Nadide, died on Jan. 10, 1983, from gunshot wounds to the head. The Justice Commandos of the Armenian Genocide took credit.
June 7: According to Radio Moscow reports, the Alliance of the Lao Reactionary Group Fronts had been established and several training camps for the rebels had been opened in China.
June 8: In Gaza, one died and eight were injured by a grenade that was thrown but missed the intended target, an army patrol.
June 10: Police officer Rocco Polimeni, alleged chief of Prima Linea, was discovered dead in Milan, Italy.
June 10: Eight were wounded by a bomb blast on a bus traveling in Belfast.
June 11: In Northern Ireland, David Reeves, RUC detective constable, died and two other RUC members were wounded by a bomb that had been planted in a stolen television set in Shantallow.
June 12: Close to Crossmaglen, County Armagh, Ire., a bomb, likely intended for British patrollers, was discovered and disarmed.
June 13: At Pasajes, Spain, a civil guard was slain during the night.
June 15: ETA terrorists allegedly abducted the wife of a businessman.
June 15: In Teheran, three were injured and possibly slain when the car of Ahmad Khomeini, son of the ayatollah, was assaulted with gunfire and grenades.
June 15: In Strabane, Ire., UDR member Alexander Cummings was fatally shot. The West Tyrone Brigade took credit.
June 15: At Apastepeque, El Sal., two Salvadoran army soldiers died and three were injured when their convoy was assaulted by leftists.
June 15: In New York, Edwin Wilson, ex-CIA agent, was arrested and charged with illegally sending explosives to Libya. He also allegedly operated training facilities for terrorists.
June 16: Nazeh Mattar, Lebanese newspaper free-lancer and student, was shot dead in Rome. The Jewish Armed Resistance of the Jewish Defense League claimed credit.
June 17: A report in the New York *Times* related the type of PLO weapons found by Israeli forces when they attacked Lebanon.
June 17: Deputy director of the PLO in Rome, Kamal Hussein, was murdered by a car bomb in Rome. The Jewish Armed Resistance of the Jewish Defense League claimed credit.
June 18: In Newry, Ire., Albert White, Irish police inspector, was in a car when he was shot dead near his home.
June 18: Simon Wiesenthal's house in suburban Vienna was bombed, causing about $40,000 damage. Neo-Nazis have used similar explosives against Jews in West Germany.
June 18: Three died and others were injured in Santo Domingo, Dom., by a grenade blast at meeting of an election board, which was inquiring into allegations of improprieties during a May 16 election. The Armed Nationalist Revolutionary Group took credit.
June 19: China committed to giving $1 million to the PLO to help after Israel attacked Lebanon.
June 22: Rebel chiefs in Cambodia agree to help each other in their fight against Vietnamese in Cambodia.
June 22: In Derry, Ire., a gas tank at a Shell station was firebombed. Another firebomb failed.
June 22: Colm and Eamon Meehan and Andrew Duggan, all charged with conspiring to sent arms to Ireland, went before a New York federal

judge. For $50,000 personal bonds apiece, they were remanded.
June 22: In Guatemala City, Victor Kaire Bassin, family member of well-known bankers, and Julio Flores Toledo, coffee merchant, were abducted.
June 23: Guerrillas kidnapped Gloria Lara de Echeverry, director of Community Action, in Bogota. Her body was found in November.
June 23: At the University of San Carlos, Guat., Ricardo Mendez, son of the minister of the interior, was abducted.
June 23: According to news reports, enormous stockpiles of PLO weapons were found in Lebanon.
June 23: At the Karachi Airport, a car bomb exploded near a place where Dom Mintoff, prime minister of Malta, was expected. However, Mintoff had been delayed.
June 24: The house of Robert Mugabe, prime minister of Zimbabwe, and the Borrowdale house of Enos Nkala, senator and minister of national supplies, were assaulted. The intended victims were not injured.
June 24: In Rome, a policeman standing guard by the house of Nimer Hammad, PLO official, was fatally shot. Rightists took credit.
June 24: An editor of the Managua, Nic., *La Prensa*, Horacio Ruiz, was abducted at gunpoint and beaten. The paper did not favor the left-wing Nicaraguan government.
June 24: Staale Gundhus, a Norwegian reporter accompanying rebels in Afghanistan, was slain during a skirmish.
June 24: The American Center Library in Calcutta, India, was attacked by about 300 members of the Democratic Youth Federation, a branch of the Indian Marxist Communist Party, who were against the invasion of Lebanon by Israel. No one was critically injured.
June 25: In Belfast, twenty-five were wounded by a bomb planted in a car. IRA Provos claim responsibility.
June 25: In Rome, the Hebrew Immigrant Aid Society and the Italian-Israeli Chamber of Commerce were bombed, causing minor damage.
June 25: Shiite Muslims exploded two car bombs in Beirut.
June 26: Ten people were killed by three bomb explosions in Kampala, Uganda.
June 28: In Ulster, 300 homes were damaged by a bomb which exploded as authorities were attempting to defuse it.
June 28: Protestants were responsible for the bombing of a Catholic church in Belfast.
June 30: An Alitalia flight was hijacked by a 33-year-old drug trafficker shortly after take-off from New Delhi. The siege ended in Bangkok when $300,000 was paid and he was given safe passage with his wife and child.
June 30: A time bomb exploded in Kampala, Uganda, damaging a hotel and vehicles in the surrounding area.
June 30: A power station was dynamited by guerrillas in San Salvador.
June 30: A bomb exploded at an army base in Londonderry, Ire.
July 2: The offices of American Express and the Chase Manhattan Bank were bombed in Athens by members of the Revolutionary Popular Struggle.
July 2: The home of an Austrian journalist and television host was bombed in Vienna.
July 2: Four people, including Ayatollah Mohammed Sadduqi were killed when a grenade thrown by members of the Mujahedeen Khalq exploded at a prayer meeting in Iran.
July 3: During the playoffs of the World Cup, three bombs exploded near the arena in Seville, Spain.
July 3: A bomb exploded at the Honduran Airline office in San Jose, Costa Rica.
July 4: Two power stations in Tegucigalpa, Honduras, were severely damaged by a dozen explosions.
July 4: A Yugoslav travel agency was bombed in Queens, New York.
July 4: A pipe bomb was discovered near a Yugoslavian Airline office in mid-town Manhattan.
July 8: A group called "The Angry Merchants" bombed a collections office in La Tour-du-Pin, France.
July 12: A police officer was killed and three others were wounded when terrorists attacked a police station in the Trujillo province of Peru.
July 13: A large cache of explosives was confiscated by the Royal Ulster Constabulary in Belfast, Ire.
July 14: Dutch police thwarted a Moluccan plot to kidnap Queen Beatrix and Prime Minister Andries van Agt.
July 14: Terrorists bombed a car belonging to tourists in Ajaccio, Corsica.
July 15: Two police officers were shot to death by members of the Red Brigades in Naples, Italy.
July 15: A bomb placed by members of the Red Placard exploded at a factory in Lyon, France.
July 15: Members of the Angry Metallurgists bombed a chateau in the Ardennes, Fr.
July 15: Seventeen bombs placed by members of ETA exploded at public buildings in northern Spain.
July 16: A tobacco company executive was murdered by ETS terrorists in Spain.
July 16: A man, Colm Carey, bled to death after being shot in the knee by an IRA gunman in Derry, Ire.
July 17: More than twenty bombs placed by Basque terrorists, exploded in four cities in Spain.
July 17: Callera Peru district governor Zenon Palomino Flores was shot to death after being kidnapped and convicted by fifteen terrorists.
July 18: A Honeywell office was bombed by Communist Front for Counter Power terrorists in Padua, Italy.
July 18: Members of the Communist Front for Counter Power bombed an art exhibit at the Israeli pavilion in Venice.
July 19: American University of Beirut President David Dodge was kidnapped by two gunmen.
July 19: A bomb exploded at an Israeli bank branch office in Paris.
July 19: Fifteen people were injured when a bomb placed by Armenian terrorists exploded at a crowded cafe in the Latin Quarter of Paris.
July 19: A corporation with Israeli business interests was bombed in Paris.
July 20: Members of the Red Panthers bombed the Society Ganco Electronic in Paris.
July 20: Two British soldiers were killed when a Provisional IRA remote-control car bomb exploded in London.
July 20: Six army musicians were killed by a Provisional IRA bomb that exploded beneath a bandstand in London.
July 20: A British Army helicopter was damaged by IRA machine-gun fire at Crossmaglen, Ire.
July 20: Members of the neo-Nazi Ludwig group clubbed two priests to death in Milan, Italy.
July 20: The offices of Shell France were bombed in Lyon.
July 20: A bomb exploded at a Maghrebian bar in Bastia, Corsica.
July 21: Members of the French Revolutionary Brigades bombed the Paris apartment previously rented by Bolivian guerrilla Regis Debray.
July 21: Irish terrorists threatened to bomb the British Armed Forces Radio station in Cologne, West Germany.
July 21: Two Dutch police officers were shot to death by terrorists attempting to kill the Turkish Consul General in Rotterdam.
July 22: The home of Prime Minister Leabua Jonathan was attacked by guerrillas in Leribe, Lesotho.
July 22: Two men armed with a can of gasoline hijacked a flight from Miami to Havana. Upon landing, they were arrested by Cuban authorities.
July 23: Six tourists were kidnapped by twelve terrorists in western Zimbabwe.
July 23: Deputy PLO Director Fadel el-Dani was killed when three terrorists tossed a bomb into his car in Paris.
July 23: Three bombs exploded in the Corsican cities of Ajaccio and Bastia.
July 24: Three more bombs exploded in the Corsican cities of Ajaccio and Bastia.
July 24: Two people were injured in Paris, when a bomb placed by the Orly Armenian terrorist organization exploded at the Pub St. Germain.
July 24: Nicaraguan rebels slaughtered fifteen peasants at San Francisco del Norte.
July 24: An Israeli civilian was shot to death at close range as he shopped at a market in Bethlehem.
July 24: One person was killed as three guerrillas attempted to rob a hotel in Matabeleland, Zimbabwe.
July 25: A Coca-Cola bottling plant was bombed in Lima, Peru.
July 25: Red Brigades informant Ennio Di Rocco was strangled and stabbed to death at a prison in Trani, Italy.
July 25: Five factory workers armed with dynamite attempted to divert a Chinese domestic flight between Xian and Shanghai, to Hong Kong. The attempt failed when after a stick of dynamite exploded, the hijackers were overpowered and detained by other passengers.
July 25: Two people were injured by two bombs that exploded in Ajaccio, Corsica.
July 26: The villa of a wealthy industrialist was bombed in Sanary, France.
July 26: Seven bombs exploded in Bastia, Corsica.
July 27: Four buildings, including the home of the British ambassador, were bombed in Lima, Peru.
July 27: A bomb destroyed a radio studio in Menilmontant, France.
July 28: Salvadoran Industry Assn. manager Mauricio Cuellar and his daughter were kidnapped near their home in Roma, El Sal.
July 28: A bomb exploded near the Legislative Palace in Lima, Peru.
July 28: Nine bombs exploded in the Corsican cities of Ajaccio and Bastia.
July 29: A bomb exploded near a reviewing stand in Lima, where the President of Peru had watched a military parade ten minutes earlier.
July 29: A pro-Palestinian radio station was bombed in Paris.
July 30: Orly Group terrorist Pierre Gulumian was killed when the bomb he was assembling exploded at his apartment in Gagny, Fr.
July 30: An attempt to divert a Chinese airline domestic flight after takeoff from Shanghai was foiled when the hijackers were overpowered by other passengers and crew members.
July 30: A police vehicle and a bar were bombed in Bastia, Corsica.
July 31: Three bombs exploded at buildings in Ajaccio, Corsica.
July 31: Architect Beruardo Dewerchin was killed by terrorists in Santiago Texacuangos, El Sal.
July 31: Seven people, including two police officers, were injured when a bomb exploded at the airport in Munich.
July 31: Four businesses were bombed over the course of a week in Bastia, Corsica.
Aug. 1: Employees were killed when a car-bomb exploded at the Iraqi Planning Ministry in Baghdad.
Aug. 1: A bank owned by Jews was firebombed in Vienna, Aust.

Aug. 1: The Communist Party office was hit by sniper fire in Antony, France.
Aug. 2: Eight people were injured when a bomb exploded at the airport in Lahore, Pak.
Aug. 3: San Lorenzo Mayor Ramiro Ponce was killed by rebels in El Salvador.
Aug. 3: A merchant was shot to death by terrorists in Corsica.
Aug. 3: An explosion damaged a military vehicle at the U.S. Army base in Schwabisch-Gmund, West Germany.
Aug. 4: A hijacker was overpowered in Amritsar, India, after failing to divert an Indian Airlines flight to Lahore, Pak.
Aug. 4: An IBM branch office was bombed in Tegucigalpa, Hond., by members of the Lorenzo Zelaya Front.
Aug. 4: Six people were wounded when bombs exploded at two airline offices in Honduras.
Aug. 5: The officer's club was bombed at the U.S. military base in Karlsruhe, Ger.
Aug. 5: A bomb exploded at the Alexandre Hotel in East Beirut, Leb.
Aug. 5: Members of INLA bombed the home of a former Royal Ulster Constabulary member in Belfast, Ire.
Aug. 5: Four bombs went off in Corsica.
Aug. 6: Bombs exploded at public buildings in five Corsican cities.
Aug. 6: A time bomb was discovered in the shopping district of downtown Vienna, Aust.
Aug. 7: Nine people, including three police officers and a terrorist were killed, and seventy-two people were injured when a bomb placed by two members of the Armenian Secret Army for the Liberation of Armenia, exploded at the airport in Ankara, Turk.
Aug. 7: A bomb placed by members of Direct Action, exploded at the Discount Bank in Paris.
Aug. 8: Members of Direct Action bombed a store owned by Jewish merchants in Paris.
Aug. 8: A Bank of America branch office was bombed in Madrid, Spain.
Aug. 8: A Sears, Roebuck store was bombed in Barcelona, Spain.
Aug. 8: Terrorists bombed a pier in San Sebastian, Spain.
Aug. 8: Members of the Orly Group attempted to bomb the central telephone exchange in Paris.
Aug. 8: Three car-bombs exploded in Corsica.
Aug. 9: A dynamite blast damaged an apartment in Corsica.
Aug. 9: Fifteen South African soldiers were killed in a helicopter crash and more than 200 SWAPO guerrillas died during clashes in Angola.
Aug. 9: Five police officers and a British soldier were injured during demonstrations throughout Northern Ireland.
Aug. 9: Ten people were injured when a hand grenade exploded at a shopping center in the Philippine province of Mindinao.
Aug. 9: Six people were killed and another twenty-two were wounded when terrorists, armed with grenades and machine-guns, attacked a Jewish restaurant in Paris.
Aug. 9: Four students seized and held for a week the Central African embassy in Beijing.
Aug. 10: Terrorists vandalized a television station and a tour bus in Corsica.
Aug. 10: Fourteen people were killed and fifty were wounded when members of the Mozambique Resistance Movement attacked a train with bazooka fire near the city of Beira.
Aug. 11: Six people were injured when a truck bomb exploded at the Iraqi embassy in Paris.
Aug. 11: Two people were injured when a bombs placed by members of Direct Action, exploded at two banks in Paris.
Aug. 11: One person was killed and fifteen were injured, when a bomb exploded on a Pan Am flight en route from Tokyo to Honolulu.
Aug. 11: Members of the Direct Action group bombed an Israeli connected importing company in Paris.
Aug. 12: IRA terrorists bombed a train near Belfast, and an insurance company office in Londonderry.
Aug. 14: A firebomb exploded at a synagogue in Paris.
Aug. 16: Eight members of the Mozambican National Resistance were killed by South African soldiers at a camp in Chitequeteque.
Aug. 17: African National Congress member Ruth First was killed by a letter bomb explosion in Maputo, Mozambique.
Aug. 18: Four people were wounded when a car-bomb exploded at a Palestinian research center in Beirut.
Aug. 19: A car-bomb was discovered before it detonated at a government ministry in Beirut, Leb.
Aug. 19: A magazine office in Paris was bombed by members of the Direct Action terrorist group.
Aug. 19: A soldier was killed and six people, including a UPI reporter were wounded, during a guerrilla attack in El Salvador.
Aug. 19: Hundreds of people were killed or wounded when rebels attacked a government rally in Pagman, Afg.
Aug. 19: Lima, Peru suffered a blackout when rebels bombed strategic power lines.
Aug. 19: Five people were executed by firing squad after failing in their attempt to hijack a Chinese airlines domestic flight.
Aug. 20: Thirty people, including the chief minister, were injured when a hand grenade exploded at a school in Punjab.
Aug. 20: Nearly 100 public buildings were bombed by members of the Corsican National Liberation Front.
Aug. 20: Four farmers were killed by guerrillas in Conopa, Peru.
Aug. 20: A Sikh hijacker was killed by sharpshooters, after diverting a Bombay to New Delhi Indian Airlines flight to Amritsar.
Aug. 20: Members of the Sendero Luminosa bombed Peruvian power lines, causing a three-day blackout in Lima.
Aug. 21: Two Parisienne police officers were killed when a car-bomb exploded near the Eiffel Tower.
Aug. 22: Twenty Sendero Luminosa guerrillas and six police officers were killed during a clash in the Ayacucho province of Peru.
Aug. 24: A bomb was discovered before it detonated on a Pan Am Airlines flight between Miami and Rio de Janeiro.
Aug. 25: Two men were arrested after they hijacked a LOT Polish airliner to Munich.
Aug. 26: Two men were killed when a bomb they were attempting to defuse, exploded in Munguia, Spain.
Aug. 26: A man named Francis McClusky was shot to death by two gunmen in Belfast.
Aug. 26: A member of the Royal Ulster Constabulary was wounded when a bomb exploded in his car.
Aug. 27: British troops clashed with IRA terrorists near the border of Northern Ireland.
Aug. 27: Turkish Military Attache Atilla Altikat was shot to death in Ottawa, Canada, by a member of the Justice Commandos of the Armenian Genocide.
Aug. 28: Authorities seized a huge cache of explosives in Northern Ireland.
Aug. 29: Three leaders of the Irish National Liberation Army were arrested in Paris.
Aug. 29: A soldiers was killed and four people were wounded when Salvadoran guerrillas bombed power lines and a freight train.
Aug. 30: The deputy minister of agriculture was one of three people shot to death by guerrillas in Kampuchea.
Aug. 31: Six Bulgarian engineers were kidnapped by Mozambican guerrillas.
Sept. 1: A member of Northern Ireland's DUP organization was shot by two men in Belfast.
Sept. 1: A police officer was killed and buildings were burned by Salvadoran guerrillas in Yamabal.
Sept. 3: Anti-mafia police chief Carlo Alberto Dalla Chiesa, his wife, and a bodyguard, were killed in Palermo, Sicily, by members of the Guerrilla Party and the Proletariat Organized Group.
Sept. 4: Members of Al-Zulfikar were the primary suspects for a fire that was set near a courthouse in Lahore, Pakistan.
Sept.5; Terrorists attempted to bomb the home of a Pakistani government official.
Sept. 6: Twenty people were killed and more than 100 wounded when a Mujahedeen Khalq truck bomb exploded in Teheran, Iran.
Sept. 6: Salvadoran guerrillas destroyed a railway bridge in San Juan.
Sept. 6: Thirteen hostages were taken by terrorists who occupied the Polish embassy in Bern, Switz. The siege ended three days later as Swiss police stormed the building.
Sept. 9: Turkish Consulate attache Bora Suelkan was shot to death in Bulgaria, by members of the Secret Army for the Liberation of Armenia and the Justice Commandos of the Armenian Genocide.
Sept. 10: Two ranchers were executed after being sentenced by a guerrilla "people's court" in Matara, Peru.
Sept. 11: Two people were killed and twenty-five wounded, when a bomb exploded at a government building in Manila.
Sept. 13: Pakistani Advisory Council member Zahur Hassan Bhopali was shot to death in Karachi.
Sept. 14: Lebanese President Bashir Gemayal was killed by an explosion in Beirut.
Sept. 14: Four police officers were killed and a fifth was wounded during an ambush near San Sebastian, Spain.
Sept. 14: Kuwaiti Embassy Acting Consul Hamad Jutaili was wounded by terrorists in Karachi, Pakistan.
Sept. 16: The branch office of Sperry Corporation was bombed by pro-Palestinian terrorists in West Berlin.
Sept. 16: Two people were killed and five injured when a pipe bomb, placed by INLA members, exploded in Belfast.
Sept. 16: Kuwaiti Embassy employee Najeeb Sayeb Refai was shot to death in Madrid, Spain, by an Abu Nidal terrorist.
Sept. 17: One person was injured when a bomb exploded near the Israeli embassy in Paris.
Sept. 17: The Guatamalan government ordered the execution of four members of the Guerrilla Army of the Poor.
Sept. 17; One person was killed and two were wounded, as members of the Cinchonero Popular Liberation Movement took 100 people hostage as they seized the Chamber of Commerce building in San Pedro Sula, Honduras.
Sept. 18: A bomb exploded at a department store in Hong Kong.
Sept. 18: Two people were arrested after a small bomb exploded at a Hilton hotel in Manila.
Sept. 18: A car of an Israeli diplomat was bombed by members of the Leftist Direct Action in Paris. Police later arrested fourteen members of the group and confiscated a large cache of arms and explosives.
Sept. 18: Four people were wounded when a terrorist sprayed machine-

gun fire at a crowd in a Brussels synagogue.
Sept. 20: Bombs placed by Basque terrorists exploded at six banks in Spain.
Sept. 20: Members of the INLA were the primary suspects in the bombing of a radar station in Schull, Ire.
Sept. 20: A British soldier was killed and four people were injured when a rocket exploded at a Royal Ulster Constabulary station in west Belfast.
Sept. 25: A man was overpowered by an Alitalia flight crew in Catania, Italy, after hijacking a flight from Algiers. The pilot was denied permission to land at Tripoli and Malta.
Sept. 26: Spanish police killed a Basque guerrilla and arrested three others, following a gun battle in San Sebastian.
Sept. 27: PLO leader Abu Walid was killed and several other PLO officials were wounded in an ambush in Lebanon.
Sept. 27: The office of Sperry Corp. was bombed in West Berlin.
Sept. 27: A British soldier was killed when a bomb exploded at a barrier in Belfast.
Sept. 27: One person was killed and another injured by bombs that exploded at a Pan Am office and two travel agencies in Frankfurt, Ger.
Sept. 28: A crowded stadium in Brisbane, Aus., was evacuated because of a bomb threat during the Commonwealth Games.
Sept. 28: Four soldiers were killed and two others wounded when members of the New People's Army ambushed a patrol in the Philippines.
Sept. 28: Terrorists attempted to bomb the Philippines Airline office in Frankfurt, West Germany.
Sept. 29: A bomb exploded at a synagogue in Milan, Italy.
Sept. 29: Sixteen bombs placed by leftist terrorists exploded at government buildings and industrial plants throughout Spain.
Sept. 29: A firebomb exploded during the construction of a prison in Pesaro, Italy.
Sept. 30: One person was killed and another arrested, after the bomb they were carrying exploded in Santiago, Chile.
Oct. 1: Sixty people were killed and more than 700 were injured when a bomb exploded in a crowded public square in Teheran, Iran.
Oct. 2: Fourteen soldiers were killed by Salvadoran guerrillas in the San Vincente, Cuscatlin, and Usulutan provinces.
Oct. 3: Six Israeli soldiers died and sixteen were wounded in an ambush near Beirut, Leb.
Oct. 3: A woman was arrested in Hamburg, Ger., after threatening to bomb a Lufthansa flight en route to Munich.
Oct. 3: Four people who hijacked an Iranian military transport were apprehended after they were refused asylum by three countries and were forced to return to Iran.
Oct. 4: Deputy commander A.S. Malik was shot to death following Hindu and Muslim rioting in Meerut, India.
Oct. 4: A Varig Airline flight from Rio de Janeiro to New York was detained because of a bomb threat.
Oct. 4: Twenty-three Red Flag leftists were killed by government troops in Anzoategui, Venez.
Oct. 5: A member of the police reserves was shot to death in Londonderry, Ire.
Oct. 7: A UDR corporal was shot to death and another man died during a subsequent collision in Armagh, Ire.
Oct. 7: A TWA flight carrying the Portuguese prime minister was forced to return to New York because of a bomb threat.
Oct. 8: One person died and another was injured when a bomb exploded at a department store in Kaohsiung, Taiwan.
Oct. 8: Italian police arrested forty members of the Armed Revolutionary Nucleus, including the son of the Undersecretary of Justice.
Oct. 8: Five members of the Armed Revolutionary Nucleus robbed a bank in Rome.
Oct. 9: A child was killed and thirty-five people were injured during a machine-gun attack at a synagogue in Rome.
Oct. 10: Fifteen Salvadoran soldiers were wounded as rebels destroyed power lines and seized the town of Las Vueltas.
Oct. 11: A Chinese was arrested after he failed in his attempt to hijack a plane from Xian to Taiwan.
Oct. 13: U.S. citizen Michael Kline was killed after being removed from a bus by soldiers in El Salvador.
Oct. 14: A flight attendant was wounded during the hijacking of Bulgarian Airlines flight from Warsaw to Burgas.
Oct. 14: Several houses were damaged when a remote-controlled bomb exploded in Belfast.
Oct. 15: Senior cleric Ayatollah Ashrafi Isfahani was killed when a hand grenade exploded at a basque in Bahtaran, Iran.
Oct. 15: A bomb exploded at a Litton Corporation plant in Toronto, Can.
Oct. 16: A grenade failed to detonate when it was shot toward the provincial governor's residence in Vitorio, Spain.
Oct. 17: Nine bombs exploded at Socialist Party offices throughout Spain.
Oct. 18: A man was wounded when a bomb placed by the INLA exploded during a Bible class in Northern Ireland.
Oct. 20: A bomb exploded at the Lebanese embassy in Rome, shortly before the arrival of Lebanese President Gemayel.
Oct. 20: A bomb was defused near the home of the Official Unionist Party leader in Northern Ireland.
Oct. 20: A firebomb placed by members of the INLA exploded at the headquarters of the Official Unionist Party.
Oct. 21: Eighteen public buildings were bombed by Basque terrorists in northern Spain.
Oct. 22: A Salvadoran civil defense minister was wounded and his three daughters were killed when rebels attacked their home in Apopa.
Oct. 23: A large cache of Soviet arms was confiscated by police in Pakistan.
Oct. 24: A bomb caused extensive damage to an office building in Kabul, Afghanistan.
Oct. 26: Hundreds of people were killed when Islamic fundamentalists rioted in Nigeria.
Oct. 26: A Nirankari Sikh sect district leader was shot to death by three gunmen on motorcycles east of Amritsar, India.
Oct. 27: Three police officers, a prisoner, and a terrorist were killed during a rebel attack on a police station on the Jaffa peninsula of Sri Lanka.
Oct. 28: A preacher and his four sons were murdered by terrorists in El Jicaro, Nicaragua.
Oct. 31: Twenty vehicles were destroyed by a car-bomb which exploded on a U.S. military base in Giessen, Ger.
Nov. 1: Two terrorist bombs destroyed a railway bridge in the Tecoluca province of El Salvador.
Nov. 3: Three men attempted to kidnap the publisher of *Quorum* magazine in Buenos Aires, Arg.
Nov. 3: The Turkish Consulate in Cologne, Ger., was seized by gunmen, who took eighty people hostage. The siege ended after sixteen hours when police stormed the building.
Nov. 4: An oil pipeline was severed by guerrillas near Dasht-i-Kelagai, Afghanistan.
Nov. 4: While driving in Madrid, Spanish General Victor Lago Roman was assassinated and his driver wounded, by two machine-gun wielding terrorists.
Nov. 5: A Turkish travel agency in Amsterdam was seized by ten members of the Turkish Revolutionary Left group.
Nov. 7: The pilot was stabbed and two passengers were injured, as three men hijacked a Soviet domestic flight to Turkey.
Nov. 7: Rebels severed an oil pipeline at Charikar, Afghanistan.
Nov. 7: One person died and four were wounded when a grenade thrown at an Israeli jeep exploded on a street in Gaza.
Nov. 7: Three police officers, a former cabinet minister and his son, and an army officer, were killed by a rebel near the British embassy in Afghanistan.
Nov. 8: UNITA rebels captured the town of Gago Coutinho, Angola.
Nov. 8: An IRA member was shot to death as he left a pub in Londonderry, Ire.
Nov. 12: Salvadoran guerrillas bombed power lines, causing a blackout in most of El Salvador.
Nov. 13: U.S. newsman Clifford Krauss was wounded during guerrilla crossfire in El Salvador.
Nov. 14: More than twenty people were killed when bombs exploded at four restaurants in Kabul.
Nov. 14: The Armed Struggle Organization took credit for the military building collapse in Tyre, Israel, in which eighty-nine people were killed.
Nov. 16: A bomb placed by members of the Workers Army of the Welsh Republic, exploded at a government building in Swansea, Wales.
Nov. 19: An Israeli soldier was killed and three others wounded, when members of the Lebanese National Resistance attacked a military base in Siddon, Leb.
Nov. 19: A leftist rocket attack damaged the Columbian Defense Ministry in Bogota.
Nov. 20: Members of the Bakunin-Gdansk terrorist group bombed a trading company and a chemical firm in Paris.
Nov. 21: A woman was injured when a bomb exploded at a railway station in Tel Aviv.
Nov. 22: A LOT Polish Airlines flight was hijacked to West Berlin by one of its own security guards. The guard was arrested by West German police after being wounded during the hijacking effort.
Nov. 25: A bomb destroyed a building near Beirut, killing six people and injuring twenty others.
Nov. 25: Five people were killed and thirty-two injured when two bombs exploded at a shopping center in Kabul, Afghanistan.
Nov. 26: Rebel leader Adamson Mushala was shot to death at the Lunga National park in Zambia.
Nov. 27: Ku Klux Klan counter-demonstrators vandalized areas of Washington D.C., during a Klan rally near the White House.
Nov. 27: A man was arrested in Warsaw, Poland, as he was attempting to hijack a Hungarian Airlines flight to Budapest.
Nov. 29: The body of a Columbian Senator's wife was discovered near a church in Bogota. She had been kidnapped by guerrilla rebels on June 23, 1982.
Nov. 30: A garage at an apartment complex for U.S. military personnel, was destroyed by arson fire near Frankfurt, Ger.
Nov. 30: Members of the Animal Rights Militia sent letter bombs to the British Prime Minister, as well as four other government leaders. One security officer was burned by a blast, while the others failed to detonate.
Dec. 1: Four people, including a police officer were killed, and thirty-

eight were injured when terrorists attempted to kill Druse Muslim leader Walid Jumblatt with a remote-controlled car bomb.
Dec. 3: Lima, Peru, suffered a blackout after guerrillas bombed two power stations.
Dec. 4: Six people were killed when government troops raided a Communist Party meeting in the Philippines.
Dec. 5: A bomb exploded at a travel agency in Nicosia, Cyprus.
Dec. 5: October 1 Anti-Fascist Revolutionary Group leader Juan Martin Luna was killed in a shootout with police in Barcelona, Spain.
Dec. 5: More than 125 people were taken hostage at a soccer stadium by Salvadoran guerrillas.
Dec. 6: Seventeen people were killed and another sixty-six injured when a Irish National Liberation Army bomb exploded in Ballykelly, Ire.
Dec. 7: Nine people were killed by two car-bomb explosions in Lebanon.
Dec. 8: A man was shot to death by police sharpshooters after seizing and threatening to blow up the Washington Monument.
Dec. 9: Forty-two people were killed, including four African National Congress leaders, during a raid by South African troops on a ANC camp in Lesotho, S. Afri.
Dec. 12: Two Israeli soldiers were injured by hand grenade explosions in Nabatiye, Leb.
Dec. 12: A National Guardsman was shot to death by two machine-gun wielding Basque ETA terrorists in Tolosa, Spain.
Dec. 14: Members of the Revolutionary Movement kidnapped the daughter of Honduran President Roberto Suazo Cordova. She was released on Dec. 22, 1982.
Dec. 14: A bus was evacuated shortly before it was destroyed by an explosion in Tel Aviv.
Dec. 14: A bomb destroyed the car of a U.S. soldier in Butzbasch, Ger.
Dec. 15: Seven people were killed when a car bomb exploded near a news agency in Baghdad, Iraq.
Dec. 15: A U.S. military officer was injured when a bomb exploded as he entered his car in Darmstadt, Ger.
Dec. 16: Members of the Freedom Front/Revolutionary Fighting Group were the primary suspects for the bombings of a South African airline office and an IBM facility near New York City.
Dec. 17: Terrorists issued bomb threats at IBM facilities in New York and Chicago.
Dec. 18: Members of the African National Congress detonated two bombs at a power plant construction site near Cape Town.
Dec. 19: Bombs damaged police stations in Gottingen and Wolfenbuttel, Ger.
Dec. 21: Peruvian Cultural Institute director Walter Wong was shot to death in Ayacucho.
Dec. 21: Afghan rebels bombed a number of government buildings in Kabul.
Dec. 23: Three people were injured when a bomb exploded at the Israeli Consulate in Sydney, Aus.
Dec. 23: Two Israeli soldiers were killed and three people were injured when a bomb exploded at a refugee camp at Siddon, Leb.
Dec. 26: A power line was bombed by Salvadoran guerrillas, severing power to four provinces in El Salvador.
Dec. 29: Two Afghan airports and numerous buildings were bombed by rebel forces.
Dec. 31: Three New York City police officers were seriously injured when bombs placed by FALN and PLO terrorists exploded at four government building.

1983

Jan. 5: Anti-government guerrillas blew up a primary oil pipeline in Mozambique.
Feb. 13: South African terrorists blew up an oil storage tank in Lesotho, S. Afri.
Feb. 14: More than eighty people were killed during rioting between Hindu and Moslem factions in the Assam province of India. Subsequent violence claimed as many as 2,000 lives in ten days.
Feb. 21: During the previous week, ninety-six SWAPO guerrillas were killed by South African troops in Nambia.
Mar. 9: Two gunmen shot and killed Galip Balkar, the Turkish ambassador to Yugoslavia, while in his car. The chauffeur and one assailant were injured. The Justice Commandos of the Armenian Genocide took responsibility for the assault.
Apr. 10: In Portugal, Abu Nidal terrorists assassinated PLO leader Issam Sartawi.
Apr. 18: Forty-seven people were killed when Jihad terrorists bombed the U.S. embassy in Beirut.
May 22: Eighteen people were killed and more than 200 injured when a African National Congress car-bomb exploded at an Air Force base in Pretoria, S. Afri.
May 26: A U.S. deputy military commander was shot to death in San Salvador, El Sal.
July 3: Provisional IRA members fire-bombed the home of former government official Gerry Fitt in West Belfast, Ire.
July 23: Thirteen soldiers were killed by Tamil separatists near Jaffna, Sri Lanka. More than 100 persons were reportedly killed in subsequent rioting.
Aug. 21: Philippine politician Benigno Aquino was assassinated in Manila, as he was returning from a three-year exile.
Sept. 25: A prison guard was killed and several injured when thirty-eight IRA terrorists escaped from the Maze prison in Belfast, Ire.
Oct. 9: Twenty-one people were killed, including four South Korean Cabinet ministers, when a North Korean terrorist bomb exploded in Rangoon, Burma.
Oct. 23: Suicide truck bombers attacked U.S. and French military installations in Beirut, Leb., killing 241 Marines and fifty-eight French soldiers.
Nov. 4: Sixty people were killed when a truck exploded at an Israeli military installation in Tyre, Leb.
Nov. 20: Three church elders were shot to death near Darkley, Ire. Members of the Irish National Liberation Army were believed to be responsible.
Dec. 12: Four people were killed and sixty injured, when six terrorist bombs exploded in Kuwait.
Dec. 17: Six people died and more than ninety were injured when a Provisional IRA car-bomb exploded outside Harrods department store in London.

1984

Feb. 18: The Jordanian embassy was attacked and burned by a mob in Tripoli, Libya.
Mar. 14: National Conciliation Party leader Hector Flores Larin was shot to death in El Salvador.
Apr. 2: A Hindu politician was murdered by Sikh terrorists in Punjab.
Apr. 3: Three people were killed and sixteen injured when a car bomb allegedly planted by the ANC exploded in Durban, S. Afri.
Apr. 8: The daughter of a Northern Ireland magistrate was shot to death by Provisional IRA terrorists.
Apr. 9: Nine soldiers were wounded when a Tamil separatist bomb exploded in Jaffna, Sri Lanka.
May 10: A former High Priest of the Amritsar Golden Temple was murdered by Sikh extremists in Punjab.
May 12: A newspaper editor was murdered by Sikh extremists in Punjab.
May 17: Newspaper editor Jim Campell was shot and wounded in Belfast, Ire., after publishing a series of articles attacking paramilitary organizations.
May 18: Two British soldiers were killed and eleven people injured when a Provisional IRA car-bomb exploded in Enniskillen, Ire.
May 18: Two Royal Ulster Constabulary members were killed and another was injured when a Provisional IRA landmine exploded in South Armagh, Ire.
May 30: Rebel leader Eden Pastora was injured by a bomb which exploded during a press conference in Nicaragua.
June 2: More than 1,000 Sikh extremists, including a leader named Bhindranwale, were killed in four days of violence by Indian Army troops in Punjab.
July 5: Former Nigerian official Umaru Dikko was discovered alive in a packing crate bound for Nigeria, after he was abducted from his London home.
Aug. 12: One person was killed and twenty were injured as Royal Ulster Constabulary members attempted to arrest a Noraid leader in West Belfast, Ire.
Sept. 20: Fourteen people were killed when a truck bomb exploded at the U.S. embassy in Beirut, Leb.
Oct. 19: Four people were killed when a Provisional IRA bomb exploded at a Brighton, Eng., hotel, during the stay of British Prime Minister Margaret Thatcher.
Oct. 31: Indian Prime Minister Indira Ghandi was assassinated by two of her Sikh bodyguards.
Dec. 4: A Kuwaiti airliner was hijacked to Teheran by five Arab terrorists seeking the release of Shiite prisoners. Two U.S. hostages were killed before the others were released on Dec. 9, when Iranian troops stormed the aircraft.
Dec. 29: Two Black June terrorists murdered PLO official Fahd Qawasma in Jordan.

1985

Feb. 17: Prison official Patrick Kerr was shot to death by Provisional IRA terrorists as he walked from mass with his children, in Armagh, Ire.
Feb. 20: Royal Ulster Constabulary member Frank Murphy was killed by Provisional IRA terrorists as he drove near Armagh, Ire.
Feb. 23: Three Provisional IRA terrorists were shot to death by police in Strabane, Ire.
Feb. 26: Nine members of the Royal Ulster Constabulary were killed by a Provisional IRA mortar attack in Newry, Ire.
Mar. 3: Royal Ulster Constabulary member Hugh McCormac was shot to death as he walked to mass with his family in Enniskillen, Ire.

1987

Jan. 12: A French journalist and a Saudi diplomat were kidnapped in Beirut, Leb.
Jan. 17: West German businessman Rudolf Cordes was kidnapped in Beirut, Leb.
Jan. 20: West German engineer Alfred Schmidt was kidnapped in Beirut, Leb. He was released on Sept. 7, 1987.
Jan. 20: Anglican church envoy Terry Waite was abducted in Beirut, Leb.
Jan. 22: Twelve people were killed and another 100 injured when government troops attacked Communist protesters in Manila.
Jan. 24: Four professors at American University in Beirut, Leb., were abducted.

Mar. 18: A bomb exploded beneath a bandstand in the Philippines where President Aquino was to appear four days later.
Mar. 20: Air Force General Licio Giorgieri was killed by terrorists in Italy.
June 1: Lebanese premier Rashid Karami was killed when a bomb exploded in his helicopter.
June 2: Thirty-three people were killed when Tamil guerrillas attacked a bus in Sri Lanka.
June 18: Ali Osseiran, the son of the Lebanese defense minister and Charles Glass, a U.S. journalist, were kidnapped in Beirut, Leb. Osseiran was released on June 24.
July 7: Sikh extremists killed at least 100 people in one week of violence in Punjab.
July 24: A Shiite terrorist, seeking the release of a political prisoner, hijacked a plane to Geneva, Switz. One passenger was killed when police stormed the plane.
July 30: Sixty-eight people were injured when a bomb exploded at a barracks in Johannesburg, S. Afri.
Aug. 18: One person died and fifteen were injured when a bomb exploded at the Parliament House in Sri Lanka.
Oct. 28: Three U.S. citizens were killed at the Clark Air Force Base in the Philippines by members of the New People's Army.
Nov. 8: Eleven people were killed and sixty-one injured when a bombed exploded in Northern Ireland during services for Remembrance Day.
Nov. 29: All 115 people on board were killed when a KAL South Korean plane crashed near the border of Thailand and Burma. North Korean terrorists were suspected of sabotaging the flight.

1988

Feb. 14: Three PLO senior officers were killed when a car bomb exploded in Limassol, Cyprus.
Mar. 6: In Gibraltar, three unarmed IRA members were shot to death when they were suspected of possessing a remote control explosive detonator, by members of the British Special Air Service.
Mar. 7: Three Palestinian terrorists seized an Israeli bus near a nuclear power plant in Dimona. All three were killed, as well as three passengers during an ensuing gun battle with Israeli commandos.
Mar. 11: At least seventeen passengers were killed by gunfire and hand grenades when Tamil rebels attacked a bus near Anuradhapura, Sri Lanka.
Mar. 16: Three people were killed and dozens wounded at an IRA funeral in Belfast, Ire., by a Protestant terrorist who threw four hand grenades into a crowd of 5,000 mourners.
Mar. 19: Two British soldiers were beaten and killed by mourners at an IRA funeral after their vehicle was trapped by the crowd.
Mar. 20: Six bombs placed by the Farabundo Marti National Liberation Front exploded in San Salvador, El Sal., halting highway traffic and severing power lines, on the eve of the El Salvadoran national elections.
Mar. 29: African National Congress member Dulcie September was shot to death near her office in Paris. South African assassination squads were suspected.
Apr. 5: A Kuwaiti airliner bound for Kuwait was hijacked shortly after taking off in Thailand, by eight Arab gunmen, who diverted the plane to Iran. They demanded the release of seventeen imprisoned Arab terrorists. On April 8, the plane was flown to Cyprus where two Kuwaiti passengers were killed. On April 13, the plane was flown to Algeria. Six days later the hostages were released, and the hijackers were allowed to leave the country.
Apr. 7: South African lawyer Albie Sachs was wounded when a car-bomb exploded in Maputo, Mozambique. South African assassination squads were suspected.
Apr. 14: Five people were killed when a car bomb exploded near a U.S. servicemen's club in Naples, Italy. The Japanese Red Army was thought to be responsible.
Apr. 16: PLO senior military officer Abu Jihad was killed at his home near Tunis, Tunisia. Israeli commandos were the primary suspects.
Apr. 23: More than forty people were killed when a truck bomb exploded at a crowded market in Tripoli, Leb.
June 18: Turkish Prime Minister Turgut Ozal was wounded while making a speech, by Kartal Demirag a member of the ultra-right Grey Wolves.
July 11: Nine people were killed and more than eighty injured when a Greek ferry boat was attacked by Iranian terrorists.
Aug. 17: Pakistani President Mohammed Zia-ul-Haq was one of thirty people thought to be victims of sabotage when a military plane crashed shortly after takeoff in Pakistan.
Aug. 30: Three IRA members died after being ambushed by British Special Air Service members in Northern Ireland.
September: Four members of the Lesotho Liberation Army hijacked a bus with seventy passengers en route to see Pope John Paul II. Three terrorists and two hostages were killed in the rescue attempt.
Dec. 21: A bomb exploded on a Pan Am flight from London to New York City, killing 259 passengers, as well as eleven others on the ground, when it crashed into a small village in Scotland. Scotland Yard and the FBI determined that the plane was destroyed by plastic explosives.

TERRORIST ORGANIZATIONS

A

AAA: see Argentine Anticommunist Alliance.
AALA: see Afro-American Liberation Army.
AAPRA: see All-African People's Revolutionary Army.
Abdala: an anti-Castro terrorist organization, active in New York City during the 1970s.
Abu Abbas: a Syrian terrorist organization, aligned with the Fatah faction of the Palestine Liberation Front.
Abu Musa: a Syrian terrorist group, a faction of the Fatah organization.
Abu Nidal Faction (Fatah Revolutionary Council): A Middle Eastern terrorist organization based in Libya and Syria.
Acao Libertadora Nacional (ALN): a Brazilian terrorist organization.
Action Directe (Direct Action, (AD): an anti-Nato terrorist organization headquartered in France. AD was responsible for the murder of Georges Besse in 1986.
Action Organization for the Liberation of Palestine: a terrorist organization credited with the February, 1970 attack on Israeli passengers at the Munich airport.
Action pour la Renaissance de la Corse (Corsican Resistance Action, ARC): Founded in 1967, the ARC was created to protect the regional identity of Corsica. It has been responsible for various bombings throughout Corsica.
AD: see Action Directe.
African National Congress (ANC): an organization devoted to the anti-apartheid movement in South Africa.
Afro-American Liberation Army (AALA): a terrorist organization, active in Los Angeles during the 1970s.
AIM: see American Indian Movement.
Al-Asifa: a European terrorist organization active during the 1980s.
Al Dawa (The Call): An Islamic Shiite organization consisting of Ayatollah Khomeini supporters and Iraqi dissidents, Al Dawa took credit for the Baghdad bombing of the British embassy.
Al Fatah: a Middle East terrorist organization active for the past three decades.
Al Jihad Al Mudaddas Front: a Lebanese terrorist organization active during the 1980s.
Al Zulifikar: a Pakistani terrorist organization active during the 1980s.
ALF: see Arab Liberation Front.
Aliens of America: a U.S. terrorist organization, based in Los Angeles during the 1970s.
All-African People's Revolutionary Army (AAPRA): an African terrorist organization.
All-India Communist Party: a terrorist organization, active during the 1980s.
Alliance of the Lao Reactionary Group Fronts: a terrorist organization formed in China during 1982.
ALN: see Acao Libertadora Nacional.
Alpha 66: an anti-Castro terrorist organization, active in the Miami area during the 1980s.
ALQ: see Armee de Liberation Quebecois.
Amal (Islamic Hope): A Shiite organization of 5000 members, headed by Nabih Berri, Amal was founded as the Movement of the Disinherited.
American Indian Movement (AIM): Founded to preserve Indian reservations in the upper Plains, AIM is best known for the 1973 occupation of Wounded Knee, which resulted in several shootouts with federal marshals and FBI agents.
Americans for Justice: a U.S. terrorist organization, active on the West Coast during the 1970s.
ANC: see African National Congress.
Angry Merchants: a terrorist organization, responsible for bombings in France during 1982.
Animal Rights Militia: a group responsible for numerous letter bombing incidents in Britain, during the 1980s.
ANM: see Arab Nationalist Movement.
Anti-Communist Commandos: a terrorist organization, active in Puerto Rico during the 1970s.
AOLP: see Action Organization for the Liberation of Palestine.
April 19 Movement: see Movimiento 19 Abril (M 19).
April 6 Liberation Movement: a Philippine terrorist organization during the 1980s.
ARC: see Action pour la Renaissance de la Corse.
Arab Brigades Movement: a terrorist organization, active in India during the 1980s.
Arab Communist Organization: a Middle Eastern terrorist organization during the 1970s.
Arab Liberation Front (ALF): a terrorist organization founded in Iraq in 1968 for the purpose of attacking Israeli interests.
Arab National Youth for the Liberation of Palestine: a Middle Eastern terrorist organization during the 1970s.
Arab Nationalist Movement: a Middle Eastern terrorist organization.
Arab Revolution Vanguards: a Middle Eastern terrorist organization during the 1980s.
Arab Steadfastness Front: a terrorist organization, active in Egypt during the 1980s.
ARENA: see Nationalist Republican Alliance.
Argentine Anticommunist Alliance (AAA): an Argentine terrorist organization.
Argentinian Revolutionary Workers Party: a Latin American terrorist organization active during the 1980s.
Armed Commandos of Liberation: a Puerto Rican terrorist organization, responsible for bombings during the 1970s.
Armed Communist Formations: an Italian terrorist organization active during the 1970s.
Armed Communist League: a terrorist organization, active in Mexico during the 1970s.
Armed Forces of National Loberation of Puerto Rico.
Armed Forces of National Resistance (FARN): a terrorist organization based in El Salvador.
Armed Nationalist Reactionary Group: a Dominican terrorist organization, active during the 1980s.
Armed Nationalist Revolutionary Group.
Armed Nuclei for Popular Autonomy (NAPAP): a terrorist organization based in France.
Armed Proletarian Nuclei: see Nuclei Armati Proletari.
Armed Revolution Squads: an Italian right-wing terrorist organization during the 1980s.
Armed Revolutionary Nuclei (NAR): an Italian terrorist organization during the 1980s.
Armed Revolutionary Vanguard-Palmares: see Vanguarda Armada Revolucionaria-Palmares.
Armed Struggle: a Middle Eastern terrorist organization, active during the 1980s.
Armed Vanguard of the Proletariet: a Mexican terrorist organization during the 1970s.
Armee de Liberation Quebecois (ALQ): a separatist terrorist organization in Quebec, responsible for the 1964 invasion of a Montreal armament factory.
Armenian Orly Group: a terrorist organization, active in Paris during the 1980s.
Armenian Secret Army for the Liberation of Armenia (ASALA): an Armenian nationalist terrorist organization.
ASALA: see Armenian Secret Army for the Liberation of Armenia.
As-Sa'iqa (Thunderbolt): a Palestinian group which is headquartered in Damascus, the Sa'iqa aligns itself with the Syrian Baath party.
AUTOP: see Workers Autonomy.
Azedegan: an Iranian pro-monarcharist terrorist organization, active during the 1980s.

B

Baader-Meinhof Gang (B-Ms): a terrorist organization founded in West Germany by Andreas Baader and Ulrike Meinhof in the 1970s, supported by East Germany and Moscow.
Bakunin-Gdansk: a terrorist organization, active in Paris during the 1980s.
BAMM: see Black Afro Militant Movement.
Basque Fatherland and Liberty Group.
Basque Nationalists: see Euzkadi Ta Azkatazuna-Basque Homeland and Liberation.
Bay Bombers: a terrorist organization in the San Francisco area during the 1970s.
BFO: a Middle Eastern terrorist organization, active during the 1970s.
BLA: see Black Liberation Army.
Black Afro Militant Movement: a U.S. terrorist organization.
Black June: a Middle East terrorist organization active during the 1970's.
Black Liberation Army (BLA): An offshoot of the Black Panthers, founded in 1971, the BLA was accused of murdering several police officers in New York and San Francisco. Within two years, most of the group's members were imprisoned or had been shot to death.
Black Muslims: Originally a black separatist organization based on the teachings of Elijah Muhammad, the Muslims occasionally resorted to violence to perpetuate their religious and commercial empire. They have been involved in numerous shootouts with police and were responsible for fourteen murders in San Francisco known as the Zebra killings.
Black Nation of Islam (BNI): a U.S. terrorist organization.
Black Panther Party (BPP): A black militant organization founded in Oakland, Calif. in 1966, by Huey Newton and Bobby Seale, the BPP was active in both campus and ghetto protests. They were accused of numerous shooting and bombing incidents until the mid-70s when they turned their activities to the formation of black private enterprise.
Black Revolutionary: a terrorist organization active in New York City during the 1970s.
Black September (BSO): a terrorist organization, based in the Middle East, Black September was founded in 1970 and is believed to be

responsible for the massacre at the Munich Olympics.

B-Ms: see Baader-Meinhof Gang.

BNI: see Black Nation of Islam.

Bozkurtlar: see Grey Wolves.

BPP: see Black Panther Party.

BPR: see Popular Revolutionary Bloc.

Breakthrough: A Detroit-based reactionary group headed by Donald Lobsinger, Breakthrough was known to attack participants at many left-wing rallies in the mid-1970s.

Brigate Rosse: see Red Brigades.

Brotherhood of Aleppo: a Middle Eastern terrorist organization during the 1980s.

BSO: see Black September Organization.

C

CAL: see Commandos Armados de Liberacion.

Carlos Aguero Echevarria: a Costa Rican terrorist organization during the 1980s.

CCC: see Cellules Communistes Combattantes.

Cellules Communistes Combattantes: a terrorist organization headquartered in Belgium.

Chicano Liberation Front (CLF): Founded in the Los Angeles barrio in the early 1970s to protest the deaths of Chicanos at anti-war rallies, the CLF was accused of numerous attacks in public buildings, and of at least one death in a bombing incident.

Chukaku-Ha: a Japanese terrorist organization.

CLF: see Chicano Liberation Front.

COLINA: see Comando da Libertacao Nacional.

Comando da Libertacao Nacional (National Liberation Commandos, COLINA): a South American terrorist organization.

Comite Argentino de Lucha Anti-Imperialista: an Argentine terrorist organization active in the 1970s.

Commando Boudia: the operational name for the terrorist Carlos, in London and Paris, named for Algerian terrorist Mohammed Boudia.

Commandos Armados de Liberacion (CAL): a terrorist organization based in Puerto Rico.

Communist Armed Nuclei: an Italian terrorist organization during the 1980s.

Communist Front for Counter Power: a terrorist organization, active in Italy during the 1980s.

Communist Groups for Proletarian Internationalism: a terrorist organization, active in Italy during the 1980s.

Continental Revolutionary Army: a U.S. terrorist organization, active in the Denver area during the 1970s.

Coordination of United Revolutionary Organizations (CORU): a consortium of Spanish terrorist organizations.

Corsican National Liberation Front (FLNC): a Corsican terrorist organization.

CORU: see Coordination of United Revolutionary Organizations.

Croatian Revolutionary Brotherhood (Hrvatsko Revolucionarno Bratsvo, HRB) : a nationalist terrorist organization based in Yugoslavia.

Crypto: a Malaysian terrorist organization, active during the 1980s.

Cuban Action Commandos: Founded in Los Angeles in the late 1960s, the Cuban Action Commandos were responsible for bombing the embassies of countries friendly to Fidel Castro. In 1975, they bombed a series of left-wing bookstores.

Cuban Power: see El Poder Cubano.

Cuban Revolutionary Directorate: an Anti-Castro terrorist organization, active in Europe during the 1970s.

D

Democratic Front Against Repression: a Latin American terrorist organization during the 1980s.

Democratic Front for the Liberation of Palestine (DFLP): a terrorist organization, formed in 1969 by breakaway exremists from the PFLP. The DFLP was responsible for a 1974 attack which killed 22 Israeli children.

Democratic Popular Front (DPF): a terrorist organization.

DEV SOL: a leftist terrorist organization headquartered in Turkey.

DFLP: see Democratic Front for the Liberation of Palestine.

DGI: see Directoria General de Inteligencia.

Direct Action: see Action Directe.

Directoria General de Inteligencia (DGI): a Cuban intelligence organization, supported by the KGB, and aligned with Western European terrorist activities.

DPF: see Democratic Popular Front.

E

Eagles of National Unity: a Middle Eastern terrorist organization, active during the 1970s.

Eagles of the Revolution: a Middle Eastern terrorist organization, active during the 1980s.

Eagle Warrior Society: a U.S. terrorist organization, active on Indian Reservations during the 1970s.

EAN: a Greek anti-dictatorial youth terrorist organization.

Easter Commandos: a terrorist faction of the Black September Organization.

Eelam Revolutionary Organization of Students (EROS): a terrorist organization based in Sri Lanka.

EGP: a Guatemalan terrorist organization during the 1980s.

Ejercito de Libercion National (ELN): a Peruvian terrorist organization.

Ejercito Popular de Liberacion (EPL): a Columbian terrorist organization.

Ejercito Revolucionario del Pueblo (ERP): an Argentine and Salvadoran terrorist organization, active during the 1970s.

El Poder Cubano (Cuban Power): an anti-Castro terrorist organization, active in the U.S.

El Salvador Democratic Revolutionary Front: an anti-government terrorist organization during the 1980s.

ELF: see Eritrean Liberation Front.

ELN: see Ejercito de Liberacion National.

ELS: see Southern Liberation Army.

Emiliano Zapata Unit (EZP): Based in San Francisco, the EZP was responsible for four bombings in 1975 and 1976. They later merged with the New Dawn Collective.

English Republican Army: a terrorist organization during the 1980s.

Enlightened Path: a Peruvian terrorist organization during the 1980s.

EOKA: see Ethniki Organosis Kyprion Agoniston.

EPL: see Ejercito Popular de Liberacion.

EPLF: see Eritrean People's Liberation Front.

Eritrean Liberation Front (ELF): an Ethiopian terrorist organization.

Eritrean People's Liberation Front (EPLF): An Ethiopian secessionist group which sabotaged food shipments to the starving nation during the 1980s.

Eros: see Eelam Revolutionary Organization of Students.

ERP: see Ejercito Revolucionario del Pueblo.

ETA: see Euzkadi Ta Azkatazuna-Basque Homeland and Liberation.

Ethniki Organosis Kyprion Agoniston (EOKA): a terrorist organization based in Cyprus.

Euzkadi Ta Azkatazuna-Basque Homeland and Liberation (ETA): a terrorist organization, active in Spain since the late 1950's, seeking independence for the Basque provinces.

EZP: see Emiliano Zapata Unit.

F

FAL: see Frente Argentino de Liberacion.

Falangists: a Bolivian right-wing terrorist organization during the 1980s.

FALN: see Fuerzas Armadas de Liberacion Nacional Puertoriquena.

Family of Jihad: a terrorist faction of the Al Fatah.

FANE: see Federation National Europe.

FAP: see Fuerzas Armadas Peronistas.

FAR: see Fuerzas Armadas Rebeldes.

Farabundo Marti National Liberation Front (FMLN): an El Salvadoran terrorist group active in the 1980's.

FARC: see Fuerzas Armadas Revolucionarias de Columbia.

FARL: see Lebanese Armed Revolutionary Faction.

FARN: see Armed Forces of National Resistance.

Fatah Revolutionary Council: see Abu Nidal, Harat Tahrir Filastin.

Fedaj Khalq: a terrorist organization headquartered in Iran.

Fedayeen: a Middle Eastern terrorist organization active during the 1970s.

Federation National Europe (FANE): a neo-fascist terrorist organization, active during the 1980s.

FFI: see Fighters for the Freedom of Israel.

Fighters for the Freedom of Israel (FFI): an Israeli terrorist organization.

15th of May Arab Movement for the Liberation of Palestine: a Middle Eastern terrorist active during the 1980's.

Fighting Communist Formation: an Italian terrorist organization during the 1970s.

FIN Cuban National Front: an anti-Castro terrorist organization, active in New York City during the 1970s.

FINC-Youth of the Stars: a terrorist organization active in the Miami area during the 1970s.

First Line Armed Cell: an Italian terrorist organization during the 1980s.

First of October Autonomous Revolutionary Group (GRAPO): a left-wing terrorist organization, active in Spain during the 1970s.

FLB-ARB: see Front de Liberation de la Bretagne-Armee Revolutionnaire Bretonne.

FLN: see Front de Liberation National.

FLN: see Front de Liberation of Algeria.

FLNC: see Corsican National Liberation Front.

FLNC-Cuban Anti-Communist League: a terrorist organization, active in the Miami area during the 1970s.

FLOSY: see Front for the Liberation of Occupied South Yemen.

FLQ: see Front du Liberation du Quebec.

FMLN: see Farabundo Marti National Liberation Front.

FMPR: see Manuel Rodriguez Patriotic Front.

Forcas Populares do 25 Abril (FP 25): a terrorist organization headquartered in Portugal.

FP 25: see Forcas Populares do 25 Abril.

FRAP: see Frente Revolucionario AntiFascista y Patriotica.

FRAP: see Fuerzas Revolucionarias Armadas del Pueblo.

Freedom Front/Revolutionary Fighting Group: a U.S. terrorist organization, active in New York City during the 1980s.

French Revolutionary Brigades: a terrorist organization, active during the 1980s.

Frente Argentino de Liberacion (FAL): an Argentine terrorist organization.

Frente Revolucionario AntiFascista y Patriotica (FRAP): a Spanish terrorist organization, founded in 1971.

Frente Sandinista de Liberacion Nacional (FSLN): a terrorist organization based in Nicaragua.

Frente Urbana Zapatista (ZAPATISTA): a terrorist organization based in Mexico.

Front de Liberation de la Bretagne-Armee Revolutionnaire Bretonne (FLB-ARB): a terrorist organization, founded in France in 1969.

Front de Liberation of Algeria (FLN): an Algerian terrorist organization, active during the 1980s.

Front de Liberation National: a separatist terrorist organization, active in Quebec during the 1960s.

Front du Liberation du Quebec (FLQ): a Canadian terrorist organization, based in the province of Quebec, founded in 1963.

Front for the Liberation of Lebanon: a right-wing terrorist organization during the 1980s.

Front for the Liberation of Occupied South Yemen (FLOSY): a Middle Eastern terrorist organization.

Front Line: an Italian terrorist organization, which served as a companion organization to the Red Brigades.

FSLN: see Frente Sandinista de Liberacion Nacional.

Fuerzas Armadas de Liberacion Nacional Puertorriquena (Armed Forces of Puerto Rican National Liberation, FALN): Formed to lobby for Puerto Rican independence, the FALN resorted to violence with the bombings of five New York banks in 1974. Other bombings in public places from New York to Chicago resulted in four deaths and scores of injuries.

Fuerzas Armadas Peronistas (FAP): an Argentine terrorist organization.

Fuerzas Armadas Rebeldes (FAR): a Guatemalan terrorist organization, aligned with the Communist Party.

Fuerzas Armadas Revolucionarias de Colombia (FARC): a terrorist organization based in Colombia.

Fuerzas Revolucionarias Armadas del Pueblo (FRAP): a Mexican terrorist organization.

G

German People's Socialist Movement (USBD): a West German terrorist organization active during the 1980s.

George Jackson Brigade: a U.S. terrorist organization, active in the Pacific Northwest during the 1970s.

Ghassan Kanafi: an Italian terrorist organization during the 1970s.

GRAPO: see First of October Autonomous Revolutionary Group.

Greek Anti-Dictatorial Youth.

Greek Armed Group for the Support of the Northern Irish Struggle: a terrorist organization in Greece during the 1980s.

Greek People: a Greek anti-government terrorist organization during the 1970s;

Grey Wolves (BOZKURTLAR): a Turkish terrorist organization.

Groupe de Liberation Armee of La Guadaloupe: a terrorist organization, active in Paris during the 1980s.

Groupe de Liberation de la Martinique: a terrorist organization that was responsible for the 1981 bombing of the Palace of Justice in Martinique.

Guatemalan Committee of Patriotic Unity: a terrorist organization, formed in 1982 by combining four terrorist factions.

Guatemalan Labor Party's National Directorate Nucleus.

Guatemalan National Revolutionary Unity: a terrorist consortium formed in 1982, by combining the EGP, FAR, OPRA, and National Directorate Nucleus terrorist factions.

Guatemalan Work Party: a Latin American terrorist organization during the 1980s.

Guerrilla Army of the Poor: a Guatemalan terrorist organization during the 1980s.

Guerrilla Party: a Sicilian terrorist organization during the 1980s.

Guerrilleros Del Cristo Rey (Warriors of Christ The King): a terrorist organization, based in Spain during the 1970s.

H

Habash Front: a terrorist organization, active in Europe during the 1970s.

Hanafi Muslims: a terrorist organization during the mid 1970s in Washington, D.C.

Harakat Tahrir Filastin: see Fatah.

Hawatmah Front: a Turkish terrorist organization, active during the 1970s.

Hizbollah (Party of God): a pro-Iranian Shiite organization founded in 1982, that was responsible for the 1985 hijacking of a TWA flight in Beirut. The Hizbollah are affiliated with Amal and the Soldiers of God.

HRB: see Croatian Revolutionary Brotherhood.

Hrvatsko Revolucionarno Bratstvo: see Croation Revolutionary Brotherhood.

I

IMRO: see Inner Macedonian Revolutionary Organization.

Independence, Liberation, Resistance Organization: a Greek terrorist organization, active during the 1970s.

INLA: see Irish National Liberation Army.

Inner Macedonian Revolutionary Organization (IMRO): a terrorist organization based in the Balkan regions of Greece and Yugoslavia.

Invisible Ones: a Colombian terrorist organization, responsible for the 1969 kidnapping of the Swiss consul.

Iparretarrak: a terrorist organization, active in Europe during the 1980s.

IRA: see Irish Republican Army.

Iraqi Islamic Revolution: a dissident exile organization, based in Iran which supports such splinter groups as the Iraqi Dawa and the Iraqi Mujaheddin.

Irgun Zvai Leumi (Irgun, IZL): a Palestinian terrorist organization.

Irish National Liberation Army (INLA): a terrorist organization based in Northern Ireland.

Irish Republican Army (IRA): a terrorist organization, active against the British occupation of Northern Ireland.

Islamic Amal: Headquartered in Baalbek, Leb., the Islamic Amal is a Shiite terrorist organization splintered from the larger Amal group.

Islamic Jihad: Best known for the suicide bombings of U.S. Marine barracks in Beirut, and the U.S. embassies in Lebanon and Kuwait, the Islamic Jihad is an affiliation of various Lebanese, Iraqi and Iranian Shiite terrorist organizations dedicated to the Islamic Revolution in the Middle East.

Islamic Resistance Movement: a title used by various terrorists with Shiite affiliations, the Islamic Resistance Movement is primarily active against the Israelis and their allies.

Islamic Revolutionary Guards: a Middle Eastern terrorist organization during the 1980s.

Islamic Unification Movement (Tawhid): Based in Tripoli, Lebanon, the Islamic Unification Movement is a group of fundamentalist Sunni Moslems.

Islamic Unity of the Mujahedeen.

IZL: see Irgun Zvai Leumi.

J

January 31 Popular Front: a Guatemalan terrorist organization during the 1980s.

Japanese Red Army: See Red Army.

JCAG: see Justice Commando of the Armenian Genocide.

JDL: see Jewish Defense League.

Jewish Armed Resistance: a U.S. terrorist organization active during the 1970s.

Jewish Defense League (JDL): Formed by rabbi Meir Kahane and lawyer Bert Zweibon in 1968 to protest the treatment of Soviet Jews, the JDL evolved into a counteractive terrorist organization, being attributed with several bombings in the Middle East, as well as many in New York City.

Jewish Underground Army: a U.S. terrorist organization, based in New York City during the 1970s.

Jibril Front: a Palestinian terrorist organization suspected of the 1970 bombing of a Swissair flight.

JIN: an anti-Castro terrorist organization, active in the Miami area during the 1970s.

JRA: See Japanese Red Army.

June 9 Organization: an Armenian terrorist organization, during the 1980s.

Justice Commando of Armenian Genocide (JCAG): an Armenian terrorist organization.

JVP-People's Liberation Front: a terrorist organization active in Sri Lanka during the 1980s.

K

Kabataang Makabayan: a Philippine student terrorist organization active during the 1970s.

KGB: the Russian secret intelligence service.

KKK: see Ku Klux Klan.

Ku Klux Klan (KKK): The 20th century's most visible symbol of racism and hatred, the KKK has been practicing lynching, bombing, beating, and cross burning in the rural South for decades. Their movements became more surreptitious during the 1960s Civil Rights movement, but as bigotry continued to fester, the KKK practiced its random violence, such as the bombing of school buses in Pontiac, Mich. in 1971.

L

Lebanese Armed Revolutionary Brigades.

Lebanese Armed Revolutionary Faction (Fractions armeés révolutionnaires libanaises) (FARL): a Christian Lebanese terrorist organization created to attack Americans and Israelis.

Lebanese National Resistance Front: a blanket name for various Middle Eastern terrorist organizations, active during the 1980s.

Lebanese Socialist Revolutionary Organization: a Middle Eastern terrorist organization during the 1970s.

Leftist Patriotic Honduran Front: a terrorist organization during the 1980s.

Legion of Justice: A reactionary group based in Chicago between 1969 and 1971, the Legion of Justice members attacked anti-war protesters and communist sympathizers.

LEHI: see Lohame Herut Israel.

Lesotho Liberation Army: a terrorist organization, active during the 1980s.

Liberation Tigers of Tamil Eelam (LTTE): a secessionist terrorist organization based in Sri Lanka.

Lohame Herut Yisrael (LEHI): an Israeli terrorist organization.

Lorenzo Zelaya Popular Revolutionary Command: a terrorist organization, active in Honduras during the 1980s.

LTTE: see Liberation Tigers of Tamil Eelam.

M

M 19: see Movimiento 19 Abril.

Macheteros: a Puerto Rican terrorist organization during the 1980s.

Manipur: a terrorist organization, active in India during the 1980s.

MANO: see Movimiento Argentino Nacional Organisacion.

Mano Blanco: a Guatamalan terrorist organization.

Manuel Rodriguez Patriotic Front (FMPR): a Chilean terrorist organization.

MAR: see Movimiento de Accion Revolucionaria.

Masada Action and Defense Movement: a terrorist organization active in Europe, during the 1970s.

Menominee Warrior Society: a U.S. Indian terrorist organization during the 1970s.

Mexican People's Revolutionary Army.

Militant Jewish Defense League.

Military Sports Group Hoffman: a neo-Nazi terrorist organization based in West Germany and suspected of violence during the 1980s in France and England.

Minutemen: Following the Red scare of the 1950s, the turn to the more liberal presidency of John Kennedy, and the emergence of Fidel Castro, the right-wing paramilitary Minutemen organization was formed by Robert DuPugh, who had been given a medical discharge for psychosis during WWII. They amassed huge arsenals and paraded their weaponry for five years until nineteen members were arrested in October 1966, while preparing to attack three liberal organizations in New York. The group's activity declined when DuPugh was convicted for a Federal firearms violation.

MIR: see Movimiento de la Izquierda Revolucionaria.

MIRA: see Movimiento Independista Revolucionario Armada.

MLN: see Tupamaros-Movimiento de Liberacion Nacional.

Montoneros: an Argentine terrorist organization named after Juan Jose Valle Montoneros.

MoPoCo: a terrorist organization based in Paraguay.

MOVE: a radical terrorist organization, active in the Philadelphia area during the 1980s.

Movement for the Restoration of Democracy: a Pakistani terrorist organization during the 1980s.

Movement of Youthward Brothers: a pro-Palestinian terrorist organization, active in Europe during the 1970s.

Movimiento Argentino Nacional Organisacion (MANO): a terrorist organization headquartered in Argentina.

Movimiento de Accion Revolucionaria (MAR): a Mexican terrorist organization active during the 1970s.

Movimiento de la Izquerda Revolucionaria (MIR): a terrorist organization in Chile, Peru, and Venezuela.

Movimiento Independista Revolucionario Armada (MIRA): a Puerto Rican terrorist organization responsible for bombings during the 1970s.

Movimiento 19 Abril (April 19 Movement, M 19): a Colombian terrorist organization.

Movimiento Revolucionario do Octobre 8 (MR-8): a terrorist organization affiliated with the Brazilian Communist Party; responsible for the 1969 kidnapping of the U.S. ambassador.

Movimiento Revolucionario Alejandro de Leon 13 Noviembre (MR-13): a Trotskyite Guatemalan terrorist organization, named after an unsuccessful military coup on Nov. 13, 1960.

Mozambican National Resistance: a terrorist organization during the 1980s.

MPLA: an Angolan terrorist organization active in the 1970s.

MR-8: see Movimiento Revolucionario do Octobre 8.

MR-13: see Movimiento Revolucionario Alejandro de Leon 13 Noviembre.

MRTA: see Tupac Amaru Revolutionary Movement.

Mujaheddin: a terrorist organization based in Iran.

Mushala Gang: a terrorist organization, active in Zambia during the 1980s.

Muslim Brotherhood: a Middle Eastern terrorist organization during the 1980s.

N

NAP: see Nuclei Armati Proletari-Armed Proletarian Nuclei.

NAPAP: see Armed Nuclei for Popular Autonomy.

NAR: see Armed Revolutionary Nuclei.

Nat Turner-John Brown Faction: a terrorist faction of the New World Liberation Front.

National Arab Youth for the Liberation of Palestine (NAYLP): a Middle Eastern terrorist organization, active during the 1970s.

National Committee to Combat Fascism: a terrorist organization active in Detroit during the 1970s.

National Directorate Nucleus: a terrorist faction of the Guatemalan Labor Party during the 1980s.

National Fatherland Front: a terrorist organization, active in Kabul during the 1980s.

National Liberation Armed Forces: a Venezuelan terrorist organization during the 1970s.

National Liberation Army: a Colombian terrorist organization responsible for the 1970 kidnapping of a foreign minister.

National Liberation Commando: see Comando da Libertacao Nacional.

National Liberation Front (NLF): a terrorist organization based in South Yemen, and aligned with the PFLP and PDFLP.

National Liberation Movement: a Guatemalan terrorist organization during the 1980s.

National Peasant Movement: a Honduran terrorist organization during the 1980s.

National Resistance Army: an Ugandan terrorist organization during the 1980s.

National Socialist Liberation Front (NSLF): A reactionary group led by Joseph Tommasi, the NSLF bombed four left-wing organizations in Los Angeles in 1975, before Tommasi was shot to death by Nazis, disbanding the group.

National Youth Resistance Organization: a Greek terrorist organization, active in the 1970s.

Nationalist Group for the Liberation of Palestine: a Middle Eastern terrorist organization active during the 1970s.

Nationalist Republican Alliance (ARENA): A Salvadoran conservative organization suspected of death squad activities.

NAYLP: see National Arab Youth for the Liberation of Palestine.

New Dawn Collective: a U.S. terrorist organization, active in Northern California during the 1970s.

New Organization: a terrorist organization, active in Greece during the 1980s.

New People's Army (NPA): A leftist terrorist organization which attacks police officers and U.S. soldiers in the Philippines.

New World Liberation Front (NWLF): A 1970s west coast terrorist organization, the NWLF was responsible for eight bombings in 1974, and twenty-two a year later. Espousing the views of Brazilian revolutionary Carlos Marighella, they acted as a shelter organization for the splintered factions of other leftist groups such as the SLA, Red Guerrilla Family, and the Chicano Liberation Front.

19th of May: a Latin American terrorist organization during the 1980s.

NLF: see National Liberation Front.

NOA: see Nueva Organizacion Anticommunista.

November 17 Terrorist Group: a Greek terrorist organization founded in the 1970s.

N.P.A.: see New People's Army.

NSLF: see National Socialist Liberation Front.

Nuclei Armati Proletari-Armed Proletarian Cells (NAP): an Italian terrorist organization during the 1970s.

Nueva Organizacion Anticommunista (NOA): a Guatamalan terrorist organization.

NWLF: see New World Liberation Front.

O

October 1 Anti-Fascist Revolutionary Group: a terrorist organization, active in Spain during the 1980s.

OPRA: a Guatemalan terrorist organization, active during the 1980s.

OPR-33: see Organization of the Popular Revolution - 33.

Order, The: a U.S. terrorist organization during the 1980s.

Organization for Victims of Zionist Occupation: a Palestinian terrorist organization responsible for the 1972 hijacking of a Lufthansa airliner.

Organization of the National Confrontation Front: a Middle Eastern terrorist organization, active during the 1980s.

Organization of the Oppressed on Earth: A Lebanese terrorist group composed of pro-Iranian Shiite Moslems, which was responsible for the 1988 kidnapping of U.S. Marine officer William Higgins.

Organization of the Popular Revolution - 33 (OPR-33): a terrorist organization based in Uruguay, active in the early 1970s.

Orly Group: see Armenian Orly Group.

P

Palestine Liberation Army (PLA) : a terrorist organization, serving as the military component of the PLO.

Palestine Liberation Organization (PLO): a Middle Eastern terrorist organization, headed by Yasser Arafat.

Palestinian Communist Party.

Palestinian Popular Struggle Front.

Partido Revolucionario Dominican (PRD): a terrorist organization based in the Dominican Republic.

Party of God: see Hizbollah.

Pattani Liberation Front: a Muslim separatist terrorist organization, based in Thailand during the 1970s.

PDFLP: see Popular Democratic Front for the Liberation of Palestine.

Peace and Freedom Fighters: A reactionary group composed of Hungarian exiles based in Los Angeles, the Peace and Freedom Fighters were suspected of several attacks against left-wing organizations in the 1970s.

People's Army: a Philippine terrorist organization founded in 1987.

People's Forces Unit IX: a terrorist faction of the New World Liberation Army.

People's Front 31st January: a Latin American terrorist organization during the 1980s.

People's Liberation Army: a terrorist organization, active in Burma during the 1980s.

People's Liberation Forces: a Salvadoran terrorist organization during the 1980s.

People's Redemption Council: a Liberian terrorist organization during the 1980s.

People's Revolutionary Armed Forces.

People's Revolutionary Army: a Latin American terrorist group, active during the 1970s.

People's Revolutionary Army: an Ugandan terrorist organization during the 1980s.

People's Revolutionary Front: a Philippine terrorist organization during the 1970s.

People's Revolutionary Party (PRP): a terrorist organization active in Northern California during the 1970s.

Peykar Group: a left-wing Iranian terrorist organization during the 1980s.

PFLP: see Popular Front for the Liberation of Palestine.

PFLP-GC: see Popular Front for the Liberation of Palestine - General Command.

PIRA: see Provisional Irish Republican Army.

PLA: see Palestine Liberation Army.

PLF: Popular Liberation Forces.

PLO: see Palestine Liberation Organization.

Polisario Front.

Popular Democratic Front for the Liberation of Palestine (PDFLP): a Middle Eastern terrorist organization, founded by Nayef Hawatmeh; a splinter group of the PFLP.

Popular Forces of April 25: a Portuguese terrorist organization during the 1980s.

Popular Front for the Liberation of Palestine (PFLP): a Middle Eastern terrorist organization founded in 1967.

Popular Front for the Liberation of Palestine - General Command (PFLP-GC): a branch of the Popular Front for the Liberation of Palestine, supported by Syria.

Popular League: a left-wing Salvadoran terrorist organization during the 1980s.

Popular Liberation Forces (PLF): a component of the PLO terrorist organization, serving as the commando wing of the PLA.

Popular Resistance Group: a Greek terrorist organization, active during the 1970s.

Popular Revolutionary Bloc (BPR): a Salvadoran terrorist organization during the 1970s.

Popular Revolutionary Struggle: a Greek terrorist organization during the 1980s.

Popular Struggle Front: a Turkish terrorist organization during the 1970s.

Posse Commitatus: A vigilante group founded in 1968 by Mike Beach in Portland, Ore., the Posse Commitatus was menacing without being particularly violent.

P.P.S. Okrezeva: a Polish socialist terrorist organization which in 1905 attempted to kill the police chief of Warsaw.

PRD: see Partido Revolucionario Dominican.

Prima Linea: an Italian terrorist organization during the 1980s.

Progressive Labor Party: a reactionary terrorist organization, based in Southern California during the 1970s.

Proletarian Action Group: a terrorist organization, active in Italy during the 1970s.

Proletariat Organized Group: a terrorist organization, active in Sicily during the 1980s.

Proud Eagle Tribe: a terrorist faction of the Weather Underground, responsible for bombing incidents in the Boston area during the 1970s.

Provisional Irish Republican Army (PIRA): A Northern Ireland terrorist organization beginning in 1969.

PRP: see People's Revolutionary Party.

Puerto Rican Armed Resistance Group: a terrorist organization, active in the New York City area during the 1980s.

Puerto Rican Liberation Front: a U.S. terrorist organization active on the East Coast during the 1970s.

Puerto Rican Resistance Movement: a terrorist organization active in the 1970s.

Puerta Rican Revolutionary Workers: a Puerto Rican terrorist organization.

Purple Sunshine: a U.S. terrorist organization in Northern California during the 1970s.

Q

Quarter Moon Society: a U.S. terrorist organization responsible for bombings in the Seattle area during the 1970s.

Quebec Separatists Movement: a Canadian terrorist organization founded in the 1960s.

R

RAF: see Rote Armee Fraktion.

RAM: see Revolutionary Action Movement.

Red Army (Rengo Sekigun) (United Red Army) (Japanese Red Army) (JRA): a left wing Japanese terrorist organization founded in 1969, aligned with the PFLP in the attack on Tel Aviv's Lod Airport in 1972.

Red Brigades: an Italian terrorist organization headed by Renato Curcio during the 1970s.

Red Cloud Group: a U.S. Indian terrorist organization during the 1970s.

Red Flag: a Venezuelan terrorist organization, active during the 1970s.

Red Guerrilla Family (RGF): The RGF was responsible for numerous bombings in the San Francisco area in the mid-1970s.

Red Hand Commandos: a Northern Ireland terrorist organization during the 1980s.

Red Panthers: a terrorist organization, active in Paris during the 1980s.

Red Placard: a terrorist organization, active in France during the 1980s.

Rengo Sekigun: see Red Army.

Republic of New Africa (RNA): A black militant group founded in 1968, mostly by former members of RAM. Eleven members were charged with murder and assault for sporadic violence in Mississippi in the summer of 1970.

Revolutionare Zellen (RZ): a West German terrorist organization.

Revolutionary Action Movement (RAM): Active on the East Coast between 1963 and 1968, RAM espoused a militant Black independence. Sixteen members were arrested and a large cache of weapons was seized in June 1967, by police in New York and Philadelphia. Later, four other members were arrested in Philadelphia for attempting to poison the water supply.

Revolutionary Anti-Capitalist Action: a terrorist organization, active in Greece during the 1980s.

Revolutionary Armed Action: a Portuguese terrorist organization active during the 1970s.

Revolutionary Armed Forces: a Guatemalan terrorist organization responsible for the 1970 kidnapping of a foreign minister.

Revolutionary Cells: a terrorist organization, active in West Germany during the 1980s.

Revolutionary Commandos for Solidarity: a Costa Rican terrorist organization during the 1970s.

Revolutionary Council: a terrorist organization active in Northern Africa during the 1970s.

Revolutionary Force 9: a terrorist organization responsible for the 1970 bombings of several corporate headquarters in New York City.

Revolutionary Force 7: a terrorist organization responsible for the 1970 bombing of several embassies in Washington, D.C.

Revolutionary Justice Organization: A pro-Iranian terrorist group responsible for the kidnappings of a television technician and a journalist in 1986.

Revolutionary Left Movement.

Revolutionary Movement: a Honduran terrorist organization during the 1980s.

Revolutionary Popular Forces - Lorenzo Zelaya.

Revolutionary Organization of the People in Arms: a Guatemalan terrorist organization during the 1980s.

Revolutionary Party of Central American Workers: a Latin American terrorist organization during the 1970s.

Revolutionary Popular Struggle: a terrorist organization responsible for numerous bombings in Greece during the 1980s.

Revolutionary Student Brigade: a U.S. terrorist organization, active on the East Coast during the 1970s.

Revolutionary Sympathizers Union: a Turkish terrorist organization during the 1980s.

RGF: see Red Guerrilla Family.

RNA: see Republic of New Africa.

Rote Armee Fraktion (RAF): a terrorist organization, dominated by the Baader-Meinhof Gang, in West Germany.

RZ: see Revolutionare Zellen.

S

S.A.O. Terrorists: a French terrorist organization founded in 1962.

Scottish National Liberation Army: a terrorist organization during the 1980s.

SDS: see Students for a Democratic Society.

Second of June Movement: a West German terrorist organization.

Secret Anti-Communist Army: A pro-government paramilitary "death squad" in El Salvador, that tortures and mutilates non-combative civilians.

Secret Army for the Liberation of Armenia: an Armenian terrorist organization during the 1980s.

Secret Army Organization (SAO): A reactionary group that harassed student protesters in Arizona and Southern California, the SAO was suspected of being funded by the FBI.

Secret Cuban Government: an anti-Castro terrorist organization, active in New York City during the 1970s.

SEEK: a student terrorist organization, perpetrating violence on several New York City campuses during the 1960s.

Self Defense Against All Authority: a French terrorist organization during the 1980s.

Sendero Luminoso (Shining Path): a Peruvian terrorist organization.

September 23 Communist League: A Mexican terrorist group responsible for murders and kidnappings during the 1970s.

Seventh Suicide Squad: a Greek terrorist group that claimed responsibility for a 1973 attack on Athens Airport.

Shield Society: A terrorist group of extreme nationalists, led by writer Yukio Mishima, in Japan during the 1960s.

Shining Path: see Sendero Luminoso.

Sidamo Liberation Movement: an Ethiopian terrorist organization during the 1980s.

Skinheads: a U.S. terrorist organization founded in 1988.

SLA: see Symbionese Liberation Army.

SNCC: see Student Nonviolent Coordinating Committee.

Socialist People's Movement: a right-wing terrorist organization, active in West German during the 1980s.

Socialist White People's Party: a reactionary terrorist organization active in Southern California during the 1970s.

Society for International Involvement: a terrorist organization, active in California during the 1970s.

Sons of Liberty: a terrorist organization active in the Boston area during the 1970s.

South Moluccas: a terrorist organization based in the Netherlands.

Southern Liberation Army (ELS): a Mexican terrorist organization.

Spanish Basque Battalion: a terrorist organization, active in Europe during the 1980s.

Stern Gang: see Lohame Herut Yisrael.

Student Nonviolent Coordinating Committee (SNCC): Originally formed in the 60s as a Southern voter registration group, SNCC through the leadership of Stokely Carmichael and H. Rap Brown emerged as one of the more strident advocates of Black equal rights. The group was involved in occasional violence, most often on college campuses in the 60s and early 70s.

Students for a Democratic Society (SDS): Founded in 1959 to influence the Democratic Party, SDS emerged as the foremost campus anti-war protest group of the 1960s. After a 1965 protest march, and the Spring 1968 occupation of Columbia University, the group splintered following the 1968 Democratic Convention in Chicago. The militant Weathermen was formed by members seeking a more immediate and less peaceful solution to national problems.

SWAPO: a South African terrorist organization during the 1980s.

Symbionese Liberation Army (SLA): Founded in 1973, the group was responsible for the murder of Oakland school superintendent Marcus Foster, before becoming nationally known for the Feb. 4, 1974 kidnapping of heiress Patricia Hearst. Six members died in a gun battle with Los Angeles police in May 1974, and the group dissipated after Bill and Emily Harris, and Patricia Hearst were apprehended in September, 1975.

T

Takfir Wal Hijra: an Egyptian terrorist organization, implicated in the assassination of President Anwar Sadat.

Tamil Eelam Liberation Organization (TELO): a terrorist organization headquartered in Sri Lanka.

The Movement For The Restoration of Democracy.

TELO: see Tamil Eelam Liberation Organization.

Terror Brigade: a Russian terrorist organization in 1905.

Third Force: a Protestant terrorist organization in Northern Ireland, during the 1980s.

Third Position: a terrorist organization, active in Padua during the 1980s.

3-X: a U.S. terrorist organization during the 1930s.

Thunderbolt: see As-Sa'iga.

TPLA: see Turkish People's Liberation Army.

TPLF: see Turkish People's Liberation Front.

Tupac Amaru Revolutionary Movement (MRTA): a Peruvian terrorist organization.

Tupamaros-Movimiento de Liberacion Nacional (MLN): an ultra-left Marxist terrorist organization based in Uruguay, Chile and Guatemala during the 1970s.

Turkish People's Liberation Army (TPLA): a Turkish militant terrorist organization founded in the 1970s.

Turkish People's Liberation Front (TPLF): a terrorist organization based in Turkey.

Turkish Revolutionary Left Group: a Turkish terrorist organization during the 1980s.

28 February Popular League: a Salvadoran terrorist organization during the 1980s.

23rd of September Communist League: a terrorist organization, active in Mexico during the 1970s.

U

UDA: see Ulster Defence Association.

UFF: see Ulster Freedom Fighters.

Ugandan Freedom Movement: an African terrorist organization, active during the 1980s.

Ugandan Patriotic Movement: an African terrorist organization during the 1980s.

Ulster Defence Association (UDA): a terrorist organization headquartered in Northern Ireland.

Ulster Freedom Fighters (UFF): a terrorist organization headquartered in Northern Ireland.

Ulster Volunteer Forces (UVF): a terrorist organization headquartered in Northern Ireland.

Umkonto Wesizwe: a terrorist faction of the African National Congress, active during the 1980s.

Union de Travailleurs Agricoles: a terrorist organization, active in Guadalupe, during the 1980s.

UNITA: an Angolan terrorist organization, active during the 1980s.

United Anti-Reelection Command: a left-wing terrorist organization in the Dominican Republic that kidnapped a U.S. military officer in 1970.

United Front for Guerrilla Action: a Colombian terrorist organization active during the 1970s.

United Front of the Revolution: a terrorist organization in Guatemala during the 1970s.

United Popular Liberation Army: a Mexican terrorist organization during the 1970s.

United Red Army: see Red Army.

United Revolutionary Front: a Guatemalan terrorist organization during the 1980s.

USBD: see German People's Socialist Movement.

U.S. Cultural Organization (US): A black power group best known for its' clashes with other black organizations in the late 1960s. They are accused of murdering at least three Black Panther members.

UVF: see Ulster Volunteer Forces.

V

Vanguard Group: a U.S. terrorist organization during the 1970s.

Vanguarda Armada Revolucionaria-Palmares: a terrorist organization that was formed by the merger of COLINA and VPR.

Vanguarda Popular Revolucionaria (VPR): a Brazilian terrorist organization, that participated in the 1970 kidnappings of the Japanese consul and the West German ambassador.

VAR-Palmares: see Vanguarda Armada Revolucionaria-Palmares.

Vieques Group: a Puerto Rican terrorist organization, active during the 1980s.

VPR: see Vanguarda Popular Revolucionaria.

W

Warriors of Christ the King: see Guerrilleros Del Cristo Rey.

Way of Eternal Bliss: a terrorist organization which hijacked a flight in Oslo, Norway in 1979.

Weathermen: a U.S. terrorist organization founded in the 1960s.

Weather Underground Organization Weathermen, (WU): Responsible for many terrorist bombings between 1969 and 1974, the WU was formed by former SDS members. In October 1969, they staged the Days of Rage protests in Chicago coinciding with the trial of the Chicago Seven, and shortly after, another protest after two Black Panther members were murdered. In 1970, three members were killed in their bomb factory in New York's Greenwich Village. The WU was responsible for nineteen bombings, including one at the U.S. Capitol in 1971, and the Pentagon in 1974.

White Panthers: a U.S. terrorist organization during the 1970s.

WOG: see Wrath of God.

Workers Army of the Welsh Republic: a terrorist organization, active in Wales during the 1980s.

Workers Autonomy: an Italian terrorist organization.

Workers Self Defense: a Colombian terrorist organization during the 1980s.

Wrath of God (WOG): a group of European Zionists, formed to avenge the Israeli massacre at the 1972 Olympics in Munich.

WU: see Weather Underground Organization.

Y

Young Croatian Republican Army: a terrorist organization during the 1970s.

Youth Action Group: a terrorist organization, active in Paris during the 1970s.

Youth Council: a black commando terrorist organization, active in Milwaukee during the 1960s.

Youth League to Crush the Y and P System: A terrorist group comprised of Japanese nationalists, who in 1977 seized the headquarters of Keidanren, a business and industry federation.

Young Lords: a New York City terrorist organization, comprised of Puerto Rican youths, during the late 1960s.

Z

Zapata Urban Front (ZUF): a terrorist organization.

Zapatista: see Frente Urbana Zapatista.

ZAPU Patriotic Front: a Zimbabwe terrorist organization, active during the 1980s.

Zengakuren: a Japanese terrorist organization comprised of left-wing students.

Zero: a pro-Castro terrorist organization, active in the Miami area during the 1970s.

ZUF: see Zapata Urban Front.

TOXICOLOGY (POISONINGS)

The study of poisons, their harmful long-term effects on the human body, and their legal control is known as toxicology. Standard classifications distinguish four categories of poisons according to their effects on the human body: (1) those that impair the blood's oxygen-carrying capacity (e.g., cyanide and carbon monoxide); (2) those which irreversibly damage the nervous system and hasten kidney failure (e.g., arsenic, mercury, antimony, and poisonous plants, such as hyoscine and strychnine); (3) those that burn the mouth or perforate the stomach (e.g., corrosive acids and alkaloids), and (4) those which destroy the blood and tissue but leave no trace of entry (e.g., ricin, nitrobenzene, and arsine).

There is a commonly held assumption that women are most likely to employ poison to eliminate an adversary or a husband. This stereotype was reinforced by such Victorian poisoners as Mary Ann Cotton, Cordelia Botkin, and Florence Maybrick, but women certainly had no monopoly on this deadly business. In fact, if there was any group that seemed to rely on deadly poisons to hasten a victim's demise, it was the medical profession. Such famous killers as Dr. Hawley Harvey Crippen, Neill Cream, and more recently Dr. Carl Coppolino, have been convicted of murder using toxic substances.

Statistics show that most fatal poisonings are accidental or suicidal. Indeed, less than 6 percent of all murders are attributable to poisoning. Still, the government of Britain, for example, has implemented strong measures to control the availability of dangerous chemicals to the public. The Pharmacy Act of 1852 limited the number of persons allowed to sell and dispense poison to the general public. In 1868 the act was further revised to require all pharmacists to keep accurate records showing the names of their customers who bought poison. The Pharmacy and Poisons Act of 1933 was the first tough measure aimed at controlling the manufacture, supply, storage, and distribution of poisons. The Dangerous Drugs Act of 1951 and subsequent measures passed in 1968 and 1971, have further curtailed the availability of poisons.

ACONITINE

Aconitine is derived from the leaves and root of wolfsbane or monkshood (*Aconitum napellus*). It was once used medicinally in liniments to relieve rheumatism, toothache, and neuralgia, but its extreme toxicity prevented any but minute doses. From fatal amounts (one to two milligrams), death usually occurs within eight minutes, during which the victim experiences numbness in the mouth, nausea, vomiting, and loss of vision and muscular strength. Death results from heart or respiratory failure as paralysis sets in. The drug can be administered internally or externally through the skin.

Aconitine has been used by murderers since ancient times. It was known to ancient Greek political figures as a means of eliminating rivals, and the Roman Emperor Trajan outlawed the growing of wolfsbane in gardens. As recently as a century ago, aconitine could not be traced in postmortem examination.

ADIPOCERE

When body fats solidify in a damp environment, adipocere, a yellow waxy substance is formed, and adheres to the skeletal structure. Through a process known as saponification, the neutral body fats are decomposed into a combination of fatty acids and soap. Adhering to the face, limbs, and chest wall, the adipocere keeps the body shape intact for years. Because of its preservation qualities, adipocere becomes a valuable tool for forensic scientists. In 1913, police solved the murders of two young brothers who were found at the bottom of a water-filled Scottish quarry. Analyzing their stomachs, preserved through adipocere, police were able to determine the time of death and their likely last meal. These determinations led to the arrest and conviction of the suspected murderer, the boys' widowed father.

ANTIMONY

A tasteless, colorless, odorless poison, antimony can cause death even though it has also been used for medicinal purposes. It can relieve constipation and dehydration, as well as cure fits of coughing. But taken in larger doses, antimony reduces respiratory action, causing a death similar to heart failure. When given to an unsuspecting victim, it is usually administered in the form of tarter emetic. Antimony is an irritant, similar to arsenic, and its symptoms are often misdiagnosed as gastroenteritis.

ARSENIC

Another poison known from ancient times, arsenic was the reason prominent Romans had food tasters. It was also the favorite murder weapon of the Borgias. Arsenic is a white, odorless powder that can pass for flour in a poisoner's pantry, and it is flavorless in a victim's food. During the industrial revolution, so many legitimate uses were found for it—in cosmetics, dyes, glassmaking, taxidermy, and poisons for household pests, for example—that it had a place in almost any 19th-century household. In addition, the primary symptoms of arsenic poisoning, vomiting, diarrhea, and, in chronic cases, discoloration and gastrointestinal pain, are common to so many other causes that murder by this means was easy to conceal.

James Marsh, an English chemist, discovered a method of tracing arsenic poisoning in 1836. It involved converting the arsenic in body tissues into arsine gas and collecting it on a piece of metal. The test detected down to a fiftieth of a milligram, and by measuring the amount of arsenic left in tissues pathologists could tell whether a person had been murdered by arsenic or not.

Development of the Marsh Test led to the Arsenic Act of 1851, which made the poison available only to persons over the age of twenty-one and personally known to the shopkeeper selling it. Purchases of arsenic were to be recorded in a poisons book, and the chemical itself had to be diluted with soot so that it couldn't be mistaken for a comestible.

The Marsh Test is still used by some toxicologists, although most prefer either the more easily conducted Reinsch or the Gutzeit tests.

The most famous of the many cases of arsenic poisoning was that of Napoleon I. Samples of his hair were subjected to the modern process of neutron activation in the 1950s and found to contain thirteen times the amount of trace arsenic normally found in human hair, strong evidence that he was probably murdered.

BACTERIAL POISONING

Exposing unsuspecting victims to germs has been under scrutiny since World War I. French financier Henri Girard killed Louis Pernotte in 1912 for an insurance benefit by causing him to contract typhoid, only to be "cured" with fatal doses of camomile. In 1918 Girard murdered a woman with poisoned mushrooms. After being taken into custody, he committed suicide with one of his concoctions. In 1915, Arthur Warren Waite, a dentist in New York, attempted to collect an inheritance by murdering his in-laws by poisoning them with a nasal spray containing anthrax, diphtheria, influenza, tuberculosis, and typhoid germs. Waite was caught and sent to the electric chair. Texas socialite Joan Robinson Hill was killed by her husband in 1969 with injections of human excretions mixed with antibiotics. John Hill was brought to trial by his second wife, but was shot to death before he could be convicted.

CHLOROFORM

A powerful narcotic discovered in 1831 in Germany by Baron von Liebig, chloroform is a clear and volatile liquid. Through internal consumption or inhalation as a vapor, its properties can cause stimulation similar to "glue sniffing," or ease irritations such as vomiting and coughing spells. In larger ingestions or inhalations, chloroform will cause death due to poisonous accumulations in the heart and liver. As a poison it can be detected by its powerful odor. Criminals often use a cloth soaked with chloroform to place over their victims' noses and mouths to temporarily disable them. When carefully monitored, chloroform is an excellent anaesthetic with few side effects.

CYANIDE

The ingestion of cyanide can cause death within ten seconds, a characteristic making it a favored poison for suicides. In the form of prussic acid, it interrupts the oxygen flow in the blood stream, weakening the pulse, causing convulsions, and paralyzing the respiratory core of the brain. Cyanide salts work a bit slower, reacting with the stomach's gastric juices to release a fatal hydrocyanic acid. Almonds, cherries, and peaches, as well as many leaves, contain cyanide as a natural vegetable acid. Indeed, the characteristic odor is that of bitter almonds, a smell that has alerted many a coroner that poison will be in the body's internal cavities. Splotchy pink areas of the skin are the only external evidence of cyanide poisoning. The fast-acting hydrogen cyanide is the favored gas in those states employing the gas chamber in the execution of death penalties.

DIGITALIS

Discovered in 1775 by an English physician named Dr. Withering, digitalis is an extract from the leaves of the poisonous purple foxglove plant. Taken in small doses, it can regulate the rhythm of the heart, but larger quantities will reduce the heart rate, causing cardiac arrest within three hours. Victims experience nausea, diarrhea, convulsions, disturbed vision, and respiratory problems.

HYOSCINE

Also known as scopolamine, hyoscine is a depressant taken from the leaves and seeds of henbane. It has medicinal purposes, such as soothing nerves and treating motion sickness. As medicine it is administered in small doses. In slightly larger doses, it also slows reflexes and causes hallucinations. Because individual sensitivity to hyoscine varies, it is difficult to prescribe a proper amount. In most cases a quarter to half a grain will be fatal.

The most famous case of hyoscine poisoning was that of Dr. H. H. Crippen, a British homeopath, who was hanged for his wife's murder in 1910. Crippen is remembered for having been the first fugitive apprehended due to transatlantic radio communications when he attempted to flee to the U.S. It has been suggested that he may not have intended to kill his wife, but misjudged the amount of the dangerous drug he gave her, and panicked when he found she had died.

INSULIN

A clear, colorless hormone, insulin is manufactured by the pancreas and secreted into one's bloodstream to regulate the amount of sugar. When an insulin deficiency occurs, the quantity of sugar increases causing diabetes. That person is prescribed commercial insulin, usually taken from the pancreas of an ox or pig. When properly administered, it will lower blood sugar levels for about five hours. But from larger doses, a person can lapse into a coma and die due to hypoglycemia. Symptoms of a blood sugar imbalance are dilated pupils, weakness, sweating accompanied by an ashen pallor, and lack of concentration.

LSD

Lysergic acid diethylamide, or LSD, is a powerful, toxic hallucinogen, twenty-five micrograms of which is enough to alter the brain's capacity to register sensory input accurately. One milligram may be enough to block vital functions sufficiently to cause death. It was discovered by a Swiss chemist in 1943. Despite its nonaddictiveness, LSD has a tendency to cause "flashbacks," momentary periods in which the user re-experiences the state of mind the drug has induced up to three weeks earlier.

One of LSD's most significant characteristics is its unpredictability, providing seemingly timeless euphoric visions one time and nightmarish morbidity another. Although its euphoric and hallucinatory properties caused it to be the center of a vogue of drug experimentation during the late 1960s, LSD has also been associated with psychotic and violent behavior in those on "bad trips."

MERCURY

While mercury has extensive agricultural and industrial uses, it is also poisonous and has been used in many murders and suicides. Mercury poisoning can be administered in a variety of ways, as its vapor can be inhaled, it can be absorbed through the skin, and it can be taken internally. It can also be fatal in various doses, causing different symptoms depending on whether a large dose is taken all at once, or whether tiny amounts accumulate chronically. As little as three to five grains can cause death by heart failure in a short time, but a chronic case features symptoms such as anemia, kidney failure, stomach problems, mercurial palsy, and gum shrinkage, the last of which leaves a distinctive, identifying mark on the gums.

MORPHINE

Discovered in 1806 by German chemist Friedrich Serturner, morphine is a powerful alkaloid of opium. Combined with water to form morphine hydrochloride, the liquid is administered with a syringe to those in great pain. However, the resultant addiction becomes a larger problem than the initial pain, as subsequent treatments require increasingly larger doses. Before lapsing into narcosis and a coma, the victim of morphine poisoning experiences a slower pulse, the lowering of body temperature, and the loss of reflex ability. Death is caused by respiratory failure. The victims pupils will be dilated, and the smell of morphine evident on their breath or in the contents of their stomachs.

PHOSPHORUS

Extremely volatile, phosphorus will ignite when exposed to air. It is a yellow, waxy material that glows in the dark, and must be kept under water. It has been used commercially as a rodent poison and as the activator on match sticks. A small dose in tea or medication can cause a slow death, preceded by the feeling of nausea and vomiting caused by internal hemorrhaging. Even if a victim survives an initial dosage, the symptoms can recur within a few days. The substance is revealed in autopsies by an acrid smell and a glow in bodily excretions. Nonfatal doses damage the liver and kidneys, cause sudden weight loss and anorexia, and necrosis in the jaw bone, which causes teeth to fall out.

RICIN

An extremely toxic substance, ricin is lethal enough for a single gram to kill more than 30,000 people. The castor-oil bean derivative was isolated during World War II. Its use has often been threatened in chemical warfare, although the World Health Organization warned of its dangers in 1970. Ricin is quickly absorbed into the bloodstream, causing red corpuscles to congeal and multiply, resulting in death due to toxemia. Victims usually succumb when a small pellet of ricin is prodded into their body. Bulgarian defector, Georgi Markov was killed in London on Sept. 7, 1978, after an assassin was thought to have poked him with an umbrella containing the minute pellet. He died four days later, after appearing to be suffering from the flu.

STRYCHNINE

An alkaloid extracted from the seeds of the East Indian tree, *Strychnos nux-vomica*, strychnine is a violent poison. Discovered in 1817, the colorless, crystalline powder is used medicinally as a stimulant for invalids with debilitating illnesses. Larger doses are absorbed quickly into the bloodstream, causing disruption to the central nervous system. The victim convulses, spasms occur, arching the spine and stiffening muscles, while breathing becomes difficult. One can die within an hour from respiratory paralysis or complete exhaustion. Strychnine has a bitter taste that must be disguised in a strong liquid if administered to an unsuspecting victim.

WAR CRIMES

A war crime is a violation of an existing international law or treaty that governs the conduct of opposing nations during time of war. Since the end of WWII, the term has connoted three major categories: (1) acts of aggression, waged by one nation against another for purposes of conquest; (2) persecution of a people for religious, ethnic, racial, or philosophical reasons before or during the actual war, including forced internment of civilians or acts of genocide; and (3) ill treatment, deportation, or murder of prisoners of war or civilians in an occupied territory.

These stipulations were established during the 1945 Nürnberg war crimes trials of Nazi leaders. Prior to this time, nations wrestled with this issue in an effort to find a workable set of rules to govern conduct in time of war. In antiquity there were rules to protect the lives of prisoners and government emissaries. During the Middle Ages, wars were often the result of religious and family differences, for which the church established the boundaries. In the 10th century, for example, the "Truce of God" provided church people, women, tradesmen, peasants, pilgrims, and livestock immunity on the Holy days and the Sabbath, and violations of this edict often resulted in excommunication.

By the 17th century international law had progressed to the point that ministers of nations could meet in a formal setting and promulgate workable codes. In 1625 the Dutch jurist Hugo Grotius drafted a landmark treatise, *De Jure Belli ac Paris* (On the Law of War and Peace), which distinguished just war from unjust war and attempted to set forth rules based on religious concepts and issues of national importance. In 1864 the first Red Cross convention was held, in which guidelines were established for the care and treatment of sick and wounded prisoners. Two years later, the St. Petersburg Declaration outlawed certain types of weapons. The next significant code came out of the Hague conferences of 1899 and 1907, which drafted laws governing naval and land warfare, some of which are still in effect today. The Kellogg-Briand Pact of 1928, which established the law making aggressive war illegal, was ratified by Germany in that year, thus forming the legal basis on which the Nazi war criminals were tried seventeen years later. The famous Geneva Convention of 1929 spelled out the proper treatment for prisoners of war. Meeting again in Geneva in 1949, delegates further resolved that wars of national liberation, civil wars, and guerrilla wars should be subject to the same code of conduct as those fought between nations.

A

Abetz, Heinrich Otto, 1903-58, Ger., ambassador in Paris, was sentenced in France to twenty years but was released in 1954. He died in an auto collision.

Abrial, Jean Marie, Fr., admiral, was tried at Versailles in 1946.

Altstötter, Josef, Ger., Justice Ministry official, was sentenced for being in a criminal organization by a U.S. military tribunal.

Ambros, Otto, Ger., I. G. Farben official, was sentenced by U.S. military tribunal.

Antonescu, Ion, 1882-1946, Rom., marshal, was executed.

Antonescu, Mihai, d.1946, Rom., was executed.

Artukovic, Andrija, 1900- , Croatian, minister of justice and internal affairs, came to America in 1948 and was under investigation in 1976 on suspicion of murdering thousands of Serbs, Jews, and Gypsies.

B

Bach, Erich von dem, Ger., chief of Anti-Partisan Units and Higher SS and Police Leader Russia Center, was sentenced by denazification court. In 1952, he criticized his past actions as mass murder and was sentenced in 1961 in Nuremburg for his participation in the 1934 purge.

Backe, Herbert, d.1947, Ger., Acting Food Minister, killed himself in 1947.

Baer, Richard, Ger., Auschwitz I commander, was arrested in 1961 after a reward for his capture was posted.

Baier, Hans, Ger., WVHA official, was sentenced by U.S. military tribunal.

Baky, Laszlo, d.1946, Hung., Interior Ministry official, was executed in Hungary.

Barbie, Klaus, 1913- , Fr., gestapo officer, was condemned in absentia in French court in 1954 for the torture death of DeGaulle's deputy Jean Moulin. He was extradited to France from Bolivia in 1983 and convicted of war crimes in 1987. He is now serving a life sentence.

Bardossy, Laszlo, d.1946, Hung., prime minister, was executed in Hungary.

Beckerle, Adolf Heinz, Ger., ambassador to Bulgaria and Police President of Frankfurt, was arrested in West Germany in 1960.

Berger, Friedrich, Ger., Gestapo intelligence officer in France.

Berger, Gottlob, 1897-1975, Ger., SS official, was sentenced to twenty-five years by U.S. tribunal, but his sentence was reduced to ten years by Clemency Board.

Best, Robert H., Am., broadcaster, was convicted of treason and sentenced to life by American court in 1948. During the war he had made radio appearances to disseminate Nazi propaganda and undermine American morale.

Best, Werner, Ger., Plenipotentiary in Denmark, was sentenced to death in Denmark, but he was released in 1951.

Biberstein, Ernst, Ger., Einsatzgruppe C official, was condemned to death by U.S. military tribunal, but the sentence was commuted to life by Clemency Board.

Biebow, Hans, d.1947, Ger., Lodz ghetto administration official, was executed in Poland.

Blaskowitz, Johannes, 1883-1948, Ger., field marshal, killed himself during his trial for murdering civilians and prisoners of war in Poland.

Blobel, Paul, d.1951, Ger., Einsatzgruppe C official, was executed.

Blome, Kurt, Ger., Party Main Office Health official, was acquitted by U.S. military tribunal.

Blume, Walter, Ger., Einsatzgruppe B official, was condemned to death by U.S. military tribunal, but the sentence was commuted to life by Clemency Board.

Bobermin, Hans, Ger., WVHA official, was sentenced by U.S. military tribunal. His sentence was reduced by the tribunal, and he was freed by the Clemency Board in 1951.

Boger, Wilhelm, 1907- , Ger., Auschwitz intelligence officer, was sentenced to life in German court in 1965.

Böhme, Franz, Ger., Military Commander in Serbia, committed suicide while under indictment at Nuremburg.

Bormann, Martin Ludwig, 1900-c. 1945, Ger., Party Chancellor, is believed to have been killed in the Battle of Berlin in 1945, but rumors have persisted for decades that he escaped and stills lives in a South American jungle fortress. He was found guilty in absentia and condemned at Nuremberg.

Böttcher, Herbert, d.1950, Ger., SS and Police Leader in Radom, Poland, was extradited from British zone in Germany to Poland in 1947 and hanged.

Bouhler, Philipp, d.1945, Ger., Führer Chancellory official, committed suicide.

Brack, Viktor, d.1948, Ger., Führer Chancellory official, was condemned to death by U.S. military tribunal and executed.

Brandt, Karl, d.1948, Ger., Plenipotentiary for Health, was condemned to death by U.S. military tribunal and executed.

Brandt, Rudolf, d.1948, Ger., secretary of Heinrich Himmler, was condemned to death by U.S. military tribunal and executed.

Brauchitsch, Heinrich Alfred Hermann Walter von, 1881-1948, Ger., Commander-in-Chief of the army, died in a British army hospital while awaiting trial.

Braune, Werner, d.1951, Ger., Einsatzgruppe D official, was sentenced to death by U.S. military tribunal and executed.

Braunsteiner-Ryan, Hermine, Ger., Majdanek prison guard, married an American GI at the end of the war and lived in America until her 1973 extradition to West Germany, where she was sentenced to life.

Brinon, Fernand de, d.1947, Fr., Vichy official, was executed by firing squad.

Brunner, Alois, Ger., SS deportation expert in France, Salonika, and Slovakia, remains missing.

Bruno, Karl, 1911- , Yug., was a Belgrade merchant who accepted a store confiscated from a Jewish merchant. He was ordered to pay reparation by an American court in 1980.

Buhler, Joseph, d.1948, Ger., Generalgouvernement official, was executed in Poland.

Bunke, Heinrich, Ger., doctor, was convicted in Frankfurt in 1987 of taking part in euthanasia of the handicapped in 1940-41.

Bütefisch, Heinrich, Ger., I. G. Farben official, was sentenced by U.S. military tribunal.

C

Calotescu, Corneliu, Rom., Governor of Bukovina, was condemned to death in Romania, but King Mihai granted an indefinite stay of execution.

Caruso, Pietro, d.1944, Italian, police chief of Rome, was executed by firing squad.

Catlos, Josef, Slovakian war minister, deserted to insurgent territory in 1944 and was reportedly killed by the Soviets.

Chack, Paul, 1876-1945, Fr., collaborator, was charged with and convicted of creating pro-nazi propaganda during the occupation and executed.

Christov, Dmitri, Bul., interior minister, killed himself when Turkey refused him entry.

Clauberg, Carl, d.1957, Ger., medical experimenter at Auschwitz, was released by Soviets in 1955. Clauberg died of apoplexy while awaiting trial.

Clodius, Karl, Ger., economist, was jailed in USSR.

Cubage, Granville, Am., serviceman, was accused in 1946 of having abused prisoners.

D

Daluege, Kurt, d.1946, Ger., ORPO and Protektorat official, was executed in Czechoslovakia.

Dannecker, Theodor, Ger., SS deportation expert in France and Bulgaria, remains missing.

Darnand, Joseph, d.1945, Fr., chief of Vichy police, was executed by firing squad.

Delfau, Denise, Fr., collaborator, was tried in 1952.

Demjanjuk, John (Ivan Demjanjuk), 1921- , Pol., came to America in 1952, but was brought under suspicion in 1974 when a death camp guard's identity card bearing his name was found in Soviet archives. He lost his U.S. citizenship in 1981 and was deported to Israel for trial in 1986. In 1988 he was sentenced to hang for running the gas chamber at Treblinka.

Detlavs, Karlis, Latvian, came to America in 1950 and faced deportation proceedings in 1976 due to accusations of transporting Latvian Jews.

Deutscher, Albert, d.1981, Ger., took American citizenship after the war and lived in Brookfield, Ill., until he was accused of membership in a Nazi paramilitary group during the war. He was hit by a train and killed the day of the accusation.

Dietrich, Joseph (Sepp Dietrich), b. 1893, Ger., commander of Hitler's bodyguards, was sentenced by International Military Tribunal to twenty-five years. After his release in 1955, he stood trial again for political murders committed in 1934 and was sentenced to eighteen months.

Dietrich, Otto, Ger., Hitler's press secretary, was sentenced at Nuremberg in 1949.

Doihara Kenji, d.1948, general, condemned by International Military Tribunal and hanged.

Dönitz, Karl Doenitz, 1891-1980, Ger., president, minister of war, succeeded Hitler as Führer and surrendered to end the war in Europe. He was sentenced by International Military Tribunal and freed from prison in 1956. He published his memoirs in 1958.

Dostler, Anton, d.1945, Ger., general, was condemned by U.S. military tribunal and shot.

Dürrfeld, Walter, Ger., Auschwitz official, was sentenced by U.S. military tribunal.

E

Eichmann, Karl Adolf, 1906-62, Ger., SS official, escaped from internment camp in U.S. zone in 1946. He was captured by Israeli agents in Argentina in 1960, and was executed in Israel.

Eirenschmalz, Franz, Ger., WVHA official, was condemned to death by U.S. military tribunal. The sentence was commuted to nine years by Clemency Board.

Endre, Laszlo, d.1946, Hung., interior minister, was executed in Hungary.

Ennis, Leonard, Am., serviceman, was accused in 1946 of having abused prisoners.

Epp, Franz von, Ger., Bavarian political leader, was arrested in Austria in 1945.

F

Falkenhausen, Alexander von, Ger., Military Commander in Belgium, was sentenced in Belgium to twelve years, but was released in 1951.

Fanslau, Heinz, Ger., WVHA official, was sentenced by U.S. military tribunal.

Fellgiebel, Erich, d.1944, Ger., OKW official, was purged and executed.

Felmy, Helmut, Ger., was sentenced by U.S. military tribunal and released in 1952.

Fendler, Lothar, Ger., Einsatzgruppe C official, was sentenced by U.S. military tribunal.

Ferenczy, Laszlo, d.1946, Hung., Gendarmerie official, was executed in Hungary.

Filov, Bogdan, d.1945, Bul., prime minister, was executed in Bulgaria.

Finta, Imre, Hung., lived in Canada after WW II until he was brought to trial in Toronto in 1989 for transporting Hungarian Jews in 1944.

Fischer, Franz, Ger., SS sergeant major, was sentenced to life at Nuremberg in 1946 for transporting Dutch Jews. He was released in 1989.

Fischer, Ludwig, d.1947, Ger., Gouverneur of Warsaw, was executed in Poland.

Flick, Friedrich, Ger., Mitteldeutsche Stahlwerke official, was sentenced by U.S. military tribunal.

Forster, Albert, d.1948, Ger., Gauleiter of Danzig-West Prussia, was executed in Poland.

Frank, August, Ger., WVHA official, was sentenced to life by U.S. military tribunal. The sentence was reduced to fifteen years by the Clemency Board.

Frank, Hans, 1900-1946, Ger., generalgouverneur, was sentenced to death by International Military Tribunal and hanged.

Frank, Karl-Hermann, d.1946, Ger., protektorat official, was executed in Czechoslovakia.

Frauenfeld, Alfred, Ger., Generalkommissar of Melitopol, was arrested for neo-Nazi activities and freed after investigation by a German court in 1953.

Freisler, Roland, d.1944, Ger., justice ministry official, was reported killed in an air raid.

Frey, Willi, 1924-47, Ger., secret service officer, was hanged.

Frick, Wilhelm, 1877-1946, Ger., interior minister and reichsprotektor of Bohemia and Moravia, was sentenced to death by International Military Tribunal and hanged.

Friedenberg, Hans Georg von, d.1945, admiral, took poison after surrendering to Sir Bernard Montgomery.

Fritzsche. Hans, 1899-1953, Ger., propaganda deputy to Göbbels, was acquitted at Nuremberg in 1946, but sentenced to nine years by a German court. He was released in 1950.

Fuenten, Ferdinand aus der, Ger., SS officer, was sentenced to life at Nueremberg for transporting Dutch Jews. He was released after forty-three years in 1989.

Funk, Walther, 1890-1960, Ger., Economy Minister, was discovered hiding among Japanese embassy personnel and sentenced to life by International Military Tribunal. He was released in 1957 for health reasons.

Fünten, Ferdinand aus der, Ger., official in Central Office for Jewish Emigration in Holland, was condemned to death in the Netherlands. His sentence was commuted to life in 1951 after alleged intervention by Konrad Adenaur.

G

Gebhardt, Karl, d.1948, Ger., SS chief clinician, was sentenced to death by U.S. military tribunal and hanged.

Genzken, Karl, Ger., SS medical officer, was sentenced to life by U.S. military tribunal. His sentence was reduced to twenty years by Clemency Board.

Globocnik, Odilo, d.1945, Pol., SS and Police Leader of Lublin, killed himself.

Glücks, Richard, Ger., WVHA official, remains missing.

Göbbels, Paul Josef Goebbels, 1897-1945, Ger., Propaganda Minister and Gauleiter of Berlin, killed himself.

Göring, Hermann Wilhelm Goering, 1893-1946, Ger., head of storm troopers, killed himself while under sentence of death by Nuremberg court.

Grabowsky, Peter, Bul., minister of interior, reputedly persecuted Jews and was expelled from Turkey in September 1944.

Grawitz, Ernst, d.1945, Ger., SS Reich physician, killed himself.

Greifelt, Ulrich, d.1949, Ger., Main Office official, was sentenced to life by U.S. military tribunal.

Greiser, Artur, d.1946, Ger., Gauleiter of Wartheland, was executed in Poland.

Grese, Irma, 1923-45, Ger., Auschwitz administrator, was sentenced to death by British court and executed.

Günther, Rolf, Ger., RSHA official, is missing but believed to be dead.

H

Hácha, Emil, 1872-1945, Ger., president of Czechoslovakia and jurist, died while awaiting trial.

Haensch, Walter, Ger., Einsatzgruppe C official, was sentenced to death by U.S. military tribunal. The sentence was reduced by Clemency Board to fifteen years.

Halder, Franz, Ger., 1884-1972, General Staff chief, was indicted before a Bavarian denazification court, but exonerated in 1948.

Handloser, Siefried, Ger., Armed Forces Medical Service chief, was sentenced to life by U.S. military tribunal. His sentence was reduced to twenty years by Clemency Board.

Hartjenstein, Fritz, Ger., Auschwitz administrator, was sentenced to life by British court. None of the charges brought against him involved his activities at Auschwitz.

Haussmann, Emil, d.1948, Ger., major, killed himself midway through his trial.

Hazners, Vilis, Latvian, came to America in 1956 and was under investigation in 1976 on suspicion of taking part in Latvian police atrocities.

Heissmayer, Josef Heiszmaier, Ger., head of ubergestapo, was arrested in 1948 and sentenced in 1949.

Henlein, Konrad, 1898-1945, Ger., Sudetenland gauleiter, killed himself upon capture.

Hess, Rudolf (Walther Richard Rudolf Hess), 1894-1987, Ger., deputy führer, was sentenced to life in Spandau prison, where he died at 93.

Heydrich, Reinhardt Tristan Eugen (AKA: **der Henker**), 1904-42, Ger., RSHA official and reichsprotektor, was assassinated in Prague. In retaliation for his death, Lidice, Czech., was destroyed by Nazis.

Hildebrandt, Richard, Ger., RuSHA chief and higher SS and police leader of Danzig, was sentenced by U.S. military tribunal to twenty-five years, but was reportedly free in 1955.

Himmler, Heinrich, 1900-45, Ger., head of SS and gestapo, killed himself upon capture by British officials.

Hindenburg, Oskar von, d.1960, Ger., commander of prisoner of war camps in East Prussia, was fined by denazification courts.

Hirota Koki, d.1948, Japanese, premier 1936-37, was condemned by

International Military Tribunal and hanged.

Hirt, August, Ger., medical officer, ran a laboratory at Struthof-Natzweiler where people were experimented on.

Hitler, Adolf, 1889-1945, Ger., chancellor, killed himself at the end of the war.

Hoffman, Heinrich, Ger., Hitler's photographer, aided the prosecution at Nuremberg, but was sentenced to ten years in denazification court for profiteering on photographs of Hitler.

Höfle, Hans, Ger., SS and Police Leader in Lublin, was reportedly under arrest in Salzburg, Austria, in 1961.

Höfle, Hermann, Ger., Higher SS and Police Leader in Slovakia, was sentenced to death in Czechoslovakia in 1948.

Hofmann, Otto, Ger., RuSHA official, was sentenced to twenty-five years by U.S. military tribunal. The sentence was reduced to fifteen years by Clemency Board.

Hohberg, Hans, Ger., WVHA official, was sentenced to ten years by U.S. military tribunal. The sentence was reduced by Clemency Board in 1951 to time served.

Homma Masaharu (Honma), Japanese, general, was convicted by U.S. Military Tribunal and executed, primarily for his role in the Bataan Death March.

Höppner, Erich, d.1944, Ger., commander of Fourth Panzer Army, Army Group North, was purged and executed during the war.

Höss, Rudolf Francis Ferdinand Hoess, 1900-47, Pol., Auschwitz commander and deputy inspector of all concentration camps, was hanged in Auschwitz on a gallows constructed to face the camp crematoria.

Hössler, Franz, d.1945, Ger., Auschwitz administrator, was condemned to death by a British court and executed.

Hoth, Hermann, Ger., commander of Panzer Group 3, Army Group Center, and commander of 17th Army, Army Group South, was sentenced by U.S. military tribunal.

Houdremont, Eduard, Ger., Krupp Essen official, was sentenced to ten years by U.S. military tribunal. His sentence was reduced by Clemency Board in 1951 to time served.

Hoven, Waldemar, d.1948, Ger., Buchenwald camp doctor, was condemned by U.S. military tribunal and executed.

Hunsche, Otto, Ger., RSHA official, was captured in Frankfurt in 1957, tried twice, and ultimately acquitted.

I

Ihn, Max Otto, Ger., Krupp personnel officer, was sentenced to nine years by U.S. military tribunal. The sentence was reduced by Clemency Board to time served in 1951.

Ilgner, Max, Ger., I. G. Farben official, was sentenced by U.S. military tribunal.

Imredy, Béla, 1891-1946, Ger., economy minister, was executed in Hungary.

Ishii Shiro, Japanese, medical experimenter, ran a chemical warfare installation and concentration camp in Pingfan, Manchuria from 1937-45, where he experimented on prisoners of war. He plea bargained with U.S. officials in 1947 to give information on the camp in return for safety for himself and his staff.

Isopescu, Modest, Rom., Transnistrian official, was condemned to death in Romania, but King Mihai granted an indefinite stay of execution was granted.

Itagaki Seishiro, d.1948, Japanese, war minister, was condemned by International Military Tribunal and hanged.

J

Jarosz, Andor, d.1946, Hung., interior minister, was executed in Hungary.

Jeckeln, Friedrich, d.1946, Ger., SS and Police Leader in Ostland, was executed in the USSR.

Jodl, Alfred, 1890-1946, Ger., headed German operations personnel, was sentenced to death by International Military Tribunal and hanged.

Jost, Heinz, Ger., Einsatzgruppe A commander, was sentenced to life by U.S. military tribunal. His sentence was reduced to ten years by Clemency Board.

Joyce, William, AKA: "Lord Haw-Haw", Brit., broadcaster who made propaganda to undermine British morale, was under sentence of death in 1945.

K

Kaduk, Oswald, Ger., Auschwitz guard, served nine years in East Germany and was then tried in West Germany in 1964.

Kairys, Luidas, Lithuanian, gained U.S. citizenship in 1957 but was tried in 1982 for being a member of the SS Wachmannschaft and a guard at Treblinka.

Kaltenbrunner, Ernst, d.1946, Ger., RSHA official, was condemned by International military tribunal and hanged.

Kaminskas, Bronius, Lithuanian, came to America in 1947 and was investigated in 1976 on suspicion of shooting 200 people and transporting 400 others.

Kammler, Hans, Ger., WVHA official, reportedly killed himself in 1945.

Kappler, Herbert, Ger., SS and police official in Rome, was sentenced to life by an Italian military court.

Kasche, Siegfried, d.1947, Ger., Minister to Croatia, was executed in Yugoslavia.

Kastner, Rudolf, Hung., Isr., accused collaborator, brought suit for libel against his accuser in Israeli court in 1955. (He had attempted to save lives by dealing with the Nazis; no charges were brought against him.)

Katzmann, Fritz, d.1957, Ger., SS and Police Leader in Galicia, died in Darmstadt.

Kehrl, Hans, Ger., economy and armament ministry official, was sentenced to fifteen years by U.S. military tribunal. In 1951, the sentence was reduced by Clemency Board to time served.

Keitel, Wilhelm, 1882-1946, Ger., field marshal, was condemned by International military tribunal and hanged.

Kemeny, Baron Gabor, Hung., foreign minister, was arrested in 1945.

Keppler, Wilhelm, Ger., economic advisor and Foreign Office official, was sentenced to ten years by U.S. military tribunal. In 1951, the sentence was reduced by Clemency Board to time served.

Kesselring, Albert, 1885-1960, Ger., field marshal, was condemned by a British court, but his sentence was commuted to life, then reduced to 21 years. He was released in 1952.

Kiefer, Max, Ger., WVHA official, was sentenced to life by U.S. military tribunal, which then reduced the sentence to twenty years. It was further reduced by Clemency Board in 1951 to time served.

Killinger, Manfred von, d.1944, Ger., minister to Romania, killed himself in Bucharest.

Kimura Heitaro, d.1948, Japanese, general, was condemned by International Military Tribunal and hanged.

Klein, Fritz, d.1945, Ger., Auschwitz camp doctor, was condemned by British court and executed.

Kleist, Ewald von, Ger., Panzer Group 1, Army Group South officer, was extradited in 1949 from Yugoslavia to the USSR, where he was reported to have died in 1954.

Klemm, Herbert, Ger., Justice Ministry official, was sentenced to life by U.S. military tribunal. The sentence was reduced by Clemency Board to twenty years.

Klingelhöfer, Waldemar, Ger., Vorkommando Moskau officer, was condemned by U.S. military tribunal, but his sentence was commuted to life by Clemency Board.

Klingenfuss, Karl Otto, Ger., Foreign Office official, was reported in Argentina in 1951. West Germany's request for his extradition from Argentina was reportedly rejected in 1958.

Klopfer, Gerhard, Ger., Party Chancellory official, was reportedly at liberty in 1960.

Knochen, Helmut, Ger., BdS France official, was condemned in France in 1954, but in 1958 his sentence was commuted to life.

Koch, Erich, Ger., reichskommissar in the Ukraine, was seized by the British in 1949 and extradited to Poland in 1950. He was brought to trial in 1958 and sentenced to death in 1959, but his execution was indefinitely postponed due to ill health.

Koch, Heinz Hermann, Ger., military officer, was tried by USSR court at Minsk in 1946 for personally executing 5000 people.

Koppe, Wilhelm, Ger., Generalgouvernement official and Higher SS and Police Leader in Wartheland, spent the postwar years as director of a chocolate factory in Bonn until his arrest in 1960.

Korechika Anami, d.c.1945, Japan, war minister, was reportedly allowed to commit hara-kiri.

Körner, Paul, Ger., Four-Year Plan official, was sentenced to fifteen years by U.S. military tribunal, but in 1951 the sentence was reduced by Clemency Board to time served.

Korschan, Heinrich Leo, Ger., Krupp Markstadt official, was sentenced to six years by U.S. military tribunal. In 1951 the sentence was reduced by Clemency Board to time served.

Kowalczuk, Mikola, Ukrainian, came to America in 1950. He and his brother Serge were under investigation in 1976 on suspicion of murder in Lubomil, Ukraine.

Kowalczuk, Serge, Ukrainian, came to America in 1950. He and his brother Mikola were under investigation in 1976 on suspicion of murder in Lubomil, Ukraine.

Kramer, Josef, d.1945, Ger., Auschwitz II and Bergen-Belsen commander, was condemned by British court and executed.

Krauch, Carl, Ger., General Plenipotentiary of the Chemical Industry, was sentenced by U.S. military tribunal.

Krosigk, Schwerin von, Ger., Finance Minister, was sentenced to ten years by U.S. military tribunal. In 1951 his sentence was reduced by Clemency Board to time served.

Krüger, Friedrich, Ger., Higher SS and Police Leader and Generalgouvernement official, was reportedly killed in action in 1945.

Krumey, Hermann, Ger., Einsatzkommando Eichmann, was pronounced a lesser offender by a denazification court in 1948, but was reportedly under arrest again in 1958.

Krupp, Alfried, Ger., munitions manufacturer who used concentration camp prisoners to staff his factories, was sentenced by U.S. military tribunal to twelve years and deprivation of property. The Clemency Board reduced his sentence to time served and gave him back his money.

Kube, Wilhelm, d.1943, Ger., Generalkommissar of Byelorussia, was assassinated.

Küchler, Georg von, Ger., 18th Army and Army Group North commander, was sentenced by U.S. military tribunal to twenty years. His sentence was reduced to twelve years by Clemency Board due to his age.

Kuntze, Walter, Ger., Commander-in-chief of the Southeast, was sentenced to life by U.S. military tribunal.

Kvaternik, Eugen, Croatian, Interior Ministry official, was reported in Argentina in 1950.

L

Lages, Willy, Ger., Security Police and SD official in Amsterdam, was sentenced to death in the Netherlands in 1949, but the sentence was commuted to life in 1952.

Laipenieks, Edgars, Latvian, police official, came to America in 1960 and was under investigation in 1976 for taking part in murders in Riga prison in 1941.

Lammers, Hans Heinrich, Ger., Reich Chancellory official, was sentenced to twenty years by U.S. military tribunal in 1949. The sentence was reduced to ten years by Clemency Board, and he was released in 1952.

Landfried, Friedrich, d.1953, Ger., Economy Ministry official, was released from custody due to his mental condition.

Lange, Otto, Ger., KdS official in Latvia, was said to have escaped from British detention to Buenos Aires in 1949.

Lantier, Germain, Fr., Gestapo agent, deserted from the French army and defected, rising to a Lieutenancy in the Gestapo. He escaped from a military hospital at the end of the war, was condemned in absentia for treason, and was recaptured in 1951.

Lanz, Hubert, Ger., 22nd Corps officer in Greece and Hungary, was sentenced to twelve years by U.S. military tribunal. In 1951 his sentence was reduced by Clemency Board to time served.

Laval, Pierre, 1883-1945, Fr., Premier, was executed for treason.

Leeb, Wilhelm von, Ger., Army Group North commander, was sentenced by U.S. military tribunal.

Ley, Robert, 1890-1945, Ger., labor minister and head of Nazi party, was indicted for war crimes. He committed suicide on October 25, 1945, before coming to trial.

Lie, Jonas, d.1945, Nor., police chief, killed himself.

Liebenhenschel, Arthur, d.1948, Ger., Auschwitz commander, was condemned and executed in Poland.

Lindow, Kurt, Ger., RSHA official, was arrested by German officials in 1950 but apparently not brought to trial.

Linkomies, Edwin, Fin., premier, was sought as a war criminal by USSR in 1944.

Linnas, Karl, Estonian, came to America in 1951 and took citizenship in 1960. He was under investigation in 1976 on suspicion of administering a concentration camp at Tartu, Estonia. He was condemned by Soviet court in absentia in 1962.

List, Siegmund Wilhelm Walther, 1880-1971, Ger., Southeast Wehrmacht commander, was sentenced to life by U.S. military tribunal, but released on medical parole in 1951.

Löhr, Alexander, d.1945, Ger., Southeast Army Group E officer, was executed in Yugoslavia.

Lohse, Hinrich, Ger., Ostland Reichskommissar, was sentenced to ten years by denazification court, but he was released in 1951 due to ill health.

Lorenz, Werner, Ger., VOMI official, was sentenced by U.S. military tribunal to twenty years. The sentence was reduced to fifteen years by Clemency Board.

Lorkovic, d.1944, Croatian, Foreign Minister, was purged and executed by Croatian government.

Lörner, Georg, Ger., WVHA official, was sentenced to death by U.S. military tribunal, which then commuted the sentence to life. The Clemency Board reduced that sentence to fifteen years. He was released in 1954, and then was acquitted by a Bavarian denazification court.

Lörner, Hans, Ger., WVHA official, was sentenced to ten years by U.S. military tribunal. In 1951 the sentence was reduced by Clemency Board to time served.

Löser, Ewald, Ger., Krupp official, was sentenced to seven years by U.S. military tribunal. In 1951 the sentence was reduced by Clemency Board to time served.

Ludin, Hans Elard, Ger., Minister to Slovakia, was sentenced to death in Czechoslovakia in 1946.

M

Mach, Sano, Slovakian, interior minister, was sentenced in Czechoslovakia to 30 years.

Mackensen, Eberhard von, Ger., commander in Rome, was sentenced to death by a British court, but was released in 1952.

Macs, Edmund Gustav, Latvian, came to America in 1949 and was under investigation in 1976 on suspicion of murder in Lumbazu, Latvian.

Maelzer, Kurt, Ger., former Italian general and governor of Rome, was condemned in Rome in 1946.

Maikovskis, Boleslavs, Latvian, police official, entered United States in 1951. He was under investigation in 1976 for transporting Jews in 1941-43. He was also condemned in absentia by Soviet court in 1965.

Manstein, Fritz Erich von AKA: Lewinski, 1887-1973, Ger., field marshal, was sentenced to eighteen years by a British court, but the sentence was reduced to twelve years and he was released in 1952.

Marquis, André, Fr., admiral, was tried for conspiracy at Versailles in 1946.

Matsui Iwane, d.1948, Japanese, general, was condemned by International Military Tribunal and hanged.

Maurras, Charles, Fr., collaborator, was sentenced to life at hard labor in 1945.

Mengele, Josef, d.1979, Ger., Auschwitz camp doctor, was protected from extradition to West Germany from Argentina in 1959 and 1960, and was subsequently reported in hiding in Brazil and Argentina. He drowned in the Atlantic Ocean off the coast of South America.

Merten, Max, Ger., Chief of military administration in Salonika, was not arrested until 1959, when he was sentenced to twenty-five years. He was released before conclusion of the indemnification agreement between West Germany and Greece the same year.

Meyer, Alfred, d.1945, Ger., East Ministry official, killed himself.

Meyer, Kurt, Ger., major general, was condemned to firing squad by a Canadian court in 1946.

Mihailovich, Draja, Yug., war minister, was held for trial in 1945.

Milch, Eberhard, 1892-1972, Ger., Air Force and Jägerstab officer, was sentenced to life by U.S. military tribunal. The sentence was reduced to fifteen years by Clemency Board.

Mrugowsky, Joachim, d.1948, Ger., SS Hygienic Institute chief, was condemned by U.S. military tribunal and executed.

Müller, Erich, Ger., Krupp official, was sentenced to twelve years by U.S. military tribunal. In 1951 the sentence was reduced by Clemency Board to time served

Müller, Heinrich, Ger., RSHA official, remains missing.

Mummenthey, Karl, Ger., WVHA official, was sentenced to life by U.S. military tribunal, but the sentence was reduced to twenty years by Clemency Board.

Mussert, Anton, Dutch, Nazi leader, was jailed at The Hague in 1945.

Muto Akira, d.1948, Japanese, general, was condemned by International Military Tribunal and hanged.

N

Naumann, Erich, d.1951, Ger., Einsatzgruppe B commander, was condemned by U.S. military tribunal and executed.

Nedic, Milan, Serbian, head of state, killed himself.

Neubacher, Hermann, d.1960, Ger., mayor of Vienna and Southeast Economic Plenipotentiary, was sentenced in Yugoslavia to twenty years but was granted amnesty after seven years.

Neurath, Konstantin von (Constatin), 1873-1956, Ger., Foreign Minister and Reichsprotektor, was sentenced to fifteen years by International Military Tribunal but released in 1954.

Noske, Gustav, 1868-1946, Ger., defense minister, was sentenced to life by U.S. military tribunal, but the sentence was reduced to ten years by Clemency Board.

Novak, Franz, Ger., RSHA official, was arrested in Vienna in 1961 shortly after a reward was offered by the State Prosecutor in Frankfurt.

O

Oberg, Karl Albrecht, Ger., SS and police leader in Galicia and Higher SS and Police Leader in France, was sentenced to death in France in 1954, but the sentence was commuted to life in 1958.

Ohlendorf, Otto, d.1951, Ger., Einsatzgruppe D commander, was condemned by U.S. military tribunal and executed.

Okawa Shunei, Japanese, railroad agent of Manchuria, was tried by International Military Tribunal in Tokyo in 1946.

Oshima Hiroshi, Japanese, ambassador to Germany, was tried by International Military Tribunal in Tokyo in 1946.

Ott, Adolf, Ger., Einsatzgruppe B official, was sentenced to death by U.S. military tribunal, but the sentence was commuted to life by Clemency Board.

P

Panzinger, Friedrich, d.1959, Ger., RSHA official, was released from Soviet captivity in 1955. He collapsed and died in his Munich apartment when West German police came to arrest him.

Papen, Franz von, 1879-1969, Ger., diplomat and deputy chancellor, was acquitted at Nuremberg in 1945 but sentenced to eight years by a German court. On appeal in 1949, he was released and fine His memoirs were published in 1952.

Pavelic, Ante, d.1959, Croatian, head of state, was in Argentina until 1957, but died in Madrid.

Pétain, Henri Philippe, 1856-1951, Fr., Marshal of France, was arrested in absentia by France in 1944, condemned in person in 1945, but had his sentence commuted to life in solitary confinement. He was never released.

Pleiger, Paul, Ger., Hermann Göring Works official, was sentenced by U.S. military tribunal to fifteen years. The sentence was reduced to nine years by Clemency Board.

Pohl, Oswald, d.1951, Ger., WVHA official, was condemned by U.S. military tribunal and executed.

Pokorny, Adolf, Ger., sterilization plan author, was acquitted by U.S. military tribunal.

Pook, Hermann, Ger., WVHA official, was sentenced by U.S. military tribunal, but the sentence was reduced in 1951 by Clemency Board to time served.

Prützmann, Hans, d.1945, Ger., Ukraine Higher SS and Police Leader, killed himself.

Puhl, Emil, Ger., Reichsbank official, sentenced by U.S. military tribunal.

R

Rademacher, Karl, Ger., Foreign Office official, was arrested by German authorities in 1949 and sentenced in March, 1952, but skipped bail that August and was reported to have arrived in South America the following month. He was reported to be in Egypt in 1959.

Radetzky, Waldemar von, Ger., Einsatzgruppe B official, was sentenced by U.S. military tribunal to twenty years. In 1951 the sentence was reduced by Clemency Board to time served.

Raeder, Erich, 1876-1960, Ger., grand admiral, was sentenced to life in 1946 for rebuilding the German navy in the 1930s in contravention of the Treaty of Versailles. He was released due to poor health in 1955.

Rasch, Otto, Ger., Einsatzgruppe Commander, was indicted before U.S. military tribunal, but was too ill to stand trial.

Rasche, Karl, Ger., Dresdner Bank official, was sentenced to seven years by U.S. military tribunal, but was released in 1950.

Rascher, Sigmund, Ger., Dachau medical experimenter, was purged and was rumored to have been shot in Dachau in 1945.

Rauter, Hans Albin, d.1949, Ger., Higher SS and Police Leader in Holland, was condemned in the Netherlands and executed.

Reinecke, Hermann, Ger., OKW official, was sentenced to life by U.S. military tribunal.

Reinhardt, Hans, Ger., Panzer Group 3, Army Group Center, and 3rd Panzer Army commander, was sentenced to fifteen years by U.S. military tribunal.

Rendulic, Lothar, Ger., 52nd Infantry Division commander at the Russian front, was sentenced to twenty years by U.S. military tribunal. The sentence was reduced to ten years by Clemency Board, and he was released in 1952.

Ribbentrop, Joachim von, 1893-1946, Ger., foreign minister, was condemned by International Military Tribunal and hanged.

Ritter, Karl, Ger., foreign office official, was sentenced to four years by U.S. military tribunal.

Roatta, Mario, Ital., chief of staff and secret police chief, was sentenced to life but escaped in 1945.

Rogstad, Henrik, d.1945, Nor., SS security police chief, killed himself.

Roques, Karl von, d.1949, Ger., Rear Area Army Group South commander, was sentenced by U.S. military tribunal.

Rose, Gerhard, Ger., Robert Koch Institute/Division of Tropical Medicine official, was sentenced to life by U.S. military tribunal. The sentence was reduced to fifteen years by Clemency Board.

Rosenbaum, Wilhelm, Ger., SS officer, was sentenced to life in 1961 but released for health reasons in 1976.

Rosenberg, Alfred, 1893-1946, Ger., east minister, was condemned by International Military Tribunal and hanged.

Rothaug, Oswald, Ger., judiciary official, was sentenced to life by U.S. military tribunal. The sentence was reduced to twenty years by Clemency BoarHe was pensioned upon his release.

Rothenberger, Curt, Ger., justice ministry official, was sentenced to seven years by U.S. military tribunal, then pensioned upon his release.

Röthke, Heinz, Ger., SS deportation expert in France, remains missing.

Ruehl, Felix, Ger., Einsatzgruppe D official, was sentenced to ten years by U.S. military tribunal. The sentence was reduced by Clemency Board to time served.

Ryti, Risto, Fin., premier, was sentenced by Finnish court in 1946.

S

Salmuth, Hans von, Ger., 30th Corps, 11th Army and Second Army, Army Group Center commander, was sentenced to twenty years by U.S. military tribunal. The sentence was reduced to twelve years by Clemency Board.

Sandberger, Martin, Ger., Einsatzgruppe A official, was condemned by U.S. military tribunal. His sentence was commuted to life by Clemency Board.

Sauckel, Fritz (Saukel), d.1946, Ger., Labor Plenipotentiary, was condemned by International Military Tribunal and hanged.

Schacht, Hjalmar Horace Greeley, 1877-1970, Ger., Reichsbank official, was acquitted in 1946 by International Military Tribunal.

Schäfer, Emanuel, Ger., BdS official in Serbia, was sentenced by both denazification court and German criminal court.

Scheide, Rudolf, Ger., WVHA official, was acquitted by U.S. military tribunal.

Schellenberg, Walter, d.1952, Ger., RSHA official, was sentenced by U.S. military tribunal but released before serving sentence. He died in Italy.

Schellong, Conrad Heinrich, Ger., gained U.S. citizenship in 1962, but was tried in 1982 for having hidden his military record of being stationed at both Sachsenburg and Dachau in the 1930s. He was deported in 1988.

Schirach, Baldur von, 1907-1974, Ger., Vienna Reichsstatthalter, was sentenced to twenty years by International Military Tribunal.

Schlegelberger, Franz, Ger., Justice Ministry official, was sentenced to life by U.S. military tribunal. He was released on medical grounds in 1951 by Clemency Board recommendation

Schmidt, Paul, Ger., Foreign Office press official, was arrested in Salzburg, Austria in 1945.

Schmitz, Hermann, Ger., I. G. Farben official, was sentenced by U.S. military tribunal. By 1955, he was chairman of Aufsichtsrat, Rheinische Stahlwerke.

Schnitzler, Georg von, Ger., director of I. G. Farben, was sentenced by U.S. military tribunal and released in 1949.

Scholtz-Klink, Gertrud, Ger., leader of German women, was arrested in 1948 and sentenced to nineteen months, which she had already served, in 1949.

Schöngarth, Karl, Ger., BdS Holland and BdS Generalgouvernement, was condemned in 1946 by British court

Schröder, Oskar, Ger., Air Force Medical Service official, was sentenced to life by U.S. military tribunal. The sentence was reduced to fifteen years by Clemency Board.

Schubert, Heinz Hermann, Ger., Einsatzgruppe D official, was condemned by U.S. military tribunal. His sentence was commuted to ten years by Clemency Board.

Schulz, Erwin, Ger., Einsatzgruppe C official, was sentenced to twenty years by U.S. military tribunal. His sentence was reduced to fifteen years by Clemency Board.

Seibert, Willi, Ger., Einsatzgruppe D official, was condemned by U.S. military tribunal. His sentence was commuted to fifteen years by Clemency Board.

Seidl, Siegfried, Ger., Theresienstadt commander, was condemned by Austrian court in 1946.

Seyss-Inquart, Artur, 1892-1946, Aus., conspirator to effect Austrian annexation and later Netherlands high commissioner, was condemned by International Military Tribunal and hanged.

Shigemitsu Mamoru, 1887-1957, Japanese, foreign minister, was indicted for war crimes and appeared before the International Military Tribunal in Tokyo.

Sievers, Wolfram, d.1948, Ger., Ahnenerbe official, was condemned by U.S. military tribunal and hanged.

Simon, Gustav, Ger., Luxembourg chief of civil administration, killed himself sometime after his arrest in 1945.

Six, Franz, Ger., Vorkommando Moskau official, was sentenced to twenty years by U.S. military tribunal. The sentence was reduced to ten years by Clemency Board.

Sokolov, Vladimir, Rus., publisher, edited Russian-language Nazi newspaper in occupied USSR. He came to America after the war and fled to Canada in 1986 to avoid deportation proceedings.

Sollmann, Max, Ger., Lebensborn official, was sentenced to time served for membership in a criminal organization by U.S. military tribunal.

Sommer, Karl, Ger., WVHA official, was condemned by U.S. military tribunal, with the sentence commuted to life by Military Governor. The sentence was further reduced to twenty years by Clemency Board.

Speer, Albert, 1905-1981, Ger., armament and munitions minister, was sentenced to twenty years by International Military Tribunal at Nuremberg. He was released from Spandau prison in West Berlin in 1966.

Speidel, Wilhelm, Ger., military commander in Greece, was sentenced to twenty years by U.S. military tribunal. In 1951, his sentence was reduced by Clemency Board to time served.

Sporrenberg, Ger., SS and Police Leader in Lublin, was condemned in Poland in 1950.

Stahlecker, Franz Walter, d.1942, Ger., Einsatzgruppe A commander, was killed in action.

Steengracht von Moyland, Adolf, Ger., Foreign Office official, was sentenced by U.S. military tribunal. His sentence was reduced to five years when his conviction for aggression was overturned, and he was released in 1950.

Steimle, Eugen, Ger., Einsatzgruppe B official, was condemned by U.S. military tribunal. His sentence was commuted to twenty years by Clemency Board.

Steinbrinck, Otto, Ger., Mitteldeutsche Stahlwerke official, was sentenced by U.S. military tribunal.

Strauch, Eduard, Ger., Einsatzgruppe A official, was condemned both by U.S. military tribunal and Belgian court, but execution was stayed due to his insanity.

Streicher, Julius, 1885-1946, Ger., publisher of *Der Stürmer*, was condemned by International Military Tribunal and hanged.

Strippel, Arnold, Ger., Majdanek prison guard, lived in United States until his extradition to West Germany, where he was sentenced in 1981.

Stroop, Jurgen, d.1951, Ger., SS and Police Leader in Warsaw, was condemned by Polish court and executed.

Stuckart, Wilhelm, d.1953, Ger., Interior Ministry official, was sentenced by U.S. military tribunal to time served due to his ill health. He was also fined by denazification court. He was killed in an automotive accident.

Stülpnagel, Otto von, d.1948, Ger., military commander in France, killed himself in a French prison.

Szálasi, Ferenc, 1897-1946, Hung., head of state, was executed in Hungary.

Sztojay, Döme, d.1946, Hung., prime minister, was executed in Hungary.

T

Takejiro Onishi, d.c.1945, Japan, vice admiral, devised the Kamikaze, and was reportedly permitted to commit hara-kiri.

Tanner, Väinö (AKA: **Alfred Tanner**), 1881-1966, Fin., finance minister, opposed Soviet aggression in thirties and forties. He was imprisoned on Soviet insistence and released in 1949.

Ter Meer, Fritz, Ger., I. G. Farben official, was sentenced by U.S. military tribunal. He was released in 1950.

Terboven, Josef, d.1945, Ger., Nazi commissioner for Norway, killed himself with dynamite.

Thadden, Eberhard von, Ger., foreign office official, was indicted at Nuremberg in 1948, but escaped to Cologne. Extradition was refused in 1949-50, and he was reported to be still there in 1953.

Thierack, Otto, d.1946, Ger., justice minister, killed himself.

Thomas, Max, Ger., BdS official in Ukraine, is believed to have been killed in action in 1944.

Thyssen, Fritz, 1873-1951, Ger., industrialist, was an early supporter of Hitler who turned against him when he led Germany into war. In 1940, Thyssen moved to France, where the Vichy government later arrested him. Although he was interned at Dachau, he was convicted and fined by a denazification court of being a minor Nazi.

Tiso, Jozef (Josef, Joseph), d.1947, Slovakian, president, hid out in Bavarian monastery under Cardinal's protection until his capture by American troops in 1945. He was extradited to Czechoslovakia and hanged.

Tojo, Hideki, d.1948, Japanese, prime minister, was condemned by International Military Tribunal and hanged.

Tokuda Hisakichi, Japanese, Shinagawa Prison medical officer, was condemned by U.S. military court in 1948.

Trifa, Valerian, Rom., came to U.S. after war and rose to Bishop in the Romanian Orthodox church. He was ordered deported in 1982 for concealing his participation in atrocities in Bucharest in 1941.

Tschentscher, Erwin, Ger., WVHA official, was sentenced to ten years by U.S. military tribunal. In 1951, his sentence was reduced by the Clemency Board to time served.

Tuka, Vojtech, Slovakian, prime minister, was condemned in Czechoslovakia in 1946.

Turner, Harald, Serbian, military governor official, was condemned in Yugoslavia in 1947.

U

Ulrich, Aquilin, Ger., doctor, was convicted in Frankfurt in 1987 of taking part in euthanasia of the handicapped in 1940-41.

V

Vallat, Xavier, Fr., anti-Jewish commissioner in France, was sentenced to ten years by French court. He was released in 1950.

Vishinksky, Andrei, Rus., Soviet occupation leader, was responsible for the murder of 979 Latvians in Riga in 1940-41. In 1953, he was the USSR's chief UN delegate.

Volk, Leo, Ger., WVHA official, was sentenced to ten years by U.S. military tribunal. His sentence was reduced to eight years by Clemency Board.

W

Wada Shusuke, Japanese, translator, was sentenced to life by U.S. military court in 1948 for mistreatment of prisoners aboard troopship on which only 450 of 1619 men survived.

Wagner, Horst, Ger., Foreign Office official, fled to Spain, then Italy to avoid arrest in 1949. He returned to Germany in 1960 and was arrested when he applied for a government pension.

Wagner, Robert, d.1946, Ger., Chief of Civil Administration in Alsace and Reichsstatthalter of Baden, was executed in France.

Waiter, Edward, d.1945, Ger., Dachau commander, killed himself.

Waldheim, Kurt, Aus., army lieutenant, was stationed in Greece during the war. In the 1980s he has served as both secretary-general of the United Nations and president of Austria, during which time there have been repeated allegations of complicity in deportation of Greek Jews to death camps. Evidence of this is questionable, and he has never been brought to trial.

Walther, Fritz, d.1946, Ger., railroad switchman who deliberately threw a wrong switch to run a train into another, killing eighteen Red Army occupation personnel.

Walus, Frank, Pol.-U.S., was accused in 1977 of war crimes and exonerated in American court in 1980.

Warlimont, Walter, Ger., OKW official, was sentenced to life by U.S. military tribunal. The sentence was reduced to eighteen years by Clemency Board.

Weichs, Maximilian von, Ger., 2nd Army, army group center commander and Southeast commander-in-chief, was indicted by U.S. military tribunal, but was too ill for trial.

Weidemann, Fritz, Ger., counsel-general in San Francisco and spy for Third Reich, was brought back to U.S. in 1945, apparently to testify at war crimes trials.

Weizsäcker, Ernst von, d.1951, Ger., Foreign Office official, was sentenced to seven years by U.S. military tribunal in 1949, but the sentence was reduced to five years by the overturn of conviction for aggression. He was released in 1950.

Wilhaus, Gustav, Ger., Janovsky concentration camp officer, was tried at Nuremberg in 1946.

Winkler, Max, d.1961, Ger., main trusteeship office east official, was exonerated by denazification court in 1949.

Wisliceny, Dieter, d.1948, Ger., SS deportation expert in Greece, Hungary, and Slovakia, was executed in Czechoslovakia.

Wöhler, Otto, Ger., 11th Army officer, was sentenced to eight years by U.S. military tribunal.

Wolff, Karl, Ger., Himmler's chief of staff, was sentenced by denazification court in 1949 to time served.

Wörmann, Ernst, Ger., foreign office official, was sentenced to seven years by U.S. military tribunal, but the sentence was reduced to five years on the overturn of conviction for aggression.

Wüster, Karl, Ger., I.G. Farben official, was acquitted by U.S. military tribunal.

Z

Zhdanov, Andrei, d.1948, Rus., Soviet occupation leader, was responsible for 200 Estonians murdered in 1940-41.

Zirpins, Walter, Ger., Lodz criminal police official, was arrested when discovered working as Hannover Polizeidirecktor in 1960.

WESTERN LAWMEN

The task of enforcing the laws of the U.S. in the untamed 19th-century Western frontier was often left to the marshals and sheriffs of the respective areas. The word "marshal" was originally a corruption of the German "marah" and "calc," which together mean "horsekeeper," but the status of marshals gradually improved until by the Middle Ages the rank of marshal was for the commander of great armies.

In the U.S., the office of marshal, adopted from the earlier British model, was attached to each federal district court. The marshal was authorized to carry out all "lawful precepts," as determined by the federal bench. The president appointed the marshal with the consent of the Senate. They were originally compensated from an inadequate fee system, which was revised over time so that the marshal could charge a municipality a fee equal to that of a state office. The federal marshals who were sworn to uphold the law on the frontier faced many obstacles, notably Congress' failure to assess stiff penalties to those who violently resisted arrest. By the 1850s, federal marshals policed a vast stretch of territory, assisted by county sheriffs, city marshals, and precinct constables. They had "acquired the primary duty of enforcement within the territories" and were "the sole police power in pioneer communities."

The Texas Rangers were organized in the 1830s to protect American settlers from Indian attacks. During the Texas war for independence this paramilitary force served as a border patrol. Though they refused to wear any kind of uniform, or even salute their superior officers, the Rangers were a highly disciplined outfit noted for their marksmanship. They adopted the Colt six-shooter as their preferred weapon, and in time the gun became synonymous with the settlement of the West. With the taming of the frontier, the Texas Rangers became less important, so that by 1935 they were absorbed into the state highway patrol, but they will always be prominent in the legend and folklore of the Old West.

A

Abeyta, Agapito, a lawman of Mora County, in the New Mexico Territory, implicated in the murder of John Doherty.

Adams, Charles, a detective for the postal service who led several posses throughout the New Mexico Territory, capturing several bandits during the Lincoln County War.

Adams, J.H., a New Mexico deputy marshal who was killed with Marshal Cornelius Finley on Sept. 2, 1878.

Alarid, Eugenio, a lawman and outlaw, was a policeman in Las Vegas, N.M., in the 1890s and a member of Silva's White Caps.

Alexander, E.M., a lawman, served as a captain of the Texas State Police from 1870 to 1873.

Allee, Alfred Y., appointed deputy sheriff of Karnes County, Texas, in 1882, made deputy sheriff of Frio County, Texas. He shot and killed train and bank robber Brack Cornett in 1888.

Allen, Abe, a lawman, was a deputy U.S. marshal for the Indian Nations working out of Judge Isaac Parker's court in the 1880s and 1890s.

Allison, Charles, a lawman and outlaw, was appointed deputy sheriff of Conjos County, Colo., but soon organized a band of outlaws that almost exclusively robbed stagecoaches.

Allison, Dave, a lawman, was the sheriff of Pecos City, Texas, in the 1890s.

Alston, Fielding, a lawman, served as a lieutenant in the Texas Rangers in 1847.

Alvord, Albert (Burt, Bert), a lawman and outlaw, was deputy sheriff in Cochise County, Ariz., under Sheriff John Slaughter in 1886. He became town constable of Fairbank in the early 1890s, then town constable of Wilcox where he killed Bill King. Alvord later led a band of train robbers.

Anderson, Bernard, a deputy marshal in the New Mexico Territory.

Anderson, J.E., a New Mexico deputy marshal, who had previously served as assistant secretary of the territory.

Anderson, William H., appointed U.S. deputy marshal in Dallas after the Civil War, tracked Bill Collins into Canada where they shot and killed each other in a gunfight.

Andrew, Robert, a detective and lawman, was a deputy sheriff in Oklahoma. He arrested Ragged Bill and discovered the Doolin Gang hideout.

Andrews, Captain **M.**, a lawman, commanded the Texas Rangers in 1837.

Archibald, Albert W., was appointed marshal of New Mexico on Sept. 13, 1861, but decided against accepting the position and moved to Colorado.

Armstrong, Charles, a lawman, served as a Texas Ranger and fought Mexicans on the border during WWI.

Armstrong, John Barclay, enlisted with the Travis Rifles in 1871 and joined the Texas Rangers in 1875. He helped capture King Fisher in 1874 and tracked and captured John Wesley Hardin in 1877. He retired as a captain in 1883 and died May 1, 1913.

Arrington, George W., joined the Texas Rangers in 1875, and brought in sixteen alleged murderers and twenty other felons from the Panhandle in July 1878. He was appointed captain of Company C, and later served as sheriff of Wheeler County for eight years. He died at his ranch on Mar. 31, 1923.

Ascarate, Guadalupe, a sheriff in the New Mexico Territory who was eventually replaced by Pat Garrett.

Aten, Edwin, joined the Texas Rangers after his brother Ira Aten and was assigned to Company D.

Aten, Ira D., joined the Texas Rangers in 1883, and became captain of Company D. He was elected sheriff of Castro County in 1890 and 1893. He tracked and shot down outlaw Judd Robberts and two cattle rustlers, Alvin Odle and Will Odle.

B

Baca, Elfego, was a prominent lawman in New Mexico for several years as well as an attorney and prosecutor. He was involved in a shootout at John Slaughter's ranch.

Bailey, Marvin E., a lawman, was a Texas Ranger in 1907.

Baird, P.C., a lawman, served as sergeant of Company D, Texas Rangers for several years and in 1888 was elected sheriff of Mason County. He served for ten years and died on Mar. 9, 1928.

Baker, A.R., a lawman, served as a Texas Ranger under Captain Frank Johnson in 1906.

Baker, Frank, an outlaw and lawman, served as a deputy sheriff in the Lincoln County War and rode in the posse that killed John Tunstall. He was killed by Billy the Kid on Mar. 10, 1878.

Baker, J.H., a lawman, served in Company C of the Texas Rangers around 1907.

Ballard, Charles, a deputy marshal, serving at Roswell, New Mexico.

Barela, Mariano, the sheriff of Mesilla, New Mexico, who later became a deputy U.S. marshal.

Barker, Dudley S., a lawman, served in Company B as a Texas Ranger in 1896 and helped break up a gang terrorizing the town of San Saba in 1897.

Barler, W.L., a lawman, served as a Texas Ranger and as the sheriff and tax collector of Terrell County.

Barringer, J.C., a lawman, served as a Texas Ranger in 1886 under Captain G.H. Schmidt.

Bartley, C.C., a lawman, was the sheriff of Val Verde County, Texas, in 1909.

Barton, Charles, a lawman, served in Company D of the Texas Rangers in 1887.

Bassett, Charles E. (AKA: **Senator**), a lawman, served as deputy sheriff of Ford County, Kan., in 1878, and was made marshal of Dodge City after Ed Masterson was killed. He appointed Wyatt Earp special deputy.

Bauman, Wes, a lawman, was a deputy U.S. marshal for the Indian Nations working out of Judge Isaac Parker's court in the 1880s and 1890s.

Baylor, George Wythe, a West Texas confederate soldier turned lawman, served with the Texas Rangers from 1879 to 1885, attaining the rank of major. He was a legislator and judge before he died on Mar. 27, 1916.

Bean, Roy, the "Law West of Pecos," served as a California Ranger before his election as justice of the peace of Pecos County in 1882. Bean died on Mar. 16, 1903.

Bean, Samuel G., a sheriff and deputy marshal in the New Mexico Territory.

Beckner, Frederick (Burckner), a lawman, who was appointed sheriff of Dona Ana County, N.M., on Mar. 28, 1863.

Beckwith, John H., a lawman and brother of Robert, was a deputy sheriff under Sheriff William Brady during the Lincoln County War of New Mexico, and was killed in the fighting.

Beckwith, Robert W., a lawman and brother of John, was a deputy sheriff under Sheriff William Brady during the Lincoln County War of New Mexico, and was killed during the battle at the McSween house.

Behan, John H., an Arizona lawman, was a deputy under Sheriff Shibbell in Tombstone and was elected sheriff of Cochise County. He killed Dick Tolby and disarmed two of the Clantons before the OK Corral gunfight. He died in Tucson in 1917.

Bell, Bob, a lawman, served in Company D of the Texas Rangers in 1887.

Bell, Hamilton B. (AKA: **Ham**), the sheriff of Ford County, Kan., for thirty years following Bat Masterson, he arrested more alleged outlaws, with a warrant, than any other lawman in the West. He lived past the age of ninety.

Bell, J.W. (AKA: **Lone Bell**), a lawman, was a Texas Ranger in the mid 1870s, and a deputy sheriff under Pat Garrett during the Lincoln County War. He was killed by Billy the Kid while he was guarding the outlaw in the Lincoln courthouse on Apr. 28, 1881.

Bell, James W., a lawman, served as a Texas Ranger in the 1890s and in 1897 helped break up a gang terrorizing citizens in San Saba. Bell was killed by Billy the Kid in a jailbreak.

Berstein, Morris, a deputy sheriff in the New Mexico Territory.

Best, Phil, a lawman, was a Texas Ranger, Company B in 1889 under Captain Sam McMurry.

Bingham, George, a lawman, was a Texas Ranger killed by Jesse Evans.

Birchfield, Steve, a lawman, served as deputy sheriff of Cochise County, Ariz., under Sheriff C.S. Fly. He rode with the posse that battled the Black Jack Ketchum Gang at Mud Springs.

Blackburn, Leslie, a deputy sheriff at Tombstone, Arizona.

Blackwell, C.J., a lawman, served as a Texas Ranger in 1919.

Blumner, Charles, was appointed Marshal of the New Mexico Territory on Dec. 10, 1853.

Bobbitt, A.A. (AKA: **Gus**), a lawman and gunman, was a deputy U.S. marshal in Oklahoma but returned to ranching. He feuded with cattlemen in Pontotoc County, was arrested, and lynched in February 1909.

Boles, Thomas, a lawman, was a U.S. marshal for the western district of Arkansas. He was appointed by President Chester Arthur in 1882.

Boston, Riley, a lawman, served in Company D of the Texas Rangers in 1887.

Bowers, Edward G., a lawman who served as sheriff of Yavapai County, New Mexico.

Bracken, J.W., a lawman, was a Texas Ranger, Company B in 1889 under Captain Sam McMurry.

Brady, William, a lawman and outlaw, was appointed sheriff of Lincoln County in 1878. He deputized Murphy's employees, formed a posse, and killed John Tunstall. He was ambushed and killed by Billy the Kid and other Tunstall Regulators shortly after.

Breakenridge, William M. (Billy, Billie), a lawman, served as deputy under Sheriff John Behan of Tombstone, Ariz., in the early 1880s. He later worked as a detective for the SP Railroad and died on Jan. 31, 1931.

Brent, James R., a buffalo hunter and lawman, served as chief deputy to John Poe when Poe succeeded Pat Garrett as sheriff of Lincoln County. Brent was deputy in the mid-1880s.

Brewer, Richard M., a gunman and lawman, worked for John Tunstall as leader of the Regulators in the Lincoln County War. As deputy sheriff, he captured the Jesse Evans Gang. Brewer was killed at Blazer's Mill by Buckshot Roberts on Apr. 4, 1878.

Briant, Elijah S. (Lige), a lawman, was the druggist and sheriff of Sonora, Sutton County, Texas. In a gun battle, he killed Will Carver and George Kilpatrick on Apr. 2, 1901. He served as a county judge and died on Dec. 22, 1932.

Bridges, Jack L., a lawman, served in Hays City, Kan., as a deputy U.S. marshal in 1869, and was later assigned to Wichita where he killed horse thief J.E. Ledford. He became marshal of Dodge City, Kan., in the early 1870s.

Britton, Ed, a lawman, was a Texas Ranger, Company B in 1889 under Captain Sam McMurry.

Brooks, J.A., a lawman, served as a sergeant in the Texas Rangers in 1919.

Brooks, James Abijah, a lawman, joined the Texas Rangers in 1882 and served with Company F and A. He was made a captain in May 1889, resigned in 1906, and died on Jan. 15, 1944.

Brooks, William (AKA: **Buffalo Billy**), a lawman and gunman, was the first town marshal of Newton, Kan., in the early 1870s, and participated in the Newton War. He was the assistant town marshal of Dodge City in 1872 where he killed or wounded fifteen men.

Brown, A.W., a lawman, was a Texas Ranger in Company B in 1909.

Brown, Angus (AKA: **Arapaho, Red**), a lawman, was the sheriff of Buffalo, Wyo., in 1892. He was killed by two young cowboys.

Brown, George S., a lawman, served as city marshal of Caldwell, Kan., and was killed on June 22, 1882, by Jim Bean.

Brown, Henry Newton (Hendry), an outlaw and lawman, was a Regulator in the Lincoln County War and then deputy sheriff of Tascosa. In Caldwell, Kan., he was assistant town marshal and then marshal on Dec. 2, 1882. With Ben Wheeler and others, he robbed the bank at Medicine Lodge on Apr. 30, 1884, and was killed by a mob.

Brown, Neal (AKA: **Skinny**), a lawman in Dodge City, Kan., in the late 1870s, was a deputy under Bill Tilghman in Oklahoma. Brown was with Tilghman when he chased the Doolin Gang.

Bruner, Heck, a lawman, was a deputy U.S. marshal for the Indian Nations working out of Judge Isaac Parker's court in the 1880s and 1890s.

Brunner, Neal, a lawman, was a deputy U.S. marshal in Indian Territory in the late 1890s, working out of Judge Parker's federal court at Fort Smith.

Bryant, Ed, a lawman, served as a Texas Ranger in 1896.

Burke, A.F., a deputy sheriff in Tombstone, Ariz., in the 1880s.

Burke, J.S. (Steve), a lawman, served under E.D. Nix as a deputy U.S. marshal in the Fourth District, Texas. He helped capture Cattle Annie and Little Britches. Burke later became an evangelist.

Burroughs, W.H., a lawman, was a deputy sheriff in Nacogdoches County, Texas, under Sheriff Milton Mast. He aided in the capture of Wild Bill Longely.

Bursum, Holm O., a lawman, who in the 1890s, served as sheriff of Sorocco County, in the New Mexico Territory.

Burts, Matthew (Matt), an outlaw and lawman, robbed a train with a gang led by Burt Alvord and served briefly as a deputy town constable in Pearce, Ariz., in 1899. He was imprisoned for robbery, and killed by a ranching neighbor in November 1925.

Burwell, W.M., a lawman, served as a Texas Ranger in 1896.

Buttner, A.F., a deputy marshal in the New Mexico Territory.

C

Cameron, John, a lawman, served in Company E as a Texas Ranger in 1892.

Campbell, J.E, a lawman, was a sergeant in the Arizona Rangers in 1903.

Canton, Frank M., a lawman and gunman, was elected deputy sheriff of Jacksboro, sheriff of Johnson County, Wyo., in 1882, and served as a deputy U.S. marshal in Oklahoma under Marshal Nix. Canton captured Teton Jackson in 1887 while sheriff of Buffalo and was later appointed adjutant general of four states by the governors.

Carlyle, James, a lawman, was a deputy sheriff in Las Vegas, N.M., and was killed by Billy the Kid on Dec. 1, 1880.

Carnes, H.A., a lawman, served in Company C of the Texas Rangers around 1907.

Carr, "Bat", a gambler and businessman, was made city marshal of Caldwell, Kan., and appointed Willis Metcalf and Hendry Brown as his deputies.

Carr, T. Jeff, a lawman, was made the first sheriff of Laramie County, Wyoming Territory, in 1869. He made Wild Bill Hickok check his guns in Cheyenne and in 1876 arrested Jack McCall, the man who shot Hickok.

Carson, Joe, a lawman, was the constable of Las Vegas, N.M., wounded James Lowe in a shootout, and was killed by outlaw John Dorsey on Jan. 22, 1884.

Carson, Thomas, a lawman, served in Company D and E of the Texas Rangers and fought the Chris Evans Gang in 1880.

Carson, Tom, a lawman and nephew of Kit Carson, was a deputy city marshal of Abilene, Kan., under Wild Bill Hickok. He was killed at Dodge City, Kan.

Caruthers, L.B., a lawman, served with the Texas Rangers during the Higgins-Horrell feud and fought the Evans Gang in 1880.

Castle, Kit, a lawman, was elected sheriff of Unitah County, Wyo., killed two horse thieves, and, while serving as mayor pistolwhipped five men into returning to their cell.

Charlton, John B. (Jack), a soldier in the Indian Territory, who chased several outlaws, including Red McLaughlin.

Chavez, Francisco (Frank), a lawman, who served as sheriff of Santa Fe, N.M.

Chew, Bob, a lawman, served as a Texas Ranger in 1896.

Christianson, Willard Erastus (AKA: **Matt Warner, Ras Lewis**), an outlaw and brother-in-law of outlaw Tom McCarty, robbed trains and banks with Butch Cassidy, Elza Lay, and McCarty from 1878, served a prison sentence, became a lawman, and died Dec. 21, 1938.

Clark, Ben, a lawman at Clifton, Ariz., who killed Black Jack Christian in April 1897.

Clark, G.H., a lawman, served as a Texas Ranger in 1886 under Captain G.H. Schmidt.

Clements, Emanuel, Jr. (Mannie), a lawman, served under Sheriff Dave Allison as deputy sheriff at Pecos City, Texas, from 1894. He later worked for Jim Miller during the Miller-Frazer feud and served as constable of El Paso.

Clements, W.T. (AKA: **Slick**), a lawman, served as a Texas Ranger in Company D in the 1870s.

Clever, Charles P., a lawman born in Prussia, who in the 1850s, served as marshal in the New Mexico Territory.

Coalson, Doug, a lawman, served as a Texas Ranger in Company D in the 1870s.

Coe, Chas, a lawman and outlaw, killed two men in Grayson County, Texas, in 1884 and was indicted for murder.

Colbert, Paden, a lawman, served out of Fort Smith, Ark., as a deputy U.S. marshal for the Indian Territory in the 1880s and 1890s. He led the posse that killed Ned Christie.

Colcord, Charles F., a lawman, served as a deputy U.S. marshal for the Indian Territory in the 1880s and 1890s. A friend of Bill Tilghman, he was elected city marshal of Oklahoma City in August 1890.

Coldwell, Captain **Neal**, a soldier and lawman, was made captain of Company F of the Texas Rangers under Major John B. Jones in June 1874, captain of Company A in 1876, and resigned in 1883 to become a rancher.

Coleman, Dan, a lawman, served as a Texas Ranger in 1894 as a private in Company E.

Coleman, E.E., a lawman, served as a Texas Ranger in 1894 as a private in Company F.

Collier, W.W., a lawman, was made a Texas Ranger at the age of eighteen.

Collins, John, a New Mexico lawman, who was a deputy marshal in Santa Fe.

Conklin, Charles, a deputy marshal in Las Vegas, N.M., whose pursuit of twelve train robbers in 1879, led to their arrests.

Conley, Ed, a lawman, served as a Texas Ranger in 1896.

Connell, Ed, a lawman, served as a Texas Ranger in 1894 as a private in Company B.

Connelly, Charles T., a lawman, was city marshal of Coffeyville, Kan., when the Dalton Gang attempted to rob the town's two banks. Connelly was the fifth person the Daltons killed.

Cook, Thalis T., a lawman, served as a Texas Ranger for several years in the 1880s and 1890s and killed many outlaws including Fine Gilliland and the Friar brothers.

Cooke, C.G., a lawman, served as a Texas Ranger in 1894 as a private in Company F.

Cooley, Corydon E., a deputy marshal in Springerville, N.M., who rid his jurisdiction of desperadoes in 1877.

Cooley, Scott, a lawman and gunman, killed deputy sheriff John Wohrle during the Mason County War in Texas in 1875 to avenge Wohrle's killing Tim Williamson. He formed a gang that continued to terrorize Mason County until he mysteriously fell dead in 1876.

Cooper, Harry, a deputy marshal in New Mexico, who was accused of stealing courtroom evidence in 1899.

Copeland, Charles, a lawman, was a deputy U.S. marshal for the Indian Nations working out of Judge Isaac Parker's court in the 1880s and 1890s.

Costley, Solon, a lawman, served as a Texas Ranger in the early 1890s.

Cottle, A.R., a lawman, was appointed Chief deputy U.S. marshal of the northern district of Oklahoma on July 1, 1903, and served several decades.

Cotton, Mitchell, a lawman, served on the Texas state police and killed D.C. Applewhite on Sept. 30, 1871.

Courtright, Timothy Isaiah (AKA: **Long Haired Jim**), a lawman and outlaw, was elected city marshal of Fort Worth, Texas, in 1876, and named Bill Woody deputy. As deputy U.S. marshal in 1883 under Marshal Johnson, Courtright became a fugitive after his posse killed two ranchers. He was later acquitted.

Craighead, Charlie, a lawman, was a deputy sheriff of Val Verde County, Texas, in 1909.

Crawford, Ed, a lawman, served on the Ellsworth, Kan., police force in the early 1870s. He was discharged for killing suspected murderer Cad Pierce, and was later killed by Pierce's brother.

Culver, Martin S., a member of Major Tobin's Rangers, who fought numerous battles along the Rio Grande.

Cummings, Samuel M. (AKA: **Doc**), a lawman, was the deputy marshal of El Paso, Texas, in 1881 under Dallas Stoudenmire and was killed by Jim Manning on Feb. 14, 1882.

Cunningham, William P., a lawman in the New Mexico Territory during the 1890s.

Cury, W.S., a lawman, was the sheriff of Pima County, Ariz., from 1873 to 1877.

Cutler, Abraham, was brought from Kansas to serve as marshal of the New Mexico Territory, beginning Aug. 16, 1862.

D

Dake, Albert, a lawman during the 1880s, in the New Mexico Territory.

Dake, Crawley P., became marshal of the New Mexico Territory in 1878.

Dallam, Richard, a miner and merchant, who became marshal of the New Mexico Territory in 1846.

Dalton, Bob, a lawman turned outlaw, formed the Dalton Gang in 1891 with his brothers and robbed banks throughout Kansas. He and most of the gang were killed attempting to simultaneously rob two banks at Coffeyville on Oct. 5, 1892.

Dalton, Frank, a deputy U.S. Marshal, stationed at Fort Smith, in the Indian Territories, who later became an outlaw with his brothers.

Dalton, Gratton, a deputy U.S. Marshal, who became an outlaw member of the Dalton Gang.

Daniels, Ben F., a lawman, served in Arizona as a deputy sheriff and later joined Theodore Roosevelt's Rough Riders. In 1901 he was appointed U.S. Marshal of Arizona and New Mexico territories.

Davidson, James, a corrupt lawman, commanded the Texas state police as adjutant general from 1870 to 1873.

Davis, E.K., a lawman, served as deputy sheriff of Custer County, Mont., in 1880, and was part of a group of famous Montana manhunters.

Davis, Levi, a lawman, was a Texas Ranger in 1907.

Delling, M.G. (AKA: **Blaze**), a lawman, served as a Texas Ranger in Company B from September 1900 to December 1906.

Delony, Lewis S., a lawman and deputy, became a Texas Ranger in 1877. Served as deputy sheriff in Clinton.

Dibrell, John L., a lawman, served as a Texas Ranger in Company C for five years and as a deputy U.S. marshal for thirteen years.

Dickason, Isaac Q., a lawman, was appointed marshal of the New Mexico Territory on Apr. 15, 1871.

Doherty, John, a lawman, served as sheriff of Mora County, N.M., and was later murdered.

Dolan, Patrick, a lawman, joined the Texas Rangers in 1874, was made a lieutenant in 1876, and in January 1878, was appointed captain of Company F by Major Jones.

Donahue, Cornelius (AKA: **Lame Johnny**), a lawman and an outlaw, moved to Texas to become a cowboy, but a physical impairment led him to horse thievery. Left Texas and became deputy sheriff of Deadwood. Was arrested as horse thief, and returned to Deadwood, but on return trip a masked man abducted him. Was found hung from a tree in 1878.

Donley, Ed, a lawman, served as a Texas Ranger in 1896.

Donnelly, Dr., a lawman, served as a Texas Ranger in the 1890s and in 1897 helped break up a gang terrorizing San Saba.

D'Orgenay, Francis J.L., was the first western marshal, appointed to jurisdiction of the Orleans Territory in 1804.

Dow, E.A., a lawman in Lincoln County, N.M., during the 1870s.

Dow, J. Leslie, a lawman and gunman, killed Zack Light in a gunfight in the late 1880s, became sheriff of Eddy County, Texas, on Nov. 27, 1896, and was killed shortly thereafter by the former sheriff, Dave Kemp.

Dow, Luke, a lawman, served as a Texas Ranger in Company E from 1890 to 1892 and was later sheriff of Maverick County.

Downing, William, a lawman, was deputy sheriff of Willcox, Ariz., under Burt Alvord in the late 1890s, and allowed Alvord and his gang to escape.

Duffield, Milton B., a lawman from West Virginia, who was appointed marshal of Arizona on Mar. 10, 1863.

Dunavan, C.T., a chief deputy marshal who investigated the robbery of an Army paymaster in Graham County, N.M. on May 11, 1889.

Dunman, William Hickman, a lawman, joined the Texas Rangers in 1874. He died in 1905.

Dunn, Amasa G., was a deputy marshal during the 1860s, in the New Mexico Territory.

Durbin, Walter, a lawman, served as a corporal in Company D of the Texas Rangers in 1886 and 1887.

Durham, George P., a lawman, was one of McNelly's Rangers from 1875 to 1878, and then became foreman on the King ranch.

Durst, S.O. (AKA: **Sod**), a lawman, joined Company F of the Texas Rangers in 1918 and served two years. He joined Company A in 1921 and quit in 1922. He was elected sheriff of Kimble County and later served as special ranger for the Gulf Oil Corporation.

E

Earp, Morgan S., a lawman and gunman, was city marshal of Butte, Mont., when he killed Billy Brooks. He was appointed sheriff of Pima County, Ariz., in 1879, and a policeman in Tombstone in 1880. He was shot through a window and killed on Mar. 18, 1882.

Earp, Virgil W., a lawman and gunman, was appointed city marshal of Tombstone, Ariz., in 1880, lost an election, and later was appointed marshal again. Virgil died Oct. 19, 1906.

Earp, Wyatt, a lawman and gunman, was appointed marshal of Ellsworth, Kan., in 1873, marshal of Wichita in 1874, and marshal of Dodge City in 1876. He was appointed deputy city marshal in 1880 by Virgil. Wyatt died on Jan. 13, 1929.

Edwards, W.R., a lawman, was a deputy sheriff of Val Verde County, Texas, in 1909.

Ervin, Christopher Columbus, a lawman, was a court officer in the Choctaw Nation in the 1870s.

Evans, Joseph, a deputy marshal in the New Mexico Territory.

Evans, Rut, a lawman, served in Company E as a Texas Ranger in 1892.

Evetts, J.H., a lawman, was a Texas Ranger in 1896.

Ezekiels, Alexander, a lawman and expert manhunter during the 1890s, in the New Mexico Territory.

F

Faber, Charles, deputy sheriff and town constable of Las Animas, Colo., in the 1870s. Shot and killed by Clay Allison in 1876 at a town dance when he attempted to remove Clay's and John Anderson's guns.

Fain, William, a Kansas lawman, who in 1858, organized his own "army" of possemen, until federal authorities ordered them to disband.

Fall, Philip, a rustler turned lawman, who in the 1890s served as a deputy marshal in Las Cruces, N.M.

Farr, Edward, a lawman, was elected sheriff of Walsenburg, Colo., in 1897. He was killed by Will Carver when Farr's posse encountered the Ketchum-Carver Gang in 1899.

Farr, Jeff B., a lawman and brother of Edward, served as sheriff of Huerfano County, Colo., for several years.

Ferguson, Andy, a lawman, was a Texas Ranger in 1896.

Finley, Cornelius, a New Mexico lawman, who was murdered by outlaws on Sept. 2, 1878.

Fisler, John King (AKA: **King Fisher**), a lawman and a gunman, served as sheriff in Uvalde County. Killed in shootout with Ben Thompson in 1884.

Flapp, George W., a lawman, was the first marshal of Caldwell, Kan., in 1880. He was disliked and shot dead in the back in 1885.

Flint, Ed, a lawman, was a Texas Ranger in 1896.

Foraker, Charles, a rancher who became a deputy marshal in New Mexico Territory in February 1903.

Foraker, Creighton M., a rancher with his brother Charles, he was appointed U.S. Marshal of New Mexico Territory on July 22, 1897.

Forbes, Harry, a lawman who served as Chief Deputy of Roswell, New Mexico.

Forbes, William R., a deputy marshal in the New Mexico Territory.

Ford, John Salman (AKA: **Rip**), a lawman and legislator, was made captain of the Texas Rangers in 1849, killed Chief Buffalo Hump, and fought many bandits, including Cortina. He died on Nov. 3, 1897.

Fornoff, Fred, a lawman, was the captain of the New Mexico Mounted Police during the state's territorial days.

Forsyth, J.P., a lawman, was sheriff of Panola County, Texas, for eighteen years and never carried a pistol.

Frazer, George A. (AKA: **Bud**), a lawman, joined the Texas Rangers and later served as deputy sheriff of Fort Stockton, Texas. He was elected sheriff of Pecos City in 1890 and 1892, and was killed in a saloon on Sept. 14, 1896, by rival marshal James Miller.

Fulgam, James, a lawman, was a Texas Ranger in 1896.

Fullerton, C.B., a lawman, served as a Texas Ranger in 1894 as a private in Company B.

Fusselman, Charles H., a lawman, served in Company D of the Texas Rangers in 1887.

G

Gabriel, Peter, a lawman, was sheriff of Pima County, Ariz., in 1883 and 1885. He pursued the Red Jack Gang and shot and killed ex-deputy Joe Phy in a duel on May 3, 1888.

Gardner, Raymond Hatfield (AKA: **Arizona Bill**), a lawman, was born in 1846 and became a deputy U.S. marshal and later an Arizona Ranger. He buffaloed Doc Holliday in 1881.

Garrett, Buck, a lawman and nephew of Pat Garrett, fought in the Johnson County War in 1892, was deputy U.S. marshal in the Chickasaw Nation, and sheriff of Ardmore. He led the posse that killed outlaw Bill Dalton.

Garrett, Patrick Floyd, a lawman, was made sheriff of Lincoln County in November 1880 and killed Tom O'Folliard, Charles Bowdre, and later Billy the Kid in July 1881. He became a Texas Ranger, resigned in 1885, and was killed on Feb. 28, 1908.

Gildea, Augustus M. (Gus), a lawman and cowboy, was a part-time Texas Ranger in Company D and F, and was a deputy sheriff from 1881 to 1889. He died on Aug. 10, 1935.

Gillett, James Buchanan, a lawman, joined Captain Roberts' Texas Rangers in 1875, killed outlaw Dick Dublin, served as sheriff of El Paso, and as sheriff of Brewster County in the 1890s. In 1937, he was the first person appointed a lifetime captain of the Rangers.

Gilliland, Jim, appointed a deputy marshal of the New Mexico Territory in 1893, he was suspected of cattle rustling a year later.

Gilson, Bill, a lawman, served as a peace officer in northern Texas in 1874.

Glasgow, Mr., a lawman, was a deputy sheriff of Georgetown, N.M., and killed outlaw Boyd Dempster on Dec. 26, 1881.

Goodlet, Bill, a lawman turned gunman, was a member of the Dodge City Gang in Las Vegas, N.M.

Goodnight, Charles, a lawman and gunman, was a Texas Ranger in 1857 and drove cattle after the Civil War. He fought outlaws and Indians for many years in Texas, New Mexico, and California. He died in Tucson, Ariz., on Dec. 12, 1929, at the age of ninety-three.

Goodwin, Francis H., a lawman who served as U.S. Marshal of the New Mexico Territory between February, 1875 and July, 1876.

Gosling, Harold L., a lawman, was appointed U.S. marshal of the Western District of Texas in 1884 and was killed by two stage robbers in his custody en route to a prison on a train.

Graham, Dayton, a lawman who became a sergeant in the Arizona Rangers. Killed Bill Smith in a shootout.

Graham, Samuel, a lawman, joined Company A of the Texas Rangers in July 1878, was discharged in 1880, and later reenlisted. He led the posse that captured Albert Gross.

Green, George, a lawman, was a New Mexico marshal in 1907.

Gregory, Walter, a lawman, serving as a marshal in the Arizona Territory in 1905.

Greigo, Francisco (AKA: **Pancho**), a lawman and gunman, was city marshal of Santa Fe, N.M., and was killed by Clay Allison in 1875.

Griffith, William M., a lawman who served as marshal of the Arizona Territory between June 15, 1897, and June 6, 1901.

Grimes, A.C., a lawman, served as a lieutenant of the Texas Rangers in 1886 under Captain G.H. Schmidt.

Guyse, Buck, a lawman and outlaw, deserted from the Texas Rangers and fled to New Mexico Territory and was arrested by Pat Garrett.

H

Hall, Edward L., a lawman who was appointed marshal of the New Mexico Territory on May 16, 1893.

Hall, Frank W., a deputy marshal in the New Mexico Territory during the 1890s.

Hall, Jesse Lee, a lawman, served as city marshal of Sherman, Texas, joined the Texas Rangers in 1876.

Hall, Jesse Leigh (AKA: **Lee, Red, Colorado Grande**), a lawman, became deputy sheriff of Grayson County, Texas, in 1876 and later joined the Texas Rangers. He was in the Pat Garrett posse that killed Charles Bowdre and captured Billy the Kid.

Hall, T.L., a lawman, as deputy sheriff led a posse that killed outlaw train robber Mitch Lee.

Hamer, Frank, a lawman, joined the Texas Rangers in 1906, served as city marshal of Navasota, two years later, rejoined the Rangers in 1915, and was made captain of Company C. Hamer tracked down fugitives Clyde Barrow and Bonnie Parker and organized the ambush that killed them in May 1934.

Hanson, William, a lawman, served as a captain of the Texas Rangers in 1919.

Harkey, D.R. (Dee), a lawman, served as deputy sheriff in San Saba County, Texas, under his brother Joe and at the age of seventeen, arrested Jim Miller. He held several other positions as a peace officer in Texas and New Mexico.

Harrell, Jack, a lawman, served as a Texas Ranger in the 1890s and in 1897 helped break up a gang terrorizing San Saba.

Harris, James, a gunman and former lawman, was killed while dueling Bob Majors at Santa Cruz, Calif., in the 1880s.

Harrison, Richard, served as a special deputy beginning in September 1886, at La Marcia, in the Arizona Territory.

Harwell, Jack, a lawman, served as a Texas Ranger in 1896.

Hawkins, Jack, a lawman, served in Company D of the Texas Rangers and was a member of the famous Montana manhunters.

Hayden, Carl, a lawman in the Arizona Territory, who in 1910 became one of the first officers to use an automobile.

Hays, John Coffee (Jack), a lawman, became a captain in the Texas Rangers in 1840 and fought several battles with Indians. He was elected the first sheriff of San Francisco in April 1850, and died on Apr. 25, 1883.

Head, Lafayette, served as a deputy marshal in the New Mexico Territory, beginning in 1858.

Heirs, C.F., a lawman, served as a Texas Ranger in 1896.

Helm, Jack, a lawman and outlaw, was appointed a special officer by the state police in 1869 and fought in the Sutton-Taylor feud. He led the posse that killed Hays Taylor on Aug. 23, 1869, and was killed by Wes Hardin and Jim Taylor in July 1873.

Hereford, Frank H., a lawman, who served as a deputy marshal in the New Mexico Territory.

Herredia, Clato, a lawman, scouted for the Texas Rangers in 1880 during the Jesse Evans Gang roundup.

Hess, John, a lawman, served as a Texas Ranger in 1896.

Hickey, Mike, a lawman, who in 1885 served as vice-president of the Anti-Chinese Labor Assn. in Arizona.

Hickman, Tom, a lawman, served as a Texas Ranger in the 1880s and 1890s for more than twelve years in Company B and later as captain of Company C.

Hickok, James Butler (AKA: **Wild Bill**), a gunman and lawman, served as a constable in the 1860s and as town marshal of Abilene, Kan., in 1872. He was credited with killing thirty to eighty-five men including Sam Strawhorn, Bill Mulvey, Bill Thompson, and David McCandles. On Aug. 2, 1876, Jack McCall shot and killed Hickok in Deadwood, S.D.

Higgins, Fred, a lawman, served as a deputy sheriff of Globe, Ariz., in 1895 and led the attack on the Black Jack Christian hideout in which Christian was killed. He fought the Black Jacks in 1896 under Sheriff C.S. Fly.

Hildreth, William (Billy), a lawman, was made a deputy when John Slaughter was elected sheriff of Tombstone, Ariz. He fought the Black Jacks as a deputy of Sheriff C.S. Fly and was a friend of Burt Alvord.

Hill, John, a lawman, who during 1860s served as a deputy marshal at Albuquerque, N.M.

Hill, Tom, a lawman, serving as a New Mexico deputy marshal, who was a member of the posse that killed John Tunstall on Feb. 18, 1878.

Hindman, George, a lawman and gunman, was a deputy sheriff in Lincoln County under Sheriff William Brady and rode in the posse that killed John Tunstall. He was killed by Billy the Kid and John Middleton on Apr. 1, 1878.

Holliday, John Henry (Doc), was deputized by Virgil Earp to abet the efforts against the Clanton Gang, which culminated with a gunfight at the O.K. Corral on Oct. 26, 1881. He died in a sanatarium in 1885.

Hollister, Cassius M. (AKA: **Cash**), lawman and deputy U.S. marshal. Shot in 1884 while attempting to arrest an adulterer.

Holmes, W.A. (AKA: **Hunky Dory**), a lawman, served as a deputy sheriff under Sheriff Glen Reynolds of Gila County, Ariz. While transporting the western outlaw Apache Kid, he had a heart attack and died.

Hopkins, Arthur A., a lawman, who served as a deputy marshal in the Arizona Territory.

Hopkins, Gilbert W., a lawman and mining engineer who became a deputy marshal in the New Mexico Territory in 1864.

Horn, Tom, worked as Pinkerton detective, during which time he was charged with and convicted of murdering a Wyoming boy. Horn was hanged on Nov. 20, 1903, in Cheyenne, though many still believe he was innocent.

Horton, George, a lawman, was a Texas Ranger in 1896 as a private in Company D.

Houston, Tom, a lawman, served as Oklahoma law officer during early 1890s. Killed in shootout with Doolin gang.

Hudson, R.M. (AKA: **Duke**), a lawman, served in Company C of the Texas Rangers in 1907.

Hughes, John Reynolds, a lawman, joined the Texas Rangers, Company D, in 1887 and was made captain in 1893. He arrested and killed numerous outlaws and committed suicide in 1946, at the age of eighty-nine.

Hume, James B., a Wells Fargo detective, investigated more than 350 stagecoach and train robberies.

Hunnicut, J.R., a lawman, served as a Texas Ranger in 1919.

Hunnicutt, M.P., a lawman, served as a captain of the Texas State Police from 1870 to 1873.

Hunt, Frank, a lawman, served as a deputy sheriff of Caldwell, Kan., under Sheriff George Flapp in the late 1870s. In a gunfight with four outlaws, he and the four outlaws were killed.

I

Irvan, Tom, a lawman, served as sheriff of Custer County, Mont., and was one of the famous Montana manhunters.

J

Jefferson, Dunk, a lawman, served as a Texas Ranger in 1877 under Pat Dolan and was one of his most efficient men.

Jennings, Napoleon Augustus, lawman. Became a Texas Ranger in 1876 and was with Lee Hall when the Rangers ended the Sutton-Taylor feud.

Johnson, Charles, a lawman, served in Company E as a Texas Ranger in 1892.

Johnson, Jack (AKA: **Turkey Creek**), lawman and gunman. Former Dakota goldminer, he moved to Arizona after killing his partners. Was deputy marshal to Wyatt Earp and part of posse that killed Frank Stillwell.

Johnson, John (AKA: **Liver Eating**), a lawman and friend of Buffalo Bill Cody, was constable of Coulson, Mont., in the 1870s and was deputy sheriff of Coulson in 1880.

Johnson, Tom, a lawman, served in Company B of the Texas Ranger in 1896 and was a deputy U.S. marshal for the Indian Nations working out of Judge Isaac Parker's court in the 1880s and 1890s.

Johnson, William H., lawman and gunman. Confederate captain in Civil War. Made deputy to Sheriff William Brady during the Lincoln County War.

Jones, Frank, a lawman, served in Company A, Company F in 1874, and Company D in 1878 of the Texas Rangers. He served as captain in 1887 and was killed by outlaws on June 30, 1893.

Jones, Fred, a lawman, was a deputy sheriff of Val Verde County, Texas, in 1909.

Jones, Gus (AKA: **Buster**), a lawman, was a Texas Ranger stationed in Alice, Texas, in 1906.

Jones, John B., a lawman, joined the Texas Rangers before the Civil War and was commissioned as the commander of the Frontier Battalion of the Rangers during the Texas reconstruction. In 1877, Jones ended the Horrell-Higgins feud, and died on June 19, 1881.

Jones, John G., a lawman, who on Mar. 12, 1851, became the first U.S. Marshal under civilian rule, of the New Mexico Territory.

Jones, Nat B. (AKA: **Kiowa**), a lawman, joined the Texas Rangers under Captain Bill McDonald. He died around 1928.

Jones, Walter, a lawman, served in Company D of the Texas Rangers in 1887.

K

Karnes, Quill, a lawman, was a Texas Ranger stationed in Alice, Texas, in 1906.

Kaseman, George A., a lawman who served as a deputy marshal in the New Mexico Territory.

Kemp, Dave, an outlaw, shot and killed a man in Texas, moved to New Mexico, killed Sheriff Les Dow, and later served as a lawman in Eddy County, N.M.

Kennon, Louis, a lawman, who in the 1880s served as a deputy marshal at Silver City, New Mexico.

Kimball, George, a lawman. who served as sheriff and deputy marshal of Lincoln County, N.M., beginning in 1879.

King, Frank, a lawman, was a deputy sheriff of Phoenix, Ariz., and a guard at Yuma prison in 1889. He fought the Black Jack Gang in 1896 at Nogales.

King, Jim, a lawman, served in Company D of the Texas Rangers in 1887.

King, Lou, a lawman, served as deputy sheriff of Custer County, Mont., in 1880, and was part of a group of famous Montana manhunters.

Kirchner, Karl, a lawman, served as a sergeant in Company D of the Texas Rangers in 1894.

Kosterlitsky, Emilio, a Mexico lawman, was the head of the Rurales at the turn of the century.

Krummeck, Charles, a lawman, was a deputy sheriff of Santa Cruz, N.M., where he shot and killed a man in December 1880.

Kuhley, Charles, a lawman, served as a Texas Ranger in 1886 under Captain G.H. Schmidt.

L

Lambert, Charles Frederick (AKA: **Kid Lambert**), a lawman, arrested three killers at sixteen and was made a deputy sheriff. He was appointed to the New Mexico Mounted Police and pursued the "Hole in the Wall" Gang and Black Jack Ketchum's gang. He was made a U.S. special officer, and after WWII, became a deputy sheriff.

Landrum, James David, a lawman, served as a Texas Ranger, as a deputy sheriff of Haskell County in 1901, and then as deputy sheriff of Abilene. He served on the Waco police force from 1912 to 1917 and later on the Dallas police force and died in 1942.

Lane, Van, a lawman, served as a Texas Ranger in the 1890s and in 1897 helped break up a gang terrorizing San Saba.

Langford, N.P., a lawman, was known as a "law and order officer" in Montana at the time of Sheriff Plummer's Innocents Gang.

Larkin, Sam, a lawman, served in Company C of the Texas Rangers around 1907.

Larn, John M., an outlaw turned lawman, killed a rancher in Colorado and a sheriff in New Mexico. He rustled cattle while sheriff of Shackleford County, Texas, in the late 1870s.

Latham, James V., a lawman, enlisted in the Texas Rangers, Company D in 1880, 1884, and 1893 and fought the Evans Gang. He served as a deputy sheriff of El Paso County for two years and as a deputy in New Mexico. He died on Nov. 17, 1936.

Latta, Oscar, a lawman, served as a Texas Ranger in the 1890s, and was a deputy sheriff of Kimble County, Texas, in February 1897. He was later elected sheriff and helped defeat the Crane-Knight Gang. He rejoined the Texas Rangers in 1939.

Laughlin, J.T. (Tom), a lawman, was a Texas Ranger in 1907.

Leatherwood, Robert N., a lawman, was sheriff of Pima County, Ariz., in 1883 and captured a train-robbing gang.

Ledbetter, Bud, a lawman, was a deputy U.S. marshal in the 1880s and then town marshal of Vinita, Okla., in 1893. As a deputy U.S. marshal under E.D. Nix, he captured the Al Jennings Gang. He was police chief of Muskogee, Okla., and then county sheriff.

Lee, Oliver, a lawman who became a deputy marshal in the New Mexico Territory in 1894.

Lefors, Joseph, a detective in Wyoming who fought battles with the Hole-in-the-Wall Gang, he was later appointed a deputy U.S. marshal.

Lewis, Lon, a lawman, served briefly as a Texas Ranger in 1889 before his appointment as deputy U.S. marshal of Oklahoma and the Indian Territory. He was the first sheriff of Tulsa County, Okla.

Lewis, W.W., a lawman, served in Company D, Texas Rangers under Captain Dan W. Roberts. He became a merchant and died in 1934.

Long, John (AKA: **Rivers**), a lawman, was deputized for a raid upon the McSween house on July 19, 1878, during the Lincoln County War.

Long, Steve (AKA: **Big Steve**), a lawman and outlaw, ran the "Bucket of Blood" saloon in Laramie City, Wyo., and appointed himself assistant marshal. Long and his two partners were lynched on Oct. 28, 1868.

Loomis, A.W., a lawman, served as a deputy marshal in the New Mexico Territory.

Loomis, H.W., a lawman, was a chief deputy U.S. marshal in New Mexico Territory and killed train robber Cole Estes on Oct. 2, 1896.

Love, H.M., a lawman, who serving as a deputy marshal in New Mexico, was wounded while in pursuit of Samuel Ketchum, on July 16, 1899.

Love, Harry, a lawman, served as a Texas Ranger in the 1850s, and allegedly brought in the head of Murieta, the Mexican outlaw.

Lowe, Joseph (AKA: **Red Joe, Rowdy Joe, Monte Joe**), a lawman, a gambler and one-time lawman, served as a Texas Ranger at Camp San Saba in 1866.

Lozier, Doctor, a lawman, served as a Texas Ranger in 1896.

M

McCall, Thomas P., a lawman, was the first sheriff of Medina County, Texas, in 1858, and was later a deputy sheriff in Bexar County. McCall became sheriff and served for a decade.

McCauley, William, a lawman, served as a Texas Ranger in the 1890s and in 1897 helped break up a gang terrorizing San Saba.

McClure, Robert, a lawman, served as a Texas Ranger in the 1890s and in 1897 helped break up a gang terrorizing San Saba.

McCord, Myron, a lawman, who was appointed Marshal of the Arizona Territory on June 6, 1901.

McCuiston, O.W., a lawman, who while sheriff of Raton, Ariz., in 1894, became embroiled in a railway strike.

McDonald, William Jesse (AKA: **Captain Bill**), a lawman, was a deputy sheriff at Wood County and then sheriff of Wichita County. He served as a special Texas Ranger and was appointed captain in 1893. Appointed a deputy U.S. marshal of northern Texas and southern Kansas and he was made captain of Company B, Texas Rangers before becoming a U.S. marshal.

McIntosh, T.W., a lawman, who served as a deputy marshal at Prescott, Ariz.

McIntire, James (Jim McIntyre), a Texas gunman and lawman from 1860, was at different times a Texas Ranger, city marshal of Las Vegas, deputy sheriff, cowboy, hunter, gambler, and outlaw with a $1,000 reward on his head for the deaths of two men in American Valley, N.M.

McKidrict, Joe, a lawman, was a Texas Ranger and shot and fatally wounded deputy U.S. marshal, Bass Outlaw.

McKinney, Thomas L., a lawman, was a deputy sheriff under Pat Garrett, and was present when Garrett killed Billy the Kid. McKinney killed Bob Edwards on May 8, 1881, in a shootout.

McMahon, Francis Marion, a lawman, joined Company D of the Texas Rangers under J.R. Hughes in September 1893 and arrested Bass Outlaw on Apr. 4, 1894. He was a deputy U.S. marshal under Dick Ware, and died on Mar. 6, 1940.

McMillan, Private, a lawman, served as a Texas Ranger in 1919.

McMurry, Sam A., a lawman, served for several years in the 1880-90s as captain of Company B, Texas Rangers.

McNeel, J.S., Jr., a lawman, served in Company E as a Texas Ranger in 1892.

McNeel, P.J., a lawman, served in Company E as a Texas Ranger in 1892.

McNelly, Leander H., a lawman, was commissioned as captain of the state police on July 1, 1870, and commanded the "Special Ranger Force" in 1874 which patrolled the Mexico border. He died on Sept. 4, 1877.

McNew, William, a lawman, served as deputy marshal of Dona Ana County, New Mexico.

Maddox, Allen R., a lawman, served in Company B of the Texas Ranger in 1896.

Madsen, Chris, a lawman, served as chief deputy U.S. marshal under Marshal William Grimes in the Territories in 1889, and then under E.D. Nix in the 1890s, John Shelby from 1897 to 1898, Marshal Hamner till 1902, and marshals Paden Colbert and Abernathy. In 1910 he was appointed Marshal, and died in 1947.

Mahorn, Tom, a lawman, was a Texas Ranger, Company B, in 1889 under Captain Sam McMurry.

Maledon, George, a lawman, was a policeman at Fort Smith, Ark., and a deputy sheriff in Sebastian County. He later served as the hangman of the Federal Court at Fort Smith.

Marsden, Crosby, a lawman, was a Texas Ranger in 1907.

Martinez, Romulo, a lawman, was sheriff of Santa Fe County, N.M., between 1881 and 1884.

Mason, Barney, a gunman and lawman, killed John Farris in self defense at Fort Sumner, N.M., in 1880. He was a deputy to Sheriff Garrett.

Mast, Milton, the sheriff of Nacogdoches County, Texas, who captured Wild Bill Longley on June 26, 1877.

Masterson, Edward J. (AKA: **Little Ed**), a lawman and brother of Bat Masterson, was the Dodge City, Kan., town marshal and was killed by cowboys on Apr. 9, 1878.

Masterson, James H., a lawman and brother of Bat Masterson, was a law officer in Dodge City, Kan., in 1885, deputy sheriff of Colfax County, and then a deputy U.S. marshal in Indian Territory, serving under E.D. Nix. He fought the Doolin Gang and was part of the posse that forced Arkansas Tom to surrender.

Masterson, Robert (AKA: **Smiling Bob**), a lawman and brother of Bat Masterson, was marshal of Trinidad, Colo., in 1882 and reportedly killed twenty-one men.

Masterson, William Barclay (AKA: **Bat**), a famous lawman, was deputy town marshal of Dodge City, Kan., was elected Ford County sheriff in the 1870s, and was later city marshal of Dodge City, Kan., when he helped capture outlaw Dave Rudabaugh. Appointed deputy U.S. marshal of the New York district in 1905, he resigned in 1907 and died on Oct. 25, 1921.

Mather, David (AKA: **Mysterious Dave**), an outlaw and lawman, was one of the Dodge City Gang in Las Vegas, N.M. On Jan. 26, 1880, as assistant marshal of Las Vegas, he killed Joe Costillo.

Matthews, Frank, a lawman, served as a Texas Ranger in 1919.

Matthews, Jacob B. (Billy), a gunman and lawman, served in the Tennessee Cavalry in the Civil War, and was a deputy sheriff under Sheriff Brady during the Lincoln County War. He died in 1903.

Meade, William Kidder, a lawman, was appointed U.S. Marshal for the Arizona Territory on July 8, 1885.

Middleton, C.P., a lawman, was a Texas Ranger in Company B in 1909.

Miles, Hod, an outlaw turned deputy sheriff, who in January 1888, killed Jake Gibson, purported to be his fifth victim.

Millard, George, a lawman, served as a Texas Ranger in 1919.

Miller, James B. (Jim), an outlaw and lawman, was a deputy sheriff in Pecos, Texas, in the 1890s, was appointed town constable, and later served as a Texas Ranger. He killed Sheriff Bud Frazier and was suspected of forty other killings including Pat Garrett and A.A. Bobbitt. A mob lynched him on Apr. 19, 1909, at Ada, Okla.

Miller, John, a lawman, a deputy marshal Tucson, Ariz., during the 1870s.

Milton, Jefferson Davis, a lawman, served as city marshal of El Paso, Texas, and became a deputy U.S. marshal at Fairbanks, Ariz. He captured outlaw William E. Walters (AKA: **Bronco Bill**) and killed John Patterson (AKA: **Three-Fingered Jack**).

Montgomery, David, a lawman, serving in 1878 as chief deputy marshal of Lincoln County, N.M.

Moore, George, a lawman, served as a Texas Ranger.

Moore, Jeff B., a lawman, mercenary, and cowboy, fought Indians in Argentina before he served several terms as sheriff of Crockett County, Texas.

Moore, John, a lawman, served as a Texas Ranger in 1896.

Morgan, Joe, a gunman and lawman, fought deputy sheriff Ben Williams in Las Cruces, N.M., on Sept. 15, 1895, with Albert Fall. He was later a deputy sheriff and Oliver Lee supporter.

Morris, Brack, a lawman, served in Company D as a Texas Ranger in 1882 and was sheriff of Karnes County, Texas, when he was killed on June 13, 1901.

Morrison, Alexander L., Jr., a lawman, served as chief deputy to his father in Santa Fe County, N.M.

Morrison, Alexander L., Sr., a lawman, was appointed marshal of Santa Fe, N.M., on Mar. 2, 1882.

Mossman, Burton C., a lawman, was the first captain of the Arizona Rangers.

Mowbray, George W., a lawman, was a posseman under Heck Thomas, Bill Tilghman, and Chris Madsen in the early 1890s and was appointed deputy U.S. marshal by E.D. Nix. He fought the Cook Gang, the Doolin Gang, the Buck Gang, and the Cherokee Bill Gang.

Murchison, Ivan, a lawman, served as a Texas Ranger under Captain Frank Johnson in 1906.

N

Nagle, David, a lawman and one of the fastest gunfighters, killed Judge David Terry while serving as a deputy U.S. marshal in California. He was deputy sheriff of Tombstone, Ariz., in the late 1870s.

Natus, Joe, a lawman, served as a private in Company F of the Texas Rangers in 1894.

Neal, Doc, a lawman, served as a Texas Ranger in 1896.

Neal, Edgar T., a lawman, served as a Texas Ranger in Company B in the 1890s and was elected sheriff of San Saba County for several terms.

Neeley, A.A., a lawman, served as a Texas Ranger in 1894 as a private in Company B.

Neil, Edgar, a lawman, served as a Texas Ranger in 1896.

Neis, Tony, a lawman, who in 1881 was assigned to escort Billy the Kid to trial at Mesilla, N.M.

Nevill, Charles L., a lawman, served as a Texas Ranger, and was lieutenant of Company E in 1879, and later captain. Arrested a wounded Sam Bass in 1878, broke up the Jesse Evans gang, and captured the Potter Gang. Served as sheriff of Presidio County from 1885 to 1888.

Newell, J. Benson, a lawman and nephew of Creighton Foraker, was appointed a U.S. marshal in New Mexico Territory in 1907.

Newhall, James T., a lawman, serving during the 1870s, as a deputy marshal in the New Mexico Territory.

Newman, Jim, a lawman and outlaw, consorted with Wes Hardin in the 1860s. He later lived in Texas and New Mexico Territory.

Newton, J.O., a lawman, was the adjutant general of the Texas Rangers in 1907.

Nichols, Frank P., a lawman, was deputy sheriff of Springer, N.M., and shot and killed outlaw John Scott on May 17, 1883.

Nix, Everett Dumas, a lawman, was the U.S. Marshal of Oklahoma and the Indian nations in the 1890s. He employed over 100 deputies who arrested and jailed several thousand suspected criminals.

O

O'Grady, John, a lawman, served as a Texas Ranger in the early 1890s.

Olinger, Charles Robert, an outlaw, crooked U.S. marshal, and deputy sheriff of Lincoln County, N.M., was indicted for his participation in the Lincoln County War, and was killed by Billy the Kid on Apr. 28, 1881.

O'Neill, John H. "Jack", a lawman at Fort Thomas, N.M. during the late 1880s.

Osborn, William S., a lawman, serving as a deputy marshal at Precott, Ariz. during the 1870s.

Outlaw, Bass L., a lawman, joined Company E of the Texas Rangers in 1885 and changed to Company D in 1887, resigned in 1894 after shooting up the town of Alpine, and was appointed deputy U.S. marshal. Outlaw was killed by Ranger John Selman on Apr. 4, 1894.

Owens, Will, a lawman, served as a Texas Ranger in 1886 under Captain G.H. Schmidt.

P

Palmer, Edward, a lawman, served in Company D of the Texas Rangers in 1894.

Parker, F.D., a lawman, served as deputy marshal at Prescott, Ariz., who in 1876, apprehended an Army clerk attempting to steal a payroll.

Paul, John V., a lawman, serving as an Arizona marshal, who in 1890 was accused of deporting Chinese laborers.

Paul, Robert H., a lawman, was sheriff and constable of Calaveras County, Calif., from 1854 to 1861. He became a deputy U.S. marshal in Tucson, Ariz., and arrested Pony Deal in 1881. As sheriff of Pima County, he battled Red Jack and Charles Hensley.

Pauli, Louis, a lawman, served as a Texas Ranger in 1892.

Payne, Ransom, a lawman, served as a deputy U.S. marshal in the 1890s in Indian Territory and pursued the Dalton Gang.

Peak, Junius (June), a lawman, served as a deputy sheriff of Dallas, Texas, after the Civil War and became one of the special Rangers recruited to breakup the Bass Gang, which they did in 1878. He resigned on Mar. 15, 1880, and died in Dallas in 1934.

Penwell, E.S., a lawman, served as a deputy marshal in the Arizona Territory during the 1870s.

Peppin, George, a lawman and gunman, was the sheriff of Lincoln County, Ariz., during the Lincoln County War.

Perry, Cicero R. (AKA: **Rufe**), a lawman and Indian fighter, joined the Texas Rangers under Jack Hays in 1844 and became commander of Company D in 1874. He resigned several years later and died on Oct. 7, 1898.

Perry, Ollie, a lawman, served as a Texas Ranger in the 1890s, and in 1897 helped break up a gang terrorizing San Saba.

Phelps, E.M., a lawman, served as a colonel in Company C of the Texas Rangers in 1907.

Phelps, Edward, a lawman, served as U.S. Marshal of the Arizona Territory beginning June 1866.

Phillipowski, Lyon, a lawman and Dolan factionist, was a deputy sheriff of Lincoln County, N.M., and killed William Burns, a clerk at Murphy store, in a duel.

Phillips, Charles A., a lawman, served as a deputy marshal in the Arizona Territory during the 1860s.

Phy, Josephus, a lawman, served as deputy sheriff of Pinal County, Ariz., under Pete Gabriel and was discharged in 1885. Phy ran for sheriff and Gabriel killed him in a gunfight.

Pickard, E.B., a lawman, served as a marshal in the New Mexico Territory during the 1890s.

Pickett, Sam, a lawman, served as a Texas Rangers in 1886 under Captain G.H. Schmidt.

Pickett, Thomas, an outlaw and lawman, stole cattle and was captured with Billy the Kid in New Mexico on Dec. 20, 1880. He later served as a ranger and died on May 14, 1934, in Arizona.

Pinkerton, Allen, the founder of the famous detective agency, who was hired privately to track down criminals, including the James Gang.

Platt, Rudd, a lawman, was a Texas Ranger, Company B, in 1889 under Captain Sam McMurry.

Platt, Sam, a lawman, was a Texas Ranger, Company B, in 1889 under Captain Sam McMurry.

Platt, Tom, a lawman, was a Texas Ranger, Company B, in 1889 under Captain Sam McMurry.

Plummer, Henry, an outlaw leader and lawman, organized in Idaho in early 1860 the worst gang of cutthroats in the West. Plummer and over thirty members of the gang were lynched by vigilantes in 1864. He was about to become U.S. marshal of the Territory.

Poe, John W., a gunman and lawman, was town marshal and deputy U.S. marshal of Fort Griffin, Kan., became a deputy sheriff, and helped Sheriff Pat Garrett track Billy the Kid. He was elected sheriff of Lincoln County, N.M., in 1882 and died in July 1925.

Porterie, J.A., a lawman, served as a marshal in New Mexico Territory, who in 1907, was accused but exonerated of killing an Hispanic.

Potter, Dell, a lawman, served as deputy marshal at Dona Ana County, N.M., during the 1890s.

Pratt, John, a lawman, served as U.S. Marshal of the New Mexico Territory between March 1866 and May 1876.

Premont, Charles, a lawman, served in Company E as a Texas Ranger in 1892.

Price, Sterling, a lawman, was a Texas Ranger, Company B, in 1889 under Captain Sam McMurry.

Pridgen, Bolivar Jackson, a senator from 24th District from Price Creek Settlement, DeWitt County, Texas.

Putts, Henry, a lawman, served as a Texas Ranger in 1886 under Captain G.H. Schmidt.

Q

Queen, Lee, a lawman, served as a Texas Ranger in 1896.

R

Rader, Bud, a lawman, served in Company E as a Texas Ranger in 1892.

Rankin, John, a lawman, was a marshal in Texas and helped kill outlaw William Whitley.

Redus, Roscoe, a lawman, served as a sergeant in Company B of the Texas Rangers in 1909.

Reid, F.J., a lawman, was a deputy sheriff of Val Verde County, Texas, in 1909 under Sheriff C.C. Bartley.

Reynolds, N.O. (AKA: **Nage**), a lawman, commanded Company E of the Texas Rangers in 1878. He helped break up the Horrell-Higgins feud and warned Rangers of an attack at Round Rock by Sam Bass.

Rigdon, Terrell, a lawman, served in Company E as a Texas Ranger in 1892.

Roberts, Buckshot (AKA: **Bill Williams, William Albert Roberts, Andrew L. Roberts, Bill Roberts**), a Texas Ranger, outlaw, and member of King Fisher's gang in New Mexico, was killed in the gun battle at Blazer's Mill in 1878 after having killed Dick Brewer.

Roberts, Daniel Webster, a lawman, joined the Texas Rangers and served under Rufe Perry in 1874. He was made captain in 1878 and broke up outlaw gangs such as the Mason County Mob, the Potter boys, and the Jesse Evans Gang. He resigned in 1914.

Roberts, Ross, a lawman, was a deputy sheriff of Val Verde County, Texas, in 1909 under Sheriff C.C. Bartley.

Robinson, D.S., a lawman, served in Company E as a Texas Ranger in 1892.

Robinson, Jim R., a lawman, served as a Texas Rangers in 1886 under Captain G.H. Schmidt.

Rogers, C.L. (AKA: **Kid**), a lawman, served as a Texas Ranger in 1896.

Rogers, Ernest, a lawman, served in Company D of the Texas Rangers in 1887.

Rogers, Ike, a lawman, was a deputy under U.S. Marshal Crum, and captured Cherokee Bill on Jan. 29, 1895. He was killed at Fort Gibson in 1897.

Rogers, J.H., a lawman for fifty years, joined the Texas Rangers in 1882, was appointed U.S. marshal, but returned to the Rangers and served as a captain in Company C in 1907.

Rogers, L.T., a lawman, served as a colonel in Company C of the Texas Rangers in 1907.

Romero, Bernardo, a lawman, the nephew of Trinidad Romero, served as a deputy marshal in the New Mexico Territory.

Romero, Cleofes, a lawman and sheriff of San Miguel County, N.M., during the 1890s.

Romero, Miguel A., a lawman, served as deputy marshal at Las Vegas, N.M.

Romero, Secundino, a lawman, served as U.S. Marshal of New Mexico beginning in 1912.

Romero, Trinidad, a lawman, served as U.S. Marshal of the New Mexico Territory beginning Nov. 7, 1889.

Rosenthal, William, a lawman, served as a deputy in the New Mexico Territory during the 1870s.

Ross, T.M., a lawman, served as a private in Company F of the Texas Rangers in 1894 and as captain of Company B of the Texas Rangers in 1909.

Roundtree, Oscar J., a lawman, served as a Texas Ranger under Captain Frank Johnson in 1906.

Rucker, E.C., a lawman, was deputy sheriff of Tularosa, N.M., and sided with John Good in the Tularosa feud.

Rudabaugh, David, an outlaw and briefly city marshal of Las Vegas, N.M., rode with the Roark Gang, Doc Holliday, and Billy the Kid. He was shot and beheaded by vigilantes in Mexico.

Rudd, W.L. (AKA: **Colorado Chico, Little Red**), a lawman, served under Lee Hall in McNelly's Rangers in the 1870s and was elected sheriff of Karnes County in the 1880s. He died at age ninety-four in 1938.

Rumley, Charles S., a lawman, served as U.S. Marshal of the New Mexico Territory beginning Apr. 5, 1853.

Rusk, Dave, a lawman, was a deputy U.S. marshal for the Indian Nations working out of Judge Isaac Parker's court in the 1880s and 1890s.

Russell, Richard Robertson (Dick), a lawman, joined the Texas Rangers in 1880, served as sheriff of Menard, Texas, from 1886 to 1896, and died on June 28, 1922.

Russell, Stillwell, a lawman, served in the New Mexico Territory during the 1870s.

Rynning, Thomas Harbo, a lawman, commanded the Arizona Rangers in the 1890s and 1900s.

S

Sallis, W.F., a lawman, served in Company B of the Texas Rangers in 1909.

Saunders, J.W., a lawman, served in Company D of the Texas Rangers in 1894.

Scarborough, George, a lawman, was elected sheriff of Jones County, Texas, in 1885, served for several terms. He killed John Selman in 1895 while a deputy U.S. marshal of El Paso. He was killed by the Will Carver Gang on Apr. 5, 1900.

Schmidt, Frank, a lawman, served in Company D of the Texas Rangers in 1887 under Captain Frank Jones.

Schmidt, G.S., a lawman, was the captain of a company of Texas Rangers in 1886.

Schmidt, Will, a lawman, served in Company D of the Texas Rangers in 1894.

Scotten, Ed H., a lawman, served under Jim Gillett as assistant city marshal of El Paso in 1882, and died on Sept. 2, 1884.

Seale, James, a lawman, served in Company B of the Texas Rangers in 1909.

Selman, John, a Texas lawman and outlaw, allegedly rustled with John Larn around Fort Griffin, Texas. He befriended Billy the Kid during the Lincoln County War, and killed Wes Hardin in August 1895. George Scarborough killed him on Apr. 6, 1896.

Selman, John, Jr., a lawman, deputized as a Arizona marshal in 1899.

Sena, George, a lawman, was removed as a sheriff of Lincoln County, N.M., in 1896, for failure to enforce the law.

Sena, Jose D., a lawman, served as a deputy marshal of Santa Fe County, N.M., during the 1860s.

Sena y Baca, Jesus Maria, a lawman, became a deputy marshal in the New Mexico Territory in 1858.

Shaffenburg, M.A., a lawman, served as a marshal in the Colorado Territory during the 1860s.

Sharp, Mike, a lawman, was a deputy sheriff of Val Verde County, Texas, in 1909 under Sheriff C.C. Bartley.

Sheridan, J.J., a lawman, served as a deputy marshal in the New Mexico Territory, during the 1890s.

Shibell, Charles, a lawman, served as sheriff of Pima County, Ariz., from 1877 to 1879 and appointed Wyatt Earp as deputy to replace Virgil Earp. Deputy Sheriff John Behan replaced Shibell as sheriff.

Sieber, Albert, a lawman and Indian scout, commanded a scout and police force as a deputy U.S. marshal, employing at different times the

Apache Kid, Frank Leslie, and Tom Horn. He died in 1907.

Sieker, Edward A., a lawman and one of the Sieker brothers, served as a Texas Ranger in Company D under Dan Roberts and led the attack against the Jesse Evans Gang in 1880.

Sieker, Frank, a lawman and one of the Sieker brothers, joined the Texas Rangers and served on Company B. He was shot and killed in a battle with Mexican horse thieves in May 1885.

Sieker, Lamartine P. (AKA: **Lamb**), a lawman and one of the Sieker brothers, joined Company D of the Texas Rangers and in 1884 was made Quartermaster general. He served as a Ranger for nineteen years and died in 1914.

Sieker, Tom, a lawman and one of the Sieker brothers, served on the Texas Rangers and lived in Dallas.

Simms, Pink, a lawman and cowboy, served as a lawman in Texas and hunted individual outlaws of the Wild Bunch with Charles Siringo.

Sippy, Benjamin, a lawman, served as city marshal of Tombstone, Ariz., in January 1881, and was replaced by Virgil Earp who lost the following election to Sippy.

Siringo, Charles, a gunman, was a cowboy detective who pursued outlaws and rustlers throughout the West. He joined the Pinkerton Agency in the 1890s and worked for them for twenty-two years.

Sitters, Joe, a lawman, served in Company D of the Texas Rangers in 1894.

Slaughter, John, a lawman, was sheriff of Cochise County, Ariz., during the 1880s.

Smith, Colonel, a lawman, was the colonel of the Texas Rangers of Headquarters Company of Austin, Texas, in 1919.

Smith, J.H., a lawman, served as a deputy marshal in the New Mexico Territory, and was shot to death while in pursuit of the outlaw Samuel Ketchum.

Smith, Simeon H., a lawman, served as a deputy marshal in the New Mexico Territory during the 1850s.

Smith, Thomas J. (AKA: **Bear River**), a lawman, served as a police officer in Bear River, Wyo., during the "Bear River troubles." He was appointed the first marshal of Abilene, Kan., in 1870. Known as the "No gun marshal," he was shot and killed on Nov. 2, 1870.

Smith, William, a lawman, was a deputy U.S. marshal for the Indian Nations working out of Judge Isaac Parker's court in Fort Smith, Ark., in the 1880s and 1890s.

Snearly, W.J., a lawman, served as a Texas Ranger in 1877 under Pat Dolan and was one of his most efficient men.

Sowell, A.J., a lawman, served as a Texas Ranger in 1870-71, and later wrote and published several Texas history books. He died in 1922.

Spradley, A.J. (John), a lawman, served as deputy sheriff of Nacogdoches County, Texas, in 1880 under Sheriff Dick Orton and was elected sheriff in 1882. He served for several years, solved many murder cases such as the Truitt murder, and tracked outlaws.

Standefer, Wiley W., a lawman, served as U.S. Marshal of the Arizona Territory from Aug. 15, 1876, until June 12, 1878.

Stephens, R.M., a lawman, served as a sheriff in the New Mexico Territory during the 1850s.

Stiles, William (Billie), an outlaw, rode with Burt Alvord as a lawman and outlaw in Arizona in the 1890s and 1900s, and was killed in 1908.

Stillwell, F.C. (Frank), a gunman and lawman, was a deputy sheriff under Sheriff Behan in Tombstone, Ariz., and was shot and killed in 1881 during the grand jury investigation of Morgan Earp's shooting death.

Stillwell, Simpson (AKA: **Commanche Jack, John**), a gunman and lawman, scouted for the Army in Texas, served as a deputy U.S. marshal in the Indian Nations, and brought in several outlaws.

Stockton, William Porter (AKA: **Porter Stogden**), an outlaw, lawman, and brother of Ike, shot and killed Juan Gonzales in October 1876 in Cimarron, N.M., and was killed on Jan. 10, 1881, by Alfred Graves.

Stoudenmire, Dallas, a lawman and gunman, joined Company A of the Texas Rangers in 1874, was city marshal of El Paso in 1881, and killed several men before his death in the early 1880s.

Sullivan, W. John L., a lawman, served as a sergeant in Company B of the Texas Rangers in 1889 and 1896.

Sunday, Jesse, a lawman, served as sheriff of the Sabine district, Cherokee Nation in the late 1880s.

T

Taylor, Creed, a lawman, joined the Texas Rangers under Captain Hays, fought in many battles, and died Dec. 27, 1906, at eighty-six years old.

Terrell, Arthur, a lawman, was a Texas Ranger, Company B, in 1889 under Captain Sam McMurry.

Therringer, T.M., a lawman, served as a deputy marshal in the Arizona Territory during the 1870s.

Thomas, Heck, a lawman and one of the "Three Guardsmen," served in the Indian Nations as a deputy U.S. marshal in 1877, and as a special Texas Ranger in 1883. He helped break up the Dalton, Doolin, and Casey gangs, and captured the Lee Gang. He died on Aug. 15, 1912.

Thompson, Ben (AKA: **Shotgun Ben**), a gunman and lawman in Texas, served as city marshal of Austin, Texas. He killed thirty-two men, and was killed in ambush with King Fisher in March 1884. Bat Masterson called him the West's greatest gunfighter.

Throckmorton, Sergeant, a lawman, served as a sergeant in the Texas Rangers in 1896.

Tidball, Zan L., a lawman, was appointed U.S. Marshal of the Arizona Territory on July 18, 1882.

Tilghman, Bill, a lawman, served as marshal of Dodge City, Kan., as sheriff of Ford County, and was the first city marshal of Perry, Okla. He became a deputy U.S. marshal under E.D. Nix and brought in outlaws Bill Doolin and Henry Starr. He was killed by prohibition officer Wylie Lynn on Nov. 1, 1924.

Tolbit, John, a lawman, was a deputy U.S. marshal for the Indian nations working out of Judge Isaac Parker's court in the 1880s and 1890s.

Townsend, Everett E., a lawman, served in Company E as a Texas Ranger in 1892.

Townsley, Bob, a lawman, served in Company E as a Texas Ranger in 1892.

Townsley, Forest, a lawman, served in Company E as a Texas Ranger in 1892.

Trentham, Charles, a lawman, was a Texas Ranger who killed a man in Marfa, Texas, and escaped to New Mexico with a friend.

Tucker, George, a lawman, served in Company D of the Texas Rangers in 1894 and 1896.

Tucker, Thomas, a lawman and gunfighter, served as deputy marshal in Las Cruces, N.M., during the 1850s.

Turnbo, L.S. (Kirk), a lawman, served under Colonel Baylor as a Texas Ranger and made first lieutenant before he became sheriff of Reeves County, Texas, on Aug. 20, 1885.

Turner, George, a lawman and Arizona deputy marshal, was shot to death by Indians in September 1881.

Turner, Marion, a gunman and lawman, was a part-time assistant sheriff under Sheriff Peppin of Lincoln County, N.M., who led an army of men against Billy the Kid and his Regulator who were in hiding.

Tyner, Andrew, a lawman, served as sheriff of Yuma County, Ariz., during the 1870s.

Tyng, George, a lawman, served as sheriff of Yuma County, Ariz., during the 1860s.

U

Updyke, David, a lawman, was elected sheriff of Ada County, Idaho, in 1865. He was lynched on Apr. 14, 1866, for allegedly aiding horse thieves and murderers.

Utting, Charles, a lawman, served as a deputy marshal in the Arizona Territory.

V

Valdez, Antonio Jose (AKA: **El Mico, El Patas de Rana**), an outlaw and lawman, was one of Silva's White Caps of Las Vegas, N.M., shot and killed Vicente Silva from behind, and later became city marshal of Wagon Mound, N.M.

Vandenburg, B.C. (Bob), a lawman and U.S. cavalryman, served as deputy sheriff of Ford County in 1872 and as marshal of Dodge City, Kan., from 1881 to 1883.

W

Wakefield, Lyman, a lawman, served as the sheriff of Cochise County, Ariz., in the 1890s. He shot and killed outlaw Pedro Chavez.

Wallace, William Alexander Anderson (AKA: **Bigfoot**), a lawman, fought Mexicans for several years before joining the Texas Rangers under Captain Hays. He was made captain in 1858 and fought outlaws along the border. Bigfoot Wallace died on Jan. 7, 1899.

Ware, R.C. (Dick), a lawman, served as a Texas Ranger in 1878 and shot Sam Bass at Round Rock. He served as sheriff of Mitchell County, Texas, 1880-81, 1887-88, as U.S. Marshal of West Texas in 1884, and was killed by constable John Selman at El Paso.

Webb, John Joshua (AKA: **Samuel King**), an outlaw, member of the Dodge City Gang in Las Vegas, N.M., and city marshal of Las Vegas, murdered Michael Kelliher on Mar. 2, 1880, was condemned to hang, but escaped from jail with David Rudabaugh in 1881 and died of smallpox the following year.

Welch, John, a lawman, was Judge Roy Bean's deputy in 1893.

Welles, Justus P., a lawman, served as a deputy marshal in the Arizona Territory.

Wernett, John, a lawman, was a deputy sheriff of Val Verde County, Texas, in 1909 under Sheriff C.C. Bartley.

West, Duval, a lawman, was a Texas deputy U.S. marshal in 1886 to 1888, and helped kill outlaw William Whitley. He was later a federal judge.

Weston, Parker, a lawman, served as a Texas Ranger under Captain Frank Johnson in 1906.

Wheeler, Ben, a lawman and outlaw, was a companion of Billy the Kid during the Lincoln County War, robbed the Medicine Lodge, Kan., bank with Marshal Hendry Brown and others on Apr. 30, 1884, and was lynched.

Wheeler, Harry, a lawman, served as an Arizona Ranger and then as sheriff of Cochise County, Ariz., for several years.

White, Coley, a lawman, served as the deputy sheriff of Travis County, Texas,in 1907.

White, Dudley, a lawman, served as a Texas Ranger in 1907.

White, Fred, a lawman, the marshal of Tombstone, Ariz., who was killed by "Curley Bill" Brocius in October 1880.

White, G.S., a lawman, served as a deputy U.S. marshal out of Fort Smith, Ark., in the 1890s.

White, Golf, a lawman, served in Company C of the Texas Rangers in 1907.

White, J.C. (AKA: **Doc**), a lawman, served as Texas Ranger in 1907.

White, Jack, a lawman, was once sheriff of Cochise County, Ariz.

White, Scott, a lawman and politician, served as sheriff of Cochise County, Ariz., from 1892 to 1901.

White, Tom B., a lawman, served as a Texas Ranger under Captain Frank Johnson in 1906.

White, Will, a lawman, served as the sheriff of Wilson County, Texas, in 1907.

Whitney, Chauncey B., a lawman, was the first city marshal of Ellsworth, Kan., in 1871, and became sheriff of the county in 1872. He was killed on Aug. 18, 1873, by Billy Thompson, who claimed his gun fired by accident.

Widenmann, Robert A., a lawman, served as a deputy marshal in the New Mexico Territory during the 1870s.

Wiley, John M., a lawman, served as a deputy marshal in the New Mexico Territory.

Williams, Ben, a lawman, was the deputy sheriff of Las Cruces, N.M., and fought Joe Morgan and Albert Fall in a shootout on Sept. 15, 1895.

Wilson, Vernon Coke, a lawman, joined Company A, Texas Rangers in 1876 under Neal Coldwell and alerted the Rangers that Sam Bass was at Round Rock in 1878. He was chief of the Mounted Inspectors of Arizona and New Mexico Territories in 1885. As a deputy U.S. marshal assigned to track Chris Evans and John Sontag, he was killed by Evans on Sept. 13, 1892.

Wilson, William (AKA: **Buffalo Billy**), an outlaw, lawman, was arrested with Billy the Kid, served time in prison, received a pardon in 1896, and became sheriff of Terrell County, N.M. He was killed in 1911.

Wohrle, John (John Worley), a lawman and outlaw, was deputy sheriff in Mason County, Texas, and involved in the Hoodoo War in 1875. He was shot, stabbed, and scalped by Scott Cooley to avenge Wohrle's part in the death of Tim Williamson.

Wright, Milam, a lawman, was a deputy sheriff of Val Verde County, Texas, in 1909 under Sheriff C.C. Bartley.

Wright, Will, a lawman, served as a captain in the Texas Ranger during WWI.

WESTERN OUTLAWS AND GUNMEN

The homesteaders and fortune seekers who moved west into previously ungoverned Indian lands during the mid-19th century faced enormous perils, including the many colorful gunfighters and desperados who etched their names into history in the fifty years before the Western frontier officially "closed" in 1890. The exploits of these men have been greatly exaggerated in the popular culture of the late 20th century. There really was a Billy the Kid, for example, though it is doubtful that he killed twenty-two men, one for every year of his life; according to his friend George Coe, this figure never exceeded nine. Similarly, Ben Thompson of Texas was said to have gunned down thirty men single-handedly, and John Wesley Hardin thirty-five.

Lawlessness in the Old West was not confined to the main streets of wide-open towns like Abilene or Dodge City. The worst incidents of gun play often occurred in the era's range wars and personal feuds that sprang up in New Mexico, Arizona, and Texas. The Mason County War in particular was characterized by a violent clash between German homesteaders and native Texans. Their differences harkened back to the Civil War, when the Germans espoused the cause of the Union, and the natives took the side of the Confederacy. Erupting between them in 1875, a shooting war resulted in many casualties on both sides before the Texas Rangers restored order.

The era of the gunfighter was over by the turn of the century. Improvements in transportation, the encroachments of civilization, and a more efficient deployment of law enforcement personnel put an end to this colorful but violent chapter in U.S. history.

Adamson, Carl, an outlaw who rode with Jim Miller, helped kill Pat Garrett in New Mexico on Feb. 28, 1908.

Adkins, Dave, an outlaw, was a member Black Jack Ketchum's Gang.

Aguelari, Epeminto, an outlaw, killed Jose A. Samora at Wallace, N.M., on Apr. 20, 1884.

Aguilar, Ceberiano, an outlaw, fought and died in the Harrold War of Lincoln County, N.M., in 1874.

Aguilar, Donaciano, an outlaw, was sentenced to life imprisonment in New Mexico on Nov. 24, 1909.

Aguilar, Reymundo, an outlaw, fought and died in the Harrold War of Lincoln County, N.M., 1874.

Aguillan, Felix, an outlaw, was a member of the Castillo Gang.

Aguirre, Jermin, a gunman, was shot on Aug. 8, 1875, near San Augustin Ranch, N.M.

Ake, Jeff was a Texas Reconstruction gunman.

Ake, William, a gunman and brother of Jeff Ake, fought in the Mason County feud in the 1870s in Texas.

"Alamosa Bill", an outlaw, was killed at El Paso, Texas, in April 1888.

Alarid, Eugenio, a lawman and outlaw, was a member of the Las Vegas, N.M., police force and a member of Vincente Silva's White Caps, also in Las Vegas.

Alarid, Nasario, an outlaw, was sentenced to ninety-nine years in prison in New Mexico on Sept. 17, 1906.

Alexander, John, an outlaw, stole horses in Texas and was shot and killed by a mob on May 25, 1874, in Belton.

Alford, George, an outlaw, was imprisoned five years for killing a sheriff in 1880 at Fort Worth, Texas.

Allen, Bill, a Texas outlaw and robber, occasionally rode with the Jesse Evans Gang.

Allen, Billy (AKA: **The Kid**), a gunman in Deadwood, S.D., and New Mexico, killed several men.

Allen, "Bladder", an outlaw in Lincoln County, was jailed for stabbing a man in White Oaks, N.M.

Allen, Chas, an outlaw, robbed and killed a group of people in Virginia City for which he was hanged.

Allen, Frank, a gunman, was shot and killed in El Paso, Texas, in March 1881.

Allen, James, an outlaw, killed James Moorehead in Las Vegas, N.M., for ordering eggs on Mar. 2, 1880, and was killed by a posse after escaping prison.

Allen, John, a outlaw member of the Dodge City gang, operating around Las Vegas, New Mexico.

Allen, Joseph, a gunman, was hanged on Apr. 19, 1909, at Ada, Okla., for his participation in a feud.

Allen, Mal, an outlaw, killed two men in the Chickasaw Nation and was hanged at Fort Smith on Apr. 19, 1889.

Allison, Charles, a former deputy sheriff turned outlaw, robbed stages between Colorado and New Mexico. He was captured in 1881 by sheriff Matt Kyle, then by Frank Hyatt, and released in 1890.

Allison, Clay, a rancher quick-draw artist from Cimarron, N.M., lethally dangerous while drinking.

Allison, Robert A., a quick-draw gunman who killed at least fifteen men, moved between Colorado, New Mexico, and Texas as a cowhand. He led several lynch mobs and died on July 1, 1887, when a wagon wheel crushed his head.

Almer, Jack (Jack Averill, AKA: **Red Jack)**, an outlaw and leader of the Red Jack Gang, was killed on Oct. 4, 1883, by a posse near Wilcox, Ariz.

Alsup, Wade, an outlaw, was lynched by fifteen masked men in Blue, Texas, on June 27, 1877.

Altman, Perry, a New Mexico gunman and the half-brother of Oliver Lee.

Alvarid, Juan, an outlaw, was lynched in Socorro, N.M., on Aug. 16, 1882, for raping an 8-year-old girl.

Alverson, Leonard, a cowboy and gunman, was accused, with two others, of a Dec. 9, 1897, robbery at Steins Pass, N.M. They were imprisoned, but in 1899, Sam Ketchum confessed to the crime and the three men were freed.

Alvord, Burt, a deputy sheriff turned outlaw, led a gang that robbed trains in Arizona. Captured in Mexico by Arizona Rangers, he served two years in prison and died in 1912 in Honduras.

Amador, Martin, an outlaw, was hanged for murder in Deming, N.M., on Jan. 13, 1908.

Amos, Fred was an outlaw and highwayman in California in the late 1860s.

Anderson, Ham, a gunman and cousin of Wes Hardin, used his guns in Dodge City, Kan., and Texas before he was killed in 1874.

Anderson, Jim, an outlaw with Bill Anderson's guerilla band, was killed in Texas in the 1860s.

Anderson, Reese, a gunman and cowboy who led a vigilante sweep of the Lower Judith Basin in Montana, 1884, captured and hanged twenty-three horse thieves.

Anderson, Scott, L., the trusted guard for the Northwestern Stage and Transportation Company, which transported gold in the Dakotas, killed Boston Joe when the stage robber attempted to take over $100,000 in gold.

Anderson, Tom, a gunman, was the brother of Black Jack Christian.

Anderson, William, a resident of Delano, the vice district of Wichita, Kan., was a drunken gunman who in 1873 was blinded in a shootout. Anderson died begging coins outside saloons.

Andrews, Hank, an outlaw, was lynched by vigilantes in February 1884, near Tularosa, N.M.

Anthony, Ernest, an outlaw horse thief, was jailed in Springer, N.M., in March 1885.

Apache Kid (Zenogalache, AKA: **The Crazy One)**, an outlaw Apache Indian, along with a band of warriors, raided ranches and wagon trains throughout New Mexico and Arizona territories. A rancher presumably killed him during a raid on Sept. 10, 1905.

Apodaca, Maximo, an outlaw and convicted murderer of the Nesmith family in White Sands, N.M., committed suicide in prison on Nov. 4, 1885.

Applegate, Bill, an outlaw, led a gang of rustlers in New Mexico Territory in the 1870s. He was nearly captured by Seven Rivers.

Aragon, Serefin, a New Mexico Territory outlaw and cattle rustler.

Arajo, Justin, an outlaw in California, was lynched for shooting a man to death on July 12, 1877.

Arango, Doroter (AKA: **Francisco "Pancho" Villa)**, an outlaw, cattle rustler, and Mexican revolutionist, successfully raided the U.S. border several times. He was killed on July 20, 1923, at Parral, Mex.

Archer Brothers, outlaws, robbed travelers, trains, and stages throughout Orange and Marion Counties of Indiana. Tom, Mort, and John Archer were lynched by vigilantes in March 1886 and Sam Archer was hanged July 10, 1886.

Arguello, A., an outlaw, murdered Asher Jones at Clayton, N.M., in 1881.

"Arizona Jack", a gunman and teamster, was lynched at Wagon Bed Springs, Kansas Territory, for shooting to death another teamster.

"Arkansas Bill", a gunman of Dodge City, Kan., in the late 1870s claimed he killed twenty-two men.

Armstrong, Jack, an outlaw of Las Vegas, N.M., killed a bartender over the price of a drink.

Arquello, David, an outlaw, was hanged in Raton, N.M., on May 25, 1906.

Arrington, Willis, a Texas outlaw, was charged in 1881 with rustling cattle.

Ashby, George, an outlaw, stole horses in Montana and Texas, and killed a sheriff near Powder River and Little Missouri, Mont.

Asque, Joe (Joe Askew), an outlaw, rustled cattle near Hillsboro, N.M., around 1877 and cut himself down from a hangman's noose.

Atkins, David, an outlaw and member of the Black Jack Ketchum Gang, robbed trains throughout New Mexico, West Texas, and Arizona.

Augustine, Robert, a cowboy and gunman, was arrested in 1863 for hurrahing San Antonio, Texas. He was lynched after the court acquitted him.

Averill, James, and **Watson, Ella**, outlaws, rustled cattle. Their deaths in July 1860 at the hands of rival ranchers began the bloody Johnson County War.

Avila, Genovevo (AKA: **El Cochumeno)**, a Mexican native who was a member of Vincente Silva's Forty Thieves.

Ayers, Thomas G. a gunman, was killed by the Dalton Gang in the Coffeyville, Kan., bank robberies on Nov. 5, 1892, while attempting to shoot a rifle.

Baca, Abran, an outlaw, murdered A.M. Conklin of Socorro, N.M., with others on Christmas Eve 1880. He was acquitted in 1881.

Baca, Antonio, an outlaw, murdered A.M. Conklin with others in 1880. He was killed attempting to escape jail on Dec. 29, 1880.

Baca, Celso, a murderer who beat Jose de la Cruz Sandoval to death in 1884 at Santa Rosa, N.M.

Baca, Cruz, an outlaw, murdered W.H. Allen of Hillsboro, N.M., in February 1887.

Baca, Jose, an outlaw and multiple offender, was sent to prison on Nov. 19, 1906, for the fifth time.

Baca, Manuel, an outlaw and member of Silva's White Caps in the 1890s, was the "judge" who ordered the execution of disloyal gang members.

Baca, Onofre, an outlaw, murdered A.M. Conklin with others in 1880 and was lynched on Mar. 31, 1881.

Baca, Patricio, an outlaw and the most notorious horse thief in northern New Mexico Territory, was killed in Chimayo in December 1875.

"Bad Nell", a Texas outlaw and cowboy. She operated around Fort Griffin in the 1870s.

Bader, Pete was a gunman in the Mason County "Hoodoo War" of Texas. His brother, Charles Bader, was killed by John Ringo.

Bailey, John, an outlaw and rustler, was shot and killed by Ranger P.C. Baird in Edward County, Texas, on July 29, 1884.

Baker, Chas, a gunman in the Lincoln County War and brother of Frank Baker, was captured by Ranger Jim Gillett in Texas and imprisoned for twenty-five years.

Baker, Cullen Montgomery, an outlaw and veteran guerilla soldier, fought reconstructionist soldiers and terrorized Texas for four years after the war. He was killed on Jan. 6, 1869, having killed twenty-six men in his fifteen years as a soldier.

Baker, Frank, an outlaw and member of the Jesse Evans Gang, helped kill John Tunstall during the Lincoln County War. Billy the Kid killed Baker in March 1878 in retaliation.

Baldwin, Thurman (AKA: **Skeeter**), an outlaw and member of the Cook Gang in Indian Territory, was captured after a bank robbery.

Ballard, Charles, a gunman, rode with the posse that captured Black Jack Ketchum in September 1896.

Ballew, Steve, a gunman, in 1870, shot and killed Jim Golden in Collin County, Texas, and was executed.

Bangs, "Cherokee", an outlaw and cattle rustler in Utah, led a gang in the 1890s which included Matt Warner.

Barbee, Claude, an outlaw, shot and killed deputy sheriff Hamilton on Gene Rhodes ranch.

Barbour, John, an outlaw, was a member of the Brack Cornett Gang of Texas in the 1880s. He was killed in the Indian Nations.

Barela, Manuel, a New Mexico gunman who killed a man in Las Vegas, only to be hanged by vigilantes in 1879.

Barela, Santos, an outlaw, was hanged on May 20, 1881, in Mesilla, N.M.

Barela, Ysabel, a gunman, was shot and killed by John Kinney in Mesilla, N.M., on Nov. 2, 1877.

Barkley, Clinton, an outlaw wanted for murder, was a Horrell gunman in the Horrell-Higgins feud.

Barnes, Johnny was an Arizona and New Mexico outlaw.

Barnes, Seaborne (Sebe, AKA: **Nubbin's Colt**), an outlaw, joined the Sam Bass Gang in 1874, was indicted for assault, and killed with Bass at Round Rock, Texas, in 1878.

Barnett, Wes, an outlaw in the Indian Nations in the 1880s, was killed by police in 1889. He terrorized the Creek Indian capital.

Barrera, Calisto, an outlaw, murdered John D. Bohn on Aug. 16, 1882, near Sapello, N.M.

Barter, Richard (AKA: **Rattlesnake Dick; Dick Woods**), a California outlaw, stole horses and robbed mining camps. He was killed in July 1859 while his gang robbed a mule train.

Barton, Jerry, a gunman, ran a saloon in Charleston, Ariz., killed his partner, and was jailed for killing a Mexican in 1881.

Barton, "Kid", an outlaw, led a stage robbing gang that operated at Raton Pass. He killed several people and was hanged in the late 1860s.

Basham, Tucker, an outlaw, was a member of Jesse James' gang.

Bass, Samuel (Sam), an outlaw who robbed stages in the Dakotas, organized a gang in Texas and robbed trains. He and another gang members were killed by Texas Rangers at Round Rock, Texas, in July 1878.

Basset, Harry, a gunman, was shot on Nov. 20, 1879, in Otero, N.M.

Baugh, Captain **Andrew T.**, a Texas outlaw and cattle rustler, was lynched in the 1880s when caught with a herd of stolen cattle.

Baxter, Dan, a gunman, was shot and killed in August 1884 by Frank Thurmond in Deming, N.M.

Beach, Charles, a gunman, shot and killed a man who stabbed him in the Prescott, Ariz., court room on Dec. 3, 1883.

Beard, Edward T., a gunman in California, Oregon, and Arizona, ran a par in Wichita, Kan., and died on Nov. 11, 1873, from wounds received from a shoot-out with rival saloon owner and gunman Rowdy Joe Lowe.

Beard, John, a gunman in the Mason County, Texas, "Hoodoo War," participated in the Horrell-Higgins feud.

Beard, Mose, brother of John, was a gunman in the Mason County, Texas, "Hoodoo War."

Beck, Frank, an outlaw, helped murder Joe Hickson on Oct. 28, 1884, at Good Hope, N.M.

Beck, H.O. (AKA: **Welch, Ed**), an outlaw, was a cell mate of Ben Kilpatrick of the Wild Bunch and wanted to join the gang. He was shot and killed Mar. 13, 1912, during a train robbery in which Kilpatrick was also killed.

Beck, William Ellison (AKA: **Cyclone Bill**), an outlaw, who became a suspect in the robbery of an Army paymaster on May 11, 1889.

Beckwith, Henry, a gunman in the Lincoln County War, shot-gunned his son-in-law on Aug. 16, 1878.

Beckwith, John, a gunman and son of Henry, participated in the Lincoln County War.

Beckwith, Robert W., gunman in the Lincoln County War, was a member of the posse that killed John Tunstall. He was killed in the McSween fight July 19, 1878.

Bell, C.S., a gunman, lawman, and former Union spy, claimed he killed over thirty men.

Bell, "Choctaw", an outlaw, was a member of the Langford Gang of Texas in the early 1880s. He was shot by a posse in 1881.

Bell, Tom, a California outlaw, robbed stages with a gang he led, and was lynched by a sheriff in 1856.

Belmont, Courtney, a gunman, rode with Matt Zimmerman in the 1880s in Nebraska.

Belmont, Dick, a gunman, rode with Matt Zimmerman but went to Kansas after Matt was killed. Belmont was shot dead in Stockton.

Benavides, Santos, an outlaw, murderer and horse thief, was lynched in Albuquerque, N.M., Dec. 29, 1880.

Bennett, George, a outlaw and member of the Bill Dalton Gang, was killed in 1893 at Longview, Texas, during a bank robbery.

Bentley, Charley, an outlaw, escaped from jail at White Oaks, N.M., in March 1881.

Berry, James, an outlaw and member of the Sam Bass Gang, was caught by lawmen after the train robbery at Big Spring.

Bewley, Jim, a gunman, was killed in Oregon attempting to break the small-pox quarantine.

Bickerstaff, Benjamin F., an outlaw and guerilla soldier, looted Federal supplies and fought soldiers throughout Texas. He was shot and killed by citizens of Alvarado in April 1869.

Bideno, Juan, an outlaw, killed the trail boss during a cattle drive from Texas to Kansas. A posse which included Wes Hardin pursued Bideno, and Hardin killed him in Bluff Creek, Kan.

"Big Sandy" was an outlaw in California in the 1850s.

Bill, Charles, an outlaw, was run out of the territory of New Mexico on Feb. 6, 1906.

Billee, John, an outlaw, murdered W.P. Williams with the help of Thomas Willis. Billee and Willis were captured by deputies Will Ayers, James Wilkerson, and Perry DuVall, and hanged on Jan. 16, 1890.

Billy the Kid (William H. Bonney, Jr., William Johnson), a notorious outlaw, one of the "Regulators" in the Lincoln County War, 1870s-1880s. He ambushed Sheriff Brady, and was slain on July 14, 1881, at Fort Sumner by Pat Garrett in the home of Pete Maxwell.

Bishop, Miles was an outlaw in New Mexico, in the mid-1860s.

Bishop, Pete, a gunman and saloon owner, killed two men in December 1871.

Bivins, Bill, a Wyoming outlaw, was jailed for train robbery near Atlantic City in 1877.

Bivins, Lige, an outlaw, was a member of a gang of raiders in Bell, Texas, during the Civil War.

Black, Blackie, a gunman and teamster, killed several men in Texas in the early 1850s.

Black, Isaac, an outlaw and member of the Doolin Gang, was killed by a posse near Enid, Okla., on Aug. 1, 1895.

Black, Jim, a train robber in the New Mexico Territory.

Black, John, a train robber in the New Mexico Territory.

Black, Pope, an outlaw, was shot and killed in the Florida Mountains, N.M., while resisting arrest, December 1882.

Black, Robert (AKA: **Arkansaw**), an outlaw, eluded lynching by challenging the vigilantes to a fight.

Blackburn, Duncan (AKA: **Tom**), an outlaw, robbed stages in 1877 in Deadwood, Dakota Territory. He disappeared after Boone May killed four bandits.

Blackwell, James, an outlaw, shot and killed W.B. Foster in Raton, N.M., on Aug. 8, 1882.

Blain, Joe, an outlaw, shot and killed Joe Pitman in Luna Valley, N.M., on Feb. 18, 1888.

Blake, John, (AKA: **Tulsa Jack**), an outlaw and member of the Doolin-Dalton Gang, was killed by lawmen following the Rock Island train robbery near Dover, Okla., in 1895.

Blevins, John, a gunman, fought in the Pleasant Valley, Ariz., War and against the Tewksburys in their feud with the Grahams.

Blevins, M. (AKA: **F.C. Marklin**), an outlaw, escaped from the Texas penitentiary in 1884, at the age of twenty.

Blind Joe, a gunman, was killed on the Mescalero Apache Reservation in January 1908.

Blue Duck, a gunman, friend of Belle Starr, and half-breed Indian, allegedly killed a farmer in 1886 and was sentenced to die. He was later pardoned.

Blun, Kenry, an outlaw, shot George C. Quaries on Sept. 20, 1884, at Fairview, N.M.

Bobbitt, A.A. (Gus), a gunman and former lawman, led a faction in the Pontotoc County War against cattlemen Jesse West and Joseph Allen. He was killed in ambush in February 1909.

Bogan, Dan, an outlaw, was wanted in Wyoming and indicted for murder in Texas in 1881.

Boggs, Thomas O., a gunman and a mountain man around Taos, N.M., in 1844, was a friend and associate of Kit Carson.

Boles, Charles E. (AKA: **Black Bart**), an outlaw, successfully robbed twenty-seven stages in California in the early 1880s. He was captured in 1883 and sent to San Quentin prison. He was released on Jan. 23, 1888, and disappeared.

Bolt, William James, an outlaw, was hanged in Lincoln on June 18, 1886.

Boot, Joseph, an outlaw, was captured and imprisoned in 1899 after attempting his first stage robbery with Pearl Hart.

Born, Dutch Henry, an outlaw, and the leader of a group of horse and mule thieves in the 1870s throughout Texas, Kansas, and the Indian Nations.

Bothwell, Albert J., a gunman and head of the cattle barons of Sweetwater, Wyo., Bothwell ordered the lynching of Jim Averill and Ella Watson, precipitating the Johnson County War. He was driven out of the county by other ranchers and disappeared.

Boucher, William, an outlaw and cowboy of Tombstone, Ariz., was suspected of stage robbery and killed on Mar. 25, 1888, by Sheriff Billy Breakenridge's posse.

Bowdre, Charles, an outlaw and right hand to Billy the Kid in the Lincoln County War, was killed on Dec. 20, 1880, awaiting trial for the murder of Buckshot Roberts.

Bowers, George, gunman, was killed in the Lincoln County War on July 19, 1878.

Boyce, Mart, a gunman and faro dealer in Caldwell, Kan., in 1883 was killed by Marshal H. Brown.

Boyce, Reuben H. (AKA: **Rube**), an outlaw in Kimble County, Texas, led a gang of rustlers. He was arrested for murder on Jan. 24, 1878, and died on May 23, 1927, in Texas.

Boyd, Thomas M. Jr., an outlaw, shot and killed John Foundation in Lake Valley, N.M., on Aug. 15, 1884.

Boyle, Andrew was a gunman in the Lincoln County War.

Boyle, Robert H. (AKA: **Hornsburg**), an outlaw, shot Pat Slavin in Magdalena, N.M., on May 28, 1881.

Boyle, "Sport", a gunman, was a member of the Dodge City Gang in Las Vegas, N.M.

Brady, Jack, an outlaw in 1892, stole $50,000 from a Wells-Fargo coach and was killed by a detective.

Brady, William, the outlaw sheriff of Lincoln County during the war in 1878, formed the posse of deputies and known outlaws that killed John Tunstall. He was ambushed and shot by Billy the Kid and others shortly after.

Brann, William Cowper (AKA: **the Iconoclast**), a newspaperman, engaged Captain T.E. Davis in a gunfight on Apr. 1, 1898, in which both men were killed.

Brazel, Wayne, a gunman, confessed to the Feb. 28, 1908, shooting of Pat Garrett. He was acquitted following a trial.

Brazelton, William, an outlaw, robbed stagecoaches in Arizona, while wearing various disguises. He was killed in August 1878.

Brent, Henry, an outlaw, was run out of Bannack, Mont., by vigilantes and killed during a fight with Indians.

Brewer, Richard M. (Dick), a gunman formerly of the Murphy-Dolan faction in the Lincoln County War, was named leader of the regulators in 1878 and led a posse after Tunstall's murderers. Brewer was killed in the Blazer's Mill battle.

Brinster, Joseph, an outlaw, was hanged in Isleta, Texas, on July 5, 1883.

Broadwell, Richard (Dick, AKA: **Texas Jack)**, an outlaw and member of the Dalton Gang, robbed banks and trains throughout Kansas and Oklahoma, and was killed during the Coffeyville, Kan., raid on Oct. 5, 1892.

Brocius, William (AKA: **Curley Bill; Graham**), an outlaw leader in Tombstone, Ariz., shot and killed the Haslett brothers with Johnny Ringo in June 1881 at Hachita, N.M. He was reportedly shot-gunned by Wyatt Earp.

Brock, Leonard Calvert, an outlaw, was a member of the Rube Burrow Gang that robbed trains in Texas and Alabama. He was captured and died on Nov. 10, 1890, after jumping from the fourth floor of the jail upon confessing to train robbery.

Broderick, David C., a gunman and politician in California, was killed by Judge David S. Terry in a duel in the 1850s.

"Bronco Charlie", an outlaw, was lynched near Miles City, Mont., in the late 1880s.

Brooks, William L. (AKA: **Buffalo Billy**), a lawman and gunman, participated in the Newton War in Kansas during which fourteen men were killed. He was killed in 1877 by Morgan Earp.

Brophy, Hank, an outlaw, rustled cattle in New Mexico.

Brown, Billy (AKA: **Long-Haired Sam**), a gunman, killed his best friend on Aug. 19, 1880, near Fort Sill, was arrested in Texas, and hanged in Fort Smith.

Brown, Bob, an outlaw, attempted to rob a train at Fairbanks, Ariz., with a gang. He was captured and served a prison term in Yuma, Ariz.

Brown, Henry Newton (Hendry), an outlaw and member of Billy the Kid's gang who went to Arizona, became the city marshal of Caldwell, Kan. He led a gang that robbed a bank in Medicine Lodge on Apr. 30, 1884. He was captured and hanged.

Brown, Robert C., an outlaw, attempted to rob a train with his gang at Fairbanks, Ariz., on Feb. 20, 1900. He was captured, imprisoned in Yuma, and disappeared after his release.

Brown, Sam (AKA: **Long-Haired Sam**), a gunman in the Nevada mining camps, killed fifteen men and was shot and killed on July 7, 1861.

Brown, W.E., an outlaw, was shot and killed by Sheriff Turnbo on Sept. 6, 1887, in Pecos, Texas.

Browning, William (AKA: **Browney**), an outlaw and train robber in Illinois in the 1900s, was killed in Texas while robbing a bank.

Brunton, "Tex", an outlaw, fled from Texas, California, and Oklahoma.

Bryant, Charles (AKA; **Black Face Charlie; Black Eyed Charlie**), an outlaw and member of the Dalton-Doolin Gang, was killed in a duel with a lawman named Short in Hennessey, Okla., in 1891.

Buck Gang, the infamous outlaw Indian gang of Okmulgee, Cherokee Nation, raped, murdered, and robbed for thirteen days. They were captured and hanged on July 1, 1896. Led by Rufus Buck, the gang was Sam Sampson, Maomi July, Lewis Davis, and Lucky Davis.

Buckley, James (AKA: **Coal Oil Jimmy**), an outlaw stage robber and murderer, was killed in January 1871.

Bull, John C., a gunman, killed a farmer in Montana in 1867. He was tried, acquitted in 1882, and died in 1928.

Bullion, Laura, the girlfriend of several outlaws including Bill Carver and Ben Kilpatrick, helped Kilpatrick rob a train with and was imprisoned in 1901 for currency forgery.

Bunch, Eugene, an outlaw, robbed an express car in Texas and was killed on Aug. 21, 1892, near Franklin.

Burbridge, William, an outlaw, shot and killed William Heine on Apr. 12, 1881, in San Marcial, N.M.

Burleson, Pete, an outlaw, shot and killed Tom Driscoll in Springer, N.M.. on Jan. 16, 1884. Driscoll died sixteen days later.

Burrows, James Buchanan, an outlaw and brother of Rube, James robbed trains with his brother in 1886-87 and was captured in 1888. He died in the Montgomery, Ala., jail of natural causes.

Burrows, Reuben Houston (AKA: **Rube; Charles Davis**), a famed outlaw leader and train robber who's gang operated in Texas, Arkansas, Missouri, and Alabama. He was killed on Nov. 17, 1890, in Linden, Ala.

Burt, Sam, an outlaw, was lynched by the Committee of 601 on Dec. 17, 1875, in Montana Territory.

Burts, Matthew (Matt), a lawman and part-time Arizona outlaw, rode with Burt Alvord, Billie Stiles, and the Owens brothers. He ranched in California, and was murdered in 1925 during a dispute over water rights.

Buster, John, an outlaw and member of the silver gang, killed William Holland in Seven Rivers in December 1884.

Caballero, Guadalupe (AKA: **The Owl**), an outlaw and the chief spy and rustler for Vicente Silva's White Caps in Las Vegas, N.M., he was sentenced to ten years as an accessory to Pat Maes' hanging.

Cameron, Andrew, an outlaw, shot and killed Donaciano Tafoya on Apr. 25, 1881, in New Mexico.

Campbell, William, an outlaw, rode with Jesse Evans, killed Thomas King on Dec. 6, 1896, and was acquitted of murder.

Campbell, William, a Texas gunman and cowboy, was killed in a gun battle with Babe and Andy Moye on the streets of Ogalalla, Neb., after insulting Babe.

Campbell, William (AKA: **The Kid**), an outlaw, was a member of the Ashly Gang of Montana in 1884. He was killed by lawmen.

Canton, Frank M., a gunman and lawman, was a rancher, cowboy, sheriff, and adjunct general of four states. He lived in Oklahoma, Wyoming, Alaska, and Montana.

Capehart, Tom, an outlaw, was a member of the Black Jack Ketchum Gang.

Carbajal, Antonio, a gunman, fatally wounded Bernardino Chavez on Dec. 8, 1897, at Mesilla, N.M.

Cardenas, Manuel, a gunman, was suspected of murder in November 1875 at Cimarron, N.M.

Cardis, Louis, an outlaw, led the Mexican faction in the El Paso Salt War, and was killed by Judge Howard in 1877.

Carl, Peter, an outlaw, shot and killed Harry Huber in a saloon in Rincon, N.M., on Aug. 31, 1884.

Carlile, William L., an outlaw and the last of the old west train robbers, was captured and imprisoned in the 1900s.

Carlisle, John, a Texas outlaw, was hanged in 1893 for conspiracy to commit murder.

Carmondy, Patric, an outlaw, was jailed with Mexican conspirators Jagola and Gonzales, for killing William Wiggins. The three escaped from jail in Socorro, N.M., in October 1888.

Carrhert, George, a gunman, was killed in Bannack, Mont., during a duel in 1863.

Carrolla, Jose M. (AKA: **Portuguese Jo**), an outlaw and member of the "Wild" Bill Martin Gang, was shot and killed by John Perry on June 19, 1877.

Carson, Christopher (AKA: **Kit**), the legendary scout, mountain man, and Indian fighter, ranged throughout the west and lived on the Santa Fe Trail near Cimarron, N.M.

Carson, Joe, a gunman and city marshal of Las Vegas, N.M., was a member of the Dodge City Gang in Las Vegas and was killed in a saloon gunfight.

Carter, "Tex", a gunfighter for Jim Lacy, Opium Bob, and Dutch Charley Bates, escaped a lynch mob on Mar. 22, 1881, at Rawlins, Wyo., and later became a sheriff in Nebraska.

Carver, William, an outlaw and a Texas cowboy, rode with the Black Jacks, the Wild Bunch, and the High Five Gang. While robbing with the Kilpatrick brothers, he was killed by a posse led by Sheriff Lige Briant in 1901 outside of Sonora, Texas.

Casey, Joe, an outlaw, was jailed by Sheriff Bob Paul in 1882 in Tucson, Ariz., escaped several times, and was hanged.

Casey, John P., an outlaw horse thief, was apprehended in the Black Hills of New Mexico in June 1889.

Casharago, James, an outlaw and prison escapee, was hanged in Fort Smith on July 30, 1896, for the murder of Zack Thatch.

Cassidy, Butch, See: **Parker, George Leroy.**

Castillo, Candido, an outlaw with rewards for him totaling $2400, was shot and killed by a posse near Espanola, N.M., in 1884.

Castillo, Manuel was Candido's younger brother.

Catfish Kid, an outlaw, reportedly killed deputy Sheriff L.S. Pierce and others in a gunfight, and was imprisoned for murder. He was present when three LS cowboys were killed in March 1886 at Tascosa, Texas.

Catron, Jim (AKA: **The Pagnas Stage Robber**), an outlaw, was shot and killed by a guard in the 1880s at Fort Garland, Colo.

Cattle Annie (Annie McDoulet; McDougal), an outlaw, at eighteen, associated with the Doolin Gang and was suspected of stealing livestock and selling whiskey. Steve Burke captured her and Bill Tilghman caught her partner Little Britches and they were sent to reform school.

Chaco, Icnacio, an outlaw, was a member of the Castillo Gang.

Chacón, Augustin (AKA: **Paludo; Peledo; the Hairy One**), an outlaw, led a gang who murdered and robbed in Arizona and escaped jail and execution twice before he was captured by the deputy sheriff of Cochise County, Burt Alvord. He was hanged on Nov. 23, 1901.

Chadwell, William (AKA: **Happy Bill**), an outlaw and member of the James-Younger Gang, was killed on Sept. 7, 1876, during the First National Bank of Northfield, Minn., robbery.

Chamberlain, Samuel E. (AKA: **Peloncillo Jack**), a gunman and soldier of fortune in the 1840s, later became a general in the Civil War, and died in Worcester, Mass, in 1908.

Champion, Nathan D., an outlaw and rustler, was killed with Nick Ray by cattleman in their cabin in Kaycee, Wy.

Chaves, Juan, a New Mexico outlaw and horsethief, was captured by the 9th Cavalry in February 1876.

Chaves, Paz, an outlaw, stole horses around Boquilla, N.M.

Chavez, Antonio, an outlaw, was shot and killed during a hold-up outside San Simon, N.M., on May 21, 1880.

Chavez, Carlos, an outlaw, was hanged for slaying Yum Kee in Silver City, N.M., in 1884.

Chavez, Fernando, an outlaw, was lynched in Las Lunas, N.M., on Oct. 6, 1881.

Chavez, Josefito, an outlaw and horsethief, was a gunman in the Lincoln County War.

Chavez, Pedro, an outlaw and member of Augustin Chacon's gang in the 1890s, was arrested for robbery, escaped prison at Tuscon, Ariz., and was killed in a gun battle with Sheriff Wakefield.

Chavez y Baca, Jose was a gunman in the Lincoln County War.

Chavez y Chavez, Jose, an outlaw and member of Vicente Silva's White Caps, was the last surviving member of the gang. He was sentenced to life imprisonment.

Chenowith, Otto, a Wyoming outlaw and horsethief, was placed in a sanatarium in the east.

"Cherokee Bob" was a gunman in the 1860s in mining camps of Idaho an Montana.

Cherry (AKA: **The Kid**), an outlaw, was a member of Ike Stockton's gang. Dyson Eskridge shot him in the back.

Chilton, Fred, a cowboy and gunman, was one of three cowboys killed by Len Woodward on Mar. 21, 1886, at Tascosa, Texas.

Choalt, Frank, an outlaw, escaped from a prison train on Apr. 16, 1906.

Christian, Will (AKA: **Black Jack**), an outlaw who committed several robberies throughout Oklahoma, Arizona, and New Mexico, he was ambushed and killed at his hideout near Clifton, Ariz.

Christianson, Willard Erastus (AKA: **Matt Warner; Ras Lewis**), an outlaw and brother-in-law of outlaw Tom McCarty, robbed trains and banks with Butch Cassidy, Elza Lay, and McCarty from 1878, served a prison sentence, became a lawman, and died Dec. 21, 1938.

Christie, Ned, an outlaw Cherokee Indian, killed Marshal Dan Maples and others, stole horses, and was killed by a large posse on Nov. 1, 1892, in the Cherokee Nation.

Claiborne, William F. (AKA: **Billy the Kid**), a gunman and cowhand, moved to Cochise County, Ariz., when John Slaughter bought the old McLowery ranch. He survived the O.K. Corral gunfight and was killed by N.F. Leslie in Tombstone in November.

Clancy, John, an outlaw, allegedly robbed a stage in September 1879 near Tecolote, N.M., and was tried and acquitted.

Clanton, Isaac (Ike), a gunman who was a member of the Clanton family in Cochise County, Ariz. He was unarmed when the Earps and Doc Holliday advanced on them at the O.K. Corral. His brother Billy, who carried a gun, was killed.

Clanton, N.H. (AKA: **Old Man**), the head of the Clanton clan in Cochise County, N.M., was accused by the Earps of rustling, ambushing smugglers, and harboring rustlers. He was never prosecuted or arrested for these alleged crimes.

Clanton, Phineas, although not as active an outlaw as his brothers, he did serve a prison sentence for cattle stealing.

Clanton, Robert, a gunmen who killed Jerome and Dick Maddox and Lew Coates in a gunfight in Portland, Mo., in 1863, escaped to Texas, but was arrested twenty-five years later for murder.

Clanton, William (Billy), a gunman, took a horse Wyatt Earp claimed belonged to him, and thus precipitated the gunfight at the O.K. Corral in which Billy, sixteen, was killed along with Frank and Tom McLaury.

Clark, Benjamin, a gunman and Indian scout, fought and killed renegade and hostile Indians most of his life. He served with Bat Masterson and scouted for General Nelson Miles in the Indian Wars, 1874.

Clark, Jap, was a New Mexico gunman, who lasted into the 20th century, until his imprisonment in 1908.

Clark, Thomas (AKA: **Pennsylvania Butch**), an outlaw, was a member of the gang that held up a train outside Marcus, Ill. He was arrested and sent to the prison at Joliet.

Clements, Emanuel, Jr. (AKA: **Mannie**), a lawman, gunman, and son of Emanuel Sr. of Gonzales County, Texas, participated in the Miller-Frazer feud in Pecos, Texas, in 1891 and was killed in El Paso while a lawman on Dec. 29, 1908.

Clements, Emanuel, Sr. (AKA: **Mannen**), an outlaw, cousin, and cohort of Wes Hardin, killed two men in July 1871 in Indian Territory, jailed in Kansas by Bill Hickok, and released on request of Hardin. He was killed at Ballinger, Texas, on Mar. 29, 1887.

Clements, James, a gunman, brother of Emanuel Sr., and cousin of Wes Hardin, drove cattle with Hardin and helped him kill six Mexican herders near Newton, Kan., in 1871.

Clements, John Gibson (AKA: **Gip**), a gunman and youngest of the Clements brothers, helped cousin Wes Hardin disarm several deputies of Bill Hickok in 1871, and send them back to Abilene, Kan., pantless. He died in Runnels County, Texas.

Clements, Joseph, a cowboy, gunman, and one of the Clements brothers, trailed Wes Hardin's herd in 1874 to Comanche County.

Cleveland, George, a black outlaw, was a member of Kit Joy's gang and was killed by the gang after escaping from jail at Silver City, N.M., on March 1884.

Clifton, Daniel (AKA: **Dynamite Dick**), outlaw and member of the Doolin-Dalton Gang, participated in several train and bank robberies and escaped from the Guthrie, Okla., jail, freeing thirteen prisoners including Bill Doolin.

Clum, John P., a gunman and Apache Indian agent in Arizona, sided with the Earps against the "cowboys" in Tombstone.

Clyde, Charles, an outlaw, was arrested for stealing mules in April 1884.

Coal Oil Jimmie, a rustler and stage robber, who was also involved in the Cimarron War.

Cockerill, Tilton, an outlaw and former army officer, led the group that robbed a train at Verdi, Neb., on Nov. 4, 1870.

Cockrane, Thomas, a gunman in the Lincoln County War, was a member of the posse that killed John Tunstall.

Coe, Chas, a lawman and outlaw, killed two men in Grayson County, Texas, in 1884, and was indicted for murder.

Coe, Frank, a gunman in the Lincoln County War, was charged with the murder of Buckshot Roberts with Billy the Kid and others.

Coe, George Washington, a gunman in the Lincoln County War, was charged with the murder of Buckshot Roberts, received amnesty, and died in Roswell in 1942.

Coe, Phillip Haddox, called the greatest gunfighter of Texas, was killed by Bill Hickok in 1871 at Abilene, Kan.

Collins, George, an outlaw train robber and partner of Bill Rudolph, killed a Pinkerton detective and was hanged on Mar. 26, 1904.

Collins, Henry, a gunman and cousin of Joel, allegedly helped Sam Bass rob a train in 1878 at Mesquite, Texas.

Collins Joel, an outlaw, joined Sam Bass in a train robbery near Big Springs, Neb., and was killed by soldiers near Hays City, Kan.

Collins, William, an outlaw, joined Sam Bass after his brother, Joel, was killed and participated in a train robbery. He was arrested, escaped, and fled to Canada where he and U.S. Marshal Bill Anderson shot and killed each other.

Colville, James, an outlaw and rustler, was apprehended in March 1883 by the militia of A.J. Fountain.

Connor, Al, an outlaw, was one of five brothers chased by Texas Rangers for many months in the 1880s.

Connor, Bill, an outlaw, was one of five brothers chased by Texas Rangers for many months in the 1880s.

Connor, Fred, an outlaw, was one of five brothers chased by Texas Rangers for many months in the 1880s.

Connor, John, an outlaw, was one of five brothers chased by Texas Rangers for many months in the 1880s.

Connor, Willis, an outlaw, was one of five brothers chased by Texas Rangers for many months in the 1880s.

Cook, Jim, an outlaw and brother of William Cook, was wounded while resisting arrest in the Cherokee Nation.

Cook, William Tuttle (Bill), leader of the outlaw Cook Gang, committed several bold robberies throughout the Indian Territory. He was arrested Jan. 11, 1895, and sentenced to forty-five years' imprisonment in the federal prison at Albany, N.Y.

Cooley, Scott, a lawman and gunman, killed deputy sheriff John Worley during the Mason County War in Texas, in 1875, to avenge the death of Tim Williamson. He formed a gang that continued to seek vengeance for Williamson's death until Major John B. Jones and his Texas Rangers ended the violence.

Cooper, Ira, a gunman, helped end the Lee-Good feud in Tularosa, N.M.

Cooper, Jim, a gunman and rancher, participated in the Lee-Good feud in Tularosa, N.M.

Cooper, Tom (AKA: **Tom Kelly**), an outlaw, rustled cattle in Hillsboro, N.M., in 1877.

Copeland, James, an outlaw, led the most successful gang which robbed, killed, and rustled cattle throughout the South and Texas. He was captured and executed at Augusta, Miss., on Oct. 30, 1857.

Corman, Burt, an outlaw, shot and killed Matt Craig on Dec. 27, 1886, in Fairview, N.M.

Corna, Silveria, an outlaw, murdered Tavian Pacheco on July 15, 1882, in Sabinal, N.M.

Cornett, Brack, an outlaw and member of the Bill Whitley Gang, robbed banks and trains throughout Texas. Whitley was killed on Sept. 25, 1888, and Cornett was tracked and killed by Sheriff Alfred Allee.

Cortez, Gregorio, a Texas rustler and outlaw, killed Karnes County sheriff Morris, then killed Gonzales County sheriff Dick Glover, was jailed for eight years, and pardoned.

Cortina, Juan Nepomucena (AKA: **Cheno**), a Mexican bandit chieftain, led raids against towns north of the Rio Grande River during the 1850s. He captured the U.S. Army garrison at Brownsville, Texas. After Texas rangers killed several of his leaders, the Mexican bandit retired and died in 1894.

Costillo, Can, a New Mexico outlaw, was wanted for murder.

Coughlin, Pat, an outlaw cattle rustler and friend of Billy the Kid, was apprehended by John W. Poe but released after the only witness was gunned down.

Coulter, Ed, an outlaw, was lynched by vigilantes in New Mexico in October 1881.

Courtright, Timothy Isaiah (AKA: **Longhaired Jim**), a notorious gunman, participated in the May 1883 American Valley murders. He was killed in an accidental shooting in February 1887.

Craft, James H., an outlaw and partner of Charles G. Walrath, murdered William Shook by Ojo Caliente, N.M., and was lynched on June 30, 1879, with Walrath.

Crane, Jim, an outlaw in Arizona and New Mexico, may have died in 1881, but a rustler named Jim Crane was killed in a shootout in 1897. It is not clear whether or not they were the same person.

Cravens, Ben, a lone Oklahoma outlaw, rustled cattle and escaped jail several times. He was captured in July 1894 and given a long prison term but escaped by killing a guard. Recaptured in November 1876, he was imprisoned for life.

Crawford, Foster, an outlaw who rode with Elmer "The Slaughter Kid" Lewis, robbed and murdered in Texas. The pair were captured by Texas Rangers, jailed, and lynched on Feb. 27, 1896.

Crawford, "Salecooler" was a gunman in the Lincoln County War, and died at Fort Stanton in 1878.

Crockett, David, a gunman said to be related to Davy Crockett, escaped from the Texas prison in 1872. He and an accomplice allegedly killed three black soldiers in cold blood. The two were shot dead while attempting to escape arrest.

Crompton, Zacariah, an outlaw and horsethief, on Dec. 20, 1873, with several others, killed Isidoro Patron, Isidoro Padilla, Dario Balazar, and Jose Candelaria in Lincoln County.

Crosthwaite, Charles H., a gunman and newspaperman, was hanged for killing George W. Johnson in January 1889.

Crowe, Patrick, an outlaw, robbed a train in 1894 and stole diamonds in Denver. He was captured in Cincinnati and sentenced to three years in prison.

Cruz, Florentino (AKA: **Indian Charlie**), an outlaw in Arizona and New Mexico, was killed by Wyatt Earp in 1882.

Cullin, Ed (AKA: **Shoot 'em Up Dick**), an outlaw and member of Black Jack Ketchum's gang, was killed during a train robbery in December 1897.

Cummins, James Robert (AKA: **James Johnson; Old Jim**), an outlaw and member of the James Gang, he was present during several robberies, and eventually settled in Missouri where the law forgot about him. He published a book about his life in 1903.

Curry, George L. (AKA: **Flat Nose George; Tom Dilly**), an outlaw, rustler, and member of the Wild Bunch, taught the skills of robbery to Harvey Logan, whom he raised. He was shot and killed after a bank robbery in 1900, by the sheriff of Vernal, Utah.

Curry, John, an outlaw, was killed along with Dick Rodgers on Mar. 13, 1885, attempting to help a prisoner escape from the Springer jail.

Cush, Old John, an outlaw and member of the Black Jack Ketchum Gang, was captured by Jeff Milton and sent to prison.

Dalton, Christopher (AKA: **Kit; Charles Bell; Thomas Mabry**), an outlaw and second cousin of the Dalton brothers, robbed and looted along the North-South border during the Civil War and claimed he rode with the James Gang and the Bass Gang. He died in 1920.

Dalton, Emmett (AKA: **Charley McLaughlin**), an outlaw and member of the Dalton Gang, survived the raid on Coffeyville but was apprehended while attempting to rescue his brother Bob. He served over fourteen years in prison, moved to Hollywood, Calif., and wrote *When the Daltons Rode*.

Dalton, Grattan, a Kansas deputy marshal and outlaw, robbed trains, and was killed during the Coffeyville bank robbery attempt on Oct. 5, 1892.

Dalton, J. Frank (AKA: **Happy Jack**), an outlaw, was wanted in Limestone County, Texas, in 1886 for horse theft. He later claimed he was Jesse James.

Dalton, Robert, a lawman turned outlaw, formed the Dalton Gang in 1891, with his brothers. The Daltons robbed banks throughout Kansas. He and most of the gang were killed attempting to simultaneously rob two banks at Coffeyville on Oct. 5, 1892.

Dalton, William (Bill), an outlaw and a member of the California legislature, joined Bill Doolin's gang after the death of his brothers, and became a leader of the Doolin-Dalton Gang. Lawmen killed him September 1895.

Daly, James, an outlaw and member of Three-Fingered Jack McDowell's gang, ran a gambling house and saloon in Aurora and killed at least two men in cold blood. When vigilantes captured Daly and three other gang members, he took poison but they lynched him anyway.

Damewood, Boston, a California outlaw and highwayman, was lynched by a mob of 200 in Los Angeles.

Daniels, Bill, led a gang of outlaws who robbed the Tucumcari, N.M., bank and shot a boy who was holding his hands in the air.

Daugherty, Roy (AKA: **Tom Jones; Arkansaw Tom**), an outlaw and member of the Doolin-Dalton Gang, was captured at Ingalls, Okla., and served seventeen years in prison. He returned to crime and was killed by law officers on Aug. 16, 1924.

Davenport, Jim, a Texas outlaw and cowboy, was accused of killing Elk Hereford, fought with Texas Rangers, and was killed by Ranger Wright in Cotulla, Texas, in 1899.

Davis, George, an outlaw and member of the Jesse Evans Gang, was a gunman in the Lincoln County War.

Davis, Hog, a gunman who killed Peter Hildreth and was in return shot to death in 1872.

Davis, Jack, an outlaw, was a friend of Bill Longley and robbed trains with Sam Bass and Joel Collins.

Davis, "Lucky", a half-black Creek Indian and member of the infamous Buck Gang, was hanged on July 1, 1896.

Day, Alfred, a gunman in the Taylor faction in the Sutton-Taylor feud and a friend of Wes Hardin, he allegedly shot Bill Sutton in the back in 1876. He wrote a book on his life in the 1930s.

Dayson, Curtis, an outlaw, was a member of the Cook Gang in Indian Territory. He was captured after a bank robbery.

Dedrick, Sam, a gunman and rancher, lived in White Oaks, N.M., and was a friend of Billy the Kid.

Delaney, William E. (AKA: **Bill Johnson, Morman Bill**), an outlaw suspected of murder in Pennsylvania, was a member of a gang in Arizona. He was captured by deputy Ben Daniels and hanged in Tombstone on Mar. 8, 1884.

Deloach, Tom, shot and killed Joe Holland in September 1885 outside of El Paso, Texas.

Demmons, Dan, an outlaw, led a gang in Texas and New Mexico in the 1870s. He was captured in 1880.

Dempster, Boyd, an outlaw, was shot and killed in Georgetown, N.M., on Dec. 26, 1881, by Deputy Sheriff Glasgow.

de Rana, Patas (AKA: **El Coyote**), an outlaw and member of Silva's White Caps, shot and killed Vicente Silva by orders of the gang on May 19, 1895. The gang's breakup came after one of them was ordered hanged by the gang court.

Devine, James (AKA: **Jones; James Johnson; Curran**), an outlaw, was lynched in Raton, N.M., on Apr. 16, 1881.

Dial, J.I., a gunman, allegedly killed a freighter on Mar. 14, 1872, in Mexico. He was killed near El Paso.

Diehl, "Pony", a Dodge City gunman, participated in several robberies in Tombstone, Ariz., in 1887.

Dilion, Jerry, an outlaw, killed Captain Paul Dowlin on May 5, 1877, by Fort Stanton, N.M.

Dodds, John, a gunman, was a companion of Dick Rogers of Raton, N.M.

Dolan, James J., a gunman and businessman, led the Murphy-Dolan faction in the Lincoln County War and was suspected of riding with the posse that killed John Tunstall. He was charged with the murder of H.J. Chapman on Feb. 18, 1879.

Doolin, William (Bill, AKA: **Will Barry)**, an outlaw, led a gang of unemployed cowboys who robbed trains and banks in Oklahoma, New Mexico, Missouri, and Kansas. He either died of tuberculosis or was shot and killed by lawman Heck Thomas in August 1896.

Doran, Major **A.S.**, a gunman and soldier, killed about ten men and was shot dead in Hot Springs, Ark., in 1888.

Dorsey, John, an outlaw, was lynched for killing Constable Joe Carson in Las Vegas, N.M., on Jan. 22, 1884.

Dow, J. Leslie, a gunman and lawman, shot and killed Zack Light during an argument while bartender at Seven Rivers, N.M., in the late 1880s. He later became sheriff of Eddy County and was killed by former sheriff Dave Kemp at Carlsbad.

Dowd, Daniel, an outlaw companion of Bill Delaney, was hanged on Mar. 8, 1884, in Tombstone and buried on Boot Hill.

Downing, Bill, an outlaw and member of the Alvord-Stiles Gang, was deputy sheriff of Willcox, Ariz., who allowed the gang to escape after a train robbery. He killed over thirty men and was shot dead by Sheriff Billy Speed in August 1900 at Willcox.

Dublin, Dell, an outlaw, was captured in Coryell, Texas, for murder.

Dublin, Dick, an outlaw and brother of Dell, was captured in Coryell, Texas, for murder.

Duboise, E. Leon, an outlaw, was imprisoned in February 1886.

Dudley, Nathan Augustus Monroe, a gunman and lieutenant colonel stationed at Fort Stanton, N.M., sided with the Murphy-Dolan faction during the Lincoln County War and besieged the McSween house. He was tried and acquitted for his actions.

Duffy, Thomas, an outlaw, was jailed for killing Thomas Bishop in Liberty, N.M., on Sept. 19, 1880, and was shot and killed while attempting to escape the Las Vegas jail.

Dugi, Giovanni (AKA: **Dagi; Duque**), an outlaw, was lynched on June 4, 1879, in Las Vegas, N.M.

Duke, Frank, an outlaw and cattle rustler, was imprisoned in the Socorro, N.M., jail in 1884.

Duncan, Dick, an outlaw and nephew of the Ketchums, was hanged for murder in 1891 at Eagle Pass, Texas.

Dunlop, John (AKA: **Three Fingered Jack**), an outlaw, train robber, and member of Black Jack Christian's gang, was shot by a guard in 1881, left for dead by the gang, and taken to Tombstone where he informed on the others.

Dupont, John, an outlaw, shot and killed Bartole Garcia on Jan. 14, 1883, in La Joya, N.M.

Dwindle, Charlie, a gunman, was arrested for the murder of John Byers, near Springer, N.M., in March 1883.

Earhart, William (Bill), a gunman, fought with Oliver Lee in the feud in Tularosa, N.M. He was killed in Pecos, Texas, Fall 1896.

Edwards, Joseph M. (AKA: **Bob**), an outlaw, was killed by Sheriff Thomas L. McKinney in Rattlesnake Springs, N.M., on May 8, 1881.

Elliott, Frank, an outlaw and part-time member of the Dalton Gang, was arrested and charged with robbery on Oct. 27, 1891.

Elliott, James, a gunman, shot and killed James Fay on February 1884, in Lake Valley, N.M.

Ellis, Charles, a Texas outlaw, was charged with train robbery and murder in 1898

Ellis, William, a gunman, shot and killed J.S. McAlpin on Apr. 18, 1886, in La Luz, N.M.

Elmoreau (AKA: **Frenchy**), an outlaw and member of Ike Stockton's gang, was lynched in October 1881 in Socorro, N.M.

"El Pollo", a notorious horsethief, was captured near Socorro and shot by a lynch mob on Feb. 8, 1869.

Elvard, Juan, an outlaw, was lynched in August 1882 in Socorro, N.M.

Enbree, Jack, a gunman, shot and wounded Laramie, Wy., rancher E.M. Dixon and was imprisoned for two years. He was killed on Jan. 23, 1889, when he returned to threaten Dixon.

Escobar, Rafael, an outlaw, was lynched by a vigilance committee at Jackson, Calif., in the early 1850s.

Eskridge, Dyson, an outlaw and murderer, was a member of Ike Stockton's gang.

Eskridge, Harg, an outlaw rustler and brother of Dyson, was a member of Ike Stockton's gang.

Espinosa, Juan, the oldest of the outlaw "Bloody Espinosas," robbed and killed in the 1850s-60s with his brother in New Mexico and Colorado. Mountain man Tom Tobin killed Juan and his nephew in 1863.

Espinosa, Vivian, the younger of the outlaw "Bloody Espinosas," was killed by posseman Joe Lamb near Cripple Creek, Colo., in 1863.

Espinoso, Selzo, an outlaw, was lynched on Oct. 6, 1881, in Las Lunas, N.M.

Espolin, Jose, a gunman, was accused of murdering Mescalero merchant A.H. Howe in 1886.

Estabol, Tranquellano, a gunman, shot-up Phoenix, Ariz., in 1895 and was arrested by Sheriff Cicero Stewart and Dee Harkey.

Estes, Cole, a gunman who was shot to death robbing a train on Oct. 2, 1896.

Evan, Tom, an outlaw, robbed a bank with three others in Limestone, Indian Territory, on Jan. 23, 1888, and was killed.

Evans, Chris (AKA: **Bill Powers**), an outlaw, led a train robbing gang after the railroad took his land. He was caught by a posse in 1893, charged with murder, escaped jail, was captured again, and sent to prison for life. Paroled in 1911, he died in 1917.

Evans, Dan, an outlaw, who killed a cowboy in the Creek Nation and was hanged at Fort Smith in 1875.

Evans, Jesse, outlaw leader of the Evans Gang, fought on the Murphy-Dolan side in the Lincoln County War of New Mexico, and was a friend and foe of Billy the Kid. He was sent to prison for rustling but escaped in 1882, and was never heard from again.

Falkner, Frederick, an outlaw, was hanged Aug. 19, 1892.

Fall, Albert, a gunman, lawyer, Congressman, and rancher in New Mexico, fought Ben Williams on Sept. 15, 1895, on the streets of Las Cruces, N.M.

Fall, Philip, the brother of Albert, a cattle rustler and outlaw, who later became a deputy marshal.

Fallon, Charles, a cowboy and gunman, with companion Long Haired Owens, fought one of the fiercest gun battles known in the West on July 4, 1884, at Lewistown, Mont., against the Stuart cowboy-vigilantes. Fallon was killed, shot nine times.

Farley, Hutch, an Indian scout, killed the Indian that killed his father at the battle at Beecher's Island, Colo., in November 1868.

Farrington, Hilary, an outlaw and train robber, served under Quantrell in 1870 and was captured in Vinita, Indian Territory.

Farrington, Levi, an outlaw and train robber, brother of Hilary, served under Quantrell in 1870 and was captured in Vinita, Indian Territory.

Farris, William, an outlaw, was a member of the Cook Gang in the Indian Territory. He was captured after a bank robbery.

Felshaw, Jake, an outlaw, who participated in a train robbery near Bowie, N.M. on Jan. 6, 1894.

Ferris, Henry, a Colorado gunman and lawyer, was killed in Sterling in 1873.

Fields, Tom, an outlaw, robbed a train near Samuels, Texas, in 1891, was captured by Rangers, and received a life sentence.

Finch, Bill, an outlaw, stole two horses and two guns in Fort Sill, Texas, in 1882 and was hanged in Fort Smith in 1883 after killing two soldiers.

Finley, Jim, an outlaw, stole cattle around Socorro, N.M., and was killed by Joel Fowler.

Finnessy, Tom was a gunman and friend of M'Rose.

Fisher, Bill, a Texas outlaw, was wanted in 1886 for killing J.S. Vaughn. He was arrested and tried.

Fisher, Dick, an outlaw, was wanted in Texas and found dead near Cimarron, N.M., in 1871.

Fisher, John K. (King), a gunman and suspected outlaw gang leader, became deputy sheriff of Uvalde, and was killed by a concealed assassin in March 1884.

Fitzpatrick, Mike, an outlaw, shot Judge Halliday in the 1870s and was killed by Marshal Jack Johnson.

Flint, John, an outlaw, killed several men in the year following the Civil War in Doaksville, Indian Territory, and was convicted of murder and hanged by federal authorities.

Floyd, Henry, an outlaw and member of Bill Henderson's gang in 1876, was arrested in Dodge City and lynched in June at Albany, Texas.

Floyd, W.S. (AKA: **William Wardell; Taylor; Simmons**), an outlaw, was killed in May 1884 near Flora Vista, N.M.

Flynt, John, an outlaw and member of the Wallington Gang, robbed a train in 1891 in Val Verde County, Texas, and killed himself in a battle.

Follett, Lyman, an outlaw who was involved in the robbery of an Army paymaster on May 11, 1889.

Follett, Warren, the brother of Lyman, who was involved in the robbery of an Army paymaster on May 11, 1889.

Folsom, Tandy, an outlaw, killed a man on the Indian Territory border in February 1881 and was hanged at Fort Smith.

Fooy, Sam, an outlaw, was hanged on Sept. 3, 1875, in Fort Smith for robbing and killing a school teacher.

Ford, Charles, an outlaw, member of the James Gang, and brother of Robert Ford, committed suicide in his home on May 6, 1884.

Ford, Robert, a gunman, shot Jesse James in the back of the head on Apr. 3, 1882, and was pardoned by Governor T.T. Crittenden. He was killed in June 1892.

Foster, Joseph, a gunman and gambler, was shot and killed by King Fisher in San Antonio, Texas, in 1884 when Fisher and Ben Thompson were shot by unknown gunmen.

Fountain, Albert J., a gunman, soldier, editor, and lawyer, killed B.F. Williams on Dec. 7, 1870, in El Paso, Texas, and defended Billy the Kid in his first trial in Mesilla, N.M. He disappeared in the White Sands on Feb. 1, 1896.

Fowler, Joel, a gunman, gambler, and rancher, killed over twenty men, and was lynched on Jan. 22, 1884, in Socorro, N.M.

Freeman, Frank, a New Mexico gunman and a factor in the Lincoln County War, was killed in Cimarron in late 1876.

French, James (Jim), an outlaw, member of the Cook Gang, and gunman in the Lincoln County War, ambushed Brady and Hindman on Apr. 1, 1878, with Billy the Kid. He was killed by lawmen.

Frescan, Cesario, an outlaw, shot and killed Nicanor Garcia near La Mesilla, N.M., on Dec. 10, 1886.

Frink, D.B., a gunman and member of the Truckee, Calif., Committee of "601," was accidentally killed in November 1874.

Gagen, Richard F., an outlaw, was one of the conspirators in the June 17, 1877, murder of Captain R.N. Calhoun.

Gallagher, Bill (Barney), an outlaw, was shot and killed in Fall 1876 by John Slaughter in South Springs, N.M.

Gallagher, J.G., a gunman, shot and killed Alberto Martinez in January 1883 in the Steeple Rock district of New Mexico.

Gallagher, "Three Fingered Jack", an outlaw and member of the Plummer Gang was hanged by vigilantes on Jan. 13, 1864, in the Montana Territory.

Gallegos, Jose Trujillo, a gunman, killed Miguel Montano in March 1885 at Pederval, N.M.

Gallegos, Leandro, an outlaw, was a member of Vicente Silva's White Caps in Las Vegas, N.M.

Gallegos, Nestor, an outlaw, was a member of Vicente Silva's White Caps in Las Vegas, N.M.

Gallegos, Pantaeleon, a gunman in the Lincoln County War, rode in the posse that killed John Tunstall on Feb. 18, 1878.

Galvin, John, a gunman in the Lincoln County War, was indicted in 1879 for his participation.

Garfias, Pete, an outlaw, allegedly robbed a train in 1883 and was killed in a battle.

Garrett, Joe, an outlaw, was a member of Ike Stockton's gang.

Garza, Catarino, a gunman and self-styled rebel, organized a gang of over 300 men, crossed the border into Mexico, fought against Diaz, and was defeated. Arrested for violating International Law, he was killed in Cuba during a revolution.

George, Joe, an outlaw, allegedly robbed an SP train near Wilcox with Grant Wheeler.

German, Joe, a gunman, was killed by Frank Leslie in Eureka, N.M., on June 22, 1881.

Gibbons, James, a gunman, was charged with murder in 1891 at Clayton, N.M.

Gibbs, Bill (AKA: **The Panther of the Boston Mountains**), an outlaw, killed five men and was shot and killed by a lawman.

Gibson, Con, a gunman in the Miller-Frazer feud of Reeves County, Texas, was killed in the 1890s in Phoenix, N.M.

Gibson, Volney, a gunman, shot and killed Kyle Terry in 1889 at the courthouse in Galveston, Texas, for killing L.E. Gibson.

Gilbreth, Bud (AKA: **Cook**), an outlaw, was a companion of Ike Stockton.

Gilliand, Jim, an accused rustler, joined the Oliver Lee faction in the Good-Lee feud in Tularosa, N.M.

Gilliland, Fine, a cowboy, shot and killed Henry Harrison Powe on a roundup. He was shot and killed by lawmen, including Thalis Cook, Jim Gillett, and Ranger Jim Putman.

Gilson, Chris, a gunman, participated in the Newton, Kan., gunfight in 1867 which left fourteen gunmen dead.

Gladden, George, a gunman in the "Hoodoo War" in Mason County, Texas, was arrested on charges that included a jail break, received a 99-year sentence, was pardoned, and died "somewhere in the west."

Glanton, John Joel, a gunman. was outlawed by Sam Houston when he fought on both sides in the Regulator-Moderator War in East Texas. He was arrested, escaped, and led a gang of scalp hunters. He was killed by Indians in 1850 at Yuma, Colo.

Golden, John, a gambler and gunman, was lynched by a mob in 1876 outside Fort Griffin, Texas.

Goldensen, an outlaw, was hanged in September 1888 for the murder of Mami Kelley.

Goldsby, Crawford (AKA: **Cherokee Bill**), an outlaw and killer, he was also a member of the Cook Gang. He was hanged for murder on Mar. 17, 1896.

Gomez, Juan, an outlaw, escaped from prison and was recaptured on Feb. 16, 1907.

Gonzales, Marcus, an outlaw, was jailed in La Veta, Colo., and lynched by a mob in July 1877.

Gonzolez, Gabriel, a gunman, killed Adolf Harmon in Springer, N.M., in Aug. 1, 1907, and started a feud.

Gonzolez, Juan, an outlaw, stole horses and was killed in Albuquerque, N.M., in October 1876.

Gonzolez y Blea, Manuel (AKA: **El Mellado**), an outlaw, was a member of Vicente Silva's White Caps of Las Vegas.

Gonzolez y Blea, Martin (AKA: **El Moro**), an outlaw, was a member of Vicente Silva's White Caps of Las Vegas.

Good, Isham was the brother of John H. Good.

Good, John H., gunman and rancher, along with others, shot and killed Charles Dawson on Dec. 8, 1885, in La Luz, N.M., and feuded with Oliver Lee.

Good, Lee was the son of John H. Good.

Good, Walter, a gunman and son of John Good, started the Good-Lee feud by ambushing George McDonald on June 13, 1888. He was found dead in the White Sands of New Mexico.

Goodlet, Bill, a lawman turned gunman, was a member of the Dodge City Gang in Las Vegas, N.M.

Goodman, William, an outlaw, escaped from the Las Vegas jail along with Rudabaugh and Webb, on Dec. 3, 1881.

Goodnight, Charles, a lawman, was a Texas Ranger in 1857 and drove cattle after the Civil War. He fought outlaws and Indians for many years in Texas, New Mexico, and California, and died in Tucson, Ariz., on Dec. 12, 1929, at the age of ninety-three.

Gordon, Lon, an outlaw and member of the Bill Cook Gang in Oklahoma, was killed near Sapulpa, Okla., after the Chandler bank robbery.

Gordon, Mike, a gunman, was shot in Las Vegas, N.M., on July 19, 1879.

Gordon, Tom, an outlaw, was lynched in Socorro on Mar. 10, 1881.

Grady, Tom, an outlaw, rustled cattle and killed John Carney on Dec. 14, 1885, in Lake Valley, N.M.

Graham, Albert (**Abbs**; AKA: **Charles Graves; Ace Carr**), an outlaw and member of the Jesse Evans Gang, robbed throughout New Mexico and West Texas. He was arrested, but either died or left the country, as he never appeared in court.

Graham, Charles (AKA: **Bud Davis**), an outlaw and member of the Jesse Evans Gang and brother of Abbs, was captured and accused of killing a man while shooting up Jonesboro.

Graham, Dollay (AKA: **George Davis; George Graves**), an outlaw and one of the Graham brothers who rode with Jesse Evans in Lincoln County, N.M., was killed when the gang was captured in West Texas.

Graham, John D., a gunman in the feud with the Tewksburys in Pleasant Valley, Ariz., was killed in Holbrook in September 1887.

Graham, Thomas H., a gunman in the feud with the Tewksburys and brother of John, was ambushed and killed at Tempe, Ariz., in August 1892.

Grant, Joe, a gunman and bounty hunter, attempted to bring in Billy the Kid. The Kid shot him, and he died on Jan. 10, 1880.

Graves, Mit, a gunman, allegedly killed two members of the Truitt family in connection with a feud in Hood County, Texas, in 1874.

Graves, "Whiskey Bill", an outlaw and member of the Plummer Gang, was lynched by vigilantes at Bitter Root in January 1864.

Greathouse, James (AKA: **Whiskey Jim**), a former deputy sheriff labelled an outlaw by ranger Patrick Garrett, ran a way station on the White Oaks-Las Vegas, N.M., road. He was shot to death southeast of Socorro.

Green, Thomas, a gunman in the Lincoln County War, rode with the posse that killed John Tunstall on Feb. 18, 1878.

Green, Tom, an outlaw, was indicted for murder in 1877 at Parker County, Texas.

Grey, Dick was an outlaw in Arizona and New Mexico.

Griego, Francisco (AKA: **Poncho**), an outlaw and former city marshal of Santa Fe, N.M., was killed by Clay Allison on Nov. 1, 1875, at Cimarron, N.M.

Griffin, George a Texas and New Mexico gunman, was given to shooting up a town while drunk.

Griffith, Ben, a guerilla outlaw under Cullen Baker in the Texas reconstruction war, was killed by three citizens of Glarkville in 1868.

Gross, Albert (AKA: **John Gunter**), an outlaw and member of the Evans Gang, was captured by rangers near Shafter, Texas, on July 3, 1880. He escaped jail but was recaptured by Ranger Sam Graham.

Guyse, Buck, a lawman and outlaw, deserted the Texas Rangers and fled to New Mexico where he was arrested by Pat Garrett.

Halderman, Bill, an outlaw, was hanged with his brother Tom in Tombstone, Ariz., on Nov. 16, 1900, for killing a man.

Halderman, Tom, an outlaw, was hanged with his brother Bill in Tombstone, Ariz., on Nov. 16, 1900, for killing a man.

Hale, John, a gunman and foreman of the Manning ranch near El Paso, Texas, shot and killed Gus Krempkau in 1881 and was killed by Marshal Stoudenmire.

"Halfbreek Jack", an outlaw, was lynched near Yellowstone by the Montana Stranglers in 1884 for rustling cattle.

Hall, Bill, an outlaw, was the first prisoner of Yuma Prison in 1875.

Hall, Charles (AKA: **Tex**), rustled cattle near Hillsboro, N.M., in 1877.

Hanks, Orlando Camillo (AKA: **Charley Jones; Deaf Charley**), an outlaw and the last and toughest of Butch Cassidy's Wild Bunch, robbed trains in Montana and New Mexico from the 1880s. He was killed in 1902 by Sheriff Pink Taylor after killing a lawman.

Hannah, James (AKA: **Socorro Jim**), a gunman, was shot on Mar. 17, 1883, in Middle Camp, N.M.

Hardin, Bill, a gunman and first cousin to Wes Hardin, was lynched by a mob after killing a man near Engle, N.M., in the 1880s.

Hardin, John Wesley (Wes), Texas's most deadly gunman, killed over thirty people. Hardin fought for the Taylors in the Sutton-Taylor feud. Captured by Ranger John Armstrong in 1877, he was released in 1894 after eighteen years in prison. He was killed by Constable John Selman in El Paso, Texas, in August 1895.

Hardin, Joseph, the brother of Wes. Although not active as a criminal, he was lynched in June 1874, after he brandished a shotgun in his brother's defense.

Hardin, Mart, an outlaw, was charged with conspiracy in the murder of Bud Frazer committed in 1893 by Jim Miller.

Harlin, JJ (AKA: **Off Wheeler**), an outlaw, was named on a Las Vegas, N.M., poster reading: "Notice! To Thieves, Thugs, Fakirs and Bunko-Steerers...you have until ten p.m. to leave town, or be invited to Attend a Grand Neck-Tie Party."

Harmon, Adolf, an outlaw, was shot and killed by Gabriel Gonzolez, ten years after Harmon killed Deputy Sheriff Esteban Trujillo on Jan. 22, 1897.

Harmon, Albert, a gunman, shot and killed Tomas Salazar in January 1908 at Springer, N.M.

Harmon, Augustin, a gunman, was sentenced to twenty-five years in prison for killing Ricardo Lovato of Springer, N.M.

Harper, Chas, an outlaw and member of the Plummer Gang, was hanged at Florence, Idaho, in 1891.

Harrington, Frank E., the conductor of the Fort Worth Express train, shot and critically wounded Tom Ketchum on Aug. 16, 1899. Harrington was wounded in the forearm and Ketchum was captured the following day and later executed at Clayton, N.M.

Harris, James, a gunman and former lawman, was killed while dueling Bob Majors at Santa Cruz, Calif., in the 1880s.

Harrold, Benjamin, a gunman and one of five Harrold brothers of Lampasas County, Texas, was killed while resisting arrest on Dec. 20, 1873, leading to an earlier Lincoln County War.

Harrold, Martin was one of the five Harrold brothers.

Harrold, Merritt was one of the five Harrold brothers.

Harrold, Samuel was one of the five Harrold brothers.

Harrold, Thomas, one of the five Harrold brothers, moved back to Texas with his three brothers due to escalating violence.

Hart, Pearl (Pearl Taylor), an outlaw and mother of two children, a miner, committed the "comic opera" stage hold-up between Globe and Riverside with Joe Boot. Hart was arrested, sent to prison, and released after five years.

Hartnett, Splay Foot, an outlaw, was lynched by the Montana Stranglers in 1884.

Haslett, Bill, gunman and rancher, with his brother Ike, ambushed and killed two men on June 12, 1881, who were attempting to take over his ranch. Both were killed in Eureka by Leslie on June 22.

Haslett, Ike, a gunman, was the brother of Bill Haslett.

Hasley, Sam, an outlaw, killed several men and joined the war against the Texas reconstructionists in Bell County.

Hassells, Samuel (Bob Hayes), an outlaw and member of the Black Jack Ketchum Gang, was killed in a battle with lawmen.

Hawkins, Henry, who led a band of outlaws named the "Mesa Hawks", robbing trains in the New Mexico Territory in 1897.

Hawks, George, a gunman, shot and killed John M. Berry on Jan. 18, 1887, in Flagstaff, Ariz.

Hawley, C.B., an outlaw, confessed to stage robbery in 1882 near Globe, Ariz., and was lynched.

Hays, Bob, an outlaw and member of Black Jack Christian's gang, was killed on Aug. 6, 1896, after an aborted bank robbery at Nogales, Ariz.

Head, Harry (AKA: **Harry the Kid**), a Tombstone outlaw, was accused by Wyatt Earp of robbing the Benson stage when Bud Philpot was killed. He was killed by the Haslett brothers and Billy Leonard in 1881.

Hedgepeth, Marion C., an outlaw in Missouri, Montana, Colorado, and Wyoming, was a rustler, horse thief, and bank robber. He was killed in 1910 in Chicago, Ill., while attempting a robbery.

Hedges, William (AKA: **Pawnee Bill**), an outlaw, was listed in the Las Vegas, N.M., poster warning all "Thieves, Thugs, Fakirs and Bunko-Steerers" to leave town before ten p.m. or be invited to "a Grand Neck-Tie Party."

Hefferman, Art, an outlaw, shot a man at Virginia City in March 1871 and was lynched by vigilantes.

Heffridge, Bill, an outlaw and member of the Sam Bass Gang in 1877, was killed in Kansas during a gun battle.

Heffron, Augustus (Gus), an outlaw and friend of Dave Crockett, was captured in the gun battle with lawmen at Cimarron, N.M., in October 1876 where Crockett was killed. He escaped and was not heard from again.

Heith, John, an alleged outlaw, was charged with robbery and murder at Tombstone, Ariz. A mob lynched him after he was convicted of second-degree murder and robbery on Feb. 21, 1884.

Helm, Boone, an outlaw, murderer, and robber, was a member of several gangs, including the "Destroying Angels" and the Plummer Gang. He was hanged in Virginia City by vigilantes on Jan. 14, 1864.

Helm, Charles, a gunman and cowboy buried in Tombstone's Boot Hill, was shot and killed by Billie McCauley in 1882 after arguing about whether to drive cattle fast or slow.

Helm, Jack, a lawman and outlaw, fought for the Suttons in the Sutton-Taylor feud and terrorized DeWitt and surrounding counties. His posse killed Hays Taylor on Aug. 23, 1869. Wes Hardin and Jim Taylor killed him in July 1873.

Henderson, Bill, an outlaw, robbed stages, trains, and stole horses in Texas and New Mexico in the 1880s and was lynched in Texas.

Henderson, Wall, an outlaw, was shot and killed on Nov. 14, 1871, by John W. Stinson in Elizabethtown, N.M.

Hernandez, Mariano, an outlaw, allegedly killed a man and was lynched at San Jose, Calif., in 1850.

Herndon, Al, an outlaw and member of the Sam Bass Gang, was captured in 1878.

Herrera, Nestor, an outlaw, was one of Vicente Silva's White Caps in Las Vegas, N.M.

Herring, Bob, a Texas outlaw and member of Joe Baker's gang, stole horses from 1885-1894 and was imprisoned for thirty-five years after a gunfight at Dallas in 1899.

Hetherington, Joe, an Englishman outlaw, was lynched by vigilantes in San Francisco, Calif., on July 29, 1856.

Hicks, Milt was an outlaw in Arizona and New Mexico.

Hilderman, George (AKA: **The Great American Pie-Eater**), an outlaw, was a member of the Plummer Gang.

Hill, Frank, an outlaw and rustler who was killed by a posse in New Mexico in March, 1880.

Hill, George W., a gunman, shot and killed Pooler and Juan Romero in March 1884 in the Vermejo Valley, N.M., and was captured in 1879 by Sheriff Pete Burleson.

Hill, Joe, a gunman, was friends with Jim Hughes, John Ringo, and Curly Bill. He died when a horse fell on him.

Hill, Tom (AKA: **Tom Chelson**), an outlaw and member of the Jesse Evans Gang, rode with the posse that killed John Tunstall on Feb. 18, 1878.

Hindman, George, a lawman and gunman who rode in the posse that killed John Tunstall, was ambushed and killed by Billy the Kid and two others on Apr. 1, 1878.

Hinton, John,, an outlaw in the New Mexico Territory in 1896.

Hite, Clarence, an outlaw and relative of Wood Hite, allegedly helped the James Gang rob a train at Winston, Mo., in the 1870s.

Hite, Robert (AKA: **Wood**), an outlaw and cousin of Jesse James, robbed trains with the James Gang and was killed in 1881 by Dick Liddell in 1881.

Hoges, Henry, a gunman, was arrested for the March 1883 murder of John Byers.

Holden, "Judge", a gunman, fought in the Mexican War and was a member of the scalp-hunting Glanton Gang.

Holliday, John Henry (AKA: **Doc; Tom McKey; John Powers**), the gunman and companion of Wyatt Earp, followed the Earps from Dodge City to Tombstone, and joined O.K. Corral gunfight. Holliday died in 1885 at a sanitarium in Glenwood Springs, Colo.

Holloway, Russ, an outlaw, killed a man in 1879 in Earth County, Texas, and fled. He returned in 1927 and surrendered himself but was released as no indictment was standing.

Holzhay, Reimund (AKA: **Black Bart**), a German immigrant and outlaw, was captured in 1889 while robbing a train single handedly. He received a life sentence.

Horan, John (AKA: **Pete**), was a gunman and miner, and was hanged by Sheriff Henry Plummer for murder in 1863.

Horn, Thomas, the famous lawman, gunman, and scout, initially worked in the frontier as a gunman for hire. He was hanged at Cheyenne, Wyo., on Nov. 20, 1903, for murdering a 14-year-old boy from ambush.

Horrell, Sam, a New Mexico rancher and outlaw.

House, Eddie, an outlaw, was charged with the murder of a Lincoln County sheepherder but was acquitted in 1881.

House, Thomas Jefferson (AKA: **Tom Henry**), an outlaw and horse thief, killed Joe Carson, constable of Las Vegas, N.M., on Jan. 22, 1880. He was lynched on Feb. 7.

Houston, Temple Lea, a gunman, state senator, and son of Texas governor Sam Houston, killed Ed Jennings in Woodward, Okla., was acquitted of murder, and died in Woodward, Aug. 15, 1905.

Hovey, Walter (AKA: **Fatly Ryan**), an outlaw, was a member of the Black Jack Ketchum Gang.

Howard, Charles, an outlaw and member of the later Robert McKimie Gang, was captured in 1878 along with Little Reddie.

Howard, James (**Tex;** AKA: **Tex Willis, Jack Howard**), an outlaw, was the scout for a Bisbee, Ariz., robbery in 1883 during which several people were killed. He was arrested and hanged in 1884.

Howard, Joe, an alleged outlaw and horse thief, was lynched in 1873 at Franklin, Mo.

Howard, Joe, a gunman in Lincoln County, N.M., in 1877, killed Chihuahua, a Cherokee Indian.

Howell, Bennett, a gunman and cowboy, was killed with two others by Billy the Kid on June 5, 1881, in John Chisum's camp.

Howland, Big Dan, an outlaw, murdered J.W. Lacy, a relative of Ike Stockton in May 1881 at the insistence of the vigilantes in Farmington, N.M.

Hoyt, George R., a gunman and cowboy, was shot by Wyatt Earp while "hurrahing" Dodge City. His arm was amputated and he died.

Hubert, Joe (AKA: **Joe Roberts**), an outlaw, rustled cattle in 1877 near Hillsboro, N.M., and was convicted of mail robbery.

Hudgens, John, a gunman, shot and killed Louis Montjeau in January 1885 at White Oaks.

Hudson, Hugh, a Peacock gunman in the late 1860s Peacock-Lee feud, was shot and killed after he was accused of killing a man.

Hughes, Jim, an Arizona and New Mexico outlaw, died on Nov. 2, 1899.

Hughes, Wilson (AKA: **Texas Jack**), an outlaw, was a member of the Ike Stockton Gang.

"Human Tiger, The", an outlaw and rustler, was killed while attempting to escape from A.J. Fountain's militia in 1877.

"Humpy Jack", an alleged outlaw, was shot and killed in his cabin in 1884 by the vigilante Montana Stranglers.

Hunt, Richard (AKA: **Zwing Hunt**), an outlaw, robbed the Tombstone Mining and Milling Company with Billy "the Kid" Grounds and killed M.C. Peel. Deputy Billy Breakenridge killed Billy and Hunt was badly wounded. He disappeared while jailed at Tombstone.

Hunter, Bill (AKA: **Tex**), an outlaw, was a member of Ike Stockton's gang.

Hunter, Bill, an outlaw and member of the Plummer Gang in the 1860s, was the last of the gang, lynched by vigilantes.

Hurley, John, a gunman in the Lincoln County War, rode with the posse that killed John Tunstall on Feb. 18, 1878.

Irwin, Nat (AKA: **Tex**), an outlaw, rustled cattle in New Mexico and was captured by A.J. Fountain's militia in March 1883.

Isom, Ben, an outlaw, shot a man at Howe Station, Texas in 1885 and was killed by the sheriff.

Ivers, Alice (AKA: **Poker Alice**), a woman gambler well-known from Tombstone to Deadwood, carried a pistol in her vest and wounded a man who attempted to stab her husband. She witnessed the killing of Bill Hickok.

Ives, George, an outlaw and a member of the Plummer Gang of Montana Territory, was hanged on Jan. 3, 1864, at Alder Gulch.

Jackson, Frank (Blocky), one of the toughest outlaws of Texas, joined Sam Bass in 1877. After Texas Rangers killed Bass and Sebe Barnes on July 20, 1878, Jackson moved to Arizona.

Jackson, James, a gunman, killed James Williams on May 12, 1884, in Lake Valley, N.M.

Jackson, Tom, an outlaw who was involved in a train robbery at Bowie, New Mexico, on Jan. 6, 1894.

Jacobs, Ben, a gunman, killed John Findlay on Nov. 5, 1882, in White Oaks, N.M.

James, Alexander Franklin (AKA: **Buck; Frank Vaughn**), an outlaw and brother of Jesse James, rode with the James-Younger Gang on most of their robberies. He surrendered to Governor T.T. Crittenden after Jesse was killed. He was acquitted of murder and robbery, lived peacefully in Kearny, and died on Feb. 19, 1915.

James, Jesse Woodson, the famous outlaw and leader of the James-Younger Gang, robbed banks and trains for sixteen years. Born on Sept. 4, 1847, he was shot in the back of the head by Robert Ford in his home in St. Joseph, Mo., on Apr. 3, 1881.

Jamieson, George, an outlaw, stole horses around Folsom, N.M., in the early 1900s.

Janes, John, an outlaw, was hanged in Lincoln, N.M., on June 18, 1886.

Jenkins, James Gilbert, an outlaw, stole horses, and robbed and killed strangers, companions, law officers, and Indians throughout the U.S. between 1846 and 1864. He was hanged in Napa County, Calif., in 1864.

Jenkins, Tom, a gunman from Dawson, N.M., shot a prostitute for shooting his brother on Aug. 15, 1907.

Jennings, Aphonso (Al), an outlaw, led the Jennings Gang, beginning his fourteen week criminal career after Temple Houston killed his brother Ed. Captured by Marshal Bud Ledbetter, Al served five years in prison and became a lawyer after his release.

Jennings, Frank, an outlaw and brother of Al, was a member of the train robbing gang. He was captured with Al and imprisoned.

Johnson, "Arkansas", an outlaw and member of the Sam Bass Gang, was killed at Salt Creek, Texas, by rangers on June 12, 1878.

Johnson, Bill, a gunman who rode with Bronco Bill Walters, was killed by Jeff Milton and George Scarborough.

Johnson, Chas, an outlaw and member of the Backus Gang, was lynched by the "Hoodoos" on June 12, 1878, in Mason County, Texas.

Johnson, Dan, an outlaw and accomplice of Jim Nite, was apprehended by deputy U.S. marshal Dee Harkey near Sacramento Sinks, N.M., in 1908.

Johnson, DeWitt C., an outlaw, was hanged in Lincoln, N.M, on Nov. 19, 1886.

Johnson, Jack (AKA: **Turkey Creek**), a gunman, joined the Earps in Tombstone in 1881 and was indicted for murder. He left town and was later killed.

Johnson, Otter, an outlaw, shot and killed Norman Buck in Deming, N.M., and received a three-year prison sentence.

Johnson, Peter (AKA: **Toppy**), an outlaw, rustled cattle in New Mexico and served a prison sentence in Santa Fe.

Johnson, Richard (Dick), a Lee gunman in the Lee-Peacock feud in Grayson County, Texas, in the late 1860s, may have been Peacock's murderer on July 1, 1871.

Johnson, Samuel (AKA: **Rattlesnake Sam**), an outlaw in Canoncito, N.M., was killed by a bartender on Dec. 3, 1879.

Johnson, "Swede", an outlaw, rode with Butch Cassidy in the Powder River bunch, killed a cowboy in 1899, and was killed by lawmen.

Johnson, Tobe, an outlaw, rustled cattle around Hillsboro, N.M., in 1877.

Johnson, W.H., a gunman in the Lincoln County War, was indicted in 1879 for his participation.

Jones, "Acorn Head", an outlaw, stole horses and was lynched by vigilantes in Sumner County, Kan., on July 27, 1874.

Jones, "Chubby", an outlaw and member of Dutch Henry's gang, was lynched with eight others at Sweet Water Creek, Texas.

Jones, John, a gunman in the Lincoln County War, was charged, along with Marion Turner with the July 19, 1879, murder of Alexander A. McSween.

Jones, John, an outlaw for eight years, was killed with his brother Jim after robbing a train near Hugo, Colo.

Jones, John, an outlaw who stabbed George Wagstaff to death in Blossburg, N.M., in 1897.

Jones, "Ranger", a Texas gunman, was shot from his horse and killed in ambush near Buffalo, Wyo., during the Cattleman's War.

Jones, Tom was a gunman in the Lincoln County War of New Mexico.

Jones, William (AKA: **Canada Bill**), a gunman, was allegedly one of the hidden snipers that shot and killed Ben Thompson and John Fisher in San Antonio, Texas, in 1884.

Jordan, Francisco, an outlaw, was lynched on Nov. 25, 1881, in Cuchilla Negra, N.M.

Joseph, Martin (AKA: **Bully Josey**), a gunman, was hanged at Fort Smith in 1882 for killing a woman.

Joy, Christopher (AKA: **Kit**), an noted outlaw, robbed trains with his gang before his capture in March 1884. He escaped jail once and was sent to prison.

July, Maomi, an outlaw Creek Indian and member of the Buck Gang, was hanged on July 1, 1896.

Kay, Jim, an outlaw, rustled cattle near Socorro, N.M., and was killed by Joel Fowler.

Kearney, Frank, an outlaw, escaped from the Las Vegas, N.M., jail on Dec. 3, 1881, with outlaws Dave Rudabaugh and John Webb.

Keaton, Pierce, a Texas cowboy and outlaw, attempted to hold up a train on June 9, 1898, at Coleman Junction, and was captured in Sutton County. He was imprisoned, pardoned about 1916, and died in 1931.

Kellam, William (AKA: **Cherokee Bill**) was a gunman for Oliver Lee in the Good-Lee feud in Tularosa, N.M.

Kelly, Bill, an outlaw, broke out of jail, killed a deputy, and was charged with murder in 1885 at Brazos County, Texas.

Kelly, Dan (AKA: **Yorky**), an outlaw, raided Bisbee, Ariz., with a gang on Dec. 7, 1883. Several people were killed, and Yorky was tried, convicted of murder, and hanged on Mar. 8, 1884.

Kelly, Edward O. (AKA: **Red**), on June 8, 1892, shot and killed Bob Ford, the murderer of Jesse James, in Ford's saloon in South Creede, Colo. He was released from prison after eighteen years and was killed in Oklahoma City by a lawman in 1904.

Kelly, Jack, an outlaw, escaped from the Las Vegas, N.M., jail on Dec. 3, 1881, with outlaws Dave Rudabaugh and John Webb.

Kemp, Dave, an outlaw, shot and killed a man in Texas, moved to New Mexico, killed Sheriff Les Dow, and later served as a lawman in Eddy County, N.M.

Kennedy, Charles, a mountain man and outlaw according to his wife, killed his baby daughter and robbed and killed many travelers near Eagle Nest, N.M. He was lynched on Oct. 7, 1870.

Kenny, Robert, a gunman, shot and killed Julius Lancleve in March 1878 at Palomas, N.M.

Ketchum, Samuel, an outlaw, joined the Black Jacks in the mid-1890s and led the gang in his brother's absence in 1899. He was captured and died on July 24, 1899.

Ketchum, Thomas E. (AKA: **Black Jack**), an outlaw and the youngest of the Ketchum brothers, led a gang which robbed trains in New Mexico, West Texas, and Arizona. He was hanged on Apr. 26, 1901.

Kettle Jack, an outlaw, led a gang in the Big Horn Basin, Wyo.. His gang was lynched by 150 vigilantes in 1889, but he got away.

Kilmartin, Jack, a gunman and civilian Indian scout, pursued rustlers and outlaws around Fort Sill, Okla., and was killed while spying on rustlers.

Kilpatrick, Benjamin (AKA: **The Tall Texan**), an outlaw and member of the Wild Bunch and the Black Jacks, robbed trains and banks in Nevada, Missouri, Montana, and Texas. He was killed on Mar. 13, 1912 while robbing the SP train stopped at Sanderson Draw, Texas.

King, "Cowboy Bill", a gunman and ranch foreman in Sonorra, N.M., was killed by Burt Alvord in the 1890s.

King, Ed, a gunman and cowboy at the LS ranch in Oldham county, Texas, was killed in a shoot-out with Len Woodruff, an LX cowboy.

King, Luther, an outlaw, was accused by the Earps of robbing the Benson stage and killing the driver, Bud Philpot.

King, Sandy, an outlaw and member of Curly Bill's gang in Arizona and New Mexico, was hanged by the Shakespeare, N.M., vigilance committee on Jan. 1, 1881, for stealing a horse and being "a damned nuisance."

Kingsbury, Jack, an outlaw, killed a cowboy at Calabasas, Ariz., in 1882, and fled to Mexico where he was killed by lawmen.

Kinney, John, a gunman for hire and a cattle rustler, fought in the El Paso Salt War in 1877 and for Dolan in the Lincoln County War. He served five years in prison for rustling, and died in Arizona in 1919.

Kirby, Andrew, an outlaw who was implicated in the stage coach robbery at Wickenburg, Ariz., on Apr. 19, 1978.

Kirk, George, an outlaw, was lynched on July 13, 1881, at Virginia City, Nev.

Kitt, George, a gunman in the Lincoln County War, rode with the posse that killed John Tunstall on Feb. 18, 1878.

Kloehr, John Joseph, a gunman and resident Coffeyville, Kan., was credited with killing Bob Dalton, Bill Broadwell, Grat Dalton, and Texas Jack, and wounding Emmet Dalton during the Dalton Gang's attempted raid on Coffeyville. He died in 1927.

Knight, Jim, an outlaw, robbed the Longview, Texas, bank with his brother Jourdan on Feb. 6, 1897. He was captured by a posse and received a life sentence.

Knight, Jourdan, an outlaw, robbed the Longview, Texas, bank with his brother Jim on Feb. 6, 1897, and was killed in Bear Creek, Texas, by a law officer.

Kosterlitsky, Colonel **Emilo**, a former U.S. army soldier and the commander of the Mexican Rurales in Sonora, Mex., hated bandits and lynched several while in command in the 1900s.

Kresling, Charles, a gunman in the Lincoln County War, was indicted for his participation.

Kuhns, Marvin (AKA: **J.W. Wilson**, an outlaw, was jailed on Dec. 12, 1890, in Fort Wayne, Ind., with five gunshot wounds.

Lacy, Robert, a gunman and gambler, killed a man and was the alleged leader of a group of gunmen. He was lynched in Rawlins, Wyo., in 1877.

Lamb, Thomas N., an outlaw who was involved in the robbery of an Army paymaster in Graham County, N.M. on May, 11, 1889.

"Lame Johnny", an outlaw, allegedly robbed a stage in 1878 and was hanged in Deadwood, S.D., in 1879.

Lane, "Cubfoot George", an outlaw and deputy under outlaw sheriff Henry Plummer of Virginia City, Montana Territory. He was hanged on Jan. 13, 1864, with Boone Helm.

Lang, Bill was an outlaw in Arizona and New Mexico.

Langston, Sell,a gunman, along with John B. Schlaepfer killed two men and wounded another during a shoot-out in March 1884.

Langworthy, Charles, a gunman, shot John Jackson on June 15, 1885.

Lara, Ruperto, an outlaw, participated in the killing of George Nesmith's family on Aug. 17, 1882, in White Sands, N.M.

L'archeveque, Sostenes, an outlaw and immigrant from France, operated in the 1870s, around West Texas and New Mexico, and was killed in Texas.

Largo, Jesus, an outlaw and horsethief, was lynched in August 1877 outside Lincoln, N.M.

Largo, Juan, an outlaw, led a gang of horse thieves around the Boquilla, N.M., and was lynched in August 1877.

Larn, John M., a outlaw turned lawman, killed a rancher in Colorado and a sheriff in New Mexico. He rustled cattle while sheriff of Shackleford County, Texas, in the late 1870s.

Latterner, Charles, a New Mexico criminal wanted for forgery in 1893.

Lawless, Bill, a cowboy and outlaw, killed a man in McLennon County, Texas, in 1870 and was killed near Cameron.

Lay, William Ellsworth (AKA: **Elzy; William McGinnis**), an outlaw and member of the Wild Bunch, robbed a train with the Black Jack Ketchum Gang. He was captured and served several years in prison. The last of the Wild Bunch, he died many years after his release.

Layton, G.I., an outlaw, alleged robber, and killer, was lynched by a vigilance committee on June 17, 1852, at Sonora, Calif.

Layton, Juan, a gunman, killed Alejandro Maes on Oct. 23, 1881, in Canoncito, N.M.

Lea, Smith, a gunman, killed Catarino Romero in June 1885 at Lincoln, N.M.

Lee, B.B., an outlaw, was killed by Joe Farr in 1868 at Hempstead, Texas.

Lee, Bob, a gunman, was a companion of Dick Rogers in Raton, N.M., and attempted to break a friend out of jail in Springer.

Lee, Clem, an outlaw and leader of a gang that robbed the Reno stage, was arrested in Virginia City, Mont.

Lee, James, an outlaw, led a gang in the 1880s that stole horses around Cooke County, Texas. He and his brother Pink were killed on Dec. 7, 1885, by a posse led by Heck Thomas and Jim Taylor.

Lee, Mitch, an outlaw and member of the Kit Joy Gang, was killed by Deputy Sheriff T.L. Hall on Mar. 13, 1884.

Lee, Oliver, one of the best gunmen, was the primary agitator in the Good-Lee feud in Tularosa. He allegedly had A.J. Fountain killed, and was an enemy of Pat Garrett.

Lee, Pink, an outlaw and brother of James Lee, stole horses and was killed with his brother on Dec. 7, 1885.

Lee, Robert E. (AKA: **Bob Curry**), an outlaw and cousin of Harvey Logan, was a member of the Curry Gang and the Wild Bunch. He robbed a train in Wyoming on June 2, 1899, and was arrested, imprisoned, and released in February 1907.

Lee, Robert E., an outlaw, was involved in reconstruction troubles in North Texas after the Civil War. After several confrontations with the federal authorities and soldiers, he was killed in ambush in Hopkins County on June 26, 1869.

Leland, William (AKA; **Butch**), an outlaw and rustler in New Mexico, was killed by A.J. Foundation's militia in March 1888.

Lemons, Dan, a rustler and outlaw who was arrested in March 1880, at Lincoln County, New Mexico.

Lenta, Antonio, an outlaw aligned with the Clayton, and served time for killing Hop Lee in 1891.

Leonard, Bill, an outlaw and stage robber in Arizona, was killed by the Haslett brothers in June 1881.

Leroy, Billy, an outlaw, robbed stages and was lynched in 1881.

Le Roy, Kitty, a gunfighter and gambler, was one of the West's best women gamblers. In 1876 she ran a saloon in Deadwood. Her many lovers included Sam Bass and Bill Hickok. Her fourth husband grew jealous and killed her in 1878.

Leslie, N. Frank (AKA: **Buckskin Frank**), a deadly gunman in Arizona, killed ten to thirteen men including Mike Killeen and Billy Claibourne in 1881, and claimed he killed John Ringo. He served several years in Yuma prison for murder in 1889.

Levy, Jim, a gunman and a gambler, shot and mortally wounded C.H. Harrison in 1877 at Deadwood, S.D.

Lewis, Bill, an outlaw, stole horses in Parker County, Texas, in 1881, and was imprisoned for life for robbing the U.S. Mail.

Lewis, Elmer (AKA: **Slaughter Kid; Mysterious Kid**), an outlaw, robbed the bank at Wichita Falls, Texas, with Foster Crawford. He was arrested by Ranger Bill McDonald and hanged by a mob.

Lewis, Jim (AKA: **Arizona Bill**), an outlaw, attempted to "run the town" of Crested Butte, Colo., and was killed by Marshal Hatch on Sept. 30, 1881.

Leyba, Marino, an outlaw, led a gang of horse thieves and robbers who killed Colonel Charles Potter and was killed in Golden, Colo.

Liddell, James Andrew (AKA: **Dick**), an outlaw who robbed with Kit Dalton and the James Gang, turned himself in to Sheriff Timberlake after Jesse James was killed, served several years in prison, and died a natural death in 1893.

Liddil, Dick, a outlaw, was a member of the Jesse James Gang. He opened a saloon with Bob Ford in Las Vegas, N.M.

Light, Zachary, a gunman and one of the best shots in Mason County, Texas, wounded "Judge" Adams, and was shot and killed by Les Dow in Seven Rivers, N.M., while attempting to rob him.

Little Britches (Jennie Stevens, Jennie Metcalf), an outlaw connected with the Doolin Gang, rustled cattle and horses in the Osage Nation with Cattle Annie McDougal. She was arrested in 1894 and sent to the Federal Reformatory in Framingham, Mass.

Lockhart, Del, a New Mexico outlaw, was lynched in October 1881.

Logan, Harvey (AKA: **Kid Curry; Harvey Curry; Ed Howard; Charles Johnson**), a cowboy and rustler, participated in all the Wild Bunch train robberies, later joined the Black Jacks, and allegedly killed nine men. He either killed himself after a train robbery near Parachute, Colo., or absconded to South America.

Logan, Lonnie, an outlaw and member of the Wild Bunch Gang and brother of Harvey Logan, was killed by a posse on Feb. 28, 1900, outside Dodson, Mont.

Logwood, William, a gunman, shot and killed Juan Chavez y Pino on July 11, 1882, in the Nogal Mountains.

Long, John, an outlaw, was wanted for killing Marshal George Wellman in 1892 in Johnson County, Wyo.

Long, John (AKA; **Rivers**) was a gunman in the Lincoln County War. He died in Arizona.

Long, Steve (AKA: **Big Steve**), a lawman and outlaw, ran the "Bucket of Blood" saloon in Laramie City, Wyo., and appointed himself assistant marshal. Long and his two partners were lynched on Oct. 28, 1868.

Longbaugh, Harry (AKA: **The Sundance Kid; Henry Brown**), an outlaw and horse wrangler from Colorado who worked in Sundance, Wyo. He rode with the "Wild Bunch of Robbers' Roost." He and Butch Cassidy fled to South America where they were reportedly killed by government soldiers in either Bolivia or Argentina in 1908.

Longley, William Preston (AKA: **Wild Bill; Rattling Bill; Tom Jones; Jim Patterson, Jim Webb, Bill Black; Bill Henry, Bill Jackson**), a romantic gunfighter, allegedly killed more men than Wes Hardin. Not an outlaw, he was hanged Oct. 11, 1878.

Love, Harry, a lawman and former Texas Ranger, was allegedly a Mexican outlaw in the 1850s.

Loving, Frank (AKA: **Cock-eyed Frank**), a Dodge City gambler, killed Levie Richardson, and was gunned down by another gambler three years later in Trinidad, Colo.

Lowe, James (AKA: **James West**), an outlaw and horsethief, was lynched in Las Vegas, N.M., on Feb. 7, 1886.

Lowe, Joseph (AKA: **Red Joe; Rowdy Joe; Monte Joe**), gunman and former Ranger, consorted with Sam Bass and Joel Collins and was reputedly violent and a good gunfighter. He was killed in Feb. 11, 1899, by E.A. Kimmel, an ex-police officer, while unarmed.

Lucas, Elmer (AKA: **Chicken**), an outlaw and part-time member of the Bill Cook Gang, was captured in Indian Territory, after a bank robbery. He received a fifteen-year sentence in Detroit's federal prison.

Lucero, Aban, a gunman, shot and killed a man in Galisteo, N.M., on Feb. 9, 1891.

Lucero, Cecilio, an outlaw in Silva's White Caps, killed two cousins, Benizno Martinez and Juan Gallegos, and was lynched.

Lucero, Francisco, an outlaw, was jailed in 1891 in Clayton, N.M.

Lucero, Quinia, an outlaw, shot and killed Jose A. Samora on Apr. 20, 1884, in Wallace, N.M.

Lucero, Sostenes, an outlaw in Silva's White Caps, with Juan Romero, shot and killed gang member Antonio Rael.

Lucero, Tomas, an outlaw in Silva's White Caps of Las Vegas, N.M., died in the 1940s.

Lujan, Martiniano, a gunman, shot and killed Martias Mirival on Feb. 21, 1890, near Lincoln, N.M.

Luna, Melchior, a gunman, shot Manuel Sanchez on Feb. 20, 1883, in Belen, N.M.

Luttrell, Charles, an outlaw, killed a witness in 1880 to Sam Sparks's murder in Lee County, Texas, and fled to Denison. Captured in 1893, he was hanged after attempting escape several times.

Lyons, Haze, an outlaw and deputy under outlaw Sheriff Henry Plummer in Silver City, Montana Territory, was lynched on Jan. 14, 1864.

McCall, Jim, an outlaw, rustled cattle near Springer, N.M., in the 1880s.

McCall, John (**Jack**; AKA: **Broken-Nose Jack; Curly; Buffalo Curly**), a gunman, shot and killed Bill Hickok on Aug. 2, 1876. He was hanged for murder on Mar. 1, 1877.

McCandles, David C., a gunman, was killed by Bill Hickok on July 12, 1861, at Red Rock Ranch in Nebraska.

McCarty, Bill, an outlaw, brother of Tom McCarthy, and brother-in-law of Matt Warner, joined Butch Cassidy and the Wild Bunch, and was killed during the Delta, Colo., bank robbery.

McCarty, Henry (AKA: **Billy the Kid**), an outlaw and member of the Aelbee Gang in South Dakota, was frequently confused with New Mexico's Billy the Kid.

McCarty, Tom, an outlaw, brother of Bill McCarthy, and brother-in-law of Matt Warner, joined Butch Cassidy and the Wild Bunch and was killed during a gunfight in Montana.

McCauley, Hamp, an outlaw, was lynched by vigilantes in Napa, Calif., after he was tried for murder in 1851.

McCloskey, Andy, a gunman and buffalo hunter, dueled with another man at Camp Supply, Texas, in 1872. Both men were killed.

McCloskey, Sam, a gunman, was injured in the Lincoln County War.

McCoy, "One-Legged-Jim", an outlaw, killed Sheriff Charles McKinney in La Salle County, Texas, and was hanged in San Antonio in 1887.

McCullough, Green, an outlaw, was lynched in San Antonio, Texas.

McDaniels, J., an outlaw and member of the Pitts-Yeager Gang, was killed in 1884 in Texas.

McDaniels, Jim, a gunman in the Lincoln County War, participated in the McSween gunfight on July 19, 1879.

McDaniels, William (AKA: **Bud**), an outlaw and former guerilla soldier, rode with the James Gang.

McDonald, J., a gunman, shot and killed his friend Robert Taylor on Jan. 13, 1890, in Clayton, N.M.

McDonald, Walter, a gunman, shot Thomas Richards in 1884 in Coeur de'Alene, N.M.

McDowell, Jack (AKA: **Three-Fingered Jack**), an outlaw, led a gang of outlaws and was lynched in Aurora, Nev., in February 1864.

McGrand, Ed, a gunman, received a life sentence in 1876 for killing a man in Nebraska.

McGuire, Edward, an outlaw, sheltered horse thieves on his New Mexico ranch and was caught.

McIntire, James, a Texas gunman and lawman from 1860, was Ranger, city marshal of Las Vegas, deputy sheriff, cowboy, hunter, gambler, and outlaw with a $1,000 reward on his head for the deaths of two men in American Valley, N.M.

McIntyre, Chas, a gunman, was jailed in 1874 at Belmont, Neb., for drawing his pistol, and was later lynched.

McKeague, Neal, a gunman and gambler, was killed at Church's Ferry, Dakota Territory in 1890 by a bar-keeper.

McKimie, Robert (AKA: **Little Reddie from Texas**), an outlaw and member of the Sam Bass Gang of the Dakotas in the 1870s, joined other outlaw gangs.

McKinney, Thomas L., a New Mexico gunman, who was also a lawman, accompanied Pat Garrett to the shootout with Billy the Kid on July 14, 1881.

McLaughlin, M. (AKA: **Red**), an outlaw and robber, escaped jail in Springer, N.M., on July 4, 1884.

McLowery, Frank, a gunman, was one of the three cowboys killed by the Earps in the O.K. Corral shoot-out on Oct. 26, 1881.

McLowery, Thomas, a gunman and the brother of Frank, was killed in the O.K. Corral shoot-out by the Earps.

McMains, Oscar P., a New Mexico reverend who was active in the disorder surrounding the Maxwell Land Grant.

McManus, Irving, an outlaw, rode with the Black Jack Ketchum Gang in the 1890s.

McMasters, Sherm, an outlaw, rode with Wyatt Earp from 1879 to 1881, stole a horse, and was killed in the Texas Panhandle.

McNab, Frank, a gunman in the Lincoln County War, was killed in Bonito, N.M. in 1878.

McNew, Bill, a gunman and accused rustler, fought with Oliver Lee in the Good-Lee feud in Tularosa, N.M.

M'Rose, Martin, an outlaw, rustled cattle and was killed by El Paso city marshal Jeff Milton.

McWilliams, Sam (AKA: **the Verdigris Kid**), an outlaw and member of the Cook Gang in the Indian Territory, was killed by lawmen in 1895.

Mace, Cal, an outlaw and Gunnison, Colo., gambler, was wanted for killing two men in Texas, and was killed by Jim McClease at Gunnison in the 1890s.

Mace. John, a gunman in the Lincoln County War, was indicted in 1878 for his participation. He was killed by a posse in 1880.

Maes, Juanito, an outlaw, stole horses around Boquilla, N.M.

Maes, Patricio, an outlaw and member of the White Caps, was hanged by the gang on Oct. 23, 1892, as a suspected traitor.

Maes, Zenon, an outlaw, was a member of Silva's White Caps.

Maestas, German (Herman), an outlaw and member of Silva's White Caps, was hanged on May 25, 1894, in Las Vegas for killing his common-law wife and her lover.

Mahoney, John, an outlaw, was one of the gang that killed Jock Harriman on Dec. 10, 1883, in Wallace, N.M.

Majors, Robert, a gunman, shot and killed ex-Texas Ranger James Harris in a shoot-out at Santa Cruz, Calif., in the early 1880s.

Maldonado, Manuel, an outlaw, was a member of Silva's White Caps.

Mallory, L.P., a youthful troublemaker who was wanted for forgery in 1886.

Malone, James, an outlaw, executed for murder on Mar. 15, 1878, in the Arizona Territory.

Mamby, Henry, a gunman, shot and killed D.B. Griffin on May 11, 1884, in Vermijo, N.M.

Mancy, Mitchell E. (AKA: **Mitch; Mike Manning**), a gunman, shot and killed Juan Patron in Puerto de Luna, N.M., on Apr. 12, 1884.

Mankiller, Smoker, an outlaw Cherokee Indian, was hanged for killing a man at Fort Smith, Indian Territory, on Sept. 3, 1875.

Manning, A.E., a merchant in Northfield, Minn., and gunman, shot Cole Younger and Bill Chadwell on Sept. 7, 1876, while the James-Younger Gang robbed the bank.

Manning, James, a gunman, was one of the brothers in an El Paso feud with Marshal Dallas Stoudenmire. In 1882, James shot Stoudenmire in the head and was acquitted of murder.

Mansker, Jim, a gunman, was killed at Miles City, Mont., in 1894 during a gunfight.

Mares, Hilario, an outlaw, was a member of Silva's White Caps.

Marlow Brothers, outlaw brothers, Boone, Albert, Llewellen, Charles, and George were horse thieves who killed a sheriff in 1889. They battled a lynch mob, killed four people, and the mob killed two brothers. Boone was poisoned, and last two fled to California.

Marshall, Charles, a gunman in the Lincoln County War, rode with the posse that killed John Tunstall on Feb. 18, 1878.

Martin, Chàrles, a gunman in the Lincoln County War, was indicted in 1878 for his participation.

Martin, Robert, an outlaw, who in 1879, led a gang in the Arizona Territory.

Martin, William (AKA: **Hurricane Bill**), a gunman, was jailed for playing cards, matching Holliday, and assault. He fled to Castroville, Texas, after he was forced to marry a prostitute.

Martin, William (AKA: **Wild Bill; Jones**), an outlaw in Lincoln County, was killed by John Perry in June 1887.

Martinez, Atanacio, a gunman, claimed he shot and killed Morris J. Bernstein in Lincoln County, a shooting credited to Billy the Kid.

Mason, Barney, a gunman, lawman, and Sheriff Garrett's deputy, killed John Farris in self defense at Fort Sumner, N.M., in 1880.

Massagee, George, an outlaw, convicted of robbing a post office in the New Mexico Territory.

Masterson, Edward J. (AKA: **Little Ed**), Bat Matterson's brother, Edward served as town marshal in Dodge City, Kan., and was killed by two cowboys on Apr. 9, 1878.

Masterson, James, a gunman and brother of Bat Masterson, was run out of Raton, N.M., in March 1885.

Masterson, Robert (AKA: **Smiling Bob**), another brother of Bat, Robert was marshal in Trinidad, Colo., in 1882. He reportedly killed twenty-one men.

Masterson, William Barclay (AKA: **Bat**), served as sheriff of Ford County, Kan., city marshal in Dodge, and deputy U.S. marshal for the New York District. Bat killed one of the men who murdered his brother and helped apprehend Dave Rudabaugh and his gang. He died working as a newspaper sports writer in 1921.

Mathers, David (AKA: **Mysterious Dave**), an outlaw, was one of the Dodge City Gang in Las Vegas, N.M.

Mathias, Oscar, a gunman, shot John Coddington on Sept. 30, 1882, at Three Rivers, N.M.

Matthews, Jacob B., a gunman, served in the Tennessee Cavalry in the Civil War, and was a gunman employed by L.G. Murphy during the Lincoln County War, as deputy sheriff. He died in 1903.

Maxwell, Peter Menard, a cowboy and gunman, was a friend of Billy the Kid in Lincoln County. Pat Garrett shot and killed the Kid in Maxwell's bedroom in July 1881. He died on June 21, 1898.

May, D. Boone, a gunman and stage guard in Deadwood, S.D., and Cheyenne, Wyo., killed several stage robbers in the 1870s.

Meade, William, a gunman, shot J.E. "Dobe" Johnson on Feb. 24, 1884, in Hillsboro, N.M.

Means, Colonel **Thomas**, a gunman, was lynched on Jan. 1, 1867, for attempting to murder his father-in-law in Taos, N.M.

Medlock, John, an outlaw, was hanged on May 25, 1906, in Raton.

Medran, Florentino, an outlaw, was a member of Silva's White Caps.

Meeks, Henry Wilbur (Bub), an outlaw and member of the Wild Bunch, was imprisoned in the 1900s, and died in an insane asylum on Nov. 22, 1912, in the State Hospital in Evanston, Wyo.

Menczer, Augustus (Gus), a gunman and Texas saloon owner, killed several men after a shoot-out with his business partner in Raton, N.M., in 1882. A mob lynched him on June 28, 1882.

Meras, Nica, an outlaw, stole horses in Lincoln County and was shot in 1877.

Merideth, Charles, an outlaw, killed "Red" Dent Kyes in Clayton, N.M, in March 1890.

Merrill, David, an Oregon outlaw, rode with Harry Tracy who killed him in 1899, after a prison escape.

Mes, Cruz, an outlaw and horsethief, was killed with Roman and Pancho on a road near White Sands, N.M., in 1876.

Mes, Felipe, a gunman in the Lincoln County War, rode with the posse that killed John Tunstall on Feb. 18, 1878.

Mes, Pancho, an outlaw horse thief, was killed with Roman and Cruz on a road near White Sands, N.M., in 1876.

Mes, Roman, an outlaw horse thief, was killed with Pancho and Cruz on a road near White Sands, N.M., in 1876.

Metcalfe, "Wild Bill", an outlaw, fled Loma Parda, N.M., in November 1877 after killing a man. He was jailed and lynched by a mob.

Middleton, Chas, an outlaw, was wanted by the sheriff of Bastrop County, Texas, in 1886.

Middleton, John, an outlaw and cousin of Jim Reed, rode with Quantrell and killed Sheriff J.H. Black in Texas, and was shot and killed southwest of Fort Smith.

Middleton, John, an outlaw and gunman with Billy the Kid in Lincoln County, ambushed Sheriff William Brady and George Hindman on Apr. 1, 1878, and was charged with the murder of Buckshot Roberts.

Middleton, Thomas (Doc), led an outlaw gang of horse thieves in Nebraska, 1870s-1890s. He died in 1913.

Miera, Pantaleon, an outlaw, stole horses and killed men in New Mexico. He was lynched in Albuquerque, N.M., on Dec. 29, 1880.

Miller, Clell, an outlaw in the James-Younger Gang, was active in the 1870s, before his death during the robbery of the First National Bank at Northfield, Minn., in September 1876.

Miller, Eli (AKA: **Slick**), an New Mexico outlaw, was captured by A.J. Foundation.

Miller, James P., a gunman, professional killer, and occasional lawman in Pecos, Texas, in the 1890s, killed Sheriff Bud Frazier and was suspected of forty other killings including Pat Garrett and A.A. Bobbitt. A mob lynched him in 1909 at Ada, Okla.

Miller, Jesse (AKA: **Jesse Williams; Jeff Davis**), an outlaw, was a member of the Cole Estes Gang of train robbers in New Mexico.

Miller, Captain **John**, a gunman, killed thirty-two men in his life before he was killed in 1888 by John Ables, a tenant on his farm in Jonesboro, Indian Territory, who claimed Miller attacked him.

Miller, S.C., a gunman, shot John Saun in November 1885 in San Marcial, N.M.

Miller, "Wild Bill", an outlaw, was killed by lawmen in Corwell County, Texas, on Jan. 13, 1869.

Mills, Alexander H., a gunman and murderer, rode with the posse that killed John Tunstall on Feb. 18, 1878.

Miner, Bill, an outlaw, robbed stages for forty years and died in a Georgia prison in 1913.

Mitchell, Bill (AKA: **John W. King**), an outlaw, killed men in the Hood County, Texas, feud, and received a ninety-nine-year sentence in 1912 in Texas. He escaped from jail at the age of seventy.

Montoya, Jose F., an outlaw, was a member of Silva's White Caps.

Montoya, Narciso, an outlaw, killed Luis Gallegos and was lynched in Taos, N.M., on June 10, 1881.

Montoya, Ramon, a gunman in the Lincoln County War, rode with the posse that killed John Tunstall on Feb. 18, 1878.

Moon, Jim, an outlaw, led a gang that stole mules from Texas and New Mexico army posts in 1870.

Moore, Lester, a gunman, was buried on Boothill in Tombstone, Ariz. His tombstone reads "Here lies Lester Moore, Four Slugs from a .44, No Les, No More.

Moore, Thomas, a gunman in the Lincoln County War, rode with the posse that killed John Tunstall on Feb. 18, 1878.

Moore, W.C. (AKA: **Bill**), an outlaw, horsethief, and murderer, rode with John Casey in New Mexico and later moved to Alaska.

Morgan, Frank, an outlaw, held up the San Marcial, N.M., stage on May 15, 1881, and was killed.

Morgan, Joe, a gunman and lawman, fought Deputy Sheriff Ben Williams in Las Cruces, N.M., on Sept. 15, 1895, with Albert Fall. He was later a deputy sheriff and Oliver Lee supporter.

Morrell, Ed, an outlaw and author of a book, aided the escape of Chris Evans from a California jail in 1893.

Morris, Harvey, a gunman in the Lincoln County War, was killed during the McSween gunfight on July 19, 1878.

Morris, W.C., a gunman, dueled with "Editor Shannan" and killed him at Visalia, Calif., in 1860.

Morrissey, Peter, a New Mexico outlaw, was killed in June 1877 by a posse.

Morton, William, a gunman in the Lincoln County War, rode with the posse that killed John Tunstall in February. He was killed by Billy the Kid in March 1878.

Mosely, "Scar Face", an outlaw, was killed by the Montana Stranglers close to Glendive, Mont., in 1884.

Mosier, Henry, a gunman who participated in the killing of Jock Harriman in Wallace, N.M. on Dec. 10, 1883.

Moyer, Ace, a gunman and founder of Laramie, Wyo., was hanged with his brother Con in 1868.

Moyer, Con, a gunman and founder of Laramie, Wyo., was hanged with his brother Ace in 1868.

Munson, Henry, an outlaw and member of the Bill Cook Gang of Oklahoma, was killed on Aug. 2, 1894, during a battle at Sapulpa, Okla.

Murieta, Joaquin, the half-mythical "King of the California Outlaws," reportedly killed Texas Ranger Harry Love before he was killed in 1853, by a posse.

Murietta, Procopio, an outlaw and nephew of Joaquin Murieta, once terrorized Santa Cruz, Calif., and rode with Timbucio Vasquez in the late 1860s.

Murillo, Zeke, an outlaw, led a gang of rustlers headquartered in Shakespeare, N.M.

Murphy, John, an outlaw, sentenced for train robbery at Las Vegas, N.M. in 1905.

Murphy, Lawrence Gustave, an immigrant from Ireland who became a judge, shopkeeper, and post trader in Lincoln County, died on Oct. 20, 1878, during the height of the Lincoln County War, which he started.

Muskgrove, George, an outlaw, was a member of the Black Jack Ketchum Gang in the 1890s in New Mexico.

Muskgrove, L.H., an outlaw, led a gang in the 1860s after the Civil War in Colorado.

Muskgrove, M., an outlaw, was a member of Black Jack Christian's gang.

Nangway, Charles, an outlaw, murdered a rancher on June 3, 1885, near Lake Valley, N.M.

Nash, Joe, a gunman in the Lincoln County War, was indicted for his participation in 1878.

Neel, John S., a gunman, shot J.N. New on June 19, 1883, on the Penasco.

Neill, H.G. (AKA: **Hoodoo Brown**), an outlaw and justice of the peace, was one of the Dodge City Gang, and was run out of Las Vegas, N.M.

Nelson, Bob, an outlaw, was a member of Wild Bill Martin's gang in Lincoln, N.M.

Nelson, Mart, a gunman, killed seven people in Bonito, N.M., on May 4 1885.

Newcombe, George (AKA: **Bitter Creek; The Slaughter Kid**), an outlaw and member of the Dalton and Doolin gangs of Oklahoma in 1890s, was killed near Pawnee, Okla.

Newman, Bud, an outlaw with the Taylor Gang of West Texas, was captured in 1898, and killed in an escape attempt.

Newman, Jim, a lawman and outlaw, consorted with Wes Hardin in the 1860s. He later lived in Texas and New Mexico.

Nicholson, William (AKA: **Flap Jack Bill**), an outlaw, was lynched on Oct. 1, 1881, in Sanders, N.M.

Nite, Jim, an outlaw and member of the Dalton Gang, was apprehended by deputy U.S. Marshal Dee Harkey near Sacramento Sinks, N.M., in 1908 along with Dan Johnson.

Nolan, Francisco, an outlaw, was a member of the Castillo Gang.

Noranjo, Aristotle, an outlaw, was lynched on Oct. 6, 1881, in Las Lunas, N.M.

Norfleet, J. Frank, a gunman and rancher in Gonzales county, Texas, tracked, captured, and sent to prison a gang that conned him out of more than $100,000.

O'Day, Tom, an outlaw, robbed banks in the Black Hills in the 1890s and was imprisoned in 1903 for horse theft.

O'Dell, Bill, a gunman, was killed with his brother Tom by lawmen in Texas in December 1880.

O'Dell, Tom, a gunman, was killed with his brother Bill by lawmen in Texas in December 1880.

Odle, Al, an outlaw, escaped from the Burnet, Texas, jail with his brother William in 1889, fled to Mexico, and was later killed by rangers Outlaw and Hughes in Edwards County, Texas.

Odle, William, an outlaw, escaped from the Burnet, Texas, jail with his brother Al in 1889, fled to Mexico, and was later killed by rangers Outlaw and Hughes in Edwards County, Texas.

O'Folliard, Thomas, an outlaw, friend of Billy the Kid, and cohort in the Lincoln County War, was killed in ambush by Pat Garrett's posse on Dec. 19, 1880. He is buried with Billy the Kid.

O'Laughlin, Jimmy, an outlaw, broke out of jail on June 1885.

Olinger, J. Wallace, a gunman in the Lincoln County War and brother of Robert, was indicted for his participation.

Olinger, Robert, an outlaw, crooked U.S. marshal, and deputy sheriff of Lincoln county, was indicted for his participation in the Lincoln County War, and was killed by Billy the Kid on Apr. 28, 1881.

Omohundro, John B. (AKA: **Texas Jack**), a scout and gunman, tracked horsethieves and led massacres of Indian tribes in the 1850s-60s, in Texas, Kansas, Arizona, and New Mexico. He died in 1888.

O'Neill, Thomas, a gunman, killed Walter Byers in Dawson, N.M.

Orr, John (AKA: **Donaldson**), an outlaw and member of Wild Bill Martin's gang, was killed by a gang led by John Perry in June 1877.

Owens, George, an outlaw and member of the Alvord-Stiles Gang of Arizona, was imprisoned for a train robbery committed in 1899.

Owens, Lewis, an outlaw and brother of George, robbed trains with a gang, and was captured and imprisoned in 1900.

Padilla, Pablo, an outlaw, stole horses and cattle around Valencia County, N.M., and was lynched in January 1872.

Paine, John, a Texas gunfighter, fought for the Grahams in the Tonto Basin, Ariz., war in the 1880s.

Paine, Manfred, an outlaw and son of a suspected killer, shot and killed his father in Washington, as well as the lawman who arrested him.

Palmeter, Page, a gunman, shot and killed Harry Walters on Oct. 27, 1883. in Raton, N.M.

Parker, George Leroy (AKA: **Butch Cassidy**), an outlaw, led the Wild Bunch which robbed trains and banks in Utah, Nevada, Wyoming, Colorado, New Mexico, and other states. He and Harry Longbaugh, the Sundance Kid, were allegedly killed in Bolivia or Argentina, in 1908.

Parrott, George (AKA: **Big Nose George**), an outlaw, led a gang in a train robbery in 1878 but was thwarted. Captured in 1880, he was lynched after receiving a death sentence from the court.

Pate, James, an outlaw, was arrested on Nov. 17, 1906, for murder.

Patterson, Ferd, an outlaw, was killed either in a barber's chair or in a hotel lobby in Idaho or Walla Walla, Wash., in the 1860s.

Patterson, Frank was an outlaw in Arizona and New Mexico.

Paxton, Louis, a gunman in the Lincoln County War, was indicted in 1879 for his participation.

Peacock, Lewis, a western outlaw and gunman.

Pearl, William S., a gunman, killed a soldier in Fort Stanton, N.M., and was lynched on Jan. 23, 1883, by other soldiers.

Pell, Henry (AKA: **Henry Thompson; Long Henry**), a gunman who lived in Missouri, Texas, and Montana, killed seven men before he was gunned down in 1902.

Peppin, George, a lawman who aligned himself with outlaws during a feud in Lincoln County, N.M. on July 19, 1879.

Perkins, Louis, an outlaw, was captured with Charlie Allison in Albuqerque, N.M., in June 1881.

Perry, Samuel R., a gunman in the Lincoln County War, was indicted in 1879 for his participation.

Petal, Gabriel, an outlaw, was a member of Silva's White Caps.

Phillipowski, Lyon, a lawman who was involved in a shootout with a store clerk in Lincoln County, N.M. on Oct. 21, 1874.

Pickett, Thomas, an outlaw and lawman, stole cattle and was captured with Billy the Kid in New Mexico on Dec. 20, 1880. He later served as a Ranger and died on May 14, 1934, in Arizona.

Pierce, Charles, an outlaw, joined the Dalton Gang and later the Doolin Gang, in Oklahoma in the 1890s. He was killed on May 2, 1895, near Pawnee, along with George Newcombe.

Pino y Pino, Pablo, a gunman in the Lincoln County War, was indicted in 1879 for his participation.

Pipkin, Red, an outlaw, rode with Bronco Bill Walters.

Pitman, Joe, a gunman, shot and killed Dick Blain on Feb. 18, 1888, in Luna Valley, N.M.

Pitts, Charles, an outlaw and member of the Younger Gang, was killed after the failed robbery of the Northfield, Minn., bank on Sept. 7, 1876.

Plummer, Henry, an outlaw leader and lawman, organized the worst gang of cutthroats in the West, in early 1860. Plummer and over thirty members of the gang were lynched by vigilantes in 1864. He was about to become U.S. marshal of the Territory.

Poe, John W., a gunman and deputy to Pat Garrett, was with Garrett when he killed Billy the Kid on July 14, 1881.

Polanco, Librado, an outlaw, was the secretary of Silva's White Caps, and received a life sentence for robbery.

Porter, Frank, an outlaw, was killed eighty miles west of Albuquerque, N.M., in April 1888, by a posse.

Potter, Andrew Jackson, an outlaw turned Methodist preacher, scouted and fought hostiles in New Mexico and Texas from 1847, and died in October 1895.

"Powder Bill", an outlaw, was hired to kill A.J. Foundation but did not attempt the murder.

Powell, Buck, a gunman in the Lincoln County War, was indicted for his participation.

Power, William (Bill, AKA: Joe; Tim Evans), an outlaw and member of the Dalton Gang, was killed by John Kloehr in the Coffeyville, Kan., bank robbery, in 1892.

Powers, Doc, a New Mexico gunman, who killed a man in Council Springs, on June 27, 1888.

Price, Elmer, an outlaw, was sent to prison. He was refused pardon twice; first on Feb. 6, 1909, and then on Apr. 27, 1912.

Putman, Ed (AKA: **Ed Sibley**), an outlaw killed by Texas Rangers on Dec. 1, 1906, at Del Rio, Texas, during a shoot-out. Putman was wanted for killing two men over a sheep deal.

Quantrell, William Clark, an outlaw, commanded group of guerrilla fighters in the Civil War that raided towns in the 1860s. Known for the raids on Centralia and Lawrence, the Dalton, James, and Younger brothers rode with him, and was killed in Kentucky after May 1865.

Queen, Richard, an outlaw, was jailed in Socorro, N.M., on Aug. 17, 1906.

Queen, Vic, an outlaw, rode with Martin M'Rose in New Mexico.

Quinlan, Tom (AKA: **Tex**), an outlaw, escaped from the Las Vegas jail with Webb and Rudabaugh on Dec. 3, 1881.

Radigan, Thomas, an outlaw, rode with Ike Stockton's gang.

Rael, Antonio, an outlaw, was a member of Silva's White Caps, and was killed by gang members Juan Romero and Sostenas Lucero.

Raidler, William (AKA: **Little Bill**), an outlaw, joined the Dalton-Doolin Gang in Oklahoma in 1892, and was captured in 1895. After his release from prison, Raidler quit crime.

Randall, William, an outlaw and horsethief, shot and killed Constable Joe Carson on Jan. 22, 1880, and was himself killed in Las Vegas.

Rande, Frank (AKA: **Charles Van Zandt**), an outlaw in Iowa, Illinois, and Indiana in the 1870s, was shot and killed by guards while in prison in March 1884.

Rascon, Eugenio, a gunman, shot and killed Demas Garcia in New Mexico on Nov. 18, 1883.

Ray, Charles (AKA: **Pony Diehl; Deal**), a well known outlaw frequenting Lincoln and Tombstone, was hanged in 1884.

Raynolds, Joseph, stole a horse from Captain Jack Crawford and served eighteen months in prison.

Real, Acasio, an outlaw, was a member of Silva's White Caps.

Real, Procopio, an outlaw, was a member of Silva's White Caps.

Realis, Pablo, an ax murderer who killed his wife and sister-in-law on July 19, 1848, in Santa Fe, N.M., was the first murderer reported in the first English newspaper in New Mexico Territory.

Redding, Robert, a New Mexico gunman, shot and killed a Central City, Colo., man in October 1888.

Redfield, Len, a suspected outlaw in Arizona, was lynched in 1877 for allegedly robbing a stagecoach.

Reed, Ed, the son of Belle Starr and Jim Reed, he was a suspected stagecoach and train robber.

Reed, Jim, an outlaw and husband of Belle Starr, was wanted in Central Texas for robbery. He was killed in 1874.

Reese, James, a gunman in the Lincoln County War, fought in the McSween gun battle July 19, 1879.

Remine, Richard, an outlaw, was hanged at Silver City, N.M., in March 1881.

Reynolds, Laris, an outlaw, rode with Ike Stockton's gang.

Richardson, Robert, a gunman, shot and killed Louis Lesser on Nov. 12, 1881, in Teseque, N.M.

Riggs, Barney, an outlaw in Texas in the 1880s, he was killed at Fort Stockton in the 1890s.

Riley, John Henry, a gunman and immigrant from Ireland, was a leader of the Murphy-Dolan faction in the Lincoln County War in New Mexico. He died in 1916.

Ringo, John (John Ringgold), a gunman prominent in Texas, Arizona, and New Mexico, killed several men before his bootless body was found outside Tombstone on July 14, 1882.

Rivera, Petronilio, a gunman, killed a man on Oct. 23, 1884, in Tularosa, N.M.

Roach, John was a gunman and gambler in Kingston, N.M.

Roberts, Buckshot (AKA: **Bill Williams; William Albert Roberts; Andrew L. Roberts; Bill Roberts**), a Texas Ranger, outlaw, and member of King Fisher's gang in New Mexico, killed Dick Brewer was killed in the gunbattle at Blazer's Mill in 1878.

Robertson, William, a gunman, was shooting at an enemy when police killed him in April 1880.

Rodriguez, Jesus, a gunman and horsethief, participated in the Lincoln County War.

Rogers, Annie, girlfriend of outlaw Kid Curry, was charged with Curry as an accomplice, imprisoned in the Tennessee Penitentiary, and released on June 19, 1902.

Rogers, Bob, an Indian Territory outlaw from 1893, was killed by a posse south of Coffeyville on Mar. 13, 1896.

Rogers, David, an outlaw, arrested in 1889 for complicity in the robbery of an Army paymaster in the New Mexico Territory.

Rogers, Dick, an outlaw, attempted to break a friend from jail on Mar. 13, 1885, and was killed.

Romero, Cristobel, an outlaw, was lynched in 1884 near Los Lunas.

Romero, Damon, an outlaw and murderer, was hanged in Springer, N.M., on Feb. 2, 1883.

Romero, Juan, an outlaw and member of Silva's White Caps, killed gang member Antonio Rale with Sostenas Lucero. He died in Raton in 1931.

Romero, Ricardo (AKA: **El Romo**), an outlaw, was Silva's first lieutenant in the White Caps.

Romero, Torevio, a gunman, killed Francisco Martinez on Mar. 25, 1886, in Rio Quemado, N.M.

Romero, Vicente, a gunman in the Lincoln County War, was killed in the McSween gunfight on July 19, 1879.

Rose of Cimarron, an outlaw, lover of George Newcomb, and friend of the Dalton-Doolin Gang, helped Newcomb escape from a gunbattle outside Ingalis, Indian Territory, and served time in a U.S. reformatory.

Roth, Fred, a gunman, shot and killed James Spurlock in Spring 1885 on John Chisum's Ranch.

Rucker, E.C., a New Mexico lawman, but also aligned with the outlaw, John Good.

Rudabaugh, David, an outlaw and briefly city marshal of Las Vegas, N.M., rode with the Roark Gang, Doc Holliday, and Billy the Kid. He was shot and beheaded by vigilantes in Mexico.

Rudolph, Bill (AKA: **The Missouri Kid**), an outlaw and murderer, robbed banks in Missouri with George Collins the 1900s, and was captured in 1904. He was imprisoned and hanged on May 8.

Ruff, Rufus (AKA: **Windy**), an outlaw, was lynched in Mora County, N.M., for killing Charles Norton.

Rush, Matt, an outlaw and suspected rustler, was killed by Tom Horn on July 9, 1900, near Brown's Hole, Wyo.

Russell, T.N., a gunman and citizen of Coffeyville, Kan., killed Dick Broadwell when the Dalton Gang attempted to robbed two banks on Oct. 5, 1892.

Ryan, "Fatty", an outlaw, was an early hold-up artist in Arizona.

Ryan, P., a gunman, shot and killed Charles Walker on June 23, 1881, in San Marcial, N.M.

Rynerson, William L., a gunman and legislator, killed Territorial Chief Justice John P. Slough in Santa Fe, N.M., and was acquitted. Later, he was a Dolan gunman in the Lincoln County War.

Sage, Lee, an outlaw, rustled cattle and was born in Robber's Roost country.

Sagolia, Manuel, a gunman in the Lincoln County War, rode with the posse that killed John Tunstall on Feb. 18, 1878.

Said, John (AKA: **Rattlesnake Jack**), an Idaho outlaw, was shot and killed by the sheriff and posse in Weiser City in November 1882.

Sais, Carlos, an outlaw, was sentenced to be hanged for murder on Dec. 17, 1906.

Saiz, Doroteo, an outlaw and John Kinney's right hand man, was killed while attempting escape.

Salas, Justo, a New Mexico gunman who was involved in a 1900 shootout at a dance hall.

Salazar, Yginio was a gunman in the Lincoln County War.

Sample, Omer W., an outlaw and member of the Heith Gang, was hanged in Tombstone for robbery on March 8, 1884.

Sampson, Sam, an outlaw and member of the Buck Gang in the Indian Territory, was hanged on July 1, 1896.

Sanders, George, an outlaw, was a member of the Cook Gang in the Indian Territory. He was killed by lawmen.

Sandobal, Juan, an outlaw, was lynched on Dec. 15, 1871, in Las Lunas, N.M.

Sandoval, Anastacio, a gunman, shot and killed Cypriano Montoya on Mar. 20, 1884, in Anton Chico, N.M.

Sandoval, Remigio (AKA: **El Gavilan**), an outlaw, was a member of Silva's White Capes in New Mexico.

Sanez, Doroteo, an outlaw, was a lieutenant in John Kinney's gang of professional gunmen. He was killed in July 1877 by A.J. Fountain's militia.

Santleben, August, a gunman, ran a stage line from 1867 between Texas and Mexico and killed several Mexican outlaw and hostile Indians. He died on Sept. 19, 1911.

Saunders, William, a gunman, shot Sid Moore in June 1885 in White Oaks, N.M.

Schroeder, S., an outlaw, was jailed in Las Vegas, N.M., and escaped on Dec. 3, 1881, with David Rudabaugh and John Webb.

Scorgins, John (Bill), a gunman in the Lincoln County War, was indicted for the murder of Buckshot Roberts.

Scott, E., a wanted outlaw with a reward for his arrest, killed several men on Dec. 20, 1873, in Lincoln County, N.M.

Scott, John, an outlaw, shot by Springer, N.M., Deputy Sheriff Frank P. Nichols on May 17, 1883.

Scurlock, Josiah, G. (AKA: **Doc**), a gunman and friend of Billy the Kid, left when he was indicted for the murder of Buckshot Roberts, but later returned to New Mexico. In 1882, during an argument, Fred Roth shot and killed him.

Seaman, Carey, a gunman and resident of Coffeyville, Kan., wounded Dick Broadwell and shot Emmett Dalton when the Dalton Gang attempted to rob the two Coffeyville banks on Nov. 5, 1892.

See, James, a Texas outlaw, murderer, and rustler in the 1860s, died in California in 1887.

Segura, Jose, an outlaw and leader of a gang of horse thieves, was lynched by vigilantes on July 10, 1876, near Fort Stanton.

Selman, John, a Texas lawman and gunman, allegedly rustled with John Larn around Fort Griffin, Texas. He befriended Billy the Kid during the Lincoln County War, and killed Wes Hardin in August 1895. George Scarborough killed him on Apr. 6, 1896.

Sharp, Milton A., a California outlaw, robbed the Bodie stage four times in June and September 1880.

Shears, John, a gunman, killed W.W. Pruner on June 2, 1888.

Sheedy, Ben, an outlaw, was shot while attempting to escape arrest in Lincoln, N.M., in September 1887.

Sheehan, Larry, an outlaw, led a group of train robbers in 1887, in the New Mexico Territory.

Sheet Iron Jack, a California outlaw known as a "Robinhood," was lynched by vigilantes from Idaho and Montana.

Short, Luke, a gunfighter who killed two men, was one of the Dodge City Gang that followed Wyatt Earp to Tombstone, Ariz. He died in December 1893.

Sias, Carlos, an outlaw and murderer, was hanged in January 1907 in Socorro, N.M.

Silva, Vicente, an outlaw, led the White Caps, a gang of robbers and murderers in Las Vegas, N.M. He was killed by White Caps members in 1895.

Simms, W.H. (AKA: **Billy**), a saloon keeper in San Antonio, who in 1884, was suspected of killing King Fisher and Ben Thompson.

Siringo, Charles A., a gunman and cowboy detective, chased outlaws and rustlers throughout Texas, New Mexico, and the Montanas in the 1890s. He died in California in 1928.

Sisneros, Dionicio (AKA: **Candelas**), an outlaw, was a member of Silva's White Caps. He was sentenced to life imprisonment.

Slade, Joseph A. (AKA: **Captain Jack**), a gunman in Montana, Idaho, and Colorado territories, was hanged by vigilantes in 1864.

Slaughter, John Horton (AKA: **Little Black John**), a gunman, rancher in South Arizona, and one time sheriff of Cochise County, killed two men in Tombstone in 1882, and was suspected of train robbery. He died on Feb. 15, 1922.

Smith, Billie, a Kansas cowboy turned outlaw, robbed the Medicine Lodge bank with a gang led by Marshal Hendry Brown and killed two men on Apr. 30, 1884. He was lynched while awaiting trial.

Smith, James, a gunman, on Feb. 18, 1894, shot C.F. Hilton.

Smith, Joe, an Texas outlaw, was arrested for murder in New Mexico by Texas Rangers.

Smith, Sam (AKA: **Fred Wyat**) was a gunman in the Lincoln County War.

Smith, Six Shooter, a New Mexico gunmen who enjoyed wounding people without killing them.

Snider, William (AKA: **Bill Caveness**), an outlaw, arrested at Springerville, Ariz. in November, 1877.

Snow, Bud was an outlaw in Arizona and New Mexico.

Snow, Charles (AKA: **Johnson**), a gunman, was killed in New Mexico on Aug. 12, 1881.

Snyder, Jess, an outlaw, was a member of the Cook Gang in the Indian Territory. He was captured after a bank robbery.

Sontag, George C. (AKA: **George Bohm**), an outlaw in the 1880s and 1890s, robbed several trains in California with Chris Evans and was released from prison in 1908.

Sontag, John, an outlaw and brother of George, robbed trains in Illinois and California in the 1890s with Chris Evans. He was in a shoot-out with police officers in 1893 near Visalia, Calif.

Spawn, George (AKA: **Buffalo Bill**), a New Mexico outlaw and cattle rustler.

Spence, Pete, a gunman and friend of the Clantons in Tombstone, Ariz., in the early 1880s, reportedly killed Morgan Earp.

Spencer, Charles, an outlaw, horse thief, and murderer, was jailed in Silver City, N.M., and escaped in March 1884 with the Kit Joy Gang.

Sperry, Sam was a gunman in the Lincoln County War.

Starr, Belle, wife of outlaws Sam Starr, Jim Reed, and Bruce Younger, and gunman Jim Starr, had a $10,000 reward on her head, and spent one year in a reformatory with Sam Starr. She was killed on Feb. 2, 1889.

Starr, Henry (AKA: **Frank Jackson**), an outlaw nephew of Belle Starr who robbed banks from the 1890s, was killed on Feb. 18, 1921, while attempting to rob a bank.

Stevens, Stephens, a gunman in the Lincoln County War, was charged with the murder of Buckshot Roberts.

Stiles, William (Billy), an outlaw, rode with Burt Alvord as a lawman and outlaw in Arizona in the 1890s and 1900s, and was killed in 1908.

Stillwell, Simpson (AKA: **Commanche Jack**), a gunman and lawman, scouted for the Army in Texas, and brought in several outlaws.

Stillwell, T.C. (Frank), a gunman, lawman, and cowboy in Texas and Tombstone, Ariz., was shot down in 1882 during the grand jury investigation of the killing of Morgan Earp.

Stinson, J.W., a gunman, shot William McCann in June 1886.

Stockton, Isaac (AKA: **Ike**), an outlaw and leader of a gang of robbers in northern New Mexico, was shot, captured, and died after having his leg amputated on Sept. 27, 1881.

Stockton, Thomas, a rancher who owned a popular overnight stage stop near Trinidad, Colo., killed several rustlers in the 1870s and was allegedly tried for murder.

Stockton, William Porter (AKA: **Porter Stogden**), an outlaw, lawman, and brother of Ike, shot and killed Juan Gonzales in October 1876 in Cimarron, N.M., and was killed on Jan. 10, 1881, by Alfred Graves.

Storms, Charlie, a gunman, gambler, and friend of Bat Masterson in Kansas and Arizona, was killed by Luke Short in 1880.

Stoudenmire, Dallas, a lawman and gunman in New Mexico and Texas, shot and killed several men before his death in the early 1880s.

Sullivan, James, a gunman, who in April 1884, killed John Houston, at Black Hawk, New Mexico.

Swilling, Hank was an outlaw in Arizona and New Mexico.

Taggart, Frank, an outlaw and member of the train robbing Kit Joy Gang, was killed on Mar. 13, 1884, by a posse led by Deputy Sheriff T.L. Hall.

Tattenbaum, William (AKA: **Russian Bill**), a gunman in Tombstone, Ariz., was lynched on Jan. 1, 1881, for horse theft.

Taylor, Jack Hays, a gunman and brother of Phillip Taylor, killed a cavalry soldier and became a fugitive in the Sutton-Taylor feud of South Texas. A Sutton posse ambushed and killed him near the Taylor home on Aug. 23, 1889.

Taylor, Jack J., an outlaw, led a gang of train robbers and killers in Arizona and New Mexico. He received a life sentence for train robbery in 1888.

Taylor, James M., a gunman and son of Pitkin Taylor, led the Taylor faction in the Taylor-Sutton feud in 1873 in South Texas. He gunned down several men and was killed in December 1875.

Taylor, Phillip (AKA: **Doboy**), a gunman and brother of Pitkin and William Taylor, participated in the Sutton-Taylor feud, and was gunned down in November 1871, near Kerrville, Texas.

Taylor, Pitkin, a gunman, led the Taylors in the Taylor-Sutton feud which began in 1867. He was gunned down outside his home by the Suttons in October 1872 and died in March 1873.

Taylor, Steve, an outlaw, stole money at Custer County, Mont., in 1884, and was arrested in New Mexico.

Taylor, William, the son of Pitkin Taylor, participated in the Taylor-Sutton feud and killed men with his brother, James. He rode with their relative, Wes Hardin, and was imprisoned in 1877.

Telfrin, Count **Feador** (AKA: **Russian Bill**), an outlaw and son of a Russian Countess, was hanged in November 1881 at Shakespeare for rustling cattle.

Telles, Jose, an outlaw, was executed on Apr. 3, 1903, in Santa Fe, N.M.

Telles, Octoviano, a New Mexico outlaw who eluded authorities until his arrest on Aug. 13, 1907.

Terry, Kyle, a gunman, killed Henry Williams in February 1886 at Houston, Texas, shotgunned Ned Gibson on Jan. 21, 1888, at Wharton. Volney Gibson shot and killed Terry on Jan. 21, 1890, in Galveston.

Tewksbury, Edwin, a gunman in the Graham-Tewksbury feud in Globe County, Ariz., helped kill John Graham and was arrested. He became constable of Globe County and later deputy sheriff of Gila County.

Tewksbury, Jim, a gunman in the feud and brother of Edwin Tewksbury, killed several members of the Graham faction, and died of consumption in 1888.

"Texas Jack", an outlaw, was shot and killed in February 1881 in Rincon, N.M.

Thomas, Charles was an outlaw and cattle rustler in New Mexico.

Thompson, Ben (AKA: **Shotgun Ben**), a gunman and lawman in Texas, killed thirty-two men, and was ambushed with King Fisher in March 1884. Bat Masterson called him the West's greatest gunfighter.

Thompson, John (AKA: **Kid**), an outlaw, twice robbed a train near Los Angeles, Calif., in December 1893 and February 1895 with a man named Johnson. He was imprisoned in Summer 1895.

Thompson, William (AKA: **Texas Billy**), a gunman and brother of Ben, engaged in several gunbattles with lawmen and ranchers in Kansas, Texas, and Nebraska. He was killed in Laredo, Texas.

Thurmond, Frank, a gunman, shot and killed Dan Baxter in August 1881 in Deming, N.M.

Tobin, Thomas, a famous frontiersman, gunman, and mountain man, was shot by Kit Carson's son, and died in 1902.

Todd, Captain **George W.**, an outlaw, fought along side Cole Younger in Bill Anderson's guerilla army and was killed after the war.

Towerly, William, an outlaw horsethief, in less than a month, killed two law officers and was himself shot dead by U.S. Marshal Bill Moody in December 1887.

Tracy, Harry, an outlaw who rode with the Hole-in-the-Wall-Gang and Dave Merrill in Washington, killed Merrill during a prison escape and committed suicide in 1902.

Trentham, Charles, an outlaw and Texas Ranger, killed a man in Marfa, fled to New Mexico, and then the Indian Territory.

Trujillo, Antonio Maria, an outlaw in New Mexico, was hanged for high treason on Feb. 18, 1883.

Trujillo, Julian, an outlaw, was one of Silva's White Caps.

Tucker, Jim, an outlaw and murderer, poisoned W.F. Fletcher and was shot and killed on May 20, 1882, in Pinos Altos, N.M., by Deputy Sheriff Henry Barton.

Tucker, Tom, a gunman in the Graham-Tewkesbury feud in Arizona, joined Oliver Lee in his feud in Tularosa, N.M.

Turner, Ben, a gunman employed by the Horrell brothers in the Horrell-Higgins feud in the 1870s, was gunned down by angry citizens in December 1873, following the jailbreak of Matt Horrell and Jerry Scoot.

Turner, Marion, a gunman in the Lincoln County War and deputy sheriff in Lincoln, was indicted with John Jones on July 19, 1878, for the murder of Alexander McSween.

Ulibarri, Francisco, an outlaw and Comanche Indian, was a member of Silva's White Caps.

Updyke, Dave, stage coach robber in and around the Idaho Territory.

Urieta, Leandro, an outlaw, was shot in Mesilla, N.M., on Nov. 2, 1877, by Sheriff Mariano Barela.

Utter, Charles (AKA: **Sentimental Charley; Colorado Charley**), a gunman, friend, and cohort of Bill Hickok, made Hickok's tombstone and dealt cards at Socorro, N.M., and El Paso, Texas.

Valdez, Antonio Jose (AKA: **El Patas de Rana**), an outlaw and member of Silva's White Caps, shot Vicente Silva in the back and was jailed. He was later appointed Marshal of Wagon Mound.

Valley, Frank, a gunman and cowboy on the LS ranch in Tascosa, Texas, was killed by Len Woodruff in 1886.

Varela, Marcos, an outlaw, was a member of Silva's White Caps and a nephew of Vicente Silva.

Vasquez, Tiburcio, a California outlaw and member of Murietta's gang, was captured and hanged for raiding Santa Cruz, Calif., in 1875.

Vega, Cruz, an outlaw, was lynched by a mob in Cimarron, N.M., on Oct. 30, 1875, for allegedly murdering Reverend F.J. Tolby.

Vialpando, J.M. was an outlaw member of Silva's White Caps.

Vialpando, Juan de Dios, an outlaw and member of Silva's White Caps, killed two men and was hanged on Nov. 19, 1895, in Santa Fe.

Wade, "Kid", an outlaw and horse thief in northern Nebraska and the Dakotas, rode with Doc Middleton, and later formed his own gang. He was lynched in February 1884 at Bassett, Neb.

Wait, Frederick T. (AKA: **Dash Wait**), a gunman and a quarter-blood Cherokee Indian, was employed by John Tunstall in the Lincoln County War, riding with Billy the Kid as a "Regulator." He died in 1895 at the age of forty-two in Indian Territory.

Wakefield, E.H., a gunman in the Lincoln County War, rode with the posse that killed John Tunstall on Feb. 18, 1878.

Walker, Joe, an outlaw, rustled cattle with the Robbers Roost outlaws in Utah, and robbed banks with Butch Cassidy and the Wild Bunch before a posse shot him to death in May 1898 at Thompson.

Walker, Thomas J., a gunman, shot and killed Albert Kjellstrom in January 1885 in Socorro, N.M.

Walker, William, a gunman and mercenary commander, attempted to conquer the western section of Mexico, led a private army to Nicaragua in 1855, became president of Nicaragua in 1857, and was captured and executed in Trujillo, Honduras, on Sept. 12, 1860.

Walker, William, an outlaw and alleged leaders of the "Bald Knobbers," a gang of over 400 members, was hanged in May 1889 at Ozark, Mo.

Wall, William, an outlaw, was a member of the Wild Bunch. He was imprisoned and then released on Jan. 11, 1900, with Matt Warner.

Wallace, Dan (AKA: **Texas Dan**), an outlaw, robbed and killed a rancher near San Antonio, Texas, and was captured in the late 1880s.

Wallace, William Alexander Anderson (AKA: **Bigfoot**), a gunman and Texas Ranger, fought Mexicans in throughout mid and early 1800s to avenge the deaths of his brother and cousin. He rode shotgun on a Texas stage line, and died near Austin on Jan. 7, 1899.

Walrath, Charles G., an outlaw, shot and killed William Shook, and was hanged.

Walters, William E. (AKA: **Bill Anderson; Billy Brown; Bronco Bill**), an outlaw, rode with the Black Jack Ketchum Gang in the late 1890s. Released from prison in 1917, he died a few years later.

Warderman, Bill, an outlaw, was a member of the Black Jack Ketchum Gang.

Warner, M. (AKA: **Doc**), an outlaw, murdered Thomas Colligan on Feb. 20, 1883, near Rio Quemado, N.M.

Warner, Matt (**Willard Erastus Christianson**, AKA: **Morman Kid**), an outlaw, bank robber, and friend to Butch Cassidy and the Wild Bunch, became a justice of the peace, a deputy sheriff, and then a policeman in Price, Utah. He died in 1938 at age seventy-four.

Warren, James, a gunman, shot W.F. Markham on Sept. 2, 1886.

Washington, George, an outlaw, was lynched in June 1882 in Lincoln, N.M.

Waters, Buck was a gunman in the Lincoln County War.

Watson, Sam, a gunman and saloon keeper in Folsom, N.M., shot and killed a gambler named Fred Brown.

Watts, Henry, an outlaw and horse thief, was captured in June 1881 with Charlie Allison in Albuquerque, N.M.

Watts, John, an outlaw and rustler who was killed by the militia in New Mexico in March 1883.

Webb, Gilbert, an outlaw, arrested for complicity in the robbery of an Army paymaster at Fort Thomas, Arizona, on May 11, 1889.

Webb, John Joshua (AKA: **Samuel King**), an outlaw, member of the Dodge City Gang in Las Vegas, N.M., and city marshal of Las Vegas, murdered Michael Kelliher on Mar. 2, 1880, was condemned to hang, but escaped from jail with David Rudabaugh in 1881 and died of small pox the following year.

Webb, Wilfred, an outlaw, arrested for complicity in the robbery of an Army paymaster at Fort Thomas, on May 11, 1889.

Weightsman, George (**Waightman**, AKA: **Red Buck**), an outlaw and member of the Doolin Gang, was captured and imprisoned by Heck Thomas in 1889. He was killed in a gunfight with lawmen near Arapaho, Okla., in either October or March 1896.

Wells, Charles Knox Polk, an admitted outlaw and murderer, robbed banks and trains, and allegedly killed over thirty men including an uncle and a jailer. He was convicted of murder in May 1882 and received a life sentence.

Welsh, Tom, an outlaw, killed Joe Hickson in Good Hope, N.M., on Oct. 28, 1884.

Wesley, John (AKA: **Harry Hill**), a cowboy and outlaw, attempted to rob the Medicine Lodge Bank on Apr. 30, 1884, with Marshal Hendry Brown and two others. Brown was killed attempting to escape a lynch mob.

West, James (AKA: **James Lowe**), an outlaw, shot and killed Constable Joe Carson in Las Vegas, N.M., on Jan. 22, 1880, and was lynched.

West, Richard (AKA: **Little Dick**), an outlaw and member of the Doolin Gang, was the last of the gang to die. He joined the Jennings Gang and was killed in 1896 either by U.S Marshal William Fosset or Bill Tilghman.

Whealington, Tom (AKA: **Red River Tom**), an outlaw, was shot and killed with Dick Rogers while attempting to break a friend out of jail in Springer, N.M., on Mar. 13, 1885.

Wheeler, Ben, a lawman and outlaw, was a companion of Billy the Kid during the Lincoln County War, robbed the Medicine Lodge, Kan., bank with Marshal Hendry Brown and others on Apr. 30, 1884, and was lynched.

Wheeler, Grant, an outlaw, robbed trains in the 1890s and was trailed by George Scarborough and Billy Breakenridge. He killed himself on Apr. 25, 1895, at Mancos, Colo., after he was wounded and cornered by lawmen.

Wheeler, James, an outlaw, shot and killed Adolph Davidson in Chance City, N.M., in April 1886.

White, Ham, a murderer and stage robber on the road between San Antonio and Austin, Texas.

Whitley, William, an outlaw and member of Brack Cornett's gang, was killed on Sept. 25, 1888, at Floresville, Texas.

Wiggin, W., an outlaw, was lynched in San Marcial, N.M., in Sept. 1882.

Williams, Ben, a lawman who was involved in a shootout with fellow lawmen, Albert Fall and Joe Morgan, at Las Cruces, N.M., on Sept. 15, 1895.

Williams, Charles, an outlaw, was lynched near Harshaw, N.M., in November 1883.

Williams, Jess, an outlaw, was a member of the Black Jack Christian's gang.

Willis, Thomas, an outlaw, murdered W.P. Williams with the help of John Billee. Billee and Willis were captured by deputies Will Ayers, James Wilkerson, and Perry DuVall, and hanged on Jan. 16, 1890.

Wilson, Jim, an outlaw, shot and killed Dane Williams in Central City, N.M., on Mar. 20, 1886.

Wilson, William (AKA: **Buffalo Bill**), an outlaw, lawman, was arrested with Billy the Kid, served time in prison, received a pardoned in 1896, and became sheriff of Terrell County, N.M. He was killed in 1911.

Wilson, William, an outlaw, shot and killed Robert Casey in Lincoln, N.M., and was hanged twice on Dec. 10, 1875.

Wohrle, John, a lawman and outlaw, was deputy sheriff in Mason County and involved in the Hoodoo War in 1875. He was shot, stabbed, killed, and scalped by Scott Cooley to avenge Wohrle's part in the death of Tim Williamson.

Wolcott, Major **Frank**, a gunman and mercenary commander, led an army of gunfighters and soldiers to quell the Johnson County War in April 1892. The U.S. army ended the war and the mercenaries were arrested and later acquitted.

Wolz, Charles, a gunman in Lincoln County, N.M., was part of the posse that shot and killed John Tunstall on Feb. 18, 1878.

Woodruff, Len, a cowboy and gunman, was wounded in the gunfight between LX and LS cowboys on Mar. 21, 1886, in Oldham County, Texas.

Worthington, Nick, a New Mexico and Colorado outlaw, stole horses and killed several men before he was shot and killed by civilians in Cimarron, N.M., on June 18, 1878.

Wyatt, Nelson Ellsworth (Zip, AKA: **Dick Yeager: Wild Charlie)**, the self-claimed greatest Oklahoma outlaw, stole livestock and robbed post offices before he was wounded, captured, and imprisoned in Enid, where he died from his wounds on Apr. 5, 1895.

Yager, Erastus (AKA: **Red**), an outlaw and messenger for Henry Plummer's gang, the Innocents, revealed the identities of Plummer and the Innocents. He was lynched in December 1863.

Young, Cole (AKA: **Cole Estes**, an outlaw and member of the Black Jack Ketchum Gang of Arizona and New Mexico, was killed by Marshal Loomis during a bank robbery in Nogales on Oct. 8, 1896.

Young, William, an outlaw, was hanged in March 1881 in Silver City, N.M.

Younger, James (Jim), an outlaw and member of the Younger Gang, robbed banks and trains with his brothers Cole, John, and Bob, and cousins Jesse and Frank James. He was captured and imprisoned after the failed Northfield, Minn., bank raid on Sept. 21, 1876, and released on July 14, 1901. He killed himself in October 1902.

Younger, John, an outlaw, Younger brother, and member of the Younger Gang, was killed by Pinkerton detectives Louis Lull and Jim Duckworth in St. Clair County, Mo., in March 1874.

Younger, Robert (Bob), an outlaw, a member of the gang, and youngest of the Younger brothers, was severely wounded in the 1876 Northfield raid. He was captured and imprisoned in Stillwater, Minn., and died of his wounds on Sept. 16, 1889.

Younger, Thomas Coleman (Cole), an outlaw, Younger brother, and leader of the Younger Gang, was wounded and captured following the Northfield bank raid, and pardoned on July 10, 1901. He died of a heart condition at Lee's Summit, Mo., in March 1916.

Yountis, Oliver (AKA: **Crescent Sam**), an outlaw and member of the Dalton-Doolin Gang, was killed by lawmen at his home near Orlando, Okla., by Chris Madsen after the gang's first bank robbery in the early 1890s.

Zamora, Francisco, a gunman for McSween in the Lincoln County War, was killed during the McSween gunbattle on July 19, 1878.